MW00753271
DOMI MINA
NVS TIO
ILLV MEA

THE
NEW SHORTER
OXFORD ENGLISH
DICTIONARY

THE NEW SHORTER OXFORD ENGLISH DICTIONARY

ON HISTORICAL PRINCIPLES

EDITED BY

LESLEY BROWN

VOLUME 1

A–M

CLARENDON PRESS · OXFORD

Oxford University Press, Walton Street, Oxford OX2 6DP
Oxford New York
Athens Auckland Bangkok Bombay
Calcutta Cape Town Dar es Salaam Delhi
Florence Hong Kong Istanbul Karachi
Kuala Lumpur Madras Madrid Melbourne
Mexico City Nairobi Paris Singapore
Taipei Tokyo Toronto
and associated companies in
Berlin Ibadan

Oxford is a trade mark of Oxford University Press

Published in the United States by
Oxford University Press Inc., New York

© *Oxford University Press 1973, 1993*

First Edition 1933
Second Edition 1936
Third Edition 1944
Reprinted with Revised Etymologies and Enlarged Addenda 1973
This Edition 1993

All rights reserved. No part of this publication may be reproduced, stored in a retrieval system, or transmitted, in any form or by any means, without the prior permission in writing of Oxford University Press. Within the UK, exceptions are allowed in respect of any fair dealing for the purpose of research or private study, or criticism or review, as permitted under the Copyright, Designs and Patents Act, 1988, or in the case of reprographic reproduction in accordance with the terms of the licences issued by the Copyright Licensing Agency. Enquiries concerning reproduction outside these terms and in other countries should be sent to the Rights Department, Oxford University Press, at the address above

British Library Cataloguing in Publication Data
Data available

Library of Congress Cataloging in Publication Data
Data available

ISBN 0–19–861134–X Plain Edition
ISBN 0–19–861271–0 Thumb Index Edition
ISBN 0–19–863142–1 Luxury Edition
ISBN 0–19–195804–2 Leather Bound Edition

7 9 10 8

Printed in the United States of America
on acid-free paper

CONTENTS

EDITOR-IN-CHIEF Lesley Brown

GENERAL EDITORS A. M. Hughes (1984–), John Sykes (1989–)

ASSOCIATE EDITOR William R. Trumble (1980–91)

SENIOR EDITORS Georgia Hole (1986–), Elizabeth M. Knowles (1983–)
Helen Liebeck (1989–), Freda J. Thornton (1985–92)

SENIOR ASSISTANT EDITORS Jeremy H. Marshall (1988–), Richard Palmer (1984–)
Catherine I. Soanes (1989–), Angus Stevenson (1988–)

ASSISTANT EDITORS Gerard O'Reilly (1988–), David B. Shirt (1990–)

D. B. W. Birk (1983–6), M. A. Cooper (1983–6), D. Greene (1988–90), H. Kemp (1986–8)
F. McDonald (1985–9), J. Paterson (1986–8), S. C. Rennie (1989–91)

SUPPLEMENTARY EDITING E. S. C. Weiner (1991–)

Administrative Assistant Rena Jones (1990–)
Text Editing Assistant Steven Siddle (1990–)

PREFACE

THE *New Shorter Oxford English Dictionary* is a historical dictionary of modern English. It sets out the main meanings and semantic developments of words current at any time between 1700 and the present day: those which have been in regular literary or colloquial use at some point in their history; slang or dialect words which are nevertheless likely to be generally encountered through accessible literature or the modern mass media; and in addition a wide range of scientific and technical words such as may be of interest to serious amateurs or advanced students. Every headword is traced back to the time of its first known use, however early, in many cases to the manuscript records of the Old and Middle English periods.

Words which have fallen into disuse during the past three centuries are included if they meet the other general criteria. Words which became obsolete before 1700 appear if they are significant in the formation or history of some other headword in the text, or if they remain familiar from the works of Shakespeare, the 1611 Authorized Version of the Bible, and a small number of other influential literary sources (notably the poems of John Milton and Edmund Spenser's *Faerie Queene*).

This work is a replacement for the third edition of the *Shorter Oxford English Dictionary*, but not a direct revision of its text. The *New SOED* editors returned to the *Oxford English Dictionary* itself (in later stages the second edition of 1989, originally the first edition of 1884–1928 and its four-volume *Supplement* of 1972–86), and reabridged, conflated, revised, restructured, added, and updated. Every entry has been written afresh, taking into account the linguistic evidence of the Dictionary Department's extensive quotation files and computer databases. Many new words and senses have been added, and all have been reviewed in the light of social and political changes.

A more strictly chronological basis for entry structure has been adopted than in previous editions (which followed the *OED* more directly). Senses within major semantic and grammatical units are arranged according to the period or date range within which the first known example of each falls (for the definition of date ranges used see p. xvi). In many cases dates are at variance with those in the *OED* because earlier and later examples have now been identified. For the *New SOED*, researchers have systematically scrutinized historical dictionaries such as the *Middle English Dictionary* in progress in Ann Arbor, Michigan, the *Dictionary of the Older Scottish Tongue*, the *Scottish National Dictionary*, the *Dictionary of American English*, the *Dictionary of Americanisms*, and the *Australian National Dictionary*, looking for examples which would affect dates or descriptive labels. New information was sought in other known relevant publications, such as Jürgen Schäfer's *Documentation in the O.E.D.* and articles in *Notes and Queries*. Unresolved first dates in the *OED* were pursued and clarified. Several million paper slips in the English Dictionary Department's files were scanned for individual antedatings or postdatings. The editors of the *Middle English Dictionary* have further provided some information from their drafts of later parts of the alphabet which have not yet been published, and a number of unpublished earlier uses have been verified in the files of the *Dictionary of the Older Scottish Tongue*. New significant information will continue to come to light, but every effort has been made to present the most accurate and up-to-date record possible at the time of going to press.

The *New SOED* is founded in the *OED*, and shares its coverage of many words and senses from North America, Australia, New Zealand, South Africa, the Indian subcontinent, and elsewhere within the English-speaking world. Many of the entries for recent vocabulary are based on as yet unpublished additions prepared by members of the *OED*'s New Words section.

The main senses of the headwords are illustrated by 83,000 quotations, drawn from the Dictionary Department's quotation files and computerized databases. Their primary function here is to illuminate semantic distinctions and exemplify possible grammatical constructions. Defined phrases and combinations, and derivatives and minor words related to a headword, cannot receive such expansive treatment and are not illustrated. Where possible and historically appropriate, modern sources have been used, but real examples are notoriously ambiguous or resistant to intelligible abridgement, and the undeniable quotability of Defoe, Macaulay, and Dickens has ensured the use of many earlier quotations directly from the *OED*.

Pronunciations are provided in symbols of the International Phonetic Alphabet, and represent a style of British Received Pronunciation. Coverage of the wide regional, social, and other differences in spoken English in Britain and throughout the world would require more space and a more complex technical apparatus than would be suitable, given the emphases and intended non-specialist readership of the *New SOED*.

Editorial work on this completely new edition of the *SOED* began in 1980, with a build-up of staff from late 1983. Until well into the letter I, entries were handwritten on 6-by-4-inch paper slips. Then in 1987 the availability of the second edition of the *OED* in electronic form prompted a radical revision of editorial procedures. A complex specification was drawn up for the automatic modification of the *OED* text: certain categories of entry and types of information were omitted, senses and structural units were reordered, old-fashioned modes of expression were modified, and many other changes were made to bring it closer to the spirit and style of the *New SOED*. This provisional abridged and transformed *OED* was made a reality as an electronic database and in proofed paper form on editors' desks by members of the Reference Computing team at Oxford University Press and members of the Centre for the New OED at the University of Waterloo in Ontario, Canada. Thereafter a team of keyboarders made the lexicographers' substantial alterations and additions directly to the central database.

Meanwhile International Computaprint Corporation (ICC) in Pennsylvania, who had undertaken data-capture of the second edition of the *OED*, keyed the handwritten slips for *A* to *interwreathe*, converting their conventional typographical mark-up into a generic form which identified the start and end points of the many different elements of dictionary structure. The tagging of the output was then refined and enhanced by programs written within OUP. Soon the sections of dictionary text produced by such contrasting means were formally indistinguishable.

Almost every member of the lexicographical team took part in the first round of editing. Proofs of the results were sent out to advisers for criticisms and suggestions, and many individual entries were also submitted to subject specialists. Comments from both these sources were then fed into a revision of the whole text by senior lexicographers. But for the requirement of publication, this revision could continue for ever.

A project of the size and duration of the *New Shorter Oxford English Dictionary* inevitably draws upon the time and expertise of members of many different departments within Oxford University Press. The editors thank them all. In particular the Reference Computing team helped transform working methods and perceptions and provided the support to sustain the transformation. From outside the organization we wish to mention Hazel Wright and Deborah Honoré, for general critical reading of the text; Dr Clive Upton, for advising on pronunciation and checking phonetic transcriptions; G. Elizabeth Blake, for the programs for preliminary shortening of the *OED*; Julia Cresswell, for historical research in published materials; Ralph Bates, for bibliographical and other library research; Lidie Howes and Barbara Grant, for information from the *Middle English Dictionary* materials; Lorna Pike, for quotations from the *DOST* collections; Helen De Witt, Sara Hawker, Rachel James, Marcia Slater, Jerry Spring, Jeremy Trevett, Penny Trumble, Penny Waddell, Carl Watson, Seren Wildwood, and Jane Windebank, for data-capture and structural tagging; Patricia Moore, for this and on-line regularization of stylistic inconsistencies; Fabia

Claris, Louise Keegan, Christina Malkowski-Zaba, Helen Marriage, Margaret McKay, and Coralie O'Gorman, for proofreading and checking of underlying structure; Dorothy McCarthy, for establishing proofreading procedures; Patricia Greene, Lisa Johnston, and Sandy Vaughan, for cross-reference checking; Fred Gill and Peter Gibbs, for checking final page-proofs; Peter Robinson, Catherine Bates, Stephen Shepherd, Lynda Mugglestone, Alexandra Barratt, and Rod McConchie, particularly for searching files for dating and usage information; Margaret Davies, for file-searching and research for the list of authors and publications; Philippa Berry, for work on the authors' list and for identifying potential cross-references for inclusion; Clare Todd, particularly for research for the authors' list, for identifying cross-references, and for quotation abridgement and copying; Kate Batchelor, Mary Burns, and Katie Weale, for quotation copying and for other clerical and administrative help; Colinette Dorey, for file-searching and for filing and clerical help; Kay Pepler, particularly for keying information for the authors' list; Clare Senior, for clerical and filing assistance; Carol Percy, for bibliographical research; Anna Taylor, for distributing proofs. At various earlier stages of the project Karen Cooper, Hania Porucznik, and Annabella Duckit were project administrative assistants, and M. A. Mabe, K. Atherton, and M. C. Palmer contributed to early editorial work.

For specific advice on particular languages and areas of knowledge, we are indebted to Mrs A. J. Allott, Dr Philip Baker, Mr David Barrett, Professor Tomás de Bhaldraithe, Mr R. J. Bowater, Dr Savile Bradbury, Dr Jean Branford, Mr David Bunker, Mr Andrew Burrows, Miss Penelope Byrde, Dr Stanley Chapman, Mr Howard Colvin, Mr Yassin Dutton, Mr Colin Dyson, Mr Elwyn Hartley Edwards, Mr D. H. Fowler, Mr J. B. Franks, Mr Alan J. Gamble, Professor Bryan Garner, Dr Ives Goddard, Mr Noël Goodwin, Mrs Judy Gray, Dr Anne Grinter, Dr P. T. Harries, Mr Andrew Hawke, Professor Tony Honoré, Mr Simon James, Dr W. J. Johnson, Dr Russell Jones, the late Mr Peter Kemp, Professor Harriet Klein, Dr Ann Lackie, M. Pierre-Yves Lambert, Professor J. D. Latham, Professor G. L. Lewis, Professor Robert E. Lewis, Dr Andrew Louth, Professor J. B. McMillan, Dr C. M. MacRobert, Dr F. H. C. Marriott, Professor P. H. Matthews, Dr M. J. Morris, Mr James Mosley, Professor P. Nailor, Mr David Parlett, Professor Andrew Pawley, Ms Jenny Putin, Dr D. A. Roe, Dr H. M. Rosenberg, Captain A. B. Sainsbury, Dr Geoff Sharman, Mr Jonathan Spencer, Professor N. S. Sutherland, Professor M. Twyman, Professor J. O. Urmson, Professor Geza Vermes, Miss Freda Walker, Lord Walton of Detchant, Mr Harry D. Watson, Ms Niki Watts, Dr M. Weitzman, Mr Ken Whyld, Mr Thomas Woodcock, Professor Clifford Wright, Mrs Hazel Wright, and Dr R. David Zorc.

L.B.

March 1993

GUIDE TO THE USE OF THE DICTIONARY

1 Purpose

The following guide aims to explain to the user the kind of information that is available in the *New Shorter Oxford English Dictionary*, and to assist in the finding of particular information. It outlines the types of entry which appear in the dictionary, lists the possible places where certain kinds of words or phrases may be found, details the different features which may occur in an entry, and explains some of the conventions the dictionary uses.

2 The dictionary entry

2.1 TYPES OF ENTRY

There are four basic types of entry in this dictionary: standard entries, combining entries, letter entries, and variant entries.

2.1.1 *Standard entries.* The majority of entries are standard entries. In these the headword, or word being defined, does not belong to any of the other three entry types below. The typical standard entry has a headword (in **bold** type), pronunciation (in the International Phonetic Alphabet), part of speech (in *italic* type), date (expressed as a period of part of a century), etymology (in square brackets [ ]), and definition section. The definition section may be accompanied by one or more small-type paragraphs containing illustrative quotations, phrases which contain the headword, compounds whose first element is the headword, or derivatives consisting of the headword and a suffix. Usage indicators (labels), variant spellings, and grammatical or other information may also appear in the entry. More information on all these features is given in section 4 below.

2.1.2 *Combining entries.* In these entries the headword either begins or ends with a hyphen, and in use generally occurs joined to another word (either hyphenated or as a solid word). Combining entries include affixes of three types: suffixes (like *-ly, -ness*), prefixes (like *re-, un-*), and combining forms (like *hyper-, kilo-*). See further under section 6 below.

2.1.3 *Letter entries.* Each letter of the alphabet has an entry which contains a brief account of the history of the letter and a selection of abbreviations and acronyms which begin with that letter. See further under section 7 below.

2.1.4 *Variant entries.* A variant entry refers an alternative spelling or grammatical form of a headword to the standard or combining entry with the main form and all other information. See further under section 8 below.

2.2 ORDERING OF ENTRIES

Entries are listed in strict alphabetical order. Those with hyphens or spaces follow otherwise identical words written solid; a headword with an accent or diacritic over a letter follows one consisting of the same sequence of letters without. Capital and lower-case letters are regarded as equivalent. Strict alphabetical order applies also to prefixes of titles and names (such as *Mc-*, *St* (saint)) which in other contexts may conventionally be placed elsewhere.

The order of headwords which are spelled the same way but have different parts of speech is as follows:

noun	(abbreviated *n.*)
pronoun	(abbreviated *pron.*)
adjective	(abbreviated *a.*)
verb	(abbreviated *v.*)
adverb	(abbreviated *adv.*)
preposition	(abbreviated *prep.*)
conjunction	(abbreviated *conj.*)
interjection	(abbreviated *int.*)
prefix/combining form	(abbreviated *pref./comb. form*)
suffix	(abbreviated *suff.*)

Entries are positioned in the headword sequence by their first part of speech. The order of headwords with the same spelling and the same (first) part of speech is chronological (according to date ranges: see 4.8 below), with variant entries following any full entries: see 4.4 below.

Subcategorizations of parts of speech, such as participial (*ppl*) of adjectives, verbal (*vbl*) of nouns, or personal (*pers.*) of pronouns, are disregarded in determining entry order.

3 How to find a word or phrase

Look in the obvious alphabetical place in the main sequence of entries. If the item sought is not there, consider the following:

(i) Is it formed from a prefix or a combining form (as *dis-*, *Euro-*)? If so, is it included in the entry for that prefix or combining form? It may be listed (in italics) as an example there, or be treated in a small-type paragraph.

(ii) Is it a derivative, i.e. does it end with a suffix (as *-ly*,

-ness)? If so, is it included at the end of the entry for the word from which it is derived? For example, *befitting* appears under **befit** *v.*, *disclosing* under **disclose** *v.*, and *lacelike* and *lacery* under **lace** *n.* & *a.*: none would be found in its own alphabetical place.

(iii) Is it a phrase or combination, or other compound? If so, is it included in a small-type paragraph in the entry for one of the words which it contains? For example, *three cheers* and *sling mud* are respectively under **cheer** *n.*[1] and **mud** *n.*[1], *colour-blind* is under **colour** *n.*, and *infant prodigy* is under **infant** *n.*[1] & *a.* Sometimes an entry for one word in a phrase or compound will contain a cross-reference to one of the other elements, under which the definition will be found. For two-word compounds it is probably most reliable to look initially under their first element. For further information see 4.14 below.

(iv) Is it very similar to a word included as a headword? If so, and especially if it is an uncommon or obsolete word, it may also be included in the small-type derivative block at the end of the entry for that word. (See 4.16 below for more information on derivatives.)

(v) Is it an acronym or an abbreviation? If so, and particularly if it is pronounced as a set of initials and not as a word, it may be under the entry for the letter it begins with. For example *LAN*, *l.b.w.*, and *Lincs.* are under **L, l**, *RIP* is under **R, r**, but **ANZAC** and **Nimby** are main entries in their own alphabetical places.

4 The features of a standard dictionary entry

This section describes the elements which may appear in a standard dictionary entry, in the order in which they most usually occur. Some, such as labels or phrases, can occur in several places: this is mentioned, and the range of places indicated, later in the guide in the section for the feature in question. Many of the characteristics of standard entries are shared by the other types of dictionary entry.

4.1 HEADWORD

Every entry opens with a headword, printed in bold type. The headword is the word whose meaning, etymology, history, pronunciation, etc., are the subject of the entry.

If the headword is obsolete (i.e. no longer in use in current English) it is preceded by a dagger: †.

If the headword is a word (or phrase) which, although used in English, is still regarded as essentially foreign, it is printed in bold italics. In their normal contexts such items are often written or printed in light italics or within quotation marks, and many may still usually be pronounced in a foreign way.

Where a word has more than one spelling, the spelling used for the headword is usually the one regarded as the dominant or preferred current form. Other spellings may be given later in the entry, as variants (see 4.6 below). Historical considerations occasionally require a form which is less usual for some senses to be chosen as the headword, but in such cases current usage is made clear.

4.2 PRONUNCIATION

4.2.1 The pronunciations shown are those which can safely be regarded as allowable in British English at the present time, within the form of received pronunciation that does not give rise to any negative social judgement when heard by most native speakers. An attempt has been made to represent the English spoken by the current generation, older forms being discarded where necessary, but absence of a variant need not indicate that it is completely unacceptable, and the order of variants need not be one of decreasing frequency.

Pronunciations are given, between slashes, in the symbols of the International Phonetic Alphabet (IPA). The symbols and conventions used are intended to provide sufficient information for accurate production of the appropriate sounds, without needless detail.

4.2.2 *Vowels.* In a conventional vowel diagram (representing the position and degree of raising of the tongue in articulating each sound), the vowel symbols used in this dictionary appear as follows:

	Front	*Central*	*Back*
High	i y		u
	ɪ		ʊ
	e ø	ə	o
Mid			
	ɛ œ	ʌ	ɔ
Low	a		ɑ ɒ

Lengthening is indicated by ː

Nasality is indicated by the superscript diacritic ˜

The front vowels with lip-rounding, /y/, /ø/, and /œ/, occur only in words which are not fully naturalized. See further the Key to the Pronunciation.

The English vowel sounds are

Short			*Long*		
a	as in	**cat**	ɑː	as in	**arm**
ɛ		**bed**	əː		**her**
ɪ		**sit**	iː		**see**
i		**cosy**	ɔː		**saw**
ɒ		**hot**	uː		**too**
ʌ		**run**	ɛː		**hair**
ʊ		**put**			
ə		**ago**			

Diphthongs

ʌɪ	as in	**my**	ʌɪə	**tire**
aʊ		**how**	aʊə	**sour**
eɪ		**day**		
əʊ		**no**		
ɪə		**near**		
ɔɪ		**boy**		
ʊə		**poor**		

4.2.3 *Consonants and semivowels.* The following sounds are recorded in this dictionary:

Plosives: p, b, t, d, k, g

Fricatives: f, v, θ, ð, s, z, ʃ, ʒ, ç, x, h

Affricates: tʃ, dʒ

Liquids and nasals: l, ʎ, m, n, ɲ, ŋ, r

Semivowels: j, w, ɥ

Of these, b, d, f, h, k, l, m, n, p, r, s, t, v, w, and z have their usual English values. Other symbols are used as follows:

ɡ as in **get**
tʃ **chip**
dʒ **jar**
ŋ **ring**
θ **thin**
ð **this**
ʃ **she**
ʒ vision
j **yes**;

in some Scottish and foreign words

x as in lo**ch**, German a**ch**;

and only in respect of words which are not fully naturalized

ç as in German ni**ch**t
ʎ as in Spanish **ll** or Italian **gl** in *gli*
ɲ as in Spanish **ñ**, French **gn**, Italian **gn** in *gnocco*
ɥ as in French n**u**it.

See further the Key to the Pronunciation.

4.2.4 Primary stress is indicated by superscript ˈ before the stressed syllable, secondary stress by subscript ˌ. Primary stress is shown for words with two or more syllables; secondary stress only where its marking is needed to avoid doubt. Word stress is not a significant feature of the French language, and no stress is marked in words retaining a true French pronunciation. See further 4.2.6 below.

4.2.5 Unstressed vowels are reduced to /ə/ unless they are likely to have their full phonetic value when the word is pronounced in isolation.

4.2.6 Optional sounds, sometimes pronounced, sometimes not, are enclosed within round brackets.

E.g. **prompt** /prɒm(p)t/
delivery /dɪˈlɪv(ə)ri/.

The bracketing of schwa, (ə), before /l/, /m/, and /n/ shows that these consonants are often syllabic in the words concerned.

4.2.7 An explicit pronunciation is given for a derivative only if it differs in some unpredictable way from that of the headword or from that usual in combination with the suffix in question. If the derivative bears primary stress on a different syllable from the headword (and consequently has a predictably different pronunciation) this is indicated by a primary stress mark before the stressed syllable within the actual bold form; any secondary stress is assumed to fall on the syllable bearing primary stress in the headword unless otherwise marked.

E.g. (S.V. FALSIFY) **falsifiable** bears no stress mark so is stressed like *falsify* on the first syllable, but **falsiˌfiaˈbility.**

Among predictable changes associated with the position of primary stress are

ə or (ə) → a in nouns in *-ality* formed from adjectives in *-al* (e.g. **practiˈcality** and not the full phonetic transcription /praktɪˈkalɪti/ is given under **practical** /ˈpraktɪk(ə)l/);

əʊ or ə(ʊ) → ɒ in derivatives of combining forms in *-o* or words formed from them (e.g. **maˈcropterous** and not the full phonetic transcription /maˈkrɒpt(ə)rəs/ is given under **macro-** /ˈmakrəʊ/).

A final *-r* is pronounced in derivatives formed with a suffix beginning with a vowel.

E.g. **authoress** under **author** /ˈɔːθə/ is to be understood as /ˈɔːθərɪs/.
cellarage under **cellar** /ˈsɛlə/ is to be understood as /ˈsɛlərɪdʒ/.

An exception to this is the suffix *-ed*, which results in a pronunciation /əd/ not /-ərəd/ after /ə/.

The pronunciation of *-icity* in derivatives of adjectives in *-ic* (/-ɪk/) is /-ɪsɪti/.

4.2.8 A second or subsequent pronunciation is often abbreviated so as to show just the part where it differs from the first; the same applies to pronunciations of variant or inflected forms.

4.2.9 An alternative non-Anglicized pronunciation may be given for a word which is largely but not fully naturalized. Such pronunciations are preceded by *foreign.* The first (or only) pronunciation of any non-naturalized word, phrase, or form (printed in italic bold) from one of the more familiar modern European languages will represent the foreign pronunciation but will have no specifying label. A second or subsequent fully Anglicized pronunciation will often be given.

4.2.10 A hyphen may be used in a phonetic transcription to clarify or emphasize that the divided sounds are to be separately pronounced, for example where they could be mistaken for a diphthong or single affricate, or where /l/ is repeated when *-less* or *-ly* is added to a word ending in *-l.*

E.g. **Mazdaism** /ˈmazdə-ɪz(ə)m/
potsherd /ˈpɒt-ʃəːd/
drolly /ˈdrəʊl-li/
moralless /ˈmɒr(ə)l-lɪs/.

Most often, however, hyphens simply open or close truncated pronunciations.

4.2.11 Additional examples of words illustrating particular sounds are to be found in the Key to the Pronunciation, and the main English sounds are summarized at the foot of the page throughout much of the dictionary.

4.3 PART OF SPEECH

A part of speech is given for all entries, except letter entries. It appears in italics, in abbreviated form (see 2.2 above and the Abbreviations List on pp. xxiii–xxvi), after the pronunciation, or after the headword if no pronunciation is shown.

All the parts of speech of a headword are listed at the beginning of an entry, e.g. *a.* & *adv.*; *n.*, *a.*, & *v.* Sometimes parts of speech are treated together, but more often they are in separate sections, in which case each section is headed with a capital initial followed by the part(s) of speech being treated in that section, e.g. A *n.*, B *adj.*

Plurals of abbreviated parts of speech are usually formed by the simple addition of *-s*, but for clarity *a.* becomes *adjs.* After sense numbers, and in some other contexts (especially when in roman type), *adj.* is also preferred to *a.* for 'adjective'.

If the headword consists of two or more separate words, it may be specified as a phrase (*phr.*). For example, *n. phr.*, or *adv. phr.*, or (when parts of speech are combined) *n.* & *a. phr.*

If the headword is a verb, the part of speech may be followed by an indication of the verb's transitivity (e.g. *v.i.*, *v.t.*). For more information about transitivity see 4.11.1 below.

Parts of speech are also given for some of the items in combination and other subentry blocks (see 4.14 below) and for derivatives (see 4.16 below).

4.4 HOMONYMS

If two or more headwords have the same spelling and part of speech, but each has a different origin and meaning, the headwords are homonyms. They are distinguished by a superscript number after the relevant part of speech. In this dictionary, homonyms include headwords whose only difference is an initial capital, but not headwords which differ in respect of hyphenation, spacing, or letters with accents or diacritics. If the first part of speech of two or more homonyms is the same, the entries are presented in chronological order (according to date range: see 4.8 below). If successive entries have more than one part of speech, homonym numbers of later parts of speech are allocated in the order in which the entries appear in the text. E.g. if *n.*[1] & *a.*[1] is followed by *n.*[2] & *a.*[2], it is to be understood that the second noun is recorded later (or at least no earlier) than the first, but nothing is implied about the relative first dates of the adjectives. Homonyms which are variant entries follow all standard- or combining-entry homonyms of the same (first) part of speech.

E.g. **cupper** . . . *n.*[1] . . . ME.
cupper . . . *n.*[2] . . . E20.
cupper *n.*[3] var. of CUPPA.

Only the simple part of speech is relevant in allocating homonym numbers. Qualifications such as *vbl* and *ppl* are disregarded (cf. last paragraph of 2.2 above).

E.g. **picking** *n.*[1]
picking *vbl n.*[2]

In cross-references to combining entries the part of speech is omitted and the homonym number is attached to the small-capital form, e.g. -ER[1], -Y[6].

4.5 LABELS AND SYMBOLS

4.5.1 *Subject and status labels.* Restrictions in the usage of words or senses are frequently conveyed by the use of labels (usually in italic). These can show restriction to the English of a particular geographical area (e.g. *dial.*, *Sc.*, *US*, *Austral.*), to a specific style or register of language (e.g. *colloq.*, *poet.*, *slang*), to a particular branch of knowledge or field of activity (e.g. *Cricket*, *Her.*, *Law*, *Naut.*), or can denote frequency or extent of use (e.g. *rare*).

Subject labels precede any definition (or partial definition) or any variant spelling or form to which they apply. (If they apply to a complete entry they therefore follow the etymology.)

E.g. **infauna** /ɪnˈfɔːnə/ *n.* E20. [. . .] *Zool.* The animal life . . .
(s.v. COLOUR *n.*) 8 *Mining.* (A particle of) gold. M19.
(s.v. OCCLUDE *v.*) 5 *v.i. Meteorol.* Of a front . . .

If a subject label is immediately adjacent to an italic phrase or combination, the subject label is distinguished by roman type.

E.g. (s.v. ACETIC *a.*) 1 Chem. *acetic acid*, a weak acid . . .

Geographical, stylistic, and frequency labels (together here referred to as 'status labels') applying to the whole entry appear at the top of the entry after the part of speech.

E.g. **peripherial** /pɛrɪˈfɪərɪəl/ *a. rare.* L17.

In a main definition section a status label applying to a complete dated sense follows the definition and immediately precedes the date.

E.g. (s.v. CHIP *v.*[1] 9) **b** *v.t.* Tease, chaff. *colloq.* L19.

Within dated senses, a status label applying to only part of a definition generally precedes that part to which it applies. If the definition has formal divisions (as (*a*), (*b*), etc.) the label always precedes the part it qualifies; if there is no formal division, the label follows the first part of the definition but precedes any later parts.

E.g. (s.v. OVERLANDER *n.*) **1** A person who journeyed from one part of Australia to another (*obs.* exc. *Hist.*); a person who drives livestock overland; *slang* a tramp.

In small-type subentries (as combinations or derivatives) labels of any kind precede the relevant definition or partial definition.

E.g. (s.v. BASE *n.*[1]) **base hit** *Baseball* a hit enabling the batter to reach a base safely.
(s.v. LOCAL *a.*) **local talent** the talented people or (*colloq.*) the attractive women or men of a particular locality.
(s.v. PUPPET *a.* & *n.*) **puppetish** *a.* (*rare*) pertaining to . . .
(s.v. JESSED) wearing jesses; *Her.* having jesses of a specified tincture.

Status labels precede any variant spelling or form to which they apply.

E.g. **kiln** /kɪln/ *n.* & *v.* Also (now *Sc.*) **kill** . . .

Interests of clarity may produce some variation of label positioning, particularly in subentries and individual parts of definitions.

Labels can be combined with other labels, of either the same or a different type. Combined subject and status labels are positioned as for the latter. Labels can also be qualified by words like 'Now' or 'Only'.

E.g. Now *rare* or *obs.*
Somewhat *derog.*
Chiefly *US.*
obs. exc. *Hist.*

These are largely self-explanatory. 'Long' (as in 'long *rare* or *obs.*') implies for several centuries, usually from before the eighteenth.

Certain italic labels can also be used to link or clarify the relationship between (parts of) definitions, e.g. *esp.*, *spec.*, *fig.*, *gen.*, *transf.* The abbreviations used in these labels also appear in other contexts. (The specification *esp.* is in italics if it introduces a complete definition, but in romans if introducing a parenthetical part of a larger definition.)

4.5.2. *Status symbols.* Two symbols are used to express status: a dagger (†) and an asterisk (*).

The dagger indicates that a word, sense, form, or construction is obsolete. It is placed before the relevant word(s) or relevant sense number.

The asterisk indicates that a spelling or form is now used primarily in the United States, and elsewhere where US spelling conventions are followed. The asterisk does not exclude the possibility that the form was standard or common in British use in the past. It is placed before the form it qualifies.

E.g. (s.v. FAVOURITE) Also ***favorite**.

Very occasionally an American pronunciation is given, in which case an asterisk is similarly used.

4.6 VARIANT SPELLINGS

If a headword has a significant alternative spelling, this is given, in bold type, before the date (and inflection if appropriate) at the top of the entry. Variants are generally preceded by 'Also', or sometimes 'Orig.', and are often further qualified in some respect.

E.g. **defence** ... *v.t.* Also **defense**.
locale ... *n.* Also †**local**.
jaunty ... *a.* Also (earlier) †**janty**.
disc ... *n.* Also (*US* & *Computing* now the usual form) **disk**.
set ... *n.*[1] Also (now chiefly in senses 16, 23, 24, 32, 33) **sett**.

Frequently the difference from the headword is highlighted by abbreviating the variant to the significant part, the missing part(s) being indicated by a hyphen.

E.g **emigre** ... *n.* Also **é-**.
dislikeable ... *a.* Also **-likable**.
Amerikan ... *a.* Also **-kkk-**.

If a variant form is current and has a different pronunciation from the headword, this is given.

E.g. **McCoy** /məˈkɔɪ/ *n.* ... Also **Mackay** /məˈkʌɪ/.

Variants differing only in initial capitalization are not usually given except for proprietary terms, for nouns from modern German, and for words passing into names or titles. If the capitalization difference applies only to certain senses, it can be specified under those senses.

E.g. **La** /la/ *a.* (*def. article*). Also **la**.
(s.v. BEAUTY *n.* 1) **b** (**B-**.) This quality personified.

Many compounds can be (or, in the past, have been) written in several different ways: as two or more words, hyphenated, or (increasingly) as one solid word. In most cases one form (the usual modern form) is given, but this does not mean that the others are unacceptable or even, in some cases, uncommon.

This dictionary follows the tradition of Oxford University Press in using *-ize* (and corresponding *-ization*, *-izer*, etc.) rather than *-ise* for verbs (and corresponding nouns etc.) derived from Greek *-izein* or Latin *-izare*, and for words modelled on these forms. The *-s-* variants are specified for headwords and are to be assumed for derivatives.

Variants with the ligatures *æ* and *œ* are to be assumed for words (usually of classical origin) written in this dictionary with *ae* and *oe*.

Not all possible variants (current or obsolete) of a headword are listed, but only those of particular significance. Among these are variants which are used in the works of a major author (such as Shakespeare), variants which are important for the development or current spelling of the headword or for the etymology of another word, obsolete variants which were widely current up to the modern period, and current variants which are usual in the United States.

A variant entry in the main alphabetical sequence cross-refers the user to the full entry for the word except where the two would be immediately adjacent (see further under 8 below).

4.7 INFLECTIONS

Three kinds of inflected forms may be specified:

1. plurals of nouns (and very occasionally of French adjectives)
2. forms of verbs (according to person, tense, aspect, etc.)
3. comparatives and superlatives of adjectives.

Inflections are specified only if they are unpredictable or irregular in some way, or if there are several alternative inflections for one headword.

4.7.1 *Nouns.* No plural form is given for nouns which simply add *-s* or (in the case of those ending in *-s*, *-x*, *-z*, *-sh*, or soft *-ch*, or in *-j*) *-es*, including those in which final *-y* inflects as *-ies*. Other plural forms are specified, and they include those for:

nouns ending in *-o* (as the plural may vary between *-os* and *-oes*);

nouns ending in Latinate forms such as *-a* and *-um*;
nouns with more than one plural form;
nouns whose plural involves a change in the stem (as **foot, feet**);
nouns whose plural and singular are the same (as **sheep**; in such cases the formula used is 'Pl. same').

'Pl. pronounced same' with no specified form implies a regular inflection.

4.7.2 *Verbs*. Inflections which are regarded as regular and are not specified are (i) third person singular forms adding *-s* or *-es* (when the stem ends in *-s*, *-x*, *-z*, *-sh*, or soft *-ch*), including most of those in which *-y* inflects as *-ies*; (ii) past tenses and past participles adding *-ed* and, where appropriate, dropping a final silent *-e*, (as **changed, walked**); (iii) present participles adding *-ing* and, again where appropriate, dropping a final silent *-e* (as **changing, walking**); (iv) regular archaic *-est* and *-eth* in older verbs. Other inflections are specified, and they include:

inflections where a final consonant is doubled (as **bat, batted, batting**; in such cases the formula used is 'Infl. **-tt-**');
inflections for the past tense and past participle which involve a change in the stem (as **drink, drank, drunk** and **go, went, gone**).

4.7.3 *Adjectives*. Adjectives which add *-er* and *-est* to form the comparative and superlative, including those which drop a final silent *-e* (e.g. **braver, bravest**), or replace a final *-y* by *-i-* (e.g. **happier, happiest**), are regarded as regular and their inflections are not specified. Single-syllable adjectives which double a final consonant (as **hot, hotter, hottest**) do have their inflections specified (the formula used is 'Compar. & superl. **-tt-**'), as do adjectives with irregular inflections (as **good, better, best**).

4.7.4 Inflected forms are given in bold type, usually at the top of the entry before the date. Frequently only the part of a form which differs from the headword is specified. Pronunciations are not given for the most regular forms. The pronunciations of *-ed*, *-s*, and *-es* vary according to the preceding letter(s) or sound(s): for fuller details see the entries for **-ed** *suff.*[1], **-s** *suff.*[1], and **-s** *suff.*[2]

E.g. **hoof** /huːf/ *n.* Pl. **hoofs, hooves** /huːvz/.
canephora /kəˈnɛf(ə)rə, -ˈniː-/ *n.* Pl. **-rae** /-riː/.
fly /flʌɪ/ *v.* Pa. t. **flew** /fluː/; pa. pple **flown** /fləʊn/.
learn /ləːn/ *v.* Pa. t. & pple **learned** /ləːnd/, **learnt** /ləːnt/.
learned ... *a.* Compar. (*arch.*) **learneder**; superl. (*arch.*) **learnedest**.

4.7.5 Inflectional information usually follows any variant forms, except where it does not apply to the variant(s).

E.g. **defer** /dɪˈfəː/ *v.*[1] Infl. **-rr-**. Also † **differ**.

If an entry has several parts of speech, and an inflection applies to only one of them, the inflection is usually specified at the beginning of the section for that part of speech.

E.g. **lasso** ... *n.* & *v.* ... A *n.* Pl. **-o(e)s**.

4.8 DATES

Provision of information about the age of all words included, and of their principal senses, is one of the distinctive features of this dictionary. The date of first (and, if relevant, last) recorded uses is given in terms of date ranges: after the Middle English period (and the introduction of printing) according to a tripartite division of centuries into early, middle, and late; in earlier times, where dating depends on less secure manuscript sources, according to broader divisions. The date ranges are defined and abbreviated as follows.

OE	Old English	-1149
LOE	late Old English	1000–1149
ME	Middle English	1150–1349 or, in some contexts, 1469
LME	late Middle English	1350–1469
L15	late fifteenth century	1470–1499
E16	early sixteenth century	1500–1529
M16	mid sixteenth century	1530–1569
L16		1570–1599
E17		1600–1629
M17		1630–1669
L17		1670–1699
E18		1700–1729
M18		1730–1769
L18		1770–1799
E19		1800–1829
M19		1830–1869
L19		1870–1899
E20		1900–1929
M20		1930–1969
L20		1970–

Every standard entry bears at least one date, indicating the earliest recorded use of the word. Combining entries are also sometimes individually dated for the combining form.

The word's earliest recorded date is given at the top of the entry, immediately before the etymology. Exceptions to this are Old English words which are presumed to be older than the written record (for example because of the existence of parallel words in other Germanic languages) or for which the exact Old English form is considered to be significant. In these cases OE (or Late OE) and a specified form begin the etymology and the date is not repeated immediately before the opening etymological bracket.

Old English words and senses are usually only specified as 'late' if use earlier in the period (for which written records are scarce) seems unlikely.

Every main numbered or lettered sense in the large-type section of an entry also bears a date, at the end of the definition and after any labels.

4.8.1 *Obsolete words and senses*. If a word or sense is obsolete, the date of its last recorded use is given, linked to the opening date by a dash (e.g. LME–E18). If an obsolete headword has only one sense, or if all senses have exactly the same period of currency, a final date is given with the opening date at the top of the entry. In other cases final dates are given after the opening dates at the end of each obsolete sense.

Currency for only one date range, or for one main period or century, is indicated by 'Only in'. For example, 'Only in L16', 'Only in ME' (either only between 1150 and 1349 or only in the Middle English period as a whole, 1150 to 1469), 'Only in 17' (in all three parts of the 17th century only). If a word or sense is current for two consecutive date ranges in the same century, the century is given only in the closing date, e.g. E-M17; M-L18.

4.8.2 *Dates for derivatives.* Derivatives at the end of a standard entry and in most combining entries are also dated. Each bears a single date of first (or, if obsolete, first and last) use at the end of its entry. The dates of individual senses or parts of speech are not distinguished.

4.9 ETYMOLOGY

All entries which are not simply variant entries contain etymological information, explaining the origin and formation of the headword. In standard entries and some combining entries, this information is generally placed in square brackets after the first date. In some combining entries and all letter entries the etymological information is not formally distinguished, but forms part of a general description of the head form.

Within an entry a particular sense or subentry may also have its own additional etymology.

Etymologies in square brackets frequently contain a great deal of information, usually in a highly abbreviated form. Recourse to the Abbreviations List will often clarify an etymology, but various conventions of presentation are used. This section aims to explain only those most likely to require clarification.

4.9.1 *Basic etymological forms and facts.* If a word is formed from one or more other words (as by contraction or combination, or by the addition of a prefix or suffix) the etymology gives the words from which it is formed and often explains the nature of the formation.

E.g. **Amerindian** ... *n.* ... [Contr. of *American Indian.*]
fatuous ... *a.* ... [f. L *fatuus* foolish ... + -OUS.]
initial ... *v.* ... [f. the n.]
jama ... *n.*[2] ... [Abbrev.] Pyjama.
matchmake ... *v.i.* ... [Back-form. f. MATCHMAKER *n.*]
outswinger ... *n.* ... [f. OUT- + SWINGER *n.*[1]]

If a word is an adoption from another language, the etymology opens with a specification of the language of origin and, if it differs from the English spelling of the headword, the form of the word in the foreign language.

E.g. **scandal** ... *n.* ... [(O)Fr. *scandale* ...]
bigot ... [Fr., of unkn. origin.]

'From' ('f.') is widely used to open etymologies where the headword is formed from several combined elements or from another headword. The formula 'f. as' (usually followed by a cross-reference) indicates that the headword is from the same principal or initial word as the other word mentioned.

E.g. **colotomy** ... [f. as COLON *n.*[1] + -TOMY.]—the etymology of **colon** *n.*[1] (L f. Gk *kolon*) is also valid for the *colo-* part of **colotomy.**

References to other headwords are in the usual cross-reference style of small capitals (see section 5), unless the headword is adjacent to the entry in question, when it is often referred to as 'prec.' (for 'preceding entry') or 'next' (for 'next entry').

A half bracket can be used to exclude part of a word in an etymology that is not represented in the headword.

E.g. **Politbureau** ... [Russ. *politbyuro*, f. *polit(icheskoe* political + *byuro* bureau.]

Foreign forms from languages which do not use the Roman alphabet (as Greek, Russian, Sanskrit, Hebrew, Arabic, and Chinese) are transliterated. The transliteration system used for Chinese is Pinyin, although the Wade-Giles transliteration is also given if it sheds light on the English form. Transliteration tables for Greek and Russian are on p. xxii.

4.9.2 *References and cross-references in etymologies.* Etymologies often contain cross-references to other entries, frequently at the end of the etymology, preceded by either 'see' or 'cf.'

E.g. **nitrogen** ... [Fr. *nitrogène*, f. as NITRO-: see -GEN.]
lecherous ... [OFr. *lecheros*, f. *lecheor*: see LECHER *n.*[1], -OUS.]
buffalo ... [Prob. immed. f. Port. **bufalo** ... Cf. BUFF *n.*[2], BUFFLE.]

If 'see' is used to refer to another entry, the etymology of the entry referred to directly extends or elaborates on the first etymology, and there is usually an identifiable point of contact, often a shared foreign form. For example in **lecherous** above there is a reference 'see LECHER *n.*[1]', and under **lecher** *n.*[1] the etymology runs [OFr. *lichiere* (nom.), *lecheor*, *-ur* (accus.), f. *lechier* live in debauchery ...]. The point of contact is the form *lecheor* and the etymology of **lecher** *n.*[1] contains more information about that form.

'Cf.' simply draws attention to some parallel or point of interest shared by etymologies.

A reference beginning 'See also' usually refers to a word derived from, or from the same source as, the headword.

4.10 DIVISIONS IN AN ENTRY

Every standard entry has a possible maximum of five hierarchical levels of formal sense division, though in practice two levels (those designated by bold arabic numerals and bold lower-case letters) are most frequent. The five levels are as follows:

A, B, etc.—Bold capital letters are used in entries with more than one part of speech, each of which is treated separately. The section for each is designated by a capital letter. A statement of the part(s) of speech being treated in that section immediately follows the letter: **A** *n.*, **B** *attrib.* or as *adj.*

I, II, etc.—Bold capital roman numerals are used to indicate major grammatical or semantic divisions of the same part of speech, especially in long or complex entries. The basis of the division may be specified after the roman numeral.

1, 2, etc.—Bold arabic numerals divide different basic meanings of the same part of speech. These are the most common sense divisions.

a, b, etc.—Within basic senses identified by arabic numerals, related subsenses are designated by bold lower-case letters. The first division, **a**, may be unmarked if further subsenses are subdivisions of or subordinate to the first definition.

(a), ***(b)***, etc.—Bold italic lower-case letters in brackets are used to designate minor divisions in a main sense and senses of phrases, derivatives, and other subentries.

The first, third, and fourth of these levels are individually dated, and the second is implicitly dated from the next following sense. Within each dated level senses and divisions are ordered chronologically. The dagger for obsolete uses is usually attached to the highest relevant sense level and not repeated for each of the ranks below.

4.11 GRAMMATICAL INFORMATION

Many definitions (and other parts of entries) contain grammatical information about the word being defined. Much of this information is straightforward, and this section aims only to explain some features which may require further clarification.

4.11.1 *Transitivity of verbs.* All verbs have a specification of transitivity, according to the two main categories transitive and intransitive: *v.t.* and *v.i.* Fully established uses of fundamentally transitive verbs with an object understood are in this dictionary classed as intransitive.

If a verb has the same transitivity in all its senses, a single indication of transitivity is given. This will be at the top of the entry beside the part of speech if the headword is a verb only, or has no part-of-speech divisions, and after a bold capital if the entry is divided into separate parts of speech. If transitivity varies among senses, it is shown after each relevant sense number or letter, before the definition. Possibilities are *v.t.*, *v.i.*, and, where the definition covers both transitive and intransitive uses, *v.t. & i.* or *v.i. & t.* (either the older or the more frequent being specified first).

Reflexive senses may be marked by *refl.*, alone if the verb is otherwise only transitive, as *v.refl.* if transitivity is mixed.

If a sense of a transitive verb occurs only in the passive, the definition is expressed in the passive form, preceded by 'in *pass.*'

If transitivity is the basis of major divisions within an entry, it is specified after each roman numeral, and not at the lower sense divisions.

4.11.2 *Plurality of nouns.* A use or sense of a noun may be specified as 'In *pl.*'. This means that the following definition relates to the plural form of the noun.

E.g. **acoustic** *n.*, sense 1 opens 'In *pl.*' and the definition which follows is of *acoustics*.
gubbin *n.*, sense 3 opens 'In *pl.* (treated as *sing.*)' and the definition which follows ('A fool') is of *gubbins*.

By contrast *pl.* alone implies no change of form (as in PEOPLE *n.*, **2 a** *pl.* The persons belonging to a particular place . . . , where the use defined is of *people* not *peoples*).

4.11.3 *Constructional information.* Many definitions contain information about the constructions which the headword takes or the contexts in which it is habitually used. Most of this information is in the form of self-explanatory statements of fixed or typical phrases, but in entries for verbs and for limited-set grammatical words (such as determiners) details can be more complex. Often the focus is on what the headword is followed by: either a general category of grammatical construction, for example 'w. double object' (as *envied her her job*), 'Foll. by inf. without *to*' (as *shall go*), or a particular word (especially an adverb or preposition) specified in italics, as 'Foll. by *out*'. In these contexts *to do* stands for any infinitive, *doing* stands for any gerund, and *that* stands also for object clauses without explicit *that* ('I said I would' as well as 'I said that I would').

Constructional information can appear before or after a definition, or can form an integral part of it. If the constructional statement precedes the definition, the definition is of the whole construction. If it follows the definition, the definition is of the headword only.

E.g. (s.v. LAY *v.*[1] 18) **b** *Naut.* Foll. by *aboard*: run into or alongside (a ship), usu. for boarding.
—the definition is of *lay aboard* and in this use *lay* is always followed by *aboard.*

(s. v. LIVE *v.*) **5** *v.i.* Continue in life . . . Also foll. by *on.*
—the definition is of *live* but *live on* means the same and is also covered.

(s.v. REFER *v.*) **2** Assign *to* a particular class . . .
—when *refer* means 'assign' it is always followed by *to.*

(s.v. ENCLOSE *v.*) **3** Surround with or *with* a wall, fence, etc.
—*enclose* means 'surround with a wall etc.' and may or may not be followed by a specifying phrase beginning *with.*

Following elements which occur frequently (but not always) and which extend the meaning of the headword are shown in brackets or preceded by 'Also'.

E.g. (s.v. PRELUDE *v.* **2 b**) be introductory (*to*)
(s.v. LIKENESS) **4** The quality or fact of being like . . . (Foll. by *between, to,* † *with.*)
(s.v. RACKET *v.*[2]) **3** *v.i.* Make a racket, esp. by noisy movement. Also foll. by *about, along, around.*

Verbal transitivity can be qualified by constructional information.

E.g. (s.v. HARE *v.*) **2** *v.i. & t.* (w. *it*). Run or move with great speed.
—the verb is used either intransitively, or transitively in the form *hare it.*

(s.v. LICK *v.* 1) †**b** *v.t.* & *i.* (w. *of*, *on*). Lap with the tongue; drink, sip, (a liquid).

—*lick of* and *lick on* mean the same here as *lick* with a direct object.

4.12 USE OF BRACKETS

Brackets are used in many places and for many purposes, and this section does not cover all of these.

A specified direct object of a verb is bracketed.

E.g. (s.v. LIMB *v.t.*) 3 Remove branches from (a tree).

Definitions in such a form may, when the usage of the verb permits, be designated both transitive and intransitive. In such cases the intransitive definition is to be understood by mentally removing the brackets from around the direct object.

The referent of an adjective or subject of a verb is bracketed when it applies to only part of a sense or to a subsense.

E.g. (s.v. GREEN *a.*) 2 Covered with herbage or foliage; (of a tree) in leaf.

(s.v. GO *v.*) (*b*) (of a firearm etc.) explode.

(If the referent applies to a whole main sense it opens the definition and is followed by a colon.

E.g. (s.v. FOUL *a.*) 4 Of speech etc.: indecent, obscene.)

Brackets are frequently used in definitions to combine information and avoid repetition.

E.g. (s.v. CHEEP *n.*) A shrill feeble sound (as) of a young bird.

(s.v. LEAVE *v.*) 1 *v.t.* a (Arrange to) transfer possession of at one's death . . .

(s.v. COLOUR *n.*) 8 *Mining*. (A particle of) gold.

(s.v. BEEP *v.t.* & *i.*) (Cause to) emit a beep or beeps.

(s.v. MINNESOTAN *n.* & *a.*) (A native or inhabitant) of Minnesota . . .

(s.v. LACK *v.*) **lackland** *a.* & *n.* (designating) a person owning no land . . .

(s.v. COLOUR *n.*) **colour-wash** *n.* & *v.t.* (paint with) coloured distemper.

In such cases, separate definitions are obtained by including and excluding the bracketed section.

A clarifying or reinforcing part of a definition, which may be useful but is not essential, may also be bracketed.

E.g. (s.v. CYLINDER *n.*) 2 A (solid or hollow) body . . .

4.13 ILLUSTRATION BLOCKS

Any main definition section in an entry may be followed by a small-type paragraph containing illustrative quotations and phrases linked to individual senses.

4.13.1 *Illustrative quotations*. The purpose of the illustrative quotations is to complement the definitions by clarifying sense distinctions, illustrating constructions, and representing common collocations. Consequently, quotations are selective and many words and senses are not illustrated. The first quotation for any use is not the first known example.

All quotations in this dictionary are from published sources.

The first quotation included for any sense (when an entry has more than one sense) is preceded by the number (and letter) of that sense, in bold type. If an entry has more than one quotation for a sense, these are arranged in basically chronological order. If a quotation illustrates a type of usage not explicity covered by the definition, the quotation may be preceded by a qualification, such as *attrib.*:, *fig.*:.

The source of a quotation is given immediately before the quotation text. This is usually either an author (in small capitals except for true capitals) or a published newspaper, journal, etc. (in italics). No quotation from a periodical dates from before the nineteenth century, and the great majority are from the twentieth. With a few exceptions titles of individual works are given only for Shakespeare. Chapter and verse are given for books of the Bible.

E.g. (s.v. CHEER *n.*[1]) 6 *Times* The market took cheer . . and marked the shares up 3p.

(s.v. RAIN *v.*) 3 SHAKES. *Twel. N.* The rain it raineth every day.

(s.v. DISCIPLE *n.*) 1 AV *John* 20:20 Then were the disciples glad, when they saw the Lord.

Quotations specified 'OED' reproduce examples included in the *Oxford English Dictionary* but attributed to no particular source and usually described as 'Modern'. They belong to the late nineteenth or early twentieth century.

Omissions from quotations are indicated by ellipses.

See also the list of Authors and Publications Quoted.

4.13.2 *Other illustrative material*. Illustration blocks can also contain defined phrases and cross-references to phrases defined elsewhere. Typical or common types of uses of a headword may be illustrated by italic examples rather than quotations from specified sources.

E.g. (s.v. ANALYSIS) **1 in the final, last, ultimate, analysis** after all due consideration, in the end.

(s.v. BUTCHER *n.*) 1 FAMILY *butcher*.

(s.v. RHYME *n.*) 3 *double rhyme, eye rhyme, imperfect rhyme, treble rhyme*, etc.

4.14 PHRASES AND COMPOUNDS

Phrases and compounds (collectively referred to here as subentries) are usually included (either listed or defined) in small-type blocks in the main entry for one of their significant words. The small-type blocks in which they appear are located after a definition section and any illustration block. These blocks are of several kinds, and each has an italic heading, as

Phrases:
Comb.:
Attrib. & comb.:
Special collocations: (only of adjectives)
With advs. (or *preps.*) *in specialized senses*: (only of verbs)

or some combination of these. Within such blocks subentries are in alphabetical order. Defined items are in bold type, and there may also be cross-references to similar phrases containing the headword but defined under another entry (see section 5). Subentries in these blocks are not dated. Separate senses or parts of speech of a subentry can be divided by a bracketed bold italic lower-case letter: ***(a)***, ***(b)***, etc. Any status labels and symbols at the top of an entry apply also to the subentries in these blocks.

4.14.1 *Phrases*. Phrases can appear in several places in an entry: in a small-type block headed *Phrases*:, in an illustration block (see 4.13.2), in a main definition, or (occasionally) in another subentry block as a phrase of a compound. The examples below illustrate the latter two of these:

(s.v. KIBOSH *n.*) 1 *put the kibosh on*, put an end to, dispose of finally.

(s.v. LEG *n.*) **leg-of-mutton** *a.* resembling a leg of mutton, esp. in shape; *leg-of-mutton sail*, a triangular mainsail; *leg-of-mutton sleeve*, . . .

Phrases are usually treated in the entry for their first significant word, but if a later word in the phrase has particular importance, the phrase can be treated under that word.

E.g. **ship of the line** is treated under LINE *n.*[2], not under SHIP *n.*

4.14.2 *Combinations*. A combination is a compound (usually a two-word compound) the first element of which is the headword. A combination most often consists of two nouns, but may also be made up of a noun and some other part of speech (especially an adjective), a verb plus a noun object or adverb, or an adjective plus any part of speech other than a (separately written) noun (when the formation is classed as a special collocation: see 4.14.3 below). If a combination is a noun only, no part of speech is given. Otherwise a part of speech is specified.

If a noun is particularly frequently used attributively in a certain manner or sense, a combination paragraph may be headed *Attrib.* & *comb.*:, and may open with a statement of the headword's attributive use(s) and some italic examples.

E.g. (s.v. LAND *n.*[1]) *Attrib.* & *comb.*: In the senses . . 'situated or taking place on land . .', 'living on land . .', as *land-battle*, *-bird*, . . *-journey*, *-monster* . . etc. Special combs., as **land-agency** . . .

If the first word of the definition of a combination would simply repeat the second word of the combination, a colon may be subsituted.

E.g. (s.v. CREAM *n.*[2]) **cream bun, cake**: filled with cream.

4.14.3 *Special collocations*. A special collocation is a compound (written as two words) consisting of an adjective (the headword) and a following noun used in a fixed way or in a way which is not simply determinable from the separate meanings of its two elements.

No part of speech is given; all special collocations are nouns.

4.14.4 *Verbs with adverbs/prepositions in specialized senses*. A verbal phrase consisting of a verb headword plus a preposition or adverb, whose meaning is not simply the sum of its parts, has a 'specialized sense', and such phrases may be treated (in verb entries) in a small-type block headed

With advs. in specialized senses:
With preps. in specialized senses:
With advs. & preps. in. specialized senses:
etc.

Adverbs in such verbal constructions are sometimes referred to in grammatical literature as 'particles', and with transitive verbs can typically both precede and follow a direct object: *phone her up*, *phone up her father*.

A small-type block like this is normally created only when the uses with adverbs or prepositions are numerous. Isolated or specific examples can be treated under numbered senses or in an illustration block.

E.g. (s.v. LIGHT *v.*[1]) 4 *v.t.* & *i. Naut.* Move or lift (a sail etc.) *along* or *over*.

11 *v.i.* Foll. by *out*: depart, get out.

Transitivity for items in these blocks is not usually specified unless a definition is ambiguous or transitivity varies among senses.

4.15 NOTES

Information of relevance or interest, usually relating to a whole entry, which does not fit obviously into the normal entry structure appears in a small-type note at the end of an entry (but before any derivative block). Such a note opens with a paragraph sign ¶.

Notes can be on a range of subjects, including dating, pronunciation, etymology, usage, and other relevant entries.

E.g. (s.v. SERENDIPITY) ¶ Rare bef. 20.

(s.v. PORT *n.*[1]) ¶ See also CINQUE PORTS.

(s.v. LUNCH *n.* & *v.*) ¶ As a synonym of LUNCHEON *n.* 2, *v.*, now the usual word exc. in specially formal use & in certain combs., though formerly objected to as vulgar.

4.16 DERIVATIVES

A derivative is formed by adding a suffix (such as *-able*, *-ly*, *-ness*) to a word. Many such formations are treated as main entries, but many others, especially if they are fairly simple, with few senses and without further derivatives or compounds of their own, are placed in a small-type derivative block at the end of an entry.

A derivative block always comes last in its entry. Derivatives themselves are in bold type and always have a part of speech and one date, but regular formations with readily deducible meanings (e.g. those with the adverbial suffix *-ly* or the noun suffix *-ness*) may be left undefined.

Derivatives appear in alphabetical order. Alphabetically adjacent items with the same part of speech, definition, and date may be combined.

E.g. (s.v. METAPSYCHICS) **metapsychic(al)** *adjs.* E20.

(s.v. NEW JERSEY) **New Jerseyan, New Jerseyite** *ns.* a native or inhabitant of New Jersey M20.

If a derivative is divided into formal senses or parts of

speech, or if it has a compound definition (i.e. its definition contains a semicolon), its date is separated from its definition(s) by a colon.

A variant of a derivative may be given after the main form, abbreviated to its differing element.

E.g. (s.v. CONTEST *v.*) **contester, -or** *n.* a person who contests L19.

As long as historically appropriate, any variant spellings specified for the headword occur also in its derivatives. Status and subject labels given at the top of an entry and applying to all its senses are assumed also to apply to any derivatives.

A derivative preceded by 'Also' is a synonym of the headword.

E.g. (s.v. CONVALESCENCE) Also **convalescency** *n.* (*rare*) M17.

Minor words which are not formal derivatives of the headword but which are etymologically related to it may also be included in the derivative block.

Derivatives are cross-referred to in small capitals (the same style as for headwords).

For pronunciation of derivatives see section 4.2.6.

5 Cross-references

A standard style is used in this dictionary to refer from one dictionary entry to another. For main entries and derivatives (including words defined within combining entries) the word being referred to is represented in small capitals (though any true large capitals are retained). The part(s) of speech may follow in italics (with any homonym number), and a particular branch or sense number may be specified.

E.g. À LA CARTE
FREE *a.*
ORTHOPTER I
POST *n.*²

Phrases, combinations, and special collocations which constitute cross-references are given in italic type. Direction to the entry or subentry at which the definition appears is made explicitly by 'see' or implicitly (when the direction is to a unique head form and no individual sense number) by printing the relevant headword or derivative in small roman capitals in context within the italic phrase.

E.g. *abjure the realm*: see ABJURE 3.
FLANDERS *poppy*.

Explicit cross-references may be made from one subentry to another. The subentry to which direction is made appears in italics followed by 's.v' (when reference is to another entry) or 'above' or 'below' (when reference is to another subentry or sense within the same entry).

E.g. *catch cold*: see *catch a cold* above.
Cornish moneywort: see *moneywort* s.v. MONEY *n.*

A definition may consist of an equation of one word, sense, or phrase with another. An equals sign is followed by a small capital or italic cross-reference, as described above.

E.g. (s.v COON *n.*) **1** = RACOON.
(s.v. FIN *n.*¹) **fin-back** = *fin whale* below.
(s.v. GUN *n.*) **6** = *electron gun* s.v. ELECTRON *n.*²
(s.v. LINE *n.*² 17) **c** A particular policy .. which a politician may maintain or expect others to follow; = *party line* s.v. PARTY *n.*

When a cross-reference constitutes the only definition, the item cross-referred to is the more common or important one in that sense.

A cross-reference simply to a headword or part of speech equates the item being defined with all senses of that referred to.

6 Combining entries

In combining entries the headword is an affix, either beginning or ending with a hyphen and generally used joined to another word. Combining entries treat affixes of three types: suffixes, prefixes, and combining forms.

The dividing line between prefixes and combining forms is not always clear cut, and for ordering and cross-reference purposes they are regarded as a single part of speech. In this dictionary combining forms generally represent either (i) modified forms of independent words in English or the source language, often in, or in imitation of, Latin and Greek forms and ending in *-i-* or *-o-* (e.g. **Anglo-**, **auto-**) or (ii) identical and closely related independent English words combining more or less freely with others and in combination not always readily differentiable one from the other (e.g. **after-**, **back-**). All other initial word-forming elements are classed as prefixes (e.g. **ex-**, **non-**, **re-**).

7 Letter entries

Each of the twenty-six letters of the alphabet is treated in its own entry. These entries contain the majority of the abbreviations included in this dictionary.

The headword consists of an upper- and lower-case representation of the initial letter, separated by a comma.

E.g. **A, a.**

The headword is followed by a pronunciation and a description and brief history of the letter.

This is typically followed by three branches: the first covering senses relating to the letter itself and to its shape or size; the second covering symbolical uses; the third containing a selection of abbreviations which begin with the letter. These abbreviations appear in alphabetical order in bold type. Each abbreviation is followed by an equals sign (any label applying to all the expansions appears in brackets before the equals sign). The expansions of each abbreviation follow the equals sign, also in alphabetical order.

E.g. (s.v. V, v) **VC** = Vice-Chairman; Vice-Chancellor; Vice-Consul; Victoria Cross; Viet Cong.

Some digraphs and ligatures, such as **ch**, **ph**, **æ**, and **œ**, are also included as headwords.

8 Variant entries

Variant spellings or inflectional forms specified at the top of an entry will usually also be mentioned in their proper alphabetical sequence. Exceptions are those which would be alphabetically adjacent to the headword, noun plurals in *-os* or *-oes*, regular inflections specified because there is an (irregular) alternative, inflections deducible from statements of consonant doubling, and inflections stated to be the same as those of the root (as in the case of some minor or obsolete words, such as † **acknow** which is 'Infl. as KNOW *v.*').

In a variant entry the headword (in bold) is referred to the word under which it is mentioned (in small capitals) by means of the direction 'see' or by means of a statement of its relationship with the word referred to, as 'var. of', 'pa. t. & pple of'.

If a form is obsolete or foreign, this is reflected in the variant entry by a dagger or italicization as appropriate. Other qualifications are restricted to the main entry, which the user is directed to 'see'.

Headwords in variant entries may be combined if they are alphabetically adjacent and are for the same entry or for several correspondingly adjacent entries. If many related words share the same spelling variation, not all will necessarily be listed in the variant entry.

E.g. **honyock, honyocker** *ns.* vars. of HUNYAK.
labored *a.*, **laborer** *n.*, **laboring** *a.* see LABOURED *a.* etc.
serjeant, -antcy, *ns.*, etc., vars. of SERGEANT etc.

Variant entries which are homonyms follow all the main entries for that homonym.

TRANSLITERATION

TRANSLITERATION OF GREEK

a	α	i	ι	ō	ω	t	τ
b	β	k	κ	p	π	th	θ
d	δ	kh	χ	ph	φ	u	υ
e	ε	l	λ	ps	ψ	x	ξ
ē	η	m	μ	r	ρ	z	ζ
g	γ	n	ν	rh	ῥ		
h	ʽ (rough breathing) over a following vowel	o	ο	s	σ, ς		

TRANSLITERATION OF RUSSIAN

a	а	i	и	r	р	ya	я
b	б	ĭ	й	s	с	yu	ю
ch	ч	k	к	sh	ш	z	з
d	д	kh	х	shch	щ	zh	ж
e	е	l	л	t	т	ʼ	ь
é	э	m	м	ts	ц	ʺ	ъ
ë	ё	n	н	u	у		
f	ф	o	о	v	в		
g	г	p	п	y	ы		

ABBREVIATIONS AND SYMBOLS

In this list the abbreviations are printed in the type and with the capitalization that is normally used for them, but variation according to context will be found. Some general abbreviations, such as those for units of measurement or points of the compass, are not listed here, but can be found under the main dictionary entry for the initial letter.

a.	adjective
abbrev.	abbreviated, abbrevation (of)
abbrevs.	abbreviations
abl.	ablative
abl. absol.	ablative absolute
Aborig.	Aboriginal
absol.	in absolute use, absolutely
accus.	accusative
act.	active, -ly
adj.	adjective, adjectival
adjs.	adjectives
adv.	adverb
advb.	adverbial, -ly
advs.	adverbs
Aeronaut.	Aeronautics
Afk.	Afrikaans
Afr.	African, Africa
agent-n(s).	agent-noun(s)
Agric.	Agriculture
AL	Anglo-Latin
Alch.	Alchemy
allus.	allusion
allus.	allusively
alt.	altered, alteration
Amer.	American, America
AN	Anglo-Norman
anal.	analogy
Anat.	Anatomy
Anglo-Ind.	Anglo-Indian
Anglo-Ir.	Anglo-Irish
Ant. & Cl.	Antony and Cleopatra
Anthropol.	Anthropology
Antiq.	Antiquities
aphet.	aphetic, aphetized
app.	apparently
approx.	approximately
Arab.	Arabic
Aram.	Aramaic
arch.	archaic
Archaeol.	Archaeology
Archit.	Architecture
assim.	assimilated, -ation
assoc.	associated, -ation
Assyr.	Assyrian
Astrol.	Astrology
Astron.	Astronomy
Astronaut.	Astronautics
attrib.	attributive, -ly
Attrib. & comb.	in attributive uses and combinations
augm.	augmentative
Austral.	Australian, Australia
aux.	auxiliary (verb etc.)
AV	Authorized Version
Avest.	Avestan
A.Y.L.	As You Like It
back-form(s).	back-formation(s)
Bacteriol.	Bacteriology
Balto-Slav.	Balto-Slavonic
bef.	before
Bibliogr.	Bibliography
Biochem.	Biochemistry
Biol.	Biology
Bot.	Botany
Brit.	British
Burm.	Burmese
c	*circa*, 'about'
Campanol.	Campanology
Canad.	Canadian
Canad. Polit.	Canadian Politics
cap(s).	capital(s)
Catal.	Catalan
Celt.	Celtic
cent.	century
cents.	centuries
cf.	*confer*, 'compare'
Ch.	Church
Chem.	Chemistry
Chin.	Chinese
Chr. Ch.	Christian Church
Chr.L	Christian Latin
Chron.	Chronicles
Chr. Theol.	Christian Theology
Cinemat.	Cinematography
cl.	clause
Class.	Classical
Class. Antiq.	Classical Antiquities
Class. Archit.	Classical Architecture
Class. Hist.	Classical History
Class. Mythol.	Classical Mythology
Class. Pros.	Classical Prosody
cl.Gk	classical Greek
cl.L	classical Latin
cogn. (w.)	cognate (with)
Col.	Colossians
collect.	collective, -ly
colloq.	colloquial, -ly
comb. (form)	combining (form)
Comb.	(in) combination
combs.	combinations
Com. Err.	Comedy of Errors
Comm.	Commerce, Commercial
compar(s).	comparative(s)
compl.	complement
Conchol.	Conchology
conf. (w.)	confused with
conj.	conjunction, conjunctive
conjs.	conjunctions
conn. (w.)	connected (with)
contempt.	contemptuous, -ly
contr.	contracted, contraction
Cor.	Corinthians
Coriol.	Coriolanus
Corn.	Cornish
correl.	correlative
corresp.	corresponding
corrupt.	corruption
cross-refs.	cross-references
Cryst.	Crystallography
Cymb.	Cymbeline
Cytol.	Cytology
d.	died
Da.	Danish
Dan.	Daniel
dat.	dative
def.	definite
demonstr.	demonstrative
deriv(s).	derivative(s), derivation(s)
derog.	derogatory
Deut.	Deuteronomy
devel.	development
dial.	dialect, dialectal, -ly
Dicts.	(in) Dictionaries
dim(s).	diminutive(s)
distrib.	distributive
Du.	Dutch
E	early (in dates)
Eccl.	Ecclesiastical
Eccles.	Ecclesiastes
eccl.Gk	ecclesiastical Greek
Eccl. Hist.	Ecclesiastical History
eccl.L	ecclesiastical Latin
Ecclus	Ecclesiasticus
Ecol.	Ecology
Econ.	Economics
Educ.	Education, -al
EFris.	East Frisian
EGmc	East Germanic
Egyptol.	Egyptology

Electr.	Electricity
Electr. Engin.	Electrical Engineering
elem(s).	element(s)
ellipt.	elliptical, -ly
Embryol.	Embryology
Encycl. Brit.	Encyclopaedia Britannica
Eng.	English
Eng. Hist.	English History
Engin.	Engineering
Entomol.	Entomology
Eph.	Ephesians
equiv.	equivalent
erron.	erroneous, -ly
Esd.	Esdras
esp.	especially
etym.	etymology
euphem.	euphemistic, -ally
exc.	except
exclam(s).	exclamation(s)
Exod.	Exodus
exp	exponential
expr.	expressing, expressive of
Ezek.	Ezekiel
f.	from
f. as	from the same (initial or principal) word as
fem.	feminine
fig.	in figurative use, figuratively
Finn.	Finnish
fl.	*floruit*, 'flourished'
Flem.	Flemish
foll.	followed
Fortif.	Fortification
Fr.	French
Frank.	Frankish
freq.	frequent, -ly
frequent.	frequentative
Fr. Hist.	French History
Fris.	Frisian
G	German (language)
Gael.	Gaelic
Gal.	Galatians
gen.	general, -ly
Gen.	Genesis
genit.	genitive
Geogr.	Geography
Geol.	Geology
Geom.	Geometry
Ger.	German
Gk	Greek
Gk Antiq.	Greek Antiquities
Gk Archaeol.	Greek Archaeology
Gk Archit.	Greek Architecture
Gk Gram.	Greek Grammar
Gk Hist.	Greek History
Gk Mythol.	Greek Mythology
Gk Orthodox Ch.	Greek Orthodox Church
Gk Pros.	Greek Prosody
Gk Rhet.	Greek Rhetoric
Gmc	Germanic
Goth.	Gothic
Gram.	Grammar
Hab.	Habbakuk
Haml.	Hamlet
Haw.	Hawaiian
Heb.	Hebrew
Heb.	Hebrews
Heb. Gram.	Hebrew Grammar
Hen.	Henry
Her.	Heraldry
HG	High German
Hind.	Hindustani
Hist.	Historical, History
Histol.	Histology
Hist. Sci.	History of Science
Hort.	Horticulture
hyperbol.	hyperbolically
Icel.	Icelandic
Ichthyol.	Ichthyology
IE	Indo-European
imit.	imitative, -ly
immed.	immediately
imper.	imperative, -ly
impers.	impersonal, -ly
indef.	indefinite, -ly
indic.	indicative
inf.	infinitive
infl.	inflected, influenced
Inorg. Chem.	Inorganic Chemistry
instr.	instrumental
int.	interjection
interrog.	interrogative, -ly
intrans.	intransitive, -ly
ints.	interjections
Ir.	Irish
Ir. Antiq.	Irish Antiquities
Ir. Hist.	Irish History
Ir. Mythol.	Irish Mythology
iron.	ironical, -ly
irreg.	irregular, -ly
Isa.	Isaiah
It.	Italian
Jap.	Japanese
Jav.	Javanese
Jer.	Jeremiah
joc.	jocular, -ly
Josh.	Joshua
Judg.	Judges
Jul. Caes.	Julius Caesar
L	Latin
L	late (in dates)
Lam.	Lamentations
lang(s).	language(s)
Law L	Law Latin
Ld	Lord
LDu.	Low Dutch
Lev.	Leviticus
LG	Low German
Ling.	Linguistics
lit.	literal, -ly
lit. & fig.	in literal and figurative use, literally and figuratively
Lith.	Lithuanian
L.L.L.	Love's Labour's Lost
LME	late Middle English
LOE	late Old English
Lucr.	Lucrece
M	Middle (before language names)
M	mid (in dates)
(M)	Middle and Modern (before language names)
Macb.	Macbeth
Macc.	Maccabees
masc.	masculine
Math.	Mathematics
Matt.	Matthew
MBret.	Middle Breton
MDa.	Middle Danish
MDu.	Middle Dutch
(M)Du.	Middle and Modern Dutch
ME	Middle English
Meas. for M.	Measure for Measure
Mech.	Mechanics
Med.	Medicine
med.	medieval
med.Gk	medieval Greek
med.L	medieval Latin
Merch. V.	Merchant of Venice
Merry W.	Merry Wives (of Windsor)
Metall.	Metallurgy
Meteorol.	Meteorology
Mex.	Mexican
Mex. Sp.	Mexican Spanish
MFlem.	Middle Flemish
(M)Flem.	Middle and Modern Flemish
MHG	Middle High German
(M)HG	Middle and Modern High German
Microbiol.	Microbiology
Mids. N. D.	Midsummer Night's Dream
Mil.	Military
Min.	Mineralogy
MIr.	Middle Irish
(M)Ir.	Middle and Modern Irish
mistr.	mistranslation (of), mistranslating
MLG	Middle Low German
(M)LG	Middle and Modern Low German
mod.	modern
mod.Da.	modern Danish
mod.Du.	modern Dutch
mod.Fr.	modern French
mod.G	modern German

mod.Gk modern Greek
mod.Heb. modern Hebrew
mod.Icel. modern Icelandic
mod.Ir. modern Irish
mod.L modern Latin
mod.Prov. modern Provençal
mod.Skt modern Sanskrit
MSw. Middle Swedish
(M)Sw. Middle and Modern Swedish
Mus. Music
Mycol. Mycology
Mythol. Mythology

n. noun
N. Afr. North Africa(n)
N. Amer. North America(n)
N. Amer. Hist. North American History
Naut. Nautical
NEB New English Bible
neg. negative
neut. neuter
NFris. Northern Frisian
N. Ir. Northern Ireland, Irish
nom. nominative
north. northern
north. northern (dialect)
Northumb. Northumbrian
Norw. Norwegian
ns. nouns
Num. Numbers
Numism. Numismatics
NZ New Zealand

O Old (before language names)
(O) Old and Modern (before language names)
Obad. Obadiah
obj. object, -ive
obl. oblique
obs. obsolete
occas. occasional, -ly
Oceanogr. Oceanography
OCorn. Old Cornish
(O)Corn. Old and Modern Cornish
OE Old English
OED Oxford English Dictionary
OFr. Old French
(O)Fr. Old and Modern French
OFris. Old Frisian
OHG Old High German
(O)HG Old and Modern High German
OIr. Old Irish
(O)Ir. Old and Modern Irish
OIt. Old Italian
(O)It. Old and Modern Italian
OL Old Latin
Old Ch. Slav. Old Church Slavonic
OLFrank. Old Low Frankish
OLG Old Low German
ON Old Norse
ONFr. Old Northern French
(O)NFr. Old and Modern Northern French
OPers. Old Persian
Ophthalm. Ophthalmology
OPol. Old Polish
opp. opposed (to)
OProv. Old Provençal
OPruss. Old Prussian
Org. Chem. Organic Chemistry
orig. original, -ly
Ornith. Ornithology
ORuss. Old Russian
OS Old Saxon
OSp. Old Spanish
(O)Sp. Old and Modern Spanish
OSw. Old Swedish
Oth. Othello
OTurk. Old Turkish
OWelsh Old Welsh

pa. past
Palaeogr. Palaeography
Palaeont. Palaeontology
pa. ppl past (or passive) participial
pa. pple past (or passive) participle
pass. passive, -ly
pa. t. past tense
Per. Pericles
perf. perfect
perh. perhaps
pers. personal
Pers. Persian
Pet. Peter
Petrogr. Petrography
Pharm. Pharmacology
Phil. Philippians
Philol. Philology
Philos. Philosophy
Phonet. Phonetics
phonet. phonetic, -ally
Phonol. Phonology
Photogr. Photography
phr. phrase
Phrenol. Phrenology
phrs. phrases
Physiol. Physiology
pl. plural
pls. plurals
poet. poetical
Pol. Polish
Polit. Politics
pop. popular, -ly
pop.L popular Latin
Port. Portuguese
possess. possessive
ppl participial
ppl a. participial adjective
pple participle
prec. preceding (headword or main entry)
pred. predicate
pred. predicative, -ly
pred. a. predicative adjective
pref. prefix
prefs. prefixes
prep. preposition, -al
prep. preposition
preps. prepositions
pres. present
pres. ppl present participial
pres. pple present participle
pres. t. present tense
prob. probably
pron. pronominal, pronoun
pron. pronoun
prons. pronouns
pronunc. pronunciation
Pros. Prosody
Prov. Provençal
Prov. Proverbs
Ps. Psalms
Psychol. Psychology

RC Ch. Roman Catholic Church
redupl. reduplicated, -ation(s)
ref. reference
refash. refashioned, -ing
refl. reflexive
rel. relative
rel. related
repl. replaced, -ing
repr. representative (of), represented, representing, representation(s)
Rev. Revelation
Rhet. Rhetoric
rhet. rhetorical, -ly
Rich. Richard
Rom. Roman
Rom. Romans
Rom. & Jul. Romeo and Juliet
Rom. Antiq. Roman Antiquities
Rom. Hist. Roman History
Rom. Mythol. Roman Mythology
Russ. Russian
Russ. Hist. Russian History
RV Revised Version

S. Afr. South Africa(n)
Sam. Samuel
S. Amer. South America(n)
Sc. Scottish, Scots, Scotch
Scand. Scandinavian
Sc. Hist. Scottish History
Sci. Science
sci. scientific
Seismol. Seismology
Shakes. Shakespeare
sing. singular
Skt Sanskrit
Skt Gram. Sanskrit Grammar

Slav.	Slavonic
Sociol.	Sociology
S. of S.	Song of Solomon (or Songs)
Sonn.	Sonnets
sp.	spelling
Sp.	Spanish
spec.	specific, -ally
Stock Exch.	Stock Exchange
str.	strong
subj.	subject
subjunct.	subjunctive
subord. (cl.)	subordinate (clause)
subsp.	subspecies
suff.	suffix
suffs.	suffixes
superl.	superlative
Suppl.	Supplement
Surg.	Surgery
Sus.	Susanna
s.v.	*sub voce*, 'under the word'
Sw.	Swedish (language)
Swed.	Swedish
syll.	syllable
synon.	synonymous
t.	tense
Tam. Shr.	Taming of the Shrew
Taxon.	Taxonomy
techn.	in technical use
Telegr.	Telegraphy
Teleph.	Telephony
Temp.	Tempest
Theatr.	Theatrical
Theol.	Theology
Thess.	Thessalonians
Tib.	Tibetan
Tim.	Timothy
Times Lit. Suppl.	Times Literary Supplement
Tit.	Titus
Tit. A.	Titus Andronicus
tr.	translation (of), translating
Tr. & Cr.	Troilus and Cressida
trans.	transitive, -ly
transf.	transferred
transf. & *fig.*	transferred and figurative
Turk.	Turkish
Twel. N.	Twelfth Night
Two Gent.	Two Gentlemen (of Verona)
Typogr.	Typography
ult.	ultimate, -ly
unexpl.	unexplained
Univ.	University
Univs.	Universities
unkn.	unknown
US	United States
USA	United States of America
US Hist.	United States History
US Polit.	United States Politics
usu.	usually
v.	verb
var.	variant (of), variety
vars.	variants (of)
vb	verb
vbl	verbal
vbl n.	verbal noun
vbs	verbs
Ven. & Ad.	Venus and Adonis
Vet.	Veterinary
Vet. Med.	Veterinary Medicine
v.i.	intransitive verb
voc.	vocative
v.refl.	reflexive verb
vs.	verbs
v.t.	transitive verb
w.	with
wd(s)	word(s)
WFlem.	Western Flemish
WFris.	West Frisian
WGmc	West Germanic
W. Indies	West Indies
Wint. T.	Winter's Tale
Wisd.	Wisdom (of Solomon)
wk	weak
wk vb	weak verb
WS	West Saxon
Zech.	Zechariah
Zeph.	Zephaniah
Zool.	Zoology

Symbols

†	obsolete
*	now chiefly in the United States (see p. xv)
¶	introduces a note (see p. xx)

The printing of hyphens

Hyphens introduced at line-breaks in words or formulae not otherwise hyphenated are printed ‐.
The regular form - represents a hyphen which would occur in any circumstance in the text.

NOTE ON PROPRIETARY STATUS

THIS dictionary includes some words which have, or are asserted to have, proprietary status as trade marks. Their inclusion does not imply that they have acquired for legal purposes a non-proprietary or general significance or otherwise nor any other judgement concerning their legal status. In cases where the editorial staff have some evidence that a word has proprietary status this is indicated in the entry for that word but no judgement concerning the legal status of such words is made or implied thereby.

KEY TO THE PRONUNCIATION

Vowels

a	*as in*	cat, plait
ɛ		bed, death
ɪ		sit, myth, begin, theology
i		cosy, eerie, anemone, *Spanish* si
ɒ		hot, wash, trough
ʌ		run, son, glove, rough
ʊ		put, good, should, ambulance
ə		ago, gather, flavour, cheetah, thorough, lemon, success, mistaken
ɑː		arm, calm, locale, brahmin
əː		her, earn, bird, spur, myrrh
ɛː		hair, dare, pear, there, vary
iː		see, pea, seize, decent, foetus, paeon
ɔː		saw, ball, board, horse, thought, applaud
uː		too, glue, fruit, route, through, shrewd, rheum, lunatic

ʌɪ	*as in*	my, high, ice, sign, seismic, bonsai
aʊ		how, plough, sound, kraut
eɪ		day, gate, daisy, they, rein, deign, maelstrom, sachet
əʊ		no, cocoa, soul, roe, though, glow, beau, mauve, yeoman
ɪə		near, beer, theory, query, severe, emir, grenadier
ɔɪ		boy, spoil, Freudian
ʊə		poor, rural, dour, liqueur
ʌɪə		tire, byre, choir, quiet, diaphragm
aʊə		sour, flower, coward

ɑ	*as in*	*French* pas
e		*French* été, *Italian* verde
ɔ		*French* homme, *Italian* donna, *German* Gott
o		*French* eau, mot, *Italian* figlio
u		*French* tout
ø		*French* bleu, *German* spötteln
œ		*French* bœuf
y		*French* du, *German* fünf
eː		*German* Ehre
oː		*German* Boot
øː		*German* Höhle
œː		*French* douleur
yː		*German* Führer
aɪ		*German* ein, frei
ɔy		*German* Häuser

ː indicates length

~ indicates nasality

ɒ̃	*as in*	cordon bleu
ɒ̃ː		Lyons
ɑ̃		*French* en
ɑ̃ː		*French* blanche
ɛ̃		*French* vin
ɛ̃ː		*French* cinq
ɔ̃		*French* mon
ɔ̃ː		*French* monde
œ̃		*French* un

Consonants and Semivowels

b, d, f, h, k, l, m, n, p, r, s, t, v, w, z have their usual English values

g	*as in*	get, exact
tʃ		chip, ditch, cello, Czech, culture, question
dʒ		jar, hedge, urge, logic, gentle, privilege, soldier
ŋ		ring, bank, conquer, junction
θ		thin, throne, birth, health, tooth
ð		this, clothe, smooth, swarthy
ʃ		she, ash, chef, station, mission, spacious, herbaceous
ʒ		vision, erasure, aubergine, bourgeois
j		yes, tune, new, eulogy
x		loch, *German* ach, *Spanish* Rioja
ç		*German* nicht, Kirche
ʎ		*Spanish* olla, llamar, *Italian* gli
ɲ		*French* mignon, *Spanish* piña, *Italian* gnocco
ɥ		*French* nuit

Stress

ˈ indicates primary stress on the following syllable

ˌ indicates secondary stress on the following syllable

For further details see pp. xii–xiii

A

A, a /eɪ/, the first letter of the modern Eng. alphabet and of the ancient Roman one, corresp. to Gk *alpha*, Heb. *aleph*. The sound orig. represented by the letter, in Eng. as in L, was a low back vowel, articulated with the tongue as low as possible in the mouth, considerable separation of the jaws, and spreading of the lips. For its principal mod. sounds see the Key to the Pronunciation. Pl. **A's, As.**

I 1 The letter and its sound. **2** The shape of the letter.

1 A per se A by itself, esp. as a word; *fig.* the first, best, or unique person or thing. **A to Z** a comprehensive manual. **from A to Z** over the entire range, completely. **2 A-frame** (a house or other structure supported by) a frame shaped like a capital A. **A-line** (a garment) having a narrow waist or shoulders and a somewhat flared skirt. **A-shaped** *a.* having a shape or a cross-section like the capital letter A. **A tent** a tent with sides sloping down to the ground from a ridge pole.

II Symbolical uses. **3** Used to denote serial order; applied e.g. to the first group or section, sheet of a book, etc. **4** *Mus.* (Cap. A.) The sixth note of the diatonic scale of C major, or the first of the relative minor scale of C. Also, the scale of a composition with A as its keynote. **5** *Logic.* (Cap. A.) A universal affirmative proposition. **6** The first hypothetical person or example. **7** *Math.* (Usu. italic *a.*) The first known quantity. **8** (Usu. cap. A.) Designating the first or highest class (of road, academic marks, population as regards affluence, etc.). **9** (Cap. A.) The blood group characterized by the presence of the agglutinogen designated A and the absence of that designated B. **10** (Cap. A.) Designating a series of international standard paper sizes with a fixed shape and twice the area of the next size, as *A0, A1, A2, A3, A4*, etc. **11** *Anat.* & *Zool.* [Initial letter of *anisotropic.*] *A band*, a dark transverse band in a myofibril, consisting of interdigitating filaments of actin and myosin.

6 from A to B from any one place to some other place. **8 A No. 1** *US colloq.* excellent, first-rate. **A 1** in Lloyd's Register of Shipping, used of ships in first-class condition as to hull (A) and stores (1); *colloq.* excellent, first-rate. **A-side** (the music of) the more important side of a gramophone record. **A Special** *Hist.* a member of a full-time special police force in Northern Ireland. **9 AB** the blood group characterized by the presence of both A and B agglutinogens. **ABO** *a.* designating or pertaining to the system in which blood is divided into four types (A, AB, B, and O) on the basis of the presence or absence of certain inherited antigens.

III 12 Abbrevs.: (A small selection only is given here. Those all in caps. or small caps. also occur with a full stop after each letter; some of those all in caps. also occur (i) with initial cap. only, (ii) in small caps.) **A.** = Academician; Academy; Associate. **A** = (*Hist.*) adult (as a film classification); advanced (in *A level*, *A/S level*, of the General Certificate of Education examination); all (in *A-OK*, *A-okay* (colloq.) in perfect order or condition); ampere; atom(ic) (in *A-bomb* etc.). **a.** = accepted (on bills of exchange); active (of verbs); adjective; [L] *ante* before (with dates; also *a*). **a** = (as *pref.*) atto-. **Å** (*Physics*) = angstrom. **AA** = Alcoholics Anonymous; anti-aircraft; Automobile Association. **AAA** = Amateur Athletic Association; American or Australian Automobile Association; (*US*) anti-aircraft artillery. **A. & M.** = (Hymns) Ancient and Modern. **A. & R.** = artists and recording (or repertoire). **AAU** (*US*) = Amateur Athletic Union. **AB** = able (seaman); [L] *Artium Baccalaureus* Bachelor of Arts (*US*, cf. *BA*). **ABC** = American Broadcasting Corporation; Australian Broadcasting Corporation (formerly Commission). **ABH** = actual bodily harm. **ABM** = anti-ballistic missile. **ABS** = anti-lock braking system (for motor vehicles). **abt.** = about. **ABTA** /ˈabtə/ = Association of British Travel Agents. **AC** = air-conditioned (esp. in India); aircraftman; alternating current. **A/C** = account current. AC = [L] *ante Christum* before Christ. **a.c.** = alternating current. **Ac** (*Chem.*) = actinium. **ACAS** /ˈeɪkas/ = Advisory, Conciliation, and Arbitration Service. **AC/DC** = alternating current/direct current, *fig.* (*slang*) bisexual. **ACT** = Australian Capital Territory. **ACTH** = adrenocorticotrophic hormone. **ACV** = air-cushion vehicle. **ACW** = Aircraftwoman. AD = [L] *anno domini* in the year of our Lord, of the Christian era. **ADC** = aide-de-camp; analogue-digital converter. **ADH** = antidiuretic hormone. **ADP** = (*Biochem.*) adenosine diphosphate; automatic data processing. **AEEU** = Amalgamated Engineering and Electrical Union. **AEF** = American Expeditionary Forces (esp. in Europe during the war of 1914–18). **AEU** (*Hist.*) = Amalgamated Engineering Union. **AF** = audio frequency. **AFC** = Air Force Cross; Association Football Club. **AFM** = Air Force Medal. **AG** = Adjutant-General; Attorney-General. **Ag** (*Chem.*) = [L] *argentum* silver. **AGM** = annual general meeting. **AGR** = advanced gas-cooled (nuclear) reactor. **AH** = [L] *anno Hegirae* in the year of the Hegira (the Muslim era). **AI** = artificial insemination; artificial intelligence. **AID** = artificial insemination by donor. **AIH** = artificial insemination by husband. **AIR** = All-India Radio. **AK** = Alaska. **a.k.a.** = also known as. **AL** = Alabama; Anglo-Latin; autograph letter. **Al** (*Chem.*) = aluminium. **Ala.** = Alabama. **Alas.** = Alaska. **ALP** = Australian Labour Party. **ALS** = autograph letter signed. **Alta.** = Alberta. **ALU** (*Computing*) = arithmetic and logic unit. **AM** = amplitude modulation; [L] *Artium Magister* Master of Arts (*US*, cf. *MA*). AM = [L] *anno mundi* in the year of the world. **Am** (*Chem.*) = americium. **a.m.** = *ante meridiem*. **AMA** = American Medical Association. **AMDG** = [L] *ad maiorem Dei gloriam* to the greater glory of God. **AMGOT** = Allied Military Government of Occupied Territory, an organization first set up in Sicily during the war of 1939–45. **AMP** = adenosine monophosphate. **a.m.u.** = atomic mass unit. **AN** = Anglo-Norman. **ANC** = African National Congress. **ANZUS** = Australia, New Zealand, and United States (treaty). **AOB** = any other business (at the end of agenda for a meeting). **AOC** = [Fr.] *appellation d'origine contrôlée*. **APB** (*US*) = all-points bulletin. **API** = American Petroleum Institute (used *spec.* w. ref. to a scale for expressing the relative density of oil, with higher values corresponding to lower densities). **APL** = Associative Programming Language (a specific programming language). **Apoc.** = Apocalypse (New Testament); Apocrypha. **Apocr.** = Apocrypha. **APR** = annual percentage rate (of interest on money lent). **Apr.** = April. **APT** = Advanced Passenger Train. **AR** = Arkansas; Autonomous Republic. **Ar** (*Chem.*) = argon. **ARA** = Associate of the Royal Academy. **ARC** = Agricultural Research Council; (*Med.*) Aids-related complex. **Ariz.** = Arizona. **Ark.** = Arkansas. **ARP** = air-raid precautions. **AS** = Anglo-Saxon. **As** (*Chem.*) = arsenic. **A/S** = advanced supplementary (in *A/S level*, of the General Certificate of Education examination). **ASA** = Amateur Swimming Association; American Standards Association. **a.s.a.p.** = as soon as possible. **ASB** = Alternative Service Book (of the Church of England). **ASC** = Army Service Corps. **ASCII** /ˈaski/ = American Standard Code for Information Interchange. **ASEAN** /ˈasɪan/ = Association of South East Asian Nations. **ASH** = Action on Smoking and Health. **ASL** = American Sign Language. **ASLIB** = Association of Special Libraries and Information Bureaux. **ASM** = air-to-surface missile; assistant stage-manager. **ASSR** (*Hist.*) = Autonomous Soviet Socialist Republic. **Asst.** = Assistant. **AST** = Atlantic Standard Time. **At** (*Chem.*) = astatine. **ATC** = air traffic control; Air Training Corps. **ATM** = automated or automatic teller machine. **atm** = atmosphere. **ATP** (*Biochem.*) = adenosine triphosphate. **ATS** /*colloq.* ats/ = Auxiliary Territorial Service (for women in Britain, 1938–48); members of this. **attn.** = attention, for the attention of. **Atty.** = Attorney. **AU** = angstrom unit; astronomical unit. **Au** (*Chem.*) = [L] *aurum* gold. AUC = [L] *ab urbe condita* from the foundation of the city (of Rome, in 753 BC); [L] *anno urbis conditae* in the year of the founding of the city. **Aug.** = August. **AUT** = Association of University Teachers. **AV** = audiovisual; Authorized Version (of the Bible). **AVC** = additional voluntary contributions (to a pension scheme). **Ave.** = Avenue. **AWACS** /ˈeɪwaks/ (*Mil.*) = airborne warning and control system, an airborne long-range radar system for detecting other aircraft and controlling weapons directed against them. **AWOL** /*colloq.* ˈeɪwɒl/ = absent without (official) leave. **AZ** = Arizona. **AZT** (*Pharm.*) = azidothymidine.

a /ə/ *pron. obs.* exc. *dial.* ME. [Unstressed form of *ha* he, *heo* she, *hi* they, etc.] He, she, it, they.

SHAKES. *Haml.* Now 'a is a-praying. TENNYSON Doctors, they knaws nowt, for a says what's nawways true.

a /ə; *stressed* eɪ/ *a.* (usu. called the *indefinite article*; in mod. usage also classed as a *determiner*). Bef. a vowel sound (see below) **an** /ən; *stressed* an/. [OE *ān* one, weakened to proclitic form in early ME.] **I 1** One, some, any, (the oneness, or indefiniteness, being implied rather than asserted). OE. **b** One like. LME. **2** Bef. quantifiers: some, a matter of, about. *obs.* exc. *dial.* and in *a few*, *a great* (or *good*) *many*. OE. **3** A certain, a particular. ME. **b** A single; the same. M16.

1 SHAKES. *Wint. T.* I have . . said many A prayer upon her grave. KEATS I had a dove and the sweet dove died. C. TOMLINSON As good a student As any in the house. M. LASKI They had passed and repassed each other a dozen times. J. BETJEMAN In Ealing on a Sunday Bell-haunted quiet falls. **b** SHAKES. *Merch. V.* A Daniel come to judgment. TENNYSON Shall I weep if a Poland fall? **2** WILLIAM TURNER Stepe them a fiue or sixe dayes in vineger. **3** *Notes & Queries* It was popularized by a Mr. Trudgen. *once upon a time*. **b** SHAKES. *Haml.* These foils have all a length? E. DICKINSON I'll tell you how the Sun rose—A ribbon at a time.

II 4 In, to, or for, each. (Orig. the prep. *a*, OE *an*, *on*, defining time, as in twice *a* day; afterwards identified with the indef. article, and extended from time to space, measure, weight, number: see A *prep.*[1] 3.) OE.

4 DEFOE Four pieces of eight a man. YEATS But always went to chapel twice a week. *Oxford Times* Teams of six a side, each member of the one team fighting a duel with the six members of the other. J. STALLWORTHY Roast chestnuts, a shilling / a bag.

¶*An* is freq. bef. a consonant to end of 13, bef. sounded *h* until 18. In standard English *an* is now used bef. a vowel sound (including *h* mute), as *an egg*, *an honour*; *a* bef. a consonant (including sounded *h* and *eu-*, *u-* pronounced /jʊ, juː/) as *a pen*, *a host*, *a eunuch*, *a unit*. But bef. an unaccented syll., some retain *an* bef. sounded *h*, as *an historian*, a smaller number bef. *eu-*, *u-*, as *an university*.

a /ə/ *v.t.* & *i.* Now chiefly *slang*. ME. [Unstressed var.] = HAVE *v.* Freq. written joined to a preceding aux. vb, as *coulda*, *mighta* (= -A[5]).

¶Common 13-17. After 17 reduced HAVE *v.* was freq. written *ha*, *ha'*, though no *h* was pronounced.

a /ə/ *prep.*[1] *arch.* & *dial.* See also A-[2]. OE. [Unstressed form of ON *prep.*: cf. O' *prep.*[1]] = ON *prep.* in various senses current before the 18th cent. **1** Position or direction: on, on to, at, in, towards. OE. **2** Partition: in, into. OE. **3** Time: in, on, by. Esp. with advs. of repetition (taken as the indef. article: see A *a.* 4). OE. †**4** Manner: in, with. OE–L17. †**5** Capacity: in (someone's name). OE–E18. **6** State: in. OE. **7** Process (with a vbl n. taken pass.): in course of, undergoing. LME. **8** Action (with a vbl n. taken act.): **a** With *be*: engaged in. E16. **b** With a vb of motion: to, into. E16.

1 LD BERNERS The quene was brought a bedde. SHAKES. *Hen. V* Stand a tip-toe. C. TOURNEUR That's enow a' conscience! Compounds.: *aback*, *abed*, *aboard*, *afield*, *afoot*, *ashore*, etc. **2** SHAKES. *Hen. VIII* Torn a pieces. *asunder*. **3** CHAUCER Ful ofte a day. BUNYAN The bold villain . . haunts . . honest men's houses a nights. D. RUNYON A sure thing that is coming up a Monday. Compound.: *nowadays*. **4** C. MARLOWE Stands here a purpose. **5** SHAKES. *Rich. II* A God's name, let it go. **6** AV *2 Chron.* 2:18 To set the people a worke. Compounds.: *afloat*, *alive*, *asleep*, etc. **7** AV *1 Pet.* 3:20 When the Arke was a preparing. **8** ROBERT BURTON He would burst out a laughing. R. BENTLEY To set them a going. OED Such positions rarely go a begging.

a /ə/ *prep.*[2] Now chiefly *slang*. LME. [Var.] = OF *prep.* (cf. O' *prep.*[2]). Now freq. written joined to a preceding word, as *cuppa*, *kinda*, *loadsa*, *lotsa*, *lotta*, (= -A[6]).

a *int.* see AH *int.*

a' /ɔː/ *a.*, *n.*, & *adv.* *Sc.* Also †**a**; **aw** & other vars. LME. [Form of ALL, w. *l* vocalized.] = ALL.

a- /ə/ *pref.*[1] (not productive). OE *ā-*, orig. *ar-*, away, on, up, out, chiefly forming vbs, as *abide*, *arise*. Sometimes conf. w. A-[5].

a- /ə/ *pref.*[2] OE. [Proclitic var.] = A *prep.*[1]

a- /ə/ *pref.*[3] (not productive). OE. Reduced form of OE *of* off, from, of (see A *prep.*[2]), as *anew*.

a- /ə/ *pref.*[4] Now *dial.* ME. Reduced form of I-[1], Y- (f. OE *ġe-*). Also written as a separate word.

a- /ə/ *pref.*[5] (not productive). ME. Repr. Fr. *a-*, *à* f. L *ad(-)* w. the sense of motion to, change into, addition, or intensification, as *abandon*, *alarm*, *amass*, *avenue*: see AD-.

a- /ə/ *pref.*[6] (not productive). ME. Repr. Fr. *a-* f. L *ab(-)* off, away, from (see AB-), as *abridge*. Sometimes refash., as *abstain*, or conf. w. A-[5] and respelt, as *assoil*.

a- /ə/ *pref.*[7] (not productive). ME. Repr. AN *a-*, OFr. *e-*, *es-* f. L *ex-* out, utterly (see EX-[1]), as *abash*.

a- /ə/ *pref.*[8] (not productive). Repr. L *a-* reduced form of *ad-* bef. *sc*, *sp*, *st*, as *ascend*: see AD-.

a- /ə/ *pref.*[9] (not productive). Repr. L *a-* reduced form of *ab-* bef. *v*: see AB-.

a- /ə, eɪ, *stressed* a/ *pref.*[10] Repr. Gk *a-* used bef. a consonant for *an-* without, not (see AN-[5]), as *abyss*, *apetalous*. A productive pref. of negation and privation w. words of Gk and also L origin, as *agnostic*, *amoral*.

†**a-** *pref.*[11] Prefixed (esp. by Spenser and other archaists) to words where it had no historical or etymological basis. Often treated like A-[8] and spelt *ad-*, *ac-*, *af-*, etc.

-a /ə/ *suff.*[1] Repr. Gk & L nom. sing. ending of fem. ns., as *idea*, *arena*: cf. -IA[1].

-a /ə/ *suff.*[2] Repr. mod. Romance (It., Port., & Sp.) ending of fem. ns., as *stanza*, *duenna*.

-a /ə/ *suff.*[3] Repr. Gk & L pl. ending of neut. ns., adopted unchanged as Eng. pl., as *phenomena*, *data*: cf. -IA[2].

-a /ə, ɑː/ *suff.*[4] Appended to lines in burlesque poetry and other pop. verse for metrical reasons.

-a *suff.*[5] see A *v.*

-a *suff.*[6] see A *prep.*[2]

aa /ˈɑːɑː/. *n.* M19. [Haw. *'a-'a*.] *Geol.* Rough, clinkery, scoriaceous lava. Cf. PAHOEHOE.

aam /ɑːm, ɔːm/ *n. obs.* exc. *Hist.* Also **aum** /ɔːm/. LME. [Du. *aam* = G *Ahm*, *Ohm* ult. f. Gk *amē* bucket.] A Dutch and German liquid measure of varying capacity, 170-200 litres (approx. 37-44 gallons), used in England for Rhine wine.

aandblom /ˈɑːntblɒm/ *n.* *S. Afr.* Also **avondbloem** /ˈɑːvɒntbluːm/. L18. [Afk. *aandblom*, f. *aand* evening + *blom* flower, Du. *avondbloem*.] Any of several sweet-scented plants of the iris family with flowers which tend to open in the evening, *esp.* one belonging to the genus *Hesperantha*. Also = AFRIKANER 2.

aardvark /ˈɑːdvɑːk/ *n.* L18. [Afk. *aardvark(en)* (now *erdvark*), f. *aarde* earth + *varken* pig.] A nocturnal, insectivorous, badger-sized mammal, *Orycteropus afer*, having large ears, a long snout, and a long extensile tongue, native to sub-Saharan Africa.

aardwolf /ˈɑːdwʊlf/ *n.* Pl. **-wolves** /-wʊlvz/. M19. [Afk., f. *aarde* earth + *wolf* wolf.] A largely insectivorous southern African quadruped, *Proteles cristatus*, related to the hyenas, and having an erectile crest.

Aaronic /ɛːˈrɒnɪk/ *a.* M17. [f. *Aaron* (see below) + -IC.] Pertaining to Aaron, the first Jewish high priest; Levitical; resembling or characteristic of a high priest.

Aaronical *a.* E17.

Aaron's beard /ˌɛːr(ə)nz ˈbɪəd/ *n. phr.* E19. [*Ps.* 133:2.] Any of various plants suggestive of beards; *esp.* the rose of Sharon, *Hypericum calycinum*, which has tufts of hairlike stamens.

Aaron's rod /ˌɛːr(ə)nz ˈrɒd/ *n. phr.* M18. [*Num.* 17:8.] Any of various tall upright plants; *esp.* the great mullein, *Verbascum thapsus*.

aasvogel /ˈɑːsfəʊɡ(ə)l/ *n.* *S. Afr.* M19. [Afk. (now *aasvoël*), f. *aas* carrion + *vogel* bird.] A vulture.

Ab /ab/ *n.*[1] Also **Av** /av/. L18. [Heb. *'āḇ*.] In the Jewish calendar, the eleventh month of the civil and fifth of the religious year, usu. coinciding with parts of July and August. Also, the twelfth month of the Syriac calendar.

ab /ab/ *n.*[2] *Body-builders' slang.* M20. [Abbrev.] An abdominal muscle. Usu. in *pl.*

ab- /əb, ab/ *pref.* Repr. L *ab* off, away, from. In mod. formations, = position away from, as *abaxial*.

ab'apical *a.* (*Biol.*) pertaining to or designating the side or part remote from or opposite to the apex M20.

aba /ˈabə/ *n.* Also **abba**. E19. [Arab. *'abā'*.] A sleeveless outer garment of various forms, worn by Arabs. Cf. ABAYA.

abaca /ˈabəkə/ *n.* M18. [Sp. *abacá* f. Tag. *abaká*.] Manila hemp; the plant yielding this.

abaci *n.pl.* see ABACUS.

abaciscus /abəˈsɪskəs/ *n.* Pl. **-sci** /-skʌɪ/, **-scuses**. M18. [L f. Gk *abakiskos* dim. of *abakos* ABACUS.] A tile or square in a mosaic pavement.

abacist /ˈabəsɪst/ *n.* LME. [med.L *abacista*, f. as ABACUS: see -IST.] A person who makes calculations with an abacus.

aback /əˈbak/ *adv.* [OE *on bæc*: see A *prep.*[1] 1, BACK *n.*[1], and note below.] **1** Backwards; away, to a distance. OE. **2** In the rear, behind; at a distance, aloof. OE. **3** *Naut.* Of square sails: laid back against the mast by a head wind. Of a ship: with sails thus. L17.

2 **aback of, o'** *arch.* & *dial.* at the back of, behind. **3** **take aback** disconcert by a sudden check, discomfit. **taken aback** *Naut.* caught with the sails aback suddenly, through bad steering or a shift of wind, and driven astern.

¶The prep. and n., long written separate, were at length treated as one word. Already in 13 the pref. began to be dropped, leaving *back* as the ordinary mod. form of the word, *aback* being chiefly confined to naut. lang. Cf. *adown* and *down*, *around* and *round*, etc.

abackward /əˈbakwəd/ *adv. arch.* ME. [f. prec. + -WARD.] = BACKWARD *adv.*

abacost /ˈabəkɒst/ *n.* L20. [Zairean Fr., contr. of *à bas le costume* down with the (Western) suit.] A Zairean man's suit consisting of a short-sleeved collarless jacket and loose trousers.

†**abactor** *n.* M17–E19. [L, f. *abact-* pa. ppl stem of *abigere* drive away: see -OR.] A person who steals cattle in large numbers.

abacus /ˈabəkəs/ *n.* Pl. **-ci** /-sʌɪ/, **-cuses**. LME. [L, f. Gk *abakos*, *abax* slab, orig. drawing-board covered with dust, f. Semitic: cf. Heb. *'āḇāq* dust.] †**1** A board strewn with sand, for drawing figures, etc. Only in LME. **2** *Archit.* The upper member of a capital, supporting the architrave. M16. **3** A calculating frame, *esp.* one with balls sliding on wires. L17. **4** *Class. Antiq.* A sideboard. L18.

Abaddon /əˈbad(ə)n/ *n.* LME. [Heb. *'ăḇaddōn* (the place of) destruction.] **1** Apollyon, 'the angel of the bottomless pit' (*Rev.* 9:11); the Devil. LME. **2** The pit itself, Hell. L17.

abaft /əˈbɑːft/ *adv.* & *prep.* ME. [f. A *prep.*[1] 1 + BAFT *adv.*] Chiefly *Naut.* **A** *adv.* †**1** Backwards. ME–L15. **2** In the rear; in the stern half of the ship. E17.

B *prep.* Behind; nearer the stern than. L15.

abaft the beam: see BEAM *n.* 10c.

abaht /əˈbɑːt/ *adv.* & *prep.* *dial.* M19. [Repr. a pronunc.] = ABOUT.

†**abaisance** *n.* L17–M18. [OFr. *abaissance*, f. as ABASE + -ANCE.] A low bow.

abalone /abəˈləʊni/ *n.* Orig. *N. Amer.* M19. [Amer. Sp. *abulón* f. Shoshonean *aulun*.] An edible gastropod mollusc of the genus *Haliotis*, having an ear-shaped shell lined with mother-of-pearl.

†**aband** *v.t.* Only in L16. [Contr.] = ABANDON *v.* 3, 4.

SPENSER Enforst the kingdome to aband.

abandon /əˈband(ə)n, *foreign* abɑ̃dɔ̃/ *n.* E19. [Fr., f. *abandonner* ABANDON *v.*] Surrender to natural impulses; freedom from constraint or convention. Cf. ABANDONMENT 4.

abandon /əˈband(ə)n/ *v.t.* LME. [OFr. *abandoner*, f. *à bandon*, f. *à* at, to (see A-[5]) + *bandon* jurisdiction, control, etc.] †**1** Bring under control, subdue. LME–M16. **2** Give up to the control of another person or agent, surrender *to*. LME. **3** Cease to hold, use, or practise; give up, renounce. LME. **4** Desert; leave behind; leave without help. L15. †**5** Banish, expel. M16 M17. **6** Relinquish a claim to (property insured) to underwriters. M18.

1 J. SKELTON Fortune to her law cannot abandune me. **2** DRYDEN Abandoning his charge to fate. ARNOLD BENNETT Like a schoolgirl abandoning herself utterly to some girlish grief. J. LE CARRÉ The boiling month of August, when Parisians by tradition abandon their city to the scalding sunshine and the bus-loads of packaged tourists. **3** V. BRITTAIN I abandoned in despair the Greek textbooks that Roland had lent me. J. BRAINE I might as well abandon that idea. J. GROSS He turned his back on teaching and abandoned mathematics, except as a pastime. **4** C. G. SELIGMAN The aged were abandoned to perish of hunger. L. URIS As quickly as each truck was unloaded it was driven off toward the mountains . . to be abandoned. **abandon ship** take to the lifeboats and leave a ship in imminent danger of sinking, burning, or exploding. **5** SHAKES. *Tam. Shr.* Abandon'd from your bed.

abando'nee *n.* a person, esp. an underwriter, to whom anything is formally abandoned M19. **abandoner** *n.* L16.

abandoned /əˈband(ə)nd/ *ppl a.* LME. [f. prec. + -ED[1].] **1** Having given oneself up *to* (now always to evil). LME. **b** *absol.* Given up to evil influences, profligate. L17. **2** Forsaken, cast off. L15.

abandonedly *adv.* E18.

abandonment /əˈband(ə)nm(ə)nt/ *n.* L16. [OFr. *abandonnement*, f. as ABANDON *v.* + -MENT.] **1** The action of abandoning; the condition of being abandoned. L16. **2** *Law.* The relinquishment of an interest in property or of a claim. E19. **3** The surrender of oneself to an influence etc.; self-abandonment. M19. **4** = ABANDON *n.* M19.

1 J. WAIN She had submerged her will in Robert's, but without any abject abandonment of her own personality. **3** A. SILLITOE The hasty abandonment of making love. **4** DISRAELI His manner was frank even to abandonment.

abanet *n.* var. of ABNET.

abase /əˈbeɪs/ *v.t.* LME. [OFr. *abaissier*, f. A-[5] + *baissier* to lower, ult. f. late L *bassus* short of stature. Infl. by BASE *a.*] **1** Lower (physically); stoop. *arch.* LME. **2** Lower in rank, office, etc.; humiliate, degrade. LME. †**3** Lower in price or value; debase (coin). M16–M18.

1 SHAKES. *Rich. III* Will she yet abase her eyes on me. A. S. BYATT A half-moon from abased nape to rounded buttocks. 2 E. A. FREEMAN This famous refusal of Rolf to abase himself.

abasedly /-sɪdli/ *adv.* in an abased manner LME. **abaser** *n.* L16.

abasement /əˈbeɪsm(ə)nt/ *n.* M16. [f. prec. + -MENT, or f. Fr. *abaissement.*] The action of abasing; the condition of being abased.

abash /əˈbaʃ/ *v.* ME. [AN *abaïss-* = OFr. *esbaïss-* lengthened stem of *e(s)baïr* (mod. *ébahir*), f. ES- + *baïr* astound: see A-[7].] **1** *v.t.* Destroy the self-possession of, disconcert with sudden shame, consciousness of error or presumption, etc. ME. †**2** *v.i.* Lose self-possession through surprise, shame, etc. LME–L16.

abashedly /-ʃɪdli/ *adv.* in an abashed manner E19. **abashedness** *n.* (*rare*) the state or quality of being abashed, abashment M16. **abashless** *a.* (*poet.*) unabashed M19. **abashment** *n.* confusion from shame etc. LME.

abask /əˈbɑːsk/ *adv.* & *pred. a.* M19. [f. A-[2] + BASK *v.*] Basking.

†**abastardize** *v.t.* Also **-ise.** L16–L17. [OFr. *abastardir, -issant*, f. as A-[5], BASTARD: refash. after vbs in -IZE.] Render bastard; debase.

Also †**abastard** *v.t.* E–M17.

†**abate** *n.*[1] LME–L17. [f. ABATE *v.*[1]] = ABATEMENT *n.*[1]

abate /əˈbɑːti, *foreign* abˈbaːte/ *n.*[2] Also **abb-.** E18. [It. f. L *abbat-* ABBOT.] An Italian abbot or other ecclesiastic. Cf. ABBÉ.

abate /əˈbeɪt/ *v.*[1] ME. [OFr. *abatre* ult. f. L *batt(u)ere* to beat: see A-[5].] **1** *v.t.* Put an end to. *obs.* in *gen.* sense. ME. **b** *v.t. spec.* in *Law*. Cause (a nuisance, an action) to cease. ME. **c** *v.i.* Become null and void. L15. †**2** *v.t.* & *i.* Bring down (a person) physically, socially, or mentally; depress, humble; fall, be humbled. ME–M17. **b** *v.t.* Curtail, deprive, *of.* LME–M19. **3** *v.t.* & *i.* Reduce in size, amount, or value. *arch.* ME. **4** *v.t.* & *i.* Lessen in force or intensity; moderate, diminish. ME. **5** *v.t.* Take away (a part of something), deduct. LME. **b** *fig.* Bar, except. L16. **6** *v.t.* Beat down. Formerly also, destroy, level with the ground. LME. †**7** *v.t.* Blunt. Cf. BATE *v.*[2] 6. M16–L17.

1c DEFOE Commissions shall not abate by the death of his majesty. 2 CHAUCER The hyer that they were in this present lyf, the moore shulle they be abated and defouled in helle. b SHAKES. *Lear* She hath abated me of half my train. 3 AV *Gen.* 8:3 The waters were abated. DEFOE As wages abate to the poor, provisions must abate in the market. J. GALSWORTHY It's much more paying to abate a price than to increase it. 4 T. S. ELIOT As soon as relief has abated our rage. A. POWELL The rain had to some extent abated. 5 DEFOE Rather than abate a farthing of the price they had asked. B. FRANKLIN She would abate me two shillings a week. b S. JOHNSON Abating his brutality, he was a very good master. 6 R. FABYAN Ye gates of Bruges . . were abated. 7 BACON To abate the edge of envy.

With preps. in specialized senses: **abate of** *arch.* deduct something from, lessen.

abatable *a.* LME. **abater** *n.*[1] E17.

abate /əˈbeɪt/ *v.*[2]*i.* & (less commonly) *refl.* LME. [AN *abatre*, earlier usu. *enbatre*, *em-*. Conf. w. prec.] *Law* (now *Hist.*). Thrust oneself tortiously into a tenement between the death of the owner and the accession of the legal heir.

abater *n.*[2] M17.

abatement /əˈbeɪtm(ə)nt/ *n.*[1] LME. [OFr., f. as ABATE *v.*[1] + -MENT.] **1** The action of abating; the state of being abated. LME. **2** The result of abating; the amount by which anything is abated; decrease, deduction, drawback. L15.

1 O. CROMWELL Much abatement of my hopes. W. BLACKSTONE The abatement, or removal, of Nusances. JOYCE Abatement of wind.

abatement /əˈbeɪtm(ə)nt/ *n.*[2] ME. [AN, f. as ABATE *v.*[2] + -MENT.] *Law* (now *Hist.*). The action of abating in an inheritance.

abatis /ˈabətɪs/ *n.* Also **abattis** /əˈbatɪs/. Pl. **abat(t)is, -ises.** M18. [Fr., f. as ABATE *v.*[1]] *Mil.* A defence formed by placing felled trees lengthwise one over the other with their branches towards the enemy's line. Also, a barricade of barbed wire.

abat(t)ised /-st/ *a.* M19.

abator /əˈbeɪtə/ *n.*[1] L16. [Late AN *abato(u)r*, f. as ABATE *v.*[1] + -OR.] A person who or thing which abates; *esp.* in *Law*, a person who abates a nuisance, an action, etc.

abator /əˈbeɪtə/ *n.*[2] M16. [Late AN *abato(u)r*, f. as ABATE *v.*[2] + -OR.] *Law* (now *Hist.*). A person who abates in an inheritance.

abattis *n.* var. of ABATIS.

abattoir /ˈabətwɑː/ *n.* E19. [Fr., f. *abattre* to fell: see -ORY[1].] A slaughterhouse.

abature /ˈabətjʊə/ *n.* L16. [(O)Fr., f. as ABATE *v.*[1] + -URE.] *Hunting*. A trace left by a stag in the underwood. Usu. in *pl.*

abaxial /abˈaksɪəl/ *a.* M19. [f. AB- + AXIAL.] *Bot.* Off or away from the axis; (of the surface of a leaf etc.) initially facing away from the stem.

†**abay** *n.* ME–L17. [OFr. *abai* (mod. *aboi*): see BAY *n.*[1]] Baying of dogs upon their prey, esp. when closing round it.

stand at abay: said of the dogs. **be at abay**: said of the hunted animal.

abaya /əˈbeɪjə/ *n.* M19. [Arab. *ʿabāya.*] = ABA.

Abaza /əˈbɑːzə/ *n.* & *a.* E19. [Abaza.] **A** *n.* **1** A member of a people inhabiting the north-west Caucasus. E19. **2** The language of this people. M20. **B** *adj.* Of or pertaining to the Abazas or their language. M19.

abb /ab/ *n.* OE. [f. A-[1] + WEB *n.*[1]] (Coarse wool used for) the woof or weft in a web.

attrib.: A. S. BYATT Knitting abb wool into comforters.

Abba /ˈabə/ *n.*[1] LME. [eccl.L f. New Testament Gk f. Aram. *ʾabbā* father.] *Chr. Ch.* **1** *Abba, father*: an invocation to God as Father (*Mark* 14:36 etc.). LME. **2** A title given to bishops and patriarchs in the Syrian Orthodox and Coptic Churches. M17.

abba *n.*[2] var. of ABA.

abbacy /ˈabəsi/ *n.* LME. [eccl.L *abbacia*, *abbatia*, f. *abbat-* ABBOT: see -ACY.] The office, jurisdiction, or tenure of an abbot or abbess.

Also †**abbatie** *n.* ME–M17.

Abbasid /əˈbasɪd, ˈabəsɪd/ *a.* & *n.* Also **-ide** /-ʌɪd/, **-ss-.** M18. [f. *ʿAbbās* (566–652) uncle of Muhammad + -ID[3].] Of or pertaining to, a member of, the dynasty (750–1258) of caliphs of Baghdad claiming descent from ʿAbbās.

abbate *n.* var. of ABATE *n.*[2]

abbatial /əˈbeɪʃ(ə)l/ *a.* L17. [Fr., or med.L *abbatialis* f. *abbat-* ABBOT: see -IAL.] Of or pertaining to an abbacy, abbot, or abbess.

Also †**abbatical** *a.* M17–M19.

Abbe /ˈabə/ *n.* L19. [Ernst *Abbe* (1840–1905), Ger. physicist.] *Optics*. Used *attrib.* and in *possess.* to designate optical instruments and concepts in optical theory introduced or popularized by Abbe.

Abbe condenser a condenser for compound microscopes in the form of a wide-aperture compound lens. **Abbe number** the reciprocal of the dispersive power of a transparent substance. **Abbe refractometer** an instrument for directly determining the refractive index of a small sample of liquid.

abbé /ˈabeɪ, *foreign* abe (*pl. same*)/ *n.* M16. [Fr. f. eccl.L *abbat-* ABBOT.] In France: an abbot, a secular priest, or *loosely* anyone, with or without official duties, who is entitled to wear ecclesiastical dress.

abbess /ˈabɛs/ *n.* ME. [(O)Fr. *abbesse* f. eccl.L *abbadissa, -tissa*, f. *abbat-* ABBOT: see -ESS[1].] **1** The female superior of an abbey of nuns. ME. †**2** The mistress of a brothel. *slang.* L16–L19.

Abbevillian /abˈvɪlɪən/ *a.* & *n.* M20. [Fr. *Abbevillien*, f. *Abbeville* in northern France: see -IAN.] (Of) the earliest palaeolithic period in Europe.

abbey /ˈabi/ *n.* ME. [OFr. *ab(b)eïe* (mod. *abbaye*) f. med.L *abbatia*: see ABBACY, -Y[3].] **1** The jurisdiction or office of an abbot or abbess. ME. **2** A community of monks governed by an abbot or of nuns governed by an abbess. ME. **3** The building(s) occupied by such a community. ME. **b** A church or house that was once an abbey or part of one. M16.

Comb.: †**abbey-lubber** a lazy monk (used after the Reformation).

abbot /ˈabət/ *n.* OE. [eccl.L *abbat-*, *abbas* f. Gk *abbas* f. Aram. *ʾabbā* ABBA *n.*[1]] The head or superior of an abbey of monks. After the dissolution of the monasteries also occas., a layman to whom an abbey's revenues were impropriated.

Abbot (of) Unreason: see UNREASON *n.* *titular abbot*: see TITULAR *a.* 1.

†**abbatess, -otess** *n.* [eccl.L: see ABBESS] = ABBESS OE–L17. †**abbotric(k)** *n.* [OE *rīce* realm, rule] = ABBACY OE–E18. **abbotship** *n.* = ABBACY LME.

abbreviate /əˈbriːvɪət/ *a.* & *n.* LME. [Late L *abbreviatus* pa. pple, f. as next: see -ATE[2].] **A** *adj.* †**1** Shortened, cut short. LME–L17. **2** *Bot.* & *Zool.* Relatively short. M19. **B** *n.* An abridgement. Now only *Sc. Law*, a brief notice registering a petition for the sequestration of a bankrupt. M16.

abbreviate /əˈbriːvɪeɪt/ *v.* LME. [L *abbreviat-* pa. ppl stem of *abbreviare*, f. *ab* AB- or *ad* AD- + *breviare*, f. *brevis* short, BRIEF *a.*: see -ATE[3].] †**1** *v.t.* Shorten by omitting details; epitomize. LME–L17. †**b** *v.i.* Speak or write briefly. L16–E17. **2** *v.t.* Cut short. LME. **b** *esp.* Shorten (a word, phrase, or symbol). L16.

abbreviatory *a.* M19.

abbreviation /əbriːvɪˈeɪʃ(ə)n/ *n.* LME. [Fr. *abbréviation* or late L *abbreviatio(n-)*, f. as prec.: see -ATION.] **1** The result of abbreviating; a reduced form; an abridgement. LME. **b** *esp.* A shortened form of a word, phrase, or symbol. L16. **2** The action of abbreviating. M16.

abbreviator /əˈbriːvɪeɪtə/ *n.* E16. [med.L *abbreviator*, f. as ABBREVIATE *v.*: see -OR.] **1** A person who abbreviates. E16. **2** *Hist.* An officer who composed briefs for the Pope. M16.

abbreviature /əˈbriːvɪətjʊə/ *n.* Now *rare* or *obs.* L16. [f. as ABBREVIATE *v.* + -URE. Cf. Fr. †*abréviature.*] **1 a** An abridgement. L16. †**b** *gen.* An abbreviated state or form. E–M17. **c** = ABBREVIATION 1b. M17. †**2** = ABBREVIATION 2. M–L17.

ABC /eɪbiːˈsiː/ *n.* Formerly also as a simple word †**absey** etc. ME. [The first three letters of the alphabet.] **1** The alphabet. ME. †**2** An alphabetical acrostic, list, or table. LME–M17. **3 a** A spelling-book, a reading primer. LME–M17. **b** *fig.* The first elements (*of* a subject). M16.

1 as easy as ABC *colloq.* very easy.

abdicate /ˈabdɪkeɪt/ *v.* M16. [L *abdicat-* pa. ppl stem of *abdicare* renounce, f. *ab* AB- + *dicare* proclaim: see -ATE[3].] †**1** *v.t.* Disown; *esp.* disinherit (a child). M16–E19. †**2** *v.t.* a *refl.* Cut oneself off *from* (an office or dignity); divest oneself of an office. M16–L17. **b** Depose. Chiefly as *abdicated* ppl a. E17–L18. †**3** *v.t.* Discard. M16–L17. **4** *v.t.* Give up (a right, responsibility, trust, office, or dignity) either formally or by default. M17. **5** *v.i.* Renounce sovereignty. E18.

abdicable *a.* able to be abdicated L19. **abdicant** *a.* & *n.* (*a*) *adj.* (*rare*) abdicating; (*b*) *n.* a person who abdicates: M17. **abdicator** *n.* †(*a*) a person who is in favour of another abdicating; (*b*) a person who abdicates: L17.

abdication /abdɪˈkeɪʃ(ə)n/ *n.* M16. [L *abdicatio(n-)*, f. as prec.: see -ATION.] †**1** The action of formally disowning. M16–M17. **2** Resignation or renunciation of something. E17. **b** *spec.* Renunciation of sovereignty. L17. †**c** *Law.* = ABANDONMENT 2. Only in M18. †**3** Deposition from sovereignty. *rare.* Only in M17.

abditory /ˈabdɪt(ə)ri/ *n.* *rare.* M17. [med.L *abditorium*, f. *abdere* to hide: see -ORY[1].] A concealed repository.

abdomen /ˈabdəmən, abˈdəʊmən/ *n.* M16. [L *abdomen, -min-*, of unkn. origin.] †**1** Fat round the belly. M16–L17. 2 *Anat.* The belly; the part of the body containing the digestive organs; the cavity of the trunk below the diaphragm, usu. including the pelvic cavity. E17. 3 The posterior division of the body in insects, spiders, and some other arthropods. L18.

¶The variation in pronunc. has existed since 18.

abdominal /əb'dɒmɪn(ə)l/ *a.* & *n.* M18. [mod.L *abdominalis*, f. as prec.: see -AL[1].] A *adj.* 1 Of or pertaining to the abdomen. M18. 2 *Ichthyol.* a (Of a fish) having the ventral fins posterior to the pectoral, in the belly region; (of a vertical fin) so situated. M19. b Of a fin: ventral. L19.

1 *abdominal leg*: see LEG *n.*

B *n.* An abdominal muscle. Usu. in *pl. colloq.* M20.

abdominally *adv.* in the abdomen, with reference to the abdomen L19.

abdominous /əb'dɒmɪnəs/ *a.* M17. [f. as ABDOMEN + -OUS.] Corpulent.

abduce /əb'djuːs/ *v.t.* M16. [L *abducere*, f. *ab* AB- + *ducere* to lead.] 1 = ABDUCT. *arch.* M16. 2 Infer partly from observation or experience. M20.

abducens /ab'djuːs(ə)nz/ *n.sing.* E19. [mod.L use as n. of L pres. pple: see next.] *Anat.* An abducent nerve. Also *abducens nerve.*

abducent /əb'djuːs(ə)nt/ *a.* L17. [L *abducent-*, *abducens* pres. pple of *abducere*: see ABDUCE, -ENT.] *Anat.* Of a muscle or nerve: concerned with abduction (sense 2); *spec.* designating or pertaining to the sixth pair of cranial nerves, which supply the muscles concerned with the lateral movement of the eyeballs.

abduct /əb'dʌkt/ *v.t.* E17. [L *abduct-* pa. ppl stem of *abducere* ABDUCE.] 1 Lead or take away (a person, esp. a woman or child) by illegal force or fraud. E17. 2 *Anat.* Bring about abduction of (a limb etc.). E17.

abduction /əb'dʌkʃ(ə)n/ *n.* E17. [Late L *abductio(n-)*, f. as prec.: see -ION.] 1 *gen.* A leading away. E17. 2 *Anat.* Movement of a limb etc. outward from the median line. Opp. ADDUCTION 2. M17. 3 *Logic.* A syllogistic argument, with the major premiss certain, the minor only probable. L17. 4 The act of illegally carrying off or leading away a person, esp. a woman or child. M18.

abductive /əb'dʌktɪv/ *a.* M19. [f. (as) ABDUCT + -IVE.] 1 Of or pertaining to abduction. M19. 2 Chiefly *Philos.* & *Ling.* Of, pertaining to, or proceeding by inference from observation or experience; (of an argument) having the major premiss known, the minor only probable. E20.

abductively *adv.* E20.

abductor /əb'dʌktə/ *n.* E17. [mod.L, f. as ABDUCT: see -OR.] 1 *Anat.* A muscle which brings about abduction (sense 2). Also *abductor muscle.* E17. 2 A person who abducts. M19.

a-be /ə'biː/ *adv. Sc.* E18. [Perh. = *let be* s.v. BE *v.* on the analogy of *let* (or *leave*) *alone.*] *let a-be*, let alone.

abeam /ə'biːm/ *adv.* & *pred. a.* M19. [f. A-[2] + BEAM *n.*] On a line at right angles to a ship's or aircraft's course; opposite the middle *of* (a ship etc.).

abear /ə'bɛː/ *v.* & *n.* [OE *aberan*, f. A-[1] + BEAR *v.*[1]; later prob. a new form. on the analogy of *abide.*] A *v.t.* Infl. as BEAR *v.*[1] (obs.) †1 Bear, carry. OE–ME. 2 Endure. (Now always with *cannot* etc.) Now chiefly *dial.* OE. †3 *refl.* Comport oneself. Only in L16.

2 DICKENS She couldn't abear the men, they were such deceivers. 3 SPENSER Thus did the . . knight himselfe abeare.

†B *n.* Bearing, behaviour. ME–M17.

H. VAUGHAN Noting well my vain abear.

abearance *n.* (now *rare*) behaviour M16. †**abearing** *n.* behaviour L15–E18.

abeat /ə'biːt/ *adv.* & *pred. a.* Chiefly *poet.* L19. [f. A-[2] + BEAT *n.*[1] or *v.*[1]] Beating.

abecedarian /,eɪbiːsiː'dɛːrɪən/ *n.* & *a.* E17. [f. as next: see -ARIAN.] A *n.* 1 A person learning the alphabet or the rudiments of a subject. E17. 2 A person teaching these. *arch.* E17. B *adj.* 1 Pertaining to the alphabet; arranged alphabetically. M17. 2 (Pertaining to a person) learning the alphabet. M17.

abecedary /eɪbiː'siːdəri/ *n.* & *a.* Now *rare* or *obs.* LME. [Sense A.1 f. med.L *abecedarium*, senses A.2 and B f. late L *abecedarius*; f. the names of the letters *a, b, c, d*: see -ARY[1].] A *n.* 1 A book containing the alphabet; a primer. Long *rare.* LME. 2 = ABECEDARIAN *n.* L16. B *adj.* = ABECEDARIAN *a.* L16.

abed /ə'bɛd/ *adv. arch.* ME. [f. A *prep.*[1] I + BED *n.*] In bed; laid up.

abeigh /ə'biːx, ə'beɪx/ *adv. Sc.* Now *rare* or *obs.* M16. [Origin unkn.] At a distance because of shyness; aloof.

abele /ə'biːl, 'eɪb(ə)l/ *n.* ME. [Orig. f. OFr. *aubel*, *abel* f. med.L *albellus* dim. of *albus* white; later (L16) f. Du. *abeel* f. OFr.] The white poplar, *Populus alba.*

abelia /ə'biːlɪə/ *n.* M19. [mod.L (see below), f. Clarke *Abel* (1780–1826), Brit. botanist: see -IA[1].] Any of several hardy evergreen shrubs of the genus *Abelia*, of the honeysuckle family, having small pink or white flowers and native to eastern Asia.

abelian /ə'biːlɪən/ *a.* M19. [f. *Abel* (see below) + -IAN.] *Math.* Of a form arising from work by the Norwegian mathematician Niels H. Abel (1802–29); *spec.* designating groups in which the operation is commutative.

Abenaki *n.* & *a.* var. of ABNAKI.

abeng /a'bɛŋ/ *n.* L19. [Twi.] An animal's horn used as a wind instrument to send messages by Maroons of the W. Indies.

Aberdeen /abə'diːn/ *n.* M19. [A city and former county in the Grampian Region of Scotland.] 1 *Aberdeen Angus*, (an animal of) a Scottish breed of black polled beef cattle. Also called *Angus.* M19. 2 *Aberdeen terrier*, (an animal of) a rough variety of Scottish terrier. L19.

aberdevine /'abədəvʌɪn/ *n. dial.* (now *rare* or *obs.*). M18. [Origin unkn.] The siskin.

¶Appears to have had little real currency although regularly listed as an alternative name in ornithological texts.

Aberdonian /abə'dəʊnɪən/ *n.* & *a.* M17. [f. med.L *Aberdonia* ABERDEEN: see -IAN.] A native of, of or pertaining to, Aberdeen in NE Scotland.

Abernethy /abə'nɛθi, -'niːθi/ *n.* M19. [Prob. John *Abernethy*, Eng. surgeon (1764–1831).] In full *Abernethy biscuit.* A hard biscuit flavoured with caraway seeds.

aberr /ə'bəː/ *v.* M16. [L *aberrare*, f. *ab* AB- + *errare* wander, err.] †1 *v.i.* Go astray (chiefly *fig.*). M16–M17. 2 *v.t.* = ABERRATE 2. *rare.* L19.

2 G. B. SHAW I should have put on a pair of abnormal spectacles and aberred my vision.

aberrance /ə'bɛr(ə)ns/ *n.* M17. [f. next: see -ANCE.] The action of straying; vagary.

aberrancy *n.* the quality or condition of being aberrant M17.

aberrant /ə'bɛr(ə)nt/ *a.* M16. [L *aberrant-* pres. ppl stem of *aberrare*: see ABERR, -ANT[1].] †1 Deviating *from.* M16–E17. 2 Straying from the right path (*lit.* & *fig.*). M18. 3 Chiefly *Bot.* & *Zool.* Deviating from the normal type. M19.

aberrantly *adv.* L19.

aberrate /'abəreɪt/ *v.* M18. [L *aberrat-* pa. ppl stem of *aberrare*: see ABERR, -ATE[3].] 1 *v.i.* Produce aberration; go astray; deviate *from.* M18. 2 *v.t.* Distort, cause aberration of. Chiefly as *aberrated* ppl a. L19.

1 W. FAULKNER He regrets having to aberrate from being a gentleman.

aberration /abə'reɪʃ(ə)n/ *n.* L16. [L *aberratio(n-)*, f. as prec.: see -ATION.] 1 A deviation or divergence from the straight, correct, or recognized path (*lit.* & *fig.*). L16. 2 The failure of rays of light to converge to a focus. M18. 3 *Astron.* An apparent displacement of a celestial object from its true position, arising from the relative motion of the observer and the object. M18. 4 An abnormal state of an intellectual faculty. E19. 5 Chiefly *Bot.* & *Zool.* Deviation from the normal type; an instance of this. M19.

1 SIR W. SCOTT The slightest aberration would plunge him into a morass. GEO. ELIOT A pattern from which she was careful to allow no aberration. 2 **chromatic aberration**: due to the different refrangibilities of the components of white light. **spherical aberration**: arising from the surface geometry of a spherical lens or mirror. 3 **annual aberration**: due to the earth's orbital motion. **diurnal aberration**: due to the earth's axial rotation. **planetary aberration**: due to the motion of a planet during the time taken for its light to reach the earth. 4 *Midnight Zoo* Mental aberrations. 5 J. FOWLES Rare species and aberrations.

aberrational *a.* M19. **aberrationally** *adv.* L20.

abessive /ə'bɛsɪv/ *a.* & *n.* L19. [f. L *abesse* be away, f. *ab* AB- + *esse* be + -IVE.] *Gram.* A *adj.* Designating, being in, or pertaining to a case in Finnish and other languages expressing the absence of something. L19. B *n. The* abessive case; a word, form, etc., in the abessive case. L19.

†**abet** *n.* ME. [OFr., f. as next.] 1 Fraud, cunning. Only in ME. 2 Abetment. LME–E18.

abet /ə'bɛt/ *v.t.* Infl. **-tt-**. LME. [OFr. *abeter*, f. A-[5] + *beter* hound on, cogn. w. BAIT *v.*[1]] 1 †a Urge on to do something good or desirable. LME–E17. b Incite or encourage (*in* a crime or offence, †*to* commit an offence). LME. 2 a Support, uphold, (a good cause, opinion, etc.). *arch.* L16. b Encourage or countenance (a crime, offence, etc.), in *Law* by active assistance (chiefly in *aid and abet*). L18.

abettance *n.* (*rare*) abetment E19. **abetter** *n.* a person who abets an offence or an offender LME.

abetment /ə'bɛtm(ə)nt/ *n.* LME. [AN *abetement*, f. as prec.: see -MENT.] The action or fact of abetting (usu. an offence).

abettor /ə'bɛtə/ *n.* LME. [AN *abettour*, f. as ABET *v.* + -OR.] 1 A person who abets an offender. (In *Law* preferred to ABETTER.) LME. 2 A supporter, an adherent, an advocate, (now almost always of something or someone undesirable or reprehensible). L16.

ab extra /ab 'ɛkstrə/ *adv. phr.* M17. [Late L.] From outside.

abeyance /ə'beɪəns/ *n.* L16. [AN *abeiance*, OFr. *abeance* aspiration to a title, f. *abeer* aspire after: cf. BAY *n.*[3] and see -ANCE.] 1 *Law.* The position of being without a claimant or owner but available to the rightful owner. L16. 2 A state of suspension or temporary disuse; dormant condition liable to revival. Chiefly in *in abeyance* or *fall into abeyance.* M17.

abeyant *a.* in a state of abeyance M19.

abhisheka /əb(h)ɪ'ʃeɪkə, ʌb-/ *n.* L19. [Skt *abhiṣeka*, f. *abhi* upon, over + *sic* sprinkle.] In Hinduism etc.: (a ceremony involving) ritual sprinkling or anointing.

†**abhominable** *a.*, **-ation** *n.* vars. of ABOMINABLE, -ATION.

abhor /əb'hɔː/ *v.* Infl. **-rr-**. LME. [L *abhorrere*, f. *ab* AB- + *horrere* stand aghast. Partly from Fr. *abhorrer.*] 1 *v.t.* Regard with disgust and hatred. LME. †2 *v.t.* Cause horror or disgust to. Usu. *impers.* in (*it*) *abhors* etc. M16–E17. †3 *v.i.* Shrink with horror or repugnance *from.* M16–M17. †4 *v.i.* Differ entirely *from.* M16–L17.

1 POPE My soul abhors to stay. R. C. TRENCH To abhor evil is to have it in moral detestation. 2 SHAKES. *Oth.* It does abhor me. 4 EVELYN Abhorring from the genuine and rational sense of the text.

abhorred *a.* (*a*) detested; †(*b*) *rare* horrified: L16. **abhorrer** *n.* (*a*) a person who abhors; (*b*) *Eng. Hist.* a person who signed an address of abhorrence: E17. **abhorrible** /əb'hɒrɪb(ə)l/ *a.* (now *rare* or *obs.*) detestable M17. **abhorring** *n.* = ABHORRENCE I, 3 M16.

abhorrence /əb'hɒr(ə)ns/ *n.* M17. [f. as next + -ENCE.] 1 The action of abhorring; detestation. M17. 2 An expression of abhorrence; *spec.* any of certain addresses presented to Charles II. *obs.* exc. *Hist.* L17. 3 A detested thing. M18.

†**abhorrency** *n.* L16. [f. next + -ENCY.] 1 = ABERRANCY. *rare.* Only in L16. 2 The quality of being abhorrent; the feeling of abhorrence. E17–E18. 3 A thing which excites abhorrence. Only in E18.

abhorrent /əb'hɒr(ə)nt/ *a.* L16. [L *abhorrent-* pres. ppl stem of *abhorrere* ABHOR: see -ENT.] 1 (*pred.*) *abhorrent from*, opposed to, far removed from, inconsistent with. L16. 2 *pred.* Inherently repugnant (*to*); contrary *to*. M17. 3 Having or showing abhorrence (*of*). *arch.* M18. 4 Inspiring disgust; detestable. E19.

1 BURKE The persons most abhorrent from blood, and treason. C. MERIVALE The simple theory of the Gospel . . was . . abhorrent from the prejudices of the heathen. 2 F. A. KEMBLE Not abhorrent to nature. 3 GLADSTONE Temperate and abhorrent of excess. 4 ISAAC TAYLOR Pride, abhorrent as it is.

abhorrently *adv.* E19.

Abib /'eɪbɪb, 'ɑː-/ *n.* M16. [Heb. *'ābīb* ear of corn.] *Hist.* In the Jewish calendar, = NISAN.

abidance /ə'bʌɪd(ə)ns/ *n.* E17. [f. next + -ANCE.] 1 Abiding; dwelling. E17. 2 *abidance by*, conformity to. E19.

abide /ə'bʌɪd/ *v.* Pa. t. & pple **abided**, **abode** /ə'bəʊd/; pa. pple also **abidden** /ə'bɪd(ə)n/ (now *rare*). [OE *ābīdan*, f. A-[1] + BIDE; cogn. w. Goth. *usbeidan*.] I *v.i.* †1 Remain in expectation, wait. OE–M17. †2 Pause, delay, stop. ME–M17. 3 Stay, remain, (in a place or in some state: w. advb. or adj. complement, or absol.). ME. b Reside, dwell. *arch.* LME. 4 Endure, stand firm. LME.

1 AV *Gen.* 22:5 Abide you here with the asse. 3 LD BERNERS The towne abode frenche. W. COWPER He within his ships Abode the while. TENNYSON Tho' much is taken, much abides. b TOLKIEN Ulmo . . abode not in Valinor. 4 COVERDALE *Ps.* 91:7 But thou Lorde . . abydest worlde without ende.

II *v.t.* 5 Wait for, watch for, expect. OE. 6 Face, encounter, withstand. ME. †7 Suffer, endure. ME–E18. 8 Await submissively; submit to. LME. 9 Tolerate, put up with. (Chiefly & now only in neg. & interrog. contexts.) L15.

5 T. ELYOT He abode an answer thereof. TINDALE *Acts* 20:23 Bondes and trouble abyde me. 6 A. THWAITE He [Shakespeare] abides Our questioning syllabus still. 7 J. MOXON Not . . strong enough to abide tough Work. 8 SHAKES. *Rich. II* To abide Thy kingly doom. 9 GOLDSMITH I can't abide to disappoint myself. L. LEE They were far more alike than unalike, and could not abide each other.

With preps. in specialized senses: **abide by** remain with, remain faithful to, (pa. t. & pple now usu. *abided*).

¶Occas. conf. w. ABY (= pay for, suffer for): SHAKES. *Jul. Caes.* Some will dear abide it.

abider *n.* LME.

abiding /ə'bʌɪdɪŋ/ *n.* ME. [f. prec. + -ING[1].] 1 The action or state of a person who abides. ME. †2 An abode. LME–E17.

Comb.: **abiding-place** place of abode.

abiding /ə'bʌɪdɪŋ/ *a.* LME. [f. as prec. + -ING[2].] Enduring, permanent.

M. L. KING An abiding faith in America.

¶See also *law-abiding* s.v. LAW *n.*[1]

abidingly *adv.* LME. **abidingness** *n.* M19.

abietic /abɪ'ɛtɪk/ *a.* M19. [f. L *abiet-*, *abies* fir + -IC.] Chem. *abietic acid*, a crystalline terpenoid acid, $C_{20}H_{30}O_2$, that is a component of rosin.

abigail /'abɪgeɪl/ *n.* Also **A-**. M17. [A character in *The Scornful Lady* by Beaumont and Fletcher: cf. *1 Sam.* 25.] A lady's maid.

†abiliment *n.* var. of HABILIMENT.

ability /ə'bɪlɪti/ *n.* Also **†h-**. LME. [OFr. *ablete* f. L *habilitas*, f. *habilis*: see ABLE *a.*, -ITY.] †1 Suitableness. LME–L17. 2 Suitable or sufficient power; capacity (*to do*, †*of doing* something). LME. b Legal competency (to act). M17. 3 Bodily power. Now *Sc. dial.* LME. 4 Pecuniary power. *arch.* E16. 5a A special power of the mind, a faculty. Usu. in *pl.* L16. b Mental power; talent, cleverness. E17.

2 T. S. ELIOT Dryden is distinguished . . by his *poetic* ability. E. HEMINGWAY Cowardice . . is . . a lack of ability to suspend the functioning of the imagination. *to the best of one's ability*: see BEST *a.* etc. 3 E. TOPSELL Complaining of bodily weakness where is no want of ability. 4 SHAKES. *Twel. N.* Out of my lean and low ability I'll lend you something. 5a J. B. WATSON I'll train him to become any type of specialist . . regardless of his . . abilities. b E. GLASGOW Men with ability never stayed in a village.

-ability /ə'bɪlɪti/ *suff.* [Fr. *-abilité* f. L *-abilitas*.] Forming ns. chiefly from adjs. in -ABLE: see -ITY.

†abime *n.* var. of ABYSM.

ab initio /ab ɪ'nɪʃɪəʊ/ *adv. phr.* E17. [L.] From the beginning.

ab intra /ab 'ɪntrə/ *adv. phr.* L17. [mod.L.] From inside.

abiogenesis /,eɪbʌɪə'dʒɛnɪsɪs/ *n.* L19. [f. Gk *abios*, f. *a-* A-[10] + *bios* life + -GENESIS.] The production of organic matter or compounds, other than by the agency of living organisms; *esp.* the supposed spontaneous generation of living organisms.

abi'ogenist *n.* a believer in the spontaneous generation of living organisms L19.

abiogenic /,eɪbʌɪə'dʒɛnɪk/ *a.* L19. [f. as prec. + -GENIC.] Not involving or produced by living organisms.

abiogenically *adv.* M20.

abiological /,eɪbʌɪə'lɒdʒɪk(ə)l/ *a.* M19. [f. A-[10] + BIOLOGICAL.] Not associated with living organisms; non-biological.

abiologically *adv.* L19.

abiotic /eɪbʌɪ'ɒtɪk/ *a.* L19. [f. A-[10] + BIOTIC.] Devoid of or inimical to life; inanimate, abiological.

abiotically *adv.* in the absence of life M20.

Abitur /abi'tuːr/ *n.* Also **a-**. M20. [G, abbrev. of *Abiturientenexamen* leavers' examination.] In Germany, a set of examinations taken in the final year of secondary school (success in which formerly ensured a university place).

Abiturient /abituri'ɛnt/ *n.* [G, f. mod.L *abiturire* wish to leave] a candidate for the *Abitur* M19.

abject /'abdʒɛkt/ *a.*, *v.*, & *n.* LME. [L *abjectus* pa. pple of *abjicere* reject, f. *ab* AB- + *jacere* throw.] A *adj.* (orig. *pa. pple*). †1 Cast off, rejected. LME–E17. 2 Brought low in position, condition, or status. LME. 3 In low repute; lacking courage; despicable; self-abasing. LME.

2 F. TROLLOPE The most abject poverty is preferable to domestic service. LD MACAULAY The abject heirs of an illustrious name. 3 SHAKES. *2 Hen. VI* Paltry, servile, abject drudges. J. THURBER He lived in abject fear of the cold, overbearing, and ruthless police lieutenant. C. HAMPTON He was so abject He kept apologizing all the time.

†B *v.t.* Cast off or down (*lit.* & *fig.*). LME–L17.

C *n.* An outcast; a degraded person. L15.

¶At first, like its L original, a pple and adj., stressed on second syllable.

abjectly *adv.* LME. **abjectness** *n.* L16.

abjection /ab'dʒɛkʃ(ə)n/ *n.* LME. [(O)Fr., or L *abjectio(n-)*, f. as prec. see -ION.] 1 The condition of a person cast down; degradation; low status. LME. †2 Something cast off; refuse. Chiefly *fig.* LME–M16. †3 The action of casting down. E16–M17. †4 The action of casting off; rejection. E–M17.

abjuration /abdʒʊə'reɪʃ(ə)n/ *n.* LME. [(O)Fr., or late L *abjuratio(n-)*, f. *abjurat-* pa. ppl stem of *abjurare*: see next, -ATION.] 1 Renunciation on oath; recantation, esp. of heresies. LME. 2 Official repudiation on oath of any ecclesiastical or political principle. M17.

1 **abjuration of the realm** etc.: an oath taken to leave the realm etc. for ever. 2 **Oath of Abjuration**, **abjuration oath** (*obs.* exc. *Hist.*): disclaiming allegiance to James, son of James II, or his descendants as claimants to the British throne.

abjure /əb'dʒʊə/ *v.t.* LME. [L *abjurare* deny on oath, f. *ab* AB- + *jurare* swear.] 1 Renounce on oath; recant. LME. 2 Cause to recant. *obs.* exc. *Hist.* LME. 3 Disclaim solemnly; reject on oath. LME.

1 SHAKES. *Temp.* This rough magic I here abjure. 2 F. THYNNE All such must be burned, or ellis ab-Iuryd. 3 *absol.*: MILTON Say and unsay, feign, flatter, and abjure. **abjure the realm** etc.: swear to leave the realm etc. for ever.

abjurer *n.* L18.

Abkhazian /əb'kɑːzɪən, əb'keɪzjən/ *n.* & *a.* Also **-sian**. M19. [f. *Abkhaz(ia)*: see below, -IAN.] A *n.* A member of a Caucasian people living in Abkhaz, a territory in the Caucasus; the NW Caucasian language of this people. M19. B *adj.* Of or pertaining to Abkhaz or its inhabitants. M19.

Abkhaz *n.* = ABKHAZIAN *n.* M19.

ablactation /ablak'teɪʃ(ə)n/ *n.* LME. [Late L *ablactatio(n-)*, f. *ablactat-* pa. ppl stem of *ablactare* wean, f. *ab* AB- + *lactare* suckle: see -ATION.] 1 Weaning. LME. †2 *Hort.* Inarching. L17–E19.

†ablaqueate *v.t.* LME–M18. [L *ablaqueat-* pa. ppl stem of *ablaqueare* disentangle: see -ATE[3].] Expose the roots of (a tree) by loosening or removing soil.

†ablaqueation *n.* LME–M18.

ablate /ə'bleɪt/ *v.* L15. [L *ablat-* pa. ppl stem of *auferre* take away: see -ATE[3]. In mod. use as back-form. f. next.] 1 *v.t.* Take away, remove, *spec.* by ablation (sense 3); erode by ablation. L15. 2 *v.i.* Undergo ablation (sense 3). M20.

ablator *n.* (a layer of) a material which undergoes ablation (sense 3) M20.

ablation /ə'bleɪʃ(ə)n/ *n.* LME. [Fr., or late L *ablatio(n-)*, f. as prec.: see -ATION.] 1 The action of taking away, removal. *obs.* in *gen.* sense. LME. 2 *Med.* Removal by surgical or other means, esp. of a tumour. LME. 3 The wearing away or removal of surface material from a solid body; *esp.* (*a*) the wasting of a glacier, iceberg, etc. by melting and other processes; (*b*) the melting and evaporation of outer surface material from a spacecraft by friction with the atmosphere. M20.

ablative /'ablətɪv/ *a.* & *n.* LME. [(O)Fr. *ablatif*, *-ive* or L *ablativus*: see ABLATE, -IVE.] A *adj.* 1 *Gram.* Designating, being in, or pertaining to a case in Latin and other languages expressing direction from a place, or time, and variously also the source, cause, instrument and agent, manner, and sometimes place and time of an action or event. LME. †2 Of or pertaining to taking away or removing. M16–E18. 3 Producing, removed by, or pertaining to ablation (senses 2, 3). M20.

2 JOSEPH HALL Ablatiue directions are first needfull to vnteach error.

B *n.* 1 *Gram. The* ablative case; a word, form, etc., in the ablative case. LME. 2 An ablative material. M20.

1 **ablative absolute** *Latin Gram.* an ablative case of a noun or pronoun with a participle (expressed or implied) in concord, grammatically independent of the main clause, and expressing the time, occasion, or circumstance of a fact stated.

ablatival /-'tʌɪv(ə)l/ *a.* pertaining to the ablative case M19. **ablatively** *adv.* M19.

ablaut /'ablaʊt/ *n.* M19. [G, f. *ab* off + *Laut* sound.] *Philol.* Vowel change in related words, *esp.* that in Indo-European, which survives in English in, e.g., *sing, sang, sung, song*.

ablaut SERIES.

ablaze /ə'bleɪz/ *adv.* & *pred. a.* E19. [f. A-[2] + BLAZE *n.*[1]] On fire; *fig.* glittering, excited.

able /'eɪb(ə)l/ *a.* See also HABILE. LME. [OFr. *(h)able* f. L *habilis*, f. *habere* to hold.] I *pass.* †1 Easy to handle or use. LME–M18. †2 Suitable, competent. LME–L18. 3 *pred.* Liable *to*. *obs.* exc. *dial.* LME.

1 T. BETTERTON The Hands are the most habil members of the body. 2 R. BROME To the next able Tree with him. 3 MONMOUTH A spectacle able to make a man die for anger.

II *act.* 4 Having the qualifications for, and means of, doing something; having sufficient power (*to do*); (*pred.* foll. by *to do* esp. used with parts of *be* to supply the deficiencies of *can*). LME. b Legally qualified. E18. c Of a seaman: able to perform all duties; *spec.* in the Royal Navy, having a rating between leading and ordinary seaman. L18. 5 Physically strong; vigorous. *obs.* exc. *dial.* LME. †6 Wealthy. M16–L19. 7 Having mental power; talented, clever. M16.

4 O. FELTHAM An able servant out of imployment. G. M. TREVELYAN A vast population able to read but unable to distinguish what is worth reading. E. O'NEILL You won't be able to drag out the old bottle quick enough. **able for** *Anglo-Ir.* fit to cope with. *be able to use*: see USE *v.* *be able to wait*: see WAIT *v.* 5 SHAKES. *All's Well* Of as able body as when he numbered thirty. 6 S. PEPYS A very able citizen in Gracious Street. 7 DRYDEN Those able heads expound a wiser way. M. EDGEWORTH By no means so able a boxer. E. HEMINGWAY The bastard must be fairly able to have run this band successfully.

Comb.: **able-bodied** *a.* (*a*) having a body free from disability and fit for service; (*b*) = sense 4c above.

ableism *n.* prejudice or discrimination against disabled persons L20. **ableness** *n.* (now *rare*) LME.

†able *v.t.* ME. [f. the adj.: cf. (O)Fr. *habiller* in same senses.] 1 Fit, make ready, (esp. *to*). ME–L16. 2 Make capable, enable, (*to do*). Latterly *dial.* LME–L19. 3 Attire, dress. LME–L15. 4 Empower, strengthen, confirm. LME–M17. b Warrant; vouch for. L16–E17.

4 DONNE And life, by this death abled, shall controule Death. b SHAKES. *Lear* None does offend, none . . ; I'll able 'em.

-able /əb(ə)l/ *suff.* [Fr. f. L *-abilis* adj. suff., the form taken by the suff. *-bilis* (see -BLE) when added to vbs in *-are*, Fr. *-er*; extended in Fr. to vbs of all conjugations and also (as occas. in post-classical L, e.g. *amicabilis* AMICABLE, f. *amicus* friend) to ns., as in *charitable*, *équitable*.] Forming adjs. Orig. found in Eng. only in words from Fr. or L, as *separable* (f. Fr. *séparable* or L *separabilis*), but subsequently used to form many adjs. direct from the stem of Eng. vbs in *-ate*, as *appreciable* from *appreciate*, *educable* from *educate*, *extricable* from *extricate*. Later, prob. by confusion w. the unrelated adj. ABLE *a.*, freely used to form adjs. from vbs of all types, as *bearable*, *reliable*, from ns., as *clubbable*, *saleable*, and from vbl phrs., as *get-at-able*. In new formations now always passive in sense but earlier freq. active, as in *comfortable*, *suitable*.

abled /ˈeɪb(ə)ld/ *a.* L20. [Back-form. f. DISABLED.] Able-bodied, not disabled. Chiefly w. preceding adv., as *differently*: endowed with abilities in the manner specified (as a euphemistic substitute for *disabled*).

ablins /ˈeɪblɪnz/ *adv. Sc.* & *north.* (now *literary*). Also **aiblins**. E17. [f. ABLE *a.*: see -LING[2].] Possibly; perhaps.

abloom /əˈbluːm/ *adv.* & *pred. a.* M19. [f. A-[2] + BLOOM *n.*[1]] In or into bloom.

ablush /əˈblʌʃ/ *adv.* & *pred. a.* M19. [f. A-[2] + BLUSH *n.* or *v.*] Blushing.

ablute /əˈbluːt/ *v.t.* & *i. colloq.* L19. [Back-form. f. next.] Wash (oneself).

ablution /əˈbluːʃ(ə)n/ *n.* LME. [(O)Fr., or late L *ablutio(n-)*, f. *ablut-* pa. ppl stem of *abluere*, f. *ab* AB- + *luere* to wash: see -ION.] 1 The act of washing clean: †a *Alch.* & *Chem.* The purification of substances by the use of liquids. LME–M18. b *sing.* & (usu.) in *pl.* The washing of the body as a religious rite. M16. c *sing.* & (usu.) in *pl.* Ordinary personal washing. Freq. *joc.* M18. d *Chr. Ch.* The ceremonial washing of sacred vessels after, or of the celebrant's fingers before, during, and after, the Eucharist. L19. 2 The water etc. used in ablution. E18. 3 In *pl.* The building containing washing-places etc. in a camp, ship, etc. M20.

ablutionary *a.* M19.

ably /ˈeɪbli/ *adv.* LME. [f. ABLE *a.*: see -LY[2].] In an able manner.

-ably /əbli/ *suff.* [f. -ABLE: see -LY[2].] Forming advs. corresp. to adjs. in *-able*.

Abnaki /abˈnaki/ *n.* & *a.* Also **Abenaki** /abəˈnaki/. E18. [Fr. *Abénaqui* f. Montagnais *ouabanăkionek* people of the eastern country.] A *n.* Pl. same, -s. 1 A member of a grouping of N. American Indian peoples living chiefly in Maine and Quebec. E18. 2 Either of the two Algonquian languages of these peoples. E20. B *adj.* Of the Abnaki or their languages. E19.

abnegate /ˈabnɪgeɪt/ *v.t.* E17. [L *abnegat-* pa. ppl stem of *abnegare*, f. *ab* AB- + *negare* deny: see -ATE[3].] 1 Deny oneself (something); renounce (a right or privilege). E17. 2 Abjure (a belief etc.). M18.

abnegator *n.* M17.

abnegation /abnɪˈgeɪʃ(ə)n/ *n.* LME. [Fr., or L *abnegatio(n-)*, f. as prec.: see -ATION.] 1 Denial; rejection (of a doctrine etc.). LME. 2 Self-denial; self-sacrifice; an instance of this. (*Self* now often expressed.) LME.

1 J. KNOX Abnegation of Christe. SOUTHEY Abnegation of the opinion imputed to the heretics. M. BRADBURY A vast degeneration, a major abnegation of any regard for the quality of human life. 2 E. BLUNDEN His gallantry in going through . . the abnegations of service.

abnet /ˈabnət/ *n.* Also **abanet** /ˈabənət/. E18. [Heb. *'aḇnēṭ* belt.] *Jewish Antiq.* A girdle of fine linen worn esp. by priests.

Abney level /ˈabnɪ ˌlɛv(ə)l/ *n. phr.* L19. [Sir William *Abney* (1844–1920), Eng. scientist.] A kind of clinometer consisting of a sighting tube, spirit level, and graduated scale.

abnormal /əbˈnɔːm(ə)l/ *a.* M19. [Alt. of ANORMAL after L *abnormis*: see ABNORMOUS.] 1 Deviating from the type; contrary to the rule or system; unusual. M19. 2 Of or pertaining to what is abnormal. E20.

1 C. DARWIN The wing of a bat is a most abnormal structure. E. O'NEILL The spell of abnormal quiet. 2 **abnormal psychology**: dealing with persons having abnormal (esp. undesirable) traits.

abnorˈmality *n.* the quality or state of being abnormal; an abnormal feature or act: M19. **abnormalize** *v.t.* make abnormal L19. **abnormally** *adv.* M19. **abnormalness** *n.* (*rare*) M19.

abnormity /əbˈnɔːmɪti/ *n.* M18. [Late L *abnormitas*, f. *abnormis*: see next, -ITY.] 1 The quality of being abnormal. M18. 2 A monstrosity. M19.

abnormous /əbˈnɔːməs/ *a.* M18. [f. L *abnormis*, f. *ab* AB- + *norma* rule + -OUS.] Irregular; misshapen.

abo /ˈabəʊ/ *n.* & *a. Austral. slang* (now considered *derog.*). Also **A-**. Pl. of n. **-os**. E20. [Abbrev. of ABORIGINAL.] (An) Australian Aboriginal.

aboard /əˈbɔːd/ *adv.* & *prep.*[1] LME. [f. A *prep.*[1] 1 + BOARD *n.*, partly after (O)Fr. *à bord.*] A *adv.* 1 On or on to or into a ship, train, aircraft, etc. LME. b On or on to the back of a horse etc. L19. c *Baseball.* On base. M20. d In or into a group, team, etc.; in an enterprise. M20. 2 Alongside. LME.

1 **all aboard**: the cry to warn passengers to get aboard a vessel, train, etc., about to start. 2 CAPT. COOK Keeping the coast . . aboard. *fall aboard*: see FALL *v. lay aboard*: see LAY *v.*[1] 18b.

B *prep.* 1 On, on to, or into (a ship, train, aircraft, etc.). LME. b On or on to the back of (a horse etc.). M20. †2 Alongside of. E16–L17.

2 T. FULLER Hard aboard the shore.

abob /əˈbɒb/ *adv.* & *pred. a.* E20. [f. A-[2] + BOB *n.*[2] or *v.*[3]] 1 Bobbing, afloat. E20. 2 Foll. by *with*: in which specified objects are bobbing. E20.

abode /əˈbəʊd/ *n.*[1] ME. [vbl n. of ABIDE.] †1 The action of waiting. ME–E17. †2 A temporary stay. LME–M18. 3 Habitual residence; a house or home. LME.

1 SHAKES. *Merch. V.* Your patience for my long abode. 3 *no fixed abode*.

†abode *n.*[2] L16–L17. [f. A-[1] + BODE *n.*[2]] An omen, a prognostication.

†abode *v.*[1] L16. [f. A-[1] + BODE *v.*[1]] 1 *v.t.* Presage, forebode. L16–M17. 2 *v.i.* Be ominous. M–L17.

†aboding *n.* (a) foreboding L16–E18.

abode *v.*[2] pa. t. of ABIDE.

†abodement *n.* L16–M17. [f. ABODE *v.*[1] + -MENT.] An omen; a foreboding.

aboil /əˈbɔɪl/ *adv.* & *pred. a.* M19. [f. A-[2] + BOIL *n.*[2] or *v.*] Boiling, seething, (*lit.* & *fig.*).

abolish /əˈbɒlɪʃ/ *v.t.* LME. [(O)Fr. *aboliss-* lengthened stem of *abolir* f. L *abolere* destroy: see -ISH[2].] Put an end to, annul, demolish, destroy; (now only institutions, customs and practices). (Formerly foll. by *from*, *out of*.)

abolishable *a.* M17. **abolisher** *n.* M17. **abolishment** *n.* = ABOLITION M16.

abolition /abəˈlɪʃ(ə)n/ *n.* E16. [Fr., or L *abolitio(n-)*, f. *abolit-* pa. ppl stem of *abolere*: see prec., -ITION.] 1 The act of abolishing something; the fact or state of being abolished; destruction. E16. b *spec.* The abolition of (*a*) *Hist.* the slave-trade; (*b*) capital punishment; (*c*) *Austral. Hist.* convict transportation. L18. †2 A putting out of memory; an amnesty. E17–E19.

1 B. RUSSELL No one would advocate the abolition of competition in games. C. HAMPTON The reintroduction . . , after seventy-five years of abolition, of the death penalty. b F. A. KEMBLE The late abolition movement.

abolitionism *n.* support for abolition (ABOLITION 1b) E19. **abolitionist** *n.* & *a.* (*a*) *n.* a person who aims at abolition; (*b*) *adj.* of or pertaining to abolitionists or abolitionism: L18.

abomasum /abəʊˈmeɪsəm/ *n.* Pl. **-sa** /-sə/. Also **†-sus**, pl. **-si**. L17. [f. AB- + OMASUM.] The fourth stomach of a ruminant.

abominable /əˈbɒm(ə)nəb(ə)l/ *a.* Also **†abhom-**. ME. [OFr. f. L *abominabilis*, f. *abominari*: see ABOMINATE *v.*, -ABLE. Var. w. *-h-* (in med.L, OFr., & Eng.) as if f. L *ab* + *homin-*, *homo* a human, signifying 'inhuman'.] 1 Exciting disgust; offensive; odious. ME. 2 Very unpleasant. *colloq.* M19.

1 SHAKES. *Meas. for M.* Their abominable and beastly touches. **Abominable Snowman** = YETI. 2 G. B. SHAW What an abominable smell of garlic!

abominableness *n.* E16. **abominably** *adv.* loathsomely; *colloq.* very badly: LME.

abominate /əˈbɒmɪnət/ *a.* Now *rare* or *obs.* L16. [L *abominatus* pa. pple, f. as next: see -ATE[2].] Abominable, detested.

abominate /əˈbɒmɪneɪt/ *v.t.* M17. [L *abominat-* pa. ppl stem of *abominari*, f. *ab* AB- + *omin-*, *omen* omen: see -ATE[3].] 1 Feel extreme disgust towards; abhor; express abhorrence of. M17. 2 Dislike strongly. *colloq.* L19.

abominator *n.* L17.

abomination /əbɒmɪˈneɪʃ(ə)n/ *n.* Also **†abhom-**. ME. [(O)Fr. f. L *abominatio(n-)*, f. as prec.: see -ATION.] 1 An abominable act; a degrading vice. ME. 2 A feeling of disgust and hatred; loathing. LME. †3 A state exciting disgust; pollution. LME–L15. 4 An object that excites disgust and hatred (*to*, *unto*). LME.

1 SHAKES. *Ant. & Cl.* Antony, most large In his abominations. 4 AV *Prov.* 12:22 Lying lippes are abomination to the Lord.

†abominationly *adv.* abominably L16–E18.

†abomine *v.t.* E16–E18. [Fr. *abominer* f. L *abominari*: see ABOMINATE *v.*] = ABOMINATE *v.*

abondance *n.* see ABUNDANCE.

abonnement /abɔnmɑ̃/ *n.* Pl. pronounced same. L19. [Fr., f. *abonner* subscribe: see -MENT.] A subscription, as for a newspaper etc.; a season ticket.

abonné /abɔne (*pl. same*)/ *n.* [pa. pple of *abonner*] a subscriber, a season-ticket holder L19.

aboon *adv.*, *prep.*, & *n.* var. of ABUNE.

aboral /abˈɔːr(ə)l/ *a.* M19. [f. AB- + ORAL *a.*] *Zool.* Pertaining to the part furthest from the mouth.

aborally *adv.* L19.

abord /əˈbɔːd/ *n. arch.* E17. [Fr., f. as next.] Approach; way of approach.

abord /əˈbɔːd/ *v.t.* Now *rare* or *obs.* LME. [(O)Fr. *aborder*: see ABOARD.] †1 Approach; land on. LME–L17. 2 Accost. E17.

abordage /əˈbɔːdɪdʒ/ *n. rare.* M16. [Fr.] An attack on a ship by boarding it.

aboriginal /abəˈrɪdʒɪn(ə)l/ *a.* & *n.* M17. [Irreg. f. ABORIGINES + -AL[1].] A *adj.* 1 First or earliest known; primitive; indigenous. M17. b Existing in a land before the arrival of (European) colonists. L17. 2 Of or pertaining to aborigines, esp. (usu. **A-**) to those of Australia or their languages. L18.

1 J. HEATH-STUBBS An aboriginal Filipino pygmy. 2 E. MORRIS Such and such a word is not Aboriginal. E. BIRNEY The . . curator has left me alone / in the closed wing of the aboriginal section.

B *n.* An aboriginal inhabitant or the aboriginal language of a place, esp. (usu. **A-**) of Australia. M18.

ˌaborigiˈnality *n.* the quality of being aboriginal M19. **aboriginally** *adv.* from or in the earliest known times E19.

aborigine /abəˈrɪdʒɪniː/ *n.sing.* Also **A-**. M19. [Back-form. f. ABORIGINES.] An aboriginal inhabitant.

¶See also ABORIGINES.

ab origine /ab əˈrɪdʒɪni/ *adv. phr.* M16. [L, f. *ab* from + *origine* abl. of *origo* beginning, source.] From the beginning; from the creation of the world.

aborigines /abəˈrɪdʒɪniz/ *n.pl.* E16. [L *aborigines* pl., prob. f. prec.] 1 The original inhabitants of a country (orig. of Italy and of Greece). E16. 2 Indigenous plants or animals. L17. 3 The inhabitants of a land before the arrival of

(European) colonists, esp. (usu. **A-**) those of Australia. E18.

†aborigen, -gin *n.* = ABORIGINE E17–M19.

aborning /əˈbɔːnɪŋ/ *adv.* & *pred. a.* Chiefly *N. Amer.* M20. [f. A-² + *borning* vbl n. of BORN *v.*: see -ING¹.] (While) being born or produced.

abort /əˈbɔːt/ *n.* LME. [L ABORTUS.] †**1** A miscarriage (*lit.* & *fig.*). LME–M17. **2** The product of a miscarriage. Now *rare.* E17. **3** *Aeronaut.* & *Astronaut.* An aborted flight by a rocket etc.; a rocket etc. that fails; *transf.* any unsuccessful enterprise. M20.

abort /əˈbɔːt/ *v.* M16. [L *abort-* pa. ppl stem of *aboriri* miscarry, f. *ab* AB- + *oriri* come into being.] **1** *v.i.* Of a pregnant woman: miscarry, with loss of the foetus, esp. (& *Med.*) in the period before a live birth is possible. (In pop. use often with an implication of deliberate induction.) M16. **b** *Aeronaut.* & *Astronaut.* Abandon or fail to complete a flight. M20. **2** *v.t.* Cause abortion of; cause to abort; *fig.* bring to a premature or fruitless termination. L16. **b** *Aeronaut.* & *Astronaut.* Terminate (a flight); stop, abandon, or destroy (a rocket etc.). M20. **3** *v.i. Biol.* Of an organ: undergo arrestment of development. M19.

1b *American Speech* If trouble develops on the take-off roll.., it is possible to abort and stop the aircraft. **2** *Church Times* The 800,000 unborn children aborted under the 1967 Abortion Act. *Listener* Scruffy girls in jeans being aborted after men with sideburns.. had got them in the family way.

abor'tee *n.* a woman who undergoes an abortion M20. **abortifacient** /əbɔːtɪˈfeɪʃ(ə)nt/ *a.* & *n.* [-FACIENT] (a drug or other agent) causing abortion M19. **†abortment** *n.* abortion E17–L19. **abortorium** /abɔːˈtɔːrɪəm/ *n.*, pl. **-ia** /-ɪə/, a hospital or hospital department that specializes in performing abortions M20.

aborti *n.pl.* see ABORTUS.

abortion /əˈbɔːʃ(ə)n/ *n.* M16. [L *abortio(n-)*, f. as prec.: see -ION.] **1** The act of giving premature birth with loss of the foetus, esp. (& *Med.*) in the period before a live birth is possible; (the procuring of) induced termination of pregnancy to destroy a foetus. M16. **b** *fig.* Failure (of an aim, promise, etc.). E18. **2** The imperfect offspring or product of a miscarriage; a person or thing dwarfed or misshapen. L16. **3** *Biol.* Arrestment of development of any organ, esp. of a seed or fruit. M18.

1 *contagious abortion*: see CONTAGIOUS 3. *missed abortion*: see MISS *v.*¹

abortional *a.* (*rare*) of abortion, abortive M19. **abortionist** *n.* a person who procures or induces abortion; a person who favours permitting abortion: L19.

abortive /əˈbɔːtɪv/ *n.*, *a.*, & *v.* ME. [(O)Fr. *abortif*, *-ive* f. L *abortivus*, f. as prec.: see -IVE.] †**A** *n.* **1** A stillborn child or animal. ME–M18. **2** An imperfect result of an action. E17–E18.

B *adj.* †**1** Of or pertaining to abortion; born prematurely; causing or experiencing abortion. LME–M18. **2** Fruitless, unsuccessful. L16. **3** *Biol.* Arrested in development. M18.

1 SHAKES. *Rich. III* If ever he have child, abortive be it. **2** SCOTT FITZGERALD An abortive attempt at a laugh. T. PYNCHON An abortive firing, a warhead that didn't explode. **3** *fig.*: S. SPENDER An abortive tower at one corner.

†**C** *v.t.* Cause abortion of; render fruitless. Only in 17.

abortively *adv.* M16. **abortiveness** *n.* E17.

abortus /əˈbɔːtəs/ *n.* Pl. **-ti** /-tʌɪ/, **-tuses**. M19. [L = miscarriage: see ABORT *v.*] *Med.* **1** Abortion. M19. **2** An aborted foetus. E20.

Comb.: **abortus fever** brucellosis in humans, *spec.* that caused by *Brucella abortus*.

abosom *n.* pl. of OBOSOM.

abought *v.* pa. t. & pple of ABY.

aboulia /əˈbuːlɪə/ *n.* Also **abulia** /əˈbjuːlɪə/. M19. [Gk, f. A-¹⁰ + *boulē* will: see -IA¹.] Absence of will-power, or inability to act decisively, as a symptom of mental illness.

aboulic *a.* suffering from aboulia L19.

abound /əˈbaʊnd/ *v.i.* LME. [OFr. *abunder*, *abonder* f. L *abundare*, f. *ab* AB- + *undare*, f. *unda* a wave. 14–16 spelt *hab-* by assoc. w. L *habere* have.] **1** Overflow, be plentiful. LME. †**2** Be rich, have possessions to overflowing. LME–M18. **3** Be wealthy *in*; teem *with*. Also foll. by †*of*. LME. †**4** Be at liberty; revel *in*. LME–L18.

1 J. MCCOSH The discontent which abounds in the world. E. WAUGH English titles abounded now in Hollywood. **2** AV *Phil.* 4:18 I have all and abound. **3** E. M. FORSTER Those grey-brown streets.. in which the eastern quarter of the city abounds. W. STEVENS The vegetation still abounds with forms. **4** **†abound in one's own sense** follow one's own opinion.

abounder *n.* a person who has plenty M18. **aboundingly** *adv.* in an abounding manner, plentifully LME.

about /əˈbaʊt/ *adv.* & *prep.* [OE *onbūtan*, f. *on* in, on (see A *prep.*¹ I) + *būtan* outside of (see BUT *prep.*).] **A** *adv.* **1** Around the outside; on or towards every side; all round. OE. **b** In circumference. *arch.* LME. **2** Up and down; here and there. OE. **b** On the move, astir; prevailing (as a disease). ME. **3** In rotation or revolution; in the course of events; in succession. OE. **4** Near in number, scale, degree, etc., (hovering between adv. and prep.: cf. sense B.4 below); *colloq.* often in iron. understatement or comparison. OE. **5** On any side; somewhere near. ME. **6** Half round or less; facing in the opposite direction. ME. **b** *Naut.* On or to the opposite tack. L15. **7** With inf. (also occas. with vbl n.). †**a** Preparing, planning. ME–L18. **b** (Passing into prep.: cf. sense B.6 below.) On the point of, going *to*. In neg. contexts: intending *to*, prepared *to* (chiefly *N. Amer. colloq.*). E16.

1 W. OWEN A mead Bordered about with warbling water brooks. *fig.*: SHAKES. *Rom. & Jul.* Be wary, look about. **b** SHAKES. *Merry W.* In the waist two yards about. **2** YEATS Tumbled and blown about. E. BOWEN About on the low tables stood high alabaster lamps. *know one's way about*: see WAY *n.* **b** **out and about** (of a person, esp. after an illness) engaging in normal outdoor activity. *up and about*: see UP *adv.*² & *a.*² **3** L. STERNE Let the heralds officers twist his neck about if they will. **bring about** cause to revolve or happen, bring to pass. **come about** revolve (as time); happen, come to pass. *turn and turn about*: see TURN *n.* **4** DICKENS You're about right respecting the bond. *Tablet* We stopped firing at about seven o'clock. SCOTT FITZGERALD Her family is one aunt about a thousand years old. S. KAUFFMANN Desire and poignant affection, in about equal parts, sprang up in him. *stand about*: see STAND *v.* **5** *hang about* etc. **6** *right about*: see RIGHT *adv. the other way about*: see WAY *n.* **7b** CARLYLE England seems about deserting him. DYLAN THOMAS The conversation of prayers about to be said. M. RUSS I ain't about to work that hard for no reason. **†go about to** endeavour to (do something).

B *prep.* **1** On the outside of; on or towards every side of; all round. OE. **2** Around less definitely: **a** In attendance on. OE. **b** Somewhere on or near the person. ME. **c** Somewhere near *gen.*; in or near. Also *fig.* (in ref. to mental faculties etc.). LME. **3** Round (as opp. to across, over, into, etc.). *arch.* OE. **4** Approximately at; close to. OE. **5** Here and there in, over, or upon. ME. **b** Frequenting. L16. **6** In connection with; appertaining to; dealing or occupied with; touching; concerning; on the subject of; in relation to. ME.

1 J. HELLER A paisley kerchief.. was knotted rakishly about his neck. **2a** SHAKES. *Jul. Caes.* Let me have men about me that are fat. **b** E. WHARTON You don't happen to have a cigarette about you? **c** CHESTERFIELD Have.. your ears and your eyes about you. R. S. THOMAS There was a coldness / about his heart. **3** W. WOLLASTON Revolution.. about the sun. *beat about the bush*: see BUSH *n.*¹ **4** SHAKES. *Merry W.* Be you in the Park about midnight. J. I. M. STEWART A slight.. figure of about my own age. H. PINTER About the best convenience they had. *about time*: see TIME *n. along about*: see ALONG *adv.* 2b. *just about*: see JUST *adv.* **5** C. MEW She does the work about the house As well as most. K. MANSFIELD Tables and basket chairs scattered about the veranda. **b** *man about town*: see TOWN *n.* **6** AV *Luke* 2:49 I must be about my fathers businesse. P. LARKIN Scraps of songs about love. **how about** what is the news concerning; how do you dispose of the question of; what do you think of; I suggest. **how about that?** isn't that good, surprising, etc.? **how's about** *colloq.* = *how about* above. **what about** = *how about* above. *what something is all about*: see ALL *adv.* I.

aboutness *n.* E20.

†aboutes *adv.* & *prep.* var. of ABOUTS.

about-face /əbaʊtˈfeɪs/ *v.i.* & *n.* E20. [f. mil. command (*right*) *about face!*] = ABOUT-TURN.

†abouts *adv.* & *prep.* Also **-tes**. LME–L17. [f. ABOUT + -S³.] = ABOUT.

¶ Survives in *hereabouts* etc.

about-turn /əbaʊtˈtəːn/ *n.* & *v.i.* M20. [f. mil. command (*right*) *about turn!*] (Make) a reversal of direction, opinion, policy, or behaviour.

above /əˈbʌv/ *adv.*, *prep.*, *a.*, & *n.* OE. [f. A *prep.*¹ I repr. OE *on* + *bufan* BOVE. For illustration of senses, *a* and *bove* are here taken together: see note below.] **A** *adv.* **1** Overhead; vertically up; on high. OE. **b** In or to heaven. ME. **2** Higher on a sheet or page; earlier in a book or article. OE. **3** In a higher place; further up. ME. **4** In a higher rank, position, or station. ME. **5** In addition, besides. ME. **6** More in number or quantity. (Almost always with numeral following, passing into prep.: see sense B.8 below.) LME. **b** Above zero; above freezing point. M20.

1 DICKENS A wooden stair leading above. M. SPARK Mary cast her eyes around her and up above. *Heavens above*: see HEAVEN *n.* **b** TENNYSON Trust in things above. **2** *above-cited*, *-mentioned*, *-named*, *-quoted*, *-said*, *-written*, etc. **3** GEOFFREY HILL The tough pig-headed salmon strove.. To reach the steady hills above. **5** OVER AND ABOVE *adv. phr.*

B *prep.* **1** Over; vertically up from; on the top of. OE. **2** In a higher place than; further up from; further north than. OE. **3** Rising or appearing beyond the level or reach of. ME. **4** Superior to (the influence of); not condescending to. ME. **5** Higher in rank, position, etc. than. ME. **6** Higher in degree or quality than. ME. **7** In addition to; besides. ME. **8** Surpassing in quantity, amount, or number. (Passing into adv.: see sense A.6 above.) LME.

1 E. ST V. MILLAY Above the world is stretched the sky. *above one's head*: see HEAD *n. above water*: see WATER *n. keep one's head above water*: see WATER *n.* **2** E. HEMINGWAY The attack would cross the river above the narrow gorge. *above ground*: see GROUND *n. above the gangway*: see GANGWAY *n.* 3b. *above the salt*: see SALT *n.*¹ **3** L. HUGHES This college on the hill above Harlem. *fig.*: J. B. PRIESTLEY Even above the screeching.., voices can be heard. **4** M. MOORE Till the poets among us can be.. above insolence and triviality. **5** J. HELLER You'll be marrying far above you. **6** **above all** beyond everything, chiefly. *above measure*: see MEASURE *n.* **above oneself** lacking self-control because of high spirits etc. *above price*: see PRICE *n. above reproach*: see REPROACH *n. above suspicion*: see SUSPICION *n.* **7** **above and beyond** more than and different from. OVER AND ABOVE *prep. phr.* **8** SHAKES. *Haml.* It was never acted; or, if it was, not above once. *above par*: see PAR *n.*¹

C *n.* & *adj.* **1** Ellipt. after preps. (chiefly *from*): a higher place; heaven. ME. **2** Attrib. & absol.: w. ellipsis of a pple as *said, mentioned*, etc. M18.

1 AV *James* 1:17 Euery perfect gift is from aboue. **2** G. B. SHAW Reading the above after a lapse of 28 years. T. STOPPARD During the above speech French is becoming increasingly agitated.

Comb.: **aboveground** *a.* & *n.* (*a*) *adj.* that is above ground; that is not underground (*lit.* & *fig.*); (*b*) *n.* the part of society that is not underground.

¶ In OE *abufan* was north. and only advb., but by the end of 13 it had acquired the prep. uses of and generally replaced *bufan* BOVE, which became obs. in 15.

above-board /əbʌvˈbɔːd/ *adv.* & *pred. a.* L16. [f. ABOVE *prep.* + BOARD *n.*] Open(ly); fair(ly); without concealment.

¶ Orig. a gambling term.

ab ovo /ab ˈəʊvəʊ/ *adv. phr.* L16. [L = from the egg.] From the (very) beginning.

abox /əˈbɒks/ *adv.* & *pred. a.* E19. [f. A-² + BOX *v.*²] *Naut.* Of head-yards: in a position with only the head-sails laid aback.

abracadabra /ˌabrəkəˈdabrə/ *n.* M16. [L, first found in Q. Serenus Sammonicus (2nd cent.), ult. f. Gk.] A cabbalistic word, supposed when written triangularly, or in some other forms, to be a charm against fevers etc.; now used as a pretended conjuring word; a spell; gibberish.

abrade /əˈbreɪd/ *v.t.* L17. [L *abradere*, f. *ab* AB- + *radere* to scrape: cf. ABRASE *v.*] **1** Rub or wear off (a part *from*). L17. **2** Wear down or injure by rubbing. (*lit.* & *fig.*) M18.

abrader *n.* something that abrades a surface L19.

Abraham /ˈeɪbrəham/ *n.* & *a.* Also (*arch.*) **Abram** /ˈeɪbrəm/. OE. [The biblical patriarch (*Gen.* 11:26–25:18 etc.).] A *n.* 1 *Abraham's bosom*, †*barm* [*Luke* 16:23], heaven, the place of rest for the souls of the blessed. OE. 2 *sham Abraham* [see *Abraham-man* below], feign illness or insanity. L18.
Comb.: **Abraham-man** (*obs.* exc. *Hist.*) [perh. alluding to the beggar in *Luke* 16], after the dissolution of the religious houses (which had provided charity), a beggar feigning insanity.
†B *adj.* [Alt.] = AUBURN *a.* OE–E17.
Abrahamic /eɪbrəˈhamɪk/ *a.* of, pertaining to, or characteristic of the patriarch Abraham E19.

†**abraid** *v.* [OE *abreġdan*, f. A-[1] + BRAID *v.*[1]] 1 *v.t.* Wrench out (a sword). OE–ME. 2 *v.i.* & *t.* Start or startle out of sleep, a faint, etc. ME–E17. 3 *v.i.* & *t.* Shout out. LME–L16. 4 *v.i.* Rise nauseously in the stomach. Chiefly *dial.* M16–M19.

Abram *n.* & *a.* see ABRAHAM.

†**abrase** *a.* Only in 17. [L *abrasus* pa. pple, f. as next.] Rubbed smooth or clear; blank.

abrase /əˈbreɪz/ *v.t. rare.* L15. [L *abras-* pa. ppl stem of *abradere* ABRADE.] = ABRADE.

abrasion /əˈbreɪʒ(ə)n/ *n.* M17. [L *abrasio(n-)*, f. as prec.: see -ION.] 1 Rubbing or scraping off; wearing away. M17. b *Geol.* The wearing away of rock by the mechanical action of rock fragments carried by ice, water, or wind. M19. †2 Debris. Only in M18. 3 An abraded area; a graze. M19.
abrasional *a.* pertaining to or formed by abrasion M20.

abrasive /əˈbreɪsɪv/ *n.* & *a.* M19. [f. as ABRASE *v.* + -IVE.] A *n.* An abrasive substance or body. M19. B *adj.* Abrading; capable of polishing by rubbing or grinding; tending to graze the skin; *fig.* tending to hurt the feelings or annoy. L19.

abrazo /aˈbraθo, əˈbrɑːzəʊ/ *n.* Pl. **-os** /-ɔs, -əʊz/. E20. [Sp.] An embrace, a hug, esp. as a salutation.

abreaction /abrɪˈakʃ(ə)n/ *n.* E20. [f. AB- + REACTION after G *Abreagieren.*] *Psychoanalysis.* The relief of anxiety by the expression and release of a previously repressed emotion, through reliving the experience that caused it.
abreact *v.t.* eliminate by abreaction E20. **abreactive** *a.* M20.

abreast /əˈbrɛst/ *adv.* LME. [f. A *prep.*[1] 1 + BREAST *n.*] 1 With breasts or fronts in a line; side by side (in advancing). Formerly also after *in, of, on.* LME. b *Naut.* With ships equally distant, and parallel. L17. 2 Foll. by *of, with*: parallel to, alongside. Freq. *fig.* M17.
1 D. H. LAWRENCE They.. passed in on to the grass, four abreast. J. IRVING Three policemen came down the hall abreast, in step. *line abreast*: see LINE *n.*[2] 2 *keep abreast of* or *with*: see KEEP *v.*

†**abrecock** *n.* see APRICOT.

†**abrenounce** *v.t.* M16–M17. [f. AB- + RENOUNCE *v.*: cf. med.L *abrenunciare.*] Renounce; contradict.

abrenunciation /ˌabrɪnʌnsɪˈeɪʃ(ə)n/ *n. arch.* M16. [OFr. *abrenonciation* or late L *abrenuntiatio(n-)*, f. as AB- + *renuntiatio(n-)* RENUNCIATION.] Renunciation; retractation.

abri /əˈbriː/ *n.* E19. [Fr.] A shelter; *spec.* in *Archaeol.*, an overhanging rock affording shelter.

abridge /əˈbrɪdʒ/ *v.t.* ME. [OFr. *abreg(i)er* f. L *abbreviare*: see ABBREVIATE *v.*] 1 Deprive (a person) *of*; (*rare*) debar *from. arch.* ME. 2 Shorten in duration. Now *rare.* LME. 3 Make shorter in number of words, while retaining the sense; epitomize. (Foll. by *from.*) LME. 4 Cut short; reduce to a small size. Now *rare* of material things. LME. 5 Curtail (rights, privileges, etc.). LME.
2 SHAKES. *Two Gent.* Thy staying will abridge thy life. 4 SIR W. SCOTT To what purpose serve these abridged cloaks?
abridger *n.* M16.

abridgement /əˈbrɪdʒm(ə)nt/ *n.* Also **-dgm-**. LME. [(O)Fr. *abrégement*, f. as prec.: see -MENT.] 1 The act or process of abridging; shortening; curtailment; an instance of this. LME. 2 An epitome or compendium of a larger work, or of a subject that might be treated more fully. LME.

abrim /əˈbrɪm/ *adv.* & *pred. a.* L19. [f. A-[2] + BRIM *n.*[1]] Full to the brim; brimming.

abrin /ˈeɪbrɪn/ *n.* L19. [f. mod.L *Abrus* (see below) + -IN[1].] *Chem.* A poisonous protein present in the jequirity bean (*Abrus precatorius*).

abroach /əˈbrəʊtʃ/ *adv.* & *pred. a.* LME. [AN *abroche*, f. OFr. *abrochier*, f. as A-[5] + BROACH *n.*[1], *v.*[1]] Chiefly in *set abroach* 1 Of a cask etc.: broached; pierced, so as to let the liquor run. LME. 2 In a state to be diffused or propagated; astir. E16.
2 SHAKES. *Rom. & Jul.* Who set this ancient quarrel new abroach?

abroad /əˈbrɔːd/ *adv.* & *n.* ME. [f. A *prep.*[1] 1 + BROAD *n.*] A *adv.* 1 Widely, over a broad surface; widely scattered; widespread. ME. 2 Out of one's house or abode. ME. 3 In or into foreign countries; out of one's native land. LME. 4 At large, freely moving about, (*lit.* & *fig.*). L15. 5 Confused; dazed; astray; wide of the mark. E19.
1 AV *Rom.* 5:5 The loue of God is shed abroad in our hearts. SHAKES. *Tit. A.* The.. wind Will blow these sands like Sibyl's leaves abroad. LONGFELLOW Stretched abroad on the seashore. *send abroad*: see SEND *v.*[1] 2 HENRY MILLER The greatest delight.. was ..to walk the streets at night when no one was abroad. 3 W. PLOMER A pleasant old buffer,.. Who believed that.. an umbrella might pacify barbarians abroad. 4 LD MACAULAY The suspicions which were abroad. 5 THACKERAY At the twelfth round the.. champion was all abroad.
B *n.* 1 *from abroad*, from another country. M19. 2 Somewhere outside one's homeland; foreign countries. L19.
2 K. GRAHAME Somewhere over in that beastly abroad. R. MACAULAY Abroad is getting fuller.

abrogable /ˈabrəgəb(ə)l/ *a.* L16. [f. L *abrogare* (see ABROGATE *v.*) + -ABLE.] Able to be abrogated.

abrogate /ˈabrəgət/ *a.* (orig. *pa. pple*) *arch.* LME. [L *abrogatus* pa. pple, f. as next: see -ATE[2].] Repealed; abolished by authority.
¶In earlier use than the vb (see next), whence also (M16) a new pple *abrogated*, now more generally used.

abrogate /ˈabrəgeɪt/ *v.t.* E16. [L *abrogat-* pa. ppl stem of *abrogare*, f. *ab* AB- + *rogare* propose a law: see -ATE[3].] Repeal (a law, custom, etc.); abolish authoritatively or formally; *gen.* do away with.
abrogator *n.* L16.

abrogation /abrəˈgeɪʃ(ə)n/ *n.* M16. [Fr., or L *abrogatio(n-)*, f. as prec.: see -ATION.] Repeal; abolition by authority.

†**abrood** *adv.* & *pred. a.* ME–L19. [f. A *prep.*[1] 1 + BROOD *n.*] On its brood; hatching eggs, *fig.* mischief etc.

abrook /əˈbrʊk/ *v.t. rare.* L16. [f. A-[11] + BROOK *v.*] Brook, endure.
¶First recorded in Shakes.

abrupt /əˈbrʌpt/ *a.*, *n.*, & *v.* L16. [L *abruptus* broken off, steep, pa. pple of *abrumpere*, f. *ab* AB- + *rumpere* break.] A *adj.* †1 Broken away (from restraint). *rare.* Only in L16. 2 Characterized by sudden interruption or change; sudden, hasty; curt in manner. L16. †3 Broken off. E17–M18. 4 Precipitous, steep. E17. 5 *Bot.* Truncated. E19.
2 SHAKES. *1 Hen. VI* The cause of your abrupt departure. E. O'NEILL Talking in.. abrupt sentences. 4 O. SITWELL The abrupt and mountainous grey background.
B *n.* An abrupt place; an abyss. *literary.* M17.
MILTON Upborn with indefatigable wings Over the vast abrupt.
C *v.t.* Break off; interrupt suddenly. M17.
M. INNES To abrupt his journey in a strange town.
abruptly *adv.* L16. **abruptness** *n.* E17.

abruption /əˈbrʌpʃ(ə)n/ *n.* E17. [L *abruptio(n-)*, f. as prec.: see -ION.] 1 A breaking off; an interruption. *arch.* E17. 2 A snapping; the sudden breaking away of a portion from a mass. M17.

abruptio placentae /əˌbrʌptɪəʊ plәˈsɛntiː, əˌbrʌpʃɪəʊ/ *n. phr.* E20. [mod.L, f. as ABRUPTION + PLACENTA.] *Med.* Premature separation of the placenta from the uterine wall during pregnancy.

abs- /əbs, abs/ *pref.* (not productive). Repr. L *abs-*, the form of *ab-* AB- used bef. *c, q, t.*

abscess /ˈabsɪs, -sɛs/ *n.* M16. [L *abscessus*, f. *abscedere*, f. ABS- + *cedere* CEDE.] A localized collection of pus within the body.
abscessed *a.* affected by an abscess or abscesses M19.

abscind /əbˈsɪnd/ *v.t. arch.* E17. [L *abscindere*, f. *ab* AB- + *scindere* cut asunder.] Cut off (*lit.* & *fig.*).

abscise /əbˈsʌɪz/ *v.* E17. [L *abscis-* pa. ppl stem of *abscidere*, f. ABS- + *caedere* to cut.] 1 *v.t.* Cut off or away. E17. 2 *v.i. Bot.* Separate by abscission; fall off. E20.

abscisic /abˈsɪsɪk/ *a.* M20. [f. ABSCIS(SION + -IC.] Biochem. *abscisic acid*, a plant hormone which promotes seed and bud dormancy and inhibits germination.

abscision /əbˈsɪʒ(ə)n/ *n.* LME. [L *abscisio(n-)*, f. as ABSCISE: see -ION.] A cutting off or away.
¶Conf. in Eng. (as already in L) w. ABSCISSION.

absciss /ˈabsɪs/ *n.* In *Math.* now usu. in L form **abscissa** /abˈsɪsə/, pl. **-ssae** /-siː/, **-ssas**. L17. [mod.L *abscissa* use as n. (sc. *linea* line) of fem. pa. pple of *abscindere*: see ABSCIND.] 1 *Math.* Orig., the portion of a line between a fixed point on it and the point of intersection with an ordinate. Now, the distance of a point from the *y*-axis measured parallel to the *x*-axis. L17. 2 Bot. *absciss layer*, a distinctive layer of cells at which separation occurs on leaf-fall. L19.

absciss /əbˈsɪs/ *v.t.* & *i.* M19. [Back-form. f. next.] = ABSCISE.

abscission /əbˈsɪʃ(ə)n/ *n.* E17. [L *abscissio(n-)*, f. *absciss-* pa. ppl stem of *abscindere* ABSCIND: see -ION.] 1 A cutting off. E17. †2 The state of being cut off. Only in M17. 3 *Bot.* The natural separation of a leaf or other part from a plant. L19.

abscond /əbˈskɒnd/ *v.* M16. [L *abscondere*, f. as ABS- + *condere* put together, stow.] 1 *v.i.* & *refl.* Hide (oneself); leave hurriedly and secretly; flee from justice. M16. 2 *v.t.* Hide away, conceal. L16.
abscondence *n.* (*rare*) L19. **absconder** *n.* E18. **absconsion** *n.* (*rare*) M17.

abseil /ˈabzʌɪl, -seɪl/ *n.* & *v.i.* M20. [G *abseilen*, f. *ab* down + *Seil* rope.] 1 *Mountaineering.* (Make) a descent of a steep rock-face by means of a doubled rope fixed at a higher point. M20. 2 (Make) a similar descent from a helicopter. L20.

absence /ˈabs(ə)ns/ *n.* LME. [(O)Fr. f. L *absentia*, f. as ABSENT *a.* & *n.*: see -ENCE.] 1 The state of being away from a place or person; the time or duration of being away. LME. 2 Non-existence or lack *of.* LME. 3 Inattention due to thinking of other things. Esp. in *absence of mind.* E18. b *Med.* Sudden temporary loss of consciousness occurring without the awareness of the subject, esp. in petit mal; an episode of this (also *absence seizure*). M20.
1 B. BEHAN I was.. sentenced to death in my absence, so I said they could shoot me in my absence. B. PYM Her absences.. were spent in mysterious ploys of her own. *leave of absence*: see LEAVE *n.*[1] 2 **in the absence of something** when or as something is not present or available. 3 ADDISON The little absences and distractions of mankind.

absent /ˈabs(ə)nt/ *a.* & *n.* LME. [(O)Fr. f. L *absent-*, *absens* functioning as pres. pple of *abesse*, f. *ab* AB- + *esse* be: see -ENT.] A *adj.* 1 Away; not present. LME. 2 Not existing; lacking. LME. 3 Preoccupied; paying no attention to present objects etc. E18.
1 JAS. MILL Absent officers were summoned. **absent voter** a person who votes by post because absent from the normal voting-place. 3 SMOLLETT I.. became absent and thoughtful. I. COMPTON-BURNETT Duncan gave an absent nod towards the bed, as if he hardly heard.
Phrases: **absent from** not present in or at.
†B *n.* = ABSENTEE 1. LME–E19.
absently *adv.* with absence of mind M19. **absentness** *n.* absent-mindedness M19.

absent /abˈsɛnt/ *v.* LME. [(O)Fr. *absenter* or late L *absentare* keep or be away, f. as prec.] 1 *v.t.* Keep away. Now only *refl.* go or stay away.

LME. †2 *v.i.* Stay away; withdraw. LME–L18. 3 *v.t.* Leave. Long *rare*. LME.

1 D. RUNYON If he absents himself from her side.

absen'tation *n.* the action of absenting oneself E19. **absenter** *n.* a person who absents himself or herself L16.

absentee /abs(ə)n'tiː/ *n.* & *a.* M16. [f. prec. + -EE¹.] A *n.* 1 A person who is absent on some occasion. M16. b *spec.* An absent voter. E20. 2 A person who lives away from his or her country or home; *esp.* a landowner who lives away from his or her property. E17.

B *attrib.* or as *adj.* That is an absentee; of or pertaining to absentees. M19.

E. A. FREEMAN A foreign and absentee king. *New York Times* Laws governing absentee voting.

absenteeism *n.* the practice of being an absentee; the practice of workers, pupils, etc., of absenting themselves from work, esp. frequently or without good reason: E19. **absenteeship** *n.* (now *rare*) absenteeism, esp. of landowners L18.

absent-minded /abs(ə)nt'mʌɪndɪd/ *a.* M19. [f. ABSENT *a.* + MINDED.] = ABSENT *a.* 3.

absent-mindedly *adv.* L19. **absent-mindedness** *n.* L19.

†**absey** *n.* var. of ABC.

absinth /'absɪnθ/ *n.* Also (in sense 2 usu.) **-the**. LME. [Fr. *absinthe* f. L *absinthium* f. Gk *apsinthion* wormwood.] 1 Wormwood, the plant *Artemisia absinthium* or its essence; *fig.* bitterness, sorrow. LME. 2 A green liqueur made (at least orig.) from wine and wormwood. M19. b A green colour resembling that of the liqueur. L19.

absinthium /əb'sɪnθɪʌm/ *n.* Now *rare* or *obs.* OE. [L: see prec.] The plant absinth or wormwood.

†**absis** *n.* see APSIS.

absit omen /'absɪt 'əʊmən/ *int.* L16. [L = may this (evil) omen be absent.] May the suggested foreboding not become fact.

absolute /'absəluːt/ *a.* & *n.* LME. [L *absolutus* freed, completed, pa. pple of *absolvere* ABSOLVE; partly infl. by OFr. *absolu*.] A *adj.* †I Detached, disengaged. 1 Absolved *from*. LME–M17. 2 Disengaged from accidental or special circumstances. Only in LME. 3 Absorbed *in* (an occupation). Only in L15.

II In quality or degree. 4 Finished; perfect. *arch.* LME. 5 Pure, mere; in the strictest sense. M16. 6 Complete, entire. L16.

4 G. SANDYS Where mariners be English: who are the absolutest .. in their profession. 5 P. HAWKER The gale increased to an absolute tornado. **absolute alcohol** ethanol containing less than one per cent of water by weight. **absolute music** self-dependent instrumental music without literary or other extraneous suggestions. 6 ARNOLD BENNETT Performed with absolute assurance and perfection. N. BLAKE If he wasn't such an absolute ass. D. LESSING Your decree [of divorce] was absolute last week.

III In position or relation. 7 *Gram.* Not in the usual grammatical relation or construction; (of a form) uninflected. LME. 8 Of ownership or authority: unrestricted, independent. L15. 9 Having absolute power; arbitrary, despotic. L16. 10 Viewed without relation to or comparison with other things of the same kind; real, actual. E17.

7 *ablative absolute*: see ABLATIVE *n.* 1. *accusative absolute*: see ACCUSATIVE *n. dative absolute*: see DATIVE *n. genitive absolute*: see GENITIVE *n. nominative absolute*: see NOMINATIVE *n.* 8 **absolute majority** a majority over all rivals combined, more than half. 10 *absolute* HUMIDITY. *absolute* MAGNITUDE. **absolute pitch** a fixed standard of pitch defined by the rate of vibration; ability to recognize or reproduce the exact pitch of a note. **absolute temperature** temperature measured from absolute zero. *absolute term*: see TERM *n.* **absolute unit** a unit which can be defined in terms of mass, length, and time. **absolute value** *Math.* of a real number: its value irrespective of sign; of a complex number $a+ib$: the positive square root of a^2+b^2. *absolute viscosity*: see VISCOSITY 2. *absolute zero*: see ZERO *n.* 2b.

IV Without condition or mental limitation. 11 Of a person or prediction: free from doubt or uncertainty. *arch.* E17. 12 Of a statement etc.: free from conditions or reservations. E17. 13 *Philos.* Existing or able to be thought of without relation to other things. L18.

11 SHAKES. *Cymb.* I am absolute 'Twas very Cloten.

B *n.* 1 *the Absolute*, that which is absolute, that which exists or is able to be thought of without relation to other things. M19. 2 An absolute thing; an absolute principle or truth. M19.

absolutely *adv.* in an absolute manner or degree; also (stressed on 3rd syll.) used as an emphatic affirmative: yes, quite so: LME. **absoluteness** *n.* M16.

absolution /absə'luːʃ(ə)n/ *n.* ME. [(O)Fr. f. L *absolutio(n-)*, f. as prec.: see -ION.] 1 Remission of sins, declared by ecclesiastical authority. ME. b (An utterance of) the formula by which this is declared. LME. 2 Forgiveness of sins generally. ME. 3 More widely: any absolving or formal setting-free (*from* guilt, sentence, or obligation); remission (*of* sin or penance). LME. 4 Esp. *Rom. Law.* A judgement for the defendant. E17.

absolutise *v.* var. of ABSOLUTIZE.

absolutism /'absəluːtɪz(ə)m, -ljuː-/ *n.* M18. [f. ABSOLUTE *a.* + -ISM, after Fr. *absolutisme*.] 1 *Theol.* The doctrine that God acts absolutely in the matter of salvation. M18. 2 *Polit.* The principle of absolute government; despotism. E19. 3 *Philos.* The philosophy of the Absolute. L19.

absolutist /'absəluːtɪst, -ljuː-/ *n.* & *a.* M19. [f. as prec. + -IST, after Fr. *absolutiste*.] A *n.* 1 *Polit.* A person who is in favour of absolute government. M19. 2 *Philos.* A person who maintains the absolute identity of subject and object. M19. 3 A person who maintains certain principles to be absolute, an uncompromising person; *spec.* (*Hist.*) a conscientious objector in the war of 1914–18 who refused to perform any compulsory service. E20. B *adj.* Practising or supporting absolutism; despotic; uncompromising. M19.

absolu'tistic *a.* M19.

absolutize /'absəluːtʌɪz, -ljuː-/ *v.t.* Also **-ise**. M20. [f. ABSOLUTE *a.* + -IZE.] Make absolute.

absoluti'zation *n.* M19.

absolve /əb'zɒlv/ *v.t.* LME. [L *absolvere* free, acquit, f. *ab* AB- + *solvere* loosen: cf. ASSOIL.] 1 Set free, discharge, (*from* or *of* obligations, liabilities, etc.). LME. †2 Clear up, solve, resolve. L15–M17. 3 Pronounce free (*from* blame, guilt, the consequences of crime or sin, etc.). M16. 4 Esp. *Rom. Law.* Pronounce not liable or not guilty. M16. 5 Give absolution or remission of sins to. M16. 6 Remit, give absolution for, (a sin or crime). L16. †7 Discharge, finish, (a task etc.). L16–E19.

1 CONAN DOYLE We had come without our spoon-bait for jack, which absolved us from fishing for the day. L. A. G. STRONG It absolved him of all responsibility to them in the realm of financial speculation. 2 EVELYN Phenomena already absolved. 4 POPE Absolves the just, and dooms the guilty souls. 5 SHAKES. *Rom. & Jul.* To make confession, and to be absolv'd. M. R. MITFORD One's conscience may be pretty well absolved for not admiring this man. C. KINGSLEY I dare not absolve him of robbing a priest. 6 S. SASSOON Who shall absolve the foulness of their fate? 7 MILTON The work begun, how soon absolved.

absolvable *a.* E19. **absolver** *n.* L16.

absolvitor /ab'sɒlvɪtɔː/ *n.* M16. [L = let him or her be acquitted, 3rd pers. imper. pass. of *absolvere*: see prec.] *Sc. Law.* A judgement for the defender.

absonant /'abs(ə)nənt/ *a.* Now *rare*. M16. [f. L *ab* AB- + *sonant-* pres. ppl stem of *sonare* sound, on the analogy of *consonant*, *dissonant*, etc.] Harsh, discordant; *fig.* unreasonable, unnatural.

Also †**absonous** *a.* E17–M18.

absorb /əb'zɔːb, -'sɔːb/ *v.t.* Pa. pple **absorbed**, (*arch.*) **absorpt** /-ɔːpt/. LME. [(O)Fr. *absorber* or L *absorbere*, f. *ab* AB- + *sorbere* suck in.] 1 Include or take (a thing) in so that it no longer has separate existence; incorporate. LME. †2 Of water, mire, etc.: engulf. L15–L18. 3 Suck or drink in. E17. 4 Take up (a substance, energy, etc.) by chemical or physical action; gain energy from and reduce the intensity of (light or other radiation, sound, etc.). E18. 5 Engross (a person, a person's attention, etc.). L18. 6 Occupy or consume (time). M19. 7 Assimilate mentally. L19.

1 E. O'NEILL The conquered Chinese .. have already begun to absorb their conquerors. G. STEINER The realistic novel reached out to absorb every new quality and locus of experience. **be absorbed by** lose one's identity in. 2 T. BURNET To be absorpt .. in a lake of fire and brimstone. 7 R. CHURCH Life .. had more to offer me than I could absorb.

absorba'bility *n.* the quality of being absorbable L18. **absorbable** *a.* able to be absorbed L18. **absorbance** *n.* the logarithm of the reciprocal of transmittance; optical density: M20. **absorbancy** *n.* the ratio of the optical density of a solution to that of a similar body of pure solvent M20. **absorbed** *a.* that has been absorbed; *esp.* engrossed, intensely interested: M18. **absorbedly** /-bɪdli/ *adv.* M19. **absorbedness** /-bɪdnɪs/ *n.* L19. **absorber** *n.* a person who or thing which absorbs M19. **absorbing** *a.* that absorbs; *esp.* engrossing, all-engaging: M18. **absorbingly** *adv.* M19.

absorbent /əb'zɔːb(ə)nt, -'sɔːb-/ *a.* & *n.* E18. [L *absorbent-* pres. ppl stem of *absorbere*: see prec., -ENT.] A *adj.* Absorptive; having a tendency to absorb. E18.

absorbent cotton *N. Amer.* cotton wool.

B *n.* 1 A substance which absorbs. E18. 2 *Physiol.* In *pl.* The organs through which absorption occurs. Now *rare* or *obs.* M18.

absorbency *n.* †(*a*) the action of absorbing; (*b*) the quality of being absorbent: M19.

absorpt *v.* see ABSORB.

absorptance /əb'zɔːpt(ə)ns/ *n.* M20. [f. L *absorpt-* (see ABSORPTION) + -ANCE, after *reflectance*.] *Physics.* The degree to which a surface or object absorbs radiation incident on it, measured by the ratio of the absorbed to the incident flux.

absorptiometer /əbˌzɔːpʃɪ'ɒmɪtə, -ˌsɔːp-/ *n.* L19. [f. next + -OMETER.] 1 An analytical device which measures the amount of gas absorbed by a reagent. L19. 2 An instrument for measuring the absorption of light or other radiation. M20.

abˌsorptio'metric *a.* E20.

absorption /əb'zɔːpʃ(ə)n, -'sɔːp-/ *n.* L16. [L *absorptio(n-)*, f. *absorpt-* pa. ppl stem of *absorbere* ABSORB: see -ION.] †1 The swallowing up or engulfing of bodies. L16–M18. 2 Disappearance through incorporation in something else. M18. 3 The chemical or physical process of absorbing substances, energy, light, etc. M18. b *Physiol.* The taking up of fluids or dissolved substances by living tissue; *esp.* the taking of digested contents of the intestine into the blood and lymphatic system. M18. 4 Engrossment of the mind or faculties. M19. 5 Mental assimilation. M20.

Comb.: **absorption spectrum** a spectrum of electromagnetic radiation transmitted through a substance, characteristically showing lines or bands due to absorption at particular wavelengths.

absorptive /əb'zɔːptɪv, -'sɔːp-/ *a.* M17. [f. as prec. + -IVE.] Having the quality of absorbing.

absorp'tivity *n.* the property of being absorptive; a measure of this: M19.

absquatulate /əb'skwɒtjʊleɪt/ *v.i. joc.* Orig. *US.* M19. [After *abscond*, *squattle* (depart), *perambulate*, etc.] Depart, decamp.

absquatu'lation *n.* M19.

abstain /əb'steɪn/ *v.* LME. [AN *astener* = OFr. *abstenir* f. L *abstinere*, f. as ABS- + *tenere* to hold.] †1 *v.refl.* Keep or withhold oneself (*of*, *from*). LME–M16. 2 *v.i.* Refrain (*from*); *esp.* fast (*obs.*), refrain from alcohol, decline to use one's vote. LME. †3 *v.t.* Keep back or off. E16–M17.

3 MILTON Whether he abstain men from marying.

abstainer *n.* a person who abstains, esp. from eating or drinking particular things; in older religious writings, = NAZARITE *n.*²: LME.

abstemious /əb'stiːmɪəs/ *a.* E17. [f. L *abstemius*, f. ABS- + base of *temetum* intoxicating drink: see -OUS.] Sparing, moderate, not self-indulgent, esp. in food and drink.

P. MASSINGER Abstemious from base and goatish looseness. SIR W. SCOTT The meal of the Saracen was abstemious. J. UPDIKE The devout and abstemious Muslim he became.

abstemiously *adv.* E18. **abstemiousness** *n.* E17.

abstention /əb'stɛnʃ(ə)n/ *n.* E16. [Fr., or late L *abstentio(n-)*, f. *abstinere* ABSTAIN: see -ION.] †1 The act of keeping back or restraining. E16–M17. 2 The act or state of abstaining or refraining (*from*). E17. **b** *spec.* The action or an act of declining to cast one's vote. L19.

2 M. ARNOLD The character of abstention and renouncement. H. A. L. FISHER The fasting in the month of Ramadan, .. the abstention from wine. **b** H. KISSINGER In 1969 the Important Question resolution had passed by a wide margin of 71 in favor, 48 against, and 4 abstentions.

abstentionism *n.* the fact or policy of abstaining, *spec.* in a vote E20. **abstentionist** *n.* a person who abstains or believes in abstaining L19.

absterge /əbˈstəːdʒ/ *v.t.* Now *rare.* E16. [(O)Fr. *absterger* or L *abstergere*, f. ABS- + *tergere* wipe.] Wipe away; cleanse.

abstergent *a.* & *n.* (*a*) *adj.* cleansing; (*b*) *n.* a cleansing substance: E17.

abstersion /əbˈstəːʃ(ə)n/ *n.* LME. [(O)Fr., or med.L *abstertio(n-)*, f. L *absters-* pa. ppl stem of *abstergere*: see prec., -ION.] The act or process of cleansing or purging.

absterse *v.t.* (*rare*) = ABSTERGE LME. **abstersive** *a.* & *n.* = ABSTERGENT LME. **abstersiveness** *n.* M17.

abstinence /ˈabstɪnəns/ *n.* ME. [OFr. f. L *abstinentia*, f. as next: see -ENCE.] **1** Forbearance of any indulgence of appetite; sexual continence (the oldest sense); fasting; abstention from alcohol. ME. **2** *gen.* The action or practice of abstaining *from* (or †*of*) anything. LME.

1 *total abstinence*: see TOTAL *a.* 2 †**abstinence of war** a truce.

Comb.: **abstinence syndrome** *Med.* the physical symptoms that appear when a person abruptly stops taking a drug to which he or she is addicted.

abstinency *n.* the practice of abstaining from pleasure, food, etc.; a fast: L16.

abstinent /ˈabstɪnənt/ *a.* & *n.* LME. [(O)Fr. f. L *abstinent-* pres. ppl stem of *abstinere* ABSTAIN: see -ENT.] **A** *adj.* Practising abstinence. LME. **B** *n.* A person who abstains; a faster. LME.

abstinently *adv.* L16.

abstract /ˈabstrakt/ *a.* & *n.* LME. [OFr., or L *abstractus* pa. pple of *abstrahere*, f. as ABS- + *trahere* draw.] **A** *adj.* †**1** Derived, extracted. LME–L15. **2** = ABSTRACTED 1. Now *rare* or *obs.* LME. **3** Separated from matter, practice, or particular examples; not concrete; ideal; abstruse. LME. **b** Of art etc.: free from representational qualities. M19. **4** = ABSTRACTED 3. Now *rare.* E16.

3 R. CUDWORTH Pure, Abstract, Incorporeal Substances. E. HEMINGWAY Abstract words, such as glory, honour, courage, or hallow were obscene. **abstract noun**: denoting a quality or state. **b abstract expressionism** a movement or style of painting, originating in New York in the 1940s, and often using techniques such as action painting to allow the artist spontaneous freedom of expression. 4 D. H. LAWRENCE White and abstract-looking, he sat and ate his dinner.

B *n.* **I 1 a** An abridgement or summary of a book, document, etc. LME. **b** *gen.* Something that concentrates in itself the qualities of another greater thing or other things. M16. **2** An abstraction; an abstract term. M16. **3** An abstract painting or other work of art. M20.

1b SHAKES. *Ant. & Cl.* A man who is the abstract of all faults That all men follow.

II 4 *absol.* That which is abstract; the ideal or theoretical way of regarding things. E17.

¶At first a pple as well as adj., stressed on 2nd syll.; as pple replaced by *abstracted.*

abstractly *adv.* LME. **abstractness** *n.* L16.

abstract /əbˈstrakt/ *v.* LME. [Partly f. prec.; partly f. L *abstract-* pa. ppl stem of *abstrahere*: see prec.] **1** *v.t.* Separate, disengage, *from.* LME. **2** *v.t.* Withdraw, take away; *euphem.* steal. L15. †**b** *v.t.* Esp. *Chem.* Extract, distil. E17–E18. **3** *v.t.* Summarize, abridge. L16. **4** *v.t.* Separate in mental conception; consider abstractly. E17. **5** *v.refl.* & *i.* Withdraw oneself, retire *from*, (*lit.* & *fig.*). M17.

1 A. COWLEY The Importunities of Company or Business, which would abstract him from his Beloved [Poetry]. 2 H. MARTINEAU The public burdens, which .. abstract a large proportion of profits and wages. F. HOYLE Living plants abstract carbon dioxide and add oxygen to the atmosphere. **b** J. MARSTON Poison from roses who could e'er abstract? 4 GIBBON To abstract the notions of time, of space, and of matter. G. W. KNIGHT To abstract the skeleton of logical sequence which is the story of the play. 5 **abstracting from** *arch.* leaving out of consideration.

abstractable *a.* L19. **abstracter** *n.* a person who abstracts; a person who makes an abstract or abstracts: L17. **abstractor** *n.* an abstracter; *spec.* (now *Hist.*) as a title of a grade of clerks in the British Civil Service: M17.

abstracted /əbˈstraktɪd/ *a.* M16. [f. prec. + -ED[1].] **1** Drawn off, removed; separate, apart *from.* M16. **2** = ABSTRACT *a.* 3. Now *rare.* E17. **3** Withdrawn from the contemplation of present objects; absent in mind. E17.

2 S. JOHNSON Abstracted ideas of virtue. 3 S. KAUFFMANN Perry turned to him a little thoughtfully, in that abstracted manner which indicates that the subject has to be recalled from a distance.

abstractedly *adv.* M17. **abstractedness** *n.* M17.

abstraction /əbˈstrakʃ(ə)n/ *n.* LME. [(O)Fr., or late L *abstractio(n-)*, f. *abstract-*: see ABSTRACT *v.*, -ION.] **1** The act of taking away; withdrawal; *euphem.* stealing. LME. **2** A state of withdrawal from worldly things or things of the senses. LME. **b** Absence of mind. L18. **3a** The act of considering something independently of its associations, attributes, or concrete accompaniments; the state of being so considered. L16. **b** A thing so considered; a thing which exists only in idea; something visionary. L16. **4** Freedom from representational qualities in art; an abstract work of art. E20.

1 C. LAMB He robs .. the revenue,—an abstraction I never greatly cared about. 2 E. WAUGH Dennis awoke from a deep abstraction. **b** BOSWELL Wrapped up in grave abstraction. 3a J. WAIN We had been asked to drink a toast to success, in abstraction—not success to this or that person, but success itself. *vicious abstraction*: see VICIOUS *a.* **b** B. RUSSELL 'The State' is an abstraction; it does not feel pleasure or pain, it has no hopes or fears. 4 M. SHADBOLT The paintings were not .. abstractions. They were landscapes, more or less.

abstractional *a.* M19. **abstractionism** *n.* the pursuit of abstraction(s); *esp.* the principles or pursuit of abstract art: E20. **abstractionist** *n.* a person who deals with abstractions; an advocate or practitioner of abstract art: M19.

abstractive /əbˈstraktɪv/ *a.* LME. [med.L *abstractivus*, f. L *abstract-*: see ABSTRACT *v.*, -IVE.] †**1** *Gram.* Of a noun: abstract. Only in LME. **2** Of abstracting character or tendency (in senses 1, 4, 5 of ABSTRACT *v.*). L15.

abstractively *adv.* (long *rare*) in an abstract manner, in the abstract E17.

abstractum /əbˈstraktəm/ *n.* Usu. in pl. **-ta** /-tə/. M19. [mod.L, neut. of *abstractus*: see ABSTRACT *a.* & *n.*] *Philos.* = ABSTRACT *n.* 2.

abstruse /əbˈstruːs/ *a.* L16. [Fr. *abstrus(e)* or L *abstrusus* pa. pple of *abstrudere* conceal, f. as ABS- + *trudere* thrust.] †**1** Hidden, secret. L16–M18. **2** Difficult to conceive of or apprehend; recondite. L16.

abstrusely *adv.* E17. **abstruseness** *n.* M17. **abstrusity** *n.* (*arch.*) abstruseness; something abstruse: M17. **abstrusive** *a.* (*rare*) of abstruse quality or tendency M17.

†**absume** *v.t.* L16–M18. [L *absumere*, f. *ab* AB- + *sumere* take.] Consume gradually.

absurd /əbˈsəːd/ *a.* & *n.* M16. [Fr. *absurde* or L *absurdus.*] **A** *adj.* **1** Out of harmony with reason or propriety; incongruous; inappropriate; unreasonable; ridiculous, silly. M16. †**2** Inharmonious, out of tune. Only in E17.

B *n.* †**1** An absurd thing. E–M17. **2** *absol.* That which is absurd; *esp.* human existence in a purposeless, chaotic universe. E20.

2 *Theatre of the Absurd*: see THEATRE *n.*

absurdism *n.* the belief that human beings exist in a purposeless chaotic universe in which attempts to impose order are frustrated M20. **absurdist** *a.* & *n.* (*a*) *adj.* of or pertaining to absurdism; (*b*) *n.* an adherent of absurdism; *esp.* a writer who deals with absurdist themes: M20. **absurdly** *adv.* M16. **absurdness** *n.* M16.

absurda *n.* pl. of ABSURDUM.

absurdity /əbˈsəːdɪti/ *n.* LME. [Fr. *absurdité* or L *absurditas*: see prec., -ITY.] †**1** Lack of harmony, dissonance. *rare.* LME–L17. **2** Something absurd; an absurd action, statement, etc. L15. **3** The state or quality of being absurd; folly. E16.

absurdum /əbˈsəːdəm/ *n.* Pl. **-da** /-də/. M19. [L, neut. sing. of *absurdus* ABSURD used as n.] An absurd or illogical conclusion or condition. See also REDUCTIO AD ABSURDUM.

abubble /əˈbʌb(ə)l/ *adv.* & *pred. a.* M20. [f. A-[2] + BUBBLE *n.* or *v.*] Bubbling over (with excitement etc.).

abuilding /əˈbɪldɪŋ/ *adv.* & *pred. a.* Now *arch.* exc. *US.* M16. [f. A *prep.*[1] 7 + BUILDING *n.*] In the process of being built.

abulia *n.* var. of ABOULIA.

Abuna /əˈbuːnə/ *n.* E17. [Amharic f. Arab. *'abūnā* our father.] (The title of) the Patriarch of the Ethiopian Orthodox Church.

abundance /əˈbʌnd(ə)ns/ *n.* In sense 5 also **abon-**. ME. [OFr. *(h)abundance* (mod. *abondance*) f. L *abundantia*, f. as next: see -ANCE.] **1** A large quantity, plenty; occas. a large number. ME. **2** Overflowing state or condition; superfluity; plentifulness. LME. **3** Affluence, wealth. LME. **4** The relative quantity or number (of a plant, a substance, etc.) present. L19. **5** A call undertaking to take nine or more tricks in solo whist. L19.

1 DEFOE Abundance of good things for our comfort. H. FIELDING There are abundance .. who want a morsel of bread. 2 AV *Ps.* 105:30 The land brought foorth frogs in abundance. DE QUINCEY My thoughts .. are from the abundance of my heart. 3 AV *Ecclus* 5:12 The abundance of the rich will not suffer him to sleepe. 4 S. WEINBERG A truly primordial deuterium abundance. 5 **declared abundance**: undertaking to take thirteen tricks with no trump suit. **royal abundance**: with the suit of the turned-up card as trumps.

abundancy *n.* M16.

abundant /əˈbʌnd(ə)nt/ *a.* LME. [L *abundant-* pres. ppl stem of *abundare* ABOUND: see -ANT[1].] **1** Overflowing; more than sufficient; plentiful. LME. **2** *pred.* Possessing something in superfluity, wealthy. (Foll. by *in*, †*of.*) LME. **3** *Math.* Of a number: exceeded by the sum of its divisors (including 1 but not the number itself). Opp. DEFICIENT *a.* 3b. M16.

abundantly *adv.* LME.

abune /əˈbuːn/ *adv.*, *prep.*, & *n.* *Sc.* & *north.* Also **aboon**. LME. [Alt.] = ABOVE.

abura /əˈbjʊərə/ *n.* E20. [Yoruba.] (A soft pale wood obtained from) the tree *Mitragyna ciliata* of tropical W. Africa.

a-burton *adv.* see BURTON *n.*[1] 2.

abuse /əˈbjuːs/ *n.* LME. [(O)Fr. *abus* or L *abusus*, f. as next.] **1** An improper usage; a corrupt practice. LME. **2** Improper use, perversion, (*of*). M16. **b** *Rhet.* Catachresis. Now *rare* or *obs.* L16. †**3** An imposture; a delusion. M16–M17. **4** Reviling; abusive language. Formerly also, a verbal insult. M16. **5** Injury, maltreatment. L16. **6** Violation; defilement. Now only in *self-abuse.* L16.

1 W. R. INGE Dickens was careful to castigate abuses which were being reformed. 2 J. COLLIER The abuse of a thing is no argument against the use of it. *drug abuse* etc. 3 SHAKES. *Haml.* Or is it some abuse, and no such thing? 4 R. DAHL A torrent of abuse and obscenity as he had never heard before. 5 *child abuse* etc.

†**abuseful** *a.* full of abuse, abusive E17–E18. **abusefully** *adv.* in an abusive manner M16.

abuse /əˈbjuːz/ *v.t.* LME. [(O)Fr. *abuser* ult. f. L *abus-* pa. ppl stem of *abuti*, f. *ab* AB- + *uti* to use.] **I 1** Misuse; make a bad use of; wrongly take advantage of. LME. **b** *spec.* Take (a drug) for a purpose other than a therapeutic one. M20. **2** Violate (a person); defile. *arch.* LME. †**3** Misrepresent; adulterate. LME–M18. †**4** Misuse the confidence of; impose upon; deceive. L15–E19. **5** Maltreat, injure, esp. repeatedly. M16. **6** Speak insultingly or unkindly to or of; malign. E17.

1 M. FRAYN I'm in a position of trust and privilege .. and I take care not to abuse it. 3 H. FIELDING He hath been .. grossly abused to you. 4 MILTON A misguided and abus'd Multitude. 5 T. FULLER He that abuseth his servants, giving them too little food or sleep. R. S. THOMAS Storming at him / .. with the eloquence / of the abused heart. *Times* A girl .. was being sexually abused by her father. 6 YEATS Ever and always curse him and abuse him.

†II 7 Disuse. *Sc.* L15–M16.

abusable *a.* M17. **abusage** *n.* abuse, misuse, (*obs.* after M17, revived M20 by Eric Partridge) M16. **abuser** *n.*[1] a person who abuses someone or something LME. †**abuser** *n.*[2] [-ER[4]] illegal or wrongful use M17–M18.

†**abusion** *n.* LME–L17. [OFr. f. L *abusio(n-)*, f. as prec.: see -ION.] = ABUSE *n.*

abusive /əˈbjuːsɪv/ *a.* M16. [(O)Fr. *abusif*, *-ive* or late L *abusivus*, f. as prec.: see -IVE.] 1 Misapplied; improper; *Rhet.* catachrestic. *arch.* M16. 2 Full of abuses. *arch.* L16. 3 Employing insulting language; scurrilous. E17. †4 Deceitful. E–M17. †5 Given to misusing. Only in M17.

1 W. HAMILTON The Reproductive Imagination (or Conception, in the abusive language of the Scottish philosophers). 2 T. NASHE The abusive enormities of . . our times. 4 S. DANIEL Th' abusive Shews of Sense.

abusively *adv.* M16. **abusiveness** *n.* M17.

abustle /əˈbʌs(ə)l/ *adv.* & *pred. a.* M20. [f. A-[2] + BUSTLE *n.*[1] or *v.*] Bustling (*with*), busy.

abut /əˈbʌt/ *v.* Infl. **-tt-**. LME. [Sense 1 f. AL *abuttare*, f. as A-[8] + BUTT *n.*[2]; sense 2 f. (O)Fr. *abouter*, †*abuter*, f. as A-[5] + BUTT *v.*[1]] 1 *v.i.* Of an estate, country, etc.: end at, border on. Foll. by (*up*)*on*, †*to*. LME. 2 *v.i.* Of part of a building etc.: end *on* or *against*; lean (*up*)*on* at one end. L16. 3 *v.t.* Abut on (in either sense). M19.

abuttal *n.* abutment; in *pl.*, the parts where land abuts on neighbouring lands: E17. **abutter** *n.* a person who or thing which abuts; *spec.* an owner of contiguous property: L17.

abutilon /əˈbjuːtɪlɒn/ *n.* L16. [mod.L f. Arab. *ūbūtīlūn* Indian mallow.] A plant or shrub of the chiefly tropical genus *Abutilon* (belonging to the mallow family), of which there are numerous species bearing showy, usu. yellow, red, or mauve flowers.

abutment /əˈbʌtm(ə)nt/ *n.* M17. [f. ABUT + -MENT: cf. (O)Fr. *aboutement.*] 1 A point of junction, esp. of a support and the thing supported. M17. 2 *Archit.* The solid part of a pier, wall, etc., which supports the lateral pressure of an arch. M18. 3 Something on which another thing abuts or leans. M18.

abuzz /əˈbʌz/ *adv.* & *pred. a.* M19. [f. A-[2] + BUZZ *n.*[1] or *v.*[1]] In a buzz (of excitement); filled with buzzing.

aby /əˈbʌɪ/ *v. arch.* Also **abye**. Pa. t. & pple **abought** /əˈbɔːt/. [OE *ābyċġan*, f. A-[1] + BUY *v.*, corresp. to Goth. *usbugjan.*] †1 *v.t.* Buy, pay for. OE–E16. 2 *v.t.* Pay the penalty for, atone for. OE. †b *v.i.* Pay the penalty, atone. ME–L16. 3 *v.t.* Pay as a penalty; suffer. LME. 4 = ABIDE (with which *aby* became formally confused): †a *v.i.* Endure, remain. LME–L16. b *v.t.* Endure, experience; tolerate. *obs.* exc. *Sc.* L16.

2 E. R. EDDISON You shall bitterly aby it. 3 W. MORRIS Thou wouldst abye A heavy fate. 4a SPENSER Nought that wanteth rest can long aby. b R. L. STEVENSON I never could abye the reek of them.

abysm /əˈbɪz(ə)m/ *n.* Also (earlier) †**abime**. ME. [OFr. *abi(s)me* (mod. *abîme*) f. med.L *abysmus* alt. of *abyssus* ABYSS by assim. to Gk *-ismos* -ISM.] 1 = ABYSS 1. *arch.* or *poet.* ME. 2 = ABYSS 2. Now chiefly *literary.* L15.

abysmal /əˈbɪzm(ə)l/ *a.* M17. [f. prec. + -AL[1].] 1 Of, pertaining to, or resembling an abyss. Now *rare* in *lit.* sense. M17. 2 *fig.* Bottomless; *colloq.* extremely bad. E19.

abysmally *adv.* L19.

abyss /əˈbɪs/ *n.* Orig. in L form †**abyssus**. LME. [Late L *abyssus* f. Gk *abussos*, f. *a-* A-[10] + *bus(s)os* depth.] 1 The great deep believed in the old cosmogony to lie beneath the earth; the primal chaos; the bowels of the earth; the infernal pit, hell. LME. 2 A bottomless chasm; any unfathomable cavity or void space. Freq. *fig.* L16.

abyssal /əˈbɪs(ə)l/ *a.* M17. [Late L *abyssalis*, f. as prec.: see -AL[1].] 1 Characteristic of an abyss; unfathomable. M17. 2 Of or pertaining to the ocean depths. M19. 3 *Geol.* Pertaining to or occurring at considerable depths in the earth's crust; plutonic. L19.

Abyssinia /abɪˈsɪnɪə/ *int. slang.* M20. [Alt., after the country (see next).] I'll be seeing you! (said on parting).

Abyssinian /abɪˈsɪnɪən/ *n.* & *a.* M18. [f. *Abyssinia* (see below) + -AN.] A *n.* 1 A native or inhabitant of Abyssinia, a country (now officially called Ethiopia) in NE Africa. M18. 2 = *Abyssinian cat* below. L19.

B *adj.* Of or pertaining to Abyssinia or its inhabitants. L18.

Abyssinian banana = ENSETE. **Abyssinian cat**: of a breed having long ears and short brown hair flecked with grey.

Earlier †**Abyssian** *n.*: only in E17. †**Abyssin(e)** *a.* & *n.* M17–M18.

†**abyssus** *n.* see ABYSS.

abzyme /ˈabzʌɪm/ *n.* L20. [f. A(NTI)B(ODY + EN)ZYME.] *Biochem.* An antibody (usu. synthetic) having some of the catalytic properties of an enzyme.

ac- /ak, *unstressed* ək/ *pref.* (rarely productive). Assim. form of L AD- bef. *c* (*k*) and *qu*. In OFr., L *acc-* was reduced to *ac-*, which appears in ME adoptions, but in later Fr., and hence in Eng., *acc-* was restored by Latinization, as *account*, *acquit*. Hence extended to some words of different origin, as *accloy*, *accurse*, *acknowledge*, *acquaint*.

-ac /ak/ *suff.* Also †**-ack**, †**-aque**. [Fr. *-aque* or L *-acus* or (the source of both) Gk *-akos*, *-akē*, *-akon* forms of the adj. suff. *-kos* of or belonging to, in comb. w. ns. in *-ia*, *-ios*, *-ion*, as *kardiak-os* of the heart.] Forming adjs., as *elegiac*, *maniac*, some of which are often also (or only) used as ns. See also -ACAL.

acacia /əˈkeɪʃə, -sjə/ *n.* LME. [L f. Gk *akakia* shittah tree.] 1 Any of numerous freq. thorny leguminous trees and shrubs constituting the genus *Acacia*, found esp. in arid regions of Australia and tropical Africa, with small flowers in spikes or globular clusters. Formerly also (*Med.*), the congealed juice of unripe seed-pods of the Egyptian acacia, *A. nilotica*, formerly used as an astringent. Also, a substitute for this made from the juice of green sloes. LME. b Gum arabic. Also *gum acacia*. E19. 2 More fully *false acacia*. A robinia tree; spec. *Robinia pseudoacacia*, native to N. America and grown in Britain for its scented white flowers. M17.

academe /ˈakədiːm/ *n. literary.* Also **A-**. L16. [Partly f. L *academia*; partly f. transf. use of Gk *Akadēmos*: see ACADEMY.] 1 = ACADEMY 1, 3. L16. 2 = ACADEMIA. Esp. in *the grove(s) of Academe.* M19. 3 = ACADEMIC *n.* 2. M20.

1 SHAKES. *L.L.L.* Our court shall be a little Academe.

academese /əkadəˈmiːz/ *n.* Usu. somewhat *derog.* M20. [f. ACADEMIC etc. + -ESE.] The style or language of academic scholarship.

academia /akəˈdiːmɪə/ *n.* M20. [L: see ACADEMY.] The world of academics; the academic environment or community.

†**academian** *n.* M16–L17. [f. as prec. + -AN.] A disciple of Plato; an academic or academician.

academic /akəˈdɛmɪk/ *n.* & *a.* In senses A.1, B.1 also **A-**. M16. [(O)Fr. *académique* or L *academicus*, f. *academia*: see ACADEMY, -IC.] A *n.* 1 A Platonist. M16. 2 A (now *spec.* senior) member of a university or similar institution; a person engaged or excelling in scholarly pursuits. L16. b In *pl.* = ACADEMICAL *n.* (the more usual term). E19. 3 = ACADEMICIAN 1. *rare.* M18. 4 In *pl.* Academic studies. *US.* L20.

B *adj.* 1 Of the school or philosophy of Plato; sceptical. L16. 2 Of or belonging to a university or other institution of higher learning; scholarly. L16. 3 Abstract, unpractical, merely theoretical. L19. 4 *Art.* Conventional; idealizing; excessively formal. L19.

2 OED Such students wear a distinctive academic dress. H. CECIL The judge had succeeded at the practical side of the law and the professor at the academic. **academic year** a period of nearly a year reckoned from the time of the main student intake, usu. from the beginning of the autumn term to the end of the summer term. 3 H. G. WELLS All this discussion . . is—academic The war has begun already. S. HILL Guessing how long they'd been dead as a question of academic interest. 4 E. H. GOMBRICH The programme of idealizing, of 'beautifying' nature, according to the standards set by the classical statues. We call it the neo-classical or 'academic' programme.

academicism /-sɪz(ə)m/ *n.* (*a*) a tenet of academic philosophy; (*b*) the state or quality of being academic: E17. **academicize** /-sʌɪz/ *v.t.* render (undesirably) academic M20.

academical /akəˈdɛmɪk(ə)l/ *a.* & *n.* L16. [f. prec. + -AL[1].] A *adj.* 1 = ACADEMIC *a.* 1. *rare.* L16. 2 = ACADEMIC *a.* 2. L16. B *n.* In *pl.* Academic dress. E19.

academically *adv.* L16.

academician /əkadəˈmɪʃ(ə)n/ *n.* M18. [Fr. *académicien*, f. as ACADEMIC: see -ICIAN.] 1 A member of an academy (sense 5), esp. of the Royal Academy of Arts, the Académie française, or the former USSR Academy of Sciences. M18. 2 = ACADEMIC *n.* 2. *rare.* M18.

Academy /əˈkadəmi/ *n.* Also **a-**. LME. [Fr. *académie* or L *academia* f. Gk *akadēm(e)ia* adj., f. *Akadēmos* the man or demigod from whom Plato's garden was named: see -Y[3].] 1 The name of a garden near Athens where Plato taught. LME. 2 Plato's followers or philosophical system. M16. 3 An institution of higher learning, e.g. a university; also (esp. *Sc.*) a secondary school. Now retained chiefly in names of existing institutions. M16. †b *fig.* The knowledge taught in an academy; a treatise on this. E17–M18. 4 A place of training, esp. in a special art, as the Royal Military Academy. L16. 5 A society for the cultivation of literature, art, science, etc., of which membership is an honour, *esp.* the Royal Academy (of Arts). E17.

2 **Middle Academy** the school of philosophy of Arcesilaus, head of the Academy in the 3rd cent. BC. **New Academy** the school of philosophy of Carneades of Cyrene, head of the Academy in the 2nd cent. BC. **Old Academy** the school of philosophy founded by Plato in the 4th cent. BC.

Comb.: **academy figure** a drawing, usu. half life-size, in crayon or pencil, from the nude.

¶ Formerly stressed on 3rd syllable.

Academism *n.* †(*a*) *rare* Academic philosophy; (*b*) (**a-**) = ACADEMICISM (b): M18. **Academist** *n.* an Academic philosopher; a member or student of an academy: M17.

Acadian /əˈkeɪdɪən/ *n.* & *a.* Chiefly *N. Amer.* E18. [f. *Acadia* (see below), Fr. *Acadie* + -AN. Cf. CAJUN.] A *n.* A native or inhabitant of Acadia, a former French colony on the N. American Atlantic coast which included the present Nova Scotia and some adjacent areas; *spec.* a French-speaking descendant of early settlers in Acadia, living esp. in the Maritime Provinces of Canada or in Louisiana. E18. B *adj.* Of, pertaining to, or originating from Acadia. E19.

acajou /ˈakəʒuː/ *n.* L16. [Fr.: see CASHEW.] The cashew tree; the cashew-nut.

-acal /ək(ə)l/ *suff.* [f. -AC + -AL[1].] Forming adjs. from adjs. and ns. in -AC (as *hypochondriacal*) and occas. from adjs. with no corresp. n. (as *heliacal*); often used to distinguish ns. from adjs. (as *maniac*, *maniacal*).

acalculia /eɪkalˈkjuːlɪə/ *n.* E20. [f. A-[10] + L *calculare* CALCULATE + -IA[1].] *Med.* A diminished ability to calculate, as a symptom of cerebral disorder.

acanthite /əˈkanθʌɪt/ *n.* M19. [f. as next + -ITE[1].] *Min.* A monoclinic or orthorhombic form of silver sulphide, occurring as slender black prisms with a metallic lustre.

acantho- /əˈkanθəʊ/ *comb. form* of Gk *akantha*: see next, -O-.

acantho'cephalan *a.* & *n.* [Gk *kephalē* head] *Zool.* (designating) a parasitic worm of the phylum Acanthocephala, with a thornlike proboscis for attachment to the gut of vertebrates L19. **acan'thodian** *a.* & *n.* (designating or pertaining to) a small spiny-finned fossil fish belonging to the subclass Acanthodii, found esp. in Devonian rocks M19. **a͵canthopte'rygian** *a.* & *n.* [Gk *pterugion* fin, dim. of *pterux* wing] *Zool.* (designating) a spiny-finned fish belonging to the superorder Acanthopterygii M19. **acan'thosis** *n.* (*Med.*) abnormal thickening of the prickle-layer of the skin L19.

acanthus /əˈkanθəs/ *n.* M16. [L f. Gk *akanthos*, f. *akantha* thorn, perh. f. *akē* sharp point.] 1 Any of several erect herbaceous plants belonging to the genus *Acanthus* (family Acanthaceae), having decorative spiny leaves; esp. *Acanthus spinosus*, native to the Mediterranean region. M16. 2 *Archit.* A conventionalized acanthus leaf used to decorate Corinthian and Composite capitals. M18.

acan'thaceous *a.* of the type of acanthus; of or pertaining to the family Acanthaceae: M18. **acanthine** *a.* of or pertaining to acanthus M18.

a cappella /a kə'pɛlə, ɑː/ *a.* & *adv. phr.* L19. [It. = in chapel style.] Of choral music or choirs: unaccompanied.

acari *n.* pl. of ACARUS.

acariasis /akə'rʌɪəsɪs/ *n.* Pl. **-ases** /-əsiːz/. E19. [f. mod.L *acari* pl. of ACARUS + -IASIS.] *Med.* Disease, esp. of the skin, caused by mites.

acaricide /'akərɪsʌɪd/ *n.* L19. [f. as prec. + -CIDE.] A substance poisonous to mites or ticks.

acari'cidal *a.* poisonous to mites or ticks M20.

acarid /'akərɪd/ *n.* L19. [f. as ACARUS + -ID[3].] A mite of the family Acaridae.

acarine /'akərʌɪn/ *a.* & *n.* E19. [f. as prec. + -INE[1].] A *adj.* Pertaining to or caused by mites or ticks. E19. B *n.* An arachnid belonging to the order Acari; a mite, a tick. L19.

acaroid /'akərɔɪd/ *n.* Also **acc-**. M19. [Origin unkn.] In full *acaroid resin, gum.* A resin obtained in Australia from certain kinds of grass-tree or blackboy, and used in making varnish etc.

acarology /akə'rɒlədʒi/ *n.* E20. [f. as ACARIASIS + -OLOGY.] The branch of science that deals with mites and ticks.

acarologist *n.* L19.

acarus /'akərəs/ *n.* Pl. **-ri** /-rʌɪ/. M17. [mod.L f. Gk *akari.*] A mite, a tick.

acatalectic /a,katə'lɛktɪk/ *a.* & *n.* L16. [Late L *acatalecticus*, f. Gk *akatalēktos*, or f. A-[10] + CATALECTIC.] *Pros.* (A line of verse that is) not catalectic, complete in its syllables.

acatalepsy /a'katəlɛpsi/ *n.* E17. [med.L *acatalepsis* f. Gk *akatalēpsia*, f. *a-* A-[10] + *kata* thoroughly + *lēpsis* a seizing: see -Y[3].] *Sceptic Philos.* Incomprehensibility, as a property of the thing thought of.

a,cata'leptic *a.* (*rare*) relating to acatalepsy; incomprehensible: M18.

†acate *n.* Also **ach-**. LME. [Early OFr. & AN *acat* (later OFr. *achat*), f. *ac(h)ater* buy, ult. f. L *captare* seize.] 1 Purchasing; contract, bargain. LME–L17. 2 In *pl.* & *collect. sing.* Things purchased; provisions not made in the house; dainties. LME–L17.

¶In sense 1 *achate* became the regular form, but in sense 2 *acates* predominated and was aphetized to *cates* (see CATE).

†acater *n.* see ACATOUR.

acathisia *n.* var. of AKATHISIA.

†acatour *n.* Also **-ter, ach-**. ME–M18. [AN & early OFr. *acateor* (later OFr. *achatour*), f. *ac(h)ater*: see prec., -OUR.] A purchaser of provisions; a purveyor; a caterer.

¶*Achatour* came to be restricted to the title of an officer in the royal household; *acatour, -er* passed into common use and was aphetized to CATER *n.*[1]

†acatery, achatry *n.* provisions purchased; the storeroom for such provisions: LME–M18.

acaulescent /akɔː'lɛs(ə)nt/ *a.* M19. [f. A-[10] + CAULESCENT.] *Bot.* Stemless or apparently so.

acausal /eɪ'kɔːz(ə)l, a-/ *a.* M20. [f. A-[10] + CAUSAL *a.*] Not causal; not causally related.

acau'sality *n.* M20.

Accadian *a.* & *n.* var. of AKKADIAN.

accaroid *n.* var. of ACAROID.

accede /ək'siːd/ *v.i.* LME. [L *accedere*, f. *ad* AC- + *cedere* CEDE: cf. (O)Fr. *accéder.*] 1 Come forward, approach, arrive (at a place or state). Now *rare* in *gen.* sense. LME. 2 Give one's adhesion; join a group, become part of a country etc.; assent or agree (*to*). LME. 3 Enter upon an office or dignity, esp. a throne. (Foll. by *to.*) L17.

2 C. THIRLWALL Potidæa had already acceded to the confederacy. W. S. MAUGHAM Veiled threats to induce the Florentines to accede to his demands. 3 J. H. BURTON The Emperor Julian . . had just acceded to the purple. JOYCE Queen Victoria (born 1820, acceded 1837).

accedence *n.* the action of acceding L16.

accelerando /əksɛlə'randəʊ, ətʃɛl-/ *adv.*, *a.*, & *n.* E19. [It.] *Mus.* A *adv.* & *adj.* (A direction:) with gradual increase of speed. E19. B *n.* Pl. **-dos, -di** /-di/. A gradual increase of speed; a passage (to be) played with a gradual increase of speed. L19.

accelerate /ək'sɛləreɪt/ *v.* E16. [L *accelerat-* pa. ppl stem of *accelerare*, f. *ad* AC- + *celer* swift: see -ATE[3].] 1 *v.t.* Hasten the occurrence of. E16. 2 *v.t.* Quicken, increase the speed of, (a motion or a thing in motion). E17. 3 *v.i.* Become swifter; begin to move more quickly; cause a vehicle etc. to move more quickly. M17.

1 J. B. S. HALDANE A spot of laughter, I am sure, Often accelerates one's cure. 2 JAS. WOOD When the successive portions of space . . continually increase, the motion is said to be accelerated. J. CHEEVER Paul accelerated the car happily when they escaped from the narrow streets of the village. 3 J. R. SEELEY England's rapidly accelerating decline. A. BURGESS Crabbe accelerated, gave the car all speed.

accelerative *a.* tending to increase speed, quickening E17.

acceleration /əksɛlə'reɪʃ(ə)n/ *n.* L15. [(O)Fr., or L *acceleratio(n-)*, f. as prec.: see -ATION.] 1 The action of accelerating; the state or condition of being accelerated. L15. b Increased speed. M16. c Of a vehicle: ability to gain speed. E20. 2 The extent to which anything is accelerated; the rate of change of velocity per unit time. M17.

accelerator /ək'sɛləreɪtə/ *n.* M19. [f. ACCELERATE + -OR.] I *gen.* 1 A person who or thing which accelerates. M19. II *spec.* 2 A substance used to increase the rate of a chemical process. M19. 3 A device, usu. a pedal, for controlling the speed of the engine of a motor vehicle. E20. 4 *Physics.* An apparatus for accelerating charged particles to high energies by means of electric or electromagnetic fields. M20.

accelerograph /ək'sɛlərəgrɑːf/ *n.* E20. [f. ACCELER(ATE + -O- + -GRAPH.] An accelerometer which produces a graphical record of its measurements.

accelerogram *n.* a graphical record produced by an accelerograph M20.

accelerometer /əksɛlə'rɒmɪtə/ *n.* E20. [f. ACCELER(ATE + -OMETER.] An instrument for measuring the acceleration experienced by a moving or vibrating body.

†accend *v.t.* LME–M19. [L *accendere* rel. to *candere* to shine: see AC-.] Kindle, set on fire, (*lit.* & *fig.*).

†accensed *ppl a.* M16–M18. [L *accensus* pa. pple of *accendere* (see prec.) + -ED[1].] Kindled, set on fire.

accension /ək'sɛnʃ(ə)n/ *n.* Now *rare* or *obs.* M17. [L *accensio(n-)*, f. as prec.: see -ION.] The action of kindling; the state of being kindled.

accent /'aks(ə)nt/ *n.* LME. [(O)Fr., or L *accentus*, f. *ad* AC- + *cantus* song.] 1 The way in which something is said; tone; modulation expressing feeling. LME. 2 Prominence given to a syllable by stress or (in some languages) by pitch. L15. 3 A mark used with a letter to show the nature and position of the spoken accent of a word, to show metrical stress, to distinguish the quality of a vowel, to distinguish homonyms, etc. L16. 4 The mode of pronunciation peculiar to an individual, locality, or nation. L16. b Without defining word; a regional English accent. M20. 5 A significant tone or sound; a word; in *pl.* also, speech, language. *poet.* L16. 6 *Pros.* Rhythmical stress in verse or prose. L16. b *Mus.* Stress recurring at intervals generally fixed, but variable by syncopation. M17. 7 *fig.* a Intensity, emphasis; distinctive character; a contrasting detail. M17. b An accentuating touch of light, colour, etc. M19.

1 DRYDEN Mild was his accent. L. M. MONTGOMERY Somebody said in muffled accents: 'Merciful goodness!' 3 *acute accent, circumflex accent, grave accent*, etc. 4 G. GREENE He spoke with the faintest foreign accent. D. ABERCROMBIE R. P. is, within England, a non-regional accent. 5 SHAKES. *Jul. Caes.* In states unborn and accents yet unknown. BYRON In thy gasping throat The accents rattle. 7a W. GURNALL That which gave accent to Abraham's Faith. F. MEYNELL The design of the components . . will show local accents. b E. BOWEN The face had only accents of shadow.

accent /ək'sɛnt/ *v.* M16. [OFr. *accenter*, f. as prec.] 1 *v.i.* (*rare*) & *t.* Pronounce with accent or stress; emphasize; *Mus.* stress (a note etc.). M16. 2 *v.t.* Mark with written accents. M17. 3 *v.t.* Pronounce, utter, intone. *arch.* M17. 4 *v.t.* = ACCENTUATE 3. M17.

1 J. PALSGRAVE I can not accent aryght in the latyn tonge. H. W. FOWLER Accenting the last syllable in the adjective. 3 SIR W. SCOTT These solemn sounds, accented by a thousand voices.

accentor /ək'sɛntə/ *n.* E19. [Late L, f. *ad* AC- + *cantor* singer.] Any bird of the Eurasian genus *Prunella* (formerly *Accentor*), which includes the dunnock and other small songbirds.

accentual /ək'sɛntjʊəl/ *a.* E17. [f. L *accentus* ACCENT *n.* + -UAL.] Of or pertaining to accent.

accentually *adv.* M19.

accentuate /ək'sɛntjʊeɪt/ *v.t.* M18. [f. med.L *accentuat-* pa. ppl stem of *accentuare*, f. as prec.: see -ATE[3]. Cf. Fr. *accentuer.*] 1 = ACCENT *v.* 1 (the commoner term). M18. 2 = ACCENT *v.* 2. *rare.* M19. 3 *fig.* Mark emphatically; heighten; make conspicuous. M19.

accentuation /əksɛntjʊ'eɪʃ(ə)n/ *n.* L15. [In isolated early use f. med.L *accentuatio(n-)*, f. as prec.; later (E19) f. prec. + -ION.] 1 The marking of accent or stress in speech. L15. 2 Mode of pronunciation; vocal modulation. E19. 3 The notation of accents in writing. M19. 4 *fig.* Emphasizing, bringing into prominence. L19.

1 O. JESPERSEN Children . . learn the accentuation as well as the sounds of each word. 2 SIR W. SCOTT A strong provincial accentuation.

accept /ək'sɛpt/ *v.t.* & (*arch.*) *i.* foll. by *of.* Pa. pple **accepted**, (earlier) **†accept**. LME. [(O)Fr. *accepter* or L *acceptare* frequent. of *accipere*, f. *ad* AC- + *capere* take.] 1 Take or receive with consenting mind; receive with favour or approval. LME. 2 Receive as adequate or valid; admit; believe; tolerate; submit to. LME. 3 Undertake (an office), take upon oneself as a responsibility. E16. 4 *Comm.* Acknowledge the receipt of and agree to pay (a bill or draft). M17. 5 Of an inanimate object: physically receive or accommodate, absorb, (another object, energy, data, etc.). E20.

1 M. PATTISON The husband she had thoughtlessly accepted. JOYCE Mr Mulligan accepted of the invitation. E. O'NEILL Accept my gratitude for your warning. *absol.*: T. S. ELIOT A great many more accepted Than we thought would want to come. *accept the person of, accept persons*: see PERSON *n.* 2 GEO. ELIOT These fellow-mortals . . must be accepted as they are. G. B. SHAW Parents and priests may forbid knowledge to those who accept their authority. *Times* The report is by a working party . . and has yet to be accepted by the council itself. B. LOVELL The theory of general relativity was accepted half a century ago. *accept a wooden nickel, wooden money*: see WOODEN *a.* **accept service of a writ** agree to consider a writ validly served. 4 *absol.*: T. HOOD I'm free to give my I.O.U., Sign, draw, accept, as majors do. 5 *British Medical Bulletin* The computer can accept data only in a highly structured (digital) form. *Railway Magazine* The ceiling . . is designed to accept the fluorescent lighting tubes.

accepted, †accept *adjs.* †(*a*) acceptable; (*b*) well received, approved: LME. **acceptedly** *adv.* L16. **accepter** *n.* M16. **acceptingly** *adv.* in an accepting manner L19. **acceptive** *a.* suitable for acceptance; ready to accept, receptive: L15.

acceptability /əksɛptə'bɪlɪti/ *n.* M17. [Late L *acceptabilitas*, f. *acceptabilis*: see next, -ITY; later f. next: see -ABILITY.] The quality of being acceptable.

acceptable /ək'sɛptəb(ə)l/ *a.* LME. [(O)Fr. f. late L *acceptabilis*, f. *acceptare* ACCEPT *v.*: see -ABLE.] Worth accepting; likely to be accepted; pleasing, welcome; tolerable.

the acceptable face of: see FACE *n.*

¶Orig., and in poetry until 20, stressed on 1st syllable.

acceptableness *n.* E17. **acceptably** *adv.* M16.

acceptance /ək'sɛpt(ə)ns/ *n.* M16. [OFr.: see ACCEPT *v.*, -ANCE.] 1 Favourable reception (of persons, things, or ideas); approval; assent, belief. M16. 2 *gen.* The act or fact of accepting, whether as a pleasure, a satisfaction of claim, or a duty. L16. 3 Acceptableness. L16. 4 The state or condition of being accepted. M17. 5 *Comm.* A formal engagement to pay a bill when due; an accepted bill. L17. 6 = ACCEPTATION 4. *rare.* E18.

1 SHAKES. *Merch. V.* I leave him to your gracious acceptance. M. FARADAY The assertion finds acceptance in every rank of society. †**acceptance of persons** = ACCEPTION *of persons.* 2 E. A. FREEMAN William . . may . . have pressed the acceptance of the crown on Eadward. E. O'NEILL Her face now a fatalistic mask of acceptance. 3 BROWNING A man of such acceptance. 4 J. SELDEN She first brought Austin into acceptance with the King.

acceptancy *n.* favourable reception; willingness to receive: E19.

acceptant /ək'sɛpt(ə)nt/ *n.* & *a.* L16. [Fr., pres. pple of *accepter* ACCEPT *v.*: see -ANT[1].] †A *n.* A person who accepts. L16–L17. B *adj.* Willingly accepting (*of*); submissive. M19.

acceptation /aksɛp'teɪʃ(ə)n/ *n.* LME. [(O)Fr. f. late L *acceptatio(n-)*, f. as ACCEPT *v.*: see -ATION.] 1 = ACCEPTANCE 1. LME. †2 = ACCEPTANCE 2. LME–L17. 3 = ACCEPTANCE 4. *arch.* L16. 4 A particular sense, or the generally recognized meaning, of a word or phrase. E17. †5 = ACCEPTANCE 5. Only in E17.

acceptilation /aksɛptɪ'leɪʃ(ə)n/ *n.* Now *rare.* M16. [L *acceptilatio(n-)*, f. *acceptum* receipt + *latio* the formal proposal of a law.] *Rom. Law.* Release from a debt by an acquittance without payment. Also *fig.* free remission of sins.

acception /ək'sɛpʃ(ə)n/ *n.* Now *rare.* LME. [L *acceptio(n-)*, f. as ACCEPT *v.*: see -ION. Partly f. OFr.] 1 The action of accepting. LME. 2 = ACCEPTATION 4. M16.

1 †**acception of persons** or **faces** favourable reception of personal advances, favouritism.

acceptor /ək'sɛptə/ *n.* LME. [In earliest use f. AN *acceptour* f. L *acceptor*; later replaced by or refash. as ACCEPTER, but restored esp. in specialized senses: see ACCEPT *v.*, -OR.] 1 A person who accepts. *rare* in *gen.* sense. LME. b *spec.* A person who accepts a bill. M17. 2 *Chem.* & *Physics.* An atom or molecule which receives electrons or which can combine with another (specified) atom or molecule. E20. b An impurity atom in a semiconductor which has fewer valency electrons than the majority of atoms and effectively contributes a conducting hole to the material. M20.

access /'aksɛs/ *n.* & *v.* ME. [(O)Fr. *accès* or L *accessus*, f. *access-* pa. ppl stem of *accedere* ACCEDE.] A *n.* 1 A (sudden) coming on of illness. ME. †b *spec.* An ague fit. (Chiefly *dial.* after 16.) LME–L19. †2 Coming into the presence of or into contact with (foll. by *to*); approach, entrance. LME–E19. 3 Admittance (*to* the presence or use of). LME. b *spec.* The action of process of obtaining stored documents, data, etc. M20. 4 Being approached. LME. †5 Coming to work or business. L16–M17. 6 A coming as an addition. *arch.* (replaced by ACCESSION). L16. 7 Coming towards someone or something; advance. *arch.* E17. 8 A way or means of approach or entrance (*lit.* & *fig.*). E17. †9 = ACCESSION 6. M17–M18. 10 [After Fr.] An outburst *of* anger or other emotion. L18.

1 E. F. BENSON A violent access of hay-fever. 2 POPE Safe from access of each intruding power. 3 D. HALBERSTAM The few favored reporters who gained access to him and to his inner circle. K. AMIS He had access to as much drink as was good for him. b *open access, random access,* etc. 4 BOSWELL Lord Chesterfield's . . easiness of access. 5 T. MAY The Accesse and meeting again of the Parliament. 6 MILTON I from the influence of thy looks receive Access in every virtue. 7 J. HEALEY The Sunnes accesse and departure. 8 R. ADAMS The only access to the lower city is through the Peacock Gate. W. STEVENS Knowledge is . . The only access to true ease. 9 CHARLES I: Our Accesse to the Crowne. 10 J. HELLER An access of powerful fresh feelings.

Comb.: **access broadcasting, television**: undertaken by members of the public by arrangement with broadcasting companies; **access course** an educational course enabling those without traditional qualifications to become eligible for higher education; **access road** a road giving access to a place or to another road; a slip-road; *access television*: see *access broadcasting* above; **access time** *Computing* the time needed to retrieve stored information.

B *v.t.* Gain access to (*spec.* data etc. held in a computer or computer-based system, or such a system). M20.

¶The mod. stressing is attested from the beginning, but stress on the 2nd syll. was prevalent 16–18.

accessary /ək'sɛsəri/ *n.* & *a.* LME. [med.L *accessarius*, f. L *access-*: see prec., -ARY[1].] A *n.* 1 = ACCESSORY *n.* 2. LME. 2 = ACCESSORY *n.* 1. M16. B *adj.* †1 = ACCESSORY *a.* 1. M16–L17. 2 = ACCESSORY *a.* 2. L16.

¶Etymologically, *accessary* is the n. and *accessory* the adj., but the two have been used interchangeably in Eng. from the beginning. ACCESSORY is now increasingly used in all contexts.

accessible /ək'sɛsɪb(ə)l/ *a.* LME. [(O)Fr., or late L *accessibilis* f. L *access-*: see ACCESS, -IBLE.] 1 Able to be reached, entered, influenced, understood, etc. LME. 2 Able to be used as an access. Now *rare.* E17.

1 **accessible to** able to be reached etc. by; open to the influence of. 2 MILTON With one ascent Accessible from earth.

accessi'bility *n.* M18. **accessibleness** *n.* E19. **accessibly** *adv.* L19.

accession /ək'sɛʃ(ə)n/ *n.* & *v.* L16. [(O)Fr., or L *accessio(n-)*, f. *access-*: see ACCESS, -ION.] A *n.* I Result. 1 Something which is added; an augmentation, an increase. L16. 2 Adherence; assent; formal acceptance of a treaty etc. E17. 3 Joining; addition. M17. 4 *Law.* Artificial improvement or natural growth of a property. M18.

1 S. JOHNSON He will be a very honourable accession [to the club]. 3 T. ADAMS The accession of piety to patience.

II Action. 5 The action of coming near, approach; admittance. Formerly also, advance, arrival. E17. 6 Entering upon an office or dignity (esp. a throne) or condition. M17.

5 T. STANLEY The accession of the Sun from Tropick to Tropick.

†III 7 An onset of illness, powerful feeling, etc. E17–E19.

B *v.t.* Record the addition of (a book etc.) to a library. L19.

accessional *a.* M17.

accessory /ək'sɛs(ə)ri/ *n.* & *a.* LME. [med.L *accessorius* adj., f. L *access-*: see ACCESS, -ORY[2]. Partly through (O)Fr. *accessoire.*] A *n.* 1 An additional or subordinate thing; an adjunct, an accompaniment; a minor fitting or attachment; a small article of (usu. a woman's) dress. Now usu. in *pl.* LME. 2 A person who helps in or is privy to any act, esp. a crime. LME.

2 **accessory before, after, the fact** *Law* (now *Hist.*) a person who helps to plan, conceal, a crime.

B *adj.* 1 Of a thing: additional; subordinately contributing, dispensable; adventitious. E17. 2 Of a person: acceding *to*; participant, privy (*to*, esp. a crime). E17.

1 **accessory mineral** *Geol.* a constituent mineral present in small quantity and not taken into account in identifying a rock. **accessory nerve** *Anat.* either of the eleventh pair of cranial nerves, which supply certain muscles in the neck and shoulder.

¶See note s.v. ACCESSARY.

accessorial /aksɛ'sɔːrɪəl/ *a.* of the nature of an accessory; supplementary: E18. **accessorily** *adv.* additionally; in the manner of an accessory LME. **accessorize** *v.t.* & *i.* provide or provide (oneself) with an accessory or accessories M20.

acciaccatura /ətʃakə'tʊərə, *foreign* at ˌtʃakka'tuːra/ *n.* Pl. **-s**, **-ture** /-'tuːre/. E19. [It., f. *acciaccare* to crush.] *Mus.* A grace-note performed quickly before an essential note of a melody.

accidence /'aksɪd(ə)ns/ *n.*[1] Now *rare* or *obs.* LME. [OFr. f. late L *accidentia*: see next, -ENCE.] Chance; a fortuitous circumstance, a mishap.

accidence /'aksɪd(ə)ns/ *n.*[2] E16. [Late L *accidentia* neut. pl. pres. pple of *accidere* taken as fem. sing.: see next, -ENCE.] 1 The part of grammar which deals with the variable forms of words (inflections etc.). E16. 2 The rudiments of any subject. M16.

accident /'aksɪd(ə)nt/ *n.* LME. [(O)Fr. f. L *accident-* pres. ppl stem of *accidere* happen, f. *ad* AC- + *cadere* to fall: see -ENT.] I A thing that happens. 1 An event. *obs.* in *gen.* sense. LME. b An event that is without apparent cause or unexpected; an unfortunate event, *esp.* one causing injury or damage. LME. 2 Chance, fortune. LME. †3 *Med.* An unfavourable symptom. LME–L17. †4 A casual appearance or effect. LME–M18. 5 An irregularity in the landscape. M19.

1b C. DAY Our race may be an accident, in a meaningless universe. M. SPARK She . . had been killed in an accident. **the chapter of accidents** the unforeseen course of events. 2 S. JOHNSON Nature probably has some part in human characters and accident has some part. **by accident** by chance, unintentionally. 5 J. R. LOWELL Accidents of open green.

II Something present but not necessarily so, and therefore non-essential. 6 *Logic.* A property or quality not essential to a substance or object. LME. 7 *Gram.* A change of form to which words are subject, as to express number, case, gender, etc. Usu. in *pl. arch.* M16. 8 *gen.* A non-essential accompaniment; a mere accessory. E17.

8 DISRAELI With all the brilliant accidents of birth, and beauty, and fortune. W. W. GREG The 'accidents' of presentation, . . the spelling, punctuation, and other scribal or typographical details.

Comb.: **accident-prone** *a.* predisposed or likely to cause or suffer an accident.

accidented *a.* characterized by accidents L19. **accidently** *adv.* (now *rare* exc. as misspelling) accidentally LME.

accidental /aksɪ'dɛnt(ə)l/ *a.* & *n.* LME. [Late L *accidentalis*, f. *accident-*: see prec., -AL[1].] A *adj.* 1 *Logic.* Not essential to a substance or object. LME. 2 *gen.* Incidental; subsidiary. LME. 3 Pertaining to chance; casual; occasional. E16. 4 Happening by chance, undesignedly, or unexpectedly. L16.

2 S. JOHNSON Those accidental benefits which prudence may confer on every state. **accidental sharp, flat, natural** *Mus.*: signs attached to a single note to mark a temporary change in pitch, not in the key signature. 3 SHAKES. *Meas. for M.* Thy sin's not accidental, but a trade. 4 JOYCE Matthew F. Kane (accidental drowning, Dublin Bay).

B *n.* 1 Something non-essential or subsidiary. E17. 2 *Mus.* An accidental sharp, flat, or natural. M19. 3 *Ornith.* = VAGRANT *n.* 3. M20.

acciden'tality *n.* the quality or fact of being accidental M17. **accidentally** *adv.* †(*a*) non-essentially; (*b*) by accident: LME. **accidentalness** *n.* L17.

accidie /'aksɪdi/ *n.* ME. [AN = OFr. *accide* f. med.L *accidia* alt. of late L ACEDIA.] Sloth, torpor, apathy. Now also, black despair.

¶Obs. after E16; revived in L19.

accidious *a.* (*rare*) LME.

accinge /ək'sɪndʒ/ *v.refl.*. Now *rare.* M17. [L *accingere* gird (oneself).] Prepare for action; apply oneself.

accipiter /ak'sɪpɪtə/ *n.* E19. [L = hawk, bird of prey.] †1 A bandage for the nose, resembling a hawk's claw. Only in 19. 2 *Ornith.* Orig., any bird of prey of the order Accipitres (now called Falconiformes), which excludes owls. Now, any of the relatively short-winged, long-legged birds of prey belonging to the genus *Accipiter* and typified by the sparrowhawk and the goshawk. E20.

accipitral *a.* hawklike; rapacious; keen-sighted: M19.

accipitrine /ak'sɪpɪtrʌɪn/ *a.* M19. [Fr., f. L *accipiter*: see prec., -INE[1].] 1 *Ornith.* Pertaining to or designating birds of the family Accipitridae, which includes most birds of prey other than owls, falcons, and New World vultures. M19. 2 Accipitral. L19.

†**accite** *v.t.* L15. [L *accit-* pa. ppl stem of *accire*, f. *ad* AC- + *ciere* to call: see CITE *v.*] 1 Summon. L15–L17. 2 Excite. L16–M17. 3 Quote. Only in M17.

1 G. CHAPMAN Our heralds . . accited all that were Endamag'd. 2 JONSON To accite So ravenous . . an Appetite. 3 DONNE Accited for examples . . in the Scriptures.

acclaim /ə'kleɪm/ *v.* & *n.* E16. [L *acclamare*, f. *ad* AC- + *clamare* to shout, with spelling assim. to CLAIM *n.*, *v.*] A *v.* †1 *v.t.* Lay claim to. *Sc.* & *north.* E16–E18. 2 *v.i.* Express approval; shout applause. E17. 3 *v.t.* Applaud, welcome enthusiastically, extol. M17. b *v.t.* (w. compl.) Hail as. M18. 4 *v.t.* Shout, call out. L17. B *n.* †1 A claim. *Sc.* M16–M17. 2 Acclamation; enthusiastic praise; a shout of applause or welcome. M17.

acclaimer *n.* M19.

acclamation /akləˈmeɪʃ(ə)n/ *n.* M16. [L *acclamatio(n-)*, f. *acclamat-* pa. ppl stem of *acclamare*: see prec., -ATION.] 1 An act of acclaiming; a shout of approbation or welcome. Now usu. in *pl.* M16. b An election by acclamation (see sense 3 below). *N. Amer.* M20. †2 *Rhet.* A brief isolated sentence emphasizing what precedes it. M16–M17. 3 The action of acclaiming; loud or eager assent or approval; shouting in a person's honour. L16.

3 **by acclamation** (chiefly *N. Amer.*) unanimously, without need for a vote.

acclamatory /əˈklamət(ə)ri/ *a.* expressing acclamation L17.

acclimate /əˈklʌɪmət/ *v.t.* & *i.* Now chiefly *US.* L18. [Fr. *acclimater*, f. as A-[5] + CLIMATE.] = ACCLIMATIZE.

acclimaˈtation *n.* (now *rare*) = ACCLIMATIZATION M19. **acclimatement** *n.* (*rare*) E19. **acclimation** /aklɪˈmeɪʃ(ə)n/ *n.* = ACCLIMATIZATION E19.

acclimatize /əˈklʌɪmətʌɪz/ *v.t.* & *i.* Also **-ise.** M19. [f. as prec. + -IZE.] Habituate, become habituated, to a new climate or environment.

acclimatiˈzation *n.* M19. **acclimatizer** *n.* M19.

acclivity /əˈklɪvɪti/ *n.* E17. [L *acclivitas*, f *acclivis*, *-us*, f. *ad* AC- + *clivus* a slope: see -ITY.] An ascending slope.

acclivitous *a.* E19. **acclivous** *a.* (now *rare*) [f. L *acclivus*: see -OUS] M18.

accloy /əˈklɔɪ/ *v.t.* Now *arch. rare.* LME. [OFr. *encloer* f. med.L *inclavare*, f. *clavus* a nail.] †1 Prick (a horse) with a nail in shoeing; lame. LME–E18. 2 Stop up (an aperture); obstruct, clog, choke. LME. †3 Overfill; burden, oppress. LME–E17. 4 Disgust, become offensive to. M16.

†**accoast** *v.* var. of ACCOST *v.*

†**accoil** *v.i. rare* (Spenser). Only in L16. [OFr. *acoillir* (mod. *accueillir*).] Gather together, collect.

accolade /ˈakəleɪd, akəˈlɑːd, -kəʊl-/ *n.* & *v.* E17. [Fr. f. Prov. *acolada*, ult. f. L *ad* AC- + *collum* neck: see -ADE.] A *n.* 1 The salutation marking the bestowal of knighthood, at different times an embrace, a kiss, or (now the usual form) a stroke on the shoulder with the flat of a sword; *fig.* the bestowal of praise, an acknowledgement of merit. E17. 2 *Mus.* A vertical line or brace, used to couple two or more staves. E19.

1 M. BEADLE A Nobel Prize is the top accolade a scientist can receive.

B *v.t.* 1 Embrace or kiss in salutation. *rare.* M19. 2 Confer an accolade on (*lit.* & *fig.*). M20.

†**accoll** *v.t.* LME–M16. [OFr. *acoler*, (later) *accoller*, (mod. *accoler*): cf. prec.] Throw the arms round the neck of, embrace.

accolled /əˈkɒld/ *a.* E18 [f. as prec. + -ED[1].] *Her.* Wreathed, esp. about the neck; gorged.

accollée /əˈkɒli/ *a.* E18. [Fr., fem. pa. pple of *accoller*: see ACCOLL.] *Her.* †1 = ACCOLLED. E18–L19. 2 Of two shields: placed side by side. L19.

†**accommodate** *a.* E16–L18. [L *accommodatus* pa. pple, f. as next: see -ATE[2].] Suited; suitable, fitting.

accommodate /əˈkɒmədeɪt/ *v.* M16. [L *accommodat-* pa. ppl stem of *accommodare*, f. *ad* AC- + *commodus* fitting: see -ATE[3].] †1 *v.t.* Ascribe fittingly (a thing to a person). M16–L17. 2 *v.t.* Adapt (one thing or person *to* another). M16. †b *v.i.* Adapt oneself *to.* L16–L17. c *v.t.* Adapt to; allow for; take account of; satisfy (a need etc.). L18. 3 *v.t.* Equip or supply (esp. a person, *with*). L16. b *v.t.* Provide lodging or room for; allow space or time for. L16. c *v.t.* Oblige, confer a favour on. M17. 4 *v.t.* Reconcile (things or persons); settle (differences etc.); bring to agreement. L16. b *v.i.* Come to terms. M17. 5 *v.t.* Show the correspondence of (one thing to another); make or make appear consistent. Foll. by *to* (†or *unto, with*). E17. †6 *v.t.* Fit (a thing) for use; repair. E17–E19. †7 *v.t.* Facilitate, aid. E17–E18.

2 D. BREWSTER The power of accommodating the eye to different distances. R. W. CHAPMAN *Persien* . . was accommodated to the regular *-ian.* C. FREEMAN The reason she had no social life was . . because she couldn't accommodate herself to anyone. 3 DEFOE Wax candles . . to accommodate us with light. b J. CONRAD The other buildings . . served only to accommodate the numerous household. B. PYM The space that had once accommodated the four of them. *Independent* Television programmes . . are always about 29 minutes long to accommodate announcements, links, etc. c M. L. KING I was having press conferences three times a week—in order to accommodate the reporters and journalists. 4 LD MACAULAY The dispute had been accommodated. b EVELYN They must accommodate with His Majesty.

accommodable *a.* (now *rare*) able to be accommodated, suitable L16. **accommodating** *a.* obliging; easy to deal with; compliant: L18. **accommodatingly** *adv.* E19. **accommodative** *a.* tending or able to accommodate M19. **accommodativeness** *n.* M19. **accommodator** *n.* a person who or thing which accommodates; *US* a temporary domestic help: M17. **accommoˈdatory** *a.* characterized by accommodation or adaptation E20.

accommodation /əkɒməˈdeɪʃ(ə)n/ *n.* E17. [(O)Fr., or L *accommodatio(n-)*, f. as prec.: see -ATION.] 1 Something which supplies a want or ministers to one's comfort. E17. 2 *sing.* & (now *US*) in *pl.* Room and provision for the reception of people, lodgings; living premises. E17. 3 An arrangement of a dispute; a settlement; a compromise. M17. 4 The action of accommodating or the process of being accommodated; adaptation, adjustment. M17. 5 Adaptation to a different purpose, function, or meaning. E18. 6 Self-adaptation; obligingness; a favour. M18. 7 The action of supplying with what is requisite. *rare.* M18. 8 Pecuniary aid in an emergency; a loan. L18.

1 J. REYNOLDS The regular progress of cultivated life is from necessaries to accommodations, from accommodations to ornaments. 2 A. POWELL The accommodation was a bit . . squalid. 3 H. WILSON Trying to reach an accommodation with the Liberal leader. 4 D. BREWSTER The accommodation of the eye to the distinct vision of external objects. 6 W. FAULKNER Wherever you could take us, it would be a big accommodation. 8 D. RUNYON I do not care to extend such accommodations over any considerable period.

Comb.: **accommodation address**: used on letters to a person unable or unwilling to give a permanent address; **accommodation bill**: for raising money on credit; **accommodation ladder**: allowing access between a ship's decks, or to and from a small boat etc. alongside; **accommodation paddock** *Austral.* & *NZ*: for drovers to keep stock in overnight; **accommodation road**: giving access to a place not on a public road.

accommodational *a.* †(*a*) affording (good) accommodation; (*b*) of or pertaining to accommodation: E19.

accompaniment /əˈkʌmp(ə)nɪm(ə)nt/ *n.* E18. [(O)Fr. *accompagnement*, f. as next: see -MENT.] 1 *Mus.* The subsidiary part(s), usu. instrumental, supporting a solo instrument or voice, a choir, etc. E18. 2 *gen.* Something that accompanies; an appendage. M19.

accompanist /əˈkʌmpənɪst/ *n.* M19. [f. next + -IST.] A person who or thing which accompanies; *esp.* the performer taking the accompanying part in music.

accompany /əˈkʌmpəni/ *v.* LME. [(O)Fr. *accompagner*, f. as A-[5] + COMPANION *n.*[1], later assim. to COMPANY *v.*] †1 *v.t.* Add or join *to.* LME–L16. 2 *v.t.* Join or unite (a thing, †a person) *with*, supplement *with.* LME. †b *refl.* Associate or unite oneself *with.* LME–M17. †3 *v.i.* & *t.* Keep company (*with*); cohabit (*with*). LME–M18. 4 *v.t.* Convoy, escort, attend, go with (*lit.* & *fig.*). LME. 5 *v.t. Mus.* Support (a singer, player, melody, etc.) by performing a subsidiary, usu. instrumental, part. L16. 6 *v.t.* Go with as an attribute or attendant phenomenon; characterize. L17.

2 JOYCE With what meditations did Bloom accompany his demonstration? 3 LD BERNERS Suche as accompanyeth with man-killers. P. SIDNEY To bid her go home and accompanie her solitarie father. 4 A. CHRISTIE He got up to accompany his patient to the door. *fig.*: P. G. HAMERTON A . . *déjeuner à la fourchette*, accompanied by half a bottle of . . Bordeaux. 5 DAY LEWIS Knos would sing, accompanying herself on the harmonium. S. HILL A harmonica, which he used to accompany their songs.

accompanable *a.* (now *arch. rare*) sociable, companiable M16. **accompanied** *a.* (*a*) *Mus.* having an instrumental accompaniment; (*b*) escorted; *Mil.* (of a tour etc.) on which families are allowed to accompany military personnel: L18. **accompanier** *n.* M18. **accompanyist** *n.* = ACCOMPANIST M19.

accomplice /əˈkʌmplɪs, əˈkɒm-/ *n.* M16. [Alt. of COMPLICE, prob. by assoc. w. prec.] An associate in guilt; a partner in crime.

joc.: SHAKES. *1 Hen. VI* Success unto our valiant general, and happiness to his accomplices!

accompliceship *n.* (*rare*) the state of being an accomplice; criminal assistance: E19.

accomplish /əˈkʌmplɪʃ, əˈkɒm-/ *v.* LME. [OFr. *acompliss-* lengthened stem of *acomplir* (mod. *acc-*), ult. f. L *ad* AC- + *complere* fill, complete: see -ISH[2].] 1 *v.t.* Fulfil, perform, carry out. LME. †b *v.i.* Carry out a design. *rare.* L15–E16. 2 *v.t.* Bring to an end, complete, (a work). LME. b Reach the end of (a time, a distance). L16. 3 *v.t.* Perfect in mental acquirements or personal graces; finish off. LME. 4 *v.t.* Equip completely. *arch.* L16.

1 AV *Prov.* 13:19 The desire accomplished is sweet to the soule. S. KAUFFMANN He had seen the man for only an hour or so, but he'd accomplished enough to make the memorandum sound as if it covered an afternoon. 2 R. HOLINSHED The abbeie of Abington also he accomplished. b AV *Dan.* 9:2 He would accomplish seuentie yeeres in the desolations of Ierusalem. W. H. PRESCOTT He had accomplished half a league or more. 3 T. FULLER Nothing accomplisheth a man more than learning. 4 SHAKES. *Hen. V* The armourers accomplishing the knights.

accomplishable *a.* able to be accomplished L18. **accomplished** *a.* fulfilled; completed; perfect, esp. in acquirements; clever; well trained or educated: LME. **accomplisher** *n.* E17.

accomplishment /əˈkʌmplɪʃm(ə)nt, əˈkɒm-/ *n.* LME. [f. prec. + -MENT, after Fr. *accomplissement.*] 1 Fulfilment, completion, consummation. LME. 2 Perfection. *arch.* M16. 3 An achievement, an attainment; an acquired skill. L16. 4 Something that finishes off or equips completely (formerly including bodily equipment); now usu. a social skill or grace (passing into sense 3). E17.

accompt *n.*, *v.*, **-ant** *a.* & *n.* see ACCOUNT *n.*, *v.*, ACCOUNTANT.

accord /əˈkɔːd/ *n.* ME. [OFr. *acord* (mod. *acc-*), f. as next.] 1 Reconciliation; concurrence of opinion, will, or action. ME. 2 A formal act of reconciliation; a treaty. ME. 3 Harmonious correspondence, as of colours or tints; agreement in pitch and tone; harmony. LME. 4 Assent; consent. Long *obs.* exc. in *of* (†*by*, †*on*) *one's own accord*, of one's own volition. LME. 5 *Law.* An agreement to accept something in exchange for giving up the right of action. E17.

1 W. COWPER Harmony and family accord. WORDSWORTH With due accord Of busy hands and back and forward steps. †**be of** (or **at**) **accord** (**with**) agree (with). **with** (or †**of**) **one accord** with unanimity. 3 E. BOWEN I did not put place or time of the funeral in *The Times*; in accord with general feeling that it should be strictly private.

accord /əˈkɔːd/ *v.* OE. [OFr. *acorder* (mod. *acc-*), f. L *ad* AC- after *concordare* CONCORD *v.*] †1 *v.t.* Bring (persons) into agreement; reconcile (a person, oneself) *with* another. OE. 2 *v.i.* Come to an agreement or to terms; be at one; agree. OE. 3 *v.t.* Settle (a quarrel, a difference). *arch.* ME. †4 *v.i.* Agree, assent, consent, *to.* ME–E19. 5 *v.i.* Of things: be in harmony, be consistent, (*with*). ME. †6 *v.i. impers.* in *it accords, it accorded*, it is or was suitable or proper. LME–M16. †7 *v.t.* Agree upon, arrange. LME–L17. 8 *v.t.* Agree to, grant (a request etc., *to* a person); award. LME. †9 *v.t.* Attune (*to*). L16–M17.

accordable *a.* †(*a*) accordant; (*b*) reconcilable: LME. **accorder** *n.* a person who agrees or bestows M19. **accordment** *n.* (now *rare*) reconcilement ME.

accordance /əˈkɔːd(ə)ns/ *n.* ME. [OFr. *acordance*, f. as prec.: see -ANCE.] 1 Agreement; conformity; harmony. Esp. in *in accordance with*. ME. 2 The action of granting. M19.

accordancy *n.* a condition or state of agreement; harmony: L18.

accordant /əˈkɔːd(ə)nt/ *a.* ME. [OFr. *acordant* pres. pple, f. as prec.: see -ANT[1].] 1 In accordance or agreement *with*; compatible *with*. Also (now *rare*) foll. by *to*. ME. 2 *absol.* †a Agreeing in character or circumstances; suitable. ME–E17. b Agreeing in external action or motion; *esp.* (of sounds) harmonious. LME. †c Agreeing or concurring in mind. Only in L16.

accordantly *adv.* LME.

according /əˈkɔːdɪŋ/ *a.* & *adv.* ME. [f. ACCORD *v.* + -ING[2].] A *adj.* †1 *pred.* Corresponding *to*. ME–M16. 2 *absol.* Agreeing in nature or action. LME. †3 Appropriate, fitting. LME–L17.

2 TENNYSON Harder the times were . . , and the according hearts of men Seemed harder too.

B *adv.* 1 *according to*, in a manner consistent with or a degree proportioned to; as formulated by, as stated by. LME. b *absol.* According to circumstances. *colloq.* M19. 2 = ACCORDINGLY 3. Now *rare*. L15. 3 *according as*, exactly as, just as; in proportion as; in a manner depending on which of certain alternatives is true. E16.

1 *according to Cocker*: see COCKER *n.*[4] *according to plan*: see PLAN *n.* 2 L. MACNEICE In the second taxi . . the clock showed sixpence extra; he tipped according.

accordingly /əˈkɔːdɪŋli/ *adv.* ME. [f. prec. + -LY[2].] †1 Harmoniously, agreeably. ME–E16. 2 Becomingly, duly, properly. Long *rare*. LME. 3 In accordance with the logical premises; correspondingly. L16. 4 In natural sequence, in due course; so. L17.

Phrases: **accordingly as** according as.

accordion /əˈkɔːdɪən/ *n.* & *a.* M19. [G *Akkordion*, f. It. *accordare* tune (an instrument).] A *n.* A portable musical instrument consisting of bellows, metal reeds, and a keyboard and/or buttons. M19.

See also *piano accordion*.

B *attrib.* or as *adj.* Folding like the bellows of an accordion. L19.

accordion pleat, *-pleated* adj., *accordion wall*, etc.

accordionist *n.* L19.

accost /əˈkɒst/ *v.* & *n.* L16. [Fr. *accoster* f. It. *accostare*, ult. f. L *ad* AC- + *costa* rib, side. Assoc. w. *coast*.] A *v.* Also †**accoast**. †1 *v.i.* & *t.* Lie alongside, border (on). L16–M17. †2 *v.t.* Go alongside of. L16–E17. 3 *v.t.* Approach for any purpose; assail, face. *arch.* L16. 4 *v.t.* Approach and speak to, esp. boldly; address. L16. b *v.t.* & *i.* Of a prostitute: solicit in the street. L19. B *n.* An address, a salutation. E17.

accostable *a.* approachable, accessible E17. **accoster** *n.* M19.

accouchement /əˈkuːʃmɒ̃, *foreign* akuʃmɑ̃/ *n.* L18. [Fr., f. *accoucher*, f. as A-[5] + COUCH *v.*: see -MENT.] Childbirth.

accouche *v.i.* give birth; act as midwife: E19.

accoucheur /akuːˈʃəː; *foreign* akuʃœːr (*pl.* same)/ *n.* M18. [Fr., f. as prec. + *-eur* -OR.] A man (formerly also a woman) who acts as midwife.

accoucheuse /-əːz; *foreign* -øːz (*pl. same*)/ *n.* a midwife E19.

account /əˈkaʊnt/ *n.* Also (*arch.*) **accompt**. ME. [AN *acunt*, OFr. *acont*, later *a(c)compt*, f. as next.] 1 Counting, reckoning, calculation. ME. 2 A statement of moneys, goods, or services received and expended, or other receipts and outgoings, with calculation of the balance. Also, a business arrangement involving the reckoning of debit or credit; *esp.* (*a*) one involving deferment of payment or (*Stock Exch.*) deferment of completion of a transaction until the next account day; (*b*) one involving the keeping of money or other assets in a bank etc., with the depositor having the option of withdrawal; (*c*) a credit arrangement with a firm, shop, etc. Also, a sum of money owed or one deposited in a bank etc. but subject to withdrawal. ME. b A customer having such an arrangement. M20. c In *pl.* The department of a firm etc. that deals with accounts. M20. 3 A statement as to the discharge of any responsibility; an answering for conduct. ME. 4 Estimation, importance; consideration. LME. 5 A particular statement of the administration of money in trust or required by a creditor. E16. 6 *Law.* A writ or action against a bailiff, receiver, partner, etc., who wrongfully refuses to render account of money received. E16. 7 A narration, a report, a description; a performance (*of* a piece of music etc.). E17. 8 A reckoning in one's favour; advantage. E17. 9 The preparing of a statement of money transactions. M17.

1 T. HARDY My accompt of years outscored her own. 2 THACKERAY Pen thought of opening an account with a banker. 4 JONSON A Scholler . . of good accompt. STEVIE SMITH You are only one of many And of small account if any. 5 GOLDSMITH To give in his accompts to the masters of the temple. 7 E. V. LUCAS Has any reader ever found perfect accuracy in the newspaper account of any event of which he himself had inside knowledge? 9 GIBBON The actual account employed several hundred persons.

Phrases: †**account current** = *current account* below. **budget account** an account at a shop etc. with revolving credit and regular payments. **by all accounts** in everyone's opinion. *call to account*: see CALL *v.* **cast accounts** make calculations. **current account** an account at a bank allowing withdrawal of money on demand, now usu. also providing the depositor with means of authorizing withdrawal of money by others. **deposit account** an account at a bank usu. paying interest and not able to be drawn upon without notice or requiring the depositor to apply for repayment in person. **for account of** to be accounted for to (a person). **for the account** *Stock Exch.* not for cash, but for settlement on the next account day. **give a good account of** be successful with; do justice to. **go to one's account** die. **joint account**: held by two or more people in conjunction. **keep accounts** record expenditure for comparison with income. **lay one's account with (on, for)** (orig. *Sc.*) reckon upon, expect. **leave out of account** not take into consideration, disregard. †**make account** reckon, resolve, expect (*that*, *to do*). **make account of** esteem. **money of account** a denomination of money used in reckoning, but not current as coins etc. *nominal account*: see NOMINAL *a.* *numbered account*: see NUMBER *v.* **on account** to be accounted for at the final settlement; not to be paid for immediately; as interim payment. **on account of** (*a*) because of; †(*b*) concerning. **on no account** under no circumstances; certainly not. **on one's own account** for one's own purpose and at one's own risk. **on someone's account** so that it is chargeable to him or her; to benefit him or her. **render, send in, an account** give a statement of money due. **settle** or **square accounts (with)** receive or pay the balance due (from or to); *fig.* have revenge (on). **take account of, take into account** take into consideration, notice. *turn to (good) account*: see TURN *v.* *unit of account*: see UNIT *n.*[1] *vote on account*: see VOTE *n.* 5.

Comb.: **account book** a book prepared for the keeping of accounts; **account day** a day of reckoning; *Stock Exch.* the day on which accounts are settled; **accounts department** = sense 2c above; **account(s) executive** a business executive, esp. in advertising, who manages a client's account.

account /əˈkaʊnt/ *v.* Also (*arch.*) **accompt**. ME. [OFr. *acunter*, *aconter*, f. as A-[5] + COUNT *v.*] I†1 *v.t.* Count, enumerate. ME–E17. b *v.i.* Perform the act of counting. LME–L18. 2 *v.i.* Render or receive an account. ME. b *v.t.* Render account of. E17. 3†a *v.t.* Calculate, compute; include in a reckoning. LME–E19. b *v.t.* Reckon, credit, *to*, *unto*. LME. 4 *v.t.* Reckon, estimate (to be so and so), consider, regard as. LME.

1b ADAM SMITH Able to read, write, and account. 2 BURKE Paymasters . . who have never been admitted to account. b M. PATTISON All receipts should be accounted to a finance committee. 3a TREVISA The Grekes acounte tyme and yeres fro the fyrst Olympias. SOUTHEY Wales, Scotland, and Ireland ought to be accounted with England. 4 AV *Rom.* 8:36 We are accounted as sheepe for the slaughter. A. HECHT Trajan, of his imperial peers Accounted 'the most just'.

†II 5 *v.t.* & *i.* Recount, narrate. ME–L16.

With preps. in specialized senses: **account for** (*a*) give a reckoning of (money held in trust); answer for (conduct, performance of duty, etc.); (*b*) explain the cause of, serve as an explanation of; (*c*) constitute a specified total, proportion, etc., in a reckoning; (*d*) be responsible for the death, defeat, dismissal, etc., of. **account of** esteem, value; think (*much*, *little*, *nothing*, etc.) of; (now only in *pass.*). **account to** put (something) to the credit of, attribute to.

†**accounter** *n.* ME–M17.

accountable /əˈkaʊntəb(ə)l/ *a.* LME. [AN *accountable* (OFr. *acomptable*): see prec., -ABLE.] 1 Liable to be called to account; responsible (*to* persons, *for* things). LME. †2 Able to be computed. Only in L16. †3 To be counted on. E17–E18. 4 Explicable; able to be accounted *for*. M17. †5 Attributable *to*. Only in L17.

accountaˈbility *n.* L18. **accountableness** *n.* M17. **accountably** *adv.* M17.

accountancy /əˈkaʊnt(ə)nsi/ *n.* M19. [f. next: see -ANCY.] The profession or duties of an accountant.

creative accountancy: see CREATIVE I.

accountant /əˈkaʊnt(ə)nt/ *a.* & *n.* Also (*arch.*) **accompt-**. LME. [Law Fr., use of pres. pple of OFr. *aconter*: see ACCOUNT *v.*, -ANT[1].] †A *adj.* Giving or liable to give an account. (*rare* after M17.) LME–E19. B *n.* 1 A person who is accountable or responsible; *Law* the defendant in an action of account. LME. 2 A professional keeper and inspector of accounts; an officer in a public office who has charge of the accounts. LME. 3 *gen.* A person who reckons or calculates. *arch.* M17.

2 *certified (public) accountant*, *chartered accountant*. *turf accountant*: see TURF *n.*

accountantship *n.* (*a*) the position or employment of an accountant; †(*b*) accountancy: M17.

accounting /əˈkaʊntɪŋ/ *n.* LME. [f. ACCOUNT *v.* + -ING[1].] 1 Reckoning, counting. Now *spec.* the process or art of keeping and verifying accounts. LME. 2 Foll. by *for*: giving a satisfactory explanation of, answering for. L18.

1 *cost accounting*: see COST *n.*[2] *creative accounting*: see CREATIVE I. *current cost accounting*: see CURRENT *a.* 2 *Proverb*: There is no accounting for tastes.

Comb.: **accounting period** a period of time for which accounts are presented.

†**accouple** *v.t.* L15–M17. [OFr. *acopler* (mod. *accoupler*), f. as A-[5], COUPLE *v.*] Join (one thing) to another, couple.

accouplement /əˈkʌp(ə)lm(ə)nt/ *n.* Now *rare*. L15. [f. prec. + -MENT.] (A) coupling, esp. in marriage.

†**accourage** *v.t.* M–L16. [OFr. *aco(u)ragier* var. of *encouragier* ENCOURAGE.] Encourage.

†**accourt** *v.t.* *literary*. L16–E17. [f. A-[1] + COURT *v.*] Court.

accoutre /əˈkuːtə/ *v.t.* Also ***-ter**. M16. [(O)Fr. *accoutrer*, f. as A-[5] + COUTURE.] Attire, equip, esp. with special costume. Chiefly as *accoutred* ppl a.

accoutrement /əˈkuːtəm(ə)nt, -trə-/ *n.* Also ***-ter-** /-tə-/. M16. [Fr., f. as prec.: see -MENT.] 1 *sing.* & (usu.) in *pl.* Apparel, equipment, trappings; *Mil.* a soldier's outfit other than arms and garments. M16. 2 The process of accoutring or being accoutred. L16.

1 M. MCCARTHY A mere padded form . . on which clothes and other accoutrements were tried. I. FLEMING The usual accoutrements of a busy organization—In and Out baskets, telephones.

†**accoy** *v.t.* LME–M17. [OFr. *acoier*, f. as A-[5] + COY *a.*] Calm, quiet; coax; daunt.

accra /ˈakrə, əˈkrɑː/ *n.* Also **akkra, akara** /əˈkarə/, & other vars. L19. [Yoruba *àkàrà* bean cake.] A W. African and W. Indian fritter made with black-eyed peas or a similar pulse. Also, a W. Indian fritter made with mashed fish.

accredit /əˈkrɛdɪt/ *v.t.* E17. [Fr. *accréditer*, f. as A-[5] + CREDIT *n.*] 1 Gain belief or influence for; set forth as credible; vouch for; recommend to official recognition. E17. 2 Furnish (a person) with credentials; authorize as an envoy. L18. 3 Attribute *to*; credit *with*. M19.

accrediˈtation *n.* recommendation to credit or official recognition E19. **accredited** *a.* officially recognized; generally accepted, orthodox; having guaranteed quality: M17.

†**accresce** *v.i.* Orig. *Sc.* M16. [L *accrescere*, f. *ad* AC- + *crescere* grow.] 1 Increase or grow by addition. M16–M18. 2 Fall or accrue *to*. L16–L19.

accrescent /əˈkrɛs(ə)nt/ *a.* M19. [L *accrescent-* pres. ppl stem of *accrescere*: see prec., -ENT.]

Growing continuously; *spec.* in *Bot.*, continuing to grow after flowering.

accrescence *n.* continuous growth; an accretion: M17. **accrescency** *n.* an accretion M17.

accrete /əˈkriːt/ *v.* L18. [L *accret-* pa. ppl stem of *accrescere*: see ACCRESCE.] **1** *v.i.* Grow together, combine; grow by adhesion or coalescence of or *from* smaller bodies; adhere or become attached *to* or *on to*. L18. **2** *v.t.* Cause to grow or unite *to*; draw or attract to oneself or itself. L19.

accrete *a.* formed by accretion; made up, factitious: E19. **accretive** *a.* accretionary M17.

accretion /əˈkriːʃ(ə)n/ *n.* E17. [L *accretio(n-)*, f. as prec.: see -ION.] **1** Growth by organic enlargement. E17. **2** Growth by external addition. E17. **3** The growing of separate things into one. M17. **b** The product of such growing together. L19. **4** A thing that adheres so as to cause increase; an extraneous addition. M17. **5** The adhesion of external matter or things so as to cause increase. E18. **6** *Law.* **a** = ACCESSION 4. M19. **b** The increase of an inheritance or legacy by the addition of the share of a failing co-heir or co-legatee. L19.

Comb.: **accretion disc** *Astron.* a rotating disc of matter which may form around a large star etc., esp. one in a binary system, under the influence of gravity.

accretionary *a.* characterized or formed by accretion M19.

accroach /əˈkrəʊtʃ/ *v.* ME. [OFr. *acrochier* (later *acc-*) hook in: see A-[5] and cf. OFr. *croche* a hook.] **1** *v.t.* Draw to oneself, acquire. Now *rare* or *obs.* exc. in *accroach to oneself*, seize what is not one's own, usurp (authority etc.). ME. **2** *v.i.* Encroach. *rare.* LME.

accroachment *n.* E17.

accrue /əˈkruː/ *v.* LME. [Prob. f. AN *accru(e)*, OFr. *accreu(e)* pa. pple of *acreistre* f. L *accrescere*: see ACCRESCE.] **1** *v.i.* Come (*to* a person) as a natural growth or increment, or as an accession or advantage. LME. **2** *v.i.* Arise or spring (*from*, †or *by*, *of*) as a natural growth or result. Used esp. of interest on invested money and (*Law*) of the coming into existence of a possible cause of action. L16. **3** *v.t.* Gather up, collect. L16. †**4** *v.i.* Grow, increase. Only in 17.

accrual *n.* accruement; *Law* = ACCRETION 6b: L19. **accruement** *n.* the action of accruing; a thing that accrues or has accrued: E17. **accruer** *n.* (*Law*) = ACCRETION 6b M19.

accubation /akjʊˈbeɪʃ(ə)n/ *n.* M17. [L *accubatio(n-)*, f. *ad* AC- + *cubat-* pa. ppl stem of *cubare* to lie: see -ATION.] †**1** The posture of reclining, esp. at table. M–L17. **2** = ACCOUCHEMENT. *rare.* L19.

acculturation /əkʌltjʊˈreɪʃ(ə)n, -tʃə-/ *n.* L19. [f. AC- + CULTURE *n.* + -ATION.] Adoption of or adaptation to an alien culture.

a,culturali'zation *n.* = ACCULTURATION M20. **a'cculturate** *v.t.* & *i.* (cause to) undergo acculturation M20. **acculturational** *a.* M20. **a'cculturative** *a.* involving or producing acculturation M20. **a,culturi'zation** *n.* = ACCULTURATION L20. **a'cculturize** *v.t.* cause to undergo acculturation L19.

accumbent /əˈkʌmbənt/ *n.* & *a.* M17. [L *accumbent-* pres. ppl stem of *accumbere*, f. *ad* AC- + *-cumbere*: see CUMBENT.] **A** *n.* A person who reclines, or *gen.* is, at table. *rare.* M17. **B** *adj.* **1** Reclining at table. *rare.* E18. **2** *Bot.* Of a cotyledon: lying edgewise against the folded radicle in the seed. Cf. INCUMBENT *a.* E19.

†**accumber** *v.t.* ME–M17. [Var. of ENCUMBER *v.*] Encumber, overwhelm, crush.

accumulate /əˈkjuːmjʊlət/ *a.* M16. [L *accumulatus* pa. pple, f. as next: see -ATE[2].] Heaped up, collected.

¶Formerly adj. and pple; as pple now replaced by *accumulated.*

accumulate /əˈkjuːmjʊleɪt/ *v.* L15. [L *accumulat-* pa. ppl stem of *accumulare*, f. *ad* AC- + *cumulus* a heap: see -ATE[3].] **1** *v.t.* Heap up; gradually get an increasing number or quantity of; produce or acquire thus. Freq. *fig.* L15. **2** *v.t.* Take (degrees) by accumulation. Now *rare.* L17. **3** *v.i.* Form an increasing mass or quantity (*lit.* & *fig.*). M18.

accumulation /əkjuːmjʊˈleɪʃ(ə)n/ *n.* L15. [L *accumulatio(n-)*, f. as prec.: see -ATION. Cf. (O)Fr. *accumulation.*] **1** The action of accumulating something. L15. **2** The process of growing in amount or number; *spec.* the growth of capital by the continued addition of interest. L15. **3** An accumulated mass; a quantity formed by successive additions. L15. **4** The combination of several acts or exercises into one; *spec.* the taking of higher and lower university degrees together. M18.

1 *primitive* (*socialist*) *accumulation*: see PRIMITIVE *a.* & *n.*

accumulative /əˈkjuːmjʊlətɪv/ *a.* M17. [f. ACCUMULATE *v.* + -IVE.] **1** Arising from accumulation; cumulative. M17. **2** Given to accumulating or hoarding. E19. **3** So constituted as to accumulate. M19.

accumulatively *adv.* M17. **accumulativeness** *n.* M19.

accumulator /əˈkjuːmjʊleɪtə/ *n.* E17. [f. as prec. + -OR.] **1** A person who accumulates things. E17. **2** A person who takes degrees by accumulation. L17. **3** A thing that accumulates something; *spec.* (*a*) a rechargeable electric cell, a secondary battery; (*b*) a storage register in a computer. M19. **4** A bet placed on a sequence of events, the winnings from each being staked on the next. E20.

accuracy /ˈakjʊrəsi/ *n.* M17. [f. next: see -ACY.] **1** The state of being accurate; precision, correctness. M17. **2** The degree of refinement in measurement or specification, as given by the extent of conformity with a standard or true value. Cf. PRECISION *n.* 2C. M20.

accurate /ˈakjʊrət/ *a.* L16. [L *accuratus* pa. pple & adj., f. *accurare*, f. *ad* AC- + *cura* care: see -ATE[2].] **1** Of a thing or a person: exact or correct, as the result of care. L16. †**2** *gen.* Executed with care. E17–M18. **3** Of a thing: in exact conformity with a standard or with truth. M17.

accurately *adv.* with careful exactness; without error or defect: E17. **accurateness** *n.* E17.

†**accurre** *v.i.* & *t.* M16–M17. [L *accurrere*, f. *ad* AC- + *currere* run.] Run together, meet.

accurse /əˈkəːs/ *v.t.* *arch.* Pa. pple **accursed**, **-st**. ME. [f. A-[1] + CURSE *v.*] Utter against (a person or thing) words intended to consign their object to destruction, divine vengeance, misery, etc. (= CURSE *v.* 1).

accursed /-sɪd, -st/, **-st** *a.* under a curse; deserving or bringing a curse or misery; execrable, detestable; (= CURSED *a.* 1, 2, 3): ME. **accursedly** /-ɪdli/ *adv.* E17. **accursedness** /-ɪdnɪs/ *n.* L16.

†**accurtation** *n.* L15–L18. [med.L *accurtatio(n-)*, f. *accurtat-* pa. ppl stem of *accurtare*, f. *ad* AC- + *curtus* short: see -ATION.] = ABBREVIATION.

accusant /əˈkjuːz(ə)nt/ *n.* Now *rare.* LME. [Obs. Fr., or L *accusant-*, *accusans* pres. pple (used as n.) of *accusare* ACCUSE: see -ANT[1].] An accuser.

accusation /akjʊˈzeɪʃ(ə)n/ *n.* LME. [OFr. f. L *accusatio(n-)*, f. *accusat-* pa. ppl stem of *accusare* ACCUSE: see -ATION.] **1** The act of accusing; the state of being accused. LME. **2** A charge of an offence or crime; an indictment. LME.

accusative /əˈkjuːzətɪv/ *a.* & *n.* LME. [(O)Fr. *accusatif*, *-ive* or L *accusativus* (sc. *casus* case), f. *accusat-*: see prec., -IVE.] **A** *adj.* **1** *Gram.* Designating, being in, or pertaining to a case in inflected languages expressing primarily destination, hence a case expressing the object of transitive verbs (i.e. the destination of the verbal action); in uninflected languages occas. designating the relation in which the object stands. LME. **2** [f. ACCUSE.] Accusatory. *rare.* LME.

B *n. Gram. The* accusative case; a word, form, etc. in the accusative case. LME.

accusative absolute (*a*) in German, a construction comprising an accusative noun and a predicate with no finite verb, usu. able to be construed as a modifier of the main verb; (*b*) in English, a colloquial form of the nominative absolute construction with a pronoun in the objective case. *cognate accusative*: see COGNATE *a.*

accusatival /-ˈtaɪv(ə)l/ *a.* pertaining to the accusative case M19. **accusatively** *adv.* M18.

accusatorial /əkjuːzəˈtɔːrɪəl/ *a.* E19. [f. as next + -AL[1].] Of a system of criminal procedure: in which the facts are ascertained by the judge or jury from evidence presented by the prosecution and the defence. Opp. *inquisitorial.*

accusatorially *adv.* in an accusatorial manner; by means of a formal accuser: M19.

accusatory /əˈkjuːzət(ə)ri/ *a.* LME. [L *accusatorius*, f. *accusat-*: see ACCUSATION, -ORY[2].] Of the nature of an accusation; accusatorial.

accuse /əˈkjuːz/ *v.* & *n.* ME. [OFr. *acuser*, (also mod.) *accuser* f. L *accusare* call to account, f. *ad* AC- + *causa* CAUSE *n.*] **A** *v.t.* **1** Charge with a fault; blame. ME. **2** Charge with the crime or fault *of* (†or *for*, *in*, *upon*, *with*). ME. **3** Betray, disclose. *arch.* LME.

1 AV *Prov.* 30:10 Accuse not a seruant vnto his master. **2** M. DRABBLE You..accused me of affectation. **3** MILTON This wording..accuses the whole composure to be conscious of some other Author.

†**B** *n.* (An) accusation. LME–M17.

accusable *a.* liable to be accused; open to an accusation *of*: E16. **accusal** *n.* accusation L16. **accused** *ppl a.* & *n.* (*a*) *adj.* charged with a crime or fault; (*b*) *n. the* prisoner at the bar: L15. †**accusement** *n.* the action of accusing; an accusation: LME–E18. **accuser** *n.* a person who accuses or blames someone; *esp.* a person who accuses someone in a court of justice: ME. **accusing** *a.* blaming, reproachful L16. **accusingly** *adv.* L16.

accustom /əˈkʌstəm/ *v.* & *n.* LME. [AN *acustumer*, OFr. *acost-* (mod. *accout-*), f. as A-[5] + CUSTOM *n.*] **A** *v.* **1** *v.t.* Foll. by *to*, †*with*: make (oneself or another, or a thing) used to or familiar with. LME. †**b** *v.i.* Be wont *to*. M16–M17. †**2** *v.t.* Make customary or familiar; practise habitually. Usu. in *pass.* L15–M18. †**3** *v.i.* Become or be familiar; mix or act familiarly. M16–L17.

1 G. B. SHAW Time to accustom myself to our new relations. V. WOOLF The eyes accustom themselves to twilight and discern the shapes of things in a room. M. MCCARTHY We accustomed him to noise. **b** EVELYN Those..who..accustom to wash their heads. **2** C. MARLOWE Such ceremonious thanks, As parting friends accustom on the shore. **3** †**accustom to** frequent. †**accustom with** consort or cohabit with.

†**B** *n.* Custom; habituation. LME–M17.

†**accustomable** *a.* habitual, customary LME–M18. †**accustomably** *adv.* habitually, customarily LME–E19. †**accustomance** *n.* customary use or practice LME–M19. **accustomary** *a.* (*arch.*) usual, customary M16. **accusto'mation** *n.* (*rare*) habitual practice or use; being accustomed *to*: E17.

accustomed /əˈkʌstəmd/ *a.* LME. [f. ACCUSTOM *v.* + -ED[1].] **1** Made customary; wonted, used; usual. LME. †**2** Frequented by customers. L17–L19.

1 SHELLEY The accustomed nightingale still broods On her accustomed bough. **accustomed to** used to, in the habit of. **2** SMOLLETT A well accustomed shop.

accustomedly *adv.* E17. **accustomedness** *n.* M17.

ace /eɪs/ *n.*, *v.*, & *a.* ME. [(O)Fr. *as* f. L *as* unity.] **A** *n.* **1** The 'one' on dice, later also on playing-cards or dominoes; a throw of 'one', or a card etc. so marked (in some card-games reckoned as of the highest value). ME. **b** In Tennis etc.: an unreturnable stroke, *esp.* a service that an opponent fails to touch; a point scored. E19. **c** *Golf.* A hole in one. E20. **2** *fig.* A single point; a jot, a particle, an atom; a hair's breadth. E16. **3a** In the wars of 1914–18 and 1939–45: a pilot who brought down many enemy aircraft. E20. **b** *gen.* A person who excels at something. E20.

1 AMBS-ACE. **deuce ace** [OFr.] two aces at one throw (now taken as *deuce* + *ace* = 2 + 1; so *trey ace*, *sice ace*, etc.). **an ace up one's sleeve**, *N. Amer.* **an ace in the hole** something effective in reserve. **play one's ace** use one's best resource. **2 bate an ace** *arch.* make the slightest abatement. **within an ace of** on the very point of, within a hair's breadth of. **3b** P. G. WODEHOUSE George Bevan's all right. He's an ace.

Comb.: **ace-high** *a.* (*N. Amer. colloq.*) highly valued.

B *v.* **1** *v.t.* **a** In Tennis etc.: score an ace against (an opponent). L19. **b** *Golf.* Complete (a hole) in one stroke. M20. **2** *v.t.* & *i.* Achieve the top grade in (an examination etc.). Also foll. by *out*. *N. Amer. slang.* M20.

2 ace it achieve the top grade.

C *adj.* First-class, excellent. *colloq.* M20.

-acean /ˈeɪʃ(ə)n/ *suff.* [f. L *-acea* neut. pl. of *-aceus* -ACEOUS + -AN.] Forming adjs. or ns. from names of zoological classes etc. ending in *-acea*, as *crustacean*.

acedia /əˈsiːdɪə/ *n.* E17. [Late L *acedia* f. Gk *akēdia*, f. *a-* A-[10] + *kēdos* care, concern.] = ACCIDIE.

Aceldama /əˈkɛldəmə, əˈsɛl-/ *n.* M17. [Gk *Akeldama* f. Aram. *hăqel dĕmā* field of blood: see *Acts* 1:19.] A field of bloodshed; a scene of slaughter.

acellular /eɪˈsɛljʊlə/ *a.* M20. [f. A-[10] + CELLULAR.] Not divided into cells.

acentric /eɪˈsɛntrɪk/ *a.* M19. [f. A-[10] + CENTRIC.] Without a centre.

-aceous /ˈeɪʃəs/ *suff.* [f. L *-aceus* of the nature of, belonging to: see -EOUS, -OUS.] Forming adjs. from L wds in *-aceus* etc., *spec.* in *Bot.* from names of plant families ending in fem. pl. form *-aceae*.

Acephali /əˈsɛfəlʌɪ -liː/ *n.pl.* L16. [med.L (Isidore), pl. of *acephalus*: see next.] 1 Imaginary men or animals without heads. Now *rare* or *obs.* L16. 2 *Eccl. Hist.* Any of various Christian bodies which owned either no leader or no earthly head. L16.

acephalous /eɪˈsɛf(ə)ləs, -ˈkɛf-/ *a.* M18. [f. med.L *acephalus* f. Gk *akephalos*, f. *a-* A-[10] + *kephalē* head: see -OUS.] 1 *gen.* Headless. M18. 2 Having or recognizing no governing head or chief. M18. 3 *Zool.* Having no part of the body organized as a head. M18. 4 Lacking the beginning, as an imperfect manuscript or verse. M18.

aceˈphalic *a.* = ACEPHALOUS M17. **acephaly** *n.* absence of a head, esp. as a congenital malformation M20.

acer /ˈeɪsə/ *n.* L19. [L = maple.] A tree or shrub of the large genus *Acer*, which includes the maples and the European sycamore.

aceramic /eɪsɪˈramɪk/ *a.* M20. [f. A-[10] + CERAMIC *a.*] *Archaeol.* Of a culture: having no pottery.

acerb /əˈsəːb/ *a.* E17. [L *acerbus*: cf. Fr. *acerbe.*] = ACERBIC.

acerbly *adv.* M20.

acerbate /əˈsəːbət/ *a.* M19. [f. as next: see -ATE[2].] Embittered; exasperated.

acerbate /ˈasəbeɪt/ *v.t.* M18. [L *acerbat-* pa. ppl stem of *acerbare*, f. as ACERB: see -ATE[3].] Sour, embitter; exasperate.

acerbic /əˈsəːbɪk/ *a.* M19. [f. as ACERB + -IC.] Astringently sour, harsh-tasting; *fig.* bitter and sharp, esp. in speech, manner, or temper.

acerbically *adv.* L20.

acerbity /əˈsəːbɪti/ *n.* L16. [Fr. *acerbité* or L *acerbitas*: see ACERB, -ITY.] 1 Bitterness and sharpness, keen harshness, (of character, manner, speech, etc.). L16. 2 Sourness of taste, with astringency. E17.

acerebral /eɪˈsɛrɪbr(ə)l/ *a.* M20. [f. A-[10] + CEREBRAL *a.*] Brainless; unintelligent; unthinking.

acerose /ˈasərəʊs/ *a.* E18. [L *acerosus*, f. *acer-*, *acus* chaff: see -OSE[1]. In sense 2 erron. referred to *acus* needle, or *acer* sharp.] †1 Chaffy. Only in Dicts. E18–L19. 2 *Bot.* Needle-shaped and rigid. Now *rare.* M18.

acervation /asəˈveɪʃ(ə)n/ *n.* L17. [L *acervatio(n-)*, f. *acervat-* pa. ppl stem of *acervare* heap up, f. *acervus* heap: see -ATION.] The action of heaping up; an accumulation.

acervate /əˈsəːvət/ *a.* heaped, growing in clusters M19. **acervuline** /əˈsəːvjʊlʌɪn/ *a.* in the form of little heaps M19.

acervulus /əˈsəːvjʊləs/ *n.* Pl. **-li** /-lʌɪ, -liː/. E19. [mod.L, dim. of L *acervus* heap: see -ULE.] 1 *Anat.* In full *acervulus cerebri* /ˈsɛrɪbrʌɪ/. = *brain-sand* s.v. BRAIN *n.* Now *rare* or *obs.* E19. 2 *Bot.* A flat mass of fungal conidiophores embedded in the tissue of the host plant. L19.

acescent /əˈsɛs(ə)nt/ *a.* M18. [Fr., or L *acescent-* pres. ppl stem of *acescere* become sour: see -ESCENT.] Turning sour; tending to turn acid; somewhat sour (*lit.* & *fig.*).

acescence *n.* the act of turning sour, acetous fermentation L17. **acescency** *n.* tendency to sourness; incipient or slight acidity: M18.

acet- *comb. form* see ACETO-.

acetable /ˈasɪtəb(ə)l/ *n.* Now *rare* or *obs.* L15. [f. as next.] = next.

acetabulum /asɪˈtabjʊləm/ *n.* Pl. **-la** /-lə/. LME. [L, f. *acetum* vinegar + *-abulum* denoting a container.] 1 *Rom. Antiq.* A cup to hold vinegar at table; a liquid measure of the capacity of such a cup. LME. 2 *Anat.* a The socket of the hip-bone, with which the head of the femur articulates. L16. b A sucker possessed by some cephalopods, tremarodes, etc. M17.

acetal /ˈasɪtal/ *n.* M19. [f. ACET(IC + -AL[2].] *Chem.* 1 An odoriferous liquid, $CH_3CH(OC_2H_5)_2$, formed by reaction of acetaldehyde and ethyl alcohol. Also, any other compound with one hydrogen atom and two alkoxy groups attached to the same carbon atom. Also *gen.* = KETAL. M19. 2 = POLYOXYMETHYLENE. M20.

acetaldehyde /asɪtˈaldɪhʌɪd/ *n.* M19. [f. ACET(IC + ALDEHYDE.] *Chem.* A volatile pungent liquid, CH_3CHO, obtained by the oxidation of ethyl alcohol; ethanal.

acetamide /əˈsiːtəmʌɪd, əˈsɛt-/ *n.* M19. [f. ACET(YL + AMIDE.] *Chem.* The amide of acetic acid, a crystalline solid, CH_3CONH_2.

acetanilide /asɪtˈanɪlʌɪd/ *n.* M19. [f. ACET(YL + ANIL(INE + -IDE.] *Chem.* A crystalline solid, $C_6H_5NHCOCH_3$, obtained by acetylation of aniline.

acetate /ˈasɪteɪt/ *n.* L18. [f. ACET(IC + -ATE[1].] 1 *Chem.* A salt or ester of acetic acid. L18. 2 The cellulose ester of acetic acid, in the form of an artificial fibre or a plastic. E20. b A disc coated with cellulose acetate, for direct recording by a cutting stylus; any direct-cut disc. M20. c A clear plastic film of cellulose acetate, used in photography, as a display medium, etc.; a sheet of this. M20.

2 Freq. *attrib.*, as *acetate fibre, rayon, silk.*

acetic /əˈsiːtɪk, əˈsɛt-/ *a.* L18. [Fr. *acétique*, f. L *acetum* vinegar: see -IC.] 1 Chem. *acetic acid*, a weak acid, CH_3COOH, of which vinegar is a crude dilute solution, and which when pure and anhydrous (*glacial acetic acid*) can be obtained as colourless crystals melting at 16.7°C; ethanoic acid. L18. 2 Pertaining to or producing acetic acid. L19.

2 **acetic anhydride** a liquid, $(CH_3CO)_2O$, the anhydride of acetic acid.

acetify /əˈsɛtɪfʌɪ, əˈsiːt-/ *v.t.* M19. [f. L *acetum* vinegar + -I- + -FY.] Subject to fermentation producing acetic acid; convert into vinegar.

acetifiˈcation *n.* the process of acetifying M18. **acetifier** *n.* an apparatus in which vinegar is produced M19.

aceto- /əˈsiːtəʊ, ˈasɪtəʊ/ *comb. form* of ACETIC, ACETYL: see -O-. Bef. a vowel also **acet-**.

acetoaˈcetic *a.*: *acetoacetic acid*, an acid, CH_3COCH_2COOH, present in the urine of diabetics, and when pure a viscous unstable liquid L19. **acetoˈacetate** *n.* a salt or ester of this acid L19. **acetoˈnitrile**, **†-il** *n.* a toxic odoriferous liquid, CH_3CN; methyl cyanide: M19.

acetobacter /əˌsiːtə(ʊ)ˈbaktə, asɪ-/ *n.* M20. [mod.L (see below), f. as ACETO- + BACTER(IUM.] A bacterium that oxidizes organic compounds to acetic acid (as in vinegar formation), *esp.* one of the genus *Acetobacter*.

acetogenic /əˌsiːtə(ʊ)ˈdʒɛnɪk, asɪt-/ *a.* L20. [f. ACETO- + -GENIC.] *Microbiol.* Forming or producing acetic acid, esp. as a metabolic by-product.

acetone /ˈasɪtəʊn/ *n.* M19. [f. ACET(IC + -ONE.] *Chem.* A fragrant volatile liquid ketone, CH_3COCH_3, obtained chiefly by the dehydrogenation of isopropyl alcohol and widely used as a solvent; propanone.

acetoˈnaemia *n.* (*Med.*) = KETOSIS M19. **acetoˈnuria** *n.* (*Med.*) = KETONURIA L19.

acetous /əˈsiːtəs/ *a.* LME. [f. late L *acetosus*, f. *acetum* vinegar: see -OUS.] Having the qualities of vinegar; producing vinegar; sour.

¶ Rare bef. L18.

acetyl /ˈasɪtʌɪl, -tɪl/ *n.* M19. [f. ACET(IC + -YL.] *Chem.* The radical $\cdot COCH_3$, derived from acetic acid. Usu. in *comb.*

Comb.: **acetylcholine** the acetyl ester of choline and a major neurotransmitter; *acetylcholinesterase*, a cholinesterase that causes rapid hydrolysis of acetylcholine after transmission of an impulse; **acetyl coenzyme A** the acetyl ester of coenzyme A, involved as an acetylating agent in many biochemical processes; abbrev. *acetyl CoA*; **acetylsalicylic acid** the acetyl derivative of salicylic acid, $C_9H_8O_4$ (cf. ASPIRIN); **acetyl silk** acetate silk.

acetylation /əsɛtɪˈleɪʃ(ə)n/ *n.* L19. [f. prec. + -ATION.] *Chem.* A reaction or process in which one or more acetyl groups are introduced into a molecule.

aˈcetylate *v.t.* subject (a compound) to acetylation L19. **aˈcetylator** *n.* (*Biochem.*) an individual capable of metabolic acetylation (at a specified characteristic rate) M20.

acetylene /əˈsɛtɪliːn/ *n.* M19. [f. as prec. + -ENE.] *Chem.* A gaseous hydrocarbon, C_2H_2, which burns with a bright flame, used in welding and (esp. formerly) for illumination; ethyne.

acetyˈlenic *a.* containing the carbon-carbon triple bond characteristic of acetylene and the alkynes E20. **acetylide** *n.* a saltlike derivative of acetylene formed by replacement of one or both of the hydrogen atoms by a metal M19.

ach /ɑːx, *foreign* ax/ *int.* L15. [Celt., G, & Du.] Ah!

Achaean /əˈkiːən/ *a.* & *n.* Also **Achaian** /əˈkʌɪən/. M16. [f. L *Achaeus* f. Gk *Akhaios*, f. *Akhaia* Achaea, + -AN.] Of or pertaining to, a native or inhabitant of, Achaea (in Homer a name of Greece generally, later a district of the Peloponnese).

Achaemenian /akɪˈmɛnɪən/ *a.* & *n.* E18. [f. L *Achaemenius*, f. Gk *Akhaimenēs* Achaemenes, reputed ancestor of Cyrus: see -IAN.] Of or pertaining to, a member of, the dynasty that ruled in ancient Persia from the time of Cyrus the Great (d. 529 BC) until the death of Darius III (330 BC).

Also **Achaemenid** /əˈkiːmənɪd/ *a.* & *n.* [-ID[3]] E20.

Achaian *a.* & *n.* var. of ACHAEAN.

achalasia /akəˈleɪzjə/ *n.* E20. [f. A-[10] + Gk *khalasis*, f. *khalan* relax: see -IA[1].] *Physiol.* Failure of the muscles of the lower part of the oesophagus to relax, which prevents food from passing into the stomach.

achar /əˈtʃɑː/ *n.* L16. [Ult. f. Pers. *āchār.*] Pickles, as prepared in the Indian subcontinent.

†a-char *adv.* & *pred. a.* var. of AJAR *adv.*[1] & *pred. a.*[1]

acharnement /aʃarnəmɑ̃, əˈʃɑːnmɒ̃/ *n.* M18. [Fr., f. *acharner* give a taste of flesh (to dogs etc.): see -MENT.] Bloodthirsty fury; ferocity; gusto.

acharya /ɑːˈtʃɑːrjə/ *n.* E19. [Skt *ācārya* master, teacher.] In the Indian subcontinent, (a title given to) a spiritual teacher or leader; *transf.* an influential mentor.

achate /ˈakət/ *n.*[1] *arch.* ME. [OFr. *ac(h)ate* f. L *achates*: see AGATE *n.*] An agate.

†achate *n.*[2] var. of ACATE.

†achater *n.* var. of ACATOUR.

Achates /əˈkeɪtiːz/ *n. literary.* L16. [The faithful friend of Aeneas (Virgil *Aeneid* VI. 158 etc.).] A devoted follower; a loyal friend and companion.

Also FIDUS ACHATES.

†achatour, -try *ns.* see ACATOUR.

ache /eɪk/ *n.*[1] [OE *æće*, f. ACHE *v.*: see note below.] A continuous or prolonged dull pain, physical or mental.

aches and pains *colloq.* minor ailments and physical discomforts.

¶ The hist. pronunc. is /-tʃ/, with palatalization as in parallel n. forms (*bake, batch, speak, speech*, etc.). This was prevalent until E19, though the n. began to be conf. w. the vb as /-k/ about 1700. In the north, where there was no palatalization, *ake* as the n. is evidenced in LME. See also note s.v. ACHE *v.*

†ache *n.*[2] ME–E17. [(O)Fr. f. L *apium* parsley, f. *apis* bee (attracted to the plant).] Smallage; parsley.

†ache *n.*[3] var. of AITCH.

ache /eɪk/ *v.i.* Also (*arch.*) **ake**. [OE *acan*, corresp. to forms in WGmc; possible cognates in other IE langs. are Gk *agos* sin, guilt, Skt *āgas*. See note below.] Suffer or be the source of continuous or prolonged dull pain or mental distress.

S. RICHARDSON Does not your heart ake for your Harriet? S. ANDERSON I ached to see that race. T. SHARPE The joints in his knees ached.

¶Orig. a strong vb like *take, shake*, but with weak inflections since ME. Historically the vb is *ake*, the n. *ache* (see note s.v. ACHE *n.*[1]). Dr Johnson is mainly responsible for the mod. spellings, as he erroneously derived them from Gk *akhos* 'pain' and declared them 'more grammatically written *ache*'.

achingly *adv.* so as to cause continuous dull pain M19.

achene /əˈkiːn/ *n.* M19. [f. mod.L *achaenium*, irreg. f. Gk *a-* A-[10] + *khainein* gape.] *Bot.* A small dry one-seeded fruit which does not open to liberate the seed.

Acheron /ˈakərɒn/ *n.* E16. [L *Acheron(t-)* f. Gk *Akherōn*.] In Gk mythology, one of the rivers of Hades; the infernal regions.

Acheˈrontic *a.* of or pertaining to Acheron, infernal; gloomy; on the brink of death: L16.

Acheulean /əˈʃuːlɪən/ *a.* & *n.* Also **-ian**. E20. [Fr. *Acheuléen*, f. St-*Acheul* near Amiens, France.] (The culture or industry) of an early palaeolithic period in Europe, the Middle East, Africa, and India, preceding the Mousterian, and distinguished in particular by the manufacture of stone hand-axes.

à cheval /a ʃəval, ɑː ʃəˈvaːl/ *adv. phr.* M19. [Fr. = on horseback.] With one foot on each side; in command of two lines of communication; with a stake risked equally on two chances.

achieve /əˈtʃiːv/ *v.* ME. [(O)Fr. *achever* come or bring to a head or end, f. phr. *a chief*: see A-[5], CHIEF *n.*] **1** *v.t.* Accomplish; carry out successfully. ME. †**2** *v.t.* Finish, terminate. LME–L16. †**3** *v.i.* Come to an end; result, turn out. LME–M16. **4** *v.t.* Succeed in gaining; acquire by effort; reach (an end etc.). LME. **5** *v.i.* **a** Be successful; attain a desired end or level of performance. L15. †**b** Attain successfully *to*. L15–L16.

1 A. NEWMAN She had achieved a lot in the last twenty-four hours. DAY LEWIS Insurgents who have achieved a revolution before one has even suspected a conspiracy. **2** SHAKES. *Hen. V* Bid them achieve me, and then sell my bones. **3** LD BERNERS All your busynes shall acheue the better. **4** SHAKES. *Twel. N.* Some are born great, some achieve greatness. S. GIBBONS All the ingredients for success were present, and success was achieved. **5a** *Church Times* Intelligent people . . who had not achieved academically.

achievaˈbility *n.* the quality or state of being achievable E20. **achievable** *a.* able to be achieved M17. **achiever** *n.* L16.

achievement /əˈtʃiːvm(ə)nt/ *n.* L15. [f. prec. + -MENT or f. (O)Fr. *achèvement*.] **1** Completion, accomplishment. L15. **2** *Her.* Orig., an escutcheon or armorial device, *esp.* one granted in memory of a distinguished feat; also = HATCHMENT. Now, a representation of all the armorial devices to which a bearer of arms is entitled. L16. **3** Something achieved; a feat. L16.

Comb.: **achievement motivation** motivation to attain a desired end or level of performance, competitiveness.

achillea /akɪˈliːə, aˈkɪlɪə/ *n.* L16. [L *achillea, -eos* f. Gk *Akhilleios* a plant supposed to have been used medicinally by Achilles (see next).] Any of various plants of the genus *Achillea*, of the composite family, with flower-heads usually in corymbs; *spec.* a common garden perennial, *A. filipendulina*, with yellow flower-heads on tall stems. Cf. MILFOIL, *sneezewort* s.v. SNEEZE, YARROW.

Achilles /əˈkɪliːz/ *n.* E17. [L f. Gk *Akhilleus*, a hero in Homer's *Iliad*, invulnerable except in the heel.] A person like Achilles in point of valour, invulnerability, etc.

Comb.: **Achilles** or **Achilles' heel** one's only vulnerable spot, a weak point; **Achilles tendon** the tendon attaching the heel to the calf muscles.

Achillean *a.* resembling Achilles, invulnerable L16.

achimenes /əˈkɪmɪniːz/ *n.* Pl. same. M19. [mod.L (see below), perh. f. Gk *akhaimenis* a kind of plant or f. Gk *a-* A-[10] + *kheimainein* expose to cold.] Any of various herbaceous perennial plants of the Central American genus *Achimenes* (family Gesneriaceae), cultivated for their tubular or trumpet-shaped flowers.

Achinese /atʃəˈniːz/ *n.* & *a.* Also **Atjehnese**. L17. [f. *Acheh, Atjeh* a territory in northern Sumatra + *-n-* + -ESE.] **A** *n.* Pl. same. **1** A member of a Muslim people of northern Sumatra. L17. **2** The Austronesian language of this people. L19. **B** *adj.* Of or pertaining to the Achinese or their language. L18.

achiote /atʃɪˈɒti/ *n.* M17. [Sp. f. Nahuatl *achiotl*.] = ANNATTO.

achiral /eɪˈkaɪər(ə)l/ *a.* M20. [f. A-[10] + CHIRAL.] Of a crystal, molecule, etc.: superposable on its mirror image.

achiˈrality *n.* L20.

achkan /ˈatʃk(ə)n/ *n.* E20. [Hind. *ackan*.] A knee-length coat, buttoned in front, worn by men in the Indian subcontinent.

achlamydeous /akləˈmɪdɪəs/ *a.* M19. [f. A-[10] + Gk *khlamud-*, *khlamus* cloak + -EOUS.] *Bot.* Of a flower: lacking both calyx and corolla.

achlorhydria /eɪklɔːˈhaɪdrɪə, a-/ *n.* L19. [f. A-[10] + CHLOR-[1] + HYDRO- + -IA[1].] *Med.* Absence of hydrochloric acid in the gastric secretions.

achlorhydric *a.* exhibiting achlorhydria M20.

achlorophyllous /eɪklɒːˈrɒfɪləs/ *a.* L19. [f. A-[10] + CHLOROPHYLLOUS.] *Bot.* Lacking chlorophyll.

Acholi /əˈtʃəʊli/ *n.* & *a.* Also †**Shooli**. L19. [Acholi.] **A** *n.* Pl. same. A member of a farming and pastoral people of northern Uganda and southern Sudan; the Nilotic language of this people. L19. **B** *adj.* Of or pertaining to the Acholi or their language. L19.

acholuric /akəˈljʊərɪk, eɪ-/ *a.* E20. [Fr. *acholurique*, f. Gk *kholē* bile: see A-[10], -URIC.] *Med.* Designating a form of jaundice characterized by the absence of bile pigments in the urine.

achondrite /əˈkɒndraɪt/ *n.* E20. [f. A-[10] + CHONDRITE.] A stony meteorite containing no chondrules.

achondritic /akənˈdrɪtɪk/ *a.* E20.

achondroplasia /əkɒndrəˈpleɪzjə, eɪˌkɒn-/ *n.* L19. [f. Gk *akhondros*, f. *a-* A-[10] + *khondros* cartilage: see -PLASIA.] *Med.* A hereditary disease in which bone growth by production and ossification of cartilage at the epiphyses of the long bones is retarded, and which results in a form of dwarfism, with short limbs, a normal trunk, and a small face.

achondroplasiac -plasic, -plastic *adjs.* & *ns.* (*a*) *adj.* affected with or pertaining to achondroplasia ; (*b*) *n.* a person with achondroplasia : E20.

achromatic /akrəʊˈmatɪk/ *a.* & *n.* L18. [Fr. *achromatique*, f. as A-[10], CHROMATIC.] **A** *adj.* Free from colour; transmitting light without decomposing it into its constituent colours. L18. **B** *n.* An achromatic lens. L18.

ˈachromat *n.* [-AT[2]] an achromatic lens E20. **achromatically** *adv.* M19. **ˌachromaˈticity** *n.* M19. **aˈchromatism** *n.* the quality of being achromatic L18. **aˈchromatize** *v.t.* make achromatic M19.

achromatopsia /ˌeɪkrəʊməˈtɒpsɪə, ˌa-/ *n.* Also **-psy** /-psi/. M19. [f. Gk *akhrōmatos* without colour (*khrōmat-*, *khrōma* colour) + *-opsia*, f. *opsis* sight: see A-[10], -IA[1], -Y[3].] *Med.* Total colour-blindness.

achromatopsic *a.* & *n.* (*a*) *adj.* pertaining to or exhibiting achromatopsia; (*b*) *n.* a person with achromatopsia: L20.

achromatous /eɪˈkrəʊmətəs/ *a. rare.* L19. [f. as prec. + -OUS.] Colourless; *esp.* lacking the normal colour.

achromic /eɪˈkrəʊmɪk/ *a. rare.* M18. [f. A-[10] + Gk *khrōma* colour + -IC.] Free from colour; having no colour except black, white, or intermediate shades of grey.

achronical *a.* see ACRONYCHAL.

achronological /ˌeɪkrɒnəˈlɒdʒɪk(ə)l/ *a.* L20. [f. A-[10] + CHRONOLOGICAL.] Not following chronological order, = UNCHRONOLOGICAL I.

achy /ˈeɪki/ *a.* L19. [f. ACHE *n.*[1] + -Y[1].] Full of or suffering from aches.

achiness *n.* L20.

achylia /əˈkaɪlɪə/ *n.* L19. [mod.L, f. Gk *akhulos*, f. *a-* A-[10] + *khulos* juice, chyle, + -IA[1].] *Med.* Freq. more fully *achylia gastrica* /ˈgastrɪkə/. Absence of gastric secretion.

acicula /əˈsɪkjʊlə/ *n.* Pl. **-lae** /-liː/, **-las**. Also **-lum** /-lʌm/, pl. **-la** /-lə/; **-lus** /-lʌs/, pl. **-li** /-lʌɪ, -liː/; & Anglicized (esp. *Bot.*) as **acicle** /ˈasɪk(ə)l/. M19. [Late L, dim. of *acus* needle: see -CULE.] *Bot.* & *Zool.* A slender needle-like structure, such as a spine or prickle.

acicular /əˈsɪkjʊlə/ *a.* E18. [f. as prec. + -AR[1].] Needle-like (esp. of crystals).

aciculˈlarity *n.* M20. **acicularly** *adv.* in needle-like forms E18.

aciculate /əˈsɪkjʊlət/ *a.* M19. [f. as prec. + -ATE[2].] Covered with aciculae; marked or striated as if with a needle. Also = prec.

aciculum *n.* see ACICULA.

acid /ˈasɪd/ *n.* L17. [f. the adj.] **1** A sour substance; *spec.* in *Chem.*, any of a large class of substances that contain hydrogen replaceable by metals, and neutralize and are neutralized by alkalis, the most familiar examples being sour corrosive liquids able to dissolve metals. Also, in mod. use, any species capable of donating protons or of accepting pairs of electrons. L17. **2** The drug LSD. *slang.* M20.

1 *nitric acid, oxalic acid, phosphoric acid*, etc. *acid of sugar*: see SUGAR *n.* & *a.* **come the acid** *slang* be unpleasant or offensive, speak in a caustic or sarcastic manner. *conjugate acid*: see CONJUGATE *a.* **put the acid on** *Austral.* & *NZ slang* seek to extract a loan, favour, etc., from.

Comb.: **acid-head** *slang* a user of the drug LSD; **Acid House**, **acid rock** types of rock music associated with (the effects of) the taking of hallucinogenic drugs; **acid-test** a test for gold which involves nitric acid; *fig.* a crucial test.

aciˈdaemia *n.* (*Med.*) a condition of abnormally low pH of the blood E20. **aˈcidophil(e)**, **aˌcidoˈphilic**, **aciˈdophilous** *adjs.* readily stained with acid dyes; growing best in acid conditions: E20. **acidy** *a.* resembling or suggestive of acid, somewhat acid, esp. in taste M20.

acid /ˈasɪd/ *a.* E17. [Fr. *acide* or L *acidus*, f. *acere* be sour.] **1** Sour, tart, sharp to the taste; tasting like vinegar. E17. **b** *fig.* Biting, severe, unpleasant. L18. **c** Of a colour: intense. E20. **2** *Chem.* Having the essential properties of an acid; derived from or characteristic of an acid. E18. **3** *Geol.* Of an igneous rock: rich in silica. L19. **b** *Metall.* Pertaining to, resulting from, or designating steel-making processes involving silica-rich refractories and slags. L19.

1 **acid drop** a kind of sweet with an acid taste. **b** DISRAELI Rather an acid expression of countenance. W. S. MAUGHAM He had a certain acid humour. **c** D. H. LAWRENCE You acid-blue metallic bird. **2** **acid air** air containing a high proportion of acidic pollutants. *acid* AMIDE. **acid dye** a dye which is a metallic salt of an acid and is usu. applied in an acid medium or as a cytological strain. **acid house** synthesized music with a simple repetitive beat. **acid rain** rain made acidic by atmospheric pollution. **acid salt** a salt derived from an acid by incomplete exchange of the replaceable hydrogen. *acid tide*: see TIDE *n.*

¶In techn. senses opp. BASIC *a.*

acidly *adv.* sourly L19. **acidness** *n.* M17.

acidic /əˈsɪdɪk/ *a.* L19. [f. ACID *n.* + -IC.] **1** *Geol.* = ACID *a.* 3. L19. **2** *Chem.* Of, pertaining to, or having the properties of an acid; having a pH lower than 7. L19.

acidify /əˈsɪdɪfʌɪ/ *v.t.* L18. [f. as prec. + -I- + -FY.] Convert into an acid (now *rare*); make acid; add acid to.

aˌcidifiˈcation *n.* the act or process of acidifying L18.

acidimetry /asɪˈdɪmɪtri/ *n.* M19. [f. as prec. + -I- + -METRY.] *Chem.* The measurement of the strengths of acids.

†**acidimeter** *n.* an instrument for acidimetry M–L19. **aˌcidiˈmetric(al)** *adjs.* of or pertaining to acidimetry M19.

acidise *v.* var. of ACIDIZE.

acidity /əˈsɪdɪti/ *n.* E17. [Fr. *acidité* or late L *aciditas*: see ACID *a.*, *n.*, -ITY.] **1** The quality, state, or degree of being acid (*lit.* & *fig.*). E17. **2** Excess of acid in the stomach. M18.

1 W. S. MAUGHAM The vicar answered with some acidity.

acidize /ˈasɪdʌɪz/ *v.t.* Also **-ise**. E20. [f. ACID *n.* + -IZE.] Treat with acid; *spec.* pump acid into (an oil-well) as a means of stimulating flow.

acidiˈzation *n.* M20.

acidosis /asɪˈdəʊsɪs/ *n.* Pl. **-doses** /-ˈdəʊsiːz/. E20. [f. ACID *n.* + -OSIS.] *Med.* A condition of abnormally low pH of the body fluids.

acidotic /asɪˈdɒtɪk/ *a.* E20.

acidulate /əˈsɪdjʊleɪt/ *v.t.* M18. [f. as next + -ATE[3].] Make somewhat acid or sour; flavour with an acid.

fig.: LD MACAULAY Scarcely any compliment not acidulated with scorn.

aciduˈlation *n.* the process or state of being acidulated M19.

acidulous /əˈsɪdjʊləs/ *a.* M18. [f. L *acidulus*, f. *acidus* sour: see ACID *a.*, -ULOUS.] Somewhat sour or acid (*lit.* & *fig.*).

CARLYLE He becomes . . gloomy and acidulous.

acidulent *a.* = ACIDULOUS M19. **acidulously** *adv.* L19.

aciduria /asɪˈdjʊərɪə/ *n.* M20. [f. ACID *n.* + -URIA.] *Med.* The presence of excessive acid in the urine.

acinaciform /asɪˈnasɪfɔːm, əˈsɪnə-/ *a.* M18. [mod.L *acinaciformis*, f. Gk *akinakēs* scimitar: see -FORM.] Chiefly *Bot.* Scimitar-shaped.

acinus /ˈasɪnəs/ *n.* Pl. **-ni** /-nʌɪ/. M18. [L = a berry growing in a cluster, a kernel.] 1 *Bot.* A small berry growing in a cluster or as part of a compound fruit; a seed of such a berry. Now *rare* or *obs.* M18. 2 *Anat.* Any of a number of small rounded terminal sacs in a gland, the cells of whose walls secrete into the central cavity. M18.

acinar *a.* = ACINOUS M20. **aˈciniform** *a.* resembling a grape or a bunch of grapes M19. **acinous** *a.* (*Anat.*) consisting of or pertaining to acini M19.

-acious /ˈeɪʃəs/ *suff.* [Repr. Fr. *-acieux*, or f. L *-acis*, *-ax* added chiefly to vbl stems to form adjs. + -OUS.] Forming adjs. meaning 'given to, inclined to' or 'having much', as *audacious*, *pugnacious*, *vivacious*.

-acity /ˈasɪti/ *suff.* [Fr. *-acité* or its source L *-acitas*, *-tatis*: see prec., -TY[1].] Forming ns. of quality corresp. to adjs. in -ACIOUS.

ack /ak/. L19. *Hist.* Arbitrary syllable used for the letter *a* in spoken telephone communications and in the oral spelling of messages.

ack-ack [= *AA*] anti-aircraft (gunfire, regiment, etc.). **ack emma** [= *a.m.*] ante meridiem, air mechanic.

†-ack *suff.* var. of -AC.

ackee /ˈaki/ *n.* Also **akee**. L18. [Prob. f. a Kru lang.] The fruit, edible when cooked, of the tree *Blighia sapida*, native to W. Africa and introduced elsewhere, esp. in the W. Indies; the tree itself.

ackers /ˈakəz/ *n.pl. slang* (orig. *Mil.*). M20. [Prob. alt. of PIASTRE: orig. used by British and allied troops in Egypt.] Coins, notes, money; *spec.* piastres.

†acknow *v.t.* Infl. as KNOW *v.* OE. [f. A *prep.*[1] + KNOW *v.*: for the spelling with *ac-* see AC-.] 1 Recognize. OE–LME. 2 Acknowledge, confess, (*that*). (*dial.* after 16.) OE–M19. 3 *be acknown*, be (self-)recognized in relation to anything, avow or confess (*to* a person). ME–M17.

¶Rare after OE exc. as *acknown* pa. pple.

acknowledge /əkˈnɒlɪdʒ/ *v.t.* L15. [Prob. f. KNOWLEDGE *v.* on the analogy of the relation of ACKNOW and KNOW *v.*: see AC-.] 1 Recognize or confess (a person or thing to be something); own the claims or authority of. L15. 2 Own with gratitude or as an obligation. E17. b Announce receipt of (a letter etc.). M17. c Register recognition of; take notice of. L19. 3 Own the knowledge of; confess; admit the truth of. M17. 4 Own as genuine, or valid in law; avow or assent to, in legal form. L19.

1 AV *Wisd.* 12:27 They acknowledged him to be the true God. T. DREISER I acknowledge the Furies, I believe in them. *acknowledge the corn*: see CORN *n.*[1] 2c J. HELLER He acknowledged with a surly nod the greetings of his colleagues. 3 SHAKES. *Much Ado* He loved . . your daughter, and meant to acknowledge it this night.

acknowledgeable *a.* M19. **acknowledged** *ppl a.* recognized; admitted as true, valid, or authoritative: L16. **acknowledgedly** *adv.* M17. **acknowledger** *n.* M16.

acknowledgement /əkˈnɒlɪdʒm(ə)nt/ *n.* Also **-dgm-**. L16. [f. prec. + -MENT.] 1 The act of admitting or confessing; avowal. L16. 2 The act of recognizing the authority or claims of. L16. 3 The owning or due recognition of a gift or benefit received, or of a message etc.; something given or done in return for a favour or message; (esp. in *pl.*) an author's statement of indebtedness to others. E17. 4 A declaration or avowal of an act or document so as to give it legal validity. M17.

1 SHAKES. *Hen. V* With this acknowledgement, That God fought for us. 2 JAS. MILL All such places as owe acknowledgement to the Dutch. 3 H. E. BATES She waited at the door for a word of acknowledgement, of thanks, of simple recognition, for the things she had done. JOYCE General applause. Edward the Seventh lifts the bucket graciously in acknowledgement.

aclinic /əˈklɪnɪk/ *a.* Now *rare.* M19. [f. Gk *aklinēs*, f. *a-* A-[10] + *klinein* to bend, lean + -IC.] *aclinic line*, = *magnetic* EQUATOR.

†a clock *adv.* see O'CLOCK.

acme /ˈakmi/ *n.* L16. [Gk *akmē* highest point. Long consciously used as a Gk wd and written in Gk letters.] 1 *gen.* The highest point; the point or period of perfection. L16. 2 *spec.* †a The period of full growth; the flower or full bloom of life. L16–M19. b The crisis of an illness. *arch.* M17.

acmite /ˈakmʌɪt/ *n.* M19. [f. as prec. + -ITE[1].] *Min.* A variety of aegirine having pointed crystal terminations.

acne /ˈakni/ *n.* M19. [Erron. Gk *aknas*, a misreading for *akmas* accus. pl. of *akmē* facial eruption, ACME.] *Med.* Severe seborrhoea complicated by pustule formation in the hair follicles, esp. of the face.

acne ROSACEA.

acned *a.* (*colloq.*) afflicted with acne M20.

acock /əˈkɒk/ *adv.* & *pred. a.* E19. [f. A-[2] + COCK *n.*[1] or *v.*[1]] Turned upward; cocked.

fig.: J. FOWLES What had really knocked him a-cock was Mary's innocence.

a-cock-bill *adv.* see COCK-BILL *n.*

a-cock-horse /əˈkɒkhɔːs, əkɒkˈhɔːs/ *adv.* M16. [f. A *prep.*[1] I + COCK-HORSE.] 1 Mounted (as) on a cock-horse; astride; = COCK-HORSE *adv.* M16. †2 In an exalted position, in a place of triumph. M17–E19.

acoelomate /əˈsiːləmeɪt/ *a.* L19. [f. A-[10] + COELOMATE.] *Zool.* Lacking a coelom.

acold /əˈkəʊld/ *a. arch.* ME. [Prob. orig. pa. pple of ACOOL, with short vowel bef. two consonants or by assim. to COLD *a.*] Chilled, cold.

acolyte /ˈakəlʌɪt/ *n.* ME. [OFr. *acolyt* (mod. *-yte*) or eccl.L *acolytus*, *-it(h)us* f. Gk *akolouthos* following, follower.] 1 *Eccl.* A person who attends a priest and performs subordinate duties as bearing candles etc. ME. 2 An attendant, an assistant, a novice. E19.

Also **acolythist** *n.* (*arch.*) E17.

acone /ˈeɪkəʊn/ *a.* L19. [G: see A-[10], CONE *n.*] *Entomol.* Of an insect's eyes: lacking cones.

aconite /ˈakənʌɪt/ *n.* Also in L form **†aconitum**. M16. [Fr. *aconit* or L *aconitum* f. Gk *akoniton*.] 1 Any of numerous poisonous plants belonging to the genus *Aconitum*; *esp.* monkshood or wolfsbane, *A. napellus*. M16. b In full *winter aconite*. Any small plant of the genus *Eranthis*, esp. *E. hyemalis*, bearing yellow flowers early in the year. L16. 2 An alkaloidal extract from monkshood or the like used as a poison or in pharmacy; *poet.* deadly poison. M16.

aconitine /əˈkɒnɪtiːn/ *n.* M19. [f. prec. + -INE[5].] *Chem.* A colourless crystalline alkaloid, the toxic principle of monkshood and certain other plants of the genus *Aconitum*.

†aconitum *n.* see ACONITE.

à contrecœur /a kɔ̃trəkœːr/ *adv. phr.* E19. [Fr., lit. 'against the heart'.] Against one's will, reluctantly.

†acool *v.i.* & *t.* OE–M16. [f. A-[1] + COOL *v.*] Cool.

¶The pa. pple may survive in ACOLD.

acorn /ˈeɪkɔːn/ *n.* [OE *æcern* = MLG *ackeren* (Du. *aker*) acorn, MHG *ackeran*, *eckern* oak or beech mast, ON *akarn* acorn, Goth. *akran* fruit, produce; rel. to ACRE. Later forms assoc. with OAK and CORN *n.*[1]] †1 Fruit generally, mast. OE–E17. 2 The fruit of the oak, an oval nut growing in a cupule. OE. b An object or decorative device in the shape of an acorn. LME.

Comb.: **acorn barnacle** a barnacle that does not possess a stalk; *esp.* a member of the genus *Balanus*; **acorn-cup** the cupule of an acorn; **acorn shell** = *acorn barnacle* above; **acorn squash** *N. Amer.* a variety of squash with a longitudinally ridged rind; **acorn worm** a wormlike hemichordate of the class Enteropneusta, having an acorn-shaped anterior end to its body.

acorned *a.* furnished with or bearing acorns; fed with acorns: E17. **acorning** *n.* hunting for or gathering acorns E19.

acosmism /əˈkɒzmɪz(ə)m/ *n.* Also **akosm-**. M19. [f. A-[10] + COSMOS *n.*[1] + -ISM.] Denial of the existence of the universe, or of a universe distinct from God.

acosmist *n.* a person who professes acosmism M19.

acotyledon /əkɒtɪˈliːd(ə)n/ *n.* Now *rare* or *obs.* M18. [f. mod.L pl. *acotyledones*: see A-[10], COTYLEDON.] *Bot.* A plant forming no distinct cotyledons, such as a fern, moss, etc.

acotyledonous *a.* E19.

acouchi /əˈkuːtʃi/ *n.* L18. [Fr. f. Tupi.] A S. American rodent of the genus *Myoprocta*, resembling an agouti.

acoustic /əˈkuːstɪk/ *a.* & *n.* E17. [Gk *akoustikos*, f. *akouein* hear: see -IC.] A *adj.* 1 Pertaining to the sense of hearing, or to audible sound. E17. 2 Of a material, a device, etc.: sound-absorbent. E20. 3 Of a musical instrument, gramophone, etc.: not electrically amplified. M20.

1 *acoustic coupler*: see COUPLER 4. *acoustic* IMPEDANCE. **acoustic mine** a mine designed to be detonated by sound waves. 2 **acoustic hood** a sound-absorbent cover used esp. to reduce noise from a machine or appliance.

B *n.* 1 In *pl.* (usu. treated as *sing.*). The branch of science that deals with sound and the phenomena of hearing. L17. †2 A medicine or appliance used to aid hearing. Only in 18. 3 In *pl.* The acoustic properties of a building, room, etc., esp. one in which music or drama is performed. Now also in *sing.*, *esp.* the acoustic properties or ambience of a sound recording or of a recording studio. L19.

acoustician /-ˈstɪʃ(ə)n/ *n.* an expert in acoustics M19.

acoustical /əˈkuːstɪk(ə)l/ *a.* E19. [f. prec. + -AL[1].] Of or pertaining to audible sound or the science of acoustics.

acoustically *adv.* L19.

acoustics *n.* see ACOUSTIC *n.*

acousto- /əˈkuːstəʊ/ *comb. form.* M20. [f. ACOUSTIC *a.* + -O-.] Forming chiefly adjs. w. the sense 'involving acoustic and — effects', as *acousto-electric*, *-optic*.

†acover *v.* see COVER *v.*[1]

acquaint /əˈkweɪnt/ *a.* (orig. *pa. pple*). *arch.* ME. [OFr. *acointe*, f. as next. Cf. QUAINT.] Acquainted (*with*).

acquaint /əˈkweɪnt/ *v.* ME. [OFr. *acointier* make known f. late L *accognitare*, f. L *accognit-* pa. ppl stem of *accognoscere*, f. *ad* AC- + *cognoscere* know.] †1 *v.refl.* Make oneself known, become known (*to*). ME–L15. b *v.i.* Become acquainted or familiar (*with*). LME–L18. 2 *v.refl.* Give or gain for oneself personal knowledge: foll. by *with* a person. Now only in *pass.* as ACQUAINTED. ME. 3 *v.t.* (& *refl.*) Give (oneself or another) experimental knowledge: foll. by *with* a thing. LME. 4 *v.t.* Inform, make cognizant or aware. (Foll. by *with*, *that*, †*of*.) M16. †b Make known, tell. Only in 17. †5 *v.t.* Familiarize, accustom. Foll. by *with*, *to do*. L16–M17.

1b HOR. WALPOLE Though the Choiseuls will not acquaint with you. 2 AV *Job* 22:21 Acquaint now thyselfe with him. 3 OED Acquaint yourself with the duties of your new sphere. 4 H. FIELDING He was acquainted that his worship would wait on him. R. B. SHERIDAN I shall certainly acquaint your father. F. RAPHAEL I'm here to acquaint you with the facts. b S. ROWLANDS Acquaint thy name in private unto me. 5 J. BRINSLEY Acquaint them to pronounce some speciall examples.

acquaintance /əˈkweɪnt(ə)ns/ *n.* ME. [OFr. *acointance*, f. as prec.: see -ANCE.] 1 The state of being acquainted; mutual knowledge. Foll. by *with* (†*of*) or w. *genit.* (as *her acquaintance*, *our acquaintance*). ME. 2 Orig. *collect.*, those with whom one is acquainted. Now usu. (with *pl.*), a person with whom one is acquainted. LME. 3 Knowledge that is more than mere recognition but usu. less than intimacy. (Foll. by *with*, †*of*.) LME.

1 *bowing acquaintance*: see BOW *v.*[1] 6. *nodding acquaintance*: see NOD *v.* 2 *casual acquaintance*: see CASUAL *a.* 3 **knowledge by (or of) acquaintance** *Philos.*: by direct experience. **make the acquaintance of** come to know.

Comb.: **acquaintance rape** rape of a woman by a man known to her.

acquaintanceship *n.* = ACQUAINTANCE I E19. †**acquaintant** *n.* = ACQUAINTANCE 2 E17–L18.

acquainted /əˈkweɪntɪd/ *a.* ME. [f. ACQUAINT *v.* + -ED[1].] 1 Familiar, through being known. *obs.* of persons, *arch.* of things. ME. 2 Personally known (to another); having mutual knowledge. (Foll. by *with.*) ME. 3 Having personal or experimental knowledge. Foll. by *with*, (occas.) *of.* L15. †4 Accustomed (*with*, *to*). M16–L17.

acquaintedness *n.* the state or degree of acquaintance M17.

acquest /əˈkwɛst/ *n.* E17. [Fr. †*acquest* (OFr. *aquest*, mod. *acquêt*), ult. f. as ACQUIRE.] 1 A thing acquired; *spec.* (*Law*, now *Hist.*) property gained otherwise than by inheritance. E17. †2 = ACQUIST I. E17–L18.

acquiesce /akwɪˈɛs/ *v.i.* E17. [L *acquiescere*, f. *ad* AC- + *quiescere* to rest. See also QUIET *a.*] 1 Remain at rest or in quiet subjection; rest satisfied. (Foll. by *in*, *under.*) Now *rare.* E17. 2 Agree, esp. tacitly; concur (*in*); raise no objections (*to*). (Also foll. by †*with.*) E17.

acquiescing *a.* assenting, silently compliant L18. **acquiescingly** *adv.* M19.

acquiescence /akwɪˈɛs(ə)ns/ *n.* E17. [f. prec. + -ENCE. Cf. Fr. *acquiescence.*] 1 The action or condition of acquiescing (sense 1); resting satisfied. *arch.* E17. 2 Silent or passive assent to, or compliance with, measures or proposals. (Foll. by *in*, *to*, †*with.*) M17.

acquiescency *n.* the quality or condition of being acquiescent M17.

acquiescent /akwɪˈɛs(ə)nt/ *a.* & *n.* E17. [L *acquiescent-* pres. ppl stem of *acquiescere* ACQUIESCE: see -ENT.] A *adj.* Acquiescing; disposed to acquiesce. E17. B *n.* A person who acquiesces. *rare.* E19.

acquiescently *adv.* L17.

acquire /əˈkwʌɪə/ *v.t.* LME. [OFr. *aquerre*, Eng. sp. Latinized *c*1600 under influence of its ult. source L *acquirere* get in addition, f. *ad* AC- + *quaerere* seek.] 1 Gain or get as one's own, by one's own exertions or qualities. LME. 2 Come into possession of. L16. 3 Of radar, a radar operator: begin receiving signals from, locate. M20.

1 W. FAULKNER The gun . . which he had acquired . . at the sacrifice of actual food. E. BIRNEY They had acquired piety & table manners. 2 S. JOHNSON The Idler acquires weight by lying still.

acquirable *a.* M17. **acquiˈree** *n.* (chiefly *Comm.*) a person, company, etc., acquired M20. **acquirer** *n.* M18. **acquiring** *n.* the action of obtaining for oneself; the thing obtained: M17.

acquired /əˈkwʌɪəd/ *ppl a.* E17. [f. prec. + -ED[1].] Obtained by one's own exertion; gained, as opp. to innate or inherited; esp. *Biol.* & *Med.*, developed after birth through the influence of the environment.

B. RUSSELL Man has improved in knowledge, in acquired skill, and in social organization, but not . . in congenital intellectual capacity. **acquired immune deficiency syndrome** = AIDS. **acquired taste** (an object of) liking gained by experience.

acquirement /əˈkwʌɪəm(ə)nt/ *n.* M17. [f. as prec. + -MENT.] 1 The action of acquiring. M17. 2 Something which is acquired; a personal attainment of body or mind (as opp. to a material *acquisition*, or a natural *gift*). M17.

†**acquisite** *pple* & *ppl a.* E16–L17. [L *acquisitus* pa. pple, f. *acquisit-*: see next.] Acquired.

acquisition /akwɪˈzɪʃ(ə)n/ *n.* LME. [L *acquisitio(n-)*, f. *acquisit-* pa. ppl stem of *acquirere*: see ACQUIRE *v.*, -ION.] 1 The action of acquiring something or someone. LME. 2 A thing gained or acquired; a useful or welcome addition. L15.

acquisitional *a.* L19.

acquisitive /əˈkwɪzɪtɪv/ *a.* M17. [f. L *acquisit-* (see prec.) + -IVE; partly through Fr. *acquisitif*, *-ive* f. late L *acquisitivus.*] †1 Belonging to one by acquisition. Only in M17. 2 Acquiring; keen to acquire things. M19.

acquisitively *adv.* in an acquisitive manner; in a manner expressing acquisition: M16. **acquisitiveness** *n.* the quality of being acquisitive; desire of possession: E19.

acquist /əˈkwɪst/ *n.* E17. [Var. of ACQUEST, after L *acquisitum*, med.L *acquistum*, It. *acquisto.*] 1 The action of acquiring, acquisition. E17. †2 A thing acquired. M17–M19.

¶There has been a tendency to use *acquist* for the action, *acquest* for the result.

†**acquit** *n.* LME–L18. [f. the vb.] The act of acquitting; acquittance.

acquit /əˈkwɪt/ *v.* Infl. **-tt-**. Pa. pple & ppl a. **-tted**, (*arch.*) **acquit**. ME. [OFr. *a(c)quiter* (Prov. *aquitar*) f. med.L *acquitare*, f. *ad* AC- + *quitare* QUIT *v.*] I Quit a claim. 1 *v.t.* Discharge, pay, (a claim, debt, or liability). *arch.* ME. 2 *v.t.* Requite (a benefit or injury). *arch.* ME. †3 *v.t.* & *i.* Atone for (an offence). ME–E17. †4 *v.t.* Discharge the duties of (an office), perform, accomplish. LME–L17. II Clear or discharge a debtor. †5 *v.t.* Pay or cancel the debt of and free. ME–M17. 6 *v.t.* Set free, release *of* or *from* a duty, obligation, or burden. *arch.* ME. 7 *v.t.* Clear from a charge; declare not guilty (*of*, †*from*, an offence). LME. †8 *v.refl.* Deliver, rid oneself, *of.* LME–M18. 9 *v.refl.* Discharge oneself (*of* duty or responsibility); perform one's part in a specified manner. LME. III Satisfy a creditor. †10 *v.t.* Pay off (a person in respect *of* a debt due to him or her); be quits with. LME–L16.

acquitment *n.* (now *rare* or *obs.*) acquittal, release LME. **acquitter** *n.* E17.

acquittal /əˈkwɪt(ə)l/ *n.* LME. [f. prec. + -AL[1].] †1 Payment, requital, amends. LME–M18. 2 = ACQUITTANCE 2. Now *rare* or *obs.* LME. 3 Discharge (of duty); performance. LME. 4 Deliverance from a charge by verdict or other legal process. L15.

acquittance /əˈkwɪt(ə)ns/ *n.* & *v.* ME. [OFr. *aquitance*, f. as ACQUIT *v.* + -ANCE.] A *n.* 1 The action of clearing off debt or other obligation. ME. 2 Release or discharge from a debt or obligation. ME. 3 A release in writing; a receipt in full. LME. 4 = ACQUITTAL 3. *rare.* L15. †B *v.t.* Give an acquittance to, discharge. *rare.* LME–L16.

acral /ˈakr(ə)l/ *a.* E20. [f. as ACRO- + -AL[1].] Pertaining to a tip or apex; *spec.* (*Med.* & *Vet. Med.*) affecting the extremities.

acraldehyde /əˈkraldɪhʌɪd/ *n.* M19. [f. as ACRID + ALDEHYDE.] *Chem.* = ACROLEIN.

†**acrasy** *n.* L16–L18. [Gk, confusing two wds *akrasia*, (i) lack of proper mixing, f. *akratos* unmixed, untempered, intemperate, (ii) lack of self-command, f. *akratēs* powerless, incontinent.] Irregularity, disorder, intemperance.

¶Personified in Spenser's *Faerie Queene.*

acrawl /əˈkrɔːl/ *adv.* & *pred. a.* M19. [f. A-[2] + CRAWL *n.*[2] or *v.*] Crawling (*with*).

acre /ˈeɪkə/ *n.* [OE *æcer* = OFris. *ekker*, OS *akkar* (Du. *akker*), OHG *ackar* (G *Acker*), ON *akr*, Goth. *akrs*, f. Gmc f. IE base repr. also by L *ager*, Gk *agros*, Skt *ajra* field; rel. to ACORN, ACT *v.*] 1 A piece of tilled or arable land, a field. *obs.* exc. in *God's Acre* [f. mod.G] a churchyard, in proper names, as *Great Acre*, and *rhet.* in *pl.*, lands, estates, etc. OE. 2 A measure of land, orig. as much as a yoke of oxen could plough in a day, later limited by statute to a piece 220 yards long by 22 broad (= 4840 sq. yards or about 4047 sq. metres) or of equivalent area (now largely superseded by the hectare); *loosely* a large extent. OE.

2 CARLYLE Acres of despatches. *Cheshire acre*: see CHESHIRE 3. (*land of*) *the broad acres*: see BROAD *a.* 2.

Comb.: †**acre breadth** a linear measure equal to 22 yards or about 20 metres; **acre-foot** a unit of volume one acre in area and one foot in depth; †**acre length** a linear measure equal to a furlong or about 201 metres.

acreable *a.* (now *rare*) per acre M18. **acreage** *n.* extent of acres; acres collectively or in the abstract: M19. **acred** *a.* possessing landed estates (mostly in *comb.*, as *large-acred*) M18.

acrid /ˈakrɪd/ *a.* E18. [Irreg. f. L *acri-*, *acer* sharp, pungent + -ID[1], prob. after *acid.*] 1 Bitterly pungent to the organs of taste or smell, or to the skin etc.; irritating; corrosive. E18. 2 Bitterly irritating to the feelings; of bitter and irritating temper or manner. L18.

aˈcridity *n.* the quality of being acrid E19. **acridly** *adv.* L18. **acridness** *n.* (now *rare*) acridity E18.

acridid /ˈakrɪdɪd/ *n.* & *a.* M20. [mod.L *Acrididae* (see below), f. Gk *akrid-*, *akris* locust: see -ID[3].] *Entomol.* A *n.* A grasshopper or locust of the family Acrididae, characterized by the possession of relatively short antennae. M20. B *adj.* Of, pertaining to, or designating this family. M20.

aˈcridian *n.* & *a.* = ACRIDID L19. **aˈcridiid** *n.* & *a.* = ACRIDID E20.

acridine /ˈakrɪdiːn/ *n.* L19. [G *Acridin*, f. as ACRID: see -IDINE.] *Chem.* A colourless crystalline heteroaromatic compound, $C_{13}H_9N$, obtained from coal tar and from which the structures of many dyes and pharmaceuticals are derived.

acriflavine /akrɪˈfleɪvɪn, -iːn/ *n.* E20. [f. ACRI(DINE + FLAVINE.] *Pharm.* A bright orange-red derivative of acridine, used as an antiseptic.

Acrilan /ˈakrɪlan/ *n.* M20. [f. ACR(YLIC + -I- + L *lana* wool.] (Proprietary name for) a synthetic acrylic fibre used for clothing, blankets, etc.

acrimonious /akrɪˈməʊnɪəs/ *a.* E17. [f. next + -OUS.] 1 = ACRID I. *arch.* E17. 2 Bitter and irritating in tone or manner. L18.

1 SIR T. BROWNE A rough and acrimonious kinde of salt. 2 E. WAUGH An acrimonious dispute about the date of the Battle of Hastings.

acrimoniously *adv.* L18. **acrimoniousness** *n.* E19.

acrimony /ˈakrɪməni/ *n.* M16. [Fr. *acrimonie* or L *acrimonia*, f. as ACRID: see -MONY.] 1 Bitter pungency to the organs of taste or smell, or to the skin etc. M16. 2 Bitterness of tone or manner. E17.

†**acrious** *a.* L17–E18. [f. as ACRID + -OUS.] = ACRID I.

acritarch /ˈakrɪtɑːk/ *n.* M20. [f. Gk *akritos* uncertain, confused + *arkhē* origin.] *Palaeont.* Any single-celled fossil whose true affinities are unknown.

†**acritude** *n. rare.* L17–M19. [L *acritudo*, f. as ACRID: see -TUDE.] Acridity.

acro- /ˈakrəʊ/ *comb. form* of Gk *akros* tip, peak: see -O-.

acroˈcarpous *a.* (of a moss) bearing the archegonia and capsules at the tip of a stem or main branch (opp. PLEUROCARPOUS) M19. **acroˈcentric** *a.* (*Cytol.*) (of a chromosome) having the centromere close to the end M20. **acrodont** *a.* (*Zool.*) having the teeth attached to the ridge of the jaw, as in certain lizards M19. **acrogen** *n.* (*Bot.*) a cryptogam with a distinct permanent stem; a fern, a moss: M19. **acrolect** *n.* [-LECT] *Ling.* the dialect or variety of any language with the greatest prestige M20. **acrolith** *n.* (*Gk Antiq.*) a statue with the head and extremities of stone, the trunk usu. of wood M19. **acroˈlithic** *a.* of or pertaining to an acrolith M19. **acromeˈgalic** *a.* & *n.* pertaining to acromegaly; (a person) affected with acromegaly: E20. **acroˈmegaly** *n.* (*Med.*) abnormal enlargement of the hands, feet, and face; disease caused by excessive growth-hormone secretion, of which this is a symptom: L19. **ˌacroparaesˈthesia**, ***-paresˈthesia** *n.* (*Med.*) paraesthesia of the extremities L19. **aˈcropetal** *a.* [L *petere* seek] *Bot.* characterized by successive development of parts from below upwards L19. **a'cropetally** *adv.* in an acropetal manner L19. **acrophobe** *n.* a person afflicted with acrophobia M20. **acro'phobia** *n.* irrational fear of heights L19. **acro'phobic** *a.* pertaining to or affected with acrophobia M20.

acroamatic /ˌakrəʊəˈmatɪk/ *a.* & *n.* M17. [Gk *akroamatikos* adj., f. *akroama(t-)* what is heard, f. as next: see -IC.] A *adj.* Communicated by oral teaching; esoteric. M17. B *n.* Something so communicated; *spec.* in *pl.* (A-), Aristotle's lectures on the esoteric parts of his philosophy. M17.

acroamatical *a.* (now *rare*) L16.

acroatic /akrəʊˈatɪk/ *a.* & *n.* M17. [Gk *akroatikos* adj., f. *akroasthai* hear: see -IC.] = ACROAMATIC.

acrobat /ˈakrəbat/ *n.* E19. [Fr. *acrobate* f. Gk *akrobatēs*, f. *akrobatos* walking on tiptoe, f. as ACRO- + base of *bainein* walk.] A performer of daring gymnastic feats, as rope-walking; a tumbler; *fig.* a person who changes position nimbly in argument, performance, etc.

acrobacy *n.* (now *rare*) = ACROBATISM E20. **acro'batic** *a.* & *n.* (*a*) *adj.* of or characteristic of an acrobat; (*b*) *n.* in *pl.*, (the performing of) acrobatic feats: M19. **acro'batically** *adv.* L19. **acrobatism** *n.* the art of the acrobat; the performing of gymnastic feats: M19.

acrolein /ˈakrəliːn/ *n.* M19. [f. as ACRID + *oleum* oil: see -IN[1].] *Chem.* A colourless, acrid, liquid aldehyde, CH_2:CHCHO, obtained by dehydration of glycerol; propenal.

acromion /əˈkrəʊmɪən/ *n.* L16. [Gk *akrōmion*, f. as ACRO- + *ōmos* shoulder.] *Anat.* The lateral extremity of the posterior projection or spine of the upper part of the shoulder-blade. Also *acromion process*.

acromial *a.* of or pertaining to the acromion M19. **acromiocla'vicular** *a.* of or pertaining to the articulation of the acromion and the lateral end of the clavicle M19.

acronychal /əˈkrɒnɪk(ə)l/ *a.* Also **achronical** & other vars. (freq. erron. as if f. Gk *khronos* time). M16. [f. Gk *akronukhos* at nightfall, f. as ACRO- + *nux* night, + -AL[1].] Happening at nightfall (applied esp. to the rising or setting of stars).

acronych *a.* = ACRONYCHAL M16. **acronychally** *adv.* L16.

acronym /ˈakrənɪm/ *n.* & *v.* M20. [f. ACRO- + -NYM.] A *n.* A word formed from the initial letters or parts of other words; *loosely* an abbreviation composed of initial letters. M20. B *v.t.* Abbreviate as an acronym. M20.

acro'nymic *a.* M20. **acro'nymically** *adv.* L20. **a'cronymize** *v.t.* = ACRONYM *v.* M20.

acrook /əˈkrʊk/ *adv.* & *pred. a.* LME. [f. A *prep.*[1] I + CROOK *n.*] In a bend or curve; awry.

acropolis /əˈkrɒpəlɪs/ *n.* E17. [Gk *akropolis*, f. as ACRO- + *polis* city.] The citadel or elevated fortified part of a Greek city, esp. of Athens.

acrospire /ˈakrəspʌɪə/ *v.* & *n.* Chiefly *dial.* (orig. *Sc.*). LME. [f. OE (Northumb.) *æhher, eher* EAR *n.*[2] + SPIRE *v.*[1], assim. to ACRO-.] A *v.i.* Of malt: sprout. LME. B *n.* The first leaf-shoot or a cereal plant. L17.

across /əˈkrɒs/ *adv.*, *prep.*, & *a.* ME. [OFr. *a croix*, *en croix*, in, on a cross (see CROSS *n.*), assim. to native formations in A *prep.*[1] I.] A *adv.* 1 In the form of a cross, crosswise, crossed. *arch.* ME. 2 Transversely; from side to side, or corner to corner. ME. b (Filling or to fill spaces) along a horizontal line of a crossword puzzle. Usu. following the number of the word or clue (passing into *adj.*). E20. 3 Obliquely; awry; amiss. *obs.* exc. *dial.* M16. 4 On the other side. E19.

1 W. H. AUDEN Sheep-dogs . . slumber on with paws across. 2 G. B. SHAW The nurse rushes across behind the head of the bed. DYLAN THOMAS My heart is cracked across. **come across as** give the impression of being. **come across (with)** *slang* hand over, contribute (money, information, etc.). **get** or **come across (to)** succeed in communicating (with), convey the desired information or impression (to). *last across*: see LAST *a.* *put across*: see PUT *v.*[1] 3 JOSEPH HALL The squint-eyed pharisees looke a-crosse at all the actions of Christ. 4 OED At this rate we shall soon be across. SCOTT FITZGERALD I'm right across from you. *across the tracks*: see TRACK *n.*

B *prep.* 1 Motion: from side to side of; over, in any direction but lengthwise. L16. 2 Direction: transverse to; at an angle with; sideways or obliquely against. E17. b Indirectly or unintentionally into contact with. E19. 3 Position: on the other side of, beyond. M18. 4 Distribution: throughout, all over. *colloq.* M20.

1 TENNYSON After dinner talk Across the walnuts and the wine. T. STOPPARD I once took a train journey right across America. *across country*: see COUNTRY *n.* *across lots*: see LOT *n.* *across the board*: see BOARD *n.* 2 W. STEVENS The shawl across one shoulder. b *come, run, across*: see COME *v.*, RUN *v.* 3 J. CHEEVER The shores of West Chop, across the Sound. 4 *Newsweek* Newsweek bureaus across the U.S. reported the story.

C *adj.* Of a crossword clue or answer: that fills or is intended to fill the spaces along a horizontal line of the puzzle. Cf. sense A.2b above. E20.

acrostic /əˈkrɒstɪk/ *n.* & *a.* Also †**-ich**. L16. [Fr. *acrostiche* f. Gk *akrostikhis*, f. as ACRO- + *stikhos* row, line of verse: assim. to -IC.] A *n.* 1 A poem or other composition in which the initial (*single acrostic*), the initial and final (*double acrostic*), or the initial, middle, and final (*triple acrostic*) letters of the lines make words. L16. b A word-puzzle so made. L19. †2 The beginning or end of a verse. E17–M18. 3 A poem in which the consecutive lines or verses begin with the successive letters of the alphabet. L17. B *adj.* Of the nature of or in the form of an acrostic. M17.

acrostical *a.* = ACROSTIC *a.* M19. **acrostically** *adv.* M19.

acroterion /akrəˈtɪərɪən/ *n.* Also **akro-**. Pl. **-ia** /-ɪə/. Also **acroter** /ˈakrətə/, pl. **-ters**; **acroterium** /-ˈtɪərɪəm/, pl. **-ia** /-ɪə/. M17. [Gk *akrōtērion* extremity, f. as ACRO-. Vars. f. Fr. *acrotère* and (its source) L *acroterium* f. Gk.] 1 *Archit.* †a *collect. sing.* & (usu.) in *pl.* Ornaments in ranges on roofs of classical buildings. M17–L19. b A pedestal for a statue or the like on the centre or side of a pediment. E18. †2 *Med.* In *pl.* The extremities of the body. E–M18.

acroterial *a.* (*Archit.*) E18.

acrow /əˈkrəʊ/ *adv.* & *pred. a. poet.* L19. [f. A-[2] + CROW *v.*] Crowing.

acrylamide /əˈkrɪləmʌɪd/ *n.* L19. [f. ACRYL(IC + AMIDE.] *Chem.* The amide of acrylic acid, CH_2:CHCONH$_2$, a colourless crystalline solid which readily yields water-soluble polymers.

acrylate /ˈakrɪleɪt/ *n.* M19. [f. next + -ATE[1].] 1 *Chem.* A salt or ester of acrylic acid. M19. 2 = ACRYLIC *n.* Also *acrylate resin*. M20.

acrylic /əˈkrɪlɪk/ *a.* & *n.* M19. [f. ACR(OLEIN + -YL + -IC.] A *adj.* 1 Chem. *acrylic acid*, a liquid, CH_2:CHCOOH, orig. obtained by oxidizing acrolein and easily polymerized; propenoic acid. M19. 2 Designating or made from resins, plastics, artificial fibres, etc., which are polymers of acrylic acid or its derivatives. M20. B *n.* An acrylic fibre, plastic, etc. M20.

acrylonitrile /ˌakrɪləˈnʌɪtrʌɪl/ *n.* L19. [f. prec. + -O- + NITRILE.] *Chem.* A pungent, toxic liquid, CH_2:CHCN, the nitrile of acrylic acid, from which artificial fibres and other polymeric materials can be made; propenenitrile.

act /akt/ *n.* LME. [Mainly f. L *actus* doing, playing a part, dramatic action, act of a play, *actum* public transaction, (in pl.) records, register, f. *act-* (see next); partly through Fr. *acte* f. L.] 1 A thing done; a deed. LME. b An operation of the mind. L17. c A thing done as an outward sign of a condition etc. M18. †2 Fact or reality, as opp. to intention, possibility, etc. LME–L17. †3 An active principle. LME–M18. 4 Something transacted in council or in a deliberative assembly; a decree passed by a legislative body etc.; a statute. LME. 5 A record of decrees etc.; a verificatory document. LME. 6 The process of doing; action, operation. L15. 7 a Each of the main divisions of a play. E16. †b An interlude in a play. E–M17. c Each of a series of short performances in a variety programme, circus, etc.; the performer(s) of one of these. M19. d A piece of acting; a pretence (of being what one is not); a display of exaggerated behaviour; *Austral. slang* a fit of temper, a tantrum. E20. 8 A thesis publicly defended by a candidate for a university degree. *obs.* exc. *Hist.* M16.

1 MILTON Victorious deeds Flam'd in my heart, heroic acts. **act of contrition** a penitential prayer. *act of faith*: see FAITH *n.* *act of grace*: see GRACE *n.* **the act** *colloq.* sexual intercourse. b A. J. AYER The realist analysis of our sensations in terms of subject, act, and object. c L. VAN DER POST This . . act of trust between them and the harsh desert earth. 2 SHAKES. *John* If I in act, consent, or sin of thought, Be guilty. 4 *Act of Parliament*: see PARLIAMENT *n.* *Act of Toleration*: see TOLERATION 4. *Act of Uniformity*: see UNIFORMITY I. 5 **Acts (of the Apostles)** (treated as *sing.*) a New Testament book immediately following the Gospels. **act and deed**: part of a formula used in concluding a legal transaction by signing a document. 6 **in the act (of)** in the process (of), in the very doing of; on the point of. 7a *fig.*: SCOTT FITZGERALD There are no second acts in American lives. c W. TREVOR The act he'd devised for the Spot the Talent competition. a **hard act to follow** *transf.* a person or thing difficult to be more impressive or successful than. *do a* (or *the*) *disappearing act*: see DISAPPEAR. **get in on** or **into the act** *slang* become a participant, esp. for profit. *get one's act together*: see GET *v.* d D. LODGE Will you stop putting on this concerned parent act. **put on an act** *colloq.* show off, talk for display, pretend.

Other phrases: **Act of God** the operation of uncontrollable natural forces; an instance of this.

Comb.: **act-drop** in a theatre, a curtain let down between acts; *act-tune*: see TUNE *n.* 2c.

act /akt/ *v.* LME. [L *act-* pa. ppl stem of *agere*: see AGENT. Prob. infl. by prec.] †1 *v.t.* Decide judicially (a case at law). LME–L15. †2 *v.t.* Enact, decree; record. Chiefly *Sc.* L15–M18. †3 *v.t.* Perform, bring about (a thing or process). L16–L18. 4 *v.t.* Carry out or represent in mimic action; perform (a play etc.); *fig.* simulate, counterfeit. L16. 5 *v.i.* Perform a play or part; be an actor or actress. L16. b *v.i.* Of a play: be able to be performed (well, or in a specified manner). M17. 6 *v.t.* Carry out in action. *arch.* E17. †7 *v.t.* Put in motion; actuate, animate. E17–M18. 8 *v.t.* Perform the part of (a character in a play); behave like (a specified kind of person). M17. 9 *v.i.* Perform actions; behave. L17. b *v.i.* Do the duties of a particular employment temporarily. E19. 10 *v.i.* Of a thing: exert influence (*on*), produce an effect. M18.

3 DEFOE Had Satan been able to have acted anything by force. 4 DAY LEWIS He would act the biblical stories on which he was commenting. J. SQUIRE To ask trite questions and act indifference. *act a lie*: see LIE *n.*[1] **act a part, act the part of** play the part of (a character in a play); simulate; fulfil the character or duties of. 5 T. CORYAT I saw women acte, a thing that I neuer saw before. b BYRON My plays won't act . . my poesy won't sell. 6 SHAKES. *Temp.* To act her . . abhorr'd commands. 7 POPE Self-love . . acts the soul. 8 *act the fool*: see FOOL *n.*[1] *act the goat*: see GOAT. 9 T. S. ELIOT What it is to act or suffer. J. D. SALINGER I act quite young for my age. **act (up)on** regulate one's conduct according to. **act up to** come up to (an assumed standard), carry out in practice. b **act as** do the work of (a particular employment etc.), serve as. **act for**: on someone's behalf or in his or her absence. 10 T. H. HUXLEY A fall of snow . . acts like a mantle.

With advs. in specialized senses: **act out** (*a*) *v.phr.t.* translate (ideas etc.) into action, represent in action; (*b*) *v.phr.t.* & *i.* express (repressed or unconscious feelings) in overt behaviour. **act up** *colloq.* misbehave, give trouble or pain.

actable /ˈaktəb(ə)l/ *a.* M19. [f. prec. + -ABLE.] Able to be acted (on the stage) or carried out in practice.

¶ Earlier (E19) in the negative UNACTABLE.

acta'bility *n.* M19.

acte gratuit /akt gratwiː/ *n. phr.* Pl. **-s -s** (pronounced same). M20. [Fr. (A. Gide).] A gratuitous or inconsequent action performed on impulse.

actin /ˈaktɪn/ *n.* M20. [f. Gk *aktin-*, *aktis* ray + -IN[1].] *Biochem.* A protein which with myosin forms the contractile filaments of muscle fibres.

acting /ˈaktɪŋ/ *n.* L16. [f. ACT *v.* + -ING[1].] 1 Performance; execution. L16. 2 The performance of deeds; in *pl.*, doings, practices, etc. *arch.* E17. 3 The performing of plays etc.; the art or occupation of performing parts in plays, films, etc.; simulation. M17. 4 The putting forth of energy, activity, etc.; operation. M17.

2 SIR W. SCOTT The great actings which are now on foot.

Comb.: **acting copy** a copy of a play etc. specially prepared for actors' use, with stage-directions, cuts, etc.; **acting part, play** a part or play with good dramatic qualities; **acting version** = *acting copy* above.

acting /'aktɪŋ/ *a.* L16. [f. ACT *v.* + -ING[2].] 1 That acts or has power to act. L16. 2 *spec.* (Freq. bef. a title etc.) Doing duty temporarily (as *Acting Captain*); doing alone duties nominally shared with others (as *Acting Manager*). L18.

actinia /ak'tɪnɪə/ *n.* Pl. **-iae** /-ɪiː/, **-ias.** M18. [mod.L, f. as ACTIN + -IA[2].] A sea anemone of the genus *Actinia*, esp. *A. equina*, a common British species; *loosely* any sea anemone.

actinian *n.* a sea anemone of the genus *Actinia* L19.

actinide /'aktɪnʌɪd/ *n.* M20. [f. ACTINIUM + *-ide* after LANTHANIDE.] Any of the series of radioactive chemical elements having atomic numbers between 89 (actinium) and 103 (lawrencium) inclusive, which form part of the group of transition metals.

actinism /'aktɪnɪz(ə)m/ *n.* M19. [f. as ACTIN + -ISM.] The property by which light or other electromagnetic radiation causes chemical change, as in photography.

ac'tinic *a.* of or pertaining to actinism; (of light etc.) having the ability to cause chemical change: M19.

actinium /ak'tɪnɪəm/ *n.* E20. [f. as prec. + -IUM.] A radioactive metallic chemical element, atomic no. 89, which is the first element of the actinide series and is found in small quantities in pitchblende. (Symbol Ac.)

actinoid, actinon *ns.* = ACTINIDE M20.

actino- /'aktɪnəʊ, ak'tɪnəʊ/ *comb. form* of Gk *aktin-*, *aktis* ray: see -O-.

,actino'morphic *a.* (*Bot.*) (of a flower) characterized by radial symmetry (opp. *zygomorphic*) L19. **,actino'mycin** *n.* an antibiotic obtained from actinomycetes M20. **,actinomy'cosis** *n.* a disease of animals (esp. cattle), and sometimes of people, caused by infection with actinomycetes and most commonly affecting the mouth, jaw, or neck L19. **,actinomy'cotic** *a.* pertaining to or suffering from actinomycosis E20. **,actinopte'rygian** *a.* & *n.* [Gk *pterugion* fin, dim. of *pterux* wing] (designating or pertaining to) a ray-finned fish, a fish belonging to the subclass Actinopterygii, which includes most living bony fishes L19. **,actino'therapy** *n.* treatment of disease by means of ultraviolet radiation E20. **,actino-u'ranium** *n.* the uranium isotope of mass 235 E20.

actinolite /ak'tɪnəlʌɪt/ *n.* L18. [f. ACTINO- + Gk *lithos* stone: see -ITE[1]. Named in ref. to the rayed masses of crystals it often forms.] *Min.* A green amphibole mineral containing calcium, magnesium, and ferrous iron, forming elongated monoclinic crystals or fibrous masses, and found esp. in many metamorphic rocks and as a form of asbestos.

,actino'litic *a.* M19.

actinometer /aktɪ'nɒmɪtə/ *n.* M19. [f. ACTINO- + -METER.] An instrument for measuring the heating or actinic power of radiant energy.

,actino'metric *a.* of or pertaining to actinometers or their use M19. **,actino'metrical** *a.* = ACTINOMETRIC L19. **actinometry** *n.* M19.

actinomycete /,aktɪnə(ʊ)'mʌɪsiːt/ *n.* Orig. only in pl. **-mycetes** /-'mʌɪsiːts, -mʌɪ'siːtiːz/. E20. [Anglicized sing. of mod.L *actinomycetes*, f. as ACTINO- + Gk *mukēs* pl. of *mukēs* fungus.] A filamentous bacterium of the order Actinomycetales.

actio /'aktɪəʊ/ *n.* L17. [L.] (An) action.

actio in distans /ɪn 'dɪstanz/ [= on something apart] = *action at a distance* s.v. ACTION *n.*

action /'akʃ(ə)n/ *n.* & *v.* ME. [(O)Fr. f. L *actio(n-)*, f. as ACT *v.*: see -ION.] A *n.* 1 The taking of legal steps to establish a claim or obtain remedy; the right to institute a legal process. ME. b A legal process or suit. LME. 2 The process or condition of acting or doing; the exertion of energy or influence; working, agency, operation. LME. 3 A thing done, a deed, an act (usu. viewed as occupying some time in doing); (in *pl.*) freq. habitual or ordinary deeds, conduct. LME. 4 Mode of acting. a Gesture, esp. in oratory or acting. M16. b The management of the body or limbs in movement. L16. c The way in which an instrument acts; the mechanism effecting this. M19. d A film director's command to begin a scene. M20. †5 The celebration of a sacrament. Chiefly *Sc.* M16–L19. 6a An engagement with the enemy; a fight. L16. b Active operation against, or engaging, an enemy; fighting. E17. †7 The acting of plays, performance. E17–E18. †8 A share in a joint-stock company. L17–M19. 9 The event or series of events represented in a drama or forming the subject of a poem or other composition. L17. 10 *Physics.* The product (or a corresponding integral) of momentum and distance or (equivalently) of twice the kinetic energy and time. Now also, the product (or integral) of the difference between kinetic energy and potential energy, and time. E19. 11 Activity; *the* exciting or important events etc. Freq. in *where the action is. slang.* M20.

2 JOYCE The corrosive action of coppers. G. SANTAYANA Trust the man who hesitates in his speech and is quick and steady in action. DELAYED-*action*. 6a S. SASSOON The Division had now been in action for a week. E. BOWEN A month when enemy action was not severe.

Phrases: **action at a distance** the exertion of force by one body on another separated from it by space; *fig.* the exertion of influence from a distance. **action front!, action rear!**: commands in an artillery regiment to prepare for action in front of, behind, the guns. **action of a verb, verbal action** the thing asserted by the verb, strictly action but also state, existence, etc. *action of* DECLARATOR. *action of* TROVER. *action rear!*: see *action front!* above. *chose in action*: see CHOSE *n. clear the decks for action*: see CLEAR *v.* 8. *direct action*: see DIRECT *a.* **go into action** begin a military action or attack; *gen.* begin work, begin operating. **in action** (*a*) (of property) not in possession, but recoverable by legal process; (*b*) in practical or effective operation. *industrial action*: see INDUSTRIAL *a. join action*: see JOIN *v. live action*: see LIVE *a. man of action*: see MAN *n.* **out of action** not working. *principle of* LEAST *action*. *suit the action to the word*: see SUIT *v.* **take action** institute legal proceedings; *gen.* begin to act, act effectively. *transitory action*: see TRANSITORY 3. *unity of action*: see UNITY *n.*[1] 8. *verbal action*: see *action of a verb* above.

Comb.: **action committee, group**: formed to take active steps, esp. in politics; **action-noun** *Gram.*: expressing an action; **action-packed** *a.* (*colloq.*) full of action or excitement; **action painting** (a painting produced by) spontaneous or random application of paint; **action point** a point or issue on which there is a need or a decision to take action; **action potential** *Biol.* the change in electrical potential associated with the passage of an impulse along the membrane of a muscle cell or nerve cell; **action replay** a playback of a televised incident, esp. in a sports match, just after it has taken place; **†action sermon** in the Scottish Presbyterian Church, a discourse at the Eucharist or other sacrament; **action song** a (children's) song involving also some dramatic movement, esp. of the hands; **action stations** positions taken up by troops etc. before going into action; *transf.* positions for beginning any activity.

B *v.t.* 1 Bring a legal action against. M18. 2 Take action on, put into effect. M20.

actional *a.* of or pertaining to action(s); actionable: M17.

actionable /'akʃ(ə)nəb(ə)l/ *a.* L16. [f. prec. + -ABLE.] Affording ground for an action at law.

actiona'bility *n.* L19. **actionably** *adv.* E19.

activate /'aktɪveɪt/ *v.t.* E17. [f. ACTIVE *a.* + -ATE[3].] 1 Make active, cause to act. Freq. *techn.* E17. 2 *spec.* Make radioactive. M20.

1 **activated carbon, charcoal** charcoal which has been treated so as to increase its adsorptive power. **activated sludge** aerated sewage containing aerobic bacteria.

activator *n.* a thing which or (*rare*) a person who activates E20.

activation /aktɪ'veɪʃ(ə)n/ *n.* E20. [f. prec.: see -ATION.] The action of activating; the state of being activated.

Comb.: **activation analysis** *Chem.* a technique of analysis in which atoms of a particular element in a sample are made radioactive (esp. by irradiation with neutrons) and their concentration is then determined radiologically.

active /'aktɪv/ *a.* & *n.* ME. [L *activus*, f. as ACT *v.* + -IVE; partly f. Fr. *actif, -ive*.] A *adj.* 1 Given to action rather than contemplation or speculation; practical. ME. 2 Originating or communicating action. LME. 3 *Gram.* Designating, being in, involving, or pertaining to a voice comprising all forms of intransitive verbs, and those forms of transitive verbs that attribute the action of the verb to the person or thing whence it proceeds (the logical subject, in this case coinciding with the grammatical subject). Opp. *passive*, and in some languages *middle*. LME. 4 Energetic; diligent; brisk; busy. LME. 5 Working, effective; not quiescent or extinct. M17. b Radioactive. E20. c *Electronics.* Of a circuit: containing a source of power. Opp. *passive.* M20. d *Electronics* & *Mech.* Of a system: capable of modifying its state or characteristics automatically in response to input or feedback. M20.

1 Esp. in *active life* [L *vita activa*]. 2 **active citizen** a member of the public who actively takes the initiative in crime prevention etc. 4 SHAKES. *2 Hen. IV* The most active fellow in Europe. DAY LEWIS Sunday was . . the most active day of the week. 5 BOSWELL Instances of his active benevolence. **active carbon, charcoal** activated carbon. **active driveway** *US*: in use by vehicles etc. **active layer** *Physical Geogr.* a seasonally thawed surface layer above permafrost. **active list** a list of officers in the armed forces liable to be called on for service. **active service** actual participation in warfare; full-time service in armed forces. **active volcano** a volcano that is erupting or has erupted in historical times. *optically active*: see OPTICALLY. d *Autocar* A sensational prototype with a . . turbo-engine, four-wheel drive, active suspension.

B *absol.* as *n.* 1 A person devoted to the active life. LME. 2 *Gram. The* active voice; an active form of a verb. M16.

actively *adv.* LME. **activeness** *n.* the quality of being active; *esp.* = ACTIVITY 2: E16.

activism /'aktɪvɪz(ə)m/ *n.* E20. [f. ACTIVE *a.* + -ISM.] 1 *Philos.* The theory that everything whatsoever is active. Now *rare.* E20. 2 A policy of vigorous action, esp. in politics. E20.

activist *n.* & *a.* (*a*) *n.* an advocate of activism; (*b*) *adj.* of or pertaining to activists or activism: E20.

activity /ak'tɪvɪti/ *n.* LME. [Fr. *activité* or late L *activitas*, f. as ACTIVE: see -ITY.] 1 The state of being active; the exertion of energy, action. LME. b The degree to which an enzyme or other substance exhibits its characteristic property. L19. c Radioactivity. E20. d *Chem.* A thermodynamic quantity which is a measure of the effective concentration of a substance in a system. E20. 2 Brisk or vigorous action; energy; diligence; liveliness. L15. †3 Gymnastics, athletics; a gymnastic exercise. M16–E18. 4 An active force or operation; an occupation, a pursuit. M17. b In *pl.* Things that a person, animal, or group chooses to do. E20.

1c *specific activity*: see SPECIFIC *a.* 2 *optical activity*: see OPTICAL. 4b H. W. FOWLER A regrettable by-product of their activities. *Listener* The widespread activities of the state security police.

actomyosin /aktə(ʊ)'mʌɪəsɪn/ *n.* M20. [f. ACTIN + -O- + MYOSIN.] *Biochem.* A complex of actin and myosin.

acton /'aktən/ *n. obs.* exc. *Hist.* Also **aketon.** ME. [OFr. *auqueton* (mod. *hoqueton*), ult. f. Sp. Arab. *alkuṭūn* the cotton.] A jacket of quilted cotton worn under mail; a mail-plated jacket of leather etc.

actor /'aktə/ *n.* LME. [L, f. as ACT *v.* + -OR. Cf. (O)Fr. *acteur.*] 1 An agent, *esp.* an administrator; a person who acts on behalf of another. *obs.* exc. *Rom. Law* (15–17 chiefly *Sc.*). LME. †2 The plaintiff or complainant in a legal action; a pleader. LME–M18. 3 A person who performs or takes part in any action; a doer. (Now usu. w. allus. to sense 4.) M16. 4 A person who personates a character, or acts a part; a person whose occupation is acting in plays, films, etc. L16.

4 *character actor, utility actor*, etc.

actorish, actorly *adjs.* appropriate to or characteristic of a dramatic actor; affectedly theatrical: M20. **actorship** *n.* the quality or position of a dramatic actor L16. **actory** *a.* = ACTORISH E20.

actress /'aktrɪs/ *n.* L16. [f. prec. + -ESS[1].] †1 A

female doer. L16–E18. 2 A female actor in plays, films, etc. E18.

actressy *a.* pertaining to or characteristic of an actress L19.

actual /'aktjʊəl, -tʃʊəl/ *a.* & *n.* ME. [(O)Fr. *actuel* f. late L *actualis* active, practical, f. *actus* ACT *n.*: see -AL[1]. The spelling *-al* is by assim. to L.] A *adj.* 1 Pertaining to or exhibited in acts; practical, active. *obs.* exc. as below. ME. 2 Existing in act or fact; real. LME. 3 In action or existence at the time; present, current. L16.

1 **actual grace** *Theol.* a divine influence inspiring some good act. **actual sin** *Theol.* a sin resulting from an individual act of free will (opp. *original sin*). 2 S. HILL He had no illusions about himself as actual or potential soldier. A. BURGESS Too late to attend the actual ceremony. *actual cautery*: see CAUTERY 1. 3 J. BRAINE Husbands were chosen as much on eventual as actual salary.

B *n.* In *pl.* Actual qualities, actualities. M16.

actualism *n.* (*a*) (now *rare*) the theory that nothing is merely passive; (*b*) realism: M19. **actualist** *n.* an advocate of actualism M19. **actua'listic** *a.* of the nature of actualism; realistic: L19. **actualness** *n.* = ACTUALITY LME.

actualise *v.* var. of ACTUALIZE.

actuality /aktjʊ'alɪti, -tʃʊ-/ *n.* LME. [OFr. *actualité* or med.L *actualitas*, f. *actualis*: see prec., -ITY.] †1 Capacity of action, activity. LME–L17. 2 Reality; existing objective fact. M17. 3 In *pl.* Existing conditions or circumstances. M17. 4 Realism in description or presentation. M19.

4 *attrib.*: L. MACNEICE The radio dramatist . . must select his actuality material with great discrimination.

actualize /'aktjʊəlʌɪz, -tʃʊ-/ *v.t.* Also **-ise**. E18. [f. ACTUAL *a.* + -IZE.] Make actual or real; realize in action or description.

actuali'zation *n.* E19.

actually /'aktjʊəli, -tʃʊ-/ *adv.* LME. [f. ACTUAL *a.* + -LY[2]: partly after late L *actualiter*, Fr. *actuellement*.] †1 With deeds; actively. LME–M17. 2 As a fact; really. LME. 3 As a present fact, at present, for the time being. E16. 4 As a matter of fact; indeed; even (strange as it may seem). M18.

2 GEO. ELIOT With a fixed look, seeing nothing that was actually present. 3 OED The party actually in power. 4 E. O'NEILL You feel no shame, but actually boast you are planning to dishonour yourself and your family. D. HEFFRON We think it's quite all right, actually.

actuarial /aktjʊ'ɛːrɪəl, -tʃʊ-/ *a.* M19. [f. next + -AL[1].] Of or pertaining to actuaries or their profession.

actuarially *adv.* in relation to actuarial principles; on an actuarial basis: L19.

actuary /'aktjʊəri, -tʃʊ-/ *n.* M16. [L *actuarius*, f. *actus* ACT *n.*: see -ARY[1].] 1 A registrar, a clerk; an officer who records the acts of a court. *obs.* exc. in the Convocation of the Province of Canterbury (Ch. of England). M16. 2 An officer who manages the deposits in a savings bank. E19. 3 A person who compiles statistics of mortality, accidents, etc., and calculates insurance risks and premiums. M19.

actuate /'aktjʊeɪt, -tʃʊ-/ *v.* L16. [med.L *actuat-* pa. ppl stem of *actuare*, f. *actus* ACT *n.*: see -ATE[3].] †1 *v.t.* Carry out in practice. (*rare* after 17.) L16–L19. 2 *v.t.* Give life to, enliven, vivify; stir into activity, excite. Now *rare* or *obs.* L16. 3 *v.i.* Exert activity, act. E17. 4 *v.t.* Communicate motion to (a machine etc.); cause the operation of (an electrical device etc.); be the motive for (an action). M17. 5 *v.t.* Be the motive for action of (a person). M18.

actuator *n.* a person who or thing which actuates L19.

actuation /aktjʊ'eɪʃ(ə)n, -tʃʊ-/ *n.* E17. [In early use f. med.L *actuatio(n-)*, f. as prec.; later f. prec.: see -ATION.] A communication of motion; a bringing into action; impulse, movement.

acuate /'akjʊət/ *a.* LME. [med.L *acuatus* pa. pple of *acuare* var. of L *acuere*: see ACUTE, -ATE[2].] Made sharp or pungent; sharp-pointed.

†**acuate** *v.t.* M16–M18. [f. prec.: see -ATE[3].] Make sharp or pungent.

acuity /ə'kjuːɪti/ *n.* LME. [(O)Fr. *acuité* or med.L *acuitas*, f. *acuere*: see ACUTE, -ITY.] Sharpness (*lit.* & *fig.*, as of a needle, the sight or hearing, wit, etc.).

visual acuity: see VISUAL *a.*

aculeate /ə'kjuːlɪət/ *a.* & *n.* M17. [L *aculeatus*, f. *aculeus* dim. of *acus* needle: see -ATE[2].] A *adj.* 1 *Zool.* Bearing a sting; *spec.* designating hymenopterous insects of the section Aculeata, which comprises bees, ants, and wasps. M17. 2 *fig.* Pointed, incisive, stinging. M17. B *n.* An aculeate insect. L19.

aculeated /-eɪtɪd/ *a.* sharply pointed; armed with prickles; incisive: M17.

acumen /'akjʊmən, ə'kjuːmən/ *n.* L16. [L *acumen*, *-min-* point, acuteness, f. *acuere*: see ACUTE.] 1 Sharpness of wit; penetration of perception; keenness of discrimination. L16. 2 *Bot.* A tapering point. L18.

¶The older and etymological pronunc. is /ə'kjuːmən/.

acuminate /ə'kjuːmɪnət/ *a.* L16. [Late L *acuminat-* pa. ppl stem of *acuminare* sharpen to a point, f. as prec.: see -ATE[2].] *Bot.* & *Zool.* Tapering to a point.

acuminate /ə'kjuːmɪneɪt/ *v.* L16. [f. as prec.: see -ATE[3].] 1 *v.t.* Sharpen; give poignancy or keenness to. L16. 2 *v.i.* Rise or taper to a point. Chiefly as *acuminating* ppl a. M17.

acumi'nation *n.* sharpening or giving point to (*lit.* & *fig.*); tending towards a point; a tapering point: M17.

acupressure /'akjʊprɛʃə/ *n.* M19. [f. L *acu* with a needle + PRESSURE *n.*] *Med.* 1 The prevention of bleeding from an artery by compressing it with one or more needles inserted through the adjacent tissue. M19. 2 The application of pressure with the fingers to points on the body, for therapeutic purposes, = SHIATSU. (Now the usual sense.) M20.

acupuncture /'akjʊpʌŋktʃə/ *n.* L17. [f. as prec. + PUNCTURE *n.*] Pricking with a needle; *spec.* the insertion of needles into living tissues for remedial purposes, other than for the injection of drugs.

acupunctu'ation *n.* (now *rare*) = ACUPUNCTURATION M19. **acupunctu'ration** *n.* the practice or process of acupuncture M18. **acupuncturist** *n.* a person who practises acupuncture M20.

acushla /ə'kʊʃlə/ *n.* *Anglo-Ir.* M19. [Ir., short for *a chuisle mo chroí* O pulse of my heart. Cf. CUSHLA-MACHREE, MACUSHLA.] As a form of address: darling, dear heart.

acutance /ə'kjuːt(ə)ns/ *n.* M20. [f. ACUTE *a.* + -ANCE.] Sharpness of a photographic or printed image; a measure of this.

acute /ə'kjuːt/ *a.*, *n.*, & *v.* LME. [L *acutus* pa. pple of *acuere* sharpen, f. *acus* needle.] A *adj.* 1 *Med.* Of a disease, symptoms of disease: of short duration (and usu. severe). Cf. CHRONIC *a.* 1. LME. b Of a medical facility: designed or reserved for the treatment of acute illness. M20. c *fig.* Of controversy, difficulty, shortage, etc.: critical, serious. M20. 2a Of an angle: less than a right angle. M16. b Sharp at the end; coming to a point. L16. 3 Of a sound: shrill, high (*Phonet.* as a classificatory feature, opp. *grave*). M16. 4 Of the intellect: penetrating, sharp-witted, shrewd. Cf. CUTE *a.*[1] L16. †5 Of tastes or odours: sharp, pungent. E–M17. 6 Of pain, pleasure, etc.: keen, intense. M17. 7 Of the senses, the nervous system: responsive or sensitive to impressions; finely-strung. M18.

3 **acute accent** the mark ´ placed over letters in some languages to show quality, vowel length, pronunciation, etc.

Comb.: **acute-angled** *a.* having an acute angle or angles.

B *n.* An acute illness, tone, etc.; *esp.* an acute accent. LME.

†C *v.t.* Sharpen; mark with an acute accent. Chiefly as *acuted* ppl a. M17–L18.

acutely *adv.* L16. **acuteness** *n.* E17.

-acy /əsi/ *suff.* [A branch of -CY.] Forming ns. of quality, state, or condition. 1 Repr. L *-acia*, f. adjs. in *-aci-*, *-ax*, as *fallacy*. 2 Repr. L *-atia* (med.L often *-acia*), f. ns. in *-at-*, *-as*, as *abbacy*, *primacy*; similarly *supremacy*. 3 Repr. med.L *-atia*, f. ns. in *-atus*, as *advocacy*, *prelacy*; hence f. ns. in -ATE[1], as *confederacy*, and adjs. in -ATE[2], as *accuracy*, *obstinacy*. 4 Repr. Gk ns. in *-ateia*, as *piracy*. See also -CRACY.

acyclic /eɪ'sʌɪklɪk, -'sɪk-/ *a.* L19. [f. A-[10] + CYCLIC.] Not cyclic.

acyl /'eɪsʌɪl, 'asɪl/ *a.* L19. [G, f. L *acidum* acid: see -YL.] *Chem.* A radical (RCO·) derived from an organic acid by loss of hydroxyl from the carboxy group. Usu. in *comb.*

acylate *v.t.* introduce an acyl radical into (a compound) E20. **acy'lation** *n.* E20.

ad /ad/ *n.* *colloq.* M19. [Abbrev.] An advertisement; advertising.

small ad: see SMALL *a.*

Comb.: **adman** a person who produces advertisements commercially; **admass** the section of the community regarded as readily influenced by advertising etc.

adless *a.* without advertisements, carrying no advertisements E20.

ad- /ad, *unstressed* əd/ *pref.* 1 Repr. L *ad* prep. 'to', with sense of motion to or direction towards, addition, adherence, increase. The *d* was assim. to following *c*, *f*, *g*, *l*, *n*, *p*, *q*, *r*, *s*, *t* (see AC-, AF-, etc.); *ad-* was reduced to *a-* before *sc*, *sp*, *st* (see A-[8]). In OFr. the double consonant of *acc-*, *add-*, etc., were reduced to single ones, and *adv-* became *av-*, and OFr. words were adopted with such forms in Eng.; but in 14 these began to be refash. after L, as *address*. Opp. to *ab-* away from, as in *adaxial*, *abaxial*, *ad-* is recent. 2 At the same time *ad-* was substituted for *a-* of different origin, as in *advance*, *addebted*, *admiral*.

-ad /ad, əd/ *suff.*[1] [Repr. L f. Gk *-ad-*, *-as*.] 1 Forming collect. numerals, as *monad*, *myriad*, etc. 2 Forming fem. patronymics (var. of -ID[2]) as *dryad*, *naiad*, etc. 3 In names of epic poems, as *Dunciad*, *Rosciad*, after *Iliad*. 4 *Bot.* Forming names of members of some taxonomic groupings, as *bromeliad*, *cycad*.

-ad /əd/ *suff.*[2] Repr. Fr. *-ade*, as *ballad*, *salad*, etc.: see -ADE.

-ad /ad/ *suff.*[3] E19. [f. L *ad* to: cf. AD-.] *Anat.* Invented to form adjs. and advs. in the sense of 'nearer to' or 'towards' (the part denoted by the main element of the word), as *dorsad* etc.

†**adad** *int.* Also **adod**. M17–M18. [f. as AGAD, EGAD, etc.] = EGAD.

adage /'adɪdʒ/ *n.*[1] M16. [Fr. f. L *adagium*, f. *ad* AD- + an early form of *aio* I say.] A traditional maxim, a proverb of common experience.

adagial /ə'deɪdʒɪəl/ *a.* of the nature of an adage L17. †**adagy** *n.* [L *adagium*] an adage M16–M18.

adage /adaːʒ/ *n.*[2] Pl. pronounced same. M20. [Fr., f. as next.] = ADAGIO *n.* 2.

adagio /ə'dɑːdʒɪəʊ/ *adv.*, *a.*, & *n.* L17. [It., f. *ad agio* at ease.] *Mus.* A *adv.* & *adj.* In slow time, leisurely. L17. B *n.* Pl. **-os**. 1 A musical piece or movement in slow time. M18. 2 A dance or ballet movement in slow time. M18.

Adam /'adəm/ *n.* ME. [Heb. *'ādām* man, later interpreted as a name.] 1 The first man in Hebrew tradition. ME. 2 More fully (now the only form) *old Adam*. Unregenerate human nature. E16.

1 **not know from Adam** have no knowledge of the appearance of (a person). *second Adam*: see SECOND *a.*

Comb. (chiefly genitival): **Adam-and-Eve** *dial.* any of various plants, *esp.* any of certain orchids (from the supposed resemblance of the tubers to a human couple); **Adam's ale**, (Sc. & north.) **wine** *joc.* water; **Adam's apple** (*a*) any of various fruits, *esp.* a variety of lime; (*b*) the projection formed in the neck by the thyroid cartilage, esp. when prominent in men; **Adam's needle** yucca, esp. *Y. filamentosa*.

A'damic *a.* = ADAMICAL M18. **A'damical** *a.* pertaining to or resembling Adam M17.

Adam /'adəm/ *a.* L19. [A surname.] Designed or built by, or in the style of, the brothers Robert and James Adam, 18th-cent. Scottish architects and designers.

Ada'mesque *a.* resembling the work of the Adam brothers M20.

adamant /'adəm(ə)nt/ *n.* & *a.* OE. [OFr. *adamaunt-* f. L *adamant-*, *-ma(n)s* f. Gk *adamant-*, *-mas* hardest iron or steel, diamond, orig. adj. 'invincible', f. *a-* A-[10] + *daman* tame. The sense 'magnet, lodestone' arose from assoc. of med.L *adamas* with L *adamare* have a strong liking for. Cf. DIAMOND *n.* & *a.*] A *n.* An alleged rock or mineral, to which many (often contradictory) properties have been attributed, formerly sometimes identified with the diamond or with the lodestone or magnet. Now only *poet.* & *rhet.* as an embodiment of impregnable hardness. OE. B *adj.* Unshakeable, unyielding to requests. M20.

¶The point at which the n. use passed into the adj. is not determinable: M20 represents the date of the first indubitably adj. examples.

adamance *n.* adamantine quality; refusal to yield: M20. **adamantly** *adv.* M20.

adamantane /adə'manteɪn/ *n.* M19. [Fr., f. as prec. + -ANE.] *Chem.* A crystalline alicylic hydrocarbon, $C_{10}H_{16}$, in the molecule of which the carbon atoms are arranged in three six-sided rings as in the crystal structure of diamond.

adamantine /adə'mantʌɪn/ *a.* ME. [L *adamantinus* f. Gk *adamantinos*, f. *adamant-* ADAMANT: see -INE[2].] Made of, or having the qualities of, adamant; unbreakable, impregnable, unshakeable.

POPE To count them all, demands . . A throat of brass, and adamantine lungs. C. P. SNOW An adamantine will for success.

¶Rare bef. 16. The historical pronunc. is /-tɪn/.

Also †**adamantean** *a.* (*rare*, Milton): only in L17.

adamellite /adə'mɛlʌɪt/ *n.* L19. [f. Monte *Adamello* in northern Italy + -ITE[1].] *Geol.* A quartz-bearing plutonic igneous rock containing roughly equal proportions of orthoclase and plagioclase.

Adamite /'adəmʌɪt/ *n.*[1] & *a.* M16. [eccl.L *Adamita*: see ADAM *n.*, -ITE[1].] A *n.* 1 A person who goes naked like Adam; *esp.* a member of any of various sects advocating nakedness. M16. 2 A human being regarded as a descendant of Adam. M17. B *adj.* Descended from Adam; human. M19.

Ada'mitical *a.* pertaining to an Adamite or Adamites; naked like Adam: M17. **Adamitism** *n.* (*rare*) the beliefs and practices of Adamites M19.

adamite /'adəmʌɪt/ *n.*[2] M19. [f. G. J. *Adam* (1795–1881), Fr. mineralogist + -ITE[1].] *Min.* A basic zinc arsenate occurring as yellow, green, or colourless orthorhombic crystals or crystal aggregates.

adance /ə'dɑːns/ *adv.* & *pred. a.* E19. [f. A-[2] + DANCE *n.* or *v.*] Dancing.

adangle /ə'daŋg(ə)l/ *adv.* & *pred. a.* M19. [f. A-[2] + DANGLE *v.*] Dangling.

adapt /ə'dapt/ *v.* Pa. pple & ppl a. **adapted**, †**adapt**. LME. [Fr. *adapter* f. L *adaptare*, f. *ad* AD- + *aptare*, f. *aptus* fit, APT.] 1 *v.t.* Fit, adjust, (*to*); make suitable (*to* or *for*). LME. 2 *v.t.* Alter or modify to fit for a new use, new conditions, etc. L18. 3 *v.i.* Undergo modification to fit a new use, new conditions, etc. M20.

1 W. S. MAUGHAM She . . was unable to adapt her expenditure to her altered circumstances. 2 C. HAMPTON The account of the Beiços-de-Pau tribe . . is adapted from his diaries. 3 H. WOUK Rhoda adapted merrily to diplomatic life.

adaptative *a.* = ADAPTIVE E19. **adaptedness** *n.* the state of being adapted L17. **adaption** *n.* = ADAPTATION M17. **adaptitude** *n.* (*rare*) specially produced aptitude M19.

adaptability /ədaptə'bɪlɪti/ *n.* M17. [f. prec.: see -ABILITY.] The state or quality of being adaptable.

adaptable /ə'daptəb(ə)l/ *a.* E19. [f. as prec. + -ABLE.] Able to be adapted (*to, for*) or to adapt oneself.

adaptableness *n.* M19.

adaptation /adəp'teɪʃ(ə)n/ *n.* E17. [Fr. f. late L *adaptatio(n-)*, f. *adaptare*: see ADAPT, -ATION.] 1 The action or process of fitting or suiting one thing *to* another. E17. b Modification to fit a new use, new conditions, etc. L18. c *Biol.* Modification by which an organ, organism, or species becomes better fitted for its environment or mode of existence. M19. 2 The condition of being adapted; suitableness. L17. 3 An instance of adapting; something adapted. M19.

1b L. BLOOMFIELD Adaptation . ., in which the foreign form is altered to meet the fundamental phonetic habits of the language. c B. J. WILLIAMS The pelvis and limbs of *Oreopithecus* indicate an adaptation to upright posture. 2 J. MARTINEAU The adaptation of immortality to our true wants. 3 L. HELLMAN *Monserrat*, an adaptation I made from the French play by Emmanuel Roblès.

adaptational *a.* L19.

adapter /ə'daptə/ *n.* Also **-or**. M18. [f. ADAPT *v.* + -ER[1], -OR.] 1 A device allowing connection of pieces of equipment, e.g. chemical apparatus, unable to be connected directly. M18. b *spec.* An electrical fitting of this nature, usu. one enabling more than one plug to be connected to the same socket. E20. 2 A person who adapts. E19.

¶*Adapter* is now more usual for a person, *adaptor* for a device.

adaptive /ə'daptɪv/ *a.* E19. [f. ADAPT *v.* + -IVE.] Characterized by or given to adaptation.

adaptive RADIATION.

adaptively *adv.* by way of adaptation; to suit special conditions: M19. **adaptiveness** *n.* M19.

adaptor *n.* see ADAPTER.

Adar /a'dɑː/ *n.* LME. [Heb. *'ădār.*] In the Jewish calendar, the sixth month of the civil and twelfth of the religious year, usu. coinciding with parts of February and March; in leap years, either of two successive months, *First Adar* and *Second Adar* (coinciding with parts of March and April).

adat /'adat/ *n.* L18. [Malay f. Arab. *'āda.*] Custom, or customary law, in the Islamic regions of SE Asia, esp. in contrast to Islamic religious law. Also *adat law*.

adatom /'adat(ə)m/ *n.* M20. [Contr. of *adsorbed atom*: see ADSORB *v.*, ATOM.] *Physical Chem.* An atom adsorbed on a surface.

†**adaunt** *v.t.* ME–L16. [Prob. AN: cf. AN *adant(e)üre* training, breaking in (of a horse) and see DAUNT.] Quell, subdue.

S. DANIEL Wherewith the Rebell rather was the more Incourag'd than addaunted.

†**adaw** *v.t.* LME–M17. [f. adv. phr. *a* (*o, of*) *dawe*, f. A *prep.*[2] + *dawe* obs. form of DAY *n.*, = OE *of dagum* from days, from life.] Subdue, daunt.

SPENSER Like one adawed with some dreadfull spright.

adaxial /a'daksɪəl/ *a.* E20. [f. AD- + AXIAL.] *Bot.* Toward the axis; (of the surface of a leaf etc.) initially facing toward the stem.

a-day /ə'deɪ/ *adv.* ME. [Orig. two wds, f. A *prep.*[1] 3 + DAY *n.*] †1 By day. Only in ME. 2 Daily. (The *a* now identified with the indef. article: see A *a.* 4.) See also NOWADAY. ME.

a-days /ə'deɪz/ *adv.* LME. [f. A *prep.*[1] 3 + genit. sing. of DAY *n.* (used alone advb. in OE in sense 'by day', and later blended with prec.).] †1 By day. LME–M18. 2 At the present time. Chiefly & now only with *now*: see NOWADAYS. LME.

adazzle /ə'daz(ə)l/ *adv.* & *pred. a.* M19. [f. A-[2] + DAZZLE *v.* & *n.*] Dazzling.

ad captandum vulgus /ad kap'tandəm 'vʌlgəs/ *adv.* & *a. phr.* M18. [L = for alluring the crowd.] (Designed) to appeal to the emotions (of the rabble). Also *ad captandum*.

add /ad/ *v.* LME. [L *addere*, f. *ad* AD- + base of *dare* put, give.] 1 *v.t.* Join or unite (one thing *to* another) as an increase or supplement. LME. †b *v.t.* Give by way of increased possession (*to*). M16–E18. 2 *spec.* a *v.t.* Unite (a number *to* another) to get a number equal to their total amount. LME. b *v.i.* Perform the arithmetical process of addition. L15. c *v.t.* Unite (two or more numbers, freq. *together*) into one sum. L17. 3 *v.t.* Say or write in addition; go on to say. LME. 4 *v.i.* Foll. by *to*: increase, augment. L16.

1 TENNYSON Yet this grief Is added to the griefs the great must bear. b AV *Matt.* 6:33 All these things shalbe added vnto you. 2 **add in** include in a sum. **add up** (*a*) *v.phr.t.* & *i.* find the sum of (a series of numbers); (*b*) *v.phr.i.* make the desired or correct total; amount *to*; *colloq.* make sense. 3 POPE But let me add, Sir Robert's mighty dull. 4 S. DELANEY You've got enough bad habits without adding to your repertoire.

Comb.: **add-on** *a.* & *n.* (something) that has been or can be added to what already exists.

addax /'adaks/ *n.* L17. [L f. an African wd (quoted by Pliny).] A large, stocky antelope, *Addax nasomaculatus*, with twisted horns, native to the N. African desert.

†**addebted** *pa. pple* & *ppl a. Sc.* E16–E19. [f. as INDEBTED, refash. w. AD-.] Indebted.

†**addeem** *v.t. literary.* Only in L16. [f. DEEM *v.* after *adjudge*: see A-[11].] Adjudge.

addend /'adɛnd/ *n.* L17. [L *addendus* masc. gerundive (sc. *numerus* number) of *addere* ADD: see -END. Cf. next.] A number which is to be added to another.

addendum /ə'dɛndəm/ *n.* Pl. **-da** /-də/. L17. [L, neut. gerundive of *addere* ADD: cf. prec.] 1 A thing to be added, esp. because of omission; an appendix, an addition; *sing.* & (esp.) in *pl.* (occas. treated as *sing.*), additional matter at the end of a book. L17. 2 *Mech.* The radial distance from the pitch-circle of a cog-wheel, worm-wheel, etc., to the crests of the teeth or ridge. M19.

adder /'adə/ *n.*[1] [OE *nǣd(d)re*, corresp. to OS *nādra* (MDu. *nadre*, Du. *adder*), OHG *nātara* (G *Natter*), and (with a different vowel-grade) ON *naðr*, *naðra*, Goth. *nadrs*; perh. rel. to L *natrix* water snake, OIr. *nathir*, Welsh *neidr* snake, viper. The initial *n* was lost in ME (14–15) through the erroneous division of *a naddre* as *an addre*, as in *apron*, *auger*, etc.] †1 A serpent, a snake; *fig. the* Devil. OE–E16. 2 A small poisonous snake, a viper; *spec.* the common European viper, *Vipera berus*. OE. b Any of various other poisonous snakes, belonging esp. to the family Viperidae. Usu. w. specifying wd. See also *deaf adder* s.v. DEAF *a.* OE.

2 **deaf as an adder** completely deaf. b *death adder*, *night adder*, *puff adder*, etc.

Comb.: **adderbolt** (now *dial.*) a dragonfly; **adder-stone** (now *dial.*) an ancient amulet or bead; a perforated stone; **adderwort** bistort; **adder's grass** the early purple orchid, *Orchis mascula*; **adder's mouth** *N. Amer.* an orchid of the genus *Malaxis*; **adder's tongue** any of several plants; *spec.* a fern of the genus *Ophioglossum*.

adder /'adə/ *n.*[2] L16. [f. ADD + -ER[1].] A person who or thing which adds (*rare* in *gen.* sense); *spec.* in a computer, a unit which adds together two input variables.

addict /'adɪkt/ *n.* E20. [f. ADDICT *v.*] A person who is addicted to a drug (usu. specified by prefixed wd); *colloq.* an enthusiastic devotee of a sport or pastime (usu. specified by prefixed wd).

drug addict, *heroin addict*, *jazz addict*, etc.

†**addict** *ppl a.* E16. [L *addictus* pa. pple of *addicere*, f. *ad* AD- + *dicere* appoint, allot.] 1 Formally made over or bound *to*. Only in 16. 2 Attached by inclination *to*, devoted *to*. M16–L19.

¶Replaced by ADDICTED.

addict /ə'dɪkt/ *v.t.* M16. [Back-form. f. next.] †1 *refl.* Attach or devote oneself as a servant or adherent (*to* a person or cause). M16–L17. 2 Devote or apply habitually or compulsively (*to* a practice). L16. †3 Deliver over formally by judicial sentence *to*; *fig.* make over, give up. L16–L19.

2 SHAKES. *2 Hen. IV* To addict themselves to sack. SIR W. SCOTT The researches to which your taste addicts you.

addicting *a.* = ADDICTIVE M20.

addicted /ə'dɪktɪd/ *a.* M16. [f. ADDICT *ppl a.* + -ED[1], the vb being inferred later.] †1 Voluntarily attached *to* (a person or party). M16–E18. 2 Attached by inclination *to* (a practice); devoted *to*; doing or using something, esp. a drug, as a habit or compulsively. M16. †3 In *Rom. Law*, delivered over by judicial sentence *to*; *fig.* destined, bound *to*. M16–L19. †4 *absol.* Devoted (freq. in subscribing letters). L16–M17.

1 JAMES II Addicted to the Royal Interest. 2 L. A. G. STRONG The only form of music to which he was addicted. J. H. BURN Those who are addicted to cocaine often take it in the form of powder like snuff. 3 P. HOLLAND Addicted and destined to death. 4 MILTON The same addicted fidelity.

addictedness *n.* M17.

addiction /ə'dɪkʃ(ə)n/ *n.* L16. [L *addictio(n-)*, f. as ADDICT *ppl a.*; later senses f. ADDICT *v.*: see -ION.] 1 The way in which one is addicted; inclination; what one is addicted to. Now *rare*. L16. †2 *Rom. Law.* A formal giving over by sentence of court; hence, a dedication of a person to a master. E17–L19. 3 The state of being addicted *to* a habit or pursuit; *esp.* the state of dependence on a drug to the extent that it cannot be withdrawn without adverse effects. M17.

1 G. EWART A public whose addiction / is mainly romantic fiction.

addictive /əˈdɪktɪv/ *a.* M20. [f. ADDICT *v.* + -IVE.] Tending to cause addiction or dependence.

addio /adˈdiːo/ *int.* L18. [It., f. *a* to + *Dio* god: cf. ADIEU, ADIOS.] Goodbye. (Formerly in general use in the subscription of letters etc.).

Addisonian /adɪˈsəʊnɪən/ *a.*[1] L18. [f. *Addison* (see below) + -IAN.] Pertaining to or characteristic of the English essayist, poet, and dramatist Joseph Addison (1672–1719) or his works.

Addisonian /adɪˈsəʊnɪən/ *a.*[2] E20. [f. as next + -IAN.] *Med.* 1 *Addisonian anaemia*, pernicious anaemia. E20. 2 Suffering from or pertaining to Addison's disease. M20.

Addison's disease /ˈadɪs(ə)nz dɪˌziːz/ *n. phr.* M19. [Thomas *Addison* (1793–1860), Eng. physician.] *Med.* A condition associated with a deficiency of adrenal corticosteroids, which is characterized by weakness, low blood pressure, and brown pigmentation of the skin.

additament /ˈadɪtəm(ə)nt/ *n.* LME. [OFr. *additement* or L *additamentum*, f. as next: see -MENT.] A thing added or appended.

addition /əˈdɪʃ(ə)n/ *n.* LME. [(O)Fr., or L *additio(n-)*, f. *addit-* pa. ppl stem of *addere* ADD: see -ION.] 1 The action or process of adding. LME. b *Chem.* The combination of one molecule with another to form a larger molecule with no other products. L19. 2 A thing added; an appendix, an accession. LME. b *spec.* A phrase, prefix, etc., added to a person's name to distinguish him or her by rank, place of origin, etc. L15.

1 W. S. MAUGHAM A few sums in simple addition. **in addition** as an added thing (*to*), as well. **note** (or **point**) **of addition** *Mus.* (now *Hist.*) a dot on the right of a note signifying that it is to be lengthened by half (a second dot increasing its value by a further fourth; cf. DOT *n.*[1] 4b, *double dot* s.v. DOUBLE *a.* & *adv.*). 2 E. O'NEILL Expecting an addition to the family.

Comb.: **addition reaction** *Chem.*: in which addition occurs.

additional /əˈdɪʃ(ə)n(ə)l/ *n.* & *a.* E17. [f. prec. + -AL[1].] A *n.* Something added; an extra. Now *rare.* E17. B *adj.* Existing in addition; added; supplementary. M17.

additionally *adv.* M17.

addititious /adɪˈtɪʃəs/ *a. rare.* M18. [Late L *additicius* (Tertullian), f. as ADDITION + -ITIOUS[1].] Due to, or of the nature of, an addition.

additive /ˈadɪtɪv/ *a.* & *n.* L17. [Late L *additivus*, f. as ADDITION + -IVE. Cf. Fr. *additif, -ive.*] A *adj.* 1 Characterized by addition; to be added. L17. 2 Of or pertaining to the reproduction of colours by the superimposition of primary colours. E20.

B *n.* Something that is added; *esp.* a substance added to another to give it specific qualities. M20.

additively *adv.* M19. **addiˈtivity** *n.* E20.

additory /ˈadɪt(ə)ri/ *a.* & *n.* Now *rare.* M17. [f. L *addit-* (see ADDITION) + -ORY[2].] (Something) tending to add.

addle /ˈad(ə)l/ *n.*, *a.*, & *v.*[1] [OE *adela* = MLG *adele*, MDu. *adel* (Du. *aal*), G *Adel* mire, puddle, OSw. *-adel* in *koadel* cow's urine. *addle egg* tr. med.L *ovum urinae* egg of urine, alt. of *ovum urinum* repr. Gk *ourion ōon* wind-egg.] A *n.* Stinking urine or liquid filth; mire. *obs.* exc. *dial.* (after OE in literary use only in the north). OE.

B *attrib.* or as *adj.* 1 Of an egg: rotten or putrid; producing no chicken. ME. 2 *fig.* Empty, idle, muddled, unsound. L15.

2 J. LYLY His addle head. DRYDEN His brains grow addle. *addle-brain(ed)*, *-head(ed)*, *-pate(d)*, etc.

C *v.* 1 *v.t.* Make addle; confuse; make abortive. L16. 2 *v.i.* Grow addle (*lit.* & *fig.*). E19.

1 H. FIELDING My muddy brain is addled like an egg.

addleness *n.* L16.

addle /ˈad(ə)l/ *v.*[2] *north.* ME. [ON *ǫðla*, refl. *ǫðlask*, f. *óðal* property: see UDAL.] 1 *v.t.* Acquire as one's own; earn. ME. 2 *v.i.* Of crops: yield. L16.

1 D. H. LAWRENCE Get thy money, Sam, tha's addled it.

†addoom *v.t. rare* (Spenser). Only in L16. [f. A-[11] + DOOM *v.*] Adjudge.

addorsed /əˈdɔːst/ *a.* L16. [f. L *ad* to + *dorsum* back + -ED[1]. Cf. Fr. *adossé.*] Orig. & chiefly *Her.* Turned back to back.

address /əˈdrɛs/ *n.* M16. [Partly f. next, partly f. (O)Fr. *adresse.*] I Direction. 1 The act of approaching or applying to anyone; *esp.* (and now only, in *pl.*) dutiful or courteous approach, courtship. M16. †2 The action of sending or dedicating something written. M17–E18. 3 A discourse delivered to an audience; a formal speech of congratulation, thanks, etc. M17. 4 Manner in conversation. *arch.* L17. 5 The superscription of a letter etc.; the name of the place to which anyone's letters etc. are directed; one's place of residence. E18. b *Computing.* A sequence of bits which identifies a particular location in a data processing system. M20. 6 The action of dispatching (esp. a ship, to a person or place). L19.

1 GOLDSMITH Farmer Williams . . had paid her his addresses. 3 A. WILSON The judge's address to the jury was . . different. *public address system*: see PUBLIC *a.* & *n.* 4 W. STEVENS A funny foreigner of meek address. 5 JOYCE The partially obliterated address and postmark. E. HEMINGWAY I got into the cab and gave the driver the address of Simmons. **form of address** a name, title, etc., used in addressing a person. b *direct address*: see DIRECT *a.* *relative address*: see RELATIVE *a.* & *n.* *symbolic address*: see SYMBOLIC *a.*

II Preparation. †7 Attire, dress. L16–M17. 8 General preparedness; skill, dexterity. L16. †9 The action of making ready; preparation. M17–L18.

8 P. G. WODEHOUSE He saved me with the most consummate address from a large shaggy dog. 9 MILTON She makes address to speak.

Addressograph *n.* (proprietary name for) a machine for printing addresses E20.

address /əˈdrɛs/ *v.* ME. [(O)Fr. *adresser*, ult. f. as AD- + DIRECT *a.*] I Make straight or right. †1 *v.t.* Erect, raise, set up. ME–E17. †2 *v.t.* Put straight or to rights; set in order. LME–L17. †3 *v.t.* & *i.* Prepare, make ready. (Cf. branch III below.) LME–M19. 4 *esp.* †a *v.t.* Apparel or attire for a special purpose; (later simply) clothe. LME–L17. b *v.t.* Put on (a garment). *arch.* E16.

2 P. HOLLAND Forced for to addresse themselues, and range a nauall battell in order. MILTON A Parlament being call'd, to addres many things. 3 ELIZ. I: We will that you shall . . address several Schedules. SHAKES. *Tr. & Cr.* Let us address to tend on Hector's heels. H. L'ESTRANGE He . . did addresse himself for the stroke of death. 4 J. JEWEL Tecla sometime addressed her selfe in Mans apparell. b BROWNING I have addressed a frock of heavy mail.

II Direct. 5 *v.t.* Guide, direct; aim. *obs.* exc. *Golf*, take aim at (the ball). ME. 6 *v.t.* †a *refl.* Betake oneself. LME–L17. b Direct to go (*to*); introduce; send, dispatch. *obs.* exc. w. a ship as obj. L15. 7 *v.t.* Send as a written message *to* (a person); inscribe. Also, write directions for delivery on (an envelope etc.). LME. b *Computing.* Specify a location in (memory) or location of (data) by means of an address, with a view to transferring data or executing an operation. M20. 8a *v.t.* Direct spoken words (*to* a person; w. the words or oneself as obj.). L15. †b *v.i.* Speak directly, present a formal address, pay addresses, *to.* E17–M18. c *v.t.* Speak directly to; deliver a speech to; present a formal address to; pay addresses to. E18. 9 *v.t.* Use a particular (specified) form of words in speaking or writing to. L18.

5 TENNYSON Bent their . . faces toward us and address'd Their motion. 6 EVELYN I addressed him to Lord Mordaunt. 7 G. GREENE All the notes she had once addressed to me. E. BOWEN Recollecting, as she addressed the envelope, that she had no stamp. 8a SCOTT FITZGERALD To address cordial remarks to the passers-by. G. B. SHAW You should address yourself to His Majesty. b SHAKES. *Lear* My Lord of Burgundy, We first address toward you. c POPE And, calling Venus, thus address'd his child. E. O'NEILL You'd think you were going to address an audience of literary critics. 9 J. MASTERS Subalterns address field officers as 'Sir'. W. TREVOR He wished the boy would address him by his correct name.

III f. sense 3, infl. by sense 6. †10 *v.t.* Apply or turn to some object or purpose. LME–L16. 11a *v.refl.* Apply oneself, direct one's skill or energies, *to.* LME. †b *v.i.* Turn one's attention *to.* M17–M18. c *v.t.* Turn one's attention to (a topic etc.); approach, face, (a problem). E19.

11a M. H. ABRAMS Johnson addresses himself to a general examination of Shakespeare's dramas. b MILTON Which I shall forthwith addresse to prove. c *Guardian Weekly* The agreement . . does not address every aspect of every subproblem.

addressable *a.* (*Computing*) pertaining to or designating a memory unit in which all locations can be separately accessed M20. **addressee** *n.* a person to whom something (esp. a letter) is addressed E19. **addresser** *n.* L17. **addressing** *n.* (*a*) the action of the vb; (*b*) *Computing* the method of or system for identifying, referring to, or allocating locations in one or more computers: E16. **addressor** *n.* a person who signs a formal address or addresses a formal document M17.

addressed /əˈdrɛst/ *ppl a.* Also (*arch.*) **addrest**. LME. [f. prec. + -ED[1].] †1 Prepared. LME–M17. 2 Attired, dressed. *arch.* LME. †3 Well ordered; accomplished. L15–L16. 4 Erect, raised. *arch. rare.* L16. 5 Directed, dispatched. L16. 6 Superscribed with directions for delivery. L19.

3 SPENSER Full jolly knight he seemde, and wel addrest. 4 T. S. ELIOT Sweeney addressed full-length to shave. 5 SOUTHEY The shaft, unerringly addrest.

adduce /əˈdjuːs/ *v.t.* LME. [L *adducere*, f. *ad* AD- + *ducere* lead, bring.] Bring forward for consideration; cite as a proof or instance.

adducer *n.* E19. **adducible** *a.* L18.

adducent /əˈdjuːs(ə)nt/ *a.* L17. [L *adducent-* pres. ppl stem of *adducere*: see prec., -ENT.] *Anat.* Concerned with adduction (sense 2).

adduct /ˈadʌkt/ *n.* M20. [G *Addukt* f. as ADD(ITION + PRO)DUCT *n.*] *Chem.* A product of an addition reaction.

adduct /əˈdʌkt/ *v.t.* M19. [Back-form. f. next.] *Anat.* Bring about adduction (sense 2) of (a limb etc.).

adduction /əˈdʌkʃ(ə)n/ *n.* LME. [Fr., or late L *adductio(n-)*, f. *adduct-* pa. ppl stem of *adducere*: see ADDUCE, -ION.] 1 The action of bringing a thing to something else; *spec.* an alleged bringing of Christ's body and blood into the Eucharistic elements. LME. 2 *Anat.* Movement of a limb etc. towards the median line. Opp. ABDUCTION 2. M17. 3 The action of adducing. M18.

adductive /əˈdʌktɪv/ *a.* Now *rare.* M17. [f. L *adduct-* (see prec.) + -IVE.] Bringing to something else, *spec.* Christ's body and blood into the elements (see ADDUCTION 1).

adductor /əˈdʌktə/ *n.* E17. [mod.L, f. as prec.: see -OR.] *Anat.* A muscle which brings about adduction towards the median line; *spec.* one which closes the shell of a bivalve mollusc. Also *adductor muscle.*

†adduice *v.t.* L15–E18. [OFr. *ad(d)oulcir* (mod. *adoucir*) f. late L *addulcire*, f. *ad* AD- + *dulcis* sweet.] Sweeten, make palatable; soothe, mollify, (a person).

-ade /eɪd/ *suff.* Forming ns. 1 Repr. Fr. *-ade* f. Prov., Sp., Port. *-ada*, It. *-ata*, meaning (i) an action done, as *crusade, parade*; (ii) the body concerned, as *brigade, comrade*; (iii) the product of an action or process, as *arcade, marmalade.* b In or after new Fr. formations, as *cannonade, harlequinade, lemonade.* 2 Repr. Fr. *-ade* f. Gk *-ad-a* (nom. *-as*), as in *decade.* 3 Repr. Sp., Port. *-ado*, It. *-ato*, masc. of 1, as in *brocade, renegade.*

¶In limited use in Eng. as a living suff. (examples are *blockade, gingerade*).

adeem /əˈdiːm/ *v.t.* M19. [f. ADEMPTION, after *redeem, redemption.*] Take away; *spec.* in *Law*, revoke (a grant or bequest) by prior disposal.

Adelantado /ˌadelanˈtaðo, ˌadəlanˈtɑːdəʊ/ *n.* Also *a-*. Pl. **-os** /-ɒs, -əʊz/. L16. [Sp.] Chiefly *Hist.* A Spanish grandee; a lord-lieutenant or governor of a Spanish province or colony.

ademption /əˈdɛm(p)ʃ(ə)n/ *n.* L16. [L *ademptio(n-)*, f. *adimere*, f. *ad* AD- + *emere* take: see -ION.] The action of taking away; *spec.* in *Law*, revocation of a grant or bequest by prior disposal.

adenine /ˈadɪniːn/ *n.* L19. [f. Gk *adēn* gland + -INE[5].] *Biochem.* A derivative of purine which is one of the bases of nucleic acids, paired with thymine in double-stranded DNA; 6-aminopurine, $C_5H_5N_5$.

adenitis /adɪˈnʌɪtɪs/ *n.* M19. [f. Gk *adēn* gland + -ITIS.] *Med.* Inflammation of glands, *spec.* of lymph nodes.

adeno- /ˈadɪnəʊ/ *comb. form* of Gk *adēn* gland: see -O-. Bef. a vowel **aden-**.

adenocarciˈnoma *n.*, pl. **-mas**, **-mata** /-mətə/, *Med.* a malignant epithelial tumour of glandular form L19. **adenohyˈpophysis** *n.*, pl. **-physes** /-fɪsiːz/, *Anat.* the anterior lobe of the hypophysis (pituitary gland) M20. **adeˈnoma** *n.*, pl. **-mas**, **-mata** /-mətə/, *Med.* a benign epithelial tumour of glandular form L19. **adeˈnomatous** *a.* pertaining to or resembling an adenoma L19. **adenoˈvirus** *n.* (*Med.*) any of a class of viruses (the first examples of which were discovered in adenoid tissue), most of which cause respiratory diseases M20.

adenoid /ˈadɪnɔɪd/ *a.* & *n.* M19. [f. Gk *adēn* gland + -OID.] A *adj. Med.* Glandular; like a gland. M19. B *n. sing.* (*rare*) & in *pl.* A collection of lymphoid tissue in the wall of the nasopharynx, usu. becoming less prominent in early adult life; *colloq.* an enlarged condition of this tissue, hindering speech and breathing. L19.

adeˈnoidal *a.* (*a*) *rare* = ADENOID *a.*; (*b*) suffering from enlarged adenoids; characteristic or suggestive of this condition: L19. **adenoiˈdectomy** *n.* (an instance of) surgical removal of the adenoids E20. **adenoidy** *a.* (*colloq.*) = ADENOIDAL (b) E20.

adenosine /əˈdɛnəʊsiːn/ *n.* E20. [Blend of ADENINE and RIBOSE.] *Biochem.* A nucleoside (adenine riboside), found in living tissue in the form of nucleotides (see below).

Comb.: **adenosine di-**, **mono-**, **triphosphate**: nucleotides involved in many physiological processes, the breakdown of the triphosphate to the diphosphate providing energy, e.g. for muscular contraction (see also next).

adenylic /adɪˈnɪlɪk/ *a.* L19. [f. ADEN(INE + -YL + -IC.] Biochem. *adenylic acid*, a nucleotide composed of a phosphoric acid ester of adenosine, present in most DNA and RNA.

adeps /ˈadɛps/ *n.* LME. [L.] Animal fat; lard.

adept /ˈadɛpt; *as adj. also* əˈdɛpt/ *a.* & *n.* M17. [L *adeptus* pa. pple of *adipisci* attain, acquire.] A *adj.* Thoroughly proficient (*at*, *in*). M17. B *n.* (Orig. in L form **†adeptus**, pl. **-ti**.) A person who is proficient in or at anything. M17.

†adeption *n.* obtaining M16–M17. **adeptly** *adv.* M20. **aˈdeptness** *n.* M19. **adeptship** *n.* (*rare*) thorough proficiency; the state or condition of an adept: E19.

adequacy /ˈadɪkwəsi/ *n.* E19. [f. next: see -ACY. Cf. earlier INADEQUACY.] The state or quality of being adequate.

adequate /ˈadɪkwət/ *a.* E17. [L *adaequatus* pa. pple, f. as next: see -ATE[2].] (Foll. by *to*, †*with*.) †1 Equal in magnitude or extent. E17–M18. 2 Commensurate in fitness; sufficient, satisfactory. E17. b Barely sufficient. E20. 3 *Logic.* Of an idea or concept: fully and clearly representing its object. L17.

adequately *adv.* E17. **adequateness** *n.* M17. **adequative** *a.* adequate, equivalent E19.

adequate /ˈadɪkweɪt/ *v.t.* L16. [L *adaequat-* pa. ppl stem of *adaequare*, f. *ad* AD- + *aequus* equal: see -ATE[3].] Make or be equal or equivalent (*to*).

JOYCE Let them continue as is meet To adequate the balance-sheet. T. EAGLETON No text literally . . adequates its signifiers to some signified distinct from them.

adequation /adɪˈkweɪʃ(ə)n, -ʒ(ə)n/ *n.* L16. [L *adaequatio(n-)*, f. as prec.: see -ATION.] †1 The action of equalling. Only in L16. 2 The result of making equal or adequate; an equivalent. E17. 3 The action of equalizing or making equivalent; the fact of being equalized or made equivalent. E17. 4 *Ling.* A change in meaning due to the influence of typical contexts. M20.

adespota /əˈdɛspətə/ *n.pl.* L19. [Gk, neut. pl. of *adespotos* adj., f. *a-* A-[10] + *despotēs* master.] *Bibliogr.* Literary works not attributed to, or not claimed by, an author.

Adessenarian /ədɛsɪˈnɛːrɪən/ *n.* M18. [f. mod.L *adessenarii*, f. L *adesse* be present: see next, -ARIAN.] *Eccl. Hist.* A person who believed in the real presence of Christ's body in the Eucharist, but not by transubstantiation.

adessive /əˈdɛsɪv/ *a.* & *n.* M19. [f. L *adesse* be present, f. *ad* AD- + *esse* be + -IVE.] *Gram.* A *adj.* Designating, being in, or pertaining to a case in Finnish and other languages expressing position in or presence at a place. M19. B *n. The* adessive case; a word, form, etc., in the adessive case. M19.

ad eundem /ad ɪˈʌndəm/ *adv. phr.* E18. [L = to the same (degree).] (Admitted) to the same degree or rank at another university or institution.

à deux /a dø/ *adv.* & *a. phr.* L19. [Fr.] Of, for, or between, two.

adhere /ədˈhɪə/ *v.i.* L15. [(O)Fr. *adhérer* or L *adhaerere*, f. *ad* AD- + *haerere* to stick.] 1 Attach oneself *to* a person or party; be a follower. L15. 2 Stick fast (*to* a substance or object). E16. 3 Give support to, or continue to maintain or observe, an opinion, practice, rule, etc. Foll. by *to*. M16. †4 Be consistent with itself or circumstances. L16–E17.

1 LD MACAULAY These people . . adhered to the Church of Rome. 2 T. REID The parts of a body adhere so firmly. A. WILSON The ends of her fat, sticky fingers to which the chocolate had adhered. *fig.*: GIBBON Flattery adheres to power. 3 W. S. MAUGHAM He had adhered scrupulously to the terms of the capitulation. 4 SHAKES. *Macb.* Nor time nor place Did then adhere.

adherer *n.* (now *rare*) M16.

adherence /ədˈhɪər(ə)ns/ *n.* LME. [(O)Fr. *adhérence* f. late L *adhaerentia*, f. as prec.; later f. prec.: see -ENCE.] 1 The action of adhering (*to*). LME. 2 An instance of adhering; something adherent. (*rare* after 17.) M16.

adherency /ədˈhɪər(ə)nsi/ *n. arch.* L16. [f. ADHERE + -ENCY. Cf. prec.] 1 The quality or state of being adherent. L16. †2 An adhering party; a following. L16–M17. †3 Something adherent. Only in 17.

adherend /ədˈhɪərənd/ *n.* M20. [f. ADHERE + -END.] An object bonded to another by an adhesive, or to which an adhesive adheres.

adherent /ədˈhɪər(ə)nt/ *a.* & *n.* LME. [(O)Fr. *adhérent* f. L *adhaerent-* pres. ppl stem of *adhaerere* ADHERE: see -ENT.] A *adj.* †1 Attached in sympathy or as a follower (*to*). LME–E17. 2 Attached materially (*to*); sticking; adhering *to* (an opinion, a rule, etc.). M16. 3 Attached as an attribute or circumstance. L16.

1 W. FULBECKE To be adherent to the King's enemies. 2 A. BURGESS A perceptible shaking in the adherent custard.

B *n.* 1 A supporter or follower (*of*). LME. †2 Something which adheres. E–M17.

1 W. S. CHURCHILL He was tried and hanged with four of his adherents. 2 MILTON Not a true limb . . but an adherent.

adherently *adv.* (*rare*) E17.

adhesion /ədˈhiːʒ(ə)n/ *n.* L15. [Fr. *adhésion* or L *adhaesio(n-)*, f. *adhaes-* pa. ppl stem of *adhaerere* ADHERE: see -ION.] 1 The action of adhering to a person, party, tenet, etc. L15. 2 The action of sticking (together or *to* something); an instance of this; *spec.* in *Physics*, the sticking together of unlike materials (cf. COHESION). M17. b The frictional grip of a wheel on a rail, road surface, etc. M19. 3 *Med.* The union of normally separate parts due to inflammation or injury; a mass of tissue joining normally separate parts; *rare* benign union of tissue as in healing. M17.

adhesive /ədˈhiːsɪv, -zɪv/ *a.* & *n.* L17. [f. as prec. + -IVE.] A *adj.* 1 Apt or tending to adhere (*fig.*), cling to, or persevere in. L17. 2 Having the property of adhering (*lit.*); sticky; prepared so as to adhere. L18.

2 **adhesive tape** opaque or transparent paper, plastic, etc., coated with an adhesive and used for fastening, sticking, masking, or insulating.

B *n.* Something which adheres; an adhesive substance. L19.

adhesively *adv.* M19. **adhesiveness** *n.* M18.

adhibit /ədˈhɪbɪt/ *v.t.* E16. [L *adhibit-* pa. ppl stem of *adhibere*, f. *ad* AD- + *habere* have, hold.] 1 Take in, let in, admit. E16. 2 Put to, put upon, affix. M16. 3 Apply, employ, esp. as a remedy. L16.

adhibition /adhɪˈbɪʃ(ə)n/ *n.* the action of adhibiting M17.

ad hoc /ad ˈhɒk/ *adv.* & *a. phr.* M17. [L, lit. 'to this'.] For this particular purpose; special(ly).

adhoc(k)ery *n.* (*colloq.*) (an) improvisation M20. **adhocism** *n.* the policy of improvisation, adhocery M20.

ad hominem /ad ˈhɒmɪnɛm/ *adv.* & *a. phr.* L16. [L = to the person.] Of an argument etc.: directed to the individual, personal; appealing to feeling not reason.

adhort /ədˈhɔːt/ *v.t.* Now *rare* or *obs.* L15. [L *adhortari*, f. *ad* AD- + *hortari* incite.] Urge, exhort.

ˌadhorˈtation *n.* exhortation M16.

adhortative /adˈhɔːtətɪv/ *a.* M19. [f. as prec.: see -ATIVE.] *Gram.* Of a verbal mood: expressing exhortation.

adiabatic /ˌeɪdʌɪəˈbatɪk, ˌadɪə-/ *a.* & *n.* L19. [f. Gk *adiabatos* impassable, f. *a-* A-[10] + *dia* through + *batos* passable: see -IC.] *Physics.* A *adj.* Involving or allowing neither gain nor loss of heat; pertaining to such conditions; (of a curve, line, etc.) obtained by plotting the relative changes in pressure and volume of a gas during a process of this kind. L19. B *n.* An adiabatic curve; the relationship expressed by an adiabatic curve. L19.

adiabat /eɪˈdʌɪəbat/ *n.* = ADIABATIC *n.* M20. **adiabatically** *adv.* with neither gain nor loss of heat L19.

adiaphanous /adɪˈaf(ə)nəs/ *a.* M17. [f. A-[10] + DIAPHANOUS.] Not translucent; opaque.

adiaphora *n.* pl. of ADIAPHORON *n.*

adiaphorist /adɪˈaf(ə)rɪst/ *n.* M16. [mod.L *adiaphorista*, f. Gk *adiaphoros*: see ADIAPHOROUS, -IST.] 1 *Eccl. Hist.* A moderate Lutheran who held some things, condemned by Luther, to be unimportant. M16. 2 A person who is uninterested in points of theological discussion. E17.

adiaphorism *n.* theological unconcern E17.

adiaphoron /adɪˈaf(ə)rən/ *n.* & *a. arch.* Pl. of n. **-ra** /-rə/. L16. [Gk, neut. of *adiaphoros*: see next.] *Chr. Ch.* (A thing) inessential in the eyes of the Church.

adiaphorous /adɪˈaf(ə)rəs/ *a.* E17. [Gk *adiaphoros*, f. *a-* A-[10] + *diaphoros* differing: see -OUS.] Making no difference; non-essential; neutral.

ad idem /ad ˈɪdɛm/ *adv. phr.* L16. [L = to the same thing.] On the same point, in agreement.

adieu /əˈdjuː/ *int.* & *n.* LME. [AN *adeu*, (O)Fr. *adieu*, f. *à* to + *Dieu* god: cf. ADDIO, ADIOS.] A *int.* Goodbye. *arch.* LME. B *n.* Pl. **adieus**, **adieux** /əˈdjuːz/. A leave-taking; a parting word; a farewell. LME.

Adi Granth *n. phr.* see GRANTH.

ad infinitum /ad ɪnfɪˈnʌɪtəm/ *adv.* & *a. phr.* E17. [L, lit. 'to infinity'.] Without limit, for ever.

ad interim /ad ˈɪntərɪm/ *adv.* & *a. phr.* L18. [L, *ad* to + *interim* adv. 'meanwhile' used as n.] For the meantime.

adios /adɪˈəʊs, adɪˈɒs/ *int.* M19. [Sp. *adiós*, f. *a* to + *Dios* god: cf. ADIEU, ADDIO.] Goodbye.

adipic /əˈdɪpɪk/ *a.* M19. [f. L *adip-*, ADEPS (from the acid having first been prepared by oxidizing fats) + -IC.] Chem. *adipic acid*, a crystalline acid, $HOOC(CH_2)_4COOH$, used in the manufacture of nylon.

adipocere /adɪpə(ʊ)ˈsɪə/ *n.* E19. [Fr. *adipocire*, f. as prec. + Fr. *cire* wax.] A greyish-white fatty substance generated in dead bodies subjected to moisture.

adipocyte /ˈadɪpəsʌɪt/ *n.* M20. [f. as next + -o- + -CYTE.] *Physiol.* A cell specialized for the storage of fat, found in connective tissue.

adipose /ˈadɪpəʊs, -z/ *a.* & *n.* M18. [mod.L *adiposus*, f. as ADIPIC + -OSE¹.] A *adj.* Of or pertaining to animal fat. Of tissue: concerned with the storage of fat. M18.

adipose fin a small, rayless, fleshy, dorsal fin present in certain fishes, notably in the salmon family.

B *n.* Adipose tissue. M19.

adiˈposity *n.* fatness, obesity M19. **adipous** *a.* = ADIPOSE *a.* in less techn. contexts M17.

adit /ˈadɪt/ *n.* E17. [L *aditus* approach, entrance, f. *adit-* pa. ppl stem of *adire*, f. *ad* AD- + *ire* go.] 1 A horizontal passage leading into a mine, for the purpose of entrance or drainage. E17. 2 Entrance, access. *rare.* M19.

adivasi /ɑːdɪˈvɑːsi/ *n.* Also A-. M20. [mod.Skt (nom.) *ādivāsī*, f. *ādi* the beginning + *vāsin* inhabitant.] A member of any of the aboriginal tribes of India.

adj. /adʒ/ *n.*¹ M17. [Abbrev.] *Gram.* An adjective.

Adj. /adʒ/ *n.*² *colloq.* M20. [Abbrev.] = ADJUTANT *n.* 2.

adjacency /əˈdʒeɪs(ə)nsi/ *n.* M17. [L *adjacentia* neut. pl. (in sense 2), f. as next; in mod. use f. next: see -ENCY.] 1 A thing which lies near; in *pl.*, adjacent places, environs. M17. 2 The fact, quality, or state of being adjacent. M18.

adjacence *n.* = ADJACENCY 2 E17.

adjacent /əˈdʒeɪs(ə)nt/ *a.* & *n.* LME. [L *adjacent-* pres. ppl stem of *adjacere*, f. *ad* AD- + *jacere* lie down: see -ENT.] A *adj.* Lying near (*to*), adjoining, contiguous (*to*). LME.

adjacent angles *Geom.* the two angles defined on the same side of a line when it is intersected by another line.

†B *n.* = ADJACENCY 1. M16–M19.

†adject *ppl a.* & *n.* LME. [L *adjectus* pa. pple of *ad(j)icere*, f. *ad* AD- + *jacere* lay, throw.] A *ppl a.* Annexed, joined. LME–E17. B *n.* An addition; an adjunct. L17–E18.

adject /əˈdʒɛkt/ *v.t.* LME. [L *adjectare* frequent. of *ad(j)icere*: see prec.] Add, join, annex.

adjection /əˈdʒɛkʃ(ə)n/ *n.* ME. [L *adjectio(n-)*, f. *adject-*: see ADJECT *ppl a.* & *n.*, -ION.] †1 A thing which is added; an addition. ME–L18. 2 The action of adding or joining. LME.

ˌ**adjecˈtitious** *a.* additional M17.

adjectival /adʒɛkˈtʌɪv(ə)l/ *a.* & *n.* L18. [f. next + -AL¹.] A *adj.* 1 *Gram.* Forming an adjunct to a noun; dependent on a noun and as an attribute; of the nature or quality of an adjective. L18. 2 Of style etc.: characterized by many adjectives. E20. 3 *euphem.* Bloody, damned, etc. *colloq.* E20.

3 D. L. SAYERS An adjectival . . watering-place like Wilvercombe.

B *n. Gram.* = ADJECTIVE *n.* 1. Also, a phrase, clause, etc., with an adjectival function. L19.

adjectivally *adv.* M19.

adjective /ˈadʒɪktɪv/ *a.*, *n.*, & *v.* LME. [(O)Fr. *adjectif*, *-ive* f. late L *adjectivus*, *-iva*, f. *adject-*: see ADJECT *ppl a.* & *n.*, -IVE. First in *noun adjective* rendering late L *nomen adjectivum* (Priscian) tr. Gk *onoma epitheton*.] A *adj.* 1 *Gram.* = ADJECTIVAL *a.* 1. Now *rare.* LME. 2 *gen.* Dependent; attached. E17. 3 Of law: relating to enforcement or procedure, as opp. to rights and duties. Cf. SUBSTANTIVE *a.* 3a. L18. 4 = ADJECTIVAL *a.* 3. *colloq.* M19.

1 **noun adjective** = sense B.1. 2 G. GROTE The women were treated . . as adjective beings. W. H. AUDEN Pastors adjective / to rustic flocks. **adjective dye**: needing a mordant to fix it. 4 DICKENS I won't . . have no adjective police . . in my adjective premises.

B *n.* 1 *Gram.* A word designating an attribute and added to a noun, to describe the thing etc. more fully. (One of the parts of speech.) LME. 2 *gen.* A dependent; an accessory. E17.

2 T. FULLER Subjects should be adjectives, not able to stand without their prince.

C *v.t.* Make adjectival; provide with an adjective. M17.

adjectively *adv.* in an adjectival manner M16. **adjectivize** *v.t.* make into an adjective E20.

adjoin /əˈdʒɔɪn/ *v.* ME. [OFr. *ajoi(g)n-* stem of *ajoindre* (mod. *adj-*) f. L *adjungere*: see ADJUNCT.] 1 *v.t.* Join, unite (*to* or *unto*). *arch.* ME. †b *v.i.* Come into union or contact. LME–L17. 2 *v.i.* a Lie close, be contiguous *to*, *with*. *obs.* exc. absol. as *adjoining* ppl a. ME. b Lie close to each other. L19. 3 *v.t.* Lie close or be contiguous to. ME.

1 SHAKES. *Haml.* A massy wheel, . . To whose huge spokes ten thousand lesser things Are mortis'd and adjoin'd. 2a POPE Close to the bay great Neptune's fane adjoins. W. FAULKNER He came from the adjoining county. b N. SHUTE Two adjoining cabins with a communicating door.

adjoint /ˈadʒɔɪnt/; *in sense A.2 also foreign* adʒwɛ̃, *pl. same*/ *n.* & *a.* L16. [Fr., pa. pple of *adjoindre*: see prec., ADJUNCT.] A *adj.* †1 A helper; an adjunct. L16–E18. 2 A French civil officer who assists the mayor. Also, an assistant professor in a French college. M19. 3 *Math.* An adjoint matrix, function, etc. L19. B *adj. Math.* Of a function, quantity, etc.: related to a given function, quantity, etc., by a particular process of transposition; *gen.* designating or pertaining to such a relationship; *spec.* (of a matrix) being the transpose of the cofactors of a given square matrix. L19.

¶In sense A.2 often italicized.

adjourn /əˈdʒəːn/ *v.* ME. [OFr. *ajorner* (mod. *ajourn-*), f. phr. *à jorn (nomé)* to a day (appointed).] †1 *v.t.* Appoint (a person) a day to appear; cite or summon for a particular day. ME–M17. 2 *v.t.* Defer, put off. LME. 3 *v.t.* Break off (a meeting etc.) for later resumption. L15. 4 *v.i.* Of people met together: suspend proceedings and disperse; transfer a meeting to another place. L15.

2 R. W. EMERSON I adjourn what I have to say on this topic. 3 T. STOPPARD Meeting adjourned for ten minutes. 4 D. LODGE They adjourned to a nearby pub to continue the conversation.

adjournal *n.* (*obs.* exc. *Sc. Law*) adjournment L15.

adjournment /əˈdʒəːnm(ə)nt/ *n.* LME. [OFr. *ajornement*, f. *ajorner*: see prec., -MENT.] The act of adjourning; the state of being adjourned.

Comb.: **adjournment debate**: on the motion that the House of Commons adjourn (often used as an opportunity to raise various matters).

adjudge /əˈdʒʌdʒ/ *v.t.* LME. [OFr. *ajuger* (mod. *adj-*) f. L *adjudicare*: see next.] 1 Settle or decide (a matter) judicially. LME. 2 Pronounce or decree by judicial sentence (something *to be*, *that* something is). LME. 3 Determine in one's own judgement, consider. LME. 4 Condemn (*to* a penalty, *to do*). *arch.* LME. 5 Award, grant, or impose judicially (something *to* a person). L15. †6 Try judicially; pass sentence on. E16–M17.

adjudg(e)ment *n.* the act of adjudging; a decree, an award: M16. **adjudger** *n.* †(*a*) a person to whom something is adjudged; (*b*) a person who awards judicially: E18.

adjudicate /əˈdʒuːdɪkeɪt/ *v.* E18. [L *adjudicat-* pa. ppl stem of *adjudicare*, f. *ad* AD- + *judic-*, *judex* a judge: see -ATE³.] †1 *v.t.* Award judicially (*Sc. Law* esp. a debtor's estate). E18–E19. 2 *v.t.* Try and determine judicially (a claim etc.); pronounce (a person *to be*). L18. 3 *v.i.* Act as a judge in a court, a tribunal, a competition, etc. M19.

adjudicative *a.* having the character of adjudicating M19. **adjudicator** *n.* a person who settles a question or awards a prize M19. **adjudicature** *n.* the process of adjudicating M19.

adjudication /ədʒuːdɪˈkeɪʃ(ə)n/ *n.* E17. [Fr., or late L *adjudicatio(n-)*, f. as prec.: see -ATION.] 1 *Sc. Law.* An award of a heritable estate as security or to fulfil an obligation. E17. 2 The act of adjudicating; an awarding or settling by judicial decree. M17. 3 A judicial sentence or award. L18. 4 *Law.* More fully *adjudication order*. An order declaring bankruptcy. M19.

†adjument *n.* L16–E18. [L *adjumentum* contr. of *adjuvamentum*, f. *adjuvare*: see ADJUVANT, -MENT.] Help; a helper.

adjunct /ˈadʒʌŋkt/ *a.* & *n.* E16. [L *adjunctus* pa. pple of *adjungere*, f. *ad* AD- + *jungere* join.] A *adj.* Joined, added; subordinate. E16. B *n.* 1 Something joined to something else and auxiliary to or dependent on it, something subordinate or incidental (*to*, *of*). L16. 2 A qualifying addition to a word or name. L16. 3 *Gram.* A word or words amplifying or modifying the meaning of another word or words in a sentence. L16. 4 *Logic.* A non-essential attribute. L16. 5 A personal addition or enhancement. E17. 6 A person joined to another in some (esp. temporary) service or office. M17.

aˈdjunctive *n.* & *a.* †(*a*) *n.* = ADJUNCT *n.*; (*b*) *adj.* contributing *to*, forming an adjunct: L17. **aˈdjunctively** *adv.* as an adjunct E19.

adjunction /əˈdʒʌŋkʃ(ə)n/ *n.* L16. [L *adjunctio(n-)*, f. as prec.: see -ION.] The act of joining on or adding (*to*).

adjuration /adʒʊəˈreɪʃ(ə)n/ *n.* LME. [Fr., or L *adjuratio(n-)*, f. as next: see -ATION.] The action of adjuring; an earnest appeal, *spec.* in exorcism.

adjuratory /əˈdʒʊərət(ə)ri/ *a.* containing a solemn charge or appeal E19.

adjure /əˈdʒʊə/ *v.t.* LME. [L *adjurare*, f. *ad* AD- + *jurare* swear, f. *jur-*, *jus* oath.] †1 Put (a person) on oath; bind under penalty of a curse. LME–M17. 2 Charge or entreat solemnly or earnestly, as if under oath or under the penalty of a curse. Foll. by *to do* (†or *that*). LME.

1 AV *Josh.* 6:26 Ioshua adiured them . . , saying, Cursed be the man . . that [etc.]. 2 L. A. G. STRONG Adjuring each other to have fresh cups of tea.

adjust /əˈdʒʌst/ *v.* E17. [Fr. †*adjuster* (now *aj-*) refash., after *juste* JUST *a.*, of OFr. *ajoster* (mod. *ajouter* add), ult. f. L *ad* AD- + *juxta* close to.] 1 *v.t.* Arrange, compose, harmonize, (differences, discrepancies, accounts); assess (loss or damages). E17. †b *v.i.* Come to terms. M17–M18. 2 *v.t.* Arrange suitably in relation to something else or to some standard or purpose. (Foll. by *to*.) M17. b *v.i.* Adapt oneself (*to*); get used to changed circumstances etc. E20. 3 *v.t.* Arrange (something) suitably in relation to its parts; put in order; regulate. M17. b *v.i.* Admit of being so arranged. E20.

2 BURKE They have adjusted the means to that end. S. LEWIS The . . rug was adjusted so that his bare feet would strike it. J. S. HUXLEY The individual . . can adjust himself . . to the ethical standards of his society. b S. KING She needs time to adjust. 3 M. MCCARTHY As he . . adjusted the handkerchief in his pocket.

adjustaˈbility *n.* L19. **adjustable** *a.* L18. **adjuster** *n.* L17. **adjustive** *a.* concerned with adjustment L19.

adjustment /əˈdʒʌs(t)m(ə)nt/ *n.* M17. [OFr. *adjustement* (mod. *aj-*), f. as prec.: see -MENT.] 1 The process of adjusting. M17. 2 *Comm.* The settlement among various parties of claims, liabilities, or payments. M17. 3 The state of being adjusted; settlement. L17. 4 An arrangement whereby things are adjusted. M18.

Comb.: **adjustment centre** *US* a section of a prison reserved for the solitary confinement of refractory prisoners.

adjutage /ˈadʒʊtɪdʒ, əˈdʒuːt-/ *n.* Also **aj-**. E18. [Fr. *aj(o)utage*, f. *ajouter*: see ADJUST, -AGE.] A tube added to or inserted into an aperture to control the outflow of water, as a pipe at the mouth of an artificial fountain.

adjutant /ˈadʒʊt(ə)nt/ *n.* & *a.* E17. [L *adjutant-* pres. ppl stem of *adjutare* frequent. of *adjuvare*: see ADJUVANT, -ANT¹.] A *n.* 1 An assistant, a helper. Now *rare* in *gen.* sense. E17. 2 *Mil.* an officer who assists superior officers by communicating orders, conducting correspondence, etc. E17. 3 Either of two large black and white storks of the genus *Leptoptilos*, *L. dubius* (in full *greater adjutant*), and *L. javanicus* (in full *lesser adjutant*), native to India and SE Asia. Also *adjutant bird*, *stork*. L18.

2 **Adjutant-General**: a high-ranking Army administrative officer.

B *adj.* Helping. *rare.* L17.

adjutancy *n.* the rank or office of an adjutant M18.

adjutator /ˈadʒʊteɪtə/ *n.* M17. [Alt. of AGITATOR after *adjutant* etc.] *Eng. Hist.* = AGITATOR 1.

adjutor /ˈadʒʊtə/ *n.* Now *rare.* M16. [L *adjutor*, f. *adjut-* pa. ppl stem of *adjuvare*: see ADJUVANT, -OR.] = ADJUTANT *n.* 1.

adjuvant /ˈadʒʊv(ə)nt/ *a.* & *n.* L16. [Fr., or L *adjuvant-* pres. ppl stem of *adjuvare*, f. *ad* AD- + *juvare* help: see -ANT¹.] A *adj.* 1 Helpful, auxiliary. L16. 2 *Med.* Designating therapy applied after the initial treatment of cancer, esp.

to suppress secondary tumour formation. L20. B *n.* 1 A help; a helper. E17. 2 *Med.* Something given to augment the effect of a drug or other agent; now *esp.* a substance which enhances the body's immune response to an antigen. M19.

Adlerian /ad'lɪərɪən/ *a.* & *n.* M20. [f. *Adler* (see below) + -IAN.] Pertaining to, a disciple of, the Austrian psychologist Alfred Adler (1870–1937) or his school of analytic psychology, which was based on such concepts as the inferiority complex and the desire for power.

ad lib /ad 'lɪb/ *adv., a., v.,* & *n.* Also (esp. as attrib. adj. & vb) **ad-lib.** E19. [Abbrev. of next.] A *adv.* At one's pleasure; to any desired extent. E19. B *adj.* Extemporized; spontaneous. E20. C *v.t.* & *i.* Infl. **-bb-**. Speak extempore, improvise. E20. D *n.* An ad-lib remark, an extemporized speech; something improvised. M20.

ad libitum /ad 'lɪbɪtəm/ *adv.* & *a. phr.* E17. [L = according to pleasure.] = AD LIB *adv. phr., a.*

ad litem /ad 'lʌɪtɛm/ *adv.* & *a. phr.* M18. [L.] *Law.* Of a guardian, etc.: appointed to act, in a lawsuit, on behalf of a child or other incapable person.

†**adlocution** *n.* var. of ALLOCUTION.

admeasure /əd'mɛʒə/ *v.t.* ME. [OFr. *amesurer* f. med.L *admensurare*: see AD-, MEASURE *v.*] †1 Keep in measure; limit, control. ME–E17. †2 Apply a measure to; measure out. L15–L19. 3 Apportion; assign in due shares. M17.

admeasurement /əd'mɛʒəm(ə)nt/ *n.* Now *rare.* E16. [OFr. *amesurement*, f. as prec.: see -MENT.] 1 Ascertainment and apportionment of just shares. E16. 2 The process of applying a measure in order to ascertain dimensions. E17. 3 Size, dimensions. L18.

admensuration /ədmɛnsjʊ'reɪʃ(ə)n/ *n.* Now *rare.* L17. [Late L *admensuratio(n-)*, f. *admensurare*, f. *ad* AD- + *mensura* a measure: see -ATION.] = prec.

admin. /'admɪn/ *n. colloq.* M20. [Abbrev.] Administration.

adminicle /əd'mɪnɪk(ə)l/ *n.* M16. [L *adminiculum* prop, support, f. *ad* AD- + dim. *-culum* -CULE on an obscure base.] 1 Something that helps. M16. 2 *Sc. Law.* Supporting or corroboratory evidence; a writing tending to prove the existence and tenor of a lost deed. L16.

ˌadmiˈnicular *a.* helpful, corroboratory L17.

adminiculate /admɪ'nɪkjʊleɪt/ *v.t.* M16. [L *adminiculat-* pa. ppl stem of *adminiculare*, f. as prec.: see -ATE[3].] Help, support; *Sc. Law* support by corroboratory evidence.

administer /əd'mɪnɪstə/ *v.* LME. [OFr. *aministrer* f. L *administrare*: see AD-, MINISTER *v.* Orig. *am-*, refash. after Latinized (O)Fr. *administrer*.] I *v.t.* 1 Manage as a steward; carry on or execute (an office, affairs, etc.). LME. 2 *Law.* Manage and dispose of (the estate of a deceased person) under a will or by official appointment. LME. 3 Execute or dispense (justice). LME. 4 Furnish, supply, give, (orig. something beneficial, *to*). LME. 5 Execute or perform (offices of religion); dispense (a sacrament). L15. 6 Formerly, apply (a branch of medicine). Now, give (medicine, *to*). M16. 7 Offer (an oath) for swearing (*to* a person). L16.

1 W. HOLTBY Once the laws have been passed, we only can administer them. P. G. WODEHOUSE Your aunt . . decided to take over the family finances and administer them herself. 4 STEELE The Joy which this Temper of Soul administers. JOYCE Even a fellow on the broad of his back could administer a nasty kick.

II *v.i.* 8 Act as an administrator. E17. 9 Minister *to. arch.* E18.

administrable *a.* able to be administered E19. †**administrer** *n.* L15–L17.

administrant /əd'mɪnɪstr(ə)nt/ *a.* & *n. rare.* E17. [Fr., pres. pple of *administrer*: see prec., -ANT[1].] A *adj.* Managing affairs, executive. E17. B *n.* An acting officer. E17.

administrate /əd'mɪnɪstreɪt/ *v.t.* & *i.* M16. [L *administrat-* pa. ppl stem of *administrare*: see ADMINISTER, -ATE[3].] = ADMINISTER.

administration /ədmɪnɪ'streɪʃ(ə)n/ *n.* ME. [(O)Fr., or L *administratio(n-)*, f. as prec.: see -ATION.] 1 The action of administering something (a sacrament, justice, remedies, an oath, etc.) to another. ME. 2 The action of administering in any office; attendance; performance (*of*). *obs.* in *gen.* sense. LME. 3 Management (*of* any business). LME. 4 *Law.* The management and disposal of a deceased person's estate. LME. b The management of an insolvent company under a court order. L20. 5 *ellipt.* The management of public affairs; government. E16. 6 The executive part of the legislature; the ministry; the Government. E18. b A period of office of a President of the United States. L18.

4 **letters of administration** authority to administer the estate of an intestate (cf. *probate*). 5 *Parliamentary Commissioner for Administration*: see PARLIAMENTARY *a.*

administrative /əd'mɪnɪstrətɪv/ *a.* & *n.* M18. [Fr. *administratif, -ive* or L *administrativus*, f. as ADMINISTRATE: see -ATIVE.] A *adj.* Pertaining to management of affairs; executive. M18. B *n.* An administrative body; an administrator. *rare.* L19.

administratively *adv.* M19.

administrator /əd'mɪnɪstreɪtə/ *n.* LME. [L, f. as ADMINISTRATE + -OR. Cf. Fr. *administrateur.*] 1 A manager of business or public affairs; a person capable of organizing. LME. 2 *Law.* a A person appointed to administer an estate in default of an executor, or to manage an insolvent company. LME. b A person authorized to manage an estate for the legal owner during his or her minority, absence, etc.; *Sc. Law* (in full *administrator in law*) a person empowered to act for another, *spec.* for a child. M16. 3 A person who administers something (a sacrament, justice, etc.) to another; an applier or giver (*of*). M16.

administratorship *n.* L16. **administratress** *n.* (*rare*) a female administrator L18.

administratrix /ədmɪnɪ'streɪtrɪks/ *n.* Pl. **-trixes, -trices** /-trɪsiːz/. M16. [f. prec.: see -TRIX. Cf. Fr. *administratrice.*] A female administrator, *spec.* of an estate in default of an executor.

admirable /'adm(ə)rəb(ə)l/ *a.* & *adv.* LME. [(O)Fr. f. L *admirabilis*, f. *admirari*: see ADMIRE, -ABLE.] A *adj.* 1 To be wondered at. *obs.* exc. in *Admirable* CRICHTON. LME. 2 Causing pleased surprise, or wonder united with approbation; (by degrees losing the idea of wonder) excellent, to be warmly approved. L16.

1 MILTON Not only strange and admirable, but lamentable to think on.

†B *adv.* Admirably. E17–E18.

admirableness *n.* E17. **admirably** *adv.* L16.

admiral /'adm(ə)r(ə)l/ *n.* ME. [(O)Fr. *amiral*, †*admira(i)l* f. (through med.L) Arab. *amīr* commander (see AMIR, EMIR) + *-al* -AL[1]: assoc. w. prec.] †1 An emir or prince under the Sultan; a Saracen commander. ME–E16. 2 The commander-in-chief of a country's navy. LME. 3 A naval officer of high rank, *spec.* of the rank next below Admiral of the Fleet; the commander of a fleet or squadron. LME. 4 The ship which carries the admiral; the flagship. L16. 5 Any of various nymphalid butterflies, *spec.* a red or white admiral. E18.

2 **Lord High Admiral**: a title of the British monarch (formerly of an officer who governed the Royal Navy and had jurisdiction over maritime causes). 3 **Admiral of the Fleet,** (*US*) **Fleet Admiral**: the highest grade of such officers. *High Admiral*: see HIGH *a. rear admiral*: see REAR *a.*[1] VICE ADMIRAL. *yellow admiral*: see YELLOW *a.* 5 *red admiral*: see RED *a. white admiral*: see WHITE *a.*

admiraˈlissimo *n.* (*colloq.*) [after GENERALISSIMO] the supreme commander of (combined) naval forces E20. **admiralship** *n.* the position or rank of admiral; ability to perform the duties of an admiral: L16.

admiralty /'adm(ə)r(ə)lti/ *n.* LME. [OFr. *admiral(i)té* (mod. *amirauté*), f. as prec.: see -TY[1].] 1 The jurisdiction or office of an admiral. LME. †2 The department under command of the admiral. LME–E17. 3 The department administering the Navy. *obs.* exc. *Hist.* and in titles. LME. 4 The maritime branch of the administration of justice. LME. 5 *rhet.* Command of the seas. L19.

1 *Droit of Admiralty*: see DROIT *n.*[1] I. 3 **the Admiralty**: the building from which the British navy is administered. **the Board of Admiralty,** (since 1964) **the Admiralty Board**: appointed to administer the British navy. 5 R. KIPLING If blood be the price of admiralty Lord God, we ha' paid in full!

admiration /admə'reɪʃ(ə)n/ *n.* LME. [(O)Fr., or L *admiratio(n-)*, f. *admirat-* pa. ppl stem of *admirari*: see next, -ATION.] 1 The action of wondering or marvelling; wonder. *arch.* LME. 2 An object of admiration. L15. 3 Wonder mingled with reverence, esteem, approbation; pleased contemplation, warm approval. M16. †4 Admirableness. M16–M17. 5 An exclamation mark (= *note of admiration* below). *arch.* L16.

1 T. FULLER Admiration is the daughter of ignorance. **note of admiration** *arch.* an exclamation mark. 2 M. W. MONTAGU The young prince . . is the admiration of the whole court. 3 *mutual admiration society*: see MUTUAL *a.* **to admiration** in an admirable manner, excellently. 4 SHAKES. *Temp.* Admir'd Miranda! Indeed the top of admiration.

ˈ**admirative** *a.* characterized by admiration L15.

admire /əd'mʌɪə/ *v.* L15. [Isolated early use f. OFr. *amirer*; later (L16) f. Fr. *admirer* or L *admirari*, f. *ad* AD- + *mirari* to wonder.] 1 *v.t.* Regard with pleased surprise, respect, or approval. L15. b Express admiration of. M19. 2 *v.i.* Feel or express surprise or astonishment. *arch.* L16. 3 *v.t.* View with wonder or surprise; marvel at. *arch.* L16. 4 *v.t.* Astonish, surprise. *rare.* M17.

1 DAY LEWIS I always admired Auden for . . his certainties. J. HELLER You admire money and you idolize the people who have it. 2 SWIFT She admir'd as much at him. DICKENS Mrs. Chick admires that Edith should be . . such a perfect Dombey. **admire to** *US colloq.* be pleased to (do something), like to. 3 ADDISON How can we sufficiently admire the stupidity or Madness of these Persons?

admirer *n.* a person who admires; a suitor, a lover: L16. **admiring** *ppl a.* showing or feeling admiration L16. **admiringly** *adv.* E17.

ad misericordiam /ad mɪzərɪ'kɔːdɪam/ *adv.* & *a. phr.* E19. [L.] Of an appeal, argument, etc.: to mercy, to pity.

admissible /əd'mɪsɪb(ə)l/ *a.* E17. [Fr., or med.L *admissibilis*, f. as next: see -IBLE.] 1 Of an idea or plan: worthy of being accepted or considered. E17. b *Law* Allowable as evidence. M19. 2 Worthy or able to be admitted (*to* an office or position, or the use of a place). L18.

admissable *a.* = ADMISSIBLE L19. **admissiˈbility** *n.* L18.

admission /əd'mɪʃ(ə)n/ *n.* LME. [L *admissio(n-)*, f. *admiss-* pa. ppl stem of *admittere*: see next, -ION.] 1 The action of admitting or the fact of being admitted (*to* or *into* a place, office or position, class, etc.); a charge or ticket for this. LME. 2 The admitting (*of* something) as proper, valid, or true; acknowledging, conceding. M16. b A concession, an acknowledgement. E19.

1 BACON The admission of poor suitors without fee. R. BRAUTIGAN Fifty-cents admission for their flea circus. 2 A. G. GARDINER Wars . . only end with the admission of defeat. b J. BRAINE Shocking her into an admission that she still cared what happened to him.

admissive /əd'mɪsɪv/ *a.* characterized by admitting, tending to admit L18.

admit /əd'mɪt/ *v.* Infl. **-tt-**. LME. [L *admittere*, f. *ad* AD- + *mittere* send; but some early forms reflect semi-pop. OFr. *amettre*.] I As a voluntary agent. 1 *v.t.* & †*i.* w. *of.* Let in, permit (a person etc.) entrance or access (*to* or *into* a place, office or position, class, etc.), *spec.* in *Law* (now *Hist.*) into the possession of a copyhold estate. LME. 2 *v.t.* & †*i.* w. *of.* Consent to, permit; accept as valid or true; acknowledge, confess; concede (*that*). LME. b *v.i.* Foll. by *to*: acknowledge (a weakness etc.), confess to. M20.

1 E. M. FORSTER Admitting into her kindly voice a note of exasperation. B. RUSSELL The Orphic communities . . admitted slaves on equal terms. G. GREENE The office had two waiting-rooms, and I was admitted alone into one. †**admit of**: into the number or fellowship of. *admit to bail*: see BAIL *n.*[1] 2 SHAKES. *Twel. N.* She will admit no kind of suit. JAS. MILL Tippoo . . had admitted no delay. E. O'NEILL The old veldt has its points, I'll admit, but it isn't home. A. BURGESS I made a mistake, I freely admit it.

II As an involuntary agent. 3 *v.*†*t.* & *i.* with *of.* Be open to or compatible with; leave room for. M16. 4 *v.t.* Afford entrance to; have room for. L16.

3 SHAKES. *Tr. & Cr.* My love admits no qualifying dross. G. B. SHAW Public medical work . . admits of organization. 4 A. SILLITOE The gap in the fence would have admitted an armoured division.

admittable *a.* able to be admitted (now usu. to a place or as a fact) M16. **admittedly** *adv.* as is acknowledged (by a person, or by people generally) to be true E19. **admitter** *n.* L16. †**admittible** *a.* LME–M17. **admitting** *a.* that admits someone or something, responsible for the admissions to a hospital etc. E20.

admittance /əd'mɪt(ə)ns/ *n.* M16. [f. prec. + -ANCE.] 1 The action of admitting or the fact of being admitted (now usu. to a place); entrance given or allowed. M16. **b** = ADMISSION 2. L16. 2 *Electr.* The reciprocal of impedance. L19.

¶The fig. ideas connected with *admit* are now usu. expressed by ADMISSION.

admix /'admɪks/ *n.* M20. [f. the vb.] An admixture, a mix.

admix /əd'mɪks/ *v.t.* & *i.* Orig. & chiefly as ppl a. **admixt**, (now) **admixed** /-kst/. LME. [Orig. ppl a. f. L *admixtus* pa. pple of *admiscere*, f. *ad* AD- + *miscere* mix; vb (E16) as back-form. or f. AD- + MIX *v.*] Mingle (*with* something else); add as an ingredient.

admixtion *n.* (now *rare* or *obs.*) = ADMIXTURE 1 LME.

admixture /əd'mɪkstʃə/ *n.* E17. [f. AD- + MIXTURE.] 1 The action of admixing; the fact of being admixed. E17. 2 Something mixed with something else; a minor ingredient. M17.

admonish /əd'mɒnɪʃ/ *v.t.* ME. [OFr. *amonester* ult. f. L *admonere*, f. *ad* AD- + *monere* advise; assim. to -ISH². Early *am-* was Latinized to *adm-*.] 1 Charge authoritatively, urge, (*to do*, *that* one should do). ME. 2 *gen.* Put in mind of duties; counsel; warn. Also, reprimand, rebuke. LME. 3 Warn or caution against danger or error. Usu. foll. by *of*. M16. 4 Remind; apprise, inform. *arch.* L16.

admonisher *n.* L16. **admonishingly** *adv.* in an admonishing manner, so as to admonish M19. **admonishment** *n.* the action of admonishing, the fact of being admonished; a reproof, an admonition. ME.

admonition /admə'nɪʃ(ə)n/ *n.* LME. [OFr. *amonition* (mod. *adm-*) f. L *admonitio(n-)*, f. *admonit-* pa. ppl stem of *admonere*: see prec., -ION.] 1 The action of admonishing; authoritative counsel; warning, reproof. LME. 2 An act of admonishing; a statement of counsel or reproof. LME.

admonitory /əd'mɒnɪt(ə)ri/ *a.* L16. [med.L *admonitorius*, f. as prec.; in mod. use. f. prec.: see -ORY².] Giving or conveying admonition; warning.

admonitor *n.* (now *rare*) a person who admonishes M16. **admonitorial** /ədmɒnɪ'tɔːrɪəl/ *a.* (*rare*) = ADMONITORY M19. **admonitorily** *adv.* M19.

adnate /'adneɪt/ *a.* M17. [L *adnatus* var. of *agnatus* AGNATE, due to assoc. w. AD-.] Now chiefly *Bot.* Joined by having grown together.

ad'nation *n.* (*Bot.*) adnate condition M19.

ad nauseam /ad 'nɔːzɪam, -sɪam/ *adv. phr.* M17. [L, lit. 'to sickness'. Cf. earlier USQUE AD NAUSEAM.] To a disgusting or tiresome extent.

adnexa /ad'nɛksə/ *n.pl.* L19. [L, neut. pl. of *adnexus* joined, pa. pple of *adnectere*, f. as AD- + *nectere* to tie, fasten: cf. ANNEX *v.*] *Anat.* The parts adjoining an organ.

adnexal *a.* E20.

†**adnihilate** *a.*, *v.*, **-ation** *n.*, vars. of ANNIHILATE *a.* & *v.*, -ATION *n.*

adnominal /əd'nɒmɪn(ə)l/ *a.* & *n.* M19. [f. L *adnomin-*, *-men* (var. of AGNOMEN) + -AL¹.] *Gram.* (A word or phrase) modifying a noun.

†**adnoun** *n.* M18–L19. [f. AD- + NOUN, after *adverb*.] *Gram.* An adjective.

ado /ə'duː/ *n.* LME. [f. next, the advs. in *much ado* etc. being taken as adjs.] 1 Pl. **ado(e)s**. Action, business; fuss; *rare* a fuss. LME. 2 Labour, trouble, difficulty. LME.

1 without more ado forthwith.

ado /ə'duː/ *v.* (*inf.*) & *a.* Now *arch.* & *dial.* (chiefly *north.* & *Sc.*). LME. [Reduced form of *at do*, f. adoption of ON *at* as sign of inf. + DO *v.*, corresp. to native *to-do* (see DO *v.*).] A *v.* (*pres. inf.*) To do. Exc. *north.* only in *have ado*. LME. B *adj.* Being done, in process, astir. M16.

-ado /'eɪdəʊ, 'ɑː-/ *suff.* Forming ns. 1 Repr. Sp. & Port. *-ado* (f. L *-atus* -ATE²) masc. pa. ppl ending of vbs in *-ar*, as *desperado*, *tornado*. 2 Refash. of Fr. words in *-ade* (see -ADE 1), Sp. words in *-ada*, and It. words in *-ata*, as *bravado*.

adobe /ə'dəʊb(ɪ)/ *n.* M18. [Sp., f. *adobar* to plaster, f. Arab. *aṭ-ṭūb*, f. *al* the + *ṭūb* bricks.] 1 An unburnt brick dried in the sun. M18. **b** A house built of such bricks. *US.* E19. 2 Clay or earth prepared for making into such bricks or suitable for this purpose. L18.

1 *attrib.*: I. SHAW A Mexican peasant woman . . sitting in front of an adobe wall.

†**adod** *int.* var. of ADAD.

adoing /ə'duːɪŋ/ *adv.* & *pred. a. arch.* M16. [f. A *prep.*¹ 7 + DOING *vbl n.*] Being done; in the process of happening.

adolescence /adə'lɛs(ə)ns/ *n.* LME. [(O)Fr. f. L *adolescentia*, f. *adolescent-*: see next, -ENCE.] The process or condition of growing from childhood to manhood or womanhood; the period of growing up.

adolescency *n.* the quality or state of being adolescent L15.

adolescent /adə'lɛs(ə)nt/ *n.* & *a.* LME. [(O)Fr. f. L *adolescent-* pres. ppl stem of *adolescere*, f. *ad* AD- + *alescere* grow up, f. *alere* nourish: see -ENT.] A *n.* A person in the age of adolescence. LME.

B *adj.* Growing from childhood to maturity; in the age of adolescence. L18.

M. PEAKE Their adolescent faces. *fig.*: E. O'NEILL This adolescent country.

adolesce *v.i.* reach or pass through adolescence E20. **adolescently** *adv.* M20.

Adonai /adɒ'nʌɪ, -'neɪʌɪ/ *n.* LME. [Heb. *'ădōnāy*: see JEHOVAH.] In Judaism (and in the Old Testament): (a name of) God.

Adonic /ə'dɒnɪk/ *a.* & *n.* L16. [Fr. *adonique* f. med.L *adonicus*, f. Gk *Adōnis*: see next, -IC.] A *adj.* Of or relating to Adonis; *Class. Pros.* designating a metre consisting of a dactyl and a spondee. L16. B *n.* An Adonic verse or line. L16.

Adonian /ə'dəʊnɪən/ *a.* = ADONIC *a.* M17.

Adonis /ə'dəʊnɪs/ *n.* L16. [Gk *Adōnis*, a youth loved by Aphrodite in Gk mythol., ult. f. Phoenician *'adōnī* my lord, *'adōn* lord.] 1 A plant of the genus *Adonis*; pheasant's eye. L16. 2 A handsome young man. E17.

Comb.: **Adonis blue** a European butterfly, *Lysandra bellargus*.

adonization /adənʌɪ'zeɪʃ(ə)n/ *n.* (*arch.*) dandification E19. **adonize** *v.t.* & *i.* (*arch.*) dandify (oneself) E17.

†**a-doors** *adv.* E16–L19. [Contr.: see A *prep.*²] Of doors; at doors.

adopt /ə'dɒpt/ *v.t.* L15. [(O)Fr. *adopter* or L *adoptare*, f. *ad* AD- + *optare* choose.] 1 Take (a person) voluntarily into a relationship (usu. foll. by *as*), esp. (*a*) as one's child, (*b*) as a candidate for membership of the House of Commons. L15. **b** Of a local authority: accept responsibility for the maintenance of (a road etc.). M19. 2 Take (a practice, idea, etc.) from someone else. E17. **b** *Philol.* Take (a foreign word) into use without (intentionally) changing its form. L19. 3 Choose for one's own practice, take up, (something that need not be another's). M18. 4 Approve, accept (a report etc.). E20.

1 SHAKES. *Oth.* I had rather to adopt a child than get it. S. JOHNSON Those whom he happens to adopt as favourites. **b** J. BETJEMAN By roads 'not adopted', by woodlanded ways. 2 R. GRAVES I adopted the Stoic way of looking at things. 3 J. BERGER The ruling class adopted new tactics towards the workers and the peasantry. 4 J. GALSWORTHY I propose . . that the report and accounts be adopted.

adoptable *a.* M19. **adop'tee** *n.* an adopted person L19. **adopter** *n.* L16.

adoption /ə'dɒpʃ(ə)n/ *n.* ME. [(O)Fr., or L *adoptio(n-)*, f. as *adoptare*: see prec., -ION.] 1 The action of taking or the fact of being taken into any relationship; *esp.* the action of taking a minor who is not one's offspring into the legal relationship of child. ME. 2 The action of taking up and treating as one's own an idea etc.; the fact of being so taken up; an idea etc. so taken. L16. **b** *Philol.* The taking of a foreign word into use without (intentionally) changing its form; a word so taken. L19. 3 Approval, acceptance (of a report etc.). L19.

Adoptionist *n.* & *a.* (*Eccl. Hist.*) (*a*) *n.* a person who maintained that Christ is the son of God by adoption only; (*b*) *adj.* of or pertaining to Adoptionists or their beliefs: M19. †**adoptious** *a.* (*rare*, Shakes.) pertaining to adoption: only in E17.

adoptive /ə'dɒptɪv/ *a.* LME. [(O)Fr. *adoptif*, *-ive* f. L *adoptivus*: see ADOPT, -IVE.] 1 Due to adoption; having the specified familial relation by adoption. LME. 2 Inclined to or in the habit of adopting. *rare.* M19.

1 *adoptive brother, child, father, mother, sister*, etc. 2 G. A. SALA Surely the English language is the . . most swiftly adoptive in the world.

adoptively *adv.* by way of adoption M19.

adorable /ə'dɔːrəb(ə)l/ *a.* E17. [Fr., or L *adorabilis*, f. *adorare* ADORE: see -ABLE.] 1 Worthy of divine worship. Now *rare.* E17. 2 Worthy of passionate attachment; *colloq.* very pleasing. E18.

1 BURKE The adorable wisdom of God. 2 E. M. FORSTER Look at that adorable wine-cart!

adora'bility *n.* M17. **adorableness** *n.* L17. **adorably** *adv.* E19.

adoral /ad'ɔːr(ə)l/ *a.* L19. [f. AD- 1 + ORAL.] *Zool.* Situated at or near the mouth.

adorally *adv.* towards or near the mouth L19.

adoration /adə'reɪʃ(ə)n/ *n.* E16. [(O)Fr., or L *adoratio(n-)*, f. *adorare*: see next, -ATION.] 1 The act of worshipping or honouring as divine. E16. 2 (The exhibition of) profound regard or love. L16. 3 *RC Ch.* A method of electing a pope by a low reverence before the same candidate from two thirds of the voters present. L16.

adore /ə'dɔː/ *v.* LME. [(O)Fr. *adourer* (now *adorer*), earlier *ao(u)rer* f. L *adorare*, f. *ad* AD- + *orare* speak, pray.] 1 *v.t.* Worship as divine. Now chiefly *poet.* LME. **b** *v.t. RC Ch.* Offer reverence to (the Host etc.). L16. 2 *v.t.* Regard with deep respect and affection; *colloq.* like greatly. LME. 3 *v.i.* Offer prayers or entreaties; offer worship. *arch.* E16.

1 POPE Be crown'd as Monarchs, or as Gods adored. 2 O. SITWELL Her mother, whom plainly she adored. D. RUNYON If there is one thing he adores it is spare-ribs. 3 J. M. FAULKNER How the chieftains starlit To Bethlehem came to adore.

adorant *a.* (*poet.*) adoring E19. **adorative** *a.* (now *rare*) pertaining to adoration, adoring M17. **adorer** *n.* a worshipper, an ardent admirer E17. **adoringly** *adv.* in an adoring manner E19.

†**adorn** *a. rare* (Milton). Only in M17. [It. *adorno*, ult. f. as next.] Adorned, ornate.

adorn /ə'dɔːn/ *v.t.* LME. [(O)Fr. *adorner*, earlier *ao(u)rner* f. L *adornare*, f. *ad* AD- + *ornare* furnish, deck.] 1 Be an ornament to, add beauty or lustre to. LME. 2 Provide with ornament(s); embellish (*with*). LME.

1 MILTON A garland to adorn her tresses. LEIGH HUNT The following might have adorned the pages of Spenser. CONAN DOYLE A butler who would have adorned a bench of bishops. 2 SHAKES. *1 Hen. VI* Adorn his temples with a coronet. BURKE The many great vertues with which he has adorned his mind.

adorner *n.* E16. **adornment** *n.* the action of adorning; a thing which adorns, an ornament: L15.

adown /ə'daʊn/ *adv.* & *prep.* Now *arch.* or *poet.* [OE *adūn(e)*, f. as A *prep.*², DOWN *adv.* & *a.* Aphet. to DOWN *adv.*] A *adv.* Downward, down. OE. B *prep.* Downwards upon or along. LME.

†**adownright** *adv.* (aphet. to DOWNRIGHT) straight down, downright: only in ME. †**adownward** *adv.* & *prep.* (aphet. to DOWNWARD) OE–LME.

adoze /ə'dəʊz/ *adv.* & *pred. a.* M19. [f. A-² + DOZE *n.*] In a doze, dozing.

ad personam /ad pɜː'səʊnam/ *adv.* & *a. phr.* M20. [L, lit. 'to the person'.] Personal(ly); on an individual basis.

adpressed /ad'prɛst/ *a.* E19. [f. L *adpress-* pa. ppl stem of *adprimere*, f. *ad* AD- + *premere* press + -ED¹.] *Bot.* Lying close to the stem, the ground, etc.

adrad /əˈdrad/ *a. arch.* Earlier †**of-**. OE. [pa. pple of *ofdrǣdan*, f. OFF- + base of DREAD *v.* Weakened to *a-* in ME after which *ofdrad* is not recorded.] Frightened, terrified.

†**adragant** *n.* Only in 18. [Fr. *adragant(e)* pop. alt. of *tragacanthe* TRAGACANTH. Cf. earlier DRAGANT.] Tragacanth. Also *gum adragant.*

†**adread** *v.* see DREAD *v.*

adream /əˈdriːm/ *adv.* & *pred. a. poet.* M19. [f. A-[2] + DREAM *n.*[2]] In a dream, dreaming.

†**adreamed** *pple* & *ppl a.* M16–L19. [Prob. f. A-[4] + DREAM *n.*[2] or *v.*] *be adreamed*, to dream.

ad referendum /ad rɛfəˈrɛndəm/ *adv. phr.* L18. [mod.L, lit. 'for reference'.] Subject to the assent of a higher authority.

ad rem /ad rɛm/ *adv.* & *a. phr.* L16. [L, lit. 'to the matter'.] To the point; to the purpose.

adrenal /əˈdriːn(ə)l/ *a.* & *n.* L19. [f. AD- I + RENAL.] *Anat.* A *adj.* Situated above the kidney, suprarenal; *spec.* designating or pertaining to the adrenals (see sense B. below). L19.

adrenal cortex the outer part of an adrenal gland, secreting corticosteroids and some other hormones. **adrenal medulla** the central part of an adrenal gland, secreting adrenalin and noradrenaline. *adrenal rest*: see REST *n.*[3] 6.

B *n.* Either of the two small suprarenal glands, which secrete certain hormones, notably adrenalin and corticosteroids. Usu. in *pl.* L19.

adrenaˈlectomy *n.* (an instance of) surgical removal of the adrenal glands E20. **adrenaˈlectomized** *ppl a.* that has undergone adrenalectomy E20.

adrenalin /əˈdrɛnəlɪn/ *n.* Also **-ine.** E20. [f. prec. + -IN[1].] A hormone, $(HO)_2C_6H_3\cdot CHOH\cdot CH_2NHCH_3$, secreted by the adrenal medulla of people and animals under stress, which has a range of physiological effects, e.g. on circulation, breathing, muscular activity, and carbohydrate metabolism; (also *US* **A-** as proprietary name) this hormone extracted from animals or prepared synthetically for medicinal purposes.

adrenergic /adrɪˈnəːdʒɪk/ *a.* M20. [f. prec. + -ERGIC.] *Physiol.* Releasing, involving, or resembling adrenalin or noradrenaline as a neurotransmitter. Cf. CHOLINERGIC.

adreno- /əˈdriːnəʊ, əˈdrɛnəʊ/ *comb. form.* [f. ADRENAL and ADRENALIN: see -O-.] Adrenal; adrenalin.

adrenoˈcortical *a.* of, pertaining to, or secreted by the adrenal cortex M20. **aˌdrenocorticoˈtrop(h)ic** *a.* stimulating or controlling the adrenal cortex; *adrenocorticotrophic hormone*, a hormone of this nature secreted by the pituitary: M20. **adrenoˈlytic** *a.* inhibiting the action of adrenalin or the adrenergic transmission of nerve impulses M20.

Adriatic /eɪdrɪˈatɪk/ *a.* & *n.* E17. [L *Adriaticus*, *Ha-*, f. *Adria*, *Ha-* Etruscan settlement in NE Italy: see -IC.] A *adj.* Designating or pertaining to a sea between Italy and the Balkan peninsula (an arm of the Mediterranean). E17. B *n. The* Adriatic Sea. L18.

adrift /əˈdrɪft/ *adv.* & *pred. a.* L16. [f. A *prep.*[1] I + DRIFT *n.*] Drifting; subject to control by wind and tide, or (*fig.*) by circumstances; *colloq.* unfastened, out of touch, away from what is expected or desired.

cast adrift: see CAST *v.*

adrip /əˈdrɪp/ *adv.* & *pred. a.* M19. [f. A-[2] + DRIP *n.* or *v.*] Dripping.

adrogate /ˈadrəgeɪt/ *v.t.* & *i.* M17. [L *adrogat-* pa. ppl stem of *adrogare*, f. *ad* AD- + *rogare* ask: see -ATE[3] and cf. ARROGATE.] *Rom. Law.* Adopt (a person who is at the time his or her own master or *sui juris*).

adroˈgation *n.* E18. **adrogator** *n.* a person who adrogates another L19.

adroit /əˈdrɔɪt/ *a.* M17. [(O)Fr., f. adv. phr. *à droit* according to right, properly.] Physically or mentally resourceful; dexterous, skilful.

adroitly *adv.* M18. **adroitness** *n.* M18.

†**adrop** *n.* L15–M18. [Misreading of Arab. *usrubb* lead f. Pers. †*usrup* (now *surb*).] *Alch.* A substance from which mercury was to be extracted for the philosopher's stone; the philosopher's stone.

adry /əˈdrʌɪ/ *adv.* & *pred. a.* L16. [f. DRY *a.* after *acold*, *athirst*, etc.] In a dry condition; thirsty.

†**ads** *n.* L17–E19. [Alt.] God's: used in oaths. Cf. OD *n.*[1]

adscititious /adsɪˈtɪʃəs/ *a.* Also (now *rare*) **asc-** /as-/. E17. [f. L *a(d)scit-* pa. ppl stem of *adsciscere* admit, adopt + -ITIOUS[1], after *adventitious*.] Adopted from without; supplemental.

adscript /ˈadskrɪpt/ *n.* & *a.* L17. [L *adscriptus* pa. pple of *adscribere*, f. *ad* AD- + *scribere* write.] A *n.* †1 *Math.* The tangent of an angle. L17–M19. 2 An adscript serf (see sense B.1 below). M19. 3 A comment or note added to a manuscript. L19. B *adj.* 1 [For med.L *adscriptus glebae* attached to the soil.] Of a feudal serf: hereditarily pertaining to an estate and transferred with it. E19. 2 Written after (opp. *subscript*). L19.

adscription /adˈskrɪpʃ(ə)n/ *n. rare.* M17. [L *adscriptio(n-)*, f. as prec.: see -ION.] †1 The circumscribing or inscribing of geometrical figures. Only in M17. 2 = ASCRIPTION. M19. 3 Attachment as an adscript serf. L19.

adsignification /adˌsɪgnɪfɪˈkeɪʃ(ə)n/ *n.* Now *rare.* E17. [med.L *adsignificatio(n-)*, f. *adsignificare*, f. *ad* AD- + *significare* SIGNIFY: see -ATION.] *Logic* & *Gram.* (The signification of) a meaning additional to the basic meaning of a word, phrase, etc.

adsorb /ədˈsɔːb/ *v.* L19. [Back-form. f. next.] *Chem.* 1 *v.t.* Collect (a substance) by adsorption. L19. 2 *v.i.* Undergo adsorption (*on, on to, to*, a surface). E20.

adsorbaˈbility *n.* the degree to which a substance is adsorbable E20. **adsorbable** *a.* able to be adsorbed E20. **adsorbate** *n.* an adsorbed substance E20. **adsorbent** *n.* a substance on which adsorption occurs E20.

adsorption /ədˈsɔːpʃ(ə)n/ *n.* L19. [Blend of AD- and ABSORPTION.] *Chem.* The adhering of atoms or molecules of gases, liquids, or solutes to exposed surfaces (usu. of solids).

adsorptional, **adsorptive** *adjs.* E20. **adsorptively** *adv.* M20.

adstratum /ˈadstrɑːtəm, adˈstrɑːtəm/ *n.* Pl. **-ta** /-tə/. M20. [mod.L, f. L AD- + *stratum* STRATUM.] *Ling.* (Elements or features of) a language responsible for change in a neighbouring language. Cf. SUBSTRATUM, SUPERSTRATUM.

†**adstrict** *v.*, **-ion** *n.* etc., vars. of ASTRICT etc.

†**adstringe** *v.* var. of ASTRINGE.

adsuki *n.* var. of ADZUKI.

adsum /ˈadsʌm/ *int.* L16. [L.] I am present (as an answer in a roll-call etc.).

†**adub** *v.t.* LME. [OFr. *ad(o)ub(b)er*, f. as A-[5] + DUB *v.*[1]] 1 Knight, dub. LME–E17. 2 Equip, array. LME–L16.

adularia /adjʊˈlɛːrɪə/ *n.* L18. [f. Fr. *adulaire* adj., f. *Adula* a group of peaks in the Lepontine Alps, Switzerland: see -IA[1].] *Min.* A low-temperature form of potassium feldspar forming colourless or white prisms.

adulation /adjʊˈleɪʃ(ə)n/ *n.* LME. [(O)Fr., or L *adulatio(n-)*, f. *adulari* fawn upon: see -ATION.] Servile flattery; hypocritical praise.

ˈ**adulate** *v.t.* flatter obsequiously M18. ˈ**adulator** *n.* a servile or hypocritical flatterer LME. **adulatory** *a.* servilely or fulsomely flattering E17.

Adullamite /əˈdʌləmʌɪt/ *n.* LME. [f. *Adullam* (see below) + -ITE[1] I.] 1 A native or inhabitant of the Canaanite city of Adullam. LME. 2 A frequenter of the cave of Adullam (see *1 Sam.* 22:1, 2); *fig.* a member of a group of Liberal rebels in the House of Commons in 1866; a member of any dissident political group. M19.

adult /ˈadʌlt, əˈdʌlt/ *a.* & *n.* M16. [L *adultus* pa. pple of *adolescere* (see ADOLESCENT); cf. Fr. *adulte* (L16).] A *adj.* 1 Grown up; having reached the age of maturity; fully developed. M16. 2 [Orig. attrib. use of n.] Of, pertaining to, or for adults. E19. b Sexually explicit. M20.

2 H. G. WELLS Exhaustive character study is an adult occupation. **adult education**: for those over the usual school age.

B *n.* An adult person; a person who has reached maturity. M17.

consenting adult: see CONSENT *v.* 2.

adulthood *n.* M19. **adultly** *adv.* M20. **adultness** *n.* M18.

†**adulter** *n.* For early forms see ADULTERER. ME–M17. [Orig. OFr. *a(v)outre* f. L *adulter*; later assim. to L.] An adulterer.

adulter /əˈdʌltə/ *v.* Now *rare* or *obs.* For earliest forms see ADULTERER. LME. [Orig. OFr. *a(v)outrer* f. L *adulterare* (see ADULTERATE *v.*); later assim. to L.] 1 *v.i.* Commit adultery. LME. †2 *v.t.* Corrupt, debase. LME–M18.

1 R. MACAULAY Ye're nought but an adultering wumman, when all's said.

adulterant /əˈdʌlt(ə)r(ə)nt/ *a.* & *n.* M18. [L *adulterant-* pres. ppl stem of *adulterare*: see ADULTERATE *v.*, -ANT[1].] (A substance) used in adulterating.

adulterate /əˈdʌlt(ə)rət/ *a.* E16. [L *adulteratus* pa. pple, f. as next: see -ATE[2].] 1 Spurious; base in origin or by admixture. E16. 2 Stained by adultery, in origin or conduct; adulterous. M16.

adulterate /əˈdʌltəreɪt/ *v.* M16. [L *adulterat-* pa. ppl stem of *adulterare* debauch, corrupt: see -ATE[3].] 1 *v.t.* Render spurious; debase, esp. by admixture of other substances. M16. †2 *v.i.* Commit adultery (*with*). L16–M19. †3 *v.t.* Defile by adultery; debauch. Only in 17.

adulterator *n.* a person who adulterates E17.

adulteration /ədʌltəˈreɪʃ(ə)n/ *n.* E16. [L *adulteratio(n-)*, f. as prec.: see -ATION.] 1 The action of adulterating; debasement. E16. 2 An adulterated condition, product, or substance. M17.

adulterer /əˈdʌlt(ə)rə/ *n.* For early forms see below. LME. [f. ADULTER *v.* + -ER[1].] 1 A person who commits adultery. LME. †2 = ADULTERATOR. LME–M17.

¶The series *adulter*, *adulterer*, *adulteress*, *adulterous*, *adultery* emerged in 15 or 16 and finally superseded earlier *avouter* adulterer, *avoutre* commit adultery, *avout(e)rer* adulterer, *avoutres* adulteress, *avoutrous* adulterous, *avoutrie* adultery, all of which were from regular phonetic derivs. in OFr. of L *adulterare* (see ADULTERATE *v.*). The forms in *avout-* had vars. in *advout-* (after later OFr.), which facilitated adoption of forms in *adult-* after L.

adulteress /əˈdʌlt(ə)rɪs/ *n.* For early forms see prec. LME. [Orig. OFr. *a(v)outresse*, f. as ADULTER *n.* + -ESS[1]; later assim. to L.] A woman who commits adultery.

adulterine /əˈdʌlt(ə)rʌɪn/ *a.* M16. [L *adulterinus*, f. *adulter* adulterous, adulterer: see -INE[1].] 1 Spurious; due to adulteration. M16. 2 Illegal, unlicensed. M17. 3 Born of adultery. M18. 4 Of or pertaining to adultery. M19.

adulterize /əˈdʌltərʌɪz/ *v.i. arch.* Also **-ise.** L16. [f. as next + -IZE.] Commit adultery.

adulterous /əˈdʌlt(ə)rəs/ *a.* L15. [f. ADULTER *n.* + -OUS.] 1 Pertaining to or characterized by adultery. L15. †b = ADULTERINE I. L16–E17. 2 Pertaining to or characterized by adulteration. *arch.* M16.

adulterously *adv.* L16.

adultery /əˈdʌlt(ə)ri/ *n.* For early forms see ADULTERER. ME. [Orig. OFr. *avout(e)rie*, f. as ADULTER *n.* + -Y[3]; later assim. to L.] 1 Voluntary sexual intercourse of a married person other than with his or her spouse. ME. b Occas. extended in biblical and theological use: any irregular sexual intercourse or forbidden marriage; idolatry. LME. †2 Adulteration. Only in 17.

1 Vbl action now usu. expressed by *commit adultery*. b AV *Jer.* 3:9 Shee . . committed adultery with stones and with stockes.

adumbrate /ˈadʌmbreɪt/ *v.t.* L16. [L *adumbrat-* pa. ppl stem of *adumbrare*, f. *ad* AD- + *umbrare*, f. *umbra* shade: see -ATE[3].] †1 Shade (a sketch) and so complete it. *rare.* Only in L16. 2 Represent in outline, give a faint indication of. L16. 3 Shadow forth, typify; foreshadow, prefigure. L16. 4 Overshadow; obscure. L16.

2 JAS. MILL Its duties were . . not defined . . , but only adumbrated. 3 T. GALE Noah . . is adumbrated to us . . in Prometheus. 4 W. STYRON Her happy

reminiscence . . had . . become adumbrated by the consciousness of something else.

a'dumbrative *a.* having the attribute of adumbrating M19.

adumbration /adʌm'breɪʃ(ə)n/ *n.* M16. [L *adumbratio(n-)*, f. as prec.: see -ATION.] †1 Shading in painting. *rare.* Only in M16. 2 Representation in outline; an outline, a slight sketch or description. M16. 3 Symbolic representation typifying or prefiguring the reality. E17. 4 Overshadowing; obscuration. M17.

adunation /adjʊ'neɪʃ(ə)n/ *n.* M16. [eccl.L *adunatio(n-)*, f. *adunat-* pa. ppl stem of *adunare*, f. *ad* AD- + *unare*, f. *unus* one: see -ATION. Cf. OFr. *adunation.*] Union.

adunc /ə'dʌŋk/ *a.* E17. [L *aduncus*, f. *ad* AD- + *uncus* hook.] Hooked.

aduncity /-sɪtɪ/ *n.* (now *rare* or *obs.*) hookedness, crookedness L16. **aduncous** *a.* hooked, incurved M17.

†adure *v.t.* & *i.* LME–M17. [L *adurere*: see next.] Burn (something) completely, scorch.

adust /ə'dʌst/ *a.* & *v. arch.* LME. [Fr. *aduste* or L *adustus* pa. pple of *adurere*, f. *ad* AD- + *urere* burn.] A *adj.* 1 Orig. (*Med.*), exhibiting or pertaining to a supposed hot, dry, atrabilious quality of the body and its humours. Now *obs.* exc. in *gen.* sense, sallow, melancholic. LME. 2 Scorched; calcined; parched. LME. 3 Brown, as if scorched; sunburnt. L16.

1 POPE No meagre muse-rid mope adust and thin. *choler adust*: see CHOLER 2. 2 E. BLUNDEN So adust, red-dry / the rock-drift soil was. 3 SMOLLETT Arabia's scorching sands he crossed . . Conductor of her Tribes adust.

B *v.t.* Scorch, dry up with heat. Chiefly as *adusted* ppl a. Long *arch. rare.* LME.

†adustion *n.* the action of scorching or parching; the state of being scorched or parched: LME–M19.

adust /ə'dʌst/ *adv.* & *pred. a. rare.* E19. [f. A-[2] + DUST *n.*] In a dusty condition.

ad valorem /ad və'lɔːrɛm/ *adv.* & *a. phr.* L17. [L = according to the value.] Of taxes: in proportion to the estimated value of goods.

advance /əd'vɑːns/ *n.* & *a.* ME. [Partly f. Fr. *avance*, f. as next; partly f. next.] A *n.* †1 = ADVANCEMENT 3. Only in ME. 2 Progress; a step forward. LME. 3 Payment beforehand, or on security; an anticipatory payment; a loan. L16. 4 The state or position of being before, to the front, or above. (Usu. as below.) M17. 5 Forward motion; progression (in space). L17. 6 A personal approach; a friendly or amorous overture. Freq. in *pl.* L17. 7 A rise in amount, value, or price. L17.

2 B. LOVELL The tortuous nature of scientific advance. B. RUSSELL This development . . is indubitably an advance. 3 G. VIDAL They'll give you an advance for a book. J. CARY An . . advance to enable her to go to Paris and study music. 4 **in advance** (**of**) ahead (of) in place or time. 5 CLARENDON The manner of the enemy's advance. H. FAST The fire was brought under control and its advance was halted. 6 LD MACAULAY Frederic had . . made advances towards a reconciliation with Voltaire. L. P. HARTLEY Irma had rejected the crude advances of the three young men. 7 JOYCE Any advance on five shillings?

B *attrib.* or as *adj.* Being, going, supplied, or acquired in advance. L16.

advance booking: made before the day of a performance, journey, etc. **advance copy** a copy of a book etc. supplied before the date of publication. **advance guard**: preceding the main body of an army. **advance man** *N. Amer.*: preparing the way for a visit by a politician etc.

advance /əd'vɑːns/ *v.* ME. [(O)Fr. *avancer*, ult. f. late L *abante*, f. *ab* AB- + *ante* before. For sp. *adv-* see AD- 2.] 1 *v.t.* Forward, help on, (a process, plan, etc.). ME. 2 *v.t.* Raise or promote (a person) in rank or office; put in a better position. ME. 3 *v.t. Law.* Give as an advancement. LME. 4 *v.t.* Move, put or push, forward (physically, or in time). LME. 5 *v.t.* Raise or lift up (*lit.* & *fig.*). *arch.* LME. †6 *v.t.* Extol; *refl.* boast. LME–M17. 7 *v.t.* Make earlier (an event or date). L15. 8 *v.t.* Bring forward (a statement, claim, etc.) for notice. E16. 9 *v.i.* Move forward, proceed. E16. b *fig.* Make progress in life or any course. L17. c *fig.* Go on towards completion or perfection. M19. d Of a colour: stand out. L19. 10 *v.t.* Pay (money) before it is due; lend (money). L16. 11a *v.t.* Raise in rate or price. L17. b *v.i.* Rise in rate or price. L19.

1 M. FONTEYN Those who have advanced the art by contributing to its evolution. 2 V. WOOLF At the office they advanced him to a post of considerable responsibility. 4 POPE Who spread their bucklers and advance their spears. E. BROCK All / the family advanced their watches by two minutes. 5 SHAKES. *Temp.* The fringed curtain of thine eye advance. 8 W. TREVOR She advanced the opinion that the bird wouldn't last much longer. 9 A. WILSON His companion . . advanced towards them. ALDOUS HUXLEY In Africa the Sahara is advancing. b W. S. GILBERT If you wish in this world to advance, Your merits you're bound to enhance. c CONAN DOYLE You will feel even less humorous as the evening advances.

advancer *n.* a person who or thing which advances, *spec.* a second branch of a buck's horn: L15.

advanced /əd'vɑːnst/ *a.* LME. [f. prec. + -ED[1].] †1 Promoted. LME–L17. 2 *fig.* Far on in life or time, or in any course of action, or march of ideas. M16. †3 Raised (physically). L16–E18. 4 Moved forward, being to the front. E18. 5 Raised in amount, increased. L18.

2 P. G. WODEHOUSE The day was already well advanced. SCOTT FITZGERALD Everybody thinks so—the most advanced people. **advanced degree**: one superior to a bachelor's. **advanced level** an examination (formerly the higher of the two main levels) of the General Certificate of Education in England and Wales. **advanced studies**: in the higher branches of a subject. 4 Esp. Mil. *advanced guard, post, works.*

advancement /əd'vɑːnsm(ə)nt/ *n.* ME. [(O)Fr. *avancement*: see ADVANCE *v.*, -MENT.] I 1 Promotion, preferment, (of a person). ME. 2 *Law.* The promotion of children in life, esp. by the gift of part or all of their prospective share in property to be distributed at a later time under a settlement or will. LME. 3 Furtherance of a thing in progress; improvement. L15. 4 A going forward (*lit.* & *fig.*). Now *rare.* M18. 5 Advancing or forward condition. M18. †II 6 Extolment; boasting. ME–M17.

advantage /əd'vɑːntɪdʒ/ *n.* ME. [(O)Fr. *avantage*, f. *avant* before: see -AGE. For sp. *adv-* see AD- 2.] I Superior position. 1 The position, state, or circumstance of being ahead of another, or of having the better of him or her; superiority, esp. in contest or debate. ME. 2 A favouring circumstance; something which gives one a better position. ME. †3 A vantage-ground. LME–L17. †4 A favourable occasion, a chance. LME–M17. 5 *Tennis.* The next point won after deuce (gaining a temporary superiority, but not the game). M17.

1 **have** (or **get**, **give**, etc.) (**an**) **advantage over** (**of**, **†on**) have etc. a better position than. **have the advantage of** be in a better position than; *spec.* have a personal knowledge of (another) which is not reciprocal. 2 **make one's, an, advantage of** = *take advantage of* below. **take advantage**(**s**) avail oneself of circumstances, use one's opportunities, esp. unfairly. **take advantage of** avail oneself of (a circumstance), outwit (a person), esp. unfairly. **take at advantage** *arch.* take (a person) by surprise. 3 W. RALEIGH Upon the advantage of a mountain-side. 4 SHAKES. *Ven. & Ad.* Make use of time, let not advantage slip.

II The result of a superior position. 6 Benefit; increased well-being or convenience; a resulting benefit. ME. †7 Increased quantity or number; excess. ME–E18. †8 Pecuniary profit; interest on money lent. LME–M17.

6 SHAKES. *1 Hen. IV* Those blessed feet Which . . were nail'd For our advantage on the bitter cross. P. SCOTT The advantages people like us enjoy over those who . . have to make do without servants. *mechanical advantage*: see MECHANICAL *a.* **to advantage** in a way such as to exhibit merits. 8 SHAKES. *Merch. V.* You neither lend nor borrow Upon advantage.

Comb.: **advantage game, set**: one in which advantage is part of the scoring system.

advantage /əd'vɑːntɪdʒ/ *v.t.* LME. [f. the n., or f. (O)Fr. *avantager.*] 1 Give an advantage or superiority to; benefit, profit. LME. †2 Add to the amount or value of. L15–L17. 3 Further the progress of, promote. L16.

advantaged *a.* placed at advantage; socially or financially privileged: L16.

advantageous /adv(ə)n'teɪdʒəs/ *a.* L16. [f. ADVANTAGE *n.* + -OUS: cf. Fr. *avantageux, -euse.*] Profitable, opportune, favourable, (*to, for*).

advantageously *adv.* E17. **advantageousness** *n.* E17.

advection /əd'vɛkʃ(ə)n/ *n.* E20. [L *advectio(n-)*, f. *advehere*, f. *ad* AD- + *vehere* carry: see -ION.] Flow of matter within the atmosphere, the oceans, or in any fluid, esp. horizontally; transfer of heat etc. brought about by such motion.

advect *v.t.* convey (fluid, heat, etc.) by advection M20. **advective** *a.* of, pertaining to, or brought about by advection E20.

advene /əd'viːn/ *v.i.* E17. [OFr. *avenir* (mod. *adv-*) or L *advenire*: see ADVENT.] Accede or come (*to*); be superadded.

advenient /əd'viːnɪənt/ *a.* L16. [L *advenient-* pres. ppl stem of *advenire*: see next, -ENT.] Superadded; adventitious.

advent /'adv(ə)nt, -vɛnt/ *n.* In sense 1 **A-**. OE. [OFr., refash. after L of *auvent* (mod. *avent*) f. L *adventus* arrival, f. *advent-* pa. ppl stem of *advenire*, f. *ad-* AD- + *venire* come.] 1 The season before Christmas in the ecclesiastical calendar, now four weeks in length. OE. 2 *Chr. Theol.* The coming of Christ on earth. LME. 3 The arrival of an important person or thing. M18.

2 *second advent*: see SECOND *a.*

Comb.: **Advent calendar** a calendar for the days of Advent with a hidden picture or gift to be revealed on each day; **Advent Sunday** the first Sunday in Advent, the Sunday nearest to the 30 November.

adventist /'adv(ə)ntɪst/ *n.* Also **A-**. M19. [f. prec. + -IST.] A member of any of various sects holding millenarian views.

Second Adventist = MILLERITE *n.*[1] **Seventh-day Adventist** a member of a millenarian sect who observe Saturday as the Sabbath.

adventism *n.* the beliefs of adventists M19.

adventitious /adv(ə)n'tɪʃəs/ *a.* E17. [f. med.L *adventitius* alt. of L *adventicius*, f. *advent-*: see ADVENT, -ITIOUS[1].] 1 Coming from without, accidental, casual. E17. 2 *Law.* Of property: coming from a stranger or by collateral, not direct, succession. Opp. *profectitious.* M17. 3 Formed in an unexpected place anatomically; *esp.* in *Bot.* (of roots, buds, etc.) arising from a part other than that usual in plants generally. L17.

adventitiously *adv.* M18.

adventive /əd'vɛntɪv/ *a.* E17. [f. L *advent-* (see ADVENT) + -IVE, after prec.] 1 = ADVENTITIOUS 1. *rare.* E17. 2 *Bot.* & *Zool.* Present spontaneously in a region but not native to it. L19.

1 L. DURRELL So . . tenderly had he captured the adventive minute.

adventure /əd'vɛntʃə/ *n.* ME. [(O)Fr. *aventure* ult. f. L *adventurus* future pple of *advenire*: see ADVENT, -URE. For sp. *adv-* see AD- 2.] †1 Chance, fortune, luck. ME–E18. †2 A chance occurrence, an accident. ME–E18. 3 Chance of danger or loss; risk, jeopardy. *arch.* exc. *Maritime Insurance.* ME. 4 Hazardous activity. ME. 5 A hazardous enterprise or performance. ME. b An unexpected or exciting incident. L16. c An instance of adventurism in foreign policy. M20. †6 A hazard, a venture, an experiment. LME–L18. 7 A pecuniary venture, a commercial speculation. L15.

1 DRYDEN She . . wished me fair adventure. 2 SWIFT An hope, that this adventure might . . help to deliver me. 4 V. WOOLF He, bound for adventure; she, moored to the shore. 5 JOYCE Friend Sinbad and his horrifying adventures. b C. BRONTË To walk alone in London seemed of itself an adventure. 6 SHAKES. *John* To try the fair adventure of to-morrow. **at adventure**(**s**) at hazard, recklessly. **at all adventure**(**s**) at any risk; at all events. 7 BACON He that puts all vpon Aduentures, doth often times brake, and come to Pouerty. *joint adventure*: see JOINT *a.*

Comb.: **adventure playground**: with apparatus for children to climb on and functional materials for building with etc.

adventuresome *a.* given to running risks; adventurous: E17.

adventure /əd'vɛntʃə/ *v.* ME. [(O)Fr. *aventurer*, f. as prec.] 1 *v.t.* Take the chance of; venture upon. *arch.* ME. 2 *v.t.* Risk the loss of;

imperil. *arch.* ME. 3 *v.i.* Incur risk; dare to go or come (*into, upon*, etc., a place); dare to enter (*up*)*on* (an undertaking); go so far as *to do.* ME. b *v.t.* Venture to say. L19.

adventurer /əd'vɛntʃ(ə)rə/ *n.* L15. [Fr. *aventurier*, †*adv-*, f. as ADVENTURE *n.*: see -ER[2].] †1 A gamester. *rare.* Only in L15. 2 A person who seeks adventures; *esp.* a mercenary soldier. E16. 3 A person who undertakes or shares in commercial adventures; a speculator. E16. 4 A person who lives by his or her wits. M17.
adventuress *n.* a woman who lives by her wits M18.

adventurism /əd'vɛntʃərɪz(ə)m/ *n.* M19. [f. ADVENTURE *n.* + -ISM.] 1 The principles and practice of an adventurer. *rare.* M19. 2 A tendency to take risks in foreign policy etc. M20.
adventurist *n.* & *a.* (*a*) *n.* a person inclined to adventurism; (*b*) *adj.* of or pertaining to adventurists or adventurism: E20.

adventurous /əd'vɛntʃ(ə)rəs/ *a.* ME. [OFr. *aventureus*, -*o*(*u*)*s*, f. as ADVENTURE *n.*: see -OUS.] 1 In search of adventures; enterprising; full of adventure. ME. †2 Full of risk or peril. ME–M17. 3 Rash, venturesome. LME. †4 Fortuitous. LME–L15.
adventurously *adv.* ME. **adventurousness** *n.* M16.

adverb /'advəːb/ *n.* LME. [Fr. *adverbe* or L *adverbium*, f. *ad* AD- + *verbum* VERB.] *Gram.* A word that qualifies or modifies another, esp. an adjective, a verb, or another adverb, so as to express a relation of place, time, circumstance, manner, cause, degree, etc. (One of the parts of speech.)

adverbial /əd'vəːbɪəl/ *n.* & *a.* L16. [Late L *adverbialis* or Fr.: see prec., -AL[1].] *Gram.* A *n.* A word or phrase of the nature of an adverb. L16. B *adj.* Of, pertaining to, or of the nature of an adverb. L16.
adverbialize *v.t.* make (another type of word) into an adverb E19. **adverbially** *adv.* L15.

adversaria /advə'sɛːrɪə/ *n.pl.* E18. [L, use as n. of neut. pl. (sc. *scripta* writings) of *adversarius* facing one (see ADVERSARY).] Miscellaneous remarks and observations; *collect. sing.* a commonplace-book.

adversarial /advə'sɛːrɪəl/ *a.* E20. [f. next + -AL[1].] Of or pertaining to opposition; involving adversaries; adversary.

adversary /'advəs(ə)ri/ *n.* & *a.* ME. [OFr. *adversarie* (mod. -*aire*) f. L *adversarius* opposed, opponent, f. *adversus*: see ADVERSE, -ARY[1].] A *n.* An opponent, an antagonist, an enemy. ME.
the Adversary the Devil.
B *adj.* Opposed, antagonistic. LME.
¶In Shakes. stressed on 1st syll.; in Milton on 1st or on 2nd.

adversative /əd'vəːsətɪv/ *a.* & *n.* LME. [Fr. *adversatif, -ive* or late L *adversativus* (Priscian), f. *adversari*, f. *adversus*: see next, -ATIVE.] A *adj.* Expressive of opposition, contrariety, or antithesis. LME. B *n.* An adversative word or proposition. M16.
adversatively *adv.* L16.

adverse /'advəːs/ *a.* LME. [OFr. *advers*, earlier *av-* f. L *adversus* against, opposite, pa. pple of *advertere*: see ADVERT *v.*] 1 Acting in opposition; actively hostile. (Foll. by *to*.) LME. 2 Hurtful, injurious. LME. 3 Opposite in position. *arch.* E17.
adversely *adv.* E17. **adverseness** *n.* E17.

adversity /əd'vəːsɪti/ *n.* ME. [(O)Fr. *adversité*, earlier *av-* f. L *adversitas*, f. as prec.: see -ITY.] 1 The condition of adverse fortune; distress, trial, affliction. ME. 2 An adverse circumstance; a misfortune, a calamity, a trial. ME. †3 Opposition; contrariety. LME–L15. †4 Perversity. L15–E17.

advert /'advəːt/ *n. colloq.* M19. [Abbrev.] An advertisement.

advert /əd'vəːt/ *v.* LME. [(O)Fr. *avertir*, †*advertir* ult. f. L *advertere*, f. AD- + *vertere* to turn. Cf. ANIMADVERT.] 1 *v.t.* Turn towards. *rare.* LME. 2 *v.i.* Turn one's attention; take heed. Foll. by *to*, †*on*, †*that. arch.* LME. †3 *v.t.* Take note of, observe, heed, (a thing). LME–L17. †4 *v.t.* Turn the attention of (another) to, warn of. *rare.* E16–L17. 5 *v.i.* Refer *to* in speech or writing. L18.
1 F. R. LEAVIS The facts, to the adverted eye, are obvious. 2 F. O'BRIEN I walked down to the centre of the town without adverting to my surroundings. 3 R. SANDERSON Frailties and infirmities .. not hitherto by them adverted, because never suspected. 5 L. STRACHEY After referring to the death of the Princess, .. the Duke adverted to his own position.
advertent *a.* attentive LME. **advertently** *adv.* L19. (Both chiefly repr. in neg. *inadvertent*(*ly*).)

advertence /əd'vəːt(ə)ns/ *n.* LME. [OFr. *a*(*d*)*vertence*, f. *a*(*d*)*vertir*: see prec., -ENCE and cf. med.L *advertentia*.] The action of adverting; observation, attention, consideration. Also, advertency.
¶Now chiefly repr. in the neg. *inadvertence, -ency.*
advertency *n.* attentiveness, heedfulness M17.

advertise /'advətʌɪz/ *v.* LME. [OFr. *a*(*d*)*vertiss-* lengthened stem of *a*(*d*)*vertir* ADVERT *v.*] †1 *v.i.* = ADVERT *v.* 2. LME–E16. †2 *v.t.* = ADVERT *v.* 4. LME–E17. 3 *v.t.* Notify, admonish (a person *of* or *concerning* a thing, *that*; (arch.) *absol.*). LME. 4 *v.t.* Give notice of; make generally or publicly known. LME. b *v.t.* Call attention to by a published announcement; describe or present (goods, services) publicly with a view to promoting sales. E18. 5 *v.i.* Give warning or information (*of*). *obs.* in *gen.* sense. E17. b *v.i.* Make an announcement in a public place; describe or present goods publicly with a view to promoting sales. L18.
3 SHAKES. *3 Hen. VI* We are advertis'd .. That they do hold their course toward Tewksbury. 4 R. P. WARREN I wouldn't go around advertising this visit. E. BOWEN The .. chintz .. advertised its original delicacy by being .. always a little soiled. b JOYCE Corsets .. advertised cheap in the Gentlewoman. J. C. POWYS So widely had John's clever circulars advertised this event, that .. every available lodging .. was crowded. **5b advertise for** ask for by public notice.
advertiser *n.* a person who advertises; a journal publishing advertisements: M16. **advertising** *n.* (*a*) the action of the vb; (*b*) the practice or profession of preparing and issuing public advertisements: M18.

advertisement /əd'vəːtɪzm(ə)nt/ *n.* LME. [Fr. *avertissement*, †*adv-*, f. as prec.: see -MENT.] †1 Admonition, instruction. LME–E18. †2 Information, notification. LME–E18. 3 A (written) statement calling attention to something; a notice to readers in a book etc. *arch.* LME. †4 Attention, observation. L15–M17. 5 A public announcement (formerly by the town-crier, now usu. in newspapers, on posters, by television, etc.). L16. b Foll. by *for* (w. adj. of quality or degree): a means of conveying the merits or demerits of. *colloq.* M20.
5 *small advertisement*: see SMALL *a.* b *New Yorker* She has been a splendid advertisement for the benefits of a happy marriage.
advertisemental *a.* L18.

advertorial /advəː'tɔːrɪəl/ *n.* Orig. *US.* M20. [Blend of ADVERTISEMENT and EDITORIAL *n.*] An advertisement offering information about a commercial or industrial product or activity in the style of editorial comment.

advice /əd'vʌɪs/ *n.* ME. [(O)Fr. *avis* ult. f. L *ad* AD- + *visum* neut. pa. pple of *videre* see. For sp. *adv-* see AD- 2.] †1 The way in which a matter is looked at; opinion, judgement. ME–L17. †2 Forethought, wisdom. LME–E16. †3 Consideration, consultation, reckoning. LME–M17. 4 An opinion given or offered as to action; counsel. LME. †5 The result of consultation; determination, plan. LME–E18. 6 Information given, news; formal notice of a transaction; in *pl.* also, communications from a distance. LME.
1 G. HERBERT All things .. joyn with one advise To honour thee. 3 SHAKES. *Merch. V.* Bassanio, upon more advice, Hath sent you here this ring. 4 E. O'NEILL I need your advice—your *scientific* advice this time, .. Doctor. JOYCE If I went by his advices. 5 DRYDEN You may, but 'twill not be your best Advice. 6 STEELE A mail from Holland, which brought me several advices.
Phrases: *letter of advice*: see LETTER *n.*[1] **take advice** †(*a*) deliberate; (*b*) seek advice, esp. from a legal or other expert; (*c*) act upon advice given.
†**adviceful** *a.* thoughtful; skilful as an adviser: LME–E17.

†**adview** *v.* var. of AVIEW.

advisable /əd'vʌɪzəb(ə)l/ *a.* LME. [Isolated early use f. (O)Fr. *avisable*; later (M17) f. next + -ABLE.] 1 To be recommended; expedient. LME. 2 Open to advice. M17.
advisa'bility *n.* the quality of being advisable; expediency: M19. **advisableness** *n.* (*a*) *rare* readiness to be advised; (*b*) advisability: L17. **advisably** *adv.* M19.

advise /əd'vʌɪz/ *v.* ME. [(O)Fr. *aviser* ult. f. L *ad* AD- + *visere* frequent. of *videre* see. For sp. *adv-* see AD- 2.] †1 *v.t.* Look at, observe; watch for. ME–E17. †2 *v.t.* Purpose, devise. ME–E17. †3 *v.refl.* & *i.* Bethink oneself; consider, reflect. ME–L17. 4 *v.t.* Consider, think of. Now only *Sc. Law*, deliberate upon, review, revise, (a case). LME. 5 *v.i.* Consider in company, hold a consultation. *obs.* exc. in *advise with*, consult with (now chiefly *US*). LME. 6a *v.t.* Give advice to, caution. LME. b *v.t.* Recommend. E17. 7 *v.i.* Offer counsel, give advice. LME. 8 *v.t.* Inform, notify. Foll. by *of, that.* L16.
3 SHAKES. *Twel. N.* Advise you what you say. MILTON Advise Forthwith how thou oughtst to receive him. 6a R. ELLISON I am trying to advise you what is best for you. J. HELLER I advised him to put most of the money into an annuity. b D. DAVIE The guidebook cheats: the green road it advises In fact misled. 8 M. BRADBURY The headlines advise him of many indignities and wrongs.
advi'see *n.* the person advised E19. **adviser** *n.* a person who gives advice E17. **advisor** *n.* (chiefly *US*) an adviser L19.

advised /əd'vʌɪzd/ *a.* ME. [f. prec. + -ED[1].] †1 Purposed, determined. ME–L15. †2 Of a person: a Having considered something. LME–M17. b Deliberate, wary. LME–E18. 3 Of a thing: deliberate, considered. LME. 4 Counselled. L16. 5 Apprised. L16.
2 †**be advised** consider, reflect. 3 **ill-advised** injudicious, imprudent.
advisedly /-zɪdli/ *adv.* in an advised manner; *esp.* deliberately: LME. **advisedness** /-zɪdnɪs/ *n.* (now *rare*) the quality of being advised, prudent consideration LME.

advisement /əd'vʌɪzm(ə)nt/ *n.* ME. [(O)Fr. *avisement* (later OFr. also *adv-*), f. as ADVISE: see -MENT and cf. med.L *a*(*d*)*visamentum*.] †1 The process of looking at or viewing something. ME–E17. 2 Consideration, deliberation; consultation. ME. 3 Advice, counsel; an instruction how to act. *arch.* LME.
2 **under advisement** under or into (esp. official or formal) consideration.

adviso /əd'vʌɪzəʊ/ *n.* Now *arch. rare.* Pl. **-o(e)s.** L16. [f. as AVISO, infl. by L and cognate Eng. wds.] = AVISO.

advisory /əd'vʌɪz(ə)ri/ *a.* & *n.* L18. [f. ADVISE + -ORY[2].] A *adj.* Giving advice; consisting in giving advice. L18. B *n.* A statement giving advice or information. *N. Amer.* M20.

advocaat /'advəkɑː, -kɑːt/ *n.* M20. [Du. = ADVOCATE *n.*] A liqueur of eggs, sugar, and spirit; a drink of this.

advocacy /'advəkəsi/ *n.* LME. [OFr. *a*(*d*)*vocacie* f. med.L *advocatia*, f. as ADVOCATE *v.*[2]: see -ACY.] The function of an advocate; pleading in support *of*.

advocate /'advəkət/ *n.* ME. [(O)Fr. *avocat* f. L *advocatus* use as n. of pa. pple of *advocare*: see ADVOKE, -ATE[1]. For sp. *adv-* see AD- 2.] 1 A person whose profession is to plead causes in courts of law (now chiefly *Sc.*); *US* any lawyer. ME. 2 *gen.* A person who pleads, intercedes, or speaks for another. ME. †3 = ADVOWEE 2. LME–M18. 4 A person who speaks in favour *of*, †*for*, a proposal etc. M18.
1 *devil's advocate*: see DEVIL *n. judge advocate, Judge Advocate General*: see JUDGE *n.* **Faculty of Advocates** the Scottish bar. **Lord Advocate** the principal law officer of the Crown in Scotland.
Comb.: **Advocate-Depute** each of several officers assisting the Lord Advocate in prosecutions; **Advocate-General** each of several officers assisting the judges in the European Court of Justice.
advocateship *n.* M16. **advocatess** *n.* a female advocate LME. **advocatory** /'advəkeɪt(ə)ri/ *a.* of or pertaining to an advocate M19. †**advocatrice** *n.* [OFr.] = ADVOCATESS LME–L16.

advocate /ˈadvəkeɪt/ *v.*[1] E16. [L *advocat-* pa. ppl stem of *advocare*: see ADVOKE, -ATE[3].] Chiefly *Sc. Law*. = ADVOKE.

advocate /ˈadvəkeɪt/ *v.*[2] L16. [f. ADVOCATE *n*.] **1** *v.t.* Plead in favour of, defend; recommend publicly. L16. **2** *v.i.* Act as advocate *for*. Now *rare*. M17.

advocation /advəˈkeɪʃ(ə)n/ *n*. LME. [OFr. *a(d)vocacion* f. L *advocatio(n-)*, f. as ADVOCATE *v.*[1]: see -ATION.] †**1** A summoning. LME–L15. †**2** The function or office of an advocate. LME–M18. **3** The calling of an action before itself by a superior court, *spec.* the papal court or a Scottish criminal (formerly also civil) court. E16. †**4** An appeal for aid or defence. L16–M18.

advocator /ˈadvəkeɪtə/ *n*. L15. [In early use f. late L *advocator*, f. as ADVOCATE *v.*[1]; in mod. use f. ADVOCATE *v.*[2]: see -OR.] †**1** A patron (saint). L15–L16. **2** A person who advocates something. M18.

advocatus diaboli /advəˌkɑːtəs diːˈabəliː, advəˌkeɪtəs dʌɪˈabəlʌɪ/ *n. phr.* E19. [mod.L.] = *devil's advocate* s.v. DEVIL *n*.

advoke /ədˈvəʊk/ *v.t.* M16. [L *advocare*, f. *ad* AD- + *vocare* call.] Call (a cause) to a higher tribunal.

advowee /advaʊˈiː/ *n*. ME. [AN *a(d)vowé* patron (mod.Fr. *avoué* solicitor) f. L *advocatus* ADVOCATE *n*.: assim. to -EE[1].] †**1** A patron, a protector; *esp.* a patron saint. ME–L15. **2** A person who holds the advowson of an ecclesiastical house or benefice. E17.

advowson /ədˈvaʊz(ə)n/ *n*. ME. [AN *a(d)voweson*, *a(d)voeson*, OFr. *avoeson* f. L *advocatio(n-)*: see ADVOCATION.] Orig., the guardianship or patronage of an ecclesiastical house or benefice. Now, the right of presentation to a benefice.

adytum /ˈadɪtəm/ *n*. Pl. **-ta** /-tə/. E17. [L f. Gk *aduton* use as n. of neut. sing. of *adutos* impenetrable.] The innermost part of a temple; a private chamber, a sanctum.

adze /adz/ *n*. & *v*. Also ***adz**. [OE *adesa*, of unkn. origin.] **A** *n*. A tool like an axe with an arched blade at right angles to the handle, for cutting away the surface of wood. OE. **B** *v.t.* Cut or dress with an adze. M19.

adzuki /ədˈzuːki/ *n*. Also **ads-**, **az-**. E18. [Jap. *azuki*.] A bushy leguminous plant, *Vigna angularis*, cultivated in China and Japan; the edible bean of this plant. Also *adzuki bean*.

Æ, æ, a ligature. **1** OE 'ash' (see ASH *n.*[1] 3), the symbol of a simple vowel intermediate between *a* and *e*. In early ME short *æ* was replaced by *a* (sometimes *e*), long *æ* by *e* or *ee*. **2** From 16 used in forms derived from L *æ* and Gk *ai*. When thoroughly Anglicized and popularized this becomes *e*; *æ*, now usu. (and in this dictionary) written as a digraph *ae*, is retained only in some Gk and L proper names, terms of Gk and Rom. Antiquities, and some scientific and techn. terms (where, however, *e* is usual in the US).

-ae /iː/ *pl. suff.* Repr. pl. ending of L ns. of 1st declension in *-a* and romanized form of Gk (*-ai*) in pl. of ns. In all words completely popularized it yields to *-as*.

aecidium /ɪˈsɪdɪəm/ *n*. Pl. **-dia** /-dɪə/. M19. [mod.L, f. Gk *aikia* injury + -IDIUM.] *Mycol.* = AECIUM; *spec.* a cup-shaped aecium.

aecidial *a*. L19. **aecidiospore** *n*. = AECIOSPORE L19.

aecium /ˈiːsɪəm/ *n*. Pl. **-cia** /-sɪə/. E20. [mod.L, f. as prec. + -IUM.] *Mycol.* A fruiting body of a rust fungus, in which aeciospores are produced.

aecial *a*. E20. **aeciospore** *n*. any of the first binucleate spores to develop in a rust fungus, often produced on one host and germinating on another E20.

aedicule /ˈiːdɪkjuːl, ˈɛd-/ *n*. Also **ed-**, & in L form **-cula** /-kjʊlə/, pl. **-lae** /-liː/. M19. [L *aedicula* dim. of *aedes* dwelling: see -CULE.] A small structure or room, *esp.* one used as a shrine; (a small structure over) a niche for a statue etc.

aeˈdicular *a*. M20.

aedile /ˈiːdʌɪl/ *n*. M16. [L *aedilis* adj. & n., f. *aedes*, *-is* building: see -ILE.] *Rom. Hist.* Any of several magistrates who superintended public buildings, policing, and other matters.

aedileship, **aeˈdility** *ns.* the position or term of office of an aedile M16.

Aegean /iːˈdʒiːən, ɪ-/ *a*. E17. [f. L *Aegaeus* f. Gk *Aigaios*: see -EAN.] Designating, of, or pertaining to the sea between Greece and Asia Minor.

aegirine /ˈiːdʒɪriːn, ˈɛdʒ-/ *n*. M19. [f. *Aegir*, Norse god of the sea + -INE[5].] *Min.* A silicate of iron and sodium occurring in many alkaline igneous rocks and belonging to the pyroxene minerals.

Also **aegirite** *n*. M19.

aegis /ˈiːdʒɪs/ *n*. Also ***egis**. E17. [L f. Gk *aigis* shield of Zeus.] **1** A shield, defensive armour, *esp.* that of Jupiter or Minerva. E17. **2** *fig.* Protection; an impregnable defence. L18.

2 under the aegis of under the auspices of.

aegophony /ɪˈgɒfəni/ *n*. M19. [f. Gk *aig-*, *aix* goat + -O- + -PHONY.] *Med.* A tremulous nasal resonance of the voice, sometimes heard with the stethoscope in pleurisy.

aegophonic /iːgəˈfɒnɪk/ *a*. M19.

aegrotat /ʌɪˈgrə(ʊ)tat, ˈiː-, iːˈgrə(ʊ)-/ *n*. L18. [L *aegrotat* 3 sing. pres. indic. of *aegrotare* be ill, f. *aegr-*, *aeger* sick, ill.] In universities, a certificate that a student is too ill to attend an examination etc., an examination pass or (*N. Amer.*) a credit awarded to a student having such a certificate.

-aemia /ˈiːmɪə/ *suff.* Also ***-emia**. [f. Gk *haima* blood + -IA[1].] Forming ns. denoting conditions of the blood, as *acidaemia*, *leukaemia*, *septicaemia*, etc.

aeneolithic *a*. var. of ENEOLITHIC.

†**aenigma** *n*. var. of ENIGMA.

Aeolian /iːˈəʊlɪən/ *a*. Also ***Eo-** & (in sense 2) with lower-case initial. L16. [f. L *Aeolius* + -IAN.] **1** Of or pertaining to Aeolis or Aeolia, an ancient district of Asia Minor. L16. **2** Of or pertaining to Aeolus, mythical god of the winds; of, produced by, or borne on the wind. E17.

1 Aeolian mode *Mus.* (*a*) an ancient Greek mode; (*b*) the ninth of the church modes (with A as final and E as dominant). **2** A. HOLMES Contrasts between water-laid and Aeolian sands. **aeolian harp** a stringed instrument producing musical sounds on exposure to a current of air.

Aeolic /iːˈɒlɪk/ *a*. & *n*. Also ***Eo-**. L17. [L *Aeolicus* f. Gk *Aiolikos*: see prec., -IC.] **A** *adj.* = AEOLIAN 1. L17. **B** *n*. The Greek dialect of Aeolia. E18.

aeolienne *n*. var. of ÉOLIENNE.

aeolipyle /ˈiːə(ʊ)lɪpʌɪl, iːˈɒl-/ *n*. Also **-pile**. M17. [Fr. *éolipyle* (16) f. L *Aeoli pylae* (= Gk *pulai*) the doorway of Aeolus.] An instrument illustrating the force with which vapour generated by heat in a closed vessel escapes by a narrow aperture.

aeolotropy /iːə(ʊ)ˈlɒtrəpi/ *n*. Now *rare*. L19. [f. Gk *aiolos* changeful + -TROPY.] = ANISOTROPY.

aeolotropic /iːˌəʊləˈtrəʊpɪk, -ˈtrɒpɪk/ *a*. M19.

aeon /ˈiːən/ *n*. Also (the usual form in *Geol.*) **eon**. M17. [eccl.L f. Gk *aiōn* age.] **1** An age of the universe; an immeasurable period of time; eternity; *colloq.* a very long time. M17. **b** *Geol.* The largest division of geological time, composed of several eras. M20. **c** *Astron.* & *Geol.* One thousand million years. M20. **2** The personification of an age; *Gnostic Philos.* a power existing outside time, an emanation or phase of the supreme deity. M17.

1 P. G. WODEHOUSE Six-thirty seemed æons ahead.

aeonial /iːˈəʊnɪəl/ *a*. = AEONIAN M19. **aeonian** /iːˈəʊnɪən/ *a*. eternal, everlasting M18. **aeonic** /iːˈɒnɪk/ *a*. lasting an aeon L19.

aepyornis /iːpɪˈɔːnɪs/ *n*. M19. [mod.L, f. Gk *aipus* high + *ornis* bird.] An extinct giant flightless bird of the genus *Aepyornis*, known from remains found in Madagascar. Also called *elephant-bird*.

†**aequi-** *comb. form* var. of EQUI-.

†**aera** *n*. see ERA.

aerate /ˈɛːreɪt/ *v.t.* L18. [f. L *aer* air + -ATE[3], after Fr. *aérer*.] **1** Expose to the action of air. L18. **2** Charge with air or another gas (esp. carbon dioxide), usu. so as to produce effervescence. L18.

aerated *a*. (*a*) that has been aerated; (*b*) *slang* angry, agitated: E19. **aeˈration** *n*. M19. **aerator** *n*. something which aerates; a device for aerating: M19.

aerenchyma /ɛːˈrɛŋkɪmə/ *n*. L19. [f. Gk *aēr* air + *egkhuma* infusion.] *Bot.* Soft cellular tissue containing air spaces, found in many aquatic plants.

aerenˈchymatous *a*. L20.

aerial /ˈɛːrɪəl/ *a*. & *n*. L16. [f. L *aerius* f. Gk *aerios*, f. *aēr* air: see -AL[1].] **A** *adj.* **1** Thin as air, ethereal; immaterial, imaginary. L16. **2** Light as air, airy. E17. **3** Of, pertaining to, or produced in the air; atmospheric. E17. **4** Existing, moving, or happening in the air. E17. **b** Growing above ground (opp. *subterranean*). M19. **c** By or from aircraft etc. L19. **5** Placed at an airy height, elevated (*lit.* & *fig.*). E17. **6** Composed of air; gaseous. M17.

3 aerial perspective: in which distant objects are shown as fainter. **4** A. SILLITOE Full clouds drifting like an aerial continent of milk-white mountains. **aerial ping-pong** *Austral. slang* Australian Rules football. *aerial* PLANKTON. **b** ANTHONY HUXLEY Aerial roots as in ivy are produced on the dark side of the stem. **c** G. B. SHAW The British refusal to bar aerial bombardment . . made the air battles of the world war lawful. **aerial top-dressing** *NZ* crop-dusting. *aerial torpedo*: see TORPEDO *n*. 2b. **5 aerial cableway**, **railway**, **ropeway** a system of overhead cables from which cars or containers are suspended for transport, usu. driven electrically.

B *n*. A metal wire, rod, or other structure used to transmit or receive radio waves. Cf. ANTENNA 4. E20.

¶ Formerly, & still sometimes in poetry where the metre calls for 4 syllables, with pronunc. /eɪˈɪərɪəl, eɪˈɛːrɪəl/.

aerialist *n*. (*a*) *rare* a stylite; (*b*) a high-wire or trapeze artist: M19. **aerially** *adv*. E19.

aerie *n*. var. of EYRIE.

aeriferous /ɛːˈrɪf(ə)rəs/ *a*. L17. [f. L *aer* air + -I- + -FEROUS.] Bearing or conveying air.

aeriform /ˈɛːrɪfɔːm/ *a*. L18. [f. as prec. + -I- + -FORM.] Of the form of air, gaseous; unsubstantial, unreal.

aero- /ˈɛːrəʊ/ *comb. form* of Gk *aēr* air: see -O-. Often *spec.* w. ref. to aeroplanes and aviation.

aero-ˈallergen *n*. an airborne allergen M20. **aerobioˈlogical** *a*. of or pertaining to aerobiology M20. **aerobiˈologist** *n*. an expert in or student of aerobiology M20. **aerobiˈology** *n*. the branch of knowledge that deals with the nature and distribution of the living organisms, spores, pollen, and seeds carried by the air M20. **aeroeˈlastic** *a*. of or pertaining to aeroelasticity M20. **aeroelaˈsticity** *n*. the science of the interaction between aerodynamic forces and non-rigid structures M20. **aero-engine** *n*. an engine for propelling an aircraft M20. **aeroˈgenerator** *n*. a wind-powered electric generator M20. **aerogram**, **-gramme** *n*. a message sent through the air; esp. = *air letter* s.v. AIR *n.*[1]: L19. **aeˈrographer** *n*. a meteorologist L19. **aeˈrography** *n*. the description of the atmosphere; meteorology: M18. **aeromagˈnetic** *a*. of, or pertaining to, or derived from the measurement of the earth's magnetism by means of airborne instruments M20. **ˌaeromagneˈtometer** *n*. an instrument for making aeromagnetic measurements M20. **aeromancy** *n*. divination or augury by the air; later, weather-forecasting: LME. **aeˈrometry** *n*. (*a*) the measurement of the properties of the air; †(*b*) pneumatics: M18. **aeˈrophagy** *n*. (*Med.*) the swallowing of air E20. **aerophobe** *n*. a person who is afraid of air travel M20. **aeroˈphobia** *n*. fear of air travel L20. **aerospace** *n*. (the technology of flight in) the earth's atmosphere and outer space M20. **aerothermodyˈnamic** *a*. of or pertaining to aerothermodynamics M20. **ˌaerothermodyˈnamics** *n*. (the branch of science that deals with) the thermodynamic behaviour of flowing gases M20. **aero-towing** *n*. the towing of a glider in the air by a powered aircraft M20.

aerobatics /ɛːrəˈbatɪks/ *n.pl.* E20. [f. AERO- after *acrobatics*.] Feats of expert aviation; spectacular flying.

ˈaerobat *n*. a person who performs aerobatics E20. **aerobatic** *a*. of or pertaining to aerobatics E20.

aerobic /ɛːˈrəʊbɪk/ *a*. L19. [f. AERO- + Gk *bios* life + -IC.] **1** *Biol.* Normally dependent for life upon the presence of free oxygen; taking place in or characterized by the presence of free oxygen. L19. **2** Of, pertaining to, or resulting from aerobics. M20.

ˈaerobe *n.* an organism unable to survive in the absence of free oxygen L19. **aerobically** *adv.* (*a*) in the presence of free oxygen; (*b*) by means of aerobics: L19.

aerobics /ɛːˈrəʊbɪks/ *n.* M20. [f. prec.: see -ICS.] (The practice of) physical exercises for producing beneficial changes in the respiratory and circulatory systems by activities which can be sustained by virtue of their low oxygen demand.

aerodrome /ˈɛːrədrəʊm/ *n.* L19. [f. AERO- + -DROME; in sense 1 f. Gk *aerodromos* traversing the air.] †1 An aeroplane. L19–E20. 2 An area of open level ground, together with runways, hangars, and other installations, for the take-off, landing, and maintenance of aircraft. E20.

aerodynamics /ˌɛːrə(ʊ)dʌɪˈnamɪks/ *n.pl.* (usu. treated as *sing.*). M19. [f. AERO- + DYNAMICS.] The branch of science that deals with the properties of air or other gases in motion and the interaction between the air and solid bodies (esp. aircraft) moving through it. Also, the aerodynamic properties of an aircraft etc.

aerodynamic *a.* of or pertaining to aerodynamics or the phenomena with which it is concerned L19. **aerodynamical** *a.* = AERODYNAMIC E20. **aerodynamically** *adv.* as regards aerodynamics E20. **aerodynamicist** /-sɪst/ *n.* an expert in aerodynamics M20.

aerofoil /ˈɛːrəfɔɪl/ *n.* E20. [f. AERO- + FOIL *n.*[1]] A structure which gives rise to a lift force when moving through the air, e.g. a wing of an aircraft; a similar structure causing downward pressure on a road vehicle.

aerolite /ˈɛːrəlʌɪt/ *n.* E19. [f. AERO- + -LITE.] A meteorite; *spec.* a stony meteorite.

aerolitic /-ˈlɪtɪk/ *a.* M19.

aerology /ɛːˈrɒlədʒi/ *n.* M18. [f. AERO- + -LOGY.] The branch of knowledge that deals with the atmosphere, now *spec.* with atmospheric conditions away from ground level.

aeroˈlogical *a.* M19.

aeronaut /ˈɛːrənɔːt/ *n.* L18. [Fr. *aéronaute*, f. *aéro-* AERO- + Gk *nautēs* sailor.] A traveller through the air; a balloonist, a pilot.

aeronautic /ɛːrəˈnɔːtɪk/ *a.* L18. [f. prec. + -IC.] Of or pertaining to aeronauts or aeronautics.

aeronautical *a.* E19.

aeronautics /ɛːrəˈnɔːtɪks/ *n.pl.* (usu. treated as *sing.*). E19. [mod.L *aeronautica*, f. as prec.: see -ICS.] The science, art, or practice of controlled flight through the air.

aeronomy /ɛːˈrɒnəmi/ *n.* M20. [f. AERO- + -NOMY.] The branch of science that deals with the upper regions of the atmosphere, where dissociation and ionization of air molecules are important.

aeronomer *n.* an expert in aeronomy M20. **aeroˈnomic(al)** *adjs.* of or pertaining to aeronomy M20. **aeronomist** *n.* = AERONOMER M20.

aerophone /ˈɛːrəfəʊn/ *n.* M20. [f. AERO- + -PHONE.] A musical instrument which employs a column of air to produce the sound.

aeroplane /ˈɛːrəpleɪn/ *n.* & *v.* M19. [In sense A.1 f. AERO- + PLANE *n.*[3]; in sense A.2 f. Fr. *aéroplane*, f. *aéro-* AERO- + Gk *-planos* wandering.] A *n.* †1 An aerofoil. M19–E20. 2 An aircraft that is heavier than air and has fixed (non-rotating) wings. L19. B *v.i.* Fly like or in an aeroplane. E20.

aeroplanist *n.* (*rare*) a person who flies an aeroplane E20.

aerosol /ˈɛːrəsɒl/ *n.* & *v.* E20. [f. AERO- + SOL *n.*[5]] A *n.* 1 A colloidal suspension of particles in air or another gas. E20. 2 A substance packed under pressure and able to be released as a fine spray; a container holding such a substance. M20. B *v.t.* & *i.* Spray with an aerosol. M20.

aerosoliˈzation *n.* the action of aerosolizing something M20. **aerosolize** *v.t.* make into an aerosol, disperse as an aerosol M20.

aerostat /ˈɛːrəstat/ *n.* L18. [Fr. *aérostat*, f. *aéro-* AERO- + Gk *statos* standing.] 1 Any craft which is sustained in the air by buoyancy, e.g. a balloon, an airship. L18. †2 An aeronaut. L18–L19.

aerostation /-ˈsteɪʃ(ə)n/ *n.* (now *rare*) [Fr.] flight by lighter-than-air craft L18.

aerostatic /ɛːrəˈstatɪk/ *a.* L18. [Fr. *aérostatique*, f. as prec.: see -IC.] 1 Of or pertaining to aerostatics. L18. 2 Of or pertaining to aerostats and their use. L18.

aerostatical *a.* (*rare*) L17.

aerostatics /ɛːrəˈstatɪks/ *n.pl.* (usu. treated as *sing.*). L18. [mod.L *aerostatica*, f. as prec.: see -ICS.] The science of the equilibrium and pressure of the air and other gases, and of the behaviour of bodies supported in them.

aeruginous /ɪəˈruːdʒɪnəs/ *a.* E17. [L *aeruginosus*, f. as next: see -OUS.] Of the nature or colour of verdigris.

aerugo /ɪəˈruːgəʊ/ *n.* M16. [L, f. *aer-*, *aes* bronze.] = *crystallized* VERDIGRIS.

aery *n.* var. of EYRIE.

aery /ˈɛːri/ *a. poet.* L16. [L *aerius*, f. *aer* air, the suff. assoc. w. -Y[1].] Aerial; ethereal, incorporeal.

Aeschylean /iːskɪˈliːən/ *a.* M19. [f. L *Aeschylus* f. Gk *Aiskhulos*: see -EAN.] Of, pertaining to, or characteristic of the Athenian tragic poet Aeschylus (525–456 BC), or his works, style, etc.

Aesculapius /iːskjʊˈleɪpɪəs/ *n. joc. arch.* L16. [L *Aesculapius*, Roman god of medicine.] A physician.

Aesculapian *a.* of or pertaining to Aesculapius, medicine, or physicians E17.

Aesopian /iːˈsəʊpɪən/ *a.* L17. [f. *Aesop* (see next) + -IAN.] 1 = AESOPIC 1. L17. 2 [tr. Russ. *ézopovskiĭ*.] Designating or pertaining to Russian or Soviet Communist language or writing in which (esp. political) dissent is expressed ambiguously or allegorically, to avoid official censorship etc. M20.

Aesopic /iːˈsɒpɪk/ *a.* E18. [Late L *Aesopicus*, f. *Aesopus* f. Gk *Aisōpos*: see -IC.] 1 Pertaining to or characteristic of Aesop, a semi-legendary Greek fabulist of the 6th cent. BC. E18. 2 = AESOPIAN 2. E20.

Aesopical *a.* (*rare*) L16.

aesthesis /ɛsˈθiːsɪs/ *n.* Also ***es-**. E18. [Gk *aisthēsis* a perceiving: see AESTHETIC.] The perception of the external world by the senses.

aesthesiˈometer *n.* an instrument for measuring tactile sensitivity M19.

aesthete /ˈiːsθiːt, ˈɛs-/ *n.* Also ***es-**. L19. [f. next, after *athlete*, *athletic*, or f. Gk *aisthētēs* a person who perceives, f. as next.] A person who professes a superior appreciation of what is beautiful; in British universities, a studious person (opp. *hearty*).

aesthetic /iːsˈθɛtɪk, ɛs-/ *a.* & *n.* Also ***es-**. L18. [Gk *aisthētikos*, f. *aisthēta* things perceptible by the senses, f. *aisthesthai* perceive: see -IC. Current senses derived through G from A. T. Baumgarten's *Æsthetica* (1750). Senses B.1 & 2 in sing. through G *Ästhetik*, Fr. *esthétique*.] A *adj.* †1 Pertaining to perception by the senses. Only in L18. 2 Of or pertaining to the appreciation or criticism of the beautiful or of art. E19. 3 Of a person etc.: having appreciation of the beautiful; refined. Of a thing: in accordance with the principles of good taste; beautiful. M19. 4 *spec.* Designating, of, or pertaining to a 19th-cent. movement of artists and writers who advocated 'art for art's sake'. M19. 5 = COSMETIC *a.* 2. E20.

B *n.* 1 *sing.* & (usu.) in *pl.* (treated as *sing.*). The science of sensuous perception. (Used only w. ref. to the works of Kant.) E19. 2 *sing.* & (usu.) in *pl.* (treated as *sing.*). The philosophy of the beautiful or of art; a system of principles for the appreciation of the beautiful etc. E19. 3 An aesthete; an adherent of the aesthetic movement. L19.

2 M. H. ABRAMS The concept that art is imitation . . played an important part in neo-classic aesthetics. W. STEVENS Tests of the strength of his aesthetic, his philosophy.

aesthetical *a.* = AESTHETIC *a.* (esp. sense 2) L18. **aesthetically** *adv.* E19. **aesthetician** /-ˈtɪʃ(ə)n/ *n.* a person versed in aesthetics E19. **aestheticism** /-sɪz(ə)m/ *n.* the quality of being aesthetic; susceptibility to aesthetic influences: M19. **aestheticist** /-sɪst/ *n.* an aesthetician M19. **aestheticize** /-sʌɪz/ *v.t.* render aesthetic M19.

aestival /ˈiːstɪv(ə)l, iːˈstʌɪv(ə)l; ɛ-/ *a.* Also ***est-**. LME. [(O)Fr. *estival* f. L *aestivalis*, f. as AESTIVE: see -AL[1].] Belonging to or of summer or the summer solstice; appearing in summer.

aestivate /ˈiːstɪveɪt, ˈɛst-/ *v.i.* Also ***est-**. E17. [L *aestivat-* pa. ppl stem of *aestivare*, f. as AESTIVE: see -ATE[3].] Spend the summer, *spec.* (*Zool.*) in a state of torpor. Cf. HIBERNATE.

aestivator *n.* an animal that aestivates E20.

aestivation /iːstɪˈveɪʃ(ə)n, ɛst-/ *n.* Also ***est-**. E17. [f. as prec.: see -ATION.] †1 The spending of summer; summer residence. E17–M18. 2 *Bot.* The arrangement of the parts of a flower inside its bud before opening. Cf. VERNATION 1. E19. 3 *Zool.* The act of spending the summer in a state of torpor. Cf. HIBERNATION. M19.

aestive /ˈiːstɪv/ *a.* Also ***est-**. E17. [L *aestivus*, f. *aestus* heat: see -IVE.] Aestival; hot and burning.

†**aestuary** *n.* var. of ESTUARY.

†**aestuation** *n.* Also **est-**. L15–M18. [L *aestuatio(n-)*, f. *aestuare* boil up, f. *aestus* heat: see -ATION.] Feverish disturbance, ebullition.

†**aestuate** *v.i.* boil; surge up: E17–M18.

aetatis /ʌɪˈtɑːtɪs, iːˈteɪtɪs/ *a.* Usu. abbrev. **aet.** /ʌɪt, iːt/, ***aetat*** /ˈʌɪtat, ˈiːteɪt/. E19. [L.] Of or at the age of.

W. OWEN His son, aetat 13, learned in nothing.

aetheling *n.* var. of ATHELING.

aether *n.* see ETHER *n.*[1]

aethereal, -rial *adjs.* see ETHEREAL.

†**Aethiop, -ian** *ns.* & *adjs.* etc., vars. of ETHIOP etc.

aetiology /iːtɪˈɒlədʒi/ *n.* Also **et-**. M16. [med.L *aetiologia* (Isidore) f. Gk *aitiologia*, f. *aitia* cause + *logia* -LOGY.] 1 The assignment of a cause; (occas.) the cause assigned. M16. 2 The philosophy of causation; the part of a science which treats of the causes of its phenomena. Now *rare* or *obs.* M17. 3 *Med.* The causation of disease (usu., of a specified disease), esp. as a subject for investigation. L17.

ˌ**aetioˈlogical** *a.* M18. ˌ**aetioˈlogically** *adv.* M19.

aetites /iːˈtʌɪtiːz/ *n.* L16. [L f. Gk *aetitēs* adj. (used as n.), f. *aetos* eagle.] A stone with a loose nucleus, formerly believed to be found in eagles' nests and to have magical and medicinal properties.

†**aetna** *n.* var. of ETNA.

aeviternity /iːvɪˈtəːnɪti/ *n.* Now *rare.* Also **e-**. L16. [f. L *aeviternus* eternal + -ITY.] Eternal existence; everlasting duration.

af- /af, *unstressed* əf/ *pref.* (rarely productive). Assim. form of L *ad-* bef. *f*. In OFr., L *aff-* was reduced to *af-*, which appears in early adoptions, but in later Fr., and hence in Eng., *aff-* was restored by Latinization, as *affair*, *affront*. Hence extended to some words of different origin, as *affray*, *affright*.

afanc /aˈvaŋk/ *n.* M19. [Welsh *afanc* beaver; cogn. w. Ir. *abac* beaver, dwarf.] *Celtic Mythol.* An aquatic monster.

Afar /ˈafɑː/ *n.* & *a.* Pl. of n. same. M19. [Afar *qafar*.] = DANAKIL.

afar /əˈfɑː/ *adv.* ME. [f. A *prep.*[1] 1 & A *prep.*[2] + FAR *adv.*] 1 From a distance. Now only in *from afar*. ME. 2 At or to a distance. Now usu. foll. by *off*. ME.

afara /əˈfɑːrə/ *n.* E20. [Yoruba.] = LIMBA *n.*[2]

afear /əˈfɪə/ *v.t.* Now *dial.* OE. [f. A-[1] + FEAR *v.*] Frighten.

afear(e)d *ppl a.* (superseded in general use by AFRAID) OE.

afebrile /eɪˈfiːbrʌɪl/ *a.* L19. [f. A-[10] + FEBRILE.] *Med.* Unaccompanied by fever; not feverish.

affable /ˈafəb(ə)l/ *a.* LME. [(O)Fr. f. L *affabilis*, f. *affari*, f. *ad* AF- + *fari* speak: see -ABLE.] Easy to approach and converse with; courteous, esp. with inferiors; kindly and polite.

affaˈbility *n.* L15. **affably** *adv.* E17.

affair /əˈfɛː/ *n.* ME. [AN *afere*, OFr. *afaire* (mod. *affaire*), f. *à faire* to do: cf. ADO *n.* See also EFFEIR.] 1 What one has to do; business; a concern, a matter. ME. 2 *spec.* In *pl.* Ordinary pursuits of life; business dealings; public matters. L15. 3 A (usu. temporary) sexual relationship outside marriage; a love affair. E18. 4 A thing; an incident; an occasion; *spec.* a notorious incident, a scandal. *colloq.* E19.

1 SHAKES. *Haml.* What is your affair in Elsinore? **affair of honour** *arch.* a duel to settle a question of honour. 2 S. SMILES Men of affairs, trained to business. N. MITFORD They chatted . . about local affairs. *state of affairs*: see STATE *n.* *statement of affairs*: see STATEMENT *n.* 3 C. HAMPTON I did have an affair with a gypsy when I was about fifteen. 4 JOYCE The annual dinner you know. . . Boiled shirt affair. R. RENDELL The neighbouring front door, a far more trendy and ambitious affair.

affaire /afɛːr/ *n.* Pl. pronounced same. E19. [Fr.] In full *affaire de* (or *du*) *cœur* /də, dy, kœːr/ [lit. 'of the heart']. = AFFAIR 3.

affairé /afere/ *a.* E20. [Fr.] Busy; involved.

†**affamish** *v.t.* & *i.* M16–M17. [Fr. *affamer*: see A-[5], FAMISH.] Starve.

affamishment /əˈfamɪʃm(ə)nt/ *n. arch.* L16. [f. prec. + -MENT.] Starvation.

affect /ˈafɛkt/ *n.* LME. [L *affectus* n. of completed action f. *afficere*: see AFFECT *v.*[2] Sense 2 through G *Affekt*.] †1 Mental or physical disposition or constitution. LME–L17. 2 *Psychol.* An emotion, a mood. L19.

affectless *a.* without emotion, incapable of feeling emotion M20. **affectlessness** *n.* M20.

†**affect** *ppl a.* LME–L17. [L *affectus* pa. pple of *afficere*: see AFFECT *v.*[2]] = AFFECTED II, III.

affect /əˈfɛkt/ *v.*[1]*t.* LME. [Fr. *affecter* or L *affectare*, f. *affect-*: see next.] 1 Like, love. *arch.* LME. b *esp.* Like to use, practise, wear, or frequent. M16. †2 Aim at, seek. L15–L18. 3 Use or display ostentatiously; assume the character of; take upon oneself (*to do*), profess. L16. 4 Of things: have or display a natural tendency towards. E17. 5 Assume a false appearance of; pretend. E17.

1 EVELYN Some affect to have it fry'd a little broun and crisp. R. KIPLING [He] . . did not much affect the Major. *absol.*: SHAKES. *Ant. & Cl.* Making peace or war As thou affects. b M. BRADBURY He took to wearing the black leather jackets that most of his colleagues . . affected. 2 SHAKES. *2 Hen. VI* Have I affected wealth or honour? T. JEFFERSON He has affected to render the military independent of . . the civil power. 3 POPE Spenser himself affects the obsolete. CARLYLE He affected the freethinker. D. MAHON And once (he affected communism) He brought the whole crew out on strike. 5 SIR W. SCOTT He tired, or affected to tire. G. VIDAL I affected an even deeper sincerity.

affecter *n.* M16.

affect /əˈfɛkt/ *v.*[2]*t.* LME. [Fr. *affecter* or L *affect-* pa. ppl stem of *afficere*, f. *ad* AD- + *facere* do; sense I may be f. L *affectare* and so a branch of prec.] 1 Attack as a disease. LME. 2 Move, touch, (in mind or feelings); influence; make a material impression on. L16. 3 In *pass.* Be assigned *to*. *arch.* E17.

affectaˈbility *n.* ability to be affected L19. **affectable** *a.* able to be affected M18.

affectation /afɛkˈteɪʃ(ə)n/ *n.* M16. [Fr., or L *affectatio(n-)*, f. *affectare*: see AFFECT *v.*[1], -ATION.] †1 An aiming at; earnest pursuit. M16–E18. 2 An ostentatious fondness; studied display. Foll. by *of*. M16. 3 Artificiality of manner; (a) pretence. L16. †4 Affection, liking. (Foll. by *of*.) E17–L18.

affected /əˈfɛktɪd/ *a.* M16. [Branch I f. AFFECT *v.*[1] + -ED[1]; branch II f. AFFECT *ppl a.* + -ED[1]; branch III f. AFFECT *v.*[2] + -ED[1]: senses to some extent confused through formal identity.] I 1 Artificially assumed or displayed; pretended; (of language) stilted. M16. 2 Of a person: full of affectation, artificial. L16. †3 Sought after, aimed at. L16–M17. †4 Fondly held; loved. L16–E18. II 5 Disposed, inclined (usu. w. adv. of manner). M16. †6 *esp.* Favourably disposed, partial, (*to*). M16–L17. III 7 Attacked by a disease, afflicted. E17. 8a Mentally influenced; moved, touched in the feelings, (*by*, †*with*). E17. b Of a thing: influenced, acted upon, (*by*). M18. 9 Specially allotted. E17.

affectedness *n.* = AFFECTATION 3 E17.

affectedly /əˈfɛktɪdli/ *adv.* L16. [f. AFFECTED I + -LY[2].] †1 Intentionally, earnestly. L16–M18. †2 Affectionately. L16–E17. 3 With studied art; artificially. L16. 4 With studied simulation; hypocritically. M17.

affecting /əˈfɛktɪŋ/ *ppl a.* L16. [Branch I f. AFFECT *v.*[1], branch II f. AFFECT *v.*[2] + -ING[2].] I †1 Using affectation. L16–E17. †2 Loving, affectionate. Only in E17. II †3 Impressive. M17–L18. 4 Touching the emotions; moving. E18.

affectingly *adv.* M18.

affection /əˈfɛkʃ(ə)n/ *n.* ME. [(O)Fr. f. L *affectio(n-)*, f. *affect-*: see AFFECT *v.*[2], -ION.] I Of the mind. 1 A mental state; an emotion, a feeling. ME. †b *esp.* Feeling as opp. to reason; passion, lust. ME–M18. 2 Disposition towards something, bent, inclination. *arch.* ME. †b *gen.* Mental tendency, disposition. M16–M18. 3 Goodwill, kindly feeling, love. LME.

1b SPENSER Most wretched man, That to Affections does the bridle lend! 3 R. D. LAING Love lets the other be, but with affection and concern. L. P. SMITH Unrequited affections are in youth unmitigated woes. *alienation of affection*: see ALIENATION 1. *walk into a person's affections*: see WALK *v.*[1]

II Of the body. 4 A bodily state; *esp.* a malady, a disease. M16.

4 A. P. HERBERT Her voice was permanently husky from some old affection of the throat.

III Of substances or essences. 5 A non-essential state; a mode of being; a property or attribute. M16.

5 INJURIOUS *affection*.

IV *gen.* 6 The action of affecting; the state of being affected. L16. b *Celtic Philol.* Mutation or umlaut of a vowel under the influence of a following sound. E20.

6 J. S. MILL The affection of our bodily organs from without.

V [AFFECT *v.*[1] confused w. *v.*[2]] †7 = AFFECTATION 2, 3. L16–E19.

7 COLERIDGE The gaudy affections of style which passed current . . for poetic diction.

affectional *a.* of or having affections M19. **affectioned** *a.* (now *rare* or *obs.*) = AFFECTIONATE *a.* M16.

affection /əˈfɛkʃ(ə)n/ *v.t. arch.* L16. [(O)Fr. *affectionner*, f. as prec.] Like, love.

affectionate /əˈfɛkʃ(ə)nət/ *a.* L15. [f. Fr. *affectionné* beloved, or its source med.L *affectionatus* devoted: see AFFECTION *n.*, -ATE[2].] †1 Mentally disposed (*to*). L15–M17. †2 Biased, prejudiced. L15–E17. †3 Passionate, wilful. M16–E18. †4 Well-disposed, favourable, (*to*). M16–M18. 5 Loving, fond; (of a thing) expressing or indicating affection. L16. †6 Eager, ambitious. L16–M18.

†**affectionated** *a.* = AFFECTIONATE *a.* M16–M19. **affectionately** *adv.* M16. **affectionateness** *n.* M17.

affective /əˈfɛktɪv/ *a.* LME. [Fr. *affectif*, *-ive* f. late L *affectivus*, f. *affect-*: see AFFECT *v.*[2], -IVE.] †1 Tending to affect or influence. LME–E18. 2 Of or pertaining to the affections; emotional. LME.

affectively *adv.* M17. **affecˈtivity** *n.* emotional susceptibility E20.

affectual /əˈfɛktjʊəl, -tʃʊəl/ *a.* L15. [OFr. *affectuel* f. med.L *affectualis*, f. as AFFECT *n.*: see -AL[1].] †1 Earnest, ardent. L15–L16. 2 = AFFECTIVE 2. M17.

affectually *adv.* LME.

†**affectuous** *a.* ME–L19. [Fr. *affectueux*, f. as AFFECT *n.*: see -OUS.] Eager, earnest; affectionate; emotional.

†**affectuously** *adv.* LME–E20.

affeer /əˈfɪə/ *v.t.* ME. [OFr. *aforer*, *afeurer*, AN *aferer* f. med.L *afforare* fix the price, f. *ad* AF- + *forum* market.] *Hist.* Assess (an amercement); reduce to a fair amount.

affeerment *n.* the action of affeering M17. **affeeror** *n.* a person who affeers an amercement LME.

affenpinscher /ˈafənpɪnʃə/ *n.* E20. [G, f. *Affe* ape, monkey + *Pinscher* terrier.] (An animal of) a toy breed of dog related to the griffon and having a profuse wiry coat.

afferent /ˈaf(ə)r(ə)nt/ *a.* M19. [L *afferent-* pres. ppl stem of *afferre*, f. *ad* AF- + *ferre* bring: see -ENT.] *Anat.* Conducting inwards (of a nerve: towards the central nervous system; of a blood-vessel: towards an organ). Opp. EFFERENT.

affettuoso /əfɛtjʊˈəʊzəʊ, -tʊ-/ *adv.*, *a.*, & *n.* E18. [It.] *Mus.* A *adv.* & *adj.* (A direction:) with feeling, tender(ly). E18.

B *n.* Pl. **-si** /-zi/, **-sos**. A movement expressing tenderness. *rare.* L18.

fig.: BURKE The tender, soothing strains, in the affettuoso of humanity.

affiance /əˈfʌɪəns/ *n. arch.* ME. [OFr. *afiance*, f. as AFFY: see -ANCE.] 1 Trust, faith, (*in*, occas. *on*). ME. †2 Confidence, assurance. LME–M18. 3 The pledging of faith, esp. in marriage. LME. †4 Affinity. L15–E17.

affiance /əˈfʌɪəns/ *v.t.* L15. [OFr. *afiancer*, f. as prec.] Promise solemnly, esp. in marriage. Usu. in *pass.* foll. by *to*.

affiant /əˈfʌɪənt/ *n. US.* E19. [Fr.: see AFFY, -ANT[1].] *Law.* A person who makes an affidavit.

affiche /afiʃ (*pl. same*); əˈfiːʃ/ *n.* E19. [Fr.] A notice affixed to a wall etc.; a poster.

affidavit /afɪˈdeɪvɪt/ *n.* M16. [3 sing. perf. indic. of med.L *affidare* declare on oath: see AFFY.] *Law.* A written statement, confirmed by oath or affirmation, to be used as evidence.

¶In legal phr. the deponent *swears* an affidavit, the judge *takes* it; but in pop. use the deponent *makes* or *takes* it.

affiliate /əˈfɪlɪət/ *ppl a.* & *n.* M19. [L *affiliatus* pa. pple, f. as next: see -ATE[1].] A *ppl a.* Affiliated. *rare.* M19. B *n.* Someone or something affiliated; *esp.* an affiliated organization or company. L19.

affiliate /əˈfɪlɪeɪt/ *v.* E17. [med.L *affiliat-* pa. ppl stem of *affiliare*, f. *ad* AF- + *filius* son; prob. after Fr. *affilier*: see -ATE[3].] †1 *v.t.* Adopt as a son. Only in Dicts. Only in E17. 2 *v.t.* Adopt as a subordinate member of a society, branch of an organization or company, etc.; attach *to* or connect *with* an organization etc. M18. b *v.i.* Connect oneself *with*. M19. 3 *v.t.* In *Law*, fix the paternity of an illegitimate child *on* the putative father (for the purpose of maintenance); *gen.* ascribe (a child) *to* his or her proper parent; *fig.* father (*up*)*on*, attribute *to*. E19.

affiliative *a.* pertaining to affiliation or social relationships; sociable, sympathetic: M20.

affiliation /əfɪlɪˈeɪʃ(ə)n/ *n.* E17. [Fr. f. med.L *affiliatio(n-)*, f. as prec.: see -ATION.] 1 Adoption of a son. *rare.* E17. 2 Adoption by a society etc. of branches; union with a central organization. L18. b (A) connection, association. Freq. in *pl.* M19. 3 The fixing of the paternity of a child; *fig.* the fathering of a thing upon anyone, the assignment of a thing to its origin. M19.

2b F. D. ROOSEVELT I have not the slightest idea what your political affiliations are. S. ROBERTSON The closest affiliations of English . . are . . with the Low German languages.

Comb.: **affiliation order** a legal order that the putative father of an illegitimate child must help to support him or her.

affinal /əˈfʌɪn(ə)l/ *a.* M19. [f. L *affinis* (see AFFINITY) + -AL[1].] Related by marriage; pertaining to marriage.

affine /əˈfʌɪn/ *n.* & *a.* E16. [f. as prec. or OFr. *afin* (mod. *affin*).] A *n.* A relation by marriage; a kinsman, a kinswoman. E16. B *adj.* 1 Closely related. M17. 2 *Math.* That allows of or preserves parallelism. E20.

affined /əˈfʌɪnd/ *ppl a.* L16. [f. (as) prec. + -ED[1], perh. after OFr. *afiné*.] 1 Related, connected. L16. 2 Bound by any tie. *rare.* E17.

1 W. STEVENS Portentous enunciation, syllable To blessed syllable affined. 2 SHAKES. *Oth.* Whether I . . am affin'd To love the Moor.

affinity /əˈfɪnɪti/ *n.* ME. [OFr. *afinité* (mod. *aff-*) f. L *affinitas*, f. *affinis*, f. *ad* AF- + *finis* border: see -ITY.] I By position. 1 Relationship, esp. by marriage; *collect.* relations, kindred. ME. 2 *fig.* Similarity of character suggesting relationship; family likeness. LME. 3 Structural resemblance (between languages, animals, plants, etc.) suggestive of a common stock or type. L16.

II By inclination or attraction. †4 Voluntary social relationship. LME–E17. 5 *fig.* Liking, attraction; a person having attraction for another. E17. 6 *Chem.* The tendency of a substance to combine with another. M18.

4 AV *2 Chron.* 18:1 Jehosaphat . . ioyned affinitie with Ahab. 5 D. CECIL There is no affinity more perfect than that founded on similar tastes and complementary temperaments. W. FAULKNER A woman's affinity and instinct for secrecy. 6 JOYCE The incalculable trillions . . of imperceptible molecules contained by cohesion of molecular affinity in a single pinhead.

Comb.: **affinity card** (*a*) *US* a discount card issued to members of an affinity group; (*b*) a bank card for which the bank donates to a specified charity etc. a portion of the money spent using the card; **affinity group** *US* an association of people with a common interest or aim.

affinitive *a.* characterized by affinity; closely related: M17.

affirm /əˈfəːm/ *v.* ME. [OFr. *afermer* (mod. *affirmer*) f. L *affirmare*, f. *ad* AF- + *firmus* firm.] †1 *v.t.* Make firm, strengthen; support. ME–M17. 2 *v.t. Law.* Confirm or ratify (a judgement, a contract). LME. †3 *v.t.* Confirm or maintain (a statement). LME–M17. 4 *v.t.* Assert strongly, state as a fact. LME. b *Law.* Make an affirmation because unwilling to take an oath. (Foll. by *that.*) LME. c *Logic.* State to be true. L17. 5 *v.i. Logic & Gram.* Make a statement in the affirmative. *rare.* M16.

1 LD BERNERS The goddis assure & affirme euerything. 2 LD MACAULAY Twenty-three peers voted for reversing the judgment; thirty-five for affirming it. 3 SHAKES. *Hen. V* I said so . . and I must not blush to affirm it. 4 A. STORR If a man holds beliefs that are unpopular . . he will look for people with whom he can identify himself in order to affirm his own identity. J. MONTAGUE Against her choice, I still affirm That nothing dies. 5 P. SIDNEY Grammer sayes . . That in one speech two Negatiues affirme.

affirmable *a.* E17. **affirmant** *a.* & *n.* (*a*) *adj.* affirming; (*b*) *n.* a person who affirms: L16. **affirmer** *n.* LME.

affirmance /əˈfəːm(ə)ns/ *n.* LME. [OFr. *af(f)ermance*, f. as prec.: see -ANCE.] 1 An assertion; a strong declaration. LME. 2 A confirming. E16.

affirmation /afəˈmeɪʃ(ə)n/ *n.* LME. [Fr., or L *affirmatio(n-)*, f. *affirmare*: see AFFIRM, -ATION.] 1 Confirmation. LME. 2 Assertion as true. Also, something which is affirmed; a positive statement. LME. 3 *Law.* A solemn declaration by a person who conscientiously declines taking an oath. L17.

aˈffirmatory *a.* giving affirmation, assertive (*of*) M17.

affirmative /əˈfəːmətɪv/ *a.*, *n.*, & *int.* LME. [(O)Fr. *affirmatif*, *-ive* f. late L *affirmativus*, f. as prec.: see -ATIVE.] A *adj.* 1 Assertive; positive. LME. 2 Asserting that a fact is so; answering 'yes'. L15. b *Logic.* Asserting that something is true of the subject of a proposition. L16. †3 Corroborative, confirmatory. E16–M17.

1 **affirmative action** positive action towards a goal, *esp.* the employment of minority groups and women. 3 CLARENDON The affirmative advice of all the Judges of England.

B *n.* Something which affirms; an affirmative word, statement, or proposition; an affirmative reply. LME.

answer in the affirmative answer 'yes', or that it is so. **vote in the affirmative** vote in favour of a proposal.

C *int.* Yes. Chiefly *N. Amer.* (orig. *Mil.*). L19.

affirmatively *adv.* LME.

affix /ˈafɪks/ *n.* L16. [L *affixus* pa. pple of *affigere*, f. *ad* AF- + *figere* fasten.] 1 An appendage, an addition. L16. †2 = AFFICHE. L16–L19. 3 *Gram.* A grammatical element prefixed, infixed, or suffixed to the root of a word. E17.

affixal *a.* (*Gram.*) pertaining to or involving an affix L19.

affix /əˈfɪks/ *v.t.* LME. [(O)Fr. *affixer* or med.L *affixare*, f. *ad* AF- + *fixare* fix.] 1 Fix, fasten, (*to*, *on*, *upon*). LME. †2 Fix upon, determine, settle. E16–E18. 3 Impress (a seal, stamp); add in writing (a signature, postscript, etc.). M17. b *fig.* Attach as a stigma (*to*), stigmatize (*with*). M17.

1 JOYCE An exotically . . accorded . . tinkle gatebell affixed to left lateral gatepost. *fig.*: SPENSER She affixed had Her hart on knight so goodly-glorifyde. 2 POPE The land, affix'd . . To end his toils.

affixer *n.* M19.

affixation /afɪkˈseɪʃ(ə)n/ *n.* E17. [Sense 1 f. AFFIX *v.*, sense 2 f. AFFIX *n.*: see -ATION.] 1 Affixture. E17. 2 *Gram.* Addition of an affix. E20.

affixture /əˈfɪkstʃə/ *n.* L18. [f. AFFIX *v.*, after *fixture.*] The action of affixing; the state of being affixed; attachment.

afflate /əˈfleɪt/ *v.t. rare.* L16. [L *afflat-*: see next, -ATE[3].] Blow or breathe upon; inspire. Chiefly as *afflated* ppl a.

afflation *n.* M17.

afflatus /əˈfleɪtəs/ *n.* M17. [L, f. *afflat-* pa. ppl stem of *afflare*, f. *ad* AF- + *flare* to blow.] The communication of supernatural knowledge; divine impulse; (esp. poetic) inspiration.

†**afflict** *ppl a.* Also **afflight**. ME–L16. [OFr. *aflit* f. L *afflictus* pa. pple of *affligere*: see next.] Afflicted.

afflict /əˈflɪkt/ *v.t.* LME. [L *afflictare*, or *afflict-* pa. ppl stem of *affligere*, f. *ad* AF- + *fligere* strike; partly through prec. Cf. OFr. *afflicter.*] †1 Cast down; deject, humble. LME–M17. 2 Distress with bodily or mental suffering; trouble grievously. M16.

1 MILTON Reassembling our afflicted Powers. 2 S. JOHNSON They are afflicted with the head-ach. B. RUSSELL A more general trouble afflicting all large organizations.

afflicter *n.* L16. **afflictingly** *adv.* in an afflicting manner, so as to afflict E19.

affliction /əˈflɪkʃ(ə)n/ *n.* ME. [(O)Fr. f. L *afflictio(n-)*, f. *afflict-*: see AFFLICT *v.*, -ION.] †1 The infliction of grievous pain or trouble; self-mortification. ME–E17. 2 The state of being afflicted; misery, distress. LME. 3 A pain, a calamity; a cause of misery or distress. LME.

afflictive /əˈflɪktɪv/ *a.* E17. [(O)Fr. *afflictif*, *-ive* f. med.L *afflictivus*, f. *afflict-*: see AFFLICT *v.*, -IVE.] Tending to afflict; painful; trying. (Foll. by *to.*)

afflictively *adv.* L17.

†**afflight** *ppl a.* var. of AFFLICT *ppl a.*

affluence /ˈafluəns/ *n.* LME. [Fr. f. L *affluentia*, f. as next: see -ENCE.] 1 A plentiful flow (*of*); profusion, abundance. LME. 2 Abundance of worldly possessions, wealth. L16. 3 A flowing towards a particular place; a concourse. L16.

1 LONGFELLOW Winter . . with its affluence of snows. 2 D. LODGE At a time of increasing general affluence they had to be content with cramped, poorly furnished accommodation. 3 CARLYLE Great affluence of company.

Also **affluency** *n.* (long *rare*) M17.

affluent /ˈafluənt/ *a.* LME. [(O)Fr. f. L *affluent-* pres. ppl stem of *affluere*, f. *ad* AF- + *fluere* flow: see -ENT.] †1 Flowing towards a particular place. LME–M18. 2 Flowing freely; copious, abundant. LME. 3 Having plenty of money; wealthy. M18.

2 T. NASHE So affluent an argument. GOLDSMITH Possessed of a very affluent fortune. SOUTHEY O'er his shoulders broad the affluent mane Dishevell'd hung. 3 **affluent society**: in which material wealth is widely distributed.

affluently *adv.* L17.

afflux /ˈaflʌks/ *n.* E17. [med.L *affluxus*, f. *afflux-* pa. ppl stem of *affluere*: see prec. Cf. Fr. *afflux.*] 1 = AFFLUENCE 1. E17. 2 An accession. *rare.* M17.

Also **affluxion** *n.* M17.

affodill /ˈafədɪl/ *n.* Now *rare* or *obs.* LME. [med.L *affodilus* var. of L *asphodilus* ASPHODEL.] †1 = ASPHODEL 1. LME–E17. 2 = DAFFODIL 2. *dial.* M16.

afforce /əˈfɔːs/ *v.t.* ME. [OFr. *aforcier*, f. as A-[5] + FORCE *n.*[1]] †1 Apply force to; *refl.* try. ME–E16. †2 Add force to. Only in LME. 3 Strengthen (a deliberative body etc.) by the addition of new members. E19.

afforcement *n.* †(*a*) a fort; (*b*) reinforcement of a deliberative body etc.: M18.

afford /əˈfɔːd/ *v.t.* [Late OE *ġeforþian*, f. *forþian* to further, f. as FORTH: see A-[4]. For the change of /θ/ to /d/ cf. *burden*, *murder.*] †1 Advance; perform; accomplish. LOE–LME. 2 Manage *to do*. With *can*, *be able to*: have the means or be rich enough *to do*, be in a position *to do*; spare; bear the expense of. LME. 3 Provide, furnish, grant; of things: be capable of yielding, yield naturally. L16.

2 O. MANNING We cannot afford to go to expensive restaurants every night. G. GREENE I had won the game already, and I could afford to feel a certain pity for my victim. E. O'NEILL I paid a lot of money I couldn't afford. F. M. FORD She could not . . afford a maid . . since every penny was of importance to her. 3 SHAKES. *Rom. & Jul.* The world affords no law to make thee rich. J. IRVING The great privacy afforded us by speaking English in a German-speaking tavern.

affordaˈbility *n.* ability to be afforded L20. **affordable** *a.* able to be afforded M19. **affordably** *adv.* L20. **afforder** *n.* L16.

afforest /əˈfɒrɪst/ *v.t.* E16. [med.L *afforestare*, f. *ad* AF- + *foresta* FOREST *n.*] Convert into forest; plant with trees.

afforestable *a.* E20. **afforeˈstation** *n.* the action or result of converting an area into forest E17.

afformative /əˈfɔːmətɪv/ *a.* & *n.* E19. [f. AF- + FORMATIVE.] Chiefly *Semitic Gram.* (A particle) suffixed as a formative element. Cf. PREFORMATIVE.

affranchise /əˈfran(t)ʃʌɪz/ *v.t.* L15. [OFr. *afranchiss-* lengthened stem of *afranchir* (mod. *aff-*), f. *à* A-[5] + *franc* free. Cf. ENFRANCHISE.] Release from servitude or from an obligation etc.

affranchisement *n.* L18.

affray /əˈfreɪ/ *n.* ME. [AN *affrai*, OFr. *effrei*, *esf-* (mod. *effroi*), f. as next.] †1 An attack, an assault. ME–L16. †2 Alarm, fright, terror. ME–L16. 3 A disturbance, a noisy outburst; a fray. *obs.* in *gen.* sense. ME. b *esp.* A breach of the peace by fighting or rioting. L15.

affray /əˈfreɪ/ *v.t. arch.* Pa. pple & ppl a. **affrayed**, AFRAID. ME. [AN *afrayer*, OFr. *effreer*, *esf-* (mod. *effrayer*), f. as A-[7] + base ult. f. Gmc (cogn. w. FRITH *n.*[1]). Aphet. to FRAY *v.*[1]] 1 Disturb, startle. ME. 2 Alarm, frighten. ME. 3 Frighten away. LME.

affrayer *n.* a person who affrays; a disturber of the peace: L15.

affrayed *pred. a.* see AFRAID.

affreightment /əˈfreɪtm(ə)nt/ *n.* M18. [Fr. *affrètement* (earlier written *affrét-*), f. *affréter*, f. *à* A-[5] + *fret* freight; sp. assim. to FREIGHT *n.*: see -MENT.] The hiring of a ship to carry cargo.

affricate /ˈafrɪkət/ *n.* L19. [L *affricatus* pa. pple, f. as next: see -ATE[1].] *Phonet.* A combination of a plosive with an immediately following homorganic fricative or spirant as one phoneme (as in the first and last consonants of *church* and *judge*).

Also **aˈffricative** *n.* L19.

affricate /ˈafrɪkeɪt/ *v.t.* M17. [L *affricat-* pa. ppl stem of *affricare*, f. *ad* AF- + *fricare* rub: see -ATE[3].] †1 Rub (on or against). *rare.* M17–E18. 2 *Phonet.* Convert into an affricate. L19.

affrication /afrɪˈkeɪʃ(ə)n/ *n.* E18. [L *affricatio(n-)*, f. as prec.: see -ATION.] †1 Rubbing on or against. *rare.* Only in E18. 2 *Phonet.* Conversion into an affricate; pronunciation as an affricate. L19.

†**affriended** *pa. pple* & *ppl a. rare* (Spenser). Only in L16. [f. A-[11] + FRIEND *n.* + -ED[1].] Made friends, reconciled.

affright /əˈfrʌɪt/ *n. arch.* L16. [f. the vb, on the analogy of *fright* n. & vb.] 1 Terror, fright. L16. 2 The action of frightening; a cause of fear. E17.

affrightful *a.* (*arch.*) frightening, terrifying E17.

affright /əˈfrʌɪt/ *ppl a.* Long *arch. rare.* [OE *āfyrhted* pa. pple: see A-[1], FRIGHT *v.*, -ED[1]. Cf. next.] Frightened.

affright /əˈfrʌɪt/ *v.t. arch.* or *poet.* LME. [Rare early use f. as prec.; later (L16) f. FRIGHT *v.* by vague form-association.] Frighten, terrify.

affrighted *ppl a.* frightened (replacing AFFRIGHT *ppl a.*) E17. **affrightedly** *adv.* E17. **affrighten** *v.t.* = AFFRIGHT *v.* M17. **affrightment** *n.* †(*a*) = AFFRIGHT *n.* 1; (*b*) = AFFRIGHT *n.* 2: L16.

affront /əˈfrʌnt/ *n.* L16. [f. the vb. Cf. Fr. *affront.*] 1a An open insult; an intentionally disrespectful word or act. L16. b An instance of offence to one's self-respect or modesty. E17. †2 An encounter; an attack, an assault. L16–L17. †3 A position of hostility; an obstacle. Only in M17.

1a BUNYAN They had offered great affronts to his person. b A. G. GARDINER She . . looked indignant, almost hurt, as though she had received some secret personal affront. 2 MILTON Dreaded On hostile ground, none daring my affront.

affront /ə'frʌnt/ *v.t.* ME. [OFr. *afronter* (mod. *aff-*) ult. f. L phr. *ad frontem* to the face: see AF-, FRONT *n.*] 1 Insult to the face or openly. ME. 2 Offend the modesty or self-respect of. ME. 3 Face in defiance; confront. M16. †4 Put oneself in the way of, accost. E-M17. 5 Face in position; look towards. *arch.* E17.

affronter *n.* L16. **affrontingly** *adv.* in an affronting manner, so as to affront L17. **affrontive** *a.* affronting in character or tendency M17.

affronted /ə'frʌntɪd/ *ppl a.* L16. [f. prec. + -ED¹; sense 2 tr. Fr. *effronté.*] 1 Fronted; faced. Also = AFFRONTY. *rare.* L16. †2 Impudent; full of effrontery. Only in M17. 3 Insulted, offended. E18.

1 D. DAVIE Two birds affronted with a human head Between their beaks.

†**affrontedly** *adv.* with effrontery E17-M18.

affrontee /afrʌn'tiː/ *n. rare.* E19. [f. AFFRONT *v.* + -EE¹.] An affronted person; the person affronted.

affronty /ə'frʌnti/ *a.* M16. [Fr. *affronté* pa. pple of *affronter*: see AFFRONT *v.*] *Her.* Looking towards the spectator.

affuse /ə'fjuːz/ *v.t.* Now *rare.* E17. [L *affus-* pa. ppl stem of *affundere*, f. *ad* AF- + *fundere* pour.] Pour (*upon*).

affusion /-ʒ(ə)n/ *n.* a pouring on or into, as of water on the body in one method of baptism E17.

affy /ə'fʌɪ/ *v. arch.* ME. [OFr. *afier* (later *aff-*) f. med.L *affidare*, f. *ad* AF- + *fidare* to trust.] †1 *v.t.* & *i.* Trust, confide, (*in*, *on*). ME-M17. †2 *v.t.* Affirm on one's faith. L15-E17. 3 *v.t.* Make fast by a solemn promise; espouse; affiance. L15.

Afghan /'afgan/ *n.* & *a.* L18. [Pashto *afghānī.*] A *n.* 1 A native or inhabitant of Afghanistan, a country lying N. of Pakistan; the language (Pashto) of the people of Afghanistan. L18. 2 (**a-**.) A knitted and sewn woollen blanket or shawl; (in the Indian subcontinent) a quilt, a coarse rug. M19. 3 = *Afghan hound* below. M20. 4 = *Afghan coat* below. L20.

B *attrib.* or as *adj.* Of or pertaining to Afghanistan or the Afghans. L18.

Afghan coat a kind of sheepskin coat with the skin side outside, sometimes embroidered and usu. having a shaggy border. **Afghan hound** (an animal of) a tall breed of hunting dog with long silky hair, originating in Afghanistan.

afghani /af'gɑːni/ *n.* the basic monetary unit of Afghanistan, equal to 100 puls E20.

aficionado /afɪsjə'nɑːdəʊ, *foreign* afiθjo'naðo/ *n.* Pl. **-os** /-əʊz, *foreign* -os/. M19. [Sp. = amateur, use as n. of pa. pple of *aficionar* become fond of, f. *afición* f. L: see AFFECTION *n.*] 1 A devotee of bullfighting. M19. 2 An ardent follower of any activity. L19.

afield /ə'fiːld/ *adv.* ME. [f. A *prep.*¹ 1 + FIELD *n.*] 1 In or to the field. ME. 2 Away from home; to or at a distance. LME.

1 SHAKES. *Tr. & Cr.* Æneas is a-field. W. MORRIS Afield he never went, Either to hunting or the frontier war. E. POUND High grain a-field, hundred-fold yield. 2 C. KINGSLEY I had . . never been further afield than Fulham.

†**afingered** *a.* var. of OFHUNGERED.

afire /ə'fʌɪə/ *adv.* & *pred. a.* ME. [f. A *prep.*¹ 6 + FIRE *n.*] On fire, burning, (*lit.* & *fig.*).

aflame /ə'fleɪm/ *adv.* & *pred. a.* M16. [f. A *prep.*¹ 6 + FLAME *n.*] In flames; in a glow (*lit.* & *fig.*).

aflare /ə'flɛː/ *adv.* & *pred. a.* L19. [f. A-² + FLARE *n.*¹] Flaring; spread out; blazing, glowing.

aflat /ə'flat/ *adv.* & *pred. a. arch.* ME. [f. A *prep.*¹ 1 + FLAT *n.*²] In a flat position.

aflatoxin /aflə'tɒksɪn/ *n.* M20. [f. mod.L *A(spergillus fla(vus)* (see below) + TOXIN.] Any of a class of carcinogenic toxins produced by moulds of the *Aspergillus flavus* group.

aflaunt /ə'flɔːnt/ *adv.* & *pred. a. arch.* M16. [f. A *prep.*¹ 6 + FLAUNT *n.*] Flaunting.

afloat /ə'fləʊt/ *adv.* & *pred. a.* OE. [f. A *prep.*¹ 6 + FLOAT *n.*; in ME partly after ON *á flot(i)*, and OFr. *en flot*; from 16 prob. a new formation.] I *lit.* 1 Floating (as if) in water; at sea; on board ship. OE. 2 Floating in the air. M16. 3 In a state of overflow or submersion. L16.

1 S. JOHNSON Whatever is afloat in the stream of time. M. INNES Enough to stock all the smoke-rooms of all the liners afloat. 2 BROWNING Carelessly passing with your robes afloat. 3 F. MARRYAT The main deck was afloat.

II *fig.* 4 Unembarrassed, out of debt. M16. 5 Fully started; in full swing. M16. 6 In general circulation; current. L16. 7 Unsettled; adrift. E17.

6 J. BRIGHT Various rumours were afloat. J. AUSTEN Whatever money he might come into . . it is, I dare say, all afloat, all employed in his stock, and so forth.

aflow /ə'fləʊ/ *adv.* & *pred. a.* M19. [f. A-² + FLOW *n.*¹ or *v.*] Flowing.

aflower /ə'flaʊə/ *adv.* & *pred. a.* L19. [f. A-² + FLOWER *n.*] Flowering; in bloom.

aflutter /ə'flʌtə/ *adv.* & *pred. a.* E19. [f. A-² + FLUTTER *n.*] Fluttering; in a flutter.

afoam /ə'fəʊm/ *adv.* & *pred. a.* E19. [f. A-² + FOAM *n.*] Foaming.

afocal /eɪ'fəʊk(ə)l/ *a.* M20. [f. A-¹⁰ + FOCAL.] *Optics.* Designating or involving a lens or lens system with a focal power of zero (so that rays entering parallel emerge parallel).

à fond /a fɔ̃/ *adv. phr.* E19. [Fr., lit. 'to bottom'.] Thoroughly, fully.

afoot /ə'fʊt/ *adv.* & *pred. a.* ME. [f. A *prep.*¹ 1 + FOOT *n.*, partly after ON *á fótum.*] 1 On foot, on one's own feet. *arch.* ME. 2 Astir, on the move; in operation or employment. M16.

1 R. KIPLING The lama and Mahbub Ali, both afoot, walking cautiously. 2 W. S. CHURCHILL The Hungarians were in revolt . . and the Turks were once more afoot. M. SPARK A new plot which is afoot to force me to resign.

afore /ə'fɔː/ *adv.*, *prep.*, & *conj.* Now chiefly *dial.* & *Naut.* [OE *onforan*; later (14) f. ON *prep.* + FORE *adv.* & *prep.*] A *adv.* 1 Of place: in front; in or into the forepart. OE. 2 Of time: before. ME.

Comb.: With pa. pples forming adjs., as *aforesaid*, *afore-mentioned*, etc.

B *prep.* 1 Of time: before. OE. 2 Of place: in front of; in advance of; in or into the presence of. ME. 3 Of rank etc.: in precedence of. LME.

C *conj.* Before, sooner than. ME.

aforehand /ə'fɔːhand/ *adv.* & *pred. a. arch.* LME. [f. AFORE *prep.* + HAND *n.*, after earlier *beforehand.*] A *adv.* In anticipation, in advance. LME. †B *pred. a.* Prepared or provided for the future. E16-M18.

aforethought /ə'fɔːθɔːt/ *n.* & *ppl a.* ME. [f. AFORE *adv.* + THOUGHT *n.*¹ and *thought* pa. pple of THINK *v.*²] A *n.* Forethought, premeditation. *rare.* ME.

B *ppl a.* Thought before; premeditated. L15.

malice aforethought [after *malice prepensed* s.v. PREPENSE *v.*] *Law* wrongful intent that was in the mind beforehand, esp. as an element in murder.

aforetime /ə'fɔːtʌɪm/ *adv.* & *a. arch.* LME. [f. AFORE *prep.* + TIME *n.*, after earlier *beforetime.*] Before in time; former(ly).

aforetimes *adv.* (*rare*) L16.

a fortiori /eɪ fɔːtɪ'ɔːrʌɪ/ *adv. phr.* E17. [L.] With yet stronger reason; more conclusively.

afoul /ə'faʊl/ *adv.* & *pred. a.* Now chiefly *N. Amer.* E19. [f. A-² + FOUL *a.*, *n.*] In a tangle; in collision; foul. Esp. in *run* or *fall afoul of.*

afraid /ə'freɪd/ *pred. a.* Also (*arch.*) **affrayed**. ME. [pa. pple of AFFRAY *v.* used as adj. after AN *afrayé.*] Frightened, alarmed, in a state of fear. (Foll. by *of* a person or thing, *of doing*; *to do*; *that* or (somewhat *arch.*) *lest* w. subjunct. (an unpleasant possibility); *that* w. indic. (an unpleasant probability or contemplated reality).)

SWIFT I was affraid of trampling on every traveller that I met. POPE Willing to wound, and yet afraid to strike. J. AUSTEN I am afraid you do not like your pen. G. H. LEWES Afraid lest the poetical spirit should be swept away. J. M. SYNGE A man who is not afraid of the sea will soon be drowned. T. S. ELIOT I have seen the eternal Footman hold my coat, and snicker, And in short, I was afraid. SCOTT FITZGERALD I was afraid . . that my house was on fire. W. STEVENS Mother was afraid I should freeze in the Parisian hotels. **I am afraid (that)** *colloq.* I say or admit with regret.

afraidness *n.* (*rare*) M17.

afreet /'afriːt/ *n.* Also **afrit**, **efreet** /'ɛfriːt/. L18. [Arab. *'ifrīt*, colloq. *'afrīt.*] A powerful jinnee in Arabian stories and Muslim mythology.

afresh /ə'frɛʃ/ *adv.* L15. [f. A-³ + FRESH *a.*, after *anew.*] Anew; with a fresh beginning.

Afric /'afrɪk/ *a. arch.* or *poet.* L16. [L *Africus*: see next.] African.

African /'afrɪk(ə)n/ *n.* & *a.* [OE (only pl.) *Africanas* f. L *Africanus* (Cicero), f. *Africa* use as n. of fem. (sc. *terra* land) of *Africus*, f. *Afri* pl. (sing. *Afer*) ancient people of N. Africa: see -AN.] A *n.* 1 A dark-skinned native or inhabitant of the continent of Africa; an African Black. OE. b *Hist.* An American Black of African origin or descent. E18. 2 A White inhabitant of Africa. E19.

B *adj.* Of or pertaining to Africa; belonging to or characteristic of the Blacks of Africa or (*Hist.*) of America. M16.

African American an American Black; of or pertaining to American Blacks. **African blackwood** = MPINGO. *African cypress*: see CYPRESS *n.*¹ 1b. **African daisy** a yellow-flowered plant of the composite family, *Lonas annua*, which is native to the Mediterranean region and N. Africa and is a naturalized weed elsewhere. *African* ELEPHANT. **African hemp** = SPARMANNIA. **African mahogany** (the wood of) a W. African tree, *Khaya senegalensis* (family Meliaceae). *African peach*: see PEACH *n.*¹ 2. *African pepper*: see PEPPER *n.* *African* POMPANO. *African* SWINE *fever*. *African* TEAK. **African violet** = SAINTPAULIA. **African walnut** (the wood, resembling mahogany, of) a tropical African tree, *Lovoa trichilioides* (family Meliaceae).

¶See also *South African* s.v. SOUTH.

Afri'cana *n.pl.* publications or other items concerning or associated with Africa E20. **Africanism** *n.* an African mode of speech, idiom, etc.; African character; African nationalism: M17. **Africanist** *n.* & *a.* (*a*) *n.* a specialist in things African; an African nationalist; (*b*) *adj.* of or pertaining to Africanists or Africanism: L19. **Afri'canity** *n.* = AFRICANNESS M20. **Africanize** *v.t.* make African in character; *spec.* (*a*) place under the control of African Blacks; (*b*) hybridize (honeybees) with a stock of African origin to give an unusually aggressive strain: E19. **Africanness** /-n-n-/ *n.* the quality or condition of being African M20.

Africander *n.* etc., see AFRIKANER.

Afrikaans /afrɪ'kɑːns/ *n.* & *a.* E20. [Du. = African.] (Of) a modified form of the Dutch language used in South Africa.

Afrikander *n.* etc., see next.

Afrikaner /afrɪ'kɑːnə/ *n.* Also **Africander**, **-kander** /-'kandə/. E19. [Afk., f. *Afrikaan* an African + *-(d)er* pers. suff., after *Hollander* Dutchman.] 1 An Afrikaans-speaking White person in South Africa, *esp.* one of Dutch descent. E19. 2 (Also **a-**.) A South African gladiolus belonging to any of several species. E19. 3 (Also **a-**.) (An animal of) a long-horned South African breed of cattle, or the indigenous South African breed of sheep. M19.

¶In general, the *-nder* forms are recorded earlier than those in *-ner*. However, except in sense 3 (breeds of cattle and sheep), where both are still common, *Afrikaner* is now dominant, and its derivs. are used exclusively.

Afrikan(d)erdom *n.* the Afrikaner people; the beliefs of Afrikaners; Afrikaners collectively: L19. **Afrikan(d)erism** *n.* an Afrikaans word or idiom used in South African English L19. **Afrikan(d)erize** *v.t.* bring under the influence or control of Afrikaners; make like an Afrikaner: E20. **Afri,kaneri'zation** *n.* the process of Afrikanerizing M20.

afrit *n.* var. of AFREET.

Afro /'afrəʊ/ *a.* & *n.* M20. [f. next, or f. AFR(ICAN + -O.] A *adj.* African, Afro-American; *spec.* (of a hairstyle) long and bushy, as naturally grown by some Blacks. M20. B *n.* Pl. **-os.** 1 An Afro-American; a Black. M20. 2 An Afro hairstyle. L20.

Afro- /'afrəʊ/ *comb. form.* Bef. a vowel occas. **Afr-**. M19. [L *Afr-*, *Afer* African: see -O-.] Forming adjs. and ns. w. the senses 'African (and)', as *Aframerican*, *Afro-American*, *Afro-Asian*, *Afro-Brazilian*, *Afro-Caribbean*, *Afro-Cuban*, and 'of or pertaining to Africa', as *Afrocentric.*

Afro-Asiatic /ˌafrəʊeɪʃɪˈatɪk, -eɪʒ-/ *a.* & *n.* M20. [f. prec. + ASIATIC *a.*] (Designating or pertaining to) a language family of N. Africa and SW Asia including Semitic languages, Egyptian, Berber, Chadic, and Cushitic.

afront /əˈfrʌnt/ *adv.* & *prep.* Now *dial.* or *obs.* LME. [f. A *prep.*[1] I + FRONT *n.*] **A** *adv.* †**1** Face to face, opposite. LME–E17. †**2** In a front; abreast. LME–E17. **3** In front. L16. **B** *prep.* In front of. M16.

afrormosia /afrɔːˈməʊzɪə/ *n.* M20. [mod.L, f. as AFRO- + *Ormosia*, a related genus, f. Gk *hormos* necklace: see -IA[1].] (The wood of) a N. and W. African leguminous tree of the genus *Pericopsis* (formerly *Afrormosia*).

aft /ɑːft/ *adv.* & *a.* E17. [Prob. alt. of earlier ABAFT, BAFT *adv.*, after LG, Du. *achter* abaft, after.] *Naut.* & *Aeronaut.* In or near or to or towards the stern or tail.

after /ˈɑːftə/ *n. colloq.* L19. [Abbrev.] Afternoon.

after /ˈɑːftə/ *a.* [OE *æfter(r)a*, corresp. to OHG *aftaro*. Later AFTER *adv.* etc. in attrib. use.] †**1** Second. OE–ME. **2** Next, subsequent. Later freq. in *comb.*: see AFTER-. OE. **3** Nearer the rear; (chiefly *Naut.*) nearer the stern. ME.

aftermost *superl. a.* (*Naut.*) nearest the stern of a ship E18. **afterness** *n.* (now *rare*) the quality of being after or later L16.

after /ˈɑːftə/ *adv.*, *prep.*, & *conj.* [OE *æfter*, corresp. to OFris. *efter*, OS, OHG *aftar*, ON *aptr*, Goth. *aftra*; prob. compar. deriv., rel. to Gk *apo* away from or *opisō* behind.] **A** *adv.* **1** Behind in place or order. OE. **2** Later in time. OE. **b** *spec.* Contrasted w. *before* (see BEFORE *adv.* 2b): following an event or (*esp.*) the use of a remedy, cosmetic, or other product. M18.

1 J. STALLWORTHY Stiffly he walked out / and his audience shuffled after. **2** SHAKES. *Jul. Caes.* I do fawn on men . . , And after scandal them. W. STEVENS The lilacs came long after.

B *prep.* **I** Of place. **1** In the rear of, behind. OE. **2** In pursuit or quest of; in the direction of someone or something moving away; about, concerning. OE.

1 JOYCE He filed out of the study-hall after the others. **after you**: a formula used in yielding precedence. **2** LD MACAULAY He was greedy after power. J. WAIN What most of the Sixth were after was a scholarship at Oxford or Cambridge. J. CHEEVER 'Merry Christmas, Charlie!' both the Fullers called after him. J. P. DONLEAVY A Mr. Skully, a former landlord, is after me for money. **be after doing** (chiefly *Anglo-Ir.*) (*a*) be intending to do, be on the point of doing; freq. *pleonastic*, be doing; (*b*) have just done. **see after** attend to.

II Of time. **3** Following in time, in succession to. OE. **4** Following the interval of, at the close of. OE. **5** Subsequent to or later than (a point in time). OE. **b** Past, beyond (a specified hour). Now chiefly *dial.* & *N. Amer.* M18. **6** Subsequent to and in consequence of. OE. **7** Subsequent to and notwithstanding. E17.

3 SPENSER Sleep after toil, port after stormy seas, Ease after war, death after life does greatly please. COLERIDGE Day after day, day after day, We stuck, nor breath nor motion. **after you with** *colloq.* may I have the next turn at. *time after time*: see TIME *n.* **4** S. HEANEY After eleven years I was composing Loveletters again. **5** S. HILL Only a little after ten-thirty. **after hours** after the regular hours of work or of opening (of a public house etc.). *after the event*: see EVENT *n.* **b** A. MILLER It's twenty after twelve. **6** T. S. ELIOT After such knowledge what forgiveness? **7** SHAKES. *Meas. for M.* Hark how the villain would close now, after his treasonable abuses! **after all** in spite of all that has happened or been said; in spite of one's exertions, expectations, etc.

III Of manner. **8** According to; in a manner consistent with. OE. **9** In a manner proportionate to. *arch.* OE. **10** In imitation of; in allusion to. ME. **11** At (the rate of). *arch.* LME.

8 DICKENS Handsome after its kind. *after a fashion*: see FASHION *n.* *after a sort*: see SORT *n.*[2] **9** H. LATIMER Cut thy cloth after the mesure. **10** GIBBON After his oracle, Dr. Johnson, my friend . . denies all original genius. R. MAYER Van Gogh's drawing after Millet's *The Reapers*. R. BRAUTIGAN It's good to name creeks after people. *after the fashion of*: see FASHION *n.*

IV Of order. **12** Next to in order or importance. ME.

12 DRYDEN Codrus after Phœbus sings the best.

C *conj.* **1** In or at the time subsequent to that when. Also (*arch.*) *after that*. OE. †**2** According as. Also *after that*, *as*. ME–M17.

1 AV *Jer.* 36:27 After that the king had burnt the roule. LD MACAULAY A few days after the Revolution had been accomplished.

after- /ˈɑːftə/ *comb. form.* OE. [AFTER *adv.* & *prep.*, *a.*] Forming combs., fixed or transitory, with ns., adjs., and vbs, in various relations and senses, as 'rear', 'subsequent(ly)', 'eventual(ly)', 'subordinate(ly)'.

after-born *a.* born after one's father's death or last will; younger. †**after-burden** = AFTERBIRTH. **afterburner** a fitment for burning extra fuel in the exhaust of a jet engine as a means of increasing thrust. **afterburning** the action or use of an afterburner. †**after-burthen** = AFTERBIRTH. **after-care** attention given after a stay in hospital, prison, etc. **afterclap** an unexpected stroke after the recipient has ceased to be on his or her guard; a surprise happening after a matter is supposed to be at an end. **aftercomer** a successor; in *pl.*, posterity. **after-course** †(*a*) a later course at dinner; (*b*) a subsequent course. **aftercrop** a second crop in one season. **after-damp** (gas rich in) carbon monoxide occurring in a mine after an explosion. **after-days** later or subsequent days. **after-effect** an effect that follows after an interval or after the primary action of something. **after-game** a second game played to improve on the result of the first; a new plan to meet an unforeseen development. **afterglow** a glow (*lit.* or *fig.*) that remains after the removal or disappearance of its source. **aftergrass** = AFTERMATH I. **after-growth** (*a*) = AFTERMATH I; (*b*) growth afterwards. **after-guard** *Naut.* on a sailing ship, the men stationed on the quarterdeck and poop to work the sails aft of the mainmast. **after-image** an impression of a vivid (esp. visual) sensation retained after the cause has been withdrawn. **after-knowledge** knowledge after the event. **afterlife** life at a later time or after death. **afterlight** an afterglow; hindsight. **aftermarket** (*a*) a market for spare parts and components; (*b*) a market in shares after their original issue. **after-pain** a pain which follows later; *spec.* in *pl.*, uterine contractions occurring after childbirth. **afterpiece** *Hist.* a farce or other short piece after a play; *fig.* a subsequent dramatic event. **after-reckoning** a subsequent or final account. **after-sensation** an after-image (less commonly visual). **aftershave** *a.* & *n.* (a lotion) for use after shaving. **after-shock** a lesser shock following the main shock of an earthquake. **aftersight** hindsight. **aftertaste** a taste remaining or recurring after eating or drinking. **afterthought** something that is thought of or added later. **after-time(s)** a later or future time. **aftertouch** *Mus.* the resonant effect produced when a pianist sustains the pressure on a key after striking it; (the facility provided by) a programmable device for reproducing this on an electronic keyboard etc. **after-wit** *arch.* wisdom after the event. **afterword** a concluding comment in a book, esp. by a person other than the author. **after-world** the world later in time; a world after death. †**after-wort** *Brewing* the second run of beer. **after-years** later years, years to come.

afterbirth /ˈɑːftəbəːθ/ *n.* M16. [Perh. directly f. G *Afterbürde* (Luther, *Deut.* 28:57), also *Aftergeburt*: cf. Icel. *eftirburður*, OSw. *efterbörd*, Da. *efterbyrd*, and see AFTER-, BIRTH *n.*[1]] The placenta and foetal membranes expelled from the womb after the birth of offspring.

aftermath /ˈɑːftəmaθ/ *n.* L15. [f. AFTER- + MATH *n.*[1] Cf. LATTERMATH.] **1** A second or later mowing; a crop of grass growing after mowing or harvest. Now *dial.* L15. **2** *fig.* An effect or condition arising from an (esp. unpleasant) event. M19.

1 J. BUCHAN Meadowland from which an aftermath of hay had lately been taken. **2** W. S. CHURCHILL The life and strength of Britain . . will be tested to the full, not only in the war but in the aftermath of war. M. L. KING The aftermath of nonviolence is the creation of the beloved community.

afternoon /ɑːftəˈnuːn/ *n.* ME. [f. AFTER *prep.* + NOON *n.*: cf. L *post meridiem*.] **1** The time from midday or lunch-time to evening; this time spent in a particular way. ME. **2** *ellipt.* As *int.* Good-afternoon. *colloq.* E20.

1 TENNYSON In the afternoon they came unto a land In which it seemed always afternoon. **this afternoon** (during) the afternoon of today. **2** E. O'NEILL Afternoon, Harriet. . . Afternoon, Ma.

Comb.: *afternoon tea*: see TEA *n.* 5(a).

afternoons /ɑːftəˈnuːnz/ *adv.* *N. Amer.* L19. [Pl. of prec.: cf. DAYS, EVENINGS, NIGHTS, etc. (earlier uses of -S[3] being identified w. -S[1]).] During the afternoon, every afternoon.

afters /ˈɑːftəz/ *n.pl. colloq.* E20. [f. AFTER *adv.* or *a.*] The course following the main course of a meal.

afterward /ˈɑːftəwəd/ *adv.* [Late OE *æfterweardе*: see AFTER-, -WARD.] †**1** Of place: behind; *Naut.* towards the stern. LOE–E17. **2** = AFTERWARDS. Now chiefly *US*. ME. †**3** Of order: next. ME–L16.

afterwards /ˈɑːftəwədz/ *adv.* ME. [f. prec.: see -WARDS.] At a later time, subsequently.

ag /ag/ *a.* & *n.* Chiefly *N. Amer. colloq.* E20. [Abbrev.] **A** *adj.* Agricultural. E20. **B** *n.* Agriculture. M20.

ag /ax/ *int.* *S. Afr.* M20. [Afk. f. Du. *ach*.] = ACH.

ag- /ag, *unstressed* əg/ *pref.* (not productive). Assim. form of L AD- bef. *g*. In OFr., L *agg-* was reduced to *ag-*, which appears in ME adoptions, but in later Fr., and hence in Eng., *agg-* was restored by Latinization, as *aggrandize*, *aggrieve*, except in *agree*.

aga /ˈɑːgə/ *n.*[1] Also **agha**. M16. [Turk. *ağa* master, lord f. Mongolian *aqa*.] An Ottoman title, now abolished, for (orig.) a military commander and (later) officials of various ranks. Now, a title of respect for landowners among Turkish village people.

Aga Khan the spiritual leader of the Khoja branch of Ismalian Muslims.

Aga /ˈɑːgə/ *n.*[2] M20. [Acronym, f. Sw. Svenska *A*ktiebulaget *Ga*sackumulator, the original manufacturer.] (Proprietary name for) a type of large domestic stove for cooking and for heating water.

agacerie /agasəri/ *n.* Pl. pronounced same. E19. [Fr.] (An) allurement; coquetry.

†**agad** *int.* L17–M18. [f. AH *int.* + GAD *n.*[2]] = EGAD.

Agadic /əˈgadɪk/ *a.* L19. [f. *Agada* Latinized form of HAGGADAH + -IC.] = HAGGADIC.

again /əˈgɛn, əˈgeɪn/ *adv.*, *prep.*, & *conj.* [OE (WS) *ongē(a)n*, later *aġēn*, (Anglian) *ongæġn*, *-ġegn*, corresp. to OS *angegin*, OHG *ingagan*, *ingegin(i)* (G *entgegen* opposite), ON *í gegn* against. ME forms in *aȝ-*, *ay-* were superseded by those in *ag-* from north. dialects (of Scand. origin).] **A** *adv.* **1** In the opposite direction; back to the point of starting. *obs.* exc. *dial.* & in *return*, *come back*, etc., *again* (passing into sense 2). OE. **2** Back in or into a former position or state. OE. **3** In accordance or response; later extended to indicate intensity of action. Now chiefly *arch.* & *dial.* ME. **4** Another time; once more. ME. **b** Once repeated. L16. **5** Anywhere besides. *arch.* M16. **6** On the other hand; further, besides. M16.

1 to and again to and fro. **2** S. HILL They have moved us back again to where we were before. **3** DICKENS He laughed till the glasses in the sideboard rang again. WILKIE COLLINS She gallops . . till the horse reeks again. **4** A. E. HOUSMAN Now, of my threescore years and ten, Twenty will not come again. **again and again** repeatedly. BREATHE **again**. *come again*: see COME *v.* *ever and again*: see EVER. *here we go again*: see HERE *adv.* NEVER *again!* **now and again** occasionally. **over (and over) again** repeatedly, many times. *think again*: see THINK *v.*[2] **time and (time) again** repeatedly. **b as much** (or **many**) **again** twice as much or many. **half as much** (or **many**) **again** one-and-a-half times as much or many. (*the*) *same again*: see SAME *pron.* & *n.* **6** S. RICHARDSON But now again, see what succeeds to this. *English Studies* The use of traditional diction is one thing; improvisation is something else again. B. PYM I might decide to live here, and again I might not.

B *prep.* Also **agen**, (& *joc.*) **agin** /əˈgɪn/. = AGAINST *prep.* Now *dial.* OE.

C *conj.* = AGAINST *conj.* Now *dial.* ME.

†**againward** *adv.* again ME–L16.

against /əˈgɛnst, əˈgeɪnst/ *prep.* & *conj.* ME. [f. prec. + -S[3] + *t* as in *amidst*, *amongst*, etc.] **A** *prep.* **I** Of motion or action in opposition. **1** In hostility or active opposition to; in competition with; to the disadvantage of. ME. **b** *Betting.* In expectation of the failure of. With specified odds: with that likelihood of failure of. Also *ellipt.* M19. 2 In resistance to, as protection from. ME. 3 In opposition in tendency or character to; contrary to. ME. 4 Towards with hostile intent. *arch.* ME. 5 In the opposite direction to, counter to. LME.

1 AV *Gen.* 16:12 His hand will be against euery man. G. J. WHYTE-MELVILLE I rode a race against Bob Dashwood. E. WAUGH Even his good qualities of geniality and impetuosity counted against him, for his parties . . got talked about. D. H. LAWRENCE Effie sided with Tom against Frank. K. AMIS No Welsh witness would testify against them. b DISRAELI I'll take the odds against Caravan. D. RUNYON All life is six to five against. 2 MILTON Here only weak Against the charm of beauty's powerful glance. B. BAINBRIDGE The men with the sacks over their shoulders against the rain. 3 COLERIDGE No power on earth can oblige me to act against my conscience. 4 AV *Luke* 14:31 To meete him that commeth against him with twentie thousand. 5 J. STALLWORTHY Walking against the wind.

II Of position. 6 Directly opposite, facing. Now chiefly in *over against* s.v. OVER *adv.* ME. †b Exposed to (light, cold, etc.). LME–E18. †7 In the sight or presence of. ME–E16. 8 *fig.* With respect to. *arch.* LME. 9 Near, adjoining. Now *dial.* LME.

6b SHAKES. *Sonn.* Those boughs which shake against the cold.

III Of mutual opposition or relation. 10 In return for; instead of. ME. 11 Weighed in the opposite scale to (*lit.* & *fig.*). ME. 12 *fig.* In contrast with. Also *as against*. ME.

10 H. MARTINEAU To exchange wheat against bullocks. 11 A. THWAITE Seven hundred years of labour-saving gadgets Weigh little in the balance put against you.

IV Of time. 13 Drawing towards, close to. *obs.* exc. *dial.* ME. 14 In anticipation of, in preparation for. ME.

14 L. DURRELL Comestibles specially prepared against a feast-day.

V Of motion towards, or contact with. 15 Towards, to meet. Long *obs.* exc. *dial.* ME. 16 Into contact with, into collision with. LME. 17 In contact with, supported by. L16. 18 Of something seen: in front of, having as background. E19.

16 W. TREVOR Breakers crashed against the wall of the promenade. 17 W. OWEN Under his helmet, up against his pack, . . Sleep took him by the brow and laid him back. R. CHANDLER There was a bar against the right hand wall. 18 J. BETJEMAN Still I see Twigs and serrated leaves against the sky.

Phrases: *against nature*: see NATURE *n.* **against the clock, against time** so as to complete a task by a certain time, with a time-limit. *against the grain*: see GRAIN *n.*[1] *against the hair*: see HAIR *n.* *against the world*: see WORLD *n.* **run up against** *colloq.* meet accidentally. *up against*: see UP *adv.*[2] & *a.*[2]

B *conj.* Before the time that; in anticipation of the time that. *arch.* ME.

THACKERAY Shutting his shutters . ., against service commenced.

agal /a'gɑːl/ *n.* M19. [Repr. Bedouin pronunc. of Arab. *'ikāl* bond, rope for hobbling a camel.] A fillet worn by Bedouin Arabs to keep the keffiyeh in position.

agallochum /ə'galəkəm/ *n.* Also **agalloch**. L16. [Late L f. Gk *agallokhon*; ult. rel. to AGILA.] Aloes wood.

agalmatolite /agəl'matəlʌɪt/ *n.* M19. [f. Gk *agalmat-*, *agalma* statue, image + -O- + -LITE.] A soapstone or other soft mineral, *esp.* one in which Chinese figures are carved.

agama /ə'gɑːmə/ *n.* L18. [Perh. f. Carib.] A lizard resembling an iguana, belonging to *Agama* or a related genus.

¶Orig. including some American lizards, the genus has been restricted to Old World species by reclassification.

agamid *a.* & *n.* (designating or pertaining to) a lizard of the Old World family Agamidae, to which the agamas belong L19.

agami /ə'gɑːmi/ *n.* M18. [Fr., f. Galibi *agamy.*] The chestnut-bellied heron, *Agamia agami*, of northern S. America.

agamic /ə'gamɪk/ *a.* M19. [f. Gk *agamos* unmarried + -IC.] *Biol.* Asexual; reproducing asexually. Formerly also, unfertilized; cryptogamic.

Also **agamous** /'agəməs/ *a.* M19.

agamogenesis /ˌagəmə'dʒɛnɪsɪs/ *n.* Now *rare.* M19. [f. as prec. + -GENESIS.] *Biol.* Asexual reproduction; *spec.* parthenogenesis.

ˌ**agamoge'netic** *a.* L19.

agapanthus /agə'panθəs/ *n.* L18. [mod.L, f. Gk *agapē* love + *anthos* flower.] A lily-like plant of the southern African genus *Agapanthus*, bearing umbels of blue or white flowers.

agape /'agəpi/ *n.* Pl. **-pae** /-piː/, **-pes.** E17. [Gk *agapē* brotherly love.] 1 A love-feast held by early Christians in connection with the Eucharist; *transf.* a parochial feast at a festival time. E17. 2 Christian love, charity. M19.

agape /ə'geɪp/ *adv.* & *pred. a.* M17. [f. A *prep.*[1] 6 + GAPE *n.*] Gaping; open-mouthed with wonder or expectation.

agapemone /agə'piːməni, -'pɛm-/ *n.* M19. [Irreg. f. Gk *agapē* love + *monē* abode: orig. (w. cap. initial) the name of a community founded in Somerset, England *c* 1850.] An abode of love; an establishment where free love is practised.

agar-agar /eɪgɑːr'eɪgɑː/ *n.* In sense 2 usu. simply **agar.** E19. [Malay.] 1 Any of certain SE Asian seaweeds from which a gelatinous substance is extracted; *esp.* Ceylon moss, *Gracilaria lichenoides.* E19. 2 The substance itself, used esp. to make soups and to form biological culture media. M19.

agarose /'agərəʊz, -s/ *n.* [-OSE[2]] *Biochem.* a polysaccharide containing L- and D-galactose residues which is the main constituent of agar and is used in making gels for electrophoresis etc. M20.

agaric /'ag(ə)rɪk, ə'gɑːrɪk/ *n.* LME. [L *agaricum* (Pliny) f. Gk *agarikon* tree fungus. Cf. Fr. *agaric* (15).] †1 Any of various bracket fungi having medicinal or other uses; esp. *Fomes officinalis*, a cathartic, and *Phellinus ignarius*, used to check bleeding, etc. LME–M19. 2 A gill-bearing mushroom or toadstool, any member of the order Agaricales. E18.

2 *fly agaric*: see FLY *n.*[1]

agasp /ə'gɑːsp/ *adv.* & *pred. a.* E19. [f. A-[2] + GASP *n.*] Gasping.

†**agast** *v.t.* Latterly *dial.* Also **aghast.** Pa. pple & ppl a. **agast,** AGHAST *a.*, **agasted.** ME–M19. [f. A-[1] (intensifier) + GAST *v.* & *a.*] Frighten, terrify.

agate /'agət/ *n.* L15. [(O)Fr. *agate*, †*-the* f. L *achates* f. Gk *akhatēs.* Cf. ACHATE *n.*[1]] 1 A hard semi-transparent variegated chalcedony, having colours usu. arranged in bands. L15. †2 *fig.* A diminutive figure (from those cut in agates for seals). Only in L16. 3 *Typogr.* Ruby type. *US.* M19. 4 A coloured toy marble resembling an agate. M19.

Comb.: **agateware** a kind of pottery coloured to resemble agate.

agatized *pa. pple* & *ppl a.* converted into or made to resemble agate M17.

agate /ə'geɪt/ *adv.* & *pred. a. Sc.* & *north.* M16. [f. A *prep.*[1] 1 + GATE *n.*[2]] On the way; on the road; in motion, astir.

agathodemon /agəθə'diːmən/ *n.* Also **-daemon.** M18. [Gk *agathodaimōn*, f. *agathos* good + *daimōn* a spirit.] A good divinity or genius.

agave /ə'geɪvi/ *n.* L18. [L *Agave* pers. name in mythol. f. Gk *Agauē* proper fem. of *agauos* illustrious.] Any of numerous spiny-leaved plants of the American genus *Agave* (family Agavaceae), most members of which, e.g. the American aloe, *Agave americana*, take several years to mature and flower only once.

agaze /ə'geɪz/ *adv.* LME. [f. A *prep.*[1] 6 + GAZE *n.*] Gazing.

†**agazed** *ppl a.* LME–E19. [Perh. var. of *agast* AGHAST *a.* infl. by prec.] Frightened; astounded.

agba /'agbə/ *n.* E20. [Yoruba.] (The wood of) a tall W. African leguminous tree, *Gossweilerodendron balsamiferum.*

age /eɪdʒ/ *n.* ME. [OFr. (mod. *âge*) ult. f. L *aetat-*, *aetas*, f. *aevum* age of time. Cf. AEON.] I A period of existence. 1 The length of past life or of existence; the ordinary duration of life. ME. 2 The duration of life which naturally or conventionally qualifies for something; *esp.* the duration of life which ordinarily brings maturity, or which by custom or law is fixed as such. ME. 3 A period or stage of life. ME. 4 *esp.* The latter part of life; old age. ME. 5 The effects of age; senility; maturity (of things). LME.

1 **act one's age** = *be one's age* below. **ages with** *Sc.* of the same age as. **be one's age** act sensibly (chiefly as imper.). *full age*: see FULL *a.* *great age*: see GREAT *a.* **look one's age** look as old as one really is. *mental age*: see MENTAL *a.*[1] **of an age to** old enough to. **of an age with** of the same age as. *reading age*: see READING *n.*[1] *the awkward age*: see AWKWARD *a.* 3b. **the moon's age** the time elapsed since the new moon. 2 *age of consent*: see CONSENT *n.* 1. **come of age** reach adult status, *esp.* in *Law* in Britain and US at 18 (formerly 21). **over age** old enough; too old. **under age** not old enough; *esp.* not yet of adult status. 3 SHAKES. *A.Y.L.* One man in his time plays many parts, His acts being seven ages. *age of* DISCRETION. See also MIDDLE AGE, *old age* s.v. OLD *a.* 5, *third age* s.v. THIRD *a.* 4 E. WAUGH Having for many years painfully feigned youth, he now aspired to the honours of age.

II A period of time. 6a A distinctive period of human history, real or mythical. ME. b *Geol.* A division of geological time; *spec.* a subdivision of an epoch, corresponding to a stratigraphic stage. M19. 7 The generation to which someone belongs. ME. 8 A long but indefinite period of time (*gen.* & *colloq.* (esp. in *pl.*) in exaggeration). LME. b A century. *rare.* L16. 9 A generation (as a measure of time). E16.

6a *Age of Aquarius, Age of Chivalry, age of gold, brazen age, Bronze Age, Dark Age(s), golden age, Iron Age, Middle Age(s), New Age, silver age, Stone Age, three ages,* etc. *in this day and age*: see DAY *n.* *the age of reason*: see REASON *n.*[1] b *ice age.* 7 ARNOLD BENNETT He had survived into another and a more fortunate age than his own. 8 J. AUSTEN The two ladies . . called it an age since they had met. JOYCE He died of galloping drink ages ago. J. BERRYMAN Across the ages certain blessings swarm. 9 HOBBES The Writers of the New Testament lived all in lesse then an age after Christ's Ascension.

Comb.: **age gap** a difference in age, esp. as a source of disharmony or misunderstanding; **age-group** a number of persons or things classed together as of similar age; **age-hardening** *Metall.* spontaneous hardening occurring on storage at ambient temperature, or on mild heat treatment, following quenching; **age-long** *a.* as long as an age; lasting for a very long time; **age-old** *a.* having existed for a very long time; **age-mate** a person of the same age.

ag(e)ism *n.* prejudice or discrimination against people of a particular age, esp. against the elderly M20. **ag(e)ist** *a.* & *n.* (*a*) *adj.* of ageism; (*b*) *n.* a person who practises ageism: L20. **ageless** *a.* without limits of duration; never growing or appearing old or outmoded: M17. **agelessness** *n.* E20. **ager** *n.* a person living in or having a specified age (as 2nd elem. of comb.) M20.

age /eɪdʒ/ *v.* Pres. pple **ageing, aging.** LME. [f. the n.] 1 *v.i.* Grow old, mature, show the effects of the passage of time; begin to appear older; undergo ageing (see below). LME. 2 *v.t.* Cause or allow to grow old, mature, begin to appear older, undergo ageing, etc. M16. 3 *v.t.* Calculate or determine the age of. L19.

ageing, aging *vbl n.* the action or process of growing or causing to grow old etc.; a process of change, usu. gradual and spontaneous, in the properties of a material; age-hardening: M19.

-age /ɪdʒ/ *in a few words* ɑːʒ/ *suff.* [Repr. (O)Fr. *-age* f. late L *-aticum* neut. of adjs. in *-aticus* -ATIC. Later a living Eng. formative.] Forming ns. w. gen. sense of appurtenance or collectives. The meanings are typified by *baggage, carriage, cartage, damage, dotage, hermitage, homage, language, luggage, marriage, passage, tillage, tonnage, vicarage, village.*

aged /*in senses A.1, 2, B,* 'eɪdʒɪd; *in senses A.1b, 3, 4,* eɪdʒd/ *a.* & *n.* LME. [f. AGE *v.* + -ED[1], after Fr. *âgé.*] A *adj.* 1 Having lived long; old. LME. b Of a horse, farm animal, etc.: over a certain age, as (usu.) 6 or 7 for a horse, 3 or 4 for cattle. M19. 2 Belonging to old age. *rare.* L16. 3 Of or at the age of. L16. 4 Of a material: subjected to ageing. M19.

1 DICKENS You don't object to an aged parent, I hope? 2 SHAKES. *Tit. A.* The aged wrinkles in my cheeks. 3 DYLAN THOMAS Among those Killed in the Dawn Raid was a Man Aged a Hundred.

B *absol.* as *n.pl. The* old or elderly people as a class. E20.

agedly /ˈeɪdʒɪdli/ *adv.* after the manner of an aged person M16. **agedness** /ˈeɪdʒɪdnɪs/ *n.* the quality of being of advanced age or of a specified age LME.

agee *adv.* & *pred. a.* var. of AJEE.

ageing *pres. pple* & *vbl n.* see AGE *v.*

agelast /ˈadʒɪlast/ *n. rare.* L19. [Gk *agelastos*, f. *a-* A-[10] + *gelastos*, f. *gelan* to laugh.] A person who never laughs.

agen *prep.* see AGAIN *prep.*

agency /ˈeɪdʒ(ə)nsi/ *n.* M17. [med.L *agentia*: see AGENT, -ENCY.] **1a** Active operation, action. M17. **b** Intervening action towards an end. M17. **c** Action personified; a source of action towards an end. L18. **2** The function or position of an agent (sense 2). M17. **3** The headquarters or business establishment of an agent (sense 2); a specialized department of the United Nations. E19.

1a N. SHUTE There may be human agency behind that power. b F. M. FORD If he could smile again through her agency. c P. H. JOHNSON As though some outside agency is at work. 3 *adoption agency*, *employment agency*, *news agency*, etc.

Comb.: **agency shop** *US* (an establishment operating) a system whereby a recognized trade union receives a sum of money from non-members equivalent to the subscriptions of members.

agenda /əˈdʒɛndə/ *n.pl.*, also used as *sing.* Less commonly in sing. **agendum** /-dəm/; †**agend**. E17. [L, pl. of *agendum* use as n. of gerundive of *agere*: see AGENT.] **1** *pl.* Things to be done; matters of practice. E17. **2** *collect. sing.* A memorandum book. *arch.* M18. **3** As *pl.*, items of business to be considered at a meeting or to be otherwise attended to. As *sing.*, a list of such items. L19.

3 B. BAINBRIDGE She hadn't a spare moment. She had a busy agenda.

agenesis /əˈdʒɛnɪsɪs, eɪ-/ *n.* M19. [f. A-[10] + -GENESIS.] *Med.* Congenital absence or imperfect development of a part of the body.

agent /ˈeɪdʒ(ə)nt/ *n.*, *a.*, & *v.* LME. [L *agent-* pres. ppl stem of *agere* act, do, cogn. w. Gk *agein*, Skt *ajati*: see -ENT. Rel. to ACT *v.*, AGILE, AGONY.] **A** *n.* **1** A person who or thing which produces an effect; (the cause of) a natural force or effect on matter. LME. **2** A person who acts for another in business, politics, etc. M16. **3** The material cause or instrument. L16. **4** A person who or thing which acts or exerts power; *spec.* in *Gram.*, the entity performing the action of the verb. Opp. *patient* or *instrument*. L16.

1 I. ASIMOV Hydrogen, like carbon, is a reducing agent. *Agent Orange*: see ORANGE *n. uncoupling agent*: see UNCOUPLE 3. VACUOLATING *agent*. *V-agent*: see V, v 3b. 2 P. G. WODEHOUSE Pongo will handle the whole affair, acting as your agent. E. BOWEN This kitchen was, by agents' definition, a kitchenette. R. HOGGART Agents for one of the great Clothing or General Credit Clubs. G. VIDAL A special agent of the Central Intelligence Agency. **agent-general** the representative of an Australian State or a Canadian province (or, formerly, a South African province) in London or other major foreign city. *double agent*: see DOUBLE *a.* & *adv.* **law agent** *Sc. Hist.* a solicitor. *literary agent*: see LITERARY *a. secret agent*: see SECRET *a. treble agent*: see TREBLE *a. triple agent*: see TRIPLE *a.* & *adv. universal agent*: see UNIVERSAL *a.* 3 R. SCRUTON The Church was the principal agent of charity. 4 **free agent** a person whose actions are not subject to another's control.

B *adj.* Acting, exerting power. *arch.* L16.

C *v.t.* Act as agent in. M17.

Comb.: **agent-noun**, **agent-suffix** *Gram.*: denoting an agent or agency.

agential /əˈdʒɛnʃ(ə)l/ *a.* of or pertaining to an agent or agency L19. **agentive** /əˈdʒɛntɪv/ *a.* & *n.* (*Gram.*) (a noun, suffix, case, etc.) indicating an agent or agency M19. **agentship** *n.* = AGENCY 2 E17.

agent provocateur /aʒɑ̃ prɔvɔkatœːr/ *n. phr.* Pl. ***-s -s*** (pronounced same). L19. [Fr. = provocative agent.] An agent employed to tempt suspected persons into committing an incriminating act.

ageostrophic /eɪdʒɪəˈstrɒfɪk/ *a.* M20. [f. A-[10] + GEOSTROPHIC.] *Meteorol.* Not geostrophic: *spec.* designating the wind component which when added to a geostrophic wind gives the actual wind.

ageratum /əˈdʒɛrətəm, adʒəˈreɪtəm/ *n.* Sense 1 also †**-ton**. M16. [mod.L f. L *ageraton* f. Gk, neut. of *agēratos*, f. *a-* A-[10] + *gērat-*, *gēras* old age.] **1** An everlasting flower, known to the ancients. M16. **2** Any of a number of plants of the American genus *Ageratum*, bearing long-lasting composite flowers. M18.

ageusia /əˈgjuːzɪə, -sɪə/ *n.* M19. [f. A-[10] + Gk *geusis* sense of taste: see -IA[1] and cf. Gk *ageustia*.] *Med.* Inability to distinguish taste.

agey /ˈeɪdʒi/ *a. arch.* Also **agy**. M16. [f. AGE *n.* + -Y[1].] Aged.

Aggadah *n.* var. of HAGGADAH.

agger /ˈadʒə/ *n.* LME. [L.] *Archaeol.* A mound; *esp.* the rampart of a Roman camp or a raised Roman road or causeway.

aggeration /adʒəˈreɪʃ(ə)n/ *n. rare.* L17. [L *aggeratio(n-)*, f. *aggerare* heap up, f. as prec.: see -ATION.] The raising of a heap or mound.

aggiornamento /addʒornaˈmento, ədʒɔːnəˈmɛntəʊ/ *n.* M20. [It.] Bringing up to date, esp. of Roman Catholic Church policy by and after the Second Vatican Council (1962–5).

agglomerate /əˈglɒmərət/ *ppl a.* & *n.* E19. [L *agglomeratus* pa. pple, f. as next: see -ATE[1].] **A** *ppl a.* Collected into a mass. E19. **B** *n.* **1** An agglomerated mass. M19. **2** *Geol.* A coarse mass of pyroclastic fragments, freq. consolidated by heat. Cf. CONGLOMERATE *n.* 1. M19.

agglomerate /əˈglɒməreɪt/ *v.t.* & *i.* L17. [L *agglomerat-* pa. ppl stem of *agglomerare* add or join to, f. *ad* AG- + *glomerare*, f. *glomer-*, *glomus* ball: see -ATE[3].] Collect into a mass; accumulate in a disorderly way.

agglomeˈration *n.* the action of agglomerating; an agglomerated mass: L18. **agglomerative** *a.* pertaining to agglomeration; tending to agglomerate: E19.

agglutinant /əˈgluːtɪnənt/ *a.* & *n.* Now *rare.* L17. [L *agglutinant-* pres. ppl stem of *agglutinare*: see next, -ANT[1]. Perh. partly through Fr.] (A substance) that agglutinates or causes agglutination.

agglutinate /əˈgluːtɪnət/ *a. rare.* M16. [L *agglutinatus* pa. pple, f. as next: see -ATE[2].] **1** United as with glue; glued together. M16. **2** *Philol.* Of or formed by agglutination. *arch.* M19.

agglutinate /əˈgluːtɪneɪt/ *v.* M16. [L *agglutinat-* pa. ppl stem of *agglutinare*, f. *ad* AG- + *glutinare*, f. *gluten* glue: see -ATE[3].] **1** *Biol.* & *Med.* **a** *v.t.* Orig., cause to adhere. Now, cause agglutination of. M16. **b** *v.i.* Undergo agglutination. E20. **2** *v.t. gen.* Unite as with glue. L16. **3** *v.t. Philol.* Compound (words) by agglutination. M19.

aˌgglutinaˈbility *n.* the quality or property of being agglutinable E20. **agglutinable** *a.* (chiefly *Biol.* & *Med.*) able to cause or undergo agglutination E20. **agglutinating** *a.* that agglutinates; *Philol.* agglutinative: M17.

agglutination /əˌgluːtɪˈneɪʃ(ə)n/ *n.* M16. [Fr., or L *agglutinatio(n-)*, f. as prec.: see -ATION.] **1** The action of agglutinating; the state of being agglutinated. M16. **b** *Philol.* The combining of grammatical elements (roots or affixes) into complex words with little or no change of form. M19. **c** *Biol.* & *Med.* The induced adhering together or coalescence of cells, esp. bacteria or blood corpuscles. L19. **2** A thing which is agglutinated; a mass, a group. L16.

agglutinative /əˈgluːtɪnətɪv/ *a.* L16. [Fr. *agglutinatif*, *-ive* or f. AGGLUTINATE *v.* + -IVE.] **1** Of or pertaining to agglutination; adhesive, cementing. L16. **2** *Philol.* Characterized by agglutination. M17.

agglutinin /əˈgluːtɪnɪn/ *n.* L19. [f. AGGLUTIN(ATE *v.* + -IN[1].] *Biol.* & *Med.* An antibody, lectin, or other substance which causes agglutination of cells.

agglutinogen *n.* an antigenic substance present in blood cells, bacteria, etc., which stimulates the formation of an agglutinin in blood serum E20.

aggrace /əˈgreɪs/ *v.* & *n. rare.* L16. [f. A-[1] + GRACE *v.*] **A** *v.t.* †**1** Favour. Only in L16. **2** Grace. *arch.* E19. †**B** *n.* Favour, grace. Only in L16.

aggradation /agrəˈdeɪʃ(ə)n/ *n.* L19. [f. AG- + DE)GRADATION *n.*[1]] *Physical Geogr.* The deposition of material by a river, stream, or current.

aggradational *a.* of or pertaining to aggradation L19. **aggrade** /əˈgreɪd/ *v.t.* & *i.* [back-form.] build up by deposition E20.

aggrandise *v.*, **-ment** *n.* vars. of AGGRANDIZE, -MENT.

aggrandize /əˈgrandʌɪz/ *v.* Also **-ise**. M17. [(O)Fr. *agrandiss-* lengthened stem of *agrandir* prob. f. It. *aggrandire*, f. L *grandis* GRAND *a.*[1]; assim. to vbs in -IZE.] **1** *v.t.* Increase, magnify, intensify, (a thing). Now *rare* in *gen.* sense. M17. †**2** *v.i.* Become greater. M17–E18. **3** *v.t.* Increase the power, wealth, or rank of (a person or State). L17. **4** *v.t.* Make appear greater than the reality. L17.

aggrandiˈzation *n.* (now *rare*) = AGGRANDIZEMENT M17. **aggrandizer** *n.* a person who aggrandizes something M18.

aggrandizement /əˈgrandɪzm(ə)nt/ *n.* Also **-ise-**. M17. [Fr. *agrandissement*: see prec., -MENT.] **1** The action of aggrandizing. M17. **2** The state or condition of being aggrandized. M18.

†**aggrate** *v.t.* L16. [It. †*aggratare* (Florio, now *aggradare*), f. *a* AG- + *grato* pleasing: cf. AGREE.] **1** Gratify. L16–M18. **2** Thank. Only in M17.

†**aggravate** *a.* L15. [L *aggravatus* pa. pple, f. as next: see -ATE[2].] **1** Weighed down (*lit.* & *fig.*). L15–E16. **2** Under ecclesiastical censure. Only in L15. **3** Made more serious as an offence. M16–M18.

aggravate /ˈagrəveɪt/ *v.t.* M16. [L *aggravat-* pa. ppl stem of *aggravare* f. *ad* AG- + *gravare*, f. *gravis* heavy (prob. through (O)Fr. *aggraver*): see -ATE[3].] **I** Put weight upon. †**1** Load (someone or something *with*, something heavy or serious *upon*); bring as a charge (*against*). M16–L18. **II** Add weight to. **2** Strengthen, increase, or magnify. Now *rare* in *gen.* sense. M16. **3** Increase the gravity of (something evil, an offence, etc.). L16. **4** Exasperate, provoke, (a person). *colloq.* L16. **III** Add weight unduly. **5** Exaggerate. *obs.* exc. as an extension of sense 3. M16.

aggravating *a.* that aggravates; *colloq.* exasperating, irritating: M17. **aggravatingly** *adv.* L17. **aggravator** *n.* L16.

aggravation /agrəˈveɪʃ(ə)n/ *n.* L15. [Fr. f. med.L *aggravatio(n-)*, f. as prec.: see -ATION.] †**1** Oppression. Only in L15. **2** *RC Ch.* An ecclesiastical censure which if repeated can lead to excommunication. M16. **3** The act of increasing or the fact of being increased in gravity or seriousness. M16. **4** An extrinsic circumstance which increases the gravity of a crime, calamity, etc. M16. †**5** Exaggeration. E17–M18. †**6** Accusation. M–L17. **7** The act of irritating or provoking; aggressive behaviour; trouble. *colloq.* L19.

aggregate /ˈagrɪgət, -geɪt/ *a.* & *n.* LME. [L *aggregatus* pa. pple, f. as next: see -ATE[2].] **A** *adj.* **1** (Orig. *pple.*) Collected into one body. LME. **2** Constituted by the collection of many particles or units into one body; collective, total. E17. †**3** *Gram.* Collective. L17–M18. **4** *Taxon.* That is an aggregate (see sense B.4 below). L19.

2 J. K. GALBRAITH A fall in the aggregate demand . . for buying the output of the economy. *corporation aggregate*: see CORPORATION 2.

B *n.* **1** Sum total. LME. **2** A complex whole, mass, or body formed by the union of numerous units or particles; an assemblage. LME. **3a** A material, esp. a rock, consisting of fragments or particles grouped or loosely held together. L18. **b** Sand, gravel, slag, or the like used in making concrete etc. L19. **4** *Taxon.* A group of several species elsewhere treated as one species. Cf. SEGREGATE *n.* L19.

1 **in (the) aggregate** as a whole.

aggregately *adv.* collectively, in the aggregate M18.

aggregate /ˈagrɪgeɪt/ *v.* LME. [L *aggregat-* pa. ppl stem of *aggregare*, f. *ad* AG- + *greg-*, *grex* flock: see -ATE[3].] **1** *v.t.* & *i.* Gather into one whole, mass. LME. **2** *v.t.* Unite (an individual) *to* an association or company; add as a member. M17. **3** *v.t.* Amount to (a specified total). *colloq.* M19.

aggregable *a.* able to be aggregated (*with*) L16.

aggregation /agrɪˈgeɪʃ(ə)n/ *n.* LME. [med.L *aggregatio(n-)*, f. as prec., or f. Fr. †*aggrégation* (now *agr-*): see -ATION.] 1 The action of aggregating, or of adding one particle *to* an amount; the state of being aggregated. LME. 2 A whole or mass formed by aggregating items. M16.

aggregative /ˈagrɪgətɪv/ *a.* LME. [In isolated early use f. med.L *aggregativus*; later f. Fr. *agrégatif, -ive*: see AGGREGATE *v.*, -ATIVE.] †1 *Med.* Having the tendency to close wounds. Only in LME. 2 Of or pertaining to aggregation. M17. 3 Having the tendency to collect particulars into wholes or particles into masses. E18. 4 Associative, social. *rare.* M19.

aggregometer /agrɪˈgɒmɪtə/ *n.* L20. [f. AGGREGATION + -OMETER.] An instrument for measuring the rate or degree of spontaneous aggregation of blood platelets.

aggress /əˈgrɛs/ *v.* L16. [Fr. †*aggresser* (OFr. *agr-*) f. L *aggress-* pa. ppl stem of *aggredi* attack, f. *ad* AG- + *gradi* proceed, step.] †1 *v.i.* Approach. Only in L16. 2 *v.t.* Attack, assault. M17. 3 *v.i.* Make an attack (*on*); begin a quarrel or war (*against*). E18.

aggression /əˈgrɛʃ(ə)n/ *n.* E17. [Fr. *agression* or L *aggressio(n-)*, f. *aggress-*: see prec., -ION.] 1 An unprovoked attack; an assault. Now *rare.* E17. 2 The act of beginning a quarrel or war. E18. 3 Behaviour intended to injure another person or animal. E20. b Self-assertion, forcefulness. M20.

1 SIR W. SCOTT An unjust aggression upon their ancient liberties. H. MACMILLAN Egypt had been the victim of an aggression by Israel. 2 G. B. SHAW The protection of Ireland against foreign aggression. INDIRECT *aggression.* 3 A. STORR The most deplorable manifestations of aggression share identical roots with valuable and essential parts of human endeavour.

aggressive /əˈgrɛsɪv/ *a.* E19. [f. L *aggress-* (see AGGRESS) + -IVE. Cf. Fr. *agressif, -ive.*] 1 Of or pertaining to aggression; offensive. E19. 2 Disposed to attack others; characterized by aggression (sense 3). M19. b Self-assertive, forceful. Chiefly *N. Amer.* M20. 3 Of a chemical: strongly corrosive, promoting corrosion. M20. 4 Of a disease or condition: developing or spreading very rapidly within the body. L20.

1 E. A. FREEMAN An aggressive war, as distinguished from mere plundering inroads. 2 N. MAILER If he were aggressive, he would swear at her. b P. ROTH An ad promising high commissions to aggressive salesmen.

aggreˈssivity *n.* aggressive quality, aggressiveness M20. **aggressively** *adv.* E19. **aggressiveness** *n.* M19.

aggressor /əˈgrɛsə/ *n.* M17. [Late L, f. as prec.: see -OR. Cf. Fr. *agresseur.*] A person who makes an assault or unprovoked attack; the person or nation beginning a quarrel or war.

attrib.: GEORGE VI To continue the fight against the aggressor nations.

aggri *n.* var. of AGGRY.

aggrievance /əˈgriːv(ə)ns/ *n.* Now *rare* or *obs.* LME. [OFr. *agrevance*, f. as next. Sp. assim. to next.] †1 A hardship or burden; a grievance. LME–M18. †2 Aggravation, making more serious. Only in E16. 3 The action of aggrieving or troubling; oppression. L16.

aggrieve /əˈgriːv/ *v.t.* Now *rare* (exc. as AGGRIEVED) or *obs.* ME. [OFr. *agrever* make heavier, ult. f. L *aggravare*: see AGGRAVATE *v.* Sp. assim. to GRIEVE *v.*] 1 Grieve, distress; oppress, treat unfairly. ME. †2 Aggravate, make more serious. Only in 16.

aggrievement *n.* M19.

aggrieved /əˈgriːvd/ *a.* ME. [f. prec. + -ED¹.] †1 Distressed, troubled, grieved. ME–L16. †2 Aggravated, made more serious. E–M16. †3 Injured physically. L16–L18. 4 Injured or wronged in one's rights etc.; having a grievance. L16.

aggrievedly /-vɪdli/ *a.* L19.

aggro /ˈagrəʊ/ *n. colloq.* Also **agro.** M20. [Abbrev. of AGGRAVATION or AGGRESSION: see -O.] Deliberate troublemaking; aggression; aggravation.

aggroup /əˈgruːp/ *v.t.* & *i.* Now *rare.* L17. [Fr. *agrouper*, f. It. *aggroppare*, f. *groppa* group.] Form into a group or groups.

aggroupment *n.* M19.

aggry /ˈagri/ *a.* & *n.* Also **-ri.** E18. [Prob. f. an Afr. lang.] (Designating) a type of ancient variegated glass bead found buried in the ground in Ghana.

agha *n.* var. of AGA *n.*¹

aghast /əˈgɑːst/ *a.* LME. [Var. of *agast* pa. pple & ppl a. of AGAST *v.*, infl. by *ghost* etc.] Terrified; struck with amazement. (Foll. by *at* the object, *with* the emotion; *to do.*)

aghastness *n.* the state of being aghast, horror L19.

†**aghast** *v.* var. of AGAST.

agila /ˈagɪlə/ *n.* Also **aguila.** L16. [Port. *aguila* f. Tamil *akil.* Cf. AGALLOCHUM.] Aloes wood. Also *agila wood.*

agile /ˈadʒʌɪl/ *a.* LME. [(O)Fr. f. L *agilis*, f. *agere* do: see -ILE.] Quick-moving, nimble, active.

agile gibbon a gibbon, *Hylobates agilis*, which has variable coloration and is found in the Malay peninsula, Borneo, and Sumatra.

agilely *adv.* L19.

agility /əˈdʒɪlɪti/ *n.* LME. [(O)Fr. *agilité* f. L *agilitat-, -tas*, f. as prec.: see -ITY.] The quality of being agile; readiness, nimbleness.

agin *prep.* see AGAIN *prep.*

aging *pres. pple* & *vbl n.* see AGE *v.*

agio /ˈadʒɪəʊ/ *n.* Pl. **-os.** L17. [It. *ag(g)io.*] 1 The percentage charged for changing paper money into cash, or an inferior for a more valuable currency; the excess value of one currency over another. L17. 2 *loosely.* Money-changing. E19.

agiotage /ˈadʒɪətɪdʒ/ *n.* L18. [Fr., f. *agioter* speculate, f. *agio* f. as prec.: see -AGE.] Money-changing business; speculation in stocks; stock-jobbing.

agist /əˈdʒɪst/ *v.* LME. [OFr., AN *agister*, f. as A-⁵ + *gister*, f. *giste* lodging.] †1 *v.t.* Use or grant use of (land etc.) for pasture for a stated time or at a certain rate. LME–E17. 2 *v.t.* Orig., admit (livestock) for a stated time into a forest. Later, take in (livestock) to remain and feed at a certain rate. L15. 3 *v.i.* Of livestock: remain and feed for a stated time etc. *rare.* L16. 4 *v.t.* Charge (land or its owner) with any public burden. L17.

agister *n.* var. of AGISTOR.

agistment /əˈdʒɪs(t)m(ə)nt/ *n.* LME. [OFr. *agistement*, f. as AGIST: see -MENT.] 1 The action or process of agisting livestock. LME. 2 A rate levied upon the owner or occupier of pasture-land. Esp. in *agistment tithe* (Hist.). E16. 3 The rate levied or profit made by agisting another's livestock. L16. 4 The herbage of a forest, or the right to it. L16.

agistor /əˈdʒɪstə/ *n.* Also **-er.** L15. [AN *agistour*, f. as AGIST: see -OR.] A person who agists or supervises the agistment of livestock.

agitant /ˈadʒɪt(ə)nt/ *n. rare.* M17. [Fr., use as n. of pres. pple of *agiter* stir up f. L *agitare*: see AGITATE *v.*, -ANT ¹.] A person who agitates; a thing which causes agitation.

†**agitate** *a.* (orig. *pa. pple*). Chiefly *Sc.* LME–L17. [L *agitatus* pa. pple, f. as next: see -ATE².] Agitated.

agitate /ˈadʒɪteɪt/ *v.* LME. [L *agitat-* pa. ppl stem of *agitare* frequent. of *agere* drive: see -ATE³.] I Move, excite. †1 *v.t.* Drive away. Only in LME. 2 *v.t.* Disturb, perturb, excite (the thoughts, feelings, etc.). L16. 3 *v.t.* Move to and fro, shake (something material). L16. †4 *v.t.* Communicate action or motion to. E17–M18. 5 *v.t.* Perturb or excite (a person etc.) in mind or feelings. E19.

2 D. J. ENRIGHT Too much coffee agitates the nerves. 3 B. PYM He agitated his tea-bag with a spoon. 4 J. THOMSON Who.. surrounds, informs, and agitates the whole. 5 W. S. CHURCHILL Constant bickering agitated the two countries.

II Be active or busy. †6 *v.t.* & *i.* Manage as an agent. Only in M17. 7 *v.t.* Discuss, debate; push forward as a plan. M17. 8 *v.t.* Revolve in the mind; contrive busily. *arch.* M17. 9 *v.i.* Keep a political or other object continually under discussion, keep up an agitation (*for* or *against*). E19.

7 BURKE Before an appeal was so much as agitated.

agitatedly *adv.* in an agitated manner E19. **agitating** *ppl a.* that agitates; *Eng. Hist.* acting as an agitator in the Parliamentary army: L17. **agitatingly** *adv.* E19. **agitative** *a.* tending to agitate E16.

agitation /adʒɪˈteɪʃ(ə)n/ *n.* M16. [Fr., or L *agitatio(n-)*, f. as prec.: see -ATION.] †1 Action, exercise of activity. M16–E18. 2 The action of moving to and fro, shaking. L16. 3 Mental tossing of a matter to and fro, debate, consideration. L16. 4 The state of being agitated; commotion, disturbance (mental or physical). E17. †5 Busy devising, scheming. E17–E19. 6 The keeping of a political or other object constantly before public attention; public excitement. E19.

agitational *a.* M19.

agitato /adʒɪˈtɑːtəʊ/ *adv., a.,* & *n.* E19. [It.] *Mus.* A *adv.* & *adj.* (A direction:) in an agitated manner. E19. B *n.* Pl. **-ti** /-ti/, **-tos.** A passage (to be) played or sung in an agitated manner. *rare.* E19.

agitator /ˈadʒɪteɪtə/ *n.* M17. [L *agitator*, f. as AGITATE *v.*: see -OR.] 1 *Eng. Hist.* A delegate of the private soldiers of the Parliamentary army 1647–9. (Also alt. to ADJUTATOR.) M17. 2 A person who agitates, esp. politically. M18. 3 A device for stirring, shaking, or mixing. E19.

agitprop /ˈadʒɪtprɒp, ˈag-/ *n.* Also **A-.** E20. [Russ., f. *agit(atsiya* agitation + *prop(aganda* propaganda.] *Hist.* Soviet Communist propaganda; the system or activity of disseminating this.

aglare /əˈglɛː/ *adv.* & *pred. a.* L19. [f. A-² + GLARE *n.*¹] In a glare, glaring.

agleam /əˈgliːm/ *adv.* & *pred. a.* L19. [f. A-² + GLEAM *n.*¹] Gleaming.

aglet /ˈaglət/ *n.* Also **ai-** /ˈeɪ-/. LME. [(O)Fr. AIGUILLETTE.] 1 The metal tag of a lace. LME. 2 A metallic tag, pendant, or spangle, worn as an ornament. E16. b *spec.* A tagged point hanging from the shoulder upon the breast of some uniforms. Now usu. AIGUILLETTE. M19. 3 A catkin. L16.

agley /əˈgleɪ, əˈgliː/ *adv.* & *pred. a. Sc.* L18. [f. A-² + GLEY *v.*] Askew, awry.

aglimmer /əˈglɪmə/ *adv.* & *pred. a.* E19. [f. A-² + GLIMMER *n.*¹] Glimmering.

aglisten /əˈglɪs(ə)n/ *adv.* & *pred. a.* L19. [f. A-² + GLISTEN *v.*] Glistening.

aglitter /əˈglɪtə/ *adv.* & *pred. a.* E19. [f. A-² + GLITTER *n.*] In a glitter, glittering.

aglomerular /eɪglɒˈmɛrʊlə, a-/ *a.* E20. [f. A-¹⁰ + GLOMERULAR.] Chiefly *Ichthyol.* Lacking (kidney) glomeruli (as certain fishes).

agloo *n.* see IGLOO.

aglow /əˈgləʊ/ *adv.* & *pred. a.* E19. [f. A-² + GLOW *n.*] In a glow (of warmth, colour, excitement, etc.).

aglu *n.* see IGLOO.

aglycone /əˈglʌɪkəʊn/ *n.* Also (see below) **aglu-** /əˈgluː-/. E20. [G *Aglykon*, f. as A-¹⁰ + GLYCO- + -ONE.] *Chem.* The compound remaining when the sugar is removed from a glycoside. Also called *aglucone* when the sugar is glucose.

aglyphous /ˈaglɪfəs/ *a.* L19. [f. A-¹⁰ + Gk *gluphē* carving + -OUS.] *Zool.* Of a snake's tooth: solid, without a hollow or groove for venom. Of a snake: lacking fangs; not venomous.

aglyph *n.* an aglyphous snake E20.

agma /ˈagmə/ *n.* M20. [Late Gk f. Gk = fragment.] The velar nasal consonant /ŋ/; a letter or symbol representing this.

agnail /ˈagneɪl/ *n.* [OE *angnægl*, corresp. to OFris. *ongneil*, OHG *ungnagel* (G dial. *Anneglen, Einnegeln*), f. a Gmc base meaning 'compressed, tight, painful' + as NAIL *n.* The application of the wd has been much infl. by pop. etym.] †1 A corn on the toe or foot. OE–L19. 2 A painful swelling around the toe- or fingernail. L16. 3 A strip of torn skin at the root of the fingernail. M19.

agnamed /ˈagneɪmd/ *pa. pple* & *ppl a.* Chiefly *Sc.* M17. [f. AG- + *named*, f. NAME *v.*, on the analogy of AGNOMEN.] Styled or called, in addition to the given personal name and surname; nicknamed.

agnate /ˈagneɪt/ *n.* & *a.* L15. [L *agnatus*, f. *ad* AG- + (*g*)*natus* born.] **A** *n.* A descendant, esp. by male links, from the same male ancestor. L15. **B** *adj.* Descended from the same male ancestor, esp. by male links; of the same clan or nation; *fig.* akin. E17.

agnatic /əgˈnatɪk/ *a.* pertaining to agnates; related on the father's side: M18. **agˈnation** *n.* descent from a common male ancestor, esp. through male links only; kinship by descent: L16.

agnathan /agˈneɪθ(ə)n/ *n.* & *a.* M20. [f. mod.L *Agnatha* (see below), f. Gk A-[10] + *gnathos* jaw: see -AN.] **A** *n.* A primitive jawless vertebrate of the superclass Agnatha (or Marsipobranchii), which includes the lampreys, the hagfishes, and many fossil fishes. M20. **B** *adj.* Of, pertaining to, or characteristic of Agnatha. L20.

agnise *v.* var. of AGNIZE.

agnition /agˈnɪʃ(ə)n/ *n.* Now *rare.* LME. [L *agnitio(n-)*, f. *agnit-* pa. ppl stem of *agnoscere*, f. *ad* AG- + (*g*)*noscere* know: see -ION.] Recognition, acknowledgement.

agnize /əgˈnʌɪz/ *v.t. arch.* Also **-ise**. M16. [f. L *agnoscere* (see prec.) after *cognize*, *recognize*: see -IZE.] †1 Recognize in any capacity, own *for*, *as*, *to be*, etc. M16–M18. 2 Recognize the existence of, confess. M16. †3 Own the authority or claims of. L16–M18. 4 Recognize, remember. E17.

Agnoetae /agnəʊˈiːtiː/ *n.pl.* M18. [med.L *agnoetae* f. late Gk *agnoētai*, f. *agnoein* be ignorant.] *Eccl. Hist.* A Monophysite sect of the 6th cent. holding that Jesus was ignorant of some things.

Agnoite /ˈagnəʊʌɪt/, **-ete** /-iːt/ *ns.* a member of the Agnoetae L16.

agnomen /agˈnəʊmɛn/ *n.* M17. [L *agnomen*, f. *ad* AG- + (*g*)*nomen* name.] A name given or acquired during the course of one's life, a nickname; *Rom. Hist.* a fourth name occas. given as an honour.

agnominate /agˈnɒmɪneɪt/ *v.t. rare.* Also **annom-** /aˈnɒm-/. L16. [L *agnominat-* pa. ppl stem of *agnominare*, f. as prec.; forms w. *ann-* f. Fr. f. med.L: see -ATE[3].] Give an agnomen to, call, nickname.

agnomination /əgnɒmɪˈneɪʃ(ə)n/ *n.* Now *rare.* Also **annom-** /ənɒm-/. M16. [L *agnominatio(n-)*, f. as prec.; forms w. *ann-* f. Fr. f. med.L: see -ATION.] *Rhet.* 1 Paronomasia. M16. 2 Alliteration. M16.

agnosia /əgˈnəʊsɪə/ *n.* E20. [Gk *agnōsia* ignorance, f. A-[10] + *gnōsis* knowledge: -IA[1].] *Med.* A diminished ability to recognize objects by one or other of the senses.

visual agnosia: see VISUAL *a.*

agnosic *a.* pertaining to or affected with agnosia M20.

agnostic /agˈnɒstɪk/ *n.* & *a.* M19. [f. A-[10] + GNOSTIC.] **A** *n.* A person who holds the view that nothing can be known of the existence of God or of anything beyond material phenomena. Also, a person who is uncertain or noncommittal about a particular thing. M19. **B** *adj.* Of or pertaining to agnostics or agnosticism. L19.

¶Coined by T. H. Huxley (OED); but occurs earlier in a letter of 1859 from Isabel Arundell.

agnostical *a.* L19. **agnostically** *adv.* L19. **agnosticism** /-sɪz(ə)m/ *n.* the doctrine or tenets of agnostics, an agnostic attitude L19.

Agnus /ˈagnʊs, -nəs, ˈanjʊs/ *n.* LME. [Abbrev.] = AGNUS DEI.

agnus castus /ˈagnəs ˈkastəs/ *n. phr.* Now *rare* or *obs.* exc. (w. hyphen) as mod.L specific epithet. LME. [L, f. *agnus* f. Gk *agnos*, name of the tree, conf. w. *hagnos* chaste, + *castus* chaste.] The chaste-tree, *Vitex agnus-castus*.

Agnus Dei /ˈagnʊs ˈdeiːː, *in sense 1 also* ˈanjʊs; ˈagnəs ˈdiːʌɪ/ *n. phr.* LME. [L = Lamb of God.] *Chr. Ch.* 1 Part of the Mass beginning with the words *Agnus Dei*; a musical setting of this. LME. 2 A figure of a lamb bearing a cross or flag, as an emblem of Christ. LME. **b** A cake of wax stamped with such a figure and blessed by the Pope. L16.

ago /əˈgəʊ/ *ppl a.* & *adv.* Also (*arch.*) **agone** /əˈgɒn/. ME. [pa. pple of next, orig. in use as adj. qualifying a n. of time.] 1 *adj.* (now always *postpositive* and also interpreted as *adv.*). Past, gone by. ME. 2 *adv.* In *long ago* (†occas. w. other advs. w. similar meaning): long since. ME.

1 SHAKES. *Twel. N.* He's drunk, . . an hour agone. DICKENS Ay, a goodish bit ago. E. BISHOP A slight landslide occurred . . / about an hour ago.

†ago *v.i.* See also prec. OE. [f. A-[1] + GO *v.*] 1 Go on, proceed. OE–ME. 2 Of time: pass. OE–M16. 3 Go away. ME–L17.

agog /əˈgɒg/ *adv.* & *pred. a.* M16. [Prob. (w. substitution of A *prep.*[1]) repr. late OFr. *en gogues*, f. *en* in + pl. of *gogue* merriment, pleasantry.] In eager readiness, expectant.

agogic /əˈgɒdʒɪk/ *a.* & *n.* L19. [G *agogisch*, f. Gk *agōgos* leading, f. *agein* to lead: see -IC.] *Mus.* **A** *adj.* Designating or pertaining to accent effected by lengthening the time-value of the note. L19. **B** *n.* In *pl.* (treated as *sing.*) The theory or use of agogic accents; the deliberate modification of time-values in a musical performance. L19.

a gogo /ə ˈgəʊgəʊ/ *adv.* & *postpositive a. phr. colloq.* M20. [Fr. *à gogo*.] In abundance, galore.

agon /ˈagəʊn/ *n.* Pl. **agones** /əˈgəʊniːz/. E17. [Gk *agōn* contest.] *Gk Hist.* 1 A public celebration of games; a contest for the prize at the games or *transf.* elsewhere. E17. 2 A verbal contest between two characters in a play. L19.

agonal /ˈag(ə)n(ə)l/ *a.* L18. [Sense 1 f. prec., sense 2 f. AGONY: see -AL[1].] 1 Pertaining to an agon. L18. 2 Pertaining to or occurring during agony, esp. death agony. E19.

agone *ppl a.* & *adv.* see AGO *ppl a.* & *adv.*

agonic /əˈgɒnɪk/ *a.* M19. [f. Gk *agōn(i)os*, f. *a-* A-[10] + *gōnia* angle, + -IC.] *agonic line*, the imaginary line joining points on the earth's surface where the magnetic declination is zero.

agonise *v.* var. of AGONIZE.

agonism /ˈagənɪz(ə)m/ *n.* M17. [In sense 1 f. Gk *agōnisma*, f. *agōnizesthai* (see AGONIZE); in sense 2 f. next: see -ISM.] 1 A contest; a prize. *rare* (only in Dicts.). M17. 2 *Biochem.* The action of an agonist (AGONIST 4). L20.

agonist /ˈagənɪst/ *n.* E17. [Gk *agōnistēs* contestant, f. as AGON: see -IST.] 1 A person who competes for prizes. *rare.* E17. 2 A protagonist in a drama (*lit.* & *fig.*). E20. 3 *Physiol.* A muscle whose contraction is directly responsible for the movement of a part. Cf. ANTAGONIST 2. E20. 4 *Biochem.* A chemical which combines with a receptor and initiates a physiological response. Cf. ANTAGONIST 3. M20.

agonistes /agəˈnɪstiːz/ *postpositive a.* L17. [f. as prec.] Who is an agonist.

¶First used in Milton's *Samson Agonistes*

agonistic /agəˈnɪstɪk/ *a.* M17. [Late L *agonisticus* f. Gk *agōnistikos*, f. as AGONIST: see -IC.] 1 Pertaining to (orig. ancient Greek) athletic contests or to athletic feats. M17. 2 *Rhet.* Polemic, combative. M17. 3 Striving for effect. M19. 4 *Zool.* Of animal behaviour: associated with conflict between individuals. M20.

agonistical *a.* (now *rare*) = AGONISTIC 1, 2 M17. **agonistically** *adv.* (*rare*) polemically M19.

agonize /ˈagənʌɪz/ *v.* Also **-ise**. L16. [Fr. *agoniser* or late L *agonizare* (after Gk *agōnizesthai*, f. as AGON): see -IZE.] 1 *v.t.* Subject to agony. L16. 2 *v.i.* Suffer agony; writhe in anguish; be in the throes of death. L16. 3 *v.i.* Contend in the arena; wrestle. Chiefly *fig.*, *esp.* worry intensely *about*, *over*, etc. L16. 4 *v.i. fig.* Make desperate efforts for effect. M19.

agonized *ppl a.* subjected to or expressing agony L16. **agonizedly** /-zɪdli/ *adv.* M19. **agonizing** *ppl a.* causing agony; expressing agony; *arch.* suffering agony: L16. **agonizingly** *adv.* E19.

agonothete /əˈgəʊnəθiːt/ *n.* Also **-thet** /-θɛt/. E17. [Gk *agōnothetēs*, f. as AGON + *thetēs* disposer.] *Gk Hist.* A director of the public games.

agony /ˈagəni/ *n.* LME. [(O)Fr. *agonie* or late L *agonia* f. Gk *agōnia*, f. as AGON: see -Y[3].] 1 Extreme mental suffering; a paroxysm of grief or anguish. LME. **b** A paroxysm of pleasure. *arch.* E18. 2 *spec.* The mental anguish of Jesus in Gethsemane. LME. 3 The convulsive throes or pangs of death. Exc. *Med.* now *rare* without specification. LME. 4 Extreme bodily suffering; writhing or throes of the body produced by this. E17. 5 A severe struggle or contest. (Usu. w. suggestion of sense 4.) L17.

1 COLERIDGE Never a saint took pity on My soul in agony. **b** POPE With cries and agonies of wild delight. 3 *death agony*, *last agony*, *mortal agony*, etc. 4 MILTON Here in perpetual agony and pain. W. OWEN We hear the mad gusts tugging on the wire, Like twitching agonies of men.

Phrases: *pile on the agony*: see PILE *v.*[2]

Comb.: **agony aunt** *colloq.* a female writer of an agony column (sense b); **agony column** (*a*) a personal column of a newspaper etc.; (*b*) a newspaper etc. feature of readers' questions about personal difficulties, with answers and advice; **agony uncle** *colloq.* a male writer of an agony column (sense b).

agora /ˈagɒrə/ *n.*[1] Pl. **-rae** /-riː/, **-rai** /-rʌɪ/, **-ras**. L16. [Gk.] *Gk Hist.* An assembly; a place of assembly, *esp.* a market-place.

agora /agəˈrɑː/ *n.*[2] Pl. **-rot** /-rəʊt/, **-roth** /-rəʊθ/. M20. [Heb. *ʾăgōrāh* a small coin.] A monetary unit of Israel, equal to one-hundredth of a shekel (initially of a pound or lira).

agoraphobia /ag(ə)rəˈfəʊbɪə/ *n.* L19. [f. Gk AGORA *n.*[1] + -PHOBIA.] Irrational fear of open spaces.

ˈagoraphobe *n.* = AGORAPHOBIC *n.* M20. **agoraphobic** *a.* & *n.* (a person) affected with agoraphobia; pertaining to agoraphobia: L19.

agorot, -oth *ns.* pls. of AGORA *n.*[2]

agouti /əˈguːti/ *n.* Also **aguti**. M16. [Fr., or Sp. *aguti* f. Tupi-Guarani *akutí*.] 1 A long-legged rodent belonging to the genus *Dasyprocta*, native to Central and South America. M16. 2 (An animal having) a fur type in which each hair has alternate bands of light and dark pigmentation, usu. producing a grizzled or salt-and-pepper appearance. L19.

agraffe /əˈgraf/ *n.* M17. [Fr. *agrafe*, f. *agrafer* to hook.] A hook which fastens to a ring and is used as a clasp.

agrammatism /əˈgramətɪz(ə)m/ *n.* L19. [f. Gk *agrammatos* illiterate, f. as A-[10] + *grammata* letters, + -ISM.] *Med.* An inability to form sentences grammatically, as a symptom of cerebral disease or mental illness.

agranulocytosis /əˌgranjʊlə(ʊ)sʌɪˈtəʊsɪs/ *n.* Pl. **-toses** /-ˈtəʊsiːz/. E20. [f. A-[10] + GRANULOCYTE + -OSIS.] *Med.* A deficiency of granulocytes in the blood, causing increased vulnerability to infection.

agranulocytic /-ˈsɪtɪk/ *a.* E20.

agrapha *n.* pl. of AGRAPHON.

agraphia /əˈgrafɪə/ *n.* M19. [f. A-[10] + Gk *-graphia* writing.] *Med.* Inability to write, as a symptom of cerebral disease or damage.

agraphic *a.* characterized by agraphia L19.

agraphon /ˈagrəfɒn/ *n.* Pl. **-pha** /-fə/. L19. [Gk, neut. of *agraphos* unwritten, f. as A-[10], -GRAPH.] A saying attributed to Jesus but not in the canonical Gospels. Usu. in *pl.*

agrarian /əˈgrɛːrɪən/ *a.* & *n.* E17. [f. L *agrarius*, f. *agr-*, *ager* land: see -ARIAN.] **A** *adj.* 1 *Rom. Hist.* Designating a law (L *Lex agraria*) for the division of conquered lands. E17. 2 Of or pertaining to landed property. E18. 3 Of or pertaining to cultivated land or the cultivation of land. L18. **B** *n.* 1 An agrarian law. *rare.* M17. 2 An advocate of the redistribution of landed property. E19.

agrarianism *n.* (advocacy of or agitation for) the redistribution of landed property or reform of the conditions of tenure of land E19.

agree /əˈgriː/ *v.* Pa. t. & pple **agreed**. LME. [(O)Fr. *agréer* ult. f. L *ad* AG- + *gratus* pleasing, agreeable. Cf. GREE *n.*[2]] I Please, be pleased. †1 *v.t.* Please. LME–L15. †2 *v.t.* Be pleased with, accept. LME–M17.

II Make agreeable or harmonious. †3 *v.t.* & *i.* Pay (a person); settle an account *with*. Only in LME. 4 *v.t.* Arrange, settle; reach agreement concerning; consent to, approve of. LME. †5 *v.t.* Reconcile (persons), cause to be friends. L15–L17. 6 *v.t.* Bring into harmony (things that differ; now only discrepant accounts etc.). M17.

4 SPENSER Some troublous uprore, Whereto he drew in haste it to agree. POPE Did I for this agree The solemn truce?

III Become well-disposed. 7 *v.i.* Give consent, accede. (Foll. by *to, to do, that.*) LME. †8 *v.refl.* Accede, consent *to*. LME–L16. †9 *v.i.* Accede *to* the opinion of. E16–M17.

7 SHAKES. *1 Hen. VI* Post . . to France; Agree to any covenants. LD MACAULAY He reluctantly agreed . . that some indulgence should be granted. G. B. SHAW Theyve agreed to come to the breakfast. SCOTT FITZGERALD 'All right,' I agreed, 'I'll be glad to.'

IV Come into harmony. 10 *v.i.* Come into accord as to something; come to terms. (Foll. by †*for* a payment or price; *on, as to,* †*of* a matter or point; *to do* something; or *that.*) LME. 11 *v.i.* Make up differences; become friends. Now *dial.* LME.

10 **agree to differ, agree to disagree** no longer try to convince each other.

V Be in harmony. 12 *v.i.* Of things: accord (*together*); coincide in any respect (*with*); be consistent (*with,* †*to*). L15. 13a *v.i.* Be of the same mind as to particular points; concur *with* a person *in, on, as to, about, that,* †such *to be*. L15. b *v.i.* Feel or state one's thoughts to be in accordance (*with* an opinion or statement). M16. c *v.t.* Say in agreement. M19. 14 *v.i.* Do well *with*: a Of a person: be suited by (a food, climate, etc.). *obs.* exc. *dial.* E16. b Of food, a climate, etc.: suit the constitution of (a person). E17. †15 *v.i.* Be suitable or appropriate *to*. M16–L17. 16 *v.i.* Be in sympathy; live or act together harmoniously. (Foll. by *together, with.*) M16. 17 *v.i. Gram.* Have the same number, gender, case, person, etc. (Foll. by *with.*) M16.

12 SHAKES. *Tam. Shr.* At last . . our jarring notes agree. SWIFT The constitution of the English government . . to which the present establishment of the church doth so happily agree. YEATS If his tale agrees with yours, then I am clear. 13a **I couldn't agree (with you) more** *colloq.* I am in complete agreement (with you). 14a G. BURNET Fagius, not agreeing with this air, died soon after. b K. AMIS Spirits don't seem to agree with you. 16 T. FULLER It is probable that in Noahs Ark the wolf agreed with the lambe.

agreeance *n.* (now *rare*) agreement E16. **agreeing** *ppl a.* †(*a*) according *to*; (*b*) that agree(s) (*with* etc.): E16. **agreeingly** *adv.* (now *rare*) (*a*) in an agreeing manner; †(*b*) according *to*: M16. **agreer** *n.* a person who or thing which agrees M16.

agreeability /əgriːəˈbɪlɪti/ *n.* LME. [Isolated early use f. OFr. *agreableté*, f. as next; re-formed L18 f. next: see -ABILITY.] Agreeableness, esp. of disposition.

agreeable /əˈgriːəb(ə)l/ *a., adv.,* & *n.* LME. [(O)Fr. *agréable*, f. as AGREE: see -ABLE.] A *adj.* 1 To one's liking; pleasing (*to*). LME. 2 Conformable, corresponding, suitable, consistent. Foll. by *to, unto,* †*with*, or †*absol.* LME. 3 Kindly disposed; willing to agree (*to* a thing, *to do*). Now *colloq.* LME. †4 Of one mind. L15–E17.

1 **make oneself agreeable to** behave so as to please (a person).

B *adv.* In a way that corresponds *to*; according *to*. *arch.* M16.

C *n.* †1 An agreeable person or thing. *rare.* E18–E19. 2 *absol.* A pleasing or polite thing. Esp. in *do the agreeable. arch.* E19.

agreeableness *n.* †(*a*) conformity (*to*), consistency (*with*); (*b*) pleasingness, pleasantness: M16. **agreeably** *adv.* (*a*) pleasantly; (*b*) in a manner corresponding *to*; in accordance *with*; †(*c*) correspondingly, in the same way: LME.

agreed /əˈgriːd/ *a.* LME. [f. AGREE + -ED^1.] †1 Made pleasing. Only in LME. †2 Pleased, contented. LME–M16. 3 Arranged or settled by common consent. Now usu. foll. by *on*. L15. b As a rejoinder: consented to. M16. 4 United in feeling or sentiment. M16. 5 Having come to be, or of, the same opinion. E17.

agreement /əˈgriːm(ə)nt/ *n.* LME. [OFr. (mod. *agrément*), f. as AGREE: see -MENT.] 1 A mutual understanding; a covenant, a treaty. LME. 2 *Law.* A legally binding arrangement between two or more parties. LME. 3 Mutual conformity of things; harmony, affinity. LME. †4 Pleasing; satisfaction. L15–L16. †5 Consent. Only in L15. †6 Atonement. E–M16. 7 Accordance in sentiment, opinion, action, etc. E16. 8 *Gram.* The condition of having the same number, gender, case, person, etc. M16. 9 An agreeable quality, circumstance, etc. Usu. in *pl.* (= now more usual AGRÉMENT 1). L17.

1 *conditional agreement*: see CONDITIONAL *a.* 1. *gentleman's* or *gentlemen's agreement*: see GENTLEMAN. 2 *Net Book Agreement*: see NET *a.*^{2} & *adv.*

agrémens *n.pl.* see AGRÉMENT.

agrément /agremɑ̃/ *n.* Pl. ***-ments, -mens***, (pronounced same). E18. [Fr.: see AGREEMENT.] 1 In *pl.* Agreeable qualities, circumstances, etc. E18. 2 *Mus.* In *pl.* Grace-notes; embellishments. L18. 3 Official approval given to a diplomatic representative of another country. E20.

agrestal /əˈgrɛst(ə)l/ *a.* M19. [f. as next.] *Bot.* Growing wild in cultivated fields.

agrestial /əˈgrɛstɪəl/ *a.* E17. [f. as next + -AL^1.] Of, pertaining to, or inhabiting the fields or open country.

agrestic /əˈgrɛstɪk/ *a.* E17. [f. L *agrestis*, f. *agr-*, *ager* field, + -IC.] Rural, rustic; uncouth.

agribusiness /ˈagrɪbɪznɪs/ *n.* M20. [f. AGRI(CULTURE + BUSINESS.] The production, distribution, etc., of farming produce and agricultural equipment and supplies; (any of) the group of industries engaged in this; agriculture as a business using advanced technology.

Comb.: **agribusinessman** a man who engages in agribusiness.

agrichemical /agrɪˈkɛmɪk(ə)l/ *a.* & *n.* M20. [f. AGRI(CULTURAL + CHEMICAL.] A *adj.* Agricultural and chemical; of or pertaining to agrochemicals. M20. B *n.* A chemical used or produced in agribusiness; an agrochemical. M20.

†**agricole** *n. rare.* M17–L19. [(O)Fr. f. L *agricola*, f. *agr-*, *ager* field + *-cola* tenant.] A farmer; a rustic.

†**agricolist** *n.* an agriculturist M–L18. †**agricolous** *a.* (*joc.*) agricultural: only in 19.

†**agricultor** *n.* LME–M19. [L, f. as next + *cultor* tiller.] A person who cultivates; a farmer.

¶Rare bef. L18.

agriculture /ˈagrɪkʌltʃə/ *n.* LME. [Fr., or L *agricultura*, f. *agr-*, *ager* field + *cultura* CULTURE *n.*] The science or practice of cultivating the soil and rearing animals; farming; occas. *spec.* tillage.

agriˈcultural *a.* of or pertaining to agriculture L18. **agriˈculturalist** *n.* a person engaged in agriculture E19. **agriˈculturally** *adv.* with regard to agriculture E19. †**agriculturer** *n.* an agriculturalist E–M19. **agriˈculturist** *n.* (*a*) a person who studies agriculture; (*b*) an agriculturalist: M18.

agrimensorial /ˌagrɪmɛnˈsɔːrɪəl/ *a.* L19. [f. L *agrimensor*, f. as prec. + *mensor* surveyor, + -IAL.] Of or pertaining to land-surveying.

agrimi /əˈgriːmi/ *n.* Pl. **-mia** /-mɪə/, **-mis**. M19. [mod.Gk.] In Crete and in Minoan art, the wild goat.

agrimony /ˈagrɪməni/ *n.* LME. [Early forms f. (O)Fr. *aigremoine*; later mod. form f. L *agrimonia* misreading for *argemonia* (Pliny, Celsus) f. Gk *argemōnē* poppy.] 1 Any plant of the genus *Agrimonia*; esp. *A. eupatoria*, a common perennial bearing spikes of yellow flowers. LME. 2 Any of a number of other plants, esp. = HEMP *agrimony*. L16.

agrin /əˈgrɪn/ *adv.* & *pred. a.* E19. [f. A-^{2} + GRIN *n.*^{2}] Grinning.

agriology /agrɪˈɒlədʒi/ *n.* L19. [f. Gk *agrios* wild, savage + -OLOGY.] The branch of knowledge that deals with the history and customs of non-literate peoples.

agriologist *n.* L19.

†**agriot** *n.* Also **eg-**. E16–L19. [OFr. *agriote* (mod. *griotte*).] A sour kind of cherry.

agriproduct /ˈagrɪprɒdəkt, -dʌkt/ *n.* L20. [f. *agri-* in AGRIBUSINESS + PRODUCT *n.*] A product of agribusiness.

†**agrise** *v.* [OE *āgrīsan*, f. A-^{1} + vb f. base also of GRISLY *a.*] 1 *v.i.* Tremble; be terrified. OE–L16. 2 *v.t.* Make tremble; terrify. Orig. *impers.* in (*it*) *agrises* etc. ME–M17. 3 *v.t.* Shudder at, loathe. Only in LME.

agro *n.* var. of AGGRO.

agro- /ˈagrəʊ/ *comb. form.* [f. Gk *agros* land, field: see -O-.] Agricultural; agriculture and.

agrobioˈlogical *a.* of or pertaining to agrobiology M20. **agrobiˈologist** *n.* an expert in or student of agrobiology M20. **agrobiˈology** *n.* the branch of knowledge that deals with soil science and plant nutrition and its application to crop production M20. **agrobusiness** *n.* = AGRIBUSINESS M20. **agroˈchemical** *n.* a chemical used in agriculture; a chemical fertilizer, pesticide, weedkiller, etc.: M20. **agro-cliˈmatic** *a.* of or pertaining to the relationship between climate and agriculture M20. **agro-ecoˈlogical** *a.* of or pertaining to the relationship between ecology and agriculture M20. **agro-inˈdustrial** *a.* of or pertaining to agro-industry M20. **agro-industry** *n.* industry connected with agriculture; agriculture developed along industrial lines: M20. **agrotechˈnology** *n.* the application of technology in agriculture M20.

agrology /əˈgrɒlədʒi/ *n.* E20. [f. prec. + -LOGY. Cf. Fr. *agrologie*.] 1 Soil science in relation to crops. *rare.* E20. 2 *Canad.* The application of science to agriculture. M20.

agrologist *n.* (*Canad.*) M20.

agronomic /agrəˈnɒmɪk/ *a.* & *n.* E19. [Fr. *agronomique*, f. *agronome*: see next, -IC.] A *adj.* Of or pertaining to agronomy. E19. B *n.* In *pl.* (usu. treated as *sing.*). = AGRONOMY. M19.

agronomical *a.* M19. **agronomically** *adv.* M20.

agronomy /əˈgrɒnəmi/ *n.* E19. [Fr. *agronomie*, f. *agronome* agriculturist, f. Gk *agros* land + *-nomos* arranging, f. *nemoein* arrange: see -NOMY.] The science of soil management and crop production.

agronome /ˈagrənəʊm/ *n.* [Fr.] an agronomist M19. **agronomist** *n.* a person engaged in agronomy E19.

aground /əˈgraʊnd/ *adv.* & *pred. a.* ME. [f. A *prep.*^{1} 1 + GROUND *n.*] †1 On the ground; on or to the earth. Latterly *dial.* ME–L19. 2 Of a ship: on the bottom of shallow water. Opp. *afloat.* L15.

1 J. CLARE She furious stampt her shoeless foot aground. 2 BYRON One bark blew up, a second near the works Running aground, was taken by the Turks.

aguardiente /aˌgwardiˈente, əˌgwɑːdɪˈɛnti/ *n.* E19. [Sp., f. *agua* water + *ardiente* fiery, ARDENT.] Coarse Spanish brandy; in Spanish-speaking areas of America, a similar distilled liquor, *esp.* one made from sugar cane.

ague /ˈeɪgjuː/ *n.* & *v.* ME. [(O)Fr. f. med.L *acuta* use as n. (sc. *febris* fever) of fem. of L *acutus* ACUTE.] A *n.* 1 An acute fever. Now *dial.* *rare* in *gen.* sense. ME. 2 *esp.* A malarial fever with cold, hot, and sweating stages (at first *esp.* the hot stage, later *esp.* the cold). LME. 3 Any shivering fit. L16.

2 WALCHEREN *ague.*

Comb.: †**ague-cake** the spleen or another organ so enlarged as to be perceptible externally; **ague-tree** sassafras.

B *v.t.* Affect (as) with ague. Chiefly as *agued* ppl a. E17.

aguila *n.* var. of AGILA.

†**aguise** *v.t.* Only in L16. [f. GUISE *v.*, *a-* opp. *dis-* in *disguise* (cf. *accord, discord*, etc.).] Dress, array.

SPENSER Sometimes her head she . . would aguize With gaudy girlonds.

aguish /ˈeɪgjuːɪʃ/ *a.* E17. [f. AGUE *n.* + -ISH^1.] 1 Subject to ague. E17. 2 Tending to produce ague. E17. 3 Of the nature of or characteristic of an ague; shaky; intermittent. M17.

aguishly *adv.* M17. **aguishness** *n.* (*rare*) E18.

aguti *n.* var. of AGOUTI.

agy *a.* var. of AGEY.

ah /ɑː/ *pers. pron. dial.* & *US Black English.* L19. [Repr. a pronunc.] = I *pers. pron.*

ah /ɑː/ *int., n.,* & *v.* Also (earlier, now *rare*) **a.** ME. [OFr. *a(h)* (mod. *ah*); cf. It., Sp. *ah*, L *a(h)*, Gk *a(a)*, etc.] A *int.* Expr.: sorrow, regret; entreaty, remonstrance; surprise, pleasure, admiration; realization, discovery; dislike, boredom, contempt, mockery. ME.

SHAKES. *2 Hen. VI* Ah, villain, thou wilt betray me. TENNYSON Ah! when shall all men's good Be each man's rule. YEATS Ah me! I cannot reach them. SCOTT

FITZGERALD 'Ah,' she cried, 'you look so cool.' T. STOPPARD Ah!—I knew there was something.

B *n.* An utterance of 'ah!'. E18.

C *v.i.* Say 'ah!'. L19.

¶ See also OOH *n.*, *v.*

aha /əˈhɑː, ɑːˈhɑː/ *int.* ME. [f. AH *int.* + HA *int.*] Expr.: surprise; triumph, satisfaction; mockery, irony.

Comb.: **aha experience, moment, reaction**, etc.: of sudden insight or discovery.

ahead /əˈhɛd/ *adv.* Orig. *Naut.* M16. [f. A *prep.*[1] 1 + HEAD *n.*] **1** Of motion: straight forwards; headlong. M16. **2** Pointing forwards; *fig.* into the future. L16. **3** At the head (of a moving company); in advance, in front (*lit.* & *fig.*). E17. **4** In the line of one's forward motion; further forward in space or time. L17.

1 BROWNING Galloping straight a-head. *go ahead*: see GO *v.* See also GO-AHEAD. **2** J. F. COOPER One who looked on a-head to the wants of posterity. **3** E. O'NEILL Navy has drawn ahead—half a length—looks like Navy's race. L. HUGHES I am the man who never got ahead, The poorest worker bartered through the years. **4** W. H. AUDEN When courage fails, when hopes are fading, Think on the victory ahead.

Phrases: **ahead of** in front of, further advanced than, (*lit.* & *fig.*). *line ahead*: see LINE *n.*[2] *one jump ahead*: see JUMP *n.*[1]

aheap /əˈhiːp/ *adv.* & *pred. a. literary.* E19. [f. A-[2] + HEAP *n.*] In a heap; all of a heap.

a-height /əˈhʌɪt/ *adv. arch.* E17. [f. A *prep.*[1] 1 + HEIGHT *n.*] On high, aloft.

ahem /əˈhɛm/ *int.* M18. [Lengthened form of HEM *int.*] Expr. desire to attract attention, gain time, or show disapproval.

ahey /əˈheɪ/ *int.* L17. [f. AH *int.* + HEY *int.*] Expr. desire to attract attention or show surprise.

ahigh /əˈhʌɪ/ *adv. arch.* ME. [f. A *prep.*[1] 1 + HIGH *n.*] †**1** In loud tones. ME–L15. **2** On high, aloft. LME.

ahimsa /əˈhɪmsɑː/ *n.* L19. [Skt, f. *a* non- + *hiṁsā* violence.] *Hindu, Buddhist, & Jain Philos.* The doctrine that there should be no violence or killing.

ahind /əˈhɪnd, əˈhʌɪnd/ *adv.* & *prep. Sc.* & *dial.* Also **ahint** /əˈhɪnt/. M18. [f. A-[2] + *-hind* as in *behind*: see HIND *a.*] Behind.

ahistoric /eɪhɪˈstɒrɪk/ *a.* M20. [f. A-[10] + HISTORIC.] Not historic; unrelated to history.

ahistorical *a.* M20.

ahold /əˈhəʊld/ *n. colloq.* & *dial.* L19. [Prob. f. A *a.* + HOLD *n.*[1]] Hold, grasp, *of*, *on*, etc.

†**ahold** *adv.* Only in E17. [f. A *prep.*[1] 6 + HOLD *n.*[1]] *Naut.* Close to the wind, so as to hold to it.

SHAKES. *Temp.* Lay her a-hold, a-hold.

-aholic /əˈhɒlɪk/ *suff.* Also **-oholic**. M20. [f. ALCOHOLIC *n.*] Forming ns. w. the sense 'a person addicted to —', as *workaholic* etc.

a-horseback /əˈhɔːsbak/ *adv. arch.* & *dial.* L15. [f. A *prep.*[1] 1 + HORSEBACK.] On horseback.

Also **a-horse** *adv.* E19.

ahoy /əˈhɔɪ/ *int.* M18. [f. AH *int.* + HOY *int.*] *Naut.* Used in hailing.

land ahoy!: see LAND *n.*[1]

ahull /əˈhʌl/ *adv.* L16. [f. A *prep.*[1] 6 + HULL *n.*[2]] *Naut.* With sails taken in and the helm lashed on the lee side, to weather a storm.

ahunger /əˈhʌŋɡə/ *adv.* & *pred. a.* LME. [f. A *prep.*[1] 6 + HUNGER *n.*] In a famished state, hungry.

ahungered /əˈhʌŋɡəd/ *a. arch.* LME. [Prob. var. of OFHUNGERED.] Famished, very hungry.

ahungry *a.* famished, hungry LME.

ahunt /əˈhʌnt/ *adv.* & *pred. a.* L19. [f. A-[2] + HUNT *n.*[2]] On the hunt.

ai /ˈɑːi/ *n.* E17. [Tupi, repr. the animal's cry, prob. through Port. *aï*, Fr. *aï* (†*hay*, †*haiit*).] The three-toed sloth *Bradypus tridactylus*, of S. America.

aiblins *adv.* var. of ABLINS.

aid /eɪd/ *n.* LME. [OFr. *aïde* (mod. *aide*) ult. f. pa. pple of L *adjuvare*: see ADJUVANT.] **1** Help, succour, relief. LME. **b** *Eng. Law* (now *Hist.*). Help in defending an action, legally claimed from someone who has a joint interest in the defence. E16. **c** Material help given by one country to another. M20. **2 a** *Eng. Hist.* A grant of a tax or subsidy to the Crown; an exchequer loan. LME. **b** *Eng. Hist.* A pecuniary contribution paid by a feudal vassal to his lord. L16. **c** *Fr. Hist.* In *pl.* Customs dues. E18. **3** A helper, an assistant; an auxiliary. LME. **b** = AIDE. *N. Amer.* L18. **4** Something helpful; a material source of help. L16.

1 in aid of in support of; *colloq.* about, concerned with, esp. in *what's* (*all*) *this* etc. *in aid of? legal aid*: see LEGAL *a. Voluntary Aid Detachment*: see VOLUNTARY *a.* **b** *pray in aid* (*of*): see PRAY *v.* **4** G. BROOKE During the period that the novice is riding his first mount, he should learn the aids (correct and combined applications of his hands and legs). R. HOGGART A life with few modern aids such as vacuum cleaners and electric washers. *visual aid*: see VISUAL *a.*

Comb.: **aid-prayer** an appeal for aid.

aidful *a.* helpful L16. **aidless** *a.* E17.

aid /eɪd/ *v.t.* LME. [OFr. *aïdier* (mod. *aider*) f. L *adjutare* frequent. of *adjuvare*: see ADJUVANT.] Help, give support to; further the progress of.

AV *1 Macc.* 8:26 Neither shal they . . aide them with victuals, weapons, money, or ships. SHAKES. *Wint. T.* All the instruments which aided to expose the child. JOYCE Reclining in a state of supine repletion to aid digestion. *absol.*: COLERIDGE Saints will aid if men will call.

aidable *a.* (*rare*) †(*a*) helpful; (*b*) able to be helped: L16. **aidance** *n.* aid L16. **aider** *n.* E16.

aidant /ˈeɪd(ə)nt/ *a.* & *n.* LME. [OFr. *ai*(*d*)*ant* pres. pple, f. as prec.: see -ANT[1].] **A** *adj.* Assisting, auxiliary. LME. **B** *n.* A helper, an auxiliary. *rare.* LME.

aid-de-camp *n.* var. of AIDE-DE-CAMP.

aide /eɪd/ *n.* L18. [Abbrev. of next.] **1** = AIDE-DE-CAMP. L18. **2** *gen.* An assistant, an ancillary worker. Orig. *US.* M19.

aide-de-camp /eɪddəˈkɒ̃, *foreign* ɛddəkɑ̃/ *n.* Also ***aid-**. Pl. **aides-de-camp, *aids-**, /eɪdz-, *foreign* ɛd-/. L17. [Fr. = camp adjutant.] *Mil.* An officer acting as a confidential assistant to a senior officer, or assisting on a ceremonial occasion.

aide-mémoire /ˌeɪdmɛmˈwɑː; *foreign* ɛd memwaːr (*pl. same*)/ *n.* M19. [Fr., f. as AID *v.*, MEMORY.] (A book or document serving as) an aid to the memory; (in diplomats' use) a memorandum.

Aids /eɪdz/ *n.* Also **AIDS**. L20. [Acronym, f. *acquired immune deficiency syndrome*.] A syndrome marked by severe loss of cellular immunity as a result of infection with a virus transmitted in sexual fluids and in blood, leaving the patient susceptible to certain opportunistic infections and malignancies.

Comb.: **Aids-related complex** a set of symptoms including lymphadenopathy, fever, weight loss, and malaise, that seems to precede the full development of Aids.

aiel /ˈeɪ(ə)l/ *n.* Long *obs.* exc. *Hist.* Also **aile, ayle**. LME. [OFr. *aiol*, *aiuel* (mod. *aïeul*) f. Proto-Romance dim. of L *avus* grandfather. Cf. BESAIEL.] *Law.* A grandfather.

writ of aiel an action by a party based on the seisin of a grandfather for the recovery of land of which that party had been dispossessed.

aiglet *n.* var. of AGLET.

aigre-doux /ɛɡrədu, ɛɡrəˈduː/ *a.* Also ***-douce*** /-dus, -ˈduːs/. LME. [Fr.] Compounded of sweet and sour; bitter-sweet.

aigrette /ˈeɪɡrɛt, eɪˈɡrɛt/ *n.* M18. [Fr.: see EGRET.] An egret's plume; a tuft of feathers or hair; a spray of gems etc. worn on the head.

†**aigue-marine** *n.* L16–M19. [Fr. f. as AQUAMARINE.] = AQUAMARINE 1.

aiguille /ˈeɪɡwiːl/ *n.* M18. [Fr. = needle. Cf. next.] A sharply pointed peak of rock, esp. in the Alps.

aiguillette /eɪɡwɪˈlɛt/ *n.* M16. [(O)Fr., dim. of prec.: see -ETTE.] = AGLET, esp. sense 2b.

aikido /ʌɪˈkiːdəʊ/ *n.* M20. [Jap. *aikidō*, f. *ai* together, unify + *ki* spirit + *dō* way.] A Japanese form of self-defence and martial art, developed from ju-jitsu and involving holds and throws.

ail /eɪl/ *n.*[1] Long *dial.* [OE *eġl*, cogn. w. G dial. *Egel*, *Agel*.] The awn of barley or other corn.

ail /eɪl/ *n.*[2] Now *arch.* & *dial.* ME. [f. the vb.] Trouble; illness; an ailment.

ail /eɪl/ *v.* [OE *eġl*(*i*)*an* rel. to Goth. *agls* disgraceful, *aglo* oppression, *us*)*agljan* oppress.] **1** *v.t.* Trouble, afflict. Chiefly & now only w. indef. subj. in *what* etc. *ails* etc. OE. **2** *v.i.* Be troubled or adversely affected (mentally, *obs.* or *dial.*); be ill. ME. †**3** *v.t. impers.* in *what* etc. *ails* etc. Obstruct, prevent. LME–E19.

1 AV *1 Sam.* 11:5 What aileth the people that they weep? HENRY MILLER He was supposed to be suffering from ulcers of the stomach, though nobody was quite sure exactly what ailed him. **2** G. HEYER They never ail, though they did have the measles . . when they were small. *Times* An improvement in the ailing United States economy.

ailing *n.* (*a*) the action of the vb; (*b*) an ailment: M19. **ailment** *n.* a disorder, a (usu. slight) illness E18.

ailanthus /eɪˈlanθəs/ *n.* E19. [mod.L (also *ailantus*) f. Fr. *ailanthe*, (usu.) *ailante* f. Amboinese *ailanto* lit. 'tree of heaven': infl. by names ending w. *-anthus* f. Gk *anthos* flower.] A tree of the mainly Asian genus *Ailanthus* (family Simaroubaceae); esp. the tree of heaven, *A. altissima*, an ornamental and shade tree.

aile *n.* var. of AIEL.

aileron /ˈeɪlərɒn/ *n.* E20. [Fr., dim. of *aile* wing.] A movable aerofoil used to control the balance of an aircraft in flight, usu. a hinged flap in the trailing edge of a wing.

ailette /eɪˈlɛt/ *n.* LME. [Fr., f. as prec.: see -ETTE.] *Hist.* A steel shoulder-piece worn by a soldier.

ailurophile /ʌɪˈljʊərəfʌɪl/ *n.* Also **-phil** /-fɪl/. M20. [f. Gk *ailouros* cat + -PHILE.] A lover of cats.

ailurophobia /ˌʌɪljʊərəˈfəʊbɪə/ *n.* E20. [f. as prec. + -PHOBIA.] Irrational fear of cats.

aiˈlurophobe *n.* a person affected with ailurophobia E20. **ailurophobic** *a.* E20.

aim /eɪm/ *n.* ME. [f. the vb.] **1** A thing aimed at, a mark, a butt, (*lit.*). Long *rare.* ME. †**2** Conjecture; a guess. Latterly *dial.* LME–L19. **3** The directing of a weapon, missile, etc., at its mark. LME. †**4** Course, direction. M16–L17. †**5** Direction given, guidance. E17–E18. **6** An end aimed at, an objective; design, intention, purpose. E17. **7** A person who aims in a specified manner. *colloq.* L19.

1 SHAKES. *Rich. III* A garish flag To be the aim of every dangerous shot. **2** SHAKES. *Jul. Caes.* What you would work me to, I have some aim. **3** †**cry aim**: in order to encourage archers about to shoot; *gen.* in encouragement of anything. *level one's aim*: see LEVEL *v.*[1] **take aim** direct a weapon, a missile, etc., at its mark. **5** MILTON Posts of direction for Travellers . . to give you ayme. **6** C. HAMPTON We have kidnapped you in order to achieve certain political aims. J. BARTH It is my aim to learn all that can be learned of my father's life.

aimful *a.* (*rare*) full of purpose M19. **aimless** *a.* without means of taking aim; without purpose: E17. **aimlessly** *adv.* M19. **aimlessness** *n.* M19.

aim /eɪm/ *v.* ME. [Partly f. OFr. *amer* dial. var. of *esmer* f. L *aestimare* (see ESTIMATE *v.*); partly f. OFr. *ae*(*s*)*mer* ult. f. L *ad* AD- + *aestimare*.] †**1** *v.t.* Calculate (a number or value); take account of; esteem; evaluate. Only in ME. †**2** *v.t.* Guess, conjecture. Long *dial.* ME–L19. **3** *v.i.* Direct one's course, make it one's object to attain, intend, try, (foll. by *at*, (occas.) *for*, *to do*); *transf.* be directed *at*, be intended *to do*. ME. †**4** *v.t.* Arrange, plan. LME–E17. **5** *v.t.* & *i.* Direct (a missile, blow, remark, act, †missive, etc.) *at*; point or level (a firearm etc., *at*). LME.

3 aim high show ambition. **5** J. RHYS I asked her who had taught her to aim so well.

aimer *n.* L16.

Aino *n.* & *a.* var. of AINU.

ain't *v.* see BE *v.*, HAVE *v.*

Ainu /ˈeɪnuː, ˈʌɪ-/ *n.* & *a.* Also **-no** /-nəʊ/. E19. [Ainu, lit. 'man', 'person'.] **A** *n.* Pl. same, **-s**. **1** A member of (the people descended from) an aboriginal people of Japan, living also in neighbouring parts of Asia. E19. **2** The language of this people. L19. **B** *attrib.* or as *adj.* Of or pertaining to the Ainu or their language. M19.

aioli /ʌɪˈəʊli, *foreign* ajɔli/ *n.* E20. [Fr., f. Prov. *ai* garlic + *oli* oil.] Mayonnaise seasoned with garlic.

air /ɛː/ *n.*[1] Also (*obs.* exc. as in sense 11b) **ayre**. ME. [Branch I f. (O)Fr. *air* f. L *aer* f. Gk *aēr* (rel. to AURA); branch II f. Fr. *air* prob. repr. OFr. *aire* place, site, disposition, f. L *ager*, *agri*- infl. by L *area* AREA (rel. to EYRIE); branch III repr. It. ARIA.] **I 1** The invisible gaseous substance which envelops the earth and is breathed by all land animals and plants, one of the four elements of the ancients, now known to be a mixture of oxygen, nitrogen, carbon dioxide, and traces of other gases. ME. **b** This considered as a medium for the transmission of radio waves. E20. **2** A special state or condition of the atmosphere, as affected by contaminating exhalations, temperature, moisture, etc., or as modified by time or place. ME. **b** *spec.* The fresh unexhausted air of the outer atmosphere, as opp. to that in confined spaces. LME. **3** The body of air surrounding the earth; the (apparently) free or unconfined space in the atmosphere. ME. **b** This considered as a medium for operations with aeroplanes etc.; aircraft, aerial power. E20. **†4** Breath; inspiration; confidential information. LME–E18. **5** Now chiefly *Sailing*. A breeze, a light wind. M16. **†6** Any gas or vapour. M17–M19.

1 *hot air*: see HOT *a.* *live on air*: see LIVE *v.* *thin air*: see THIN *a.* **tread** or **walk** (**as if**) **on air** feel elated. *upper air*: see UPPER *a.* *vital air*: see VITAL *a.* **b off the air** not broadcasting. **on the air** broadcast(ing) by radio or television. *university of the air*: see UNIVERSITY 1. 2 POPE Content to breathe his native air In his own ground. F. NIGHTINGALE His goods are spoiled by foul air and gas fumes. A. J. LERNER All I want is a room somewhere, Far away from the cold night air. BREATH *of fresh air*. **change of air** variety of climate, esp. as secured by travel. **b take the air** go out of doors. 3 AV *Eccles.* 10:20 A bird of the aire shall carry the voyce. LONGFELLOW The sun is bright—the air is clear. *beat the air*: see BEAT *v.*[1] 1. **build** (**castles**) **in the air** form unsubstantial or visionary projects (see also CASTLE *n.*[1]). CHÂTEAU *in air*. *clear the air*: see CLEAR *v.* 8. **give a person the air** *US slang* dismiss a person. **in the air** (of opinions etc.) spreading about, everywhere met with; (of projects etc.) uncertain, unfixed. *open air*: see OPEN *a.* *saw the air*: see SAW *v.*[1] 1. **take air** become widely known. *with one's nose in the air*: see NOSE *n.* **b by air** in or by aircraft. 4 SHAKES. *Wint. T.* Still, methinks, There is an air comes from her. What fine chisel Could ever yet cut breath? BACON The airs, which the princes and states abroad received from their ambassadors. 5 POPE Let vernal airs thro' trembling osiers play. *Times* We've got a yacht which does very well as long as there's reasonable airs.

II Manner, appearance. **7** Outward appearance, manner, style. L16. **8** A person's bearing, gesture, or manner, now usu. as expressive of a specified personal quality or emotion; *absol.* a confident or stylish bearing. L16. **†b** Attitude, expression, (*of* a part of the body). M17–M18. **†c** Disposition, mood. *rare.* M17–E18. **9** *Horsemanship.* An artificial or practised movement in *haute école*. E17. **10** An affected manner. Usu. in *pl.* M17.

7 SCOTT FITZGERALD There was an unmistakable air of natural intimacy about the picture. S. LEWIS It had the air of being a very good room in a very good hotel. 8 SHAKES. *Wint. T.* Your father's image is so hit in you, His very air. S. JOHNSON He . . excites curiosity by an air of importance. BYRON But her air, If not her words, tells me she loves another. D. LODGE Telling the truth with a jesting air was . . the safest way of protecting your secrets. **b** HOR. WALPOLE The variety of attitudes and airs of heads. 10 *airs and graces*: see GRACE *n.* **give oneself**, **put on**, etc., **airs** be pretentious.

III *Mus.* **11** An expressive succession of musical sounds, songlike music; a melody; a tune. L16. **b** *spec.* A part-song, usu. with lute accompaniment; a light or sprightly tune or song. L16.

11 SHAKES. *Mids. N. D.* Your tongue's sweet air More tuneable than lark to shepherd's ear. J. THURBER Two bagpipers were playing Scottish airs near the water's edge.

Comb.: **air-bag** a bag inflated with air; **air-ball** *arch.* a toy balloon; **airbase** a centre for the operation of military aircraft; **air-bed** an inflated mattress; **air-bell** a small bubble of air; **air bladder** an air-filled sac in an animal or plant; *esp.* a fish's swimming-bladder; **airborne** *a.* carried through the air; in flight; carried by or employing aircraft; **air-brake** (*a*) a brake operated by compressed air; (*b*) a movable flap or other device used to increase the drag of an aircraft; **air-brick** a brick perforated for ventilation; **air-bridge** a portable bridge used at airports to connect a passenger terminal and an aircraft; **airbrush** a device for spraying paint etc. by means of compressed air; **air-burst** the explosion of a bomb etc. in the air; **Airbus** (proprietary name for) an aircraft designed to carry a large number of passengers economically over relatively short routes; **air-castle** a castle in the air (see CASTLE *n.*[1]); **air-cell** = *air-sac* (a) below; **Air Chief Marshal**: a high rank in the Royal Air Force, next above Air Marshal; *air commodore*: see COMMODORE 4; **air-conditioned** *a.* having air-conditioning; **air-conditioner** an apparatus for air-conditioning; **air-conditioning** the process of cleaning air and controlling its temperature and humidity before it enters a room, building, etc.; apparatus for this; **air-cooled** *a.* cooled by means of a current of air; **air corridor** a route to which aircraft are restricted; **aircrew** an aeroplane's crew; also (pl. same), a member of an aeroplane's crew; **air-cushion** *n.* & *a.* (*a*) *n.* a cushion inflated with air; a body of air supporting a vehicle such as a hovercraft; (*b*) *adj.* having an air-cushion; **air-cushioned** *a.* inflated or cushioned with air, having an air-cushion; **airdrome** *US* = AERODROME 2; **air-drop** *n.* & *v.* (*a*) *n.* the dropping of supplies, troops, etc., by parachute; (*b*) *v.t.* & *i.* drop (supplies etc.) by parachute; **air-dry** *a.* not giving off any moisture on exposure to air; **air ferry** a service of aircraft carrying cars etc. across water; **airfield** an area of land set aside for the take-off, landing, and accommodation of (esp. non-commercial) aircraft; *air-filter*: see FILTER *n.* 4; **airflow** the flow of air, *esp.*. that encountered by a moving aircraft or vehicle; **airfoil** *US* = AEROFOIL; **air force** a large force of war-planes; the branch of a country's armed forces which conducts operations primarily by means of aircraft; (in the UK) *Royal Air Force* s.v. ROYAL *a.*); **airframe** the basic structure of an aircraft; **air-freight** *n.* & *v.* (*a*) *n.* freight conveyed by aircraft; (*b*) *v.t.* convey (freight) by aircraft; **air-freshener** a substance or device for freshening the air in a room; **airglow** radiation emitted by the upper atmosphere; **airgun** a gun firing pellets etc. by compressed air; **air gunner** an aircrew-member whose job is to operate a gun; **airhead** (*a*) an airbase established in enemy territory; (*b*) *slang* a foolish, unintelligent, or empty-headed person; **air-hole** a hole admitting air, *esp.* one formed in ice or water; **air hostess** a stewardess in a passenger aircraft; **air-kiss** *v.t.* & *i.* purse the lips as if to kiss, without making contact; simulate a kiss (to); **air lane** a route designated for use or regularly used by aircraft; **air-layering** *Hort.* a form of layering in which the branch is wrapped in moist earth etc., or potted, to promote root growth; **air letter** a letter conveyed by air; *esp.* (one written on) a special folding sheet of lightweight paper; **airlift** *n.* & *v.* (*a*) *n.* the transportation of supplies, troops, etc. by air; (*b*) *v.t.* transport (supplies, troops, etc.) by air; **airliner** a large passenger aircraft; **airlock** (*a*) an antechamber giving access to a chamber which is kept at a regulated pressure (usu. above that of its surroundings); (*b*) a stoppage of the flow of liquid in a pipe etc. due to a bubble of air; **airman** a man who is engaged in the operation of aircraft, esp. as a crew-member; in Royal Air Force usage, an enlisted man as distinct from a commissioned officer; **airmanship** skill in flying an aircraft; **Air Marshal**: a high rank in the Royal Air Force, equivalent to Lieutenant General and Vice Admiral; the highest rank in the Royal Australian Air Force; **airmobile** *a.* (of troops etc.) readily moved about by air; **air officer** any Royal Air Force officer above the rank of Group Captain; **air-pipe** a pipe conveying air; a bronchial tube; **air piracy** skyjacking; **air pirate** a skyjacker; **air pistol** a pistol firing pellets etc. by compressed air; **airplane** (now chiefly *N. Amer.*) an aeroplane; **air plant** any epiphytic plant; any plant growing naturally without soil, *spec.* the life plant, *Kalanchoe pinnata*, which produces young plants from its leaf margins; **airplay** broadcast playing (of recorded music); **air-pocket** a local atmospheric condition causing an aircraft to lose height suddenly; **airport** an aerodrome catering for passenger travel, *esp.* a large one with customs facilities; *air potato*: see POTATO *n.* 3; **air power** ability to defend and attack by means of aircraft etc.; **air-pump** (*a*) a device for pumping air in or out; (*b*) (usu. **A-**) *the* constellation Antlia; **air raid** an attack by aircraft, esp. bombers; **air-rifle** a rifle firing pellets etc. by compressed air; **air-sac** (*a*) *Anat.* a lung compartment containing air; (*b*) *Zool.* an air-filled extension of a bird's lung or an insect's trachea; **airscrew** an aircraft's propeller; **air-sea rescue** rescue from the sea by aircraft; **air-shaft** a straight, usu. vertical passage admitting air into a mine, tunnel, building, etc; **airship** a dirigible powered balloon, *esp.* one having a rigid elongated structure; also occas. (chiefly *N. Amer.*) any aircraft; **air-shot** *colloq.* (*a*) a missed stroke at a ball etc.; (*b*) a recording made from broadcast music etc.; **air show** a show at which aircraft are on view and featuring aerial displays; **airsick** *a.* affected with airsickness; **airsickness** nausea caused by the motion of an aircraft; **airside** *n.*, *a.*, & *adv.* (designating or pertaining to, to or towards) the side or sections of an airport to which only passengers and airport personnel have admittance; **airspace** the air above a country etc., esp. considered as subject to its jurisdiction; **airspeed** the speed of an aircraft or other flying body relative to the surrounding air; **airstrip** a strip of land on which aircraft may take off and land; **air terminal** a place in a town where facilities for the reception of passengers and transport to and from an airport are provided; **airtight** *a.* impermeable to air; *fig.* invulnerable, unassailable; **air-time** broadcasting time available for a given purpose; **air-to-air** *a.* from one aircraft to another in flight; **air-to-ground** *a.* from an aircraft in flight to the ground; **air-to-surface** *a.* from an aircraft in flight to the surface of the sea etc.; **air-twist** a decorative spiral in the stem of a wineglass; **air-vessel** an air-filled vessel, esp. in an animal or plant; **Air Vice-Marshal**: a high rank in the Royal Air Force or Royal Australian Air Force, next below Air Marshal; **airwave** a wave in the atmosphere; *esp.* (in *pl.*) broadcast radio waves; **airwoman** a woman engaged in the operation of aircraft, esp. as a crew-member.

airified *a.* made airy, given to assuming airs M19. **airless** *a.* without air or other atmosphere; stuffy; breezeless, still: E17. **airlessness** *n.* M19. **airlike** *a.* resembling (that of) air M16. **airward** *adv.* toward or up into the air E19.

air /ɛː/ *n.*[2] E18. [ON *eyrr*.] A gravelly beach; a sandbank.

air /ɛː/ *v.* M16. [f. AIR *n.*[1]] **1** *v.t.* Expose to the open air, ventilate. M16. **2** *v.t.* Finish drying or warm at a fire, in a heated cupboard, etc. M16. **3** *v.refl.* & (*arch.*) *i.* Take the air, go out in the fresh air. E17. **4** *v.t.* Wear openly; parade ostentatiously; make public; talk openly about. E17. **5** *v.t.* & *i.* (Become) broadcast; transmit, be transmitted, by radio or television. M20.

1 M. EDGEWORTH To keep the room aired and swept. 2 D. L. SAYERS The clean sheets, . . all laying aired and ready. 4 SHAKES. *Cymb.* I beg but leave to air this jewel. E. BLUNDEN I began to air my convictions that the war was useless and inhuman. 5 *Publishers Weekly* After the tape was aired . . we received hundreds of calls from listeners. *Broadcasting* Only two episodes have aired.

airer *n.* a person who or thing which airs; *spec.* a frame for drying off clothes etc.: L18.

air /ɛː/ *adv.* *Sc.* LME. [Parallel to OR *adv.* Cf. ERE.] **†1** Formerly. LME–M16. **2** Early, soon. E16.

aircraft /ˈɛːkrɑːft/ *n.* Pl. **-craft**, **†-crafts**. M19. [f. AIR *n.*[1] + CRAFT *n.*] A machine that can be flown in the air; now *spec.* an aeroplane or helicopter; such machines collectively.

Comb.: **aircraft carrier** a warship designed to serve as a base for aircraft; **aircraftman**, **-woman** the lowest rank in the (Women's) Royal Air Force (*leading aircraftman*: see LEADING *ppl a.*).

†aire *n.* ME–E18. [OFr.: see EYRIE.] = EYRIE.

Airedale /ˈɛːdeɪl/ *n.* L19. [A district in West Yorkshire, England.] In full *Airedale terrier*. (A dog of) a breed of large terrier having a short dense coat.

airing /ˈɛːrɪŋ/ *n.* E17. [f. AIR *v.* + -ING[1].] **1** Ventilating; exposure to heat in order to finish drying. E17. **2** A walk, ride, drive, etc., to take air or exercise. E17. **3** Exposure to public notice. L19. **4** Broadcasting; a radio or television transmission. M20.

Comb.: **airing cupboard** a cupboard for airing linen and clothing.

airish /ˈɛːrɪʃ/ *a.* LME. [f. AIR *n.*[1] + -ISH[1].] **1** Aerial; like the air. Now *rare*. LME. **2** Cool, fresh, breezy. Now *dial.* M17.

airline /ˈɛːlaɪn/ *n.* Also **air-line**. E19. [f. AIR *n.*[1] + LINE *n.*[2]] **1** A direct line, a beeline. *N. Amer.* E19. **2** A regular succession of aircraft plying between certain places; a company or other body operating aircraft in public service. E20. **3** A pipe or tube conveying (compressed) air. E20.

airmail /ˈɛːmeɪl/ *n.* & *v.* E20. [f. AIR *n.*[1] + MAIL *n.*[3]] **A** *n.* Mail conveyed by air; the conveyance of mail by air. E20.

Comb.: **airmail paper** etc.: lightweight and suitable for dispatching by air.

B *v.t.* Send (a letter, parcel, etc.) by air. M20.

airt /ɛːt/ *n.* & *v. Sc.* As n. also †**art**. ME. [Gael. *àird* f. OIr. *aird*.] **A** *n.* A quarter of the compass; a direction. ME. **B** *v.* **1** *v.t.* Direct, guide. L18. **2** *v.i.* Direct one's way, make *for*. M19.

airway /ˈɛːweɪ/ *n.* M19. [f. AIR *n.*[1] + WAY *n.*] **1** **a** A passage for ventilation in a mine. M19. **b** *Med.* The normal passage for air into the lungs; an artificial device replacing or supplementing this. E20. **2** A route through the air, *esp.* one regularly followed by commercial aircraft. L19. **b** A company etc. operating aircraft, an airline. Usu. in *pl.* E20. **3** A radio broadcasting channel. *N. Amer.* M20.

airworthy /ˈɛːwəːði/ *a.* E19. [f. AIR *n.*[1] + -WORTHY.] Of an aircraft: in a fit condition for flight.

airworthiness *n.* E20.

airy /ˈɛːri/ *a.* LME. [f. AIR *n.*[1] + -Y[1]. Cf. AERY *a.*] **I** Of the atmosphere. †**1** Atmospheric; living in the air. LME–L17. **2** Placed high in the air; lofty; heavenly. Now *poet.* L16. **3** Exposed to the open air; breezy. L16. **4** Performed or taking place in the air. E17. **II** Of the substance air. **5** Composed of air; of the nature of air; airlike. LME. **6** *depreciative.* Unsubstantial as air, vain; immaterial, unreal; visionary; superficial, flippant. L16. **7** *appreciative.* Light or buoyant as air in texture or movement; lively, sprightly; delicate in fancy. L16. **III** [AIR *n.*[1] II.] **8** Assuming airs, pretentious. *rare.* E17.

Comb.: **airy-fairy** *a.* (*colloq.*) delicate or light as a fairy; nonchalant; *depreciative* fanciful, unsubstantial.

airily *adv.* M18. **airiness** *n.* L16.

aisle /ʌɪl/ *n.* Also †**ele** (earliest), †**i(s)le**. LME. [OFr. *ele* (mod. *aile*) f. L *ala* wing; conf. w. *isle*, *island* and infl. by Fr. *aile* wing.] **1** A wing or lateral division of a church; a part parallel to, and usu. divided by pillars from, the main nave, choir, or transept. See also CROSS-AISLE. LME. **2** A passage between rows of pews or seats; a passage between cabinets and shelves of goods in a supermarket etc. M18. **3** Any architectural division of a church. M18.

1 *fig.*: KEATS Through the dark pillars of those sylvan aisles. **2** N. BAILEY *Isles*, Certain straight Passages between Pews within a Church. J. HELLER A wooden stool in the aisle of the locker room. **have** etc. **people (rolling) in the aisles** *colloq.* make an audience laugh uncontrollably, be very amusing.

aisled *a.* furnished with an aisle or aisles M16. **aisleless** /-l-l-/ *a.* without an aisle or aisles M19.

ait /eɪt/ *n.*[1] See also EYOT. [OE *iġġaþ*, *iġ(e)oþ*, *īġ(e)þ*, ult. f. *īeġ* island + dim. suff.] A small island, esp. in a river.

ait *n.*[2] see OAT *n.*

aitch /eɪtʃ/ *n.* Also †**ache**. M16. [OFr. *ache*, perh. f. a Proto-Romance wd exemplifying the sound.] The letter H, h.

drop one's aitches fail to pronounce initial *h* in words.

aitchless *a.* lacking an *h*; (esp. of a person or speech) characterized by a failure to pronounce initial *h*'s: L19.

aitchbone /ˈeɪtʃbəʊn/ *n.* L15. [f. as NACHE + BONE *n.*, with loss of *n* as in *adder*, *apron*.] (A cut of beef lying over) the buttock or rump bone.

aith *n.* see OATH *n.*

aiver *n.* var. of AVER *n.*

aixies /ˈeɪksɪz/ *n.pl. Sc.* & *north.* Also **aixes**, **exies** /ˈɛksɪz/. L16. [Dial. form of ACCESS *n.*] A fit of ague. Also, hysterics.

ajar /əˈdʒɑː/ *adv.*[1] & *pred. a.*[1] Also †**a-char**. L17. [f. A *prep.*[1] 6 + CHAR *n.*[1]] Of a door etc.: partly open.

ajar /əˈdʒɑː/ *adv.*[2] & *pred. a.*[2] M19. [f. A-[2] + JAR *n.*[1]] Out of harmony.

ajee /əˈdʒiː/ *adv.* & *pred. a. Sc.* & *dial.* Also **agee**. E18. [f. A *prep.*[1] 6 + JEE *n.*] Off the straight (*lit.* & *fig.*); aside; ajar; disturbed, mildly deranged.

ajog /əˈdʒɒg/ *adv.* & *pred. a.* E17. [f. A *prep.*[1] 6 + JOG *n.*[1]] Moving mechanically up and down; jogging.

ajutage *n.* var. of ADJUTAGE.

Akali /əˈkɑːliː/ *n.* E19. [Panjabi *akālī*, f. mod.Skt *Akāla* the Immortal One + Panjabi -*ī* follower of.] A member of a militant sect of Sikhs; a member of a Sikh political party.

Akan /ˈɑːkən/ *n.* & *a.* Pl. of n. same, **-s**. L17. [Twi *akaŋ*.] (A member of, of or pertaining to) a people inhabiting southern Ghana and adjacent parts of Ivory Coast; (of) the group of Twi and Fante languages spoken by this people.

akara *n.* var. of ACCRA.

akasha /ɑːˈkɑːʃə/ *n.* Also **-sa**. M19. [Skt *ākāśa*.] Ether, atmosphere, as one of the five elements in Hindu philosophy.

akathisia /eɪkəˈθɪsɪə, a-/ *n.* Also **ac-**. E20. [f. A-[10] + Gk *kathisis* sitting + -IA[1].] *Med.* Irrational fear of sitting; restlessness preventing sitting still.

ake *v.* see ACHE *v.*

ake-ake /ˈakɪaki/ *n.* *NZ.* M19. [Maori.] A hardwood evergreen tree or shrub, *Dodonaea viscosa*, of the soapberry family. Also, any of certain trees or shrubs of the genus *Olearia* (Compositae), with tinted foliage.

akee *n.* var. of ACKEE.

akela /ɑːˈkeɪlə/ *n.* E20. [*Akela*, a wolf in Kipling's *Jungle Book* and *Second Jungle Book*.] An adult leader of a pack of Cub Scouts.

aketon *n.* var. of ACTON.

akimbo /əˈkɪmbəʊ/ *adv.* LME. [Prob. f. ON phr. = bent in a curve; assim. to A *prep.*[1]] Of the arms: with hands on hips and elbows turned outwards.

akin /əˈkɪn/ *pred. a.* M16. [f. A *prep.*[2] + KIN *n.*] **1** Of the same kin; related by blood. M16. **2** Of the same kind; similar in character or properties. M17.

akinesia /eɪkɪˈniːsɪə, a-/ *n.* M19. [Gk *akinēsia* quiescence, f. *a-* A-[10] + *kinēsis* motion.] *Med.* Loss or impairment of the power of voluntary movement.

akinetic /-ˈnɛtɪk/ *a.* of, pertaining to, or displaying akinesia L19.

akita /əˈkiːtə/ *n.* E20. [*Akita*, a district in northern Japan.] (An animal of) a Japanese breed of dog, a kind of spitz.

Akkadian /əˈkeɪdɪən/ *a.* & *n.* Also **Acc-**. M19. [f. *Akkad*, a city and district in ancient Babylonia + -IAN.] **A** *adj.* Of or pertaining to an eastern Semitic language of northern Babylonia, known from cuneiform inscriptions, and having two dialects, Assyrian and Babylonian; of or pertaining to the people of northern Babylonia. M19. **B** *n.* **1** The Akkadian language. L19. **2** A native or inhabitant of Akkad or northern Babylonia. L19.

akkra *n.* var. of ACCRA.

aknee /əˈniː/ *adv. arch.* Also †**-s**. ME. [f. A *prep.*[1] + KNEE *n.*] On one's knee or knees.

akosmism, -ist *ns.* vars. of ACOSMISM, -IST.

akroterion *n.* var. of ACROTERION.

akvavit *n.* var. of AQUAVIT.

al- /al, *unstressed* əl/ *pref.*[1] (not productive). Assim. form of L AD- bef. *l*. In OFr. L *all-* was reduced to *al-*, which appears in ME adoptions, but in later Fr., and hence in Eng., *all-* was restored by Latinization, as *allegation*, *alliterate*. Hence extended to some words of different origin, as *allay*.

al- /al/ *pref.*[2] (not productive). The Arab. def. article *al*, forming an essential element of many words of Romance (esp. Sp. and Port.) origin adopted in Eng., as *alcohol*, *alcove*, *algebra*, *alkali*.

-al /əl/ *suff.*[1] **1** [Repr. L *-alis* adj. suff. or Fr. *-el* (later refash. after L).] Forming adjs. w. the sense 'of the kind of, pertaining to', f. L (*central*, *general*, *oral*, *providential*, etc.), on L bases (*basal* etc.), f. Gk (*baptismal*, *colossal*, *tropical*, etc.: cf. -IAL, -ICAL), or f. Eng. ns. (*tidal* etc.). **2** [Repr. Fr. *-ail(le)*, *-al* or f. or after L *-alis* etc. used as n.] Forming ns. (*animal*, *cardinal*, *rival*, etc.), esp. of vbl action (*arrival*, *proposal*, *withdrawal*, etc.).

-al /al, əl/ *suff.*[2] [f. AL(COHOL, AL(DEHYDE.] *Chem.* Forming the names of substances which are aldehydes or occas. other derivatives of alcohols, as *acetal*, *chloral*, *retinal*, etc. Also used in *Pharm.* with little or no chemical significance, as in *barbital*, *Veronal*.

ala /ˈeɪlə/ *n.* Pl. **alae** /ˈeɪliː/. M18. [L = wing.] **1** *Anat.* A winglike process; *esp.* either of the lateral cartilages of the nose, enclosing the nostrils. M18. †**2** *Bot.* An axil; also, a lateral petal of a papilionaceous flower, a wing of a seed. M18–M19.

à la /ɑː lɑː, *foreign* a la/ *prep. phr.* L16. [Fr., abbrev. of À LA MODE.] In the manner, method, or style of (usu. w. Fr., but also nonce w. Eng., ns.).

à la broche /brɒʃ, *foreign* brɔʃ/, **brochette** /brɒˈʃɛt, *foreign* brɔʃɛt/ (cooked) on a spit or skewer. À LA CARTE. **à la daube** /dəʊb, *foreign* doːb/ [DAUBE] (of beef etc.) stewed, braised. **à la Florentine** /ˈflɒr(ə)ntiːn, *foreign* flɒrɑ̃tin/ = FLORENTINE *a.* 2. **à la fourchette** /fʊəˈʃɛt, *foreign* furʃɛt/ (of a meal) requiring the use (only) of a fork. À LA PAGE. **à la russe** /ruːs, *foreign* rys/ in the Russian manner.

Alabaman /aləˈbamən/ *n.* & *a.* Also **-mian** /-mɪən/. M19. [f. *Alabama* (see below) + -AN.] A native or inhabitant of, of or pertaining to, the State of Alabama, USA.

†**alabandine** *n.* LME–M17. [med.L *alabandina* (sc. *gemma* gem), f. *Alabanda* a city of Caria in ancient Asia Minor.] = ALMANDINE.

Alabarch /ˈaləbɑːk/ *n.* M17. [Dissimilated form of L *arabarches* (Juvenal) f. Gk *arabarkhēs*, *ala-*.] (The title of) the chief magistrate of the Jews at Alexandria under the Ptolemies and Romans.

alabaster /ˈaləbɑːstə, aləˈbɑːstə/ *n.* & *a.* Also †**alablaster**. LME. [OFr. *alabastre* (mod. *albâtre*) f. L *alabaster*, *-trum* f. Gk *alabastos*, *-tros*.] **A** *n.* **1** A fine-grained, translucent, ornamental form of gypsum, usu. white but sometimes tinted or clouded with yellow, red, or other colours; also occas., calcite of similar appearance and use. LME. **2** A box made of alabaster, esp. for holding unguents. LME.

1 *fig.*: E. LINKLATER The lovely creature with . . a brow of alabaster.

B *adj.* Of alabaster; like alabaster in whiteness or smoothness. E16.

alaˈbastrine *a.* of or like alabaster L16.

alabastron /aləˈbɑːstrɒn/ *n.* M19. [Gk.] = ALABASTER *n.* 2.

†**alablaster** *n.* & *a.* var. of ALABASTER.

à la carte /ɑː lɑː ˈkɑːt, *foreign* a la kart/ *adv.* & *a. phr.* E19. [Fr.: see À LA, CARTE *n.*[1]] By the bill of fare; ordered as a separately priced item or as separately priced items from a menu, not as part of a table d'hôte meal.

alack /əˈlak/ *int. arch.* LME. [f. AH *int.* + LACK *n.*[1], after ALAS.] Expr. dissatisfaction, deprecation, regret, surprise. Freq. in *alack the day*, *alack-a-day*.

†**alacrious** *a.* E17–E18. [f. L *alacris* var. of *alacer* (see next) + -OUS.] Brisk, lively, active.

†**alacriously** *adv.*: only in 17.

alacrity /əˈlakrɪti/ *n.* LME. [L *alacritas*, f. *alacr-*, *alacer* brisk: see -ITY.] Briskness, cheerful readiness, liveliness.

alacritous *a.* (*rare*) brisk, lively, active L19. **alacritously** *adv.* (*rare*) L19.

Aladdin /əˈladɪn/ *n.* E19. [Arab. *ʿAlā' al-dīn*, a character in the *Arabian Nights' Entertainments*.] **1** *Aladdin's lamp*, a talisman enabling the holder to gratify any wish. E19. **2** *Aladdin's cave*, a place of great riches. L19.

alalia /əˈleɪlɪə, eɪ-/ *n.* M19. [Gk, f. *a-* A-[10] + -LALIA.] *Med.* Absence or loss of the ability to utter speech sounds.

alameda /aləˈmeɪdə/ *n.* L18. [Sp.] In Spain and Spanish-speaking areas: a public walk, shaded with trees.

Alamire /eɪləˈmiːreɪ/ *n. obs.* exc. *Hist.* Also **A la mi re**. LME. [f. *A* as a pitch letter + *la*, *mi*, *re* designating tones in the solmization of Guido d'Arezzo (*c* 990–1050).] *Medieval Mus.* The note A in Guido d'Arezzo's 2nd, 3rd, 4th, 5th, 6th, and 7th hexachords, where it was sung to the syllables *la*, *mi*, or *re*. Cf. ARE *n.*[1], BEFA, CEFAUT, etc.

à la mode /ɑː lɑː ˈməʊd, *foreign* a la mɔd/ *adv.*, *a.*, & *n.*, *phr.* Also **alamode**. L16. [Fr. = in the fashion.] A *adv.* & *adj.* (*phr.*) **1** In or according to the fashion; fashionable. L16. **2** *Cookery*. **a** Of beef: braised or made into a rich stew, usu. with wine. M17. **b** Of food: served with ice-cream. Chiefly *US*. E20. **B** *n.* (*phr.*) Usu. as one wd. †**1** A fashion, a temporary mood. M–L17. **2** A thin light glossy usu. black silk. M17

alamoˈdality *n.* (*rare*) the quality of being à la mode M18.

alamort /aləˈmɔːt/ *adv.* & *a. arch.* Also ***à la mort*** /a la mɔːr, ɑː lɑː ˈmɔːt/. L16. [Fr. *à la mort* to the death. See also AMORT.] **A** *adv.* To the death; mortally. L16. **B** *adj.* Mortally sick; dispirited. L16.

Alan /ˈalən/ *n.*[1] & *a.* Pl. of n. **Alani** /əˈlɑːni, əˈleɪni/, **Alans**. LME. [L *Alanus*.] (A member of, of or pertaining to) an ancient Scythian people, first mentioned as dwelling near the Caspian Sea.

alan *n.*[2] var. of ALANT.

aland *n.* var. of ALANT.

aland /əˈland/ *adv. arch.* OE. [f. A *prep.*[1] 1 + LAND *n.*[1]] †**1** In the land, in the country. Long *dial.* OE–L19. **2** On dry land. ME. **3** To the land or shore. ME.

alanine /ˈalənɪːn/ *n.* M19. [G *Alanin*: see ALDEHYDE, -INE[5]; *-an-* is app. for euphony.] *Biochem.* A hydrophobic amino acid, $CH_3CH(NH_2)COOH$, which occurs in proteins; 2-aminopropanoic acid.

β-alanine an amino acid, $(NH_2)CH_2CH_2COOH$; 3-aminopropanoic acid.

alanna /əˈlanə/ *n. Anglo-Ir.* Also **-ah**. M19. [Ir. *a leanbh* O child.] My child: used as a form of address or as a term of endearment.

alant /əˈlɑːnt/ *n. obs.* exc. *Her.* Also †**alan, aland,** †**alaun(t)**. ME. [OFr. *alan(t)*.] A large hunting dog; a wolfhound; *Her.* also, a short-eared mastiff.

alap /ɑːˈlɑːp/ *n.* Also **-pa** /-pə/, **-pana** /-pənə/. L19. [Hind. *alāp*.] *Indian Mus.* An improvisation on a raga as a prologue to its formal expression.

à la page /a la paːʒ, ɑː lɑː ˈpɑːʒ/ *adv.* & *a. phr.* M20. [Fr., lit. 'at the page'.] Up to date, up to the minute.

alapana *n.* var. of ALAP.

Alar /ˈeɪlɑː/ *n.* M20. [Origin unkn.] (Proprietary name for) a growth retardant used as a spray on fruit and vegetables to enhance the quality of the crop.

alar /ˈeɪlə/ *a.* M19. [L *alaris*, f. as ALA: see -AR[1].] Alary; wing-shaped; *Bot.* axillary.

alarm /əˈlɑːm/ *n.* Also (exc. in sense 6 somewhat *arch.*) **alarum** /əˈlɑːrəm, -ˈlɛːr-, -ˈlar-/. LME. [f. the adv. in phrs. such as *cry alarm*.] **1** Frightened anticipation of danger; a state of frightened surprise; apprehension. LME. **2** A frightening loud noise or disturbance. *arch.* E16. **3** A signal calling upon people to arm; news of approaching hostility. M16. †**4** A sudden attack; a surprise. L16–L17. **5** A sound to warn of danger or to attract attention, arouse from sleep, etc.; a warning. L16. **6** A mechanism that sounds the alarm; an apparatus that rings, bleeps, etc., at a set time; an alarm clock. L16.

1 S. LEWIS Babbitt roused, his stomach constricted with alarm. *take alarm*: see TAKE *v.* 2 KEATS What divinity Makes this alarum in the elements? 3 SOUTHEY From east and west . . the breathless scouts Bring swift alarums in. W. OWEN No alarms of bugles, no high flags, no clamorous haste. **alar(u)ms and excursions** *joc.* [from an old stage-direction] confused noise and bustle. 4 DRYDEN The doubtful nations watch his arms, With terror each expecting his alarms. 5 V. SACKVILLE-WEST The vixen, prick-eared for the first alarm. *false alarm*: see FALSE *a.* 6 J. CHEEVER The alarm began ringing at six in the morning. *burglar alarm*, *fire alarm*, etc.

Comb.: **alarm bell** a bell rung as a signal of danger; **alarm bird** any of various birds with strident cries; *esp.* (*Austral.*) the kookaburra; **alarm call** (*a*) a bird's or animal's cry when startled; (*b*) a telephone call notifying the person called that a previously agreed time has arrived; **alarm clock**, **watch**: with an apparatus that rings or bleeps at a set time; **alarm-post** *Mil.* a post appointed to be resorted to in the event of an alarm; *alarm watch*: see *alarm clock* above.

alarmism *n.* alarmist behaviour or tendency M19. **alarmist** *n.* & *a.* (*a*) *n.* a person who raises alarm on slight grounds, a panic-monger; (*b*) *adj.* of or pertaining to alarmism or alarmists: L18.

alarm /əˈlɑːm/ *v.* Also †**alarum**. L16. [f. the n.] **1** *v.i.* & †*t.* Call to arms. Long *rare*. L16. †**2** *v.t.* Rouse to action. E17–M18. **3** *v.t.* Rouse to a sense of danger. M17. **4** *v.t.* Agitate with sudden fear or apprehension; disturb. M17. **5** *v.t.* Fit or protect with an alarm. Chiefly as *alarmed* ppl a. M20.

alarmable *a.* liable to be alarmed or excited E19. **alarmingly** *adv.* in an alarming manner L18.

alarm /əˈlɑːm/ *adv.* Long *arch.* Also **alarum** /əˈlɑːrəm, -ˈlɛːr-, -ˈlar-/. LME. [(O)Fr. *alarme* f. It. *allarme* = *all' arme* to arms!] As a call to prepare for fighting.

LD BERNERS The townes all about range their belles alarum. SHAKES. *Rich. III* Strike alarum, drums! G. B. SHAW *Auxiliaries*. Alarm! Alarm! *Centurion*. What now? has the old woman attacked you again?

alarum *n.*, *v.*, *adv.* see ALARM *n.*, *v.*, *adv.*

alary /ˈeɪləri/ *a.* M17. [L *alarius*, f. as ALA: see -ARY[1].] Of or pertaining to wings or alae.

alas /əˈlas, əˈlɑːs/ *int.* & *n.* ME. [OFr. *a las(se)* (mod. *hélas*), f. *a* AH *int.* + *las(se)* f. L *lassus* weary.] **A** *int.* Expr. unhappiness, grief, pity, or concern. ME.

SHAKES. *Oth.* Alas the heavy day! Why do you weep. DAY LEWIS I had a vision of eternity in my sleep—a vision, alas, far different from Vaughan's 'I saw eternity the other night'. NEB *Luke* 22:22 Alas for that man by whom he is betrayed.

B *n.* An utterance of 'alas!'. E17.

Alaska /əˈlaskə/ *n.* L19. [The northernmost State in the US.] In full *baked Alaska*. Sponge cake and ice-cream in a rapidly cooked meringue covering; a dish of this.

Alaskan /əˈlask(ə)n/ *a.* & *n.* M19. [f. prec. + -AN.] **A** *adj.* Of or pertaining to Alaska or its inhabitants. M19. **B** *n.* A native or inhabitant of Alaska. L19.

Alastor /əˈlɑːstə, -ˈlast-/ *n.* Also **a-**. L16. [Gk *alastōr*, f. *a-* A-[10] + *last-* f. *lathein* forget.] An avenging god, a nemesis.

alate /ˈeɪleɪt/ *a.* M17. [L *alatus*, f. as ALA: see -ATE[2].] Having wings or winglike appendages.

alate /əˈleɪt/ *adv. arch.* LME. [f. A *prep.*[2] + LATE *n.*[2]] Of late, lately.

alated /ˈeɪleɪtɪd/ *a.* L16. [f. as ALATE *a.* + -ED[1].] = ALATE *a.*

alaternus /aləˈtəːnəs/ *n.* Now *rare*. Also †**alatern**. E17. [L: cf. Fr. *alaterne*.] An evergreen shrub, *Rhamnus alaternus*, of the buckthorn family.

†**alaun(t)** *ns.* vars. of ALANT.

†**alay** *v.* var. of ALLAY *v.*[3]

alb /alb/ *n.* OE. [eccl.L *alba* use as n. of fem. of L *albus* white.] A white vestment reaching to the feet, worn by Christian priests.

alba /ˈalbə/ *n.* E19. [Prov., ult. f. L *albus* white.] A medieval Provençal song at dawn.

albacore /ˈalbəkɔː/ *n.* L16. [Port. *albacor(a)*, f. Arab. *al-bakūra* perh. f. *al* the + *bakūr* premature, precocious.] The long-finned tunny, *Thunnus alalunga*; *loosely* any related fish.

Albanian /alˈbeɪnɪən/ *n.*[1] & *a.*[1] L16. [f. *Albania* (see below) + -AN.] **A** *n.* A native or inhabitant of the country of Albania in the western part of the Balkan peninsula; the language of Albania, constituting a separate branch of the Indo-European family. L16. **B** *adj.* Of or pertaining to the country of Albania, its inhabitants, or their language. L16.

Albanian /alˈbeɪnɪən/ *n.*[2] & *a.*[2] L16. [f. *Albania* (see below) + -AN.] *Hist.* **A** *n.* A native or inhabitant of Albania, an ancient province on the Caspian sea; the language of the province of Albania. L16. **B** *adj.* Of or pertaining to the province of Albania, its inhabitants, or their language. E17.

albarello /albəˈrɛləʊ/ *n.* Pl. **-lli** /-liː/, **-llos**. L19. [It. *alberello* pot, phial.] A majolica jar used esp. as a container for drugs.

albata /alˈbeɪtə/ *n.* M19. [L, fem. of *albatus* clothed in white, f. *albus* white.] White metal, German silver.

albatross /ˈalbətrɒs/ *n.* L17. [Alt. of ALCATRAS, app. by assoc. w. L *albus* white.] **1** Any of several large, long-winged, tube-nosed oceanic birds constituting the family Diomedeidae. L17. **b** *fig.* (usu. w. allusion to Coleridge's *Ancient Mariner*: see below). A heavy burden, a disadvantage, a hindrance. M20. †**2** A frigate-bird. Cf. ALCATRAS. Only in M18. **3** *Golf.* A hole played in three strokes under par. M20.

1 COLERIDGE Instead of the cross, the albatross About my neck was hung.

†**albe** *conj.* LME–E19. [Contr.] = ALBEIT.

albedo /alˈbiːdəʊ/ *n.* Pl. **-os**. M19. [eccl.L = whiteness, f. L *albus* white.] The proportion of incident radiation reflected by a surface, esp. of a planet or moon.

albeit /ɔːlˈbiːɪt/ *conj.* Now *literary*. LME. [f. ALL *adv.* + BE + IT *pron.*, = although it be (that).] Even though (it be *that*).

R. KNOLLES Albeit that a great number of them were slain. M. MEAD In Iatmul a man is a master in his own house, albeit he has to fight for it. M. DRABBLE She was going to Paris, albeit in a school raincoat.

albergo /alˈbɛrgo, alˈbəːgəʊ/ *n.* Pl. ***-ghi*** /-gi, -giː/. E17. [It.: cf. AUBERGE.] An Italian inn.

Albers-Schönberg disease /albəzˈʃəːnbəːg dɪˌziːz/ *n. phr.* Also **Albers-Schönberg's disease**. E20. [H. E. *Albers-Schönberg* (1865–1921), Ger. radiologist.] *Med.* Osteopetrosis, esp. in a delayed form.

albert /ˈalbət/ *n.* Also **A-**. M19. [Prince *Albert* (1819–61), consort of Queen Victoria of England.] **1** In full *albert chain*. A watch-chain with a crossbar. M19. **2** *Albert Medal*: (*a*) instituted in 1864 by the Royal Society of Arts for 'distinguished merit in promoting Arts, Manufactures, and Commerce'; (*b*) instituted in 1866 (though no longer awarded) for 'gallantry in saving life at sea or on land'. M19.

Albertine /ˈalbətʌɪn/ *a.* M18. [f. *Albert* (see below) + -INE[1].] *Hist.* Designating or pertaining to the younger of the two lines of the house of Frederick the Gentle, Elector of Saxony, which originated with his son Albert III (1443–1500) and to which the electoral title was transferred in 1547. Cf. ERNESTINE.

albertite /ˈalbətʌɪt/ *n.* M19. [f. *Albert* County, New Brunswick, Canada + -ITE[1].] *Min.* A black, almost infusible form of bitumen.

albescent /alˈbɛs(ə)nt/ *a.* E18. [L *albescent-* pres. ppl stem of *albescere* become white, f. *albus* white: see -ESCENT.] Growing white; shading into white.

albespine /ˈalbəspʌɪn/ *n. arch.* Also **-yne**. LME. [OFr. *albespine* (mod. *aubépine*) f. L *alba spina* white thorn.] Whitethorn, hawthorn.

Albigenses /albɪˈgɛnsiːz, -ˈdʒɛn-/ *n.pl.* E17. [med.L, f. *Albiga* L name of Albi, a city in SW France.] A Manichaean sect in southern France between the 11th and 13th cents.

Albigensian *n.* & *a.* a member of, pertaining to, the Albigenses E17.

albino /alˈbiːnəʊ/ *n.* & *a.* E18. [Sp. & Port., f. *albo* white + *-ino* (-INE[1]): orig. applied by the Portuguese to albinos among African Blacks.] **A** *n.* Pl. **-os**. **1** A human being having a congenital deficiency of pigmentation in the skin and hair, which are white, and the eyes, which are usu. pink. E18. **2** An abnormally white animal or plant. E19. **B** *adj.* Congenitally lacking in pigmentation; abnormally white. E19.

albiness /-bɪˈnɛs/ *n.* a female albino E19. **albinism** /ˈalbɪnɪz(ə)m/ *n.* the condition of being an albino M19. **albinistic** /-bɪˈnɪstɪk/ *a.* = ALBINOTIC L19. **albinoid** /ˈalbɪnɔɪd/ *a.* being or resembling an albino M20. **albinoism** *n.* = ALBINISM M19. **albinotic** /-bɪˈnɒtɪk/ *a.* pertaining to, affected with, albinism L19.

Albion /ˈalbɪən/ *n. poet.* & *rhet.* OE. [L f. Celt.; prob. cogn. w. L *albus* white (w. allus. to the white cliffs of Britain).] (Orig. the Gk and Roman name for) Britain.

perfidious Albion [tr. Fr. *la perfide Albion*] England (w. ref. to her alleged treachery to other nations).

albite /ˈalbʌɪt/ *n.* E19. [f. L *albus* white + -ITE¹.] *Min.* A sodium-rich plagioclase, usu. white, occurring widely in silicate rocks; sodium feldspar.

albitic /-ˈbɪtɪk/ *a.* of the nature of or containing albite M19. **albitization** /-bɪtʌɪˈzeɪʃ(ə)n/ *n.* conversion into (a form containing) albite L19. **albitize** /ˈalbɪtʌɪz/ *v.t.* convert into (a form containing) albite E20.

albitite /ˈalbɪtʌɪt/ *n.* L19. [f. prec. + -ITE¹.] *Geol.* Intrusive rock consisting largely of albite.

albititic /-ˈtɪtɪk/ *a.* of the nature of or containing albitite M20.

albugo /alˈbjuːgəʊ/ *n.* Now *rare.* LME. [L *albugo*, *-gin-* whiteness, f. *albus* white.] = LEUCOMA.

albugineous /albjʊˈdʒɪnɪəs/ *a.* (now *rare* or *obs.*) of or pertaining to white fibrous tissue; also, albuminous: M16.

album /ˈalbəm/ *n.* E17. [L = blank tablet, use as n. of neut. of *albus* white; first in Eng. f. G use of L phr. *album amicorum* album of friends, and in L forms.] I A blank book for the insertion of collected items. 1 A blank book in which people other than the owner insert autographs, memorial verses, etc. E17. 2 A blank book for the insertion of stamps, photographs, etc. M19. II 3 A holder for a set of discs or tape recordings; an integral set of discs or tapes; a disc or tape comprising several pieces of music etc. E20.

3 *double album*: see DOUBLE *a.* & *adv.*

albumen /ˈalbjʊmɪn/ *n.* L16. [L *albumen*, *-min-*, f. *albus* white.] 1 The white of an egg. L16. 2 *Bot.* = ENDOSPERM. L17. 3 Soluble protein, such as that in egg-white. Cf. ALBUMIN. E19.

alˈbumenize *v.t.* coat or impregnate with albumen M19.

albumin /ˈalbjʊmɪn/ *n.* M19. [Fr. *albumine*, f. as prec.: see -IN¹.] *Biochem.* Any protein which is readily soluble in water and coagulable by heat; *spec.* (*Med.*) the soluble protein present in blood serum. Cf. ALBUMEN 3.

albuminoid /alˈbjuːmɪnɔɪd/ *a.* & *n.* M19. [f. as ALBUMEN + -OID.] A *adj.* Of the nature of, resembling, or containing albumen. M19. B *n.* A protein; *esp.* a scleroprotein. L19.

albuminous /alˈbjuːmɪnəs/ *a.* M17. [f. as prec. + -OUS.] Of the nature of, resembling, or containing albumen or albumins.

albuminuria /ˌalbjʊmɪˈnjʊərɪə/ *n.* M19. [f. as prec. + -URIA.] *Med.* The presence of albumins or other proteins in the urine.

albuminuric *a.* characterized by albuminuria L19.

alburnum /alˈbəːnəm/ *n.* M17. [L, f. *albus* white.] Sapwood.

alburnous *a.* (now *rare*) E19.

alcabala *n.* var. of ALCAVALA.

alcade *n.* var. of ALCALDE.

alcahest *n.* var. of ALKAHEST.

alcaic /alˈkeɪɪk/ *a.* & *n.* Also **A-**. M17. [Late L *alcaicus* f. Gk *alkaikos*, f. *Alkaios* Alcaeus: see -IC.] A *adj.* Of or pertaining to Alcaeus, a lyric poet of Mytilene (*c* 600 BC); *esp.* of a verse metre in a four-line stanza invented by him. M17. B *n.* In *pl.* Alcaic verses. M17.

alcaide /alˈkʌɪdi, *foreign* alˈkaide/ *n.* Also **†-caid, -cayde.** E16. [Sp. f. Arab. *al-ḳā'id* the leader, the commander: see AL-².] The governor of a Spanish, Portuguese, Moorish, etc., fortress; a jailer.

alcalde /alˈkaldi, *foreign* alˈkalde/ *n.* Also **alcade** /alˈkɑːd, *foreign* alˈkad/. M16. [Sp. *alcalde* (Fr. *alcade*) f. Arab. *al-ḳāḍī* the judge: see AL-², CADI.] A mayor, magistrate, or similar administrative officer in Spain, Portugal, and parts of S. America and the south-western US.

alcanna /əlˈkanə/ *n.* Also **alk-**. LME. [Sp. *alcana*, *alcaña* f. Arab. *al-ḥinnā'* HENNA.] Henna; also, alkanet.

alcaptonuria *n.* var. of ALKAPTONURIA.

alcarraza /alkəˈrɑːzə, *foreign* alkaˈrraθa/ *n.* E19. [Sp. f. Arab. *al-karrāz* the water-cooling jug: see AL-².] A porous earthenware vessel.

alcatras /ˈalkətras/ *n.* Now *rare.* M16. [Sp. *alcatraz* pelican, Port. *alcatraz* frigate-bird, (formerly) pelican, f. Arab. *al-ġaṭṭās* the diver: see AL-².] Any of various large water-birds, *esp.* a pelican or a frigate-bird.

alcavala /alkəˈvɑːlə/ *n.* Also **-bala** /-ˈbɑːlə/. L16. [Sp. *alcabala*, Port. *-vala* f. Arab. *al-ḳabāla* the tax, duty: see AL-². Cf. GABELLE.] *Hist.* In Spain and Spanish colonies: an *ad valorem* tax, orig. of ten per cent, chargeable at every sale or exchange of goods.

alcayde *n.* var. of ALCAIDE.

alcazar /alkəˈzɑː, *foreign* alˈkaθar/ *n.* Pl. **-zars** /-ˈzɑːz/, **-zares** /-θares/. E17. [Sp. *alcázar* f. Arab. *al-ḳaṣr* the castle: see AL-².] A Spanish palace or fortress.

†alce *n.* M16–L18. [L.] An elk.

†alchahest *n.* var. of ALKAHEST.

alchemical /alˈkɛmɪk(ə)l/ *a.* Also **†alchym-**. M16. [f. ALCHEMY + -ICAL.] Of or pertaining to alchemy.

alchemic *a.* = ALCHEMICAL E19. **alchemically** *adv.* E17.

alchemist /ˈalkɪmɪst/ *n.* Also **†alchym-**. E16. [OFr. *alkemiste*, med.L *alchemista*: see ALCHEMY, -IST.] A person who studies or practises alchemy.

†alchemister *n.* = ALCHEMIST LME–L16. **alcheˈmistic** *a.* L17. **alcheˈmistical** *a.* M16. **†alchemistry** *n.* alchemy M16–E19. **alchemize** *v.t.* [after *baptist*, *baptize*] change (as) by alchemy L16.

alchemy /ˈalkɪmi/ *n.* Also **†alchymy**. LME. [OFr. *alkemie*, *-kamie* (mod. *alchimie*) f. med.L *alchimia*, *-chemia* f. Arab. *al-kīmiyā'*, f. *al* AL-² + *kīmiyā'* f. Gk *khēm(e)ia* art of transmuting metals (Suidas). The var. w. *-chym-* by assoc. w. Gk *khymeia* infusion.] 1 The chemistry of the Middle Ages and the 16th cent.: now usu. connoting the pursuit of the transmutation of baser metals into gold, and the search for the elixir of life, etc. LME. b *fig.* Miraculous power of transmutation or extraction. E17. 2 A composition, mainly of brass, imitating gold. *obs.* exc. *Hist.* LME. †b *fig.* Glittering dross. L16–M17. †c A trumpet made of alchemy or similar metal. *literary.* M17–E19.

1b SHAKES. *Sonn.* Gilding pale streams with heavenly alchemy. 2b DONNE Compared to this All honour's mimic, all wealth alchemy. c MILTON Four speedy cherubim Put to their mouths the sounding alchymie.

alchera /ˈaltʃərə/ *n.* M20. [Aborig.] = next.

alcheringa /altʃəˈrɪŋgə/ *n.* L19. [Aranda = in the dream-time.] A golden age in the mythology of some Australian Aborigines.

alchymical *a.*, **-ist** *n.*, etc., vars. of ALCHEMICAL etc.

alcid /ˈalsɪd/ *n.* L19. [f. mod.L *Alcidae* (see below), f. *Alca* genus name, f. as AUK: see -ID³.] *Zool.* A bird of the auk family, Alcidae. Cf. AUK.

Alcmanian /alkˈmeɪnɪən/ *a.* & *n.* M19. [f. L *Alcmanius*, f. *Alcman* f. Gk *Alkman* a Greek lyric poet of the 7th cent. BC: see -AN.] *Class. Pros.* (A verse) of four dactyls.

Also **Alcmanic** /-ˈmanɪk/ *a.* M19.

†alcoate *n.* Only in 19. [Contr.] Alcoholate.

alcohol /ˈalkəhɒl/ *n.* M16. [Fr. (now *alcool*) or med.L f. Arab. *al-kuḥl* the kohl: see AL-², KOHL.] †1 A fine powder produced by grinding or esp. by sublimation. M16–M18. †2 *spec.* = KOHL *n.* E17–E19. 3 A liquid essence or spirit obtained by distillation. *obs.* in *gen.* sense. M17. 4 Pure spirit of wine, the intoxicating component of fermented or distilled liquors; = ETHANOL. M17. b Intoxicating drink. L19. 5 *Chem.* Any organic compound containing one or more hydroxyl groups bonded to an aliphatic radical. M19.

3 *fig.*: COLERIDGE Intense selfishness, the alcohol of egotism. 4 *absolute alcohol*: see ABSOLUTE *a.* 5 *ethyl alcohol*, *methyl alcohol*, etc.

alcoholate *n.* an alkoxide; a compound containing alcohol of crystallization: M19.

alcoholic /alkəˈhɒlɪk/ *a.* & *n.* L18. [f. prec. + -IC.] A *adj.* 1 Of, pertaining to, or caused by alcohol; containing alcohol. L18. 2 Suffering from alcoholism. E20. B *n.* A person addicted to alcoholic drink. L19.

Alcoholics Anonymous an association for the mutual support and rehabilitation of alcoholics.

alcoholically *adv.* L19.

†alcoholimeter *n.* var. of ALCOHOLOMETER.

alcoholise *v.* var. of ALCOHOLIZE.

alcoholism /ˈalkəhɒlɪz(ə)m/ *n.* M19. [f. ALCOHOL + -ISM.] The diseased condition caused by chronic overindulgence in alcoholic drink; addiction to alcohol.

alcoholist *n.* an alcoholic; a drinker of alcohol: L19.

alcoholize /ˈalkəhɒlʌɪz/ *v.t.* Also **-ise**; **†alcol-**. M17. [Fr. *alcooliser*: see ALCOHOL, -IZE.] †1 Sublimate, pulverize; refine to an essence, rectify. M17–L18. 2 Saturate or otherwise treat with alcohol. M19.

alcoholiˈzation *n.* L17.

alcoholometer /alkəhɒˈlɒmɪtə/ *n.* Also **†-imeter; alcoholmeter, alcoometer.** M19. [f. ALCOHOL + -OMETER.] An instrument for measuring the proportion of alcohol in a liquor.

ˌalcoholoˈmetric *a.* M19. **alcoholometry** *n.* M19.

†alcolize *v.* var. of ALCOHOLIZE.

alcoometer *n.* var. of ALCOHOLOMETER.

Alcoran /alkəˈrɑːn, ˈalkəran/ *n. arch.* Also **Alkoran**. LME. [(O)Fr. f. Arab. *al-ḳur'ān*: see AL-², KORAN.] The Koran.

Alcoranic *a.* M19. **†Alcoranish** *a.* M17–M18. **Alcoranist** *n.* a person who adheres to the original text of the Koran E17.

alcove /ˈalkəʊv/ *n.* L16. [Fr. *alcôve* f. Sp. *alcoba* f. Arab. *al-ḳubba* the vault, the vaulted structure: see AL-².] 1 A vaulted or arched recess in a room-wall, formerly *esp.* one for a bed. L16. 2 A recess in a garden-wall or hedge; *arch.* a bower, a summer-house. E18.

alcoved *a.* made as an alcove; vaulted, arched: M19.

alcyonarian /alsɪəˈnɛːrɪən/ *n.* & *a.* L19. [f. mod.L *Alcyonaria* (see below), f. *alcyonium* f. Gk *alkuoneion* a coral said to resemble a halcyon's nest (Dioscorides): see HALCYON, -ARIAN.] *Zool.* A *n.* An anthozoan of the subclass Alcyonaria, which includes colonial soft corals whose polyps bear eight pinnate tentacles. L19. B *adj.* Of, pertaining to, or designating this subclass. L19.

†ald *n.* see OLD *n.*¹

ald- *comb. form* see ALDO-.

aldea /alˈdeɪə, *foreign* alˈdeia/ *n.* E17. [Port. *aldeia*, †*-ea*, Sp. *aldea* f. Arab. *al-ḍay'a*, f. *al* AL-² + *ḍay'a* agricultural village, farm.] A small village or a farm in Portugal, Spain, or one of their former territories.

aldehyde /ˈaldɪhʌɪd/ *n.* M19. [f. L *al(cohol) dehyd(rogenatum)* dehydrogenated alcohol.] *Chem.* †1 = ACETALDEHYDE. M–L19. 2 Any of a class of compounds, typified by acetaldehyde, which contain the group ·CH·O and are formed by the partial oxidation of primary alcohols. M19.

aldeˈhydic *a.* pertaining to or characteristic of an aldehyde L19.

al dente /al ˈdɛnti, *foreign* al ˈdɛnte/ *adv.* & *a. phr.* M20. [It., lit. 'to the tooth'.] Of pasta, vegetables, etc.: (cooked) so as to be still firm when bitten.

alder /ˈɔːldə/ *n.* [OE *alor*, *aler*, rel. to MLG *aller*, MDu. *else*, OHG *elira*, *erila* (G *Erle*), ON *ǫlr*, conn. w. L *alnus*. Forms with *d* recorded from 14.] 1 Any tree of the genus *Alnus*, related to the birch; esp. *A. glutinosa*, common in wet places. Also *alder tree*. OE. b Any of several similar trees and shrubs of other genera. Also *alder tree*. L16. 2 An alder-fly. E19.

1b **black alder** (*a*) = *alder buckthorn* below; (*b*) *N. Amer.* a winterberry, *Ilex verticillata*. **red alder** (*a*) *S. Afr.* = ROOI-ELS; (*b*) a tree of western N. America, *Alnus oregona*. **white alder** (*a*) *N. Amer.* any of several pepperbushes; (*b*) *S. Afr.* a tree, *Platylophus trifoliatus*, allied to the rooi-els but with trifoliate leaves.

Comb.: **alder buckthorn** a deciduous shrub, *Frangula alnus*, of the buckthorn family, growing on peaty soils and bearing red or (when ripe) black berries; **alder-fly** a neuropteran insect of the genus *Sialis*, found near streams; **alder kitten** a kitten-moth, *Furcula bicuspis*; *alder tree*: see sense 1 above.

†alder- *pref.* ME–M17. [Later devel. of OE *alra* genit. pl. of ALL.] Of all, as *alderliefest* dearest of all.

alderman /ˈɔːldəmən/ *n.* Also (*Hist.*) **ealdor-**. Pl. **-men**. [OE *aldormann*, f. *aldor*, *ealdor* chief, prince (f. as OLD *a.*) + MAN *n.*] **1** A man of noble or high rank. Long *obs.* exc. *Hist.* OE. **2** The chief officer or warden of a guild. Long *obs.* exc. *Hist.* OE. **3** Chiefly *Hist.* A magistrate of a borough; a municipal officer next in dignity to a mayor, for a long time (and still in the City of London) representing a ward, more recently (up to 1974) a co-opted member of an English or Welsh county or borough council; *N. Amer.* & *Austral.* an elected member of a city council. (The status and conditions of appointment of aldermen have varied with time and place.) OE.

3 **honorary alderman**: a title which, since 1974, can be given to past English or Welsh councillors.

alder'manic *a.* of, pertaining to, or like an alderman M18. **alder'manity** *n.* (*rare*) (*a*) *joc.* aldermanship; (*b*) the body of aldermen: E17. **aldermanlike** *a.* resembling (that of) an alderman E17. **aldermanly** *a.* like, or becoming to, an alderman E18. **aldermanry** *n.* (*a*) *Hist.* a district having its own alderman; (*b*) the dignity or rank of an alderman: LME. **aldermanship** *n.* the office, position, or quality of an alderman LME. **alderwoman** *n.* (*rare*) †(*a*) an alderman's wife; (*b*) *N. Amer.* a female alderman: M16.

Alderney /'ɔːldəni/ *a.* & *n.* L18. [One of the Channel Islands.] **A** *adj.* Designating (an animal of) a breed of dairy cattle belonging to Alderney or to the Channel Islands in general. L18. **B** *n.* An animal of the Alderney breed. E19.

Aldine /'ɔːldʌɪn/ *a.* & *n.* E19. [mod.L *Aldinus*, f. *Aldus*: see below, -INE[1].] (A book or edition) printed by Aldus Manutius (1450–1515), a Venetian printer or his successors; (in) a style of printing type made for him, or an imitation of it.

Aldis /'ɔːldɪs/ *n.* E20. [A. C. W. *Aldis* (1878–1953), Brit. inventor.] In full *Aldis lamp*. (Proprietary name for) a hand lamp for signalling in Morse code.

aldo- /'aldəʊ/ *comb. form* of ALDEHYDE: see -O-. Bef. a vowel **ald-**.

aldo'sterone *n.* (*Biochem.*) an adrenocortical steroid hormone important in electrolyte metabolism M20. **aldo'steronism** *n.* (*Med.*) excessive secretion of aldosterone M20. **al'doxime** *n.* (*Chem.*) an oxime of an aldehyde, a compound of the general formula RCH=NOH (where R is an alkyl group) L19.

aldol /'aldɒl/ *n.* L19. [f. ALD(EHYDE + -OL.] *Chem.* A viscous liquid, $CH_3CH(OH)CH_2CHO$, obtained when acetaldehyde dimerizes in dilute alkali or acid; 3-hydroxybutanal.

Comb.: **aldol condensation** an addition reaction typified by the formation of aldol from acetaldehyde, undergone by most aldehydes and ketones.

aldose /'aldəʊz, -s/ *n.* L19. [f. ALD(EHYDE + -OSE[2].] *Chem.* Any sugar which is also an aldehyde.

†**aldress** *n.* M16–E18. [Perh. contr. of ALDERMAN + -ESS[1].] An alderman's wife.

aldrin /'ɔːldrɪn/ *n.* M20. [f. K. *Alder* (1902–58), Ger. chemist, + -IN[1].] A chlorinated polycyclic hydrocarbon, $C_{12}H_8Cl_6$, formerly used as an insecticide.

ale /eɪl/ *n.* [OE (*e*)*alu* = OS *alo-*, OHG *al-*, ON *ǫl*, f. Gmc.] **1** Beer, formerly esp. of unhopped or paler-coloured kinds, a type of this, a drink of this, now chiefly in *real ale* & as a trade wd. Also (usu. w. specifying wd) a similar drink made from other ingredients. Cf. BEER *n.*[1], PORTER *n.*[2] OE. **2** Chiefly *Hist.* A festival or gathering at which much ale is drunk. OE.

1 *brown ale*, *light ale*, *mild ale*, *pale ale*, (trade terms). *cakes and ale*: see CAKE *n. ginger ale*: see GINGER *n. real ale*: see REAL *a.*[2] *twopenny ale*: see TWOPENNY *a.* 1. *yard of ale*: see YARD *n.*[2]

Comb.: **ale-bench** a bench in or at the front of an alehouse; **aleberry** (*obs.* exc. *dial.*) ale boiled with spice, sugar, and sops of bread; porridge made with ale; **aleconner** an inspector of ale (still a titular office in some boroughs); **alecost** [COST *n.*[1]] = COSTMARY; †**ale-draper** an alehouse-keeper; **ale firkin** a small barrel of ale; an old unit of liquid capacity equal to 9 (earlier 8) gallons; **ale gallon** an old unit of liquid capacity equal to 282 cu. in. (4.62 litres); **alehouse** (chiefly *Hist.*) a house where ale is retailed; †**ale-knight** a frequenter of alehouses, a tippler; **ale-taster** an aleconner; **ale-wort** the fermenting infusion of malt.

aleatico /alɪ'atɪkəʊ/ *n.* Also **A-**. E19. [It.] A sweet Italian red wine.

aleatory /'eɪlɪət(ə)ri/ *a.* L17. [L *aleatorius*, f. *aleator* dice player, f. *alea* a die: see -Y[2].] Depending on the throw of a die or on chance; depending on uncertain contingencies; *Mus.* & *Art* involving random choice by the composer, performer, or artist.

Also **aleatoric** /ˌeɪlɪə'tɒrɪk/ *a.* M20.

alec *n.* see SMART ALEC.

alecithal /eɪ'lɛsɪθ(ə)l/ *a.* L19. [f. A-[10] + Gk *lekithos* yolk + -AL[1].] Of an egg or egg cell: having little or no yolk.

aleck *n.* see SMART ALEC.

†**alectoria** *n.* Also **-ius**. LME–M19. [L, f. as next.] A precious stone said to be found in the gizzard of cocks.

†**alectorian** *n.* & *a.* L16–L19.

alectryomancy /ə'lɛktrɪəmansi/ *n.* Also **-toro-**, †**-tro-**. M17. [f. Gk *alectruōn*, *-tōr* cock + -MANCY.] Divination by means of a cock with grains of corn.

alee /ə'liː/ *adv.* & *pred. a.* LME. [f. A *prep.*[1] 1 + LEE *n.*[1], partly after ON *á hlé*.] *Naut.* On the lee or sheltered side of a ship; to leeward.

aleft /ə'lɛft/ *adv. arch.* ME. [f. A *prep.*[1] 1 + LEFT *n.*] On or to the left.

alegar /'eɪlɪgə/ *n.* LME. [f. ALE, after VINEGAR.] Sour ale; malt vinegar.

ale-hoof /'eɪlhuːf/ *n.* Now *dial.* ME. [Prob. alt. of earlier *hayhove* s.v. HAY *n.*[2]] Ground ivy, *Glechoma hederacea*.

Alemannic /alɪ'manɪk/ *a.* & *n.* Also **-manic**, **Alle-**. L18. [Late L *Alemannicus*, f. *Alemanni* pl. (Gk *Alamanoi*) a Gmc tribe, f. Gmc (prob. f. as ALL + MAN *n.*, denoting a wide alliance of peoples): see -IC.] **A** *adj.* Of or pertaining to a confederation of Germanic tribes occupying the territory between the Rhine, the Main, and the Danube, or the (modern representatives of the) dialects of these people. L18. **B** *n.* The group of Old High German dialects spoken by these people; the modern representatives of these in Alsace, Switzerland, and SW Germany. E19.

Alemannian *a.* & *n.* = ALEMANNIC L19. **Alemannish** *a.* & *n.* †(*a*) German; (*b*) = ALEMANNIC: ME.

alembic /ə'lɛmbɪk/ *n.* & *v.* ME. [OFr. f. med.L *alembicus* f. Arab. *al-'anbīk*, the still cap f. Gk *ambix*: see AL-[2]. Aphet. to LIMBECK.] **A** *n.* An obsolete kind of still consisting of a gourd-shaped vessel or *cucurbit*, and a cap or *alembic* proper having a long beak for conveying the products to a receiver. ME.

fig.: BURKE The hot spirit drawn out of the alembic of hell.

†**B** *v.t.* Distil (as) in an alembic. Earlier as LIMBECK *v.* M17–M18.

alembicated *a.* (of ideas, expression, etc.) overrefined, subtilized L18. **alembi'cation** *n.* overrefinement of expression etc.; concentration: L19.

alembroth /ə'lɛmbrɒθ/ *n. obs.* exc. *Hist.* ME. [Origin unkn.] (A name of the alchemists for) mercury ammonium chloride. Freq. also *sal alembroth*.

alength /ə'lɛŋθ/ *adv.* & *pred. a.* Now *dial.* LME. [f. A *prep.*[1] 1 + LENGTH.] Lengthwise; forward (freq. *fig.*).

aleph /'ɑːlɛf/ *n.* ME. [Heb. *'ālep* lit. 'ox'. Cf. ALPHA.] **1** The first letter of the Hebrew, Phoenician, and other Semitic alphabets. ME. **2** *Math.* A transfinite cardinal numeral. E20.

Comb.: **aleph-null**, **-zero** *Math.* the smallest transfinite cardinal numeral, the cardinal of the set of positive integers.

†**alepine** *n.* M18–M19. [Fr. *alépine* f. Arab. *halabī* from Aleppo.] A mixed fabric of wool and silk, or mohair and cotton.

alerce /ə'ləːsi/ *n.* M19. [Sp. = LARCH *n.*[1]] (The wood of) a Patagonian conifer, *Fitzroya cupressoides*.

alerion /ə'lɪərɪən/ *n.* Also **alle-**. L15. [Fr. *alérion* = med.L *alario*.] *Her.* An eagle with spread wings but without beak or feet.

alert /ə'ləːt/ *adv.*, *a.*, *n.*, & *v.* Also †**alerte**. L16. [Fr. *alerte*, earlier *allerte*, *à l'airte* f. It. *all' erta*, f. *alla* at the + *erta* lookout (tower).] **A** *adv.* & *adj.* **1** *adv.* & *pred. a.* Orig. *Mil.* On the lookout; watchful, vigilant. L16. **2** *adj.* Quick in attention or motion; lively, nimble. E18.

B *n.* A sudden attack or surprise; a warning call, an alarm; (the period of) a warning of an air raid etc. L18.

on the alert on the lookout against danger or attack. *red alert*: see RED *a. yellow alert*: see YELLOW *a.*

C *v.t.* Make alert, warn. M19.

alertly *adv.* L18. **alertness** *n.* E18.

aleuromancy /ə'ljʊərəmansi/ *n. rare.* M17. [Fr. *aleuromancie*, f. as next: see -MANCY.] Divination by means of meal or flour.

aleurone /ə'ljʊərəʊn/ *n.* Also **-on** /-ɒn/. M19. [Gk *aleuron* flour.] *Bot.* Protein stored as granules within the cells of seeds.

Aleut /ə'ljuːt, 'alɪuːt/ *n.* & *a.* L18. [Origin unkn.] **A** *n.* **1** A native or inhabitant of the Aleutian Islands (see next); a speaker of the language of the Aleutian Islands. L18. **2** The language of the Aleutian Islands, other islands in the Bering Sea, and parts of western Alaska, related to Eskimo (Inuit and Yupik). L19. **B** *attrib.* or as *adj.* Of or pertaining to the Aleutian Islands, their inhabitants, or their language. M20.

¶ See also ESKIMO-*Aleut*.

Aleutian /ə'ljuːʃ(ə)n/ *a.* & *n.* L18. [f. prec. + -IAN.] **A** *adj.* Designating a group of islands off the west coast of Alaska; of or pertaining to the Aleutian Islands, = ALEUT *a.* L18. **B** *n.* = ALEUT *n.* E19.

¶ See also ESKIMO-*Aleutian*.

alevin /'aləvɪn/ *n.* M19. [(O)Fr., ult. f. L *allevare* set up, raise up.] A young fish fresh from the spawn.

alewife /'eɪlwʌɪf/ *n.* Pl. **-wives** /-wʌɪvz/. LME. [f. ALE + WIFE *n.* (in sense 'woman').] **1** A woman who keeps an alehouse. *arch.* LME. **2** A fish of the herring family, *Alosa pseudoharengus*, found on the Atlantic coast of N. America. M17.

Alexander /alɪg'zɑːndə/ *a.* M20. [f. the surname *Alexander*: see below.] Designating or pertaining to the principle or technique of using the body and postural alignment advocated by the Australian-born physiotherapist Frederick Matthias Alexander (1869–1955).

†**Alexander** *v.t.* M17–E18. [f. as ALEXANDRIAN *a.*[2] & *n.*[2]] Treat in a manner characteristic of or appropriate to Alexander the Great.

alexanders /alɪg'zɑːndəz/ *n.* OE. [f. med.L *alexandrum*; in ME also f. OFr. *alissa(u)ndre*, *-derie*.] An umbelliferous plant, *Smyrnium olusatrum*, formerly used for salads; *N. Amer.* any of certain other umbellifers.

Alexandrian /alɪg'zɑːndrɪən/ *n.*[1] & *a.*[1] M16. [f. *Alexandria* (see below), founded by Alexander the Great, + -AN.] **1** A native or inhabitant of, of or pertaining to, the Egyptian city of Alexandria. M16. **2** Belonging or akin to, a member or follower of, any of the schools of philosophy in ancient Alexandria, *esp.* the Neoplatonic school of Plotinus and others or that of the Christian fathers Clement of Alexandria and Origen. M18. **3** Belonging or akin to, a member or imitator of, the school of Greek literature, esp. poetry, which flourished at Alexandria under the Ptolemies; (of a writer) imitative, or fond of recondite learning. M19.

Alexandrianism *n.* the philosophical method or doctrine or the literary style of the Alexandrians M19.

Alexandrian /alɪg'zɑːndrɪən/ *a.*[2] & *n.*[2] In senses A.1 & B also **a-**. M18. [f. *Alexander* the Great (356–323 BC), king of Macedonia, + -IAN.] **A** *adj.* **1** = ALEXANDRINE *a.*[2] M18. **2** Of, pertaining to, or characteristic of Alexander the Great. E19.

2 **Alexandrian laurel** (*a*) a shrub of SW Asia, *Danae racemosa*, of the lily family, sometimes grown for its evergreen leaves and red berries; (*b*) a large Indo-Malayan evergreen tree, *Calophyllum inophyllum* (family Guttiferae), with glossy leaves, fragrant white flowers, and round green fruit; also called *poon tree*.

B *n.* = ALEXANDRINE *n.*[2] M18.

Alexandrine /alɪg'zɑːndrɪn, -ʌɪn/ *n.*[1] & *a.*[1] L15. [Fr. *alexandrin*, f. as ALEXANDRIAN *n.*[1] & *a.*[1]: see -INE[1].] = ALEXANDRIAN *n.*[1] & *a.*[1]; also, a type of embroidery associated with Alexandria.

alexandrine /alɪg'zɑːndrɪn, -ʌɪn/ *a.*[2] & *n.*[2] Also **A-**. L16. [Fr. *alexandrin*, f. *Alexandre* Alexander (the Great), eponymous hero of a famous OFr. romance in which the metre is used.] *Pros.* A *adj.* Designating or pertaining to an iambic line of twelve syllables or six feet. L16.

B *n.* An alexandrine line or verse. M17.

POPE A needless Alexandrine ends the song That like a wounded snake, drags its slow length along.

alexandrite /alɪgˈzɑːndrʌɪt/ *n.* M19. [f. *Alexander* II (1818–81), Tsar of Russia + -ITE[1].] *Min.* A gem variety of chrysoberyl which appears green in daylight and red in artificial light.

alexia /əˈlɛksɪə, eɪ-/ *n.* L19. [Irreg. f. A-[10] + Gk *lexis* speech (conf. w. L *legere* read) + -IA[1].] *Med.* Inability to read, or to understand written words, as a result of brain disorder. Cf. DYSLEXIA.

alexic *a.* E20.

alexin /əˈlɛksɪn/ *n.* Also **-ine**. L19. [f. Gk *alexein* ward off + -IN[1].] *Physiol.* = COMPLEMENT *n.* 4e.

alexipharmic /əlɛksɪˈfɑːmɪk/ *n.* & *a.* Now *rare* or *obs.* Also †**-mac**. M17. [Fr. *alexipharmaque* f. mod.L *alexipharmacum* f. Gk *alexipharmakon* neut. sing. (as n.) of adj. f. *alexein* ward off + *pharmakon* poison: assim. to -IC.] A *n.* An antidote against poison. M17. B *adj.* Having the quality or nature of an antidote. M17.

alexipharmacon, -cum *n.* = ALEXIPHARMIC *n.* M16. †**alexipharmical, -acal** *a.* & *n.*: only in 17.

†**alexiteric** *a.* & *n.* L17–L19. [f. med.L *alexiterium* remedy, f. Gk *alexitērion* safeguard, + -IC.] (A substance) having the power to ward off contagion, or act as an antidote.

†**alexiterial** *a.* & *n.* E17–M19. †**alexiterical** *a.* M17–L18. †**alexitery** *a.* & *n.* E17–E18.

alexithymic /eɪ,lɛksɪˈθʌɪmɪk/ *a.* & *n.* L20. [f. A-[10] + Gk *lexis* speech + *thumos* soul + -IC.] *Psychol.* (A person) lacking the ability to recognize and express emotions.

alexithymia *n.* an affective disorder characterized by an inability to recognize and express emotions L20.

aley *a.* var. of ALY.

alfa /ˈalfə/ *n.* Also **ha-** /ˈha-/. M19. [Arab. *ḥalfā'*, colloq. *ḥalfa*.] Esparto grass.

alfalfa /alˈfalfə/ *n.* M19. [Sp. f. Arab. *al-fasfaṣa* a green fodder.] = LUCERNE *n.*[2]

alfaqui /alfəˈkiː, *foreign* alfaˈki/ *n.* Now *rare*. Pl. **-quis** /-ˈkiːz/, **-quies** /-ˈkiɛs, *foreign* -ˈkies/. E17. [Sp. *alfaquí* f. Arab. *al-fakīh*, f. *al* AL-[2] + *fakīh* a person skilled in Islamic jurisprudence.] A Muslim expert in religious law.

alferez /alˈfɛrəz, *foreign* alˈfereθ/ *n.* Also †**-res**. Pl. **-rezes** /-rəzɪz/, **-reces** /-rəsɪz, *foreign* -reθes/. L16. [Sp. *alférez*, OSp. & Port. *-res* f. Arab. *al-fāris* the horseman, the skilled fighter on horseback: see AL-[2].] In Spanish, and formerly in Portuguese, armies: an ensign, a standard-bearer; a second lieutenant.

alfilaria /alfɪləˈriːə/ *n.* *US.* M19. [Mex. Sp., f. Sp. *alfiler* pin, w. ref. to the long-beaked carpels.] = *pin clover* s.v. PIN *n.*[1]

alfin /ˈalfɪn/ *n.* Long *obs.* exc. *Hist.* Also **-phin**. LME. [OFr. *aufin*, later also *alphin* (med.L *alphinus*) f. Sp. & Port. *alfil* f. Arab. *al-fīl* the elephant: see AL-[2].] A chess piece similar in function to the present-day bishop.

Alfisol /ˈalfɪsɒl/ *n.* M20. [f. arbitrary 1st elem. + -SOL.] *Soil Sci.* A soil of an order comprising leached basic or slightly acid soils with a clay-enriched B horizon.

alforja /alˈfɔːhə, *foreign* alˈfɔrxa/ *n.* Also †**-rge**. E17. [Sp. *alforja*, Port. *-rge* f. Arab. *al-ḵurj* saddle-bag: see AL-[2].] 1 In Spain, Portugal, Latin America, and other areas of Spanish influence (as the south-western US): a wallet, a saddle-bag. E17. †2 A cheek-pouch. E–M18.

Alfredian /alˈfriːdɪən/ *a.* E19. [f. *Alfred* (see below) + -IAN.] Pertaining to or characteristic of Alfred the Great (849–99), king of the West Saxons, or his writings.

alfresco /alˈfrɛskəʊ/ *adv.* & *a.* M18. [It. *al fresco*: see FRESCO.] A *adv.* 1 In the open air. M18. 2 *Art.* In fresco. M18. B *adj.* Open-air. E19.

Alfvén /ˈalfveɪn, -vən/ *n.* M20. [Hannes *Alfvén* (1908–95), Swed. physicist.] *Physics.* Used *attrib.* with ref. to Alfvén's discoveries.

Alfvén speed or **velocity** the speed of an Alfvén wave in a plasma of given properties. **Alfvén wave** a transverse magnetohydrodynamic wave travelling in the direction of the magnetic field in a magnetized plasma.

alga /ˈalgə/ *n.* Pl. **algae** /ˈaldʒiː, ˈalgiː/. M16. [L = seaweed.] Orig., seaweed; now, any of a large group of non-vascular mainly aquatic cryptogams capable of photosynthesis, including seaweeds and many unicellular and filamentous organisms. Also *collect.*, the mass formed by such organisms.

blue-green alga: see BLUE *a.* *brown alga*: see BROWN *a.* *green alga*: see GREEN *a.* *red alga*: see RED *a.*

algal /ˈalg(ə)l/ *a.* & *n.* M19. [f. prec. + -AL[1].] A *adj.* Of or pertaining to algae; of the nature of an alga. M19. B *n.* An alga. *rare.* M19.

algarroba /algəˈrəʊbə/ *n.* L16. [Sp. f. Arab. *al-ḵarrūb(a)*: see AL-[2], CAROB.] 1 (The pod of) the carob tree. L16. 2 (The fruit of) any of certain mesquites. M18.

algate /ˈɔːlgeɪt/ *adv.* Long *obs.* exc. *dial.* Also **-gates** /-geɪts/. ME. [f. ALL + GATE *n.*[2]; *-s* analogical.] †1 Always, continually. ME–L16. 2 Anyhow; by all or any means. ME. †3 At any rate, at all events. ME–E17. †4 All the way, altogether. ME–E17. 5 Nevertheless, after all. ME. 6 Everywhere. *north.* L19.

algebra /ˈaldʒɪbrə/ *n.* LME. [It., Sp., med.L, f. Arab. *al-jabr*, f. *al* AL-[2] + *jabr* reunion of broken parts, f. *jabara* set broken bones, reunite, restore. The term achieved currency in the title of a book, *ʻilm al-jabr wa'l-mukābala* 'the science of restoring what is missing and equating like with like', by the mathematician al-Ḵwārizmī (cf. ALGORISM).] †1 The surgical treatment of fractures. LME–M16. 2 The part of mathematics which investigates the relations and properties of numbers or other mathematical structures by means of general symbols; a system of this based on given axioms. M16.

algebraist /-breɪɪst/ *n.* a person versed in algebra E17. **algebraize** *v.* (*a*) *v.t.* express in algebraic form; (*b*) *v.i.* perform algebra: M19. †**algebrician** *n.* = ALGEBRAIST L16–L17. **algebrist** *n.* = ALGEBRAIST L17.

algebraic /aldʒɪˈbreɪɪk/ *a.* M17. [f. prec. + -IC.] Of, pertaining to, or occurring in algebra; *spec.* (of a function, etc.) able to be produced by the simple algebraic operations (opp. TRANSCENDENTAL *a.*).

C. S. OGILVY The famous equation . . $e^{\pi i} = -1$, is not algebraic.

algebraical *a.* of or relating to algebra L16. **algebraically** *adv.* in terms of, by means of, algebra M17. **algebraicize** /-saɪz/ *v.t.* express in algebraic form L19.

algedonic /aldʒɪˈdɒnɪk/ *a.* L19. [f. Gk *algos* pain + *hēdonē* pleasure + -IC.] Pertaining to or characterized by pleasure and pain, or reward and punishment.

Algerian /alˈdʒɪərɪən/ *n.* & *a.* E17. [f. *Algeria* (see below) + -AN.] A *n.* 1 A native or inhabitant of the country of Algeria or the town of Algiers, in N. Africa. E17. 2 Wine from Algeria. M20. B *adj.* Of or pertaining to Algeria or Algiers. L19.

Algerine /ˈaldʒəriːn/ *n.* & *a.* (*arch.*) = ALGERIAN; *esp.* (characteristic of) a pirate from Algiers: M17.

-algia /ˈaldʒə/ *suff.* [f. Gk *algos* pain + -IA[1].] Forming ns. denoting pain in a specified part, as *neuralgia*.

-algic *suff.*: forming corresp. adjs.

algicide /ˈaldʒɪsʌɪd, ˈalgɪ-/ *n.* E20. [f. ALGA + -I- + -CIDE.] A substance poisonous to algae.

algid /ˈaldʒɪd/ *a.* E17. [L *algidus*, f. *algere* be cold: see -ID[1].] Cold, chilly; *Med.* characterized by a feeling of coldness.

alˈgidity *n.* (*rare*) M17.

algin /ˈaldʒɪn/ *n.* L19. [f. ALGA + -IN[1].] Alginic acid or any of its salts.

alginic /alˈdʒɪnɪk/ *a.* L19. [f. prec. + -IC.] Chem. *alginic acid*, an insoluble gelatinous carbohydrate found (chiefly as salts) in many brown algae.

ˈalginate *n.* a salt of alginic acid L19.

Algol /ˈalgɒl/ *n.* M20. [f. ALGO(RITHMIC *language*.] (The name of) an early high-level programming language.

algolagnia /algəʊˈlagnɪə/ *n.* E20. [f. Gk *algos* pain + *lagneia* lust.] *Psychiatry.* The practice of obtaining sexual pleasure from pain inflicted on oneself or another.

algology /alˈgɒlədʒi/ *n.* M19. [f. ALGA + -OLOGY.] The branch of science that deals with algae.

algoˈlogical *a.* M19. **algologist** *n.* M19.

Algonkian /alˈgɒŋkɪən/ *a.* & *n.* L19. [Var. of ALGONQUIAN.] 1 *Geol.* = PROTEROZOIC. L19. 2 = ALGONQUIAN. E20.

Algonkin *n.* & *a.* var. of ALGONQUIN.

Algonquian /alˈgɒŋkwɪən, -kɪ-/ *a.* & *n.* See also ALGONKIAN. L19. [Irreg. f. next + -IAN.] A *adj.* Of or pertaining to a large group of N. American Indian peoples including the Algonquins proper, or to their languages and dialects. L19. B *n.* A member of, any of the languages or dialects of, this group of peoples. L19.

Algonquin /alˈgɒŋkwɪn, -kɪn/ *n.* & *a.* Also **-kin** /-kɪn/. E17. [Fr., contr. of †*Algoumequin*: cf. Micmac *algoomeaking* at the place of spearing fish and eels.] A *n.* A member of a N. American Indian people of the districts of Ottawa and Quebec; the language of this people; more widely = ALGONQUIAN *n.* E17. B *attrib.* or as *adj.* Of or pertaining to the Algonquin or their language; more widely = ALGONQUIAN *a.* E18.

†**algor** *n.* LME–L19. [L.] Cold, chilliness, esp. at the onset of fever.

algorism /ˈalgərɪz(ə)m/ *n.* Also †**augrim** & similar forms. ME. [OFr. *augori(s)me*, *algorisme* f. med.L *algorismus* f. Arab. *al-Ḵwārazmī* the man of *Ḵwārazm* (Khiva), agnomen of the mathematician Abū Jaʻfar Muhammad ibn Mūsā (fl. *c*800–47), author of widely translated works on arithmetic and algebra.] 1 The Arabic or decimal system of writing numbers; *gen.* arithmetic. ME. 2 = ALGORITHM 2. *rare.* M20.

algoˈrismic *a.* (*rare*) M19.

algorithm /ˈalgərɪð(ə)m/ *n.* L17. [Var. of ALGORISM after Gk *arithmos* number.] 1 = ALGORISM I. L17. 2 A procedure or set of rules for calculation or problem-solving, now esp. with a computer. E19.

algoˈrithmic *a.* expressed as or using an algorithm or algorithms L19. **algoˈrithmically** *adv.* L20.

alguacil /algwəˈsɪl, *foreign* algwaˈθil/ *n.* Pl. **-cils** /-ˈsɪlz/, **-ciles** /-ˈθiles/. Also **-zil** /-ˈzɪl, *foreign* -ˈθil/, pl. **-zils** /-ˈzɪlz/, **-ziles** /-ˈθiles/. E16. [Sp. (earlier *-zil*) f. Arab. *al-wazīr*, f. *al* AL-[2] + *wazīr* VIZIER.] 1 In Spain: an officer of justice, a warrant-officer, a sergeant. In Latin America or other areas of Spanish influence: a sheriff, a constable. E16. 2 A mounted official at a bullfight. E20.

algum /ˈalgʌm/ *n.* Pl. **-im** /-ɪm/, **-s**. L16. [Heb. *'algūm*: cf. ALMUG.] A tree, not definitely identified, mentioned in the Bible. Also *algum tree*.

Al-Hadj *n.* var. of AL-HAJJ.

alhagi /alˈhɑːdʒi/ *n.* M18. [mod.L, f. Arab. *al-ḥāj*: see AL-[2].] A spiny leguminous shrub of the genus *Alhagi*, members of which yield a kind of manna.

alhaji /alˈhadʒi/ *n.* As a title **A-**. M20. [Hausa, f. as next.] In W. Africa: a Muslim who has been to Mecca as a pilgrim.

Al-Hajj /alˈhadʒ/ *n.* Also **-Hadj**. M19. [Arab., f. as AL-[2] + HAJJ.] As a title: a Muslim who has undertaken the hajj. Cf. HAJJI.

Alhambresque /alhamˈbrɛsk/ *a.* M19. [f. *Alhambra* (see below) + -ESQUE.] In the architectural style of the Alhambra, the palace of the Moorish kings at Granada in Spain; like the Alhambra.

†**alhidada** *n.* var. of ALIDADE.

alias /ˈeɪlɪəs/ *adv.* & *n.* LME. [L = at another time, otherwise.] A *adv.* Otherwise called or named; called at other times. LME.

E. O'NEILL It sounds to me like Bacchus, alias the Demon Rum, doing the talking.

B *n.* †1 *Law.* A second writ, containing the words *sicut alias praecipimus*, issued after the first has failed. LME–E19. 2 A name by which a person is or has been called on other occasions; an assumed name. E17.

Ali Baba /ˈali ˈbɑːbə, ˈbɑːbɑː/ *n. phr.* M20. [Arab. *ʿAlī Bābā*, a character in the *Arabian Nights' Entertainments*.] In full *Ali Baba basket*. A tall basket with a rounded body and a flat base.

alibi /ˈalɪbʌɪ/ *adv., n., & v.* L17. [L = elsewhere.] †**A** *adv.* Elsewhere. L17–L18. **B** *n.* A plea by the person accused of an act that he or she was elsewhere when it took place; evidence to support such a plea; *colloq.* an excuse of any kind. L18. **C** *v.t.* & *i.* Provide an alibi, offer an excuse, (for). E20.

alible /ˈalɪb(ə)l/ *a. rare.* M17. [L *alibilis*, f. *alere* nourish: see -IBLE.] Nutritive, nourishing.

Alicante /alɪˈkanti/ *n.* Also †**-cant**, †**-gant**. L15. [A city in Spain.] A red wine exported from or produced near Alicante in SE Spain.

Alice /ˈalɪs/ *n.* E20. [Female forename.] **1** [*Alice* Roosevelt Longworth, daughter of the US President Theodore Roosevelt.] *Alice blue*, a light greenish-blue colour. E20. **2** [Heroine of two books by Lewis Carroll.] a *Alice-in-Wonderland* adj., fantastic, absurd. E20. **b** *Alice band*, a type of band to hold back the hair. M20.

alick *n.* see SMART ALEC.

alicyclic /alɪˈsʌɪklɪk, -ˈsɪk-/ *a.* L19. [f. ALI(PHATIC + CYCLIC.] *Chem.* Of an organic compound: cyclic but not aromatic. Also, of or pertaining to such a compound.

alidade /ˈalɪdeɪd/ *n.* Also †**allidatha**, †**alhidada**, †**alidad**. LME. [Orig. f. Arab. *al-ʿiḍāda*, perh. f. *al* AL-² + *ʿadud* upper arm; in mod. form f. Fr. f. Sp.] A sighting device or pointer for angular measurement, usu. for use with (orig.) a quadrant, astrolabe, etc., or (now) a plane table.

alien /ˈeɪlɪən/ *a.* & *n.* ME. [OFr. f. L *alienus* belonging to another, f. *alius* other.] **A** *adj.* **1** Belonging to another person, family, place, context, or world. ME. **b** *esp.* Of a foreign nation, under foreign allegiance. LME. **c** Of a plant: introduced from another country and subsequently naturalized. M19. **2** Foreign in nature, character, or origin; out of harmony. LME. **b** Foll. by *from*: differing in nature from, inconsistent with. LME. **c** Foll. by *to*: repugnant to, opposed to; out of character with. E18.

1 KEATS The sad heart of Ruth, when, sick for home, She stood in tears amid the alien corn. *Guardian* Was this an alien attempt to establish life on this planet? b **Alien Priory**: owing obedience to a mother-abbey in a foreign country. 2 A. G. GARDINER The Fifth Symphony.. creates a state of mind, a spiritual atmosphere, that is destroyed by any intrusive and alien note.

B *n.* **1** A stranger, a foreigner. ME. **b** *esp.* A non-naturalized foreigner. ME. **c** A being from another world. M20. **2** A person separated or excluded *from*. *arch.* M16. **3** *Bot.* A plant orig. introduced from another country and later naturalized. M19. **4** *Philol.* A word from one language used but not naturalized in another. L19.

1 *fig.*: SHAKES. *1 Hen. IV* Almost an alien to the hearts Of all the court. b M. MCCARTHY It was against the law for an alien to interfere in the domestic affairs of a foreign country. c K. AMIS Some excellent stories have been written about non-communicating aliens. 2 J. H. NEWMAN As if aliens from God's mercies.

Comb.: **alien-enemy**, **-friend** *Law* an alien owing allegiance to a country at war with, at peace with, his or her country of residence.

alienage *n.* the condition or legal standing of an alien E19. **alienness** /-n-n-/ *n.* E20.

alien /ˈeɪlɪən/ *v.t.* Now *rare*. In sense 2 also **-ene** /-iːn/. LME. [(O)Fr. *aliener* f. L *alienare*: see ALIENATE *v.*] **1** = ALIENATE *v.* 1. LME. **2** = ALIENATE *v.* 2. LME.

alie'nee *n.* a person to whom the ownership of property is transferred. M16. **alienor** *n.* a person who transfers property to another M16.

alienable /ˈeɪlɪənəb(ə)l/ *a.* E17. [f. prec. + -ABLE. Cf. Fr. *aliénable*.] Able to be alienated.

aliena'bility *n.* L18.

†**alienate** *a.* & *n.* LME. [L *alienatus* pa. pple, f. as next: see -ATE².] **A** *adj.* **1** Estranged. LME–E19. **2** Alienated. E16–M17. **3** Foreign in nature or character. M16–M17. **B** *n.* An alien, a stranger. L15–M16.

alienate /ˈeɪlɪəneɪt/ *v.t.* E16. [L *alienat-* pa. ppl stem of *alienare*, f. *alienus*: see ALIEN *a.* & *n.*, -ATE³.] **1** Estrange; turn away in feelings or affection. E16. **2** Transfer to the ownership of another. E16. **3** *gen.* Turn away, divert. L16.

alienator *n.* L17.

alienation /eɪlɪəˈneɪʃ(ə)n/ *n.* LME. [OFr., or L *alienatio(n-)*, f. as prec.: see -ATION.] **1** The act of estranging or state of estrangement in feeling or affection. LME. **b** *Theatr.* Objectivity of a spectator's reaction, sought by some dramatists. M20. **2** Loss of mental faculties, insanity. Now usu. more fully *mental alienation*. LME. **3** The action of transferring ownership of anything. LME. **b** The state of being held by other than the proper owner. *arch.* E19. **4** Diversion of something to a different purpose. L18.

1 BURKE They grow every day into alienation from this country. E. KAMENKA The philosophico-ethical conceptions that underlie the younger Marx. Chief among these conceptions is that of 'alienation': the notion that in modern capitalistic society man is estranged or alienated from what are properly his functions and creations and that instead of controlling them he is controlled by them. **alienation of affection(s)** *US Law* transfer of a person's affection from one with rights or claims to it to another held responsible for the estrangement. 3 J. BRAMHALL The alienation of Lands to the Church. 4 H. WILSON He [Gladstone] was particularly concerned to strengthen the safeguards against 'alienation', that is, diverting to another purpose.. moneys that had been specifically voted by Parliament for a particular use.

aliene *v.* see ALIEN *v.*

alienism /ˈeɪlɪənɪz(ə)m/ *n.* L18. [f. ALIEN *n.* + -ISM.] **1** The position of being an alien; foreign status. Now *rare*. L18. **2** The study and treatment of mental illness. Now *rare* or *obs.* L19.

alienist /ˈeɪlɪənɪst/ *n.* Now chiefly *US*. M19. [Fr. *aliéniste*: see ALIENATION 2, -IST.] An expert in mental illness, esp. from a legal standpoint.

†**alife** *adv.* M16–L17. [Prob. f. LIEF, conf. w. LIFE *n.*] *love alife*, love dearly.

aliform /ˈeɪlɪfɔːm/ *a.* E18. [mod.L *aliformis*, f. L *ala* wing: see -FORM.] Wing-shaped.

†**Aligant** *n.* var. of ALICANTE.

alight /əˈlʌɪt/ *v.i.* Pa. t. & pple **alighted**, (*arch.* or *poet.*) **alit** /əˈlɪt/; pa. pple also †**alight**. OE. [f. A-¹ + LIGHT *v.*¹] **1** Spring lightly down, dismount, *from* (or †*of*) a horse; descend *from* or *out of* a conveyance. OE. †**b** Spring lightly *on* or *upon*. LME–E16. †**2** *gen.* Go or come down. ME–L15. **3** Get down from a horse or conveyance; land, stop. ME. **4** Descend and settle; come to earth from the air. ME. **5** Descend and strike; fall *on* or *upon*, as a blow. *arch.* ME. **6** Come by chance *on*, *upon*. M19.

1 CLARENDON His Majesty alighted out of his Coach. JOYCE Our travellers.. alighted from their palfreys. B. PYM Elegantly dressed people were alighting from cars. 3 SHAKES. *Merch. V.* Madam, there is alighted at your gate A young Venetian. 4 V. WOOLF That moment.. when if a feather alight in the scale it will be weighed down. G. ORWELL A thrush had alighted on a bough not five metres away. *Times* We were about to alight along the centre-line of the runway. *fig.*: SCOTT FITZGERALD So far his suspicions hadn't alighted on Tom. 6 S. GILLESPIE His eye immediately alighted on a Degas.

alight /əˈlʌɪt/ *adv.* & *pred. a.* LME. [Prob. f. phr. †*on a light* (= *lighted*) *fire*.] On fire; lighted up.

†**alighten** *v.t.* M16–L18. [Irreg. after LIGHTEN *v.*¹] Lighten, relieve.

align /əˈlʌɪn/ *v.* Also (earlier) **aline**. LME. [OFr. *alignier* (mod. *aligner*), f. phr. *à ligne* into line: see A-⁵, LINE *n.*²] †**1** *v.t.* Of a male animal: copulate with (a female animal). Only in LME. **2** *v.t.* Place or lay in a line; bring into line; *esp.* bring (points) into a straight line. L17. **3** *v.i.* Fall into line (*with*). L19. **4** *v.t. fig.* Bring into a relation of (esp. political) agreement or alliance (*with*). M20.

alignment /əˈlʌɪnm(ə)nt/ *n.* Also **aline-**. L18. [(O)Fr. *alignement*, f. as prec.: see -MENT.] **1** Arrangement in a line or lines. L18. **b** *spec.* Arrangement of soldiers in a line or lines; a military line. L18. **2** The drawing of a straight line through a point or points. M19. **3** Bringing into line, straightening. L19. **4** Bringing into (esp. political) agreement or alliance; a grouping of parties, powers, etc. M20.

Comb.: **alignment chart** = NOMOGRAM.

alike /əˈlʌɪk/ *a.* (now usu. *pred.*). [OE *ġelīċ* = OFris. *gelīk*, OS *gelīc* (Du. *gelijk*), OHG *galīh* (G *gleich*), ON *glíkr*, Goth. *galeiks*, f. Gmc: see A-⁴, LIKE *a.* Reinforced by ON *álíkr* (w. pref. as AN-¹).] Like one another; similar; indistinguishable.

SHAKES. *Com. Err.* Male twins, both alike. E. BOWEN Their alike profiles. D. PARKER They looked alike, though the resemblance did not lie in their features.

alikeness *n.* LME.

alike /əˈlʌɪk/ *adv.* [OE *ġelīċe*, f. as prec. + advb. suff. *-e* (corresp. forms in OHG and Goth.): see A-⁴, LIKE *adv.* Reinforced by ON *álíka* (w. pref. as AN-¹).] In like manner; equally; similarly.

GOLDSMITH Nature, a mother kind alike to all. R. WEST The curtains,.. the wallpapers, which alike were a rich-coloured paste of little flowers. *share and share alike*: see SHARE *n.*², *v.*²

aliment /ˈalɪm(ə)nt/ *n.* L15. [Fr., or L *alimentum*, f. *alere* nourish: see -MENT.] **1** Nutriment, food. L15. **2** *fig.* Support, mental sustenance. M17 **3** *Sc. Law* & *gen.* Provision for maintenance; alimony. M17.

ali'mental *a.* of or pertaining to aliment; nutritive: L16. **ali'mentally** *adv.* (*rare*) M17.

aliment /ˈalɪmɛnt/ *v.t.* L15. [Fr. *alimenter* f. late L *alimentare*, f. *alimentum*: see prec.] **1** Supply with food. *rare.* L15. **2** *Sc. Law* & *gen.* Make provision for the maintenance of, provide alimony for. E17. **3** *fig.* Sustain, support, nourish. M17.

ali'mentative *a.* (*rare*) connected with the supply of aliment L19. **ali'mentativeness** *n.* (*rare*) feeding instinct, desire for food M19. **alimenter** *n.* (*rare*) a person who receives or provides aliment E19. **ali'mentive** *a.* (*rare*) = ALIMENTATIVE M19. **ali'mentiveness** *n.* = ALIMENTATIVENESS E19.

alimentary /alɪˈmɛnt(ə)ri/ *a.* L16. [L *alimentarius*, f. as prec.: see -ARY¹.] **1** Concerned with or performing functions of nutrition. L16. **2** Of the nature of aliment, nourishing. E17. **3** Concerned with or providing maintenance. M18.

1 **alimentary canal** the whole passage through the body, from mouth to anus, by which food is received, digested, etc.

alimentation /ˌalɪm(ə)nˈteɪʃ(ə)n/ *n.* L16. [Fr., or med.L *alimentatio(n-)*, f. *alimentare*: see ALIMENT *v.*, -ATION.] **1** Maintenance, support. L16. **2** The process of being nourished; the mode of receiving nourishment. E17. **3** The action or process of nourishing. M17.

alimony /ˈalɪməni/ *n.* E17. [L *alimonia*, f. *alere* nourish: see -MONY.] **1** Nourishment, maintenance; means of subsistence. E17. **2** *spec.* An allowance made to a woman (occas. to a man) by her (or his) (ex-)spouse after divorce or legal separation, or during proceedings for these. Now chiefly *US* (in Britain all such allowances are now called *maintenance*). M17.

aline *v.*, **-ment** *n.* vars. of ALIGN, -MENT.

aliphatic /alɪˈfatɪk/ *a.* L19. [f. Gk *aleiphat-*, *-phar* unguent, fat + -IC: orig. used of the fatty acids.] *Chem.* Of an organic compound: having an open-chain structure; not aromatic. Also, of or pertaining to such compounds.

aliquot /ˈalɪkwɒt/ *a.* & *n.* L16. [Fr. *aliquote* f. L *aliquot* some, several, f. *alius* one of two + *quot* how many.] Orig. *Math.* **A** *adj.* That is contained in the whole an integral number of times. Chiefly in *aliquot part*. Cf. QUANTAL *a.* 1. L16. **B** *n.* An aliquot part, integral factor; *loosely* any fraction of a whole, a sample. E17.

alisma /əˈlɪzmə/ *n.* L16. [L f. Gk.] A plant of the genus *Alisma*; a water plantain.

alisphenoid /alɪˈsfiːnɔɪd/ *a.* & *n.* M19. [f. L *ala* wing + SPHENOID *a.*] *Anat.* & *Zool.* (Forming or pertaining to) one of the lateral bones of the cranium (in the human skull either of the greater wings of the sphenoid bone).

alisphe'noidal *a.* M19.

alit *v.* see ALIGHT *v.*

aliter /ˈalɪtə/ *adv.* L17. [L.] Chiefly *Law*. Otherwise.

aliterate /eɪˈlɪt(ə)rət/ *a.* & *n.* M20. [f. A-[10] + LITERATE.] **A** *adj.* Unwilling to read, despite being able to do so. M20. **B** *n.* An aliterate person. L20.
aliteracy *n.* L20.

-ality /ˈalɪti/ *suff.* [f. -AL[1] + -ITY.] Forming ns., with senses as -ITY.

aliunde /alɪˈʌndi/ *adv.* M17. [L.] From elsewhere; from another source.

alive /əˈlʌɪv/ *adv.* & *a.* (usu. *pred.*). [OE phr. *on life*: see A *prep.*[1] 6, LIFE *n.*] **1** Living; in life; while still living. OE. **2** Unextinguished, undiminished, unforgotten. E17. **3** In a sentient or susceptible condition; fully aware; sensitive or responsive *to*. E17. **4** Full of energy or animation; active, lively, brisk. M18. **b** *Electr.* = LIVE *a.* 5b. L19. **5** In a state of commotion; swarming. Foll. by *with*. L18.
1 SHAKES. *Merch. V.* Is my boy—God rest his soul!—alive or dead? STEELE The most contented happy man alive. DICKENS Why, bless my heart alive, my dear, how late you are! 2 E. F. BENSON For two years she had . . kept that illusion undeniably alive. R. JARRELL This print of mine, that has kept its colour Alive through many cleanings. A. S. BYATT The fire was still alive in the hearth. 3 A. G. GARDINER You cannot be alive unless you take life gallantly. J. CONRAD I was perfectly alive to the difficulty of stopping him from going there. 4 K. NORWAY Group Captain Hurst is the most alive man I know. 5 L. VAN DER POST The swamp was alive with crocodile and hippo. T. STOPPARD The air is alive with bells and sirens.
Phrases etc.: **alive and kicking** *colloq.* very active. **alive and well (and living in —)** *colloq.* not (as has been suggested) ill or dead, and to be found in (the place named). **alive oh** [from a fish-sellers' cry] very much alive and active. *burn alive*: see BURN *v.* 8. *dead-(and-)alive*: see DEAD *a.* & *adv.* *Heavens alive*: see HEAVEN *n.* **look alive!** *colloq.* be brisk. **man alive!** *colloq.*: an expletive. *sakes alive!*: see SAKE *n.*[1] *snakes alive!*: see SNAKE *n.* 1C.
aliveness *n.* M19.

alizarin /əˈlɪz(ə)rɪn/ *n.* Also **-ine**. M19. [Fr. *alizarine* f. *alizari* madder, perh. f. colloq. Arab. *al-ʿiṣāra* the juice or sap pressed out: see AL-[2], -IN[1].] *Chem.* The red colouring matter of madder root; 1,2-dihydroxyanthraquinone, $C_{14}H_8O_4$.
Comb.: **alizarin red, yellow**: (the colours of) synthetic dyestuffs derived from or resembling alizarin.

Al-kaaba *n.* see KAABA.

alkahest /ˈalkəhɛst/ *n.* Also **†alc(h)-**. M17. [Prob. invented by Paracelsus, after Arab.] The universal solvent sought by the alchemists. Also *fig.*, anything universally applicable.

alkalaemia /alkəˈliːmɪə/ *n.* E20. [f. ALKALI + -AEMIA.] *Med.* A condition of abnormally raised pH of the blood.

alkalescent /alkəˈlɛs(ə)nt/ *a.* Now *rare*. M18. [f. ALKALI + -ESCENT.] Slightly alkaline; conducive or tending to alkalinity.
alkalescence, -ency *ns.* tendency to alkalinity, slight alkaline character M18.

alkali /ˈalkəlʌɪ/ *n.* Pl. **-s, -es**. LME. [med.L f. Arab. *al-kalī* the calcined ashes of *Salsola* etc.: see AL-[2].] **1** A saline substance extracted from the calcined ashes of plants such as saltwort (genus *Salsola*) or glasswort (genus *Salicornia*); soda ash. LME. **2** A plant from which soda ash is obtained; saltwort, glasswort. Now *rare* or *obs.* L16. **3** Any substance which neutralizes or effervesces with acids and forms a caustic or corrosive solution in water; a water-soluble base, *esp.* a hydroxide. E17. **4** A soluble salt or mixture of such salts existing in excess in the soil; terrain characterized by this. Freq. *attrib.* *N. Amer.* M19.
3 VOLATILE *alkali*. 4 S. E. WHITE The limitless alkali of the Arizona plains. *attrib.*: J. H. BEADLE Little to see but . . alkali flats and sand-hills.
Comb.: **alkali metal** *Chem.* any of the elements occupying group IA of the periodic table (namely lithium, sodium, potassium, rubidium, caesium, francium), which are soft, reactive metals forming soluble hydroxides.
alkalify /-ɪfʌɪ/ *v.t.* make alkaline M19. **†alkalious** *a.* = ALKALINE L17–M18.

alkalic /alˈkalɪk/ *a.* M18. [f. prec. + -IC.] **1** Alkaline. *rare*. M18. **2** *Geol.* Of a rock or mineral: richer in alkali metals, esp. sodium and potassium, than the average for the group it belongs to. E20.

alkalide /ˈalkəlʌɪd/ *n.* L20. [f. ALKALI + -IDE.] *Chem.* A binary ionic compound in which the anion is an alkali metal.

alkalimetry /alkəˈlɪmɪtri/ *n.* E19. [f. as prec. + -METRY.] *Chem.* The measurement of the strengths of alkalis.
alkalimeter *n.* an instrument for alkalimetry E19. **alkaliˈmetric(al)** *adjs.* M19.

alkaline /ˈalkəlʌɪn/ *a.* L17. [f. ALKALI + -INE[1].] Of, pertaining to, or of the nature of alkalis; rich in alkali; *Chem.* having a pH greater than 7.
alkaline earth *Chem.* any of the strongly basic oxides of the metals calcium, strontium, barium, and radium; *loosely* any of these elements, which are placed in group IIA of the periodic table. **alkaline metal** = ALKALI *metal*. *alkaline tide*: see TIDE *n.*
alkalinity /-ˈlɪnɪti/ *n.* alkaline character or quality L18. **alkalinization** /alkəlɪnʌɪˈzeɪʃ(ə)n/ *n.* making alkaline; reduction of acidity: M20. **alkalinize** /-lɪn-/ *v.t.* make alkaline E19.

alkalize /ˈalkəlʌɪz/ *v.t.* Also **-ise**. M17. [f. ALKALI + -IZE.] Make alkaline, treat with alkali.
†alkalizate *a.* alkaline E17–M18. **alkaliˈzation** *n.* L17.

alkaloid /ˈalkəlɔɪd/ *a.* & *n.* E19. [G: see ALKALI, -OID.] *Chem.* (Designating or pertaining to) any of a class of complex organic bases of vegetable origin which have pronounced physiological actions on man (e.g. morphine, strychnine, nicotine).
vinca alkaloid: see VINCA *n.*[1]
alkaˈloidal *a.* of the nature of an alkaloid; pertaining to alkaloids: L19.

alkalosis /alkəˈləʊsɪs/ *n.* Pl. **-loses** /-ˈləʊsiːz/. E20. [f. ALKALI + -OSIS.] *Med.* A condition of abnormally raised pH of the body fluids.

alkane /ˈalkeɪn/ *n.* L19. [f. ALKYL + -ANE.] *Chem.* Any of the saturated hydrocarbons (e.g. methane, butane) which form a series having the general formula C_nH_{2n+2}. Cf. PARAFFIN.

alkanet /ˈalkənɛt/ *n.* ME. [Colloq. Arab. *al-ḥanna(t)* = classical Arab. *al-ḥinnāʾ* ALCANNA.] **1** A red dye obtained from the roots of certain plants of the genus *Alkanna*, of the borage family, esp. *A. lehmannii*. ME. **2** Any plant of the genus *Alkanna*; any of several related plants having roots which can be used in similar ways, esp. *Anchusa officinalis* of Europe, with violet or occas. yellow or white flowers. Also (more fully *green* or *evergreen alkanet*), a coarse blue-flowered garden plant, *Pentaglottis sempervirens*, native to SW Europe. ME.

alkanna *n.* var. of ALCANNA.

alkaptonuria /al,kaptəˈnjʊərɪə/ *n.* Also **alc-**. L19. [f. G *Alkapton*, *Alc-* homogentisic acid, f. *alkali* ALKALI + Gk *kapton* neut. pres. pple of *kaptein* swallow greedily, + -URIA.] *Med.* A hereditary metabolic disorder characterized by an accumulation of homogentisic acid in certain tissues and its excretion in the urine.
alkaptonuric *a.* & *n.* (a person) suffering from alkaptonuria L19.

alkekengi /alkɪˈkɛndʒi/ *n.* LME. [med.L f. Arab. *al-* & Pers. *kākanj*: see AL-[2].] An ornamental plant, *Physalis alkekengi*, native to southern Europe and Asia, bearing red berries enclosed by an inflated orange calyx. Also called *Chinese lantern*, *winter cherry*, and other names.

alkene /ˈalkiːn/ *n.* L19. [f. ALKYL + -ENE.] *Chem.* Any of the unsaturated hydrocarbons with one double bond, which form a series having the general formula C_nH_{2n}; = OLEFIN.

alkermes /alˈkəːmiːz, -ɪz/ *n.* M16. [Fr. *alkermès* f. Arab. *al-kirmiz*: see AL-[2], KERMES.] **1** A confection or cordial containing the kermes insect; a sweet cordial coloured with cochineal. M16. **†2** = KERMES 2. E17–M18.

alkie *n.* var. of ALKY.

†alkin *a.* Long *dial.* ME–L19. [f. genit. of ALL + genit. of KIN *n.* & *a.*, orig. as prenominal phr., later treated as adj.] Of every kind; every kind of.

alkine *n.* see ALKYNE.

Alkoran *n.* var. of ALCORAN.

alkoxide /alˈkɒksʌɪd/ *n.* L19. [f. ALKOXY- + -IDE.] *Chem.* A salt or simple compound containing an alkoxyl radical.

alkoxy- /alˈkɒksi/ *comb. form.* Also as attrib. adj. **alkoxy**. L19. [f. ALKALI + OXY-.] Used to denote the presence of an alkoxyl group.

alkoxyl /alˈkɒksʌɪl, -sɪl/ *n.* L19. [f. as prec. + -YL.] The radical RO· derived from an organic alcohol. Usu. in *comb.*

alky /ˈalki/ *n.* *slang*. Also **alkie**. M19. [Abbrev.: see -Y[6], -IE.] **1** = ALCOHOL. M19. **2** = ALCOHOLIC *n.* M20.

alkyd /ˈalkɪd/ *n.* E20. [f. ALKYL + ACID *n.*] *Chem.* Any of a class of synthetic polyester resins. Usu. more fully *alkyd resin* etc.

alkyl /ˈalkʌɪl, -kɪl/ *n.* L19. [G, f. *Alkohol* ALCOHOL: see -YL.] *Chem.* Any radical derived from an alkane by removal of a hydrogen atom; a compound of a metal, e.g. lead, with a number of such radicals. Freq. in *comb.*
alkylate *v.t.* introduce an alkyl radical into (a compound) L19. **alkyˈlation** *n.* E20.

alkyne /ˈalkʌɪn/ *n.* Orig. **-ine**. E20. [f. ALKYL + -YNE.] *Chem.* Any of the series of unsaturated hydrocarbons containing one triple bond and having the general formula C_nH_{2n-2}, e.g. acetylene.

all /ɔːl/ *a.* (in mod. usage also classed as a *determiner*), *pron.*, *n.*, & *adv.* [OE *(e)all* = OFris. *al*, *ol*, OS, OHG *al* (Du. *al*, G *all*), ON *allr*, Goth. *als*.] **A** *adj.* **1** With *n.sing.* The whole amount, quantity, extent, or compass of. (Preceding the n. and any determiners (the def. article, †the indef. article, demonstratives, possessives, etc.) and other adjs.; following the head n. (always so with pers. prons. without adjunct); or with *be* (*arch. rare* with other vbs) following the vb.) OE. **2** With *n.pl.* The entire number of; the individual constituents of, without exception. (Positioned as for sense 1; after n. (though not pers. pron.) *poet.*; †preceding *we*.) OE. **3** With *n.sing.* Every. (Preceding the n. only.) Long *obs.* exc. as below. OE. **4** With *n.sing.* Any whatever. (In universally exclusive sentences or clauses; preceding the n. only.) LME. **5** With *n.sing.* The greatest possible. (Preceding the n. only.) L16.
1 AV *1 Pet.* 1:24 All flesh is as grasse. G. WASHINGTON All this looks very well on paper. LD MACAULAY All Devonshire had been gathered together to welcome him. K. MANSFIELD This all sounds very strenuous and serious. E. WAUGH All day the heat had been barely supportable. S. KAUFFMANN I still need all the love I can get. R. MILLAR But one desire—to give all my might to letters. A. AYCKBOURN It was all rather pathetic. *all day (long)*: see DAY *n.* *all night (long)*: see NIGHT *n.* *all that*: see THAT *demonstr. pron.* etc. *all the best*: see BEST *a.*, *n.*, & *adv.* *all the day (long)*: see DAY *n.* *all the night (long)*: see NIGHT *n.* *all the time*: see TIME *n.* *all the way*: see WAY *n.* *all the world and his wife*: see WORLD *n.* *for all the world*: see WORLD *n.* *get away from it all*: see GET *v.* *have seen it all before*: see SEE *v.* *of all the cheek* etc.: see OF *prep.* *to all* APPEARANCE(*s*). 2 AV *Isa.* 53:6 Alle we like sheepe haue gone astray. MILTON Hear all ye Angels. E. YOUNG All men think all men mortal, but themselves. G. CRABBE My senses fail not all. KEATS They are all here to-night. *Daily News* All you who mean to follow in the same old way. YEATS Come gather round me, players all. R. MILNER A fellow from the B.B.C. Symphony Orchestra, of all outfits. J. BOWEN Cast all lean one way. C. HAMPTON May all your troubles be lexicological ones. J. OSBORNE Do you want us to all go? R. MAUGHAM All three men were stone dead when you left? *all and singular*: see SINGULAR *a.* 2. *all comers*: see COMER 1. **All Fools' Day** 1 April, popularly appropriated to practising upon people's credulity. ALL FOURS. ALL HALLOWS. **all kinds** or **sorts of** many different kinds of. **All Saints' (Day)** 1 November, on which there is a general commemoration of the saints. **all-sorts** a miscellany, esp. of liquorice sweets. *all sorts of*: see *all kinds of* above. **All Souls' Day** 2 November, on which the Roman Catholic Church makes supplications on behalf of the dead. *all systems go*: see SYSTEM *n.* *at all costs*: see COST *n.*[2] *at all hours*: see HOUR *n.* *at all points*: see POINT *n.*[1] **be all things to all men** be able to please everybody. *fire* (or *function* etc.) *on all cylinders*: see CYLINDER 3. *of all others*: see OTHER *pron.* & *n.* *of all things*: see THING *n.*[1] *till all hours*: see HOUR *n.* *to all appearances*: see APPEARANCE. *you-all*: see YOU. 3 **all kind** or **manner of** = *all kinds of* (sense 2 above).

†**all thing** everything; also = ALL *adv.* I. See also ALKIN, and cf. *all-weather, work* in Comb. below. 4 LONGFELLOW Without all guile or Suspicion . . was he. C. FRY But by no right does this Briton Break in and ruffle them beyond all hope. J. ORTON If you run into trouble I shall deny all knowledge of you. 5 SHAKES. *Rich. III* I in all haste was sent.

B *pron.* & *n.* **I** *pron.* **1** As antecedent to a relative, in senses A.I, 2 (the earliest use as pron.); (freq.) the limit of what, the only thing(s) *that*. OE. **2** *pl.* All people; all persons concerned. OE. **3** *sing.* Everything; the totality. OE. **4** Distributed to each member or part of the whole: see phrases below. ME. **5** Foll. by *of*: every one of; the whole of; *colloq.* as much as. L16. **6** In games, of a score: for each side. M18.

1 SHAKES. *Timon* To have his pomp, and all what state compounds. D. D. EISENHOWER I call upon all who love freedom to stand with us now. DAY LEWIS All I can remember of it is that there was a fire lit in my bedroom and a too heavy eiderdown. B. BERMANGE We will do . . all that our means will allow. 2 P. BARNES The rest is drowned out as all start shouting angrily. *all aboard*: see ABOARD *adv.* I. *free-for-all*: see FREE *a.* 3 MILTON What though the field be lost? All is not lost. S. GRAY I assumed you were coming back, that's all. *above all*: see ABOVE *prep.* 6. *after all*: see AFTER *prep.* 7. **all but** *adv. phr.* everything short of, almost. **all in all** (*a*) *advb.* taken as a whole; (*b*) *pred.* of supreme importance. *all in the* or *a day's work*: see DAY *n. all told*: see TELL *v.* **at all** in any way, to any extent, on any occasion (usu. in neg., interrog., or hypothet. contexts). BE-ALL. **bugger, damn,** etc., **all** *coarse slang* absolutely nothing. *crown all*: see CROWN *v.*[1] 5. END-ALL. *first of all*: see FIRST. *for all it* or *one is worth*: see WORTH *a.* **for all (that)** notwithstanding (that) (with n. passing into adj., and *that* conj. into pron.). *for good and all*: see GOOD *n.* **in all** in total number. *in all but name*: see NAME *n. least of all*: see LEAST *a., n.,* & *adv. not at all*: see NOT *adv.* †**of all** most of all, beyond all. ONCE (*and*) *for all. the devil and all to do*: see DEVIL *n. warts and all*: see WART. See also WITHAL. 4 **all and each** *arch.*, **all and every, all and some** *arch.*, **all and sundry, one and all** all collectively and individually. 5 K. LAFFAN It's not all of us have the stuff of martyrdom. A. SHAFFER He wasn't at his cottage all of Saturday. M. TWAIN It must have been all of fifteen minutes . . of dull, homesick silence.

II *n.* **7** *The* (or *this*) whole system of things; the universe. L16. **8** (Usu. with possess. pron.) Everything that one has or that pertains to one; one's whole property, interest, energy, etc. Also in *pl.* in *pack up one's alls* (now *dial.*) [perh. an alt. of *awls*]. E17. **9** Whole being, entirety, totality. M17.

7 CARLYLE The wide circle of the All where God's Laws are not. 8 BURKE We are, as I think, fighting for our all. P. ROTH I gave my all to his cross-examination. **one's little all** the little that one has. 9 J. MASEFIELD Ah, but that ben't the all of love.

Other phrases: **and all** and everything or everyone else (*boots and all*: see BOOT *n.*[2]; *warts and all*: see WART *n.*).

C *adv.* **1** Modifying an adj. or adv. (phr.) (orig. the adj. separated from the n. phr. and app. referring to the predicate): wholly, completely; altogether, quite. OE. **b** *hyperbol.* Very. *colloq.* M20. †**2** Modifying a particle combined with a vb, esp. *to-*. Hence *all to*, *alto-* with other vbs: wholly, completely: OE–L17. **3** Modifying an adv. or prep. of place: in all directions, in every part, everywhere. ME. **4** Even *if*, even *though*. Also with conj. omitted, although. Long *obs.* exc. in ALBEIT (cf. also ALBE), ALTHOUGH. ME. **5** Just, merely, even. Passing into a mere intensive. *arch.* L16. **6** With advb. *the* and compar.: by that amount, to that extent. L16. **7** Modifying a vb: wholly, completely. *arch. rare.* E18.

1 DISRAELI His Royal Highness all smiles, and his Consort all diamonds. BROWNING All a-gog to have me trespass. JOYCE How, all of a sudden, she had broken out into a peal of laughter. E. O'NEILL She remains like this all during the scene. SCOTT FITZGERALD I'm all out of practice. T. FRISBY This place'll be all empty. **All Black** *colloq.* a member of the New Zealand international rugby union team; freq. in *pl. all ears*: see EAR *n.*[1] *all fingers and thumbs*: see FINGER *n.* **all for** *colloq.* entirely in favour of. ALL IN. *all in* or *of a tremble*: see TREMBLE *n.* I. *all of a* —: see OF *prep. all of a piece*: see PIECE *n.* **all one** quite the same, a matter of indifference (*to*), (*all* here passing into n.). ALL OUT. ALL RIGHT. *all square*: see SQUARE *a.* 6b. **all there** *colloq.* not deficient in intellect etc. *all the same*: see SAME *a., adv. all wool and a yard wide*: see WOOL *n.* **all yours** *colloq.* your responsibility. †*call all to naught*: see NAUGHT *pron.* & *n. go all unnecessary*: see UNNECESSARY *a.* I. *not all that* —: see NOT *adv.* **what something is all about**: its essential nature. b ALDOUS HUXLEY We will assume that the Indians have gone all hygienic. 3 *all along*: see ALONG *adv.* 7. ALL OVER. ALL ROUND. ALL UP. *walk all over*: see WALK *v.*[1] 5 SIR W. SCOTT He . . Gave them a chain of twelve marks' weight All as he lighted down. 6 V. WOOLF One liked Mr Ramsay all the better for thinking that if his little finger ached the whole world must come to an end. 7 P. J. BAILEY Gazing o'er thee, I all Forget the bounds of being.

Comb.: With n. in adj. sense (see sense A. above, ALLSPICE, etc.) and in advs. which were orig. n. phrs. (ALGATE, ALWAYS, etc.); also attrib., as *all-night, -time*, etc. With n. in sense 'of all, universal', as *all-creator, -destroyer, -father, -giver*, etc. With n. (usu. attrib.) in advb. sense 'wholly, altogether, made wholly of', as *all-male, -star, -wool*, etc. With adj. in advb. sense 'wholly, infinitely', as *all-beauteous, -holy, -merciful, -powerful*, etc. With adj. in sense 'representative of the whole of', as *all-Russian* etc. With pres. ppl a. as the obj. of vbl action, sometimes also w. the sense 'wholly, infinitely', as *all-absorbing, -encompassing, -judging, -pervading, -seeing*, etc. With pa. ppl a. in advb. sense 'wholly, completely', also 'by all', as *all-accomplished, -honoured, -praised*, etc. Hence w. corresp. and deriv. ns., as *all-alikeness, -inclusiveness, -pervadingness, -powerfulness, -sufficiency*, etc. Special combs., as **all-American** *a.* (*a*) representing the whole of, or only, America or the USA; (*b*) *colloq.* truly American; **all around** *a.* (*US*) = ALL ROUND *a.*; **all clear** a signal that danger or difficulty is over; **all-electric** *a.* using only electricity for heating and lighting; **all-fired** *a.* & *adv.* (*slang*, chiefly *US*) [euphem. for *hell-fired*] infernal(ly), extreme(ly); **all-firedly** *adv.* (*slang*, chiefly *US*) infernally, extremely; **allgood** = *Good King Henry* s.v. GOOD *a.*; **all hail** *int., n. phr.*, & (with hyphen) *v.* (*arch.*) (a greeting of, greet with the words) [I wish you] all health; **all-heal** (*a*) any of various plants having medicinal uses, esp. valerian, *Valeriana officinalis*; †(*b*) a panacea; †**all-hid** the game of hide-and-seek; **all-important** *a.* of vital importance; **all-in-one** *n.* & *a.* (a garment etc.) made in a single connected piece; **all-might** *arch.* omnipotence; **all-nighter** *colloq.* a task etc. that takes all night; **all-or-none** (or **-nothing**) **law** *Physiol.*: that the magnitudes of certain responses (esp. nerve impulses), once evoked, are independent of the strength of the stimuli; **all-points** *a.* & (without hyphen) *n.* (*N. Amer.*) (a request, bulletin, etc., esp. for the apprehension of a wanted person) issued generally; **all-pro** *a.* & *n.* (*a*) *adj.* designating or pertaining to either of two nominated American football teams made up of the best players of the season; (*b*) *n.* a player nominated to an all-pro team; **all-purpose** *a.* with numerous uses; **all-red** *a.* (*Hist.*) entirely on British territory (usu. coloured red in maps); **allseed** any of a number of small plants producing much seed for their size, esp. *Polycarpon tetraphyllum*, of the pink family, and *Radiola linoides*, of the flax family; **all-weather** *a.* suitable for use whatever the weather; **allwhere(s)** *arch.* everywhere; **all work** work, esp. domestic work, of all kinds; *maid of all work*: see MAID *n.*

allness *n.* universality M17.

alla breve /alə 'breɪvi, *foreign* alla 'brɛve/ *adv., a.,* & *n., phr.* M18. [It. = according to the breve.] *Mus.* With increased speed, at two minim beats in a bar instead of four crotchets; such a tempo or time signature.

alla cappella /ˌalə kə'pɛlə/ *adv.* & *a. phr.* M18. [It.] = A CAPPELLA.

Allah /'alə, ə'lɑː/ *n.* L16. [Arab. *'allāh* prob. contr. of *al-'ilāh* the god, f. *al* AL-[2] + *'ilāh* god.] The name of God among Arabs and Muslims.

alla marcia /ˌalə 'mɑːtʃə/ *adv., a.,* & *n. phr.* L19. [It.] *Mus.* (A piece, movement, etc.) in the style of a march.

†**allanerly** *adv.* & *a.* var. of ALLENARLY.

allanite /'alənʌɪt/ *n.* E19. [f. T. *Allan* (1777–1833), Sc. mineralogist + -ITE[1].] *Min.* A brownish-black monoclinic mineral of the epidote group containing rare-earth metals, aluminium, and iron.

allantoid /ə'lantɔɪd/ *a.* & *n.* M17. [Gk *allantoeidēs* (Galen), f. *allant-*, *allas* sausage (named from its form in a calf): see -OID.] *Anat.* (Of or pertaining to) the allantois.

allantoin /ə'lantəʊɪn/ *n.* M19. [f. next + -IN[1]: it was discovered in the allantoic fluid of cows.] *Chem.* A crystalline base formed in the nitrogen metabolism of many mammals (excluding primates); 5-ureidohydantoin, $C_4H_6N_4O_3$.

allantois /ə'lantəʊɪs/ *n.* Pl. **-toides** /-təʊɪdiːz/. M17. [mod.L, spurious form evolved from *allantoides* ALLANTOID.] *Anat.* The foetal membrane lying beneath the chorion in mammals, birds, and reptiles.

allan'toic *a.* of or pertaining to the allantois M19.

allargando /alɑː'gandəʊ/ *adv., a.,* & *n.* L19. [It. = broadening.] *Mus.* **A** *adv.* & *adj.* (A direction:) getting slower and slower and often also fuller in tone. L19. **B** *n.* Pl. **-di** /-di/, **-dos**. A passage (to be) so played. M20.

allative /'alətɪv/ *a.* & *n.* M19. [f. L *allat-* pa. ppl stem of *afferre* bring to, f. *ad* AF- + *ferre* carry + -IVE.] *Gram.* **A** *adj.* Designating, being in, or pertaining to a case in Finnish and other languages denoting motion to or towards. M19. **B** *n.* *The* allative case; a word, form, etc., in the allative case. E20.

†**allay** *n.*[1] ME. [ONFr. *aley*, *alai*, f. as ALLAY *v.*[2]] **1** = ALLOY *n.* I. ME–E19. **2** = ALLOY *n.* II. L16–L18.

1 LD BERNERS Money . . of the same forme and alay as is in Paris. BACON Mixture of Falshood, is like Allay in Coyne of Gold and Siluer. T. D'URFEY Those that know finest metal say, No Gold will coin without Allay. 2 CLARENDON The Committee . . prepared other Votes of a brighter allay. F. BURNEY Good-nature gives pleasure without any allay.

†**allay** *n.*[2] LME. [f. ALLAY *v.*[1], infl. by prec.] **1** Dilution. LME–M17. **2** Abatement, tempering of the force of something. LME–M18. **3** Repression, hindrance. M17–E18. **4** Alleviation. Only in M19.

allay /ə'leɪ/ *v.*[1] [OE *alecġan*, f. A-[1] + LAY *v.*[1]; = OHG *irleggen* (G *erlegen*), Goth. *uslagjan*. The sense-development has been infl. by formal identity w. (in ME) ALLEGE *v.*[1], *v.*[2] and w. ALLAY *v.*[2]] **I** *v.t.* †**1** Lay down, lay aside; annul, abolish; abandon. OE–LME. †**2** Bring low (a person). OE–LME. †**3** Put down, quash, (a principle, personal attribute, etc.). OE–M17. **4** Quell (a disturbance, a strong feeling, etc.), appease. ME. **5** Diminish, weaken, mitigate. ME. **6** Assuage, relieve, alleviate. LME. †**7** Temper (iron, steel, etc.). LME–L15. †**8** Dilute. LME–E19. **9** Make less severe (wind, hot weather, etc.); cause (water, a storm, dust, etc.) to subside. L15. **10** Temper or abate (a pleasure, advantage) by the association of something unpleasant. E16.

4 P. GALLICO Had insisted they follow the usual tourist route to allay suspicion. 5 CHESTERFIELD Neither envy, indignation, nor ridicule, will obstruct or allay the applause which you may really deserve. 6 P. G. WODEHOUSE A secret sorrow which the spectacle of Judson did nothing to allay. W. GOLDING The water did not satisfy thirst so much as allay it. 9 SHAKES. *Temp.* If by your art . . you have Put the wild waters in this roar, allay them. M. LOWRY The street where no one had allayed the dust. 10 S. JOHNSON Benefits are allayed by reproaches.

II *v.i.* †**11** Subside, abate, become mild. E16–E18.

allayer *n.* E17.

†**allay** *v.*[2] LME. [ONFr. var. of OFr. *al(e)ier* ALLY *v.*] **1** = ALLOY *v.* 2. LME–L18. **2** = ALLOY *v.* 3. LME–M18. **3** = ALLOY *v.* I: completely identified w. ALLAY *v.*[1] LME.

†**allayment** *n.* (*rare*, Shakes.) admixture: only in E17.

allay /ə'leɪ/ *v.*[3]*t.* Long *arch.* Also †**alay**. L15. [Origin unkn.] Carve (a pheasant).

allective /ə'lɛktɪv/ *n.* & *a.* Now *rare* or *obs.* LME. [med.L *allectivus*, f. *allect-* pa. ppl stem of *allicere* allure: see -IVE.] (Something) alluring or enticing.

allée /ale/ *n.* Pl. pronounced same. M18. [Fr.: see ALLEY *n.*[1]] = ALLEY *n.*[1] 2.

allegate /'alɪgeɪt/ *v.* LME. [Sense 1 f. L *allegat-* pa. ppl stem of *allegare* allege: see -ATE[3]; sense 2 back-form. f. next.] †**1** *v.t.* = ALLEGE *v.*[1] LME–M17. **2** *v.i.* Argue; make allegations against each other. *Anglo-Ir.* L19.

allegator *n.* (*rare*) L17.

allegation /alɪˈgeɪʃ(ə)n/ *n.* LME. [(O)Fr. *allégation* or L *allegatio(n-)*, f. as prec.: see -ATION.] 1 The action of making a charge before a legal tribunal; a charge so made. LME. †2 An excuse, a plea, an alleged reason. LME–E17. 3 An assertion, *esp.* one made without proof. M16. †4 The action of citing an author or document; a quotation. M16–L17.

allege /əˈlɛdʒ/ *v.*[1]*t.* ME. [AN *alegier* = OFr. *esligier* (see A-[7]), ult. f. L EX-[1] + *lit-*, *lis* lawsuit; conf. in sense w. L *allegare*.] 1 Declare upon oath at a tribunal; bring forward as a legal ground or plea. *obs.* exc. as passing into senses 2 and 4. ME. 2 Affirm, assert, esp. without proof. ME. 3 Cite, quote, (*for* or *against*). *arch.* LME. 4 Advance as an argument or excuse. LME.

1 T. CROMWELL I have no merits or good works which I may alledge before thee. STEELE The Prosecutor alledged, That he was the Cadet of a very ancient Family. 2 GIBBON Where much is alleged, something must be true. G. B. SHAW It is simply unscientific to allege or believe that doctors do not under existing circumstances perform unnecessary operations. J. ORTON He is alleged to have misconducted himself with a party of schoolchildren. 3 MILTON With what face or conscience can they alleage Moses . . for tithes? 4 GOLDSMITH Refused to lend a farthing, alledging a former resolution against lending. J. R. SEELEY England would give nothing beyond arms and ammunition, alleging that her Spanish enterprise occupied her wholly.

allegeable *a.* M16. †**allegeance** *n.* = ALLEGATION 1 LME–E18. **alleged** *ppl a.* (*a*) *arch.* cited, quoted; (*b*) asserted as provable, asserted but not proved; (*c*) adduced as a legal ground, or as an excuse: LME. **allegedly** /-dʒɪdli/ *adv.* (used esp. in statements for which the author disclaims responsibility) L19. **allegement** *n.* the act of alleging, an allegation E16. **alleger** *n.* L16.

†**allege** *v.*[2]*t.* ME. [OFr. *alegier* f. late L *alleviare*: see ALLEVIATE.] 1 Lighten (a person) *of* a burden. ME–L15. 2 Lighten (something); alleviate, diminish, (a burden, grief, pain); abate, repress. (Replaced by ALLAY *v.*[1], some parts of the two vbs being formally identical in ME.) ME–L16.

2 SPENSER The joyous time now nigheth fast, That shall alegge this bitter blast.

allegiance /əˈliːdʒ(ə)ns/ *n.* LME. [AN var. of OFr. *ligeance* (f. as LIEGE), perh. due to assoc. w. AL *alligantia* alliance.] †1 The status of a liege lord. Only in LME. 2 The relation or duty of a liegeman to his liege lord; the tie or obligation of a subject to his or her monarch or government. LME. 3 Loyalty; the recognition of the claims which someone or something has to respect or duty. M18.

2 *oath of allegiance*: see OATH *n.*

allegiancy *n.* L16. **allegiant** *a.* & *n.* (*a*) *adj.* giving allegiance, loyal; (*b*) *n.* a person who owes or gives allegiance: M16.

allegoric /alɪˈgɒrɪk/ *a.* LME. [Late L *allegoricus* f. Gk *allēgorikos*: see ALLEGORY, -IC.] = ALLEGORICAL (which is now more usual).

allegorical /alɪˈgɒrɪk(ə)l/ *a.* E16. [f. prec. + -AL[1].] Of or pertaining to allegory; of the nature of an allegory; consisting of or containing an allegory.

allegorically *adv.* M16.

allegorise *v.* var. of ALLEGORIZE.

allegorist /ˈalɪg(ə)rɪst/ *n.* L17. [Fr. *allégoriste* f. Gk *allēgoristēs*: see ALLEGORY, -IST.] A person who constructs allegories, or writes allegorically; occas., a person who expounds allegorically.

allegorism *n.* the use of allegory, allegorical interpretation L19.

allegorize /ˈalɪg(ə)rʌɪz/ *v.* Also **-ise**. LME. [Late L *allegorizare*, f. *allegoria*: see ALLEGORY, -IZE. Cf. Fr. *allégoriser*.] †1 *v.t.* Interpret allegorically. Only in LME. 2 *v.i.* Give allegorical explanations, expound allegorically; also, construct allegories. L16. 3 *v.t.* Make or treat as allegorical; turn into, or explain as, an allegory. L16.

allegoriˈzation *n.* M19. **allegorizer** *n.* L17.

allegory /ˈalɪg(ə)ri/ *n.* LME. [(O)Fr. *allégorie* f. L *allegoria* f. Gk *allēgoria*, f. *allos* other + *-agoria* speaking.] 1 Narrative description of a subject under the guise of another having points of correspondence with it; symbolic representation. LME. 2 An instance of such description; an extended or continued metaphor. M16. 3 An emblem; a picture in which meaning is symbolically represented. M17.

allégresse /alegrɛs, alɪˈgrɛs/ *n.* Now *rare.* M17. [Fr.] Gaiety, sprightliness.

allegretto /alɪˈgrɛtəʊ/ *adv.*, *a.*, & *n.* M18. [It., dim. of ALLEGRO.] *Mus.* A *adv.* & *adj.* (A direction:) in fairly quick time, but not as quick(ly) as allegro. M18. B *n.* Pl. **-ttos**, **-tti** /-ti/. A movement or piece in fairly quick time. Also, a short movement or piece in quick time. L19.

allegro /əˈleɪgrəʊ, -ˈlɛg-/ *adv.*, *a.*, & *n.* L17. [It. = lively, gay.] *Mus.* A *adv.* & *adj.* (A direction:) in quick time; *transf.* (of forms of words and phrases) used in speech and shortened (e.g. *we'll* for *we will*). L17. B *n.* Pl. **-gros**, **-gri** /-griː/. A movement or piece in quick time. M18.

allele /ˈaliːl/ *n.* M20. [G *Allel* abbrev. of next.] *Biol.* Any of a number of alternative forms of one gene.

aˈllelic *a.* of, pertaining to, or of the nature of an allele M20. **aˈllelism** *n.* the occurrence of, or relationship between, alleles M20.

allelomorph /əˈliːləʊmɔːf/ *n.* E20. [f. Gk *allēl-* one another + -O- + -MORPH.] *Biol.* = ALLELE.

alleloˈmorphic *a.* E20. **alleloˈmorphism** *n.* E20.

alleluia /alɪˈluːjə/ *int.* & *n.* Also **-uya**. OE. [eccl.L f. (Septuagint) Gk *allēlouia* f. as HALLELUJAH.] A *int.* Praise the Lord (occurring in many psalms and hymns). OE. B *n.* 1 *Eccl.* A liturgical chant consisting of or containing the word 'Alleluia'; *spec.* (usu. **A-**) the one that follows the Gradual in the Eucharist. ME. 2 Wood sorrel (in allusion to its flowering between Easter and Whitsun). LME. 3 A song of praise to God. L16.

alleluˈiatic *a.* M19.

allemande /ˈalmɑːnd; almɑ̃d (*pl. same*)/ *n.* M17. [Fr. = German (fem.): see ALMAIN.] †1 (**A-**.) A German woman. *rare.* Only in M17. 2 A piece of music for a German dance or in its rhythm, *esp.* one which forms a movement of a suite. L17. 3 Any of various German dances. E18. b A figure in square dancing in which adjacent dancers link arms or join hands and make a full or partial turn. Also used as a call to dancers to execute this figure turning in the specified direction. E19.

Allemanic, **Allemannic** *adjs.* & *ns.* vars. of ALEMANNIC.

Allen /ˈalən/ *n.* M20. [The *Allen* Manufacturing Co., Hartford, Connecticut, US.] *Allen screw*, (proprietary name for) a screw which has a head furnished with a hexagonal recess and can be turned by means of an *Allen key*, *wrench*, etc., of corresponding cross-section.

allenarly /əˈlɛnəli/ *adv.* & *a. north.* (*obs.*) & *Sc.* Also **-an-**. ME. [f. ALL *adv.* + as ANERLY.] A *adv.* Solitarily, alone; solely, merely. ME. B *adj.* †1 Only, sole. Only in 16. 2 Alone, lonely. *rare.* E20.

allene /ˈaliːn/ *n.* L19. [f. ALLYLENE.] *Chem.* A gaseous hydrocarbon, propadiene, $CH_2{:}C{:}CH_2$. Also, any derivative of this with two adjacent double bonds.

allergen /ˈalədʒ(ə)n/ *n.* E20. [f. as next + -GEN.] *Med.* A substance which produces an allergic reaction.

allerˈgenic *a.* producing an allergic reaction E20.

allergic /əˈləːdʒɪk/ *a.* E20. [f. next + -IC.] 1 Pertaining to, characterized by, or suffering from allergy. E20. 2 *fig.* Antipathetic. M20.

1 G. DURRELL He was only allergic to . . the pollen of the lilac flowers, cats, and horses. 2 S. HEANEY Allergic equally to Pearse and Pope.

allergy /ˈalədʒi/ *n.* E20. [G *Allergie*, f. Gk *allos* other, different, after *Energie* ENERGY.] 1 *Med.* Altered reactivity of the body towards an antigen; *esp.* hypersensitivity towards a particular foreign substance such as a type of food, pollen, or micro-organism. E20. 2 *fig.* Antipathy. M20.

allergist *n.* a specialist in the field of allergy M20.

allerion *n.* var. of ALERION.

allers *adv.* see ALLUS.

alleviate /əˈliːvɪeɪt/ *v.t.* Pa. pple & ppl a. **-ated**, †**-ate**. LME. [Late L *alleviat-* pa. ppl stem of *alleviare* lighten, f. L *allevare*, f. *ad* AL-[1] + *levare* raise, infl. by *levis* light: see -ATE[3].] 1 Make less burdensome or severe; relieve, mitigate. LME. †2 Diminish the weight of. L15–M17. †3 Extenuate (an offence). L17–L18.

alleviative *a.* & *n.* (*rare*) (something) tending to alleviate L16. **alleviator** *n.* a person who or thing which alleviates M17. **alleviatory** *a.* of an alleviating nature or tendency M19.

alleviation /əliːvɪˈeɪʃ(ə)n/ *n.* LME. [OFr., or med.L *alleviatio(n-)*, f. as prec.: see -ATION.] The action of lightening weight, gravity, severity, or pain; relief, mitigation.

alley /ˈali/ *n.*[1] LME. [OFr. *alee* (mod. ALLÉE) walking, passage, f. *aler* (mod. *aller*) go f. L *ambulare* to walk.] †1 A passageway in or into a house. LME–E17. 2 A walk or passage in a garden, park, etc., usu. bordered by trees or bushes; an avenue. LME. 3 A passage between buildings; a narrow street, a lane. LME. b A back-lane running parallel with a main street. *US.* E18. 4 A passage between the rows of pews or seats in a church (= AISLE 3). Now *dial.* LME. 5 An enclosure for skittles, bowling, etc. L15. 6 A passage or free space between two lines of any kind. M18.

3 *blind alley*: see BLIND *a.* **up one's alley** *colloq.* = (*right*) *up one's street* s.v. STREET *n.*

Comb.: **alley cat** (chiefly *N. Amer.*) a stray town cat; **alleyway** a narrow passage.

alleyed *a.* laid out as an alley, or with alleys LME.

alley *n.*[2] see ALLY *n.*[2]

alley-oop /alɪˈuːp/ *int.*, *n.*, & *a. colloq.* Also **allez-**. E20. [Origin uncertain: perh. f. Fr. *allez* (imper.) go on! come on! + repr. of a supposedly Fr. pronunc. of UP *advs.*] A *int.* Encouraging or drawing attention to the performance of some physical, esp. acrobatic, feat. E20. B *n.* & *a. US Sports.* (Designating) a high lob or pass caught by a leaping teammate, or a score made by the catcher of such a pass. M20.

all fours /ɔːl ˈfɔːz/ *n. phr.* Sense 1 also †**four**. L15. [f. ALL *a.* + FOUR, sense 1 *sc.* limbs etc., sense 2 *sc.* points.] 1 All four limbs (the legs of a quadruped, the arms and legs of a human etc.). L15. 2 A game of cards, called after the winning four points ('high', 'low', 'Jack', and 'the game'). L17.

1 **on all fours** (*a*) *esp.* on hands and knees; (*b*) *fig.* even *with*, completely analogous or corresponding.

All Hallows /ɔːl ˈhaləʊz/ *n. phr. arch.* Also **Hallow**. OE. [f. ALL *a.* + HALLOW *n.*[1] + -S[1].] 1 All saints; the saints in heaven collectively. OE. 2 *ellipt.* (Now freq. with hyphen.) All Hallows' Day or Allhallowmass. LME.

Comb.: **All Hallow Eve** the eve of All Saints (= HALLOWE'EN); **Allhallowmass** the feast of All Saints; †**All-hallown summer** (*rare*, Shakes.) a season of fine weather in the autumn, an Indian summer; **All Hallows' Day** All Saints' Day, 1 November; **Allhallowtide** the season of All Saints.

alliable /əˈlʌɪəb(ə)l/ *a.* L16. [f. ALLY *v.* + -ABLE. Cf. Fr. *alliable*.] Able to be allied; able to enter into alliance or union.

alliaceous /alɪˈeɪʃəs/ *a.* L18. [f. ALLI(UM + -ACEOUS.] Characteristic of or resembling garlic.

alliance /əˈlʌɪəns/ *n.* & *v.* ME. [OFr. *aliance* (mod. *all-*), f. as ALLY *v.*: see -ANCE.] A *n.* 1 A union by marriage; kinship, consanguinity. ME. 2 Combination in pursuit of common interests, esp. by sovereign States or political groups; a league, an association. ME. 3 Community in nature or qualities; affinity; a group of related things. LME. †4 *collect.* People united by kinship or friendship. LME–M17. †5 A kinsman, a kinswoman; an ally. LME–L18. 6 *Ecol.* A group of closely related plant associations. M20.

1 M. LASKI The ladies settled the details of the coming alliance between their two families. 2 G. ORWELL We were not at war with Eastasia at all. We were in alliance with them. W. S. CHURCHILL An alliance of the four Great Powers already existed. *Holy Alliance*: see HOLY *a.* **the Alliance** (**Party**): *spec.* (*a*) of Roman Catholic and Protestant moderates in Northern Ireland; (*b*) of the British Liberal and Social

Democratic Parties. *triple alliance*: see TRIPLE *a.* & *adv.* *unholy alliance*: see UNHOLY *a.* I. 3 T. SHERLOCK Corrupt Principles . . have no Alliance with Reason. J. LINDLEY Classes, sub-classes, groups, alliances, and orders.

B *v.t.* & *i.* Join in alliance, ally. *rare.* M16.

allice *n.* var. of ALLIS.

allicholly /'alɪkəli/ *n.* *joc.* L16. [Alt.] Melancholy.

¶ First recorded in Shakes.

allicient /ə'lɪʃɪənt/ *a.* & *n.* *rare.* E17. [L *allicient-* pres. ppl stem of *allicere* entice to: see -ENT.] (A thing) that attracts.

alliciency *n.* (long *rare* or *obs.*) attractive power M17.

†**allidatha** *n.* var. of ALIDADE.

allied /ə'lʌɪd, *esp. attrib.* 'alʌɪd/ *ppl a.* ME. [f. ALLY *v.* + -ED[1].] 1 United, joined, esp. by marriage or kindred or by league or formal treaty; of or pertaining to allied forces or States; *spec.* (usu. **A-**) of or pertaining to the Allies in the wars of 1914–18, 1939–45, and later. ME. 2 Connected by nature or qualities; having affinity. LME.

1 LD MACAULAY A German Princess nearly allied to the Imperial House. P. FUSSELL Allied troops landed on the beach at Salerno in September, 1943. 2 DRYDEN Great wits are sure to madness near allied. C. HAMPTON Literature and the allied arts.

alligation /alɪ'geɪʃ(ə)n/ *n.* Now *rare* or *obs.* M16. [L *alligatio(n-)*, f. *alligat-* pa. ppl stem of *alligare* bind to: see -ATION.] 1 The action of attaching; the state of being attached. M16. †2 *Math.* The arithmetical solution of problems concerning the mixing of different things. M16–M19.

alligator /'alɪgeɪtə/ *n.* L16. [Sp. *el lagarto* the lizard, prob. ult. f. L *lacerta* LIZARD. Cf. LAGARTO.] 1 Either of two crocodilians of the genus *Alligator*, the American *A. mississippiensis*, and *A. sinensis*, native to China. Also *loosely*, any New World crocodilian; (by confusion) a crocodile. L16. 2 Alligator skin. Freq. *attrib.* L19.

Comb.: **alligator clip** = *crocodile clip* s.v. CROCODILE *n.*; **alligator gar** a large holostean freshwater fish of the southern US, *Lepisosteus spatula*; **alligator pear** *N. Amer.* = AVOCADO; **alligator snapper, snapping turtle, tortoise**, etc., a large freshwater snapping turtle, *Macroclemys temmincki*, native to the region of the Gulf of Mexico; **alligator weed** an ornamental aquatic plant, *Alternanthera philoxeroides*, native to S. America and introduced elsewhere.

alligatoring *n.* (the development of) intersecting cracks in paint, varnish, etc., caused by contraction E20.

all in /ɔːl 'ɪn/ *a. phr.* Also **all-in.** L19. [Sense 1 f. ALL *n.*, sense 2 f. ALL *adv.*, + IN *adv.*] 1 *attrib.* (With hyphen.) Inclusive of all; *Wrestling* with few or no restrictions. L19. 2 *pred.* (Without hyphen.) a Tired out. *colloq.* E20. b Completely or wholeheartedly involved. E20.

allis /'alɪs/ *n.* Also **-ice,** †**alose.** L16. [(O)Fr. *alose* f. late L *alausa* (Ausonius), a small fish in the Moselle.] An anadromous European fish of the herring family, *Alosa alosa*. Now usu. more fully *allis shad*.

allision /ə'lɪʒ(ə)n/ *n.* M17. [Late L *allisio(n-)*, f. *allis-* pa. ppl stem of *allido* dash against: see -ION.] The action of dashing against or striking with violence upon something; now only of one ship upon another stationary ship.

alliterate /ə'lɪtəreɪt/ *v.* L18. [Back-form. f. next: see -ATE[3].] 1 *v.t.* Compose with alliteration. Chiefly as *alliterated* ppl a. L18. 2 *v.i.* Of a word or words: manifest or produce alliteration. E19. 3 *v.i.* Use alliteration, compose alliteratively. E19.

alliterator *n.* (*rare*) a person who uses alliteration M18.

alliteration /əlɪtə'reɪʃ(ə)n/ *n.* E17. [med.L *alliteratio(n-)*, f. L *ad* AL-[1] + *littera* letter + -ATION.] 1 *gen.* The commencement of adjacent or closely connected words with the same sound or letter. E17. 2 As a principle of versification: in Old and Middle English and other Germanic poetry, the commencement of certain accented syllables of a verse with the same consonant or consonantal group, or with any vowel sounds; in some Celtic poetry also, commencement with consonants related by mutation. L18.

2 *transverse alliteration*: see TRANSVERSE *a.*

†**alliteral** *a.* = ALLITERATIVE, as applied to Xhosa languages M19–E20. **alliterational** *a.* (*rare*) = ALLITERATIVE M19.

alliterative /ə'lɪt(ə)rətɪv/ *a.* M18. [f. ALLITERATE *v.* + -IVE.] Pertaining to or marked by alliteration.

alliteratively *adv.* E19. **alliterativeness** *n.* (*rare*) E19.

allium /'alɪəm/ *n.* E19. [L = garlic.] A plant of the genus *Allium*, such as garlic, leek, onion, etc.

allo- /'aləʊ/ *comb. form.* [Gk, f. *allos* other, different: see -O-.] Forming wds w. the sense 'other, different'; *spec.* in *Genetics*, used in comb. w. -PLOID (and also *-ploidy*) to refer to hybrid individuals whose chromosome sets are derived from different species (cf. AUTO-[1]), as *allodiploid*, *allopolyploid*, etc.

alloantibody *n.* (*Immunol.*) = ISOANTIBODY M20. **alloantigen** *n.* (*Immunol.*) = ISOANTIGEN M20. **allo'centric** *a.* centred in external objects, interested in objects for themselves E20. **a'llogamy** *n.* (*Bot.*) cross-fertilization L19. **allograft** *n.* & *v.t.* (*Med.*) (a) graft between genetically dissimilar individuals of the same species M20. **allo'patric** *a.* [Gk *patra* fatherland] (*Biol.*) (of species, speciation, etc.) occurring in different areas; not overlapping in distribution: M20. **allo'patrically** *adv.* (*Biol*) by means of allopatric speciation; in physical isolation: M20. **a'llopatry** *n.* (*Biol.*) allopatric speciation; the occurrence of allopatric forms: M20. **allo'purinol** *n.* [PURINE, -OL] *Pharm.* a synthetic purine which inhibits uric acid formation in the body and is used to treat gout and related conditions M20. **allo'steric** *a.* (*Biochem.*) of, pertaining to, or characterized by the alteration of the activity of an enzyme by means of a conformational change induced by a different molecule M20. **allosterically** *adv.* (*Biochem.*) in an allosteric manner M20. **allostery** *n.* (*Biochem.*) allosteric behaviour M20. **allo'tetraploid** *a.* & *n.* (*Genetics*) (designating) an individual with two diploid sets of chromosomes, each from different species M20. **allo'tetraploidy** *n.* (*Genetics*) the condition of being allotetraploid M20.

†**allocate** *ppl a.* & *pa. pple. Sc.* M16–M18. [f. as next: see -ATE[2].] Allocated, allotted, assigned.

allocate /'aləkeɪt/ *v.t.* M16. [med.L *allocat-* pa. ppl stem of *allocare*, f. L *ad* AL-[1] + *locare* LOCATE: see -ATE[3].] †1 Allow (an item) in an account; authorize payment for. M–L16. 2 Assign, allot, devote, (*to* a person as a special share, responsibility, etc.; *to* a special purpose). M17. 3 Assign to a place. *rare.* M19. 4 Fix the locality of. *rare.* L19.

2 DE QUINCEY That very sum which the Manchester Grammar School allocated to every student. H. R. F. KEATING Determined not to allocate men of the Bombay police to any duties at the mere whim of this Rajah.

allocable *a.* able to be allocated E20. **allocator** *n.* M20.

allocation /alə'keɪʃ(ə)n/ *n.* LME. [med.L *allocatio(n-)*, f. as prec.; later f. Fr. or f. prec.: see -ATION.] †1 Authorization. Only in LME. †2 A contribution levied on revenue etc. for a specific purpose. M16–M17. 3 The action of allowing an item in an account; an item so allowed. Now *rare* or *obs.* M17. 4 The action of adding one thing to another. *arch.* M17. 5 The action of apportioning or assigning to a special person or purpose; allotment; a portion so allocated. M19. 6 Fixing in position; placing; arrangement. M19.

5 J. K. GALBRAITH Military considerations have induced a large allocation of resources to research. *Times* Allocations will be based on the actual sales made by the butchers.

allochthonous /ə'lɒkθənəs/ *a.* E20. [f. G *allochthon*, f. as ALLO- + Gk *khthōn*, *khthonos* earth, soil: see -OUS.] *Geol.* Consisting of or formed from transported material originally accumulated elsewhere; not formed *in situ*.

allochthon *n.* an allochthonous rock formation M20.

allocution /alə'kjuːʃ(ə)n/ *n.* Also †**adl-.** E17. [L *allocutio(n-)*, f. *allocut-* pa. ppl stem of *alloqui* address, f. *ad* AL-[1] + *loqui* speak: see -ION.] 1 A formal or hortatory address. E17. b *spec. Rom. Hist.* An address or exhortation by a general to his soldiers. L17. †2 An instance of being addressed or spoken to. M17–L18.

allod /'alɒd/ *n.* Also **alod.** L17. [f. as ALLODIUM.] = ALLODIUM.

†**allodge** *v.t.* & *i.* ME–E17. [OFr. *alogier*, f. as A-[5] + LODGE *v.*] Lodge; pitch (a tent, camp, etc.).

†**allodgement** *n.* [after It. *allogiamento* (now *-gg-*)] lodging; in *pl.*, soldiers' quarters: L16–M18.

allodial /ə'ləʊdɪəl/ *a.* & *n.* Also **alod-.** M17. [med.L *al(l)odialis*, f. as next: see -AL[1].] *Hist.* A *adj.* 1 Of an estate etc.: held in absolute ownership. M17. 2 Of or pertaining to the absolute ownership of land. M18. 3 Owning an allodium. M19. B *n.* 1 In *pl.* Allodial lands. L17. 2 = ALLODIALIST. *rare.* L18.

allodialism *n.* the allodial system of land tenure M19. **allodialist** *n.* an allodial proprietor E19. **allodially** *adv.* by allodial tenure L18.

allodium /ə'ləʊdɪəm/ *n.* Also **alod-.** E17. [med.L *al(l)odium* (Domesday Book), f. Frank., f. as ALL + *ōd* estate, wealth.] *Hist.* An estate held in absolute ownership, without acknowledgement to a superior.

allodiary *n.* = ALLODIALIST L19. **allodifi'cation** *n.* conversion to allodialism L19.

allogeneic /ˌalə(ʊ)dʒə'niːɪk, -'neɪɪk/ *a.* M20. [f. ALLO- + Gk *genea* race, stock + -IC.] *Immunol.* Genetically dissimilar, and hence immunologically incompatible, although belonging to (individuals of) the same species. Also, involving tissue of this nature.

allogeneous /alə'dʒiːnɪəs/ *a.* *rare.* Also **allogenous** /ə'lɒdʒɪnəs/. M19. [f. Gk *allogenēs*, f. as ALLO- + *genos* kind, + -OUS.] Diverse in kind; of a different kind, race, etc.

allogeneity /-dʒə'niːɪti/ *n.* (*rare*) difference of nature E19.

allogenic /alə'dʒɛnɪk/ *a.* L19. [f. ALLO- + -GENIC.] 1 *Geol.* Originating elsewhere (applied esp. to a river or the sediment a river carries). L19. 2 *Ecol.* Caused by external factors. M20.

allograph /'aləgrɑːf/ *n.* M20. [f. ALLO- + GRAPH(EME).] *Ling.* 1 Each of two or more alternative forms of a minimal distinctive unit of a writing system, as a letter of an alphabet. M20. 2 Either of two or more letters or letter-combinations representing a single phoneme in different words etc. M20.

allo'graphic *a.* M20.

allometry /ə'lɒmɪtri/ *n.* M20. [f. ALLO- + -METRY.] *Biol.* Growth of a part at a rate different from that of the body as a whole (or of some other standard). Cf. ISOMETRY 2.

allo'metric *a.* pertaining to or exhibiting allometry M20.

allomone /'aləməʊn/ *n.* M20. [f. ALLO- after PHEROMONE.] *Biol.* A chemical secreted and released by an organism which causes a specific response when detected by an organism of another species, *esp.* one that is to the advantage of the releasing organism (cf. KAIROMONE).

allomorph /'aləmɔːf/ *n.* M20. [f. ALLO- + MORPH(EME).] *Ling.* Each of two or more alternative forms of a morpheme.

allo'morphic *a.* M20.

allonge /ə'lɒndʒ; *foreign* alɔ̃ːʒ (*pl. same*)/ *n.* In sense 1 also †**elonge.** E18. [Fr. = lengthening, drawing out, f. *allonger*, f. *long* LONG *a.*[1]] 1 = LUNGE *n.*[2] 1. (Only in Dicts.) E18. 2 A slip of paper attached to the end of a bill of exchange etc. to give room for further endorsements. M19.

allopathy /ə'lɒpəθi/ *n.* M19. [f. ALLO- + -PATHY.] *Med.* The treatment of disease by inducing an opposite condition (i.e. in the usual way). Opp. HOMOEOPATHY.

'allopath, allopathist *ns.* a person who practises allopathy M19. **allo'pathic** *a.* of or pertaining to allopathy M19. **allo'pathically** *adv.* M19.

allophane /'aləfeɪn/ *n.* E19. [f. ALLO- + Gk *phainein* show, appear: the mineral loses its colour on heating.] *Min.* An amorphous, usu. pale blue, clay mineral consisting essentially of hydrated aluminium silicate.

allophone /'aləfəʊn/ *n.* M20. [f. ALLO- + PHONE(ME).] *Ling.* Each of two or more alternative sounds realizing a phoneme.

allophonic /aləˈfɒnɪk/ *a.*[1] *rare.* E20. [f. ALLO- + Gk *phōnē* voice + -IC.] Speaking with a different accent etc.

allophonic /aləˈfɒnɪk/ *a.*[2] M20. [f. ALLOPHONE + -IC.] *Ling.* Of or pertaining to an allophone or allophones.

allophylian /aləˈfɪlɪən/ *a.* & *n. arch.* M19. [f. L *allophylus* f. Gk *allophulos*, f. as ALLO- + *phulē* tribe, + -IAN.] Of or pertaining to languages, esp. in Europe or Asia, which are neither Indo-European nor Semitic; of or pertaining to, a member of, a people speaking any such language.

allot /əˈlɒt/ *v.* Infl. **-tt-**. L15. [OFr. *aloter* (mod. *allotir*), f. as A-[5] + *lot* LOT *n.*] **1** *v.t.* Distribute by lot; apportion authoritatively. L15. **2** *v.t.* Assign as a lot, appoint, *to* (without the idea of distribution); appropriate to a special purpose. M16. †**3** *v.t.* Make it the lot of (a person *to do*). L16–L17. †**4** *v.t.* Attribute as due or proper. L16–M18. **5** *v.i.* Determine *upon*, choose or intend *to*. *colloq.* (orig. *US*). E19.

1 GOLDSMITH I allotted to each of my family what they were to do. W. S. GILBERT See how the Fates their gifts allot, For A is happy—B is not. S. JOHNSON Ten years I will allot to the attainment of knowledge. 2 W. FAULKNER What the Lord has seen fit to allot you. C. S. LEWIS Three other officers and I were allotted a compartment. 3 SHAKES. *1 Hen. VI* Thou art allotted to be ta'en by me. 4 S. JOHNSON Scarce any man is willing to allot to accident, friendship, etc... the part that they may justly claim in his advancement. 5 D. STOREY Had allotted.. to go in for languages.

allottable *a.* M19. **alloˈttee** *n.* a person to whom an allotment is made M19. **allotter** *n.* a person who allots something M17. †**allottery** *n.* (*rare*, Shakes.) an allotted share: only in L16.

allotheism /alə(ʊ)ˈθiːɪz(ə)m/ *n.* M16. [f. ALLO- + THEISM *n.*[1]] The abnormal worship of other gods.

allotment /əˈlɒtm(ə)nt/ *n.* M16. [f. ALLOT + -MENT.] **1** a A share or portion of land assigned to a particular person or appropriated to a special purpose; *spec.* a small portion of usu. public land let out for cultivation. M16. b *gen.* A share allotted to someone. E17. **2** The action of allotting or assigning as a share; apportionment. L16. **3** One's lot in life. L17.

1a *attrib.*: DICKENS Certain allotment-gardens by the road-side. b W. BLACKSTONE The elder sons.. migrate from their father with a certain allotment of cattle. 2 R. GORDON Long voyages and young wives don't mix. You leave the allotment of your pay, [etc.]. 3 H. FIELDING No man is born into the world without his particular allotment.

allotmenˈteer *n.* a person who holds or rents an allotment of land E20.

allotrope /ˈalətrəʊp/ *n.* L19. [Back-form. f. next.] *Chem.* An allotropic form of a substance.

allotropy /əˈlɒtrəpi/ *n.* M19. [f. Gk *allotropos* of another form: see ALLO-, -TROPY.] *Chem.* The existence in the same state of more than one form of the same element with different properties.

alloˈtropic /-ˈtrəʊpɪk, -ˈtrɒpɪk/ *a.* pertaining to or displaying allotropy M19. **allotropism** *n.* = ALLOTROPY M19.

allotype /ˈalətʌɪp/ *n.* E20. [f. ALLO- + TYPE *n.*] **1** *Taxon.* A paratype of the opposite sex to the holotype. E20. **2** *Immunol.* An allotypic variant of a protein or antigen. M20.

alloˈtypic *a.* (*Immunol.*) of or pertaining to allotypes or allotypy M20. **allotypy** *n.* (*Immunol.*) the occurrence of an antibody or other protein in antigenically distinct forms in different individuals of a species M20.

all out /ɔːl ˈaʊt/ *adv. phr.* & *a.* Also **all-out**. ME. [f. ALL *adv.* + OUT *adv.*] **1** *adv.* Entirely, completely, quite. Now *arch.* & *dial.* ME. **2** *adv.* & (w. hyphen) *adj.* To the fullest extent of someone or something's strength, power, resources, etc.; at full speed. L19.

2 E. F. NORTON Irvine.. was willing.. to 'go all out', as he put it, in an utmost effort to reach the top. M. L. KING The time has come for an all-out world war against poverty.

all over /ɔːl ˈəʊvə/ *adv.* & *prep. phr.*, *a.*, & *n.* Also **all-over**, (as n.) **allover**. ME. [f. ALL *adv.* + OVER *adv.*, *prep.*] **A** *adv. phr.* †**1** To the full extent. Only in ME. **2** Over the whole extent; in every part; in or on one's whole body etc. LME. **3** In all respects; as regards characteristic attitude, behaviour, etc. E18. **4** Completely finished. M18.

2 H. P. BROUGHAM Such an exertion.. I already *ache all over* with it. JOYCE I often felt I wanted to kiss him all over. 3 J. GALSWORTHY She's not a bit like me. She's your mother all over. Obstinate as a mule! 4 H. NELSON I am a dead man, Hardy... I am going fast:—it will be all over with me soon. J. LE CARRÉ And then I asked him, 'Is this goodbye?'—whether it was all over.

B *prep. phr.* Everywhere on or in; all through. E17.

DEFOE The People.. began to be allarm'd all over the Town. L. HUGHES In the middle of the winter, Snow all over the ground. **be all over** display great affection towards (someone), be excessively attentive to (someone).

C *adj.* (*attrib.*) (With hyphen.) **1** Generally indisposed. *rare.* M19. **2** Covering every part. M19. **3** Overall. M20.

1 H. MAYHEW An all-over sort of feeling. 2 *Times Lit. Suppl.* At least six 'original' bindings, ranging from all-over boards with label, through half-cloth and full-cloth. 3 *Irish Press* The Irish people.. have given Fianna Fáil its all-over majority. *Notes & Queries* His all-over conclusion is [etc.].

D *n.* (In senses 1 and 2 with hyphen or as one wd.) **1** (Something with) a pattern that covers every part uniformly, without conspicuous features. M19. **2** In *pl. the all-overs*, a feeling of nervousness or revulsion. *US slang.* L19. **3** After preps. (chiefly *from*): everywhere, many different places. E20.

3 *Time* There were a lot of young people from all over—Colorado, Illinois, Tennessee, Georgia, Brazil, Canada.

all-ˈoverish *a.* & *adv.* (*colloq.*) (*a*) *adj.* generally ill, indisposed all over; nervous; also, ubiquitous; (*b*) *adv.* over the whole extent: M19. **all-ˈoverishness** *n.* (*colloq.*) a general sense of illness or indisposition E19. **all-ˈoverness** *n.* (*colloq.*) (*a*) = ALL-OVERISHNESS; (*b*) the quality of covering every part: E19.

allow /əˈlaʊ/ *v.* ME. [OFr. *alouer* (later *all-*) partly f. L *allaudare*, f. as AL-[1] + LAUD *v.*, partly f. med.L *allocare* ALLOCATE *v.*] **I** *v.t.* †**1** Praise, commend. ME–L18. **2** Approve of, sanction; accept. *arch.* ME. †**3** Assign as a right or due. ME–L16. †**4** Place to someone's credit in an account. ME–L17. **5** Accept as true or valid; acknowledge, admit, grant; concede. LME. †**6** Give an allowance to, pay. LME–E18. **7** Give or let have as a share or as appropriate to needs. LME. †**8** Remit, deduct. LME–M16. **9** Not prevent the occurrence of; not prevent (a person) from doing something; permit. M16. b With ellipsis of inf. bef. adv. (phr.): permit to go, come, be, etc. M19. c *Physics.* As *allowed* pa. pple & ppl a.: designating or involving a transition between two quantum-mechanical states that conforms to a certain selection rule. E20. **10** Add or deduct in consideration of something. M17. **11** *refl.* Indulge oneself *in*. *arch.* E18. **12** Consider, assert, (*that*). *Eng.* & *US dial.* E19.

1 G. CRABBE Proud To find the triumphs of his youth allow'd. 2 AV *Luke* 11:48 Truely ye beare witnesse that ye allowe the deeds of your fathers. 3 SHAKES. *Merch. V.* And you must cut this flesh from off his breast. The law allows it and the court awards it. 5 COVERDALE If any man allowe not the vnderstanding of Rome by Babylon. MILTON I suppose it will be allowed us that marriage is a human society. R. B. SHERIDAN They'll not allow our friend.. to be handsome. JOYCE What was their civilisation? Vast, I allow: but vile. 6 STEELE The Father who allows his Son to his utmost ability. 7 POPE Allow him but his plaything of a pen. G. B. SHAW His trustees cannot.. allow him more than £800 a year. B. ENGLAND You really must allow me a moment or two to rest. 9 H. S. MERRIMAN He would not allow himself the luxury of being the first arrival. E. F. BENSON We give here plays that the censor would not allow on the London stage. J. B. PRIESTLEY As long as society allows me to hunt, I shall hunt. D. J. ENRIGHT Is it not allowed to stand here? b R. BROOKE We were allowed ashore from 5 to midnight. 10 BURKE To allow on their account as much as added to the losses of the conqueror, may amount to a million of deaths. A. AYCKBOURN It's only a five minute walk... No, but they have to allow a bit longer. 11 J. RUSKIN It refuses to allow itself in any violent or spasmodic passion. 12 B. HARTE I allows one thing, he allows another, and this yer man gives me the lie and I stabs him!

II *v.i.* **13** Foll. by *of*: accept the truth or validity of, acknowledge. E16. **14** Foll. by *of*, (arch. & dial.) (*up*)*on*: approve of, not prevent the occurrence or existence of, admit of. M16. **15** Foll. by *for*: make due allowance for, take into consideration. M17. **16** *absol.* Give an opportunity, not prevent something. M18.

13 J. R. LOWELL Jortin is willing to allow of other miracles. 14 S. JOHNSON She tacitly allows of his future visits. 15 G. B. SHAW Unfortunately he did not allow for the precession of the equinox. I had to correct some of his results accordingly. 16 *if circumstances, conditions*, etc., *allow*.

allowedly /əˈlaʊɪdli/ *adv.* by general allowance or admission, admittedly E17. **allower** *n.* L16.

allowable /əˈlaʊəb(ə)l/ *a.* LME. [OFr. *alouable* (later *all-*), f. as prec.: see -ABLE.] †**1** Praiseworthy. LME–E18. **2** Appropriate; satisfactory, acceptable. Long *arch.* LME. **3** Intellectually admissible; valid; probable. LME. **4** Able to be added or deducted in consideration of something. E16. **5** Permissible, tolerable, legitimate. M16.

allowableness *n.* (now *rare*) L17. **allowably** *adv.* L16.

allowance /əˈlaʊəns/ *n.* & *v.* LME. [OFr. *alouance* (later *all-*), f. as ALLOW *v.*: see -ANCE.] **A** *n.* †**1** a Praise. LME–M17. b Approbation; sanction; voluntary acceptance. *arch.* LME. **2** The act of allotting a sum as payment or expenses. LME. **3** A limited quantity or sum, esp. of money or food, granted to cover expenses or other requirements. LME. †**4** The act of granting as a right or due. Only in L15. †**5** A balance, remainder. E–M16. **6** a A sum or item put to someone's credit; deduction, discount. M16. b *fig.* Addition or deduction in consideration of something; the act of taking (esp. mitigating circumstances) into consideration. Esp. in *make allowance(s) for*. L17. †**7** Acknowledgement, admission. L16–M18. **8** Permission, tolerance (*of*). E17.

1b G. CRABBE He look'd smiling on And gave allowance where he needed none. 2 BACON Illiberalitie of Parents in allowance towards their children. 3 MILTON In such a scant allowance of starlight. F. MARRYAT They had but their allowance of bread and grog for one day. A. KOESTLER The Committee now paid him a small weekly allowance on which he could manage to live. **at no allowance** *arch.* & *dial.* without stint or limitation. *compassionate allowance*: see COMPASSIONATE *a.* 1b. *family allowance*: see FAMILY *n.* 7 SHAKES. *Haml.* The censure of the which one must, in your allowance, o'erweigh a whole theatre of others. 8 E. A. FREEMAN The allowance of slavery in the South. P. V. WHITE I would ask your allowance that I may write to your Uncle.. for your hand.

B *v.t.* **1** Put (a person or animal) on a limited allowance. L18. **2** Limit the amount of (a commodity) supplied. M19.

alloxan /aˈlɒks(ə)n/ *n.* M19. [f. ALL(ANTOIN + OX(ALIC + -AN.] *Chem.* An acidic heterocyclic compound, $C_4H_2N_2O_4$, obtained by oxidation of uric acid and isolated as an efflorescent crystalline hydrate.

alloy /ˈalɔɪ, (*in branch II always*) əˈlɔɪ/ *n.* L16. [(O)Fr. *aloi*, f. *aloier*, earlier *al(e)ier* ALLY *v.* Replacing ALLAY *n.*[1]] **I** *lit.* †**1** Agio of exchange. L16–L17. **2** The comparative purity of gold or silver. E17. **3** Orig., a mixture of a precious metal with a baser one. Now *gen.*, a metallic substance made by combining two or more elements at least one of which is a metal, esp. to give greater strength, resistance to corrosion, etc. M17. **4** An inferior metal mixed with one of greater value. E18.

3 *ferro-alloy*, *Wood's alloy*, etc.

II *fig.* †**5** Intrinsic standard or character, quality. L16–L17. **6** Admixture of something which diminishes character or value; an alien element, something which debases. E17.

5 SIR T. BROWNE A Soull of the same alloy as our owne. 6 J. AUSTEN Disadvantages which threatened alloy to her many enjoyments. V. WOOLF The fatal alloy in his genius, the great clod of clay that has got itself mixed up with the purity of his inspiration.

Comb.: **alloy steel** steel containing one or more added elements.

alloy /ˈalɔɪ, (*in senses 1, 3 always*) əˈlɔɪ/ *v.* M17. [Fr. *aloyer*, f. as prec. Replacing ALLAY *v.*[2]] **1** *v.t.* Moderate, modify. Cf. ALLAY *v.*[1] M17. **2** *v.t.* Mix with a baser metal. L17. **3** *v.t. fig.* Debase by admixture. E18. **4** *v.t.* Mix (metals). E19. **5** *v.i.* Of a metal or metals: enter into combination (*with*). E19.

all right /ɔːl ˈrʌɪt/ *adv., a., & n. phr.* Also **alright**. E17. [f. ALL *adv.* + RIGHT *adv., a.*] **A** *adv. phr.* As desired; duly; satisfactorily; certainly, indeed. E17.

E. FITZGERALD I got your letter all right. M. LOWRY Boy, but it was hot all right. T. STOPPARD The Minister said up here—he'll find us alright.

B *adj. phr.* **1** In good condition; safe and sound; satisfactory, acceptable. Usu. *pred.* but occas. (with hyphen) *attrib.* E18. **2** As *int.* Expr. acquiescence, assent, or acknowledgement. M19.

1 R. CHANDLER *The Big Sleep* is very unequally written. There are scenes that are all right. J. P. DONLEAVY Don't cry anymore now. Its all right. M. PROCTER He seemed an all-right bloke to me. **all right by** or **with** acceptable to (a person). *I'm all right, Jack*: see JACK *n.*[1] 2 DICKENS 'Stand firm, Sam,' said Mr. Pickwick...'All right, sir,' replied Mr. Weller. A. LURIE 'I want to go. I want to see the animals!' 'All *right*, Markie. I'll take them outside and let them run around for a while, Katherine.'

C *n. phr. a bit of all right*, someone or something very pleasing. *colloq.* L19.

¶The spelling *alright* is often considered erroneous, but cf. analogous *already, although*, etc.

all round /ɔːl ˈraʊnd/ *adv., prep., & a. phr.* Also **all-round**. E18. [f. ALL *adv.* + ROUND *adv., prep.*] **A** *adv. phr.* Everywhere around; in all respects; for all concerned. E18.

H. P. TRITTON Work was scarce and wages low, and conditions all-round were tough.

B *prep. phr.* Around all the parts of, round in every direction. E19.

C *adj.* (*phr.*) (Freq. with hyphen.) Encompassing everything; affecting everything or everyone; having ability in many departments. M19.

W. JAMES The all-round men like Washington. *Economist* An all-round increase in the rates payable for workmen's compensation. *New Statesman* An excellent all-round performance by the Guildford Repertory Company.

all-ˈrounder *n.* †(*a*) a collar which fits all round; (*b*) a person with ability in many departments: M19. **all-ˈroundness** *n.* L19.

allspice /ˈɔːlspʌɪs/ *n.* E17. [f. ALL + SPICE *n.*, as combining several flavours.] **1** (The aromatic dried ground berry of) the W. Indian tree *Pimenta dioica*, of the myrtle family. Also called *pimento* and *Jamaica pepper*. E17. **2** Any of various other aromatic shrubs, esp. *Calycanthus fertilis* and *C. floridus* (both called *Carolina allspice*). M18.

allude /əˈluːd, əˈljuːd/ *v.* L15. [L *alludere*, f. *ad* AL-[1] + *ludere* to play.] †**1** *v.t.* Hint (at), suggest. L15–L17. **2** *v.i.* Have or make an oblique, covert, transient, or indirect reference, *to*; *pop.* refer in any manner *to*. M16. †**3** *v.t.* Play with, mock. M–L16. †**4** *v.i.* & *t.* Play upon words; refer by play of words ((*un*)*to*); pun. M16–E17. †**5** *v.t.* & *i.* Refer (something) fancifully or figuratively, have fanciful or figurative reference, *to*. L16–M17. †**6** Refer (something) as applicable, appropriate, or belonging, *to*. E–M17.

2 STEELE Quotations which allude to the Perjuries of the Fair. E. M. FORSTER He would allude to her, and hear her discussed, but never mentioned her by name. G. VIDAL He had star quality, an element often alluded to in Arlene's circle of show-biz friends.

allumette /aluːˈmɛt; *foreign* alymɛt (*pl. same*)/ *n.* E17. [Fr., f. *allumer* set light to: see -ETTE.] A match for lighting or setting things alight.

pommes allumettes: see POMME *n.*

¶Rare bef. 19.

all up /ɔːl ˈʌp/ *a. phr.* Also **all-up**. E19. [Sense 1 f. ALL *adv.*, sense 2 f. ALL *n.*, + UP *adv.*[2]] **1** *pred.* Completely done or finished; almost over. Chiefly *impers.* as below. E19. **2** *attrib.* (With hyphen.) **a** Of the weight of an aircraft: total, including crew, passengers, cargo, etc., when in the air. M20. **b** Of a postal service, mail, etc.: (with all items) sent by air though charged at a surface-mail rate. M20.

1 **it is all up with someone**: he or she will shortly die, be defeated, etc. **it is all up with something**: it has no prospect of continuation or success.

allure /əˈljʊə/ *n.*[1] M16. [f. the vb.] Enticement; personal charm; attractiveness.

allure /alyːr, əˈljʊə/ *n.*[2] Now *rare*. Pl. pronounced same. M19. [Fr.] Bearing, mien, air.

allure /əˈljʊə/ *v.t.* LME. [AN *alurer*, OFr. *aloirrier, aleurier*, f. as A-[5] + *luere* LURE *n.*[1]] **1** Attract or tempt by something advantageous, pleasant, or flattering; entice, win over. LME. †**2** *gen.* Draw or attract towards oneself or itself; elicit. M16–L18. **3** Fascinate, charm. E17.

1 W. RALEIGH To allure the principall of them to his partie. BUNYAN Things that seem to be hid in words obscure, Do but the Godly mind the more alure, To study. J. CONRAD He went to Sambir.. allured.. by the fact that there was no Dutch resident on the river. JOYCE Those whose eyes tempted and allured them from the path of virtue. P. G. WODEHOUSE Alluring the public with a rich smell of mixed foods. 3 BURKE Some were allured by the modern, others reverenced the ancient.

allurance *n.* allurement, enticement L16. **allurer** *n.* M16. **alluring** *a.* tempting, seductive, attractive L16. **alluringly** *adv.* L16. **alluringness** *n.* (*rare*) E17.

allurement /əˈljʊəm(ə)nt/ *n.* M16. [f. prec. + -MENT.] **1** The means of alluring; a lure, a bait. M16. **2** The action or process of alluring; temptation, enticement. M16. **3** Alluring faculty or quality; fascination, charm. L16.

allus /ˈɔːləz/ *adv. dial.* Also **allers**. M19. [Repr. a pronunc.] Always.

allusion /əˈluːʒ(ə)n, -ˈljuː-/ *n.* M16. [Fr., or late L *allusio(n-)*, f. *allus-* pa. ppl stem of *alludere* ALLUDE *v.*: see -ION.] †**1** A play on words, a pun. M16–M18. †**2** A metaphor, a parable, an allegory. M16–L18. **3** A covert, passing, or indirect reference (*to*); *pop.* any reference *to*. E17.

allusive /əˈluːsɪv, -ˈljuː-/ *a.* L16. [f. as prec. + -IVE.] **1** Symbolical, metaphorical, figurative. *arch.* L16. **2** Containing an allusion (*to*); containing many allusions. E17. **3** Playing on a word, punning. *rare* exc. *Her.*, designating arms in which the charges suggest or pun on the bearer's name or title. M17.

allusively *adv.* M17. **allusiveness** *n.* M17.

alluvial /əˈluːvɪəl, -ˈljuː-/ *a.* & *n.* E19. [f. ALLUVIUM + -AL[1].] **A** *adj.* Of, pertaining to, or consisting of alluvium. E19. **B** *n.* An alluvial deposit; alluvium; *Austral.* gold-bearing alluvial soil. M19.

alluvian *a.* (*rare*) = ALLUVIAL *a.* L18. **alluvious** *a.* (*rare*) = ALLUVIAL *a.* M18.

alluvion /əˈluːvɪən, -ˈljuː-/ *n. arch.* exc. in sense 4. M16. [Fr. f. L *alluvio(n-)*, f. as next: see -ION.] **1** The wash of water against the shore or a river-bank. M16. **2** An inundation; a flood, esp. when the water carries much suspended material. M16. **3** The matter deposited by a flood or a river; alluvium. M18. **4** *Law.* The action of flowing water in forming new land by deposition (cf. AVULSION 3). M18.

alluvium /əˈluːvɪəm, -ˈljuː-/ *n.* Pl. (now *rare*) **-ia** /-ɪə/, **-iums**. M17. [L, neut. of *alluvius* washed against, f. *ad* AL-[1] + *luv-*, *luere* to wash.] A deposit of clay, silt, sand, etc., left by flowing water, as in a river valley or delta.

alluviate *v.t.* cover or build up with deposits of alluvium (chiefly as *alluviated* ppl a.) E20. **alluviˈation** *n.* the deposition of alluvium M19.

ally /ˈalʌɪ/ *n.*[1] LME. [Partly f. OFr. *alié* use as n. of pa. pple of *alier* ALLY *v.*; partly f. ALLY *v.*] †**1** Kinship; confederation, alliance. LME–L16. †**2** *collect.* Kindred, relatives; associates, confederates. LME–L16. **3** A relative; a kinsman, a kinswoman. *arch.* LME. **4** A person, State, etc., united to another by treaty or league or combined with another for a special purpose. LME. **b** *the Allies*, the States in alliance against Germany and her allies in the wars of 1914–18 and 1939–45; Britain and the States in alliance with her in later wars. E20. **5** Something akin to another thing by community of nature or properties, or placed near it in classification. L17.

¶The pronunc. /əˈlʌɪ/, formerly general, is now not commonly heard.

ally /ˈali/ *n.*[2] Also **alley**. E18. [Perh. dim. of ALABASTER.] A choice playing-marble, orig. of marble or alabaster, later also of glass or other material.

make one's ally good *Austral. slang* exploit one's advantage, confirm one's position. **pass** or **toss in one's ally** *Austral. slang* give in, die.

ally /əˈlʌɪ, ˈalʌɪ/ *v.* See also ALLIED. ME. [OFr. *al(e)ier* f. L *alligare*, f. *ad* AL-[1] + *ligare* to bind. Cf. ALLAY *v.*[2], ALLOY *n., v.*] **1** *v.t.* Combine or unite, esp. for a special purpose, *to, with*. Chiefly of marriage, alliance with foreign States, and union of nature or spirit. ME. **2** *v.i.* Unite, enter into alliance. *arch.* ME. †**3** *v.t.* Combine or mix (ingredients). LME–L15.

-ally /əli/ *suff.* Forming advs. f. adjs. in -AL[1]: see -LY[2].

allyl /ˈalʌɪl, -lɪl/ *n.* M19. [f. ALLIUM + -YL.] *Chem.* The monovalent radical $CH_2{=}CHCH_2{\cdot}$. Freq. in *comb.*

Comb.: **allyl plastic, resin** any synthetic resin which is a polymer of an allyl compound.

allylene /ˈalɪliːn/ *n.* a gaseous hydrocarbon, $CH_3C{\equiv}CH$, propyne; formerly = ALLENE: M19. **allylic** /aˈlɪlɪk/ *a.* of or pertaining to an allyl radical or compound M19.

alma /ˈalmə/ *n.* Also **almah, alme**. Pl. same, **-s**. L18. [Arab. *ʿālima* (colloq.) singer, orig. (fem. adj.) brained, learned, f. *ʿalima* know.] Any of a class of Egyptian singing- and dancing-girls who entertain at festivals and act as mourners.

almacantar *n.* var. of ALMUCANTAR.

almadia /alməˈdiːə/ *n. obs.* exc. *Hist.* Also **-made** /-ˈmɑːd/, **-madie** /-məˈdiː/. M16. [Arab. *al-maʿdiya* the ferry-boat: see AL-[2]. Vars. f. Fr. f. Port.] An African canoe made of bark or of a hollowed tree-trunk. Also, a long swift Indian riverboat.

almagest /ˈalmədʒɛst/ *n.* Also **A-**. LME. [OFr. *almageste* ult. f. Arab. *al-mijistī*, f. as AL-[2] + Gk *megistē* greatest (sc. composition).] A great astronomical treatise by Ptolemy (translated into Arabic in the 9th cent.); any of various other early textbooks of astrology and alchemy.

†**almagra** *n.* L16–E19. [Sp., f. Arab. *al-magra*, *-muġra* red ochre: see AL-[2].] A deep red ochre found in Spain.

almah *n.* var. of ALMA.

Almain /ˈalmeɪn/ *n.* & *a.* Now *arch.* or *Hist.* Also **-aine**, †**-an**, **-ayn**, & other vars. ME. [OFr. *aleman* (mod. *allemand*) f. late L *Alemanni*: see ALEMANNIC.] **A** *n.* **1** A German. ME. †**2** The German language. LME–M16. **3** = ALLEMANDE 3. L16. **4** = ALLEMANDE 2. L16.

B *adj.* German. L15.

Almain rivets a kind of flexible light armour with overlapping plates sliding on rivets.

Alma Mater /ˌalmə ˈmɑːtə, ˈmeɪt-/ *n. phr.* Pl. **Alma Maters**, (*rare*) **Almae Matres** /ˌalmʌɪ ˈmɑːtrɛz, ˌalmiː ˈmeɪtriːz/. M17. [L = bounteous mother, a title given to various Roman goddesses, esp. Ceres and Cybele.] **1** Someone or something providing nourishment and care. M17. **2** *esp.* A university or school as regarded by its past and present members. L17.

†**Alman** *n.* & *a.* var. of ALMAIN.

almanac /ˈɔːlmənak, ˈɒl-/ *n.* Also (*rare*) **-ack**. LME. [med.L *almanac(h)* f. late Gk *almenikhiaka* of unkn. origin.] An annual table, or book of tables, containing a calendar of months and days, usu. with astronomical data and other information, formerly including astrological and astrometeorological forecasts.

NAUTICAL *almanac*.

almandine /ˈalməndiːn, -dʌɪn/ *n.* LME. [Fr. (obs.), alt. of ALABANDINE.] An aluminium iron garnet of a violet or amethyst tint.

Also **almandite** *n.* (*Min.*) M19.

Almayn *n.* & *a.* var. of ALMAIN.

alme *n.* var. of ALMA.

almeira, -ah *ns.* vars. of ALMIRAH.

almery *n.* see AUMBRY.

almighty /ɔːlˈmʌɪti/ *a., n., & adv.* [OE *ælmihtiġ*, f. ALL *adv.* + MIGHTY *a.*; corresp. to OFris.

elmachtich, OS *alomahtig*, OHG *alamahtīc* (G *allmächtig*), ON *almáttigr*.] A *adj.* 1 Having all possible power (orig. as an attribute of God). OE. 2 Very great. *slang*. E19.

1 *God Almighty*: see GOD *n*.

B *n. the Almighty*, God. OE.

C *adv.* Exceedingly. *slang*. M19.

almightiness *n.* LME. †**almightiship** *n.* (*rare*) M17–E18.

almirah /əlˈmʌɪrə/ *n.* Also **-meira(h)**. E19. [Hind. *almārī* f. Port. *almario* f. L *armarium*: see AUMBRY.] In the Indian subcontinent: a wardrobe, a movable cupboard.

almoign /əlˈmɔɪn/ *n.* Also **-oin**. ME. [Late AN *almoin*, OFr. *almone* (mod. *aumône*), ult. f. as ALMS.] †1 Ecclesiastical possession. Only in ME. 2 Tenure by spiritual service, or by the performance of some religious duty. Chiefly in FRANKALMOIGN. E16.

almond /ˈɑːmənd/ *n.* ME. [OFr. *alemande*, *a(l)mande* f. med.L *amandula* f. Gk *amugdalē*.] 1 The kernel, oval with pointed ends, of the stone-fruit of the tree *Prunus dulcis*, of which there are two varieties, the sweet and the bitter. ME. 2 The tree itself, allied to the plum, cherry, etc. Also *almond tree*. LME. 3 Something having the shape or appearance of an almond. LME. b In *pl.* The tonsils; also, the lymph nodes below the ear. Freq. more fully *almonds of the throat, ears*, etc. *arch.* L16. 4 The delicate pink colour of almond blossom or the light brown colour of an almond kernel. Freq. *attrib.* M18.

1 BURNT *almond*. *butter of almonds*: see BUTTER *n.*[1] 2.

Attrib. & *comb.*: Attrib. in senses 'resembling the almond' as *almond pink* etc. (see also sense 4 above); 'made with or containing almonds', as *almond cake, paste*, etc. Special combs., as **almond eye**: with the eyelids forming an almond-shape; **almond-eyed** *a.* having almond eyes; **almond milk** a soothing medicine made with blanched almonds, sugar, and water, or similar ingredients; **almond oil** the expressed oil of bitter almonds, consisting chiefly of benzaldehyde; *almond tree*: see sense 2 above.

almondy *a.* like an almond or almonds M19.

almoner /ˈɑːmənə, ˈalm-/ *n.* ME. [AN *aumoner*, OFr. *-ier*, earlier *a(u)lmosnier* (mod. *aumônier*) ult. f. as ELEEMOSYNARY; assoc. w. wds in AL-[1].] 1 An official distributor of alms on behalf of an individual, as a monarch, or an institution, as a religious house. (Holders of particular offices may also have other duties.) ME. b A social worker attached to a hospital, seeing to the after-care etc. of patients and orig. also to patients' payments. (Not now an official title.) L19. †2 *gen.* An alms-giver. ME–L19.

1b B. PYM The almoner, or medical social worker as they called it now, at the hospital.

almonership *n.* the position or office of an almoner L16.

almonry /ˈɑːmənri, ˈalm-/ *n.* LME. [Orig. f. OFr. *au(l)mosnerie* (mod. *aumônerie*), f. as prec.; later f. prec.: see -ERY, -RY.] A place where alms are or were distributed; an office responsible for the distribution of alms.

†**almose** *n.* var. of ALMS.

almost /ˈɔːlməʊst, -məst/ *adv.* & *a.* OE. [f. ALL + MOST *adv.*] †1 *adj.* or *adv.* Mostly all; for the most part. OE–M17. 2 *adv.* Very nearly; all but; as the nearest thing to. ME. b *adv.* or *adj.* Close to being, near. *arch.* M16. †c Used to intensify a rhetorical interrogative. L16–M18.

1 R. ASCHAM Thies giuers were almost Northmen. 2 DONNE One might almost say, her body thought. SWIFT Eyes with Reading almost blind. R. WATSON His affairs almost never prospered. BYRON To lose the hour would make her quite a martyr, And they had wasted now almost a quarter. V. WOOLF Almost one might imagine them . . questioning and wondering. E. HEMINGWAY I stood until it had almost passed, then jumped and caught the rear hand-rods. W. TREVOR A single window reached almost to the floor. b SOUTHEY I am . . an almost Quaker. c R. SOUTH Whom almost can we see who opens his arms to his enemies?

alms /ɑːmz/ *n.* Also †**almose**, (*Sc.* & *dial.*) **almous**, (*Sc.*) **awmous**. [OE *ælmyssa*, *-messe*, corresp. to ON *almusa*, *ǫlmusa* (from which the Sc. vars. derive), OFris. *ielmisse*, OS *alamosna* (Du. *aalmoes*), OHG *alamuosan* (G *Almosen*); Gmc ult. f. alt. (prob. through L *alimonia* ALIMONY) of Chr.L *eleemosyna* (see ELEEMOSYNARY).] 1 Charitable relief of the poor, orig. and esp. as a religious duty. As a count n. (infl. pl. long *obs.*): *sing.* a charitable donation, *pl.* things given in charity. OE. †2 A good deed; a charity. Often *iron.* Latterly *Sc.* OE–E19. 3 = ALMOIGN 2. OE.

1 ADDISON A Beggar Man that had asked an Alms of him. W. S. MAUGHAM Her nuns lived entirely upon alms. W. DE LA MARE This chance-come outcast had Asked for alms a crust of bread. *do, make, work*, etc., *alms*; *give, bestow*, etc., *alms*. 2 R. SANDERSON If he be hungry, it is alms to feed him. 3 **free alms** = FRANKALMOIGN.

Comb.: **alms-deed** *arch.* (*a*) an act of almsgiving, a charitable deed; †(*b*) the practice of almsgiving; **almsfee** *Hist.* Peter's pence, Rome-scot; **almsfolk** people supported by alms; **almsgiver** a person who gives alms; **almsgiving** the giving of alms; **almshouse** (*a*) a house founded by charity for the reception or support of the poor; †(*b*) a house belonging to a monastery where alms and hospitality were dispensed; **almsman** (*a*) a person supported by alms; (*b*) *arch.* an almsgiver; **almswoman** a woman supported by alms.

almucantar /almәˈkantə/ *n.* Also **alma-**. ME. [med.L *almucantarath* or Fr. †*almicantarat*, †*almucantara* f. Arab. *al-mukanṭarāt* (pl.) circles of celestial latitude, f. as AL-[2] + *ḳanṭara* arch.] *Astron.* 1 A circle on the celestial sphere parallel to the horizon; a parallel of altitude. Usu. in *pl.* ME. 2 A telescope mounted on a float resting on mercury, used to determine stellar altitude and azimuth. L19.

almug /ˈalmʌɡ/ *n.* Pl. **-im** /-ɪm/, **-s**. E17. [Heb. *ʾalmug* (Ugaritic *ʾalmg*): cf. ALGUM.] = ALGUM. Also *almug tree*.

¶First recorded in AV.

†**almuten** *n.* L16–E18. [Alt. of (OFr. *almutaz* f.) Arab. *al-muʿtazz*, f. *al* AL-[2] + *muʿtazz* powerful, proud.] *Astrol.* The ruling planet in the horoscope.

alnage, **-er** *ns.* vars. of AULNAGE, -ER.

alod *n.*, **-ial** *a.* & *n.*, **-ium** *n.* etc., vars. of ALLOD etc.

aloe /ˈaləʊ/ *n.* [OE *al(e)we* f. L *aloe* f. Gk *aloē*; in LME reinforced by OFr. *aloes* (mod. *aloès*) or its source as in LIGN-ALOES, whence freq. use in pl.] 1 In *pl.* The fragrant resin or (also *aloes wood*) heartwood of the trees *Aquilaria agallocha* and *A. malaccensis*, from the Far East. OE. 2 A plant of the genus *Aloe* of the lily family, which includes succulent herbs, shrubs, and trees, bearing erect spikes of flowers and yielding bitter sap. LME. 3 *sing.* & (usu.) in *pl.* A bitter, nauseous purgative, made from the juice of the plant. LME. 4 Any of several other plants resembling those of the genus *Aloe*; *esp.* (more fully *American aloe*) a stemless agave, *Agave americana*, with long spiny leaves which flowers only once in many years (also called *century plant*). M17.

1 NEB *Ps.* 45:8 Your robes are all fragrant with myrrh and powder of aloes. 3 *fig.*: S. HIERON The bitter aloes of the law.

aloetic /aləʊˈɛtɪk/ *n.* & *a.* (now *rare*) (a drug) containing or of the nature of the purgative aloes M17.

aloft /əˈlɒft/ *adv.*, *pred. a.*, & *prep.* ME. [ON *á lopt(i)* f. *á* in, on, to + *lopt* air, sky, LOFT *n.* (corresp. to OE LIFT *n.*[1], OHG *luft*, Goth. *luftus* air).] A *adv.* & *pred. a.* 1 *gen.* Of position: high up, at a relatively great elevation. ME. 2 *gen.* Of direction: into the air; upward. ME. 3 In or to heaven. *arch.* exc. as below. ME. 4 *Naut.* On or to a higher part of a ship; into the rigging. ME. †5 In the sky, above the horizon. ME–L16. †6 In the ascendant, prevailing. LME–E17. †7 On the top, on the surface. LME–E18. †8 In a loud voice; in a lofty tone. LME–E17.

3 *go aloft*: see GO *v.*

B *prep.* Above, over; high up in. Long *rare.* LME.

SHAKES. *John* I was amaz'd Under the tide; but now I breathe again Aloft the flood. M. PEAKE A pale sun . . was hung aloft an empty and faded sky.

alogical /eɪˈlɒdʒɪk(ə)l/ *a.* L17. [f. A-[10] + LOGICAL *a.* Cf. Fr. *alogique*.] Non-logical; opposed to logic.

aloha /əˈləʊhə/ *int.* & *n.* E19. [Haw.] Love, affection: used in Hawaii esp. at greeting or parting; an utterance of this.

Comb.: **aloha shirt** a loose brightly coloured Hawaiian shirt; **Aloha State** *US* Hawaii.

alone /əˈləʊn/ *a.* (chiefly *pred.*) & *adv.* ME. [f. ALL *adv.* + ONE *a.* etc. Aphet. to LONE *a.*, *adv.*] 1 Quite by oneself, itself, or themselves; unaccompanied; without other companions. Occas. *attrib.*, solitary, lonely. ME. 2 Having no one else sharing in one's action, feeling, or position. (Usu. in neg. contexts.) ME. 3 As distinct from anyone or anything else; only, exclusively. ME. 4 Taken or acting by itself; of itself, without anything more. †Also *attrib.* LME. 5 *pred.* & *attrib.* Having no equal; being the only example; unique, exclusive. Now *rare.* M16.

1 COLERIDGE Alone on a wide wide sea! J. M. FAULKNER I am left alone in the sitting, With none to sit beside. D. H. LAWRENCE This morning Pancrazio and Giovanni had gone off somewhere, Alvina and Cicio were alone on the place. E. BOWEN Two rather alone people. DAY LEWIS The whiteness of the cup, standing alone on the grass, is dazzling. **go it alone** act without assistance. **leave** or **let alone** (*a*) leave to himself or herself, not have dealings with, not attend to or interfere with; *leave* or *let well alone*: see WELL *a.*; (*b*) in *imper.* (*colloq.*) (now usu. *let alone*): not to mention, far less or more. 2 C. P. SNOW Rose was not alone in that room in having a generalized dislike of scientists. 3 AV *Dan.* 10:7 I Daniel alone saw the vision. SHAKES. *Haml.* 'Tis not alone my inky cloak, good mother, . . That can denote me truly. TENNYSON Wisdom . . which not alone had guided me, But served the seasons that may rise. 4 S. JOHNSON He that hopes by philosophy and contemplation alone to fortify himself against that. LD MACAULAY The appointment of a ruined gambler would alone have sufficed to disgust the public. 5 SHAKES. *Two Gent.* All I can is nothing To her, whose worth makes other worthies nothing; She is alone. G. HERBERT Christ is my onely head, My alone onely heart and breast.

aloneness *n.* LME.

alonely /əˈləʊnli/ *adv.* & *a.* Long *arch.* ME. [f. ALL *adv.* + ONLY *a.*] 1 *adv.* & *pred. a.* Only, solely; without anyone or anything else; solitarily. ME. †2 *attrib. adj.* Sole, onely; unique; solitary. L15–E17.

along /əˈlɒŋ/ *a.*[1] *arch.* & *dial.* [OE *ġelang*, corresp. to forms in WGmc, OS *gilang* ready, OHG *gilang* neighbouring: see A-[4], LONG *a.*[1]] Foll. by *of* (†*on*): pertaining to; owing to; on account of; together with.

along /əˈlɒŋ/ *a.*[2], *prep.*, & *adv.* [OE *andlang*, corresp. to OS *antlang*. See LONG *a.*[1] and cf. ENDLONG.] †A *adj.* Extending lengthwise; livelong. Only in OE (later merged in *all long*, as *all night long*). OE.

B *prep.* (Orig. the adj. used absol. or advb. w. genit.) From end to end of; through any part of the length of; parallel to the length of. OE.

SIR W. SCOTT Along the bridge Lord Marmion rode. TENNYSON We roam'd along the dreary coast. T. HARDY Along a shelf at one side were ranged bottles and canisters. W. OWEN He sings along the march Which we march taciturn. S. HILL Men sat along trestle tables lined down the church hall.

C *adv.* 1 In a line with the length (of something understood); longitudinally. Now only with *by* and as in sense 2. ME. 2 Onward in the course or line of motion or in the course of life etc.; progressively on; further on in a row. ME. b To or at a place, having come from another. M19. c Further on (or *back*) in time. *N. Amer.* M19. †3 At a distance, afar. ME–L16. †4 At full length. LME–L19. †5 In full, at length. LME–L16. 6 Foll. by *with*: onward with, in company with; together with, in conjunction with; also *ellipt.*, with a person etc. L16. 7 *all along*, all the time, throughout, continuously. E17.

1 V. WOOLF They were sailing so fast along by the rocks that it was very exciting. 2 JOYCE Shuffling along for a yard or so . . in an old pair of blue canvas shoes. W. STEVENS As if the sky was a current that bore them along. K. AMIS He bustled round the taxi he had secured, hurrying the baggage-porter along. b J. WYNDHAM Any time now they'd be along with pneumatic drills. S. GRAY Mr Keyston says kindly send him along to the office. c **along about** at about (a specified time). 4 SHAKES. *Rom. & Jul.* Under yond yew trees lay thee all along. 6 YEATS He was seen coming here along with you. E. HUXLEY Along with

coal, steel, woollens, whisky and pedigree bulls, for many years we exported people. A. BURGESS Love is something you learn along with the other duties of marriage. G. B. SHAW Bring your sabre along. J. BOWEN Sharks is still there, mind. They're always there. Patient. Tagging along. *play along, string along*, etc. 7 J. IRVING He must be waiting . . for me to tell him he was right all along.

Comb.: **alongshore** *adv.* & *a.* by the shore, along and on the shore (see also LONGSHORE).

alongside /əlɒŋ'sʌɪd/ *adv.* & *prep.* E18. [f. ALONG *prep.* + SIDE *n.*] **A** *adv.* **1** Along, parallel to, or close to the side (of a ship or something else understood). E18. **2** Foll. by *of*: side by side with (*lit.* & *fig.*). L18.

1 COLERIDGE The naked hulk alongside came. S. HILL Manor house, it was, and a farm alongside. 2 N. HAWTHORNE Alongside of a sheet of water. C. HAMPTON Alongside of preaching the Gospel . . there are other ways in which we have to change the lives of these savages.

B *prep.* Side by side with, parallel to. L18.

alongst /ə'lɒŋst/ *prep.* & *adv.* *obs.* exc. *Sc.* & *dial.* ME. [f. ALONG *prep.* & *adv.* + -S[3] + *t* as in *against*, *amidst*, etc.] **A** *prep.* **1** Down or through the length of (in contrast to *across*, *athwart*). ME. **2** Close by, parallel to. L16. †**B** *adv.* **1** = ALONG *adv.* I. M–L16. **2** Lengthwise (in contrast to *athwart*). M16–L18. **3** Foll. by *with*: = ALONG *adv.* 6. E18–E19.

aloof /ə'luːf/ *adv.*, *a.*, & *prep.* M16. [f. A *prep.*[1] I + LUFF *n.*[1], prob. after Du. *te loef*.] **A** *adv.* **1** *Naut.* †**a** As *int.* To windward! (expr. an order to turn or keep the ship's head as close as possible to the wind). M16–L18. **b** Away to windward. M16. **2** Away at a distance (*from*), apart. M16. **3** From a distance. *arch.* M16.

1a *fig.*: R. B. SHERIDAN I thought that dragon's front of thine would cry aloof to the sons of gallantry. b POPE With all our force we kept aloof to sea. 2 *hold, keep, sit, stand*, etc., *aloof (from)*. 3 MILTON The lion and fierce tiger glared aloof. TENNYSON Purple cliffs, aloof descried.

B *adj.* Distant; detached, unsympathetic. E17.

D. CECIL She . . hid her true self behind the shield of an aloof formality. G. MAXWELL Mijbil was neither hostile nor friendly; he was simply aloof and indifferent.

†**C** *prep.* Away from, apart from. *rare* (Milton). Only in M17.

aloofly *adv.* E20. **aloofness** *n.* M17.

alopecia /alə'piːʃə/ *n.* LME. [L f. Gk *alōpekia* lit. 'fox-mange', f. *alōpek-*, *alōpēx* fox: see -IA[1].] *Med.* Hair loss, baldness.

†**alose** *n.* var. of ALLIS.

aloud /ə'laʊd/ *adv.* ME. [f. A *prep.*[1] 4 + LOUD *a.*] In a loud voice, loudly (*arch.*); audibly, not silently or in a whisper.

think aloud: see THINK *v.*[2]

à l'outrance *adv. phr.* var. of À OUTRANCE.

alow /ə'ləʊ/ *adv.*[1] *Sc.* & *north.* ME. [f. A *prep.*[1] 6 + LOW *n.*[2]] Ablaze.

alow /ə'ləʊ/ *adv.*[2] & *prep.* LME. [f. A *prep.*[1] + LOW *a.*; mod. Sc. prob. after BELOW.] **A** *adv.* **1 a** *gen.* Low down, below; downwards. Now *arch.* & *dial.* LME. **b** *Naut.* In or into a lower part of a vessel. E16. †**2** *fig.* In a low condition or estate. LME–M16. †**3** In a low voice. LME–E16. **B** *prep.* Below, low down in or on. *obs.* exc. *Sc.* M16.

alp /alp/ *n.*[1] Also **A-**. LME. [Orig. pl., f. Fr. *Alpes* f. L f. Gk *Alpeis* of unkn. origin.] **1** (**A-**.) In *pl.*, the high mountain range occupying much of Switzerland and adjacent regions; *sing.* a peak in this range. LME. **2** Any high, esp. snowcapped, mountain(s). LME. **3** In Switzerland: an area of green pasture on a mountainside. E19.

2 **Southern Alps** the high mountain range of South Island, New Zealand.

Comb.: **Alp-horn** = ALPENHORN.

alp /alp/ *n.*[2] *obs.* exc. *dial.* LME. [Origin unkn.] A bullfinch.

alpaca /al'pakə/ *n.* L18. [Sp. f. Aymara *allpaca*.] A domesticated Peruvian animal, *Lama pacos*, resembling the llama, with long fine woolly hair and usu. brown and white colouring; the wool of the alpaca; fabric or a garment made from this.

alpargata /alpɑː'gɑːtə/ *n.* E19. [Sp.] = ESPADRILLE.

alpeen /'alpiːn/ *n.* Also **-ine**. E19. [Ir. *ailpín*.] In Ireland: a cudgel, a stout-headed stick.

alpenglow /'alpənglәʊ/ *n.* L19. [Partial tr. G *Alpenglühen* lit. 'Alp-glow'.] The rosy light of the setting or rising sun seen on high mountains.

alpenhorn /'alpənhɔːn/ *n.* L19. [G = Alp-horn.] A long wooden horn used by Alpine herdsmen.

alpenrose /'alpənrəʊz/ *n.* E20. [G = Alp-rose.] Either of two pink-flowered rhododendrons, *Rhododendron ferrugineum* and *R. hirsutum*, native to the region of the Alps.

alpenstock /'alpənstɒk/ *n.* E19. [G = Alp-stick.] A long iron-tipped staff used in mountain-climbing.

alpha /'alfə/ *n.* ME. [L f. Gk.] **1** The first letter (*A*, *α*) of the Greek alphabet; the beginning of anything. ME. **2** Denoting the first in a numerical sequence. E17. **b** *attrib.* *Sci.* Freq. written *α*: (*a*) *Astron.* (preceding the genitive of the L name of the constellation) designating the chief star in a constellation; (*b*) *Chem.* designating the first of a number of isomeric forms of a compound, or of allotropes of an element, etc.; (*c*) designating a positively-charged particle now known to be a helium nucleus, which is one of the three main types of decay product emitted by radioactive substances; also designating decay, emission, radiation, rays, etc., associated with such a particle; (*d*) *alpha rhythm*, *waves*, the normal rhythmic electrical activity of the conscious brain, consisting of oscillations having a frequency of 8 to 13 hertz; (*e*) Med. *alpha receptor*, one of two kinds of adrenergic receptor in the sympathetic nervous system, stimulation of which results esp. in increased blood pressure; *alpha-adrenergic* adj., pertaining to or involving alpha receptors; *alpha-blocker*, a drug preventing stimulation of alpha receptors; (*f*) *alpha test*, a test of machinery, software, etc., in course of development, carried out by the developer before it is made available for beta testing; *alpha-test* v.t., perform an alpha test on. M18. **c** A first-class mark in an examination etc. E20.

1 **Alpha and Omega** the beginning and the end (orig. as a title of God). 2b *alpha* GLOBULIN. c **alpha minus** a mark just in the first class. **alpha plus** a superlatively good mark.

alphabet /'alfəbɛt/ *n.* & *v.* LME. [Late L *alphabetum*, (Tertullian) *alphabetos*, f. Gk f. ALPHA, BETA, the first two letters of the alphabet, taken to represent the whole. Cf. ABC.] **A** *n.* †**1** Knowledge acquired from written works. *rare*. Only in LME. **2** A set of letters used in writing a language; a set of symbols or signs used for these letters. E16. **b** *Computing*. A set of characters or symbols used in representing data. M20. **3** An index in alphabetical order. Now *rare*. M16. **4** *fig.* The key to a branch of knowledge; the first rudiments of a subject. *arch.* L16. **5** *fig.* A long or complete series. L16.

2 *initial teaching alphabet*: see INITIAL *a.* **phonetic alphabet** a set of symbols used to represent speech sounds (*International Phonetic Alphabet*: see INTERNATIONAL *a.*).

Comb.: **alphabet soup** clear soup containing letter-shaped pieces of macaroni paste etc.; *fig.* a muddle.

B *v.t.* = ALPHABETIZE. Chiefly *US*. L17.

alphabetarian /-'tɛːrɪən/ *n.* (now *rare*) (*a*) = ABECEDARIAN *n.* 1; (*b*) a person who studies alphabets: E17. **alpha'betic** *a.* = ALPHABETICAL M17. **alpha'betical** *a.* (of the order of letters or words) corresponding to that of the alphabet; of or pertaining to an alphabet; employing an alphabet: M16. **alpha'betically** *adv.* in alphabetical order; by means of an alphabet: M16. **alpha'betiform** *a.* shaped like the letters of an alphabet E20. **alphabeti'zation** *n.* the process of arranging in alphabetical order; an alphabetical series or list: L19. **alphabetize** *v.t.* arrange in alphabetical order L18.

alphametic /alfə'mɛtɪk/ *n.* M20. [Blend of ALPHABETIC and ARITHMETIC *n.*[1]] A mathematical puzzle in which numerical values are to be deduced from an equation or the like in which they are represented by letters.

alphanumeric /ˌalfənjuː'mɛrɪk/ *a.* & *n.* M20. [f. ALPHA(BET + NUMERIC.] **A** *adj.* Consisting of or employing both letters and numerals. M20. **B** *n.* In *pl.* Alphanumeric symbols or expressions. M20.

alphin *n.* see ALFIN.

Alphonsine /əl'fɒnsʌɪn/ *a.* M17. [f. *Alphonso* (see below) + -INE[1].] *Hist.* Designating astronomical tables prepared in Toledo for Alphonso X, 'the Wise' (1226–84), King of Castile.

†**alpieu** *n.* L17–M18. [Fr. *alpiou* f. It. *al più* for the more, for most.] In the card-game basset: the bending of one corner of a card to indicate that the punter raises the stake on it after winning.

alpine *n.*[1] var. of ALPEEN.

Alpine /'alpʌɪn/ *a.* & *n.*[2] Also **a-**. LME. [L *alpinus*: see ALP *n.*[1], -INE[1].] **A** *adj.* **1** Of, pertaining to, or characteristic of the Alps or high mountains in general; growing in or inhabiting such mountains above the tree line; in *Hort.* now designating any small plant suitable for rockeries. LME. **2** Designating a subgroup of the Caucasoid division of humankind associated mainly with central and eastern Europe. L19.

1 *alpine chough*: see CHOUGH 2. **alpine fir** a tall conifer, *Abies lasiocarpa*, native to western N. America. **alpine rose** = ALPENROSE. *alpine* STRAWBERRY. *alpine* WOODSIA.

B *n.* **1** An alpine plant. E19. **2** A member of the Alpine division of humankind. E20.

Alpinist /'alpɪnɪst/ *n.* Also **a-**. L19. [Fr. *alpiniste*, f. as ALPINE *a.*: see -IST.] An Alpine climber.

Alpinism *n.* Alpine climbing L19.

already /ɔːl'rɛdi/ *a.* & *adv.* ME. [f. ALL *adv.* + READY *a.*] †**A** *adj.* (*pred.* & *compl.*). Fully prepared. ME–E16.

B *adv.* **1** Beforehand, in anticipation; before this or that time; as early as this or that. ME. **2** In speech infl. by Yiddish, used at the end of a phrase or sentence as an intensive, to express impatience, etc. *N. Amer.* E20.

1 G. ORWELL The best books . . are those that tell you what you know already. G. GREENE He didn't even hear what I said: he was absorbed already. 2 M. SHULMAN 'This story has helped a great many people, and I hope it will help you.' 'So tell it already'.

alright *a.*, *adv.*, & *n.* see ALL RIGHT.

†**als** *adv.* see ALSO.

†**Alsacian** *a.* & *n.* var. of ALSATIAN.

Alsatia /al'seɪʃə/ *n.* *obs.* exc. *Hist.* L17. [med.L = Alsace (as being a much disputed territory).] The precinct of White Friars in London as a sanctuary for debtors and criminals.

Alsatian /al'seɪʃ(ə)n/ *a.* & *n.* Also †**-cian**, (in sense B.3) **a-**. L17. [f. as prec. + -AN.] **A** *adj.* **1** Of or pertaining to White Friars in London or any other place as a sanctuary for debtors and criminals. *obs.* exc. *Hist.* L17. **2** Of or pertaining to Alsace, an area of Europe now forming part of France bordering Germany and Switzerland. L19.

2 †**Alsatian wolfdog, wolfhound** = sense B.3 below.

B *n.* **1** A debtor or criminal in sanctuary. *obs.* exc. *Hist.* L17. **2** A native or inhabitant of Alsace. E19. **3** (An animal of) a breed of wolfhound; a German shepherd dog. E20.

†**alse** *adv.* see ALSO.

al segno /al 'semjəʊ/ *adv. phr.* L18. [It. = to the sign.] *Mus.* A direction: go back (= DAL SEGNO) or continue to the point indicated by the sign.

alsike /'alsɪk/ *n.* M19. [*Alsike* near Uppsala, Sweden.] In full *alsike clover*. Clover of the species *Trifolium hybridum*, widely cultivated for fodder.

also /'ɔːlsəʊ/ *adv.* Also (chiefly *north.* & *Sc.*) †**als(e)**. See also AS *adv.* etc. [OE *alsurā*, (WS) *ealsurā*, f. ALL *adv.* + SO; corresp. to OFris. *alsa*, Du. *alzoo* thus, consequently, OHG *alsō* even so, as (G *also* therefore).] **I** Demonstrative. †**1** In that degree; to that extent; equally. OE–L16. †**2** Wholly so; in this or that very manner. OE–LME. **3** In like manner, similarly. (Passing into sense 4.) *arch.* OE. **4** Further, in addition, besides, too. ME.

3 NEB *Luke* 14:33 So also none of you can be a disciple of mine without parting with all his possessions. 4 SHAKES. *1 Hen. IV* I do not only marvel where thou spendest thy time, but also how thou art accompanied. MILTON They also serve who only stand and wait. JOYCE Saturday and Sunday being free days some boys might be inclined to think that Monday is a free day also. SCOTT FITZGERALD Also from New York were the Chromes and Backhyssons. **also-ran** *n.* a horse or dog not placed (in the first three, *US* the first two) in a race; a person who fails to win distinction, a failure.

II Correlative. †5 So, as. Latterly *Sc.* ME–E18.

III Relative and conjunctive. †6 As, as though. Only in ME.

alstonia /al'stəʊnɪə/ *n.* M19. [mod.L, f. Charles *Alston* (1683–1760), Sc. botanist and physician + -IA[1].] A tree or shrub of the genus *Alstonia*, found chiefly in SE Asia and the Pacific islands, some of whose members yield a soft light timber.

alstonite /'ɔːlstənʌɪt/ *n.* M19. [f. *Alston*, a town in Cumbria, England + -ITE[1].] *Min.* A carbonate of barium and calcium, occurring as white, orthorhombic, usu. bipyramidal crystals.

alstroemeria /alstrə'mɪərɪə/ *n.* L18. [mod.L, f. K. von *Alstroemer* (1736–96), Swed. naturalist + -IA[1].] Any of various ornamental plants constituting the S. American genus *Alstroemeria*, of the lily family, of which several species are cultivated for their showy lily-like flowers; *esp.* the Chilean *A. aurea*, with bright orange flowers. Also called *Peruvian lily*.

alt /alt/ *n.* M16. [It. ALTO.] Mus. *in alt*, in the octave above G at the top of the treble stave; *fig.* in an exalted mood. Cf. ALTISSIMO.

Altaic /al'teɪɪk/ *a.* & *n.* M19. [f. *Altai* (see below) + -IC. Cf. Fr. *altaïque*.] A *adj.* 1 Of or pertaining to the Altai Mountains in central Asia. M19. 2 Of, pertaining to, or designating a group or language family including Turkish, Mongolian, and Tungus, among others. M19. B *n.* The Altaic group or language family. M20.

Phrases: Ural-Altaic: see URAL *a.*

Also **Altaian** *a.* & *n.* E19.

altar /'ɔːltə, 'ɒl-/ *n.* [OE *altar*, *-er*, corresp. to OFris. *altare*, *-er*, OS, OHG, ON *altari*, *-eri*; Gmc f. late L *altar(e)*, *-ium*, f. L *altus* high.] 1 A flat-topped block or other raised structure on which to make offerings to a god. OE. 2 *Chr. Ch.* A raised structure or table at which the Eucharist is celebrated. ME. 3 (Usu. **A-**.) *The* constellation Ara. M16.

1 *fig.*: M. L. KING High places where men are willing to sacrifice truth on the altars of their self-interest. 2 *high altar*: see HIGH *a.* **lead to the altar** marry (a woman).

Comb.: **altar-boy** *Eccl.* a boy acolyte; **altar-bread** bread used in celebrating the Eucharist; **altar-cloth**: covering an altar during the Eucharist; **altarpiece** a reredos, esp. in the form of a painting; **altar-stone** a stone forming part of or used as an altar; **altar-tomb** a raised tomb resembling an altar.

altarage *n.* (*obs.* exc. *Hist.*) offerings or an endowment for the maintenance of an altar and a priest to say mass LME. **altarist** *n.* a person who prepares an altar for a Eucharist M16. **altarless** *a.* L19. **altarwise** *adv.* after the manner or in the position of an altar M16.

altazimuth /al'tazɪməθ/ *n.* M19. [f. ALT(ITUDE) + AZIMUTH.] *Astron.* A telescope having a mounting enabling it to move in azimuth about a vertical axis and in altitude about a horizontal axis. Usu. *attrib.*, as *altazimuth mounting*, *telescope*. Cf. EQUATORIAL.

alter /'altə/ *n.* L19. [L = other.] *Psychol.* The individual's conception of another person; a person with whom one has a social interaction.

alter /'ɔːltə, 'ɒl-/ *v.* LME. [(O)Fr. *altérer* f. late L *alterare*, f. L *alter* other.] 1 *v.t.* Make otherwise or different in some respect; change in characteristics, position, etc.; modify. LME. b *v.t.* Castrate, spay. *US* & *Austral.* E19. 2 *v.i.* Become otherwise; undergo some change. L15. †3 *v.t.* Affect mentally, disturb. M16–L17.

1 SHAKES. *Merch. V.* There is no power in Venice Can alter a decree established. E. M. FORSTER Marriage was to alter her fortunes rather than her character. J. GALSWORTHY She was altering the lace on a collar. L. P. HARTLEY Being with Alec had altered her idea of what became her. **altered chord** *Mus.*: in which one or more notes are chromatically changed. 2 AV *Dan.* 6:12 The law of the Medes and Persians which altereth not. A. J. CRONIN Stephen saw his expression alter imperceptibly.

alterant *a.* & *n.* (now *rare*) (something) producing alteration; formerly *spec.*, an alterative medicine: E17. †**alterate** *v.t.* & *i.* = ALTER *v.* LME–E18. **alterer** *n.* a person who or thing which alters or causes alteration LME.

alterable /'ɔːlt(ə)rəb(ə)l, 'ɒl-/ *a.* LME. [(O)Fr. *altérable* or med.L *alterabilis*: see prec., -ABLE.] †1 Liable to alter or vary. LME–L17. 2 Able to be altered. L16.

altera'bility *n.* L17. **alterableness** *n.* (*rare*) M17.

alteration /ɔːltə'reɪʃ(ə)n, ɒl-/ *n.* LME. [(O)Fr. *altération* or late L *alteratio(n-)* f. *alterat-* pa. ppl stem of *alterare*: see ALTER *v.*, -ATION.] 1 The action of altering. LME. †b *Mus.* Extension (usu. doubling) of the value of a note. E16–E17. 2 A change in character or appearance; an altered condition. LME. †b *spec.* A change for the worse; a distemper. M16–M17.

1 *chromatic alteration*: see CHROMATIC *a.* 1.

Comb.: **alteration hand** one employed to alter or remake clothes.

alterative /'ɔːlt(ə)rətɪv, 'ɒl-/ *a.* & *n.* LME. [med.L *alterativus*, f. *alterat-*: see prec., -ATIVE.] A *adj.* Tending to produce alteration; *Med.* (*arch.*) improving bodily function, digestion, etc. LME. B *n.* An alterative medicine or treatment. *arch.* LME.

altercate /'ɔːltəkeɪt, 'ɒl-/ *v.i.* M16. [L *altercat-* pa. ppl stem of *altercari* wrangle: see -ATE[3].] Dispute vehemently or angrily; wrangle.

†**altercative** *a.* characterized by altercation M–L18.

altercation /ɔːltə'keɪʃ(ə)n, ɒl-/ *n.* LME. [(O)Fr. f. L *altercatio(n-)*, f. as prec.: see -ATION.] 1 The action of disputing vehemently or angrily. LME. b The conduct of a legal case by question and answer. L18. 2 A vehement or angry dispute; a noisy controversy. LME.

alter ego /ˌaltər 'ɛgəʊ, ˌɒlt-, 'iːg-/ *n. phr.* Pl. **alter egos**. M16. [L = other self.] A person's second self; an intimate friend; a representative of another person.

alterity /al'tɛrɪti, ɒl-/ *n.* LME. [Early uses f. late L *alteritas*, later also f. Fr. *altérité*: see ALTER *v.*, -ITY.] †1 An alteration. Only in LME. 2 The state of being other or different, otherness. M17.

altern /ɒl'təːn; 'ɔːltən, -təːn/ *a.* & *adv.* *arch.* L16. [L *alternus* every other, f. *alter* other. Cf. Fr. *alterne*.] A *adj.* Alternate, alternating. L16. B *adv.* In turns, one after the other. M17.

alternance /ɔːl'təːnəns, ɒl-/ *n.* E20. [Fr., f. as next: see -ANCE.] Chiefly *Philol.* Alternation, variation.

alternant /ɔːl'təːnənt, ɒl-/ *a.* & *n.* M17. [L *alternant-* pres. ppl stem of *alternare*: see ALTERNATE *v.*, -ANT[1].] A *adj.* Alternating, changing from one to the other. M17. B *n.* 1 An alternating quantity. *rare.* L19. 2 *Logic.* Either component of an alternation. L19. 3 *Philol.* An alternative form, a variant. E20.

alternate /ɔːl'təːnət, ɒl-/ *a.*, *adv.*, & *n.* E16. [L *alternatus* pa. pple, f. as next: see -ATE[2].] A *adj.* 1 Of things of two kinds, from two sources, etc.: coming each after one of the other kind etc. E16. 2 Of things of the same kind: occurring first on one side and then on the other of an axial line. Used *esp.* in *Bot.* of leaves (opp. *opposite*) and in *Geom.* of angles. L16. 3 Alternative. (*rare* bef. 20.) Chiefly *N. Amer.* L16. 4 Of a sequence etc.: consisting of things of two kinds etc. coming each after one of the other kind. M17. 5 (With *pl.*) Every other, every second, of a sequence of. L17. 6 (With *pl.*) Of things of the same kind etc. in two sets: taken or coming each after a member of the other set. E19.

1 W. STEVENS A wheel spoked red and white In alternate stripes. A. LURIE The family's alternate feasts and famine whenever his father got work or was laid off. 3 G. SARTON Modern editions include four books, the fourth having an alternate title. *Dictionaries* The inclusion of numerous alternate spellings. 4 G. CRABBE Smooth alternate verse. 5 W. FAULKNER The afternoons of practice (soon he was excused from this on alternate days, which afternoons he spent raking leaves in the five yards). 6 OED The minister and the people read alternate verses.

B *adv.* One after the other; by turns. *arch.* E18.

POPE Wane and wax alternate like the moon. SIR W. SCOTT Massive arches . . That rose alternate row and row.

C *n.* 1 Something alternative to something else. Now chiefly *N. Amer.* E18. 2 A deputy; someone to substitute for someone else. Chiefly *N. Amer.* M19.

1 R. M. PIRSIG The best ones [roads] . . have an alternate that gets you there quicker. *Tucson Magazine* Fresh fruit as an alternate to potatoes with entrees. 2 *Transatlantic Review* I was the alternate in case he got sick.

alternate /'ɔːltəneɪt, 'ɒl-/ *v.* L16. [L *alternat-* pa. ppl stem of *alternare* do things by turns, f. as ALTERN: see -ATE[3].] 1 *v.t.* Arrange or perform (two different things or two sets of things) alternately; cause to occur in alternation. L16. 2 *v.i.* Of two (occas. more than two) things: succeed each other by turns. E18. 3 *v.i.* Of a whole: consist of alternations *between*. Of an individual person or thing: move *between*; fluctuate in opinion, resolution, etc., *between*. E19. 4 *v.i.* Of one thing or one class of things: appear or occur alternately *with* another. M19. 5 *v.t.* Interchange (one thing) alternately *with* (occas. *by*) another. M19.

1 MILTON Who in their course Melodious Hymns about the sovran Throne Alternate all night long. 2 T. STOPPARD Though chickens and eggs may alternate back through the millennia. 3 DISRAELI A land which alternates between plains of sand and dull ranges of monotonous hills. N. MITFORD He . . had not, like me, alternated between faith and black moods of scepticism. 4 G. MAXWELL Eating them like a stick of Edinburgh rock, always with five crunches of the left-hand side of the jaw alternating with five crunches on the right. 5 F. RAPHAEL Isidore alternated promises of fur coats with threats of excommunication.

alternately /ɔːl'təːnətli, ɒl-/ *adv.* LME. [f. as ALTERNATE *a.* + -LY[2].] 1 In alternate order; by turns. LME. 2 In alternate positions; on each side in turn. M18.

alternating /'ɔːltəneɪtɪŋ, 'ɒl-/ *a.* M19. [f. ALTERNATE *v.* + -ING[2].] 1 Occurring alternately with something else. M19. 2 *Electr.* Of a current, potential, etc.: that reverses its polarity at regular intervals, esp. sinusoidally; associated with or producing an alternating current, potential, etc. Cf. DIRECT *a.* 6. M19.

alternatingly *adv.* L19.

alternation /ɔːltə'neɪʃ(ə)n, ɒl-/ *n.* LME. [Partly f. L *alternatio(n-)*, partly f. Fr.: see ALTERNATE *v.*, -ATION.] 1 The action of two things succeeding each other by turn; alternate succession, occurrence, or performance. LME. 2 Successive change because of alternating phenomena. M17. 3 The position or state of being in alternate order. M19. 4 *Logic.* The function of alternative propositions, symbolized by v (L *vel* or) and corresponding to the inclusive sense of 'or' (and/or); a statement of such alternatives. L19.

1 **alternation of generations** *Biol.* the occurrence in alternate generations of different forms of an organism having different (usu. sexual and asexual) reproductive processes.

alternative /ɔːl'təːnətɪv, ɒl-/ *a.* & *n.* M16. [Fr. *alternatif*, *-ive* or med.L *alternativus* f. as ALTERNATE *v.*: see -ATIVE.] A *adj.* 1 Characterized by alternation; alternating; alternate. Now *rare.* M16. 2 Stating or offering either of two things; expressing alternation; disjunctive. L16. 3 Of two things: mutually exclusive. Of one or more things: available in place of another. M19. b *spec.* Designating a mode of life, system of knowledge and practice, organization, etc., purporting to represent a preferable and cogent alternative to that of the established social order. M20.

3 **Alternative Service Book**: for use in the Church of England as an alternative to the *Book of Common Prayer*. b *the alternative society*. *alternative birthing*, *alternative medicine*, *alternative technology*, etc. **alternative comedian**, **comedienne**: performing alternative comedy. **alternative comedy**: rejecting certain established (esp. racist and sexist) comic stereotypes and having a strong political component.

alternative energy: (*a*) not from nuclear fuel; (*b*) not from fossil fuel.

B *n.* 1 A proposition containing two or more mutually exclusive statements; a statement or offer of two or more mutually exclusive things; liberty to choose between two or more things. E17. †2 Alternative course; alternation. M–L18. 3 Each of the components of an alternative proposition; each of two or more possibilities; the other or remaining course; a thing available in place of another. E19.

1 J. S. MILL The alternative seemed to be either death, or to be permanently supported by other people, or a radical change in the economical arrangements. 2 J. WEDGWOOD They bear sudden alternatives of heat and cold. 3 T. HARDY Warren's was a sort of clubhouse, used as an alternative to the inn. B. ENGLAND You leave me no alternative I give you twenty-four hours in which to prove your theories correct. J. ORTON You have the choice. What is it to be? Either madness or death? .. Neither of your alternatives would enable me to continue to be employed by Her Majesty's Government. J. IRVING 'You have four alternatives,' Vigneron said.

alternatively *adv.* †(*a*) by turns; (*b*) in a way that offers an alternative; as or by way of an alternative: L16. **alternativeness** *n.* (*rare*) M18.

alternator /'ɔːltəneɪtə, 'ɒl-/ *n.* M19. [f. ALTERNATE *v.* + -OR.] 1 A person who causes alternation. *rare.* M19. 2 An electric generator producing an alternating power supply. L19.

alternity /ɔːl'təːnɪti, ɒl-/ *n. rare.* M17. [Fr. *alternité* or med.L *alternitas* f. as ALTERN: see -ITY.] Being alternate; alternation.

althaea /al'θiːə/ *n.* Also **-thea**. LME. [L f. Gk *althaia* marshmallow, f. *althein* heal.] A plant of the genus *Althaea* of the mallow family, *esp.* marshmallow. Also, the ornamental shrub *Hibiscus syriacus* (formerly *A. frutex*).

Althing /'ɔːlθɪŋ, 'ɒl-/ *n.* L18. [Icel. *alþing* f. ON *alþingi*, f. *allr* ALL *a.* + *þing* THING *n.*[2]] *Hist.* The general assembly of Iceland.

altho' *conj.* see ALTHOUGH.

althorn /'althɔːn/ *n.* M19. [G, f. as ALT, HORN *n.*] *Mus.* A wind instrument of the saxhorn family.

although /ɔːl'ðəʊ, ɒl-/ *conj.* Also (*informal*) **altho'**. ME. [f. ALL *adv.* + THOUGH.] Even though; notwithstanding the fact that; and yet, nevertheless.

E. O'NEILL I think she's much better, don't you—although she won't admit it. G. EWART Although he giggled Dominic was shocked.

alti *n.* pl. of ALTUS *n.*

alti- /'alti/ *comb. form* of L *altus* high and *alte* highly: see -I-.

altipla'nation *n.* (*Geol.*) the production of terraces or other flat surfaces by periglacial processes such as solifluction E20.

altimeter /'altɪmiːtə/ *n.* E19. [f. ALTI- + -METER.] †1 An instrument for measuring altitudes geometrically. Only in Dicts. E–M19. 2 An instrument used to determine altitude attained, esp. a barometric or radio-echo device fitted in an aircraft etc. E20.

altimetry /al'tɪmɪtri/ *n.* LME. [med.L *altimetria*: see ALTI-, -METRY.] The measurement of height or altitude.

alti'metric *a.* E20.

altiplano /altɪ'plɑːnəʊ, *foreign* alti'plano/ *n.* E20. [Sp.] The high tableland of central S. America.

altisonant /al'tɪsənənt/ *a. arch.* E17. [f. L *altisonus*, f. as ALTI- + *sonare* to sound + -ANT[1].] High-sounding, pompous, loud.

altissimo /al'tɪsɪməʊ/ *n.* L18. [It., superl. of ALTO.] Mus. *in altissimo*, in the second octave above G at the top of the treble stave. Cf. ALT.

†altitonant *a.* L16–M17. [L *altitonant-*, *-ans*, f. as ALTI- + pres. pple of *tonare* to thunder: see -ANT[1].] Thundering from on high: an epithet of Jove (Jupiter).

altitude /'altɪtjuːd/ *n.* LME. [L *altitudo*, *-din-*, f. *altus* high: see -TUDE.] 1 *Astron.* Angular distance above the horizon. Cf. ZENITH *distance*. LME. 2 Height or depth, as dimensions of space. LME. 3 Height above the ground or above sea level; loftiness. LME. 4 (As a count n.) A height; in *pl.*, great heights. LME. †b In *pl. fig.* Lofty feelings, airs, phrases, etc. E17–E19. 5 *fig.* Eminence; high or exalted position. L15. 6 *Geom.* The height of a triangle or other figure, measured by a perpendicular from a vertex to the base or base produced. L16.

Comb.: **altitude sickness** illness caused by ascent to high altitude, characterized chiefly by nausea and exhaustion.

alti'tudinal *a.* relating to height or degree of elevation L18. **alti'tudinous** *a.* high, lofty M19.

altivolant /al'tɪvəl(ə)nt/ *a. rare.* M17. [L *altivolant-*, *-ans*, f. as ALTI- + pres. pple of *volare* to fly: see -ANT[1].] Flying on high.

alto /'altəʊ/ *n.* & *a.* L16. [It. = high (*sc.* song) f. L ALTUS.] *Mus.* A *n.* Pl. **-os**. 1 a The highest adult male voice, with range above the tenor, the counter-tenor voice; a part written for such a voice. L16. b A female voice of similar range, a contralto voice; a part written for such a voice. E19. 2 A person who has a counter-tenor or contralto voice. L18. 3 An alto wind instrument (see sense B. below). L19.

B *adj.* Designating, pertaining to, or intended for a counter-tenor or contralto voice. Also, designating that member of a group of similar instruments with a range or relative pitch comparable to an alto voice (among wind instruments usu. the second or third highest member of the family). E18.

alto clef: placing middle C on the middle line of the stave. **alto horn** (*a*) = ALTHORN; (*b*) *US* an alto saxophone.

alto- *pref.* see ALL *adv.* 2.

altocumulus /altəʊ'kjuːmjʊləs/ *n.* Pl. **-li** /-lʌɪ, -liː/. L19. [f. mod.L *alto-*, f. *altus* high, + CUMULUS.] *Meteorol.* A cloud or cloud-type resembling cumulus but occurring at medium altitude (usu. 2 to 7 km, 6500 to 23,000 ft).

altogether /ɔːltə'gɛðə, ɒl-/ *n.* & *adv.* OE. [f. ALL + TOGETHER.] A *n.* †1 The whole together; the total; everything. OE–E16. 2 *for altogether*, for ever, for good. *arch.* M16. 3 A whole; an overall effect. Now *rare*. M18. 4 *The* nude. *colloq.* L19.

1 TINDALE *1 Cor.* 7:19 Circumcision is nothynge .. but the keppynge of the commaundmentes of god is altogether.

B *adv.* 1 Totally; entirely; in all respects. OE. 2 All in a company; all inclusively. From 17 usu. *all together*. ME. 3 In all; in total amount. L18. 4 On the whole; taking everything into account. E19.

1 H. T. BUCKLE In Greece, we see a country altogether the reverse of India. S. HILL It is getting altogether too hot to walk back to Cliff House. 2 E. RAYMOND A medical officer .. and the whole of his Sick Parade ran altogether. 3 J. AUSTEN Altogether, they will have five hundred a-year amongst them. 4 W. E. COLLINSON Altogether I cannot think of any modern writer who has exercised so far-reaching an influence on our every-day speech.

altogetherness *n.* (now *rare*) wholeness, unity L17.

alto-relievo /ˌaltəʊrɪ'liːvəʊ/ *n.* Also **-rilievo** /-rɪ'ljeɪvəʊ/. Pl. **-os**. M17. [It. *alto-rilievo*: see ALTO, RELIEVO *n.*[1]] (A sculpture, moulding, carving, etc., in) high relief.

altostratus /altəʊ'strɑːtəs, -'streɪtəs/ *n.* L19. [f. mod.L *alto-*, f. *altus* high, + STRATUS.] *Meteorol.* A cloud or cloud-type resembling stratus or cirrostratus but occurring at medium altitude (usu. 2 to 7 km, 6500 to 23,000 ft).

altricial /al'trɪʃ(ə)l/ *a.* L19. [f. mod.L *Altrices*, a former division of birds, pl. of *altrix* fem. of *altor* nourisher, f. *alere* nourish: see -IAL.] *Zool.* (Having young which are) helpless at birth; nidicolous. Cf. PRECOCIAL.

altruism /'altrʊɪz(ə)m/ *n.* M19. [Fr. *altruisme* (A. Comte), f. It. *altrui* somebody else: see -ISM.] Regard for others as a principle of action; unselfishness.

altruist *n.* an altruistic person M19. **altru'istic** *a.* of, pertaining to, or practising altruism; unselfish: M19. **altru'istically** *adv.* M19.

altus /'altʌs/ *n.* & *a.* Pl. of n. **-ti** /-tʌɪ, -tiː/. L16. [L = high.] *Early Mus.* = ALTO.

aludel /'aljʊdɛl/ *n.* LME. [OFr. *alutel*, later *aludel*, f. Sp. f. Arab. *al-'uṯāl* the sublimation-vessel: see AL-[2].] A pear-shaped earthenware or glass pot, open at both ends so that a series could be fitted one above another, formerly used in sublimation.

alula /'aljʊlə/ *n.* Pl. **-lae** /-liː/. L18. [mod.L, dim. of *ala* wing.] 1 *Ornith.* A bastard wing. L18. 2 *Entomol.* A small lobe at the base of a wing or elytron, present in certain insects. E19.

alum /'aləm/ *n.* & *v.* LME. [OFr. f. L *alumen* rel. to *aluta* tawed leather.] A *n. Chem.* 1 A hydrated double sulphate of aluminium and potassium, forming colourless octahedral crystals and having astringent properties; $KAl(SO_4)_2{\cdot}12H_2O$. LME. 2 Any of various substances resembling this; now *spec.* any of a series of isomorphous double sulphates in which other elements or radicals may replace aluminium or potassium. LME.

2 With specifying wd indicating the characteristic element or source, as *ammonium alum*, *chrome alum*, *ferric alum*, *iron alum*, *potash alum* (= sense 1), *rock alum*, *Roman alum*, *soda alum*, etc.

Comb.: **alum-rock** (*a*) = ALUNITE; (*b*) alum-shale; **alum-root** *N. Amer.* any of various plants with astringent roots, *esp.* heuchera; **alum-schist**, **-shale**, **-slate** argillaceous rock impregnated with alum; **alum-stone** = ALUNITE.

B *v.t.* Treat or impregnate with alum. LME.

alumina /ə'luːmɪnə/ *n.* L18. [f. L *alumin-*, *alumen* ALUM, after *soda*, *magnesia*, etc.] Aluminium oxide, Al_2O_3, a white refractory solid which is a major constituent of many rocks, esp. clays, and is found crystallized as corundum, sapphire, etc.

†alumine *n.* [Fr.] = ALUMINA L18–M19. **aluminate** *n.* (*Chem.*) a salt formed (as) from alumina and a base M19.

aluminium /aljʊ'mɪnɪəm/ *n.* & *a.* Also ***aluminum** /ə'luːmɪnəm/. E19. [f. ALUMINA + -IUM.] A *n.* A light silvery ductile and malleable metal, not readily tarnished by air, which is a chemical element, atomic no. 13. (Symbol Al.) E19.

B *attrib.* or as *adj.* Of aluminium; made with or containing aluminium. M19.

aluminium bronze an alloy of aluminium with copper (and sometimes other metals). **aluminium foil** aluminium in very thin sheets, used as wrapping material etc.

aluminize /ə'ljuːmɪnʌɪz/ *v.t.* coat with aluminium E20.

alumino- /ə'luːmɪnəʊ/ *comb. form* of ALUMINA and ALUMINIUM: see -O-.

alumino'silicate *n.* a silicate containing aluminium, *esp.* one in which aluminium replaces some of the silicon in the ion SiO_4^-; *spec.* any of the numerous minerals of this kind, e.g. the clay minerals and feldspars: E20. **alumino'thermic** *a.* of or pertaining to aluminothermy E20. **alumino'thermy** *n.* the production of high temperatures (for welding, smelting, etc.) by means of the oxidation of powdered aluminium E20.

aluminous /ə'luːmɪnəs/ *a.* LME. [f. L *aluminosus*, f. *alumin-*, *alumen* ALUM: see -OUS.] Of the nature of or containing alum or alumina.

aluminum *n.* see ALUMINIUM.

alumna /ə'lʌmnə/ *n.* Pl. **-nae** /-niː/. L19. [L, fem. of next.] A female graduate or former student of a school, college, university, or other educational institution.

alumnus /ə'lʌmnəs/ *n.* Pl. **-ni** /-nʌɪ/. M17. [L = nursling, pupil, f. *alere* nourish.] Formerly, a pupil. Now *spec.*, a (male) graduate or former student of a school, college, university, or other educational institution.

alunite /'aljʊnʌɪt/ *n.* M19. [Fr., f. *alun* f. as ALUM + -ITE[1].] *Min.* A hexagonal basic sulphate of potassium and aluminium, used in alum manufacture.

alunogen /ə'ljuːnədʒ(ə)n/ *n.* M19. [Fr. *alunogène*, f. as prec.: see -GEN.] *Min.* A hydrated aluminium sulphate, usu. occurring as masses of feathery or fibrous triclinic crystals.

alure /'aljə/ *n.* Now *arch.* & *dial.* ME. [OFr. *alëor*, later *alëeur*, AN *aleür* passage, gallery, etc., esp. in fortifications.] A passage, gallery, or cloister to walk in, *esp.* one behind battlements or on the roof of a church.

alveary /'alvɪəri/ *n.* Now *rare* or *obs.* L16. [f. L

alvearium set of beehives, f. *alveus* beehive: see -ARY[1].] A beehive.
fig.: J. BARET An alvearie or quadruple dictionarie.

alveolar /al'vɪələ/ *a.* & *n.* L18. [f. ALVEOLUS + -AR[1].] **A** *adj.* Of or pertaining to an alveolus or alveoli; *Phonet.* (of a consonant) articulated with the tip of the tongue at or near the ridge of the upper teeth. L18.
alveolar ridge the ridge that contains the sockets of the upper teeth.
B *n.* **1** *Anat.* An alveolar process. *rare.* L19. **2** *Phonet.* An alveolar consonant. L19.
alveolarity /-'larɪti/ *n.* (*Phonet.*) the quality of being alveolar M20.

alveolo- /al'vɪələʊ, alvɪ'əʊləʊ/ *comb. form.* L19. [f. next: see -O-.] Of or pertaining to the sockets of the teeth or the alveolar ridge; *Phonet.* alveolar and, as *alveolo-palatal* etc.

alveolus /al'vɪələs, alvɪ'əʊləs/ *n.* Pl. **-li** /-lʌɪ, -liː/. L17. [L, dim. of *alveus* cavity.] Chiefly *Anat.* A small cavity or depression; *esp.* (*a*) the socket of a tooth; (*b*) any of the terminal air-sacs of the lungs; (*c*) an acinus.
al'veolate *a.* pitted with small cavities E19. **'alveole** *n.* [Fr.] = ALVEOLUS M18.

alveus /'alvɪəs/ *n.* L17. [L.] The channel or bed of a river, the trough of the sea. Also, beach ground between the high- and low-water marks.

alvine /'alvʌɪn/ *a.* Now *rare.* M18. [mod.L *alvinus*, f. *alvus* belly: see -INE[1].] Of or pertaining to the bowels.

alway /'ɔːlweɪ, ɔːl'weɪ/ *adv.* Now *arch.* & *poet.* OE. [Orig. two wds, f., ALL + WAY *n.* (= *all the way*).] **1** = ALWAYS 2. OE. **2** = ALWAYS 1. LME. †**3** = ALWAYS 3. LME-L15.

always /'ɔːlweɪz, -ɪz/ *adv.* ME. [Prob. distrib. genit., f. as prec. + -S[3].] **1** On all occasions; invariably; repeatedly; at every available opportunity; whenever appropriate or possible. ME. **2** Throughout all (the) time; for ever; continually; from as far back as can be remembered. LME. **3** Whatever the circumstances; in any event; anyway. LME.
1 MILTON And Love hath oft, well meaning, wrought much wo, Yet always pity or pardon hath obtain'd. ADDISON She is always seeing Apparitions. SHELLEY None slow enough for sadness: till we came Homeward, which always makes the spirit tame. YEATS I always said you could not trust these Moors. J. D. SALINGER She was somebody you always felt like talking to on the phone. **2** DONNE But what thy thorny crowne gain'd, that give mee, A crowne of Glory, which doth flower alwayes. F. J. FURNIVALL Since I first saw the Boxes . . , I always meant to have a turn at them. SCOTT FITZGERALD In a real dark night of the soul it is always three o'clock in the morning. W. H. AUDEN It wasn't always like this? Perhaps it wasn't, but it is. DAY LEWIS The smell of bacon and the smell of breadcrumbs have always been closed memories for me. **3** GEO. ELIOT Fred had always (at that time) his father's pocket as a last resort.

alwise /'ɔːlwʌɪz/ *adv. arch.* ME. [f. ALL *a.* + -WISE, = *in all wise*; assoc. w. prec.] In every way; in any way; at all events; *Sc.* always.

aly /'eɪli/ *a.* Also **aley.** M16. [f. ALE + -Y[1].] Of or like ale.

alyssum /'alɪs(ə)m, ə'lɪs(ə)m/ *n.* Also (in sense 2) **alison** /'alɪs(ə)n/. M16. [mod.L (see below), f. L *alysson* f. Gk *alusson*, f. *a-* A-[10] + *lussa* rabies.] **1** Any of several cruciferous plants belonging to the chiefly yellow-flowered genus *Alyssum* or formerly included in it. M16. **2** *spec.* In full *sweet alyssum.* A small Mediterranean plant, *Lobularia maritima*, much grown for its fragrant white flowers. E19.

Alzheimer's disease /'altshʌɪməz dɪˌziːz/ *n. phr.* E20. [f. Alois *Alzheimer* (1864–1915), Ger. neurologist.] *Med.* Mental deterioration occurring in middle or old age, owing to progressive generalized degeneration of the brain; (premature) senile dementia. Also *Alzheimer's.*

am *v.* see BE *v.*

ama /'amə/ *n.* Pl. same. M20. [Jap.] A Japanese woman who dives for shellfish and edible seaweed.

amability /amə'bɪlɪti/ *n.* Now *rare* or *obs.* E17. [Fr. *amabilité* or L *amabilitas*, f. *amabilis* lovely, f. *amare* to love: see -ITY.] Lovableness.

amacrine /'aməkrʌɪn, -krɪn/ *a.* & *n.* E20. [f. A-[10] + Gk *makros* MACRO- + *in-*, *is* sinew, strip.] *Histol.* **A** *adj.* Designating a type of small nerve cell within the retina having dendrites but no axon. E20. **B** *n.* An amacrine cell. E20.

amadavat *n.* see AVADAVAT.

amado /'amado/ *n.* Pl. same. L19. [Jap., f. *ame* rain + *to* door.] (Each of) a set of shutters on the outer side of the veranda of a Japanese house.

amadou /'amədu:/ *n.* L18. [Fr., of unkn. origin.] A kind of tinder made from either of the bracket fungi *Fomes fomentarius* and *Phellinus igniarius*, soaked in saltpetre.

amah /'ɑːmə/ *n.* M19. [Port. *ama* nurse.] In parts of the Indian subcontinent and the Far East: a wet-nurse, a children's nurse, a house-servant.

amain *v.* var. of AMAINE.

amain /ə'meɪn/ *adv. arch.* M16. [f. A *prep.*[1] 4 + MAIN *n.*[1]] **1** In or with full force; vehemently, violently. M16. **2** At full speed; without delay. M16. **3** Exceedingly, greatly. L16.

†**amaine** *v.* Also **amain.** M16. [(O)Fr. *amener*, f. as A-[5] + *mener* bring.] **1** *v.t.* Direct, guide. *rare.* Only in M16. **2** *Naut.* **a** *v.t.* Lower (a sail etc., esp. the topsail). Only in E17. **b** *v.i.* Lower the topsail as a sign of yielding; *gen.* yield. E17–M19.

Amal /ə'mɑːl, *foreign* 'amal/ *n.* L20. [Arab. *'amal* hope.] A political and paramilitary organization of Shiite Muslims founded in Lebanon in 1975.

amalgam /ə'malgəm/ *n.* L15. [Fr. *amalgame* or med.L *amalgama*, prob. ult. f. Gk *malagma* emollient.] **1** *Chem.* Orig., a soft mass formed esp. by combination (of gold, etc.) with mercury. Now, any alloy with mercury. L15. **2** An intimate plastic mixture of substances. E17. **3** *fig.* A combination of various elements. L18. **4** An ingredient in an amalgam or alloy. Now *rare* or *obs.* M19.
1 N. V. SIDGWICK Another peculiarity of mercury is its power of forming liquid metallic solutions or amalgams. **3** M. FONTEYN His perfect amalgam of virtuosity and elegance. **4** J. H. BURTON No tin or other amalgam.

amalgam /ə'malgəm/ *v. arch.* LME. [med.L *amalgamare*, f. as prec.] **1** *v.t.* Amalgamate (*lit.* & *fig.*). LME. †**2** *v.i.* Form an amalgam. L16–L17.
amalgamable *a.* L17.

amalgamate /ə'malgəmeɪt/ *v.* Pa. pple & ppl a. **-ated,** (*arch.*) **-ate** /-ət/. E17. [med.L *amalgamat-* pa. ppl stem of *amalgamare*: see prec., -ATE[3].] **1** *Chem.* **a** *v.t.* Soften by combining with mercury; alloy with mercury. E17. **b** *v.i.* Combine with mercury. M18. **2** *v.t.* & *i.* Unite, mix together; combine in a homogeneous whole. L18.
2 COLERIDGE [The Romans] were ordained . . to conquer and amalgamate the materials of Christendom. A. CRUMP Two banks of issue had amalgamated. P. H. GIBBS The old *Daily Post*, afterwards amalgamated with another journal. A. J. P. TAYLOR A reorganization commission was to devise schemes for closing the less efficient pits and amalgamating the others.
amalgamater *n.* (*rare*) = AMALGAMATOR M19. **amalgamative** *a.* tending to or characterized by amalgamation M19. **amalgamator** *n.* a person who or thing which amalgamates; an apparatus used in amalgamating; a person involved in an amalgamation: M19.

amalgamation /əmalgə'meɪʃ(ə)n/ *n.* E17. [f. as prec., perh. through Fr.: see -ATION.] **1** *Chem.* The action or process of amalgamating; the state of being alloyed with mercury. E17. **2** The action of combining into one uniform whole. L18. **3** A homogeneous union. E19.
2 A. J. P. TAYLOR The amalgamation of public assistance with the local councils. E. F. SCHUMACHER The amalgamation of many small family farms into large agricultural units operated as if they were factories. **3** G. B. SHAW Her dialect is now a spirited amalgamation of the foreign accents of all the waiters she has known.

amand *n.* see AMEND *n.*

Amandebele *n.pl.* see NDEBELE *n.*

amandine /ə'mandʌɪn/ *n.* & *a.* M19. [Fr., f. *amande* ALMOND: see -INE[4].] (Something) prepared or served with almonds.

amang *prep.* & *adv.* see AMONG.

amanuensis /əˌmanjʊ'ɛnsɪs/ *n.* Pl. **-enses** /-'ɛnsiːz/. E17. [L (Suetonius), f. *a manu* in *servus a manu* slave at hand + *-ensis* belonging to: see -ESE.] A person who writes from dictation or copies manuscript; a literary assistant.
amanuense *v.i.* (*rare*) act as an amanuensis M19.

Amapondo *n.* & *a.* see PONDO.

amaracus /ə'marəkəs/ *n.* Now *rare* or *obs.* LME. [L f. Gk *amarakos* marjoram.] An aromatic plant, dittany of Crete (*Origanum dictamnus*).

amaranth /'amərанθ/ *n.* Also **-ant** /-ant/ & in L forms **-ant(h)us** /-ʌs/. M16. [Fr. *amarante* or mod.L *amaranthus*, alt. after names in *-anthus* (Gk *anthos* flower) of L *amarantus* f. Gk *amarantos* unfading, f. *a-* A-[10] + *maran-*, *marainein* wither.] **1** Any of various plants of the family Amaranthaceae and esp. of the genus *Amaranthus*, characterized by chaffy spikes of small flowers and often by coloured foliage. M16. **2** An imaginary flower that never fades. E17. **3** The purple colour of *Amaranthus* leaves. L17. **b** A red dye used esp. to colour food. L19. **4** = *purpleheart* s.v. PURPLE *a.* E20.
1 globe amaranth an erect annual, *Gomphrena globosa*, bearing long-lived globular flower-heads. **green amaranth** a pigweed, *Amaranthus hybridus.* **purple amaranth** *Amaranthus cruentus*, bearing purple flowering spikes.

amaranthine /amə'ranθʌɪn, -θɪn/ *a.* Also **-tine** /-t-/, †**-tin.** M17. [f. prec. + -INE[1].] **1** Of or pertaining to the everlasting flower amaranth. M17. **2** Fadeless, undying. L18. **3** Of the colour amaranth. *rare.* L19.
¶ First recorded in Milton.

amaryllid /amə'rɪlɪd/ *n.* M19. [L *Amaryllid-*, *Amaryllis*: see next, -ID[2].] *Bot.* Any plant of the large family Amaryllidaceae, which includes many bulbous plants, such as amaryllis, daffodil, snowdrop, etc.
ˌ**amarylli'daceous** *a.* of or pertaining to the family Amaryllidaceae M19.

amaryllis /amə'rɪlɪs/ *n.* L18. [mod.L, use of L *Amaryllis* f. Gk *Amarullis*, a country girl in Theocritus, Virgil, and Ovid.] A bulbous plant of the genus *Amaryllis*, or formerly of this genus, which now contains only one species (the southern African *A. belladonna*, belladonna lily).
¶ Many species have been transferred to other genera, notably *Hippeastrum*.

amasi *n.* see MAAS.

amass /ə'mas/ *v.* & *n.* L15. [(O)Fr. *amasser* or med.L *amassare*, ult. f. as AD- + MASS *n.*[2]] **A** *v.* **1** *v.t.* **a** Accumulate (wealth or other resources) as one's own. L15. **b** *gen.* Heap together, pile up, collect. Now *rare.* L16. **2** *v.i.* Gather, assemble. *arch.* L16.
1a C. V. WEDGWOOD The son of a small landowner whose family had first amassed, and then lost, considerable wealth. G. GREENE A detective must find it as important as a novelist to amass his trivial material before picking out the right clue. **b** DONNE This last lesson, in which hee amasses and gathers all his former Doctrine. T. BLOUNT Cromwell had amass'd togither a numerous Body of Rebels. M. LASKI The bonfire that the children had been amassing all day. **2** D. G. ROSSETTI Billowing skies that scatter and amass.
†**B** *n.* An accumulation; a collection. M16–M18.
amasser *n.* L17. **amassment** *n.* the action or result of amassing M17.

amastigote /eɪ'mastɪgəʊt/ *n.* & *a. rare.* L20. [f. A-[10] + Gk *mastig-*, *mastix* whip + *-ote* (cf. -OT[2]).] *Zool.* & *Med.* (Designating) a parasitic protozoan of the genus *Leishmania* in the leishmanial or non-flagellated form. Opp. PROMASTIGOTE.

†**amate** *v.*[1]*t.* ME–M19. [OFr. *amater*, ult. f. as MATE *a.*] Cast down; deject.

†**amate** *v.*[2]*t.* L16–M17. [f. A-[11] + MATE *v.*[2]] Be a mate to; match, equal.

amateur /'amətə, -tjʊə/ *n.* & *a.* L18. [Fr. f. It. *amatore* f. L *amator* lover (see AMATORY).] **A** *n.* **1** A person who is fond *of* something; a person who has a taste for something. L18. **2** A person who practises something, esp. an art or game, only as a pastime; an unpaid player, performer, etc. (opp. *professional*); also (*depreciative*), a dabbler. L18. **B** *attrib.* or as *adj.* Done by amateurs, not professional; also (*depreciative*), unskilful, amateurish. E19.

amateurish *a.* characteristic of an amateur, having the faults of amateur work, unskilful M19. **amateurishly** *adv.* L19. **amateurishness** *n.* M19. **amateurism** *n.* the characteristic practice of an amateur M19. **amateurship** *n.* the quality or character of an amateur E19.

Amati /ə'mɑːti/ *n.* M19. [See below.] In full *Amati cello, violin*, etc. A stringed instrument from the workshops of the Amati family in Cremona (*c*1550–1700).

amative /'amətɪv/ *a.* M17. [med.L *amativus*, f. L *amat-* pa. ppl stem of *amare* to love: see -ATIVE.] Disposed to loving.

amativeness *n.* (*Phrenol.*) propensity to love or to sexual passions E19.

amatol /'amətɒl/ *n.* E20. [Irreg. f. AM(MONIUM + TOL(UENE.] A high explosive consisting of a mixture of TNT and ammonium nitrate.

amatory /'amət(ə)ri/ *a.* L16. [L *amatorius*, f. *amator* lover, f. *amare* to love: see -ORY[2].] Of or pertaining to a lover, lovemaking, or sexual love generally.

amatorial /-'tɔːrɪəl/ *a.* amatory E17. **amatorious** /-'tɔːrɪəs/ *a.* amatory; amorous: E17.

amaurosis /amɔː'rəʊsɪs/ *n.* M17. [Gk *amaurōsis*, f. *amauroun* darken: see -OSIS.] *Med.* Partial or total blindness, without apparent change in the eye. Freq. in *amaurosis fugax* /'fjuːgaks/ [see FUGACIOUS], a transient loss of vision.

amaurotic /-'rɒtɪk/ *a.* affected or characterized by amaurosis E19.

amaze /ə'meɪz/ *n.* LME. [f. the vb.] †**1** = AMAZEMENT 1. LME–M18. **2** = AMAZEMENT 3. Now *arch.* or *poet.* L16. †**3** = AMAZEMENT 2. E17–M18.

†**amazeful** *a.* causing amazement; struck with amazement: M16–E17.

amaze /ə'meɪz/ *v.* [OE *āmasian*, f. A-[1] + base perh. as in Norw., Da. *mase* be busy or active (Norw. dial. *masast* lose consciousness). Aphet. to MAZE *v.*] †**1** *v.t.* Stun, stupefy; infatuate, craze; bewilder, perplex. OE–E18. †**2** *v.t.* Terrify, alarm. M16–L18. **3** *v.t.* Overwhelm with wonder, astonish greatly. L16. **4** *v.i.* Be astounded or stupefied. *arch.* L16.

1 MARVELL How vainly men themselves amaze, To win the palm, the oak, or bays. 2 I. WALTON The sight of any shadow amazes the fish. 4 B. TAYLOR Men amaze thereat.

amazed /ə'meɪzd/ *a.* ME. [f. prec. + -ED[1].] †**1** Stunned, stupefied; bewildered; thrown into confusion; terrified, alarmed. ME–E18. **2** Lost in wonder or astonishment. L16.

amazedly /-zɪdli/ *adv.* L16. **amazedness** /-zɪdnɪs/ *n.* M16.

amazement /ə'meɪzm(ə)nt/ *n.* L16. [f. AMAZE *v.* + -MENT.] †**1** *gen.* Loss of one's wits or self-possession; mental stupefaction; bewilderment, perplexity. L16–M18. †**2** *spec.* Overwhelming fear or apprehension. L16–M18. **3** *spec.* Overwhelming wonder, extreme astonishment. E17.

amazing /ə'meɪzɪŋ/ *a.* & *adv.* LME. [f. AMAZE *v.* + -ING[2].] **A** *adj.* †**1** Causing stupefaction; confusing; terrifying, dreadful. LME–L18. **2** Astonishing, wonderful. E18. **B** *adv.* Astonishingly, wonderfully. Now *rare.* L18.

amazingly *adv.* in an amazing manner; *colloq.* very, exceedingly: L17. **amazingness** *n.* M19.

Amazon /'aməz(ə)n/ *n.* Also (esp. in sense 3) **a-**. LME. [L f. Gk *Amazōn*, explained by the Greeks as meaning 'breastless' (as if f. A-[10] + *mazos* breast) but prob. of foreign origin. Sense 4 f. the River *Amazon*.] **1** Any of a race of female warriors once thought to exist in Scythia and elsewhere. Usu. in *pl.* LME. **2** Any female warrior. E16. **3** A very strong, tall, or athletic woman. E17. **4** In full *Amazon parrot.* Any of several short-tailed, chiefly green Central and South American parrots constituting the genus *Amazona.* L19.

Comb.: **amazon ant** an ant of the genus *Polyergus*, the members of which depend on slave ants of other species, captured as pupae; *Amazon parrot*: see sense 4 above; **amazon-stone** [f. the River *Amazon*] an opaque green variety of microcline, used for amulets, beads, etc.; a piece of this.

Amazonic /amə'zɒnɪk/ *a.* = AMAZONIAN *a.* 1 L19. **Amazonism** *n.* Amazonian character or condition, in which women are dominant L19.

Amazonian /amə'zəʊnɪən/ *a.* & *n.* L16. [f. L *amazonius*: see prec., -AN.] **A** *adj.* **1** Of, pertaining to, resembling, or befitting the Amazons or an Amazon; warlike as a woman; very strong, tall, or athletic as a woman. L16. **2** Of the River Amazon in S. America or its basin. E17. **B** *n.* = AMAZON 1. *rare.* E17.

amazonite /'amaz(ə)nʌɪt/ *n.* E17. [f. AMAZON + -ITE[1]; in sense 2 f. Fr.] †**1** = AMAZON 1. E–M17. **2** Amazon-stone. L19.

ambages /am'beɪdʒiːz, 'ambɪdʒɪz/ *n.pl.* Formerly, esp. in sense 1, also sing. †**ambage**. LME. [(O)Fr. f. L *ambages*, f. *amb-* both ways + *agere* to drive (cf. AMBIGUOUS). Naturalized f. Fr. until 17, but latterly treated as L.] **1** Roundabout or indirect modes of speech, for deceit, concealment, or delay. Now *rare* exc. as coinciding with fig. uses of sense 2. LME. **2** Indirect or roundabout paths, circuitous ways. Now chiefly *fig.* (lit. *arch.*). M16.

1 CHAUCER If Calkas lede us with ambages, That is to seyn, with dowble wordes slye. A. BEHN Without more ambages, Sir, I have . . consented to marry him. *Observer* Popular literature is happiest when it can evade the ambages of language and fulfil itself in some unequivocal visual form like the cinema. 2 BACON He shall, by Ambages of diets, bathings, anointings, etc. prolong life. SWIFT The other cost me so many strains and traps and ambages to introduce. S. PEGGE You will find it, through the windings and ambages, eight, or perhaps nine miles.

ambagious /am'beɪdʒəs/ *a.* full of ambages, roundabout L16.

ambari /am'bɑːri/ *n.* M19. [Hind. *ambārā*, *ambārī*.] In the Indian subcontinent: a hibiscus, *Hibiscus cannabinus*; (more fully *ambari hemp*) the brown fibre of this plant, used to make ropes and coarse cloth.

ambash *n.* var. of AMBATCH.

†**ambassade** *n.* & *adv.* Also **em-**. LME. [Fr. (15, superseding OFr. *ambassée* EMBASSY) f. It. *ambasciata* f. Prov. *ambaisado* embassy, ult. f. as AMBASSADOR: see -ADE.] **A** *n.* **1** The mission, function, or business of an ambassador or embassy. LME–M19. **2** An ambassador; a deputation sent to a monarch etc. LME–E18. **3** A message carried by an ambassador or embassy. LME–L16. **B** *adv.* On an embassy. *rare.* Only in 16.

Also †**ambassiat(e)** *n.* [med.L *ambassiata*] LME–L16.

ambassador /am'basədə/ *n.* Also (common 17–18, latterly *US*) **em-** /ɛm-/; †**-dour**, †**-to(u)r**, & other vars. LME. [Fr. *ambassadeur* f. It. *ambasciator* ult. f. med.L *ambactia*, *-axia* (Salic and Burgundian Laws) f. Gmc (Goth. *andbahts* servant, OE *ambeht* servant, messenger, OHG *ambaht*) f. L *ambactus* servant, vassal (Ennius, Caesar), a Gaulish wd.] **1a** An appointed or official messenger. Now *rare* in *gen.* sense exc. *fig.* LME. **b** *spec.* A diplomat sent by one monarch or State on a mission to another. LME. **2** A diplomat of the highest rank permanently representing a monarch or State at a foreign court or government. L16.

Phrases & *comb.*: **ambassador-at-large** *US*: appointed to perform special duties, and not accredited to any one monarch or State. **ambassador extraordinary** = sense 1b above. †**ambassador leger** = sense 2 above. **ambassador plenipotentiary**: with full powers to sign treaties or otherwise act for the monarch or State. **ordinary** or **resident ambassador** = sense 2 above.

ambassadorial /-'dɔːrɪəl/ *a.* of or pertaining to an ambassador M18. **ambassa'dorially** /ˌambasə-/ *adv.* L19. **ambassadorship** *n.* the position or function of an ambassador M19.

ambassadress /am'basədrɪs/ *n.* Also (now *rare*) **em-** /ɛm-/. L16. [f. prec. + -ESS[1].] **1** A female ambassador. L16. **2** The wife of an (esp. resident) ambassador. M17.

ambassadrice /-driːs/, †**-trice** *n.* (*rare*) an ambassadress M17. **ambassadrix** /-drɪks/, †**-trix** *n.* (*rare*) an ambassadress M17.

ambassage *n.* see EMBASSAGE.

†**ambassato(u)r** *ns.* vars. of AMBASSADOR.

ambassy *n.* see EMBASSY.

ambatch /'ambatʃ/ *n.* Also **-ash** /-aʃ/. M19. [App. of Ethiopic origin.] The pith tree, *Aeschynomene elaphroxylon.*

amber /'ambə/ *n.*, *a.*, & *v.* LME. [(O)Fr. *ambre* f. Arab. *'anbar* (orig.) AMBERGRIS, (later) amber.] **A** *n.* †**1** = AMBERGRIS. LME–E18. **2** A translucent, usu. yellow, fossil resin, used for ornaments etc. and easily electrified by rubbing. LME. †**b** An amulet made of amber. Only in 17. **3** An alloy of four parts of gold with one of silver. LME. **4** = LIQUIDAMBAR 1. Also *liquid amber.* M16. **5** The yellow colour of amber; a substance having this colour. M18. **b** A yellow road traffic light shown as a caution between green (= *go*) and red (= *stop*). E20. **6** *Biol.* [tr. G *Bernstein*, app. name of a friend of the discoverers.] The nonsense codon UAG; a mutant fragment of genetic material containing this. Freq. *attrib.* M20.

2 A. ALVAREZ Two lives preserved in amber, unmoving. *fly in amber*: see FLY *n.*[1] **oil of amber** a resinous liquid distilled from amber or colophony. b T. DEKKER Pearles and Ambers, shall not draw me to their Chambers.

B *adj.* Having the yellow colour of amber; *spec.* designating the intermediate cautionary light in road traffic signals. E16.

fig.: A. WILSON I regard this as the amber warning.

amber-fish, **amberjack** (chiefly *N. Amer.*) any of a number of brightly coloured marine fishes of the genus *Seriola* (cf. YELLOWTAIL *n.* 2); esp. *S. dumerili*, of the W. Atlantic and *S. lalandi* of S. Africa.

C *v.t. rare.* Chiefly as *ambered* ppl a. [Cf. Fr. *ambrer*, pa. pple *ambré*.] †**1** Perfume with ambergris. E17–M18. **2** Cause to have the yellow colour of amber. E19. **3** Preserve in amber. L19.

ambergris /'ambəgrɪs, -iːs/ *n.* Also †**-grease** & other vars. LME. [(O)Fr. *ambre gris* grey amber, as distinct from the later *ambre jaune* yellow amber (the resin): cf. AMBER *n.*] An odoriferous pale grey waxlike substance, which originates as a secretion in the intestines of the sperm whale and is found floating in tropical seas.

amberoid /'amb(ə)rɔɪd/ *n.* Also **ambroid**. L19. [f. AMBER *n.* + -OID.] Amber moulded by heat and pressure.

ambi- /'ambi/ *comb. form.* [L *ambi-*, *ambo.*] Forming adjs. and ns. w. the sense 'both, on both sides, both ways', as *ambilingual*, *ambisexual(ity)*, etc.

ambiance /ɑ̃bjɑ̃s/ *n.* M20. [Fr., f. *ambiant*: see AMBIENT, -ANCE.] = AMBIENCE; also *spec.*, the combination of the surrounding and accessory elements of a painting to support the main effect of a piece.

ambidexter /ambɪ'dɛkstə/ *n.* & *a.* Now *rare.* LME. [Late L, f. L AMBI- + *dexter* right-handed.] **A** *n.* **1** A double-dealer; *spec.* in *Law*, a person who takes bribes or fees from both sides. LME. **2** A person able to use left and right hands equally well; *fig.* a person of unusual dexterity. L16. **B** *adj.* **1** = AMBIDEXTROUS 2. L16. **2** = AMBIDEXTROUS 1. M17. **3** Two-sided. E19.

ambidexterity /ˌambɪdɛk'stɛrɪti/ *n.* L16. [f. prec. + -ITY, after DEXTERITY.] **1** The ability to use left and right hands equally well; *fig.* unusual dexterity, many-sidedness. L16. **2** Double-dealing. M18.

ambidextrous /ambɪ'dɛkstrəs/ *a.* Also **-terous** /-t(ə)rəs/. M17. [f. as prec. + -OUS.] **1** Able to use left and right hands equally well; *fig.* more than usually dexterous or clever, versatile. M17. **2** Double-dealing; trying to please both parties. M17.

ambidextrously *adv.* E19. **ambidextrousness** *n.* E18.

ambience /'ambɪəns/ *n.* L19. [f. next: see -ENCE. Cf. AMBIANCE.] Environment, surroundings; atmosphere.

ambient /'ambɪənt/ *a.* & *n.* L16. [Fr. *ambiant* or L *ambient-* pres. ppl stem of *ambire* go round,

a cat, ɑː **arm**, ɛ bed, əː **her**, ɪ sit, i cosy, iː **see**, ɒ hot, ɔː **saw**, ʌ run, ʊ put, uː **too**, ə ago, ʌɪ **my**, aʊ **how**, eɪ **day**, əʊ **no**, ɛː **hair**, ɪə **near**, ɔɪ **boy**, ʊə **poor**, ʌɪə **tire**, aʊə **sour**

f. as AMBI- + *ire* go: see -ENT.] A *adj.* 1 Surrounding, encircling, encompassing; enveloping. L16. 2 Moving round (something), circling about (something). *rare.* M17.

1 MILTON Opening to the ambient light. BOSWELL A captive in thy ambient arms. E. F. BENSON A life that should be less idle . . than that of the ambient world. 2 DISRAELI Ye ambient Winds, That course about the quarters of the globe.

B *n.* 1 An encompassing circle or sphere. L16. 2 *Astrol.* The ambient air or sky. L17.

ambiente /ambi'ente, ambɪ'ɛnti/ *n.* E20. [It. & Sp., f. L *ambient-*: see prec.] = AMBIENCE.

†**ambigu** *n.* L16. [Fr., use of adj. = AMBIGUOUS.] 1 = AMBIGUITY 4. Only in L16. 2 A banquet at which a medley of dishes are served together. L17–M18.

ambiguity /ambɪ'gjuːɪti/ *n.* LME. [(O)Fr. *ambiguité* or L *ambiguitas*, f. as next: see -ITY.] †1 Hesitation, doubt, uncertainty as to one's course. LME–L16. 2 Ability to be understood in more than one way, ambiguousness. LME. †3 An uncertainty. L16–M17. 4 An instance of double meaning; an expression having more than one meaning. L16.

2 *latent ambiguity*: see LATENT *a. systematic ambiguity*: see SYSTEMATIC *a.*

ambiguous /am'bɪgjʊəs/ *a.* E16. [L *ambiguus* doubtful, shifting, f. *ambigere* go round, f. as AMBI- + *agere* to drive: see -OUS, -UOUS.] 1 Indistinct, obscure, not clearly defined. E16. 2 Admitting more than one interpretation or explanation; having a double meaning or reference; equivocal. M16. 3 Using words with doubtful or double meaning. M16. †4 Uncertain as to course or conduct, hesitating. M16–M17. 5 Doubtful as regards classification; indeterminate. E17. 6 Uncertain as regards outcome or tendency. E17. 7 Unreliable. M18.

1 J. RUSKIN Even the most dexterous distances of the old masters . . are ambiguous. 2 MILTON Answers . . dark, Ambiguous, and with double sense deluding. G. GREENE Notes for rendezvous made ambiguous in case they fell into the wrong hands. G. MAXWELL Calum Murdo MacKinnon is always given both his Christian names, for there are so many Calum MacKinnons in the district that Calum alone would be ambiguous. 3 POPE Antinous . . Constrain'd a smile and thus ambiguous spoke. E. J. HOWARD 'Well—once more then.' She was deliberately ambiguous about whether it was forgiveness or another cup of tea. 4 MILTON Thus shall they be too and fro, doubtfull and ambiguous in all thir doings. 5 J. FLORIO Mungrell and ambiguous shapes. T. STOPPARD Four of them carry a machine of ambiguous purpose: it might be a television camera. 6 SIR W. SCOTT The eddying tides of conflict wheeled Ambiguous. 7 BURKE The taste, that most ambiguous of the senses.

ambiguously *adv.* L16. **ambiguousness** *n.* L17.

ambilingual /ambɪ'lɪŋgw(ə)l/ *a.* & *n.* M20. [f. AMBI- + LINGUAL.] (A person who is) bilingual in all situations.

ambisextrous /ambɪ'sɛkstrəs/ *a. colloq.* E20. [Blend of AMBIDEXTROUS and SEX *n.*] = next.

ambisexual /ambɪ'sɛksjʊəl, -ʃʊəl/ *a.* M20. [f. AMBI- + SEXUAL *a.* Cf. AMBOSEXUAL.] Sexually attracted to individuals of both sexes.

ambisexu'ality *n.* E20.

ambisonic /ambɪ'sɒnɪk/ *a.* & *n.* L20. [f. AMBI- + SONIC *a.*] A *adj.* Designating or pertaining to a high-fidelity audio system that reproduces the directional properties (direct and reverberant) of recorded sound. L20. B *n.* In *pl.* (treated as *sing.*). Ambisonic reproduction. L20.

ambisonically *adv.* L20.

ambit /'ambɪt/ *n.* LME. [L *ambitus* circuit, compass, f. *ambit-*: see next.] 1 a A space surrounding a house, castle, town, etc.; precincts. LME. b A circuit, a compass, a circumference. L16. c The confines, bounds, or limits of a district etc. M19. 2 *fig.* Extent, scope, sphere, (*of*). L17.

2 W. S. CHURCHILL Both motor boats and lawn-mowers came into the ambit of this modest indulgence.

ambition /am'bɪʃ(ə)n/ *n.* ME. [(O)Fr. f. L *ambitio(n-)*, f. *ambit-* pa. ppl stem of *ambire*: see AMBIENT, -ION.] 1 An ardent (orig. inordinate) desire for distinction. ME. †2 Ostentatious display, pomp; an instance of this. LME–M17. †3 Personal solicitation of honours. M16–L17. 4 An aspiration *to be*, *to do* (†*of*, †*for*). E17. 5 An object of ardent desire or aspiration. E17.

1 SHAKES. *Jul. Caes.* I thrice presented him a kingly crown, Which he did thrice refuse. Was this ambition? 2 DONNE Costly and expensive ambitions at Court. 3 MILTON I, on the other side, Used no ambition to commend my deeds. 4 BURKE The pitiful ambition of possessing five or six thousand more acres. M. LASKI Sheila's present ambition was to be Senior Mathematics Mistress. G. EWART The ambition of the wealthy was . . to do absolutely nothing but to drink, to ride, to dance, to flirt. 5 W. GOLDING A beautiful woman is her own ambition.

ambitionist *n.* (*rare*) a person who is ruled by ambition M17. **ambitionless** *a.* E19.

ambition /am'bɪʃ(ə)n/ *v.t.* Now *rare.* E17. [Fr. *ambitionner*, f. as prec.] †1 Make desirous. Only in E17. 2 Be ambitious of, desire strongly. E17.

2 HOR. WALPOLE The Bishop of Chester had ambitioned the Bishopric of Winchester. T. JEFFERSON Who ambitioned to be his correspondent. H. SMART Ambitioning that her lover should make his mark.

ambitious /am'bɪʃəs/ *a.* LME. [(O)Fr. *ambitieux* or L *ambitiosus*, f. as AMBITION *n.*: see -OUS.] 1 Ardently desiring distinction, full of ambition. LME. 2 Strongly desirous *of* or †*for* a thing, *to be* or *to do* something. LME. 3 Rising, swelling, towering. *arch.* E17. 4 Showing or requiring ambition. M18.

3 POPE Helps th' ambitious hill the heav'ns to scale. 4 E. O'NEILL You can afford to make bigger, more ambitious plans now. E. WAUGH Sebastian set me to draw it. It was an ambitious subject for an amateur.

ambitiously *adv.* LME. **ambitiousness** *n.* L15.

ambivalence /am'bɪv(ə)l(ə)ns/ *n.* E20. [G *Ambivalenz*, after *Äquivalenz* EQUIVALENCE.] The coexistence in one person or one work of contradictory emotions or attitudes towards the same object or situation.

A. A. BRILL The synchronous laughing and crying are a partial manifestation of schizophrenic ambivalence. L. TRILLING Rousseau's *Confessions* had laid the ground for the understanding of emotional ambivalence. A. L. ROWSE There is much to be said for a certain judicious ambivalence.

Also **ambivalency** *n.* E20.

ambivalent /am'bɪv(ə)l(ə)nt/ *a.* E20. [f. prec., after EQUIVALENT.] Of, pertaining to, or characterized by ambivalence.

B. RUSSELL Christianity . . has always had an ambivalent attitude towards the family.

ambivalently *adv.* M20.

ambiversion /ambɪ'vəːʃ(ə)n/ *n.* E20. [f. AMBI- after *extroversion*, *introversion*.] *Psychol.* A condition of balance between extrovert and introvert features in the personality.

'**ambivert** *n.* a person whose personality displays ambiversion E20. '**ambiverted** *a.* E20.

amble /'amb(ə)l/ *v.* & *n.* ME. [(O)Fr. *ambler* f. L *ambulare* to walk.] A *v.i.* 1 Of a horse, mule, etc.: move lifting each foot individually and both on one side before those on the other; move with a smooth or easy gait. ME. 2 Of a person: ride an ambling horse etc.; ride at an easy pace. LME. 3 Of a person: move on foot at a smooth or easy pace; proceed in a leisurely fashion. L16.

3 ADDISON She has . . play'd at an Assembly, and ambled in a Ball or two. HARPER LEE They ambled across the square, shuffled in and out of the stores around it, took their time about everything. C. HAMPTON The ability to create essentially frivolous entertainments, which were enjoyed by enough essentially frivolous people for me to be able to amble comfortably through life.

B *n.* 1 The gait of an ambling horse, mule, etc. LME. 2 A movement suggestive of the gait of an ambling horse; a leisurely pace. E17.

ambler *n.* a horse, mule, etc., that ambles; an ambling person: LME.

ambligon *a.* & *n.* var. of AMBLYGON.

amblygon /'amblɪgɒn/ *a.* & *n.* Now *rare* or *obs.* Also **ambli-**. L16. [Fr. *amblygone* or late L *ambligonius* f. Gk *amblugōnios*, f. *amblus* blunt + *gōnia* angle.] †A *adj.* Obtuse-angled. L16–L18. B *n.* Also (earlier) in L form †**-gonium**. An obtuse-angled figure, esp. a triangle. L16.

amblygonite /am'blɪg(ə)nʌɪt/ *n.* E19. [f. as prec. + -ITE[1].] *Min.* A triclinic basic phosphate of aluminium, lithium, and sodium occurring as white or faintly coloured prisms.

amblyopia /amblɪ'əʊpɪə/ *n.* E18. [Gk *ambluōpia* dim-sightedness, f. *ambluōpos*, f. *amblus* blunt: see -OPIA.] *Med.* Impaired vision, without apparent change in the eye.

amblyopic *a.* M19. †**amblyopy** *n.* = AMBLYOPIA E18–E19.

ambo /'ambəʊ/ *n.* Pl. **-os**; also in L form **ambones** /am'bəʊniːz/. M17. [med.L *ambo(n-)* f. as AMBON.] The pulpit or reading-desk in early Christian churches; an oblong enclosure with steps at both ends.

Amboinese /ambɔɪ'niːz/ *n.* & *a.* Also **-bon-** /-bən-/, **-boyn-**. M19. [f. *Amboina* (see below) + -ESE.] A native or inhabitant of, of or pertaining to, Amboina (Ambon), an island in the Moluccas. Also, (of) the Austronesian language of Amboina.

ambon /'amb(ə)n/ *n.* E18. [Gk *ambōn* rim or edge of a cup, (med.Gk) pulpit.] = AMBO.

ambones *n.pl.* see AMBO.

Ambonese *n.* & *a.* var. of AMBOINESE.

ambosexual /ambəʊ'sɛksjʊəl, -ʃʊəl/ *a.* L18. [f. L *ambo* both + SEXUAL *a.* Cf. AMBISEXUAL.] Of or pertaining to both sexes; bisexual, ambisexual.

¶In isolated use bef. 20.

amboyna /am'bɔɪnə/ *n.* Also **A-**. M19. [Var. of *Amboina*: see AMBOINESE.] The wood of the SE Asian tree *Pterocarpus indicus*. Also called *amboyna wood*, *Burmese rosewood*, *lingoa*, *narra*.

Amboynese *n.* & *a.* var. of AMBOINESE.

ambrette /am'brɛt/ *n.* E18. [Fr., f. as AMBER: see -ETTE.] †1 A pear having a musky odour. E–M18. 2 The seeds of the musk mallow, *Abelmoschus moschatus*, which yield an oil used in perfumery. Also *ambrette seed.* M19.

ambroid *n.* var. of AMBEROID.

†**ambrose** *n.* LME. [(O)Fr. *ambroise* f. as next.] 1 Wood sage, *Teucrium scorodonia*; occas. some other herb. LME–M19. 2 = AMBROSIA 1. *rare.* Only in E17.

ambrosia /am'brəʊzjə/ *n.* M16. [L f. Gk = immortality, elixir of life, f. *ambrotos* immortal; in Dioscurides and Pliny applied to one or more herbs.] I 1 *Class. Mythol.* The food, drink, or unguent of the gods. M16. 2 = *bee-bread* (b) s.v. BEE *n.*[1] E17. 3 Something divinely sweet to taste or smell. M17. 4 Water, oil, and fruits mixed as a libation; also, a perfumed or flavoured drink. L17. 5 A fungal product which forms the food of the pinhole borer. L19. II 6 Any of various plants (cf. AMBROSE 1). Now only as mod.L name of a genus of plants of the composite family which includes ragweed. M16.

Comb.: **ambrosia beetle** the adult form of the pinhole borer.

ambrosial /am'brəʊzɪ(ə)l/ *a.* L16. [f. L *ambrosius*, f. as prec. + -AL[1].] Of or like ambrosia; divinely fragrant or delicious. Also, of or pertaining to the immortal gods, heaven, or paradise.

ambrosially *adv.* (*rare*) M19.

ambrosian /am'brəʊzj(ə)n/ *a.*[1] E16. [f. as prec. + -AN.] = prec.

Ambrosian /am'brəʊzj(ə)n/ *a.*[2] E17. [Late L *ambrosianus*, f. *Ambrosius* Ambrose: see -AN.] Of, pertaining to, or instituted by St Ambrose (d. 397), Bishop of Milan.

ambrotype /'ambrətʌɪp/ *n.* Orig. *US.* M19. [Origin unkn.] A photograph on glass, with lights given by the silver, and shades by a dark background showing through.

ambry *n.* see AUMBRY.

ambs-ace /amz'eɪs/ *n. arch.* ME. [OFr. *ambes as*, f. L *ambo* both + *as* ACE *n.*] A pair of aces, the lowest throw at dice; *fig.* bad luck, worthlessness, next to nothing.

†**within ambs-ace of** on the very verge of.

ambulacrum /ambjʊ'leɪkrəm, -'lakrəm/ *n.* Pl. **-cra** /-krə/. E19. [L = walk, avenue, f. *ambulare* to walk.] *Zool.* In an echinoderm, each of the radially-arranged bands, together with their underlying structures, through which the double rows of tube-feet protrude.

ambulacral *a.* of or pertaining to an ambulacrum E19.

ambulance /ˈambjʊl(ə)ns/ *n.* E19. [Fr., replacing *hôpital ambulant* mobile (horse-drawn) field ambulance, f. as next: see -ANCE.] 1 A mobile hospital following an army. E19. 2 A conveyance for sick or injured persons. M19.

Comb.: **ambulance-chaser** *N. Amer. slang* a lawyer who makes a business of raising actions for personal injury.

ambulant /ˈambjʊl(ə)nt/ *a.* E17. [L *ambulant-* pres. ppl stem of *ambulare* walk: see -ANT[1].] 1 Walking, moving about; *spec.* in *Med.*, walking about or able to walk about although ill or injured. E17. 2 *Med.* Of a disease or treatment: not confining the patient to bed. E20.

1 BACON Sir Edward Coke was at Friday's hearing, but in his night-cap; and complained to me he was ambulant and not current. CARLYLE An ambulant 'Revolutionary Army' .. shall perambulate the country at large. *fig.*: COLERIDGE Discriminating offence from merit by such dim and ambulant boundaries.

ambulate /ˈambjʊleɪt/ *v.i.* E17. [L *ambulat-* pa. ppl stem of *ambulare* walk: see -ATE[3].] Walk, move about.

ambulative *a.* (now *rare* or *obs.*) = AMBULATORY *a.* LME. **ambulator** *n.* (*rare*) a walker M17.

ambulation /ambjʊˈleɪʃ(ə)n/ *n.* M16. [L *ambulatio(n-)*, f. as prec.: see -ATION.] †1 The spreading of gangrene. M16–M18. 2 The action of walking; moving about. Now *rare* exc. *Med.*, after an injury or illness. L16.

ambulatory /ˈambjʊlət(ə)ri/ *n.* M16. [med.L *ambulatorium* use as n. of neut. of *ambulatorius*: see next, -ORY[1].] A place for walking; an arcade, esp. in an apse; a cloister.

ambulatory /ˈambjʊlət(ə)ri/ *a.* E17. [L *ambulatorius*, f. as AMBULATE: see -ORY[2].] 1 Moving from place to place; movable. E17. 2 Of or pertaining to walking. E17. 3 *fig.* Shifting, temporary, not fixed, mutable. E17. 4 Adapted or fitted for walking. M19. 5 *Med.* = AMBULANT 2. L19. 6 = AMBULANT 1. M20.

1 JER. TAYLOR Their ambulatory life. W. BURKITT The tabernacle was an ambulatory temple. 2 A. HELPS When that man has an object, it is astonishing what ambulatory powers he can develop. 3 W. LAUD Nor is this ceremony Jewish or ambulatory, to cease with the law. H. L. PIOZZI They learn to think virtue and vice ambulatory. 4 J. D. DANA Feet ambulatory or prehensile. 6 M. MCCARTHY The ambulatory mothers who wanted to were allowed to go into the diet kitchen. A. SHAFFER 'An ambulatory tun of port with the face of Father Christmas.' That's how I describe him.

ambury *n.* var. of ANBURY.

ambuscade /ambəˈskeɪd/ *n.* & *v.* L16. [Fr. *embuscade* f. It. *imboscata* or Sp. *emboscada*, Port. *embuscada*: see AMBUSH *n.*, -ADE.] A *n.* = AMBUSH *n.* L16. B *v.i.* & *t.* = AMBUSH *v.* L16.

ambuscader *n.* = AMBUSHER L17.

ambuscado /ambəˈskeɪdəʊ/ *n.* *arch.* Pl. **-os**. L16. [Refash. of prec. after Sp.: see -ADO 2. Usual in 17.] = AMBUSH *n.*, AMBUSCADE *n.*

ambush /ˈambʊʃ/ *n.* L15. [OFr. *embusche*, f. as next.] (A military disposition of) troops concealed in a wood or other place in order to surprise an enemy; an attack from such concealment. Also *transf.* & *fig.*, (a disposition of) someone or something lying in wait; a surprise attack from concealment.

SHAKES. *Rich. II* Once did I lay an ambush for your life. S. JOHNSON He that perishes in the ambushes of envy. DAY LEWIS These flowers .. hummed all day with ambushes of bees and wasps. S. NAIPAUL An American congressman .. had been shot and killed in an ambush at a remote jungle airstrip.

ambush /ˈambʊʃ/ *v.* ME. [OFr. *embuschier*, ult. f. as IM-[1], BUSH *n.*[1]] 1 *v.t.* Dispose (troops etc.) in concealment among bushes or elsewhere, in order to surprise an enemy. Now *rare* or *obs.* ME. 2 *v.i.* Lie in ambush; lie in wait, lurk. E17. 3 *v.t.* Attack from an ambush; waylay. M17.

1 COLERIDGE The ambushed soldier must not fire his musket. *refl.*: SIR W. SCOTT To ambush us in greenwood bough. 2 M. ARNOLD The archest chin Mockery ever ambush'd in. 3 A. HALEY He had organized a war party .. to track and ambush a detachment of the U.S. Army.

ambusher *n.* a person who lays an ambush L19.

ambushment /ˈambʊʃm(ə)nt/ *n.* *arch.* ME. [OFr. *embuschement*, f. as prec. + -MENT.] = AMBUSH *n.*

¶ Formerly pronounced w. stress on 2nd syll.

ameba *n.*, **-bean** *a.*, **-bic** *a.* see AMOEBA, -BEAN, -BIC.

âme damnée /ɑːm dɑne/ *n. phr.* Pl. ***-s -s*** (pronounced same). E19. [Fr. = damned soul.] A devoted adherent; a tool.

ameer *n.* see AMIR.

amel /ˈam(ə)l/ *n.* & *v.* Also **aumail** /ɔːˈmeɪl/. LME. [AN *amail* = OFr. *esmail* (see A-[7]), f. Gmc.] A *n.* = ENAMEL *n.* Long *arch.* & *dial.* LME. †B *v.t.* = ENAMEL *v.* Chiefly as *amelled* ppl a. LME–E18.

amelanchier /amәˈlaŋkɪə/ *n.* M18. [Savoy dial. *amelancier* medlar.] A tree or shrub of the chiefly N. American genus *Amelanchier*, of the rose family, typified by the Juneberry, service-berry, or shadbush, *A. canadensis*.

amelcorn /ˈam(ə)lkɔːn/ *n.* Now *rare* or *obs.* L16. [Du. & G *Amelkorn*, f. L *amylum* starch + *korn* corn.] = EMMER *n.*[1]

ameliorate /əˈmiːlɪəreɪt/ *v.* M18. [Alt. of earlier MELIORATE after Fr. *améliorer* (refash. after L *melior* better of OFr. *ameillorer*, f. *meilleur* better).] 1 *v.t.* Make better, improve. M18. 2 *v.i.* Become better. L18.

ameliorator *n.* a person or thing which ameliorates something M19.

amelioration /əˌmiːlɪəˈreɪʃ(ə)n/ *n.* M17. [Fr.: see prec. and cf. MELIORATION.] 1 The action of making something better; the condition of being made better; improvement; *Ling.* development of a more favourable meaning or connotation, melioration (opp. *pejoration*). M17. 2 An improvement. *rare.* L18.

1 T. PYLES Amelioration .. is well illustrated by *knight*, which used to mean 'servant'. E. F. SCHUMACHER The size of the problem puts it beyond any kind of little amelioration, any little reform, improvement, or inducement. 2 ADAM SMITH The buildings, drains, enclosures, and other ameliorations.

ameliorative /əˈmiːlɪərətɪv/ *a.* & *n.* E19. [f. AMELIORATE + -IVE.] A *adj.* Tending to ameliorate something, improving; *Ling.* meliorative. E19. B *n.* *Ling.* = MELIORATIVE *n.* M20.

ameloblast /əˈmɛləʊblast/ *n.* L19. [f. EN)AMEL *n.* + -O- + -BLAST.] *Anat.* Any cell in the layer of columnar cells which secrete enamel in the teeth.

amen /ɑːˈmɛn, eɪ-/ *int.*, *adv.*, *n.*, & *v.* OE. [eccl.L *amen* f. Gk *amēn* f. Heb. *ʼāmēn* certain(ty), f. base *ʼmn* be firm, be certain; adopted in Gk by the Septuagint, whence in New Testament and in early Chr. use in Gk and L.] A *int.* or *adv.* 1 In biblical translations, simply transf. f. L: finis. OE. 2 At the end of a prayer or wish: so be it. ME. 3 In translations of the Creed: it is so in truth. ME. 4 In biblical translations: truly, verily. LME.

2 **amen corner** *US* the part of a meeting-house formerly occupied by persons who would affirm the preacher's utterances with occasional responses. **Amen glass** an 18th-cent. drinking-glass with part of the Jacobite version of 'God Save the King', concluding with 'Amen', engraved upon the bowl.

B *n.* 1 (The saying of) the word 'amen' at the end of a prayer etc. ME. 2 As a title of Christ (*Rev.* 3:14): the faithful one. LME. 3 An expression of assent; an assertion of belief. L16. 4 A concluding word or act; conclusion. *rare.* L17.

C *v.t.* Say 'amen' to (chiefly *fig.*). *rare.* E19.

amenable /əˈmiːnəb(ə)l/ *a.* Also (earlier) †**amesn-**. L16. [Presumably legal AN, f. OFr. *amener* bring to, f. *a* AD- + *mener* bring, lead f. pop.L *minare* drive (animals) for L *minari* threaten: see MENACE *n.*, -ABLE.] Foll. by *to* or *absol.* 1 Of a person: liable to answer (*to* a law, tribunal, etc., or *fig.*); responsible, liable, subject, (*to*). L16. 2 Of a thing (foll. by *to*): liable to the legal authority of; *gen.* subject or liable to. M18. 3 Disposed to respond or submit (*to*); responsive, susceptible, (*to*); tractable. E19.

1 SPENSER Not amenable to Law. COLERIDGE The sufficiency of the conscience to make every person a moral and amenable being. E. MELLOR The next witness .. is amenable to the same imputation. JOYCE Amenable under section two of the Criminal Law Amendment Act. 2 JAS. MILL All offences against the act were rendered amenable to the courts of law. DICKENS Your property .. being amenable to all claims upon the company. 3 CONAN DOYLE She is quite amenable to her father's will. A. J. P. TAYLOR Churchill determined to restore confidence by changing the leaders. Maybe he hoped, too, to get more amenable ones. C. SAGAN The hypothesis .. is amenable to experimental testing. D. STOREY You're young, you're flexible, you're amenable to new ideas.

amenaˈbility *n.* the quality of being amenable (*to*) L18. **amenableness** *n.* the quality or state of being amenable (*to*) M19. **amenably** *adv.* M19.

†**amenage** *v.t.* *rare* (Spenser). Only in L16. [Fr. *aménager*, f. *a* AD- + MÉNAGE.] Domesticate.

†**amenance** *n.* Also **-aunce**. L16–M18. [OFr., f. *amener*: see AMENABLE, -ANCE.] Conduct, bearing, mien.

amend /əˈmɛnd/ *n.* *obs.* exc. *Hist.* Also (*Sc.*) **amand** /əˈmɑːnd/. Pl. AMENDS. L15. [Fr.: see AMENDE, AMENDS.] †1 Reparation, compensation. L15–M17. 2 A fine. Chiefly *Sc. Law.* *rare.* L16.

amend /əˈmɛnd/ *v.* ME. [(O)Fr. *amender*, ult. f. as EMEND with prefix-substitution. Cf. MEND *v.*] I *v.t.* †1 Correct, reform, convert, (a person). ME–E18. 2 Free (a thing) from faults; correct (what is faulty); rectify. *arch.* in *gen.* sense. ME. b *spec.* Correct errors in (the text of a document etc.); correct (a textual error); emend. LME. 3 Repair or make good (what is broken or damaged), restore. (Now MEND *v.*) *arch.* ME. †4 Heal (a sick person); cure (a disease). ME–E19. †5 Make amends for. ME–M17. 6 Better, improve; *spec.* make minor improvements in (a parliamentary bill, a motion etc. under discussion). LME. †7 Improve upon, surpass. LME–L15.

1 SHAKES. *L.L.L.* God amend us, God amend! We are much out o' th' way. 2 AV *Jer.* 7:3 Amend your wayes, and your doings.

II *v.i.* †8 Recover from illness. ME–E17. †9 Make amends. ME–L16. 10 Reform oneself; abandon one's faults or evil ways. LME.

amendable *a.* ME. **amendatory** *a.* (*US*) of or pertaining to amendment; tending to amend: M19. **amender** *n.* a person or thing which amends (usu. foll. by *of*) LME.

amende /amɑ̃ːd/ *n.* Pl. pronounced same. E18. [Fr.: see AMENDS. In sense 2 abbrev. of next.] †1 A compensatory payment. Only in E18. 2 = next. E19.

amende honorable /amɑ̃ːd ɔnɔrabl/ *n. phr.* Pl. ***-s -s*** (pronounced same). E17. [Fr. = honourable reparation.] Public or open apology and reparation; an instance of this.

amendment /əˈmɛn(d)m(ə)nt/ *n.* ME. [(O)Fr. *amendement*: see AMEND *v.*, -MENT.] 1 Removal of faults or errors; (self-)reformation; correction; emendation. ME. 2 Improvement in health, recovery from illness. *arch.* ME. 3 General improvement; betterment. ME. b *spec.* Improvement of the soil; fertilizer, manure. Long *dial.* LME. c *spec.* (A) minor improvement in a parliamentary bill, a motion before a meeting, etc.; a proposed alteration, a change or addition to a document. L17. †4 Amends-making, reparation. Only in ME. †5 Repair, mending (of things damaged). Only in 17.

3c *reasoned amendment*: see REASON *v.* 4b. *take the Fifth Amendment*: see FIFTH. *wrecking amendment*: see WRECK *v.*[1]

amends /əˈmɛn(d)z/ *n.* (*sing.* & *collect. sing.*; in sense 1 also †*pl.*). See also AMEND *n.* ME. [OFr. *amendes* pecuniary fine, penalties, pl. of *amende* reparation, f. as AMEND *v.*] †1 Moneys paid or things given to make reparation; a fine. ME–L18. 2 Reparation, restitution, compensation, satisfaction. Esp. in *make amends*. ME. 3 Improvement, betterment. Esp. in *thole amends*. Now *dial.* L16. †b *spec.* Improvement in health, recovery. L16–L17.

2 SOUTHEY I looked forward to an honourable amends.

amene /ə'miːn/ *a.* Now *rare.* LME. [OFr. (implied in *amenement* pleasantly) f. L *amoenus* pleasant; later directly f. L.] Pleasant, agreeable.

amenity /ə'miːnɪti, -'mɛn-/ *n.* LME. [(O)Fr. *aménité* or L *amoenitas*, f. *amoenus* pleasant: see -ITY.] **1** Pleasantness, agreeableness. LME. **2** A pleasure; a delight; a pleasant feature; a desirable facility. Usu. in *pl.* M17. **3** A pleasantry; a civility. Usu. in *pl.* L19.

1 T. CORYAT For amenity of situation . . it doth farre excel all other cities. T. F. DIBDIN Who does not love the amenity of Erasmus? W. S. MAUGHAM The smile died on her lips and she gave me a glance that was totally lacking in amenity. 2 HOR. WALPOLE A country so profusely beautiful with the amænities of nature. DISRAELI Amenities of authors. P. FITZGERALD The new Library was an important amenity.

Comb.: **amenity bed** a bed available in hospital to give more privacy for a small payment.

amenorrhoea /əmɛnə'riːə/ *n.* Also ***-rrhea.** E19. [f. A-[10] + MENO- + -RRHOEA.] *Med.* Abnormal absence of menstruation.

amenorrhoeal *a.* of, pertaining to, or affected with amenorrhoea E19. **amenorrhoeic** *a.* of, pertaining to, or affected with amenorrhoea L19.

a mensa et thoro /eɪ ˌmɛnsaː ɛt 'tɔːrəʊ/ *adv.* & *a. phr.* E17. [L = from table and bed.] *Law.* Formerly (bef. 1857) of a divorce: decreed by an ecclesiastical court on grounds sanctioned by law (having the effect of a modern judicial separation).

ament /ə'mɛnt/ *n.*[1] Also (earlier) in L form **amentum** /-təm/, pl. **-ta** /-tə/. M18. [L *amentum* thong, strap.] A catkin.

amen'taceous *a.* of the nature of or bearing catkins M18. **amental, amen'tiferous** *adjs.* bearing catkins M19.

ament /'eɪmɛnt, ə'mɛnt/ *n.*[2] L19. [L *ament-*: see next.] A person with amentia.

amentia /eɪ'mɛnʃə, ə-/ *n.* LME. [L = madness, f. *ament-*, *amens* mad, f. *a-* A-[9] + *ment-*, *mens* mind: see -IA[1].] *Med.* The condition of having a mental handicap.

¶Rare bef. E19.

amentum *n.* see AMENT *n.*[1]

Amerasian /amə'reɪʃ(ə)n, -ʒ(ə)n/ *a.* & *n.* M20. [f. AMER(ICAN + ASIAN.] (A person) of mixed American and Asian parentage; *esp.* (a child) fathered by an American serviceman stationed in Asia.

amerce /ə'məːs/ *v.t.* Orig. †**amercy.** LME. [AN *amercier*, orig. in *estre amercié* be placed at the mercy of another (as to the amount of a fine), f. *à merci* at (the) mercy.] Impose a discretionary (as opp. to fixed) fine on (a person); mulct (a person); punish in any way; (with the penalty or amount expressed as second obj. or foll. by *in, with*). Also, deprive *of.*

amerciable *a.* liable to be amerced E17. †**amerciate** *pa. pple* & *v.t.* (*Sc.*) amerce(d) LME–M19.

amercement /ə'məːsm(ə)nt/ *n.* LME. [AN *amerciment*, f. as prec.: see -MENT.] **1** Imposition of a discretionary penalty or fine (orig. one lighter than a fixed fine). LME. **2** A discretionary penalty or fine. LME.

amerciament /ə'məːsɪəm(ə)nt/ *n.* Now *rare.* LME. [med.L *amerciamentum*, f. *amerciare* Latinization of AN *amercier* AMERCE: see -MENT.] = prec.

†**amercy** *v.* see AMERCE.

Amerenglish /'amərɪŋglɪʃ, amər'ɪŋglɪʃ/ *n.* Also **AmerEnglish.** L20. [Contr.] American English.

American /ə'mɛrɪk(ə)n/ *n.* & *a.* M16. [mod.L *Americanus*, f. *America* f. Latinized form of the name of *Amerigo* Vespucci (1451–1512), It. navigator: see -AN.] **A** *n.* **1** An aboriginal inhabitant of the continent of America. Now only as *Native American* s.v. NATIVE *a.* M16. **2** A native or inhabitant of (esp. North) America of Old-World descent. E18. **3** With specifying wd: a native or inhabitant of the specified part of the continent of America. M18. **4** The English language as used in the United States of America. L18. **5** A citizen of the United States of America. E19. **6** *ellipt.* An American ship etc.; in *pl.*, American stocks, shares, etc. E19.

2 *Irish American*: see IRISH *a.* 3 *Central American*: see CENTRAL *a. Latin American*: see LATIN *a. Middle American*: see MIDDLE *a. North American*: see NORTH *adv.* etc. *South American*: see SOUTH *adv.* etc. 4 **General American** American English with few regional peculiarities. 5 *Middle American*: see MIDDLE *a. quiet American*: see QUIET *a.* & *adv. Ugly American*: see UGLY *a.*

B *adj.* **1** Of, pertaining to, or characteristic of any part of the continent of America or its inhabitants. L16. **2** *spec.* Of, pertaining to, or characteristic of the United States of America (formerly to the British colonies in N. America) or its inhabitants. M17. **3** With specifying wd: of, pertaining to, or characteristic of the specified part of the continent of America or its inhabitants. Cf. sense A.3 above. L18.

3 MESO-AMERICAN.

Special collocations: *American aloe*: see ALOE 4. **American bar** a bar serving drinks in an allegedly American style, esp. from a counter at which customers sit. *American bitter-sweet*: see BITTER-SWEET *n.* 4. **American cloth** a cotton cloth with a coated or waterproofed surface. *American cowslip*: see COWSLIP 1. *American crow*: see CROW *n.*[1] 1. **American dream** the ideal of a democratic and prosperous society, regarded as the aim of the American people. *American elk*: see ELK *n.*[1] *American elm*: see ELM 1. **American English** = sense A.4 above. **American football** football played with an oval ball which may be carried, thrown, or kicked, in which in order to maintain possession of the ball a team must advance at least 10 yards towards the goal in four opportunities. *American* IPECACUANHA. *American* INDIAN. *American jute*: see JUTE *n.*[2] **American marten** a N. American marten, *Martes americana*, which is brown with a buff throat. *American* MISTLETOE. *American olive*: see OLIVE *n.*[1] 1b. **American organ** a reed-organ in which the air is drawn inwards to the reeds, instead of being blown outwards. *American* PENNYROYAL. **American plaice** = *rough dab* s.v. ROUGH *a.* **American plan** *N. Amer.* a method of charging for a hotel room inclusive of meals. **American Revolution** the overthrow of British supremacy in America by the War of Independence, 1775–81 (*Daughters of the American Revolution*: see DAUGHTER). *American robin*: see ROBIN *n.*[1] 1b. **American Sign Language** a form of sign language developed for the use of the deaf in the US. **American tea** a social function for raising funds, to which guests contribute by bringing or buying food and drink. **American tiger** the jaguar. **American tournament** a sporting tournament in which each competitor plays all the others in turn. *American turtle*: see TURTLE *n.*[2] 2. *American wayfaring tree*: see WAYFARING *n.* **American whitewood** = TULIP-*wood* (a). *American woodcock*: see WOODCOCK 1.

Ameri'cana *n.pl.* publications or other items concerning or associated with America M19. **America'nese** *n.* (somewhat *derog.*) American English, English full of Americanisms L19. **Americanist** *n.* a specialist in or student of subjects pertaining to America L19. **Americanly** *adv.* M19. **Americanness** /-n-n-/ *n.* L19.

Americani /əmɛrɪ'kɑːni/ *n.* Also **Mer(c)kani** /məː'kɑːni/. M19. [Kiswahili, alt. of AMERICAN *a.*] In Africa: a kind of (esp. white) cotton cloth.

Americanise *v.* var. of AMERICANIZE.

Americanism /ə'mɛrɪk(ə)nɪz(ə)m/ *n.* L18. [f. AMERICAN + -ISM.] **1** A word, sense, or phrase peculiar to or originating from the United States of America. L18. **2** Attachment to or sympathy with the United States of America. L18. **3** American quality or character. M19.

Americanize /ə'mɛrɪk(ə)nʌɪz/ *v.* Also **-ise.** L17. [f. as prec. + -IZE.] **1** *v.t.* Make American in character; naturalize as an American. L17. **2** *v.i.* Become American in character. M19.

Americani'zation *n.* M19.

americium /amə'rɪsjəm/ *n.* M20. [f. *America* (see AMERICAN) + -IUM.] A radioactive metallic chemical element of the actinide series, atomic no. 95, which is produced artificially. (Symbol Am.)

Americo- /ə'mɛrɪkəʊ/ *comb. form.* L18. [f. *America* (see AMERICAN) + -O-.] Of America, as *Americomania*, *-phobia*, a passion for, fear of, America or things American.

Amerikan /ə'mɛrɪk(ə)n/ *a.* Chiefly *US.* Also **-kkk-.** M20. [f. *Amerik(kk)a* alt. of *America* (see AMERICAN) after G *Amerika*, *-kkk-* after *Ku Klux Klan*: see -AN.] Of or pertaining to the United States of America regarded as a racist, fascist, or oppressive country, esp. by Blacks.

Amerind /'amərɪnd/ *n.* & *a.* L19. [f. (as) next.] = next.

Amerindian /amə'rɪndɪən/ *a.* & *n.* L19. [Contr. of *American Indian.*] **A** *adj.* Of or pertaining to American Indians. L19. **B** *n.* An American Indian. E20.

à merveille /ɑ mɛrvɛːj/ *adv. phr.* M18. [Fr. = to a marvel.] Admirably, wonderfully.

âmes damnées *n. phr.* pl. of ÂME DAMNÉE.

Ameslan /'amɪslan/ *n.* L20. [Acronym.] American Sign Language.

†**amesnable** *a.* see AMENABLE.

amethocaine /a'mɛθə(ʊ)keɪn/ *n.* M20. [Perh. f. Gk *amethustus* (see next) or blend of AMINO- + METHYL: see -O-, -CAINE.] A cyclic amino ester, $C_{15}H_{24}N_2O_2$, related to procaine which is used as a local anaesthetic, esp. in the eye. Also called *tetracaine.*

¶A proprietary name for this substance is PANTOCAIN.

amethyst /'amɪθɪst/ *n.* & *a.* ME. [OFr. *ametiste*, L *amethystus* f. Gk *amethustos* use as n. (sc. *lithos* stone) of adj., f. *a-* A-[10] + *methuein* be intoxicated: so called because it was supposed to prevent intoxication.] **A** *n.* **1** A precious variety of quartz, of a clear purple or bluish-violet colour owing to the presence of iron. ME. **2** *Her.* The tincture purpure in the fanciful blazon of arms of peers. *obs.* exc. *Hist.* L16. **b** The colour of amethyst. E19. **B** *attrib.* or as *adj.* Of or resembling amethyst; violet-purple. L15.

amethystine /amɪ'θɪstʌɪn/ *a.* L17. [L *amethystinus* f. Gk *amethustinos*: see prec., -INE[2].] **1** Of or containing amethyst. L17. **2** Amethyst-coloured, violet-purple. L17.

ametropia /amɪ'trəʊpɪə/ *n.* M19. [f. Gk *ametres* irregular (f. as A-[10] + *metron* measure) + -OPIA.] *Med.* Any abnormal condition of the refraction of the eye.

ametropic /-'trəʊpɪk, -'trɒpɪk/ *a.* M19.

†**ameve** *v.* var. of AMOVE *v.*[1]

Amharic /am'harɪk/ *n.* & *a.* M18. [f. *Amhara* (see below) + -IC.] **A** *n.* **1** A native or inhabitant of Amhara, a central province of Ethiopia. *rare.* M18. **2** The Semitic language of Amhara, the principal language of modern Ethiopia. M19. **B** *adj.* Of or pertaining to Amhara, its people, or its language. E19.

amiable /'eɪmɪəb(ə)l/ *a.* LME. [(O)Fr. f. late L *amicabilis* AMICABLE; later infl. in sense by mod.Fr. *aimable* lovable, likeable.] **1** Friendly; kind in action. *obs.* exc. as passing into sense 3. LME. **2** Lovable, lovely. *obs.* exc. as passing into sense 3. LME. **3** (Combining senses 1 and 2.) Having a friendly disposition that inspires friendliness in return. M18.

amia'bility *n.* the quality of being amiable E19. **amiableness** *n.* M16. **amiably** *adv.* LME.

amianth /'amɪanθ/ *n.* Now *poet.* Also **-ant** /-ant/. E17. [Fr. *amiante* or L *amiantus*: see next.] = next.

amianthus /amɪ'anθəs/ *n.* Also **-tus** /-təs/. E17. [L *amiantus* f. Gk *amiantos*, f. *a-* A-[10] + *miainein* defile.] Asbestos, esp. of a fine, silky quality suitable for weaving into cloth.

amianthine *a.* of the nature of amianthus M17.

amicable /'amɪkəb(ə)l/ *a.* LME. [Late L *amicabilis*, f. L *amicus* friend: see -ABLE.] **1** Of a thing: pleasant, kindly, benign. *obs.* exc. as below. LME. **2** Friendly; done in a friendly spirit. L15.

1 **amicable numbers** *Math.* any pair of numbers having the property that each is the sum of the factors of the other, e.g. 220 and 284. 2 POPE Each mild, each amicable guest. P. V. WHITE The most amicable thing about their marriage was their parting.

amica'bility *n.* the quality of being amicable M17. **amicableness** *n.* M17. **amicably** *adv.* LME.

amical /'amɪk(ə)l/ *a.* Now *rare.* L16. [L *amicalis*, f. *amicus*: see prec., -AL[1].] Friendly.

amice /'amɪs/ *n.*[1] LME. [med.L *amicia*, *-sia*, of obscure formation. Superseding AMIT *n.*] A scarf, kerchief, or other loose wrap; *spec.* (*Eccl.*)

a white linen vestment worn by celebrant priests, formerly on the head, now on the neck and shoulders.

amice /'amɪs/ *n.*[2] LME. [OFr. *aumusse* f. med.L *almucia, -ium*, of unkn. origin.] **1** A cap, hood, hooded cape, or badge of a religious order, made of or lined with grey fur. LME. †**2** The fur of the marten or grey squirrel, used for such a garment. M–L16.

amicus curiae /a,mʌɪkəs 'kjʊərɪiː/ *n. phr.* Pl. **amici curiae** /a'mʌɪsʌɪ/. E17. [mod.L = friend of the court.] *Law.* A disinterested adviser who assists the court by drawing attention to points that might otherwise fail to be mentioned.

amid /ə'mɪd/ *adv.* & *prep.* ME. [f. A *prep.*[1] I + MID *a.*] †**A** *adv.* In the middle, in the midst. ME–L16.

B *prep.* **1** *lit.* In or near the middle or centre of; in the interior of; surrounded by. Now chiefly *poet.* ME. **2** *fig.* In the middle of (a state or condition); in the course of. LME.

1 LONGFELLOW Like Ruth amid the golden corn. J. S. BLACKIE A certain part of his work . . must be done amid books. **2** TOLKIEN It was not easy to get any clear account out of him, amid his mumblings and squeakings, and the frequent interruptions. K. AMIS Mr. Parry sat rock-like amid the storm of introductions.

amide /'eɪmʌɪd, 'amʌɪd/ *n.* M19. [f. AM(MONIA + -IDE.] *Chem.* A derivative of ammonia in which a hydrogen atom is replaced by an acid radical (orig. by any radical) or a metal. In *Org. Chem.*, any compound containing the group $\cdot CO\cdot NH_2$ (which may be further substituted); also *acid amide*. Cf. AMINE.

amidated /'amɪdeɪtɪd/ *ppl a.* (now *rare* or *obs.*) converted into an amide M19. **a'midic** *a.* L19. †**amidogen** *n.* the radical $\cdot NH_2$ M–L19.

†**amidine** *n.*[1] Also **amidin**. M–L19. [f. L *amylum* starch + -IN[1], -INE[5].] *Chem.* The soluble matter in starch granules; dissolved starch.

amidine /'amɪdiːn/ *n.*[2] L19. [f. AMID(E + -INE[5].] *Chem.* Any compound containing the group $\cdot C(NH_2)NH$, or a substituted derivative of this.

amido- /ə'mʌɪdəʊ/ *comb. form* of AMIDE (orig. = AMINO-): see -O-. Also as attrib. adj. **amido**. M19.

amidships /ə'mɪdʃɪps/ *adv.* Also *****-**ship**. L17. [f. A *prep.*[1] I + MIDSHIPS *n.*] In or into the middle of a ship; *fig.* in or into the middle.

amidst /ə'mɪdst/ *prep.* & *adv.* ME. [f. AMID + -S[3] + *t* as in *against*, *amongst*, etc.] **A** *prep.* **1** *lit.* = AMID *prep.* 1. ME. **2** *fig.* = AMID *prep.* 2. LME. **B** *adv.* = AMID *adv.* (Foll. by *of.*) *arch.* LME.

amigo /ə'miːgəʊ/ *n. colloq.* (chiefly *US*). Pl. **-os**. M19. [Sp.] A friend, a comrade: freq. as a form of address.

amil /'ɑːmɪl/ *n.* Now *Hist.* Also **aum-** /'ɔːm-/. M18. [Urdu & Arab. *'āmil* operator, agent, f. *'amila* do: see next.] = next.

amildar /'ɑːmɪldɑː/ *n.* Also **aum-** /'ɔːm-/. L18. [Pers. & Urdu *'amal-dār*, f. Arab. *'amal* work, administration + Pers. *-dār* holding, holder. Sp. infl. by prec.] Formerly, a non-European factor in the Indian subcontinent, *esp.* a collector of revenue. Now, the official in charge of a taluk in Karnataka.

aminded /ə'mʌɪndɪd/ *pa. pple* & *ppl a.* Long *dial.*, now *rare.* L16. [f. A-[4] + MINDED.] Minded, disposed, inclined.

amine /'eɪmiːn/ *n.* M19. [f. AM(MONIA + -INE[5].] *Chem.* Any derivative of ammonia in which one or more hydrogen atoms are replaced by alkyl or aryl groups.

amino- /ə'miːnəʊ, ə'mʌɪnəʊ, 'amɪnəʊ/ *comb. form.* Also as attrib. adj. **amino**. [f. AMINE + -O-.] *Chem.* Designating or containing the group $\cdot NH_2$.

aminoa'cetic *a.* designating the acid glycine L19. **aminoben'zoic** *a.*: *aminobenzoic acid*, an acid, $NH_2\cdot C_6H_4\cdot COOH$, with three isomers, one of which is anthranilic acid E20. **amino-'plastic** *n.* any synthetic resin made by copolymerizing urea, melamine, or a related compound with an aldehyde (esp. formaldehyde) M20.

amino acid /ə,miːnəʊ 'asɪd, ə,mʌɪn-/ *n. phr.* Also **aminoacid, amino-acid**. L19. [f. prec. + ACID *n.*] *Chem.* An organic compound containing both an amino and a carboxyl group; *spec.* any of about twenty such compounds which occur widely in living organisms and are the building blocks of proteins.

amir /ə'mɪə/ *n.* Also **ameer**. L16. [Pers. & Urdu f. Arab. *'amīr* commander, governor, prince, f. *amara* to command. Cf. ADMIRAL, EMIR.] A title of various Muslim rulers.

amirate *n.* = EMIRATE M20.

Amish /'amɪʃ, 'ɑː-, 'eɪ-/ *a.* & *n.* M19. [App. f. G *amisch*, f. Jacob *Amen* or *Amman* a Swiss Mennonite preacher (fl. end of 17): see -ISH[1].] **A** *adj.* Of, pertaining to, or characteristic of a strict US Mennonite sect. M19. **B** *n.pl.* *The* members of the Amish sect. L19.

amiss /ə'mɪs/ *adv.*, *pred. a.*, & *n.* ME. [ON *á mis* so as to miss or not to meet, f. *á* on + *mis* rel. to MISS *v.*[1]] **A** *adv.* & *pred. a.* Out of order; astray, awry; erroneous(ly); defective(ly); wrong(ly); inappropriate(ly). ME.

CAXTON Our Archyers shet neuer arowe amys. S. JOHNSON It is good to speak dubiously about futurity. It is likewise not amiss to hope. H. MARTINEAU Apt to see wrong and speak amiss. D. H. LAWRENCE Ursula wondered if something was amiss, and if the wedding would yet all go wrong. S. J. PERELMAN Slight dizzy spell this afternoon. . . I wonder if anything could be amiss with my hearing. **take amiss**: now *esp.* take offence at.

†**B** *n.* An error, a fault, a misdeed. L15–L17.

amissible /ə'mɪsɪb(ə)l/ *a.* L17. [eccl.L *amissibilis*, f. *amiss-* pa. ppl stem of *amittere* AMIT *v.*: see -IBLE. Cf. earlier INAMISSIBLE.] Liable to be lost.

amissi'bility *n.* (*rare*) M17.

amissing /ə'mɪsɪŋ/ *ppl a.* Chiefly *Sc.* L16. [f. A *prep.*[1] 8 + MISSING *ppl a.*: cf. AWANTING.] Missing, wanting.

†**amission** *n.* LME–M18. [(O)Fr., or L *amissio(n-)*, f. *amiss-*: see AMISSIBLE, -ION.] Loss, a loss.

†**amit** *n.* ME–E19. [OFr. (mod. *amict*): see AMICE *n.*[1]] = AMICE *n.*[1]

†**amit** *v.t.* & *i.* foll. by *of*. E16–M19. [L *amittere*, f. as A-[6] + *mittere* send.] Lose.

amitotic /eɪmʌɪ'tɒtɪk, am-/ *a.* L19. [f. A-[10] + MITOTIC.] *Biol.* Pertaining to or designating the division of a cell nucleus without mitosis.

amitosis *n.*, pl. **-toses** /-'təʊsiːz/, amitotic division L19. **amitotically** *adv.* L19.

amitriptyline /amɪ'trɪptɪliːn/ *n.* M20. [f. AMI(NO- + TRI- + HE)PTYL + -INE[5].] *Pharm.* A tricyclic antidepressant and sedative drug, $C_{20}H_{23}N$, given usu. as the hydrochloride.

amity /'amɪti/ *n.* LME. [(O)Fr. *amitié*, ult. f. L *amicus* friend: see -ITY.] *sing.* & (*arch.*) in *pl.* Friendship; friendly relations, esp. of a public character between States or individuals.

ammeter /'amɪtə/ *n.* L19. [f. AM(PERE + -METER.] An instrument for measuring electrical current, esp. in amperes.

ammine /'amiːn/ *n.* L19. [f. AMM(ONIA + -INE[5].] *Chem.* A coordination compound of ammonia with a metal.

ammo /'aməʊ/ *n. colloq.* E20. [Abbrev. of AMMUNITION: see -O.] Ammunition, esp. for small arms.

ammocoete /'aməʊsiːt/ *n.* M19. [mod.L *Ammocoetes*, f. Gk *ammos* sand + *koitē* bed.] The larva of a lamprey (orig. believed to be a distinct creature and given its own genus, *Ammocoetes*).

†**ammodyte** *n.* E17. [L *ammodytes* f. Gk *ammodutēs* sand-burrower, f. *ammos* sand + *duein* to dive.] **1** A southern European venomous snake, the sand-natter (*Vipera ammodytes*). E17–L18. **2** A sand eel. (*Ammodytes* is a genus of sand eels.) L17–M19.

¶The mod.L generic and specific names remain current.

ammonal /'amən(ə)l/ *n.* E20. [f. AMMON(IUM + AL(UMINIUM.] A high explosive consisting chiefly of ammonium nitrate, with some powdered aluminium and occas. other ingredients.

ammonia /ə'məʊnɪə/ *n.* L18. [mod.L, f. *sal ammoniacus* sal ammoniac: see next, -IA[1].] A colourless pungent gas, NH_3, which is extremely soluble in water giving a strongly alkaline solution; an aqueous solution of this gas.

ammoniate *v.t.* treat with ammonia (chiefly as *ammoniated* ppl a.) E19.

ammoniac /ə'məʊnɪak/ *a.* & *n.* Also as n. in L form **-iacum** /-ɪakəm/; †**arm-**. ME. [OFr. *armoniac* (14), *amm-* (15) f. L *ammoniacus*, *-um* f. Gk *ammōniakos*, *-on* of Ammon, used as n. for the salt and the gum, which were said to be obtained (the former from camel dung) from near the temple of Jupiter Ammon, Siwa, Egypt.] **A** *adj.* **1** *sal ammoniac*, ammonium chloride, a hard white crystalline salt. ME. **2** *gum ammoniac*, a bitter, odoriferous gum resin obtained from certain N. African or Asian umbelliferous plants, and having some medicinal use; *esp.* that from *Dorema ammoniacum*, native to Persia. LME. **3** Ammoniacal. Now *rare* or *obs.* M17. **B** *n.* Gum ammoniac. LME.

ammoniacal /amə(ʊ)'nʌɪək(ə)l/ *a.* M18. [f. prec. + -AL[1].] Of the nature of or containing ammonia.

ammoniacum *n.* see AMMONIAC.

ammonification /ə,məʊnɪfɪ'keɪʃ(ə)n/ *n.* L19. [f. AMMONIA + -FICATION.] The production of ammonia or ammonium compounds, esp. by micro-organisms; treatment with or conversion into ammonia.

a'mmonify *v.t.* (freq. as *ammonifying* ppl a.) E20.

ammonio- /ə'məʊnɪəʊ/ *comb. form.* [f. AMMONIUM: see -O-.] Indicating the presence of the ammonium ion (esp. in names of minerals).

ammonite /'amənʌɪt/ *n.* M18. [mod.L *ammonites*, f. med.L *cornu Ammonis* horn of Ammon, name given to these fossils from their supposed resemblance to the involuted horn of Jupiter Ammon: see -ITE[1].] *Palaeont.* Any of numerous fossil cephalopods of the order Ammonoidea, which have a chambered shell usu. coiled into a plane spiral, and occur mainly in Mesozoic rocks.

ammo'nitic *a.* pertaining to or characteristic of ammonites; (of shell suture lines) highly convoluted: M19. **ammoni'tiferous** *a.* containing ammonites M19. **ammonoid** *n.* any fossil cephalopod belonging to Ammonoidea, which comprises the ammonites and similar forms M19.

ammonium /ə'məʊnɪəm/ *n.* E19. [f. AMMONIA + -IUM.] *Chem.* The ion NH_4^+, which occurs in the salts formed by ammonia and in ammonia solutions.

ammunition /amjʊ'nɪʃ(ə)n/ *n.* & *v.* L16. [Fr. †*am(m)unition*, f. division of *la munition* the MUNITION as *l'amunition*.] **A** *n.* **1** Military stores or supplies, formerly of all kinds, now restricted to projectiles (bullets, shells, grenades, etc.) and propellants (powder etc.). L16. **2** *fig.* Facts, arguments, etc., used in attack or defence. M17. **B** *v.t.* Supply with ammunition. Chiefly as *ammunitioned* ppl a. M17.

amnesia /am'niːzjə/ *n.* L18. [Gk *amnēsia* forgetfulness.] Loss of memory.

amnesiac *n.* a person suffering from amnesia E20. **amnesic** *a.* M19. **amnestic** *a.* & *n.* (*a*) *adj.* pertaining to, suffering from, or characterized by amnesia; (*b*) *n.* an amnesiac: L19.

amnesty /'amnɪsti/ *n.* & *v.* L16. [Fr. †*amnestie* (now *-istie*) or L *amnestia* f. Gk *amnēstia* forgetfulness: cf. prec.] **A** *n.* An act of forgetfulness; an intentional overlooking; a general pardon, esp. for a political offence. L16.

Amnesty International an organization upholding and campaigning for the human rights of prisoners of conscience.

B *v.t.* Give an amnesty to. E19.

amnio /'amnɪəʊ/ *n. colloq.* Pl. **-os**. L20. [Abbrev.] An amniocentesis.

amnio- /'amnɪəʊ/ *comb. form* of AMNION: see -O-.

amniocentesis /-sen'tiːsɪs/ *n.*, pl. **-teses** /-'tiːsiːz/, [Gk *kentēsis* pricking, f. *kentein* prick] *Med.* the sampling of amniotic fluid during pregnancy by insertion of a hollow needle into the uterus M20. **amni'otomy** *n.* (*Med.*) rupture of the foetal membranes in order to induce birth M20.

amnion /'amnɪən/ *n.* Pl. **-nia** /-nɪə/, **-nions**. M17. [Gk = caul, dim. of *amnos* lamb.] An inner membrane that forms round a developing foetus in mammals, birds, and reptiles.

Also †**amnios** *n.* M17–M19.

amniotic /amnɪˈɒtɪk/ *a.* E19. [Irreg. f. AMNIOS + -OTIC, perh. through Fr. *amniotique*. Cf. *chaos*, *chaotic*.] *Anat.* Of or pertaining to the amnion.

amniotic cavity the fluid-filled cavity inside the amnion, in which the foetus develops. **amniotic fluid** the fluid contained in the amniotic cavity.

amniote *n.* & *a.* (of or designating) any animal whose embryo develops within an amnion and chorion and has an allantois (a mammal, bird, or reptile) E20.

amoeba /əˈmiːbə/ *n.* Also ***ameba**. Pl. **-bas**, **-bae** /-biː/. M19. [mod.L f. Gk *amoibē* change, alternation.] A single-celled aquatic protozoan, characterized by a constantly changing shape.

amoeˈbiasis *n.*, pl. **-ases** /-əsiːz/, *Med.* infection with amoebas, esp. as causing dysentery E20. **amoebicide** *n.* a substance that kills amoebas E20. **amoebiform** *a.* resembling an amoeba M19. **amoebocyte** *n.* a cell resembling an amoeba, *esp.* a leucocyte in some invertebrates L19. **amoeboid** *a.* resembling or characteristic of an amoeba M19.

amoebean /amiːˈbiːən/ *a.* Also **-baean**, ***ameb-**. M17. [f. L *amoebaeus* f. Gk *amoibaios* interchanging + -AN. Cf. prec.] Esp. of verse dialogue: alternately answering; responsive.

amoebic /əˈmiːbɪk/ *a.* Also ***amebic**. L19. [f. AMOEBA + -IC.] Pertaining to, of the nature of, or caused by an amoeba or amoebas.

amok /əˈmɒk/ *a.*, *n.*, & *adv.* Also **amuck** /əˈmʌk/, (earliest) †**am(o)uco**. E16. [(Port. *am(o)uco* f.) Malay *amuk* fighting furiously, in a homicidal frenzy. See also MUCK *n.*[2]] †**A** *adj.* In a homicidal frenzy. *rare.* Only in E16. **B** *n.* **1** A Malay in a homicidal frenzy. M17. **2** A homicidal frenzy; an act of running amok. M19. **C** *adv. run amok*, run about in a frenzied thirst for blood; go on a destructive rampage; rush wildly and heedlessly. L17.

amole /əˈməʊli/ *n.* M19. [Mex. Sp.] The root of any of several plants of Mexico and the southern US, used as a detergent; any of these plants, *esp.* the soap-plant, *Chlorogalum pomeridianum*, and the lechuguilla, *Agave lecheguilla*.

amomum /əˈməʊməm/ *n.* LME. [L name of some aromatic shrub, f. Gk *amōmon*.] An aromatic plant belonging to the genus *Amomum*, of the ginger family.

¶The name was used orig. for a variety of spice plants, the *amomum* of the ancients being of uncertain identity. The genus *Amomum* has also been reduced: it formerly included all cardamoms (most now *Elettaria*) and grains of Paradise (now *Aframomum*).

among /əˈmʌŋ/ *prep.* & *adv.* Also (*obs.* exc. *north.*) **amang**; †**emong**. [OE *on(ġe)mang*, *-mong*, f. ON *prep.* (see A *prep.*[1] 6) + *ġemang* MONG *n.*[1]] **A** *prep.* **1** With *n.pl.*: in the assemblage of, surrounded by and grouped with. With *n.sing.* (exc. *collect.* now chiefly *Sc.* & *Anglo-Ir.*): surrounded by the separate members, components, or particles of; amid. OE. **b** Through the assemblage of; through the midst of. M19. †**2** During; in the course of. OE–L17. **3** In company or association with; in the house, city, country, etc., of. ME. **4** In the number or class of; in comparison with. ME. **5** In the general practice or views of; with or by generally. ME. **6** Divided between, to be shared by, (collectively or distributively); in portions to each of. ME. **7** By the joint action of. ME. **8** As a reciprocal action of. ME.

1 SIR W. SCOTT Among the bubbling blood. LONGFELLOW He saw once more his dark-eyed queen Among her children stand. YEATS And saplings root among the broken stone. D. DU MAURIER If I heard it, even among a thousand others, I should recognise her voice. DAY LEWIS There is a screech from among the gooseberry bushes. †**among the hands of** under the charge of, while being attended by. **b** E. WAUGH Sauntering and skipping among the trim gravel walks. G. GREENE Picking among the dry seaweed for cigarette ends. S. HILL Colds spread like a forest fire among the old. **2** CAXTON Saynt ambrose . . gaue up his ghoost emonge the wordes of his prayers. **3** G. CRABBE Susan . . had some pride Among our topmost people to preside. SCOTT FITZGERALD It's a great advantage not to drink among hard-drinking people. **4** TREVISA Amonge all elementes water is prouffytablest. LD BERNERS Your folkes haue brent my house, the whiche I loued among all other. W. STEVENS Among the old men that you know, There is one, unnamed, that broods On all the rest. **5** ADDISON I pass among some for a disaffected Person. J. BOWEN Among the criminal classes, the word 'bird' . . is used to mean 'lady friend' and also a stretch in prison. J. G. FARRELL With a reputation among the young men of that circle. **6** OED That leaves five shillings among us. M. MCCARTHY She was one of many readers he had to distribute manuscripts among. **7** SHAKES. *Much Ado* You have among you kill'd a sweet and innocent lady. **8** E. O'NEILL The three girls . . stand around the entrance to the bar, chatting excitedly among themselves.

†**B** *adv.* **1** Meanwhile, at the same time. ME–L16. **2** From time to time, now and then. ME–E17. **3** Together, along with something else. Only in E17.

amongst /əˈmʌŋst/ *prep.* ME. [f. prec. + -S[3] + *t* as in *against*, *amidst*, etc.] = AMONG *prep.*

amontillado /əmɒntɪˈlɑːdəʊ, -ˈljɑː-/ *n.* Also **A-**. Pl. **-os**. E19. [Sp., f. *Montilla* a town in southern Spain + -ADO I. Cf. MONTILLA.] Formerly, a wine of the sherry type produced in Montilla. Now, a medium sherry of a matured type. Also, a drink or glass of either of these wines.

amora /əˈmɔːrə/ *n.* Pl. **-im** /-ɪm/. E18. [Heb. *ʾămōrā* interpreter f. Aram. *ʾămōrā*.] *Jewish Hist.* Any of the religious teachers in the 3rd to 5th cents. who expounded the Mishnah and thus contributed to the completion of the Gemara.

amoraic /amɔːˈreɪɪk/ *a.* of or pertaining to the amoraim E20.

amoral /eɪˈmɒr(ə)l/ *a.* L19. [f. A-[10] + MORAL *a.*] Unconcerned with or outside morality; non-moral.

amoralism *n.* the practice of disregarding morality E20. **amoralist** *n.* E20. **amoˈrality** *n.* amoral quality E20.

†**amoret** *n.* LME. [OFr. *amoret(te)* (mod. AMOURETTE *n.*) dim. of *amor* f. L *amor* love: see -ET[1], -ETTE.] **1** A sweetheart; a lover. LME–L18. **2** A love-knot. Only in LME. **3** A love-sonnet or -song. Only in L16. **4** In *pl.* Amorous glances; dalliances. L16–M17.

amoretto /aməˈrɛtəʊ, *foreign* amoˈretto/ *n.* Pl. **-tti** /-t(t)i/, **-tto(e)s** /-təʊz/. L16. [It., dim. of *amore* love.] †**1** = AMORET 1, 3. L16–E18. **2** A cupid. E17.

amorino /aməˈriːnəʊ, *foreign* amoˈriːno/ *n.* Pl. **-ni** /-ni/, **-nos**. M19. [It., dim. of *amore* love.] = AMORETTO 2.

amorist /ˈamərɪst/ *n.* L16. [f. L *amor* or Fr. *amour* love + -IST.] **1** A person who avows (esp. sexual) love. L16. **2** A person who writes about love. M17.

Amorite /ˈamərʌɪt/ *n.* & *a.* M16. [f. Heb. *ʾĕmōrī* f. Akkadian *ʾamurrū* + -ITE[1].] **A** *n.* A member of any of a group of Semitic tribes whose semi-nomadic culture flourished in Mesopotamia, Palestine, and Syria in the third millennium BC and who are described in biblical texts as inhabiting the land of Canaan before the arrival of the Israelites; the language of these people. M16. **B** *adj.* Of or pertaining to the Amorites or their language. L19.

amoroso /aməˈrəʊzəʊ/ *n.*, *adv.*, & *a.* E17. [Sp. & It. f. med.L *amorosus* AMOROUS.] **A** *n.* Pl. **-si** /-si/, **-sos**. †**1** A lover; a gallant. E17–E19. **2** A type of sweetened oloroso sherry. L19. **B** *adv.* & *adj. Mus.* (A direction:) tender(ly). L18.

amorous /ˈam(ə)rəs/ *a.* ME. [OFr. (mod. *amoureux*) f. med.L *amorosus*, f. L *amor* love: see -OUS.] **1** Habitually inclined to (esp. sexual) love. ME. **2** In love, enamoured. (Foll. by *of*, †*on*.) ME. **3** Showing (esp. sexual) love; loving. LME. **4** Of or pertaining to (esp. sexual) love. LME. †**5** Lovable; lovely. LME–E17.

amoˈrosity *n.* love, fondness LME. **amorously** *adv.* LME. **amorousness** *n.* LME.

amorphism /əˈmɔːfɪz(ə)m/ *n.* M19. [f. Gk *amorphos* AMORPHOUS + -ISM.] Absence of regular form; amorphous quality.

Also **amorphy** *n.* (*rare*) E18.

amorphous /əˈmɔːfəs/ *a.* M18. [mod.L *amorphus* f. Gk *amorphos*, f. as A-[10] + *morphē* shape: see -OUS.] **1** Having no determinate shape or structure; shapeless; unorganized. M18. **2** *Chem.* & *Min.* Of a solid: not crystalline, or not apparently so. E19.

2 J. J. LAGOWSKI The so-called amorphous forms of carbon . . are actually composed of microcrystals.

amorphousness *n.* L19.

amort /əˈmɔːt/ *adv.* & *pred. a. arch.* L16. [Misconstruction of Fr. *à la mort* ALAMORT as ALL + *amort*.] Orig. & chiefly in *all amort*. As dead; lifeless, inanimate; spiritless, dejected.

amortise /əˈmɔːtʌɪz/ *v.t.* Also **-ize**. LME. [OFr. *amortiss-* lengthened stem of *amortir* ult. f. L AD- + *mort-*, *mors* death. The spelling *-ize* is due to med.L *amortizare*.] †**1** Deaden; destroy. LME–M17. **2** *Hist.* Transfer (property) to a corporation in mortmain. LME. **3** Extinguish or wipe out (a debt etc.), usu. by means of a sinking fund; gradually write off the initial cost of (assets). L19.

amortisable /-tɪzəb(ə)l/ *a.* extinguishable as a liability L19. **amortiˈsation** *n.* M17. **amortisement** /-tɪzm(ə)nt/ *n.* = AMORTISATION LME.

amosite /ˈeɪməsʌɪt, ˈam-/ *n.* E20. [f. initial letters of *A*sbestos *M*ines *o*f *S*outh Africa + -ITE[1].] *Min.* An iron-rich amphibole asbestos, mined in South Africa.

amotion /əˈməʊʃ(ə)n/ *n. arch.* LME. [L *amotio(n-)*, f. *amot-* pa. ppl stem of *amovere* AMOVE *v.*[2]: see -ION.] **1** Removal, esp. of a person from office; ousting. LME. **2** Deprivation of possession. M17.

†**amouco** *a.*, *n.*, & *adv.* see AMOK.

amount /əˈmaʊnt/ *n.* E18. [f. the vb.] **1** The total to which anything amounts; the total quantity or number. E18. **b** *spec.* The sum of the principal and interest on a loan. L18. **2** *fig.* The full value, effect, significance, etc. Now *rare*. M18. **3** A quantity or sum viewed as the total reached. M19.

2 J. LINGARD What the real amount of that statement may be. **3** E. A. FREEMAN The amount of resistance which William met with. W. S. MAUGHAM I knew a certain amount of French before. E. BOWEN Quite an amount of people . . have genuinely no idea who I am. A. LURIE Probably the stuff is harmless in small amounts, but what is a small amount? **any amount of** *colloq.* a great quantity of. **no amount of** *colloq.* not even the greatest possible amount of.

amount /əˈmaʊnt/ *v.* ME. [OFr. *amunter*, *amo(u)nter*, f. *amont* upward f. L *ad montem*: see AD-, MOUNT *n.*[1]] †**1** *v.i.* Go up, ascend, mount. ME–M17. †**2** *v.i.* Mount up, increase. ME–E18. **3** *v.†t.* & *i.* with *to*. Be equivalent in total to (a specified number or quantity). ME. **4** *v.†t.* & *i.* with *to*. Be equivalent to in significance etc. ME. †**5** *v.i.* Arise from addition; result. M16–M17. †**6** *v.t.* Cause to rise; elevate. M16–M17.

3 SHAKES. *Com. Err.* Which doth amount to three odd ducats more Than I stand debted to this gentleman. **4** D. H. LAWRENCE There was a strange freedom, that almost amounted to anarchy, in the house. STEVIE SMITH Although I collect facts I do not always know what they amount / to. P. NICHOLS We'd gathered that she wasn't ever going to amount to much.

amour /əˈmʊə, *foreign* amuːr/ *n.* ME. [(O)Fr. f. L *amor* love, rel. to *amare* to love.] **1** Love; affection. Now *rare* exc. in AMOUR COURTOIS, AMOUR PROPRE. ME. †**2** In *pl.* Sexual or romantic love. LME–E18. **3** A love affair, *esp.* a secret one. L16.

1 K. AMIS Now and then an ill-printed book, Letters in female hands: the thin Detritus of amour. **3** DRYDEN Intrigue, that's an old phrase; I have laid that word by: amour sounds better. J. BARTH My high-school amours were limited to hot, open-mouthed kisses and much risqué conversation.

amour courtois /amuːr kurtwa/ *n. phr.* L19. [Fr.] = *courtly love* s.v. COURTLY *a.*

amourette /amʊəˈrɛt; *foreign* amurɛt (*pl. same*)/ *n.* E19. [Fr.: see AMORET.] **1** A brief or unimportant love affair. E19. **2** = AMORETTO 2. M19.

amour propre /ˌamʊə ˈprɒpr(ə), *foreign* amur prɔpr/ *n. phr.* Also **amour-propre**. L18. [Fr.] Self-esteem; vanity.

†**amove** *v.*[1] Long *dial.* Also **ameve**. ME. [OFr. *ameuv-* tonic stem of *amo(u)voir*, f. *a* AD- + *moveir* MOVE *v.*; cf. med.L *admovere*, *amm-*. App. infl. by OFr. *esmo(u)voir* (see EMOVE).] **1** *v.t.* Set

in motion; stir up; rouse; *esp.* move the feelings of. ME–L19. **2** *v.i.* Be roused or moved. ME–L15.

†amove *v.²t.* LME. [OFr. *amover* or L *amovere*, f. *a* AB- + *movere* move.] **1** Remove from a position; dismiss (a person) from an office. LME–L19. **2** Remove, put away, (things immaterial). M16–M17.

Amoy /əˈmɔɪ/ *a.* & *n.* M19. [The conventional western name for the island of Xiamen (see below).] (Designating, of, or pertaining to) the form of Chinese of the Min group spoken by the people of Xiamen in Fujian province, China.

amp /amp/ *n.*[1] *colloq.* L19. [Abbrev.] = AMPERE.

amp /amp/ *n.*[2] *colloq.* M20. [Abbrev.] = AMPLIFIER 2.

ampelopsis /ampɪˈlɒpsɪs/ *n.* Pl. same. E19. [mod.L, f. Gk *ampelos* vine + *opsis* appearance.] A climbing plant of the genus *Ampelopsis*, belonging to the vine family.

amper /ˈampə/*n.* Long *dial.* OE. [Origin unkn.: cf. ANBURY.] A tumour, a swelling; a varicose vein.

ampere /ˈampɛː/ *n.* L19. [f. André-Marie *Ampère* (1775–1836), Fr. physicist.] A unit of electric current (now a base unit in the SI) equal to a flow of one coulomb per second. (Symbol A.)

Comb.: **ampere-hour** a quantity of electricity equivalent to a current of one ampere flowing for one hour; **ampere-turn** a unit of magnetomotive force when expressed as the product of the number of turns in a coil and the current in amperes flowing through it.
amperage /ˈamp(ə)rɪdʒ/ *n.* the strength of an electric current measured in amperes; the rated current of a fuse or other electrical component: L19.

ampersand /ˈampəsand/ *n.* M19. [Alt. of '& per se (i.e. by itself) *and*', the old way of naming and explaining the character.] The sign & (= *and*, L *et*).

amphetamine /amˈfɛtəmiːn/ *n.* M20. [f. *a*lpha-*m*ethyl-*phe*ne*t*hyl*amine*.] A synthetic drug, $C_6H_5CH_2CH(CH_3)NH_2$, used as a decongestant and central nervous system stimulant; a tablet of an amphetamine salt.

¶A proprietary name for this drug is BENZEDRINE.

amphi- /ˈamfi/ *comb. form.* [Gk.] Both, of both kinds, about, around.

amphiarˈthrodial *a.* (*Anat.*) of or pertaining to amphiarthrosis M19. **amphiarˈthrosis** *n.* (*Anat.*) a form of joint which allows limited movement, the bones being joined by fibrous tissue, fibrocartilage, or hyaline cartilage M18. **amphiarˈthrotic** *a.* = AMPHIARTHRODIAL M20. **amphiˈcoelous** *a.* (*Anat.* & *Zool.*) (esp. of vertebral centra) concave on both sides M19. **amphiˈdiploid** *a.* & *n.* (*Genetics*) = ALLOTETRAPLOID M20. **amphiˈdiploidy** *n.* (*Genetics*) = ALLOTETRAPLOIDY M20. **amphiˈdromic** *a.* designating a point in a system of tides where the tidal range is zero E20. **amphiˈpathic, -ˈphilic** *adjs.* (*Chem.*) having both a hydrophilic and a hydrophobic part; consisting of such molecules: M20. **amphiˈprotic** *a.* (*Chem.*) (of a solvent) able both to accept and to donate protons M20.

amphibia *n.pl.* see AMPHIBIUM.

amphibian /amˈfɪbɪən/ *a.* & *n.* M17. [f. AMPHIBIUM + -AN.] **A** *adj.* **1** Of double or doubtful nature. *rare.* M17. **2** Of or pertaining to the Amphibia. M19. **3** Of a vehicle or other conveyance: able to operate both on land and water. E20.

1 A. TATE Mr. Eliot is amphibian and, if 'neither living or dead', is likewise neither American nor English; he is both. 3 H. G. WELLS Enormous amphibian tanks crawl up out of the water. M. INNES An amphibian plane could come and go in darkness.

B *n.* **1** An animal belonging to the class Amphibia. M19. **2** A person having a double nature or mode of existence. E20. **3** A vehicle or other conveyance able to operate both on land and on water. E20.

1 *fig.*: G. SARTON The Greeks were . . restless amphibians sailing across the Mediterranean or caravaning across foreign lands.

amphibious /amˈfɪbɪəs/ *a.* M17. [f. next + -OUS.] **1** Living both on land and in water. M17. **2** Of, pertaining to, or suited for both land and water; (of a vehicle etc.) = AMPHIBIAN *a.* 3. M17. **b** *spec.* Of a military operation: involving cooperation of sea, land, and air forces. Of forces: trained for such operations. M20. **3** Occupying two positions; having a double nature or mode of existence. M17.

2 R. CAMPBELL Since half the country consists of water and reeds, everybody leads an amphibious life.

amphibium /amˈfɪbɪəm/ *n.* Pl. **-bia** /-bɪə/, (in branch I) **-biums**. E17. [mod.L f. Gk *amphibion* use as n. of neut. of adj. *amphibios*, f. AMPHI- + *bios* life.] **I 1** A creature that lives both in water and land. E17. **2** *fig.* A being that has an ambiguous position or a double existence. M17. **II** In *pl.* only. *Zool.* Also **A-**. **3 a** *Hist.* The reptiles, including mod. Amphibia (Linnaeus). M18. **b** A class of vertebrates, including frogs, newts, salamanders, etc., which as adults are air-breathing and mainly terrestrial, but whose young have gills and are aquatic. E19.

amphibole /ˈamfɪbəʊl/ *n.* E17. [Fr. (both senses) f. L *amphibolus* ambiguous f. Gk *amphibolos*, f. AMPHI- + *ballein* to throw.] **†1** = AMPHIBOLOGY 1. E–M17. **2** *Min.* Orig., hornblende. Now, any of a large class of silicate and aluminosilicate rock-forming minerals which form fibrous or columnar crystals (they are characterized by a crystal structure based on cross-linked double chains of SiO_4 tetrahedra). E19.

amphibolic /amfɪˈbɒlɪk/ *a.* E19. [f. prec. or AMPHIBOLY + -IC.] **1** *Geol.* Of, pertaining to, or of the nature of amphibole. E19. **2** Ambiguous, equivocal. *rare.* L19.

amphibolite /amˈfɪbəlʌɪt/ *n.* E19. [f. AMPHIBOLE + -ITE[1].] *Geol.* A metamorphic rock consisting chiefly of hornblende and plagioclase.
amphiboˈlitic *a.* E20.

amphibology /amfɪˈbɒlədʒi/ *n.* Also in L form **†-gia**. LME. [(O)Fr. *amphibologie* f. late L *amphibologia* for cl.L *amphibolia* AMPHIBOLY: see -OLOGY.] **1** An ambiguity; a quibble. LME. **2** Ambiguous wording; equivocation. L16.
amˌphiboˈlogical *a.* ambiguous, quibbling L16.

amphiboly /amˈfɪbəli/ *n.* L16. [L *amphibolia*: see AMPHIBOLE, -Y[3]. Cf. Fr. *amphibolie.*] **1** = AMPHIBOLOGY 2. L16. **2** = AMPHIBOLOGY 1. E17.

amphibrach /ˈamfɪbrak/ *n.* Orig. in L form **†-chus, †-chys**. L16. [L *amphibrachys* (later *-us*) f. Gk *amphibrakhus* short at both ends, f. as AMPHI- + *brakhus* short.] *Pros.* (orig. *Class.*). A foot consisting of one long syllable between two short syllables or (in English etc.) one stressed syllable between two unstressed syllables.
amphiˈbrachic *a.* E19.

amphictyon /amˈfɪktɪən/ *n.* Also **-ion**; (*Gk Hist.*) **A-**. L16. [Gk *amphiktuones* pl. (orig. *-ion-*) dwellers around f. *ktizein* to found: see AMPHI-.] A delegate to an amphictyonic council, orig. and esp. that of ancient Greece. Usu. in *pl.*
amphictyˈonic *a.* of or pertaining to an amphictyony M18. **amphictyony** *n.* an association of States for the common interest, orig. and esp. in ancient Greece M19.

amphigouri /amfɪˈɡʊəri/ *n.* Also **amphigory** /ˈamfɪɡəri/. E19. [Fr., app. a learned (joc.) formation f. Gk AMPHI- + *allégorie* ALLEGORY.] A nonsensical burlesque composition; a piece of nonsense-verse.

amphilogy /amˈfɪlədʒi/ *n. rare.* LME. [Gk *amphilogia* dispute, f. *amphilogos* disputed, uncertain: see AMPHI-, -OLOGY.] Ambiguity, equivocation.

amphimacer /amˈfɪməsə/ *n.* L16. [L *amphimacrus* f. Gk *amphimakros* long at both ends, f. as AMPHI- + *makros* long.] *Class. Pros.* A foot consisting of one short syllable between two long syllables (= CRETIC *n.*). Occas. *transf.*, a foot consisting of one unstressed syllable between two stressed syllables.

amphioxus /amfɪˈɒksəs/ *n.* Pl. **-oxi** /-ˈɒksʌɪ/. M19. [mod.L, f. Gk AMPHI- + *oxus* sharp.] A lancelet of the genus *Branchiostoma* (formerly *Amphioxus*).

amphipod /ˈamfɪpɒd/ *n.* & *a.* M19. [f. mod.L *amphipoda* (sc. *animalia*), f. Gk AMPHI- + -POD.] (A crustacean) of the largely marine order Amphipoda, members of which, e.g. sand-hoppers, have seven pairs of thoracic legs, some specialized for feeding and others for swimming. Cf. ISOPOD.

amphiprostyle /amˈfɪprəstʌɪl/ *n.* & *a.* E18. [L *amphiprostylus* f. Gk *amphiprostulos*, f. as AMPHI- + PROSTYLE.] *Archit.* (A building, esp. a temple) with a portico at each end.

amphisbaena /amfɪsˈbiːnə/ *n.* LME. [L (Pliny) f. Gk *amphisbaina*, f. *amphis* both ways, AMPHI- + *bainein* go, walk.] **1** A fabled serpent with a head at each end and able to move in either direction. LME. **2** A wormlike burrowing lizard of the genus *Amphisbaena*. M19.
amphisbaenian *a.* & *n.* (being or pertaining to) a reptile of the kind typified by *Amphisbaena* L19. **amphisbaenid** *n.* = AMPHISBAENIAN *n.* L19.

Amphiscii /amˈfɪʃɪʌɪ/ *n.pl. arch.* E17. [med.L f. Gk *amphiskioi*, f. as AMPHI- + *skia* shadow.] The inhabitants of the tropics (whose shadows at one time fall northward, at another southward).
Also **Amphiscians** *n.pl.* (*arch.*) E17.

amphitheatre /ˈamfɪθiːətə/ *n.* Also ***-theater**. LME. [L *amphitheatrum* f. Gk *amphitheatron*, f. as AMPHI- + THEATRE. Cf. Fr. *amphithéatre.*] **1** An oval or circular building with seats rising in tiers around a central open space. LME. **†2** A joined pair of theatres. E–M17. **3** The scene of a contest. M17. **†4** The surrounding scene. M17–E18. **5** A piece of level ground surrounded naturally by rising slopes; a large circular hollow. L18. **6** A semicircular rising gallery in a theatre. M19.
amphitheˈatric *a.* = AMPHITHEATRICAL E17. **amphitheˈatrical** *a.* of, pertaining to, or resembling an amphitheatre L16. **amphitheˈatrically** *adv.* E18.

Amphitryon /amˈfɪtrɪən/ *n.* M19. [A character in Molière's play *Amphitryon.*] A host at dinner.

amphora /ˈamf(ə)rə/ *n.* Pl. **-rae** /-riː/, **-ras**. Also **†amphore**. ME. [L f. Gk *amphoreus*, or Fr. *amphore.*] **1** A Greek or Roman two-handled vessel. ME. **2** A Greek or Roman liquid measure of varying capacity. LME.
amphoral *a.* of, pertaining to, or resembling an amphora M17. **amˈphoric** *a.* (*Med.*) (of respiratory sounds heard in auscultation) suggesting the resonance produced by blowing across the mouth of an amphora M19.

amphoteric /amfəˈtɛrɪk/ *a.* M19. [f. Gk *amphoteros* compar. of *amphō* both + -IC.] Acting both ways (*rare* in *gen.* sense); *spec.* in *Chem.*, having both acidic and basic properties.

amphtrac(k) *ns.* vars. of AMTRAC.

ampicillin /ampɪˈsɪlɪn/ *n.* M20. [f. AM(INO- + P(EN)ICILLIN.] *Pharm.* A semisynthetic penicillin used esp. to treat infections of the urinary and respiratory tracts.

¶A proprietary name for this drug is PENBRITIN.

ample /ˈamp(ə)l/ *a.* & *adv.* LME. [(O)Fr. f. L *amplus* large, capacious, abundant.] **A** *adj.* **1** Of immaterial things: large in amount, extensive, abundant, excellent. LME. **2** Extending far and wide; large in dimensions, proportions, capacity, or volume; spacious; capacious; *euphem.* (of a person) stout. L15. **3** Of writing or speech: copious; treating of matters at full length. E16. **4** Quite enough; large enough to satisfy all demands; liberal, unsparing. M16. **†B** *adv.* Amply. M16–E17.
ampleness *n.* (*arch.*) M16. **amply** *adv.* in an ample manner LME.

amplexicaul /amˈplɛksɪkɔːl/ *a.* M18. [f. mod.L *amplexicaulis*, f. as next + *caulis* stem.] *Bot.* Of sessile leaves: embracing the stem.

amplexus /amˈplɛksəs/ *n.* M20. [L = embrace.] *Zool.* The mating position of frogs and toads, in which the male clasps the female about the back.

ampliation /amplɪˈeɪʃ(ə)n/ *n. arch.* E16. [(O)Fr., or L *ampliatio(n-)*, f. *ampliat-* pa. ppl stem of *ampliare*, f. *amplus* AMPLE: see -ATION.] **1** Enlarging; amplification. E16. **2** An enlargement, an extension. L16. **3** *Law* (now *Hist.*). Deferring of judgement for further consideration. M17.

ampliative /ˈamplɪətɪv/ *a.* M17. [Fr. *ampliatif* (med.L *ampliativus*), f. as prec.: see -ATIVE.] Amplificatory; *spec.* (*Logic*) enlarging a simple conception by predicating of it something which is not directly implied in it (now chiefly in *ampliative induction*).

amplification /ˌamplɪfɪˈkeɪʃ(ə)n/ *n.* E16. [(O)Fr., or L *amplificatio(n-)*, f. *amplificat-* pa. ppl stem of *amplificare*: see AMPLIFY, -FICATION.] 1 The action of amplifying something; enlargement; augmentation; enhancement; *Rhet.* elaboration to increase effect or add importance. E16. 2 The result of amplifying; something which has been extended or elaborated. E16. 3 A thing which amplifies; an addition. E18.

amplificatory *a.* tending or serving to amplify something L18.

amplifier /ˈamplɪfʌɪə/ *n.* M16. [f. next + -ER[1].] 1 A person who amplifies; *esp.* a person who amplifies a statement or narrative. M16. 2 A device for amplifying input electrical signals, esp. in sound reproduction. E20.

amplify /ˈamplɪfʌɪ/ *v.* LME. [Fr. *amplifier* f. L *amplificare* enlarge, f. *amplus* AMPLE: see -FY.] 1 *v.t.* Enlarge, increase, augment; enhance; elaborate on (a statement or narrative); exaggerate. LME. b *spec.* Increase the strength or amplitude of (an electrical signal or other physical quantity). E20. 2 *v.i.* Expatiate, speak largely, (*arch.* also foll. by *on*, *upon*). M16. 3 *v.i.* Become larger, increase. *rare.* E17.

amplitude /ˈamplɪtjuːd/ *n.* M16. [Fr., or L *amplitudo*, f. *amplus* AMPLE: see -TUDE.] 1 Physical extent; largeness; bulk; *esp.* width, breadth. M16. 2 Excellence, grandeur, splendour. *arch.* M16. 3 Copiousness; abundance; wide range. M16. †4 *Astron.* Angular distance from the eastern or western point of the horizon at rising or setting. E17–M19. 5 The maximum extent of vibration or oscillation from an equilibrium position; the maximum extent of deviation from the mean value of an alternating electrical signal or other oscillatory phenomenon. M19.

1 T. NASHE It cuts out an Island of some amplitude. C. LAMB An amplitude of form and stature, answering to her mind. T. WALKER And exploiting his great strength, / hurls his amplitude the length / of a pond too small for him. 2 R. COKE To the greater amplitude and glory of God. 3 BACON All works are overcommen by amplitude of reward .. and by the conjunction of labours. LD MACAULAY His mind is .. distinguished by the amplitude of its grasp.

Comb.: **amplitude modulation** variation of the amplitude of a radio or other wave as a means of carrying information such as an audio signal.

ampliˈtudinous *a.* ample, copious E20.

ampoule /ˈampuːl/ *n.* M17. [mod.Fr.: see AMPUL.] 1 = AMPULLA 2. *rare.* M17. 2 A small sealed glass vessel for holding sterilized materials for injection, poisons, air-sensitive chemicals, etc. E20.

ampster /ˈam(p)stə/ *n. Austral. slang.* Also **ams-** /ˈams-/. M20. [Origin unkn.] A showman's or trickster's accomplice who starts the buying of tickets, goods, etc.

amptman *n.* var. of AMTMAN.

ampul /ˈampuːl, -p(ə)l/ *n.* Now *rare* or *obs.* OE. [OFr. *ampo(u)le* (mod. *ampoule*) f. L AMPULLA.] †1 *gen.* A small bottle or flask; a phial. OE–L15. 2 *spec.* = AMPULLA 2. LME.

ampulla /amˈpʊlə/ *n.* Pl. **-llae** /-liː/. LME. [L, dim. of *ampora* var. of AMPHORA.] 1 *Rom. Antiq.* A small two-handled globular flask or bottle. LME. 2 A vessel for holding consecrated oil or for other sacred uses. L16. 3 *Anat.* A vessel or cavity shaped like the ancient ampulla. M19.

3 **ampulla of Lorenzini** /lɒr(ə)nˈziːni/ [Stefano *Lorenzini*, 17th-cent. It. physician] *Ichthyol.* a saclike sensory structure sensitive to electric fields, which occurs in numbers in the heads of certain fishes, esp. elasmobranchs. VATER'*s ampulla.*

ampullar *a.* of the form or character of an ampulla (sense 3) M19.

amputate /ˈampjʊteɪt/ *v.* M16. [L *amputat-* pa. ppl stem of *amputare*, f. *am-* for *amb-* around + *putare* prune, lop: see -ATE[3].] 1 *v.t.* Cut off, lop off; prune. *obs.* exc. as *fig.* use of sense 2. M16. 2 *v.t.* & *i. spec.* Cut off from an animal body (some part, esp. a limb because of injury or disease). M17.

amputator *n.* a person who amputates E19. **ampuˈtee** *n.* a person who has lost a limb or other part of the body by amputation E20.

amputation /ampjʊˈteɪʃ(ə)n/ *n.* E17. [f. as prec.: see -ATION.] 1 A cutting or lopping off; a pruning. *obs.* exc. as *fig.* use of sense 2. E17. 2 *spec.* The operation of cutting off a limb or other part of an animal body. E17.

Amratian /amˈreɪʃ(ə)n/ *a.* E20. [f. El *Amra* a district in Egypt + *-t-* + -IAN.] Designating or pertaining to an early period of the ancient predynastic culture in Egypt.

amrita /amˈriːtə, *foreign* ˈʌmritə/ *n. poet.* Also **-reeta.** L18. [Skt *amṛta* an immortal, nectar.] Ambrosia.

amster *n.* var. of AMPSTER.

amtman /ˈamtman/ *n.* Now *Hist.* Also **ampt-**. Pl. **-men.** L16. [G *Amtmann*, Du., & Scand.] In Germany, Scandinavia, etc.: a person in charge; a bailiff, steward, magistrate, etc.

amtrac /ˈamtrak/ *n. US.* Also **amph-** /ˈamf-/; **-ck.** M20. [f. AM(PHIBIOUS + TRAC(TOR.] An amphibious tracked vehicle for landing assault troops.

amuck, †**amuco** *a.*, *n.*, & *adv.* see AMOK.

amulet /ˈamjʊlɪt/ *n.*[1] L16. [L *amuletum* (Varro, Pliny) of unkn. origin.] Something worn as a charm against evil, disease, witchcraft, etc.; *fig.* a preservative, a protection, a charm.

amuletic /-ˈlɛtɪk/ *a.* M18.

†**amulet** *n.*[2] see OMELETTE.

amuse /əˈmjuːz/ *v.* L15. [(O)Fr. *amuser* entertain, †deceive, f. *à* AD- + *muser* MUSE *v.*[2]] I 1 *v.t.* Divert the attention of (a person) in order to mislead; delude, deceive. (The usual sense 17–18.) *arch.* L15. †2 *v.t. gen.* Engage the attention of. E17–L18. 3 *v.t.* Divert from seriousness, give pleasure to, with something trifling, ludicrous, or entertaining; make laugh or smile. M17.

1 MARVELL And all to amuse men from observing. H. NELSON Their Fleet was to amuse ours whilst they cross from Leghorn. 2 P. HOLLAND Why art thou amused upon the course of the stars? SIR T. BROWNE Hairs which have most amused me have not been in the face or head, but on the back. 3 G. B. SHAW It amuses him to be treated in this fashion: he chuckles secretly. D. DU MAURIER I've a mass of things to see to this morning, do you think you can amuse yourself? S. BARSTOW The door flies open and young Dorothy and Angela catch me without pants. This amuses them no end.

†II 4 *v.i.* Muse intently; gaze in astonishment. M16–L17. 5 *v.t.* Cause to muse; confound, bewilder, puzzle. E17–M18.

¶ Rare bef. 17. Not in Shakes.

amusable *a.* E19. **amusedly** /-zɪdli/ *adv.* in an amused manner, with amusement M19. **amuˈsee** *n.* (*rare*) a person amused or to be amused M19. **amuser** *n.* L16. **amusingly** *adv.* in an amusing manner E19. **amusingness** *n.* the state or quality of being amusing E19.

amusement /əˈmjuːzm(ə)nt/ *n.* E17. [Fr., f. as prec.: see -MENT.] †1 Musing; mental abstraction. E17–E18. 2 Distraction or diversion of the attention; beguiling, deception; an instance of this. *arch.* E17. †3 Distracting bewilderment. M–L17. 4 A pastime; a means of recreation; something amusing. (Orig. *depreciative*.) M17. 5 Pleasurable occupation of the attention without seriousness; (orig., idle time-wasting) entertainment, recreation; the causing of laughter or smiles; humour aroused by something droll or grotesque. L17.

4 J. H. NEWMAN To take .. pleasure in our families rather than to seek amusements out of doors. V. WELBURN Roll-up, roll-up. .. Amusements. .. Candy-floss. .. Roundabouts. 5 POPE Amusement is the happiness of those that cannot think. COLERIDGE The same craving for amusement, i.e. to be away from the Muses for relaxation. G. GREENE His old Italian face showed few emotions but a mild amusement. A. J. P. TAYLOR Lloyd George derived a malicious amusement from the way in which the spokesmen of these two democratic countries .. defied Wilson. S. HILL To the amusement of her mother and sisters. T. STOPPARD A little team I run, mainly for our own amusement.

Comb.: **amusement arcade** a place for recreation containing automatic game-playing machines, etc.

amusette /amjʊˈzɛt/ *n.* M18. [Fr. = plaything: see AMUSE, -ETTE.] *Hist.* A type of light field-cannon.

amusive /əˈmjuːzɪv/ *a.* E18. [f. AMUSE + -IVE.] †1 Deceitful, illusive. E–M18. †2 Affording recreation. Only in M18. 3 Affording pleasing entertainment; causing laughter or smiles. M18. 4 Having amusement as an object. *rare.* L18.

amusively *adv.* L18. **amusiveness** *n.* (*rare*) E19.

amygdala /əˈmɪgdələ/ *n.* Pl. **-lae** /-liː/. Long Anglicized as †**-dal**; also †**-dale.** OE. [L f. Gk *amugdalē* almond; some uses & form *-dale* f. Fr.] †1 An almond. OE–LME. 2 *Anat.* Orig. = ALMOND *n.* 3b. Now, either of two of the basal ganglia of the brain adjoining the optic tract. LME.

amygdale /əˈmɪgdeɪl/ *n.*[1] L19. [Fr. f. as prec.] *Geol.* A vesicle in an igneous rock, containing secondary minerals.

amygdule *n.* a small amygdale L19.

†**amygdale** *n.*[2] var. of AMYGDALA.

amygdalin /əˈmɪgdəlɪn/ *n.* M19. [f. L AMYGDALA + -IN[1].] *Chem.* A bitter crystalline glycoside found in bitter almonds and the stones of peaches, apricots, etc.

amygdaline /əˈmɪgdəlʌɪn/ *a. rare.* L17. [L *amygdalinus* f. Gk *amugdalinos* of almonds: see AMYGDALA, -INE[2].] Of or pertaining to almonds; almond-shaped.

amygdaloid /əˈmɪgdəlɔɪd/ *a.* & *n.* M18. [f. L AMYGDALA + -OID.] A *adj.* Almond-shaped; like almonds; *Geol.* containing numerous amygdales. M18.

amygdaloid nucleus *Anat.* an amygdala of the brain.

B *n. Geol.* An igneous rock containing numerous amygdales. L18.

amygdaˈloidal *a.* (*Geol.*) E19.

amyl /ˈeɪmʌɪl, ˈamɪl/ *n.* M19. [f. L *amylum* starch + -YL.] *Chem.* Pentyl; *spec.* the primary straight-chain radical $C_5H_{11}\cdot$. Usu. in *comb.*

amylene *n.* pentene; *amylene hydrate*, tertiary pentyl alcohol, an anaesthetic: M19.

amylase /ˈamɪleɪz/ *n.* L19. [f. as prec. + -ASE.] An enzyme which hydrolyses starch.

amylo- /ˈamɪləʊ/ *comb. form* of L *amylum* starch, or of AMYL: see -O-.

amyloˈbarbitone *n.* a narcotic and sedative barbiturate, 5-ethyl-5-isopentyl-barbituric acid; (a proprietary name for the drug is AMYTAL): M20. **amyˈlolysis** *n.* the breakdown of starch to sugars L19. **amyloˈlytic** *a.* of or pertaining to amylolysis L19. **amyloˈpectin** *n.* the amorphous form of starch, consisting of branched polysaccharide chains E20. **amyˈlopsin** *n.* a pancreatic enzyme which converts starch to sugars L19. **amylose** *n.* the crystallizable form of starch, consisting of long unbranched polysaccharide chains L19.

amyloid /ˈamɪlɔɪd/ *a.* & *n.* M19. [f. as prec. + -OID.] A *adj.* 1 Resembling (the chemical structure of) starch. M19. 2 *Med.* Of or pertaining to amyloid. L19. B *n. Med.* A glycoprotein (orig. thought to be akin to starch) deposited in connective tissue in certain diseases. L19.

amyloiˈdosis *n.* deposition of amyloid in the tissues E20.

amyotrophy /amɪˈɒtrəfi/ *n.* L19. [f. A-[10] + Gk *mu-*, *mus* muscle + -O- + -TROPHY.] *Med.* Atrophy of muscle.

amyotrophic /-ˈtrəʊfɪk, -ˈtrɒfɪk/ *a.* characterized by amyotrophy; *amyotrophic lateral sclerosis* = LOU GEHRIG'S DISEASE: L19.

Amytal /ˈamɪt(ə)l/ *n.* E20. [f. AMYL + euphonic *-t-* + -AL[2].] (Proprietary name for) amylobarbitone.

an *a.* (*indef. article*) see A *a.*

an /an, ən/ *prep. arch.* Also as *pref.* (= AN-[1]). OE. [Orig. form of ON *prep.*; later a var. of ON *prep.* bef. vowels: cf. A *prep.*[1]] = ON *prep.*

an /(ə)n/ *conj.* & *n.* Now *arch.* & *dial.* (see also A.1 below). Also **an'**. ME. [Weakened form of AND *conj.*[1] & *n.*] A *conj.* 1 = AND *conj.*[1] I (coordinating). Now *rare* as a written form exc. *an'* as repr. illiterate or dial. use, though the pronunc. is common in informal speech. ME. 2 = AND *conj.*[1] II (conditional). M16. B *n.* = AND *n.* M19.

an- /ən/ *pref.*[1] (not productive). OE. [Proclitic var.] = AN *prep.*, as *anent*, *anon*. Cf. A-[2].

an- /ən/ *pref.*[2] (not productive). ME. Repr. AN *an-*, OFr. *en-* f. L in, into (see IN-[2]), as *anoint*.

an- /ən/ *pref.*[3] (not productive). ME. Repr. L *an-* assim. form of AD- bef. *n*, directly, or indirectly through Fr. (OFr. *a-* refash. after L in Fr. itself or after adoption in Eng.), as *annex*, *announce*, *annul*.

an- /an/ *pref.*[4] (not productive). Repr. Gk ANA- bef. a vowel, as *aneurysm*.

an- /an, *unstressed* ən/ *pref.*[5] Repr. Gk privative *an-* without, lacking, not, the original form of A-[10] retained bef. vowels, as *anecdote*, *anonymous*. A productive pref. of negation and privation in mod. techn. terms, as *analgesia*, *anachoic*, *anhydrous*.

-an /*in sense 1* (ə)n, *in sense 2* -an/ *suff.* 1 Repr. L *-anus*, *-na*, *-num* of or belonging to, as *urban*, *silvan*, directly, or indirectly through Fr. *-ain(e)* later refash. A productive suff., forming *adjs.* (often used as *ns.*), esp. f. names of places (as *American*, *Chilean*), systems (as *Anglican*), zoological classes or orders (as *crustacean*), and founders (as *Lutheran*). Already in L added so commonly to *-ius*, forming *-ianus*, that -IAN is in use merely a euphonic var. of -AN (as *Russian*, *Presbyterian*, *crocodilian*, *Christian*). 2 [G: cf. -ANE.] *Chem.* Used more or less arbitrarily to form names of organic compounds, esp. polysaccharides (as *dextran* etc.).

ana /'ɑːnə/ *n.*[1] M18. [f. -ANA.] 1 As *sing.* (with pl. **-s**). A collection of a person's memorable sayings. M18. 2 As *pl.* Publications or other items concerning or associated with a person, place, activity, etc. M18.

ana /'anə/ *adv.* & *n.*[2] Long *obs.* exc. in Dicts. LME. [med.L f. Gk *ana* again.] A *adv.* In recipes for drugs etc.: of each, of every one alike. LME. †B *n.* An equal quantity or number (of each ingredient in a recipe); an instruction to use this. M–L17.

ana- /'anə/ *pref.* Bef. a vowel usu. **an-**. Repr. Gk *ana-* up, back, again, anew.

ana'genesis *n.* (*Biol.*) species formation without branching of the evolutionary line of descent (cf. CLADOGENESIS) L19. **anage'netic** *a.* of or pertaining to anagenesis L19. **anaphase** *n.* (*Biol.*) the stage of cell division in which daughter chromosomes separate towards opposite poles of the spindle L19. **ana'plasia** *n.* (*Biol.*) loss of specialized characteristics by cells, as in the formation of tumours dedifferentiation E20. **ana'plastic** *a.* (*Med.*) †(*a*) of or pertaining to plastic surgery (only in Dicts.); (*b*) pertaining to or characterized by anaplasia: L19. †**anaplasty** *n.* (*Med.*) plastic surgery (Dicts.): only in L19.

-ana /'ɑːnə/ *suff.* [L, neut. pl. ending of adjs. in *-anus*: see -AN 1.] Forming pl. ns. w. the sense 'publications or other items concerning or associated with a person, place, or topic', as *Americana*, *cricketana*, *railwayana*, *Shakespeariana*, *Victoriana*. Occas. as euphonic var. of -IANA, after L wds ending in *-iana*.

anabaptise *v.* var. of ANABAPTIZE.

Anabaptism /anə'baptɪz(ə)m/ *n.* Also (in sense 2 usu.) **a-**. M16. [eccl.L *anabaptismus* (Augustine) f. Gk *anabaptismos*, f. as ANA- + *baptismos* BAPTISM.] 1 *Hist.* The doctrines of the 16th-cent. Continental Anabaptists or (opprobriously) of the later Baptists (see next). M16. 2 Rebaptism. Now *rare*. M17.

Anabaptist /anə'baptɪst/ *n.* Also **a-**. M16. [Fr. *anabaptiste* or mod.L *anabaptista*, f. as prec.: see -IST.] *Hist.* 1 A member of any of various 16th-cent. religious groups in Germany, Switzerland, and the Low Countries, who recognized the baptism of (adult) believers only. M16. 2 (Used more or less opprobriously for) a Baptist (see BAPTIST *n.* 2). Also *loosely*, a person who rejected other Anglican doctrines. L16.

ˌ**Anabap'tistic** *a.* M17. ˌ**Anabap'tistical** *a.* M16. ˌ**Anabap'tistically** *adv.* M16. †**Anabaptistry** *n.* = ANABAPTISM 1 M16–E18.

anabaptize /anəbap'tʌɪz/ *v.t.* Now *rare*. Also **-ise**. M17. [med.L *anabaptizare* f. Gk *anabaptizein*, f. as ANA- + *baptizein* BAPTIZE.] Rebaptize; rechristen; rename.

anabasis /ə'nabəsɪs/ *n.* *literary*. Pl. **-ases** /-əsiːz/. E18. [Gk = going up, f. as ANA- + *basis* going. Cf. KATABASIS.] A military advance, an up-country march, *esp.* that of Cyrus the Younger into Asia, as narrated by Xenophon.

anabatic /anə'batɪk/ *a.* M19. [Gk *anabatikos*, f. *anabatēs* a person who ascends, f. *anabainein* go up: see ANA-, -IC.] 1 *Med.* Of or pertaining to the course of a disease to its climax. Only in Dicts. M19. 2 *Meteorol.* Of a wind: caused by local upward motion of warm air. Opp. KATABATIC. E20.

anabiosis /anəbʌɪ'əʊsɪs/ *n.* L19. [Gk *anabiōsis* a return to life, f. *anabioein* come to life again: see ANA-, -OSIS.] *Biol.* Revival from a state of suspended animation. Also, that state itself.

anabiotic *a.* L19.

anabolic /anə'bɒlɪk/ *a.* L19. [f. as next + -IC.] *Biol.* Pertaining to, involved in, or characterized by anabolism. Opp. CATABOLIC.

anabolic steroid any of a class of synthetic steroid hormones used to increase muscle size.

anabolism /ə'nabəlɪz(ə)m/ *n.* L19. [f. Gk *anabolē* a throwing up, ascent, f. *anaballein*, f. as ANA- + *ballein* to throw: see -ISM.] *Biol.* Constructive metabolism; the metabolic synthesis of complex substances and their incorporation into body tissue. Opp. CATABOLISM.

anabranch /'anəbrɑːn(t)ʃ/ *n.* Chiefly *Austral.* M19. [f. *anastomosing* pres. pple of ANASTOMOSE *v.* + BRANCH *n.*] A stream that leaves a river and re-enters it downstream.

anacard /'anəkɑːd/ *n.* Now *rare* or *obs.* Also in L forms **-dium** /-dɪəm/, †**-dus**. LME. [med.L *anacardus*, mod.L *-dium* f. Gk *anakardion*, f. *ana* like + *kardion* heart-shaped ornament.] A cashew-nut.

anachoret *n.* see ANCHORITE.

anachronic /anə'krɒnɪk/ *a.* E19. [f. next, after pairs such as *synchronism*, *synchronic*: see -IC. Cf. Fr. *anachronique*.] Erroneous in date or order; involving anachronism.

anachronically *adv.* E19.

anachronism /ə'nakrənɪz(ə)m/ *n.* M17. [Fr. *anachronisme* or Gk *anakhronismos*, f. *anakhronizesthai* refer to a wrong time, f. as ANA- + *khronos* time: see -ISM.] 1 An error in computing time or fixing dates; the relating of an event, custom, or circumstance to a wrong period of time. M17. 2 Something or someone out of harmony with the time. E19.

1 T. HEARNE Virgil making Dido and Æneas Cotemporaries, whereas they lived at Three Hundred Years distance . . committed an Anachronism. H. B. STOWE Some anachronisms with regard to the time of the session of courts have been allowed. 2 V. SACKVILLE-WEST He had thought of Chevron as a dead thing, an anachronism, an exquisite survival . . with its . . servants and luxury. M. MCCARTHY She herself was a smoldering anachronism, a throwback to one of those ardent young women of the Sixties, Turgenev's heroines. S. J. PERELMAN Anachronisms in the script . . , like penicillin and the atomic bomb.

anachro'nistic *a.* of the nature of or involving anachronism L18. **anachronous** *a.* = ANACHRONISTIC E19.

anaclasis /ə'nakləsɪs/ *n.* Also **-klasis** & (orig.) in Gk characters. Pl. **-ases** /-əsiːz/. L18. [Gk *anaklasis* bending back, f. *anaklaein*: see next.] *Class. Pros.* In Ionic metre: an interchange of the final long syllable of the first foot with the opening short syllable of the second.

anaclastic /anə'klastɪk/ *a.* M18. [f. Gk *anaklastos*, f. *anaklaein* bend back, refract, f. as ANA- + *klaein* break, + -IC.] 1 Springing back. *rare*. M18. 2 *Optics*. Pertaining to or produced by refraction. *rare*. L18. 3 *Class. Pros.* Of, pertaining to, or involving anaclasis. L19.

anacoluthon /anəkə'luːθɒn, -θ(ə)n/ *n.* Pl. **-tha** /-θə/. E18. [Late L f. Gk *anakolouthon* neut. sing. of adj. = lacking sequence, f. as AN-[5] + *akolouthos* following.] A sentence or construction lacking grammatical sequence.

anacoluthia *n.* = ANACOLUTHON M19. **anacoluthic** *a.* M19.

anaconda /anə'kɒndə/ *n.* Also †**-do**. M18. [Unexpl. alt. of L *anacandaia* python, for Sinhalese *henakandayā* whip snake, perh. f. *hena* lightning + *kanda* stem.] Orig., a large python of Ceylon (Sri Lanka). Now, a S. American boa of the genus *Eunectes*, esp. the very large, semi-aquatic *E. murinus*. Also *loosely*, any large constricting snake.

anacreontic /anakrɪ'ɒntɪk/ *a.* & *n.* E17. [Late L *anacreonticus*, f. Gk *Anakreōn*, *-ont-* Anacreon: see -IC.] A *adj.* After the manner of the Greek lyric poet Anacreon (*c* 570–490 BC); convivial, amatory. E17. B *n.* A poem after the manner of Anacreon; an erotic poem. M17.

anacrusis /anə'kruːsɪs/ *n.* Pl. **-cruses** /-'kruːsiːz/. M19. [mod.L f. Gk *anakrousis* prelude, f. *anakrouein*, f. as ANA- + *krouein* to strike.] 1 *Pros.* An unstressed syllable at the beginning of a verse. M19. 2 *Mus.* An unstressed note or unstressed notes before the first strong beat of a phrase. E20.

anadem /'anədɛm/ *n.* *poet.* E17. [L *anadema* f. Gk = head-band. Cf. DIADEM.] A wreath for the head, usu. of flowers; a chaplet, a garland.

anadiplosis /anədɪ'pləʊsɪs/ *n.* Pl. **-ploses** /-'pləʊsiːz/. M16. [Gk *anadiplōsis*, f. *anadiploun* to double: see ANA-, DIPLO-, -OSIS.] *Rhet.* Reduplication; the beginning of a sentence, line, or clause with the concluding, or any prominent, word of the one preceding; an instance of this.

anadromous /ə'nadrəməs/ *a.* M18. [f. Gk *anadromos* running up (of fish entering a river): see ANA-, -OUS.] *Zool.* Of fish: that ascend rivers from the sea to spawn.

anaemia /ə'niːmɪə/ *n.* Also ***anemia**. E19. [mod.L f. Gk *anaimia*, f. as AN-[5] + *haima* blood: see -IA[1].] *Med.* A deficiency of red blood cells or their haemoglobin, often causing pallor.

pernicious anaemia: see PERNICIOUS *a.*[1]

anaemic /ə'niːmɪk/ *a.* Also ***anemic**. M19. [f. prec. + -IC.] Pertaining to or exhibiting anaemia; *fig.* spiritless, weak.

anaerobic /anɛː'rəʊbɪk/ *a.* L19. [f. AN-[5] + AEROBIC.] *Biol.* Living or taking place in the absence of free oxygen; lacking free oxygen.

a'naerobe *n.* an organism which lives in anaerobic conditions L19. **anaerobically** *adv.* in the absence of free oxygen L19. **anaerobi'osis** *n.* life under anaerobic conditions L19.

anaesthesia /anɪs'θiːzjə/ *n.* Also ***anes-**. E18. [mod.L f. Gk *anaisthēsia*, f. as AN-[5] + *aisthēsis* sensation: see -IA[1].] Absence of sensation; *esp.* artificially induced inability to feel pain.

general anaesthesia: involving the whole body (with loss of consciousness). **local anaesthesia**: involving a limited part of the body.

anaesthesi'ologist *n.* an expert in or student of anaesthesiology M20. **anaesthesi'ology** *n.* the branch of knowledge that deals with anaesthesia; the practice of anaesthesia: E20. **anaesthesis** *n.* (*rare*) anaesthesia M19.

anaesthetic /anɪs'θɛtɪk/ *a.* & *n.* Also ***anes-**. M19. [f. Gk *anaisthētos* without feeling: see prec., -IC.] A *adj.* Of, pertaining to, or producing anaesthesia. M19.

B *n.* A substance which produces anaesthesia. M19.

B. MALAMUD He cut into the pussing sores with a scalpel, without anaesthetic. **general anaesthetic, local anaesthetic** an agent which produces general, local, anaesthesia.

anaesthetically *adv.* as or in the manner of an anaesthetic M19.

anaesthetize /ə'niːsθətʌɪz/ *v.t.* Also ***anes-**; **-ise**. M19. [f. as prec. + -IZE.] Deprive of feeling; administer an anaesthetic to.

fig.: A. KOESTLER Deformities . . will only appear as comic if sympathy is anaesthetized.

anaesthetist *n.* a person who administers anaesthetics L19. **anaestheti'zation** *n.* M19.

anaglyph /'anəglɪf/ *n.* L16. [Gk *anagluphē* work in low relief, f. as ANA- + *gluphein* carve.] 1 An embossed ornament in low relief. L16. 2 A composite stereoscopic picture printed in superimposed complementary colours. L19.

ana'glyphic *a.* = ANAGLYPTIC M17.

Anaglypta /anə'glɪptə/ *n.* Also **a-**. L19. [L *anaglypta* work in low relief: see next.] (Proprietary name for) a thick embossed wallpaper.

anaglyptic /anə'glɪptɪk/ *a.* M17. [Late L *anaglypticus* f. Gk *anagluptikos*: see ANAGLYPH,

-IC.] Of or pertaining to embossed anaglyphs or the art of carving in low relief; embossed in low relief.

anagnorisis /anəg'nɒrɪsɪs/ *n.* Pl. **-rises** /-rɪsiːz/. L18. [Gk *anagnōrisis*.] Recognition; the dénouement in a drama.

†anagnost *n.* E17–E18. [L *anagnostes* f. Gk *anagnōstēs* reader.] A reader, esp. aloud; a prelector.

anagogy /'anəgɒdʒi/ *n.*LME. [Analogical alt. of eccl.L f. Gk *anagōgē* (religious or ecstatic) elevation, mystical feeling, f. *anagein* lift up, f. as AN-[4] + *agein* to lead.] 1 Spiritual, mystical, or allegorical interpretation. LME. †2 Spiritual elevation, esp. to understand mysteries. *rare.* Only in E18.

anagoge /anə'gəʊdʒi/ *n.* [eccl.L] = ANAGOGY 1 M16. **ana'gogic** *a.* = ANAGOGICAL LME. **ana'gogical** *a.* having a spiritual, mystical, or allegorical interpretation E16. **ana'gogically** *adv.* L16.

anagram /'anəgram/ *n.* & *v.* L16. [Fr. *anagramme* or mod.L *anagramma*, f. Gk ANA- + *gramma* letter.] A *n.* 1 A transposition of the letters of a word or phrase to form another word or phrase. L16. †2 *transf.* & *fig.* A transposition; a mutation. M17–E18. B *v.t.* Infl. **-mm-**. = ANAGRAMMATIZE. *rare.* M17.

anagra'mmatic *a.* = ANAGRAMMATICAL E19. **anagra'mmatical** *a.* of or pertaining to an anagram; performed or produced by transposition of letters: E17. **anagra'mmatically** *adv.* E17. **ana'grammatism** *n.* the formation of anagrams E17. **ana'grammatist** *n.* a maker of anagrams E17. **ana'grammatize** *v.t.* transpose so as to form an anagram; change into another word or phrase by a different arrangement of letters: L16.

anaklasis *n.* var. of ANACLASIS.

anal /'eɪn(ə)l/ *a.* M18. [mod.L *analis*: see ANUS, -AL[1]; cf. Fr. *anal.*] 1 Of or pertaining to the anus; situated near the anus. M18. 2 *Psychol.* Designating or pertaining to a stage of infantile psychosexual development that is thought to involve a preoccupation with the anus and defecation; of or pertaining to a personality supposed to be the result of fixation at this stage. E20.

Special collocations & *comb.*: **anal-erotic** *a.* & *n.* (*Psychol.*) (*a*) *adj.* pertaining to or characterized by eroticism associated with the anal region; (*b*) *n.* a person characterized by such eroticism. **anal retentive** *Psychol.* (a person) displaying excessive orderliness and parsimony (interpreted as the result of conflict over toilet-training in infancy). **anal sadism** *Psychol.* abnormal aggressive and destructive tendencies thought to be caused by fixation at the anal stage of development. **anal sadistic** *a.* (*Psychol.*) displaying anal sadism.

a'nality *n.* (*Psychol.*) anal quality or character M20. **anally** *adv.* L20.

analcime /ə'nalsiːm/ *n.* E19. [Fr. f. Gk *analkimos* weak, f. as AN-[5] + *alkimos* stout, brave: the mineral was found to be weakly electrified by friction.] *Min.* A zeolite occurring as white or faintly coloured trapezohedral crystals.

Also **analcite** *n.* M19.

analects /'anəlɛkts/ *n.pl.* Also in L form **analecta** /anə'lɛktə/. LME. [L *analecta* f. Gk *analekta* things gathered up, f. *analegein*, f. as ANA- + *legein* gather.] †1 Crumbs, gleanings. LME–E18. 2 *spec.* Literary gleanings. M17.

analemma /anə'lɛmə/ *n.* Pl. **-mae** /-miː/, **-mas.** M17. [L (Vitruvius) = sundial, f. Gk *analēmma* support, (base of a) sundial.] 1 (An astronomical instrument incorporating) an orthographic projection of the sphere on the plane of the meridian. M17. 2 A figure representing the sun's daily declination and the difference between the right ascension of the mean sun and that of the true sun, drawn esp. on terrestrial globes. M19.

analeptic /anə'lɛptɪk/ *a.* & *n.* L16. [Late L *anale(m)pticus* f. Gk *analēptikos* restorative: see -IC. Cf. Fr. *analeptique.*] *Med.* A *adj.* 1 Restorative, strengthening. L16. 2 Able to stimulate the central nervous system. M20. B *n.* 1 A restorative medicine or food. L17. 2 A stimulant of the central nervous system. M20.

analgesia /an(ə)l'dʒiːzjə/ *n.* E18. [Gk *analgēsia* painlessness, ult. f. as AN-[5] + *algeein* feel pain.] *Med.* Absence or reduction of ability to feel pain; relief of pain, esp. by drugs.

analgesic /-sɪk/ *a.* & *n.* (*a*) *adj.* pertaining to analgesia; (*b*) *n.* an analgesic drug tending to remove pain: L19.

analog *n.* see ANALOGUE.

analogate /ə'naləgət/ *n.* M17. [f. ANALOG(OUS + -ATE[1].] A thing, concept, etc., shown to be analogous; an analogue.

analogic /anə'lɒdʒɪk/ *a.* M17. [Fr. *analogique* or L *analogicus* f. Gk *analogikos*: see ANALOGUE, -IC.] Of or pertaining to analogy.

analogical /anə'lɒdʒɪk(ə)l/ *a.* L16. [f. as prec. + -AL[1].] †1 *Math.* Proportional; in exact ratio. Only in L16. 2 Of the nature of analogy; according to analogy. E17. 3 Expressing an analogy. E17. 4 = ANALOGOUS 1. *arch.* M17. 5 Of or pertaining to analogy. M19.

analogically *adv.* L16. **analogicalness** *n.* (*rare*) M18.

analogise *v.* var. of ANALOGIZE.

analogist /ə'nalədʒɪst/ *n.* M19. [f. next + -IST.] A person who argues from or seeks analogies.

analogize /ə'nalədʒaɪz/ *v.* Also **-ise.** M17. [Gk *analogizesthai* reckon up; later f. ANALOGY: see -IZE.] 1 *v.i.* Employ analogy. M17. 2 *v.t.* Represent by analogy. M18. 3 *v.i.* & *t.* (Show to) be in harmony *with.* M18.

analogon /ə'naləg(ə)n/ *n.* Now *rare.* Pl. **-ga** /-gə/. E19. [Irreg. use as n. of neut. sing. of Gk *analogos*: see ANALOGY.] = ANALOGUE *n.* 1.

analogous /ə'naləgəs/ *a.* M17. [f. L *analogus* (Varro) f. Gk *analogos*: see ANALOGY, -OUS.] 1 Having analogy; similar in certain attributes, circumstances, relations, or uses; parallel. (Foll. by *to, with.*) M17. 2 = ANALOGICAL 3. *rare.* L17.

analogously *adv.* in a manner analogous (*to, with*); by or according to analogy: M17.

analogue /'anəlɒg/ *n.* & *a.* Also (*US* & also *gen.* in *Computing*) **-log.** E19. [Fr. f. Gk ANALOGON.] A *n.* 1 An analogous or parallel word or thing; a representative in different circumstances; something or someone performing a corresponding part. E19. 2 *Chem.* A compound with a molecular structure closely similar to that of another. M20. 3 A synthetic food product resembling a natural food in taste and texture. L20. B *attrib.* or as *adj.* Designating, pertaining to, or operating with signals or information represented by a continuously variable quantity, such as spatial position, voltage, etc. Opp. DIGITAL *a.* 1. M20.

analogy /ə'nalədʒi/ *n.* LME. [Fr. *analogie* or L *analogia* (Varro) f. Gk = equality of ratios, proportion (orig. Math.), f. *analogos* proportionate, conformable.] †1 Appropriateness; correlation; correspondence or adaptation of one thing to another. LME–L18. 2 Mathematical proportion; agreement of ratios. M16. 3 Equivalence or likeness of relations; agreement, parallelism; a similarity. (Foll. by *to, with, between.*) M16. 4 A figure of speech involving a comparison; a simile, a metaphor. M16. 5 Grammatical patterning; similarity of formative or constructive linguistic processes. M16. b *spec.* Imitation of existing words in forming (the inflections or constructions of) others, without the existence of corresponding intermediate stages of formation. L19. 6 *Logic.* Resemblance of relations or attributes forming a ground of reasoning; the process of reasoning from parallel cases. E17. 7 = ANALOGUE *n.* 1. M17. 8 *Biol.* Resemblance of form or function without fundamental identity. E19.

1 GOLDSMITH Some philosophers have perceived so much analogy to man in the formation of the ocean, that they have not hesitated to assert its being made for him alone. 3 BACON Which three parts active have a correspondence and analogy with the three parts speculative. SIR T. BROWNE Who from some analogy of name conceive the Ægyptian Pyramids to have been built for granaries. D. BREWSTER There is still one property of sound, which has its analogy also in light. 4 HOBBES According to the same analogy, the Dove, and the Fiery Tongues . . might also be called Angels. D. M. THOMAS The Church's dogmas, he said, smiling, were the whalebone of the soul. The analogy delighted her. 5b JOYCE Unusual polysyllables of foreign origin she interpreted phonetically or by false analogy. 6 W. STUBBS Analogy . . is not proof, but illustration. 7 LYTTON The child is the analogy of a people yet in childhood.

Phrases: **by analogy** after an established pattern or model, by extension. **by analogy with, on the analogy of** on the model of, in imitation of. **draw an analogy (between)** make a comparison (between), point out similarities or parallelism (in).

analphabet /an'alfəbɛt/ *a.* & *n.* As n. also **-bete.** L16. [L *analphabetus* f. Gk *analphabētos*, f. as AN-[5] + ALPHABET.] A *adj.* Totally illiterate. *rare.* L16.

B *n.* A person who is totally illiterate; (in extended use) a person without knowledge of a particular subject etc. L19.

R. V. JONES They were very weak on matters concerning science and technology, since . . the average S.I.S. agent was a scientific analphabet.

analphabetic /analfə'bɛtɪk/ *a.* L19. [f. Gk *analphabētos* (see prec.) + -IC.] 1 = ANALPHABET *a. rare.* L19. 2 *Phonet.* Representing sounds by composite signs, not by single letters or symbols. L19.

†analyse *n.* M17–M18. [Fr. f. as ANALYSIS.] = ANALYSIS.

analyse /'an(ə)laɪz/ *v.t.* Also ***-lyze.** L16. [Perh. orig. f. as prec.; later infl. by Fr. *analyser.*] I *gen.* 1 Ascertain the elements of (something complex); examine minutely the constitution of. L16. †2 Dissect, decompose, (material things). E17–L18. II *spec.* 3 Examine critically (a literary or musical composition) in order to bring out essential elements or structure. E17. 4 *Chem.* Ascertain the constituents of (a sample of a mixture or compound) or their amounts. M17. 5 *Gram.* Resolve (a sentence, phrase, etc.) into smaller grammatical elements. E18. 6 *Philos.* Subject to logical or philosophical analysis. E20. 7 *Psychol.* Subject to psychological analysis; *spec.* = PSYCHOANALYSE. E20.

With advs. in specialized senses: **analyse out** discover or isolate by analysis, work out.

analysa'bility *n.* the quality of being analysable E20. **analysable** *a.* able to be analysed M19. **analysand** /ənalɪ'zand/ *n.* a person undergoing psychological analysis M20. **analysandum** /ənalɪ'zandəm/ *n.*, pl. **-da** /-də/, *Philos.* that which is to be analysed or clarified E20. **analysans** /ənalɪ'zanz/ *n.* (*Philos.*) the clarifying expression in a philosophical analysis M20. **analy'sation** *n.* (now *rare*) analysis M18.

analyser /'an(ə)laɪzə/ *n.* Also ***-lyzer.** E17. [f. prec. + -ER[1].] 1 A person who analyses; an analyst. E17. 2 An instrument or device for performing analysis; *spec.* a device able to transmit only light polarized in a given direction. M19.

analysis /ə'nalɪsɪs/ *n.* Pl. **-lyses** /-lɪsiːz/. L16. [med.L f. Gk *analusis*, f. *analuein* unloose, f. as ANA- + *luein* loosen.] I *gen.* 1 The resolution or breaking up of something complex into its various simple elements; the exact determination of the elements or components of something complex. L16. 2 A statement of the result of such an operation. M17.

1 **in the final, last, ultimate, analysis** after all due consideration, in the end. *dimensional analysis*, *harmonic analysis*, *linguistic analysis*, *prosodic analysis*, etc. *retrograde analysis*: see RETROGRADE *a.* 2 **bowling analysis** *Cricket* a statement of a bowler's performance record (overs and maiden overs bowled, runs conceded, wickets taken, etc.).

II *spec.* 3 Critical examination of a literary or musical composition in order to bring out essential elements or structure. L16. 4 *Philos.* a The resolution, by application of logic etc., of complex structures, facts, propositions, and concepts into their elements. L16. b The tracing of things to their source and the resolution of knowledge into its original principles; the discovery of general principles underlying concrete phenomena. E18. c The finding of an expression exactly equivalent to a given word, phrase, or sentence, for the purposes of clarification. E20. 5 *Gram.* The resolution of a sentence, phrase, etc., into smaller grammatical elements. E17. 6 *Chem.* The qualitative or quantitative determination by chemical or instrumental means of the constituents of a substance, or of particular components (e.g. contaminants) of a substance. M17. 7 *Math.* Orig., resolution into simpler propositions already proved or admitted; later, algebra. Now, the part of mathematics which embraces the theory of functions, the use of limits, continuity, and the operations of calculus. M17. 8 *Psychol.* Treatment by the examination of memories, dreams, etc.; *spec.* = PSYCHOANALYSIS. E20.

4a **philosophical analysis** *spec.* the branch of philosophy that deals with the clarification of existing concepts and knowledge. 6 *gravimetric analysis, qualitative analysis, quantitative analysis, thermal analysis*, etc. 8 *lay analysis*: see LAY *a.* *transactional analysis*: see TRANSACTIONAL 2.

¶In various senses contrasted with *synthesis*.

analyst /ˈan(ə)lɪst/ *n.* M17. [Fr. *analyste*, f. *analyser* ANALYSE *v.*, after ns. in *-iste* -IST f. vbs in *-iser* -IZE.] 1 A person engaged or skilled in analysis. M17. 2 *Psychol.* A person who practises or has been trained in psychological analysis; *spec.* = PSYCHOANALYST. E20.

1 N. G. CLARK The days are past when every chemist was his own analyst. *Computers & the Humanities* Computational analysts of style. *Times* Analysts say the market may drift for a while. 2 W. STYRON My analyst said that my transference problem has passed from the hostile to the affectionate stage. *lay analyst*: see LAY *a.*

analytic /anəˈlɪtɪk/ *n.* & *a.* L16. [f. L *analytica* f. Gk *analutika* use as n. of neut. pl. adj. by Aristotle as a title of his treatises on logic; as adj. f. late L *analyticus* f. Gk *analutikos*, f. *analuein*: see ANALYSIS, -IC.] A *n.sing.* & (usu.) in *pl.* (treated as *sing.*). The use of analysis; *spec.* the part of logic which deals with analysis. Now only w. ref. to Aristotle's works. L16.

B *adj.* 1 Of or pertaining to analysis. E17. 2 = ANALYTICAL I. E19. 3 *Ling.* Of a language: = ISOLATING. E19. 4 *Psychol.* Seeking to analyse ideas and their origins; of, pertaining to, or employing psychological analysis; *spec.* = PSYCHOANALYTIC. M19. 5 *Math.* = HOLOMORPHIC. L19.

1 **analytic proposition** *Philos.* a proposition the truth of which depends on the definition of the terms employed, a self-evident proposition. 2 M. MITCHELL So still was her face as she stared at Stuart that he, never analytic, took it for granted that she was merely surprised. 3 M. L. SAMUELS The largest grammatical restructuring known in the history of most European languages—the so-called change from synthetic to analytic structure.

analyticity /an(ə)lɪˈtɪsɪti/ *n.* the property of being analytic M20.

analytical /anəˈlɪtɪk(ə)l/ *a.* E16. [f. late L *analyticus* (see prec.) + -AL[1].] 1 Employing analysis; employing the methods of analysis. E16. 2 = ANALYTIC I. M17. 3 = ANALYTIC 3. E19. 4 *Psychol.* = ANALYTIC 4. M19.

1 **analytical geometry** geometry involving the use of algebra; coordinate geometry. 4 **analytical psychology**: *spec.* that of Jung.

analytically *adv.* M17.

analyze *v.*, **analyzer** *n.* see ANALYSE *v.*, ANALYSER.

Anamese *a.* & *n.* var. of ANNAMESE.

anamnesis /anəmˈniːsɪs/ *n.* Pl. **-neses** /-ˈniːsiːz/. L16. [Gk *anamnēsis* remembrance.] 1 The recalling of things past; reminiscence. L16. 2 *Chr. Ch.* That part of the Eucharistic canon in which the sacrifice of Christ is recalled. L19. 3 A patient's account of his or her medical history. L19.

anamnestic /-ˈnɛstɪk/ *n.* & *a.* †(*a*) *n.* a medicine to aid the memory; (*b*) *adj.* recalling to mind, aiding the memory; pertaining to or of the nature of anamnesis: E18.

anamorphic /anəˈmɔːfɪk/ *a.* E20. [f. ANA- + Gk *morphē* form + -IC.] 1 Of or pertaining to an anamorphosis. E20. b Of a lens: that produces an image distorted in one dimension. M20. 2 *Bot.* & *Zool.* Characterized by anamorphosis. M20.

anamorphosis /anəˈmɔːfəsɪs/ *n.* Pl. **-phoses** /-fəsiːz/. E18. [Gk *anamorphōsis* transformation: see ANA-, MORPHOSIS.] 1 A distorted projection or drawing of anything, which appears normal when viewed from a particular point or by means of a suitable mirror. E18. 2 *Bot.* & *Zool.* Progression to a higher type. Now *spec.* development of the adult form through a series of small changes. M19.

anamorphoscope *n.* a mirror designed to give a correct image of an anamorphosis L19.

†**anan** *adv.* var. of ANON *adv.*

ananas /əˈnɑːnəs/ *n.* L16. [Fr. & Sp. f. Port. *ananás* f. Guarani *naná*.] The pineapple plant (*Ananas comosus*) or fruit.

anandrous /əˈnandrəs/ *a.* M19. [f. Gk *anandros* without males, f. *an-* AN-[5] + *andr-*, *anēr* man + -OUS.] *Bot.* Having no stamens.

anapaest /ˈanəpiːst, -pɛst/ *n.* Also ***-pest**. Also (earlier) in L form †**-p(a)estus**. L16. [L *anapaestus* f. Gk *anapaistos* reversed, f. as ANA- + *paiein* to strike: so called because it is the reverse of a dactyl.] *Pros.* 1 A foot consisting of two short syllables followed by one long syllable or, in English etc., of two unstressed syllables followed by a stressed syllable. L16. 2 A verse composed of or containing such feet. M19.

anapaestic /anəˈpiːstɪk, -ˈpɛst-/ *a.* & *n.* Also ***-pest-**. L17. [Late L *anapaesticus* f. Gk *anapaistikos*: see prec., -IC.] *Pros.* A *adj.* Composed of or containing anapaests; of or pertaining to an anapaest or anapaests. L17. B *n.* An anapaestic verse or line. Usu. in *pl.* L17.

anapaestus *n.*, **anapest** *n.*, **anapestic** *a.* & *n.*, †**anapestus** *n.* see ANAPAEST, ANAPAESTIC *a.* & *n.*

anaphora /əˈnaf(ə)rə/ *n.* L16. [Branch I f. L f. Gk = repetition, f. as ANA- + *pherein* carry; branch II f. late Gk.] I 1 *Rhet.* The repetition of the same word or phrase in several successive clauses. L16. 2 *Ling.* The use of an expression which refers to or stands for an earlier word or group of words. M20. II 3 *Chr. Ch.* The part of the Eucharist at which the oblation is made. M18.

anaphoric, **-ical** /anəˈfɒrɪk, -ɪk(ə)l/ *adjs.* of, pertaining to, or constituting grammatical anaphora; referring to or standing for an earlier word or words: E20. **anaˈphorically** *adv.* M20.

anaphrodisiac /anafrəˈdɪzɪak/ *a.* & *n.* E19. [f. AN-[5] + APHRODISIAC.] (A drug) that reduces sexual desire.

anaphylaxis /anəfɪˈlaksɪs/ *n.* E20. [mod.L, f. Gk ANA- + *phulaxis* watching, guarding.] *Med.* An acute allergic reaction to an antigen on reintroduction.

anaphylactic *a.* of or pertaining to anaphylaxis; *anaphylactic shock*, extreme reaction to a second dose of an antigen: E20. **anaphylactoid** *a.* resembling anaphylaxis or anaphylactic shock E20.

anaplasmosis /anəplazˈməʊsɪs/ *n.* Pl. **-moses** /-ˈməʊsiːz/. E20. [f. mod.L *Anaplasma* (see below) + -OSIS.] *Vet. Med.* A disease of cattle and other animals due to infection with micro-organisms of the genus *Anaplasma*, and characterized chiefly by anaemia.

anaplerosis /anəplɪˈrəʊsɪs/ *n. rare.* Pl. **-roses** /-ˈrəʊsiːz/. L17. [Gk *anaplērōsis*, f. *anaplēroun* fill up: see -OSIS.] The filling up of a deficiency (†*spec.* (*Med.*) of tissue).

anaplerotic *a.* & *n.* (*a*) *adj.* promoting anaplerosis; †(*b*) *n.* an anaplerotic medicine: E18.

anapsid /əˈnapsɪd/ *a.* & *n.* M20. [mod.L *Anapsida* pl. (see below), f. as AN-[5] + Gk (*h*)*apsid-*, (*h*)*apsis* arch: see -ID[3].] *Zool.* A *adj.* Of, pertaining to, or characteristic of the subclass Anapsida of reptiles lacking temporal openings in the skull. M20. B *n.* An anapsid reptile. M20.

anaptyxis /anəpˈtɪksɪs/ *n.* L19. [mod.L f. Gk *anaptuxis* unfolding, f. as ANA- + *ptuxis* folding.] *Phonet.* The development of a vowel between two consonants.

anaptyctic *a.* L19.

anarch /ˈanɑːk/ *n.* M17. [Gk *anarkhos* without a chief, f. as AN-[5] + -ARCH.] 1 An instigator of anarchy, a leader of revolt. *poet.* M17. 2 An anarchist. L19.

aˈnarchal *a.* (*rare*) = ANARCHICAL E19.

anarchism /ˈanəkɪz(ə)m/ *n.* M17. [In early use f. as prec. + -ISM; later after Fr. *anarchisme*.] The principles or practice of anarchy or anarchists.

anarchist /ˈanəkɪst/ *n.* M17. [In early use f. as prec. + -IST; later after Fr. *anarchiste*.] An advocate of anarchy; a person who believes that all government should be abolished.

anarˈchistic *a.* associated with or tending to anarchy L19.

anarchy /ˈanəki/ *n.* M16. [med.L *anarchia* f. Gk *anarkhia*, f. as ANARCH: see -Y[3].] 1 Absence of government in a society (orig. as a source of civil disorder, later also as a political ideal); a state of political or social confusion; absolute freedom of the individual. M16. 2 *transf.* & *fig.* Absence or non-recognition of authority in any sphere; moral or intellectual conflict; a state of disorder; chaos. M17.

1 CARLYLE Without sovereigns, true sovereigns, temporal and spiritual, I see nothing possible but an anarchy; the hatefullest of things. C. V. WEDGWOOD Meanwhile the country, lacking any accepted government, slipped towards anarchy. G. K. ROBERTS *Anarchy* The organisation of society on the basis of voluntary cooperation, and especially without the agency of political institutions, i.e. the state. 2 A. COWLEY Thousand worse Passions then possesst The Interregnum of my Breast. Bless me from such an Anarchy! CHESTERFIELD Our language is . . in a state of anarchy. M. BEERBOHM An anarchy of small curls.

aˈnarchial *a.* (now *rare*) = ANARCHICAL E18. **aˈnarchic** *a.* = ANARCHICAL L18. **aˈnarchical** *a.* of or pertaining to anarchy; disorderly; unregulated: L16. **aˈnarchically** *adv.* L19. **anarchize** *v.t.* (*rare*) reduce to anarchy E19. **aˈnarcho-** *comb. form* [-O-] involving anarchy and, used esp. in *anarcho-syndicalism, -ist* ns. (a supporter of) a movement aiming at the transfer of the means of industrial production to unions of workers M20.

anarthria /əˈnɑːθrɪə/ *n.* L19. [Gk = lack of vigour, f. as next: see -IA[1].] *Med.* Inability to articulate in speech, usu. as a result of cerebral disease.

anarthrous /əˈnɑːθrəs/ *a.* E19. [f. Gk AN-[5] + *arthron* joint, definite article + -OUS.] *Gk Gram.* Of a noun: used without the article.

anasarca /anəˈsɑːkə/ *n.* Now *rare.* LME. [med.L *anasarc(h)a* f. Gk *anasarx* adj. (Galen) = *ana sarka* (*ana-* up, *sarx* flesh).] *Med.* A generalized oedema of subcutaneous tissue, usu. with accumulation of fluid in serous cavities.

fig.: DISRAELI An aged power . . which . . looked with complacency on its own unnatural greatness, its political anasarca.

anasarcous *a.* of the nature of or exhibiting anasarca L17.

anastatic /anəˈstatɪk/ *a. obs.* exc. *Hist.* M19. [f. Gk *anastatos* ppl formation on *anistanai* set up + -IC.] Designating a lithographic process of printing reproductions from slightly raised metallic plates.

anastigmatic /anəstɪgˈmatɪk/ *a.* L19. [f. AN-[5] + ASTIGMATIC.] Of a lens or lens system: free from astigmatism.

aˈnastigmat *n.* [-AT[2]] an anastigmatic lens or lens-system L19.

anastomosis /anəstəˈməʊsɪs/ *n.* Pl. **-moses** /-ˈməʊsiːz/. L16. [Gk *anastomōsis*, f. *anastomoun* furnish with a mouth or outlet, f. ANA- + *stoma* mouth: see -OSIS.] (A) cross-connection between two vessels, channels, branches, etc. (orig., blood-vessels). Also (*Med.*), (a) surgical formation of an interconnecting passage between blood-vessels, hollow viscera, etc.

aˈnastomose *v.t.* (now *rare*) & *i.* connect or communicate by anastomosis L17.

anastomotic /anəstəˈmɒtɪk/ *a.* & *n.* M17. [Gk *anastomōtikos* proper for opening: see prec., -OTIC.] A *adj.* †1 Of a medicine: designed to open the mouths of vessels. M17–M19. 2 Of or pertaining to anastomosis. M19. †B *n.* An anastomotic medicine. Only in E18.

anastrophe /əˈnastrəfi/ *n.* M16. [Gk *anastrophē* turning back, f. as ANA- + *strephein* to turn.] *Rhet.* Inversion or unusual order of words or clauses.

anatase /ˈanəteɪz/ *n.* E19. [Fr. f. Gk *anatasis* extension, f. as ANA- + *teinein* to stretch: w. allus. to the length of the crystals.] *Min.* One of the tetragonal forms of titanium dioxide (cf. RUTILE), found usu. as brown dipyramidal crystals.

anathema /əˈnaθəmə/ *n.* Pl. **-mas**, in sense 3 also **anathemata** /anəˈθiːmətə/. E16. [eccl.L (as senses 1 and 2) f. Gk orig. 'a thing devoted' (sense 3), later 'an accursed thing' (see *Rom.* 9:3), orig. var. of *anathēma* votive offering, f. *anatithenai* set up.] 1 Something or someone accursed or assigned to damnation; something or someone detested. E16. 2 The formal act or formula of consigning to damnation; the curse of God; the curse of the Church, excommunicating a person or denouncing a doctrine etc.; a denunciation of alleged impiety, heresy, etc.; an imprecation. L16. 3 [Gk *anathēma*.] Something devoted or consecrated to divine use. Now *rare*. L16.

1 BACON He would wish to be an Anathema from Christ, for the Salvation of his Brethren. J. GALSWORTHY Let them go! They are as much anathema to me as I, no doubt, am to them. **anathema maranatha** /marəˈneɪθə/ [Gk *Maran atha* = Aram. *māran ʼăṯā* come, Lord] (taken as) a portentously intensified anathema. 2 BURKE The divine thunders out his anathemas. LYTTON 'Confound the man!' was my mental anathema. GLADSTONE The Pope . . has condemned the slave trade—but no more heed is paid to his anathema than to the passing wind. W. FAULKNER Gaunt, fanaticfaced country preachers thundered anathema from the rustic pulpit at his oblivious and unregenerate head. 3 S. BIRCH The little figures . . may have been votive offerings to the gods, such anathemata being offered by the poor.

†**anathem** *n.* = ANATHEMA 1, 2 M16–L18. **anatheˈmatical** *n.* & *a.* (*rare*) †(*a*) *n.* = ANATHEMA 2; (*b*) *adj.* of the nature of an anathema: L16. **anathematism** *n.* a statement of anathema, an ecclesiastical denunciation M16. ˈ**anatheme** *n.* (now *rare*) = ANATHEMA 3 M17. **anathemize** *v.t.* (*rare*) = ANATHEMATIZE 1 L17.

anathematize /əˈnaθəmətʌɪz/ *v.* Also **-ise**. M16. [(O)Fr. *anathématiser* f. eccl.L *anathematizare* f. Gk *anathematizein*, f. *anathema*: see prec., -IZE.] 1 *v.t.* Pronounce an anathema against; denounce; curse. M16. 2 *v.i.* Pronounce anathemas; curse. M18.

a,nathematiˈzation *n.* M16. **anathematizer** *n.* (*rare*) M17.

anatocism /əˈnatəsɪz(ə)m/ *n.* Now *rare* or *obs.* M17. [L *anatocismus* (Cicero) f. Gk *anatokismos*, f. *tokos* interest: see ANA-, -ISM.] Compound interest.

Anatolian /anəˈtəʊlɪən/ *a.* & *n.* Also †**Nat-**. L16. [f. *Anatolia* (cf. Gk *anatolē* east) Asia Minor + -AN.] A *adj.* Of or pertaining to Anatolia, now the Asian portion of Turkey, or its inhabitants. L16. B *n.* A native or inhabitant of Anatolia. L16.

Also **Anatolic** *a.* M19.

anatomical /anəˈtɒmɪk(ə)l/ *a.*L16. [f. Fr. *anatomique* or late L *anatomicus*: see ANATOMY, -ICAL.] 1 Of or pertaining to the study or practice of anatomy. L16. 2 Of or pertaining to the anatomy; structural. E18.

anatomic *a.* anatomical L17. **anatomically** *adv.* M17. **anatomico-** *comb. form* [-O-] anatomical and, as *anatomico-physiological* adj.: L18.

anatomise *v.* var. of ANATOMIZE.

anatomist /əˈnatəmɪst/ *n.* M16. [Fr. *anatomiste* or med.L deriv. of *anatomizare* ANATOMIZE: see -IST.] 1 A dissecter of dead bodies; a person skilled in (esp. human) anatomy. M16. 2 *fig.* A dissecter of anything, an analyser. L16.

anatomize /əˈnatəmʌɪz/ *v.* Also **-ise**. LME. [Fr. *anatomiser* or med.L *anatomizare*: see ANATOMY, -IZE.] 1 *v.t.* & *i.* Dissect; cut up (an animal or vegetable body) in order to display the position, structure, and relations of its various parts. LME. 2 *v.t. fig.* Reveal in detail; analyse. L16. †3 *v.t.* Analyse chemically. E–M17.

anatomiˈzation *n.* M17. **anatomizer** *n.* M17.

anatomy /əˈnatəmi/ *n.* LME. [(O)Fr. *anatomie* f. late L *anatomia* f. Gk, f. as ANA- + -TOMY.] 1 The science of the structure of the bodies of humans, animals, and plants; a treatise in this field. LME. 2 Anatomical structure. LME. †3 A body or part anatomized; a subject for dissection. L15–M18. 4 The artificial separation of the parts of a human, animal, or vegetable body, in order to discover their position, structure, and relations; dissection. M16. 5 *fig.* Detailed examination or analysis; structure, organization. M16. †6 A model or drawing of the human body as dissected. M16–M18. 7 A skeleton; a corpse of skin and bone, a mummy; an emaciated being. Cf. ATOMY *n.*[1] *arch.* L16. 8 The bodily frame. Chiefly *joc.* L16. †9 Chemical analysis. E17–E18.

1 C. P. SNOW The anatomy they learn is sheer unscientific nonsense. MORBID *anatomy*. 4 ADDISON Curious observations which he had lately made in an anatomy of an human body. 5 ROBERT BURTON The Anatomy of Melancholy: what it is [etc.]. A. SAMPSON Anatomy of Britain. 7 DISRAELI Death in the Gothic form of a gaunt anatomy parading through the universe. CARLYLE The thread-paper Duchess of Kendal . . poor old anatomy. *fig.*: J. A. FROUDE What lean and shrivelled anatomies the best of such descriptions would seem! 8 J. G. LOCKHART Brown leathern gaiters buttoned upon his nether anatomy. T. H. WHITE You may grow old and trembling in your anatomies.

anatopism /əˈnatəpɪz(ə)m/ *n. rare.* E19. [f. Gk ANA- + *topos* place + -ISM.] A putting of a thing out of its proper place.

anatropous /əˈnatrəpəs/ *a.* M19. [f. as AN-[5] + ATROPOUS.] *Bot.* Of an ovule: inverted on its funicle.

anatta *n.* var. of ANNATTO.

Anaxagorean /anək,sagəˈriːən/ *a.* L16. [f. L *Anaxagoras* (see below) + -EAN.] Of or pertaining to the Greek philosopher Anaxagoras (fl. during the 5th cent. BC), who taught that matter was eternal but was combined into bodies by a supreme intelligence.

anbury /ˈanb(ə)ri/ *n.* Now *dial.* Also **am-** /ˈam-/. L16. [Perh. f. *ang-* in OE *angnægl* AGNAIL, *angseta* carbuncle, pimple + BERRY *n.*[1] in the sense of a red mark or pustule.] 1 A soft tumour or spongy wart on horses, oxen, etc. L16. 2 Club-root of turnips or cabbages. M18.

-ance /(ə)ns/ *suff.* [Fr. f. L (i) *-antia*, f. pres. ppl stems in *-ant-* -ANT[1], (ii) *-entia*: see -ENCE.] Forming ns. of quality (or instances of it), as *arrogance*, *relevance*, or of action, as *assistance*, *penance*. Since 16 many wds ending in *-ance* f. Fr. have been altered back to *-ence* after L, and more recent wds have taken *-ance* or *-ence* according to the L vowel (hence much inconsistency, as *dependence*, *-ance*, *resistance*, *subsistence*). Through such pairs as *appear*, *appearance* it became to some extent a living suff. and was appended to vbs of non-Romance origin, as *forbear*, *forbearance*, *hinder*, *hindrance*, *rid*, *riddance*. Now a common formative element in techn. terms, as *absorbance*. Cf. -ANCY.

ancestor /ˈansɛstə/ *n.* ME. [OFr. *ancestre* (mod. *ancêtre*) f. L *antecessor*, f. as ANTE- + *cess-* pa. ppl stem of *cedere* go: assim. to -OR.] 1 A person, usu. more remote than a grandparent, from whom one is descended; a forefather. Also *transf.* & *fig.*, an animal from which another is (remotely) descended; a source, a precursor. ME. 2 *Law.* A person who precedes another in the course of inheritance. E17. 3 An animal or other organism from which another has evolved. M19.

1 H. H. MILMAN St. Peter . . the spiritual ancestor of the Bishop of Rome. M. C. SELF It is believed that his [the Suffolk's] ancestors were the horses of the Norsemen. F. FITZGERALD In the rites of ancestor worship the child imitated the gestures of his grandfather. 3 B. J. WILLIAMS The reptilian ancestors of mammals.

anceˈstorial *a.* (now *rare*) = ANCESTRAL M17. **ancestress** *n.* a female ancestor L16.

ancestral /anˈsɛstr(ə)l/ *a.* LME. [OFr. *ancestrel* (mod. *-al*), f. as prec. + -AL[1].] 1 Of, pertaining to, or inherited from ancestors. LME. 2 Of, pertaining to, or constituting an evolutionary ancestor; earlier in a line of (evolutionary) development. (Foll. by *to*.) M19.

1 COLERIDGE Kubla heard from far Ancestral voices prophesying war. G. ORWELL Why should one feel it to be intolerable unless one had some kind of ancestral memory that things had once been different? 2 D. MORRIS In the Old World . . ancestral apes were spreading over a wide forest area.

ancestrally *adv.* L19.

ancestrula /ənˈsɛstrʊlə/ *n.* Pl. **-lae** /-liː/, **-las**. E20. [mod.L, irreg. f. Fr. ANCESTRAL + L *-ula* fem. dim. suff.] *Zool.* The original zooecium in a bryozoan colony.

ancestry /ˈansɛstri/ *n.* ME. [Alt. of OFr. *ancesserie* after ANCESTOR: see -Y[3], -RY.] 1 Ancestral lineage or descent; *spec.* noble, aristocratic, or ancient descent. Also *fig.*, origin, background. ME. 2 *collect.* One's ancestors. *arch.* ME.

1 ADDISON Title and ancestry render a good man more illustrious. W. S. GILBERT I can trace my ancestry back to a protoplasmal primordial atomic globule. M. C. SELF Somewhere in the ancestry of Janus there must have been a happy 'nick' which gave him the peculiar characteristics of the Quarter horse. J. K. GALBRAITH The explanation of consumer behaviour has its ancestry in a much older problem. 2 W. COWPER Our ancestry, a gallant Christian race.

anˈcestrial *a.* (*rare*) = ANCESTRAL M17.

anchor /ˈaŋkə/ *n.*[1] [OE *ancor*, *-cer*, *-cra* (= OFris., (M)LG, MDu. *anker*, late OHG *anchar* (G *Anker*), ON *akkeri*) f. L *ancora* f. Gk *agkura*. In ME reinforced by (O)Fr. *ancre*. The present sp. follows the erron. L *anchora*.] 1 An appliance for holding a ship etc. fixed in a particular place by mooring it to the bottom of the sea or river, or for similarly holding a balloon etc. by mooring it to the ground; a heavy metal structure traditionally composed of a long shank with a ring at one end for the cable and at the other end two arms or flukes, tending upwards, with barbs on each side. OE. 2 *fig.* A ground or source of confidence or security. LME. 3 Any contrivance or instrument that fulfils a purpose similar to that of an anchor. M16. b In *pl.* The brakes of a vehicle. *colloq.* M20. 4 Something resembling an anchor in shape, as an architectural moulding. M17. 5 In full *anchorman*, *anchorperson*, *anchorwoman*. A person playing a vital part, as the end member of a tug-of-war team, the last runner in a relay race, the compère of a broadcast programme, etc. E20.

1 *kedge anchor*, *mushroom anchor*, etc.

Phrases: **at anchor** moored by an anchor. **bring to anchor** moor with an anchor. **cast, come to, anchor** let down the anchor(s). *crown and anchor*: see CROWN *n.* **drop anchor** = *cast anchor* above. *foul anchor*: see FOUL *a.* *fouled anchor*: see FOUL *v.* SHEET ANCHOR. **weigh anchor** take up the anchor(s).

Comb.: **anchor-hold** *n.*[1] the hold or grip that an anchor takes; a place for anchoring; *fig.* a firm hold, a point clung to, a ground of confidence, security, etc.; *anchorman*, *-person*: see sense 5 above; **anchor-plate** a heavy piece of timber or metal serving as a support, e.g. for the cables of a suspension bridge; **anchor-ring** (*a*) the ring through which the cable is attached to an anchor; (*b*) *Geom.* a torus of circular cross-section; *anchorwoman*: see sense 5 above.

anchorless *a.* without an anchor; *fig.* without a firm hold, drifting: M19.

anchor /ˈaŋkə/ *n.*[2] Long *arch.* or *Hist.* [OE *ancra*, *ancor*, *-cer* perh. through OIr. *anchara*, *angciore* f. eccl.L *anchoreta* ANCHORITE.] An anchorite; an anchoress.

Comb.: **anchor-hold** *n.*[2] the cell or retreat of an anchorite.

anchor /ˈaŋkə/ *v.* ME. [(O)Fr. *ancrer* = med.L *anc(h)orare*: see ANCHOR *n.*[1]] 1 *v.t.* Secure (a ship etc.) by means of an anchor; place at or bring to anchor. ME. 2 *v.t. transf.* & *fig.* Fix as with an anchor, fix firmly. ME. 3 *v.i.* Cast anchor; come to anchor; be moored by means of an anchor. L16. 4 *v.t.* & *i.* Act as anchorperson of (a broadcast programme). M20.

1 SOUTHEY It was not possible to anchor the fleet. SCOTT FITZGERALD An enormous couch on which two young women were buoyed up as though upon an anchored balloon. 2 SHAKES. *Rich. III* Till that my nails were anchor'd in thine eyes. E. O'NEILL Green seaweed anchored to a rock. J. B. PRIESTLEY I didn't feel quite right in my mind, I wasn't firmly anchored to reality. 3 MILTON Sea-faring men . . whose Bark by chance Or Pinnace anchors in a craggy Bay. *fig.*: SHAKES. *Meas. for M.* Heaven hath my empty words, Whilst my invention . . Anchors on Isabel.

anchorage /ˈaŋk(ə)rɪdʒ/ *n.*[1] ME. [f. ANCHOR *n.*[1] + -AGE. Cf. Fr. *ancrage*.] 1 A toll or charge for anchoring. *arch.* ME. 2a Conditions admitting of anchoring; a place at which to anchor. L16. b

For other words beginning with *ana-* see the entry for **ana-**

transf. & *fig.* A point of support or rest; a hold; something on which to depend or repose. L17. 3 A set of anchors. *rare.* L16. 4 The action or process of anchoring; the condition of lying at anchor. E17.

2b J. A. FROUDE The Church anchorage no longer tenable in the change of wind, and the new anchorage in the Bible as yet partially discovered and imperfectly sounded. J. TYNDALL I crossed the fissure, obtained the anchorage at the other side, and helped the others over. 3 SHAKES. *Tit. A.* The bark.. Returns with precious lading to the bay From whence at first she weigh'd her anchorage.

anchorage /'aŋk(ə)rɪdʒ/ *n.*[2] Now *arch.* or *Hist.* L16. [f. ANCHOR *n.*[2] + -AGE. Cf. *hermitage*, *parsonage*.] The cell or retreat of an anchorite.

anchoress /'aŋkərɛs/ *n.* Also (*arch.*) **ancress** /'aŋkrɛs/. LME. [f. ANCHOR *n.*[2] + -ESS[1].] A female anchorite; a nun.

anchorite /'aŋkərʌɪt/ *n.* Also **anchoret** /'aŋkərɪt/, (esp. in sense 2) **anachoret** /ə'nakərɪt/. LME. [med.L *anc(h)orita*, eccl.L *anchoreta* f. eccl.Gk *anakhōrētēs*, f. *anakhōrein* retire, retreat, f. as ANA- + *khōrein* withdraw, f. *khōra*, *khōros* place. Superseding ANCHOR *n.*[2]] 1 A person who has withdrawn from the world, usu. for religious reasons; a hermit, a recluse. LME. 2 *Eccl. Hist.* A recluse of the early Eastern Church. L16. 3 *gen.* A person of solitary or secluded habits. E17.

ancho'retic *a.* M17. **anchoritic** /-'rɪt-/ *a.* M19. **anchoritical** /-'rɪt-/ *a.* M17.

anchoveta /antʃə'vɛtə/ *n.* M20. [Sp., dim. of *anchova*: see next.] A Pacific anchovy, *Cetengraulis mysticetus*, used as bait or to make fish-meal.

anchovy /'antʃəvi, an'tʃəuvi/ *n.* L16. [Sp. & Port. *ancho(v)a*, of unkn. origin.] A small, mainly Mediterranean fish of the herring family, *Engraulis encrasicholus*, which has a rich flavour and is usu. eaten pickled or in pastes, sauces, etc. Also, any of numerous related fishes.

Comb.: **anchovy pear** (the edible fruit of) the W. Indian tree *Grias cauliflora*.

anchusa /ən'ku:sə, -'tʃu:-/ *n.* M16. [L (Pliny) f. Gk *agkhousa*, *egkh-*.] Any plant of the genus *Anchusa*, of the borage family; *esp.* the plant *A. azurea*, grown for its deep blue flowers.

anchylose *v.*, **-osis** *n.* vars. of ANKYLOSE, -OSIS.

†**anciency** *n.* M16–L19. [Alt. of ANCIENTY as if ANCIENT *a.* were of ppl origin, after *decent*, *decency*, etc.] Ancientness; antiquity.

ancien régime /ɑ̃sjɛ̃ reʒim/ *n. phr.* L18. [Fr. = former regime.] The system of government in France before the Revolution of 1789. Also *transf.*, the old system or style of things.

ancient /'eɪnʃ(ə)nt/ *n.*[1] In senses 2, 6 also **A-**. LME. [f. the adj.] 1 An old man (or animal); a patriarch. *arch.* LME. 2 A person who lived in times long past; a Greek or Roman of classical antiquity, esp. an author. Freq. in *the ancients.* L15. †3 A senior, *one's* superior in age. M16–M17. †4 An ancestor. *rare.* M16–E19. 5 A person holding a senior position, an elder, a dignitary. *arch.* M16. 6 *the Ancient of Days*, God. M16.

ancient /'eɪnʃ(ə)nt/ *n.*[2] *arch.* M16. [Alt. of ENSIGN *n.* by assoc. w. early forms of prec.] 1 A standard or flag; in *pl.*, insignia, colours. M16. 2 A standard-bearer. L16.

ancient /'eɪnʃ(ə)nt/ *a.* LME. [AN *auncien*, (O)Fr. *ancien*, ult. f. L ANTE- + *-anus* -AN.] 1a Belonging to times long past. LME. b Former, earlier, bygone, (not necessarily referring to *long* ago). *arch.* L15. c *spec.* (Also **A-**.) Belonging or pertaining to the period before the fall of the Western Roman Empire in AD 476. E17. 2 Having lived long; old, aged; having the experience or wisdom of age; venerable. LME. 3 That has been many years in some rank, position, or capacity; veteran. *arch.* LME. 4 Of early origin or formation; going far back in history; long-established; time-worn. L15.

1a D. H. LAWRENCE The grand, pagan twilight of the valleys, .. with a sense of ancient gods. *ancient Briton*: see BRITON *n.* 2. *ancient Greek*: see GREEK *n.* & *a.* b BUNYAN Thy antient kindness. POPE They mourn'd their ancient leader lost. c ADDISON Statuary and Architecture both Ancient and Modern. **ancient history** *fig.* something already long familiar. 2 SHAKES. *Rom. & Jul.* Farewell, ancient lady. S. JOHNSON The precepts of ancient experience. J. GROSS Saintsbury .. looked the more ancient of the two, with his black skull-cap and his patriarchal beard. 3 K. DIGBY Seuerall of our ancientest seamen .. were sea sicke. 4 ARNOLD BENNETT The fine and ancient borough. M. PEAKE These dwellings, by ancient law, were granted this chill intimacy. M. DRABBLE They were very upper, but not a bit like an ancient family. *ancient demesne*: see DEMESNE *n.* **ancient lights** a window that a neighbour must not deprive of light by erecting a building. **ancient monument** an old building etc. protected by Act of Parliament from damage or destruction.

anciently *adv.* (*a*) in ancient times, long ago; (*b*) from ancient times, for a long time: L15. **ancientness** *n.* M16.

ancientry /'eɪnʃ(ə)ntri/ *n. arch.* M16. [f. ANCIENT *n.*[1], *a.* + -RY.] †1 *collect.* Older people, elders. M16–E17. 2 The quality or condition of being ancient. L16. 3 Time long past, antiquity. M18.

†**ancienty** *n.* LME. [AN *auncienté*, (O)Fr. *ancienneté*: see ANCIENT *a.*, -TY[1].] 1 The quality of having lived or existed for a long time. LME–M17. 2 The time long past; antiquity. Long *rare.* LME–E19. 3 Distance in past time. L15–L16. 4 Seniority, priority. L15–L18.

ancile /an'sʌɪli/ *n.* Pl. ***-lia*** /-lɪə/. L16. [L.] The sacred tutelary shield of ancient Rome, said to have fallen from heaven.

ancilla /an'sɪlə/ *n. rare.* Pl. **-llae** /-li:/, **-llas**. L19. [L, fem. dim. of *anculus* servant.] A maidservant, a handmaid (*lit.* & *fig.*).

ancillary /an'sɪləri/ *a.* & *n.* M17. [L *ancillaris*, f. as prec.: see -ARY[2].] A *adj.* 1 Subservient, subordinate; auxiliary, providing support; now *esp.* providing essential support or services to a central function or industry, esp. to hospital medical staff. (Foll. by *to*.) M17. 2 Of or pertaining to maidservants. *rare.* M19.

1 R. FRY It is an adjectival and ancillary beauty scarcely worthy of our prolonged contemplation. H. WILSON A period of great anxiety in the medical profession and occupations ancillary to medicine. *Financial Times* Its latest offer of 7.5 per cent for nurses and 6 per cent for ancillary staff and other grades. 2 THACKERAY The ancillary beauty was the one whom the Prince had selected.

B *n.* An auxiliary, an accessory; an ancillary worker. M19.

†**ancle** *n.* var. of ANKLE.

†**ancome** *n.* L16–L19. [Prob. var. of ONCOME *n.* Cf. INCOME *n.*[2], UNCOME *n.*] A boil forming unexpectedly. Also, a whitlow.

ancon /'aŋkɒn, -k(ə)n/ *n.* Pl. **ancones** /aŋ'kəuni:z/, **ancons**. E18. [L f. Gk *agkōn* nook, bend, elbow.] *Archit.* †1 The corner or quoin of a wall, cross-beam, or rafter. Only in E18. 2 A console, usu. of two volutes, apparently supporting a cornice. M18.

Ancona /ən'kəunə/ *n.*[1] M19. [A town in Italy.] (A bird of) a breed of poultry having black and white mottled plumage.

ancona /an'ko:na, an'kəunə/ *n.*[2] Pl. ***-ne*** /-ne, -ni/. L19. [It. = med.L, of uncertain origin: perh. alt. of Gk *eikona* accus. of *eikōn* ICON.] An altarpiece, *esp.* one consisting of a group of paintings connected by architectural structure.

ancone *n.* pl. of ANCONA *n.*[2]

ancones *n.pl.* see ANCON.

ancress *n.* see ANCHORESS.

-ancy /(ə)nsi/ *suff.* [f. or after L *-antia* -ANCE. Cf. -ENCY.] Forming ns. of quality, as *relevancy*, or state, as *expectancy*, but not of action (cf. -ANCE). Many wds orig. in *-ance* have been refash., as *constancy*.

ancylostomiasis /,aŋkɪləustə'mʌɪəsɪs, ,ansɪ-/ *n.* Pl. **-ases** /-əsi:z/. Also **ank-** /,aŋk-/. L19. [f. mod.L *Ancylostoma* (see below) f. Gk *agkulos* crooked + *stoma* mouth, + -IASIS.] *Med.* Hookworm infection of the small intestine, esp. by *Ancylostoma duodenale* or *Necator americanus*, often leading to anaemia. Also called *uncinariasis*.

and /ənd, (ə)n, *stressed* and/ *conj.*[1], *adv.*, & *n.* [OE *and*, *ond*, corresp. to OFris. *and(a)*, *ande*, *end(a)*, *en*, OS *ande*, *endi* (Du. *en*), OHG *anti*, *enti* (G *und*), Skt *atha* thereupon, also. See also AN *conj.*] A *conj.* I Coordinating. Introducing a wd, phr., cl., or sentence which is to be taken side by side with, along with, or in addition to, that which precedes. 1 Simply additive. (When connecting three or more members it is expressed only with the last in ordinary prose but formerly, & still *colloq.* & *rhet.* for emphasis, with every member.) OE. b Introducing an adversative cl.: on the other hand, yet, but. *arch.* & *rhet.* OE. †c Before either of two members connected. ME–E16. 2 Connecting occurrences of the same member, expressing continuous or indefinite repetition. OE. 3 Introducing a consequence, actual or predicted; after an imperative: in the case or circumstance that you do so. OE. 4 Introducing an explanation, amplification, or parenthesis. OE. 5 Connecting two vbs approaching the sense of *to* with the inf., esp. after *go, come, try.* OE. 6 Continuing a narration from a previous sentence or from implied assent to a previous question or opinion. OE. 7 Expr. a difference of quality between things of the same name or class. M16. 8 Connecting two adjs. or an adj. and an adv., of which the former approaches an advb. relation to the latter, esp. in *good and, nice and.* L16. 9 Expr. surprise at, or asking the truth of, what one has already heard. L18.

1 SHAKES. *Com. Err.* My master and his man are both broke loose. AV *Ps.* 90:10 The days of our yeres are threescore yeeres and ten. MILTON My three-and-twentieth year. ADDISON We do in our Consciences believe two and two make four. T. MOORE Six hundred and eighty-five ways to dress eggs. KEATS Dance, and Provençal song, and sunburnt mirth! BYRON Through life's road, so dim and dirty, I have dragged to three and thirty. R. KIPLING Oh it's Tommy this, an' Tommy that, an' 'Tommy, go away'. G. B. SHAW My lunch will cost me one [shilling] and sixpence. B. RUSSELL The present holders of power are evil men, and the present manner of life is doomed. JOYCE He saw the priest bend down and kiss the altar and then face about and bless all the people. S. SASSOON Allgood was quiet, thoughtful, and fond of watching birds. P. SCOTT Susy removed the mirror and only set it up again when she had finished. *and all, hit and run, now and then, once and for all, smash and grab, still and all, time and again, to and fro*, etc. **and/or** either together or as an alternative. *but and*: see BUT *conj.* b AV *Matt.* 22:30 Hee said, I goe sir, and went not. 2 SHAKES. *2 Hen. IV* A hundred mark is a long one for a poor lone woman to bear; and I have borne, and borne, and borne. BYRON I have lived for months and months on shipboard. YEATS Eternity is passion, girl or boy, Cry at the onset of their sexual joy 'For ever and for ever'. *two and two*: see TWO *n.* 1. 3 A. E. HOUSMAN Their shoulders held the sky suspended; They stood, and earth's foundations stay. D. L. SAYERS Spray with Sanfect and you're safe. 4 SHAKES. *Temp.* I heard a humming, And that a strange one too. THACKERAY A regular bang-up chap, and no mistake. DICKENS Scrooge signed it: and Scrooge's name was good upon 'Change. LD MACAULAY He and he alone has done all this. G. K. CHESTERTON The French would certainly have recovered the stolen French provinces whenever they could; and quite right too. 5 G. B. SHAW Without waiting for them to come and ask for these things. SCOTT FITZGERALD Here's your money. Go and buy ten more dogs with it. E. O'NEILL Try and use your brains! 6 AV *John* 21:21 Peter seeing him saith to Jesus, Lord, and what shall this man do? C. KINGSLEY And why could not you run away, boy? 7 BROWNING Alack, there be roses and roses, John! 8 *Blackwood's Magazine* They shall drive nice and slowly. J. LONDON The lawyers .. waded into me good and hard for the cash. E. O'NEILL It's nice and quiet out here. 9 W. J. MICKLE And are ye sure the news is true? And are ye sure he's weel?

II Conditional. 10 Provided that; on condition that. Also *and if.* Now *arch.* & *dial.* ME. 11 Even if; although. Now *arch.* & *dial.* LME. †12 As if, as though. LME–E17. †13 *indirect interrog.* Whether. L16–E17. B *adv.* [A Latinism.] Also, even. Long *arch.* LME.

C *n.* 1 An instance of the conj. 'and' (esp. conditional); an expression of condition or doubt. E16. 2 (Usu. **AND.**) *Computing.* A

Boolean operator which gives the value unity if and only if all the operands are unity, and is otherwise zero. Usu. *attrib.* M20.

1 J. ASHFORD As my old aunt used to say, 'If ifs and ands were pots and pans, there'd be no work for tinkers' hands.'

Comb.: **AND gate** a circuit which produces an output only when signals are received simultaneously through all input connections.

†and *conj.*[2] (after *compars.*). LME–L16. [Erron. expansion of north. dial. var. (cf. 'N *conj.*[2]) of THAN *conj.*[2], formally conf. w. AN *conj.* = prec.] = THAN *conj.*[2]

-and /and/ *suff.* Repr. L *-andus, -da, -dum* of the gerundive of L vbs in *-are*, forming ns. usu. w. the sense 'person (or thing) to be treated in a specified way', as *analysand, multiplicand*. The neut. gerundial ending is sometimes retained, as in *memorandum*.

Andalusian /andəˈluːzjən, -sjən/ *a.* & *n.* Also **-zian.** E17. [f. *Andalusia* (see below) + -AN.] **A** *adj.* Of or pertaining to Andalusia, a region in the southernmost part of Spain, its inhabitants, or its language. E17.

Andalusian HEMIPODE.

B *n.* **1** A native or inhabitant of Andalusia. E17. **2** The variety of Spanish spoken in Andalusia. L19.

andalusite /andəˈluːsʌɪt/ *n.* E19. [f. *Andalusia* (see prec.) + -ITE[1].] *Min.* A metamorphic aluminium silicate occurring as elongated rhombic prisms sometimes of gem quality.

Andaluzian *a.* & *n.* var. of ANDALUSIAN.

Andaman /ˈandəmən/ *a.* & *n.* E19. [See below.] Of or pertaining to the Andaman Islands in the Bay of Bengal or their inhabitants; (of or pertaining to) the Indo-Pacific language of the Andaman Islands.

Andaman Islander a native or inhabitant of the Andaman Islands.

Andaˈmaner *n.* an Andaman Islander E18. **Andamaˈnese** *n.* & *a.* = ANDAMAN, ANDAMANER M19.

andante /anˈdanti/ *adv., a.,* & *n.* E18. [It., pres. pple of *andare* go.] *Mus.* **A** *adv.* & *adj.* (A direction:) (orig.) distinct(ly); (now) moderately slow(ly). E18. **B** *n.* A moderately slow movement or piece. L18.

andantino /andanˈtiːnəʊ/ *adv., a.,* & *n.* E19. [It., dim. of prec.] *Mus.* **A** *adv.* & *adj.* (A direction:) (orig.) rather slower than andante; (now usu.) with less of andante, i.e. rather quicker than andante. E19. **B** *n.* Pl. **-os.** A movement or piece rather quicker (orig. slower) than andante. M19.

Andean /ˈandɪən/ *a.* M19. [f. *Andes* (see below) + -AN.] Of, pertaining to, or resembling the Andes, a mountain range in S. America.

Andean CONDOR.

Anderson shelter /ˈandəs(ə)n ˌʃɛltə/ *n. phr.* M20. [Sir John *Anderson*, UK Home Secretary (1939–40) when the shelter was adopted.] A small prefabricated air-raid shelter.

andesine /ˈandɪziːn/ *n.* M19. [f. *Andes* (see ANDEAN) + -INE[5].] *Min.* A plagioclase occurring in igneous rocks such as andesite and diorite.

andesite /ˈandɪzʌɪt/ *n.* M19. [f. as prec. + -ITE[1].] *Geol.* A fine-grained, usu. porphyritic, volcanic rock consisting chiefly of plagioclase and biotite, hornblende, or pyroxene.

andeˈsitic *a.* of, pertaining to, or characterized by andesite M19.

andiron /ˈandʌɪən/ *n.* ME. [f. OFr. *andier* w. assim. of 2nd syll. to IRON *n.*] A metal stand for supporting burning wood on a hearth etc.; a firedog.

Andorran /anˈdɔːr(ə)n/ *a.* & *n.* M19. [f. *Andorra* (see below) + -AN.] Of or pertaining to, a native or inhabitant of, Andorra, a small independent State in the eastern Pyrenees.

andouille /ɑ̃duːj/ *n.* Pl. pronounced same. E17. [(O)Fr., of unkn. origin.] A kind of pork sausage, usually served as an hors d'oeuvre.

andouillette /ɑ̃dujɛt/ *n.* Pl. pronounced same. Also **†-llet.** E17. [Fr., dim. of prec.] A sausage made from a paste of minced veal, bacon, and other ingredients.

andr- *comb. form* see ANDRO-.

andradite /ˈandrədʌɪt/ *n.* M19. [f. J. B. de *Andrada* e Silva (*c*1763–1838), Brazilian geologist & statesman + -ITE[1].] *Min.* Calcium iron garnet, occurring in various colours, of which some types are used as gemstones.

Andrew /ˈandruː/ *n. Naut. slang.* L16. [Male forename.] In full *Andrew Millar* or *Miller.* **†1** A ship, *esp.* a warship. L16–M19. **†2** A government authority. Only in M19. **3** The Royal Navy. E20.

¶See also *merry Andrew* s.v. MERRY *a.*, *St Andrew's cross* s.v. SAINT *n.* & *a.*

andro- /ˈandrəʊ/ *comb. form* of Gk *andr-, anēr* man: see -O-. Bef. a vowel also **andr-.**

androˈcentric *a.* having man or the male as its centre E20. **androcracy** /anˈdrɒkrəsi/ *n.* the rule of man or the male, male supremacy E20. **androˈcratic** *a.* pertaining to or involving androcracy L19. **androdiˈoecious** *a.* (*Bot.*) having male and hermaphrodite flowers on separate individuals L19. **androdiˈoecism** *n.* (*Bot.*) the condition of being androdioecious L19. **androˈgenesis** *n.* fertilization of the egg by the sperm, and development of the embryo, without the participation of the female nucleus and chromosomes; male parthenogenesis: E20. **androgeˈnetic** *a.* of or pertaining to androgenesis E20. **andromoˈnoecious** *a.* (*Bot.*) having male and hermaphrodite flowers on the same individual L19. **andromoˈnoecism** *n.* (*Bot.*) the condition of being andromonoecious L19. **androsphinx** *n.* a sphinx whose human portion is male E17. **androspore** *n.* the zoospore that in some algae produces the male reproductive organs M19.

androconium /andrəˈkəʊnɪəm/ *n.* Pl. **-nia** /-nɪə/. L19. [f. prec. + Gk *konia* dust + -IUM.] *Entomol.* A scent-producing scale, numbers of which are found on the wings of certain male butterflies and moths.

androconial *a.* E20.

androecium /anˈdriːsjəm/ *n.* Pl. **-cia** /-sjə/. M19. [mod.L f. Gk ANDRO- + *oikion* house: see -IUM.] *Bot.* The stamens of a flower collectively.

androgen /ˈandrədʒ(ə)n/ *n.* M20. [f. ANDRO- + -GEN.] A male sex hormone.

androˈgenic *a.* of or pertaining to an androgen; of the nature of an androgen: M20.

androgyne /ˈandrədʒʌɪn/ *n.* & *a.* M16. [Fr., or L *androgynus, -gyne* f. Gk *androgunos, -gunē*, f. as ANDRO- + *gunē* woman.] **A** *n.* An androgynous individual. M16. **B** *adj.* = ANDROGYNOUS. M19.

¶Recorded in OE & ME in L & Gk forms.

anˈdrogynal *a.* (*rare*) M17. **anˈdrogyny** *n.* hermaphroditism M19.

androgynous /anˈdrɒdʒɪnəs/ *a.* E17. [f. L *androgynus* (see prec.) + -OUS.] **1** Uniting the (physical) characters of both sexes; hermaphrodite. Also, of ambiguous sex; partly male and partly female in appearance. E17. **2** *Astrol.* Of a planet: sometimes hot, sometimes cold. M17. **3** *Bot.* Bearing stamens and pistils on the same inflorescence, or on the same plant. M18.

1 *Time* I heard androgynous characters sing unintelligible lyrics to an endlessly repetitive beat.

android /ˈandrɔɪd/ *n.* & *a.* Orig. in L form **†-oides.** E18. [mod.L *androides*, f. Gk ANDRO- + *-eidēs* -OID.] **A** *n.* An automaton resembling a human being; *Sci. Fiction* a synthetic human being. E18. **B** *adj.* Resembling (that of) a male. L19.

Andromeda /anˈdrɒmɪdə/ *n.* M16. [L f. Gk *Andromedē*: see PERSEUS.] **1** (The name of) a constellation of the northern hemisphere between Perseus and Pegasus. M16. **2** (**a-.**) Either of two low pink-flowered shrubs of northern bogs, *Andromeda polifolia* and (*N. Amer.*) *A. glaucophylla*, of the heath family. Also called *bog rosemary.* M18.

Andromedid *n.* & *a.* [-ID[3]] *Astron.* (designating) any of a shower of meteors (now rarely seen) which appear to radiate from the constellation Andromeda L19.

androsace /anˈdrɒsəsi, -ki/ *n.* L19. [med.L *androsaces* f. Gk *androsakes* (Dioscurides), name of an unidentified marine plant or zoophyte, f. as ANDRO- + *sakos* shield.] Any of numerous dwarf tufted alpine plants of the genus *Androsace*, belonging to the primula family and bearing red or white flowers.

androsterone /andrə(ʊ)ˈstɪərəʊn, anˈdrɒstərəʊn/ *n.* M20. [f. ANDRO- + -STERONE.] *Biochem.* A relatively inactive metabolite of testosterone.

ˈandrostane *n.* [-ANE] a saturated hydrocarbon of which testosterone and related compounds are derivatives M20. **ˌandrosten(e)ˈdione** *n.* [-ENE + DI-[2] + -ONE] an isomer of testosterone which accompanies the latter in androgenic secretions, in some animals being the predominant male hormone M20.

-androus /ˈandrəs/ *suff.* [f. mod.L *-andrus* f. Gk *-andros*, f. as ANDRO-: see -OUS.] *Bot.* Having male reproductive organs of an indicated kind or number, as *gynandrous, monandrous*, etc.

ane /eɪn/ *a.* & *n. Sc.* & *north.* ME. [Var. of ONE *a.* etc.] = ONE *a.* & *n.* (now only as absol. form of the numeral).

-ane /eɪn/ *suff.* **1** Var. of -an, usu. w. differentiation, as *humane, urbane*, but also alone, as *mundane*. **2** *Chem.* Forming names of paraffins and other saturated hydrocarbons, as *methane, octane*, etc., and of hydrides of other elements, as *silane*, and more or less arbitrarily of other organic compounds, as *lindane*.

anear /əˈnɪə/ *v. arch.* M16. [f. A-[1] + NEAR *v.*] **†1** *v.i.* Draw or be near *to*. M–L16. **2** *v.t.* Approach. L16.

anear /əˈnɪə/ *prep.* & *adv. arch.* M16. [f. A-[1] + NEAR *adv.*[2] & *prep.*[2]] **A** *prep.* Near to, close to. M16. **B** *adv.* **1** Nearly, almost. E17. **2** Near, close by. L18.

aneath /əˈniːθ/ *prep.* & *adv. Sc.* & *north.* M18. [Alt. of *beneath* after *afore* and *before, aside* and *beside.*] = BENEATH.

anecdota *n.pl.* see ANECDOTE.

anecdotage /ˈanɪkdəʊtɪdʒ/ *n.* L18. [Sense I f. next + DOTAGE; sense 2 f. next + -AGE.] **1** Garrulous old age. *joc.* L18. **2** Anecdotes; anecdotic literature. E19.

anecdote /ˈanɪkdəʊt/ *n.* In sense I also (earlier) in L pl. form **anecdota** /əˈnɛkdə(ʊ)tə/. L17. [Fr., or mod.L *anecdota* f. Gk *anekdota* things unpublished, neut. pl. of *anekdotos*, f. as AN-[5] + *ekdotos*, f. *ekdidōnai* publish, give out.] **1** In *pl.* Secret or hitherto unpublished details of history. L17. **2a** A narrative of an amusing or striking incident (orig. an item of gossip). E18. **b** *Art.* (The portrayal of) a small narrative incident; a painting portraying a small narrative incident. M20.

anecˈdotal *a.* of, pertaining to, or consisting of anecdotes M19. **anecˈdotalism** *n.* (*a*) a propensity for telling anecdotes; (*b*) anecdotal quality: E20. **anecˈdotalist** *n.* a person given to or adept in telling anecdotes E20. **anecˈdotic** *a.* (*a*) = ANECDOTAL; (*b*) inclined to tell anecdotes: L18. **anecˈdotical** *a.* = ANECDOTIC M18. **anecˈdotically** *adv.* in an anecdotic manner, with use of anecdotes M19. **anecdotist** /ˈanɪkdəʊtɪst, əˈnɛkdətɪst/ *n.* a teller of anecdotes M19.

anechoic /anɪˈkəʊɪk/ *a.* M20. [f. AN-[5] + ECHO *n.* + -IC.] Free from echo.

anelastic /anɪˈlastɪk/ *a.* M20. [f. AN-[5] + ELASTIC.] *Physics.* Not elastic.

ˌanelasˈticity *n.* M20.

anele /əˈniːl/ *v.t. arch.* ME. [f. AN-[1] + *elien* to oil, f. OE *ele* f. L *oleum* oil.] Anoint; give extreme unction to.

anemia *n.*, **anemic** *a.* see ANAEMIA, ANAEMIC.

anemo- /əˈnɛməʊ, anɪˈmɒ/ *comb. form* of Gk *anemos* wind: see -O-.

aˈnemochore *n.* [Gk *khorein* to spread] a plant whose seeds are dispersed by the wind E20. **aˈnemogram** *n.* a record produced by an anemograph L19. **aˈnemograph** *n.* an instrument for recording the speed, and sometimes also direction, of the wind M19. **anemoˈgraphic** *a.* of or pertaining to an anemograph L19. **aneˈmology** *n.* (*rare*) the science of the winds L18. **aneˈmophilous** *a.* (*Bot.*) wind-pollinated L19. **aneˈmophily** *n.* pollination by the wind L19. **aˈnemoscope** *n.* an instrument for indicating wind direction and strength E18.

anemometer /anɪˈmɒmɪtə/ *n.* E18. [f. ANEMO- + -METER.] **1** An instrument for measuring the speed or force of the wind, or of any gas in motion. E18. **2** An apparatus for indicating wind-pressure in an organ. M19.

anemometry *n.* the measurement of wind speed; the use of anemometers: M19.

anemone /əˈnɛməni/ *n.* M16. [L f. Gk *anemōnē*, f. *anemos* wind.] 1 A plant of the genus *Anemone*, of the buttercup family; *esp.* (also *wood anemone*) *A. nemorosa*, a common woodland plant bearing delicate white flowers in early spring (also called *windflower*). Also, a flower of such a plant. M16. 2 More fully *sea anemone*. An anthozoan belonging to the order Actiniaria, having a radiating array of tentacles around the mouth. M18.

1 *Japanese anemone*: see JAPANESE *a.* PLUMOSE *anemone*. *St Brigid('s) anemone*: see SAINT *n.* & *a.*

Comb.: **anemone fish** any of a number of damselfishes (esp. of the genus *Amphiprion*), which live in commensal association with sea anemones.

anencephalic /ˌanɛnsɪˈfalɪk, -kɛˈfalɪk/ *a.* M19. [f. Gk *anegkephalos* without brain (Galen) (f. AN-[5] + *egkephalos* brain) + -IC.] *Med.* Having all or most of the brain congenitally absent.

anenˈcephalous *a.* = ANENCEPHALIC E19. **anenˈcephaly**, †**-lia** *n.* anencephalic condition M19.

anent /əˈnɛnt/ *prep.* & *adv.* Now chiefly *dial.* [OE *on ef(e)n*, *emn*, f. as ON *prep.* + EVEN *a.* & *n.*, = OS *an eban*, MHG *eneben*, *nebent*, (also mod.) *neben*. Form-hist. not fully explained.] A *prep.* 1 In line with; in company with. OE. 2 In the sight of, before. ME. †3 Against, towards, fronting. ME–M19. 4 In respect of; with reference to; concerning, about. Now *Sc.* & *arch.* ME. B *adv.* Opposite. E16.

-aneous /ˈeɪnɪəs/ *suff.* [f. L *-aneus*: see -EOUS, -OUS.] Forming adjs. from L wds in *-aneus*, as *cutaneous*, *miscellaneous*.

anergy /ˈanədʒi/ *n.* Orig. in L form †**-gia**. L19. [mod.L *anergia* f. Gk, f. AN-[5] + *ergon* work: see -Y[3].] *Med.* 1 Abnormal lack of energy. L19. 2 (The usual sense.) Absence of response to a given antigen or allergen. E20.

aˈnergic *a.* characterized by anergy L19.

†**anerly** *adv.* & *a.* *Sc.* & *north.* ME–L19. [f. ANE; the *-er-* is unexpl., but cf. FORMERLY, ALLENARLY.] Alone, only; solitary.

aneroid /ˈanərɔɪd/ *a.* & *n.* M19. [Fr. *anéroïde*, f. Gk A-[10] + *nēros* wet, damp: see -OID.] (A barometer) that depends on the action of air pressure on the elastic top of a box containing a vacuum.

anesthesia *n.*, **-thetic** *a.*, **-thetize** *v.*, etc., see ANAESTHESIA etc.

anestrus *n.* see ANOESTRUS.

anethole /ˈanɪθəʊl/ *n.* Also (earlier) †**-ol.** M19. [f. L *anethum* anise + -OLE[1].] *Chem.* An aromatic ether which is the major constituent of certain oils, e.g. anise, fennel; *p*-1-propenylphenyl methyl ether, $C_{10}H_{12}O$.

aneuploid /ˈanjʊplɔɪd/ *a.* E20. [f. AN-[5] + EUPLOID.] *Biol.* Not euploid.

aneuploidy *n.* aneuploid condition E20.

aneurin /əˈnjʊərɪn, ˈanjʊrɪn/ *n.* M20. [f. A(NTI- + POLY)NEUR(ITIS + VITAM)IN.] = THIAMINE.

aneurysm /ˈanjʊrɪz(ə)m/ *n.* Also **-ism.** LME. [Gk *aneurusma* dilatation, f. *aneurunein* widen out, f. AN-[4] + *eurunein*, f. *euros* wide.] *Med.* A morbid dilatation of the wall of a blood-vessel, usu. an artery.

dissecting aneurysm: see DISSECT *v.* 1.

aneuˈrysmal *n.* & *a.* †(*a*) *n.* (*rare*) = ANEURYSM; (*b*) *adj.* characterized by or of the nature of an aneurysm: LME.

anew /əˈnjuː/ *adv.* ME. [f. A-[3] + NEW *a.*] 1 Afresh, once more. ME. 2 In a new way. LME. †3 Recently. LME–E16.

anfractuosity /ˌanfraktjʊˈɒsɪti/ *n.* L16. [Fr. *anfractuosité*, f. as next: see -OSITY.] Sinuosity, circuitousness, intricacy, (*lit.* & *fig.*); as count n. in *pl.*, tortuous passages etc., involutions, intricacies.

anfractuous /anˈfraktjʊəs/ *a.* L16. [f. late L *anfractuosus*, f. L *anfractus* a bending: see -OUS. Sense 2 f. Fr. *anfractueux*.] 1 Winding, sinuous; roundabout, circuitous. L16. 2 Rugged, craggy. *rare.* E20.

1 DAY LEWIS A gorge of a street, anfractuous, narrow. 2 T. S. ELIOT Paint me the bold anfractuous rocks Faced by the snarling and yelping seas.

angareb /ˈaŋgəreɪb/ *n.* Also **-reeb**, & other vars. M19. [Yemeni Arab. *ʿangarīb*.] A stretcher or light bedstead used in Aden, Egypt, Sudan, and Ethiopia.

angary /ˈaŋgəri/ *n.* L19. [Fr. *angarie* f. It. or late L *angaria* forced service, f. Gk *aggareia* f. *aggaros* courier f. Pers.] *Law.* In full *right of angary*. A belligerent's right (subject to compensation for loss) to seize or destroy neutral property under military necessity.

angekok /ˈaŋgɪkɒk/ *n.* M18. [Eskimo (Greenlandic) *angakkoq*.] An Eskimo sorcerer or medicine man.

angel /ˈeɪndʒ(ə)l/ *n.* & *v.* [OE *engel*, corresp. to OFris. *angel*, *engel*, OS *engil*, OHG *angil*, *engil* (Du., G *Engel*), ON *engill*, Goth. *aggilus* (perh. immed. f. Gk), one of the earliest Gmc adoptions from L; superseded in ME by forms f. OFr. *angele* f. Chr.L *angelus* f. Gk *aggelos* messenger.] A *n.* 1 *Theol.* A spiritual being more powerful and intelligent than a human being, *esp.* in Jewish, Christian, Muslim, and other theologies, one acting as a messenger, agent, or attendant of God; in Christian theology also *spec.*, a member of the ninth and lowest order of the ninefold celestial hierarchy, ranking directly below the archangels (usu. in *pl.*). OE. 2 *Theol.* Any of the fallen spirits who rebelled against God; a devil. *arch.* exc. more fully *fallen angel*. OE. b In full *Hell's Angel*. A member of a group of motorcyclists in California, orig. notorious for disturbances of civil order; a member of a similar group elsewhere. M20. 3 A guardian or attendant spirit (used both with and without implication of belief in such). Also *fig.*, a person like such a spirit. ME. 4 A person regarded as a messenger of God; a prophet, a preacher; a pastor or minister, esp. (in biblical translations, as at *Rev.* 2:1) in the early Church, and in some modern sects, as the Catholic Apostolic Church. ME. 5 A messenger. *gen. poet.* (now *rare* exc. as *fig.* use of sense 1). LME. 6 A conventional representation of a celestial angel, figured with wings and usu. a long robe. LME. 7 *Hist.* In full *angel-noble*. A gold coin having as its device the archangel Michael piercing the dragon (cf. ANGELOT 1). LME. 8 An angelic person; a lovely or innocent being; an obliging or loving person; a person of exemplary conduct. L16. 9 A financial backer of an (esp. theatrical) enterprise. *slang.* L19. 10 An unexplained radar echo. M20.

1 SHAKES. *Macb.* Angels are bright still, though the brightest fell. POPE Man seems to be placed as the middle Link between Angels and Brutes. BYRON For the Angel of Death spread his wings on the blast. J. C. OATES The Indians had always feared the Spirit of Lake Noir, as an angel of mischief and death. *on the side of the angels*: see SIDE *n.* *recording angel*: see RECORD *v.* 2 AV *Matt.* 25:41 Euerlasting fire, prepared for the deuill and his angels. 3 ROBERT BURTON Every man hath a good and a bad angel attending him in particular all his life long. TENNYSON I to her became Her guardian and her angel. G. B. SHAW I am sure we all owe you the happiness of our lives. You are our good angel. *familiar angel*: see FAMILIAR *a.* 1. *guardian angel*. *ministering angel*: see MINISTER *v.* 5 JONSON The dear good angel of the spring, The nightingale. 6 JOYCE Mr Bloom walked . . by saddened angels, crosses, broken pillars, family vaults. 8 THACKERAY 'Tis strange what a man may do, and a woman yet think him an angel. V. WOOLF Prue, a perfect angel with the others. P. BARRINGTON I'm no angel . . but I'd never let anyone else swing for a crime they didn't commit.

Comb.: **angel cake** a very light and pale sponge cake; **angel dust** *colloq.* the drug phencyclidine; **angelfish** any of various fishes with winglike or elongated fins; *spec.* (*a*) = *monkfish* (a) s.v. MONK *n.*[1]; (*b*) a tropical marine fish of the family Pomacanthidae; (*c*) an aquarium fish of the S. American cichlid genus *Pterophyllum*, usu. silver and black; **angel food** = *angel cake* above; *angel-noble*: see sense 7 above; **angel's eye(s)**, **angels' eyes** *dial.* germander speedwell; **angel-shark** a shark of the family Squatinidae, with winglike pectoral fins; *spec.* = *monkfish* (a) s.v. MONK *n.*[1]; **angels on horseback** simmered oysters individually wrapped in bacon, served on toast; **angel-skin** [tr. Fr. *peau d'ange*] a fabric with a smooth waxy finish; **angel-sleeve** a long loose sleeve.

B *v.t.* Infl. **-ll-**. Back or finance (an enterprise, esp. a theatrical production). E20.

angelhood *n.* M19. **angelize** *v.t.* (*arch.*) = ANGELICIZE L16. **angeˈlolatry** *n.* the worship of angels M19. **angeˈlology** *n.* theological doctrine concerning angels M19. **angeˈlophany** *n.* a visible manifestation of angels M19. **angelship** *n.* (*a*) (with possess. adj., as *your* etc. *angelship*) a mock title of respect for an angel; (*b*) the condition of being an angel: L16.

Angeleno /andʒəˈliːnəʊ/ *n.* Pl. **-os.** L19. [Amer. Sp.] A native or inhabitant of Los Angeles, California.

angelet /ˈeɪndʒ(ə)lɪt/ *n.* LME. [Alt. of (O)Fr. ANGELOT: see -ET[1].] 1 *Hist.* A gold coin, half the value of an angel. LME. 2 A little angel; a cherub. E19.

angelic /anˈdʒɛlɪk/ *a.*[1] LME. [(O)Fr. *angélique* f. late L *angelicus* f. Gk *aggelikos*: see ANGEL, -IC.] 1 Of or pertaining to angels; of the angel kind. LME. 2 Like an angel; of superhuman beauty; of sublime power. LME.

1 *the angelic* SALUTATION. 2 **the Angelic Doctor** St Thomas Aquinas.

angelicize *v.t.* make into or like an angel M19.

angelic /anˈdʒɛlɪk/ *a.*[2] M19. [f. next + -IC.] Chem. *angelic acid*, an unsaturated acid present as esters in the roots of angelica and related plants; 2-methyl-*cis*-but-2-enoic acid, $C_5H_8O_2$.

angelica /anˈdʒɛlɪkə/ *n.*[1] E16. [med.L, short for *herba angelica* angelic plant.] 1 A robust umbelliferous plant of northern and eastern Europe, *Angelica archangelica*, grown esp. for its seeds and stems, which are used as flavouring. Also (more fully *wild angelica*), a related Eurasian plant of streamsides etc., *A. sylvestris*. E16. 2a The root of angelica; an aromatic essence obtained from it. M16. b The candied stalk of angelica, used in cookery. L19.

Comb.: **angelica tree** a prickly tree, *Aralia spinosa*, of the ginseng family, native to the eastern US.

angelica *n.*[2] var. of ANGÉLIQUE.

angelical /anˈdʒɛlɪk(ə)l/ *a.* LME. [f. ANGELIC *a.*[1] + -AL[1].] = ANGELIC *a.*[1]

angelically *adv.* M17. **angelicalness** *n.* (*rare*) M17.

angelin /ˈandʒ(ə)lɪn/ *n.*[1] Also **-im** /-ɪm/. L17. [Port. *angelim*.] (The hard wood of) a leguminous tree, *Andira inermis*, native to tropical America and W. Africa.

angelin *n.*[2] var. of ANGILI.

angélique /andʒɪˈliːk, *foreign* ɑ̃ʒelik (*pl. same*)/ *n.* Also **angelica** /anˈdʒɛlɪkə/. M17. [Fr. & L = ANGELIC *a.*[1]] *Early Mus.* An instrument of the lute family.

angelot /ˈandʒəlɒt/ *n.* E16. [(O)Fr., dim. of OFr. *angele* ANGEL: see -OT[1]. Cf. ANGELET.] 1 *Hist.* A French gold coin having as its device the archangel Michael piercing the dragon. E16. 2 In full *angelot cheese*. A small rich cheese made in Normandy. Long only in Dicts. L16. 3 = ANGÉLIQUE. *rare.* L17.

angelus /ˈandʒ(ə)ləs/ *n.* M17. [L, f. the opening wds *Angelus domini* the angel of the Lord.] 1 A devotional exercise commemorating the Incarnation, said by Roman Catholics at morning, noon, and sunset. M17. 2 = *angelus bell* below. M19.

Comb.: **angelus bell**: rung at the times for the angelus.

angely *n.* var. of ANGILI.

anger /ˈaŋgə/ *n.* ME. [ON *angr* grief, f. the base repr. also by ON *ǫngr*, Goth. *aggwus*, and OE *enge*, OS, OHG *engi* (Du., G *eng*) narrow. Rel. to L *angere* (see ANGUISH *n.*).] 1 Trouble, affliction, vexation, sorrow. Long *obs.* exc. *Sc.* (now *dial.*). ME. 2 Extreme or passionate displeasure, wrath. ME. 3 Physical pain, inflamed condition. Long *dial.* LME.

angerful *a.* (*rare*) †(*a*) careful, anxious, grievous; (*b*) full of anger, wrathful: ME. **angerless** *a.* free from anger M16. **angerly** *adv.* †(*a*) hurtfully, painfully; †(*b*) violently, extremely; (*c*) *arch.* = ANGRILY: LME. **angersome** *a.* (*obs.* exc. *Sc.*) troublesome, irritating M17.

anger /ˈaŋgə/ *v.* ME. [ON *angra* grieve, vex, f. as prec.] †1 *v.t.* Distress, trouble, vex. ME–E16. 2 *v.i.* Become angry. Chiefly *Sc.* Now *rare.* ME. 3 *v.t.* Make angry, enrage. LME. 4 *v.t.* Irritate or inflame (a sore etc.). Long *dial.* LME.

3 POPE It anger'd Turenne . . To see a footman kick'd that took his pay. S. JOHNSON You have both

pleased and angered me. SOUTHEY It angers me when people . . depreciate the Spaniards. A. J. P. TAYLOR Some Englishmen were angered at his supposed desertion of the French.

Angevin /ˈandʒəvɪn/ *n.* & *a.* M17. [Fr. f. med.L *Andegavinus*, f. *Andegavum* Angers, capital of Anjou.] (A native or inhabitant) of Anjou, a former province of France; *Eng. Hist.* (of, pertaining to, or characteristic of) any of the Plantagenet monarchs descended from Geoffrey, Count of Anjou, i.e. Henry II to Richard II.

angili /ˈandʒɪli/ *n.* Also **angelin** /ˈandʒ(ə)lɪn/, **angely**. M17. [f. Tamil *añcali*.] A tree of southern India, *Artocarpus hirsuta*, of the mulberry family; (in full *angili-wood*) the hard timber of this tree.

angina /anˈdʒʌɪnə/ *n.* M16. [L = quinsy f. Gk *agkhonē* strangling, assim. to L *angere* (see ANGUISH *n.*).] *Med.* **1** A condition marked by a suffocating, oppressive pain or discomfort; *esp.* quinsy. Now *rare*. M16. **2** In full *angina pectoris* /ˈpɛktərɪs/ [L = of the chest]. Severe pain in the chest, and often also the arms and neck, due to inadequate blood supply to the heart muscles. M18.

anginal *a.* of, pertaining to, or characterized by angina (usu. angina pectoris) E19. **ˈanginoid** *a.* = ANGINAL L19.

angio- /ˈandʒɪəʊ/ *comb. form.* [Gk *aggeio-*, f. *aggeion* vessel: see -O-.] Used chiefly in terms relating to blood- or seed-vessels.

angioblast *n.* a cell from which blood-vessel tissue evolves L19. **angioˈgenesis** *n.* the development of new blood-vessels L19. **angiogram** *n.* a radiograph made by angiography M20. **angioˈgraphic** *a.* of or pertaining to angiography M20. **angiˈography** *n.* radiography of blood and lymph vessels, carried out after introduction of a radio-opaque substance M20. **angiˈology** *n.* the branch of anatomy that deals with the blood-vessels E18. **angiˈoma** *n.*, pl. **-mas, -mata** /-mətə/, a tumour or swelling produced by a proliferation of blood-vessels L19. **angiˈomatous** *a.* pertaining to or of the nature of an angioma L19. **angioneuˈrotic** *a.* (of oedema) marked by swelling and itching of areas of skin, and usu. allergic in origin L19. **angioplasty** *n.* (an instance of) the surgical repair of a damaged blood-vessel E20.

angiosperm /ˈandʒɪəspəːm/ *n.* E19. [f. ANGIO- + Gk *sperma* seed.] *Bot.* A plant which bears its seeds enclosed in a seed-vessel, i.e. a flowering plant. Cf. GYMNOSPERM.

angioˈspermal *a.* = ANGIOSPERMOUS M19. **angioˈspermous** *a.* pertaining to or being an angiosperm M18.

angiotensin /ˌandʒɪə(ʊ)ˈtɛnsɪn/ *n.* M20. [f. ANGIO- + HYPER)TENS(ION + -IN[1].] *Biochem.* A protein whose presence in the blood promotes aldosterone secretion and tends to raise blood pressure.

angle /ˈaŋg(ə)l/ *n.*[1] *arch.* [OE *angul* = OS, OHG *angul* (G *Angel*), ON *ǫngull*.] A fishing-hook. Also, a rod and line.

I. WALTON I am, Sir, a Brother of the Angle. *fig.*: COVERDALE *Eccles.* 7:26 A woman is bytterer then death: for she is a very angle, hir hert is a nett.

Angle /ˈaŋg(ə)l/ *n.*[2] OE. [L *Anglus*, pl. *-li*, in Tacitus *-lii* f. Gmc, = the people of *Angul* (mod. *Angeln*), a district of Schleswig (now in N. Germany), so called f. its shape, f. as ANGLE *n.*[1] Cf. ENGLISH *n.*] A member of a tribe from Schleswig that invaded and settled in eastern Britain in the 5th cent.

angle /ˈaŋg(ə)l/ *n.*[3] LME. [(O)Fr., or L *angulus* corner.] **1** The indefinite space between two lines or planes that meet. LME. **2** The meeting-point of two lines not in the same direction. LME. **3** *Astrol.* Each of the four mundane houses (the 1st, 4th, 7th, and 10th of the twelve divisions of the heavens) which extend anticlockwise from the cardinal points of the compass. LME. **4** A corner viewed internally as a receding space; a sharp-cornered recess; *arch.* an out-of-the-way place, a nook. LME. **5** A corner viewed externally or as a projection; a sharp projection. M16. **6** The amount of inclination of two lines to each other, or of one line to a horizontal or vertical base-line. L16. **7** The point or direction from which something is viewed or approached (*lit.* & *fig.*); a standpoint; the direction from which a photograph etc. is taken. L19.

4 SHAKES. *Temp.* Whom I left . . In an odd angle of the isle. MILTON To search the tenderest angles of the heart. E. THOMAS I sat among the boughs of the fallen elm That strewed the angle of the fallow. 5 BURKE There is nothing more prejudicial to the grandeur of buildings than to abound in angles. E. K. KANE We trod on the fractured angles of upturned ice. 6 ARNOLD BENNETT The angle of the slatternly bag across his shoulders. B. ENGLAND Thirty feet below the crest, the angle of ascent increased so drastically that they were forced to crawl. J. IRVING He came in at too steep an angle, attempted to correct his position with a weak veer, . . and struck the pond like a stone. 7 R. LEHMANN Her face at this new angle had a look of pathos. R. MACAULAY Curious how we always seem to see Waterloo from the French angle and count it a defeat. A. BURGESS I'm concerned with the linguistic angle Then there's the angle of inter-racial relations.

Phrases: *acute angle*: see ACUTE *a.* 2b. *angle of attack*: see ATTACK *n.* *angle of* FRICTION. *angle of repose*: see REPOSE *n.* *angle of weather*: see WEATHER *n.* 3. *complementary angles*: see COMPLEMENTARY 2. *conjugate angle*: see CONJUGATE *a.* CRITICAL *angle*. *exterior angle*: see EXTERIOR *a.* *facial angle*: see FACIAL *a.* 2. *interior angle*: see INTERIOR *a.* *reverse angle*: see REVERSE *a.* *right angle*: see RIGHT *a.* *solid angle*: see SOLID *a.* SPHERICAL *angle*. *straight angle*: see STRAIGHT *a.*[1] *supplementary angle*: see SUPPLEMENTARY *a.* *trihedral angle*: see TRIHEDRAL *a.* *vergence angle*: see VERGENCE 1. *vertical angle*: see VERTICAL *a.* *visual angle*: see VISUAL *a.*

Comb.: **angle bracket** *Typogr.* etc. a bracket (used alone and in pairs) composed of two lines making an angle, thus < >; **angledozer** a type of bulldozer with an obliquely set blade; **angle-iron** a piece of iron with an L-shaped cross-section used to strengthen a framework; **Anglepoise** (proprietary name for) a type of swivelled reading-lamp with a sprung and jointed arm; **angle-wing** (*N. Amer.*) any of various nymphalid butterflies of the genus *Polygonia*, allied to the comma.

angled *a.* [-ED[2]] having an angle or angles; usu. as 2nd elem. of comb. (of the specified type or number): L16. **anglewise** *adv.* after the manner of an angle, at an angle; angularly: L16.

angle /ˈaŋg(ə)l/ *v.*[1] LME. [f. ANGLE *n.*[1]] **1** *v.i.* Fish with a hook and bait. (Foll. by *for*, †*to*, a fish.) LME. **2** *fig.* **a** *v.i.* Use artful, indirect, or wily means to obtain something. Foll. by *for*. L16. †**b** *v.t.* Seek to obtain artfully etc. L16–L17.

1 I. WALTON The fish which we are to Angle for. C. MERIVALE He would . . listlessly angle in the placid waters. 2a J. BRAINE If you're hungry and someone's preparing a good meal, you'll naturally angle for an invitation. b P. SIDNEY If he spake courteously, he angled the people's hearts.

angle /ˈaŋg(ə)l/ *v.*[2] LME. [f. ANGLE *n.*[3]] **1** *v.t.* Place so as to converge or meet at an angle. *rare*. LME. **2** *v.t.* Drive or direct into an angle or corner; *spec.* in *Billiards, Snooker*, etc., cause (a ball) to come to rest behind the cushion in the jaws of a pocket. L16. **3** *v.i.* Move obliquely; make an angular turn; lie in an oblique direction. M18. **4** *v.t.* Move, turn, hit, or direct at an angle; place obliquely. L19. **5** *v.t.* Present (news etc.) with an inclination towards a particular viewpoint. M20.

3 R. CHANDLER Two davenports angled across the corners of the room and there was one gold chair. 4 A. UPFIELD Bony had walked like a white man, angling his feet at twenty-five minutes to five. I. ASIMOV He angled the chair so that it faced more away from Baley than towards him. 5 M. DICKENS You . . almost never see the proprietor, although you feel his presence, because you have to angle your writing his way. C. MACINNES The leader columns are angled at the more intelligent portions of the population.

angleberry /ˈaŋg(ə)lb(ə)ri, -bɛri/ *n.* *Sc.* & *dial.* L16. [Perh. var. of ANBURY or *ang-berry*.] = ANBURY 1.

angler /ˈaŋglə/ *n.* ME. [f. ANGLE *v.*[1] + -ER[1].] **1** A person who angles (*lit.* & *fig.*). ME. **2** Any of numerous predatory fishes, constituting the order Pediculati (or Lophiiformes), that lure small fish to them by movements of specialized dorsal spines; spec. *Lophius piscatorius*, found in British waters. Usu. more fully *angler-fish*. M17.

anglesite /ˈaŋg(ə)lzʌɪt/ *n.* M19. [f. *Anglesey*, Wales + -ITE[1].] *Min.* Lead sulphate, occurring as white or colourless orthorhombic prisms, or in massive form.

Anglian /ˈaŋglɪən/ *a.* & *n.* E18. [f. L *Angli* (see ANGLE *n.*[2]) + -AN.] **A** *adj.* **1** Of or pertaining to the Angles or the Old English dialects of Northumbria and Mercia; *East Anglian*, of or pertaining to the East Angles or East Anglia, the region now comprising Norfolk and Suffolk, or its dialect. E18. **2** *Geol.* Designating or pertaining to a Pleistocene glaciation in Britain, identified with the Elsterian of northern Europe (and perhaps the Mindel of the Alps). M20. **B** *n.* **1** The Anglian dialect of Old English; *East Anglian*, a native or inhabitant, or the dialect, of East Anglia. L19. **2** *Geol.* The Anglian glaciation or its deposits. M20.

Anglic /ˈaŋglɪk/ *n.* M20. [f. ANGL(O- + -IC.] A simplified form of English spelling devised by the Swedish philologist R. E. Zachrisson (1880–1937) and intended for use as an international auxiliary language.

Anglic /ˈaŋglɪk/ *a.* M19. [f. med.L *Anglicus* f. L *Angli*: see ANGLE *n.*[2], -IC.] = ANGLIAN *a.* 1.

Anglican /ˈaŋglɪk(ə)n/ *a.* & *n.* E17. [med.L *Anglicanus* (*Anglicana ecclesia* in Magna Carta), f. as prec.: see -AN.] **A** *adj.* **1** Of or pertaining to the reformed Church of England or any Church in communion with it. E17. **2** *gen.* English. *rare*. M19. **B** *n.* An adherent of the reformed Church of England. L18.

Anglicanism *n.* (adherence to) Anglican doctrine and practice M19. **Anglicanize** *v.t.* (*a*) *rare* make English; (*b*) make Anglican in doctrine, character, etc.: E19.

anglice /ˈaŋglɪsi/ *adv.* Also **A-**. E17. [med.L, f. L *Anglus*: see ANGLE *n.*[2], -ICE[2].] In (plain) English.

Anglicise *v.* var. of ANGLICIZE.

Anglicism /ˈaŋglɪsɪz(ə)m/ *n.* M17. [f. med.L *Anglicus* (see ANGLIC *a.*) + -ISM.] **1** Anglicized language; an English idiom. M17. **2** Englishness; imitation of or support for what is English. L18.

Anglicist *n.* (*a*) an advocate or favourer of Anglicism; (*b*) = ANGLIST: M19.

Anglicize /ˈaŋglɪsʌɪz/ *v.t.* Also **-ise, a-**. E18. [f. as prec. + -IZE.] Make English in form or character. Also, in *pass.*, be formed by Anglicization (*from*).

Angliciˈzation *n.* L19.

Anglify /ˈaŋglɪfʌɪ/ *v.t.* Now *rare*. M18. [f. L *Angli* (see ANGLE *n.*[2]) + -FY.] = prec.

Anglist /ˈaŋglɪst/ *n.* L19. [G f. L *Anglus*: see ANGLE *n.*[2], -IST.] A student of or scholar in English language or literature, esp. on the mainland of Europe.

Anˈglistics *n.pl.* M20.

Anglo /ˈaŋgləʊ/ *n.* & *a.* E19. [Independent use of next.] **A** *n.* Pl. **-os**. A person of English or British or N. European origin or descent; a non-Hispanic white American in the south-western US; an English-speaking Canadian. E19. **B** *adj.* Of English or British origin or character; of or pertaining to Anglos. M19.

Anglo- /ˈaŋgləʊ/ *comb. form.* [f. L *Anglus* (see ANGLE *n.*[3]) + -O-.] English, of English origin; English or British and —, England or Britain in connection with —.

Anglo-ˈFrisian *a.* & *n.* (of or pertaining to) the hypothetical parent language of Old English and Old Frisian L19. **Anglo-ˈGallic** *a.* pertaining, relating, or common to both England and France M18. **Anglo-ˈGallicism** *n.* a French word or phrase adopted into English E19. **Anglo-ˈLatin** *a.* & *n.* (of or pertaining to) Anglicized Latin or medieval Latin as used in England L18. **Anglo-ˈRoman** *a.* (*a*) English Roman Catholic; (*b*) of or pertaining to England and Rome: M19. **Anglo-verˈnacular** *a.* (*Anglo-Ind.*) pertaining to or consisting of English and an Indian language L19.

Anglo-American /aŋgləʊəˈmɛrɪk(ə)n/ *n.* & *a.* L18. [f. ANGLO- + AMERICAN.] **A** *n.* An American of English or British origin. L18. **B** *adj.* **1** Of or pertaining to Americans of English or British origin. L18. **2** Of or belonging to both England (or Britain) and America. E19.

Anglo-Catholic /aŋgləʊˈkaθ(ə)lɪk/ *a.* & *n.* M19. [f. ANGLO- + CATHOLIC.] (A member) of a party holding that the Church of England is a branch of the Catholic Church and rejecting its Protestant elements.

Anglo-Caˈtholicism *n.* M19.

Anglocentric /aŋgləʊ'sɛntrɪk/ *a.* L19. [f. ANGLO- + -CENTRIC.] Centred on England or Britain.

Anglo-French /aŋgləʊ'frɛn(t)ʃ/ *n.* & *a.* E19. [f. ANGLO- + FRENCH *a.* & *n.*] A *n.* 1 Anglicized French. E19. 2 = ANGLO-NORMAN *n.* 2. E20. B *adj.* Of or belonging to both England (or Britain) and France. M19.

Anglo-Indian /aŋgləʊ'ɪndɪən/ *n.* & *a.* E19. [f. ANGLO- + INDIAN.] A *n.* 1 A person of mixed British and Indian descent resident in the Indian subcontinent. E19. 2 A person of British birth resident, or once long resident, in the Indian subcontinent. M19. B *adj.* Of, pertaining to, or being an Anglo-Indian or Anglo-Indians; of, pertaining to, or characteristic of India under British rule; (of a word) adopted into English from an Indian language. M19.

Anglo-Irish /aŋgləʊ'ʌɪrɪʃ/ *n.* & *a.* L18. [f. ANGLO- + IRISH.] A *n.* 1 *collect.* Persons of English descent born or resident in Ireland or of mixed English and Irish parentage. L18. 2 The English language as used in Ireland. E20.

B *adj.* 1 Of or pertaining to the Anglo-Irish; of mixed English and Irish parentage. M19. 2 Of or belonging to both Britain and the Republic of Ireland. E20.

2 *Economist* Off to Dublin to discuss such an Anglo-Irish deal.

Anglomania /aŋgləʊ'meɪnɪə/ *n.* M18. [f. ANGLO- + -MANIA, after Fr. *anglomanie.*] Excessive admiration for what is English.

Anglomaniac *n.* & *a.* M19.

Anglo-Norman /aŋgləʊ'nɔːmən/ *n.* & *a.* M18. [f. ANGLO- + NORMAN *n.*[1] & *a.*] A *n.* 1 A native or inhabitant of England after the Norman Conquest who was of Norman descent. M18. 2 The variety of Norman French used in England after the Norman Conquest. M19. B *adj.* Of or pertaining to the Anglo-Normans or Anglo-Norman. M18.

Anglo-Nor'manic *a.* & *n.* (now *rare*) E18.

Anglophile /'aŋglə(ʊ)fʌɪl/ *a.* & *n.* Also **-phil** /-fɪl/. M19. [Fr., f. as ANGLO- + -PHILE.] (A person who is) friendly to England (or Britain) or to what is English (or British).

Anglo'philia *n.* friendliness to England (or Britain) L19.

Anglophobia /aŋglə(ʊ)'fəʊbɪə/ *n.* L18. [f. ANGLO- + -PHOBIA.] Intense fear or hatred of England (or Britain) or of what is English (or British).

'Anglophobe *n.* & *a.* (a person who is) afraid of or hostile to England (or Britain) or what is English (or British) M19. **Anglophobic** *a.* M19.

anglophone /'aŋglə(ʊ)fəʊn/ *n.* & *a.* Also **A-**. E20. [f. ANGLO- + Gk *phōnē* voice.] (A person who is) English-speaking.

Anglo-Saxon /aŋgləʊ'saks(ə)n/ *n.* & *a.* E17. [mod.L *Anglo-Saxones* pl. for med.L *Angli Saxones*, after OE *Angulseaxe, -seaxan.*] A *n.* I Applied to people. 1 An English Saxon (as distinct from one of the Old Saxons of Continental Europe); a (Germanic) native or inhabitant of England before the Norman Conquest. E17. 2 A person of English (or British) descent wherever found. M19. II Applied to language. 3 The language of England before the Norman Conquest; Old English. L18. 4 The English language (of any period); *colloq.* plain, esp. crude, forthright English. *N. Amer.* M19. B *adj.* Of or pertaining to the Anglo-Saxons or their language (Old English); *spec.* designating, of, or pertaining to the period between the 5th-cent. conquest of Britain by the Saxons, Jutes, and Angles, and the Norman Conquest. E18.

Anglo-Saxondom *n.* the collective body of people of English or British descent M19. †**Anglo-Saxonic** *a.* & *n.* (of) the Anglo-Saxon language L17–L18. **Anglo-Saxonism** *n.* (*a*) the feeling of identity of Anglo-Saxondom; (*b*) a word, idiom, etc., deriving from Anglo-Saxon: M19.

angola *n.* & *a.* see ANGORA.

Angolan /aŋ'gəʊlən/ *n.* & *a.* E17. [f. *Angola* (see below) + -AN.] (A native or inhabitant) of Angola, a country on the south-west coast of Africa.

angon /'aŋgɒn/ *n.* L19. [med.L f. Gk *aggōn.*] *Archaeol.* A type of iron spear with a double barb.

†**angor** *n.* LME–M18. [OFr. f. L = a squeeze, a strangling: see -OR.] (A feeling of) anguish or constricting pain.

angora /aŋ'gɔːrə/ *n.* & *a.* Also **-gola** /-'gəʊlə/, **A-**. E19. [*Angora*, mod. Ankara, in Turkey; *angola* is a corruption.] I 1 In full *angora cat.* A long-haired variety of cat. E19. 2 In full *angora goat.* A long-haired variety of goat. E19. 3 In full *angora rabbit.* A variety of rabbit with long white hair. M19. II *transf.* 4 Fabric made from the hair of the angora goat; mohair. Also designating a garment etc. made from this. M19. 5 Fabric made from a mixture of sheep's wool and angora rabbit hair. Also designating a garment etc. made from this. M20.

angostura /aŋgə'stjʊərə/ *n.* Also **-gust-**, **A-**. L18. [*Angostura*, now Ciudad Bolívar, a town in Venezuela.] 1 *angostura bark*, an aromatic bark formerly used as a febrifuge and tonic. L18. 2 (**A-**.) (In full *Angostura Bitters.* (Proprietary name for) a type of aromatic bitters orig. made in Angostura. L19.

angry /'aŋgri/ *a.* & *v.* LME. [f. ANGER *n.* + -Y[1].] A *adj.* †1 Troublesome, vexatious. LME–M17. †2 Troubled, vexed. LME–L15. 3 Feeling anger or resentment, enraged, extremely displeased. (Foll. by usu. *at, about* a thing; *at, with* a person; *that.*) LME. 4 Of a mood or action: moved or excited by anger. LME. 5 Revealing or expressing anger; *fig.* seeming to express anger. LME. b Having the colour of an angry face, red. *rare.* M17. 6 Hot-tempered, irritable. *arch.* LME. 7 Of a wound, sore, etc.: inflamed, smarting. L15.

3 JONSON Where it concerns himself, Who's angry at a slander makes it true. H. E. BATES I had never been angry with her before—annoyed sometimes, . . but never more. D. STOREY I was angry with him, angry that he should allow me to talk to him like this. C. HAMPTON I was still very angry about your not letting me stay. **angry young man** a young man dissatisfied with and outspoken against existing social and political structures, *spec.* any of several British playwrights and novelists of the 1950s expressing such dissatisfaction. 4 TENNYSON A man's own angry pride Is cap and bells for a fool. 5 DRYDEN He sheathes his paws, uncurls his angry mane. J. TYNDALL Angry masses of cloud. D. DU MAURIER The angry colour flooded her dead white face. W. FAULKNER His face was not grim and neither cold nor angry. B. MALAMUD He heaved a last angry shovelful into the gutter. b C. LAMB His waistcoat red and angry. 6 N. ROWE Honour, This busie, angry thing, that scatters Discord.

B *v.t.* Make angry. *rare.* LME.

angrily *adv.* LME. **angriness** *n.* (*rare*) LME.

angst /aŋst/ *n.* E20. [G.] Anxiety, neurotic fear; guilt, remorse.

angstrom /'aŋstrəm/ *n.* Also **ångström**, **A-**, **Å-**. L19. [A. J. *Ångström* (1814–74), Swed. physicist.] A unit of length equal to one hundred-millionth of a centimetre; 10^{-10} m. Also *angstrom unit.*

Anguillan /an'gwɪlən/ *n.* & *a.* M20. [f. *Anguilla* (see below) + -AN.] (A native or inhabitant) of the island of Anguilla in the W. Indies.

anguilliform /əŋ'gwɪlɪfɔːm/ *a.* L17. [f. L *anguilla* eel + -I- + -FORM.] Eel-shaped; eel-like.

anguine /'aŋgwɪn/ *a.* M17. [L *anguinus*, f. *anguis* snake: see -INE[1].] Of a snake or serpent; snakelike.

an'guineous *a.* (*rare*) M17.

anguish /'aŋgwɪʃ/ *n.* ME. [OFr. *anguis* (mod. *angoisse*) f. L *angustia*, in pl. straits, distress, f. *angustus* narrow, tight, ult. f. as *angere* squeeze, strangle: see -ISH[2]. Cf. ANGER *n.*, ANGINA, ANGOR.] Severe bodily or mental pain, intense suffering.

A. J. CRONIN The beauty of the scene appeased the anguish of his heart. R. LEHMANN When I went to see her after Rickie's death she was in anguish. I. MURDOCH My head was heavy with pain and any movement brought twinges of anguish.

†**anguishous** *a.* (long *dial.*) (*a*) causing anguish; (*b*) oppressed with anguish; (*c*) anxious: ME–L19.

anguish /'aŋgwɪʃ/ *v.* ME. [OFr. *anguissier* (mod. *angoisser*) f. eccl.L *angustiare* to distress, f. L *angustia*: see prec., -ISH[2].] 1 *v.t.* Distress with severe bodily or mental pain. Now chiefly as ANGUISHED. ME. 2 *v.i.* Suffer severe bodily or mental pain. Now *rare.* ME.

anguished *ppl a.* suffering or expressing anguish E17. **anguishment** *n.* (*rare*) severe distress; an affliction: L16.

angular /'aŋgjʊlə/ *a.* LME. [L *angularis*, f. *angulus* ANGLE *n.*[3]: see -AR[1]. Cf. Fr. *angulaire.*] 1 *Astrol.* Of or pertaining to each of the four houses at the cardinal points. *rare.* LME. 2 Constituting an angle, sharp corner, or apex; placed in or at an angle; measured by angle. L15. 3 Having an angle or angles; sharp-cornered. L16. 4 Having the joints and bony protuberances prominent; jerky, awkward; lacking suavity, unaccommodating. M19.

2 **angular momentum** the quantity of rotation of a body, equal to the product of its moment of inertia and angular velocity. **angular velocity** rate of change of angular position. 4 J. S. BLACKIE Their movements were slow, their gesticulations abrupt and angular. DICKENS As a particularly angular man, I do not fit smoothly into the social circle. V. WOOLF All well grown, angular, ruthless youngsters.

angu'larity *n.* (*a*) the quality or state of being angular; (*b*) in *pl.*, angular outlines, sharp corners: M17. **angularly** *adv.* in an angular manner; obliquely, diagonally: L15.

angulated /'aŋgjʊleɪtɪd/ *a.* L15. [f. L *angulatus* pa. pple of *angulare*, f. *angulus* ANGLE *n.*[2] + -ED[1].] Chiefly *Bot.* & *Zool.* Formed with angles or corners.

Also **angulate** *a.* M18.

angulation /aŋgʊ'leɪʃ(ə)n/ *n.* L17. [f. as prec.: see -ATION.] †1 An oblique or diagonal movement. Only in L17. 2 Angular or cornered formation or position. M19.

angulous /'aŋgjʊləs/ *a.* Long *obs.* exc. in Dicts. LME. [f. L *angulosus* or Fr. *anguleux*: see ANGLE *n.*[3], -ULOUS.] Having angles or corners; angular.

Angus /'aŋgəs/ *n.* M19. [A district in the Grampian Region of Scotland.] = *Aberdeen Angus* s.v. ABERDEEN I.

angustura *n.* var. of ANGOSTURA.

angwantibo /əŋ'gwɒntɪbəʊ/ *n.* Pl. **-os**. M19. [Efik.] A small rare primate, *Arctocebus calabarensis*, related to the potto and loris, and native to western central Africa. Also called *golden potto.*

anharmonic /anhɑː'mɒnɪk/ *a.* E19. [f. AN-[5] + HARMONIC *a.*] Chiefly *Physics.* Not harmonic.

ˌanharmo'nicity *n.* deviation from harmonic behaviour E20.

anhedonia /anhɪ'dəʊnɪə/ *n.* L19. [Fr. *anhédonie*, f. Gk AN-[5] + *hēdonē* pleasure: see -IA[1].] *Psychiatry.* Inability to feel pleasure.

anhedral /an'hiːdr(ə)l, -'hɛd-/ *a.* & *n.* L19. [f. AN-[5] + -HEDRAL.] A *adj.* 1 *Min.* Of a crystal: not having plane faces. L19. 2 *Aeronaut.* Negatively dihedral. M20. B *n. Aeronaut.* A downward inclination of a wing, tailplane, etc.; negative dihedral. M20.

anhedron *n.* an anhedral crystal L19.

anhelation /anhɪ'leɪʃ(ə)n/ *n.* Now *rare.* E17. [Fr. *anhélation* or L *anhelatio(n-)*, f. *anhelat-* pa. ppl stem of *anhelare* pant: see -ATION.] Shortness of breath, a difficulty with breathing; *fig.* panting, aspiration (*after* an object of desire).

anhidrosis /anhɪ'drəʊsɪs/ *n.* Also **ani-** /anɪ-/. L19. [Gk *anidrōsis*, f. AN-[5] + *hidrōs* sweat: see -OSIS.] *Med.* Abnormal absence of sweating.

anhidrotic *a.* & *n.* characterized by anhidrosis; (a drug) tending to reduce sweating: L19.

anhinga /an'hɪŋgə/ *n.* M18. [Port. f. Tupi *áyinga.*] A long-necked fish-eating bird of the genus *Anhinga*; *esp.* the snake bird, *A. anhinga*. Cf. DARTER 4.

an-hua /an'hwɑː/ *n.* & *a.* E20. [Chin. *ànhuā*, f. *àn* obscure + *huā* flower.] (Of) a type of decoration of Chinese porcelain or fabrics that is visible only by transmitted light.

anhungered /ən'hʌŋgəd/ *a. arch.* ME. [Alt. of AHUNGERED by prefix-substitution.] Famished, hungry; *fig.* longing (*for*).

anhydride /an'hʌɪdrʌɪd/ *n.* M19. [f. as ANHYDROUS + -IDE.] *Chem.* A compound derived from an acid (usu. specified) by the removal of one or more molecules of water; *spec.* (*Org. Chem.*) a compound containing the group ·COO·CO·.

anhydrite /an'hʌɪdrʌɪt/ *n.* E19. [f. as prec. + -ITE[1].] *Min.* Anhydrous calcium sulphate, an orthorhombic mineral which is an important constituent of many evaporites and other sedimentary deposits.

anhydro- /an'hʌɪdrəʊ/ *comb. form* of next, esp. in names of minerals: see -O-.

anhydrous /an'hʌɪdrəs/ *a.* E19. [f. Gk *anudros* waterless, f. AN-[5] + *hudr-*, *hudōr* water: see -OUS.] Chiefly *Chem.* Lacking water, esp. water of crystallization.
Also **anhydric** *a.* (*rare*) L19.

anhypostasia /ˌanhʌɪpə'steɪzɪə/ *n.* L19. [mod.L f. Gk *anhupostasia* unsubstantiality, f. AN-[5] + as HYPOSTASIS: see -IA[1].] *Theol.* Absence of a substantial or personal existence in the human nature of Christ.
anhypostasis /-'pɒstəsɪs/ *n.* = ANHYPOSTASIA M19. **anhypo'static** *a.* having no independent or personal existence M20. **anhypo'statical** *a.* = ANHYPOSTATIC M19.

ani /'ɑːni/ *n.* E19. [Sp. *aní* & Port. *anum*, f. Tupi *anũ*.] Any of several glossy black large-billed birds of the genus *Crotophaga*, of the cuckoo family, found in Central and S. America.

aniconic /anʌɪ'kɒnɪk/ *a.* L19. [f. AN-[5] + ICONIC.] Of an idol, symbol, etc.: not in human or animal form. Of worship: not involving such idols etc.

anicut /'anɪkʌt/ *n.* Also **ann-**. L18. [Tamil *aṇai-kkaṭṭu* dam-building.] A river-dam in southern India built for irrigation purposes.

anidrosis *n.* var. of ANHIDROSIS.

anigh /ə'nʌɪ/ *adv.* & *prep. arch.* ME. [f. A-[1] + NIGH *adv.*: cf. AFAR, ANEAR *prep.* & *adv.*] A *adv.* Near. ME. B *prep.* Near to. L18.
¶ Obs. or rare after LME; re-formed L18.

anil /'anɪl/ *n.* L16. [Fr. or Port., f. Arab. *an-nīl*, f. as AL-[2] + Arab. & Pers. *nīl* f. Skt *nīlī* indigo, f. *nīla* dark blue. Cf. NIL *n.*[1]] 1 The dye indigo. L16. †2 The indigo shrub. E18–M18. 3 *Chem.* Any imine derived from aniline. Orig. more fully *anil-compound.* L19.

anile /'eɪnʌɪl/ *a.* M17. [L *anilis*, f. *anus* old woman: see -ILE.] Of or like an old woman; imbecile.

anilic /ə'nɪlɪk/ *a.* M19. [f. ANIL + -IC.] Chem. *anilic acid*, nitrosalicylic acid, indigotic acid.

aniline /'anɪliːn, -lɪn/ *n.* M19. [f. ANIL + -INE[5]: it was orig. prepared by distilling indigo with alkali.] *Chem.* A colourless basic oily liquid, $C_6H_5NH_2$, that is present in coal tar and was the basis of the earliest synthetic dyes.
attrib. (usu. w. ref. to or in names of dyes): *aniline black, colour, dye*, etc.
anilide *n.* any substituted amide having a phenyl group bonded to the nitrogen atom M19.

anility /ə'nɪlɪti/ *n.* E17. [L *anilitas*, f. as ANILE: see -ITY.] Old-womanishness; dotage; (an instance of) foolishness.

anima /'anɪmə/ *n.* E20. [L = (i) air, breath, life; (ii) mind, soul.] *Psychoanalysis.* The inner self (opp. *persona*). Also, the source of the feminine component of a personality. Cf. ANIMUS.
¶ See also ANIMA MUNDI.

animadversion /ˌanɪməd'vəːʃ(ə)n/ *n.* M16. [Fr., or L *animadversio(n-)*, f. *animadvers-* pa. ppl stem of *animadvertere*: see next, -ION.] †1 Judicial punishment; a penal visitation. M16–M19. 2 Censure, reproof, blame. L16. 3 A criticism; a (usu. censorious) comment. L16. †4 The action or faculty of observation. E17–L18. †5 A notice, a warning. M17–E18.
1 A. ALISON A power whose lightest measure of animadversion would be banishment. 2 S. JOHNSON No weakness of the human mind has more frequently incurred animadversion. 3 W. STYRON His complaints grew louder and his animadversions more serious and cutting. 4 M. HALE The due animadversion and inspection of their own Minds. J. GLANVILL In an infinite Life as God is, there can be no distraction, his animadversion necessarily being infinite. 5 CLARENDON They all knew Caesar's fate, by contemning, or neglecting such animadversions.

animadvert /ˌanɪməd'vəːt/ *v.* LME. [L *animadvertere*, f. *animum* the mind + *advertere* ADVERT *v.*] †1 *v.t.* Pay attention to, observe. LME–L17. 2 *v.i.* Pay attention *to*; observe, remark, consider, (*that*). M16. 3 *v.i.* Pass criticism or censure *on* (occas. *against*). M17. 4 *v.i.* Pass judgement, take punitive action, (*against*, (*up*)*on*). *arch.* L17.
1 I. NEWTON The light . . shall in comparison not be strong enough to be animadverted. 2 H. FIELDING Animadvert that you are in the house of a great lady. 3 POPE Your grace very justly animadverts against the too great disposition of finding faults. H. JAMES He . . inclined a critical head to either quarter, and . . animadverted to his companion on this passage and that. 4 JAS. MILL It is for the tribunal before which he offends to animadvert upon his conduct.
animadverter *n.* M17.

animal /'anɪm(ə)l/ *n.* & *a.* ME. [As adj. f. (O)Fr., or L *animalis* having vital breath, (in med.L) bestial, f. ANIMA: see -AL[1]; partly attrib. use of the n. As n. ult. f. L *animal* for *animale* use as n. of neut. adj.] A *n.* A living organism having sensation and voluntary motion, without rigid cell walls, and dependent on organic substances for food; *spec.* (*a*) an animal other than a human being; (*b*) *colloq.* a land animal as opp. to a fish or a bird; (*c*) *colloq.* a four-legged animal as opp., e.g., to an insect or a worm. Also, a brutish person, a person regarded as without human attributes. ME.
no such animal *colloq.* no such person or thing. **the animal** the animal nature in humans.
B *adj.* †1 Connected with sensation, innervation, or will. LME–L18. 2 Of, pertaining to, or characteristic of animals; not intellectual, moral, or spiritual. LME. 3 *Embryol.* Designating or pertaining to that pole of the ovum or embryo that contains the more rapidly dividing cells in the early stages of development. Opp. *vegetal*, *vegetative*. M19.
Special collocations: **animal black**, **animal charcoal** charcoal obtained from calcined bones. **animal electricity**: that generated within animals, e.g. as nerve impulses. †**animal flower** a sea anemone. *animal husbandry*: see HUSBANDRY *n.* 2. **animal kingdom** animals collectively, as one of the three (or more) major divisions of the natural world. **animal liberation** the freeing of animals from exploitation by humans. **animal magnetism** *Hist.* mesmerism. *animal oil*: see OIL *n.* **animal rights** the natural rights of animals to live a free life. **animal spirits** †(*a*) the supposed principle of sensation and voluntary motion; †(*b*) nerve, physical courage; (*c*) natural exuberance.
ani'malic *a.* (*rare*) L17. **animally** *adv.* E17.

animalcule /anɪ'malkjuːl/ *n.* Also in L form †**-culum**, pl. **-la**. L16. [mod.L *animalculum*, dim. of *animal*: see prec., -CULE.] †1 A small or tiny animal, as a mouse or an invertebrate. L16–M19. 2 A microscopic animal. L17.
animalcular *a.* of or pertaining to animalcules M18.

animalise *v.* var. of ANIMALIZE.

animalism /'anɪm(ə)lɪz(ə)m/ *n.* M19. [f. as prec. + -ISM.] 1 Animal activity, physical exercise and enjoyment; sensuality. M19. 2 The doctrine that humans are merely animals. M19. 3 A merely sensual being. *rare.* M19.
animalist *n.* (*a*) a person who practises or adheres to animalism; (*b*) a person who depicts animals; (*c*) a supporter of animal liberation or animal rights: M19. **anima'listic** *a.* L19.

animality /anɪ'malɪti/ *n.* E17. [Fr. *animalité*: see ANIMAL, -ITY.] 1 The sum of animal qualities and functions; animal nature; merely animal nature, sensuality. E17. 2 The animal kingdom. L18.

animalize /'anɪm(ə)lʌɪz/ *v.t.* Also **-ise**. E17. [f. ANIMAL + -IZE; partly through Fr. *animaliser*.] †1 Inspire, actuate. *rare.* Only in E17. 2 Represent in animal form. M18. 3 Convert to animal substance. L18. 4 Sensualize. E19.
animali'zation *n.* M18.

anima mundi /ˌanɪmə 'mʌndʌɪ, 'mʊndiː/ *n. phr.* L16. [med.L (Abelard) = soul of the world; app. formed to render Gk *psukhē tou kosmou*.] A power supposed to organize the whole universe and to coordinate its parts.

†**animastic** *a.* M17–M19. [med.L *animasticus* pertaining to the soul, f. L ANIMA: cf. ONOMASTIC.] Spiritual (as opp. to *material*). Also, animate.

animate /'anɪmət/ *a.* LME. [L *animatus* pa. pple, f. as next: see -ATE[2].] 1 Endowed with life, living. LME. 2 Lively; full of activity. E19. 3 *Gram.* Pertaining to or denoting living beings. E19.
1 CARLYLE That men should have worshipped . . stocks and stones, and all manner of animate and inanimate objects. F. B. YOUNG A shoal of flying-fish Spurts out like animate spray. 2 SOUTHEY A courser More animate of eye, Of form more faultless never had he seen. B. ENGLAND The entire area was animate with dozens of villagers running about in a state of great excitation. 3 J. LYONS Most transitive verbs tend to occur with an animate noun as their subject in active sentences.
animatism *n.* the ascription of psychic qualities to inanimate as well as animate objects E20.

animate /'anɪmeɪt/ *v.t.* L15. [L *animat-* pa. ppl stem of *animare* give life to, f. ANIMA: see -ATE[3].] 1 Breathe life into, quicken, vivify, enliven. L15. b Give (a film, cartoon figure, etc.) the appearance of showing movement, by using a quick succession of gradually varying images. L19. 2 Fill with boldness, courage, or spirit; excite (a person) to action; inspire, actuate. M16. b Put in motion (a thing). *arch.* exc. as *fig.* use of sense 2. M17.
1 R. W. EMERSON The soul in man is not an organ, but animates and exercises all the organs. O. HENRY Then his eyes get animated, and I see he's got some great scheme in his mind. K. CLARK About ten years later this stiff antiquarian style is animated by a turbine of creative energy. 2 DRYDEN The shouting animates their hearts. SIR W. SCOTT Desperate men, animated by the presence of two or three of the actors in the primate's murder. E. H. GOMBRICH The spirit of creative research that animated the young painters of the nineteenth century. b J. TYNDALL Motion . . which animates the bullet projected from the gun.
animated *a.* alive; lively, vivacious: M16. **animatedly** *adv.* L18. **animater** *n.* (*rare*) M17. **animator** *n.* a person who or thing which animates something; *Cinemat.* an artist who prepares animated cartoons: M16.

animation /anɪ'meɪʃ(ə)n/ *n.* M16. [L *animatio(n-)*, f. as prec.: see -ATION.] †1 Encouragement, inspiration. M16–L17. †2 a The action of imparting life, vitality, or motion. L16–E18. b Preparation or production of animated films, visual images, etc. L19. 3 The state of being alive, animateness. *arch.* E17. 4 Vivacity, ardour. L18. 5 Enlivenment; enlivening operation or influence. E19.
1 HENRY MORE An intimation and animation to us to follow his example. 3 M. SHELLEY Capable of bestowing animation on lifeless matter. *suspended animation*: see SUSPENDED *ppl a.* 4 A. FRASER Her attraction lay in her animation and in particular her sparkling black eyes. 5 SIR W. SCOTT The animation of the chase and the glow of the exercise.

animé /'anɪmeɪ/ *n.* L16. [Fr., f. Tupi *wana'ni*.] Any of various resins; *spec.* that from the W. Indian tree *Hymenaea courbaril*, used in making varnish. Also *gum animé*.

animism /'anɪmɪz(ə)m/ *n.* M19. [f. L ANIMA + -ISM.] 1 The doctrine of the *anima mundi*. M19. 2 The attribution of a living soul to plants, inanimate objects, and natural phenomena. M19.
animist *n.* E19. **ani'mistic** *a.* M19.

animosity /anɪ'mɒsɪti/ *n.* LME. [(O)Fr. *animosité* or late L *animositas*, f. *animosus* spirited, f. as next: see -OSITY.] 1 Spiritedness, courage. Long *rare. dial.* LME. 2 A spirit of enmity (*against, between, towards*). E17.

animus /'anɪməs/ *n.* E19. [L = spirit, mind.] 1 Actuating feeling, animating spirit, usu. hostile; animosity shown in speech or action. E19. 2 *Psychoanalysis.* The source of the masculine component of a personality. Cf. ANIMA. E20.

anion /'anʌɪən/ *n.* M19. [f. AN(ODE or ANA- + ION.] A negatively-charged ion, i.e. one which would be attracted to an anode. Opp. CATION.
ani'onic *a.* of or pertaining to anions; of the nature of an anion: E20.

aniridia /anɪ'rɪdɪə, anʌɪ-/ *n.* M19. [f. Gk AN-[5] + *irid-*, *iris* IRIS + -IA[1].] *Med.* Congenital or traumatic absence of the iris.

anis /ani(s)/ *n.* L19. [Fr.: see ANISE.] A liqueur or aperitif flavoured with aniseed; occas., aniseed.

anis- /'anɪs/ *comb. form* of L *anisum* ANISE, used in *Chem.*

ani'saldehyde *n. p*-methoxybenzaldehyde, a fragrant liquid, $CH_3O{\cdot}C_6H_4{\cdot}CHO$, used in perfumery M19. **anisic** /ə'nɪzɪk/ *a.*: *anisic acid*, *p*-methoxybenzoic acid, $CH_3O{\cdot}C_6H_4{\cdot}COOH$, a crystalline acid obtained by oxidizing anethole M19. **anisole** *n.* methoxybenzene, $C_6H_5OCH_3$, a colourless liquid ether M19. **anisyl** *n.* the *p*-methoxybenzyl radical, $CH_3O{\cdot}C_6H_4{\cdot}CH_2{\cdot}$ M19.

anise /'anɪs/ *n.* ME. [(O)Fr. *anis* f. L *anisum*, f. Gk *anison* dill, anise.] 1 (The aromatic seed of) an umbelliferous plant, *Pimpinella anisum*, native to the eastern Mediterranean region. Anciently confused with dill, which was prob. the 'anise' of the Bible. ME. 2 Any of several trees and shrubs of the Asian and American genus *Illicium*, which bear fruit with the odour of aniseed; *esp.* (*a*) (more fully *Japanese* or *Chinese anise*) = SHIKIMI; (*b*) = *star-anise* s.v. STAR *n.*[1] & *a.* Also, the fruit of these plants. E18.

anisated *a.* mixed or flavoured with aniseed L17.

aniseed /'anɪsiːd/ *n.* LME. [f. prec. + SEED *n.*] The seed of anise, used to flavour liqueurs and sweets.

Comb.: **aniseed tree** a tree or shrub of the genus *Illicium* (see ANISE 2).

aniseikonia /anʌɪsʌɪ'kəʊnɪə/ *n.* M20. [f. ANIS(O- + Gk *eikon-*, *eikōn* image + -IA[1].] *Med.* A defect of vision in which the image seen with one eye is larger than that seen with the other.

aniseikonic *a.* M20.

anisette /anɪ'zɛt/ *n.* M19. [Fr., dim. of ANIS: see -ETTE.] A liqueur flavoured with aniseed.

aniso- /'anʌɪsəʊ/ *comb. form* of Gk *anisos* unequal, forming esp. negatives (see AN-[5]) of corresp. terms in ISO-.

aniso'coria *n.* (*Med.*) inequality in the sizes of the pupils of the eyes E20. **anisocy'tosis** *n.* (*Med.*) abnormal variation in the size of red blood cells E20. **aniso'gamete** *n.* (*Biol.*) either of two unequal gametes L19. **ani'sogamous** *a.* (*Biol.*) characterized by anisogamy L19. **ani'sogamy** *n.* (*Biol.*) union of unequal gametes L19. **anisome'tropia** *n.* inequality of refractive power of the eyes L19. **anisometropic** /-'trəʊpɪk, -'trɒpɪk/ *a.* characterized by anisometropia L19.

anisotropic /ˌanʌɪsə'trəʊpɪk, -'trɒp-/ *a.* L19. [f. ANISO- + Gk *tropos* turn + -IC.] Of a material, a body: having physical properties which have different magnitudes in different directions. Of a property: varying with direction. Opp. ISOTROPIC.

anisotropically *adv.* M20. **ani'sotropy** *n.* anisotropic behaviour or quality L19.

anker /'aŋkə/ *n. obs.* exc. *Hist.* ME. [LG & Du., f. med.L *anc(h)eria* of unkn. origin.] (A cask containing) a measure of wines and spirits, about 8 gallons or 36 litres.

ankerite /'aŋkərʌɪt/ *n.* M19. [f. M. J. *Anker* (1772–1843), Austrian mineralogist + -ITE[1].] *Min.* Iron-rich dolomite; *spec.* that in which iron predominates over magnesium.

ankh /aŋk/ *n.* L19. [Egyptian = life, soul.] An object resembling a cross, but with a loop in place of the upper limb, used in ancient Egyptian art as a symbol of life. Also called *crux ansata*.

ankle /'aŋk(ə)l/ *n.* & *v.* Also †**ancle**. [OE *anclēow* superseded in ME by forms f. ON *ǫkkla*, OSw. *ankol* corresp. to OFris. *ankel*, MLG *enkel*, MDu. *ankel*, OHG *anchal*, *enchil* (G *Enkel*), f. IE base repr. also by ANGLE *n.*[3]] A *n.* The joint which connects the foot with the leg; the slender part between this and the calf. OE.

Comb.: **ankle-bone** *Anat.* = TALUS *n.*[1]; **ankle boot**, **sock**: just covering the ankle.

B *v.i.* 1 Use the ankles to good effect in cycling. L19. 2 Walk, go. *slang.* E20.

anklet /'aŋklɪt/ *n.* E19. [f. prec. + -LET, after *bracelet*.] An ornament or fetter for the ankle; also (*US*) an ankle sock.

ankus /'aŋkəs/ *n.* L19. [Hind. *āṅkus*, *aṅkas* f. Skt *aṅkuśa*.] In the Indian subcontinent: an elephant-goad.

ankylosaur /'aŋkɪləsɔː/ *n.* L20. [mod.L *Ankylosaurus* genus name, f. Gk *agkulōsis* ANKYLOSIS: see -SAUR.] Any of a group of broad short-legged ornithischian dinosaurs with heavy armour of bony plates, of the Jurassic and Cretaceous periods worldwide.

ankylo'saurus *n.*, pl. **-ruses**, **-ri** /-rʌɪ, -riː/, a large ankylosaur of the late Cretaceous genus *Ankylosaurus* E20.

ankylose /'aŋkɪləʊz/ *v.* Also **anch-**. L18. [Back-form. f. next.] 1 *v.t.* Join or stiffen by ankylosis. Usu. in *pass.*, be solidly united bone to bone. L18. 2 *v.i.* Become joined or stiffened by ankylosis. M19.

1 **ankylosing spondylitis** spinal arthritis that eventually causes ankylosis of vertebral and sacro-iliac joints.

ankylosis /aŋkɪ'ləʊsɪs/ *n.* Also **anch-**. Pl. **-loses** /-'ləʊsiːz/. E18. [Gk *agkulōsis*, f. *agkuloun* to crook, f. *agkulos* crooked: see -OSIS.] The stiffening of a joint by fibrosis or by the fusion of the separate bones.

ankylostomiasis *n.* var. of ANCYLOSTOMIASIS.

anlace /'anləs/ *n. arch.* ME. [Origin unkn.] A short tapering two-edged dagger.

anlage /'anlɑːgə, -leɪdʒ/ *n.* Pl. **-lagen** /-lɑːgən/, **-lages** /-leɪdʒɪz/. L19. [G = foundation, basis.] *Biol.* The rudimentary basis of an organ or other part, esp. in an embryo.

anlaut /'anlaʊt/ *n.* L19. [G, f. *an* on + *Laut* sound.] *Philol.* The initial sound of a word.

†**anlet** *n.* var. of ANNULET.

ann /an/ *n.* E17. [Abbrev. of *annat* ANNATE 1.] *Sc. Law* (now *Hist.*). A half-year's (orig. a year's) salary legally due to the executors of a deceased minister of religion in addition to the ordinary stipend.

anna /'anə/ *n.* E17. [Hind. *ānā* (Panjabi *ānnā*).] A former monetary unit of the Indian subcontinent, equal to one-sixteenth of a rupee.

annabergite /'anəbəːgʌɪt/ *n.* M19. [f. *Annaberg*, a town in Saxony + -ITE[1].] *Min.* A monoclinic hydrated nickel arsenate, occurring usu. as an apple-green crust on nickel ores.

annal /'an(ə)l/ *v.* & *n.* E17. [Back-form. f. ANNALS.] A *v.i.* & *t.* Record (events) in annals, chronicle. *rare.* E17. B *n.* The annals of one year; the record of one item in a chronicle. L17.

annalist /'an(ə)lɪst/ *n.* M16. [f. next + -IST.] A writer of annals.

anna'listic *a.* M19.

annals /'an(ə)lz/ *n.pl.* M16. [Fr. *annales* or L *annales* use as n. of masc. pl. of *annalis* yearly, f. *annus* year: see -AL[1].] 1 A narrative of events year by year; historical records. M16. †2 *RC Ch.* Masses said for the space of a year. M16–M18.

Annamese /anə'miːz/ *a.* & *n.* Now *Hist.* Also **Anam-**. E19. [f. L *Annam* (see below) + -ESE.] A *adj.* Of or pertaining to Annam, a former empire and later French protectorate in SE Asia, its inhabitants, or its language. E19. B *n.* 1 Pl. same. A native or inhabitant of Annam. E19. 2 The Mon-Khmer language of Annam. L19.

Annamite /'anəmʌɪt/, **-mitic** /-'mɪtɪk/ *adjs.* & *ns.* = ANNAMESE M19.

annate /'aneɪt/ *n.* In sense 1 also **annat** /'anət/. E16. [Fr. f. med.L *annata* a year's space, work, or proceeds, f. *annus* year.] 1 *Sc. Law* (now *Hist.*). = ANN. E16. 2 *RC Ch.* In *pl.* The first year's revenue of a see or benefice, paid to the Pope. M16.

annatto /ə'natəʊ/ *n.* Pl. **-os**. Also **anatta**, **annotto**, **arn-** /ɑːn-/. E17. [Carib name of the tree.] An orange-red dye obtained from the seed-coat of the tropical American tree *Bixa orellana* and much used as a food colouring. Also, the tree itself; its fruit.

anneal /ə'niːl/ *v.* [OE *onǣlan*, f. *on* (see AN *prep.*) + *ǣlan* kindle, burn, bake, f. *āl* fire, burning, = OS *ēld*, ON *eldr*.] †1 *v.t.* Set on fire, inflame. OE–LME. †2 *v.t.* Subject to the action of fire; fire, bake, fuse, glaze. LME–M17. †3 *v.t.* Burn colours into (glass, earthenware, etc.), enamel by an encaustic process. LME–L18. 4 *v.t.* Toughen (glass or metal) by heating and usu. slow cooling. Cf. TEMPER *v.*[1] 12b. M17. b *fig.* Toughen, temper. L17. 5 *v.t.* & *i. Biol.* Combine to form double-stranded nucleic acid. M20.

3 G. HERBERT When thou dost anneal in glasse thy storie. 4b SIR W. SCOTT To press the rights of truth, The mind to strengthen and anneal.

annealer *n.* M17.

†**annect** *v.t.* LME–M18. [L *annectere*: see ANNEX *v.*] = ANNEX *v.*

annectent /ə'nɛkt(ə)nt/ *a.* E19. [f. as prec.: see -ENT.] Chiefly *Biol.* Connecting, joining.

annelid /'an(ə)lɪd/ *n.* & *a.* M19. [Fr. *annélide* or f. mod.L *annelida* (see below), f. Fr. *annelés* ringed (sc. *animaux* animals) (Lamarck), use of ppl a. of *anneler*, f. OFr. *anel* ring f. L *anellus* dim. of *anulus*: see ANNULUS, -ID[3].] *Zool.* A *n.* An animal of the phylum Annelida, members of which (e.g. marine worms, earthworms, and leeches) have bodies made up of annular segments. M19. B *adj.* Of or pertaining to Annelida or an annelid. M19.

Also **a'nnelidan** *n.* & *a.* M19.

annex *n.* var. of ANNEXE.

annex /ə'nɛks/ *v.t.* LME. [(O)Fr. *annexer*, f. L *annex-* pa. ppl stem of *annectere*, f. *ad* AN-[3] + *nectere* tie, fasten.] (Foll. by *to*.) I Without the idea of subordination. 1 Join, unite. *arch.* LME.

II With the idea of subordination. 2 Append, affix; attach as an accessory or annexe. LME. 3 Add (a territory etc.) to existing possessions, esp. (*colloq.*) without right; appropriate to one's use. LME. 4 Join or attach as an attribute, condition, or consequence. LME.

2 R. BOYLE To which he annexes a Disquisition of the Scurvey. F. A. KEMBLE To each settlement is annexed a cook's shop. N. FREELING This prissy building annexed to the Ministry of Social Affairs. 3 W. BLACKSTONE Appropriators may annex the great tithes to the vicarages. E. M. FORSTER Margaret was all for sightseeing, and . . annexed a motor. G. B. SHAW When Germany annexed Poland in 1939, half of it was snatched out of her jaws by Soviet Russia. 4 HOBBES It is annexed to the Soveraignty, to be Iudge. D. HUME He, though he granted him the commission, annexed a clause, that it should not empower him [etc.]. M. ARNOLD Salvation is not annexed to a right knowledge of geometry.

annexable, †**-ible** *a.* E17. **annexment** *n.* (*rare*) = ANNEXURE E17. **annexure** *n.* something annexed, an adjunct, a supplement L19.

annexation /anɛk'seɪʃ(ə)n/ *n.* LME. [med.L *annexatio(n-)* f. *annexat-* pa. ppl stem of *annexare* f. L *annectere*: see prec., -ATION.] The action of annexing; *esp.* the action of attaching as an additional privilege, possession, or territorial dependency.

annexationist *n.* a person who advocates the annexation of a territory M19.

annexe /'anɛks/ *n.* Also **annex.** E16. [Fr. f. L *annexum* use as n. of pa. pple of *annectere*: see ANNEX *v.*] 1 *Sc. Law.* An appurtenance. *rare.* E16. †2 An adjunct, an accessory. M16–L17. 3 An addition to a document, an appendix. M17. 4 A supplementary building, esp. for extra accommodation. M19.

annexion /ə'nɛkʃ(ə)n/ *n.* Now *rare.* L15. [Late L *annexio(n-)*, f. L *annex-*: see ANNEX *v.*, -ION.] 1 = ANNEXATION. L15. †2 = ANNEXURE. L16–M18.

annexionist *n.* (now *rare*) = ANNEXATIONIST M19.

annicut *n.* var. of ANICUT.

annihilate /ə'nʌɪlət/ *a. arch.* Also †**adn-**. LME. [Late L *annihilatus* pa. pple of *annihilare* (Jerome), *adn-*, f. *ad* AN-[3] + *nihil* nothing: see -ATE[2].] 1 Reduced to nothing, blotted out of existence. LME. †2 Made null and void, of no effect. LME–L16.

annihilate /ə'nʌɪleɪt/ *v.* Also †**adn-**. Pa. pple **-ated**, (*arch.*) **-ate** /-ət/. E16. [f. as prec.: see -ATE[3].] 1 *v.t.* Make null and void, cancel, abrogate (laws, treaties, rights, etc.). *arch.* E16. 2 *v.t.* Treat as non-existent, set at naught. *arch.* M16. 3 *v.t.* Destroy largely or completely; blot out of existence. M16. 4 *v.t. fig.* Reduce to insignificance or powerlessness; silence or humiliate completely. M17. 5 *v.t.* (usu. in *pass.*) & *i. Physics.* Convert or be converted into electromagnetic radiation; subject to or undergo annihilation. M20.

1 W. FULKE To adnihilate the sacraments ministred by heretikes. 2 SMOLLETT To usurp your name, and annihilate your exploits. 3 DEFOE God can no more be the author of evil, than he can annihilate himself, and cease to be. T. PENNANT The vestiges of the Roman camp .. are almost annihilated. WELLINGTON That event has totally annihilated all order and discipline. M. BORN The human race has today the means for annihilating itself. 4 BYRON Thou who with thy frown Annihilated senates. J. B. PRIESTLEY All the years between Peter De Wint and myself were annihilated in a flash; he pointed and I saw, he spoke and I heard. 5 S. WEINBERG Nuclear reactions, in which a fraction of the mass of atomic nuclei is annihilated.

†**annihil** *v.t.* [(O)Fr.] = ANNIHILATE *v.* 1, 3 L15–L17. **annihilable** *a.* L17. **annihilative** *a.* (*rare*) such as to annihilate, crushing E19. **annihilator** *n.* L17.

annihilation /ənʌɪɪˈleɪʃ(ə)n/ *n.* Also †**adn-**. M16. [(O)Fr., f. as prec.: see -ATION.] Destruction, complete or effective; *Physics* the conversion of matter (*esp.* the mutual conversion of a particle and its antiparticle) into electromagnetic radiation.

BURKE The annihilation of our trade, the ruin of our credit. J. B. MOZLEY When reason itself has opened a view into immortality, to put up contentedly with annihilation,—what a dreadful stupefaction of the human spirit. H. ARENDT The final catastrophe which brought the Jews so near to complete annihilation. H. WOUK Unescorted bombers ran a high risk of annihilation.

annihilationism *n.* (*Theol.*) belief in the destruction of the souls of the wicked as well as their bodies L19. **annihilationist** *n.* (*Theol.*) an adherent of annihilationism L19.

anniversary /anɪˈvəːs(ə)ri/ *n.* & *a.* ME. [L *anniversarius* returning yearly, f. *annus* year + *versus* turning + *-arius* -ARY¹; used as n. in med.L *anniversaria* (sc. *dies* day), *-arium* (sc. *festum* feast); cf. (O)Fr. *anniversaire.*] A *n.* 1 The yearly return of a noteworthy date; the day on which some event of ecclesiastical, national, or personal interest is annually commemorated; the celebration of this. ME. †2 *RC Ch.* A commemorative mass said for the space of a year. E17–M18. B *adj.* 1 Returning or commemorated on the same date each year; annual, repeated each year. *arch.* L15. †2 Enduring for or completed in a year. E17–E18.

anniversarily *adv.* at the yearly return M17.

Anno Domini /ˈanəʊ ˈdɒmɪnʌɪ/ *adv.* & *n. phr.* M16. [L = in the year of the Lord.] A *adv.* Of the Christian era. Usu. written AD (see A, A III). M16.

B *n.* 1 A particular year. L17. 2 Advanced or advancing age. *colloq.* L19.

1 DRYDEN The *Anno Domini* of your new sovereign's coronation. 2 E. V. LUCAS When the time came for A to take the bat he was unable to do so. *Anno Domini* asserted itself.

annominate *v.*, **-ation** *n.* vars. of AGNOMINATE, -ATION.

annotate /ˈanəteɪt/ *v.* L16. [L *annotat-* pa. ppl stem of *annotare*, f. *ad* AN-³ + *nota* mark: see -ATE³.] †1 *v.t. gen.* Make a mark on. *rare.* Only in L16. 2 *v.t.* Add notes to (a book etc.). M18. 3 *v.i.* Add or make notes (*on, upon*). M18.

annotation /anəˈteɪʃ(ə)n/ *n.* LME. [Fr., or L *annotatio(n-)*, f. as prec.: see -ATION.] 1 A note by way of explanation or comment. LME. †2 Chronological reckoning or notation. L15–M17. 3 The action of annotating. L16.

1 R. QUIRK Annotations in margins and endpapers. 2 T. GALE There was anciently no annotation of historie among them [the Grecians].

annotator /ˈanəteɪtə/ *n.* M17. [f. as ANNOTATE + -OR: cf. Fr. *annotateur* (16), med.L *annotator.*] A person who annotates a text.

annotto *n.* var. of ANNATTO.

announce /əˈnaʊns/ *v.* & *n.* L15. [Fr. *annoncer* f. L *annuntiare*, f. *ad* AN-³ + *nuntiare*, f. *nuntius* messenger.] A *v.t.* 1 Make publicly known, proclaim as news. L15. b Proclaim the arrival or approach of; publicly introduce. M18. 2 Make known (without words) to the senses or mind. L18.

1 E. O'NEILL I take this opportunity to publicly announce the betrothal of my daughter. R. ELLISON A huge electric sign announced its message. O. MANNING The wireless announced that the King would address his subjects in Rumanian. b SCOTT FITZGERALD Before I could reply that he was my neighbor dinner was announced. P. V. WHITE Do not forget to announce Mr Voss on showing him into the room. 2 GIBBON His feeble efforts announced his degenerate spirit. SIR W. SCOTT Gold buckles in his shoes, etc... announced him to be a domestic of trust and importance. JOYCE He announced his presence by that gentle .. cough which so many have tried .. to imitate.

†B *n.* = ANNOUNCEMENT. L18–M19.

announcement *n.* the action of announcing; a public notice, a proclamation: L18. **announcer** *n.* a person who makes an announcement or announcements, *spec.* in *Broadcasting* of the subjects of programmes, and items of news E17.

annoy /əˈnɔɪ/ *n.* Now *arch.* & *poet.* ME. [OFr. *anui, anoi* (mod. *ennui*) ult. f. L *in odio* in *mihi in odio est* it is hateful to me.] 1 = ANNOYANCE 2. ME. 2 = ANNOYANCE 3. LME.

†**annoyous** *a.* (latterly *dial.*) troublesome, vexatious, harmful LME–L19.

annoy /əˈnɔɪ/ *v.* ME. [OFr. *anuier, anoier* (mod. *ennuyer*), ult. f. as prec. (cf. late L *inodiare*).] †1 *v.i.* Be hateful *to*, be a cause of trouble *to*. Only in ME. †2 *v.t.* in *pass.* Foll. by *of*: be troubled, irked, or wearied by. ME–M16. 3 *v.t.* Cause slight anger or mental distress to. ME. 4 Molest, injure, harass. LME. †5 Damage (something material). Latterly *dial.* LME–L19.

3 **be annoyed** be somewhat angry *with* a person, *about* or *at* a thing, *that*, or *to do*.

annoyer *n.* L16. **annoyingly** *adv.* in an annoying manner M19. **annoyment** *n.* (*rare*) = ANNOYANCE 1, 2 L15.

annoyance /əˈnɔɪəns/ *n.* LME. [OFr. *anoiance*, f. as prec.: see -ANCE.] 1 The action of annoying; vexing, molestation. LME. 2 The state of being annoyed; vexation, trouble. E16. 3 Something that annoys, a nuisance. E16.

1 G. WHITE To secure these nests from the annoyance of sheperd boys. 2 A. NEWMAN Annoyance made her tactless. 3 S. BELLOW There are the standard rooming-house annoyances: cooking odours, roaches, and peculiar neighbors.

¶ Sense 3 earlier as NOYANCE.

annoyancer *n.* (*rare*) a person who or thing which causes annoyance M17.

annual /ˈanjʊəl/ *a.* & *n.* LME. [(O)Fr. *annuel* f. late L *annualis* for L *annuus* and *annalis*, f. *annus* year: see -AL¹.] A *adj.* 1 Reckoned, payable, or engaged by the year. LME. 2 Lasting for one year. LME. 3 Pertaining to a year's events. (Now chiefly of publications and freq. interpreted as sense 4.) E16. 4 Recurring once every year. M16.

1 SHAKES. *Haml.* Gives him threescore thousand crowns in annual fee. JOYCE The balance .. repayable quarterly in equal annual instalments. 2 BACON The dying in winter of the roots of plants that are annual. MILTON Whether the Civil Government be an annual Democracy or a perpetual Aristocracy. J. A. FROUDE The annual course of the sun was completed in 365 days and six hours. W. FAULKNER As the holder of the annual commuters' ticket sits on his accustomed bench. **annual general meeting**: of members or shareholders to elect officers, report on the past year, etc. 4 P. GALLICO She established the birthday interview as an annual custom.

B *n.* †1 *RC Ch.* A commemorative mass said for a year after, or on the anniversary of, a person's death; a payment for this. LME–M18. †2 A yearly payment. Latterly *Sc.* LME–M19. 3 A plant that lives for one year only, perpetuating itself by seed. M17. 4 A book etc. forming part of a series published successively at the same time each year; a book etc. reviewing the events of the past year. L17.

3 *hardy annual*: see HARDY *a.* *tender annual*: see TENDER *a.*

annualize *v.t.* convert (a quantity) to its value for one year from that for a shorter period M20. **annually** *adv.* L16.

annuity /əˈnjuːɪti/ *n.* LME. [Fr. *annuité* f. med.L *annuitas*, f. *annuus*: see prec., -ITY.] 1 A yearly grant or allowance; a sum of money payable in respect of a particular year. LME. 2 An investment of money entitling the investor to a series of equal annual sums. L17.

2 *consolidated annuities*: see CONSOLIDATE *v.* 1. *deferred annuity*: see DEFER *v.*¹ 2.

annuitant *n.* [after *accountant*] a person who holds or receives an annuity E18.

annul /əˈnʌl/ *v.t.* Infl. **-ll-**. LME. [OFr. *a(d)nuller* (mod. *annuler*) f. late L (Vulgate) *annullare*, f. *ad* AN-³ + *nullum* nothing, neut. sing. of *nullus* NULL *a.*] 1 Cause to exist no longer; do away with; abolish; cancel. LME. 2 Declare invalid; *spec.* declare (a marriage) to have had no legal existence. LME.

1 MILTON Light .. to me is extinct, And all her various objects of delight Annulled. R. W. EMERSON Intellect annuls Fate. So far as a man thinks, he is free. K. AMIS You, Who cannot annul a sparrow's footprint. 2 LD MACAULAY A bill, which should at once annul all the statutes passed by the Long Parliament.

annullable *a.* (*rare*) L17.

annular /ˈanjʊlə/ *a.* L16. [Fr. *annulaire* or L *annularis*, f. as ANNULUS: see -AR¹.] 1 Of or pertaining to a ring or rings; ringlike. L16. 2 Bearing a ring or rings (designating the fourth finger of the left hand). M17.

1 **annular eclipse** an eclipse of the sun in which the moon, seen projected on the solar disc, leaves a ring of light visible. **annular thickening** *Bot.* (in the tracheary elements of xylem) a thickening of the cell wall taking the form of isolated rings.

annuˈlarity *n.* annular condition or form M19. **annularly** *adv.* E18. **annulary** *a.* & *n.* (*a*) *adj.* = ANNULAR; (*b*) *n.* the ring finger: E17.

annulate /ˈanjʊlət/ *a.* E19. [L *annulatus*, f. as ANNULUS: see -ATE².] Having or marked with a ring or rings; consisting of rings.

annulated /ˈanjʊleɪtɪd/ *a.* M17. [f. as prec. + -ED¹.] = prec.

annuˈlation *n.* the formation of rings or ringlike divisions; a ringlike structure: E19.

annulene /ˈanjʊliːn/ *n.* M20. [f. ANNULUS + -ENE.] *Chem.* Any cyclic hydrocarbon whose molecule is a ring having alternate double and single bonds.

Freq. with numeral specifying number of carbon atoms, as [*18*]-*annulene*.

annulet /ˈanjʊlɪt/ *n.* Also †**anlet** & other vars. LME. [OFr. *anelet* (mod. *ann-*) dim. of *anel* f. L *anellus* dim of *anulus*, refash. (L16) after L: see ANNULUS, -ET¹.] 1 *gen.* A small ring. LME. 2 *Her.* A charge in the form of a small ring. L16. 3 *Archit.* A small fillet or other flat moulding encircling a column. E18.

annulment /əˈnʌlm(ə)nt/ *n.* L15. [f. ANNUL + -MENT.] 1 Total destruction; abolition. L15. 2 Invalidation; *spec.* declaration of a marriage as having had no legal existence. Also, a decree of invalidity. M17.

2 M. MCCARTHY In your place, I'd get a divorce or an annulment.

annulose /ˈanjʊləʊs/ *a.* E19. [mod.L *annulosus*, f. as next + -OSE¹.] Ringlike; annulate.

annulus /ˈanjʊləs/ *n.* Pl. **-li** /-lʌɪ, -liː/. M16. [L, late form of *anulus* dim. of *anus* ring (see ANUS).] Chiefly *Math.* & *Bot.* A ring, a circle that is not filled in; *spec.* a partial veil forming a collar round the stalk in some agarics; the ring of thickened cells surrounding the sporangium of a fern.

†**annumerate** *v.t.* LME. [L *annumerat-* pa. ppl stem of *annumerare*, f. *ad* AN-³ + *numerare* to number: see -ATE³.] 1 Reckon as an addition *to*. LME–L18. 2 Enumerate, adduce. Only in E19.

annunciate /əˈnʌnsɪeɪt/ *v.t.* Also (now *rare*) **-tiate**. Pa. pple †**-ate** (earlier), **-ated**. LME. [Orig. pa. pple, f. med.L *annunciat-* for L *annuntiat-* pa. ppl stem of *annuntiare*: see ANNOUNCE, -ATE³.] Proclaim; indicate as coming or ready.

annunciative *a.* (*rare*) characterized by or proper to annunciation M17.

annunciation /ənʌnsɪˈeɪʃ(ə)n/ *n.* ME. [(O)Fr. *annonciation* f. late L *annuntiatio(n-)*: see prec., -ATION.] 1 The action of announcing; an announcement. ME. 2 *spec.* (**A-**.) The announcement of the Incarnation, made by Gabriel to Mary; the festival commemorating this, Lady Day, 25 March. LME.

annunciator /əˈnʌnsɪeɪtə/ *n.* M18. [Late L *annunciator*: see ANNUNCIATE, -OR.] An announcer; an audible or visible indicator of where a bell has been rung, the position of a train, etc.

annunciatory *a.* of an announcer or announcing M19.

annuntiate *v.* see ANNUNCIATE.

annus mirabilis /ˌanəs mɪˈrɑːbɪlɪs/ *n. phr.* M17. [mod.L = wonderful year.] A remarkable or auspicious year.

ano- /ˈeɪnəʊ/ *comb. form* of ANUS: see -O-.

anoˈgenital *a.* of or pertaining to the anus and genitals M20.

anoa /əˈnəʊə/ *n.* M19. [A name in Sulawesi.] A small wild bovine, *Anoa depressicornis*, native to Sulawesi (Celebes), Indonesia.

anode /ˈanəʊd/ *n.* M19. [f. Gk *anodos* way up, f. ANA- + *hodos* way.] A positive electrode or terminal. Opp. CATHODE.

anodal *a.* of or pertaining to an anode L19. **anodize** *v.t.* give (a metal, esp. aluminium) a protective oxide coating by means of an electrolytic process in which it forms the anode M20. **anodizer** *n.* M20.

anodic /əˈnɒdɪk/ *a.* M19. [f. prec. + -IC.] Of or pertaining to an anode or anodizing.

anodically *adv.* E20.

anodyne /ˈanədʌɪn/ *a.* & *n.* M16. [L *anodynus* (Celsus) f. Gk *anōdunos* free from pain, f. AN-[5] + *odunē* pain; as n. f. Gk *anōdynon*, late L *anodynum*.] A *adj.* 1 *Med.* Having the power of easing pain. M16. 2 *fig.* Soothing, comforting; bland, inoffensive. L18. B *n.* 1 *Med.* A medicine that eases pain. M16. 2 *fig.* Something that soothes the feelings, allays anxiety, etc. M16.

aˈnodynous *a.* (*rare*) M17.

anoesis /anəʊˈiːsɪs/ *n.* E20. [f. A-[10] + Gk *noēsis* understanding.] *Psychol.* Consciousness with sensation but without thought and without understanding of the environment.

anoetic /-ˈɛtɪk/ *a.* (*a*) (*rare*) unthinkable; (*b*) of or pertaining to anoesis: M19.

anoestrus /aˈniːstrəs/ *n.* Also ***anest-**. E20. [f. AN-[5] + OESTRUS.] A sexually inactive or unreceptive state in animals. Opp. OESTRUS.

anoestrous *a.* of or pertaining to anoestrus E20.

anoint /əˈnɔɪnt/ *v.t.* ME. [AN (see AN-[2]), OFr. *enoint* pa. pple of *enoindre* f. L *inungere*, f. IN-[2] + *ungere* anoint.] 1 Smear or rub over with oil or ointment, esp. as a religious ceremony at baptism or on consecration as a priest or monarch. (Foll. by *with*.) ME. 2 Smear or rub with any other substance. LME. 3 Thrash soundly, baste. Now *dial.* L15.

1 AV *Exod.* 28:41 Thou . . shalt annoint them, and consecrate them . . that they may minister vnto mee in the Priests office. GIBBON The salutary custom of bathing the limbs in water and of anointing them with oil. D. ATTENBOROUGH The bird takes the oil . . with its beak and anoints its feathers individually. **the Lord's Anointed** (*a*) Jesus Christ; (*b*) a monarch by divine right. 2 R. CONQUEST While she's proceeding to anoint The sting with sal ammoniac.

anointer *n.* L16. **anointment** *n.* (*arch.*) the action of anointing; an ointment: LME.

anole /əˈnəʊli/ *n.* Also **-lis** /-lɪs/. E18. [Carib: cf. Fr. *anolis*.] Any of numerous, chiefly arboreal, iguanid lizards belonging to the American genus *Anolis*, esp. the green *A. carolinensis*.

anomalism /əˈnɒm(ə)lɪz(ə)m/ *n. rare.* M17. [f. as next + -ISM.] Anomalousness; an anomaly.

anomalistic /ənɒməˈlɪstɪk/ *a.* M18. [f. Gk *anōmalos* ANOMALOUS + -ISTIC.] *Astron.* Of or pertaining to anomaly.

anomalistic month the period between successive perigees of the moon. **anomalistic year** the period between successive perihelia of the earth or another planet.

Also †**anomalistical** *a.*: only in 18.

anomalous /əˈnɒm(ə)ləs/ *a.* M17. [f. late L *anomalus* f. Gk *anōmalos*, f. AN-[5] + *homalos* even, + -OUS.] 1 Unconformable or dissimilar *to*. *arch.* M17. 2 Irregular; abnormal. M17.

anomalously *adv.* M17. **anomalousness** *n.* L17.

anomalure /əˈnɒməljʊə/ *n.* L19. [f. mod.L *Anomalurus*, f. Gk *anōmalos* ANOMALOUS + *oura* tail.] = *scaly-tailed squirrel* s.v. SCALY *a.*

anomaly /əˈnɒm(ə)li/ *n.* L16. [L *anomalia* (Varro) f. Gk *anōmalia*, f. *anōmalos*: see ANOMALOUS, -Y[3].] 1 Irregularity of condition, motion, behaviour, etc.; an anomalous thing or being, an exceptional circumstance. L16. 2 *Astron.* The angular distance of a planet or the moon from its last perihelion or perigee. M17.

1 *magnetic anomaly*: see MAGNETIC *a.* 2 **eccentric anomaly** the actual anomaly in an elliptical orbit. **mean anomaly** the corresponding angle in an imaginary circular orbit.

Also †**anomal** *n.* M16–M17.

anomer /ˈanəmə/ *n.* M20. [f. Gk *anō* upwards + -MER.] Either of two isomers of a cyclic carbohydrate which differ only in the configuration about the hemi-acetal carbon atom.

anoˈmeric *a.* M20.

anomic /əˈnɒmɪk/ *a.* L19. [Partly f. as next + -IC, partly Fr. *anomique*.] 1 Obeying no known law; not concerned with law. L19. 2 Characterized by anomie. M20.

anomie /ˈanəmi/ *n.* M20. [Fr. f. Gk *anomia*, f. *anomos* lawless: cf. ANOMY.] Lack of the usual social standards in a group or person.

Anomoean /anəˈmiːən/ *a.* & *n.* L17. [f. mod.L *Anomoeus*, f. Gk *anomoios*, f. AN-[5] + *homoios* like, similar, + -AN.] *Eccl. Hist.* Pertaining to, a member of, an extreme Arian sect which held that the Father and the Son are unlike in essence.

anomuran /anəˈm(j)ʊər(ə)n/ *n.* & *a.* L19. [f. mod.L *Anomura* (see below), f. Gk *anomos* irregular + *oura* tail + -AN: the abdomen in Anomura is irregular in size or form.] *Zool.* A *n.* Any member of the section Anomura of decapod crustaceans, including certain kinds of crab, notably hermit crabs. L19. B *adj.* Of or pertaining to Anomura or an anomuran. L19.

anomy /ˈanəmi/ *n.* L16. [Gk *anomia*: see ANOMIE, -Y[3].] †1 Disregard of (esp. divine) law. L16–L17. 2 = ANOMIE. M20.

anon /əˈnɒn/ *a.* & *n.* Also **anon.** (point), **A-**. M18. [Abbrev.] Anonymous; (a designation for a person, esp. a writer or composer) whose name is unknown or not stated.

anon /əˈnɒn/ *adv.* Now *arch.* & *literary*. In sense 4 also **anan.** [OE *on ān* into one, *on āne* in one: see ON *prep.*, ONE *a.*] †1 In or into one body, state, course, etc. OE–LME. 2 At once, instantly. Long *obs.* exc. as occas. deliberately revived. OE. 3 Soon, in a short time; for a little. LME. 4 As *int.* (To a person calling for attention) in a moment! coming! Also, at your service!; what did you say? eh? Long *dial.* M16. 5 Now again; now at this time (in contrast to another). L16.

2 AV *Matt.* 12:20 He that heareth the word, & anon with ioy receiueth it. 3 R. L. STEVENSON At our concerts, of which more anon. SCOTT FITZGERALD Good night, Mr. Carraway. See you anon. 4 SHAKS. *1 Hen. IV* Francis! . . Anon, anon, sir. C. J. LEVER 'Such little events are not unfrequent down here, then? 'Anan!' said she, not understanding his question. 5 J. TYNDALL The avalanche rushed, hidden at intervals, and anon shooting forth.

anonym /ˈanənɪm/ *n.* Also **-nyme**. E19. [Fr. *anonyme* f. Gk *anōnumos* ANONYMOUS: see -NYM.] 1 An anonymous person or publication. E19. 2 A pseudonym. M19.

anonymity /anəˈnɪmɪti/ *n.* E19. [f. as next + -ITY.] The state of being anonymous; impersonality.

A. B. GROSART The anonymity of the poem on Felton. K. AMIS Every face Had taken on the flat anonymity of pain. J. FRAME The languorous anonymity of the big overseas cities.

anonymous /əˈnɒnɪməs/ *a.* & *n.* L16. [Late L *anonymos*, *-mus* f. Gk *anōnumos*, f. as AN-[5] + *onuma* name (see -NYM) + -OUS.] A *adj.* 1 Nameless; of unknown name; impersonal, not individuated. L16. 2 Of unknown or undeclared source or authorship. L17.

1 ALDOUS HUXLEY No longer anonymous, but named, identified. O. MANNING He could not be recognised among the anonymous dark-clad figures within. D. STOREY Like all the other big towns—socialist, impersonal, anonymous. D. LESSING The men making announcements . . had had the anonymous voices of officialdom. *Alcoholics Anonymous*: see ALCOHOLIC *n.* 2 JOYCE A volume . . entitled *Sweets of Sin*, anonymous, author a gentleman of fashion. J. LE CARRÉ Are you used to receiving anonymous gifts of a thousand pounds?

B *n.* An anonymous person. Now *rare.* E17.

¶In earliest uses as a pseudonym; at first freq. in Gk or L forms.

anonymously *adv.* M18. **anonymousness** *n.* E19. **anonyˈmuncule** *n.* [after L HOMUNCULUS] a petty anonymous writer M19.

anopheles /əˈnɒfɪliːz/ *n.* L19. [mod.L f. Gk *anōphelēs* unprofitable, useless.] A mosquito of the genus *Anopheles*, which includes species that carry the parasites of malaria and other diseases.

anopheline *a.* & *n.* (pertaining to or designating) a mosquito of a group that contains this genus but not *Culex* E20.

anoplothere /əˈnɒpləθɪə/ *n.* Also in L form †**-therium**. E19. [Fr. *anoplothère*, f. Gk *anoplos* unarmed, f. AN-[5] + *hoplon* weapon + *thērion* wild animal.] *Palaeont.* An extinct hornless artiodactyl of the family Anoplotheriidae, found as fossils of Eocene and Oligocene age.

anopsia /əˈnɒpsɪə/ *n. rare.* Orig. †**-sy.** M17. [f. Gk AN-[5] + *opsis* sight + -IA[1].] Sightlessness, blindness.

anorak /ˈanərak/ *n.* E20. [Eskimo (Greenlandic) *annoraaq*.] A skin or cloth hooded jacket worn by Eskimos and so by others in polar regions; a similar weatherproof garment worn elsewhere.

anorectic /anəˈrɛktɪk/ *a.* & *n.* L19. [f. Gk *anorektos*, f. as AN-[5] + *orexein* to desire: see -IC.] A *adj.* Characterized by a lack of appetite, *spec.* by anorexia nervosa; producing a loss of appetite. L19. B *n.* 1 An anorectic agent. M20. 2 A person with anorexia. L20.

Also **anoretic** *a.* & *n.* E20.

anorexia /anəˈrɛksɪə/ *n.* Also †**-exy.** L16. [Late L f. Gk, f. AN-[5] + *orexis* appetite: see -IA[1].] *Med.* Absence of appetite; *pop. spec.* anorexia nervosa (see below).

anorexia nervosa /nɔːˈvəʊsə/ chronic anorexia induced by emotional disturbance.

anorexiant *a.* & *n.* (a drug) producing anorexia M20. **anorexic** *a.* & *n.* (*a*) *adj.* = ANORECTIC *a.*; (*b*) *n.* = ANORECTIC *n.* 2: M20. **anorexiˈgenic** *a.* producing anorexia M20.

anormal /eɪˈnɔːm(ə)l, ə-/ *a.* M16. [Isolated early use f. Fr., var. of *anomal* (see ANOMALY); later (M19) f. A-[10] + NORMAL *a.*] Irregular, not usual.

¶Without the depreciatory overtones of *abnormal*.

anorthic /əˈnɔːθɪk/ *a.* Now *rare* or *obs.* M19. [f. AN-[5] + Gk *orthos* straight, right + -IC.] *Cryst.* = TRICLINIC.

anorthite /əˈnɔːθʌɪt/ *n.* M19. [f. as prec. + -ITE[1].] *Min.* A calcium-rich plagioclase occurring in many basic igneous rocks; calcium feldspar.

anorthoclase /əˈnɔːθəkleɪz/ *n.* L19. [f. as prec. + Gk *klasis* breaking, cleavage.] *Min.* A triclinic sodium-rich alkali feldspar occurring in many alkalic lavas.

anorthosite /əˈnɔːθəsʌɪt/ *n.* M19. [f. Fr. *anorthose* plagioclase, (now) anorthoclase + -ITE[1]: see ANORTHIC.] *Geol.* A granular igneous rock composed largely of a plagioclase (usu. labradorite).

anorthoˈsitic *a.* of the nature of anorthosite M20.

anosmia /aˈnɒzmɪə/ *n.* E19. [f. AN-[5] + Gk *osmē* smell + -IA[1].] *Med.* Loss of the sense of smell.

anosmic *a.* & *n.* (a person) suffering from anosmia E20.

another /əˈnʌðə/ *pron.* & *a. sing.* (in mod. usage also classed as a *determiner*). ME. [f. AN *a.* (see A *a.*) + OTHER *a.* In two wds as late as 16. Cf. NOTHER *a.*[2], 'NOTHER.] 1 A second, further, additional (one, specified number (of)). ME. b A second in likeness, character, or attributes. L16. 2 A different (one, specified number (of)); some or any other. ME.

1 F. M. FORD At meals she would feel an intolerable desire to drink a glass of wine, and then another and then a third. S. BARSTOW Another five minutes goes by while he reckons to look it over. A. THWAITE A stream, a fence, a hedge, another fence. *ask me another*: see ASK *v.* **such another** another of the same sort. *tell me another*: see TELL *v.* **you're another** *colloq.*: applying an accusation to the person who makes it; also as a vaguely contemptuous retort. b YEATS Another Troy must rise and set, Another lineage feed the crow, Another Argo's painted prow Drive to a flashier bauble yet. 2 SAKI Do you suppose we shall all get appropriate punishments in another world for our sins

in this? V. WOOLF Whose day had slipped past in one quick doing after another. R. G. COLLINGWOOD A patron who buys a picture of a fox-hunt or a covey of partridges does not buy it because it represents that fox-hunt or that covey and not another. G. GREENE He'd got to close her mouth one way or another. D. DU MAURIER I am not she who left him five minutes ago... I am another woman, older, more mature. R. P. WARREN Two men, the one who had fired the shot and another, .. ran to the fallen man. T. S. ELIOT One year is a year of rain, Another a year of dryness. I. MURDOCH Well, I'll be off. I can easily see Catherine another time. R. WEST George Willoughby, like many another naval officer, had his reasons for liking a quiet mount. *one and another, one another, one with another*: see ONE *a.* etc. *one way and another*: see WAY *n.*

Special collocations & comb.: †**anothergates** *a.* (*attrib.*) [f. genit. of GATE *n.*[2]] = *anotherguess* below. **anotherguess** *a.* (*attrib.*) *arch.* [alt. of *anothergates* above: cf. GUESS *a.*] of another sort or kind. **another place** the other House of Parliament (used in the Commons to refer to the Lords, and vice versa).

anovulatory /ˌanɒvjʊˈleɪt(ə)ri/ *a.* M20. [f. AN-[5] + OVULATORY.] *Med.* Of menstruation etc.: not accompanied by ovulation.

aˈnovulant *a.* & *n.* (a drug etc.) that suppresses ovulation M20.

anoxaemia /anɒkˈsiːmɪə/ *n.* L19. [f. as next + -AEMIA.] *Med.* = HYPOXAEMIA.

anoxia /aˈnɒksɪə/ *n.* M20. [f. AN-[5] + OX- + -IA[1].] = HYPOXIA.

anoxic *a.* characterized by anoxia E20.

ansa /ˈansə/ *n.* Pl. **-sae** /-siː/ Also Anglicized as †**anse**. M17. [L = handle (of a vessel).] *Astron.* Either extremity of Saturn's ring system as seen projecting like a handle from the planet's disc.

Ansafone, ansaphone *ns.* see ANSWERPHONE.

ansated /ˈanseɪtɪd/ *a. rare.* M18. [f. L *ansatus* pa. pple of *ansare*, f. as ANSA, + -ED[1].] Having (something resembling) handles.

Anschauung /ˈanʃaʊʊŋ/ *n.* Pl. ***-en*** /-ən/. M19. [G = looking at.] **1** *Philos.* (esp. *Kantian*). A sense-perception, an intuition, an immediate apprehension by sense. M19. **2** An outlook, an attitude, a point of view. E20.

Anschluss /ˈanʃlʊs/ *n.* E20. [G, f. *anschliessen* join, annex.] Union, annexation; *spec.* the annexation of Austria by Germany in 1938.

†**anse** *n.* see ANSA.

Anselmian /anˈsɛlmɪən/ *a.* L19. [f. St *Anselm* (see below) + -IAN.] Of or pertaining to St Anselm (1033–1109), Archbishop of Canterbury and scholastic philosopher, esp. to his ontological argument for the existence of God and his view of the atonement.

Also **Anselmic** *a.* L19.

anserine /ˈansərʌɪn/ *a.* M19. [L *anserinus*, f. *anser* goose: see -INE[1].] Of or like a goose; silly.

Also **anserous** *a.* E19.

an sich /an zɪç/ *a.* & *adv. phr.* M19. [G.] In itself; in the abstract; not in relation to anything else. See also DING AN SICH.

answer /ˈɑːnsə/ *n.* [OE *andswaru* corresp. to OFris. *ondser*, OS *antswōr*, ON *andsvar*, f. Gmc, f. pref. meaning 'against, opposite' + base found also in SWEAR *v.*] **I** Something said or done in order to deal with what has preceded. **1** A reply to a question. OE. **2** A reply to a charge; a defence. ME. **3** A reply to an objection; a rebuttal. ME. **4** A reply to an appeal, address, communication, etc.; an acknowledgement; a rejoinder. ME. **5** The solution of a problem; a response to a test of knowledge etc. ME.

1 G. VIDAL People started asking him vague questions to which there were no sensible answers. *the short answer is*: see SHORT *a.* **2** SHAKES. *2 Hen. VI* Call these foul offenders to their answers. **3** SIR T. MORE The Answer to the First Part of the Poysoned Booke. T. STOPPARD Everything has to begin somewhere and there is no answer to *that*. **4** AV *Job* 19:16 I called my seruant, and he gaue me no answere. W. FAULKNER I've had no answer to the last two letters. E. WAUGH I wrote long letters to Sebastian and called daily at the post-office for his answers. *not take no for an answer*: see NO *n.*[1] **5** L. HENSLEY The Scholar's Arithmetic, with Answers to the Examples. J. BETJEMAN His written answers .. Pleased the examiners. S. HILL For many people a hospital of this kind is not the answer. **know all the answers** *colloq.* be very experienced, be knowing.

II Something said or done as a reaction to what has preceded. **6** A reply to an implied question; a decision upon a point at issue. LME. **7** *Mus.* A repetition or echoing of a phrase, theme, etc.; also = ANTIPHON 2. LME. **8** A practical reply; a responsive, corresponding, or resulting action. M16. **b** An equivalent or rival *to*. *colloq.* M20.

6 TENNYSON There must be answer to his doubt. E. O'NEILL Remember our offer. Give us your answer tomorrow. **8** SHAKES. *Haml.* If Hamlet give the first or second hit, Or quit in answer of the third exchange. C. DARWIN The answer was given by a volley of musketry. **b** *Times* Smirking juveniles being mobilized by a Seattle's answer to Harry Lauder.

answerless *a.* (*rare*) having no answer; unanswerable: M16.

answer /ˈɑːnsə/ *v.* [OE *andswarian*, f. prec.: cf. OFris. *ondswera*, ON *andsvara*.] Orig. *v.i.* w. *dat.*, through levelling of inflections later *v.t.* in nearly every sense. **I** Make an answer to a charge. **1 a** *v.i.* Reply to a charge or accusation. OE. **b** *v.t.* Defend oneself against (a charge etc.); justify. M16. **2** *v.i.* Be responsible or accountable *for*; vouch *for*. ME. **3** *v.i.* foll. by *for* (†*to*) & †*v.t.* Suffer, atone, make amends, (for). ME. **4** *v.*†*i.* & *t.* Rebut (an objection, an argument). ME. **5** *v.t.* †**a** Satisfy (a person) *of* or *for* a pecuniary claim. LME–M16. **b** Satisfy (a pecuniary claim), discharge (a debt); be sufficient for (a pecuniary liability). L15. †**6** *v.t.* Prove a satisfactory return for (an investment) or to (an investor). E16–L18. **7** *v.t.* Satisfy or fulfil (wishes, hopes, expectations, etc.). M16. **8** *v.t.* Accomplish (an end); suit (a purpose); satisfy the requirements of. M17. **9** *v.i.* Serve the purpose; prove a success; turn out (in a specified manner); be satisfactory *to* (a person). M18.

1a SHAKES. *Much Ado* It is proved already that you are little better than false knaves... How answer you for yourselves? **b** C. MARLOWE We were best look that your devil can answer the stealing of this same cup. G. B. SHAW This court has summoned all the dictators to .. answer charges brought against them. **2** AV *Gen.* 30:33 So shall my righteousnesse answere for me. E. GASKELL I'll answer for it Mrs. Goodenough saw Molly. G. B. SHAW Waiting nervously in the Hammersmith Police Court to answer for his breach of the peace. **3** SHAKES. *Jul. Caes.* If it were so, it was a grievous fault; And grievously hath Caesar answer'd it. **4** E. O'NEILL He can answer all your arguments easy—with things right out of the Bible! **5a** LD BERNERS We wolde demaunde good hostages and sufficient, to answere vs of our horses agayne. R. HOLINSHED He would be answered for such summes of monie as king Richard had taken. **b** SHAKES. *1 Hen. IV* This proud king, who studies day and night To answer all the debt he owes to you. H. MARTINEAU A few shillings .. to answer any sudden occasion. **6** SWIFT The maid will .. sell more butter and cheese than will answer her wages. **8** H. FIELDING I applied a fomentation .. which highly answered the intention. SIR W. SCOTT He offered him a beast he thought wad answer him weel eneugh. **9** W. COWPER Their labour was almost in vain before, but now it answers. LYTTON If Beatrice di Negra would indeed be rich, she might answer to himself as a wife. G. B. SHAW I tried the experiment of treating a scarlet fever case with a sample of hydrophobia serum .., and it answered capitally.

II Make an answer to a question, remark, etc. **10** *v.i.* & *t.* Reply to (a question, remark, appeal, request, or other expression of desire or opinion); speak or write in reply (to). OE. **b** Reply impertinently (to). Also (*colloq.*) *answer back*. E16. **11** *v.t.* & *i.* Respond antiphonally or canonically (to); make a responsive sound, echo. OE. **12** *v.i.* & *t.* Act in response to (a signal), acknowledge (a signal); react to a summons from (a knock, bell, etc.). L16. **13** *v.t.* & *i.* Reply favourably to (a petitioner, a petition). L16. **14** *v.t.* & *i.* Solve (a problem); respond to (a test of knowledge etc.). M18.

10 TINDALE *Luke* 13:25 He shall answer and saye vnto you: I knowe you not. AV *Job* 23:5 The words which he would answere me. R. BENTLEY Mr. B. here answers to a Question, that never was ask'd him. POPE The mighty Czar might answer, he was drunk. TENNYSON Will she answer if I call? JOYCE Answering an ad? .. Yes, Mr Bloom said. Town traveller. SCOTT FITZGERALD 'Where is he from, I mean? And what does he do?' 'Now *you're* started on the subject,' she answered with a wan smile. R. GRAVES I wrote, but he did not answer. R. P. WARREN I said I would like to answer any questions they had. S. BELLOW Everybody asks the same questions. You get tired of answering. W. FAULKNER Have they got him? Answer me. L. DURRELL Melissa still writes the spirited nonchalant letters which I have such difficulty in answering. **b** LYTTON Hush, Frank, never answer your father. H. G. WELLS The King .. admonishes him with evident severity... Against all etiquette he answers back. **11** AV *1 Sam.* 18:7 The women answered one another, as they played. DRYDEN Both alike inspir'd To sing, and answer as the Song requir'd. POPE The woods shall answer, and their echo ring. **12** JOYCE Last look at mirror always before she answers the door. S. HILL She went to answer the ringing telephone. A. AYCKBOURN I ring someone up and when they answer I say is that 2467. M. KEANE She pressed the .. bell on the table, and when Breda answered it .. she said: 'What did I want?' **answering machine** a tape recorder which supplies a recorded answer to a telephone call and sometimes also takes messages. **answering service** a business that receives and answers telephone calls for its clients. **answer to (the name of)** respond when addressed as, be called. **13** AV *Ps.* 27:7 Haue mercie also vpon mee, and answere me. TENNYSON The Gods have heard it, O Icenian! .. Doubt not ye the Gods have answer'd. O. WILDE When the gods wish to punish us they answer our prayers. **14** A. J. CRONIN When he began the written part of the examination .., he found himself answering the papers with a blind automatism.

III Correspond. **15 a** *v.i.* Correspond *to*. ME. **b** *v.t.* Correspond to. *arch.* exc. in *answer the description*. M16. †**16** *v.t.* Return the (esp. hostile) action of. LME–L16. **17** *v.t.* Give back in kind, return. L16. **18** *v.t.* & *i.* Act in sympathy or conformity (with); be responsive (to). E17.

15a AV *Gal.* 4:25 This Agar .. answereth to Ierusalem, which now is. **b** J. LOCKE The Terms of our Law .. will hardly find Words that answer them in the Spanish, or Italian. **17** SPENSER Well did the squire perceive himselfe too weake To aunswere his defiaunce in the field. J. KEBLE Answering love for love. **18** SHAKES. *Temp.* I come To answer thy best pleasure. DICKENS The girl instantly answered to the action in her sculling.

answerer *n.* E16. **answeringly** *adv.* (*rare*) correspondingly LME.

answerable /ˈɑːns(ə)rəb(ə)l/ *a.* E16. [f. prec. + -ABLE.] **1** Liable to be answered; able to be answered. E16. **2** Liable to answer, responsible, (*to* an authority, *for* a person or thing). L16. **3** Corresponding (*to*); suitable, fitting, proper, (*to*); commensurate, equivalent, (*to*). *arch.* L16.

2 SHAKES. *1 Hen. IV* If he have robb'd these men He shall be answerable. DEFOE She would be answerable for her on all accounts. SIR W. SCOTT I will be answerable that this galliard meant but some Saint Valentine's jest. E. A. FREEMAN For the good administration of which the magistrate .. was answerable to the power which appointed him. **3** J. LYLY If the courtesie of Englande be aunswerable to the custome of Pilgrimes. P. SIDNEY A likeness .. answerable enough in some features and colours, but erring in others. MILTON If answerable style I can obtaine Of my Celestial Patroness. J. REYNOLDS Render your future progress answerable to your past improvement. WELLINGTON The revenue of that Island will [not] be found answerable to its necessary expenditure.

answeraˈbility *n.* liability to be called to account, responsibility E20. **answerableness** *n.* (*a*) *arch.* correspondency, conformity; (*b*) = ANSWERABILITY: L16. **answerably** *adv.* in an answerable manner, conformably (*to*) E17.

answerphone /ˈɑːnsəfəʊn/ *n.* Also (proprietary) **Ansafone**; **ansaphone**. M20. [f. ANSWER *v.* + PHONE *n.*[2]] = *answering machine* s.v. ANSWER *v.*

ant /ant/ *n.* & *v.* [OE *æmet(t)e* = MLG *āmete*, *ēmete*, OHG *ā̆meiza* (G *Ameise*), f. WGmc, f. pref. meaning 'off, away' and base meaning 'cut, hew'. The OE forms gave two ME types, (i) *am(e)te*, whence *ant* (the prevailing standard form) and (ii) *emete* (see EMMET).] **A** *n.* **1** Any of numerous small hymenopterous insects constituting the family Formicidae, usu. wingless except in the mating season, living in complex social colonies, and proverbial for their industriousness. Cf. *velvet ant* s.v. VELVET *n.* & *a.* OE. **2** = *white ant* (a) s.v. WHITE *a.* L17.

1 *black ant, honey-pot ant, red ant, wood ant*, etc. **have ants in one's pants** *colloq.* be fidgety, be restless.
Comb.: **ant-bear** (*a*) the giant anteater, *Myrmecophaga tridactyla*; (*b*) = AARDVARK; **antbird** any of numerous insectivorous birds belonging to the neotropical family Formicariidae, usu. with dark plumage; **ant eggs, ants'-eggs** pupae or larvae of ants, used as animal food; †**ant-fly** a winged ant; **ant-heap, anthill, ant-hillock** a nest built by ants or termites in the form of a mound; **ant-lion** [tr. Gk *murmēko-leōn* in the Septuagint] any of numerous predatory insects of the neuropterous family Myrmeleontidae, whose larvae live beneath pits in which they trap small insects; **ant-orchid** a terrestrial Australasian orchid, *Chiloglottis gunnii*, with antlike flowers; **ant-plant** any of various plants (e.g. certain acacias) having hollow parts in which ants live in symbiosis with the plant; **ant-thrush** (*a*) orig., any antbird; now, any of several large antbirds; (*b*) each of four African thrushes of the genus *Neocossyphus*; (*c*) = PITTA *n.*[1]

B *v.i.* & *refl.* Of a bird: rub ants (or occas. other insects or substances) on its plumage. M20.

antlike *a.* resembling (that of) an ant L19.

an't *v.* see BE *v.*, HAVE *v.*

ant- *pref.* see ANTI-.

-ant /(ə)nt/ *suff.*[1] [Fr., or its source L *-ant-* pres. ppl stem of vbs of the 1st conjugation, or *-ent-* (see -ENT).] Forming adjs. denoting existence of action, as *pendant, repentant*, or state, as *arrogant, expectant*, and ns. denoting an agent, as *assistant, celebrant, deodorant*, usu. f. vbs. Conflicting Eng., Fr., & L analogies have produced much inconsistency of use of *-ant* and *-ent*.

-ant /(ə)nt/ *suff.*[2] (not productive). [Alt. (in OFr. & AN) of wds in *-an*.] Forming ns., as *pheasant, tyrant*, etc.

anta /'antə/ *n.* Pl. **-tae** /-tiː/, **-tas**. L16. [L.] *Archit.* A square pilaster at either side of a door or at the corner of a building. Cf. ANTES.

Antabuse /'antəbjuːs/ *n.* M20. [f. ANTI- + ABUSE *n.*] (Proprietary name for) disulfiram.

antacid /ant'asɪd/ *a.* & *n.* M18. [f. ANT- + ACID *n.*] (A substance) corrective or preventive of acidity, esp. in the stomach.

antae *n.pl.* see ANTA.

antagonise *v.* var. of ANTAGONIZE.

antagonism /an'tag(ə)nɪz(ə)m/ *n.* E19. [Fr. *antagonisme*: see next, -ISM.] 1 Mutual resistance of opposing forces; active opposition; a feeling of hostility or opposition. E19. b *Biochem.* Inhibition of or interference with the action of a substance or organism by another. L19. 2 An opposing force or principle. M19.

1 R. COBDEN The Government had not placed itself in antagonism to them. E. O'NEILL In their whole tense attitudes is clearly revealed the bitter antagonism between them. A. LURIE The antagonism we felt for the audience. A. J. P. TAYLOR The general strike seems to have produced a lessening of class antagonism. b M. C. GERALD Atropine's antagonism of acetylcholine. 2 DE QUINCEY As if resulting from mighty and equal antagonisms.

antagonist /an'tag(ə)nɪst/ *n.* & *a.* L16. [Fr. *antagoniste* or late L *antagonista* (Jerome) f. Gk *antagōnistēs*, f. as next: see -IST.] A *n.* 1 An opponent, an adversary; an opposing force. L16. 2 *Physiol.* A muscle whose action counteracts that of another. Cf. AGONIST 3. L17. 3 *Biochem.* A substance or organism which interferes with or inhibits the action of another. Cf. AGONIST 4. L19.

1 E. GLASGOW Some have said that Nature is the antagonist of happiness. C. V. WEDGWOOD The outbreak of the second war convinced the King's more ruthless antagonists that no peace could be made while he lived.

B *attrib.* or as *adj.* = ANTAGONISTIC. Now *rare.* L17.

MILTON None daring to appear antagonist. COLERIDGE Antagonist forces are necessarily of the same kind.

antago'nistic *a.* actively opposed, of the nature of an antagonist M17. **antago'nistical** *a.* (*rare*) = ANTAGONISTIC E17. **antago'nistically** *adv.* E17.

antagonize /an'tag(ə)nʌɪz/ *v.t.* Also **-ise**. M17. [Gk *antagōnizesthai*, f. as ANT- + *agōnizesthai* struggle, f. as AGON: see -IZE.] †1 Vie with, rival. Only in M17. 2 Struggle against, contend with. *arch.* M18. 3 Counteract, tend to neutralize (a force etc.). M18. 4 Render antagonistic, evoke antagonism in. M19.

1 T. HERBERT The Dodo which for shape and rarenesse may antigonize the Phoenix of Arabia. 2 KEATS Like one huge Python Antagonising Boreas. 3 R. W. EMERSON If Fate follows and limits power, power attends and antagonizes Fate. G. H. LEWES The body is balanced by an incessant shifting of the muscles, one group antagonising the other. J. G. FARRELL Our first object must be to antagonize the poison. 4 J. HELLER They conducted their duties humbly and reticently . . and went to great lengths not to antagonize anyone.

antagoni'zation *n.* L19.

antanaclasis /antə'naklәsɪs/ *n.* Pl. **-ases** /-əsiːz/. L16. [Gk: see ANT-, ANACLASIS.] *Rhet.* Repetition, esp. of a word in different or contrary senses.

antapex /ant'eɪpɛks/ *n.* Orig. †**anti-apex**. L19. [f. ANT- + APEX *n.*[1]] *Astron.* The point on the celestial sphere away from which the sun is moving. Cf. APEX *n.*[1] 4.

antaphrodisiac /ˌantafrə'dɪzɪak/ *a.* & *n.* Now *rare* or *obs.* M18. [f. ANT- + APHRODISIAC.] = ANAPHRODISIAC.

†**antapology** *n.* M17–E18. [f. ANT- + APOLOGY *n.*[1]] A reply to an apology.

Antarctic /an'tɑːktɪk/ *a.* & *n.* Also **a-**; orig. †**-art-**. LME. [OFr. *antartique* (mod. *-arct-*) or L *antarcticus* f. Gk *antarktikos* opposite to the north: see ANT-, ARCTIC.] A *adj.* 1 Orig., southern. Now usu. opposite to the Arctic; pertaining to the continent of Antarctica or the south polar regions in general. LME. †2 *fig.* Opposite, contradictory, (*to*). M17–E18.

1 **Antarctic Circle** the parallel of latitude 66° 33′ S. **Antarctic convergence** the zone of the Southern Ocean (marking a distinct climatic and ecological boundary) where the cold Antarctic surface water sinks beneath the warmer waters to the north. **Antarctic Ocean** = *Southern Ocean* s.v. SOUTHERN *a.*

B *n.* *The* south polar regions; Antarctica. LME.

ante /'anti/ *n.* & *v.* Chiefly *N. Amer.* E19. [f. as next.] A *n.* 1 In poker and similar games: a stake put up by a player before drawing cards. E19. 2 *transf.* An advance payment; a sum of money for a payment. L19.

1 *penny ante*: see PENNY *a.*

B *v.t.* Put up as ante; *transf.* bet, stake, pay *up.* M19.

ante- /'anti/ *pref.* [L *ante* prep. & adv. = before.] Forming *ns.* and *adjs.* (from adjs. or ns.) w. the sense 'before, preceding, (in place, time, or order)'.

ante-chapel *n.* the outer part at the west end of a college chapel E18. **Ante-Co'mmunion (Service)** *n.* the earlier portion of the Anglican Communion service said when there is no Eucharist E19. **ante'cubital** *a.* (*Anat.*) of or pertaining to the inner surface of the forearm L19. *ante-orbital* adj. var. of ANTORBITAL. **ante-post** *a.* (of racing odds or betting) made before the competitors' starting-numbers are known E20. **antetype** *n.* a preceding type, an earlier example E17.

anteater /'antiːtə/ *n.* M18. [f. ANT *n.* + EATER.] Any of a number of edentate mammals constituting the neotropical family Myrmecophagidae, having long, sticky, threadlike tongues and feeding chiefly on ants and termites. Also (*pop.*) any of certain other insectivorous mammals (see below).

banded anteater = NUMBAT. **Cape anteater** = AARDVARK. **giant anteater** = TAMANOIR. **scaly anteater** = PANGOLIN. **spiny anteater** = ECHIDNA.

ante-bellum /antɪ'bɛləm/ *a.* M19. [L *ante bellum* before the war.] Occurring or existing before a particular war, esp. (*US*) the American Civil War.

antebrachial /antɪ'breɪkɪəl/ *a.* M19. [f. ANTE- + BRACHIAL.] *Anat.* Of or pertaining to the forearm.

antecede /antɪ'siːd/ *v.* LME. [L *antecedere*, f. as ANTE- + *cedere* go.] †1 *v.i.* Go before, come first. LME–L17. 2 *v.t.* Precede in place, time, or order. E17.

antecedence /antɪ'siːd(ə)ns/ *n.* LME. [L *antecedentia*, f. as prec.: see -ENCE.] †1 Something which precedes; *spec.* = ANTECEDENT *n.* 2a. LME–L16. †2 *Astron.* Retrograde motion. M17–L18. 3 Precedence, priority. L17.

antecedency *n.* (*a*) = ANTECEDENCE 3; †(*b*) an antecedent condition or event: L16.

antecedent /antɪ'siːd(ə)nt/ *n.*, *a.*, & *adv.* LME. [(O)Fr. *antécédent* adj. & n. or L *antecedent-* pres. ppl stem (also in philosophy as n.) of *antecedere*: see ANTECEDE, -ENT.] A *n.* 1 *gen.* A preceding thing or circumstance. LME. 2 *spec.* a *Logic.* The statement upon which a consequence logically depends; the part of a conditional proposition on which the other part depends. LME. b *Gram.* A noun, clause, sentence, etc., to which a (usu. following and esp. relative) pronoun or adverb refers. LME. c *Math.* The first of two quantities which are linked by some relationship or operation, e.g. a ratio. L16. †3 An usher. E–M17. 4 In *pl.* The events of the past history *of* (esp. a person). M19. B *adj.* 1 Preceding in time or order. Also *pred.* & *adv.*, prior *to.* M16. 2 Presumptive, a priori. L18. 3 *Geol.* Of (systems of) streams etc.: with courses determined before the establishment of the present topography and essentially unchanged by later geological processes. L19.

antece'dental *a.* (*rare*) L18. **antecedently** *adv.* M17.

antecessor /'antɪsɛsə, antɪ'sɛsə/ *n.* LME. [L: see ANCESTOR.] A predecessor.

antechamber /'antɪtʃeɪmbə/ *n.* Orig. †**anti-**. M17. [Fr. *antichambre* f. It. *anticamera*: see ANTE-, CHAMBER *n.*] A room leading to a more important one.

antedate /'antɪdeɪt/ *n.* LME. [f. ANTE- + DATE *n.*[2]] 1 A date (affixed to a document, assigned to an event, etc.) earlier than the true one. LME. †2 A feeling of anticipation. Only in E17.

antedate /'antɪdeɪt, antɪ'deɪt/ *v.t.* L16. [f. the n.] 1 Affix an earlier than the true date to (a document). L16. 2 Carry back to an earlier time or date. *arch.* L16. 3 Anticipate. *arch.* E17. 4 Assign (an event etc.) to an earlier date; find an earlier instance of. M17. 5 Bring about at an earlier date, accelerate. *arch.* M17. 6 Precede in time, come before (something) in date. M17.

1 G. BURNET He got the king to antedate it, as if it had been signed at Oxford. 2 E. B. BROWNING That rage Barbaric, antedates the age. 3 POPE Our joys below it can improve, And antedate the bliss above. 4 DONNE Wilt thou then antedate some new-made vow? 5 SIR W. SCOTT Seem'd . . that Fate Would Camlan's ruin antedate. 6 DEFOE As if design'd by Instinct to be Great, His Judgment seem'd t'o antidate his Wit. R. V. JONES 'The Hobnails' which . . he had managed to prove antedated (1474) the first mention of hobnails in the Oxford English Dictionary (1594).

antedating *n.* (*a*) the action of marking with or assigning to an earlier date; anticipating; (*b*) an earlier instance: L16.

antediluvian /ˌantɪdɪ'luːvɪən/ *a.* & *n.* M17. [f. ANTE- + L *diluvium* DELUGE + -AN.] A *adj.* 1 Belonging, referring, or appropriate to the time before the Flood described in Genesis. M17. 2 Utterly out of date, very antiquated. *colloq.* E18. B *n.* A person who lived before the Flood; an old-fashioned or very old person. L17.

Also **antediluvial** *a.* E19.

antefix /'antɪfɪks/ *n.* Also in L form **-fixum** /-fɪksəm/, pl. **-fixa** /-fɪksə/. M19. [L *antefixum*, f. as ANTE- + use as n. of *fixus*: see FIX *v.*] *Class. Archit.* An ornament on an eave or cornice to conceal the ends of tiles; also, an ornamental head etc. making a spout from a gutter. Usu. in *pl.*

ante'fixal *a.* M19.

anteflexion /antɪ'flɛkʃ(ə)n/ *n.* M19. [f. ANTE- + FLEXION.] *Anat.* = ANTEVERSION.

'anteflexed *a.* (of the uterus) anteverted L19.

antelope /'antɪləʊp/ *n.* Pl. same, **-s**. LME. [OFr. *antelop* or med.L *ant(h)alopus* f. med.Gk *antholops* of unkn. origin and meaning.] 1 A fierce mythical creature with long serrated horns, said to haunt the banks of the Euphrates; a heraldic animal resembling this. LME. 2 Any of the more deerlike members of the ruminant family Bovidae (e.g. chamois, gnu, gazelle). Also, the pronghorn of N. America. E17.

antelopine *a.* var. of ANTILOPINE.

antelucan /antɪˈluːk(ə)n/ *a.* M17. [L *antelucanus*, f. as ANTE- + *luc-*, *lux* light: see -AN.] Of or pertaining to the hours before dawn; happening before dawn.

ante meridiem /ˌantɪ məˈrɪdɪəm/ *a.* & *adv. phr.* M16. [L: see MERIDIAN *a.*] Before midday; between midnight and the following noon. Abbrev. *a.m.*

anteme'ridian *a.* (*rare*) pertaining or appropriate to the forenoon or morning M17.

†antemetic *n.* & *a.* var. of ANTI-EMETIC.

ante-mortem /antɪˈmɔːtəm/ *a.* L19. [L *ante mortem* before death.] Made before death.

antemundane /antɪˈmʌndeɪn/ *a.* M18. [f. ANTE- + L *mundus* world + -ANE I.] Existing or occurring before the creation of the world.

antenatal /antɪˈneɪt(ə)l/ *a.* E19. [f. ANTE- + NATAL *a.*[1]] 1 Happening or existing before birth. E19. 2 *Med.* Pertaining to or concerned with the health and well-being of women during pregnancy. L19.

antenatally *adv.* L19.

antenna /anˈtɛnə/ *n.* Pl. **-nnae** /-niː/, (esp. sense 4) **-nnas**. M17. [L, alt. of *antemna* sailyard, used in pl. as tr. of Aristotle's *keraioi* 'horns' (of insects).] 1 *Zool.* Either of a pair of sensory appendages on the heads of insects, crustaceans, and some other arthropods; a feeler. M17. 2 *fig.* In *pl.* Receptive senses, means of exploration. M19. 3 *Bot.* Either of a pair of projections on the male flowers of certain orchids of the genus *Catasetum*, which when touched cause the ejection of the pollinia. M19. 4 = AERIAL *n.* Chiefly *US* & *techn.* E20.

1 G. DURRELL A weird creature . . , a pear-shaped body, long antennae that twitched indignantly. 2 E. POUND My soul's antennæ are prey to such perturbations. L. LEE Antennae of eyes and nose and grubbing fingers. 4 J. CHEEVER A north wind was howling in the television antennas. T. PYNCHON A radio transmitting station was set up on the cliff, antennas aimed at the Continent. *V antenna*: see V, V 2.

antennal, antennary *adjs.* of, pertaining to, or of the nature of antennae M19. **ante'nniferous** *a.* bearing antennae E19. **antenniform** *a.* of the form of antennae M19. **antennule** *n.* a small antenna M19.

antenuptial /antɪˈnʌpʃ(ə)l/ *a.* E19. [Late L *antenuptialis*, f. as ANTE- + NUPTIAL.] Born, occurring, etc., before marriage.

ante-orbital *a.* var. of ANTORBITAL.

antepagment /antɪˈpagm(ə)nt/ *n.* Also in L form **-pagmentum** /-pagˈmɛntəm/, pl. **-ta** /-tə/. L17. [L *antepagmentum*, f. as ANTE- + *pangere* fasten: see -MENT.] *Archit.* Each of the jambs or moulded architraves of a door. Usu. in *pl.*

antepartum /antɪˈpɑːtəm/ *a.* L19. [L *ante partum* before birth.] *Med.* Occurring not long before childbirth.

antepast /ˈantɪpɑːst/ *n. arch.* L16. [f. ANTE- + L *pastus* food: cf. REPAST *n.*, ANTIPASTO.] A first course to whet the appetite, an hors d'oeuvre; a foretaste.

antependium /antɪˈpɛndɪəm/ *n.* Also **†anti-**. L16. [med.L, f. as ANTE- + L *pendere* hang.] A veil or hanging for the front of an altar.

antepenult /antɪpɪˈnʌlt/ *a.* & *n.* L16. [Abbrev. of next.] = ANTEPENULTIMATE.

antepenultima /ˌantɪpɪˈnʌltɪmə/ *n.* Pl. **-mae** /-miː/, **-mas**. L16. [Late L (*syllaba*) *antepaenultima*, f. as ANTE- + PENULTIMA.] *Pros.* The last syllable but two of a word or verse.

antepenultimate /ˌantɪpɪˈnʌltɪmət/ *a.* & *n.* L17. [f. as ANTE- + PENULTIMATE.] A *adj.* The last but two. L17. B *n.* = prec. E18.

anteposition /ˌantɪpəˈzɪʃ(ə)n/ *n. rare.* M18. [f. ANTE- + POSITION *n.*, as if f. L *anteponere* place before: cf. POSTPOSITION.] The placing of anything in front, *esp.* (*Gram.*) in front of a word which usually precedes.

anteprandial /antɪˈprandɪəl/ *a.* E19. [f. ANTE- + L *prandium* dinner + -AL[1].] Before-dinner.

anter *n.* & *v.* see AUNTER.

ante rem /ˈantɪ rɛm/ *a.* & *adv. phr.* L19. [med.L (Albertus Magnus) = before the thing.] *Philos.* Prior to the existence of something else; *spec.* (of a universal) prior to the particular; of or pertaining to the theory that the universal is logically prior to the particular. Cf. IN RE 2, POST REM.

anterior /anˈtɪərɪə/ *a.* M16. [Fr. *antérieur* or L *anterior*, compar. f. *ante* before: see -IOR.] 1 Fore, more to the front; *esp.* in *Anat.*, situated in the front of the body, or nearer to the head, forepart, etc.; in the case of humans and other erect animals, = VENTRAL. M16. b *Bot.* Situated further away from the axis. E19. 2 Former, earlier, prior (*to*). L16.

2 R. L. STEVENSON News of their anterior home. M. LOWRY From what conceivable standpoint of rectitude did she imagine she could judge what was anterior to her arrival?

anteri'ority *n.* E18. **anteriormost** *a.* (chiefly *Biol.*) in the furthest forward position, nearest to the anterior M20. **anteriorly** *adv.* L16.

antero- /ˈantərəʊ/ *comb. form* of ANTERIOR, used (chiefly *Anat.*) to form adjs. and corresp. advs.: see -O-.

anterograde *a.* directed forwards in time; *spec.* (of amnesia) involving inability to remember new information: L19. **antero'lateral** *a.* both anterior and lateral M19. **anteropo'sterior** *a.* pertaining to front and back; directed forwards and backwards: M19. **anteropos'teriorly** *adv.* in an anteroposterior direction, frontwards and backwards M19.

ante-room /ˈantɪruːm, -rʊm/ *n.* M18. [f. ANTE- + ROOM *n.*[1], after ANTECHAMBER.] A room leading to another.

antes /ˈantiːz/ *n.pl.* L16. [Fr. repr. L *antae* pl. of ANTA.] *Archit.* Antae.

ante-temple /ˈantɪtɛmp(ə)l/ *n.* E18. [med.L *antetemplum* tr. Gk PRONAOS: see ANTE-, TEMPLE *n.*[1]] A portico of a church or ancient temple.

anteversion /antɪˈvəːʃ(ə)n/ *n.* M19. [f. ANTE- + VERSION.] *Anat.* Forward inclination of the uterus.

antevert /ˈantɪvəːt/ *v.t.* M17. [L *antevertere* anticipate, prevent, f. as ANTE- + *vertere* turn.] 1 Avert beforehand, prevent, anticipate. *rare.* M17. 2 Turn forward. Chiefly as *anteverted* ppl a. (*Anat.*, of the uterus) inclined forward. M19.

anth- /anθ/ *pref.* (no longer productive). Var. of Gk ANTI- bef. an aspirate.

anthelion /anˈθiːlɪən/ *n.* Pl. **-lia** /-lɪə/. L17. [Gk *anthēlion* neut. of *anthēlios*, earlier *antēlios* opposite to the sun, f. ANTH- + *hēlios* sun.] A parhelion opposite to the sun in the sky. Also, a glory, a halo.

anthelix /anˈθiːlɪks/ *n.* Also **antihelix** /ˈantɪhiːlɪks/. E18. [Gk: see ANTH-, HELIX 3.] *Anat.* The curved elevation within the helix of the ear.

anthelmintic /anθ(ə)lˈmɪntɪk/ *a.* & *n.* Also **-thic** /-θɪk/. L17. [f. ANTH- + Gk *helminth-*, *-mins* worm + -IC.] *Med.* A *adj.* Active against parasitic worms. L17. B *n.* An anthelmintic medicine. E18.

anthem /ˈanθəm/ *n.* & *v.* OE. [eccl.L *antiphona* ANTIPHON: sp. w. *-th-* dates from 15.] A *n.* 1 = ANTIPHON *n.* I. *arch.* OE. 2 A composition in non-metrical prose (usu. from the Scriptures or Liturgy) set to music for sacred use. LME. 3 Any song of praise and gladness; *esp.* a song (sometimes strictly a hymn) adopted by a nation to express patriotism or loyalty (usu. more fully *national anthem*). LME. B *v.t.* Celebrate in an anthem. E17.

anthemion /anˈθiːmɪən/ *n.* Pl. **-mia** /-mɪə/. M19. [Gk = flower.] A figure or ornament resembling honeysuckle.

anther /ˈanθə/ *n.* Orig. in (in sense I only in) L form **†-era**, pl. **-erae**. E16. [Fr. *anthère* or mod.L *anthera*, in cl.L medicine extracted from flowers, f. Gk *anthēra*, fem. of *anthēros* of flowers, f. *anthos* flower.] **†1** A medicine extracted from flowers, used to treat sore gums. E16–L17. 2 *Bot.* The part of the stamen in which pollen is contained and from which it is shed when mature. E18.

antheral *a.* L18.

antheridium /anθəˈrɪdɪəm/ *n.* Pl. **-dia** /-dɪə/. M19. [mod.L: see prec., -IDIUM.] *Bot.* A male reproductive organ in a cryptogam.

antheridial *a.* M19.

antherozoid /ˌanθ(ə)rəˈzəʊɪd/ *n.* Also **-zooid** /-ˈzəʊɔɪd/. M19. [f. ANTHER + -O- + ZO(O)ID.] *Bot.* A motile male gamete produced by a cryptogam or gymnosperm.

anthesis /anˈθiːsɪs/ *n.* M19. [Gk *anthēsis* flowering, f. *anthein* to blossom.] *Bot.* The time when a flower opens, or becomes sexually functional.

antho- /ˈanθəʊ/ *comb. form* of Gk *anthos* flower: see -O-.

an'thography *n.* (*rare*) scientific description of flowers L19. **antho'mania** *n.* an extravagant passion for flowers L18. **antho'maniac** *n.* (*rare*) a person with anthomania M19. **an'thophilous** *a.* (of insects etc.) frequenting flowers L19. **anthophore** *n.* (*Bot.*) a stalk which raises the receptacle above the calyx M19. **antho'xanthin** *n.* (*Chem.*) any yellow flavonoid pigment found in plants M19.

anthocyanin /anθəˈsʌɪənɪn/ *n.* Orig. **†-cyan**. M19. [G *Anthocyan*, f. Gk ANTHO- + *kuanos* blue: see -IN[1].] *Chem.* Any of a large class of blue, violet, or red flavonoid pigments found in plants.

anthocy'anidin *n.* any of the pigments of which the anthocyanins are glycosides E20.

anthology /anˈθɒlədʒi/ *n.* M17. [Fr. *anthologie* or med.L *anthologia* f. Gk, f. *anthos* flower: see -LOGY.] 1a A collection of poems by various authors, chosen as being especially fine or appropriate. M17. b A collection of other literary works or of paintings, songs, etc. L18. 2 A collection of flowers. *rare.* M18.

antho'logical *a.* †(*a*) treating of flowers; (*b*) of or relating to an anthology: E17. **anthologist** *n.* the compiler of an anthology E19. **anthologize** *v.t.* & *i.* compile an anthology (of); use in an anthology: E19.

Anthony /ˈantəni/ *n.* LME. [Name of the patron saint of swineherds, to whom one of each litter was traditionally vowed.] The smallest pig of a litter. Also *Anthony pig, hog*, etc.

See also *St Anthony('s) cross, St Anthony's fire* s.v. SAINT *n.* & *a.*, TANTONY.

Anthony Eden /ˌantənɪ ˈiːd(ə)n/ *n.* M20. [Eng. statesman, 1897–1977.] A black Homburg hat.

anthophyllite /anθəˈfɪlʌɪt, anˈθɒfɪlʌɪt/ *n.* E19. [f. mod.L *anthophyllum* clove + -ITE[1]: so called from its typical clove-brown colour.] *Min.* An orthorhombic ferromagnesian amphibole which occurs usu. as fibrous or asbestiform masses.

anthozoan /anθəˈzəʊən/ *n.* & *a.* L19. [f. mod.L *Anthozoa* (see below), f. Gk *anthos* flower + *zōia* animals + -AN.] A *n.* Any animal of the class Anthozoa of marine coelenterates, which includes sea anemones, corals, and sea-pens. L19. B *adj.* Of or pertaining to Anthozoa. L19.

anthracene /ˈanθrəsiːn/ *n.* M19. [f. Gk *anthrak-*, *anthrax*, coal + -ENE.] *Chem.* A tricyclic aromatic hydrocarbon, $C_{14}H_{10}$, found in coal tar and isolated as colourless crystals.

anthracite /ˈanθrəsʌɪt/ *n.* & *a.* L16. [Gk *anthrakitēs*, f. as prec.: see -ITE[1].] **†1** A gem described by Pliny, supposedly hydrophane. L16–M18. 2 A hard, non-bituminous kind of coal consisting of relatively pure carbon. Also *anthracite coal*. E19. 3 (Of) the dark grey colour of this coal. L19.

anthra'citic *a.* of, pertaining to, or of the nature of anthracite coal M19.

anthracnose /anˈθraknəʊs/ *n.* L19. [Fr., f. Gk *anthrak-*, *anthrax* coal + *nosos* disease.] A fungal disease of plants, characterized by dark lesions.

anthracoid /ˈanθrəkɔɪd/ *a.* L19. [f. Gk *anthrak-*, ANTHRAX + -OID.] Of a bacterium: of the kind typified by the anthrax bacillus.

anthracosis /anθrəˈkəʊsɪs/ *n.* Pl. **-coses** /-ˈkəʊsiːz/. M19. [f. as prec. + -OSIS.] *Med.* Pneumoconiosis caused by inhalation of coal dust.

anthracotic *a.* suffering from anthracosis M19.

anthracothere /ˈanθrəkəθɪə/ *n.* M19. [Fr. *anthracothère* f. Gk *anthrak-*, *anthrax* coal + *thērion* wild animal: its remains were first found in coal-bearing strata.] *Palaeont.* An extinct artiodactyl of the family Anthracotheriidae, resembling a pig, found as fossils of Middle Tertiary age.

anthranilic /anθrəˈnɪlɪk/ *a.* M19. [f. Gk *anthrax* coal + ANIL + -IC: app. so called because of a dark blue-black substance intermediate in its first preparation.] Chem. *anthranilic acid*, a colourless or yellow crystalline compound first obtained by alkaline hydrolysis of indigo; *o*-aminobenzoic acid, $C_7H_7NO_2$.
anˈthranilate *n.* a salt or ester of this acid M19.

anthraquinone /ˈanθrəkwɪnəʊn/ *n.* L19. [f. ANTHRA(CENE + QUINONE.] *Chem.* A yellow crystalline quinone, $C_{14}H_8O_2$, which is obtained by oxidation of anthracene, and is the basis of many natural and synthetic dyes. Also, any of various other quinones with similar structures.

anthrax /ˈanθraks/ *n.* LME. [L = carbuncle, f. Gk *anthrax, anthrak-* coal, carbuncle.] *Med.* **1** A carbuncle, a pustule. Now *rare* or *obs.* LME. **2** Infection with the bacterium *Bacillus anthracis*, which in animals (esp. sheep and cattle) usu. takes the form of a fatal acute septicaemia, and in humans usu. affects the skin, causing development of a pustule, or the lungs, causing woolsorters' disease, a form of pneumonia. L19.

anthropic /anˈθrɒpɪk/ *a.* M19. [Gk *anthrōpikos*, f. as next: see -IC.] Of or pertaining to humankind; human.
anthropic principle the cosmological principle that theories of the origin of the universe are constrained by the necessity to allow individual human existence.

anthropo- /ˈanθrəpəʊ/ *comb. form* of Gk *anthrōpos* human being: see -O-.
anthropoˈgenic *a.* (*a*) of or pertaining to anthropogeny; (*b*) originated by humans: L19. **anthroˈpogeny** *n.* the investigation of the origin of humans M19. **anthropogeoˈgraphical** *a.* of or pertaining to anthropogeography M17. **anthropogeˈography** *n.* human geography; geographical anthropology: L19. **†anthropography** *n.* an anatomical or ethnographic description L16–M19. **anthroˈpolatry** *n.* worship of a human being M17. **anthroˈponymy** *n.* the study of persons' names M20. **anthropoˈpsychism** *n.* the ascription of human mental characteristics to a divine being or agencies at work in nature L19. **anthropoˈsophical** *a.* of or pertaining to anthroposophy E20. **anthroˈposophy** *n.* (*a*) the knowledge of the nature of humans; human wisdom; (*b*) a movement inaugurated by Rudolf Steiner (1861–1925) to develop the faculty of cognition and the realization of spiritual reality: M18. **anthropoˈtomical** *a.* (now *rare*) of or in human anatomy M19. **anthroˈpotomist** *n.* (now *rare*) a person who studies human anatomy M19. **anthroˈpotomy** *n.* (now *rare*) the anatomy of the human body M19.

anthropocentric /ˌanθrəpəˈsɛntrɪk/ *a.* M19. [f. prec. + -CENTRIC.] Centring in humans; regarding humanity as the central fact of the universe.
anthropocentrically *adv.* M20. **anthropocentricism** /-sɪz(ə)m/, **-centrism** *ns.* an anthropocentric view or doctrine E20.

anthropoid /ˈanθrəpɔɪd/ *a.* & *n.* M19. [Gk *anthrōpoeidēs*, f. as ANTHROPO-: see -OID.] **A** *adj.* **1** Of human shape; *spec.* of or pertaining to the primate suborder Anthropoidea, comprising humans, apes, and monkeys. M19. **2** Apelike. *colloq.* M20.
1 anthropoid ape a large ape of the family Pongidae; a gorilla, orang-utan, or chimpanzee.
B *n.* A being that is human in form only; *esp.* an anthropoid ape. M19.
anthroˈpoidal *a.* M19.

anthropolite /anˈθrɒp(ə)lʌɪt/ *n.* Now *rare* or *obs.* L18. [f. ANTHROPO- + -LITE.] A petrified human being; a human fossil.

anthropological /ˌanθrəpəˈlɒdʒɪk(ə)l/*a.* E19. [f. as next + -ICAL.] Of, pertaining to, or connected with anthropology; relating to the nature of humankind.
anthropologic *a.* anthropological L17. **anthropologically** *adv.* L19.

anthropology /anθrəˈpɒlədʒi/ *n.* L16. [f. ANTHROPO- + -LOGY.] The science of humankind, in the widest sense.
cultural or **social anthropology**, the science of human social and cultural behaviour and its development. **physical anthropology**, the science of human zoology, evolution, and ecology. *social anthropology*: see *cultural anthropology* above.
¶For a time (18–19), commonly restricted essentially to human biology. Subsequently regaining its original scope, and becoming divided into the two branches defined above.
anthropologist *n.* L18. **anthropologize** *v.i.* (*colloq.*) study anthropology M20.

anthropometric /anθrəpəˈmɛtrɪk/ *a.* & *n.* L19. [f. next + -IC.] **A** *adj.* Of or pertaining to anthropometry. L19. **B** *n.* In *pl.* (treated as *sing.*). Anthropometry, now esp. as used in designing furniture and machinery. L19.
anthropometrical *a.* L19. **anthropometrically** *adv.* L19.

anthropometry /anθrəˈpɒmɪtri/ *n.* M19. [f. ANTHROPO- + -METRY.] The branch of science that deals with the measurement and proportions of the human body and their variation.
anthropometer *n.* an instrument used in anthropometry L19. **anthropometrist** *n.* a person engaged in anthropometry L19.

anthropomorph /anˈθrɒpəmɔːf, ˈanθrə-/ *n.* L19. [f. as ANTHROPOMORPHOUS.] *Art.* A representation of the human form.

anthropomorphic /anθrəpəˈmɔːfɪk/ *a.* E19. [f. as prec. + -IC.] **1** Of the nature of anthropomorphism. E19. **2** Having or representing a human form. L19.
anthropomorphical *a.* M19. **anthropomorphically** *adv.* M19.

anthropomorphise *v.* var. of ANTHROPOMORPHIZE.

anthropomorphism /anθrəpəˈmɔːfɪz(ə)m/ *n.* M18. [f. as ANTHROPOMORPHOUS + -ISM.] Ascription of human form, attributes, or personality to God, a god, an animal, or something impersonal.
anthropomorphist *n.* a person who uses anthropomorphism M19.

anthropomorphite /anθrəpəˈmɔːfʌɪt/ *n.* & *a.* Also **A-**. LME. [eccl.L *anthropomorphitae* pl. f. eccl.Gk *anthrōpomorphitai*, f. as ANTHROPOMORPHOUS: see -ITE[1].] (Designating) a member of a religious sect ascribing a human form to God.
anthropomorˈphitic *a.* M19. **†anthropomorphitical** *a.* L17–M18. **anthropomorphitism** *n.* the doctrine of anthropomorphites; anthropomorphism: M17.

anthropomorphize /anθrəpəˈmɔːfʌɪz/ *v.* Also **-ise**. M19. [f. as next + -IZE.] **1** *v.t.* Render or regard as human in form. M19. **2** *v.i.* Use anthropomorphism. M19.
anthropomorphiˈzation *n.* L19.

anthropomorphous /anθrəpəˈmɔːfəs/ *a.* M18. [f. Gk *anthrōpomorphos*, f. as ANTHROPO- + *morphē* form: see -OUS.] Of human form.

anthropopathy /anθrəˈpɒpəθi/ *n.* M17. [f. ANTHROPO- + -PATHY.] Ascription of human emotions to God.
anthropopathism *n.* = ANTHROPOPATHY M19. **anthropoˈpathic** *a.* E19. **anthropoˈpathically** *adv.* M19.

anthropophagi /anθrəˈpɒfəgʌɪ, -dʒʌɪ/ *n.pl.* Sing. (*rare*) **-gus** /-gəs/. M16. [L *anthropophagus*, *-gi* f. Gk *anthrōpophagos* man-eating, f. as ANTHROPO-: see -PHAGOUS.] Cannibals.
†anthropophaginian *n.* (*rare*, Shakes.) a cannibal: only in L16. **anthropophagite** *n.* a habitual cannibal M16.

anthropophagy /anθrəˈpɒfədʒi/ *n.* M17. [Gk *anthrōpophagia*, f. as prec.: see -Y[3].] Cannibalism.
anthropophagous /-gəs/ *a.* cannibal M19.

†anthypophora *n.* M16–M18. [L f. Gk *anthupophora*, f. as ANTH- + *hupophora* allegation.] *Rhet.* A counter-inference, a contrary allegation.

anti- /ˈanti/ *pref.* Also **ant-** bef. a vowel or aspirate (see ANTH-). [Gk = opposite, against, in exchange, instead, representing, rivalling, simulating.] Used in wds adopted (ult.) f. Gk and in Eng. wds modelled on these, and as a freely productive pref. w. the sense 'opposite, against, preventing', forming (*a*) ns. f. ns., as *antibody, -climax, -democrat*; also w. the senses 'rival, pseudo-', as *Antichrist, antipope*, 'the reverse of, unlike the conventional', as *anti-hero, antinovel*, and (w. suff. *-ism, -ist*) '(the doctrine of) a person opposed to', as *anti-Americanism, antidisestablishmentarianism* (a factitious long word), *anti-feminism, -feminist, -imperialism, -imperialist, -militarism, -militarist, -papist, -socialist, -vivisectionism, -vivisectionist*, (those in *-ist* also used attrib. or as adj.); in *Physics* designating an antiparticle of a specified particle, as *antineutrino, -proton, -quark*; in *Biol.* & *Med.* designating substances which counteract or inhibit the effect of another substance, as *anticholinesterase, -hormone, -vitamin*; in *Chem.* (usu. italicized) designating geometrical isomers of organic compounds containing C=N or N=N in which the principal atoms or groups attached to the doubly bonded atoms are on opposite sides of the plane of the double bond (opp. *syn-*); (*b*) adjs. f. adjs., the pref. acting as a prep. governing the n. implied, as *anti-American, -colonial, -inflationary, -malarial, -natural, -papal, -parliamentary, -revolutionary, -Semitic, -totalitarian, -traditional, -utilitarian*, (these can further form advs. where appropriate); these adjs. can be used ellipt. as ns., esp. *Med.* designating a drug or other agent counteracting the n. implied, as *anticonvulsant, -depressant*; (*c*) adjs. f. ns. in attrib. use, as *anti-apartheid* (demonstration etc.), *-combination* (laws etc.), *-court* (party etc.), *-missile* (missile etc.), *-noise* (regulations etc.), *-roll* (bar etc.), *-slavery* (society etc.), *-union* (feeling etc.), *-war* (literature, party, etc.).
anti-aˈbortion *a.* opposed to abortion on demand L20. **anti-aˈbortionist** *n.* & *a.* (a person who is) anti-abortion L20. **anti-ˈaircraft** *a.* & *n.* (a gun etc.) for defence against hostile aircraft E20. **anti-ˈattrition** *n.* (now *rare*) something which resists the effects of friction E19. **antibacˈterial** *a.* active against bacteria E20. **antiˈbilious** *a.* (now *rare*) of use against biliousness E19. **Anti-ˈBirmingham** *n.* (*Eng. Hist.*) an opponent of the 1680 Exclusion Bill, a Tory (cf. BIRMINGHAM) L17. **Antiˈburgher** *n.* (*Hist.*) a member of the section of the Secession Church in Scotland which held it unscriptural to take the burgess oath (cf. BURGHER 2) M18. **anti-ˈbusing, *-bussing** /-bʌsɪŋ/ *a.* (*US*) opposed to the counteracting of racial segregation by transporting pupils in buses to more distant schools M20. **antiˈcathode** *n.* in an X-ray tube, the target on which electrons from the cathode impinge, producing X-rays E20. **antiˈcatholic, anti-ˈCatholic** *a.* & *n.* (a person) opposed to what is catholic or (*esp.*) Roman Catholic M17. **anti-ˈchoice** *a.* opposed to granting choice, *spec.* to granting pregnant women the right to choose abortion L20. **antiˈclerical** *a.* & *n.* (a person who is) opposed to clerical rule or influence, esp. in politics M19. **antiˈclericalism** *n.* opposition to clerical rule or influence L19. **antiˈclockwise** *a.* & *adv.* in a direction of movement opposite to that of the hands of a clock, moving in a curve from right to left as seen from a central position L19. **antiˈcodon** *n.* (*Biochem.*) a triplet of nucleotides forming a unit of genetic code in transfer RNA, corresponding to a complementary codon in messenger RNA. **anticoˈdonic** *a.* of or pertaining to an anticodon L20. **anticonˈvulsant** *a.* & *n.* (a medicine) that prevents or retards convulsions M20. **antideˈpressant** *a.* & *n.* (a drug) that alleviates the symptoms of depression M20. **antidiuˈretic** *a.* & *n.* (a drug) that tends to inhibit the secretion of urine (*antidiuretic hormone* = VASOPRESSIN; abbrev. *ADH*) E20. **antifeˈbrific** *a.* & *n.* (now *rare*), **antiˈfebrile** *n.* & *a.* (a medicine) of use against fever M17. **antiform** *n.* (*Geol.*) a fold that is convex upwards, irrespective of the chronological sequence of the strata (opp. *synform*) M20. **antifreeze** *a.* & *n.* (designating) a chemical agent added to water in order to lower the freezing point, esp. for use in the radiator of an engine E20. **antiˈfriction** *n.* & *a.* (a substance) that reduces friction M19. **anti-ˈGallican** *a.* & *n.* (a person) opposed to what is French M18. **anti-ˈGallicanism** *n.* opposition or aversion to the French E19. **anti-god** *n.* (*a*) a rival god; (*b*) an evil demon or devil: M17. **anti-hero** *n.* a person, esp. the chief character in a novel etc., who is the opposite of or unlike a conventional hero E18. **anti-heroine** *n.* an untypical or unconventional heroine E20. **antiˈhistamine** *n.* & *a.* (a drug) that counters the physiological effects of histamine, esp. in some allergies M20. **ˌantihistaˈminic** *a.* & *n.* = ANTIHISTAMINE M20. **antihyˈsteric** *n.* & *a.* (now *rare*) (a medicine) of use against hysteria M18. **antihyˈsterical** *a.* (*rare*) = ANTIHYSTERIC *a.* M17. **anti-ˈJacobin** *a.* & *n.* (a person) opposed to the Jacobins (1789) or to the French

Revolution E19. **antiknock** *n.* & *a.* (designating) a substance added to motor fuel to prevent detonation in the engine E20. **anti-life** *n.* & *a.* (a principle or attitude) opposed to living fully and harmoniously with the natural order E20. **anti-lock(ing)** *a.* (of a vehicle braking system) designed to prevent the wheels from locking L20. **antima'larial** *a.* & *n.* (a drug) of use against malaria M20. **antimatter** *n.* (*Physics*) matter whose elementary particles are the antiparticles of those (electrons, protons, etc.) making up normal matter M20. **antime'tabolite** *n.* a substance resembling a metabolite and interfering with normal metabolic processes M20. †**antimonarchial** *a.* = ANTIMONARCHICAL L17–M18. †**antimonarchic** *a.* = ANTIMONARCHICAL M17–M18. **antimo'narchical** *a.* opposed to monarchy E17. **anti'monarchist** *n.* a professional opponent of monarchs and monarchy M17. **anti-'national** *a.* opposed to one's own nation or to a national party E19. **antineo'plastic** *n.* & *a.* (a drug) that suppresses neoplasia M20. †**antinephritic(al)** *adjs.* & *ns.* (a medicine) of use against kidney disease M17–M19. **antinode** *n.* (*Physics*) a point or line at which the amplitude of a vibrating system is a maximum L19. **antinovel** *n.* a novel of an unconventional or untraditional, often experimental, type M20. **anti-'nuclear** *a.* opposed to nuclear weapons M20. **anti-odon'talgic** *a.* (*rare*) of use against toothache E19. **anti'oxidant** *n.* & *a.* (an agent) that inhibits oxidation M20. **anti'parallel** *a.* (chiefly *Physics*) parallel but moving or oriented in opposite directions M17. **antiparticle** *n.* (*Physics*) an elementary particle having the same mass as a given particle but an opposite electrical charge, or (in the case of an uncharged particle) an opposite magnetic moment; a particle of antimatter: M20. **antiperi'staltic** *a.* (*Physiol.*) acting contrary to peristaltic motion E18. **anti-perso'nnel** *a.* (of bombs, weapons, etc.) designed to kill, injure, or obstruct human beings M20. **anti'perspirant** *n.* & *a.* (a substance) tending to inhibit perspiration M20. †**antipestilential** *a.* of use against pestilence M17–E19. **antipole** *n.* the opposite pole; *fig.* the direct opposite: E19. **antipru'ritic** *n.* & *a.* (a substance) that relieves itching L19. **antipsy'chotic** *n.* & *a.* (a drug) used to treat psychotic disorders L20. **antipy'retic** *n.* & *a.* (a medicine) that tends to reduce fever L17. **antira'chitic** *a.* (*Med.*) preventing or curing rickets M19. **anti'resonance** *n.* (*Physics*) a condition in which an interaction or a response has a minimum value E20. **ˌantisabba'tarian** *a.* & *n.* (a person) opposed to the observance of the Sabbath M17. **antiscor'butic** *a.* & *n.* (a medicine) that prevents or cures scurvy M17. †**antiscorbutical** *a.* = ANTISCORBUTIC *a.* M17–M18. **anti'scriptural** *a.* opposed to Scripture L17. †**antiscripturist** *n.* a person who denies the truth and authority of Scripture M17–M18. **anti-self** *n.* an adopted persona that is the opposite of the conscious normal self E20. **anti-'Semite** *n.*, **anti-Se'mitic** *a.* (a person) hostile to Jews L19. **anti-'Semitism** *n.* hostility or opposition to Jews L19. **antiserum** *n.*, pl. **-ra**, *Med.* a serum containing antibodies, usu. for a particular antigen E20. **antispas'modic** *a.* & *n.* (*Med.*) (a medicine) of use against involuntary-muscle spasm L17. **anti'static** *a.* counteracting the effects of static electricity M20. **ˌantisyphi'litic** *n.* & *a.* (a medicine) of use against syphilis M19. **antite'tanic** *n.* & *a.* (a drug) that counteracts or prevents tetanus L19. **anti'theism** *n.* opposition to belief in the existence of a god M19. **anti'theist** *n.* a person opposed to belief in the existence of a god M19. **antithe'istic** *a.* of or pertaining to antitheists, opposed to belief in a god M19. **anti'toxic** *a.* (*Physiol.*) of the nature of, pertaining to, or containing an antitoxin L19. **antitoxin** *n.* (*Physiol.*) an antibody effective against an antigenic (usu. bacterial) toxin L19. **antitrade (wind)** *n.* (*phr.*) (*Meteorol.*) orig., any of the prevailing westerly winds of middle latitudes; now, a contrary wind blowing at a high altitude above the trade wind: M19. **antitragus** *n.* (*Anat.*) a small cartilaginous projection above the lobe of the ear, opposite the tragus M19. **ˌantitrini'tarian** *n.* & *a.* (a person) opposed to the doctrine of the Trinity E17. **anti-'trust** *a.* (*US*) opposed to trusts or similar monopolistic combinations L19. **antive'nene** *n.* an antiserum for a snake venom or other animal poison L19. **anti'venin** *n.* = ANTIVENENE E20. **anti'viral** *a.* acting against viruses L20. **anti'virus** *n.* an antiviral agent M20.

†**anti-apex** *n.* see ANTAPEX.

antibiosis /ˌantɪbʌɪˈəʊsɪs/ *n.* L19. [f. ANTI- + SYM)BIOSIS *n.*] *Biol.* Antagonism between organisms (opp. *symbiosis*); *esp.* the action of antibiotics.

antibiotic /ˌantɪbʌɪˈɒtɪk/ *a.* & *n.* M19. [f. ANTI- + Gk *biōtikos* fit for life, f. *bios* life: see -OTIC.] A *adj.* †1 Doubting the possibility of life (in a particular environment). M–L19. 2 Injurious to or destructive of living matter, esp. micro-organisms; of or pertaining to antibiotics. L19. B *n.* A substance which is capable of destroying or inhibiting the growth of bacteria or other micro-organisms; *spec.* one that is produced by another micro-organism (or is a synthetic analogue of a microbial product), and is used therapeutically. M20.

¶ Rare bef. M20.

antibody /ˈantɪbɒdi/ *n.* E20. [f. ANTI- + BODY *n.*, tr. G *Antikörper*.] *Physiol.* A protein produced in the body which reacts with a given antigen (whose introduction usu. stimulates its formation).

Comb.: **antibody-negative, -positive** *adjs.* in which antibodies associated with a particular antigen (esp. with HIV) are absent or present.

antic /ˈantɪk/ *n.*, *a.*, & *v.* Also †**antique**. See also ANTIQUE. E16. [It. *antico* ancient, f. L *antiquus*, *anticus* ANTIQUE, used in Eng. = *grottesco*: see GROTESQUE.] A *n.* 1 A grotesque or absurd posture or action. Usu. in *pl.* E16. †2 *Archit.* & *Art.* A grotesque or fantastic ornamental representation of a person, animal, or thing; a gargoyle's grotesque face. M16–M19. 3 A clown; a mountebank; a merry-andrew. *arch.* M16. †4 A grotesque pageant or theatrical representation. L16–L17.

1 J. MONTAGUE For an instant / you smile to see / his antics. 2 C. MARLOWE To make his monks . . stand like apes, And point like antics at his triple crown. 3 DEFOE Dancing and hallooing like an antic. 4 SHAKES. *L.L.L.* Some delightful ostentation, or show, or pageant, or antic, or firework.

B *adj.* 1 Grotesque, bizarre, fantastically incongruous. *arch.* M16. †2 Of the face or features: grotesquely distorted (see sense A.2 above). L16–L17.

1 E. HALL A fountayne of embowed woorke . . ingrayled with anticke woorkes. SHAKES. *Haml.* How strange or odd some'er I bear myself—As I perchance hereafter shall think meet To put an antic disposition on. SWIFT Two rows of guards . . dressed after a very antic manner. WORDSWORTH An antic pair Of monkeys on his back. E. LINKLATER Juan was moved to something between fear and antic laughter.

C *v.* Infl. **-ck-**. 1 *v.i.* & *t.* w. *it.* Perform antics, act as an antic. *arch.* L16. †2 *v.t.* Make grotesque. *rare* (Shakes.). Only in E17.

anticly *adv.* (*arch.*) grotesquely M16.

†**antichamber** *n.* see ANTECHAMBER.

Antichrist /ˈantɪkrʌɪst/ *n.* OE. [OFr. *antecrist* (mod. *antéchrist*) or eccl.L *antichristus* f. Gk *antikhristos* (1 John 2:18), f. as ANTI- + CHRIST.] 1 A great personal opponent of Christ, expected by the early Church to appear before the end of the world. OE. 2 Any opponent of Christ. ME.

antichristian /antɪˈkrɪstʃ(ə)n, -tɪən/ *a.* & *n.* Also **A-**. M16. [f. prec. after CHRISTIAN *n.*, *a.*; senses A.2 and B.2 w. extended meaning, as if f. ANTI- + CHRISTIAN *n.*, *a.*] A *adj.* 1 Of or pertaining to Antichrist. M16. 2 Opposed to what is Christian or to Christianity. L16. B *n.* †1 A follower of Antichrist. Only in M16. 2 An opponent of Christianity. E17.

antichristianism *n.* (*a*) the system of Antichrist; (*b*) the quality of being opposed to Christianity; an antichristian act or belief: L16. **antichristi'anity** *n.* (long *rare*) = ANTICHRISTIANISM M16. †**antichristianize** *v.i.* oppose Christ M17–E18. **antichristianly** *adv.* L16.

†**antichronism** *n.* E17–E18. [Gk *antikhronismos* use of one tense for another, f. as ANTI- + *khronos* time, tense + *-ismos* -ISM.] Contradiction of true chronology; anachronism.

antichthon /anˈtɪkθəʊn/ *n.* Pl. (in sense 1) †**-ones**. M16. [Gk *antikhthōn* use as n. of adj. (sc. *gē* earth), f. as ANTI- + *khthōn* earth, ground.] †1 The antipodes; in *pl.*, their inhabitants. M16–M18. 2 *Hist. Sci.* A supposed counterpart of the earth in the heavens. M17.

anticipant /anˈtɪsɪp(ə)nt/ *a.* & *n.* *arch.* E16. [L *anticipant-* pres. ppl stem of *anticipare*: see next, -ANT[1].] A *adj.* 1 Acting in advance. E16. 2 Apprehending beforehand, expectant. L18. B *n.* A person who anticipates something. M19.

anticipate /anˈtɪsɪpeɪt/ *v.* M16. [L *anticipat-* pa. ppl stem of *anticipare*, f. as ANTE- + *cip-* var. of base of *capere* take: see -ATE[3]. Partly after Fr. *anticiper*.] 1 *v.t.* Take into consideration or mention before the due time. M16. b *v.i.* Consider something too soon; raise a matter too soon. E18. 2 *v.t.* Observe or practise in advance of the due time; cause (a future event) to be a reality beforehand; cause to happen earlier, accelerate. M16. †3 *v.i.* Occur earlier. L16–M17. †4 *v.t.* Seize or take possession of beforehand. L16–L18. 5 *v.t.* Take action in advance regarding; forestall. E17. 6 *v.t.* Use or spend in advance. L17. 7 *v.t.* Look forward to; *colloq.* expect. M18.

1 R. BAXTER You shall not again tempt me to anticipate the question of effectual Grace. b JOYCE I understand you to suggest there was misconduct with one of the brothers. . . But perhaps I am anticipating? 2 SIR W. SCOTT To anticipate by half an hour the usual time of his arrival. BYRON Some leap'd overboard . . As eager to anticipate their grave. C. BRONTË Some real lives do . . actually anticipate the happiness of Heaven. A. J. P. TAYLOR Both British and French tried to anticipate the future. 3 SIR T. BROWNE The Equinoxes had anticipated. 4 W. COWPER To soar, and to anticipate the skies. 5 M. MCCARTHY It was the job of a good servant to read his master's mind and anticipate his wishes. J. LE CARRÉ I'm sorry—do go on. I do not mean to anticipate you. DAY LEWIS To sustain the singer, . . and anticipate every change of volume and tempo. 6 CLARENDON To carry on that vast Expence, the Revenue of the Crown had been Anticipated. 7 G. K. CHESTERTON The interview which was promised him . . he anticipated with a particular pleasure. S. LEWIS I don't anticipate we'll have any more real cold weather now. A. TOFFLER In the future, we can anticipate networks that broadcast for such specialized occupational groups as engineers, accountants and attorneys. A. EDEN They would anticipate that . . their descendents would work on the estate for many generations.

anticipatingly *adv.* with anticipation M19. **anticipative** *a.* (*a*) of the nature of anticipation; (*b*) given to anticipation, expectant: M17. **anticipatively** *adv.* E17. **anticipator** *n.* a person who anticipates something L16. **anticipatorily** *adv.* (*rare*) in anticipation, beforehand L19. **anticipatory** *a.* of the nature of anticipation M17.

anticipation /antɪsɪˈpeɪʃ(ə)n/ *n.* LME. [Fr., or L *anticipatio(n-)*, f. as prec.: see -ATION.] 1 Introduction in advance, *spec.* in *Mus.* of part of a chord which is about to follow. LME. †2 Occurrence in advance of the expected time. LME–M19. 3 Prior action that meets beforehand, provides for, or precludes the action of another; forestalling of an event. LME. 4 Intuition; presentiment. *arch.* M16. 5 The using of money before it is at one's disposal; a sum so used in advance. M16. †6 Prepossession, prejudice. M17–E18. 7 Contemplation or consideration in advance; the action of looking forward to something; (esp. eager or pleasurable) expectation. E18.

anticlimax /antɪˈklʌɪmaks/ *n.* E18. [f. ANTI- + CLIMAX *n.*] 1 *Rhet.* The addition of a particular which, against expectation, suddenly lowers the effect; the opposite of climax. E18. 2 An ineffective end where a climax is expected; a descent contrasting with a previous rise. E19.

ˌanticli'mactic *a.* of the nature of an anticlimax L19. **ˌanticli'mactically** *adv.* E20.

anticlinal /antɪˈklʌɪn(ə)l/ *a.* E19. [f. ANTI- + Gk *klinein* to lean, slope + -AL[1].] 1 *Geol.* Pertaining to or of the nature of an anticline. Opp. *synclinal*. E19. 2 *Anat.* Of a vertebra: having an upright spine, towards which the spines of adjacent vertebrae incline. L19. 3 *Bot.* Of a cell wall etc.: perpendicular to the surface of the meristem. Of growth: taking place by the formation of anticlinal walls. Opp. *periclinal*. L19.

anticlinally *adv.* M19.

anticline /ˈantɪklʌɪn/ *n.* M19. [f. as prec. after INCLINE *n.*] *Geol.* A fold from whose axis the strata incline downwards on either side. Opp. SYNCLINE.

anticli'norium *n.*, pl. **-ria** /-rɪə/, a system of folds which has an overall anticlinal form L19.

anticoagulant /ˌantɪkəʊˈagjʊl(ə)nt/ *a.* & *n.* E20. [f. ANTI- + COAGULANT.] (A substance) that inhibits coagulation of the blood.

anticoagulate *v.t.* treat with an anticoagulant M20. **anticoagu'lation** *n.* M20.

anticyclone /antɪ'sʌɪkləʊn/ *n.* M19. [f. ANTI- + CYCLONE.] *Meteorol.* A pressure system characterized by a high central barometric pressure and a slow clockwise (northern hemisphere) or anticlockwise (southern hemisphere) circulation.

anticy'clonic *a.* of, pertaining to, of the nature or characteristic of an anticyclone L19. **anticy'clonically** *adv.* L19.

antidoron /antɪ'dɔːrɒn/ *n.* M19. [Gk *antidōron*, f. as ANTI- + *dōron* gift.] *Orthodox Ch.* The unconsecrated bread remaining after the Eucharistic Liturgy, blessed by the priests and given to non-communicants as well as communicants.

†antidotary *n.* & *a.* LME. [med.L *antidotarius*, *-um*, f. *antidotum*: see next, -ARY[1]. Cf. Fr. *antidotaire*.] **A** *n.* A book describing antidotes; also, a dispensary. LME–E18. **B** *adj.* Of the nature of an antidote. L16–M17.

antidote /'antɪdəʊt/ *n.* LME. [Fr., or L *antidotum* f. Gk *antidoton* use as n. of neut. of *antidotos*, f. as ANTI- + *do-* stem of *didonai* give.] **1** A medicine given to counteract the effects of a poison (or, formerly, a disease). (Foll. by *against*, *for*, *to*.) LME. **2** *fig.* Something which counteracts an evil. (With constructions as sense 1.) M16.

antidotal *a.* pertaining to or of the nature of an antidote M17.

antidote /'antɪdəʊt/ *v.t.* M17. [f. prec., after med.L *antidotare*, Fr. *antidoter*.] **†1** Provide with an antidote; fortify against an evil. M17–E18. **2** Administer an antidote against; counteract (a poison, an evil). M17.

antidromic /antɪ'drəʊmɪk/ *a.* E20. [f. ANTI- + Gk *dromos* running + -IC.] *Physiol.* Of an impulse: travelling in the opposite direction to that normal in a nerve fibre. Opp. ORTHODROMIC 2.

antidromically *adv.* E20.

anti-emetic /ˌantɪɪ'mɛtɪk/ *n.* & *a.* Also **†antemetic**. E18. [f. ANTI- + EMETIC.] (A medicine) serving to prevent vomiting.

antiferromagnetic /ˌantɪfɛrəʊmag'nɛtɪk/ *a.* M20. [f. ANTI- + FERROMAGNETIC.] *Physics.* Designating or exhibiting a form of magnetism characterized by an antiparallel alignment of adjacent electron spins in a crystal lattice.

'antiferro,magnet *n.* an antiferromagnetic substance M20. **antiferro'magnetism** *n.* M20.

anti-g /antɪ'dʒiː/ *a.* M20. [f. ANTI- + *g* = acceleration due to gravity.] Of clothing (for pilots etc.): designed to counter the effects of high acceleration.

antigen /'antɪdʒ(ə)n/ *n.* E20. [G f. Fr. *antigène*, f. as ANTI-, -GEN.] *Physiol.* A foreign substance which, when introduced into the body, stimulates the production of an antibody.

anti'genic *a.* of the nature of or pertaining to an antigen E20. **anti'genically** *adv.* M20. **antige'nicity** *n.* M20.

antigorite /an'tɪgərʌɪt/ *n.* M19. [f. *Antigorio*, a valley in Piedmont, Italy + -ITE[1].] *Min.* A magnesium silicate mineral of the serpentine group, occurring usu. as thin green plates.

antigravity /antɪ'gravɪti/ *a.* & *n.* E20. [f. ANTI- + GRAVITY.] **A** *adj.* Acting in opposition to the effects of gravity or of high acceleration; (of muscles) serving to maintain the erect posture of the body. E20. **B** *n.* A (hypothetical) force opposed to that of gravity. M20.

Also **anti-grav** *a.* & *n.* (*colloq.*) M20.

Antiguan /an'tiːg(w)ən/ *a.* & *n.* M19. [f. *Antigua* (see below) + -AN.] (A native or inhabitant) of the W. Indian island of Antigua, part of the country Antigua and Barbuda.

antihelix *n.* var. of ANTHELIX.

Antillean /an'tɪlɪən/ *a.* L19. [f. *Antilles* (see below) + -AN.] Of or pertaining to the Antilles, a group of islands in the W. Indies.

antilog /'antɪlɒg/ *n.* *colloq.* E20. [Abbrev.] = next.

antilogarithm /antɪ'lɒgərɪð(ə)m/ *n.* M17. [f. ANTI- + LOGARITHM.] *Math.* **†1** The logarithm of the complementary trigonometrical function (to a sine etc.), or the complement of the logarithm of a sine etc. *rare.* M17–L18. **2** The number to which a given logarithm belongs. L17.

ˌantiloga'rithmic *a.* of or pertaining to antilogarithms M18.

antilogism /an'tɪlədʒɪz(ə)m/ *n.* E20. [f. Gk *antilogia* (see next) + -ISM: cf. late Gk *antilogismos*.] *Logic.* A set of three propositions which cannot be true together.

antilogy /an'tɪlədʒi/ *n.* E17. [Fr. *antilogie* (= med.L *antilogium*, *-gia*) f. Gk *antilogia* contradiction, f. ANTI- + *-logia* -LOGY.] A contradiction in terms or ideas.

antilopine /an'tɪləpʌɪn/ *a.* Also **ante-**. E19. [f. mod.L *antilopus* ANTELOPE + -INE[1].] Pertaining to or characteristic of an antelope; of the nature of or resembling an antelope.

antimacassar /ˌantɪmə'kasə/ *n.* Now chiefly *Hist.* M19. [f. ANTI- + MACASSAR.] A cover put over the backs (and arms) of chairs etc. as a protection against grease or as an ornament.

antimacassared *a.* covered or adorned with an antimacassar E20.

antimasque /'antɪmɑːsk/ *n.* Also **-mask**. E17. [f. ANTI- + MASQUE *n.*] A grotesque interlude as a contrast, given between the acts of a masque.

antimasquer *n.* a performer in an antimasque M17.

antimeric /antɪ'mɛrɪk/ *a.* L19. [f. Gk ANTI- opposite + *meros* part + -IC.] Characterized by the existence of or designating forms which are mirror-images of each other.

'antimer(e) *n.* either of a pair of antimeric forms; an enantiomorph: L19.

antimonate /'antɪməneɪt, antɪ'məʊneɪt/ *n.* M19. [f. ANTIMONY + -ATE[1].] *Chem.* A salt of antimonic acid.

Also **anti'moniate** *n.* (now *rare*) E19.

antimonial /antɪ'məʊnɪəl/ *a.* & *n.* E17. [f. ANTIMONY + -AL[1].] **A** *adj.* Of or pertaining to antimony; containing antimony. E17. **B** *n.* A medicine containing antimony E18.

antimonian *a.* = ANTIMONIAL *a.*; *esp.* (*Min.*) containing antimony: M17.

antimonic /antɪ'mɒnɪk/ *a.* E19. [f. ANTIMONY + -IC.] *Chem.* Of pentavalent antimony.

antimonic acid a colloidal acid, $HSb(OH)_6$ (approx.), formed e.g. when antimony pentachloride is hydrolysed.

antimonide /'antɪmənʌɪd, antɪ'məʊ-/ *n.* M19. [f. ANTIMONY + -IDE.] *Chem.* A compound of antimony with a more electropositive element.

antimonious /antɪ'məʊnɪəs/ *a.* E19. [f. ANTIMONY + -OUS.] *Chem.* Of trivalent antimony.

antimonious acid the hypothetical parent acid of antimonites.

antimonite /'antɪmənʌɪt, antɪ'məʊnʌɪt/ *n.* E19. [f. ANTIMONY + -ITE[1].] **1** *Chem.* A salt formed (as) by reaction of antimony trioxide with alkalis. E19. **2** *Min.* = STIBNITE. *rare.* M19.

antimony /'antɪməni/ *n.* LME. [med.L *antimonium*, of unkn. origin.] **1** The mineral stibnite, Sb_2S_3. *obs.* exc. as in phrs. below. LME. **2** A brittle silvery-white metalloid chemical element, atomic no. 51, of which stibnite is the chief ore, used in many alloys (e.g. type-metal). (Symbol Sb.) E19.

Phrases: **black antimony** (*a*) *arch.* stibnite; (*b*) an unstable non-metallic allotrope of antimony. *glass of antimony*: see GLASS *n.* **grey antimony** *arch.* stibnite. REGULUS *of antimony*. **white antimony** *arch.* antimony trioxide, Sb_2O_3.

Comb.: **antimony ochre** cervantite or a similar mineral; antimony tetroxide, Sb_2O_4.

anti'moniated *a.* combined or impregnated with antimony E18.

antinomian /antɪ'nəʊmɪən/ *a.* & *n.* M17. [f. med.L *Antinomi*, name of the sect, f. as next, + -AN.] **A** *adj.* Opposed to the obligatoriness of moral law; of or pertaining to the antinomians. M17. **B** *n.* A person who maintains that the moral law is not binding on Christians; *spec.* a member of a 16th-cent. sect in Germany alleged to hold this opinion. M17.

antinomianism *n.* M17.

antinomy /an'tɪnəmi/ *n.* L16. [L *antinomia* f. Gk, f. as ANTI- + *nomos* law: see -Y[3]. Cf. Fr. *antinomie*.] **1** A contradiction in a law, or between two laws; a conflict of authority. L16. **†2** A contradictory law or principle. Only in M17. **3** (After Kant.) A paradox; intellectual contradictoriness. L18.

anti'nomic *a.* (*rare*) M19. **anti'nomical** *a.* (*rare*) L19.

Antiochene /an'tʌɪəkiːn/ *n.* & *a.* M19. [L *Antiochenus*, f. *Antiochia* Antioch.] *Eccl. Hist.* (An adherent) of the theological school represented by the church at Antioch in Syria in the 4th and 5th cents.

Also **Antiochian** /antɪ'ɒkɪən/ *a.* & *n.* M19.

†antipape *n.* see ANTIPOPE.

antipasto /antɪ'pɑːstəʊ/ *n.* Pl. **-ti** /-ti/, **-tos**. E17. [It., f. as ANTEPAST.] An appetizer, an hors d'oeuvre.

¶ Rare bef. M20.

antipathetic /ˌantɪpə'θɛtɪk/ *a.* M17. [f. as ANTIPATHY, after PATHETIC.] Having an antipathy or constitutional aversion; opposed in nature or tendency (*to*).

antipathetical *a.* E17. **antipathetically** *adv.* M17.

antipathic /antɪ'paθɪk/ *a.* M19. [f. next + -IC.] Of or pertaining to antipathy; of a contrary nature or character (*to*).

antipathy /an'tɪpəθi/ *n.* L16. [Fr. *antipathie* or L *antipathia* f. Gk *antipatheia*, f. *antipathēs* opposed in feeling, f. as ANTI- + PATHOS: see -Y[3].] **†1** Contrariety of feeling, nature, or disposition (*with* a thing, *between* things). L16–L17. **2** Constitutional or settled aversion (*against*, *for*, *to*; *between* persons). E17. **†3a** Something contrary to nature. Only in E17. **b** An object of constitutional or settled aversion. L17.

antipathist *n.* (*rare*) a person possessed by an antipathy, a natural enemy E19. **†antipathize** *v.* (*a*) *v.i.* feel or show antipathy; (*b*) *v.t.* render antipathetic: M17–L18. **antipathous** *a.* (*rare*) antipathetic E17.

†antipendium *n.* var. of ANTEPENDIUM.

antiperistasis /ˌantɪpə'rɪstəsɪs/ *n.* *arch.* L16. [Gk, f. as ANTI- + *peristasis* standing round. Cf. Fr. *antiperistase* (16).] Opposition or contrast of circumstances; resistance, reaction.

antiphlogistic /ˌantɪflə'dʒɪstɪk, -'gɪst-/ *a.* & *n.* Now *rare.* M18. [f. ANTI- + PHLOGISTIC.] **A** *adj.* **1** *Med.* Counteracting inflammation. M18. **2** *Hist.* Opposed to the theory of phlogiston. L18. **B** *n.* A medicine counteracting inflammation. M18.

antiphlo'gistian *n.* & *a.* (*Hist.*) (a person) opposed to the theory of phlogiston L18.

Antiphlogistine /ˌantɪflə'dʒɪstiːn/ *n.* Also **a-**; **-in** /-ɪn/. E20. [f. prec. + -INE[5].] (Proprietary name for) a kind of kaolin poultice.

antiphon /'antɪf(ə)n/ *n.* LME. [eccl.L *antiphona* fem. sing. f. Gk neut. pl. of *antiphōnos* responsive, f. as ANTI- + *phōnē* sound. Cf. ANTHEM.] **1** A composition consisting of passages or verses sung or recited responsively by a choir. LME. **2a** A versicle or sentence sung by one choir in response to another. M17. **b** *transf.* A response, an echo, an answer. M17.

anti'phonic *a.* (*rare*) antiphonal, mutually responsive M19. **anti'phonically** *adv.* M19.

antiphonal /an'tɪfən(ə)l/ *n.* & *a.* E16. [f. prec. + -AL[1]. Cf. OFr. *antiphonal*.] **A** *n.* = ANTIPHONARY. E16. **B** *adj.* **1** Of the nature of an antiphon; sung alternately. L17. **2** Responsive (*to*). M19

antiphonally *adv.* M18.

antiphonary /an'tɪf(ə)nəri/ *n.* E17. [eccl.L *antiphonarium*, f. as ANTIPHON: see -ARY[1].] A book of antiphons; a collection of antiphons.

antiphoner /an'tɪf(ə)nə/ *n.* *arch.* LME. [OFr. *antiphonier* f. as prec.: see -ER[2].] = prec.

antiphony /an'tɪf(ə)ni/ *n.* M16. [f. ANTIPHON + -Y[3], partly through OFr. *antiphonie*.] **1** = ANTIPHON 2a. M16. **b** = ANTIPHON 2b. M17. **2** Opposition of sound, antiphonal effect. E17. **3** Antiphonal singing. M18.

antiphrasis /an'tɪfrəsɪs/ *n.* Pl. **-ases** /-əsiːz/. M18. [Late L f. Gk, f. *antiphrazein* express by the opposite, f. as ANTI- + *phrazein* indicate, declare, tell.] *Rhet.* Use of words in a sense opposite to their customary meaning.

For other words beginning with *anti-* see the entry for **anti-**

antipodal /an'tɪpəd(ə)l/ *a.* & *n.* M17. [f. ANTIPODES + -AL[1].] A *adj.* 1 Of or pertaining to the antipodes; situated on the opposite side of the earth (*to*). M17. 2 Diametrically opposite (*to*). M17. 3 *Bot.* Designating cells formed at the chalazal end of the embryo sac. L19. B *n. Bot.* An antipodal cell. M20.

antipode /'antɪpəʊd/ *n.* Pl. of sense 3 pronounced /'antɪpəʊdz/. E17. [Back-form. f. ANTIPODES.] †1 An inhabitant of the opposite side of the earth. (For pl. see ANTIPODES 1.) Only in E17. 2 The exact opposite (*of, to*). (For pl. see ANTIPODES 3.) M17. 3 *Chem.* An enantiomorphic compound. L19.

antipodean /ˌantɪpə'diːən/ *a.* & *n.* M17. [Irreg. f. next + -AN.] A *adj.* 1 Diametrically opposite (*to*). M17. 2 Using the feet rather than the hands; upside down. E19. 3 Of or pertaining to the opposite side of the earth, *esp.* Australasian. M19. B *n.* 1 A person who lives on the opposite side of the earth; a native or inhabitant of the antipodes. M17. 2 A juggler with the feet. L19. 3 An exact opposite (*to*). E20.

antipodes /an'tɪpədiːz/ *n.pl.* (sense 3 also treated as *sing.*). Also A-. LME. [Fr., or late L f. Gk pl. of *antipous* having the feet opposite, f. as ANTI- + *pous, pod-* foot.] †1 Those who live on the opposite side of the earth to each other or to oneself. LME–M19. b *fig.* Those in any way resembling the inhabitants of the opposite side of the earth. Only in 17. 2 Places on the surface of the earth directly or diametrically opposite to each other; a place diametrically opposite to another, *esp.* Australasia as the region on the opposite side of the earth to Europe. M16. 3 Exact opposites. Also as *sing.*, = ANTIPODE 2. (Foll. by *of, to.*) E17. 4 See ANTIPODE 3.

1b BACON He will neuer be one of the Antipodes, to tread opposite to the present world. 2 SHAKES. *Much Ado* I will go on the slightest errand now to the Antipodes. A. R. WALLACE New Zealand, almost the antipodes of Britain. 3 SIR T. BROWNE Fools . . are antipodes unto the wise. O. HENRY Passengers . . saw them seated together, and wondered at the conflux of two such antipodes. E. B. TITCHENER Common sense is the very antipodes of science.

¶Formerly trisyllabic '*antipodes*; later pronunc. after Gk & L.

antipope /'antɪpəʊp/ *n.* Also A-; orig. †-pape. LME. [Fr. *antipape* f. med.L *antipapa* (after *antichristus* ANTICHRIST), later assim. to POPE *n.*[1]] A person set up as Pope in opposition to one (held by others to be) canonically chosen.

antiquarian /antɪ'kwɛːrɪən/ *n.* & *a.* E17. [f. as ANTIQUARY: see -ARIAN.] A *n.* = ANTIQUARY *n.* 2. E17. B *adj.* Of or connected with the study of antiquities or antiques. L18.

antiquarianism *n.* the profession or pursuits of the antiquarian; taste for or devotion to antiquities: L18. **antiquarianize** *v.i.* (*colloq.*) pursue antiquarianism E19.

antiquary /'antɪkwəri/ *n.* & *a.* M16. [L *antiquarius*, f. *antiquus*: see ANTIQUE, -ARY[1]. Cf. Fr. *antiquaire.*] A *n.* 1 An official recorder or custodian of antiquities. Long *obs.* exc. *Hist.* M16. 2 A student or collector of antiquities or antiques. L16. †3 A person of great age. *rare.* L16–M17. B *adj.* Of antiquity; ancient; antique. *rare.* E17.

antiquate /'antɪkwət/ *a. arch.* LME. [L *antiquatus* pa. pple of *antiquare* restore (a thing) to its former condition, in eccl.L make old, f. *antiquus*: see ANTIQUE, -ATE[2].] = ANTIQUATED.

antiquate /'antɪkweɪt/ *v.t.* Now *rare* exc. as ANTIQUATED. L16. [f. prec.: see -ATE[3].] 1 Make old or out of date; make obsolete; abolish as out of date. L16. 2 Make conform with earlier usage etc. E19.

anti'quation *n.* (now *rare*) the action of antiquating; the state of being antiquated: E17.

antiquated /'antɪkweɪtɪd/ *a.* L16. [f. prec. + -ED[1].] 1 Grown old, of long standing, inveterate. *arch.* L16. 2 Out of use by reason of age; obsolete. *arch.* E17. 3 Old-fashioned; out of date. L17. 4 Of a person: advanced in age, superannuated. Now *rare* exc. as coinciding w. sense 3. L17.

1 ISAAC TAYLOR Prejudice and antiquated jealousy did not easily yield themselves up. 2 JONSON Neat Terence, witty Plautus now not please; but antiquated and deserted lye. 3 J. MARQUAND I paused at the door to grope for the antiquated light switch, for electrical appliances are not modern in Peking. A. KOESTLER We are like children, . . eager to learn from their elders all sorts of useful tricks, while at the same time laughing at their antiquated outlook. 4 ADDISON A maiden Aunt . . one of these Antiquated Sybils.

antique /an'tiːk/ *a., n.,* & *v.* Also (*arch.*) **antic** /'antɪk/. See also ANTIC. L15. [Fr., or L *antiquus, anticus*, f. as ANTE-.] A *adj.* 1 Having existed since old times, old, aged, venerable. L15. 2 Belonging to former times; ancient, olden. E16. 3 Of, belonging to, or after the manner of ancient Greece and Rome; in the style of classical antiquity. M16. 4 Old-fashioned, antiquated; in the style of an earlier age; archaic. M17.

1 SPENSER A nation so antique, as that no monument remaines of her beginning. D. DUNN They have an antique goldfish, a cat called Sly. 2 A. H. CLOUGH The antique pure simplicity with which God and good angels communed undispleased. L. LEE The village . . was like a deep-running cave still linked to its antic past. TED HUGHES Not utterly fantastical I expected (As in some antique tale depicted). 3 BYRON And thus they form a group that's quite antique, Half naked, loving, natural, and Greek. K. CLARK Virgil, that great mediator between the antique and the medieval world. 4 LONGFELLOW There stood the broad-wheeled wains and the antique ploughs and the harrows. C. BRONTË Looking down on a fine antique street.

B *n.* 1 A relic of ancient art; a relic of old times; an item of furniture, china, etc., valued by collectors because of its age. M16. †2 A person of ancient times; in *pl.* the ancients. M–L16.

1 GOLDSMITH His own business . . was to collect pictures, medals, intaglios and antiques of all kinds. K. CLARK He made imitations of Graeco-Roman sculpture, one of which . . was actually sold as an antique.

C *v.t.* 1 Bind (a book) in the style of an earlier period. M18. 2 Make (furniture etc.) appear antique by artificial means. E20.

antiqueness *n.* M17.

antiquity /an'tɪkwɪti/ *n.* ME. [(O)Fr. *antiquité* f. L *antiquitas*, f. *antiquus*: see prec., -ITY.] 1 The ancient times; *spec.* the period before the Middle Ages. ME. 2 *collect.* The people (esp. authors) of ancient times; the ancients. LME. 3 The quality of having existed from ancient times; ancientness. LME. †b Old age; seniority. L16–L17. 4 In *pl.* & *collect. sing.* Customs, precedents, or events of ancient times; ancient records. (Formerly also *sing.* of an individual custom etc.) LME. 5 An ancient relic; an antique. Usu. in *pl.* E16.

1 J. S. BLACKIE The coolest and most practical thinker of all antiquity . . Aristotle. B. RUSSELL In antiquity all large States, except Egypt, suffered from a lack of stability. **Christian antiquity** the early period of the Christian era, the early centuries of the Church. **classical antiquity** the time of the ancient Greeks and Romans. 2 MILTON That indigested heap, and frie of Authors, which they call Antiquity. 3 J. I. M. STEWART Anderman was a baronet and his family of some antiquity. b SHAKES. *2 Hen. IV* Is not your voice broken, your wind short, . . and every part about you blasted with antiquity? 4 J. PRIESTLEY Whiston . . was certainly well read in Christian antiquity. K. E. DIGBY The subject belongs entirely to the antiquities of our law. 5 BACON Antiquities are history defaced, or some remnants of history which have casually escaped the shipwreck of time. T. JEFFERSON The Pont du Gard, a sublime antiquity, and well preserved. D. ASH Reputable dealers in antiquities . . will give a written guarantee of authenticity if required.

anˌtiqui'tarian *n.* a person attached to the practices or opinions of antiquity M17.

antirrhinum /antɪ'rʌɪnəm/ *n.* M16. [L f. Gk *antirrhinon*, f. *anti-* counterfeiting + *rhin-, rhis* nose.] Any of numerous plants constituting the genus *Antirrhinum*, of the figwort family, bearing usu. showy tubular two-lipped flowers; *spec.* the snapdragon, *A. majus.*

antiscion /an'tɪʃ(ə)n/ *n.* Pl. **-scia** /-ʃə/, **-scions.** L16. [App. repr. Gk *antiskion* (sc. *zōidion* sign of the zodiac), f. as ANTI- + *skia* shadow.] *Astrol.* A sign of the zodiac at the same distance from Cancer or Capricorn as another and on the opposite side of it.

antisepsis /antɪ'sɛpsɪs/ *n.* L19. [f. ANTI- + SEPSIS.] *Med.* The practice or principles of antiseptic treatment.

antiseptic /antɪ'sɛptɪk/ *n.* & *a.* E18. [f. ANTI- + SEPTIC.] A *n.* An antiseptic substance (see sense B.). E18.

B *adj.* Preventing sepsis, esp. by chemically destroying or retarding the growth of bacteria; scrupulously clean, sterile. M18.

fig.: CARLYLE Not divine men, yet useful antiseptic products of their generation.

antiseptically *adv.* M19.

antisocial /antɪ'səʊʃ(ə)l/ *a.* L18. [f. ANTI- + SOCIAL *a.*] 1 Averse to society or companionship; not sociable. L18. 2 Opposed to the practices, principles, and instincts on which society is based. E19.

antisocialism *n.* = ANTISOCIALITY M19. **antisociality** /ˌantɪsəʊʃɪ'alɪti/ *n.* the quality or condition of being antisocial E19. **antisocially** *adv.* E20.

antispastic /antɪ'spastɪk/ *n.* & *a.* E17. [Gk *antispastikos*, f. *antispan* draw in the opposite direction: see ANTI-, SPASTIC.] *Class. Pros.* (A foot, line, etc.) composed of, or containing feet composed of, an iamb and a trochee.

antistrophe /an'tɪstrəfi/ *n.* M16. [Late L f. Gk *antistrophē*, f. *antistrephein* turn against: see ANTI-, STROPHE.] 1 *Rhet.* The repetition of words in inverse order. M16. 2 The returning movement, from left to right, in Greek choruses and dances, answering to the strophe; the lines of choral song recited during this movement; *transf.* any choral response. E17. 3 An inverse relation or correspondence. E17.

antistrophic /-'strəʊfɪk/ *n.* & *a.* (*a*) *n.* in *pl.*, the lyrical part of Greek dramas; (*b*) *adj.* of or pertaining to antistrophes: E19.

antistrophon /an'tɪstrəf(ə)n/ *n.* Pl. **-pha** /-fə/. E17. [Gk, neut. sing. of *antistrophos*, f. as prec.] *Rhet.* An argument that is retorted upon an opponent.

antisymmetric /ˌantɪsɪ'mɛtrɪk/ *a.* E20. [f. ANTI- + SYMMETRIC.] *Math.* & *Physics.* Of a function: changed in sign but not in magnitude by the exchange of two variables. Also, able to be represented by such a function.

antisymmetrical *a.* = ANTISYMMETRIC E20. **anti'symmetrize** *v.t.* make antisymmetric M20. **antiˌsymmetri'zation** *n.* M20. **anti'symmetry** *n.* E20.

antithesis /an'tɪθəsɪs/ *n.* Pl. **-eses** /-əsiːz/. LME. [Late L f. Gk, f. *antitithenai*, f. as ANTI- + *tithenai* to set, place: cf. THESIS.] †1 *Gram.* a The substitution of one case for another. Only in LME. b The substitution of one sound for another. L16–M17. 2 *Rhet.* (An) opposition or contrast of ideas, expressed by parallelism of words which are the opposites of, or strongly contrasted with, each other. Also, repetition of the same word at the end of successive clauses. E16. 3 The second of two opposed clauses or sentences; a counter-thesis. M16. 4 Direct or striking opposition of character or function (*of, between* two things). E17. 5 The direct opposite, a complete contrast, (*of, to*). M17. 6 In Hegelian philosophy, the negation of the thesis as the second stage in the process of dialectical reasoning. Cf. SYNTHESIS 2C, THESIS 2. L19.

antithet /'antɪθɛt/ *n.* E17. [L *antitheton* f. Gk, neut. sing. of *antithetos*: see ANTITHETICAL.] An instance of antithesis; an antithetical statement.

antithetical /antɪ'θɛtɪk(ə)l/ *a.* L16. [f. Gk *antithetikos*, f. *antithetos* placed in opposition, f. as ANTITHESIS: see -ICAL.] 1 Of the nature of antithesis; containing or using antithesis. L16. 2 Characterized by direct opposition (*to*). M19.

antithetic *a.* antithetical E17. **antithetically** *adv.* E19.

antitype /'antɪtʌɪp/ *n.* E17. [Late L *antitypus* f. Gk *antitupos* adj., corresponding as an impression to the die, f. as ANTI- + *tupos* TYPE *n.*] 1 Something which a type or symbol represents. E17. 2 A person or thing of the opposite type. E20.

For other words beginning with *anti-* see the entry for **anti-**

anti'typical *a.* of the nature of or pertaining to an antitype M17.

antler /ˈantlə/ *n.* LME. [AN var. of OFr. *antoillier* (mod. *andouiller*), of unkn. origin.] A branch of either of the two deciduous outgrowths on the head of a male deer (or a reindeer of either sex), consisting when fully grown of dead bone; orig. *spec.* the lowest (forward-directed) branch. Also, this branched structure as a whole.

Comb.: **antler-moth** a small noctuid, *Cerapteryx graminis*, with white branched wing markings.

antlered *a.* bearing antlers; adorned with stags' horns: E19. **antlerless** *a.* without antlers L19.

antlia /ˈantlɪə/ *n.* E19. [L f. Gk = instrument for raising water.] 1 The spiral proboscis of butterflies and moths. E19. 2 (Usu. **A-**.) (The name of) an inconspicuous constellation of the southern hemisphere between Hydra and Vela; = *air-pump* (b) s.v. AIR *n.*[1] M19.

†antoeci *n.pl.* E17–L18. [Late L f. Gk *antoikoi*, f. as ANTI- + *-oikos* dwelling.] Persons living on the same meridian at equal latitudes on opposite sides of the equator. Cf. PERIOECI.

Antonian /anˈtəʊnɪən/ *a.* & *n.* E20. [f. L *Antonius* Anthony + -IAN.] = ANTONINE *n.* 1, *a.* 2.

Antonine /ˈantənʌɪn/ *n.* & *a.* M16. [L *Antoninus*, f. as prec.: see -INE[1].] A *n.* 1 A disciple or follower of St Anthony of Egypt (*c*251–356). M16. 2 In *pl.* *The* Roman emperors Antoninus Pius (reigned 138–161) and Marcus Aurelius Antoninus (161–180). L17.

B *adj.* 1 Of or pertaining to the Antonines (sense A.2 above). L18. 2 Of or pertaining to St Anthony of Egypt. L19.

1 **the Antonine Wall** a Roman frontier wall in Britain from the Forth to the Clyde, built for Antoninus Pius.

antonomasia /ˌantənəˈmeɪzɪə/ *n.* M16. [L f. Gk, f. *antonomazein* name instead, f. as ANTI- + *onoma* name: see -IA[1].] The substitution of an epithet etc. or the name of an office or dignity, for a proper name (e.g. *the Iron Duke* for Wellington). Also, conversely, the use of a proper name to express a general idea (e.g. *a Solomon* for 'a wise man').

antonym /ˈantənɪm/ *n.* M19. [Fr. *antonyme*, f. Gk ANTI- + *onuma* name: see -NYM.] A term of opposite meaning to another.

an'tonymous *a.* opposite in meaning M20. **an'tonymy** *n.* M20.

antorbital /anˈtɔːbɪt(ə)l/ *a.* Also **ante-orbital** /antɪˈɔːbɪt(ə)l/. M19. [f. ANT(E- + ORBITAL *a.*] *Anat.* Situated in front of the eyes.

antra *n.* pl. of ANTRUM.

antre /ˈantə/ *n. poet.* E17. [Fr. f. L ANTRUM.] A cave, a cavern.

antrorse /anˈtrɔːs/ *a.* M19. [mod.L *antrorsus*, f. L ANTERO- + *versus* towards, after *extrorsus* etc.: see EXTRORSE.] Directed forward or upward.

antrum /ˈantrəm/ *n.* Pl. **antra** /ˈantrə/. E19. [L f. Gk *antron* cave.] *Anat.* A cavity, *esp.* one with bony walls. Also, the part of the stomach adjacent to the pylorus.

antral *a.* of or pertaining to an antrum L19.

antrustion /anˈtrʌstjən/ *n.* E19. [Fr., or med.L *antrustio(n-)* (in Salic Law etc.) f. OFrank. (= OHG *trōst* help, protection).] *Hist.* A member of the voluntary personal guard of the Merovingian rulers in early medieval Europe.

antsy /ˈantsi/ *a. N. Amer. colloq.* M20. [f. ANT *n.* + -SY.] Irritated, impatient; fidgety, restless.

Antwerp /ˈantwəːp/ *n.* M19. [A city in Belgium.] 1 *Antwerp blue*, a pale Prussian blue. M19. 2 *Antwerp edge, edging stitch*, an embroidery stitch used for decorating and finishing edges and hems. L19.

anucleate /eɪˈnjuːklɪət/ *a.* M20. [f. A-[10] + NUCLEATE *a.*] *Biol.* Of a cell: having no nucleus.

anuran /əˈnjʊər(ə)n/ *n.* & *a.* L19. [f. mod.L *Anura* (see below), f. Gk AN-[5] + *oura* tail: see -AN.] *Zool.* A *n.* Any of the tailless amphibians, constituting the order Anura; a frog, a toad. L19. B *adj.* Of or pertaining to this order. E20.

anuria /əˈnjʊərɪə/ *n.* M19. [f. AN-[5] + -URIA.] *Med.* Failure of the kidneys to produce urine.

anuric *a.* displaying or pertaining to anuria L19.

anus /ˈeɪnəs/ *n.* LME. [L *anus*, orig. 'ring'.] The posterior excretory opening of the alimentary canal.

anvil /ˈanvɪl/ *n.* & *v.* [OE *anfilte* (earlier *onfilti*), *anfealt* = MDu. *aenvilte*, OHG *anafalz*, ult. f. Gmc base of ON *prep.* + vbl stem meaning 'beat' (cf. FELT *n.*).] A *n.* 1 A block (usu. of iron) on which a smith hammers and shapes metal. OE. 2a *Anat.* = INCUS *n.* 1. E17. b *Meteorol.* A horizontally extended top of a cumulonimbus cloud. L19.

1 *fig.*: BURKE He has now on the anvil another scheme.

Comb.: **anvil cloud** a cloud with a horizontally extended top.

B *v.* Infl. **-ll-**. 1 *v.t.* Fashion on an anvil. Freq. *fig.* L16. 2 *v.i.* Work at an anvil. L19.

anxiety /aŋˈzʌɪəti/ *n.* E16. [Fr. *anxiété* or L *anxietas*, f. as ANXIOUS: see -TY[1].] 1 The quality or state of being anxious; uneasiness, concern; a cause of this. E16. †2 *Med.* A condition of distress accompanied by precordial tightness or discomfort. M17–M19. 3 Earnest or solicitous desire *for* a thing, *to do* something. M18. 4 *Psychiatry.* A morbid state of excessive or unrealistic uneasiness or dread. L19.

1 *Nature* Finance has been a constant anxiety. 4 Freq. attrib., as *anxiety complex, neurosis, state.*

anxiolytic /ˌaŋzɪəˈlɪtɪk/ *a.* & *n.* M20. [f. prec. + -O- + -LYTIC.] *Med.* (A drug) that reduces anxiety.

anxious /ˈaŋ(k)ʃəs/ *a.* E17. [L *anxius*, f. *anx-* pa. ppl stem of *angere* choke, oppress: see ANGUISH *v.*, -IOUS.] 1 Troubled in mind about some uncertain event; concerned, solicitous; being in disturbing suspense. (Foll. by *for, about.*) E17. 2 Distressing, worrying; fraught with trouble. M17. 3 Full of desire and endeavour; eager *for* a thing, *to do* something. M18.

1 LD MACAULAY Anxious for their own safety. G. B. SHAW The most anxious man in a prison is the governor. E. M. FORSTER She was anxious about Leonard, for whom they certainly were responsible. 2 A. UTTLEY It was always an anxious time, a slip and a man and mare might be killed. 3 K. AMIS All seemed pleased with the performance and anxious for another of the same sort. S. KING You must be anxious to see your folks.

anxiously *adv.* L17. **anxiousness** *n.* (*rare*) M17.

any /ˈɛni/ *a.* (in mod. usage also classed as a *determiner*), *pron.*, & *adv.* [OE *ǣnig* = OFris. *ēnich*, OS *ēnig*, MLG *einich*, MDu. *ēnich* (Du. *eenig*), OHG *einag* (G *einig*), ON *einigr*, Goth. *ainaha*, f. Gmc: see ONE, -Y[1].] A *adj.* 1 *gen.* As *sing.*, a —, some —, no matter which, or what. As *pl.*, some — no matter which, of what kind, or how many: a Used primarily in interrog., hypothet., and condit. contexts. OE. b With a preceding negative (expressed or implied): none at all of, no — of any kind etc.; not even one. OE. c In affirmative senses: every one of (the sort named). ME. 2 With quantitative emphasis: a A quantity or number of, however great, or however small. E16. b A large or considerable (number, amount, etc.). *colloq.* M19. 3 With qualitative emphasis: of any kind or sort whatever; one or some, however imperfect. M19.

1 AV *John* 1:46 Can there any good thing come out of Nazareth? LD MACAULAY The best governed country of which he had any knowledge. J. STEINBECK If there were any water at all, it would be there. *any day*: see DAY *n. any old (how)*: see OLD *a. any old thing*: see THING *n.*[1] **any road** (chiefly *north.*) = ANYWAY 2. *at any cost*: see COST *n.*[2] *at any price*: see PRICE *n.* **at any rate, in any case** whatever the circumstances may be. b SHAKES. *Haml.* Thou canst not then be false to any man. BURKE It ought not to be done at any time. DAY LEWIS They know so little of any life but their own. E. WAUGH None of these people you go about with pull any weight in their own colleges. c I. WALTON I love any discourse of rivers, and fish and fishing. DICKENS Any object they think can lay their thieving hands on. E. BOWEN The two of them would be gabbing up to any hour of the night. 2a *Daily Chronicle* An animal with little, if any, fat on it. *Nursery rhyme*: Black sheep, have you any wool? b R. KIPLING It is not a good idea to live in the East for any length of time. *Academy* The pigeon-hole form of mind collecting any quantity of conclusions and facts. 3 M. PATTISON The danger is . . that any reform should be adopted because some reform is required.

B *pron.* 1 Any person; as *pl.*, any persons. OE. 2 One or more, or some, of the n. expressed already or after following *of.* ME. 3 Either (of two). Long *dial.* LME.

1 KEATS Unknown . . to any, but those two alone. T. S. ELIOT I wouldn't have danced like that with any but you. NEB *James* 1:5 If any of you falls short in wisdom, he should ask God for it. 2 SHAKES. *Wint. T.* If there be any of him left, I'll bury it. W. S. GILBERT He exercises of his brains, that is, assuming that he's got any. A. J. P. TAYLOR The real failure, if any, was his. **not having any** *colloq.* wanting no part in something; rejecting a proposition; refusing to tolerate a situation.

C *adv.* 1 With compar. adjs. and advs.: in any degree, at all. OE. 2 (Not qualifying another wd.) At all. *colloq.* M18.

1 T. HARDY A happy Providence kept it from being any worse. K. AMIS I'm not answering any more questions about whales or tigers. 2 M. TWAIN It is a good tune—you can't improve it any. A. CHRISTIE We're used to responsibility. Doesn't worry us any.

anybody /ˈɛnɪbɒdi/ *pron.* Orig. two wds. ME. [f. prec. + BODY *n.*] A person, no matter who; whichever person.

J. PARKER Anybody can attach himself to a mob. J. RUSKIN I am never angry with anybody unless they deserve it. **anybody's game** etc. *colloq.* a finely balanced contest. **anybody's guess** *colloq.* a totally unpredictable matter. **anybody who is anybody** (or similar phr.) *colloq.* any person of rank or importance.

anyhow /ˈɛnɪhaʊ/ *adv.* Orig. two wds. L17. [f. ANY + HOW *adv.*] 1 In any way or manner whatever; in any way however imperfect; haphazardly, carelessly. L17. 2 At any rate, in any case, at least. E19.

1 H. G. WELLS His rather crisp brown hair seemed to grow anyhow. 2 G. MACDONALD They went, anyhow, whether they had to do it or not.

any more /ɛnɪ ˈmɔː/ *adv. phr.* Also **anymore**. LME. [f. ANY + MORE *adv.*] To any greater extent; any longer.

MRS H. WARD If Westall bullies him any more he will put a knife into him. E. HEMINGWAY I am not lucky anymore. J. P. DONLEAVY Don't cry anymore now. It's all right. A. GLYN It didn't matter any more. The game was over.

anyone /ˈɛnɪwʌn/ *pron.* Orig. two wds. E18. [f. ANY + ONE *n.* & *pron.*] Any person; = ANYBODY.

anyplace /ˈɛnɪpleɪs/ *adv. N. Amer. colloq.* Also as two wds. M20. [f. ANY + PLACE *n.*[1], after ANYWHERE.] = ANYWHERE.

anything /ˈɛnɪθɪŋ/ *pron.*, *adv.*, & *n.* Orig. two wds. OE. [f. ANY + THING *n.*[1]] A *pron.* Something, no matter what; whatever thing. OE.

E. WAUGH 'Anything wrong?' he asked. IRVING BERLIN Anything you can do I can do better. DAY LEWIS I have never been anything but a poor sight-reader. **anything but** *colloq.* by no means, on the contrary. *anything in* TROUSERS. **(as) — as anything** *colloq.* extremely —. **if anything** if in any degree, perhaps even. **like anything** *colloq.* to a great extent etc.; exceedingly. **too — for anything** *colloq.* extremely —. *try anything once*: see TRY *v. would give anything*: see GIVE *v.*

B *adv.* In any measure; to any extent. *arch.* OE.

C *n.* A thing of any kind. L16.

SHAKES. *Tam. Shr.* She is my house, . . my ox, my ass, my any thing.

anything'arian *n.* (*contempt.*) a person who professes no creed in particular E18.

any time /ˈɛnɪ tʌɪm/ *adv. phr. colloq.* Also **anytime**. LME. [f. ANY + TIME *n.*] At any time; whenever.

OED I will leave the basket; you can send it round any time. *Guardian* Any time you're stuck for a meal, come around.

anyway /ˈɛnɪweɪ/ *adv.* Orig. two wds. ME. [f. ANY + WAY *n.*: cf. next.] 1 In any way or manner; anyhow. ME. 2 At any rate, in any case. (Freq. used in resuming after a digression.) M19.

1 ADDISON All those who are any way concerned in works of literature. 2 C. P. SNOW She couldn't wish

for that. Anyway, she took it for granted that she wouldn't get him.

anyways /ˈɛnɪweɪz/ *adv.* Now *dial.* Orig. two wds. ME. [f. ANY + -WAYS.] = prec.

anywhen /ˈɛnɪwɛn/ *adv. rare* exc. *dial.* Orig. two wds. M16. [f. ANY + WHEN.] At any time, ever.

anywhere /ˈɛnɪwɛː/ *adv.* Orig. two wds. LME. [f. ANY + WHERE.] In or to any place; whichever place.

anywhere from — to — (orig. *N. Amer.*) at any point within specified limits of variation. **not anywhere near** = *nowhere near* s.v. NOWHERE *adv.* 1. **not get anywhere** = *get nowhere* s.v. NOWHERE *adv.* 3. **not go anywhere** = *go nowhere* s.v. NOWHERE *adv.* 3.

anywhither /ˈɛnɪwɪðə/ *adv. arch.* Orig. two wds. E17. [f. ANY + WHITHER *adv.*] To or towards any place.

anywise /ˈɛnɪwʌɪz/ *adv. arch.* Orig. two wds. OE. [f. ANY + -WISE.] In any manner, way, or case; at all.

Anzac /ˈanzak/ *n.* E20. [Acronym of the corps name (see below).] A member of the Australian and New Zealand Army Corps (1914–18); an Australian, a New Zealander, esp. a serviceman.

Comb.: **Anzac biscuit**: made from wheat flour, rolled oats, desiccated coconut, and golden syrup; **Anzac Day** 25 April, the date of the landing of the corps on the Gallipoli peninsula in 1915.

Anzus /ˈanzəs/ *n.* Also **ANZUS**. M20. [Acronym of the country names (see below).] The combination of Australia, New Zealand, and the United States for the security of the Pacific.

ao dai /aʊ dʌɪ/ *n. phr.* M20. [Vietnamese.] A Vietnamese woman's long-sleeved tunic with ankle-length panels at front and back, worn over trousers.

Aonian /eɪˈəʊnɪən/ *a.* E17. [f. L *Aonia* (see below) f. Gk + -AN.] Of or pertaining to Aonia, a region of Boeotia in ancient Greece containing Mount Helicon, sacred to the Muses.

aorist /ˈeɪərɪst/ *a.* & *n.* L16. [Gk *aoristos* indefinite (sc. *khronos* time), f. A-[10] + *horistos* delimited, f. *horizein* define: cf. HORIZON.] *Gram.* (Designating) a past tense of verbs, in ancient Greek and some other languages, denoting simple occurrence, with none of the limitations of the other past tenses.

aoˈristic *a.* undefined; of or pertaining to the aorist tense: M19. **aoˈristically** *adv.* M17.

aorta /eɪˈɔːtə/ *n.* Pl. **-tae** /-tiː/, **-tas**. M16. [Gk *aortē*, by Hippocrates used in pl. for the branches of the windpipe, by Aristotle for the great artery, f. base of *aeirein* raise: cf. ARTERY.] *Anat.* The great artery or trunk of the arterial system, from its origin in the left ventricle of the heart to its division into the left and right common iliac arteries.

aortal *a.* aortic E19. **aortic** *a.* of or pertaining to the aorta; *aortic arch*, the section of the aorta which loops over and behind the heart: L18.

aortography /eɪɔːˈtɒgrəfi/ *n.* M20. [f. prec. + -O- + -GRAPHY.] X-ray examination of the aorta.

aoudad /ˈɑːʊdad/ *n.* Also **udad** /ˈuːdad/. E19. [Fr. f. Berber *udād*.] A sheep, *Ammotragus lervia*, native to N. Africa. Also called *Barbary sheep*.

aoul *n.* var. of AUL.

à outrance /a utrɑ̃ːs/ *adv. phr.* Also ***à l'outrance*** /a l-/, ***à toute outrance*** /a tut/. E17. [Fr., f. *à* to + OUTRANCE.] To the death; to the bitter end.

ap- /əp, *stressed* ap/ *pref.*[1] (not productive). Assim. form of L AD- bef. *p*. In OFr., L *app-* was reduced to *ap-*, which appears in ME adoptions, but in later Fr., and hence in Eng., *app-* was restored by Latinization, as *apparel*, *appear*.

ap- *pref.*[2] see APO-.

apace /əˈpeɪs/ *adv.* Now *literary.* LME. [OFr. *à pas*: see A-[8], PACE *n.*[1]] 1 At a considerable pace; swiftly. LME. †2 At once, promptly. LME–E18.

1 AV *Ps.* 68:12 Kings of armies did flee apace. M. ARNOLD The field . . and the elms Fade into dimness apace. BOSW. SMITH The news . . reached Rome apace.

Apache /*in senses A.1, B.1* əˈpatʃi; *in senses A.2, B.2* əˈpaʃ, *foreign* apaʃ (*pl. of n. same*)/ *n.* & *a.* Senses A.2, B.2 also **a-**. M18. [Mex. Sp., prob. f. Zuñi *Ápachu* lit. 'enemy'. Senses A.2, B.2 through Fr.] A *n.* Pl. **-s**, same. 1 A member of an Athapaskan Indian people of New Mexico and Arizona; the language of this people. M18. 2 A violent street ruffian, orig. in Paris. E20. B *attrib.* or as *adj.* 1 Of or pertaining to the Apache or their language. M19. 2 Designating a vigorous dance for two associated with street ruffians or apaches. E20.

Apachean *a.* & *n.* (*a*) *adj.* of or pertaining to the Apache Indians or their language; (*b*) *n.* an Apache Indian; the Apache language: M20.

apagoge /apəˈgəʊdʒi/ *n. rare.* E18. [Gk *apagōgē* leading away, f. *apagein* lead off.] *Logic.* 1 In Aristotelian logic: = ABDUCTION 3. E18. 2 A *reductio ad absurdum*. M18.

apagogic *a.* (*rare*) = APAGOGICAL L17. **apagogical** *a.* of the nature of apagoge E18.

†**apaid** *v.* pa. pple of APAY.

Apalachee /apəˈlatʃi/ *n.* Also **App-**. Pl. **-s**, same. E18. [Sp. *Apalache* perh. f. Choctaw *apelachi* helper, ally.] A member of a Muskogean Indian people formerly inhabiting parts of Georgia, Alabama, and Florida. Also, the language of this people.

apanage *n.* var. of APPANAGE.

aparejo /apəˈreɪhəʊ/ *n. US.* Pl. **-os**. M19. [Sp. = preparation, harness, tackle.] A pack-saddle.

apart /əˈpɑːt/ *adv.* LME. [OFr. (mod. *à part*) f. L *a parte* at the side: see A-[6], PART *n.*] (Foll. by *from*.) 1 To one side, aside; to or at a place removed from the general body. LME. 2 Away from each other; parted, separated; in pieces, asunder. LME. 3 Separately, independently, individually. LME. b Used adjectivally, with ellipsis of vb: separate, distinct. L18. 4 Away from all consideration or use. LME. b In absol. phrs.: laid aside, excepted; put out of the question. M18. 5 Away from common use for a special purpose. E17.

1 SHAKES. *Jul. Caes.* Thy heart is big, get thee apart and weep. H. P. BROUGHAM The precise period at which the Commons first sat apart from the Lords is unknown. V. S. PRITCHETT Their experience had set them apart and the effect was to make me feel childish and cut off. 2 J. M. BARRIE My mother and I were hundreds of miles apart. A. P. HERBERT So far apart were their worlds, though they had slept on the same floor. J. BETJEMAN Red Admirals basking with their wings apart. J. CHEEVER He had the rifle apart and was cleaning it. *poles apart*: see POLE *n.*[2] *tear apart*: see TEAR *v.*[1] 3 J. SELDEN Their power . . was exercised either collectively, or apart and severally. C. LUCAS Let us view each ingredient apart. **tell apart** distinguish between. b G. B. SHAW The passionately religious are a people apart. 4 AV *James* 1:21 Wherefore lay apart all filthinesse. b DISRAELI However, jesting apart, get your hat. A. J. P. TAYLOR His distribution of honours, wartime leaders apart, had been no greater than that of Asquith. 5 ADDISON Families that set apart an Hour in every Morning for Tea.

With preps. in specialized senses: **apart from** other than; except for, in addition to.

apartness *n.* the quality of standing apart; aloofness: M19.

apartheid /əˈpɑːtheɪt/ *n.* M20. [Afk., lit. 'separateness', f. Du. *apart* APART + *heid* -HOOD.] The South African (policy of) racial segregation of the White inhabitants from the remainder. Also *transf.* & *fig.*, any other form of (esp. racial) segregation.

petty apartheid: see PETTY *a.*

apart-hotel *n.* var. of APARTOTEL.

apartment /əˈpɑːtm(ə)nt/ *n.* M17. [Fr. *appartement* f. It. *appartamento*, f. *appartare* to separate, f. *a parte* APART: see -MENT.] 1 a A suite of rooms allotted to the use of an individual or group. *arch.* M17. b A suite of rooms forming one residence in a building containing a number of these; a flat. Chiefly *N. Amer.* L19. †2 Place of abode; quarters. L17–E18. †3 A compartment. L17–M19. 4 A single room in a house; usu. in *pl.*, = sense 1a. E18.

Comb.: **apartment block, building, house** (chiefly *N. Amer.*) a building divided into flats.

apartˈmental *a.* (*rare*) E19.

apartotel /əˈpɑːtəʊtɛl/ *n.* Also **apart-hotel** /əˈpɑːt(h)əʊtɛl/. M20. [f. prec. + HOTEL.] An apartment building with privately-owned suites available for short-term renting.

apatheia /apəˈθiːə/ *n.* L19. [Gk: see APATHY.] Stoical apathy.

apathetic /apəˈθɛtɪk/ *a.* M18. [f. next after PATHETIC.] Of or characterized by apathy; not feeling emotion; uninterested, indifferent, (*towards* or *about* something).

apathetically *adv.* E19.

apathy /ˈapəθi/ *n.* E17. [Fr. *apathie* f. L *apathia* f. Gk *apatheia*, f. *apathēs* without feeling: see A-[10], PATHOS, -Y[3].] Insensibility to suffering or emotion; passionless existence; lack of interest or emotion; stolid indifference.

G. H. LEWES Apathy was considered by the Stoics as the highest condition of Humanity. A. TATE A failure resulting from the apathy of responsible classes of society. G. MAXWELL Days when a kind of apathy would settle down upon me.

apathist *n.* a person habitually given to apathy M17.

apatite /ˈapətʌɪt/ *n.* E19. [f. Gk *apatē* deceit + -ITE[1]: so named from its diversity of form and colour.] *Min.* Any of a series of hexagonal calcium phosphate minerals of wide occurrence, having the general formula $Ca_5(PO_4)_3$(F, Cl, OH); freq. = FLUORAPATITE.

†**apay** *v.t.* Pa. pple **apaid**. ME. [OFr. *apaier*, ult. f. L *ad* A-[5] + *pacare* please, satisfy, (orig.) pacify, f. *pac-*, PAX: see PAY *v.*[1]] Usu. in *pass.* or *pa. ppl a.* 1 Satisfy, please. ME–L19. 2 Repay, requite. LME–M18.

ape /eɪp/ *n.*, *a.*, & *v.* [OE *apa* masc., *ape* fem. = OS *apo* (Du. *aap*), OHG *affo*, *affe* (G *Affe*), ON *api*, f. Gmc.] A *n.* 1 a An animal of the monkey tribe (suborder Simiae or Anthropoidea): the generic name before 'monkey', and still occas. so used, esp. w. ref. to resemblance to and mimicry of humans. OE. b *spec.* A member of the family Pongidae, which includes the gorilla, chimpanzee, orang-utan, and gibbon, and is characterized by the absence of a tail and cheek-pouches. L17. 2 *fig.* An (esp. inferior or mindless) imitator; a mimic. ME. 3 An apelike person; a fool. Also as a gen. term of abuse. ME. †4 *sea-ape*, the thresher or fox-shark, *Alopias vulpinus*. E17–M19.

1a *Barbary ape*: see BARBARY *n.* *Japanese ape*: see JAPANESE *a.* **lead apes in hell** *arch.* (the supposed consequence of dying an old maid). †**play the ape** indulge in (poor) imitation. b **the naked ape** humankind. 2 SHAKES. *Cymb.* O sleep, thou ape of death. HOR. WALPOLE Every genius has his apes. 3 S. RICHARDSON That she should instigate the titled ape her husband to write to me.

Comb.: **apeman** an extinct primate intermediate between ape and man; an apelike human.

B *adj.* †1 *attrib.* Foolish, silly. Only in LME. 2 *pred.* Crazy. Esp. in *go ape*. (*slang*, orig. *N. Amer.*) M20.

C *v.t.* Imitate, esp. pretentiously or absurdly. M17.

apelike *a.* resembling an ape in appearance or behaviour; resembling that of an ape: M19. **ˈapeling** *n.* (*rare*) a young or small ape M18.

apeak /əˈpiːk/ *adv.* & *pred. a.* Orig. †**apike**. L16. [Fr. *à pic*: see A-[5], PEAK *n.*[1]] *Naut.* In a vertical position; vertical; (of an anchor) with the ship directly over it; (of oars) held vertically.

Apelles /əˈpɛliːz/ *n.* E17. [Gk painter of the 4th cent. BC.] A master artist.

apepsia /əˈpɛpsɪə/ *n.* Now *rare* or *obs.* Also **-sy** /-si/. L17. [Gk, f. A-[10] + *peptein* to digest: see -IA[1].] *Med.* Lack of digestive power.

aperçu /apɛrsy (*pl. same*), apɛːˈsjuː/ *n.* E19. [Fr.] A summary, a conspectus; an insight, a revealing glimpse.

aperient /əˈpɪərɪənt/ *a.* & *n.* E17. [L *aperient-* pres. ppl stem of *aperire* to open: see -ENT.] A *adj.* Opening the bowels; laxative. E17. B *n.* A laxative medicine or food. L17.

aperiodic /ˌeɪpɪərɪˈɒdɪk/ *a.* L19. [f. A-[10] + PERIODIC *a.*[1]] Not periodic, esp. owing to strong damping of vibration; irregular.

aperiodically *adv.* L19. **aperioˈdicity** *n.* L19.

aperitif /əˈpɛrɪtiːf, əpɛrɪˈtiːf/ *n.* Also ***apéritif*** /aperitif (*pl. same*)/. L19. [Fr. *apéritif* (n. & adj.) f. med.L *aperitivus* (adj.) var. of late L *apertivus*,

f. *apertus*: see APERT, -IVE.] An alcoholic drink taken as an appetizer.

†aperitive *a.* & *n.* E16–M19. [f. med.L *aperitivus*: see prec.] (A medicine or food) that opens; *spec.* = APERIENT.

apert /əˈpəːt/ *a.* & *adv.* Long *arch.* ME. [OFr. f. L *apertus* pa. pple of *aperire* to open: cf. PERT *a.*] **A** *adj.* 1 Open, public; overt. ME. †2 Evident, plain. ME–L17. †3 Straightforward; brisk, bold. Only in ME. †4 Outspoken; insolent. ME–L17. †5 Clever, ready, expert. ME–L16. †**B** *adv.* Openly, publicly; plainly. ME–L17.
†**apertion** *n.* an opening; the action of opening: L16–M18. †**apertive** *a.* = APERITIVE *a.*, APERIENT *a.* M16–E18. **apertly** *adv.* openly, evidently; boldly: ME. **apertness** *n.* (now *rare* or *obs.*) openness, frankness E17.

aperture /ˈapətjʊə, -tʃ(ʊ)ə/ *n.* LME. [L *apertura*, f. *apert-* pa. ppl stem of *aperire* to open: see -URE.] †1 The process of opening. LME–M18. 2 An opening; a gap, a cleft, a hole. LME. 3 A space through which light passes in an optical instrument; *esp.* that provided by the lens diaphragm of a camera. Also, the diameter of this. M17.
2 C. DARWIN The size and shape of the apertures in the sternum. R. L. STEVENSON Raising my head to an aperture among the leaves, I could see clear down into a little green dell. R. P. WARREN She opened the door . . a little way, and slipped through the aperture.
aˈpertural *a.* (*rare*) M19.

apery /ˈeɪpəri/ *n.* E17. [f. APE *n.* + -ERY.] 1 Apelike behaviour; pretentious or silly mimicry. Also, an instance of this. E17. 2 A collection or colony of apes. *rare.* E19.

apetalous /eɪˈpɛt(ə)ləs, ə-/ *a.* E18. [f. mod.L *apetalus* f. Gk *apetalos* leafless: see A-[10], PETAL, -OUS.] *Bot.* Having no petals.

apex /ˈeɪpɛks/ *n.*[1] Pl. **apexes, apices** /ˈeɪpɪsiːz/. E17. [L.] 1 The small rod at the top of a flamen's cap. *rare.* E17. 2 The tip, top, peak, or pointed end of anything; the vertex of a triangle, cone, etc.; *Bot.* the growing point of a shoot etc. E17. †3 A horn on a Hebrew letter; *fig.* a tittle, a jot. M–L17. 4 *Astron.* The point on the celestial sphere towards which the sun is moving. Also *solar apex.* L18.
2 S. GIBBONS A sick plunge at the apex of your stomach. P. G. WODEHOUSE He sailed in and knocked them base over apex into a pile of Brussels sprouts. M. KEANE Our house stood at the apex of two carriage drives. *fig.*: R. H. TAWNEY A community penetrated from apex to foundation by the moral law.

Apex /ˈeɪpɛks/ *n.*[2] Also **APEX**. L20. [f. *advance-purchase excursion.*] A type of reduced-price airline ticket or fare, requiring advance booking and acceptance of certain other limiting conditions.

apfelstrudel /ˈapf(ə)lʃtruːd(ə)l/ *n.* M20. [G, f. *Apfel* APPLE + STRUDEL.] = *apple strudel* s.v. APPLE *n.*

aphaeresis /əˈfɪərɪsɪs/ *n.* Also ***apher-**. Pl. **-eses** /-ɪsiːz/. M16. [Late L f. Gk *aphairesis*, f. *aphairein* take away, f. APH- + *hairein* take.] The loss of a letter or syllable at the beginning of a word.
aphaeretic /afɪˈrɛtɪk/ *a.* of the nature of aphaeresis L19.

aphakia /əˈfeɪkɪə/ *n.* M19. [f. A-[10] + Gk *phakos* lentil + -IA[1].] *Med.* Absence of the lens of the eye.
aphakic *a.* pertaining to or displaying aphakia L19.

aphanite /ˈaf(ə)nʌɪt/ *n.* E19. [f. Gk *aphanēs* unseen + -ITE[1].] *Geol.* Orig., a very fine-grained diabase. Now, any igneous rock in which crystalline grains cannot be distinguished with the unaided eye.
aphaˈnitic *a.* consisting or characteristic of aphanite M19.

aphasia /əˈfeɪzɪə/ *n.* M19. [Gk, f. *aphatos* speechless, f. A-[10] + *phanai* speak: see -IA[1].] Loss or impairment of the faculty of speech or of understanding of language (or both), due to cerebral disease or damage.
BROCA's *aphasia.* SEMANTIC *aphasia. sensory aphasia*: see SENSORY *a.* WERNICKE's *aphasia.*
aphasiac *a.* & *n.* (*rare*) = APHASIC M19. **aphasic** *a.* & *n.* (a person) affected with aphasia; of or pertaining to aphasia: M19. **aphasiˈology** *n.* the study and treatment of aphasia M20.

aphelion /apˈhiːlɪən, əˈfiːlɪən/ *n.* Also **†-lium.** Pl. **-lia** /-lɪə/. M17. [Graecized form of mod.L *aphelium*, f. Gk APH- + *hēlios* sun, after L *apogaeum* APOGEE.] *Astron.* The point in the orbit of a planet, comet, etc., at which the furthest distance from the sun is reached.

aphemia /əˈfiːmɪə/ *n.* Now *rare.* M19. [f. A-[10] + Gk *phēmē* voice + -IA[1].] *Med.* A form of aphasia in which words can be understood but not uttered.

apheresis *n.* see APHAERESIS.

aphesis /ˈafɪsɪs/ *n.* Pl. **-eses** /-ɪsiːz/. L19. [Gk = letting go, f. *aphienai*, f. APH- + *hienai* let go, send.] Aphaeresis; *spec.* the loss of an unaccented vowel at the beginning of a word (e.g. of *e* from *esquire* to form *squire*).
aˈphetic *a.* pertaining to or resulting from aphesis L19. **aˈphetically** *adv.* L19. **aphetism** *n.* (a word formed by) aphesis L19. **aphetize** *v.t.* shorten by aphesis L19.

apheta /ˈafɪtə/ *n.* M17. [L f. Gk *aphetēs* starter, sender off.] *Astrol.* = HYLEG.

aphid /ˈeɪfɪd/ *n.* L19. [Back-form. f. *aphides*, pl. of next.] A small soft-bodied insect of the homopteran family Aphididae, whose members live on plant juices and include many plant pests, e.g. a greenfly or a blackfly.
rose aphid: see ROSE *n.* & *a. woolly aphid*: see WOOLLY *a.*
aphiˈdivorous *a.* feeding on aphids E19.

aphis /ˈeɪfɪs/ *n.* Pl. **-ides** /-ɪdiːz/. L18. [mod.L f. Gk, prob. a misreading (αφ *aph* for κορ *kor*) of *koris* bug.] = prec.
aphicide *n.* an insecticide used against aphids L19.

aphonia /eɪˈfəʊnɪə, ə-/ *n.* Orig. **†aphony.** L17. [mod.L f. Gk *aphōnia* speechlessness, f. A-[10] + *phōnē* voice: see -PHONIA.] *Med.* Loss or absence of voice through a defect in the vocal organs. Cf. ANARTHRIA, APHASIA.
aphonic *a.* without voice or sound E19.

aphorise *v.* var. of APHORIZE.

aphorism /ˈafərɪz(ə)m/ *n.* & *v.* E16. [Fr. *aphorisme* or late L *aphorismus* f. Gk *aphorismos* definition, f. *aphorizein* define, f. APH- + *horizein* set bounds to: see HORIZON, -ISM.] **A** *n.* 1 A concise statement of a scientific principle, usu. by a classical author. E16. 2 Any pithily expressed precept or observation; a maxim. L16. **B** *v.t.* & *i.* Utter as an aphorism; aphorize. *rare.* E17.
aphorisˈmatic *a.* (now *rare*) = APHORISMIC E19. **aphoˈrismic** *a.* of the nature of an aphorism L18.

aphorist /ˈafərɪst/ *n.* E18. [f. prec. + -IST.] A person who writes or utters aphorisms.
aphoˈristic *a.* of or pertaining to an aphorist; of the nature of an aphorism: M18. **aphoˈristical** *a.* (*rare*) L17. **aphoˈristically** *adv.* in an aphoristic manner M17.

aphorize /ˈafərʌɪz/ *v.i.* Also **-ise.** M17. [f. as prec. + -IZE.] Write or speak in aphorisms.

aphotic /eɪˈfəʊtɪk, ə-/ *a.* L19. [f. A-[10] + PHOTIC.] *Oceanogr.* Not reached by sunlight.

aphrodisiac /afrəˈdɪzɪak/ *n.* & *a.* E18. [Gk *aphrodisiakos*, f. *aphrodisios*, f. *Aphroditē*: see next, -AC.] **A** *n.* A food, drug, etc., which stimulates sexual desire. E18.
fig.: J. RAE Medals, promotion, fame, the thrill of taking risks and taking life; all the natural and artificial aphrodisiacs to keep the soldiers keen.
B *adj.* Of the nature of an aphrodisiac; arousing sexual desire. M19.
aphrodisiacal /-ˈzʌɪək(ə)l/ *a.* E18.

Aphrodite /afrəˈdʌɪti/ *n.* M17. [Gk *Aphroditē* the goddess of love, the Grecian Venus, lit. 'foam-born', f. *aphros* foam.] 1 A goddess of love; a beautiful woman. M17. 2 = SEA *mouse.* Now only as mod.L genus name. L18.

aphtha /ˈafθə/ *n.* Pl. **-thae** /-θiː/. M17. [L f. Gk, mostly in pl.; conn. w. *haptein* set on fire.] *Med.* A small usu. white ulcer occurring in groups in the mouth or on the tongue; *rare* the occurrence of such ulcers. Usu. in *pl.*
¶Orig. applied esp. to the ulcers associated with candidiasis, but now usu. excluding these.
aphthous *a.* of the nature of or characterized by aphthae M18.

aphyllous /əˈfɪləs/ *a.* E19. [f. mod.L *aphyllus* f. Gk *aphullos*, f. A-[10] + *phullon* leaf: see -OUS.] Without leaves; *Bot.* inherently leafless.

apian /ˈeɪpɪən/ *a.* E19. [L *apianus*, f. *apis* bee: see -AN.] Of or pertaining to bees.

apiarian /eɪpɪˈɛːrɪən/ *a.* & *n.* E19. [f. as next + -AN.] **A** *adj.* Of or pertaining to bee-keeping. E19. **B** *n.* = APIARIST. Now *rare* or *obs.* E19.

apiary /ˈeɪpɪəri/ *n.* M17. [f. L *apiarium*, f. *apis* bee: see -ARY[1].] A place where bees are kept.
apiarist *n.* a person who keeps an apiary; a bee-keeper: E19.

apical /ˈeɪpɪk(ə)l, ˈap-/ *a.* E19. [f. L *apic-*, APEX *n.*[1] + -AL[1].] 1 Of or pertaining to an apex; situated at the tip or summit. E19. 2 *Phonet.* Of a sound etc.: made using the tip of the tongue. L19.
apically *adv.* at or towards the apex L19.

Apician /əˈpɪʃ(ə)n/ *a.* Now *rare.* E17. [f. *Apicius* Roman epicure of the early 1st cent. AD + -AN.] Of or pertaining to luxurious eating; epicurean.

†a pick-pack *adv. phr.* see PIGGYBACK *adv.*

apico- /ˈeɪpɪkəʊ, ˈap-/ *comb. form.* E20. [f. APICAL + -O-.] Forming adjs. & ns. (esp. in *Phonet.*) w. the sense 'apical and', as *apico-alveolar, -dental, -palatal.*

apiculate /əˈpɪkjʊlət/ *a.* E19. [f. as APICULUS + -ATE[2].] Chiefly *Bot.* Terminating in a minute point.

apiculi *n.* pl. of APICULUS.

apiculture /ˈeɪpɪkʌltʃə/ *n.* M19. [f. L *apis* bee + -CULTURE.] Bee-keeping, bee-rearing.
apiˈcultural *a.* L19. **apiˈculturist** *n.* a person who practises apiculture L19.

apiculus /əˈpɪkjʊləs/ *n.* Now *rare.* Pl. **-li** /-lʌɪ, -liː/. M19. [mod.L, dim. of APEX *n.*[1]: see -CULE.] A minute point or tip.

apiece /əˈpiːs/ *adv.* LME. [f. A *a.* + PIECE *n.*] For each piece, article, or person; each, severally.
E. WAUGH Each sold its thousand copies at five guineas apiece. J. T. STORY We now sat up on the bunk, sipping a large scotch apiece.

a-pieces /əˈpiːsɪz/ *adv. obs.* exc. *dial.* M16. [f. A *prep.*[1] 2 + PIECE *n.* + -S[1].] In pieces; to pieces.

†apike *adv.* & *pred. a.* see APEAK.

apish /ˈeɪpɪʃ/ *a.* LME. [f. APE *n.* + -ISH[1].] 1 Of the nature or appearance of an ape. LME. 2 Apelike in manner; foolish, silly, affected. M16. 3 Unintelligently imitative. L16.
apishly *adv.* L16. **apishness** *n.* M16.

aplanatic /apləˈnatɪk/ *a.* L18. [f. Gk *aplanētos* free from error, f. A-[10] + *planan* wander, + -IC.] Free from spherical aberration.
ˈaplanat *n.* [-AT[2]] an aplanatic compound lens L19. **aˈplanatism** *n.* freedom from spherical aberration M19.

aplasia /əˈpleɪzɪə/ *n.* L19. [f. A-[10] + -PLASIA.] *Med.* Congenital absence or defectiveness of an organ or tissue.
aplastic /-ˈplas-/ *a.* pertaining to or characterized by aplasia; unable to form new tissue: M19.

aplenty /əˈplɛnti/ *adv.* M19. [f. A-[2] + PLENTY *n.*] In plenty, in abundance.

aplite /ˈaplʌɪt/ *n.* L19. [G *Aplit*, f. Gk *haplous* simple (named on account of its composition): see -ITE[1].] *Geol.* A light-coloured hypabyssal igneous rock having a characteristic saccharoidal texture and usu. granitic composition.
aˈplitic *a.* consisting or characteristic of aplite E20.

aplomb /əˈplɒm/ *n.* L18. [Fr., f. *à plomb* according to the plummet.] 1 Perpendicularity; steadiness. Now *rare* or *obs.* L18. 2 Self-possession, coolness; assurance. E19.

aplustre /əˈplʌstri/ *n.* Pl. **-tra** /-trə/, **-tria** /-trɪə/. E18. [L f. Gk *aphlaston.*] The curved and ornamented stern of an ancient Greek or Roman ship.

apnoea /apˈniːə/ *n.* Also ***apnea.** E18. [mod.L f. Gk *apnoia*, f. *apnous* breathless: see -IA[1].] *Med.* Interruption or cessation of breathing.
apnoeic *a.* characterized by or suffering from apnoea L19.

apo- /ˈapəʊ/ *pref.* Bef. a vowel or *h* usu. **ap-**. [Repr. Gk *apo-* off, from, away, quite.] A productive pref., chiefly in *Sci.*, esp. w. the senses 'separate', 'away from', 'other than', as *apocarpous*, *apocrine*, *apogamy*. In *Astron.* forming ns. denoting the point in the orbit of a body at which it is furthest from the primary about which it revolves (opp. PERI-).

aˈpastron *n.* [Gk *astron* star] *Astron.* the point furthest from a star in the path of a body orbiting that star E20. **apoˈapsis** *n.*, pl. **-apses** /-ˈapsiːz/, *Astron.* the point in the path of an orbiting body at which it is furthest from the primary L20. **apojove** *n.* (*Astron.*) the point furthest from Jupiter in the orbit of any of Jupiter's satellites M19.

Apocalypse /əˈpɒkəlɪps/ *n.* In sense 2 also **a-**. OE. [(O)Fr. f. eccl.L *apocalypsis* f. Gk *apokalupsis*, f. *apokaluptein* uncover, f. APO- + *kaluptein* cover.] **1** The supposed revelation of the future made to St John in the island of Patmos; the book of the New Testament relating this. OE. **2** Any vision or prophecy, esp. of violent or climactic events comparable with those foretold in the book *Revelation of St John*. Also, the events themselves. LME.

apocalypst *n.* (*rare*) = APOCALYPTIST E19.

apocalyptic /əpɒkəˈlɪptɪk/ *n.* & *a.* E17. [Fr. *apocalyptique* adj. f. Gk *apokaluptikos*, f. *apokaluptein*: see prec., -IC.] **A** *n.* **1** The writer of the Apocalypse, St John the Divine; the author or revealer of any comparable vision of the future. E17. **2** Apocalyptic teaching, philosophy, or literature. L19.

1 P. JOHNSON All societies contain not only creators and builders but apocalyptics. 2 R. H. CHARLES Prophecy and Apocalyptic . . both claim to be a communication through the Divine Spirit of the character and will and purposes of God. *Scrutiny* A periodical which has previously discussed the problems of the relation between culture and the coming social-economic revolution mainly in terms of the crudest Marxian apocalyptic.

B *adj.* **1** Of, pertaining to, or concerned with the Revelation of St John. M17. **2** Of a person: concerned with or given to (similar) visions of the future. M17. **3** Resembling the Apocalypse; revelatory, prophetic. L17.

1 D. MASSON Meade was at the head of the Apocalyptic commentators. 2 R. SOUTH That some apocalyptick ignoramus . . must . . pick it out of some abused, martyred prophecy of Ezechiel. *Time* As for where the current turmoil is leading Portugal, Lagoa is increasingly apocalyptic. 3 A. C. SWINBURNE The recognition of the apocalyptic fact that a workman can only be known by his work.

apocalyptical *a.* M17. **apocalyptically** *adv.* after the manner or by means of revelation or of the Apocalypse M18. **apocalypticism** /-sɪz(ə)m/, **-tism** *ns.* belief in an imminent apocalypse L19.

apocalyptist /əpɒkəˈlɪptɪst/ *n.* M19. [f. Gk *apokaluptein* (see APOCALYPSE) + -IST.] The author of the Apocalypse or a similarly prophetic work; a commentator on the Apocalypse.

apocarpous /apəˈkɑːpəs/ *a.* M19. [f. APO- + Gk *karpos* fruit + -OUS.] *Bot.* Of a gynoecium: having separated carpels. Opp. SYNCARPOUS.

apocatastasis /ˌapə(ʊ)kəˈtastəsɪs/ *n.* Also **-kat-**. L17. [L f. Gk *apokatastasis* re-establishment, f. as APO- + CATASTASIS.] Restoration, renewal, return; *spec.* in *Theol.*, the ultimate salvation of all moral beings.

apocentre /ˈapə(ʊ)sɛntə/ *n.* Also ***-ter**. E20. [f. APO- + CENTRE *n.*] The point in the path of a body revolving round a centre at which it is furthest from the centre.

apochromatic /ˌapə(ʊ)krəˈmatɪk/ *a.* L19. [f. APO- + CHROMATIC.] Corrected for chromatic aberration at three wavelengths. Cf. ACHROMATIC.

ˈapochromat *n.* [-AT[2]] an apochromatic lens or lens system E20.

apocope /əˈpɒkəpi/ *n.* M16. [Late L f. Gk *apokopē*, f. *apokoptein* cut off, f. APO- + *koptein* to cut.] The loss of one or more letters or syllables at the end of a word.

apocopate *v.t.* remove or shorten by apocope E19. **apocoˈpation** *n.* M18.

apocrine /ˈapəkrʌɪn, -krɪn/ *a.* E20. [f. APO- + Gk *krinein* to separate.] *Physiol.* Designating or pertaining to glands which lose some of their cytoplasm during secretion, *esp.* sweat glands opening into hair follicles (e.g. in the armpits and pubic region). Cf. ECCRINE, HOLOCRINE, MEROCRINE.

apocrisiary /apəˈkrɪzɪəri/ *n.* Also **-sary** /-zəri/. LME. [med.L *apocrisiarius*, f. Gk *apokrisis* answer: see -ARY[1].] A person appointed as a representative; *spec.* a papal nuncio.

Apocrypha /əˈpɒkrɪfə/ *a.* & *n.* Also **a-**. LME. [eccl.L, neut. pl. (sc. *scripta* writings) of *apocryphus* f. Gk *apokruphos* hidden, f. *apokruptein* to hide: see APO-.] †**A** *adj.* = APOCRYPHAL *a.* 1, 2. LME–L17. **B** *n.* (Usu. treated as *sing.*; rarely as *pl.*, w. *sing.* **-phon** /-fɒn/.) A writing or statement of doubtful authorship or authenticity; *spec.* (*a*) those Old Testament books included in the Septuagint and Vulgate which are not included in the Hebrew Scriptures, and which were excluded from the Protestant canon at the Reformation; (*b*) *New Testament Apocrypha*, various early Christian writings parallel to but excluded from the New Testament canon. LME.

apocryphal /əˈpɒkrɪf(ə)l/ *a.* & *n.* In sense A.2 also **A-**. L16. [f. prec. + -AL[1].] **A** *adj.* **1** Of a writing, statement, story, etc.: of doubtful authenticity; spurious, false, mythical. L16. **2** Of or pertaining to the Apocrypha. E17. **3** Sham, counterfeit. E17.

1 V. BRITTAIN We collected all the tales of her, both authentic and apocryphal, that we could gather together. 3 JONSON A whoreson, upstart, apocryphal captain.

†**B** *n.* An apocryphal writing. Only in 17.

apocryphally *adv.* without authenticity M19.

apocynthion /apə(ʊ)ˈsɪnθɪən/ *n.* M20. [f. APO- + neut. of Gk *Kunthios* (adj.) designating Mount Cynthus: see CYNTHIA.] *Astron.* The point at which a spacecraft in lunar orbit is furthest from the moon's centre, after having been launched from the earth. Cf. APOLUNE.

†**apod** *a.* Also **-ode**. Only in 19. [f. as next: cf. Fr. *apode*.] *Zool.* Apodous; apodal.

apodal /ˈapəd(ə)l/ *a.* & *n.* Now *rare* or *obs.* M18. [f. Gk *apod-*, *apous* without feet, f. A-[10] + *pous* foot, partly through mod.L *Apoda*, *Apodes* (taxonomic groupings): see next, -AL[1].] *Zool.* **A** *adj.* Lacking feet; (of fish) lacking ventral fins. M18. **B** *n.* = next. M19.

apodan /ˈapəd(ə)n/ *n.* L19. [f. mod.L *Apoda*, an order (usu. called Gymnophiona) + -AN: see prec.] *Zool.* = CAECILIAN.

†**apode** *a.* var. of APOD.

apodeictic *a.* etc., **-deixis** *n.*, see APODICTIC etc., -DIXIS.

apodeme /ˈapədiːm/ *n.* M19. [mod.L *apodema*, f. Gk APO- + *demas* body, frame.] *Zool.* A hollow invagination of the cuticle of an arthropod, which serves as a point of attachment for muscle.

apodictic /apəˈdɪktɪk/ *a.* Also **-deictic** /-ˈdʌɪktɪk/. M17. [L *apodicticus* f. Gk *apodeiktikos*, f. *apodeiknunai* demonstrate, f. APO- + *deiknunai* show.] Clearly demonstrated or established.

apod(e)ictical *a.* (*arch.*) based on necessary truth, apodictic L16. **apod(e)ictically** *adv.* E17.

apodixis /apə(ʊ)ˈdɪksɪs/ *n.* *rare.* Also **-deixis** /-ˈdʌɪksɪs/. L16. [L f. Gk *apodeiksis*, f. *apodeiknunai*: see prec.] Demonstration; proof.

apodosis /əˈpɒdəsɪs/ *n.* Pl. **-oses** /-əsiːz/. E17. [Late L f. Gk, f. *apodidonai* give back, f. APO- + *didonai* give.] *Gram.* & *Rhet.* The concluding clause of a sentence; *spec.* the consequent clause of a conditional sentence. Opp. PROTASIS 2.

apodous /ˈapədəs/ *a.* E19. [f. as APODAL + -OUS.] *Zool.* Without feet; having only rudimentary feet.

apodyterium /ˌapədɪˈtɪərɪəm/ *n.* Pl. **-ria** /-rɪə/. E17. [L f. Gk *apodutērion*, f. *apoduein* to strip.] *Class. Hist.* A room adjacent to a bath or palaestra where clothes were deposited.

apoenzyme /apəʊˈɛnzʌɪm/ *n.* M20. [f. APO- + ENZYME.] *Biochem.* The protein part of an enzyme, which is inactive unless combined with a coenzyme.

apogamy /əˈpɒgəmi/ *n.* L19. [f. APO- + -GAMY.] *Bot.* Asexual reproduction; *spec.* the production in some ferns etc. of a sporophyte directly from a prothallus without the union of gametes.

apogamous *a.* characterized by or of the nature of apogamy L19. **apogamously** *adv.* L19.

apogee /ˈapədʒiː/ *n.* Formerly also in L & Gk forms. L16. [Fr. *apogée* or mod.L *apog(a)eum* f. Gk *apogaion*, *-geion* use as n. (sc. *diastēma* distance) of neut. of *apogaios*, *-geios* far from the earth, f. APO- + *gaia*, *gē* earth.] (Opp. PERIGEE.) **1** *Astron.* The point furthest from the earth in the path of a body orbiting the earth. (Orig. also used w. ref. to the sun and planets, viewed geocentrically.) L16. †**2** The point in the sky at which the sun has the highest altitude at noon (i.e. at the summer solstice). E–M17. **3** *fig.* The furthest or highest point; the culmination, the climax. M17.

3 P. A. SCHOLES Beethoven's Ninth Symphony remains the apogee of the orchestral art. E. BOWEN This conversation we're having now . . seems to me the apogee of bad taste.

†**apoga(e)ic** *a.* M–L19. **apoˈgeal** *a.* (now *rare* or *obs.*) M18. **apoˈgean** *a.* of or pertaining to apogee (*lit.* or *fig.*) M17.

apograph /ˈapəgrɑːf/ *n.* M17. [Gk *apographon*, f. *apographein* to copy f. as APO- + *graphein* write.] An exact copy or transcript.

à point /a pwɛ̃/ *adv. phr.* E20. [Fr. = to the point.] Esp. *Cookery.* At or to exactly the right point; just enough, without overcooking or undercooking.

apokatastasis *n.* var. of APOCATASTASIS.

apo koinou /ˌapəʊ ˈkɔɪnuː, ˈkɔɪnaʊ/ *a.* & *adv. phr.* L19. [Gk, lit. 'in common'.] *Gram.* Designating a construction comprising two clauses having an unrepeated word or phrase in common; so as to form such a construction.

apolar /eɪˈpəʊlə/ *a.* M19. [f. A-[10] + POLAR *a.*] Not polar; having no poles.

apoˈlarity *n.* E20.

apolaustic /apəˈlɔːstɪk/ *a.* M19. [Gk *apolaustikos*, f. *apolauein* enjoy: see -IC.] Given to enjoyment; self-indulgent.

apolausticism /-sɪz(ə)m/ *n.* L19.

apolitical /eɪpəˈlɪtɪk(ə)l/ *a.* M20. [f. A-[10] + POLITICAL *a.*] Unconcerned with or detached from politics.

Apollinarian /əpɒlɪˈnɛːrɪən/ *n.* & *a.* L16. [f. L *Apollinaris* of Apollo, also as pers. name: see -ARIAN.] **A** *n.* *Eccl. Hist.* An adherent of the heretical views of Apollinaris of Laodicea (4th cent. AD), who held that Christ assumed a human body but not a human soul. L16. **B** *adj.* **1** *Eccl. Hist.* Of or pertaining to Apollinaris or his beliefs. M17. **2** Sacred to or in honour of Apollo. Cf. APOLLONIAN *a.* 1. M18.

Apollinarianism *n.* the doctrine of the Apollinarians L19. **Apollinarist** *n.* (now *rare* or *obs.*) = APOLLINARIAN *n.* LME.

Apollinaris /əpɒlɪˈnɛːrɪs/ *n.* L19. [f. *Apollinarisburg* (see below).] An effervescent mineral water from Apollinarisburg in the Rhineland of Germany.

Apolline /əˈpɒlʌɪn, -lɪn/ *a.* E17. [L *Apollineus*, f. *Apollin-*, *Apollo*.] Of, pertaining to, or resembling Apollo (see APOLLONIAN *a.* 1).

Apollinian /apəˈlɪnɪən/ *a.* E20.

Apollonian /apəˈləʊnɪən/ *a.* & *n.* E17. [f. L *Apollonius* f. Gk. *Apollōnios* of Apollo, also as pers. name: see -IAN.] **A** *adj.* **1** Of, pertaining to, or resembling Apollo, the sun-god of the Greeks and Romans, patron of music and poetry; *spec.* (of character etc.) serene, rational, self-disciplined (opp. *Dionysian*). E17. **2** *Math.* Of Apollonius of Perga, Alexandrine mathematician of the 3rd cent. BC, esp. w. ref. to his work on conic sections. E18. **B** *n.* A follower or worshipper of Apollo; a person of Apollonian character. E17.

Apoˈllonic *a.* = APOLLONIAN *a.* 1 E19.

Apollonicon /apəˈlɒnɪk(ə)n/ *n.* E19. [f. as prec. after HARMONICON.] *Hist.* An organ of great power and complexity, exhibited in London in the early 19th cent.

Apollyon /ə'pɒlɪən/ *n.* LME. [late L (Vulgate) f. Gk *Apolluōn* destroyer (tr. ABADDON, *Rev.* 9:11), use as n. of pres. pple of *apollunai* intensive of *ollunai* destroy.] The Devil as destroyer.

apologetic /əpɒlə'dʒɛtɪk/ *n.* & *a.* LME. [Fr. *apologétique* or late L *apologeticus* f. Gk *apologētikos* fit for defence, f. *apologeisthai*: see APOLOGY *n.*[1], -IC.] A *n.* 1 A formal defence or justification of a person, doctrine, action, etc. LME. 2 *sing.* & (usu.) in *pl.* Reasoned defence, esp. of Christian belief. M18. B *adj.* 1 Of the nature of a defence; vindicatory. M17. 2 Regretfully acknowledging or excusing fault or failure; diffident. M19.

apologetical *a.* L16. **apologetically** *adv.* in an apologetic manner; by way of apology: M17.

apologia /apə'ləʊdʒɪə/ *n.* L18. [L: see APOLOGY *n.*[1]] A written defence of one's opinions or conduct.

†apological *a.* E17–M19. [f. as prec. + -ICAL.] Of the nature of an apology or defence; apologetic.

apologise *v.* var. of APOLOGIZE.

apologist /ə'pɒlədʒɪst/ *n.* M17. [Fr. *apologiste*, f. Gk *apologizesthai*: see next, -IST.] A person who defends another, a belief, etc., by argument; a literary champion.

apologize /ə'pɒlədʒʌɪz/ *v.* Also **-ise**. L16. [Gk *apologizesthai* render an account, f. *apologos*: see next, -IZE. Now assoc. w. APOLOGY *n.*[1]] 1 *v.i.* Make an apology (*for* a person, circumstance, action, etc.). L16. 2 *v.t.* †a Make an apology for (an action etc.) E17–M18. b Acknowledge, and express regret, *that* (something has occurred etc.). M20.

1 HENRY MORE I can justly apologize for my self that Necessity has no law. E. WAUGH His friends bore him to the gate and . . his host . . returned to apologize. S. NAIPAUL The head waiter, admitting his fault, apologized profusely for the oversight. 2a SWIFT T'apologise his late offence. b A. J. P. TAYLOR Lloyd George apologizing to the house of commons that misplaced personal loyalty . . had made him cling to an incompetent minister.

apologizer *n.* a person who apologizes M17.

apologue /'apəlɒg/ *n.* Orig. **†-logy** M16. [Fr., or late L *apologus* f. Gk *apologos* story, account, f. APO- + *logos* discourse: see -LOGUE.] A moral fable, *esp.* one having animals or inanimate things as its characters.

apology /ə'pɒlədʒi/ *n.*[1] M16. [Fr. *apologie* or late L *apologia* f. Gk = speech in defence, f. *apologeisthai* speak in one's own defence: see -LOGY.] 1 A formal defence or vindication against an (actual or potential) accusation or imputation. M16. 2 A justification, an explanation, an excuse. L16. 3 A frank acknowledgement of fault or failure, given by way of reparation; an explanation that no offence was intended, with regret for any given or taken. L16. 4 *an apology for*, a poor substitute for (a thing), a poor or inadequate specimen of. M18.

1 T. SHERLOCK And before the same great Court of Areopagites Paul made his Apology. C. CONNOLLY The book closes with a long and reasoned apology for the pursuit of happiness. 2 DEFOE The consequence . . will be the best apology for my conduct. 3 G. K. CHESTERTON I am afraid my fury and your insult are too shocking to be wiped out even with an apology. G. B. SHAW Sitting down again with a gesture of apology. A. SHAFFER I wonder if all her jewellery was inscribed with apologies for your bully boy behaviour. **with apologies to —**: used to introduce a parody or adaptation. 4 C. HAMPTON It never begins to dribble across your apology for a mind that half a million children under five starved to death in Brazil last year.

†apology *n.*[2] var. of APOLOGUE.

apolune /'apə(ʊ)luːn/ *n.* M20. [f. APO- + L *luna* moon.] *Astron.* The point at which a spacecraft in lunar orbit (esp. one launched from the moon) is furthest from the moon's centre. Cf. APOCYNTHION.

apomixis /apə'mɪksɪs/ *n.* E20. [f. APO- + Gk *mixis*, *mikt-* mingling.] *Bot.* Asexual reproduction, esp. in a form outwardly resembling a sexual process.

'apomict *n.* [back-form. f. APOMICTIC] a plant which reproduces by apomixis M20. **apomictic** *a.* characterized by or of the nature of apomixis E20. **apomictically** *adv.* E20.

apomorphine /apə'mɔːfiːn/ *n.* L19. [f. APO- + MORPHINE.] *Chem.* A white crystalline compound, $C_{17}H_{17}NO_2$, which was originally derived from morphine and is used as an emetic and in the treatment of Parkinsonism.

Also **†apomorphia** *n.* M–L19.

aponeurosis /apənjʊ'rəʊsɪs/ *n.* Pl. **-roses** /-'rəʊsiːz/. L17. [mod.L f. Gk *aponeurōsis*, f. APO- + *neuron* sinew + -OSIS.] *Anat.* A sheet of pearly-white fibrous tissue which takes the place of a tendon in sheetlike muscles having a wide area of attachment.

aponeurotic *a.* pertaining to or of the nature of an aponeurosis M18.

a-poop /ə'puːp/ *adv.* L17. [f. A *prep.*[1] 1 + POOP *n.*[1]] *Naut.* On the poop; astern.

apopetalous /apə'pɛt(ə)ləs/ *a.* M19. [f. APO- + PETAL + -OUS.] *Bot.* Having the petals separate.

apophatic /apə'fatɪk/ *a.* M19. [Gk *apophatikos* negative, f. *apophasis* denial, f. as APO- + *phanai* speak: see -IC.] *Theol.* Of knowledge of God: obtained through negation. Opp. CATAPHATIC.

†apophlegmatic *a.* & *n.* E–M18. [Gk *apophlegmatikos*, f. as APO- + *phlegmatikos*: see PHLEGMATIC.] *Med.* (An) expectorant.

†apophlegmatism *n.* an apophlegmatic agent or action E17–M18.

apophony /ə'pɒfəni/ *n.* L19. [Fr. *apophonie*, f. as APO-: see -PHONY.] *Philol.* = ABLAUT.

apo'phonic *a.* M20.

apophthegm /'apəθɛm/ *n.* Also ***apothegm**. M16. [Fr. *apophthegme* or mod.L *apophthegma* f. Gk, f. *apophtheggesthai* speak one's opinion plainly, f. as APO- + *phtheggesthai* speak.] A terse saying; a pithy maxim.

apophthegmatic /-θɛg'mat-/ *a.* = APOPHTHEGMATICAL L18. **apophthegmatical** /-θɛg'mat-/ *a.* pertaining to or of the nature of an apophthegm; pithy, sententious; given to the use of apophthegms: L16. **apophthegmatically** /-θɛg'mat-/ *adv.* M17. **apophthegmatize** /-'θɛgmət-/ *v.i.* write or speak in apophthegms M17.

apophyge /ə'pɒfɪdʒi/ *n.* M16. [Gk *apophugē* lit. 'escape', f. *apophugein* flee away.] *Archit.* The part of a column where it springs out of its base, or joins its capital, usu. moulded into a concave sweep or cavetto.

apophyllite /ə'pɒfɪlʌɪt/ *n.* E19. [f. APO- + Gk *phullon* leaf + -ITE[1].] *Min.* A tetragonal hydrated silicate and fluoride of calcium and potassium, related to zeolites and occurring usu. as white prisms with a vitreous lustre.

apophysis /ə'pɒfɪsɪs/ *n.* Also **†-physe**. Pl. **-physes** /-fɪsiːz/. L16. [mod.L f. Gk *apophusis* offshoot, f. APO- + *phusis* growth.] 1 *Anat.* & *Zool.* A protuberance from a bone or other hard tissue. L16. 2 *Bot.* A dilatation of the base of the sporangium in some mosses. L18.

apo'physeal, -ial *a.* pertaining to or of the nature of an apophysis L19.

apoplectic /apə'plɛktɪk/ *a.* & *n.* E17. [Fr. *apoplectique* or late L *apoplecticus* f. Gk *apoplēktikos*, f. as APOPLEXY: see -IC.] A *adj.* 1 Of or pertaining to apoplexy; causing or conducive to apoplexy. E17. †2 Of use against apoplexy. L17–M18. 3 Suffering from or liable to apoplexy. E18.

1 DICKENS One of your stiff-starched apoplectic cravats. *apoplectic stroke*: see STROKE *n.*[1] 2b. 3 J. AUSTEN A short-necked, apoplectic sort of fellow.

B *n.* A sufferer from apoplexy; a person liable to apoplexy. L17.

†apoplectical *a.* E17–E19. **apoplectically** *adv.* L19. **apoplectiform** *a.* (now *rare* or *obs.*) having the form of apoplexy M19.

apoplex /'apəplɛks/ *n.* & *v. arch.* M16. [Late L *apoplexis* f. Gk, var. of *apoplēxia*: see next.] A *n.* Apoplexy. M16. B *v.t.* Strike with apoplexy; benumb. E17.

apoplexy /'apəplɛksi/ *n.* LME. [(O)Fr. *apoplexie* f. late L *apoplexia* f. Gk *apoplēxia*, f. *apoplēssein* disable by a stroke, f. APO- + *plēssein* strike.] 1 A sudden loss of sensation and movement due to a disturbance of blood supply to the brain; a stroke. LME. 2 With specifying wd: a haemorrhage or failure of blood supply in another organ or part. Now *rare* or *obs.* M19.

apoptosis /apəp'təʊsɪs/ *n.* E19. [Gk *apoptōsis* lit. 'falling away or off', f. as APO- + PTOSIS.] 1 *Med.* Loosening (of a bandage, ligament, etc.); the loosening and falling off of a scab or crust. *rare* (only in Dicts.). E19. 2 *Med.* & *Biol.* The controlled destruction of cells, as in the growth and development of an organism; the type of cell lysis characteristic of this. L20.

apoptotic /-'tɒtɪk/ *a.* L20.

aporetic /apə'rɛtɪk/ *a.* E17. [Fr. *aporétique* f. Gk *aporētikos*, f. *aporein* be at a loss, f. A-[10] + *poros* passage: see -IC.] Full of doubts and objections; inclined to doubt.

aporia /ə'pɔːrɪə, ə'pɒrɪə/ *n.* M16. [Late L f. Gk, f. *aporos* impassable, f. A-[10] + *poros*: see prec., -IA[1].] 1 *Rhet.* The expression of doubt. M16. 2 A doubtful matter, a perplexing difficulty. L19.

aport /ə'pɔːt/ *adv.* & *pred. a.* M16. [f. A *prep.*[1] 1 + PORT *n.*[5]] *Naut.* On or towards the port side of the ship.

put the helm aport port the helm, i.e. move the rudder to starboard, causing the vessel to turn to the right.

aposematic /ˌapəʊsɪ'matɪk/ *a.* L19. [f. APO- + SEMATIC.] *Zool.* Of coloration, markings, etc.: serving to warn or repel.

aposiopesis /ˌapəsʌɪə'piːsɪs/ *n.* Pl. **-peses** /-'piːsiːz/. L16. [L f. Gk *aposiōpēsis*, f. *aposiōpan* be silent.] *Rhet.* (A) sudden breaking-off in speech.

aposiopetic /-'pɛtɪk/ *a.* M17.

apospory /ə'pɒsp(ə)ri/ *n.* L19. [f. APO- + Gk *sporos* seed + -Y[3].] *Bot.* In some cryptogams: the growth of a gametophyte directly from a sporophyte, without spore production.

aposporous *a.* characterized by or of the nature of apospory L19. **aposporously** *adv.* L19.

apostasy /ə'pɒstəsi/ *n.* Also **†-acy**. ME. [eccl.L *apostasia* f. late Gk alt. of *apostasis* defection: see -Y[3].] 1 Abandonment or renunciation of one's religious faith or moral allegiance. ME. b Renunciation of religious vows without dispensation. ME. 2 The abandonment of principles, beliefs, or party. L16.

apostate /'apəsteɪt/ *n.* & *a.* Also **†-ata**. ME. [(O)Fr., or eccl.L *apostata* f. late Gk *apostatēs* apostate, runaway slave, f. as APO- + *stat-* rel. to *histanai* cause to stand.] A *n.* 1 A person who abandons his or her religious faith or moral allegiance. ME. b A person who renounces religious vows without dispensation. LME. 2 *gen.* A person who deserts his or her principles or allegiance; a turncoat, a renegade. LME. B *adj.* 1 Unfaithful to religious principles or creed, or to moral allegiance; unbelieving, infidel. LME. 2 *gen.* Unfaithful, renegade. L17.

apo'static *a.* = APOSTATICAL L16. **apo'statical** *a.* of the nature of apostates or apostasy; heretical: M16. **a'postatism** *n.* apostasy L16.

apostatize /ə'pɒstətʌɪz/ *v.i.* Also **-ise**. M16. [med.L *apostatizare* (earlier *apostatare*), f. *apostata*: see prec., -IZE.] 1 Become an apostate (*from* a religion etc.). M16. 2 *gen.* Abandon a principle etc.; transfer one's allegiance (*from* a cause, party, etc.). M17.

†apostem *n.* var. of APOSTUME.

†apostemate *v.*, **-ation** *n.* vars. of APOSTUMATE, -ATION.

†aposteme *n.* var. of APOSTUME.

a posteriori /eɪ, ɑː, pɒˌstɛrɪ'ɔːrʌɪ, pɒˌstɪə-/ *adv.* & *a. phr.* E17. [L = from what comes after.] 1 Of reasoning: (by) proceeding from effects to causes; inductive(ly), empirical(ly). Opp. A PRIORI. E17. 2 From behind; on the buttocks. *facetious.* M18.

†aposthumate *v.*, **-ation** *n.* vars. of APOSTUMATE, -ATION.

†aposthume *n.* var. of APOSTUME.

apostil /ə'pɒstɪl/ *n.* & *v.* As n. also **-ille**. E16. [OFr. *apostil(le)* n., f. *apostiller* vb, f. as POSTIL *n.*, *v.*] A *n.* A marginal note, an annotation. E16. B *v.t.* Annotate; inscribe with marginal notes. M17.

apostle /əˈpɒs(ə)l/ *n.* Also **A-** (the usual sp. in biblical usage & in sense 5). OE. [eccl.L *apostolus* f. Gk *apostolos* messenger, f. *apostellein* send forth: infl. by OFr. *apostle.*] 1 In biblical translations: a person sent, a messenger; *spec.* Christ. OE. 2 Each of the twelve witnesses whom Jesus sent out to preach his gospel. Also, Barnabas or Paul. OE. 3 Any person who imitates or is held to resemble the Apostles; a pioneering missionary. LME. b An advocate or follower of a cause, activity, etc.; a leader of reform. E19. †4 Any of the books of Acts and Epistles of the Apostles. LME–M19. 5 *Hist.* A member of an exclusive conversazione society ('The Apostles') at Cambridge University. E19.

1 NEB *Heb.* 3:1 Think of the Apostle and High Priest of the religion we profess. 3 A. MACLAINE Boniface has gained the title of the Apostle of Germany. b A. J. P. TAYLOR The members of Milner's kindergarten were, in the nineteen-thirties, apostles of appeasement. M. KEANE When I was twenty, foxhunting was Wholly Holy and everybody was an apostle or disciple.

Comb.: **apostle-bird** *Austral.* any of various birds often seen in flocks of about twelve; *spec.* a grey magpie-lark, *Struthidea cinerea*; **Apostles' Creed** the simplest and prob. earliest form of the Christian creed, anciently ascribed to the Apostles; **apostle spoon**: with the figure of an Apostle at the end of the handle.

apostlehood *n.* OE. **apostleship** *n.* E16. †**apost(o)less** *n.* a female apostle LME–E19. **apostolize** *v.t.* & *i.* (*rare*) proclaim (a message); act like an apostle: M17.

apostolate /əˈpɒstələt/ *n.* LME. [eccl.L *apostolatus* f. *apostolus*: see prec., -ATE¹.] 1 The position or office of an apostle. LME. 2 The Apostles collectively; a group comparable to or associated with the Apostles. LME.

apostolic /apəˈstɒlɪk/ *a.* & *n.* Also **A-**. ME. [Fr. *apostolique* or eccl.L *apostolicus* f. Gk *apostolikos*, f. *apostolos*: see APOSTLE, -IC.] A *adj.* 1 Of or pertaining to the Apostles; contemporary with the Apostles. ME. 2 Of or pertaining to the Pope as successor of St Peter; papal. LME. 3 Of the nature or character of the Apostles; befitting an apostle. M16. 4 *Hist.* Of or pertaining to the Cambridge Apostles. M19.

1 **Apostolic Fathers** the early leaders of the Christian Church. **apostolic succession** the uninterrupted transmission of spiritual authority through a succession of Popes and bishops from the Apostles. CATHOLIC (*and*) *Apostolic Church.* 3 VICAR *apostolic.*

B *n.* A member of any of various sects seeking to imitate the Apostles. L16.

apostolical *a.* LME. **apostolically** *adv.* E17. **apostolicity** /-ˈlɪsɪti/ *n.* apostolic character or origin E19.

apostrophe /əˈpɒstrəfi/ *n.*¹ M16. [L f. Gk *apostrophē*, f. *apostrephein* turn away, f. as APO- + *strephein* to turn.] *Rhet.* Sudden exclamatory address; an exclamatory passage addressed to a particular person (freq. absent or dead) or thing.

apostrophe /əˈpɒstrəfi/ *n.*² Also †**-phus.** M16. [Fr., or late L *apostrophus* f. Gk *apostrophos* mark of elision, use as n. (sc. *prosōdia* accent) of adj. 'turned away', f. *apostrephein*: see prec.] †1 The omission of one or more letters in a word. M16–M17. 2 A sign (') used to indicate the omission of one or more letters or numerals (as in *can't*, *o'er*, *'cello*; *spirit of '76* (i.e. 1776)), or in marking the possessive case (*man's*, *boys'*). L16.

apostrophic /apəˈstrɒfɪk/ *a.* L18. [f. APOSTROPHE *n.*¹, *n.*² + -IC.] 1 Of or pertaining to the sign called an apostrophe. L18. 2 Of or pertaining to a rhetorical apostrophe; given to apostrophe. E19.

apostrophize /əˈpɒstrəfaɪz/ *v.t.* & *i.* Also **-ise.** E17. [f. APOSTROPHE *n.*¹, *n.*² + -IZE.] 1 Mark the omission in letters in (a word) with an apostrophe; omit one or more letters in a word. *rare.* E17. 2 Address (someone or something) in a rhetorical apostrophe; use apostrophe. E18.

†**apostrophus** *n.* var. of APOSTROPHE *n.*²

†**apostumate** *v.* Also **-tem-, -thum-.** Pa. pple & ppl a. **-ate** (earlier), **-ated.** LME. [med.L *apostemat-* pa. ppl stem of *apostemari*, f. *apostema* APOSTUME: see -ATE³. Cf. IMPOSTUMATE.] 1 *v.t.* & *i.* Form into a cyst or abscess; fester. LME–L17. 2 *v.t.* In *pass.* Be affected by a cyst or abscess. L16–L17.

†**apostematous** *a.* festering; characterized by abscesses: M17–M19.

†**apostumation** *n.* Also **-tem-, -thum-.** LME. [OFr. *apostemation*, *apostumacion* f. med.L *apostematio(n-)*, f. as prec.: see -ATION. Cf. IMPOSTUMATION.] 1 The formation of a cyst or abscess; festering. LME–L17. 2 A cyst, an abscess. M16–M18.

†**apostume** *n.* Also **-tem(e), -thume.** LME–M18. [OFr. *aposteme*, *-ume* f. L *apostema* f. Gk = separation of pus into an abscess, f. *aposta-*, *apostēnai* withdraw: cf. IMPOSTUME.] A gathering of pus; a large abscess.

apotelesmatic /ə,pɒt(ə)ləzˈmatɪk/ *a.* M17. [Gk *apotelesmatikos*, f. *apotelesma*, f. *apotelein* bring to an end, f. as APO- + *telein* finish: see -IC.] Of or pertaining to the casting of horoscopes.

apothecary /əˈpɒθɪk(ə)ri/ *n. arch.* LME. [OFr. *apotecaire*, *-icaire* (mod. *apothicaire*) f. late L *apothecarius* storekeeper, f. *apotheca* f. Gk *apothēkē* storehouse: see -ARY¹.] 1 A person who prepares and sells drugs and other medicinal substances; a pharmaceutical chemist. LME. †2 Drugs collectively; a store or list of drugs; treatment by drugs. E16–E17.

1 **apothecaries' measure, weight** sets of units formerly used in pharmacy for liquid volume (with one fluid ounce = 8 drachms = 480 minims) and for weight (with one ounce = 8 drachms = 24 scruples = 480 grains) respectively.

apothecium /apəˈθiːsɪəm/ *n.* Pl. **-ia** /-ɪə/. E19. [mod.L f. Gk *apothēkē*: see prec., -IUM.] *Bot.* An open cup- or disc-shaped fruiting body borne by many lichens and ascomycetous fungi.

apothecial *a.* L19.

apothegm *n.* etc.: see APOPHTHEGM etc.

apothem /ˈapəθɛm/ *n. arch.* L19. [f. Gk *apotithenai* deposit, after *thema*, f. *tithenai* to place: see THEME *n.*] *Geom.* A perpendicular from the centre of a regular polygon to a side.

apotheosis /əpɒθɪˈəʊsɪs/ *n.* Pl. **-oses** /-ˈəʊsiːz/. L16. [eccl.L f. Gk *apotheōsis*, f. *apotheoun* deify, f. APO- + *theos* god.] 1 (Elevation to) divine status. L16. 2 Glorification or exaltation of a person, principle, or practice; canonization; idealization. E17. 3 Ascension to glory, resurrection, triumph; highest development, culmination. M17.

1 F. W. FARRAR The early Emperors rather discouraged . . this tendency to flatter them by a premature apotheosis. 2 COLERIDGE The apotheosis of familiar abuses . . is the vilest of superstitions. T. HARDY Thus a mild sort of apotheosis took place in his fancy, whilst she still lived and breathed within his own horizon. T. P. O'CONNOR The meeting developed into an apotheosis of the Marquis of Chandos. 3 C. WALKER His Majesties Speech upon the Scaffold, and this Death or Apotheosis. J. BRAINE An actor-manager whom I knew . . as the apotheosis of wholesome masculinity. J. G. FARRELL At any moment the pageant would begin, the triumphant apotheosis of the Empire's struggle for Peace.

a'potheose *v.t.* (now *rare*) = APOTHEOSIZE L17. **a'potheosize** *v.t.* deify; exalt; idealize: M18.

†**apotome** *n.* E16. [Gk *apotomē* cutting off, f. *apotemnein* cut off: see APO-, -TOME.] 1 *Mus.* A variety of semitone. E16–E19. 2 *Math.* A difference of two quantities which are commensurable only when raised to a power, e.g. $(\sqrt{2} - 1)$. L16–L18.

apotropaic /apətrəˈpeɪk/ *a.* L19. [f. Gk *apotropaios* averting evil, f. *apotrepein* turn away (see APO-), + -IC.] Intended to avert evil influence; considered to have the power to avert evil influence or ill luck.

a-pout /əˈpaʊt/ *adv.* & *pred. a.* L19. [f. A-² + POUT *v.* & *n.*³] Pouting.

†**apozem** *n.* LME–L19. [(O)Fr. *apozème* or late L *apozema* f. Gk, f. *apozein* boil off, f. APO- completely + *zein* to boil.] *Med.* A decoction, an infusion.

†**appair** *v.* see IMPAIR *v.*

appal /əˈpɔːl/ *v.* Also †**-pale**; ***-ll.** Infl. **-ll-.** ME. [OFr. *apal(l)ir*, f. A-⁵ + *palir* (mod. *pâlir*) PALE *v.*²] †1 *v.i.* Grow pale, fade; become enfeebled; lose flavour. ME–M19. †2 *v.t.* Make pale; cause to fade; weaken, impair. LME–E18. 3 *v.t.* Dismay, terrify; horrify, scandalize. Freq. in *pass.* LME.

3 SHAKES. *Macb.* A bold one that dare look on that Which might appal the devil. J. B. PRIESTLEY The waste of money appalled him, but he could not help being delighted by the dash and importance of it all. I. MURDOCH I was utterly appalled that Otto could have laid hands upon his wife. S. HILL I was so appalled at the broken buildings and so little worried by the broken bodies. *absol.*: J. KEBLE Thoughts that awe but not appal.

appalling *a.* dismaying, shocking; unpleasant: E19. **appallingly** *adv.* E19. **appalment** *n.* (*rare*) L16.

Appalachee *n.* var. of APALACHEE.

Appalachian /apəˈleɪtʃ(ə)n/ *a.* & *n.* L17. [f. (as) APALACHEE + -AN.] A *adj.* 1 Designating the extensive system of mountain ranges in the eastern US. Also, of, pertaining to, or characteristic of this system, its region as a whole, or that region's inhabitants. L17. 2 Designating the Apalachee and other Indian peoples of the eastern US; pertaining to or characteristic of these peoples. M18.

1 *Appalachian* DULCIMER.

B *n.* 1 In *pl.* The Appalachian mountains, or the region in general. M19. 2 An Appalachian Indian. L19.

appale, appall *v.* see APPAL.

Appaloosa /apəˈluːsə/ *n.* E20. [Prob. f. *Palouse*, a river in Idaho, USA.] (An animal of) a N. American breed of horse, usu. white with many spots of colour.

appanage /ˈap(ə)nɪdʒ/ *n.* Also **apan-.** E17. [(O)Fr. *apanage*, f. *apaner* dower (a daughter) f. med.L *appanare* provide with means of subsistence, f. L *ad* AP-¹ + *panis* bread: see -AGE.] 1 The provision made for the maintenance of the younger children of kings, princes, etc. (usu. a province, jurisdiction, or office). E17. 2 A natural accompaniment; a special attribute. M17. 3 A dependent territory or property. E19. 4 A perquisite. M19.

1 E. A. FREEMAN His son received . . the apanage of Cumberland. 2 SWIFT Had he thought it fit, That wealth should be the appennage of wit. 3 SYD. SMITH Ireland . . the most valuable appanage of our empire. *fig.*: T. E. HULME Landscape was still a toy or an appanage of figure-painting when Turner and Constable arose to reveal its independent power. 4 LYTTON Its revenues and its empire will become the appanage of the hardy soldier.

appanaged *a.* endowed with an appanage M18.

apparat /apəˈrɑːt/ *n.* M20. [Russ. f. G f. as APPARATUS.] The Communist Party machine in the former USSR and other countries.

apparatchik /apəˈratʃɪk/ *n.* Pl. **-i** /-i/, **-s.** M20. [Russ., f. prec.] 1 A member of the *apparat*; a Communist agent. M20. 2 *transf.* An implementer of party etc. policy; an executive officer. L20.

apparatus /apəˈreɪtəs/ *n.* Pl. **-uses,** (*rare*) same. E17. [L, f. *apparare* make ready, f. *ad* AP-¹ + *parare* PREPARE *v.*] 1 The things collectively necessary for the performance of some activity or function; the equipment used in doing something; a machine, a device. E17. 2 *spec.* a Equipment used for scientific experimentation or processes. M17. b The organs etc. by which a natural process is carried on. L17. c In full *critical apparatus*, = APPARATUS CRITICUS. E18. d Equipment used in athletic, gymnastic, or sporting activities. L19. †3 Preparation. M17–L18. 4 An organization within a political party or State; *esp.* = APPARAT. M20.

2a KIPP'S APPARATUS. b *Weberian apparatus*: see WEBERIAN *a.*¹

apparatus criticus /apə,reɪtəs ˈkrɪtɪkəs/ *n. phr.* Pl. ***apparatus critici*** /apə,reɪtəs ˈkrɪtɪsaɪ/. M19. [mod.L: see prec., CRITICAL.] A collection of material, as variant readings and other palaeographical and critical matter, for the textual study of a document.

apparel /əˈpar(ə)l/ *n.* ME. [OFr. *apareil* (mod. *app-*), f. as next.] 1 Furnishings, trappings; accoutrements, equipment. *arch.* ME. †b The outfit or rigging of a ship. ME–L19. †2 Physical or moral attributes; bearing, stature. ME–E16. 3 Personal outfit or attire; clothing, raiment. Now *literary*. LME. 4†a Ornamentation, embellishment. LME–L15. b An ornament embroidered on certain ecclesiastical vestments. M19. †5 The work of making ready; preparations. LME–L15.

1 J. GALSWORTHY The scarlet and green drawing-room, whose apparel made so vivid a setting for their unaccustomed costumes. 3 A. G. GARDINER He decked himself out in brave apparel to show the world that he was a person of consequence. J. BALDWIN From their apparel the sinfulness of their lives was evident. *fig.*: ADDISON The rude Stile and evil Apparel of this antiquated Song.

apparel /əˈpar(ə)l/ *v.t. arch.* Infl. **-ll-**, ***-l-**. ME. [OFr. *apareiller* (mod. *app-*), ult. f. L *ad-* AP-[1] + dim. of *par* equal.] †1 Make ready, prepare (*for*); put into proper order. ME–M17. 2 Provide with necessary things; equip. LME. †b *spec.* Equip for fighting. LME–L17. 3 Array with proper clothing; attire, clothe. LME. †4 Embellish, adorn; trick out, dress up (speciously). LME–M18.

2 LONGFELLOW Never . . owned a ship so well apparelled. 3 AV *Luke* 7:25 They which are gorgeously apparelled, and liue delicately, are in kings courts. *fig.*: WORDSWORTH When meadow, grove, and stream, To me did seem Apparelled in celestial light. 4 *fig.*: SHAKES. *Com. Err.* Apparel vice like virtue's harbinger.

apparelment *n.* (*rare*) clothing, garb; equipment, trappings: LME.

apparency /əˈpar(ə)nsi/ *n.* Now *rare*. LME. [f. OFr. *aparence*, *-a(u)nce*, f. as APPEAR, or f. late L *apparentia* APPEARANCE: see -ENCY.] 1 Outward appearance. LME. 2 The quality or state of being apparent to the senses, or to the mind; visibility. E17. 3 The position of being heir apparent. M18.

apparent /əˈpar(ə)nt/ *a.* & *n.* LME. [OFr. *aparant*, *-ent* (mod. *apparent*) f. L *apparent-* pres. ppl stem of *apparere* APPEAR: see -ENT.] A *adj.* 1 Open to sight; plainly visible. *arch.* LME. 2 Manifest to the understanding; evident, obvious; palpable. LME. †3 Likely, probable. E16–M18. 4 Seeming; that appears to the mind or senses, as distinct from (but not necessarily opposed to) what really is. Often contrasted w. *real*. M17.

1 G. WITHER An Owl-eyed buzzard that by day is blinde, And sees not things apparant. 2 C. HAMPTON The man had no taste at all, as was apparent by the morons he'd already chosen. B. ENGLAND His disapproval of the Court is quite apparent. S. HILL It was not apparent how he died, he seemed to have no injuries. **heir apparent** a person whose right of inheritance cannot be superseded by the birth of another (cf. *heir presumptive* s.v. PRESUMPTIVE *a.* 1). 4 GIBBON His real merit, and apparent fidelity, had gained the confidence both of the prince and people. D. H. LAWRENCE Her nature, in spite of her apparent placidity and calm, was profoundly restless. *apparent* MAGNITUDE. **apparent (solar) time**: as calculated by the apparent motion of the sun (cf. *mean solar time* s.v. MEAN *a.*[2]).

†B *n.* = *heir apparent* above. LME–M17.

apparentness *n.* (*rare*) L16.

apparently /əˈpar(ə)ntli/ *adv.* LME. [f. APPARENT *a.* + -LY[2].] †1 Visibly, openly. LME–M17. 2 Evidently to the understanding; clearly, plainly. *arch.* E16. 3 Seemingly; in external appearance; as far as one can judge; (parenthetically or modifying a sentence) it would seem (that); (as a comment on a statement or a reply to a question) so it appears. M16.

1 HOBBES The Prophets . . who saw not God apparently like unto Moyses. 2 F. QUARLES When thou knowest not apparently, judge charitably. 3 T. HARDY An elderly woman, apparently his wife. J. B. PRIESTLEY Winter had set in and apparently taken possession for ever. C. S. FORESTER There was a long delay; apparently the officer had some difficulty in getting up the ship's side. DAY LEWIS The great singer had met something of the same difficulty in this apparently simple song.

apparition /apəˈrɪʃ(ə)n/ *n.* LME. [(O)Fr., or L. *apparitio(n-)* attendance, service, f. *apparit-* pa. ppl stem of *apparere* APPEAR: see -ITION.] 1 The action of appearing or becoming visible, esp. where this is unexpected or unusual. LME. b *Astron.* The appearance of a comet or other body after a period of invisibility; the period during which it is visible. M16. †c The Epiphany of Christ; the festival commemorating it. E17–E18. †2 Semblance, appearance; aspect. LME–M17. 3 Something which appears, esp. if remarkable or unexpected; a phenomenon. L15. b *spec.* A ghost, a phantom; a supernatural appearance. L16. †4 An illusion; a sham. Only in 17.

1 SIR W. SCOTT Presbyterian divines put to the rout by a sudden apparition of the foul fiend. H. G. WELLS The Arabic chroniclers note their apparition upon the Caspian, and give them the name of Russians. V. WOOLF The silent apparition of an ashen-coloured ship. b C. SAGAN In 1301, Giotto . . witnessed another apparition of Comet Halley. 2 R. BOYLE By their whiteishness, to emulate in some measure the apparition of Light. MILTON A dream, Whose inward apparition gently moved My fancy. 3 GIBBON So strange an apparition excited his surprise and indignation. b SHAKES. *Jul. Caes.* I think it is the weakness of mine eyes That shapes this monstrous apparition. J. CLAVELL I thought that I was seeing another apparition, . . a ghost.

apparitional *a.* of or pertaining to an apparition; spectral, subjective: E19.

apparitor /əˈparɪtə/ *n.* ME. [L = public servant, f. *apparit-*: see prec., -OR.] 1 A servant or attendant of an ecclesiastical or civil court. ME. 2 *Rom. Hist.* A public servant of a Roman magistrate. M16. 3 A herald, an usher. M16.

appassionate /əˈpaʃ(ə)nət/ *a.* Long *arch.* L16. [It. *appassionato* (now rare) adj., f. as AD- + *passione* PASSION *n.*: see -ATE[2].] Impassioned.

†**appassionate** *v.t.* M16–M17. [f. as prec.: see -ATE[3].] Inflame with passion.

appeach /əˈpiːtʃ/ *v.* Long *arch.* ME. [AN *enpecher* (see A-[7]), OFr. *empechier* IMPEACH *v.* Aphet. to PEACH *v.*] 1 *v.t.* Charge, accuse, impeach (*of* or *with* an offence etc.). ME. †2 *v.t.* Impugn, discredit (a person's honour etc.); denounce, inform against (a crime etc.). LME–E18. †3 *v.i.* Give accusatory evidence. *rare* (Shakes.). Only in E17.

appeal /əˈpiːl/ *n.* ME. [OFr. *apel* (mod. *appel*), f. as next.] 1 The submission of a case to a higher court in the hope of altering the judgement of a lower one; a request to higher authority for alteration of a decision. ME. 2 A call to an authority for vindication or support, or to a witness for corroboration etc.; a call for help, an entreaty, a supplication. ME. b *Cricket.* A call to an umpire for a decision, *esp.* a request for a batsman to be given out. M19. c A request for public donations to support a charity or cause. L19. 3 A calling to account before a legal tribunal; *spec.* a criminal accusation made by a person undertaking to prove it. *obs.* exc. *Hist.* LME. †4 A challenge to defend one's honour by fighting. LME–E19. 5 An address *to* a principle, characteristic, etc., in the expectation of a favourable response. M19. 6 Attractive power or influence. E20.

1 *appeal to the country*: see COUNTRY *n.* **Court of Appeal** or (*US*) **Appeals** a court which hears cases previously tried in lower courts. *Lord Justice of Appeal*: see JUSTICE *n.* *Lord of Appeal* (*in Ordinary*): see LORD *n.* 2 BACON The casting up of the eyes . . is a kind of appeal to the Deity. D. STOREY There was real appeal in her voice. . . She was crying. J. OSBORNE A very moving appeal to all Christians to do all they can to assist in the manufacture of the H-bomb. c C. HAMPTON I saw that TV appeal you did a few weeks ago. 5 M. R. MITFORD Slavery . . must not be treated by appeals to the passions. T. FRISBY I like the appeal to my old-fashioned feminine instincts. 6 W. DEEPING She was standing close to him, . . and Kit was conscious of the sudden shock of her appeal. L. DEIGHTON The shape of his face . . would have little appeal to a portraitist.

Comb.: **Appeal Court** = *Court of Appeal(s)*, sense 1 above.

appeal /əˈpiːl/ *v.* ME. [OFr. *apeler* (mod. *app-*) call, f. L *appellare* accost, accuse, impeach, appeal to, f. *ad-* AP-[1] + *pell-* stem of *pellere* to drive.] I *v.i.* (Foll. by *to* a court, person, etc.) 1 Make request to a higher court or authority for alteration of the decision of a lower one; take a case, question, etc., *from* one court, authority, etc., *to* another; make an appeal *against* a verdict etc. ME. 2 Call on an authority for a decision in one's favour. LME. b *Cricket.* Call on an umpire for a decision; *esp.* request an umpire to give a batsman out. M18. 3 Call *to* a witness for corroboration; call attention *to* some evidence for confirmation. LME. 4 Make entreaty or earnest request (*to* a person *for* something, *to do* something). M16. 5 Address oneself *to* a principle, characteristic, etc., in the expectation of a favourable response from a person or group; seek to be attractive or acceptable *to* a particular group. L18. 6 Be attractive or pleasing. L19.

1 G. O. TREVELYAN The Revising Barrister's . . decisions have never been appealed against. A. J. P. TAYLOR Thus Lloyd George appealed from the ruling classes to 'the people'. *appeal from Philip drunk to Philip sober*: see DRUNK *a.* 1. *appeal to the country*: see COUNTRY *n.* 2 A. J. P. TAYLOR The Chinese appealed to the League of Nations against Japan. *appeal to Caesar*: see CAESAR 1. 3 SHAKES. *2 Hen. VI* To heaven I do appeal How I have lov'd my King and commonweal. E. WAUGH Her resistance ended when I appealed to the mysteries of my trade. 4 T. CROMWELL I appell to your Highnes for mercy. D. H. LAWRENCE She had managed to get his address, so that she could appeal to him in time of distress. *Daily Telegraph* He appealed for anyone who attended the pool . . to come forward. 5 G. B. SHAW The Sunday papers . . appealed almost exclusively to the lower middle class. I. MURDOCH Appealing to Dora's better nature may turn out to be a difficult operation. 6 *Smart Set* The speciousness of Betty's words appealed. T. S. ELIOT I happen to know of a vacancy In my own parish . . If it should appeal to you. V. S. PRITCHETT Gothic inevitably appealed to the disorderly minds of the young.

II *v.t.* 7 Call (a person) to answer before a tribunal; accuse (*of* a crime, esp. treason), impeach. *obs.* exc. *Hist.* LME. 8 Challenge to defend one's honour by fighting. Long *arch.* LME. 9 Submit (a case etc.) to a higher court; make an appeal against (a decision etc.). L15. †10 Call to witness. Only in M17.

7 SHAKES. *Rich. II* Hast thou sounded him If he appeal the Duke on ancient malice, Or worthily. W. PRYNNE I . . appeale you to the Tribunall of that high Judge above. T. KEIGHTLEY They came before the king . . and appealed of treason the Archbishop of York. 8 SIR W. SCOTT Man to man will I appeal the Norman to the lists. 9 C. MARLOWE To patient judgments we appeal our plaud. J. BARTH The young barrister . . didn't even think of appealing the judgment until it was too late. 10 MILTON He hath presum'd to appeale . . the testimony of God.

appealaˈbility *n.* the state or quality of being appealable M20. **appealable** *a.* able to be appealed against E17. **appealer** *n.* a person who makes an appeal LME. **appealing** *a.* that appeals; *esp.* attractive, pleasing: L16. **appealingly** *adv.* imploringly; attractively: M19.

appear /əˈpɪə/ *v.* & *n.* ME. [OFr. *aper-* tonic stem of *apareir* (mod. *apparoir*) f. L *apparere*, f. *ad* AP-[1] + *parere* come into view.] A *v.i.* 1 Come into view, as from concealment, or from a distance; become visible; become evident. ME. 2 Be visible; be displayed; be located, occur; manifest itself (*as*). LME. 3 Present oneself formally before an authority; come before a court etc. Also, act as legal representative *for* someone. LME. 4 Present oneself publicly; put in an appearance. LME. b *spec.* Come before the public as an author. L17. c Be published, be issued, become available. E18. d *spec.* Come before the public as an actor, performer, participant in a broadcast, etc. E18. 5 Be clear or evident to the understanding; be manifest. LME. 6 (In some uses as copular vb.) Seem to the mind, be perceived as, be considered; seem outwardly or superficially (but not be in reality). Foll. by *to be*, *to do*, *that*, *as if*, *as though*. Also *impers.* w. *it*. LME.

1 AV *Luke* 1:11 There appeared vnto him an Angel of the Lord. C. S. FORESTER A row of four or five swarthy faces had appeared at the stern of the galley. P. A. SCHOLES When he was about thirty the first signs of deafness appeared. A. KOESTLER Hipparchus . . had seen a new star appear in the sky. B. MALAMUD Then one day . . there appeared a sign in the empty store window. 2 D. H. LAWRENCE A wide plate-glass door, . . in the round arch of which the words: 'Manchester House' should appear large and distinguished. C. CAUDWELL In him the revolt of the heart against

reason appears as the revolt of the hero against circumstance. R. V. JONES It was no artefact for it appeared on two separate photographs. 3 STEELE Many.. are known to have Ill-will to him for whom I appear. E. WAUGH Bound over to appear in a week's time. J. LE CARRÉ I supposed he didn't want any mud raked up by Mundt appearing at the Old Bailey. 4 D. DU MAURIER 'You can't possibly not appear' 'No.., I'm not coming down. I can't face them.' S. HILL Kathleen did not appear to tea, and Isabel was sent in search of her. b *appear in print*: see PRINT *n*. c E. WAUGH Many years later, there appeared the first massive volume of his.. work on Byzantine Art. E. F. SCHUMACHER The existence of 'goods' which never appear on the market. d A. JACOBS Italian tenor who.. appeared in Britain from 1902, U.S.A. from 1903. A. S. BYATT I think he will ask you to appear on his programme. *Encycl. Brit.* Garrick appeared.. in Thomas Southerne's *Oroonoko* as Aboan, a noble savage. 5 SHAKES. *Merch. V.* It doth appear you are a worthy judge. MILTON Our greatness will appear Then most conspicuous. 6 D. HUME Solely, as it appears, for what you believe to be for our advantage. J. TYNDALL Raindrops which descend vertically appear to meet us when we move swiftly. T. HARDY Oak, not to appear unnecessarily disagreeable, stayed a little while. H. FRENCH They appear as though they had been written in red. G. ORWELL He caught a glimpse of the girl,.. at the far end of the room. She appeared not to have seen him. HARPER LEE He could.. appear tall if height was part of the devilry required. D. STOREY If you must appear the busy executive, you must. S. BARSTOW It appears they live in Essex and this is the first time they've stayed on the Yorkshire coast. *appear in the light of*: see LIGHT *n*.

B *n*. Appearance. *rare*. E17.

appearer *n*. E17. **appearingly** *adv*. (*obs.* exc. *dial.*) †(*a*) visibly; (*b*) apparently: LME.

appearance /əˈpɪər(ə)ns/ *n*. LME. [OFr. *aparance*, *-ence* (mod. *apparence*) f. late L *apparentia*, f. L *apparent-* pres. ppl stem of *apparere*: see prec. (to which assim. in form). Cf. APPARENCY.] 1 The action of coming into view or becoming visible or evident. LME. 2 The action of appearing formally at any proceedings, e.g. in court. LME. 3 The action or state of seeming or appearing to be (to the eyes or mind); semblance. LME. †b Likelihood, probability. LME–L18. †c Viewpoint, opinion. LME–E17. 4 State or form as perceived; look, aspect; in *pl*., circumstances as they appear, the look of things in general. LME. 5 Outward show or aspect (opp. *reality*). LME. 6 Something which appears; a phenomenon; an apparition. L15. †7 A gathering of people; an attendance. L16–L18. 8 A conspicuous display; show. L16. 9 The action or an instance of coming before the world or the public in any way; being present, participating. L17. b Publication, issue, being made available. L19. 10 Visible occurrence; a manifestation. M19.

1 E. A. FREEMAN The appearance of the fleet was unlooked for. J. BUCHAN I had not seen him approach, and the sudden appearance made me start. 2 B. ENGLAND His appearance before this court will in no way affect his official knowledge of these proceedings. 3 AV *1 Thess.* 5:22 Abstaine from all appearance of euill. P. H. JOHNSON They gave every appearance of happiness, of a problem solved, but I felt sure that another problem lay behind it. 4 SOUTHEY All appearances Denote alarm and vigilance. A. WILSON Isobel was deeply distressed at her brother's tired, grey appearance. J. LE CARRÉ He took less care of his appearance and less notice of his surroundings. 5 G. ORWELL We bring him over to our side, not in appearance, but genuinely, heart and soul. S. HILL Alida appears to be a new woman, but is it only an appearance? 6 SHAKES. *2 Hen. IV* Whose well-labouring sword Had three times slain th' appearance of the King. W. COWPER I am.. a great observer of natural appearances. 7 EVELYN An innumerable appearance of gallants. 8 STEELE I gratify the vanity of all who pretend to make an Appearance. 9 J. SULLIVAN 'The first great event in history,' says Berosus, 'was the appearance of Oannes.' B. JAMES The match featured the first appearance of.. Bobby Charlton. G. ABRAHAM Increasing deafness.. inhibited Beethoven's appearances as a virtuoso. b F. PALGRAVE The appearance of his first book. 10 E. A. FREEMAN The single appearance of the word in Domesday is the earliest instance.

Phrases: **keep up appearances** maintain artificially an outward show of normality etc. so as to conceal the true state of affairs. **make, put in, an appearance** be present, esp. briefly; turn up. **save appearances** = *keep up appearances* above. **to all appearance(s)** so far as can be seen.

Comb.: **appearance money**: paid to a performer merely for taking part in a particular event.

appeasable /əˈpiːzəb(ə)l/ *a*. M16. [OFr. *apaisable*, f. *apaisier*: see next, -ABLE.] Able to be appeased.

appease /əˈpiːz/ *v*. ME. [AN *apeser*, OFr. *apaisier* (mod. *apaiser*), f. A-[5] + *pais* PEACE *n*.] 1 *v.t.* Bring to peace, settle (strife, disorder); calm, pacify (persons in conflict). ME. 2 *v.t.* Assuage, allay (anger, displeasure); propitiate (a person who is angry etc.). LME. 3 *v.t.* Relieve, soothe (pain, suffering; †the part suffering, †the sufferer). LME. 4 *v.t.* Satisfy (a demand, appetite, prejudice, etc.); pacify or placate (a person) by acceding to his or her demands etc. (Cf. APPEASEMENT 1b.) LME. †5 *v.i.* Be pacified, calmed; abate. LME–M17.

appeaser *n*. a person who or thing which appeases; *spec*. a person who supports a policy of appeasement: LME. **appeasive** *a*. tending to appease; propitiatory: E17.

appeasement /əˈpiːzm(ə)nt/ *n*. LME. [OFr. *apaisement*, f. *apaisier*: see prec., -MENT.] 1 The action or process of appeasing. LME. b *Polit.* A policy of making concessions to a potential aggressor in order to preserve peace; *spec*. such a policy pursued by Britain towards Nazi Germany prior to the outbreak of war in 1939. Often *derog.* E20. †2 A means of appeasing. M16–L17. 3 A state of pacification or satisfaction. *arch.* L16.

appellant /əˈpɛl(ə)nt/ *a*. & *n*. LME. [OFr. *apelant* pres. pple of *apeler* APPEAL *v*.: see -ANT[1].] A *adj.* 1 Making an appeal; *esp*. appealing to a higher court; *Hist.* accusing, challenging. Freq. *postpositive*. LME. 2 Concerned with appeals; appellate. L18.

B *n*. 1 A person who formally accuses another of treason or felony (*Hist.*), or of negligence etc. in a maritime court. LME. †b A challenger. LME–L17. 2 A person who makes an appeal to a higher court or authority. E17. 3 *gen.* A person who makes an entreaty or request. E18.

1 *Lords Appellant(s)*: see LORD *n*.

appellate /əˈpɛlət/ *a*. LME. [L *appellatus* pa. pple, f. as next: see -ATE[2].] †1 Appealed against, accused. *rare*. LME–E18. 2 Appealed to; concerned with appeals. M18.

†**appellatory** *a*. & *n*. (*a*) *adj.* pertaining to an appellant; of the nature of an appeal; (*b*) *n*. a letter of appeal: L16–M18.

appellate /ˈapəleɪt/ *v.t.* *rare*. M18. [L *appellat-* pa. ppl stem of *appellare* APPEAL *v*.: see -ATE[3].] Call, designate.

appellation /apəˈleɪʃ(ə)n/ *n*. LME. [(O)Fr. f. L *appellatio(n-)*, f. as prec.: see -ATION.] 1 The action of appealing (esp. in legal senses); an appeal. *arch.* LME. 2 A designation, a name, a title. LME. b The action of calling by a name; nomenclature. L16.

appellation contrôlée /apɛlasjɔ̃ kɔ̃trole/ *n*. *phr.* M20. [Fr. = controlled appellation.] (A guarantee of) the description of a bottle of French wine (or other item of food) in conformity with statutory regulations as to its origin. Also *appellation d'origine contrôlée* /dɔriʒin/.

appellative /əˈpɛlətɪv/ *a*. & *n*. LME. [Late L *appellativus*, f. as APPELLATE *v*.: see -ATIVE.] A *adj.* 1 Designating a class of things, people, etc., in general; (of a noun) common (opp. *proper*). LME. †2 Of the nature of a descriptive name or appellation. L16–M17. 3 Of or pertaining to the giving of names. *rare*. M19. B *n*. 1 A common noun. L16. 2 An appellation or descriptive name. L16.

appellatively *adv*. as an appellative E17.

appellee /apəˈliː, əpɛˈliː/ *n*. M16. [f. Fr. *appelé* pa. pple of *appeler* APPEAL *v*.: see -EE[1].] *Law.* 1 A person who is formally accused or challenged by another. Now *arch.* exc. in a maritime court. M16. 2 The defendant in a case taken to a higher court. Cf. RESPONDENT. Chiefly *US*. E17.

appellor /apəˈlɔː, əˈpɛlɔː/ *n*. Now *arch.* or *Hist.* LME. [AN *apelour* = OFr. *apeleor* f. L *appellator*, f. as APPELLATE *v*. + -OR.] *Law.* A person who formally accuses or challenges another.

append /əˈpɛnd/ *v.t.* LME. [L *appendere* hang to, f. *ad* AP-[1] + *pendere* hang.] 1 Hang on, attach as a pendant, affix. LME. 2 Join on, annex. L18. 3 Add, esp. in writing. M19.

1 CARLYLE A Conquering Hero, to whom Fate has malignantly appended a tin-kettle of Ambition. 2 S. JOHNSON Hales-Owen.. was appended.. to a distant county. 3 J. S. MILL Some additional remarks.. are appended. SCOTT FITZGERALD 'They carried him into my house,' appended Jordan, 'because we lived just two doors from the church.' M. MUGGERIDGE He even appended his signature to a memorandum calling for drastic action on the Government's part.

†**appension** *n*. the action or process of appending LME–E18.

appendage /əˈpɛndɪdʒ/ *n*. M17. [f. prec. + -AGE.] Something attached; a subsidiary adjunct; an addition; an accompaniment.

W. CAVE Confirmation.. ever was a constant appendage to Baptism. W. DERHAM Clothing, another necessary Appendage of Life. JOYCE A strong suspicion of nose-paint about the nasal appendage. G. B. SHAW Rather than be reduced to a mere appendage of a big American concern, we might fight for our independence.

appendaged *a*. furnished with or having an appendage L18.

appendance /əˈpɛnd(ə)ns/ *n*. Also **-ence**. E16. [OFr. *apendance*, f. *apendre*: see next, -ANCE.] †1 A dependent possession. E16–M17. †2 An appendage. M16–L17. 3 *Law.* The fact of being appendant. M19.

appendancy, **-ency** *n*. (now *rare*) †(*a*) = APPENDANCE 1, 2; (*b*) = APPENDANCE 3: E17.

appendant /əˈpɛnd(ə)nt/ *a*. & *n*. Also **-ent**. LME. [OFr. *apendant* (mod. *app-*), f. *apendre* depend on, belong to, f. as APPEND: see -ANT[1].] A *adj.* (Foll. by *to*, *on*.) 1 *Law.* Attached or belonging to a possession or tenure as an additional but subsidiary right. LME. 2 Pertinent, attendant, consequent. E16. 3 Hanging attached. M16. 4 Attached in a subordinate capacity; annexed. L16. B *n*. *arch.* 1 *Law.* A lesser right or property attached by prescription to one more important. L15. 2 An addition, an adjunct, an appendage, an appendix; a dependency. L16. 3 A dependant. L16. 4 A natural consequence; a corollary. L16.

appendectomy /ap(ə)nˈdɛktəmi/ *n*. Chiefly *N. Amer.* L19. [f. APPENDIX + -ECTOMY.] *Med.* = APPENDICECTOMY.

appendence *n*., **-ent** *a*. vars. of APPENDANCE, -ANT.

appendical /əˈpɛndɪk(ə)l/ *a*. Now *rare*. M19. [f. as next + -AL[1].] Of, pertaining to, or of the nature of an appendix.

appendicectomy /əpɛndɪˈsɛktəmi/ *n*. L19. [f. L *appendic-*, APPENDIX *n*. + -ECTOMY.] Surgical removal of the vermiform appendix; an instance of this.

appendices *n.pl.* see APPENDIX *n*.

appendicitis /əpɛndɪˈsʌɪtɪs/ *n*. L19. [f. as prec. + -ITIS.] Inflammation of the vermiform appendix.

appendicle /əˈpɛndɪk(ə)l/ *n*. E17. [L *appendicula* dim. of *appendic-*, APPENDIX *n*.: see -CULE.] A small appendix or appendage.

appendicular /ap(ə)nˈdɪkjʊlə/ *a*. M17. [f. as prec. + -AR[1].] 1 Of, pertaining to, or of the nature of an appendage or appendicle. M17. 2 Of or pertaining to a limb or limbs. L19.

appendicularian /ˌap(ə)ndɪkjəˈlɛːrɪən/ *n*. & *a*. L19. [f. mod.L *Appendicularia*, a typical genus, f. as prec., + -AN.] *Zool.* A *n*. A member of the class Larvacea of minute free-swimming planktonic tunicates. L19. B *adj.* Of or pertaining to this class. L19.

appendiculate /ap(ə)nˈdɪkjʊlət/ *a*. E19. [f. as APPENDICLE + -ATE[2].] *Biol.* Having appendages or appendicles; forming an appendage or appendicle.

appendix /əˈpɛndɪks/ *n*. & *v*. M16. [L *appendix*, *-dic-*, f. as APPEND.] A *n*. Pl. **-dices** /-dɪsiːz/, **-dixes**. 1 An addition to a book or document, having some contributory value, but not essential to completeness. M16. †2 A subsidiary non-material addition, accompaniment, or consequence. M16–L17. 3 A subsidiary external adjunct; a dependent possession or territory. L16. 4 *Anat.* A small process developed from the surface of an organ; *spec.* (more fully *vermiform appendix*) the short thin blind tube extending from the caecum. E17.

2 ROBERT BURTON Idleness is an appendix to nobility. 3 CONAN DOYLE I am a brain, Watson. The rest of me is a mere appendix. L. DURRELL The whole island is geologically simply an appendix to the Anatolian continent which has at some time been broken off and set free to float. 4 SIR T. BROWNE The appendices or beards in the calicular leaves. G. B. SHAW The surgeon . . can remove the appendix or the uvula, and leave the patient none the worse.

B *v.t.* Add as an appendix. *rare.* M18.

apperceive /apəˈsiːv/ *v.t.* ME. [OFr. *aperceveir* (mod. *apercevoir*) ult. f. L *ad* AP-[1] + *percipere* perceive.] 1 Observe, notice, perceive. Long *rare.* ME. 2 *Psychol.* Comprehend by apperception. L19.

apperception /apəˈsɛpʃ(ə)n/ *n.* M18. [Fr. *aperception* or mod.L *apperceptio(n-)* (Leibniz), f. as AP-[1] + PERCEPTION.] 1 The mind's perception of itself. M18. 2 Mental perception, recognition. M19. 3 *Psychol.* The active mental process of assimilating an idea (esp. one newly perceived) to a body of ideas already possessed, and thereby comprehending it. L19.

3 *Thematic Apperception Test*: see THEMATIC *a.*

apperceptive *a.* (*Psychol.*) of or pertaining to apperception L19.

†**apperil** *n. rare.* E17–M19. [f. A-[11] + PERIL.] Peril.

appertain /apəˈteɪn/ *v.* LME. [OFr. *apartenir* (mod. *app-*) f. Proto-Romance var. of late L *appertinere*, f. as AP-[1] + PERTAIN.] I *v.i.* Foll. by *to.* 1 Be related, be akin. *arch.* LME. 2 Belong as a possession, right, or privilege. LME. 3 Belong naturally, be appropriate. LME. 4 Pertain, relate. LME.

1 AV *Num.* 16:32 All the men that appertained vnto Korah. 2 HOBBES Shall not all Judicature appertain to Christ? R. FIRBANK Prior to the Reformation the farm buildings . . had appertained . . to the Abbots of St. Veronica. 3 SHAKES. *Much Ado* Do all rites That appertain unto a burial. D. LESSING Psychological characteristics that are considered as appertaining to one sex rather than another. *absol.*: AV *1 Esd.* 1:12 They rosted the Passeouer with fire, as appertaineth. 4 CHAUCER A certein nombre of conclusions apertenyng to the same instrument. J. CONRAD All that appertained to her haunted me . . , her whole form in the familiar pose, her very substance in its colour and texture.

II *v.t.* †5 Belong to, become, befit. LME–E17.

†**appertainance** *n.* = APPURTENANCE E16–M19.

appertinent *a.* & *n.* see APPURTENANT.

appetence /ˈapɪt(ə)ns/ *n.* E17. [Fr. *appétence* or f. as next: see -ENCE.] = APPETENCY 2.

appetency /ˈapɪt(ə)nsi/ *n.* E17. [L *appetentia* longing after, f. *appetere*: see APPETITE, -ENCY.] 1 Natural tendency, affinity; instinctive inclination or propensity. *arch.* E17. 2 The state or action of desiring; passion; an appetite, a craving. (Foll. by *after, for,* †*of.*) M17.

2 I. D'ISRAELI Fanaticism and robbery . . will satiate their appetency for blood and plunder. D. MASSON An appetency after literary distinction. M. INNES The magical and irrational appetencies which make up nine-tenths of the content of the human mind.

appetent /ˈapɪt(ə)nt/ *a.* LME. [L *appetent-* pres. ppl stem of *appetere*: see APPETITE, -ENT.] Eagerly desirous. (Foll. by *after, of.*)

appetible /ˈapɪtɪb(ə)l/ *a.* Now *rare* or *obs.* L15. [L *appetibilis* desirable, f. *appetere*: see APPETITE, -IBLE.] †1 Impelling. Only in L15. 2 Desirable. E17.

†**appetibility** *n.* desirableness E17–E19.

appetise *v.*, **-iser** *n.*, **-ising** *a.* vars. of APPETIZE etc.

appetite /ˈapɪtʌɪt/ *n.* ME. [OFr. *apetit* (mod. *appétit*) f. L *appetitus* desire towards, f. *appetit-* pa. ppl stem of *appetere* seek after, f. *ad* AP-[1] + *petere* seek.] Foll. by *for* (†*of*, †*to*, †*to do*). 1 (A) desire to satisfy a natural need, esp. for food or for sexual pleasure; an instinctive craving; capacity for food, sexual activity, etc. ME. 2 *gen.* A desire, an inclination, a disposition. LME. †3 A natural tendency of a thing towards a state etc. LME–M17. 4 An object of desire or longing. *arch.* LME.

1 ADDISON The most violent Appetites in all Creatures are Lust and Hunger. P. G. WODEHOUSE I can't explain till I've had something to eat. You idle rich don't realize it, but working gives one an appetite. J. HERSEY He gained back some of the weight he lost, but his appetite remained only fair. J. HELLER She picked without appetite at her small salad. R. GRAYSON Suji's sexual appetite is formidable. 2 J. LYLY I have an appetite it were best for me to take a nap. G. GROTE Obeying without reflection the appetite of the moment. K. TYNAN A pitiful spectacle which has bred in modern audiences an appetite for pathos that amounts to an addiction. 3 BACON In all Bodies, there is an Appetite of Union. 4 WORDSWORTH The mountain, and the deep and gloomy wood . . were then to me An appetite.

appeˈtitious *a.* (*rare*) belonging to appetite, appetizing M17.

appetition /apəˈtɪʃ(ə)n/ *n.* E17. [L *appetitio(n-)* strong desire after, f. *appetit-*: see prec., -ITION.] Chiefly *Philos.* The directing of any kind of desire towards an object or purpose.

appetitive /əˈpɛtɪtɪv/ *a.* M16. [Fr. *appétitif* or med.L *appetitivus*, f. *appetit-*: see APPETITE, -IVE.] Characterized by appetite.

appetize /ˈapɪtʌɪz/ *v.t.* Chiefly *Sc.* & *north.* Also **-ise.** M18. [Back-form. f. APPETIZING.] Give an appetite to. Chiefly as *appetized* ppl a.

appetizer /ˈapɪtʌɪzə/ *n.* Also **-iser.** M19. [f. APPETIZE + -ER[1].] Something eaten or drunk to stimulate the appetite.

appetizing /ˈapɪtʌɪzɪŋ/ *a.* Also **-ising.** M17. [f. (O)Fr. *appétissant* w. ending assim. to -IZE, -ING[2].] Exciting a desire, esp. for food; stimulating the appetite.

appetizingly *adv.* L19.

applaud /əˈplɔːd/ *v.* L15. [Partly f. L *applaudere*, f. *ad* AP-[1] + *plaudere* to clap, partly after Fr. *applaudir.*] 1 *v.t.* Express approval of, as by clapping hands; approve of, praise. L15. †2 *v.i.* Assent *to*; give approbation *to.* M16–L17. 3 *v.i.* Express approval in a loud or lively manner, esp. by clapping hands. L16.

1 ADDISON They . . applaud themselves for the Singularity of their Judgment. M. EDGEWORTH I applaud him for standing forward in defence of his friend. A. PATON John Kumalo sits down, and the people applaud him, a great wave of shouting and clapping. J. K. GALBRAITH Audiences of all kinds most applaud what they like best. 2 SPENSER The people standing all about . . doe thereto applaud. 3 J. B. PRIESTLEY The enraptured audience would not stop applauding.

applauder *n.* L16. **applaudingly** *adv.* with applause or loud commendation M18.

applause /əˈplɔːz/ *n.* LME. [L *applausus*, f. *applaus-* pa. ppl stem of *applaudere*: see prec.] 1 Approbation loudly expressed, esp. by clapping hands; marked approval. LME. †2 An acclamation; a commendation. E17–L18. †3 An object of approval. *rare.* Only in E17.

1 WELLINGTON He has always conducted himself in such a manner as to gain my applause. D. M. THOMAS They took their bows to warm, if not tumultuous, applause. 2 POPE Loud applauses rend the vaulted sky. 3 JONSON The applause! delight! the wonder of our Stage.

applausive *a.* (*a*) (loudly) expressive of approval; †(*b*) worthy of approval: L16. **applausively** *adv.* (*rare*) M18.

apple /ˈap(ə)l/ *n.* & *v.* [OE *æppel*, corresp. to OFris., OS, (M)Du. *appel*, OHG *apful* (G *Apfel*), ON *epli*, Crimean Goth. *apel*, f. Gmc.: cognates in other IE langs.] A *n.* 1 The round firm fruit of a tree of the rose family, *Malus domestica*, cultivated in innumerable varieties in the temperate zones. Also, an apple tree. OE. 2 Any fruit, *esp.* one which in some respects resembles an apple. Also, a gall. Usu. w. specifying wd in particular names, e.g. *oak-apple*, *thorn-apple.* OE. 3 The forbidden fruit of the tree of knowledge of good and evil (*Gen.* 3:6). OE. 4 Something resembling an apple in form or colour. OE.

2 *balsam apple*, *crab-apple*, *custard-apple*, *May-apple*, *oak-apple*, *pineapple*, etc.

Phrases: *Adam's apple*: see ADAM *n.* **apple of discord** a subject of dissension (from the golden apple inscribed 'for the fairest' contended for by Hera, Athene, and Aphrodite). **apple of love** = *love-apple* s.v. LOVE *n.* **apple of one's** (or **the**) **eye** †(*a*) the pupil; (*b*) the person or thing most cherished. **apple of Peru** (*a*) a Peruvian plant of the nightshade family, *Nicandra physalodes*, bearing bluish flowers and round brown fruit; (*b*) *N. Amer.* the thorn-apple, *Datura stramonium.* **apple of Sodom, Sodom apple** = DEAD SEA *fruit.* **apples (and pears)** *rhyming slang* stairs. **(as) sure as God made little apples** *colloq.* with complete certainty. *Sodom apple*: see *apple of Sodom* above. **the (Big) Apple** *US slang* New York City. WAGENER *apple* See also APPLES.

Comb.: **apple-bee** *dial.* a wasp; **apple brandy** spirit distilled from cider; **apple-butter** *N. Amer.* a spread of spiced stewed apple, usu. made with cider; **apple-cart** a cart for carrying apples; *upset someone's* (or *the*) *apple-cart* (fig.), spoil someone's plans, ruin an undertaking; **apple-green** yellowish green; **apple-head** a domed head of a toy dog; **applejack** (*a*) *N. Amer.* apple brandy; (*b*) *dial.* sliced apple baked in pastry; †**apple-john** [said to be ripe on St John's Day] a kind of apple eaten when much withered; **apple-peru** *N. Amer.* = *apple of Peru* (b) above; **apple-polisher** *N. Amer.* a toady; **apple sauce** (*a*) apples stewed to a pulp; (*b*) *N. Amer.* insincere flattery, nonsense; †**apple-squire** a pimp; **apple strudel** baked spiced apples in flaky pastry; **apple tree** (*a*) a tree which bears apples; (*b*) *Austral.* any of various indigenous trees, chiefly eucalypts; **apple-woman** a woman who sells apples from a stall.

B *v.* 1 *v.t.* & *i.* Form or turn into apples; bear apples. OE. b Of a turnip: swell into globular shape. Now *rare* or *obs.* E18. 2 *v.i.* Gather apples. L18.

apple-pie /ap(ə)lˈpʌɪ; *as adj.* ˈap(ə)lpʌɪ/ *n.* & *a.* L16. [f. prec. + PIE *n.*[2]] A *n.* 1 A pie with a filling of apples. L16. 2 The great willowherb, *Epilobium hirsutum.* Also *apple-pie-plant.* (From the odour of its flowers and shoots.) *dial.* M19.

Comb.: **apple-pie bed** a bed made as a practical joke, with sheets so folded that one's legs cannot be stretched out; **apple-pie order** perfect order.

B *attrib.* or as *adj.* Representing or displaying homespun conservative virtues regarded as traditionally American. M20.

apples /ˈap(ə)lz/ *a. Austral.* & *NZ slang.* M20. [Pl. of APPLE *n.*] Satisfactory, all right, fine.

T. A. G. HUNGERFORD How's it going, Wally? Everything apples?

Appleton layer /ˈap(ə)lt(ə)n ˌleɪə/ *n. phr.* M20. [Edward V. *Appleton* (1892–1965), Brit. physicist.] = *F-layer* s.v. F, F 7.

appliable /əˈplʌɪəb(ə)l/ *a. arch.* LME. [f. APPLY + -ABLE.] †1 Compliant, accommodating, favourably disposed; ready and willing. Cf. PLIABLE. LME–L17. 2 Able to be applied; having reference, pertinent. L15.

applial /əˈplʌɪəl/ *n. rare.* M16. [f. as prec. + -AL[1].] Application; a request.

appliance /əˈplʌɪəns/ *n.* M16. [f. APPLY + -ANCE.] 1 The bringing to bear of some technique or agency; application, use, putting into practice. *arch.* M16. 2 A thing applied as means to an end; a device, a utensil, an apparatus. L16. b *spec.* A fire engine. L19. †3 Compliance; (an act of) subservience. Only in E17.

1 CARLYLE The human soul . . could be acted-on . . by the appliance of birch-rods. 2 SHAKES. *Hen. VIII* Ask God for temp'rance; that's th' appliance only Which your disease requires. J. CHEEVER Neither of them understood the mechanics of radio—or of any of the other appliances that surrounded them. 3 SHAKES. *Meas. for M.* Too noble to conserve a life In base appliances.

applianced *a.* equipped with domestic appliances M20.

†**appliant** *a.* LME. [OFr. *apliant* pres. pple of *aplier* APPLY: see -ANT[1].] 1 Favourably disposed, willing, compliant; diligent. LME–M17. 2 Applicable, pertinent *to. rare.* M16–M19.

applicable /ˈaplɪkəb(ə)l, əˈplɪk-/ *a.* M16. [(O)Fr., or med.L *applicabilis*, f. *applicare*: see APPLY, -ABLE.] †1 = APPLIABLE 1. M16–M18. 2 Able to be applied (*to* a purpose etc.); having reference, relevant. L16. 3 Suitable, appropriate. M19.

applica'bility *n.* the quality of being applicable; pertinence: M17. **applicableness** *n.* (*rare*) M17. **applicably** *adv.* (*rare*) so as to be applied; pertinently, suitably: M18.

applicant /'aplɪk(ə)nt/ *n.* E19. [f. APPLICATION + -ANT[1].] A person who applies or makes request, esp. formally.

applicate /'aplɪkət, -keɪt/ *pa. pple* & *ppl a. arch.* LME. [L *applicatus* pa. pple, f. *applicat-*: see next, -ATE[2].] Applied; applicable.

application /aplɪ'keɪʃ(ə)n/ *n.* LME. [(O)Fr. f. L *applicatio(n-)*, f. *applicat-* pa. ppl stem of *applicare*: see APPLY, -ATION.] 1 The action of bringing something into material or effective contact with something else; *esp.* the putting on or administration of a medicament. Also, a remedy so applied. LME. b *Geom.* The placing of a line or figure in contact with another. E18. 2 Use with special reference (*to*); use, employment; a specific use or purpose to which something is put. LME. 3 The bringing of a general or figurative statement, a theory, principle, etc., to bear upon a matter; applicability in a particular case, relevance; the bringing of something to bear practically in a matter, practical operation. Also, a practical lesson or moral. LME. 4 *Astron.* & *Astrol.* The action of approaching. L16. 5 The action of applying oneself closely (*to* a task etc.); assiduous effort, attention, diligence. E17. †6 An obsequious deference or soliciting of favour. Only in E17. 7 (The making of) a request, esp. of a formal nature. M17.

1 J. ABERNETHY I began again to try some medicated applications. J. SCOFFERN The application of heat to the bulb. ANTHONY HUXLEY Well-farmed soils . . contain two to four times more phosphate and potassium than is needed by most crops, following past years of regular application. 2 S. HILL The forceful novelty of this application of such a difficult word, to himself. C. SAGAN The idea of a code, at least in the usual military intelligence application, is to make a message difficult to read. 3 HOBBES The application of the Law to the present case. J. BUTLER A fable or a parable, related without any application or moral. E. O'NEILL He quotes with great sentiment, if with slight application. A. J. P. TAYLOR A lesson . . which had its application in the wider field of international relations. E. F. SCHUMACHER A fascination with novelties . . which insists on their application long before their long-term consequences are even remotely understood. 5 POPE I am obliged . . to give up my whole application to Homer. A. FRASER He was obviously capable of great application when his interest was aroused. 7 G. BURNET Frequent applications to God in prayer. ALDOUS HUXLEY Applications for bank credit had been rather disappointing. J. LE CARRÉ A firm . . showed interest in his application for the post of assistant manager and personnel officer.

applicative /'aplɪkeɪtɪv, -kətɪv/ *a.* M17. [f. L *applicat-* (see prec.) + -IVE.] Characterized by being applied in some way; practical.

applicator /'aplɪkeɪtə/ *n.* M17. [f. as prec. + -OR.] A thing which or (*rare*) a person who applies; *esp.* a device for the application of a medication or other substance.

applicatory /'aplɪkət(ə)ri/ *a. arch.* M16. [f. as prec. + -ORY[2].] 1 Having the property of applying something to practical use. Also, applicable. M16. †2 Making application or request. M–L17.

applied /ə'plʌɪd/ *a.* E16. [f. APPLY + -ED[1].] †1 Folded. Only in E16. 2 Put to practical use; having or concerned with practical application. (Opp. *abstract*, *pure*, or *theoretical.*) M17. 3 *Needlework.* Laid on as appliqué. L19.

applier /ə'plʌɪə/ *n.* M16. [f. APPLY + -ER[1].] A person who or thing which applies.

appliqué /ə'pliːkeɪ/ *n.* & *v.* M18. [Fr., use as n. of pa. pple of *appliquer* f. L *applicare*: see APPLY.] Chiefly *Needlework.* **A** *n.* (A piece of) ornamental work cut out from one material and affixed to the surface of another; the technique of ornamenting in this way. M18. **B** *v.t.* Decorate in this way. Chiefly as *appliquéd* ppl a. L19.

applot /ə'plɒt/ *v.t. arch.* Infl. **-tt-**. M17. [f. PLOT *n.*, app. after *lot*, *allot.*] Divide into plots or parts; apportion.

applotment *n.* division into plots M17.

apply /ə'plʌɪ/ *v.* LME. [OFr. *aplier* f. L *applicare*, f. *ad* AP-[1] + *plicare* to fold.] I Of a thing in contact with another. 1 *v.t.* Put close or in contact. (Foll. by *to.*) LME. b *Geom.* Bring or construct (a figure etc.) in contact. Foll. by *to* (a line etc.). M17. 2 *v.t.* Place (a plaster, ointment, etc.) in effective contact with the body (foll. by *to*); administer (a remedy etc., *to*); *transf.* & *fig.* bring effectively to bear on something (foll. by *to*). LME. †3 *v.i.* Come or be close; come into or be in contact. Foll. by *to*. LME–L18. 4 *v.t.* Put *to* a special use or purpose; devote, appropriate, *to*; use in special reference *to*. LME. 5 *v.t.* Put to use; employ; dispose of. LME. 6 *v.t.* Give a specific reference to (a general, theoretical, or figurative statement); use as relevant or suitable; bring to bear practically, put into practical operation. (Foll. by *to.*) LME. †7 *v.t.* Refer, ascribe, *to*. LME–E18. 8 *v.i.* Have a practical bearing; have relevance; refer; be operative. (Foll. by *to*, †*for.*) (*rare* bef. L18.) L15. †9 *v.t.* Compare, liken, *to*. L16–M17.

1 JOYCE He applies his handkerchief to his mouth. *apply the brakes*: see BRAKE *n.*[7] 2 SPENSER To Guyon . . Their pleasaunt tunes they sweetly thus applyde. BACON He that will not apply new remedies must expect new evils. T. FULLER To apply comfort to him who is not . . ready for it. JAS. MILL They applied coercion to the English resident. V. WOOLF Unless you apply some balm to the anguish of this hour. P. NICHOLS I undressed her and applied a suppository. M. LEITCH There was little or no splintering . . and no real sign on the outside that force had been applied. 4 MARVELL The Poll money hath likewise been applyd to the use of the warre. G. B. SHAW I wonder why the epithet robber is applied only to barons. You never hear of robber dukes. 5 STEELE Knife or a pistol, if he finds stomach to apply them. S. HILL It's not a word you tend to apply. 6 S. JOHNSON Knowledge which he cannot apply will make no man wise. J. FORDYCE I leave you to apply the remark. W. FAULKNER How false the most profound book turns out to be when applied to life. T. S. ELIOT A test . . which can only be slowly and cautiously applied. A. J. P. TAYLOR His ideas would have had to be applied by civil servants and industrialists who had no faith in them. 7 POPE Thus Wit, like Faith, by each man is apply'd To one small sect, and all are damn'd beside. 8 W. PALEY This test applies to every supposition. V. WOOLF Perhaps what he was saying did not apply to pictures. E. O'NEILL Arthur hangs back, as if the designation 'kids' couldn't possibly apply to him. M. SPARK She is above the common moral code, it does not apply to her. A. J. P. TAYLOR The Anglo-Polish alliance specifically did not apply against Russia.

II Of a person in close contact with an activity. 10 *v.t.* Give or devote (a faculty etc., oneself) assiduously *to*, *to do*. LME. 11 *v.i.* Attend assiduously (*to*). *arch.* L15. †12 *v.t.* Devote one's energy to; wield; practise. L15–M17. †13 *v.t.* Supply persistently *with*. M16–L16.

10 COVERDALE *Ps.* 89:12 That we maye applie oure hertes vnto wyssdome. J. RAY I applyed my mind to consider . . the physical reason of it. V. NABOKOV With rising appetite, Lo applied herself to the fruit. 11 SHAKES. *Macb.* Let your remembrance apply to Banquo. C. BRONTË I found my pupil . . disinclined to apply. 12 T. ELYOT Quintius . . repaired again to his plough and applied it diligently. MILTON The birds thir quire apply.

III Bend, direct. †14 *v.t.* Bend (the mind, oneself) *to*; *refl.* conform *to*, be subservient *to*, adapt *to*. LME–E17. †15 *v.i.* Comply, adapt, *to*. LME–E17. †16 *v.i.* & *refl.* Land, arrive, (*at*, *to*); steer, proceed, go, (*to*). LME–E19. †17 *v.t.* Go to, visit. *rare.* Only in 16. †18 *v.t.* Bring (a ship) to land; direct, steer. L16–E17. 19 *v.i.* & †*refl.* a Appeal *to*, address oneself *to*, give attention *to*. *obs.* in *gen.* sense. M17. b Address oneself for information, help, a service, etc., *to*; make a formal request (*to* someone, *for* or *to do* something); make or submit an application (*to* someone, *for* something). M17. †20 *v.t.* Direct (words) *to*. M17–M18.

14 BACON They fail sometimes in applying themselves to particular persons. P. HEYLIN Applying themselves unto the times, they were alwaies favourable to the strongest. 15 J. FOXE If she would applie to his request, she should be . . set at libertie. BACON The precedent state or disposition, unto which we do apply. 17 G. CHAPMAN He applied each place so fast. 18 SPENSER To whom his course he hastily applide. W. RALEIGH Light things apply themselves upwards. 19a S. BUTLER Those who apply to Men's Fancies and Humours. J. SMEATON On applying to the bridle . . we found that the chain was dragging upon the rocks. b ADDISON An old Woman applied herself to me for my charity. E. WAUGH Sebastian . . had applied to be taken on as a missionary lay-brother. J. LE CARRÉ A notice came round inviting linguists to apply for specialist service abroad. . . I was fed up with soldiering, so I applied. S. HILL There are state agencies to help you, you must apply to them. J. ORTON Have you applied for compensation? 20 MILTON God at last To Satan . . his doom apply'd, Though in mysterious terms.

appoggiatura /əpɒdʒə'tʊərə/ *n.* M18. [It., f. *appoggiare* lean upon, rest.] *Mus.* A grace-note just above or below a primary note, which it precedes and delays; the use of such notes.

appoint /ə'pɔɪnt/ *v.* LME. [OFr. *apointer*, f. *à point* to a point, into condition: see POINT *n.*[1]] I Come, or bring matters, to a point. †1 *v.t.* (in *pass.*) & *v.i.* Agree, settle, arrange definitely. Usu. w. inf. or *that*. LME–M17. 2 *v.i.* & †*refl.* Make up one's mind, resolve, determine. *arch.* LME. 3a *v.i.* Make an appointment *to do* something. *arch.* E16. b *v.t.* Arrange the time or place of (a meeting); arrange to meet (a person). *arch.* E16.

2 AV *2 Sam.* 17:14 The Lord had appointed to defeate the good counsell of Ahithophel. 3a DICKENS Mr. Bentley went away thanking him and appointing to call again. b SHAKES. *Tit. A.* Appoint the meeting Even at his father's house. J. GAY I appointed him at this hour.

II Determine authoritatively; ordain, decree. 4 *v.t.* Prescribe, fix (a time or place) for an action. Freq. in *pass.* Cf. APPOINTED 1. LME. 5 *v.t.* Decree, prescribe, fix *that* a thing shall be; ordain (something). Freq. in *pass.* LME. 6 *v.t.* Nominate, ordain (a person) *to* an office, *to* act in some capacity; give (a person) an official position; nominate, set up someone as (an officer, trustee, etc.). LME. 7 *v.t.* Destine, ordain, (*to* a fate or purpose, *to* do or suffer something). *arch.* L15. †8a *v.t.* Assign or grant authoritatively (a thing *to* a person). L15–M18. b *v.t.* & *i.* *Law.* Declare the destination of (property), in exercise of a power conferred for that purpose. E16.

4 SHAKES. *1 Hen. IV* We will . . appoint them a place of meeting. DEFOE The time appointed for execution. 5 CARLYLE Strangely . . it is appointed that Sound . . should be the most continuing of all things. J. MCCOSH The laws . . are appointed by God. 6 C. MERIVALE The Roman citizens appointed to all the higher magistracies. W. S. CHURCHILL President Davis appointed him Commander-in-Chief. A. S. NEILL I appoint teachers and ask them to leave if I think they are not suitable. J. LE CARRÉ A committee of enquiry . . appointed by the Praesidium to investigate and report upon a certain . . subject. 7 AV *1 Thess.* 5:9 God hath not appointed vs to wrath. DEFOE Next day I was appointed to be tried.

III 9 *v.t.* Put into proper order, make ready; *esp.* equip completely, furnish, accoutre. *obs.* exc. as *pa. pple.* LME.

9 BURKE The house of commons . . is miserably appointed for that service. SIR W. SCOTT Thus appointed . . he was in readiness to depart.

IV †10 *v.t.* Point to; point out. Only in M16. †11 *v.t.* Attribute *to*; attribute blame to. *rare.* Only in 17.

10 H. SURREY A blazing sterne . . By a long tract appointing vs the way. T. CRANMER As well as if you had appointed me with your finger. 11 MILTON Appoint not heavenly disposition, father. Nothing of all these evils hath befallen me But justly.

appointable *a.* M16. **appoin'tee** *n.* †(*a*) [Fr. *appointé*] a long-serving soldier with a special rate of pay; (*b*) a person who is appointed or nominated to an office; (*c*) *Law* a person in whose favour a power of appointment is executed: E18. **appointer** *n.* a person who ordains or nominates E16. **appointive** *a.* (orig. *N. Amer.*) pertaining to appointment; that is filled by appointment: L19. **appointor** *n.* (*Law*) a person who exercises the power of appointment L19.

appointed /ə'pɔɪntɪd/ *ppl a.* L15. [f. prec. + -ED[1].] 1 Settled or fixed beforehand; ordained.

L15. 2 (W. qualifying adv.) Equipped, fitted out. M16.

1 A. KOESTLER Last year's moth which had miraculously and uselessly survived its appointed life-term. R. SUTCLIFF He arrived at the appointed meeting ground . . to find the other waiting for him. 2 JOYCE They would have a beautifully appointed drawing-room with pictures and engravings . . and chintz covers for the chairs.

appointment /əˈpɔɪntm(ə)nt/ *n.* LME. [OFr. *apointement*, f. as APPOINT: see -MENT.] †1a Agreeing, coming to an arrangement; an agreement, a contract. LME–M18. b *spec.* (Terms of) capitulation. LME–E17. 2 An agreement or arrangement for a meeting; a prearranged meeting. LME. 3a The action of ordaining or directing what is to be done; ordinance, decree. *arch.* LME. b *Law.* The act of declaring the destination of any property, in exercise of a power conferred for that purpose. E17. c The action of nominating to or placing in an office or post; the position so given. M17. †4 Purpose, resolution. E16–E17. 5 (An item of) equipment; outfit, furnishing. Now usu. in *pl.* L16. †6 An allowance paid, esp. to a public official. E18–E19.

2 SHAKES. *Merry W.* For missing your meetings and appointments. N. MITFORD If people did not keep their appointments with him well before the specified time he always counted them as being late. J. BARTH I'd like an appointment to see Dr. Rose just before lunch. 3a J. BUTLER According to a natural order or appointment. c N. SHUTE It meant a new appointment, his first work for five months. H. MACMILLAN My appointment as Chancellor of the Exchequer . . was announced on 21 December 1955. **by appointment** by or as by royal warrant. 5 I. MURDOCH The room . . was spartan in its appointments.

apport /əˈpɔːt/ *n.* & *v.* LME. [OFr. *aport* action of bringing, f. *aporter* bring to.] A *n.* †1 Demeanour; bearing. LME–E17. †2 Something brought; an offering, revenue. Usu. in *pl.* LME–M16. 3 The production of material objects by supposedly occult means at a seance; an object so produced. Usu. in *pl.* L19. B *v.t.* †1 Bring. L16–E17. 2 Produce or transport by supposedly occult means. M20.

apportion /əˈpɔːʃ(ə)n/ *v.t.* L16. [(O)Fr. *apportionner* or med.L *apportionare* f. *ad* AP-[1] + *portionare*: see PORTION *v.*] 1 Assign (*to*) as a due portion; allot. L16. 2 Share, portion out. L16. †3 Adjust in due proportion. E17–E19.

apportionable *a.* E17. **apportionate** *v.t.* (now *rare* or *obs.*) = APPORTION E16. **apportioner** *n.* E17. **apportionment** *n.* the action or result of apportioning M16.

†**appose** *v.*[1]*t.* ME. [OFr. *aposer* var. of *oposer* OPPOSE. Aphet. to POSE *v.*[2]] 1 Confront with objections or hard questions: examine, interrogate. ME–M17. 2 *spec.* Examine as to accounts; audit. E17–M18.

†**apposal** *n.* a searching question; enquiry, investigation, esp. legal examination of accounts: LME–E19. †**apposer** *n.* a person who apposes; *spec.* an Exchequer officer who audited sheriffs' accounts: LME–M19.

appose /əˈpəʊz/ *v.*[2]*t.* L16. [f. L *apponere* after *compose*, *expose*, etc.: see next, POSE *v.*[1]] 1 Put or apply (a thing) *to* another. L16. 2 Place in apposition or juxtaposition. E19.

apposite /ˈapəzɪt/ *a.* & *n.* L16. [L *appositus* pa. pple of *apponere* apply, f. *ad-* AP-[1] + *ponere* to place, put.] A *adj.* 1 Well put or applied; appropriate, suitable. L16. †2 Of a person: ready with apt remarks. M17–L18.

1 W. S. MAUGHAM He rehearsed to himself a number of apposite speeches.

B *n.* Something placed beside or in apposition. *rare.* L17.

appositely *adv.* M17. **appositeness** *n.* M17.

apposition /apəˈzɪʃ(ə)n/ *n.*[1] LME. [Fr., or late L *appositio(n-)*, f. *apposit-* pa. ppl stem of *apponere*: see prec., -ION.] 1 The action of putting or applying one thing to another; application. *arch.* LME. 2 *Gram.* The placing of a term in syntactic parallelism with another; *esp.* the declarative or distinguishing addition of one noun to another without explicit coordination; the position of the term added. LME. 3 *gen.* The placing of things side by side or in close proximity; the fact or condition of juxtaposition or parallelism. E17.

1 J. AYLIFFE By the Apposition of a Publick Seal. 2 L. BLOOMFIELD In English we have also *close* apposition without a pause-pitch, as in *King John*, *John Brown*, *John the Baptist*, *Mr. Brown*, *Mount Everest*. B. RUBENS 'My son, a linguist'—the apposition was a habit with her. 3 W. S. LANDOR He places strange and discordant ideas in close apposition. C. LYELL These layers must have accumulated one on the other by lateral apposition.

appositional *a.* & *n.* (*a*) *adj.* of, pertaining to, or standing in apposition; (*b*) *n.* a term standing in apposition: L17. **appositionally** *adv.* in apposition L19.

apposition /apəˈzɪʃ(ə)n/ *n.*[2] E16. [OFr. *aposicion*, *apposition* var. of OPPOSITION: see APPOSE *v.*[1]] †1 An objection; opposition. E16–E17. 2 (The name given to) speech- or prize-day at St Paul's School, London. M17.

appositive /əˈpɒzɪtɪv/ *a.* & *n.* L17. [Late L *appositivus* subsidiary, f. *apposit-*: see APPOSITION *n.*[1], -IVE.] A *adj.* = APPOSITIONAL *a.* L17. B *n.* = APPOSITIONAL *n.* M19.

appositively *adv.* = APPOSITIONALLY L16.

appraise /əˈpreɪz/ *v.t.* LME. [Alt., by assim. to PRAISE *v.*, of APPRIZE *v.*[1]] 1 Assign a monetary value to, fix a price for, esp. as an official valuer. LME. 2 Estimate the amount, quality, or excellence of; assess; *spec.* conduct a usu. regular formal review of the work performance of (an individual). M19.

appraisable *a.* able to be valued or assessed M19. **appraisal** *n.* the act of appraising; a setting of price; an estimate of worth; *spec.* (a) usu. regular formal review of an individual's work performance, an interview or meeting with this purpose: E19. **apprai'see** *n.* a person whose work performance receives a formal review M20. **appraisement** *n.* valuation, estimation; an estimated value: M17. **appraiser** *n.* a person who appraises something or someone; an official valuer of goods or property: LME. **appraisingly** *adv.* so as to make a valuation or assessment L19. **appraisive** *a.* involving or concerned with appraisal M20.

appreciable /əˈpriːʃəb(ə)l, -ʃɪə-/ *a.* LME. [(O)Fr. *appréciable*, f. *apprécier*: see next, -ABLE.] †1 Worth esteeming. Only in LME. 2 Able to be estimated or judged; perceptible; considerable. E19.

appreciably *adv.* to an appreciable extent, considerably M19.

appreciate /əˈpriːʃɪeɪt, -sɪ-/ *v.* Also †**-tiate**. M16. [Late L *appretiat-* (med.L *-ciat-*) pa. ppl stem of *appretiare* set a price on, f. L *ad* AP-[1] + *pretium* PRICE *n.*: see -ATE[3]. Cf. (O)Fr. *apprécier*.] 1 *v.t.* Estimate rightly; perceive the full force of, understand, recognize *that*; be sensible or sensitive to; esteem adequately; recognize as valuable or excellent; be grateful for. M16. 2 *v.t.* Make or form an estimate of worth, quality, or amount of. *arch.* M18. 3 *v.t.* Raise in value. L18. 4 *v.i.* Rise in value. L18.

1 E. O'NEILL You been kind as kind can be to me and I certainly appreciate it—only don't spoil it all now. O. SITWELL It is fatal to be appreciated in one's own time. E. HEMINGWAY You don't appreciate what a fine wife you have. G. GREENE I could appreciate the obstinate stand at Khartoum—the hatred of the safe politicians at home. T. S. ELIOT I'd like to learn about music. I wish you would teach me how to appreciate it. K. AMIS I hope you appreciate these Portuguese wines? 2 BURKE Let us calmly . . appreciate those dreadful and deformed gorgons and hydras. 3 H. H. GIBBS The resumption of specie payments in Gold, thus appreciating that metal. 4 R. H. TAWNEY They were compelled to repay loans in an appreciating currency.

appreciatingly *adv.* with appreciation L19.

appreciation /əpriːʃɪˈeɪʃ(ə)n, -sɪ-/ *n.* Also †**-tiat-**. LME. [Fr. *appréciation* f. late L *appretiatio(n-)*, f. as prec.: see -ATION.] †1 Appraised value. *rare.* Only in LME. 2 Estimation; judgement; an assessment. E17. 3 Adequate or high estimation; sympathetic recognition; perception, understanding; gratitude. M17. 4 The action of setting a money value upon something; valuation. Chiefly *Sc.* L18. 5 A rise in value. L18.

2 A. POWELL There had been a number of appreciations of his work in the literary papers. B. ENGLAND He settled back and tried to make a proper military appreciation of their situation. 3 J. GALSWORTHY The appreciation of enough persons of good taste was what gave a work of art its permanent market value. JOYCE His appreciation of the importance of inventions now common but once revolutionary. E. WAUGH In token of her appreciation the chief purser had been asked to our party.

appreciative /əˈpriːʃ(ɪ)ətɪv/ *a.* Also †**-tiat-**. L17. [f. APPRECIATE + -IVE.] Involving (esp. sympathetic) estimation, understanding; showing adequate or great appreciation, grateful.

¶Rare bef. M19.

appreciatively *adv.* M17. **appreciativeness** *n.* M19.

appreciator /əˈpriːʃɪeɪtə/ *n.* L18. [f. APPRECIATE + -OR.] †1 *Sc. Law.* An appraiser of impounded goods. Only in L18. 2 A person who forms an adequate estimate; a person who recognizes the excellence (*of*); a person with understanding (*of*). E19.

appreciatory /əˈpriːʃ(ɪ)ət(ə)ri/ *a.* E19. [f. as prec. + -ORY[2].] Of or befitting an appreciator; appreciative.

apprehend /aprɪˈhɛnd/ *v.* LME. [Fr. *appréhender* or L *apprehendere*, f. *ad* AP-[1] + *prehendere* seize.] I Mentally. †1 *v.t.* & *i.* Learn, gain knowledge (of). LME–L17. 2 *v.t.* & (*occas.*) *i.* Perceive with the intellect; understand. L15. †3 *v.t.* Feel emotionally, be sensible of. L16–L17. 4 *v.t.* Perceive with the senses, become conscious of (an external impression). E17. 5 *v.t.* Anticipate, esp. with fear or dread; be apprehensive *that*. E17.

1 S. BUTLER Children . . Improve their nat'ral Talents without Care, And apprehend, before they are aware. 2 J. WESLEY I apprehended myself to be near death. STEELE I cannot apprehend where lyes the trifling in all this. T. REID What it is to think, to apprehend. LD MACAULAY The nature of the long contest between the Stuarts and their parliaments, was indeed very imperfectly apprehended by foreign statesmen. GLADSTONE The eternal laws, such as the heroic age apprehended them. BROWNING Each man . . avails him of what worth He apprehends in you. 3 JONSON Dead. Lord! how deeply, sir, you apprehend it. 4 A. BAIN If I see . . two candle flames, I apprehend them as different objects. I. MURDOCH The birds could still be vaguely apprehended, close overhead. 5 SHAKES. *Meas. for M.* A man that apprehends death no more dreadfully but as a drunken sleep. N. HAWTHORNE I sometimes apprehend that our institutions may perish. I. MURDOCH More danger was to be apprehended from shock than from anything else. D. M. WALKER At common law any private person may arrest where . . a breach of the peace has been or is actually being committed or is reasonably apprehended.

II Physically. †6 *v.t.* Lay hold upon, seize or grasp physically. LME–M19. †7 *v.t.* Seize (goods etc.) as a legal act; take possession of. *Sc.* L15–L17. †8 *v.t.* Come upon, find, esp. in wrongdoing or in the wrong place. *Sc.* L15–E17. 9 *v.t.* Seize (a person) in the name of the law, arrest. E16. †10 *v.t.* Seize or embrace (an offer, opportunity, etc.). L16–M17.

6 E. TOPSELL His dogs . . apprehending the garments of passengers. *absol.*: S. RUTHERFORD A lame hand that cannot apprehend. 9 A. FRASER Their priests in particular were in danger of death if apprehended.

apprehender *n.* M16.

apprehensible /aprɪˈhɛnsɪb(ə)l/ *a.* L15. [Late L *apprehensibilis*, f. *apprehens-*: see next, -IBLE.] †1 Capable of attaining (*to*). Only in L15. 2 Able to be apprehended; able to be grasped by the intellect or senses. (Foll. by *by*, *to*.) E17.

apprehensi'bility *n.* E19. **apprehensibly** *adv.* (*rare*) L17.

apprehension /aprɪˈhɛnʃ(ə)n/ *n.* LME. [Fr. *appréhension* or late L *apprehensio(n-)*, f. *apprehens-* pa. ppl stem of *apprehendere* APPREHEND: see -ION.] I Mental. †1 The action of learning, acquirement of knowledge. LME–M17. 2 The intellectual faculty; understanding. L16. 3 The action of perceiving with the intellect, conception. L16. 4 A conception, an idea; a view, a notion, an opinion. L16. 5 The action of perceiving with the senses. Long *arch.* L16. †6 Emotional consciousness. E-M17. 7 Anticipation, esp. with fear or dread; uneasiness; an anxiety, a foreboding. E17.

2 T. DEKKER O the quick apprehension of women. 3 J. GLANVILL Simple apprehension denotes no more than the soul's naked intellection of an object. 4 R. BAXTER Fix not too rashly upon your first apprehensions. H. JAMES The great question meanwhile was what Chad thought of his sister, which was naturally ushered in by that of Sarah's apprehension of Chad. 5 SHAKES. *Mids. N. D.* Dark night, that from the eye his function takes, The ear more quick of apprehension makes. 7 SHAKES. *Meas. for M.* The sense of death is most in apprehension. M. BEERBOHM I had on the way a horrible apprehension What if the Duke . . had taken the one means to forgetfulness. V. BRITTAIN My apprehensions for his safety had been lulled by the long quiescence of the Italian front. L. URIS Each of those dozen people who knew of the scheme went around with hearts heavy with apprehension A thousand things could go wrong.

II Physical. 8 The seizure of a person, a ship, etc., in the name of the law; an arrest. L16. 9 The action of laying hold of physically, prehension. *rare.* M17. 10 *Law.* The taking of actual possession. *arch.* M19.

8 *Scientific American* About a million apprehensions were made per year for violations of immigration law.

apprehensive /aprɪˈhɛnsɪv/ *a.* LME. [Fr. *appréhensif, -ive* or med.L *apprehensivus*, f. *apprehens-*: see prec., -IVE.] 1 Pertaining to perception by the intellect or the senses. LME. 2 Intelligent, perceptive, discerning. *arch.* E17. 3 Realizing, conscious, sensible. Foll. by *of, that. arch.* E17. 4 Anticipative of something adverse; uneasy in mind, fearful. (Usu. foll. by *of, that, for.*) E17. †5 In the habit of seizing; ready to seize (an offer, opportunity, etc.). E-M17.

1 MILTON Thoughts, my tormentors, armed with deadly stings, Mangle my apprehensive tenderest parts. 2 SHAKES. *Jul. Caes.* Men are flesh and blood, and apprehensive. ROBERT BURTON If the Imagination be very apprehensive, intent, and violent. BROWNING The lower phrase that suits the sense O' the limitedly apprehensive. 3 J. SPEED The King apprehensiue of his meaning, called his Lords. J. H. NEWMAN Miracles . . wrought . . by instruments but partially apprehensive that they are such. 4 R. BOYLE Why should I be more apprehensive for my Body than my Mind. SWIFT Being apprehensive it might spoil the sale of the book. BURKE More apprehensive from his servants . . than from the hired blood-thirsty mob without. CARLYLE Physically of a timid apprehensive nature. ARNOLD BENNETT She was apprehensive about future dangers and her own ability to cope with them; but she was always apprehensive. J. FRAME In spite of our training and position we were . . rather apprehensive of our own safety.

apprehensively *adv.* M17. **apprehensiveness** *n.* E17.

apprentice /əˈprɛntɪs/ *n.* & *v.* ME. [OFr. *aprentis* (mod. *apprenti*) nom. of *aprentif*, f. *aprendre* learn f. L *apprendere* contr. of *apprehendere* APPREHEND: see -IVE, -ICE[1].] A *n.* 1 A learner of a craft, bound to serve, and entitled to instruction from, his or her employer for a specified term. ME. 2 A barrister-at-law of less than sixteen years' standing. *obs.* exc. *Hist.* LME. 3 A beginner, a novice. L15.

1 *attrib.*: W. OWEN A poor apprentice-tailor.

B *v.t.* Bind as an apprentice. L16.

apprenticehood *n.* (now *rare*) = APPRENTICESHIP LME. **apprenticement** *n.* (*rare*) apprenticing, apprenticeship E19.

†apprenticeage *n.* see APPRENTISSAGE.

apprenticeship /əˈprɛntɪsʃɪp/ *n.* L16. [f. prec. + -SHIP.] 1 The position of an apprentice; service as an apprentice; initiatory training. L16. 2 The period for which an apprentice is bound; *spec.* (*arch.*) a period of seven years. M17.

1 *articles of apprenticeship*: see ARTICLE *n.* 4.

†apprentissage *n.* Also **-iceage**. L16–L18. [Fr., f. as APPRENTICE + -AGE.] = prec.

appress /əˈprɛs/ *v.t.* E17. [L *appress-* pa. ppl stem of *apprimere*, f. *ad* AP-[1] + *premere* press.] Press close to each other or to a surface etc. Cf. ADPRESSED.

appressorium /aprɛˈsɔːrɪəm/ *n.* Pl. **-ria** /-rɪə/. L19. [f. as prec. + -ORIUM.] *Bot.* A pad of mycelium by which certain parasitic fungi attach themselves to their hosts.

†appretiate *v.*, **-tiation** *n.*, etc., vars. of APPRECIATE, -CIATION, etc.

apprise /əˈprʌɪz/ *v.*[1]*t.* Also **-ize**. L17. [Fr. *appris(e)* pa. pple of *apprendre* teach (causative), learn: see APPRENTICE.] Inform, acquaint. (Foll. by *of.*)

be apprised of be aware of, know.

apprise *v.*[2] see next.

apprize /əˈprʌɪz/ *v.*[1]*t. arch.* Also (esp. in sense 2) **-ise**. LME. [OFr. *aprisier*, f. as A-[5] + *pris* PRICE *n.*, assim. to PRIZE *n.*[1]] 1 Value; esteem. LME. 2 *Sc. Law.* Put a selling price upon; put up for sale to pay a creditor. *obs.* exc. *Hist.* M16.

apprizement, (esp. *Sc. Law*) **-isement** *n.* (now *arch.* & *Hist.*) the action of apprizing LME. **apprizer**, (esp. *Sc. Law*) **-iser** *n.* (now *arch.* & *Hist.*) a person who apprizes LME.

apprize *v.*[2] var. of APPRISE *v.*[1]

appro /ˈaprəʊ/ *n. colloq.* L19. [Abbrev. of APPROVAL or APPROBATION.] *on appro*, on approval.

approach /əˈprəʊtʃ/ *n.* LME. [f. the vb.] 1 The act of coming near(er) in space. LME. b The descent of an aircraft to the landing area. Freq. *attrib.* M20. 2 Power of approaching; access. *arch.* E16. 3 A drawing near in time or circumstances; a coming near in quality, character, etc.; an approximation. L16. 4 A movement towards establishing personal relations with someone, an overture, an advance; an application. Freq. in *pl.* M17. 5 A means or way of approaching; a passage, avenue, channel, etc., giving access; (freq. in *pl.*). Also *fig.*, a way of addressing a task, dealing with a subject, etc.; an attitude. M17. b *Mil.* In *pl.* Entrenchments or other works by which besiegers draw closer to the besieged. *obs.* exc. *Hist.* M17. 6 *Hort.* Inarching. Chiefly in *by approach.* M17. 7 *Golf.* The play of the ball (other than from the tee) towards or on to the green. Usu. *attrib.* L19.

1 W. WHISTON The approach of a Comet to the Earth. GEO. ELIOT Casson's thoughts were diverted by the approach of the horseman. R. P. WARREN Upon nearer approach, he saw that a very dim light showed . . at one window. b *missed approach*: see MISS *v.*[1] 2 BACON Honour hath in it . . the approach to kings and principal persons. 3 SHAKES. *2 Hen. VI* Where death's approach is seen so terrible! POPE Thus sung the shepherds till th' approach of night. BURKE Some sort of approach towards infinity. E. O'NEILL The nearest approach to feeling he has shown in many a long night. 4 D. ROGERS Thy timorous and weake approaches toward his grace. A. J. P. TAYLOR Harris . . promoted his strategy by personal approach to the minister of defence. 5 W. COWPER Mastiffs in gold and silver lined the approach. K. AMIS Some fishing-boats were doing something in the approaches to Cascais Harbour. J. ORTON The present enlightened approach to the mentally sick. *Western Approaches*: see WESTERN *a.*

Comb.: **approach road** a road leading up to a place, a slip-road leading on to a motorway etc.

approachless *a.* (*literary*) unapproachable, inaccessible M17.

approach /əˈprəʊtʃ/ *v.* ME. [OFr. *aproch(i)er* (mod. *approcher*) f. eccl.L *appropiare*, f. *ad-* AP-[1] + *propius* nearer, compar. of *prope* near.] I *v.t.* 1 Come near to in space; move towards. ME. 2 Come near(er) to in time, quality, rank, etc.; be nearly equal to; move towards in thought, set about (a problem etc.). LME. 3 Be so situated or arranged that the parts lie successively nearer to (a line, point, etc.). Also (*arch.*), adjoin, neighbour. LME. 4 Come into the presence of (someone), or (*arch.*) into (someone's presence); seek a meeting or relationship with; make overtures, advances, proposals, etc., to; *spec.* seek to influence or bribe. LME. 5 Bring near(er); make closer in quality, character, etc. *arch.* LME. 6 *Mil.* Work forward towards by means of entrenchments. *obs.* exc. *Hist.* L17.

1 E. WAUGH Two policemen quickened their stride and approached us. A. SHAFFER A minstrels gallery which . . is approached by a winding staircase. 2 E. A. FREEMAN Vigorous youths fast approaching manhood. C. FRY It was approaching dusk, last evening. T. S. ELIOT Let us approach the question from another angle. S. WEINBERG Velocities approaching that of light. 3 ADDISON Trees rising one higher than another in proportion as they approach the centre. *Encycl. Brit.* The curve and its asymptote approach one another ever more closely but never quite meet except at infinity. 4 STEELE I cannot approach her without Awe. *Congressional Record* Everything that is said about public men being corrupted or approached. J. BUCHAN Twenty days of hiding before I could venture to approach the powers that be. J. P. DONLEAVY I was once approached by a talent scout in summer stock. J. BARTH The Colonel approached me . . on ten different occasions with offers of business. J. BOWEN The sinner approaches your presence, high priest. 5 SIR W. SCOTT He approached to the fire a three-footed stool. C. MERIVALE His object was . . to approach the Gaulish provincials to Rome.

II *v.i.* 7 Come nearer in space; draw near; *arch.* come near(er) *to* a place, person, etc. ME. 8 Draw near in time, befall; come near(er) *to* something in quality, magnitude, etc. LME. 9 Be so situated or arranged that the parts lie successively closer (*to* something). Also (*arch.*), be situated nearby. LME. 10 Come into someone's presence; make an overture or advance. (Foll. by *to.*) *arch.* LME.

7 AV *2 Sam.* 11:20 Wherefore approched ye so nigh vnto the city when yee did fight? TOLKIEN Before long they saw the marching line approaching: the Ents were swinging along with great strides down the slope towards them. 8 G. GASCOIGNE I thinke How ioyes approch, when sorrowes shrinke. B. STEWART The coefficients of dilation . . approach more nearly to equality. SAKI With money behind one, the problem of where to live approaches more nearly to the simple question of where do you wish to live. A. J. P. TAYLOR Perhaps they were conscious that a general election was approaching. 9 D. HARTLEY The ventricles of the brain approach towards each other. 10 T. J. MATHIAS To the Peers approach with awe.

approacher *n.* (*arch.*) L16. **approaching** *ppl a.* & *adv.* (*a*) *adj.* that approaches; (*b*) *adv.* nearly: LME. **approachment** *n.* (now *rare*) the action or state of approaching M16.

approachable /əˈprəʊtʃəb(ə)l/ *a.* L16. [f. prec. + -ABLE.] Able to be approached; accessible (*lit.* & *fig.*), affable.

S. JOHNSON He that regards the welfare of others should make his virtue approachable. HOR. WALPOLE The town was . . approachable only by a narrow causeway. T. ROETHKE Irish writers of the non-sullen and approachable variety.

approachaˈbility *n.* M19. **approachableness** *n.* (*rare*) M18.

approbate /ˈaprəbeɪt/ *v.t.* Pa. pple & ppl a. **-ated**, **†-ate**. LME. [L *approbat-* pa. ppl stem of *approbare*: see APPROVE *v.*[2], -ATE[3].] 1 Approve expressly or formally; sanction, approve of. Now only *N. Amer.* LME. 2 *Sc. Law.* Assent to. L18.

2 **approbate and reprobate** take advantage of the favourable parts of a deed while repudiating the rest.

approˈbatory *a.* = APPROBATIVE M16.

approbation /aprəˈbeɪʃ(ə)n/ *n.* LME. [(O)Fr. f. L *approbatio(n-)*, f. as prec.: see -ATION.] †1 Confirmation, proof. LME–E18. 2 The action of formally or authoritatively declaring good or true; sanction, endorsement. LME. 3 Approval or satisfaction expressed or felt. M16. †4 Probation, trial. E–M17.

1 SHAKES. *Cymb.* Would I had put my estate . . on th' approbation of what I have spoke! 2 T. KEIGHTLEY Received the royal approbation. 3 W. BLAKE Advertisements in Newspapers are no proof of Popular approbation, but often the Contrary. ALDOUS HUXLEY The Controller nodded his approbation 'I like your spirit, Mr Watson'. **on approbation** = *on* APPROVAL. 4 SHAKES. *Meas. for M.* This day my sister should the cloister enter, And there receive her approbation.

approbative /ˈaprəbeɪtɪv/ *a.* E17. [Fr. *approbatif, -ive* or med.L *approbativus*, f. as APPROBATE + -IVE.] Expressing approbation or approval.

approbativeness *n.* (now *rare*) (*a*) tendency to approve, approbative quality; (*b*) *Phrenol.* love of approbation: M19.

approof /əˈpruːf/ *n. arch.* E17. [f. APPROVE *v.*[1] after PROOF *n.*] 1 The act of proving, trial; proven quality. E17. 2 Approbation, approval. E17.

appropinquate /aprəˈpɪŋkweɪt/ *v.i.* & *†t. arch.* L16. [L *appropinquat-* pa. ppl stem of *appropinquare* to approach, f. *ad* AP-[1] +

propinquus neighbouring, f. *prope* near: see -ATE[3].] Approach; come near *to*.

appropinque /-ˈpɪŋk/ *v.t.* & *i.* (*rare*) = APPROPINQUATE M17. **appropinquity** *n.* (*rare*) nearness M17.

appropinquation /əprɒpɪŋˈkweɪʃ(ə)n/ *n. arch.* LME. [L *appropinquatio(n-)*, f. as prec.: see -ATION.] The action of coming or bringing near; approach.

appropriable /əˈprəʊprɪəb(ə)l/ *a.* M17. [f. APPROPRIATE *v.* + -ABLE.] Able to be appropriated.

appropriate /əˈprəʊprɪət/ *a.* (& †*pa. pple*). LME. [Late L *appropriatus* pa. pple, f. as next: see -ATE[2].] **1** Attached or belonging (*to*) as an attribute, quality, or right; peculiar (*to*); inherent, characteristic; specially suitable (*for*, *to*); proper, fitting. LME. **2** Annexed or attached (*to*) as a possession, appropriated; *esp.* (*Eccl.*) annexed as a benefice to a monastery. Now *rare* or *obs.* L16.

1 COLERIDGE To charm away .. *Ennui*, is the chief and appropriate business of the poet. M. MEAD Some peoples think of women as too weak to work out of doors, others regard women as the appropriate bearers of heavy burdens. J. BOWEN They must behave in a manner appropriate to the myth in which they were participating. A. LURIE Actually, he looks lots better when he isn't dressed as he thinks appropriate for dinner at Illyria. B. ENGLAND At an appropriate moment I shall strike the gong. T. STOPPARD He makes a wordless noise appropriate to male approval of female pulchritude. D. JACOBSON He was dressed in a tweed suit appropriate either to countryman or academic. G. BOYCOTT The music on the radio was turned off; somehow a bit of quiet seemed more appropriate.

appropriately *adv.* †(*a*) specially, peculiarly; (*b*) in an appropriate manner, fittingly: M16. **appropriateness** *n.* M17.

appropriate /əˈprəʊprɪeɪt/ *v.t.* Pa. pple & ppl a. **-ated**, †**-ate** (see prec.). LME. [L *appropriat-* pa. ppl stem of *appropriare* make one's own, f. *ad* AP-[1] + *propius* own, proper: see -ATE[3].] **1** Take *to* oneself as one's own property or for one's own use. LME. †**2** Make over *to* a person, institution, etc., as his, her, or its own or for his, her, or its use. LME–E18. **3** Devote, set aside, or assign, *to* the use of a person or institution, *to* or *for* a special purpose or use. LME. **4** Assign or attribute as properly pertaining *to*; attribute specially or exclusively *to*. *arch.* LME. **5** Make, or select as, appropriate or suitable (*to*). *arch.* LME. **6** Take possession of; use as one's own, esp. without permission. L16.

1 G. ANSON Appropriating the whole ships provisions to themselves. E. MELLOR The name 'priesthood' .. was never appropriated by apostles to themselves. **2** COVERDALE *Micah* 4:13 Their goodes shalt thou appropriate vnto the Lorde. T. BLOUNT It was lawful to appropriate the whole Fruits of a Benefice to an Abbey or Priory. **3** M. PATTISON The revenue is appropriated to the payment of University officers. *Time* Economic Opportunity Act .. appropriates almost $948 million for ten programs including job training, work-study programs, [etc.]. **4** J. STRUTT These amusements .. were appropriated to the season of Lent. COLERIDGE The word presumption I appropriate to the internal feeling. **5** R. PLOT The best methods of Cultivating, appropriating seeds and manures, and cureing the diseases of land. H. HALLAM The subject chosen is appropriated to the characteristic peculiarities of the poet. **6** J. K. JEROME He comes in quietly .., appropriates the most comfortable chair. P. V. WHITE Some man, a kind of *bushranger*, .. rode up to their vehicle, and appropriated every single valuable the unfortunate couple had upon them. A. J. P. TAYLOR The Conservatives appropriated patriotism.

appropriative *a.* of appropriating character or tendency M17. **appropriator** *n.* a person who or thing which appropriates; *esp.* (*Eccl. Hist.*) the monastery etc. to which a benefice is assigned: M17. †**appropr(i)e** *v.t.* = APPROPRIATE *v.* ME–E17.

appropriation /əprəʊprɪˈeɪʃ(ə)n/ *n.* LME. [(O)Fr. f. late L *appropriatio(n-)*, f. as prec.: see -ATION.] **1** The making over (*of* a thing) into one's own or (*arch.*) another's possession; the taking of a thing for one's own use, esp. without permission. LME. **2** *Eccl. Hist.* The transference to a body or individual (*spec.* to a monastery) of the tithes and endowments of a parish. LME. †**3** Attribution, application; a special attribute. LME–L17. **4** The assignment of something to a special purpose. Also, the thing so assigned; *esp.* a sum of money allocated officially for a particular use. M18.

Comb.: **appropriation bill** a legislative bill allocating public revenue to the purposes for which it may be used.

approval /əˈpruːv(ə)l/ *n.* E17. [f. APPROVE *v.*[2] + -AL[1].] The action of approving; sanction.

on approval (of goods supplied) to be returned if not satisfactory; for examination, without obligation to purchase.

approvance /əˈpruːv(ə)ns/ *n. arch.* L16. [OFr. *aprovance*, f. as APPROVE *v.*[2] + -ANCE.] = APPROVAL.

approve /əˈpruːv/ *v.*[1]*t.* Also †**approw**. ME. [OFr. *apprower*, *appro(u)er*, f. *à* A-[5] + *pro(u)* advantage, profit; later form (17) by interpretation of *u* in *approuer* as = *v*. Cf. IMPROVE *v.*[2]] *Law.* Increase one's profit from (land); *esp.* increase the value of (common land) by appropriation or enclosure, as permitted to the lord of a manor by the Statute of Merton, 1235.

approve /əˈpruːv/ *v.*[2] ME. [OFr. *aprover* (mod. *approuver*) f. L *approbare* make good, assent to as good, f. *ad* AP-[1] + *probus* good, just.] **I** †**1** *v.t.* Show to be true, demonstrate. ME–L17. †**2** *v.t.* Corroborate, attest. LME–M19. **3** *v.t.* Confirm authoritatively; sanction. LME. **4** *v.t.* & *i.* (foll. by *of*, †*on*). Pronounce or consider to be good or satisfactory; commend; be in sympathy or agreement. LME. **5** *v.t.* Display, exhibit, make proof of. *arch.* E16. **b** Show (esp. oneself) to be. *arch.* M16. **6** *v.t.* Recommend (oneself, one's qualities, etc.) as worthy of approval. *arch.* E17.

1 T. HEYWOOD This aproves unto us, that order is a cheefe rule in memorie. T. FULLER To approve the truth .. thereof against some one who questioned. MARVELL Mr. Onslow was approved not to have been culpable. **2** CLARENDON The success has approved this judgement. GIBBON The trembling emperor .. solemnly approved the innocence and fidelity of their assassins. **3** CHARLES JAMES The colonel or commanding officer approves the sentence of a regimental court-martial. A. J. P. TAYLOR On 28 January the naval plan was approved by the war council. **approved school** *Hist.* an institution for young offenders, a community home. **4** E. HEMINGWAY You cannot marry me and I understand that, although I do not approve it. B. BAINBRIDGE Things go on here that I don't approve of, but I neither interfere nor criticize. *absol.*: J. GALSWORTHY We've never cared whether the world approves or not. **5** BYRON 'Tis an old lesson; Time approves it true. LD MACAULAY When he approved himself ripe for military command. R. W. EMERSON Many opportunities to approve his stoutness and worth. **6** ISAAC TAYLOR If anticipations such as these approve themselves to reason.

†**II 7** *v.t.* Put to the proof or test of experience. LME–L18. **8** *v.t.* Find by experience. L16–M17.

7 SHAKES. *1 Hen. IV* Nay, task me to my word; approve me, lord.

approvable *a.* able to be approved; worthy of approval: LME. **approvableness** *n.* (*rare*) E19. **approvedly** /-vɪdli/ *adv.* (*rare*) †(*a*) in a tried and tested manner; (*b*) in a sanctioned or commended manner: LME. **approvingly** *adv.* in an approving manner E19.

approvement /əˈpruːvm(ə)nt/ *n.*[1] Also †**appowment**. LME. [OFr. *apro(u)ement*, *aprowe-* profit, f. as APPROVE *v.*[1] + -MENT.] *Law.* The action of increasing one's profit by approving land.

approvement /əˈpruːvm(ə)nt/ *n.*[2] E17. [OFr. *aprovement* (later *approuve-*), f. as APPROVE *v.*[2] + -MENT.] †**1** A proof. Only in E17. †**2** Approbation, approval. E17–M19. **3** The action of convicting another by turning informer. Now *arch.* & *Hist.* M18.

†**approver** *n.*[1] Also **apprower**. LME–M18. [AN *aprouour*, f. as APPROVE *v.*[1] + -OUR; suff. later interpreted as and replaced by -ER[1].] A person who manages land for the owner; a steward or bailiff; an agent in any business.

approver /əˈpruːvə/ *n.*[2] LME. [f. APPROVE *v.*[2] + -ER[1]. Cf. OFr. *aproveur.*] **1** A person who proves or offers to prove another guilty, an informer; latterly *spec.* one who turns King's, Queen's, or State's evidence. Now *arch.* & *Hist.* LME. †**2** A person who proves, tests, or tries someone. M16–L17. **3** A person who confirms, sanctions, pronounces good, or commends something. M16.

†**approw** *v.*, **-er** *n.*, **-ment** *n.* vars. of APPROVE *v.*[1], APPROVER *n.*[1], -MENT *n.*[1]

approximant /əˈprɒksɪm(ə)nt/ *a.* & *n.* M17. [L *approximant-* pres. ppl stem of *approximare*: see APPROXIMATE *v.*, -ANT[1].] †**A** *adj.* Approaching closely, resembling. *rare.* Only in M17. **B** *n.* **1** *Math.* A function, series, etc., which is an approximation to the solution of a given problem. M20. **2** *Phonet.* A non-fricative continuant. L20.

approximate /əˈprɒksɪmət/ *a.* (†*pa. pple*) & *n.* LME. [Late L *approximatus* pa. pple, f. *approximat-*: see next, -ATE[2].] **A** *adj.* (*pa. pple.*) †**1** Brought or placed close. Only in LME. **2** Very near in position or character; close together; similar. *arch.* LME. **3** Fairly or reasonably correct; near to the actual. E19.

3 very approximate more or less correct; fairly near to the actual.

B *n.* An approximate result or quantity. *rare.* L18.

approximately *adv.* nearly, with near approach to accuracy M19.

approximate /əˈprɒksɪmeɪt/ *v.* M17. [f. prec. or late L *approximat-* pa. ppl stem of *approximare* (Tertullian) draw near to, f. *ad* AP-[1] + *proximus* very near, next: see -ATE[3].] **1** *v.t.* Bring close or near, cause to approach or be near (*to*). (Chiefly of non-physical relationships). M17. **2** *v.i.* Come near or close (*to*, esp. in quality, number, etc., rarely physically). L18. **3** *v.t.* Come close to, approach closely, (used as sense 2). L18.

1 S. JOHNSON Shakespeare approximates the remote, and familiarizes the wonderful. E. H. GOMBRICH He must purify the world of matter, erase its flaws, and approximate it to the idea. J. G. FARRELL A compress .. placed on the palm after the edges of the wound had been evenly approximated. **2** JOHN ROSS The shores gradually approximate. A. G. GARDINER There are times when the dog approximates so close to our intelligences that he seems to be of us. E. J. HOWARD Pleasing meant approximating to the man's idea of the sort of woman his position and intelligence owed him. **3** J. SULLIVAN We may yet approximate .. a certainty that is demonstrative. E. POUND Progress lies rather in an attempt to approximate classical quantitative metres (NOT to copy them) than in a carelessness regarding such things.

approximator *n.* (*rare*) a person who approximates *to* M19.

approximation /əprɒksɪˈmeɪʃ(ə)n/ *n.* LME. [Late L *approximatio(n-)*, f. as prec.; later f. prec.: see -ATION.] **1** The action of bringing or coming near in place, time, or any conception to which ideas of space apply; the state of being near, proximity. LME. **2** A coming or getting near to identity in quantity, quality, or degree; the result of such a process; a value or quantity that is nearly but not exactly correct. M17.

approximative /əˈprɒksɪmətɪv/ *a.* E19. [f. APPROXIMATE *v.* + -IVE: cf. Fr. *approximatif.*] Of approximate character; nearly but not exactly reaching accuracy.

approximatively *adv.* M19.

appui /əˈpwiː, *foreign* apɥi/ *n. arch.* L16. [Fr.] **1** †**a** *gen.* Support; a stay, a prop. L16–L17. **b** *Mil.* Defensive support. L18. †**2** *Horsemanship.* The tension of the reins; the response of the horse's mouth to the control through the reins. E18–E19.

1b point of appui = *point d'appui* s.v. POINT *n.*[2] 2.

appulse /əˈpʌls/ *n.* E17. [L *appulsus* a driving towards, f. *appuls-* pa. ppl stem of *appellere*, f. *ad* AP-[1] + *pellere* drive.] **1** A driving or energetic motion towards a place; a strong impulse towards something. *arch.* E17. **2** *Astron.* An apparent close approach (falling short of occultation) by a planet etc. to a star or other body. M17.

appurtenance /əˈpəːt(ɪ)nəns/ *n.* ME. [AN *apurtenaunce*, OFr. *apartenance*, *apert-*, ult. f. late L *appertinere* (see APPERTAIN) + -ANCE.] **1** A minor property, right, or privilege, subsidiary or incidental to a more important one; an appendage. Usu. in *pl.* ME. 2 A contributory adjunct, an accessory. Usu. in *pl.* LME. 3 The fact or state of appertaining. *rare.* M19.

1 C. SANDBURG The land and all appurtenances thereto and all deposits of oil and gold. 2 SHAKES. *Haml.* Th' appurtenance of welcome is fashion and ceremony. L. STRACHEY The bonnet with its jet appurtenances. M. MUGGERIDGE It had now become a grammar school, with all the usual appurtenances in the shape of houses, prefects, blazers, a school song, and so on. 3 W. D. WHITNEY The word is a token of the most indefinite appurtenance.

appurtenant /əˈpəːt(ə)nənt/ *a.* & *n.* Also (esp. in sense A.2, *arch.*) **appertinent**. LME. [OFr. *apartenant* pres. pple of *apartenir* APPERTAIN: see -ANT[1].] A *adj.* 1 Belonging (*to*) as a (subsidiary or incidental) property, right, or privilege. LME. 2 Appertaining (*to*); appropriate (*to*); relating, pertinent. LME. B *n.* An appurtenance. Now *rare.* LME.

apraxia /əˈpraksɪə/ *n.* L19. [G *Apraxie* f. Gk *apraxia* inaction.] *Med.* Inability to perform given purposive actions, as a result of cerebral disorder.

après /ˈapreɪ, *foreign* ɑprɛ/ *prep.* M19. [Fr. = after.] 1 *après coup* /ku/ [lit. 'after stroke'], after the event; as an afterthought. M19. 2 *après-ski* /skiː/ *n.* & *a.*, (worn, done, etc., at) the time when skiing is over for the day at a resort. M20. b Used w. Eng. wds in imitation of *après-ski*, as *après-bath, -sex*, etc. M20.

apricate /ˈaprɪkeɪt/ *v. rare.* L17. [L *apricat-* pa. ppl stem of *apricari* bask in the sun, f. *apricus* exposed (to the sun): see -ATE[3].] 1 *v.i.* Bask in the sun. L17. 2 *v.t.* Expose to sunlight. M19.

apricot /ˈeɪprɪkɒt/ *n.* Orig. †**abrecock**, †**apricock**. M16. [Port. *albricoque* or Sp. *albaricoque* f. Sp. Arab. *al-barḳūḳ*, f. AL-[2] + *barḳūḳ* f. late Gk *praikokion* f. L *praecoquum* n., f. neut. of var. of *praecox* early-ripe. Assim. to Fr. *abricot* and perhaps infl. by L *apricus* ripe.] 1 The juicy stone-fruit of the tree *Prunus armeniaca*, of the rose family. M16. 2 The tree itself, cultivated in the warmer temperate regions and orig. native to China. M16. 3 The pinkish-yellow colour of the ripe fruit. L19.

1 *Irish apricot*: see IRISH *a.*

Comb.: **apricot plum** (the edible yellow stone-fruit of) a tree of the rose family, *Prunus simonii*, which is native to China and bears white blossom.

April /ˈeɪpr(ɪ)l/ *n.* OE. [L *Aprilis* use as n. of adj. (sc. *mensis* month).] The fourth month of the year in the Gregorian calendar. Also *fig.*, w. allusion to April's position in spring or to bright changeable weather with showers, considered characteristic of the month in Britain and elsewhere in the northern hemisphere.

TENNYSON Half-opening buds of April. *attrib.*: SHAKES. *Two Gent.* The uncertain glory of an April day. *fig.*: P. SIDNEY In the April of your age. SHAKES. *Ant. & Cl.* The April's in her eyes. It is love's spring.

Comb.: **April fool** a person upon whom a joke is played on the first of April (called *April Fool's* (or †*Fool*) *Day*).

¶Rare until LME, bef. which the usual sp. was *Averil*. At first (and long in dial. use) stressed on 2nd syll., which rhymed with *mile*.

a priori /eɪ praɪˈɔːraɪ, ɑː priˈɔːri/ *adv.* & *a. phr.* L16. [L *a priori* from what is before.] 1 Of reasoning: (by) proceeding from causes to effects; deductive(ly). Opp. A POSTERIORI. L16. 2 *loosely.* Presumptive(ly); without previous investigation; as far as one knows. E19. 3 *Philos.* Of knowledge or concepts: not derived from sensory experience; innate(ly). M19.

apriority *n.* (*a*) innateness in the mind; (*b*) = APRIORISM: M19.

apriorism /eɪpraɪˈɔːrɪz(ə)m/ *n.* L19. [f. prec. + -ISM.] The doctrine of the existence of a priori knowledge or concepts. Also, (an example of) reasoning a priori.

apriorist *n.* an adherent of apriorism; a person given to reasoning a priori: L19. **aprioˈristic** *a.* L19.

apron /ˈeɪpr(ə)n/ *n.* & *v.* Orig. †**n-**. ME. [OFr. *naperon* (mod. *napperon*), f. *nap(p)e* tablecloth f. L *mappa* napkin: initial *n* lost by misdivision as in *adder, auger*, etc.] A *n.* I 1 An article of dress. 1 A garment, orig. of linen, worn in front of the body to protect the clothes from dirt or damage, or simply as a covering. ME. 2 A similar garment worn as part of official dress, e.g. by a bishop, dean, Freemason, etc. LME.

1 SHAKES. *Jul. Caes.* Where is thy leather apron and thy rule? E. JONG I changed into a blue Gown with my prettiest embroider'd Apron and a Tucker of white Lace.

II A structure like an apron in form or function. 3 A protective or decorative layer of brickwork etc., esp. beneath a window. E17. b A strengthening timber behind the stem of a wooden ship. E18. 4 The skin covering the belly of a roast duck or goose, enclosing the stuffing. M18. 5 A protective covering for the legs in an open carriage. L18. 6 The folded abdomen of a crab. M19. 7 An endless conveyor consisting of overlapping plates (usu. called *apron conveyor*); each of these plates. M19. 8 *Geol.* An extensive outspread deposit of sediment, esp. at the foot of a glacier or mountain. L19. 9 *Theatr.* A projecting strip of stage for playing scenes in front of the curtain. E20. 10 A hard-surfaced area used for the (un)loading, manoeuvring, etc., of aircraft at an airfield. E20.

Comb.: *apron conveyor*: see sense 7 above; †**apron-man** a mechanic, a workman; **apron stage** = sense 9.

B *v.t.* Cover with an apron; cover or surround in the manner of an apron. M19.

DICKENS I mean to apron it and towel it. B. RUBENS All the villas looked exactly alike, red-brick structures, aproned by patios and well laid-out gardens.

aproned *a.* having an apron (formerly regarded as a symbol of a working man) E17. **apronful** *n.* the quantity that can be held in an apron M17.

apron-string /ˈeɪpr(ə)nstrɪŋ/ *n.* M16. [f. APRON *n.* + STRING *n.*] A string with which an apron is tied on.

Comb. & *phrases*: **apron-string hold, tenure** *arch.* tenure of property in virtue of one's wife, or during her lifetime only; **tied to the apron-strings of** unduly controlled by (a wife, mother, etc.).

apropos /aprəˈpəʊ, ˈaprəpəʊ/ *adv., a., n.,* & *prep.* Also ***à propos*** /a prɔpo/. M17. [Fr. *à propos*, f. *à* to + *propos* purpose.] A *adv.* 1 To the point; fitly, opportunely. M17. 2 In respect or as a relevant association *of* (now less commonly, *to*). (Cf. sense D. below.) M18. b *absol.* Incidentally, by the way. M18.

1 DRYDEN The French . . use them with better judgment, and more àpropos. ADDISON Stanhope and Earl arrived very àpropos. 2 G. CLARE Apropos of nothing she declared that love must be wonderful. b SMOLLETT But a-propos! Hast thou seen the girl?

B *adj.* Pertinent, appropriate, opportune. (Foll. by *of, to.*) M17.

POPE A tale extremely apropos. J. WOODFORDE Mr. Johnson gave us a very excellent Sermon indeed, very apropos to the times.

C *n.* †1 An opportune or pertinent occurrence. Only in L18. 2 Relevance, pertinency. M19.

2 GEO. ELIOT I fail to see the à propos.

D *prep.* Concerning, with regard to (cf. sense A.2 above). *colloq.* M20.

Phrases: ***à propos de bottes*** /də bɔt/ [Fr. = with regard to boots, i.e. to something quite irrelevant] without serious motive, without rhyme or reason.

aprosexia /aprəˈsɛksɪə/ *n.* L19. [Gk = lack of attention, f. A-[10] + *prosekhein* turn (one's mind): see -IA[1].] Abnormal inability to concentrate.

aprosopia /aprəˈsəʊpɪə/ *n. rare.* M19. [f. Gk A-[10] + *prosōpon* face + -IA[1].] *Med.* Absence or imperfect development of the face.

aprotic /eɪˈprəʊtɪk/ *a.* M20. [G *aprotisch*, f. as A-[10], PROTON, -IC.] *Chem.* Of a solvent: having little or no ability to exchange protons with the solute.

aps *n.* see ASP *n.*[1]

apsara /ˈʌpsərɑː/ *n.* Also **up-**. M19. [Hindi *apsarā* f. Skt *apsarās*.] *Hindu Mythol.* Any of a class of celestial nymphs, freq. regarded as the wives of the gandharvas or heavenly musicians.

apse /aps/ *n.* E19. [f. as APSIS.] 1 *Astron.* = APSIS *n.* 2. E19. 2 *Archit.* A large semicircular or polygonal structure, often roofed with a semi-dome, situated esp. at the end of the choir, nave, or an aisle of a church. M19.

apsidal /ˈapsɪd(ə)l/ *a.* M19. [f. as next + -AL[1].] 1 *Archit.* Of the form or nature of an apse. M19. 2 *Astron.* Of or pertaining to the apsides. M19.

apsis /ˈapsɪs/ *n.* Also †**absis** (orig. the usual spelling). Pl. **apsides** /əpˈsʌɪdiːz, ˈapsɪdiːz/. E17. [L *apsis, absis, -sid-* f. Gk (*h*)*apsis* arch, vault, (rim of a) wheel, perh. f. *haptein* fasten, join.] †1 Circumference, circuit; orbit (of a planet). E17–E18. 2 *Astron.* Either of the two points in the elliptical orbit of a planet or other body at which it is respectively nearest to and furthest from the primary about which it revolves. M17. 3 *Archit.* = APSE *n.* 2. Now *rare* or *obs.* E18.

apˈsidiole *n.* (*Archit.*) a small apse L19.

apso /ˈapsəʊ/ *n.* Pl. **-os**. M20. [Tib. *a-sob* /ˈapso/.] In full *Lhasa apso, Tibetan apso.* (An animal of) a breed of small long-coated dog, often gold or grey and white, originating at Lhasa.

apt /apt/ *a.* LME. [L *aptus* pa. pple of *apere* fasten, attach. Cf. Fr. *apte*.] 1 Suited, fitted, adapted, prepared, ready, *for*, †*to*. *arch.* LME. 2 Habitually liable, customarily disposed, likely, prone, *to do* something. E16. b Inclined, disposed, *to think*, in a particular instance. *arch.* L17. 3 Suitable, appropriate, apposite. M16. 4 Ready to learn, quick-witted, prompt, (*at*). M16.

1 SHAKES. *Jul. Caes.* Live a thousand years, I shall not find myself so apt to die. BACON States . . apt to be the Foundations of Great Monarchies. W. MORRIS Tall was he, slim, made apt for feats of war. E. WAUGH The time was apt for reminiscence. 2 N. COWARD I'm so apt to see things the wrong way round. C. MACKENZIE When Hugh did that onlookers were apt to be impressed. R. SUTCLIFF When you get men into that state there is apt to be trouble coming. S. KING Her morning routine was as set as a single person's is apt to be. 3 SHAKES. *Mids. N. D.* In all the play There is not one word apt. WORDSWORTH To give me human strength, by apt admonishment. DISRAELI The prompt reply or the apt retort. Q. CRISP The day I was there was Columbus day. This I thought was an apt coincidence. 4 DEFOE He was the aptest scholar that ever was. H. MARTINEAU Men . . are . . apt at devising ways of easing their toils.

aptly *adv.* LME. **aptness** *n.* E16.

apterous /ˈapt(ə)rəs/ *a.* L18. [f. Gk *apteros* f. A-[10] + *pteron* wing, + -OUS.] Chiefly *Entomol.* Wingless.

apterygote /apˈtɛrɪgəʊt/ *a.* & *n.* E20. [mod.L *Apterygota* (see below), f. Gk A-[10] + *pterugōtos* winged.] *Entomol.* A *adj.* Pertaining to or designating insects of the subclass Apterygota, which includes primitive orders in which wings are totally lacking, e.g. bristletails, springtails. E20. B *n.* An apterygote insect. E20.

apteryx /ˈaptərɪks/ *n.* Now *rare.* E19. [mod.L, f. Gk A-[10] + *pterux* wing.] = KIWI I.

aptitude /ˈaptɪtjuːd/ *n.* LME. [(O)Fr. f. late L *aptitudo* (Boethius), f. as APT: see -TUDE. Cf. ATTITUDE.] 1 Natural tendency, propensity, or disposition. LME. 2 Fitness, suitability, appropriateness. M16. 3 Natural ability; a talent (*for*); capacity to acquire a particular skill. M16. †4 = ATTITUDE I. M17–E18.

1 R. OWEN The aptitude of the Cheiroptera . . to fall like Reptiles into a state of true torpidity. 2 T. WARREN They lose their aptitude for heaven. A. HELPS In any comparison so frequently used there must be some aptitude. 3 R. CHURCH I had no aptitude for figures. A. TOFFLER People who share the same interests and aptitudes on the basis of which friendship may blossom. *attrib.*: M. MCCARTHY By the use of aptitude tests, psychological questionnaires, . . he hoped to discover a method of gauging student potential.

†**aptote** *n.* L16–L18. [Late L *aptotus* f. Gk *aptōtos* without cases, f. A-[10] + *ptōsis* case.] *Gram.* An indeclinable noun.

Apulian /əˈpjuːlɪən/ *a.* & *n.* E17. [f. L *Apulia* (see below) + -AN.] A *adj.* Of or pertaining to the ancient province or the modern district of Apulia in S. Italy, or its inhabitants. E17. B *n.* A native or inhabitant of Apulia. E17.

Apus /ˈeɪpəs/ *n.* E18. [L *apus* a kind of bird f. Gk *apous*.] (The name of) an inconspicuous circumpolar constellation of the southern hemisphere; = *bird of paradise* (b) s.v. BIRD *n.*

apyretic /eɪpʌɪˈrɛtɪk, apɪ-/ *a.* Now *rare.* M19. [f. A-[10] + PYRETIC.] *Med.* = APYREXIAL.

apyrexia /apʌɪˈrɛksɪə, eɪ-/ *n.* Also †**-exy.** M17. [mod.L f. Gk *apurexia*; partly through Fr. *apyrexie* (16).] *Med.* Absence of fever.
apyrexial *a.* free from fever L19.

aqua /ˈakwə/ *n.*[1] M20. [Abbrev.] The colour aquamarine.

aqua /ˈakwə/ *n.*[2] M20. [L.] 1 *Chem.* The water molecule, H_2O, as a neutral ligand. Usu. *attrib.* Also called *aquo.* M20. 2 *gen.* Water. L20.
1 *aqua complex, salt,* etc. 2 *aqua birth, park, pool,* etc.

aqua- /ˈakwə/ *comb. form.* [L *aqua* water.] Forming ns. w. the sense 'water', esp. w. ref. to aquatic entertainment.

aquaculture /ˈakwəkʌltʃə/ *n.* Also **aqui-** /ˈakwɪ-/. M19. [f. prec. + -CULTURE.] The rearing of aquatic animals or the cultivation of aquatic plants, for food.
aquaˈcultural *a.* L19.

aqua fortis /ˌakwə ˈfɔːtɪs/ *n. phr. arch.* Also **aquafortis.** L15. [L = strong water.] Nitric acid; orig., any powerful solvent.

aquake /əˈkweɪk/ *adv.* & *pred. a. poet.* L19. [f. A-[2] + QUAKE *n.* or *v.*] Quaking.

Aqua Libra /ˌakwə ˈliːbrə/ *n. phr.* L20. [L *aqua* water + *libra* balance.] (Proprietary name for) a beverage made from flavoured mineral water and fruit juices; a drink of this.

aqualung /ˈakwəlʌŋ/ *n.* & *v.* Also (US proprietary name) **Aqua-Lung.** M20. [f. AQUA- + LUNG.] A *n.* A portable breathing-apparatus for divers, comprising cylinders of compressed air strapped on the back, feeding air automatically to a mask or mouthpiece. M20. B *v.i.* Use an aqualung. M20.

aquamanile /ˌakwəməˈnʌɪli, -ˈniːli/ *n.* L19. [Late L f. L *aquaemanalis* hand-basin, f. *aquae* genit. sing. of *aqua* water + *manale* ewer.] A water vessel or ewer, freq. in the form of an animal or bird.

aquamarine /ˌakwəməˈriːn/ *n.* & *a.* E18. [f. L *aqua marina* seawater.] A *n.* 1 A bluish-green variety of beryl. E18. 2 The colour of this. M19. B *adj.* Having the colour of aquamarine. M19.
¶The earlier equivalent was AIGUE-MARINE f. Fr.

†**aqua mirabilis** *n. phr.* L16–E19. [L = wonderful water.] A cordial distilled from a mixture of various spices with alcohol.

aquanaut /ˈakwənɔːt/ *n.* L19. [f. AQUA- + Gk *nautēs* sailor.] An underwater swimmer or explorer.

aquaplane /ˈakwəpleɪn/ *n.* & *v.* E20. [f. AQUA- + PLANE *n.*[3]] A *n.* A board on which a person rides, towed behind a speedboat. E20. B *v.i.* 1 Ride standing on an aquaplane. E20. 2 Of a vehicle: glide uncontrollably on water covering a road surface. M20.

aqua regia /ˌakwə ˈriːdʒə/ *n. phr.* Also †**aqua regis.** E17. [L = royal water.] *Chem.* A concentrated mixture of nitric and hydrochloric acids, able to dissolve gold, platinum, etc.

aquarelle /akwəˈrɛl/ *n.* M19. [Fr. f. It. *acquarella* watercolour, f. *acqua* f. L *aqua* water.] A style of painting in thin, usu. transparent, watercolours; a painting in this style.
aquarellist *n.* an artist in aquarelle L19.

aquaria *n.pl.* see AQUARIUM.

Aquarian /əˈkwɛːrɪən/ *n.* & *a.* L16. [f. L *aquarius* pertaining to water, AQUARIUS, f. *aqua* water, + -AN.] A *n.* 1 *Eccl. Hist.* A member of an early Christian sect who used water instead of wine at the Eucharist. L16. 2 (**a-**.) = AQUARIST. M19. 3 A person born under the sign Aquarius. E20. B *adj.* 1 (**a-**.) Of or pertaining to an aquarium. M19. 2 Of or pertaining to the sign Aquarius; (characteristic of a person) born under Aquarius. M20.

aquarist /ˈakwərɪst/ *n.* Also †**-iist.** L19. [f. next + -IST.] A person who keeps an aquarium.

aquarium /əˈkwɛːrɪəm/ *n.* Pl. **-ria** /-rɪə/, **-riums.** M19. [Use as n. of neut. sing. of L *aquarius* (see AQUARIAN), after VIVARIUM.] An artificial pond or tank (usu. with transparent sides) for keeping live aquatic plants and animals; a place containing such tanks.

Aquarius /əˈkwɛːrɪəs/ *n.* OE. [L = water-carrier, use as n. of adj.: see AQUARIAN.] 1 (The name of) a constellation on the ecliptic just south of the celestial equator, next to Capricorn; *Astrol.* (the name of) the eleventh zodiacal sign, usu. associated with the period 20 January to 18 February (see note s.v. ZODIAC); the Water-carrier. OE. 2 A person born under the sign Aquarius; = AQUARIAN *n.* 3. M20.
1 *attrib.*: E. KIRK Aquarius people are remarkable spiritual healers. **Age of Aquarius** an astrological age characterized by (esp. sexual) freedom and brotherhood.

aquarobics /akwəˈrəʊbɪks/ *n.pl.* (treated as *sing.* or *pl.*). L20. [Blend of AQUA- and AEROBICS.] (A system of) aerobic exercises performed in water.
¶Proprietary name in the US.

aquatic /əˈkwatɪk, -ˈkwɒt-/ *a.* & *n.* L15. [(O)Fr. *aquatique* or L *aquaticus*, f. *aqua* water: see -ATIC. Cf. AQUATILE.] A *adj.* †1 Watery; rainy. L15–L17. 2 Growing or living in or near water. M17. 3 Of a sport: conducted on or in water. M19. B *n.* 1 An aquatic plant or animal. L17. b A swimmer, a bather. *joc.* E19. 2 In *pl.* Aquatic sports. M19.

aquatile /ˈakwətʌɪl, -tɪl/ *a.* & *n. arch.* E17. [L *aquatilis*, f. *aqua* water: see -ATILE.] A *adj.* = AQUATIC *a.* 2. E17. †B *n.* = AQUATIC *n.* 1. M17–M18.

aquatint /ˈakwətɪnt/ *n.* & *v.* As n. also **aquatinta** /akwəˈtɪntə/. L18. [Fr. *aquatinte*, It. *acquatinta* coloured water: cf. TINT *v.*[1]] A *n.* A method of etching on copper with nitric acid, which produces shaded effects as well as lines; an engraving made by this method. L18. B *v.i.* & *t.* Etch in aquatint. E19.
aquatinter *n.* M19.

aquavit /akwəˈviːt/ *n.* Also **akva-** /akvə-/. L19. [Norw., Sw., Da. *akvavit* AQUA VITAE.] An alcoholic spirit distilled from potatoes or other starch-containing plants.

aqua vitae /ˌakwə ˈvʌɪtiː, ˈviːtʌɪ/ *n. phr.* Also **aqua-vitae.** LME. [L = water of life: cf. Fr. *eau de vie*, USQUEBAUGH.] Alcoholic spirits, esp. of the first distillation.

†**-aque** *suff.* var. of -AC.

aqueduct /ˈakwɪdʌkt/ *n.* M16. [Fr. †*aqueduct* (now *-duc*) or its source L *aquae(-)ductus*, f. genit. of *aqua* water + *ductus* conveying.] 1 An artificial channel, esp. an elevated structure of masonry, for the conveyance of water. M16. 2 *Anat.* A small fluid-filled canal; *spec.* that connecting the third and fourth ventricles of the brain. E18.

aqueous /ˈeɪkwɪəs/ *a.* & *n.* M17. [f. med.L *aqueus*, f. *aqua* water: see -EOUS.] A *adj.* 1 Of the nature of water; watery. M17. 2 Connected with or relating to water. M18.
1 **aqueous humour** the clear fluid occupying the space between the lens and cornea of the eye. 2 **aqueous solution**: of a substance dissolved in water.
B *n.* The aqueous humour. L19.

aquiculture *n.* var. of AQUACULTURE.

aquifer /ˈakwɪfə/ *n.* E20. [f. L *aqui-* comb. form of *aqua* water + -FER.] *Geol.* A water-bearing stratum of permeable rock.

aquiferous /əˈkwɪf(ə)rəs/ *a.* M19. [f. as prec.: see -FEROUS.] Conveying or yielding water.

Aquila /ˈakwɪlə, əˈkwɪlə/ *n.* M16. [L *aquila* eagle.] (The name of) a constellation on the celestial equator, lying in the Milky Way near Cygnus; the Eagle.

aquilegia /akwɪˈliːdʒə/ *n.* Also †**-lege.** L16. [med.L *aquilegia*, *-leia*, prob. f. L *aquilegus* water-collecting.] Any plant of the genus *Aquilegia* of the buttercup family, bearing showy flowers whose five petals have backward-directed hollow spurs; a columbine.
¶Rare bef. 19 exc. as mod.L genus name.

aquiline /ˈakwɪlʌɪn/ *a.* M17. [L *aquilinus*, f. *aquila* eagle, prob. after Fr. *aquilin*: see -INE[1].] 1 Of or belonging to an eagle. M17. 2 Like an eagle; *esp.* (of the nose or features) curved like an eagle's beak. M17.
2 BURKE A penetrating aquiline eye. ALDOUS HUXLEY The aquiline good looks of a rather long and narrow face. M. DRABBLE She has a . . tall, stiletto . . figure . . . at the worst he could call her aquiline.

†**Aquilon** *n.* LME–E17. [(O)Fr. f. L *aquilo(n-)*.] The north or north-north-east wind.

aquiver /əˈkwɪvə/ *adv.* & *pred. a.* L19. [f. A-[2] + QUIVER *n.*[2] or *v.*[1]] In a quiver, trembling.

aquo /ˈakwəʊ/ *n.* E20. [f. as AQUA *n.*[2] + -O-.] *Chem.* = AQUA *n.*[2] 1. Usu. *attrib.*

aquose /ˈakwəʊs/ *a. rare.* LME. [L *aquosus*, f. *aqua* water: see -OSE[1].] Watery; full of fluid.

aquosity /əˈkwɒsɪti/ *n.* LME. [Late L *aquositas*, f. as prec.: see -ITY.] 1 The quality of being moist or watery. LME. †2 Moisture, liquid, fluid. LME–E18.

ar /ɑː/ *n.* LME. [Repr. pronunc.] The letter R (r).

ar- /ar, *unstressed* ər/ *pref.* (not productive). Assim. form of L AD- bef. *r.* In OFr., L *arr-* was reduced to *ar-*, which appears in ME adoptions, but in later Fr., and hence in Eng., *arr-* was restored by Latinization, as *arrange*, *arrest.*

-ar /ə/ *suff.*[1] 1 [Repr. L *-aris* adj. suff., synon. w. *-alis* (-AL[1]) but used where *l* preceded, or OFr. *-aire*, *-ier* (later refash. after L).] Forming adjs. w. the sense 'of the kind of, pertaining to', as *angular, lunar, molecular, stellar, titular,* etc. Also forming ns., as *scholar.* 2 [Repr. L *-ar(e)* neut. of *-aris*, or Fr. *-er.*] Forming ns., as *pillar.*

-ar /ə/ *suff.*[2] (not productive). [Repr. L *-arius*, *-ium* (usu. repr. by -ER[1], -ARY[1]) or Fr. *-aire*, or *-ier.*] Forming ns., as *bursar, exemplar, vicar,* etc.

-ar /ə/ *suff.*[3] (not productive). Alt. of -ER[1], -ER[2], or -OR, as *beggar, liar, pedlar,* etc.

Ara /ˈɑːrə/ *n.* L17. [L *ara* altar.] (The name of) a small constellation of the southern hemisphere in the Milky Way, near Scorpius; the Altar.

Arab /ˈarəb/ *n.* & *a.* In sense A.3 also **a-.** LME. [Fr. *Arabe* f. L *Arabs* f. Gk *Araps*, *Arab-* f. Arab. *ʿarab.*] A *n.* 1 A member of the Semitic people orig. inhabiting the Arabian peninsula and neighbouring lands, and now the Middle East generally. LME. 2 An Arabian horse (prized for pure breeding and swiftness). M17. 3 More fully *street arab.* A homeless vagrant child. (By some regarded as racially offensive.) M19. B *adj.* Of or pertaining to Arabia or the Arabs; Arabian. E19.
¶Rare bef. 17, the usual wd being ARABY earlier.
Arabdom *n.* Arabs collectively; the Arab world: M20.

araba /əˈrɑːbə/ *n.* E19. [Turk. f. Arab. *ʿarrāda* gun-carriage.] Chiefly *Hist.* An ox-drawn or horse-drawn carriage used in Turkey and the Middle East.

arabesque /arəˈbɛsk/ *n., a.,* & *v.* M17. [Fr. f. It. *arabesco*, f. *arabo* Arab: see -ESQUE.] A *n.* 1 Decorative work of a kind which originated in Arabic or Moorish art, consisting of flowing lines of branches, leaves, scrollwork, etc., fancifully intertwined; an ornamental design of this kind. M17. †2 Vernacular Arabic. Only in L18. 3 *Ballet.* A posture in which the body is bent forwards and supported on one leg with the other leg extended horizontally backwards, with the arms extended one forwards and one backwards. M19. 4 *Mus.* A passage or composition with fanciful ornamentation of the melody. M19
1 *fig.*: LONGFELLOW Not Art but Nature . . carved this graceful arabesque of vines.
B *adj.* Of ornamental design: decorated in arabesque, of the nature of arabesque. L18.
fig.: DICKENS Surrounded by this arabesque work of his musing fancy.
C *v.t.* Ornament in arabesque. M19.
¶Arabesque decoration often incorporates representations of living creatures, but these are absent from Moorish arabesque *sensu stricto.*

Arabian /əˈreɪbɪən/ *a.* & *n.* LME. [f. OFr. *arabi* ARABY or L *Arab(i)us* f. Gk *Arabios*, f. as ARAB: see -AN, -IAN.] A *adj.* Of or pertaining to Arabia, a large peninsula in SW Asia. LME.
Arabian bird a phoenix, a unique specimen. *Arabian camel*: see CAMEL 1. *Arabian* JASMINE. *Arabian* ORYX.

B *n.* 1 A native or inhabitant of Arabia. LME. 2 An Arabian horse. Cf. ARAB *n.* 2. L18.

Arabic /ˈarəbɪk/ *a.* & *n.* Also **a-**. ME. [OFr. (mod. *arabique*) f. L *Arabicus* f. Gk *Arabikos*, f. as ARAB: see -IC.] A *adj.* 1 From Arabia. Chiefly in *gum arabic*, a water-soluble gum exuded by certain acacias (esp. *Acacia senegal*). ME. 2 Of the Arabs; of or pertaining to the language and literature of the Arabs. LME.

2 arabic numerals the figures 1, 2, 3, 4, etc.

B *n.* The Semitic language originally of the Arabs, now spoken in much of the Middle East and N. Africa. LME.

Arabicism /əˈrabɪsɪz(ə)m/ *n.* an Arabic idiom or peculiarity of language E19. **Arabicize** /əˈrabɪsʌɪz/ *v.t.* make like Arabic; make conform to Arabic usage: L19.

arabica /əˈrabɪkə/ *n.* Also **A-**. E20. [L, specific epithet (see below), fem. of *arabicus*: see prec.] More fully *arabica coffee*. A coffee-plant of the most widely grown species, *Coffea arabica*; beans or coffee obtained from such a plant.

arabinose /ˈarəbɪnəʊz, -s/ *n.* L19. [f. prec. + -IN[1] + -OSE[2]: it was first obtained from gum arabic.] *Chem.* A pentose sugar which is a constituent of many plant gums.

arabis /ˈarəbɪs/ *n.* E17. [med.L f. Gk, use as n. of fem. of *Araps* ARAB.] A cruciferous plant of the genus *Arabis*, with white, pink, or purple flowers.

Arabise *v.* var. of ARABIZE.

Arabism /ˈarəbɪz(ə)m/ *n.* E17. [f. ARAB + -ISM.] 1†a Arabic. Only in E17. b An Arabicism. M18. 2 Arab culture or its influence; (support for) Arab nationalism or political self-assertion. L19.

Arabist *n.* (*a*) an expert in or student of the Arabic language or other aspects of Arab culture; (*b*) a supporter of Arabism: M18.

Arabize /ˈarəbʌɪz/ *v.t.* Also **-ise**. L19. [f. ARAB + -IZE.] Make Arab; give an Arabic character to.

Arabiˈzation *n.* M20.

arable /ˈarəb(ə)l/ *a.* & *n.* LME. [(O)Fr., or L *arabilis*, f. *arare* to plough: see -ABLE.] A *adj.* Of land: ploughed or fit for ploughing. Also, (of crops) suitable for cultivation on arable land; (of farming) given over largely to growing crops on arable land. LME. B *n.* Arable land; arable farming. L16.

araˈbility *n.* suitability for being used as arable land L19.

Araby /ˈarəbi/ *n.* & *a.* Long *arch.* & *poet.* ME. [OFr. *ar(r)abi* adj., prob. f. Arab. *ʿarabī* f. *ʿarab* ARAB; in sense A.3 f. (O)Fr. *Arabie* f. L *Arabia* f. Gk.] A *n.* †1 An Arabian horse. Cf. ARAB *n.* 2. Only in ME. †2 An Arab. LME-L16. 3 Arabia. LME. B *adj.* Arabian; Arabic. Now *rare* or *obs.* LME.

†**arace** *v.t.* ME-M16. [OFr. *aracier*, f. as A-[6] + *rais* root: see RACE *n.*[2] Aphet. to RACE *v.*[1]] Pull up by the roots; pull violently away.

arachide /ˈarəʃiːd/ *n.* M20. [Fr.] = ARACHIS.

arachidic /arəˈkɪdɪk/ *a.* M19. [f. mod.L *arachid-*, ARACHIS *n.* + -IC.] Chem. *arachidic acid*, a straight-chain saturated fatty acid, $C_{19}H_{39}COOH$, present in peanut oil. Also called *eicosanoic acid*.

arachidonic /arakɪˈdɒnɪk/ *a.* E20. [Unsystematically f. prec. + -ON(E + -IC.] Chem. *arachidonic acid*, a polyunsaturated fatty acid, $C_{20}H_{32}O_2$, found in animal fats and considered essential in animal metabolism.

arachis /ˈarəkɪs/ *n.* M19. [mod.L f. Gk *arak(h)os*, *-kis* some leguminous plant.] The groundnut plant, *Arachis hypogaea*.

Comb.: **arachis oil** peanut oil.

arachnean /arəkˈniːən/ *a.* *rare.* L16. [f. Gk *arakhnaios*, f. *arakhnē* spider: see -AN.] Of spiders or their webs; gossamer.

arachnid /əˈraknɪd/ *n.* & *a.* M19. [Fr. *arachnide* or mod.L *Arachnida* (see below), f. Gk *arakhnē* spider: see -ID[3].] *Zool.* (Designating or pertaining to) an arthropod belonging to the class Arachnida, which includes spiders, scorpions, mites, ticks, etc.

Also **arachnidan** *n.* & *a.* (now *rare*) E19.

arachnoid /əˈraknɔɪd/ *a.* & *n.* M18. [mod.L *arachnoides* f. Gk *arakhnoeidēs* like a cobweb, f. as prec.: see -OID.] A *adj.* 1 *Anat.* Designating or pertaining to a fine delicate membrane which is the middle of the three meninges enveloping the brain and spinal cord. M18. 2 *Bot.* Covered with or consisting of cobweblike hairs. E19. 3 Like an arachnid; arachnean. M19.

B *n.* *Anat.* The arachnoid membrane. E19. *pia-arachnoid*: see PIA *n.*[1]

arachˈnitis *n.* = ARACHNOIDITIS E19. **arachˈnoidal** *a.* = ARACHNOID *a.* 1 M19. **arachnoiˈditis** *n.* inflammation of the arachnoid membrane M19.

arachnology /arəkˈnɒlədʒi/ *n.* M19. [f. Gk *arakhnē* spider + -OLOGY.] The branch of zoology that deals with arachnids.

arachnoˈlogical *a.* M19. **arachnologist** *n.* E19.

arachnophobia /əraknə(ʊ)ˈfəʊbɪə/ *n.* E20. [f. as prec. + -O- + -PHOBIA.] Irrational fear of spiders.

aˈrachnophobe *n.* a person who is frightened of spiders E20.

†**araeometer** *n.* var. of AREOMETER.

arage *n.* see AVERAGE *n.*[1]

Aragonese /arəgəˈniːz/ *a.* & *n.* Also †**Arr-**. E16. [Sp. *aragonés*, f. *Aragón* Aragon (see below): see -ESE.] A *adj.* Of or pertaining to Aragon, its region and former kingdom of NE Spain, its inhabitants, or their dialect. E16. B *n.* Pl. same. 1 A native or inhabitant of Aragon. E19. 2 The dialect of Spanish spoken there. L19.

aragonite /ˈarəg(ə)nʌɪt/ *n.* Also †**arr-**. E19. [f. *Aragon* (see prec.) + -ITE[1].] *Min.* A low-temperature orthorhombic form of calcium carbonate.

Arahat *n.* var. of ARHAT.

arain /ˈar(ə)n/ *n.* Long *dial.* Also **arrand** /ˈar(ə)nd/. LME. [(O)Fr. *araigne* f. L *aranea*.] A spider.

†**araise** *v.t.* ME-E17. [f. A-[1] + RAISE *v.*] Raise, lift up; raise from the dead, arouse.

SHAKES. *All's Well* A medicine . . whose simple touch Is powerful to araise King Pepin.

arak *n.* var. of ARRACK.

Arakanese /arəkəˈniːz/ *a.* & *n.* E19. [f. *Arakan* (see below) + -ESE.] A *adj.* Of or pertaining to Arakan, a district on the west coast of Myanmar (Burma), its inhabitants, or their dialect. E19. B *n.* Pl. same. 1 A native or inhabitant of Arakan. E19. 2 The dialect of Burmese spoken there. L19.

Araldite /ˈar(ə)ldʌɪt/ *n.* M20. [Origin unkn.] (Proprietary name for) any of a series of epoxy resins used esp. as strong cements.

aralia /əˈreɪlɪə/. *n.* M18. [mod.L, of unkn. origin.] A plant of the genus *Aralia* (family Araliaceae), which includes a number of American and Asian trees and shrubs, e.g. wild sarsaparilla *A. nudicaulis*.

araliˈaceous *a.* of or pertaining to the family Araliaceae, which includes ivy, ginseng, wild sarsaparilla, and other plants, besides the aralias M19.

Aramaean /arəˈmiːən/ *a.* & *n.* Also **-mean**. M19. [f. as next + -AN.] A *adj.* Of or pertaining to the country or language of Aram (now Syria). M19. B *n.* A native or inhabitant of Aram. Also, Aramaic. M19.

Aramaic /arəˈmeɪɪk/ *a.* & *n.* M19. [f. Gk *Aramaios* f. Heb. *ʾărām* Aram, biblical name of Syria: see -IC.] A *adj.* Of or pertaining to Aram (now Syria); *spec.* designating or pertaining to a Semitic language of ancient Syria, the official language of the Persian Empire from the 6th cent. BC, widely used as a lingua franca by Jews and others in the Near East, and later developing into dialects, including Syriac, Mandaean, and one used by Christian Palestinians. M19. B *n.* The ancient Aramaic language; any of the dialects developed from it. L19.

Aramean *a.* & *n.* var. of ARAMAEAN.

Aran /ˈar(ə)n/ *a.* M20. [The *Aran* islands off the west coast of Ireland.] Designating a type of knitwear with patterns traditionally used in the Aran islands, esp. involving raised cable stitch and large diamond designs, or a sweater or pullover of this type.

Aranda /əˈrandə/ *n.* & *a.* Also **-ta** /-tə/, **Arunta** /əˈrʌntə/. L19. [Aborig.] A *n.* Pl. same, **-s**. 1 A member of an Aboriginal people of central Australia. L19. 2 The language of this people. M20. B *attrib.* or as *adj.* Of or pertaining to the Aranda or their language. L19.

araneid /əˈreɪnɪɪd/ *n.* & *a.* L19. [mod.L *Araneida* (see below), f. as next: see -ID[3].] *Zool.* (An arachnid) of the order Araneida or the family Araneidae; a spider.

Also **araneidan** /arəˈniːɪd(ə)n/ *n.* & *a.* = ARANEID *n.* M19.

araneology /areɪnɪˈɒlədʒi/ *n.* L18. [f. L *aranea* spider + -OLOGY.] The branch of zoology that deals with spiders.

araneologist *n.* L19.

araneous /əˈreɪnɪəs/ *a.* Now *rare* or *obs.* M17. [f. L *araneosus*, f. as prec.: see -OUS.] Arachnean; arachnoid.

Aranta *n.* & *a.* var. of ARANDA.

Arapaho /əˈrapəhəʊ/ *n.* & *a.* Pl. of n. same, **-s**. E19. [Crow *alappahó* lit. 'many tattoo marks'.] A member of, of or pertaining to, an Algonquian Indian people of the plains of N. America; (of) the language of this people.

arapaima /arəˈpʌɪmə/ *n.* M19. [Tupi.] A very large S. American freshwater food fish, *Arapaima gigas*. Also called *paiche*, *pirarucú*.

araroba /arəˈrəʊbə/ *n.* L19. [Port. f. Tupi.] 1 *Pharm.* = GOA *powder*. L19. 2 A leguminous tree of Brazil, *Andira araroba*, from which Goa powder is obtained. E20.

aration /əˈreɪʃ(ə)n/ *n. rare.* M17. [L *aratio(n-)*, f. *arat-* pa. ppl stem of *arare* to plough: see -ATION.] Ploughing, tillage.

arational /eɪˈraʃ(ə)n(ə)l/ *a.* M20. [f. A-[10] + RATIONAL *a.*] Unconcerned with or outside rationality; non-rational.

Araucanian /arɔːˈkeɪnɪən/ *a.* & *n.* E19. [f. Sp. *Araucania* a region of Chile + -AN.] A *adj.* Of or pertaining to an Indian people of central Chile and adjacent parts of Argentina, or their language. E19. B *n.* An Araucanian Indian; the Araucanian language. E19.

araucaria /arəˈkɛːrɪə/ *n.* M19. [mod.L, f. Sp. *Arauco* a province of Araucania, Chile: see -ARY[1].] A member of the genus *Araucaria* of tall evergreen conifers native to the southern hemisphere and including several trees valuable for their timber; *esp.* the monkey-puzzle, *A. araucana*.

araucarian *a.* of the genus *Araucaria* M19.

Arawak /ˈarəwak, -ɑːk/ *n.* & *a.* M18. [Carib *aruac*.] A *n.* A member of a group of Arawakan Indian peoples now chiefly inhabiting the NE coast of S. America; the language of these peoples. M18. B *attrib.* or as *adj.* Of or pertaining to these peoples or their language. M18.

Arawakan /arəˈwak(ə)n, -wɑːk-/ *a.* & *n.* E20. [f. prec. + -AN.] A *adj.* Designating or pertaining to a widespread family of languages of S. America, including Arawak; designating or belonging to a people speaking an Arawakan language. E20. B *n.* 1 A member of an Arawakan people. E20. 2 The Arawakan family of languages. M20.

arb /ɑːb/ *n.* *colloq.* L20. [Abbrev.] = ARBITRAGEUR.

arbalest /ˈɑːbəlɛst/ *n.* *obs.* exc. *Hist.* Also **-balist** /-bəlɪst/, **-blast** /-blɑːst/. OE. [OFr. *arbaleste*, *arbe-* (mod. *arbalète*) f. late L *arcuballista*, f. *arcus* bow: see ARC *n.*, BALLISTA.] 1 A crossbow with a wooden shaft and special drawing mechanism, used for discharging arrows, bolts, stones, etc. OE. 2 = ARBALESTER. ME.

arbalester *n.* a soldier armed with an arbalest; a crossbowman: ME. **arbaˈlestrier** *n.* (*Hist.*) = ARBALESTER M19.

†**arber** *n.* Also **er-**. ME-E18. [OFr. *(h)erbier(e)*, *arb-* (mod. *herbier*), f. *(h)erbe* rumen.] The windpipe, the gullet; (sometimes extended to) the whole pluck of an animal.

make the arber *Hunting* remove the pluck, the first stage in disembowelling.

arbiter /ˈɑːbɪtə/ *n.* LME. [L = judge, supreme ruler.] 1 A person whose opinion or decision is authoritative in a matter of debate; a judge, arbitrator, or umpire appointed to decide a dispute. LME. 2 A person with complete authority over or control *of* (a matter). E17.

1 W. H. DIXON Appointed arbiter of the dispute. *fig.*: MILTON Twilight.. short Arbiter 'Twixt Day and Night. 2 D. HALBERSTAM Her taste was impeccable, she was not so much an arbiter of fashion as she was fashion herself.

Phrases: **arbiter elegantiarum** /ˌɛlɪɡantɪˈɑːrəm/, **elegantiae** /ɛlɪˈɡantɪʌɪ/ [L = judge of elegance] an authority on matters of taste or etiquette.

arbitrable /ˈɑːbɪtrəb(ə)l/ *a.* Now chiefly *US*. M16. [f. L *arbitrari*: see ARBITRATE, -ABLE.] Subject to or capable of settlement by an arbiter.

arbitrage /ˈɑːbɪtrɪdʒ; *Comm. also* ɑːbɪˈtrɑːʒ, ˈɑːbɪtrɑːʒ/ *n.* & *v.* LME. [(O)Fr., f. *arbitrer* f. L *arbitrari*: see ARBITRATE, -AGE. Commercial use f. mod.Fr.] A *n.* †1 Exercise of individual authoritative judgement; self-determination. LME–E19. 2 Decision by an arbitrator or arbitrators; the process of arbitration. *arch.* L15. 3 *Comm.* Trade in bills of exchange or stocks in different markets to take advantage of their different prices. L19. B *v.i. Comm.* Engage in arbitrage. E20.

arbitrageur /ˌɑːbɪtrɑːˈʒəː/ *n.* L19. [Fr., f. as prec. + *-eur* -OR.] *Comm.* A person who engages in arbitrage.

arbitral /ˈɑːbɪtr(ə)l/ *a.* L15. [(O)Fr., or late L *arbitralis*, f. as ARBITER: see -AL[1].] Of or pertaining to arbitrators or arbitration.

arbitrament /ɑːˈbɪtrəm(ə)nt/ *n.* Also **-ement**. LME. [OFr. *arbitrement* f. med.L *arbitramentum*, f. *arbitrari*: see ARBITRATE, -MENT.] †1 The right or capacity to decide for oneself; free will. LME–E19. 2 The power to decide for others; absolute authority. *obs.* exc. as approaching sense 3. LME. 3 The deciding of a dispute by arbitration. LME. 4 The authoritative decision reached or the sentence pronounced by an arbiter. LME. †5 Agreement reached by arbitration; amicable compromise. M16–E17.

1 MILTON To stand or fall Free in thine own Arbitrament it lies. 2 W. S. MAUGHAM He decided to leave the matter to the arbitrament of God. 3 GLADSTONE An immediate resort to the arbitrament of war. D. BREWSTER In the arbitraments of science it has always been a difficult task to adjust the rival claims of competitors. 4 LYTTON I will not abide by the arbitrement of a pope. 5 BACON As if they would make an Arbitrement, betweene God and Man.

arbitrary /ˈɑːbɪt(rə)ri/ *a.* & *n.* LME. [L *arbitrarius*, f. as ARBITER (perh. after Fr. *arbitraire*): see -ARY[1].] A *adj.* 1 Dependent on will or pleasure; *Law* (now *Hist.*) dependent on the decision of a legally recognized authority; discretionary. LME. 2 Based on mere opinion or preference as opp. to the real nature of things; capricious, unpredictable, inconsistent. M17. 3 Unrestrained in the exercise of will or authority; despotic, tyrannical. M17. 4 *Printing*. Of a character: used occasionally to supplement the letters and other characters which constitute an ordinary font of type. E19.

1 JOSEPH HALL It is not left arbitrary to you that you may doe good if you will. 2 H. G. WELLS Those arbitrary standards by which we classify people into moral and immoral. J. HELLER His moods were arbitrary and unpredictable. P. USTINOV His internal policy was as arbitrary as his mother's had been consistent. 3 H. MARTINEAU No tyrant, no arbitrary disposer of the fortunes of his inferiors. H. MACMILLAN Arbitrary action without consultation or notice, in breach of solemn undertakings, .. revealed the true character of the regime.

B *n.* Something arbitrary; *spec.* in *Printing*, an arbitrary character. LME.

arbitrarily *adv.* E17. **arbitrariness** *n.* M17. †**arbitrarious** *a.* = ARBITRARY 1, 2, 3 L16–E19.

arbitrate /ˈɑːbɪtreɪt/ *v.* M16. [L *arbitrat-* pa. ppl stem of *arbitrari* examine, give judgement, f. as ARBITER: see -ATE[3].] 1 *v.t.* Settle by or submit to arbitration. M16. †2 *v.t.* & *i.* Give an authoritative decision (*that*). L16–L17. 3 *v.t.* Give an authoritative decision with regard to. *arch.* E17. 4 *v.i.* Mediate or act as arbitrator (*in* a dispute, *between* contending parties). E17.

1 A. MILLER He was called upon to arbitrate disputes as though he were an unofficial judge. 2 H. SWINBURNE He did arbitrate and awarde, that.. the cooke should bee recompensed. R. SOUTH The mind .. with an universal Superintendence, arbitrates .. upon them all. 3 JOHN TAYLOR Now swordes, not wordes, doe kingdoms arbitrate. 4 R. SANDERSON The blessed Apostle taketh upon him to arbitrate and to mediate in the business. LD MACAULAY He must relinquish all thought of arbitrating between contending nations.

arbitrated *ppl a.* settled by arbitration; *spec.* in *Comm.*, determined or conducted by arbitration of exchange: L16.

arbitration /ɑːbɪˈtreɪʃ(ə)n/ *n.* LME. [(O)Fr. f. L *arbitratio(n-)*, f. as prec.: see -ATION.] †1 = ARBITRAMENT 1, 2. LME–M17. 2 The settlement of a dispute or debate by an arbitrator; the process of arbitrating a dispute. LME. 3 *arbitration of exchange*, the determination of the rate of exchange to be obtained between two countries or currencies, when the operation is to be conducted through an intermediary or intermediaries, in order to ascertain the most profitable method of drawing bills. Cf. ARBITRAGE 3. E19.

arbitrator /ˈɑːbɪtreɪtə/ *n.* LME. [Late L, f. as ARBITRATE: see -OR. Cf. OFr. *arbitrateur.*] 1 A person chosen by the opposing parties in a dispute to decide the differences between them; an arbiter. LME. 2 A person who decides according to his or her own absolute pleasure; a supreme ordainer. L16.

1 J. L. MOTLEY In case of their inability to agree, they were to appoint arbitrators. 2 W. WHISTON God is the arbitrator of success in war.

arbitratorship *n.* the position or function of an arbitrator M17. **arbitratrix** *n.* (now *rare*) a female arbitrator, an arbitress L16.

arbitrement *n.* var. of ARBITRAMENT.

†**arbitrer** *n.* Also **-or**. LME–E19. [AN *arbitrour*, OFr. *-eor*, f. as prec.] = ARBITRATOR.

arbitress /ˈɑːbɪtrɪs/ *n.* ME. [OFr. *arbitresse* fem. of *arbitre* ARBITER: see -ESS[1].] A female arbiter.

S. RICHARDSON The arbitress of the quarrels of unruly spirits. DISRAELI The arbitress of fashion is one who is allowed to be singular, in order that she may suppress singularity.

†**arbitror** *n.* var. of ARBITRER.

arblast *n.* var. of ARBALEST.

arbor /ˈɑːbə/ *n.*[1] M17. [Fr. *arbre* tree, principal axis, assim. in sp to L *arbor.*] *Mech.* An axle, beam, or spindle on which something revolves; *esp.* a tool-holder or mandrel on a lathe.

arbor *n.*[2] see ARBOUR.

Arbor Day /ˈɑːbə deɪ/ *n. phr.* Orig. *US*. L19. [f. L *arbor* tree + DAY *n.*] A day set apart annually in the US, Australia, New Zealand, and elsewhere for the planting of trees.

arboreal /ɑːˈbɔːrɪəl/ *a.* M17. [f. L *arboreus*, f. *arbor* tree, + -AL[1].] 1 Pertaining to or of the nature of trees. M17. 2 Connected with, haunting, or inhabiting trees. M19.

ˈ**arboral** *a.* (*rare*) = ARBOREAL 1 M17. **arboreˈality** *n.* (*Zool.*) the state or condition of living primarily in trees; cf. TERRESTRIALITY: L20.

arboreous /ɑːˈbɔːrɪəs/ *a.* M17. [f. as prec. + -OUS.] 1 Having many trees, wooded. M17. 2 = ARBOREAL. M17. 3 Treelike. M18.

arborescent /ɑːbəˈrɛs(ə)nt/ *a.* L17. [L *arborescent-* pres. ppl stem of *arborescere* grow into a tree, f. *arbor* tree: see -ESCENT. Cf. Fr. *arborescent.*] 1 Treelike in growth or size; having a woody stem. L17. 2 a Treelike in appearance; branching. L17. b *Archit.* Of ornamentation: branching from and sustained by its support. M19.

arborescence *n.* treelike growth or formation M19.

arboret /ˈɑːbərɛt/ *n. arch.* L16. [f. L *arbor* tree + -ET[1].] A little tree, a shrub.

arboretum /ɑːbəˈriːtəm/ *n.* Pl. **-ta** /-tə/, (chiefly *N. Amer.*) **-tums**. E19. [L = place with trees f. *arbor* tree.] A place devoted to the cultivation and exhibition of rare trees; a botanical tree-garden.

arborical /ɑːˈbɒrɪk(ə)l/ *a. rare*. M17. [f. as next + -ICAL.] = ARBOREAL 1.

arboricide /ɑːˈbɔːrɪsʌɪd/ *n.* L19. [f. as next + -CIDE.] The wanton destruction of trees.

arboriˈcidal *a.* given to arboricide M19.

arboriculture /ˈɑːb(ə)rɪkʌltʃə, ɑːˈbɔːr-/ *n.* E19. [f. L *arbor* tree + -I- + -CULTURE.] The cultivation of trees and shrubs.

ˌ**arboriˈcultural** *a.* of or pertaining to arboriculture E19. ˌ**arboriˈculturist** *n.* a person who practises arboriculture E19.

arborisation *n.* var. of ARBORIZATION.

arborist /ˈɑːb(ə)rɪst/ *n.* L16. [f. L *arbor* tree + -IST. Cf. ARBOUR 2.] †1 A person who cultivates or studies herbs or other flowering plants. Only in L16. 2 A scientific student or cultivator of trees. M17.

arborization /ˌɑːb(ə)rʌɪˈzeɪʃ(ə)n/ *n.* Also **-isation**. L18. [f. as prec. + -IZATION.] (The production of) a treelike structure or appearance; *esp.* (*Anat.*) the ramification of the ends of certain nerve cells.

ˈ**arborize** *v.* (*a*) *v.t.* make treelike in structure or appearance (chiefly as *arborized* ppl a.); (*b*) *v.i.* develop arborization: E19.

arborous /ˈɑːb(ə)rəs/ *a.* M17. [f. as prec. + -OUS.] Of, belonging to, or consisting of trees.

arborvirus *n.* var. of ARBOVIRUS.

arbor vitae /ˌɑːbə ˈvʌɪtiː, ˈviːtʌɪ/ *n. phr.* Also (esp. in sense 1) **arborvitae**. Pl. same. E17. [L = tree of life.] 1 Any of a number of N. American or Far Eastern evergreen conifers, belonging chiefly to the genus *Thuja*. E17. 2 *Anat.* The arborescent appearance of the white matter in a sagittal section of the cerebellum. Also called *tree of life*. E19.

arbour /ˈɑːbə/ *n.* Also ***arbor**; †**harbour**; (orig.) **herber** (long *obs.* exc. *Hist.*), †**erber**. ME. [AN *erber*, OFr. *erbier* (mod. *herbier*), f. *erbe* herb + *-ier* f. as -ARIUM: see -OUR. The mod. spelling was furthered by assoc. w. L *arbor* tree.] †1 A garden lawn or green. ME–L15. 2 A herb or flower garden; a flower-bed. Long *obs.* exc. *Hist.* ME. 3 A bower or shady retreat, with sides and roof formed mainly by trees and climbing plants. ME. †b A covered alley or walk. L16–E18. †4 A garden of fruit trees; an orchard. LME–L16. †5 Trees or shrubs trained on trellis-work; espaliers. LME–M17.

arboured *a.* placed in or as in an arbour; furnished with arbours: L16.

arbovirus /ɑːbəˈvʌɪrəs/ *n.* Also **-bor-** /-bɔː-/. M20. [f. *ar*thropod-*bo*rne + VIRUS *n.*] *Med.* Any of a class of pathogenic viruses which are transmitted by arthropods (mainly mosquitoes and ticks).

arbuscle /ˈɑːbʌs(ə)l/ *n. rare*. M17. [L *arbuscula* dim. of *arbor*, *arbos* tree: see -CULE.] A dwarf tree, a treelike shrub.

arbutus /ɑːˈbjuːtəs, ˈɑːbjʊtəs/ *n.* M16. [L.] 1 An evergreen tree or shrub of the genus *Arbutus*, of the heath family, *esp.* the strawberry tree, *A. unedo*. M16. 2 A N. American evergreen trailing shrub, *Epigaea repens*, of the heath family, bearing white or pink flowers. Also more fully *trailing arbutus*. Also called *ground-laurel*, *mayflower*. L18.

Also **arbute** /ˈɑːbjuːt/ *n.* (*arch.* & *poet.*) M16.

arc /ɑːk/ *n.* LME. [(O)Fr., f. L *arcus* bow, arch, curve.] 1 *Astron.* The part of a circle which a celestial object, esp. the sun, appears to follow from horizon to horizon. Now *rare* or *obs.* LME. †2 An arch. M16–M18. 3 *gen.* Part of the circumference of a circle or other curve; something having the form or appearance of this. L16. 4 *Electr.* A luminous discharge produced between electrodes in a gas. E19. 5 *Physiol.* The connected set of nerves involved in the production of a reflex action. Usu. more fully *reflex arc*. M19.

1 **diurnal, nocturnal, arc** the path of the sun above, below, the horizon. 2 POPE Turn arcs of triumph to a garden-gate. 3 F. O'BRIEN He lifted it in the air, slowly describing an arc of forty-five degrees. TED HUGHES Porpoises .. With arcs And plungings. B. LOVELL The Moon subtends an angle of 31 minutes of arc. *island arc*: see ISLAND *n.*

Attrib. & *comb.*: Designating devices and methods using an electric arc as a source of light or heat, as *arc furnace, lamp, light, welding*; *Math.* preceding a trigonometrical function, designating the angle having a given value of that function, as *arc sine* (also *arcsine*), *arc tangent* (*arctangent*). Special combs., as **arc** minute *Astron.* a unit of angular measure equal to 1/60 degree; **arc second** *Astron.* 1/60 arc minute.

arc /'ɑːk/ *v.i.* L19. [f. the n.] **1** Form an electric arc. Chiefly as *arcing* vbl n. L19. **2** Move or fly in an arc. M20.

arcade /ɑː'keɪd/ *n.* L17. [Fr. f. Prov. *arcada* or It. *arcata*, ult. f. L *arcus* ARC *n.*: see -ADE.] **1** A passage arched over; any covered walk or avenue, esp. with shops etc. along one or both sides. L17. †**2** An arched opening or recess. M18–E19. **3** *Archit.* A series of arches supporting or along a wall. L18.

1 WORDSWORTH And shades Of trellis-work in long arcades. THACKERAY A garden, with trim lawns, green arcades and vistas of classic statues. K. CLARK These light, sunny arcades with their round arches . . under their straight cornices. AMUSEMENT *arcade*. *video arcade*: see VIDEO *a.* & *n.*

arcaded *a.* furnished with or formed into an arcade L18. **arcading** *n.* an arrangement of arcades M19.

Arcades ambo /'ɑːkədiːz 'ambəʊ/ *n. phr.* Freq. *derog.* E19. [L (Virgil) = both Arcadians, i.e. both pastoral poets or musicians.] Two people of the same tastes, profession, or character.

Arcadia /ɑː'keɪdɪə/ *n.* Also (*poet.*) **Arcady** /'ɑːkədi/. LME. [L f. Gk *Arkadia* a mountainous district in the Peloponnese.] (Used as a name for) an ideal region of rural contentment.

Arcadian /ɑː'keɪdɪən/ *n.* & *a.*[1] L16. [f. L *Arcadius*, f. as prec., + -AN.] **A** *n.* An inhabitant of Arcadia; an ideal rustic. L16. **B** *adj.* Of or pertaining to Arcadia; ideally rustic. E17.

Arcadianism *n.* pastoral simplicity E19.

arcadian /ɑː'keɪdɪən/ *a.*[2] *rare.* L19. [f. ARCADE + -IAN.] Of, pertaining to, or furnished with arcades.

Arcadic /ɑː'keɪdɪk/ *n.* & *a.* E19. [f. ARCADIA + -IC.] (Of) the ancient Greek dialect of Arcadia.

Arcady *n.* see ARCADIA.

arcana *n.* pl. of ARCANUM.

arcane /ɑː'keɪn/ *a.* M16. [(O)Fr., or L *arcanus*, f. *arcere* shut up, f. *arca* chest: see -ANE I.] Hidden, secret; mysterious; abstruse.

J. CHEEVER An old Turkey carpet, multicolored and scattered with arcane symbols. W. STYRON Sophie loses track of much of the arcane detail. B. MASON Art was therefore something arcane: if not precisely forbidden, then heavy with the possibility of discovery and guilt.

arcanum /ɑː'keɪnəm/ *n.* Pl. **-na** /-nə/. L16. [L, use as n. of neut. sing. of *arcanus*: see prec.] Usu. in *pl.* **1** A hidden thing; a mystery, a profound secret. L16. **2** *spec.* Any of the supposed secrets of nature sought by alchemists; a marvellous remedy, an elixir. *arch.* E17.

arcanist *n.* a person who has knowledge of a secret process of manufacture E20.

arc-boutant /arkbutɑ̃/ *n.* Pl. pronounced same. M18. [Fr.] *Archit.* An arched or flying buttress.

arch /ɑːtʃ/ *n.*[1] ME. [(O)Fr. *arche* ult. f. L *arcus* ARC *n.*] **I1** A curved structure spanning an opening, either acting as a support for a bridge, roof, wall, floor, etc., or as a monument, or as an ornamental feature. ME. †**2** Any part of a curve. LME–M19. **3** A thing resembling an arch as described in senses 1 and 2 in form or function; *Anat.* & *Zool.* = GIRDLE *n.*[1] 4. L16. **b** Each of the arched structures formed by the tarsal and metatarsal bones of the foot. M19. **4** An arched roof, a vault; an archway; *fig.* the heavens. E17. **5** Curvature in the shape of an arch. M19.

1 BYRON For *this* the conqueror rears The arch of triumph! E. M. FORSTER The immense viaduct, whose arches span untroubled meadows and the dreamy flow of Tewin Water. L. T. C. ROLT A bridge with two of the largest and flattest arches. J. BRONOWSKI The Romans always made the arch as a semicircle. M. GIROUARD Two large studio windows under the gables, crowned with Gothic pointed arches. **Court of Arches** *Eccl.* the court of appeal for the province of Canterbury, orig. held in the church of St Mary-le-bow (or 'of the Arches'). **Dean of the Arches** *Eccl.* the lay judge of the Court of Arches having jurisdiction over thirteen London parishes exempt from the authority of the Bishop of London. *skew arch*: see SKEW *a.* *straight arch*: see STRAIGHT *a.*[1] & *adv.*[1] *triumphal arch*: see TRIUMPHAL *a.* 1. **2** SIR T. BROWNE An Arch of the Horizon. **3** ADDISON His head is encompassed with . . an arch of glory. J. RUSKIN God's arch, the arch of the rainbow. *aortic arch*, *visceral arch*, *zygomatic arch*, etc. **b** A. S. BYATT Mrs Bruce said her feet hurt, sat down . . and rubbed her arches. **fallen arch** an arch of the foot that has flattened. **4** SIR W. SCOTT While the deep arch with sullen roar Return'd their surly jar. **5** F. Y. GOLDING The hollowness or arch of the waist [of a shoe].

II6 In *pl.* In names of various moths, as *buff arches*, *dark arches*, *silvery arches*. M18.

Comb.: **archway** a vaulted passage, an arched entrance.

archlet *n.* a little arch E19. **archwise** *adv.* in the form of an arch L16. **archy** *a.* (*rare*) arched, arching, suggestive of an arch M17.

arch /ɑːtʃ/ *a.* & *n.*[2] M16. [ARCH- used independently; sense A.2 f. use w. *rogue*, *wag*, etc.] **A** *adj.* **1** Chief, principal, pre-eminent. Now *rare* without hyphen (see ARCH-). M16. **2** Clever, roguish, waggish; (now usu.) consciously or affectedly playful or teasing. M17.

1 SHAKES. *Rich. III* The most arch deed of piteous massacre. LYTTON Thou mayest have need of thy archest magic to protect thyself.

†**B** *n.* A chief. *rare.* Only in E17.

SHAKES. *Lear* The noble Duke my master, My worthy arch and patron.

archly *adv.* M17. **archness** *n.* E18.

arch /ɑːtʃ/ *v.*[1] ME. [f. ARCH *n.*[1] Cf. OFr. *archer.*] **1** *v.t.* Form into or provide with an arch. ME. **2** *v.i.* Form an arch. E17. **3** *v.t.* Span like an arch. M17.

1 BACON Fine Deuices, of Arching Water without Spilling. SIR T. BROWNE Dinocrates began to Arche the Temple . . with Load stone. A. SILLITOE The lane was arched with trees. D. M. THOMAS The cat arched her back and spat at the man. **2** BACON The sound . . archeth over the wall. B. MOORE The rainbow arched up and away from this place. **3** SOUTHEY The vine that arch'd His evening seat. R. W. EMERSON The rude bridge that arched the flood.

arching *n.* an arched structure L16.

arch /ɑːtʃ/ *v.*[2]*i.* M17. [Back-form. f. ARCHER, ARCHERY.] Engage in archery.

arch- /ɑːtʃ/ *pref.* [L f. Gk *arkhi-* etc., f. *arkhos* chief, or OFr. *arche-* f. L *arch-*. Cf. ARCHI-.] **1** In titles of office, rank, or dignity, w. the sense 'principal, -in-chief, superior', as *archbishop*, *-deacon*, *-druid*, *-duke*, etc. **2** In descriptive appellations of people, w. the sense 'a person pre-eminent as, greatest, chief, leading' as *arch-critic*, *-defender*, etc., and now esp. 'worst of, out-and-out, extremely bad', as *arch-conspirator*, *-criminal*, *-heretic*, *-rebel*, *-scoundrel*, *-tempter*, *-thief*, *-traitor*, *villain*, etc. Cf. GRAND *a.*[1] 2. **3** In descriptive appellations of people, w. the sense 'first in time, original', as *arch-father*, *-founder*. All either *obs.* or *arch.* **4** Of things: **a** With the sense 'chief, principal, prime', as *archdiocese* etc. **b** With the sense 'primitive, original', as *arch-house*, *-see*, etc. All either *arch.* or *obs.*

archabbey *n.* [4a] the head abbey of a Benedictine congregation L19. **archabbot** *n.* [1] the chief abbot of a Benedictine congregation L19. **arch-chanter** *n.* (*obs.* exc. *Hist.*) [1] a precentor LME. ˌ**archconfra'ternity** *n.* [1] *RC Ch.* a confraternity with power to incorporate or affiliate other similar confraternities M17. **archdean** *n.* (chiefly *Sc.*, *obs.* exc. *Hist.*) [1] a chief dean, an archdeacon LME. **arch'deanery** *n.* (chiefly *Sc.*, *obs.* exc. *Hist.*) [4a] the jurisdiction, rank, or office of an archdean L15. **arch'diocese** *n.* [4a] the see or jurisdiction of an archbishop E19. **arch-'enemy** *n.* [2] a chief enemy; the Devil: M16. **arch-fiend** *n.* [2] a chief fiend, the Devil M17. **arch-flamen** *n.* (now *arch.* & *Hist.*) [med.L *archiflamen*] a chief flamen or priest, an archbishop LME. **arch-foe** *n.* [2] an arch-enemy, the Devil E17. †**arch-poet** *n.* [1] a chief or first poet, a poet laureate E17–M18. **arch-prelate** *n.* [1] a chief prelate, an archbishop L16.

-arch /ək, ɑːk/ *suff.* (not productive). [Repr. Gk *-arkhos*, *arkhēs* ruling, rel. to *arkhē* rule, *arkhein* begin, take the lead.] In ns. denoting kinds of ruler, as *monarch*, *ethnarch*, *tetrarch*, etc.

Archaean /ɑː'kiːən/ *a.* & *n.* Also ***Archean.** L19. [f. Gk *arkhaios* ancient + -AN.] *Geol.* (Designating or pertaining to) the earlier part of the Precambrian era (before the Proterozoic).

¶Sometimes used only to refer to rocks of this period.

archaebacterium /ˌɑːkɪbak'tɪərɪəm/ *n.* Pl. **-ia** /-ɪə/. L20. [f. ARCHAEO- + BACTERIUM.] *Microbiol.* Any of a diverse group of micro-organisms, believed to be of very ancient origin, which are similar to ordinary bacteria in size and simplicity of structure, but radically different in molecular organization.

archaebacterial *a.* L20.

archaeo- /'ɑːkɪəʊ/ *comb. form.* Also ***archeo-**, †**archaio-**. [f. Gk *arkhaios* ancient, primitive: see -O-.] Forming terms relating to archaeology or prehistoric times.

archaeo-a'stronomy *n.* the archaeological investigation of astronomical knowledge in prehistoric cultures L20. **archaeography** /ɑːkɪ'ɒgrəfi/ *n.* (*arch.*) the systematic description of antiquities E19. ˌ**archaeomag'netic** *a.* of or pertaining to archaeomagnetism M20. ˌ**archaeo'magnetism** *n.* the investigation of the magnetic properties of archaeological remains, esp. for the purpose of dating; magnetism possessed by such materials: M20. **archaeo'metric** *a.* of or pertaining to archaeometry L20. **archaeometry** /ɑːkɪ'ɒmətri/ *n.* the application of scientific techniques to the dating of archaeological remains M20. **Archaeo'zoic** *a.* & *n.* (*Geol.*) (pertaining to or designating) the Archaean period or (orig.) that part of it in which primitive life existed L19.

archaeology /ɑːkɪ'ɒlədʒi/ *n.* Also ***archeo-**, †**archaio-**. E17. [mod.L *archaeologia* f. Gk *arkhaiologia*, f. as ARCHAEO- + -LOGY.] **1** Ancient history. *arch.* E17. **2** The systematic description or study of human antiquities, esp. as revealed by excavation. M19.

archaeo'logian *n.* (now *rare*) = ARCHAEOLOGIST M19. **archaeo'logic** *a.* = ARCHAEOLOGICAL M18. **archaeo'logical** *a.* of or pertaining to archaeology L18. **archaeo'logically** *adv.* L18. **archaeologist** *n.* E19. **archaeologize** *v.i.* study or practise archaeology L19. **archaeologue** /'ɑːkɪəlɒg/ *n.* (*arch.*) [Fr.] an archaeologist, an antiquarian M19.

archaeopteryx /ɑːkɪ'ɒptərɪks/ *n.* M19. [f. ARCHAEO- + Gk *pterux* wing.] *Palaeont.* The oldest known fossil bird, dating from the late Jurassic and having several reptilian features such as teeth, forelimb claws, and vertebrate tail.

archaic /ɑː'keɪɪk/ *a.* M19. [Fr. *archaïque* f. Gk *arkhaikos*, f. *arkhaios* ancient: see -IC.] **1** Of a word, language, etc.: no longer in ordinary use though retained by individuals or for special purposes (e.g. poetical, liturgical). M19. **2** Designating or belonging to an early or formative period of culture, art, etc. M19. **3** *gen.* Primitive; antiquated. L19.

archaical *a.* (*rare*) archaic; of or pertaining to what is archaic: E19. **archaically** *adv.* in an archaic style; with regard to archaism: L19. **archaicism** /-sɪz(ə)m/ *n.* archaic style or quality M19. **archaicist** /-sɪst/ *n.* (*rare*) a person who employs archaism L19.

†**archaio-** *comb. form*, †**archaiology** *n.*, etc., vars. of ARCHAEO-, ARCHAEOLOGY, etc.

archaise *v.* var. of ARCHAIZE.

archaism /'ɑːkeɪɪz(ə)m/ *n.* M17. [mod.L *archaismus* f. Gk *arkhaismos*, f. *arkhaizein* copy the ancients in language etc., f. *arkhaios* ancient: see -ISM.] **1** The retention or imitation of what is old or obsolete, esp. in language or art. M17. **2** An archaic word or expression; an archaic feature. M17.

archaist *n.* (*a*) *rare* an antiquary; (*b*) a person who employs archaism: M19. **archa'istic** *a.* of or pertaining to an archaist; imitatively archaic, affectedly antique: M19. **archa'istically** *adv.* L19.

archaize /'ɑːkeɪʌɪz/ *v.* Also **-ise**. M19. [Gk *arkhaizein*: see prec., -IZE.] **1** *v.i.* Imitate the archaic. M19. **2** *v.t.* Render archaistic. M20.

archaizer *n.* L19.

archangel /'ɑːkeɪndʒ(ə)l, ɑːk'eɪn-/ *n.* Also (esp. in titles) **A-**. OE. [AN *archangele* f. eccl.L *archangelus* f. eccl.Gk *arkhaggelos*, f. Gk *arkhi-* ARCH- + *aggelos* (see ANGEL).] **1** An angel of the highest rank; a member of the eighth order of the ninefold celestial hierarchy, ranking directly below the principalities and above the angels (usu. in *pl.*). OE. **2** Any of various dead-nettles (genus *Lamium* and allied plants); *esp.* (more fully *yellow archangel*) *Lamiastrum galeobdolon*, a yellow-flowered woodland plant of Europe and western Asia. LME.

archan'gelic *a.* of, pertaining to, or resembling archangels; of the nature of an archangel: LME. **archan'gelical** *a.* = ARCHANGELIC M17.

archbishop /ɑːtʃ'bɪʃəp, *esp. in titles* 'ɑːtʃ-/ *n.* Also (esp. in titles) **A-**. OE. [f. ARCH- (replacing *hēah* high in OE *hēah-biscop*) + BISHOP *n.*] The chief bishop of a province.

archbishophood *n.* (*rare*) the rank or office of an archbishop LME. **archbishopric** *n.* [OE *rīce* realm, rule] the diocese or jurisdiction of an archbishop; the rank or office of an archbishop: OE. **archbishopship** *n.* (*rare*) = ARCHBISHOPRIC M16.

archdeacon /ɑːtʃ'diːkən, *esp. in titles* 'ɑːtʃ-/ *n.* Also (esp. in titles) **A-**. OE. [eccl.L *archidiaconus* (Jerome) f. eccl.Gk *arkhidiakonos*: see ARCH-, DEACON *n.*] A chief deacon; a member of the Anglican clergy next below a bishop; a dignitary of similar rank in other Churches.

arch'deaconess *n.* (now *rare*) the wife of an archdeacon M19. **arch'deaconry** *n.* the jurisdiction or district under the ecclesiastical control of an archdeacon; the rank or office of an archdeacon: LME.

archducal /ɑːtʃ'djuːk(ə)l/ *a.* Also **†archi-**. E17. [Fr. *archiducal*: see ARCHDUKE, -AL[1].] Of or pertaining to an archduke or archduchy.

archduchess /'ɑːtʃdʌtʃɪs/ *n.* Also (esp. as a title) **A-**. E17. [Fr. *archiduchesse*: see ARCH-, DUCHESS.] *Hist.* The wife of an archduke. Also, a woman with an archducal title in her own right, *spec.* as a daughter of the Emperor of Austria.

archduchy /'ɑːtʃdʌtʃi/ *n.* L17. [Fr. †*archeduché* (now *archi-*): see ARCH-, DUCHY.] *Hist.* The territory subject to an archduke or archduchess.

archduke /'ɑːtʃdjuːk/ *n.* Also (esp. as a title) **A-**. E16. [OFr. *archeduc* (mod. *archi-*) f. Merovingian L *archidux, -duc-*: see ARCH-, DUKE *n.*] *Hist.* A chief duke; *spec.* (the title of) a son of the Emperor of Austria.

archdukedom *n.* (now *rare*) = ARCHDUCHY M16.

Archean *a.* & *n.* see ARCHAEAN.

archegonium /ɑːkɪ'gəʊnɪəm/ *n.* Pl. **-ia** /-ɪə/. M19. [mod.L, f. Gk *arkhegonos* progenitor, f. *arkhe-* ARCHI- + *gonos* race: see -IUM.] *Bot.* The female reproductive organ borne by mosses, ferns, and some other plants.

archegonial *a.* of or pertaining to an archegonium M19. **archegoniate** *a.* bearing archegonia L19.

archei *n.* pl. of ARCHEUS.

archenteron /ɑː'kɛntərɒn/ *n.* L19. [f. Gk *arkhē* beginning + *enteron* intestine.] *Zool.* The rudimentary alimentary cavity of a gastrula.

archeo- *comb. form*, **archeology** *n.*, etc., see ARCHAEO-, ARCHAEOLOGY, etc.

archer /'ɑːtʃə/ *n.* ME. [AN *archer*, OFr. *archier* (mod. *archer*), ult. f. L *arcus* bow: see -ER[2].] 1 A person who shoots with bow and arrows. ME. 2 (Usu. **A-**.) *The* constellation and zodiacal sign Sagittarius. LME. 3 *Chess.* A bishop. Long *obs.* exc. *Hist.* M16. 4 Usu. more fully *archer-fish*. Any of several small SE Asian percoid fishes of the genus *Toxotes* (family Toxotidae) which have the ability to knock insect prey off vegetation by spitting water. M19.

archeress *n.* (now *rare*) a female archer M17.

archery /'ɑːtʃəri/ *n.* LME. [OFr. *archerie*, f. *archier*: see prec., -ERY.] 1 The practice or art of shooting with bow and arrows; skill as an archer. LME. 2 *collect.* An archer's equipment; bows, arrows, etc. Now *rare*. LME. 3 *collect.* A company or corps of archers. *arch.* LME.

Arches /'ɑːtʃɪz/ *n.* Now *rare*. E17. [f. ARCH- 4.] *Naut.* *the Arches*, the Archipelago (the Aegean Sea); any specific archipelago.

archesporium /ɑːkɪ'spɔːrɪəm/ *n.* Pl. **-ia** /-ɪə/. L19. [f. Gk *arkhe-* ARCHI- + SPORE + -IUM.] *Bot.* A cell or group of cells from which spore-producing or other reproductive cells are developed.

archesporial *a.* L19.

archetype /'ɑːkɪtʌɪp/ *n.* Also (earlier) in L form **†-typum**. M16. [L *archetypum* f. Gk *arkhetupon* use as n. of neut. of adj. 'first moulded as a model', f. *arkhe-* ARCHI- + *tupon* model. Cf. Fr. *archétype*.] 1 The original pattern or model from which copies are made; a prototype; a typical specimen. M16. 2 *spec.* a *Zool.* & *Bot.* An idealized typical specimen or original form of a particular grouping of living organisms. M19. b In Jungian psychoanalysis, a primordial mental concept inherited by all from the collective unconscious. E20. c A pervasive or recurrent idea or symbol in legend, etc. M20.

1 LD MACAULAY The House of Commons, the archetype of all the representative assemblies which now meet. A. STORR During the thirty-one years of his residence in Cambridge, he was a recluse; the very archetype of the absent-minded, solitary scholar.

archetypal *a.* of the nature of or constituting an archetype; of or pertaining to an archetype; primitive, original: M17. **arche'typical** *a.* = ARCHETYPAL M18.

archeus /'ɑːkɪəs/ *n.* Pl. **-ei** /-ɪʌɪ/. M17. [mod.L *archaeus* f. Gk *arkhaios* ancient.] *Hist. Sci.* The immaterial principle supposed by the Paracelsians to govern animal and vegetable life; a vital force.

archi *n.pl.* see ARCO.

archi- /'ɑːki/ *pref.* [L f. Gk *arkhi-*: see ARCH-.] 1 = ARCH-: a Forming ns., as *archiepiscopate*, *archipresbyter*, etc. b Forming adjs., as *archiepiscopal* etc., freq. corresp. to ns. in ARCH-, as *archidiaconal* etc. 2 *Biol.* With the sense 'archetypal, primitive', as *archinephros* etc. 3 *Anat.* Designating the phylogenetically oldest parts of the brain, as *archipallium*, *-striatum*, etc.

archiater /ɑːkɪ'eɪtə/ *n.* E17. [Late L f. Gk *arkhiatros*, f. *arkhi-* ARCHI- + *iatros* physician. Cf. Fr. *archiatre*.] *Hist.* The chief physician of a monarch; the court physician.

Archibald /'ɑːtʃɪbɔːld/ *n.* *slang* (now *Hist.*). E20. [Male forename: f. the refrain of a pop. music hall song.] An anti-aircraft gun, *esp.* one used by the Germans in the war of 1914–18.

archidiaconal /ˌɑːkɪdʌɪ'ak(ə)n(ə)l/ *a.* LME. [med.L *archidiaconalis*: see ARCHI-, DIACONAL.] Of, pertaining to, or holding the position of an archdeacon.

archidiaconate *n.* = ARCHDEACONRY M18.

†archiducal *a.* var. of ARCHDUCAL.

Archie /'ɑːtʃi/ *n.* & *v.* *slang* (now *Hist.*). E20. [Dim. of ARCHIBALD.] A *n.* = ARCHIBALD. E20. B *v.t.* Fire at with an anti-aircraft gun. E20.

archiepiscopacy /ˌɑːkɪɪ'pɪskəpəsi/ *n.* M17. [f. eccl.L *archiepiscopus* f. Gk *arkhiepiskopos* (Athanasius) archbishop f. as ARCHI-, BISHOP *n.*, + -ACY.] 1 The system of Church government by archbishops. M17. 2 = ARCHIEPISCOPATE. M17.

archiepiscopate *n.* an archbishop's tenure of office; an archbishopric: L18.

archiepiscopal /ˌɑːkɪɪ'pɪskəp(ə)l/ *a.* E17. [f. as prec. + -AL[1].] Of, pertaining to, or of the nature of an archbishop.

archiepiscopally *adv.* M19.

archil /'ɑːtʃɪl, 'ɑːkɪl/ *n.* M16. [Var. of ORCHIL.] The dye orchil, or any of the lichens which yield this.

Archilochian /ɑːkɪ'ləʊkɪən/ *a.* M18. [f. L *Archilochius*, f. Gk *Arkhilokhos* Archilochus (see below) + -AN.] Of, pertaining to, or derived from the Greek satiric poet Archilochus (7th cent. BC), the alleged originator of iambic metre.

archilute *n.* var. of ARCHLUTE.

archimage /'ɑːkɪmeɪdʒ/ *n.* Now chiefly *poet.* Also **†-mago**, **†-magus**. L16. [Gk *arkhimagos* chief of the magi: see ARCHI-, MAGE, MAGUS, and cf. Fr. *archimage*.] A chief magician; a great wizard.

archimandrite /ɑːkɪ'mandrʌɪt/ *n.* M17. [Fr., or eccl.L *archimandrita* f. eccl.Gk *arkhimandritēs*, f. *arkhi-* ARCHI- + *mandra* enclosure, stable, monastery: see -ITE[1].] The superior of a large monastery in the Orthodox Church; also used as an honorary title of a monastic priest.

Archimedean /ɑːkɪ'miːdɪən/ *a.* E19. [f. late L *Archimedeus* (f. as next) + -AN.] Of, pertaining to, or invented by Archimedes.

Archimedean drill a drill in which to-and-fro motion along the axis of the drill produces alternating rotary motion of the bit. **Archimedean screw** an instrument for raising water by the turning of an inclined screw within a cylinder.

Archimedes /ɑːkɪ'miːdiːz/ *n.* M17. [Gk *Arkhimēdēs*, a celebrated mathematician (*c*287–212 BC).] 1 A person like Archimedes, esp. in making scientific discoveries. M17. 2 *Archimedes' principle*, (arch.) *principle of Archimedes*: that a body immersed in a fluid is subject to an upward force equal in magnitude to the weight of fluid it displaces. M19.

archimime /'ɑːkɪmʌɪm/ *n.* Also **arch-mime** /'ɑːtʃ-/. M17. [L *archimimus* f. Gk *arkhimimos*: see ARCHI-, MIME *n.*] *Rom. Hist.* The chief mimic who imitated the deceased in a funeral procession.

archinephros /ɑːkɪ'nɛfrəs/ *n.* L19. [f. ARCHI- + Gk *nephros* kidney.] *Zool.* The archetypal primitive kidney of the earliest vertebrates.

archinephric *a.* L19.

archipelago /ɑːkɪ'pɛləgəʊ/ *n.* Pl. **-o(e)s**. Also **†-gus**. E16. [It. *arcipelago* (13), f. Gk *arkhi-* ARCHI- + *pelagos* sea.] 1 *the Archipelago*, the Aegean Sea. *arch.* E16. 2 A sea or other stretch of water like the Aegean in having many islands; a group of islands. M16.

archipelagic /-pə'ladʒɪk/ *a.* M19.

archiphoneme /'ɑːkɪfəʊniːm/ *n.* M20. [Fr. *archiphonème*: see ARCHI-, PHONEME.] *Ling.* A phonological unit comprising the sum of distinctive features common to two or more neutralized phonemes.

archipho'nemic *a.* M20.

archipresbyter /ɑːkɪ'prɛzbɪtə/ *n.* Also **archpresbyter** /'ɑːtʃ-/. M16. [Late L f. Gk *arkhipresbuteros*: see ARCHI-, PRESBYTER.] = ARCHPRIEST.

ˌarchipres'byterate *n.* [med.L *archipresbyteratus*] the position or term of office of an archpriest; the order of archpriests: E20.

†archisynagogue *n.* ME–L18. [eccl.L *archisynagogus* f. Gk *arkhisunagōgos* (New Testament): see ARCHI-, SYNAGOGUE.] A president of a synagogue.

architect /'ɑːkɪtɛkt/ *n.* & *v.* M16. [Fr. *architecte* f. It. *architetto*, or their source L *architectus* f. Gk *arkhitektōn*, f. *arkhi-* ARCHI- + *tektōn* builder.] A *n.* 1 A designer of buildings, who prepares plans, and superintends construction. M16. b In full *naval architect*. A designer of ships etc. M19. 2 A designer of any complex structure. L16. 3 A person who plans, devises, or contrives the achievement *of* a desired result. L16.

2 T. REID Plato made the causes of things to be matter, ideas, and an efficient architect. G. GROTE The inference that Peisistratus was the first architect of the Iliad and Odyssey. **the Architect** the Creator. 3 MILTON The architects of their own happiness. J. HELLER The architect of an illicit and secret policy of detente.

B *v.t.* Design and build; plan and bring about (a desired result). M17.

architective *a.* of or pertaining to architecture; fitted for or characterized by construction: E17. **†architector** *n.* †(*a*) a superintendent; (*b*) = ARCHITECT: L15–E18. **architectress** *n.* (now *rare*) a female architect E17.

architectonic /ˌɑːkɪtɛk'tɒnɪk/ *a.* & *n.* M17. [L *architectonicus* (Vitruvius) f. Gk *arkhitektonikos*, f. *arkhitektōn*: see prec., -IC.] A *adj.* 1 Of or pertaining to architecture or architects. M17. 2 Of or pertaining to construction. L17. 3 Directive, controlling. L17. 4 Pertaining to the systematization of knowledge. L18. B *n.sing.* & (freq.) in *pl.* (treated as *sing.*). 1 The science of architecture. M17. 2 The science of the systematic arrangement of knowledge. L18.

architectonical *a.* (now *rare*) E17. **architectonically** *adv.* with regard or in relation to architectonics M17.

architecture /'ɑːkɪtɛktʃə/ *n.* & *v.* M16. [Fr., or L *architectura*: see ARCHITECT, -URE.] A *n.* 1 The art or science of building; *esp.* the art or practice of designing and building edifices for human use, taking both aesthetic and practical factors into account. M16. 2 Architectural work; something built. L16. 3 A style of building; mode, manner, or style of construction or organization; structure. E17. b The conceptual structure and logical organization of a computer or computer-based system. M20. 4 The action or process of building; construction. *arch.* E17.

1 **marine architecture, naval architecture** the design and building of ships etc. 2 J. H. BURTON

Architecture, especially if it be of stone. M. PEAKE An eccentric notion translated into architecture. 3 J. RUSKIN Many other architectures besides Gothic. *Discovery* The architecture of molecules. D. COOKE We speak of the 'architecture' of a symphony. M. GIROUARD They moved on . . to revive elements from the homelier brick architecture of the seventeenth and eighteenth centuries. 4 SIR T. BROWNE [If] the great Cities Anchiale and Tarsus were built . . both in one day . . Certainely, it was the greatest Architecture of one day.

B *v.t.* Design as architect. E19.

archi'tectural *a.* of, relating to, or according to architecture; resembling architecture: L18. **archi'tecturally** *adv.* in an architectural manner; as regards architecture: M19.

architrave /ˈɑːkɪtreɪv/ *n.* M16. [Fr. f. It., f. *archi-* ARCHI- + *trave* f. L *trab-*, *trabs* beam.] *Archit.* 1 The lowest part of an entablature, resting immediately upon the abacus on the capital of a column. M16. 2 The various parts surrounding a door or window. M17. 3 Moulding around the exterior of an arch. M19.

architraved *a.* furnished with an architrave M17.

archive /ˈɑːkʌɪv/ *n.* & *v.* E17. [Fr. *archives* pl. f. L *archi(v)a* f. Gk *arkheia* public office or records, use as n. of neut pl. of *arkheios* governmental, f. *arkhē* government.] **A** *n.* 1 *sing.* & in *pl.* A place in which collected public or corporate records are kept; a repository for documents etc.; a data bank. E17. 2 In *pl.* & †*sing.* Records so kept. M17. **B** *v.t.* Place or store in an archive; *spec.* (*Computing*) transfer to a store of infrequently used files, or to a memory at a lower hierarchical level (e.g. from disc to tape). L19.

ar'chival *a.* of or pertaining to archives M19. **archivist** /ˈɑːkɪvɪst/ *n.* a keeper of archives M18.

archivolt /ˈɑːkɪvəʊlt/ *n.* Also †**-volto**. M17. [It. *archivolto* (whence med.L *archivoltum*) or Fr. *archivolte* ult. f. as ARC *n.* + VAULT *n.*[1]] *Archit.* The lower curve of an arch, from impost to impost; the band of mouldings on this.

archlute /ˈɑːtʃl(j)uːt/ *n.* Also **archi-** /ˈɑːtʃɪ-/. M17. [Fr. *archiluth*, It. *arciliuto*: see ARCH-, LUTE *n.*[1]] A theorbo.

arch-mime *n.* var. of ARCHIMIME.

archon /ˈɑːkən/ *n.* Pl. **archons, archontes** /ɑːˈkɒntiːz/. L16. [Gk *arkhōn*, *arkhont-* ruler, use as n. of pres. pple of *arkhein* to rule.] 1 The chief magistrate, or, after the time of Solon, each of the nine chief magistrates, of ancient Athens. L16. 2 A ruler, a president. M18. 3 A power subordinate to God, held by some of the Gnostics to have created the world. M18.

archonship *n.* the position or tenure of office of an Athenian archon L17. **archontate** *n.* the tenure of office of an Athenian archon M18. **ar'chontic** *n.* & *a.* (*a*) *n.* a member of a sect of Gnostics who believed that the world was created by archons; (*b*) *adj.* of or pertaining to an archon: L16.

archosaurian /ɑːkəˈsɔːrɪən/ *a.* & *n.* L19. [f. mod.L *Archosauria* (see below), f. Gk *arkhos* chief or *arkhōn*: see prec., -SAUR, -IAN.] *Zool.* **A** *adj.* Belonging to or characteristic of the subclass Archosauria of living and extinct reptiles, which includes the dinosaurs, pterosaurs, and crocodilians. L19. **B** *n.* Any archosaurian reptile. E20.

Also **'archosaur** *n.* M20.

archpresbyter *n.* var. of ARCHIPRESBYTER.

archpriest /ˈɑːtʃpriːst/ *n.* LME. [OFr. *archeprestre* (mod. *archiprêtre*) f. late L ARCHIPRESBYTER, later assim. to ARCH-, PRIEST.] A chief priest; formerly, a chief assistant or vicar to a bishop in a cathedral. Also, a rural dean.

archpriesthood *n.* the position or office of an archpriest L17. †**archpriestship** *n.* = ARCHPRIESTHOOD LME–L17.

-archy /əki, ɑːki/ *suff.* (not productive). [Repr. Gk *arkh(e)ia* government, leadership, f. as -ARCH: see -Y[3].] In abstract ns. corresp. to personal ns. in -ARCH, as *monarchy*, *oligarchy*, *tetrarchy*, etc.

arco /ˈarko, ˈɑːkəʊ/ *n.*, *adv.*, & *a.* M18. [It.] *Mus.* **A** *n.* Pl. ***archi*** /ˈarki/, ***arcos*** /ˈɑːkəʊz/. A bow for a stringed instrument. M18. **B** *adv.* & *adj.* (A direction:) resuming use of the bow after a pizzicato passage. E19.

Arctic /ˈɑːktɪk/ *a.* & *n.* Also **a-**; (earlier) †**Art-**. LME. [OFr. *artique* (mod. *arct-*) f. L *ar(c)ticus* f. Gk *arktikos*, f. *arktos* bear, the Great Bear (constellation): see -IC.] **A** *adj.* 1 Of or pertaining to the north pole, or the north polar regions. Formerly also *gen.*, northern. LME. b Designating animals and plants of northern species. L18. c (Usu. **a-**.) Characterized by or typical of the very cold climate of the north polar regions. L19. 2 *fig.* Bitterly cold. Formerly also, extreme, remote. L17.

1 **Arctic Circle** the parallel of latitude 66° 33′ N. **Arctic Ocean** the (chiefly ice-covered) ocean bounded by the north coasts of Eurasia and N. America. b *Arctic char*, *Arctic cisco*, *Arctic grayling*, *Arctic skipper*, *Arctic skua*, *Arctic willow*, etc. **Arctic fox** a small fox, *Alopex lagopus*, whose coat turns white in winter and which occurs on the tundra of Eurasia and N. America; the fur of this fox. **Arctic hare** (*a*) a hare, *Lepus arcticus*, of Greenland and Arctic Canada, whose coat is brown in summer and white in winter; (*b*) = MOUNTAIN *hare*. **Arctic tern** a migratory tern, *Sterna paradisaea*, which breeds mainly in northern Eurasia and N. America but winters mainly in antarctic regions.

B *n.* 1 *The* north polar regions. LME. 2 In *pl.* (**a-**.) Thick waterproof overshoes. *N. Amer.* M19.

arcual /ˈɑːkjʊəl/ *a.* M17. [f. L *arcus* ARC *n.* + -AL[1].] = next.

arcuate /ˈɑːkjʊət/ *a.* LME. [L *arcuatus* pa. pple, f. *arcuat-*: see next, -ATE[2].] Bent like a bow, curved, arched.

arcuated /-eɪtɪd/ *a.* (*a*) = ARCUATE; (*b*) *Archit.* characterized by arches: M18.

arcuation /ɑːkjʊˈeɪʃ(ə)n/ *n.* LME. [Fr., or L *arcuatio(n-)* (Frontinus), f. *arcuat-* pa. ppl stem of *arcuare* to curve, f. *arcus* ARC *n.*: see -ATION.] 1 Curving in the shape of an arch; incurvation. LME. 2 The use of the arch in building; arched work. M18.

arcubalist /ˈɑːkjʊbəlɪst/ *n.* *obs.* exc. *Hist.* LME. [Late L *arcuballista*: see ARBALEST.] = ARBALEST 1.

arcubalister *n.* = ARBALESTER L16.

arcus senilis /ˌɑːkəs sɪˈnʌɪlɪs/ *n. phr.* L18. [L, lit. 'senile bow'.] *Med.* A narrow opaque band encircling the cornea, common in old age.

ard /ɑːd/ *n.* M20. [ON *arðr* plough: see ARDER.] *Archaeol.* A primitive light plough.

-ard /əd, *occas.* ɑːd/ *suff.* 1 Repr. (O)Fr. *-ard*, †*-art* f. G *-hart*, *-hard* 'hardy' in ns., as *haggard*, *mallard*, *placard*, etc., freq. depreciatory, as *bastard*, *coward*, etc., and formerly a suff. productive of similar English ns. esp. w. the sense 'a person who does to excess, or does what is discreditable', as *dotard*, *drunkard*, *laggard*, *niggard*, *sluggard*, *wizard*. See also -ART. 2 Repr. endings of various origin, as *bustard*, *hazard*, *leopard*, *standard*, *tankard*, etc.

ardeb /ˈɑːdɛb/ *n.* E19. [Arab. *ʼirdabb*, *ʼar-*, ult. f. Gk *artabē*.] An Egyptian unit of capacity, usu. equal to about 198 litres (5.44 bushels).

ardency /ˈɑːd(ə)nsi/ *n.* M16. [f. next + -ENCY.] Burning quality; *fig.* warmth of feeling or desire, ardour.

ardent /ˈɑːd(ə)nt/ *a.* ME. [OFr. *ardant* (mod. *ardent*) f. L *ardent-* pres. ppl stem of *ardere* to burn: see -ANT[1], -ENT.] 1 Flammable. *obs.* exc. in *ardent spirit(s)*, alcoholic spirits (now usu. interpreted as sense 2, w. ref. to their taste). ME. 2 Burning, fiery; parching; glowing like fire, gleaming. LME. 3 *fig.* Burning with passion or desire; fervent, eager, zealous. LME.

2 POPE From rank to rank she darts her ardent eyes. M. ARNOLD There are some, whom a thirst Ardent, unquenchable, fires. 3 R. BURNS A faltering ardent kiss he stole. W. OWEN Children ardent for some desperate glory. S. LEWIS She passed from a feeble disgust at their closer relations into what promised to be ardent affection. M. MUGGERIDGE We were ardent co-op supporters.

ardently *adv.* ME.

arder /ˈɑːdə/ *n.* Long *obs.* exc. *dial.* E16. [Prob. f. ON *arðr* plough f. L *aratrum*.] Ploughing, tilth; land ploughed and left fallow; (a strip of land used for) one stage of a crop rotation.

ardour /ˈɑːdə/ *n.* Also *****-or**. LME. [OFr. (mod. *ardeur*) f. L *ardor*, f. *ardere* to burn.] 1 (A feeling of) ardent passion or desire; eagerness, intensity of feeling. LME. 2 (A) fierce or burning heat; fire. *arch.* LME. †3 A radiant spirit. *poet.* Only in M17.

1 L. STRACHEY Affection, gratitude, . . such feelings possessed him, but the ardours of reciprocal passion were not his. P. H. GIBBS The war had been a horror after the first ardour with which he had come out in time for the Somme. E. F. BENSON His love for her was of an ardour she had not contemplated. 2 C. COTTON To qualifie the excessive ardours of the Sun. 3 MILTON The wingéd Saint . . from among Thousand Celestial ardors . . up springing light.

arduous /ˈɑːdjʊəs/ *a.* M16. [f. L *arduus* steep, difficult + -OUS.] 1 Hard to achieve or overcome; difficult, laborious. M16. 2 High; steep. *arch.* E18. 3 Of an effort etc., or a person making an exertion: energetic, strenuous. M19.

1 LD MACAULAY Such an enterprise would be in the highest degree arduous and hazardous. J. HILTON The next stage . . was less arduous than he had been prepared for, and a relief from the lung-bursting strain of the ascent. M. MUGGERIDGE She found riding or pushing her bicycle uphill too arduous. 2 *fig.*: STEELE To forgive is the most arduous pitch human nature can arrive at. 3 J. TYNDALL An arduous climber. A. J. CRONIN The chapel . . was the product of prolonged and arduous effort. *Partisan Review* The arduous theorists of the SPD were steeped in German pedantry.

arduously *adv.* laboriously, strenuously; with difficulty: E18. **arduousness** *n.* M18.

ardurous /ˈɑːdjʊrəs/ *a. poet. rare.* M18. [Irreg. f. as prec., infl. by ARDOUR.] Ardent, full of ardour.

Are /eɪˈreɪ/ *n.*[1] *obs.* exc. *Hist.* Also **A re**. LME. [f. *A* + *re*: see ALAMIRE.] *Medieval Mus.* The note A in Guido d'Arezzo's 1st hexachord, where it was sung to the syllable *re*. Cf. ALAMIRE, BEFA, CEFAUT, etc.

are /ɑː/ *n.*[2] L18. [Fr. f. as AREA.] A metric unit of area equal to 100 sq. metres (about 119.6 sq. yards). Cf. HECTARE.

are *v.* see BE *v.*

area /ˈɛːrɪə/ *n.* Pl. **areas,** (occas.) †**areae**. M16. [L = vacant piece of level ground.] **I** A particular extent of ground or of another surface. 1 A piece of ground, or space within a building, that is not built on or occupied, or is enclosed or reserved for a particular purpose. M16. b A sunken enclosure giving access to the basement of a house. E18. 2 A particular tract of the earth's (or another planet's) surface; a region; a neighbourhood, a vicinity. M18. 3 A particular part of any other surface (e.g. of a living organism), usu. distinguished by coloration, structure, or function. Also, a part of a solid body; *esp.* a region of the brain of specified function. E19.

1 J. LELAND In the west Part of this Street is a large Area invironed with meetly good Buildinges. E. WAUGH One could not normally go further into it than a small roped area around the door. *Lore & Language* The two tarmac play areas would nowadays be considered cramped. b DICKENS Pulling the caps from the heads of small boys and tossing them down areas. 2 H. GEORGE There are still in India great areas uncultivated. F. RAPHAEL I should have a scout round the area, get your bearings. C. SAGAN We imagined . . that the bright areas that retain frost on Mars are . . low. 3 R. T. PETERSON A very large white stork with . . extensive black wing areas and black tail. A. H. COTTRELL The formation of rust layers on the cathodic areas of the metal surface. J. Z. YOUNG The brain areas involved in speech. *Broca's area*, *language area*, *motor area*, *Wernicke's area*, etc.

II Extent. 4 Superficial or two-dimensional extent; the amount of this contained within given limits. L16.

4 STEELE The Area of my Green-House is a Hundred Paces long, Fifty broad. J. UPDIKE In area Kush measures 126,912,180 hectares. F. HOYLE A retreat of the ice sheet at its margin, a shrinkage of its area and decrease in its thickness.

III *fig.* 5 A part of anything conceived as having superficial extent; a field (of study etc.), a range of topics etc.; scope, extent. E17.

5 G. GREENE Whole areas of both our lives were blank like an early map, to be filled in later. D. DAVIE The images serve to indicate roughly the area of

experience that the poet is dealing with. G. FABER The feeling . . was strongly rooted in a still hateful area of memory.

Phrases: *special area*: see SPECIAL *a.* *twilight area*: see TWILIGHT *a.* *utility area*: see UTILITY *a.*

Comb.: **area bishop** in the Church of England, a bishop who has much of the authority of a diocesan bishop within a particular part of a diocese, by delegation from the diocesan; **area bombing** the indiscriminate bombing of an extended area; **area code** *N. Amer.* a telephone dialling code for another part of the country; **area defence**: designed to protect an entire area against air attack; **area linguistics** areal linguistics; **areaway** *N. Amer.* a sunken passageway; *esp.* = sense 1b above.

†areach *v.* Infl. as REACH *v.*[1] [OE *arǣcan*, f. as A-[1] + REACH *v.*[1]] **1** *v.t.* Get at; get possession of. OE–L16. **2** *v.t.* Hand, deliver, (a thing to a person). OE–M16. **3** *v.i.* Stretch, extend (*to*). ME–M16.

1 SPENSER Till his ambitious sonnes vnto them twaine Arraught the rule.

aread /əˈriːd/ *v.* & *n.* Long *arch.* Also **arede, areed.** Pa. t. & pple **areaded, ared** /əˈrɛd/. [OE *arēdan*, f. as A-[1] + READ *v.* Branch A.II f. A-[1] + READ *v.*] **A** *v.t.* **I†1** Divine, prophesy; make known, declare. OE–M17. **2** Divine the meaning of; interpret, solve. OE. **3** Guess, conjecture. ME.

2 W. MORRIS So is thy dream areded. 3 SOUTHEY Rightly he ared the Maid's intent.

II 4 Counsel, advise. M16. **5** Decide, adjudge. L16.

4 MILTON Let me arreed him, not to be the foreman of any mis-judg'd opinion. 5 SPENSER Thereby Sir Artegall did plaine areed That unto him the horse belong'd.

†B *n.* Counsel, advice. L16–E19.

areal /ˈɛːrɪəl/ *a.* L17. [f. AREA + -AL[1].] **1** Of, pertaining to, or of the nature of an area. L17. **2** *Ling.* Of or pertaining to geographical factors as determinants of the relationship or development of languages or dialects. M20.

2 **areal linguistics** a school of linguistics emphasizing geographical factors in language development and distribution.

areally *adv.* with regard to area M20.

arear /əˈrɪə/ *adv.* & *pred. a. rare.* M19. [f. A-[2] + REAR *n.*: cf. ARREAR *adv.*] In the rear.

areca /ˈarɪkə, əˈriːkə/ *n.* L16. [Port. f. Malayalam *aṭekka*.] (The fruit of) a tropical Asian palm of the genus *Areca*, esp. *A. catechu*, which yields astringent seeds often chewed with betel leaves.

Comb.: **areca nut** an astringent seed of *A. catechu*.

arecoline /əˈriːkəliːn, -lɪn/ *n.* L19. [f. prec. after QUINOLINE.] *Chem.* An alkaloid obtained from areca nuts, which has some use in veterinary medicine as an anthelmintic.

ared, arede, areed *v.* see AREAD.

areg *n.* pl. of ERG[2].

arena /əˈriːnə/ *n.* E17. [L (*h*)*arena* sand, sand-strewn place.] **1** The central part of an amphitheatre, bullring, stadium, etc., in which the action occurs; the building as a whole. E17. **2** *fig.* Any scene of open conflict, a sphere of action. L18.

2 H. ROGERS Howe seldom entered the arena of controversy. J. K. GALBRAITH Economic society was an arena in which men met to compete. N. GORDIMER A landscape without theatricals except when it became an arena for summer storms.

Comb.: **arena stage** *Theatr.* a stage placed amid the audience; **arena theatre** theatre-in-the-round.

arenaceous /arɪˈneɪʃəs/ *a.* M17. [f. L *arenaceus*, f. as prec.: see -ACEOUS.] Having the appearance or consistency of sand; sandy; living or growing in sand.

arenaceous rock = ARENITE.

arenavirus /əˈriːnəvʌɪrəs/ *n.* Also **areno-.** L20. [f. L *arenosus* sandy f. as ARENA, + VIRUS.] *Med.* Any of a class of viruses (e.g. that of Lassa fever), which appear under an electron microscope to contain sandlike granules.

arene /ˈariːn/ *n.* M20. [f. AR(OMATIC + -ENE.] *Chem.* An aromatic hydrocarbon.

arenite /ˈarɪnʌɪt/ *n.* E20. [f. as ARENA + -ITE[1].] *Geol.* A sandstone or other sedimentary rock made up very largely of sand-sized particles.

arenose /ˈarɪnəʊs/ *a.* LME. [L *arenosus*, f. as ARENA: see -OSE[1].] Sandy, gritty.

Also **†arenous** *a.* LME–M18.

arenovirus *n.* var. of ARENAVIRUS.

aren't *v.* see BE *v.*

areo- /ˈarɪəʊ/ *comb. form* of Gk *Arēs* Mars: see -O-.

areo'centric *a.* (*Astron.*) having the planet Mars as centre L19.

areola /əˈriːələ/ *n.* Pl. **-lae** /-liː/. M17. [L *areola* dim. of AREA.] Chiefly *Anat.* **1** A small space or interstice, esp. within body tissue such as bone. M17. **2** A small circular area; *spec.* the area of pigmented skin surrounding a nipple. L17.

areolar *a.* containing many areolae (sense 1); *areolar tissue*, loose connective tissue found beneath the skin and around muscles, organs, etc.: E19. **'areole** *n.* an areola; *esp.* a small area bearing spines or hairs on a cactus: E19.

†areometer *n.* Also **araeo-.** L17–L19. [Fr. *aréomètre*, f. Gk *araios* thin: see -METER.] = HYDROMETER *n.* 1.

Areopagi *n.* pl. of AREOPAGUS.

Areopagite /arɪˈɒpəgʌɪt, -dʒʌɪt/ *n.* LME. [L *areopagites* f. Gk *areiopagitēs*: see next, -ITE[1].] *Gk Hist.* A member of the court of Areopagus (see next).

areopagitic /ˌarɪɒpəˈdʒɪtɪk/ *n.* & *a.* †(*a*) *n.* a speech imitating that of Isocrates addressed to the court of Areopagus; (*b*) *adj.* of or pertaining to the Areopagus or its court: M17. **areopagitical** /ˌarɪɒpəˈdʒɪtɪk(ə)l/ *a.* L16.

Areopagus /arɪˈɒpəgəs/ *n.* Pl. **-gi** /-gʌɪ/. M17. [L, f. Gk *Areios pagos* hill of Ares (Mars), where the highest judicial court of ancient Athens held its sittings, hence the court itself.] An important tribunal.

†aret *v.t.* Also **-tt.** LME. [OFr. *aret(t)er* f. *à* A-[5] + *reter* f. L *reputare* REPUTE *v.*] **1** Adjudge, reckon (to be). LME–L15. **2** Impute (esp. as a fault) *to*; charge *upon*. LME–E17. **3** Accuse, indict, (*of*). LME–L17. **4** Entrust, deliver. L16–E17.

4 SPENSER The charge, which God doth unto me arrett, Of his deare safety I to thee commend.

¶Sense 4 was orig. a misunderstanding by Spenser of *aret to the charge of* repr. sense 2.

aretalogy /arɪˈtalədʒi/ *n.* E20. [Gk *aretalogia*, f. *aretē* excellence, miracle: see -LOGY.] A narrative of the miracles performed by a god or semi-divine hero.

areta'logical *a.* L19.

arête /əˈrɛt, əˈreɪt/ *n.* E19. [Fr. f. L *arista* ear of corn, fish-bone or -spine. Cf. ARRIS.] A sharp mountain ridge with steep sides.

Aretine *a.* var. of ARRETINE.

†arett *v.* var. of ARET.

'arf /ɑːf/ *n.*, *a.*, & *adv. slang.* M19. [Repr. a pronunc.] = HALF *n.*, *a.* & *adv.*

arfvedsonite /ɑːfˈvɛdś(ə)nʌɪt/ *n.* E19. [f. J. A. *Arfvedson* (1792–1841), Swed. chemist + -ITE[1].] *Min.* An iron-rich sodium amphibole which occurs as black or dark green monoclinic crystals.

argal *n.* var. of ARGOL *n.*[2]

argal /ˈɑːg(ə)l/ *adv. arch.* E17. [Alt. of L *ergo* therefore.] Therefore.

SHAKES. *Haml.* He drowns not himself: Argal, he that is not guilty of his own death shortens not his own life.

†argala *n.* M18–M19. [Hind. *hargīlā* lit. 'bone-swallower'.] The greater adjutant stork.

argali /ˈɑːg(ə)li/ *n.* L18. [Mongolian.] The large wild sheep of eastern central Asia, *Ovis ammon*; *loosely* the bighorn or other similar animal.

argan /ˈɑːg(ə)n/ *n.* E17. [Moroccan Arab. f. Berber *argān*).] **1** The olive-like fruit of the argan tree (see sense 2). *rare.* E17. **2** *argan tree*, an evergreen tree or shrub, *Argania spinosa*, native to Morocco. E19. **3** *argan oil*, an edible oil from the seeds of the argan tree. L19.

Argand /ˈɑːgənd/ *n.* L18. [A Fr. surname.] **1** *Hist.* [A. *Argand* (1755–1803), Fr. physicist.] a *Argand burner*, a kind of cylindrical burner for oil or gas, allowing air to pass both inner and outer surfaces of the flame. L18. **b** In full *Argand lamp*. A lamp fitted with such a burner. E19. **2** *Math.* [J. R. *Argand* (1768–1822), Fr. mathematician.] *Argand diagram*, a diagram on which complex numbers are represented geometrically using Cartesian axes. E20.

argent /ˈɑːdʒ(ə)nt/ *n.* & *a.* LME. [(O)Fr. f. L *argentum* silver.] **A** *n.* **†1** Silver coin; money, cash. LME–M18. **2** The metal silver. Now *arch.* & *poet.* M16. **3** *Her.* The tincture silver or white in armorial bearings. M16.

B *adj.* Chiefly *Her.* Silver, white. L15.

W. DE LA MARE Wan as the argent moon. T. H. WHITE The cognizance was argent, a tall cross gules.

argen'tiferous *a.* yielding silver L18. **argentry** *n.* (*rare*) silver plate E17.

'argentaffin /ɑːˈdʒɛntəfɪn/ *a.* E20. [Fr. *argentaffine*, f. L *argentum* silver + *affinis* akin.] Readily stained black by silver salts; *spec.* (*Anat.*, now *arch.*) designating numerous isolated endocrine cells situated in the intestinal epithelium.

argentaffi'noma *n.*, pl. **-mas, -mata** /-mətə/, *Med.* an intestinal tumour whose tissue stains like argentaffin cells, from which it is thought to develop M20.

argentic /ɑːˈdʒɛntɪk/ *a.* E19. [f. L *argentum* silver + -IC.] *Chem.* Of or pertaining to divalent silver.

¶Orig. designating monovalent compounds (cf. ARGENTOUS).

argentine /ˈɑːdʒ(ə)ntʌɪn/ *a.*[1] & *n.*[1] LME. [(O)Fr. *argentin(e)*, f. as ARGENT + -INE[1].] **A** *adj.* **1** Of, made of, or containing silver. LME. **2** Silvery. LME. **B** *n.* **1** Silver; material simulating silver. Now *rare* or *obs.* L16. **2** A small silvery marine fish of the salmoniform genus *Argentina*. M18.

Argentine /ˈɑːdʒ(ə)ntʌɪn/ *a.*[2] & *n.*[2] E19. [Sp. *Argentina* (in *República*, formerly *Confederación*, *Argentina*) lit. 'silvery', named from the Rio de la Plata (Sp. *plata* silver).] **A** *adj.* Of, pertaining to, or designating the federal republic which occupies the greater part of the southern end of S. America, extending from Chile in the west to the Brazilian and Uruguayan borders and the Atlantic Ocean in the east, and bordering Bolivia and Paraguay in the north (now usu. called *Argentina*). E19.

Argentine ant a S. American ant, *Iridomyrmex humilis*, which has been introduced and become a pest elsewhere.

B *n.* **1** A native or inhabitant of Argentina. E19. **2** *the Argentine*, Argentina. L19.

Argentinian /ɑːdʒ(ə)nˈtɪnɪən/ *a.* & *n.* (*a*) *adj.* of or pertaining to Argentina; (*b*) *n.* = ARGENTINE *n.*[2] 1: E20.

argentite /ˈɑːdʒ(ə)ntʌɪt/ *n.* M19. [f. L *argentum* silver + -ITE[1].] *Min.* A form of silver sulphide crystallizing in the cubic system and occurring as dark grey crystals with a metallic lustre.

argento- /ɑːˈdʒɛntəʊ/ *comb. form* of L *argentum* silver: see -O-.

argentophil(e), -'philic *adjs.* = ARGYROPHILIC M20.

argentous /ɑːˈdʒɛntəs/ *a.* M19. [f. as prec. + -OUS.] *Chem.* Of or pertaining to monovalent silver.

¶Orig. designating certain compounds apparently of a lower valency (cf. ARGENTIC).

Argie /ˈɑːdʒi/ *n.* & *a. slang. derog.* Also **Argy.** L20. [Abbrev. of ARGENTINE *a.*[2] & *n.*[2] or ARGENTINIAN: see -IE.] (An) Argentine, (an) Argentinian.

argil /ˈɑːdʒɪl/ *n.* LME. [OFr. *argille* f. L *argilla* f. Gk *argillos* clay.] Clay, *esp.* potter's clay.

argillaceous /ɑːdʒɪˈleɪʃəs/ *a.* L17. [f. L *argillaceus*, f. *argilla* clay, + -OUS: see prec., -ACEOUS.] Of the nature of clay; largely composed of clay; clayey.

argillite /ˈɑːdʒɪlʌɪt/ *n.* L18. [f. L *argilla* clay + -ITE[1].] *Geol.* An indurated argillaceous rock that is harder than shale and does not split easily.

arginase /ˈɑːdʒɪneɪz/ *n.* E20. [f. next + -ASE.] *Biochem.* An enzyme which hydrolyses arginine to urea and ornithine.

arginine /ˈɑːdʒɪniːn/ *n.* L19. [G *Arginin*, perh. f. Gk *arginoeis* bright-shining, white: see -INE[5].] *Biochem.* A basic amino acid, $HN{=}C(NH_2)NH(CH_2)_3CH(NH_2)COOH$, which occurs in many proteins, is essential in the diet of vertebrates during periods of intensive growth, and is involved in urea synthesis; guanidine aminovaleric acid.

Argive /ˈɑːɡʌɪv, -dʒʌɪv/ *n.* & *a.* M16. [L *Argivus* (Gk *Argeios*) pertaining to Argos (see below).] A *n.* A native or inhabitant of Argos, a city-state of ancient Greece, or the surrounding territory of Argolis; (in Homeric and later classical use) a Greek. M16. B *adj.* Of or pertaining to Argos or Argolis. Also, Grecian, Greek. L16.

argle /ˈɑːɡ(ə)l/ *v. obs.* exc. *dial.* L16. [Alt. of ARGUE, w. *-le* as in *haggle*.] 1 *v.t.* Argue about. L16. 2 *v.i.* = ARGY-BARGY *v.* E19.

argle-bargle /ˈɑːɡ(ə)lˈbɑːɡ(ə)l (*main stress variable*)/ *v.* & *n. dial.* & *colloq.* E19. [Redupl. of prec.] A *v.* 1 *v.t.* Exchange (words) in argument. *rare.* E19. 2 *v.i.* = ARGY-BARGY *v.* E19. B *n.* = ARGY-BARGY *n.* L19.

Argo /ˈɑːɡəʊ/ *n.* M16. [L: cf. ARGONAUT.] (The name of) a large constellation of the southern hemisphere now divided into Carina, Puppis, Vela, and Pyxis; the Ship. Also *Argo Navis* /ˈneɪvɪs/ [L *navis* ship].

argol /ˈɑːɡɒl, -ɡ(ə)l/ *n.*[1] ME. [AN *argoile*, of unkn. origin.] = TARTAR *n.*[1] I.

argol /ˈɑːɡ(ə)l/ *n.*[2] Also **argal**. M19. [Mongolian.] Dried cattle dung used as fuel in the steppes of central Asia.

argon /ˈɑːɡɒn/ *n.* L19. [Gk, neut. of *argos* idle, inactive, f. A-[10] + *ergon* work.] A colourless odourless gaseous chemical element, atomic no. 18, which is one of the noble gases and is present in air to the extent of about one per cent by volume. (Symbol Ar.)

Argonaut /ˈɑːɡ(ə)nɔːt/ *n.* L16. [L *argonauta* f. Gk *argonautēs* sailor (*nautēs*) in the ship Argo.] 1 Any of the legendary sailors who travelled with Jason in the Argo in quest of the Golden Fleece. L16. b *transf.* (Also **a-**.) An adventurer with a quest, esp. for gold; an explorer. E19. 2 (Now usu. **a-**.) An octopod of the genus *Argonauta*, the female of which possesses a thin coiled shell into which the eggs are laid. Also called *paper nautilus*. M19.

argo'nautic *n.* & *a.* (*a*) *n.* a poem concerning the Argonauts; an epic story; (*b*) *adj.* of or pertaining to the Argonauts; epic: L16.

argosy /ˈɑːɡəsi/ *n. Hist.* & *poet.* Also (earlier) †**ragusye**. L16. [App. f. It. *Ragusea* use as n. of fem. adj. (sc. *nave* ship, etc.) 'of Ragusa'.] A merchant-vessel of the largest size and burden, *esp.* one of Ragusa or Venice.

fig.: T. W. HIGGINSON Wagons of sea-weed just from the beach . . each weed an argosy.

argot /ˈɑːɡəʊ/ *n.* M19. [Fr., of unkn. origin.] The jargon, slang, or peculiar phraseology of a social class or group; orig., rogues' and thieves' cant.

argue /ˈɑːɡjuː/ *v.* ME. [(O)Fr. *arguer* f. L *argutari*, frequent. of *arguere* make clear, prove, assert, accuse.] I Bring reasons, reason, dispute. 1 *v.i.* Discuss, reason, debate; contend, dispute. (Foll. by *with*, *against*, an opponent; *for*, *against*, *about*, †*of*, a proposition). ME. 2 *v.t.* Discuss the pros and cons of; bring forward reasons for or against (a proposition). L15. 3 *v.t.* Maintain, by adducing reasons, *that*. M16. 4 *v.t.* Adduce as a reason or argument. *arch.* E17. 5 *v.t.* Persuade (a person) *into* or *out of* a course of action, opinion, intention, etc. M17.

1 MILTON Of good and evil much they argu'd then. M. W. MONTAGU I am not . . arguing for an equality of the two sexes. P. G. WODEHOUSE One cannot argue about personality. Its compelling power has to be accepted as a fact. A. S. EDDINGTON We do not argue with the critic who urges that the stars are not hot enough for this process; we tell him to go and find a hotter place. J. GROSS A well-drilled child of the Scottish Enlightenment, a debater trained to argue back to first principles. 2 G. B. SHAW Fifty civilians . . to support two skilled judges in trying her case . . and to argue it out with her at sitting after sitting. J. BUCHAN We refused no challenge, but argued any question anywhere with anyone. 3 M. L. KING A few hours later, before Judge Carter, the city argued that we were operating a 'private enterprise' without a franchise. 4 DEFOE He told me the same thing, which I argued for my staying . . was the strongest Repulse to my Pretensions. 5 W. CONGREVE A sort of poetical logic to argue you into a protection of this play.

II Bring evidence, prove, indicate. †6 *v.t.* Convict (*of*), prove an accusation against. LME–E18. †7 *v.t.* Accuse (*of*); call in question. LME–L17. 8 *v.t.* Be evidence of; indicate or prove (a thing, a person or thing *to be*, *that* something is). LME.

7 SIR T. BROWNE Nor would we argue the definitive sentence of God. 8 SHAKES. *3 Hen. VI* Which argued thee a most unloving father. J. LOCKE Contrary choices that Men make in the World, do not argue that they do not all pursue Good. H. MAUNDRELL Which seem to argue it to be ancient. J. AGATE The principal star is one Ethel Waters, and her enthusiastic reception argues talent.

Phrases: *argue the toss*: see TOSS *n.* **argue well for** (usu. in neg.) make a good case for.

arguable *a.* able to be argued, debatable, open to disagreement E17. **arguably** *adv.* as may be shown by argument or made a matter of argument L19. **arguer** *n.* LME. **arguing** *n.* (*a*) the action or process of the vb; †(*b*) an accusation; (*c*) an argument: LME.

arguendo /ɑːɡjʊˈɛndəʊ/ *adv.* M18. [L, abl. of *arguendum* gerund of *arguere*: see prec.] Chiefly *Law*. In the course of the argument; for the sake of argument.

argufy /ˈɑːɡjʊfʌɪ/ *v. colloq.* & *dial.* L17. [f. prec. + -FY. Cf. *speechify*.] †1 *v.t.* = ARGUE 2. Only in L17. 2 *v.i.* Dispute, wrangle, argue. M18. 3 *v.i.* Prove or be evidence of something; be of importance or consequence; signify. M18. 4 *v.t.* Worry with argumentation. L18.

argufier *n.* E19.

argument /ˈɑːɡjʊm(ə)nt/ *n.* ME. [(O)Fr. f. L *argumentum*, f. *arguere*: see ARGUE, -MENT.] 1 A connected series of statements or reasons intended to establish a position; a process of reasoning or disputation; argumentation. ME. b *spec.* Any of a number of lines of reasoning that seek to prove the existence of God. E19. 2 A statement or fact advanced to influence the mind; a reason urged in support of a proposition. Formerly *spec.* in *Logic*, the middle term in a syllogism. LME. 3 Proof, evidence; a token, an indication. *arch.* LME. 4 *Math.* etc. An independent quantity (orig., *Astron.*, an angle) on which the value of a function depends or on which an operator acts. LME. 5a Statement of the pros and cons of a proposition; discussion, debate (esp. contentious); a verbal dispute, a quarrel. L15. †b Subject of contention. L16–E17. †6 Subject, theme of debate or discussion, either verbal or written. L15–M19. 7 A summary of the subject-matter of a book; an index, table (of contents), etc. *arch.* M16.

1b *argument from design*, *cosmological argument*, *ontological argument*, etc. 2 HENRY MORE But that the Beast that was, and is not, is not the Devil, we shall now evince by other arguments. C. M. YONGE Well provided with golden arguments. F. L. WRIGHT To hold snow on the roof is always a good, wise provision and a good argument for a flat roof. 3 T. SHERIDAN Beating the Desk and biting of Nails were Arguments of taking Pains. 5a MILTON In argument with men a woman ever Goes by the worse. SHAFTESBURY So intent in upholding their own side of the argument. K. AMIS Just assume for the sake of argument that he's a fake. V. S. PRITCHETT Grandmother, Grandfather and Father were shouting in angry argument across the table, about God and 'that Eddy woman'. A. HAILEY Their discussion . . had quickly developed into an argument. b SHAKES. *Hen. V* And sheath'd their swords for lack of argument. 6 DISRAELI The throbbing deed Shall make thy name a household argument. 7 POPE Argument to Book the First.

argu'mental *a.* (now *rare*) L16.

†**argument** *v.* LME. [f. the n. or (O)Fr. *argumenter* f. L *argumentari*, f. *argumentum*: see prec.] 1 *v.i.* Adduce arguments (*for*); argue. LME–M19. 2 *v.t.* Provide proof, establish, (*that*); argue for. M16–M19. 3 *v.t.* Make the subject of debate. M18–E19.

argumentation /ˌɑːɡjʊmɛnˈteɪʃ(ə)n/ *n.* LME. [(O)Fr. f. L *argumentatio(n-)*, f. *argumentat-* pa. ppl stem of *argumentari*: see prec., -ATION.] 1 The action or process of arguing; methodical employment or presentation of arguments; logical or formal reasoning; interchange of argument, discussion, debate. LME. 2 An argument advanced; a sequence of arguments, a process of reasoning. LME.

argumentative /ɑːɡjʊˈmɛntətɪv/ *a.* LME [OFr., or late L *argumentativus* (Donatus), f. *argumentari*: see prec., -ATIVE.] 1 Characterized by argument; controversial; logical. LME. †2 Of the nature of an argument (*for*); of weight as evidence (*of*). M–L17. 3 Given to argumentation; capable or fond of arguing. M17.

argumentatively *adv.* M17. **argumentativeness** *n.* M18.

argumentator /ˌɑːɡjʊmɛnˈteɪtə/ *n.* Now *rare.* M17. [L: see ARGUMENT *v.*, -ATOR.] A person who conducts an argument, a reasoner.

argumentive /ɑːɡjʊˈmɛntɪv/ *a. rare.* M17. [f. ARGUMENT *v.* + -IVE.] = ARGUMENTATIVE.

argumentum ad hominem /ɑːɡjʊˌmɛntəm ad ˈhɒmɪnɛm/ *n. phr.* M17. [L: see ARGUMENT *n.*, AD HOMINEM.] An argument, usu. vilificatory, appealing to the personal circumstances or character of an opponent rather than to sound reasoning.

argumentum e silentio /ɑːɡjʊˌmɛntəm eɪ sɪˈlɛntɪəʊ, -ʃɪəʊ/ *n. phr.* M20. [L = argument from silence.] A conclusion based on silence, i.e. on lack of contrary evidence.

Argus /ˈɑːɡəs/ *n.* In senses 2 & 3 also **a-**. LME. [L f. Gk *Argos*, a mythological person with a hundred eyes.] 1 A very vigilant watcher, a guardian. LME. 2 Any of certain butterflies bearing eyespots, esp. *Aricia agestis* (in full *brown argus*) or *A. artaxerxes* (in full *Scotch argus*). E18. 3 Either of two large SE Asian pheasants, both of which have long tails with numerous eyespots, *Argusiana argus* (in full *great argus*) and *Rheinardia ocellata* (in full *crested argus*). M18.

Comb.: **Argus eye** (*a*) in *pl.*, sharp eyes, acute observation; (*b*) each of the eyelike markings on the tail of a peacock (to which Argus' eyes were said to be transferred by Hera after his death); **Argus-eyed** *a.* extremely vigilant, sharp-sighted.

argute /ɑːˈɡjuːt/ *a.* Now *literary.* LME. [L *argutus* pa. pple of *arguere* make clear, ARGUE.] †1 Of taste: sharp. Only in LME. 2 Of a person, faculty, action, etc.: quick, subtle, shrewd. L16. 3 Of sound: shrill. E18.

argutely *adv.* L16. **arguteness** *n.* M17.

Argy *n.* & *a.* var. of ARGIE.

argy-bargy /ˌɑːɡɪˈbɑːɡi, ˌɑːdʒɪˈbɑːdʒi/ *v.* & *n. dial.* & *colloq.* L19. [Alt. & redupl. of ARGUE: cf. ARGLE-BARGLE.] A *v.i.* Dispute, wrangle. L19. B *n.* Disputatious argument; a wrangle, a dispute. L19.

argyle /ɑːˈɡʌɪl/ *n.* Also **-gyll**, **A-**. L18. [*Argyll* (*Argyle*), a former county of Scotland and a family name.] 1 A vessel, usu. of silver or other metal and resembling a small coffee-pot, in which to serve hot gravy. *obs.* exc. *Hist.* L18. 2 A knitting pattern with diamonds of various colours on a single background colour, based on the tartan of the Argyll branch of the Campbell clan. Also, a garment (esp. in *pl.*, socks) in this pattern. Chiefly *N. Amer.* M20.

argyro- /ˈɑːdʒɪrəʊ/ *comb. form* repr. Gk *arguro-*, f. *arguros* silver: see -O-. Bef. a vowel also **argyr-**.

ar'gyria *n.* (*Med.*) silver poisoning, esp. as causing a greyish-blue discoloration of the skin L19. **ar'gyrodite** *n.* [Gk *argurōdēs* rich in silver] *Min.* a sulphide of silver and germanium crystallizing in the cubic system and occurring as black crystals with a metallic lustre L19. **'argyrophil(e)** *a.* = ARGYROPHILIC E20. **argyro'philia** *n.* the property of being argyrophilic M20. **argyro'philic** *a.* readily stained black by silver salts M20.

Arhat /ˈɑːhat/ *n.* Also **Arahat** /ˈarəhat/, **a-**. L19. [Skt *arhat*, Pali *arahat* meritorious.] *Buddhism* & *Jainism*. A saint of one of the highest ranks.

Ar(a)hatship *n.* the state of an Arhat L19.

arhythmic *a.* var. of ARRHYTHMIC.

aria /ˈɑːrɪə/ *n.* E18. [It. f. L *aera* accus. of *aer*: see AIR *n.*[1]] *Mus.* A long song for one voice usu. with accompaniment; *esp.* such a song in an opera, oratorio, etc.

Arian /ˈɛːrɪən/ *a.*[1] & *n.*[1] LME. [eccl.L *Arianus*, f. *Arius* f. Gk *Arios*, *Areios* (d. 336), a presbyter of Alexandria: see -AN.] **A** *adj.* Designating the heretical doctrine of Arius, who denied that Christ was consubstantial with God; of, pertaining to, or holding this doctrine. LME. **B** *n.* A holder of this doctrine. LME.

Arianism *n.* the Arian doctrine L16. **Arianize** *v.* (*a*) *v.i.* follow the doctrine of Arius; (*b*) *v.t.* convert to Arianism: E17. **Arianizer** *n.* L17.

Arian /ˈɛːrɪən/ *a.*[2] & *n.*[2] E20. [f. ARIES + -AN.] **A** *adj.* Of or pertaining to the zodiacal sign Aries; (characteristic of a person) born under Aries. E20. **B** *n.* A person born under Aries. E20.

Arian *a.*[3] & *n.*[3] var. of ARYAN.

-arian /ˈɛːrɪən/ *suff.* [f. L *-arius* -ARY[1] + -AN.] Forming adjs. or corresp. ns. of which the earliest (gen. formations) are *disciplinarian* (n.), *antiquarian*, *proletarian*; (numeral adjs.) *quinquagenarian*; commonly in terms denoting religious or moral tenets, as *Millenarian*, *sectarian*, *Unitarian*, on the anal. of which were formed *humanitarian*, *utilitarian*, etc., and joc. formations as *anythingarian*.

arid /ˈarɪd/ *a.* M17. [Fr. *aride* or L *aridus*, f. *arere* be dry or parched: see -ID[1].] †**1** Of a substance, the skin, etc.: dry, parched, withered. M17–E19. **2** Of the ground, climate, etc.: dry, parched; barren, bare; *Geogr.* too dry to support vegetation. M17. **3** *fig.* Uninteresting, dull; unfruitful, barren, jejune. Cf. ARIDITY *n.* 2. E19.

2 A. KOESTLER The mountains underneath were arid as craters on the moon. E. ROOSEVELT It looked like good farming country, in contrast to the arid appearance of the land in so many parts of Greece. 3 T. C. WOLFE A dry campaign over an arid waste of Latin prose. H. E. BATES I felt rather stupid; and then a little flat and arid from fears that had decayed.

aˈridify *v.t.* make arid E20. **aridly** *adv.* L19. **aridness** *n.* M18.

Aridisol /əˈrɪdɪsɒl/ *n.* M20. [f. prec. + -I- + -SOL.] *Soil Sci.* A soil of an order comprising often saline or alkaline soils with very little organic matter, characteristic of arid regions.

aridity /əˈrɪdɪti/ *n.* L16. [Fr. *aridité* or L *ariditas*, f. as ARID: see -ITY.] **1** Arid state or quality; dryness, barrenness; parched condition. L16. **2** *fig.* Lack of interest, dullness; unproductiveness. L17.

ariel /ˈɛːrɪəl/ *n.* M19. [Arab. *ʾaryal*.] A Middle Eastern and African gazelle, *Gazella arabica*.

Aries /ˈɛːriːz/ *n.* OE. [L *aries* ram.] **1** (The name of) a constellation of the northern hemisphere, on the ecliptic near Andromeda; *Astrol.* (the name of) the first zodiacal sign, usu. associated with the period 21 March to 20 April (see note s.v. ZODIAC); the Ram. OE. **2** A person born under the sign Aries; = ARIAN *n.*[2] M20.

1 *attrib.*: E. KIRK It is almost impossible to hide anything from an Aries individual who has recognized his or her power of intuition. **first point of Aries** the point of the vernal equinox (now actually located in Pisces, owing to precession).

†**arietation** *n.* E17–L18. [L *arietatio(n-)*, f. *arietat-* pa. ppl stem of *arietare* butt like a ram, f. *aries*, *ariet-* ram: see -ATION.] The action of butting like a ram; ramming, battering, bombardment, (*lit.* & *fig.*).

arietta /arɪˈɛtə/ *n.* E18. [It., dim. of ARIA.] *Mus.* A short tune or song.

Also **ariette** *n.* [Fr.] E19.

aright /əˈrʌɪt/ *adv.* [OE *on riht*, *ariht*: see A *prep.*[1] 1, RIGHT *n.*[1]] **I** Of manner. **1** In a right manner, rightly; justly, correctly. OE. †**2** Immediately; at once. ME–L15. †**3** Directly; in a straight line. ME–E17. **4** Exactly, just; indeed. Long *arch.* LME.

1 COVERDALE *Ps.* 77:8 A generacion that set not their herte aright. M. INNES And if I remember aright, sir, it was just then that the horse stopped nodding—sudden-like. 4 E. B. BROWNING Is it true besides—Aright true?

II Of direction. **5** On or to the right hand. *arch. rare.* ME.

5 SOUTHEY Aright, aleft, The affrighted foemen scatter from his spear.

arightly *adv.* (now *rare* or *obs.*) = ARIGHT 1 L16. †**arights** *adv.* (*rare*) = ARIGHT 1: only in L16.

aril /ˈarɪl/ *n.* Also in L form **arillus** /-əs/, pl. **-lli** /-lʌɪ, -liː/. M18. [mod.L *arillus* of unkn. origin; med.L *arilli* = dried grape-pips.] *Bot.* An additional envelope, often fleshy, developed around the seed in certain plants (e.g. yew).

arillate *a.* having an aril E19.

Arimasp /ˈarɪmasp/ *n.* Pl. **Arimasps**, **Arimaspi** /arɪˈmaspʌɪ/. L16. [L *Arimaspi* pl., Gk *Arimaspoi*, said to mean 'one-eyed' in Scythian.] Any of a mythical race of one-eyed men in northern Europe who tried to take gold guarded by griffins.

Also **Ariˈmaspian** *n.* M17.

arioso /arɪˈəʊzəʊ, ɑː-/ *a.*, *adv.*, & *n.* E18. [It., f. ARIA.] *Mus.* **A** *adj.* Melodious, songlike, cantabile; having something of the quality of an aria. Also as *adv.* as a direction. E18. **B** *n.* Pl. **-os**. A piece of vocal or instrumental music of this kind. L19.

ariose /ɑːrɪˈəʊs/ *a.* = ARIOSO *a.* E18.

-arious /ˈɛːrɪəs/ *suff.* [f. L *-arius* -ARY[1] + -OUS.] Forming adjs., as *vicarious*, *gregarious*, etc.

aripple /əˈrɪp(ə)l/ *adv.* & *pred. a.* E19. [f. A-[2] + RIPPLE *n.*[3]] In a ripple, rippling.

arise /əˈrʌɪz/ *v.i.* Pa. t. **arose** /əˈrəʊz/; pa. pple **arisen** /əˈrɪz(ə)n/. [OE *ārīsan*, (Northumb.) *arrīsa* = OS *ārīsan*, OHG *ur-*, *ar-*, *irrīsan*, Goth. *us-*, *urreisan*: see A-[1], RISE *v.* Largely replaced by *rise* except in senses in branch III.] **I** Rise from sitting, repose, inaction, etc. Now *arch.* & *poet.* **1** Get up from sitting or kneeling; stand up. OE. †**2** Get up from a fall. OE–M17. **3** Get up from sleep or rest. OE. **4** Of the sun, moon, etc.: come above the horizon. Of the day, morning, etc.: dawn, begin. OE. **5** Rise from the dead. OE. **6** Rise from inaction or quiet, esp. in hostility or rebellion. OE. **7** Rise in agitation or violence, as the wind, sea, etc.; boil up. OE. **8** Of a sound: become audible, be heard. ME.

1 AV *John* 14:31 Arise, let us go hence. 2 MILTON Awake, arise, or be for ever fall'n. 3 GOLDSMITH Nash generally arose early in the morning. 4 SHAKES. *Rom. & Jul.* Arise, fair sun, and kill the envious moon. 5 AV *Matt.* 27:52 Many bodies of the saints which slept arose. 6 SHAKES. *Oth.* Arise, black vengeance, from the hollow hell. 7 TENNYSON A wind arose and rush'd upon the South. 8 AV *Acts* 23:9 There arose a great cry.

II Go or come higher. **9** Go or come up; ascend, mount. Now *poet.* OE. †**10** Rise in height, eminence, quantity, value, etc.; grow, swell up; amount or attain *to*. ME–L18.

9 KEATS A mist arose, as from a scummy marsh. 10 SWIFT Stocks arose three per cent. upon it in the city. T. R. MALTHUS The number arising annually to the age of puberty.

III Spring up; come into existence. **11** Spring out from its source, as a river etc. (*arch.*); originate, result (*from*, †*of*); proceed *out of* as a consequence. OE. **12** Of a person: be born; come into the world of events. OE. **13** Of a thing: spring up, be raised or built. *poet.* OE. **14** Come into existence or notice; present itself, occur. OE.

11 SHAKES. *Hen. V* Some sudden mischief may arise of it. R. G. COLLINGWOOD Other philosophers discussed problems arising out of distinctions I thought false. F. HOYLE The forces arising from the weight of the ice are . . greatest at the bottom of the glacier. 12 COVERDALE *Deut.* 34:10 There arose no prophet more in Israel like vnto Moses. J. BRYCE In the fourteenth century there arose in Italy the first great masters of painting and song. 13 TENNYSON So long, that mountains have arisen since With cities on their flanks. 14 LD MACAULAY All questions which arose in the Privy Council. D. ATTENBOROUGH If we want to consider how life arose, we have to look back a further thousand million years.

arisings *n.pl.* materials forming secondary or waste products of a process E20.

arista /əˈrɪstə/ *n.* Pl. **-tae** /-tiː/. L17. [L = awn or ear of grain.] *Zool.* & *Bot.* A bristly or beardlike process.

aristate *a.* furnished with aristae; awned, bearded: E19.

Aristarch /ˈarɪstɑːk/ *n.* Also †**-chus**. M16. [L *Aristarchus* f. Gk *Aristarkhos* (2nd cent. BC), a severe critic of Homeric poetry.] A severe critic.

aristo /əˈrɪstəʊ/ *n. colloq.* Pl. **-os**. M19. [Fr., abbrev. of *aristocrate* ARISTOCRAT.] An aristocrat.

aristocracy /arɪˈstɒkrəsi/ *n.* L15. [(O)Fr. *aristocratie* f. Gk *aristokratia*, f. *aristos* best: see -CRACY.] **1** The government of a State by its best citizens. L15. **2** Government of a State by those who are most distinguished by birth and wealth; oligarchy; a State so governed. L16. **3** A ruling body of nobles, an oligarchy. E17. **4** The class to which such rulers belong, the nobility; the patrician or privileged class, regardless of the form of government. M17. **5** *transf.* & *fig.* The best representatives of any quality, skill, etc.; any privileged or élite group. M19.

5 G. B. SHAW The plays which constitute the genuine aristocracy of modern dramatic literature. G. M. TREVELYAN The working class aristocracy, the engineers and the men of other skilled trades. B. BAINBRIDGE He was convinced that physicians were an ignorant aristocracy kept afloat by witchcraft.

aristocrat /ˈarɪstəkrat, əˈrɪst-/ *n.* L18. [Fr. *aristocrate* (a wd of the Fr. Revolution) f. *aristocratie*, *-tique*: see prec., next, -CRAT.] A member of an aristocracy or of the nobility, orig. of the French aristocracy in the French Revolution of 1790 (cf. DEMOCRAT *n.* 1). Also (*rare*), an advocate of aristocratic government.

ariˈstocratism *n.* aristocratic conduct; haughty exclusiveness: L18. **ariˈstocratize** *v.t.* make aristocratic L18.

aristocratic /ˌarɪstəˈkratɪk/ *a.* E17. [Fr. *aristocratique* f. Gk *aristokratikos*: see ARISTOCRACY, -IC.] **1** Of or pertaining to an aristocracy; attached to or favouring aristocracy. E17. **2** Befitting an aristocrat; grand, stylish, distinguished. M19.

aristocratical *a.* oligarchical; aristocratic: L16. **aristocratically** *adv.* L16. **aristocraticalness** *n.* (*rare*) M18.

aristolochia /ˌarɪstəˈləʊkɪə/ *n.* OE. [med.L *aristologia*, Fr. *aristoloche*, f. L *aristolochia* f. Gk *aristolokhia*, *-eia*, f. *aristolokhos* well-born (from its medicinal repute).] Any of numerous climbing shrubs or other plants of the genus *Aristolochia* (family Aristolochiaceae), bearing tubular, often bizarre, flowers; esp. *A. clematitis*. Also called *birthwort*.

aristology /arɪˈstɒlədʒi/ *n.* M19. [f. Gk *ariston* breakfast, luncheon + -LOGY.] The art or science of dining.

aristoˈlogical *a.* L19. **aristologist** *n.* M19.

Aristophanic /ˌarɪstəˈfanɪk/ *a.* & *n.* E19. [L *Aristophanicus*, Gk *Aristophanikos*, f. *Aristophanēs* (see below): see -IC.] **A** *adj.* Of, pertaining to, or characteristic of the Athenian comic dramatist Aristophanes (d. *c*380 BC). E19. **B** *n. Class. Pros.* A logaoedic tripody beginning with a dactyl. M19.

Aristotelian /ˌarɪstəˈtiːlɪən/ *a.* & *n.* L16. [f. L *Aristotelius*, *-eus* f. Gk *Aristoteleios*, f. *Aristotelēs* Aristotle (see below): see -AN.] **A** *adj.* Of or pertaining to the Greek philosopher Aristotle (d. 322 BC) or his philosophical system based on the theory of syllogism, and on the choice of matter, form, potentiality, and actuality as basic concepts; logical, deductive. L16. **B** *n.* An adherent or student of Aristotle's philosophy. L16.

Aristotelean /ˌarɪstɒtɪˈliːən/ *a.* & *n.* (now *rare*) = ARISTOTELIAN E17. **Aristotelianism** *n.* the philosophical system or any doctrine of Aristotle E18. **Aristotelic** /ˌarɪstəˈtɛlɪk/ *a.* = ARISTOTELIAN *a.* E17. †**Aristotelical** *a.* L16–L17.

Aristotle's lantern *n. phr.* see LANTERN *n.* 7b.

Arita /əˈriːtə/ *a.* L19. [A town in S. Japan.] Designating Japanese porcelain of a distinctive style made in or near Arita, typically with unsymmetrical floral designs in blue and white underglaze or polychrome enamel.

arithmancy /ˈarɪθmansi/ *n.* L16. [f. Gk *arithmos* number + -MANCY.] Divination by numbers.

arithˈmantical *a.* M16.

arithmetic /əˈrɪθmətɪk/ *n.*[1] Also (earlier) †**arsmet(r)ike** & similar vars. ME. [OFr. *arismetique* ult. f. L *arithmetica* f. Gk *arithmētikē* (*tekhnē*) counting (art), f. *arithmein* reckon, f. *arithmos* number. Early forms were infl. by L *ars metrica* 'measuring art': conformation to orig. L and Gk forms took place in 16.] **1** The science of numbers; (the branch of mathematics that deals with) the properties and manipulation of numbers; calculation, reckoning. ME. 2 A treatise on this. L15.

1 BINARY *arithmetic*. *decimal arithmetic*: see DECIMAL *a*. *mental arithmetic*: see MENTAL *a*.[1] *universal arithmetic*: see UNIVERSAL *a*.

Comb.: **arithmetic (and logic) unit** a unit in a computer which carries out arithmetical and logical operations.

arithmetic /arɪθ'mɛtɪk/ *n*.[2] & *a*. M17. [Fr. *arithmétique*: see prec.] †A *n*. An arithmetician. Only in M17.

B *adj*.. Of, pertaining to, or connected with arithmetic; according to the rules of arithmetic. M17.

arithmetic mean (of *n* numbers): their sum divided by *n*. **arithmetic progression, series**: in which there is a constant (positive or negative) difference between successive quantities, as 2, 5, 8, 11.

arithmetical /arɪθ'mɛtɪk(ə)l/ *a*. M16. [f. L *arithmeticus* f. Gk *arithmētikos*: see ARITHMETIC *n*.[1], -AL[1].] = ARITHMETIC *a*.

arithmetical ratio: see RATIO *n*. 2a.

arithmetically *adv*. according to arithmetic; by calculation: L15.

arithmetician /ərɪθmə'tɪʃ(ə)n, ˌarɪθ-/ *n*. M16. [Fr. *arithméticien* f. L *arithmetica*: see ARITHMETIC *n*.[1], -ICIAN.] A person skilled in arithmetic.

arithmetize /ə'rɪθmətʌɪz/ *v*. Also **-ise**. M17. [f. ARITHMETIC *n*.[1] + -IZE.] 1 *v.i.* & *t*. Use arithmetic; calculate. *rare*. M17. 2 *v.t.* Express arithmetically; reduce to arithmetical form. L19.

arithmeti'zation *n*. E20.

arithmo- /ə'rɪθməʊ/ *comb. form* of Gk *arithmos* number: see -O-.

arith'mology *n*. the science of numbers; (a) writing on this subject: L16. **arithmo'mania** *n*. a pathological desire to count objects or make calculations L19. **arithmo'maniac** *n*. a person affected with arithmomania L19. **arith'mometer** *n*. (now *rare* or *obs*.) a calculating instrument E19.

arity /'arɪti/ *n*. M20. [f. -ARY[1] (in *binary*, *ternary*, etc.) + -ITY.] *Math*. The number of elements by virtue of which something is unary, binary, etc.

-arium /'ɛːrɪəm/ *suff*. Pl. **-ariums, -aria** /'ɛːrɪə/. [L, neut. of adjs. in *-arius*: see -ARY[1].] Forming ns. w. the sense 'a thing connected with or employed in, a place for', as *herbarium*, *honorarium*, *planetarium*, *vivarium*, etc., freq. (after *aquarium*) 'a place for keeping and exhibiting something', as *dolphinarium* etc.

Arizonian /arɪ'zəʊnɪən/ *a*. & *n*. Also **-nan** /-nən/. M19. [f. *Arizona* (see below) + -IAN.] Of or pertaining to, a native or inhabitant of, the State of Arizona, USA.

arjun /'ɑːdʒʌn, -uːn/ *n*. M19. [Skt *arjuna*.] = KUMBUK.

ark /ɑːk/ *n*. In senses 2, 3 also **A-**. [OE *ærc* (*eark*) corresp. to OFris. *erke*, OHG *arc(h)a*, ON *ǫrk*, *ark-*, Goth. *arka* f. L *arca* chest, box, coffer.] 1 A chest, coffer, basket, or similar receptacle; (chiefly *dial*.) a chest or bin for storing meal, fruit, or other foodstuffs. OE. 2 *spec*. The wooden chest which contained the tables of Jewish law and was kept in the holiest place of the Tabernacle and of the First Temple in Jerusalem (also more fully *Ark of the Covenant*, *Ark of Testimony*). Now also, the chest or cupboard housing the Torah scrolls in a synagogue (also more fully *Holy Ark*). OE. 3 The large floating covered vessel in which Noah, his family, and animals were said to be saved from the Flood. Also *fig*., a place of refuge. OE. 4 A ship, boat, etc.; *esp*. (*N. Amer*.) a large flat-bottomed riverboat. L15.

1 AV *Exod*. 2:3 She tooke for him an arke of bul-rushes. 2 **lay hands on, touch, the ark** treat irreverently what is held to be sacred. 3 *fig*.: H. FAST They stood on the deck as the ancient, rusty ship that had been their home and ark for seventeen days wore into Ellis Island. **have come out of the Ark** *colloq*. be very antiquated. 4 BYRON No more he said: but . . commits him to his fragile ark. M. TWAIN Drifting arks and stone-boats.

Comb.: **ark shell** (a shell of) a small bivalve belonging to *Arca* or a related genus.

arkite *a*. (*rare*) of or pertaining to Noah's ark L18.

†**Arkansa** *n*. & *a*. var. of ARKANSAS.

Arkansan /ɑː'kanz(ə)n/ *n*. & *a*. M19. [f. *Arkansas* (see below), f. as next: see -AN.] A native or inhabitant of, of or pertaining to, Arkansas, a State of the US.

Also **Arkansian** *n*. & *a*. M19.

Arkansas /'ɑːk(ə)nsɔː/ *n*. & *a*. Also †**-sa(w)**. Pl. of n. same. L17. [Fr. f. Illinois *akansea*: cf. OZARK.] = QUAPAW.

†**Arkansaw** *n*. & *a*. var. of ARKANSAS.

arkose /'ɑːkəʊs, -z/ *n*. M19. [Fr., prob. f. Gk *arkhaios* ancient.] *Geol*. A coarse-grained sandstone which is at least 25 per cent feldspar.

ar'kosic *a*. E20.

arles /ɑːlz/ *n*. *Sc*. & *north*. ME. [App. repr. med.L dim. of L ARRHA: cf. OFr. *ere*, pl. *erres*, *arres*, (16) *arrhes*.] Money given to bind a bargain; earnest-money. Also *fig*., an earnest, a foretaste.

Comb.: **arles-penny** a sum of money given as earnest.

arm /ɑːm/ *n*.[1] [OE *arm*, *earm* = OFris. *arm*, *erm*, OS, OHG (Du., G) *arm*, ON *armr*, Goth. *arms* f. Gmc.] I A limb. 1 Either of the upper limbs of the human body, from the shoulder to the hand (the part from the elbow downwards being the *forearm*); (in *pl*.) the space enclosed by a person's arms. OE. 2 *fig*. Might, power, authority; a prop, a support. OE. 3 The forelimb of an animal; a flexible limb or other appendage of an invertebrate. LME. b *Falconry*. The leg of a hawk from thigh to foot. L16. 4 A sleeve. L18.

1 G. STEIN He got up and put his arm around her like a brother. J. CONRAD Outside I met Therese with her arms full of pillows and blankets. D. LODGE Allowing his long, gorilla-like arms to hang loosely over the edge of his seat. 2 AV *Jer*. 17:5 Cursed be the man that trusteth in man, and maketh flesh his arme. D. BREWSTER No period of his life can be named when his intellectual arm was shortened. 3 D. MORRIS The anthropoid apes differ from the true monkeys in that they are tailless and have elongated arms. D. ATTENBOROUGH These creatures appear to be crinoids that . . are lying in an inverted position with . . their five arms outstretched.

II Something resembling an arm. 5 A narrow strip of water or land projecting from a larger body. OE. 6 Each of the branches into which a main trunk divides, e.g. of a tree, road, nerve, etc. ME. 7 A part of an apparatus which resembles an arm in shape, disposition, or function. See also YARD-ARM. M16. b The middle segment of the bucket of a water-wheel. E17. 8 A side part of a chair or sofa upon which the sitter's arm may rest. M17. 9 *Astron*. Any of the luminous bands of stars and gas which form the outer parts of a spiral galaxy. L19.

5 C. DARWIN The islands, though in sight of each other, are separated by deep arms of the sea. P. LARKIN I dreamed of an out-thrust arm of land Where gulls blew over a wave. 6 I. MURDOCH A great tree spread its arms over a circle of grass. D. STOREY The road divided, one arm leading to the Dell, the other to the station. 7 G. F. FIENNES The arm had fallen off the Up starter at Tottenham. *Encycl. Brit*. That device . . directs the robot's arm and hand to repeat a specific sequence of movements. G. J. KING The modern pickup consists of an arm and a cartridge. 8 J. D. SALINGER He came over and sat down on the arm of Stradlater's chair.

Phrases: **an arm and a leg** *fig*. a large sum, something of high value to one, (esp. in *cost an arm and a leg*, *give an arm and a leg for*). **arm in arm** (of two or more people) with arms interlinked. *a shot in the arm*: see SHOT *n*.[1] **as long as my, your, arm** *colloq*. very long. **at arm's length** as far as the arm can reach; *fig*. without undue familiarity; (of dealings) with neither party controlled by the other. *chance one's arm*: see CHANCE *v*. 3. **give, offer, one's arm (to)** allow or invite (someone) to walk arm in arm with one, or to lean on one's arm. **have a good arm** (esp. *Cricket*) be a strong thrower. **in arms** (of a child) too young to walk (BABE *in arms*). **in a person's arms** embraced by him or her. *left arm*: see LEFT *a*. *offer one's arm* (*to*): see *give one's arm to* above. **on one's arm**: supported by it. *right arm*: see RIGHT *a*. *secular arm*: see SECULAR *a*. TREM *arm*. *tremolo arm*: see TREMOLO *n*. 2b. *twist a person's arm*: see TWIST *v*. **under one's arm**: between it and the body. **within arm's reach** near enough to reach by extending one's arm; *fig*. readily available. **with open arms** cordially, eagerly.

Comb.: **armband** a band worn round the arm; **arm-bone** (now *rare* or *obs*.) the humerus; ARMCHAIR; **armhole** (*a*) (*obs*. exc. *dial*.) an armpit; (*b*) a hole through which the arm is put into the sleeve of a garment or out of which it is put in a sleeveless garment; **armlock** a close hold by the arm in wrestling or judo; **armpit** (*a*) the hollow under the arm where it is joined to the trunk; the axilla; (*b*) the corresponding region of other animals; (*c*) *fig*. (*N. Amer*. *colloq*.) a disgusting or contemptible place or part; the lowest place; **armrest** something to support the arm of a seated person; **armstrong** *a*. (long *arch*.) having strong arms; **arm-twisting** *fig*. (persuasion by) the use of physical force or moral pressure; **arm-wrestle** *v.t.* & *i*. engage in arm-wrestling (with); **arm-wrestling**: in which two people sit opposite each other at a table, and each places one elbow on the tabletop, grips the other's hand, and tries to force the other's arm down on to the table.

armful *n*. as much as one arm, or both arms, can hold LME. **armless** *a*.[1] without arm or branch LME. **armlet** *n*. (*a*) an ornament or band worn round the arm; (*b*) a small arm of the sea, branch of a river, etc.: M16. **armlike** *a*. resembling (that of) an arm L19.

arm /ɑːm/ *n*.[2] ME. [(O)Fr. *armes* pl. f. L *arma* (no sing.).] I Something used in fighting. 1 In *pl*. Defensive covering for the body; armour, mail. Now *poet*. ME. 2 A weapon. Usu. in *pl*., instruments used in fighting, weapons, armaments. ME. 3 In *pl*. Defensive or offensive parts of animals or plants. *rare*. LME.

1 SHAKES. *Rich. II* Boys . . clap their female joints In stiff unwieldy arms. 2 R. GRAVES As a final arm for use when even the lance failed they carried a heavy broadsword. H. MACMILLAN As regards defence, Pakistan wanted more arms, especially tanks and bombers. *fig*.: SIR T. BROWNE Unable to wield the intellectual arms of reason.

II Elliptical senses. 4 In *pl*. The exercise of arms; fighting, war. ME. 5 In *pl*. The practice or profession of arms; soldiering. ME. 6 In *pl*. Feats of arms; valiant deeds. *poet*. LME. 7 Each kind of troops in an army, as cavalry, infantry, etc. (orig. these two only); a branch of the armed forces, or (*transf*.) of any organization. (Occas. understood as a fig. use of ARM *n*.[1]) L18.

4 SHAKES. *Rich. II* Thou art a banish'd man, and here art come . . In braving arms against thy sovereign. STEELE It is a barbarous Way to extend Dominion by Arms. 5 G. B. SHAW A patrician keeping a shop instead of following arms! 6 DRYDEN Arms and the man I sing. 7 G. R. GLEIG They numbered about 12,000 of all arms. H. G. WELLS The Emperor . . placed him in control of the new aeronautic arm of the German forces. *Daily Telegraph* Opel, the European arm of General Motors.

III 8 In *pl*. Heraldic insignia or devices, borne orig. on the shields of knights or barons to distinguish them in battle, which later became the hereditary possessions of their families; armorial bearings. Also, the insignia of a country, corporation, company, etc. (Freq. also in names of inns and public houses.) ME.

8 J. BETJEMAN Balkan Sobranies in a wooden box, The college arms upon the lid. G. HEYER An impressive vehicle which bore its noble owner's arms emblazoned on the door-panels. DYLAN THOMAS It is always opening time at the Sailors Arms.

Phrases etc.: *assault-at* (or *-of*)*-arms*: see ASSAULT *n*. 1. **bear arms** be armed, serve as a soldier; have a coat of arms. *coat of arms*: see COAT *n*. *College of Arms*: see COLLEGE *n*. *companion in arms*: see COMPANION *n*.[1] *firearms*: see FIREARM *n*. **in arms** armed, prepared to fight. **in arms with** *Her*. quartered with. *King of* (or *at*) *Arms*: see KING *n*. **lay down (one's) arms** cease fighting, surrender. **man-at-arms** (or †**-of-arms**) *arch*. a soldier, *esp*. one heavily armed. **master-at-arms** the chief police officer on a man-of-war or merchant vessel. *office of arms*: see OFFICE *n*. *passage of* (or *at*) *arms*: see PASSAGE *n*. 15b. *place of arms*: see PLACE *n*.[1] *small arms*: see SMALL *a*. **take up arms** arm oneself, begin fighting. **to arms!** prepare to fight! **under arms** ready for war or battle. **up in arms** actively rebelling; *fig*. strongly protesting.

Comb.: **arms control** international agreement to limit or reduce armaments; **arms race** competition between nations in the development and accumulation of weapons.

armless *a*.[2] (*arch*.) without arms; unarmed: E17.

arm /ɑːm/ *v*.[1] ME. [(O)Fr. *armer* f. L *armare*, f. *arma*: see prec.] I *v.t.* 1 Provide with weapons or (*arch*.) armour; equip for war. ME. 2 Provide with equipment, qualities, advantages, etc., for a task; prepare, make ready. ME. 3 Provide (an animal etc.) with organs of offence or defence. Usu. in *pass.* LME. 4 *Her.* (Earlier as ARMED *a.*[1] 2.) Represent as wearing armour; represent (an animal) with distinct teeth, talons, etc. LME. 5 Plate, coat, cover, or furnish with something providing strength, protection, etc. Usu. in *pass.* LME. †6 Provide (a magnet) with an armature. M17–M19. 7 Make (a weapon) ready for immediate use; activate the fuse or firing device of (a bomb etc.). E20.

1 G. K. CHESTERTON Enough swords, pistols, partisans, cross-bows, and blunderbusses to arm a whole irregular regiment. P. GALLICO Armed themselves, fought and won battles against their hostile neighbours. 2 SHAKES. *Mids. N. D.* Look you arm yourself To fit your fancies to your father's will. I. WALTON First you must arm your hook. 5 DRYDEN Ceres . . armed with Iron Shares the crooked Plough. **arm the lead** *Naut.* cover the base of the sounding-weight with tallow (to pick up a sample from the bottom). 7 *Country Life* When the airship made an attack . . it was the pilot who had to arm the bombs, take a sight, and drop them. J. CLAVELL He had broken open some of the crates of muskets and had set those who could to arming them with powder and with shot.

II *v.i.* 8 Take up arms; provide oneself with weapons or (*arch.*) armour; prepare oneself. ME.

8 BURKE It certainly cannot be right to arm in support of a faction, though it is most laudable to arm in favour of our country. G. B. SHAW Protestant Ulster . . armed against the rest of Ireland and defied the British Parliament. J. KIRKUP If we permit our governments to arm for peace, We sanction war.

arming *vbl n.* (*a*) the action of the vb; †(*b*) arms, armour; (*c*) a defensive or protective covering; a part which protects, strengthens, or fits for a purpose: ME.

arm /ɑːm/ *v.*[2] M16. [f. ARM *n.*[1]] †1 *v.i.* Project like an arm. Only in M16. 2 *v.t.* Embrace; put one's arm(s) round. *rare.* E17. 3 *v.t.* Give one's arm to; conduct by walking arm in arm. E17.

armada /ɑːˈmɑːdə/ *n.* Also †**-ado**. M16. [Sp. f. Proto-Romance *armata* ARMY: see -ADE.] 1 A fleet of warships. M16. b *spec.* (**A-**.) = *Spanish Armada* s.v. SPANISH *a.* L16. †2 A single warship. L16–M17. 3 *transf.* & *fig.* A large army or airborne force; a large fleet of vessels of any kind. E18.

3 LYTTON Nor was the naval unworthy of the land armada. C. RYAN As the long sky trains swarmed out over the English Channel . . a new kind of expectancy began to permeate the armada.

¶Formerly pronounced /ɑːˈmeɪdə/.

armadilla /ɑːməˈdiːljə, *foreign* armaˈðiʎa/ *n.* Also †**-illo**. L17. [Sp., dim. of prec.] A small (Spanish) fighting ship. Also, a small naval squadron.

armadillo /ɑːməˈdɪləʊ/ *n.*[1] Pl. **-os**. L16. [Sp., dim. of *armado* armed man, f. L *armatus* pa. pple of *armare* ARM *v.*[1]] Any of a number of burrowing edentate mammals native to S. and Central America, which have bodies encased in bony plates and are able to roll themselves into a ball when threatened.

†**armadillo** *n.*[2] var. of ARMADILLA.

†**armado** *n.* var. of ARMADA.

Armageddon /ɑːməˈgɛd(ə)n/ *n.* E19. [The place of the last battle at the Day of Judgement: see *Rev.* 16:16 (AV).] (The scene of) a decisive conflict on a great scale.

Armagnac /ˈɑːm(ə)njak/ *n.* M19. [Former name of a district of SW France (department of Gers).] A brandy made in the former Armagnac district.

armalcolite /ɑːˈmalkəlʌɪt/ *n.* L20. [f. Neil A. *Arm*strong, Edwin E. *Al*drin, and Michael *Col*lins, US astronauts, + -ITE[1].] *Min.* An orthorhombic titanate of iron and magnesium first found in lunar rocks.

armament /ˈɑːməm(ə)nt/ *n.* L17. [L *armamentum* (in cl.L only pl.), f. *armare* ARM *v.*[1]: see -MENT.] 1 A force (esp. naval) equipped for war. *arch.* L17. 2 *sing.* or in *pl.* Military weapons and equipment; (usu. *sing.*) the weapons mounted on a warship, aircraft, tank, etc. E18. 3 The process of equipping for war. E19.

1 TOLKIEN Ar-Pharazôn . . prepared then the greatest armament that the world had seen, and when all was ready he sounded his trumpets and set sail. 2 M. ARNOLD-FORSTER Throughout the rest of 1940 . . Britain imported the food and armaments she needed from the United States in her own ships. J. G. FARRELL Fleury looked to his armament, which . . included a sabre, . . a couple of wavy-bladed daggers from Malaya, and another, Indian, dagger. D. HOWARTH Going in to attack, the *Exeter* drew the fire of the *Graf Spee*'s main armament. 3 A. J. P. TAYLOR Armament on a large scale was begun after the general election of 1935.

armamentarium /ɑːməmɛnˈtɛːrɪəm/ *n.* Pl. **-ia** /-ɪə/. L19. [L = arsenal, armoury.] The medicines, equipment, and techniques available to a medical practitioner.

armature /ˈɑːmətjə/ *n.* LME. [Fr. f. L *armatura*, f. *armat-* pa. ppl stem of *armare* ARM *v.*[1]: see -URE.] 1 Arms, armour. *arch.* LME. †2 Armed troops. LME–M18. †3 The art of fighting with armour. LME–E18. 4 Defensive covering (or occas. offensive apparatus) of animals or plants. E18. 5a A keeper for a magnet. M18. b The iron core of an electromagnetic machine together with the windings which carry the induced electromotive force. Also, the moving part of a relay, electric bell, or similar device. M19. 6 An internal framework to support a sculpture during construction. E20.

1 *fig.*: SIR T. BROWNE Not the armour of Achilles, but the Armature of St. Paul.

armazine *n.* var. of ARMOZEEN.

armchair /ɑːmˈtʃɛː; *as adj.* ˈɑːmtʃɛː/ *n.* & *a.* Also **arm-chair**. L16. [f. ARM *n.*[1] + CHAIR *n.*[1]] A *n.* A chair with arms or side supports. L16.

B *attrib.* or as *adj.* Confined to an armchair; *fig.* theorizing rather than participating; lacking or not involving first-hand experience. E19.

E. A. POWELL After . . the arm-chair historians have settled down to the task of writing a connected account of the campaign. *Discovery* Armchair travel becomes easier and more pleasant every day. DAY LEWIS We don't want big talk from an armchair critic.

Armco /ˈɑːmkəʊ/ *n.* Pl. **-os**. E20. [Acronym, f. *A*merican *R*olling *M*ill *Co*mpany.] 1 (Proprietary name for) a very pure soft iron. E20. 2 (Proprietary name for) a motorway or motor-racing track crash barrier. M20.

arme blanche /arm blɑ̃ːʃ/ *n. phr.* Pl. **-s -s** (pronounced same). L19. [Fr., lit. 'white arm'.] A cavalry sword or lance; the cavalry.

armed /ɑːmd/ *a.*[1] ME. [f. ARM *v.*[1] + -ED[1].] 1 Equipped with weapons. ME. 2 *Her.* Of a charge: having teeth or talons of a specified tincture. LME.

1 *fig.*: F. RAPHAEL At last she felt armed against the empty bourgeois life of Cricklewood. E. HEATH We were armed with the addresses of youth hostels. **armed bullhead** the pogge *Agonus cataphractus*, a fish with a broad spined head and a tapering body covered with bony plates. **armed camp** a town, territory, etc., fully armed for war. *armed forces*: see FORCE *n.*[1] **armed neutrality**: with weapons kept available. *armed services*: see SERVICE *n.*[1] *armed to the teeth*: see TOOTH *n.*

armed /ɑːmd/ *a.*[2] E17. [f. ARM *n.*[1] + -ED[2].] Having upper limbs, or extensions resembling these. Chiefly as 2nd elem. of comb., as *long-armed*, *nine-armed*, *open-armed*, etc.

Armenian /ɑːˈmiːnɪən/ *a.* & *n.* M16. [f. L *Armenia* f. Gk f. OPers. *Armina*, *Arminiya* + -IAN.] A *adj.* Of or pertaining to Armenia, a country of SW Asia; of or pertaining to the people of this region, their language, or the ancient Christian community established there. M16.

Armenian bole: see BOLE *n.*[2] I.

B *n.* 1 A native or inhabitant of Armenia; a member of the Armenian church. M16. 2 The Indo-European language of Armenia. E18.

Armeniac *a.* = ARMENIAN *a.* LME. **Armenoid** /ˈɑːmənɔɪd/ *a.* of or pertaining to an eastern branch of the Alpine racial group L19.

armes blanches *n. phr.* pl. of ARME BLANCHE.

armet /ˈɑːmɪt/ *n.* E16. [Fr. (infl. by *armes*: see ARM *n.*[2]) f. Sp. *almete* or It. *elmetto* HELMET.] *Hist.* A round iron helmet with visor, beaver, and gorget.

armiger /ˈɑːmɪdʒə/ *n.* M16. [L = bearing arms, f. *arma* arms: see ARM *n.*[2], -GEROUS.] An esquire: orig., a person who attended a knight to bear his shield; now, a person entitled to heraldic arms.

arˈmigerous *a.* entitled to heraldic arms M18.

armil /ˈɑːmɪl/ *n.* L15. [Partly f. (O)Fr. *armille* f. L ARMILLA; partly a more recent adaptation of L.] 1 A bracelet. *rare.* L15. 2 A stole of cloth of gold put on the monarch at the coronation. L15. 3†a *armil sphere*, an armillary sphere. M16–E17. b = ARMILLA *n.* I. M19.

armilla /ɑːˈmɪlə/ *n.* Pl. **-llae** /-liː/, **-llas**. M17. [L, dim. of *armus* shoulder.] 1 An ancient astronomical instrument consisting of a graduated ring or hoop fixed in the plane of the equator (*equinoctial armilla*), sometimes crossed by another in the plane of the meridian (*solstitial armilla*). M17. 2 = ARMIL 2. L17. 3 Chiefly *Archaeol.* A bracelet, an armlet. E18.

armillary /ɑːˈmɪləri/ *a.* & *n.* M17. [mod.L *armillaris*, f. as prec.: see -ARY[2].] A *adj.* Of or pertaining to armillae; *armillary sphere*, a skeleton celestial globe, consisting of a number of graduated rings or hoops representing the principal celestial circles, which revolves on an axis within a wooden horizon. M17. B *n.* An armillary sphere. M19.

Arminian /ɑːˈmɪnɪən/ *a.* & *n.* E17. [f. *Arminius* Latinized form of *Harmensen* (see below) + -AN.] A *adj.* Of or pertaining to the Dutch Protestant theologian Arminius (Jakob Harmensen, 1560–1609) or his doctrines, which opposed those of Calvin, esp. regarding predestination. E17. B *n.* An adherent of the doctrines of Arminius. E17.

Arminianism *n.* (adherence to) the Arminian doctrines E17. **Arminianize** *v.* (*a*) *v.i.* teach Arminianism; (*b*) *v.t.* make Arminian: E17.

armipotent /ɑːˈmɪpət(ə)nt/ *a.* LME. [L *armipotent-*, *-ens*, f. *arma* arms + *potens* powerful.] Mighty as a warrior (orig. an epithet of Mars).

armistice /ˈɑːmɪstɪs/ *n.* E18. [Fr., or mod.L *armistitium*, f. *arma* arms + *-stitium* stoppage, after *solstitium* SOLSTICE.] A cessation from hostilities; a short truce.

Comb.: **Armistice Day** (an anniversary of) 11 November 1918, when an armistice was concluded which ended the war of 1914–18; (since 1945 superseded by Remembrance Sunday and Veterans' Day).

armoire /ɑːˈmwɑː/ *n.* L16. [Fr.: see AUMBRY.] A cupboard, a wardrobe; *esp.* one that is ornate or antique.

†**armoniac** *a.* & *n.* var. of AMMONIAC.

armor *n.* & *v.*, **-ed** *ppl a.*, **-er** *n.*, see ARMOUR etc.

armorial /ɑːˈmɔːrɪəl/ *a.* & *n.* L16. [f. ARMORY *n.*[1] + -AL[1].] A *adj.* 1 Pertaining to or of the nature of heraldic arms. L16. 2 Of porcelain etc.: bearing heraldic arms. E20. B *n.* A book of coats of arms. M18.

armorially *adv.* E17.

Armorican /ɑːˈmɒrɪk(ə)n/ *a.* & *n.* L15. [f. L *Armoricae* (Caesar) the north-western provinces of Gaul (mod. Brittany), f. Gaulish *are* in front of + *mor* sea, + -AN.] A *adj.* 1 Of or pertaining to Armorica (Brittany), its inhabitants, or their language (Breton). L15. 2 *Geol.* = HERCYNIAN *a.* 2b. E20. B *n.* A native or inhabitant of Armorica; the Breton language. *rare.* M17.

†**Armoric** *a.* & *n.* M17–M18.

armory /ˈɑːməri/ *n.*[1] LME. [OFr. *armoi(e)rie* (mod. *armoiries* pl.), f. *armoier* blazon, f. *arme* ARM *n.*[2]: see -Y[3]. Cf. ARMOURY.] 1 Heraldry. LME. 2 Armorial bearings. *arch.* L15.

armorist *n.* a person skilled in heraldry L16.

armory *n.*[2] see ARMOURY.

armour /ˈɑːmə/ *n.* & *v.* Also *** -or**. ME. [(O)Fr. *armure*, earlier *armëure*, f. L *armatura* ARMATURE: see -OUR.] A *n.* I Corresp. to ARM *n.*[2] I, II. 1 *Hist.* Defensive covering for the body worn when fighting; mail. ME. †2 *sing.* & in *pl.* The whole apparatus of war; arms. ME–E19. 3 A suit of mail. *arch.* LME. †4 The exercise of arms; fighting, warfare. LME–E17. 5 Protective or defensive covering of animals or plants. M17. 6

A diver's suit. E19. 7 Sheathing or cladding usu. of metal plates protecting a warship, tank, etc., from projectiles. M19. 8 Tanks and other armoured vehicles collectively. M20.

1 SHAKES. *Hen. V* The sun doth gild our armour; up, my lords! T. H. WHITE Sir Ector was dressed in 'sensible' leather clothes—it was not considered sporting to hunt in armour. *fig.*: MILTON And also arme With spiritual Armour. BYRON Suspicion is a heavy armour. *hog in armour*: see HOG *n.* **in armour** *fig.* (*arch. slang*) wearing a condom. *shining armour*: see SHINING *a.* 2 R. HOLINSHED The people . . were up in armour against the King. 3 CAXTON He had . . armours ynowe for to garnysshe with seuen thousand men. 5 D. MORRIS In contrast to all other armadillos . . the body armour is connected to the animal's back only down the mid-line. 7 C. RYAN Gliders were without protective armour, except in the cockpits. R. V. JONES Such charges could be used in bombs against battleships, where they would easily penetrate the deck armour. 8 M. RICHLER In response to an Egyptian attack, Israeli armour had gone into action.

II Corresp. to ARM *n.*[2] III. 9 Blazonry, heraldic arms. *obs.* exc. in *coat armour* s.v. COAT *n.* LME.

Comb.: **armour-bearer** *Hist.* a person who carried a warrior's armour; a squire; **armour-clad** *a.* provided with armour, *esp.* armour-plated; **armour-piercing** *a.* (of a shell etc.) designed to penetrate the armour of a warship, tank, etc., before exploding; **armour-plate** (a plate of) the protective metal sheathing of a warship, tank, etc.; **armour-plated** *a.* provided with armour-plate; **armour-plating** (the material of) armour-plate.

B *v.t.* Put armour on; furnish with protective or defensive covering. Freq. in *pass.* LME.

R. GRAVES In battle the nobler men wear leather coats armoured in front with overlapping plates. *fig.*: N. HAMPSON There are no killers here, whom crusted pride Armours against their own humanity.

armouring *n.* an external covering, usu. of steel wire, to protect electric cables etc. E20. **armourless** *a.* without armour, defenceless LME.

armoured /ˈɑːməd/ *ppl a.* Also ***-ored**. E17. [f. ARMOUR *v.* + -ED[1].] 1 Clad in armour; having a natural protective or defensive covering. E17. 2 Of a ship, vehicle, cable, etc.: furnished with armour-plate, armouring, or other protective covering. M19. 3 Of glass: toughened. M20. 4 Of a military force: equipped with tanks and other armoured vehicles. Of warfare: fought with tanks etc. M20.

2 **armoured car, train**: protected with armour-plate and usu. equipped with guns.

armourer /ˈɑːmərə/ *n.* Also ***-orer**. ME. [AN *armurer*, (O)Fr. *armurier*, f. as ARMOUR *n.*: see -ER[2].] 1 A maker or repairer of armour or weapons. ME. 2 A person who assisted warriors in putting on their armour. *obs.* exc. *Hist.* LME. 3 An official who has charge of the arms of a warship, regiment, etc. M18.

¶ First recorded as a surname.

armoury /ˈɑːməri/ *n.* Also ***-ory**. ME. [OFr. *armoi(e)rie* ARMORY *n.*[1], assim. to ARMOUR.] 1 Arms or armour collectively (*arch.*); an array of weapons or (*fig.*) resources etc. ME. 2 A place where arms and armour are kept or (chiefly *US*) made; an arsenal; *N. Amer.* a drill hall. LME.

1 WORDSWORTH In our halls is hung Armoury of the invincible Knights of old. *fig.*: J. WAIN It was only the presence of the two visitors . . that stopped her from setting about him with the full armoury of feminine weapons. C. SAGAN I was outfitted under my raincoat with a full armory of shirt, tie, and jacket. 2 J. CHEEVER Touch a suit of chain mail in the armory and your hand comes away black with rust. *fig.*: COLERIDGE Language is the armoury of the human mind; it . . contains the trophies of its past and the weapons of its future conquests.

armozeen /ɑːməˈziːn/ *n.* Also **armazine** & other vars. E16. [Fr. *armoisin*, (16) *tafetas armoisy*, *armezin*, f. It. *ermesino* f. Egyptian Arab. *'irmiz*, Arab. *ḳirmiz* KERMES.] Orig. †*armozeen taffeta*. A heavy plain silk, usu. black, used esp. for clerical gowns and for mourning.

armure /ˈɑːmjʊə/ *n.* L19. [Fr.] A fabric made of wool, silk, or both, with a twilled or ribbed surface.

army /ˈɑːmi/ *n.* In sense 3 also **A-**. LME. [(O)Fr. *armée* f. Proto-Romance *armata* use as n. of fem. pa. pple of L *armare* ARM *v.*[1]: see -Y[5].] I *lit.* †1 An armed expedition by sea or land. LME–E16. 2 An armed force whether by land or sea; a host. Without qualification, now *spec.* a force equipped to fight on land; an organized body of soldiers. LME. 3 *The* entire body of land forces of a country; *the* military service or profession. M17.

1 LD BERNERS They gette the duke of Burgoyne in great desyre to make an armye into Englande. 2 AV *S. of S.* 6:10 Terrible as an armie with banners. G. B. SHAW Whenever he won an election his opponent raised an army and attempted a revolution. A. J. P. TAYLOR The Russians had just destroyed a German army at Stalingrad. *army of* OCCUPATION. *army of reserve*: see RESERVE *n.* *land army*: see LAND *n.*[1] *private army*: see PRIVATE *a.* *Red Army*: see RED *a.* *regular army*: see REGULAR *a.* *standing army*: see STANDING *a.* *Territorial Army*: see TERRITORIAL *a.* *White Army*: see WHITE *a.* 3 SCOTT FITZGERALD A young major just out of the army and covered over with medals he got in the war. E. WAUGH Hooper had no illusions about the Army . . He had come to it reluctantly, under compulsion. . . He accepted it, he said, 'like the measles'.

II *fig.* & *transf.* 4 A large number, a multitude; an array. L15. 5 A body of people organized for a cause. M16.

4 D. LIVINGSTONE An army of locusts. E. BOWEN An army of evening shoes was drawn up under the bureau. E. F. SCHUMACHER The modern man of action may surround himself by ever-growing armies of forecasters. 5 ADDISON Latimer, one of the glorious Army of Martyrs. *Church Army*: see CHURCH *n.* *Land Army*: see LAND *n.*[1] *Salvation Army*: see SALVATION.

Comb.: **army ant** = DRIVER 6; **army corps** a main subdivision of an army in the field; **Army List** an official list of commissioned officers in the British army; **army worm** any of various moth or fly larvae occurring in destructive swarms.

arnatta, -atto, *ns.* vars. of ANNATTO.

Arnaut /ɑːˈnaʊt/ *n.* E18. [Turk.] An Albanian, *spec.* one serving in the Ottoman army.

arnica /ˈɑːnɪkə/ *n.* M18. [mod.L, of uncertain origin.] Any plant of the genus *Arnica*, of the composite family; *esp.* mountain tobacco, *A. montana*, native to central Europe. Also, a medicinal tincture prepared from this plant, and used esp. for bruises.

Arnoldian /ɑːˈnəʊldɪən/ *a.* L19. [f. *Arnold* (see below) + -IAN.] Pertaining to or characteristic of either Thomas Arnold (1795–1842), Headmaster of Rugby School, or his son Matthew Arnold (1822–88), poet and critic.

ˈ**Arnoldism** *n.* doctrine, theory or practice formed after the precepts and example of either Thomas or Matthew Arnold M19.

Arnoldist /ˈɑːn(ə)ldɪst/ *n.* M17. [f. *Arnold* (see below) + -IST.] *Eccl. Hist.* A follower of Arnold (or Arnaldus) of Brescia, a religious reformer in the 12th cent.

arnotto *n.* var. of ANNATTO.

aroar /əˈrɔː/ *adv.* & *pred. a.* *arch.* LME. [A *prep.*[1] 6 + ROAR *n.*[1]] In a roar, roaring.

aroid /ˈɛːrɔɪd/ *n.* & *a.* L19. [f. ARUM *n.* + -OID.] *Bot.* (A plant) belonging to the family Araceae, exemplified by the arums.

aroint /əˈrɔɪnt/ *v.t.* *arch.* Also **-oynt**. E17. [Origin unkn.] 1 *aroint thee!* avaunt! begone! E17. 2 Drive away with an execration. M19.

1 SHAKES. *Macb.* 'Aroint thee, witch!' the rump-fed ronyon cries. 2 BROWNING That Humbug, whom thy soul aroints.

¶ First recorded in Shakes.

arolla /əˈrɒlə/ *n.* L19. [Swiss Fr. *arol(l)e*.] The Swiss stone pine, *Pinus cembra*. Also *arolla pine*.

aroma /əˈrəʊmə/ *n.* Pl. **-mas**, (*rare*) **-mata** /-mətə/. Orig. †**-mat**. ME. [L *aroma*, *-mat-* f. Gk *arōma* spice; earlier form f. OFr. *aromat* (mod. *-ate*) f. L pl. *aromata*.] †1 A fragrant plant, spice. Usu. in *pl.* ME–M18. 2 The distinctive fragrance of a spice, plant, etc., an agreeable odour. E19. 3 A subtle pervasive quality or charm. M19.

Comb.: **aromatherapeutic** *a.* of or pertaining to aromatherapy; **aromatherapist** an advocate or promoter of aromatherapy; **aromatherapy** the use of essential oils and other plant extracts to promote personal health and beauty.

aromal *a.* M19.

aromatic /arəˈmatɪk/ *a.* & *n.* LME. [(O)Fr. *aromatique* f. late L *aromaticus* f. Gk *arōmatikos*: see prec., -IC.] A *adj.* 1 Fragrant, pungent, spicy, sweet-smelling. LME. 2 *Chem.* (Of a compound) possessing one or more planar conjugated rings of the form typified by the benzene molecule; designating or pertaining to such a compound. M19. B *n.* 1 A substance or plant emitting a spicy odour; a fragrant drug. LME. 2 *Chem.* An aromatic compound. E20.

†**aromatical** *a.* = AROMATIC *a.* 1 LME–E19. **aromatically** *adv.* with aromatic odour or taste; spicily: E17. **aromaticity** /-ˈtɪsɪti/ *n.* (*Chem.*) aromatic character or condition M20. **aromaticness** *n.* the quality of being aromatic LME.

aromatize /əˈrəʊmətʌɪz/ *v.t.* Also **-ise**. LME. [(O)Fr. *aromatiser* f. late L *aromatizare* f. Gk *arōmatizein* to spice: see AROMA, -IZE.] 1 Render aromatic or fragrant; flavour or season with spice. LME. 2 *Chem.* Make aromatic (AROMATIC *a.* 2). M20.

aromatiˈzation *n.* (*a*) the action or process of rendering aromatic; *Chem.* conversion into an aromatic compound; (*b*) aromatic flavouring: E17. **aromatizer** *n.* L17.

†**aron** *n.* see ARUM.

around /əˈraʊnd/ *adv.* & *prep.* ME. [Prob. f. A *prep.*[1] 1 + ROUND *n.*[1]: cf. OFr. *a la reond* in the round, Fr. *en rond* in a circle, *au rond de* round about (16).] A *adv.* 1 In circumference; in a circle; so as to surround. ME. 2 Along the periphery, on or along the circuit or surface, (of something round). ME. 3 On every side; in every direction or in various directions from a fixed point. E18. 4 Here and there; at, in, or to various places; all about; at random; with no definite direction or aim. L18. 5 With more or less circular motion; with return to the starting point after such motion; with rotation; with change to the opposite position; with regard to relative position; to a particular place, point, or state. E19. 6 To all points of a circumference or within a given area; to all members of a company etc. L19. 7 Near at hand; somewhere in the vicinity. *colloq.* L19.

1 JOYCE The players closed around, flushed and muddy. W. STEVENS A blue pigeon it is, that circles the blue sky, . . around and round and round. 2 DRYDEN All their heads around With chaplets green of cerrial-oak were crowned. 3 POPE While op'ning blooms diffuse their sweets around. G. B. SHAW Every stick and stone for miles around falling and crumbling. 4 DAY LEWIS What shall I do this afternoon?—attach myself, probably, to Keyes and follow him around in a daze of pure satisfaction. J. BOWEN If you want to do exercises, then do them. Don't hang around hinting. C. HAMPTON I haven't been sitting around brooding about it for days. T. STOPPARD He has been looking around for a place to put his pants. *go around, play around, sleep around*, etc. **have been around** *colloq.* have gained worldly experience. 5 SCOTT FITZGERALD Turning me around by one arm. DYLAN THOMAS The weather turned around. J. CHEEVER She waited in the rain for him to bring their car around. S. HILL He could not reach around to find his water bottle. S. GRAY I shall find out later which way around it is. *get around (to)*. 6 *know one's way around*: see WAY *n.* 7 G. VIDAL Well, I'll see you around, Cy. J. F. KENNEDY These very qualities . . have in times of peace caused him to be considered 'dangerous', and a little uncomfortable to have around. J. CHEEVER When I got downstairs, Lawrence wasn't around, but the others were all ready for cocktails. *stick around*: see STICK *v.*[1]

B *prep.* 1 On or along the circuit or periphery of; at points on the circumference of; so as to make a circuit of. LME. 2 On all sides of; in all or various directions from or with regard to; so as to centre or have a basis in. M17. 3 So as to surround; enveloping. E19. 4 Here and there in or near; to various places in; from one member of (a company) to another; all about. E19. 5 So as to double or pass in a curved course; having passed in a curved course; in a position that would result from passing in a curved course. Chiefly *N. Amer.* M19. 6 In the vicinity of; near; close to. M19. 7 At approximately, at about. Chiefly *N. Amer.* L19.

1 MILTON No war or battle's sound Was heard the world around. JOYCE Lifted from the dish the heavy cover pearled around the edge with glistening drops. SCOTT FITZGERALD Her own party . . were spread around a table on the other side of the garden. W. STEVENS Perhaps The truth depends on a walk around

a lake. S. GRAY There are a few hard-backed chairs around the walls. 2 J. TYNDALL The air around and above us was . . clear. SCOTT FITZGERALD I saw Jordan Baker and talked over and around what had happened to us together. K. AMIS There's a lot of stuff in and around Lisbon we've still got to see. B. LOVELL Planetary systems around stars other than the Sun. 3 E. O'NEILL Tenderly solicitous now, puts an arm around her. A. BURGESS Fussing as if she thought he ought to have rugs around him and his feet in a footcosy. W. TREVOR His short pale hair was plastered around his head. 4 JOYCE He looked around the little class of students. H. MACLENNAN He had been walking around Halifax all day. 5 P. SHAFFER I know it's just around the corner, that's not the point. ANNE STEVENSON You watch a workman wheel his bicycle around a stile. *get around.* 6 B. SCHULBERG That's why I took this job, so I can be around writers. 7 W. G. McADOO The convention adjourned around four o'clock. E. BOWEN Last May, around that time of the funeral.

arouse /ə'raʊz/ *v.* L16. [f. A-[11] + ROUSE *v.*[1], after *rise, arise*, etc.] 1 *v.t.* Raise or stir up (a person or animal) from sleep or inactivity; excite sexually. L16. 2 *v.t.* Stir up into activity (principles of action, emotions, etc.); bring into existence. E18. 3 *v.i.* Wake up. E19.

1 D. RUNYON The noise of John Wangle's yelling . . arouses many of the neighbors. R. ELLISON Such an effective piece of eloquence . . you aroused them so quickly to action. P. H. JOHNSON She was still sleeping, and now she looked so serene, so peaceful, that I hated to arouse her. 2 G. GREENE I wondered whether Miss Smythe was so convenient a sister as Henry was a husband, and all my latent snobbery was aroused by the name—that y, the final e. T. CAPOTE A case like the Clutter case, crimes of that magnitude, arouse the interest of lawmen everywhere. A. STORR Everyone knows that anger, once thoroughly aroused, takes time to subside. 3 J. THURBER Always a deep sleeper, slow to arouse.

arousable *a.* L19. **arousal** *n.* the action of arousing or fact of being aroused M19. **arouser** *n.* M19.

arow /ə'rəʊ/ *adv.* & *pred. a.* ME. [f. A *prep.*[1] 1 + ROW *n.*[1]] 1 In a row, rank, or line. ME. †2 In succession. ME–L16.

aroynt *v.* var. of AROINT.

arpeggio /ɑː'pɛdʒɪəʊ/ *n.* Pl. **-os.** E18. [It., f. *arpeggiare* play on the harp, f. *arpa* HARP *n.*] *Mus.* The sounding of the notes of a chord in (usu. rapid upward) succession, not simultaneously; a chord so sounded.

arpeggiated *a.* played or sung in arpeggio E20. **arpeggi'ation** *n.* playing or singing in arpeggio L19.

arpeggione /ɑːpɛdʒɪ'əʊni, *foreign* arpe'dʒoːne/ *n.* L19. [G, f. as prec.] An early 19th-cent. bowed musical instrument, resembling a guitar.

arpent /'ɑːp(ə)nt; *foreign* arpɑ̃ (*pl. same*)/ *n. obs.* exc. *Hist.* Also **arpen** /-p(ə)n; *foreign* -pɑ̃ (*pl. same*)/. M16. [(O)Fr.] An old French measure of land, of varying amount but freq. equal to about two-fifths of a hectare (approx. one acre).

¶Used in parts of Canada and other areas of French influence, as well as in France itself.

arquebus *n.* var. of HARQUEBUS.

arra *n.* var. of ARRHA.

arrack /'arək/ *n.* Also **arak.** E17. [Arab. *'arak* sweat, esp. in *'arak at-tamr* fermented and distilled juice of dates. Aphet. to RACK *n.*[7]] In Eastern countries: an alcoholic spirit of local manufacture, esp. distilled from the sap of the coco palm or from rice.

†**Arragonese** *a.* & *n.*, †**arragonite** *n.* vars. of ARAGONESE, ARAGONITE.

arrah /'arə/ *int. Anglo-Ir.* L17. [Ir. *ara, arú.*] Expr. emotion or excitement.

arraign /ə'reɪn/ *v.*[1] & *n.* LME. [AN *arainer, areiner*, OFr. *araisnier, areisnier*, ult. f. L *ad* AR- + *ratio(n-)* account, REASON *n.*[1]] A *v.t.* 1 Call on (a person) to answer a criminal charge before a court; call to account, indict, accuse. LME. 2 Find fault with, censure, call in question (an action, statement, etc.). L17.

1 BARONESS ORCZY He was arraigned for treason against the nation, and sent to the guillotine. A. MILLER As though arraigning the entire clock industry, she adds: 'I've got six or eight clocks in this house, and none of them work'. 2 GIBBON He boldly arraigned the abuses of public and private life.

B *n.* = ARRAIGNMENT. M17.

arraigner *n.* E19. **arraignment** *n.* the act of arraigning or fact of being arraigned; indictment, accusation, censure: LME.

†**arraign** *v.*[2] LME–E19. [AN *arraigner, arainer*, alt. of *aramer* = OFr. *arami(e)r* f. med.L *arramire* guarantee, decide, f. *ad* AR- + Frank. *hramjan* appoint a place or time.] *Law.* Appeal to, claim, demand, (an assize).

arrand *n.* var. of ARAIN.

arrange /ə'reɪndʒ/ *v.* LME. [OFr. *arangier, arengier* (mod. *arranger*), f. A-[5] + *rangier* RANGE *v.*[1]] I *v.t.* 1 Draw up in ranks or in lines of battle. *obs.* exc. as passing into sense 2. LME. 2 Put into proper or requisite order; dispose; adjust. M18. 3 Plan or settle beforehand the details of (something to be done); give instructions for, cause to take place. L18. 4 *Mus.* Adapt (a composition) for instruments or voices other than those for which it was written. E19. 5 Settle (a dispute, claim, etc.). M19. 6 Adapt (a play etc.) for performance, esp. for broadcasting. M20.

1 LD BERNERS There he araynged his men in the stretes. 2 G. B. SHAW Each atom . . arranging itself by attraction and repulsion in orderly crystalline structure. J. C. POWYS Crummie had . . taken to helping old Mrs. Robinson arrange the flowers for the church altar. C. ISHERWOOD A plateful of jam tarts arranged in the shape of a star. S. BELLOW The room where the old woman lay, her white hair arranged in a fringe that nearly met her brow. A. WILSON He had read . . that the process of arranging one's thoughts in good order was often helped by an equally careful ordering of external objects. E. J. HOWARD He . . took off his scarf and arranged it . . round her neck. *Encycl. Brit.* Mendeleyev arranged all the known elements according to their atomic weights on what he called a periodic table. M. KEANE She seemed less well arranged than usual—her hair not so crisply set, her jersey and cardigan not twins. 3 LD MACAULAY The details of a butchery were frequently discussed, if not definitely arranged. T. HARDY They had arranged that their meeting should be at the holm-tree. SCOTT FITZGERALD Why didn't he ask you to arrange a meeting? **arranged marriage** a marriage planned and agreed by the families or guardians of the couple concerned, who have little or no say in the matter themselves. 5 G. B. SHAW I have arranged that little difficulty with Trench. It was only a piece of mischief made by Lickcheese.

II *v.i.* 7 Get into order; fall into place. *rare.* E16. 8 Come to an agreement or understanding (*with* a person, *about* something); settle or determine matters, take steps, make plans, (*about, for, to do*). L18.

8 BURKE We cannot arrange with our enemy in the present conjuncture. N. HAWTHORNE To arrange about my passport. J. B. PRIESTLEY Next morning I was up in good time, for I had arranged to go round the Fish Market. E. O'NEILL I shall arrange for places in the stage. B. ENGLAND If you find your duties too arduous . . I can arrange to have you relieved of them.

¶Rare bef. L18; not in AV, Shakes., Milton's poetry, or Pope.

arrangeable *a.* M19. **arranger** *n.* a person who arranges something (esp. music) L18.

arrangement /ə'reɪndʒm(ə)nt/ *n.* L17. [f. prec. + -MENT.] 1 The action of arranging; the fact of being arranged. L17. 2 A manner of being arranged; an orderly disposition. M18. 3 A disposition or preparation for a future event (freq. in *pl.*); something planned or agreed; a settlement or agreement between parties. M18. 4 A number of objects arranged or combined in a particular way. E19. 5 A setting of a piece of music for instruments or voices other than those for which it was originally written; a piece so arranged. M19.

2 C. DARWIN I believe that the arrangement of the groups within each class . . must be strictly genealogical. E. O'NEILL Her general appearance, the arrangement of her hair and clothes, has the disheveled touch of the fugitive. 3 BURKE Arrangements with the Rajah . . for the better government and management of his Zemindary. LD MACAULAY It was impossible to make an arrangement that would please everybody. G. STEIN Mrs. Kreder and Mrs. Haydon . . made all the arrangements for the wedding. A. KOESTLER His staying in the flat was a reasonable and practical arrangement. 4 B. PYM An expensive florist's arrangement of white chrysanthemums had been placed at the side of the altar.

arrant /'ar(ə)nt/ *a.* LME. [Var. of ERRANT *a.* Sense 2 developed f. its use to designate an outlawed, roving thief.] †1 = ERRANT *a.* 1. LME–M17. 2 Of a thief, wrongdoer, etc., or w. gen. terms of opprobrium: openly criminal, professed; public, notorious; downright, unmitigated. (Earlier as ERRANT *a.* 2a.) M16. b Of an (undesirable) action, opinion, quality, etc.: unmitigated, utter, blatant. M17. 3 (Without opprobrious force.) Thorough, complete; genuine, inveterate. L16. †4 Thoroughly bad, wicked; good-for-nothing. L16–M18.

2 SWIFT Every servant an arrant thief as to victuals and drink. H. FIELDING The arrantest villain that ever walked upon two legs. W. HOWITT The inhabitants of solitary houses are often most arrant cowards. b R. BENTLEY They cover the most arrant Atheism under the mask and shadow of a Deity. W. GERHARDIE The guest, a Russian general, was talking arrant nonsense. 3 G. B. SHAW Nobody but an arrant cockney would dream of calling it a brogue now.

arrantly *adv.* L16.

arras /'arəs/ *n.* LME. [*Arras*, a town in Artois, NE France, famous for the fabric.] 1 A rich tapestry fabric, in which figures and scenes are woven in colours. Freq. *attrib.* LME. 2 *Hist.* A screen of this hung round the walls of a room. L16.

arrased /'arəst/ *a.* hung or covered with arras E17.

array /ə'reɪ/ *n.* ME. [AN *arai* f. OFr. *arei* (mod. *arroi*), f. as next.] 1 A state of special preparedness esp. for war, festivities, etc.; preparation. Now *poet.* ME. 2 Arrangement in line or ranks, esp. martial order; orderly disposition. LME. 3 *Hist.* The mustering of an armed force; the arming of a militia. LME. 4 A military force, an armed host; *esp.* (*Hist.*) the militia of a county etc. LME. 5 Attire, dress; (an) outfit. Now *poet.* LME. †6 Plight, condition; state of affairs. LME–M16. 7 *Law.* The order of empanelling a jury; the panel itself. L16. 8 An imposing or well-ordered series of persons or things; an assemblage, an arrangement. E19. b *Math.* A matrix or other ordered arrangement of quantities. M19. c *Computing.* A set of memory locations or data items of which each member is identified by a common identifier together with one or more subscripts. M20.

1 POPE The pomp, the pageantry, the proud array. 2 R. HOLINSHED They found them out of araie in following the chase. K. AMIS What howls of dismay From his fans in their dense array. *fig.*: AV *Job* 6:4 The terrors of God doe set themselues in aray against mee. 3 **Commission of Array** a body of officials responsible for raising a militia. 4 LD MACAULAY The whole array of the city of London was under arms. 5 SHAKES. *Tam. Shr.* We will have rings and things, and fine array. T. H. WHITE A Man or a Power set upon Lancelot . . and clothed him in another array which was full of knots. 8 *Nature* An array of particle detectors laid out in a suitable pattern. W. TREVOR He drew back his lips, displaying a small array of teeth. F. WELDON A really magnificent show of sports trophies to join her own array of cups and shields. D. HALBERSTAM He filled his bureau with a stunning array of the best reporters in America.

arrayal *n.* the process of arraying, muster; array: E19.

array /ə'reɪ/ *v.t.* ME. [AN *araier*, OFr. *areer*, ult. f. L *ad* AR- + a Gmc base meaning 'prepare' (cf. READY *v.*).] 1 Set or place in order of readiness (orig. esp. for battle); marshal, dispose, arrange. ME. †2 Make ready, prepare; equip, fit out. ME–M16. 3 Attire, dress, esp. with display; *fig.* adorn, embellish, furnish (*with*). LME. †4 Discomfit, thrash; afflict; disfigure, dirty. *iron.* LME–L16. 5 *Law.* Empanel (a jury). L16.

1 LD MACAULAY A force of thirteen thousand fighting men were arrayed in Hyde Park. J. LONDON He saw arrayed around his consciousness endless pictures from his life. A. WILSON Three sorts of ink—blue, red and green—were carefully arrayed before her. 3 K. GRAHAME Mr. Toad, arrayed in goggles, cap, gaiters, and enormous overcoat, came swaggering down the steps. W. S. MAUGHAM I was taking them to a very smart restaurant and expected to

find Isabel arrayed for the occasion. W. S. CHURCHILL Mary had arrayed herself superbly for the final scene. *fig.*: EARL RIVERS Arraye you withe iustice. R. ELLISON A panel arrayed with coils and dials.

arrayer *n.* a person who arrays; *esp.* (*Hist.*) a person who musters armed men: LME. **arrayment** *n.* (*a*) dress, accoutrement; an outfit; (*b*) the act of arraying; the state of being arrayed: LME.

arrear /əˈrɪə/ *n.* ME. [f. the adv.] **I** *in arrear(s)*. †**1** In the past. Only in ME. **2** Behind in time; behind in the discharge of duties or liabilities; *esp.* behindhand in payment. E17. †**3** Behind in position. Only in M17. **4** Behind as to state or condition. (Foll. by *of*.) M19.

2 STEELE The World is in Arrear to your Virtue. A. KNOX I am two or three letters in arrear to different persons. S. RAVEN For years we've had a system whereby we pay tradesmen a term in arrears. A. BRINK Others . . had been evicted from their homes . . because they'd fallen in arrears with the rent. 4 R. FORD The arts of medicine and surgery are somewhat in arrear in Spain.

II Without *in*. **5** Something in which one has fallen behind; something remaining to be done; a duty or liability undischarged; an outstanding debt. Now usu. in *pl.* LME. **6** The rear, esp. of a train or procession. Long *arch.* E17. †**7** A portion held back; something held in reserve. M17–M18.

5 BURKE Having so faithfully and so fully acquitted towards me whatever arrear of debt was left undischarged. F. MARRYAT To obtain my arrears of pay, and some prize-money which I find due. DICKENS To you . . I owe a long arrear of thanks. J. BUCHAN If I were you I would go to bed, for you must have considerable arrears of sleep to overtake. E. F. BENSON The arrears of general events were soon cleared off, . . and the talk became more intimate.

†**arrear** *adv.* ME–E19. [OFr. *ar(i)ere* (mod. *arrière*) f. med.L *adretro*, f. L *ad* AR- + *retro* backward, behind. Cf. AREAR.] In or to the rear; behind; overdue.

arrear-band: see ARRIÈRE-BAN. *arrear-guard*: see ARRIÈRE-GUARD.

arrearage /əˈrɪərɪdʒ/ *n.* ME. [OFr. *arerage* (mod. *arrérage*), f. *arere*: see prec., -AGE.] **1** = ARREAR *n.* 5. Now usu. in *pl.* Now *US.* ME. †**2** The state or condition of being in arrears in payment; indebtedness, debt. ME–L17. **3** *gen.* The state or condition of being behind; backwardness. L16.

2 in arrearages in arrears in payment.

†**arrear-guard** *n.* var. of ARRIÈRE-GUARD.

arrect /əˈrɛkt/ *ppl a. arch.* M17. [L *arrectus* pa. pple of *arrigere* raise up, f. *ad* AR- + *regere* straighten.] Upright, pricked up (as of the ears of an animal); *fig.* attentive, alert.

arrent /əˈrɛnt/ *v.t.* Now *arch.* & *Hist.* LME. [OFr. *arentir*, f. *à* A-[5] + *rente* RENT *n.*[1], or Fr. *arrenter*.] Let out or farm at a rent; *spec.* allow the enclosure of (forest land) for a yearly rent.

arren'tation *n.* the action or the privilege of arrenting land E16.

arrest /əˈrɛst/ *n.* LME. [OFr. *areste* stoppage, and *arest* (mod. *arrêt*) act of arresting, f. as next.] †**1** The act of standing still or stopping in one's course; halt; delay. LME–L16. **2** The act of stopping something; stoppage; check. LME. **b** *Med.* A sudden, sometimes temporary, cessation of function of an organ or system, esp. (more fully *cardiac arrest*) the heart. L19. **3** The act of catching and holding, seizure, (*lit.* & *fig.*); legal apprehension. LME. **4** The state of having been arrested; custody, imprisonment, detention. LME. †**5** An abode. LME–L15. †**6** A resting-place for the butt of a lance on a piece of armour. LME–L15. †**7** = ARRÊT. E16–E18.

2 BACON Some Checke or Arrest in their Fortunes. J. H. BURN Arrest of the patient's respiration might sometimes assist the surgeon. **arrest of judgement** *Law* a stay of proceedings after a verdict, on the ground of error. 3 C. LAMB The first arrests of sleep. GEO. ELIOT This strong arrest of his attention made him cease singing. *citizen's arrest*: see CITIZEN *n. false arrest*: see FALSE *a.* **under arrest** legally arrested. 4 BYRON The Forty hath decreed a month's arrest. *house arrest*: see HOUSE *n.*[1] **under** (†**an**) **arrest** under legal restraint.

arrest /əˈrɛst/ *v.* LME. [OFr. *arester* (mod. *arrêter*), ult. f. L *ad* AR- + *restare* stop behind (REST *v.*[3]).] **I** *v.i.* †**1** Stop, stay, remain, rest. LME–E17.

1 J. GOWER A wilde beast, In whom no reson might areste. CAXTON Without arestyng for to helpe them. DONNE We must arrest awhile vpon the nature, and degrees, and effects of charity.

II *v.t.* **2** Stop; detain; retard. (Cf. sense 6.) LME. **3** Apprehend (a person, a ship) by legal authority. LME. **b** Seize (property) by legal warrant. Now only *Sc.* & *Admiralty Law.* L15. †**c** *fig.* Take as security. *rare* (Shakes.) L16–E17. **4** *gen.* Catch, lay hold on. *obs.* exc. as *fig.* use of sense 3. L15. †**5** Fix, engage; keep (one's mind, oneself) on a subject. L15–M17. **6** Catch and fix (one of the senses, the attention, mind, etc.); catch and fix the attention of. (Passing into sense 2.) E19.

2 DRYDEN My Dogs with better speed Arrest her flight. GIBBON In the pursuit of greatness he was never arrested by the scruples of justice. GEO. ELIOT Her tears were arrested. J. GALSWORTHY He found Irene seated at the piano with her hands arrested on the keys. D. L. SAYERS Peter made a movement to go back, but a strong conviction that he could only make matters worse for her arrested him. S. SPENDER A famous educationist whose interest in education seemed to stop or be arrested when it came to governing his own college. K. WATERHOUSE I caught his eye and waved to him, a half-wave arrested before it began. H. KISSINGER The Soviet advance was first arrested and finally reversed. **arrest judgement** *Law* stay proceedings after a verdict, on the ground of error. 3 D. LODGE Sixteen people . . were arrested . . for stealing used bricks from the demolition site. **b** D. H. LAWRENCE The Unholy Inquisition has arrested all my pictures. 4 SPENSER Whenas Morpheus had with leaden mace Arrested all that courtly company. J. RUSKIN We cannot arrest sunsets nor carve mountains. 5 JER. TAYLOR We may arrest our thoughts upon the divine mercies. 6 BYRON The gleaming turret . . and yon solitary palm arrest the eye. T. HARDY He was about to leave his hole of espial . . when he was arrested by the conversation. E. WHARTON Miss Bart was a figure to arrest even the suburban traveller rushing to his last train. A. J. CRONIN His gaze instantly arrested by the smudged grey headlines. H. READ A work of art must be dynamic—it must arrest the attention of the onlooker, move him, infect him.

arrestable *a.* (*a*) liable to be arrested; (*b*) (of an offence etc.) such that the offender may be arrested without warrant: M16. **arre'station** *n.* the action of arresting, an arrest L18. **arre'stee** *n.* (*a*) *Sc. Law* the person in whose hands another's earnings or other assets are attached; (*b*) a person being legally arrested: M18. **arrester** *n.* (*a*) a person who arrests someone or something; (*b*) something which arrests; *esp.* a device for retarding an aircraft by a hook and cable on landing, esp. on an aircraft carrier: LME. **arrestingly** *adv.* in a manner that arrests the attention, strikingly L19. **arrestive** *a.* tending to arrest the attention etc., striking M19. **arrestor** *n.* = ARRESTER LME.

arrestment /əˈrɛs(t)m(ə)nt/ *n.* LME. [OFr. *arestement* or med.L *arrestamentum*: see prec., -MENT.] **1** The action of apprehending a person by legal authority; arrest. Chiefly *Sc.* LME. **2** A seizure of property by legal authority; *Sc. Law* attachment of earnings or other assets held by a third party. M16. **3** The action or result of stopping or checking. M19.

arrêt /arɛ (*pl. same*), əˈrɛt/ *n.* M17. [Fr.: see ARREST *n.*] An authoritative sentence or decision, *spec.* of the monarch (*Hist.*) or parliament of France.

Arretine /ˈarətʌɪn/ *a.* Also **Aret-**. L18. [L *Ar(r)etinus*, f. *Ar(r)etium*: see below, -INE[1].] Of or pertaining to Arretium (mod. Arezzo), an ancient city in central Italy; *spec.* designating fine red pottery made at Arretium and elsewhere from *c* 100 BC until the late 1st cent. AD.

arrha /ˈarə/ *n.* Also **arra**. Pl. **arr(h)ae** /ˈariː/. L16. [L *arr(h)a* (Gellius) abbrev. of *arr(h)abo* (Plautus) f. Gk *arrabōn* earnest-money. Cf. ARLES.] Chiefly *Rom.* & *Sc. Law.* Money given to bind a bargain, earnest-money.

arrhenotoky /arɪˈnɒtəki, ˌarənəˈtəʊki/ *n.* L19. [f. Gk *arrenotokos* bearing male children + -Y[3].] *Zool.* Parthenogenesis in which unfertilized eggs give rise to males. Cf. THELYTOKY.

arrhenotokous *a.* L19.

arrhythmia /əˈrɪðmɪə/ *n.* L19. [Gk *arruthmia* lack of rhythm: see A-[10], RHYTHM, -IA[1].] *Med.* Deviation from the normal rhythm of the heart.

arrhythmic /əˈrɪðmɪk/ *a.* Also **arh-**. M19. [f. A-[10] + RHYTHMIC, after Gk: see prec.] Not rhythmic; without rhythm or regularity.

¶The spelling *arrh-* predominates in *Med.*; *arh-* is used more frequently in *Mus.* & *Pros.*

arrhythmical *a.* L19. **arrhythmically** *adv.* L19.

arrhythmy /ˈarɪðmi/ *n.* M19. [f. as ARRHYTHMIA: see -Y[3].] Lack of rhythm or regularity.

arriage *n.* see AVERAGE *n.*[1]

arride /əˈrʌɪd/ *v.t. arch.* L16. [L *arridere* smile upon, f. *ad* AR- + *ridere* to laugh, smile.] **1** Please, gratify, delight. L16. †**2** Smile at, laugh at. E–M17.

arrière-ban /arjɛrbɑ̃, ˈarɪəban/ *n.* Also Anglicized as †***arrear-band***. E16. [Fr. *arrière-ban*, OFr. *ariereban* alt. of *arban*, *herban* f. a Frank. wd (= OHG *heriban* call-up for military service), f. *hari*, *heri* army + *ban* proclamation, BAN *n.*[1]] *Hist.* (The order of a Frankish or French king for) the calling together of vassals summoned for military service; the body of vassals thus summoned or liable to be summoned.

arrière-guard /ˈarɪəgɑːd/ *n.* Also †**arrear-**. L15. [Fr. †*arrière-guarde* (now *-garde*): see ARREAR *adv.*, GUARD *n.*] A rearguard.

arrière-pensée /arjɛrpɑ̃se/ *n.* Pl. pronounced same. E19. [Fr., lit. 'behind-thought'.] A concealed thought or intention; an ulterior motive; a mental reservation.

arriero /ariˈero/ *n.* Pl. **-os** /-ɒs/. E19. [Sp.] In Spain and Spanish-speaking countries: a muleteer.

arris /ˈarɪs/ *n.* L17. [Alt. of early mod.Fr. *areste* sharp ridge, ARÊTE.] Esp. *Archit.* The sharp edge formed by the angular contact of two plane or curved surfaces.

arris-ways *adv.* (*arch.*) so as to present a sharp edge, diagonally L17.

arrival /əˈrʌɪv(ə)l/ *n.* LME. [AN *arrivaile*, f. as next: see -AL[1].] **1** The act of arriving; appearance upon the scene. LME. **2** A person who or thing which has arrived. E19.

1 ADDISON Our Time lies heavy on our Hands till the Arrival of a fresh mail. G. GISSING She had been in the house since her arrival the day before yesterday. OED There was long debate, but no arrival at any agreement. G. B. SHAW The arrival of western civilization in the Balkans. A. C. CLARKE She gave birth to Peter, and with the arrival of his son it seemed to Franklin that the old chapter of his life had finally closed. S. HILL Your sister . . may well be dead upon arrival at the hospital. 2 E. O'NEILL The crowd of people has been steadily augmented by new arrivals. **new arrival** *spec.* (*colloq.*) a newborn child.

arrive /əˈrʌɪv/ *v.* ME. [OFr. *ariver* (mod. *arriver*), ult. f. L *ad* AR- + *ripa* shore. Cf. RIVER *n.*[1]] **1** *v.i.* Come to the end of a journey (orig. by water); reach one's destination or a specified point on a journey; make one's appearance, come on the scene; (of a child, *colloq.*) be born. (Foll. by *at*, *in*, *(up)on*, †*into*, †*to*.) ME. **b** Of a thing: be brought or conveyed. M17. †**2** *v.t.* Bring (orig. a ship, its crew or passengers) to a destination; land. LME–M18. **3** *v.i.* Come to a position or state of mind; reach an object; attain, achieve, compass, something. Foll. by *at*, †*to*, †*to do*. LME. **4** *v.i.* Come to a certain stage of development by natural growth, lapse of time, etc. Foll. by *at*, †*to*. L16. **b** Of time: come, so as to be present. M18. **5** *v.t.* Come to, reach, land at. *arch.* E17. **6** *v.i.* Come about, occur, happen. (Foll. by *to*.) *obs.* exc. as passing into sense 4. M17. †**b** *v.t.* Happen to, befall. Only in M17. **7** *v.i.* [After mod.Fr.] Be successful, establish one's position or reputation. L19.

1 P. SIDNEY We arrived upon the verge of his estate. O. CROMWELL Yesterday arrived to me hither your Majesties servants. J. BUCHAN He arrived before eight o'clock every morning and used to depart at seven. D. H. LAWRENCE Already the middle of September was here, and the baby had not arrived. T. S. ELIOT Perhaps she won't even arrive by this plane. DAY LEWIS Arriving at the church, he found it filled with a whole tribe of tinkers. L. HELLMAN Bethe arrived in

New Orleans long before I was born. **b** DRYDEN Let the rest arrive to the Audience by narration. R. GRAVES Augustus . . had reached Athens when the news arrived. A. J. CRONIN Parcels of books began to arrive periodically. **2** G. CHAPMAN And made the sea-trod ship arrive them near The grapeful Crissa. **3** SHAKES. *Timon* Many so arrive at second masters Upon their first lord's neck. SWIFT If such gentlemen arrive to be great scholars. H. SPENCER The same conclusion is thus arrived at. T. S. ELIOT Contending and contentious orators, who have not even arrived at the articulation of their differences. **4** SHAKES. *Hen. V* Grandsires, babies, and old women, Either past or not arriv'd to pith and puissance. ADDISON They were each of them arrived at Years of Discretion. **b** SMOLLETT At length the hour arrived. **5** MILTON Ere he arrive The happy Ile. SHELLEY While I ask and hear Whence coming they arrive the Ætnean hill. **6** HOBBES Causes of all things that have arrived hitherto, or shall arrive hereafter. H. FIELDING Any such event may arrive to a woman. **b** MILTON Let him also forbear force . . lest a worse woe arrive him. **7** *English Studies* The book was Herrick's greatest success. . . With *Together* Herrick arrived.

†**arrivance** *n.* = ARRIVAL E17–L19. **arriver** *n.* E17.

arriviste /arivist/ *n.* Pl. pronounced same. E20. [Fr., f. as prec.: see -IST.] An ambitious or self-seeking person.

arrivisme /-ism/ *n.* the behaviour or character of an *arriviste* M20.

arroba /əˈrəʊbə/ *n.* M16. [Sp. f. Arab. *ar-rubʿ*, f. AL-[2] + *rubʿ* quarter (being a quarter of a quintal).] A unit of weight formerly used in Spain, Portugal, and Latin America, varying locally between 11 and 16 kg (approx. 24 to 35 lb).

arrogance /ˈarəg(ə)ns/ *n.* ME. [(O)Fr. f. L *arrogantia*, f. *arrogant-*: see next, -ANCE.] Arrogant manner or behaviour; aggressive conceit or presumption.

arrogancy *n.* (*a*) = ARROGANCE; †(*b*) an arrogant act or assumption: E16.

arrogant /ˈarəg(ə)nt/ *a.* & *n.* LME. [(O)Fr. f. L *arrogant-* pres. ppl stem of *arrogare*: see next, -ANT[1].] **A** *adj.* Unduly appropriating authority or importance; aggressively conceited or presumptuous; haughty, overbearing. LME.

C. DARWIN The arrogant man looks down on others, and with lowered eyelids hardly condescends to see them. D. H. LAWRENCE Gudrun could see in Gerald an arrogant English contempt for a foreigner. ALDOUS HUXLEY Bernard gave his orders in the sharp, rather arrogant and even offensive tone of one who does not feel himself too secure in his superiority.

B *n.* An arrogant person. *rare.* L15.

arrogantly *adv.* M16.

arrogate /ˈarəgeɪt/ *v.t.* M16. [L *arrogat-* pa. ppl stem of *arrogare* claim for oneself, f. *ad* AR- + *rogare* ask: see -ATE[3] and cf. ADROGATE.] **1** Appropriate, assume, or claim (*to oneself*) unduly or without justification. M16. **2** Ascribe or attribute *to* (a person †or thing) without just reason. E17. †**3** *Rom. Law.* = ADROGATE. Only in M17.

1 MILTON Will arrogate Dominion undeserv'd Over his brethren. C. STEAD He arrogated every honor to himself, he went out of his way to push into official circles. H. MACMILLAN The illegal but effective authority which the Assembly of the United Nations seemed now to have arrogated to itself. **2** COLERIDGE To antiquity we arrogate many things, to ourselves nothing.

arroˈgation *n.* †(*a*) *Rom. Law* = ADROGATION; (*b*) the action of claiming and assuming without just reason; an unwarrantable assumption: L16.

arrondissement /arɔ̃dismɑ̃/ *n.* Pl. pronounced same. E19. [Fr., f. *arrondiss-* lengthened stem of *arrondir* make round: see -MENT.] An administrative subdivision of a French city or department.

†**arrouse** *v.t.* L15–M17. [Fr. *arrouser* (now *arroser*) f. L *adrorare*, f. *ad* AR- + *ror-*, *ros* dew. Aphet. to ROUSE *v.*[2]] Sprinkle, moisten.

arrow /ˈarəʊ/ *n.* & *v.* [OE *ar(e)we* f. ON, rel. to Goth. *arhwazna*, f. Gmc base f. IE, whence L *arcus* bow, ARC *n.*] **A** *n.* **1** A slender pointed missile shot from a bow, usu. feathered and barbed. OE. **b** A dart as used in the game of darts. *colloq.* M20. **2** A mark or symbol shaped like an arrow (e.g. one indicating direction on a map, diagram, etc.) or arrowhead (esp. in *broad arrow* s.v. BROAD *a.*). M16. **3** The leading shoot of a plant or tree, *esp.* the flowering stem of the sugar cane. L16. **4** (Usu. **A-**.) *The* constellation Sagitta. E18. **5** *Surveying.* A metal pin (orig. a real arrow) for driving into the ground at the end of a chain. M18.

1 *fig.*: S. JOHNSON A mark to the arrows of lurking calumny. E. NEWMAN One wants to have a number of arrows in one's quiver. **arrow of time, time's arrow**, the direction of travel from past to future in time considered as a physical dimension. *have an arrow left in one's quiver*: see QUIVER *n.*[1] *straight arrow*: see STRAIGHT *a.*[1] & *adv.*

Comb.: **arrow arum** a N. American arum, *Peltandra virginica*, of wet ground, with arrow-shaped leaves; also called *tuckahoe*, *wake-robin*; **arrow-back** *N. Amer.* (the back of) a type of Windsor chair with arrow-shaped spindles; **arrow bamboo** = METAKE; **arrow-grass** either of two grasslike marsh plants of the genus *Triglochin*, bearing a slender flowering spike, *T. palustre* (more fully *marsh arrow-grass*) and *T. maritimum* (more fully *sea arrow-grass*); **arrowhead** (*a*) the pointed end of an arrow; (*b*) an aquatic or marsh plant of the genus *Sagittaria*, esp. the European *S. sagittifolia*, bearing white flowers and sagittate leaves; **arrow-headed** *a.* shaped like an arrowhead; *spec.* = CUNEIFORM; **arrow-slit** = LOOPHOLE *n.* 1; **arrowsmith** a maker of iron arrowheads; **arrow-wood** *N. Amer.* any of various shrubs having straight tough shoots, esp. *Viburnum dentatum*; **arrow worm** = CHAETOGNATH.

B *v.* **1** *v.t.* Pierce, shoot like an arrow. *rare.* E17. **2** *v.i.* Move swiftly, like an arrow in flight; dart. E19.

arrowed *a.* provided or marked with arrows; *poet.* made into an arrow, pierced with arrows: M17. **arrowy** *a.* (*a*) consisting of or containing arrows; (*b*) like an arrow, in shape, motion, etc.: E17.

arrowroot /ˈarəʊruːt/ *n.* L17. [Alt. of Arawak *aru-aru* lit. 'meal of meals', by assim. to ARROW *n.* and ROOT *n.*[1], the tubers having been used to absorb poison from arrow wounds.] **1** A plant of the genus *Maranta*, *esp.* the W. Indian *M. arundinacea* with fleshy tuberous rhizomes. L17. **2** Pure edible starch prepared from the tubers of *M. arundinacea*, or from other plants. E19.

2 PORTLAND *arrowroot*. TAHITI *arrowroot*.

arroyo /əˈrɔɪəʊ/ *n.* *N. Amer.* Pl. **-os.** M19. [Sp.] A gully, a watercourse.

arse /ɑːs/ *n.* Now *coarse slang.* Also ***ass** /as, ɑːs/. [OE *ærs* (*ears*) = OFris. *ers*, MLG *ars*, *ers*, MDu. *aers*, *e(e)rs* (Du. *(n)aars*), OHG *ars* (G *Arsch*), ON *ars*, *rass*, f. Gmc f. IE. Rel. to Gk *orros* rump.] **1** The buttocks, the rump; the anus. OE. **b** (Women regarded as a source of) sexual gratification. M20. **2** *transf.* & *fig.* The lower or hinder end; the bottom; the fag end, the tail. LME. **b** = *arse-hole* (b) below. M20.

1 **arse over tip** or **tit** head over heels. **drag** or **haul ass** *N. Amer.* move fast, hurry, leave. *kick (a person's) arse*: see KICK *v.*[1] *kiss a person's arse, my arse*: see KISS *v.* *lick a person's arse*: see LICK *v.* **not know one's arse from one's elbow** be totally ignorant or incompetent. *pain in the arse*: see PAIN *n.*[1] SMART-ARSE. *tit(s) and arse*: see TIT *n.*[1] **work** etc. **one's arse off** work etc. very hard. **b** *piece of arse*: see PIECE *n.*

Comb.: †**arse-foot** a grebe, or other bird with feet placed well back; **arsehole** (*a*) the anus; (*b*) *slang* a stupid or despicable person; **arse-kisser** a toady; **arse-kissing** *vbl n.* & *ppl a.* toadying; **arse-licker** a toady; **arse-licking** *vbl n.* & *ppl a.* toadying; **arsesmart** (now *dial.*) water-pepper, *Persicaria hydropiper*.

arsed *a.* having buttocks or a rump (of a specified kind) OE. †**arseward(s)** *adv.* & *a.* backward, perverse(ly) LME–L19.

arse *v.* see ASS *v.*

arsedine /ˈɑːsɪdiːn, -dʌɪn/ *n.* Also **orsedue** /ˈɔːsɪdjuː/ & other vars. LME. [Origin unkn.] A gold-coloured alloy of copper and zinc, used as leaf.

arsen- *comb. form* see ARSENO-.

arsenal /ˈɑːs(ə)n(ə)l/ *n.* E16. [Fr. *arsenal*, †*archenal* or its source It. †*arzanale*, (now) *arsenale*, f. Venetian It. *arzanà* ult. (w. unexpl. loss of *d*) f. Arab. *dār-(aṣ-)ṣināʿa* workshop, f. *dār* house + AL-[2] + *ṣināʿa* art, manufacture, f. *ṣanaʿa* make, fabricate.] †**1** A dock equipped for the reception, construction, repair, and fitting of ships. E16–M19. **2** A government establishment for the storage or manufacture of weapons and ammunition; a store of weapons (*lit.* & *fig.*). L16.

2 GIBBON Offensive weapons of all sorts, and military engines, which were deposited in the arsenals. J. K. JEROME I collected a small arsenal—two or three pieces of coal, a few hard pears, . . an empty soda-water bottle, and a few articles of that sort—and . . bombarded the spot from where the noise appeared to come. M. H. ABRAMS Aristotle bequeathed an arsenal of instruments for technical analysis of poetic forms and their elements.

arsenate /ˈɑːs(ə)neɪt/ *n.* E19. [f. next + -ATE[1].] *Chem.* A salt or ester of any oxoacid of arsenic (orig. only of arsenic acid, H_3AsO_4).

Also **arseniate** /ɑːˈsiːnɪeɪt/ *n.* (now *rare*) E19.

arsenic /ˈɑːs(ə)nɪk/ *n.* & *a.*[1] LME. [(O)Fr. f. L *arsenicum* f. Gk *arsenikon* yellow orpiment, (identified w. *arsenikos* male, but in fact) f. Arab. *az-zarnīḵ*, f. as AL-[2] + *zarnīḵ* orpiment f. Pers., f. *zar* gold.] **A** *n.* **1** Yellow orpiment, arsenic sulphide, As_2S_3 (more fully *yellow arsenic*). Also, realgar, AsS (more fully *red arsenic*). Now *rare*. LME. **2** Arsenic trioxide, As_2O_3 (more fully *white arsenic*). Also, this or any other arsenic compound used as a poison; *fig.*, poison. LME. **3** The chemical element common to these, in its usual form a brittle steel-grey metalloid, atomic no. 33. (Symbol As.) E19. **B** *attrib.* or as *adj.* Of arsenic, arsenical. LME.

arsenicated /ɑːˈsɛnɪkeɪtɪd/ *a.* (now *rare* or *obs.*) treated, mixed, or combined with arsenic L18. †**arseniuret** *n.* = ARSENIDE M19–E20. **arseniuretted** /ɑːˈsɛnjʊrɪtɪd/ *a.* (*arch.*) combined with arsenic E19.

arsenic /ɑːˈsɛnɪk/ *a.*[2] E19. [f. prec., the ending being identified with -IC.] *Chem.* Of pentavalent arsenic.

arsenic acid a weak acid, H_3AsO_4, with oxidizing properties.

arsenical /ɑːˈsɛnɪk(ə)l/ *a.* & *n.* E17. [f. ARSENIC *n.* + -AL[1].] **A** *adj.* Of the nature of, pertaining to, or containing arsenic. E17. **B** *n.* A compound (esp. organic) of arsenic. L19.

arsenide /ˈɑːs(ə)nʌɪd/ *n.* M19. [f. ARSENIC *n.* + -IDE.] *Chem.* A compound of arsenic with a more electropositive element.

arsenious /ɑːˈsiːnɪəs/ *a.* E19. [f. ARSENIC *n.* + -IOUS.] *Chem.* Of trivalent arsenic.

arsenious acid a weak acid, H_3AsO_3, formed when arsenic trioxide dissolves in water.

Also **ˈarsenous** *a.* E19.

arsenite /ˈɑːs(ə)nʌɪt/ *n.* E19. [f. ARSENIC *n.* + -ITE[1].] *Chem.* A salt of arsenious acid.

arseno- /ˈɑːs(ə)nəʊ, ɑːˈsɛnəʊ/ *comb. form.* Also (in some mineral names) **arsen-**. [f. ARSENIC *n.* + -O-.] Forming names of compounds and derivatives of arsenic.

arˈsenolite *n.* (*Min.*) a form of arsenic trioxide crystallizing in the cubic system, occurring usu. as colourless octahedra M19. **arsenoˈpyrite** *n.* (*Min.*) an arsenide and sulphide of iron (and usu. also cobalt), occurring as silvery-grey monoclinic prisms; mispickel: M19.

arses *ns.* pls. of ARSE *n.*, ARSIS.

arshin /ɑːˈʃiːn/ *n.* Also **-shine.** M16. [Russ., of Turkic origin.] A Russian and Turkish unit of length, equal to about 70 cm.

arsine /ˈɑːsiːn/ *n.* L19. [f. ARS(ENIC *n.* + -INE[5].] *Chem.* A highly poisonous gas, AsH_3. Also, any substituted derivative of this.

arsis /ˈɑːsɪs/ *n.* Pl. **arses** /ˈɑːsiːz/. LME. [Late L f. Gk = lifting, raising, f. *airein* raise.] The syllable or part of a metrical foot that is stressed (orig., *Class. Pros.*, by raised pitch or volume); the unstressed beat in barred music. Opp. THESIS.

†**arsmet(r)ike** *n.* see ARITHMETIC *n.*[1]

arson /ˈɑːs(ə)n/ *n.* L17. [Legal AN & OFr., f. med.L *arsio(n-)*, f. L *ars-* pa. ppl stem of *ardere* to burn.] The malicious setting on fire of a house, ship, forest, etc.

arsonist *n.* a person who commits arson M19.

arsphenamine /ɑːsˈfɛnəmiːn, -ɪn/ *n.* E20. [f. ARS(ENIC *n.* + PHEN- + AMINE.] A toxic synthetic bicyclic arsenic compound, $C_{12}H_{12}As_2N_2O_2{\cdot}2HCl$, formerly used to treat syphilis, yaws, etc. Cf. SALVARSAN.

arsy-versy /ɑːsɪˈvəːsi/ *adv.* & *a.* Now *dial.* & *coarse slang* M16. [f. ARSE *n.* + L *versus* turned,

w. -Y[1] added to both elems. to make a jingle.] A *adv.* Backside foremost; upside down; contrariwise; perversely. M16. †B *adj.* Contrary; perverse. Only in 17.

art /ɑːt/ *n.*[1] ME. [(O)Fr. f. L *art-*, *ars*, f. a base meaning 'put together, join, fit'.] I Skill. (As a non-count n.) 1 Skill as the result of knowledge and practice. ME. †b *spec.* Technical or professional skill. ME–L17. c Human skill, as opp. to nature. LME. 2 The learning of the schools; scholarship. Now *arch.* & *Hist.* ME. 3 The application of skill according to aesthetic principles, esp. in the production of visible works of imagination, imitation, or design (painting, sculpture, architecture, etc.); skilful execution of workmanship as an object in itself; the cultivation of the production of aesthetic objects in its principles, practice, and results. E17.

1 POPE The copious accents fall with easy art. LD MACAULAY The potato, a root which can be cultivated with scarcely any art. b SHAKES. *Macb.* Tell me, if your art Can tell so much. c DRYDEN Art may err, but nature cannot miss. 2 LONGFELLOW Art is long, and time is fleeting. 3 T. TRAHERNE Art . . more frequently appears in fiddling and dancing, then in noble deeds. DRYDEN From hence the rudiments of art began, A coal or chalk first imitated man. J. RUSKIN High art differs from low art in possessing an excess of beauty in addition to its truth. A. C. SWINBURNE The well-known formula of art for art's sake . . has, like other doctrines, a true side to it, and an untrue. G. B. SHAW The Renascence of antique literature and art in the sixteenth century.

II Something in which skill may be obtained or displayed. (As a count n.) 4 In *pl.* Certain branches of (esp. university or school) study serving as a preparation for more advanced studies or for later life, now esp. languages, literature, philosophy, history, etc., as distinguished from the sciences or technological subjects. (In the Middle Ages the elements of a course of seven sciences, the trivium, consisting of grammar, logic, and rhetoric, and the quadrivium, consisting of arithmetic, geometry, music, and astronomy.) ME. †b *sing.* Each of the subjects of the medieval trivium or quadrivium. Only in ME. 5 A practical application of any science; *esp.* an industrial pursuit of a skilled nature, a craft. LME. b A guild or company of craftsmen. *rare.* M19. 6 A pursuit or occupation in which skill is directed towards the production of a work of imagination, imitation, or design, or towards the gratification of the aesthetic senses; the products of any such pursuit. L16. 7 An acquired faculty; a knack. M17.

4 SHAKES. *Per.* My education been in arts and arms. JOYCE Through the matriculation, first arts second arts and arts degree courses at the royal university. 5 ADDISON The Fisher-men can't employ their Art with so much success in so troubled a Sea. E. TERRY Only a great actor finds the difficulties of the actor's art infinite. E. LINKLATER They grew . . technical about such obscure arts as splicing, seizing, gaffing, and pointing. K. CLARK Another development of the art of printing was nourishing the imagination: the woodcut. 6 J. REYNOLDS All arts having the same general end, which is to please. C. MACKENZIE It is a dying art and only to be heard in perfection from old men and old women. K. CLARK The very narrowness of primitive society gives their ornamental art a peculiar concentration and vitality. 7 A. G. GARDINER The art of the business is to work easily and with a light hand. C. S. FORESTER Curzon had partly acquired the art . . of being uncommunicative without being rude. V. S. PRITCHETT A clever journalist explains to another the art of writing short sketches.

III Skilful or crafty conduct. 8 Cunning; artfulness. ME. 9 An artifice, a stratagem, a wile, a cunning device. Usu. in *pl.* LME.

8 POPE Smile without Art, and win without a Bribe. 9 J. AUSTEN The arts which ladies sometimes condescend to employ for captivation. LD MACAULAY No art was spared which could draw Monmouth from retreat.

Phrases: **art-and-crafty** *a.* = *artsy-(and-)craftsy* below. *art and mystery*: see MYSTERY *n.*[2] **art and part, art or part** (orig.) contrivance and/or execution; *have art or part in*, share in, be involved in; *be art and part in*, be an accessory or participant in. **arts and crafts** decorative design and handicraft, orig. as encouraged by the Arts and Crafts Exhibition Society. **artsy-(and-)craftsy** *adjs.* pertaining to or characteristic of the arts-and-crafts movement, esp. in its more pretentious manifestations; *spec.* (of furniture) remarkable for artistic style rather than for usefulness or comfort. **Bachelor of Arts** (a person who has been awarded) a degree (usu. the lowest, below a master's degree) in an arts subject or arts subjects. *black art*: see BLACK *a.* **decorative arts**: those which involve the production of high-quality objects which are both useful and beautiful. *fine arts*: see FINE ART. **graphic arts**: those which involve graphic representation or writing, printing, etc. **imitative arts** painting and sculpture. **liberal arts** the medieval trivium and quadrivium; (chiefly *N. Amer.*) arts subjects as opp. to science and technology. MARTIAL *art.* **Master of Arts** (a person who has been awarded) a degree (usu. above a bachelor's degree) for a high level of proficiency in an arts subject or arts subjects. *object of art*: see OBJECT *n.* **performing arts**: those, such as drama, dancing, etc., which involve public performance. **plastic arts**: those which involve modelling, as sculpture etc. *pop art*: see POP *a.* *state of the art*: see STATE *n.* **the arts** the fine arts (see FINE ART). *the gentle art*: see GENTLE *a.* *the noble art*: see NOBLE *a.* *will to art*: see WILL *n.*[1] **work of art** a fine picture, sculpture, poem, building, etc.

Attrib. & *comb.*: Pertaining to the use of artistic skill, designed to produce an artistic effect, composed with conscious artistry, as *art cinema, film, furniture, music, needlework, song, theatre*, etc. Special combs., as *art* DECO; **art editor** a person who is responsible for illustrations and design, or for the section devoted to the arts, in a book, magazine, etc.; **art form** [cf. G *Kunstform*] (*a*) an established form of composition (e.g. novel, sonata, sonnet, triptych); (*b*) a medium of artistic expression; **art gallery** (a portion of) a building devoted to the exhibition of works of art; **art object** = OBJET D'ART; **art paper** paper coated with china clay or the like to give a smooth surface; **artsman** (*a*) *arch.* = ARTIST; (*b*) a student of or graduate in arts; **artsy-fartsy** *a.* (*colloq.*) pretentiously artistic; **art therapy** painting, sculpture, or other artistic activity engaged in as a form of occupational therapy; **art union** a union of people for the purchase of works of art, usu. to be distributed by lottery; *Austral.* & *NZ* any public lottery; **art work**, (esp. senses b, c) **artwork** (*a*) a work of art; (*b*) (an example of) graphic art or design; illustrative or decorative matter in a printed text; (*c*) prepared or camera-ready copy.

¶Cf. CRAFT *n.*

†art *n.*[2] var. of AIRT.

art /ɑːt/ *v.*[1] *rare.* E17. [f. ART *n.*[1]] †1 *v.t.* Obtain by art. Only in E17. †2 *v.t.* Make artificial. Only in E17. †3 *v.t.* foll. by *it.* Use art or artifice. Only in M17. †4 *v.t.* Instruct in an art or arts. Only in M17. 5 *v.t.* & *i.* Foll. by *up*: make arty; decorate in an arty fashion. E20.

art *v.*[2] see BE *v.*

-art /ət/ *suff.* Occas. var. of -ARD, as in *braggart* etc.

artefact /ˈɑːtɪfakt/ *n.* Also **arti-**. E19. [f. L *arte* abl. of *ars* art + *factum* neut pa. pple of *facere* make.] 1 A product of human art or workmanship; *Archaeol.* a product or by-product of prehistoric or aboriginal workmanship, as opp. to a natural object. E19. 2 Something observed in a scientific investigation, experiment, etc., that is not naturally present but originates in the preparative or investigative procedure or extraneously. L19.

arteˈfactual *a.* of or pertaining to an artefact or artefacts M20. **arteˈfactually** (*a*) as an artefact; (*b*) by extraneous means: M20.

artel /ɑːˈtɛl/ *n.* L19. [Russ. *artel'*.] A Russian or Soviet collective enterprise of craftsmen or skilled workers.

artemisia /ɑːtɪˈmɪzjə/ *n.* ME. [L f. Gk, = wormwood, f. *Artemis* the goddess Diana, to whom it was sacred.] Any of numerous aromatic or bitter-tasting plants of the genus *Artemisia*, of the composite family, which includes wormwood, mugwort, sagebrush, etc.

artemisinin /ɑːtɪˈmiːsɪnɪn/ *n.* L20. [f. prec. + QUININE.] = QINGHAOSU.

arterial /ɑːˈtɪərɪəl/ *a.* LME. [med.L *arterialis*: see ARTERY, -AL[1].] 1 Of, pertaining to, or of the nature of an artery; (of blood) oxygenated in the lungs and of a bright red colour (opp. VENOUS). LME. 2 Resembling an artery, esp. as a main road or other important route of transport or communication. M19.

1 **arterial system** the system of arteries by which oxygenated blood is conveyed from the heart and lungs to the various parts of the body. **†arterial vein** the pulmonary artery.

arterialiˈzation *n.* the action or process of arterializing blood M19. **arterialize** *v.t.* oxygenate (blood) in the lungs M19. **†arterious** *a.* = ARTERIAL M17–E19.

arterio- /ɑːˈtɪərɪəʊ/ *comb. form.* [Gk *artērio-*: see ARTERY, -O-.] Of or pertaining to an artery.

arteriˈotomy *n.* (an instance of) surgical incision into an artery M17. **arterioˈvenous** *a.* of, pertaining to, or affecting an artery and a vein L19.

arteriography /ɑːˌtɪərɪˈɒgrəfi/ *n.* M19. [f. ARTERIO- + -GRAPHY.] *Med.* 1 Systematic description of the arteries. Only in Dicts. M19. 2 Radiography of an artery, carried out after injection of a radio-opaque substance. E20.

arˈteriogram *n.* an image obtained by arteriography E20.

arteriole /ɑːˈtɪərɪəʊl/ *n.* M19. [Fr. *artériole* dim. of *artère* ARTERY: see -OLE[1].] A small artery adjoining capillaries.

arteriˈolar *a.* M20.

arteriosclerosis /ɑːˌtɪərɪəʊsklɪəˈrəʊsɪs, -sklə-/ *n.* Pl. **-roses** /-ˈrəʊsiːz/. L19. [f. ARTERIO- + SCLEROSIS.] *Med.* Abnormal thickening and hardening of the walls of arteries.

arteriosclerotic *a.* pertaining to or affected by arteriosclerosis L19.

arteritis /ɑːtəˈrʌɪtɪs/ *n.* M19. [f. ARTERY + -ITIS.] *Med.* Inflammation of the walls of an artery.

artery /ˈɑːtəri/ *n.* LME. [L *arteria* f. Gk *artēria*, prob. f. *airein* raise: see -Y[3].] †1 The windpipe. LME–M17. 2 Any of the muscular-walled tubes forming part of the system of vessels by which blood (usu. oxygenated) is conveyed from the heart to all parts of the body. LME. †3 A ligament. E–M17. 4 An important channel of communication or transport; a major road, railway, river, etc. M19.

2 *coronary artery, pulmonary artery*, etc.

artesian /ɑːˈtiːzjən, -ʒ(ə)n/ *a.* M19. [Fr. *artésien* lit. 'of Artois' (OFr. *Arteis*), a region of NE France where wells of this type were first made: see -IAN.] Of a well: made by a perpendicular boring into a confined aquifer, the water rising spontaneously above the water table (strictly, to the surface). Also, of, pertaining to, or obtainable by such a well.

†artetik *a.* & *n.* see ARTHRITIC.

artful /ˈɑːtfʊl, -f(ə)l/ *a.* E17. [f. ART *n.*[1] + -FUL.] 1 Of a person, action, etc.: skilful, clever, (*arch.*); (passing into) crafty, deceitful. E17. †2 Of a person: learned, wise. Only in 17. 3 Of a thing: artificial, imitative, unreal. *arch.* E18.

artfully *adv.* E17. **artfulness** *n.* E18.

arthame *n.* var. of ATHAME.

arthralgia /ɑːˈθraldʒə/ *n.* M19. [f. Gk *arthron* joint + -ALGIA.] *Med.* Pain in a joint.

arthritic /ɑːˈθrɪtɪk/ *a.* & *n.* Orig. **†artetik** & similar vars. LME. [OFr. *artetique* f. med.L *arteticus* f. L *arthriticus* f. Gk *arthritikos*: later assim. to L.] A *adj.* Of, pertaining to, or affected with arthritis. LME. B *n.* †1 Disease of the joints. LME–L15. 2 An arthritic person. E19.

†arthritical *a.* E16–L18.

arthritis /ɑːˈθrʌɪtɪs/ *n.* Pl. **-tides** /-tɪdiːz/. M16. [L f. Gk, f. *arthron* joint: see -ITIS.] An inflammatory or painful condition of a joint; *spec.* (*a*) = RHEUMATOID *arthritis*; (*b*) = OSTEOARTHRITIS.

arthro- /ˈɑːθrəʊ/ *comb. form* of Gk *arthron* joint: see -O-.

arˈthrodesis *n.* [Gk *desis* binding together] *Surg.* surgical fusion of bones at a joint E20. **arˈthrography** *n.* (*a*) systematic description of the joints (Dicts.); (*b*) examination of joints by radiography: L19. **arˈthropathy** *n.* any disease affecting joints L19. **arthroplasty** *n.* (an instance of) surgical reconstruction of a joint L19.

arthrodia /ɑːˈθrəʊdɪə/ *n.* L16. [Gk *arthrōdia*, f. *arthrōdēs* well-jointed: see -IA[1].] *Anat.* & *Zool.* A form of articulation in which bony surfaces slide freely over each other.

arthrodial *a.* (of a joint) having this form of articulation M19. **arthrodic** *a.* = ARTHRODIAL L19.

arthropod /ˈɑːθrəpɒd/ *n.* L19. [f. mod.L *Arthropoda* (see below), f. Gk *arthron* joint + -POD.] *Zool.* Any animal of the phylum Arthropoda, members of which (e.g. insects, arachnids, and crustaceans) are characterized by segmented bodies and jointed limbs.

arthrosis /ɑːˈθrəʊsɪs/ *n.* Pl. **-roses** /-ˈrəʊsiːz/. M17. [L f. Gk *arthrōsis*: see ARTHRO-, -OSIS.] 1 Connection by a joint, articulation. M17. 2 *Med.* Any disease affecting joints. E20.

Arthurian /ɑːˈθjʊərɪən/ *a.* & *n.* E17. [f. *Arthur* (see below) + -IAN.] A *adj.* Of, pertaining to, or resembling the legendary British king Arthur, his court, his knights, or the romances in which these figure. E17. B *n.* A knight of the Round Table, a follower of King Arthur. E20.

¶Rare bef. M19.

artic /ˈɑːtɪk/ *n.*[1] *colloq.* M20. [Abbrev.] An articulated lorry.

†Artic *a.* & *n.*[2] see ARCTIC *a.* & *n.*

artichoke /ˈɑːtɪtʃəʊk/ *n.* M16. [North. It. *articiocco*, *arci-* alt. of OSp. *alcarchofa* f. Arab. *al-ḵaršūf(a)*.] 1 (The edible flower-head of) a plant of the composite family, *Cynara scolymus*, resembling a thistle and native to the Mediterranean region. Also more fully *French* or *globe artichoke*. M16. 2 *Jerusalem artichoke* [alt. of It. *girasole* sunflower], (the edible tuberous root of) a sunflower, *Helianthus tuberosus*. E17. 3 *Chinese artichoke*, *Japanese artichoke*, (the edible tuber of) a plant of the mint family, *Stachys affinis*, cultivated esp. in the Far East. E20.

article /ˈɑːtɪk(ə)l/ *n.* & *v.* ME. [(O)Fr. f. L *articulus* dim. of *artus* joint, f. base also of ART *n.*[1]: see -CLE.] A *n.* I A separate portion of something written. 1 A separate clause or statement of the Apostles' Creed; an item of a summary of faith. ME. 2 A separate clause or provision of a statute, constitution, code, etc.; an item in a rule-book, a regulation. ME. 3 Each of the distinct charges or counts of an accusation or indictment. *arch.* LME. 4 Each of the distinct heads or points of an agreement or treaty; in *pl.*, a formal agreement, a period of apprenticeship, now esp. as a solicitor. LME. b In *pl.* Terms, conditions. *arch.* M17. c A formal agreement. *arch.* M18. 5 *gen.* A paragraph, section, or distinct item of any document. LME. 6 A non-fictional literary composition forming part of a newspaper, magazine, or other publication, but independent of others in the same publication. E18.

1 **the Thirty-nine Articles** statements of doctrine in the *Book of Common Prayer* to which those taking orders in the Church of England had formerly to assent. 2 **Lords of the Articles** *Sc. Hist.* a standing committee of the Scottish Parliament, who drafted and prepared the measures submitted to the House. 4 H. FIELDING Articles of separation were soon drawn up, and signed between the parties. T. JEFFERSON To prepare an article defining the extent of the powers over commerce. E. JONG When our Time was up at Sea, an' our Articles were at their End, we went into the Priggism Trade in London. A. N. WILSON He had just finished his articles at a London firm of solicitors. **articles of apprenticeship** terms of agreement between an apprentice and employer. *articles of association*: see ASSOCIATION 1. *articles of* CONFEDERATION. 6 *leading article*: see LEADING *a.* *turnover article*: see TURNOVER *a.*

II A particular item. 7 A particular item of business; a concern, a matter, a subject. *obs.* exc. in *in the article of* (arch.), so far as concerns, with regard to. LME. †8 An item in an account, list, etc. Only in 18. 9 A particular of a subject, action, or proceeding; a distinct detail. M18. 10 A particular material thing (*of* a specified class); a commodity; a piece of goods or property. L18. b A person regarded (usu. disparagingly) as a commodity etc. E19.

7 S. RICHARDSON To say, there was no article so proper for parents to govern in, as this of marriage. 9 **article of faith** a basic point of belief. 10 W. C. MACREADY Called at several shops and priced various articles of furniture. JOYCE Pitcher and night article (on the floor, separate). D. L. SAYERS There was one article of diet which was partaken of by Philip Boyes alone, and that was a bottle of Burgundy. A. PATON The manufacturers will be able to make more articles. J. D. SALINGER He was putting away all his crumby toilet articles. *article of virtu*: see VIRTU *n.* 1. **genuine article** something authentic of its kind. b A. TROLLOPE She's the very article for such a man as Peppermint. A. HIGGINS Isn't she the incompetent article all the same? . . She couldn't crack an egg without spilling it on the floor.

III A portion of time. 11 A specific juncture in time; the critical point or moment. *arch.* LME.

11 W. WOLLASTON An infirm building, just in the article of falling. **the article of death** the moment of death.

IV *Gram.* 12 A member of a small set of words (in English two, traditionally regarded as adjectives, now also classed as determiners) that give definiteness or indefiniteness and specificness or genericness to the application of a noun. LME.

12 *definite article*, *indefinite article*.

V *Math.* †13 The number 10, or any multiple of it. LME–M18.

VI *Anat.* †14 A joint, a limb. LME–L17.

B *v.* †1 *v.t.* Formulate in articles, particularize; claim *that*. LME–E17. 2a *v.t.* & *i.* Set forth (offences) in articles *against*; make a charge or accusation *against*. *arch.* LME. b *v.t.* Indict, charge. *arch.* E17. †3 *v.t.* & *i.* Arrange by treaty or stipulation (w. *direct obj.*, *that*, *to do*; *with* a person, *for* a thing). LME–E19. 4 *v.t.* Bind by articles of apprenticeship. L18. 5 *v.t.* Provide with articles of faith. *rare.* E19.

4 **articled clerk** a person training to be a solicitor.

articulable /ɑːˈtɪkjʊləb(ə)l/ *a.* M19. [f. ARTICUL(ATE *v.* + -ABLE.] That can be articulated.

articulacy /ɑːˈtɪkjʊləsi/ *n.* M20. [f. ARTICULATE *a.*: see -CY. Cf. earlier INARTICULACY.] The quality or state of being articulate.

articular /ɑːˈtɪkjʊlə/ *a.* LME. [L *articularis*, f. *articulus*: see ARTICLE *n.*, -AR[1].] 1 Of or pertaining to the joints. LME. 2 *Gram.* Of the nature of an article (ARTICLE *n.* 12); having an article preposed. M18.

†articularly *adv.* article by article, in separate heads or divisions. LME–M18.

articulate /ɑːˈtɪkjʊlət/ *a.* M16. [L *articulatus* pa. pple, f. as next: see -ATE[2].] †1 Charged or specified in articles; formulated in articles. M16–E18. 2 Of sound: with clearly distinguishable parts, each having meaning. Of speech, expression, etc.: fluent and clear. Of a person: able to express himself or herself fluently and clearly. M16. b *transf.* Of other sensations: distinct. E17. 3 Jointed; united by a joint; composed of segments united by joints. L16. 4 Distinctly jointed; having the parts distinctly recognizable. M17.

2 MILTON Beasts . . Created mute to all articulate sound. K. GRAHAME The water's own noises . . were more apparent than by day . . ; and constantly they started at what seemed a sudden clear call from an actual articulate voice. M. H. ABRAMS Poetry consists of a sequence of articulate sounds in time rather than of forms and colours fixed in space. H. ARENDT Its most articulate spokesman, Ludwig von der Marwitz . . submitted a lengthy petition to the government. M. SHADBOLT Just a note. Will write again. Not very articulate at present. b A. BAIN The discriminative or articulate character of the sense of touch. 4 W. IRVING A miserable horse, whose ribs were as articulate as the bars of a gridiron. CARLYLE Added to the firm land of articulate History.

articulately *adv.* M16. **articulateness** *n.* M18.

articulate /ɑːˈtɪkjʊleɪt/ *v.* M16. [L *articulat-* pa. ppl stem of *articulare*, f. *articulus*: see ARTICLE, -ATE[3].] I Cf. ARTICLE *v.* 1 *v.t.* Formulate in an article or articles; particularize. *arch.* M16. †2 *v.t.* & *i.* Charge; bring a charge *against*. M16–E17. †3 *v.i.* Come to terms; capitulate. L16–M17. †4 *v.t.* Arrange by articles or conditions. Only in 17.

1 T. NASHE If I articulate all the examples of their absurdeties that I could. 2 M. DRAYTON Gainst whom, at Pomfret, they articulate. 3 SHAKES. *Coriol.* Send us to Rome The best, with whom we may articulate For their own good and ours. 4 W. FULBECKE Articulating peace with the Albanes.

II 5 *v.t.* Pronounce distinctly; give utterance to; express in words; express clearly and fluently. M16. 6 *v.t.* Modify (the air, a pulmonary air-stream, etc.) to produce a speech sound, word, etc. *arch.* L16. 7 *v.i.* Utter words; speak distinctly; pronounce words. M17. 8 *transf.* Make distinct to sight etc. M19.

5 DISRAELI The lady . . began to articulate a horrible patois. D. H. LAWRENCE 'You do as you like—you can leave altogether if you like,' he managed to articulate. J. CARY Partly from breathlessness, partly from agitation, he could not articulate any single word. R. ELLISON We need a good speaker for this district. Someone who can articulate the grievances of the people. P. GOODMAN There is complaint later that they do not know how to articulate their thoughts. M. FRENCH She discovered only gradually, for Carl never articulated it, just what he expected of her. I. MCEWAN She drew breath sharply, and held it for several seconds, then articulated from the back of her throat a strangled, hard C. 7 V. KNOX The capricious modes of dressing, articulating and moving. LD MACAULAY His agitation was so great that he could not articulate. 8 L. A. G. STRONG The powerful light . . beat down on it, throwing it into relief, articulating with dark shadow the long slender fingers.

III 9 *v.t.* Attach by a joint; connect with joints; mark with apparent joints; construct (esp. a vehicle) of flexibly connected sections. Usu. in *pass.* Earlier as ARTICULATED 2. E17. 10 *v.i.* Form a joint (*with*). M19.

9 ST G. J. MIVART The most movable joints are those in which the adjacent bones are articulated on the principle either of a pivot, or of a hinge. 10 T. H. HUXLEY The hollow of the cup articulates with a spheroidal surface furnished by the humerus.

articulated /ɑːˈtɪkjʊleɪtɪd/ *ppl a.* M16. [f. prec. + -ED[1].] 1 Formulated in an article or articles. *arch.* M16. 2 Attached by a joint; connected by joints; having segments united by joints. L16. b Of a vehicle: consisting of flexibly connected sections. E20. 3 Uttered as articulate sound; distinctly spoken. E18.

2 G. ROLLESTON An ossicle articulated to its apex. b *Times* Joe had a brand-new articulated truck, . . (where the driving cab is separately joined to the lorry). 3 COLERIDGE The same words may be repeated; but in each second of time the articulated air hath passed away.

articulation /ɑːˌtɪkjʊˈleɪʃ(ə)n/ *n.* LME. [Fr., or L *articulatio(n-)*, f. as prec.: see -ATION.] I 1 The action or process of joining; the state of being jointed; a mode of jointing. LME. 2 A joint; *esp.* a structure whereby two bones, or parts of an invertebrate skeleton, are connected in the body, whether rigidly or flexibly. LME. 3 Movement by a flexible joint. *rare.* M16. 4 Each of the segments of a jointed body; the part between two joints. M17.

3 E. LINKLATER As if the American hip and knee gave free articulation all round the circle.

II 5 The production or formation of speech sounds, words, etc.; articulate utterance or expression; speech. E17. 6 A speech sound; an articulate utterance. M18. 7 Articulacy, distinctness. *rare.* L18.

5 T. S. ELIOT Contending and contentious orators, who have not even arrived at the articulation of their differences. J. LYONS The oldest, and still the most common, method of phonetic description is that made in terms of 'articulation' by the speech-organs. J. BARNES He had a whiny, imprecise voice . . ; what seemed at first a regional inflection turned out to be only casual articulation. **manner** or **mode of articulation** *Phonet.*: with or without voicing, friction, etc. **place** or **point of articulation** *Phonet.* the place at which obstruction of the air passage takes place in the production of a consonant. 7 W. COWPER The looks and gestures of their griefs and fears Have all articulation in his ears.

articulative /ɑːˈtɪkjʊlətɪv/ *a.* E19. [f. ARTICULATE *v.* + -IVE.] Of or pertaining to articulation.

articulator /ɑːˈtɪkjʊleɪtə/ *n.* L18. [f. ARTICULATE *v.* + -OR.] I 1 A person who articulates words, speech sounds, etc.; a person who gives utterance to or expresses something. L18. 2 A mobile organ of speech, as the tongue. M20.

1 BOSWELL An elderly housekeeper, a most distinct articulator, showed us the house. *Dictionaries* A recent articulator of this need is Professor Fred C. Robinson of Yale University.

II 3 A person who articulates bones and mounts skeletons. M19.

articulatory /ɑːˈtɪkjʊlət(ə)ri, ɑːˌtɪkjʊˈleɪt(ə)ri/ *a.* E19. [f. prec.: see -ORY[2].] 1 = ARTICULAR I. *rare.* E19. 2 Of or pertaining to the articulation of speech. M19.

artifact *n.* var. of ARTEFACT.

artifice /ˈɑːtɪfɪs/ *n.* LME. [(O)Fr. f. L *artificium*, f. *arti-*, *ars* ART *n.*[1] + *fic-* var. of *fac-* stem of *facere* make.] †1 Technical skill; art; workmanship; the making of something by art or skill. LME–L18. †2 Mode or style of workmanship. L16–M18. 3 Skill in designing and employing expedients; address, cunning, trickery. E17. 4 An ingenious expedient; a cunning trick; a device, a contrivance. E17. †5 A work of art. Only in 17. 6 (The products of) human skill as opp. to what is natural. M19.

1 SIR T. BROWNE Though they abounded in milk, they had not the Artifice of Cheese. D. HUME Does it not counterwork the artifice of nature? 2 BURKE Examine . . into the artifice of the contrivance. 3 DEFOE All the artifice and sleight of hand they were masters of. J. BRAINE A noisy snuffle, without grace or artifice. 4 A. G. GARDINER He monopolises the applause as he monopolises the limelight; and by these artifices he has persuaded the public that he is an actor. R. H. TAWNEY Every shift and artifice most repugnant to the sober prudence of plain-dealing men. 6 E. H. GOMBRICH Men turned from the admiration of artifice to the worship of nature. R. WILBUR Trusting in God, mistrusting artifice, He would not graft or bud the stock he sold.

artificer /ɑːˈtɪfɪsə/ *n.* LME. [AN (cf. med.L *artificiarius*), prob. alt. of OFr. *artificien*, f. as prec.: see -ER[2].] 1 A person who makes things by art or skill; a craftsman; an artist. LME. b *gen.* A maker. *arch.* M17. †2 A crafty or artful person; a trickster. LME–E17. 3 A contriver, an inventor, a deviser, (*of*). E17. 4 *Mil.* & *Naut.* A skilled technician. M18.

artificial /ɑːtɪˈfɪʃ(ə)l/ *a.* & *n.* LME. [(O)Fr. *artificiel* or L *artificialis*, f. *artificium*: see ARTIFICE, -AL[1].] A *adj.* I Opp. *natural.* 1 Made by or resulting from art or artifice; constructed, contrived; not natural (though real). LME. 2 Not real; imitation, substitute. L16. 3 Affected, insincere; factitious; feigned. L16.

1 J. R. MCCULLOCH To give an artificial stimulus to population. J. C. POWYS You are confusing natural, instinctive happiness and the artificial social pride that we get from private property. F. L. WRIGHT Artificial lighting is nearly as important as daylight. **artificial insemination** injection of semen into the uterus by other than the natural means. **artificial language** a composite language, esp. for international use, made from the words and other elements in several languages. *artificial person*: see PERSON *n.* 5. **artificial respiration** the restoration or initiation of breathing by manual or mechanical means. 2 A. CARTER She made me instant coffee . . there was artificial cream made from corn-syrup solids to go with it. W. MAXWELL When my brother undressed at night he left his artificial leg leaning against a chair. A. GRAY Jam-jars of artificial flowers, some made of plastic, some of coloured wax, some of paper. **artificial horizon** a gyroscopic instrument or a fluid (esp. mercury) surface used to provide a horizontal reference plane for navigational measurement. **artificial intelligence** (the field of study that deals with) the capacity of a machine to simulate or surpass intelligent human behaviour. *artificial* KIDNEY. *artificial mother*: see MOTHER *n.*[1] II. **artificial silk** *arch.* rayon. **artificial stone** concrete or a similar substance made to resemble stone, used esp. in building. 3 S. JOHNSON Endeavour to kindle in myself an artificial impatience. F. W. ROBERTSON Some will have become frivolous and artificial. T. WILLIAMS Blanche has a tight, artificial smile on her drawn face.

†II Displaying special art or skill. 4 Cunning, deceitful. LME–E18. 5 Displaying skill; skilful. L15–M18. 6 Displaying education or training; scholarly. Only in E17.

4 MILTON This is the artificialest piece of finesse to perswade Men to be Slaves, that the wit of Court could have invented. 5 R. FABYAN An horologe or a clocke . . of a wonder artyficiall makyng. R. HAKLUYT They are very artificiall in making of images. 6 DONNE Scholastique and artificiall men use this way of instructing.

†III Of art(s). 7 According to the rules of art or science; technical. LME–E19.

B *n.* Something artificial; *spec.* (*a*) an artificial flower; (*b*) an artificial bait used in fishing. E17.

artificialism *n.* an artificial principle or practice M19. **artificialize** *v.t.* L17. **artificially** *adv.* LME. **artificialness** *n.* L16.

artificiality /ˌɑːtɪfɪʃɪˈalɪti/ *n.* M16. [f. prec. + -ITY.] †1 Craftsmanship; artifice. M–L16. 2 The quality or state of being artificial. M18. 3 An artificial thing, characteristic, etc. M19.

artify /ˈɑːtɪfʌɪ/ *v.t.* L18. [f. ART *n.*[1] + -I- + -FY; mod. uses partly f. ARTY *a.*] Modify or adorn by art; render arty.

¶ Rare bef. 20.

artillery /ɑːˈtɪləri/ *n.* LME. [(O)Fr. *artillerie*, f. *artiller* alt. (after *art*) of OFr. *atillier* equip, arm, prob. by-form of *atirier*, f. *à* A-[5] + *tire* order: see TIER *n.*[1], -ERY.] †1 Warlike munitions; implements of war. LME–L18. 2 Engines for discharging missiles: formerly including catapults, slings, bows, etc.; now *spec.*, large guns used in fighting on land. LME. †3 Missiles discharged in war. M16–M19. 4 The science or practice of using artillery. Formerly *spec.*, archery, now *spec.* gunnery. M16. 5 Thunder and lightning. *poet.* L16. 6 The branch of the army that uses large guns. L18.

Comb.: **artilleryman** a man whose military duty it is to serve a large gun, a man who belongs to a regiment of artillery; **artillery plant** a tropical American plant, *Pilea microphylla*, of the nettle family, whose mature anthers throw out clouds of pollen.

artillerist *n.* a user of artillery, an artilleryman; a person who studies the principles of artillery: L16.

artiodactyl /ɑːtɪə(ʊ)ˈdaktɪl/ *a.* & *n.* Also (earlier) †**-yle**. M19. [mod.L *Artiodactyla* pl., f. Gk *artios* even + *daktulos* finger, toe.] *Zool.* (Designating or pertaining to) any living or extinct mammal belonging to the order Artiodactyla of even-toed ungulates, including camels, pigs, and ruminants.

artisan /ɑːtɪˈzan, ˈɑːtɪzan/ *n.* Also **-zan**. M16. [Fr. f. It. *artigiano*, ult. f. L *artitus* pa. pple of *artire* instruct in the arts, f. *art-*, *ars* ART *n.*[1]: see -AN.] 1 A skilled (esp. manual) worker; a mechanic; a craftsman. M16. †2 A person who practises or cultivates an art. L16–L18.

artisanal *a.* of or pertaining to artisans; involving manual skill: M20. **artisanate** *n.* artisans collectively, the body or class of artisans M20. **artisanship** *n.* the work and activity of an artisan or of artisans E19.

artist /ˈɑːtɪst/ *n.* E16. [(O)Fr. *artiste* f. It. *artista*, f. *arte* ART *n.*[1]: see -IST.] †1 A person who is master of the liberal arts; a learned person. E16–M18. †2 A person who is master of a practical science or pursuit; a medical practitioner, astrologer, astronomer, alchemist, professor of occult sciences, chemist, etc. M16–L19. 3 A person who cultivates or practises one of the fine arts, now esp. painting. L16. 4 A person who practises one of the performing arts; an artiste. L16. 5 *gen.* A skilled performer; a connoisseur. Now only in a specified or understood activity. L16. b A person, a fellow; (usu. w. specifying wd) a devotee, an indulger in something. *slang.* L19. 6 = ARTISAN I. *obs.* exc. as infl. by sense 3, a person who makes his or her craft a fine art. M17. †7 A person who practises artifice; a schemer, contriver. M17–E19.

1 SHAKES. *Tr. & Cr.* The wise and fool, the artist and unread. 2 W. ROWLEY The artists . . That seek the secrets of futurity. MILTON The Moon, whose Orb Through Optic Glass the Tuscan Artist views. SMOLLETT Luckily my wounds were not mortal, and I fell into the hands of a skilful artist. 3 **artist's proof** a copy of an engraving taken for the artist and valued as fresher than ordinary copies. 4 ADDISON That excellent Artist . . having shewn us the Italian Musick in its Perfection. C. BRONTË He told me his opinion of . . the actress: he judged her as a woman, not an artist. 5 I. WALTON I will give you more directions concerning fishing; for I would fain make you an Artist. DEFOE The mate was an excellent sea artist, and an experienced sailor. A. S. BYATT Cassandra was . . an artist in not being on speaking terms. b D. M. DAVIN A real artist for the booze, isn't he? HENRY MILLER Neither of us is a booze artist. 6 POPE Then from his anvil the lame artist rose. SOUTHEY Greek artists in the imperial city forged That splendid armour. H. L. MENCKEN And yet the man was a superb artist in words, a master-writer. 7 DEFOE The young artist that has done this roguery.

artistlike *a.* & *adv.* (in a manner) befitting an artist, artistic(ally) E18. **artistly** *adv.* (now *rare*) artistically, in the manner of an artist M18. **artistry** *n.* artistic ability, artistic characteristics M19.

artiste /ɑːˈtiːst/ *n.* E19. [Fr.: see prec.] A performing artist; a professional singer, dancer, actor, etc.

artistic /ɑːˈtɪstɪk/ *a.* M18. [f. ARTIST + -IC.] Of or pertaining to art or artists; made or done with art; appreciative of or having natural skill in art.

artistical *a.* E19. **artistically** *adv.* in an artistic manner; from an artistic point of view: M19.

artizan *n.* var. of ARTISAN.

artless /ˈɑːtlɪs/ *a.* L16. [f. ART *n.*[1] + -LESS.] 1 Without art or skill; unskilled, ignorant; unartistic, uncultured. L16. 2 Rude, clumsy, crude. L16. 3 Natural, simple. L17. 4 Guileless, ingenuous. E18.

1 S. JOHNSON The work in which I engaged is generally considered . . as the proper toil of artless industry. J. RUSKIN A shadowy life—artless, joyless, loveless. 2 S. JOHNSON Brogues, a kind of artless shoes. 3 C. BROOKS It is like the daffodils, or the mountain brooks, artless, and whimsical, and 'natural' as they. 4 W. IRVING The delightful blushing consciousness of an artless girl.

artlessly *adv.* E17. **artlessness** *n.* M18.

art nouveau /ɑː nuːˈvəʊ, *foreign* aːr nuvo/ *n. phr.* E20. [Fr., lit. 'new art'.] An art style of the late 19th cent. characterized by ornamented and flowing lines.

arty /ˈɑːti/ *n. slang.* M20. [Abbrev.] Artillery.

arty /ˈɑːti/ *a. colloq.* E20. [f. ART *n.*[1] + -Y[1].] Pretentiously or quaintly artistic.

G. ORWELL They were arty-looking houses, another of those sham-Tudor colonies. N. FREELING And those exercise-books . . . virulent plastic covers . . : they'd got arty lately in a jazzy style, he had noticed.

Comb.: **arty-(and-)craftiness** arty-crafty quality or characteristics; **arty-(and-)crafty** *adjs.* = *artsy-(and)-craftsy* s.v. ART *n.*[1]; **arty-farty** *a.* = *artsy-fartsy* s.v. ART *n.*[1]

artiness *n.* E20.

arum /ˈɛːrəm/ *n.* Also in Gk form †**aron**. LME. [L f. Gk *aron*.] Any of various monocotyledonous plants constituting the genus *Arum* (family Araceae), which have insignificant flowers in a club-shaped spike (or spadix) enclosed in a large leafy bract (or spathe); *esp.* (more fully *wild arum*) *A. maculatum*, a common plant of woods and hedges.

arrow arum, *dragon arum*, etc.

Comb.: **arum lily** a plant of the related southern African genus *Zantedeschia*, esp. *Z. aethiopica*, bearing a tall white spadix.

arundinaceous /ərʌndɪˈneɪʃəs/ *a.* M17. [f. L *arundinaceus*, f. (*h*)*arundo* reed: see -ACEOUS.] Reedlike, reedy.

Also **arunˈdineous** *a.* M17.

Arunta *n.* & *a.* var. of ARANDA.

†**aruspex** *n.* see HARUSPEX.

arval /ˈɑːv(ə)l/ *n. north.* Also **arvill** /-ɪl/. LME. [ON *ervi-ǫl*, f. *arfr* inheritance + *ǫl* ALE, banquet.] A funeral feast, a wake.

arvo /ˈɑːvəʊ/ *n. Austral.* & *NZ slang.* Pl. **-os**. M20. [Repr. of voicing of consonants in *af-* of *afternoon* + -O.] = AFTERNOON.

-ary /əri/ *suff.*[1] [f. L *-arius*, (fem.) *-aria*, (neut.) *-arium* connected with, or Fr. *-aire*: see -Y[3].] Forming adjs., as *arbitrary*, *budgetary*, *contrary*, *primary*, etc., and ns., as *adversary*, *dictionary*, *fritillary*, *January*, etc.

-ary /əri/ *suff.*[2] [f. L *-aris* -AR[1] I or Fr. *-aire*: see -Y[3].] Forming adjs., as *capillary*, *military*, etc., and occas. ns., as *preliminary*.

Aryan /ˈɛːrɪən/ *n.* & *a.* Also **Arian**. L15. [f. Skt *ārya* noble (applied earlier as a national name) + -AN; sense A.1 through L *Ariani* inhabitants of Ariana (see below).] A *n.* †1 A native or inhabitant of Ariana, the eastern part of ancient Iran. L15–E17. 2 A member of any of the peoples who spoke the parent language of the Indo-European (or esp. Indo-Iranian) family, or one of their descendants. *arch.* M19. b (Esp. in Nazi Germany) a Caucasian not of Jewish descent. M20. 3 The parent language of the Indo-

European (or esp. Indo-Iranian) family. L19. **B** *adj.* **1** Designating or pertaining to the parent language of the Indo-European (or esp. Indo-Iranian) family; *arch.* belonging to the Indo-European (or esp. Indo-Iranian) language family. M19. **2** Aryan-speaking; of or pertaining to the Aryan-speaking peoples or their descendants. M19. **b** (Esp. in Nazi Germany) of or pertaining to the 'Aryan race'; non-Jewish Caucasian. M20.

¶The idea of an 'Aryan race' corresponding to the parent Aryan language was taken up by several 19th.-cent. writers, esp. by de Gobineau, who linked it with theories of racial superiority. Although the existence of any such superior race had been generally rejected, the idea was revived by Hitler for political purposes, and became part of the anti-Semitic doctrine of the Nazis.

Aryanism *n.* belief in an 'Aryan race' and esp. in the theory of its racial and cultural superiority L19. **Aryani'zation** *n.* the act of Aryanizing, the fact of being Aryanized L19. **Aryanize** *v.t.* make Aryan; *esp.* (in Nazi Germany) bring within 'Aryan' control or status: M19.

aryballos /arɪ'baləs/ *n.* M19. [Gk *aruballos* bag, purse, oil-flask.] *Gk Antiq.* A globular flask with a narrow neck used to hold oil or unguent.

aryl /'arʌɪl, -rɪl/ *n.* E20. [f. AR(OMATIC *a.* + -YL.] *Chem.* Any radical derived from an aromatic hydrocarbon by removal of a hydrogen atom. Usu. in *comb.*

arytenoid /arɪ'tiːnɔɪd/ *a.* & *n.* Also †**-taen-**. E18. [mod.L *arytaenoides* f. Gk *arutainoeidēs*, f. *arutaina* funnel: see -OID.] *Anat.* **A** *adj.* Designating, pertaining to, or associated with either of two pyramidal cartilages situated at the back of the larynx and articulating with the cricoid. E18. **B** *n.* Either of these cartilages. M19.

aryte'noidal *a.* (*rare*) = ARYTENOID L17.

as /as/ *n.* Pl. **asses** /'asɪz/. M16. [L: see ACE *n.*] *Rom. Antiq.* A copper coin which was orig. of twelve ounces but was reduced in stages to half an ounce.

as /əz, *stressed* az/ *adv.*, *conj.*, & *rel. pron.* Also **'s** /z/. ME. [Reduced form of OE *alswā* ALSO. Cf. OFris. *asa*, *as(e)*, *is.*] **A** *adv.* (In a main cl., introducing (w. *as*, †*so*) an expressed or understood subord., esp. compar., cl.) †**1** Of manner or quality: in the (same) way that. ME–L15. **2** Of quantity or degree: in the same degree; to that extent (in or to which); (w. ellipsis of rel. cl.) equally. ME.

2 W. WOTTON He was as covetous as cruel. STEELE Chance has . . thrown me very often in her way, and she as often has directed a discourse to me. R. B. SHERIDAN I'd as lieve let it alone. LD MACAULAY He used it, as far as he dared. (See also similes under B.1.)

B *rel. adv.* or *conj.* (In a subord. cl.) **I** Of quantity or degree (preceded by an adj. or adv.). **1** With antecedent *as* or *so* (see sense A.2): in which degree, to what extent; (*arch.*, in comparison w. a hypothetical act or state) as if, as though; (in parenthetical clauses) though, however. ME. **2** Without antecedent *as* or *so* (giving emphasis or absoluteness to the attribute or qualification); *esp.* (in parenthetical clauses), though, however. ME. **3** After a compar.: than. *obs.* exc. *dial.* LME.

1 SHAKES. *John* The day shall not be up so soon as I. S. RICHARDSON To think I should act so barbarously as I did. SOUTHEY As certain of success As he had made a league with victory. SIR W. SCOTT You have never so much as answered me. LONGFELLOW So long as you are innocent fear nothing. B. CLEARY As much as he longed to stop . . , he would not let himself. M. BISHOP As tired as he was, he was too hyper to stretch out for some shut-eye. *as black as jet, as old as the hills, as safe as houses, as warm as toast*, etc. 2 MILTON Soon as they forth were come. G. CRABBE Fair as she is, I would my widow take. T. S. ELIOT Consider Phlebas, who was once handsome and tall as you. J. STALLWORTHY 'Here comes Sir George.' / Yes, here he comes, punctual as nine o'clock. 3 LD BERNERS They coude do no better . . as to make to their capitayne sir Eustace Damlreticourt. SIR W. SCOTT I rather like him as otherwise.

II Of quality or manner (preceded by a vb). **4** With antecedent *so* (†*as*) or equiv. phr. w. *such, same*, etc.: **a** In the manner that. *arch.* ME. **b** With the clauses transposed for emphasis: in what manner ... (in that manner); in the way that. LME. **c** Even as, just as; both ... and; equally ... and. *arch.* E17. **5** Without antecedent *so* etc., in subord. cl.: **a** In the way or manner that; to the same extent that; in proportion as; according as. ME. **b** Introducing a supposition: as if, as though. *arch.* ME. **c** Introducing a cl. attesting a statement or adjuring someone: in such manner as befits the prayer, anticipation, belief, profession, etc., that. LME. **d** In antithetical or parallel clauses: as on the other hand, even as, whereas, whilst. E16. **6** Without antecedent *so* etc., in phr. (part of subord. cl. understood): **a** In the same way as, as if, as it were; after the manner of; in the likeness of; like. ME. **b** In the character, capacity, function, or role of. E16. **7** Modifying the whole main cl. or some part other than its predicate: in accordance with what (is); in the way that. ME.

4a AV *Gen.* 18:5 So doe, as thou hast said. OED The committee was not so constituted as he had expected. **b** DRYDEN As the Cold Congeals into a Lump the liquid Gold; So 'tis again dissolv'd by Summer's Heat. **c** W. HAMILTON As some philosophers have denied to vision all perception of extension . . so others have equally refused this perception to touch. 5a AV *John* 15:12 That ye love one another, as I have loved you. G. BERKELEY Which, as they are pleasing or disagreeable, excite the passions of love, hatred, etc. J. CONRAD She turned right round as a marionette would turn. R. DAVIES Boy died as he lived: self-determined and daring. S. MENASHE As streams spread Through a delta Veins on the instep Reach the toes. **b** COLERIDGE He looks as he had seen a ghost. **c** SHAKES. *Rich. II* This swears he, as he is a prince, is just; And as I am a gentleman I credit him. LD MACAULAY Admonished to speak with reverence of their oppressor . . as they would answer it at their peril. **d** THACKERAY It has its prejudices to be sure, as which of us has not? 6a SPENSER His angry steede did chide his foming bitt, As much disdayning to the curbe to yield. AV *Heb.* 12:7 God dealeth with you as with sonnes. BYRON I . . Behold the tall pines dwindled as to shrubs. KEATS To sit upon an Alp as on a throne. TENNYSON His . . hand Caught at the hilt, as to abolish him. W. OWEN What passing-bells for these who die as cattle. H. CORBY Think of them. You did not die as these / caged in an aircraft that did not return. **b** SIR W. SCOTT He as truth received What of his birth the crowd believed. J. RUSKIN The lesson which men receive as individuals, they do not learn as nations. D. H. LAWRENCE When Van Gogh paints sunflowers, he reveals, or achieves, the vivid relationship between himself, as man, and the sunflower, as sunflower, at that quick moment of time. *Times*: *Toad of Toad Hall*, with Mr. Leo McKern as the irrepressible Toad. DAY LEWIS I feel more at home as a guest than as a host. E. BURROWS I come to tell you that my son is dead. / Americans have shot him as a spy. *seem, appear, rank*, etc., *as*; *view, regard, represent, treat, acknowledge, know, consider, accept*, etc., *as.* 7 ADDISON This project, as I have since heard, is postponed 'till the Summer Season.

III Of time or place. **8** At or during the time that; when, while; whenever. ME. **9** At the place that, in which, where. *obs.* exc. as passing into sense 8. ME.

8 OED The thought occurred to me as I was watching the procession. STEVIE SMITH As I write this / I can hear Arthur roaming overhead. A. MCCOWEN As a small boy I was somewhat tormented by God and Jesus.

IV Of reason. **10** In conformity with, in consideration of, the fact that; it being the case that; since. ME.

10 J. MOXON The whole Work will be spoiled, as being smaller than the proposed Diameter. M. DRABBLE She found everything easy, as her memory for facts was remarkable.

V Of result or purpose. **11** Without antecedent *so* or with *so* conjoined with *as* in the subord. cl.: with the result or purpose that. Foll. by inf. (†finite vb). ME. **12** With antecedent *so*, †*such*, †*that*, in the main cl.: (in such a manner, to such a degree, of such a kind, etc.) that. Foll. by inf. (†finite vb). LME.

11 C. MARLOWE The bright shining of whose glorious acts Lightens the world with his reflecting beams, As . . it grieves my soul I never saw the man. HOBBES He miscarried by unskilfulness so as the loss can no way be ascribed to cowardice. OED Put on your gloves, so as to be ready. 12 R. HAKLUYT This so amazed our men . . as they forsooke their Commanders. MILTON I gained a son, And such a son as all men hailed me happy. ADDISON I am not so vain as to think.

VI Introducing an attrib. or subord. cl. or phr.: passing into *rel. pron.* **13** After *such, same*, etc.: that, who, which. Also (now *dial.* & *slang*) w. *such* etc. omitted or replaced by *that, those*, etc. ME. **b** In parenthetic affirmations: that; (referring to the whole statement) a thing or fact which. M16. **14** Like and including, such as, for instance. ME. **15** Added to demonstr. and interrog. advs. to give conjunctive force. *obs.* exc. in *when as* (arch.) and WHEREAS (where the local sense is lost). ME. **16** Introducing a subord. cl.: that, whether, how. *obs.* exc. *dial.* L15.

13 SHAKES. *Rom. & Jul.* That kind of fruit As maids call medlars. STEELE Such a passion as I have had is never well cured. CARLYLE Never shall we again hear such speech as that was. **b** M. EDGEWORTH He was an Englishman, as they perceived by his accent. LYTTON Crouch! wild beast as thou art! 14 ADDISON I pluck'd aboue Five different Sorts . . as Wild-Time, Lauender, etc. J. P. DONLEAVY 'Yes. And what do you feel now?' 'The good things.' 'As?' 'Joy. Relief.' 16 STEELE That the Fop . . should say, as he would rather have such-a-one without a Groat, than me with the Indies. H. B. STOWE I don't know as you'll like the appearance of our place.

VII Used preceding preps. and advs. **17** Restricting or specially defining the ref. of preps.; sometimes almost pleonastic. ME. **18** Restricting the force of advs. Now *dial.* exc. in *as yet.* ME.

17 AV *1 Cor.* 8:1 As touching things offered unto idols, we know. *Listener* There are strongly convergent tendencies as between industrial societies. 18 LD BERNERS I vnderstode so as then.

Phrases: **as and when** to the extent and at the time that; *absol.* (*colloq.*) if and when, in due time. **as a rule** usually, more often than not. *as best one can* or *may*: see BEST *a., n., & adv. as far as*: see FAR *adv.* **as for** with regard to. **as from** from, after, (in formal dating). **as good as** practically. **as how?** *arch.* how? **as if** as the case would be if (with cl. containing an explicit or understood past subjunct. or an inf. expressing purpose or destination). **as (it) is** in the existing state, things being what they are. *as it stands*: see STAND *v.* **as it were** to a certain extent, as if it were actually so. *as long as*: see LONG *adv.* **as much** that quantity etc.; the same; what practically amounts to that, so. **as of** (orig. *US*) = *as from* above. *as of right*: see RIGHT *n.*[1] *as per*: see PER *prep. as regards*: see REGARD *v. as soon as*: see SOON *adv.* **as such** as being what has been named. **as that** *arch.* (in such a manner, to such a degree, of such a kind) that. **as though** as if, as the case would be if. **as to** with respect to. **as usual** as is or was usually the case. **as was** in the previously existing state. *as well (as)*: see WELL *adv.* **as who** *arch.* as one would who, like one who, as if one. **as yet** up to this or that time (though perhaps not at some later time). **as you were!** (an order, esp. *Mil.*, to) return to a previous position.

Comb.: **as-new** *a.* not yet soiled or impaired by use, as good as new; **as-told-to** *a.* & *n.* (a book, article, etc.) written with the help of a professional author.

as- /as, *unstressed* əs/ *pref.*[1] (not productive). Assim. form of L AD- bef. *s.* In OFr., L *ass-* was reduced to *as-*, which appears in ME adoptions, but in later Fr., and hence in Eng., *ass-* was restored by Latinization, as *assent, assign*, etc.

as- /as, *unstressed* əs/ *pref.*[2] (not productive). Var. of OFr. ES- f. L EX-[1]. Adoptions w. *as-* were usu. altered back or aphetized, but sometimes retained, as *assay, astonish.*

asafoetida /asə'fiːtɪdə, -'fɛt-/ *n.* Also **assa-**, ***-fet-**. LME. [med.L, f. *asa* (f. Pers. *āzā* mastic) + *foetida* (fem.), *-us* FETID *a.*] An acrid gum resin with a strong smell like that of garlic, obtained from certain Asian plants of the umbelliferous genus *Ferula*, and used in condiments. Also, a plant yielding this.

asail /ə'seɪl/ *adv.* & *pred. a.* L19. [f. A-[2] + SAIL *v.*[1]] Sailing.

Asante *n.* var. of ASHANTI.

asarabacca /'asərəbakə/ *n.* E16. [Syncopated f. L *asarum* (f. Gk *asaron*) + *bacc(h)ar* (f. Gk *bakk(h)ar* Lydian name for the same plant) or *bacc(h)aris* (f. Gk *bakkaris*) unguent made from it.] A plant of the birthwort family, *Asarum europaeum.*

asbestos /az'bɛstɒs, as-; -təs/ *n.* Orig. †**-ton**. Also †**-tus**; (*poet.*) **asbest**. OE. [OFr. *a(l)beston* f. L f. Gk *asbeston* (accus.), *-os* unquenchable (applied by Dioscurides to quicklime), f. A-[10] + *sbestos* quenched.] †1 A mineral reputed to be unquenchable when set on fire. OE–M18. 2 Any of various fibrous silicate minerals which can be woven, *esp.* chrysotile and certain amphiboles; incombustible fabric or other material made from such minerals. E17. †3 An allegedly incombustible flax. E17–M18.

2 *fig.*: K. AMIS Beauty . . is a dangerous thing, Whose touch will burn, but I'm asbestos, see? *blue asbestos*: see BLUE *a.* *serpentine asbestos*: see SERPENTINE *n.*

asbestiform *a.* having the form or appearance of asbestos L18. **asbestine** *a.* of, pertaining to, or resembling asbestos; incombustible: M17. **asbestosis** /-'stəʊsɪs/ *n.* lung disease caused by inhalation of asbestos particles E20.

ascariasis /askə'rʌɪəsɪs/ *n.* Pl. **-ases** /-əsiːz/. L19. [f. next + -IASIS.] *Med.* Disease due to infestation by the nematode *Ascaris lumbricoides*, esp. in the intestine.

ascaris /'askərɪs/ *n.* Pl. (in use long bef. sing.) **ascarides** /ə'skarɪdiːz/. LME. [mod.L f. Gk *askaris*, pl. *-ides*, intestinal worm.] A parasitic nematode worm of the genus *Ascaris*; esp. *A. lumbricoides*, parasitic in man.

Also **ascarid** *n.* [back-form. f. pl. *ascarides*] L17.

ascend /ə'sɛnd/ *v.* LME. [L *ascendere*, f. *ad* AS-[1] + *scandere* to climb.] I *v.i.* 1 Go up, come up; rise, soar; be raised. Occas. foll. by *up*. LME. b Of a planet, zodiacal sign, etc.: move towards the zenith, *esp.* come above the horizon; move northwards. LME. 2 Slope or extend upwards; *poet.* rise by growth or construction, be reared. LME. 3 Of sound: rise in pitch, go up the scale. LME. 4 Proceed from inferior to superior; rise in quality, station, degree, etc. LME. 5 Go back in time, or in order of genealogical succession. L16.

1 AV *John* 6:62 What and if yee shall see the sonne of man ascend vp where hee was before? MILTON The noise Of riot ascends above their loftiest Towrs. L. DEIGHTON I don't know when you last ascended from your cellar. b W. CONGREVE I was born, Sir, when the Crab was ascending. **ascending node** *Astron.* the point at which the moon's or a planet's orbit crosses the ecliptic from south to north. 2 GOLDSMITH Far to the right, where Apennine ascends. G. B. SHAW On both sides of this passage steps ascend to a landing. 4 J. JORTIN A rash desire to ascend to a rank—for which God's providence has not designed us. J. MCCOSH We shall ascend . . beyond laws to a lawgiver.

II *v.t.* 6 Go up, climb; climb to the summit of; move upstream along (a river etc.). LME. 7 Get up on to, mount; *arch.* go up into. L16.

6 GIBBON Their galleys ascended the river. C. DARWIN We ascend the lofty peaks of the Cordillera and we find an alpine species of bizcacha. B. MOORE Ascending and descending these winding turret stairs. 7 SHAKES. *Rom. & Jul.* Go, get thee to thy love, . . Ascend her chamber, hence and comfort her. E. O'NEILL He ascends the dais and places her on the table as on a bier. **ascend the throne** become king or queen.

ascendable *a.* (*rare*) M18.

ascendancy /ə'sɛnd(ə)nsi/ *n.* Also **-ency**; (sense 2) **A-**. E18. [f. next + -ANCY.] 1 Supremacy, paramount influence (*over*), dominant control; the state or quality of being in the ascendant. E18. 2 *spec.* (*Hist.*) (Usu. w. def. article.) The domination by the Anglo-Irish Protestant minority in Ireland esp. in the 18th and 19th cents.; the dominant class itself. Also more fully *Protestant ascendancy*. L18.

ascendance *n.* = ASCENDANCY 1 M18.

ascendant /ə'sɛnd(ə)nt/ *a.* & *n.* Also (now *rare*) **-ent**. LME. [(O)Fr. f. L *ascendent-* pres. ppl stem of *ascendere* ASCEND: see -ANT[1].] A *adj.* 1 Of a planet etc.: rising towards the zenith; *Astrol.* just rising above the eastern horizon. LME. 2 *gen.* Rising, ascending. M16. 3 Having ascendancy; predominant, superior. M17.

2 BACON A double scale or ladder, ascendent and descendent. SOUTHEY Distended like a ball . . The body mounts ascendant. 3 A. KNOX To quicken, exalt, and make ascendant all that is rational and noble in us. G. GROTE An ascendent position in public life.

B *n.* 1 *Astrol.* The point of the ecliptic or sign of the zodiac which at a given moment (esp. at a person's birth) is just rising above the eastern horizon. LME. †2 *gen.* A person who or thing which ascends or rises; a slope, a rise, a peak; a flight of steps. M16–E18. 3 = ASCENDANCY *n.* 1. Now only in *in the ascendant*, supreme, dominating; *pop.* rising; (freq. w. fig. reference to sense 1). L16. 4 A person who precedes in genealogical order; an ancestor. E17.

1 **house of the ascendant** the celestial house immediately below the eastern horizon. **lord of the ascendant** a planet within the house of the ascendant. 2 T. NASHE Pryde can endure no Superiours, no equals, no ascendants. MILTON A Lordly Ascendant . . from Primate to Patriarch, and so to Pope. 3 MARVELL Having gained this Ascendent upon him. E. A. FREEMAN The star of Harold was fairly in the ascendant. C. S. FORESTER There was one ruling motive still in the ascendant and that was a passionate desire not to make himself conspicuous. 4 JOYCE Traces of elephantiasis have been discovered among his ascendants.

ascendency *n.* var. of ASCENDANCY.

ascendent *a.* & *n.* see ASCENDANT.

ascender /ə'sɛndə/ *n.* E17. [f. ASCEND + -ER[1].] 1 A person who or thing which ascends. E17. 2 *Typogr.* & *Palaeogr.* An ascending letter; a part or stroke projecting above letters such as x. M19.

ascending /ə'sɛndɪŋ/ *a.* E17. [f. ASCEND *v.* + -ING[2].] 1 Rising, mounting, increasing; sloping upwards. E17. 2a *Anat.* Directed upwards; *spec.* (of a nerve etc.) passing up the spinal cord to the brain. E18. b *Bot.* Of a stem etc.: inclined upwards, esp. with steepness increasing from the base. M19. 3 Going backwards in genealogical order. E18.

1 DRYDEN Bak'd in the Sunshine of ascending Fields. POPE Dark o'er the fields th' ascending vapour flies. F. A. G. OUSELEY The diminished fifth . . should be prepared by a sixth, with an ascending bass. A. J. P. TAYLOR Three tasks in ascending order of difficulty. **ascending letter** *Typogr.* & *Palaeogr.* a letter with a part or stroke projecting above letters such as x. 3 BURKE The ascending collateral branch was much regarded amongst the ancient Germans.

ascension /ə'sɛnʃ(ə)n/ *n.* In sense 1 also **A-**. ME. [(O)Fr. f. L *ascensio(n-)*, f. *ascens-* pa. ppl stem of *ascendere* ASCEND: see -ION.] 1 The ascent of Christ to heaven on the fortieth day after the Resurrection. Also, Ascension Day. ME. 2 *Astron.* & *Astrol.* The rising of a celestial object; a measure of this. Usu. in special collocations (see below). LME. 3 *gen.* The act or process of ascending; ascent, rise; *arch.* a path for ascending. LME. †4 Distillation, evaporation. LME–E19. †5 A going back in genealogical succession; reversion to an ancestor. L16–E17.

2 **oblique ascension** (of a star, etc.) the arc intercepted between the first point of Aries and the point of the celestial equator which rises with the star in an oblique sphere. **right ascension** angular distance measured (in hours, minutes, seconds) eastwards along the celestial equator from the first point of Aries. 3 SOUTHEY Round and round The spiral steps in long ascension wound. C. MACKENZIE We stayed on deck until the funicular had made its last golden ascension and descension. H. F. PRINGLE The ascension to power of Woodrow Wilson. G. SARTON Gigantic mountains, the ascension of which may tax our strength to the limit.

Comb.: **Ascension Day** the day of Christ's Ascension; the Thursday on which this is commemorated; **Ascensiontide** the ten-day period between Ascension Day and the eve of Pentecost.

ascensional *a.* of or pertaining to ascension or ascent; tending upwards; *ascensional difference* (Astron.), the difference between the right ascension and oblique ascension of a celestial object: L16.

ascensive /ə'sɛnsɪv/ *a.* Now *rare*. E17. [med.L *ascensivus*, f. L *ascens-*: see prec., -IVE.] Characterized by or producing upward movement, rising; progressive, intensive.

ascent /ə'sɛnt/ *n.* L16. [f. ASCEND *v.* after *descend*, *descent*.] 1 The action or an act of ascending; upward movement, rise (*lit.* & *fig.*). L16. b *spec.* The action or an act of climbing or travelling up a mountain, slope, stair, etc. E17. †2 An eminence, a hill. L16–M18. 3 A means of ascending; a way leading upwards; a way up; an upward slope. E17. 4 A going back in time or genealogical order. E17.

1 GIBBON His ascent to one of the most eminent dignities of the republic. J. SIMMONS Stretches of relatively level line to assist the locomotive on the ascent. *Encycl. Brit.* Many manned ascents were made with both hot-air and hydrogen balloons. *Song of Ascents*: see SONG *n.*[1] b B. ENGLAND Compared to previous climbs, it was a simple ascent, and in less than two hours they were on the peak. 3 HOR. WALPOLE The ascent of steps from the hall. M. INNES Hudspith puffed as the ascent grew steeper.

Earlier †**ascence** *n.* LME–L16.

ascertain /asə'teɪn/ *v.t.* LME. [OFr. *acertain-* tonic stem of *acertener* (later *ass-*, *asc-*), f. as A-[5] + CERTAIN.] †1 Assure, convince; inform, tell; *refl.* acquire information. LME–L18. †2 Make certain; prove, demonstrate; ensure, guarantee. L15–L19. †3 Fix, determine, limit. L15–L18. b Destine, doom, (a person) *to*. Only in M17. 4 Find out or learn for a certainty; make sure of, get to know. L16.

1 CHARLES CHURCHILL Who may perhaps . . Be ascertained that Two and Two make four. G. MORRIS I wish to be ascertained of the . . intentions of the Court. 2 G. HORNE But who shall exactly ascertain to us what superstition is? BOSWELL [This] would ascertain it not to be the production of Johnson. W. GODWIN The intelligence that was brought me by no means ascertained the greatness of the danger. SIR W. SCOTT The squire's influence . . ascertained him the support of the whole class of bucks. 3 SHAFTESBURY To suppress by violence the natural Passion of Enthusiasm or to endeavour to ascertain it. J. STEPHEN Such charters ascertained what were the customs by which the citizens were to be governed. 4 W. C. WILLIAMS He went to great trouble to ascertain the depth of the water. T. CAPOTE The door was partly open; she opened it . . enough to ascertain that the office was filled only with shadow. C. JACKSON Whether he had ascertained if she was old or young.

ascertainable *a.* able to be ascertained L18. **ascertainably** *adv.* in an ascertainable manner; recognizably: M19. **ascertainment** *n.* †(*a*) fixing, settlement; assurance; (*b*) finding out; determination, discovery: M17.

ascesis /ə'siːsɪs/ *n.* L19. [Gk *askēsis* exercise, training, f. *askein* to exercise.] The practice of self-discipline.

ascetic /ə'sɛtɪk/ *a.* & *n.* M17. [med.L *asceticus* or Gk *askētikos* f. *askētēs* monk, hermit, f. *askein* to exercise: see -IC.] A *adj.* 1 Practising severe abstinence or austerity, esp. for religious or spiritual reasons; characteristic of or suggesting a person dedicated to such existence. M17. 2 = ASCETICAL *a.* (a) (which is more usual in this sense). E19.

1 SIR T. BROWNE The old Ascetick christians found a paradise in a desert. R. RENDELL He wore a perfectly plain, almost ascetic dark suit. W. TREVOR His face seeming ascetic until cheered by a smile.

B *n.* 1 A person who practises extreme self-denial or austerity; *esp.* one of those in the early Church who retired into solitude for this purpose. M17. †2 *sing.* & (usu.) in *pl.* An ascetical treatise. E–M18.

1 ARNOLD BENNETT They discovered the ascetic's joy in robbing themselves of sleep and in catching chills. R. P. JHABVALA He . . was dressed in nothing but an orange robe like an Indian ascetic.

ascetical *a.* (*a*) of or pertaining to spiritual exercises intended to lead to perfection and virtue; (*b*) = ASCETIC *a.* 1 (which is more usual in this sense): E17. **ascetically** *adv.* M19. **asceticism** /-sɪz(ə)m/ *n.* the principles or practice of ascetics; rigorous self-discipline, austerity: M17. **ascetism** *n.* = ASCETICISM M19.

asci *n.* pl. of ASCUS.

ascidian /ə'sɪdɪən/ *n.* & *a.* M19. [f. mod.L *Ascidia* pl. (genus name), f. Gk *askidion* dim. of *askos* wineskin: see -AN.] *Zool.* A *n.* Any tunicate belonging to the class Ascidiacea; a sea squirt. M19. B *adj.* Of or pertaining to this class. M19.

ascidiform /ə'sɪdɪfɔːm/ *a.* M19. [f. mod.L *ascidium* f. Gk *askidion* (see prec.) + -I- + -FORM.] Chiefly *Bot.* Shaped like a pitcher or bottle.

ascites /ə'sʌɪtiːz/ *n.* Pl. same. LME. [Late L f. Gk *askitēs* dropsy, f. *askos* wineskin.] *Med.* Abnormal accumulation of fluid in the abdomen.

ascitic /ə'sɪtɪk/ *a.* of, pertaining to, or affected with ascites L17. **ascitical** *a.* (now *rare*) = ASCITIC L17.

ascititious *a.* see ADSCITITIOUS.

asclent *adv., pred. a., & prep.* var. of ASKLENT.

Asclepiad /əˈskliːpɪad/ *n.*[1] E17. [f. late L *asclepiadeus* adj. f. Gk *asklēpiadeios*, f. *Asklēpiadēs* Gk poet of the 3rd cent. BC, who invented the form.] *Class. Pros.* A measure consisting of a spondee, two (or three) choriambi, and an iambus.

Asclepiaˈdean *a.* E18.

asclepiad /əˈskliːpɪad/ *n.*[2] M19. [f. next + -AD[1].] *Bot.* Any plant of the milkweed family Asclepiadaceae.

asclepiaˈdaceous *a.* of or pertaining to the family Asclepiadaceae M19.

asclepias /əˈskliːpɪəs/ *n.* L16. [L = swallowwort f. Gk *asklēpias*, f. *Asklēpios* AESCULAPIUS.] Any of various plants now or formerly included in the genus *Asclepias*, of the milkweed family; *esp.* swallowwort, *Vincetoxicum hirundinaria*.

asco- /ˈaskəʊ/ *comb. form* of ASCUS: see -O-.

ascocarp *n.* a fruiting body of an ascomycete, containing a number of asci L19. **aˈscogenous** *a.* producing asci L19. **ascoˈgonium** *n.* a female reproductive organ of an ascomycete L19. **ascospore** *n.* a spore produced in an ascus L19.

ascomycete /ˌaskəˈmʌɪsiːt/ *n.* Orig. only in pl. **-mycetes** /-ˈmʌɪsiːts, -mʌɪˈsiːtiːz/. M19. [Anglicized sing. of mod.L *Ascomycetes* (see below), f. prec. + Gk *mukētes* pl. of *mukēs* fungus.] *Mycol.* A fungus of the subdivision Ascomycotina (formerly the class Ascomycetes), bearing asci.

ascomyˈcetous *a.* M19.

ascon /ˈaskɒn/ *n.* L19. [mod.L genus name, f. Gk *askos* bag, sac.] *Zool.* A grade of sponge structure of the asconoid type; a stage in sponge development characterized by this structure; a sponge of this type or stage. Cf. LEUCON, SYCON.

asconoid *a.* & *n.* (*a*) *adj.* of, pertaining to, or designating the simplest sponges, which have a tubelike or baglike structure lined with choanocytes; (*b*) *n.* a sponge of this type: M20.

ascorbic /əˈskɔːbɪk/ *a.* M20. [f. A-[10] + SCORB(UT)IC *a.*] Biochem. *ascorbic acid*, the antiscorbutic vitamin (chemically an enolic lactone, $C_6H_8O_6$), which is found in citrus fruits and green vegetables and is essential in maintaining healthy connective tissue; also called *vitamin C*.

ascot /ˈaskət/ *n.* Also **A-**. E20. [*Ascot* in Berkshire, southern England, where race meetings are held.] (In full *ascot tie*) a man's broad silk necktie; a broad scarf looped under the chin.

ascribe /əˈskrʌɪb/ *v.t.* Branch I orig. also †**-ive**. ME. [L *ascribere*, f. *ad* AS-[1] + *scribere* write; forms in *-v-* f. OFr. *ascriv-* stem of *ascrire* f. It. *ascrivere*.] **I 1** Assign or impute *to* someone or something as an action, effect, product, etc., or as a quality, characteristic, or property (rarely in a material sense). ME. †**2** Reckon up, count. LME–E17.

1 R. W. EMERSON There is a depth in those brief moments which constrains us to ascribe more reality to them than to all other experiences. J. N. LOCKYER The invention of clocks is variously ascribed to the sixth and ninth centuries. J. CONRAD I ascribed this behaviour to her shocked modesty. A. KOESTLER You ascribe to me an opinion which I do not hold. W. STYRON Most of the mischief ascribed to the military has been wrought with the advice and consent of civil authority.

†**II 3** Enrol, register. LME–L17. **4** Dedicate, inscribe, *to*. Only in M16. **5** Subjoin (one's name); subjoin one's name to. E–M17.

ascribable *a.* able to be ascribed; attributable: M17.

ascription /əˈskrɪpʃ(ə)n/ *n.* L16. [L *ascriptio(n-)*, f. *ascript-* pa. ppl stem of *ascribere*: see prec., -ION.] The act of ascribing; a statement etc. that ascribes; *spec.* a formula ascribing praise to God, used at the end of a sermon.

ascriptive *a.* able to be ascribed; pertaining to ascription: M17.

ascrive *v.* see ASCRIBE.

ascus /ˈaskəs/ *n.* Pl. **asci** /ˈaskʌɪ/. M19. [mod.L f. Gk *askos* bag, sac.] *Mycol.* A sac, usu. cylindrical, in which a number of spores develop in ascomycetes.

Asdic /ˈazdɪk/ *n.* Also **a-**, **ASDIC**. E20. [f. *ASD*, prob. repr. Anti-Submarine Division + -IC.] An early form of sonar used to detect submarines.

-ase /eɪz/ *suff.* [f. DIAST)ASE.] Forming names of enzymes, as *lactase*, *maltase*, etc.

asea /əˈsiː/ *adv.* & *pred. a.* M19. [f. A-[2] + SEA *n.*] At sea, to the sea.

aseismic /eɪˈsʌɪzmɪk/ *a.* L19. [f. A-[10] + SEISMIC *a.*] **1** Resistant to the effects of earthquakes. L19. **2** *Geol.* Free from earthquakes. E20.

aseity /eɪˈsiːɪti, ə-/ *n.* L17. [med.L *aseitas*, f. L *a* from + *se* oneself: see -ITY.] *Metaphysics.* Underived or independent existence.

asepsis /eɪˈsɛpsɪs/ *n.* L19. [f. A-[10] + SEPSIS.] *Med.* The exclusion or absence of disease-causing micro-organisms in surgery etc.

aseptic /eɪˈsɛptɪk/ *a.* M19. [f. A-[10] + SEPTIC *a.*] *Med.* Free from sepsis; pertaining to or promoting asepsis.

aseptically *adv.* E20. †**asepticism** *n.* L19–E20.

asexual /eɪˈsɛksjʊəl, -ʃʊəl/ *a.* M19. [f. A-[10] + SEXUAL.] Chiefly *Biol.* Not sexual; without sex or sexuality; (of reproduction) not involving the fusion of gametes.

asexuˈality *n.* L19. **asexually** *adv.* M19.

ash /aʃ/ *n.*[1] [OE *æsć* = OS *ask* (Du. *esch*), OHG *ask* (G *Esche*), ON *askr*, f. Gmc.] **1** More fully *ash tree*. A forest tree, *Fraxinus excelsior*, with grey bark, pinnate foliage, and hard, tough, pale wood. OE. **b** Any of various related or otherwise similar trees; *esp.* any other tree of the genus *Fraxinus*. Usu. w. specifying wd. LME. **2** More fully *ash-wood*. The wood of the ash. OE. †**b** (The ashen shaft of) a spear. OE–E18. **3** The runic letter ᚨ; its romanized equivalent *æ* (see Æ, Æ 1). OE.

1b *black ash*, *ground ash*, *manna ash*, *mountain ash*, *red ash*, *white ash*, etc.

Comb.: **ash-key** the one-seeded winged fruit of the ash; **ash-plant** an ash sapling used as a stick, whip, etc.; *ash tree*: see sense 1 above; **ashweed** ground elder, *Aegopodium podagraria*, whose leaves resemble those of ash; *ash-wood*: see sense 2 above.

ashling *n.* an ash sapling M18.

ash /aʃ/ *n.*[2] Freq. in pl. **ashes** /ˈaʃɪz/. [OE *æsće*, *æxe* = MLG *asche*, Du. *asch*, OHG *asca* (G *Asche*), ON *aska*: cf. Goth. *azgo*.] **1** In *pl.* & *collect. sing.* The powdery residue, composed chiefly of earthy or mineral particles, left after the combustion of any substance. (Sometimes as a symbol of grief or repentance.) OE. **b** *sing.* A powdery residue (as above); *spec.* that left after the smoking of tobacco. LME. **2** Dust of the ground, esp. as symbolizing man's mortal constitution. OE. **3** That which remains of a human body after cremation; *poet.* mortal remains. ME. **4** Powdery matter ejected from volcanoes. M17. **5** The colour of (esp. wood) ashes; pale grey; deathlike pallor. E19.

1 E. WAUGH The fire, unattended . ., had sunk to a handful of warm ashes. B. JONES On watering-place islands / our fires of dead wood / sink rapidly to ash. *fig.*: J. A. FROUDE Where the ashes of the Sertorian rebellion were still smouldering. P. GALLICO The triumph suddenly developed the taste of ashes. **ash(es) of roses** a greyish-pink colour. *dust and ashes*: see DUST *n.* *in* SACKCLOTH *and ashes*. **lay in ashes** burn to the ground, destroy utterly. **rise from the ashes** be renewed after destruction. **turn to ashes (in a person's mouth)** become utterly disappointing or worthless. *volcanic ash*: see VOLCANIC *a.* **b** J. D. DANA Hircite . . after complete combustion leaves an ash. 3 LD MACAULAY Facing fearful odds For the ashes of his fathers And the temples of his Gods. **the Ashes** *Cricket* the mythical trophy held by the winners of a series of test matches between England and Australia (orig. w. ref. to the symbolical remains of English cricket, taken to Australia). 5 BYRON The lip of ashes, and the cheek of flame.

Comb.: **ash-bin** a receptacle for ashes and household refuse, a rubbish bin; **ash blonde** *a.* & *n.* (of hair) very fair; (a person) with very fair hair; **ashcan** (chiefly *US*) = *ash-bin* above; **ash-coloured** *a.* of the colour of ashes, pale grey; **ash-hole** a hole beneath a fireplace or furnace into which the ashes fall; **ashpan** a tray, fitted beneath a grate, in which ashes are collected and removed; **ash-pit** = *ash-hole* above; **ashtray** a receptacle for tobacco-ash etc.; **Ash Wednesday** the first day of Lent (from the custom of sprinkling ashes on or otherwise applying ashes to the heads of penitents).

ashery *n.* a place for the manufacture of potash or pearl ash M19.

ash /aʃ/ *v.t.* E16. [f. ASH *n.*[2]] **1** Sprinkle or cover with ashes; mark (a person) with ash as a sign of penitence. E16. **2** *Chem.* Remove all combustible components from (a substance) by incineration, in analysis. L19.

ashake /əˈʃeɪk/ *adv.* & *pred. a.* M19. [f. A-[2] + SHAKE *n.* or *v.*] Shaking.

ashame /əˈʃeɪm/ *v. arch.* exc. as next. [OE *āsćamian*, f. as A-[1] + SHAME *v.*] †**1** *v.i.* Feel shame. OE–M16. **2** *v.t.* Put to shame. (Cf. next.) L15.

ashamed /əˈʃeɪmd/ *a.* (usu. *pred.*). [OE *āsćamod*: see prec., -ED[1].] Affected, embarrassed, or disconcerted, by shame. (Foll. by *of* or †*for*, †*on*, the cause of shame; *for* a person, on his or her account; *that*. See also *ashamed to do* below.)

AV *Jer.* 17:13 All that forsake thee shall be ashamed. M. W. MONTAGU I am ashamed for her who wrote them. STEELE I am ashamed to be caught in this Pickle. TENNYSON Ashamed am I that I should tell it thee. ARNOLD BENNETT Maggie . . felt as though she had done something wrong and was ashamed of it. **ashamed to do** (*a*) prevented by shame from doing; (*b*) feeling shame when doing. **not ashamed to do** not prevented or deterred by shame from doing.

ashamedly /-mɪdli/ *adv.* E17. **ashamedness** /-md-, -mɪd-/ *n.* L16.

Ashanti /əˈʃanti/ *n.* & *a.* Also **Asante** /əˈsanti/. E18. [Twi *Asante*.] **A** *n.* **1** A member of one of the Akan peoples of Ghana. E18. **2** The dialect of Twi spoken by this people. L19. **B** *adj.* Of or pertaining to this people or their dialect. M19.

Also **Ashantian** *a.* E18.

ashen /ˈaʃ(ə)n/ *a.*[1] ME. [f. ASH *n.*[1] + -EN[4].] **1** Made of ash-wood. *arch.* ME. **2** Of or pertaining to an ash tree. L15.

ashen /ˈaʃ(ə)n/ *a.*[2] LME. [f. ASH *n.*[2] + -EN[4].] **1** Ash-coloured, deathly pale. LME. **2** Of ashes. M19.

Asherah /aˈʃiːrɑː/ *n.* Pl. **-rim** /-rɪm/. M19. [Heb. *ʾăšērāh*.] *Hist.* (A tree-trunk or wooden post symbolizing) a Canaanitish goddess.

ashet /ˈaʃɪt/ *n. Sc., north., & NZ.* M16. [Fr. ASSIETTE.] A large plate or dish, esp. for meat.

ashimmer /əˈʃɪmə/ *adv.* & *pred. a.* L19. [f. A-[2] + SHIMMER *n.* or *v.*] Shimmering.

ashine /əˈʃʌɪn/ *adv.* & *pred. a.* M19. [f. A-[2] + SHINE *n.* or *v.*] Shining.

ashipboard /əˈʃɪpbɔːd/ *adv.* & *pred. a. arch.* M16. [f. A *prep.*[1] 1 + SHIPBOARD.] On board ship.

ashiver /əˈʃɪvə/ *adv.* & *pred. a.* E19. [f. A-[2] + SHIVER *n.*[3] or *v.*[2]] Shivering; shivery.

Ashkenazi /aʃkəˈnɑːzi/ *n.* Pl. **-zim** /-zɪm/. M19. [mod.Heb., f. *Ashkenaz* a descendent of Japheth (*Gen.* 10:3).] A Jew of middle, northern, or eastern Europe, or of such ancestry. Cf. SEPHARDI.

Ashkenazic *a.* L19.

ashlar /ˈaʃlə/ *n.* & *v.* Also **-ler**. ME. [OFr. *aisselier* f. L AXILLA dim. of AXIS *n.*[1], *assis*, board, plank.] **A** *n.* A square-hewn stone; masonry constructed of such stones laid in horizontal courses with vertical joints; similar masonry used as a facing to rubble or brick. ME. **B** *v.t.* Face with ashlar. M19.

ashlaring *n.* (*a*) upright boarding fixed in attics from the joists to the rafters to cut off the acute angle of the roof and the floor; (*b*) ashlar masonry: E18.

ashore /əˈʃɔː/ *adv.* & *pred. a.* L16. [f. A *prep.*[1] 1 + SHORE *n.*[1]] **1** To the shore, to land. L16. **2** On shore, on land. M17.

2 *Jack ashore*: see JACK *n.*[1]

ashram /ˈaʃrəm/ *n.* E20. [Skt *āśrama* hermitage.] **1** In the Indian subcontinent: a hermitage, a place of religious retreat. E20. **2** *transf.* Any group with shared spiritual or social aims living together. M20.

Ashura /ˈaʃʊərə/ *n.* M19. [f. Arab. *ʿāšūrā* f. Aram. *ʿăśōrā*.] The tenth of Muharram, celebrated as a holy day by Sunni Muslims and as a day of mourning (the anniversary of the death of Husain) by Shiite Muslims.

ashy /'aʃi/ *a.* LME. [f. ASH *n.*[2] + -Y[1].] 1 Covered or sprinkled with ashes. LME. 2 = ASHEN *a.*[2] 1. LME. 3 Consisting of ashes. L15.
2 *ashy-grey, -pale*, etc.

Asian /'eɪʃ(ə)n, -ʒ(ə)n/ *n.* & *a.* LME. [L *Asianus* f. Gk *Asianos*, f. *Asia*: see below, -AN.] A *n.* A native or inhabitant of the continent of Asia; a person of Asian descent. LME.
KENYA *Asian. Kenyan Asian*: see KENYAN *a.* UGANDA *Asian. Ugandan Asian*: see UGANDAN *a.* 1.
B *adj.* Of or pertaining to Asia or its peoples or inhabitants; descended from Asians. E17.
Asian flu *colloq.* a kind of influenza whose virus was first identified at Hong Kong.
Asianic /eɪʃɪ'anɪk, eɪʒɪ-/ *a.* of or pertaining to Asia Minor L19. **Asianize** *v.t.* make Asian in character etc.; transfer to Asian ownership or control: L19.

Asiarch /'eɪʃɪɑːk, 'eɪʒ-/ *n.* M18. [Late L *asiarcha* f. Gk *asiarkhēs*, f. *Asia* Asia: see -ARCH.] *Hist.* An official responsible for religious rites and public games in Asia Minor under Roman rule.

Asiatic /eɪʃɪ'atɪk, eɪʒ-/ *a.* & *n.* E17. [L *Asiaticus* f. Gk *Asiatikos*, f. *Asia* Asia: see -IC.] A *adj.* 1 = ASIAN *a.* Now usu. considered *racially offensive* when applied to persons. E17. 2 Of literary style: florid and imaginative. *arch.* M18.
1 *Asiatic* CHOLERA.
B *n.* = ASIAN *n.* Now usu. considered *racially offensive.* E17.
Asiatically *adv.* in an Asiatic style or manner E19. **Asiaticism** /-sɪz(ə)m/ *n.* (*arch.*) (a) florid and imaginative expression or usage L18.

aside /ə'sʌɪd/ *adv.*, *prep.*, & *n.* ME. [f. A *prep.*[1] 1 + SIDE *n.*] A *adv.* 1 To or at the side; out of the way, away. ME. 2 Sideways, obliquely, aslant; towards one side, away from the direct line. ME. 3 Away from the general throng or main body; in or into privacy; so as not to be generally heard (freq. as a stage direction: cf. sense C.1 below). LME. 4 Away from one's person or thought; out of use or consideration; off, down; excepted, apart. LME. 5 Alongside, close by; by the side (*of*). *arch.* & *dial.* LME.
1 V. S. NAIPAUL Ganesh stood between the women, but The Great Belcher moved him aside. T. STOPPARD He throws the paper aside and picks up the Guardian. 2 CHAUCER With that he loked on me asyde, As who sayth nay, that wol not be. J. MCCRAE We have sworn and will not turn aside. K. AMIS Barbara turned the car aside on to an unmade track. 3 SCOTT FITZGERALD Sloane and the lady began an impassioned conversation aside. C. S. FORESTER 'Beggin' your pardon, sir,' said Hunter aside to Hornblower. G. GREENE He . . took my arm and led me a little aside. 4 SPENSER Her fillet she vndight, And laid her stole aside. E. O'NEILL No, all kiddin' aside, I know he'll run me down first second he sees you. A. WILSON He put aside prejudice. J. HELLER I've put aside my novel, you know. **aside from** (chiefly *N. Amer.*) = APART *from.* 5 SIR W. SCOTT From ancient vessels ranged aside.
B *prep.* †1 Past, beyond. L16–L19. 2 At the side of, beside. *obs.* exc. *dial.* E17.
C *n.* 1 Words spoken aside or in an undertone, esp. by an actor in the hearing of the audience but supposedly not of the other actors. E18. 2 An incidental writing or remark of an author etc. L19.
1 G. B. SHAW The action is not carried on by impossible soliloquys and asides. M. KEANE The laughing asides grew into a mild kind of persecution. 2 O. SACKS Other observations and asides . . have instead been placed in footnotes.

asile /ə'sʌɪl/ *n. arch.* Also **-yle**. LME. [(O)Fr. f. L ASYLUM.] = ASYLUM *n.*

asilus /ə'sʌɪləs/ *n.* L17. [L = gadfly.] *Entomol.* A robber-fly. Now only as mod.L genus name.
asilid /'asɪlɪd/ *a.* & *n.* (*a*) *adj.* of or pertaining to the family Asilidae (robber-flies); (*b*) *n.* a fly of this family: E20.

†**asinego** *n.* Also **-igo, as(s)inico**. E17–L19. [Sp. *asnico* dim. of *asno* ASS *n.*[1]] A little ass; *fig.* a dolt, a fool.

asinine /'asɪnʌɪn/ *a.* L15. [L *asininus*, f. *asinus* ASS *n.*[1]: see -INE[1].] Of or pertaining to asses; asslike; stupid, obstinate.
asininity /asɪ'nɪnɪti/ *n.* M19.

ask /ɑːsk/ *n.*[1] *rare.* OE. [f. the vb.] A request; a question.

ask /ask/ *n.*[2] *Sc.* & *north.* ME. [App. f. OE *āpexe*, cogn. w. OHG *egidehsa* (G *Eidechse* lizard).] A newt; occas. (*Sc.*) a lizard.

ask /ɑːsk/ *v.* Also (now *dial.*) **ax(e)** /aks/. [OE *āscian, ācsian, āhsian, āxian* = OFris. *āskia*, OS *ēscon*, OHG *eiscōn*, f. WGmc.] †I 1 *v.t.* Call for, call upon to come. OE–ME.
II 2 *v.t.* Call upon a person, or thing personified, for an answer or for information. As obj. the person, the thing desired (which may take the form of a n. or pron., a cl. introduced by a rel. pron. or conj., or direct or indirect speech), or both. (Foll. by †*at*, †*to*, or *of* the person; *about*, (arch.) *of* the matter in question; *after* the matter in question, esp. a person absent; *for* esp. a person whom one wishes to see.) OE. 3 *v.i.* Enquire, make enquiries. (Foll. by *about*, †*of* the thing desired; *after* a thing missing, a person absent, etc.; *for* esp. a person whom one wishes to see; †*at*, †*of* the person called upon.) OE.
2 CAXTON Asking to her why she had trespaced his commaundments. COVERDALE *Ecclus* 21.17 It is axed at the mouth of the wyse. H. LATIMER The other axed ye price, he sayed: xx. nobles. SHAKES. *2 Hen. IV* Knocking at the taverns, And asking every one for Sir John Falstaff. AV *John* 9:19 They asked them, saying, Is this your son? POPE Ask your own heart; and nothing is so plain. GOLDSMITH Ask me no questions and I'll tell you no fibs. TENNYSON Once I ask'd him of his early life. DICKENS I . . asked him what o'clock it was. G. BORROW I asked her her maiden name. GEO. ELIOT Animals are such agreeable friends—they ask no questions, they pass no criticisms. OED A farmer of whom I asked the way. R. KIPLING 'Dost *thou* give news for love, or dost thou sell it?' Kim asked. E. W. ROGERS If you want to know the time, ask a P'liceman! G. STEIN Often Jeff would ask her, did she really love him. V. WOOLF Where was he this morning, for instance? Some committee, she never asked what. G. GREENE If Hitler had come into the conversation she would have interrupted to ask who he was. L. DURRELL It was the question that Nessim asked himself repeatedly. DAY LEWIS I seldom asked my father . . about our relations near or distant. K. LAFFAN Father Patrick asked me if I'd like to be a priest. **ask me another** *colloq.* I do not know (the answer to your question). **I ask you** *colloq.*: expr. ridicule, contempt, denial, etc. **if you ask me** in my opinion. 3 AV *1 Sam.* 28:16 Wherefore then doest thou aske of me? MILTON Ask for this great deliverer now, and find him Eyeless in Gaza. G. MACDONALD To ask after their health when he met them. T. FRISBY Here, you're not kinky or anything, are you? . . Why do you ask?
III 4 *v.t.* Express to someone a desire to obtain a thing. As obj. the person, the thing desired (which may take the form of a n. or pron., a cl. introduced by *that*, or an inf. phr.), or both. (Foll. by indirect obj. or †*at*, *of*, *from* the person, *for* the thing desired.) ME. 5 *v.i.* Express a desire to obtain something. (Foll. by †*after* or *for* the thing desired.) ME.
4 EARL RIVERS I had delyte & axed to rede some good historye. SHAKES. *Com. Err.* He ask'd me for a thousand marks in gold. MILTON To stand upright Will ask thee skill. H. FIELDING I ask Mr. Blifil pardon. R. BURNS I am ashamed to ask another favour of you. J. TYNDALL I asked him to accompany me. M. ARNOLD I ask but that my death may find The freedom to my life denied. G. B. SHAW Thirty crowns is too much to ask from him. T. FRISBY I say, could I ask you a favour? C. HAMPTON I'm sure she'd marry you like a shot if you asked her. A. AYCKBOURN They keep sending them. . . I've asked them not to. *ask a blessing*: see BLESSING 1. 5 COVERDALE *Matt.* 6:7 Axe & it shalbe giuen you. SOUTHEY Could hear a famish'd woman ask for food, And feel no pity. J. LE CARRÉ We always ask for a banker's reference before giving credit.
IV Pregnant senses and special uses. †6 *v.t.* & *i.* Inquire into, examine, investigate. OE–E17. 7 *v.t.* & *i.* (foll. by *for*). Predicated of things: need, require; demand; call for. ME. 8 *v.t.* & *i.* Call for as by right; demand. (Foll. by direct obj. or *for* the thing demanded; *from* or *of* the person or thing called upon). LME. 9 *v.t.* Proclaim in church, calling upon any who have claims or objections to put them forward. Now only in *ask the banns.* LME. 10†a *v.t.* Provoke, bring upon oneself. L15–E17. b *v.i.* Foll. by *for*: provoke, bring upon oneself, lay oneself open to, (trouble etc.) E20. 11 *v.t.* Invite. Freq. foll. by adv. M19.
7 SHAKES. *Tam. Shr.* Signior Baptista, my business asketh haste. 8 W. FAULKNER Because they don't ask thirty-five cents for it. L. T. C. ROLT Once again he may have asked too much from the manufacturing resources of the day. G. F. FIENNES It would have to be an act of faith that the Pacifics would stand up to what we were going to ask of them, . . almost 500 miles a day. *New Zealand Herald* The unrealistic prices asked for by vendors. 10b *Times* Mr — had behaved as badly as anyone could and a bystander might well have taken the view that he had asked for everything he got. **ask for it** *colloq.*: for trouble. *ask for trouble*: see TROUBLE *n.* 11 DICKENS If I see him . . tomorrow, perhaps I'll ask him down. R. CROMPTON But if he asks you to his you must ask him back. J. LE CARRÉ We'll ask Sam round and perhaps one or two of the old press boys from Berlin. J. BOWEN They asked me to tea at St. Peter's Hall. **ask out** invite to accompany one to a restaurant, entertainment, etc.
askingly *adv.* (*rare*) †(*a*) as a question; (*b*) inquiringly, with entreaty: LME.

askance /ə'skans, ə'skɑːns/ *adv.*[1], *a.*, & *v.* L15. [Origin unkn.] A *adv.* & (usu. *pred.*) *a.* Sideways, oblique(ly); with a side glance, asquint. Now chiefly *fig.*, suspicious(ly), with disfavour; esp. in *look askance (at).* L15.
J. BEATTIE They meet, they dart away, they wheel askance. R. L. STEVENSON Looking askance on each other as possible enemies. T. HARDY Down there they are dubious and askance. P. G. WODEHOUSE One looked askance at that habit of his of writing poetry. E. BOWEN Looking at all this in here with a wild askance shrinking eye. V. S. PRITCHETT The habit of seeing things askance or out of the corner of his eye.
B *v.t.* Turn (one's eye) aside. *rare.* L16

†**askance** *conj.* & *adv.*[2] Also **askances**. LME–L16. [Origin unkn.: not rel. to prec.] As though, as if; *ellipt.* as much as to say.

askant /ə'skant/ *adv.* & *pred. a.* M17. [f. ASKANCE *adv.*[1], *a.*, prob. after *aslant*, *asquint*.] = ASKANCE *adv.*[1], *a.*

†**Askapart** *n.* LME–M18. [Ult. origin unkn.] A hardy warrior of a fabled Arabian race.

askari /ə'skɑːri/ *n.* Pl. **-s**, same. L19. [Arab. *'askarī* soldier.] An E. African soldier or police officer.

asker /'ɑːskə/ *n.*[1] LME. [f. ASK *v.* + -ER[1].] 1 A person who asks a question; an inquirer. LME. 2 A suppliant, a beggar. LME.

asker /'ɑːskə/ *n.*[2] *dial.* L17. [f. ASK *n.*[2]] A newt.

askew /ə'skjuː/ *adv.* & (usu. *pred.*) *a.* M16. [f. A *prep.*[1] 1 + SKEW *n.*[3]] Oblique(ly), askance, to one side; awry, crooked(ly).
SIR W. SCOTT The boy looking askew at him with his sharp gray eyes. S. SMILES Bridges of masonry . . several of them askew bridges. M. BRADBURY Collision ensued; the kiss went askew and landed in her hair. L. DEIGHTON His hair was unkempt and his club tie was, as always, askew. B. CHATWIN An old yew-tree whose writhing roots have set the paving slabs askew. **look askew** *fig.* (*arch.*) look disdainfully or as if pretending not to see.

asking /'ɑːskɪŋ/ *n.* OE. [f. ASK *v.* + -ING[1].] I 1 The action of ASK *v.* OE.
1 **for the asking** (available) upon the least request, merely to be asked for.
II 2 An inquiry, a question. Long *arch. rare.* ME. 3 A request, a supplication. *arch.* ME. †4 A demand; a claim; a price asked. LME–M17.
Comb.: **asking price** the price set by the seller.

asklent /ə'sklɛnt/ *adv.*, *pred. a.*, & *prep. Sc.* Also **ascl-**. L16. [Alt.] = ASLANT.

†**aslake** *v.* [OE *aslacian*: see A-[1], SLAKE *v.*[1]] 1 *v.i.* Become slack or feeble; grow less. OE–L16. b Grow cool. Only in E19. 2 *v.t.* Mitigate, assuage; reduce, abate. ME–E19.

aslant /ə'slɑːnt/ *adv.*, *pred. a.*, & *prep.* ME. [f. A *prep.*[1] 1 + SLANT *n.*[1] See also ASKLENT.] A *adv.* & *pred. a.* On the slant, oblique(ly). ME. B *prep.* Obliquely across; athwart. E17.
aslantwise *adv.* = ASLANT *adv.* E19.

asleep /ə'sliːp/ *adv.* & *pred. a.* ME. [f. A *prep.*[1] 6 + SLEEP *n.*] 1 In a state of sleep, sleeping. ME. 2 Into a state of sleep. Esp. in *fall asleep.* ME. 3 *fig.* In or into a state of inactivity or quiescence; idle, dormant, inattentive. ME. 4 *euphem.* Dead. ME. 5 Of a limb etc.: benumbed by pressure.

LME. 6 *Naut.* Of a sail: filled with wind just enough to prevent flapping. Now *rare* or *obs.* M19.

1 G. GREENE I had told from the irregularity of her breathing that she was not asleep. DAY LEWIS An ass which was lying asleep in the middle of the road. 2 SHAKES. *Tit. A.* A nurse's song Of lullaby to bring her babe asleep. W. GIBSON At last he cursed himself asleep. 3 SHAKES. *1 Hen. IV* And now their pride and mettle is asleep. R. WATSON Their apprehensions were laid asleep. BYRON During this inquisition Julia's tongue Was not asleep. *asleep at the switch*: see SWITCH *n.* 3. 4 TINDALE *1 Cor.* 15:18 They which are fallen a slepe in Christ.

aslope /əˈsləʊp/ *adv.* & *pred. a.* LME. [Origin uncertain: earlier than SLOPE *n.*[1], *v.*[1]] Inclined, sloping; crosswise, aslant.

†asma *n.* var. of ASTHMA.

†asmak *n.* see YASHMAK.

asmoke /əˈsməʊk/ *adv.* & *pred. a.* E19. [f. A-[2] + SMOKE *n.* or *v.*] Smoking.

Asmonean *n.* & *a.* var. of HASMONEAN.

asoak /əˈsəʊk/ *adv.* & *pred. a.* E17. [f. A *prep.*[1] 8 + SOAK *n.*[1] or *v.*] Soaking.

asocial /eɪˈsəʊʃ(ə)l/ *a.* & *n.* L19. [f. A-[10] + SOCIAL *a.*] A *adj.* Not social; antisocial; inconsiderate or hostile to others. L19. B *n.* An asocial person. *rare.* M20.

asomatous /əˈsəʊmətəs/ *a. rare.* M18. [f. late L *asomatus* f. Gk *asōmatos*, f. A-[10] + *sōmat-*, *sōma* body, + -OUS.] Disembodied, incorporeal.

asp /asp/ *n.*[1] *arch.* Also (long *dial.*) **aps** /aps/. [OE *æspe* (corresp. to OHG *aspa*), *æps* (corresp. to ON *ǫsp*), f. Gmc.] (The wood of) the aspen.

asp /asp/ *n.*[2] Orig. in L form **†aspis**, pl. **†aspides**, **†aspisses**. ME. [OFr. *aspe* or (its source) L *aspis*, *-id-* f. Gk.] 1 The Egyptian cobra, *Naja haje*, found throughout Africa. Also, a southern European viper, *Vipera aspis*. ME. 2 *loosely* & *poet.* A poisonous snake. E18.

aspalathus /əˈspaləθəs/ *n.* E17. [L f. Gk *aspalathos*.] Orig., the Middle Eastern camel-thorn, *Alhagi camelorum*, or a similar fragrant shrub. Now, an evergreen thorny leguminous shrub of the African genus *Aspalathus*.

asparagine /əˈsparədʒiːn/ *n.* Also **†-in**. E19. [f. next + -INE[5].] *Biochem.* A hydrophilic amino acid, $CONH_2 \cdot CH_2 \cdot CH(NH_2) \cdot COOH$, which is an amide of aspartic acid and occurs in proteins and (free) in plant tissues.

asparagus /əˈsparəgəs/ *n.* Orig. **†sp-**. Many pop. vars.: see SPARAGE, SPARROW-GRASS. OE. [(med.L *sparagus* f.) L *asparagus* f. Gk *asparagos*.] A plant of the genus *Asparagus*, of the lily family, spec. *A. officinalis*; the young shoots of this plant, eaten as a delicacy.

Comb.: **asparagus beetle** a small beetle of the genus *Crioceris*, which feeds on the foliage of asparagus; **asparagus fern** *Asparagus setaceus*, native to southern Africa, grown for its decorative fernlike foliage; **asparagus stone** yellow-green apatite of gem quality.

asparkle /əˈspɑːk(ə)l/ *adv.* & *pred. a.* M19. [f. A-[2] + SPARKLE *n.* or *v.*[1]] Sparkling.

aspartame /əˈspɑːteɪm/ *n.* L20. [f. next + *-ame* of unkn. origin.] A derivative of phenylalanine that contains the radical of aspartic acid and is used as a low-calorie artificial sweetener.

aspartic /əˈspɑːtɪk/ *a.* M19. [Fr. *aspartique*, formed arbitrarily on L ASPARAGUS: see -IC.] Biochem. *aspartic acid*, an acidic amino acid, $COOH \cdot CH_2 \cdot CH(NH_2) \cdot COOH$, which occurs in proteins and esp. in sugar cane, and is important in nitrogen metabolism in animals.

aspect /ˈaspɛkt/ *n.* LME. [L *aspectus*, f. *aspect-* pa. ppl stem of *aspicere* look at, f. *ad* A-[8] + *specere* to look.] I The action of looking. †1 The action of looking at something; beholding; view, gaze. LME–E19. †2 Mental looking; consideration, regard. LME–L17. 3 A look, a glance. *arch.* L16.

1 BACON The tradition . . that the basilisk killeth by aspect. STEELE The downcast Eye, and the Recovery into a sudden full Aspect. 2 J. DENHAM Those latter parts . . have not yet received your Majesties favourable Aspect. 3 SHAKES. *Com. Err.* Some other mistress hath thy sweet aspects. *fig.*: O. W. HOLMES Meeting the cold aspect of Duty.

II Way of looking, as to position or direction. 4 *Astrol.* The relative positions of the planets, etc., or the position of one with respect to the others, as they appear from the earth. LME. 5 The direction in which a thing has respect or practical bearing; bearing *upon*; reference *to*. *arch.* E16. 6 The looking, facing, or fronting of something in a given direction; the side or surface which fronts or is turned towards a given direction. M17. 7 A point of view (chiefly *fig.*); any of the ways in which something may be looked at or considered. M17. 8 Any of the ways in which something may present itself to the mind; a phase; a particular component or area of something complex. L17. 9 *Gram.* A group of forms of a verb, expressing inception, duration, completion, repetition, etc.; the quality of a verb by which it represents such features. M19.

4 SHAKES. *Tr. & Cr.* The glorious planet Sol . . , whose med'cinable eye Corrects the ill aspects of planets evil. SWIFT He Mars could join To Venus in aspect malign. 5 O. CROMWELL Divers things . . which I hope have a public aspect. 6 MILTON The setting Sun . . with right aspect Against the eastern Gate of Paradise. JOYCE A thatched . . 2 storey dwellinghouse of southerly aspect. 7 T. F. DIBDIN Their rarity and intrinsic worth render them acceptable under any aspect. C. S. FORESTER Six months ago he had been inspecting similar arrangements from a regimental aspect. 8 K. MANSFIELD There are in life as many aspects as attitudes towards it. N. MITFORD We talked about nothing else, too, round and round the subject, every aspect of it. A. WILSON They enjoyed . . showing each other little-known aspects of London—an Italianate Methodist Chapel in Lewisham, a strange formal garden in Highbury. G. VIDAL The third aspect of the one god is Siva, the destroyer. D. HALBERSTAM Lawyers were getting ready to go through every aspect of Murrow's own past, in preparation for McCarthy's counterchallenge.

III Appearance. 10 The look a person wears; expression; countenance. LME. 11 The appearance presented by an object to the eye; look. LME. b Any of a number of different lights that can be shown by a railway signal. E20. †12 A sight. E17–E18. 13 The appearance presented by circumstances etc. to the mind. E18.

10 MILTON But soon his cleer aspect Returned. BYRON Ah! he unveils his aspect; on his brow The thunder-scars are graven. J. C. OATES If he did appear, his aspect was so greatly changed she could not recognize him. 11 R. SUTCLIFF Later that evening the tumble-down shelter bore a much more cheerful aspect. 12 DEFOE That he saw such Aspects . . I never believ'd. 13 W. PENN Matters seem to look of a better aspect.

Comb. & phrases: **aspect ratio** *gen.* a ratio of height or length to width; *spec.* (of an aerofoil or a bird's wing) orig. the ratio of the span to the mean chord, now usu. the ratio of the square of the span to the surface area. *in* TRIAN *aspect*.

aspected *a.* having an aspect (usu. specified) L16. **aspectful** *a.* (*rare*) having favourable aspect, benignant E17. **a'spectual** *a.* †(*a*) *rare* of or pertaining to a planetary aspect or planetary aspects; (*b*) of or pertaining to grammatical aspect: L15.

aspect /əˈspɛkt, ˈaspɛkt/ *v.* LME. [L *aspectare* frequent. of *aspicere*: see prec.] 1 *v.t. Astrol.* Of a planet: look upon and exert influence upon (another). Usu. in *pass.* LME. †2 *v.t.* Look with favour upon. L16–M17. †3 *v.t.* Look at, face; survey, watch. L16–L17. †4 *v.i.* Look; have an aspect or bearing. Only in M17.

†aspectable *a.* (*a*) able to be seen, visible; (*b*) fit to be beheld, attractive to the eye: E17–M19.

aspen /ˈasp(ə)n/ *a.* & *n.* LME. [f. ASP *n.*[1] + -EN[4].] A *adj.* 1 (Now taken to be the n. used *attrib.*) Of or pertaining to the aspen. LME. 2 *fig.* Tremulous; timorous. LME.

2 G. CHAPMAN Possess'd with aspen fear.

B *n.* (The wood of) a European poplar, *Populus tremula*, noted for its tremulous leaves, or any of a number of similar poplars, esp. the N. American *P. tremuloides* (in full *quaking aspen*). L16.

asper /ˈaspə/ *n.*[1] *obs.* exc. *Hist.* Also **aspre**. LME. [Fr. *aspre* app. f. Turk. f. med.Gk *aspron* f. L *asper* (*nummus*) newly minted (coin).] A small silver Byzantine and Ottoman coin; later, as a monetary unit, 1/120 piastre.

asper /ˈaspə/ *n.*[2] L19. [L (sc. *spiritus* breath): see next.] *Gk Gram.* The sign (ʽ) of rough breathing.

†asper *a.* Long *dial.* Also **aspre**. LME–L19. [OFr. *aspre* (mod. *âpre*) f. L *asper* rough, harsh.] Rough; harsh, bitter; severe, stern; fierce.

asperate /ˈaspəreɪt/ *v.t.* Now *rare.* Pa. pple & ppl a. **-ate** /-ət/, **-ated**. L16. [L *asperat-* pa. ppl stem of *asperare*, f. *asper*: see prec., -ATE[3].] Make rough or harsh.

asperge /əˈspəːdʒ/ *v.t.* E16. [Fr. *asperger* or L *aspergere*, f. *ad* AS-[1] + *spargere* sprinkle.] Sprinkle, besprinkle.

asperges /əˈspəːdʒiːz/ *n.* L16. [First wd (= thou shalt purge) of L text of *Ps.* 50(51):7, recited during the sprinkling of holy water before mass.] *RC Ch.* The sprinkling of holy water before mass. Also = ASPERGILLUM.

aspergill /ˈaspədʒɪl/ *n.* M19. [Anglicized f. ASPERGILLUM.] = ASPERGILLUM.

aspergilla *n.pl.* see ASPERGILLUM.

aspergillosis /aspədʒɪˈləʊsɪs/ *n.* Pl. **-lloses** /-ˈləʊsiːz/. L19. [f. mod.L *Aspergillus* (see below), f. next, + -OSIS.] *Med.* Infection, esp. of the lungs, with a fungus of the genus *Aspergillus*.

aspergillum /aspəˈdʒɪləm/ *n.* Pl. **-lla** /-lə/, **-llums**. M17. [mod.L, f. *aspergere* (see ASPERGE) + *-illum* dim. suff.] A kind of brush or other implement for sprinkling holy water.

asperity /əˈspɛrɪti/ *n.* ME. [(O)Fr. *asperité* or L *asperitas*, f. *asper* rough, harsh: see -ITY.] 1 Hardship; rigour, severity. *arch.* ME. 2 Harshness to any of the senses; roughness, ruggedness; hardness. *arch.* LME. b A rough excrescence. *arch.* M17. 3 Harshness or sharpness of temper, esp. as displayed in tone or manner; bitterness, acrimony; in *pl.*, embittered feelings. M17.

1 HENRY MORE To . . minysh the vygour and asperite of the paynes. S. JOHNSON The nakedness and asperity of the wintry world. 2 CAXTON Fewe people wente for to see him, for the grete asprete or sharpnesse of the place. G. BERKELEY The asperity of tartarous salts. S. JOHNSON Our language, of which the chief defect is ruggedness and asperity. b J. LINDLEY Almost all Delimaceæ have the leaves covered with asperities. 3 DICKENS Demanded with much asperity what she meant. H. WILSON Intervening also to soften asperities and curb the invocation of personalities.

aspermia /eɪˈspəːmɪə, ə-/ *n.* M19. [f. A-[10] + Gk *sperma* seed + -IA[1].] *Med.* Failure to produce semen, or absence of sperms from the semen. Cf. AZOOSPERMIA.

aspermic *a.* pertaining to or characterized by aspermia E20.

asperous /ˈasp(ə)rəs/ *a.* Now *rare.* M16. [f. late L *asperosus*, f. L *asper* rough, harsh: see -OUS.] 1 Rough, rugged. M16. 2 Harsh, bitter. M16.

asperse /əˈspəːs/ *v.t.* L15. [L *aspers-* pa. ppl stem of *aspergere* ASPERGE.] 1 Besprinkle, bespatter, (a person or thing, *with*). *arch.* L15. †2 Sprinkle in as an ingredient; intermingle. M16–E17. 3 Sprinkle, scatter, (liquid, dust, etc.). *arch.* E17. 4 Attack the reputation of (a person) *with* injurious allegations etc. E17. 5 Spread false and injurious charges against; calumniate; detract from. M17.

1 H. L'ESTRANGE The child is thrice to be aspersed with water on the face. M. BEERBOHM Rain! His very mantle was aspersed. In another minute he would stand sodden. 2 E. TOPSELL Making a plaister thereof with Barley meal and a little Brimstone aspersed. 3 SOUTHEY Blood, which hung on every hair, Aspersed like dew-drops. 4 JAS. MILL The criminations with which the leaders . . appeared desirous of aspersing one another. 5 SIR W. SCOTT There were foul tongues to asperse a Douglas. L. A. G. STRONG No one is aspersing their honesty.

asperser *n.* a person who asperses someone, a calumniator E18. **aspersive** *a.* (*rare*) defamatory M17.

aspersion /əˈspəːʃ(ə)n/ *n.* LME. [L *aspersio(n-)*, f. as prec.: see -ION.] I 1 The action of sprinkling or scattering liquid, esp. in baptism. LME. †2 The sprinkling in of an ingredient; admixture. E–M17. 3 Calumniation, defamation. M17.

1 J. FOXE By the aspersion of the bloud of Jesus Christ. 2 BACON Divinity Morality and Policy, with great aspersion of all other artes. 3 W. COWPER

Aspersion is the babbler's trade, To listen is to lend him aid.

II 4 A calumny, a slander, a false insinuation. L16. 5 A shower, a spray. *arch.* E17.

4 Esp. in *cast aspersions (on)*: see CAST *v.* 5 SHAKES. *Temp.* No sweet aspersion shall the heavens let fall To make this contract grow.

aspersorium /aspə'sɔːrɪəm/ *n.* Pl. **-ria** /-rɪə/. M19. [med.L, f. as ASPERSE: see -ORIUM.] A vessel for holy water; an aspergillum.

aspersoir /a'spəːswɑː/ *n.* [Fr.] = ASPERSORIUM M19. **aspersory** /ə'spəːsəri/ *n.* = ASPERSORIUM L19.

asphalt /'asfalt, -əlt/ *n.* & *v.* LME. [(Fr. *asphalte* ult. f.) late L *asphalton, -um* f. Gk *asphalton*, of alien origin.] A *n.* Also in L form **asphaltum** /as'faltəm/. 1 Black or brownish-black, solid or viscous, bituminous pitch, of natural occurrence or produced from petroleum. LME. 2 A mixture of this with sand etc. used for surfacing paths, roads, etc. M19. B *v.t.* Cover or lay (a road etc.) with asphalt. M19.

asphalter *n.* a person who lays down asphalt L19. **as'phaltic** *a.* of the nature of or containing asphalt M17. **asphaltite** *n.* any of the naturally occurring solid forms of asphalt L19.

asphaltene /'asfaltiːn, as'faltiːn/ *n.* M19. [f. ASPHALT *n.* + -ENE.] Any of the solid organic constituents of asphalt, petroleum, etc., which are soluble in carbon disulphide but not in paraffin oil.

asphaltum *n.* var. of ASPHALT *n.*

aspheric /ə'sfɛrɪk, eɪ-/ *a.* E20. [f. A-[10] + SPHERIC *a.*] *Optics.* Not spherical (although curved); (of a lens) having one or more aspheric surfaces.

aspherical *a.* E20. **asphericity** /eɪsfɛ'rɪsɪti/ *n.* the state of being aspheric M20.

aspheterism /əs'fɛtərɪz(ə)m/ *n.* L18. [f. A-[10] + Gk *spheteros* one's own, after *spheterismos* appropriation: see -ISM.] The doctrine that there ought to be no private property; communism.

asphodel /'asfədɛl/ *n.* LME. [f. L *asphodilus, -delus* f. Gk *asphodelos.* Cf. AFFODILL.] 1 a Any plant of the genera *Asphodelus* and *Asphodeline*, of the lily family, native to the Mediterranean region, the former with white flowers, the latter (more fully *yellow asphodel*) with yellow flowers, esp. *Asphodeline lutea.* LME. b An immortal flower, said to cover the Elysian fields. *poet.* M17. 2 (With specifying wd.) Any of certain other plants of related genera. L16.

2 **bog asphodel** a yellow-flowered marsh plant of the genus *Narthecium*, esp. *N. ossifragum.* **false asphodel** *N. Amer.* = *Scotch asphodel* below (in the wider sense). **Scotch asphodel, Scottish asphodel** a white-flowered subalpine plant of the genus *Tofieldia*; *esp.* (in Britain) *T. pusilla.*

asphyxia /əs'fɪksɪə/ *n.* E18. [mod.L f. Gk *asphuxia*, f. A-[10] + *sphuxis* pulsation: see -IA[1].] *Med.* 1 Stoppage of the pulse. Only in Dicts. E18. 2 The condition of defective aeration of the blood caused by failure of the oxygen supply; suffocation. M19.

asphyctic *a.* = ASPHYXIAL L19. **asphyxial** *a.* of, pertaining to, or characterized by asphyxia M19. **asphyxiant** *a.* & *n.* (a substance) causing asphyxia L19.

asphyxiate /əs'fɪksɪeɪt/ *v.t.* M19. [f. prec. + -ATE[3].] Affect with asphyxia, suffocate.

asphyxi'ation *n.* the action of asphyxiating; asphyxia: M19.

asphyxy /əs'fɪksi/ *n.* & *v.* Now *rare.* L18. [Fr. *asphyxie*: see ASPHYXIA, -Y[3].] A *n.* = ASPHYXIA 2. L18. B *v.t.* = ASPHYXIATE. M19.

aspic /'aspɪk/ *n.*[1] Chiefly *poet.* M16. [(O)Fr., var. of OFr. *aspide* ASP *n.*[2], prob. infl. by *piquer* to sting.] = ASP *n.*[2]

aspic /'aspɪk/ *n.*[2] E17. [Fr. f. Prov. *aspic, espic* f. med.L (*lavandula*) *spica*: see SPIKE *n.*[1]] Lavender.

aspic /'aspɪk/ *n.*[3] L18. [Fr. (18), a use of *aspic* asp, ASPIC *n.*[1], the various colours of the jelly being prob. compared to those of the snake.] A savoury meat jelly used as a garnish or to contain game, eggs, etc.

†aspides *n.pl.* see ASP *n.*[2]

aspidistra /aspɪ'dɪstrə/ *n.* E19. [mod.L, f. Gk *aspid-*, *aspis* shield, after *Tupistra* a related genus.] A plant of the Far Eastern genus *Aspidistra*, of the lily family, with broad tapering leaves (freq. regarded as a symbol of dull middle-class respectability, owing to its former popularity as a house-plant).

aspidistral *a.* of or pertaining to an aspidistra; decorated with aspidistras: M20.

aspirant /ə'spʌɪər(ə)nt, 'asp(ɪ)r-/ *n.* & *a.* M18. [Fr., or L *aspirant-* pres. ppl stem of *aspirare*: see ASPIRE, -ANT[1].] A *n.* A person who aspires (*to, for, after*); a person who desires and strives to attain a position, acquire a privilege, etc. M18.

LD MACAULAY The way to greatness was left clear to a new set of aspirants. BROWNING Degrade me . . To an aspirant after fame, not truth! B. TAYLOR Aspirants for poetic honors. A. STORR A Catholic aspirant to the priesthood.

B *adj.* 1 Aspiring to a higher position, seeking distinction. E19. 2 Mounting up, ascending. Now *rare.* M19.

1 SOUTHEY I receive plenty of letters from poets aspirant. 2 A. C. SWINBURNE With flame all round him aspirant Stood flushed . . the tyrant.

aspirate /'asp(ə)rət/ *a.* & *n.* M16. [L *aspiratus* pa. pple, f. as next: see -ATE[2], -ATE[1].] A *adj.* Aspirated, pronounced with a marked flow of breath. M16. B *n.* An aspirate consonant; a consonant followed by or blended with the sound of *h*; the sound of *h.* E17.

aspirate /'aspəreɪt/ *v.* L17. [L *aspirat-* pa. ppl stem of *aspirare* ASPIRE *v.*: see -ATE[3].] I 1 *v.i.* Of a consonant: be pronounced with aspiration. *rare.* L17. 2 *v.t.* Pronounce with a marked flow of breath. E18. 3 *v.i.* Pronounce the sound of *h* at the beginning of a word. E19.

1 DRYDEN Our *w* and *h* aspirate. 2 L. BLOOMFIELD An aspirated *p, t, k,* (as we usually have it in words like *pin, tin, kick*). 3 M. EDGEWORTH Londoners [are] always aspirating where they should not, and never aspirating where they should.

II 4 *v.t.* Remove or draw (esp. a fluid) by suction; remove fluid etc. from (a cavity) by suction. L19.

4 O. SACKS She . . aspirated a chicken-bone, and choked to death on the spot. *Lancet* The ankle and an ear nodule were aspirated, but no fluid or crystals were found. *Nature* The liquid was directly aspirated into the flame of the atomic absorption spectrometer.

aspiration /aspə'reɪʃ(ə)n/ *n.* LME. [(O)Fr. f. L *aspiratio(n-)*, f. as prec.: see -ATION.] I Corresp. to ASPIRATE *v.* 1 The action of aspirating a consonant. LME. 2 = ASPIRATE *n.* Now *rare.* M16. 3 The removal or transfer of fluid etc. by suction. M19.

II Corresp. to ASPIRE. †4 Inspiration. LME–M16. 5 The action of breathing; the drawing of breath; a breath, a sigh. L15. 6 The action of desiring and striving for something; an earnest desire (*to, for, after*). E17.

5 E. TOPSELL Corrupt inflamation taking away freedom or easinesse of aspiration. R. B. SHERIDAN There is . . not an aspiration of the breeze, but hints some cause. J. F. COOPER She sighed with an aspiration so low that it was scarcely audible. 6 I. WATTS A soul inspired with the warmest aspirations after celestial beatitude. L. M. MONTGOMERY Anne's highest pinnacle of aspiration had been a teacher's provincial licence, Class First. B. BAINBRIDGE His entire life, with its small triumphs and disasters, its boundless hopes and aspirations for the future.

aspirational *a.* L19.

aspirator /'aspɪreɪtə/ *n.* E19. [f. ASPIRATE *v.* + -OR.] An instrument or apparatus for aspirating fluid etc.

aspire /ə'spʌɪə/ *v.* LME. [(O)Fr. *aspirer* or L *aspirare*, f. *ad* AS-[1] + *spirare* breathe.] I Desire. 1 *v.i.* Have an earnest desire or ambition for something; desire and seek to attain something. (Foll. by *to* (*do*), *after, at,* †*for.*) LME. †2 *v.t.* Have an earnest desire for, be ambitious of. L16–E19.

1 R. LOVELACE Aspiredst for the everlasting Crowne. GOLDSMITH Ye powers of truth, that bid my soul aspire. V. KNOX He who aspires at the character of a good man. R. LYND It is no wonder that human beings aspire after a standard pronunciation which will reduce as far as possible the chances of misunderstanding. M. L. KING We Americans have long aspired to the glories of freedom while we compromised with prejudice and servitude. *New York Review of Books* He aspired to be a Rhodes Scholar, and thus had to be an all-around man. 2 SOUTHEY And Love aspired with Faith a heavenward flight.

†II 3 *v.t.* Breathe (*in*)*to*; inspire. L15–M17.

III Rise (infl. by SPIRE *n.*[1], *v.*[1]). 4 *v.i.* Rise up, mount up, tower, rise high, (*lit.* & *fig.*). M16. †5 *v.i.* Grow up *to* (a specified age). Only in L16. †6 *v.t.* Mount up to, reach, attain. L16–E17.

4 SHAKES. *Merry W.* Lust is but a bloody fire, . . whose flames aspire, As thoughts do blow them, higher and higher. S. JOHNSON Orgilio sees the golden pile aspire. S. LEWIS The towers of Zenith aspired above the morning mist. 5 SPENSER To ryper yeares he gan aspire. 6 SHAKES. *Rom. & Jul.* That gallant spirit hath aspir'd the clouds.

aspirer *n.* L16. **aspiringly** *adv.* in an aspiring manner, so as to aspire E17. **aspiringness** *n.* the quality of being aspiring M19.

aspirin /'asp(ə)rɪn/ *n.* L19. [G, f. *acetyli(e)rte Spirsäure* acetylated salicylic acid: see ACETYL, SPIRAEA, -IN[1].] Acetylsalicylic acid, $C_9H_8O_4$, used as an analgesic and antipyretic drug; a tablet of this.

†aspis *n.*, **†aspisses** *n.pl.* see ASP *n.*[2]

asportation /aspɔː'teɪʃ(ə)n/ *n.* Now chiefly *Law.* L15. [L *asportatio(n-)*, f. *asportat-* pa. ppl stem of *asportare* carry away, f. ABS- + *portare* carry: see -ATION.] The action of carrying off; detachment or movement of property (formerly an essential in the common law crime of larceny).

a'sport *v.t.* carry away, remove feloniously E17.

asprawl /ə'sprɔːl/ *adv.* & *pred. a.* L19. [f. A-[2] + SPRAWL *n.*, *v.*] Sprawling, in a sprawling posture.

aspre *n.*, *a.* vars. of ASPER *n.*[1], *a.*

aspread /ə'sprɛd/ *adv.* & *pred. a.* L19. [f. A-[2] + SPREAD *v.*] Spread out, spread widely.

asquat /ə'skwɒt/ *adv.* & *pred. a.* L17. [f. A *prep.*[1] 6 + SQUAT *n.*[1]] Squatting.

asquint /ə'skwɪnt/ *adv.* & *pred. a.* ME. [Perh. f. A-[1] + a LG or Du. form now repr. by Du. *schuinte* obliquity, slant, f. *schuin* oblique = Fris., LG *schüns.* Aphet. to SQUINT *a.*, *v.*] 1 (Looking) to one side, or out of the corners of the eyes; oblique(ly). ME. 2 (Looking) obliquely because of a defect in the eyes, so that they look in different directions; with a squint. LME. 3 (Looking) suspiciously, askance; with bias or distortion; furtive(ly), glancing(ly). LME. 4 In contexts other than vision: oblique(ly), aslant. *rare.* L15.

Asquithian /a'skwɪθɪən/ *a.* & *n.* E20. [f. *Asquith* (see below) + -IAN.] *Hist.* A *adj.* Pertaining to, resembling, or supporting Herbert Henry Asquith (1852–1928), Brit. Prime Minister 1908–16, as leader of the Liberal Party or, later, of a faction of the divided party. E20. B *n.* A supporter of Asquith. E20.

ass /as/ *n.*[1] [OE *as(s)a* f. Celt. (Welsh *asyn* = OIr. *asan*, OCorn. *asen*, Breton *azen*) f. L *asinus.*] 1 A quadruped, *Equus asinus*, smaller than a horse, with long ears, tufted tail, and dark stripe across the shoulders; a donkey. (Proverbially regarded as the type of clumsiness, ignorance, and stupidity.) OE. b In full *wild ass.* A wild animal of the genus *Equus.* ME. 2 An ignorant or stupid person. LME.

1 **make an ass of** make (someone, oneself) look absurd or foolish. 2 **asses' bridge** *Math.* = PONS *asinorum. silly ass*: see SILLY *a.*

Comb.: **ass-head** *colloq.* a fool.

¶Except in particular contexts (e.g. scripture, history, fable), *ass* has been largely superseded as the name of the domestic animal by *donkey.*

assifi'cation *n.* (*rare*) the action of making an ass of a person, an asinine act E19. **assify** *v.t.* (*joc.*) make an ass of, turn into an ass E19. **assish** *a.* asinine, stupid L16. **assishness** *n.* L16. **asslike** *adv.* & *a.* (*a*) *adv.* in the manner of an ass; (*b*) *adj.* resembling (that of) an ass: M16.

ass *n.*[2] see ARSE *n.*

ass /as/ *v.* In sense 2b also **arse** /ɑːs/. L16. [f. ASS *n.*[1]: in recent use infl. by ASS *n.*[2], ARSE *n.*] †1 *v.t.* Call ass. Only in L16. 2 *v.i.* †a Play the ass. Only in M17. b Fool or mess *about, around. slang.* L19.

assafoetida *n.* var. of ASAFOETIDA.

assagai *n.* & *v.* var. of ASSEGAI.

assai /a'sʌɪ/ *adv.* E18. [It.] *Mus.* In directions: very.

assail /ə'seɪl/ *v.* & *n.* ME. [OFr. *asaill-* tonic stem of *asalir* (mod. *assaillir*) f. med.L *assalire* (L *assilire*), f. *ad* AS-[1] + *salire* to leap: infl. by ASSAY *v.*, esp. in sense 3.] A *v.t.* 1 Attack with physical violence; assault. ME. †2 Attack with temptation, try; woo, court. ME-E17. †3 Venture on, attempt; endeavour *to do*. ME-E17. 4 Attack with hostile speech, writing, etc.; take action against (a belief, practice, etc.). LME. 5 Seek to persuade or controvert by reasoning. LME. 6 Of a mental condition, physical state or phenomenon: come upon (a person, sense, etc.) strongly; invade, threaten to overcome; dash against, injure. LME. 7 Approach (an obstacle, task, etc.) with the intention of mastering. L17.

1 STEELE It is for the Vulgar to assail one another like brute Beasts. W. S. CHURCHILL Tribal revolts and Scottish raids continually assailed the northern frontier system. 2 SHAKES. *Cymb.* I have assail'd her with musics. 4 H. P. BROUGHAM Choosing to assail the religion of the people before he had destroyed their liberty. W. S. CHURCHILL Clive was assailed in the House of Commons. He defended himself in an eloquent speech. 5 H. MARTINEAU She assailed her husband on the subject of taking work. 6 DRYDEN New pangs of mortal fear our minds assail. J. TYNDALL We were assailed by a violent hailstorm. J. LONDON The ever-recurrent fever of expectancy assailed Martin as he took the bundle of long envelopes. M. LEITCH A smell of gun-oil assailed their nostrils. 7 POPE The thorny wilds the woodmen fierce assail. P. G. WODEHOUSE When a lazy man does make up his mind to assail a piece of work, he is like a dog with a bone. *absol.*: SHAKES. *Lucr.* When shame assail'd, the red should fence the white.

B *n.* (An) attack, (an) assault. *arch.* ME.

assailable *a.* E17. **assailer** *n.* a person who assails, an assailant LME. **assailment** *n.* (now *rare* or *obs.*) the action or power of assailing L16.

assailant /ə'seɪl(ə)nt/ *n.* & *a.* M16. [f. prec. + -ANT[1], after Fr.] A *n.* A person who or thing which assails someone or something; an attacker. M16. B *adj.* Assailing, attacking. *arch.* L16.

Assam /a'sam/ *n.* M19. [See next.] In full *Assam tea*. (A) tea grown in Assam in NE India.

Assamese /asə'miːz/ *n.* & *a.* E19. [f. *Assam* (see below) + -ESE.] A *n.* 1 Pl. same. A native or inhabitant of Assam, a State of NE India. E19. 2 The Indo-Aryan (official) language of Assam. M19. B *adj.* Of or pertaining to Assam, its people, or their language. E19.

assart /ə'sɑːt/ *n. obs.* exc. *Hist.* LME. [AN, f. as next: cf. ESSART *n.*] *Law.* 1 A piece of land converted from forest to arable. LME. 2 The action of asserting. L16.

assart /ə'sɑːt/ *v.t. obs.* exc. *Hist.* E16. [AN *assarter*, *-ier*, *-ir*, OFr. *essarter* f. med.L *ex(s)artare*, f. EX-[1] + *sart-* pa. ppl stem of *sar(r)ire* to hoe, weed: cf. ESSART *v.*] *Law.* Make (forest land) arable by grubbing up trees and bushes.

assassin /ə'sasɪn/ *n.* M16. [Fr., or med.L *assassinus* f. Arab. *ḥašīšī* hashish-eater.] A person who undertakes to assassinate somebody; *spec.* (*Hist.*) any of a band of Ismaili Muslim fanatics in the time of the Crusades who were allegedly sent on murder errands by the Old Man of the Mountains or by later leaders.

Comb.: **assassin bug** any bug of the large family Reduviidae, members of which are predacious or bloodsucking.

†**assassin** *v.t.* M17-L18. [Fr. *assassiner*, f. as prec.] = ASSASSINATE *v.*

†**assassinate** *n.* L16. [Sense 1 app. f. Fr. *assassinat* f. med.L *assassinatus*, f. as next: see -ATE[1]. Sense 2 is unexpl.] 1 An assassination. L16-M18. 2 An assassin. E17-E19.

assassinate /ə'sasɪneɪt/ *v.t.* E17. [med.L *assassinat-* pa. ppl stem of *assassinare*, f. *assassinus*: see ASSASSIN *n.*, -ATE[3].] 1 Kill (esp. a public figure such as a political or religious leader) by treacherous violence; commit a planned murder of (freq. by a person hired or instructed to commit the act). E17. †b Attempt to murder. L17-E18. 2 *fig.* Destroy or injure maliciously. E17.

1 M. SPARK If the authorities wanted to get rid of her she would have to be assassinated. H. KISSINGER Palestinian guerillas sought . . to assassinate King Hussein, attacking his motorcade. 2 E. P. WHIPPLE After his death they tried to assassinate his name.

assassinator *n.* a person who assassinates someone; an assassin: M17.

assassination /əsasɪ'neɪʃ(ə)n/ *n.* E17. [f. as prec. + -ATION.] The action of assassinating someone; (a) planned murder, esp. of a public figure.

character assassination: see CHARACTER *n.*

†**assation** *n.* L16-E19. [Fr., or med.L *assatio(n-)*, f. *assat-* pa. ppl stem of late L *assare* to roast, f. L *assus* roasted: see -ATION.] Roasting, baking.

assault /ə'sɔːlt, ə'sɒlt/ *n.* ME. [OFr. *asaut* (mod. *assaut*) ult. f. med.L *assalire*: see ASSAIL *v.*] 1 An attack with blows or weapons; a sudden military raid or offensive. ME. b *spec.* The charge of an attacking force against the walls of a fortress etc. ME. 2 An attack by spiritual enemies; temptation to evil. *obs.* exc. as passing into other fig. and transf. senses. ME. 3a *Law.* Unlawful attack upon a person whether by menacing words or deeds. LME. b *euphem.* Sexual molestation, rape. M20. 4 An attempt to overthrow institutions, opinions, etc. LME. 5 The hostile onset of a misfortune, harmful natural phenomenon, etc. LME. †6 An act of wooing. *rare* (Shakes.). L16-E17.

1 F. FITZGERALD The imperial armies disintegrated quickly under direct assault. *fig.*: E. F. BENSON The pastry resisted the most determined assaults without showing any sign of fracture. **assault-at**(or **-of**)**-arms** a display of combat by two fencers etc. b W. S. CHURCHILL Marlborough and the Margrave . . in a bloody assault stormed the strong entrenchments of the Schellenberg. 2 MILTON Hear what assaults I had, what snares besides. 3a **assault and battery** unlawful attack involving the striking of blows or other menacing physical contact. INDECENT *assault*. 4 W. S. CHURCHILL Fox had made his name by savage personal assaults on North's administration. 5 S. O'CASEY A fine old Georgian house, struggling for its life against the assaults of time.

Comb.: **assault course** a course (of instruction or of obstacles) for the training of troops in vigorous attack; **assault craft, ship** a vessel for carrying and landing attacking troops.

assault /ə'sɔːlt, ə'sɒlt/ *v.t.* LME. [OFr. *assauter*, ult. f. L *ad* AS-[1] + *saltare* frequent. of *salire* to leap.] 1 Make a violent hostile attack upon by physical means; storm (a fortress etc.); commit an assault upon the person of (*Law*: cf. ASSAULT *n.* 3a). LME. b *euphem.* Molest sexually, rape. M20. 2 Tempt, try. *arch.* E16. 3 Attack with hostile words etc.; seek to persuade or overcome with argument etc. M16. 4 = ASSAIL *v.* 6. L16.

1 AV *Acts* 17:5 But the Iewes which beleeued not . . gathered a company, and . . assaulted the house of Iason. J. K. JEROME George suggested walking back to Henley and assaulting a policeman, and so getting a night's lodging in the station-house. 3 A. TOFFLER The average American adult is assaulted by a minimum of 560 advertising messages each day. 4 GIBBON His vessel was assaulted by a violent tempest. D. WALCOTT Each spring, memories Of his own country . . Assaulted him.

assaultable *a.* M16. **assaulter** *n.* a person who makes an assault; an assailant: M16. **assaultive** *a.* liable to commit an assault M20.

assay /ə'seɪ/ *n.* ME. [OFr. *assai*, *-ay* var. of *essai* ESSAY *n.*] I Trial, testing. 1 The trial or testing of the virtue, fitness, etc., of a person or thing. (Now only as fig. use of 2.) ME. 2 The determination of the quality or purity of an ore or (esp. precious) metal; any (esp. biological) test to measure the content of a preparation. LME. b A substance to be assayed. M19. †3 Tribulation, an affliction. LME-L17. †4 (An) experiment; experience. LME-M18. 5 The trial of food, drink, or other substances by taste. *obs.* exc. *Hist.* LME. †6 Trial of weights and measures etc. by legal standard. E17-M18.

1 SHAKES. *Meas. for M.* He hath made an assay of her virtue to practise his judgment with the disposition of natures. J. RUSKIN A great assay of the human soul. 2 R. L. STEVENSON Some rock pounded for assay. *Lancet* The identification and quantitative assay of specific antibodies in parasitic and infectious diseases. 3 MILTON My way must lie Through many a hard assay even to the death. 4 TREVISA Schort witted men and litel of assay. L. STERNE 'Tis an assay upon human nature. 5 W. PRYNNE Hee made Dukes and Earles to serve him with Wine, with assay taken. **cup of assay** a small cup with which wine was tasted before being served to a noble etc.

II 7 (Good) quality or character; standard of purity etc. *arch.* ME.

7 J. GOWER That outward feignen youthe so And ben within of pouer assay. SPENSER Gold and pearle of rich assay.

III 8 An attempt, an endeavour; a tentative effort; one's best effort. *arch.* ME. †9 An assault, an attack. LME-E18.

8 J. GOWER He hath put all his assay To winne thing which he ne may get. BUNYAN She and her companions made a fresh assay to go past them. A. HECHT Surely the mind in all its brave assays Must put much thinking by. 9 SHAKES. *Hen. V* Galling the gleaned land with hot assays.

Comb.: **assay-master** the master of an assay office; **assay office** an office for the assaying of metals, ores, etc.; *spec.* (w. cap. initials) one authorized to award hallmarks on precious metal.

assay /ə'seɪ/ *v.* ME. [OFr. *assaier* var. of (O)Fr. *essayer* ESSAY *v.*] 1 *v.t.* Put to the proof; test the quality, fitness, etc., of. (Now chiefly as fig. use of 4.) ME. †b *v.i.* Make trial (*of*). LME-L16. †2 *v.t.* Learn or know by experience; examine, inquire into. ME-M17. 3 *v.t.* Attempt (a deed); try *to do* something; do one's best *to do*. *arch.* ME. †b *v.i.* & *t.* w. inf. Address or apply oneself (*to do*). ME-M17. †c Make bold, venture, *to do*. L15-L17. 4 *v.t.* Test chemically the purity of (a metal, ore, etc.); perform an assay on. LME. b Yield (a purity, value, etc.) on assay. L19. 5 *v.t.* & *i.* (foll. by *of*). Test by tasting. *obs.* exc. *Hist.* LME. †6 *v.t.* Practise by way of trial. LME-E18. †7 *v.t.* Make trial of with afflictions, temptation, etc. LME-E17. 8 *v.t.* Attack, assault, assail, (*lit.* & *fig.*). Long *arch.* LME. †b Challenge. *rare* (Shakes.). Only in E17. †9 *v.t.* Try the fit or style of (an item of clothing). Also foll. by *on*. L16-M17.

1 MILTON I shall . . his strength as oft assay. S. BELLOW I should not venture to assay the merit of the tendency without more mature consideration. 2 CHAUCER Thou hast nat yit assayed al hire wit. CAXTON The auncyent faders wold . . assaye the werkis of our Lord. S. BUTLER He knew . . Which Socrates and Chærophon In vain assaid so long agone. 3 SIR W. SCOTT Uncertain whether he should demand or assay entrance. E. A. FREEMAN He assayed to show himself in the usual kingly state. 4 N. LUTTRELL The goldsmiths are to meet to assay the new money coyned at the Tower. *Lancet* Drugs . . can be assayed . . by biological methods. J. BRONOWSKI The man who assayed gold was also more than a technician. *fig.*: SOUTHEY Sterling merit . . he can now understand and value, having . . the means of assaying it. b *Sunday Times* Ore . . assaying as high as 7.3 dwts. 6 MILTON Let him . . now assay His utmost subtlety. 7 SPENSER O, how great sorrow my sad soule assaid! W. RALEIGH Then did he assay them with goodly words, accompanied with gifts. 8 SPENSER Th' other was with Thetis love assaid. M. DRAYTON She the high Mountaynes actively assayes. HOBBES Exhorting them the Trenches to assay. b SHAKES. *Haml.* Did you assay him To any pastime?

assayable *a.* M19. **assayer** *n.* LME.

†**assecution** *n.* E16-E18. [L *assecut-* pa. ppl stem of *assequi* obtain f. *ad* AS-[1] + *sequi* follow: see -ION.] Acquisition; attainment.

assegai /'asəgʌɪ/ *n.* & *v.* Also **assa-**. E17. [Fr. †*azaguie* (now *zagaie*, *s-*) or Port. *azagaia*, Sp *azagaya*, f. colloq. Arab. *az-zaġāya*, f. *az-* AL-[2] + Berber *zaġāya* spear.] A *n.* A slender iron-tipped spear of hard wood, esp. as the missile of southern African tribesmen. E17.

Comb.: **assegai tree** a southern African hardwood tree, *Curtisia dentata*; **assegai wood** the wood of the assegai tree.

B *v.t.* Kill or pierce with an assegai. E19.

asself /ə'sɛlf/ *v.t. rare.* M17. [Irreg. f. AS-[1] + SELF *n.*] Take to oneself, appropriate.

assemblage /ə'sɛmblɪdʒ/ *n.* L17. [f. ASSEMBLE *v.* + -AGE; partly after Fr.] 1 A bringing or coming together; the state of being collected together. L17. b *spec.* The fitting or joining together of a number of components. E18. 2 A number of things grouped together; a collection, a cluster. L17. b A number of pieces fitted together; *spec.* a work of art consisting of miscellaneous objects fastened together. L19. 3 A number of people gathered together; a gathering, a concourse. M18.

1 J. LOCKE Wit lying most in the assemblage of Ideas. W. BLACKSTONE In consequence of this lucky assemblage. b *Listener* The cutting and assemblage of the recordings under the composer's care. 2 G. ANSON Opposite .. is an assemblage of rocks. J. D. CLARK The preservation of more complete faunal assemblages. 3 HOR. WALPOLE It was an assemblage of all ages and nations. J. A. MICHENER The vast assemblage prepared to make the move, which all approved.

†assemblance *n.*[1] LME–L16. [OFr.: see ASSEMBLE *v.*, -ANCE.] Assemblage, assembling.

†assemblance *n.*[2] L15–L16. [OFr.: see AS-[1], SEMBLANCE *n.*] Semblance, show.

SHAKES. *2 Hen. IV* Care I for the limb, the thews, the stature, bulk, and big assemblance of a man?

assemble /əˈsɛmb(ə)l/ *v.* ME. [OFr. *asembler* (mod. *ass-*), ult. f. L *ad* AS-[1] + *simul* together.] I *v.t.* 1 Bring together into one place, company, or mass; collect, convene. ME. 2 Put together the separate component parts of (a machine or other object). M19. 3 *Computing.* Translate (a program) from a symbolic language into machine code. M20.

1 AV *1 Kings* 8:2 All the men of Israel assembled themselves unto king Solomon. E. LONGFORD The French assembled an army along the Pyrenees. M. AMIS Now, I thought, assembling fountain-pen, inkpot and notes, I'm really going to hit the bastard with everything.

II *v.i.* 4 Come together into one place or company; congregate, meet. ME. b *spec.* in *Entomol.* Of insects: gather together; *esp.* (of male moths) gather for mating in response to a pheromone released by a female. E20.

4 V. WOOLF The audience was assembling. G. ORWELL It was inconceivable that its members could ever assemble in larger numbers than twos and threes. W. S. CHURCHILL About these two centres there slowly assembled the troops and resources for the waging of civil war.

assembler *n.* a person who or thing which assembles; *spec.* in *Computing* (*a*) a program for converting programs in a low-level language into machine code; (*b*) an assembly language: M17. **assembling** *n.* (*a*) the action of the vb; (*b*) *Entomol.* the collecting of male moths by attracting them with a captive female: LME.

assemblé /asɑ̃ble/ *n.* Pl. pronounced same. L18. [Fr., pa. pple of *assembler*: see prec.] *Ballet.* A leap in which the feet are brought together before landing.

assemblée /asɑ̃ble/ *n.* Pl. pronounced same. E18. [Fr.: see next.] = ASSEMBLY (esp. sense 2c).

assembly /əˈsɛmbli/ *n.* ME. [OFr. *asemblee* (mod. *assemblée*) use as n. of fem. pa. pple of *asembler* ASSEMBLE *v.*: see -Y[5].] 1 Gathering or putting together; the state of being collected or brought together. ME. 2 A gathering of people; a concourse, a throng. ME. b *spec.* A deliberative body; a legislative council. LME. c *spec.* A gathering (esp. public) for social purposes or recreation. L16. d A gathering (esp. of a school) for religious worship; a congregation. E17. †3 A hostile encounter, an attack. LME–M16. 4 A collection of objects; *esp.* a number of component pieces fitted together to form a whole; a device consisting of numerous parts. M17. 5 A military call to assemble, given by drum or bugle. E18.

1 J. R. GREEN A Triennial Bill enforced the assembly of the Houses every three years. *Encycl. Brit.* After final assembly it is necessary to test the completed equipment. 2 F. FITZGERALD To forbid not only demonstrations but assemblies of over seven people. UNLAWFUL *assembly*. b J. KNOX The General Assembly of the Church .. holden in December after the Queen's Arrival. A. J. P. TAYLOR Chamberlain, Stresemann, and Briand always attended the meetings of the League assembly at Geneva. *National Assembly*: see NATIONAL *a.* c P. V. WHITE Mr Bright, the dancing instructor, who was experienced in conducting Assemblies and such like. d SHAKES. *A.Y.L.* Here we have no temple but the wood, no assembly but horn-beasts. E. BLISHEN At assembly the head announced that it was going to be a fine year. 4 D. H. LAWRENCE The whole is a strange assembly of apparently incongruous parts. E. WAUGH A wireless set had now been added to Nanny Hawkins' small assembly of pleasures. L. DEIGHTON With each pull the tail assembly of Sweet's Lancaster rose higher until it was strung up .. suspended from a buttress.

Comb.: **assembly language** *Computing* a low-level language employing mnemonic symbols which correspond exactly to groups of machine instructions; **assembly line** a group of machines and workers progressively assembling some product; **assembly-man** a (male) member of a legislative assembly; **assembly program** *Computing* = ASSEMBLER (a); **assembly room** (*a*) a public room in which social functions are held (usu. in *pl.*); (*b*) = *assembly shop* below; **assembly shop** a place where a machine or its parts are assembled.

assent /əˈsɛnt/ *n.* ME. [OFr. *as(s)ent(e)*, f. as next.] 1 Consent to or compliance with a proposal, desire, etc. ME. 2 *spec.* Official or judicial sanction; an action or instrument signifying this. ME. †3 Common purpose or feeling; accord. ME–M19. †4 Opinion. LME–M16. 5 (Expression of) agreement with a statement, opinion, etc.; mental acceptance. L15.

1 G. B. SHAW The assent of the majority is the only sanction known to ethics. K. AMIS Already his silence might have been taken as assent to some proposal that he should cable the British Council in Lisbon. 2 POPE Laws, to which you gave your own assent. **royal assent** the formal consent of the British monarch to a bill passed by Parliament. 3 AV *2 Chron.* 18:12 The prophets declare good to the king with one assent. 5 J. S. MILL Our assent to the conclusion being grounded on the truth of the premises. ALDOUS HUXLEY He smiled nervously and nodded a vague and non-committal assent.

assent /əˈsɛnt/ *v.* ME. [OFr. *as(s)enter*, ult. f. L *assentire* f. *ad* AS-[1] + *sentire* feel, think.] I *v.i.* 1 Agree, give one's consent (*to* a proposal, request, etc.). ME. †2 Agree together, determine. (Foll. by *to* or *into* a proposal.) ME–E16. †3 Conform, submit *to*. ME–M17. 4 Give or express one's agreement (*to* a statement, opinion, etc., †*with*, †*unto*). ME.

1 W. S. CHURCHILL To all the actions of these zealots the King had so far assented. 4 G. B. SHAW A Roman Catholic may obey his Church by assenting verbally to the doctrine of indissoluble marriage. J. CONRAD The deep voice on the other side said: 'What an extraordinary thing,' and I assented mentally. E. F. SCHUMACHER An axiom is a self-evident truth which is assented to as soon as enunciated.

†II *v.t.* 5 Agree to, agree upon. LME–L17. 6 *refl.* Agree. LME–L15.

assentant *a.* (now *rare* or *obs.*) = ASSENTIENT *a.* LME. **assenter** *n.* a person who gives assent LME. **assentingly** *adv.* in a manner expressing assent M16. **assentment** *n.* (*rare*) assent, agreement L15. **assentor** *n.* an assenter; *spec.* a person other than the proposer and seconder who subscribes a candidate's nomination: LME.

assentation /as(ə)nˈteɪʃ(ə)n/ *n.* Now *rare.* L15. [Fr.: see prec., -ATION.] The (esp. obsequious) expression or act of assent.

assentator *n.* (*rare*) a person who assents to or connives at something M16.

assentient /əˈsɛnʃ(ə)nt, -ʃɪənt/ *a.* & *n.* M19. [L *assentient-* pres. ppl stem of *assentire* assent: see ASSENT *v.*, -ENT.] A *adj.* Assenting, approving. M19. B *n.* A person who assents. M19.

assert /əˈsəːt/ *v.t.* E17. [L *assert-* pa. ppl stem of *asserere* claim, affirm, f. *ad* AS-[1] + *serere* join. Cf. med.L *assertare.*] 1 Declare formally and distinctly; aver, affirm. E17. 2 Affirm the existence of; draw attention to the existence of. *arch.* M17. b Be evidence of. *rare.* E19. 3 Vindicate one's claim to (a right etc.); give effect to (a quality etc.). M17. b *refl.* Insist that one's rights or opinions be recognized. L19. †4 Lay claim to; claim as belonging *to* oneself or another. M17–M19. †5 Take the part of; champion, protect. M17–E19. †6 Release *to* liberty. M–L17.

1 J. RUSKIN Would you not at once assert of that mistress, that she knew nothing of her duties? E. A. FREEMAN It is not directly asserted, but it seems to be implied. H. SPENCER Common Sense asserts the existence of a reality. P. TILLICH If courage, as he asserts, is the knowledge of 'what is to be dreaded and what dared'. J. THURBER The kind of senator or congressman that boldly asserts he will be glad to repeat his remarks in private and practically never does. 2 T. S. ELIOT My necktie rich and modest, but asserted by a simple pin. b C. LAMB Their air and dress asserted the parade. 3 J. M. BARRIE Father .. assert your position as the chief person on the island. E. WAUGH I hope to assert my independence early and so get time for a little more writing. b J. WAIN If he did not assert himself now his wife would rule him for ever. *fig.*: J. BRAINE Brought out, perhaps, by the music and the dancers .., a deeply buried instinct asserted itself. 4 W. COWPER The fourth awarded lot .. Meriones asserted next. W. HAMILTON The few who assert to man a knowledge of the infinite. 5 POPE Sedition silence, and assert the throne.

asserter *n.* = ASSERTOR M17. **assertiˈbility** *n.* ability to be asserted E20. **assertible** *a.* able to be asserted M19. **assertor** *n.* a person who asserts something LME.

assertation /asəˈteɪʃ(ə)n/ *n. rare.* M16. [med.L *assertatio(n-)*, f. *assertare* assert, f. as prec.: see -ATION.] (An) assertion, affirmation.

aˈssertative *a.* (*rare*) = ASSERTIVE E19.

assertion /əˈsəːʃ(ə)n/ *n.* LME. [OFr., or L *assertio(n-)* declaration, f. as ASSERT *v.* + -ION.] 1 Positive statement; a declaration. LME. †2 The action of setting free. M16–E18. 3 The action of maintaining a cause; vindication. *arch.* M16. 4 Insistence upon a right or opinion; effective use of a power etc. M17.

1 G. B. SHAW I hear the note of breezy assertion in your voice. E. O'NEILL A profound assertion of joy in living. E. LONGFORD Greville's assertion that the Duke had nothing to do was untrue. T. SHARPE The loud assertions that passed for conversation. 3 SIR W. SCOTT Flinching from the assertion of his daughter's reputation. 4 J. R. GREEN An assertion of her right of arbitrary taxation.

assertional *a.* (*rare*) M19.

assertive /əˈsəːtɪv/ *a.* E17. [Fr. *assertif, -ive* f. med.L *assertivus*, f. as ASSERT *v.* + -IVE.] Of the nature of or characterized by assertion; tending to assert oneself; dogmatic, positive.

assertively *adv.* LME. **assertiveness** *n.* L19.

assertory /əˈsəːtəri/ *a.* E17. [med.L *assertorius*, f. as ASSERT *v.*: see -ORY[2].] Of the nature of assertion; assertive, affirmative.

assertory oath: taken in support of a statement.

asserˈtorial *a.* = ASSERTORIC M19. **asserˈtorially** *adv.* L19. **asserˈtoric** *a.* (chiefly *Logic*) of the nature of assertion, affirming that something is L19. **asserˈtorical** *a.* = ASSERTORIC M19. **asserˈtorically** *adv.* M19.

asses *ns.* pls. of AS *n.*, ASS *n.*[1], *n.*[2]

assess /əˈsɛs/ *v.* & *n.* LME. [OFr. *assesser*, f. L *assess-* pa. ppl stem of *assidere* sit by, (in med.L) levy tax, f. *ad* AS-[1] + *sedere* sit: cf. ASSIZE *n.* Aphet. to CESS *v.*[1], SESS *v.*] A *v.t.* 1 Fix the amount of (a tax, fine, etc.); impose (a specified tax etc.) (*up*)*on* a person or community. LME. 2 Impose a fine or tax on (a person or community). (Foll. by *at*, *in* the amount, or foll. by second obj.) LME. 3 Estimate officially the value of (property, income, etc.) for taxation. E19. 4 *gen.* Estimate the worth or extent of; evaluate. M20.

1 J. R. GREEN A forced loan was assessed upon the whole kingdom. *Daily Telegraph* The judge assessed total damages at £112,600. 2 H. COX John Hampden was assessed twenty shillings. 4 A. J. CRONIN Material success isn't so important... Usually it's assessed by false standards. J. HELLER Dressing at his locker, he assessed the damage to his flesh, bones, and systems. D. LESSING One of my tasks was to observe him, to assess his present state.

†B *n.* = ASSESSMENT. Cf. CESS *n.*[1] L16–L17.

assessable *a.* LME. **asseˈssee** *n.* a person whose property or income is assessed E18.

assession /əˈsɛʃ(ə)n/ *n.* LME. [L *assessio(n-)* session, (in med.L) assessment, f. *assess-*: see prec., -ION.] 1 *Law.* Assessment, assessing; *spec.* the action of assessing and leasing the lord's demesnes in the Duchy of Cornwall, done at a special court. LME. 2 A sitting beside or together; a session. Now *rare* or *obs.* M16.

assessionable *a.* let by a court of assession E19.

assessment /əˈsɛsm(ə)nt/ *n.* M16. [f. ASSESS *v.* + -MENT.] 1 The determination of the amount of a tax, fine, etc.; a scheme of taxation etc. M16. 2 Official valuation of property, income, etc. for the purpose of taxation. M16. 3 The amount of such a charge or valuation. E17. 4 *gen.* Evaluation, estimation; an estimate of worth, extent, etc. E17.

4 T. S. ELIOT It is not merely the passage of time . . that makes new assessments necessary. CONTINUOUS *assessment*.

assessor /əˈsɛsə/ *n.* LME. [OFr. *assessour* (mod. *-eur*) f. L *assessor* assistant judge, (in med.L) assessor of taxes: see ASSESS *v.*, -OR.] **I 1** A person who sits as assistant or adviser to a judge or magistrate on technical points. LME. **2** *gen.* A person who sits beside another; a person who shares another's position. Now *rare* or *obs.* M17.

2 MILTON Whence to his Son, Th' Assessor of his Throne.

II 3 A person who makes assessments for the purposes of taxation. LME. **4** *gen.* A person who makes evaluations or estimates. M19.

asseˈssorial *a.* of or pertaining to an assessor or assessors E18.

asset /ˈasɛt/ *n.* Orig. only as *collect. sing.* (now regarded as *pl.*) **assets**. M16. [Legal AN *as(s)etz* f. OFr. *asez* (mod. *assez* enough), ult. f. L *ad* to + *satis* enough, sufficiency.] **1** In *pl.* Sufficient estate or effects for an executor to discharge a testator's debts and legacies. M16. **2** In *pl.*, any property or effects available to meet the debts of a testator, debtor, or company, whether sufficient or not; *sing.* an item of property or an effect so available. L16. **3** *fig.* A thing or person of use or value. L17.

1 T. SOUTHERNE I shall fall like an Executor without assets. 2 JAS. MILL The assets or effects of the London Company in India fell short of the debts of that concern. W. PLOMER He felt that the best thing would be to store the picture against better times, as it was a great asset. *tangible assets*: see TANGIBLE *a.* 1. *wasting asset*: see WASTE *v.* 13. 3 D. LODGE Philip Swallow's chief social asset at Euphoric State turned out to be his association with Charles Boon. G. CLARE An ability to speak languages would undoubtedly have been a great asset to his work. *current asset*: see CURRENT *a.*

Comb.: **asset-stripper** an entrepreneur engaged in asset-stripping; **asset-stripping** the piecemeal sale of a company's assets by an entrepreneur for profit.

†assethe *n.* & *v.* see ASSYTHE.

assever /əˈsɛvə/ *v.t. arch.* L16. [L *asseverare*: see next.] = next.

asseverate /əˈsɛvəreɪt/ *v.t.* L18. [L *asseverat-* pa. ppl stem of *asseverare*, f. *ad* AS-[1] + *severus* grave, SEVERE: see -ATE[3].] Declare solemnly or emphatically.

asseveration /əsɛvəˈreɪʃ(ə)n/ *n.* M16. [L *asseveratio(n-)*, f. as prec.: see -ATION.] (A) solemn affirmation; (an) emphatic declaration or confirmation; an oath.

BACON Men ought . . to propound things sincerely, with more or less asseueration, as they stand in a man's own judgement. SMOLLETT Incensed at this asseveration, which he was not prepared to refute. DICKENS The sergeant rejoined with many choice asseverations that he didn't.

aˈsseverative *a.* pertaining to or of the nature of asseveration M19.

assibilate /əˈsɪbɪleɪt/ *v.t.* M19. [L *assibilat-* pa. ppl stem of *assibilare* hiss at, f. *ad* AS-[1] + *sibilare* to hiss: see -ATE[3].] *Phonet.* & *Philol.* Pronounce as or change to a sibilant or other fricative.

assibiˈlation *n.* pronunciation as or change to a sibilant or other fricative M19.

Assidean /asɪˈdiːən/ *n. arch.* E17. [f. Gk *Asidaioi* (f. as HASID) + -AN.] **1** A member of a Jewish group who opposed the attempts of Antiochus Epiphanes to introduce idolatry among them (*I Macc.* 2:42). E17. **2** A Hasid. M19.

assiduity /asɪˈdjuːɪti/ *n.* LME. [L *assiduitas*, f. as next: see -ITY. Cf. (O)Fr. *assiduité*.] **1** Persistence, unremitting application, perseverance, diligence. LME. **b** Persistent endeavour to please; in *pl.*, constant attentions. *arch.* M17. **†2** Continual recurrence; frequency. LME–M17.

¶Rare bef. 17.

assiduous /əˈsɪdjʊəs/ *a.* M16. [f. L *assiduus*, f. *assidere* (see ASSESS), + -OUS.] **1** Of an action etc.: unremitting, persistent. M16. **2** Of a person: persevering, diligent; attending closely. E17. **b** Constantly endeavouring to please. *arch.* E18.

1 MILTON To wearie him with my assiduous cries. H. MACMILLAN Selwyn Lloyd . . worked with assiduous and skilful diplomacy. 2 ADDISON Those assiduous Gentlemen who employ their whole Lives in the Chace. D. J. ENRIGHT A self-effacing, even shadowy, presence, assiduous without passion, obliging and long-suffering. b S. JOHNSON Few can be assiduous without servility.

assiduously *adv.* E17. **assiduousness** *n.* M17.

†assiege *v.t.* ME–M17. [OFr. *asegier* (mod. *assiéger*) f. Proto-Romance, ult. f. as AS-[1] + SIEGE *n.*] Besiege, beset.

†assiegement *n.* L16–M19.

assiento /asɪˈɛntəʊ, *foreign* asiˈɛnto/ *n.* Pl. **-os** /-əʊz, *foreign* -os/. E17. [Sp. (now *asiento*).] *Hist.* A contract or convention between the King of Spain and other powers, esp. for supplying the Spanish dominions in America with Black slaves (as that made between Spain and Great Britain at the peace of Utrecht).

assiˈentist *n.* a party to an assiento, a slave-trader for Spain E18.

assiette /asjɛt (*pl. same*), asɪˈɛt/ *n.* M18. [Fr. = plate, course of a meal; seat, site; bed, foundation.] **1** A prepared dish of food. M18. **2** *Bookbinding.* A composition laid on the cut edges of books before gilding. M19.

assign /əˈsʌɪn/ *n.* ME. [f. as ASSIGNEE, with which early uses are identical.] **1** = ASSIGNEE 1. ME. **†2** = ASSIGNEE 2. LME–E18. **†3** An appurtenance. *rare* (Shakes.). Only in E17.

assign /əˈsʌɪn/ *v.t.* ME. [OFr. *asi(g)ner* (mod. *assigner*) f. L *assignare*, f. *ad* AS-[1] + *signare* SIGN *v.*] **I** Allot, appoint, determine. **1** Transfer or make over formally (esp. personal property, *to*). ME. **2** Appoint or designate (a person) *to* an office, duty, fate, etc., *to do* a task etc.; set aside or designate (a thing) *for* a purpose. ME. **†b** Appoint or consign (a person) *to* a place. LME–E17. **3** Fix, determine, or appoint (a time or temporal limit). ME. **†b** Fix the time and place of (a meeting). LME–M16. **4** Allot as a share or allowance (*to*); allot or appoint (a place, *to* a person); allocate (a task, office, etc., *to*); allot as a task. LME. **5** Appoint (a person) *to* another to assist or act for him or her in some capacity. LME. **b** *Austral. Hist.* Make over (a convict) as an unpaid servant to a colonist. E19. **†6** Prescribe (a course of action). LME–E17. **7** Determine, establish. *arch.* M17.

1 S. JOHNSON I assign to him the right of copy of an Imitation of the Tenth Satire of Juvenal. 2 W. BLACKSTONE If the founder has appointed and assigned any other person to be visitor. G. CRABBE Has a small space for garden-ground assign'd. T. CAPOTE A total of eighteen men were assigned to the case full time, among them three of the F.B.I.'s ablest investigators. D. HALBERSTAM The *New York Times* . . had a large and expensive staff of reporters assigned to cover the world. b AV *2 Sam.* 11:16 He assigned Vriah vnto a place where hee knewe that valiant men were. 3 SWIFT In this month likewise an ambassador will die in London; but I cannot assign the day. 4 MILTON The work which here God hath assign'd us. GOLDSMITH I was assigned my place on a cushion on the floor. O. HENRY He assigned his men to their respective posts with discretion, and coached them carefully as to their duties. R. LARDNER The Thayers had a very pretty home and the room assigned to us was close to perfection. W. S. CHURCHILL To him was assigned what was then a lowly office, the Presidency of the Board of Trade. D. LODGE We're supposed to discuss some text I've assigned. 5 JOSEPH HALL The Lords Assigned us five very worthy Lawyers. 7 CAPT. COOK Who sailed round it, and assigned its true position.

II Point out, show. **8** Designate, specify. ME. **†9** Exhibit, display. Only in LME.

8 SIR T. MORE Folk whom I neither assigne bi name, nor as yet know not who they be.

III Ascribe, attribute. **10** Ascribe, attribute, refer, as belonging or due *to*. LME. **11** Ascribe (a reason, explanation, etc., *to* or *for*). LME. **12** Bring forward, allege, suggest, as a reason, explanation, etc. LME.

10 M. MEAD Sometimes one quality has been assigned to one sex, sometimes to the other. 12 W. PALEY I cannot assign a supposition of forgery.

IV After SIGN *v.* **†13** Sign. M16–L19.

assignable *a.* able to be assigned (*to*, *for*) LME. **assignably** *adv.* (*rare*) LME. **assigner** *n.* †(*a*) = ASSIGNEE; (*b*) a person who assigns: LME. **assignor** *n.* †(*a*) = ASSIGNEE; (*b*) the person for or by whom an assignee is appointed: LME.

assignat /asiɲa (*pl. same*), ˈasɪgnat/ *n.* L18. [Fr. f. L *assignatum* neut. pa. pple of *assignare*: see prec.] *Hist.* A promissory note issued until 1796 by the revolutionary government of France, on security of State lands. Cf. MANDAT 1.

assignation /asɪgˈneɪʃ(ə)n/ *n.* LME. [(O)Fr. f. L *assignatio(n-)*, f. *assignat-* pa. ppl stem of *assignare*: see ASSIGN *v.*, -ATION.] **†1** A command; bidding. LME–E17. **†2** Appointment to office. LME–M17. **†3** The allotment of revenue to meet claims; a mandate granting payment of a claim; a pension, an allowance. LME–M18. **4** Formal transference; a document effecting this; (= ASSIGNMENT 6). L16. **5** Allotment; apportionment; allocation; (= ASSIGNMENT 4). E17. **6** Attribution as belonging or due *to*; (= ASSIGNMENT 10). E17. **7** Appointment of a particular time and place; an appointment; a tryst, an illicit meeting. M17. **8** A promissory note secured by revenue or property; paper currency. Cf. ASSIGNAT. *arch.* L17.

assignee /asʌɪˈniː, -sɪ-/ *n.* ME. [(O)Fr. *assigné* pa. pple of *assigner* ASSIGN *v.*, used as n.: in early use identical w. ASSIGN *n.*] **1** A person (other than the heir-at-law) to whom a right or property is legally transferred. ME. **2** A person appointed to act for another; a deputy, an agent, a representative. LME. **b** *spec. Hist.* A person appointed to administer a bankrupt's property on behalf of the creditors. L17.

assigneeship *n.* the position or office of assignee E19.

assignment /əˈsʌɪnm(ə)nt/ *n.* LME. [OFr. *assignement* f. med.L *assignamentum*, f. L *assignare*: see ASSIGN *v.*, -MENT.] **†1** Command, bidding. LME–M18. **†2** = ASSIGNATION 2. LME–M19. **†3** = ASSIGNATION 3. LME–M19. **4** Allotment; apportionment; allocation; (= ASSIGNATION 5). LME. **b** *Austral. Hist.* The making over of a convict to a colonist as an unpaid servant; the condition of such service. E19. **†5** An assigned measure; a definite amount. E–M16. **6** Legal or other formal transference of a right or property; a document that effects or authorizes this; (= ASSIGNATION 4). L16. **†7** = ASSIGNATION 8. E17–E18. **8** Statement or attribution (of a reason etc.). M17. **9** Indication; specification. M17. **10** Attribution as belonging or due *to*; (= ASSIGNATION 6). L17. **11** A task assigned; a commission. M19.

assimilable /əˈsɪm(ɪ)ləb(ə)l/ *a.* M17. [med.L *assimilabilis*, f. L *assimilare*: see ASSIMILATE *v.*, -ABLE.] **1** Able to be absorbed and incorporated. M17. **2** Able to be likened or compared *to*. *arch.* M19.

assimilaˈbility *n.* E19.

assimilate /əˈsɪmɪlət/ *ppl a.* & *n. rare.* LME. [L *assimilatus* pa. pple, f. as next: see -ATE[2], -ATE[1].] **†A** *ppl a.* Like, likened, (*to*). LME–L17. **B** *n.* **†1** A similar thing. Only in L17. **2** An assimilated substance. M20.

assimilate /əˈsɪmɪleɪt/ *v.* LME. [L *assimilat-* pa. ppl stem of *assimilare*, f. *ad* AS-[1] + *similis* SIMILAR: see -ATE[3].] **I** Absorb and incorporate. **1** *v.t.* Of a living organism: convert (extraneous material) into fluids and tissues identical with its own; absorb into the system; *fig.* absorb and make one's own (ideas, influences, etc.); incorporate into one's own way of thinking or acting; take in and understand fully. LME. **2** *v.i.* Become absorbed or incorporated into the system (*lit.* & *fig.*). E17.

1 S. JOHNSON Falsehood by long use is assimilated to the mind, as poison to the body. E. WILSON Marx and Engels . . had assimilated with remarkable rapidity the social and historical thinking of their time. K. CLARK Poussin was a learned artist who had studied and assimilated the poses of antique sculpture. H. WILSON Showed a detailed knowledge of the subject matter which could not have been assimilated within so short a time. 2 CHARLES CHURCHILL He stands aloof from all . . And scorns, like Scotsmen, to assimilate. J. H. NEWMAN I am a foreign material, and cannot assimilate with the Church of England. DICKENS The nightly pint of beer, instead of assimilating naturally [etc.].

II Make or be like. (Earlier as ASSIMILATE *ppl a.*) †3 *v.t.* Resemble. L16–M17. 4 *v.t.* Make like (*to*; also, w. suggestion of incorporation, as in branch I, *with*). E17. b Bring into conformity, adapt, *to*. *arch.* M17. c *Phonol.* Make (a sound) more like another in the same or a contiguous word. M19. 5 *v.t.* Liken, compare, put into the same class. (Foll. by *to*, *with*.) *arch.* E17. 6 *v.i.* Be or become like, resemble. Foll. by *to*, (w. suggestion of incorporation, as in branch I above) *with*. *arch.* M18. b Conform *to*, act in accordance *with*. *arch.* L18.

3 J. GAULE The reason that children . . assimulate their nurses more than their mothers. 4 W. COWPER The downy flakes . . Softly alighting upon all below, Assimilate all objects. DICKENS Observe the dyer's hand, assimilating itself to what it works in. J. S. MILL Whose education and way of life assimilate them with the rich. b S. RICHARDSON This lady . . half-assimilates me to her own virtue. 5 GOLDSMITH Which we can assimilate with no shells that are known. J. HUTTON To assimilate things upon fallacious grounds. R. G. COLLINGWOOD They have been assimilating a work of art to an artifact, and the artist's work to the craftsman's. 6 W. BLACKSTONE Which revenues . . do always assimilate, or take the same nature, with the antient revenues. LYTTON Whose courage assimilated to their own. b COLERIDGE With whose prejudices and ferocity their unbending virtue forbade them to assimilate.

assimilative *a.* (*a*) of, characterized by, or tending to assimilation; (*b*) *rare* that may be or has been assimilated: LME. **assimilator** *n.* a person who or thing which assimilates M18. **assimilatory** *a.* = ASSIMILATIVE (a) M19.

assimilation /əsɪmɪˈleɪʃ(ə)n/ *n.* LME. [Fr., or its source L *assimilatio(n-)*, f. as prec.: see -ATION.] 1 Conversion into a similar substance; *esp.* conversion by a living organism of extraneous material into fluids and tissues identical with its own; the final part of this process, the incorporation of digested nutriment within the system following absorption. LME. b *fig.* Absorption and incorporation (of ideas, influences, etc.); integration with another (dominant) social, racial, or cultural group. L18. c *Psychol.* The process whereby a person acquires new ideas through comparing experience with the existing content of the mind. M19. 2 The action of making or becoming like; the state of being like. E17. b The action of conforming *to*, conformity *with*. *arch.* exc. as passing into sense 1b. L17. c *Phonol.* The process of assimilating a sound. M19.

1b BURKE Which, by a bland assimilation, incorporated into politics the sentiments which beautify and soften private society. G. H. LEWES Interpretation means mental assimilation. MALCOLM X 'Integration' is called 'assimilation' if white ethnic groups alone are involved. 2c *progressive assimilation*: see PROGRESSIVE *a.* *reciprocal assimilation*: see RECIPROCAL *a.*

assimilationist *n.* & *a.* (*a*) *n.* an advocate of racial or cultural integration; (*b*) *adj.* of or pertaining to assimilationists or their beliefs: E20.

Assiniboine /əˈsɪnɪbɔɪn/ *n.* & *a.* Also **-boin**, **Assina-**, (earlier) **†-bouet**. Pl. of n. same, **-s**. L17. [Canad. Fr. f. Ojibwa *assini:-pwa:n* lit. 'stone Sioux', f. *assin* stone + *pwa:n* (Cree *pwa:t*) Sioux Indian.] 1 A member of, of or pertaining to, a Siouan Indian people of the Great Plains of N. America. L17. 2 (Of) the language of this people. M19.

†assinico *n.* var. of ASINEGO.

Assisian /əˈsiːsɪən/ *a.* & *n.* L19. [f. *Assisi* (see below) + -AN.] (A native or inhabitant) of the town of Assisi in central Italy; *spec.* (of) St Francis of Assisi.

assist /əˈsɪst/ *n.* L16. [f. the vb.] 1 An act of helping; a help. Now chiefly *US.* L16. 2 In baseball, ice hockey, etc.: a player's action in helping to put out an opponent, score a goal, etc.; a credit for this. Chiefly *N. Amer.* L19.

assist /əˈsɪst/ *v.* LME. [(O)Fr. *assister* f. L *assistere*, f. *ad* AS-[1] + *sistere* take one's stand.] I Help. 1 *v.t.* Help (a person *in*, *to do*, *with*, etc.; a person in necessity; an action, process, or result); support, further, promote. LME. 2 *v.i.* Give help or support (*in*, †*to*, (arch.) *to do*, *with*). LME.

1 STEELE When I assist a friendless person. E. GASKELL May I assist you to potatoes? R. MACAULAY Miss Smith . . was assisted from her hammock. J. C. POWYS Mr. Geard . . permitted John to assist him to mount the platform. P. K. KEMP An assisted take-off with rockets. P. H. JOHNSON Her pelvis is very narrow and they will have to assist the birth. T. CAPOTE A young man who assisted him with the management of the farm. **assisted passage** a journey to another country at a fare reduced by a subsidy. **assisted place** a place in a fee-paying school for which State financial assistance is given. 2 DRYDEN If Heav'n assist, and Phœbus hear my call. J. A. FROUDE Barlow . . whose indiscretion had already assisted to ruin Cromwell. E. F. BENSON She had herself assisted in adding to the tediousness.

II Be present. †3 *v.t.* Stand by; attend, escort; accompany, join. L15–M17. 4 *v.i.* Be present (*at*), either as a spectator (*arch.*) or as a participant. M16.

3 SHAKES. *Temp.* The King and Prince at prayers! Let's assist them. R. CRASHAW Three vigorous virgins, waiting still behind, Assist the throne of th' iron-sceptred king. 4 THACKERAY The dinner at which we have just assisted.

assister *n.* a person who assists; an assistant: E16. **assistful** *a.* (*arch.*) helpful E17. **†assistor** *n.* (chiefly *Law*) = ASSISTER LME–L18.

assistance /əˈsɪst(ə)ns/ *n.* LME. [(O)Fr., or med.L *assistentia*, f. L *assistere*: see prec., -ANCE, -ENCE.] I 1 *sing.* & †in *pl.* The action of helping; help, aid, support. LME. †2 A helper; *collect.* a body of helpers. M16–L17.

1 *National Assistance*: see NATIONAL *a.*

II 3 *collect. sing.* (occas. *pl.*). Persons present; bystanders. *obs.* exc. as occas. readopted f. Fr. L15. 4 Presence, attendance. Long *rare.* E16.

assistant /əˈsɪst(ə)nt/ *a.* & *n.* LME. [(O)Fr., or med.L *assistent-* pres. ppl stem of *assistere*: see ASSIST *v.*, -ANT[1], -ENT.] A *adj.* 1 Helping, auxiliary, subordinate, (*to*). LME. †2 Standing by, present, accompanying. L15–L17.

1 *assistant manager, master, mistress, professor, secretary*, etc.

B *n.* 1 A helper; a supporter; a subordinate worker. LME. †2 A person who is present, a bystander, a participant. L15–M19.

1 *editorial assistant, shop assistant*, etc.

assistancy *n.* = ASSISTANTSHIP E17. **assistantship** *n.* the position or office of an assistant E17.

assize /əˈsʌɪz/ *n.* & *v.* *obs.* exc. *Hist.* ME. [OFr. *as(s)ise* use as n. of fem. of *assis* pa. pple of *asseeir* (mod. *asseoir*) sit, settle, assess, f. L *assidere*: see ASSESS *v.*] A *n.* I Uses pertaining to legislation or trial. 1 A decree or edict made by a consultative or legislative body. ME. 2a An ordinance regulating weights, measures, and the price of articles of general consumption; the regulation of weights, measures, and prices in accordance with such an ordinance. ME. b The statutory weight, measure, or price (esp. of bread and ale) ordained; customary or prescriptive standard. LME. 3 A legal proceeding of the nature of an inquest or trial; *spec.* (*sing.* & (usu.) in *pl.*) a periodical session in each county of England and Wales for the administration of civil and criminal justice. ME. b An action decided at such a trial; a writ instituting such a trial. L16. †4 Judgement; sentence. ME–M17. 5 In Scotland: a trial by jury; a jury, a panel. LME. †6 The office of judge; the action of judging. M–L17.

1 **†rent of assize** a fixed rent. 3 **the great** or **last assize(s)** the Last Judgement.

†II Other uses. 7 Custom, practice; mode, manner, fashion. ME–L15. 8 Site; situation. LME–L15. 9 Measurement, dimensions, size; measure, extent. LME–M17.

†B *v.t.* 1 Decree, ordain. LME–L15. 2 Decide, judge; try. LME–L17. 3 Assess. LME–E17. 4 Regulate (weights, measures, prices, etc.) according to an ordinance or standard. M16–M19.

assizer *n.* = ASSIZOR (b) L16. **assizor** *n.* (*a*) each of those who constituted an assize or inquest; (*b*) *Sc.* a member of a jury: ME.

associable /əˈsəʊʃɪəb(ə)l, -sɪ-/ *a.* M16. [Fr., f. *associer* f. L *associare*: see ASSOCIATE *v.*, -ABLE.] †1 Companionable. *rare.* M16–L17. 2 That may be associated (*with*) or joined in association. E19.

associate /əˈsəʊʃɪət, -sɪ-/ *a.* & *n.* LME. [L *associatus* pa. pple, f. as next: see -ATE[2], -ATE[1].] A *adj.* 1 Joined in companionship, function, or dignity; allied; concomitant. LME. 2 Sharing in responsibility, function, membership, etc., but with a secondary or subordinate status. E19.

1 C. MARLOWE With him is Edmund gone associate? R. KNOLLES Christ our Sauiour, equall and associate to his Father. POPE Amphinomus survey'd th' associate band. S. JOHNSON They want some associate sounds to make them harmonious. 2 H. F. PRINGLE The *Outlook* office where the ex-President was an associate editor. **associate professor** in N. American universities, (a person of) the academic rank immediately below (full) professor.

B *n.* 1 A partner, a comrade; a companion; an ally, a confederate; a colleague. M16. 2 A thing placed or found in conjunction with another. M17. 3 A person who belongs to an association or institution in a secondary or subordinate degree of membership. E19.

1 P. SIDNEY They persuade the king . . to make Plangus his associate in government. LD MACAULAY These men, more wretched than their associates who suffered death. W. IRVING His associates soon turned the tide of the battle. D. W. HARDING To her the first necessity was to keep on reasonably good terms with the associates of her everyday life. 2 PAIRED *associates*.

associateship *n.* the position or status of an associate E19.

associate /əˈsəʊʃɪeɪt, -sɪ-/ *v.* LME. [L *associat-* pa. ppl stem of *associare*, f. *ad* AS-[1] + *socius* sharing, allied: see -ATE[3].] 1 *v.t.* Join, unite, ally, (persons; oneself or another *with*, (arch.) *to* another or others, *in*, †*to* a common purpose, action, or condition); declare (oneself) in agreement *with*. LME. b Elect as an associate member. E19. †2 *v.t.* Join oneself to (a person); accompany; keep company with. M16–M17. 3 *v.t.* a *gen.* Join, combine, (things together; one thing *with*, *to* another or others). Chiefly *refl.* or in *pass.* *arch.* L16. b *spec.* Connect as an idea (*with*, †*to*). M18. †4 *v.t.* Of things: accompany, join. L16–L17. 5 *v.i.* Combine for a common purpose; keep company, have frequent dealings, *with*. M17.

1 SWIFT None but papists are associated against him. D. HUME The troops . . associating to them all the disorderly people. E. A. FREEMAN Arnulf associated his son with him in his government. GLADSTONE It is for me . . to associate myself with the answer previously given by the Under-Secretary. b SOUTHEY He . . was associated to the royal Academy there. 2 J. MARBECK Therfore shal man leaue father and mother and associate his wife. SHAKES. *Rom. & Jul.* A barefoot brother . . to associate me, Here in this city visiting the sick. 3 A. BAIN The muscles . . act in groups, being associated together by the organization of the nervous centres. T. H. HUXLEY This vapour is intimately associated with the other constituents of the atmosphere. b A. S. NEILL The children will leave electric lights on because they do not associate light with electricity bills. JENNIE MELVILLE She associated love and pain. 4 T. HEYWOOD Those torturing pangues That should associate death. 5 BURKE When bad men combine, good men must associate. D. RUNYON As a rule I do not care to associate with coppers, because it arouses criticism from other citizens.

associater *n.* (*rare*) = ASSOCIATOR E17. **associator** *n.* a person who or thing which associates; an associate; a confederate: L17. **associatory** *a.* having the quality of associating L19.

association /əsəʊsɪˈeɪʃ(ə)n, -ʃɪ-/ *n.* M16. [Fr., or med.L *associatio(n-)*, f. as prec.: see -ATION.] 1 The action of joining or uniting for a common purpose; the state of being so joined. M16. 2 A body of people organized for a common purpose; a society. L16. †3 A document setting out the common purpose of a number of people and signed by them. L16–M19. 4 Fellowship, companionship; social intercourse (esp. in prison). M17. 5 The conjoining or uniting of things or persons with another or others; the state of being so conjoined, conjunction. M17. 6 Mental connection between related ideas; an idea, recollection, or feeling mentally connected with another. L17. 7 *Ecol.* A group of dominant plant species occurring together; a plant community characterized by such a group. E20.

1 R. COKE A solemn oath of association for the restoring of it. CONAN DOYLE The good Watson had

at that time deserted me for a wife, the only selfish action which I can recall in our association. **articles** or **deed of association** a document giving the regulations of a limited liability company. **memorandum of association** a document giving the name, status, purposes, and capital of a limited liability company. 2 F. O'BRIEN The people who attended the College had banded themselves into many private associations. 3 LD MACAULAY Dropping the Association into a flowerpot. 4 SMOLLETT The nobility would be profaned by my association. H. ALLEN To have so pleasant and bright a companion as young Anthony sitting before the fire sped their association mightily. 5 J. REYNOLDS The spark that without the association of more fuel would have died. T. CAPOTE A tendency not to experience anger or rage in association with violent aggressive action. 6 J. LOCKE On the Association of Ideas. W. HAMILTON Our Cognitions, Feelings, and Desires are connected together by what are called the *Laws of Association* B. RUBENS The theatre, the picnics, the concerts, separately and by association, they triggered off total recall. A. STORR The dreamer's associations to all the images in the dream. B. BETTELHEIM The replacement of a word that has deep emotional associations with one that evokes hardly any. *free association*: see FREE *a.* PAIRED *association*.

Comb.: **association book, copy** a volume showing some mark of personal connection with the author or a notable former owner; **Association football** football played according to the rules of the Football Association, with a round ball which may not be handled during play except by a goalkeeper, soccer.

associational *a.* of or pertaining to (an) association E19. **associationism** *n.* (*a*) *rare* union in an association; (*b*) a theory accounting for mental phenomena by association of ideas: M19. **associationist** *n.* & *a.* (*a*) *n.* a member of an association; an adherent of associationism; (*b*) *adj.* = ASSOCIATIONISTIC: M19. **associatio'nistic** *a.* of or pertaining to associationism or associationists E20.

associative /ə'səʊʃɪətɪv, -sɪ-/ *a.* E19. [f. ASSOCIATE *v.* + -IVE.] 1 Of, pertaining to, or characterized by association (esp. of ideas). E19. 2 *Math.* Governed by or stating the condition that where three or more quantities in a given order are connected together by operators, the result is independent of any grouping of the quantities, e.g. that $(a \times b) \times c = a \times (b \times c)$. M19.

2 B. RUSSELL The associative, commutative and distributive laws.

associatively *adv.* L19. **associativeness** *n.* (*rare*) L19. **associa'tivity** *n.* (esp. *Math.*) M20.

assoil /ə'sɔɪl/ *v.t. arch.* exc. *Sc. Law* (see sense 4b). Also (*Sc.*) **assoilzie** /-l(j)i/. ME. [AN *as(s)oili(e)r*, f. OFr. *assoil-* tonic stem of *asoldre* (mod. *absoudre*) f. L *absolvere* ABSOLVE; the Sc. form derives from ME *-lȝ-*.] I With a person as obj. 1 Grant absolution to; absolve *of*, *from* a sin. ME. b Release from purgatory. LME. †2 Release from excommunication or other ecclesiastical sentence. LME–L17. †3 Release *from*, *of* obligations or liabilities. LME–M17. 4 Acquit of a criminal charge. (Foll. by *of*, *from*.) LME. b *Sc. Law* (as *assoilzie*). Hold not liable, in a civil action, by decision of court. E17. 5 *gen.* Release, set free, discharge, (*of*, *from*). LME. II With a thing as obj. †6 Clear up, solve, resolve. LME–L17. †7 Refute (an objection or argument). LME–E18. 8 Expiate, atone for. L16. †9 Get rid of, dispel. *rare* (Spenser). Only in L16.

assoilment *n.* absolution from sin, guilt, censure, accusation, etc. E17.

†**assoin** *n.*, *v.* see ESSOIN *n.*, *v.*

assonance /'as(ə)nəns/ *n.* E18. [Fr., f. L *assonare* respond to, f. *ad* AS-[1] + *sonare*, f. *sonus* sound: see -ANCE.] 1 Resemblance or correspondence of sound between two syllables. E18. 2 The rhyming of one word with another in accented vowel and those that follow, but not in consonants, or (less usually) in consonants but not in vowels. E19. 3 *transf.* Correspondence more or less incomplete. M19.

assonant *a.* & *n.* (*a*) *adj.* exhibiting assonance; (*b*) *n.* in *pl.*, words exhibiting assonance: E18. **assonantal** /-'nant(ə)l/ *a.* of or pertaining to assonance, exhibiting assonance M19.

assonate /'as(ə)neɪt/ *v.i.* E17. [L *assonat-* pa. ppl stem of *assonare*: see prec., -ATE[3].] †1 Sound like a bell. *rare.* Only in E17. 2 Correspond in sound; *spec.* exhibit assonance. M17.

¶ Only in Dicts. bef. 19.

assort /ə'sɔːt/ *v.* L15. [OFr. *assorter* (mod. *-ir*), f. *à* A-[5] (assim. to *as* AS-[1]) + *sorte* SORT *n.*[2]] 1 *v.t.* Distribute into groups; arrange in sorts. L15. b Classify, place in a group, *with*. M19. 2 *v.t.* Provide with an assortment. *arch.* M18. 3 *v.i.* Fall into a class *with*; correspond or suit (*well*, *ill*, etc.) *with*. E19. 4 *v.i.* Keep company, associate, *with*. *arch.* E19.

1 *Tait's Edinburgh Magazine* Merchants . . employ wool-sorters of their own to assort and repack it. b DICKENS He would . . assort it with the fabulous dogs . . as a monstrous invention. 2 OED We have sent orders for some white goods to assort our store. 3 W. HAMILTON Finding that it is harmonious,—that it dovetails and naturally assorts with other parts. E. LINKLATER Her cold hard voice that assorted so badly with his memory of her. 4 C. LAMB I could abide to assort with fisher-swains.

assorted *a.* (*a*) matched *to*; (*ill*, *well*, etc.) suited to one another; (*b*) of various sorts put together: L18.

assortative /ə'sɔːtətɪv/ *a.* L19. [f. prec. + -ATIVE.] *Biol.* Designating mating which is not random, but correlated with the possession by the partners of certain similar (or dissimilar) characteristics.

assortment /ə'sɔːtm(ə)nt/ *n.* E17. [f. ASSORT *v.* + -MENT, after Fr. *assortiment*.] 1 The action of assorting; the state of being assorted. *arch.* E17. 2 A set of various sorts put together. M18. 3 A group of things of the same sort. *rare.* M18.

1 OED She was engaged in the assortment of her crewels. 2 J. BRAINE A confusion of voices and an assortment of minor noises—glasses clinking, matches being struck, the central heating rumbling. 3 ADAM SMITH Those classes and assortments, which . . are called genera and species.

assot /ə'sɒt/ *v.* Long *arch. rare.* Infl. **-tt-**. ME. [(O)Fr. *assoter*, f. as A-[5] + *sot* f. med.L *sottus*: see SOT *n.*] †1 *v.i.* Behave foolishly; become infatuated. Only in ME. 2 *v.t.* Make a fool of; infatuate. Chiefly as *assotted* ppl a. LME.

assuage /ə'sweɪdʒ/ *v.* ME. [OFr. *as(s)ouagier* f. Proto-Romance, f. L *ad* AS-[1] + *suavis* sweet.] I *v.t.* 1 Mitigate, appease, allay, alleviate, relieve, (feelings, pain, appetite, desire, etc.). ME. †2 Relax, moderate, (a harsh law etc.). ME–L15. 3 Pacify, soothe, (a person). LME. 4 *gen.* Abate, lessen, diminish. *arch.* LME.

1 BACON They need medicine . . to assuage the disease. J. LONDON He had once gone three days without water . . in order to experience the exquisite delight of such a thirst assuaged. N. ALGREN Assuaging her fears by day and her lusts by night. 3 ADDISON Kindling pity, kindling rage At once provoke me, and asswage. 4 W. OWEN Of a truth All death will he annul, all tears assuage? W. S. CHURCHILL But in the name of reason irrational forces had been let loose. These were not easily to be assuaged.

II *v.i.* †5 Of passion, pain, appetite, etc.: become less violent, abate. ME–E18. 6 *gen.* Diminish, fall off, abate, subside. Long *arch.* LME.

5 DEFOE The plague being come to a crisis, its fury began to assuage. 6 AV *Gen.* 8:1 And the waters asswaged.

assuagement *n.* (*a*) the action of assuaging; the condition of being assuaged; (*b*) (now *rare*) an assuaging medicine or application: M16. **assuager** *n.* M16.

assuasive /ə'sweɪsɪv/ *a.* Now *rare.* E18. [f. AS-[1] after PERSUASIVE, conf. in sense w. prec.] Soothingly persuasive; soothing.

assubjugate /ə'sʌbdʒʊgeɪt/ *v.t. rare.* E17. [f. A-[11] (assim. to AS-[1]) + SUBJUGATE.] Reduce to subjugation.

¶ First recorded in Shakes.

assuefaction /aswɪ'fakʃ(ə)n/ *n.* Long *arch. rare.* E17. [f. L *assuefact-* pa. ppl stem of *assuefacere* habituate: see -FACTION. Perh. partly through Fr. *assuéfaction*.] The action of becoming or the state of being accustomed to something; habituation.

assuetude /'aswɪtjuːd/ *n.* E17. [L *assuetudo*, f. *assuet-* pa. ppl stem of *assuescere*, f. *ad* AS-[1] + *suescere* accustom: see -TUDE.] Accustomedness; familiarity.

assume /ə'sjuːm/ *v.t.* LME. [L *assumere*, f. *ad* AS-[1] + *sumere* take. Cf. Fr. *assumer*.] 1 Receive (a person) into association, service, or use; adopt; *spec.* receive up into heaven. *arch.* LME. †b Choose, elect, to some (elevated) position. E16–L17. 2 Take (a thing) into use; use, absorb, consume. Long *rare.* LME. 3 Take for granted; take as being true, for the sake of argument or action; suppose. LME. 4 Chiefly *Law.* Take it upon oneself, undertake, *to do*. *arch.* LME. 5 Lay claim to, appropriate, arrogate, (*to* oneself). LME. b Claim *to do*. L16. 6 Take or put on oneself (an aspect, form, or garb); take to oneself, develop, (an attribute); take to oneself formally (the insignia of office or symbol of a vocation); undertake (an office or duty). In early use foll. by *upon* oneself. M16. 7 Simulate, pretend to have. E17. 8 *Logic.* = SUBSUME 2b. *arch.* E17.

1 R. C. TRENCH Revealed religion assumes them into her service. b F. QUARLES Her Unkles love assum'd her for his own. 2 T. VENNER Let there be assumed a draught of . . Beere. D. H. LAWRENCE The pink young houses show one side bright Flatly assuming the sun. 3 E. WILSON Marx had assumed the value of Shakespeare and the Greeks and more or less left it at that. C. S. FORESTER A slight broadening of the high-road, with an avenue of trees, which Hornblower assumed must be the central square of the town. M. AMIS When you're young you assume everybody old knows what they're doing. H. KISSINGER The letter was assumed—quite correctly—to have been drafted by my staff and me. 5 O. FELTHAM Such . . think there is no way to get Honour, but by a bold assuming it. LD MACAULAY The king assumed to himself the right of filling up the chief municipal offices. b GIBBON Witnesses who had or assumed to have knowledge of the fact. 6 DRYDEN The slipp'ry God will . . various Forms assume. E. A. FREEMAN He assumed the monastic habit. D. H. LAWRENCE Gerald assumed responsibility for the amusements on the water. J. B. PRIESTLEY She had dropped the manner she had assumed at lunch. A. WILSON Bill had been the rebel of the family and inevitably had ended by assuming his father's mantle. L. DEIGHTON A line of men had formed and assumed the relaxed attitudes with which Servicemen accept inevitable delay. O. SACKS The attacks were now assuming a most frightening intensity. 7 SHAKES. *Haml.* Assume a virtue, if you have it not. D. CECIL An essay he wrote under the assumed name of Elia.

assumable *a.* M17. **assumedly** /-mɪdli/ *adv.* as is assumed, presumably L19. **assumer** *n.* E17. **assuming** *a.* taking much upon oneself, presumptuous, arrogant E17. **assumingly** *adv.* in an assuming manner, presumptuously M19.

assumpsit /ə'sʌm(p)sɪt/ *n.* L16. [L, lit. 'he has taken upon himself', 3 perf. indic. sing. of *assumere* ASSUME.] 1 An undertaking. L16. 2 *spec.* in *Law* (now *Hist.*). A promise or contract, oral or in writing not sealed, founded upon a consideration. Also (more fully *action of assumpsit*), an action to recover damages for breach or non-performance of such a contract. M17.

assumpt /ə'sʌm(p)t/ *v.* Long *arch.* Pa. pple **-ed**, †**assumpt**. LME. [L *assumpt-* pa. ppl stem of *assumere* ASSUME.] 1 *v.t.* = ASSUME 1. *obs.* exc. *spec.* receive up into heaven. LME. †b = ASSUME 1b. L16–E17. †2 *v.t.* = ASSUME 6. LME–E17. 3 *v.i.* Ascend (to heaven). LME.

3 E. CRISPIN 'B.V.M. assumpting in jakes,' he spluttered.

assumption /ə'sʌm(p)ʃ(ə)n/ *n.* ME. [OFr. *asompsion* (mod. *assomption*) or L *assumptio(n-)*, f. as prec.: see -ION.] I Reception, adoption. 1 *Chr. Ch.* (Also **A-**.) The reception of the Virgin Mary bodily into heaven; a feast held annually on 15 August in honour of this. ME. b *gen.* (An) ascent to and reception into heaven. L16. †2 Consumption, absorption. L16–M17. 3 Reception into union or association; incorporation; adoption. *obs.* exc. *Sc. Law.* E17. †4 Elevation to office or dignity. M–L17.

1b TENNYSON Can hang no weight upon my heart In its assumptions up to heaven. 2 JONSON The most gentlemanlike use of tabacco . . the delicate sweete formes for the assumption of it. 3 T. WARTON It is evident that the prose psalms of our liturgy were chiefly consulted . . by the perpetual assumptions of their words.

II Taking for or upon oneself. 5 The action or an act of laying claim to something; appropriation, arrogation, usurpation. LME. 6 The action or an act of taking upon oneself of a form, aspect, or character; formal taking of office or position. L15. 7 *Law.* A promise or undertaking, either oral or in writing not sealed, founded on a consideration. Cf. ASSUMPSIT. Now *rare.* L16. 8 Presumption, arrogance. E17. 9 The action or an act of taking of something for granted; the taking of something as being true, for the sake of argument or action; something so assumed; a supposition. E17.

5 R. CRASHAW We to the last Will hold it fast, And no assumption shall deny us. BURKE This astonishing assumption of the publick voice of England. 6 SIR T. BROWNE The assumption of humane shape, had proved a disadvantage unto Sathan. HOR. WALPOLE Before Richard's assumption of the crown. E. WILSON There is something other than romantic perversity in this assumption of a diabolic role. 8 SIR W. SCOTT His usual air of haughty assumption. 9 T. STANLEY He used Arguments not by Assumption, but by inference. E. M. FORSTER Improvements that they had made under the assumption that all would be theirs some day. J. G. FARRELL Were the Irish civilized? The Major was not prepared to risk his life on the assumption that they were. B. MAGEE We, all of us, take a great number of things for granted, and many of these assumptions are of a philosophical character.

III 10 *Logic.* = SUBSUMPTION I. *arch.* LME.

assumptive /ə'sʌm(p)tɪv/ *a.* M16. [L *assumptivus*, f. as ASSUMPT + -IVE.] 1 Characterized by assumption to oneself; adopted. M16. 2 Taken for granted; apt to take things for granted. M17. 3 Appropriative; making undue claims; arrogant. L18.

†assura *n.* see SURA *n.*[2]

assurance /ə'ʃʊər(ə)ns/ *n.* LME. [(O)Fr. (earlier *aseürance*), f. as next: see -ANCE.] 1 A formal guarantee, engagement, or pledge. LME. †b *spec.* A marriage engagement, a betrothal. LME-M17. c *spec.* A pledge of peace; in *pl.*, terms of peace. *obs.* exc. *Hist.* L16. 2 Subjective certainty; confidence, trust. LME. 3 Security, safety. *arch.* LME. †4 Objective certainty. L15-E17. 5 *Law.* The security of a title to property; (legal evidence of) the conveyance of property by deed. *arch.* L16. 6 Insurance, now esp. of life. L16. 7 Self-confidence, self-reliance; presumption, impudence. L16. 8 A positive declaration intended to give confidence; encouraging confirmation. E17.

2 SHAKES. *Macb.* But yet I'll make assurance double sure And take a bond of fate. J. BUCHAN He spoke with assurance, but I could see the dawning of a doubt in his mind. T. C. WOLFE Like an ignorant fighter . . he is exultant in the assurance of his knowledge and his power. 3 W. LAMBARDE To sende . . unto a place of most assuraunce all such as hee had taken prisoners. 7 SWIFT Several of my friends had the assurance to ask me, whether I was in jest? B. SPOCK With your second baby you have more assurance. 8 H. MACMILLAN I was able to give sufficient assurances to satisfy the Australian Cabinet. D. LODGE I'd hoped that the roses would have been some assurance that I was alive and kicking and thinking of you.

assure /ə'ʃʊə/ *v.* LME. [(O)Fr. *assurer* (earlier *asseürer*) f. Proto-Romance, f. L *ad* AS-[1] + *securus* SECURE *a.*] †1 *v.t.* Guarantee (a thing *to* a person); promise (*that*). LME-L17. 2 *v.t.* Give confidence to, confirm, encourage. LME. †b *v.i.* Have confidence or trust *in*. Only in LME. 3 *v.t.* Make (a person) sure or certain (*of, that*); *refl.* & in *pass.*, feel certain or satisfied. LME. †4 *v.t.* Make safe or secure from attack or danger; secure to oneself. LME-L17. 5 *v.t.* Make safe *from* or *against* risks; insure (esp. life). LME. 6 *v.t.* Make secure from change or overthrow; make stable, establish securely. LME. †7 *v.t.* Affiance, betroth. LME-L16. 8 *v.t.* Tell (a person) confidently (*of* a thing, its being so, *that*) as something that can be relied upon. E16. †9 *v.t.* State positively, affirm. M16-E18. †10 *v.t.* Secure the possession or reversion of; convey (property) by deed. L16-L17. 11 *v.t.* Ensure the occurrence, arrival, etc., of (an event). E17. 12 *v.t.* Make certain (a thing that was doubtful). *arch.* L17.

2 BACON Man, when he resteth and assureth himselfe, vpon diuine Protection. F. W. ROBERTSON A pure man forgives, or pleads for mercy, or assures the penitent. 3 SPENSER Assure your selfe, I will not you forsake. AV *2 Tim.* 3:14 Continue thou in the things which thou hast learned, and hast been assured of. J. S. MILL To consider how we are to assure ourselves of its truth. R. KIPLING He came in as one assured that thou wouldst not soon return. S. BELLOW I felt obliged to visit her, at first, as though to assure her that I valued her as much as ever. 4 W. RALEIGH The Romans, the better to assure themselves, cut a deep trench. 6 LYTTON The two chiefs who most assured his throne. 8 OED He assured us of his own willingness to go. J. B. PRIESTLEY Miss Trant . . was assured by Hilary that all was well with her. T. S. ELIOT You'll come to find that I'm right, I assure you. 9 COVERDALE *Jer.* 29:23 This I testifie and assure. SWIFT I cannot . . so confidently assure the events will follow exactly as I predict them. 10 C. MARLOWE And with my proper blood Assure my soul to be great Lucifers. 11 A. EDEN Vitality, charm, together with a sweeping no-nonsense air . . always assured her an eager welcome and a rapt audience. 12 DRYDEN Not to assure our doubtful way.

assurer *n.* (*a*) an insurer, an underwriter; (*b*) a person who or thing which gives assurance; (*c*) a person who insures his or her life: L16. **assuror** *n.* = ASSURER (a) E17.

assured /ə'ʃʊəd/ *a.* & *n.* LME. [f. prec. + -ED[1].] A *adj.* †1 Made safe; secure. LME-E17. 2 Made sure or certain, guaranteed. LME. †3 Engaged, covenanted, pledged. LME-L17. 4 Self-possessed, confident, bold; self-satisfied, presumptuous. LME. 5 Satisfied as to the truth or certainty of a matter. E16. 6 Certified, verified. L16. B *n.* A person whose life or goods are insured. M18.

assuredly /ə'ʃʊərɪdli/ *adv.* (*a*) certainly, undoubtedly; (*b*) confidently: L15. **assuredness** /ə'ʃʊədnɪs, ə'ʃʊərɪdnɪs/ *n.* (*a*) certainty, confidence, trust; (*b*) self-confidence, audacity: M16.

assurgent /ə'sɜːdʒ(ə)nt/ *a.* L16. [L *assurgent-* pres. ppl stem of *assurgere*, f. *ad* AS-[1] + *surgere* to rise: see -ENT.] Rising, ascending; *Bot.* rising obliquely.

assurgency *n.* the quality of being assurgent; the disposition to rise: M17.

Assyrian /ə'sɪrɪən/ *n.* & *a.* LME. [f. L *Assyrius*, f. Gk *Assurios*, f. *Assuria* Assyria (see below), + -AN.] A *n.* 1 A native or inhabitant of Assyria, an ancient empire in Mesopotamia. LME. 2 The Akkadian dialect of Assyria. L19. B *adj.* Of or pertaining to Assyria or its dialect. L16.

Assyriology /əsɪrɪ'ɒlədʒi/ *n.* L19. [f. L *Assyria* f. Gk *Assuria* (see prec.), + -OLOGY.] The branch of knowledge that deals with the language, history, and antiquities of Assyria.

Assyriologist *n.* L19.

†assythe *n.* & *v.* Also (earlier) **assethe**. LME-E17. [f. as ASSET.] A *n.* Compensation, satisfaction. LME-E17. B *v.t.* Compensate, satisfy. LME-E17.

assythement /ə'sʌɪðm(ə)nt/ *n.* M16. [f. prec. + -MENT.] *Sc. Law* (now *Hist.*). Indemnification owed by an unlawful killer to the surviving relatives of the victim.

astable /ə'steɪb(ə)l, eɪ-/ *a.* M20. [f. A-[10] + STABLE *a.*] *Electronics.* Designating or pertaining to a circuit which oscillates spontaneously between unstable states.

astarboard /ə'stɑːbəd/ *adv.* & *pred. a.* L15. [f. A *prep.*[1] I + STARBOARD *n.*] *Naut.* On or towards the starboard side of a ship.

put the helm astarboard starboard the helm, i.e. move the rudder to port, causing the vessel to turn to the left.

astare /ə'stɛː/ *adv.* & *pred. a.* M19. [f. A-[2] + STARE *n.*[2] or *v.*] Staring; prominent.

astart /ə'stɑːt/ *v.* Long *arch. rare.* ME. [f. A-[1] + START *v.*] 1 *v.i.* Start up, move suddenly. ME. †2 *v.i.* & *t.* Escape, get away, (from). ME-L16. †3 *v.i.* & *t.* Happen (to), befall. LME-L16.

astart /ə'stɑːt/ *adv.* E18. [f. A *prep.*[1] 4 + START *n.*[2]] With a start, suddenly.

astatic /ə'statɪk/ *a.* E19. [f. Gk *astatos* unstable + -IC.] *Electr.* Having no fixed position of stability; *esp.* not lining up with or otherwise responding to external magnetic fields.

astatine /'astətiːn/ *n.* M20. [f. as prec. + -INE[5].] An artificial radioactive chemical element, atomic no. 85, which belongs to the halogen group and has no long-lived isotopes. (Symbol At.)

asteer /ə'stɪə/ *adv.* & *pred. a. Sc.* M16. [f. A *prep.*[1] 6 + var. of STIR *n.*[1]] Stirring, aroused; in commotion.

asteism /'astiːɪz(ə)m/ *n.* Also in L form **-ismus** /-'ɪzməs/. M16. [Late L *asteismus* f. Gk *asteismos* refined, witty talk, f. *asteios* polite, f. *astu* city.] *Rhet.* Urbane irony, polite mockery.

aster /'astə/ *n.* E17. [L f. Gk *astēr* star.] †1 A star. E17-E18. 2a Any of numerous plants constituting the genus *Aster*, of the composite family, bearing showy radiated flowers, e.g. Michaelmas daisy; a flower of such a plant. E18. b *China aster*, a related plant, *Callistephus chinensis*, native to China and much cultivated for its showy flowers; a flower of this plant. M18. 3 *Cytol.* A star-shaped structure formed during division of the nucleus of an animal cell. L19.

2a NEW ENGLAND *aster*.

-aster /'astə/ *suff.* (not productive). [L.] Forming ns. expressing poor quality or incomplete resemblance, as *pinaster*, *poetaster*, etc.

astereognosis /əˌstɛrɪɒg'nəʊsɪs, əˌstɪər-; eɪ-/ *n.* E20. [f. A-[10] + STEREOGNOSIS.] *Med.* Inability to identify the nature, size, and shape of objects by touch, as a symptom of disorder of the central or peripheral nervous system.

Also **astereognosia** *n.* M20.

asteriated /ə'stɪərɪeɪtɪd/ *a.* E19. [f. Gk *asterios* starry + -ATE[2] + -ED[1].] *Min.* Displaying an asterism (ASTERISM *n.* 4).

asterion /ə'stɪərɪən/ *n.* OE. [L f. Gk, f. *astēr* star.] †1 A flower, of unknown identity. OE-E17. 2 *Anat.* The point at which the parietal, occipital, and temporal bones meet, situated behind the mastoid process. L19.

asterisk /'astərɪsk/ *n.* & *v.* Orig. & (sense A.2b) also in L form **-iscus** /-ɪskəs/, pl. **-isci** /-ɪskʌɪ/. LME. [Late L *asteriscus* f. Gk *asteriskos* dim. of *astēr* star.] A *n.* 1 The figure of a star (*) used in writing and printing as a reference to a footnote, as a distinguishing or dividing mark, or to replace omitted matter. LME. 2 *gen.* A little star; something starlike or star-shaped. L17. b *Orthodox Ch.* A star-shaped utensil placed above the chalice and paten to prevent the veil from touching the elements. L19. B *v.t.* Mark with an asterisk. M18.

asterism /'astərɪz(ə)m/ *n.* L16. [Gk *asterismos*, f. *astēr* star: see -ISM.] 1 A group of stars; a constellation. L16. †2 A star; something star-shaped. M17-L18. 3 An asterisk or group of asterisks, esp. three printed thus (⁂). M17. 4 *Min.* A figure of light having the form of a six-rayed star, seen in certain crystals. M19.

astern /ə'stɜːn/ *adv.*, *pred. a.*, & *prep.* LME. [f. A *prep.*[1] I + STERN *n.*[2]] Chiefly *Naut.* A *adv.* & *pred. a.* 1 Of position: in or at the stern; in the rear, behind. (Foll. by *of.*) LME. 2 Of motion: to the rear, backward; stern foremost. L17.

1 DICKENS Keeping half his boat's length astern of the other boat. N. HAMPSON Free as the petrels hovering astern. M. LOWRY If he had expected to leave British snobbery astern with his public school he was sadly mistaken. *line astern*: see LINE *n.*[2] 2 R. DAHL They'd have to put her in reverse and go full speed astern.

B *prep.* At the stern or rear of. *rare.* L17.

asteroid /'astərɔɪd/ *n.* & *a.* E19. [f. Gk *asteroeidēs* starlike, f. *astēr* star: see -OID.] A *n.* 1 *Astron.* Any of the numerous small planetary bodies which orbit the sun, mainly between the orbits of Mars and Jupiter. E19. 2 *Zool.* An echinoderm of the class Asteroidea, which includes the starfishes other than the brittle-stars. M19. B *adj.* Star-shaped; starlike. M19.

aste'roidal *a.* (*Astron.*) of or pertaining to an asteroid or asteroids; of the nature of or resembling an asteroid: E19.

asthenia /əs'θiːnɪə/ *n.* L18. [mod.L f. Gk *astheneia* weakness, f. *asthenēs* weak: see -IA[1].] *Med.* Loss of strength, weakness.

asthenic /as'θɛnɪk/ *a.* & *n.* L18. [Gk *asthenikos*, f. *asthenēs* weak: see -IC.] **A** *adj.* **1** *Med.* Of, pertaining to, or characterized by asthenia. L18. **2** (Of physique) lean, narrow-shouldered, and long-limbed; characterized by or pertaining to such a physique. Cf. STHENIC. E20.

1 **asthenic personality** *Psychol.*: characterized by low energy, lack of enthusiasm, and oversensitivity to stress.

B *n.* An asthenic person; *esp.* a person with an asthenic physique. L19.

asthenosphere /əs'θɛnəsfɪə/ *n.* E20. [f. Gk *asthenēs* weak + -O- + -SPHERE.] *Geol.* The upper layer of the earth's mantle, below the lithosphere, characterized by a relatively low resistance to plastic flow.

asthenospheric /asθɛnə'sfɛrɪk/ *a.* of or pertaining to the asthenosphere M20.

asthma /'asmə/ *n.* Also †**asma**. LME. [(med.L *asma* f.) Gk *asthma*, *-mat-*, f. *azein* breathe hard.] Difficulty of breathing; *spec.* such a condition characterized by attacks due to bronchial spasm and often of allergic origin.

Comb.: **asthma herb, weed** *Austral.* a common tropical weed, *Euphorbia pilulifera*, used to treat asthma.

asthmatic /as'matɪk/ *n.* & *a.* E16. [L *asthmaticus* f. Gk *asthmatikos*, f. *asthmat-*: see prec., -IC.] **A** *n.* A person who suffers from asthma. E16. **B** *adj.* **1** That suffers from asthma. E16. **2** Of or pertaining to asthma. E17. **3** Of medicine: of use against asthma. Now *rare*. E18. **4** *fig.* Puffing, wheezy. E19.

4 J. BERESFORD An asthmatic pair of bellows.

asthmatical *a.* = ASTHMATIC *a.* M17. **asthmatically** *adv.* E19.

asthore /əs'θɔː/ *n.* *Anglo-Ir.* E19. [Ir., f. *a* O *int.* + *stór* treasure.] As a form of address: (my) treasure, darling.

Asti /'asti/ *n.* M19. [A province in Piedmont, NW Italy.] A still or (esp.) sparkling white wine from Asti.

Asti spumante /spʊ'manti/ sparkling Asti.

astigmatic /astɪg'matɪk/ *a.* M19. [f. as next + -IC.] **1** Pertaining to or characterized by astigmatism. M19. **2** Correcting astigmatism. L19.

astigmatism /ə'stɪgmətɪz(ə)m/ *n.* M19. [f. A-[10] + Gk *stigmat-*, *-ma* point + -ISM.] A defect of the cornea or lens of the eye, or of any lens, mirror, etc., which prevents rays of light from coming to a single focus.

astilbe /ə'stɪlbi/ *n.* M19. [mod.L, f. Gk *a-* A-[10] + *stilbē* fem. of *stilbos* glittering.] A plant of the genus *Astilbe*, of the saxifrage family, bearing small inconspicuous white or pink flowers.

†**astipulation** *n.* L16–E18. [L *astipulatio(n-)*, f. *astipulat-* pa. ppl stem of *astipulari*, f. *ad* AS-[1] + *stipulari* STIPULATE *v.*: see -ATION.] Agreement, assent; a confirming statement.

astir /ə'stɜː/ *adv.* & *pred. a.* L18. [f. A-[2] + STIR *n.*[1] or *v.*: cf. ASTEER.] Stirring, esp. out of bed; in motion, excited(ly).

†**astone** *v.t.* Also **astun**. ME. [OFr. *estoner* (mod. *étonner*) f. Proto-Gallo-Romance, f. L EX-[1] + *tonare* to thunder: see ASTOUND *v.*, STUN *v.* Cf. ASTONY.] **1** Stun, stupefy. ME–M18. **2** Amaze, astound; bewilder. ME–L17.

astonied *ppl a.* see ASTONY *v.*

astonish /ə'stɒnɪʃ/ *v.t.* E16. [Prob. f. ASTONY or ASTONE + -ISH[2]: first recorded as pa. ppl a. Cf. ASTOUND *v.*] †**1** Stun mentally; drive stupid, bewilder; dismay, terrify. E16–L18. †**2** Render insensible; paralyse, benumb. M16–M17. **3** Amaze; surprise greatly. E17.

1 SHAKES. *Jul. Caes.* The most mighty gods by tokens send Such dreadful heralds to astonish us. MILTON Blind, astonished, and struck with superstition as with a planet. 2 P. HOLLAND The one smote the king upon the head, the other astonished his shoulder. 3 AV *Matt.* 7:28 The people were astonished at his doctrine. GIBBON The Romans.. astonished the Greeks by their sincere and simple performance of the most burthensome engagements. E. BLYTON Think how astonished the Sticks will be to find the little girl gone—and their dear Edgar shut up in the cave instead! *astonish the natives*: see NATIVE *n.* 5.

astonishable *a.* †(*a*) calculated to astonish, surprising; (*b*) able to be astonished: E17. **astonishedly** *adv.* in an astonished manner, with astonishment E17. **astonisher** *n.* M19. **astonishingly** *adv.* in an astonishing manner; to an astonishing degree; amazingly: M17.

astonishment /ə'stɒnɪʃm(ə)nt/ *n.* L16. [f. prec. + -MENT.] †**1** Insensibility; paralysis, numbness. L16–M17. †**2** Bewilderment, stupor; consternation, dismay, loss of presence of mind. L16–M19. **3** Amazement due to the unexpected or unaccountable; great surprise. L16. **4** An object or cause of amazement or great surprise. E17.

1 E. TOPSELL Those which are troubled with any deafness or astonishment in any part of their bodies. 2 AV *Ps.* 60:3 Thou hast made vs to drinke the wine of astonishment. 3 ADDISON We are flung into pleasing astonishment at such unbounded views. J. BARTH I shook my head in astonishment at the whole business. 4 AV *Deut.* 28:37 Thou shalt become an astonishment, a prouerbe, and a by-worde.

astony /ə'stɒni/ *v.t.* *arch.* Now only as **astonied** *pa. ppl a.* ME. [Obscure var. of ASTONE *v.*] = ASTONISH.

astoop /ə'stuːp/ *adv.* & *pred. a.* M17. [f. A *prep.*[1] 4 + STOOP *n.*[2]] In an inclined position, stooping.

astound /ə'staʊnd/ *a.* *arch.* ME. [Phonet. devel. of *astoned* pa. pple of ASTONE.] †**1** Stunned, insensible. ME–M18. **2** Astonished, amazed; confounded. LME.

astound /ə'staʊnd/ *v.t.* LME. [Earliest as *astounded* ppl a., f. prec. + -ED[1]; later back-form. f. this.] †**1** Render insensible, stupefy. LME–E18. **2** Shock with alarm or wonder; astonish, amaze. L16.

astoundingly *adv.* in an astounding manner, astonishingly E19. **astoundment** *n.* (profound) astonishment E19.

astrachan *n.* var. of ASTRAKHAN.

astraddle /ə'strad(ə)l/ *adv.* & *pred. a.* M17. [f. A *prep.*[1] 6 + STRADDLE *n.*] In a straddling position; astride (*of*).

astragal /'astrəg(ə)l/ *n.* M17. [f. next, partly through Fr. *astragale*.] **1** *Archit.* A small moulding of semicircular section, esp. placed round the top or bottom of a column. Freq. *attrib.* M17. **2** A ring or moulding round the barrel of a cannon. M17. **3** = ASTRAGALUS 1; in *pl.* also, dice (for which such bones were formerly used). E18. **4** A thin bar separating panes of glass in a window. E19.

astragalus /ə'strag(ə)ləs/ *n.* Pl. **-li** /-lʌɪ, -liː/. M16. [L f. Gk *astragalos*.] **1** *Anat.* = TALUS *n.*[1] *arch.* M16. †**2** = ASTRAGAL 1. Only in M16. **3** Any plant of the large leguminous genus *Astragalus*. Also called *milk-vetch*. M16.

astragalar *a.* (*Anat.*) of or pertaining to an astragalus M19. **astragalomancy** *n.* divination by means of dice or knuckle-bones (cf. ASTRAGAL 3) M17.

astrain /ə'streɪn/ *adv.* & *pred. a.* M18. [f. A-[2] + STRAIN *n.*[2] or *v.*[1]] On the strain, straining.

astrakhan /astrə'kan/ *n.* Also **-chan**. M18. [*Astrakhan*, a city and region in central Asia.] The dark furry fleece of very young lambs from Astrakhan; a cloth resembling this.

Red Astrachan: see RED *a.*

astral /'astr(ə)l/ *a.* & *n.* E17. [Late L *astralis*, f. *astrum* star: see -AL[1].] **A** *adj.* **1** Of, connected with, or proceeding from the stars. E17. **2** Star-shaped, starlike. L17. **3** *Theosophy.* Pertaining to or consisting of an ethereal substance supposed to be next above the material world in refinement and to pervade all space. L19. **4** *Cytol.* Of or pertaining to an aster. L19.

1 **astral spirits**: those formerly thought to inhabit celestial objects. 2 **astral lamp** *Hist.* a kind of Argand lamp. 3 **astral body** the ethereal counterpart of a human or animal body.

B *n.* **1** *Hist.* An astral lamp. M19. **2** *Theosophy.* An astral body. L19.

astrally *adv.* (*a*) according to the stars; (*b*) in or through the powers of the astral body: L17.

astrand /ə'strand/ *adv.* & *pred. a.* E19. [f. A-[2] + STRAND *v.*[1]] Stranded.

astray /ə'streɪ/ *adv.* & *pred. a.* ME. [AN var. of OFr. *estraié* pa. pple of *estraier* stray, ult. f. L *extra* out of bounds + *vagari* wander: see A-[7] and cf. STRAY *a.*] **1** Out of the right way, wandering. ME. **2** *fig.* In or into error or sin. LME.

1 SIR W. SCOTT Why urge thy chase so far astray? **go astray** be lost, be mislaid. 2 SHAKES. *Two Gent.* Nay, in that you are astray. E. A. FREEMAN Evil counsellors had led him astray. J. BALDWIN Fathers.., have you ever had a son who went astray?

astream /ə'striːm/ *adv.* & *pred. a.* M18. [f. A-[2] + STREAM *n.* or *v.*] Streaming; in a stream.

astrict /ə'strɪkt/ *v.t.* Pa. pple & ppl a. **-ed**, (earlier) †**astrict**. Also †**ad-**. LME. [Orig. pa. pple, f. L *astrict-* pa. ppl stem of *astringere* ASTRINGE.] **1** Bind, compress, constrict. *arch.* LME. **2** Bind by moral or legal obligation. *arch.* LME. **3** Restrict, limit, (*to*). M16. **4** *Sc. Law.* Restrict in tenure by an obligation to have grain ground at a particular mill. Usu. as *astricted* ppl a. *obs.* exc. *Hist.* M16.

astrictive *a.* (now *rare* or *obs.*) binding; obligatory; astringent: M16.

astriction /ə'strɪkʃ(ə)n/ *n.* Also †**ad-**. M16. [(O)Fr., or L *astrictio(n-)*, f. as prec.: see -ION.] †**1** Moral or legal obligation. M16–M17. **2** Binding together; constriction; constipation. *arch.* M16. †**3** Astringency. M16–M18. **4** Restriction; *spec.* in *Sc. Law*, restriction in tenure by an obligation to have grain ground at a particular mill. *obs.* exc. *Hist.* E17.

astride /ə'strʌɪd/ *adv.*, *a.*, & *prep.* E17. [f. A *prep.*[1] 6 + STRIDE *n.*] **A** *adv.* & (chiefly *pred.*) *a.* With the legs apart or on either side (*of*). E17.

W. COWPER The playful jockey scow'rs the room.. astride upon the parlour broom. S. SMILES Sitting astride of a house-roof. S. G. GOLDSCHMIDT Some say that astride riding is safer. *fig.*: A. ALISON Napoleon's central position astride on the Elbe.

B *prep.* Bestriding. E18.

E. M. FORSTER He sat near her, astride the parapet, with one foot in the loggia and the other dangling into the view. *fig.*: W. S. CHURCHILL Rosecrans manoeuvred Bragg out of all his defensive lines astride the Nashville-Chattanooga railway.

astringe /ə'strɪn(d)ʒ/ *v.t.* Also †**ad-**. E16. [L *astringere*, f. *ad* AS-[1] + *stringere* bind, draw tight.] †**1** Bind morally or legally; oblige. E16–M18. **2** Bind together, constrict; constipate. M16.

astringent /ə'strɪn(d)ʒ(ə)nt/ *a.* & *n.* M16. [Fr. f. L *astringent-* pres. ppl stem of *astringere*: see prec., -ENT.] **A** *adj.* **1** Causing contraction of the body tissues, styptic. M16. **2** *fig.* Severe, austere. E19. **B** *n.* An astringent medicine or substance. E17.

astringency *n.* astringent quality (*lit.* & *fig.*) E17. **astringently** *adv.* M19.

†**astrion** *n.* ME–L19. [L, dim. of Gk *astēr* star.] A certain precious stone, prob. star sapphire.

astro- /'astrəʊ/ *comb. form* of Gk *astron* star: see -O-.

astro-archae'ology *n.* = ARCHAEO-ASTRONOMY M20. **astrobi'ology** *n.* the branch of science that deals with the search for and investigation of extraterrestrial life M20. **astrobleme** /-bliːm/ *n.* [Gk *blēma* wound produced by a missile] *Geol.* an eroded remnant of a large impact crater of extraterrestrial origin M20. **astro'chemistry** *n.* the chemistry of materials present in outer space M20. **astrocompass** *n.* an instrument designed to indicate direction with respect to the stars M20. **astrocyte** *n.* (*Anat.*) a star-shaped glial cell of the central nervous system L19. **astrocy'toma** *n.*, pl. **-mas**, **-mata** /-mətə/, *Med.* a brain tumour derived from astrocytes M20. **astrodome** *n.* (*a*) a domed window in an aircraft for astronomical observations; (*b*) (chiefly *US* in proper names) a stadium with a domed roof: M20. **astrohatch** *n.* = ASTRODOME (a) M20. **astrometeoro'logical** *a.* of or pertaining to the investigation of the supposed influence of the celestial objects on the weather etc. L17. **astrometeo'rologist** *n.* an expert in or student of astrometeorology M19. **astrometeo'rology** *n.* the investigation of the supposed influence of celestial objects on the weather etc. M19. **astronavi'gation** *n.* navigation of aircraft or spacecraft by means of the stars M20. **astrophil(e)** *n.* a lover of the stars E18. **astrophoto'graphic**, **-ical** *adjs.* of or pertaining to astrophotography L19. **astropho'tography** *n.* the use of photography in astronomy M19. **astrothe'ology** *n.* theology founded on observation of celestial objects E18.

astrography /ə'strɒgrəfi/ *n.* M18. [f. ASTRO- + -GRAPHY.] Orig., the science of describing the stars. Now, the mapping of the heavens.

'astrograph *n.* a telescope designed for photographic astrography M20. **astro'graphic** *a.* of, pertaining to, used in, or produced by astrography L19.

astroid /'astrɔɪd/ *n.* L19. [f. ASTRO- + -OID.] *Math.* A hypocycloid with four cusps (resembling a square with concave sides), defined by the equation $x^{2/3} + y^{2/3} = R^{2/3}$.

†astroite *n.* Freq. in L form **astroites**. M16. [L *astroites* f. Gk *astroitēs*: see ASTRO-, -ITE[1].] 1 = ASTRION *n.* M16–M18. 2 A star-shaped mineral or fossil. E17–E18. 3 A kind of coral. L17–M19.

astrolabe /'astrəleɪb/ *n.* LME. [OFr. *astrelabe* f. med.L *astrolabium* f. Gk *astrolabon* use as n. of neut. of adj. *astrolabos* star-taking.] An instrument used to make astronomical measurements, esp. of the altitudes of stars.

astro'labic *a.* of or pertaining to the astrolabe M20. **astro'labical** *a.* (*rare*) = ASTROLABIC E17.

astrolatry /ə'strɒlətri/ *n.* L17. [f. ASTRO- + -LATRY.] The worship of celestial objects.

astrologer /ə'strɒlədʒə/ *n.* LME. [OFr. *astrologue* or *-logien* f. L *astrologus* f. Gk *astrologos*: see ASTRO-, -LOGER.] †1 An observer of the stars, a practical astronomer. LME–M18. †2 *common astrologer*, the cock. Only in LME. 3 A person who practises astrology (ASTROLOGY *n.* 2). E17.

†astrolog(ue) *n.* an astrologer LME–E18. **†astrologian** *n.* an astrologer LME–M19.

astrologic /astrə'lɒdʒɪk/ *n.* & *a.* M16. [n. f. med.L *astrologica* n.pl.; adj. f. Fr. *astrologique* or as next.] †A *n.* In *pl.* Matters or facts of astrology. M16–L17. B *adj.* = next. M17.

astrological /astrə'lɒdʒɪk(ə)l/ *a.* L16. [f. late L *astrologicus* f. Gk *astrologikos*, f. *astrologia*: see ASTROLOGY, -IC, -AL[1].] Of or pertaining to astrology.

astrologically *adv.* E17.

astrologist /ə'strɒlədʒɪst/ *n.* Chiefly *N. Amer.* M20. [f. next + -IST.] An astrologer.

astrology /ə'strɒlədʒi/ *n.* LME. [(O)Fr. *astrologie* f. L *astrologia* f. Gk: see ASTRO-, -LOGY.] †1 Astronomy, esp. in its practical aspects, as the measurement of time, prediction of natural phenomena, etc. Also more fully *natural astrology*. LME–M19. 2 The supposed art of foretelling or counselling in human affairs by interpretation of the motions of celestial objects. Also more fully *judicial astrology*. M16.

astrometry /ə'strɒmɪtri/ *n.* M19. [f. ASTRO- + -METRY.] The measurement of the positions, motions, and magnitudes of stars.

astro'metric *a.* of or pertaining to astrometry; identified by astrometry: M20. **astro'metrical** *a.* = ASTROMETRIC E20.

astronaut /'astrənɔːt/ *n.* E20. [f. ASTRO- after *aeronaut*.] A space-traveller; a member of the crew of a spacecraft.

astronautics /astrə'nɔːtɪks/ *n.* E20. [f. ASTRO- after *aeronautics*.] The science and technology of the exploration and utilization of space.

astronautical *a.* pertaining to or concerned with astronautics or astronauts E20.

astronomer /ə'strɒnəmə/ *n.* LME. [f. ASTRONOMY + -ER[1].] 1 A person who studies or practises astronomy. LME. †2 = ASTROLOGER 3. LME–E17.

1 **Astronomer Royal**: a title held by two astronomers, one in England and one in Scotland who are usu. also the directors of the Royal Observatories.

astronomical /astrə'nɒmɪk(ə)l/ *a.* M16. [f. Fr. *astronomique* or L *astronomicus* f. Gk *astronomikos*: see ASTRONOMY, -ICAL.] 1 Of or pertaining to astronomy. M16. 2 *fig.* As enormous as the distances, sizes, etc., typically encountered in astronomy; very great. L19.

1 **astronomical clock**: keeping sidereal time. *astronomical day*: see DAY *n.* **astronomical telescope** *spec.* a refractor giving an inverted image (opp. *terrestrial telescope*). **astronomical triangle** a triangle on the celestial sphere whose vertices are the north or south celestial pole, the zenith, and the position of a given celestial object. **astronomical unit** the mean distance of the earth from the sun, equal to 1.496 × 10[8] km or approx. 93 million miles. *astronomical year*: see YEAR *n.*[1] 2 P. H. GIBBS Reparations demanded from Germany—astronomical sums. ANTHONY HUXLEY Pollen production is astronomical in wind-pollinated flowers.

astronomic *a.* = ASTRONOMICAL E18. **astronomically** *adv.* M17.

astronomy /ə'strɒnəmi/ *n.* ME. [(O)Fr. *astronomie* f. L *astronomia* (Seneca) f. Gk: see ASTRO-, -NOMY.] 1 The science of celestial objects (including the earth in relation to them), of space, and of the universe as a whole. With specifying wd, any of the branches of this subject, as *radio astronomy*. ME. †2 = ASTROLOGY 2. ME–E18.

astronomize *v.i.* pursue astronomy; act or speak astronomically: L17.

†astrophel *n. rare* (Spenser). Only in L16. [Perh. alt. of *astrophyllum* star-leaf f. Gk *astron* star + *phullon* leaf.] A certain unidentified plant.

astrophysics /astrə(ʊ)'fɪzɪks/ *n.* L19. [f. ASTRO- + PHYSICS.] The branch of astronomy that deals with the physical and chemical properties of celestial objects and interstellar space.

astrophysical *a.* of or pertaining to astrophysics L19. **astrophysically** *adv.* as regards or by means of astrophysics L20. **astrophysicist** *n.* an expert in or student of astrophysics M19.

Astroturf /'astrətəːf/ *n.* M20. [f. *Astrodome*, an indoor baseball ground in Houston, Texas, where first used, + TURF *n.*] (Proprietary name for) an artificial grasslike surface.

astrut /ə'strʌt/ *adv.* & *pred. a. arch.* ME. [f. A *prep.*[1] 4 + STRUT *n.*[2]] Sticking out; puffed up; defiant.

astucious /ə'stjuːʃəs/ *a.* E19. [f. Fr. *astucieux*, f. *astuc(i)e* astuteness + *-eux* -OUS.] Astute.

astucity /-sɪti/ *n.* astuteness L18.

†astun *v.* var. of ASTONE.

Asturian /ə'stjʊərɪən/ *a.* & *n.* E17. [Sp. *asturiano*, f. *Asturias* (see below). Cf. L *Astur*, *-uris* Asturian.] A *adj.* 1 Of or pertaining to Asturias, a region of northern Spain (formerly a principality and once an independent kingdom), or its inhabitants. E17. 2 *spec.* in *Archaeol.* Designating or pertaining to a mesolithic culture whose remains are found in Asturias. E20. B *n.* 1 A native or inhabitant of Asturias. E17. 2 The Castilian dialect spoken in Asturias. L19.

astute /ə'stjuːt/ *a.* E17. [Fr. †*astut* or L *astutus*, f. *astus* crafty, cunning.] Of keen penetration, esp. as to one's own interests; shrewd; sagacious; crafty.

CONAN DOYLE He made a bad slip when he allowed my astute friend to notice the number of the seat taken for his wife. G. B. SHAW It seemed an astute stroke of German imperial tactics to send Lenin safely through Germany to Russia. **be astute to do** *Law* (of a court) exercise ingenuity to do, take pains to do.

astutely *adv.* E19. **astuteness** *n.* M19.

astylar /ə'staɪlə/ *a.* M19. [f. Gk *astulos* without columns, f. A-[10] + *stulos* column, + -AR[1].] Without columns or pilasters.

asudden /ə'sʌd(ə)n/ *adv.* L19. [f. A-[2] + SUDDEN.] Suddenly.

asunder /ə'sʌndə/ *adv.* [OE *on sundran*, *-um*: see A *prep.*[1] 2, SUNDER *a.*] †1 In or into a position separate or apart. OE–M16. 2 Apart or separate from one another in position or direction. ME. 3 Apart from one another in character, separately as objects of thought. *arch.* LME. 4 Into separate parts. LME.

1 COVERDALE But me called he a sonder to be his preacher. 2 J. A. FROUDE Wide asunder as pole and pole. J. GALSWORTHY He went up to the curtains, and .. drew them asunder. 3 **know asunder** distinguish. 4 B. BAINBRIDGE A noise .. like a piece of silk being ripped asunder.

aswarm /ə'swɔːm/ *adv.* & *pred. a.* M19. [f. A-[2] + SWARM *n.* or *v.*[1]] Swarming (*with*).

asway /ə'sweɪ/ *adv.* & *pred. a.* M19. [f. A-[2] + SWAY *n.* or *v.*] Swaying.

asweat /ə'swɛt/ *adv.* & *pred. a.* L19. [f. A-[2] + SWEAT *n.* or *v.*] Sweating.

aswim /ə'swɪm/ *adv.* & *pred. a.* M17. [f. A *prep.*[1] 6 + SWIM *n.*] Swimming, afloat.

aswing /ə'swɪŋ/ *adv.* & *pred. a.* L19. [f. A-[2] + SWING *n.*[1] or *v.*] Swinging.

aswirl /ə'swəːl/ *adv.* & *pred. a.* E20. [f. A-[2] + SWIRL *n.* or *v.*] Swirling.

aswoon /ə'swuːn/ *adv.* & *pred. a.* [OE *ġeswōgen*: see A-[4], SWOWN. Later f. A-[2] + SWOON *n.* or *v.*] In a swoon or faint.

asyle *n.* var. of ASILE.

asyllabic /eɪsɪ'labɪk, a-/ *a.* E19. [f. A-[10] + SYLLABIC *a.*] Not syllabic; not constituting a syllable.

asyllabical *a.* (*rare*) M18.

asylum /ə'saɪləm/ *n.* & *v.* LME. [L f. Gk *asulon* refuge, use as n. of neut. of *asulos* inviolable, f. A-[10] + *sulē*, *sulon* right of seizure.] A *n.* Pl. **-lums**, †**-la**. 1 A sanctuary, a place of refuge and safety, orig. and esp. for criminals. LME. 2 Sanctuary, refuge, protection. E18. 3 An institution for the shelter and support of handicapped (esp. insane) or destitute persons. Now chiefly *Hist.* & *pop.* M18.

1 A. WOOD He fled to Oxon, the common Asylum of afflicted royalists. 2 E. WILSON Weitling had been expelled from Paris .. and, seeking asylum in Switzerland, had there been convicted of blasphemy. G. MAXWELL Morag had .. given asylum to four goats left homeless by their owners' demise. G. GREENE When you claim asylum you have to make a promise not to indulge in political action. E. LONGFORD Catherine Long-Wellesley .. had found asylum with her two unmarried sisters. **political asylum** protection from arrest by another country. 3 T. PENNANT When the grievous distemper of the leprosy raged .. our ancestors erected asyla. W. TREVOR She wondered .. if this boarding-house might not be in an asylum for the mentally deprived. L. HELLMAN He had spent much of his childhood in a Philadelphia orphan asylum. LUNATIC *asylum*.

B *v.t.* Give asylum to; place in an asylum. *rare.* L18.

asymbolia /asɪm'bəʊlɪə, eɪ-/ *n.* L19. [f. A-[10] + SYMBOL *n.*[1] + -IA[1].] *Med.* Inability to understand or use visual, auditory, or other sensory symbols.

asymmetric /asɪ'mɛtrɪk, eɪ-/ *a.* L19. [f. A-[10] + SYMMETRIC.] 1 = next. L19. 2 *Chem.* Designating or containing a carbon atom which is bonded to four different substituents and is hence a cause of optical isomerism. Of a synthesis: preferentially yielding a particular optical isomer. L19.

asymmetrical /asɪ'mɛtrɪk(ə)l, eɪ-/ *a.* L17. [f. A-[10] + SYMMETRICAL.] Not symmetrical, with the parts not arranged in symmetry.

asymmetrically *adv.* L19.

asymmetry /a'sɪmɪtri, eɪ-/ *n.* M17. [Gk *asummetria*: see A-[10], SYMMETRY.] †1 *Math.* Incommensurability. M17–L18. 2 Absence of symmetry or proportion. M17. 3 *Chem.* The property of being asymmetric. L19.

asymptomatic /ə,sɪmptə'matɪk, eɪ-/ *a.* M20. [f. A-[10] + SYMPTOMATIC *a.*] *Med.* Producing or exhibiting no symptoms.

asymptote /'asɪm(p)təʊt/ *n.* M17. [mod.L *asymptota* (sc. *linea* line) f. Gk *asumptōtos* adj. (also used as n.), f. A-[10] + *sun-* SYN- + *ptōtos* apt to fall.] *Math.* A straight line which is continually approached by a given curve but does not meet it within a finite distance.

asymptotic /asɪm(p)'tɒtɪk/ *a.* of, pertaining to, or of the nature of an asymptote; pertaining to the behaviour of a function when its argument takes large values: L17. **asymp'totical** *a.* E18. **asymp'totically** *adv.* in the manner of an asymptote L17.

asynchronous /ə'sɪŋkrənəs, eɪ-/ *a.* M18. [f. A-[10] + SYNCHRONOUS.] Not synchronous.

asyndetic /asɪn'dɛtɪk/ *a.* L19. [f. as next + -IC.] 1 *Rhet.* Characterized by asyndeton, not connected by conjunctions. L19. 2 Of a catalogue, index, etc.: without cross-references. L19.

asyndeton /ə'sɪndɪt(ə)n/ *n.* M16. [mod.L f. Gk *asundeton* use as n. of neut. of *asundetos* unconnected, f. A-[10] + *sundetos* bound together.] *Rhet.* Omission of a conjunction.

asyntactic /asɪn'taktɪk, eɪ-/ *a.* E19. [f. Gk *asuntaktos* disorganized, ungrammatical + -IC, after SYNTACTIC: see A-[10].] With loose syntax, ungrammatical.

asystole /ə'sɪstəli/ *n.* L19. [f. A-[10] + SYSTOLE.] Cessation of the contractions of the heart.

at /at, *unstressed* ət/ *prep.* [OE *æt* = OFris. *et*, OS *at*, OHG *az*, ON, Goth. *at*, a Gmc prep. and vbl pref., rel. to L *ad.*] I Physical position. **1** Expr. exact, approximate, or vague spatial or local position (*lit.* or in *fig.* contexts). OE. **b** With proper names of places, esp. of towns (exc. usu. those of public or private importance, cf. IN *prep.*) and small islands. OE. **c** Expr. position or distance in relation to a point of orientation. E16. **d** Used with cardinal points of the compass to indicate parts of the country or (*Naut.*) the quarter of the wind. *US.* M17. **2** Expr. some practical connection with a place (freq. with article omitted). OE. **3** Expr. the place of occurrence of an event; assisting or present on the occasion of. OE. **4** Defining the point or part, side or direction, where anything is or is applied. OE. **5** Expr. the relation of an attribute to a particular place or part. OE. **6** Defining the point where anything enters or issues; through, by. OE. **7** Specifying the source from which anything comes and where it is sought. *obs.* exc. in *at the mouth* or *hands of.* OE. **8** With vbs of motion: expr. attainment of a position or determining the point to which motion extends; as far as. OE. **9** Governing a person: †**a** In personal contact with; in the presence or company of; *fig.* in the eyes of, in the estimation of. ME–L18. **b** Ellipt.: (w. the possess.) in the house of; (w. the possess. or simply) in the shop etc. of. M16. **c** In active or aggressive contact with; applying to, pestering. E17. **10** In the direction of, towards; so as to reach or attack. LME.

1 I. BARROW At a point given A, to make a right line AG. E. HEMINGWAY I.. found the major sitting at a table in the bare room. N. BALCHIN The young chimpanzee was sitting at the back of the cage. J. CARY She said no more except to utter a brief thanks when Joanna put her down at her door. S. ULLMANN The dog's scraping at the door. R. QUIRK I have often been at the receiving end of calls for help from this Unit. J. I. M. STEWART The cricket field at the centre of the scene. R. WILLIAMS At the very centre of a major area of modern thought and practice.. is a concept 'culture'. A. BURNETT At the start of the poem the speaker thinks he sees his dead wife brought to him; at the end only his 'night' is brought back. **b** LD MACAULAY The Parliament met at Edinburgh. GERALD MOORE I was born at Watford, Hertfordshire, in 1899. **c** MILTON To save himself against a coward arm'd At one spear's length. H. NELSON The Corsican privateers kept at such a distance. **2** DICKENS What the parson at chapel says. L. GOLDING He would put up at the village pub. A. SILLITOE Winnie enquired: had he had a good time at the camp? H. FAST Thomas was at school in the East. B. MOORE Eileen deserves better, her father was at the university. J. MORTIMER Later she taught drawing in Manchester, at a Lycée in Versailles, and at a girls' school in Natal. **3** SHAKES. *Temp.* When we were.. at the marriage of your daughter. STEELE He is at a Play. T. PYNCHON Apt.. to appear at a public function and begin a speech. **4** J. WEEVER The Seale.. hanging at the parchment by a silke string. ADDISON Liberty with Monarchy at her right hand. L. GOLDING Whenever and wherever a farmer died.., his widow would find Johnnie Hummel at her ear. W. TREVOR Your predecessor would suck at the butt of a cig. **5** SHAKES. *Haml.* 'Tis bitter cold, And I am sick at heart. J. THOMSON Withered at the root. **6** THACKERAY He looked in at the dining-room window. A. BRIDGE The air blowing in at the car windows was chill with the approach of nightfall. **7** COVERDALE *Judith* 10:7 They axed no question at her, but let her go. **8** *arrive,* (arch.) *come, end, land, stop,* etc., *at.* **9b** STEELE We had Yesterday at Sir Roger's a Set of Country Gentlemen who dined with him. P. SCOTT The memsahib was at the hairdresser. **c** OED The midges are at me again. J. HERRIOT She was at me again the next day and I had to rush out to her cottage. **10** SHAKES. *2 Hen. VI* Put forth thy hand, reach at the glorious gold. ADDISON The Parson is always preaching at the 'Squire. N. HAWTHORNE The spectator's imagination completes what the artist merely hints at. T. DREISER He had unintentionally struck at her. M. DE LA ROCHE She peered up at him from under her shaggy red brows. S. SASSOON Earth and chalk heaved up at the blue sky. G. STEINER In method and scope I am aiming at something different from literary criticism. W. STYRON Clothes like this have individuality... That's why it's fun when people stare at us. A. GRAY He pressed his lips together and frowned at the coffee cup.

II Action, engagement, occupation, condition, etc. **11** With things put for the activities of which they are the objects, centres, or instruments. OE. **12** Connecting adjs. or ns. of occupation and proficiency with a thing or action. OE. **13** With actions in or with which one is engaged, before ns. or after vbs expressing such action. ME. **14** Of state or condition of existence, posture, conditioning circumstance, mutual relations, mode, manner, measure, extent, etc. ME. **15** Of relation to someone's will or disposition. ME.

11 S. JOHNSON He must be a great English lawyer, from having been so long at the bar. T. HOOD And my right hand grows raging hot, Like Cranmer's at the stake. J. L. MOTLEY His carpets.. were disposed of at auction. OED To contest it at sword's point. *barrister-at-law, serjeant-at-arms,* etc. **12** THACKERAY I am not good at descriptions of female beauty. LD MACAULAY In agility and skill at his weapons he had few equals. G. B. SHAW I'm no good at making money. **13** SHAKES. *Two Gent.* As she sits at supper. G. CRABBE I trace the matron at her loved employ. OED To work hard at clearing a path. **14** H. FIELDING Pursue her at the hazard of his life. JOHN PHILLIPS Section at right angles to the axis. E. A. FREEMAN At all risks, at all sacrifices, to keep Normandy in full possession. B. RUSSELL Civilians stood bare-headed and soldiers at the salute. J. HELLER His round white cap was cocked at an insolent tilt. **15** LD BERNERS To make your marchaundise at your pleasure. LD MACAULAY Their votes were at his disposal. *at the mercy of*: see MERCY *n.*

III Of time, order, consequence, cause, object. **16** Of order. OE. **17** Defining the time of an event, the time indicated by an event, or a person's age at the time of an event. ME. **18** Of nearness or distance in time, interval. ME. **19** Of the number of times, turns, or occasions. ME. **20** Defining the occasion or event on which a fact or occasion ensues, and hence the occasioning circumstance or cause. ME. **21** Defining the occasion or cause (sometimes also the object) of an emotion. ME. †**22** Defining the reason or consideration. LME–L16.

16 *at first, at last, at length,* etc. **17** DEFOE Our men.. gave them a shout at parting. ARNOLD BENNETT At a quarter to seven he put his boots on. R. FULLER As on a silly marriage, he embarked / at sixty-five on a whole programme of moon / watching. H. FAST She would awaken at night in the darkness. J. JOHNSTON I played a lot of tennis at your age. **18** M. SPARK Sandy and Jenny got ink on their blouses at discreet intervals of four weeks. F. FORSYTH At the end of two hours he had secured the name he was looking for. **19** M. HALE May go far at one Essay to provide a fit law. OED To complete the business at two sittings. **20** E. WHARTON Stooping to pick up the book he had dropped at Lily's approach. J. STEINBECK Tom touched his swollen face.., and at his movement Al groaned and murmured in his sleep. **21** MILTON I sorrow'd at his captive state. E. K. KANE Impatient at the delays. D. TOPOLSKI Weary disgust.. at the self-satisfied imposition of an alien way of life and values on these people. J. CHEEVER I was cross at myself for having forgotten her birthday.

IV Relative position in a series or scale; degree, rate, value. **23** Defining a special point in a series or scale. ME. **24** Of the rate or degree at which a thing is done. ME. **25** Of price or value. ME. **26** Of reference to a standard generally; according to. LME.

23 COVERDALE *Ezek.* 9:6 Then they begane at the elders, which were in the Temple. G. O. TREVELYAN He was rewarded by seeing Johnson at his very best. K. VONNEGUT Graduating from Cornell Law School at the top of his class. E. PENNING-ROWSELL Some vineyards were practically wiped out at temperatures as low as −24 degrees C. J. GALWAY The whole might of the Berlin Philharmonic at full blast. **24** POPE If I am to go on at this rate. R. M. PIRSIG The wind, even at sixty miles an hour, is warm and humid. B. BAINBRIDGE He propelled her at a fast trot up the cobbled ramp. **25** SHAKES. *Haml.* If my love thou hold'st at aught. K. VONNEGUT Published at twenty-five cents. *at any cost*: see COST *n.*[2] **26** LD MACAULAY By land or water at their choice. L. P. HARTLEY They often reversed their roles, at the dictates of the penny.

V With inf. (cf. ON *at*). **27** Introducing the inf. of purpose. (See also ADO *v.*) Long *obs.* exc. *dial.* ME.

VI Bef. other preps. and advs. †**28** Bef. preps. LME–L16. **29** Bef. advs. Long *obs.* exc. *dial.* LME.

Phrases: (For the many phrs. in which *at* governs a n. or forms an elem. in a phrasal vb, see the ns. and vbs.) **where it's at** *slang* the (true) scene of action, the (true) state of things.

at- /at, *unstressed* ət/ *pref.* (not productive). Assim. form of L AD- bef. *t.* In OFr., L *att-* was reduced to *at-*, which appears in ME adoptions, but in later Fr., and even more commonly in Eng., *att-* was restored by Latinization, as *attainder* (cf. Fr. *atteindre*), *attorney* (Fr. *atourné*), etc.

-at /at/ *suff.*[1] (not productive). [(Fr. f.) as -ATE[1].] Forming ns., as *commisariat, concordat, format, secretariat,* etc.

-at /at/ *suff.*[2] [Back-form. after G *aplanat(isch* etc.] Forming ns. denoting lenses, etc., of the kinds specified by adjs. in *-atic*, as *achromat, aplanat,* etc.

atabal /ˈatəbal/ *n.* L16. [Sp. f. Arab. *aṭ-ṭabl* f. *al-* AL-[2] + *ṭabl* drum.] A Moorish kettledrum.

Atabrine *n.* var. of ATEBRIN.

atacamite /atəˈkɑːmʌɪt/ *n.* E19. [f. *Atacama* a province of Chile + -ITE[1].] *Min.* An emerald-green basic chloride of copper, crystallizing in the orthorhombic system, freq. as thin prisms.

atactic /əˈtaktɪk/ *a.* M19. [f. Gk *ataktos*, f. A-[10] + *taktos* arranged, + -IC.] **1** Of (a) language: without rigid word order, without syntax. Cf. ASYNTACTIC. M19. **2** *Med.* = ATAXIC *a.* L19. **3** *Chem.* Having or designating a polymeric structure in which the repeating units have no regular configuration. M20.

ataghan *n.* var. of YATAGHAN.

†**Atalantis** *n.* L18–E19. [Short title of an E18 romance (prob. itself named after Bacon's *New Atlantis*) satirizing the movers of the Glorious Revolution.] A secret or scandalous history.

ataman /ˈatəman/ *n.* M19. [Russ.] A Cossack leader. Cf. HETMAN.

atamasco /atəˈmaskəʊ/ *n.* M18. [N. American Indian.] *atamasco lily*, a plant, *Zephyranthes atamasco*, of the south-eastern US, bearing a single white lily-like flower.

atap *n.* var. of ATTAP.

ataractic /atəˈraktɪk/ *a.* & *n.* M20. [f. Gk *ataraktos* not disturbed, calm + -IC. Cf. ATARAXY.] *Med.* **A** *adj.* Of a drug: tranquillizing. M20. **B** *n.* A tranquillizing drug. M20.

ataraxia /atəˈraksɪə/ *n.* M19. [Gk: see ATARAXY.] = ATARAXY.

ataraxic /atəˈraksɪk/ *a.* & *n.* M20. [f. as next + -IC.] **A** *adj.* **1** Calm, serene. *rare.* M20. **2** *Med.* = ATARACTIC *a.* M20. **B** *n.* *Med.* = ATARACTIC *n.* M20.

ataraxy /ˈatəraksi/ *n.* E17. [Fr. *ataraxie* f. Gk *ataraxia* impassiveness, f. A-[10] + *tarassein* disturb: see -Y[3], -IA[1].] Imperturbability; stoical indifference.

ataunt /əˈtɔːnt/ *adv.* & *pred. a.* Sense 2 also **-to** /-təʊ/. LME. [Sense 1 f. (O)Fr. *autant* as much, ult. f. L *aliud* (neut.) other + *tantum* (neut.) so great; sense 2 f. A *prep.*[1] 6 + TAUNT *a.*] †**1** *adv.* As much as possible; to the full; thoroughly. LME–E16. **2** *adv.* & *pred. a.* *Naut.* With all sails set; fully shipshape. L16.

atavism /ˈatəvɪz(ə)m/ *n.* M19. [Fr. *atavisme*, f. L *atavus* great-grandfather's grandfather, forefather, f. *at-* beyond + *avus* grandfather: see -ISM.] Resemblance to more remote ancestors rather than to parents; tendency of animals or plants to revert to an ancestral type.

atavic /əˈtavɪk/ *a.* = ATAVISTIC M19. **ataˈvistic** *a.* of, pertaining to, or of the nature of atavism L19. **ataˈvistically** *adv.* L19.

ataxia /əˈtaksɪə/ *n.* L19. [mod.L f. Gk, f. A-[10] + *-taxia*, *taxis* order: see -IA[1].] *Med.* Lack of coordination of movement, esp. as causing unsteadiness of gait.

locomotor ataxia incoordination of movements, *spec.* due to syphilitic infection of the spinal cord; tabes dorsalis.

ataxic /əˈtaksɪk/ *a.* & *n.* M19. [f. next, prec. + -IC.] **A** *adj.* Of or affected with ataxia or (formerly) ataxy. M19. **B** *n.* An ataxic person. L19.

ataxy /əˈtaksi/ *n.* L16. [f. as prec.: see -TAXY.] †**1** Irregularity, disorder. L16–M18. **2** *Med.* Orig., irregularity of the animal functions or of the symptoms of disease. Later, ataxia. Now *rare*. L17.

at-bat /ət'bat/ *n.* M20. [f. AT *prep.* + BAT *n.*[1]] *Baseball.* A turn at batting.

Ate /'eɪti/ *n.* L16. [Gk *Atē*.] Infatuation, rashness, (personified by the Greeks as a destructive goddess).

ate *v.* see EAT *v.*

-ate /ət, eɪt/ *suff.*[1] [L *-atus*, *-ata* (fem.), *-atum* (neut.) n. suff. or (O)Fr. -AT[1] (earlier *-ée*).] Forming ns. denoting (*a*) office, function, state, etc., or a person, group, or thing having it, as *curate*, *doctorate*, *electorate*, *magistrate*, *mandate*, etc.; (*b*) *Chem.* salts or esters of acids (esp. of acids ending in *-ic*: cf. -ITE[1]), or other derivatives, as *acetate*, *alcoholate*, *hydrate*, *sulphate*, etc.

-ate /ət, eɪt/ *suff.*[2] [L (fem.) *-atus*, (neut.) *-ata*, *-atum* pa. ppl suff. of vbs in *-are*, or Fr. *-é*.] Forming adjs. and ns., as *affectionate*, *associate*, *caudate*, *delegate*, *Italianate*, *precipitate*, *reprobate*, *roseate*, *separate*, etc. Hence forming ns. f. Eng. vbs, denoting end-products of (esp. chemical) operations or processes, as *centrifugate*, *dialysate*, *homogenate*, etc. Many of the adjs. were orig. ppl and also served as pa. pples of vbs in -ATE[3].

-ate /eɪt/ *suff.*[3] [After or f. as -ATE[2], orig. on the basis of existing ppl adjs. in -ATE[2], later f. any L vb in *-are*; also used to Anglicize Fr. vbs in *-er* (f. L *-are*).] Forming vbs, as *assassinate*, *associate*, *fascinate*, *felicitate*, *hydrate*, *separate*, *vaccinate*, etc. Some, as *automate*, repr. back-forms. f. ns. in *-ation*.

Atebrin /'atɪbrɪn/ *n.* Also ***Atabrine**. M20. [Origin unkn.] (Proprietary name for) mepacrine.

atelectasis /atɪ'lɛktəsɪs/ *n.* M19. [f. Gk *atelēs* imperfect + *ektasis* extension.] *Med.* Incomplete dilatation of the lungs; collapse of a lung or part of a lung.
atelectatic /ˌatɪlɛk'tatɪk/ *a.* L19.

ateleiosis /ətɛlɪ'əʊsɪs, ətiːl-/ *n.* Also **-lio-**. E20. [f. A-[10] + TELEIOSIS.] *Med.* Dwarfism due to pituitary insufficiency.
ateleiotic /-'ɒtɪk/ *a.* & *n.* (*a*) *adj.* pertaining to, characterized by, or affected with ateleiosis; (*b*) *n.* a person with ateleiosis: E20.

atelier /ə'tɛlɪeɪ/ *n.* L17. [Fr.] A workshop or studio, esp. of an artist or couturier.

ateliosis *n.* var. of ATELEIOSIS.

Atellan /ə'tɛlən/ *a.* & *n.* E17. [L *Atellanus*, f. *Atella* (see below): see -AN.] **A** *adj.* Of or pertaining to Atella, a town in Campania, S. Italy, formerly famous for satirical and licentious farces; farcical, ribald. E17. **B** *n.* A farcical or ribald dramatic composition. E17.

a tempo /ɑː 'tɛmpəʊ/ *adv. phr.* M18. [It. = in time.] *Mus.* A direction: in the tempo indicated previously, before the direction to deviate from it.

atemporal /eɪ'tɛmp(ə)r(ə)l/ *a.* L19. [f. A-[10] + TEMPORAL *a.*[1]] Not temporal, free from limits of time, timeless.

Atenism /'ɑːtənɪz(ə)m/ *n.* E20. [f. *Aten* f. Egyptian *itn* a name of the sun(-god): see -ISM.] *Hist.* The worship of the sun in ancient Egypt, esp. in the reign of Amenophis IV (Akhnaten) in the 14th cent. BC.

atenolol /ə'tɛnəlɒl/ *n.* L20. [Perh. f. angina + *tension* + -O- + propran*olol*.] *Pharm.* A beta blocker given orally in the treatment of angina and hypertension.

Aterian /ə'tɪərɪən/ *a.* E20. [Fr. *atérien*, f. Bir el *Ater* in Algeria + -IAN.] *Archaeol.* Designating or pertaining to a form of middle palaeolithic culture found in N. Africa.

à terre /a tɛːr/ *adv.* & *a. phr.* E20. [Fr.] Chiefly *Ballet.* On the ground.

Athabascan, -skan *a.* & *n.* vars. of ATHAPASKAN.

athame /ə'θɑːmeɪ, ə'θeɪmi/ *n.* Also **arthame** /ɑː'θeɪmi/. M20. [Origin unkn.] A black-handled ritual dagger used in modern witchcraft.

Athanasian /aθə'neɪʃ(ə)n/ *a.* & *n.* L16. [f. *Athanasius* (see below) + -AN.] **A** *adj.* Of or pertaining to Athanasius (293–373), bishop of Alexandria in the reign of Constantine. L16.
Athanasian Creed: that beginning *Quicunque vult* 'Whosoever will', formerly attributed to Athanasius.
B *n.* An adherent of the doctrines of Athanasius. E18.

athanor /'aθənɔː/ *n.* L15. [Arab. *at-tannūr*, f. *at-* AL-[2] + *tannūr* baker's oven.] A self-feeding digesting furnace used by the alchemists, capable of maintaining a steady heat for long periods.

Athapaskan /aθə'pask(ə)n/ *a.* & *n.* Also **Athaba-** /-'ba-/; **-scan**. M19. [f. Lake *Athabaska* in western Canada f. Cree *Athapaskaw* lit. 'grass and reeds here and there', + -AN.] **A** *adj.* Of or pertaining to a widely-spread N. American Indian people speaking various closely-related languages. M19. **B** *n.* **1** A member of this people. M19. **2** Their language group. L19.

atheise *v.* var. of ATHEIZE.

atheism /'eɪθɪɪz(ə)m/ *n.* L16. [Fr. *athéisme*, f. Gk *atheos* without God, denying God, f. as A-[10] + *theos* god: see -ISM.] Disbelief in, or denial of, the existence of God or gods (opp. *theism*, (formerly) *deism*). Also, godlessness.

atheist /'eɪθɪɪst/ *n.* & *a.* L16. [Fr. *athéiste* or It. *atheista*, f. Gk *atheos*: see prec., -IST.] **A** *n.* **1** A person who denies or disbelieves the existence of God or gods. Opp. *theist*, (formerly) *deist*. L16. **2** A person who denies God morally; a godless person. L16. **B** *adj.* Denying or disbelieving the existence of God or gods; godless. L16.
athe'istic *a.* of the nature of or pertaining to atheism; of or befitting an atheist; godless, impious: M17. **athe'istical** *a.* = ATHEISTIC L16. **athe'istically** *adv.* E17.

atheize /'eɪθɪʌɪz/ *v.t.* Also **-ise**. L17. [f. Gk *atheos* (see ATHEISM) + -IZE.] Make atheistic; convert to atheism.

athel /'aθ(ə)l/ *a.* & *n.* Long *arch.* or *Hist.* Also **eth-** /'ɛθ-/. [OE *æþele* = OFris. *ethele*, OS *eþili*, OHG *edili* (Du., G *edel*) f. Gmc.] **A** *adj.* Noble; illustrious. OE. **B** *n.* A lord, a chief. ME.

atheling /'aθ(ə)lɪŋ/ *n. obs.* exc. *Hist.* Also **aeth-**. [OE *æþeling* = OFris. *etheling*, OHG *adalung*, f. WGmc, f. a base meaning 'race, family': see -ING[3].] An Anglo-Saxon prince or lord, *esp.* (*Hist.*) the heir to the throne. Often (**A-**) used as the epithet of Edgar (d. *c*1125), grandson of Edmund Ironside and putative heir of Harold II.

athematic /aθɪ'matɪk, eɪ-/ *a.* L19. [f. A-[10] + THEMATIC *a.*] **1** *Ling.* Having suffixes attached to the stem without a connecting (thematic) vowel. L19. **2** *Mus.* Not based on the use of themes. M20.

athenaeum /aθɪ'niːəm/ *n.* Also ***-neum**. M18. [L *Athenaeum* f. Gk *Athēnaion*.] **1** (**A-**.) The temple of the goddess Athene in ancient Athens, which was used for teaching. M18. **2** A reading-room, a library. L18. **b** A literary or scientific club. E19. **3** (**A-**.) As the title of various periodicals devoted to literature, science, and art. M19.

Athenian /ə'θiːnɪən/ *n.* & *a.* E16. [L *Atheniensis* adj. & n., f. *Athenae*, Gk *Athēnai* Athens.] **A** *n.* A native or inhabitant of Athens, the leading city of Greece in antiquity and its modern capital. E16. **B** *adj.* Of, pertaining to, or characteristic of Athens. L16.

atheologian /eɪθɪə'ləʊdʒɪən/ *n. rare.* E17. [f. A-[10] + THEOLOGIAN.] A person who knows no theology; a person opposed to or not admitting theology.

atheology /eɪθɪ'ɒlədʒi/ *n.* L17. [f. A-[10] + THEOLOGY.] Opposition to theology.
atheological /eɪθɪə'lɒdʒɪk(ə)l/ *a.* M17.

atheous /'eɪθɪəs/ *a.* E17. [f. Gk *atheos* (see ATHEISM) + -OUS.] †**1** Atheistic. E17–M19. **2** Not concerned with the existence of God. *rare.* L19.

atherine /'aθərʌɪn/ *n.* Also in L form **-ina** /-ʌɪnə/. M18. [mod.L *atherina* f. Gk *atherinē*: see -INE[3].] = *silverside* (b) s.v. SILVER *n.* & *a.*

atheroma /aθə'rəʊmə/ *n.* Pl. **-mas**, **-mata** /-mətə/. L16. [L f. Gk *athērōma*, f. *athērē* = *atharē* groats: see -OMA.] *Med.* **1** A sebaceous cyst. Now *rare* or *obs.* L16. **2** A deposit or the deposition of fatty material on the inside surface of an artery. Cf. next. L19.
atheromatous *a.* of the nature of or characterized by atheroma L17.

atherosclerosis /ˌaθərəʊsklɪə'rəʊsɪs, -sklə-/ *n.* Pl. **-roses** /-'rəʊsiːz/. E20. [f. as prec. + SCLEROSIS.] *Med.* A form of arteriosclerosis characterized by the deposition of fatty material in the lining of the arteries.
atherosclerotic /-'rɒtɪk/ *a.* pertaining to or characterized by atherosclerosis E20.

athetesis /aθɪ'tiːsɪs/ *n.* L19. [Gk *athetēsis*, f. *athetein*: see next.] In textual criticism: the rejection of a passage as spurious.

athetize /'aθɪtʌɪz/ *v.t.* Also **-ise**. L19. [f. Gk *athetos* (see next) + -IZE, rendering Gk *athetein*.] In textual criticism: reject (a passage) as spurious.

athetosis /aθɪ'təʊsɪs/ *n.* Pl. **-toses** /-'təʊsiːz/. L19. [f. Gk *athetos* without position or place, set aside + -OSIS.] *Med.* A form of involuntary slow writhing movement of the extremities.
athetoid /'aθɪtɔɪd/, **athetotic** /-'tɒtɪk/ *adjs.* of, pertaining to, or characterized by athetosis L19.

athirst /ə'θəːst/ *pred. a.* Now *literary*. [OE *ofþyrst* shortened f. *ofþyrsted* pa. pple of *ofþyrstan* suffer thirst: f. as OFF *adv.* + THIRST *v.*] Very thirsty; *fig.* eager, longing, (*for*).

athlete /'aθliːt/ *n.* Also in L form †**-eta**. LME. [L *athleta* f. Gk *athlētēs*, f. *athlein* contend for a prize, f. *athlon* prize.] **1** A competitor or performer in physical exercises or games. LME. **2** *fig.* & *transf.* A strong competitor; a vigorous performer. M18. **3** A person who is physically strong or fit by training and exercise; a muscular or physically robust person. E19.
1 athlete's foot ringworm infection of the foot. **2** J. R. LOWELL The long-proved athletes of debate. R. PEARL Present-day examples of sexual athletes who make Casanova . . seem a somewhat puny performer.

athletic /aθ'lɛtɪk/ *n.* & *a.* E17. [Fr. *athlétique* or L *athleticus* f. Gk *athlētikos*: see prec., -IC.] **A** *n.* **1** *sing.* & (now) in *pl.* (often treated as *sing.*). The practice of or competition in physical exercises (running, jumping, throwing, etc.); *N. Amer.* physical sports and games generally. E17. †**2** An athlete. L17–E19. **B** *adj.* **1** Of or pertaining to athletes or athletics. M17. **2** Physically powerful or fit; muscular, vigorous. M17.
athletical *a.* (long *rare*) = ATHLETIC *a.* L16. **athletically** *adv.* M18. **athleticism** /-sɪz(ə)m/ *n.* athletic quality, physical fitness; the practice of athletics: L19.

Athoan /a'θəʊən/ *a.* M19. [f. Gk *Athōos* of Athos + -AN.] Of or pertaining to Athos, a mountainous peninsula of Macedonia, or the monasteries situated upon it. Cf. ATHONITE.

Athole brose /ˌaθ(ə)l 'brəʊz/ *n. phr.* Also **Atholl**. L18. [f. *Atholl* (*Athole*) a district in Tayside, Scotland + BROSE.] Honey and whisky, often mixed with meal.

at-home /ət'həʊm/ *n.* M18. [f. *at home* (see HOME *n.*).] A reception of visitors within certain stated hours, during which the host or hostess or both have announced that they will be at home.

-athon /əθ(ə)n, əθɒn/ *suff.* After a vowel **-thon**. [f. MARATHON.] Forming ns. denoting activities of abnormal length, as *talkathon*, *radiothon*, etc.

Athonite /'aθənʌɪt/ *n.* & *a.* L19. [f. *Athon-* taken as stem of Gk *Athos* + -ITE[1].] **A** *n.* A member of an Athoan monastery. L19. **B** *adj.* Of or pertaining to Athos or (esp.) its monasteries. M20.

Athor *n.* var. of HATHOR.

athort *prep.* & *adv.* see ATHWART.

athrill /ə'θrɪl/ *adv.* & *pred. a. literary.* L19. [f. A-[2] + THRILL *n.*[2] or *v.*[1]] In a thrill, thrilled.

athrob /ə'θrɒb/ *adv.* & *pred. a. literary.* M19. [f. A-[2] + THROB *n.* or *v.*] Throbbing.

athrong /ə'θrɒŋ/ *adv.* & *pred. a.* Now *literary.* ME. [f. A *prep.*[1] 6 + THRONG *n.*] In a throng; thronged, crowded.

athwart /ə'θwɔːt/ *prep.* & *adv.* Also (*Sc.*) **athort** /ə'θɔːt/. LME. [f. A *prep.*[1] I + THWART *adv.*, prob. after ON *um þvert* over in a transverse direction.] **A** *prep.* **1** From side to side of; transversely over, across. LME. **2** Across the course or direction of, freq. so as to oppose or meet; *fig.* in opposition to; to the notice of. LME. **3** Across in various directions; to and fro over, all over. Chiefly *Sc.* M16.

1 SHAKES. *L.L.L.* Nor never lay his wreathed arms athwart His loving bosom, to keep down his heart. J. GALSWORTHY Its . . latticed window athwart which the last of the sunlight was shining. A. E. COPPARD The wind blew strongly athwart the yellow field. 2 R. HAWKINS If this Spanish shippe should fall athwart his King's armado. MILTON I have seen this present work, and finde nothing athwart the Catholick faith. SMOLLETT If you come a-thwart me, 'ware. H. A. L. FISHER The Avars, whose barbarous power . . lay athwart the middle Danube. *athwart the hawse*: see HAWSE *n.*[1] **run athwart** *Naut.* pass across the line of a ship's course.

B *adv.* **1** Across in various directions, about. *Sc.* L15. **2** Across from side to side, transversely. M16. **3** Across the course or direction of something; *fig.* in opposition, perversely, awry. L16.

1 R. BAILLIE There goes a speech athort . . dissuading the king from war with us. 2 SIR T. BROWNE The Asse having . . a crosse made by a black list down his back, and another athwart, or at right angles down his shoulders. W. FALCONER The fore-sail right athwart they brace. TENNYSON The cloud . . sweeps athwart in storms. 3 SHAKES. *Meas. for M.* The baby beats the nurse, and quite athwart Goes all decorum. W. COWPER And with his spear Advanced athwart pushed back the Trojan van.

Comb.: *athwart-hawse*: see HAWSE *n.*[1]; **athwartship** *a.*, **athwartships** *adv.* (*Naut.*) (extending, lying) from side to side of the ship.

-atic /'atɪk/ *suff.* **1** [(Fr. *-atique* f.) L *-aticus* suff. combining -IC w. vb- or n.-stems in *-at-*: cf. -AGE.] Forming adjs. and derived ns., as *aquatic*, *erratic*, *lunatic*, etc. **2** [(Late L *-aticus* f.) Gk *-atikos* suff. combining -IC w. n.-stems in *-at-*.] Forming adjs. and derived ns., as *aromatic*, *idiomatic*, *problematic*, *rheumatic*, etc.

-atile /ətʌɪl/ *suff.* [(Fr. *-atile* f.) L *-atilis* suff. combining *-ilis* -ILE w. vb- or n.-stems in *-at-*.] Forming adjs. and derived ns. expressing capability or quality, as *aquatile*, *volatile*, etc.

atilt /ə'tɪlt/ *adv.* & *pred. a.* M16. [Sense 1 f. A *prep.*[1], sense 2 f. *a-* of uncertain origin, + TILT *n.*[2]] **1** Tilted up; on the point of falling over. M16. **2** *ride, run*, etc., *atilt*: on horseback with the thrust of a lance. Chiefly *fig. arch.* L16.

1 J. HEYWOOD We apply the spigot, till tubbe stande a tilte. D. C. PEATTIE One searched for Saturn and found it, rings a-tilt, tearing out of the field of vision. 2 SHAKES. *1 Hen. VI* What will you do, good grey-beard? Break a lance, And run a tilt at death within a chair? H. TAYLOR He rode a-tilt and smote the scaly Dragon. J. H. BURTON A paper in defense of queen Mary's honour, in which he ran atilt with Buchanan.

atingle /ə'tɪŋɡ(ə)l/ *adv.* & *pred. a.* M19. [f. A-[2] + TINGLE *v.* & *n.*[3]] Tingling.

-ation /'eɪʃ(ə)n/ *suff.* [(OFr. *-aci(o)un*, mod. *-ation*, f.) L *-atio(n-)* suff. combining -(T)ION w. vb stems in *-a(t)-*.] Forming ns. denoting vbl action or an instance of it, or a resulting state or thing. Most such Eng. wds, as *creation*, *moderation*, *saturation*, etc., have corresp. vbs in -ATE[3], but some do not, as *capitation*, *constellation*, *duration*, etc. Others are formed directly on vbs in -IZE, as *civilization*, *organization*, etc. The remainder correspond to a vb without suff., derived f. Fr., as *alteration*, *causation*, *formation*, *vexation*, etc.; the suff. was thence applied to wds of various origin, as *botheration*, *flirtation*, *starvation*, etc. Cf. -FICATION.

atiptoe /ə'tɪptəʊ/ *adv.* & *pred. a.* M16. [f. A *prep.*[1] I + TIPTOE *n.*] On the tips of one's toes.

atishoo /ə'tɪʃuː/ *int.* & *n.* L19. [Imit.] (Repr.) the characteristic noises accompanying a sneeze; a sneeze.

-ative /ətɪv, 'eɪtɪv/ *suff.* [f. or after Fr. *-atif*, fem. *-ative*, or L *-ativus* suff. combining *-ivus* -IVE w. vb-stems in *-at-*.] Forming adjs., as *authoritative*, *demonstrative*, *figurative*, *imitative*, *qualitative*, *talkative*, etc.

Atjehnese *n.* & *a.* var. of ACHINESE.

atlantal /at'lant(ə)l/ *a.* E19. [f. Gk *atlant-* (see ATLAS *n.*[1]) + -AL[1].] *Anat.* †**1** Of or pertaining to the upper half of the body. E–M19. **2** Of or pertaining to the atlas vertebra. M19.

Atlantean /at'lantɪən, atlən'tiːən/ *a.* M17. [f. L *Atlanteus*, f. *Atlant-* (see ATLAS *n.*[1]): see -EAN.] Of or pertaining to the Titan Atlas; having the superhuman strength of Atlas.

atlantes /at'lantiːz/ *n.pl.* E17. [Gk, pl. of ATLAS *n.*[1]] *Archit.* Male figures used as pillars to support an entablature.

Atlantic /at'lantɪk/ *a.* & *n.* LME. [L *Atlanticus* f. Gk *Atlantikos*, f. *Atlant-*: see ATLAS *n.*[1], -IC. Branch A.I f. the Atlas mountains, II f. the Titan Atlas, III f. the island of Atlantis.] **A** *adj.* **I 1** *Atlantic Ocean*, the ocean separating Europe and Africa in the east from America in the west. Orig. restricted to the seas adjacent to the western shores of Africa (sometimes including parts of the Mediterranean). LME. **2** Of or pertaining to the Atlantic Ocean; (of or involving countries or regions) bordering the Atlantic Ocean; *fig.* (*rare*) far-reaching, distant. E17. **b** Crossing the Atlantic Ocean; transatlantic. M19. **3** Designating or pertaining to the climatic period in northern Europe or elsewhere following the boreal period. L19.

2 **Atlantic Charter** *Hist.* a declaration of common aims and principles drawn up by British Prime Minister Winston Churchill and US President Franklin D. Roosevelt at a meeting in the W. Atlantic in 1941. **Atlantic seal** = *grey seal* s.v. GREY *a.* **Atlantic States**: those forming the eastern coastline of the US. **Atlantic Time** the standard time used in eastern Canada. *Middle Atlantic States*: see MIDDLE *a.*

†**II 4** = ATLANTEAN *a.* E17–E18.

III 5 Of or pertaining to Atlantis, a mythical island placed by the Greeks in the far west; utopian. *rare.* M17.

B *n.* **1** *The* Atlantic Ocean. LME. **2** A steam locomotive of 4-4-2 wheel arrangement. E20.

Atlanticism /-sɪz(ə)m/ *n.* belief in or support for NATO or the close political relationship of western Europe and the US generally M20. **Atlanticist** /-sɪst/ *n.* & *a.* (a person) advocating or favouring Atlanticism M20.

atlanto- /at'lantəʊ/ *comb. form.* E19. [f. Gk *atlant-* (see ATLAS *n.*[1]) + -O-.] *Anat.* Forming adjs. w. the sense 'atlantal and', as *atlanto-axial*, *-occipital*, etc.

atlas /'atləs/ *n.*[1] & *v.* L16. [L *Atlas*, *Atlant-* f. Gk *Atlas*, *Atlant-*, the Titan supposed to hold up the pillars of the universe, and a mountain range in western N. Africa also regarded mythically as supporting the heavens.] **A** *n.* **1** (**A-**.) A person who supports a great burden; a mainstay. L16. **2** A collection of maps or charts bound in a volume. (Orig. published with a figure of Atlas at the front.) M17. **b** A similar collection of diagrams or illustrations in any subject. L19. **3** *Anat.* More fully *atlas vertebra*. The first or uppermost cervical vertebra, which articulates with the skull. L17. **4** (**A-**.) A large size of drawing-paper. E18.

Comb.: **atlas moth** a very large tropical saturniid, *Attacus atlas*; *atlas vertebra*: see sense 3 above.

B *v.t.* (**A-**.) Prop up or carry after the manner of Atlas. *rare.* L16.

atlas /'atləs/ *n.*[2] Now *arch.* or *Hist.* Also **-ss.** E17. [Ult. f. Arab. *'aṭlas* smooth; smooth silk cloth, satin. Cf. G *Atlas*.] An oriental satin; a piece of this; a garment made of this.

atlatl /'at(ə)lat(ə)l/ *n.* L19. [Nahuatl *ahtlatl*.] A throwing-stick used by American Indians and Eskimos.

atman /'ɑːtmən/ *n.* L18. [Skt *ātman*.] *Hindu Philos.* The self as the subject of individual consciousness, the soul; the supreme personal principle of life in the universe.

atmometer /at'mɒmɪtə/ *n.* E19. [f. Gk *atmos* vapour + -METER.] An instrument for measuring the rate of evaporation of water into the atmosphere.

atmosphere /'atməsfɪə/ *n.* & *v.* M17. [mod.L *atmosphaera*, f. Gk *atmos* vapour + *sphaira* SPHERE *n.*] **A** *n.* **1** The spheroidal gaseous envelope surrounding the earth or a celestial object; the whole quantity of such gas. M17. **b** A body of gas or vapour surrounding any object or substance, or occupying a given space. M19. †**2** A supposed region of influence surrounding a body such as a magnet. M17–M18. **3** A (unit of) pressure approximately equal to the mean pressure of the atmosphere at sea level; now, 101,325 pascal (about 14.6959 lb per sq. inch). E18. **4** The air in any particular place, esp. as regards some characteristic such as temperature, wholesomeness, etc. M18. **5** *fig.* Mental or moral environment; a pervading tone or mood; associations, effects, sounds, etc., evoking a characteristic mood. L18.

1 E. DENISON The earth's atmosphere decreases so rapidly in density, that half its mass is within 3½ miles above the sea; and at 80 miles high there can be practically no atmosphere. B. LOVELL The atmosphere of Mars contains about 95 percent carbon dioxide. W. BOYD It must be . . some trick of the atmosphere, the stillness and dryness of the air. *upper atmosphere*: see UPPER *a.* b J. K. JEROME A permanent atmosphere of paraffin, however faint, is apt to cause remark. N. CALDER The main batch of samples went into an atmosphere of sterile nitrogen. 2 B. FRANKLIN The additional quantity [of 'electrical fluid'] does not enter, but forms an electrical atmosphere. 4 N. HAWTHORNE No amount of blaze would raise the atmosphere of the room ten degrees. ANTHONY HUXLEY This plant prefers a very moist atmosphere under glass. 5 J. S. MILL Genius can only breathe freely in an atmosphere of freedom. J. B. PRIESTLEY The town seems to have no atmosphere of its own. N. SHUTE There was an atmosphere of cheerful activity in the garage that warmed his heart. J. D. WATSON These ideas . . did a great deal to liven up the atmosphere of the lab. M. FONTEYN Their [ballets'] special quality lies in their greater dependence on mood and atmosphere than on choreographic exactitude.

B *v.t.* Surround (as) with an atmosphere (*lit.* & *fig.*). Usu. in *pass.* M19.

atmospheric /atməs'fɛrɪk/ *a.* & *n.* L18. [f. prec. + -IC.] **A** *adj.* **1** Of or pertaining to the atmosphere; existing or taking place in the atmosphere; operated or produced by the action of the atmosphere. L18. **2** Possessing or evoking a particular or characteristic tone, mood, or set of associations. E20.

1 **atmospheric engine** a steam engine in which the piston is forced down by atmospheric pressure after the condensation of the steam which has raised it. **atmospheric pressure** *spec.* = ATMOSPHERE *n.* 3. **atmospheric railway**: in which motive power is provided by atmospheric pressure acting against a partial vacuum produced in a pipe laid between the rails.

B *n.* **1** In *pl.* Evocative qualities or effects, esp. in a photograph. L19. **2** In *pl.* & (*rare*) *sing.* Electrical disturbances in the atmosphere; interference with telecommunications so caused. E20.

atmospherical *a.* = ATMOSPHERIC *a.* M17. **atmospherically** *adv.* L19.

atole /ə'təʊli/ *n.* Chiefly *US.* M17. [Amer. Sp. f. Nahuatl *atolli*.] Gruel or porridge made of maize or other meal.

atoll /'atɒl, ə'tɒl/ *n.* Orig. †**atollon.** E17. [Maldivian *atoḷu*.] A coral island consisting of a ring-shaped reef enclosing a lagoon.

atom /'atəm/ *n.* & *a.* LME. [(O)Fr. *atome* f. L *atomus* smallest particle, f. Gk *atomos* use as n. of adj. 'indivisible', f. as A-[10] + *temnein* to cut. Sense 1 f. med.L: cf. eccl.Gk *atomos* moment (*1 Cor.* 15:52). Cf. ATOMY *n.*[2]] **A** *n.* †**1** The smallest medieval unit of time, equal to 15/94 second. LME–M16. **2** *Hist.* A hypothetical ultimate particle of matter, so small as to be incapable of further division. L15. **3** A speck of dust; a mote in a sunbeam. *arch.* E17. **4** A very small portion of anything; a particle, a jot. M17. **5** Anything relatively very small. *arch.* M17. **6** A particle of a chemical element which is the unit in which the elements combine and which cannot be divided into further particles all having the properties of that element now known to consist of a positively charged nucleus, containing most of the mass, surrounded by a number of electrons. E19. b A corresponding particle of a compound or radical. Now *rare* or *obs.* M19. 7 An irreducible constituent unit of something. L19.

2 SWIFT That the universe was formed by a fortuitous concourse of atoms. 3 BYRON Moted rays of light Peopled with dusty atoms. 4 HOBBES Casting atomes of Scripture, as dust before mens eyes. E. F. BENSON They haven't succeeded one atom. F. KING She was a sweet girl, there wasn't an atom of badness or meanness in her. 5 G. HERBERT The smallest ant or atome knows thy power. 6 **split the atom** *colloq.* bring about nuclear fission. 7 A. S. EDDINGTON The quantum . . is apparently an atom of action. **logical atom** *Philos.* a propositional element which cannot be analysed into simpler elements.

Comb.: **atom-smasher** *colloq.* a particle accelerator. **B** *attrib.* or as *adj.* = ATOMIC 1b. M20. *atom bomb* etc.

atomic /ə'tɒmɪk/ *a.* L17. [mod.L *atomicus*, f. *atomus*: see prec., -IC.] 1 Of or pertaining to atoms; about or concerned with atoms. L17. b *spec.* Of, pertaining to, or connected with atoms as a source of power or destructive force; nuclear; employing or driven by nuclear energy; possessing or employing nuclear weapons. E20. 2 Adhering to the doctrine of the atomism of matter. L17. 3 Like atoms in size; minute. E19. 4 Simple, elemental; *esp.* in *Philos.*, (of a proposition etc.) unanalysable, ultimate. L19. 5 Existing in the form of separate atoms. Opp. *molecular.* E20.

1 *Discovery* The quantum of action . . forms the foundation of atomic physics. N. CALDER All geology and all life are a continual reordering of the same atomic ingredients. b H. G. WELLS Destined to see atomic energy dominating every other source of power. *Daily Telegraph* How atomic power might be used to maintain the future peace. A. BOYD The arrival of the 'atomic age'. O. BRADLEY The way to win an atomic war is to make sure it never starts. A. KOESTLER The only deterrent against atomic aggression is an atomic stockpile. *Times* The Soviet atomic icebreaker Lenin left Leningrad to-day on her maiden voyage. 3 H. EDIB Flies, with atomic specks of brilliant red and green on their wings. 4 D. R. HOFSTADTER The dissection can go only so far, and then we hit the 'atomic' nature of reasoning processes.

Special collocations: **atomic bomb**: deriving its destructiveness from the release of nuclear energy. **atomic clock** an instrument which uses atomic vibrations as a standard of time. **atomic heat** the heat capacity of one gram-atom of an element. **atomic mass** = *relative atomic mass* s.v. RELATIVE *a.*; *atomic mass unit*, a unit of relative atomic mass equal to 1/12 the mass of an atom of the isotope carbon-12. **atomic number** the number of protons present in the nucleus of an atom of an element. **atomic particle** a subatomic particle. **atomic philosophy** = ATOMISM 1. **atomic pile** = PILE *n.*[4] 6. **atomic theory** (*a*) = ATOMISM 1; (*b*) the theory that chemical elements consist of atoms of definite relative weight combining with those of other elements in fixed proportions. **atomic volume** the volume occupied by one gram-atom of an element under standard conditions. **atomic weight** = *relative atomic mass* s.v. RELATIVE *a.*

atomical *a.* (now *rare*) M17. **atomically** *adv.* L17.

atomicity /atə'mɪsɪti/ *n.* M19. [f. prec. + -ITY.] 1 *Chem.* Orig., combining power, valency. Now, the number of atoms in a molecule of an element. M19. 2 The property of existing as atoms or analogous elemental units; *Philos.* the ability to be analysed into atomic propositions. E20.

atomise *v.* var. of ATOMIZE.

atomism /'atəmɪz(ə)m/ *n.* L17. [f. ATOM + -ISM.] 1 The theory that all matter consists of minute indivisible particles or atoms. L17. 2 Any doctrine or theory which propounds or implies the existence of irreducible constituent units. Also = ATOMICITY 2. M19.

2 S. BARING-GOULD Liberal atomism, the doctrine that all social and political economy must start from the individual. B. RUSSELL The philosophy which I wish to advocate may be called logical atomism or absolute pluralism, because while maintaining that there are many things, it denies that there is a whole composed of those things. **logical atomism** the theory that all propositions can be analysed into logical atoms. **psychological atomism** the theory that mental states are made up of elementary units.

atomist /'atəmɪst/ *n.* E17. [f. as prec. + -IST.] An exponent or adherent of the atomism of matter, or of any atomistic theory.

J. HEALEY Of the Atomists, some confound all, making bodies of coherent remaynders. JOHN PHILLIPS Symbols of chemical constitution, on which there is still some want of agreement among atomists. P. F. STRAWSON Atomists and Positivists alike accepted the skeleton language of the new mathematical logic.

atomistic /atə'mɪstɪk/ *a.* L17. [f. prec. + -IC.] 1 Of, pertaining to, or of the nature of atomism, in any field. L17. 2 Consisting of or of the nature of atoms or analogous elemental units. L19.

1 COLERIDGE It is the object of the mechanical atomistic philosophy to confound synthesis with synartesis. B. RUSSELL When I say that my logic is atomistic, I mean that I share the common-sense belief that there are many separate things. R. S. WOODWORTH An atomistic psychology attempts to explain any total activity by analysing it into its elements.

atomistical *a.* (*rare*) E18. **atomistically** *adv.* L19.

atomize /'atəmʌɪz/ *v.* Also **-ise.** L17. [f. ATOM + -IZE.] †1 *v.i.* Hold the doctrine of the atomism of matter. *rare.* Only in L17. 2 *v.t.* a Reduce to atoms or (*rare*) to an atom. Chiefly *fig.*, divide into small units, fragment, disunite. M19. b Convert (a liquid or solid) into fine particles or spray. M19. 3 *v.t.* Damage or destroy with nuclear weapons. *colloq.* M20.

2a J. W. N. SULLIVAN Matter, electricity, energy, they have all been atomized. I. DEUTSCHER The atomized mass of Moslem labourers did not lend itself easily to propaganda or organization. b D. BAGLEY The rain had slackened and there were no large drops, just an atomized mist. 3 A. WILSON Atomized into eternity.

atomi'zation *n.* M19. **atomizer** *n.* a device for atomizing a liquid or solid M19.

atomy /'atəmi/ *n.*[1] *arch.* L16. [f. ANATOMY by metanalysis as AN *a.* (*indef. article*) + *atomy.*] A skeleton; an emaciated body.

atomy /'atəmi/ *n.*[2] *arch.* L16. [Prob. L *atomi* pl. of *atomus* ATOM, but assoc. w. prec.] 1 An atom, a mote. L16. 2 A tiny being, a pygmy. L16.

atonal /eɪ'təʊn(ə)l, ə-/ *a.* E20. [f. A-[10] + TONAL *a.*] *Mus.* Not written in any particular key or mode.

atonalism *n.* the practice of writing atonal music E20. **atonalist** *n.* E20. **ato'nality** *n.* atonal style of composition E20. **atonally** *adv.* M20.

atone /ə'təʊn/ *v.* & *n.* ME. [Isolated early use f. *at one* (s.v. ONE *a.* etc.); later (M16) back-form. f. next.] A *v.* †1 *v.i.* Become reconciled; come into unity or concord. ME–E17. †2 *v.t.* Compose, appease, (differences, quarrels); reconcile, bring into unity or concord, (contending persons). M16–M19. †3 *v.t.* & *i.* Join in one; harmonize. E17–M19. †4 *v.t.* Conciliate, propitiate, appease, (an offended person). E17–E19. 5 *v.i.* Make propitiation or amends (*for* an offence, †*an* offender). M17. 6 *v.t.* Expiate, make amends for (an offence, †*an* offender). *arch.* M17.

1 SHAKES. *A.Y.L.* Then is there mirth in heaven, When earthly things made even Atone together. 2 MILTON The king and parliament will soon be attoned. N. ROWE Could I attone The fatal Breach 'twixt thee and Tamerlane. 3 G. CHAPMAN High built with pines, that heaven and earth attone. LD HOUGHTON Welcome such thoughts! They well atone With this more serious mood. 4 POPE So heaven atoned, shall dying Greece restore. 5 DRYDEN If sheep or oxen could atone for men. E. WAUGH The stewards . . sought to atone for ten days' neglect with a multitude of un-needed services. W. S. CHURCHILL No administrative achievements, . . no magnitude of personality, could atone to his former friends for his desertion. 6 R. B. SHERIDAN I will endeavour to atone the . . errors. LYTTON They endeavoured to atone the loss by the pursuit of Artabazus.

†**B** *n.* Atonement. L16–M19.

atoner *n.* E18.

atonement /ə'təʊnm(ə)nt/ *n.* E16. [f. *at one* (see ONE *a.* etc.) + -MENT, after med.L *adunamentum*, f. *adunare* unite, and earlier ONEMENT.] †1 Unity of feeling; harmony, concord, agreement. E16–E17. †2a Restoration of friendly relations between persons, reconciliation. E16–L17. b *Theol.* Reconciliation between God and man. E16. †3 Settlement *of* (differences, strife, etc.). Only in E17. 4 Expiation; reparation for wrong or injury; amends; *Theol.* propitiation of God by expiation of sin. E17.

1 SIR T. MORE Having more regarde to their olde variaunce then their new attonement. 2a SHAKES. *Rich. III* He desires to make atonement Between the Duke of Gloucester and your brothers. P. MASSINGER A perfect sign of your atonement with me. 4 W. BLACKSTONE No suitable atonement can be made for the loss of life, or limb. G. SAINTSBURY The admirable *Dialogues of the Dead* which make atonement in prose for the . . thing written . . to vex Dryden. N. MOSLEY It is part of Christian mythology . . that without Christ's execution there would be no atonement for the sins of the world. **Day of Atonement** the most solemn religious fast of the Jewish year, celebrated on the tenth day of Tishri.

at-oneness /at'wʌnnɪs/ *n.* L19. [f. *at one* (s.v. ONE *a.* etc.) + -NESS.] The state of being at one (*with*), harmonious relationship.

atonic /ə'tɒnɪk/ *n.* & *a.* M18. [f. A-[10] + TONIC *a.*; sense B.1 f. ATONY + -IC.] A *n.* *Pros.* (esp. *Gk*). An unaccented word, a proclitic. M18. B *adj.* 1 *Med.* Lacking tone; characterized by atony. L18. 2 *Pros.* Unaccented; not bearing the main stress. L19.

atony /'at(ə)ni/ *n.* L17. [(O)Fr. *atonie* or late L *atonia* debility f. Gk, f. *atonos* lacking tone, f. as A-[10] + *tonos* TONE *n.*: see -Y[3].] Lack of tone of muscle or other body tissue.

atop /ə'tɒp/ *adv.* & *prep.* M17. [f. A *prep.*[1] 1 + TOP *n.*[1]] A *adv.* On the top (*of*), above. M17. B *prep.* On the top of. M17.

atopy /'atəpi/ *n.* E20. [Gk *atopia* unusualness f. *atopos* unusual, f. A-[10] + *topos* place: see -Y[3].] *Med.* An allergic reaction which is associated with a hereditary predisposition to allergy in some form.

a'topic *a.* pertaining to or of the nature of atopy E20.

-ator /eɪtə/ *suff.* [f. or after (Fr. *-ateur*, †*-atour*, f.) L *-ator* suff., f. pa. ppl stems in *-at-*: see -OR.] Forming agent-ns., as *creator, denominator, dictator, mediator, spectator, translator*, etc.; also (esp. f. E19) in names of instruments, implements, and machines, as *detonator, escalator, generator, percolator, refrigerator, ventilator*, etc.

à tort et à travers /a tɔːr e a travɛːr/ *adv. phr.* M18. [Fr. = wrongly and across.] At random, haphazardly.

atour /ə'təʊə/ *prep.* & *adv.* *Sc.* & *north.* LME. [App. f. AT *prep.* + OVER *prep, adv.*] A *prep.* Over; beyond; in addition to. LME. B *adv.* Over and above, moreover, in addition. LME.

à toute outrance *adv. phr.* see À OUTRANCE.

atrabilarious /atrəbɪ'lɛːrɪəs/ *a.* L17. [f. med.L *atrabilarius* (f. as next + -ARY[1]) + -OUS.] Of or pertaining to choler adust; atrabilious.

atrabilarian *a.* (now *rare*) = ATRABILARIOUS L17. †**atrabilary** *a.* = ATRABILARIOUS L17–E18.

atrabilious /atrə'bɪlɪəs/ *a.* M17. [f. L *atra bilis* choler adust, black bile, tr. Gk *melankholia* MELANCHOLY *n.*: see -IOUS.] Orig., affected by choler adust, one of the four supposed cardinal humours of the body. Now only *gen.*: melancholy, hypochondriac; acrimonious, splenetic.

R. GRAVES He broke school bounds, he dared defy The Master's atrabilious eye. T. H. WHITE There were atrabilious hawk-masters . . quarrelling with their assistants.

atrabiliar *a.* (*rare*) = ATRABILIOUS M19. **atrabiliary** *a.* (now *rare* or *obs.*) = ATRABILARIOUS E18. **atrabiliousness** *n.* L19.

atrament /'atrəm(ə)nt/ *n.* *arch.* LME. [L *atramentum*, f. *ater* black: see -MENT.] Blacking; ink; any similar black substance.

atra'mental, -tous *adjs.* of or pertaining to ink, inky, black as ink M17.

atraumatic /eɪtrɔː'matɪk, a-; -traʊ-/ *a.* M20. [f. A-[10] + TRAUMATIC.] *Med.* Of surgical techniques or instruments: causing minimal injury to the tissues.

atraumatically *adv.* M20.

atremble /ə'trɛmb(ə)l/ *adv.* & *pred. a.* M19. [f. A-[2] + TREMBLE *n.* or *v.*] Trembling.

atresia /əˈtriːʃə, -zjə/ *n.* E19. [f. A-[10] + Gk *trēsis* perforation + -IA[1].] *Med.* 1 Absence or occlusion, esp. congenital, of a channel or opening of the body. E19. 2 Degeneration of non-ovulating ovarian follicles during the menstrual cycle. E20.

atresic /əˈtriːsɪk, -zɪk/ *a.* = ATRETIC L19. **atretic** /əˈtrɛtɪk/ *a.* pertaining to or displaying atresia E20.

atria *n.pl.* see ATRIUM.

atrip /əˈtrɪp/ *adv.* & *pred. a.* E17. [f. A *prep.*[1] 6 + TRIP *n.*[1]] *Naut.* 1 Of yards: swayed up, ready to have the stops cut for crossing. Of sails: hoisted from the cap, sheeted home, and ready for trimming. E17. 2 Of an anchor: just raised perpendicularly from the ground in weighing. M17.

atrium /ˈeɪtrɪəm/ *n.* Pl. **-ia** /-ɪə/, **-iums**. L16. [L.] 1 *Archit.* A central court, orig. that of an ancient-Roman house; a covered court or portico; (a building with) a large light-well; a central hall or glassed-in court in a building. L16. 2 *Anat.* & *Zool.* Any of various chambers into which one or more passages open; *spec.* (*a*) either of the two upper chambers of the heart (in fish, a single chamber), into which the veins conduct blood (cf. AURICLE 1); (*b*) the tympanic chamber of the ear. L19.

atrial *a.* (*Anat.* & *Zool.*) of or pertaining to an atrium M19. **atrioven'tricular** *a.* (*Anat.*) of or pertaining to the atrial and ventricular chambers of the heart; *atrioventricular bundle*, a bundle of nerves leading from the right atrium to the ventricles and serving to maintain the heartbeat: L19.

atrocious /əˈtrəʊʃəs/ *a.* M17. [f. L *atroc-*, *atrox* fierce, cruel: see -IOUS.] 1 Excessively and wantonly savage or cruel; heinously wicked. M17. †2 Stern, fierce; extremely violent. Only in M18. 3 Very bad; execrable. *colloq.* L19.

1 T. PENNANT Here all atrocious criminals were excluded. P. H. GIBBS Your pity for the world's young manhood in that atrocious war. M. LOWRY Spots where diabolical plots must be hatched, atrocious murders planned. 2 J. THOMSON The fierce, atrocious frown of sinewed Mars. 3 B. BAINBRIDGE Her knowledge of German was poor and her accent atrocious. D. M. THOMAS The weather was atrocious, and for three days we couldn't set foot outside because of a snowstorm.

atrociously *adv.* M18. **atrociousness** *n.* (now *rare*) M18.

atrocity /əˈtrɒsɪti/ *n.* M16. [(O)Fr. *atrocité* or L *atrocitas*, f. as prec.: see -ITY.] 1 Horrible or heinous wickedness; wanton cruelty. M16. 2 Fierceness, sternness. *arch.* M17. 3 An act of wanton cruelty or extreme heinousness; an atrocious deed. L18. 4 A repellent act or thing. *colloq.* L19.

1 CLARENDON They desired justice might be done upon offenders, as the atrocity of their crimes deserved. 2 S. BARING-GOULD They besiege it with atrocity, striving to break in the doors. 3 F. FITZGERALD The extortion rackets, rape, pillage, and outright military atrocities.

à trois /a trwa/ *a.* & *adv. phr.* L19. [Fr.] Shared by, or in a group of, three people.

ménage à trois: see MÉNAGE 1.

atrophy /ˈatrəfi/ *n.* E17. [Fr. *atrophie* or late L *atrophia* f. Gk, = lack of food, f. A-[10]: see -TROPHY.] 1 *Med.* Orig., wasting away of the body from lack of nourishment; emaciation. Now, wasting away of an organ or tissue, through any cause. E17. 2 *fig.* Wasting away, enfeeblement. M17.

1 *red atrophy*: see RED *a.* *yellow atrophy*: see YELLOW *a.*

atrophic /əˈtrɒfɪk/ *a.* pertaining to, affected by, or characterized by atrophy M19.

atrophy /ˈatrəfi/ *v.* L16. [Fr. *atrophier* f. as prec., or f. the n.] 1 *v.t.* Affect with atrophy. Chiefly in *atrophied* ppl a. L16. 2 *v.i.* Undergo atrophy, waste away. M19.

1 J. S. MILL Organs are strengthened by exercise and atrophied by disuse. R. FRY The pressure of commercial life has crushed and atrophied that creative impulse completely. B. PYM She was too old to learn anything new and . . her brain had become atrophied. 2 D. LIVINGSTONE The horns, mere stumps not a foot long, must have atrophied. K. VONNEGUT Foresight and the ability to reason have simply atrophied from long neglect. H. KISSINGER Causing the North Vietnamese forces in the South to atrophy owing to normal attrition.

†**atrophiated** *ppl a.* atrophied M17–M19.

atropine /ˈatrəpiːn, -ɪn/ *n.* Also **-in** /-ɪn/. M19. [f. mod.L *Atropa* (*belladonna*) deadly nightshade, fem. f. Gk *Atropos* 'Inflexible', one of the Fates, + -INE[5].] *Chem.* & *Pharm.* A poisonous alkaloid, $C_{17}H_{23}NO_3$, found in deadly nightshade, thorn-apple, and other plants, and used medicinally esp. to relax muscles and to inhibit secretion.

†**atropia** *n.* = ATROPINE: only in 19. **,atropini'zation** *n.* treatment or poisoning with atropine L19. **atropinized** *a.* treated or poisoned with atropine L19. **atropism** *n.* atropine poisoning L19.

atropous /ˈatrəpəs/ *a.* M19. [f. Gk *atropos* not turned f. A-[10] + *tropos* a turn, + -OUS.] *Bot.* Of an ovule: not inverted on its funicle; orthotropous.

Atsina /atˈsiːnə/ *n.* & *a.* Pl. of n. same, **-s**. L19. [Blackfoot, lit. 'good people'.] A member of, of or pertaining to, an Arapaho people of Montana and Saskatchewan; (of) the Arapaho dialect of this people. Also called *Gros Ventre*.

atta /ˈatə/ *n.* M19. [Hind. *āṭā*, Panjabi *āṭṭā*.] In the Indian subcontinent: wheat flour or meal.

attaboy /ˈatəbɔɪ/ *int. slang* (chiefly *N. Amer.*). E20. [Prob. repr. a pronunc. of *that's the boy!*] Expr. encouragement or admiration.

attach /əˈtatʃ/ *v.* & *n.* ME. [OFr. *atachier* (mod. *attacher*) = It. *attaccare*, Sp. *atacar*, in sense A.II, III, f. OFr. *estachier* fasten, fix = Prov., Sp. *estacar* (see A-[7]): ult. f. a Gmc base (see STAKE *n.*[1]).] A *v.* I *v.t.* 1 *Law.* Place or take (a person, goods) under the control of a court; seize or arrest by authority. ME. †2 Indict, accuse. LME–M17. †3 Seize, grasp, take hold of. M16–L17. †4 Attack. E–M17.

1 SHAKES. *Hen. VIII* For France . . hath attach'd Our merchants goods at Bordeaux. SIR W. SCOTT I attach thee of the crime of which thou hast but now made thy boast. C. M. YONGE The Earl Marshal attached Gloucester for high treason. 2 T. NASHE They shall not easily be attached of any notable absurditie. 3 SHAKES. *Temp.* Old lord, I cannot blame thee, Who am myself attach'd with weariness. J. GUILLIM The Lion . . lesse able to attach and rend his Prey.

II *v.t.* Usu. in *pass.* or *refl.* 5 Fasten or join (a thing *to* another, *to* a point). LME. 6 Join or connect functionally *to* (esp. a person *to* a group etc.); join on *to* another person as companion etc. Freq. *refl.* L17. b Allocate or join for service *to* a particular (orig. military) unit etc. E19. 7 Join in sympathy or affection *to*; bind in friendship, make devoted. Now usu. in *pass.* M18. 8 Fix *to* something or someone as a property, description, or other adjunct. E19. 9 Attribute (importance, a meaning, etc.) *to*. M19.

5 G. FENNELL The young of the oyster . . attach themselves immediately to the first clean, hard substance they meet with. J. K. JEROME Attached to the boat-hook was a line, which trailed behind them. W. TREVOR Clumps of mistletoe were attached by drawing-pin to the centre of the door-frames. 6 SIR W. SCOTT That I should seriously consider to which department of the law I was to attach myself. J. E. TENNENT A cemetery . . attached to the city. P. G. WODEHOUSE He had never speculated on any possible family that might be attached to her. DAY LEWIS What shall I do this afternoon?—attach myself, probably, to Keyes and follow him around in a daze of pure satisfaction. b A. C. CLARKE Since I've been attached to the Pacific branch of the bureau I've more or less adopted Australia as a second home. C. RYAN Ringsdorf's unit was told to report immediately to a command post. . . There, a major attached them to a company of the 21st *Panzer* Grenadier Regiment. 7 J. AUSTEN So totally unamiable, so absolutely incapable of attaching a sensible man. D. L. SAYERS She has told us herself, with great candour, how she became deeply attached to Philip Boyes. J. JOHNSTON We'll have to decide what we're going to sell and what we're going to keep. . . One becomes so attached to things. H. SEGAL Under the influence of a French governess to whom she was very attached. 8 J. BRYCE Legends which attached themselves to the name of Charles the Emperor. B. TAYLOR To this treasure a curse is attached. 9 H. KISSINGER The President . . attached the utmost importance to the avoidance of war. *attach credence to*: see CREDENCE 1.

III *v.i.* 10 Be attributable or appertain *to*; fall *upon* as an obligation etc. L18. 11 Take legal effect; come into legal operation. *arch.* E19.

10 A. W. KINGLAKE Blame attaches upon Lord Aberdeen's Cabinet for yielding. H. BELLOC There is a flavour of Fame certain to attach to his achievement. N. MITFORD She was clever enough to avoid the ridicule which often attaches to such a situation. 11 SOUTHEY Wherever they should make their settlement, there the laws of England attached. J. WILLIAMS The wife's right to dower accordingly attached.

†**B** *n.* 1 An attack (of disease etc.). LME–L17. 2 An act of legal seizure; arrest. E16–M17. 3 A thing attached; an attachment. L16–M18.

attachable *a.* liable to be attached; able to be attached (*to*): L16. **attacher** *n.* a person who attaches; a means of attaching: LME.

attaché /əˈtaʃeɪ/ *n.* E19. [Fr., pa. pple of *attacher* ATTACH *v.*] A junior official attached to the staff of an ambassador etc.; a representative of his or her government in a foreign country.

cultural attaché: see CULTURAL 2. *military attaché*: see MILITARY *a.*

Comb.: **attaché case** a small rectangular case for carrying documents etc.

attachéship *n.* M19.

attachment /əˈtatʃm(ə)nt/ *n.* LME. [(O)Fr. *attachement* f. *atachier* ATTACH *v.*: see -MENT.] 1 Apprehension or arrest, esp. for contempt of court; a writ authorizing this. LME. 2 Legal seizure of property. L16. †3 Confinement. *rare* (Shakes.). Only in E17. 4 Affection, devotion; a sympathetic, friendly, or romantic connection. E18. 5 Something attached, or intended to be attached; an adjunct. L18. 6 The action of fastening, joining, affixing, or attributing; the condition of being fastened etc. E19. 7 A means of attaching; a fastening, a bond. E19.

1 T. SHADWELL I'll follow and apprehend him, and his attachment will secure me. J. GALSWORTHY If you wish to give me your information, you can; otherwise I'm afraid we shall have to get an attachment for contempt. 2 **attachment of earnings** the payment of debts by direct deduction from the debtor's earnings, under a court order. 3 *fig.*: SHAKES. *Tr. & Cr.* Sleep kill those pretty eyes, And give as soft attachment to thy senses As infants' empty of all thought! 4 SIR W. SCOTT The lover's eye discovered the object of his attachment. J. GALSWORTHY At the most a flirtation, ending, as all such attachments should, at the proper time. H. A. L. FISHER A fierce attachment to the faith of their ancestors. E. LONGFORD The Duke's romantic attachment to the lovely Marianne Patterson was no fabrication. 5 D. NOBBS There was a hand-held shower for washing the back, and he utilized this attachment to the full. 6 R. OWEN The rest of the cranium is modified . . for the attachment of muscles to work the jaw. C. CAUDWELL Their desertion of their class and their attachment to another. F. HOYLE The attachment of mystic significance to symbols, words, and objects is still widespread today. 7 J. E. TENNENT The falling timber . . dragging those behind to which it is harnessed by its living attachments.

attack /əˈtak/ *n.* M17. [f. the vb or Fr. *attaque* f. It. *attacco*.] 1 An act of attacking with violence or weapons; an attempt to defeat, kill, or injure; offensive action. M17. 2 An assault with hostile words or other actions. M18. 3 *Chess.* A move or series of moves played with the object of checkmating, gaining a positional advantage, or capturing a man. Also, an opening or opening variation played by White. M18. 4 *Sports & Games.* An attempt to gain a scoring or other significant advantage; play, moves, or tactics aimed at gaining such an advantage; (the function of) those members of a team whose principal responsibility is to mount attacks; *Cricket* bowling or the bowlers (as opp. to batting or the batsmen); *Lacrosse* any of three players in a team whose positions are nearest the opponents' goal. L18. 5 A (sudden) bout of an illness, a mental condition, etc. E19. 6 The beginning of an arduous task; a determined attempt upon something. E19. 7 A destructive action by a physical agency; corrosion, eating away, dissolution. M19. 8 Chiefly *Mus.* The action or manner of beginning a piece, passage, etc.; brilliance or decisiveness of style. L19.

1 MILTON The dire attack Of fighting Seraphim. LD MACAULAY A night attack might be attended with success. J. G. FARRELL Not a single day had gone by without news of a raid or shooting or terrorist attack

somewhere in Ireland. 2 H. WILSON The attacks on me in the Press and in politics. 5 L. M. MONTGOMERY Anne was the victim of an overwhelming attack of stage fright. V. BRITTAIN I had been really ill with a sharp attack of influenza. *heart attack*: see HEART *n.* VASOVAGAL *attack*. 6 A. KOESTLER Kepler's first attack on the problem is described. **angle of attack**: between the wing chord of an aircraft in flight and the direction of the airflow. 8 A. L. HASKELL Riabouchinska is not a purely classical dancer, lacking the necessary hardness and attack. H. C. SCHONBERG His fortissimo attack had an almost savage quality.

attack /əˈtak/ *v.* E17. [Fr. *attaquer* f. It. *attaccare* join (battle), ATTACH *v.*] **I** *v.t.* **1** Act against with violence or force of arms; seek to kill or injure. E17. **2** Of disease: begin to affect; seize upon, afflict. E17. **3** Act against with hostile words or actions. M17. **4** *Chess.* Attempt to gain a positional advantage in relation to (a piece or square); threaten to give checkmate to or capture (a man). M18. **5** *Sports & Games.* Attempt to gain a scoring or other significant advantage over (an opponent); attempt to score points, goals, etc., against (an opponent) or in (a particular goal etc.). L18. **6** Of a physical agent: act harmfully upon, begin to destroy; corrode, dissolve. L18. **7** Begin vigorous work on (a task etc.); *Mus.* begin (a piece, passage, etc.), esp. decisively or confidently. E19.

1 W. S. CHURCHILL 673 horsemen, led by Lord Cardigan, rode up the valley under heavy fire . . to attack the Russian batteries. D. MORRIS Killers [whales] prefer to attack aquatic mammals such as dolphins, porpoises, seals, [etc.]. E. CALDWELL Several teen-age girls and young women had been attacked by a nighttime prowler. *fig.*: R. G. COLLINGWOOD I was attacked by a strange succession of emotions. 2 F. A. KEMBLE Rheumatism . . attacks indiscriminately the young and old. 3 MILTON Under colour of a pretended partie . . the Parliament is attaqued. G. GREENE There were speakers out on the Common: the I.L.P. and the Communist Party, . . a man attacking Christianity. 6 B. STEWART Hydrofluoric acid . . attacks the glass where the wax has been scratched off. 7 SHELLEY Mrs. Shelley is attacking *Latin* with considerable resolution. H. C. SCHONBERG Notes of scales could not have been more evenly matched . . ; chords could not be attacked more precisely.

II *v.i.* **8** Make or begin an attack; take the offensive; *Chess* attempt to checkmate, to gain a positional advantage, or to capture an opposing man; *Sports & Games* attempt to gain a scoring or other significant advantage, be in possession of the ball, puck, etc. E17.

8 DONNE Ere sicknesses attack, yong death is best. A. J. P. TAYLOR On 8 August the British attacked in front of Amiens, in order to protect the railway junction there. *Times* Kent attacked with fire and fury and it seemed impossible that they should fail to score.

attackable *a.* E19. **attacker** *n.* a person who attacks; an assailant; an attacking player: M17.

attain /əˈteɪn/ *v.* & *n.* ME. [AN *attain-*, *attein-*, OFr. *ataign-*, *ateign-*, stem of *ataindre*, *ateindre* (mod. *atteindre*), f. L *attingere* touch on, reach, f. *ad* AT- + *tangere* to touch.] **A** *v.* (See also ATTAINT *pa. pple* & *ppl a.*) **I** *v.t.* †**1** Convict, condemn; bring to justice. Only in ME. **2** Accomplish, achieve (an end or purpose); reach, gain (a state, rank, or quality). ME. **3** Reach or arrive at by motion in space or time, or by the passage of time. LME. †**4** Encroach on. Only in LME. †**5** Overtake, come up with, catch. LME–E17. **6** Come into the possession of, acquire, obtain, (now usu. something immaterial, passing into sense 2). LME. †**7** Get to know, find out. LME–M17. †**8** Touch, hit, strike. L15–L16.

2 J. WESLEY Let me the Life Divine attain. A. J. TOYNBEE Buenos Aires is a great modern city that has attained its present stature gradually. D. JACOBSON I never came close to attaining any of my goals. R. ADAMS She was a woman . . who had already attained a position of authority and trust. 3 SOUTHEY Now had they almost attain'd The palace portal. S. BELLOW I might be concerned with age merely because I might never attain any great age. 6 LD BERNERS To atteyne thereby the towne of Berwike. J. CONRAD At that moment I attained the knowledge of who it was I had before me. H. J. LASKI A new class of men attained control of the nation's economic power. 7 CAXTON Secretes that humayne nature may not attayne, knowe, ne understonde. 8 G. CHAPMAN Yet him beneath the eare The sonne of Telamon attain'd.

II *v.i.* Usu. with *to*, (arch.) *unto*. **9** Succeed in coming or get *to* a state, condition, goal, etc. LME. **10** Succeed in coming or get *to* a point in space; live on *to* a time or age. LME. †**11** Extend, reach; amount; matter. LME–M16. †**12** Foll. by *to*, *unto*: get to know, find out. M16–E17.

9 W. COWPER To see your trees attain to the dignity of timber. H. J. LASKI He had attained to the highest office under Anne at an exceptionally early age. J. HILTON After ten years in various parts of Asia he had attained to a somewhat fastidious valuation of places and happenings. 10 AV *Acts* 27:12 If by any meanes they might attaine to Phenice. SIR W. SCOTT Nor nearer might the dogs attain. OED He has attained to years of discretion.

B *n.* Attainment; a thing attained. *rare.* M16.

attainaˈbility *n.* attainableness E19. **attainable** *a.* able to be attained M17. **attainableness** *n.* M17.

attainder /əˈteɪndə/ *n.* LME. [AN *attainder*, *atteinder*, use as n. of inf. *atteinder*, (O)Fr. *atteindre* ATTAIN *v.*: see -ER[4].] **1** *Hist.* The action or process of attainting; *spec.* the legal consequences of a sentence of death or outlawry, i.e. forfeiture of estate, deprivation of rank or title, and loss of civil rights generally. LME. †**2** *fig.* Condemnation; dishonour; slander. L16–M18.

1 **act** or **bill of attainder**: one introduced in Parliament for attainting a person without trial. 2 SHAKES. *Rich. II* Have mine honour soil'd With the attainder of his slanderous lips. S. JOHNSON A resumption of ancestral claims, and a kind of restoration to blood after the attainder of a trade.

attainment /əˈteɪnm(ə)nt/ *n.* M16. [f. ATTAIN *v.* + -MENT.] **1** The action or process of attaining, reaching, or gaining. M16. **2** Something which is attained; an achievement, an accomplishment. M17.

2 T. F. DIBDIN A prelate and poet of very distinguished attainments.

attaint /əˈteɪnt/ *n.* ME. [OFr. *atainte*, *ateinte*, use as n. of fem. pa. pple of *ataindre*, *ateindre* ATTAIN *v.*] †**1** Exhaustion, fatigue. (Cf. ATTAINT *pa. pple* & *ppl a.* 3.) *rare.* ME–L16. **2** The act of touching or hitting, esp. in jousting. Cf. earlier TAINT *n.* 1. *arch.* E16. †**3** A contusion or wound on the leg of a horse, *esp.* one caused by overreaching. E16–M18. **4** *Law* (now *Hist.*). The process of convicting a jury for having given a false verdict, and reversing the verdict. E16. **5** †**a** (A temptation to) a dishonourable act. Only in M16. **b** Imputation or touch of dishonour; stain. L16. †**6** = ATTAINDER *n.* 1. Only in 17.

1 SHAKES. *Hen. V* He . . freshly looks, and over-bears attaint With cheerful semblance and sweet majesty. 5b D. G. ROSSETTI Among the faults . . Are two so grave that some attaint is brought Unto the greatness of his soul thereby.

†**attaint** *pa. pple* & *ppl a.* ME. [OFr. *ataint*, *ateint* pa. pple of *ataindre*, *ateindre* ATTAIN *v.*: later infl. by TAINT *v.*] **1** Convicted, attainted. ME–M18. **2** Affected with sickness, passion, etc.; infected. ME–E16. **3** Exhausted, overcome. LME–E16.

attaint /əˈteɪnt/ *v.t.* ME. [f. prec.: infl. by TAINT *v.*] †**1** Touch, reach, strike; accomplish, get at. ME–M16. †**2** Convict, prove guilty. LME–M18. **3** Subject to attainder. LME. **4** Accuse *of* crime, dishonour, etc. *arch.* E16. **5** Affect or infect with disease, contagion, corruption, etc.; sully, taint. E16.

3 HOBBES To be attainted is, that his Blood be held in Law, as stained and corrupted. H. P. BROUGHAM On Edward IV's victory, they unanimously attainted Henry IV. 4 W. D. HOWELLS Who are you to attaint me of unworthy motives? 5 J. SKELTON They be so attaynted With coveytous and ambycyon. SPENSER Lest she with blame her honour should attaint. DRYDEN The same shivering sweat his lord attaints. DE QUINCEY Even to have kicked an outsider might have been held to attaint the foot.

attaintment *n.* (*rare*) conviction, attainder M16. †**attainture** *n.* conviction; attainder; imputation of dishonour, stain: M16–M17.

†**attame** *v.t.* ME. [OFr. *atamer* f. L *attaminare* to attack: see AT-. Aphet. to TAME *v.*[2]] **1** Cut into, pierce. ME–L15. **b** Broach (a cask etc.). Only in LME. **2** Attack; meddle with. Only in LME. **3** Begin, undertake. Only in LME.

attap /ˈatap/ *n.* Also **atap**. E19. [Malay *atap* roof, thatch.] Palm fronds used in SE Asia for thatching, *esp.* those of the nipa palm; a thatch made of these. Freq. *attrib.*

attar /ˈatə/ *n.* Also (earlier) **otto** /ˈɒtəʊ/. M17. [Pers. *ʿitr*, Arab. *ʿitr*, colloq. Arab. *ʿaṭar* perfume, essence.] A fragrant volatile essence, *esp.* (more fully *attar of roses*) that obtained from rose-petals.

fig.: T. HARDY That buzz of pleasure which is the attar of applause.

Comb.: **attar-gul** /gʊl/ [Pers. *gul* roses] attar of roses.

atteal /ˈatiːl/ *n. Sc.* (esp. *Orkney*). L16. [Origin unkn.] A pochard, teal, or other small duck.

attemper /əˈtɛmpə/ *v.t. arch.* ME. [OFr. *atemprer* (mod. *attremper*) f. L *attemperare*, f. *ad* AT- + *temperare* TEMPER *v.*[1]] †**1** Regulate, control; order, arrange. ME–L18. **2** Qualify, modify, or moderate by admixture; temper. LME. **3** Make warmer or cooler. *obs.* exc. as passing into sense 2. LME. **4** Moderate, assuage (passion, harshness); soothe, appease, (a person). LME. †**5** Restrain. Usu. *refl.* LME–M16. **6** Make fit or suitable; accommodate, adapt. Foll. by *to*. LME. **7** Attune, bring into harmony. Foll. by *to*. L16.

1 T. CRANMER The Holy Ghost hath so ordered and attempered the Scriptures. 2 HOR. WALPOLE The most perfect taste in architecture, where grace softens dignity, and lightness attempers magnificence. 3 EVELYN Attemper the air with a fire of charcoal. 4 BACON How the . . Habit, To be Angry, may be attempred, and calmed. 6 E. B. PUSEY God often attempers Himself and His oracles to the condition of men. 7 POPE High airs, attemper'd to the vocal strings.

attemperament *n.* the bringing to a proper temper; mixture in due proportions: M17.

attemperate /əˈtɛmpəreɪt/ *v.t.* M16. [L *attemperat-* pa. ppl stem of *attemperare*: see prec., -ATE[3].] †**1** Moderate, regulate; accommodate or adapt *to*. M16–E18. **2** Modify in temperature as required. E17.

attempeˈration *n.* (now *rare* or *obs.*) E17. **attemperator** *n.* (*Brewing*) a system of water pipes for controlling the temperature of the fermenting wort M19. †**attemperature** *n.* attempered condition M17–M19.

attempt /əˈtɛm(p)t/ *n.* M16. [f. the vb.] **1** An act of making an effort to accomplish something uncertain or difficult; a trial, an endeavour (esp. when unsuccessful or incomplete). M16. **2** An attack, an assault; an effort to conquer or to kill (now usu. w. specification, as *an attempt on the summit of*, *on the life of*). L16. †**b** An endeavour to seduce; a temptation. E–M17. †**3** Something attempted, an aim. E17–L18. **4** Something produced in an endeavour or effort. L19.

1 SHAKES. *Macb.* They have awak'd, And 'tis not done. Th' attempt, and not the deed, Confounds us. J. M. BARRIE [He] flung away his life in a gallant attempt to save a servant who had fallen overboard. J. MARQUAND I tried to smile, but I made a rather poor attempt at it. L. DURRELL All attempts to meet her have failed so far. **make an attempt** try. 2 S. ROHMER I know that Fu-Manchu will make an attempt upon him. J. MASTERS Your adjutant has just told me about the attempt on the Karode bridge. *Encycl. Brit.* Seven successive attempts on the Northeast Ridge . . failed. b AV *Ecclus* 9:4 Vse not much the companie of a woman that is a singer, least thou be taken with her attempts. 3 W. PALEY His design and attempt was to sail . . immediately from Greece. 4 P. V. WHITE The trellis, its attempt at grapes mildewed by the humidity.

attemptless *a.* (*rare*) L16.

attempt /əˈtɛm(p)t/ *v.* LME. [OFr. *attempter*, Latinized form of *atenter* (mod. *attenter*) f. L *attemptare*, f. *ad* AT- + *temptare* TEMPT *v.*] **1** *v.t.* Try to accomplish (an action); make an effort, use one's endeavour, *to do* something. LME. **2** *v.t.* Attack, assault; try to take by force, overthrow, kill; try to take (a person's life). LME. †**b** Try to ravish or seduce. E17–M18. †**3** **a** *v.i.* Make an attack *against*, (*up*)*on*. LME–L17. **b** *v.t.* Venture (hostile action) (*up*)*on*. E17–M18. †**4** *v.t.* **a** Try with temptations; seek to win over;

tempt. LME–M19. b Try with afflictions. E16–M17. †5 *v.t.* Try to obtain or attract (friendship etc.). LME–M18. †6 *v.t.* Try to move by entreaty etc.; address urgently. M16–L17. 7 *v.t. gen.* Try to attain, venture upon, or engage with (the object of any action understood). M16.

1 SHAKES. *Oth.* If thou attempt it, it will cost thee dear. D. HUME To embolden her to attempt extorting the right of investitures. R. GRAVES Tiberius answered . . that his troops were not yet fit to attempt the task. W. TREVOR He attempted to smile back at him, but found it difficult. 2 DEFOE How I should escape from them, if they attempted me. J. MORSE Those rash hands which attempted his father's crown. J. LANGHORNE They attempted the Capitol by night. 3a W. CONGREVE Look that she attempt not on her life. b SHAKES. *Hen. VIII* If you cannot Bar his access to th' King, never attempt Anything on him. 4a SPENSER Why then will ye, fond dame, attempted bee Unto a stranger's love? MILTON God . . Hinder'd not Satan to attempt the minde of Man. b JER. TAYLOR O Pain, in vain do'st thou attempt me. 5 S. JOHNSON Shall . . No cries attempt the mercy of the skies? 6 MILTON I have attempted . . the lords With supplication prone and father's tears, To accept of ransom for my son. 7 J. RAY Courage and Hardiness to attempt the Seas. DAY LEWIS Though I was shamed . . into attempting *The Ambassadors* and the *Recherche*, I rejected these masterpieces. *Encycl. Brit.* This expedition . . was the eighth team in 30 years to attempt Everest.

attemptable *a.* (*rare*) M17. †**attemptate** *n.* an attempt; *esp.* a violent or criminal attempt, an attack, an assault: LME–E18. **attempter** *n.* a person who makes an attempt L15. **attemptible** *a.* (*rare*) attemptable E17.

attend /əˈtɛnd/ *v.* ME. [OFr. *atendre* (mod. *attendre* wait for) f. L *attendere*, f. *ad* AT- + *tendere* stretch. Aphet. to TEND *v.*[1]] I Give one's attention, efforts, or presence (to). 1 *v.t.* (*arch.*) & *i.* (w. *to*, (arch.) *unto*, or absol.). Pay attention, listen, (to); apply one's mind, give thought, (to). ME. 2 *v.i.* (w. *to*, †*to do*, (arch.) *unto*, †*upon*) & †*t.* Turn one's energies, apply oneself practically, (to). ME. 3 *v.t.* & *i.* w. *to*. Direct one's care to (a matter); look after, tend, guard, (something). LME. 4 *v.t.* & *i.* (w. *on*, (arch.) *upon*, or absol.). Wait on as a servant or attendant, or in answer to a summons; escort; follow or accompany for the purpose of rendering services. LME. 5 *v.t.* & *i.* (w. *at*, †*on*, or absol.). Be present at or go to (a meeting, function, etc., or its location); go regularly to ((a) school, (a) church, etc.). LME. 6 *v.t.* Apply oneself to the care of, tend, (a person, esp. an invalid); visit (a patient) professionally. L16. 7 *v.t.* & (*rare*) *i.* (w. *on*). Of things (usu. immaterial): accompany, occur with or as a result of; follow closely upon. E17. †8 *v.t.* Follow up or conjoin (a thing) *with* another. E17–L18. †9 *v.t.* & *i.* (w. *to*). Follow in order to counter or defeat. L17–E19.

1 SHAKES. *Cymb.* I do condemn mine ears that have So long attended thee. AV *Ps.* 17:1 O Lord, attend vnto my crie. POPE Thus Chryses pray'd: the favouring power attends. E. M. FORSTER Mrs. Honeychurch started and smiled. She had not been attending. J. W. KRUTCH Everything seems designed to be glanced at rather than attended to. 2 S. DANIEL First, he attends to build a strong conceipt Of his usurped powre. AV *Rom.* 13:6 They are Gods ministers, attending continually vpon this very thing. POPE The maids . . dispersing various tasks attend. I. COMPTON-BURNETT Well, Nance, send the servants to church, and attend to the dinner yourself. 3 POPE Leave only two the gally to attend. DAY LEWIS After the hens had been attended to, the sisters would sit . . shelling peas. 4 SHAKES. *Two Gent.* We'll both attend upon your ladyship. DRYDEN Officious Nymphs, attending in a Ring. SOUTHEY Following the deep-veil'd Bride Fifty female slaves attend. D. L. SAYERS The prisoner was brought in, attended by a female wardress. J. BUCHAN The High Commissioner and his wife . . are attended by a lady-in-waiting, by several maids of honour, and by four A.D.C.'s. 5 *Boston Transcript* To attend church tomorrow in the Bloomer costume. T. HARDY This fair was frequently attended by the folk of Weatherbury. OED He attends regularly at the City Temple. R. MACAULAY He wanted to know what churches she had been used to attend when in London. J. B. PRIESTLEY She died about ten days later, and I didn't even attend her funeral. J. WAIN He had arranged to attend the hospital as an out-patient. JO GRIMOND He never attended unless personally summoned. 6 DEFOE Hired nurses who attended infected people. G. STEIN He would not let a doctor come in to attend Melanctha. 7 SHAKES. *Tr. & Cr.* All fears attending on so dire a project. H. FIELDING Our food was attended with some ale. E. BOWEN The birth of the third of her little boys, attended by a quite serious illness. J. CHEEVER The song, attended with laughing and clapping, came from the far end of the basement. F. WELDON The shock, dismay and disagreeable nostalgia which attends any untimely and violent death. 8 G. ANSON The Governor . . had returned a very obliging answer . . and had attended it with a present of two boats. 9 CLARENDON He was . . strong enough to have stopped or attended Waller in his western expedition. H. NELSON Cruizing off Cadiz for the purpose of attending to L'Aigle, and securing the approach of our Convoy.

II Wait for. †10 *v.t.* Look forward to, expect. LME–L17. 11 *v.t.* Look out for, await (an event, time, etc.; †a person). *arch.* L15. †12 *v.i.* Wait, tarry. M16–M18.

10 J. RAY So dreadful a Tempest that all the People attended therein the very End of the World. 11 SMOLLETT Here I attend The king—and lo! he comes. T. WALKER The first breath / of a day breeze blows and quiet- / ly he attends a new night. *fig.*: J. LOCKE The state that attends all men after this. 12 L. STERNE The lady attended as if she expected I should go on.

atten'dee *n.* = ATTENDANT *n.* 3 M20. **attender** *n.* LME.

attendance /əˈtɛnd(ə)ns/ *n.* LME. [OFr.: see prec., -ANCE.] †1 = ATTENTION 1. LME–M19. †2 = ATTENTION 2. LME–L17. 3 The action or condition of waiting upon or accompanying someone to render service; ministration, assiduous service. LME. 4 The action or condition of awaiting the leisure, convenience, or decision of a superior. LME. 5 The action or fact of being present at a meeting, function, etc., or when summoned. LME. †6 Waiting; delay; expectation. LME–M17. 7 A body of attendants, a retinue. *arch.* LME. 8 The body or number of people present at any proceedings. M19.

3 DEFOE Reputation for . . good attendance on his customers. 5 POPE The King in council your attendance waits. D. L. SAYERS Whatever fantastic pictures she had . . conjured up of married life . . , none of them had ever included attendance at village concerts. P. SCOTT Her own attendances had fallen off, and she had not gone to communion for years. 6 R. HOOKER That which causeth bitterness in death, is the languishing attendance and expectation thereof. W. RALEIGH Compelled . . to put the matter in hazard without further attendance. 7 R. GRAVES He had a meagre attendance of four or five young officers, who clung to him from loyalty. 8 B. JAMES The poor attendance, only 35,000, was attributed to the strong counter-attraction of the Oxford-Cambridge Boat Race.

Phrases: **dance** (or †**wait**) **attendance** (**on**) follow about obsequiously, be deliberately kept waiting (by). **in attendance** waiting upon someone, attending.

Comb.: **attendance allowance** a social-security benefit payable to a severely disabled person needing constant attendance at home (formerly *constant attendance allowance*); **attendance centre** a place where young delinquents must attend regularly instead of being sent to prison; **attendance officer** a person whose duty it is to see that children attend school.

attendant /əˈtɛnd(ə)nt/ *a.* & *n.* LME. [(O)Fr.: see ATTEND *v.*, -ANT[1].] A *adj.* †1 Attentive. LME–M17. 2 Waiting upon, ministering; accompanying in a subordinate capacity. LME. †3 *Law.* Dependent *on*, owing service *to*. LME–M17. 4 Present at a meeting etc. *rare.* L16. 5 Closely consequent (*on*, *upon*); resulting, associated. E17.

2 MILTON Other Suns . . With thir attendant Moons thou wilt descrie. LD MACAULAY Fresh meat was never eaten by the gentlemen attendant on a great Earl. R. L. STEVENSON Alone, on the other side of the railway, stands the Springs Hotel, with its attendant cottages. 5 R. D. LAING The anxieties attendant on the schizophrenic's phantasmic omnipotence. H. MACMILLAN The . . revolt in the capital city with all its attendant horrors.

B *n.* 1 A person in attendance or providing service; a servant, assistant, subordinate companion, etc. M16. 2 A close consequence, an accompanying circumstance etc. E17. 3 A person who is present at a meeting etc. M17.

1 MILTON Least sin Surprise thee, and her black attendant, Death. BYRON Two . . ladies, who With their attendant aided our escape. SAKI He left all the parcels in charge of the cloak-room attendant. ARNOLD BENNETT An attendant . . was feeding the sheets at one end of the machine and another attendant . . taking them off at the other. 2 POPE The laugh, the jest, attendants on the bowl. 3 D. H. LAWRENCE She was . . a regular attendant at morning service.

attent /əˈtɛnt/ *n. arch.* ME. [OFr. *atente* (mod. *att-*) use as n. of fem. pa. pple of *atendre* ATTEND *v.*; in OFr. conf. w. *entente* INTENT *n.*] †1 Intention, purpose. Only in ME. †2 Attitude. ME–L15. 3 Attention; care, heed. ME.

attent /əˈtɛnt/ *a. arch.* L15. [L *attentus* pa. pple of *attendere* ATTEND *v.*] Attentive (*to*); intent (*on*).

attentat /*in sense 1 foreign* atɑ̃ta (*pl. same*); *in sense 2* əˈtɛntət/ *n.* Also (now only in sense 2) **-ate** /-eɪt/. E17. [(O)Fr., or med.L *attentatum*, f. *attentat-* pa. ppl stem of *attentare* var. of L *attemptare* ATTEMPT *v.*] 1 An attack; an attempted assassination. E17. 2 *Law.* Something wrongfully done by a judge in a proceeding, pending an appeal. E18.

attention /əˈtɛnʃ(ə)n/ *n.* LME. [L *attentio(n-)*, f. *attent-* pa. ppl stem of *attendere* ATTEND *v.*: see -ION.] 1 The action, fact, or state of attending or giving heed; the mental faculty of attending, attentiveness; application of the mind, consideration, thought. LME. 2 Practical consideration, observant care. M18. 3 The action of attending to the comfort or pleasure of others; ceremonious politeness, courtesy. Freq. in *pl.* M18. 4 Orig. *Mil.* An erect attitude of readiness; chiefly as *at* or *to attention*. Also as *int.*, a command to assume such an attitude. L18.

1 SHAKES. *Rich. II* The tongues of dying men Enforce attention like deep harmony. W. LINDGREN Brought to my attention three specimens of a mineral. DAY LEWIS I must have weakened my capacity for attention and observation. E. ROOSEVELT Whenever he read anything aloud like this, he acted it straight through, which was why he held the attention of the little children so well. *attract attention*; *draw attention to*; *give, pay attention* (*to*), etc. *call attention to*: see CALL *v.* SELECTIVE *attention*. 2 *Encounter* Please address it for the attention of John Hall. 3 CHESTERFIELD Nice and scrupulous, in points of ceremony, respect, and attention. P. ACKROYD He fed my vanity with his attentions. **pay one's attentions to** court. 4 G. B. SHAW Remember that you are in the army now. . . Attention! Left turn! Quick march. C. S. FORESTER Each officer in turn came up to attention as his name was spoken.

attentional *a.* of or pertaining to the mental faculty of attention L19.

attentisme /atɑ̃tism/ *n.* M20. [Fr., f. *attente* wait, waiting: see ATTENT *n.*, -ISM.] The policy of waiting to see what happens.

attentive /əˈtɛntɪv/ *a.* LME. [(O)Fr. *attentif*, *-ive*, f. as ATTENT *n.* + -IVE.] 1 Steadily applying one's mind or energies; intent, heedful. LME. b = ATTENTIONAL *a.* L19. 2 Assiduously attending to the comfort or wishes of others; polite, courteous. L16.

attentively *adv.* LME. **attentiveness** *n.* LME.

†**attenuant** *a.* & *n.* E17. [Fr. *atténuant* f. L *attenuant-* pres. ppl stem of *attenuare*: see next, -ANT[1].] *Med.* A *adj.* Having the property of thinning the secretions. E17–M19. B *n.* A drug or other agent credited with this property. E18–M19.

attenuate /əˈtɛnjʊət/ *a.* LME. [L *attenuatus* pa. pple, f. as next: see -ATE[2].] 1 Slender, thin; emaciated; tapering to thinness. LME. 2 Thin in consistency; weakened, rarefied, refined. *arch.* LME.

attenuate /əˈtɛnjʊeɪt/ *v.* M16. [L *attenuat-* pa. ppl stem of *attenuare*, f. *ad* AT- + *tenuare* make thin, f. *tenuis* thin: see -ATE[3].] 1 *v.t.* Make thin or slender. M16. 2 *v.t.* Make thin in consistency; dilute; rarefy. M16. 3 *v.t.* Weaken; reduce in force, effect, value, etc. M16. b *Physics.* Reduce the amplitude of (an oscillation, esp. an electrical signal). L19. c *Med.* Reduce the virulence of (pathogenic organisms) or of pathogenic organisms in (vaccines). Usu. as *attenuated* ppl a. L19. 4 *v.i.* Become slender, weaker, etc.; *esp.* (*Physics*) decrease in amplitude. M19.

1 E. YOUNG The spider's most attenuated thread. 2 C. LAMB Attenuated small beer. 3 J. GALSWORTHY 'I expect we shall be sick.' They were, and reached London somewhat attenuated. T. SHARPE My conditions are final. . . I am not prepared to attenuate them. H. ACTON Experience had attenuated and finally extinguished Nancy's Socialist sympathies.

†**attenuater** *n.* (*Med.*) = ATTENUANT *n.* L17–L18. **attenuator** *n.* †(*a*) = ATTENUANT *n.* (Dicts.); (*b*) *Physics* a device which produces attenuation: L19.

attenuation /ətɛnjʊˈeɪʃ(ə)n/ *n.* LME. [Fr. *atténuation* or L *attenuatio(n-)*, f. as prec.: see -ATION.] 1 The action of making something thin or slender; diminution of thickness, emaciation. LME. 2 The action of making something thinner in consistency; diminution of density, esp. (*Brewing*) of the wort during fermentation. L16. 3 The process of weakening; reduction in force, effect, etc. M19. b *Physics.* Reduction of the amplitude of an electrical signal or other oscillation. L19. c *Med.* Reduction of the virulence of a pathogenic organism. L19.

atter /ˈatə/ *n.* Long *obs.* exc. *dial.* (*north.*). [OE *ātr*, *āt(t)or* = OS *ettor*, OHG *eitar* (G *Eiter*), ON *eitr*.] 1 Poison, venom, *esp.* that of reptiles. OE. 2 Gall; bitterness. OE. 3 Corrupt matter, pus. LME.

attery *a.* venomous; spiteful; bitter; purulent: OE.

attercop /ˈatəkɒp/ *n.* Long *obs.* exc. *dial.* [OE *āttorcoppe*, f. as prec. + (perh.) COP *n.*[1]] 1 A spider. OE. 2 *fig.* A malevolent person. E16. 3 A spider's web. M16.

†**attermine** *v.t.* LME–E19. [OFr. *aterminer* f. late L *atterminare*, f. *ad* AT- + *terminare* TERMINATE *v.*] Settle the term or limit of; set a date for (esp. payment of a debt).

†**atterrate** *v.t.* L17–M18. [It. *atterrare*, f. *a* to + *terra* earth: see -ATE[3].] Fill up with (esp. alluvial) earth.

†**atterration** *n.* L17–M18.

attest /əˈtɛst/ *v.* & *n.* E16. [Fr. *attester* f. L *attestari*, f. *ad* AT- + *testari* to witness, f. *testis* witness.] A *v.* 1 *v.t.* Bear witness to, affirm the truth or validity of; testify, certify formally. E16. 2 *v.t.* Of things: be evidence or proof of; testify to, tend to confirm. L16. †3 *v.t.* Call to witness. E17–L19. 4 *v.t.* Put (a person) on oath; *esp.* administer an oath of allegiance to or enrol (a recruit) for military service. L17. 5 *v.i.* Bear witness, testify, *to*. L17. 6 *v.i.* Enrol oneself as ready for military service. E20.

1 SWIFT I will assert nothing here, but what I dare attest. L. A. G. STRONG As if to attest the excellence of her nursing, he began quickly to recover. D. CECIL An oath attesting him to be a member of the Church. **attested cattle, milk**: certified free from disease. *attesting witness*: see WITNESS *n.* 4. 2 GIBBON Twenty-two acknowledged concubines, and a library of sixty-two thousand volumes attested the variety of his inclinations. J. SULLIVAN Physical appearances attest the high antiquity of the globe. 3 SHAKES. *Tr. & Cr.* But I attest the gods, your full consent Gave wings to my propension. 4 WELLINGTON They are to be attested according to the following form . . I, A. B. do make oath [etc.]. 5 J. WILKINS To the reasonableness of this, several of the wisest heathens have attested. 6 *Observer* I attested for military service but was not called up.

B *n.* Testimony, evidence, attestation. E17.

attestant *n.* a person who makes a formal attestation L17. **attester** *n.* L16. **attestor** *n.* an attester M17.

attestation /atɛˈsteɪʃ(ə)n/ *n.* LME. [Fr., or late L *attestatio(n-)*, f. *attestat-* pa. ppl stem of *attestari*: see prec., -ATION.] 1 The action of bearing witness, testimony; evidence, proof, confirmation; *spec.* formal confirmation by signature or oath, esp. by a witness in verification of the execution of a will, deed, etc. LME. †2 The action of calling to witness. M16–M18. 3 The administration of an oath of allegiance, esp. to a military recruit. E19.

aˈttestative *a.* of the nature of or pertaining to attestation M19. **attestator** *n.* an attester L16.

Attic /ˈatɪk/ *a.*[1] & *n.*[1] L16. [L *Atticus* f. Gk *Attikos* of Attica: see -IC.] A *adj.* Of, pertaining to, or characteristic of Attica, a district of ancient Greece, or Athens, its chief city, or (formerly) Greece generally; (of literary style etc.) refined, elegant, classical. L16.

C. THIRLWALL A wooden theatre still sufficed for the Attic drama. M. ARNOLD Addison's prose is Attic prose. JOYCE He will never capture the Attic note. The note of Swinburne, of all poets. **Attic base** *Archit.* a column base consisting of an upper and lower torus divided by a scotia and two fillets. **Attic dialect** Greek as used by the ancient Athenians. **Attic order** *Class. Archit.* a square column or pillar. **Attic salt, wit** refined, delicate, poignant wit.

B *n.* A native or inhabitant of Attica or ancient Athens; the Attic dialect. L17.

attic /ˈatɪk/ *a.*[2] & *n.*[2] L17. [Fr. *attique* f. as prec.] A *adj.* 1 *Archit.* Designating a small order above a taller one (see sense B.1 below). *rare.* L17. 2 (Passing into *attrib.* use of the n.) Designating the highest storey of a building, under the beams of the roof, or a room in this. E18.

2 DEFOE The Rustic and Attic Stories are 12 Feet high each. CARLYLE The attic floor of the highest house. W. FAULKNER Behind a loose board in the wall of his attic room.

B *n.* 1 *Archit.* A small (usu. Attic) order (column and entablature) placed above another order of much greater height constituting the main façade. M18. 2 The highest storey of a house, usu. immediately under the beams of the roof; a room in this. E19. 3 *Anat.* The upper part of the cavity of the middle ear. *arch.* L19.

2 E. LINKLATER The servants got it first and in a drove took to their garrets and attics. E. O'NEILL It might be in an old trunk in the attic.

Atticise *v.* var. of ATTICIZE.

atticism /ˈatɪsɪz(ə)m/ *n.* Also A-. L16. [Gk *Attikismos*, f. *Attikos*: see ATTIC *a.*[1] & *n.*[1], -ISM.] 1 An ancient-Athenian idiom; an instance of elegant Greek; a well-turned phrase. L16. 2 *Hist.* Siding with or attachment to Athens. *rare.* E17.

Atticist /ˈatɪsɪst/ *n.* M17. [Gk *Attikistēs*, f. *Attikos*: see ATTIC *a.*[1] & *n.*[1], -IST.] *Hist.* A person who affected Attic literary style.

Atticize /ˈatɪsʌɪz/ *v.* Also -ise. E17. [Gk *Attikizein*, f. *Attikos*: see ATTIC *a.*[1] & *n.*[1], -IZE.] 1 a *v.i.* Affect Attic style; conform to Athenian or (in a wider sense) Greek habits, modes of thought, etc. E17. b *v.t.* Make Attic in character. M19. 2 *v.i.* Side with or favour Athens. M18.

attingent /əˈtɪndʒ(ə)nt/ *a.* *rare.* L16. [L *attingent-* pres. ppl stem of *attingere*: see ATTAIN, -ENT.] Touching, contiguous (*to*).

†**attirail** *n.* Also -al. E17–L18. [Fr., f. as ATTIRE *v.*: see -AL[1].] Apparatus, gear.

attire /əˈtʌɪə/ *n.* ME. [f. the vb.] †1 A person's complete equipment for war. Only in ME. 2 Dress, apparel; *esp.* fine, formal, or special clothing. ME. b An outfit of clothes; a style of dress. *arch.* L16. †3 Personal adornment or decoration. LME–M17. †4 Covering for the head; a head-dress, esp. for a woman. LME–E17. 5 *Hunting & Her.* A deer's antlers. M16.

2 SHAKES. *Jul. Caes.* And do you now put on your best attire? And do you now cull out a holiday? G. GISSING Her attire of subdued mourning indicated widowhood. V. S. NAIPAUL He had eaten, dressed—not in English clothes but in his normal Hindu attire. *fig.*: MILTON Earth in her rich attire Consummate lovly smil'd. b F. BURNEY Two new attires, one half, the other full dressed. G. K. CHESTERTON It seemed odd to them that men had once worn so elvish an attire. 3 T. FULLER Commonly known by her whorish attire: As crisping and curling.

attire /əˈtʌɪə/ *v.t.* ME. [OFr. *atir(i)er* arrange, equip, f. *a tire*, Prov. *a tieira* in succession or order, of unkn. origin.] †1 Equip, fit out; make ready, prepare. ME–L15. 2 Dress, esp. in fine, formal, or special clothing; clothe. Now chiefly *refl.* & as *attired* ppl a. ME. 3 Adorn, arrange, (the hair, the head). *arch.* LME. 4 *Hunting & Her.* Provide with antlers, esp. of a distinct colour. Chiefly as *attired* ppl a. L16.

2 DRYDEN His shoulders large a mantle did attire. R. KIPLING I was . . attired as a Sahib. G. HEYER Nattily attired in the correct town-dress of a gentleman of fashion. *fig.*: BURKE The rose and the apple blossom are both beautiful, and the plants that bear them are most engagingly attired. 3 SPENSER Her golden tresses, She dothe attyre vnder a net of gold. TENNYSON The women who attired her head.

attirement *n.* (*a*) an outfit, a dress, apparel; †(*b*) an ornament, an adornment: M16. **attiring** *n.* (*a*) the action of the vb; †(*b*) a dress, an outfit; a head-dress; an ornament; in *pl.* trappings: ME.

attitude /ˈatɪtjuːd/ *n.* L17. [Fr. f. It. *attitudine*, Sp. *attitud*, fitness, disposition, posture, f. late L *aptitudo*, *-din-* APTITUDE.] 1 *Fine Art.* The disposition of a figure in painting, statuary, etc.; the posture given to a figure. *obs.* exc. as passing into sense 2. L17. 2 The posture of the body proper to or implying some action or mental state. E18. b A posture or disposition of the body in dancing. E18. c The orientation of an aircraft, spacecraft, etc., relative to the direction of travel. E20. 3 Settled behaviour, as representing feeling or opinion; (also *attitude of mind*) settled mode of thinking. M19.

2 W. CATHER He stood in an attitude of self-defense, his feet well apart, his hands clenched and drawn up at his sides. P. HESKETH The fox's sculpted attitude was tense With scenting, listening. D. JACOBSON Those portraits of languid houris lying about in attitudes suggestive of inner heats. *strike an attitude*: see STRIKE *v.* 3 H. SPENCER Much depends on the attitude of mind we preserve while listening to, or taking part in, the controversy. E. WILSON Michelet's fundamental attitude is . . realistic and not romantic. R. HOGGART Characteristic working-class relationships and attitudes. G. J. WARNOCK A marked capacity for abstract thought is compatible with an 'attitude to life' entirely ordinary, or even dull. T. STOPPARD Her whole attitude in the play is one of innocent, eager willingness to please.

attiˈtudinal *a.* of or pertaining to attitudes or attitude M19. **attitudiˈnarian** *n.* a person who uses postures and poses M18. **attitudiˈnarianism** *n.* the (excessive) use of attitudes E19.

attitudinize /atɪˈtjuːdɪnʌɪz/ *v.i.* Also -ise. L16. [f. It. *attitudine* (see prec.) + -IZE.] Practise or adopt attitudes; strike an attitude; speak, write, or behave affectedly.

attitudinizer *n.* E19.

atto- /ˈatəʊ/ *comb. form.* [f. Da. or Norw. *atten* eighteen: see -O-.] Used in names of units of measurement to denote a factor of 10^{-18}, as *attowatt* etc. Abbrev. *a.*

attorn /əˈtəːn/ *v.* ME. [OFr. *atorner*, *aturner* assign, appoint, f. *a* A-[5] + *torner* TURN *v.*] †1 *v.t.* Turn; change, transform; deck out. Only in ME. 2 *v.t.* Turn over (goods, service, allegiance, etc.) to another; transfer, assign. *arch.* LME. 3 *v.i.* Transfer one's tenancy, or (*arch.*) homage or allegiance, *to* another; formally acknowledge such transfer. LME.

2 **attorn tenant (to)** *Law* formally transfer one's tenancy (*to*), make legal acknowledgement of tenancy (*to* a new landlord).

attornment *n.* the transference of bailor status, tenancy, or (*arch.*) allegiance, service, etc., to another; formal acknowledgement of such transfer: LME.

attorney /əˈtəːni/ *n.* & *v.* ME. [OFr. *atorné*, *aturné*, or (branch A.II) *atornée* (fem.), use as n. of pa. pple of *atorner*: see prec.] A *n.* I 1 *Law.* A person formally appointed to act for another in legal or business matters. Also *attorney-in-fact*, *private attorney*. ME. †b *gen.* A person appointed to act for another; an agent, a deputy, a representative. LME–M17. 2 A legal practitioner properly qualified to represent a client in a court of law (now chiefly *US*). In English law (*Hist.*), a legal practitioner entitled to conduct litigation in lower courts (distinguished from *counsel*), a solicitor (freq. *derog.*). Also *attorney-at-law*, *public attorney*. Also (A-), the title of certain law officers of the Crown, councils, etc. ME. †3 An advocate, a mediator. LME–L16.

1 †**Attorney general**: one empowered to act for his principal without restriction to specified matters. b SHAKES. *Com. Err.* I will attend my husband, . . And will have no attorney but myself. 2 **Attorney-General** the highest legal officer in Britain and some other States, empowered to act for the Crown or State in legal matters. **Attorney-Generalship** the position of Attorney-General. *district attorney*: see DISTRICT *n.* †**King's** or **Queen's Attorney** the Attorney-General. *Scotch attorney*: see SCOTCH *a.* 3 SHAKES. *Rich. III* Therefore, dear mother . . Be the attorney of my love to her.

II 4 The action or fact of appointing a person to act as one's representative in legal or business matters. Now chiefly in *power of attorney*, the authority conferred by this action; the legal document conferring such authority. LME.

4 SHAKES. *Rich. III* I, by attorney, bless thee from thy mother. **letter** etc. **of attorney** the legal document conferring power of attorney. *warrant of attorney*: see WARRANT *n.*[1]

B *v.t.* Appoint as attorney; perform etc. by attorney or proxy. *rare.* L15.

attorneydom *n.* M19. **attorneyism** *n.* (*arch.*) the practice of attorneys; unscrupulous cleverness: M19. **attorneyship** *n.* (*a*) acting as attorney, proxy; (*b*) the position of an attorney: L16.

attract /əˈtrakt/ *v.t.* LME. [L *attract-* pa. ppl stem of *attrahere*, f. *ad* AT- + *trahere* draw.] 1 (Tend to) draw to oneself or itself, cause to come near, esp. (*a*) by an invisible force such as gravity, magnetism, or electricity, (*b*) by influencing the will or actions of people or animals, (*c*) by presenting favourable conditions or opportunities. LME. †2 Draw or pull in; absorb, inhale. M16–L17. 3 Excite (pleasurable emotions) in a person towards oneself or itself; give or promise pleasure to (a person). E17. 4 Draw out and fix upon oneself or itself (the attention etc. of others). L17. 5 *euphem.* Come by dishonestly, pilfer. L19.

1 SIR T. BROWNE Jet and amber attracteth straws. J. A. FROUDE Like all other systems which have attracted followers, it addresses itself, not to the logical intellect, but to the imagination. E. F. SCHUMACHER Neither the successful farmers nor the Soil Association have been able to attract official support or recognition. M. GIROUARD The old red-brick houses and innumerable artistic associations of Hampstead attracted architects, artists, and writers. J. UPDIKE There was no population here, until your contraption attracted it. D. ATTENBOROUGH Some orchids . . attract insects by sexual impersonation. 3 MILTON Adornd She was indeed, and lovely to attract Thy Love. I. FLEMING She had the sort of firm, compact figure that always attracted him. R. DAWKINS The ability to attract loyal friends. 4 DRYDEN A wife . . Made to attract his eyes, and keep his heart. E. WAUGH Now and then I noticed him attract curious glances, but most of the party knew him too slightly to see the change in him. M. LEITCH He couldn't have attracted their attention more if he had waved a red, white and blue flag.

attractable *a.* able to be attracted L18. **attractant** *n.* an agent which attracts; *esp.* a substance used to attract insects: E20. **attractor** *n.* a person who or thing which attracts something or someone else (GREAT *attractor*; *strange attractor*: see STRANGE *a.*) M17.

attraction /əˈtrakʃ(ə)n/ *n.* LME. [Fr., or L *attractio(n-)*, f. as prec.: see -ION.] †1 *Med.* The action of a poultice etc. in drawing matter from the tissues; something applied for this purpose. LME–M17. †2 Absorption; the taking in of food; inhalation. M16–M17. 3 The action of a body in drawing another towards itself by some physical force such as gravity, magnetism, etc.; the tendency for this to occur. Opp. *repulsion.* E17. 4 An attractive quality. Freq. in *pl.* E17. 5 The action of causing people or animals to come nearer by influencing their conscious actions, providing favourable conditions, etc. M18. 6 The action or capacity of eliciting interest, affection, sympathy, etc.; attractiveness, charm, fascination. M18. 7 A thing or feature which attracts visitors, customers, etc. E19. 8 *Gram.* The influence of a word in context causing an adjacent word to be given an incorrect form, as in *one in six have* (for *has*) *this problem.* E20.

3 LONGFELLOW Every arrow that flies feels the attraction of earth. A. KOESTLER Explanation of the tides as an effect of the moon's attraction. *capillary attraction*: see CAPILLARY *a.* 3. *centre of attraction*: see CENTRE *n.* **chemical attraction** = AFFINITY 6. 4 SHAKES. *Per.* She, questionless, with her sweet harmony And other chosen attractions, would allure. DAY LEWIS A capacity for relishing the everyday and recognising the attractions in the commonplace. A. J. P. TAYLOR Here, he believed, he could win the war—with the added attraction of doing so before the Americans arrived. 5 OED The attraction of the disaffected to his standard. ROGER JOHNSON Sexual attraction has been a frequently suggested function of scent glands. 6 E. WAUGH She was daily surprised by the things he knew and the things he did not know; both . . added to his attraction. T. STOPPARD What is the attraction or the point in thinking better of oneself? E. F. SCHUMACHER Scientific . . 'solutions' which poison the environment or degrade the social structure . . are of no benefit, no matter how brilliantly conceived or how great their superficial attraction. 7 ANTHONY HUXLEY Another major flowery attraction is nectar, a . . sugar secretion . . which is of course food of a delicious kind to many insects. P. THEROUX There are few tourist attractions in Veracruz; there is an old fort and . . a beach.

attractive /əˈtraktɪv/ *a.* & *n.* LME. [Fr. *attractif*, *-ive* f. late L *attractivus*, f. as ATTRACT + -IVE.] **A** *adj.* †1 Absorptive. LME–E18. †2 *Med.* Having the property of drawing bodily humours etc. LME–L18. 3 Having the property or capacity of attracting towards itself by a physical force; of the nature of such attraction. Opp. *repulsive.* M16. 4 Having the property or capacity of attracting towards oneself or itself by influencing will and action; having the property of attracting interest, attention, affection, desire, etc.; interesting, pleasing, alluring. L16.

3 W. HERSCHEL The sun, by its attractive power, retains the planets . . in their orbits. 4 SIR W. SCOTT Interesting and attractive for those who love to hear an old man's stories of a past age. W. CATHER A gay young fellow, so attractive that the prettiest Bohemian girl in Omaha had run away with him. S. HILL What an attractive garden you have here! P. SCOTT The proposal could turn out to be financially attractive One might presume to make a small profit.

†**B** *n.* 1 *Med.* A preparation used to draw bodily humours etc. LME–L18. 2 An attractive thing or quality. L16–M19.

attractively *adv.* E17. **attractiveness** *n.* M17.

†**attrahent** *a.* & *n.* M17–L18. [L *attrahent-* pres. ppl stem of *attrahere* ATTRACT: see -ENT.] (Something) that attracts.

attrait /atrɛ/ *n.* E20. [Fr., f. *attraire* attract.] *Theol.* Vocation; inclination.

†**attrap** *v.t.* Infl. **-pp-**. L16–L17. [f. A-[1] + TRAP *v.*[1]] Provide (a horse) with trappings. Chiefly as *attrapped* ppl a.

attribute /ˈatrɪbjuːt/ *n.* LME. [(O)Fr. *attribut* or L *attributum* use as n. of neut. pa. pple of *attribuere* ATTRIBUTE *v.*] †1 *Med.* A condition of the bodily humours. Only in LME. 2 A quality or character ascribed (esp. in common estimation) to a person or thing. Also, an epithet denoting this. L15. 3 A material object recognized as appropriate to or symbolic of a person or office; a conventional symbol serving to identify a figure in a painting etc. L16. 4 An inherent characteristic quality or feature of a person or thing; a property; in *Statistics* etc., a non-quantifiable property. E17. **b** *Logic.* That which may be predicated of something. L18. †5 Distinguished quality or character; reputation, credit. Only in 17. 6 *Gram.* An attributive word or phrase. E19.

2 SHAKES. *Merch. V.* But mercy is above this sceptred sway, . . It is an attribute to God himself. T. WRIGHT It is surprising how soon historical personages become invested with romantic attributes. 3 WORDSWORTH A crown, an attribute of sovereign power. K. CLARK The Greek philosophers are represented with their attributes. Aristotle, with the severe figure of Dialectic. 4 BACON The attributes and acts of God, as far as they are revealed to man. SIR W. SCOTT Beauty was an attribute of the family. H. FAST It had all the attributes and virtues and sins that history requires of a great city. H. KISSINGER At this point I experienced for the first time two of Nixon's distinguishing attributes. S. NAIPAUL Recycling is the highest good, biodegradability the most sought-after attribute. 5 SHAKES. *Tr. & Cr.* Much attribute he hath, and much the reason Why we ascribe it to him.

†**attribute** *ppl a.* LME–L16. [L *attributus* pa. pple, f. as next.] Attributed; assigned, given.

attribute /əˈtrɪbjuːt/ *v.t.* L15. [L *attribut-* pa. ppl stem of *attribuere*, f. *ad* AT- + *tribuere* allot: cf. TRIBUTE *n.*] †1 Assign, give, or concede *to* a person as a right. L15–L18. 2 Ascribe as belonging or appropriate *to*. M16. 3 Ascribe *to* as an inherent quality or characteristic. M16. 4 Ascribe *to* as an effect or consequence. M16. 5 Ascribe *to* an author, painter, etc., as his or her work. M16. 6 Assign in one's opinion *to* its proper time and place. M16.

1 LD BERNERS These two townes were attributed to Flaunders by reason of gage. BACON What celsitude of honour Plinius Secundus attributeth to Trajan in his funeral oration. 2 MILTON God attributes to place No sanctity, if none be thither brought By men. W. S. CHURCHILL Opposition speakers were pleased to attribute to him an aim he did not possess. †**attribute much** etc. **to** attach great etc. importance or value to. 3 E. BISHOP Their gods, to which, in their present historical state of superstition and helplessness, they attribute magical powers. 4 R. L. STEVENSON It was the character of the man to attribute nothing to luck and but little to kindness. R. LYND Some writers have attributed the tendency to laugh at mispronunciations to snobbery. G. VIDAL I attributed my condition to the altitude. 5 P. GALLICO He repeated the words John had attributed to Jesus. M. GIROUARD Two more houses in Cambridge . . can be attributed to him with reasonable confidence. 6 F. H. A. SCRIVENER Several copies which may fairly be attributed to the fourth century.

attributable *a.* able to be attributed *to*, owing *to* M17.

attribution /atrɪˈbjuːʃ(ə)n/ *n.* LME. [(O)Fr. f. L *attributio(n-)*, f. as prec.: see -ION.] †1 Bestowal, awarding. LME–E19. †2 Something ascribed in estimation or opinion, as a quality, appellation, meaning, etc. L15–M18. 3 *Logic.* Predication of an attribute. E17. 4 Ascription of a quality etc. as belonging or proper to a person or thing. M17. 5 Ascription of an effect to a cause, a work to an author, etc. M17. 6 An authority or function granted to a ruler, court, etc. L18.

attributive /əˈtrɪbjʊtɪv/ *a.* & *n.* E17. [Fr. *attributif*, *-ive*, f. *attribut*: see ATTRIBUTE *n.*, -IVE.] **A** *adj.* †1 Characterized by attributing. *rare* (Shakes.). Only in E17. 2 *Logic.* That assigns an attribute to a subject. M19. 3 *Gram.* That expresses an attribute; *spec.* (opp. *predicative*) designating adjectives (or their equivalents) that premodify or occas. immediately follow nouns (e.g. *old* in *the old dog*, *a dog old in years*, but not in *the dog is old*). M19. 4 Of a work of art etc.: that is such by attribution. M19. **B** *n. Gram.* An attributive word or phrase. M18.

attributively *adv.* M19.

†**attrist** *v.t.* L17–M19. [Fr. *attrister*, f. *à* A-[5] + *triste* sad, f. L *tristis*.] Make sad, sadden.

attrit /əˈtrɪt/ *v.t. US colloq.* M20. [Back-form. f. ATTRITION: cf. ATTRITE *v.*] Wear down in quality or quantity by military attrition.

attrite /əˈtrʌɪt/ *a.* LME. [L *attritus* pa. pple, f. as next.] †1 Worn or ground down. LME–M17. 2 *Theol.* Having attrition. E17.

attrite /əˈtrʌɪt/ *v.t.* M18. [L *attrit-* pa. ppl stem of *atterere*, f. *ad* AT- + *terere* to rub.] 1 Wear down by continued friction. Chiefly as *attrited* ppl a. M18. 2 = ATTRIT. *US colloq.* M20.

attritive *a.* (*rare*) = ATTRITIONAL M19. **attritor** *n.* (*rare*) an agent which wears something down by attrition E19.

attrition /əˈtrɪʃ(ə)n/ *n.* LME. [Late L *attritio(n-)*, f. as prec.: see -ION.] 1 *Theol.* Regret for sin, e.g. through fear of punishment, falling short of true repentance or contrition. LME. 2 *Med.* Comminution; tearing; excoriation, abrasion (passing into sense 3). Now *rare* or *obs.* LME. 3 Rubbing away, wearing or grinding down, by friction. L15. 4 The action of rubbing one thing against another; mutual friction. E17. 5 The gradual wearing down of an enemy's forces in sustained warfare; loss of men or material by enemy action; *gen.* gradual loss or reduction. E20.

3 C. LYELL Pebbles and sand . . decrease in size by attrition. *fig.*: MAX-MÜLLER Contact with English society exercises a constant attrition on the system of castes. 4 J. PRIESTLEY Some . . think that heat is produced in the lungs by the attrition of the blood in passing through them. 5 H. WOUK Combat attrition was taking a steep toll, and to send green replacements into the skies was fruitless. P. F. BOLLER He [Ulysses S. Grant] was similarly resistant to retreating; he hammered stubbornly away at the enemy and wore him down by sheer attrition. *Scientific American* The resulting family of poults is subject to a high rate of attrition, owing to predators, vagaries of the weather and desertion. *Daily Telegraph* The unions said that '8,000 job cuts' would be negotiable only if the jobs could be eliminated by 'attrition' (encouraging early retirement). **war of attrition** a prolonged war characterized by continual small-scale actions rather than by decisive battles.

attritional *a.* characterized by or of the nature of attrition M19.

attune /əˈtjuːn/ *v.* L16. [f. AT- + TUNE *v.*] **1** *v.t.* Bring into musical accord. (Foll. by *to.*) L16. †**2** *v.t.* Make tuneful or melodious. M17–L18. **3** *v.t.* Bring (an instrument) to the correct pitch; tune. E18. **4** *v.t. fig.* Bring into harmony or accord; make perfectly suited or receptive *to.* E18. **5** *v.i.* Harmonize *with.* E20.

1 POPE For Phemius to the lyre attuned the strain. 2 MILTON Aires, vernal aires . . attune The trembling leaves. 4 M. L. KING My hearing was not attuned to the sound of such bitterness. C. SAGAN Life forms developed that were finely attuned to their specific environments. J. CAREY It's curious . . that a novel so attuned to the selfishness and pain behind every face should transmit such an exuberant sense of life. 5 *fig.*: R. LANGBRIDGE This might have been carefully studied so as to attune with his general appearance.

attunement *n.* M19.

atua /ˈatua, əˈtuːə/ *n.* M18. [Maori, & other Polynesian langs.] A supernatural being, god, or demon.

atwain /əˈtweɪn/ *adv.* Long *arch.* ME. [f. A *prep.*[1] 2 + TWAIN *n.*] In two; apart, asunder.

atweel /əˈtwiːl/ *adv. Sc.* M18. [Prob. contr. of *I wat weel* = I wot well.] Certainly, for sure; indeed.

atween /əˈtwiːn/ *prep.* & *adv. arch.* & *dial.* LME. [f. A *prep.*[1] 1 + stem of BETWEEN, on the analogy of *afore, before.*] **A** *prep.* Between. LME. **B** *adv.* In between. LME.

atwist /əˈtwɪst/ *adv.* & *pred. a.* M18. [f. A-[2] + TWIST *n.*[1]] Twisted, askew.

atwitter /əˈtwɪtə/ *adv.* & *pred. a.* M19. [f. A-[2] + TWITTER *n.*[2] or *v.*[1]] Twittering; aflutter.

atwixt /əˈtwɪkst/ *prep. arch.* & *dial.* ME. [f. A *prep.*[1] 1 + stem of BETWIXT: cf. ATWEEN.] Between.

atwo /əˈtuː/ *adv. arch.* & *dial.* OE. [f. A *prep.*[1] 2 + TWO.] In two; apart, asunder.

atypia /eɪˈtɪpɪə, a-/ *n.* M20. [f. A-[10] + Gk *tupos* TYPE *n.* + -IA[1].] *Med.* An atypical condition; irregularity, abnormality.

atypical /eɪˈtɪpɪk(ə)l, a-/ *a.* L19. [f. A-[10] + TYPICAL *a.*] Not typical; not conforming to type.

atypically *adv.* E20.

aubade /əʊˈbɑːd; *foreign* obad (*pl. same*)/ *n.* L17. [Fr. f. Sp. *albada*, f. *alba* (= Fr. *aube*) dawn.] A piece of music or a poem written to be heard at or appropriate to dawn.

aubaine /obɛn/ *n.* L16. [Fr., f. *aubain* foreigner, of unkn. origin.] *Hist.* In full *droit d'aubaine* /drwa dobɛn/. The right of the French monarch to claim the property of any foreigner who died in France.

auberge /əʊˈbɛːʒ; *foreign* obɛrʒ (*pl. same*)/ *n.* L16. [Fr. f. Prov. *alberga* lodging.] An inn, *esp.* one in France.

aubergiste /obɛrʒist (*pl. same*)/ *n.* the keeper of an auberge M18.

aubergine /ˈəʊbəʒiːn/ *n.* & *a.* L18. [Fr. f. Catal. *alberginia* f. Arab. *al-bādinjān*, f. AL-[2] + Pers. *bādingān, -injān* f. Skt *vātiṃgana.*] **A** *n.* **1** The fruit of the eggplant, *Solanum melongena*, eaten as a vegetable; the plant itself. L18. **2** A dark purple colour typical of the skin of the fruit. L19. **B** *adj.* Of the colour aubergine, dark purple. L19.

aubrietia /ɔːˈbriːʃə/ *n.* Also **-ta** /-tə/, **aubretia**. E19. [mod.L *Aubrieta*, f. Claude *Aubriet* (1668–1743), Fr. botanist: see -IA[1].] Any of several dwarf trailing cruciferous plants of the genus *Aubrieta*, usu. bearing violet or purple flowers.

¶*Aubrieta* is the original spelling of the name of the genus but in common parlance the form with *-tia* has been predominant.

auburn /ˈɔːbən, -bəːn/ *a.* LME. [OFr. *alborne, auborne* f. med.L *alburnus* whitish, f. L *albus* white: later assoc. with *brown* by false etymology (through forms w. metathesis).] Orig., of a yellowish- or brownish-white colour. Now, of a golden- or reddish-brown colour. (Used esp. of a person's hair.)

Aubusson /obysɔ̃/ *n.* Pl. pronounced same. E20. [A town in central France.] Tapestry or (esp.) a tapestry carpet woven at Aubusson.

aucht /ɔːxt/ *n.* Long *obs.* exc. *Sc.* Also **aught**. [OE *æht* (= OHG *ēht*, Goth. *aihts*), f. *āgan* to own, possess (pa. t. *āhte*).] Possessions, property.

aucht *v.* see OUGHT *v.*

au courant /o kurɑ̃/ *adv.* & *pred. a. phr.* M18. [Fr.] In an informed position; aware of current developments. (Usu. foll. by *with, of.*)

auction /ˈɔːkʃ(ə)n/ *n.* & *v.* L16. [L *auctio(n-)* lit. 'increase', f. *auct-* pa. ppl stem of *augere* to increase: see -ION.] **A** *n.* **1** A (usu. public) sale in which articles are sold to or reserved for the highest bidder. L16. **2** The bidding in a hand of a card-game such as bridge. Also *ellipt.*, = *auction bridge* s.v. BRIDGE *n.*[2]. E20.

1 **all over the auction** *Austral. slang* everywhere. **Dutch auction** a sale in which the price is gradually reduced by the auctioneer until a buyer is found. *mock auction*: see MOCK *a.* 2 *auction bridge*: see BRIDGE *n.*[2]

B *v.t.* Sell by auction. E19.

auctioneer /ɔːkʃəˈnɪə/ *n.* & *v.* E18. [f. prec. + -EER.] **A** *n.* A person who conducts sales by auction, *esp.* a person whose business is to do this. E18. **B** *v.i.* & *t.* Sell by auction. Chiefly as *auctioneering* vbl n. M18.

auctorial /ɔːkˈtɔːrɪəl/ *a.* E19. [f. L *auctor* AUTHOR *n.* + -IAL.] Of or pertaining to an author. Cf. AUTHORIAL *a.*

aucuba /ˈɔːkjʊbə/ *n.* L18. [mod.L f. Jap. *aokiba.*] A hardy evergreen shrub belonging to the Far Eastern genus *Aucuba*, of the dogwood family; *esp.* the Japanese laurel, *A. japonica.*

aucupate /ˈɔːkjʊpeɪt/ *v.t.* M17. [L *aucupat-* pa. ppl stem of *aucupari* lit. 'go bird-catching', f. *avis* bird + *capere* to catch: see -ATE[3].] Lie in wait for, gain by craft.

audacious /ɔːˈdeɪʃəs/ *a.* M16. [f. L *audac-, -ax* bold, f. *audere* dare: see -ACIOUS.] **1** Daring, bold, confident, intrepid. M16. **2** Openly disregarding decorum or morality; impudent, shameless. L16.

1 A. J. CRONIN Claire began to look at the paintings, seeing little . . but an audacious contrast of brilliant colours. J. BERGER The bold and audacious youth who had the fabulous vision of the Alps conquered and fleeing under his glance. 2 SHAKES. *1 Hen. VI* Such is thy audacious wickedness. DEFOE I grew more hardened and audacious than ever.

audaciously *adv.* L16. **audaciousness** *n.* = AUDACITY L16.

audacity /ɔːˈdasɪti/ *n.* LME. [f. med.L *audacitas*, f. as prec.: see -ACITY.] **1** Boldness; reckless daring. LME. **2** Effrontery; impudence. M16.

Audenesque /ɔːdəˈnɛsk/ *a.* M20. [f. *Auden* (see below) + -ESQUE.] Resembling in matter or style the works of the English poet and critic Wystan Hugh Auden (1907–73).

audible /ˈɔːdɪb(ə)l/ *a.* & *n.* L15. [Late L *audibilis*, f. *audire* hear: see -IBLE. Cf. earlier INAUDIBLE.] **A** *adj.* Able to be heard. L15.

S. RICHARDSON I had rather have their silent Prayers, than their audible ones. R. LARDNER The hubbub must have been audible to Miss Jackson outside. M. FRAYN He could hear a distant banging and shouting, but it was scarcely audible over the noise of the celebration.

B *n.* **1** A thing able to be heard. *rare.* E17. **2** *N. Amer. Football.* A play called at the line of scrimmage to replace that previously agreed on. M20.

audiˈbility *n.* the quality of being audible, audible capacity M17. **audibleness** *n.* E17. **audibly** *adv.* M17.

audience /ˈɔːdɪəns/ *n.* LME. [(O)Fr., refash. after L of †*oiance* f. L *audientia*, f. *audient-* pres. ppl stem of *audire* hear: see -ENCE. Sense 5 f. Sp. *audiencia.*] **1** Hearing; attention to what is spoken. *arch.* LME. **2** Judicial hearing. Now *arch.* & *Hist.* LME. **3** (A) formal interview, esp. with a monarch or a member of government. (Foll. by *of, with.*) LME. **4a** The persons within hearing; an assembly of listeners. LME. **b** *transf.* The readership of a book, newspaper, etc.; the whole group of spectators or viewers of a play, television programme, etc. M18. **5** *Hist.* (The territory administered by) a Spanish-American court of government or justice. E18.

1 SHAKES. *Coriol.* List to your tribunes. Audience! peace, I say. H. F. CARY Thou in his audience shouldst thereof discourse. LD MACAULAY These teachers easily found attentive audience. **give audience** give ear, listen. 2 **Court of Audience** *Hist.* an ecclesiastical court, orig. held by an archbishop, later by his auditors. 3 SHAKES. *Hen. V* The French ambassador upon that instant Crav'd audience. *Daily Telegraph* The Rt. Hon. James Callaghan . . had an audience of Her Majesty this evening. M. AMIS I had then had a brief audience with Rachel's guardians. 4a E. M. FORSTER The lecturer was a clergyman, and his audience must be also his flock. *captive audience*: see CAPTIVE *a.* 1. b A. TOFFLER Like radio broadcasters and moviemakers, publishers tended to seek the largest and most universal audience. G. EWART Opposite was the audience, to watch the total effect, / a sort of firework display.

Comb.: **audience-chamber** a reception room in a palace etc.; **audience participation** participation by the audience esp. in a broadcast programme; **audience research** investigation into the numbers and opinions of listeners or viewers of broadcast programmes.

†**audiencer** *n.* L16–M18. [(O)Fr. *audiencier* f. med.L *audientiarius*, f. *audient-*: see prec., -ER[2].] An officer in Chancery who dealt with all letters patent.

audient /ˈɔːdɪənt/ *n.* & *a.* E17. [n. f. late L *audient-, -ens* (Cyprian) catechumen; adj. f. L *audient-*: see AUDIENCE, -ENT.] **A** *n.* A hearer, a listener; *Eccl. Hist.* a hearer of the gospel, not yet a member of the Church, a catechumen. E17. **B** *adj.* Listening. M19.

audile /ˈɔːdʌɪl/ *a.* & *n.* L19. [Irreg. f. L *audire* hear + -ILE.] **A** *adj.* **1** Of, pertaining to, or predominantly involving the sense of hearing. L19. **2** *Psychol.* Of, pertaining to, or characterized by responses that involve audile imagery; (of a person) responding to perceptions more readily in terms of audile imagery than in tactile or visual terms. E20. **B** *n. Psychol.* An audile person. L19.

audio /ˈɔːdɪəʊ/ *n.* E20. [Independent use of next: orig. used attrib. or as adj.] Audible sound, esp. as electrically reproduced; sound reproduction.

Comb.: **audio frequency**: within the normal frequency range of human hearing; **audio secretary**: who does audio typing; **audio typing** typewriting directly from a tape or other sound recording; **audio typist**: who types directly from a tape or other sound recording.

audio- /ˈɔːdɪəʊ/ *comb. form* of L *audire* hear: see -O-.

audio-active *a.* (of language teaching, facilities for this) providing opportunity for listening and response M20. **audioˈgenic** *a.* caused by sound M20. **audiogram** *n.* a graphic record of sensitivity of hearing produced by an audiometer M20. **audio-lingual** *a.* pertaining to listening and speaking, as opp. to reading and writing, esp. in language teaching M20. **audiophile** *n.* a devotee of high-fidelity sound reproduction M20. **audiotape** *n.* & *v.* (*a*) *n.* (also as two wds) magnetic tape on which sound can be recorded; (a sound recording on) a length of magnetic tape; (*b*) *v.t.* record on audiotape: M20. **audioˈvisual** *a.* (esp. of aids to teaching) using or pertaining to both sight and sound M20.

audiology /ɔːdɪˈɒlədʒi/ *n.* M20. [f. prec. + -LOGY.] The branch of science that deals with hearing.

audioˈlogical *a.* M20. **audiologist** *n.* M20.

audiometer /ɔːdɪˈɒmɪtə/ *n.* L19. [f. AUDIO- + -METER.] An instrument for measuring the sensitivity of the ear to sounds of different frequencies.

audioˈmetric *a.* of or pertaining to audiometry L19. **audiomeˈtrician**, **audiometrist** *ns.* a person who specializes in audiometry M20. **audiometry** *n.* the measurement and testing of the sense of hearing L19.

audion /ˈɔːdɪən/ *n. obs.* exc. *Hist.* E20. [f. L *audire* hear + *-on.*] A triode valve of the earliest form.

audit /ˈɔːdɪt/ *n.* & *v.* LME. [f. L *auditus* hearing, f. *audit-* pa. ppl stem of *audire* hear; in med.L *auditus (compoti)* audit (of an account).] **A** *n.* **1** An official examination and verification of (orig. orally presented) financial accounts, esp. by an independent body. LME. †2 A statement of account; a balance sheet. LME–M17. 3 A hearing, an inquiry, a methodical and detailed review; *arch.* a judicial hearing or examination. LME. 4 A periodical settlement of accounts between landlord and tenants. L15. 5 *fig.* A searching examination; a reckoning, a settlement; *esp.* the Day of Judgement. M16.

3 MILTON With his orisons I meddle not, for hee appeals to a high audit. *Shell Technology* In the safety audit, an independent safety team reviews the design and construction work, concentrating on safety aspects. 5 T. DEKKER Those heapes of Siluer . . will be a passing bell . . calling thee to a fearefull Audit.

Comb.: **audit ale** an ale of special quality formerly brewed at certain colleges of English universities, orig. for use on the day of audit; **audit-house, -room** a building or room attached to a cathedral for the transaction of business; **audit trail** a system allowing tracing of the detailed transactions underlying any part of an audit record.

B *v.* 1 *v.t.* Conduct an audit of (accounts etc.); *gen.* review methodically and in detail. LME. †2 *v.i.* Draw up or render an account. M17–E18. 3 *v.t.* & *i.* Attend (a lecture, course, etc.) without intending to receive credits. *N. Amer.* M20.

1 J. A. FROUDE With subscribed funds, regularly audited. *Christian Science Monitor* Honeywell . . would audit a building, identify [energy] conservation possibilities, install the equipment, and monitor its operation. 3 A. LURIE She audited his undergraduate lectures; she waylaid him in the department office.

audition /ɔːˈdɪʃ(ə)n/ *n.* & *v.* L16. [L *auditio(n-)*, f. *audit-*: see prec., -ION.] A *n.* 1 The action, power, or faculty of hearing; listening. L16. 2 Something heard. *rare.* M17. 3 A trial hearing or viewing of an applicant for employment as a singer, actor, etc. L19.

1 E. POUND All that the critic can do for the reader or audience or spectator is to focus his gaze or audition. 2 HOR. WALPOLE I went to hear it for it is not an *apparition* but an audition. 3 J. BERGER She had the impression that everyone was waiting their opportunity to compete, like singers at an audition.

B *v.* 1 *v.t.* Give an audition to (an applicant); test by means of an audition M20. 2 *v.i.* Undergo an audition; be tested by means of an audition. M20.

auditive /ˈɔːdɪtɪv/ *a.* LME. [(O)Fr. *auditif*, *-ive*, f. L *audit-*: see AUDIT, -IVE.] = AUDITORY *a.* I.

auditor /ˈɔːdɪtə/ *n.* ME. [AN *auditour*, (O)Fr. *auditeur*, f. L *auditor*, f. *audit-*: see AUDIT, -OR.] 1 A person who conducts an audit of accounts etc.; *spec.* (more fully *auditor of court*) a taxing-master in a Scottish court. ME. 2 A hearer, a listener. LME. 3 A person who listens judicially and tries cases, esp. in an ecclesiastical court. *obs.* exc. *Hist.* LME. 4 A person who learns by oral instruction; a pupil, a disciple; a catechumen. L15. 5 A person who attends a lecture, course, etc., without intending to receive credits. *N. Amer.* M20.

1 SHAKES. *Timon* Call me before th'exactest auditors, And set me on the proof. 2 S. JOHNSON He that long delays a story, and suffers his auditor to torment himself with expectation. 3 J. AYLIFFE The Auditor, or Official of Causes and Matters in the Court of Audience of Canterbury. 4 A. WOOD Bodley . . was an auditor of Chevalerius in Hebrew.

auditorship *n.* the position of an auditor LME. **auditress** *n.* (now *rare*) a female auditor M17.

auditorial /ɔːdɪˈtɔːrɪəl/ *a. rare.* M19. [Sense I f. AUDITORY *a.* + -AL[1]; sense 2 f. prec. + -IAL.] 1 = AUDITORY *a.* I. M19. 2 Of or pertaining to auditors or an audit. L19.

auditorially *adv.* L19.

auditorium /ɔːdɪˈtɔːrɪəm/ *n.* Pl. **-riums, -ria** /-rɪə/. E17. [L, use as n. of neut. of *auditorius*: see AUDITORY *a.*, -ORIUM.] 1 *gen.* A place for hearing. *rare.* E17. 2 *spec.* The part of a theatre, lecture-hall, or other public building occupied by the audience; (*N. Amer.*) such a building as a whole. M19.

auditory /ˈɔːdɪt(ə)ri/ *n. arch.* LME. [f. L AUDITORIUM: see -ORY[1].] 1 An assembly of hearers, an audience. LME. 2 A place for hearing; an auditorium. LME. †b A lecture-room; a philosophical school. E17–L18.

auditory /ˈɔːdɪt(ə)ri/ *a.* L16. [Late L *auditorius*, f. L AUDITOR: see -ORY[2].] 1 Pertaining to the sense or organs of hearing. L16. 2 Pertaining to an auditorium. *rare.* M18.

1a *auditory scanning*: see SCANNING *n.*

audiˈtorily *adv.* by means of hearing or listening M20.

auditual /ɔːˈdɪtjʊəl/ *a.* Long *rare.* M17. [f. L *auditus* sense of hearing f. *audit-* (see AUDIT), + -AL[1].] Of or pertaining to the sense of hearing, auditory.

au fait /əʊ feɪ, *foreign* o fɛ/ *adv.* & *pred. a. phr.* M18. [Fr., lit. 'to the fact, to the point'.] Thoroughly conversant (*with*, †*of*), well instructed (*in*), expert or skilful (*at*).

†**auf(e)** *ns.* see OAF *n.*

aufgabe /ˈaʊfɡɑːbə/ *n.* E20. [G.] Chiefly *Psychol.* A task, an assignment. Cf. TASK *n.* I(d).

Aufklärung /ˈaʊfklɛːrʊŋ/ *n.* E19. [G = enlightenment.] = ENLIGHTENMENT 2.

au fond /o fɔ̃/ *adv. phr.* L18. [Fr.] At bottom, basically.

†**auge** *n.* L16–M18. [OFr. f. Arab. *'awj* peak, apogee.] *Astron.* = APOGEE, APSIS.

Augean /ɔːˈdʒiːən/ *a.* L16. [f. L *Augeas*, Gk *Augeias* (see below) + -AN.] Abominably filthy; resembling the stables of Augeas, King of Elis, that had been uncleaned for 30 years until Hercules turned the River Alpheus through them.

augelite /ˈɔːɡəlʌɪt, ˈɔːdʒ-/ *n.* M19. [f. Gk *augē* lustre + -LITE.] *Min.* A monoclinic basic aluminium phosphate occurring usu. as colourless or reddish tabular crystals.

augen /ˈaʊɡ(ə)n/ *n.pl.* L19. [G, pl. of *Auge* EYE *n.*] *Geol.* Lenticular mineral grains or aggregates present in some metamorphic rocks. Usu. *attrib.* or *comb.*, denoting the presence of these, as *augen-gneiss*.

augend /ˈɔːdʒ(ə)nd/ *n.* L19. [G f. L *augendus* gerundive of *augere* to increase: see -END.] The quantity to which an addend is added.

auger /ˈɔːɡə/ *n.*[1] Also †**n-**. [OE *nafogār*, f. *nafu* NAVE *n.*[1] + *gār* spear, piercer: corresp. to OS *nabugēr*, OHG *nabugēr*, ON *nafarr*. The initial *n* was lost by misdivision as in *adder*, *apron*, etc.] 1 A tool for boring holes in wood, having a long shank with a usu. helical cutting edge, and a transverse handle fixed to the top of the shank by means of which the tool is turned by hand. OE. 2 An instrument for boring in earth, working on a similar principle. L16. 3 More fully *auger-shell*. (The slender tapering spiral shell of) any marine gastropod of the genera *Terebra* and *Turritella*. L18. 4 A helical bit used to convey material, or to mix material and force it through an aperture. M20.

Comb.: **auger-hole** a hole drilled by an auger; *auger-shell*: see sense 3 above.

Auger /ˈəʊʒeɪ/ *n.*[2] M20. [P. V. *Auger* (b. 1899), Fr. physicist.] *Physics.* 1 *Auger effect*, the emission of an electron, rather than an X-ray photon, accompanying the filling of a vacancy in an inner electron shell of an atom. M20. 2 *Auger electron*, an electron emitted in this effect. M20.

aught *n.* var. of AUCHT *n.*

aught /ɔːt/ *pron.*, *a.*, & *adv.* Also **ought**, (*Sc.*) **ocht** /ɒxt/, (*dial.*) **owt** /aʊt/. [OE *āwiht*, *āwuht*, *āuht*, *āht*, corresp. to OFris. *āwet*, *āet*, OS *ēowiht*, OHG *eowiht*, *iewiht*, f. WGmc compound of AYE *adv.*[1] & WIGHT *n.*] A *pron.* Anything whatever; anything. OE.

B. MALAMUD For aught he meant to anyone, Yakov Bok did not exist.

†B *adj.* Worth something; worthy, doughty. Only in ME.

C *adv.* To any extent, in any respect, at all. ME.

W. OWEN Lest aught she be disturbed or grieved at all.

aught *v.* see OUGHT *v.*

augite /ˈɔːdʒʌɪt/ *n.* E19. [L *augites* a precious stone, prob. turquoise, f. Gk *augitēs*, f. *augē* lustre: see -ITE[1].] *Min.* A monoclinic mineral of the pyroxene group which occurs as black or dark green prisms esp. in many basic igneous rocks.

augitic /ɔːˈdʒɪtɪk/ *a.* pertaining to or characterized by augite E19.

augment /ˈɔːɡm(ə)nt/ *n.* LME. [(O)Fr., or late L *augmentum*, f. *augere* to increase: see -MENT.] 1 Increase. LME. 2 *Gram.* The prefixed vowel marking the past tenses of verbs in the older Indo-European languages. L17.

1 W. H. AUDEN April's rapid augment of colour.

augment /ɔːɡˈmɛnt/ *v.* LME. [(O)Fr. *augmenter* or late L *augmentare*, f. *augmentum*: see prec.] I *v.t.* 1 Make greater in size, number, amount, degree, etc.; increase. LME. 2 Raise (a person) in estimation or dignity. Now *rare.* M16. 3 *Her.* Make an honourable addition to (a coat of arms). M17.

1 SIR W. SCOTT The insurgents were intent upon augmenting and strengthening their forces. W. PLOMER I took on stray jobs of this kind to augment my income. A. J. TOYNBEE Man has been content just to live on Nature's bounty without seeking to augment it. 2 P. H. JOHNSON Certain things Rupert really loved, his wife (when he was not put to the necessity of augmenting her) and his games.

II *v.i.* 4 Become greater in size, amount, etc.; increase. LME.

4 DRYDEN The Winds redouble, and the Rains augment. J. TYNDALL The polarizing angle augments with the refractive index of the medium.

augmentable *a.* †(*a*) capable of increasing; (*b*) able to be increased: L15. **augmenter** *n.* = AUGMENTOR E18. **augmentive** *a.* & *n.* (*rare*) = AUGMENTATIVE E17. **augmentor** *n.* a person who or thing which augments something M16.

augmentation /ɔːɡmɛnˈteɪʃ(ə)n/ *n.* LME. [OFr. *au(g)mentacion* (mod. *augmentation*) f. late L *augmentatio(n-)*, f. *augmentat-* pa. ppl stem of *augmentare*: see prec., -ATION.] 1 The action or process of making or becoming greater in size, amount, etc.; enlargement, increase. LME. †2 The action or process of raising in estimation or dignity; exaltation, honouring. LME–E17. 3 Something by which anything is augmented; an addition, an increase. L15. 4 Augmented or intensified state or condition; increased size etc. M16. 5 *Her.* An honourable addition to a coat of arms. L16. 6 *Mus.* The repetition of a subject (esp. in fugues) in notes uniformly longer than those of the original. L16. 7 *Sc. Law.* An increase of clerical stipend obtained through an action in the Court of Teinds. *obs.* exc. *Hist.* M17.

1 **Court of Augmentation(s)** *Hist.* a court established in the reign of Henry VIII in order to settle the disposal of the property of monasteries upon dissolution.

augmentative /ɔːɡˈmɛntətɪv/ *a.* & *n.* LME. [(O)Fr. *augmentatif*, *-ive* or med.L *augmentativus*, f. *augmentat-*: see prec., -IVE.] A *adj.* 1 Having the property of increasing or adding to; *Logic* = AMPLIATIVE. LME. 2 *Gram.* Of an affix or derivative: intensive; *esp.* indicating something large of its kind (opp. *diminutive*). M17. B *n. Gram.* An augmentative formative or word. L17.

augmented /ɔːɡˈmɛntɪd/ *a.* E17. [f. AUGMENT *n.*, *v.*: see -ED[2], -ED[1].] 1 That has been augmented; increased. E17. 2 *Mus.* Of an interval: greater by a semitone than the corresponding major or perfect interval. Of a chord: containing such an interval. Opp. DIMINISHED 2. E19. 3 *Gram.* Having an augment. M19.

au grand sérieux /o ɡrɑ̃ serjø/ *adv. phr.* M19. [Fr.] In all seriousness. Cf. AU SÉRIEUX.

au gratin /o ɡratɛ̃/ *adv.* & *pred. a. phr.* E19. [Fr., f. *au* with the + GRATIN.] *Cookery.* Sprinkled with breadcrumbs and/or grated cheese and browned.

†**augrim** *n.* var. of ALGORISM.

augur /ˈɔːɡə/ *n.* LME. [L.] A Roman religious official who interpreted omens derived from the behaviour of birds, the appearance of entrails, etc., and gave advice in accordance with them; *gen.* a soothsayer, a diviner, a prophet.

augural /ˈɔːɡjʊr(ə)l/ *a.* (*a*) of or pertaining to augurs or augury; (*b*) significant of the future, lucky or ominous: E16. **augurate** *n.* the position of augur M18. **augurous** /ˈɔːɡjʊrəs/ *a.* (*rare*) full of foreboding, anxious E17. **augurship** *n.* = AUGURATE *n.* E17.

augur /ˈɔːɡə/ *v.* M16. [f. prec.: cf. (O)Fr. *augurer* f. L *augurari*.] 1 *v.t.* Usher in (or *in*) with auguries; inaugurate. M16. 2 *v.i.* a Take auguries; conjecture from signs, have a foreboding. M16. b (With *well, ill*, etc.) (Of a person) anticipate, (of a thing) portend, a good or bad outcome. L18. 3 *v.t.* Divine, forebode, anticipate; portend, give promise of. E17.

1 H. LATIMER Numa Pompilus, who was augured and created king [of] the Romaynes next after Romulus. 2a SIR W. SCOTT Not that he augur'd of the doom, Which on the living closed the tomb. b WELLINGTON I augur well from this circumstance. W. H. PRESCOTT A reverential deference, which augured well for the success of his mission. E. J. HOWARD Everything augured badly—they weren't meant to be together. 3 JONSON I did augur all this to him beforehand. W. SPARROW He may augur the gust is coming, but cannot prevent it. LYTTON Whose open, handsome, hardy face augured a frank and fearless nature. L. STRACHEY The strange mixture of ingenuous light-heartedness and fixed determination . . seemed to augur a future perplexed and full of dangers.

augurer *n.* = AUGUR *n.* LME.

auguration /ɔːɡjʊˈreɪʃ(ə)n/ *n.* Now *rare.* LME. [L *auguratio(n-)*, f. *augurat-* pa. ppl stem of *augurari*: see prec., -ATION.] Augury; an omen, a token.

†**augurate** *v.t.* & *i.* = AUGUR *v.* L16–M18.

augury /ˈɔːɡjʊri/ *n.* LME. [OFr. *augurie* or L *augurium*, f. as AUGUR *n.*: see -Y[3].] 1 The art of the augur; divination; *arch.* skill in this. LME. 2 An augural observance or rite. E17. 3 An omen, a portent, a token. E17. 4 Foreboding, anticipation; promise, indication. L18.

augurial /ɔːˈɡjʊərɪəl/ *a.* (*rare*) E16.

August /ˈɔːɡəst/ *n.* OE. [L *augustus* (see next): named after *Augustus* Caesar, the first Roman Emperor.] The eighth month of the year in the Gregorian calendar.

august /ɔːˈɡʌst/ *a.* M17. [(O)Fr. *auguste* or L *augustus* consecrated, venerable.] 1 Inspiring reverence and admiration; solemnly grand, stately. M17. 2 Venerable by birth, status, or reputation; eminent, dignified; (sometimes as an honorific). L17.

augustly *adv.* M17. **augustness** *n.* M18.

august /ˈɔːɡəst/ *v.t. rare.* L17. [f. AUGUST *n.*, after Fr. *aoûter*.] Ripen, bring to fruition.

Augustal /ɔːˈɡʌst(ə)l/ *a.* M17. [f. L *augustalis*, f. *Augustus*: see AUGUST *n.*, -AL[1].] *Hist.* Of or pertaining to Augustus Caesar; imperial Roman.

Augustal Prefect (the title of) the prefect of Roman Egypt.

Augustan /ɔːˈɡʌst(ə)n/ *a.* & *n.* M16. [L (sense A.1 med.L) *Augustanus*, f. (sense A.1) *Augusta* (*Vindelicorum*) Augsburg, a city in Bavaria, (sense A.2) *Augustus*: see AUGUST *n.*, -AN.] A *adj.* 1 *Eccl. Hist.* Of Augsburg, where in 1530 Luther and Melanchthon drew up their confession of Protestant principles. M16. 2 Designating or pertaining to the reign of Augustus Caesar (27 BC–AD 14), esp. as a period of outstanding refinement of Latin literature, or the corresponding period of any national literature; classical; *spec.* designating or pertaining to English literature from the mid 17th to the late 18th cent. E18. B *n.* 1 Augustan literary style. *rare.* M19. 2 A writer of the Augustan age of any literature. L19.

Augustanism *n.* Augustan principles, quality, or condition, *spec.* in English literature E20. †**Augustean** *a.* = AUGUSTAN *a.* 2: only in L17.

auguste /ˈɔːɡuːst; *foreign* ogyst (*pl. same*)/ *n.* E20. [Fr. f. G *August*, male forename, (slang) clown, fool.] A circus clown wearing ill-fitting or dishevelled clothes.

Augustine /ɔːˈɡʌstɪn/ *n.* & *a.* Also †**-in.** LME. [(O)Fr. *augustin*, f. L *Augustinus* Augustine (see below): cf. AUSTIN.] A *n.* A member of the monastic order named after St Augustine of Hippo (354–430), a Father of the Church. LME. B *adj.* Of or pertaining to St Augustine or the Augustines. LME.

Augustinian /ɔːɡəˈstɪnɪən/ *a.* & *n.* M16. [f. prec. + -IAN.] A *adj.* = AUGUSTINE *a.* M16. B *n.* = AUGUSTINE *n.* Also, an adherent of the doctrines of St Augustine. M16.

Augustinianism *n.* the doctrines of St Augustine, *esp.* those regarding predestination and grace M19.

auk /ɔːk/ *n.* L17. [ON *álka* razor-bill (orig. neck) (Sw. *alka*, Da. *alk*).] Any of several short-winged diving sea birds of the family Alcidae, native to the northern oceans, which includes razor-bills, guillemots, and puffins.

great auk a large flightless auk, *Pinguinus impennis*, of the N. Atlantic, now extinct. **little auk** a small Arctic auk, *Alle alle*.

auklet *n.* any of various small auks, chiefly of the N. Pacific L19.

aul /ˈɑːʊl/ *n.* Also **aoul.** E19. [Eastern Turkic.] A Caucasian or Tartar village or encampment.

aula /ˈɔːlə/ *n.* Pl. **-lae** /-liː/, **-las.** M18. [med.L = hall, court, college, f. Gk *aulē*.] 1 Hist. *aula regis* /ˈriːdʒɪs/, the King's Court of the Norman kings of England. M18. 2 A hall; an assembly hall, esp. at a German school or university. L19.

aulacogen /ɔːˈlakədʒ(ə)n/ *n.* L20. [f. Gk *aulak-*, *aulax* furrow + -OGEN.] *Geol.* A sediment-filled trough in continental crust representing the trace of an incipient rift which failed to develop.

aularian /ɔːˈlɛːrɪən/ *n.* & *a.* L17. [f. med.L *aularius* adj., f. *aula*: see AULA, -ARIAN.] *Oxford* & *Cambridge Univs.* A *n.* A member of a hall (as opp. to a college). L17. B *adj.* Of, pertaining to, or characteristic of a hall. M19.

auld /ɔːld, ɑːld/ *a.*, *n.*, & *adv. Sc.* LME. [Var. of OLD *a.* repr. OE (Anglian) *ald*.] = OLD *a.*, *n.*[2], & *adv.*

auld lang syne /laŋ sʌɪn/ 'old long since', the days of long ago (esp. as the title and refrain of a song sung at parting etc.). **Auld Reekie** 'Old Smoky', Edinburgh. *auld* THIEF.

aulic /ˈɔːlɪk/ *a.* E18. [Fr. *aulique* or L *aulicus*, f. Gk *aulikos*, f. *aulē* court: see -IC.] Of or pertaining to a court; courtly.

Aulic Council *Hist.* the personal council of the German Emperor; later, a council managing the war department of the Austrian Empire.

aulnage /ˈɔːlnɪdʒ/ *n.* Also **aln-**, †**aun-.** LME. [OFr. *alnage*, (mod.) *aunage*, f. *alner*, *auner* measure by the ell, f. *alne*, AUNE: see -AGE. Cf. ULNAGE.] *Hist.* The official measurement and inspection of cloth; the fee paid for this.

aulnager *n.* an officer appointed to measure and inspect cloth M16.

aum *n.* var. of AAM.

aumail *n.* & *v.* var. of AMEL.

aumbry /ˈɔːmbri/ *n.* Also **almery** /ˈɑːm(ə)ri/, **ambry** /ˈambri/. ME. [OFr. *almarie* var. of *armarie* (mod. *armoire*) f. L *armarium* closet, chest, f. *arma* utensils.] A place for keeping things; *spec.* †(*a*) a library, an archive; (*b*) (now *dial.*) a pantry, a store-closet; (*c*) a closed recess in the wall of a church; (*d*) *Hist.* a small cupboard.

R. MACAULAY The Blessed Sacrament had had to be locked in an aumbry when no one was on guard.

†**aumelet** *n.* see OMELETTE.

au mieux /o mjø/ *adv. phr.* M19. [Fr. = at the best.] On the best of, or on very intimate, terms *with* (someone).

aumil, -ildar *ns.* vars. of AMIL, -ILDAR.

aumônière /omonjɛːr/ *n.* Pl. pronounced same. E19. [Fr., fem. of *aumônier*: see ALMONER.] A purse carried at the waist.

†**aunage** *n.* var. of AULNAGE.

au naturel /o natyrɛl/ *adv. phr.* E19. [Fr.] In the natural state; cooked plainly; uncooked.

auncel /ˈɔːns(ə)l/ *n.* Long *obs.* exc. *dial.* ME. [AN, earlier *aunser*, = AL *auncella*, *a(u)nser* of unkn. origin.] A kind of balance and weight; a steelyard.

aune /ɔːn/ *n. obs.* exc. *Hist.* L15. [Fr.] An ell; a French measure of cloth.

aung *v.* var. of OUNG.

aunt /ɑːnt/ *n.* Also (esp. as a title) **A-.** ME. [AN *aunte*, OFr. *ante* (mod. *tante*) f. L *amita*. Cf. NAUNT, TANTE.] 1 The sister of one's father or mother; an uncle's wife. ME. b A woman to whom one can turn for help; an unrelated older woman friend, esp. of children. *colloq.* L18. †2 An old woman; a gossip. Only in L16. †3 A bawd, a procuress; a prostitute. E17–M19.

1 J. R. ACKERLEY My Aunt Bunny, my mother's younger sister. **Aunt Sally** a game in which players throw sticks or balls at a wooden dummy; *fig.* an object of unreasonable attack. *great-aunt*: see GREAT *a.* **my** (**giddy**, **sainted**, etc.) **aunt!** expr. surprise, disbelief, etc. *Welsh aunt*: see WELSH *a.* b H. B. STOWE These universally useful persons receive among us the title of 'aunt' by a sort of general consent. J. LE CARRÉ She . . became . . their guide, friend and universal aunt. AGONY *aunt.* 2 SHAKES. *Mids. N. D.* The wisest aunt, telling the saddest tale.

auntly *a.* having or showing the qualities of an aunt M19. **auntship** *n.* (*a*) (with possess. adj., as *your* etc. *auntship*) a pompous form of address to an aunt; (*b*) the relationship of aunt: E19.

aunter /ˈɔːntə/ *n.* & *v.t.* & *i.* Long *obs.* exc. *Sc.* & *north.* Also (*Sc.*) **anter** /ˈantə/. ME. [Contr.] = ADVENTURE *n.*, *v.*

auntie /ˈɑːnti/ *n. colloq.* Also **-ty**; (esp. in names) **A-.** L18. [f. prec. + -IE, -Y[6].] 1 = AUNT. L18. 2 (**A-.**) An institution regarded as conservative in its approach; *spec.* the BBC. M20.

1 R. BURNS My auld Auntie Katie upon me taks pity. W. FAULKNER She began to ask her old schoolmates that their children call her 'cousin' instead of 'aunty'. J. BRAINE Honestly, that woman's magazine stuff, just the sort of advice these damned aunties give. DAY LEWIS You'd better not tell your Auntie.

au pair /əʊ pɛː/ *a.* & *n. phr.* L19. [Fr. = on equal terms.] A *adj. phr.* Of arrangements between two parties: paid for (entirely or largely) by mutual services. Of a person: party to such an arrangement; *spec.* (of a (usu. foreign) girl) undertaking domestic duties in return for room and board. L19. B *n.* An au pair girl. M20.

au pied de la lettre /o pje də la lɛtr/ *adv. phr.* L18. [Fr. = to the foot of the letter.] Down to the last detail; literally.

aura /ˈɔːrə/ *n.* Pl. **-ras**, (*rare*) **-rae** /-riː/. LME. [L f. Gk = breath, breeze.] 1 A gentle breeze, a zephyr. *arch.* & *poet.* LME. 2 A subtle emanation or exhalation; a surrounding glow; *fig.* an atmosphere diffused by or attending a person, place, etc.; a distinctive impression of character or aspect. M18. 3 A premonitory sensation experienced before an epileptic fit. L18.

1 C. PATMORE I *did* respire the lonely auras sweet. 2 COLERIDGE The electrical aura of oxygen. A. MILLER There is an aura of far places about him. L. LEE A dog trotted past like a ghost in a cloud, panting his aura around him. J. G. FARRELL A dimly lit table above which a faint aura of exasperation seemed to hang.

aural /ˈɔːr(ə)l/ *a.*[1] M19. [f. L *auris* ear + -AL[1].] Of, pertaining to, or received by the ear.

aurally *adv.* L19.

aural /ˈɔːr(ə)l/ *a.*[2] M19. [f. AURA + -AL[1].] Of or pertaining to an aura.

auramine /ˈɔːrəmiːn, -ɪn/ *n.* L19. [f. L *aurum* gold + AMINE.] A synthetic yellow dyestuff of the diphenylmethane series.

aurata /ɔːˈreɪtə/ *n.* E16. [L *aurata* fem. pa. pple (used as n.) of *aurare* gild, f. *aurum* gold.] A gold-coloured marine fish, *esp.* the gilt-head, *Sparus aurata*.

aurate /ˈɔːreɪt/ *n.* E19. [f. L *aurum* gold + -ATE[1].] *Chem.* A salt derived from auric acid.

aureate /ˈɔːrɪət/ *a.* LME. [Late L *aureatus*, f. *aureus* golden, f. *aurum* gold: see -ATE[2].] 1 Golden, gold-coloured. LME. 2 Resplendent; (of literary style or diction) highly ornamented, elaborate. LME.

aure'ation *n.* the condition of being aureate in literary style E20.

aureity /ɔːˈriːɪti/ *n.* E19. [med.L *aureitas*, f. *aureus*: see prec., -ITY.] The peculiar quality of gold.

aurelia /ɔːˈriːlɪə/ *n.* L16. [It., fem. of *aurelio* golden; as n. a silkworm in its cocoon.] †1 A helichrysum, *Helichrysum stoechas*. L16–E17. 2 A chrysalis. Now *rare* or *obs.* E17. 3 A jellyfish of the common genus *Aurelia*, esp. *A. aurita*. L19.

aurelian /ɔːˈriːlɪən/ *a.* & *n.* L18. [f. prec. + -AN.] Of or pertaining to, a student or collector of, butterflies and moths.

aureola /ɔːˈriːələ/ *n.* Pl. **-lae** /-liː/, **-las.** L15. [L, fem. (sc. *corona* crown) of *aureolus* adj., dim. of *aureus* golden, f. *aurum* gold.] = AUREOLE.

aureole /ˈɔːrɪəʊl/ *n.* & *v.* ME. [(O)Fr. *auréole* f. as prec.] **A** *n.* **1** *RC Ch.* The celestial crown won by a martyr, virgin, or doctor as victor over the world, the flesh, and the devil; the special degree of glory which distinguishes these. ME. **2** The glory around the head or body in depictions of divine figures. M19. **3** A halo or ring around the sun or moon. M19. **4** *transf.* & *fig.* Something that surrounds like a halo; an aura. M19. **5** *Geol.* The zone of metamorphosed rock surrounding an igneous intrusion. L19.

4 O. W. HOLMES The aureole of young womanhood had not yet begun to fade from around her. J. AGATE One of the clowns wearing a flaming aureole of silly yellow hair. A. SILLITOE The glow of her soft features was framed and accentuated by an aureole of silence backed by the sound of the city.

B *v.t.* Encircle with or as with an aureole. Chiefly as *aureoled* ppl a. M19.

aureolin /ˈɔːrɪəlɪn, ɔːˈrɪəlɪn/ *n.* L19. [f. as AUREOLA + -IN[1].] Cobalt yellow, a transparent yellow pigment.

Aureomycin /ɔːrɪəˈmʌɪsɪn/ *n.* Also **a-**. M20. [f. mod.L (*Streptomyces*) *aureofaciens*, the source bacterium, f. *aureus* golden + *-faciens* -FACIENT, + -MYCIN.] (Proprietary name for) the antibiotic chlortetracycline.

au reste /o rɛst/ *adv. phr.* E17. [Fr.] As for the rest.

aureus /ˈɔːrɪəs/ *n.* Pl. **-rei** /-rɪʌɪ/. E17. [L, use as n. of *aureus* golden, f. *aurum* gold.] A Roman coin of the late republic and the empire, of the value of 25 silver denarii.

au revoir /o rəvwaːr, əʊ rəˈvwɑː/ *int.* & *n. phr.* L17. [Fr., lit. 'to the seeing again'.] (Goodbye) until we meet again; a farewell for the present.

auric /ˈɔːrɪk/ *a.*[1] E19. [f. L *aurum* gold + -IC.] Of or pertaining to gold, golden; *spec.* (*Chem.*) of gold in the trivalent state (cf. AUROUS).

auric acid (*a*) the weakly acidic hydroxide $Au(OH)_3$; †(*b*) auric oxide, Au_2O_3.

auric /ˈɔːrɪk/ *a.*[2] L19. [f. AURA + -IC.] = AURAL *a.*[2]

aurichalc *n.* var. of ORICHALC.

aurichalcite /ɔːrɪˈkalsʌɪt/ *n.* M19. [f. L *aurichalcum*, *orichalcum*, f. Gk *oreikhalkon* 'mountain copper', (brass or copper made from) a yellow ore, + -ITE[1].] *Min.* An orthorhombic basic carbonate of copper and zinc, occurring usu. as greenish-blue incrustations.

aurichalcum *n.* see ORICHALC.

auricle /ˈɔːrɪk(ə)l/ *n.* LME. [f. L AURICULA: see -CLE.] **1** *Anat.* A small muscular pouch situated on the upper anterior surface of each atrium of the heart. Formerly also, the atrium itself. LME. **2** *Anat.* (†The lower lobe of) the external ear. M17. **3** Chiefly *Zool.* & *Bot.* A projection or process shaped like an ear or ear-lobe. M17.

auricula /ɔːˈrɪkjʊlə/ *n.* In sense 1 orig. **†-culus**. M17. [L, dim. of *auris* ear: see -CULE.] **1** A primula, *Primula auricula*, having ear-shaped leaves. M17. †**2** = AURICLE 2. Only in L17. **3** A pulmonate mollusc of the family Ellobiidae, found in brackish marshes. Now *rare* or *obs.* L18. **4** *Zool.* A perforated projection from an ambulacral plate of an echinoid, to which jaw muscles are attached. L19.

auricular /ɔːˈrɪkjʊlə/ *a.* & *n.* LME. [Late L *auricularis*, f. as prec.: see -AR[1].] **A** *adj.* **1** Of confession: spoken into the ear, private. LME. **2** Audible. L16. †**3** Addressing, affecting, or employing the ear only (without mental apprehension). L16–M18. **4** *gen.* Of or pertaining to the ear. M17. **5** Of, pertaining to, or resembling an auricle of the heart. M19.

2 SHAKES. *Lear* I will place you where you shall hear us confer of this, and by an auricular assurance have your satisfaction. 3 C. CIBBER Not mere auricular imitators of one another. 4 **auricular finger** the little finger (see sense B.1 below). **auricular witness**: one who relates what he has heard.

B *n.* **1** The little finger (as most easily inserted into the ear). M17. **2** Any of the feathers in the tuft covering the orifice of a bird's ear. L18. **3** An ear. *rare.* M19.

auricularly *adv.* L16.

auriculate /ɔːˈrɪkjʊlət/ *a.* E18. [f. AURICULA + -ATE[2].] *Bot.* & *Zool.* Furnished with one or more auricles or earlike processes.

Also **auriculated** *a.* E18.

auriculo- /ɔːˈrɪkjʊləʊ/ *comb. form.* M19. [f. as AURICLE + -O-.] Forming adjs. w. the sense 'of the auricle and —', as *auriculo-temporal*, *-ventricular*.

†**auriculus** *n.* see AURICULA.

auriferous /ɔːˈrɪf(ə)rəs/ *a.* M17. [f. L *aurifer* gold-bearing, f. *aurum* gold, + -OUS: see -FEROUS.] Containing or yielding gold (*lit.* & *fig.*).

auriferously *adv.* (*rare*) M19.

aurify /ˈɔːrɪfʌɪ/ *v.t.* & *i.* M17. [f. L *aurum* gold + -I- + -FY.] Turn into gold.

Auriga /ɔːˈrʌɪgə/ *n.* In sense 1 **a-**. LME. [L *auriga* charioteer, Auriga, f. *aureae* bridle + *-iga* f. *agere* drive.] †**1** A charioteer; *fig.* a leader. Only in LME. **2** (The name of) a constellation of the northern hemisphere in the Milky Way, near Orion; the Charioteer, the Wagoner. M16.

aurigation /ɔːrɪˈgeɪʃ(ə)n/ *n. rare.* E17. [L *aurigatio(n-)*, f. *aurigat-* pa. ppl stem of *aurigare*, f. *auriga* a charioteer: see -ATION.] The action or art of driving a chariot or coach.

Aurignacian /ɔːrɪˈnjeɪʃ(ə)n, -ɪgˈneɪ-/ *a.* & *n.* E20. [Fr. *Aurignacien*, f. *Aurignac* in SW France, where remains of it were found.] **A** *adj.* Designating or pertaining to a culture of the palaeolithic period in Europe following the Mousterian and preceding the Solutrean. E20. **B** *n.* (A person of) this culture. E20.

†**aurigo** *n.* ME–L18. [L.] Jaundice.

aurin /ˈɔːrɪn/ *n.* Also **-ine**. M19. [f. L *aurum* gold + -IN[1].] A red synthetic dyestuff of the triphenylmethane series.

†**auripigment** *n.* Also in L form **-mentum**. LME–E19. [L *auripigmentum*: see ORPIMENT.] = ORPIMENT.

auriscope /ˈɔːrɪskəʊp/ *n.* M19. [f. L *auris* ear + -SCOPE.] *Med.* An instrument for visual examination of the ear.

aurist /ˈɔːrɪst/ *n.* L17. [f. as prec. + -IST.] *Med.* A specialist with regard to the ear.

aurivorous /ɔːˈrɪv(ə)rəs/ *a. rare.* L18. [f. L *aurum* gold + -I- + -VOROUS.] Consuming gold; avidly desirous of gold.

auro- /ˈɔːrəʊ/ *comb. form.* [f. L *aurum* gold: see -O-.] Used chiefly in *Chem.* & *Min.* to form names of substances containing gold, as *aurochloride*.

aurochs /ˈɔːrɒks, ˈaʊ-/ *n.* L18. [G, early var. of *Auerochs* (OHG *ūrohso*, f. *ūr* = OE *ūr* etc. of unkn. origin, + *ohso* OX). Cf. URE-OX, UROCHS, URUS.] The extinct wild ox, *Bos primigenius*, which is the ancestor of domestic cattle in Europe and many parts of the world. Also, the European bison.

aurora /ɔːˈrɔːrə/ *n.* Pl. **-rae** /-riː/, **-ras**. LME. [L: cf. EAST.] **1** The rising light of the morning; the dawn. Also (**A-**), a goddess in Roman mythology. LME. **b** *fig.* The beginning, the early period. M19. **2** A rich orange colour, as of the sky at sunrise. M17. **3** A luminous phenomenon, often taking the form of variable streamers or resembling drapery, seen in the upper atmosphere in high northern or southern latitudes, and caused by the interaction of charged solar particles with atmospheric gases, under the influence of the earth's magnetic field; orig. w. specifying adj. (see below). E18.

3 **aurora australis** /ɔːˈstreɪlɪs/ [southern] the aurora of the southern polar regions, the southern lights. **aurora borealis** /bɔːrɪˈeɪlɪs/ [northern] the aurora of the northern regions, the northern lights. **aurora polaris** /pə(ʊ)ˈlɑːrɪs/ [polar] either of the auroras of the polar regions, the northern or southern lights.

Comb.: **aurora snake** a non-venomous southern African snake, *Lamprophis aurora*, which is olive-green with an orange-yellow stripe.

aurorean *a.* belonging to dawn, or like it in hue E19.

auroral /ɔːˈrɔːr(ə)l/ *a.* M16. [Orig. f. Fr., or med.L *auroralis*; later f. prec. + -AL[1].] **1** Of or pertaining to the dawn; eastern; *fig.* of or pertaining to the first period of anything. M16. **2** Like the dawn; dawning, roseate. E19. **3** Of or pertaining to the aurora (borealis or australis). E19. **4** Resembling the aurora in its bright display. L19.

1 P. BAYNE Auroral splendours of promise . . which accompany all revolutions in their earlier stages. V. NABOKOV An atmosphere of . . barbecue smoke, horseplay, jazz music, and auroral swimming. 2 LONGFELLOW Her cheeks suffused with an auroral blush. 3 E. K. KANE A true and unbroken auroral arch. 4 F. T. PALGRAVE Auroral flashings of wit.

aurorally *adv.* L19.

aurothiomalate /ˌɔːrə(ʊ)θʌɪˈɒməleɪt, ˌɔːrə(ʊ)θʌɪə(ʊ)ˈmaleɪt/ *n.* M20. [f. AURO- + THIO- + MALATE.] *Pharm.* The sodium salt of a gold- and sulphur-containing derivative of succinic acid, used to treat rheumatoid arthritis.

aurous /ˈɔːrəs/ *a.* M19. [f. L *aurum* gold + -OUS.] *Chem.* Of gold in the monovalent state. Cf. AURIC *a.*[1]

aurum /ˈɔːrəm/ *n. arch.* LME. [L.] Gold.

†***aurum fulminans*** gold fulminate. ***aurum mosaicum*** /məˈzeɪɪkəm/, ***aurum musivum*** /mʊˈziːvəm/ stannic sulphide, SnS_2, formerly used as a bronzing powder. †***aurum potabile*** potable gold.

auscultate /ˈɔːsk(ə)lteɪt/ *v.* M18. [L *auscultat-* pa. ppl stem of *auscultare* hear with attention: see -ATE[3].] **1** *v.i.* Listen, hear. *rare.* M18. **2** *v.t.* *Med.* Examine by auscultation. M19.

au'scult *v.t.* & *i.* = AUSCULTATE M19. **au'scultative** *a.* (*Med.*) of or pertaining to auscultation M19. **auscultator** *n.* (*Med.*) a person who examines by auscultation M19. **auscultatory** *a.* of or pertaining to listening or (*Med.*) auscultation M17.

auscultation /ɔːsk(ə)lˈteɪʃ(ə)n/ *n.* M17. [L *auscultatio(n-)*, f. as prec.: see -ATION.] **1** The action of listening. M17. **2** *Med.* The action of listening, usu. with a stethoscope, to the heart, lungs, or other organs, as an aid to diagnosis. E19.

au sérieux /o serjø/ *adv. phr.* M19. [Fr.] Seriously. Cf. AU GRAND SÉRIEUX.

auslaut /ˈaʊslaʊt/ *n.* L19. [G, f. *aus-* denoting termination + *Laut* sound.] *Philol.* The final sound of a syllable or word.

Auslese /ˈaʊsleːzə/ *n.* Also **a-**. Pl. ***-sen*** /-zən/, ***-ses***. M19. [G, f. *aus* out + *lese* picking, vintage.] A white wine made (esp. in Germany) from selected bunches of grapes picked later than the general harvest.

Ausonian /ɔːˈsəʊnɪən/ *a.* & *n.* L16. [f. L *Ausonia* southern Italy, in poetry Italy, f. Gk, f. *Ausōn* son of Odysseus, who was said to have settled there, + -AN.] (A native or inhabitant) of ancient central and southern Italy; (an) Italian.

auspicate /ˈɔːspɪkeɪt/ *v.t.* Now *rare.* E17. [L *auspicat-* pa. ppl stem of *auspicari*, f. *auspicium*: see next, -ATE[3].] **1** Prognosticate; predict. E17. **2** Initiate with an auspicious ceremony; give a fortunate start to. E17. **3** Enter upon in a specified way or with specified consequences. E17. **4** Begin; inaugurate. M17.

auspice /ˈɔːspɪs/ *n.* M16. [Fr., or L *auspicium* taking omens from birds, f. *avis* bird + var. stem of *specere* look.] **1 a** An observation of birds for omens; a sign or token given by birds. M16. **b** *gen.* A prophetic token or premonition, esp. of a happy future; a forecast. M17. **2** *sing.* & (now) in *pl.* Patronage, favouring influence. E17.

2 Esp. in *under the auspices of*.

au'spicial *a.* auspicious; of or pertaining to auspices or augury: E17.

auspicious /ɔːˈspɪʃəs/ *a.* L16. [f. prec. + -OUS.] **1** Propitious; favourable, favouring; conducive to success. L16. **2** Giving or being an omen; *spec.* of good omen, betokening success. E17. **b** Of a person: predicting or prognosticating good. E18. **3** Prosperous, fortunate. E17.

1 SHAKES. *All's Well* Fortune play upon thy prosperous helm, As thy auspicious mistress! E. CALDWELL You might want to consult Evelyn about the most auspicious date for our wedding. 2 E. YOUNG Beneath auspicious planets born. K. AMIS But such an auspicious debut Was a little too good to be true.

a cat, ɑː arm, ɛ bed, əː her, ɪ sit, i cosy, iː see, ɒ hot, ɔː saw, ʌ run, ʊ put, uː too, ə ago, ʌɪ my, aʊ how, eɪ day, əʊ no, ɛː hair, ɪə near, ɔɪ boy, ʊə poor, ʌɪə tire, aʊə sour

A. K. RAMANUJAN A belief / in auspicious / snakes in the skylight. b C. ROSSETTI The aspect of jubilant auspicious angels.

auspiciously *adv.* L16. **auspiciousness** *n.* M17.

Aussie /'ɒzi, 'ɒsi/ *n.* & *a. colloq.* E20. [Abbrev. of AUSTRALIAN, *Australia*: see -IE. Cf. OZZIE.] A *n.* An Australian; Australia. E20. B *adj.* Australian. E20.

austenite /'ɒstɪnʌɪt, 'ɔː-/ *n.* E20. [f. Sir William Roberts-*Austen* (1843–1902), Eng. metallurgist + -ITE[1].] *Metall.* A solid solution of carbon in a non-magnetic high-temperature allotropic form of iron.

auste'nitic *a.* pertaining to or consisting principally of austenite E20.

Auster /'ɒstə, 'ɔː-/ *n.* LME. [L.] The south wind, esp. personified; the south.

austere /ɒ'stɪə, ɔː-/ *a.* ME. [(O)Fr. *austère* f. L *austerus* f. Gk *austēros* severe.] I 1 Stern in manner, appearance, or disposition; severe in judgement. ME. b Resolute in warfare. ME. 2 Severe in self-discipline; stringently moral; strict. LME. 3 Severely simple; without any luxury. L16. 4 Grave, sober, serious. M17.

1 BROWNING They would be gentle, not austere. E. O'NEILL His mask-like face is .. grimly remote and austere in death. b C. M. YONGE Simon, Count de Montfort, an austere warrior. 2 LD MACAULAY To these austere fanatics a holiday was an object of positive disgust. W. S. CHURCHILL He ruled according to the laws, and he made it known that these were to be administered in austere detachment from his executive authority. 3 R. MACAULAY I'm afraid our meals are rather austere .. Our meat ration is so tiny. J. K. GALBRAITH An austere community is free from temptation... Not so a rich one. L. DEIGHTON The white-painted office was bare and austere. 4 MILTON Eve .. With sweet austeer composure thus reply'd.

II 5 Harsh to the taste; astringent and bitter or sour. *arch.* LME.

5 W. COWPER The bramble, black as jet, or sloes austere.

austerely *adv.* LME. **austereness** *n.* LME.

austerity /ɒ'stɛrɪti, ɔː-/ *n.* LME. [(O)Fr. *austérité* f. L *austeritas*, f. *austerus*: see prec., -ITY.] 1 Sternness of manner, appearance, or disposition; severity in judgement. LME. b *transf.* Rigour. E18. 2 Severe self-discipline; moral strictness; asceticism; severe simplicity, lack of luxury or adornment; abstinence, economizing, esp. nationwide; *pl.* ascetic practices, economies. LME. 3 Harshness to the taste; astringent bitterness or sourness. *arch.* M17.

1 W. RALEIGH He gave presence .. with such austeritie, that no man durst presume to spit or cough in his sight. b BYRON Which soften'd down the hoar austerity Of rugged desolation. 2 SHAKES. *Mids. N. D.* On Diana's altar to protest For aye austerity and single life. BYRON And wherefore blame gaunt wealth's austerities? Because, you'll say, nought calls for such a trial. R. CHURCH The austerity of life in the boys' school did not improve my health. A. J. P. TAYLOR Cripps .. rejoiced at introducing measures of austerity: no petrol for pleasure motoring, the clothes ration cut down. H. ACTON In spite of the prevalent austerities he managed to conjure succulent meals for his guests.

Austin /'ɒstɪn, 'ɔː-/ *n.* & *a.* ME. [Contr. of (O)Fr. *augustin*: see AUGUSTINE.] = AUGUSTINE.

Austin Friars: see FRIAR.

austral /aʊ'strɑːl/ *n.* Pl. **-les** /-lɪz/. L20. [Sp. = southern, f. as next.] A monetary unit of Argentina replacing the peso between 1985 and 1992.

austral /'ɒstr(ə)l, 'ɔː-/ *a.* In sense 2 also **A-**. L15. [L *australis*, f. AUSTER: see -AL[1].] 1 Southern; influenced by the south wind. L15. 2 Of or pertaining to Australia or Australasia. E19.

Australasian /ɒstrə'leɪʒ(ə)n, -ʃ(ə)n; ɔː-/ *a.* & *n.* E19. [f. *Australasia* (see below) f. Fr. *Australasie*, f. as *Australia* + *Asia*, + -AN.] A *adj.* Of or pertaining to Australasia (Australia and the islands of the SW Pacific). E19.

Australasian warbler: see WARBLER 2C.

B *n.* A native or inhabitant of Australasia. E19.

Australian /ɒ'streɪlɪən, ɔː-/ *n.* & *a.* L17. [Fr. *australien*, f. L *australis* in *Terra Australis* southern land (see sense A.1 below), + -AN.] A *n.* †1 A native of the *Terra Australis*, the supposed continent and islands lying in the Great Southern Ocean, now identified as including Australasia, Polynesia, and parts of southern S. America. L17–L18. 2 A native or inhabitant of the island-continent of Australia. E19.

2 *new Australian*: see NEW *a.*

B *adj.* Of or pertaining to Australia. E19.

Australian cattle-dog *Austral.* & *NZ* a cattle-dog with a dark speckled body. **Australian crawl** a fast swimming stroke originating in Australia. **Australian football** = *Australian Rules football* below. *Australian* MAGPIE. *Australian* PRATINCOLE. **Australian Rules** (the rules governing) a form of football developed in Australia (= *Australian Rules football* below). **Australian Rules football** a form of football played on an oval pitch with a rugby ball by teams of 18 players. **Australian salmon** a large green and silver percoid fish, *Arripis trutta*, found off the coast of New Zealand and SE Australia. **Australian teak** = FLINDOSA. **Australian terrier** a wire-haired terrier of an Australian breed. *Australian warbler*: see WARBLER 2C.

Australi'ana *n.pl.* [-ANA] publications or other items concerning or associated with Australia M19. **Australianism** *n.* (*a*) a word or idiom peculiar to Australia; (*b*) = AUSTRALIANNESS: L19. **Australianize** *v.t.* make Australian in character etc. L19. **Australianness** /-n-n-/ *n.* the state or quality of being Australian M20.

australite /'ɒstrəlʌɪt, ɔː-/ *n.* E20. [f. *Australia* + -ITE[1].] *Geol.* A tektite found in the Australian strewn field.

Australoid /'ɒstrəlɔɪd, ɔː-/ *a.* & *n.* M19. [f. AUSTRALIAN + -OID.] (A person) of the ethnological type of the Australian Aborigine.

Also **Aus'tralioid** *a.* M19.

Australopithecus /,ɒstrələʊ'pɪθɪkəs, ,ɔː-/ *n.* E20. [mod.L, f. L *australis* southern + -O- + Gk *pithēkos* ape.] Any of various small-brained fossil hominids of the genus *Australopithecus*, known from remains found in Africa and southern Asia.

Au'stralopith *n.* = AUSTRALOPITHECUS M20. **australopithecine** /-siːn/ *a.* & *n.* M20.

Australorp /'ɒstrəlɔːp, ɔː-/ *n.* E20. [f. AUSTRALIAN + ORP(INGTON.] A black Orpington fowl of an Australian breed.

Austrasian /ɒ'streɪʃ(ə)n/ *a.* & *n.* L18. [f. med.L *Austrasia*, *Ost-* + -AN.] *Hist.* (A native or inhabitant) of the eastern part of the Frankish empire in the Merovingian period.

Austrian /'ɒstrɪən, ɔː-/ *a.* & *n.* E17. [f. *Austria* (= G *Österreich* Eastern kingdom) + -AN.] (A native or inhabitant) of Austria, a country in central Europe.

Austrian brier: see BRIER *n.*[1] **Austrian pine** a very hardy pine, *Pinus nigra*, of Europe and Asia Minor, with a dense branch system.

austringer /'ɔːstrɪndʒə/ *n.* Also **ost-** /'ɒst-/. L15. [Alt. of OFr. *ostruchier*, *aust-* OSTREGER: cf. *messenger*, *passenger*.] A keeper of goshawks.

Austro- /'ɒstrəʊ, 'ɔː-/ *comb. form*[1] of AUSTRIAN, as *Austro-Hungarian*, *-Prussian*, etc.: see -O-.

Austro- /'ɒstrəʊ, 'ɔː-/ *comb. form*[2] of *Austral* (AUSTRAL *a.* 2) and AUSTRALIAN, as *Austro-Asiatic*, *-Malayan*, etc.: see -O-.

Austronesian /ɒstrə(ʊ)'niːzjən, -ʒ(ə)n, ɔː-/ *a.* & *n.* E20. [f. G *austronesisch*, f. L *australis* southern + -O- + Gk *nēsos* island: see -IAN.] (Of or pertaining to) a family of agglutinative languages spoken widely in Malaysia, Indonesia, and other parts of SE Asia, and in the islands of the central and southern Pacific.

aut- *comb. form* see AUTO-[1].

autarchic /ɔː'tɑːkɪk/ *a.*[1] L19. [f. AUTARCHY *n.*[1] + -IC.] Absolute, despotic.

autarchical *a.*[1] M20.

autarchic, -ical *adjs.*[2] vars. of AUTARKIC, -ICAL.

autarchy /'ɔːtɑːki/ *n.*[1] M17. [mod.L *autarchia* after *monarchia* MONARCHY: see AUTO-[1], -ARCHY.] Absolute sovereignty, despotism.

autarch *n.* an absolute ruler, an autocrat E19.

autarchy *n.*[2] var. of AUTARKY.

autarky /'ɔːtɑːki/ *n.* Also **-archy**. E17. [Gk *autarkeia*, f. *autarkēs* self-sufficient, f. AUTO-[1] + *arkein* suffice.] Self-sufficiency, esp. in spiritual or economic matters.

au'tarkic *a.* of, pertaining to, or characterized by autarky; (economically) self-sufficient: L19. **au'tarkical** *a.* = AUTARKIC M20. **autarkist** *n.* an advocate of autarky M20.

autecious *a.* see AUTOECIOUS.

autecology /ɔːtɪ'kɒlədʒi/ *n.* E20. [f. AUTO-[1] + ECOLOGY.] *Biol.* The ecology of an individual species. Cf. SYNECOLOGY.

auteco'logical *a.* E20.

auteur /otœːr/ *n.* Pl. pronounced same. M20. [Fr. = AUTHOR.] *Cinema.* A director who so greatly influences the films directed as to be able to rank as their author.

authentic /ɔː'θɛntɪk/ *a.* & *n.* LME. [OFr. *autentique* (mod. *authentique*) f. late L *authenticus* f. Gk *authentikos* principal, genuine.] A *adj.* †1 Of authority, authoritative; entitled to obedience or respect. LME–M19. †2 Legally valid; legally qualified. LME–E18. 3 Entitled to belief as stating or according with fact; reliable, trustworthy. LME. 4 Real, actual, genuine; original, first-hand; really proceeding from its stated source, author, painter, etc. L15. †5 Own, proper. L16–M17. 6 *Mus.* Of a church mode: having sounds comprised between a final note and its octave (cf. PLAGAL). Of a cadence: perfect. E18.

1 LD BERNERS One of the moost autentyke men of the court of parlyment. SWIFT Some short plain authentick tract might be published. 2 SHAKES. *All's Well* All the learned and authentic fellows. J. FLAVEL What is done by Commission is Authentick. 3 T. NORTON To discredit so many authentike witnesses. A. J. P. TAYLOR The battles of El Alamein or Stalingrad only became fully authentic when they appeared on the [cinema] screen. *Listener* BBC1's *Tenko* was the most authentic representation to date of the Far East prisoner's life. 4 MILTON Him who had stole Joves authentic fire E. WAUGH A treasure house of period gems; pure authentic 1914. R. D. LAING To be 'authentic' is to be true to oneself, to be what one is, to be 'genuine'. 5 G. CHAPMAN Then Nestor cut the gears With his new-drawn authentic sword.

B *n.* 1 An original or authoritative document. Long *obs.* exc. as below. L15. †2 An authority. *rare.* Only in E17.

1 **the Authentics** a collection of enactments of Justinian.

authentical *a.* (now *rare* or *obs.*) = AUTHENTIC *a.* M16. **authentically** *adv.* L16. †**authenticalness** *n.* M17–M19. †**authenticly** *adv.* LME–M18. **authenticness** *n.* M16.

authenticate /ɔː'θɛntɪkeɪt/ *v.t.* E17. [med.L *authenticat-* pa. ppl stem of *authenticare*, f. late L *authenticus*: see prec., -ATE[3].] 1 Give authority or legal validity to, establish as valid. E17. 2 Establish the credibility of a statement, reported occurrence, reputed fact, etc. M17. 3 Establish as genuine or real; certify the origin or authorship of. M19.

1 R. NORTH Antiquity to authenticate their ceremonies. C. V. WEDGWOOD The minutes read in the form in which Phelps finally authenticated them on the great roll of parchment .. as a perpetual record. 2 C. LAMB A room, which tradition authenticated to have been the same. C. DARWIN I doubt whether any case of a perfectly fertile hybrid animal can be considered as thoroughly well authenticated. J. CHEEVER Letters, photographs, diplomas—anything that authenticated the past was always thrown into the fire. 3 H. T. COCKBURN We went through the whole work, authenticating all his papers. V. WOOLF The authenticated masterpiece by Michael Angelo.

authenti'cation *n.* the action or process of authenticating something; the condition of being authenticated: L18. **authenticator** *n.* a person who authenticates something M19.

authenticity /ɔːθɛn'tɪsɪti/ *n.* M17. [f. AUTHENTIC *a.* + -ITY.] The quality of being authentic.

authigenic /ɔːθɪ'dʒɛnɪk/ *a.* L19. [f. Gk *authigenēs* born on the spot, native + -IC.] *Geol.* Originating where found; formed *in situ.*

authigenesis *n.* formation *in situ* M20.

author /'ɔːθə/ *n.* & *v.* ME. [AN *autour*, OFr. *autor* (mod. *auteur*) f. L *auctor*, f. *augere auct-* increase, promote, originate.] A *n.* 1 *gen.* The person who originates, invents, gives rise to, or causes something (now only an immaterial thing, a condition, an event, exc. of God). ME. †b A person who authorizes or instigates. M16–M17. 2 A father, an ancestor. *arch.* LME. 3 The writer of a book, essay, article, etc.; a person who writes books etc. LME. **b** *ellipt.* An author's writings. E17. †**c** The editor of a journal. L17–M18. **4** A person on whose authority a statement is made; an informant. *obs.* exc. *dial.* LME.

1 W. LAMBARDE One Robert Creuequer, the authour of the Castle. J. CHEEVER Embittered by the waste that he himself was the author of. A. HAILEY He was the author of early legislation to protect minorities. **the Author (of all** etc.), **the great Author** God, the Creator. b SHAKES. *Tit. A.* The gods of Rome forfend I should be author to dishonour you! 2 C. LAMB Certainly old Walter Plumer (his reputed author) had been a rake in his days. 3b SHAKES. *Twel. N.* I will be proud, I will read politic authors. 4 W. DAMPIER Islands that abound with Gold and Cloves, If I may credit my Author Prince Jeoly.

Comb.: **author-craft** *arch.* (exercise of) skill as an author (of books etc.).

B *v.t.* **1** Originate, bring about, (an action, condition, circumstance, etc.). L16. †**2** State, declare. E–M17. **3** Write, be the author of, (a book, essay, article, etc.). Orig. *US.* E20.

1 M. LOWRY Who would ever have believed that some obscure man . . was authoring their doom. 3 *Time* Her father . . authored several successful plays and movies.

¶The spelling w. *-th-* was rare bef. 16.

authoress *n.* a female author L15. **authorial** /ɔːˈθɔːrɪəl/ *a.* of or pertaining to an author (of books etc.) L18. **authorially** *adv.* M19. **authorism** *n.* (now *rare* or *obs.*) the position or character of an author of books etc. M18. **authorless** *a.* E18. **authorling** *n.* a petty or insignificant writer L18. **authorly** *a.* proper to or characteristic of an author or authors L18.

authorise *v.*, **-ised** *a.* vars. of AUTHORIZE, -IZED.

authoritarian /ɔːθɒrɪˈtɛːrɪən/ *a.* & *n.* L19. [f. AUTHORITY + -ARIAN.] **A** *adj.* Favouring or characterized by obedience to (esp. political) authority as opp. to personal liberty; tyrannical, dictatorial. L19.

P. NICHOLS I don't want to sound authoritarian or fascist but there's only one useful approach to any human problem and that's a positive one. A. STORR A parent who is too dominant may become frightening, and no one would wish to advocate a return to the authoritarian rule of the Victorian *pater familias.* B. MAGEE Whereas a free society cannot impose common social purposes, a government with Utopian aims has to, and is bound to become authoritarian.

B *n.* A supporter of authoritarian principles or methods. L19.

authoritarianism *n.* E20.

authoritative /ɔːˈθɒrɪtətɪv, -teɪtɪv/ *a.* E17. [f. next + -ATIVE.] **1** Having authority; exercising or assuming power; imperative, commanding. E17. **2** Possessing or claiming due authority; entitled to deference or acceptance. M17. **3** Proceeding from a competent authority. E19.

1 R. NORTH He was diligent and in acting authoritative. L. W. MEYNELL Above the general chatter, a loud authoritative voice cried, 'Now, then, what's the trouble 'ere?' 2 HENRY MORE A number sufficient to constitute an Authoritative Church. E. F. SCHUMACHER If the 'rich' populations grow at . . 1¼ per cent and the 'poor' at . . 2½ per cent a year, world population will grow to about 6900 million by AD 2000—a figure not very different from the most authoritative current forecasts. 3 J. B. MARSDEN An authoritative declaration of pardon.

authoritatively *adv.* LME. **authoritativeness** *n.* M17.

authority /ɔːˈθɒrɪti/ *n.* ME. [(O)Fr. *autorité* f. L *auctoritas*, f. *auctor*: see AUTHOR, -ITY.] **I** Power to enforce obedience. **1** Power or right to enforce obedience; moral or legal supremacy; right to command or give a final decision. ME. **2** Derived or delegated power; authorization. LME. **3** Those in power or control (treated as *sing.* (abstract) or *pl.*); the governing body; a body exercising power in a particular sphere. M16.

1 J. RUSKIN If ever you find yourselves set in positions of authority. D. LODGE You conspired with the students to weaken the authority of the senior staff. **in authority** in a position of power or control. 2 COVERDALE *Ezra* 7:24 Ye shall have no auctorite to requyre taxinge & custome. CARLYLE He carries in him an authority from God. 3 *Westminster Gazette* The Port of London Authority is a thoroughly practical body of men. K. AMIS If you want to get up a charity . . , then you must first get the authorities' permission. C. P. SNOW As a natural conservative, his feelings would be on the side of authority. *local authority*: see LOCAL *a.*

II Power to influence action, opinion, belief, etc. **4** The book, quotation, etc., acknowledged or alleged to settle a question or give conclusive testimony. ME. **5** Power to inspire belief; right to be believed; testimony, statement. ME. **6** Power over the opinions of others; authoritative opinion, intellectual influence. ME. **7** Power to influence the conduct and actions of others; personal or practical influence, commanding manner etc. LME. **8** A person whose opinion or testimony is to be accepted; an expert in any subject. M17.

4 SIR T. MORE Hys fyrst authorite be these words of saynte Austyne. J. R. GREEN Giving in detail the authorities for every statement. 5 OED Do not accept news on the authority of the evening papers. G. B. SHAW I await the decision of the Church. Until that is delivered the story has no authority. 6 J. S. MILL He is either led by authority, or adopts . . the side to which he feels most inclination. W. H. DIXON I hear on good authority . . that Cardinal Wolsey is not now in favour of a divorce. 7 V. S. PRITCHETT He was a man of authority with a deep, curt sarcastic voice used to command. 8 W. H. PRESCOTT Historians in a season of faction are not the best authorities. LADY BIRD JOHNSON I became an authority on the climate of India. I knew exactly where the rain fell and where it failed to fall.

authorize /ˈɔːθərʌɪz/ *v.t.* Also **-ise**. LME. [(O)Fr. *autoriser* f. med.L *auctorizare*, f. *auctor*: see AUTHOR, -IZE.] †**1** Set up or acknowledge as having authority. LME–E17. †**2** Make legally valid. LME–L17. **3** Give formal approval to; sanction, countenance. LME. †**4** Vouch for, confirm. LME–M17. **5** Endow (a person, body, etc.) with authority; commission. LME. **6** Give legal or formal warrant to (a person or body) *to do*; empower, permit authoritatively. LME. **7** Of things: give grounds for, justify. E17. **8** Of things: give grounds to. L18.

3 ISAIAH BERLIN Why should any conduct be tolerated that is not authorized by appropriate experts? 4 SHAKES. *Macb.* A woman's story at a winter's fire, Authoriz'd by her grandam. 6 LD MACAULAY A royal message authorizing the Commons to elect another Speaker. 7 G. ANSON These reasons alone would authorize the insertion of those papers. 8 J. SULLIVAN Nothing which can authorise us to suppose it formed in the sea.

authorizable *a.* †(*a*) able to be entrusted with authority; †(*b*) having the power of authorizing; (*c*) able to be authorized: LME. **authoriˈzation** *n.* formal approval or warrant L15. **authorizer** *n.* a person who authorizes something or someone L16.

authorized /ˈɔːθərʌɪzd/ *a.* Also **-ised**. LME. [f. prec. + -ED[1].] **1** Acknowledged as authoritative; thoroughly established. *arch.* LME. **2** Endowed with authority. LME. **3** Legally or formally sanctioned or appointed. LME.

1 COLERIDGE Received and authorized opinions. 2 OED The arrangement was made by your own authorized agent. 3 **Authorized Version** the 1611 English translation of the Bible.

authorship /ˈɔːθəʃɪp/ *n.* E18. [f. AUTHOR *n.* + -SHIP.] **1** Occupation or career as a writer; the dignity or position of an author. E18. **2** Literary origin (of a writing); *gen.* origination of any action or circumstance. E19.

autism /ˈɔːtɪz(ə)m/ *n.* E20. [f. Gk *autos* self + -ISM.] *Psychiatry.* Abnormal withdrawal from the world of reality; *spec.* a condition which has its onset in childhood and is marked by severely limited responsiveness to other persons, restricted behaviour patterns, and usu. abnormal speech development.

auˈtistic *a.* & *n.* (*a*) *adj.* pertaining to, associated with, or affected by autism; (*b*) *n.* a person affected by autism: E20.

auto /ˈauto/ *n.*[1] Pl. **-os** /-ɒs/. M16. [Sp. & Port. f. L *actus* ACT *n.*] **1** = AUTO-DA-FÉ. M16. **2** A play (by a Spanish or Portuguese author). L18.

auto /ˈɔːtəʊ/ *n.*[2] & *v. colloq.* L19. [Abbrev. of AUTOMOBILE.] **A** *n.* Pl. **-os**. A motor car. L19.

Comb.: **automaker** *N. Amer.* a manufacturer of motor vehicles, a company that manufactures motor vehicles.

B *v.i.* Travel in or drive a motor car. E20.

auto- /ˈɔːtəʊ/ *comb. form*[1]. Bef. a vowel also **aut-**. [Repr. Gk *auto-*, f. *autos* self.] **1** Used in wds adopted from Gk and in Eng. wds modelled on these, and as a freely productive pref., w. the sense 'one's own, of or by oneself, by itself, independent, self-produced, spontaneous, automatic'. **2** *Genetics.* Used in comb. w. -PLOID (and also *-ploidy*) to refer to individuals whose chromosome sets are derived from a single parent species (cf. ALLO-), as *autodiploid*, *autopolyploid*, etc.

auto-ˈanalysis *n.* self-analysis L19. **auto-ˈantibody** *n.* an antibody produced by an organism in response to a constituent of its own tissues M20. **autoˈcentric** *a.* centred in the self; making oneself the centre: M19. **autoˈcephalous** *a.* [Gk *kephalē* head] independent of archiepiscopal or patriarchal jurisdiction M19. **autocode** *n.* a low-level programming language in which each instruction corresponds to an instruction in machine code M20. **autoˈcritical** *a.* critical of oneself or one's own work M17. **Autocue, a-** *n.* (proprietary name for) a device which projects a rolling script, out of camera range, in front of a speaker on television M20. **auto-destruct** *n.* & *v.* (*a*) *n.* self-destruction, esp. as a built-in feature of a machine etc.; (*b*) *v.i.* destroy oneself, self-destruct: L20. **auto-destruction** *n.* self-destruction L20. **auto-destructive** *a.* self-destructive; *spec.* designating or pertaining to art in which the art-work is destroyed as it is created: M20. **autodiˈgestion** *n.* = AUTOLYSIS L19. **autofocus** *n.* & *a.* (*Photogr.*) automatic(ally) focusing M20. **autoˈfocusing** *n.* automatic focusing M20. **autograft** *n.* (*Surg.*) a graft of skin or other tissue taken from the same individual E20. **autoharp** *n.* a musical instrument of the zither type, with dampers to facilitate the production of arpeggio effects L19. **auto-inˈfection** *n.* (*a*) self-infection; (*b*) continued infection with parasitic worms owing to their larvae maturing without leaving the body: L19. **auto-inˈfective** *a.* of or pertaining to auto-infection L19. **auto-intoxiˈcation** *n.* poisoning by a toxin formed within the body L19. **autoland** *n.* & *v.* (*a*) *n.* automatic landing; (*b*) *v.t.* & *i.* land automatically: M20. **autolatry** /ɔːˈtɒlətri/ *n.* self-worship E17. **autoˈlogical** *a.* (of a word) having the property which it denotes (opp. HETEROLOGICAL) E20. **autologous** /ɔːˈtɒləgəs/ *a.* obtained from the same individual E20. **autology** /ɔːˈtɒlədʒi/ *n.* study of oneself, self-knowledge M17. **automath** *n.* (*rare*) = AUTODIDACT M18. **autophagic** /-ˈfeɪdʒɪk/ *a.* pertaining to or concerned with (lysosomal) autophagy M20. **autophagy** /ɔːˈtɒfədʒi/ *n.* digestion of the body's own tissues; *esp.* breakdown of cell constituents within lysosomes: L19; **autopilot** *n.* = *automatic pilot* s.v. AUTOMATIC *a.* M20. **autoˈplastic** *a.* of or pertaining to autoplasty M19. **autoˈplastically** *adv.* by means of autoplasty E20. **autoplasty** *n.* plastic surgery using autografts M19. **Autoplate** *n.* (*Printing*, now chiefly *Hist.*) (proprietary name for) a machine for making curved stereotype plates; a stereotype plate made by such a machine: E20. **autopsyˈchography** *n.* psychography of oneself M19. **autoseˈmantic** *a.* & *n.* (a word or phrase) having meaning outside its context; categorematic: E20. **autoˈsexing** *a.* (of a breed of poultry) possessing sex-linked characters which enable easy identification of sexes on hatching M20. **autosoteric** /-sə(ʊ)ˈtɛrɪk/ *a.* [Gk *sōtēria* salvation] relating to salvation by one's own efforts L19. **autotelic** /-ˈtɛlɪk/ *a.* having or being an end in itself E20. **autoˈtherapy** *n.* treatment of one's own infirmity M20. **autotransˈformer** *n.* (*Electr.*) a zooidtransformer having a single winding of which part is common to both primary and secondary circuits L19. **autotransˈfusion** *n.* (*Med.*) (*a*) a transfer of blood within the body; (*b*) transfusion with a patient's own blood: E20. **autotransˈplant** *v.t.* transplant (tissue) from one site to another within the same individual E20. **ˌautotransplanˈtation** *n.* transplantation of tissue from one site to another within the same individual E20. **autozooid** /-ˈzəʊɔɪd/ *n.* (*Zool.*) a typical zooid of an anthozoan or bryozoan L19.

auto- /ˈɔːtəʊ/ *comb. form*[2]. [Abbrev. of AUTOMOBILE *a.* & *n.*: cf. AUTO *n.*[2]] Forming wds relating to motor vehicles.

autobus *n.* = BUS *n.* 1 L19. **autocade** *n.* (*US*) [after *cavalcade*] a motorcade M20. **autocar** *n.* (*arch.*) = AUTOMOBILE *n.* L19. **autocrime** *n.* theft of motor vehicles or their contents L20. **autocross** *n.* motor racing across country or on unmade roads M20. **autocycle** *n.* (*arch.*) a bicycle with an auxiliary engine E20.

autobahn /ˈɔːtəbɑːn, *foreign* ˈaʊtobaːn/ *n.* Pl. **-bahns**, ***-bahnen*** /-baːnən/. M20. [G, f. *Auto* automobile + *Bahn* road.] A German, Swiss, or Austrian motorway.

autobiographer /ˌɔːtəbʌɪˈɒɡrəfə/ *n.* E19. [f. AUTO-[1] + BIOGRAPHER.] A person who writes the story of his or her own life.

autobiographical /ˌɔːtəbʌɪəˈɡrafɪk(ə)l/ *a.* E19. [f. AUTO-[1] + BIOGRAPHICAL.] Of or pertaining to an autobiography; of the nature of autobiography, relating to one's own life story.
autobiographic *a.* = AUTOBIOGRAPHICAL E19. **autobiographically** *adv.* M19.

autobiography /ˌɔːtəbʌɪˈɒɡrəfi/ *n.* L18. [f. AUTO-[1] + BIOGRAPHY.] The writing of one's own history; a story of a person's life written by himself or herself.
autobiographist *n.* = AUTOBIOGRAPHER M19.

autocatalysis /ˌɔːtə(ʊ)kəˈtalɪsɪs/ *n.* L19. [f. AUTO-[1] + CATALYSIS.] *Chem.* Catalysis of a reaction by one of its products.
autoˈcatalyst *n.* a product effecting autocatalysis M20. **autocataˈlytic** *a.* E20. **autocataˈlytically** *adv.* M20.

autochthon /ɔːˈtɒkθ(ə)n, -θəʊn/ *n.* Pl. **-thons,** (senses 1,2) in L form **-thones** /-θəniːz/. L16. [Gk *autokhthōn* indigenous, f. AUTO-[1] + *khthōn* earth, soil.] 1 (Usu. in *pl.*) Any of the earliest known dwellers in a region; an original inhabitant, an aboriginal. L16. 2 A human being living in his or her place of origin. *rare.* M17. 3 *Geol.* An autochthonous rock formation. M20.
autochthonal *a.* = AUTOCHTHONOUS *a.* 1 E19. **autochˈthonic** *a.* = AUTOCHTHONOUS *a.* 1 M19. **autochthony** *n.* autochthonous condition M19.

autochthonous /ɔːˈtɒkθənəs/ *a.* E19. [f. prec. + -OUS.] 1 Indigenous, native, aboriginal. E19. 2 *Med.* Of a blood clot etc.: that originated where it is found, or without external agency. L19. 3 *Geol.* Formed *in situ*; consisting of indigenous material. E20.
autochthonously *adv.* L19.

autoclave /ˈɔːtəkleɪv/ *n.* & *v.* L19. [Fr., f. as AUTO-[1] + L *clavus* nail or *clavis* key: so called because self-fastening.] A *n.* 1 A pressure cooker. *rare.* L19. 2 A strong vessel used for chemical reactions at high pressures and temperatures, or for high-pressure sterilization using steam. L19. B *v.t.* Heat in an autoclave. E20.

autocorrelation /ˌɔːtə(ʊ)kɒrɪˈleɪʃ(ə)n/ *n.* M20. [f. AUTO-[1] + CORRELATION.] A correlation between the elements of a series and those respectively separated from them by a given interval.
autoˈcorrelator *n.* a machine for performing autocorrelations M20. **autoˈcorrelogram** *n.* a graphical representation of an autocorrelation M20.

autocracy /ɔːˈtɒkrəsi/ *n.* M17. [Gk *autokrateia*, f. as next: see -CRACY.] †1 Independent power; autonomy. M17–M19. 2 Absolute government; controlling authority or influence. E19. 3 Autocrats collectively. E20.

autocrat /ˈɔːtəkrat/ *n.* E19. [Fr. *autocrate* f. Gk *autokratēs*, f. AUTO-[1] + *krate-*, *kratos* power, authority.] A monarch of uncontrolled authority, an absolute ruler; a person with dictatorial powers or tendencies.
autoˈcratic(al) *adjs.* of the nature of or pertaining to an autocrat; despotic, dictatorial: E19. **autoˈcratically** *adv.* M19. **autocratism** /ɔːˈtɒkrətɪz(ə)m/ *n.* the principles or practices of autocrats M19.

autocrator /ɔːˈtɒkrətə/ *n.* *arch.* M18. [Late L = emperor, f. Gk *autokratōr* one's own master, f. AUTO-[1] + *kratōr* ruler.] An absolute monarch.
†**autocratorical** *a.* M17–E19. **autocratrix** *n.* a female autocrator, esp. *Hist.* (A-) as a title of empresses of Russia ruling in their own right M18.

auto-da-fé /ˌautodaˈfe; ˌɔːtəʊdɑːˈfeɪ, ˌaʊt-/ *n.* Pl. ***autos-da-fé*** /ˌautosdaˈfe; ˌɔːtəʊzdɑːˈfeɪ, ˌaʊtəʊz-/, ***auto-da-fés***. E18. [Port. = act of the faith.] (The execution of) a judicial sentence of the Inquisition; *esp.* the public burning of a heretic.

autodidact /ˈɔːtəʊdɪdakt/ *n.* M18. [f. Gk *autodidaktos* self-taught: see AUTO-[1], DIDACTIC.] A person who is self-taught.
autodiˈdactic *a.* self-taught; of or pertaining to self-teaching: M19.

autoecious /ɔːˈtiːʃəs/ *a.* Also ***autec-**. L19. [f. AUTO-[1] + Gk *oikia* house + -IOUS.] *Bot.* (Of a parasitic fungus) completing its life cycle on a single host; (of a bryophyte) having antheridia and archegonia on separate branches of the same plant.

auto-erotic /ˌɔːtəʊɪˈrɒtɪk/ *a.* L19. [f. AUTO-[1] + EROTIC.] *Psychol.* Of or pertaining to auto-eroticism; characterized by or given to auto-eroticism.
auto-erotically *adv.* E20.

auto-eroticism /ˌɔːtəʊɪˈrɒtɪsɪz(ə)m/ *n.* E20. [f. AUTO-[1] + EROTICISM.] *Psychol.* Sexual arousal or gratification obtained without the involvement of another person; masturbation.

auto-erotism /ɔːtəʊˈɛrətɪz(ə)m/ *n.* L19. [f. AUTO-[1] + EROTISM.] *Psychol.* = prec.

autogamy /ɔːˈtɒɡəmi/ *n.* L19. [f. AUTO-[1] + -GAMY.] *Biol.* Self-fertilization; (in some unicellular organisms) fusion of sister nuclei.
autogamic /ɔːtəˈɡamɪk/, **autogamous** *adjs.* pertaining to or characterized by autogamy L19.

autogenesis /ɔːtə(ʊ)ˈdʒɛnɪsɪs/ *n.* L19. [f. AUTO-[1] + -GENESIS.] Self-production; spontaneous formation.

autogenetic /ˌɔːtə(ʊ)dʒəˈnɛtɪk/ *a.* L19. [f. prec.: see AUTO-[1], -GENETIC.] Self-produced; spontaneously formed.
autogenetically *adv.* L19.

autogenic /ɔːtə(ʊ)ˈdʒɛnɪk/ *a.* L19. [f. AUTO-[1] + -GENIC.] Self-produced, autogenous; *Ecol.* self-generated without external influence.
autogenic training a method of learning to hypnotize oneself and then induce physiological changes in the body.

autogenous /ɔːˈtɒdʒɪnəs/ *a.* M19. [f. Gk *autogenēs*: see AUTO-[1], -GENOUS.] Self-produced; *spec.* (*a*) (of a weld, welding) formed by or involving the melting of the joined ends, without added filler; (*b*) (of a vaccine) derived from the patient's own infecting micro-organisms.
autogenously *adv.* L19.

autogiro /ɔːtəʊˈdʒʌɪrəʊ/ *n.* Also **-gyro.** Pl. **-os.** E20. [Sp., f. as AUTO-[1] + *giro* gyration.] A type of aircraft having a propeller and freely rotating horizontal rotary blades.

autograph /ˈɔːtəɡrɑːf/ *n.*, *v.*, & *a.* E17. [Fr. *autographe* or late L *autographum* f. Gk *autographon* use as n. of neut. of *autographos* written with one's own hand: see AUTO-[1], -GRAPH.] A *n.* 1 A person's own signature. E17. 2 A manuscript in an author's own handwriting; a document signed by its author. M17. 3 A person's own handwriting. M19. 4 A reproduction made by direct facsimile; *esp.* = AUTOLITHOGRAPH *n.* *arch.* M19.
1 DICKENS Left our autographs and read those of other people. 2 W. W. SKEAT The MS. of Piers Plowman . . seems to be an autograph of the author. 3 N. HAWTHORNE Poems of Tasso in his own autograph.
Comb.: **autograph album, book** a book in which a person collects the signatures of various people, often with rhymes etc.; **autograph-hunter** a person who makes a collection of signatures of celebrities.
B *v.t.* 1 Write with one's own hand. E19. 2 Write one's signature on or in; sign. M19.
2 S. LEACOCK The Prince took the pen and very kindly autographed for us seven photographs of himself. D. WELCH A book that had been signed by Walter de la Mare . . the first autographed book I had ever held.
C *adj.* Written in the author's own handwriting; (of a painting) done by the artist himself, not by a copier. M19.
P. G. WODEHOUSE You will appreciate another capture of mine, the autograph manuscript of Don Juan, Canto Nine. *Times Lit. Suppl.* Some of the Madonnas . . must be wholly or in large part autograph.

autographic /ɔːtəˈɡrafɪk/ *a.* E19. [f. prec. + -IC.] 1 Written with the author's own hand. E19. 2 Of or pertaining to reproduction by direct facsimile; *esp.* = AUTOLITHOGRAPHIC *a.* *arch.* M19.
autographical *a.* †(*a*) = AUTOBIOGRAPHICAL; (*b*) = AUTOGRAPHIC: M17. **autographically** *adv.* L17.

autography /ɔːˈtɒɡrəfi/ *n.* M17. [f. AUTOGRAPH *n.* + -Y[3].] 1 The action of writing with one's own hand; the author's own handwriting. M17. 2 = AUTOBIOGRAPHY. Now *rare* or *obs.* M17. 3 Reproduction of writing, drawing, etc., by direct facsimile; *esp.* = AUTOLITHOGRAPHY. *arch.* M19.

autogyro *n.* var. of AUTOGIRO.

autohypnosis /ˌɔːtəʊhɪpˈnəʊsɪs/ *n.* Pl. **-noses** /-ˈnəʊsiːz/. E20. [f. AUTO-[1] + HYPNOSIS.] (A) self-induced hypnosis; self-hypnotism.
autohypnotic /-hɪpˈnɒtɪk/ *a.* E20. **autoˈhypnotism** *n.* self-hypnotism L19.

autoimmunity /ˌɔːtəʊɪˈmjuːnɪti/ *n.* E20. [f. AUTO-[1] + IMMUNITY.] *Med.* †1 Immunity produced within the body. Only in E20. 2 The production or presence within the body of autoantibodies. M20.
autoimmune *a.* pertaining to, caused or characterized by autoimmunity (sense 2) M20. **ˌautoimmuniˈzation** *n.* †(*a*) = AUTOIMMUNITY 1; (*b*) the induction of autoimmunity (sense 2): E20.

autokinesis /ˌɔːtə(ʊ)kɪˈniːsɪs, -kʌɪ-/ *n.* M19. [f. AUTO-[1] + Gk *kinēsis* motion.] 1 Spontaneous motion. Only in Dicts. M19. 2 An illusion of the motion of a stationary object in an otherwise empty visual field. M20.
autokinetic *a.* L19.

autolithography /ˌɔːtə(ʊ)lɪˈθɒɡrəfi/ *n.* L19. [f. AUTO-[1] + LITHOGRAPHY.] Lithographic printing done directly from original drawings etc.
autoˈlithograph *n.* & *v.* (*a*) *n.* a picture or print made by autolithography; (*b*) *v.t.* produce or reproduce by autolithography: L19. **autolithoˈgraphic** *a.* L19.

autolysis /ɔːˈtɒlɪsɪs/ *n.* E20. [f. AUTO-[1] + -LYSIS.] *Biol.* Destruction of cells or tissues by their own enzymes, esp. as released from lysosomes.
autolysate *n.* a substance produced by autolysis E20. **ˈautolyse** /-lʌɪz/ *v.i.* & *t.* (cause to) undergo autolysis E20. **autolysin** *n.* an enzyme causing autolysis E20. **autoˈlytic** *a.* E20.

automacy /ɔːˈtɒməsi/ *n.* *rare.* M19. [f. AUTOMATIC: see -ACY.] The condition or state of being an automaton; automaticity.

automat /ˈɔːtəmat/ *n.* L17. [G f. Fr. AUTOMATE *n.*] 1 = AUTOMATON. L17. 2 A cafeteria in which food is obtained from a slot-machine; a slot-machine. Chiefly *US.* E20.

automata *n.pl.* see AUTOMATON.

†**automate** *n.* & *a.* M17. [Fr. f. L AUTOMATON.] A *n.* An automaton. M17–M18. B *adj.* Automatic. Only in E19.

automate /ˈɔːtəmeɪt/ *v.* M20. [Back-form. f. AUTOMATION.] 1 *v.t.* Convert to or equip for largely automatic operation. Freq. as *automated* ppl a. M20. 2 *v.i.* Apply or introduce automation. M20.

automatic /ɔːtəˈmatɪk/ *a.* & *n.* M18. [f. Gk *automatos* + -IC: see AUTOMATON.] A *adj.* 1 Like the action of an automaton; unintelligent, merely mechanical; done without thought, unconscious; occurring as a matter of course without debate. M18. 2 Self-acting; *esp.* (of a machine, device, etc.) working of itself, with little or no direct human actuation; (of a process etc.) working thus, involving such equipment. M18. b *spec.* Of a firearm: having a mechanism for continuous loading, firing, and ejecting until ammunition is exhausted or pressure on the trigger is released. L19. c *spec.* Of a telephone exchange: operated by automatic switches. L19. d *spec.* Of the transmission in a motor vehicle: changing gear automatically according to speed and acceleration. Of a vehicle: equipped with automatic transmission. M20. 3 Of psychic phenomena etc.: occurring subconsciously or unconsciously. L19. 4 Occurring as a necessary consequence; (esp. of a legal sanction) taking effect without further process in set circumstances. E20. 5 *Art.* Characterized by or pertaining to surrealist automatism. M20.
1 A. BAIN The winking of the eyes is essentially automatic. J. MASTERS I tossed my head—it is an automatic gesture I cannot help—and went forward again. DAY LEWIS A natural system . . under which the demands of the younger are not given automatic priority over the rights of the older. C. JACKSON The invitation was compulsive and automatic, it sprang from old habit merely. T. BAILEY As a batsman, he would have been an automatic choice for any Test

team of any period. *Lancet* Approximately a quarter of narcoleptics have frequent periods of automatic behaviour in the daytime when they are only half-awake. 2 OED A Sewing Machine with automatic tension. G. B. SHAW A box of matches will come out of an automatic machine when I put a penny in the slot. T. S. ELIOT She smoothes her hair with automatic hand, And puts a record on the gramophone. J. HEDGECOE Fully automatic metering systems set both aperture and shutter speed automatically. **automatic landing** landing of an aircraft under the control or guidance of instruments. **automatic pilot** a device for keeping an aircraft or ship on a set course. 3 **automatic writing**: done by means of a planchette etc. 4 *Washington Post* Brown was charged with a game misconduct, his fourth, and will sit out the next two games on an automatic suspension.

B *n.* 1 A machine, device, etc., operated automatically; *esp.* (*a*) an automatic firearm; (*b*) a motor vehicle with automatic transmission. L19. 2 *N. Amer. Football.* = AUDIBLE *n.* 2. M20.

automatical *a.* (now *rare* or *obs.*) L16. **automatically** *adv.* M19. **automaticity** /-mə'tɪsɪti/ *n.* automatic condition, nature, or functioning L19.

automation /ɔːtə'meɪʃ(ə)n/ *n.* M20. [Irreg. f. AUTOMATIC + -ATION.] Automatic control of a manufacturing or other process through a number of successive stages; the use of automatic devices to save mental and manual labour; the introduction of automatic methods or equipment.

automatise *v.* var. of AUTOMATIZE.

automatism /ɔː'tɒmətɪz(ə)m/ *n.* M19. [Fr. *automatisme*, f. AUTOMATE *n.*: see -ISM.] 1 The quality of being automatic, or of acting mechanically only; involuntary action; a doctrine ascribing this quality to animals. M19. 2 Mechanical, unthinking routine. L19. 3 The faculty of independently originating action. Now *rare* or *obs.* L19. 4 *Psychol.* An action that is, unusually, performed subconsciously or unconsciously; the mental state accompanying such an action. L19. 5 *Art.* A surrealist technique seeking to eliminate conscious thought from the creative process. M20.

automatist *n.* an adherent or practitioner of, or a person subject to, automatism L19.

automatize /ɔː'tɒmətʌɪz/ *v.t.* Also **-ise**. M19. [Fr. *automatiser*, f. as prec.: see -IZE.] Reduce to an automaton; make automatic; automate.

automati'zation *n.* E20.

automaton /ɔː'tɒmət(ə)n/ *n.* Pl. **-matons**, **-mata** /-mətə/. E17. [L (also *-tum*) f. Gk, use as n. of neut. of *automatos* acting of itself.] 1 Something having the power of spontaneous motion; *esp.* a living being viewed as a machine. E17. 2 A piece of mechanism with concealed motive power, *esp.* one simulating a living being; a robot. M17. 3 A living being whose actions are purely involuntary or mechanical; a person behaving without active intelligence or mechanically in a set pattern or routine. L17. 4 *Computing.* A machine whose responses to all possible inputs are specified in advance. M20.

1 R. BOYLE These living Automata, Human bodies. BURKE The perfect Drama, an automaton supported and moved without any foreign help, was formed late and gradually. T. H. HUXLEY Such a self-adjusting machine, containing the immediate conditions of its actions within itself, is what is properly understood by an Automaton. 2 EVELYN Another automaton strikes the quarters. L. MUMFORD The belief that automatons would ultimately displace human labor was common to the new Utopias. 3 J. PRIESTLEY Descartes . . made the souls of brutes to be mere automata. J. A. SYMONDS How could a Spartan, that automaton of the state . . excel in any fine art? C. S. FORESTER Last night they had staggered into the village, exhausted automata.

automatous /ɔː'tɒmətəs/ *a.* M17. [f. Gk *automatos* (see prec.) + -OUS.] 1 Of the nature of an automaton; acting mechanically. M17. 2 Acting spontaneously; having the power of self-motion. M18.

automobile /'ɔːtəməbiːl/ *a.*, *n.*, & *v.* Chiefly *N. Amer.* L19. [Fr., f. as AUTO-[1] + MOBILE *a.*] **A** *adj.* 1 Esp. of a vehicle: self-propelling (as opp. to horse-drawn). *arch.* L19. 2 [The n. used attrib.] Of or pertaining to motor vehicles. L19. **B** *n.* A motor vehicle; a car. L19. **C** *v.i.* Drive or travel in a motor vehicle. L19.

auto'mobilism *n.* (*arch.*) the use of motor vehicles L19. **auto'mobilist** *n.* (*arch.*) a motorist L19. **automo'bility** *n.* the use of motor vehicles; mobility based on this: E20.

automorphism /ɔːtəʊ'mɔːfɪz(ə)m/ *n.* M19. [f. AUTO-[1] + Gk *morphē* form + -ISM.] 1 *Math.* Any of various kinds of transformation or correspondence which relate a function etc. to itself or to another of the same kind; *spec.* an isomorphism of a structure with itself. M19. 2 The ascription of one's own characteristics to another. Now *rare* or *obs.* L19.

automorphic *a.* pertaining to, characterized by, or invariant under automorphism M19.

automotive /ɔːtə'məʊtɪv/ *n.* & *a.* M19. [f. AUTO-[1] + MOTIVE *a.*] †**A** *n.* A self-propelled vehicle. Only in M19. **B** *adj.* Of or pertaining to an automobile or automobiles. L19.

autonomic /ɔːtə'nɒmɪk/ *a.* M19. [f. AUTONOMY + -IC.] 1 Self-governing, independent. M19. 2 *Physiol.* Functioning independently of the will; *esp.* denoting the parts of the nervous system serving organs which control the normally involuntary functions of the body. L19.

autonomical *a.* (*rare*) = AUTONOMIC M17. **autonomically** *adv.* M19.

autonomous /ɔː'tɒnəməs/ *a.* E19. [f. Gk *autonomos* (see next) + -OUS.] Of, pertaining to, or characterized by autonomy; self-governing, independent; free of external influence or control.

J. REED At Helsingfors the Finnish Senate . . declared Finland autonomous, and demanded the withdrawal of Russian troops. R. G. COLLINGWOOD Consciousness is absolutely autonomous: its decision alone determines whether a given sensum or emotion shall be attended to or not. J. C. RANSOM English might almost as well announce that it does not regard itself as entirely autonomous, but as a branch of the department of history.

autonomously *adv.* L19.

autonomy /ɔː'tɒnəmi/ *n.* E17. [Gk *autonomia*, f. *autonomos* having its own laws, f. AUTO-[1] + *nomos* law: see -NOMY.] 1 The right or condition of self-government (freq. only in specified matters) of a State, community, institution, etc. E17. 2 Freedom of the will. L18. 3 *gen.* Independence, freedom from external control or influence; personal liberty. E19.

1 C. G. SELIGMAN The village is the administrative unit, to which the most complete autonomy is allowed. *Encycl. Brit.* The national autonomous regions [of China] reflect the CCP policy of seeking to . . accord cultural autonomy—but not political independence—to areas in which national minority peoples predominate. 3 A. STORR The therapist should not give advice or do anything else which might interfere with the patient's autonomy. U. LE GUIN They preserved autonomy of conscience even at the cost of becoming eccentric.

autonomism *n.* = AUTONOMY L19. **autonomist** *n.* an advocate of autonomy M19.

autonym /'ɔːtənɪm/ *n.* M19. [f. AUTO-[1] + -NYM.] (A work published under) an author's own name. Opp. PSEUDONYM.

autopista /ɔːtə'piːstə, *foreign* auto'pista/ *n.* M20. [Sp., f. *auto* automobile + *pista* track, PISTE.] A motorway in Spain and Spanish-speaking countries.

autopsy /'ɔːtɒpsi, ɔː'tɒpsi/ *n.* & *v.* Also †**-opsia**. M17. [Fr. *autopsie* or mod.L *autopsia* f. Gk, f. *autoptēs* eye-witness: see AUTO-[1], OPTIC, -Y[3].] **A** *n.* 1 Seeing with one's own eyes; personal observation. *rare.* M17. 2 Dissection of a dead body so as to determine the cause of death or the extent of disease; a post-mortem examination; *fig.* a critical dissection. M19. **B** *v.t.* Perform an autopsy on (a body). E20.

autopsic *a.* of or pertaining to an autopsy L19.

autoptical /ɔː'tɒptɪk(ə)l/ *a.* M17. [f. Gk *autoptikos*, f. *autoptēs* (see prec.), + -AL[1].] 1 Of, pertaining to, or of the nature of an eye-witness; based on personal observation. M17. 2 = AUTOPSIC. L20.

autoptic *a.* (*a*) *rare* = AUTOPTICAL 1; (*b*) = AUTOPSIC: M19. **autoptically** *adv.* M17.

autoradiograph /ɔːtəʊ'reɪdɪəgrɑːf/ *n.* & *v.* E20. [f. AUTO-[1] + RADIOGRAPH.] **A** *n.* A photograph of an object obtained using radiation from radioactive material in the object. E20. **B** *v.t.* Make an autoradiograph of. M20.

autoradiogram *n.* = AUTORADIOGRAPH *n.* M20. **autoradio'graphic(al)** *adjs.* of or pertaining to autoradiography or an autoradiograph M20. **autoradio'graphically** *adv.* M20. **autoradi'ography** *n.* the production and interpretation of autoradiographs M20.

autorotation /,ɔːtə(ʊ)rə(ʊ)'teɪʃ(ə)n/ *n.* E20. [f. AUTO-[1] + ROTATION.] *Aeronaut.* Rotation (esp. of rotor blades) not caused by engine power.

autorotate *v.i.* undergo autorotation E20.

autoroute /'ɔːtəruːt, *foreign* otorut (*pl. same*)/ *n.* M20. [Fr., f. *auto* automobile + *route* ROUTE *n.*] A French motorway.

autoschediastic /,ɔːtəʊskɛdɪ'astɪk/ *a.* E19. [Gk *autoskhediastikos*, f. *autoskhediazein* act or speak extempore, f. *autoskhedios* personally near, off-hand: see -IC.] Done on the spur of the moment, improvised.

autoscopy /ɔː'tɒskəpi/ *n.* L19. [f. AUTO-[1] + -SCOPY.] Viewing or examination of oneself; a hallucination of viewing one's own body.

'autoscope *n.* an instrument for self-observation; *esp.* any device which reveals subliminal actions (e.g. a dowsing-rod): L19. **auto'scopic** *a.* E20.

autos-da-fé *n.pl.* see AUTO-DA-FÉ.

autosome /'ɔːtəsəʊm/ *n.* E20. [f. AUTO-[1] + -SOME[3].] *Biol.* A chromosome other than a sex chromosome.

auto'somal *a.* M20.

autostrada /ɔːtə'strɑːdə, *foreign* auto'straːda/ *n.* Pl. **-stradas**, ***-strade*** /-'straːde/. E20. [It., f. *auto* automobile + *strada* road f. L STRATUM.] An Italian motorway.

auto-suggestion /,ɔːtə(ʊ)sə'dʒɛstʃ(ə)n/ *n.* L19. [f. AUTO-[1] + SUGGESTION.] *Psychol.* Suggestion to oneself; the hypnotic or subconscious adoption of an idea originating within oneself.

auto-su'ggest *v.* (*a*) *v.t.* produce, remove, influence (ideas, feelings), by auto-suggestion; (*b*) *v.i.* undergo auto-suggestion: E20. **auto-su'ggestible** *a.* able to be influenced by auto-suggestion E20. **auto-su'ggestive** *a.* of the nature of or pertaining to auto-suggestion E20.

autotheism /ɔːtəʊ'θiːɪz(ə)m/ *n.* L16. [f. eccl. Gk *autotheos* very god, f. AUTO-[1] + *theos* god, + -ISM.] 1 *Theol.* The doctrine of the self-subsistence of God or (esp.) Christ. L16. 2 Self-deification. E17.

autotheist *n.* M18. **autothe'istic** *a.* M19.

autotomy /ɔː'tɒtəmi/ *n.* L19. [f. AUTO-[1] + -TOMY.] *Zool.* The casting off of a part of the body by some animals (e.g. lizards, crabs) as a means of escape.

autotomize *v.t.* lose by autotomy E20.

autotoxin /ɔːtə(ʊ)'tɒksɪn/ *n.* L19. [f. AUTO-[1] + TOXIN.] A product of an organism's metabolism which is poisonous to the organism itself.

autoto'xaemia *n.* toxaemia due to an autotoxin L19. **autotoxic** *a.* E20.

autotrophic /ɔːtə(ʊ)'trəʊfɪk, -'trɒfɪk/ *a.* L19. [f. AUTO-[1] + -TROPHIC.] *Biol.* Of an organism: requiring only simple inorganic compounds for nutrition.

'autotroph(e) *n.* an autotrophic organism M20. **autotrophically** *adv.* M20. **au'totrophism** *n.* E20.

autotype /'ɔːtə(ʊ)tʌɪp/ *n.* M19. [f. AUTO-[1] + -TYPE.] 1 A reproduction in facsimile; a true representation of an original. M19. 2 (A facsimile produced by) a photographic printing process for monochrome reproduction. M19.

autoxidation /,ɔːtɒksɪ'deɪʃ(ə)n/ *n.* L19. [f. AUTO-[1] + OXIDATION.] *Chem.* Spontaneous oxidation by molecular oxygen.

au'toxidize *v.i.* undergo autoxidation E20. **autoxi'dizable** *a.* susceptible to autoxidation L19.

autumn /'ɔːtəm/ *n.* LME. [OFr. *autompne* (mod. *automne*), later directly f. L *autumnus*.] 1 The third season of the year, between summer and winter: in the northern hemisphere freq. regarded as comprising September, October, and November, or (*Astron.*) reckoned from the autumnal equinox to the winter solstice; in the southern hemisphere corresponding in time to the northern spring. LME. **b** The fruits of autumn; harvest. *poet.* E17. **2** *fig.* A season of maturity or incipient decay. L16.

1b MILTON On her ample square, from side to side, All Autumn pil'd. **2** J. LANGHORNE The very autumn of a form once fine Retains its beauties.

Comb.: *autumn crocus*: see CROCUS *n.*[1] 1b; **autumn equinox** = AUTUMNAL *equinox*; **autumn gentian** felwort, *Gentianella amarella*; **autumn tints** the brown and gold colours of dying leaves.

autumnity /ɔːˈtʌmnɪti/ *n.* (*rare*) autumnal quality or conditions L16. **autumny** /ˈɔːtəmi/ *a.* suggestive or characteristic of autumn E20.

autumn /ˈɔːtəm/ *v.t.* & *i.* Now *rare.* M17. [L *autumnare* bring on autumn, (med.L), f. *autumnus* AUTUMN *n.* ripen.] Bring or come to maturity; ripen.

autumnal /ɔːˈtʌmn(ə)l/ *a.* L16. [L *autumnalis*, f. *autumnus* AUTUMN *n.*: see -AL[1].] **1** Of or pertaining to autumn; characteristic of or appropriate to autumn; maturing or blooming in autumn. L16. **2** *fig.* Past the prime of life; in decline. E17.

1 MILTON Thick as Autumnal Leaves that strew the Brooks In Vallombrosa. LD MACAULAY The autumnal rains of Ireland are usually heavy. M. DRABBLE The autumnal colours were deeper . . in the sinking light. **autumnal equinox** the point in time at which the sun crosses the celestial equator in a southerly direction (approx. 22 September), or, in the southern hemisphere, in a northerly direction (approx. 21 March). **2** DONNE No Spring, nor Summer Beauty hath such grace, As I have seen in one Autumnall face. *absol.*: DICKENS Melissa might have seen five and thirty summers or thereabouts, and verged on the autumnal.

autumnally *adv.* M19.

autunite /ˈɔːtʌnʌɪt/ *n.* M19. [f. *Autun*, a town in eastern France + -ITE[1].] *Min.* A tetragonal hydrated phosphate of uranium and calcium, occurring usu. as yellow crystal aggregates or incrustations.

Auvergnat /ovɛrɲa/ *n.* Pl. pronounced same. M19. [Fr., f. *Auvergne*: see -AT[1].] A native or inhabitant of the Auvergne, a region of central France; the dialect spoken in the Auvergne.

auxanography /ɔːksəˈnɒɡrəfi/ *n.* E20. [f. as next + -OGRAPHY.] *Biol.* A technique for determining the substances required by a micro-organism for growth, in which different nutrients are distributed on a culture of the micro-organism.

auˈxanogram *n.* a plate culture used in this L19. **ˌauxanoˈgraphic** *a.* E20.

auxanometer /ɔːksəˈnɒmɪtə/ *n.* L19. [f. Gk *auxanein* to increase + -OMETER.] *Bot.* An instrument for measuring growth in plants.

auxesis /ɔːkˈsiːsɪs/ *n.* L16. [Late L f. Gk *auxēsis* increase, amplification.] **1** *Rhet.* Increase in intensity of meaning; hyperbole; amplification. L16. **2** *Biol.* Increase, growth; *esp.* increase in size by expansion of cell size or number of cells. M19.

auxetic /-ˈsɛtɪk/ *a.* M18.

auxiliary /ɔːɡˈzɪlɪəri, ɒɡ-/ *a.* & *n.* LME. [L *auxiliarius*, f. *auxilium* help: see -ARY[1].] **A** *adj.* **1** Helpful; giving support or succour; orig., (of foreign troops etc.) assisting an army at war. LME. **2** Subsidiary, additional, ancillary; (freq. in names of military or other service bodies). L17. **3** *Gram.* Used in forming words, constructions, etc. Now *spec.* (of a verb) used in forming tenses, moods, aspects, or voices, of other verbs. L17. **B** *n.* **1** (A member of) a body of foreign or allied troops etc. in the service of a belligerent nation. E17. **2** A person who or thing which assists, supports, or is subsidiary or ancillary. M17. **3** *Gram.* An auxiliary verb. L17.

†**auxiliar** *a.* & *n.* = AUXILIARY L16–M19.

auxin /ˈɔːksɪn/ *n.* M20. [f. Gk *auxein* to increase + -IN[1].] *Biochem.* Any of a class of compounds that cause the elongation of plant cells in shoots and (with cytokinins) control plant growth and development.

auxo- /ˈɔːksəʊ/ *comb. form* of Gk *auxein* to increase: see -O-.

auxochrome *n.* (*Chem.*) a polar group which when introduced into a chromogen produces a dyestuff L19; **auxoˈchromic** *a.* (*Chem.*) of or pertaining to an auxochrome L19. **auxospore** *n.* (*Bot.*) a vegetative cell formed by diatoms, usu. sexually L19.

auxotroph /ˈɔːksətrəʊf, -trɒf/ *n.* M20. [f. L *auxilium* help + -O- + Gk *trophos* feeder.] *Biol.* A mutant bacterium, fungus, etc., having an additional nutritional requirement compared with the original strain.

auxoˈtrophic *a.* M20. **auˈxotrophy** *n.* M20.

Av *n.* var. of AB *n.*[1]

ava /ˈɑːvə/ *n.* L18. [Haw. *ʻawa.*] = KAVA.

ava /əˈvɑː/ *adv. Sc.* M18. [Repr. a pronunc. of *of all.*] Of all; at all.

avadavat /ˈavədəvat/ *n.* Also (earlier) **am-** /ˈam-/. L17. [f. *Ahmadabad*, a city in western India where the birds were sold.] Either of two southern Asian waxbills, the green *Amandava formosa* and (esp.) the red *A. amandava*.

avail /əˈveɪl/ *n.* LME. [App. f. the vb, but cf. AN *avail.*] **1** Beneficial effect, advantage; assistance; value, estimation. *arch.* exc. in neg. or interrog. phrs. LME. **2** *sing.* & (usu.) in *pl.* Profits, proceeds; remuneration, perquisites. *arch.* LME.

1 *of or to little* or *no avail. to what avail? without avail.*

avail /əˈveɪl/ *v.* ME. [f. VAIL *v.*[1], app. on the analogy of pairs like *amount, mount.*] **1** *v.i.* & *t.* Be of use, help, value, or advantage, (to); have efficacy; profit. ME. **2** *v.refl.* & *i.* Make use *of*, obtain the benefit *of*, take advantage *of.* LME. †**3** *v.i.* Do well, prosper. E16–E17. **4** *v.t.* Give (a person) the advantage *of*; inform, assure, *of. US. arch.* L18.

1 CHAUCER Moore it auaileth a man to haue a good name, than for to haue grete richesses. AV *Esther* 5:13 All this auaileth me nothing, so long as I see Mordecai the Iew sitting at the kings gate. POPE Nor aught the warrior's thundering mace avail'd. SIR W. SCOTT Words avail very little with me, young man. DISRAELI What avail his golden youth, his high blood . . if they help not now? E. M. FORSTER How little, we feel, avails knowledge and technical cleverness against a man who truly feels! **2** MILTON Then shall they seek to avail themselves of names, Places, and titles. J. TYNDALL I . . availed myself of my position to make an excursion into North Wales. R. W. EMERSON Power . . must be availed of, and not by any means let off and wasted. D. LESSING This time I availed myself of the invitation to move about. **4** T. JEFFERSON It will rest, therefore, with you, to avail Mr. Barclay of that fund. F. TROLLOPE We should have got no invites, you may be availed of that.

availing *a.* advantageous, profitable, of beneficial effect LME. **availment** *n.* benefit, efficacy L17.

available /əˈveɪləb(ə)l/ *a.* LME. [f. prec. + -ABLE.] **1** Capable of producing a desired result; effectual, valid; *obs.* exc. *Law.* LME. **2** Of advantage (*to, unto*). *arch.* LME. **3** Able to be used or turned to account; at one's disposal; within one's reach, obtainable; (of a person) free for consultation, service, amorous advances, etc. E19. **4** Of a political candidate: likely to succeed in gaining office irrespective of ability, because of political associations, personal popularity, etc. *US.* M19.

3 J. TYNDALL We spent every available hour upon the ice. S. KAUFFMANN He was vividly excited by the renewed evidence that right here in the house was an available female. J. ORTON I'd like another woman present. Is your wife available? J. T. STORY To have a hire car made available for a visiting Member of Parliament. M. BRADBURY Of course Henry would elect to carry a tray when he had only one available hand.

availaˈbility *n.* (*a*) the quality of being available; (*b*) something available: E19. **availableness** *n.* L17. **availably** *adv.* LME.

avalanche /ˈavəlɑːnʃ/ *n.* & *v.* L18. [Fr. f. Romansh, alt. of Alpine Fr. dial. *lavanche* (of unkn. origin), by blending w. *avaler* descend: cf. Prov. *lavanca*, It. *valanga.*] **A** *n.* **1** A large mass of snow, rocks, and ice, moving swiftly down a mountainside. L18. **2** *transf.* & *fig.* A sudden onrush or descent; a rapidly descending mass. M19. **b** *Physics.* A process of cumulative ionization in which each electron and ion generates further charged particles. Also more fully *Townsend avalanche*. Freq. *attrib.* M20.

2 A. G. GARDINER An avalanche of indignant protests and appeals burst on him. C. MCCULLERS He grasped the scuttle . . and rattled an avalanche of coal on the fire. H. ARENDT The Nazis let loose an avalanche of laws and decrees.

Comb.: **avalanche lily** *N. Amer.* an erythronium commonly found near the snowline, esp. the yellow *Erythronium grandiflorum*.

B *v.* **1** *v.i.* Descend in or like an avalanche. L19. **2** *v.t.* Strike, carry, or envelop (as) by an avalanche. L19. **3** *v.i. Physics.* Undergo a rapid increase in conductivity due to an avalanche process. M20.

1 M. TWAIN We avalanched from one side of the stage[-coach] to the other. **2** *Daily Telegraph* Just one touch of *rustique* from a designer who used to avalanche us with folklore: cream, Aran-knit coats . . glamorised by lynx collars. P. GILLMAN He and three other men were avalanched.

avalanchy *a.* susceptible to avalanches L19.

†**avale** *v.* ME. [(O)Fr. *avaler*, f. *à val* at the bottom, down, f. L *ad vallem.* Cf. AMOUNT *v.*, DEVALL.] **1** *v.i.* Sink, drop; flow down; descend, alight. ME–L16. **2** *v.t.* Cause to descend or fall; let down, lower; remove or doff (one's headgear), open (one's visor). ME–L18. **b** *fig.* Abase, degrade. LME–M17.

avania /avəˈniːə/ *n. obs.* exc. *Hist.* Also **-iah**. L16. [Ult. f. med.Gk *abania* perh. f. Arab. *ʻawān* mischievous damage. Cf. It. *avania*, Fr. *avanie.*] A tax (esp. an extortionate one) levied by the Turkish authorities.

avanious *a.* (*arch.*) extortionate L17.

avant-courier /avɒ̃ːˈkʊrɪə/ *n.* E17. [f. Fr. *avant* forward, before + COURIER *n.*, after Fr. *avant-coureur.* Cf. earlier VAUNT-COURIER.] A person who runs or rides before; a herald; a member of the advance guard of an army.

avant-garde /avɒ̃ː(ŋ)ˈɡɑːd/ *n.* & *a.* LME. [Fr., f. *avant* forward, before + *garde* GUARD *n.*] **A** *n.* **1** The vanguard of an army. Now *arch.* or *Hist.* LME. **2** The pioneering or innovative writers, artists, etc., in a particular period. E20. **B** *adj.* Of or pertaining to the artistic avant-garde; progressive, ultra-modern. E20.

avant-gardism *n.* the characteristic quality or principles of the artistic avant-garde M20. **avant-gardist** *n.* a member of the artistic avant-garde M20.

avanturine *n.* var. of AVENTURINE.

Avar /ˈavɑː, ˈɑː-/ *n.* L18. [Avar.] A member of a people of the NE Caucasus, identified with a people prominent in SE Europe from the 6th to the 9th cent.; the language of this people.

Avarian /əˈvɑːrɪən, ɑː-/ *a.* & *n.* (*a*) *adj.* of or pertaining to the Avars; (*b*) *n.* the language of the Avars L19.

avarice /ˈav(ə)rɪs/ *n.* ME. [(O)Fr. f. L *avaritia*, f. *avarus* greedy: see -ICE[1].] Greed for gain, cupidity; *fig.* eager desire to get or keep something for oneself.

avaricious /avəˈrɪʃəs/ *a.* LME. [(O)Fr. *avaricieux*, f. as prec. + *-ieus, -ieux* -IOUS.] Manifesting avarice; grasping; greedy for wealth.

avariciously *adv.* M16. **avariciousness** *n.* M16.

avascular /əˈvaskjʊlə, eɪ-/ *a.* E20. [f. A-[10] + VASCULAR.] Characterized by or associated with an absence or deficiency of blood-vessels.

avascuˈlarity *n.* M20.

avast /əˈvɑːst/ *int.* E17. [f. Du. *hou'vast, houd vast* hold fast, with 1st syll. assim. to A *prep.*[1]] *Naut.* Stop! cease! hold!

SMOLLETT Avast there friend, none of your tricks upon travellers. F. MARRYAT 'Avast heaving,' said Gascoigne.

avatar /ˈavətɑː/ *n.* L18. [Skt *avatāra* descent, f. *ava* off, away, down + *tar-* pass over.] **1** *Hindu Mythol.* The descent of a god to earth in incarnate form. L18. **2** An incarnation or embodiment (of another person, an idea, etc.). E19. **3** A manifestation to the world as a ruling power or as an object of worship; *gen.* a manifestation, a phase. E19.

1 R. K. NARAYAN Krishna was the eighth avatar of Vishnu, incarnated to help the Five Brothers regain their kingdom. **2** Q. BELL A certain kind of beauty appears and reappears, sometimes vaguely, sometimes strikingly reincarnated from avatar to avatar. M. MCCARTHY The classic English butler, of which he personally was the avatar. **3** L. STEPHEN Wit and sense are but different avatars of the same spirit. *Listener* I knew Victor Neuburg so well during his avatar as editor of the 'Poets' Corner'.

†avaunt *v.*[1] & *n.*[1] ME. [OFr. *avanter*, *avaunter*, f. as A-[5] + VAUNT *v.*] A *v.* 1 *v.t.* Boast or brag of; praise; vaunt (oneself). ME–L16. 2 *v.i.* Boast, brag. LME–L16. B *n.* Boasting, bragging; a brag, a boast. LME–L16.

¶ VAUNT *n.*[1], *v.* partly f. this.

avaunt /ə'vɔːnt/ *adv.*, *int.*, *v.*[2] & *n.*[2] Long *arch.* LME. [AN, (O)Fr. *avant* to the front, before, onward, ult. f. L *ab* from + *ante* before.] †A *adv.* Forward; to the front. LME–E17. B *int.* Onward! go on! begone! away! LME. †C *v.* 1 *v.i.* Advance, go forward; depart, be off. LME–E17. 2 *v.t.* Raise, advance. LME–E17. †D *n.* An order to go away. L16–E18.

ave /'ɑːvi, 'ɑːveɪ/ *n.* & *int.* ME. [L as imper. sing. of *avere* be or fare well, used as an expression of greeting or farewell. In earliest use short for *Ave Maria.*] A *n.* 1 (Also **A-**.) = AVE MARIA I. ME. b A bead on a rosary (as used for counting the number of aves recited). ME. 2 A shout of welcome or farewell. E17.

Comb.: **ave-bell** a bell rung at the hours when aves are to be said.

B *int.* Hail! farewell! LME.

avellan /ə'vɛlən, 'avələn/ *n.* & *a.* Also **-l(l)ane** /-leɪn/. ME. [f. L *Avellanus* of Avella, a town in Campania, Italy: see -AN.] A *n.* A filbert, a hazelnut. ME. B *adj.* 1 *avellan nut* = sense A. above. LME. 2 *Her.* Of a cross: resembling four thin filberts joined together. E17.

Ave Maria /ˌɑːvi mə'riːə, ˌɑːveɪ/ *int.* & *n. phr.* Also **Ave Mary** /'mɛːri/. ME. [L = hail, Mary!: see AVE.] 1 The angel's greeting to the Virgin Mary combined with that of Elizabeth (cf. *Luke* 1:28 & 42), used as a devotional recitation; the prayer to the Virgin as Mother of God beginning with these words; a recitation of this devotional phrase or prayer. ME. 2 (The time of) the ave-bell. L16.

aven /'eɪv(ə)n/ *n.* L19. [Fr. dial., of Celt. origin.] A vertical shaft in limestone, closed or almost closed at the top; a swallow-hole.

avener /ə'viːnə/ *n. obs.* exc. *Hist.* ME. [AN *avener*, OFr. *avenier*, f. med.L *avenarius* use as n. of the L adj., f. *avena* oats: see -ARY[1].] A chief officer of the stable, in charge of provender for the horses.

avenge /ə'vɛndʒ/ *v.* & *n.* LME. [OFr. *avengier*, f. *a* (intensifier) + *vengier* (mod. *venger*) f. L *vindicare* VINDICATE.] A *v.* 1 *v.t.* Take vengeance, inflict retribution, exact satisfaction, on behalf of (another person, oneself), or on account of (a wrong, injury, etc.). Freq. in *pass.* Foll. by (*up*)*on*, †*of*, †*against* the offender. LME. 2 *v.i.* Take vengeance. *arch.* M16. †3 *v.t.* Take vengeance upon. Only in M17.

1 COVERDALE *Ps.* 119:84 When wilt thou be auenged of my aduersaries? MILTON Avenge, O Lord, thy slaughtered saints. W. N. MASSEY Private grudges were avenged. W. F. HOOK Edwy had the power to avenge himself upon Dunstan. A. TROLLOPE Those who offend us are generally punished . . but we so frequently miss the satisfaction of knowing that we are avenged. L. TRILLING Why Hamlet . . did not avenge upon his hated uncle his father's death. D. JACOBSON The ferocity and guile with which Absalom had avenged the rape of his sister. 2 AV *Lev.* 19:18 Thou shalt not auenge nor beare any grudge against the children of thy people.

B *n.* Retribution, vengeance. *arch.* M16.

†avengeance *n.* vengeance LME–E18. **avengeful** *a.* (*arch.*) full of vengeance, taking vengeance L16. **avengement** *n.* (*arch.*) vengeance L15. **avenger** *n.* †(*a*) a person who takes vengeance on (an offender); (*b*) a person who avenges (an injured person or an injury): LME. **avengeress** *n.* (*rare*) a female avenger L16.

avens /'eɪv(ə)nz/ *n.* ME. [OFr. *avence* = med.L *avencia*, of unkn. origin.] Any of a number of rosaceous plants belonging to the genus *Geum* or a related genus.

mountain avens a creeping alpine, *Dryas octopetala*, bearing white flowers. **water avens** *Geum rivale*, bearing bell-like flowers having dull pink petals and a purple calyx. **wood avens** *Geum urbanum*, bearing small yellow flowers; also called *herb bennet*.

aventail /'av(ə)nteɪl/ *n.* Also **-ayle**. ME. [AN = (see A-[7]) OFr. *esventail* air-hole, f. *esventer* (mod. *éventer*), ult. f. L EX-[1] + *ventus* wind: see -AL[1].] *Hist.* The movable front or mouthpiece of a helmet, which may be raised to admit air. Cf. VENTAIL 2.

aventure /ə'vɛntʃə/ *n. obs.* exc. *Hist.* E17. [OFr. = ADVENTURE *n.*] *Law.* Pure accident, as a cause of death (cf. MISADVENTURE).

aventurine /ə'vɛntʃərɪn/ *n.* Also **avan-** /ə'van-/. E18. [Fr. f. It. *avventurino*, f. *avventura* chance (from its accidental discovery): see ADVENTURE *n.*, -INE[1].] 1 A brownish ornamental glass containing sparkling particles of copper or another foreign material. Also *aventurine glass.* E18. 2 A variety of quartz or of feldspar spangled with particles of another mineral (usu. mica or haematite respectively). Also *aventurine quartz*, *feldspar.* L18.

avenue /'av(ə)njuː/ *n.* E17. [Fr., use as n. of fem. pa. pple of *avenir* arrive, approach, f. L *advenire*, f. AD- + *venire* come.] 1 A way of access or approach. Now chiefly *fig.*, a way, a means. E17. 2 A tree lined approach to a country house; lines of trees forming such an approach; a broad roadway marked by trees or other objects at regular intervals. M17. 3 A broad street; an urban street with trees. (Freq. in proper names.) L18. 4 *Zool.* = AMBULACRUM. Now *rare* or *obs.* M19.

1 H. BELLOC Cheating on a large scale was an avenue to social advancement in most of the progressive European countries. D. CARNEGIE She had found in making the breakfast food an avenue of self-expression. EXPLORE *every avenue.* 2 GEO. ELIOT Arthur Donnithorne passed under an avenue of limes and beeches. A. P. STANLEY The avenue of sphinxes leading to the huge gateway. 3 D. LESSING I'd better be getting home to 16 Plane Avenue. S. CISNEROS Down the avenue one block past the bright lights.

aver /'eɪvə/ *n.* & *v.*[1] *Sc.* & *north.* Also **aiver**. [OE *eafor*, whence AN *aver*, AL *av(e)ra*, *affrus.*] A *n.* A draught horse; an old horse, a nag. OE. †B *v.t.* Supply with horse-transport. Only in OE.

aver /ə'vəː/ *v.*[2]*t.* Infl. **-rr-**. LME. [(O)Fr. *avérer*, f. A-[5] + *veir*, *voir* f. L *verus* true.] †1 Declare true. LME–M17. †2 Prove true; confirm. LME–L17. 3 *Law.* Prove or justify (a plea etc.); make an averment *that.* LME. 4 Assert as a fact; state positively, affirm. L16. 5 Assert the existence or occurrence of. *arch.* E17.

4 P. SIDNEY How often doe the Phisitians lye, when they auer things good for sicknesses. R. BENTLEY Which being . . within the reach of my own Knowledge, I do averr to be a Calumny. COLERIDGE They all averr'd I had killed the Bird That brought the fog and mist. G. P. R. JAMES What one author avers upon the subject, another denies. BARONESS ORCZY A brilliant matrimonial prize for which, as all chroniclers aver, there had been many competitors. 5 MILTON Æsop's Chronicles auer many stranger Accidents.

averrable *a.* M16.

average /'av(ə)rɪdʒ/ *n.*[1] *obs.* exc. *Hist.* Also (*Sc.*) **arage, arriage**, /'arɪdʒ/. LME. [med.L *averagium*, f. AVER *v.*[1]: see -AGE.] A service (orig. with draught animals) owed by a tenant to a feudal superior.

average /'av(ə)rɪdʒ/ *n.*[2] L15. [f. Fr. *avarie* damage to ship or cargo, (earlier) customs duty, f. It. *avaria* f. Arab. *'awār* damage to goods: *-age* after *damage* etc.] I Maritime use. 1 A minor charge over and above the freight incurred in the shipment of goods, and payable by their owner or consignee. Also *petty average.* L15. †2 A duty charged upon goods; a customs duty etc. E16–M18. 3 (The equitable apportionment of) liability resulting from loss of or damage to an insured ship or its cargo. L16.

3 **general average**: arising from the deliberate partial sacrifice of a ship or its cargo in order to avoid total loss. **particular average**: arising from accidental partial damage or loss.

II *transf.* 4 The determination of a medial estimate or arithmetic mean. Chiefly in *on* (†*at*) (*the*, *an*) *average*, as a mean value or general rule, usually. M18. 5 The generally prevailing rate, degree, or amount; the ordinary standard; the arithmetic mean. M18. b *spec.* In *Cricket*, the mean number of runs per completed innings scored by a batsman, or the mean cost in runs per wicket achieved by a bowler, during a season, tour, etc.; in *Baseball* (more fully *batting average*), the mean number of safe hits made by a batter per time at bat. M19.

5 I. COMPTON-BURNETT I never can make out whether Father's hearing is below the average or above it. R. HOGGART Those whose husbands earned just a few shillings above the average for the street. R. DAVIES We played an average of five days a week. **law of averages** the proposition that the occurrence of one extreme will be matched by that of the other extreme so as to maintain the average. *weighted average*: see WEIGHT *v.* 3c.

Comb.: **average adjustment** the apportionment of liability due to average.

average /'av(ə)rɪdʒ/ *n.*[3] *dial.* M16. [Origin unkn.] The pasturage of arable land after harvest; land under stubble.

average /'av(ə)rɪdʒ/ *a.* L18. [f. AVERAGE *n.*[2]] Estimated or calculated as an average; medium; of the ordinary standard or kind; typical.

ARNOLD BENNETT The average age appeared to be about fifty. E. GLASGOW In a democracy . . it was safer to be average. W. H. AUDEN Average distance run per week: two hundred miles. B. PYM There was something very unattractive about the average man's pyjamas.

averagely *adv.* to an average degree; ordinarily: M19. **averageness** *n.* E20.

average /'av(ə)rɪdʒ/ *v.* M18. [f. AVERAGE *n.*[2]] 1 *v.t.* Amount to on average; do or achieve on average in any activity. M18. 2 *v.t.* Work out or estimate the average of. L18. 3 *v.t.* & *i.* (with *out*). (Cause to) result in or yield on average a moderate value, intermediate level, even distribution, etc.; even or cancel *out*; remove (variation) by calculating an average. E20.

1 D. MASSON The sale of the book . . averaged a thousand copies a year. G. GREENE Over twenty years I have probably averaged five hundred words a day for five days a week. R. LARDNER It averaged about two dollars per day for the two of us. 2 SOUTHEY His Sunday congregation was averaged at about six hundred persons. 3 *Times Lit. Suppl.* The particular obstacles will vary from time to time . . but on the whole will average out. D. W. SCIAMA The clustering might then be real, but be averaged out by this procedure. *Accountant* Those who seek to average out profits by taking profit by stages.

averager *n.* (*a*) a person whose business is average adjustment; (*b*) a small computer designed for the automatic averaging of a series of input signals: L19.

averment /ə'vəːm(ə)nt/ *n.* LME. [AN, OFr. *aver(r)ement*: see AVER *v.*[2], -MENT.] 1 The action of proving, by argument or evidence; *esp.* (*Law*) a formal statement including an offer of proof or justification. LME. 2 Assertion, affirmation; a positive declaration. E17.

Avernal /ə'vəːn(ə)l/ *a.* L16. [L *avernalis*, f. *avernus* (*lacus*) = Gk *aornos* (*limnē*) birdless (lake), f. A-[10] + *ornis* bird: see -AL[1].] Of the nature of or pertaining to Avernus, a lake in Campania, Italy, the effluvium from which was anciently said to kill overflying birds; *gen.* infernal, devilish.

Averroist /ə'vɛrəʊɪst, avə'rəʊɪst/ *n.* Also **-rrhoist**. M18. [f. *Averroes* (see below) + -IST.] Any of a sect of peripatetic philosophers in pre-Renaissance Italy, who adopted the supposed tenets of Averroes (1126–98), a Muslim philosopher from Córdoba, esp. the belief that the individual soul returns after death to a universal, immortal soul.

Averroism *n.* M18. **Averro'istic** *a.* M19. **Averro'istical** *a.* M17.

averruncate /avə'rʌŋkeɪt/ *v.t. rare* exc. in Dicts. E17. [L *averruncat-* pa. ppl stem of *averruncare* avert, f. *a* AB- + *verruncare* turn: see -ATE[3]. Erron. explained in 17 as f. L *ab* off + *eruncare* weed out.] 1 Root out, weed; prune. E17. †2 Avert, ward off. M–L17.

†averruncation *n.* M17–E19. **†averruncator** *n.* (*Hort.*) a long-handled pruning implement: only in 19.

aversation /avə'seɪʃ(ə)n/ *n. arch.* E17. [L *aversatio(n-)*, f. *aversat-* pa. ppl stem of *aversari* turn away from, frequent. of *avertere*: see AVERT, -ATION.] = AVERSION.

averse /ə'vəːs/ *a.* (usu. *pred.*) & *adv.* L16. [L *aversus* pa. pple of *avertere* AVERT.] A *adj.* 1 Turned away in thought or feeling; opposed, disinclined. (Foll. by *from*, *to*.) L16. †2 Of things: adverse. Only in 17. †3 Lying on the opposite side. *rare*. Only in M17. †4 Turned away or in the reverse direction. L17–E18.

1 AV *Micah* 2:8 As men auerse from warre. E. M. FORSTER Averse to wasting her time, she went on sewing. J. GALSWORTHY She was ever silent, passive, gracefully averse. B. PYM He wasn't averse to a bit of a rest. 2 HOBBES What Opinions and Doctrines are averse, and what conducing to Peace. 3 MILTON On the Coast averse From entrance or cherubic watch.. Found unsuspected way. 4 DRYDEN The tracks averse a lying notice gave.

†B *adv*. In the reverse or opposite direction. E17–E19.

E. TOPSELL The hair groweth averse.. forward toward his head.

aversely *adv*. M17. **averseness** *n*. E17.

aversion /əˈvəːʃ(ə)n/ *n*. L16. [Fr. or L *aversio(n-)*, f. as prec.: see -ION.] 1 The action of turning away oneself, one's eyes, etc. Long *rare*. L16. 2 A mental attitude of opposition or repugnance; a habitual dislike; antipathy, unwillingness. (Foll. by *to*, *from*, *for*, †*towards*, †*against*.) E17. 3 An object of dislike or repugnance. L17.

1 T. BERGER He might turn no female heads, but neither would he cause the aversion of faces. 2 BACON His aversion towards the house of York. ADDISON An unconquerable aversion which some stomachs have against a joint of meat. R. L. STEVENSON She had conceived at first sight a great aversion for the present writer, which she was at no pains to conceal. H. A. L. FISHER Charles had married, and on grounds of personal aversion divorced, the daughter of the Lombard king. J. GALSWORTHY Her aversion from him who had owned her body, but had never touched her spirit or her heart. W. S. CHURCHILL The Tories regarded with aversion the sending of large armies to the Continent. K. A. PORTER He had a moral aversion to poverty, an instinctive contempt and distrust of the swarming poor. 3 M. TWAIN For years my pet aversion had been the cuckoo clock.

Comb.: **aversion therapy** behaviour therapy designed to cause the patient to give up an undesirable habit by associating it with an unpleasant effect.

avert /əˈvəːt/ *v*. LME. [Partly f. OFr. *avertir*, partly directly f. L *avertere*, f. *a* AB- + *vertere* turn.] 1 *v.t.* Turn away (a person) *from* a place, course of action, etc. *arch*. LME. 2 *v.i.* Turn away (*from*). *arch*. L15. 3 *v.t.* Alienate, estrange. *arch*. M16. 4 *v.t.* Turn away (the face, eyes, thoughts, etc.). L16. 5 *v.t.* Prevent; ward off. E17. †6 *v.t.* Oppose; view with aversion. Only in M17.

1 DRYDEN Mighty Cæsar, whose victorious Arms.. Avert unwarlike Indians from his Rome. A. TROLLOPE How fatal it might be to avert her father from the cause while the trial was still pending. 2 SOUTHEY And from that hideous man Averting, to Ocellopan he turn'd. 3 L. MORRIS Appease Zeus and the averted Gods. 4 SHAKES. *Lear* I.. therefore beseech you T'avert your liking a more worthier way. R. G. COLLINGWOOD I could not bear to look at it, and passed with averted eyes. F. RAPHAEL James was asleep.., his head averted from the light of the door. 5 J. B. PRIESTLEY Elsie averted the kiss that she knew would inevitably have descended upon her a moment later. A. LURIE Time is of the essence if a frightful disaster is to be averted.

avertable *a*. = AVERTIBLE L19. **avertible** *a*. preventable M17.

Avesta /əˈvɛstə/ *n*. E19. [Pers.] (The text of) the Zoroastrian scriptures, compiled by Zoroaster as a means of reforming an older tradition. See also ZEND-AVESTA.

Avestan *a*. & *n*. (*a*) *adj*. of or pertaining to the Avesta or the ancient Iranian language in which it is written; (*b*) *n*. this language: M19. **Avestic** *a*. & *n*. = AVESTAN L19.

avgas /ˈavgas/ *n*. Orig. *US*. M20. [f. AV(IATION + GAS *n*.[2]] Aviation gasoline, petrol for aircraft.

avian /ˈeɪvɪən/ *a*. L19. [f. L *avis* bird + -AN.] Of or pertaining to birds.

aviary /ˈeɪvɪəri/ *n*. L16. [L *aviarium*, f. *avis* bird: see -ARY[1].] A large cage, building, or enclosure for keeping birds.

aviate /ˈeɪvɪeɪt/ *v*. L19. [Back-form. f. next.] 1 *v.i.* Pilot or fly in an aeroplane. L19. 2 *v.t.* Fly (an aeroplane). M20.

aviation /eɪvɪˈeɪʃ(ə)n/ *n*. M19. [Fr., irreg. f. L *avis* bird: see -ATION.] The operation of aircraft, aeronautics; the development and manufacture of aircraft.

CIVIL *aviation*.

aviator /ˈeɪvɪeɪtə/ *n*. L19. [Fr. *aviateur*, f. as prec.: see -ATOR.] 1 A pilot of an aeroplane; an airman, an airwoman. L19. †2 An aeroplane. L19–E20.

aviatrix *n*. a female aviator E20.

avicide /ˈeɪvɪsaɪd/ *n*. *rare*. M19. [f. L *avis* bird + -CIDE.] The slaughter of birds, bird-shooting.

avicularium /əˌvɪkjʊˈlɛːrɪəm/ *n*. Pl. **-ria** /-rɪə/. M19. [mod.L, f. *avicula* dim. of *avis* bird: see -CULE, -ARIUM.] *Zool*. A specialized member of an ectoproctan colony, having the form of a pair of snapping jaws resembling a bird's head.

aviculture /ˈeɪvɪkʌltʃə/ *n*. L19. [f. L *avis* bird + -CULTURE.] The breeding and rearing of birds.

aviˈculturist *n*. a person who breeds and rears birds E20.

avid /ˈavɪd/ *a*. M18. [Fr. *avide* or L *avidus*, f. *avere* long for: see -ID[1].] Eager; eagerly desirous, greedy, (*of*, *for*).

avidly *adv*. M19.

avidin /ˈavɪdɪn/ *n*. M20. [f. AVID + -IN[1].] *Biochem*. A protein found in raw egg white which combines with and inactivates biotin.

avidious /əˈvɪdɪəs/ *a*. *rare*. M16. [f. as AVID + see -IOUS.] Avid; greedy, eager.

avidiously *adv*. LME.

avidity /əˈvɪdɪti/ *n*. LME. [Fr. *avidité* or L *aviditas*, f. *avidus*: see AVID, -ITY.] 1 Extreme eagerness, greediness (*for*, *of*). LME. 2 *spec*. Graspingness, avarice. M17.

†**aview** *v.t.* Also **ad-**. L15–L16. [f. A-[11] + VIEW *v*.] Survey; reconnoitre; view.

SPENSER All which when Artegall.. well advewed.. He could no longer beare.

avifauna /ˈeɪvɪfɔːnə/ *n*. L19. [f. L *avis* bird + FAUNA.] The birds of a region collectively.

avifaunal *a*. L19.

avine /ˈeɪvʌɪn/ *a*. *rare*. L19. [f. L *avis* bird + -INE[1].] Avian; birdlike.

avionics /eɪvɪˈɒnɪks/ *n.pl.* M20. [f. AVI(ATION + ELECTR)ONICS.] 1 Treated as *sing*. Electronics as applied to aviation. M20. 2 Electronic equipment fitted in an aircraft. M20.

avionic *a*. of or pertaining to avionics M20.

avirulent /eɪˈvɪrjʊl(ə)nt, a-/ *a*. E20. [f. A-[10] + VIRULENT.] Of a micro-organism: not virulent.

avirulence *n*. M20.

avisandum *n*. var. of AVIZANDUM.

aviso /əˈvʌɪzəʊ/ *n*. *arch*. Pl. **-os**, †**-oes**. E17. [Sp.: see ADVICE.] †1 Intelligence, information; a notification, a dispatch. E–M17. 2 A boat bringing news, a dispatch-boat. E18.

avitaminosis /eɪˌvɪtəmɪˈnəʊsɪs, -ˌvʌɪt-/ *n*. Pl. **-noses** /-ˈnəʊsiːz/. E20. [f. A-[10] + VITAMIN + -OSIS.] *Med*. A vitamin deficiency disease.

†**avives** *n.pl.* var. of VIVES.

avizandum /avɪˈzandəm/ *n*. Also **-isa-**. E17. [med.L, neut. gerund of *avizare*, *-sare* consider, ADVISE.] *Sc. Law*. Further consideration, esp. out of court; private consideration by a judge etc.

avocado /avəˈkɑːdəʊ/ *n*. & *a*. M17. [Sp., alt. (after *avocado* lawyer) f. *aguacate* f. Nahuatl *ahuacatl*.] A *n*. Pl. **-os**, ***-oes**. 1 (The rough-skinned pear-shaped edible fruit of) the tree *Persea americana*, of the laurel family, native to Central America and the W. Indies. Also *avocado pear*. M17. 2 Avocado green. L20.

Comb. **avocado green** (of) the green colour of the flesh of the avocado; *avocado pear*: see sense 1 above.

B *adj*. Of avocado green. L20.

†**avocate** *v.t.* M16. [Sense 1 f. L *avocat-* (see next); sense 2 after Fr. †*avoquer* f. L *advocare* ADVOKE] 1 Call away, withdraw, (*from*). M16–M18. 2 = ADVOKE. M–L17.

avocation /avəˈkeɪʃ(ə)n/ *n*. E16. [Branch I after L *advocatio(n-)* ADVOCATION; branch II f. L *avocatio(n-)*, f. *avocat-* pa. ppl stem of *avocare*, f. *a-* AB- + *vocare* to call: see -ATION.] I 1 = ADVOCATION 3. E16.

II †2 Diversion of the thoughts. E17–M18. 3 The condition of having one's attention diverted; distraction. *arch*. M17. 4 A (less important) distraction; a minor occupation; *colloq*. (a) vocation, (a) calling. M17.

2 T. GRAY Try, by every method of avocation and amusement, whether you cannot.. get the better of that dejection. 3 S. R. MAITLAND He devoted himself, with less avocation, to prayer. 4 G. B. SHAW It was at the university that I became.. a sky pilot. When the war took me it seemed natural that I should pursue that avocation as a member of the air force. W. FAULKNER A horseman, a groom, merely by accident, but by avocation and dedication a minister of God.

avocational *a*. M20.

avocatory /əˈvɒkət(ə)ri, avəˈkeɪtəri/ *a*. M17. [med.L *avocatorius*, f. *avocat-*: see prec., -ORY[2].] Recalling; that recalls.

letters avocatory *Hist*.: by which a monarch recalled subjects from a foreign State or ordered them to desist from illegal proceedings.

avocet /ˈavəsɛt/ *n*. Also †**-set(ta)** L17. [Fr. *avocette* f. It. *avosetta*.] A wading bird of the genus *Recurvirostra*, having a long upturned beak; *esp*. the black and white *R. avosetta* of Europe.

avodiré /avəʊˈdɪəreɪ/ *n*. M20. [Fr.] (The smooth, light-coloured hardwood of) either of two W. African trees, *Turraeanthus africanus* and *T. vignei*, of the mahogany family.

Avogadro /avəˈgɑːdrəʊ/ *n*. L19. [Count Amedeo *Avogadro* (1776–1856), It. scientist.] *Chem*. 1 *Avogadro's law*: that equal volumes of gases under the same conditions of temperature and pressure contain equal numbers of molecules. L19. 2 *Avogadro('s) number* or *constant*, the number of molecules in a mole of material, 6.023×10^{23}. E20.

avoid /əˈvɔɪd/ *v*. LME. [AN *avoider* = OFr. *esvuidier*, *evuider* (see A-[7]), f. *es-* EX-[1] + *vuide* empty, VOID *a*.] I Make empty. †1 *v.t.* Empty; clear, free, rid (*of*); depart from, quit (a place). LME–E19. 2 *v.t.* Chiefly *Law*. Make void or of no effect; refute. Formerly also, defeat (pleading); invalidate, quash (a sentence etc.). LME. †3 *v.t.* Clear out, put away; eject, excrete; do away with; get rid of; expel, banish. LME–L17. 4 *v.refl.* Leave, withdraw. Long *arch*. LME. †5 *v.i.* Leave, withdraw, depart; retire, retreat. L15–M18. b Of things: escape; run out or away. L15–E17. †6 *v.i.* Fall vacant. E16–E18.

1 T. ELYOT Commanded the chambre to be avoided. 3 R. FABYAN He auoyded yͤ munkys out of the house of Aumbrisbury. R. HAKLUYT It causeth vrine to be avoided in great measure. W. PRYNNE His Images and Pictures.. should be pluckt down and avoided out of all Churches. R. BAXTER There was then no Judge of such controversies.. to avoid and end them. 4 SIR W. SCOTT Avoid thee, Fiend! 5 AV *1 Sam*. 18:11 Dauid auoided out of his presence. G. SANDYS The Musicians spent so much time in vnseasonable tuning, that he commanded them to auoid. b G. MARKHAM If you put a hollow quill therein.. the wind will auoyd the better. 6 J. AYLIFFE If a Person takes a Bishoprick, it does not avoid by Force of that Law of Pluralities, but by the antient Common Law.

II Keep (away) from, keep off. 7 *v.t.* Keep away from; shun; refrain from. Foll. by a person or thing, *doing*, †*to do*. LME. 8 *v.t.* Evade, escape; keep or get out of the way of (something coming towards one or in one's path). LME. 9 *v.t.* Keep off; prevent; obviate. E17.

7 ALDOUS HUXLEY He always does his best to avoid me; goes out of the room when I come in;.. won't even look at me. L. P. HARTLEY He avoided looking at himself in the glass, so as not to see the circles under his eyes. C. JACKSON Harry Harrison avoided the main highway as tiresome, and took an older, less direct route instead. W. MAXWELL The epidemic was raging and people were told to avoid crowds. 8 J. GALSWORTHY How, by some sort of settlement, he could best avoid the payment of those death duties which would follow his decease. C. ISHERWOOD A second journey had to be made through the living-room in the dark.., skirting the table, avoiding the chairs. W. TREVOR A red Post Office van had to swerve to avoid him. 9 CARLYLE That the Body.. be decently interred, to avoid putrescence.

avoidable *a*. (*a*) able to be avoided; †(*b*) to be shunned: LME. **avoidably** *adv*. M19. **avoidal** *n*. (*rare*) avoidance L17. **avoider** *n*. E17. **avoidless** *a*. (*poet*.) that cannot be avoided M17.

avoidance /əˈvɔɪd(ə)ns/ *n*. LME. [f. prec. + -ANCE.] †1 The action of emptying; ejection, excretion; removal; dismissal; departure (*from, out of*). LME–M17. 2 The occurrence of a vacancy (of an office, benefice, etc.); the right to fill up a vacancy. *arch.* LME. 3 The action of keeping away or refraining from something; escaping, evasion; shunning, holding aloof from someone or something; prevention. LME. 4 Chiefly *Law*. The action of making void or of no effect; invalidation, annulment. E17. †5 An outlet. Only in E17.

1 J. HAYWARD By voluntary avoidance out of the Realme. DONNE The King having made avoydance of those hee esteemed not necessary. 2 G. F. MACLEAR On each avoidance of the abbacy, to fill up the situation from founder's kin. 3 DONNE For avoydance of scandall is Divine law. *Listener* The avoidance of marked peaks and troughs in the amplitude-frequency characteristic. A. LURIE The same avoidance of all topics which might annoy them. *tax avoidance*: see TAX *n.* 4 H. H. MILMAN The obsequious clergy.. pronounced at once the avoidance of the marriage.

avoirdupois /avədə'pɔɪz, ˌavwɑːdjʊ'pwɑː/ *n.* ME. [OFr. *aveir de peis* goods of weight, f. *ave(i)r* (mod. *avoir*) use as n. of *avoir* have (f. L *habere*) + *de* of + *peis, pois* (mod. *poids*) weight, POISE *n.*[1] Substitution of *du* for *de* established 17.] †1 Merchandise sold by weight. ME–L17. 2 A system of weights based on a pound (the *avoirdupois pound*) of 16 ounces or 7,000 grains. More fully *avoirdupois weight*. L15. 3 Weight, heaviness. L16.

†avolation *n.* M17–E19. [med.L *avolatio(n-)*, f. *avolat-* pa. ppl stem of *avolare*, f. *a-* AB- + *volare* to fly: see -ATION.] The action of flying away; exhalation; evaporation.

avondbloem *n.* see AANDBLOM.

†avoset(ta) *ns.* vars. of AVOCET.

avouch /ə'vaʊtʃ/ *v.* & *n.* *arch.* & *rhet.* L15. [OFr. *avochier* f. L *advocare*: see ADVOKE. Cf. AVOW *v.*[1]] A *v.* 1 *v.t.* Declare as a thing one can prove or, formerly, on which one is an authority; testify to as a personal witness; affirm, assert. L15. 2 *v.t.* & *i.* Guarantee; vouch for or *for*. M16. 3 *v.t.* Acknowledge; take responsibility for; admit; sanction. M16. 4 *v.t.* Establish, prove. L16. †5 *v.t.* Appeal to; cite as warrant, authority, or testimony. L16–E18. †6 *v.t.* Establish upon testimony. L16–L17.

1 BYRON A report.. Avouch'd his death. C. M. YONGE His own deposition, as three Cardinals avouched that he had made it before them. J. CAREY A locket containing ringlets which he avouches, in confidence, to be relics of a Spanish girl. 2 BACON The seller must bring one to avouch his sale. DEFOE I can avouch for his reputation. H. H. MILMAN The authority of Erasmus avouches the accomplished scholarship of Pace. 3 S. DANIEL He for whom thou dost this villanie.. will not avouch thy fact. AV *Deut.* 26:17 Thou hast auouched the Lord this day to be thy God. SIR W. SCOTT The first time that I have heard one with a beard on his lip avouch himself a coward. R. C. TRENCH Milton in his prose works frequently avouches the peculiar affection to the Italian literature and language which he bore. 4 C. MARLOWE And will avouch his saying with the sword. 5 G. HARVEY Reasuns he usid none against me, but only avouchid and maintainid M. Osburns. 6 F. THYNNE Whiche I will sufficiently advouche, yf Instances be called for at my handes.

B *n.* Guarantee, assurance. E17.

avouchable *a.* L16. **avoucher** *n.* L16. **avouchment** *n.* the action of avouching; an assurance, guarantee; a positive declaration: L15.

avoué /avwe/ *n.* Pl. pronounced same. E19. [Fr.: see ADVOWEE.] 1 = ADVOWEE 2. E19. 2 A French solicitor. E19.

avow /ə'vaʊ/ *n.* *arch.* ME. [f. AVOW *v.*[2]] 1 A vow, a solemn promise. ME. †2 A votive offering. Only in LME.

avow /ə'vaʊ/ *v.*[1] ME. [OFr. *avouer* acknowledge, recognize as valid, f. L *advocare*: see ADVOKE. Cf. AVOUCH.] †1 *v.t.* Acknowledge (a person) as one's own. ME–E17. †2 *v.t.* Authorize, approve. ME–M17. 3 *v.t.* Declare as a thing one can vouch for; affirm, maintain. ME. 4 *v.t.* Admit, confess; *refl.* reveal one's identity or character. LME. †5 *v.refl.* Affiliate oneself *to*; put oneself under the patronage of (foll. by (*up*)*on*). LME–E17. 6 *v.i.* *Law.* Justify or maintain an act done, esp. a distraining for rent. *arch.* E16.

1 R. HAKLUYT Not our subiects, nor by vs any way to be advowed. 2 HOBBES Be contented to avow all the actions he shall do. 3 SIR T. MORE Ryghte worshipful folk, that before me aduowed it in his face. F. WELDON God can be worshipped anywhere, the Reverend Allbright avowed. 4 T. WILLIAMS For the first time.. I saw her beauty, I consciously avowed it to myself. W. S. CHURCHILL By a custom, openly avowed, the Paymaster was permitted to carry his balances to his private account and draw the interest on them.

avowable *a.* E17. **avowal** *n.* acknowledgement, unconstrained admission M18. **avowant** *n.* (*Law*, now *Hist.*) a challenger; a person who admits an act but believes it to be justified: E16. **avowedly** /ə'vaʊɪdli/ *adv.* with open declaration or acknowledgement L16. **avower** *n.*[1] †(*a*) a patron, a protector; (*b*) a person who declares or acknowledges something: LME. **†avower** *n.*[2] [-ER[4]] a vow; avowal: only in 16.

†avow *v.*[2] ME. [OFr. *avo(u)er* vow, f. as A-[5] + VOW *v.*] 1 *v.t.* Bind with a vow (*to, to do*); devote, consecrate, (*to*). ME–L16. 2 *v.t.* & *i.* Make a vow (*that, to* an act, *to do*); undertake solemnly, vow, (something, *to do*). LME–E19.

avowry /ə'vaʊ(ə)ri/ *n.* ME. [AN *avowrie*, OFr. *avoerie*, f. *avoeor* (f. as AVOW *v.*[1] + -OR): see -Y[3], -RY.] †1 Acknowledgement as one's own. Only in ME. †2 Authorization, approval. Only in ME. †3 Patronage, protection. Only in ME. 4 A patron, a protector; a patron saint. LME. †5 The right of presentation to a benefice; advowson. LME–M17. 6 The avowal of an act done; *esp.* in *Law* (now *Hist.*), the plea whereby a person who distrains for rent avows the act and justifies it. L15.

avoyer /ə'vɔɪə; *foreign* avwaje (*pl. same*)/ *n.* L16. [Swiss Fr. f. OFr. *avoié* corresp. to Fr. AVOUÉ.] *Hist.* In some Swiss cantons: the chief magistrate.

avulse /ə'vʌls/ *v.t.* *rare.* M18. [L *avuls-* pa. ppl stem of *avellere*, f. *a* AB- + *vellere* to pluck.] Pull or pluck off; tear away.

avulsion /ə'vʌlʃ(ə)n/ *n.* E17. [Fr., or L *avulsio(n-)*, f. as prec.: see -ION.] 1 The action of pulling off or tearing away; forcible separation. E17. 2 A part torn off; a detached portion. L17. 3 *Law.* The sudden removal of land by a change in the course of a river, flood-water, etc., to another person's estate (the land remaining the property of the original owner: cf. ALLUVION 4). M19.

avuncular /ə'vʌŋkjʊlə/ *a.* M19. [f. L *avunculus* maternal uncle, dim. of *avus* grandfather, + -AR[1].] Of, pertaining to, or resembling an uncle.

avunculate /ə'vʌŋkjʊlət/ *n.* E20. [f. as prec. + -ATE[1].] *Anthropol.* The special relationship in some societies between a maternal uncle and his sister's son.

aw *a., n.,* & *adv.* see A'.

aw /ɔː/ *int.* *N. Amer.* & *Sc.* M19. [Imit.] Expr. mild remonstrance, entreaty, commiseration, disgust, or disapproval.

awa' *adv., a.,* & *n.* see AWAY.

awabi /ə'wɑːbi/ *n.* E18. [Jap.] The Japanese abalone, *Haliotis gigantea*.

†await *n.* LME. [AN, f. as next.] 1 A waylaying with hostile intent; (an) ambush; a plot. Long *rare*. LME–M19. 2 Watching, watchfulness, caution. LME–M16.

await /ə'weɪt/ *v.* ME. [AN *awaitier* = OFr. *aguaitier*, f. as A-[5] + WAIT *v.*] †1 *v.t.* & *i.* Keep watch (on); lie in wait (for); waylay. ME–L17. †2 *v.t.* & *i.* Look (at), observe. Only in ME. †3 *v.i.* Remain (in a place); wait (*for, on*). ME–E19. 4 *v.t.* Wait for (a coming event or person); expect. ME. †5 *v.t.* Plot (harm of some kind) *to*. Only in LME. †6 *v.t.* & *i.* Attend to; take care, endeavour, (*that, to do*). LME–E17. †7 *v.t.* & *i.* Wait on (or (*up*)*on*) as a servant, attendant, etc. LME–M18. 8 *v.t.* Be in store for. L16.

1 M. DRAYTON Thou seest who doth awaite, T' intrap thy Beautie. MILTON Your ill-meaning politician lords.. Appointed to await me thirty spies. 3 SIR W. SCOTT The acclamations.. of the commons who awaited without. 4 J. AGATE On arrival, found Lady H. awaiting us with wonderful cocktails. H. INNES If this were England.. you'd be in a condemned cell awaiting execution. 7 H. SURREY Then issued she, awayted with great train. POPE On whom three hundred gold-capt youths await. 8 LD MACAULAY Honors and rewards which he little deserved awaited him.

awaiter *n.* (now *rare*) LME.

awake /ə'weɪk/ *pred. a.* ME. [Use as adj. of obs. pa. pple of next.] 1 No longer or not yet asleep. ME. 2 Vigilant; alert. E17.

2 **awake to** fully aware of.

awake /ə'weɪk/ *v.* Pa. t. **awoke** /ə'wəʊk/, **†awaked**; pa. pple **awoke, awoken** /ə'wəʊk(ə)n/, **awaked**. [OE *āwæcnan* & *āwacian*: see A *prep.*[1] 6, WAKE *v.*] I *v.i.* 1 Come out of the state of sleep; cease to sleep. OE. 2 Come out of a state resembling sleep; become active. ME. 3 Be wakeful; be vigilant. *rare*. LME.

1 AV *Judg.* 16:20 Hee awoke out of his sleepe. ADDISON I was so transported with joy that I awaked. M. MCCARTHY Terrible dreams about money, from which she would awake sweating. F. TUOHY He fell asleep and when he awoke it was bright sunshine. 2 S. JOHNSON Whenever he awakes to seriousness and reflection. E. A. FREEMAN The national spirit again awoke. **awake to** become fully aware of.

II *v.t.* 4 Rouse from sleep. ME. 5 Rouse from a state resembling sleep; stir up, make active. ME.

4 DRYDEN No dreadful Dreams awak'd him with affright. W. OWEN Move him into the sun—Gently its touch awoke him once. 5 SIR W. SCOTT But morning beam, and wild bird's call, Awaked not Mortham's silent hall. G. ORWELL The young, strong body, now helpless in sleep, awoke in him a pitying, protecting feeling.

awaker *n.* (*rare*) E17.

awaken /ə'weɪk(ə)n/ *v.* [OE *āwæcn(i)an*: see A *prep.*[1] 6, WAKEN *v.*] I *v.i.* 1 = AWAKE *v.* 1. OE. †2 Come into existence, originate. OE–ME. 3 = AWAKE *v.* 2. E18. II *v.t.* 4 = AWAKE *v.* 4. ME. 5 = AWAKE *v.* 5; *esp.* arouse *to* a sense of, make aware. ME.

awakener *n.* L16. **awakening** *n.* (a) rising, (an) arousal, from sleep, inaction, indifference, etc. L16. **awakenment** *n.* (now *rare*) an awakening M19.

awald /'ɑːw(ə)ld/ *adv.* & *pred. a.* *Sc.* Also **-lt** /-lt/. M18. [Perh. ult. f. ON *af* from + *velta* to rise.] Of an animal, esp. a sheep: on its back and unable to rise; of a person: incapacitated through intoxication, insensible.

awanting /ə'wɒntɪŋ/ *ppl a.* Chiefly *Sc.* L16. [f. A *prep.*[1] 8 + *wanting* ppl a. of WANT *v.*: cf. AMISSING.] Missing, wanting.

award /ə'wɔːd/ *n.* LME. [AN, f. as next.] I 1 A judicial decision. LME. 2 A payment, penalty, etc., appointed by a judicial decision; a prize or other honour assigned by authority. L16. †II 3 Custody, wardship. LME–L16.

2 *Tony award*: see TONY *n.*[1]

Comb.: **award wages** *Austral.* & *NZ* minimum wages fixed by an industrial court for a particular industry or occupation; **award-winning** *a.* that has won an award.

award /ə'wɔːd/ *v.*[1]*t.* LME. [AN *awarder* var. (see A-[7]) of ONFr. *eswarder*, OFr. *esguarder* consider, ordain: see EX-[1], WARD *v.*] †1 *gen.* Decide or determine (something, *that, to do*) after consideration or deliberation. LME–E18. 2 Decide judicially (a process); issue judicially (a document etc.). LME. 3 Grant, assign, (*to* a person); order to be given as a payment, penalty, prize, etc. LME. †4 Sentence, appoint, (a person, *to* custody etc., *to do*). LME–M17.

3 SHAKES. *Merch. V.* A pound of that same merchant's flesh is thine, The court awards it and the law doth give it. G. B. SHAW A Court of Discipline, which awarded him two years imprisonment and fifty lashes. A. J. CRONIN For his thesis on Dust Inhalation, he had been awarded his MD.

awardable *a.* able (esp. legally) to be awarded E17. **awarder** *n.* M16.

†award *v.*[2]*t.* M16. [f. A-[11] + WARD *v.*] 1 Guard. Only in M16. 2 Ward off (blows etc.). L16–M19.

aware /ə'wɛː/ *pred. a.* [OE *ġewær* (see A-[4], WARE *a.*) = OS *giwar* (MDu. *ghewāre*), OHG *gawar, gi-* (G *gewahr*) f. WGmc.] †1 Vigilant, cautious, on one's guard. (Foll. by *lest, of.*) OE–M19. 2 Conscious, sensible, not ignorant, having knowledge, (*of, that*); *colloq.* (occas. *attrib.*) well-informed, responsive to conditions etc., (w. specifying adv.) informed about current developments. OE.

2 R. P. WARREN It was cold in the room, and he was aware of the cold, but as knowledge, as it were, not as sensation. E. F. BENSON I am aware there are many different sorts of people in the world. J. STEINBECK Along the road the trackers would become aware that they had missed the path. J. I. M. STEWART He seemed scarcely aware of us when we did turn up. *Gay News* I think a lot of *aware* men influenced fashion. *Chicago Tribune* You'd think people would be more ecologically aware.

awareness *n.* E19.

†awarn *v.t. rare.* LME–L16. [f. A-[11] + WARN *v.*[1]] Give notice to; warn.

SPENSER That every bird and beast awarned made To shrowd themselves.

†awarrant *v.t.* LME–L19. [f. A-[11] + WARRANT *v.*] Vouch for, warrant, guarantee.

awash /əˈwɒʃ/ *adv.* & *pred. a.* M19. [f. A-[2] + WASH *n.* or *v.*] Level with the surface of water, so that it just washes over; flooded (*lit.* & *fig.*); washing about.

C. READE The rising water set everything awash. C. MACKENZIE An unpleasant black reef awash at half tide. A. SETON The glorious singing mingled with the exultant organ and the Abbey was awash with beauty of sound. J. P. DONLEAVY The bar was awash Uncontrolled pints. *Times* The stock market has suddenly become awash with takeover bids and rumours.

away /əˈweɪ/ *adv., a.,* & *n.* Also (*Sc.*) **awa'** /əˈwɑː, əˈwɔː/. [Late OE *aweg* (earlier *on weg*): see A *prep.*[1] I, ON *prep.*, WAY *n.*] A *adv.* I 1 On one's way; onward, on, along. Long *obs.* exc. *Sc.* & *north.* LOE. 2 From this or that place; to a distance (*lit.* & *fig.*). LOE. 3 From adherence, contact, or inclusion; aside, off. LOE. 4 From or out of one's personal possession. LOE. 5 Towards or into non-existence; so as to remove, reduce, eliminate, bring to an end, reach the end of, etc., something by the action of the vb. LOE. 6 Gone from a place; absent; wanting. ME. 7 Gone from existence; vanished; consumed; dead, fainted. Now *dial.* ME. 8 At a (stated) distance; in another place. LME. b With advs. w. intensive force: a considerable distance or time *back, down, up*, etc. Chiefly *N. Amer.* E19. c *Sport.* On an opponent's ground. L19. 9 In the other direction, from the place, person, etc., in question. LME. 10 Continuously, constantly, persistently. M16. 11 Without hesitation or delay; forthwith, directly. M16.

1 SHAKES. *Twel. N.* Come away, come away, death; And in sad cypress let me be laid. R. L. STEVENSON And now come awa' to your bed. 2 DRYDEN And hungry sent the wily fox away. W. COWPER Away went Gilpin, neck or nought; Away went hat and wig. DYLAN THOMAS I have longed to move away but am afraid. P. LARKIN That Whitsun, I was late getting away: Not till about One-twenty . . Did my . . train pull out. E. ROOSEVELT He had grown away from her in some ways and . . in later years they had often not been in sympathy. M. KEANE I stepped up to my reflection, then away from it. *carry, drive*, etc., *away. go, run, slip, steal*, etc. *away.* **far** or **out and away** by far, by a very large amount. 3 LONGFELLOW She folded her work, and laid it away. G. B. SHAW She touches her eyes as if to wipe away a tear. *fall away.* 4 LONGFELLOW This passing traveller, who hath stolen away The brightest jewel of my crown to-day. *give, put, take, throw, whisk*, etc., *away.* 5 AV *Job* 33:21 His flesh is consumed away. YEATS She grew pale as death and fainted away. R. HUGHES The breeze having dropped away almost to a calm. DYLAN THOMAS There could I marvel My birthday Away. *die, fade, pine, waste, wither*, etc., *away. pass away. explain away. idle, while away* (time). *do, make, away with*: see DO *v.*, MAKE *v.* 6 A. COWLEY How could it be so fair and you away? N. COWARD They're away in Tunis. 7 COVERDALE *Jer.* 31:15 Rachel mournynge for hir children, and wolde not be comforted, because they were awaye. 8 R. D. BLACKMORE His home was some miles away. YEATS Hidden away where nobody can find it. S. HEANEY Kelly's kept an unlicensed bull, well away From the road. B. PYM She had chosen a seat away from the other people. 9 J. N. LOCKYER The axis of rotation is inclined away from the Sun. A. LOOS Mr Spoffard turned on his heels and walked away. SCOTT FITZGERALD I turned my head away and wept. 10 THACKERAY He sat down and worked away, very, very hard. A. HELPS And kept 'pegging away' . . with all my might. *pound away.* 11 *fire away*: see FIRE *v. right away*: see RIGHT *adv. straight away*: see STRAIGHT *adv.*[1]

II Ellipt. uses (esp. for an imper. or inf.). 12 Go away. ME. 13 Take away; go or get away *with.* LME. 14 Get on or along *with.* L15.

12 AV *Exod.* 19:24 Away, get thee downe. R. L. STEVENSON I'm weariet, an' here I'm awa to my bed. YEATS We must away, and wait until she dies. 13 DICKENS In his honest indignation he would reply, 'Away with it!' 14 CARLYLE Idolatry . . is a thing they cannot away-with.

B *adj.* Played or taking place on an opponent's ground. E20.

away game, goal, match, win, etc.

C *n.* A match or win on an opponent's ground. M20.

aways *adv.* (long *dial.*) = AWAY *adv.* L15.

†awayward *adv.* & *a.* ME. [f. AWAY *adv.* + -WARD.] A *adv.* In a different direction; aside; away. ME–L16. B *adj.* = WAYWARD. Only in ME.

¶Aphet. to WAYWARD.

awe /ɔː/ *n.* & *v.* [OE *ege* = Goth. *agis* fear, f. Gmc.; replaced in ME by forms cognate w. ON *agi.*] A *n.* †1 Terror, dread. OE–L18. 2 Reverential fear or wonder. OE. 3 Power to inspire reverential fear or wonder. *arch.* OE.

1 W. COWPER His voice Shook the delinquent with such fits of awe. 2 J. KEBLE There is an awe in mortals' joy, A deep mysterious fear. A. S. NEILL Some parents taught their children that sex was sacred and spiritual, something to be treated with awe and wonder. V. S. PRITCHETT We walked behind them listening with awe to their astonishing man-of-the-world talk about girls. A. EDEN We boys were in considerable awe of Smitton, whose rules were strict and whose praise was sparing. 3 D. BAGLEY Clothing himself in the full awe of British majesty.

Comb.: **awestricken, awestruck** *adjs.* suddenly affected with awe.

B *v.t.* Inspire with awe; influence or control by awe. ME.

SHAKES. *Much Ado* Shall quips, and sentences, . . awe a man from the career of his humour? GIBBON He was not awed by the sanctity of the place. J. K. JEROME They awe us, these strange stars, so cold, so clear. J. B. PRIESTLEY He looked so imposing that immediately an awed silence fell on the company. A. SCHLEE Ellie, awed out of ill temper, turned shyly to face them.

aweless *a.* (*a*) without feeling awe; †(*b*) without inspiring awe: LME. **awelessness** *n.* (*rare*) L16.

aweary /əˈwɪəri/ *pred. a.* M16. [f. A-[11] + WEARY *a.*] Tired, weary, (*of*).

Also **awearied** *a.* E17.

aweather /əˈwɛðə/ *adv., pred. a.,* & *prep.* L16. [f. A *prep.*[1] I + WEATHER *n.*] *Naut.* Towards the weather or windward side (of).

aweel /əˈwiːl/ *adv. Sc.* E19. [Weakened form of *ah well!*] Well then, well.

aweigh /əˈweɪ/ *adv.* & *pred. a.* E17. [f. A *prep.*[1] 6 + WEIGH *n.*[1]] *Naut.* Of an anchor: just raised perpendicularly above the ground in weighing. Of a ship, crew, etc.: just about to set sail.

awesome /ˈɔːs(ə)m/ *a.* L16. [f. AWE *n.* + -SOME[1].] 1 Filled with awe. L16. 2 Inspiring awe. L17. 3 Outstanding, remarkable. *colloq.* M20. b Excellent, marvellous. *slang.* L20.

awesomely *adv.* (*a*) so as to inspire awe; (*b*) *colloq.* outstanding, very: L19. **awesomeness** *n.* L19.

aweto *n.* var. of AWHETO.

awful /ˈɔːfʊl, *esp. in senses A.4, B* -f(ə)l/ *a.* & *adv.* OE. [f. AWE *n.* + -FUL.] A *adj.* I Objectively. 1 Causing terror or dread; appalling. OE. 2 Worthy of or commanding profound respect or reverential fear or wonder. OE. 3 Solemnly impressive, sublimely majestic. M17. 4 Notable of its kind (esp. in badness); exceedingly bad, long, etc. *colloq.* E19.

1 W. S. CHURCHILL The grim and awful cataclysm of war. 2 ADDISON Cato's character . . is rather awful than amiable. 3 ANNE STEVENSON The great trees, as soon as they die, / immediately become ghosts, / stalk upright among the living with awful composure. 4 KEATS It is an awful while since you have heard from me. M. DRABBLE He likes such awful people. A. LURIE An awful, vulgar sport shirt . . , made of shiny green material.

II Subjectively. †5 Terror-stricken; timid. L16–M18. 6 Profoundly respectful or reverential. *arch.* L16.

5 C. MARLOWE Monarch of hell under whose black survey Great potentates do kneel with awful fear. 6 GIBBON At an awful distance they cast away their garments. J. KEBLE Towards the East our awful greetings Are wafted.

B *adv.* = AWFULLY 3. *colloq.* E19.

A. TROLLOPE It is awful lonely here, too. R. D. PAINE A prairie town . . that looks awful good to me.

awfulness *n.* †(*a*) *rare* an awe-inspiring act; †(*b*) profound reverence, awe; (*c*) the quality of inspiring with awe; impressive solemnity; terribleness; *colloq.* poor quality: LME.

awfully /ˈɔːfʊli, *esp. in sense 3* -fli/ *adv.* LME. [f. prec. + -LY[2].] I Objectively. 1 So as to cause terror. LME. 2 So as to cause reverential fear or wonder; majestically. LME. 3 Exceedingly; very much. *colloq.* E19.

3 G. B. SHAW Thanks awfully, old chap. JOYCE Pretend to want something awfully. SCOTT FITZGERALD I certainly am awfully glad to see you again.

II Subjectively. 4 With a feeling of awe; fearfully; reverentially. *arch.* L16.

awheel /əˈwiːl/ *adv.* & *pred. a.* L19. [f. A-[2] + WHEEL *n.*] On wheels; on a bicycle.

awheto /ˈɑːweɪtəʊ, ˈɑːfeɪ-/ *n. NZ.* Also **aweto** /ˈɑːweɪtəʊ/. Pl. **-os.** L19. [Maori.] A caterpillar infested with a parasitic fungus of the genus *Cordyceps*, which reduces its host to 'mummified' form. Also called *vegetable caterpillar.*

awhile /əˈwʌɪl/ *adv.* OE. [Orig. two wds, f. A *a.* + WHILE *n.*] For a short time.

awhirl /əˈwəːl/ *adv.* & *pred. a.* L19. [f. A-[2] + WHIRL *n.* or *v.*] In a whirl; whirling.

awing /əˈwɪŋ/ *adv.* & *pred. a.* E17. [f. A *prep.*[1] I + WING *n.*] On the wing; flying (*lit.* & *fig.*).

†awk *a., adv.,* & *n.* Long *dial.* LME. [ON *afugr, of-* turned the wrong way, back foremost. For the phonetic devel. cf. HAWK *n.*[1]] A *adj.* 1 In the wrong direction; back-handed. LME–M16. 2 Perverse; clumsy; awkward. LME–M19. B *adv.* Backwards, in reverse order, confusedly; esp. in *ring* (bells) *awk*: as a warning or summons. E17–M19. C *n.* 1 Awkwardness; back-handedness. M–L17. 2 An awkward person. *rare.* Only in E19.

awkward /ˈɔːkwəd/ *adv.* & *a.* LME. [f. AWK *a.* + -WARD.] A *adv.* In the wrong direction; in reverse order; in a backwards direction; upside down. Long *obs.* exc. *dial.* of an animal: on its back and unable to rise (cf. AWALD). LME.

B *adj.* †1 Oblique; back-handed. E16–M19. 2 Froward, perverse, cantankerous, (passing into sense 7). Now *dial.* M16. 3a Of a person: lacking dexterity, clumsy, bungling; ungainly, uncouth. M16. b Of things and actions: clumsy; ill-adapted for use; ungainly. E17. †4 Unfavourable; adverse. L16–M17. 5 Of things or actions: causing embarrassment; inconvenient; reflecting embarrassment. E18. 6 Of a person: embarrassed; ill at ease. E18. 7 Difficult or dangerous to deal with. M19.

3a SWIFT I have not seen a more clumsy, aukward, and unhandy people. J. IRVING Basketball and football players, great big awkward sorts of boys. *awkward squad*: see SQUAD *n.*[1] I. b J. FRAME His body uncontrolled and his gait awkward. F. ORMSBY We laughed at your awkward dress. Your half-hearted passes at a fat waitress. **the awkward age** adolescence. 4 SHAKES. *2 Hen. VI* Twice by awkward wind from England's bank Drove back again. 5 J. O'HARA Frances's father . . had caught his daughter and Snyder in an awkward position and had given Snyder the choice of marriage or death. D. LODGE It was the most awkward time, about 6, just as I was about to serve up the dinner. W. TREVOR They didn't say anything, and after a few moments the silence hardened and became awkward. 6 LEIGH HUNT He was . . beginning to feel awkward with his Whig friends. 7 J. TYNDALL We let ourselves down an awkward face of rock. G. ORWELL It was an awkward job getting the wounded down the narrow, crowded trench. B. HINES There's always someone you can't suit, who has to be awkward, who refuses to be interested in anything.

awkwardish *a.* (*colloq.*) E17. **awkwardly** *adv.* LME. **awkwardness** *n.* L17.

awl /ɔːl/ *n.* [OE *æl* = OHG *ala* (G *Ahle*), ON *alr*, of unkn. origin.] A small pointed tool for pricking or piercing holes, *esp.* such a tool used by shoemakers.

cobbler's awls: see COBBLER IC.

Comb.: **awl-bird** *dial.* (*a*) the green woodpecker; (*b*) the avocet; **awlwort** a cruciferous aquatic plant, *Subularia aquatica*, having white flowers and awl-shaped leaves.

awmous *n.* see ALMS.

awn /ɔːn/ *n.* OE. [ON *agn*- obl. stem of *ǫgn* (Sw. *agn*, Da. *avn*) corresp. to late OE *æġnan* (pl.), *eġenu* husk, chaff, OHG *agana* (G *Ahne*), Goth. *ahana* chaff.] *Bot.* A bristle-like projection; *esp.* that terminating the grain-sheath of barley, oats, and other grasses.

awned *a.*[1] having an awn E19. **awnless** *a.* L18. **awny** *a.* (chiefly *Sc.*) bearded, bristly L18.

awn /ɔːn/ *v.*[1]*t.* E19. [f. the n.] Remove the awns from.

awner *n.* a machine for awning grain. L19.

awn /ɔːn/ *v.*[2]*t.* M19. [Back-form. f. next.] Cover with an awning.

awned *a.*[2] = AWNINGED L19.

awning /ˈɔːnɪŋ/ *n.* E17. [Origin unkn.] 1 A sheet of canvas etc. forming a shelter against sun or rain, orig. on a ship's deck. E17. 2 The part of the poop-deck of a ship which is continued forward beyond the bulkhead of the cabin. M18.

awninged *a.* furnished with an awning M19.

awoke, awoken *vs.* see AWAKE *v.*

awork /əˈwəːk/ *adv.* & *pred. a.* LME. [f. A *prep.*[1] 6 + WORK *n.*] At or to work; in activity.

awrong /əˈrɒŋ/ *adv.* LME. [f. A *prep.*[1] 4 + WRONG *n.*[2]] Wrong, in a wrong way.

awry /əˈrʌɪ/ *adv.* & (usu. *pred.*) *a.* LME. [f. A *prep.*[1] 6 + WRY *n.*] 1 Oblique(ly); crooked(ly); uneven(ly); askew; askance. LME. 2 Improper(ly); wrong; distorted(ly); amiss. L15.

1 POPE Not Cynthia when her manteau's pinned awry, E'er felt such rage. C. DARWIN Some of our party began to squint and look awry. M. MITCHELL His new coat did not fit very well, for the tailor had been hurried and some of the seams were awry. I. MCEWAN The hair, so tightly drawn back before, was slightly awry. 2 E. B. BROWNING Those who think Awry, will scarce act straightly. CARLYLE Far worse, the marriage itself went awry. ARNOLD BENNETT Most invalids got their perspective awry.

ax /aks/ *n.*[1] Long *obs.* exc. *dial.* Also **axe**. [OE *eax*, *æx* = OFris. *axe*, OS, OHG *ahsa*, also ON *ǫxull* (see AXLE), f. Gmc.] = AXLE.

Comb.: **axtree** = AXLE-TREE.

ax *n.*[2], *v.*[1] vars. of AXE *n.*[1], *v.*[1]

ax *v.*[2] see ASK *v.*

axal /ˈaks(ə)l/ *a.* Now *rare* or *obs.* E19. [Irreg. f. AXIS *n.*[1] + -AL[1].] = AXIAL.

axe /aks/ *n.*[1] Also ***ax**. [OE *æx* (*eax*), *æces* = OFris. *axa*, OS *akus* (Du. *aaks*), OHG *ackus* (G *Axt*), ON *ǫx*, Goth. *aqizi*, f. Gmc.] 1 A chopping-tool, having a blade usu. of iron with a steel edge and a wooden handle. OE. 2 *spec.* a *Hist.* A battleaxe. ME. b *Hist.* An executioner's axe. LME. c *the axe* (fig.), drastic reduction or elimination of expenditure, staff, etc.; abolition; dismissal. E20. 3 *Archaeol.* A double-edged or wedge-shaped stone implement. M19. 4 A musical instrument used in jazz and rock music, *esp.* (orig.) a saxophone, (now) a guitar. *slang.* M20.

1 **an axe to grind** a private end to serve. *battleaxe*, *Danish axe*, *double axe*, *pole axe*, *tommy-axe*, etc.

Comb.: **axe-breaker** *Austral.* a tree, *Notelaea longifolia*, with very hard timber; **axe-grinding** *vbl n.* & *ppl a.* serving a private end; **axe-hammer** a tool consisting of an axe and a hammer combined; **axe-head** the cutting blade of an axe; **axeman** a person who works with an axe; *slang* a jazz or rock guitarist; **axemanship** skill in using an axe.

†axe *n.*[2] M16–L18. [Fr. f. L AXIS *n.*[1]] = AXIS *n.*[1]

axe *n.*[3] var. of AX *n.*[1]

axe /aks/ *v.*[1]*t.* Also ***ax**. L17. [f. AXE *n.*[1]] 1 Shape or trim with an axe. L17. 2 Cut down drastically (costs, services, etc.); eliminate, remove, abolish, dismiss. E20.

axe *v.*[2] see ASK *v.*

axel /ˈaks(ə)l/ *n.* Also **A-**. M20. [f. *Axel* Rudolph Paulser (1885–1938), Norwegian skater.] *Skating.* A 1½-turn jump from the forward outside edge of one skate to the backward outside edge of the other.

axenic /eɪˈzenɪk/ *a.* M20. [f. A-[10] + Gk *xenikos* alien, strange + -IC.] *Biol.* Free from living organisms of any kind other than that stated or implied.

axenically *adv.* M20.

axes *ns.* pls. of AX *n.*[1], AXE *n.*[1], AXIS *n.*[1]

axial /ˈaksɪəl/ *a.* M19. [f. AXIS *n.*[1] + -AL[1].] Of or pertaining to an axis; of the nature of or forming an axis; round or about an axis.

axial flow flow parallel to an axis of rotation (usu. (w. hyphen) *attrib.* designating turbines etc. in which such flow occurs). *axial vector*: see VECTOR *n.* 2a.

axiˈality *n.* L19. **axially** *adv.* M19.

axiate /ˈaksɪət/ *a.* E20. [f. AXIS *n.*[1] + -ATE[2].] *Zool.* = AXIAL.

axil /ˈaksɪl/ *n.* L18. [f. L AXILLA.] *Bot.* The upper angle between a leaf or petiole and the stem from which it springs, or between a branch and the trunk.

axile /ˈaksʌɪl/ *a.* E19. [f. AXIS *n.*[1] + -ILE.] Axial; *esp.* (*Bot.*) growing or occurring along an axis.

axilla /akˈsɪlə/ *n.* Pl. **-llae** /-liː/. E17. [L, dim. of *ala* wing.] 1 *Anat.* & *Zool.* The region of the armpit; the corresponding part of a bird or other creature. E17. 2 *Bot.* = AXIL. *rare.* M19.

axillant /akˈsɪl(ə)nt/ *a.* L19. [f. prec. + -ANT[1].] *Bot.* Of a leaf: growing at a particular axil.

axillar /akˈsɪlə/ *a.* & *n.* M16. [f. L AXILLA + -AR[1], after Fr. *axillaire.*] A *adj.* 1 = AXILLARY *a.* 1. M16. 2 = AXILLARY *a.* 2. *rare.* M19. B *n.* Something axillary; *spec.* †(*a*) *Anat.* an axillary vein; (*b*) *Ornith.* an axillary feather. E18.

axillary /akˈsɪləri/ *a.* & *n.* E17. [f. AXILLA + -ARY[2].] A *adj.* 1 *Anat.* & *Zool.* Of or pertaining to an axilla. E17. 2 *Bot.* Pertaining to, situated in, or growing from an axil. Opp. *terminal.* M18. B *n.* Something axillary; *esp.* (*Ornith.*) an axillary feather. L19.

axinite /ˈaksɪnʌɪt/ *n.* E19. [f. Gk *axinē* axe + -ITE[1].] *Min.* A rock-forming triclinic silicate of the epidote group containing calcium, iron, manganese, aluminium, and boron, and occurring as brown or yellow, often large, crystals.

axinomancy /akˈsɪnəmansi/ *n.* E17. [L *axinomantia* f. Gk *axinomanteia*, f. *axinē* axe: see -MANCY.] Divination by means of an axe-head.

axiology /aksɪˈɒlədʒi/ *n.* E20. [Fr. *axiologie*, f. Gk *axia* value + -OLOGY.] *Philos.* The theory of value.

axioˈlogical *a.* E20. **axioˈlogically** *adv.* E20. **axiologist** *n.* M20.

axiom /ˈaksɪəm/ *n.* L15. [Fr. *axiome* or L *axioma* f. Gk = what is thought fitting, a self-evident principle (Aristotle), f. *axios* worthy.] 1 An established or generally accepted principle; a maxim, a rule. L15. †2 *Logic.* A proposition (true or false). L16–M18. 3 *Math.* A self-evident truth; a proposition on which an abstractly defined structure is based. L16.

axiomata media /aksɪˌɒmətə ˈmiːdɪə/ *n. phr. pl.* M19. [mod.L (Bacon) = middle principles.] *Philos.* Principles above simple empirical laws but below the highest generalizations or fundamental laws.

axiomatic /aksɪəˈmatɪk/ *a.* & *n.* L18. [Gk *axiomatikos*, f. *axiomat-*, *-ma*: see AXIOM, -ATIC.] A *adj.* 1 Self-evident; indisputably true; of the nature of a maxim. L18. 2 Characterized by self-evident principles. E19. 3 Full of maxims, aphoristic. M19.

1 H. SPENCER These axiomatic truths, are truths recognized by the simplest order of reasoning. N. GORDIMER It's axiomatic the faults you see in others are often your own. 2 H. DAVY He gave an axiomatic form to the Science. 3 SOUTHEY The most axiomatic of English Poets.

B *n.* In *pl.* (usu. treated as *sing.*). A body of axioms; the study or use of axioms. E20.

axiomatical /aksɪəˈmatɪk(ə)l/ *a.* Now *rare.* L16. [f. as prec. + -AL[1].] †1 *Logic.* Pertaining to, or of the nature of, a simple statement or proposition. L16–L17. 2 Of or pertaining to maxims, self-evident truths, or accepted first principles. L17. 3 = AXIOMATIC *a.* 1. L17. 4 = AXIOMATIC *a.* 3. M18.

axiomatically /aksɪəˈmatɪk(ə)li/ *adv.* L16. [f. AXIOMATIC *a.* or prec.: see -ICALLY.] In an axiomatic manner; as an axiom.

axiomatize /aksɪˈɒmətʌɪz/ *v.* Also **-ise**. E18. [f. AXIOMAT(IC *a.* + -IZE.] 1 *v.i.* Make an axiom or axioms. *rare.* E18. 2 *v.t.* Render axiomatic; reduce to a system of axioms. M20.

axiomatiˈzation *n.* M20.

axion /ˈaksɪɒn/ *n.* L20. [f. AXIAL + -ON.] *Particle Physics.* A light neutral pseudoscalar particle postulated in order to account for the rarity of processes which break charge-parity symmetry.

axis /ˈaksɪs/ *n.*[1] Pl. **axes** /ˈaksiːz/. LME. [L, rel. to Skt *akṣa*, Gk *axōn*, Old Ch. Slav. *osĭ*, Lith. *aszis*, and AX *n.*[1]] I Of rotation. 1 The imaginary straight line about which a body such as the earth rotates; the prolongation of that of the earth on which the heavens appear to revolve. LME. 2 The imaginary line by rotation about which a plane figure is conceived as generating a solid. L16. †3 An axle. E17–E19. 4 *fig.* a A central support or pivot. E17. b An alliance between countries regarded as a pivot about which they and their associates revolve; *spec.* (**A-**) the alliance of 1939 between Germany and Italy, later extended to Japan and other countries; these countries collectively. Also *transf.*, (a link between) any two or more places, bodies, etc., acting or being considered together. M20. 5 *Anat.* More fully *axis vertebra*. The second cervical vertebra, upon which the head is turned. Formerly also, the odontoid process of this vertebra. L17.

II A line from pole to pole; a principal direction of extension. (Passing into branch III.) 6 A straight line between the poles of a magnet. M17. 7 A main line of extension or growth, esp. (*Anat.*, *Zool.*, etc.) of (a part of) a body or organism; a central structure following this. M18. b *Bot.* The central column of an inflorescence or other part; the main stem. L18. c *Geol.* The direction of a linear feature such as a ridge, mountain range, or valley; *esp.* the line of intersection of the land surface with the plane bisecting a fold. M19.

III Of symmetry or reference. 8 A straight line which divides a figure into two symmetrical parts, or with respect to which the parts of a body or system are symmetrically arranged. L17. 9 Any of various lines or directions defined by the geometry of optical systems, or by the structure and physical properties of crystals. E18. 10 Each of a set of (usu. mutually perpendicular) lines used to define a system of coordinates, as in a graph. M19.

8 *conjugate axis*, *major axis*, *minor axis*, *principal axis*, etc. 9 *crystal axis*: see CRYSTAL *a.* & *n.* *optic axis*: see OPTIC *a.* *visual axis*: see VISUAL *a.* 10 *x-axis*, *y-axis*, etc.

axis /ˈaksɪs/ *n.*[2] Pl. same. E17. [L (Pliny).] = CHITAL. Also *axis deer*.

axisymmetric /ˌaksɪsɪˈmetrɪk/ *a.* L19. [f. AXIS *n.*[1] + SYMMETRIC.] Symmetrical with respect to an axis.

axisymmetrical *a.* M20. **axiˈsymmetry** *n.* M20.

axle /ˈaks(ə)l/ *n.* ME. [f. as earlier AXLE-TREE.] 1 The centre-pin or spindle upon which a wheel revolves or which revolves along with it. Also = AXLE-TREE 1. ME. †2 = AXLE-TREE 3. M16–M19.

1 *fig.*: F. TUOHY Below them stood the Palace of Culture, an axle with the whole grey city gyrating around it. *axle tramp*: see TRAMP *n.* 3b. *wheel and axle*: see WHEEL *n.* 2 MILTON The earth . . With inoffensive pace that spinning sleeps On her soft Axle.

axled *a.* having an axle (usu. as 2nd elem. of comb., of a specified type) M17.

axle-tooth /ˈaks(ə)ltuːθ/ *n.* *obs.* exc. *dial.* Pl. **-teeth** /-tiːθ/. L15. [f. Da. *axel* molar + TOOTH *n.*: cf. Da. *axel-tand.*] A molar tooth.

axle-tree /ˈaks(ə)ltriː/ *n.* ME. [ON *ǫxultré*, f. *ǫxull* ult. f. as AX *n.*[1] + as TREE *n.*] 1 A fixed bar or rod on the ends of which a pair of wheels of a vehicle revolve. ME. †2 The spindle upon or with which a wheel revolves. LME–L17. †3 = AXIS *n.*[1] 1; *poet.* the heaven, the sky. LME–M17.

Axminster /'aksmɪnstə/ *n.* E19. [A town in Devon, SW England.] In full *Axminster carpet, rug*. A carpet or rug with a soft tufted cut pile of a type orig. manufactured at Axminster.

axo- /'aksəʊ/ *comb. form* of Gk *axōn* axis or of AXON: see -O-.

axolemma *n.* [Gk *lemma* husk, skin] *Anat.* the plasma membrane of an axon L19. **axo'nemal** *a.* (*Biol.*) of or pertaining to an axoneme M20. **axoneme** *n.* [Gk *nēma* thread] *Biol.* a central strand of a locomotor organelle such as a cilium or flagellum E20. **axoplasm** *n.* the cytoplasm of an axon E20. **axopod** *n.* = AXOPODIUM M20. **axo'podium** *n.*, pl. **-ia**, *Zool.* a rodlike pseudopodium having a central microtubular filament L19. **axostyle** *n.* (*Zool.*) a central flexible rod of microtubules present in certain flagellates E20. **a'xotomous** *a.* (*Min.*, now *rare* or *obs.*) (having a cleavage) perpendicular to the axis of growth E19.

axolotl /'aksəlɒt(ə)l/ *n.* L18. [Nahuatl, f. *atl* water + *xolotl* servant.] Any of a number of Central American salamanders of the genus *Ambystoma* (esp. *A. mexicanum*), which live in lakes and retain many larval characters, including external gills, throughout life, although capable in certain conditions of developing full adult form.

axon /'aksɒn/ *n.* Also **-one** /-əʊn/. M19. [Gk *axōn* axis.] *Anat.* †**1** The body axis. M-L19. **2** A filamentous extension of a nerve cell, serving to conduct impulses to other cells. L19.

a'xonal *a.* E20. **a'xonic** *a.* M20.

axonometric /,aks(ə)nə(ʊ)'mɛtrɪk/ *a.* E20. [f. Gk *axōn* axis + -O- -METRIC.] Of a (method of) pictorial representation: using an orthographic projection of the object on a plane inclined to each of the three principal axes of the object.

axunge /'aksʌndʒ/ *n.* Now *rare.* M16. [Fr. †*axunge* (now *axonge*) f. L *axungia* axle-grease, f. as AXIS *n.*[1] + *ung-* of *ungere* to grease.] The internal fat of the kidneys etc.; goose-grease, lard; *gen.* fat, grease.

ay *adv.*[1] & *n.*[1] var. of AYE *adv.*[1] & *n.*[1]

ay *adv.*[2], *int.*[1] & *n.*[2] var. of AYE *adv.*[2], *int.*, & *n.*[2]

ay /ʌɪ/ *int.*[2] Also (earlier) †**ey**. ME. [Natural exclam.; *ay me* is prob. modelled on OFr. *aimi* or It. *ahimè*, Sp. *ay de mi*.] **1** Expr. surprise or earnestness. Now *north.* ME. **2** *ay me!*: expr. regret, sorrow, or pity. M16.

ayah /'ʌɪə/ *n.* L18. [Port. *aia* fem. of *aio* tutor.] A nurse or maidservant, esp. of Europeans in India, SE Asia, etc.

ayatollah /ʌɪə'tɒlə/ *n.* Also (as a title) **A-**. M20. [Pers. f. Arab. *'āyatu-llāh* miraculous sign of God.] A Shiite religious leader in Iran; *fig.* a dogmatic leader, an influential or powerful person.

aye /eɪ, ʌɪ/ *adv.*[1] & *n.*[1] Now *arch.* & *Sc.* Also **ay**. ME. [ON *ei*, *ey* = OE *ā*, OS *eo*, OHG *eo*, *io* (G *je*), Goth. *aiws* age, eternity, f. Gmc, rel. to L *aevum* age, Gk *aie(i)* ever, *aiōn* AEON.] **A** *adv.* Ever, always; at all times. ME.

R. BURNS And ay the ale was growing better. OED Things grew ay the longer, the waur [worse]. L. G. GIBBON But poor folk aye have to work.

Comb.: **aye-green** *dial.* a houseleek.

B *n. for aye*, (expanded *for ever and aye*), for ever, for all time. ME.

aye /ʌɪ/ *adv.*[2], *int.*, & *n.*[2] Also **ay**; orig. †**I.** L16. [Prob. I *pron.* expr. assent.] **A** *adv.* & *int.* Yes. Now *arch.* & *dial.* exc. *Naut.* & in formal voting. L16.

BUNYAN Ai, ai, so I mean. H. E. MANNING Ay, but it was not only men who have so endured. W. OWEN Proud to see him going, aye, and glad. L. G. GIBBON There were cries *Rob, what about a song now, man?* And Rob said, *Och, ay, I'll manage that fine.* S. O'FAOLÁIN 'Did anyone come to warn me?' . . 'Aye. The girl of the Mullinses.' **aye, aye, sir!** *Naut.*: I understand and will carry out your order.

B *n.* Pl. **ayes**. An affirmative answer or vote. L16.

the ayes have it affirmative voters are in the majority.

aye-aye /'ʌɪʌɪ/ *n.* L18. [Fr. f. Malagasy *aiay.*] An insectivorous tree-dwelling primate of Madagascar, *Daubentonia madagascariensis*, which is closely related to the lemurs and has a narrow elongated finger on each hand for prising insects from bark.

ayle *n.* var. of AIEL.

Aylesbury /'eɪlzb(ə)ri/ *n.* M19. [A town in Buckinghamshire, central England.] In full *Aylesbury duck*. (A bird of) a breed of white domestic duck.

Aymara /'ʌɪmərɑː/ *n.* M19. [Bolivian Sp.: cf. Sp. *aimará*.] **1** A member of an Indian people of Bolivia and Peru near Lake Titicaca. M19. **2** The language of this people, related to Quechua. M19.

†**ayne** *n.* & *a.* var. of EIGNE.

ayont /ə'jɒnt/ *prep. dial.* Also **-nd** /-nd/. E18. [f. A-[2] + BEYOND, after *afore*, *before*.] Beyond, on the other side of.

ayre *n.* see AIR *n.*[1]

Ayrshire /'ɛːʃə/ *n.* M19. [A former county in the Strathclyde Region of Scotland.] In full *Ayrshire bull, cow, cattle*, etc. (An animal of) a breed of mainly white dairy cattle.

Ayurvedic /ɑːjə'veɪdɪk/ *a.* Also **a-**. E20. [f. Skt *āyur-veda* science of life, medicine (see VEDA) + -IC.] Of or pertaining to the Hindu medical tradition. Opp. UNANI.

aza- /'eɪzə/ *comb. form.* [f. AZO-.] Used in *Chem.* to indicate the presence of a nitrogen atom in a molecular ring or chain.

azalea /ə'zeɪlɪə/ *n.* M18. [mod.L f. Gk, use as n. of fem. of *azaleos* dry (because flourishing in dry soil).] Any of a large group of rhododendrons, most of which are deciduous.

mountain or **trailing azalea** a pink-flowered evergreen alpine shrub, *Loiseleuria procumbens*, of the heath family.

¶Orig. regarded as members of a distinct genus *Azalea*.

azan /ə'zɑːn/ *n.* M19. [Arab. *'aḏān* announcement.] The Muslim call to ritual prayer, often made by the muezzin from the minaret of a mosque.

Azande *n.* & *a.* see ZANDE.

azarole /'azərəʊl/ *n.* M17. [Fr. *azerole*, †*aza-* f. Sp. *azarolla*, *acerola* f. Sp. Arab. *az-za'rūra*: see AL-[2].] (The edible fruit of) the tree *Crataegus azarolus*, related to the hawthorn and native to the eastern Mediterranean region.

azedarac /ə'zɛdərak/ *n.* M18. [Fr. *azédarac* f. Sp. *acedaraque* f. Arab. *'āzād-diraḵt* f. Pers. *'āzād* free, *diraḵt* tree.] A tall Asian tree, *Melia azedarach* (family Meliaceae), bearing fragrant lilac flowers. Also called *bead-tree*, *China tree*.

azelaic /azɪ'leɪɪk/ *a.* M19. [f. AZO- (since nitric acid was involved in its orig. preparation) + Gk *elaion* oil + -IC.] *Chem.* *azelaic acid*, a solid fatty acid obtained by oxidizing various fats (such as castor oil) and present in rancid fat; nonanedioic acid, $HOOC(CH_2)_7COOH$.

azeotropic /,eɪzɪə'trəʊpɪk, -'trɒp-, ə,ziːə-/ *a.* E20. [f. A-[10] + Gk *zeo-*, *zein* to boil + -TROPIC.] *Chem.* Of a mixture of liquids: having a constant boiling point during distillation; of or pertaining to such a mixture.

azeotrope /'eɪzɪətrəʊp, ə'ziːə-/ *n.* an azeotropic mixture E20. **aze'otropism**, **aze'otropy** *ns.* azeotropic behaviour E20.

Azerbaijani /,azəbʌɪ'dʒɑːni/ *n.* & *a.* L19. [f. *Azerbaijan* (see below) + -I[2].] **A** *n.* A member of a people of Azerbaijan, in SW Asia; the Turkic language of this people. L19. **B** *attrib.* or as *adj.* Of or pertaining to the Azerbaijanis or their language. L19.

azide /'eɪzʌɪd/ *n.* E20. [f. AZO- + -IDE.] *Chem.* A salt or ester of hydrazoic acid, HN_3.

azidothymidine /,eɪzɪdəʊ'θʌɪmɪdiːn, eɪ,zʌɪdəʊ-/ *n.* L20. [f. prec. + -O- + THYMIDINE.] *Pharm.* An antiviral derivative of thymidine which is used to treat HIV infection and Aids; 3′-azido-3′-deoxythymidine, $C_{10}H_{13}N_5O_4$; abbrev. *AZT*. Also called *zidovudine*.

¶A proprietary name for this drug is RETROVIR.

Azilian /ə'zɪlɪən/ *a.* & *n.* L19. [f. Mas d'*Azil* in the French Pyrenees, where remains were found, + -IAN.] *Archaeol.* (Of or pertaining to) a culture of the transition period between the palaeolithic and mesolithic ages in southern France and northern Spain, following the Magdalenian.

azimuth /'azɪməθ/ *n.* LME. [(O)Fr. *azimut* f. Arab. *as-samt*, f. AL-[2] + *samt* way, direction: see ZENITH.] **1** An arc of a celestial great circle extending from the zenith to the horizon. Now only in *azimuth circle*, a great circle passing through the zenith. LME. **2** Horizontal angular distance of such an arc (usu. that passing through a given celestial object) from the north or south point. E17. **3** Horizontal angle or direction; compass bearing. M17.

azimuthal /azɪ'mjuːθ(ə)l/ *a.* of, pertaining to, or used in measuring azimuth; measured in azimuth: M17. **azi'muthally** *adv.* M19.

azine /'eɪziːn/ *n.* L19. [f. AZO- + -INE[5].] *Chem.* **1** Any organic compound containing the group =N—N=. L19. **2** Any (usu. polycyclic) organic compound containing a six-membered ring with two nitrogen atoms occupying opposite positions. Usu. *attrib.*, denoting dyestuffs based on such structures. L19.

azo- /'eɪzəʊ/ *comb. form.* [f. AZOTE.] *Chem.* Indicating the presence of nitrogen in a compound, *spec.* as the group —N=N— joined to two carbon atoms. Freq. as attrib. adj. **azo**, as *azo compound*, *group*, etc.

azo colour, **dye** *ns.* any of a large class of dyestuffs which contain the azo group, made by coupling of diazonium compounds L19. **azo'methine** *n.* any compound having the general formula $R^1R^2C{=}NR^3$; a Schiff base: L19. **azo'protein** *n.* (*Biochem.*) a protein coupled to another molecule by an azo group E20.

azoic /ə'zəʊɪk, eɪ-/ *a.*[1] M19. [f. Gk *azōos* + -IC: see A-[10], ZOIC.] Having no trace of life, or organic remains; *spec.* (*Geol.*) referring to the early Precambrian era.

azoic /eɪ'zəʊɪk/ *a.*[2] L19. [Fr. *azoïque*: see AZO-, -IC.] *Chem.* Orig. (*rare*) = AZO- used adjectivally. Now *spec.* designating a class of water-insoluble azo dyes made by coupling their components on the fibre; pertaining to or using such dyes.

azole /'eɪzəʊl/ *n.* L19. [f. AZO- + -OLE[2].] *Chem.* Any organic compound having a five-membered ring containing at least two hetero-atoms of which at least one is nitrogen.

azolla /ə'zɒlə/ *n.* L19. [mod.L, f. Gk *azein* to dry + *ollunai* slay.] A floating mosslike fern of the genus *Azolla*.

azonal /eɪ'zəʊn(ə)l, ə-/ *a.* L19. [f. A-[10] + ZONAL: cf. next.] Having no zonal arrangement or structure; *esp.* (of soils) lacking distinct horizons.

azonic /eɪ'zɒnɪk, ə-/ *a.* L18. [f. Gk *azōnos* f. as A-[10] + *zōnē* ZONE *n.*, + -IC.] Not confined to a zone, not local.

azoospermia /,eɪzəʊə'spəːmɪə, ə'zəʊ-/ *n.* L19. [f. A-[10] + ZOOSPERM + -IA[1].] *Med.* Absence of motile sperms in the semen. Cf. ASPERMIA.

azotaemia /azə'tiːmɪə/ *n.* Also ***-temia**. E20. [f. AZOTE + -AEMIA.] *Med.* The presence of excessive urea or other nitrogenous waste products in the blood.

azotaemic *a.* pertaining to or affected with azotaemia M20.

azote /'azəʊt/ *n. arch.* L18. [Fr., f. Gk A-[10] + *zōē* life.] Nitrogen.

†**azotic** *a.* of, pertaining to, or combined with nitrogen; nitric: L18-M19. **azotize** *v.t.* (now *rare*) nitrogenize E19.

azotea /aθo'tea, az-/ *n.* E19. [Sp.] The flat terrace roof of a house in Spain and Spanish-speaking countries.

azotemia *n.* see AZOTAEMIA.

azoth /'azəʊθ, 'azɒθ/ *n.* L15. [Sp. Arab. *az-zūḳ* f. Arab. *az-zāwūḳ*: see AL-[2].] (The alchemists' name for) mercury, as the first principle of metals. Also, Paracelsus' universal remedy.

azotobacter /ə'zəʊtəbaktə/ *n.* E20. [mod.L (see below), f. as AZOTE + -O- + BACTER(IUM.] An aerobic nitrogen-fixing bacterium of the genus *Azotobacter*.

azoturia /,azə'tjʊərɪə/ *n.* M19. [f. AZOTE + -URIA.] *Med.* The presence of excessive urea or other nitrogenous substances in the urine.

azoxy- /əˈzɒksi/ *comb. form.* Also as attrib. adj. **azoxy**. [f. AZO- + OXY-.] *Chem.* Designating or containing the group $\cdot N_2O\cdot$.

Aztec /ˈaztɛk/ *n.* & *a.* L18. [Fr. *Aztèque* or Sp. *Azteca*, f. Nahuatl *aztecatl* person from Aztlan (their legendary place of origin).] A *n.* 1 A member of the native American people dominant in Mexico until its conquest by Cortes in 1519. L18. 2 The language of the Aztecs. E19.

B *adj.* Of or pertaining to the Aztecs or their language. E19.

Aztec hop, revenge, two-step *slang* diarrhoea suffered by visitors to Mexico.

Aztecan *a.* L19.

azuki *n.* var. of ADZUKI.

azulejo /aθuˈlexo, azjʊˈleɪhəʊ/ *n.* Pl. **-os** /-ɒs, -əʊz/. M19. [Sp., f. *azul* blue.] A kind of glazed coloured tile used in Spanish buildings.

azulene /ˈazjʊliːn/ *n.* L19. [f. Sp. *azul* blue + -ENE.] *Chem.* A blue liquid hydrocarbon, $C_{10}H_8$, which has a molecule containing a five- and a seven-membered ring fused together, and occurs in some natural oils. Also, any hydrocarbon having this bicyclic structure.

azuline /ˈazjʊliːn/ *n.* M19. [App. f. Sp. *azulino* bluish, f. *azul* blue.] A shade of blue, esp. as a fashion colour.

azure /ˈaʒə, -ʒj(ʊ)ə, -zjʊə; ˈeɪ-/ *n.* & *a.* ME. [OFr. *asur*, (also mod.) *azur* f. med.L *azzurum*, *azolum* f. Arab. *al-lāzaward*, f. as AL-[2] + Pers. *lāžward* lapis lazuli.] A *n.* 1 A bright blue pigment or dye; ultramarine. Now *rare*. ME. 2 *Her.* Blue (represented in engraving by horizontal lines). ME. 3 The semiprecious stone lapis lazuli (from which ultramarine is made). *arch.* LME. 4 The blue colour of the unclouded sky (orig. the deep intense blue of more southern latitudes, now the soft clear bright blue of more northern latitudes). L15. 5 The unclouded vault of heaven. M17.

5 MILTON Not like those steps On Heavens Azure. *fig.*: CARLYLE Borne aloft into the azure of Eternity.

B *adj.* 1 *Her.* Blue. LME. 2 Of the colour azure. E16. 3 [After L *caeruleus*.] Designating or pertaining to a sea-god or river-god. *poet.* L17. 4 *fig.* Cloudless; serene. E19. 5 *Bookbinding.* Of a tooled or stamped design: composed of horizontal parallel lines. Of a tool: used to produce such a design. (Cf. sense A.2 above.) L19.

3 POPE An azure sister of the main.

azury *a.* of a colour resembling azure, tinted with azure E17.

azure /ˈaʒə, -ʒj(ʊ)ə, -zjʊə; ˈeɪ-/ *v.t.* ME. [f. prec.: cf. Fr. *azurer*, *azuré*.] 1 As *azured* ppl a. = AZURE *a. obs.* exc. *Bookbinding.* ME. 2 Paint, dye, or colour azure. LME.

azurine /ˈaʒʊrʌɪn, -ʒj(ʊ)ər-, -zjʊər-; ˈeɪ-/ *a.* Now *rare.* M16. [Fr. *azurin*: see AZURE *n.* & *a.*, -INE[1].] Of an azure colour.

azurite /ˈaʒʊrʌɪt, -ʒj(ʊ)ər-, -zjʊər-/ *n.* E19. [f. AZURE *n.* & *a.* + -ITE[1].] *Min.* †1 = LAZULITE. Only in E19. 2 A monoclinic basic copper carbonate found as blue prisms or crystal masses, usu. with malachite. E19.

azygos /ˈazɪgəs/ *n.* & *a.* As adj. also **-gous**. M17. [f. Gk *azugos*, f. A-[10] + *zugon* yoke: see -OUS.] Chiefly *Anat.* (An organic part, esp. a vein) that is not one of a pair.

azygos vein a large vein of the right posterior thorax, draining into the superior vena cava.

azyme /ˈazɪm, -ʌɪm/ *n.* L16. [eccl.L *azymus* adj., *-ma* n.pl. f. eccl.Gk *azumos*, *ta azuma* n. phr. pl., f. A-[10] + *zumē* leaven.] (A cake or loaf of) unleavened bread, esp. as used by Jews at Passover or by Christians of the Western Church in the Eucharist.

Azymite /ˈazɪmʌɪt/ *n.* E18. [med.L *azymita* f. med.Gk *azumitēs*, f. *azumos*: see prec., -ITE[1].] *Eccl. Hist.* (A contemptuous name used by the Orthodox Church for) a member of any of the Western Christian Churches which administer the Eucharist with unleavened bread. Cf. PROZYMITE.

B

B, b /biː/, the second letter of the modern Eng. alphabet and of the ancient Roman one, corresp. to Gk *beta*, Heb. *beth*. The sound normally represented by the letter is a voiced bilabial plosive consonant. Pl. **B's, Bs.**

I 1 The letter and its sound.

1 *not know a B from a* BATTLEDORE.

II Symbolical uses. 2 Used to denote serial order; applied e.g. to the second group or section, sheet of a book, etc. 3 *Mus.* (Cap. B.) The seventh note of the diatonic scale of C major (in German notation repr. by H, B repr. Eng. B flat). Also, the scale of a composition with B as its keynote. 4 The second hypothetical person or example. 5 *Math.* (Usu. italic *b*.) The second known quantity. 6 (Usu. cap. B.) Designating the second or second-highest class (of road, academic marks, population as regards affluence, etc.). 7 (Cap. B.) The blood group characterized by the presence of the agglutinogen designated B and the absence of that designated A. 8 (Cap. B.) Designating a series of international standard paper sizes with a fixed shape and twice the area of the next size, as *B0*, *B1*, *B2*, *B3*, *B4*, etc.

2 **B-DNA** *Biochem.* the commonest form of DNA, in which the base pairs are almost at right angles to the axis of the double helix. 4 *from A to B*: see A, A 6. 6 **B-film, -movie, -picture** a film made for use as a supporting feature in a cinema programme. **B-side** (the music of) the less important side of a gramophone record. **B Special** *Hist.* a member of a paid occasional special police force in Northern Ireland. 7 *AB*: see A, A 9.

III 9 Abbrevs.: (A small selection only is given here. Those all in caps. or small caps. also occur with a full stop after each letter; some of those all in caps. also occur (i) with initial cap. only, (ii) in small caps.) **B.** = Bachelor or [L] *baccalaureus* (in academic degrees); Blessed; British. **B** = bar (in *B-girl* (US slang) a bar-girl); (*Physics*) bel(s); (*Chess*) bishop; black (of pencil lead); (*Chem.*) boron. **b.** = (*colloq.*) bastard, bugger (as a euphemism sometimes printed *b*—); billion; born; (*Cricket*) bowled by, bye(s). **b** = (*Nuclear Physics*) barn; (*Particle Physics*) beauty, bottom. **BA** = Bachelor of Arts; British Academy; British Airways; British Association (for the Advancement of Science). **Ba** (*Chem.*) = barium. **BAA** = British Airports Authority. **BAe** /biːeɪ'iː/ = British Aerospace. **BAFTA** /'baftə/ = British Academy of Film and Television Arts. **BALPA** = British Airline Pilots' Association. **b. & b.** = bed and breakfast. **b. & w.** = black and white (television etc.). **BAOR** = British Army of the Rhine. **BB** = double-black (of pencil lead). **BBB** = treble-black (of pencil lead). **BBC** = British Broadcasting Corporation (*BBC English*, a form of standard English regarded as characteristic of BBC announcers). **bbl.** = barrels (esp. of oil). **BC** = British Columbia. BC = before Christ. **BCD** = binary coded decimal. BCE = before the Common Era. **BCF** = British Cycling Federation. **BCG** = bacillus of Calmette and Guérin (anti-tuberculosis vaccine). **BD** = Bachelor of Divinity. **Bde** = Brigade. **Bdr.** = Bombardier. **BDS** = Bachelor of Dental Surgery. **BE** = Bachelor of Education; Bachelor of Engineering; bill of exchange. **Be** (*Chem.*) = beryllium. **BEA** = British Epilepsy Association; (*Hist.*) British European Airways. **B.Ed.** = Bachelor of Education. **Beds.** = Bedfordshire. **BEF** = British Expeditionary Force, the British army on the Western Front, August–November 1914 and 1939–40. **BEM** = British Empire Medal; bug-eyed monster. **B.Eng.** = Bachelor of Engineering. **Berks.** = Berkshire. **BeV** = billion (10^9) electronvolts. **BF** (*colloq.*) = bloody fool. **b.f.** = (*colloq.*) bloody fool; (*US*) boldface (of type); brought forward; **B'ham** = Birmingham. **BHC** = benzene hexachloride. **bhp** = brake horsepower. **Bi** (*Chem.*) = bismuth. **BIM** = British Institute of Management. **Bk** (*Chem.*) = berkelium. **bk.** = book. **BL** = Bachelor of Law; bill of lading; (*Hist.*) British Leyland; British Library. **bl.** = barrel; black. **B.Litt.** = [L] *Baccalaureus Litterarum* Bachelor of Letters. **BM** = Bachelor of Medicine; British Museum. **BMA** = British Medical Association. **B.Mus.** = Bachelor of Music. **BMX** = bicycle moto-cross. **Bn.** = Battalion. **bn.** = billion. **BNF** (*Computing*) = Backus–Naur form. **BO** (*colloq.*) = body odour. **BOAC** (*Hist.*) = British Overseas Airways Corporation. **BOD** = biochemical oxygen demand. **BOP** (*Hist.*) = Boy's Own Paper. **BOSS** (*S. Afr. Hist.*) = Bureau of (*properly* for) State Security. **bot.** = botanic(al), botany; bottle; bought. **BP** = blood pressure; boiling point; British Petroleum; British Pharmacopoeia. BP = before the present (counting backwards from 1800). **Bp.** = Bishop. **b.p.** = boiling point. **BPC** = British Pharmaceutical Codex. **B.Phil.** = Bachelor of Philosophy. **bpi** (*Computing*) = bits per inch. **bps** (*Computing*) = bits per second. **Bq** (*Physics*) = becquerel(s). **BR** = British Rail (formerly, Railways). **Br.** = British; Brother. **Br** (*Chem.*) = bromine. **BRCS** = British Red Cross Society. **Brig.** = Brigadier. **Brit.** = Britain; British. **bro.** = brother. **Bros.** = Brothers. **BRS** = British Road Services. **BS** = (*US*) Bachelor of Science; Bachelor of Surgery; Blessed Sacrament; British Standard; (*slang*) bullshit. **B.Sc.** = Bachelor of Science. **BSE** = bovine spongiform encephalopathy. **BSI** = British Standards Institution. **BSL** = British Sign Language. **BST** = bovine somatotrophin; British Standard Time (1968–71); British Summer Time. **BT** = British Telecom. **Bt.** = Baronet. **B.th.u.** (*Hist.*) = British thermal unit. **B.T.U.** = (*Hist.*) Board of Trade Unit; British thermal unit. **B.t.u.** = British thermal unit. **bu.** = bushel(s). **Bucks.** = Buckinghamshire. **BVM** = Blessed Virgin Mary. **B/W** = black and white (television etc.). **BWI** (*Hist.*) = British West Indies. **BWR** = boiling-water (nuclear) reactor. **BYO** = bring your own (on a party invitation etc.); also, a restaurant etc. to which customers may bring their own alcoholic drinks. **BYOB** = bring your own bottle, booze, etc. **BYOG** (*Austral.* & *NZ*) = bring your own grog.

baa /bɑː/ *n.* & *v.* E16. [Imit.] A *n.* The bleat of a sheep or lamb. E16.

Comb.: **baa-lamb** (a child's name for) a lamb.

B *v.i.* Pa. t. & pple **baaed, baa'd**. Esp. of a sheep: bleat. L16.

Baal /'beɪəl/ *n.* Pl. **-im** /-ɪm/. LME. [Heb. *Ba'al* f. Canaanite, = lord.] A Phoenician or Canaanite god; *gen.* a false god.

Baalism *n.* the worship of Baal; idolatry: E17. **Baalist** *n.* a worshipper of Baal, an idolater E17. **Baalite** *n.* = BAALIST M17.

baas /bɑːs/ *n.* E17. [Du.: see BOSS *n.*[4]] †1 A Dutch sea-captain; a Dutch foreman etc. E–M17. 2 A (usu. White) employer, master, foreman, etc. Freq. as a form of address. *S. Afr.* L18.

baasskap /'bɑːsskap/ *n. S. Afr.* M20. [Afk. f. Du. *baasschap*, f. as prec. + *-schap* -SHIP.] Domination, esp. of non-Whites by Whites.

Baath /bɑːθ/ *n.* Also **Ba'ath** & other vars. M20. [Arab. *ba'ṯ* lit. 'resurrection'.] More fully *Baath party* etc. A pan-Arabic socialist movement founded in Syria in the early 1940s.

Baathism *n.* the beliefs of the Baath party M20. **Baathist** *n.* & *a.* (a member or supporter) of the Baath party M20.

bab *n.* see BABE.

baba /'bɑːbɑː/ *n.*[1] E19. [Fr. f. Pol., lit. 'married (peasant) woman'.] A rich sponge cake; *spec.* (more fully *rum baba*) one served in a rum syrup.

Baba /'baba/ *n.*[2] Also ***b-***. M19. [Malay.] In Malaysia, a Straits-born person of Chinese descent.

babaco /bə'bɑːkəʊ/ *n.* Pl. **-os**. E20. [S. Amer. Sp.] An Ecuadorian tree, *Carica pentagona*, related to the papaya or pawpaw; the large yellow fruit of this tree, similar in shape to a marrow.

babacoote /'babəkuːt/ *n.* L19. [Malagasy *babakoto* lit. 'father-child'.] = INDRI.

babassu /babə'suː/ *n.* Also **babaçú**. E20. [Brazilian Port. *babaçú* f. Tupi *ybá* fruit + *guasu* large.] A palm of the genus *Orbignya*, native to NE Brazil and yielding an edible oil.

babbitt /'babɪt/ *n.*[1] & *v.* Also **B-**. L19. [Isaac *Babbitt* (1799–1862), US inventor.] A *n.* Any of a group of usu. tin-based alloys used for antifriction linings in bearings. Also more fully *babbitt metal*. L19. B *v.t.* Line with babbitt. L19.

Babbitt /'babɪt/ *n.*[2] E20. [(The hero of) a novel by Sinclair Lewis, 1922.] A materialistic and complacent businessman conforming to the standards of his set.

Babbit(t)ry *n.* the Philistine behaviour of a Babbitt E20.

babblative /'bablətɪv/ *a.* L16. [f. BABBLE *v.* + -ATIVE.] Inclined to babble, loquacious.

babble /'bab(ə)l/ *n.* Also **†bable**. L15. [f. the vb. Cf. Fr. *babil*.] 1 Idle, foolish, or inopportune talk; (esp. as 2nd elem. of comb.) pretentious jargon. L15. 2 Confused murmur or noise, as of many voices heard at once, a stream, etc. E17. 3 Inarticulate speech, as of infants. M17. 4 *Teleph.* Crosstalk from conversations on other lines. M20.

1 CARLYLE A great deal of unwise babble on this subject. *psychobabble*, *technobabble*, etc. 2 W. MORRIS Nought he seemed to hear Save the brook's babble. G. F. NEWMAN The general babble of conversation didn't decrease . . but a few heads turned. P. ACKROYD The babble of voices was indescribable. 3 C. DARWIN Man has an instinctive tendency to speak, as we see in the babble of our young children.

babble /'bab(ə)l/ *v.* Also **†bable**. ME. [Prob. f. MLG (Du.) *babbelen*, or a parallel native imit. formation; cf. Fr. *babiller* prattle, f. onomatopoeic base *bab-*.] 1 *v.i.* Talk childishly, prattle; talk incoherently or foolishly; utter meaningless words. ME. 2 *v.i.* Utter inarticulate or indistinct sounds, like a child; (of a stream, bird, etc.) produce a more or less continuous succession of indistinct sounds. LME. 3 *v.i.* Talk excessively or inopportunely; prate. LME. 4 *v.t.* Repeat or utter with meaningless iteration; utter incoherently or foolishly. L15. 5 *v.t.* Reveal (a secret etc.) by talking. M16.

1 R. B. SHERIDAN They only babble who practise not reflection. 2 W. JONES Echo babling by the mountain's side. **babbling brook** *Austral.* & *NZ rhyming slang* a cook, esp. for a camp or for an isolated group of shepherds, musterers, etc. 3 E. F. BENSON Maud sat quite silent, while Lucia babbled on. J. THURBER An eccentric elderly woman who babbled of her recently inherited fortune. 4 QUILLER-COUCH His lips happily babbling the curses that the ships' captains had taught him. R. KIPLING He babbled tales of oppression and wrong till the tears ran down his cheeks. 5 I. D'ISRAELI The queen . . impatiently babbled the plot. R. DAVIES Didn't you yourself babble out all the secrets of your life to me?

babblement *n.* babble; idle chatter, incoherent or

meaningless talk: M17. **babblingly** *adv.* in a babbling manner, with babbling E17.

babbler /ˈbablə/ *n.* M16. [f. prec. + -ER[1].] 1 A foolish or idle talker, a chatterer. M16. 2 A gossip, a teller of secrets. L16. 3 A foxhound that gives tongue too freely. M18. 4 Any of a large group of Old World passerine birds (belonging to the family Timaliidae) with loud chattering voices. M19. 5 = *babbling brook* s.v. BABBLE *v.* 2. *Austral.* & *NZ slang.* E20.

babby *n.* see BABY *n.*

babe /beɪb/ *n.* Also (now *dial.*) **bab** /bab/. LME. [Prob. a contraction of an imit. form derived from childish utterance, similar to *mama*, *papa*: cf. ME *baban*.] 1 A young child, a baby. Chiefly *poet.* & *biblical.* LME. 2 A childish, inexperienced, or guileless person. E16. †3 = BABY *n.* 2. M–L16. 4 A girl or woman (freq. as a form of address). *slang* (chiefly *N. Amer.*). E20.

1 **babe in arms** a newborn baby. *babe of clouts*: see CLOUT *n.*[1] 4. *milk for babes*: see MILK *n.* 3a. 2 **babe in Christ** a person newly converted to Christianity. **babes in the wood** [with ref. to the old ballad *The Children in the Wood*] inexperienced persons.

babel /ˈbeɪb(ə)l/ *n.* & *a.* Also **B-**. E16. [*Babel*, the city and tower where the confusion of tongues took place (*Gen.* 11), = Heb. *bāḇel* Babylon, f. Akkadian *bāb ili* gate of God.] **A** *n.* 1 A confused medley of sounds; meaningless noise. E16. 2 A scene of confusion; a noisy assembly. E17. 3 (**B-**.) A lofty structure; a visionary project. M17.

1 A. ROSS Their words are a Babel whose meaning is plain—The shadow of Cain has been thrown on to Abel. TOLKIEN There was a hoot of snarling horns and a babel of baying voices. 2 SWIFT The whole babel of sectaries joined against the church. S. GIBBONS A babel broke out, in which Aunt Ada could dimly be discerned beating at everybody. 3 MILTON And still with vain designe New Babels, had they wherewithall, would build.

B *attrib.* or as *adj.* Confused, turbulent; lofty, visionary. M17.

DICKENS Babel towers of chimneys. E. H. W. MEYERSTEIN I never thought I should come round to Eliot as a poet. Here he has dropped his Poundian Babel-tongues.

babelish *a.* noisily confused E17. **babelism** *n.* noisy confusion of speech; a strange utterance: M19. **babelize** *v.t.* make a babel of E17.

†**babery** *n.* LME–L18. [Perh. var. of BABOONERY, assim. to BABE: see -ERY.] Absurdity; grotesque ornamentation.

babesiosis /bəbiːzɪˈəʊsɪs/ *n.* Pl. **-oses** /-ˈəʊsiːz/. E20. [f. mod.L *Babesia* (see below), f. Victor *Babès* (1854–1926), Romanian bacteriologist: see -IA[1], -OSIS.] *Vet. Med.* Tick-borne infection of animals (and rarely of man) with sporozoans of the genus *Babesia*. Also called *murrain*, *red-water (fever)*.

Also **babesiasis** /baːbɪˈzʌɪəsɪs/ *n.*, pl. **-ases** /-əsiːz/, M20.

Babi /ˈbaːbi/ *n.* M19. [Pers., f. Arab. *bāb* intermediary, lit. 'gate'. The title *Bāb* was assumed by the founder.] A member of a Persian eclectic sect founded in 1844, emphasizing the coming of a new prophet or messenger of God, and from which Baha'ism developed.

Babism *n.* the doctrine or practice of the Babis M19. **Babist** *n.* & *a.* (*a*) *n.* a Babi; (*b*) *adj.* of or pertaining to the Babis: M19. **Babite** *n.* a Babi E20.

babiche /bəˈbiːʃ/ *n.* *N. Amer.* E19. [Canad. Fr. f. Micmac *a:papi:č*.] Thongs or thread made of rawhide, sinew, etc.

babify /ˈbeɪbɪfʌɪ/ *v.t.* Also **babyfy**. M19. [f. BABY *n.* + -FY.] Make baby-like or babyish.

babingtonite /ˈbabɪŋtənʌɪt/ *n.* E19. [f. William *Babington* (1756–1833), Eng. mineralogist + -ITE[1].] *Min.* A triclinic basic silicate of iron and calcium, occurring as glassy greenish-black crystals.

babirusa /baːbɪˈruːsə/ *n.* Also **-r(o)ussa**. L17. [Malay, f. *babi* hog + *rusa* deer.] A wild hog, *Babyrousa babyrussa*, of the Malay archipelago, having upturned hornlike tusks.

babish /ˈbeɪbɪʃ/ *a. arch.* M16. [f. BABE + -ISH[1].] Infantile, baby-like; babyish, silly.

†**bable** *n.*, *v.* var. of BABBLE *n.*, *v.*

†**baboo** *n.* var. of BABU.

babool *n.* var. of BABUL.

baboon /bəˈbuːn/ *n.* ME. [OFr. *babuin* gaping figure, manikin, baboon, or med.L *babewynus*; perh. f. (O)Fr. *baboue* muzzle, grimace.] †1 A grotesque figure used in architecture etc. ME–L16. 2 Any of a number of large African and Arabian monkeys, having muzzles resembling those of dogs. LME. 3 An ugly or uncouth person; a stupid person. Also *gen.* as a term of abuse. L15.

2 *chacma baboon*, *gelada baboon*, *hamadryas baboon*, *sphinx-baboon*, *ursine baboon*, *yellow baboon*, etc.

baboonery *n.* †(*a*) = BABERY; (*b*) *rare* a baboon colony, a place where baboons are kept; (*c*) baboonish behaviour or condition: LME. **baboonish** *a.* resembling (that of) a baboon E19.

babouche /bəˈbuːʃ/ *n.* L17. [Fr. f. Arab. *bābūj*, Pers. *pāpūš*, f. *pā* foot + *pūš* covering.] A Turkish or oriental heelless slipper.

babu /ˈbaːbuː/ *n.* Also †**-oo**; **B-**. L18. [Hind. *bābū*.] †1 Orig., a Hindu title of respect. Later, a Hindu gentleman. L18–E19. 2 *Hist.* An Indian clerk or official who could write English; *derog.* an Indian, esp. in Bengal, who had had a superficial English education. M19.

Comb.: **babu English** *Hist.* ornate and unidiomatic English regarded as characteristic of an Indian who had learned the language from books.

babul /bəˈbuːl/ *n.* Also **-ool**. E19. [Hind. *babūl*, Bengali *bābul*, f. Skt *babbūla*.] Esp. in the Indian subcontinent: a tropical acacia, *Acacia nilotica*, introduced from Africa and used as a source of fuel, gum arabic, and (formerly) tannin. Cf. KIKAR, NEB-NEB, SUNT.

babushka /bəˈbʊʃkə/ *n.* M20. [Russ. = grandmother.] 1 In Russia: a grandmother, an old woman. M20. 2 A head-scarf folded diagonally and tied under the chin. M20.

baby /ˈbeɪbi/ *n.* & *a.* Also (*dial.*) **babby** /ˈbabi/. LME. [Prob. f. as BABE: see -Y[6].] **A** *n.* 1 An infant; a very young child, *esp.* one not yet able to walk. LME. **b** *fig.* A person's invention, achievement, or concern. L19. †2 A doll, a puppet. E16–E18. 3 A small image of oneself reflected in the pupil of another's eye. *obs.* exc. as below. L16. 4 In *pl.* [perh. orig. ornamental work w. cupids etc.] Pictures in books. Now only *north.* L16. 5 An unduly childish person. (Cf. CRY-BABY.) E17. 6 A (relatively) tiny or diminutive animal or thing; a small version of something generally larger; *esp.* a small-sized bottle, jar, etc. M19. 7 A person; a thing; a young woman, a girlfriend. Freq. as a form of address. *slang* (chiefly *N. Amer.*). M19. 8 The youngest or most junior member of a family, team, group, etc. L19.

1 *battered baby*: see BATTER *v.*[1] 1. *blue baby*: see BLUE *a.* **carry** or **hold the baby** bear an unwelcome responsibility. *jelly baby*: see JELLY *n.*[1] *surrogate baby*: see SURROGATE *a.* **throw away the baby with the bathwater** (& vars.) reject what is essential or valuable along with the inessential or useless. *wet the baby's head*: see WET *v.* **b it's your baby** you must deal with it. 2 POPE Sober over her Sampler, or gay over a jointed Baby. 3 **look babies** gaze into another's eyes. 7 C. SANDBURG My baby's going to have a new dress. A. LOMAX Some terrible environments . . inhabited by some very tough babies. *New York Times* You need that left ankle for strength when you hit the brake. That's why I couldn't drive stocks. You got to stay on the brake with those babies. **this baby** *slang* I, me.

Comb.: **baby-blue-eyes** a N. American ornamental annual plant, *Nemophila menziesii*, having saucer-shaped blue flowers with a white centre; **baby bonus** *Canad. colloq.* a family allowance; **baby boom** (the children born at a time of) a marked increase in the birth rate; **baby boomer** a person born during a baby boom; **baby-bouncer** = *baby-jumper* below; **Baby Buggy** (*a*) (proprietary name for) a kind of child's pushchair; (*b*) *N. Amer.* (w. lower-case initials) a pram; **baby bust** *colloq.* (orig. *US*) (a period of) a marked decrease in the birth rate; **baby buster** *colloq.* (orig. *US*) a person born during such a period; **baby carriage** a pram; **baby-doll** (*a*) = DOLL *n.*[1]; (*b*) an ingenuous girl or woman with pretty features like those of a doll; **baby-face** (a person with) a smooth rounded face like a baby's; **baby-farm** *derog.* a place where baby-farming is carried on; **baby-farmer** *derog.* a person engaged in baby-farming; **baby-farming** *derog.* the lodging and care of babies for payment; **baby food** a milk-substitute or light diet suitable for a baby; **Babygro** (proprietary), **babygrow** a kind of all-in-one stretch garment for babies; **baby house** (now *arch.* or *Hist.*) a doll's house; **baby-jumper** a hanging frame on springs, in which a child is fastened to exercise his or her limbs; **baby-minder** a person who looks after babies for payment, esp. while their parents or guardians are at work; **baby powder** a skin powder for babies; **baby's breath** (chiefly *N. Amer.*) any of various scented plants, esp. *Gypsophila paniculata*; **babysit** *v.t.* & *i.* look after (a child) while his or her parents or guardians are out; *fig.* look after (a thing) while its owner is away; **babysitter** a person engaged to babysit; **baby-snatcher** (*a*) a person who abducts a very young child; (*b*) *colloq.* a person who is sexually attracted to, has an amorous affair with, or marries a much younger person; **baby-snatching** the action of a baby-snatcher; **baby-talk** imperfect or contrived speech used by or to young children; **baby-walker** a device for helping a baby learn to walk.

B *attrib.* or as *adj.* Small or diminutive of its kind; young. E17.

F. A. FORBES I have in my room a baby rhododendron in full bloom. E. WAUGH Julia always drove herself, in the latest model of mass-produced baby car. *Daily Telegraph* Early pickings of baby carrots. **baby beef** flesh of young cattle older than those producing veal. **baby grand** a small grand piano.

babyhood *n.* infancy; babies collectively: M18. **babyish** *a.* resembling or characteristic of a baby; unduly childish, silly: M18. **babyishly** *adv.* M19. **babyishness** *n.* L19. **babyism** *n.* babyhood; a babyish phrase or action: M19. **babykins** *n.* (*colloq.*) (a term of endearment for) a baby M20. **baby-like** *a.* resembling (that of) a baby E19.

baby /ˈbeɪbi/ *v.t.* M18. [f. the n.] Treat as a baby; coddle, pamper.

babyfy *v.* var. of BABIFY.

Babylon /ˈbabɪlən, -lɒn/ *n.* M17. [L f. Gk *Babulōn* (f. Heb. *bāḇel* BABEL), name of the ancient Chaldean capital and also of the mystical city of the Apocalypse.] 1 A great and decadent city. Formerly *esp.* (*derog.*) Rome or the papal power. M17. 2 Among Blacks, esp. Rastafarians: White society; the representatives of this, *esp.* the police. M20.

Babyˈlonic *a.* = BABYLONIAN *a.* E17. **Babylonish** /babɪˈləʊnɪʃ/ *a.* (*a*) of or pertaining to Babylon; †(*b*) popish; (*c*) babelish, confused in language: M16.

Babylonian /babɪˈləʊnɪən/ *n.* & *a.* M16. [f. L *Babylonius* f. Gk *Babulōnios*: see prec., -IAN.] **A** *n.* 1 A native or inhabitant of Babylon. M16. †**b** A papist. L17–L18. 2 The Akkadian dialect of Babylon. L19. **B** *adj.* Of or pertaining to Babylon or its dialect; *fig.* (*a*) huge, gigantic, †(*b*) popish, (*c*) (with ref. to *Rev.* 17:4) scarlet. L16.

bac /bak/ *n.* E20. [Abbrev.] Baccarat.

bacalao /bakaˈlao/ *n.* Also ***-lhau*** /-ˈʎau/. M16. [Sp. *bacal(l)ao*, Port. *bacalhau*.] Codfish, esp. dried or salted.

Bacardi /bəˈkaːdi/ *n.* E20. [*Bacardi* & Co., Nassau, Bahamas (orig. based in Cuba).] (Proprietary name for) a dry white rum; a drink of this.

†**bacare** *int.* var. of BACKARE.

bacca /ˈbakə/ *n. colloq.* Also **baccer**, **backer**. E19. [Abbrev.] Tobacco. Cf. BACCO, BACCY.

baccalaurean /bakəˈlɔːrɪən/ *a.* M19. [f. med.L *baccalaureus* (see BACHELOR) + -AN.] Of or befitting a bachelor.

baccalaureate /bakəˈlɔːrɪət/ *n.* M17. [Fr. *baccalauréat* or med.L *baccalaureatus*, f. *baccalaureus*: see BACHELOR, -ATE[1].] 1 The university degree of bachelor. M17. 2 = BACHELOR 4. *rare.* L17. 3 *International Baccalaureate*, (a qualification awarded for satisfactory performance in) a set of examinations intended to qualify successful candidates for higher education in any of several countries. L20.

baccarat /ˈbakəraː/ *n.* Also **-ra**. M19. [Fr. *baccara*, of unkn. origin.] A gambling card-game, played between a banker and one punter, or several punters in turn, in which the best one- or two-card hand is that yielding the highest remainder when its total face value is divided by 10.

baccate /'bakeɪt/ *a.* E19. [L *baccatus*, f. *bacca* berry: see -ATE².] *Bot.* Bearing berries; berry-like.

baccer *n.* var. of BACCA.

Bacchanal /'bakən(ə)l, -nal/ *a.* & *n.* Also **b-**. M16. [L *bacchanalis*, f. BACCHUS: see -AL¹.] A *adj.* 1 = BACCHIC 1. M16. 2 = BACCHIC 2. L16. B *n.* 1 An occasion of drunken revelry; an orgy. M16. 2 A priest, priestess, or devotee of Bacchus. M16. 3 A dance or song in honour of Bacchus; *sing.* & (usu.) in *pl.*, a festival in honour of Bacchus. E17. 4 A scene of revelry painted or sculptured. M18. 5 A noisy or drunken reveller. E19.

bacchanalize *v.i.* indulge in drunken revelry M17.

Bacchanalia /bakə'neɪlɪə/ *n.pl.* Also **b-**. L16. [L *bacchanalia* neut. pl. of *bacchanalis*: see prec.] 1 The Roman festival in honour of Bacchus, the god of wine. L16. 2 Drunken revelry; an orgy. M17.

Bacchanalian /bakə'neɪlɪən/ *a.* & *n.* Also **b-**. M16. [f. L *bacchanalis* BACCHANAL + -IAN.] A *adj.* 1 Marked by, connected with, or given to drunken revelry; riotously drunken. M16. 2 Connected with or relating to the worship of Bacchus, the Greek and Roman god of wine. E17. B *n.* A Bacchant; a drunken reveller. E17.

Bacchant /'bakənt/ *n.* & *a.* Also **b-**. Pl. **Bacchants, Bacchantes** /bə'kantɪz/. L16. [Fr. *bacchante*: see next.] A *n.* A priest, priestess, or devotee of Bacchus, the Greek and Roman god of wine; a drunken reveller, a roisterer. L16. B *adj.* Bacchus-worshipping; wine-loving. E19.

Bacchantic /bə'kantɪk/ *a.* M19.

Bacchante /'bak(ə)nt, bə'kant, bə'kanti/ *n.* & *a.* Also **b-**. L18. [Fr., f. L *bacchant-* pres. ppl stem of *bacchari* celebrate the feast of Bacchus (in L only in fem. pl. *bacchantes*).] A *n.* A priestess or female devotee of Bacchus, the Greek and Roman god of wine. L18. B *attrib.* or as *adj.* Of, pertaining to, or characteristic of a Bacchante. E19.

¶The second pronunc. is after Fr.; the third is after It., influenced by the freq. Eng. pl. (of both genders) *Bacchantes* after L.

baccharis /'bakərɪs/ *n.* Also †**bacchar**. M16. [L *baccar*, *bacc(h)aris* f. Gk *bakkaris*, *bakkh-*.] Orig., a plant with an aromatic root, mentioned by the ancients and variously identified; any of several plants identified with this. Now *spec.* any American shrub of the genus *Baccharis*, which includes the groundsel tree, *B. halimifolia*.

Bacchic /'bakɪk/ *a.* Also **b-**. M17. [L *bacchicus* f. Gk *bakkhikos*: see BACCHUS, -IC.] 1 Of or pertaining to Bacchus, the Greek and Roman god of wine, or his worship. M17. 2 Frenzied like a devotee of Bacchus; riotously drunken, roistering. L17.

bacchius /bə'kaɪəs/ *n.* Pl. **bacchii** /bə'kaɪaɪ/. L16. [L f. Gk *bakkheios* (*pous* foot).] *Pros.* A metrical foot of three syllables, one short and two long.

bacchiac *a.* M18.

Bacchus /'bakəs/ *n.* LME. [L f. Gk *Bakkhos* the god of wine.] Wine or intoxicating liquor personified.

bacciferous /bak'sɪf(ə)rəs/ *a.* M17. [f. L *baccifer* (f. as next) + -OUS: see -FEROUS.] Berry-bearing; producing berries.

baccivorous /bak'sɪv(ə)rəs/ *a.* M17. [f. L *bacci-* comb. form of *bacca* berry + -VOROUS.] Berry-eating.

bacco /'bakəʊ/ *n. colloq.* L18. [Abbrev.] Tobacco. Cf. BACCA, next.

baccy /'baki/ *n. colloq.* Also **backy**. E19. [Abbrev.] Tobacco. Cf. BACCA, prec.

bach /batʃ/ *n.*¹ & *v. colloq.* Also **batch**. M19. [Abbrev. of BACHELOR.] A *n.* 1 A bachelor. *US.* M19. 2 A small makeshift hut; a small holiday house. *NZ.* E20. B *v.i.* & *t.* (w. *it*). Live alone and cater for oneself as a bachelor. *N. Amer., Austral.*, & *NZ.* L19.

bach /baːx/ *n.*² *Welsh dial.* L19. [Welsh, lit. 'little'.] Dear, beloved; little one; friend. (Chiefly *voc.* and often placed appositionally after personal names.)

A. BURGESS How different your voice sounds tonight, *bach.* R. DAVIES Time to pay back now, Dicky bach.

Bach /batʃ/ *n.*³ L20. [Edward *Bach* (1886–1936), British physician.] (Proprietary name for) a preparation of the flowers of a wild plant used in a system of complementary medicine to relieve emotional states, and a therapeutic system based on such preparations.

Here's Health He was plied with Bach flower remedies and some supplements.

Bacharach /'bakərak, *foreign* 'baxərax/ *n.* E17. [A town on the Rhine, western Germany.] A (usu. white) wine produced in the area of Bacharach.

bachelor /'batʃələ/ *n.* Also †**batch-**. ME. [OFr. *bacheler* young man aspiring to knighthood, f. Proto-Romance, of uncertain origin: in academic use the med.L form was *baccalarius*, later altered to *-laureus*, w. ref. to *bacca lauri* laurel berry.] 1 *Hist.* A young knight who followed the banner of another; a novice in arms. ME. 2 An unmarried man (usu. of marriageable age); occas. (*rare* bef. 19) an unmarried woman. ME. 3 A junior member or 'yeoman' of a trade-guild. *obs.* exc. *Hist.* LME. 4 A man or woman who has taken a degree below that of Master (usu. a first degree) at a university or other academic institution. LME. 5 A male animal, esp. a male fur-seal, which is prevented from breeding by more dominant males in a social group. L19. 6 An apartment suitable for a bachelor. Chiefly *N. Amer.* M20.

1 **knight bachelor** a knight of the lowest order; the full title of a gentleman who has been knighted. 4 *bachelor of arts, science*, etc. *determining bachelor*: see DETERMINE 4b.

Comb.: **bachelor apartment, flat**: suitable for an unmarried person; **bachelor girl** a young unmarried woman who lives independently; **bachelor party**: for men only, esp. to mark the end of a man's bachelorhood; **bachelor's button**(s) any of various double-flowered forms of plants grown for ornament, *esp.* a double form of the meadow buttercup, *Ranunculus acris*, or sneezewort, *Achillea ptarmica*; **bachelor's degree** a degree of Bachelor of Arts, Bachelor of Science, etc.; **bachelor's hall** a home presided over by a bachelor (or a man living apart from his wife); **bachelor's wife** the ideal wife of whom a bachelor theorizes or dreams.

bachelordom *n.* = BACHELORHOOD L19. **bachelo'rette** *n.* (*N. Amer.*) (*a*) = *bachelor girl* above; (*b*) an apartment suitable for a bachelor girl: M20. **bachelorhood** *n.* the state or quality of a bachelor E19. **bachelorism** *n.* a habit or peculiarity of a bachelor; the condition or behaviour of a bachelor: E19. **bachelorly** *a.* like a bachelor L16. **bachelorship** *n.* = BACHELORHOOD L16.

bachelorize /'batʃələraɪz/ *v.i.* Also **-ise**. M18. [f. prec. + -IZE.] 1 Take the degree of bachelor. *rare.* M18. 2 Live as a bachelor; *spec.* (*NZ*) = BACH *v.* M19.

Bachian /'bɑːkɪən, 'baːx-/ *n.* & *a.* E20. [f. *Bach* (see below) + -IAN.] A *n.* An interpreter, student, or admirer of the music of the German composer Johann Sebastian Bach (1685–1750). E20. B *adj.* Of, pertaining to, or characteristic of Bach or his music. M20.

bacillary /bə'sɪləri/ *a.* M19. [f. late L BACILLUS + -ARY¹.] 1 Of, pertaining to, or consisting of little rods. M19. 2 Of, pertaining to, or of the nature of bacilli; caused by bacilli. L19.

2 **bacillary white diarrhoea** = PULLORUM DISEASE.

bacillar *a.* = BACILLARY 2 L19. **bacilliform** *a.* rod-shaped M19.

bacillus /bə'sɪləs/ *n.* Pl. **-lli** /-laɪ, -liː/. L19. [Late L = little rod, dim. of *baculus* rod, stick.] Any rod-shaped bacterium; *loosely* any pathogenic bacterium.

baci'lluria *n.* (*Med.*) the presence of bacilli in the urine L19.

bacitracin /basɪ'treɪsɪn/ *n.* M20. [f. prec. + Margaret *Tracy*, an Amer. child in whom the substance was discovered in a wound + -IN¹.] An antibiotic obtained from bacteria of the *Bacillus subtilis* group.

back /bak/ *n.*¹ [OE *bæc* = OFris. *bek*, OS *bak*, (M)LG, MDu. *bak*, OHG *bah*, ON *bak*, f. Gmc.] I Orig. sense. 1 The convex surface of the body of man and vertebrate animals which is adjacent to the spinal axis and opposite to the belly, and extends from the neck and shoulders to the extremity of the backbone. OE. 2 Regarded with reference to its position or functions. *spec.* a The hinder surface of a person's body, esp. as turned away from someone else. OE. b The part of the body which bears burdens. OE. c That part of the body which is the special recipient of clothing (often repr. the whole body in this capacity). ME. d In animals, the upper surface opposite to that on which they move or rest. LME.

1 O. HENRY Down his back from his mane to his tail went a line of black. A. SCHLEE She stood with her back against the door feeling the brass handle press against a bone in her spine. 2a SHAKES. *Cymb.* The army broken, And but the backs of Britons seen. b SHAKES. *Tit. A.* Wrongs more than our backs can bear. R. V. JONES More than one careerist in the Admiralty had climbed on Butterworth's back by exploiting his work. c G. B. SHAW Give them the clothes off my back.

II *transf.* The surface of things analogous in position to the (human) back; the hinder side. 3 The side or surface of any object which answers in position to the back and is opposite to the face or front, or to the side approached or contemplated, or away from the normal direction of motion; e.g. the outer side of the hand, the underside of a leaf, the convex part of a book, the rear part of a house or vehicle. ME. 4 The side or part of any object that is away from or more remote from the spectator; the further side. M17. 5 *ellipt.* = *backblocks*, *back country* s.v. BACK-. L19. 6 In *pl.* (Also **B-**.) The grounds behind some Cambridge colleges bordering on the River Cam. L19.

3 LYTTON At the back of the cottage . . there are some fields. OED The back of the leaf is lighter in colour. F. O'CONNOR He . . wrote down the address on the back of an envelope. A. BURGESS Took three bullets straight in the back of the throat. T. STOPPARD He got into the back of the motor. 4 J. TYNDALL A plate of copper against the back of which a steady sheet of flame is permitted to play. G. B. SHAW Finally comes the band, which posts itself at the back of the square.

III Parts of things having relation, or analogous in position, to the human back. 7 The hind part, e.g. of a chair, garment, etc. LME. 8 A body of followers or supporters; backing. Now only *Sc.* M16. 9 The rear of an armed force. *arch.* L16. 10 *Football, Hockey*, etc. (The position of) a defending player stationed behind the forwards. L19.

7 LD MACAULAY The back of the chimney did not seem to be firmly fixed. J. CONRAD I grabbed the back of the nearest piece of furniture. 8 J. SPEED Scotland . . was a special backe and second to King Henry. 9 SHAKES. *2 Hen. IV* He leaves his back unarm'd. 10 *centre back*, *full-back*, *half-back*, *quarterback*, etc.

IV Surfaces or parts of things analogous to the back of animals. 11 The upper surface of anything, esp. as bearing burdens; the ridge of a hill; *poet.* the surface of water, the waves, etc. LME. 12 The keel and keelson of a ship. L17.

11 SHAKES. *Temp.* I saw him beat the surges under him, And ride upon their backs: he trod the water. N. HAWTHORNE We now rambled about on the broad back of the hill. 12 P. O'BRIAN I drove her on to the rock before Gijon. . . She was hopelessly bilged, her back broken.

Phrases etc. (see also BACK-): **at the back of** behind in support, pursuit, or concealment. **at the back of one's mind** in the memory but not consciously thought of or immediately recalled. *back and edge*: see EDGE *n.* **back of** (or **o'**) **Bourke** [*Bourke*, a town in western New South Wales] *Austral. slang* the most remote outback, the back of beyond. **back-to-back** *a.* (*a*) (of houses) built in a continuous terrace divided along its length so as to produce two terraces of houses adjoining at the rear; (*b*) *N. Amer.* (of events) consecutive. **behind one's back** in one's absence or without one's knowledge. **break the back of** *fig.* overburden, crush (a person), finish the greatest or hardest part of (a task). *claw the back of*: see CLAW *v.* 2. *fall off the back of a lorry*: see LORRY *n.* **get a person's back up** make a person angry or stubborn. **get off a person's back** *fig.* (*colloq.*) stop annoying or harassing him or her. **give a back** = *make a back* below. *have a* (or *the*) *monkey on one's back*: see MONKEY *n.* *have not a* *shirt to one's back*: see SHIRT *n.* **in back (of)** *N. Amer.* behind, in or at the back (of). **know like the back of one's hand** be thoroughly familiar or conversant with. *left (half-)back*: see LEFT *a. loose back*: see LOOSE *a.* **make a back** bend the body to provide a surface for jumping over, e.g. in leapfrog. *make a rod for one's own back*: see ROD *n. not a shirt to one's back*: see SHIRT *n.* **on one's back** laid up or ill in bed; prostrate, helpless. **on the back of** behind, immediately following; weighing upon as a burden; *fig.* harassing, annoying. *pat on the back*: see PAT *n.*[1] 3, *v.* 5. **put a person's back up** = *get a person's back up* above. **put one's back into** use all one's efforts or strength in (a particular endeavour). *right (half-)back*: see RIGHT *a. running back*: see RUNNING *ppl a. scratch my back and I will scratch yours*: see SCRATCH *v.* **see the back of** be rid of. **short back and sides** *colloq.* a short haircut. *slap on the back*: see SLAP *n.*[1] 1, SLAP *v.*[1] *stab in the back*: see STAB *n.*[1] 2, STAB *v.* 3. *the back of beyond*: see BEYOND *n. the beast with two backs*: see BEAST *n. the last straw that breaks the camel's back*: see STRAW *n. the shirt off one's back*: see SHIRT *n.* **turn one's back on** turn away from, flee, forsake, abandon. **upon the back of** = *on the back of* above. *watch one's* or *a person's back*: see WATCH *v.* WATTEAU *back*. **with one's back to the wall** hard-pressed, at bay.

backed *a.* having a back, background, or backing, (usu. as 2nd elem. of a comb., of a specified kind) LME. **backless** *a.* without a back, having no back; (of a woman's garment) cut low at the back: E19.

back /bak/ *n.*[2] L16. [Du. *bak*, LG *back* large dish: cf. med.L *bacca* 'vas aquarium' (Isidore).] A tub, a trough, a vat, esp. as used in brewing, dyeing, or pickling.

back /bak/ *a.* (*attrib.*) Superl. BACKMOST; compar. (*obs.* exc. in sense 2) **backer**. Freq. w. hyphen (see also BACK-). LME. [Attrib. use of BACK *n.*[1] or ellipt. use of BACK *adv.*] I From the n. 1 Situated at the back, behind, or away from the front; remote, obscure; inferior, subsidiary. LME. 2 *Phonet.* Of a sound: formed at the back of the mouth. M19.

1 J. Ray A small flat back claw, or toe. L. Sterne Coming unexpectedly from a back parlour into the shop. Thackeray A little morocco box, which . . contained the Major's back teeth. E. C. Shepherd The bomber . . might have to travel only 50 miles . . to the back areas of the German Army to bomb dumps. J. le Carré Leamas looked out of the back window, and saw the DKW following them. R. P. Jhabvala She lived off the main shopping district in a back lane. F. Forsyth They sat over a pot of tea in the back kitchen.

II From the adv. 3 In arrears, overdue; behindhand; belonging to the past. E16. 4 Turned back, reversed. L16.

back /bak/ *v.* LME. [f. BACK *n.*[1]] I Provide a back; cover the back; support. 1 *v.t.* †a Clothe. Only in LME. b Put a back to, line the back of. M16. 2 *v.t.* Support or help (a person or thing) materially or mechanically; support morally, esp. by argument. Also foll. by *up*. E16. 3 *v.t.* Mount, ride on, or (now *esp.*) break in (a horse or other animal). L16. 4 *v.t.* Countersign, endorse; print on the back (as well as the front) of; *US* & *Sc.* address (a letter). L17. 5 *v.t.* Support (an opinion or judgement) by a wager; bet on the success of (a horse in a race, an entrant in any contest, etc.); *fig.* be confident of (a stated outcome). L17. 6 a *v.t.* Form, lie, or stand at the back of. E19. b *v.i.* Be so situated that the back abuts *on* or *on to* a piece of land etc. L19. 7 *v.t.* Accompany (a singer or instrumentalist, esp. in popular music or jazz). M20.

1b J. Smeaton The ashler walls were backed . . with rubble stone, or with bricks. 2 E. A. Freeman Demands which had been backed by an armed force. W. Lippmann Guarantees, backed by the authority of the state. W. S. Churchill Canning had backed the Spanish national rising in 1808. 3 **backing dog** *Austral.* & *NZ* a sheepdog that jumps on to the backs of sheep to help move them. 5 Byron Most men (till by losing render'd sager) Will back their own opinions with a wager. E. Longford Bets were laid in the London clubs, many of Brooks's Whigs backing Napoleon for a win. **back the field** bet on the rest of the horses against the favourite. **back the wrong horse** *fig.* make a wrong or inappropriate choice. 6a T. H. Huxley The chalk cliffs which back the beach. M. Mitchell Turning so that she backed the corpse, she caught a heavy boot under each arm and threw her weight forward. b *Edinburgh Review* St. James' Square, on which the club backs. M. Bradbury The gardens, the houses backing onto them.

II Move or hold back. 8 *v.t.* Set or lay back; restrain, check; *esp.* (*Naut.*) lay (a sail or yard) aback to slow the ship down. LME. 9 *v.i.* Of a person, vehicle, etc.: go or move backwards; retreat. L15. 10 *v.t.* Cause to move backwards or in the opposite direction; reverse. M18. 11 *v.i.* Of the wind: change in an anticlockwise direction. Opp. *veer*. M19.

9 J. Steinbeck Ahead the truck pulled up and then backed slowly. L. P. Hartley She did not move towards it—rather, she backed away. E. L. Doctorow As the great liner backed into the river he stood at the rail and waved. **back and fill** *N. Amer.* move to and fro; *fig.* vacillate. 10 Dickens Backing his chair a little. E. Waugh Dennis locked the office and backed the car from the garage. **back water** reverse a boat's forward motion with the oars.

With advs. & preps. in specialized senses: **back down, off** *fig.* abandon a claim made, stand taken, etc. **back out** move backward out of a place; *fig.* withdraw from a commitment or difficulty. **back up** (*a*) *v.phr.t.* & *i.* (*Cricket*) (of a fielder) place oneself in readiness to stop the ball if it is missed by (another fielder); of the batsman at the bowler's end: start in readiness for a possible run made by (the striking batsman); (*b*) *v.phr.i.* & *t.* (orig. *N. Amer.*) of water, traffic, etc.: accumulate behind an obstacle etc.; of a barrier etc.: cause (water, traffic, etc.) to accumulate; (*c*) *v.phr.t.* & *i.* (orig. *N. Amer.*) drive (a vehicle etc.) backwards; move backwards; (*d*) *v.phr.t.* (*Computing*) provide backup for; make a duplicate copy of (a disk, file, program, etc.); (see also sense 2 above).

back /bak/ *adv.* LME. [Aphet. f. ABACK.] I Of motion or direction. 1 To the rear (often, esp. in the imper., with the vb *go*, *come*, etc., omitted); away from what is considered to be the front or the normal position. LME. 2 In the opposite direction, so as to return to the place originally left; to a former or normal condition, in reversal of progress or in restoration of former circumstances. M16. b Come, received, put, etc., back. M17. 3 Into the past; backward in time. L16. 4 In return or retaliation. L16. 5 Away from a promise or undertaking. L18.

1 AV *Matt.* 28:2 The angel of the Lord rolled back the stone. Sir W. Scott Back, beardless boy! Back, minion! J. D. Salinger I sort of brushed my hair back with my hand. P. Porter Looking back when at the gate. 2 E. A. Freeman The whole country fell back into heathenism. E. Hemingway She came back from wherever she had been. S. Spender Across the bay, the searchlight beams Swing and swing back across the sky. J. D. Salinger I started to get up and all,but Mr. Antolini got hold of my jacket and pulled me back down. b J. Conrad She was back from the remoteness of her meditation, very much so indeed. G. B. Shaw She'll come to no harm. She'll be back for tea. A. Rook Our toys of Monday are scarcely back on their tray. J. P. Donleavy Make a fire in the stove. I'll be back. 3 Steele If we go back to the days of Solomon. Q. Crisp Old men looking back on their lives. 4 Shakes. *Much Ado* What have I to give you back? J. Michie 'That's a dirty crooked question,' back I roared. *answer back*, *pay back*, *strike back*, etc.

II Of position: 6 At a distance, to the rear, away (*from* a specified point). LME. 7 In a state of check to forward movement or progress in condition. M16. 8 In the past; (a specified time) ago. L18.

6 Shakes. *Rich. III* My lord, stand back, and let the coffin pass. OED I left him back at the second milestone. E. Bowen The intruder had occupied a pew . . some way back from the last of the rows of relatives. 8 T. Pynchon Pierce had died back in the spring. C. Causley Got into trouble two years back With the local gentry.

Phrases etc. (see also BACK-): **back and forth** to and fro. **back of** (chiefly *N. Amer.*) behind. *back on one's heels*: see HEEL *n.*[1] **back to nature** to a simpler and supposedly more 'natural' existence. *back to square one*: see SQUARE *n. laid-back*: see LAID *ppl a.* 4.

back- /bak/ *comb. form.* OE. [Repr. BACK *n.*[1], *a.*, *adv.*, or (occas.) *v.*] In combs. in various relations (often difficult to distinguish) and senses, as 'of or on the back', 'backwards', 'reverse', 'rearmost'. (Many, esp. when *back* has an adjectival function, can be written with or without a hyphen.)

backache pain or discomfort in the back. **backacter** = *backhoe* below. **back-action** (orig. *US*) backward or reverse action, as in a machine. **back-along** *adv.* (*dial.*) = BACK *adv.* 2, 8. **back-and-forth** exchange, reciprocity. **backband** a broad strap or chain passing over a cart-saddle, and serving to support the shafts. †**backbear** *Law* the act of carrying game killed illegally (cf. BACK-BERAND *a.*). **back beat** a strongly accented beat in a position generally unaccented. **back-bench** one of the benches in an assembly (esp. the House of Commons) occupied by members not entitled to sit on the front benches. **back-bencher** a member who occupies a back bench. **backblocker** *Austral., NZ, & Canad.* a resident in the backblocks. **backblocks** *Austral., NZ, & Canad.* land in the remote and sparsely inhabited interior; land cut off from a river-front. †**back-blow** a blow struck at the back or from behind. **back-boiler** a boiler behind a domestic fire or cooking range. **back-bond** *Sc. Law* a deed qualifying the terms of another that is apparently absolute. **back-breaking** *a.* (*fig.*) extremely laborious, exhausting. *back burner*: see BURNER 3. **back-cast** *a.* cast or thrown backwards. **backchat** *colloq.* impertinent or impudent repartee, esp. to a superior. **backcomb** *v.t.* & *i.* comb (the hair) back towards the scalp. **back country** (chiefly *N. Amer., Austral., & NZ*) the country lying towards or in the rear of a settled district. **back-court** a smaller court to the rear of a house; *Tennis* the part of the court behind the service line. **back-crawl** *Swimming* a form of crawl in which the swimmer lies on his or her back. **back cross** *v.* & *n. phr.* (*a*) *v.t.* cross (a first-generation hybrid) with one of its parent strains; (*b*) *n.* an instance of back crossing, a hybrid so produced. **backdate** *v.t.* assign an earlier date to, make retrospectively valid. **back door** (*a*) a door at the back of a building or enclosure; a secondary or private entrance; (*b*) *fig.* a second (usu. secret or less conspicuous) means of entry or approach. **back-door** *a.* secret, clandestine, underhand. **back-double** *colloq.* & *dial.* a backstreet, a side road. **back-draught** a reverse draught of air or current of water. **backdrop** *Theatr.* (orig. *US*) = BACKCLOTH 1. **back emf** an electromotive force opposing that driving the current in a circuit. **back-end** the hinder of two ends; the later part of the year, late autumn. **back-fanged** *a.* (*Zool.*) = OPISTHOGLYPH *a.* **backfield** *N. Amer. Football* (the positions occupied by) the players behind the line of scrimmage. **backfill** *v.* & *n.* (*a*) *v.t.* fill (an excavation) in again with material removed earlier, e.g. around foundations; (*b*) *n.* earth etc. used for backfilling. **back-flash** the act or process of flashing back; *esp.* = *flashback* (b) s.v. FLASH *v.* **backflip** a backward somersault. **back-formation** *Philol.* the formation of what looks like a root-word from an already existing word which might be (but is not) a derivative of the former; a word so formed. **back-front** the rear boundary line or elevation of a building. **back-heel** (*a*) *v.t.* kick (esp. a ball) backwards with the heel; (*b*) *n.* such a kick. **backhoe** *N. Amer.* a mechanical excavator which operates by drawing towards itself a bucket attached to a hinged boom. **back-house** (now *dial.*) an outhouse; a privy, a lavatory. **backland** = *back country* above. **back-lift** (in various games) a backward lift given to the bat etc. before playing a stroke, or to the leg before kicking the ball. **back-lighting** *Photogr.* lighting coming from behind the subject. **back-line** (*a*) a rearmost line; *esp.* in games, a line marking the limit of play; (*b*) *Rugby Football* the players behind a scrum or line-out lined out across the field. **back-liner** *Rugby Football* a player in the back-line. **backlist** (a catalogue of) books still available but no longer recent. **backlit** *a.* illuminated from behind. **back-marker** one who starts from scratch or has the least favourable handicap in a race; a horse etc. at the rear of the field. **back number** a number of a periodical earlier than the current one; *colloq.* a person who or a thing which is out of date, behind the times, or useless. **backpack** *n.* & *v.* (chiefly *N. Amer.*) (*a*) *n.* a pack carried on the back, *esp.* a rucksack; (*b*) *v.i.* & *t.* travel with a backpack, esp. for recreation; carry in a backpack. **backpacker** a hiker, camper, etc., with a backpack. **back passage** *colloq.* the rectum. **back-pay(ment)** pay(ment) to cover a past period of time. **back-pedal** *v.i.* work the pedals of a bicycle backwards; *fig.* (try to) reverse one's previous action. **backpiece** a piece of armour protecting the back; the piece that forms the back of something. **backplate** a plate of armour for the back; a plate placed at or forming the back of something. **back-pressure** pressure opposing the normal flow of a liquid or gas. **back-projection** projection on to a translucent screen from the rear, as a means of providing a still or moving background to a scene etc. **backrest** a support for the back. **back room** a room at the back of a house or other building; *spec.* a room or premises where (esp. secret) research etc. is carried out; *backroom boy*, a person who does such research or wields influence behind the scenes. **back-rope** *Naut.* a rope leading inboard from the martingale. **back row** the rear line (of a chorus, rugby scrum, etc.). **back-saw** a saw with a blade strengthened by a metal strip at the rear. **back-scatter** *v.* & *n.* (*Physics*) (*a*) *v.t.* scatter (radiation etc.) with more or less complete reversal of direction; (*b*) *n.* back-scattering; radiation etc. so scattered. **back-scratcher** an implement for scratching one's own back; *fig.* a person who takes part in mutual services for gain. **back-scratching** the performance of such services. **back-set** a setting back, a reverse; an eddy or counter-current. **backsight** (*a*) *Surveying* a sight or reading taken backwards, or towards the point of starting; (*b*) the rearsight of a gun. **back slang** a form of slang in which words are spelt and pronounced backwards (as *yob* for *boy*). **backslapper** *fig.* a vigorously hearty person. **backslapping** slapping the back, esp. in congratulation or encouragement; *fig.* vigorously hearty behaviour. **backslash** a backward-sloping diagonal line, a reverse solidus. **back-space** *v.i.* use the back-spacer. **back-spacer** a key on a typewriter etc. that moves the printing position one space backward. **back-spin** a backward spin on a ball in motion. **back-stabber** *fig.* a person who attacks another unfairly, or behind his or her back. **back stage** *Theatr.* the rear part of a stage; the part of a theatre behind the stage or curtain, *esp.* the wings, dressing-rooms, etc. **backstage** *adv.* & *a.* at or to the back stage of a theatre; (situated, occurring, etc.) behind the scenes (*lit.* & *fig.*). **backstair(s)** *n.* & *a.* (*a*) *n.* stairs at the back of a house, a secondary staircase; the private stairs in a palace, used for other than State visitors; *fig.* a secret method of approach; (*b*) *adj.* relating to or employing underhand intrigue, back-door. **backstay** *Naut.* each of a number of ropes extending downwards and aft from the top of the mast towards the stern of the ship (usu. in *pl.*); *gen.* a stay or support at the back (*lit.* & *fig.*). **backstitch** *n.* & *v.* (*a*) *n.* a method of sewing with overlapping stitches; (*b*) *v.t.* & *i.* sew in backstitch. **back-stop** *n.* & *v.* (*a*) *n.* something or someone placed at the rear to serve as a barrier or support; *Cricket* = *longstop* S.V. LONG *a.*[1]; (*b*) *v.t.* (chiefly *US*) act as a back-stop to (chiefly *fig.*). **back-straight** the stretch along the side of a racecourse or racetrack opposite to that on which the races end. **backstreet** *n.* & *a.* (*a*) *n.* a street in a quiet part of a town etc., away from the main streets; (*b*) *adj.* taking place in a backstreet, taking place illicitly or illegally. **backstroke** a blow or stroke in return; a back-handed stroke; *Swimming* a stroke in which the swimmer lies on his or her back in the water. **backswimmer** a carnivorous aquatic bug of the family Notonectidae, a water-boatman. **back-swing** a backward swing, esp. of the arm or a golf club when about to hit a ball. **back-talk** *colloq.* (orig. *dial.*) = *backchat* above. **backtrack** *v.* (orig. *US*) (*a*) *v.i.* return, retrace one's steps; *fig.* go back *on*, withdraw; (*b*) *v.t.* trace, pursue, investigate. **backtracker** a person who backtracks. **backveld** *S. Afr.* primitive rural districts. **backvelder** *S. Afr.* (freq. *derog.*) a dweller in the backveld. **backwash** the motion of a receding wave, a backward current; *fig.* repercussions. **backwater** dammed or still water, *esp.* that beside a stream and fed by the back flow; *fig.* a remote or neglected place, (a place or condition of) intellectual stagnation. **back-way** a way leading to the back, a roundabout way. **back-winter** a return of winter after its regular time. **backwoods** wholly or partly uncleared forest; a remote or sparsely inhabited region. **backwoodsman** an inhabitant of the backwoods; *fig.* an uncouth person; a peer who very rarely attends the House of Lords. **back-word** *dial.* withdrawal from a promise or invitation; a contradictory or rude answer. **backyard** a yard or enclosure at the back of a building; *fig.* an adjacent or easily accessible area.

†backare *int.* Also **bacare**. M16–M17. [Prob. joc. f. BACK *adv.* + *-are* L inf. ending.] Go back! Give way!

back-berand /ˈbakbɛr(ə)nd/ *a. arch.* Also **-ind**. [OE *bæc-berende*, f. as BACK *n.*[1] + pres. pple of *beran* BEAR *v.*[1]] Bearing on the back. Long *obs.* exc. *Law* (of a thief) apprehended in the possession of stolen goods.

backbite /ˈbakbʌɪt/ *v.t.* Pa. t. **-bit** /-bɪt/; pa. pple **-bitten** /-bɪt(ə)n/. ME. [f. BACK *n.*[1] + BITE *v.*] Slander, speak ill of (someone) behind his or her back. Freq. as *backbiting* vbl n.

backbiter *n.* a slanderer, a secret calumniator ME.

backboard /ˈbakbɔːd/ *n.* & *v.* OE. [f. BACK *n.*[1] + BOARD *n.*] **A** *n.* **1** *Naut.* = PORT *n.*[5] Now *Sc.*, *rare* or *obs.* OE. **2** A board placed at or forming the back of anything; *esp.* (*a*) one fastened across the back of the shoulders to straighten the figure; (*b*) one behind the basket in basketball, off which the ball may rebound; (*c*) one against which tennis-strokes may be practised. M18. **B** *v.t.* Subject to the use of a backboard. M19.

backbone /ˈbakbəʊn/ *n.* ME. [f. BACK *n.*[1] + BONE *n.*] **1** The vertebral column, the spine. ME. **2** *transf.* A central support or axis; the chief substantial part; *N. Amer.* the spine of a book. L17. **3** *fig.* The main element or support; the mainstay. M19. **4** *fig.* Strength of character, stability of purpose, firmness. M19.

1 to the backbone *fig.* completely, through and through.

backboned *a.* having a backbone M19. **backboneless** *a.* M19.

backcloth /ˈbakˌklɒθ/ *n.* L19. [f. BACK- + CLOTH *n.*] **1** *Theatr.* A painted cloth hung across the back of the stage as the principal part of the scenery. Freq. *fig.* L19. **2** A cloth placed between a fabric that is being printed and the blanket, to keep the latter clean. L19.

1 *fig.*: G. S. FRASER A river, for a Restoration poet, would be primarily . . a backcloth for pastoral.

back-down /ˈbakdaʊn/ *n. colloq.* M19. [f. *back down* s.v. BACK *v.*] A surrender of a claim or claims made; a retreat from a stand taken.

backen /ˈbak(ə)n/ *v.* Now *rare*. M17. [f. BACK *a.*, *adv.* + -EN[5]: cf. LESSEN *v.*] **1** *v.t.* Put or throw back; retard. M17. **2** *v.i.* Move or draw back; *esp.* = BACK *v.* II. M18.

backer /ˈbakə/ *n.*[1] L16. [f. BACK *v.* + -ER[1].] A supporter, esp. a person who makes a bet; a person who provides financial backing.

backer-up a person who backs (up).

backer *n.*[2] var. of BACCA.

backer *a.* see BACK *a.*

backet /ˈbakɪt/ *n. Sc.* LME. [(O)Fr. *baquet* dim. of *bac* BACK *n.*[2]: see -ET[1].] A shallow wooden trough for carrying ashes, lime, salt, etc.

backfall /ˈbakfɔːl/ *n.* L17. [f. BACK- + FALL *n.*[1]] **†1** *Mus.* An accessory note a tone or a semitone above the main note. L17–L19. **2** A fall or throw on the back in wrestling. E19. **3** A lever in the coupler of an organ. L19.

backfire /ˈbakfʌɪə/ *n.* M19. [f. BACK *adv.* + FIRE *n.*] **1** A fire deliberately lighted ahead of an advancing prairie fire or bushfire in order to deprive it of fuel and so extinguish it. *N. Amer.* & *Austral.* M19. **2** A premature ignition or explosion in an internal-combustion engine or its exhaust-pipe. L19. **b** *fig.* The recoiling of a plan, scheme, etc., adversely on its originator (see BACKFIRE *v.* 2b). E20.

backfire /bakˈfʌɪə/ *v.* L19. [f. prec.] **1** *v.i.* Light a fire ahead of an advancing prairie fire in order to deprive it of fuel. *N. Amer.* L19. **2** *v.i.* Of an internal-combustion engine or its fuel: ignite or explode prematurely; also *transf.* (esp. of a firearm). L19. **b** *fig.* Of a plan, scheme, etc.: recoil adversely on its originator. E20. **3** *v.t.* Expel backwards in backfiring. E20.

backfisch /ˈbakfɪʃ/ *n.* Pl. **-e** /-ə/. L19. [G, lit. 'fish for frying'.] A girl in late adolescence, a teenage girl.

backfriend /ˈbakfrɛnd/ *n.* L15. [f. BACK- + FRIEND *n.*] **1** A pretended friend; an unavowed enemy. *obs.* exc. *dial.* L15. **2** A supporter, a backer. L16.

backgammon /ˈbakgamən/ *n.* M17. [f. BACK *adv.* + an earlier form of GAME *n.* (see GAMMON *n.*[4]).] **1** A game for two played on a special (usu. hinged) double board, with draughtsmen whose moves are determined by throws of the dice. M17. **2** *spec.* The most complete form of win at backgammon. L19.

background /ˈbakgraʊnd/ *n.* & *v.* L17. [f. BACK *a.* + GROUND *n.*] **A** *n.* **1** The ground or surface lying at the back of or behind the chief objects and foreground in a scene, picture, or description. L17. **2** *fig.* A less prominent position; obscurity, retirement. L18. **3** *fig.* Surroundings, ambience, the prevailing circumstances; *esp.* (information about) events or facts regarded as a basis on which more particular matters may be considered or apprehended. M19. **4** *fig.* A person's cultural knowledge, education, experience, environment, etc.; social surroundings. E20. **5** Adventitious radio, sound, etc., signals; the normal level of radioactivity, electromagnetic radiation, or other phenomena, arising from natural sources. E20. **6** Music or sound-effects used as an accompaniment, esp. to a film or broadcast programme. E20.

1 R. B. SHERIDAN Elvira walks about pensively in the background. J. HEDGECOE The most convenient way to photograph a silhouette is to position the subject some distance in front of a white background. **2** LD MACAULAY Political friends thought it best . . that he should remain in the background. **3** J. LE CARRÉ He told you about Mundt; gave you the background? *attrib.*: M. INNES Do some background reading in published sources. **4** C. JACKSON Who they are and where they came from—their backgrounds, I mean. T. STOPPARD Do you find it incredible that a man with a scientific background should be Archbishop of Canterbury? **5** J. NARLIKAR Penzias and Wilson found a radiation background which was isotropic . . and which corresponded to a black body temperature of ~3.5K. **6** L. FEATHER Vocals . . with fine backgrounds and solos by Bird.

Comb.: **background heater**, **heating** a heater, heating, intended for general warmth; **background music** music played in the background; *esp.* music accompanying a film etc. (cf. sense 6 above); **background noise** noise in the background; *esp.* adventitious radio etc. signals (cf. sense 5 above).

B *v.t.* **1** Form a background to. M18. **2** Put in the background. Chiefly *fig.*, treat as unimportant, give no emphasis to. L19. **3** Provide with background information or knowledge. M20.

backgrounder *n.* (*N. Amer.*) an official briefing or hand-out giving background information M20.

backhand /ˈbakhand/ *n.*, *a.*, & *v.* M17. [f. BACK- + HAND *n.*] **A** *n.* The hand turned backwards in making a stroke; *spec.* in *Tennis*, *Badminton*, and similar games, a stroke played with the arm across the body and the back of the hand facing one's opponent. M17.

on the backhand *Tennis*, *Badminton*, etc. (on the side on which one must strike) backhanded.

B *attrib.* or as *adj.* Of a stroke etc.: played backhanded. Of an area of a tennis or badminton court, etc.: in which it is usually necessary to play backhanded. L17.

C *v.* **1** *v.i.* Take an extra glass of wine out of turn: see BACKHANDER 2. *rare*. M19. **2** *v.t.* Hit with the back of one's hand. M20.

backhanded /ˈbakhandɪd/ *a.* & *adv.* E19. [f. prec. + -ED[2].] **A** *adj.* **1** Of a stroke etc.: made with the back of the hand or with the hand turned backwards; *spec.* in *Tennis*, *Badminton*, and similar games, played as a backhand (BACKHAND *n.*). E19. **2** *fig.* Indirect, ambiguous. E19.

2 K. TYNAN Is it a backhanded compliment to say that this actor is best when maddest?

B *adv.* With the back of the hand or with the hand turned backwards; with a backhand. L19.

backhandedly *adv.* L19.

backhander /ˈbakhandə/ *n.* E19. [f. as prec. + -ER[1].] **1** A blow with the back of the hand. E19. **b** *fig.* A hurtful or stinging remark. M19. **2** An extra glass of wine out of turn, the bottle being passed back. *rare*. M19. **3** A backhanded stroke or blow (cf. BACKHANDED *a.* 1). L19. **4** A tip or bribe made surreptitiously; a secret payment. *slang*. M20.

backing /ˈbakɪŋ/ *n.* M16. [f. BACK *v.* + -ING[1].] **1** The action of BACK *v.*, *esp.* the action of supporting at the back; motion in a backward direction. M16. **2** *collect.* Something which backs or forms the back, *esp.* a body of supporters; the material used to form the back or support of something. L18. **b** Instrumental or vocal accompaniment, esp. on a recording. M20.

Comb.: **backing store** *Computing* secondary storage (usu. disk) supporting the primary storage (usu. volatile); a device for this.

backlash /ˈbaklaʃ/ *n.* E19. [f. BACK *adv.* + LASH *n.*[1]] **1** An irregular recoil or excessive play in a piece of mechanism. E19. **2** *transf.* & *fig.* An excessive or violent reaction; reactionary attitudes or opinion. E20.

2 P. BRICKHILL She learned the police had searched her room. *I* caught the backlash. M. L. KING The white backlash had always existed underneath and sometimes on the surface of American life.

backlog /ˈbaklɒg/ *n.* L17. [f. BACK- + LOG *n.*[1]] 1 A large log placed at the back of a fire. Chiefly *N. Amer., Austral.,* & *NZ.* L17. 2 *fig.* a An accumulation, a reserve. L19. b Arrears of unfulfilled orders, uncompleted work, etc. M20.

backmost /ˈbakməʊst/ *a.* L18. [f. BACK *a.* after FOREMOST, HINDMOST: see -MOST.] Furthest to the back, hindmost. Opp. FOREMOST.

back seat /bak siːt/ *n. phr.* M19. [f. BACK *a.* + SEAT *n.*] 1 A seat at the back of a vehicle; an inferior seat at the back of a hall etc. M19. 2 A position of comparative obscurity or inferiority. *colloq.* M19.

2 **take a back seat** (orig. *US*) occupy a subordinate place.

Comb.: **back-seat driver** a person who rides in the back seat of a motor vehicle and gives unwanted advice to its driver; *fig.* a person who criticizes or attempts to control without responsibility.

backsheesh *n.* & *v.* var. of BAKSHEESH.

backside /bakˈsʌɪd; *in sense 4 also* ˈbaksʌɪd/ *n.* LME. [f. BACK *a.* + SIDE *n.*] 1 The hinder or back part; the back, the rear. LME. 2 The back premises of, or an outbuilding attached to, a dwelling; also, a privy, a lavatory. Now *dial.* & *US.* LME. †3 = BACK *n.*[1] 3. LME–E18. 4 The buttocks. E16. †5 *fig.* The reverse or wrong side; the opposite. M–L17.

backslide /ˈbakslʌɪd/ *v.i.* Pa. t. & pple **-slid** /-slɪd/. M16. [f. BACK *adv.* + SLIDE *v.*] Slide back (in fig. sense); fall away from attained excellence, esp. of religious faith and practice; relapse into sin or error.

backslider *n.* a person who backslides, an apostate L16.

backstone *n.* var. of BAKESTONE.

back-sword /ˈbaksɔːd/ *n. arch.* M16. [f. BACK *n.*[1] + SWORD *n.*] 1 A sword with only one cutting edge. M16. 2 A single stick used instead of a sword in fencing; (an) exercise using this. L17. 3 A fencer with a back-sword. L17.

backup /ˈbakʌp/ *n.* E20. [f. *back up* s.v. BACK *v.*] 1 Backward motion of a vehicle. *N. Amer.* E20. 2 An accumulation of water, traffic, etc., behind an obstruction. *N. Amer.* M20. 3 A reserve, a stand-by or spare; support, backing; *Computing* (the making of) a duplicate copy of a disk, file, program, etc. Freq. *attrib.* M20.

Comb.: **backup light** a reversing light.

Backus /ˈbakʌs/ *n.* M20. [John W. *Backus* (b. 1924), US computer scientist.] Computing. *Backus–Naur* /naʊə/ [Peter *Naur*, 20th-cent. mathematician] or *Backus normal form*, a form of notation used to describe context-free programming languages. Abbrev. *BNF*.

backward /ˈbakwəd/ *adv., a., v.,* & *n.* As adv. & (*rare*) adj. also **-wards** /-wədz/. ME. [Aphet. f. ABACKWARD: later assoc. with BACK *n.*[1]] A *adv.* I Towards one's back, or the back of anything. 1 Of movement: in the direction of one's back or away from one's front. ME. b With verbs of continuous motion: with the back foremost, with the face to the rear. ME. 2 Of position: towards the back or rear of a place; away from the front. *obs.* or *arch.* LME.

1 S. HILL She had fallen heavily backwards down the stairs. **bend, fall,** or **lean over backward(s)** *fig.* go to the opposite extreme to avoid possible bias etc., do one's utmost *to* oblige, accommodate, etc. b J. H. NEWMAN We walk to heaven backward. A. J. P. TAYLOR Like the country at large, they entered war socialism backwards, and were surprised at what they had done.

II Towards what is behind in position or course. 3 In the direction which (as regards one's ordinary position) is behind one, or from which one is moving. (Now more usu. expressed by *back* or *behind.*) *arch.* LME. 4 Of things: towards the place of starting, in the direction opposite to that of previous progress. (Not normally used of people or animals, where ambiguity might arise.) LME. 5 In the direction of retreat. LME. 6 *fig.* Towards or into a worse state; into decline. LME. 7 Of time: towards or in the past. (More usu. expressed by *back.*) *arch.* LME.

3 BROWNING Whom else could I dare look backward for? 4 DRYDEN Like some impetuous flood, which mastered once, With double force bends backward. **backward(s) and forward(s)** in both directions alternately, to and fro. 5 BYRON They are beaten backward from the palace. 6 G. B. SHAW He regarded that as a step backward in civilization. 7 M. MITCHELL Bitter-eyed women who looked backward, to dead times, to dead men, evoking memories that hurt and were futile.

III In the reverse direction or order. 8 In a direction opposite to the normal, in the reverse way. LME.

8 L. DURRELL Damn the word [love]. . . I would like to spell it backwards as you say the Elizabethans did God. J. LE CARRÉ Sloping his pen backwards he practised the second signature until he was satisfied with it. M. FRAYN As if in a film of a breaking vase run backwards the pieces flew miraculously together. **know something backward(s)** know something thoroughly, be very well versed in something. **ring the bells backward(s)** *arch.*: beginning with the bass bell, to give an alarm etc.

B *adj.* [Attrib. (often ellipt.) use of the adv.; but analogous to adjs. in -WARD of OE origin.] 1 Directed to the back or rear. LME. 2 Directed in the opposite way; of or pertaining to return. LME. †3 Perverse, unfavourable. L16–M18. 4 Turning or hanging back from action; reluctant, chary; shy, bashful. L16. 5 Placed towards or at the back; *obs.* exc. *Cricket* (of a fielding position) behind the line of the wicket. E17. 6 Reaching into the past; retrospective. M17. 7 Behindhand in respect of progress; late (esp. of the season or crops); slow to learn; educationally subnormal. L17. 8 Done in the reverse way; reversed. E18.

1 R. SUTCLIFF He watched her walking away without a backward glance. 2 W. C. BRYANT And takes the backward way with trembling limbs. 4 SHAKES. *Hen. V* Perish the man whose mind is backward now. **backward in coming forward** *colloq.* reluctant, shy (to do something), reticent, (freq. in neg. contexts). 5 S. JOHNSON A lodging in the backward garret of a mean house. *backward point, backward short leg,* etc. (in cricket). 6 BYRON The soul . . flies unconscious o'er each backward year. **backward masking** *Psychol.* a diminution in the response to a stimulus as a result of a second stimulus following closely after it. 7 G. GREENE I'd have gone to Oxford . . but they are very backward in technology. A. S. NEILL We do not take mentally defective children, but a child who is backward at school is a different story. A. J. TOYNBEE To help . . other still backward peoples on the outer edges of Mexico, to find their way into the modern world. 8 POPE The backward labours of her faithless hand.

C *v.t.* & *i.* Put or keep back, retard; go backward. Now *rare.* L16.

D *n.* The past portion of time. *rare.* E17.

SHAKES. *Temp.* What seest thou else In the dark backward and abysm of time?

backwardly *adv.* M16. **backwardness** *n.* L16.

backwardation /bakwəˈdeɪʃ(ə)n/ *n.* M19. [f. prec. + -ATION.] *Comm.* A premium paid by the seller of stock or commodities in some cases where delivery is to be deferred. Cf. CONTANGO *n.*

backwards *adv.* & *a.* see BACKWARD.

backy *n.* var. of BACCY.

bacon /ˈbeɪk(ə)n/ *n.* & *v.* ME. [OFr. *bacon*, *-un* = Prov. *bacon* f. Frank. *bako* ham, flitch = OHG *bahho* f. Gmc, rel. to BACK *n.*[1]] A *n.* 1 The cured back or side of a pig (formerly also the fresh flesh now called *pork*). ME. †2 The carcass of a pig. ME–M18. †3 A rustic. Cf. *chaw-bacon* s.v. CHAW *v. rare* (Shakes.). Only in L16.

1 **bring home the bacon** *fig.* (*colloq.*) achieve success. **save one's bacon** = *save one's skin* s.v. SAVE *v.*

Comb.: **bacon beetle** = LARDER *beetle.*

B *v.t.* Convert into bacon. Chiefly *N. Amer.* E19.

baconer *n.* a pig fit for being made into bacon and ham M18.

Baconian /beɪˈkəʊnɪən/ *a.* & *n.* E19. [f. *Bacon* (see below) + -IAN.] A *adj.* 1 Of or pertaining to the English philosopher Francis Bacon (1561–1626) or the experimental or inductive system of philosophy propounded by him. E19. 2 Designating or pertaining to the theory that Bacon wrote the plays attributed to Shakespeare. L19. B *n.* An adherent of Bacon's philosophical system, or of the Baconian theory of Shakespeare's plays. M19.

bacteraemia /baktəˈriːmɪə/ *n.* Also *-**remia**, -**riaemia** /-rɪˈiːmɪə/. L19. [f. BACTERIUM + -AEMIA.] *Med.* The presence of bacteria in the blood.

bacteraemic *a.* M20.

bacteria *n.* pl. of BACTERIUM.

bacteriaemia *n.* var. of BACTERAEMIA.

bacterial /bakˈtɪərɪəl/ *a.* L19. [f. BACTERIUM + -AL[1].] Of, pertaining to, or caused by bacteria.

bacterially *adv.* L19.

bactericide /bakˈtɪərɪsʌɪd/ *n.* L19. [f. as prec. + -CIDE.] A substance able to kill bacteria.

bacteriˈcidal *a.* able to kill bacteria L19. **bacteriˈcidally** *adv.* L19.

bacterio- /bakˈtɪərɪəʊ/ *comb. form* of BACTERIUM: see -O-.

bacterioˈcidal *a.* = BACTERICIDAL *a.* M20. **bacteriophage** *n.* a virus that causes lysis or prophage formation in bacteria E20. **bacterioˈphobia** *n.* irrational fear of bacteria E19. **bacteriorhoˈdopsin** *n.* (*Biochem.*) a protein pigment in the bacterium *Halobacterium halobium* which under the action of light transports protons across the cytoplasmic membrane L20. **bacteriˈosis** *n.*, pl. **-oses** /-ˈəʊsiːz/, a bacterial disease of plants L19.

bacteriocin /bakˈtɪərɪəsɪn/ *n.* M20. [Fr. *bactériocine*, f. as BACTERIO- + COLICIN.] *Bacteriol.* A protein produced by bacteria of one strain and active against those of a closely related strain.

bacterioid /bakˈtɪərɪɔɪd/ *a.* & *n.* L19. [f. BACTERIUM + -OID.] = BACTEROID.

bacteriological /bakˌtɪərɪəˈlɒdʒɪk(ə)l/ *a.* L19. [f. next + -ICAL.] Of or pertaining to bacteriology.

bacteriological warfare the deliberate use of bacteria to spread disease among an enemy.

bacteriologic *a.* = BACTERIOLOGICAL L19. **bacteriologically** *adv.* L19.

bacteriology /bakˌtɪərɪˈɒlədʒi/ *n.* L19. [f. BACTERIO- + -LOGY.] The branch of science that deals with bacteria.

bacteriologist *n.* L19.

bacteriolysis /bakˌtɪərɪˈɒlɪsɪs/ *n.* Pl. **-lyses** /-lɪsiːz/. L19. [f. BACTERIO- + -LYSIS.] †1 Artificial liquefaction of organic waste by bacteria. Only in L19. 2 The destruction of bacteria by an antibody. E20.

bacteriolysin /-ˈlʌɪsɪn/ *n.* a bacteriolytic antibody E20. **bacteriolytic** /-ˈlɪtɪk/ *a.* of, pertaining to, or capable of bacteriolysis E20.

bacteriostasis /bakˌtɪərɪəˈsteɪsɪs/ *n.* Pl. **-stases** /-ˈsteɪsiːz/. E20. [f. as prec. + Gk *stasis* stopping.] Inhibition of the proliferation of bacteria without killing them.

bacteriostat /bakˈtɪərɪəstat/ *n.* a bacteriostatic agent E20. **bacteriostatic** /-ˈstatɪk/ *a.* pertaining to or capable of bacteriostasis E20.

bacterium /bakˈtɪərɪəm/ *n.* Pl. **-ia** /-ɪə/. M19. [mod.L f. Gk *baktērion* dim. of *baktēria* staff, cane.] Any of the very widely distributed group *Bacteria* of microscopic prokaryotic mainly single-celled organisms, many of which are symbiotic or pathogenic in animals and plants.

iron bacterium: see IRON *n.* & *a.* *purple bacterium*: see PURPLE *a.* & *n.*

¶Bacteria were formerly classified as fungi, but are now usu. regarded (with blue-green algae) as constituting a distinct division of plants, or an independent kingdom.

bacterize /ˈbaktərʌɪz/ *v.t.* treat with bacteria E20. **bacteriˈzation** *n.* E20.

bacteriuria /bakˌtɪərɪˈjʊərɪə/ *n.* Also **bacteruria** /baktəˈrʊərɪə/. L19. [f. prec. + -URIA.] *Med.* The presence of bacteria in the urine.

bacteroid /ˈbaktərɔɪd/ *a.* & *n.* M19. [f. as prec. + -OID.] A *adj.* Of the nature of or resembling a bacterium. M19. B *n.* A bacteroid organism or structure; *esp.* a modified cell formed by a symbiotic bacterium in a root nodule of a leguminous plant. L19.

bacteruria *n.* var. of BACTERIURIA.

Bactrian /ˈbaktrɪən/ *n.* & *a.* LME. [Gk *Baktrianos*, L *Bactrianus*, f. *Bactria*: see below, -IAN.] A *n.* 1 *Hist.* A native or inhabitant of Bactria, an ancient country of central Asia lying between the Hindu Kush and the Oxus. LME. 2 = *Bactrian camel* s.v. CAMEL I. E17.

B *adj.* Of or belonging to Bactria. E17.

Bactrian camel: see CAMEL I.

baculine /ˈbakjʊlʌɪn/ *a. rare.* E18. [f. L *baculum*, *-us* rod, stick + -INE[1].] Of or pertaining to punishment by caning or flogging.

baculum /ˈbakjʊləm/ *n.* Pl. **-la** /-lə/. M20. [mod.L: see prec.] = *os penis* s.v. OS *n.*[1]

bad /bad/ *a.*, *n.*, & *adv.* ME. [Orig. disyllabic: perh. repr. OE *bǣddel* hermaphrodite (cf. BADLING *n.*[1]) with loss of *l* as in *much(e)*, *wench(e)* for OE *myċel*, *wenċel*.] A *adj.* Compar. WORSE, (now *non-standard*) **badder**, superl. WORST, (now *non-standard*) **baddest**. I In a privative sense: not good. 1 Of defective quality or worth; worthless, inferior, deficient, deteriorated; debased, counterfeit. ME. 2 Unfortunate, unfavourable; incurring or involving disapproval or dislike. ME. 3 *Law.* Not valid. L19.

1 T. R. MALTHUS Children perished . . from bad nourishment. E. GLASGOW All ways are long over bad roads. S. GOLDWYN Why should people go out to see bad films when they can stay at home and see bad television? K. LAFFAN I couldn't do it on the phone—his hearing's bad. 2 MILTON Perplexed and troubled at his bad success. E. WAUGH He . . could talk at length of [Vatican] policy and appointments, saying which contemporary ecclesiastics were in good favour, which in bad. *come to a bad end*: see COME *v.*

II In a positive sense: evil, noxious. 4 Morally depraved; immoral, wicked; (in weakened sense) naughty, badly behaved, blameworthy. ME. 5 Of a person: in ill health, sick, unwell; *transf.* distressed, regretful (*about* something). Of the body or a part of it: diseased, injured. ME. 6 Causing inconvenience or trouble; offensive, unpleasant; (of weather) inclement. E16. 7 Injurious, hurtful, or dangerous (*for* someone); more gen. as an intensifying word in unfavourable contexts: extreme, pronounced. M17.

4 J. FORDYCE Young people . . are often corrupted by bad books. LD MACAULAY Discreet counsellors implored the royal brothers not to countenance this bad man. S. HILL That is a bad habit which must be cured at once. P. ROTH When I am bad and rotten in small ways she can manage me herself. 5 S. RICHARDSON Still very bad with my Gout. W. H. HERNDON Tiger felt bad about the matter. E. O'NEILL You were afraid his heart was bad. 6 A. CHERRY-GARRARD Polar exploration is . . the cleanest and most isolated way of having a bad time. L. URIS The children . . smelled bad from the lack of water to wash with. J. HARVEY Barry's father saw that something serious and bad had happened. 7 LD MACAULAY He had just had a bad fall in hunting. N. MITFORD He caught a bad cold . . and stayed indoors. B. PYM Too much washing was bad for the skin. K. J. DOVER A trustfulness which admits regretfully that he made some bad mistakes.

III 8 Good, excellent. *slang* (chiefly *US*). M20.

Special collocations, phrases, & comb.: *a bad sport*: see SPORT *n. a bad taste in the mouth*: see TASTE *n.*[1] *bad bargain*: see BARGAIN *n.* 2. *bad blood*: see BLOOD *n. bad break*: see BREAK *n.*[1] **bad business** an unfortunate matter. *bad cess to*: see CESS *n.*[2] *bad coin*: see COIN *n.* 4. *bad* CONSCIENCE. **bad debt**: which cannot be recovered. **bad egg** (*a*) an egg that is inedible through deterioration; (*b*) a person or scheme that comes to no good. *bad faith*: see FAITH *n. bad form*: see FORM *n. bad hat*: see HAT *n. bad health*: see HEALTH *n.* 5. *bad job*: see JOB *n.*[1] **badland(s)** (chiefly *N. Amer.*) barren, inhospitable land with many gullies, ridges, and other erosional features, esp. in certain parts of the western US. *bad language*: see LANGUAGE *n.*[1] 2d. **bad law**: that is not sustainable or not justifiable. *bad lot*: see LOT *n.* **badman** (chiefly *N. Amer.*) a desperado, an outlaw. **bad mouth** *N. Amer. slang* malicious gossip or criticism. **bad-mouth** *v.t.* (*N. Amer. slang*) abuse, criticize maliciously. **bad news** *slang* an unwelcome guest; something undesirable. *bad penny*: see PENNY *n. bad scran to* —: see SCRAN 2. *bad show*: see SHOW *n.*[1] **bad-tempered** *a.* having a bad temper; easily angered. *come to a bad end*: see COME *v. from bad to worse*: see WORSE *a.*, *n.*, & *adv.* **go bad** decay, (esp. of food) become mouldy, sour, etc. *in a bad temper*: see TEMPER *n.* **in a bad way** ill, in trouble. *in bad repair*: see REPAIR *n.*[2] *in bad stead*: see STEAD *n. in someone's bad books*: see BOOK *n. just too bad*: see JUST *adv. keep bad time*: see TIME *n.* **not (half, so) bad** better than might have been expected, fairly good. *throw good money after bad*: see THROW *v.* **too bad** regrettable (often *iron.*). *with a bad grace*: see GRACE *n.*

B *n.* 1 Something bad; bad condition; ill fortune. LME. 2 (As a count n.) A bad thing, quality, or (*rare*) person. L16.

1 SHAKES. *Two Gent.* T'exchange the bad for better. *from bad to worse*: see WORSE *n. get in bad*: see GET *v.* **in bad** *colloq.* out of favour (*with*). **to the bad** to a bad state, to ruin; in deficit.

C *adv.* = BADLY. Now chiefly *N. Amer.* E17.

L. HELLMAN I only came cause she's so bad off. M. K. RAWLINGS She's bad hurt. B. SCHULBERG If you needed shoes that bad you could have told me. *have got it bad*: see GET *v.*

baddish *a.* M18. **baddy** *n.* (*colloq.*) a bad person, a criminal, a villain (esp. in a film or play) M20. **badness** *n.* LME.

†**bad** *v.* see BID *v.*

Badarian /bəˈdɛːrɪən, bəˈdɑːrɪən/ *a.* & *n.* E20. [f. *Badari* (see below) + -AN.] *Archaeol.* A *adj.* Designating or pertaining to an early predynastic culture of Upper Egypt, evidence for which was first found in the Badari region. E20. B *n.* (A person of) the Badarian culture. M20.

baddeleyite /ˈbad(ə)lɪʌɪt/ *n.* L19. [f. Joseph *Baddeley* (fl. 1892), Eng. traveller + -ITE[1].] *Min.* Zirconium dioxide, occurring as colourless, yellow, brown, or black monoclinic crystals.

badder *compar. a.* see BAD *a.*

baddest *superl. a.* see BAD *a.*

bade *v.* see BID *v.*

badge /badʒ/ *n.* & *v.*[1] LME. [Origin unkn.: cf. OFr. *bage*, AL *bagia*.] A *n.* 1 A distinctive device, emblem, or mark (orig. in *Her.*, a device borne for distinction by all the retainers of a noble house: cf. COGNIZANCE), worn as a sign of office or licensed employment or of membership of a society. LME. 2 A distinguishing sign, token, or emblem; *fig.* a characteristic feature revealing a quality or condition. E16. 3 *Naut.* An ornamental window-surround, or a representation of a window, at the stern of a small sailing vessel. M18.

1 T. H. WHITE There were already thousands . . who carried his badge of a scarlet fist clenching a whip. N. HAMILTON Monty's contempt for army regulations was epitomized by his adoption . . of a tank beret with two badges. *rogue's badge*: see ROGUE *n.* 2 G. W. KNIGHT Dark secrecy and night are in Shakespeare ever the badges of crime. A. HALEY Every cook . . would walk in a way to make those keys jangle as a badge of how important and trusted she was. *yellow badge*: see YELLOW *a.*

Comb.: **badge-man** a person who wears an official badge.

B *v.t.* Mark with or distinguish by a badge. LME.

badgeless *a.* L16.

badge /badʒ/ *v.*[2]*i.* & *t.* Long *obs.* exc. *dial.* M16. [Prob. back-form. f. BADGER *n.*[1]] Deal as a badger; trade in (corn etc.) as a badger.

badge *v.*[3] see BAG *v.*[2]

badger /ˈbadʒə/ *n.*[1] Long *obs.* exc. *dial.* ME. [Origin unkn.] A person who buys and sells grain or other commodities; a huckster.

badger /ˈbadʒə/ *n.*[2] & *v.* E16. [Perh. f. BADGE *n.* + -ARD, w. ref. to the distinctive head-markings.] A *n.* 1 A nocturnal burrowing Eurasian mammal, *Meles meles*, of the weasel family, having a grey coat and distinctive white facial stripes. E16. b Any of various animals of similar appearance or habits; *esp.* (*a*) the related N. American badger, *Taxidea taxus*; (*b*) *Austral.* the wombat. M17. 2 A brush, or a fishing-fly, made of badger's hair. L18.

1 **draw the badger** *fig.* entice one's opponent into the open. b *honey-badger*: see HONEY *n. stinking badger*: see STINKING *a.*

Comb.: **badger-baiting, -drawing** setting dogs to draw a badger from its set or from a cask; **badger game** *slang* luring men into (esp. sexually) compromising situations in order to blackmail them; **Badger State** *US* Wisconsin.

B *v.t.* Bait or pester as a dog does a badger; torment, tease, nag. L18.

F. O'CONNOR She began to badger him about his health. C. RYAN Badgered by Field Marshal Model to capture the Arnhem bridge quickly. L. VAN DER POST I could easily have been talked, badgered and teased out of my belief.

badgerer *n.* (*a*) a dog used for badger-baiting; (*b*) a person who badgers another: L19.

badian /ˈbɑːdɪən/ *n.*[1] M19. [Fr. *badiane* f. Pers. & Urdu *bādyān* fennel, anise.] The fruit of Chinese anise or star-anise.

Badian /ˈbeɪdɪən/ *n.*[2] & *a.* M19. [Abbrev. of BARBADIAN. See also BAJAN.] = BARBADIAN.

badigeon /bəˈdɪdʒ(ə)n/ *n.* Now *US.* M18. [Fr., of unkn. origin.] A composition used to fill up gaps in stone or wood.

badinage /ˈbadɪnɑːʒ/ *n.* & *v.* M17. [Fr., f. *badiner* to joke, f. *badin* fool f. Prov., f. *badar* gape f. Proto-Romance: see -AGE.] A *n.* Humorous banter or ridicule. M17. B *v.i.* & *t.* Banter playfully. E19.

badling /ˈbadlɪŋ/ *n.*[1] Long *obs.* exc. *dial.* [OE *bǣdling*, f. *bǣddel*: see BAD *a.*, -LING[1].] An effeminate man; a sodomite; a worthless fellow.

badling /ˈbadlɪŋ/ *n.*[2] L15. [Perh. var. of *paddling* vbl n. of PADDLE *v.*[1]] A small group of ducks.

badly /ˈbadli/ *adv.* & *a.* ME. [f. BAD *a.* + -LY[2].] A *adv.* Compar. WORSE, superl. WORST. 1 In a bad manner; inadequately; incorrectly; immorally, wickedly; severely. ME. 2 With *want*, *need*, etc.: greatly, very much. L19.

1 SHAKES. *John* How goes the day with us? . . Badly, I fear. SOUTHEY One of the Indian chiefs was badly wounded. DICKENS A mean and badly-furnished apartment. J. RUSKIN So great a painter . . would never paint badly enough to deceive. G. B. SHAW Think of the temptation to behave badly when he had us all there helpless. **badly off** in poor circumstances, lacking money. *have got it badly*: see GET *v.* 2 E. O'NEILL His blond hair, badly in need of a cut.

B *adj.* Sick, unwell; regretful. *dial.* L18.

D. H. LAWRENCE 'I want my mother.' . . 'Ay, but she's badly'. A. HALEY Kunta felt badly for having wished sometimes that he might strike the man.

badmash /ˈbʌdmɑːʃ/ *n.* M19. [Urdu f. Pers., f. *bad* evil + Arab. *maʿāš* means of livelihood.] In the Indian subcontinent: a rascal, a hooligan.

badminton /ˈbadmɪnt(ə)n/ *n.* M19. [*Badminton*, a town in Avon, SW England, and seat of the Duke of Beaufort.] 1 A summer drink of claret, soda, and sugar. M19. 2 A game played on a court (usu. indoors) across a net with rackets and a shuttlecock. L19.

Baedeker /ˈbeɪdɪkə/ *n.* M19. [See below.] Any of a series of guidebooks published by Karl Baedeker (1801–59), German publisher, or his successors; *gen.* any guidebook.

Comb.: **Baedeker raids** *Hist.* a series of German reprisal air raids in 1942 on places in Britain of cultural and historical importance.

bael /ˈbeɪl/ *n.* Also **bel** /bɛl/. E17. [Hind. *bel* f. Skt *bilva* f. Tamil *viḷavu*.] (The aromatic fruit of) a thorny Indian tree, *Aegle marmelos*. Also called *Bengal quince*.

baetyl /ˈbiːtɪl/ *n.* Also in Graecized form **baetylion** /bɪˈtɪlɪən/, pl. **-lia** /-lɪə/. M19. [L *baetulus* f. Gk *baitulos*.] A sacred meteoric stone.

baff /baf/ *n.* & *v. Sc.* E16. [Prob. f. OFr. *baffe* a slap in the face.] A *n.* A blow with something flat or soft. E16. B *v.t.* Beat, strike; *Golf* strike (the ground) with the sole of the club-head in making a stroke. E16.

baffle /ˈbaf(ə)l/ *v.* & *n.* M16. [In sense 1 perh. alt. of BAUCHLE *v.* In other senses perh. rel. to Fr. *bafouer* (16) ridicule, alt. of OProv. *bafar*: cf. Fr. †*beffler* (Rabelais) mock, deceive.] A *v.* I *v.t.* †1 Subject to public disgrace or infamy; treat with scorn. M16–L17. †2 Hoodwink, cheat. L16–E18. 3 Bewilder, confuse; reduce to perplexity, puzzle. M17. †4 Confound, bring to nought. M17–E19. 5 Defeat in one's efforts, thwart, foil (passing into sense 3); (of the weather) impede the progress of (a ship). L17. 6 Restrict by means of a baffle; equip with a baffle. L19.

1 SPENSER He by the heels him hung upon a tree And bafful'd so, that all which passed by The picture of his punishment might see. 2 DEFOE He had not a mind to cheat or baffle the poor man. 3 M. INNES

Such incongruities . . had an insidious power to paralyse the will, to baffle the intellect. W. FAULKNER He looked about with a strained, baffled gaze, as if . . trying to remember what it was he wanted to say or to do. H. E. BATES She had been a little sorry for Parker; she had been a little puzzled and baffled by him; and now she was hurt. W. H. AUDEN A murder which has the professionals baffled. 4 G. CRABBE A wish so strong, it baffled his repose. 5 E. A. FREEMAN The murderer baffled pursuit. R. L. STEVENSON The more they tried, the more obstinately fixed I grew to baffle them. H. ALLEN She had met light, baffling airs from the coast of Puerto Rico onward. W. S. CHURCHILL Hamilton, the baffled peacemaker, returned . . full of self-reproach for the advice he had given to the King.

II *v.i.* †7 Trifle, quibble. M17–M18. 8 Struggle ineffectually or futilely. *rare.* M19.

Comb.: **bafflegab** *colloq.* (chiefly *N. Amer.*) incomprehensible or pretentious verbiage or jargon.

B *n.* †1 Confusion, discomfiture; a setback; a disgrace or affront. E17–E19. 2 A state of being baffled. M19. 3 A plate or other device which serves to restrict or regulate the passage of fluid, gas, etc., or to limit the emission of sound, light, etc. Freq. *attrib.* L19.

3 *baffle-board, -plate*, etc.

bafflement *n.* the action of baffling; the state of being baffled: M19. **baffler** *n.* (*a*) a person who or thing which baffles; (*b*) = BAFFLE *n.* 3: E17. **bafflingly** *adv.* in a confusing or puzzling manner L19.

baft /bɑːft/ *n.* Also **bafta** /ˈbɑːftə/. L16. [Urdu f. Pers. *bāft* a textile, *bāfta* woven.] A coarse (usu. cotton) fabric.

baft /bɑːft/ *adv. arch.* [OE *beæftan*, f. *be* by, at + *æftan* behind. Cf. AFT.] Behind, in the rear. Latterly only *Naut.*, astern, aft.

bafta *n.* var. of BAFT *n.*

bag /bag/ *n.* ME. [Perh. f. ON *baggi* bag, bundle, of unkn. origin.] **I** 1 A receptacle made of flexible material with an open (usu. closable) top (esp. with preceding wd indicating its contents or purpose, or with such a wd understood). ME. 2 *spec.* **a** A money-bag; a handbag. LME. **b** A small pouch used to hold the back-hair of a wig. E18. **c** A mailbag. E18. **d** A diplomatic bag. E19. 3 *fig.* A concern or preoccupation; one's particular interest or distinctive style. *slang.* M20.

1 R. HAWKINS Any man that putteth himself into the enemies port, had need of Argus eyes, and the wind in a bagge. R. LAWLER She's got her bags piled up by the stairs, 'n' if she doesn't take to you by tomorrow mornin' she's shiftin' out. S. PLATH I cracked open a peanut from the ten-cent bag I had bought . . and ate it. *diplomatic bag, gamebag, handbag, mailbag, money-bag, paper bag, shoulder bag, sleeping-bag*, etc. 3 E. MCBAIN She developed a new bag after she moved, writing poetry. Wild, huh? A. GLYN He'd never do that. It's just not his bag.

II 4 A measure of quantity, varying according to the nature of the commodity (*rare* bef. 17). ME. 5 The amount of game a sportsman has shot or caught; *gen.* an amount obtained or achieved in any activity. M19. 6 In *pl.* Much or many (*of*), lots, heaps. *colloq.* E20.

5 N. MITFORD Davey . . often made little bachelor excursions into it [the wide world] from which he would return with a bag of interesting anecdotes. R. V. JONES My bag was mainly rabbits but over the years I had also shot hares, stoats, pigeons, crows, and jays. 6 J. B. MORTON It's not gay, this life, but it might be bags worse. A. WESKER We 'ad bags o' fun, bags o' it.

III 7 A fold of skin, esp. under the (human) eye; a dewlap; an udder. LME. 8 A sac in the body of an animal, containing poison, honey, etc. E16. 9 In *pl.* (Loosely fitting) trousers. *colloq.* L16. 10 A base in baseball. *N. Amer.* L19. 11 A woman, *esp.* one who is unattractive, elderly, or promiscuous. *slang. derog.* E20.

7 E. BOWEN That lamp makes Thomas's face all bags and lines. 8 *fig.*: DRYDEN The swelling poison of the several sects Shall burst its bag. 9 D. L. SAYERS Can't feed with Freddie Arbuthnot in these bags. OXFORD *bags*. 11 M. DICKENS I've never really known a pretty girl like you. At the training college they were all bags. C. JACKSON Heaven knows . . what hell the old bag would give him if she had [waited for him].

Phrases: *a hundred in the water-bag*: see WATER *n.* **bag and baggage** (with) all belongings, (of departure) entire, absolute; orig. (Mil.) *march out* (*with*) *bag and baggage*, make an honourable retreat, leave with equipment etc. intact. **bag of bones** an emaciated person or animal. **bag of mystery** *slang* a sausage. *bag of nerves*: see NERVE *n.* **bag of tricks** a stock of resources. **hold** (or **be left holding**) **the bag** be (left) in an awkward situation. **in the bag** *colloq.* virtually secured, (as good as) in one's possession or power; captured. *let the cat out of the bag*: see CAT *n.*[1] MIXED *bag*. *Petty Bag*: see PETTY *a.* *rough as bags*: see ROUGH *a.* **the whole bag of tricks** everything. *tote bag*: see TOTE *n.*[4]

Comb.: **bag job** *US slang* an illegal search of a suspect's property by a federal agent, esp. to copy or steal incriminating documents; **bag lady** (chiefly *N. Amer.*) a homeless woman, esp. an elderly one, who carries her possessions in bags; = SHOPPING-*bag lady*; **bagman** †(*a*) a maker of bags or pouches; (*b*) a person who carries a bag; *spec.*: *derog.* a commercial traveller; (*slang*, chiefly *US* & *Austral.*) a person who collects or distributes the proceeds of illicit activities; *Austral.* a tramp, a vagrant; **bag-net** a bag-shaped net for catching fish etc. **bag people** *N. Amer.* homeless people who carry their possessions in bags; **bagpudding** *arch.* a pudding boiled in a bag; **bag-shaped** *a.* shaped like a bag; *esp.* (of a fishing net) rounded and with an opening at the top; **bagstuffer** (orig. *US*) a piece of promotional literature handed to shoppers, *esp.* one put into shopping-bags at a checkout; **bagwash** (a laundry that undertakes) the rough unfinished washing of clothes; **bag-wig** an 18th-cent. wig with the back-hair enclosed in an ornamental bag; **bagworm** *US* any of various destructive moth larvae which live within a silken case covered with plant debris.

bagful *n.* as much or as many as a bag will hold; *colloq.* a lot: ME. **baglike** *a.* resembling (that of) a bag M19.

bag /bag/ *v.*[1] Infl. **-gg-**. LME. [f. the n.] 1 *v.i.* Swell out, bulge; *Naut.* drop away from the direct course. LME. **b** Hang loosely; *esp.* (of trousers) become out of shape at the knees. E19. 2 *v.t.* Put into a bag or bags. LME. 3 *v.t.* Cause to swell; cram full. LME. 4 *v.t.* Succeed in killing (so much game); *gen.* add to one's 'bag'; seize, catch; steal, appropriate. E19. **b** Claim or reserve, usu. on the ground of being the first to do so. Freq. in *bags I. slang* (esp. *Children's*). M19.

1 F. MARRYAT He was bagging to leeward like a . . barge laden with a hay-stack. 2 **bag up** store up. 3 J. SMEATON Almost all the lights [= windows] in the church, tho' not broke were bagged outward. 4 P. HAWKER To bag a dozen head of game without missing. J. DOS PASSOS He was almost bagged by a taxicab crossing the street. T. PYNCHON Slothrop's grandfather . . in typical sarcasm and guile bagged his epitaph from Emily Dickinson, without a credit line. b A. A. MILNE Bags I all the presents. B. MARSHALL Bags I do not ask about the room. R. A. KNOX The other girl bagging the hot-water pipes first.

bagger *n.*[1] a person who or a machine which puts something into bags M18.

bag /bag/ *v.*[2]*t.* Infl. **-gg-**. Also **badge** /badʒ/. L17. [Origin unkn. Cf. FAG *v.*[2]] Cut (wheat etc.) with a reaping-hook.

bagger *n.*[2] a person who harvests in this way M19.

Baganda /bəˈgandə/ *n.pl.* & *a.* L19. [Bantu, f. *ba-* pl. pref. + *ganda*. Cf. MUGANDA.] **A** *n.* Pl. of MUGANDA. L19. **B** *attrib.* or as *adj.* Of or pertaining to the Baganda. L19.

bagarre /bagaːr/ *n.* Pl. pronounced same. L19. [Fr.] A tumult; a scuffle, a brawl.

bagasse /bəˈgas/ *n.* E19. [Fr. f. Sp. *bagazo*.] The residue left after the extraction of juice from sugar cane or sugar beet.

bagassosis /bagəˈsəʊsɪs/ *n.* respiratory disease due to inhalation of bagasse dust M20.

bagatelle /bagəˈtɛl/ *n.* M17. [Fr. f. It. *bagatella* perh. dim. of L *baca* berry, or f. It. *baga* baggage.] 1 A trifle, a thing of no value or importance; a negligible amount. M17. 2 A piece of verse or music in a light style. M18. 3 A game in which small balls are struck (usu. by a mechanical striker operated by the player) towards numbered holes on a board with a semicircular end. E19.

1 C. ISHERWOOD They were well-to-do gentlemen, to whom a miserable fifty-mark note was a mere bagatelle. 3 RUSSIAN *bagatelle*.

¶Sense 3 is purely Eng. in origin and use.

bagel /ˈbeɪg(ə)l/ *n.* Also **beigel** /ˈbʌɪg(ə)l/. E20. [Yiddish *beygel*.] A usu. hard ring-shaped roll of bread.

baggage /ˈbagɪdʒ/ *n.* LME. [(O)Fr. *bagage*, f. *baguer* tie up, or f. *bagues* (pl.) bundles (thought to be f. as BAG *n.*): see -AGE.] Usu. *collect.* in senses 1 and 2 (formerly occas. with *pl.*). 1 Packages of belongings (now usu. suitcases etc.) that a traveller takes on a journey, luggage; *spec.* the portable equipment of an army (= L *impedimenta*). LME. **b** *fig.* Encumbrances, burdensome matters; (esp. mental) equipment. E17. 2 Rubbish, refuse, dirt; pus. Freq. *attrib. obs.* exc. *dial.* M16. 3 A disreputable or immoral woman; *joc.* a young woman (usu. w. *saucy*, *artful*, etc.). *colloq.* L16.

1 E. GOWERS Englishmen travel by land with *luggage* and by sea and air with *baggage* Americans, more sensibly, travel everywhere with *baggage*. *bag and baggage*: see BAG *n.* b R. FIRBANK 'Naturally', the lieutenant interposed, 'her intellectual baggage is nil—simply nil.' 3 GOLDSMITH Tell them they are two arrant little baggages. DYLAN THOMAS She's tucked her dress in her bloomers—oh, the baggage!

Comb.: **baggage car** *N. Amer.* a railway luggage-van; **baggage check** *N. Amer.* a luggage ticket; **baggage claim** = *baggage reclaim* (b) s.v. RECLAIM *n.* 1; *baggage reclaim*: see RECLAIM *n.* 1; **baggage room** *N. Amer.* a luggage-office or cloakroom; **baggage tag** *N. Amer.* a luggage label.

baggager *n.* a person who carries or has charge of baggage; an animal carrying baggage: E17.

bagging /ˈbagɪŋ/ *n.*[1] *north.* M18. [Perh. orig. a vbl n. expressing the act of carrying food in a bag.] Food eaten between meals; *spec.* a substantial afternoon tea.

bagging /ˈbagɪŋ/ *n.*[2] M18. [f. BAG *n.* + -ING[1]: cf. *sacking* etc.] Coarse woven fabric out of which bags are made.

baggit /ˈbagɪt/ *n.* M19. [Sc. form of *bagged* pa. pple & ppl a. of BAG *v.*[1]] A female salmon that has not shed its eggs when the spawning season is over. Cf. KELT *n.*[1]

baggy /ˈbagi/ *a.* & *n.* L18. [f. BAG *n.* + -Y[1].] **A** *adj.* Puffed out, hanging in loose folds. L18. **B** *n.* In *pl.* Loose wide-legged swimming-trunks, shorts, or trousers. *colloq.* M20.

bagginess *n.* M19.

bagne /baɲ/ *n.* Pl. pronounced same. M18. [Fr. f. as next.] = BAGNIO 1.

bagnio /ˈbɑːnjəʊ/ *n.* Pl. **-os.** L16. [It. *bagno* f. L *balneum* bath.] 1 An oriental prison; a slave-house. Now only *Hist.* L16. †2 A bath, a bathing-house. E17–E19. 3 A brothel. E17.

bagpipe /ˈbagpʌɪp/ *n.* ME. [f. BAG *n.* + PIPE *n.*[1]] 1 *sing.* & (freq.) in *pl.* A wind instrument having a bag as a reservoir for air, sound being emitted through a melody pipe (chanter), played with a reed, and from one to three single-note (drone) pipes. Also *set* or *pair of bagpipes*. ME. 2 *fig.* A long-winded speaker; a windbag. E17.

¶Formerly a popular instrument in rural England with distinct regional forms; now chiefly associated with the Scottish Highlands and Ireland.

bagpiper *n.* a person who plays the bagpipes (usu. called a *piper*) ME. **bagpiping** *n.* L16.

baguette /baˈgɛt/ *n.* E18. [Fr. f. It. *bacchetto* dim. of *bacchio* f. L *baculum* staff.] 1 *Archit.* A small moulding of semicircular section, like an astragal. E18. 2 A gem, usu. a diamond, cut in a long rectangular shape. E20. 3 A long narrow French loaf. M20.

bah /bɑː/ *int.* E19. [Prob. after Fr.] Expr. contempt, irritation, or annoyance.

bahada *n.* var. of BAJADA.

Bahadur /bəˈhɑːdʊə/ *n.* Also †**Bahawder**; **b-**. L18. [Urdu & Pers. *bahādur* f. Mongolian.] A brave man; a great or distinguished man. Freq. as a title appended to a name.

Baha'i /bɑːˈhɑːi/ *n.* & *a.* L19. [Pers., f. Arab. *bahā'* splendour.] **A** *n.* A member of a religious faith developed from Babism by Bahā' Allāh (1817–92) and his son 'Abd al-Bahā' (1844–1921), emphasizing the unity of humankind and its religions, and seeking world peace. L19. **B** *attrib.* or as *adj.* Of or pertaining to the Baha'is or Baha'ism. E20.

Baha'ism *n.* the doctrine or practice of the Baha'is E20. **Baha'ist**, **Baha'ite** *ns.* a Baha'i E20.

Bahamian /bəˈheɪmɪən/ *n.* & *a.* M18. [f. *Bahama* (see below) + -IAN.] **A** *n.* A native or inhabitant of the Bahama Islands in the western Atlantic. M18. **B** *adj.* Of or pertaining to the Bahama Islands or their people. L19.

Bahasa /bəˈhɑːsə/ *n.* M20. [Malay f. Skt *bhāṣā* speech, language.] Malay as the national language of the Indonesian Republic (in full *Bahasa Indonesia*) or of Malaysia (in full *Bahasa Malaysia*).

†Bahawder *n.* var. of BAHADUR.

Bahiric *n.* & *a.* var. of BOHAIRIC.

Bahraini /bɑːˈreɪni/ *n.* & *a.* Also **-eini**. L19. [f. *Bahrain* (see below) + -I[2].] **A** *n.* A native or inhabitant of Bahrain, a sheikhdom consisting of a group of islands in the Persian Gulf. L19. **B** *adj.* Of or pertaining to Bahrain or the Bahrainis. M20.

baht /bɑːt/ *n.* Pl. same. E19. [Thai *bāt*.] The basic monetary unit of Thailand, equal to 100 satangs.

bahut /bay/ *n.* Pl. pronounced same. M19. [Fr.] An ornamental chest or cabinet.

Bahutu *n.* pl. of HUTU.

bahuvrihi /bahʊˈvriːhi/ *a.* & *n.* M19. [Skt *bahuvrīhi*, f. *bahu* much + *vrīhi* rice (as a typical compound of this type).] *Gram.* (Designating) an exocentric compound adjective or noun.

baignoire /bɛɲwaːr/ *n.* Pl. pronounced same. M19. [Fr. = bath-tub.] A box at a theatre on the same level as the stalls.

bail /beɪl/ *n.*[1] ME. [OFr. *bail*, *bail(l)e* power, custody, jurisdiction, delivery, f. *baillier* take charge of, receive, hand over, deliver f. L *bajulare* bear a burden, manage, f. *bajulus* carrier. Senses 2–5 are peculiarly English, and their development is uncertain.] †1 Custody, charge, jurisdiction. ME–L16. †2 The friendly custody of a person otherwise liable to be kept in prison, upon security given for his or her appearance at a time and place assigned. LME–E19. 3 Temporary delivery or release of a prisoner who provides security to appear for trial. LME. 4 Security given for the release of a prisoner awaiting trial. L15. 5 The person(s) acting as surety (now only by financial guarantee) for a prisoner's appearance for trial. L16.

1 SPENSER Faunus, now within their baile. 5 SHAKES. *2 Hen. VI* The sons of York . . Shall be their father's bail. G. GREENE He ought to be brought before a magistrate. . . I will stand bail for any reasonable amount. *fig.*: THACKERAY Ye'll spend it like a man of spirit—I'll go bail for that.

Phrases: **admit to bail** allow to be released on bail. **deny bail** = *refuse bail* below. **forfeit (one's) bail**: by failing to appear for trial after release on bail. *give leg bail*: see LEG *n.* **grant bail** allow the prisoner to be released on bail. *hold to bail*: see HOLD *v.* **jump bail** *colloq.* fail to appear for trial after release on bail. *justify bail*: see JUSTIFY *v.* 6. **on bail** (with permission to be temporarily released from custody) on provision of security to appear for trial. **refuse bail** not allow the prisoner to be released on bail. *surrender to bail*: see SURRENDER *v.* 1d.

Comb.: **bail-bond** the bond or security entered into by a bail; **bail bondsman** = *bailsman* below; **bail-jumper** *colloq.* a person who fails to appear for trial after release on bail; **bail-jumping** *colloq.* failure to appear for trial after release on bail; **bailsman** a person who gives bail for another.

bail /beɪl/ *n.*[2] ME. [OFr. *bail*, *bail(l)e* palisade, enclosure (cf. *baillier* enclose), perh. f. L *baculum* rod. Cf. BAILEY.] 1 The wall of the outer court of a feudal castle; by extension, a wall of an inner court; one of the courts themselves; in *pl.*, an outer line of fortification formed of stakes, palisades. ME. 2†a A crossbar. Only in L16. **b** *Cricket.* Either of two wooden crosspieces (formerly a single crosspiece) placed over the stumps (cf. WICKET 3). M18. 3 A bar to separate horses standing in an open stable. M19. 4 A framework for securing the head of a cow at milking. *Austral.* & *NZ.* M19. 5 On a typewriter, a hinged bar that holds the paper against the platen. M20.

Comb.: **bail-dock** *Hist.* at the Old Bailey, a small open-topped room formed from the corner of the court and used to accommodate accused persons.

†bail *n.*[3] ME–M19. [Fr. *baille* bucket f. Proto-Gallo-Romance f. L *bajulus* carrier: cf. BAIL *n.*[1]] *Naut.* A bucket or scoop for bailing water from a boat.

bail /beɪl/ *n.*[4] LME. [Prob. f. ON *beygla* f. *beygja* = OE *bēgan*, *byġan* bend, bow.] A hoop or ring, *esp.* a half-hoop for supporting the cover of a wagon; the hoop-handle of a kettle, pail, etc.

bail /beɪl/ *v.*[1]*t.* M16. [f. BAIL *n.*[1] or (sense 3) immed. f. Fr. *baillier*.] 1 Of a magistrate etc.: grant bail to, release on bail. M16. 2 Obtain the release of (a person) by providing security for his or her later appearance; provide bail for. L16. 3 Deliver (goods) in trust for a specified purpose. M18.

2 **bail out** release from imprisonment by providing bail; *fig.* release from (esp. financial) difficulty.

bailable *a.* entitled to be released on bail; admitting of or providing for bail: M16. **bailage** *n.* (*Hist.*) a duty on delivery of goods M16. **bailment** *n.* (*a*) delivery in trust; (*b*) the action or process of bailing a person: M16.

bail /beɪl/ *v.*[2] Exc. in sense 1, only *Austral.* & *NZ.* L16. [App. f. OFr. *baillier* enclose, shut, rel. to *baille* BAIL *n.*[2]: the priority of *baille* or *baillier* is uncertain.] 1 *v.t.* Confine. *rare.* L16. 2 *v.t.* Secure the head of (a cow) in a bail while milking. Usu. foll. by *up.* M19. 3 *v.t.* Make (a person) hold up the arms to be robbed; detain or buttonhole (a person); corner (a wild animal). Usu. foll. by *up.* M19. 4 *v.i.* Surrender (by throwing up the arms). Usu. foll. by *up.* M19.

bail /beɪl/ *v.*[3] Also (esp. sense 2) **bale**. E17. [f. BAIL *n.*[3]] 1 *v.t.* & *i.* Scoop (water) out of a boat; scoop water out of (a boat). Freq. foll. by *out.* E17. 2 *v.i.* Foll. by *out*: jump out of an aircraft, make an emergency descent by parachute; (of a surfer) leave the surfboard. M20.

¶In sense 2 usu. spelt *bale*, as if the action were that of letting a bundle through a trapdoor; but also (esp. *N. Amer.*) spelt *bail*, as if the action were that of scooping out.

Ba-ila *n.* & *a.* see ILA.

bailee /beɪˈliː/ *n.* E16. [f. BAIL *v.*[1] + -EE[1].] A person to whom goods are delivered in trust.

bailer /ˈbeɪlə/ *n.*[1] M19. [f. BAIL *v.*[3] + -ER[1].] A utensil or machine for bailing water etc.

Comb.: **bailer-shell** = *melon-shell* s.v. MELON *n.*[1] & *a.*

bailer /ˈbeɪlə/ *n.*[2] Now *rare.* M19. [f. BAIL *n.*[2] + -ER[1].] *Cricket.* A ball that hits the bails.

bailer *n.*[3] var. of BAILOR.

bailey /ˈbeɪli/ *n.* ME. [Prob. f. OFr. *bail*, *bail(l)e* (whence med.L *ballium*, *ballia*): see BAIL *n.*[2]] 1 The outer wall and first line of defence of a castle; *gen.* any of a castle's defensive circuits. ME. 2 The outer court of a castle; any of the courts enclosed between the circuits of walls or defences. E16.

2 **Old Bailey** the seat of the Central Criminal Court in London, which formerly stood in the ancient bailey of the city wall between Lud Gate and New Gate.

Bailey bridge /ˈbeɪli brɪdʒ/ *n. phr.* M20. [Sir D. Coleman *Bailey* (1901–85), Eng. engineer, its designer.] A bridge of lattice steel designed for rapid assembly from prefabricated parts, used esp. in military operations.

bailie /ˈbeɪli/ *n.*[1] Also **-ll-**. ME. [OFr. *bailli(s)*: see BAILIFF.] 1 = BAILIFF. *obs.* exc. *dial.* ME. 2 *Sc.* **a** The chief magistrate of a barony or part of a county. Long *obs.* exc. *Hist.* LME. **b** A municipal councillor serving as a magistrate. Now *Hist.* exc. as an honorary title conferred on a senior councillor. LME.

bailiery /ˈbeɪlɪəri, -lɪri/ *n.* (*Sc.*, *obs.* exc. *Hist.*) the office or jurisdiction of a bailie; the district under the jurisdiction of a bailie: LME. **bailieship** *n.* (*obs.* exc. *Hist.*) = BAILIWICK LME.

†bailie *n.*[2] var. of BAILLIE *n.*[1]

bailiff /ˈbeɪlɪf/ *n.* ME. [OFr. *baillif* obl. case of *bailli(s)* f. med.L *bajulivus* (*ballivus*) adj., f. *bajulus* carrier, manager, administrator: cf. BAIL *n.*[1]] 1 *Hist.* (exc. in formal titles). A person charged with public administrative authority in a certain district; in England, a representative of the monarch, *esp.* the chief officer of a hundred; in Jersey and Guernsey, the first civil officer, appointed by the Crown. ME. 2 An officer of justice under a sheriff, who executes writs and processes, and performs distraints and arrests. ME. 3 The agent of the lord of a manor, who collects rents, etc.; the steward or manager of an estate or farm; the agent of a landlord. ME.

bailiffship *n.* the office of bailiff LME. **†bailiffwick** *n.* the office of bailiff; the district under a bailiff's jurisdiction: LME–M18.

bailiwick /ˈbeɪlɪwɪk/ *n.* LME. [f. BAILIE *n.*[1] + -WICK.] 1 A district or place under the jurisdiction of a bailiff. LME. **b** *transf.* A person's concern or sphere of operations. Chiefly *joc.* M19. 2 The office or jurisdiction of a bailiff. *obs.* exc. *Hist.* LME.

1 *Encycl. Brit.* They [the Channel Islands] are . . grouped into two distinct bailiwicks of Guernsey and Jersey, with differing constitutions. **b** E. ROOSEVELT I established the fairly well-understood pattern that affairs of state were not in my bailiwick.

bailliage /ˈbeɪlɪɪdʒ/ *n.* LME. [Fr., f. *bailli*: see BAILIFF, -AGE.] The jurisdiction or district of a bailiff (now usu. in a foreign country).

†baillie *n.*[1] Also **bailie**, **-lly**. ME–M18. [OFr., f. *baillir* have under one's jurisdiction etc.: cf. med.L *bajulia* tutelage etc.: see BAIL *n.*[1], -Y[3].] The office or jurisdiction of a bailiff; delegated authority.

baillie *n.*[2] var. of BAILIE *n.*[1]

†bailly *n.* var. of BAILLIE *n.*[1]

bailor /beɪˈlɔː/ *n.* Also **-er** /-ə/. L16. [f. BAIL *v.*[1] + -OR.] A person who delivers goods in trust. Occas. now also = *bailsman* s.v. BAIL *n.*[1]

bailout /ˈbeɪlaʊt/ *n.* In sense 1 also **bale-**. M20. [f. *bail out* s.v. BAIL *v.*[3] 2, *v.*[1] 2.] 1 An act of bailing out from an aircraft; an emergency descent by parachute. M20. 2 An act of bailing out a person or organization; a release from (esp. financial) difficulty. L20.

Baily's beads /ˈbeɪlɪz biːdz/ *n. phr.* M19. [Francis *Baily* (1774–1844), Eng. astronomer.] *Astron.* The appearance of the sun's crescent as a string of brilliant points at the beginning or end of totality in a solar eclipse.

báinín *n.* var. of BAWNEEN.

bain-marie /banməˈriː, *foreign* bɛ̃mari/ *n.* Pl. **bains-** (pronounced same). E18. [Fr., tr. med.L *balneum Mariae* tr. med.Gk *kaminos Marias* furnace of Maria, a supposed Jewish alchemist.] A vessel of hot water in which cooking-pans and their contents are slowly heated; a double saucepan. Also, a dish prepared in this.

Bairam /bʌɪˈrɑːm/ *n.* L16. [Turk. †*baïrām* (now *bayram*), ult. f. Pers. *bazrām*.] Either of two annual Muslim festivals, the *Lesser Bairam*, lasting one day, which follows the fast of Ramadan, and the *Greater Bairam*, lasting three days, seventy days later.

bairn /bɛːn/ *n.* Chiefly *Sc.*, *north.*, & *literary.* Also (*north.*) **barn** /bɑːn/. [OE *bearn* = OS, OHG, ON, Goth. *barn*, f. Gmc, rel. to BEAR *v.*[1]] A child; a young son or daughter.

Comb.: **bairn's part** *Sc. Law* = LEGITIME *n.* 2; **bairn-team, -time** *north.* a family of children.

bairnly *a.* childish, childlike M16.

†baisemain *n.* M17–M18. [Fr.] A kiss of the hands; in *pl.*, compliments, respects.

bait /beɪt/ *n.*[1] ME. [ON *beit* (neut.) pasture, *beita* (fem.) food; in part f. BAIT *v.*[1]] 1 Food placed on a hook or in a trap to entice fish or animals as prey; *fig.* an allurement, temptation. ME. 2 Food, refreshment, esp. a feed for horses or a meal for travellers on a journey. *obs.* exc. in *dial.* sense, a snack taken between meals. L15. 3 A stop on a journey for refreshment or rest. *arch.* L15.

1 I. WALTON Let your bait fall gently upon the water. DEFOE The profits of trade are baits to the avaricious shopkeeper. A. HAILEY Nim knew he . . was rising to the bait, probably just as Birdsong intended. *ground-bait*, *ledger-bait*, *spoon-bait*, etc. *smig bait* etc. *live bait*: see LIVE *a.*

bait *n.*[2] var. of BATE *n.*[4]

bait /beɪt/ *v.*[1] ME. [ON *beita* hunt or chase with dogs or hawks (= OE *bǣtan*, OHG *beizen*, G *beizen*), causative of *bíta* BITE *v.* Senses 6 & 7 prob. f. BAIT *n.*[1]] 1 *v.t.* Worry or torment (a chained or confined animal) by setting dogs at it; attack with dogs for sport. ME. 2 *v.t. fig.* Harass or persecute (a more or less helpless person) persistently; worry or torment; cause (a person) to be troubled or annoyed *with* something. ME. 3 *v.t.* & *i.* Attack with endeavour to bite and tear, as dogs attack a confined animal. LME. 4 *v.t.* Give food and drink to (an animal), esp. on a journey. *arch.* LME. b *v.i.* Of an animal: feed. *arch.* LME. 5 *v.i.* Stop on a journey to take food or rest. LME. 6 Put bait in or on (a trap, hook, fishing-place, etc.). LME. 7 *v.t.* Offer bait to; allure, entice. Chiefly *fig.* L16.

1 SHAKES. *2 Hen. VI* We'll bait thy bears to death. 2 S. JOHNSON I will not be baited with *what* and *why*. R. HUGHES There was not even any fun to be got out of baiting her; nothing seemed to ruffle her temper. 3 W. SOMERVILLE Raving he foams, and howls, and barks, and bates. 4 THACKERAY Whilst their horses were baited, they entered the public room. 5 R. B. SHERIDAN To bait here a few days longer, to recover the fatigue of his journey. *fig.*: MILTON Evil news rides post, while good news baits. 6 POPE My absent mates . . Bait the barb'd steel. *fig.*: L. DURRELL The Tripartite Conference was . . rumoured to be a trap, baited by an unacceptable constitution. 7 SHAKES. *Merch. V.* Why, . . thou wilt not take his flesh. What's that good for? To bait fish withal. E. ROOSEVELT He would . . bait me into giving an opinion by stating a point of view with which he knew I would disagree.

baiter *n.* E17.

bait *v.*[2] var. of BATE *v.*[1]

baittle *a.* see BATTLE *a.*

baity *a.* var. of BATEY.

baize /beɪz/ *n.* & *v.* L16. [Fr. *baies* fem. pl., use as n. of *bai* reddish brown, BAY *n.*[7] (so named presumably from its original colour).] A *n.* 1 A coarse usu. green woollen stuff with a long nap, used for coverings and linings. L16. 2 A curtain or covering of baize. E19.

Phrases: *green baize*: see GREEN *a.*

B *v.t.* Cover or line with baize. M19.

¶The pl. form *baies* was early taken as a sing.; the form *baize* was not established bef. 19.

bajada /bəˈhɑːdə/ *n.* Orig. *US.* Also **bah-**. M19. [Sp. = descent, slope.] A broad slope of alluvial material at the foot of an escarpment.

Bajan /ˈbeɪdʒ(ə)n/ *n.* & *a. colloq.* M20. [Repr. a pronunc. of BADIAN *n.*[2] & *a.*] = BARBADIAN.

Bajau /ˈbadʒaʊ/ *n.* & *a.* M19. [Origin unkn.] A *n.* 1 A member of a nomadic maritime people (formerly notorious as pirates) found throughout the islands and coastal areas of Kalimantan, Sulawesi, and eastern Indonesia to New Guinea and northern Australia (also called *sea gypsy*). M19. 2 The Austronesian language of this people. M19. B *attrib.* or as *adj.* Of or pertaining to the Bajaus or their language. L19.

bajra /ˈbɑːdʒrɑː/ *n.* Also **-ri** /-riː/. E19. [Hind. *bājrā*, *bājrī*.] In the Indian subcontinent: pearl millet or a similar grain.

baju /ˈbɑːdʒuː/ *n.* E19. [Malay.] A short loose jacket worn in Malaysia and Indonesia.

bake /beɪk/ *n.* M16. [f. the vb.] 1 The act or process of baking; baked food. M16. 2 A biscuit, a small cake. *Sc.* E17. 3 A social gathering, esp. for eating baked food. *US.* M19.

bake /beɪk/ *v.* Pa. ·pple **baked**, (*arch.* & *dial.*) **baken** /ˈbeɪk(ə)n/. [OE *bacan* str. vb = OHG *backan*, ON *baka*, f. Gmc f. IE; rel. to Gk *phōgein* roast, parch. The weak form *baked* appeared as a pa. t. bef. 15 and as a pa. pple by 16 (it is the only form in Shakes.).] I *v.t.* 1 Cook by dry heat acting by conduction and not by radiation, as in an oven or on a heated surface. OE. 2 Harden by heat. LME. †3 Form into a cake or mass. LME–L17. 4 Of the sun: ripen (fruit), tan (the skin). L17.

1 SMOLLETT My bread is . . baked in my own oven. DICKENS We have half a leg of mutton, baked, at a quarter before three. A. THOMAS Bake the aubergines in an oiled dish for about 45 minutes. J. BRONOWSKI The women . . bake bread—in the biblical manner, in unleavened cakes on hot stones. *bake blind*: see BLIND *adv.* 2 F. NORRIS All Tulare County . . was bone-dry, parched, and baked and crisped after four months of cloudless weather. J. C. RICH The clay form that is to be baked hard must be adequately . . dried *before* it is placed in the kiln. *transf.*: SHAKES. *Temp.* Th' earth when it is bak'd with frost. 3 DONNE The old dirt is still baked on my hands. 4 DRYDEN The Vine her liquid Harvest yields, Bak'd in the Sun-shine.

II *v.i.* 5 Cook a batch of bread, cakes, etc. ME. 6 Undergo cooking by dry heat; be cooked, hardened, or tanned by heat; *colloq.* become uncomfortably hot. LME.

5 W. FAULKNER Now that she had a stove to bake in. 6 J. R. GREEN The cakes which were baking on the hearth. OED These apples do not bake well. M. SHARP 'I'm going to bake' thought Julia . . and indeed the plain . . shimmered under a heat mist. R. CARRIER The warm and spicy smell of apple pie baking in the oven.

Comb.: **bakeapple** *Canad.* the (dried) fruit of the cloudberry; **bakehouse** a house or room with an oven for baking bread; †**bake-meat** a pie, pastry; **bakeware** vessels, trays, etc., used in baking.

baked /beɪkt/ *a.* M16. [f. prec. + -ED[1].] Cooked by dry heat; hardened by heat; *colloq.* uncomfortably hot.

baked beans haricot beans baked, and usu. tinned in tomato sauce. †**baked-meat** = *bake-meat* s.v. BAKE *v.* **baked potato** a potato baked in its skin. *half-baked*: see HALF-.

Bakelite /ˈbeɪkəlʌɪt/ *n.* Also **b-**. E20. [f. Leo H. *Baekeland* (1863–1944), Belgian-born US chemist + -ITE[1].] (Proprietary name for) a characteristically dark brown thermosetting plastic made by copolymerization of a phenol with formaldehyde.

baken *v.* see BAKE *v.*

baker /ˈbeɪkə/ *n.* [OE *bæcere*, f. as BAKE *v.* + -ER[1].] A person who bakes; *esp.* one who bakes and sells bread.

baker's bread bread baked professionally by a baker. **baker's dozen** thirteen (the 13th loaf representing the retailer's profit). *the butcher, the baker, the candlestick-maker*: see BUTCHER *n.*

bakery *n.* a baker's work, baked items; a place where baked products are made or sold: M16.

Baker day /ˈbeɪkə deɪ/ *n. phr. colloq.* L20. [f. Kenneth *Baker*, Brit. Education Secretary (1986–9), who introduced the practice.] Any of several days in the normal school year statutorily set aside for in-service training for teachers.

bakestone /ˈbeɪkstəʊn/ *n. dial.* Also **back-** /ˈbak-/. ME. [f. BAKE *v.* + STONE *n.*] A flat stone or metal plate on which cakes are baked in the oven.

Bakewell /ˈbeɪkwɛl/ *n.* M19. [A town in Derbyshire, N. England.] *Bakewell pudding, tart*, a baked tart of pastry lined with jam and filled usu. with an almond paste.

baking /ˈbeɪkɪŋ/ *n.* ME. [f. BAKE *v.* + -ING[1].] 1 The action of BAKE *v.*; cooking by dry heat, esp. of bread, cakes, etc.; hardening by heat. ME. 2 The product of baking; (a batch of) baked items, esp. bread, cakes, etc. LME.

Comb.: **baking-powder** a mixture of sodium bicarbonate, cream of tartar, etc., used instead of yeast to make cakes etc. rise; **baking sheet** a metal tray used for baking cakes etc.; *baking soda*: see SODA 2C.

baking /ˈbeɪkɪŋ/ *a.* L18. [f. BAKE *v.* + -ING[2].] That bakes; *colloq.* extremely or uncomfortably hot.

bakingly *adv.* M19.

baklava /ˈbɑːkləvə/ *n.* M17. [Turk.] A dessert made of thin pieces of flaky pastry, honey, and nuts.

baksheesh /bakˈʃiːʃ/ *n.* & *v.* Also **back-**. M18. [Ult. f. Pers. *bakšiš*, f. *bakšīdan* give.] A *n.* In Eastern countries: a gratuity, a tip. M18. B *v.t.* Give a gratuity to, tip. M19.

bal /bal/ *n. obs.* exc. *dial.* E17. [Corn. = tin-mine.] A mine in Cornwall.

Balaam /ˈbeɪlam/ *n.* M17. [The prophet in *Num.* 22–4.] 1 A person who follows religion for profit. M17. 2 Superfluous or trivial material used to fill up a column. *Journalists' slang.* E19.

Comb.: **Balaam basket** an editor's container for unwanted material.

Balaamite *n.* = BALAAM 1 M16.

Balaclava /baləˈklɑːvə/ *n.* L19. [A village near Sebastopol in the Crimea, site of a battle fought in 1854.] In full *Balaclava helmet*. A woollen covering for the head and neck, worn orig. by soldiers on active service.

balalaika /baləˈlʌɪkə/ *n.* L18. [Russ., of Tartar origin.] A musical instrument of the guitar kind, with a triangular body and from two to four strings, popular in Slavonic countries.

balance /ˈbal(ə)ns/ *n.* ME. [(O)Fr. f. Proto-Romance f. late L *bilanc-*, *bilanx* (in *libra bilanx* balance having two scales), f. *bi-* BI- + *lanx* scale.] I A physical object. 1 An apparatus for weighing, consisting of a beam poised so as to move freely on a central pivot, with a scale pan at each end. ME. b Any apparatus used in weighing, *esp.* a spring or lever substitute for the above. E19. 2 (Usu. **B-**.) *The* constellation and zodiacal sign Libra; the Scales. LME. †3 Either scale of a balance; in *pl.* (occas. w. *sing.* form) scales. LME–M17. 4 A counterpoise. *rare* in *lit.* sense. E17. 5 In full *balance-wheel*. A mechanical device which regulates the speed of a clock or watch. M17.

II Gen. *fig.* senses. 6 The metaphorical balance of justice, reason, or opinion, by which actions and principles are weighed or estimated. ME. †b Either scale of this. L16–M17. 7 The wavering of fortune or chance, by which issues hang in suspense. ME. †b Uncertainty. ME–L17. 8 Power to decide or determine. LME. 9 A thing of equal importance; a counterbalancing consideration etc.; a set-off. E17. 10 Equilibrium; the even distribution of weight or amount (of things ponderable and imponderable). M17. 11 Stability due to equilibrium between the forces within a system; (ability to maintain) steadiness of position; *transf.* mental stability. M17. 12 General harmony between the parts of anything; *esp.* in *Art* etc., harmony of proportion and design. M18. b *spec.* (The sound produced by) the adjustment of the relative positions, volume levels, etc., of sources of sound. E20. 13 The preponderating weight or amount. M18.

8 G. B. SHAW The balance is held in my constituency by the tradesmen and shopkeepers. 9 J. R. GREEN If France . . had ceased to be a balance to Spain, she found a new balance in Flanders. 10 W. DERHAM Such alterations in the æquipoise or ballance of the Atmosphere. D. H. LAWRENCE Life is so made that opposites sway about a trembling centre of balance. X. J. KENNEDY Hovering scale-pans . . Settled their balance slow as silt. T. BENN The balance between freedom and security poses special difficulty in political democracies. 11 E. K. KANE If my mind had retained its balance. E. ALBEE Her balance is none too good, and she bumps into or brushes against the door chimes by the door. N. GORDIMER He stands with his hands on his hips, for balance, looking down into the hole. 13 H. P. BROUGHAM The balance of evidence appears in favour of the due execution.

III The adjustment of accounts. 14 (The process of finding) the difference between credits and debits; a statement of the results. L16. 15 The difference between the debit and credit sides of an account. E17. 16 An equality between the total of the two sides of an account (cf. sense 10 above). M17. 17 A sum remaining (either *in hand* or *due*) after the settlement or partial settlement of an account or accounts; *colloq.* the rest, the remainder. E18.

14 L. P. HARTLEY This increase of personal worth, which the bank balance so eloquently conveyed. 15 A. CRUMP Such arrangements may continue for years without the balance ever being a credit-balance. 16 GLADSTONE While we exported £8,860,000, we imported £8,509,000. That is very nearly a balance. 17 S. UNWIN I sent for water, and after he had had a drink, spilt the balance over his head. J. CLAVELL We still haven't had a down payment, let alone the balance.

Phrases: *balance due, balance in hand*: see sense 17 above. **balance of mind** sanity. **balance of nature** a state of equilibrium in nature produced by the interaction of living organisms; ecological balance. **balance of payments** the difference of value between the payments into and out of a country, including invisible exports and imports. **balance of power** a state of international equilibrium with no nation predominant. **balance of terror** balance of power based on the possession of terrifying weapons, esp. nuclear weapons. **balance of trade** the difference between a country's exports and imports. **be** or **hang in the balance** be uncertain. **keep one's balance** not fall; maintain physical or mental stability. **lose one's**

balance fall or stumble physically; become upset mentally. **off balance** in danger of falling; confused; unprepared. **on balance** taking everything into consideration. *Roman balance*: see ROMAN *a. spiral balance*: see SPIRAL *a.*[1] **strike a balance** determine the difference between two sides of an account (*lit.* & *fig.*); arrive at a medial position or course.

Comb.: **balance sheet** a written statement of the assets and liabilities of an organization on a particular date; **balance spring** = *hairspring* s.v. HAIR *n.*; *balance-wheel*: see sense 5 above.

balance /ˈbal(ə)ns/ *v.* L16. [(O)Fr. *balancer*, f. as prec.] I *gen.* **1** *v.t.* Weigh in or with a balance. *rare* in *lit.* sense. L16. **2** *v.t.* Weigh (two or more arguments, considerations, etc.) against each other; consider with a view to making a choice. L16. **3** *v.t.* Equal in weight; neutralize the weight of; make up for. L16. **4** *v.t.* Counterbalance or match (one thing) *by, with,* or *against* another. E17. **5** *v.t.* Weigh (a matter or problem); ponder. M17. **6** *v.t.* Bring into or keep in equilibrium (*lit.* & *fig.*); keep steady or erect. M17. **b** *spec.* Adjust (sources of sound) to the correct relative positions, volume levels, etc. E20. **7** *v.i.* Waver, deliberate, hesitate. *arch.* M17. **8** *v.i.* Keep steady or erect, esp. as a feat of acrobatics or dancing. E19.

2 YEATS I balanced all, brought all to mind, The years to come seemed waste of breath. J. LE CARRÉ Do you think they sit like monks . . balancing the rights and wrongs? 3 R. LYND The craving for getting things done is balanced . . by the craving for leaving things undone. A. J. P. TAYLOR They were reinforced by Irish immigrants and made a number of intellectual converts, roughly balancing the old Catholics who lapsed. 4 J. RUSKIN A mass of subdued colour may be balanced by a point of a powerful one. T. HARDY And don't you know that a woman who loves at all thinks nothing of perjury when it is balanced against her love? 5 TENNYSON She balanced this a little, And told me she would answer us to-day. 6 DICKENS Strong men . . balancing chests of drawers . . upon their heads. G. MURRAY The future seemed about equally balanced between good and evil. SCOTT FITZGERALD He was balancing himself on the dashboard of his car. F. CHICHESTER I trimmed the tail as delicately as I could to balance the plane, but she would not stabilize. S. HILL Dorothea stood alone, . . balancing the two pots in her hand. 7 C. MERIVALE The same disposition to balance and temporize. 8 J. STRUTT Tumbling and balancing . . exhibited by the gleemen. *fig.*: *Times Lit. Suppl.* The East-West balancing act of Rapallo.

II *spec.* Of an account (*lit.* & *fig.*). **9** *v.t.* Add up and compare the debit and credit sides of (an account or set of accounts). L16. **10** *v.t.* Make entries in (an account or set of accounts) that will make the two sides equal; of an entry: make the two sides of (an account) equal. E17. **11** *v.t.* Settle (an account) by paying the amount due. M18. **12** *v.i.* Of an account: have its two sides equal. L19.

balanceable *a.* M17. **balanced** *a.* poised, in equilibrium; well arranged or disposed; with no constituent lacking or in excess: L16. **balancer** *n.* (*a*) a person who balances, *esp.* an acrobat; (*b*) a thing which balances; *spec.* = HALTERE 2: LME.

balancé /balɑ̃se/ *n.* Pl. pronounced same. L18. [Fr. = balanced (sc. *pas* step).] *Dancing.* A swaying step from one foot to the other.

balancing /ˈbal(ə)nsɪŋ/ *vbl n.* L16. [f. BALANCE *v.* + -ING[1].] The action of BALANCE *v.*

Comb.: **balancing act** an (acrobatic) act involving feats of balance; *fig.* a maintaining of equilibrium or harmony in difficult circumstances.

balanitis /baləˈnʌɪtɪs/ *n.* M19. [f. Gk *balanos* acorn, glans penis + -ITIS.] *Med.* & *Vet. Med.* Inflammation of the glans penis.

balanoid /ˈbalənɔɪd/ *a.* & *n.* M19. [f. mod.L *Balanus* genus name f. L *balanus* f. Gk *balanos* acorn, + -OID.] *Zool.* (Of, pertaining to, or being) an acorn barnacle (see ACORN).

balao /bəˈlaʊ/ *n.* Also **ballahoo** /baləˈhuː/. M19. [Sp. *balajú*.] The half-beak.

balas /ˈbaləs/ *n.* LME. [(O)Fr. *balais* f. med.L *balascus*, *-cius* f. Arab. *balakš*, f. Pers. *Badakš(ān)*, a district in Afghanistan, where it is found.] A delicate rose-red variety of the spinel ruby. Now usu. more fully *balas-ruby*.

balata /ˈbalətə, bəˈlɑːtə/ *n.* Also **ball-**, (earlier) †**barratta**. E17. [Carib *balatá*.] (The wood of) any of a number of tropical American trees of the sapodilla family, spec. *Manilkara bidentata*. Also, the dried latex of this tree, used as a substitute for gutta-percha.

¶In isolated use bef. 19.

balboa /balˈbəʊə/ *n.* E20. [f. Vasco Núñez de *Balboa* (*c*1475–1519), Sp. explorer and discoverer of the Pacific Ocean.] The basic monetary unit of Panama, equal to 100 centésimos.

Balbriggan /balˈbrɪg(ə)n/ *n.* & *a.* L19. [A town near Dublin in Ireland, where orig. made.] (Of) a knitted cotton fabric used esp. for underwear.

balcony /ˈbalkəni/ *n.* E17. [It. *balcone* (whence also Fr. *balcon*, Sp. *balcón*), prob. f. Gmc base repr. by BAULK *n.* w. augm. suff.: see -OON.] **1** A railed or balustraded platform projecting from the wall of a building, with access from an upper-floor window. E17. **2** In a theatre: formerly, a stage-box; now usu. a tier of seats above the dress circle; the gallery; *N. Amer.* the dress circle. In a cinema etc.: an upper tier of seats. E18.

¶Until E19 usually w. pronunc. /balˈkəʊni/, but /ˈbalkəni/ occurs in Swift (E18).

balconied *a.* having a balcony M18.

bal costumé /bal kɔstyme/ *n. phr.* Pl. ***bals costumés*** (pronounced same). E19. [Fr.] A fancy-dress ball.

bald /bɔːld/ *a.* ME. [Prob. f. a base meaning orig. 'white patch' + -ED[2]. In branch I perh. f. BALL *n.*[1]] †I **1** Round, ball-shaped; rotund, corpulent. Only in ME.

II **2** Lacking hair on part or all of the scalp. ME. **3** Lacking hair on other parts of the body. Of an animal etc.: hairless, featherless. ME. **4** *fig.* Devoid of force; meagre, dull, basic, unadorned; (of bad qualities) undisguised. LME. **5** Of things: without the usual or natural covering; treeless; leafless; napless; worn bare; (of a tyre, *colloq.*) having lost its tread by wear. E17.

2 J. D. SALINGER He was one of those bald guys that comb all their hair over from the side to cover up the baldness. G. VIDAL Completely bald, his neat round head shone pinkly under the indirect lights. L. DEIGHTON The crown of his head was bald, but a natural wave gave him curls across the ears and over his collar. 4 BOSWELL Tom Davies repeated, in a very bald manner, the story of Dr. Johnson's first repartee to me. H. T. COCKBURN In towns the great modern object has . . been to reduce everything to the dullest and baldest uniformity. J. R. LOWELL A bald egotism which is quite above and beyond selfishness. L. M. MONTGOMERY Just stick to bald facts. Begin at the beginning. 5 SHAKES. *A.Y.L.* Under an oak, whose boughs were moss'd with age, And high top bald with dry antiquity. E. BOWEN A bald patch in the carpet under her desk. L. SIMPSON My right front tyre is as bald as Odysseus. P. THEROUX The bald hills, stripped of all foliage, were rounded on their slopes.

III **6** Streaked or marked with white (cf. Welsh *ceffyl bal* a horse with a white streak or mark on its face). LME.

Phrases: **as bald as a coot** completely bald.

Comb. & *special collocations*: **bald coot, baldicoot** a coot (because of its white plate on the forehead); *fig.* a bald-headed person; *bald cypress*: see CYPRESS *n.*[1] 1b; **bald eagle** a white-headed, white-tailed, fish-eating eagle, *Haliaeetus leucocephalus*, the national emblem of the US; **baldhead** a person who has a bald head; *transf.* a white-crowned American wigeon, *Anas americana*; **bald-headed** *a.* = sense 2 above; *go bald-headed* (colloq.), proceed (*at, for, into*) regardless of the consequences; **bald ibis** either of two ibises of the genus *Geronticus*, which have bare heads (cf. WALDRAPP); **baldpate** = *baldhead* above.

balding *a.* going bald M20. **baldish** *a.* E19. **baldly** *adv.* in a bald, basic, or dull manner; meagrely; undisguisedly: E17. **baldness** *n.* LME. **baldy** *n.* & *a.* (*colloq.*) (*a*) *n.* a bald person; a bald head; (*b*) *adj.* (somewhat) bald: M19.

baldachin /ˈbaldəkɪn, ˈbɔːld-/ *n.* Also **-quin**. L16. [It. *baldacchino*, f. (with suff. *-ino* -INE[1]) *Baldacco* It. form of *Baghdad*, its place of origin. Cf. BAUDEKIN.] **1** A rich embroidered material, orig. woven with woof of silk and warp of gold thread; rich brocade. L16. **2** (Now the usual sense.) A canopy (orig. made of the material in sense 1), supported on columns or fixed to a roof or wall, and placed over an altar, throne, or doorway. M17.

baldachined *a.* covered with a baldachin E20.

balderdash /ˈbɔːldədaʃ/ *n.* & *v.* L16. [Origin unkn.] A *n.* †**1** Frothy liquid. *rare.* Only in L16. †**2** A jumbled mixture of liquors, e.g. of milk and beer, beer and wine, etc. Only in 17. **3** *transf.* A senseless jumble of words; nonsense, trash (spoken or written). L17. †**B** *v.t.* Make a jumbled mixture of (liquors); adulterate *with*. L17–E19.

baldicoot *n.* see s.v. BALD *a.*

baldmoney /ˈbɔːldmʌni/ *n.* LME. [Origin unkn.] **1** Gentian. *obs.* exc. *Sc.* LME. **2** = SPIGNEL. L16.

baldric /ˈbɔːldrɪk/ *n.* ME. [Cf. MHG *balderich*, of uncertain origin (doubtfully referred to L *balteus* belt); occas. early forms f. OFr. *baudré*.] **1** *Hist.* A belt or girdle, usu. richly ornamented, hung from the shoulder across the body to the opposite hip, and used to support a sword, bugle, etc. ME. †**2** A leather strap etc. by which the clapper of a church bell was suspended. LME–L19. †**3** A necklace. M16–M19.

1 *fig.*: SPENSER Those twelve signes which nightly we do see The heavens bright-shining baudricke to enchace.

bale /beɪl/ *n.*[1] *arch.* & *poet.* [OE *balu* (*bealu*) = OFris., OS *balu*, OHG *balo*, ON *bǫl*, f. Gmc.] **1** Evil, esp. as an active and destructive force; a malign influence; woe, harm, injury. In early use freq. *spec.* death. OE. **2** Evil as something suffered; physical torment, pain, misery. ME. **3** Mental suffering; misery, sorrow, grief. ME.

¶Marked obs. in Dicts. from E17; after that rare until 19.

baleless /-l-l-/ *a.* (long *arch.*) harmless, innocent OE.

bale /beɪl/ *n.*[2] *arch.* [OE *bǣl* = ON *bál* great fire, cogn. w. Skt *bhāla* lustre, Gk *phalos* shining, bright. In ME and mod. Eng. f. ON *bál*. Much confused w. BALE *n.*[1], esp. in *balefire* below).] †**1** *gen.* A great consuming fire, a conflagration. OE–E19. **2** *spec.* a A funeral pile or pyre. OE. **b** A signal- or beacon-fire. *Sc.* LME.

Comb.: **balefire** a great open-air fire, esp. a funeral pyre; a beacon-fire.

bale /beɪl/ *n.*[3] & *v.*[1] ME. [Prob. f. MDu. *bale* (Du. *baal*) f. OFr. *bale* (later and mod. *balle*); ult. identical w. BALL *n.*[1]] A *n.* **1** A package of merchandise, orig. round in shape, now usu. compressed, wrapped in canvas etc., and tightly corded or hooped; the quantity in a bale, used varyingly as a measure. ME. †**2** A set of dice. L15–E19.

Comb.: **bale-goods** merchandise in bales.

B *v.t.* Make up into a bale or bales. M18.

baler *n.* L19.

bale *v.*[2] see BAIL *v.*[3]

Balearic /balɪˈarɪk/ *a.* M17. [L *Balearicus*, f. *Balearis* adj. (*Baleares insulae* the islands listed below): see -IC.] Designating, of, or pertaining to a group of islands off the east coast of Spain, comprising Majorca, Minorca, Ibiza, and Formentera, and seven smaller islands.

Balearian *a.* & *n.* (*rare*) (*a*) *adj.* = BALEARIC; (*b*) *n.* a native or inhabitant of the Balearic Islands: E17.

balection *a.* & *n.* var. of BOLECTION.

baleen /bəˈliːn/ *n.* ME. [(O)Fr. *baleine* whale, f. L *balaena*.] †**1** A whale. ME–E17. **2** Whalebone. ME. †**3** Some kind of fish, perhaps sea bream. ME–L16.

Comb.: **baleen whale** any whale of the suborder Mysticeti, members of which yield whalebone.

baleful /ˈbeɪlfʊl, -f(ə)l/ *a.* OE. [f. BALE *n.*[1] + -FUL.] **1** Pernicious, destructive, malignant (physically or morally). OE. **2** Miserable; distressed, sorrowful. *arch.* ME.

balefully *adv.* LME. **balefulness** *n.* L16.

baleout *n.* see BAILOUT.

†**balester** *n.* var. of BALISTER.

balibuntal /balɪˈbʌnt(ə)l/ *n.* E20. [f. *Baliuag* in the Philippines, where it originated + BUNTAL.] A fine close-woven straw, used for hats.

Balinese /bɑːlɪˈniːz/ *a.* & *n.* E19. [f. *Bali* (see below) + -ESE, after Du. *Balinees*.] A *adj.* Of or pertaining to the island of Bali in Indonesia. E19.

B *n.* Pl. same. A native or inhabitant of Bali; the Indonesian language of Bali. E19.

balinger /ˈbalɪndʒə/ *n. obs.* exc. *Hist.* LME. [AN *balyngere* = med.L *balingaria*, *-gera* whaleboat, *-arius* a kind of warship, MFr. (north.) *balenghier(e)*, *balengier*, (O)Fr. *baleinier* whaler, f. as BALEEN.] A small seagoing sailing vessel without a forecastle, used mainly for coastal trade.

†**balister** *n.* Also **-est-**. ME–E18. [OFr. *balestre* = med.L *balistarius*, *-est-*, f. L BALLISTA: see -ER².] A crossbowman; = ARBALESTER.

balk *n.*, *v.* var. of BAULK *n.*, *v.*

Balkan /ˈbɒlkən, ˈbɔːl-/ *a.* & *n.* M19. [Turk. *balkan* chain of wooded mountains, name of a chain in Bulgaria: assim. to wds in -AN.] **A** *adj.* Designating, of, or pertaining to a mountain chain in Bulgaria, and (by extension) the peninsula bounded by the Adriatic, Aegean, and Black Seas, or the countries or peoples of this region. M19. **B** *n.* In *pl.* *The* Balkan mountains (formerly also *sing.*); *the* Balkan countries. M19.

Balkaniˈzation *n.* the action of Balkanizing an area E20. **Balkanize** *v.t.* divide (an area) into smaller mutually hostile States E20.

ball /bɔːl/ *n.*¹ ME. [ON *ball-*, *bǫllr* (OSw. *baller*, Sw. *båll*) f. Gmc.] **1** A globular body. ME. **b** *spec.* A planetary or celestial body. Now always w. specifying wd. ME. **2** A spheroid used in games or play, varying greatly in size, material, and degree of hardness, and inflated or solid, according to the purpose for which it is intended. ME. **b** A game played with a ball. ME. **c** A single throw, kick, or other kind of delivery of a ball in the course of a game (freq. w. specifying wd indicating the nature or quality of the movement); *Baseball* (esp.) a single delivery of the ball by a pitcher outside specified limits and not struck at by the batter. L15. **3** A globular or rounded mass of any substance. ME. **b** *spec.* A large pill or capsule of medicine. Now only in *Vet. Med.* LME. **4** In *pl.* The testicles; *fig.* (treated as *sing.*) nonsense, a muddle, an unsuccessful attempt. Now *coarse slang.* ME. **b** Manliness, power, strength; courage, nerve. *slang.* M20. **5** Any rounded protuberant part of the body, *esp.* that at the base of the thumb or the big toe. ME. †**6** An orb as a symbol of sovereignty. LME–E18. **7** A solid non-explosive missile (orig. always spherical) fired from a cannon, rifle, pistol, etc. (In small arms now usu. called *bullet*.) LME. **8** The eye within the lids and socket (formerly, the pupil). LME. **9** A small wooden or ivory sphere used in voting (cf. BALLOT *n.*). L16. **10** A leather-covered pad used by printers for inking type. *obs.* exc. *Hist.* L16. †**11** A rounded package. Cf. BALE *n.*³ L16–L18.

1 M. W. MONTAGU The . . tents . . are adorned on the top with guilded balls. R. E. VERNÈDE The sun's a red ball in the oak. R. CAMPBELL A kind of sweet known as Moor Balls, flavoured with anis. D. ATTENBOROUGH All the flagella around the sphere beat in an organised way and drive the tiny ball in a particular direction. **ball and chain, chain and ball** a heavy metal ball secured by a chain to the leg of a prisoner or convict to prevent escape; *fig.* a severe hindrance, *esp.* (*colloq.*, *derog.*, or *joc.*) one's wife. *claw-and-ball*: see CLAW *n.*¹ *red ball*: see RED *a.* **three balls** a pawnbroker's sign. **b** ADDISON What, though in solemn silence all Move round the dark terrestrial ball. **2** *billiard ball, cricket ball, rugby ball, tennis ball,* etc.; (also sense 2b) *baseball, basketball, football, handball, netball, volleyball,* etc. **be on the ball** be in contact with or playing the ball in a team game; *fig.* (*colloq.*) be competent, sharp, or alert. **have one's eye** (or **something**) **on the ball** *fig.* be paying attention, be alert. **have the ball at one's feet** *fig.* be able to take advantage of opportunity, be in a controlling position. **keep one's eye on the ball** *fig.* remain alert. **keep the ball rolling** *fig.* play one's part in a conversation, an undertaking, etc. **run with the ball** *fig.* take and maintain control, keep the initiative. *see off the new ball*: see SEE *v.* *spot-ball*: see SPOT *n.* 6b. **start the ball rolling** *fig.* initiate a conversation, an undertaking, etc. *the ball is in your court*: see COURT *n.*¹ *trap and ball*: see TRAP *n.*¹ **b play ball (with)** *fig.* (*colloq.*) act fairly, cooperate, (with). **c** S. RAVEN Nigel had sent him down some five or six balls, all of which he played correctly and neatly. C. POTOK He ignored it completely, and the umpire called it a ball. *base on balls*: see BASE *n.*¹ *no-ball*: see NO *a.* *short ball*: see SHORT *a.* *sinker-ball*: see SINKER *n.*¹ 7. **3** AV *Sus.* 1:17 Bring me oil & washing balls. F. MARRYAT You had a ball of twine. **ball of fire** (*a*) *slang* a glass of brandy; (*b*) a person of great energy or spirit. SNOWBALL *n.* 4 B. MARSHALL What do you mean by talking all that unpatriotic balls? S. BECKETT I've made a balls of the fly. BALLS-UP. **b** M. PUZO What gives you the balls to think I'd leave my wife for you? **5** J. STEINBECK One foot was to the ground, the other rested on the ball. **6** SHAKES. *Hen. V* The balm, the sceptre, and the ball, The sword, the mace, the crown imperial. **7** J. C. OATES A thirty-two-pound ball was fired by the British. F. SMYTH The leaden ball extracted from the dead man by a surgeon. *collect.*: LD MACAULAY A body of troops . . was ordered to load with ball. **8** SIR W. SCOTT Raising his sightless balls to heaven. EYEBALL. **9** *black ball, blackball*: see BLACK *a.*

Comb.: **ball(-and-socket) joint** a form of joint having a rounded end in a concave cup or socket, allowing great freedom of movement; **ball-bearing** a bearing in which friction is reduced by the use of small balls; a ball for this purpose; **ballboy** one who retrieves balls for the players in lawn tennis; **ball-breaker, -buster** *coarse slang* a sexually demanding woman, a woman who destroys men's self-confidence; **ball clay** a very adhesive clay, *esp.* a fine-textured clay used in the manufacture of earthenware; **ballcock** an automatic device with a floating ball, to control the level of water in a cistern; **ball-court** an area (such as a paved yard) for the playing of ball games; **ball flower** *Archit.* an ornament resembling a ball within the petals of a flower; **ball game** a game played with a ball; *spec.* (*N. Amer.*) a game of baseball; *colloq.* a particular affair or concern (esp. in *whole new ball game* & vars.); **ball hawk** *N. Amer. slang* a skilled ball player; a footballer etc. who is quick to get possession of the ball; *Baseball* a defensive outfielder skilled in catching fly balls; **ball-hawk** *v.i.* (*N. Amer. slang*) be quick to get possession of the ball in a game of football etc.; *ball joint*: see *ball-and-socket joint* above; **ball lightning** a rare globular form of lightning; **ballpark** *N. Amer.* a baseball ground; *colloq.* an area, a region, (*lit.* & *fig.*), esp. in *in the right ballpark*, close to one's objective, approximately correct; *ballpark figure*, a rough estimate; **ball-peen, -pein** *a.* (of a hammer) having a ball-shaped peen; **ball-point (pen)** a pen having a tiny ball as its writing point; **ball-proof** *a.* able to withstand the impact of a cannon etc. ball; **balls-aching** *a.* (*coarse slang*) annoying, boring.

ball-like *a.* resembling (that of) a ball, globular L19.

ball /bɔːl/ *n.*² E17. [(O)Fr. *bal* dance, f. †*bal(l)er* to dance f. late L *ballare* rel. to Gk *ballein* to throw (cf. Gk *ballizein* to dance).] **1** A formal social assembly for dancing, usu. with an organized programme and accompanied by special entertainment. E17. **2** A wildly enjoyable time. Esp. in *have (oneself) a ball. colloq.* M20.

1 *hunt ball*: see HUNT *n.*² MASKED *ball*. **open the ball** *fig.* begin operations.

Comb.: **ballroom** a large room in which balls are held; *ballroom dancing*, dancing of a type usual at balls (by couples, dances including the foxtrot, waltz, tango, and rumba, old-time dances, and sometimes folk-dances).

ball /bɔːl/ *n.*³ Chiefly *Anglo-Ir.* E20. [Origin unkn.] A glass *of* (an alcoholic drink).

S. O'CASEY There's nothin' like a ball o' malt occasional like.

ball /bɔːl/ *v.*¹ L16. [f. BALL *n.*¹] **1** *v.t.* Round or swell out. *rare.* L16. **2** *v.t.* Make into a ball; wind (thread) *off* into a ball; clench or screw up (the fist) tightly; roll *up* into a ball-like mass. M17. **3** *v.i.* Gather into a ball. E18. **4** *v.i.* Become clogged or blocked, esp. with snow. Also foll. by *up*; *fig.* make a mess of something, fail. M18. **5** *v.t.* Clog, block. Also foll. by *up*. M19. **b** Bring into a state of confusion or difficulty; make a mess of. Usu. foll. by *up*. *slang.* L19. **6** *v.t.* & *i.* Of a man (*v.i.* also of a woman): have sexual intercourse (with). *N. Amer. slang.* M20.

2 E. K. KANE Brooks balls off twine. P. GALLICO Small hands balled into possessive fists. E. CRISPIN This handkerchief, balled up in Mavis's hand. **3** SOUTHEY In clogs . . snow balls under the wooden sole. **5** A. BRONTË The snow . . clogged the wheels and balled the horses' feet. J. HERRIOT Not merely a few of the hair-like worms irritating the tubes, but great seething masses of them crawling everywhere, balling up and blocking the vital air passages. **b** N. COWARD You can't even do a straight walk off without balling it up. **6** G. VIDAL You can tell the world all about those chicks that you ball.

baller *n.* (chiefly *techn.*) a person who or a machine which makes balls E19. **balling** *vbl n.* (*a*) the action of the vb; (*b*) the administration of medicine to an animal in the form of a capsule (usu. *attrib.* as *balling-gun* etc., an instrument for this purpose): E18.

ball /bɔːl/ *v.*² M17. [f. BALL *n.*²] **1** *v.i.* Attend a ball or balls. M17. **2** *v.t.* Entertain at a ball. M19. **3** *v.i.* Enjoy oneself greatly, have a wildly enjoyable time. *N. Amer. slang.* M20.

ballabile /baˈlaːbile/ *n.* Pl. ***-li*** /-li/. M19. [It., f. *ballare* to dance.] A dance by the *corps de ballet* or by the chorus in an opera; a piece of music for this; any piece of instrumental music suggestive of a dance.

ballad /ˈbaləd/ *n.* & *v.* L15. [(O)Fr. *ballade* f. Prov. *balada* dance, song or poem to dance to, f. *balar* to dance: cf. BALL *n.*²] **A** *n.* **1** A light, simple song; *spec.* †(*a*) a song intended to accompany a dance; (*b*) a sentimental or romantic composition of two or more verses each sung to the same melody. L15. **b** A popular song, *esp.* one attacking persons or institutions. *obs.* exc. *Hist.* M16. **c** A popular narrative song in slow tempo. E20. †**2** A proverbial saying, usu. in the form of a couplet. E16–E17. **3** A lively poem in short stanzas, in which a popular narrative is graphically told (orig. sung). M18.

Comb.: **ballad-monger** a person who deals in ballads (used *contempt.*, orig. by Shakes.).

B *v.* **1** *v.i.* Compose or sing a ballad or ballads (*about*, †*against*). Now *rare.* L16. †**2** *v.t.* Compose or sing a ballad about. E17–E18.

1 R. GRAVES The best of all years to ballad about. **2** SHAKES. *Ant. & Cl.* Scald rhymers [will] Ballad us out o' tune.

ballaˈdeer *n.* a person who sings or composes ballads M19. **ballader** *n.* a writer of ballads L16. **baˈlladic** *a.* pertaining to or of the nature of ballads M19. **balladize** *v.i.* & *t.* compose a ballad or ballads (about) L16. **balladry** *n.* composition in ballad style L16.

ballade /baˈlɑːd/ *n.* & *v.* LME. [f. as prec., w. differentiation of application.] **A** *n.* **1** A poem (orig. for singing with accompaniment) of one or more triplets of stanzas having 7, 8, or 10 lines, each usu. ending with the same refrain line, and an envoy; more *gen.*, a poem divided into stanzas of equal length, usu. of 7 or 8 lines. Also *collect.*, poetry of this form. LME. **2** *Mus.* An extended, usu. dramatic, piece usu. for the piano. M19.

1 ballade royal = *rhyme royal* s.v. RHYME *n.*

†**B** *v.i.* Compose ballades. Only in LME.

ballahoo *n.* var. of BALAO.

ballahou /baləˈhuː/ *n.* M19. [Sp. *balahú* schooner.] *Naut.* A type of fast two-masted schooner. Also, an ungainly vessel. Cf. BALLYHOO *n.*¹

ballan /ˈbalən/ *n.* M18. [Ir. *ballán*, f. *ball* spot.] In full *ballan wrasse*. A wrasse, *Labrus bergylta*, usu. green or greenish-brown.

ballast /ˈbaləst/ *n.* & *v.* M16. [Prob. f. LG or Scand., in OSw. and ODa. *ballast*, *barlast* (taken to be from *bor* bare or *barm* hull (of a ship) + *last* burden).] **A** *n.* **1** A heavy substance, such as gravel, sand, iron, or lead, placed in the bilge of a ship to ensure its stability. M16. **b** A substance, usu. sand or water, carried in an airship or balloon-car to stabilize it, and jettisoned for higher flight. L18. **2** *fig.* That which gives stability in morals or politics; experience or principles regarded as reinforcing character. E17. **3** Gravel or coarse stone used to form the bed of a railway track or the substratum of a road. M19. **4** A passive component used in an electric circuit in order to moderate changes of current. Freq. *attrib.* E20.

1 in ballast (of a ship) laden with ballast only. **2** I. WALTON Having to his great Wit added the ballast of Learning. H. T. COCKBURN Delay is often the ballast of sound legislation.

Comb.: **ballast-tank**: that can be flooded with water to allow a submarine to dive.

B *v.t.* **1** Provide (a ship etc.) with ballast; fill or steady with ballast. M16. **2** Load with cargo; *fig.* burden or weigh down, steady. Now only *arch.* in *fig.* sense. M16. **3** Form (the bed of a railway line etc.) with ballast. M19.

ballasting *n.* (*a*) the action of the vb; (*b*) = BALLAST *n.*: M16.

ballata /ba'la:ta, bə'lɑ:tə/ *n.*[1] Pl. **-te** /-te, -ti/. M18. [It. f. Prov. *balada*: see BALLAD.] An Italian ballad; an old Italian verse-form in which the refrain occurs at the beginning and the end of each stanza.

ballata *n.*[2] var. of BALATA.

ballate *n.* pl. of BALLATA *n.*[1]

ballerina /balə'ri:nə/ *n.* Pl. **-nas**, †**-ne**. L18. [It., fem. of *ballerino* dancing-master, f. *ballare* to dance: see BALL *n.*[2]] A female ballet-dancer, *esp.* one who undertakes a leading role in classical ballet.

PRIMA BALLERINA.

ballet /'baleɪ, -li/ *n.* M17. [Fr. f. It. *balletto* dim. of *ballo* BALL *n.*[2]] 1 (A theatrical performance of) dancing and mime to music; a company performing this. M17. †2 *gen.* A dance. L18–E19.

1 ***ballet d'action*** /bale daksjɔ̃/, pl. ***ballets d'action*** (pronounced same), [Fr. = of action] a dramatic ballet, a ballet with a plot. CORPS *de ballet*. *maître de ballet*: see MAÎTRE 1a. RUSSIAN *ballet*. *symphonic ballet*: see SYMPHONIC 3.

Comb.: **ballet-master** a trainer of ballet dancers.

balletic /bə'letɪk/ *a.* of, pertaining to, or characteristic of ballet M20. **ba'lletically** *adv.* M20. **balletomane** /'balɪtəmeɪn/ *n.* an enthusiast for ballet M20. **balletomania** /,balɪtə'meɪnɪə/ *n.* enthusiasm for ballet M20.

ballist /'balɪst/ *n. rare.* LME. [f. as next.] = next.

ballista /bə'lɪstə/ *n.* Pl. **-stae** /-sti:/, **-stas**. E16. [L, ult. f. Gk *ballein* to throw.] A military engine used in antiquity for hurling stones and other missiles.

ballistic /bə'lɪstɪk/ *a.* L18. [f. prec. + -IC.] Of or pertaining to projectiles or their flight; moving under the action of no force except gravity.

ballistic galvanometer: with little or no damping, used to measure transient currents. **ballistic missile, rocket**: moving under gravity only, after an initial period of powered, guided flight.

ballistically *adv.* in a ballistic manner; as regards ballistics: L19. **ballistician** /balɪ'stɪʃ(ə)n/ *n.* an expert in ballistics E20.

ballistics /bə'lɪstɪks/ *n.* M18. [f. as prec. + -ICS.] The science of the motion of projectiles; *esp.* that part of the subject connected with firearms.

exterior, interior ballistics: dealing respectively with motion after and during the period when a projectile is subject to propulsive force or guidance. *terminal ballistics*: see TERMINAL *a.*

ballistocardiograph /bə,lɪstə'kɑ:dɪəgrɑ:f/ *n.* M20. [f. BALLISTIC *a.* + -O- + CARDIOGRAPH.] An instrument for recording the movements of the body caused by ejection of blood from the heart at each beat.

ballistocardiogram *n.* the record made by a ballistocardiograph M20. **ballistocardio'graphic** *a.* M20. **ballistocardi'ography** *n.* M20.

ballium /'balɪəm/ *n.* L18. [med.L f. as BAIL *n.*[2]] = BAILEY 1.

ballock /'bɒlək/ *n.* Now *coarse slang.* See also BOLLOCK *n.* [OE *bealluc* dim. of Gmc base of BALL *n.*[1]] 1 A testicle. Usu. in *pl.* OE. 2 *fig.* In *pl.* (treated as *sing.*) Nonsense; a mess, a muddle. Also as *int.* M20.

ballock /'bɒlək/ *v.t. coarse slang.* Also **bollock**. M20. [f. the n.] Reprimand severely. Freq. as *ballocking* vbl n.

ballon /balɔ̃/ *n.* Pl. pronounced same. M19. [Fr.: see BALLOON.] 1 Elasticity and buoyancy in dancing; smooth passage from step to step. M19. 2 = BALLOON *n.* 3b. M20.

¶See also *ballon*-SONDE.

ballon d'essai /balɔ̃ desɛ/ *n. phr.* Pl. ***ballons d'essai*** (pronounced same). L19. [Fr. = trial balloon.] An experiment to see how a new policy or project will be received; a tentative proposal.

ballonet /'balənɛt/ *n.* Also **-nn-**. E20. [Fr. *ballonnet* dim. of *ballon* BALLOON *n.*: see -ET[1].] A compartment in a balloon or airship into which air or another gas can be forced in order to maintain the craft's shape as buoyant gas is released.

ballonné /balɔne/ *n.* Pl. pronounced same. L18. [Fr., pa. pple of *ballonner* swell or puff out, distend.] A bouncing step in dancing.

ballonnet *n.* var. of BALLONET.

ballons d'essai *n. phr.* pl. of BALLON D'ESSAI.

balloon /bə'lu:n/ *n.* & *v.* L16. [Fr. *ballon* or It. *ballone* augm. of *balla* BALL *n.*[1]: see -OON.] A *n.* †1 (A game played with) a large inflated leather ball, struck to and fro with the arm protected by a bracer of wood. L16–E19. †2 A pasteboard ball filled with combustible matter, projected into the air as a firework. M17–M19. 3 A spherical glass with a narrow neck or mouth; *spec.*: †a *Chem.* A receiving-vessel of this shape. L17–M19. b A brandy goblet of this shape. M20. 4 A usu. round or pear-shaped airtight envelope designed to rise into the air when inflated with hot air or another gas that is lighter than air; *esp.* one carrying a basket or car for passengers. L18. b A small rubber pouch with a neck, which is inflated with air for use esp. as a child's toy. M19. 5 A round or pear-shaped outline containing words, *esp.* those in a cartoon or comic strip representing a person's words or thoughts and shown as issuing from the mouth or head. M19. 6 *fig.* A high hit or kick given to a ball. *colloq.* E20.

3b M. GEE Cradling brandy . . in his elegant glass balloon. 4 *fig.*: CARLYLE The hollow balloon of popular applause. *barrage balloon*: see BARRAGE *n.* *captive balloon*: see CAPTIVE *a.* 1. **(when) the balloon goes up** (when) the action, excitement, or trouble starts. 5 DICKENS Diabolical sentiments . . were represented as issuing from his mouth in fat balloons. D. L. SAYERS I'm afraid it's rather full of marginal balloons and interlineations.

Comb.: **balloon angioplasty** *Med.* a technique in which a tiny balloon is passed along a blood-vessel and inflated to remove a clot or other blockage; **balloon barrage** a connected system of balloons and cables used as a defence against hostile aircraft; **balloon-fish** a puffer-fish; **balloon-flower** = PLATYCODON; **balloon frame** *Archit.*: of light timbers nailed together; **balloon glass, goblet** = sense 3b above; **balloon sleeve** a large sleeve puffed out over the upper arm; **balloon tyre** a low-pressure pneumatic tyre with a large cross-section; **balloon vine** a tropical American vine, *Cardiospermum halicacabum*, which bears inflated pods.

B *v.* 1 *v.t.* Lift up in or as in a balloon. *rare.* L18. 2 *v.i.* Travel in a balloon. Chiefly as *ballooning* vbl n. L18. 3 *v.i.* & *t.* Swell, puff out; distend. M19. 4 *v.t.* Hit or kick (a ball) high in the air. *colloq.* E20. 5 *v.i.* Of an aircraft: rise up in the air, esp. as a result of a hard landing. E20.

3 I. MURDOCH His shirt ballooned out over his trousers. S. BRETT His face . ., ballooned out with indignation. T. KENEALLY The doctor was forced to work with a ballooning face, now half again its normal size. *fig.*: *Poetry Nation Review* What started with a perfectly defensible basis has ballooned out of all proportion.

ballooner, -ist *ns.* a person who travels in a balloon L18.

ballot /'balət/ *n.* M16. [It. *ballotta* dim. of *balla* BALL *n.*[1]] 1 A small ball used for secret voting; a ticket, paper, etc., so used. M16. 2 The system of or an instance of secret voting, orig. by means of small balls placed in an urn or box; the number of votes thus recorded. M16. 3 Lot-drawing, orig. by taking out small balls etc. from a box. L17.

2 G. M. TREVELYAN Protected by the ballot, the agricultural labourer could vote as he wished, regardless of farmer and landlord. B. CASTLE In the ballot the railwaymen voted six to one to escalate the dispute into a national strike. *second ballot*: see SECOND *a.* *short ballot*: see SHORT *a.*

Comb.: **ballot-box** a box used to contain ballot-papers etc., esp. to preserve secrecy; *fig.* election by ballot; **ballot-paper** the voting-paper used in a ballot.

ballot /'balət/ *v.* M16. [It. *ballottare*, f. as prec.] I†1 *v.t.* Vote by ballot on (a proposal, candidate, etc.). M16–L17. 2 *v.i.* Give a (usu. secret) vote (*for, against*). M16. 3 *v.t.* Take a ballot of (a body of voters). L19. II 4 *v.i.* Draw lots (*for*). E17. 5 *v.t.* Select (esp. conscripts) by the drawing of lots. L18.

balloter *n.* a voter by ballot M18.

ballottement /bə'lɒtm(ə)nt/ *n.* M19. [Fr.] *Med.* Palpation of a fluid-filled part of the body to detect a floating object, *spec.* of the uterus to discover the presence or position of the foetus.

†**ballow** *n. dial. rare.* E17–L19. [Origin unkn.] A cudgel; a truncheon.

SHAKES. *Lear* Whether your costard or my ballow be the harder.

balls /bɔ:lz/ *v.t. slang.* M20. [f. BALL *n.*[1] 4.] Mess *up.* Cf. BALL *v.*[1] 5b.

balls-up /'bɔ:lzʌp/ *n. slang.* M20. [f. prec.] A confusion or muddle, a mess.

ballsy /'bɔ:lzi/ *a. slang.* M20. [f. BALL *n.*[1] + -S[1] + -Y[1].] Manly, powerful; courageous; having or requiring nerve.

bally /'bali/ *a.* & *adv. slang.* L19. [Alt. of BLOODY *a.* & *adv.*, perh. f. the written form *bl—y.*] = BLOODY *a.* & *adv.* as a vague intensive; confounded(ly); unpleasant(ly); very.

ballyhoo /balɪ'hu:/ *n.*[1] M19. [Perh. f. as BALLAHOU.] *Naut.* More fully *ballyhoo of blazes.* A vessel that one dislikes.

ballyhoo /balɪ'hu:/ *n.*[2] & *v.* Orig. *US.* L19. [Origin unkn.] A *n.* A showman's touting speech; bombastic nonsense; extravagant or brash publicity; noisy fuss. L19. B *v.t.* Cajole by ballyhoo; praise or advertise extravagantly. E20.

ballyrag /'balɪrag/ *v. dial.* & *slang.* Also **bully-** /'bʊlɪ-/. Infl. **-gg-**. L18. [Origin unkn.] 1 *v.t.* Overawe; intimidate; maltreat by jeering at or playing practical jokes on. L18. 2 *v.i.* Jeer; indulge in horseplay or practical jokes. E19.

balm /bɑ:m/ *n.*[1] ME. [OFr. *ba(s)me* f. L *balsamum* BALSAM *n.*] 1 A fragrant and medicinal exudation from certain trees (see sense 5 below). ME. †2 An aromatic preparation for embalming. ME–E17. 3 Fragrant oil or ointment; *fig.* fragrance, perfume. LME. 4 Aromatic ointment used for soothing pain or healing wounds; *fig.* a healing or soothing influence, consolation. LME. 5 A tree yielding a fragrant and medicinal exudation; *esp.* an Asian and N. African tree of the genus *Commiphora* (family Burseraceae). LME. 6 Any of various fragrant herbs; *spec.* (more fully *lemon balm*) a labiate herb, *Melissa officinalis*, with lemon-scented leaves. LME.

3 SHAKES. *Rich. II* Not all the water in the rough rude sea Can wash the balm from an anointed king. J. THOMSON When nought but balm is breathing thro' the woods. 4 MILTON As Balm to fester'd wounds. D. WELCH The stillness in the room was balm. A. STORR No amount of recognition could have brought balm to that tortured soul.

Phrases etc.: **balm of Gilead** [*balm* in Coverdale *Gen.* 37:25, earlier rendered *resin*] (*a*) (a fragrant medicinal gum from) any of various trees, *spec.* of the genus *Commiphora*; (*b*) a balsam poplar, *Populus candicans*; (*c*) *balm of Gilead fir* = *balsam fir* s.v. BALSAM *n.* **bastard balm** a labiate herb of European woodland, *Melittis melissophyllum*, with leaves smelling of new-mown hay. MOLUCCA *balm*.

Comb.: **balm-apple** = *balsam apple* s.v. BALSAM *n.*

balm *n.*[2] var. of BARM *n.*[2]

balm /bɑ:m/ *v.*[1]*t. arch.* ME. [App. f. BALM *n.*[1]] 1 Embalm. ME. 2†a Anoint (with oil etc.). LME–E17. b Smear with something sticky; daub. *obs.* exc. *dial.* LME. 3 Soothe or alleviate (pain, sorrow, etc.). LME.

balm *v.*[2] var. of BARM *v.*

bal masqué /bal maske/ *n. phr.* Pl. ***bals masqués*** (pronounced same). M18. [Fr.] A masked ball.

balm-cricket /'bɑ:mkrɪkɪt/ *n.* Also †**baum-**. M17. [Partial tr. G *Baumgrille* lit. 'tree cricket', alt. after BALM *n.*[1]] A cicada.

Balmer /'bɑ:mə/ *n.* L19. [J. J. *Balmer* (1825–98), Swiss physicist.] *Physics.* Used *attrib.* & (now *rare*) in *possess.* to designate (the mathematical formula describing) a series of lines in the visible and ultraviolet spectrum of atomic hydrogen, between 656 and 365 nanometres.

balmoral /bal'mɒr(ə)l/ *n.* Also **B-**. M19. [f. *Balmoral* Castle, a royal residence in Grampian, Scotland.] 1 In full *Balmoral boot.* A stout front-lacing ankle boot. M19. 2 *Hist.* In full *Balmoral petticoat.* A stiff woollen or horsehair under-petticoat. M19. 3 A round flat cap worn by some Scottish regiments. L19.

bal musette /bal myzɛt/ *n. phr.* Pl. ***bals musettes*** (pronounced same). E20. [Fr.] In France, a popular dancehall (with an accordion band).

balmy /ˈbɑːmi/ *a.*^{1} LME. [f. BALM *n.*^{1} + -Y^{1}.] 1 Fragrant, aromatic, or soothing like balm. LME. 2 Deliciously soft and soothing; pleasant. E17. 3 Of the weather, air, etc.: mild and fragrant. E17. 4 Yielding or producing balm. M17.

1 M. R. MITFORD Under the shade of those balmy firs. E. IRVING The cure for a disease, is to send.. balmy medicines. 2 E. YOUNG Tir'd Nature's sweet restorer, balmy Sleep! G. CLARE Those happy and balmy days for fathers, when they and their wishes were immediately obeyed. 3 G. SANTAYANA The next spring was singularly balmy Crocuses and snowball blossoms were out in April. C. SAGAN A time.. of balmy temperatures, soft nights.

balmily *adv.* M19. **balminess** *n.* M18.

balmy *a.*^{2} var. of BARMY.

balneal /ˈbalnɪəl/ *a.* M17. [f. L *balneum* bath + -AL^{1}.] Of or pertaining to a (warm) bath or bathing.

balneary /ˈbalnɪəri/ *n.* & *a.* M17. [L *balnearium* bathing-place, use as n. of neut. of *balnearius* adj., f. *balneum* bath: see -ARY^{1}.] A *n.* A bath or bathing-place; a medicinal spring. M17. B *adj.* Of or pertaining to baths or bathing. L19.

balneo- /ˈbalnɪəʊ/ *comb. form* of L *balneum* bath: see -O-.

balneoˈlogical *a.* of or pertaining to balneology L19. **balneˈologist** *n.* an expert in or student of balneology L19. **balneˈology** *n.* the branch of knowledge that deals with the medicinal effects of bathing and mineral springs M19. **balneoˈtherapy** *n.* the treatment of disease by bathing, esp. in mineral springs L19.

Baloch, -chi *n.* & *a.* see BALUCHI.

baloney *n.* var. of BOLONEY.

baloo /bəˈluː/ *n.* & *int. obs.* exc. *dial.* Also **balow** /bəˈləʊ/. E17. [App. a nursery wd of unkn. origin.] A lullaby. As *int.*, used to lull a child to sleep.

balsa /ˈbɒlsə/ *n.* E17. [Sp. = raft.] 1 A raft or fishing boat, used chiefly on the Pacific coasts of S. America. E17. 2 A tropical American tree, *Ochroma pyramidale* (more fully *balsa tree*); its strong, very light wood, used for rafts, floats, etc. (more fully *balsa-wood*). M19.

balsam /ˈbɔːlsəm, ˈbɒl-/ *n.* OE. [f. L *balsamum* f. Gk *balsamon*, perh. of Semitic origin (cf. Arab. *balasān*).] 1 A resinous exudation from various trees, *esp.* = BALM *n.*^{1} I. OE. b *spec. Chem.* A resinous product which is insoluble in water and is a source of benzoic or cinnamic acid. L17. 2 A tree yielding balsam; = BALM *n.*^{1} 5. OE. 3 An aromatic ointment or other resinous medicinal preparation; *esp.* one of various substances dissolved in oil or turpentine. L16. b *fig.* A healing or soothing agency. E17. †4 *Alch.* A healthful preservative essence considered by Paracelsus to exist in all organic bodies. M17–M18. †5 = BALM *n.*^{1} 2; *fig.* a preservative. M17–M18. 6 Any plant of the genus *Impatiens* (see IMPATIENS), *esp.* (*a*) (more fully *garden balsam*) *Impatiens balsamina*, native to southern and eastern Asia and cultivated for its showy pink flowers; (*b*) (in full *Himalaya balsam*) *I. glandulifera*, a large Himalayan plant with purplish-pink flowers now widely naturalized along streams in Europe and N. America (also called *policeman's helmet*). M18.

1 *Canada balsam*: see CANADA I. 3 FRIAR*'s balsam*. TOLU *balsam*. b TENNYSON Was not the people's blessing.. a balsam to thy blood?

Comb.: **balsam apple** (the fruit of) the tropical gourd *Momordica balsamina*; **balsam fir** a common N. American fir, *Abies balsamea*, yielding Canada balsam; **balsam pear** (the pear-shaped fruit of) the tropical gourd *Momordica charantia*; **balsam poplar** any of several N. American poplars, esp. *Populus balsamifera*, whose buds exude a fragrant gum.

balsamic /bɔːlˈsamɪk, bɒl-/ *a.* & *n.* (*a*) *adj.* having the properties of balsam; fragrant; soothing; yielding balsam; (*b*) *n.* a soothing medicine: E17. **balsaˈmiferous** *a.* yielding balsam L17. †**balsamine** *n.* (*a*) = *balsam-apple* above; (*b*) = *garden balsam* (sense 6 above): L16–M19. **balsamy** *a.* like balsam in fragrance, balmy L17.

balsam /ˈbɔːlsəm, ˈbɒl-/ *v.t.* M17. [f. the n.] Anoint or impregnate with balsam.

†**balsamum** *n.* OE–M17. [L: see BALSAM *n.*] Balm; balsam.

bals costumés, masqués, musettes *n. phrs.* pls. of BAL COSTUMÉ etc.

Balt /bɔːlt, bɒlt/ *n.* L19. [Late L *Balthae* pl.] A native or (esp. German) inhabitant of one of the Baltic States.

balter /ˈbɒltə/ *v.*^{1}*i. obs.* exc. *dial.* LME. [Prob. f. ON: cf. Da. *baltre*, *boltre* wallow, welter, tumble.] Tumble about; walk unsteadily.

balter /ˈbɒltə/ *v.*^{2} *obs.* exc. *dial.* Also **bolter**. E17. [Perh. frequent. of BALL *v.*^{1}] 1 *v.t.* Clot, clog; tangle (the hair). E17. 2 *v.i.* Become tangled; form into lumps or balls. E17.

Balthazar /balˈθazə, ˈbalθəzɑː/ *n.* Also **-sar**, **Belshazzar** /bɛlˈʃazə/. M20. [The King of Babylon who 'made a great feast.. and drank wine before the thousand' (*Dan.* 5:1).] A very large wine bottle, usually holding the quantity of sixteen regular bottles.

Baltic /ˈbɔːltɪk, ˈbɒlt-/ *a.* & *n.* L16. [med.L *Balticus*, f. as BALT: see -IC.] A *adj.* 1 Designating, of, or pertaining to an almost land-locked sea separating Scandinavia from the rest of Europe. L16. 2 Designating a branch of the Indo-European languages comprising Lithuanian, Latvian, and Old Prussian, usu. classified with the Slavonic group (see BALTO-). L19.

1 **the Baltic States** Lithuania, Latvia, and Estonia, which border the Baltic Sea betwen Poland and Russia.

B *n. The* Baltic Sea; *the* lands bordering on it. E18.

Baltimore /ˈbɔːltɪmɔː, ˈbɒlt-/ *n.* M17. [Lord *Baltimore* (*c* 1580–1632), Eng. proprietary of Maryland, the bird's colours being those of his coat of arms.] In full *Baltimore oriole, bird*. A N. American oriole, *Icterus galbula galbula*, coloured bright orange and black.

¶See also *Lady Baltimore* (*cake*) s.v. LADY *n.* & *a.*

Balto- /ˈbɔːltəʊ, ˈbɒltəʊ/ *comb. form.* [f. BALTIC + -O-.] Forming combs. in the sense 'Baltic and —'.

Balto-Slaˈvonic *a.* & *n.* (designating, of, or pertaining to) the group of Indo-European languages which comprises the Baltic branch and the Slavonic branch. E20.

Baluchi /bəˈluːtʃi/ *n.* & *a.* Also **-lochi** /-ˈləʊtʃi/; **-ch**. E17. [Pers. *Balūč(ī)*.] A *n.* A native or inhabitant of Baluchistan, a region lying between the lower Indus and SE Iran; the Iranian language of Baluchistan. E17. B *adj.* Of or pertaining to the people or language of Baluchistan. M19.

baluster /ˈbaləstə/ *n.* E17. [Fr. *balustre* f. It. *balaustro*; so named from It. *balausta*, *balaustra* blossom of the wild pomegranate (L *balaustium*, Gk *balaustion*), which a baluster resembles in shape.] 1 A short pillar or column of circular section and with a curving outline, usu. one of a series called a balustrade. Also, a similar pillar used in a window. E17. 2 A slender upright post helping to support a rail. M17. b Usu. in *pl.* = BANISTER. M18. 3 *collect. sing.* = BALUSTRADE. *arch.* M17.

balustrade /baləˈstreɪd/ *n.* M17. [Fr. after It. *balaustrata*, Sp. *balaustrada*: see prec., -ADE.] A row of balusters surmounted by a rail or a coping as an ornamental parapet to a terrace, balcony, etc.

balustraded *a.* furnished with a balustrade L18. **balustrading** *n.* balustrade-work L19.

Balzacian /balˈzakɪən/ *a.* & *n.* L19. [f. *Balzac* (see below) + -IAN.] A *adj.* Pertaining to or characteristic of the French novelist Honoré de Balzac (1799–1850) or his works. L19. B *n.* An admirer or student of Balzac or his writing. E20.

bam /bam/ *v.* & *n. slang* & *dial.* E18. [Rel. to BAMBOOZLE: either an abbrev. of it or the source of its 1st syll.] A *v.t.* & *i.* Infl. **-mm-**. = BAMBOOZLE *v.* I. E18. B *n.* A hoax, a trick. E18.

bam /bam/ *int.* E20. [Imit.] Repr. the sound of a hard blow. Also *gen.* introducing a sudden action or occurrence.

B. HOLIDAY Then bam, they'd be drafted and end up right back in some camp in the South. M. FRENCH 'All of a sudden, bam!' She put her hand on her head. 'The lump's as big as a marble!'

bambino /bamˈbiːnəʊ, -əʊ/ *n.* Pl. ***-ni*** /-ni/, ***-nos***. E18. [It., dim. of *bambo* silly.] A young child or baby (in Italy); *spec.* an image of the infant Jesus in swaddling-clothes.

bamboo /bamˈbuː/ *n.* & *v.* Also (earlier) †**-bos**, †**b(o)us**. L16. [Du. *bamboes*, mod.L *bambusa*, ult. f. Malay *mamby*. Forms in *-s* later taken as pl.] A *n.* 1 Any of numerous, mainly tropical, giant grasses belonging to the genus *Bambusa* and various related genera; the hollow stem of such a plant, used as a stick or as material. L16. 2 Cane-coloured biscuit porcelain. L18. 3 A light yellowish brown. M19.

Comb.: **bamboo curtain** [after *iron curtain*] a political and economic barrier between China and non-Communist countries; **bamboo-fish** a small fish, *Sarpa salpa*, of the family Sparidae, found in the eastern Atlantic and the Mediterranean; **bamboo shoot** a young shoot of bamboo, eaten as a vegetable.

B *v.t.* Beat with a bamboo; provide with bamboo. E19.

bamboozle /bamˈbuːz(ə)l/ *v.* & *n. slang.* E18. [Prob. of cant origin: cf. BAM *v.* & *n.*] A *v.* 1 *v.t.* Hoax, deceive, trick, cheat. E18. 2 *v.t.* Mystify, perplex. E18. 3 *v.i.* Practise trickery. *rare.* E18.

1 N. ROWE You intend to bamboozle me out of a Beef Stake. P. ROTH She had allowed herself to be bamboozled.. into eating lobster Newburg. 2 E. GASKELL He fairly bamboozles me. He is two chaps. 3 C. CIBBER The old Rogue.. knows how to Bamboozle.

B *n.* = BAMBOOZLEMENT. *rare.* E18.

¶Mentioned in 1710 by Swift in the *Tatler* no. 230 (on 'the continual Corruption of our English Tongue') among other slang terms recently invented or brought into vogue.

bamboozlement *n.* hoaxing; cheating; tricky deception; mystification: M19. **bamboozler** *n.* E18.

†**bambos** *n.* see BAMBOO.

bamboula /bamˈbuːlə/ *n.* M19. [Louisiana creole.] An American Blacks' dance to tambourine accompaniment.

†**bamb(o)us** *ns.* see BAMBOO.

ban /ban/ *n.*^{1} See also BANNS. ME. [In branch I, partly aphet. f. ME *iban*, OE *gebann* (cf. OHG *ban*, ON *bann*), partly f. OFr. *ban* f. Gmc base of BAN *v.*, whence late L *bannus*, *bannum*. In branch II, strictly a separate wd, f. BAN *v.*] I 1 A public proclamation or edict; a summons (esp. to arms); *spec.* the gathering of the (French) King's vassals for war, or the body of vassals so assembled (orig. = ARRIÈRE-BAN). Now *arch.* & *Hist.* ME. 2 A section of an army; *esp.* in the later French system, the younger part of the population liable to serve in the militia, as distinct from the arrière-ban of reserves. E19.

II 3 A formal ecclesiastical denunciation, an interdict, an excommunication; *gen.* a curse supposed to have supernatural sanction. L15. b The invoking or utterance of a curse; an angry execration. *arch.* L16. 4 A formal or authoritative prohibition (*on* or *against* something), an interdict. M17. b A proclamation issued against a person by the civil power; a sentence of outlawry. L17. 5 A practical denunciation or prohibition not formally announced, *esp.* one tacitly effected by public opinion. M19.

4 *test ban*, etc.

ban /ban/ *n.*^{2} E17. [Pers. *bān* lord, master, introduced by the Avars who ruled in Slavonic countries subject to Hungary.] *Hist.* A viceroy and military commander of certain districts in Hungary, Slavonia, and Croatia.

ban /bɑːn/ *n.*^{3} Pl. **bani** /ˈbɑːni/. L19. [Romanian.] A monetary unit of Romania, equal to one-hundredth of a leu.

ban /ban/ *v.* Infl. **-nn-**. [OE *bannan* = OFris. *banna*, MLG, MDu. *bannen*, OHG *bannan*, ON *banna*, f. Gmc base repr. also by Gk *phanai*, L *fari* speak. Cf. BAN *n.*^{1}] †1 *v.t.* Summon by proclamation (esp. to arms). OE–LME. 2 *v.t.*

Curse or damn. *arch.* ME. **b** *spec.* Pronounce an ecclesiastical curse upon. *arch.* ME. **3** *v.i.* Utter curses. *arch.* ME. **4** *v.t.* & *i.* Chide, speak angrily (to). *dial.* ME. **5** *v.t.* Exclude or proscribe (a person, esp. *from* something); interdict or formally prohibit. LME.

2 W. MORRIS Ever she blessed the old and banned the new. 3 BYRON Yet harsh and haughty, as he lay he bann'd. 5 W. STORY He banned them from the city. A. J. P. TAYLOR The American government banned virtually all trade with Japan. E. LONGFORD His wife tried to ban his friends in the misguided belief that she was protecting her hero.

banal /bəˈnɑːl, -ˈnal; ˈbeɪn(ə)l/ *a.* M18. [(O)Fr., f. *ban*: see BAN *n.*[1], -AL[1].] **1** *Hist.* Of or belonging to compulsory feudal service. M18. **2** Commonplace, trite, trivial. M19.

¶Sense 2 developed from the intermediate French sense 'common to all'.

banalize *v.t.* M20. **banally** *adv.* M20.

banality /bəˈnalɪti/ *n.* M19. [Fr. *banalité*: see prec., -ITY.] A trite or trivial thing, a commonplace; commonplace character, triviality.

banana /bəˈnɑːnə/ *n.* L16. [Sp. & Port., f. Mande.] **1** The edible finger-shaped pulpy fruit of any of various tropical and subtropical plants of the genus *Musa* (family Musaceae), borne in clusters and yellow-skinned when ripe. L16. **2** The treelike herbaceous plant bearing this fruit, which has a stem of overlapping leaf sheaths. L17. **3** A comedian. Only in *second banana*, a supporting comedian in a show, *top banana*, a comedian who tops the bill of a show. *Theatr. slang* (orig. *US*). M20.

Phrases: **go bananas** *slang* become crazy or angry.

Comb.: **banana bird** any of various fruit-eating birds; *esp.* = *bananaquit* below; **Bananaland** *Austral. colloq.* Queensland; **Bananalander** *Austral. colloq.* a Queenslander; **bananaquit** [QUIT *n.*[1]] a tropical American passerine bird, *Coereba flaveola*; **banana republic** (usu. *derog.*) a small tropical (usu. Central or S. American) country that is economically dependent on its fruit-exporting or similar trade; **banana skin** *fig.* a cause of upset or humiliation; **banana split** a dessert of ice-cream and a split banana.

banate *n.* var. of BANNAT.

banausic /bəˈnɔːsɪk/ *a. derog.* M19. [Gk *banausikos* of or for artisans: see -IC.] Suitable for artisans; uncultivated; materialistic.

Banbury cake /ˈbanb(ə)rɪ keɪk/ *n. phr.* L16. [*Banbury* in Oxfordshire, where orig. made.] A cake of pastry filled with a currant mixture.

banco /ˈbaŋkəʊ/ *int.* L18. [Fr. f. It.: see BANK *n.*[3]] In baccarat etc.: expr. a player's willingness to meet single-handed the banker's whole stake. Cf. VA BANQUE.

band /band/ *n.*[1] *arch.* exc. as identified w. BAND *n.*[2] LOE. [ON *band* = OFris., OS *band*, OHG *bant* (Du. *band*, G *Band*), f. Gmc, f. base of BIND *v.* Cf. BAND *n.*[2], BEND *n.*[1], BOND *n.*[2]] **I** *lit.* **1** A thing with which a person is bound in restraint of personal liberty; a shackle, a chain. LOE. **2** A string with which some loose thing (esp. straw) is bound. LOE. **b** *Bookbinding.* Each of the cords or straps crossing the back of a book, to which the sheets are attached; the raised part on the spine formed by this. M18. **3** A connecting piece that holds together the parts of something. LOE. **4** A strap, chain, etc., used as a lead for a child or animal. LOE. **5** A hinge. LME. **II** *fig.* **6** The restraint on freedom of action regarded as imposed by sin, convention, sleep, etc. LOE. **7** An obligation or circumstance which restricts action or binds persons reciprocally; a tie, a restraint; a binding agreement or promise; a force effecting or maintaining union. LOE. **b** Security given; a legally executed deed. *arch.* E16. **8** A covenant, a league. *Sc. obs.* exc. *Hist.* LME. †**9** Binding quality or power. Only in E17.

bandster *n.* (*dial.*) a person who binds sheaves L18.

band /band/ *n.*[2] LME. [(O)Fr. *bande*, earlier *bende* (cf. BEND *n.*[2]) = Prov., Sp., It., med.L *benda*, f. Gmc, f. base of BIND *v.* Cf. BAND *n.*[1]] **1** A hoop; a ring of metal etc., now *esp.* one round a bird's leg to identify it. LME. **2** A flat strip of thin flexible material to contain or bind (cf. BAND *n.*[1] 2, 3) or (in later use) to identify or label; (freq. w. specifying wd) a fabric strip round or forming part of a dress, hat, etc. L15. **b** *spec.* The neckband or collar of a shirt, a collar, a ruff, (now *arch.* or *Hist.*); (now in *pl.*) the development of this into two strips hanging down in front in clerical, legal, or academic dress. M16. **c** A strip of linen etc. wrapped round (part of) the body; a bandage. *arch.* L16. **3** A stripe distinguished by colour or aspect from the surface which it crosses; a particular portion of a certain breadth crossing a surface. L15. **b** A ring or stripe around an object. M19. **c** *fig.* A range of values within a series; a scale extending between certain limits. E20. **d** A section of a disc, tape, etc., containing a specified sequence of recorded material. M20. **4** An endless belt or strap transmitting motion between two wheels, pulleys, etc. E18. **5** A narrow stratum of coal or rock. M19. **6** *Physics* etc. A broad feature in a spectrum; a range of wavelengths, energies, etc., between well-defined limits. M19.

1 H. ALLEN The rather ponderous wedding ring .. had just below it a narrow, worn, gold band. 2 AV *Ecclus* 6:30 Her bands are purple lace. W. J. LOCKE He selected a cigar, .. removed the band and clipped the point. Q. D. LEAVIS An enterprising publisher will reissue the novel with a band or new dust-jacket exhibiting the caption. M. LASKI There was a black band round the sleeve of his jacket. H. E. BATES Many pound notes, neatly folded and packed tight inside the hat, under the greasy leather band. *armband, hairband, hatband, headband, neckband, waistband*, etc. *Alice band*: see ALICE 2b. **elastic, rubber, band** a band of rubber to hold papers etc. together. b G. CRABBE Careless was he of surplice, hood, and band. J. ARCHER The official dress of the Vice-Chancellor, bands, collar, white tie and all. c *swaddling-band(s)*: see SWADDLING *vbl n.* 2. 3 GEO. ELIOT The .. sunshine .. came .. through the windows in slanting bands of brightness. S. BECKETT It seemed to have a red band or stripe running down its side. b G. K. CHESTERTON There seemed to be .. a continuous band round the earth .. a thing like the ring of Saturn. 6 R. V. JONES All we needed to do was to listen in the right frequency band. *citizens' band*: see CITIZEN *n.* *narrow band*: see NARROW *a.* *S-band*: see S, S 9.

Comb.: **bandfish** any of several elongated bottom-dwelling marine fishes of the family Cepolidae, with long continuous fins; **bandpass** the band of frequencies transmitted by a filter; **band-saw** an endless saw, consisting of a steel belt with a serrated edge running over wheels; **bandwidth** the extent of a band of frequencies, esp. of one used in telecommunications.

bandlet *n.* = BANDELET M18. **bandlike** *a.* M19.

band /band/ *n.*[3] L15. [(O)Fr. *bande* = Prov., Sp., It., med.L *banda*, prob. of Gmc origin and assoc. w. med.L *banda* scarf, *bandum* banner (cf. Goth. *bandwa* sign), also company, crowd.] **1** An organized company of people having a common purpose; *spec.* a troop of armed men, robbers, etc. L15. **2** A company of people or animals in movement. E17. **b** A herd, a flock. *N. Amer.* E19. **3** A body of musicians, now *esp.* those playing brass or wind instruments; (a section of) an orchestra. Now also, a rock or pop group. M17.

1 BYRON The 'black bands' who still Ravage the frontier. S. GIBBONS Mr. Mybug and Rennet joined the band of watchers. F. FITZGERALD The enemy in the south consisted of little more than a band of guerrillas. **Band of Hope** an association of young people pledged to total abstinence from intoxicating liquors. *sacred band*: see SACRED *a.* 2 AV *Gen.* 32:7 Hee diuided the .. camels into two bands. J. R. GREEN The little band of fugitives. 3 P. KAVANAGH I joined the Sinn Fein Pipers' Band that was started. P. SCOTT She felt and heard the thrum and drum of the band. *big band, brass band, German band, jazz band, marching band, military band, silver band, wind band*, etc. **beat the band** *fig.* (*slang*) surpass everything. *Schrammel band*: see SCHRAMMEL 2. **when the band begins to play** *fig.* when matters become serious.

Comb.: **bandmaster** the leader or conductor of a band of musicians; **band-shell** a bandstand in the form of a large concave shell with special acoustic properties; **bandsman** a member of a band of musicians; **bandstand** a covered outdoor platform on which a band plays; **bandwagon** (orig. *US*) a large wagon used by a band in a parade etc.; *fig.* as of one carrying a group of successful (political) leaders, esp. in *jump* or *climb on the bandwagon*, seek to join the party or group that is likely to succeed.

band /band/ *n.*[4] E16. [Origin unkn.] A ridge of a hill; in the Lake District of northern England, a long hill resembling a ridge, or a narrow sloping offshoot from a higher hill or mountain.

band /band/ *v.*[1] L15. [(O)Fr. *bander*, f. as BAND *n.*[2] Perh. partly f. the Eng. ns.] **1** *v.t.* Bind or fasten with a band or bands. L15. **2** *v.t.* Provide or cover with a band. *rare* in *gen.* sense. M16. **b** *spec.* Provide (a bird) with an identifying band. E20. **3** *v.t.* (chiefly *refl.*) & *i.* Join or form into a band or company; unite. M16. **4** *v.t.* Mark with a band or stripe, or with bands or stripes. Freq. as *banded* ppl a. M18. **5** *v.t.* Divide into bands or ranges based on a numerical characteristic, with a view to treating the bands differently; *Educ.* group or allocate (pupils) on the basis of ability. L20.

3 MILTON What multitudes Were banded to oppose his high Decree. R. ELLISON We have banded together in brotherhood so as to do something about it. I. COLEGATE People banding themselves together in order to work for a better world. 4 E. K. KANE An opalescent purple, that banded the entire horizon. D. ATTENBOROUGH Waving tentacles of the most delicate colours, banded, striped and patterned in many shades. *banded rudder-fish*: see RUDDER *n.* 5 *Financial Times* Making the community charge more fair by banding the rate of charge in proportion to ability to pay.

†**band** *v.*[2] L16–L17. [Abbrev. of BANDY *v.*] = BANDY *v.*

bandage /ˈbandɪdʒ/ *n.* & *v.* L16. [Fr., f. as BAND *n.*[2] + -AGE.] **A** *n.* **1** A strip of woven material used to bind up a wound or to protect an injured part of the body. L16. **2** A strip of material used for binding or covering up, esp. for blindfolding the eyes. E18. **3** A strip or band of stone, iron, etc., used to bind together and strengthen any structure. *arch.* M18. **B** *v.t.* Tie or bind up with a bandage. L18.

bandaging *n.* the applying of bandages; material for bandages: E19.

Band-Aid /ˈbandeɪd/ *n.*, *a.*, & *v.* Also **band-aid.** E20. [f. BAND *n.*[2] + AID *n.*] **A** *n.* **1** (Proprietary name for) a type of sticking-plaster with a gauze pad; a strip of this. E20. **2** *fig.* A makeshift or temporary solution to a problem etc.; a palliative. M20. **B** *adj.* Makeshift, temporary; palliative. L20. **C** *v.t.* Apply a makeshift or temporary solution to (a problem etc.). L20.

bandanna /banˈdanə/ *n.* Also **-ana**. M18. [Prob. f. Port. f. Hind. (*bā̃dhnū* method of tie-dyeing, spotted cloth, f. *bā̃dhnā* to tie).] A coloured silk or cotton handkerchief or headscarf with white or yellow spots.

bandar /ˈbʌndə/ *n.* Also **-der**. L19. [Hind. *bā̃dar* f. Skt *vānara*.] In the Indian subcontinent: the rhesus monkey.

Comb.: **bandar-log** /-ləʊg/ [Hind. *log* people f. Skt *loka*] the monkeys collectively; a body of irresponsible chatterers.

bandbox /ˈbandbɒks/ *n.* & *a.* M17. [f. BAND *n.*[2] + BOX *n.*[2]] **A** *n.* A lightweight paper-covered box for millinery (orig. for neckbands). M17.

look as if one came out of a bandbox (& vars.) look extremely smart.

B *attrib.* or as *adj.* Resembling a bandbox; providing little space; fragile, flimsy; conspicuously neat and smart. L18.

N. SHUTE It had come through the Grand Prix unscratched, in bandbox condition.

bandˈboxical *a.* resembling a bandbox, esp. in providing little space L18. **bandboxy** *a.* = BANDBOX *a.* M19.

bandeau /ˈbandəʊ, *foreign* bɑ̃do/ *n.* Pl. **-eaux** /-əʊz, *foreign* -o/. E18. [Fr. f. OFr. *bandel* dim. of *bande*: see BAND *n.*[2], -EL[2].] A band or strip of material, *esp.* one used for binding a woman's hair.

bandelet /ˈband(ə)lɪt/ *n.* Also †**-ette**. M17. [Fr. *bandelette* dim. of OFr. *bandele* fem. of *bandel*: see prec.] A small band, streak, or fillet; *Archit.* a small flat moulding, encompassing a column.

bander /ˈbandə/ *n.*[1] *arch.* M16. [f. BAND *v.*[1] + -ER[1].] A member of a league, a confederate.

bander *n.*² var. of BANDAR.

banderilla /bande'riʎa, bandə'rɪljə/ *n.* Pl. ***-as*** /-as, -əz/. L18. [Sp., dim of *bandera* banner.] A decorated dart thrust into a bull's neck or shoulders during a bullfight.

banderillero /ˌbanderi'ʎero, ˌbandərɪ'ljɛːrəʊ/ *n.* Pl. ***-os*** /-ɔs, -əʊz/. L18. [f. as prec. + *-ero* agent-suff.] A bullfighter who uses banderillas.

banderole /'bandərəʊl/ *n.* Also **-ol** /-əʊl, -(ə)l/; (esp. in sense 2, the earlier form) **bannerol** /'banərəʊl, -(ə)l/. M16. [Fr. *ban(n)erole*, later *banderole*, f. It. *banderuola* dim. of *bandiera* BANNER *n.*¹: see -OLE¹.] 1 A long narrow flag with a cleft end, flown from the masthead of a ship. M16. 2 A rectangular banner borne at the funerals of public figures and placed over the tomb. M16. 3 An ornamental streamer of the kind attached to a knight's lance. L16. 4 = BANNER *n.*¹ 4. *rare*. L16. 5 A ribbon-like scroll bearing a device or inscription. E17.

bandersnatch /'bandəsnatʃ/ *n.* L19. [Invented by Lewis Carroll; presumably a portmanteau wd.] A fabulous creature of dangerous propensities, immune to bribery and too fast to flee from; *allus.* any creature with such qualities.
C. S. LEWIS No one ever influenced Tolkien—you might as well try to influence a bandersnatch.

bandicoot /'bandɪkuːt/ *n.* L18. [Alt. of Telugu *pandikokku* lit. 'pig-rat'.] 1 A large destructive southern Asian rat, *Bandicota indica*. Also *bandicoot rat*. L18. 2 Any of various mainly insectivorous marsupials of the family Peramelidae, found in Australia and New Guinea. E19.

bandit /'bandɪt/ *n.* Pl. **bandits**, (now chiefly *Hist.*) **banditti** /ban'dɪti/. L16. [It. *bandito*, pl. *-ti*, use as n. of pa. pple of *bandire* ban = med.L *bannire* proclaim, proscribe, banish.] 1 An outlaw; a lawless robber or marauder; a gangster. L16. b In *pl.* **banditti** as *collect. sing.* A company of bandits. *arch.* E18. 2 *transf.* An enemy aircraft in action. M20.
1 J. R. GREEN The routed soldiery turned into free companies of bandits. W. H. AUDEN The bandit who is good to his mother. P. THEROUX Bandits stop this train and rob the passengers. **one-arm(ed) bandit** *slang* a fruit machine or the like operated by pulling down an armlike handle. b SIR W. SCOTT Deer-stealers . . are ever a desperate banditti.
banditism *n.* the practices of bandits L19. **banditry** *n.* = BANDITISM E20.

bandobast *n.* var. of BUNDOBUST.

bandog /'bandɒg/ *n.* ME. [f. BAND *n.*¹ + DOG *n.*] Orig., a (fierce) dog kept on a chain; a mastiff, a bloodhound. Now usu. *spec.*, a dog specially bred for fighting by crossing aggressive breeds.

bandoleer *n.* var. of BANDOLIER.

bandolero /bandə'lɛːrəʊ/ *n.* Pl. **-os.** M17. [Sp.] A Spanish bandit.

bandolier /bandə'lɪə/ *n.* Also **-eer.** L16. [Fr. *bandoulière* perh. f. Sp. *bandolera*, f. *banda* sash or f. Catal. *bandolera*, f. *bandoler* bandit.] †1 A shoulder-belt for carrying a wallet. L16–M18. 2 A shoulder-belt for holding ammunition, (*Hist.*) with small cases each containing a charge for a musket, (now) with small loops or pockets for carrying cartridges. L16. b Any of the cases containing a charge for a musket. Now *arch.* or *Hist.* E17.
bandoliered *a.* wearing a bandolier E20.

bandoline /'bandəliːn/ *n.* & *v.* Now *arch.* or *Hist.* M19. [Fr., f. as BANDEAU + L *linere* bedaub, anoint.] A *n.* A gummy preparation for setting hair. M19. B *v.t.* Set (hair) with this. M19.

bandoneon /ban'dəʊnɪən/ *n.* Also **-ion.** E20. [(Sp. *bandoneón* f.) G *Bandonion*, f. Heinrich *Band* its inventor, a 19th-cent. Ger. musician + *-on-* as in *harmonika* harmonica + *-ion* as in *akkordion* accordion.] A type of concertina used esp. in S. America.

bandore /ban'dɔː/ *n.*¹ Also **-ra** /-rə/. M16. [Origin uncertain: cf. Du. *bandoor*, Sp. *bandurria*, It. *pandora*, *-ura* f. L *pandura* f. Gk *pandoura* PANDORA *n.* Cf. BANJO, VANDOLA.] A bass stringed instrument of the cittern family, having a long neck and a scallop-shaped body.

†**bandore** *n.*² L17–E18. [Alt. of Fr. BANDEAU.] A widow's head-dress.

bandurria /ban'dʊərɪə, *foreign* ban'durria/ *n.* M19. [Sp.] A Spanish stringed instrument of the lute type.

bandy /'bandi/ *n.*¹ L16. [Obscurely rel. to BANDY *v.*] †1 A (now unknown) way of playing tennis. L16–E17. †2 A stroke with a racket; a ball, esp. a return, struck at tennis. L16–M17. 3 (A bent or curved stick used in) a form of hockey. E17.

bandy /'bandi/ *n.*² L18. [Telugu *baṇḍi*, Tamil *vaṇṭi*.] In the Indian subcontinent: a carriage, a buggy, a cart. .

bandy /'bandi/ *a.* L17. [Perh. attrib. use of BANDY *n.*¹ 3.] Of legs: curved so as to be wide apart at the knees. Of a person: bandy-legged.
bandiness *n.* M19.

bandy /'bandi/ *v.* L16. [Perh. f. Fr. *bander* take sides at tennis, f. as BAND *n.*³ Cf. It. *bandare*, Sp. *bandear*.] 1 *v.t.* Throw, pass, strike (a ball) to and fro (as in tennis etc.). Chiefly *fig.* L16. †2 *v.t.* Cast away or aside; *fig.* dismiss or reject. L16–M17. 3 *v.t.* Toss from side to side, from one to another, or *about*; esp. *fig.*, pass (words, stories, etc.) around in a circle or group, discuss in this way. L16. b Give and take (blows, words, etc.); exchange (conversation, compliments, etc.) *with* a person. L16. †4 *v.t.* (esp. *refl.*) & *i.* Band together, confederate. L16–E19. †5 *v.i.* Contend, fight. L16–E18.
1 TENNYSON To be the ball of Time, Bandied by the hands of fools. 2 C. MARLOWE The Cardinal, would bandy me away from Spain. 3 G. ANSON Thus was this unhappy vessel bandied about within a few leagues of her intended harbour. DICKENS The stories they invent . . and bandy from mouth to mouth! H. READ The poet must use words which are bandied about in the daily give-and-take of conversation. W. IRVING Your name is . . frequently bandied at table among us. b J. L. MOTLEY Bandying blows in the thickest of the fight. N. MITFORD She bandied repartee with the various Rorys and Rolys. 4 G. HERBERT Joyntly bandying, They drive them soon away. SIR W. SCOTT Here is his son already bandying and making a faction. 5 MILTON Neither did the People of Rome bandy with their Senate while any of the Tarquins liv'd.

bandy-bandy /'bandɪˌbandi/ *n.* E20. [Aborig.] A nocturnal Australian snake, *Vermicella annulata*, marked with black and white bands.

bane /beɪn/ *n.* & *v.* [OE *bana* = OFris. *bona*, OS, OHG *bano*, ON *bani*, f. Gmc: ult. connections uncertain.] A *n.* 1 A slayer, a murderer. Long *arch. rare.* OE. 2 A thing which causes death or destroys life, *esp.* poison. Long *arch.* exc. in *comb.*, as *henbane*, *wolf's bane*, etc. OE. †3 Murder, death, destruction. ME–M17. 4 Ruin, woe. Chiefly *poet.* LME. 5 A cause of ruin, harm, or trouble. L16.
2 TOLKIEN The Ring gleamed and flickered as he held it up. . . 'Behold Isildur's Bane!' said Elrond. 3 SHAKES. *Macb.* I will not be afraid of death and bane Till Birnam Forest come to Dunsinane. 4 R. GREENE That sweet boy that wrought bright Venus bane. 5 BURKE Theoretic plans of constitution have been the bane of France. C. BRONTË She who had been the bane of his life. M. M. KAYE His attentions soon became the bane of the boy's existence.
Comb.: **baneberry** any of several Eurasian and N. American plants of the genus *Actaea*, of the buttercup family; the bitter poisonous fruit of these plants; **banewort** *dial.* any of various, mainly poisonous, plants, *esp.* lesser spearwort, *Ranunculus flammula*.
B *v.t.* 1 Hurt, harm, poison. *arch.* LME. †2 Esp. of poison: kill. Only in L16.
baneful *a.* lethal; poisonous; pernicious: L16.

†**banes** *n.pl.* see BANNS.

bang /baŋ/ *n.*¹ M16. [f. BANG *v.*¹] 1 (The noise of) a heavy resounding blow; a thump. M16. 2 Impetus, energy. *rare.* L18. 3 A loud sharp noise, as the report of a gun; the sound of an explosion; a sonic boom. M19. 4 An injection of a drug. Cf. BHANG. *US slang.* E20. 5 Excitement, pleasure; a thrill. *N. Amer. slang.* M20. 6 An act of sexual intercourse. *slang.* M20.
1 *Suffolk bang*: see SUFFOLK 1. 3 *big bang*: see BIG *a.* *sonic bang*: see SONIC 2. **with a bang** *fig.* successfully; impressively, spectacularly; *go out with a bang*, make a dramatic exit, perform a final startling or memorable act. 6 *gang-bang*: see GANG *n.*

bang /baŋ/ *n.*² Orig. *US.* L19. [f. BANG *adv.*: cf. BANGTAIL.] A fringe of hair cut straight across the forehead.

†**bang** *n.*³ var. of BHANG.

bang /baŋ/ *v.*¹ M16. [Imit., perh. of Scand. origin (cf. ON *bang* hammering, *banga* hammer): LG has *bange(l)n* beat.] 1 *v.t.* Strike or shut noisily; cause to make the sound of a blow or explosion. M16. 2 *v.i.* Move impetuously, dash, jump. *dial.* L16. 3 *v.t.* Knock about, damage, (*N. Amer.* also foll. by *up*); drub, defeat (*lit.* & *fig.*). E17. 4 *v.i.* Strike or shut violently or noisily, thump; make a sudden loud noise. E18. 5 *v.t.* Surpass. Chiefly *dial.* L18. 6 *v.t.* *Stock Exch.* Depress (share prices, the market). *arch.* L19. 7 *v.t.* & *i.* Copulate (with). *slang.* L19.
1 TENNYSON Like an iron-clanging anvil banged With hammers. A. KOESTLER It was the sound of Sonia banging the bathroom-door behind her that woke him. **bang out** produce (a tune on a piano, etc.) noisily and roughly. 3 M. EDGEWORTH English Clay . . banged down to Clay-hall. SHAKES. *Oth.* The desperate tempest hath so bang'd the Turk That their designment halts. *banged to rights*: see RIGHT *n.*¹ 4 WILKIE COLLINS Taking great pains not to let the doors bang. C. JACKSON She had only to bang on the small painted drum. *bang one's head against a brick wall*: see WALL *n.*¹ 5 DICKENS The next Pickwick will bang all the others.

bang /baŋ/ *v.*²*t.* Orig. *US.* L19. [f. BANG *n.*²] Cut (hair) in a fringe straight across the forehead.

bang /baŋ/ *adv.* L18. [f. BANG *v.*¹] 1 With sudden impact; abruptly; explosively (as the conventional imitation of a shot or explosion, *lit.* & *fig.*). Freq. in *go bang*. L18. 2 Completely; exactly. Also as a mere intensive. *colloq.* E19.
1 O. W. HOLMES Bang went the magazine! T. STOPPARD Bang goes your credit at the off-licence. 2 *Times Lit. Suppl.* Bang-up-to-date neutron know-how. E. CRISPIN Gobbo certainly did leave here that evening bang on time. **bang off** *slang* immediately. **bang on** *slang* exactly right, excellent. *bang to rights*: see RIGHT *n.*¹ **bang-up** *a.* (*N. Amer. slang*) first-class, splendid.

Bangalore torpedo /baŋgə'lɔː tɔː'piːdəʊ/ *n. phr.* Pl. **Bangalore torpedoes.** E20. [f. *Bangalore*, a city in southern India.] *Mil.* A tube containing explosive used by infantry for blowing up wire entanglements etc.

bangalow /'baŋgələʊ/ *n.* E19. [Aborig.] Either of two Australian palms of the genus *Archontophoenix*, having feathery leaves. Also *bangalow palm*.

banger /'baŋə/ *n.*¹ Chiefly *colloq.* M17. [f. BANG *v.*¹ + -ER¹.] Something which makes a bang or is noisily conspicuous; *spec.* (*a*) a blatant lie; (*b*) a firework which goes off with a bang; (*c*) an enthusiastic kiss; (*d*) a sausage; (*e*) a dilapidated old car.

†**banger** *n.*² var. of BANJO.

banghy *n.* var. of BANGY.

Bangladeshi /baŋglə'dɛʃi, bʌŋ-/ *n.* & *a.* Pl. of n. same, **-s.** L20. [f. *Bangladesh* (see below) + -I².] (A native or inhabitant) of the People's Republic of Bangladesh in the north-east of the Indian subcontinent (formerly East Pakistan).

bangle /'baŋg(ə)l/ *n.* L18. [Hind. *baṅglī* (orig.) coloured glass bracelet.] A rigid ring as a bracelet or anklet.
slave bangle: see SLAVE *n.*¹ & *a.*¹
bangled *a.* wearing or adorned with bangles M19.

bangle /'baŋg(ə)l/ *v. obs.* exc. *dial.* M16. [Origin unkn.] 1 *v.i.* Flap, hang loosely; waste time, mess about. M16. 2 *v.t.* Fritter *away*, squander. E17.

Bangorian /baŋ'gɔːrɪən/ *a.* E18. [f. *Bangor*, a town in N. Wales + -IAN.] Of or pertaining to Bangor; *spec.* (*Hist.*) designating a religious controversy raised by a sermon directed against nonjurors preached before George I by the then Bishop of Bangor.

bangster /'baŋstə/ *n. Sc.* M16. [f. BANG *v.*¹ + -STER.] A bully, a ruffian; a victor in fights.
bangstry *n.* violence to person or property L16.

bangtail /'baŋteɪl/ *n.* L19. [f. BANG *v.*¹ + TAIL *n.*¹] (A horse etc. with) a tail cut straight across.

Comb.: **bangtail muster** *Austral.* a counting of cattle by cutting across the tuft of each animal's tail.

bangtailed *a.* M19.

bangy /ˈbʌŋgi/ *n.* Also **-ghy**. L18. [Hind. *bahaṅgī*, Marathi *baṅgī* (Skt *vihaṅgikā*).] In the Indian subcontinent: a shoulder-yoke with containers for carrying loads.

bani *n.* pl. of BAN *n.*[3]

bania /ˈbʌnɪə/ *n.* L18. [Hind. *baniyā* f. Skt *vāṇija*: see BANYAN.] A Hindu trader or merchant.

banian *n.* var. of BANYAN.

banish /ˈbanɪʃ/ *v.t.* LME. [OFr. *baniss-* lengthened stem of *banir* (mod. *bannir*) f. Proto-Romance f. Gmc, f. base of BAN *n.*[1]: see -ISH[2].] †1 Proclaim (a person) an outlaw. LME–E17. 2 Condemn to removal esp. to another country; exile. LME. 3 *gen.* Dismiss from one's presence or mind; expel. LME. †4 Clear out, empty. L15–L16.

2 SHAKES. *Temp.* This damn'd witch Sycorax . . from Argier . . was banish'd. J. MORSE He that shall be convicted there of is to be banished the kingdom. 3 DISRAELI Who had they dared to imitate him . . would have been banished society. E. M. FORSTER He was . . a stimulus, and banished morbidity. R. LOWELL Old lumber banished from the Temple. W. TREVOR He tried to think of something else, to banish away the face of the man who had been rude.

banisher *n.* LME. **banishment** *n.* the action of banishing; a state of exile or enforced absence; dismissal: L15.

banister /ˈbanɪstə/ *n.* Also **-nn-**, (earlier) †**barrister**. M17. [Alt. of BALUSTER, partly by assoc. w. BAR *n.*[1]] Any of the upright pillars supporting the handrail of a staircase; the whole structure of rail and uprights. Usu. in *pl.*

banjax /ˈbandʒaks/ *v.t. Anglo-Ir.* M20. [Origin unkn.] Ruin, destroy; incapacitate.

banjo /ˈbandʒəʊ/ *n.* Pl. **-o(e)s**. Also †**-ore**, †**banger**. M18. [Amer. Blacks' alt. of BANDORE *n.*[1]] 1 A stringed musical instrument with a head and neck like a guitar and a body like a tambourine, played with the fingers or with a plectrum. M18. 2 Any of various appliances resembling this instrument in shape; *Austral.* & *NZ slang* a shovel. M19.

banjoist *n.* a person who plays the banjo L19.

banjolele *n.* var. of BANJULELE.

banjolin /ˈbandʒəlɪn/ *n.* Also **-ine**. L19. [f. BANJO + MANDOLIN.] A four-stringed instrument, combining characteristics of the banjo and the mandolin.

†**banjore** *n.* var. of BANJO.

banjulele /bandʒəˈleɪli/ *n.* Also **-jo-**. E20. [f. BANJO + UKULELE.] A simplified banjo tuned as a ukulele.

bank /baŋk/ *n.*[1] ME. [ON *bakki* ridge, bank (ODa. *banke*; Sw. *backe*, Da. *bakke* hillock, ascent) f. Gmc; rel. to BENCH *n.*] 1 The sloping margin of a river, stream, etc.; ground at the side of a river etc. Also, the edge of a hollow place such as a mine shaft, ditch, etc. ME. 2 A ridge or shelf of ground with (steeply) sloping sides; a slope of such a ridge etc. ME. 3 A hill, a hillside (*dial.*); a railway incline. LME. 4 The seashore. *obs.* exc. *dial.* LME. 5 A shelving elevation in the seabed or a river-bed. L16. 6 A long flat-topped mass (of cloud, fog, snow, etc.). E17. 7 An ant-hill. *obs.* exc. *dial.* M17. 8 The lateral inclination of an aircraft when turning in flight; a lateral inclination given to a road at a curve. E20.

1 SHAKES. *Jul. Caes.* Tiber trembled underneath her banks. W. WOLLASTON Daisies on the banks of the road. *burst its banks*: see BURST *v.* 8. **left, right, bank** (of a river): respectively to left or right of someone looking down stream. *South Bank*: see SOUTH. 2 SHAKES. *Mids. N. D.* I know a bank where the wild thyme blows. E. WAUGH I . . organized lines of men to pass the stores from hand to hand down the steep bank. 3 J. A. H. MURRAY Thomas, lying on Huntley Banks, sees the lady riding by. 5 *Scottish Daily Express* The Albert had been fishing in the Belgian banks of the North Sea. *fig.*: SHAKES. *Macb.* But here upon this bank and shoal of time—We'd jump the life to come.

Comb.: **bank-barn** *N. Amer.* a barn built on a slope; **bank-full** *a.* full to the bank or brink; **bank martin** a sand-martin; **bankside** (*a*) the sloping side of a bank; (*b*) the margin of a lake, river, etc.; **banksman** *Mining* a pit-head overseer; **bank swallow** = *bank martin* above; *bank vole*: see VOLE *n.*[2]

bankless *a.* without banks or borders E17. **banky** *a.* full of banks, hilly; like a bank, inclined: E17.

bank /baŋk/ *n.*[2] ME. [(O)Fr. *banc* (= Prov. *banc*, Sp., It. *banco*), f. Proto-Romance deriv. of Gmc: see prec., BENCH *n.*] †1 A bench; a platform. (Cf. *mountebank*.) ME–L17. †2 A seat of justice. ME–L19. 3 A bench or table used in various trades, esp. in printing to receive the printed sheets. *obs.* exc. *Hist.* M16. 4 The bench occupied by the rowers of each oar in a galley; a line of oars set at the same height, esp. on either side of a galley. L16. 5 A set of similar pieces of equipment (e.g. lights, drawers) grouped together, esp. in rows or tiers. L19.

bank /baŋk/ *n.*[3] L15. [Fr. *banque* or its source It. *banca* (also *banco*), f. med.L *bancus*, *banca*, f. Gmc: cf. BANK *n.*[1], *n.*[2]] †1 The place of business of a money-dealer; the table on which such business is conducted. L15–M19. 2 An accumulated sum of money; a joint stock, esp. contributed for charitable purposes. *obs.* exc. as in sense 4 below. E16. 3 An establishment for the custody, deposit, loan, exchange, or issue of money, which it pays out on the customer's order; a building occupied by such an establishment. E17. 4 In gaming, the amount of money, chips, etc., which the keeper of the table, or one player playing against all the others, has before him or her; the proprietor as controlling this. E18. 5 A small enclosed receptacle for money. Chiefly in *piggy bank* s.v. PIGGY *n.* M20. 6 A reserve of something (e.g. blood, data) stored for future use; a place holding this. M20.

3 G. STEIN She would not let Lena touch her wages, but put it in the bank for her. G. GREENE Drawing a cheque is not nearly so simple an operation in an American bank as in an English one. **bank of issue** or **circulation**: one that issues its own notes. **central bank** a national (not commercial) bank. CLEARING-*bank*. **cry all the way to the bank** *colloq. iron.* receive ample financial compensation or reward. *Federal Reserve Bank*: see FEDERAL. **in (the) bank** *fig.* to one's credit, in reserve. *joint-stock bank*: see JOINT *a. merchant bank*: see MERCHANT *a.* **private bank**: one with not more than twenty unincorporated partners. *reserve bank*: see RESERVE *n.* & *a. savings bank*: see SAVING *n.* SWISS *bank*. **the Bank (of England)** the central bank of the UK, which acts as the Government's banker, manages the public debt, and issues legal tender. 4 *break the bank*: see BREAK *v.* 6 I. ASIMOV The time would come when unfertilised ova could be stored in banks at liquid-air temperatures and utilised for artificial insemination. *Times* We must be prepared for the day when 'banks' of different organs . . will be integral parts of all major hospitals. *bottle bank*, *paper-bank*, etc.

Comb.: **bank balance** the net amount held by a depositor in a bank, *loosely* a person's wealth; **bank-bill** (*a*) a bill drawn by one bank on another; (*b*) *N. Amer.* a banknote; **bank-book** a book supplied by a bank to a customer to provide a record of sums deposited or withdrawn; **bank card** a cheque card; **bank charge** commission charged by a bank for transactions and services; **bank holiday** a weekday on which banks are legally closed, in Britain usu. kept as a general holiday; **bank manager** the person in charge of a local branch of a bank; **banknote** a banker's promissory note, esp. from a central bank, payable to the bearer on demand, and serving as money; **Bank Rate** *Hist.* the minimum rate at which the Bank of England would agree to discount approved bills of exchange; **bankroll** *n.* & *v.* (orig. *N. Amer.*) (*a*) *n.* a roll of banknotes; funds; (*b*) *v.t.* (*colloq.*) finance, remunerate; **bank statement** a statement showing the balance of a bank account together with amounts paid in or withdrawn.

bank /baŋk/ *v.*[1] LME. [f. BANK *n.*[1]] 1 *v.t.* Confine or contain within a bank or banks; border, edge, surround. LME. 2 *v.t.* Heap or pile (*up*) into banks; build (a fire) up or *up* with tightly packed fuel so that it burns slowly. M16. †3 *v.t.* Coast, skirt. *rare* (Shakes.). Only in L16. 4 *v.t.* & *i. Watchmaking.* Limit the movement of (the escapement) in a watch; (of a watch or its escapement) impinge against its limits of movement. M18. 5 *v.i.* Rise or pile up or *up* into banks; build *up*. L18. 6 *v.t.* Assist (a train) to ascend an incline by pushing at the rear. E20. 7a *v.t.* Tilt (an aeroplane, road vehicle, etc.) sideways in making a turn; build (a road etc.) higher at one side than the other to assist fast cornering. E20. b *v.i.* Tilt in this way. E20.

1 R. GREENE A silent streame . . Banckt about with choyce of flowers. SOUTHEY A ridge of rocks that bank'd its side. M. MCCARTHY The altar was completely banked with flowers. 2 H. MARTINEAU They had banked up the snow. J. KOSINSKI Before retiring for the night women would bank up ashes to make certain that the embers would keep glowing until morning. D. BAGLEY Consoles of telemetering devices were banked fore and aft. 7a R. V. JONES Cecil, with all his old bomber pilot's reactions, banked us sharply into a turn heading directly at the fighter. b C. A. LINDBERGH I banked around in an attempt to get back to the field.

bank /baŋk/ *v.*[2] M17. [f. BANK *n.*[3]] 1 *v.i.* Keep a bank; trade in money. M17. 2 *v.i.* In gaming: act as banker. E19. b Put one's money *on* or *upon*; base one's hopes (*up*)*on*; count or rely (*up*)*on*. L19. 3 *v.i.* Keep money *at* or *with* (a particular bank etc.). M19. 4 *v.t.* Deposit (money etc.) in a bank. M19. 5 *v.t.* Store (blood, tissue, etc.) for future use. M20.

banka'bility *n.* the quality or condition of being bankable L20. **bankable** *a.* receivable at a bank; profitable, commercially feasible: E19.

banker /ˈbaŋkə/ *n.*[1] Long *arch.* & *dial.* ME. [AN *bankeur* = ONFr. *bankier*, *banquier*, f. *banc*: see BANK *n.*[2], -ER[2].] A covering for a bench or chair.

banker /ˈbaŋkə/ *n.*[2] M16. [(O)Fr. *banquier* (cf. It. *banchiere*, AL *bancarius*), f. *banque*: see BANK *n.*[3], -ER[2].] 1 A person who keeps or manages a bank (see BANK *n.*[3] 1, 3); in *pl.* also, a banking company. M16. 2 In gaming, a person who keeps the bank; the dealer in some games of chance. E19. b A particular gambling game of cards. L19. 3 In a football pool: a result which one forecasts identically in a series of entries; *gen.* a match etc. for which a specified outcome is confidently predicted. M20.

1 *merchant banker*: see MERCHANT *a.* SWISS *banker*.

Comb.: **banker's card** a cheque card; *banker's order*: see ORDER *n.*; *bankers' ramp*: see RAMP *n.*[3]

bankerly *a.* characteristic of or appropriate to a banker L20.

banker /ˈbaŋkə/ *n.*[3] M17. [f. BANK *n.*[1] or *v.*[1] + -ER[1].] 1 A ship or fisherman employed in cod-fishing on the Newfoundland banks. M17. 2 A labourer who makes banks of earth etc. *dial.* E18. 3 A river flooded to the top of its banks. *Austral.* & *NZ.* L19. 4 A locomotive used for banking (see BANK *v.*[1] 6). E20.

banker /ˈbaŋkə/ *n.*[4] L17. [f. BANK *n.*[2]; perh. alt. of It. *banco* (a statuary's) bench.] A wooden or stone bench on which bricks are dressed or stone is worked.

banket /baŋˈkɛt, ˈbaŋkɪt/ *n.* Orig. *S. Afr.* L19. [Afk. = almond toffee.] *Geol.* Compact gold-bearing conglomerate.

banking /ˈbaŋkɪŋ/ *n.* E17. [f. BANK *ns.* & *vs.* + -ING[1].] 1 The construction of banks or embankments. E17. b An embankment or artificial bank. M18. 2 The business of a banker (BANKER *n.*[2]). M18. 3 Sea-fishing on a bank, esp. on the Newfoundland banks. L18. 4 *Watchmaking.* Limitation of the motion of the balance, usu. by special pins. E19. 5 The raising of the outer side of a road etc. on a bend to facilitate cornering. E20.

2 *merchant banking*: see MERCHANT *a.*

Comb.: **banking-house** a mercantile firm engaged in banking.

bankrupt /ˈbaŋkrʌpt/ *n.*, *a.*, & *v.* Also †**-rout**. M16. [It. *banca rotta* lit. 'bench (or table) broken', infl. by Fr. *banqueroute* and assim. to L *ruptus* broken.] A *n.* †1 = BANKRUPTCY 1. M16–E18. 2 An insolvent debtor, a person who is hopelessly in debt; *spec.* an insolvent person (orig., a trader or merchant) whose estate is administered and distributed for the benefit of all his or her creditors by a court of law. M16. B *adj.* 1 Insolvent; undergoing legal process of bankruptcy. M16. 2 *fig.* At the end of one's resources; destitute or bereft *of* (a quality etc.). L16. C *v.* †1 *v.i.* Become bankrupt; fail financially. M16–L17. 2 *v.t.* Make bankrupt, reduce to insolvency; *fig.* exhaust the resources of, beggar. L16.

bankruptcy /ˈbaŋkrʌptsi/ *n.* E18. [f. BANKRUPT *a.* + -CY.] 1 The state of being, or fact of becoming, bankrupt. E18. 2 *fig.* Total loss (of a quality etc.); ruin. M18.

1 ADAM SMITH Bankruptcies are most frequent in the most hazardous trades. H. CECIL Unless Martin and his partner could raise another very substantial sum of money, they would be put into bankruptcy and their affairs investigated. 2 BURKE A general bankruptcy of reputation in both parties.

bankshall /ˈbaŋkʃɔːl/ *n.* E17. [Malay *bangsal* shed, perh. f. Skt *vaṇikśālā* merchants' hall.] In the Indian subcontinent and SE Asia: a warehouse; the office of a harbour-master etc.

banksia /ˈbaŋksɪə/ *n.* E19. [mod.L, f. Sir Joseph *Banks* (1743–1820), Eng. naturalist, or (sense 2) his wife Dorothea: see -IA[1].] 1 Any of various evergreen flowering shrubs of the proteaceous genus *Banksia*, native to Australia. E19. 2 *banksia rose*, a climbing rose, *Rosa banksiae*, native to China. L19.

banksian *a.* (*a*) *banksian rose* = BANKSIA *rose*; (*b*) *banksian pine*, the jack-pine, *Pinus banksiana*: M19.

bannat /ˈbanət/ *n.* Also **banate**. E19. [Serbo-Croat, f. as BAN *n.*[2] + -ATE[1].] *Hist.* The district under the jurisdiction of a ban.

banner /ˈbanə/ *n.*[1] & *a.* ME. [AN *banere*, OFr. *baniere* (mod. *bannière*) ult. f. med.L *bandum*: see BAND *n.*[3]] A *n.* 1 A piece of cloth attached by one side to the upper part of a pole, and used as the standard of a king, knight, army, etc.; a national flag, esp. as inspiring emotional attachment; *Her.* a flag displaying a person's arms. ME. 2 An ensign with a symbolic device, motto, etc., as the emblem of a guild, company, or other group, borne in religious, civic, or political processions; *esp.* such an ensign on two poles or a crossbar; a strip of cloth etc. with a sign or slogan, hung or outstretched for display; *fig.* something used as a symbol of principles. ME. †3 The company ranged under a particular banner. *rare.* ME–E19. †4 A fringed flag hanging on a trumpet. *rare* (Shakes.). Only in L16. 5 A flag awarded as a distinction. *US.* M19. 6 *Hist.* Any of the principal divisions of the Manchu army, each with a distinguishing flag or banner. Also, a military subdivision of Mongolian tribes. M19.

1 **follow, join, the banner of** *fig.* adhere to the cause of. *red banner*: see RED *a.* *Star-Spangled Banner*: see STAR *n.*[1] & *a.*

Comb.: **banner-cry** *arch.* a cry summoning men to join a banner, a slogan; **bannerman** (*a*) *Sc., arch.* a standard-bearer; (*b*) *Hist.* a soldier of one of the banners of the Manchu army.

B *attrib.* or as *adj.* 1 Entitled to a banner of distinction; pre-eminent, supreme. *US.* M19. 2 Conspicuous. E20.

2 V. GOLLANCZ The *Daily Herald* came out with a huge banner headline, in letters half an inch high, on its opening page.

bannerer *n.* (*obs.* exc. *Hist.*) a standard-bearer LME.

banner /ˈbanə/ *n.*[2] LME. [f. BAN *v.* + -ER[1].] A person who bans something or someone.

banner /ˈbanə/ *v.* L16. [f. BANNER *n.*[1]] †1 *v.i.* Raise a banner or standard *against*. *rare.* Only in L16. 2 *v.t.* Provide with a banner or banners. Chiefly as *bannered* ppl a. M17. 3 *v.t.* Bear or blazon on a banner. Chiefly as *bannered* ppl a. L18. 4 *v.t.* Announce in a banner headline. M20.

banneret /ˈbanərɪt/ *n.*[1] Also (as a title) **B-**. ME. [OFr. *banerez*, (later) *-et*, ult. f. as BANNER *n.*[1]] *Hist.* 1 (Also *knight banneret*) Orig., (the title of) a knight able and entitled to bring vassals into the field under his own banner (esp. a French rank). Later, (the title of) a person on whom a knighthood was conferred on the field for valour in the king's presence; hence as a rank or order of knighthood. ME. 2 = BANNERER. LME. 3 A title borne by certain officers in some of the Swiss cantons and Italian republics. L17.

banneret /ˈbanərɪt/ *n.*[2] Also **bannerette** /banəˈrɛt/. ME. [OFr. *banerete* dim. of *baniere*: see BANNER *n.*[1], -ETTE.] A small banner.

bannerol *n.* see BANDEROLE.

bannister *n.* var. of BANISTER.

†**bannition** *n.* M17–M18. [med.L *bannitio(n-)*, f. *bannit-* pa. ppl stem of *bannire* f. Proto-Romance base also of BANISH: see -ION.] Banishment, expulsion, esp. from university.

bannock /ˈbanək/ *n.* *Sc.* & *north.* [OE *bannuc* (recorded once), orig. f. a Brit. wd repr. by Welsh *ban*, Breton *bannac'h*, *banne*, Corn. *banna* drop.] A round, flat (but fairly thick) girdle-cake, usu. made of oatmeal, barley, pease, or flour; (local usage varies).

banns /banz/ *n.pl.* Also (with unexpl. lengthening of the vowel) †**banes**. ME. [Pl. of BAN *n.*[1], after med.L pl. *banna*.] 1 Notice given in church etc. of an intended marriage, read on three Sundays to give an opportunity for objections to be made. ME. 2 Proclamation of a performance of a play; a prologue. Long *obs.* exc. *Hist.* LME.

1 *ask, †bid, publish the banns*. **forbid the banns** make a formal objection to an intended marriage.

banquet /ˈbaŋkwɪt/ *n.* L15. [(O)Fr., dim. of *banc* bench, BANK *n.*[2]] 1 A sumptuous entertainment of food and drink; (now usu.) an elaborate dinner with speeches in celebration of something or to further a cause. L15. †2 A slight meal or snack between meals. Also *running banquet*. E16–M17. 3 A course of sweets, fruit, and wine; a dessert. Long *obs.* exc. *Sc.* & *north.* E16. †b A sweet confection; *collect.* sweets, confectionery foods for dessert. M16–L17. †4 A wine-drinking carousal. M16–E18.

banquet /ˈbaŋkwɪt/ *v.* L15. [Fr. *banqueter*, f. as prec.] 1 *v.i.* Take part in a banquet or banquets; feast, carouse. L15. 2 *v.t.* Entertain at a banquet or banquets; feast, regale. E16. †3 *v.i.* Take a snack, take dessert, (see BANQUET *n.* 2, 3). M16–E19.

banque'teer *n.* = BANQUETER (b) E19. **banqueter** *n.* †(*a*) the giver of a banquet; (*b*) a guest at a banquet; a feaster, a reveller: M16.

banquette /baŋˈkɛt/ *n.* E17. [Fr. f. It. *banchetta* dim. of *banca* bench, shelf.] 1 A raised step or way running along the inside of a rampart, at the bottom of a trench, etc., on which soldiers stand to fire at the enemy. E17. 2 A raised footway or sidewalk. *arch. rare* L18. 3 A long upholstered seat along a wall. M19.

banshee /banˈʃiː, ˈbanʃiː/ *n.* L17. [Ir. *bean sidhe*, OIr. *ben side*, f. *ben* woman + *side* of the fairy world.] In Irish and Scottish folklore: a female spirit whose wail portends death in a house.

bantam /ˈbantəm/ *n.* M18. [App. f. *Bantam*, a district of NW Java, but the fowls are not native there.] 1 A small kind of domestic fowl, of which the cock is a spirited fighter. M18. 2 *fig.* A small but spirited person. L18.

Comb.: **bantamweight** (of) a weight at which boxing etc. matches are made, intermediate between featherweight and flyweight, in the amateur boxing scale now being between 51 and 54 kg, though differing for professionals, wrestlers, and weightlifters, and according to time and place; (a boxer etc.) of this weight.

banteng /ˈbantɛŋ/ *n.* E19. [Malay.] An ox, *Bos banteng*, of SE Asia.

banter /ˈbantə/ *v.* & *n.* L17. [Origin unkn.] A *v.* I *v.t.* 1 Make fun of (a person), rally, esp. good-humouredly. L17. 2 Impose upon (a person), orig. in jest; delude, cheat, bamboozle. *arch.* L17. †3 Make a jest of (a subject, thing). E–M18. 4 Challenge or defy to a race, match, etc. *arch. US.* L18. II *v.i.* 5 Indulge in banter; talk jestingly. L17. B *n.* 1 Nonsense talked to ridicule a subject or person; humorous ridicule; good-natured personal remarks. L17. 2 An instance of such humorous ridicule. *arch.* E18. 3 A challenge to a race, match, etc. *arch. US.* M19.

banterer *n.* L17. **banteringly** *adv.* in a bantering manner, jestingly M19.

Banting /ˈbantɪŋ/ *n.* *arch.* Also **b-**. M19. [W. *Banting* (d. 1878), Eng. dietitian.] The treatment of obesity by abstinence from sugar, starch, and fat.

Bantingism *n.* M19.

bantling /ˈbantlɪŋ/ *n.* L16. [Perh. f. G *Bänkling* bastard, f. *Bank* bench, BANK *n.*[2]: see -LING[1] and cf. BASTARD.] A young child, a brat. Formerly also, an illegitimate child, a bastard.

fig.: BYRON The interest you have taken in me and my poetical bantlings.

Bantu /banˈtuː, ˈbantuː/ *a.* & *n.* M19. [In certain Bantu langs., pl. of *-ntu* person.] (Designating, of or pertaining to) a group of Niger-Congo languages spoken extensively in equatorial and southern Africa. Also (now usu. considered *racially offensive*), (of or pertaining to, a member of) the family of peoples speaking these languages.

Bantustan /-ˈstɑːn, -ˈstan/ *n.* (*S. Afr. colloq.*) [*-stan* as in *Hindustan* etc.] an area reserved for members of a particular ethnic or linguistic group M20.

banxring /ˈbaŋksrɪŋ/ *n.* E19. [Jav. *bangsring*.] In Java and adjacent islands: a tree shrew.

banyan /ˈbanɪən, -njən/ *n.* Also **banian**. L16. [Port. f. Gujarati *vāṇiyo* man of the trading caste, f. Skt *vāṇija* merchant.] I 1 = BANIA. L16. 2 An Indian broker or steward attached to a firm or individual; a sircar. M17. 3 In full *banyan shirt* etc. A loose flannel shirt or jacket. E18. II [Orig. applied by Europeans to a particular tree under which traders had built a pagoda.] 4 In full *banyan tree*. An Indian fig tree, *Ficus benghalensis*, the branches of which root themselves over a wide area. M17.

Comb.: **banyan-day** *arch.* (chiefly *Naut.*): on which no meat is served; *banyan shirt*: see sense 3 above; *banyan tree*: see sense 4 above.

banzai /banˈzʌɪ/ *int.* & *a.* L19. [Jap. = ten thousand years (of life to you).] A *int.* A form of acclamation used by the Japanese esp. to their Emperor, a cheer used in battle etc. L19. B *attrib.* or as *adj.* (As if) shouting 'banzai'; uproarious; (of an attack by Japanese) reckless. *slang.* E20.

banzuke /banˈzuːki/ *n.* L20. [Jap.] The ranking list of sumo wrestlers.

baobab /ˈbeɪəbab/ *n.* M17. [Prob. f. a central African lang.: first mentioned (in Ethiopia) in L by Prosper Alpinus (1592).] An African tree, *Adansonia digitata*, having an enormously thick trunk and large edible pulpy fruit that hangs down on stalks. Also *baobab tree*.

bap /bap/ *n.* L16. [Origin unkn.] A large soft bread roll.

Baphometic /bafəˈmɛtɪk/ *a.* M19. [f. Fr. *baphomet* f. med.L (for *Mahomet*), + -IC.] Chiefly *Hist.* Of or pertaining to (the worship of) Baphomet, the alleged idol of the Knights Templars.

baptise *v.* var. of BAPTIZE.

baptism /ˈbaptɪz(ə)m/ *n.* ME. [OFr. *ba(p)te(s)me* (now *baptême*) semi-pop. f. eccl.L *baptismus*, *-um* (also *-a*) f. eccl.Gk *baptismos* ceremonial washing, *baptisma* baptism, f. *baptizein* BAPTIZE. Refash. after L & Gk.] 1 The application of water to a person by immersion, pouring, or sprinkling, as a religious rite, symbolical of purification or regeneration, and, with Christians, betokening initiation into the Church, often accompanied by naming. ME. 2 The naming of church bells and of ships. L16.

1 *fig.*: **baptism of blood** martyrdom of the unbaptized. **baptism of fire** a soldier's first battle.

baptismal /bapˈtɪzm(ə)l/ *a.* M17. [med.L *baptismalis*, f. *baptismus* etc.: see prec., -AL[1].] Of, pertaining to, or connected with baptism.

baptismal name the personal or Christian name given at baptism. *baptismal vows*: see VOW *n.*

baptismally *adv.* M19.

baptist /ˈbaptɪst/ *n.* & *a.* Also (as a specific epithet and of the religious body) **B-**. ME. [(O)Fr. *baptiste* f. eccl.L *baptista* f. eccl.Gk *baptistēs*, f. *baptizein* BAPTIZE: see -IST.] A *n.* 1 A person who baptizes; *spec.* John, the forerunner of Christ (St John the Baptist). ME. 2 A member of a Protestant Christian religious body practising baptism only of believers (not infants) and by immersion (cf. ANABAPTIST 2). L16.

2 *Free Will Baptist*: see FREE WILL. *Particular Baptist*: see PARTICULAR *a.* *Primitive Baptist*: see PRIMITIVE *a.* & *n.* *Southern Baptist*: see SOUTHERN *a.*

B *attrib.* or as *adj.* Of or pertaining to the religious body of the Baptists; being a Baptist. E18.

baptistery /ˈbaptɪst(ə)ri/ *n.* Also **-try** /-tri/. ME. [OFr. *ba(p)tistere*, *-erie* (mod. *baptistère*) f. eccl.L *baptisterium* f. eccl.Gk *baptistērion*, f. *baptizein* (see next).] **1** That part of a church (or, formerly, a separate building adjacent to a church) used for baptism. ME. **2** In a Baptist chapel, a receptacle containing water for baptism by immersion. M19.

baptize /bapˈtʌɪz/ *v.* Also **-ise**. ME. [(O)Fr. *baptiser* f. eccl.L *baptizare* f. Gk *baptizein* dip, immerse, (eccl.) baptize.] **1** *v.t.* Administer baptism to. ME. **b** *v.i.* Administer baptism. ME. **2** *v.t.* Name (as in baptism), denominate, nickname. LME.

baptizable *a.* capable of or fit for baptism M17. †**baptization** *n.* = BAPTISM LME–E18. **baptizer** *n.* L15.

bar /bɑː/ *n.*[1] ME. [(O)Fr. *barre* f. Proto-Romance, of unkn. origin.] **I 1** *gen.* A straight piece of wood, metal, or other rigid material, long in proportion to its thickness. ME. **2** *spec.* **a** A rod or pole made to fasten, confine, or obstruct. ME. **b** A thick rod thrown in a trial of strength. L15. **c** = BARRE 2. L19. **d** *The* crossbar of a football goal. L19. **e** A heating element of an electric fire. E20. †**3** An ornamental (esp. transverse) band or boss. ME–M16. **4** A straight stripe, a broad band of colour etc. on a surface. LME. **5** *Her.* A narrow horizontal stripe equal to or less than one fifth of the width of the field. Cf. BARRULET. LME. **6** An oblong piece of metal or something manufactured (as soap, chocolate, etc.). L16. **b** One pound sterling. *slang.* E20. **7** In *pl.* The transverse ridged divisions of a horse's palate. E17. **8** A strip of silver below the clasp of a medal signifying an additional distinction; a distinction so signified. M19.

1 *parallel bars*: see PARALLEL *a.* *T-bar*: see T, T 2. 2a **behind bars** in prison. CROSSBAR *n.* 4 *Stars and Bars*: see STAR *n.*[1] & *a.* 5 **bar sinister** (erron. for) a bend or baton sinister, a supposed sign of bastardy.

II 9 A material structure of any shape, forming a barrier. ME. **10** *Hist. spec.* **a** A barrier or gate closing the entrance into a city. ME. **b** A toll-house gate or barrier. M16. **11** In *pl.* Prisoners' base (see BASE *n.*[2]) or a similar children's game. Cf. *prison bars* s.v. PRISON, *prisoners' bars* s.v. PRISONER. ME. **12** *Law.* A plea or objection of force sufficient to block an action or claim. LME. **13** *fig.* An obstruction, an obstacle; a restriction. M16. **14** A bank of sand, silt, etc., across the mouth of a river or harbour, obstructing navigation. L16. **15** *Mus.* Any of successive vertical lines across the staff dividing a composition into metrical groupings, often of equal time-value, and placed before the initial accent of each grouping; a section between two such lines, a measure. M17.

12 in bar of as a sufficient reason or plea against to prevent. *personal bar*: see PERSONAL *a.* 13 BURKE Thereby fixing a permanent bar against any relief. L. A. G. STRONG Disparity in years . . is not invariably a bar to harmony. 15 *double bar*: see DOUBLE *a.* & *adv.*

III Specialized uses in courts of law, legislative assemblies, etc. **16** In a court of law, the barrier or rail at which a prisoner stands. In the Inns of Court, formerly, a barrier or partition separating the seats of the benchers from the rest of the hall, to which students, after they had reached a certain standing, were 'called' (long pop. understood to refer to that in a court of justice, beyond which the King's or Queen's Counsel (and Serjeants-at-Law) have place, but not ordinary barristers). ME. **b** A tribunal (*lit.* & *fig.*); a (particular) court of law. LME. **17** *the bar*: **a** The whole body of barristers or (*US*) lawyers; *the outer bar*, barristers not King's or Queen's Counsel. LME. **b** The profession of barrister; occupation as counsel in a court of justice. M17. **18** A rail dividing off a space in a legislative assembly etc. to which non-members may be admitted on business. L16.

16 at the bar, *arch.* **at bar** in court, in open court. **be called to the bar** be admitted as a barrister. **be called within the bar** be appointed King's or Queen's Counsel. **call to the bar** admission as a barrister. *go to the bar*: see GO *v.* *inner bar*: see INNER *a.* PRISONER *at the bar*. b CARLYLE The Judgment-bar of the Most High God. H. P. BROUGHAM I have practised at the bar of the House of Lords. *New Republic* The United States may be called to account before the bar of world opinion . . for its Latin-American policy

IV Any other barrier or rail acquiring technical significance from its use. **19** A counter in a public house, hotel, etc., across which alcoholic refreshments are served; the space behind such a counter; the room or premises containing such a counter. L15. **20** With specifying wd: a place where something is served or offered across a counter; a specialized department in a large shop. M20.

19 J. HELLER He went to the bar for more bourbon. P. NORMAN Although Jack worked in a bar, it did not seem to make him tired of bars, and he and Olwen became frequent visitors . . to the pierhead pub. *lounge bar*, *public bar*, etc. *prop up the bar*: see PROP *v.* 2. *wet bar*: see WET *a.* 20 *coffee bar*, *food bar*, *snack bar*, *suchi bar*, *tapas bar*, etc. *heel bar*, *stocking bar*, etc.

Comb.: **barbell** an iron bar with a heavy ball at each end used in exercising; **bar billiards** a game (popular in public houses) using a small table similar to a billiard-table but with holes of different score values on the bed of the table, into which the balls have to be directed; **bar chart** a chart using bars to represent quantities; **bar code** a code of lines and numbers printed in a band on wrappings, packages, etc., and interpretable by an optical scanner; **bar-coding** the practice or process of marking goods etc. with bar codes; **barfly** *colloq.* (*a*) a person who frequents the bars of public houses etc.; (*b*) (more fully *barfly jumping*) the practice of taking a running jump at a specially coated hanging surface with the aim of sticking to it on impact; **bar-girl** *US* a woman employed to encourage customers to buy drinks at a bar; *bar-keel*: see KEEL *n.*[1]; **barkeep** *N. Amer.* = *bartender* below; **bar-line** *Mus.* a line across a stave marking metrical accent (see sense 15 above); *bar magnet*: see MAGNET 2; **barmaid**, **barman** a female, male, bartender; **bar-room** a room with a bar selling alcoholic refreshments; **bar soap** soap made up into bars (rather than cakes or tablets); **bartender** a person serving alcoholic refreshments at a bar; *bar* TRACERY.

†**barful** *a.* (*rare*, Shakes.) full of hindrances: only in E17.

bar /bɑː/ *n.*[2] E18. [Fr. *bar(s)* f. Du. *baars*: see BARSE, & cf. BASS *n.*[1]] = MEAGRE *n.*[1]

bar /bɑː/ *n.*[3] *US.* E19. [Louisiana Fr. *boire*.] In full *mosquito bar*. A type of mosquito netting.

bar /bɑː/ *n.*[4] E20. [Gk *baros* weight.] Chiefly *Meteorol.* A unit of pressure equal to 10^5 pascal (about 0.9870 atmosphere).

bar /bɑː/ *v.t.* Infl. **-rr-**. ME. [(O)Fr. *barrer*, f. as BAR *n.*[1]] **I** Make fast with a bar or bars. **1** Make fast (a door etc.) with a bar or bars; fasten up (a place) with a bar or bars; provide with a bar or bars. ME. **2** Fasten in, shut up, or confine securely (a person or thing) with a bar or bars; keep or shut *in* or *out*. LME. **3** *Law.* Block (a person, an action or claim) by objection. LME. **4** Hinder, prevent, or prohibit (a person) *from*; deprive or debar *of*. Also foll. by (*arch.*) 2nd obj., †*to do*. LME. **5** Stop, hinder, prevent, prohibit, (an action or event). M16. **6** Exclude from consideration, set aside, (cf. BAR, BARRING *preps.*). L16. **7** Obstruct (a way of approach, a person's progress). L16. **8** Take exception to, object to. Now *slang.* E17.

3 *statute-barred*: see STATUTE *n.* *time-barred*: see TIME *n.* 4 N. HARPSFIELD Is there anything here that barreth those that be under the patriarch of Alexandria . . to appeal to the see apostolic? SHAKES. *2 Hen. IV* I will bar no honest man my house. R. L'ESTRANGE A Disease . . barrs us of some Pleasures, but procures us others. TENNYSON Last from her own home-circle . . They barr'd her. 5 P. G. WODEHOUSE No more friendly little games with nothing barred except biting and bottles. F. RAPHAEL Its sale was barred on station bookstalls. (*with*) *no holds barred*: see HOLD *n.*[1] 2b. 6 R. HERRICK When next thou do'st invite, barre state, And give me meate.

II 9 Mark with bars or stripes; divide or make into bars. Chiefly as *barred* ppl a. LME.

9 KEATS Eyed like a peacock, and all crimson barr'd. R. G. COLLINGWOOD The Scherzo of Beethoven's C minor Symphony begins by reproducing the Finale of Mozart's G minor, differently barred.

bar /bɑː/ *prep.* E18. [Imper. of prec., prob. after *except*, *save*, etc.: cf. BARRING *prep.*] Except; excluding from consideration; but for.

bar none with no exceptions. **bar two**, **three**, etc. (in stating the odds in *Racing*) except the two, three, etc., horses already named; also *ellipt.* w. the number omitted. (*it is*) *all over bar the shouting*: see SHOUT *v.*

baracan *n.* var. of BARRACAN.

baragouin /baragwɛ̃, barəˈgwɪn/ *n.* E17. [Fr.] Gibberish; unintelligible jargon.

Baralipton /barəˈlɪpt(ə)n/ *n.* L16. [A mnemonic of scholastic philosophers, first used in med.L, A indicating a universal affirmative proposition and I a particular affirmative proposition.] *Logic.* The first indirect mood of the first syllogistic figure, in which a particular affirmative conclusion is drawn from two universal affirmative premisses.

barasingha /barəˈsɪŋgə/ *n.* M19. [Hind. *bārah-siŋgā* lit. 'twelve-tined'.] = *swamp deer* s.v. SWAMP *n.*

barathea /barəˈθiːə/ *n.* & *a.* M19. [Origin unkn.] (Of) a fine-textured twill cloth, made of wool or a man-made fibre, often with an admixture of silk, cotton, or other lighter fibre.

barathrum /ˈbarəθrəm/ *n.* *obs.* or *Hist.* Pl. **-thra** /-θrə/, **-thrums**. E16. [L f. Gk *barathron* pit, gulf.] †**1** Hell. E16–M18. †**2** An insatiable extortioner or glutton. E–M17. **3** *Hist.* A pit in Athens into which condemned criminals were thrown. M19.

baraza /bəˈrɑːzə/ *n.* L19. [Kiswahili.] In E. Africa: a place of public audience or reception; a meeting, a reception.

barb /bɑːb/ *n.*[1] In sense 1 also **barbe**. ME. [(O)Fr. *barbe* f. L *barba* beard.] **1** A piece of vertically pleated linen cloth worn over or under the chin, as by nuns. ME. **2**†**a** A man's beard. *rare.* LME–L17. **b** An appendage in an animal resembling a beard; *esp.* = BARBEL 2. L15. **3** A secondary backward-projecting point of an arrow, fish-hook, etc., making its extraction difficult. LME. **b** *fig.* A wounding quality or remark. L18. **4** *Vet. Med.* Usu. in *pl.* Any of the folds of the mucous membrane which protect the submaxillary glands of cattle and horses; (in *pl.*) inflammation of these folds. E16. **5** *Her.* A sepal (in *pl.* the calyx) of a flower. Also, the head of an arrow. L16. **6** Any of the lateral processes from the shaft of a feather. M19. **7** A sciaenid fish of the genus *Menticirrhus*, found on the N. American Atlantic and Gulf coasts; also called *kingfish*. Also, a brightly coloured tropical fish of the genus *Barbus*. L19.

Comb.: **barbwire** (chiefly *US*) = *barbed wire* s.v. BARBED *a.*[1] 2.

†**barb** *n.*[2] M16–M17. [Alt. of BARD *n.*[2]] Usu. in *pl.* = BARD *n.*[2] 1.

SPENSER His loftie steed with . . goodly gorgeous barbes.

barb /bɑːb/ *n.*[3] M17. [Fr. *barbe* f. It. *barbero* of Barbary: see BARBARY 1.] **1** (An animal of) a breed of horse from Barbary. M17. **2** (A bird of) a breed of pigeon from Barbary. E18. **3** A black kelpie dog. *Austral.* E20.

barb /bɑːb/ *v.t.* LME. [Fr. †*barber*, f. as BARB *n.*[1]] **1** Clip or trim (a fleece, cloth, coin, etc.). Long *rare.* LME. **2** Shave or trim the beard of. Long *rare.* L16. **3** Provide (an arrow, hook, etc.) with a barb or barbs. E17.

3 *fig.*: R. H. TAWNEY The needlessly sharp censures with which he barbed the fine imposed upon an enclosing landlord.

Barbadian /bɑːˈbeɪdɪən/ *n.* & *a.* E18. [f. BARBADOS, †(*the*) *Barbadoes* + -IAN.] (A native or inhabitant) of Barbados in the W. Indies. Cf. BADIAN.

†**Barbadoes** *n.* var. of BARBADOS.

†**Barbadoes** *v.t.* M17–M19. [f. (*the*) *Barbadoes*: see next] Transport to Barbados.

Barbados /bɑːˈbeɪdɒs/ *n.* Also †**-oes**. L17. [An island in the W. Indies, formerly (*the*) *Barbadoes*.] Used *attrib.* to designate things from or characteristic of Barbados, esp. plants.

Barbados cherry (the edible fruit of) a neotropical tree, *Malpighia glabra* (family Malpighiaceae). *Barbados* GOOSEBERRY. **Barbados lily** = HIPPEASTRUM. **Barbados pride** a W. Indian leguminous shrub, *Caesalpinia pulcherrima*, bearing red flowers with yellow petal margins.

barbal /ˈbɑːb(ə)l/ *a. rare.* M17. [f. L *barba* beard + -AL^{1}.] Of or pertaining to the beard.

†barbar *n.* & *a.* LME. [f. as BARBAROUS.] A *n.* = BARBARIAN *n.* LME–E18. B *adj.* = BARBAROUS. LME–E18.

Barbara /ˈbɑːbərə/ *n.* M16. [L = barbarous things, taken as a mnemonic for its three *a*'s, A indicating a universal affirmative proposition.] *Logic.* The first mood of the first syllogistic figure, in which both premisses and the conclusion are universal affirmatives.

Barbaresque /bɑːbəˈrɛsk/ *a.* & *n.* In sense A.2 **b-**. E19. [Fr. *barbaresque* f. It. *barbaresco* f. *Barbaria* Barbary: see BARBARY 1, -ESQUE.] A *adj.* 1 Of or pertaining to Barbary (see BARBARY 1). Now *arch.* or *Hist.* E19. 2 Barbarous in (esp. artistic) style. E19. B *n.* A native or inhabitant of Barbary. Now *arch.* or *Hist.* E19.

barbarian /bɑːˈbɛːrɪən/ *a.* & *n.* ME. [Fr. †*barbarien* or L, extended (after *chrétien* etc. CHRISTIAN *a.*, *n.*) f. (O)Fr. *barbare* f. as BARBAR: see -IAN.] A *adj.* 1 Foreign; *spec.* non-Hellenic, (*esp.*) non-Roman; also, pagan, non-Christian. Usu. *depreciative.* Now *arch.* or *Hist.* ME. 2 Uncivilized, savage. L16. †3 Of or pertaining to Barbary (see BARBARY 1). L16–L17.

1 SHAKES. *Tr. & Cr.* Thou art here but to thrash Trojans, and thou art bought and sold . . like a barbarian slave. POPE Barbarian blindness, Christian zeal conspire. H. T. COLEBROOKE Several other terms . . are not Sanscrit, but, apparently, barbarian. H. HALLAM Establishment of the barbarian nations on the ruins of the Roman Empire. 2 A. PATON A barbarian people, who not long since plundered and slaughtered . . under the most terrible chief of all.

B *n.* I 1 A foreigner; a person with a different language or different customs; *spec.* a non-Hellene, a non-Roman; also, a pagan, a non-Christian. Usu. *depreciative.* Now *arch.* or *Hist.* LME. 2 A savage, wild, or uncivilized person. L15. 3 An uncultured person; a person without sympathy for literary or artistic culture. M18.

1 SHAKES. *Coriol.* I would they were barbarians . . not Romans. HOBBES The Athenians . . expecting the coming of the Barbarian. J. CLAVELL Even that would not have mattered . . if he still had the barbarian in his power . . ; he would simply have handed over the foreigner. 2 DRYDEN Skins of Beasts, the rude Barbarians wear. K. CLARK Into that chaos came real barbarians like the Huns, who were totally illiterate and destructively hostile to what they couldn't understand. 3 D. HUME Cromwell, though himself a barbarian, was not insensible to literary merit.

†II 4 A native or inhabitant of Barbary (see BARBARY 1). LME–E18.

barbaric /bɑːˈbarɪk/ *n.* & *a.* LME. [Fr. †*barbarique* or L *barbaricus* f. Gk *barbarikos*, f. *barbaros* foreign: see -IC.] †A *n.* = BARBARIAN *n.* 1. Only in LME.

B *adj.* 1 Uncivilized, uncultured; savage; savagely cruel. L15. 2 Of or pertaining to barbarians; characteristic of the artistic taste or style of barbarians; unrestrained. M17. 3 = BARBARIAN *a.* 1. *arch.* M19.

1 H. J. LASKI The noble savage, on investigation, turns out to be a barbaric creature with a club and scalping knife. 2 MILTON Barbaric pearl and gold. R. LEHMANN Like one moving in a barbaric rite of dedication towards some altar. 3 G. GROTE Sending envoys to the Persian King and not to other barbaric powers.

barbarically *adv.* M19.

†Barbarin *n.* var. of BERBERINE.

†barbarious *a.* L15–M18. [f. (as) BARBARY + -OUS.] = BARBAROUS.

barbarise *v.* var. of BARBARIZE.

barbarism /ˈbɑːbərɪz(ə)m/ *n.* LME. [(O)Fr. *barbarisme* f. L *barbarismus* f. Gk *barbarismos*, f. *barbarizein* behave or speak like a foreigner: see -ISM.] 1 Uncivilized nature or condition; uncultured ignorance; absence of culture; barbaric style (in art etc.), unrestrainedness. LME. b A trait or characteristic of such uncivilized condition. M17. 2 The use of words and idioms not in accordance with the (supposed) normal standard language, esp. of those of foreign origin; absence of cultivation in language. M16. b A foreign, non-classical, or non-standard word or idiom. L16. †3 = BARBARITY 3. E–M17.

1 A. P. STANLEY The imperceptible boundary between civilisation and barbarism. K. CLARK Its sculpture is miserably crude, without even the vitality of barbarism. b J. HOWELL Plundering and other barbarismes that reign now abroad.

barbarity /bɑːˈbarɪti/ *n.* M16. [f. L *barbarus* (see BARBAROUS) + -ITY.] †1 = BARBARISM 2. M16–L18. 2 = BARBARISM 1, 1b. *arch.* L16. 3 Savage cruelty; harsh unkindness. L17. b An act of savage cruelty. E18.

barbarize /ˈbɑːbərʌɪz/ *v.* Also **-ise.** LME. [Late L *barbarizare* f. Gk *barbarizein* (see BARBARISM) or f. as next + -IZE.] 1 *v.i.* Use barbarisms in speech or writing; violate classical grammatical rules. LME. 2 *v.t.* Make (esp. language) barbarous. E17. 3 *v.i.* Become barbarous. E19.

barbariˈzation *n.* E19.

barbarous /ˈbɑːbərəs/ *a.* Also occas. in L form **†-rus.** LME. [f. L *barbarus* (f. Gk *barbaros* non-Greek, foreign, esp. of speech) + -OUS.] 1 Uncultured; uncivilized; rough; rude; coarse. LME. 2 *spec.* Of language: not Greek; not Greek or Latin; not classical or standard; having many barbarisms. M16. 3 Of a person: = BARBARIAN *a.* 1. *arch.* M16. 4 Cruelly savage; harshly unkind. M16. 5 Harsh-sounding; coarsely noisy. M17. †6 = BARBARIC *a.* 2. *rare.* Only in E18.

1 SHAKES. *Twel. N.* Ungracious wretch, Fit for the mountains and the barbarous caves, Where manners ne'er were preach'd! CARLYLE An uncultured semi-barbarous son of Nature. J. HAWKES Most of them [villas] were built by romanized Britons, sometimes even on the foundations of their old barbarous homes of wood and wattle. 2 W. COWPER The Carians, people of a barbarous speech. D. BAGLEY Formulating his phrases carefully in the barbarous French these people used. 4 H. FIELDING It would be barbarous to part Tom and the girl. G. B. SHAW England was a civilized Power and would not stand these barbarous lashings and vindictive hangings. 5 YEATS The barbarous clangour of a gong. 6 DRYDEN The trappings of his horse emboss'd with barbarous gold.

barbarously *adv.* M16. **barbarousness** *n.* M16.

Barbary /ˈbɑːbəri/ *n.* In sense 2 also **b-**. ME. [Sense 1 ult. f. Arab. *barbar* (cf. BERBER); sense 2 f. OFr. *barbarie* or L *barbaria*, *-ies* land of barbarians, f. as prec.: see -Y^{3}.] 1 (An old name for) the western part of N. Africa. ME. †2 Foreign nationality; paganism; barbarity; barbarism; foreign or non-Christian lands. LME–M17.

Comb.: **Barbary ape** a macaque, *Macaca sylvana*, of N. Africa and Gibraltar; **Barbary falcon** a falcon, *Falco pelegrinoides*, of N. Africa and the Middle East; **Barbary partridge** a N. African partridge, *Alectoris barbara*; **Barbary sheep** = AOUDAD.

barbasco /bɑːˈbaskəʊ/ *n.* Pl. **-os.** M19. [Amer. Sp., app. f. Sp. *verbasco* f. L *verbascum* mullein.] (A poison obtained from the roots of) any of various S. American plants; *esp.* = CUBE *n.*^{2}

barbastelle /bɑːbəˈstɛl, ˈbɑːbəstɛl/ *n.* L18. [Fr. f. It. *barbastello.*] Either of two bats of the genus *Barbastella*; esp. *B. barbastellus*, found in southern Britain.

barbate /ˈbɑːbeɪt/ *a.* M18. [L *barbatus* bearded, f. *barba* beard: see -ATE^{2}.] Bearded; furnished with a small hairy tuft or tufts.

barbe *n.* see BARB *n.*^{1}

barbecue /ˈbɑːbɪkjuː/ *n.* M17. [Sp. *barbacoa* perh. f. Arawak *barbacoa* raised wooden framework of sticks.] †I 1 A wooden framework for storage, sleeping on, etc. M–L17. II 2 An animal broiled or roasted whole, esp. out of doors; meat etc. cooked out of doors on a frame over an open fire. E18. 3 An outdoor entertainment at which meat is cooked on a frame over an open fire. M18. 4 A wooden or (now esp.) metal frame for cooking, smoking, or drying meat over an open fire; a (usu. portable) fireplace containing such a frame. L19. III 5 An open floor on which coffee beans etc. may be spread out to dry. M18.

Comb.: **barbecue sauce** a highly seasoned sauce used esp. w. grilled or roasted meat.

barbecue /ˈbɑːbɪkjuː/ *v.t.* M17. [f. (as) prec.] Cook, smoke, or dry (meat etc.) on a frame over an open fire, esp. out of doors; broil or roast (an animal) whole.

barbed /bɑːbd/ *a.*^{1} LME. [f. BARB *n.*^{1}, *v.*: see -ED^{2}, -ED^{1}.] †1 Wearing a barb (see BARB *n.*^{1} 1). LME–E17. 2 Furnished with a barb or barbs (see BARB *n.*^{1} 3, BARB *v.* 3). E17. 3 *Her.* Of a flower: having a calyx of a specified tincture. E17.

2 **barbed wire** wire of twisted strands with short pointed pieces inserted at intervals, used for fences and as an obstruction in war.

barbed /bɑːbd, *poet.* ˈbɑːbɪd/ *a.*^{2} Long *arch.* E16. [f. BARB *n.*^{2} + -ED^{2}.] Barded (see BARD *v.* 1).

barbel /ˈbɑːb(ə)l/ *n.* LME. [OFr. f. late L *barbellus* dim. of *barbus*, f. *barba* beard.] 1 A large European freshwater fish of the genus *Barbus*, having a number of fleshy filaments hanging from its mouth. LME. 2 A fleshy filament hanging from the mouth of any fish. E17.

barber /ˈbɑːbə/ *n.* & *v.* ME. [AN *barber*, *-our*, OFr. *barbier*, f. (O)Fr. *barbe* beard: see BARB *n.*^{1}, -ER^{2}.] A *n.* 1 A person who cuts and dresses men's hair and shaves or trims beards; a men's hairdresser; *Hist.* such a person also acting as a surgeon and dentist. ME. 2 A cutting cold wind. *colloq.* (chiefly *Canad.* & *NZ*). M19.

1 *spud barber*: see SPUD *n.*

Comb.: **barber-shop** (*a*) (now chiefly *N. Amer.*) a shop where a barber works; (*b*) *attrib.* designating (an ensemble, esp. a male quartet, singing) close harmony music; **barber's itch, rash** ringworm of the face or neck communicated by unsterilized shaving apparatus; **barber's pole** a pole spirally painted in red and white, used as a barber's sign; *barber's rash*: see *barber's itch* above.

B *v.* 1 *v.t.* Cut or trim the hair or beard of; cut (grass etc.) short. E17. 2 *v.i.* Work as a barber. Chiefly as *barbering* vbl n. M17.

barbery *n.* (now *rare*) the art or craft of a barber LME.

barberry /ˈbɑːbəri/ *n.* Also **ber-** /ˈbəː-/. LME. [OFr. BERBERIS, assim. to BERRY *n.*^{1}] 1 Any of numerous shrubs of the genus *Berberis* (family Berberidaceae), usu. thorny and with yellow wood; esp. *B. vulgaris*, bearing racemes of yellow flowers succeeded by red oblong berries. LME. 2 The berry of such a shrub. M16.

barbet /ˈbɑːbɪt/ *n.* L16. [Fr., f. *barbe* beard: see -ET^{1}.] †1 A poodle. L16–E19. 2 Any of numerous brightly coloured fruit-eating tropical birds of the family Capitonidae, which have tufts of bristles at the base of the bill. E19.

barbette /bɑːˈbɛt/ *n.* L18. [Fr., f. as prec.: see -ETTE.] A platform in a fort or ship from which guns fire over a parapet etc. and not through an embrasure.

barbican /ˈbɑːbɪk(ə)n/ *n.* ME. [(O)Fr. *barbacane* = med.L *barbacana*, *barbi-*, prob. ult. f. Arab.] An outer defence to a city or castle, *esp.* a double tower erected over a gate or bridge.

barbicel /ˈbɑːbɪs(ə)l/ *n.* M19. [It. & mod.L *barbicella* dim. of *barba* beard.] Any of the minute hooked filaments which interlock the barbules of a bird's feathers.

barbie /ˈbɑːbi/ *n. colloq.* (chiefly *Austral.*). L20. [Abbrev.: see -IE.] = BARBECUE *n.* 3, 4.

Barbie doll /ˈbɑːbɪ dɒl/ *n. phr.* Chiefly *N. Amer.* M20. [f. dim. of female personal name *Barbara* + DOLL *n.*^{1}] (Proprietary name for) a doll representing a slim, fashionably dressed, conventionally attractive young woman; *transf.* a pretty but passive or characterless woman.

barbiers /ˈbɑːbɪəz/ *n. arch.* L17. [Fr. alt. of BERIBERI.] A paralytic disease occurring in the Indian subcontinent.

barbital /ˈbɑːbɪt(ə)l/ *n. US.* E20. [f. as BARBITURIC + -AL^{2}.] = BARBITONE.

barbiton *n.* var. of BARBITOS.

barbitone /ˈbɑːbɪtəʊn/ *n.* E20. [f. as BARBITURIC + -ONE.] 5,5-Diethylbarbituric acid, or its sodium salt (usu. *barbitone sodium*), used as a hypnotic drug. Also called *veronal.*

barbitos /ˈbɑːbɪtəs/ *n.* Also **-ton** /-tən/. M16. [L f. Gk.] An ancient musical instrument with many strings, prob. a type of lute or lyre.

barbiturate /bɑːˈbɪtjʊrət/ *n.* L19. [f. next + -ATE^{1}.] A salt of barbituric acid; any of the large class of hypnotic and sedative drugs derived from barbituric acid.

barbituric /bɑːbɪˈtjʊərɪk/ *a.* M19. [Fr. *barbiturique* f. G *Barbitur(säure* acid), f. *Barbara* a woman's name: see URIC.] Chem. *barbituric acid*, malonyl urea, $C_4H_4O_3N_2$, a synthetic cyclic dibasic acid from which many hypnotic and sedative drugs are derived.

Barbizon /ˈbɑːbɪzɒn, *foreign* barbizɔ̃/ *n.* L19. [A village near the forest of Fontainebleau, France.] Used *attrib.* to designate (a member of) a mid-19th-cent. school of naturalistic painters.

barbola /bɑːˈbəʊlə/ *n.* E20. [Arbitrary formation f. next.] In full *barbola work*. Decorative work on small articles consisting of coloured models of flowers, fruit, etc., made from a plastic paste.

barbotine /ˈbɑːbətɪn, -tiːn/ *n.* M19. [Fr.] (Pottery ornamented with) a slip of kaolin clay.

Barbudan /bɑːˈbuːd(ə)n/ *n.* & *a.* L20. [f. *Barbuda* (see below) + -AN.] (A native or inhabitant) of the W. Indian island of Barbuda, part of the country Antigua and Barbuda.

barbule /ˈbɑːbjuːl/ *n.* M19. [L *barbula* dim. of *barba* beard: see -ULE.] 1 = BARBEL 2. Now *rare* or *obs.* M19. 2 A filament branching from a barb of a feather as the barb from the shaft. M19.

barcarole /ˈbɑːkərəʊl, bɑːkəˈrəʊl/ *n.* Also **-rolle** /-rɒl/. L18. [Fr. *barcarolle* f. Venetian It. *barcarola* rel. to *barcarolo* gondolier, f. *barca* BARK *n.*[3]] A song sung by Venetian gondoliers; a piece of music in imitation of such songs or suggestive of the rocking motion of a boat.

Barcelona /bɑːsɪˈləʊnə/ *n.* M18. [A city in Spain.] †1 In full *Barcelona handkerchief, neckerchief*. A handkerchief or neckerchief of soft twilled silk. M18–M19. 2 In full *Barcelona nut*. A hazelnut imported from Spain or an adjacent country. M19.

barchan /ˈbɑːk(ə)n/ *n.* Also **-ane**. L19. [Turkic *barkhan*.] A shifting crescent-shaped sand-dune, concave on the leeward side.

Barcoo /bɑːˈkuː/ *n. Austral. slang.* L19. [A river in western Queensland.] 1 *Barcoo grass*, a Queensland pasture grass. L19. 2 *Barcoo rot*, chronic ulceration of the skin. L19. 3 *Barcoo spew, vomit*, etc., illness accompanied by acts of vomiting. L19. 4 A violent storm. Also *Barcoo buster*. M20.

bard /bɑːd/ *n.*[1] ME. [Gael. *bàrd*, Ir. *bard*, Welsh *bardd*, f. Celt. (whence Gk *bardos*, L *bardus*). First used in Scotland and as a term of contempt, but idealized by Sir Walter Scott.] 1 Any of an ancient Celtic order of minstrel-poets, who composed and sang (usu. to the harp) verses celebrating the achievements of chiefs and warriors, recording historical events, traditional lore, etc. In Wales *spec.* a poet honoured at an eisteddfod. ME. b A strolling musician or minstrel. *Sc. arch.* LME. c A minstrel or poet of any other oral tradition, as an Anglo-Saxon scop, a Scandinavian scald, etc. M18. 2 Any poet; *esp.* a lyric or epic poet. *literary.* M17.

2 **the Bard (of Avon)** Shakespeare.

bardic *a.* of, pertaining to, or characteristic of a bard L18. **bardish** *a.* (somewhat *derog.*) = BARDIC E17. **bardism** *n.* the art or practice of bards E18. **bardling** *n.* a young or inexperienced poet, a poetaster M18. **bardship** *n.* the office, dignity, or character of a bard L18.

bard /bɑːd/ *n.*[2] L15. [(O)Fr. *barde* ult. f. Arab. *barda'a* saddle-cloth, stuffed saddle.] 1 *Hist.* Usu. in *pl.* A covering of armour for the breast and flanks of a warhorse; occas. an ornamental covering of velvet or the like. L15. †b Armour for men-at-arms composed of metal plates. M16–E17. 2 *Cookery.* A thin slice of bacon used in covering a fowl etc. E18.

bard /bɑːd/ *v.t.* E16. [Fr. *barder*, f. as prec.] 1 *Hist.* Arm or caparison with bards. Freq. as *barded* ppl a. E16. 2 Cover (a fowl etc.) with slices of bacon. M17.

†bardash *n.* M16–L19. [Fr. *bardache* f. It. *bardascia*, perh. f. Arab. *bardaj* slave.] A catamite.

bardee /ˈbɑːdi/ *n. Austral.* Also **-di**, **-dy**. M19. [Aborig.] The edible wood-boring grub of a beetle or moth. Also *bardee grub*.

Bardfield oxlip /ˈbɑːdfiːld ˈɒkslɪp/ *n. phr.* M19. [*Bardfield*, a village in Essex, England.] The true oxlip, *Primula elatior*.

bardi *n.* var. of BARDEE.

bardolatry /bɑːˈdɒlətri/ *n.* E20. [f. BARD *n.*[1] + -O- + -LATRY.] Excessive admiration of a poet, *spec.* of Shakespeare, 'the Bard of Avon'.

bardolater *n.* a worshipper of the Bard E20. **bardolatrous** *a.* E20.

Bardolphian /bɑːˈdɒlfɪən/ *a.* M18. [f. *Bardolph* (see below) + -IAN.] Resembling or characteristic of Bardolph, a character in Shakespeare's *Henry IV*, *Henry V*, and *Merry Wives of Windsor*, noted for his red nose.

bardy *n.* var. of BARDEE.

bare /bɛː/ *a.*, *adv.*, & *n.* [OE *bær* = OFris., OS, (O)HG *bar*, MDu. *baer* (Du. *baar*), ON *berr*, f. Gmc f. IE.] A *adj.* 1 Of the body or its parts: unclothed, naked. OE. b With the head uncovered; hatless. *arch.* LME. 2 *fig.* Open to view, unconcealed. OE. 3 Of things: without the natural covering which they have at other times; lacking vegetation, foliage, etc. OE. 4 Deprived of hair, wool, flesh, etc.; bald. ME. 5 Lacking appropriate covering; unfurnished; undecorated. ME. b Of weapons: unsheathed. Esp. of the hands: unarmed. ME. 6 Without addition; mere, simple; scant, slight. ME. †7 Unprotected, deserted; laid waste, desolate. ME–M17. 8 Destitute, empty, short, *of*; lacking *in*. ME. 9 *absol.* a Of a person: destitute, needy. *arch.* ME. b Empty; without contents. LME. 10 Spare, meagre. Chiefly of literary style etc.: plain, unelaborate. ME. †11 Poor in quality; paltry. LME–L16.

2 MILTON Bare in thy guilt how foul must thou appear! J. A. FROUDE His mind was . . in contact with the bare facts of life. 3 AV *Joel* 1:7 He hath . . barked my figge tree: he hath made it cleane bare. A. P. STANLEY Hills which are now bare were then covered with forest. R. LEHMANN Every branch was bare at last. 5 E. THOMAS No one left and no one came On the bare platform. I. MURDOCH Laid down as a covering upon the bare floorboards. S. KING The two bare, dangling light bulbs. *under bare poles*: see POLE *n.*[1] 1c. 6 ADDISON Nature indeed furnishes us with the bare Necessaries of Life. H. P. BROUGHAM A bare majority of seven to five. G. MURRAY I know only the barest outline of what took place. G. GREENE It was hard for me to show even bare politeness. 11 SHAKES. *Ven. & Ad.* What bare excuses mak'st thou to be gone! *bare bones*: see BONE *n.*

B *adv.* (With numeral adjs.) = BARELY. *arch.* ME.

C *n.* †1 A naked part of the body; a bare space or place. ME–E18. 2 *The* bare skin. LME.

Comb.: **bareback** *a.* & *adv.* (of a horse or its rider) without a saddle; **bare-backed** *a.* & *adv.* with the back bare, esp. = *bareback* above; **barefaced** *a.* with the face uncovered or clean-shaven; *fig.* undisguised, impudent, shameless; **barefacedly** *adv.* in a barefaced manner; **barefacedness** the quality of being barefaced; **barefoot** *a.* & *adv.* = *barefooted* below (*barefoot doctor* (in rural China) a paramedical worker with basic training; *dance barefoot*: see DANCE *v.*); **barefooted** *a.* & *adv.* without shoes or stockings, with naked feet; **barehanded** *a.* & *adv.* having nothing in or covering the hands, *esp.* carrying no weapon; **barehead** *a.* & *adv.* (*arch.*) = *bareheaded* below; **bareheaded** *a.* & *adv.* with the head uncovered, esp. as a sign of respect.

bar(e)ish *a.* M17. **bareness** *n.* LME.

bare /bɛː/ *v.*[1]*t.* [OE *barian* (f. as prec.) = OFris. *baria*, OHG *gibarōn*, ON *bera*: see prec.] 1 Make bare, uncover; expose to view; unsheathe (a weapon). OE. 2 *fig.* Make manifest, reveal. ME. 3 Strip, divest, denude, (*of*). LME.

1 J. R. GREEN Earl Warrenne bared a rusty sword. TENNYSON He bows, he bares his head. J. KIRKUP Scalpel bares a creamy rib. N. GORDIMER Sometimes . . she bares her teeth without smiling, a mannerism like a pleased snarl. 2 D. PARKER The intimate places of your heart . . you bared to me, as in confession. 3 D. LIVINGSTONE He quite bared his garden in feeding us.

bare *v.*[2] arch. pa. t. of BEAR *v.*[1]

bareca /bəˈreɪkə/ *n.* L18. [Sp.: cf. BARRICO.] A small cask or keg; = BREAKER *n.*[2]

barège /barɛːʒ/ *n.* & *a.* E19. [Fr., f. *Barèges* a village in SW France.] A *n.* Pl. pronounced same. (A garment made of) a gauzelike fabric of silk and wool. E19. B *adj.* Made of *barège*. M19.

barely /ˈbɛːli/ *adv.* OE. [f. BARE *a.* + -LY[2].] 1 Without concealment or disguise; nakedly; plainly, explicitly. *arch.* OE. 2 Merely, simply. *arch.* LME. 3 Scarcely, hardly; only just. L15. 4 Scantily, poorly. *arch.* M16.

1 J. HACKET Here is the Resurrection of our Saviour barely and positively affirmed. 2 JAS. MILL The only objection . . might have been easily removed, by barely prescribing what sort of evidence they ought to receive. 3 J. GALSWORTHY How much older he looked than on that day, barely two months ago, when she first saw him. A. HALEY George began singing one of Miss Malizy's songs, barely audibly, as if just for himself. C. FREEMAN At first he didn't even recognize her because he could barely see. 4 G. CRABBE Thy coat is thin; . . thou'rt barely drest.

baresark *n.* & *a.* var. of BERSERK.

barf /bɑːf/ *v.* & *n. slang* (chiefly *N. Amer.*). M20. [Prob. imit.] A *v.i.* & *t.* Vomit. M20. B *n.* An act of vomiting; vomited food etc. Also as *int.* L20.

barfam /ˈbɑːf(ə)m/ *n. dial.* Also **†bargham**, **barkum** /ˈbɑːk(ə)m/, BRECHAM, & many other vars. ME. [f. stem of OE *be(o)rgan* protect + HAME *n.*[1]] A collar for a draught horse.

bargain /ˈbɑːgɪn/ *n.* ME. [OFr. *barga(i)gne*, *-g(u)igne*: see next.] †1 Discussion between two parties over terms; haggling. ME–L16. 2 An agreement on the terms of a transaction, a compact. With specifying wd, as *good*, *bad*, etc.: a good, bad, etc., agreement from the point of view of one of the parties. ME. 3 A thing acquired by bargaining; any purchase, esp. regarded according to whether or not one obtained value for money; *spec.* an advantageous purchase. LME. †4 Contention, struggle, fight. *Sc.* & *north.* LME–L19. b An article offered at a reduced or allegedly reduced price, esp. in a special sale. L19.

2 **bargain and sale** *Law* (a contract for) a sale followed by the payment of the agreed price, *esp.* (*Hist.*) referring to the sale of an estate etc. without deeds. *drive a hard bargain*: see DRIVE *v.* *Dutch bargain*: see DUTCH *a.* **into** or (*US*) **in the bargain** over and above what is agreed; besides. *make the best of a bad bargain*: see BEST *a.* & *adv.* **make** or **strike a bargain** come to terms over a transaction. *Smithfield bargain*: see SMITHFIELD *n.*[1] *strike a bargain*: see *make a bargain* above.

Comb.: **bargain basement, counter**: where bargains are offered for sale; **bargain-hunter** a person who shops for bargains; **bargain-hunting** shopping for bargains; **bargain price** a low or (allegedly) reduced price.

bargain /ˈbɑːgɪn/ *v.* LME. [OFr. *bargaignier* trade, dispute, hesitate (mod. *barguigner* hesitate) = Prov. *barganhar*, It. *bargagnare*, med.L *barcaniare*, prob. f. Gmc, whence OHG *borgēn* look after, MHG, G *borgen* borrow: the *-a-* of the 1st syll. is unexpl.] 1 *v.i.* Discuss the terms of a transaction, negotiate; seek to secure the most favourable terms, haggle. LME. †2 *v.i.* Contend, struggle, fight. *Sc.* & *north.* LME–L19. 3 *v.i.* Arrange or agree terms; strike a bargain. Foll. by *with* a person, *for* a thing, *that*, *to do*. L15. 4 *v.t.* Agree to buy and sell; contract for; *obs.* exc. (*Law*) in *bargain and sell*. L15. 5 *v.t.* Foll. by *away*: part with in a bargain; sell cheaply. M19.

1 H. ALLEN They were congratulating him; already beginning to chaffer and bargain. R. P. JHABVALA He had to bargain quite hard in order to be quoted a reasonable price. J. M. KEYNES A system of free wage-bargaining. **bargaining chip, counter** a potential concession etc. which can be used to advantage in negotiations. *plea bargaining*: see PLEA *n.* 3 SHAKES. *Tam. Shr.* 'Tis bargain'd 'twixt us twain . . That she shall still be curst in company. ADDISON A merchant . . bargained for it, and carried it off. M. W. MONTAGU The marble was bespoke and the sculptor bargained with. 5 GEO. ELIOT The heir . . had somehow bargained away the estate. M. L. KING Fathers and mothers were sold from their children and children were bargained away from their parents.

With preps. in specialized senses: **bargain for** expect, be prepared for (usu. w. neg. or *more than*). **bargain on** *colloq.* (*a*) = *bargain for* above; (*b*) count on.

bargai'nee *n.* the purchaser in an agreement of bargain and sale L16. **bargainer** *n.* a person who bargains LME. **bargai'nor** *n.* the seller in an agreement of bargain and sale E17.

bargander *n.* var. of BERGANDER.

barge /bɑːdʒ/ *n.* & *v.* ME. [(O)Fr. *barge*, med.L *bargia*, perh. ult. f. Gk *baris* Egyptian boat: cf. BARK *n.*[3]] **A** *n.* **1** A small seagoing vessel with sails; *spec.* one next in size above a balinger. *obs.* exc. *Hist.* ME. **2** A flat-bottomed freight-boat or lighter, for canals, rivers, and harbours. LME. **3** A ceremonial vessel of state, usu. one propelled by oars; an ornamental houseboat. LME. **4** A small boat; now *spec.* a warship's boat for the conveyance of senior officers. LME. **5** A large carriage. *US.* L19.

1 *schooner barge*: see SCHOONER *n.*[1]

Comb.: **bargeman** a person who has charge of, or works on, a barge; **bargemaster** the master or owner of a barge; **bargepole** a long pole used on a barge for fending; *would not touch with a bargepole* (colloq.), would refuse to have anything to do with.

B *v.* **1** †**a** *v.t.* w. *it.* Travel by barge. Only in L16. **b** *v.i.* Travel by barge. E20. **2** *v.t.* Carry by barge. M17. **3** *v.i.* Lurch or rush heavily (*into, against, about*, etc.). L19. **b** *v.t.* Make *one's way* thus. E20. **4** *v.t.* Push or collide with heavily; cause to move thus. E20.

3 K. MANSFIELD Why should he come barging over to this exact spot? B. HINES He.. barged into the kitchen door, and bounced back when it wouldn't open. M. RICHLER The moment Joshua barged into the room, Uncle Oscar slapped the book shut. **barge in** butt in, intrude. **4** W. J. LOCKE By degrees he edged (or barged) his huge frame to the front rank. *Western Mail (Cardiff)* Uncle Owen was barged from behind, spilling his beer over the second tenor.

barge- /bɑːdʒ/ *comb. form.* [Cf. med.L *bargus* a kind of gallows (= cl.L *furca*).] Forming terms in *Archit.* relating to the gable of a building.

bargeboard *n.* a board or ornamental screen along the edge of a gable M19. **barge-couple** *n.* a strong pair of rafters at a gable-end M16. **barge-course** *n.* coping or tiles overhanging the wall of a house at a gable-end M17.

bargee /bɑː'dʒiː/ *n.* M17. [f. BARGE *n.* + -EE[1] (used irreg.).] A bargeman.

Bargello /bɑː'dʒɛləʊ/ *n.* & *a.* M20. [The *Bargello* Palace in Florence, Italy.] (Designating) a kind of embroidery worked on canvas in stitch patterns suggestive of flames.

†**bargeret** *n.* var. of BERGERETTE.

†**bargham** *n.* var. of BARFAM.

barghest /'bɑːgɛst/ *n.* M18. [Origin unkn.] A goblin in the shape of a large dog, fabled to portend death or misfortune.

†**barghmaster** *n.* var. of BARMASTER.

†**barghmote** *n.* var. of BARMOTE.

bar-goose /'bɑːguːs/ *n. dial.* Pl. **bar-geese**. L16. [*bar* app. abbrev. of BARNACLE *n.*[1] or as in *bargander* var. of BERGANDER.] A barnacle goose; a shelduck.

barilla /bə'rɪlə/ *n.* E17. [Sp. *barrilla* dim. of *barra* bar.] **1** The alkali plant, *Salsola soda.* E17. **2** Impure alkali made in Spain and neighbouring regions by burning dried plants, esp. of this species. E17.

Barisal guns /barɪ'sɑːl gʌnz/ *n. phr.* L19. [f. *Barisal*, a town in Bangladesh.] Booming sounds of unknown origin.

barite /'barʌɪt, 'bɛː-/ *n.* Also **-yte**. M19. [f. BARIUM *n.* + -ITE[1].] *Min.* = BARYTES 2.

baritone /'barɪtəʊn/ *n.* & *a.* Also †**barytone**; (sense A.2) **baryton** /'barɪtɒn/. E17. [It. *baritono* f. Gk *barutonos* deep-sounding, f. *barus* deep + *tonos* pitch: cf. BARYTONE *n.*[1] & *a.*[1]] **A** *n.* **1** The male voice between tenor and bass, ranging typically from lower A in the bass clef to lower F in the treble clef; a singer having such a voice; a part written for such a voice. E17. **2** A kind of bass viol. M17. **3** The member of a family of similar instruments pitched between tenor and bass, *esp.* a tenor saxhorn in B flat or C. L19.

B *adj.* **1** Of the voice: having a compass intermediate between bass and tenor. Hence, suited for or possessing such a voice. E18. **2** Of an instrument: pitched between tenor and bass varieties (cf. sense A.3). L19.

2 *baritone horn, oboe, saxophone*, etc.

barium /'bɛːrɪəm/ *n.* E19. [f. BARYTA + -IUM.] A reactive white chemical element, atomic no. 56, which is one of the alkaline earth metals. (Symbol Ba.)

Comb.: **barium meal** a radio-opaque mixture containing barium sulphate, taken before radiological examination of the alimentary tract.

bark /bɑːk/ *n.*[1] [OE (*ġe*)*beorc*: later f. BARK *v.*[1]] **1** The sharp explosive cry of a dog, fox, squirrel, etc. OE. **2** Any harsh, abrupt noise, as of a cannon, cough, shouted command, etc. L19.

one's bark (opp. *one's bite*) one's words as opp. to one's actions.

barkless *a.*[1] (of a dog) having no bark M20.

bark /bɑːk/ *n.*[2] ME. [ON *bark-*, *bǫrkr* (Sw., Da. *bark*), perh. rel. to BIRCH *n.*: the OE wd is RIND *n.*[1]] **1** The layer of tissue lying outside the vascular cambium in the stem of a tree or woody plant, consisting of phloem, cortex, and periderm; *esp.* the corky outer layer of this. ME. **b** *spec.* That used in dyeing, tanning, etc., or its bruised residue. LME. **c** *spec.* That of certain trees used medicinally, *esp.* cinchona. LME. **2** *gen.* or *fig.* An outer covering; a rind, a husk; the skin. Now *dial.* or *obs.* LME.

1 *bitter bark*: see BITTER *a.* *Peruvian bark*: see PERUVIAN *n.* & *a.* *red bark*: see RED *a.* SLIPPERY *elm bark*. *sweetwood bark*: see SWEET *a.* & *adv.*

Comb.: **bark beetle** a wood-boring beetle of the family Scolytidae (*typographer bark beetle*: see TYPOGRAPHER 3); **barkcloth** cloth made from the inner bark of the paper mulberry or similar tree; **bark-tree** a cinchona.

barken *a.* (chiefly *poet.*) made or consisting of bark M18. **barkless** *a.*[2] devoid of bark E17. **barky** *a.* covered with or of the nature of bark L16.

bark /bɑːk/ *n.*[3] Also (esp. sense 3) **barque**. LME. [(O)Fr., prob. f. Prov. *barca* f. late L: cf. BARGE *n.*] **1** Any small sailing vessel. Now only *poet.* LME. **2** A (large) rowing boat. Now only *poet.* L16. **3** An ocean-going sailing vessel of particular rig; *spec.* one with the aftermost mast fore-and-aft rigged and the other masts square-rigged. E17.

barkey *n.* (*colloq.*) a little bark; a ship: E18.

bark /bɑːk/ *v.*[1] [OE *beorcan* f. Gmc, perh. ult. metath. alt. of BREAK *v.*] **1** *v.i.* Of a dog, fox, etc.: utter a sharp explosive cry. OE. **2** *v.i.* Speak or cry out aggressively, petulantly, or imperiously. ME. **3** *v.t.* Utter as a bark; ejaculate with a bark. LME. **4** *v.t.* Drive *away, back, off*, by barking. E19. **5** *v.i.* Of a firearm etc.: emit a harsh explosive sound. M19. **6** *v.i.* & *t.* Call out to attract custom (for); tout. *US.* E20.

1 **barking bird** the black-throated huet-huet, *Pteroptochos tarnii*, of S. America. **barking deer** = MUNTJAC. **barking squirrel** = *prairie dog* s.v. PRAIRIE. **2** H. LATIMER It is the scripture and not the translation, that ye bark against. **3** SPENSER Cerberus, whose many mouthes doo bay And barke out flames. J. CLARE The dog bark'd a welcome. L. URIS Bill Fry stood on his bridge barking orders through a megaphone. S. BRILL He popped a few mints into his mouth, looked up and barked, 'Let's get started.' **5** S. E. WHITE The Colt's forty-five barked once, and then again.

Phrases: **bark against** (or **at**) **the moon** clamour to no effect. **bark up the wrong tree** make an effort in the wrong direction, be on the wrong track.

bark /bɑːk/ *v.*[2]*t.* LME. [f. BARK *n.*[2]] **1** Steep in an infusion of bark; tan. LME. **2a** Strip the bark from (a tree). M16. **b** Abrade skin from (a shin, knuckle, etc.). E19. **3** Enclose (as) with bark; encrust. M17.

barkentine *n.* var. of BARQUENTINE.

barker /'bɑːkə/ *n.*[1] ME. [f. BARK *v.*[2] + -ER[1].] **1** A tanner. Now *rare* or *obs.* ME. **2** A person who barks trees. E17.

barker /'bɑːkə/ *n.*[2] LME. [f. BARK *v.*[1] + -ER[1].] **1** A person who or thing which barks; *spec.* a dog. LME. **2** A noisy assailant or protester. LME. **3** Any of various wading birds with harsh cries, *esp.* a spotted redshank, avocet, or godwit. *dial.* M17. **4** A tout at an auction-room, sideshow, etc. Chiefly *N. Amer.* L17. **5** A pistol; a cannon. *arch. slang.* E19.

barkevikite /'bɑːkəvɪkʌɪt/ *n.* L19. [f. *Barkevik*, a place in Norway + -ITE[1].] *Min.* An iron-rich sodium and potassium amphibole occurring as dark brown or black monoclinic crystals.

barkle /'bɑːk(ə)l/ *v.t. dial.* E19. [f. BARK *v.*[2] + -LE[3].] Cake, encrust, (with dirt etc.).

barkum *n.* see BARFAM.

barley /'bɑːli/ *n.* [OE *bærlić* adj., f. as BERE *n.*[1] + -LY[1]: cf. ON *barr* barley, Goth. *barizeins* of barley.] (The grain of) a hardy awned cereal of the genus *Hordeum*, used as food and in making malt liquors and spirits.

four-rowed barley, pearl barley, sea barley, sprat-barley, etc.

Comb.: **barley-bird** *dial.* any of various birds which appear at the time of barley-sowing in spring, e.g. a wryneck, yellow wagtail, or nightingale; **barley-bree, -broth** strong ale; **barley-hood** (now *rare* or *obs.*) a fit of drunkenness or of bad temper brought on by drinking; **barleymow** a stack of barley; **barley sugar** a confection of boiled sugar, usu. in twisted sticks; **barley-sugar** *a.* (of columns etc.) twisted like barley sugar; **barley water** a decoction of pearl barley for invalids etc. or (esp. with some further flavouring) drunk for refreshment; **barley-wine** a wine or ale prepared from barley; *spec.* a strong English ale.

barley /'bɑːli/ *int. Sc.* & *north.* LME. [Perh. alt. of Fr. *parlez* PARLEY.] Parley, truce; (in children's games).

barley-break /'bɑːlɪbreɪk/ *n.* M16. [Perh. f. BARLEY *n.* or *int.* + BREAK *v.*] An old country catching-game, resembling prisoners' base, played by three couples, one of which had to catch the others, who were allowed to 'break' and change partners when hard-pressed.

barley-corn /'bɑːlɪkɔːn/ *n.* LME. [f. BARLEY *n.* + CORN *n.*[1]] **1** = BARLEY *n.* LME. **b** Personified as *John Barleycorn*, esp. as the source of malt liquors. E17. **2** *Hist.* The length of a grain of barley as a measure, usu. ⅓ inch. LME.

†**barling** *n.* ME–M18. [ON: cf. Sw. *bärling* pole, f. *bära* to bear.] A pole, *esp.* one on or used with a boat.

barlow /'bɑːləʊ/ *n. US.* L18. [Russell *Barlow*, 18th-cent. Eng. inventor.] In full *barlow knife*. A large single-bladed pocket knife.

barm /bɑːm/ *n.*[1] Long *obs.* exc. *dial.* in comb. [OE *barm*, *bearm* = OFris., OS, OHG *barm*, ON *barmr*, Goth. *barms*, f. Gmc, rel. to BEAR *v.*[1]] A bosom, a lap.

Abraham's barm: see ABRAHAM I.

Comb.: **barm cloth** an apron; **barm-skin** a leather apron.

barm /bɑːm/ *n.*[2] & *v.* Also **balm**. [OE *beorma* prob. f. LG: cf. OFris. *berme*, *barm*, Da. *bärme*, Sw. *bärma*, G *Bärme*.] **A** *n.* The froth on the top of fermenting malt liquors, used to leaven bread and to ferment other liquors; yeast, leaven. OE. **B** *v.t.* & *i.* Mix with yeast, leaven; rise in froth or fermentation. LME.

barmaster /'bɑːmɑːstə/ *n.* Also †**bargh-**. M16. [G *Bergmeister* f. *Berg-* mining: see MASTER *n.*[1]] An officer of a barmote.

barmbrack *n.* var. of BARNBRACK.

Barmecide /'bɑːmɪsʌɪd/ *n.* & *a.* E18. [Arab. *barmakī*, the patronymic of a prince in the *Arabian Nights' Entertainments* who feasted a beggar on a succession of empty dishes to test his humour.] **A** *n.* A person who offers imaginary food or illusory benefits. E18. **B** *attrib.* or as *adj.* Illusory, unreal; offering imaginary food or illusory benefits. M19.

Barme'cidal *a.* illusory, unreal M19.

bar mitzvah /bɑː 'mɪtsvə/ *n. phr.* Also **B-**. M19. [Heb. *bar miṣwāh* son of commandment.] (A religious initiation ceremony for) a Jewish boy aged thirteen, regarded as liable to observe the religious precepts and eligible to take part in public worship.

barmkin /'bɑːmkɪn/ *n. north.* Now *arch.* or *Hist.* LME. [Perh. alt. of BARBICAN.] (The battlement of) the outer fortification or barbican of a castle; a turret or tower on this.

barmote /'bɑːməʊt/ *n.* Also †**bargh-**. M16. [f. as BARMASTER + *mote* var. of MOOT *n.*[1]] A local court with jurisdiction as to lead-mining rights and related matters.

barmy /'bɑːmi/ *a.* Also **balmy**. L15. [f. BARM *n.*[2] + -Y[1].] **1** Of, full of, or covered with barm;

frothy. L15. 2 *fig.* Excitedly active; empty-headed, daft, crazy. Now *slang.* L16.

2 *barmy in* or *on the crumpet*: see CRUMPET 3.

barn /bɑːn/ *n.*[1] & *v.* [OE *ber(e)n*, earlier *berern*, f. as BERE *n.*[1] + *ærn*, *ern* a place.] A *n.* 1 A covered building for the storage of grain, hay, straw, flax, etc. OE. 2 A building for housing livestock, vehicles, etc. *N. Amer.* L18. 3 A large unduly plain building or room. M20. 4 *Physics.* A unit of area equal to 10^{-28} sq. metre, used in expressing nuclear cross-sections. M20.

1 *Dutch barn*: see DUTCH *a.* ROBIN HOOD's *barn*. 2 *receiving barn*: see RECEIVING *a.*

Comb.: **barn-ball** *US* a children's game involving bouncing a ball off the gable of a building; **barn dance** (*a*) an informal social occasion for country dancing (orig. one held in a barn); (*b*) a dance for a number of couples forming a line or circle, with the couples moving along it in turn; **barn door** the large door of a barn; *fig.* a target etc. too large to be missed; *nail to the barn door*: see NAIL *v.*; **barn-gallon** *Hist.* a measure of two imperial gallons, orig. used in the milk-trade; **barnlot** *US* the ground upon or around which a barn stands; **barn owl** an owl of the genus *Tyto*; esp. *T. alba*, which usu. has a white face and underside and frequently nests in farm buildings; **barnstorm** *v.i.* [back-form. f. *barnstormer*] tour etc. as a barnstormer (chiefly as *barnstorming* vbl n. or ppl a.); **barnstormer** (orig. & chiefly *N. Amer.*) (*a*) an itinerant actor; (*b*) a politician making a rapid electioneering tour; (*c*) an aviator who tours the country giving aerobatic displays, an adventurous pilot; **barn swallow** *N. Amer.* the common swallow, *Hirundo rustica*.

B *v.t.* House in a barn; garner. LME.

barn *n.*[2] var. of BAIRN.

Barnabite /ˈbɑːnəbʌɪt/ *n.* E18. [f. *Barnabas* the apostle + -ITE[1].] A member of a small religious order founded in 1530, named from its church of St Barnabas in Milan.

Barnaby /ˈbɑːnəbi/ *n.* L16. [By-form of *Barnabas* (see prec.): cf. Fr. *Barnabé*.] 1 *Barnaby bright*, *Barnaby-day*, *long Barnaby*, St Barnabas' day, 11 June, the longest day of the year, Old Style. L16. 2 *Barnaby thistle*, (*St*) *Barnaby's thistle*, the yellow star-thistle, *Centaurea solstitialis*, flowering on or near St Barnabas' day. L16.

barnacle /ˈbɑːnək(ə)l/ *n.*[1] ME. [med.L *bernaca*, of unkn. origin.] 1 A black, white, and grey goose, *Branta leucopsis*, breeding in the Arctic and visiting Britain in winter. Now usu. *barnacle goose.* ME. 2 A cirripede; *esp.* any of those which attach themselves directly or by a fleshy footstalk to rocks, ships' bottoms, or other objects. L16. 3 *fig.* A companion or follower who is difficult to shake off. E17.

¶The geese, whose breeding grounds were long unknown, were formerly fabled to grow from the shells of the cirripedes, or else from a tree or its fruit.

barnacled *a.*[1] covered with barnacles (BARNACLE *n.*[1] 2); *fig.* encrusted: L17.

barnacle /ˈbɑːnək(ə)l/ *n.*[2] LME. [Alt. of AN *bernac*, of unkn. origin.] 1 A kind of bit or twitch for restraining a horse or ass; *spec.* an instrument of two branches joined by a hinge, placed on the nose of the animal. Usu. in *pl.* LME. 2 In *pl.* Spectacles. *arch.* & *dial.* L16. 3 An instrument of torture fashioned and applied like a barnacle (sense 1 above). Usu. in *pl. obs.* exc. *Hist.* E17.

barnacled *a.*[2] (*arch.* or *dial.*) wearing spectacles E18.

Barnardo /bɑːˈnɑːdəʊ/ *n.* E20. [See below.] Used *attrib.* and in *possess.* to designate an orphan or destitute child brought up in one of the homes founded by the British philanthropist Dr Thomas John Barnardo (1845–1905).

P. HOBSON She was a Barnardo baby .. she was illegitimate. M. HARDWICK I was a Barnardo's girl... They found me in a slum in Walsall.

barnbrack /ˈbɑːnbrak/ *n. Anglo-Ir.* Also **barm-** /ˈbɑːm-/. M19. [Ir. *bairín breac* speckled cake.] A currant bun.

barnet /ˈbɑːnɪt/ *n. rhyming slang.* M19. [*Barnet*, now a borough of Greater London.] In full *barnet fair.* The hair; the head.

barney /ˈbɑːni/ *n.* & *v. colloq.* M19. [Origin unkn.] A *n.* A noisy altercation; an argument, a quarrel. M19. B *v.i.* Quarrel, argue. L19.

barngun /ˈbɑːngʌn/ *n. dial.* M18. [f. var. of BURN *v.* + var. of GOUND.] An eruption of the skin; shingles.

Barnum /ˈbɑːnəm/ *n.* M19. [Phineas T. *Barnum* (1810–91), US showman.] Humbug; empty showmanship.

Barnuˈmese *n.* inflated or sensational language L19.

barnyard /ˈbɑːnjɑːd/ *n.* & *a.* LME. [f. BARN *n.*[1] + YARD *n.*[1]] A *n.* The enclosure round a barn, a farmyard. LME.

Comb.: **barnyard grass** = COCKSPUR *grass*.

B *attrib.* or as *adj.* Typical of a barnyard; *fig.* earthy, coarse, scatological. *colloq.* M20.

baro- /ˈbarəʊ/ *comb. form* of Gk *baros* weight, usu. w. the sense 'pressure': see -O-.

barogram *n.* the record made by a barograph L19. **barograph** *n.* a self-recording barometer M19. **baroreˈceptor** *n.* (*Physiol.*) a receptor sensitive to changes in pressure M20. **barostat** *n.* an automatic device for regulating pressure M20. **baroˈthermograph** *n.* an instrument which records pressure and temperature simultaneously L19. **barotrauma** *n.* (*Med.*) ear injury due to change in ambient pressure M20.

barocco /bəˈrɒkəʊ/ *a.* & *n.* Pl. of n. **-os.** L19. [It.] = BAROQUE.

baroclinic /barəˈklɪnɪk/ *a.* E20. [f. BARO- + Gk *klinein* to bend, slope + -IC.] *Meteorol.* Characterized by or associated with an atmospheric condition in which surfaces of constant pressure intersect surfaces of constant density.

baroclinically *adv.* M20. **baroclinicity** /-ˈnɪsɪti/, **-clinity** *ns.* M20.

Baroco /bəˈrəʊkəʊ/ *n.* Also **-oko.** Pl. **-os.** M16. [A mnemonic of scholastic philosophers, first used in med.L, A indicating a universal affirmative proposition and O a particular negative proposition.] *Logic.* The fourth mood of the second syllogistic figure, in which a particular negative conclusion is drawn from a universal affirmative major premiss and a particular negative minor.

Barolo /bəˈrəʊləʊ/ *n.* L19. [A region of Piedmont, Italy.] A full-bodied red Italian wine from Barolo.

barometer /bəˈrɒmɪtə/ *n.* M17. [f. BARO- + -METER.] An instrument for measuring the pressure of the atmosphere, freq. also giving a forecast of change in the weather.

fig.: H. W. VAN LOON The arts are an even better barometer of what is happening in our world than the stock market or the debates in Congress.

barometric /barəˈmɛtrɪk/ *a.* E19. [f. BARO- + -METRIC.] Of, pertaining to, or indicated by a barometer.

barometrical *a.* = BAROMETRIC M17. **barometrically** *adv.* L18.

barometry /bəˈrɒmɪtri/ *n.* E18. [f. BAROMETER: see -METRY.] The art or science of barometric observation.

barometz /ˈbarəmɛts/ *n.* E17. [Russ. *baranets* dim. of *baran* ram.] A fabulous Russian creature, half plant and half sheep; the inverted woolly caudex etc. of the tree-fern *Cibotium barometz*, which was used to create the illusion of such a creature.

baron /ˈbar(ə)n/ *n.* ME. [AN *barun*, (O)Fr. *baron*, accus. of *ber* = Prov. *bar*, accus. *baron*, f. med.L *baro*, *-on-* man, male, warrior, prob. of Frank. origin.] I 1 *Hist.* A person who derived a title, by military or other honourable service, from the king or other superior; a noble, a peer, *esp.* any of those summoned to attend Parliament; *Sc.* a holder of a barony (sense 3). ME. 2 A member of the lowest order of the British or Irish nobility. ME. b A holder of a similar foreign title. L19. 3 Applied to Christ and the saints, or to any man out of respect. *rare.* ME. 4 *Hist.* A freeman of London, York, or certain other cities; a freeman or a burgess of the Cinque Ports. LME. 5 *Hist.* A judge of the Court of Exchequer. LME. 6 *Law* (now *Hist.*) & *Her.* Husband (conjoined with *fem(m)e*). LME. 7 A magnate in industry, finance, etc. (usu. w. specifying wd, as *beef baron*, *press baron*); *gen.* a powerful or influential person. Orig. *US.* E19. II 8 *baron of beef*, a joint consisting of two sirloins left joined at the backbone. M18.

Comb.: **baron-bailie** *Sc. Hist.* a deputy appointed by a baron to exercise the latter's jurisdiction in a court; **baron court** *Hist.* = COURT-BARON.

†**baronry** *n.* = BARONY LME–M18.

baronage /ˈbar(ə)nɪdʒ/ *n.* ME. [OFr. *barnage*, med.L *bar(o)nagium*: see prec., -AGE.] 1 The body of barons or nobles collectively. ME. †2 = BARONY. ME–M17. 3 An annotated list of barons or peers. L19.

baroness /ˈbar(ə)nɪs/ *n.* LME. [OFr. *bar(o)nesse* (AL *baronissa*, *-essa*): see BARON, -ESS[1].] The wife or widow of a baron; a woman holding the rank of baron in her own right.

baronet /ˈbar(ə)nɪt/ *n.* & *v.* LME. [AL *baronettus*: see BARON, -ET[1].] A *n.* †1 A lesser baron; *esp.* a gentleman, not a baron by tenure from the king, who was summoned to Parliament. LME–M17. 2 A member of the lowest hereditary titled British order, with the status of a commoner but able to use the prefix 'Sir'. E17. B *v.t.* Infl. **-t-**, ***-tt-**. Raise to the rank of a baronet. M18.

baronetage *n.* the rank of baronet; baronets collectively; an annotated list of baronets: E18. **baronetcy** *n.* a baronet's rank or patent E19. **baronetess** *n.* (*rare*) the wife of a baronet M17. **baronetize** *v.t.* confer a baronetcy on M19.

baronial /bəˈrəʊnɪəl/ *a.* M18. [f. next + -IAL.] 1 Of or pertaining to a baron or barons; befitting the rank of baron. M18. 2 *Archit.* Of or in the turreted style characteristic of Scottish country houses. Usu. *Scottish* (or *Scotch*) *baronial.* L19.

barony /ˈbar(ə)ni/ *n.* ME. [OFr. *baronie* (mod. *-nn-*), med.L *baronia*: see BARON, -Y[3].] 1 The domain of a baron. ME. b *Sc. Hist.* An estate held under barony (see sense 3 below). LME. c *Ir. Hist.* A division of a county. L16. †2 The barons collectively. ME–L16. 3 The tenure of a baron from the Crown; *spec.* in *Sc. Hist.*, the freehold of a chief tenant of a single unit of lands (not necessarily contiguous) with defined rights of civil and criminal jurisdiction. LME. 4 The rank or dignity of baron. L18.

baronian /bəˈrəʊnɪən/ *a.* (*rare*) = BARONIAL M17.

baroque /bəˈrɒk, -ˈrəʊk/ *a.* & *n.* Orig. *derog.* Also **B-.** M18. [Fr. (in earliest use, of pearls) f. Port. *barroco*, Sp. *barrueco*, (of architecture) It. BAROCCO: ult. origin unkn.] A *adj.* 1 Of, pertaining to, or characterized by an exuberant and ornate style prevalent in the arts (esp. in architecture and music) of the 17th and early 18th cents. Of a musical instrument etc.: belonging to or designed as in that period. M18. 2 *gen.* Elaborately or grotesquely ornate; whimsical, bizarre. M19. 3 Of a pearl: irregularly shaped. L19.

1 W. D. HOWELLS The building .. coldly classic or frantically baroque. W. S. MAUGHAM The sonorous periods and the baroque massiveness of Jacobean language. H. READ Michelangelo has been called the father of Baroque art, and the style can be actually traced to him. *Encycl. Brit.* The Baroque era reached its zenith in the work of Johann Sebastian Bach .. and George Frideric Handel. 2 S. SPENDER The baroque extravagance, the ribbons and trimmings, of Tony's conversation.

B *n.* (The style, music, or architecture of) the 17th and early 18th cents.; baroque ornamentation. L19.

J. N. SUMMERSON At Blenheim the English Baroque culminates.

barotropic /barəˈtrəʊpɪk, -ˈtrɒpɪk/ *a.* E20. [f. BARO- + -TROPIC.] *Meteorol.* Characterized by or associated with an atmospheric condition in which surfaces of equal pressure coincide with surfaces of equal density.

barotropically *adv.* M20. **baˈrotropy** *n.* E20.

Barotse /bəˈrɒtsi/ *n.* & *a. arch.* Pl. of n. same. M19. [Bantu.] = LOZI.

barouche /bəˈruːʃ/ *n.* E19. [G dial. *Barutsche* f. It. *baroccio* (Sp. *barrocho*) two-wheeled ult. f. L *birotus*, f. BI- + *rota* wheel.] Chiefly *Hist.* A four-wheeled horse-drawn carriage with a collapsible half-hood, a seat in front for the driver, and seats facing each other for passengers.

barouchet(te) *n.* a kind of light barouche E19.

barque *n.* var. of BARK *n.*[3]

barquentine /ˈbɑːkəntiːn/ *n.* Also **bark-**. L17. [f. *barque* BARK *n.*[3] after *brigantine*.] A three-masted vessel with foremast square-rigged and main and mizen masts rigged fore-and-aft.

barrable /ˈbɑːrəb(ə)l/ *a.* L15. [f. BAR *v.* + -ABLE.] Able to be legally excluded or stayed.

barracan /ˈbarək(ə)n/ *n.* Also **bara-**. M17. [Fr. *barracan*, *bouracan* f. Arab. *burrukān*, *barra-*cloak of camlet: cf. BARRAGON.] 1 A coarsely woven fabric of wool, silk, and goat's hair. M17. 2 In Eastern countries, a cloak or mantle made of this or another fabric. E19.

barrace /ˈbarəs/ *n. obs.* exc. *Hist.* LME. [OFr. pl. of *barre* BAR *n.*[1]] †1 A barrier or outwork in front of a fortress. LME–L15. 2 The scene of knightly contests; the lists. LME. †3 Contention, strife. L15–E17.

barrack /ˈbarək/ *n.*[1] L17. [Fr. *baraque* f. It. *baracca* or Sp. *barraca* soldier's tent: ult. origin unkn.] 1 A temporary hut or cabin. *obs.* exc. *north.* L17. 2 *sing.* & (usu.) in *pl.* (also treated as *sing.*) A set of buildings used as a residence for soldiers. L17. b *transf.* A large building or range of buildings in which a number of people are housed; any large, austere building suggestive of a military barracks. M19. c The regular quarters of the Salvation Army. *obs.* exc. *Hist.* L19.

1 GIBBON He lodged in a miserable hut or barrack. 2 DISRAELI His own idea of a profession being limited to a barrack in a London park. b E. GASKELL We went to .. her old town house, .. an immense barrack of an old half-fortified house. JOYCE I don't like being alone in this big barracks of a place.

Comb.: **barrack-room lawyer** a would-be knowledgeable, pompously argumentative person; **barrack-square** a drill ground near a barracks.

barrack /ˈbarək/ *n.*[2] *Austral.* & *NZ.* L19. [f. BARRACK *v.*[2]] An act, or the action, of barracking a person, team, etc.

barrack /ˈbarək/ *v.*[1]*t.* E18. [f. BARRACK *n.*[1]] Provide barracks for, locate in barracks.

barrack /ˈbarək/ *v.*[2]*i.* & *t.* Orig. & chiefly *Austral.* & *NZ.* L19. [Prob. f. N. Ir. dial.] Of spectators at games etc.: shout vociferously (*for*), jeer (at).

barracker *n.* L19.

barracoon /barəˈkuːn/ *n.* M19. [Sp. *barracón* augm. of *barraca*: see BARRACK *n.*[1], -OON.] *Hist.* An enclosure in which Black slaves etc. were confined for a limited period.

barracouta /barəˈkuːtə/ *n.* Pl. same, **-s**. L17. [Alt. of BARRACUDA.] †I1 See BARRACUDA. L17. II2 A long slender food fish, *Thyrsites atun* (family Gempylidae), of southern oceans; = SNOEK *n.* M19. 3 A small narrow loaf of bread. *NZ.* L20.

barracuda /barəˈkuːdə/ *n.* Also †**-couta**. See also BARRACOUTA. Pl. same, **-s**. L17. [Origin unkn.] 1 Any of various fishes of the family Sphyraenidae, comprising predatory perciform fishes of tropical and temperate seas. L17. 2 See BARRACOUTA.

1 **great barracuda** a large tropical barracuda, *Sphyraena barracuda*, of the western Atlantic which is readily provoked to attack humans and is valued as a game-fish; also called *picuda*.

barragan *n.* var. of BARRAGON.

barrage /ˈbarɑːʒ/ *n.* & *v.* M19. [Fr., f. as BAR *v.*: see -AGE.] A *n.* 1 A barrier constructed in a river (esp. the Nile) to increase the depth of water. M19. 2 An intensive artillery or machine-gun bombardment, employed to check an enemy, or protect one's own soldiers, in advancing or retreating. E20. b A rapid succession of questions, utterances, etc. E20. 3 A heat or deciding event in fencing, showjumping, etc. M20.

2 S. SASSOON My only idea was to collect all available ammunition and then renew the attack while the Stokes-gun officer put up an enthusiastic barrage. H. KISSINGER The North Vietnamese attacked with the heaviest artillery barrage of the war and large numbers of tanks. CREEPING *barrage*. b C. S. FORESTER They shielded Curzon .. by grouping themselves round him and surrounding him with a protective barrage of professional explanation. S. KING There was a moment's gaping pause .. and then the barrage of questions came again, everything mixed together into a meaningless stew of voices.

Comb.: **barrage balloon** a large captive balloon supporting a steel cable forming part of an anti-aircraft barrier.

B *v.t.* 1 Subject to a barrier of continuous fire. E20. 2 Bombard with questions, exclamations, etc. M20.

barragon /ˈbarəg(ə)n/ *n.* Also **-gan**. M17. [Sp. *barragán* f. Arab.: see BARRACAN.] A coarsely-woven cloth; a kind of fustian.

barramundi /barəˈmʌndi/ *n.* L19. [Aborig.] Any of various Australian freshwater food fishes; *spec.* the percoid fish *Lates calcarifer*.

barranca /bəˈraŋkə/ *n.* Also **-co** /-kəʊ/, pl. **-os**. L17. [Sp.] A narrow, winding river gorge.

barras /ˈbarəs/ *n.* Now *dial.* Also **burras** /ˈbʌrəs/. L15. [Fr. *bourras*.] A coarse linen or hessian cloth; canvas.

barrator /ˈbarətə/ *n.* Also **-er**. LME. [AN *baratour*, OFr. *barateor* cheat, trickster, f. *barater* f. Proto-Romance f. Gk *prattein* do, perform, manage, practise (sometimes dishonestly); perh. infl. by ON *barátta* contest, fighting.] 1 A person who buys or sells ecclesiastical preferment or offices of state or accepts money to influence judicial proceedings. Now *rare* exc. *Hist.* LME. †2 A person who indulges in riotous or violent behaviour, esp. for money; a hired bully. LME–L18. 3 A malicious raiser of discord; a troublemaker; *spec.* a vexatious litigant (now *Hist.*). LME.

barratry /ˈbarətri/ *n.* LME. [(O)Fr. *baraterie* deceit, f. OFr. *barat(e)* deceit, fraud, trouble, etc., f. *barater*: see prec., -ERY.] 1 *Hist.* The purchase or sale of ecclesiastical or state preferments or of judicial influence. LME. 2 The malicious incitement of discord; *spec.* the persistent practice of vexatious litigation (now *Hist.*). L16. 3 *Marine Law.* Fraud or gross or criminal negligence prejudicial to a ship's owner(s) or underwriters on the part of the master or crew. E17.

barratrous *a.* (*Marine Law*) of or pertaining to barratry M19. **barratrously** *adv.* M19.

†**barratta** *n.* see BALATA.

Barr body /bɑː ˈbɒdi/ *n. phr.* M20. [f. M.L. *Barr* (b. 1908), Canad. anatomist.] *Genetics.* A strongly heterochromatic body just inside the membrane of non-dividing cell nuclei in females, representing a condensed, inactive X chromosome and diagnostic of genetic femaleness.

barre /bɑː/ *n.* E20. [Fr.: see BAR *n.*[1]] 1 *Mus.* (A finger used as) a capotasto. E20. 2 A waist-level horizontal bar to help dancers keep their balance during some exercises. M20.

barré /bare/ *a.* & *n.* Pl. of n. pronounced same. L19. [Fr., pa. pple of *barrer* BAR *v.*] *Mus.* (A chord) played with strings stopped by a capotasto or finger.

barred /bɑːd/ *a.* LME. [f. BAR *n.*[1], *v.*: see -ED[2], -ED[1].] 1 Marked or ornamented with bars; striped; streaked. LME. 2 Secured or shut with a bar or bars. E16. 3 Of a harbour: obstructed by a sandbank. M16. 4 Having or furnished with a bar or bars (BAR *n.*[1] 1). L16. 5 *Mus.* Marked off by bars. L19.

barrel /ˈbar(ə)l/ *n.* ME. [f. (O)Fr. *baril* f. med.L *barriclus* a small cask.] 1 A wooden vessel of cylindrical form, usu. bulging in the middle, made of curved staves bound together by hoops, with flat ends; a similar vessel made of metal, plastic, etc. Cf. CASK *n.* 1. ME. 2 Such a vessel and its contents; the capacity of such a vessel as a measure for both liquid and dry goods, varying with the commodity; *spec.* a unit of capacity for oil and oil products equal to 35 imperial or 42 US gallons (about 159 litres). LME. 3 A revolving cylinder around which a chain or rope is wound as in a capstan, watch, and other machines. LME. †4 Brand, quality, sort. M16–L18. 5 The cylindrical body or trunk of an object, as a pump, a fountain-pen, etc. M17. 6 The metal tube of a gun, through which the shot is discharged. In *double-barrel*, *single-barrel*, etc., also, a gun with the specified number of barrels. M17. 7 The trunk of a horse etc. E18. 8 Money for use in a political campaign, esp. for corrupt purposes. *US slang* (now *Hist.*). L19.

1 **over a barrel** (chiefly *N. Amer.*) helpless. **scrape the barrel** be obliged to use the last available resources. 2 **a barrel of fun** or **laughs** *colloq.* (a source of) much amusement. *a barrel of monkeys*: see MONKEY *n.* 6 *lock, stock, and barrel*: see LOCK *n.*[2]

Comb.: **barrel-chested** *a.* having a large rounded chest; **barrel-fish** a large stromateoid fish, *Hyperoglyphe perciforme*, of the western Atlantic, often seen near floating wreckage or following vessels; **barrel-house** a low-class drinking saloon; forceful unrestrained jazz-playing; **barrel-organ** a musical instrument in which a handle-turned pin-studded cylinder opens pipes to act upon the keys or strikes metal tongues; **barrel vault** a vault with a roof of uniform concave structure.

barrelage *n.* the total amount of any commodity, esp. beer, as measured by barrels (during a specified period) L19.

barrel /bar(ə)l/ *v.* Infl. **-ll-**, ***-l-**. LME. [f. the n.] 1 *v.t.* Place or store in a barrel or barrels. LME. b Store *up*. L16. 2 *v.i.* Drive fast; proceed with force and speed. Freq. foll. by *along*. *N. Amer. slang.* M20.

1b MILTON All benefit and use of Scripture, as to public prayer, should be deny'd us, except what was barreld up in a Common-praier Book.

barren /ˈbar(ə)n/ *a.* & *n.* ME. [AN *barai(g)ne* f. OFr. *bar(a)haine*, *brehai(g)ne* (mod. *bréhaigne*), of unkn. origin.] A *adj.* (Foll. by *of*.) 1 Of a woman: incapable of bearing children; infertile. ME. 2 Of an animal: not pregnant at the usual season. ME. 3 Of a tree or plant: not producing fruit or seed. LME. 4 Of land: producing little vegetation; unproductive; infertile. LME. 5 Destitute of interest or attraction; arid; dull. LME. 6 Producing no result; fruitless; unprofitable. M16. 7 Of a person: unresponsive; dull. L16.

3 *barren strawberry*: see STRAWBERRY 2.

Comb.: **barrenwort** a low rhizomatous herb of the barberry family, *Epimedium alpinum*, once thought to cause sterility.

B *n.* 1 A barren woman or animal. Long *dial.* *rare.* ME. 2 A tract of barren land, esp. (freq. in *pl.* and w. specifying wd) in N. America. M17.

2 *oak-*, *pine-barrens*, etc.

barrenly *adv.* M16. **barrenness** /-n-n-/ *n.* ME.

†**barren** *v.t.* L16–E18. [f. the adj.] Make barren or unfruitful; render unproductive.

barrera /baˈrrera/ *n.* E20. [Sp. = BARRIER.] (The row of seats nearest to) the barrier encircling a bullring.

barret /ˈbarɪt/ *n.* E19. [Fr. *barette* f. It. †*bar(r)etta*: see BIRETTA.] A small flat cap, *esp.* a biretta.

barrette /baˈrɛt/ *n.* E20. [Fr. dim. of BARRE.] A bar-shaped clip or ornament for a woman's or girl's hair.

barretter /bəˈrɛtə/ *n.* E20. [App. f. BARRATOR w. the idea of exchange.] *Electr.* A device consisting essentially of a fine wire with a high temperature coefficient of resistance, used esp. for current stabilization.

barricade /barɪˈkeɪd/ *n.* L16. [Fr., f. *barrique* f. Sp. *barrica* cask, f. stem of *barril* BARREL *n.*: see -ADE. Cf. BARRICADO.] 1 A rampart constructed of barrels, stones, furniture, etc., set up across a street, esp. during revolutionary fighting or some other such civil disturbance; freq. (esp. in *pl.*) used allusively of the site of the final defences of a cause, movement, etc. L16. 2 Any barrier or defensive construction impeding passage. L16. 3 *Naut.* (now *Hist.*). A wooden fence built across the quarterdeck of a sailing man-of-war, barricaded to provide protection for those stationed there during an action. M18.

1 *fig.*: E. GLASGOW Would die upon the literary barricade of defending the noble proportions of 'War and Peace'.

barricade /barɪˈkeɪd/ *v.t.* L16. [f. the n. after Fr. *barricader*.] 1 Block (a street etc.) with a barricade, obstruct, render impassable. L16. 2 Defend (a place, a person) as with a barricade. M17.

barricading *n.* (*a*) the action of the vb; (*b*) (the materials of) a barricade: L17.

barricado /barɪˈkeɪdəʊ/ *n.* & *v. arch.* L16. [f. as BARRICADE *n.*: see -ADO.] **A** *n.* Pl. **-o(e)s.** = BARRICADE *n.* L16. **B** *v.t.* = BARRICADE *v.* L16.

barrico /bəˈriːkəʊ/ *n.* Pl. **-oes.** M16. [Sp. *barrica* cask: see BARRICADE *n.* and cf. BARECA.] A keg, a small barrel.

barrier /ˈbarɪə/ *n.* & *v.* LME. [AN *barrere*, OFr. *barriere* f. Proto-Romance f. as BAR *n.*[1]: see -IER.] **A** *n.* **1** A palisade or stockade erected to defend a gate, passage, etc.; a fortification commanding an entrance. Now chiefly *Hist.* LME. **2** *gen.* Any fence or railing barring advance or preventing access; a physical obstacle placed in the way. LME. **b** The starting-gate of a racecourse. E17. **c** The point of access to a railway platform at which tickets must be shown. M20. **3** In *pl.* The martial exercise of sword-fighting across the central railing dividing a tournament ground (freq. in *to fight at barriers*). Also, the palisades enclosing a tourney ground, the lists. *obs.* exc. *Hist.* L15. **4** Any physical, esp. natural, obstacle which prevents access or separates; *spec.* the mass of ice fringing the Antarctic coast. E18. **5** Anything immaterial that obstructs, prevents communication, or separates. E18. **b** *Physics.* A state, region, or level of high potential energy which must be surmounted (or tunnelled through) for a given physical change to occur. E20.

2 *vapour barrier*: see VAPOUR *n.* **b** S. ANDERSON Then when the barrier goes up he is off like his name, Sunstreak. **4** ISOLATING *barrier*. **5** *sonic barrier, sound barrier, thermal barrier*, etc. **b** J. A. WHEELER Odd nuclei have a higher barrier against fission than corresponding even nuclei. SCHOTTKY *barrier*.

Comb.: **barrier cream** a cream to protect the skin from damage, infection, etc.; **barrier method** a method of contraception using a device or preparation which prevents live sperm from reaching an ovum; **barrier reef** a coral reef separated by a broad deep channel from the adjacent land.

B *v.t.* Close or shut with a barrier. M18.

barring /ˈbɑːrɪŋ/ *vbl n.* LME. [BAR *v.* + -ING[1].] The action of BAR *v.*; marking with or dividing into bars.

Comb.: **barring-out** (*obs.* exc. *Hist.*) a form of schoolboy rebellion in which a master was shut out of a classroom or school by his pupils.

barring /ˈbɑːrɪŋ/ *prep.* L15. [Use of pres. pple of BAR *v.* 6: see -ING[2]. Cf. BAR *prep.*] Excluding from consideration, except.

barrio /ˈbarɪəʊ/ *n.* Pl. **-os.** M19. [Sp., perh. f. Arab.] A ward or quarter of a town or city in Spain and Spanish-speaking countries; a Spanish-speaking quarter of a US town or city.

barrister /ˈbarɪstə/ *n.*[1] LME. [f. BAR *n.*[1], perh. after LEGISTER or MINISTER *n.*] A lawyer who has been called to the bar, and has the right of representing clients in the higher courts (more fully *barrister-at-law*); *US* any lawyer.

barristerial /barɪˈstɪərɪəl/ *a.* of or pertaining to a barrister M19.

†barrister *n.*[2] see BANISTER.

barrow /ˈbarəʊ/ *n.*[1] See also BERRY *n.*[2], BURROW *n.*[3] [OE *beorg* = OFris., OS, OHG (Du., G) *berg*, f. Gmc. Cf. ON *berg*, *bjarg* rock, precipice, Goth. *bairgahei* hill country.] **1** A mountain, a hill. *obs.* exc. as forming a place-name element. OE. **2** *Archaeol.* A grave-mound or tumulus. OE.

2 *round barrow*: see ROUND *a.*

Comb.: **barrow-wight** *pseudo-arch.* a guardian spirit believed to inhabit a grave-mound.

barrow /ˈbarəʊ/ *n.*[2] *obs.* exc. *dial.* [OE *b(e)arg* = OFris., MDu. *barch* (Du. *barg*), OS, OHG *bar(u)g* (G dial. *Barch*), ON *bǫrgr* f. Gmc.] A castrated boar.

barrow /ˈbarəʊ/ *n.*[3] & *v.*[1] [OE *bearwe* f. Gmc, f. base of BEAR *v.*[1] Cf. BIER.] **A** *n.* **1** A frame for loads etc. carried by two people; a stretcher, a bier. Now usu. more fully *hand-barrow*. OE. **2** A shallow open box with shafts for pushing by hand and a wheel or wheels, for the transportation of loads; *spec.* (*a*) = WHEELBARROW *n.* 1; (*b*) a two-wheeled handcart used by a costermonger; (*c*) a metal frame with two wheels for transporting luggage etc. ME. **3** The quantity carried by a barrow; the contents of a barrow. LME.

Comb.: **barrow-boy** a costermonger.

B *v.t.* Wheel or transport in a barrow. *rare.* M16.

barrowful *n.* = BARROW *n.*[3] 3 L15.

barrow /ˈbarəʊ/ *v.*[2]*i.* *Austral.* & *NZ.* M20. [Origin uncertain: cf. Ir., Gael. *bearradh* shearing, clipping.] Of a novice shearer or shedhand: complete the shearing of or partly shear a sheep for a shearer.

Barrowist /ˈbarəʊɪst/ *n.* L16. [f. *Barrowe* (see below) + -IST.] *Hist.* A follower of (the beliefs of) Henry Barrowe, one of the founders of Congregationalism, executed in 1593 for nonconformity.

barrulet /ˈbarjʊlɪt/ *n.* M16. [Dim. of assumed AN dim. of Fr. BARRE: see -ULE, -LET.] *Her.* A narrow horizontal stripe, equal to the fourth part of a bar (see BAR *n.*[1] 5).

barruly /ˈbarjʊli/ *a.* M16. [AN *barrulé*: see prec., -Y[5].] *Her.* Of a field: crossed by ten or more bars.

barry /ˈbɑːri/ *a.* L15. [Fr. *barré* barred, striped, f. *barrer* BAR *v.*: see -Y[5].] *Her.* Of a field: divided horizontally into equal parts by eight or fewer bars of alternating tinctures. (Foll. by *of* the number of parts.)

Barsac /ˈbɑːsak/ *n.* E18. [Fr. (see below).] A sweet white wine from the district of Barsac, department of Gironde, France.

barse /bɑːs/ *n.* Long *dial.* [OE *baers*, *bears* = OS *bars*, MDu. *ba(e)rse*, Du. *baars*, MHG *bars*, G *Barsch*: cf. BAR *n.*[2], BASS *n.*[1]] A kind of fish, *esp.* a perch.

Bart /bɑːt/ *n.* Also (esp. when following a name) **Bart.** (point). L18. [Abbrev.] = BARONET.

¶ *Baronet* is preferably abbreviated *Bt.*

†Bartelemy *n.* var. of BARTHOLOMEW.

barter /ˈbɑːtə/ *n.* LME. [f. the vb.] **1** Traffic by exchange of goods. LME. **2** Goods to be bartered. M18. **3** *fig.* Exchange, interchange, (of blows, insults, talk, etc.). E19.

barter /ˈbɑːtə/ *v.* LME. [Prob. f. OFr. *barater*: see BARRATOR.] **1** *v.t.* Exchange (goods or something intangible, *for* other goods etc.). LME. **b** Foll. by *away*. Dispose of by barter, part with for a (usu. mercenary or unworthy) consideration. M17. **2** *v.i.* Trade by exchange. L15.

1 YEATS Barter gaze for gaze. L. VAN DER POST He .. replaced it with what he could buy, or barter, from Somalis. C. V. WEDGWOOD The Scots bartered him to the English Parliament in return for payment for their troops. **2** F. QUARLES With thy bastard bullion thou hast barter'd for wares of price. D. LIVINGSTONE We did not see much evidence of a wish to barter.

barterable *a.* M19. **barterer** *n.* E17.

Barthian /ˈbɑːtɪən/ *a.* & *n.* E20. [f. *Barth* (see below) + -IAN.] **A** *adj.* Of, pertaining to, or characteristic of the Swiss theologian Karl Barth (1886–1968) or his writings. E20. **B** *n.* A follower of Barth. M20.

Bartholomew /bɑːˈθɒləmjuː/ *n.* Also **†Bart(e)lemy.** LME. [Name of the apostle, f. eccl.L *Bartholomaeus*, Gk *Bartholomaios* partly through Fr. *Barthélemy*.] **1** *Bartholomew-day*, *-tide*, St Bartholomew's day, 24 August. *arch.* LME. **2** *Bartholomew Fair*, a fair held at West Smithfield annually from 1133 to 1855 around St Bartholomew's day. *Bartholomew pig* etc., a pig etc. sold at this fair. *obs.* exc. *Hist.* L16.

bartizan /bɑːtɪˈzan/ *n. obs.* exc. *Hist.* Also **-san.** M16. [Sc. form of BRATTICING found esp. in 17 and reinterpreted E19 by Sir Walter Scott.] A battlemented parapet at the top of a castle or church; *esp.* a battlemented turret projecting from an angle at the top of a tower.

bartizaned *a.* furnished with a bartizan or bartizans E19.

†Bartlemy *n.* var. of BARTHOLOMEW.

Bartlett /ˈbɑːtlɪt/ *n.* Chiefly *N. Amer.* M19. [Enoch *Bartlett* (1779–1860), US merchant who first distributed the pear in the US.] More fully *Bartlett pear*. = WILLIAMS *n.*[1]

barton /ˈbɑːt(ə)n/ *n.* [OE *bere-tūn*, f. as BERE *n.*[1] + TOWN *n.* Cf. BARN *n.*[1]] **†1** A threshing-floor. Only in OE. **2** *Hist.* A demesne farm; land on a manor not let to tenants but retained for the owner's use. ME. **3** A farmyard. *arch.* M16. **†4** A pen for poultry. M16–L18.

bartonellosis /bɑːtɒnɛˈləʊsɪs/ *n.* Pl. **-loses** /-ˈləʊsiːz/. E20. [f. mod.L *Bartonella* (see below), f. Alberto L. *Barton* (1871–1950), Peruvian physician: see -OSIS.] *Med.* Infection with the micro-organism *Bartonella bacilliformis*, endemic in parts of S. America and manifested either as an acute febrile anaemia (also called *Oroya fever*) or in wartlike eruptions of the skin (also called *verruga peruana*). Cf. CARRION'S DISEASE.

bartsia /ˈbɑːtsɪə/ *n.* M18. [mod.L *Bartsia*, f. Johann *Bartsch* (1709–38), Prussian physician and botanist: see -IA[1].] A plant of the genus *Bartsia*, of the figwort family, or formerly included in this genus; *esp.* (more fully *red bartsia*) *Odontites verna*, a common wayside weed bearing racemes of purplish-red flowers.

barwood /ˈbɑːwʊd/ *n.* L18. [Prob. f. BAR *n.*[1] + WOOD *n.*[1]] A hard red African wood, orig. that of the tree *Baphia nitida*, but now usu. padouk.

barycentric /barɪˈsɛntrɪk/ *a.* L19. [f. Gk *barus* heavy + -CENTRIC.] Of or pertaining to the centre of gravity.

ˈbarycentre *n.* the centre of gravity E20.

baryon /ˈbarɪɒn/ *n.* M20. [f. as prec. + -ON.] *Particle Physics.* Any of the heavier elementary particles (proton, neutron, and hyperons), which have half-integral spins and take part in the strong interaction.

baryˈonic *a.* M20.

barysphere /ˈbarɪsfɪə/ *n.* E20. [f. as prec. + -SPHERE.] The dense interior of the earth, under the lithosphere.

baryta /bəˈrʌɪtə/ *n.* E19. [f. BARYTES after *soda* etc.] Barium oxide or hydroxide.

baryte *n.* var. of BARITE.

barytes /bəˈrʌɪtiːz/ *n.* L18. [f. Gk *barus* heavy + *-itēs* -ITE[1].] **†1** = BARYTA. L18–M19. **2** Native barium sulphate, occurring usu. as white or colourless tabular crystals; heavy spar. L18.

barytic /-ˈrɪ-/ *a.* of, pertaining to, or containing baryta or barium L18.

baryton *n.* var. of BARITONE *n.* 2.

barytone /ˈbarɪtəʊn/ *n.*[1] & *a.*[1] M17. [Late L *barytonos* f. Gk *barutonos* not oxytone: cf. BARITONE.] *Gk Gram.* (A word) not having the acute accent on the last syllable.

†barytone *n.*[2] & *a.*[2] var. of BARITONE *n.* & *a.*

basal /ˈbeɪs(ə)l/ *a.* & *n.* E17. [f. BASE *n.*[1] + -AL[1].] **A** *adj.* **1** Of, pertaining to, situated at, or forming a base. E17. **2** *fig.* Fundamental. M19.

1 basal body a kinetosome. **basal ganglion** *Anat.* any of the ganglia situated at the base of the cerebrum, i.e. the lentiform, caudate, and amygdaloid nuclei. **basal metabolism**: of an organism completely at rest. **basal pinacoid** or **plane** *Cryst.* a pinacoid intersecting the vertical axis.

B *n.* Something pertaining to, forming part of, or situated at the base. E17.

basalt /ˈbasɔːlt, -(ə)lt; bəˈsɔːlt, -ˈsɒlt/ *n.* Orig. in L form **†basaltes.** E17. [L *basaltes* var. of *basanites* f. Gk *basanitēs* (*lithos* stone), f. *basanos* touchstone.] *Geol.* A dark, fine-grained igneous rock, often displaying columnar structure and usu. composed largely of plagioclase with pyroxene and olivine.

basaltic /bəˈsɔːltɪk, -ˈsɒlt-/ *a.* of, pertaining to, or consisting of basalt; of the nature of basalt: L18. **baˈsaltiform** *a.* having the form of basalt L18.

basan /ˈbaz(ə)n/ *n.* Also **bazan.** See also BASIL *n.*[3] L15. [(O)Fr. *basane* f. Prov. *bazana* f. Sp. *badana* (cf. med.L *bedana*, AL *basana*) f. Arab. *biṭāna* (dressed sheepskin used as) lining.] Sheepskin tanned in bark.

basanite /ˈbasənʌɪt/ *n.* L18. [L *basanites*: see BASALT, -ITE[1].] A black form of jasper or quartzite, formerly used as a touchstone; *Geol.* any basaltic rock consisting of calcic plagioclase, augite, olivine, and a feldspathoid.

bas bleu /bɑ blø/ *n. phr.* Pl. ***bas bleus*** (pronounced same). L18. [Fr., tr. from Eng.] A bluestocking.

bascinet *n.* var. of BASINET.

bascule /ˈbaskjuːl/ *n.* L17. [Fr. (earlier *bacule*) = see-saw, f. stem of *battre* to beat + *cul* buttocks.] A lever apparatus of which one end is raised when the other is lowered.

Comb.: **bascule bridge** a type of bridge raised or lowered with a counterpoise.

base /beɪs/ *n.*[1] ME. [(O)Fr., or directly f. L BASIS.] **I 1** The part of a column between the shaft and the pedestal or pavement; the pedestal of a statue. ME. **2** *gen.* Something on which a thing stands or by which it is supported. LME. **b** *Geom.* The line or surface of a plane or solid figure on which it is regarded as standing. L16. **c** *Her.* The lower part of a shield. E17. **d** *Bot.* & *Zool.* The extremity of a part or organ by which it is attached to the trunk or main part. M18. **e** *Surveying.* A known line used as a geometrical basis for trigonometry. M19. **3** *fig.* A fundamental principle; a foundation. L15. **4** The principal ingredient, the fundamental element. L15. **5** A starting-point, goal-line, or station in certain games; *esp.* in *Baseball*, each of the four stations that must be reached in turn when scoring a run. L17. **6** *Chem.* Any substance which is capable of combining with an acid to form a salt (including, but wider than, *alkali*). Also, in mod. use, any species capable of donating pairs of electrons or of accepting protons. E19. **b** *spec.* in *Biochem.* Any of the purine or pyrimidine groups present in nucleotides and nucleic acids. M20. **7** *Math.* The number from whose various powers a system of counting, logarithms, etc., proceeds. E19. **8** A town, camp, harbour, airfield, etc., from which (esp. military) operations are conducted and where stores and supporting facilities are concentrated; a centre of operations, a headquarters. M19. **9** *Gram.* A root or stem as the origin of a word or as the element from which a derivative is formed by affixation etc. M19. **10** The middle part of a transistor, between collector and emitter. M20. **11** A notional structure or entity conceived of as underlying some system of activity or operations; the resources etc. on which something draws or depends for its operation. Usu. w. specifying wd. M20.

1 *Nation* They toppled the statue of Mussolini . . and inscribed a motto on its base. 2 A. WILSON They passed the magnolia tree, around whose base lay the last fallen petals. J. IRVING There was a flat shelf at the base of the slope. 3 R. L. STEVENSON A man who has a few friends . . cannot forget on how precarious a base his happiness reposes. G. MURRAY That is my feeling, and there must be some base for it. 4 J. C. OATES He brewed a special concoction of poison, with an arsenic base. 5 G. GREENE It was like that child's game when you . . are sent back to base to start again. C. POTOK Mr Galanter always began a ball game by putting me at second base. 6 *conjugate base*: see CONJUGATE *a.* SCHIFF('*s*) *base.* SEMIDINE *base.* 7 T. LEHRER Base eight is just like base ten really—if you're missing two fingers. 8 S. SASSOON He had been two years with a fighting battalion and was now down at the Base for good. N. MONSARRAT Malta was a base for bombers as well. M. ARNOLD-FORSTER Halsey's immediate objective was the Japanese air base at Munda. E. HEATH The YMCA hostel . . provided us with a base for the next few days. NAVAL *base.* 11 *Economist* After its customer base, IBM's biggest asset is that $1 billion annual R&D budget. *database*: see DATA.

II 12 *sing.* & (usu.) in *pl.* A pleated skirt appended to a doublet, reaching from the waist to the knee; an imitation of this in mailed armour for man or horse. Also, the skirt of a woman's outer petticoat or robe. *obs.* exc. *Hist.* LME.

Phrases: **base on balls** *Baseball* a batter's advance to the first base when the pitcher has delivered four balls outside specified limits (see BALL *n.*[1] 2c). **get to first base** *N. Amer. slang* achieve the first step towards one's objective. **off base** *N. Amer. slang* (*a*) mistaken; (*b*) unprepared, unawares. **off one's base** *US slang* mistaken. *power base*: see POWER *n.* *touch base*: see TOUCH *v.*

Comb.: **baseball** a team game played with a bat and ball, in which runs are scored by reaching a number of bases in turn; now *spec.* the American field-game of this type, played by two teams of nine players, the object of which is for each batter to hit the ball delivered by the opponent's pitcher and then traverse a diamond-shaped circuit of four bases to score a run; a ball used in this game; **baseband** the waveband occupied by the modulating signals of a carrier wave, or of signals transmitted without a carrier wave; **baseboard** a board forming a base; *spec.* (*N. Amer.*) a skirting-board; **base hit** *Baseball* a hit enabling the batter to reach a base safely; **base level** *Geol.* a level representing a lower limit of erosion; **baseline** a starting-line, a reference line; *esp.* (*a*) the back line at each end of the court in tennis, badminton, etc.; (*b*) *Typogr.* the imaginary straight line through the feet of most letters in a line of type; **base load** the permanent minimum load that a power supply system is required to deliver; **baseman** *Baseball* a fielder stationed near the specified (*first*, *second*, or *third*) base. **base-pair** *Biochem.* a pair of complementary bases, one in each strand of double-stranded nucleic acid, held together by a hydrogen bond; **base pay** = *basic pay* s.v. BASIC *a.* 1b; **base rate** a standard minimum rate, esp. of interest charged or allowed by a bank (generally, or *US* in particular circumstances); **base-runner** *Baseball* a member of the batting team at a base or running between bases; **base-running** *Baseball* running between bases; **bases-loaded** *a.* (*Baseball*) made or occurring with runners occupying the first, second, and third bases; **base-stealer** *Baseball* a base-runner who advances to the next base when no hit or error has been made; **base-stealing** *Baseball* advancing to the next base when no hit or error has been made.

base /beɪs/ *n.*[2] LME. [Prob. alt. of *bars*: see BAR *n.*[1] II.] More fully *prisoners' base*. A chasing game played by two sides occupying distinct areas, the object being to catch and make prisoner any player from the other side running from his or her home area.

†**bid (a person) base** challenge (a person) to a chase in this game; *gen.* challenge.

†**base** *n.*[3] var. of BASS *n.*[2]

†**base** *n.*[4] var. of BASS *n.*[1]

base /beɪs/ *a.* LME. [(O)Fr. *bas* f. med.L *bassus*, found in cl.L as a cognomen.] **1** Low; of small height. *arch.* LME. **b** In plant-names: of low growth. L16. **2** Low-lying, esp. topographically or geographically. Now *rare* or *obs.* LME. **3** Of a sound: low, not loud; deep, bass. Now *rare* or *obs.* LME. **4** Of inferior quality, of little value; mean, poor, shabby, worthless; (of language) debased, not classical. LME. **b** Of coin etc.: alloyed, counterfeit. E16. **5** *Law.* Of feudal service, tenure, etc.: involving villeinage etc. rather than military service (*Hist.*); later (of tenure etc.), held in fee simple subject to some qualification or limitation. LME. **6** Low in the social scale, plebeian; menial, degrading. *arch.* L15. **7** Reprehensibly cowardly, selfish, or mean; despicable. M16. **8** Low in the natural scale. *arch.* M16. **9** Illegitimate. *obs.* exc. in *baseborn* below. L16.

7 W. RALEIGH A most base piece of flatterie. H. BELLOC A few base contemporaries no older than ourselves, but cads. B. RUSSELL He has thoughts and feelings and impulses which may be wise or foolish, noble or base. J. BRAINE Underneath the rough exterior their hearts were as base as anyone's. 8 SHAKES. *A.Y.L.* Civet is of a baser birth than tar—the very uncleanly flux of a cat.

Special collocations & *comb.*: **baseborn** *a.* of low birth or (*arch.*) origin; illegitimate. **base metal**: not classified as noble or precious. **base-minded** *a.* having a base mind, mean, despicable. *base relief*: see BAS-RELIEF.

basely *adv.* L15. **baseness** *n.* LME.

base /beɪs/ *v.t.* L16. [f. BASE *n.*[1]] **1** Make or act as a foundation for. *rare.* L16. **2** Found, build, or construct (*up*)*on* a given base, build up *around* a base, (chiefly *fig.*); provide with a base; establish securely. Freq. in *pass.* M19. **3** Station or deploy *at* a particular place as centre of operations or headquarters, or *on* land, the sea, etc. Freq. in *pass.* E20.

1 G. MACDONALD Great roots based the tree-columns. 2 F. RAPHAEL His pools forecasts were based entirely on what the experts said. E. J. HOWARD A whole set of false assumptions, based on sentiment, lust and . . nostalgia. *Scientific American* The roads were always carefully based and drained. *Listener* I doubt whether ten years from now this 'science-based' or technological university will be very different from any other. *Classic CD* The famous second movement . . is based around a *Ländler.* 3 E. F. NORTON No. 1 party was to . . remain based there for the purpose of getting the next camp on to the North Col. *New Scientist* United States bases in the Pacific were warned to expect a carrier-based air strike. D. FRASER The British Eastern fleet was based at Kalindini on the Kenyan coast.

base-court /ˈbeɪskɔːt/ *n.* L15. [Fr. †*basse-court* (now *basse-cour*): see BASE *a.* 2, COURT *n.*[1]] *Hist.* The lower or outer court of a castle, mansion, etc., usu. occupied by servants.

†**base dance** *n. phr.* see BASSE DANSE.

baselard /ˈbasɪlɑːd/ *n. obs.* exc. *Hist.* LME. [OFr. *baselard(e)* (more commonly *bazelaire*, *bad-*) = med.L *baselardus*, *basi-*, etc., of unkn. origin.] A dagger or hanger, worn at the girdle.

baseless /ˈbeɪslɪs/ *a.* E17. [f. BASE *n.*[1] + -LESS.] Without a base; groundless, unfounded.

baselessly *adv.* E20. **baselessness** *n.* M19.

basement /ˈbeɪsm(ə)nt/ *n.* M18. [Prob. f. Du. †*basement* foundation, in WFlem. *bazement*, perh. f. It. *basamento* base of a column etc., f. *basare* to base: see -MENT. Cf. (O)Fr. *soubassement*.] **1** A storey of a building wholly or partially below ground level. M18. **2** The lowest or fundamental part of a structure; an underlying layer. L18. **b** *Geol.* The oldest rocks underlying a given area; *spec.* an Archaean formation underlying identifiable strata. Freq. *attrib.* M19.

1 *attrib.*: T. S. ELIOT They are rattling breakfast plates in basement kitchens. J. G. BENNETT My wife and I had found a small basement flat in Bayswater. *bargain basement*: see BARGAIN *n.* 2 F. HOYLE When a glacier or ice sheet rests on a flat, slippery basement, such as sand or water, the ice can move more quickly at its base than at its surface.

Comb.: **basement membrane** *Anat.* the thin delicate membrane separating the epithelium from underlying tissue.

basenji /bəˈsɛndʒi/ *n.* M20. [Bantu.] A smallish hunting dog of a central African breed, which rarely barks.

base relief *n.* var. of BAS-RELIEF.

bases *ns.* pls. of BASE *n.*[1], BASIS.

bash /baʃ/ *n.* E19. [f. BASH *v.*[2]] **1** A heavy blow. Orig. *Sc.* E19. **2** A party, an entertainment; a spree, a drinking-bout. *slang.* E20. **3** An attempt, a go. *slang.* M20.

1 M. GEE Peg's injunction to 'give 'im a bash'. 2 K. MILLETT We were invited to the big bash for Marjory Strider's opening. N. THORNBURG A party there . . a cocktail bash for the energy conference delegates. 3 *Times* Tried some anti-rust oil? Worth a bash.

Phrases: **have a bash at** *slang* (*a*) strike a blow at; (*b*) make an attempt at. **on the bash** *slang* on a drinking-bout.

bash /baʃ/ *v.*[1] Long *obs.* exc. *dial.* LME. [Aphet. f. ABASH.] **1** *v.t.* Disconcert, dismay, abash. LME. **2** *v.i.* Be daunted; be abashed. LME.

bash /baʃ/ *v.*[2] M17. [Ult. imit.: perh. a blend of *bang* and ending of *dash*, *smash*, etc.] **1** *v.t.* Strike heavily; beat soundly (also foll. by *up*); smash *down* etc. with a heavy blow; injure by striking; *fig.* act or speak to the detriment of, criticize heavily. M17. **b** Subject to some prolonged arduous activity. Usu. as vbl n. as 2nd elem. of a comb. w. specifying wd, as *ear-bashing*, *spud-bashing*, *square-bashing*. *slang.* M20. **2** *v.i.* Strike *at* heavily and repeatedly; work *at* crudely and persistently. M19. **3** *v.i.* Carry *on* unheedingly. M20.

1 D. LESSING London's full of students rushing about bashing policemen. J. HERRIOT He had lifted a stone from the pasture and was bashing something with it. *fig.*: *Times* Voices in the Conservative Party arguing moderation rather than 'union bashing' in its approach to the closed shop. 2 J. B. PRIESTLEY It wasn't my kind of painting, and I just bashed away at it. J. RABAN Men were bashing at pavements with pickaxes and sledgehammers.

basher *n.* a person who bashes, a fighter L19. **bashing** *n.* the action of the vb; an instance of this, a heavy beating: M18.

basha /ˈbaʃə/ *n.* E20. [Bengali.] In SE Asia: a bamboo hut with a thatched roof.

†**bashalik** *n.* see PASHALIC.

bashaw /bəˈʃɔː/ *n. arch.* L15. [Var. of PASHA.] **1** = PASHA. L15. **2** *fig.* A grandee; a haughty imperious man. L16.

bashawship *n.* L17.

bashful /ˈbaʃfʊl, -f(ə)l/ *a.* L15. [f. BASH *v.*[1] + -FUL.] †**1** Lacking self-possession; daunted. L15–E18. **2** Shy, diffident, modest; shamefaced, sheepish. M16.
bashfully *adv.* M16. **bashfulness** *n.* M16.

bashi-bazouk /ˌbaʃɪbəˈzuːk/ *n.* M19. [Turk. *başı bozuk* lit. 'wrong-headed', f. *baş* head + *bozuk* out of order.] *Hist.* A mercenary of the Turkish irregulars, notorious for pillage and brutality.

Bashkir /baʃˈkɪə/ *n.* & *a.* E19. [Russ. f. Turkic *Başkurt*.] **A** *n.* Pl. **-s**, same. **1** A member of a Muslim people living in the southern Urals. E19. **2** The language of this people. L19. **B** *adj.* Of or pertaining to the Bashkirs or their language. M19.

bashlik /ˈbaʃlɪk/ *n.* L19. [Russ. *bashlyk* f. Turkic.] A kind of hood with long side-pieces, worn orig. by Russians as protection against the weather.

basho /ˈbaʃəʊ/ *n.* Pl. same, **-os**. L20. [Jap.] A Sumo wrestling tournament.

basi- /ˈbeɪsi/ *comb. form* of BASE *n.*[1], BASIS *n.*: see -I-.
basiˈbranchial *a.* (*Zool.*) of, pertaining to, or forming, the base of the branchial arch (in fishes) L19. **basiˈcranial** *a.* (*Anat.*) of, pertaining to, or forming, the base of the cranium M19. **basifixed** *a.* (*Bot.*) (of an anther) attached to its filament by the base L19. **basifugal** /beɪˈsɪfjʊg(ə)l/ *a.* (*Bot.*) tending away from the base L19. **baˈsifugally** *adv.* (*Bot.*) in a basifugal manner, away from the base L19. **basilect** /ˈbasɪlɛkt, ˈbeɪsɪ-/ *n.* [-LECT] *Ling.* the dialect or variety of any language with the lowest prestige M20. **basilectal** /basɪˈlɛkt(ə)l, beɪsɪ-/ *a.* (*Ling.*) of, pertaining to, or characteristic of the basilect L20. **basiocˈcipital** *a.* (*Anat.*) of, pertaining to, or forming, the base of the occiput M19. **basipetal** /beɪˈsɪpɪt(ə)l/ *a.* (*Bot.*) developing from the apex towards the base M19. **baˈsipetally** *adv.* (*Bot.*) in a basipetal manner, from the apex towards the base M20. **basiˈsphenoid** *a.* & *n.* (*Anat.* & *Zool.*) (forming or pertaining to) a bone of the floor of the cranium (in the human skull, the hind part of the sphenoid bone) M19.

BASIC /ˈbeɪsɪk/ *n.*[1] Also **Basic**. M20. [Acronym, f. *Beginners' All-purpose Symbolic Instruction Code*, after BASIC *a.*] The name of a high-level programming language designed for easy learning.

basic /ˈbeɪsɪk/ *a.* & *n.*[2] M19. [f. BASE *n.*[1] + -IC.] **A** *adj.* **1** Of, pertaining to, or forming a base; fundamental, essential. M19. **b** Constituting a minimum, esp. in a standardized scale (of wages, prices, etc.); at the lowest acceptable level. E20. **2a** *Chem.* Having the properties of a base; derived from or characteristic of a base. M19. **b** *Geol.* Of an igneous rock: having a relatively low silica content. L19. **c** *Metall.* Pertaining to, resulting from, or designating steel-making processes involving lime-rich refractories and slags. L19.
1 A. J. CRONIN In his complete severance from tradition he has lost sight of the basic principles of proportion. E. ROOSEVELT The basic food of the people is rice for every meal . . but there is a feast about once a week when they eat chicken and pork. J. IRVING He felt a need, almost as basic as survival, to find something he could finish. H. NEMEROV The study of symbolism, which is basic To the nature of money. **Basic English** a simplified form of English with a select vocabulary of 850 words, for international use. **basic industry** an industry of great economic importance. **b** *New York Times* Most offer basic accommodations (many don't have electricity or hot water). **basic pay** a standard rate of pay exclusive of extra payments, overtime, and allowances. **2 basic dye** a dye which is a salt of a coloured organic base. **basic salt** a salt formed by incomplete neutralization of a base. **basic slag** phosphate-rich slag from basic steel-making, freq. used as a fertilizer.
B *n.* Something basic, esp. basic pay; (**B-**) Basic English; in *pl.*, essentials, fundamental aspects. M20.
A. HACKNEY There's a job in Stores and Packing. Hundred and eighty-nine shillings basic. *Times* The Commission should ignore the grander politics and concentrate on the basics.
¶In techn. senses the adj. is opp. ACID *a.*
basically *adv.* (*a*) fundamentally, essentially, in sum; (*b*) (esp. modifying a sentence) actually, in fact: E20.

basicity /beɪˈsɪsɪti/ *n.* M19. [f. BASIC *a.* + -ITY.] Chiefly *Chem.* **1** The number of hydrogen atoms replaceable by a base in a particular acid. M19. **2** Basic character or condition. L19.

basidiomycete /bəˌsɪdɪəˈmʌɪsiːt/ *n.* Orig. only in pl. **-mycetes** /-ˈmʌɪsiːts, -mʌɪˈsiːtiːz/. L19. [Anglicized sing. of mod.L *Basidiomycetes* (see below), f. as next + -O- + Gk *mukētes* pl. of *mukēs* fungus.] *Mycol.* A fungus of the subdivision Basidiomycotina (formerly the class Basidiomycetes), which includes the agarics.
basidiomyˈcetous *a.* L19.

basidium /bəˈsɪdɪəm/ *n.* Pl. **-dia** /-dɪə/. M19. [mod.L, f. Gk BASIS: see -IDIUM.] *Bot.* A club-shaped spore-bearing structure produced by a basidiomycete.
basidiospore *n.* a spore produced by a basidium. M19.

basil /ˈbaz(ə)l, -zɪl/ *n.*[1] LME. [OFr. *basile* f. med.L *basilicum* f. Gk *basilikon*: see BASILICON.] **1** A shrubby aromatic labiate herb of the genus *Ocimum*; esp. *O. basilicum* (more fully *sweet basil*) and *O. minimum* (more fully *bush basil*), having culinary use; (in the Indian subcontinent) *O. sanctum* (more fully *holy basil*), sacred to Hindus. Also, the dried leaves of such a herb, used as flavouring. LME. **2** In full *wild basil*. An aromatic labiate herb, *Clinopodium vulgare*, of hedges and scrub. M16.
Comb.: **basil thyme** a small aromatic labiate herb, *Clinopodium acinos*, of dry arable land.

basil /ˈbaz(ə)l, -zɪl/ *n.*[2] Now *rare* or *obs.* M16. [OFr. *basile* basilisk.] †**1** = BASILISK 2. Only in M16. **2** A prisoner's ankle-iron. L16.

basil /ˈbaz(ə)l, -zɪl/ *n.*[3] Also **bazil**. E17. [App. var. of BASAN.] = BASAN.

basil *n.*[4] & *v.* var. of BEZEL.

basilar /ˈbasɪlə/ *a.* M16. [mod.L *basilaris*, irreg. f. L BASIS: see -AR[1].] Of, pertaining to, or situated at the base, esp. of the skull.
basilar membrane a membrane in the cochlea of the ear, bearing sensory cells.
basilary *a.* = BASILAR E19.

Basilian /bəˈzɪlɪən/ *a.* L18. [f. L *Basilius* Basil (see below) + -AN.] Of or pertaining to St Basil the Great (*c*330–79), Bishop of Caesarea, or the order of monks and nuns following his monastic rule.

basilic /bəˈsɪlɪk/ *n.* E18. [Fr. *basilique* or its source L BASILICA.] †**1** = BASILICA 1, 2. E18–M19. **2** In *pl.* = BASILICA 4. M18.

basilic /bəˈsɪlɪk/ *a.* LME. [(O)Fr. *basilique* or its source L *basilicus* f. Gk *basilikos* royal: see -IC.] **1** Anat. *basilic vein*, the large superficial vein of either arm. LME. **2** Kingly, royal. *rare*. E17.
basilical *a.*[1] †(*a*) = BASILIC *a.* 1; (*b*) = BASILIC *a.* 2: M17.

basilica /bəˈsɪlɪkə, -ˈzɪl-/ *n.* M16. [L: branch I lit. 'royal palace' f. Gk *basilikē* use as n. of fem. of *basilikos* royal, f. *basileus* king; branch II f. Gk *basilika* neut. pl. of *basilikos*.] **I** *sing.* (pl. **-cas**, (*rare*) **-cae** /-kiː/). **1** *Hist.* A large oblong hall or building, with double colonnades and a semicircular apse, used for courts of law and public assemblies. M16. **2** A building of this form used as a Christian church. Also, used as the title of certain churches granted privileges by the Pope. M16. †**3** *Anat.* The basilic vein (see BASILIC *a.* 1). L16–M18. **II** *pl.* **4** *Hist.* (**B-**.) *The* 9th-cent. Byzantine legal code initiated by the emperor Basil I. M17.
basilical *a.*[2] = BASILICAN E17. **basilican** *a.* of, pertaining to, or resembling a basilica L18.

†**basilicon** *n.* Also **-cum**. LME. [L *basilicum* or Gk *basilikon* use as n. of neut. of *basilikos*: see prec.] **1** = BASIL *n.*[1] LME–L15. **2** Any of several ointments supposed to possess sovereign virtues. LME–L18.

Basilidian /basɪˈlɪdɪən/ *n.* & *a.* L16. [f. L *Basilides* (see below), Gk *Basileidēs* + -IAN.] *Hist.* **A** *n.* A disciple or follower of Basilides, a 2nd-cent. AD Alexandrian Gnostic. L16. **B** *adj.* Of or pertaining to Basilides or his followers. L19.

basilisk /ˈbazɪlɪsk/ *n.* & *a.* LME. [L *basiliscus* f. Gk *basiliskos* kinglet, kind of serpent, goldcrest, dim. of *basileus* king.] **A** *n.* Also (after Sp.) †**-lisco**, (after L) †**-liscus**. **1** A fabulous reptile, whose gaze or breath is fatal, hatched by a serpent from a cock's egg (= COCKATRICE 1); *Her.* = COCKATRICE 1b. LME. **2** *fig.* A person who casts a malicious look; a person or thing with a destructive influence. L15. **3** A large brass cannon. E16. **4** A small tropical American iguanid lizard of the genus *Basiliscus*, having a prominent crest. E19.
2 C. BURNEY Satire . . becomes a basilisk in the hands of a man . . who employs it to blast the reputation of another.
B *attrib.* or as *adj.* Of a glance, eye, etc.: malicious, casting an evil influence. L15.
2 G. W. KNIGHT Fixed by the basilisk eye of a nameless terror.

basin /ˈbeɪs(ə)n/ *n.* Also (*arch.*) **bason**. ME. [OFr. *bacin* (mod. *bassin*) f. med.L *ba(s)cinus*, f. *bacca* water-container, perh. f. Gaulish.] **1** A circular vessel of greater width than depth, esp. for holding water, a bowl, a dish; a fixed shallow open container for water for washing etc. ME. **b** The quantity held by a basin; a basinful. LME. †**2** A cymbal or other metal dish struck or clashed to produce sound. ME–E17. †**3** *Anat.* = PELVIS 1, 2. Only in 18. **4** A hollow depression containing water; a land-locked harbour or bay; a large submarine depression. E18. **5** A dock with floodgates to maintain the water level; a widened part of a canal or river with wharves. E18. **6** A circular or oval valley or natural depression; *spec.* (*a*) the tract of country drained by a river, or which drains into a lake or sea; (*b*) a circumscribed geological formation in which the strata dip inwards to the centre. E19.
1 E. HEMINGWAY They were all eating, holding their chins close over the basin. J. CHEEVER The noise of the fountains whose basins were disfigured and cracked. *wash-basin*: see WASH *v.* **b** H. ALLEN He set the example by pouring himself a large basin of tea. **4** WORDSWORTH And in a basin black and small Receives a lofty waterfall. H. D. THOREAU The harbour of Quebec . . a basin two miles across. R. K. NARAYAN The villagers had made an artificial basin in sand and . . fetched water from distant wells and filled it. N. CALDER The ocean basins were known to be very deep and to constitute huge depressions in the Earth. **5** *tidal basin*: see TIDAL *a.* **6** A. P. STANLEY The traveller finds himself in a wide basin encircled by hills. L. D. STAMP The Thames breaks into the basin . . by . . Goring Gap. *Encycl. Brit.* The Amazon . . is . . the largest river in the world in volume and in area of its drainage basin.
basinful *n.* as much as a basin will hold; the contents of a basin; *colloq.* an excessive amount, a lot: L18.

basinet /ˈbasɪnɪt/ *n.* Also **bascinet**, **basnet** /ˈbasnɪt/. ME. [OFr. *bacinet* dim. of *bacin* BASIN: see -ET[1].] *Hist.* A light steel helmet usu. with a visor.

basis /ˈbeɪsɪs/ *n.* Pl. **bases** /ˈbeɪsiːz/. L16. [L f. Gk, = stepping. Cf. BASE *n.*[1]] **1** The base or bottom of something material; the foundation; a pedestal. *arch.* L16. **b** *Bot.* & *Zool.* = BASE *n.*[1] 2d. E17. †**2** *Geom.* = BASE *n.*[1] 2b. L16–M18. **3** The main constituent. E17. **4** A thing by or on which anything immaterial is supported or sustained. E17. **5** A thing on which anything is constructed and by which its constitution or operation is determined; a footing (of a specified kind); a determining principle; a set of underlying or agreed principles. E17. **6** = BASE *n.*[1] 8. *arch.* M19.
1 SHAKES. *Temp.* To th' shore, that o'er his wave-worn basis bowed, As stooping to relieve him. ADDISON Observing an English inscription upon the basis. **3** JABEZ HOGG Colouring-solutions should be always prepared with glycerine . . as a basis. **4** SHAKES. *Macb.* Great tyranny, lay thou thy basis sure. J. TYNDALL This speculation . . rested upon a basis of conjecture. **5** J. BRIGHT It is necessary therefore to have a basis for our discussion. J. GALSWORTHY She believed . . in putting things on a commercial basis. **on the basis of** using as a criterion or a principle of action; taking account of.

bask /bɑːsk/ *a. dial.* ME. [ON *beisk*.] Bitter, acrid.

bask /bɑːsk/ *v.* & *n.* LME. [Origin uncertain, perh. f. ON precursor of *baðast* refl. of *baða* BATHE *v.*] **A** *v.* †**1** *v.i.* & *refl.* Bathe; *fig.* swim in blood. LME–M16. 2 *v.t.* (usu. *refl.*). Expose to a flood of warmth, esp. sunshine. E17. 3 *v.i.* Disport oneself or revel in warmth and light, esp. of the sun, a fire, or *fig.* of love, favour, pleasant feelings. M17.

2 MILTON The lubbar fiend . . Basks at the fire his hairy strength. R. DAHL Do you like to swim and to bask yourself in the sun? 3 J. GALSWORTHY The sun now only reached the wall at the end, whereon basked a crouching cat. *fig.*: E. A. FREEMAN Traitors basking in the royal smiles. D. HALBERSTAM Everyone wanted to talk to him, to sit next to him at dinner, to bask in the excitement and originality of his mind. P. P. READ He basked in the confident feeling that should he want them they were his for the taking. **basking shark** a very large plankton-eating shark, *Cetorhinus maximus*, which habitually lies near the sea surface.

B *n.* A spell of basking; radiance etc. in which one basks. M18.

Baskerville /ˈbaskəvɪl/ *n.* E19. [See below.] *Typogr.* A typeface modelled on that designed by John Baskerville (1706–75), Eng. typefounder and printer; a book printed by Baskerville.

basket /ˈbɑːskɪt/ *n.* ME. [In AL *baskettum*, AN & OFr. *basket*, of unkn. origin.] 1 A container made of plaited or interwoven osiers, cane, rushes, wire, etc. ME. b *spec.* Such a container regarded as the model of daily or charitable provisions; alms. M16. 2 A basketful. LME. 3 Chiefly *Hist.* The overhanging back compartment on the outside of a stagecoach. L18. 4 A structure suspended from the envelope of a balloon for carrying crew, ballast, etc. L18. 5 A net fixed on a ring (or, orig., a fruit-basket) used as a goal in basketball; a goal scored in basketball. L19. 6 *fig.* A group, category; a range. E20. 7 *euphem.* = BASTARD *n. colloq.* M20.

1 †*alms-basket*, *bread basket*, *clothes-basket*, *fruit-basket*, *waste-basket*, *work-basket*, etc. *hanging basket*: see HANGING *a.* **in the basket** (of a dish of (esp. fried) food) served in a small basket lined with paper etc., not on a plate. *waste-paper basket*: see WASTE *n.* 6 HUGH WALPOLE Semyonov at this time flung Nikitin, Andrew Vassilievitch, Trenchard and myself into one basket We were all 'crazy romantics'. *Times* Sterling's effective devaluation against a basket of other currencies rose to 43.6 per cent. 7 N. COWARD Come on, Johnnie—don't argue with the poor little basket.

Comb.: **basketball** a game, in its codified form for two teams of five players, the object of which is to toss a large inflated ball through the opponent's goal, orig. a fruit-basket, now a net fixed on a ring mounted on a board (properly) ten feet above the ground at either end of the court of play, and in which players may throw the ball to each other or advance bouncing it but not run or walk with the ball in their hands; the ball used in this; **basket-boat** a boat of basketwork; **basket case** *colloq.* (freq. considered *offensive*) a person who has lost both arms and both legs; *fig.* a completely helpless person, a nervous wreck, a bankrupt country; **basket chair** a wickerwork chair; **basket clause**: of a comprehensive nature; **basket fish** a brittle-star having branched arms; **basket hilt** a sword hilt with a guard resembling basketwork; **basket-hilted** *a.* having a basket hilt; **basket-maker** a person who makes baskets; *spec.* in *Archaeol.* (w. cap. initials) used *attrib.* to designate an ancient culture in the south-western US characterized by basketwork; **basket meal**: served 'in the basket' (see sense 1 above); **basket star** = *basket fish* above; **basket weave** a style of weave whose pattern resembles basketwork; **basket-woman**: carrying goods for sale in a basket; **basketwork** (the art of making) a structure of interwoven osiers etc.

basketful *n.* the content of a basket ME. **basketing** *n.* basketwork E17. **basketry** *n.* basketwork M19.

basket /ˈbɑːskɪt/ *v.t.* L16. [f. the n.] 1 Put into, or hang up in, a basket. L16. 2 Throw into the waste-paper basket; discard, reject. E19.

Baskish *n.* & *a.* var. of BASQUISH.

basmati /basˈmɑːti, -z-/ *n.* M19. [Hind. *bāsmatī* lit. 'fragrant'.] More fully *basmati rice*. A kind of rice with very long thin grains and a delicate fragrance.

basnet *n.* var. of BASINET.

bason /ˈbeɪs(ə)n/ *n.*[1] & *v.* E18. [Origin unkn.] Chiefly *Hist.* A *n.* A bench with a hot plate, on which to harden felt in hat-making. E18. B *v.t.* Harden the felt of (a hat) on a bason. E18.

bason *n.*[2] see BASIN.

basophil /ˈbeɪsəfɪl/ *a.* & *n.* Also **-phile** /-fʌɪl/. L19. [f. Gk BASIS + -O- + -PHIL.] *Biol.* A *adj.* Readily stained by basic dyes; esp. in *basophil cell*, a kind of granulocyte having this property. L19. B *n.* A basophil cell. E20.

basoˈphilia *n.* affinity for basic dyes; the presence of abnormally large numbers of basophil cells in the blood: E20. **basoˈphilic** *a.* basophil; pertaining to or displaying basophilia: L19.

Basotho /bəˈsuːtuː/ *n.* & *a.* Also (earlier, now *arch.* or *Hist.*) **Basuto**. M19. [Sesotho, f. *ba-* pl. pref. + SOTHO.] A *n.* 1 (*erron.*) *sing.* Pl. **-os**. A member of the Sotho people, (*sing.*) a Mosotho. M19. 2 *pl.* (Members of) the Sotho people. L19. B *attrib.* or as *adj.* = SOTHO *a.* M19.

Basque /bask, bɑːsk/ *a.* & *n.* In sense B.3 usu. **b-**. E19. [Fr. f. L *Vasco*: cf. GASCON.] A *adj.* Of or pertaining to an ancient people inhabiting both slopes of the western Pyrenees, adjacent to the Bay of Biscay, or their non-Indo-European language. E19.

Basque beret, cap a beret as traditionally worn by Basque peasants. *Saut Basque*: see SAUT 1.

B *n.* 1 A native or inhabitant of the Pyrenees area adjacent to the Bay of Biscay; a member of the Basque people. M19. 2 The Basque language. M19. 3 A short continuation of a doublet, waistcoat or bodice below the waist; a bodice having this. M19.

2 PAS *de basque*.

basqued *a.* furnished with a basque (sense 3) L19.

basquine /baˈskiːn, bɑː-/ *n.* Also **-ina** /-iːnə/, **-iña** /-iːnjə/. E19. [(Fr., f.) Sp. *basquiña*, f. *basco* Basque.] 1 An ornamented outer skirt worn by Basque and Spanish women. E19. 2 A type of basqued jacket. M19.

Basquish /ˈbaskɪʃ, ˈbɑːsk-/ *n.* & *a.* Also **Baskish**. E17. [f. as BASQUE + -ISH[1].] (Of or pertaining to) the Basque language.

bas-relief /ˈbasrɪliːf, ˈbɑː(s)-/ *n.* Also **bass-relief**, **†base relief**. E17. [It. *basso-rilievo* (see BASSO-RELIEVO), assim. to Fr.] (A sculpture, moulding, carving, etc., in) low relief (see RELIEF *n.*[2]).

bass /bas/ *n.*[1] Also **basse**, **†base**. Pl. **-es** /-ɪz/, (usu.) same. LME. [Alt. of BARSE.] The common perch; any of numerous spiny-finned freshwater and marine percoid fishes related to or resembling the common perch; *esp.* a European marine fish, *Dicentrarchus labrax*.

black bass, *large-mouth(ed) bass*, *striped bass*, *white bass*, etc.

bass /beɪs/ *n.*[2] Also **†base**. LME. [f. BASE *a.*, BASS *a.*] 1 The lowest part in harmonized musical composition; the deepest male voice, or the lowest tones of an instrument or group of similar instruments, which sound this part. LME. 2 An instrument, string, etc., having such a part or compass; *spec.* a double-bass or bass guitar. M16. 3 A singer having a bass voice; a bass player. L16. 4 The low-frequency component of transmitted or reproduced sound. M20.

1 **figured bass** = THOROUGH BASS. *fundamental bass*: see FUNDAMENTAL *a.* *ground bass*: see GROUND *n.* THOROUGH BASS. *walking bass*: see WALKING *ppl a.* 2 DOUBLE-BASS. 4 attrib.: *Which?* Treble and bass controls are good enough, but you can also get a graphic equaliser.

Comb.: **bass-bar** a strip of wood glued inside the table of a stringed instrument along the line of the lowest string, to support the left foot of the bridge; **bassman** (chiefly *Jazz*) = BASSIST (b). (See also combs. of BASS *a.*, with which attrib. uses of the n. sometimes merge.)

bassist *n.* (*a*) *rare* a bass singer; (*b*) a person who plays a bass instrument, esp. a double-bass or bass guitar: L19.

†bass *n.*[3] LME–L16. [Prob. f. BASS *v.*[1] (though recorded earlier). Cf. BUSS *n.*[2]] A kiss.

bass /bas/ *n.*[4] L17. [Alt. of BAST *n.*] 1 A fibre obtained from certain palm trees or (orig.) from the inner bark of the lime or linden. L17. 2 An article made of this. E18.

Comb.: **basswood** (the wood of) the American lime or linden, *Tilia americana*.

bass /bas/ *n.*[5] L17. [Perh. for *bas-* or *base-coal*, as in *base coin* (BASE *a.* 4b).] *Mining.* Carbonaceous shale.

bass /beɪs/ *a.* LME. [f. BASE *a.*, assim. to It. BASSO.] †1 Low in sound, soft. LME–E16. 2 Deep-sounding, low in the musical scale; of, pertaining to, or suited to the bass (BASS *n.*[2]); lowest-pitched (in a series of similar instruments or strings). E16.

Comb. (partly attrib. uses of BASS *n.*[2]): **bass-baritone** *n.* & *a.* (designating) a voice higher than bass, yet of bass and not tenor quality; a singer having such a voice; **bass clef**: placing F below middle C on the second highest line of the stave; **bass drum** a large drum of indefinite low pitch; **bass-horn** an early instrument made in the shape of a bassoon but much deeper in its tones; **bass viol** (*a*) a viola da gamba for playing the bass part in older concerted music; (*b*) *US* a double-bass.

†bass *v.*[1]*t.* & *i.* L15–L16. [Prob. f. (O)Fr. *baiser* f. L *basiare*.] Kiss.

†bass *v.*[2]*t.* *rare* (Shakes.). Only in E17. [f. BASS *n.*[2]] Utter with bass sound.

bassarid /ˈbasərɪd/ *n.* M19. [L *Bassarid-*, *-aris*, f. Gk *Bassaris* a Thracian bacchanal, lit. a fox (prob. from their dress of fox-skins).] A Thracian bacchanal; a Bacchante.

basse *n.* var. of BASS *n.*[1]

basse dance *n. phr.* see BASSE DANSE.

basse danse /bas dɑ̃s/ *n. phr.* Also **basse dance**. Pl. **-s -s** (pronounced same). Orig. fully Anglicized as **†base dance**. E16. [Fr. = low dance.] *Hist.* A slow stately dance; *spec.* a court dance in duple or triple time which originated in France in the 15th cent.

basset /ˈbasɪt/ *n.*[1] M16. [Origin unkn.] The edge of a geological stratum exposed at the surface; an outcrop. Freq. *attrib.*

basset /ˈbasɪt/ *n.*[2] E17. [Fr., f. *bas* low: see -ET[1].] A short-legged hound for hunting hares etc. Also *basset-hound*.

basset /ˈbasɪt/ *n.*[3] *obs.* exc. *Hist.* Also **-ette**. M17. [Fr. *bassette* f. It. *bassetta* fem. of BASSETTO.] A card-game from which faro originated.

basset /ˈbasɪt/ *v.i.* L17. [f. BASSET *n.*[1]] Of the edge of a geological stratum: be exposed at the surface, crop out.

basse-taille /bastɑːj/ *n.* L19. [Fr., f. *basse* fem. of *bas* low (see BASE *a.*) + *taille* cut.] A technique of applying translucent enamels to metal reliefs so that the shade of the enamel is darkest where the relief is most deeply cut.

basset-horn /ˈbasɪthɔːn/ *n.* M19. [G, partial tr. Fr. *cor de basset* f. It. *corno di bassetto* (*corno* horn, *di* of, BASSETTO.] A tenor clarinet with extended compass.

bassette *n.* var. of BASSET *n.*[3]

bassetto /bəˈsɛtəʊ/ *n.* Pl. **-os**. E18. [It., dim. of BASSO.] A violoncello.

bassi *n.* pl. of BASSO, BASSUS *ns.*

bassinet /basɪˈnɛt/ *n.* Also **-ette**. L16. [Fr., dim. of *bassin* BASIN: see -ET[1].] †1 A marsh marigold; a geranium, a ranunculus. L16–E18. 2 A hooded wicker cradle or pram. M19.

basso /ˈbasəʊ/ *n.* & *a.* Pl. **bassos**, **bassi** /ˈbasi/. E18. [It. = low f. L *bassus*: see BASE *a.* (Earlier in Eng. in BASSO-RELIEVO.)] *Mus.* = BASS *n.*[2] (esp. sense 3), *a.*

Comb. & *special collocations*: **basso buffo** /ˈbʊfəʊ/, pl. **bassi buffi** /-fi/, **basso buffos**, [BUFFO] a bass singer who takes comic parts in opera; **basso cantante** /kanˈtanteɪ/, pl. **bassi cantanti** /-ti/, [lit. 'singing'] (a singer with) a voice in the upper register of the bass range; **basso continuo** /kənˈtɪnjʊəʊ/, pl. **basso continuos**, [CONTINUO] a figured bass, a thorough bass; **basso ostinato** /ɒstɪˈnɑːtəʊ/, pl. **basso ostinatos**, [OSTINATO] = *ground bass* s.v. GROUND *n.*; **basso profundo** /prəˈfʌndəʊ/ (occas. **profondo** /-ˈfɒnd-/), pl. **bassi profundi** /-di/, **basso profundos**, [lit. 'deep'] (a singer with) a very deep and rich voice.

bassoon /bəˈsuːn/ *n.* E18. [Fr. *basson* f. It. *bassone* augm. of BASSO: see -OON.] 1 (A player of) a bass instrument of the oboe family. E18. 2 An organ or harmonium stop similar in tone to this instrument. L19.

1 **double bassoon**: larger and longer than the normal bassoon and an octave lower in pitch.

bassoonist *n.* a bassoon player E19.

basso-relievo /ˌbasəʊrɪˈliːvəʊ/ *n.* Also **-rilievo** /-rɪˈljeɪvəʊ/. Pl. **-os.** M17. [It. *basso-rilievo*: see BASSO, RILIEVO.] = BAS-RELIEF.

bass-relief *n.* var. of BAS-RELIEF.

bassus /ˈbasʌs/ *n.* & *a.* Pl. of n. **-ssi** /-sʌɪ, -siː/. L16. [L: see BASE *a.*] *Early Mus.* = BASS *n.*[2], *a.*

bast /bast/ *n.* [OE *bæst*, corresp. to (M)Du., (O)HG, ON *bast* f. Gmc, of unkn. origin.] Fibrous material from the phloem of certain plants, as hemp, jute, or (orig.) the lime tree. Also (*Bot.*), the phloem or vascular tissue of a plant.
basten *a.* (now *rare* or *obs.*) made of bast OE.

basta /ˈbasta/ *int.* L16. [It.] Enough! No matter!

bastard /ˈbɑːstəd, ˈbast-/ *n.* & *a.* Also *S. Afr.* (senses A.4, B.6) **bastaard, baster** /ˈbɑːstə/. ME. [OFr. *bastart* (mod. *bâtard*) = Prov. *bastard*, It., Sp., Port. *bastardo*, f. med.L *bastardus*, prob. f. *bastum* pack-saddle: see BAT *n.*[2], -ARD.] **A** *n.* **1** A person conceived and born out of wedlock; an illegitimate child. ME. **2** A sweet Spanish wine, resembling muscatel; any sweetened wine. *obs.* exc. *Hist.* LME. **3** Something of unusual make, shape, or proportion, or of inferior quality; *esp.* (*a*) a kind of culverin; (*b*) a size of paper. L15. **4** A person of mixed Nama and European ancestry; a Griqua, a Rehobother. *S. Afr.* L18. **5** An unpleasant or unfortunate person or thing; (in weakened sense) a chap, a fellow. *colloq.* M19. **6** Bastarda script. E20.
1 *fig.*: T. FULLER Fame being a bastard or *filia populi*, 'tis very hard to find her father. 2 SHAKES. *Meas. for M.* We shall have all the world drink brown and white bastard. 5 H. G. WELLS Serve the cocky little bastard right. T. RATTIGAN Johnny, you old bastard! Are you all right? J. MACLAREN-ROSS This bastard of a bump on the back of my head. M. SHADBOLT At first Ned and Nick had to milk in the open, which was a bastard when it rained.
B *adj.* **1** Born out of wedlock. ME. **2** Hybrid; not genuine; spurious, corrupt. LME. **3** Of unusual shape or size (applied e.g. to a file intermediate between coarse and fine, to a font of type, etc.). LME. **4** Irregular, unauthorized, unrecognized. M16. **5** Having the appearance of; of an inferior kind; *esp.* (in names of animals, plants, etc.) closely resembling (the species etc. whose name follows). M16. **6** Designating, of or pertaining to, a person of mixed Nama and European race. *S. Afr.* L18. **7** Bastarda. L19.
2 DISRAELI That bastard, but picturesque style of architecture, called the Italian Gothic. J. CHEEVER It was not Italian . . it was a bastard language of a little Spanish and a little something that Clementina had never heard before. 4 BACON Usurie . . is the Bastard use of Money. 5 R. I. MURCHISON A bastard limestone charged with encrinites. *bastard balm, bastard pellitory, bastard saffron, bastard toadflax*, etc.
Special collocations & *comb.*: **bastard hartebeest** = TSESSEBI. **bastard mahogany** any of several Australian eucalypts, esp. *Eucalyptus botryoides*. **bastard sandalwood** = NAIO. **bastard title** a half-title. **bastard-trench** *v.t.* (*Hort.*) dig (ground) by digging over the lower soil with the topsoil temporarily removed. **bastard trout** *US* the silver sea trout, *Cynoscion nothus*. **bastard wing** *Ornith.* a group of small quill feathers borne by the first digit of a bird's wing.
†**bastardism** *n.* = BASTARDY L16–M18. †**bastardly** *a.* = BASTARD *a.* M16–L18.

bastarda /baˈstɑːdə/ *n.* & *a.* M20. [It. *bastardo*: see prec.] (Designating, of or pertaining to) a cursive Gothic script for vernacular use, originating in France and used in Germany and the Low Countries in the 14th and 15th cents.

bastardize /ˈbɑːstədʌɪz, ˈbast-/ *v.* Also **-ise.** L16. [f. BASTARD *n.* + -IZE.] **1** *v.t.* & *i.* (Cause to) deteriorate. L16. †**2** *v.t.* Beget as a bastard. *rare* (Shakes.). Only in E17. **3** *v.t.* Declare or stigmatize as illegitimate. E17.
bastardiˈzation *n.* E19.

bastardy /ˈbɑːstədi, ˈbas-/ *n.* LME. [AN, OFr. *bastardie* (med.L *bastardia*): see BASTARD *n.*, -Y[3].] **1** The condition of being a bastard; illegitimate birth. LME. **2** Begetting of bastards, fornication. *arch.* L16.
Comb.: **bastardy order** (now *arch.* or *Hist.*) = AFFILIATION *order*.

baste /beɪst/ *v.*[1]*t.* LME. [OFr. *bastir* tack, prepare, f. Frank. equiv. of OHG, MHG *besten* lace, sew, f. Gmc: rel. to BAST.] Sew loosely together; *esp.* tack together temporarily with long loose stitches.
fig.: SIR W. SCOTT You have . . basted up your first story very hastily and clumsily.

baste /beɪst/ *v.*[2]*t.* L15. [Origin unkn.] **1** Moisten (roasting meat) with gravy or melted fat to prevent drying. L15. †**2** Perfuse as with a liniment. L16–M18.

baste /beɪst/ *v.*[3]*t.* M16. [Perh. a fig. use of prec.] Beat soundly, cudgel, thrash.

bastel-house /ˈbast(ə)lhaʊs/ *n.* Also **bastle-.** M16. [f. var. of BASTILLE *n.* + HOUSE *n.*[1]] A fortified house.

baster *n.* & *a.* see BASTARD.

bastide /baˈstiːd/ *n.* E16. [OFr. f. Prov. *bastida* (med.L *bastida*): see next.] **1** *Hist.* A fortlet; a fortified village or town. E16. **2** A country house in southern France. E18.

bastile *n.*, *v.* var. of BASTILLE *n.*, *v.*

bastille /baˈstiːl/ *n.* Also **-ile.** LME. [(O)Fr., refash. of contemp. *bastide* f. Prov. *bastida* use as n. of fem. pa. pple of *bastir* build.] **1** *Hist.* A tower or bastion of a castle; a small fortress. LME. **2** In siege operations, a wooden tower on wheels, or an entrenched protective hut used by the besiegers. LME. **3a** (**B-**.) *The* prison-fortress built in Paris in the 14th cent., and destroyed in 1789. M16. **b** A prison. E18.
Comb.: **Bastille Day** 14 July, the date of the storming of the Bastille in 1789, celebrated as a national holiday in France.

bastille /baˈstiːl/ *v.t. arch.* Also **-ile.** L15. [Sense 1 f. OFr. *bastiller*, f. as prec.; sense 2 f. prec.] †**1** Fortify (a building). L15–E16. **2** Confine in a bastille; imprison. M18.

bastillion /baˈstɪljən/ *n.* M16. [OFr. *bastillon* dim. of BASTILLE *n.*] *Hist.* A small fortress or castle; a fortified tower.

bastinade /bastɪˈneɪd/ *n.* & *v.t. arch.* Also **-onade** /-əˈneɪd/. E17. [Refash. of next after Fr. *bastonnade*: see -ADE.] = next.

bastinado /bastɪˈneɪdəʊ/ *n.* & *v.* L16. [Sp. *bastonada*, f. *bastón* stick, cudgel: see BATON *n.*, -ADO.] **A** *n.* Pl. **-o(e)s.** **1** A blow with a stick or cudgel, *esp.* one on the soles of the feet. *arch.* L16. **2a** A beating with a stick, a cudgelling. *arch.* L16. **b** *spec.* (Punishment or torture involving) a caning on the soles of the feet. E18. **3** A stick, staff, truncheon, or similar instrument. L16. **B** *v.t.* **1** Beat with a stick; thrash. *arch.* E17. **2** *spec.* Beat or cane on the soles of the feet. L17.

bastion /ˈbastɪən/ *n.* M16. [Fr. f. It. *bastione*, f. *bastire* to build.] **1** A fortified outwork often in the form of an irregular pentagon, projecting from the main works so as to allow defensive fire in several directions. M16. **b** A similar natural rock formation. M19. **2** *fig.* An institution, person, principle, etc., serving as a defence. L17.
2 A. KOESTLER We have made our country a bastion of the new era. G. GREENE We are the true bastion against the communists.
bastioned *a.* furnished with or defended by a bastion E19.

bastite /ˈbastʌɪt/ *n.* M19. [f. *Baste* in the Harz Mountains in Germany: see -ITE[1].] *Min.* A greenish or brownish kind of serpentine occurring as foliated masses and having a characteristic schiller. Also called *schiller spar*.

bastle-house *n.* var. of BASTEL-HOUSE.

bastnäsite /ˈbastnɛɪsʌɪt/ *n.* Also **-naes-.** L19. [f. *Bastnäs*, a locality in Västmanland, Sweden, + -ITE[1].] *Min.* A yellow to brown hexagonal fluorocarbonate of cerium and other rare earth metals.

basto /ˈbɑːstəʊ, ˈbast-/ *n.* L17. [Sp. (*el*) *basto* (the ace of) clubs.] In ombre, quadrille, and related card-games, the ace of clubs in its fixed capacity as third highest trump.

baston /ˈbast(ə)n/ *n.* ME. [OFr.: see BATON *n.*] **1** A staff or stick used as a weapon or a symbol of office. *arch.* & *dial.* ME. †**2** *Her.* = BATON *n.* 3 L16–M17.

bastonade *n.* & *v.* var. of BASTINADE.

basuco /bəˈsuːkəʊ/ *n.* Also **-z-.** L20. [Colombian Sp., perh. rel. to Sp. *bazucar* shake violently.] Impure cocaine mixed with coca paste and other substances, often including tobacco and marijuana (a highly addictive preparation when smoked); *gen.* impure or low-grade cocaine.

Basuto *n.* & *a.* see BASOTHO.

bat /bat/ *n.*[1] Sense 9 also **batt.** LOE. [Perh. partly f. (O)Fr. *batte*, f. *batre*: see BATTER *v.*[1] Branch III of uncertain origin.] **I 1** A club, a cudgel; a stick or staff for support or defence. Now *arch.* & *dial.* LOE. **2** An implement with a rounded (usu. wooden) handle and a solid head, for striking a ball in cricket, rounders, baseball, table tennis, etc. E17. **b** An object like a table-tennis bat used to guide aircraft taxiing. Usu. in *pl.* M20. **3** A person who uses a bat in cricket etc.; a batter, a batsman. M18.
1 SPENSER A handsome bat he held, On which he leaned. SIR W. SCOTT I have given up . . my bat for a sword. 2 **at bat** *Baseball* taking one's turn at batting (see also AT-BAT). *beat the bat*: see BEAT *v.*[1] 5. **carry one's** or **the bat** *Cricket* be not out at the end of a side's completed innings (esp. after having batted throughout the innings). *dead bat*: see DEAD *a.* & *adv.* *hang one's bat out to dry*: see HANG *v.* **off one's own bat** *fig.* unaided, on one's own initiative. **right off the bat** *fig.* (*N. Amer.*) immediately. 3 E. LINKLATER He was an accomplished bat and . . fielded boldly at cover-point.
II 4 A firm blow as with a staff, club, etc. LME. **5** Rate of stroke or step; pace, speed. *dial.* & *slang.* E19. **6** A movement of the eyelids, a blink. M20.
5 J. WELCOME We turned on to the main . . road and started going a hell of a bat across the Cotswolds. 6 C. FRY We were at the boy in the bat of an eye.
III 7a A lump, a piece. Long *obs.* in *gen.* sense exc. in *bits and bats* (see BIT *n.*[2]). LME. **b** *spec.* A piece of brick with one end entire. *obs.* exc. in *brickbat* (see BRICK *n.*). E16. **c** *Pottery.* A small piece of baked ware separating pieces of biscuit ware in the kiln; a flattened-out piece of unfired clay. E19. **8** Shale interstratified between seams of coal, iron ore, etc. L17. **9** A felted mass used in hat-making. M19.
Comb.: **batboy** *Baseball* a boy or youth who looks after the bats of a team etc.; †**bat-fowling** catching birds by night using lights to dazzle them.

bat /bat/ *n.*[2] *obs.* exc. *Hist.* Also **bât** /bɑ/. LME. [OFr. *bat*, earlier *bast*, (mod. *bât*), f. Prov. *bast* f. med.L *bastum* pack-saddle.] A pack-saddle. Only in *comb.* as below.
bat-horse: carrying the baggage of military officers during a campaign. BATMAN *n.*[2] **bat-money** an allowance for carrying baggage in the field. **bat-mule**: used as a pack-animal in a military campaign. †**bat-needle** a packing-needle.

bat /bat/ *n.*[3] L16. [Alt. (perh. by assoc. w. med.L *b(l)atta, blacta*) of forms w. /-k/ (ME-) f. a Scand. wd repr. in MSw. *aftanbakka, natbakka* evening-, night-bat, MDa. *nat(h)bakke*.] **1** A member of the order Chiroptera of mainly nocturnal flying mammals which have forelimbs modified to support membranous wings extending to the tail. Also (*W. Indies*) *rat-bat*. L16. **2** A large moth or butterfly. Chiefly *W. Indies*. L16.
Phrases: **blind as a bat** completely blind. **have bats in the belfry** *colloq.* be crazy or eccentric. **like a bat out of hell** *slang* very quickly, at top speed. *serotine bat*: see SEROTINE *n.*[1] *vampire bat*: see VAMPIRE *n.* 3.
Comb.: **batfish** a marine fish of the family Ogcocephalidae, related to and resembling the angler-fishes; **batwing sleeve** a sleeve with a deep armhole and a tight cuff.

bat /bat/ *n.*[4] *slang.* M19. [Origin unkn.: cf. BATTER *n.*[4]] A spree, a binge.

bat /bat/ *n.*[5] *arch. slang.* L19. [Hind. *bāt* speech, language, word.] *The* colloquial language of a foreign country.
sling the bat speak the local language abroad.

†**bat** *n.*[6] var. of BATH *n.*[2]

†**bat** *n.*[7] see BATZ.

bat /bat/ *v.*[1] Infl. **-tt-**. LME. [f. BAT *n.*[1] or f. as BATTER *v.*[1]] **1** *v.t.* Strike with or as with a bat; cudgel; beat. LME. **2** *v.i.* Use a bat; have an innings at cricket, baseball, etc. M18. **3** *v.i.* Move, esp. in a casual or aimless fashion (*about*, *along*, *around*, etc.). *dial.* & *slang.* L19.

1 W. BARNES Well here . . 'S a ball for you if you can bat it. B. HINES He batted him twice about the ears, forehand left ear, backhand right. 2 H. DE SÉLINCOURT Padded and gloved, and rather nervously waiting his turn to bat. *bat on a sticky wicket*: see STICKY *a.*[2] 2.

bat /bat/ *v.*[2] Infl. **-tt-**. E17. [Var. of BATE *v.*[1], *v.*[2]] **1** *v.i.* = BATE *v.*[1] 2. E17. **2** *v.t.* Blink. E19.

2 not bat an eye(lid) (*a*) not sleep a wink; (*b*) betray no emotion.

Batak /ˈbatək/ *n.*[1] & *a.* E19. [Batak (Indonesian): cf. BATTA *n.*[3] & *a.*] **A** *n.* Pl. same, **-s**. A member of a people of the northern part of Sumatra; the Indonesian language of this people. E19. **B** *attrib.* or as *adj.* Of or pertaining to the Batak or their language. L19.

Batak /bəˈtɑːk/ *n.*[2] & *a.* Pl. of n. same, **-s**. E20. [Batak.] A member of, of or pertaining to, a people on the island of Palawan, Philippines; (of) the Austronesian language of this people.

batardeau /batardo/ *n.* Pl. ***-eaux*** /-o/. M18. [Fr., earlier *bastardeau* dim. of OFr. *bastard* of unkn. origin.] A coffer-dam. Also, a wall built across the moat or ditch surrounding a fortification.

batata /bəˈtɑːtə/ *n.* M16. [Sp. f. Taino.] = *sweet potato* s.v. POTATO *n.* 1.

Batavian /bəˈteɪvɪən/ *n.* & *a.* Now *arch.* or *Hist.* M16. [f. L *Batavia*, f. *Batavi* the people of Betawe (see below), + -AN.] **A** *n.* A member of an ancient people who inhabited the island of Betawe between the Rhine and the Waal (now part of the Netherlands). M16. **b** A Dutch person. M18.

B *adj.* Of or pertaining to the ancient people of Betawe or the people of the Netherlands. L18.

Batavian endive: see ENDIVE 2.

batch /batʃ/ *n.*[1] & *v.*[1] L15. [f. base of BAKE *v.* (cf. *watch*, *wake*). Repr. an OE wd: cf. OE *ġebæċ* baking, thing baked.] **A** *n.* †**1** The process of baking. L15–M16. **2** A baking; the quantity of bread produced at one baking. Also = *batch loaf* below. L15. **3** The quantity of flour or dough used for one baking. Long *arch.* M16. †**4** The sort or lot to which a thing belongs by origin. L16–E18. **5** A quantity produced at one operation. E18. **6** A number of things or persons coming at once and treated as a set; (less commonly) a quantity of a thing coming at one time, an instalment. L18.

3 COVERDALE A lytle leauen sowreth the whole batche, wherwith it is myngled. 4 MILTON This worthy Motto, No Bishop, no King is of the same batch, and infanted out of the same feares. 5 M. E. BRADDON That last batch of soup was excellent. 6 T. HOOD I am not going to favour you with a batch of politics. SAKI Several packages, evidently an early batch of Christmas presents. G. GORER Most of the questions were arranged in batches of 4 or 5 dealing with the same subject. A. SCHLEE The next batch of tourists was arriving at the head of the path.

Comb.: **batch loaf** a loaf baked close to others in a batch (and so not completely crusted at the sides). **batch process**: treating materials in batches, not continuously; **batch processing** (*a*) the processing of raw materials in batches in an industrial process; (*b*) *Computing* the processing of previously collected batches of data, jobs, etc., esp. offline without user intervention; **batch production** = *batch process* above.

B *v.t.* Treat or arrange in batches. L19.

batch *n.*[2] & *v.*[2] var. of BACH *n.*[1] & *v.*

†**batchelor** *n.* var. of BACHELOR.

batchy /ˈbatʃi/ *a.* *slang.* L19. [Origin uncertain: cf. BATTY.] Crazy, dotty; = BATTY 2.

†**bate** *n.*[1] Long *dial.* exc. in MAKEBATE. LME–L19. [Aphet. f. DEBATE *n.*, or f. BATE *v.*[1]] Contention, strife; an argument.

bate /beɪt/ *n.*[2] Long *dial.* LME. [f. BATE *v.*[2]] Deduction; diminution; discount.

bate /beɪt/ *n.*[3] Long *dial.* M17. [Origin unkn.] The grain of wood or stone.

bate /beɪt/ *n.*[4] (esp. *School*) *slang.* Also **bait**. M19. [f. BAIT *v.*[1]] A rage, a temper.

bate /beɪt/ *v.*[1] Also **bait**. ME. [OFr. *batre*: see BATTER *v.*[1]] †**1** *v.i.* & (*rare*) *refl.* Fight, contend, with blows or arguments. (Foll. by *on*.) *dial.* ME–M19. †**2** *v.t.* Beat, flutter, (wings etc.). *rare.* ME–M17. **3** *v.i.* *Falconry.* Beat the wings impatiently and flutter away from the fist or perch. LME. †**b** *fig.* Struggle; be restless or impatient. L16–L17.

3b DRYDEN You are eager, and baiting to be gone.

bate /beɪt/ *v.*[2] ME. [Aphet. f. ABATE *v.*[1]] †**1** = ABATE *v.*[1] 1. Only in ME. **2** *v.t.* & (*rare*) *i.* = ABATE *v.*[1] 4. Now chiefly in *bate one's breath*, restrain one's breathing through anxiety, suspense, etc. ME. †**3** *v.t.* Lower, let down; humble, depress. Cf. ABATE *v.*[1] 2. LME–M19. †**b** = ABATE *v.*[1] 2b. LME–E19. **4** *v.t.* = ABATE *v.*[1] 5. *arch.* LME. **b** = ABATE *v.*[1] 5b. *obs.* exc. as BATING *prep.* E17. †**5** *v.t.* & *i.* = ABATE *v.*[1] 3. L15–L17. **6** *v.t.* Blunt (*lit.* & *fig.*). Cf. ABATE *v.*[1] 7. Long *rare.* M16.

2 R. L. STEVENSON The pirates no longer ran separate and shouting . . , but kept side by side and spoke with bated breath. 4 ADDISON They offered . . to bate him the article of bread and butter in the tea-table account. W. IRVING I do not bate one nail's breadth of the honest truth. E. GASKELL Take the bated wage, and be thankful.

bateless *a.* (*rare*) †(*a*) that cannot be blunted; (*b*) unabating: L16.

bateau /batəʊ, *foreign* bato/ *n.* Pl. **-eaux** /-əʊz, *foreign* -o/. Also †**battoe**. E18. [Fr. = boat.] A light riverboat, esp. of a flat-bottomed kind used in Canada.

bateau-mouche /batomuʃ/, pl. ***bateaux-mouches*** (pronounced same), a boat which takes sight-seers on the Seine in Paris.

bateleur /ˈbat(ə)lɜː/ *n.* M19. [Fr., lit. 'juggler, mountebank'.] A short-tailed African eagle, *Terathopius ecaudatus*. Also *bateleur eagle*.

batement /ˈbeɪtm(ə)nt/ *n.* LME. [Aphet. f. ABATEMENT *n.*[1]] **1** *batement light*, in Gothic architecture, an upper window or opening with a sloping or curved sill (i.e. cut off at the low end to accommodate the curve of an arch etc.). LME. †**2** Reduction, diminution. L15–L17.

Batesian /ˈbeɪtsɪən/ *a.* Also **b-**. L19. [f. H. W. *Bates* (1825–92), Eng. naturalist + -IAN.] *Zool.* Designating or characterized by a form of mimicry in which an edible species is protected by its resemblance to one avoided by predators.

batey /ˈbeɪti/ *a.* *slang.* Also **baity**. E20. [f. BATE *n.*[4] + -Y[1].] In a rage; bad-tempered.

bath /bɑːθ/ *n.*[1] Pl. **baths** /bɑːðz/. In branch II **B-**. [OE *bæþ* = OFris. *beth*, OS *bað*, (O)HG *bad*, ON *bað*, f. Gmc.] **I 1** An immersion in liquid for cleansing or therapy. Also (w. specifying wd), an immersion in or copious application of any medium to produce analogous effects. OE. **2** A quantity of water or other liquid for bathing or taking a bath in. OE. †**3** A spring of water suitable for bathing in, *esp.* one that is hot or contains minerals. OE–E18. **4** A place for bathing for cleansing or therapeutic purposes; a town with mineral springs or other facilities for therapeutic bathing etc., a spa; (chiefly *N. Amer.* & in advertisements) a bathroom; *sing.* & (usu.) in *pl.*, a building for bathing or swimming in. ME. **5** A medicinal or disinfectant wash or lotion; a vessel for containing or applying such a wash etc. LME. **6** The state of being suffused with a liquid, esp. perspiration. Now *rare.* L16. **7a** (A vessel containing) a medium such as water, oil, sand, ice, or steam, in which chemical or other apparatus can be placed and subjected to a steady high or low temperature. L16. **b** (A vessel containing) a chemical in which objects can be immersed, as film for developing, etc. L18. **8** A receptacle for liquid, usu. water, for bathing or taking a bath in. E17.

1 *have a bath*, *take a bath*. *cold bath*, *hot bath*, etc. *dust-bath*, *mud-bath*, *shower-bath*, *sun-bath*, *Turkish bath*, *vaporous bath*, etc. *blood-bath*: see BLOOD *n.* **Order of the Bath** an order of knighthood, named from the bath which preceded the knight's installation. *warm bath*: see WARM *a.* 2 STEELE To rise the next Morning and plunge into the Cold Bath. C. KINGSLEY Countess, your bath is ready. 4 *municipal baths*, *swimming baths*, etc. *Russian bath*, *steam bath*, *Turkish bath*, etc. 5 *eye-bath*. 7b *nitrate bath*, *silver bath*, etc. 8 *bird-bath*, *hip-bath*, etc.

II 9 (**B-**.) A town in Avon, SW England, named from its hot springs. Also †*the Bath*. OE.

Comb.: **Bath brick** a preparation for cleaning polished metal; **Bath bun** a type of round spiced bun with currants and icing; **Bath chair** a wheeled chair for an invalid; **Bath chap** a type of pickled pig's chap; **bath cube**: of a preparation which crumbles and dissolves to soften or perfume bathwater; **bath essence** a concentrated liquid to soften or perfume bathwater; **bath-mat**: on which one stands after getting out of a bath; **Bath metal** a silvery-white alloy of zinc and copper, formerly used for tableware; **Bath Oliver** an unsweetened biscuit invented by Dr William Oliver (1695–1764) of Bath; **bathrobe** a dressing-gown, esp. of towelling; **bathroom** a room containing a bath and often other toilet facilities; *euphem.* a water-closet, a lavatory; **bath salts**: that dissolve to soften or perfume bathwater; **Bath stone** oolite from the formation near Bath, used as building stone; **bath towel** a large towel; **bath-tub** = sense 8 above; **bathwater** water in a bath (*throw out the baby with the bathwater*: see BABY *n.* 1); **Bath white** a white butterfly, *Pontia daplidice*, with greenish mottling on the underwings, which is a rare migrant to Britain.

bath /baθ/ *n.*[2] Also †**bat(us)**. LME. [Heb. *bat*; late L (Vulgate) *batus*.] *Hist.* An ancient Hebrew liquid measure equivalent to about 40 litres, or 9 gallons.

bath /bɑːθ/ *v.t.* & *i.* L15. [f. BATH *n.*[1]] Wash (a child, invalid, animal, etc., or oneself) in a bath; take a bath.

¶In early instances perh. only a variant spelling of *bathe*. Infl. forms (exc. *baths*) are usu. avoided in writing because of coincidence w. those of *bathe*.

bathe /beɪð/ *n.* M19. [f. BATHE *v.* 4.] An immersion in liquid, esp. in the sea, a river, a swimming pool, etc., for recreation.

bathe /beɪð/ *v.* [OE *baþian* = Du. *baden*, OHG *badōn* (G *baden*), ON *baða*, f. Gmc, f. base of BATH *n.*[1]] **I** *v.t.* **1** Immerse in liquid for cleansing or therapy. Also, immerse in any other medium for analogous effects. OE. **2** Wash; wet or moisten all over; apply liquid to. OE. **3** Envelop, suffuse, encompass. E16.

1 F. W. ROBERTSON The later martyr bathes his fingers in the flames. 2 J. HERVEY The laborer, bathed in sweat, drops the scythe. GIBBON The river bathed the foot of the walls. B. T. WASHINGTON Rarely was there any place provided . . where one could bathe even the face and hands. K. GRAHAME He . . bathed the Mole's shin with warm water. 3 COVERDALE *Isa.* 63:6 And thus haue I troden downe the people in my wrath, and bathed them in my displeasure. J. AGATE Changes of lighting bathe the audience in a glow of tender dawn warming to wanton sunset. P. G. WODEHOUSE If when I have finished you are not bathed in shame and remorse, you must be dead to all human feeling. S. J. PERELMAN The room was bathed in dense shadow. D. ATTENBOROUGH This mixture allowed ultraviolet rays from the sun to bathe the earth's surface with an intensity that would be lethal to modern animal life.

II *v.i.* **4** Immerse oneself in water, esp. in the sea, a river, a swimming pool, etc., for recreation. (Cf. BATH *v.*) OE. **5** *transf.* & *fig.* Bask; wallow; immerse oneself in any medium. LME.

4 **bathing beauty, belle** an attractive woman in a swimsuit. 5 C. MARLOWE Now lie the Christians bathing in their bloods. J. TRAPP Shall Christians be bathing in their beds on their Lord's day? *sun-bathe*: see SUN *n.*[1]

bather *n.* †(*a*) an attendant at a bath; (*b*) a person who bathes; (*c*) in *pl.* (esp. *Austral.*), swim-trunks, a swimming costume: M17.

bathetic /bəˈθɛtɪk/ *a.* L18. [f. BATHOS after *pathos*, *pathetic*.] Marked by bathos.

bathing /ˈbeɪðɪŋ/ *n.* LME. [f. BATHE *v.* + -ING[1].] **1** The action of BATHE *v.*; immersion in or exposure to water or some other medium; application of liquid, wetting, moistening. LME. **2** The conditions for bathers at a particular resort etc. M19.

1 *sea-bathing* etc. MIXED *bathing*.

Attrib. & *comb.*: Designating garments worn when bathing, as *bathing-costume*, *-suit*, *-trunks*, etc. Special combs., as **bathing-machine** *Hist.* a wheeled dressing-box drawn into the sea for bathing from.

bathochromic /baθəˈkrəʊmɪk/ *a.* L19. [f. Gk BATHOS + *khrōma* colour + -IC.] Causing or characterized by a shift of the absorption spectrum towards longer wavelengths.

batholith /ˈbaθəlɪθ/ *n.* E20. [f. Gk BATHOS + -LITH.] *Geol.* A large dome-shaped mass of igneous intrusive rock extending to unknown depth.
bathoˈlithic *a.* L19.

bathometer /bəˈθɒmɪtə/ *n.* L19. [f. Gk BATHOS + -OMETER.] An instrument for ascertaining the depth of water.
bathoˈmetric *a.* = BATHYMETRIC L20. **bathometry** *n.* = BATHYMETRY M20.

Bathonian /bəˈθəʊnɪən/ *a.* & *n.* M18. [f. *Bathonia* Latinized form of *Bath* (see BATH *n.*[1] II) + -AN.] 1 (A native or inhabitant) of the town of Bath in Avon. M18. 2 *Geol.* (Denoting or pertaining to) a subdivision of the Jurassic typified by formations at Bath. M19.

bathorhodopsin /baθərəˈdɒpsɪn/ *n.* L20. [f. as next + RHODOPSIN.] *Biochem.* = PRELUMIRHODOPSIN.

bathos /ˈbeɪθɒs/ *n.* M17. [Gk = depth. In purely Eng. sense 2 introduced by Pope.] 1 Depth, lowest phase, bottom. *rare.* M17. 2 *Rhet.* Ludicrous descent from the elevated to the commonplace; anticlimax. E18. 3 A comedown; an anticlimax; a performance absurdly unequal to the occasion. E19.
1 S. JOHNSON Declining . . to the very bathos of insipidity. 3 F. MARRYAT It was rather a bathos . . to sink from a gentleman's son to an under usher. L. A. G. STRONG The rest of their married life will be one hideous bathos after the glory of its start.

bathotic /bəˈθɒtɪk/ *a.* M19. [Irreg. f. prec. after *chaos, chaotic*.] = BATHETIC.

Bathurst bur /ˈbaθəːst bəː/ *n. phr. Austral.* M19. [f. *Bathurst*, a town in New South Wales + BUR *n.*[1]] (A bur from) the spiny cocklebur, *Xanthium spinosum*, naturalized in Australia.

bathy- /ˈbaθi/ *comb. form* of Gk *bathus* deep.
bathypeˈlagic *a.* pertaining to or inhabiting the depths of the sea, *spec.* below the level to which light penetrates L19. **bathysphere** *n.* a large strong submersible sphere for deep-sea observation M20. **bathyˈthermograph** *n.* an automatic instrument for recording water temperature at various depths M20.

bathyal /ˈbaθɪəl/ *a.* E20. [f. BATHY- + -AL[1].] Of or pertaining to the zone of the sea between the continental shelf and the abyssal zone.

bathybius /bəˈθɪbɪəs/ *n.* M19. [mod.L, f. as BATHY- + Gk *bios* living.] (A name given by Thomas Huxley to) a gelatinous inorganic substance obtained from the bed of the Atlantic Ocean, and at first supposed to be a formless mass of living protoplasm.

bathymetry /bəˈθɪmɪtri/ *n.* M19. [f. BATHY- + -METRY.] The measurement of depths in oceans, seas, or lakes.
bathyˈmetric(al) *adjs.* pertaining to or connected with bathymetry M19. **bathyˈmetrically** *adv.* L19.

bathyscaphe /ˈbaθɪskaf/ *n.* Also **-scaph**. M20. [Fr., f. as BATHY- + Gk *skaphos* ship.] A navigable manned submersible vessel for deep-sea diving and observation.

batik /ˈbatɪk, bəˈtiːk/ *n.* & *a.* L19 [Jav., lit. 'painted'.] A *n.* A method (orig. used in Java) of making coloured designs on textiles by waxing the parts not to be dyed; (a garment made of) a fabric dyed by this method. L19. B *attrib.* or as *adj.* Executed or ornamented by this method. E20.

bating /ˈbeɪtɪŋ/ *prep. arch.* M17. [Absol. use of pres. pple of BATE *v.*[2] 4b.] Excepting, leaving out of account.

batiste /bəˈtiːst/ *n.* & *a.* E19. [Fr. (earlier *batiche*), perh. f. base of *battre*: see BATTER *v.*[1]] (Of) a fine light cotton or linen fabric like cambric.

†batler *n. rare* (Shakes. First Folio). Only in E17. [Perh. taken as f. BATTLE *v.*[3] + -ER[1].] = next.
¶Substituted in the second (and subsequent) folios of Shakes. for the first folio's BATLER (*A.Y.L.* II) and preferred in many mod. editions.

†batlet *n. dial.* M17–L19. [f. BAT *n.*[1] + -LET.] A wooden stick for beating and stirring clothes during washing, etc.

batman /ˈbatmən/ *n.*[1] L16. [Turk. *batmān*, *batman* (whence also Russ. *batman*).] *Hist.* A weight in Turkey, Persia, etc., varying according to the locality.

batman /ˈbatmən/ *n.*[2] Pl. **-men**. M18. [f. BAT *n.*[2] + MAN *n.*] *Mil.* Formerly, a man in charge of a bat-horse and its load. Now, an officer's personal servant, an orderly.
batwoman *n.* M20.

bat mitzvah /bɑːt ˈmɪtsvə/ *n. phr.* Also **B-**. M20. [Heb. *baṯ miṣwāh* daughter of commandment, after BAR MITZVAH.] (A religious initiation ceremony for) a Jewish girl aged twelve years and one day, regarded as the age of religious maturity.

batologist /bəˈtɒlədʒɪst/ *n.* L19. [f. Gk *batos* bramble + -OLOGIST.] A botanist who specializes in the genus *Rubus*, and esp. in the microspecies of bramble (*R. fruticosus* aggregate).

baton /ˈbat(ə)n; *in senses 4 and 6 also foreign* batɔ̃ (*pl. same*)/ *n.* E16. [Fr. *bâton* (earlier *baston*) = Prov., Sp. *baston*, It. *bastone*, f. Proto-Romance f. late L *bastum* stick.] 1 A staff or stick used as a weapon; a cudgel, a club. *obs.* in *gen.* sense. E16. b In *pl.* One of the four suits (represented by cudgels or batons) in packs of playing-cards in Italy, Spain, and Spanish-speaking countries, and in some tarot packs. Cf. CLUB *n.* 4. M19. c *spec.* A police constable's truncheon, *esp.* a relatively long one. L19. 2 A staff etc. carried as a symbol of office, *esp.* that of a field marshal. L16. 3 *Her.* A narrow truncated bend. M18. 4 *Mus.* A conductor's wand for beating time etc.; a drum major's stick. L18. 5 A staff or stick used in walking. Now *rare.* E19. 6 A long loaf or stick of bread. M19. 7 A short tube or stick carried in a relay race and passed from one participant to the next. E20.
3 **baton sinister** a supposed sign of bastardy. 4 **under the baton of** conducted by.
Comb.: **baton charge** a charge by police constables with drawn truncheons; **baton-charge** *v.i.* & *t.* make a baton charge (at); **baton round** a rubber or plastic bullet.

baton /ˈbat(ə)n/ *v.t.* E17. [f. the n.] Strike with a baton.

batoon /bəˈtuːn/ *n.* & *v. arch.* M16. [f. as BATON *n.*: see -OON.] A *n.* 1 = BATON *n.* 1. M16. 2 = BATON *n.* 2. M16. †3 = BATON *n.* 3. M16–E18. B *v.t.* = BATON *v.* L16.

batrachian /bəˈtreɪkɪən/ *a.* & *n.* M19. [f. mod.L *Batrachia* former name of the order Anura, f. Gk *batrakheia* neut. pl. (sc. *zōa* animals) of adj. f. *batrakhos* frog: see -AN.] (Pertaining to, of the nature or characteristic of) a frog or toad; = ANURAN.

batracho- /ˈbatrəkəʊ/ *comb. form* of Gk *batrakhos* frog: see -O-.
batrachoˈtoxin *n.* an extremely toxic alkaloid secreted by the Colombian frog *Phyllobates aurotaenia* M20.

bats /bats/ *a.* (usu. *pred.*). *colloq.* E20. [f. *have bats in the belfry* s.v. BAT *n.*[3]] Crazy, dotty; = BATTY *a.* 2.

batsman /ˈbatsmən/ *n.* Pl. **-men**. M18. [f. BAT *n.*[1] + -'S[1] + MAN *n.*] 1 A user of a cricket, baseball, etc., bat. M18. 2 A signaller using bats to guide an aircraft. M20.
1 **batsman's wicket** a cricket pitch favouring batsmen.
batsmanship *n.* the art of batting at cricket etc.; batting performance: E20.

Batswana /bəˈtswɑːnə/ *n.* & *a.* Also (earlier, now *arch.* or *Hist.*) **Bechuana**, **-wana**, /bɛtʃʊˈɑːnə, bɛˈtʃwɑːnə/. E19. [Setswana, f. *ba-* pl. pref. + TSWANA.] A *n.* 1 (*erron.*) *sing.* Pl. **-s**. A member of the Tswana people, (*sing.*) a Motswana. E19. 2 *pl.* (Members of) the Tswana people. L19. B *attrib.* or as *adj.* = TSWANA *a.* E19.

batt *n.* see BAT *n.*[1]

batta /ˈbatə/ *n.*[1] *obs.* exc. *Hist.* E17. [Hind. *baṭṭā*.] In the Indian subcontinent: agio; discount on coins not current or of short weight.

batta /ˈbatə/ *n.*[2] *Anglo-Ind. obs.* exc. *Hist.* L17. [Indo-Port. *bata* = Kannada *bhatta* rice f. Skt *bhakta* food.] Allowance for subsistence; extra pay; *spec.* that given to officers serving in India.

Batta /ˈbatə/ *n.*[3] & *a.* L18. [Batak (Indonesian).] = BATAK *n.*[1] & *a.*

battailous /ˈbat(ə)ləs/ *a. arch.* LME. [OFr. *bataillos*, *-eus*, f. as BATTLE *n.*: see -OUS.] Fond of fighting; ready for battle.

battalia /bəˈtɑːlɪə/ *n. arch.* L16. [It. *battaglia* BATTLE *n.*] †1 = BATTALION I. L16–E19. 2 Order of battle; battle array. Esp. in *in(to) battalia*. E17.

battalia pie /bəˈtɑːlɪə pʌɪ/ *n. phr. arch.* Orig. **†beatille** etc. M17. [Fr. *béatilles*, med.L *beatillae* small blessed articles (as samplers worked by nuns, etc.), dim. of *beatus* blessed: pop. assim. to prec.] A pie of titbits such as sweetbreads, cocks' combs, etc.

battalion /bəˈtalɪən/ *n.* & *v.* L16. [Fr. *bataillon* f. It. *battaglione* augm. of *battaglia* BATTLE *n.*] A *n.* I *Mil.* 1 *gen.* A large body of men in battle array; each of the large divisions of an army. L16. 2 *spec.* A unit of infantry composed of several companies and forming part of a brigade or regiment. E18. II *transf.* & *fig.* 3 A large well-ordered group; an array; a large group of people with similar tasks etc. E17. B *v.t.* Form into a battalion or battalions. *rare.* E19.

battel /ˈbat(ə)l/ *v.†t.* & *i. arch.* Also **battle**. L16. [Cf. BATTLE *v.*[2]] At Oxford University: charge (one's provisions etc.) to a college account.
batteler, battler *n.* (*obs.* exc. *Hist.*, at Oxford University) a person who boards and lodges in college; *spec.* a member of an order of students below commoners: E17.

battels /ˈbat(ə)lz/ *n.pl.* L16. [Perh. f. BATTLE *v.*[2]] At Oxford University (formerly also elsewhere): a college account for board and provisions supplied, or for all college expenses.

battement /batmɑ̃ (*pl. same*); ˈbatmɒ̃/ *n.* M19. [Fr. = beating.] *Dancing.* Any of a number of beating leg movements.
grand battement: see GRAND *a.*[2] *petit battement*: see PETIT *a.*[2]

batten /ˈbat(ə)n/ *n.*[1] L15. [OFr. *batant* use as n. of pres. pple of *batre*: see BATTER *v.*[1], -ANT[1].] 1 A long narrow piece of squared timber. L15. 2 A strip of wood used for clamping the boards of a door etc. M17. 3 *Naut.* A strip of wood or metal for securing tarpaulin over a hatchway or for preventing chafing of masts and spars. M18. 4 A strip of wood etc. carrying electric (or formerly gas) lamps. M19.

batten /ˈbat(ə)n/ *n.*[2] M19. [Fr. *battant*.] A movable bar in a loom which closes the weft.

batten /ˈbat(ə)n/ *v.*[1] L15. [f. BATTEN *n.*[1]] 1 *v.t.* Strengthen or secure with battens. L15. 2 *v.t.* & *i. Naut.* Fasten *down* (the hatches etc.) against bad weather. M17.
1 K. DOUGLAS We dried our clothes on the exhaust . . and battened ourselves into the turret. F. WELDON Boarded up by means of a row of assorted doors battened together with railway sleepers. I. MCEWAN A kiosk, shuttered and battened for the night.
battening *n.* the application or addition of battens; strengthening or securing with battens; a structure formed with battens: L18.

batten /ˈbat(ə)n/ *v.*[2] L16. [ON *batna* improve, get better (for base cf. OE *ġebatian* get better): see -EN[5]. Cf. BATTLE *v.*[4]] 1 *v.i.* Improve in condition; *esp.* (of an animal) grow fat. L16. 2 *v.i.* Feed gluttonously *on* or *upon*. E17. 3 *v.i. fig.* Thrive, prosper, esp. at the expense of another. (Foll. by *on*.) E17. †4 *v.t.* Feed to advantage, fatten up. M17–L18.
1 JONSON It makes her fat you see. Shee battens with it. 2 E. B. BROWNING The strong carnivorous eagle shall . . batten deep Upon thy dusky liver. 3 D. LESSING There are some unscrupulous firms . . which batten on the ignorance of Africans about legal matters. 4 MILTON Battening our flocks with the fresh dews of night.

Battenberg /ˈbat(ə)nbəːg/ *n.* Also **-burg**. E20. [A town in Germany.] In full *Battenberg cake*. A marzipan-covered oblong sponge cake whose slices show four squares in two colours.

batter /ˈbatə/ *n.*[1] LME. [AN *bat(t)ure* = OFr. *bateüre* (mod. *batture*) action of beating, f. *batre*:

see BATTER v.[1], -ER[2].] I 1 A runny mixture of flour and eggs or the like beaten up with milk or water, for cooking. LME. †2 A cement or paste of flour and water. Chiefly *Sc.* LME–M19. 3 A thick paste of any kind. E17. II 4 *Printing.* A damaged area of metal type or blocks. E19.

batter /ˈbatə/ *n.*[2] M18. [f. BATTER *v.*[2]] A receding slope from the ground upwards.

batter /ˈbatə/ *n.*[3] L18. [f. BAT *v.*[1] + -ER[1].] A player using a bat.

batter /ˈbatə/ *n.*[4] *slang.* M19. [Origin unkn.: cf. BAT *n.*[4]] A spree, a debauch.

on the batter (*a*) on a spree; (*b*) engaged in prostitution.

batter /ˈbatə/ *v.*[1] ME. [OFr. *batre* (mod. *battre*) to strike, beat, fight, f. Proto-Romance devel. of L *bat(t)uere* beat: ending after vbs in -ER[5]. Cf. BATTLE *n.*] 1 *v.t.* & *i.* Strike repeatedly so as to bruise, shatter, or break; beat continuously or violently. ME. 2 *v.t.* Operate against (walls, fortifications, etc.) with artillery or (formerly) with a battering ram. L16. 3 *v.t.* & *i. fig.* Subject (a person, opinion, etc.) to heavy or persistent attack; handle severely. L16. 4 *v.t.* Beat out of shape; indent; damage by blows or other rough usage. L16.

1 SHAKES. *Temp.* With a log Batter his skull. J. REED A number of huge packing cases stood about, and upon these the Red Guards and soldiers fell furiously, battering them open with the butts of their rifles. R. GRAVES The door was battered down and in came the Palace guard. G. MAXWELL The hail roars and batters on the windows. D. LESSING I unroll the veal that I remembered to batter out flat this morning. **battered baby** a baby with signs of repeated violence by adults. **battered wife** a woman subjected to repeated violence by her husband. 2 W. S. CHURCHILL For six hours these two ironclads battered each other with hardly any injury or loss on either side. F. WARNER City now utterly destroyed, her walls, Her sanctuary battered down. 4 DICKENS The sexton's spade gets worn and battered. J. RHYS Some of the flowers were battered.

batterer *n.* E17.

batter /ˈbatə/ *v.*[2]*i.* M16. [Origin unkn.] Of a wall etc.: incline from the perpendicular; have a receding slope from the ground upwards.

†**batter** *v.*[3]*t.* L16. [f. BATTER *n.*[1]] 1 Mix into a paste or batter. L16–E17. 2 Paste, fix as with paste; cover with things stuck on. *Sc.* E17–L19.

batterie /batri/ *n.* Pl. pronounced same. E18. [Fr.: see BATTERY *n.*] 1 *Dancing.* A movement in which the feet or calves are beaten together during a leap. E18. 2 *batterie de cuisine* /də kɥizin/ [Fr. = for cookery], apparatus or utensils for serving or preparing a meal. L18. 3 = BATTERY 16. M20.

battering /ˈbatərɪŋ/ *n.* ME. [f. BATTER *v.*[1] + -ING[1].] 1 The action of BATTER *v.*[1]; a prolonged or violent assault. ME. 2 The result of BATTER *v.*[1]; a bruise, indentation, or other mark of damage from continuous or violent beating etc. L16.

Comb.: **battering-engine** *Mil. Hist.* = *battering ram* (a); **battering ram** (*a*) *Mil. Hist.* a swinging beam used for breaching walls, sometimes with a ram's-head end; (*b*) a similar object used by firemen etc. to break down doors; **battering-train** *Mil. Hist.* a number of cannon intended for siege purposes.

Battersea enamel /ˈbatəsɪ ɪˈnam(ə)l/ *n. phr.* M19. [f. *Battersea* a district of London + ENAMEL *n.*] Decorative enamel work produced at York House, Battersea, London, in the 18th cent.

battery /ˈbatəri/ *n.* ME. [OFr. *baterie* (mod. *batterie*), f. *batre*: see BATTER *v.*[1], -ERY.] I 1 (Articles of) metal, esp. (of) brass or copper, wrought by hammering. *arch.* ME.

II *Mil.* uses. 2 A number of pieces of artillery combining in action; an artillery unit of guns and men and vehicles. LME. †3 A succession of heavy blows inflicted on the walls of a city or fortress by means of artillery; a bombardment. M16–M19. 4 An emplacement for artillery on land or on a ship. L16.

2 N. MONSARRAT The Turks put batteries of their largest cannon . . on Tigré Point. A. EDEN Marjorie advocated the Royal Horse Artillery . . as that battery was already on active service. *fig.*: SMOLLETT The fellow who accused him has had his own battery turned upon himself. 3 MILTON By Batterie, Scale, and Mine, Assaulting. 4 WELLINGTON The batteries and works erecting at Cadiz. F. MARRYAT She continued her destructive fire . . from the main-deck battery.

III Physical beating of a person. 5 The action of assailing with blows; *Law* the infliction of any menacing touch to the clothes or person. M16. †6 A mark of beating; a bruise. L16–M17.

5 *assault and battery*: see ASSAULT *n.*3. 6 SHAKES. *Ven. & Ad.* For where a heart is hard they make no batt'ry.

IV Uses rel. to or devel. f. branch II. †7 A number of Leyden jars connected together so as to act simultaneously. M18–M19. 8 A device, consisting of one or more cells, in which chemical energy is converted into electricity. E19. 9 = *batterie de cuisine* s.v. BATTERIE 2. E19. 10 *Mining.* A set of stamps that work in one mortar of a stamp-mill. M19. 11 A submerged box or boat used in wildfowl shooting. *US.* M19. 12 *Baseball.* The pitcher and catcher (orig. the pitcher alone). M19. 13 *gen.* A set of connected similar units of equipment; an extensive series, sequence, or range, (*of*). L19. 14 *Psychol.* A series of tests. E20. 15 A series of cages etc. in which hens are confined for intensive laying or in which poultry or cattle are reared and fattened. M20.

8 E. J. HOWARD The battery was low in the torch and it can't have been very strong to see. J. BARNES We couldn't start the car: the heater had run the battery flat. *attrib.*: M. MCLUHAN The Bedouin with his battery radio. *solar battery*: see SOLAR *a.*[1] **recharge one's batteries** *fig.* have a period of rest and recuperation. *voltaic battery*: see VOLTAIC *a.*[1] 13 *Times* Adults were interviewed and asked a battery of questions. A. TOFFLER Lectures must inevitably give way to a whole battery of teaching techniques. F. HOYLE It would be necessary to use a battery of the largest and fastest computers. 15 *battery hen, system,* etc.

V 16 *Mus.* The percussion section of an orchestra or band. E20.

batting /ˈbatɪŋ/ *n.* E17. [f. BAT *v.*[1] + -ING[1].] 1 The action of BAT *v.*[1] E17. 2 Cotton fibre prepared in sheets for quilts etc. E19.

battle /ˈbat(ə)l/ *n.* ME. [(O)Fr. *bataille* battle (also, fortifying tower) f. Proto-Romance devel. of late L *battualia* military or gladiatorial exercises, f. *bat(t)uere* to beat: cf. BATTER *v.*[1]] I A fight; fighting. 1 A fight between (esp. large organized) opposing forces. ME. 2 A fight between two people; a single combat, a duel. ME. b A fight between two animals, esp. as providing sport. E17. 3 Fighting; conflict between enemies; war. ME. 4 *fig.* A contest; conflict. ME. †5 A war. LME–M16. 6 The victory in a fight or other contest. LME.

2 JOYCE It was a historic and a hefty battle when Myler and Percy were scheduled to don the gloves. 4 COVERDALE *Ps.* 55:21 Yet have they batell in their mynde. E. O'NEILL A perpetual battle of wits with his elder son. K. MILLETT That imposition of male authority euphemistically referred to as 'the battle of the sexes'. 6 AV *Eccles.* 9:11 The race is not to the swift nor the battle to the strong.

II (The disposition of) a body of troops. 7 = BATTALION 1. Long *arch.* ME. †8 The main body of an army or navy force. M16–M19. †9 = BATTALIA 1. Only in L16.

7 SIR W. SCOTT In battles four beneath their eye, The forces of King Robert lie.

Phrases: *battle of the giants*: see GIANT *n.* **battle royal** a battle in which several combatants or all available engage; a free fight; a general argument. **do battle** fight. **give battle** attack, engage in combat. **half the battle** a large contributory factor in success; the main effort. **join battle** enter into a combat. **line of battle** (the disposition of) troops or warships arranged for battle; *line-of-battle ship*, a ship of sufficient size to take part in a main attack, a battleship. *losing battle*: see LOSING *ppl a.* **order of battle** the disposition of sections of an army or navy force; now *spec.* (the discovery of, a tabular record of) the organization, movements, weaponry, etc., of an enemy force. *pitched battle*: see PITCHED *a.*[1] *running battle*: see RUNNING *ppl a. set battle*: see SET *a.* **trial by battle** *Hist.* the legal decision of a dispute by the issue of a single combat. *wager of battle*: see WAGER *n.* 5b.

Comb.: **battle array** the disposition of troops etc. arranged for battle; **battleaxe** (*a*) a type of broad-bladed axe used as a weapon, esp. in medieval or prehistoric times and in Africa; (*b*) *colloq.* a formidable or domineering (esp. middle-aged) woman; **battlebus** a bus or coach used as a mobile operational centre during an election campaign; **battle-cruiser** a heavy-gunned warship of higher speed and lighter armour than a battleship; **battle-cry** a war cry, a slogan; **battledress** a soldier's or airman's everyday khaki uniform of a tunic and trousers; **battle fatigue** mental illness due to stress in wartime combat (= *combat fatigue*); **battlefield, battleground** a field or ground on which a battle is fought (*lit.* & *fig.*); **battleship** [f. *line-of-battle ship* above] a warship of the most heavily armed and armoured class, of sufficient size to take part in a main attack; *battleship grey*, a slightly bluish grey (often used for warships as reducing their visibility); **battle-wagon** *slang* a battleship; an armed or armoured vehicle.

battleworthy *a.* fit for use in battle L19.

battle /ˈbat(ə)l/ *a. obs.* exc. *dial.* Also (*Sc.*) **baittle** /ˈbeɪt(ə)l/. E16. [Prob. f. base also of BATTEN *v.*[2]: see -LE[1]. Cf. BATTLE *v.*[4]] 1 Of grass or pasture: improving to sheep and cattle, fattening. E16. 2 Of soil or land: rich, fertile, productive. M16.

battle /ˈbat(ə)l/ *v.*[1] ME. [(O)Fr. *bataillier*, f. as BATTLE *n.*] 1 *v.i.* a Fight; engage in war. Now *rare* in *lit.* sense. ME. b *fig.* Contend; struggle (*against, for* an end etc., *through* a hostile environment etc., *with*, etc.); carry *on* struggling. LME. †2 *v.t.* Arrange for battle; dispose in battalions. Only in ME. 3 *v.t.* Fight or struggle against. Now chiefly *N. Amer.* LME. 4 *v.t.* w. *it.* Fight, struggle E18. 5 *v.t.* Make *one's way* fighting or struggling. L18.

1b J. R. GREEN Walpole battled stubbornly against the cry of war. D. BAGLEY A series of bloody civil wars engendered by ruthless men battling for power. H. FAST To battle through the storm and cold waves. A. MCCOWEN My little auntie Peggy battling with a complicated menu in the kitchen. A. BRINK I was just battling on blindly, not really knowing what was happening. 3 *Times Lit. Suppl.* Battling the anarchy of fragmenting cultures. 4 BYRON They battle it beyond the wall. **battle it out** fight to a conclusion.

battle /ˈbat(ə)l/ *v.*[2]*t. arch.* ME. [Later OFr. *bataillier*: see prec.] Fortify or provide with battlements. Chiefly as *battled* ppl a.

TENNYSON The valleys of grape-loaded vines that glow Beneath the battled tower.

†**battle** *v.*[3]*t. dial.* E16–L19. [Frequent. of BAT *v.*[1]: see -LE[3].] Beat (clothes) with a wooden stick (see BATTLEDORE 1).

†**battle** *v.*[4] Long *dial.* M16. [App. f. BATTLE *a.* Cf. BATTEN *v.*[2]] 1 *v.t.* Nourish (as a rich pasture does); render (soil etc.) fertile and productive. M16–M19. 2 *v.i.* Grow fat, thrive; become fertile and productive. L16–E18.

battle *v.*[5] var. of BATTEL.

battledore /ˈbat(ə)ldɔː/ *n.* LME. [Perh. f. Prov. *batedor* beater, f. *batre* to beat (see BATTER *v.*[1]): cf. BATTLE *v.*[3]] 1 A wooden usu. paddle-shaped instrument used in washing for beating, stirring, or smoothing clothes; a similarly-shaped utensil for inserting objects into an oven, kiln, etc. Now chiefly *Hist.* LME. †2 More fully *battledore book*. A hornbook, an ABC, a child's primer. (So called from its usual shape.) M17–L19. 3 A small racket used with a shuttlecock. Also (more fully *battledore and shuttlecock*) the game played with these, a forerunner of badminton. L17.

Phrases: **not know a B from a battledore** *arch.* be completely illiterate or ignorant.

battlement /ˈbat(ə)lm(ə)nt/ *n.* LME. [f. OFr. *bataillier* (see BATTLE *v.*[1], *v.*[2]) + -MENT.] Usu. in *pl.* 1 An alternately high and low parapet at the top of a wall, for the defence of a building. LME. 2 A roof enclosed by this. L16.

battlemented *a.* furnished with or surrounded by battlements E17.

battler /ˈbatlə/ *n.* ME. [Orig. f. OFr. *batailleor, -ier* warrior, f. as BATTLE *v.*[1]; in mod. use f. BATTLE *v.*[1] + -ER[1].] 1 A person who battles (usu. *fig.*); *colloq.* a person who fights against the odds or does not give up easily. ME. 2 A swagman. *Austral.* E20.

battler *n.*[2] var. of BATTELER.

†**battoe** *n.* var. of BATEAU.

battology /bəˈtɒlədʒi/ *n.* L16. [mod.L *battologia* f. Gk, f. *battos* stammerer: see -LOGY.] A needless and tiresome repetition in speaking or writing.

battologize *v.t.* & *i.* repeat (a word or phrase, words or phrases, etc.) needlessly M17.

battue /bəˈt(j)uː; *foreign* baty (*pl. same*)/ *n.* E19. [Fr., use as n. of fem. pa. pple of *battre*: see BATTER *v.*[1]] 1 A driving of game towards the guns by beaters; a shooting-party on this plan. E19. 2 *transf.* a A thorough search. M19. b A wholesale slaughter. M19.

batture /bəˈtjʊə/ *n.* *N. Amer.* E19. [Fr.] 1 A stretch of river shore, usu. formed by deposition, between the natural embankment and the low-water mark. E19. 2 *Canad.* A sand bar in a river. E19.

battuta /bəˈtuːtə/ *n.* E18. [It., f. *battere* to beat.] *Mus.* The beating of time; a strong beat; the regular beat.

a battuta a direction: return to the strict tempo.

batty /ˈbati/ *a.* L16. [f. BAT *n.*[3] + -Y[1]; for sense 2 cf. BATS.] 1 Of, pertaining to, or characteristic of a bat or bats. L16. 2 Crazy, dotty. *colloq.* E20.

†**batus** *n.* see BATH *n.*[2]

Batwa *n.pl.* see TWA *n.*[1]

batz /bats/ *n.* *obs.* exc. *Hist.* Also †**bat.** L16. [G †*Batze* (now *Batzen*); Eng. *bat* by mistaking for a pl.] A small coin of Switzerland and South Germany, worth four kreutzers.

bauble /ˈbɔːb(ə)l/ *n.* ME. [OFr. *ba(u)bel* child's toy, plaything, perh. ult. f. redupl. of *bel* beautiful: cf. BIBELOT.] 1 A showy trinket; a piece of vulgar or ostentatious jewellery. ME. 2 *Hist.* A baton surmounted by a fantastically carved head with asses' ears, carried by a jester as a rod of office. LME. 3 A plaything, a toy. *obs.* exc. as passing into other senses. LME. 4 A childish or trivial matter; something of no importance. M16.

1 SHAKES. *Tam. Shr.* It is a paltry cap, . . a bauble, a silken pie. LYTTON The knight's baubles become the alderman's badges. J. CAREY Women dripping with baubles. 4 LD MACAULAY The Right Honourable before my name is a bauble.

†**baubling** *a.* trifling, paltry E17–M19.

bauch /baːx, bɔːx/ *a.* *Sc.* E16. [Perh. f. ON *bágr* uneasy: cf. Icel. *bágur* difficult, hard, (*eiga*) *bágt* (be) poor, hard up.] Weak, poor, spineless.

bauchle /ˈbaːx(ə)l, ˈbɔː-/ *n.* *Sc.* E17. [Origin unkn.: cf. next.] 1 A spoiled or distorted thing; *spec.* an old shoe worn down at the heel. E17. 2 A ne'er-do-well. E19.

bauchle /ˈbaːx(ə)l, ˈbɔː-/ *v.t.* *Sc.* Long *dial. rare.* L15. [Origin uncertain: perh. f. BAUCH.] Subject to disgrace or ignominy, vilify; = BAFFLE *v.* 1.

baud /bəʊd, bɔːd/ *n.* Pl. **-s**, same. M20. [f. J. M. E. *Baudot* (1845–1903), Fr. engineer.] *Telecommunications & Computing.* A unit of signal transmission speed equal to one information unit per second; *loosely* a unit of data transmission speed of one bit per second.

baudekin /ˈbɔːdɪkɪn/ *n.* *obs.* exc. *Hist.* Also **baudkin** /ˈbɔːdkɪn/, & other vars. ME. [OFr. f. med.L *baldachinus* f. as BALDACHIN.] = BALDACHIN 1.

Baudelairean /bəʊdəˈlɛːrɪən/ *a.* & *n.* Also **-ian.** L19. [f. *Baudelaire* (see below) + -EAN.] A *adj.* Of, pertaining to, or characteristic of the French poet and critic Charles Baudelaire (1821–67) or his works. L19. B *n.* An admirer or student of Baudelaire or his writing. E20.

baudkin *n.* var. of BAUDEKIN.

baudrons /ˈbɔːdrənz/ *n.* *Sc.* L15. [Origin unkn.: cf. BAWD *n.*[2]] (A name for) the cat.

SIR W. SCOTT He had a beard too, and whiskers . . as long as baudrons'.

bauera /ˈbaʊərə/ *n.* M19. [mod.L, f. Franz (1758–1840) and Ferdinand (1760–1826) *Bauer*, Austrian botanical draughtsmen: see -A[1].] A small Australian evergreen shrub of the genus *Bauera*, bearing rose-coloured or purple flowers.

Bauhaus /ˈbaʊhaʊs/ *n.* E20. [G, f. *Bau* building + *Haus* house.] (The principles of) a German school of architecture and design founded by Walter Gropius in 1919 and closed in 1933.

bauhinia /bəʊˈhɪnɪə/ *n.* L18. [mod.L, f. Jean (1541–1613) and Gaspard (1560–1624) *Bauhin*, Swiss botanists: see -IA[1].] A leguminous plant of the tropical genus *Bauhinia*, of which there are many species.

baulk /bɔːlk, bɔːk/ *n.* Also **balk.** LOE. [ON *bálkr* partition, f. Gmc; rel. to OFris. *balca*, OS, OHG *balco* (Du. *balk*, G *Balken*), ON *bjálki*, f. a Gmc base meaning 'beam'.] I †1 A ridge, a mound, *esp.* a grave-mound; a dividing ridge of land. LOE–M17. 2 A ridge left in ploughing, either intentionally (esp. as a boundary line between sections) or unintentionally. LOE. †3 A mistake, a blunder; an omission. LME–L19. †4 A ridge in one's way; a stumbling-block, an obstacle. LME–M18. 5 *fig.* A hindrance, a check; a disappointment. M17. 6 *Billiards, Snooker,* etc. A marked-off area on the table from which play begins and which governs play in certain situations varying according to the game being played (for example, protecting a ball from a direct stroke); the area between the baulk line and the bottom cushion. Also (in some games), a play bringing one's own and the red ball within this area. L18. 7 *Baseball.* An illegal action by a pitcher. M19.

2 **make a baulk of good ground** waste an opportunity. 5 DEFOE This was a balk to them and put a damp to their new projects. D. LESSING The balk, the disappointment, is felt as a promise that has been broken. 6 *baulk-cushion, -end, -pocket,* etc. *give a miss-in-baulk*: see MISS *n.*[1]

II 8 A beam of timber; a tie-beam of a house (now chiefly *north.*). ME. 9 The beam of a balance. *obs.* exc. *dial.* LME.

8 J. MASTERS Each man carried a stave—a big balk of wood, rather.

Comb.: **baulk line** a line drawn on a billiard- or snooker-table parallel to the face of the bottom cushion at a distance one-fifth of the length of the playing area.

baulk /bɔːlk, bɔːk/ *v.* Also **balk.** LME. [f. the n.] †1 *v.t.* & *i.* Make baulks in (land) in ploughing. LME–E17. b *v.t. fig.* Heap up in ridges. *rare.* Only in L16. 2 *v.t.* Shirk or ignore; pass over (a topic, opportunity, etc.); avoid or refuse (a duty, thing offered, etc.). LME. †3 *v.t.* Pass by (a place); avoid, shun. L15–L18. 4 *v.i.* Stop short as at an obstacle; jib or shy (*lit.* & *fig.*). L16. †5 *v.t.* Miss by error or inadvertence. L16–E18. 6 *v.t.* Place a baulk in the way of (a person); hinder, thwart, disappoint, frustrate. L16. †7 *v.i.* & *t.* Quibble; argue; chop (logic). L16–M17.

2 SHAKES. *Twel. N.* This was look'd for at your hand, and this was baulk'd. S. JOHNSON I never . . balked an invitation out to dinner. D. H. LAWRENCE It's got to be done, so why balk it? 4 C. J. LEVER Burke . . suddenly swerved his horse round, and affecting to baulk, cantered back. B. SPOCK A baby may first balk at the transition from bottle to weaning cup. W. GOLDING Steam could lift a weight that an elephant would baulk at. 5 SPENSER They . . balk the right way, and strayen abroad. 6 POPE Balk'd of his prey, the yelling monster flies. DEFOE An enemy who is baulked and defeated, but not overcome. SWIFT The most effectual Way to baulk Their Malice, is—to let them talk. H. MARTINEAU My home affections . . all the stronger for having been repressed and baulked. H. READ A personal will to dominate material and form which refuses to be balked by any conventions.

baulkiness *n.* the quality of being baulky L19. **baulky** *a.* liable to baulk (BAULK *v.* 4); reluctant to proceed; perverse: M19.

†**baum-cricket** *n.* var. of BALM-CRICKET.

Baumé /ˈbəʊmeɪ/ *n.* Also **Beaumé.** M19. [See below.] 1 Used *attrib.* and in *possess.* to denote a kind of hydrometer invented by Antoine Baumé (1728–1804), French chemist, and an associated arbitrary scale of relative density. M19. 2 *degree Baumé*, a unit on this scale. L19.

baum marten /baʊm ˈmɑːtɪn/ *n. phr.* L19. [Partial tr. G *Baummarder* lit. 'tree marten'.] The pine marten; the fur of this animal.

bauson /ˈbɔːs(ə)n/ *n.* *arch.* & *dial.* Also **baw-.** LME. [f. next.] 1 BADGER *n.*[2] LME. 2 A fat or obstinate person. E18.

bausond /ˈbɔːs(ə)nd/ *a.* *dial.* Also **baw-.** ME. [OFr. *bausant* piebald = Prov. *bausan* (It. *balzano*, whence mod.Fr. *balzan*), f. Proto-Romance adj. (= belted, striped), f. L *balteus* belt.] Of an animal: having white spots on a black or bay ground; *esp.* having a white patch on the forehead, or a white stripe down the face.

bauxite /ˈbɔːksʌɪt/ *n.* Also †**beaux-.** M19. [Fr., orig. *beauxite*, f. *Les B(e)aux*, locality near Arles, France: see -ITE[1].] The major commercial source of aluminium, an earthy rock consisting of hydrated alumina with variable proportions of iron oxides and other impurities.

bauxitic /bɔːkˈsɪtɪk/ *a.* L19.

bavardage /bavardaːʒ/ *n.* E19. [Fr., f. *bavarder* to chatter, f. *bavard* talkative, f. *bave* saliva, drivel.] Idle gossip, chit-chat.

Bavarian /bəˈvɛːrɪən/ *a.* & *n.* E17. [f. *Bavaria* (G *Bayern*) (see below) + -AN.] A *adj.* Of or pertaining to Bavaria, formerly a kingdom of the German Empire, now a State in Germany, its natives or inhabitants, or their dialect. E17.

Bavarian cream = BAVAROISE.

B *n.* A native or inhabitant of Bavaria; the dialect of German used there. L18.

bavaroise /bavəˈwɑːz, *foreign* bavarwaːz/ *n.* Also **-ois** /-ˈwɑː, *foreign* -wa/. M19. [Fr., use as n. of fem. adj., = prec.] A dessert containing gelatin and whipped cream, served cold.

bavaroy /ˈbavərɔɪ/ *n.* *obs.* exc. *Hist.* E18. [Prob. f. Fr. *bavarois* BAVARIAN.] A type of greatcoat or cloak for men.

baviaan /bavɪˈɑːn/ *n.* *S. Afr.* M18. [Du.] = BABOON 2, 3.

bavin /ˈbavɪn/ *n.* ME. [Origin unkn.] (A bundle of) brushwood, firewood.

baw /bɔː/ *int.* *arch.* LME. [Imit.: cf. BAH.] Expr. contempt or aversion.

bawbee /ˈbɔːbiː/ *n.* Chiefly *Sc.* M16. [f. the laird of Sille*bawby*, mint-master under James V.] Orig., a silver coin worth three, later six, Scottish pennies. Now, a coin of low value.

bawcock /ˈbɔːkɒk/ *n.* *arch.* *colloq.* L16. [Fr. *beau coq* fine cock.] A good fellow.

bawd /bɔːd/ *n.*[1] LME. [Shortened f. BAWDSTROT.] A procurer, now only a female one, a woman who obtains women for prostitution.

bawd /bɔːd/ *n.*[2] *dial.* L15. [Perh. f BAUDRONS: cf. the Eng. use of *puss* and Sc. of *malkin* for both hare and cat.] A hare.

†**bawd** *v.i.* M17–E18. [f. BAWD *n.*[1]] Pander.

bawdry /ˈbɔːdri/ *n.* LME. [f. BAWD *n.*[1] + -RY.] †1 The practice of a bawd; procuring. LME–E18. †2 Immorality, fornication. LME–M17. 3 Obscenity in speech or writing. L16.

†**bawdstrot** *n.* ME–L15. [OFr. *baudetrot*, *baudestroyt*, f. *baut*, *baude* lively, gay, shameless (f. Gmc, = BOLD *a.*) + base of AN *trote* TROT *n.*[2]] = BAWD *n.*[1]

†**bawdy** *a.*[1] LME–E17. [Origin unkn., but cf. Welsh *bawaidd* dirty, vile, f. *baw* dirt.] Soiled, dirty.

†**bawdiness** *n.*[1] M16–M18.

bawdy /ˈbɔːdi/ *a.*[2] & *n.* E16. [f. BAWD *n.*[1] + -Y[1]: prob. assoc. w. prec.] A *adj.* Of or befitting a bawd, *esp.* (of language) humorously indecent. E16.

bawdy-house *arch.* a brothel.

B *n.* Humorously indecent language or talk (esp. in *talk bawdy*); licentiousness. M17.

bawdily *adv.* E17. **bawdiness** *n.*[2] lewdness, obscenity: M18.

bawl /bɔːl/ *v.* & *n.* LME. [Imit.: cf. med.L *baulare* bark, Icel. *baula* (Sw. *böla*) low, as an ox.] A *v.* 1 *v.i.* Bark, howl, etc., as an animal. *obs.* exc. *dial.* LME. 2 *v.i.* Shout, howl, etc., at the top of one's voice; weep or wail loudly. L15. 3 *v.t.* Utter with bawling, shout loudly. (Freq. foll. by *out.*) L16. 4 *v.t.* Foll. by *out.* Reprove or reprimand severely. *colloq.* (orig. *US*). E20.

1 ROBERT BURTON A barking dog that alwayes bawls, but seldome bites. 2 W. COWPER And ev'ry soul cried out, well done, As loud as he could bawl. P. G. WODEHOUSE Her Uncle George was bawling to somebody to fetch a policeman. T. CAPOTE He started to cry. Sat down and bawled like a kid. 3 SHAKES. *2 Hen. IV* Those that bawl out the ruins of thy linen

shall inherit his kingdom. THACKERAY 'I will fling you out of window' . . bawled out Mr. Pen. E. BLISHEN They all rose and bawled the final hymn. 4 L. A. G. STRONG He bawled him out. Gave him such a tongue-lashing. M. GEE They bawled each other out in the street.

B *n.* A shout at the top of one's voice; a loud prolonged cry. L18.

bawler *n.* L16.

bawley /ˈbɔːli/ *n.* L19. [Origin unkn.] A fishing-smack used on the coasts of Essex and Kent.

bawn /bɔːn/ *n.* M16. [Ir. *badún*, perh. f. *ba* cows + *dún* fortress.] **1** *Hist.* A fortified enclosure; the fortified court or outwork of a castle. M16. **2** A fold for cattle. *dial.* M19.

bawneen /ˈbɔːniːn/ *n.* Also in Ir. form **báinín** (pronounced same). E20. [Ir. *báinín* dim. of *bán* white.] Undyed off-white yarn used in Ireland for knitting (esp. in Aran wear) and weaving; a garment made of this.

bawson *n.*, **bawsond** *a.*, vars. of BAUSON, BAUSOND.

baxter /ˈbakstə/ *n.* Long *dial.* (esp. *Sc.*). [OE *bæcestre* fem. of *bæcere* BAKER: see -STER.] A baker.

bay /beɪ/ *n.*[1] ME. [OFr. *bai* or aphet. f. ABAY f. OFr. *abai* (mod. *aboi*), f. *(a)baiier* BAY *v.*[1]] **1** The deep bark of a large dog or of hounds in pursuit; *esp.* the chorus raised on drawing close to the hunted quarry. ME. **2** The position or action of a hunted animal when, unable to flee further, it turns and defends itself at close quarters. Freq. *fig.* Only in *at* or *to* (†*a*) *bay*. ME.

1 C. BRONTË Formidable-looking dogs . . all bristle and bay. 2 SHAKES. *Ven. & Ad.* The hounds are at a bay. T. H. WHITE The boar was not at bay any more, but charging Master Twyti. *fig.*: SHAKES. *Rich. II* To rouse his wrongs and chase them to the bay. D. H. LAWRENCE Gerald seemed always to be at bay against everybody. **bring to bay** come close to (the quarry). **hold, keep, at bay** keep at a distance, resist, hold off. **stand at bay** turn against one's assailants.

bay /beɪ/ *n.*[2] LME. [(O)Fr. *baie* f. L *baca* berry.] †**1** A berry, esp. of the laurel. LME–M19. **2** In full *bay tree*. An evergreen tree of the laurel family, *Laurus nobilis*, with dark green aromatic leaves. Also (*US*), any of various similarly aromatic trees and shrubs, esp. of the genera *Magnolia* and *Myrica*. M16. **3** *sing.* & (usu.) in *pl.* Leaves or twigs of bay, esp. as a wreath for a conqueror or poet; *fig.* fame. M16. **4** In the coastal states of south-eastern US: a tract of low marshy wooded ground with numerous bay trees. L18.

2 *red bay*: see RED *a.* *sweet bay*: see SWEET *a.* & *adv.*

Comb.: *bay-laurel*: see LAUREL *n.* 1; **bay-leaf** a dried leaf of sweet bay, used as flavouring; **bay rum** perfume (esp. for the hair) distilled from rum and leaves of the bayberry *Pimenta acris*.

bay /beɪ/ *n.*[3] LME. [(O)Fr. *baie* f. (O)Sp. *bahia*, perh. of Iberian origin.] **1** (A part of the sea filling) a broad, large indentation in a coastline. LME. **2** An indentation or recess in a range of hills etc. M19.

1 SHAKES. *A.Y.L.* My affection hath an unknown bottom, like the Bay of Portugal. N. CALDER Around the bay are sunken ruins of other seaports. 2 L. VAN DER POST Each bay cut in a cliff of green was ardent with white and blue lilies' hearts.

Comb.: **bayman** *N. Amer.* a person resident beside a (usu. specified) bay; *Canad.* a backwoodsman, a rustic; **bay salt**: obtained as large crystals by slow evaporation (orig. by the sun from seawater); **Bay State** *US* Massachusetts; **bay-whaler** *Austral.* & *NZ* a boat used in bay whaling; **bay whaling** *Austral.* & *NZ* whaling from land-based stations, practised when the whales come into shallow inshore waters to calve; **baywood** [*Bay* of Campeche, Mexico] mahogany from the Central American tree *Swietenia macrophylla*.

bay /beɪ/ *n.*[4] LME. [(O)Fr. *baie*, f. *bayer* (earlier *baer*, *beer*) stand open, gape f. med.L *batare*, of unkn. origin.] **1** A division (of a wall) of a room between columns, pilasters, party-walls, bookcases, etc. LME. **2** (In full *bay window*, a window across) an internal recess formed by the outward projection of a wall beyond the general line. Cf. *bow-window* s.v. BOW *n.*[1] LME. **3** A recess, a compartment; a partitioned or marked area forming a unit. Freq. w. specification of purpose, as *bomb-bay*, *loading bay*, *sickbay* L16. **4** A railway line at a station, having a closed end and acting as a terminus for a side-line; a platform adjoining this. Usu. *attrib.* E20.

1 F. R. WILSON The last two bays of the nave . . are unoccupied. J. HILTON A very delightful library . . containing a multitude of books so retiringly housed in bays and alcoves. 2 E. WALFORD A substantial brick house, the front diversified by two bays. H. FAST A slanted bay looked out over a greenery-choked backyard. 3 C. RYAN From the bays of the B-24s . . supplies began to fall haphazardly. E. CRISPIN A single-lane carriageway lined on either side with V-shaped bays in which pedestrians could take refuge. 4 A. CHRISTIE A train . . came slowly puffing in and deposited itself in a modest bay.

Comb.: *bay window*: see sense 2 above; **bay-windowed** *a.* having a bay window.

bayed *a.* (of a window) having or set in a bay E19.

bay /beɪ/ *n.*[5] LME. [Origin unkn.] An embankment, a dam.

bay /beɪ/ *n.*[6] M16. [f. BAY *a.*] **1** A bay horse. M16. **2** Hist. *The (Queen's) Bays*, the 2nd Dragoon Guards (now incorporated in the 1st Queen's Dragoon Guards), who orig. rode bay horses. M19.

bay /beɪ/ *n.*[7] *obs.* exc. *Hist.* L16. [(O)Fr. *baie* or Du. *baai*, f. *bai* BAY *a.*: see BAIZE.] Baize. Freq. in *pl.* (whence BAIZE, the mod. form).

bay /beɪ/ *n.*[8] M19. [Abbrev. of BEZ-ANTLER.] The second branch of a stag's horn, above the brow antler. Also *bay-antler*.

bay /beɪ/ *a.* ME. [(O)Fr. *bai* f. L *badius* chestnut-coloured (only of horses), rel. to OIr. *buide* yellow.] Usu. of a horse: reddish-brown and (of a horse) with black mane and tail.

bay /beɪ/ *v.*[1] LME. [OFr. *(a)baiier* (mod. *aboyer*) = It. *(ab)baiare* f. an imit. base: infl. by BAY *n.*[1]] **1** *v.i.* Esp. of a large dog: bark, howl. Freq. foll. by *at*. LME. **2** *v.t.* Bark at, assail with barking. LME. **3** *v.t.* Utter by baying, shout. L16. **4** *v.t.* Pursue with barking like a pack of hounds. L16. **5** *v.t.* Bring to bay, hold at bay. L16.

1 *fig.* P. GALLICO For twenty years they have been baying at your heels in Washington. B. MALAMUD The wind bayed at the window like starving wolves. 2 SHAKES. *Jul. Caes.* I had rather be a dog and bay the moon Than such a Roman. *fig.*: COLERIDGE Superstition and her wolfish brood Bay his mild radiance. 3 E. K. KANE These . . servants . . bayed their full-mouth welcome. 4 SHAKES. *2 Hen. IV* The French and Welsh Baying him at the heels. C. DARWIN The jaguar is killed by the aid of dogs baying and driving him up a tree. 5 SHAKES. *Jul. Caes.* We are at the stake, And bay'd about with many enemies.

bay /beɪ/ *v.*[2]*t.* L16. [Conn. w. BAY *n.*[5], either as source or (prob.) as deriv.] Obstruct, dam (water). Usu. foll. by *back*, *up*.

†**bay** *v.*[3]*t.* *rare* (Spenser). Only in L16. [App. pseudo-arch. alt. of BATHE *v.* Cf. EMBAY *v.*[2]] Bathe, immerse.

bay /beɪ/ *v.*[4]*i.* & *t.* *rare.* M17. [f. BAY *n.*[1]] Stand at bay (against).

bayadère /beɪjəˈdɛː, -ˈdɪə/ *n.* L16. [Fr. f. Port. *bailadeira*, f. *bailar* to dance, rel. to med.L *ballare* to dance.] **1** A Hindu dancing-girl (esp. at a southern Indian temple). L16. **2** A striped textile fabric. M19.

bayard /ˈbeɪɑːd/ *a.* & *n.* *arch.* ME. [OFr. *baiart*, *-ard*, f. *bai* BAY *a.*: see -ARD. Sense B.2 alludes to the name of the magic steed given (in medieval romance) by Charlemagne to Renaud de Montauban, which was celebrated as a type of blind recklessness.] **A** *adj.* Bay-coloured. ME. **B** *n.* **1** A bay horse. LME. †**2** A person blind to his or her own ignorance, a self-confident fool. E16–L17.

bayberry /ˈbeɪbɛri/ *n.* E16. [f. BAY *n.*[2] + BERRY *n.*[1]] **1** The fruit of the bay tree. E16. **2** A N. American shrub or small tree, *Myrica cerifera*, allied to the bog myrtle (also called *wax myrtle*); the fruit of this tree, which yields a wax made into candles. L17. **3** (The fruit of) a fragrant oil-bearing W. Indian tree, *Pimenta acris*. M18.

Bayes' theorem /ˈbeɪz ˌθɪərəm/ *n. phr.* M19. [The Revd Thomas *Bayes* (1702–61), Eng. mathematician.] *Math.* A theorem expressing the probability of each of a number of mutually exclusive events, given some other event *E*, in terms of the probabilities of those events independently of *E* and the probabilities of *E* given each of those events in turn.

Bayesian *a.* & *n.* (*a*) *adj.* pertaining to or employing concepts arising out of Bayes' work on calculations of probability; *esp.* designating methods of statistical inference in which use is made of prior information on the distributions of parameters; (*b*) *n.* a person who uses or advocates Bayesian methods: M20. **Bayesianism** *n.* advocacy or use of Bayesian methods L20.

bayonet /ˈbeɪənɪt/ *n.* & *v.* L17. [Fr. *baïonnette*, f. *Bayonne*, France, the orig. place of manufacture: see -ET[1].] **A** *n.* †**1** A short flat dagger. L17–E18. **2** A swordlike stabbing blade which may be fixed to a rifle muzzle for use in hand to hand fighting. E18. **b** A soldier armed with a bayonet; military force. L18. **3** A pin, plug, etc., which engages in a hole or socket by a push-and-twist action (orig. merely by pushing). Usu. *attrib.*, designating electrical fittings designed to engage in this way. L18.

2 *Spanish bayonet*: see SPANISH *a.*

B *v.t.* **1** Stab with a bayonet. L17. **2** Coerce by means of bayonets. L18.

Comb.: **bayonet-grass** *NZ* = SPANIARD *n.* 3.

bayou /ˈbʌɪuː/ *n.* *US.* M18. [Amer. Fr. f. Choctaw *bayuk*.] In the southern States: a marshy offshoot of a river, lake, etc.

bazaar /bəˈzɑː/ *n.* L16. [It. *bazarro* f. Turk. f. Pers. *bāzār* market.] **1** An oriental market. L16. **2** A large shop, or arcade of shops, selling fancy goods, bric-à-brac, etc. E19. **3** A sale of miscellaneous (usu. second-hand) goods in aid of charity. E19.

bazan *n.* var. of BASAN.

baze /beɪz/ *v.t.* Long *obs.* exc. *dial.* E17. [Origin unkn.: cf. Du. *bazen*.] Stupefy; frighten.

bazil *n.* var. of BASIL *n.*[3]

bazoo /bəˈzuː/ *n.* *US slang.* L19. [Origin unkn.: cf. Du. *bazuin* trombone, trumpet.] **1** = KAZOO. L19. **2** The mouth. E20.

bazooka /bəˈzuːkə/ *n.* M20. [App. f. prec.] **1** A crude musical instrument resembling a trombone. *US.* M20. **2** A portable tubular anti-tank rocket launcher. M20.

bazoom /bəˈzuːm/ *n.* *slang.* M20. [Prob. alt. of BOSOM *n.*] A woman's breast. Usu. in *pl.*

bazuco *n.* var. of BASUCO.

bdellium /ˈdɛlɪəm/ *n.* LME. [L f. Gk *bdellion*, of Semitic origin: cf. Heb. *bᵊḏōlaḥ*.] A tree, esp. of the genus *Commiphora*, yielding a fragrant gum resin; the resin itself.

bdelloid /ˈdɛlɔɪd/ *a.* E20. [f. Gk *bdella* leech + -OID.] Zool. *bdelloid rotifer*, a rotifer of the order Bdelloidea, resembling a leech.

be /biː/, *unstressed* bɪ/ *v.* Pres. indic.: 1 **am** /am, əm/; 2 & *pl.* **are** /ɑː, ə/; 3, (*dial.*) 1, 2, & *pl.* **is** /ɪz/; 2 (*arch.*) **art** /ɑːt, ət/; 2 & *pl.* (*arch.* & *dial.*) **be**. Past indic.: 1 & 3 **was** /wɒz, wəz/; 2 & *pl.* **were** /wəː, wɛː, wə/, (*dial.*) **was**; 2 (*arch.*) **wast** /wɒst, wəst/ or **wert** /wəːt, wət/. Pres. subjunct. (now often repl. by indic. forms): **be**; 2 *sing.* also †**beest**. Past subjunct.: **were**; 1 & 3 *sing.* (*colloq.*), & 2 & *pl.* (*arch.* & *dial.*) also **was**; 2 *sing.* also (*arch.*) **wert**. Imper.: **be**. Pres. pple **being** /ˈbiːɪŋ/. Pa. pple **been** /biːn, bɪn/. Informal abbrev. forms: **'m** = *am*; **'s** = *is*, **'re** = *are*; **aren't** /ɑːnt/ = *are not*, (interrog.) *am not*; **isn't** /ˈɪz(ə)nt/ = *is not*; **i'nt** /ɪnt/ (*non-standard*) = *is not*; **wasn't** /ˈwɒz(ə)nt/ = *was not*; **weren't** /wəːnt, wɛːnt/ = *were not*; **ain't** /eɪnt/, (*arch.*) **an't** /ɑːnt/ (*colloq.*) = *am not*, (*slang* & *joc.*) = *is not*, *are not*. OE. [An irreg. and defective vb, the full conjugation of which is made up of the surviving inflections of four bases: (i) the IE vb w. stem base also of Skt *as-*, Gk *es-*, L *es-*, *'s-*; (ii) the IE vb w. stem base also of Skt *vas-*, Goth. *wisan* to remain; (iii) the IE vb w. stem base also of Skt *bhū-*, Gk *phu-*, L *fu-*, OE *bēon* become; (iv) the old Gmc perfect formation, base of *are*, of unkn. origin.] **I** As full vb. **1** Have place in the realm of fact; exist, live. OE. **2** Come into existence, come about; happen, occur, take place. OE. **3** (With advs. and prep. phrs.) Have or occupy a given position; exist in a stated circumstance, condition, or relation; occupy oneself in a given way, hold a given opinion, etc. OE. **b** Take or direct oneself; go, come; (often w. infinitive expr. purpose); (in *pa. pple*) called, visited. M17. **4** Go on in its existing condition; remain, continue; take or last (a specified time). ME. **5** Be the case or the fact; obtain. ME. **6** Befall, pertain (*un*)*to*; (now only in exclams. and wishes). ME.

1 AV *Gen.* 5:24 Enoch walked with God: and hee was not, for God tooke him. DRYDEN Troy is no more. POPE Some nymphs there are, too conscious of their face. R. HEBER Cherubim and seraphim falling down before Thee, Which wert, and art, and evermore shall be. DICKENS There ain't anything the matter. 2 R. B. SHERIDAN Your husband that shall be. OED The flower-show was last week. 3 SHAKES. *Rich. III* Where is thy husband now? Where be thy brothers? EVELYN There was not his equal in the whole world. R. BURNS Oh, were I on Parnassus' Hill! W. S. GILBERT Peter's been at the old brown sherry. J. GALSWORTHY I thought that you . . might . . ascertain what the fellow is about. DYLAN THOMAS The House is 5 minutes from the station. ROBERT KENNEDY One fifth of the people are against everything all the time. J. I. M. STEWART I do have two daughters. They're still at school. b C. BURNEY Fanny . . had been to enquire after him 2 days ago. A. E. HOUSMAN Oh I have been to Ludlow fair. 4 SHAKES. *All's Well* Nay, I'll fit you, And not be all day neither. V. MCNABB St. Malachy was some months in reaching Clairvaux. 5 SHAKES. *2 Hen. IV* You loiter here too long, being you are to take soldiers up in counties as you go. ALDOUS HUXLEY It may be that, later on, I shall take your advice after all. 6 SHAKES. *Lear* To thine and Albany's issues Be this perpetual.

II As copular vb. **7** (With n., adj., or (passing into sense 3) adj. phr.) Have the state or quality expressed by the predicate. OE. **8** (With n.) Coincide with, be identical to; form the essential constituent of, act the part of. OE. **b** Amount to, mean; cost. ME.

7 SHAKES. *Ant. & Cl.* Be'est thou sad or merry, The violence of either thee becomes. J. GRAINGER What is fame? an empty bubble. SIR W. SCOTT Be of good courage. GEO. ELIOT I'm a stranger in Florence. E. WAUGH Aunt Julia . . lived to be eighty-eight. P. GALLICO He was an honest man, was Patrick. P. LARKIN Some must employ the scythe . . That the walks be smooth For the feet of the angel. 8 J. AUSTEN We have got a play . . and I am to be Count Cassel. G. STEIN Rose is a rose is a rose is a rose. A. J. P. TAYLOR The overriding problem was where to land. *Listener* For us during thirty years Kingsley Martin . . *was* the *New Statesman*. J. BRONOWSKI The gas was oxygen. b AV *Lam.* 1:12 Is it nothing to you, all ye that passe by? T. HARDY A genial and pleasant gentleman, whom to meet . . was to know, to know was to drink with, and to drink with was, unfortunately, to pay for. D. L. SAYERS Yours is one-and-a-penny and mine's ninepence.

III As auxiliary vb. **9** With pa. pple of v.t., forming the pass. voice. OE. **b** With pa. pple of v.i., forming perfect tenses. *arch.* (now usu. repl. by *have*). OE. **10** With pres. pple forming progressive act. tenses. OE. **b** With pres. pple, or more usu. w. *being* + pa. pple, forming progressive pass. tenses. M16. **11** With infinitive, expr. duty or obligation (often repl. by *have*), intention, possibility, destiny, or hypothesis. ME.

9 SHAKES. *Com. Err.* Ill deeds is doubled with an evil word. G. WHITE The manor of Selborne, was it strictly looked after . . would swarm with game. C. M. YONGE His parents were grown old. D. PARKER If all the girls attending it were laid end to end, I wouldn't be at all surprised. b MILTON Therefore I am returned. GOLDSMITH Silence is become his mother tongue. 10 BUNYAN He was talking of thee. DYLAN THOMAS I'll be ringing you in August. b C. LAMB A man who is being strangled. OED We stayed there while our house was building. 11 S. RICHARDSON I am to thank you . . for your kind Letter. DICKENS You was to come to him at six o'clock. E. A. FREEMAN Normandy was to be invaded on each side. J. CONRAD He was nowhere to be seen. R. A. KNOX It wasn't for him to mix himself up in political quarrels.

Phrases etc., & with advs. in specialized senses: BE-ALL. **be at** be doing, aim at, intend. **be away** leave (at once), depart, set out. **been** (**and gone**) **and —**: colloq. amplification of pa. pple expr. surprise or annoyance. **be for** be bound for, be on the side of, agree with, want. **being that** or **as** (*arch.* & *dial.*) it being the case that, since. *be me*: see ME *pers. pron.* **be off** = *be away* (freq. as command). *be that as it may*: see MAY *v.*[1] (**bride** etc.) **-to-be** a future bride etc. **for the time being** for the present, just now. HAS-BEEN. **I were better, as good,** etc. (& similar constructions) *arch.* I had better etc., it would be (or have been) better etc. for me. *let be*: see LET *v.*[1] (**Miss X**) **that was**: her maiden name being (X). *powers-that-be*: see POWER *n.* SO *being. such as it is, they are,* etc.: see SUCH *demonstr. a. & pron. tell it like it is*: see TELL *v. thanks be*: see THANK *n. that is as may be*: see MAY *v.*[1] THAT *was.* THERE *it is.* THERE *you are. time was*: see TIME *n.* TO-BE.

be- /bɪ/ *pref.* [OE *be-*, weak form of *bī-*, *biġ* BY *prep.* & *adv.*] A freely productive pref. forming vbs and adjs. **1** Forming vbs f. vbs, w. the sense 'around, all over, throughout', as *beset, besmear*, etc.; w. intensive force 'thoroughly, excessively', as *begrudge, belabour*, etc.; or (no longer productive) w. the privative sense 'off, away', as *bereave* etc. **2** Forming trans. vbs f. intrans. vbs by adding a prepositional relation, as *bemoan, bespeak, bestride*, etc. **3** Forming trans. vbs f. adjs. and ns., w. the sense 'make —', as *befoul, besot*, etc., or 'call, dub', as *bemadam* etc. **4** Forming trans. vbs f. ns., w. the sense 'surround or cover with, affect with, treat in the manner of', as *becloud, bedew, befriend, benight*, etc., or (no longer productive) 'deprive of', as *behead* etc. **5** Forming adjs. f. ns. + -ED[2], w. the sense 'having, furnished with' (often excessively or conspicuously), as *bejewelled, bespectacled, bewhiskered*, etc.

beach /biːtʃ/ *n.* M16. [Origin uncertain: perh. identical w. OE *bæċe*, *beċe* brook, stream (cf. BECK *n.*[2]), w. transf. meaning '(pebbly) river valley', surviving in many place-names as Sand*bach*, Wis*bech*.] **1** The water-worn pebbles of the seashore; sand and shingle. *arch.* M16. **2** The sandy or pebbly shore of the sea, a lake, or a large river; *esp.* that part lying between high- and low-water marks. L16.

2 **on the beach** (orig. *Naut.*) ashore, retired, unemployed. **raised beach** *Geol.* a beach now situated above water level owing to changes since its formation. *the only pebble on the beach*: see PEBBLE *n.*

Comb.: **beach-ball** a large inflatable ball for games on a beach; **beach buggy** a motor vehicle with large tyres for use on beaches; **beach bum** *slang* a loafer on or around a beach; **beach front** (chiefly *N. Amer.*) the sea front beside a beach; **beach-grass** marram, *Ammophila arenaria*; **beachhead** [after *bridgehead*] the first position established on a beach by the landing of troops; **beach-master** an officer supervising the landing of troops; **beach plum** (the edible fruit of) a straggling N. American maritime shrub, *Prunus maritima*; **beach-rock** a conglomerate consisting of beach sand cemented by calcium carbonate; **beachwear** clothes for wearing on a beach.

beached *a.* (*rare*) having a beach, covered with shingle or sand L16. **beachward(s)** *adv.* towards the beach M19. **beachy** *a.* covered with sand and shingle L16.

beach /biːtʃ/ *v.t.* M19. [f. the n.] **1** Haul or run up (a ship, whale, etc.) on the beach; freq. *refl.*, drive itself on to the beach, become stranded. M19. **2** *fig.* As *beached* ppl a. = *on the beach* s.v. BEACH *n.* 2. E20.

beachcomber /ˈbiːtʃkəʊmə/ *n.* M19. [f. BEACH *n.* + COMBER *n.*[1]] **1** A White person in the Pacific islands etc. living by collecting jetsam; a longshore vagrant. M19. **2** A long wave rolling in from the sea. M19.

beachcombing *n.* the activity of a beachcomber, searching the beach for jetsam M19.

beach-la-mar /biːtʃləˈmɑː/ *n.* E19. [Alt. of Port. *bicho do mar*: see BÊCHE-DE-MER. Cf. BISLAMA.] †**1** = BÊCHE-DE-MER 1. Only in E19. **2** (Also **B-**.) An English-based pidgin formerly used as a trade language and contact vernacular in the SW Pacific. Also = BISLAMA. L19.

beacon /ˈbiːk(ə)n/ *n.* & *v.* [OE *bēacn* = OFris. *bēcen*, *bācen*, OS *bōkan*, OHG *bouhhan*, f. WGmc (cf. BECKON *v.*), of unkn. origin.] **A** *n.* †**1** A sign, a portent; an ensign, a standard. OE–L15. **2** A signal fire lighted on a pole, a hill, or other high place. ME. **3** A signal station, a watch-tower. LME. **4** Any light or other object serving as a signal, warning, or guide, esp. at sea (a lighthouse etc.) or on an airfield. LME. **b** A radio transmitter whose signal helps to determine the position of a ship, aircraft, or spacecraft. E20. **5** A conspicuous hill suitable for the site of a signal fire. Freq. in names, as *Brecon Beacons, Dunkery Beacon*, etc. L16.

4 M. LOWRY The mariner who, sighting the faint beacon of Start Point after a long voyage, knows that he will soon embrace his wife. M. M. KAYE With the lights of the camp providing a beacon that could be seen for miles across the plains. *fig.*: SHAKES. *Tr. & Cr.* Modest doubt is call'd The beacon of the wise. BELISHA BEACON.

B *v.* †**1** *v.t.* Foll. by *up*: kindle as a beacon. Only in M17. **2** *v.t.* Provide or indicate with a beacon or beacons. L18. **3** *v.t.* Illuminate, lead, or guide in the manner of a beacon. E19. **4** *v.i.* Shine like a beacon. E19.

beaconage *n.* (*a*) a toll paid for the maintenance of beacons; (*b*) a system of beacons: E17.

bead /biːd/ *n.* OE. [Partly aphet. f. *ġebed* prayer, partly generalized f. *bedhus* house of prayer: rel. to OFris. *bede*, OS *beda* (Du. *bede*), *gibed*, OHG *beta*, *gibet* (G *Gebet*), Goth. *bida*, f. Gmc. Cf. BID *v.*] **1** *sing.* & (usu.) in *pl.* Prayer; devotions, latterly *spec.* using a rosary. *arch.* OE. **2** Each of a string of small perforated balls forming the rosary or paternoster, used for keeping count of the prayers said. LME. **3** A small rounded perforated piece of glass, metal, wood, etc., used ornamentally, either threaded with others on string or wire or sewn on fabric; (in *pl.*) a necklace of such beads. LME. **4a** A drop of liquid, or of molten metal etc. L16. **b** A bubble, esp. in sparkling wine, spirits, etc. M18. **c** A small knob forming the front sight of a gun. M19. **5a** An ornamental moulding resembling a string of beads; an individual ornament in this. L18. **b** A narrow moulding of semicircular section. E19. **6** The thickened inner edge of a pneumatic tyre, gripping the rim of the wheel. E20.

1 JOYCE Confession will be heard all the afternoon after beads. **bid a bead, say one's beads** offer a prayer. 2 **tell** or **count one's beads** say one's prayers. 4 C. P. SNOW In the warm evening, beads of sweat were standing out. R. P. WARREN The leaves and the grass . . were wet, and beads of water hung here and there, glistening in the clear light. c **draw a bead on** *N. Amer.* take aim at.

Comb.: **bead-folk** *arch.* people who pray for a benefactor, almsfolk; **bead-house** a chapel; an almshouse; **bead-plant** a small creeping plant of the madder family, *Nertera granatensis*, of the southern hemisphere, bearing round orange fruits and sometimes grown for ornament; **bead-rim** a thickened, rounded rim; **bead-roll** a (long) list of names (orig. of persons to be prayed for); **bead sedge** the bur-reed, *Sparganium erectum*; **bead-tree** = AZEDARAC; **bead-work** (*a*) ornamental work with beads, beading; (*b*) open-mesh canework in furniture.

¶ See also BAILY'S BEADS.

beadily *adv.* in a beady manner M20. **beadiness** *n.* beady quality L19. **beadlet** *n.* a small bead; *spec.* a type of sea anemone: M19. **beadlike** *a.* resembling (that of) a bead M19. **beady** *a.* (*a*) beadlike, (of eyes) small, round, and glittering; (*b*) covered or decorated with beads: E19.

bead /biːd/ *v.* L16. [f. the n.] **1** *v.t.* Provide or ornament with beads or beading. L16. **2** *v.t.* Make into beads; string together like beads. L16. **3** *v.i.* Form or grow into a bead or beads. L19.

beading *n.* (*a*) the action of the vb; (*b*) decoration in the form of or resembling beads, esp. lacelike looped edging; (*c*) bead moulding; the bead of a tyre: M19.

beadle /ˈbiːd(ə)l/ *n.* Also (now only in sense 3) **bedel(l)**. [OE *bydel* = OHG *butil* (G *Büttel*) f. Gmc base of OE *bēodan* (see BID *v.*), superseded by forms f. OFr. *bedel* (mod. *bedeau*) f. Proto-Romance f. Gmc.] †**1** A person who makes a proclamation; a court usher; a town-crier. OE–L17. †**2** A messenger or under-officer of justice. OE–E18. **3** A ceremonial usher, a mace-bearer, *spec.* in certain universities, city companies, etc. (sometimes conventionally spelt *bedel*, *-ell*); in University College, London, a porter. ME. **4a** *Hist.* A parish officer appointed by the vestry to keep order in church, punish petty offenders, etc. L16. **b** In Scotland, a church official attending on the minister. M19.

beadledom *n.* (*arch.*) stupid officiousness M19. **beadleship** *n.* the office or jurisdiction of a beadle M16.

beadsman /ˈbiːdzmən/ *n.* Orig. †**beadman**; also (*arch.*) **bedesman**. Pl. **-men**. ME. [f. BEAD *n.* + MAN *n.*: prob. altered after *almsman*.] *Hist.* 1 A person who prays for the soul of another. ME. 2 A person paid to pray for others; a pensioner bound to pray for his benefactors, an almsman; (in Scotland) a public almsman, a licensed beggar. LME. 3 A petitioner. LME.

1 †**your beadsman**: used as a conventional form when writing to a superior or patron.

beagle /ˈbiːg(ə)l/ *n.* & *v.* L15. [Perh. f. OFr. *beegueule* having the mouth open, f. *beer* open wide (cf. BAY *n.*[4]) + *gueule* throat (see GULES).] A *n.* 1 (An animal of) a breed of usu. small hound, used for hare-hunting when the field follows on foot. L15. 2 *fig.* A spy, an informer; a constable. M16.

1 *legal beagle*: see LEGAL *a.*

B *v.i.* Hunt with beagles. Freq. as *beagling* vbl n. E19.

beagler *n.* M19.

beak /biːk/ *n.*[1] ME. [(O)Fr. *bec* f. late L *beccus*, of Celt. origin.] 1 The horny projecting termination of the jaws of a bird, esp. when strong and hooked as in a bird of prey (cf. BILL *n.*[2]). ME. b The elongated head, proboscis, or sucker-mouth of certain insects, e.g. a weevil. M17. c The (freq. horny) extremities of the mandibles of some other animals, e.g. a turtle or a squid. E19. 2 A sharp point or projection, a peak. LME. b *Bot.* & *Zool.* A projecting tip; e.g. that of a carpel in a cranesbill etc., or an umbo of a shell or valve. E19. 3 A human nose, esp. when hooked. *joc.* LME. 4 = *beak-head* (a) below. M16. 5 The tapered spout of a retort, still, etc. M17.

Comb.: **beak-head** (*a*) an (ornamented) projection at the prow of an ancient warship; (*b*) the space before the forecastle of a sailing ship (in men-of-war used as a latrine); (*c*) an ornament in Norman architecture resembling a head with a beak; *beak-iron*: see BICKERN; **beak-sedge** a sedge of the genus *Rhynchospora*, in which the persistent base of the style forms a beak to the fruit; *esp.* (more fully *white beak-sedge*) *R. alba* of wet heaths and moors in Europe and N. America.

beakful *n.* as much as can be held in a bird's beak M17. **beakless** *a.* L16. **beaklike** *a.* resembling (that of) a beak M19. **beaky** *a.* furnished with a beak, beaklike E18.

beak /biːk/ *n.*[2] *slang.* L18. [Prob. orig. thieves' cant; cf. HARMAN 2.] 1 A magistrate. L18. 2 A schoolmaster. L19.

beak /biːk/ *v.* ME. [OFr. *bequ(i)er* peck, f. as BEAK *n.*[1]] 1 *v.t.* & *i.* Strike or seize with the beak; push the beak into. ME. 2 *v.i.* Project with or as with a beak. *rare.* ME.

beaked /biːkt/ *a.* LME. [f. BEAK *n.*[1] + -ED[2].] 1 Pointed or hooked. LME. 2 *Her.* Having the beak a different tincture from the body. E16. 3 Provided with a beak. E16. b *Bot.* & *Zool.* Having a beaklike projection or proboscis; rostrate. Freq. in names, as *beaked whale*. E19.

2 **beaked parsley** [from the beaked fruit] any of several plants of the genus *Anthriscus*, *esp.* cow parsley, *A. sylvestris*.

beaker /ˈbiːkə/ *n.* ME. [ON *bikarr* = OS *bikeri*, (M)Du. *bēker*, OHG *behhari* (G *Becher*), f. pop.L, perh. f. Gk *bikos* drinking-bowl: cf. PITCHER *n.*[1]] 1 A large drinking-vessel with a wide mouth and no handles, a goblet. *arch.* or *literary* in *gen.* sense. ME. b A tumbler-shaped metal or (usu.) plastic drinking-vessel; a metal or plastic mug. E20. c *Archaeol.* A type of pottery drinking-vessel without a handle, characteristic of the early Bronze Age in western Europe. Cf. *funnel beaker* s.v. FUNNEL *n.* E20. 2 The contents of a beaker. E19. 3 A lipped cylindrical glass vessel used for scientific experiments. M19.

Comb.: **Beaker Culture**, (*arch.*) **Beaker folk**, a people believed to have been the sole makers of beakers (sense 1c).

beak-iron *n.* see BICKERN.

beal /bɪəl/ *n.* & *v. obs.* exc. *dial.* LME. [App. alt. of BOIL *n.*[1]] A *n.* A pustule, a boil. LME. B *v.i.* Suppurate, fester. E16.

be-all /ˈbiːɔːl/ *n.* E17. [f. BE *v.* + ALL *pron.*] The whole being or essence (*of*). Chiefly in *the be-all and* END-ALL (after Shakes.).

SHAKES. *Macb.* That but this blow Might be the be-all and the end-all here.

beam /biːm/ *n.* [OE *bēam* = OFris. *bām*, OS *bām*, *boom*, (M)Du. *boom* (see BOOM *n.*[2]), OHG *boum* (G *Baum*), f. WGmc; obscurely rel. to Goth. *bagms*, ON *baðmr* tree.] 1 A tree. *obs.* since OE exc. in *hornbeam*, *whitebeam*, etc. OE. †2 The rood-tree, the Cross (cf. *Acts* 5:30). OE–E18. 3 A long piece of squared timber, metal, or reinforced concrete, used in building and construction esp. as a horizontal load-bearing member. (See also sense 10.) OE. 4 A wooden cylinder in a loom, on which the warp or cloth is wound. OE. 5a The chief timber of a plough. OE. †b The pole or shaft of a chariot. Only in 17. 6 A ray or pencil of light; a set of parallel light rays. OE. b A ray or pencil of radiation of any kind; a narrow directed flow of particles. M19. c A strongly directional radio transmission, esp. as used to guide aircraft, missiles, etc. E20. 7 The transverse bar of a balance; the balance itself. LME. 8 The main stem of a stag's horn, bearing the antlers. LME. 9 Radiance; a gleam, a bright glance, *esp.* a radiant or good-natured smile. L16. 10a A horizontal timber stretching from side to side of a ship. E17. b The greatest breadth of a ship. E17. c Either side of a ship; a sideways direction from a ship. E17. d *transf.* (The width of) a person's hips or buttocks. *colloq.* E20. 11 In a steam engine etc.: an oscillating pivoted shaft through which the piston movement is transmitted to the crank. M18.

3 AV *2 Kings* 6:2 Let vs . . take thence euery man a beame, and let vs make vs a place there where we may dwell. H. ALLEN The shafts . . also formed the beams of the wagon platform. M. LASKI Everything in splendid confusion was tacked to the walls, to the platform, to the beams in the ceiling. J. BRONOWSKI If we picture a beam lying across two columns, then . . the stresses in the beam increase as we move the columns farther apart. *cross-beam*, *hammer-beam*, *stretching beam*, *summer-beam*, etc. 6 D. LODGE The rain swept in great folds across the beam of the headlights. A. GRAY A beam of early morning summer sunlight shone on it and on me. c S. SPENDER He . . landed on a beam when all but the last drop of petrol was exhausted. K. KESEY Carrying the [TV] set every place the cord will reach, in search of a good beam. 9 BYRON Her cheek all purple with the beam of youth. S. GIBBONS She found her hand taken into a friendly clasp and met the beam of a wind-reddened, open, boyish countenance. S. O'FAOLÁIN Then he began to smile, slowly expanding his mouth into a wide beam of relief. 10c F. MARRYAT Land on the lee beam! d HUGH WALPOLE He stood watching disgustedly Bigges' broad beam.

Phrases: **abaft the beam** to one side and behind an imaginary line drawn across the centre of a ship. **beam in one's eye** *fig.* a fault great compared to another's (*Matt.* 7:3). **before the beam** to one side and ahead of an imaginary line drawn across the centre of a ship. **kick the beam** be greatly outweighed in the balance. *main beam*: see MAIN *a.* **off (the) beam** *colloq.* not on the right track, mistaken. **on the beam** *colloq.* on the right track, right. *post-and-beam*: see POST *n.*[1] RETRICK *one's beams*. *split beam*: see SPLIT *ppl a.* **strike the beam** = *kick the beam* above.

Comb.: **beam-compass(es)**: with the legs connected by a beam with sliding sockets, for drawing large circles; **beam-ends** the ends of a ship's beams; *on her beam-ends*, (of a ship) on its side, almost capsizing; *on one's beam-ends* (fig.), at the end of one's resources; **beam engine** a steam engine having a beam (sense 11 above); **beam sea**: one rolling against a ship's side; **beam-splitter** a device for dividing a beam of radiation into two (or more) separate beams; **beam-tree** whitebeam.

beamed *a.* (*a*) having or emitting beams of light (usu. of a specified quality); (*b*) (of a stag) having a horn of the fourth year; (*c*) built with a beam or beams: OE. **beamish** *a.* (*arch.*) shining brightly, radiant M16. **beamless** *a.* L17.

beam /biːm/ *v.* LME. [f. the n.] 1 *v.t.* Emit in beams; radiate (light, affection, etc.). LME. b Direct (radio signals etc.) to a specific area; transmit. E20. c *Sci. Fiction.* Foll. by *up*: transport (a person) to a spaceship by a directed flow of energy. M20. 2 *v.t.* Stretch (cloth, hide, etc.) over a beam. E17. 3 *v.i.* Shine brightly. M17. 4 *v.i.* Smile broadly or radiantly. L19.

1 W. SHENSTONE The genial sun . . Beams forth ungentle influences. b M. L. KING Television beamed the image of this extraordinary gathering across the border oceans. C. SAGAN A search for signals beamed in our general direction by civilizations interested in communicating with us. 3 G. M. HOPKINS Their harness beams like scythes in morning grass. JOYCE The young May moon, she's beaming, love. 4 J. M. BARRIE Her face beamed with astonishment and mirth. T. DREISER She beamed upon him in a melting and sensuous way.

beamer *n.* (*a*) a person who beams; (*b*) a person who arranges yarn on the beam of a loom; (*c*) *Cricket* a full toss aimed at the batsman's head: M19. **beamingly** *adv.* radiantly M17.

beamy /ˈbiːmi/ *a.* LME. [f. BEAM *n.* + -Y[1].] 1 Emitting beams, radiant. LME. 2 Massive as a (weaver's) beam. M17. 3 Possessing full-grown antlers. L17. 4 Of a ship: broad in the beam. L19.

beaminess *n.* radiance M18.

bean /biːn/ *n.* [OE *bēan* = MDu. *bōne* (Du. *boon*), OHG *bōna* (G *Bohne*), ON *baun*, f. Gmc.] 1a The smooth kidney-shaped edible seed, borne in long pods, of the leguminous plant *Vicia faba*; the plant itself. Also more fully *broad bean*. OE. b (The seed of) any of various related plants, *esp.* the French bean, *Phaseolus vulgaris*. M16. 2 A seed resembling the broad bean in shape, produced by any of several other plants, e.g. coffee, cocoa. LME. 3 Something resembling a bean in shape and size. M16. b The head. *slang* (orig. *US*). E20. 4 A coin, a small sum of money. Usu. in neg. contexts. *slang.* E19.

1b *black bean*, *French bean*, *haricot bean*, *kidney bean*, *Lima bean*, *navy bean*, *runner bean*, *vanilla bean*, *velvet bean*, *yellow bean*, etc.

Phrases: BAKED *beans*. **full of beans** full of energy, in high spirits. **give** (a person) **beans** deal severely with, scold. **hill of beans** (chiefly *N. Amer.*) a thing of little value (freq. in *not worth a hill of beans*, worthless). *jelly bean*: see JELLY *n.*[1] & *v.* **know how many beans make five** be intelligent. **not a bean** *slang* no money whatever. *old bean*: see OLD *a.* *spill the beans*: see SPILL *v.* 12.

Comb.: **bean-bag** a small closed bag filled with beans, used esp. in children's games; *bean-bag chair*, a chair consisting of a large bag filled with loose plastic granules, which takes the shape of the sitter; **bean ball** *Baseball slang* a ball pitched at the batter's head; **bean caper** a plant of the genus *Zygophyllum*, esp. the Mediterranean *Z. fabago*, with flower-buds used as capers; **bean curd** a paste made from soya beans; **beanfeast** (*a*) an annual dinner given to employees by their employer(s) (at which beans and bacon used to be regarded as an indispensable dish); (*b*) a festival, a celebration, a merry time; **bean goose** a grey goose, *Anser fabalis*, breeding in the Arctic and visiting Britain in small numbers in winter; **bean-meal** meal made by grinding beans; **beanpole** (*a*) a pole for beans to twine round; (*b*) *fig.* a tall thin person; **bean sprouts** the sprouts of a legume, esp. the mung bean, used esp. in Chinese cookery; **beanstalk** the stem of a bean plant; **bean trefoil** a poisonous leguminous shrub, *Anagyris foetida*, of the Mediterranean region; **bean tree** any of various trees bearing podded seeds, *esp.* laburnum.

beanery *n.* (*N. Amer. slang*) a cheap restaurant L19.

bean /biːn/ *v.t. slang* (chiefly *N. Amer.*). E20. [f. the n.] Hit on the head.

beanie /ˈbiːni/ *n.* Orig. *US*. E20. [Prob. f. BEAN *n.* 3b + -IE.] A hat; *spec.* a small close-fitting hat worn at the back of the head.

beano /ˈbiːnəʊ/ *n. slang.* Pl. **-os**. L19. [f. BEAN *n.* + -O.] = *beanfeast* s.v. BEAN *n.*

bear /bɛː/ *n.*[1] [OE *bera* = MDu. *bere* (Du. *beer*), OHG *bero* (G *Bär*), f. WGmc: rel. to ON *bjǫrn*.] 1 Any of several large heavily-built mammals constituting the family Ursidae (order Carnivora), with thick fur and a plantigrade gait. OE. b With specifying wd: an animal resembling or (fancifully) likened to a bear. E17. 2 *Astron.* *the Bear* (more fully *the Great Bear*) = URSA *Major*; *the Lesser* or *Little Bear* = URSA *Minor*. LME. 3 *fig.* A rough, unmannerly, or uncouth person. L16. 4 *Stock Exch.* etc. [Perh. w. ref. to expression 'selling the bear's skin before killing the bear'.] Orig., stock contracted to be sold at a set price at a future date, in the seller's expectation of lower market prices then. Now, a person who sells such stock, a speculator for a fall. Cf. BULL *n.*[1] 4. E18. 5 A rough or shaggy mat, *esp.* a block covered with matting for scrubbing the deck of a vessel. L18. 6 *the Bear*, Russia, the former USSR. E19. 7 A figure of a bear made as a child's toy. Cf. TEDDY. E20. 8 [ellipt. for *Smokey Bear* s.v. SMOKY.] A police officer; (*collect.*) *the* police. *slang* (orig. *US*). L20.

1 **black bear** either of two bears, (*a*) (more fully *American black bear*) *Ursus americanus*, of N. American forests; (*b*) (more fully *Asian black bear*) *Selenarctos thibetanus*, a small, mainly herbivorous bear of SE Asia. **brown bear** a bear, *Ursus arctos*, of western N. America and parts of Eurasia that is the world's largest carnivore (cf. GRIZZLY *a.*[1] 2, KODIAK). *cinnamon bear, polar bear, sloth bear, spectacled bear, white bear*, etc. b *koala bear, sea-bear, skunk bear*, etc. 3 LD MACAULAY This great soldier . . was no better than a Low Dutch bear. 6 W. S. CHURCHILL The left paw of the Bear bars Germany from the Black Sea. 8 *sky bear*: see SKY *n.*

Other phrases: **like a bear with a sore head** *colloq.* angry, ill-tempered. **loaded for bear** *US colloq.* fully prepared. **play the bear with** treat rudely and roughly. *Smokey Bear*: see SMOKY *a.*

Comb.: **bear animalcule** = TARDIGRADE *n.* 2; **bear-baiting** *Hist.* setting dogs to attack a captive bear, for sport; **bearberry** (the fruit of) an evergreen shrub or small tree of the chiefly N. American genus *Arctostaphylos*, of the heath family, with white or pinkish flowers, esp. *A. uva-ursi* (more fully *red bearberry*), a trailing moorland plant with bright red astringent berries; **bear-cat** (*a*) the red panda; (*b*) the binturong; (*c*) *N. Amer. colloq.* an aggressive or forceful person; a person of great energy or ability; **bear-covering** *Stock Exch.* the action of a bear in buying stock which he has previously contracted to sell; **beargarden** (*a*) a place set apart for bear-baiting or similar sports; (*b*) *fig.* a scene of tumult; **bear-grass** *N. Amer.* any of various plants with long, coarse, grasslike leaves, *esp.* yucca or a related plant; **bearherd** *Hist.* the keeper of a bear; one who leads a bear for show; **bear-hug** a powerful embrace; **bearleader** *fig.* a rich young man's travelling tutor; **bear market** *Stock Exch.*: in which prices are falling; **bear-pit** a sunken enclosure in which bears are kept; **bear's breech** = ACANTHUS 1; **bear's ear** = AURICULA 1; **bear's foot** stinking hellebore, *Helleborus foetidus*; **bear's garlic** ramsons, *Allium ursinum*; **bear's grease** *arch.* pomade; **bearskin** (*a*) a wrap etc. made of bear's skin; (*b*) a tall furry cap worn by Guards in the British army; **bearskinned** *a.* wearing a bearskin; **Bear State** *US* Arkansas; **bearward** = *bear-herd* above.

bearlike *adv.* & *a.* (*a*) *adv.* in the manner of a bear, roughly; (*b*) *adj.* resembling (that of) a bear: E17.

†bear *n.*[2], *n.*[3] vars. of BERE *n.*[1], *n.*[2]

bear /bɛː/ *v.*[1] Pa. t. **bore** /bɔː/, (*arch.*) **bare** /bɛː/. Pa. pple & ppl a. **borne** /bɔːn/, BORN. See also YBORN. [OE *beran* = OS, OHG *beran*, ON *bera*, Goth. *bairan*, f. Gmc f. IE base also of Skt *bharati*, Armenian *berem*, Gk *pherein*, L *ferre*.] I *v.t.* Carry, hold, possess. 1 Carry (esp. something weighty), transport; bring or take by carrying; *fig.* have, possess. Now *literary* or *formal*. OE. b *Backgammon.* Remove (a piece) from the board at the end of a game. Also foll. by *off*. M16. †c Take along as a companion; carry as a consequence. L16–E17. 2 Carry about with or upon one, esp. visibly; show, display; be known or recognized by (a name, device, etc.); have (a character, reputation, value, etc.) attached to or associated with one. OE. †b Wear (clothes, ornaments). OE–L16. 3 *refl.* Carry or conduct oneself; behave or acquit oneself. ME. 4 Wield, exercise, (power etc.); hold (an office). *arch.* ME. 5 Entertain, harbour, (a feeling etc. towards someone or something; foll. by indirect obj., *for, towards*). ME. 6 Hold or possess (a relation etc.) *to* something else. ME.

1 CHAUCER On his bak he bar . . Anchises. R. HOLINSHED This pope Leo . . bare but seauen and thirtie yeeres of age. SHAKES. *Macb.* I bear a charmed life, which must not yield To one of woman born. E. WAUGH Music was borne in from the next room. T. BLACKBURN I met a child beside a river, Who asked if I would bear him over. K. LAFFAN We all have our crosses to bear. *absol.*: SHAKES. *Rich. II* Forgiveness, horse! Why do I rail on thee, Since thou . . Wast born to bear? 2 SHAKES. *Wint. T.* If I Had servants true about me that bare eyes To see alike mine honour as their profits. STEELE Falshood . . shall hereafter bear a blacker Aspect. W. H. PRESCOTT Four beautiful girls, bearing the names of the principal goddesses. A. P. STANLEY The staff like that still borne by Arab chiefs. R. GRAVES Postumus . . now bore the rank of regimental commander. S. BRETT The old comedian's face bore a smile of unambiguous cynicism. 3 W. S. CHURCHILL Let us . . so bear ourselves that if the British Empire and its Commonwealth last for a thousand years men will still say, 'This was their finest hour'. 4 COVERDALE *1 Chron.* 27:6 Sonnes . . which bare rule in the house of their fathers. R. ASCHAM To beare some office in the common wealth. 5 SWIFT The contempt they bear for practical geometry. 6 J. LOCKE Nothing finite bears any proportion to infinite. G. GREENE I thought I could believe in some kind of a God that bore no relation to ourselves.

II Support, sustain, endure. 7 *v.t.* Sustain, support (a weight, strain, or burden). OE. b *v.t.* Sustain successfully, withstand; admit of, be fit for. E16. c *v.i.* Support a load. L17. 8 *v.t.* Sustain (something painful); (usu. in neg. or interrog. contexts) endure, tolerate, reconcile oneself to, bring oneself *to do* something. OE. b *v.i.* Foll. by *with*: be patient or put up with, make allowance for. M16. 9a *v.t.* Hold, keep, or lift *up*; prevent from falling or sinking; hold aloft, hold in position on the top etc. ME. b *v.t.* Keep going (the refrain or a part of a song). *arch.* LME. c *v.i.* Keep one's spirits or courage *up*; cheer *up*. M17. 10 *v.t.* Have written, inscribed, etc., on it; (in *pass.*) be registered or enrolled in a book etc. thus. ME. 11 *v.t.* Have or convey the meaning *that*, purport *to be*. *arch.* ME.

7 J. SMEATON Proportionate . . to the stress it was likely to bear. *fig.*: AV *Gen.* 13:6 The land was not able to beare them, that they might dwell together. E. F. SCHUMACHER A large part of the costs of private enterprise has been borne by the public authorities. C. PRIEST This, alone of all my problems, was one . . for which I bore some responsibility. b SHAKS. *Lear* Thy great employment Will not bear question. J. RUSKIN It is not less the boast of some styles that they can bear ornament. J. RABAN Only the great families of the Italian Renaissance could seriously bear comparison with the Gulf emirs. c G. WASHINGTON Attempted to go into the Neck on the Ice, but it wd. not bear. 8 AV *Gen.* 4:13 My punishment is greater then I can beare. SMOLLETT With an intrepid heart . . he bears the brunt of their whole artillery. R. L. STEVENSON Though I could, perhaps, bear to die, I could not bear to look upon my fate as it approached. W. CATHER It will take more courage to bear your going than everything that has happened before. N. COWARD *Sibyl*: I don't believe you like mother. *Elyot*: Like her! I can't bear her. V. S. PRITCHETT Father could not bear a drip of oil or grease on his own hands. b E. A. FREEMAN A foreign King had to be borne with. F. KING Sometimes he would wonder if she really liked him at all or merely bore with him out of her kindness and tolerance. 9a R. KNOLLES The Spaniards bearing themselves upon their wealth, were too proud. AV *Judg.* 16:29 The two middle pillars . . on which it was borne vp. O. CROMWELL To bear up our honour at sea. P. SHAFFER A small Queen Anne table bearing a fine opaline lamp. c BURKE Bearing up against those vicissitudes of fortune. E. B. BROWNING He bears up, and talks philosophy. 10 STEELE A long Letter bearing Date the fourth Instant. JOHN PHILLIPS Coins, bearing the effigy of the Horse. H. COX All persons borne on the books of Queen's ships in commission. 11 LEIGH HUNT A portrait . . bearing to be the likeness of a certain Erasmus Smith, Esq.

III *v.t.* Produce, give birth to. 12 Bring forth, produce, yield (fruit, crops, minerals, etc.). OE. 13 Of a woman or (less commonly) any female mammal: give birth to (a child, children, young); provide (offspring, w. the father as indirect obj. or w. *to*). See also BORN *pple* & *a.* OE.

12 SHAKES. *Timon* The oaks bear mast, the briars scarlet hips. DRYDEN India, black Ebon and white Ivory bears. ANNE STEVENSON Some beds bear nearly a thousand petunias. 13 I. MURDOCH Fanny had lived, she had married a distinguished man, she had borne children. NEB *Luke* 23:29 Happy are the barren, the wombs that never bore a child. TOLKIEN Aredhel bore to Eöl a son in the shadows of Nan Elmoth.

IV Push, move, apply. 14 *v.t.* Move onward by pressure; force, drive. ME. †15 *v.t.* Pierce, stab (*through*). ME–L15. 16a *v.i.* Press or come (*up*)*on* or †*at* with (esp. downward) force; exert or transmit mechanical pressure (*up*)*on* or *against*; apply weight, thrust. LME. b *v.t.* Bring *down* or tend to force *down* with pressure. L17. 17 *v.i.* (Try to) move in a certain direction, esp. deliberately or persistently; diverge, turn; (of a vessel) sail in a given direction. Freq. w. advs. L16. b Extend or stretch away in a given direction. E17. 18 *v.i.* Lie off or be situated in a certain direction from a given point. Cf. BEARING 5. L16. 19 *v.i.* Foll. by (*up*)*on*: exert a practical effect on; have relevance to. L17. 20 *v.i.* Of a gun: have the intended target in its line of fire, be aimed at the target. L17.

14 SOUTHEY Borne backward Talbot turns. 16a L. T. C. ROLT The frame was . . moved forward . . by horizontal jacks bearing against the newly completed brickwork behind. *fig.*: SOUTHEY While she pray'd the load of care Less heavily bore on her heart. b TENNYSON The dead weight . . bore it down. N. SHUTE He bore his weight down on the plate with her and the boat lifted sodden sails out of the water. 17 SHAKES. *Jul. Caes.* Stand back. Room! Bear back. J. SMEATON The wind being now fair for that port, we bore away for it. H. I. JENKINSON On arriving at the top of the crag, bear a little to the right. TOLKIEN They turned north and then bore to the north-west. 18 SHAKES. *Tam. Shr.* This is Lucentio's house; My father's bears more toward the market-place. P. O'BRIAN Dawn on the seventeenth instant, the Dry Salvages bearing SSE two leagues. 19 J. MASTERS We've been able to get a little information bearing . . on the accident. 20 H. NELSON Our after guns ceased to bear. CARLYLE Finck had no artillery to bear on Daun's transit through the Pass.

V Special uses of *borne* pa. pple & ppl a. 21 As 2nd elem. of a comb.: carried or transported by, as *airborne* etc. E17.

Phrases, & with advs. in specialized senses: *bear a bob*: see BOB *n.*[1] *bear a great stroke*: see STROKE *n.*[1] **bear a hand** assist, help. **bear and forbear** be patient and tolerant. **bear a part** (*a*) take part, share, (*in*); (*b*) play a part as actor or actress. *bear arms*: see ARM *n.*[2] *bear a stroke*: see STROKE *n.*[1] **bear away** carry away, win as a prize (*bear away the bell*: see BELL *n.*[1]). **bear company** accompany (a person). **bear date** be dated (as specified). **bear down** (*a*) push to the ground, overthrow, prevail against; (*b*) see sense 16b above; (*c*) exert downward force, press down *on*; (*d*) *bear down* (*up*)*on* (Naut.), sail with the wind towards; *gen.* move rapidly and purposefully towards. **bear fruit** *fig.* yield results, be productive. *bear great state*: see STATE *n.* **bear hard** (*a*) *arch.* take badly, resent; (*b*) *bear hard* (*up*)*on*, oppress, affect adversely or injuriously. **bear heavily** = *bear hard* above (now only sense b). **†bear in hand** profess falsely; delude, deceive. **bear in mind** not forget, keep in one's thoughts. **bear off** †(*a*) repel, ward off; (*b*) carry off, win as a prize; see also sense 1b above. **bear out** (*a*) *arch.* support, back up, (a person); (*b*) corroborate, tend to confirm or justify (a statement, a person making a statement). **†bear over** = *bear down* (a) above. *bear state*: see STATE *n. bear suspicion*: see SUSPICION *n. bear tack*: see TACK *n.*[1] **bear testimony** testify (*to*). *bear the bell*: see BELL *n.*[1] *bear the stroke*: see STROKE *n.*[1] **bear up** *Naut.* bring the vessel before the wind, sail to leeward; (see also senses 9a, c above). **bear witness** testify (*to*). **be borne in upon one** be impressed upon one, become one's conviction (*that*). **bring to bear** bring into effective operation, begin using, aim (a gun etc.), (*bring pressure to bear*: see PRESSURE *n.*). *grin and bear it*: see GRIN *v.*[2]

¶The pple *born* is now used only in sense 13, and there only in the pass. when not followed by *by* and the mother. In all other cases *borne* is usual.

bear /bɛː/ *v.*[2] M19. [f. BEAR *n.*[1] 4.] *Stock Exch.* etc. 1 *v.i.* Speculate for a fall. M19. 2 *v.t.* Produce a fall in the price of (stocks etc.). M19.

bearable /ˈbɛːrəb(ə)l/ *a.* LME. [f. BEAR *v.*[1] + -ABLE.] Able to be borne; endurable, tolerable.

bearableness *n.* (earlier in UNBEARABLENESS) M19. **bearably** *adv.* (earlier in UNBEARABLY) L19.

bearance /ˈbɛːr(ə)ns/ *n.* E18. [f. BEAR *v.*[1] + -ANCE.] 1 Endurance, toleration. E18. 2 = BEARING 6. *rare*. E19.

bearbind /ˈbɛːbʌɪnd/ *n. dial.* Also **-bine** /-bʌɪn/. LME. [f. *bear* var. of BERE *n.*[1] + BIND *v.*] Convolvulus or a similar twining plant.

beard /bɪəd/ *n.* [OE *beard* = OFris. *berd*, MDu. *baert* (Du. *baard*), OHG *bart*, G *Bart*, f. WGmc, rel. to Old Ch. Slav. *brada*, L *barba*.] 1 A mass of hair growing on the chin and lower face of a man (excluding the moustache and whiskers), esp. as a cultivated appendage; such hair collectively. OE. 2 The hair of the face or chin of any animal, e.g. a lion or goat. ME. b Chiefly *Zool.* Any of various animal growths suggestive of or resembling beards; *esp.* the gills of an oyster; the byssus of a mollusc; the beak-bristles of certain birds. LME. 3 *Bot.* A tuft of hairs or bristles on a plant; *esp.* the awn of a grass. LME. 4 A protruding part, esp. †(*a*) the barb of an arrow, fish-hook, etc.; (*b*) *Typogr.* the part of the type above and below the letter. E17. 5 The tail of a comet. *obs.* exc. *Hist.* M17.

1 P. BARKER Men with white beards and wing collars. *Independent* I cut a week's beard away from my face..

Phrases: *beards wag*: see WAG *v.* *Jupiter's beard*: see JUPITER. *old man's beard*: see OLD MAN. *Spanish beard*: see SPANISH *a.* *torpedo beard*: see TORPEDO *n.* *Vandyke beard*: see VANDYKE *n.* 4.

beardless *a.* having no beard; *fig.* youthful, immature: ME. **beardlet** *n.* a small beard or awn L19. **beardlike** *a.* resembling a man's beard M19. **beardy** *a.* bearded L16.

beard /bɪəd/ *v.* ME. [f. the n.] 1 *v.t.* Cut off the beard of; seize the beard of. ME. b *fig.* Oppose openly, defy; attack audaciously. E16. 2 *v.t.* Provide with a beard. Usu. in *pass.* LME. †3 *v.i.* Grow a beard. L15–L17.

1 **beard the lion in his den** (or **lair**) attack someone on his or her own ground or subject.

bearded /ˈbɪədɪd/ *a.* ME. [f. BEARD *n.*, *v.*: see -ED², -ED¹.] 1 Having a beard, awn, or similar growth. ME. 2 Of a comet etc.: having a tail. *obs.* exc. *Hist.* LME. †3 Barbed or jagged. E17–E19.

Special collocations: **bearded collie**: of a shaggy breed with long hair on the face. **bearded iris** any of several cultivated irises with beards on the falls. *bearded* REEDLING. **bearded seal** an Arctic seal, *Erignathus barbatus*, of the Arctic Ocean. **bearded tit** = REEDLING 2. **bearded vulture** = LAMMERGEYER.

beardedness *n.* L19.

beardie /ˈbɪədi/ *n.* Also **-dy**. E19. [f. BEARD *n.* + -IE.] 1 (A nickname for) a bearded man. E19. 2 A loach; a stickleback. *Sc.* E19. b The red-brown gadoid fish *Lotella callarias* of S. Australian coasts. Also called *ling*. L19. 3 A bearded collie. E20.

bearer /ˈbɛːrə/ *n.* ME. [f. BEAR *v.*¹ + -ER¹.] 1 A person who or (less commonly) thing which carries or helps to carry; a porter. ME. b *spec.* A person who helps to carry a coffin at a funeral; a pallbearer. M17. c *spec.* A palanquin-carrier; a personal servant. *Anglo-Ind.* M18. 2 A person who brings letters, a message, news, etc.; a messenger. ME. 3†a A person who supports a burden (*lit.* & *fig.*); an upholder. LME–M18. b Something which supports or sustains a burden or takes off pressure. L17. 4 A person who or thing which brings forth or produces (fruit, offspring, etc.). LME. 5 The holder of an office or rank; the possessor of a name, quality, etc. L16. 6 *Her.* A person who bears heraldic arms. L16. 7 The holder or presenter of a cheque, draft, etc.; the holder of shares in a company etc. L17.

1 AV *2 Chron.* 2:18 To be bearers of burdens. W. MORRIS Fleeces.. In their own bearer's blood were dyed. J. HILTON They travelled in bamboo sedan-chairs, swinging perilously over precipices while their bearers.. picked a way nonchalantly down the steep track. W. STEVENS Lantern without a bearer, you drift. *cupbearer*: see CUP *n.* *pallbearer*: see PALL *n.*¹ *standard-bearer*: see STANDARD *n.* *stretcher-bearer*: see STRETCHER. *train-bearer*: see TRAIN *n.*¹ c *sardar-bearer*: see SARDAR 2. 4 **good** etc. **bearer** a plant that produces well etc. 5 SHAKES. *2 Hen. IV* O majesty! When thou dost pinch thy bearer [etc.]. JOYCE The gallant young Oxonian (the bearer.. of one of the most timehonoured names in Albion's history). *office-bearer*: see OFFICE *n.*

bearing /ˈbɛːrɪŋ/ *n.* ME. [f. BEAR *v.*¹ + -ING¹.] 1 The action of BEAR *v.*¹: carrying, bringing; supporting, sustaining, enduring; giving birth, producing; thrusting, pressing. ME. 2 Manner of carrying oneself, bodily attitude; demeanour. ME. 3 A material support; a supporting surface. ME. 4 A heraldic charge or device: in *pl.*, that which is depicted on a coat of arms; a heraldic achievement, a coat of arms. M16. 5 The direction in which a place, object, etc., lies; direction of movement, orientation; in *pl.*, (knowledge of) relative position. M17. 6 *sing.* & (freq.) in *pl.* Part of a machine which bears friction, esp. between a rotating part and its housing. L18. 7 Practical relation or effect (*up*)*on*; influence, relevance. L18.

2 W. BLACK The.. courtesy of his bearing towards women. J. R. ACKERLEY Upon the platform.. was a tall, handsome, elegantly tailored young man, of military bearing. 3 J. SMEATON Each floor.. lying upon the horizontal bearings furnished by these ledges. 4 TENNYSON A gateway she discerns With armorial bearings stately. 5 L. GARFIELD On went the old gentleman, confident now in his bearings, deeper and deeper into the.. Town. H. WOUK The RAF could measure the range and bearing of a ship down to a hundred yards or less. *lose, take,* etc., *one's bearings. fig.*: DAY LEWIS A child first begins to get his bearings and realise its identity by seeing itself reflected from two opposite sides—its father and its mother. 6 *ball-bearing*: see BALL *n.*¹ FOOTSTEP *bearing*. *roller bearing*: see ROLLER *n.*¹ *split bearing*: see SPLIT *a.* 7 CONAN DOYLE We seem to be faced by a long series of inexplicable incidents with no bearing upon each other. D. M. THOMAS She could not think of any unpleasant episode which might have had a bearing on her illness.

Comb.: **bearing metal**: used for antifriction linings of bearings. **bearing rein** a fixed rein passing from the bit to the harness pad, serving to keep the horse's head up and its neck arched.

bearish /ˈbɛːrɪʃ/ *a.* M18. [f. BEAR *n.*¹ + -ISH¹.] 1 Like a bear, esp. in manner; rough, surly. M18. 2 *Stock Exch.* etc. Pertaining to, showing, or tending to produce a fall in prices; *gen.* pessimistic. L19.

bearishly *adv.* M19. **bearishness** *n.* M19.

Béarnaise /beɪəˈneɪz, *foreign* bearnɛːz/ *a.* L19. [Fr., fem. of *béarnais* of Béarn, a region of SW France.] *Béarnaise sauce* (also †*sauce béarnaise*), a rich white sauce flavoured with tarragon.

beast /biːst/ *n.* ME. [OFr. *beste* (mod. *bête*) f. pop.L *besta* f. L *bestia*.] 1 *gen.* An animal (orig. including, now as distinct from, man); a creature. Now *dial.* & *joc.* exc. as explicitly contrasted w. *man*. ME. b *The* animal nature in man. M17. 2 A quadruped mammal, as distinct from birds, reptiles, fish, insects, etc.; *esp.* a wild animal, or one hunted as game. ME. 3 A domesticated animal; *esp.* (*a*) a bovine farm animal; (*b*) a draught animal. ME. 4 A brutal, savage, or loathsome person; someone one detests or dislikes (freq. in a weakened sense). ME. b Something loathsome; an abominable or unpleasant example *of*. M19. 5 *Cards.* An obsolete game resembling nap; a penalty at this game, or at ombre or quadrille. M17.

1 AV *Rev.* 13:1 I.. saw a beast rise vp out of the sea, hauing seuen heads, and ten hornes. OED There's a little beast crawling up your back! C. HAMPTON No help at all to man or beast. 2 AV *1 Kings* 4:33 Hee spake also of beasts, and of foule, and of creeping things, and of fishes. G. B. SHAW There are wild beasts in this wood: lions, they say. 3 LD MACAULAY Travellers.. compelled to alight and lead their beasts. D. HOLLIDAY That year the farmers prospered, beasts were fat. 4 SHAKES. *Meas. for M.* O you beast! O faithless coward! O dishonest wretch! STEELE Morn' sends stagg'ring Home a Drunken Beast. E. WAUGH He's in an amorous stupor, poor beast, and doesn't quite know where he is. b W. S. GILBERT It's a beast of a name. H. C. BUNNER I've got to stay and finish my grind. It's a beast.

Phrases: **beast of burden** a draught animal. **beast of prey** an animal that kills and feeds on the flesh of other animals. *blond beast*: see BLOND *a.* **the Beast** Antichrist (*the mark of the Beast*, a sign of heresy or evil nature). **the beast with two backs, two-backed beast** a man and woman copulating. *the nature of the beast*: see NATURE *n.*

¶Orig. used to translate L *animal* (in which it replaced OE *dēor* DEER), and in turn largely supplanted by ANIMAL itself in senses 1–3.

beastie *n.* (*Sc.* or *joc.*) a small animal; an insect: L18. **beastish** *a.* (now *rare*) beastly, brutish LME. **beastlike** *a.* like a beast in nature or manner E16.

beast /biːst/ *v.t.* M17. [f. the n.] 1 Make a beast of; treat or regard as a beast. *rare.* M17. 2 *be beasted*, fail to win the game, incur a penalty, at ombre. M17.

beastings *n.pl.* var. of BEESTINGS.

beastly /ˈbiːstli/ *a.* ME. [f. BEAST *n.* + -LY¹.] †1 Unthinking, unintelligent, irrational. ME–E18. 2 Obeying animal instincts, sensual. ME. 3 Of, pertaining to, or of the nature of a beast; animal, natural. *arch.* LME. 4 Abominable, foul; disgusting, offensive; *colloq.* unpleasant, ill-natured, undesirable, detestable. L16.

1 R. RECORDE To bring the people from beastly rage to manly reason. 2 SWIFT The beastly vice of drinking to excess. 3 J. RUSKIN The 'breeding' of a man is what he gets from the Centaur Chiron; the 'beastly' part of him in a good sense. 4 DISRAELI The steam packet is a beastly conveyance. N. COWARD It was beastly of you to laugh like that, I felt so humiliated. STEVIE SMITH There goes the beastly bell Tolling us to lessons. J. JOHNSTON You must stop biting your nails. It's a beastly habit.

beastliness *n.* beastly quality or behaviour LME.

beastly /ˈbiːstli/ *adv.* LME. [f. BEAST *n.* + -LY².] †1 In a beastly manner, like a beast. LME–E17. 2 (W. adjs.) Abominably, offensively, brutally; now usu. in weakened sense: regrettably, very. M16.

beat /biːt/ *n.*¹ ME. [f. BEAT *v.*¹ Branch III perh. a different wd.] I†1 Beating, whipping. Only in ME. 2 A blow, a stroke in beating. ME. b *Fencing.* A blow struck upon the opponent's weapon. ME. c *Ballet.* = BATTEMENT. E20. 3 A stroke upon or the striking of a drum; the sound or a signal so produced. L17. 4 (The sound produced by) any recurring stroke, or a regular sequence of strokes, e.g. of the heart, the pulse, a clock, etc. E18. 5 A pulsation or periodic variation of amplitude produced by the combination of two sounds or other oscillations (e.g. radio waves) of slightly different frequencies. M18. 6 *Mus.* a A grace-note or ornament. *obs.* exc. *Hist.* E19. b (The movement of a conductor's baton indicating) the principal recurring accent of a piece of music; a unit of measurement of greater or lesser rhythmic accentuation (expressed as a certain number of beats *to* or *in the bar*). L19. c The strongly-marked rhythm of jazz or popular music. M20. 7 *US.* a Something which surpasses, excels, or outdoes something else. E19. b A journalistic scoop. L19. 8 An act or spell of beating to rouse game. L19.

4 E. GASKELL The measured beat of the waters against the sides of the boat. W. FAULKNER The dry, dust-laden air vibrated steadily to the rapid beat of the engine. J. MASTERS One of the telegraphs was ringing the call-attention beat. S. KING Her heart slowed a little and then made speed for a dozen beats or so. 6b M. KENNEDY In 12/8 time there are 12 beats to a bar if taken very slowly, or else 1 for each dotted crotchet. A. SCHLEE Charlotte heard his foot tap restlessly to the beat of the new waltz. OFFBEAT. c L. ARMSTRONG Anything played with beat and soul is jazz. *Crescendo* The jazz Messengers were.. a beat group! 7a O. HENRY I never saw the beat of him for elegance.

II 9 The course or area regularly patrolled by a police officer, sentinel, etc.; *gen.* a person's habitual round, territory, or ambit. E18. 10 A tract of country traversed by a hunter in search of game; a stretch of water fished by an angler. M19.

9 DICKENS The costermongers repaired to their ordinary 'beats' in the suburbs. W. C. WILLIAMS The cop on the beat yelled at him to halt. *fig.*: N. GORDIMER Space is conceived as trackless, but there are beats about the earth frequented by cyclones given female names.

III 11 A distance sailed, or a spell of sailing, to windward. L19.

Comb.: **beatbox** *slang* (*a*) a type of synthesizer producing percussion sounds; (*b*) a radio or radio-cassette player, as used to play loud music, esp. rap; (*c*) music, esp. rap music, with a largely percussion background; **beat frequency** the number of beats per second, equal to the difference in the frequencies of the two interacting tones or oscillations.

beaty *a.* (of jazz etc.) with a strongly marked beat M20.

beat /biːt; *dial. also* beɪt/ *n.*² Also **beet**. LME. [Perh. f. BEAT *v.*¹] A bundle of flax or hemp.

beat /biːt; *dial. also* beɪt/ *n.*³ E17. [Origin unkn.: cf. BEAT *v.*²] The rough sod or matted growth of waste or fallow land.

beat /biːt/ *a.* & *n.*⁴ LME. [Shortened f. BEATEN.] A *adj.* 1 = BEATEN. *arch.* & *dial.* exc. as below. LME. 2 Overcome with hard work or difficulty, worn out, exhausted. Cf. DEAD-BEAT *a.* M18. 3 *beat-up*, (*a*) = sense 2 above; (*b*) worn out, shabby, damaged by overuse. E20. 4 *beat generation*, young people (esp. in the 1950s and 1960s) adopting unconventional dress, culture, and behaviour as a form of self-expression and social protest. M20. b Of, belonging to, or characteristic of the beat generation. M20.

2 P. FRANKAU I was too beat and hazy to take anything in. 3 *Daily Express* We were all beat up after few days of the hardest soldiering you ever dreamt of. W. R. BURNETT The girl was sitting . . in the beat-up leather chair. 4 J. C. HOLMES It was John Kerouac . . who . . said 'You know, this is really a *beat* generation.' b A. TATE For the Beat poets, antiquity ends at about 1956.

B *n.* 1 An idle or worthless fellow, a vagrant. Cf. DEAD-BEAT *n. US.* M19. 2 A member of the beat generation. M20.

beat /biːt/ *v.*[1] Pa. t. **beat**; pa. pple **beaten** /ˈbiːt(ə)n/, (*arch. colloq.*) **beat** (esp. in sense 5). [OE *bēatan* = OHG *bōzan*, ON *bauta* f. Gmc.] I Strike repeatedly, thrash, defeat. 1 *v.t.* Strike with repeated blows. OE. 2 *v.t.* Inflict blows on with fist(s) or a weapon, thrash; punish, assault, or injure in this way. OE. 3 *v.t.* Strike (the ground etc.) in walking, tramp; make (a path) by trampling; make (one's way). OE. 4 Of natural agents or forces: a *v.t.* Dash against, impinge upon, assail. OE. b *v.i.* Impinge, fall, come violently or relentlessly (*against, at,* (*up*)*on*, etc.); freq. (esp. of the sun's rays) foll. by *down*. OE. 5 *v.t.* Overcome, conquer; defeat esp. in games or other competition; get the better of, baffle; outdo, surpass; be quicker than. (See also BEAT *a.*) ME. b *v.i.* Gain the victory, win. *arch.* L18. 6 *v.i.* Strike repeated blows, knock *against, at,* (*up*)*on*. ME. 7 *v.i.* Of the heart, pulse, etc.: throb, pulsate rhythmically; *gen.* pulsate, make rhythmic strokes or sounds. (Cf. sense 17 below.) ME. b Produce a beat (BEAT *n.*[1] 5). E19. †8 *v.t.* Assail with sound or voice. LME–L17. †9 *v.t.* Batter with missiles, bombard. LME–M17. 10 *v.t.* & *i.* a Flap (the wings) forcefully; move the wings up and down rapidly. LME. †b Strike (the eyelids or teeth) together. LME–E17. †11 *v.t.* & *i.* Hammer at (a subject); thrash out, discuss; insist repeatedly (*up*)*on*. L15–M17.

1 S. JOHNSON At what hour they may beat the door of an acquaintance. J. RHYS Then I beat my fist on a stone, forcing myself to speak calmly. **beat one's breast**: in woe or mourning. **beat the air, the wind** strive in vain. 2 J. RUSKIN My brothers would beat me to death, Sir. DAY LEWIS He never beat me, even for major crimes. A. HAILEY The businessman . . attacked the company serviceman with a pipe wrench and beat him badly. *beat into* or *to fits*: see FIT *n.*[2] 3 **beat it** *slang* go away, clear off. 4a WORDSWORTH Some island which the wild waves beat. b AV *Mark* 4:37 The waues beat into the ship. SOUTHEY We heard the rain beat hard. R. MACAULAY That place where the hot sun beat down on the fig trees. 5 STEELE He had beat the Romans in a pitched battle. C. BRONTË I have heard of love at first sight, but this beats all! W. DE LA MARE Why you should have taken so much trouble about it simply beats me. E. BOWEN You can't beat the military swagger. J. FOWLES We played chess and he let me beat him. *beat all to sticks*: see STICK *n.*[1] *beat creation*: see CREATION 4. *beat (someone) at his or her own game*: see GAME *n. beat the band*: see BAND *n.*[3] 3. **beat the bat** *Cricket* make the batsman play and miss. *beat the clock*: see CLOCK *n.*[1] **beat the gun, the pistol** = *jump the gun* s.v. GUN *n. beat the rap*: see RAP *n.*[1] **beat to it**, or **to the punch** get there before, anticipate, (a person). **can you beat it?** *slang*: expr. surprise or amazement. 6 SHAKES. *Lear* O Lear, Lear, Lear! Beat at this gate that let thy folly in. TOLKIEN Gandalf stood before the door of Orthanc and beat on it with his staff. 7 *fig.*: DRYDEN Such Rage of Honey in their Bosom beats. 8 WYCLIF *Ecclus* 43:18 The vois of his thunder schal beten the erthe. 10 SHAKES. *Tam. Shr.* These kites That bate and beat, and will not be obedient. TOLKIEN The great beast beat its hideous wings, and the wind of them was foul.

II Shape, alter, move, etc., by striking. 12 *v.t.* Pulverize with repeated blows, pound. OE. b Mix or stir vigorously, whip (eggs, cream, etc.). LME. 13 *v.t.* Work, shape, deform, by repeated blows; hammer, forge. LME. 14 *v.t.* Impel or force (a thing) to move by blows; drive (a person, army, etc.) by force *away, back, off, out of* (a place), etc. LME. 15 *v.t.* Strike (cover of any kind) in order to rouse or drive out game; range over in hunting; *fig.* work over roughly, search unceremoniously. LME. b *v.i.* Cover an area thus; go *over* or *about* an area thus. L16. †c *v.i.* Of the brain: think hard. E–M17. 16 *v.i.* & *t.* Of game: move here and there in an attempt to escape; take to (a stream etc.) to elude pursuit. LME. 17a *v.t.* Strike (a drum or other instrument) so as to make a rhythmical sound; make or express (a signal, rhythm, etc.) by striking or sounding (often of the heart, a clock, etc.: cf. sense 7 above). LME. b *v.i.* Of a drum etc.: sound when struck. Of a signal: be sounded upon a drum. M17. 18 *v.t.* Break, smash, or bring down by hard knocks. L16. 19 *v.t.* Bring down (a price) by haggling; cause (the seller) to reduce his price. Now only foll. by *down*. L16. 20 *v.t.* Strike (a carpet, a tree, etc.) repeatedly so as to loosen or shake out dust, fruit, etc.; strike repeatedly so as to put out a fire. E17.

11b J. SMEATON The mortar . . was prepared for use by being beat in a very strong wooden bucket. R. WEST She heated the fruit and . . the sugar and beat them up together for half an hour. 13 AV *Isa.* 2:4 They shall beate their swords into plow-shares. 14 DEFOE The blow . . beat the breath . . quite out of my body. W. FAULKNER A Cossack sergeant beat his brains out with the shod hooves of a horse. *fig.*: LEIGH HUNT The classics were beaten into their heads at school. *beat hell out of*: see HELL *n. beat the shit out of*: see SHIT *n. beat the* STUFFING *out of. beat the tar out of*: see TAR *n.*[1] 1. 15 **beat about the bush** *fig.* approach a subject indirectly, not come to the point. *beat one's brains*: see BRAIN *n.* **beat the bounds** trace out the boundaries of a parish, striking certain points with rods. 17a N. MASKELYNE A pendulum clock beating half seconds. LD MACAULAY The drums of Limerick beat a parley. **beat a retreat** *fig.* retreat, abandon an undertaking. **beat time** mark or follow the time of music with the feet, a baton, etc. **beat to quarters** *Naut.* summon the crew to action stations. 18 H. NELSON The man who may have his Ship beat to pieces. 20 AV *Deut.* 4:20 When thou beatest thine olive trees, thou shalt not go over the boughs again. J. HERSEY Mr. Tanimoto . . told others to beat the burning underbrush with their clothes.

III 21 *v.i.* & (*rare*) *t. Naut.* Sail to windward, make way against the wind. Freq. foll. by *up*. L17.

21 POPE The toss'd navies beat the heaving main. W. S. MAUGHAM A big schooner . . was beating up against the breeze towards the harbour. J. CLAVELL To beat to windward . . or to run before the wind.

With advs. & preps. in specialized senses: **beat down** (*a*) *v.phr.t.* force or drive down, demolish, or overthrow by beating; (see also sense 19); (*b*) *v.phr.i.* see sense 4b. **beat in** drive or smash in, or crush, with heavy blows. **beat off** drive back; overcome (a challenge etc.). **beat out** (*a*) forge, make, or remove by hammering; (*b*) extinguish (a fire) by beating; (*c*) sound (a rhythm) by beating; (*d*) *N. Amer.* defeat in a competition. **beat up** (*a*) *v.phr.t.* thrash (a person) severely, assault with blows; (*b*) *v.phr.t.* collect or attract (recruits etc.); (*c*) *v.phr.t.* pass very closely in an aeroplane; (*d*) *v.phr.i.*: see sense 21.

beatable *a.* that can be beaten E17.

beat /biːt; *dial. also* beɪt/ *v.*[2]*t.* M16. [Origin unkn.: cf. BEAT *n.*[3]] Slice off the rough turf from (uncultivated or fallow land).

beaten /ˈbiːt(ə)n/ *ppl a.* ME. [pa. pple of BEAT *v.*[1]] I *gen.* 1 That has been beaten. ME.

II *spec.* 2 Shaped by hammering; *esp.* (of metal) hammered into foil. ME. 3 Trodden, worn by repeated use. L15. †b *fig.* Trite, hackneyed. M16–M18. 4 Whipped to a uniform consistency; pulverized, pounded. M16. 5 Conquered, defeated; overcome, baffled, dejected. M16. 6 *Mil.* Of a zone: covered by gunfire. E20.

3 **beaten-up** = *beat-up* (b) s.v. BEAT *a.* 3. **the beaten track** the ordinary or usual way, the well-frequented route, well-known territory, (*lit.* & *fig.*); freq. in *off the beaten track*.

beatenest /ˈbiːt(ə)nɪst/ *a. US dial.* M19. [f. prec. or *beating* pres. pple of BEAT *v.*[1] + -EST[1].] Best, finest; most unusual.

beater /ˈbiːtə/ *n.* ME. [f. BEAT *v.*[1] + -ER[1].] 1 An implement or device for beating something. ME. b *spec.* A machine for preparing wet pulp for the making of paper. E19. 2 A person who beats something or someone. LME. b *spec.* A person engaged to rouse and drive game. E19.

1 *carpet-beater, egg-beater*, etc. 2 *panel-beater*: see PANEL *n.*[1] *world-beater*: see WORLD *n.*

beath /biːð/ *v.t.* Long *obs.* exc. *dial.* [OE *bepian* f. Gmc: rel. to BATHE *v.*] †1 Bathe, foment. OE–ME. 2 Heat (unseasoned wood) in order to straighten it. LME.

beatific /bɪːəˈtɪfɪk/ *a.* M17. [Fr. *béatifique* or L *beatificus*, f. *beatus* blessed: see -FIC.] Making blessed, imparting supreme happiness; *colloq.* (of a smile etc.) blissful, serenely happy.

beatific vision *Chr. Theol.* the first sight of the glories of heaven; the direct experience of God by those in heaven.

beatifical *a.* (now *rare*) E17. **beatifically** *adv.* E17.

beatification /bɪˌatɪfɪˈkeɪʃ(ə)n/ *n.* E16. [(O)Fr. *béatification* or eccl.L *beatificatio(n-)*, f. *beatificat-* pa. ppl stem of *beatificare*: see next, -ATION.] 1 The action of making or being made blessed. E16. 2 *RC Ch.* A declaration by the Pope that a deceased person is in a state of bliss, constituting a first step towards canonization and permitting public veneration. E17.

beatify /bɪˈatɪfʌɪ/ *v.t.* M16. [(O)Fr. *béatifier* or eccl.L *beatificare*, f. L *beatus* blessed: see -FY.] 1 Make blessed or supremely happy. M16. 2 *RC Ch.* Announce the beatification of; declare blessed. E17.

†**beatille pie** *n. phr.* see BATTALIA PIE.

beating /ˈbiːtɪŋ/ *vbl n.* ME. [f. BEAT *v.*[1] + -ING[1].] I *gen.* 1 The action of BEAT *v.*[1] ME.

II *spec.* 2 A thrashing; chastisement or assault with blows. ME. 3 A pulsation or throbbing esp. of the heart. LME. 4 A defeat; defeating, surpassing. L19.

2 **beating-up** a violent assault on a person. 4 **have the beating of** be able to defeat. **take some** or **a lot of beating** be hard to defeat or surpass.

beatitude /bɪˈatɪtjuːd/ *n.* LME. [(O)Fr. *béatitude* or L *beatitudo*, f. *beatus* blessed: see -TUDE.] 1 Supreme blessedness; bliss. LME. 2 A declaration of blessedness, a blessing; *spec.* (in *pl.*) those made by Jesus in the Sermon on the Mount (*Matt.* 5:3–11). E16. 3 *his, your, Beatitude*: an honorific patriarchal title in the Orthodox Church. M17. 4 = BEATIFICATION 2. M19.

beatnik /ˈbiːtnɪk/ *n.* M20. [f. BEAT *a.* & *n.*[4] + -NIK.] A member of the beat generation.

Beatrician /bɪəˈtrɪʃ(ə)n/ *a.* M20. [f. *Beatrice* (see below) + -IAN.] Of, pertaining to, or resembling (the vision of) Beatrice in Dante's *Vita Nuova* and *Divina Commedia*; of or concerning a revelatory or transcendental vision, experience, etc.

beatster /ˈbiːtstə/ *n.*[1] Also **beet-**. L16. [f. BEET *v.* + -STER.] A mender or mounter of fishing nets.

beatster /ˈbiːtstə/ *n.*[2] M20. [f. BEAT *a.* & *n.*[4] + -STER.] A member of the beat generation.

beau /bəʊ/ *n.* Pl. **beaux** /bəʊz/, **beaus**. L17. [Fr., use as n. of adj., ult. f. L *bellus* fine, beautiful.] 1 A fashionable man, a ladies' man; a fop, a dandy. L17. 2 A lady's male companion, a suitor; a boyfriend, a lover. Now chiefly *N. Amer.* E18.

beauish *a.* foppish, dandified L17.

beaufin *n.* see BIFFIN.

Beaufort scale /ˈbəʊfət skeɪl/ *n. phr.* M19. [Sir Francis *Beaufort* (1774–1857), Eng. admiral.] A scale of whole numbers denoting ranges of wind speed, from 0 for 0–0.2 metres per second (calm) to 12 for over 32.6 metres per second (hurricane).

¶The scale is sometimes extended to higher numbers.

beau geste /bo ʒɛst/ *n. phr.* Pl. ***beaux gestes*** (pronounced same). E20. [Fr. = splendid gesture.] A display of magnanimity; a generous act.

beau gregory /bəʊ ˈgrɛg(ə)ri/ *n. phr.* M19. [Origin unkn.] A blue and yellow percoid fish, *Eupomacentrus leucostictus* (family Pomacentridae), of the W. Indies and Florida.

beau ideal /bəʊ ʌɪˈdɪəl/ *n. phr.* E19. [Fr. *beau idéal* = ideal beauty (now often misunderstood as = beautiful ideal): see BEAU, IDEAL.] One's highest or ideal type of excellence or beauty; the perfect model.

Beaujolais /ˈbəʊʒəleɪ, *foreign* boʒɔlɛ/ *n.* M19. [See below.] A red or (less commonly) white light burgundy wine produced in the Beaujolais district of France.

Beaujolais nouveau /nuːˈvəʊ, *foreign* nuvo/ [= new]: of the latest vintage.

Beaumé *n.* var. of BAUMÉ.

beau monde /bəʊ ˈmɒnd, *foreign* bo mɔ̃ːd/ *n. phr.* L17. [Fr. = fine world.] (The world of) fashionable society.

beaumontage /bəʊmɒnˈteɪʒ/ *n.* Also **Beaumont('s) egg** /ˌbəʊmɒnt(s) ˈɛg/ & other vars. L19. [Origin unkn.] A composition used to conceal cracks and holes in metal, wood, etc.

Beaune /bəʊn, *foreign* boːn/ *n.* E19. [A town in the department of Côte d'Or, France.] A red burgundy wine produced in the district around Beaune.

beau-pot /ˈbəʊpɒt/ *n.* M18. [Alt. of *bough-pot* s.v. BOUGH *n.*] (A large vase containing) a display of cut flowers.

beau rôle /bo roːl/ *n. phr.* Pl. ***beaux rôles*** (pronounced same). L19. [Fr. = fine role.] A fine acting part; the leading part.

beau sabreur /bo sabrœːr/ *n. phr.* Pl. ***beaux sabreurs*** (pronounced same). M19. [Fr. = fine (or handsome) swordsman: orig. a sobriquet of Joachim Murat (1767–1815), Fr. cavalry officer and brother-in-law of Napoleon.] A gallant warrior, a handsome or dashing adventurer.

beaut /bjuːt/ *n.* & *a. slang.* Chiefly *N. Amer.*, *Austral.*, & *NZ.* M19. [Abbrev. of BEAUTY.] A *n.* A beautiful or outstanding person or thing. M19. B *adj.* Beautiful, first-rate. M20.

beauté du diable /bote dy djaːbl/ *n. phr.* M19. [Fr. = devil's beauty.] Superficial attractiveness; captivating charm.

beauteous /ˈbjuːtɪəs/ *a. literary.* LME. [f. BEAUTY after *bounteous*, *plenteous*.] Beautiful.

beauteously *adv.* L15. **beauteousness** *n.* M17.

beautician /bjuːˈtɪʃ(ə)n/ *n.* E20. [f. BEAUTY + -ICIAN.] A person who runs a beauty parlour; a specialist in beauty treatment.

beautification /ˌbjuːtɪfɪˈkeɪʃ(ə)n/ *n.* M17. [f. BEAUTIFY: see -FICATION.] The action of beautifying; adornment.

beautiful /ˈbjuːtɪfʊl, -f(ə)l/ *a.* & *n.* LME. [f. BEAUTY + -FUL.] A *adj.* Full of beauty, delightful to the eye or ear, or to any faculty or taste; morally or intellectually impressive or satisfying; *colloq.* that one likes very much; very good, excellent; pleasant, delightful. LME.

AV *Ps.* 48:2 Beautifull for situation, the ioy of the whole earth is mount Sion. D. HUME Another argument . . which seems to me very strong and beautiful. N. HAWTHORNE It had been the beautifullest of weather all day. P. G. HAMERTON A beautiful patience, and resignation. R. KIPLING Everybody paid in full—beautiful feelin'. E. ST V. MILLAY Sweet sounds, oh, beautiful music, do not cease! G. B. SHAW Her lover, a beautiful youth of eighteen. M. DE LA ROCHE I'll never forget how beautiful you were to me. ALDOUS HUXLEY A very nice fellow and a beautiful pianist. E. O'NEILL Your mother was one of the most beautiful girls you could ever see. DAY LEWIS It is . . a face which might be beautiful one day and plain another, but never uninteresting. **beautiful letters** *US* = BELLES-LETTRES. **beautiful people** *colloq.* (*a*) hippies, *esp.* flower people; (*b*) the fashionable rich. **the — beautiful**: w. the adj. postposed for emphasis or irony; the — in its ideal form, esp. as a cult.

B *absol.* as *n.* 1 Beautiful one. Used chiefly as a form of address. M16. 2 That which is beautiful; *the* qualities constituting beauty. M18.

beautifully *adv.* in a beautiful manner, delightfully; *colloq.* very well, excellently: M16. **beautifulness** *n.* E16.

beautify /ˈbjuːtɪfʌɪ/ *v.t.* E16. [f. next + -FY.] Make beautiful; adorn, embellish.

beautifier *n.* L16.

beauty /ˈbjuːti/ *n.* & *v.* ME. [AN *beuté*, OFr. *belte*, *beaute* (mod. *beauté*) f. Proto-Romance, f. L *bellus*: see BEAU, -TY¹.] A *n.* 1 That quality or combination of qualities which delights the senses or mental faculties; *esp.* that combination of shape, colour, and proportion which is pleasing to the eye. ME. b (B-.) This quality personified. LME. 2 A beautiful feature, a charm, an embellishment; a particular point giving pleasure or satisfaction. ME. b In *pl.* (In titles) choice examples of the work of a writer etc. *arch.* M18. 3 A beautiful person, *esp.* a beautiful woman. LME. b Beautiful persons collectively. E17. 4 A beautiful thing; a particularly good specimen of something. M18. 5 *Particle Physics.* A quark flavour associated with a charge of −⅓. Also called *bottom.* (Symbol *b.*) L20.

1 KEATS A thing of beauty is a joy for ever; Its loveliness increases: it will never Pass into nothingness. TENNYSON There sat . . All beauty compass'd in a female form, The Princess. R. W. EMERSON We ascribe beauty to that which is simple; which has no superfluous parts; which exactly answers its end. W. S. GILBERT There is beauty in the bellow of the blast, There is grandeur in the growling of the gale. T. E. LAWRENCE That trumpet call had an almost liquid beauty. M. DRABBLE Her gawky, bony clumsiness had suddenly transformed itself into dazzling beauty. *line of beauty*: see LINE *n.*² 2 AV *Ps.* 110:3 Thy people shalbe willing in the day of thy power, in the beauties of holinesse from the wombe of the morning. S. RICHARDSON That's the beauty of it; to offend and make up at pleasure. LD MACAULAY The one beauty of the resolution is its inconsistency. 3 P. S. BUCK It is better to be first with an ugly woman than the hundredth with a beauty. *bathing beauty*: see BATHE *v.* 5. *sleeping beauty*: see SLEEPING *ppl a.* b BYRON Belgium's capital had gather'd then Her Beauty and her Chivalry. 4 P. G. WODEHOUSE She . . swung her right and plugged Slingsby a perfect beauty in the eye. In names of butterflies and moths: *brindled beauty*, *Camberwell beauty*, *oak beauty*, *painted beauty*, etc.

Comb.: **beauty contest** a competition for a prize given to the woman judged the most beautiful; **beauty parlour** an establishment in which beauty treatment is practised professionally; **beauty queen** a winner of a beauty contest; **beauty salon**, (*US*) **shop** = *beauty parlour* above; **beauty sleep**: before midnight; **beauty spot** (*a*) a small patch placed on a woman's face as a foil to her complexion; (*b*) a beautiful locality; **beauty treatment** the use of cosmetics, face-massage, manicuring, hairdressing, etc., to enhance personal appearance.

B *v.t.* Beautify, adorn. *arch.* LME.

beautiless *a.* L16.

beaux *n.pl.* see BEAU.

beaux arts /boz ɑːr/ *n.* & *a. phr.* Also ***beaux-arts.*** E19. [Fr. *beaux-arts.*] A *n. phr. pl.* Fine arts. Also *ellipt.*, the *École des Beaux-Arts* in Paris. E19. B *adj. phr.* Of or pertaining to the classical decorative style maintained by the *École des Beaux-Arts* esp. in the 19th cent. E20.

beaux esprits *n. phr.* pl. of BEL ESPRIT.

beaux gestes *n. phr.* pl. of BEAU GESTE.

†**beauxite** *n.* var. of BAUXITE.

beaux rôles, ***sabreurs*** *n. phrs.* pls. of BEAU RÔLE, SABREUR.

beaux yeux /boz jø/ *n. phr.* E19. [Fr.] Beautiful eyes; admiring glances; favourable regard.

beaver /ˈbiːvə/ *n.*¹ & *a.* [OE *beofor*, *befor* = (M)LG, (M)Du. *bever*, OHG *bibar* (G *Biber*), ON *bjórr* f. Gmc, ult. f. IE base meaning 'brown'.] A *n.* 1 Pl. same, -s. A semi-aquatic rodent (of which there are two species, the Eurasian *Castor fiber* and the N. American *C. canadensis*), which has a broad flat paddle-like tail and soft fur, and is notable for its habit of making dams to maintain a supply of water, and its ability to gnaw down trees. OE. 2 The fur of the beaver. LME. 3 A hat made of beaver's fur. E16. 4 A heavy woollen cloth resembling beaver's fur. M18. 5 A shade of brown like the colour of beaver's fur. L19. 6 (B-.) A member of a group of six- to eight-year-old boys affiliated to the Scout Association. L20.

1 **eager beaver** *colloq.* a zealous or overzealous person. MOUNTAIN *beaver.* **work like a beaver** be very industrious, work hard.

B *attrib.* or as *adj.* Made of beaver's fur; coloured like beaver's fur. LME.

Comb.: **Beaverboard** *N. Amer.* (proprietary name for) a type of wood-fibre building-board; **beaver cloth** = sense 4 above; *beaver-dam*: see DAM *n.*¹ 1b; **beaver lamb** lambskin cut and dyed to resemble beaver's fur; *beaver meadow*: see MEADOW *n.* 3; **beaver-tail** a tapering wedge-shaped end.

beaver /ˈbiːvə/ *n.*² *obs.* exc. *Hist.* L15. [OFr. *baviere* orig. child's bib, f. *baver* slaver, f. Proto-Romance.] The lower face-guard of a helmet.

Beaver /ˈbiːvə/ *n.*³ Pl. -s, same. L18. [f. BEAVER *n.*¹, tr. Chipewyan *Tsa-ttine* dwellers among beavers.] A member of a group of Athapaskan peoples of northern Alberta, Canada; the language of this group.

beaver /ˈbiːvə/ *n.*⁴ *slang.* E20. [Origin unkn.] 1 A bearded man; a beard. E20. 2 The female genitals (with pubic hair); a woman, a girl (freq. considered *offensive*). Chiefly *N. Amer.* M20.

2 *split beaver*: see SPLIT *a.*

beaver *n.*⁵ see BEVER *n.*

beaver /ˈbiːvə/ *v.i.* M20. [f. BEAVER *n.*¹] *beaver away*, work very hard or persistently (*at*).

beavered /ˈbiːvəd/ *a.* E17. [f. BEAVER *n.*¹, *n.*², *n.*⁴ + -ED².] Wearing a beaver hat; bearded; (of a helmet etc.) equipped with a beaver.

bebeeru /bɪˈbɪəruː/ *n.* Also **bibira** /bɪˈbɪərə/ & other vars. M19. [Sp. *bibirú* f. Carib.] (The timber of) the greenheart tree, *Ocotea rodiaei*, of northern S. America.

bebleed /bɪˈbliːd/ *v.t.* Long *arch.* Infl. as BLEED *v.* ME. [f. BE- 2 + BLEED *v.*] Soak or stain with blood; make bloody.

†**bebless** *v.t.* Infl. as BLESS *v.*¹ L16–L18. [f. BE- 1 + BLESS *v.*¹] Cover with blessings; bless profusely.

beblister /bɪˈblɪstə/ *v.t.* L16. [f. BE- 1 + BLISTER *v.*] Blister (skin etc.) badly; cover with blisters.

beblood /bɪˈblʌd/ *v.t.* Long *arch.* L16. [f. BE- 4 + BLOOD *n.*] = BEBLEED.

beblubber /bɪˈblʌbə/ *v.t.* M16. [f. BE- 1 + BLUBBER *v.*] Smear over or suffuse with tears; disfigure with weeping. Chiefly as *beblubbered* ppl a.

bebop /ˈbiːbɒp/ *n.* Orig. *US.* M20. [Imit. of a typical musical phrase.] A kind of modern jazz characterized by complex harmony and rhythm.

¶Abbrev. as BOP *n.*²

bebopper *n.* a performer or adherent of bebop M20.

bebung /ˈbeːbʊŋ/ *n.* L19. [G = trembling.] *Mus.* A pulsating or trembling effect given to a sustained note; *spec.* such an effect produced on the clavichord by rocking the fingertip.

becall /bɪˈkɔːl/ *v.t.* ME. [f. BE- 1 + CALL *v.*] †1 Accuse *of.* Only in ME. †2 Call upon, summon, challenge. LME–L15. 3 Miscall, abuse; rail at. Long *dial.* L17.

becalm /bɪˈkɑːm/ *v.t.* M16. [f. BE- 1, 4 + CALM *v.*] 1 *Naut.* Deprive (a ship) of wind. Usu. in *pass.* M16. 2 Make calm or still, soothe, assuage. E17.

1 LD MACAULAY The fleet was becalmed off the Goodwin Sands. 2 POPE What power becalms the innavigable seas?

became *v.* pa. t. of BECOME *v.*

becard /ˈbeɪkɑːd/ *n.* M19. [Fr. *bécarde*, f. *bec* beak.] Any of numerous tyrant flycatchers of the genus *Pachyramphus*, of Central and S. America.

because /bɪˈkɒz/ *adv.* & *conj.* ME. [Orig. two wds, f. as BY *prep.* + CAUSE *n.*, after OFr. *par cause de* by reason of.] A *adv.* 1 For the reason *that* (also foll. by †*why*). *arch.* ME. 2 By reason *of*, on account *of.* LME. 3 *because why?* why? Chiefly *dial.* L19.

1 BYRON I abhor death, because that thou must die. 2 A. LURIE Clark doesn't support me because of my writing, but in spite of it. 3 D. H. LAWRENCE The painters try to paint her . . in vain. Because why?

B *conj.* 1 For the reason that, inasmuch as, since. LME. b Used ellipt. in answer to a question, implying that a fuller reply has been withheld. M18. †2 In order that, with the purpose that. L15–M17.

1 R. KIPLING I buy them because they are pretty. b M. CARROLL 'Why didn't you leave the bottle?' 'Because!' I said shortly. I wasn't going to explain my feelings on the matter. 2 ROBERT BURTON Anointing the doors and hinges with oyl, because they should not creak.

Phrases: †**for because** = senses A.1, 2, B.1 above.

beccafico /bɛkəˈfiːkəʊ/ *n.* Pl. -os. E17. [It., f. *beccare* to peck + *fico* FIG *n.*¹] Any of a number of warblers esteemed as a delicacy in the Mediterranean region.

béchamel /ˈbeɪʃəmɛl, *foreign* beʃamɛl/ *n.* M18. [f. the Marquis de *Béchamel*, steward of Louis XIV.] *Cookery.* More fully *béchamel sauce.* A fine savoury white sauce, freq. made with added cream or milk.

bechance /bɪˈtʃɑːns/ *v.* E16. [f. BE- + CHANCE *v.*] **1** *v.i.* Happen, fall out; occur by chance. E16. **2** *v.t.* Befall. M16.

becharm /bɪˈtʃɑːm/ *v.t.* ME. [f. BE- 1 + CHARM *v.*[1]] Charm, fascinate; subject to an enchantment.

bêche-de-mer /bɛʃdəˈmɛː/ *n.* Pl. same, **bêches-** /bɛʃ-/. L18. [Pseudo-Fr. f. Port. *bicho do mar* lit. 'worm of the sea'. Cf. BEACH-LA-MAR, BISLAMA.] **1** A sea cucumber eaten as a Chinese delicacy. L18. **2** = BEACH-LA-MAR 2. Also *bêche-de-mer English*. L19.

Bechuana, **-wana** *n.* & *a.* see BATSWANA.

beck /bɛk/ *n.*[1] Long *dial. rare.* [OE *becca*, perh. ult. f. Celt.: cf. Welsh *bach* hook.] An agricultural implement with two hooks, a mattock.

beck /bɛk/ *n.*[2] Long *north.* ME. [ON *bekkr* f. Gmc; rel. to G *Bach*.] A brook, a rivulet; *spec.* a mountain, hill, or moorland stream.

beck /bɛk/ *n.*[3] ME. [f. BECK *v.*] **1** A bow, a curtsy, a gesture of acknowledgement. ME. **2** A significant gesture indicating agreement, command, etc. ME.

1 A. WILSON He equally ignored all Rose Lorimer's flustered bobs, becks and smiles. 2 DEFOE With a beck of the head or hand, as we beckon to servants. **at the beck and call of** subservient to, at the absolute command of.

beck /bɛk/ *v. arch.* ME. [Shortened f. BECKON *v.*] **1** *v.i.* = BECKON *v.* 1. ME. **2** *v.t.* = BECKON *v.* 2. L15. **3** *v.i.* Make a sign of acknowledgement; bow, curtsy. Chiefly *Sc.* M16.

becket /ˈbɛkɪt/ *n.*[1] *obs.* exc. *dial.* LME. [Prob. f. obs. var. of BEAK *n.*[1] + -ET[1].] Any protruding or overhanging structure, as a corbel, a mantelpiece, etc.

becket /ˈbɛkɪt/ *n.*[2] E18. [Origin unkn.] *Naut.* A contrivance of rope-loop, hook, bracket, etc., used to secure loose ropes, tackle, or spars.

becket /ˈbɛkɪt/ *n.*[3] *dial.* M18. [f. BECK *n.*[1] + -ET[1].] A spade used in cutting peat or turf.

beckon /ˈbɛk(ə)n/ *v.* & *n.* [OE *bēcnan* (*bīecnan*) = OS *bōknian*, OHG *bouhnen*, f. WGmc, f. as BEACON *n.*] **A** *v.* **1** *v.i.* Signal with a gesture of head, hand, or finger, esp. to indicate that someone should approach. OE. **2** *v.t.* (orig. w. dat. obj.). Gesture to (a person) to approach, by a movement of head, hand, or finger; summon by such a signal. OE.

1 JOYCE The old woman, seeing that I hesitated to enter, began to beckon to me again repeatedly with her hand. *fig.*: S. BRETT The West End then beckoned, and he appeared as a solid juvenile in . . light comedies. 2 SHAKES. *Oth.* Iago beckons me; now he begins the story.

B *n.* A significant gesture, esp. one indicating assent or command. *rare.* E18.

beclad *v.* see BECLOTHE *v.*

beclip /bɪˈklɪp/ *v.t. arch.* Infl. **-pp-**. [OE *beclyppan*, f. as BE- 1 + CLIP *v.*[1]] †**1** Embrace, fold in the arms. OE-M17. **2** Enclose or wrap round; encircle. *arch.* OE. †**3** Lay hold of, grip; overtake. LME-M16.

beclog /bɪˈklɒg/ *v.t. arch.* Infl. **-gg-**. LME. [f. BE- 1 + CLOG *v.*] Encumber with a sticky substance, as mire etc; daub liberally with clotted matter. Usu. in *pass.*

beclothe /bɪˈkləʊð/ *v.t.* Pa. t. & pple **-clothed**, **-clad** /-ˈklad/. LME. [f. BE- 1 + CLOTHE *v.*] Clothe round, dress. Usu. in *pass.*

becloud /bɪˈklaʊd/ *v.t.* L16. [f. BE- 4 + CLOUD *n.*] Cover or darken with clouds or murk; make obscure or gloomy.

become /bɪˈkʌm/ *v.* Pa. t. **became** /bɪˈkeɪm/; pa. pple **become**. [OE *becuman* = OFris. *bicuma*, MLG, (M)Du. *bekomen*, OHG *biqueman* (G *bekommen*) obtain, receive, Goth. *biqiman*, f. Gmc: see BE-, COME *v.*] **I** Come —. †**1** *v.i.* Come to a place, arrive; travel, go. OE-M18. †**2** *v.i.* **a** Come in the course of time (*to be* or *do*). OE-E19. **b** Foll. by *of*: come from, originate from. ME-E17. †**3** *v.i.* w. dat. or *to*, later *v.t.* Happen, befall. OE-M17. **4** As *copula* with n. or adj. compl. or †*v.i.* w. (*in*)*to*. Come to be, begin to be. ME. **5** *v.t.* Foll. by *of*: (formerly) result from; (now) happen to, befall. Only w. *what* as subj. M16. **6** *v.i.* Come into being. *rare.* L16.

1 BACON Houses so full of Glasse, that one cannot tell, where to become, to be out of the Sunne. 2a SYD. SMITH It becomes to be loved on its own account. 4 EVELYN The Church of God, being now become, from a private family . . to a great and numerous nation. LD MACAULAY When first they became known to the Tyrian mariners. E. M. FORSTER Their pleasantry and their piety show cracks, their wit becomes cynicism, their unselfishness hypocrisy. S. BELLOW Depressives tended to form frantic dependencies and to become hysterical when cut off. R. K. NARAYAN After college, the question was whether I should become a dancer or do something else. C. MILNE You can keep tadpoles until they become frogs or toads. 5 SHAKES. *Twel. N.* What will become of this? . . My state is desperate. J. CONRAD I haven't seen him for a week. What has become of him?

II Befit. **7** *v.t.* (orig. w. dat. obj.). Accord with, be appropriate to, befit. Also *impers.* in (*it*) *becomes* etc. ME. †**8** *v.i. impers.* in *it becomes*, be appropriate or fitting (*to*, *for*, *that*). (Replaced by *is becoming*.) ME-L16. **9** *v.t.* Of a property, attribute, quality, etc.: suit, look well on or with, (its owner or subject). ME. **10** Of a person: grace (a place, position, etc.); look well in (a dress etc.). *arch.* L16.

7 DISRAELI He had that public spirit which became his station. SIR W. SCOTT I thought it became me to make public how far I was concerned. 9 SHAKES. *Macb.* Nothing in his life Became him, like the leaving it. J. K. JEROME This hat fits me sufficiently well, but . . do you consider that it becomes me? 10 STEELE A graceful man . . who became the dignity of his function. A. HELPS She with her dark hair did most become that yellow gown.

†**becomed** *ppl a.* (*rare*, Shakes.) befitting: only in L16. †**becomely** *a.* fitting ME-L15.

becoming /bɪˈkʌmɪŋ/ *vbl n.* E17. [f. prec. + -ING[1].] **1** [BECOME II.] The action of befitting or gracing; something becoming. *rare.* E17. **2** [BECOME 4.] The action of coming to be something or passing into a state. M19.

becoming /bɪˈkʌmɪŋ/ *a.* L15. [f. as prec. + -ING[2].] Fitting, suitable; characterized by grace or decorum; tending to show the wearer etc. to advantage, attractive-looking.

L. M. MONTGOMERY We are so much older . . that it isn't becoming to talk of childish matters. W. C. WILLIAMS In their crisp and becoming uniforms, they appear as beautiful young women. I. MURDOCH Her hair is permanently waved in whatever fashion is declared to be the most becoming. N. PEVSNER Wren's sense of becoming conformity in putting Tom Tower on Cardinal Wolsey's gatehouse at Christ Church. *absol.*: LD MACAULAY Selfcommand and a fine sense of the becoming.

becomingly *adv.* E17. **becomingness** *n.* M17.

becquerel /ˈbɛkərɛl/ *n.* In sense 1 **B-**. L19. [A. H. *Becquerel* (1852–1908), Fr. physicist, discoverer of radioactivity.] *Physics.* **1** *Becquerel('s) rays*, radiation from radioactive substances. *obs.* exc. *Hist.* L19. **2** The SI unit of radioactivity, equal to one disintegration per second. (Symbol Bq.) L20.

becripple /bɪˈkrɪp(ə)l/ *v.t.* M17. [f. BE- 1 + CRIPPLE *v.*] Make lame, cripple.

becross /bɪˈkrɒs/ *v.t.* M16. [f. BE- 1, 4 + CROSS *v.* or *n.*] Mark with the sign of the cross; decorate with crosses. Chiefly as *becrossed* ppl a.

becrown /bɪˈkraʊn/ *v.t.* L16. [f. BE- 1 + CROWN *v.*[1]] Surround as a crown, crown.

becudgel /bɪˈkʌdʒ(ə)l/ *v.t.* Infl. **-ll-**, ***-l-**. L16. [f. BE- 1 + CUDGEL *v.*] Cudgel soundly.

becurl /bɪˈkəːl/ *v.t.* E17. [f. BE- 1, 4 + CURL *v.* or *n.*] Form into curls; cover or deck with curls.

bed /bɛd/ *n.* [OE *bed(d)* = OFris. *bed(d)*, OS *bed*, *beddi*, MDu. *bedde* (Du. *bed*), OHG *betti* (G *Bett*), Goth. *badi*, f. Gmc.] **I** The sleeping-place of people or animals. **1** A permanent structure for sleeping or resting on, *esp.* a framework equipped with mattress and covers; also, a mattress. (In prep. phrs. usu. without article or possessive.) OE. **b** (The place of) conjugal union, sexual intimacy, or (*arch.*) procreation and childbirth. ME. **c** The use of a bed; being in bed; the time to go to bed. L15. **d** A bed and associated facilities in a hospital; a place for a patient in hospital. L19. **e** *spec.* Uninflected *pl.* after a numeral or quantifier: bedrooms. (Chiefly an advertising term.) E20. **2** Any sleeping-place; an extemporized resting-place for the night. ME. **3** (Usu. w. specifying adj. or contextual indication.) The grave. Freq. in *narrow bed*. ME. **4** The resting-place of an animal. L17.

1 CAXTON He was in his bed and a slepe on a fethyr bedde. M. W. MONTAGU I carried my own bed with me. J. CARLYLE My great comfortable four-posted bed. *bunk-bed*, *camp-bed*, *double bed*, *French bed*, *single bed*, *twin bed*, etc. *deathbed*, *hospital bed*, *marriage-bed*, *sickbed*, etc. b STEELE He betrays the Honour and Bed of his Neighbour. G. CRABBE And hoped, when wed, For loves fair favours, and a fruitful bed. J. I. M. STEWART I don't believe . . that Lawrence was any good in bed. c S. PEPYS We began both to be angry, and so continued till bed. R. FORD The traveller should immediately on arriving secure his bed. M. PATTISON Bed, with its warmth and recumbent posture, he found favourable to composition. d *Times* Twenty beds have been closed at the 52-bed post-operative Courtaulds Hospital. e P. G. WODEHOUSE A joyous suburban villa equipped with main drainage, . . four bed, . . and the usual domestic offices. 2 SHAKES. *Mids. N. D.* Find you out a bed For I upon this bank will rest my head. 3 R. BURNS Welcome to your gory bed, Or to victorie. F. O'CONNOR The desolate edges of the bog that was to be their last earthly bed. 4 DRYDEN The Water-Snake . . lyes poyson'd in his Bed.

II Other uses. **5** A garden-plot (to be) filled with plants; a place where osiers, willows, etc., are grown. OE. **6** The bottom of a sea, lake, river, or other watercourse. L16. **7** A level surface or other base upon which something rests or in which something is embedded; an extended substructure furnishing a support or foundation. L16. **b** The surface of a stone or brick that is embedded in the mortar; the underside of a slate. L17. **c** The body of a cart, wagon, or truck. *dial.* & *N. Amer.* E18. **d** The foundation of a road or railway. L19. **e** The slates or other flat surface below the cloth-cover of a billiard-table. L19. **8** A layer, *esp.* one of several; a horizontal course. E17. **b** A layer of small animals congregated in a particular spot; *esp.* a layer of oysters etc. E17. **c** A geological stratum. L17. **9** A division of the marked surface in hopscotch, shovelboard, etc.; in *pl.* (*local*), hopscotch. E19.

5 L. A. G. STRONG A small, neat front garden, with . . a circular bed containing four standard rose-trees. G. HEYER The narrow paths which separated various beds filled with vegetables and currant bushes. *flower-bed*, *onion-bed*, etc. *hotbed*: see HOT *a.* MIXED *bed*. 7 WELLINGTON The mortar beds and howitzer carriages. ARNOLD BENNETT There was another cracking sound . . beneath the bed of the machine. M. LASKI A diamond ring, . . on its cream velvet bed. V. STRAUSS The bed of the press . . is a flat, even surface on which the form is placed for printing. O. DOPPING An acoustic coupler contains a 'bed' upon which a telephone receiver is laid. 8 *New Yorker* Scallops on a bed of spinach sautéed in butter.

Phrases: **bed and board** (hospitality with) food and lodging; *arch.* full connubial relations with a husband. **bed and breakfast** overnight accommodation and breakfast next morning as offered by hotels etc.; *fig.* (*attrib.*) designating financial transactions in which shares are sold and then bought back the next morning. **bed-and-breakfast** *v.t.* sell (shares) and then buy back the next morning. **bed of justice** *Fr. Hist.* the throne of the king in the parliament of Paris; a sitting of this parliament in the presence of the king, *esp.* one to enforce the registration of one of his own decrees. **bed of nails** (*a*) a board studded with protruding nails, lain upon for self-mortification or as a display of self-control or skill; (*b*) *fig.* a hazardous or uncomfortable situation brought upon or chosen by oneself. **bed of roses** a position of ease and luxury. **bed of sickness** the state of being an invalid. **brought to bed** *arch.* delivered of (or *of*) a child. *die in one's bed*: see DIE *v.*[1] **get** (or **have got**) **out of bed on the wrong side** behave bad-temperedly during the day. **go to bed** retire for the night; have sexual intercourse *with*; of a newspaper: go to press. **in(to) bed** between the lower and upper bedclothes. *hop into bed*: see HOP *v.*[1] **keep one's bed** remain in bed because of illness etc. **lie in the bed one has made** accept the natural consequences of one's acts. **make a bed** put a bed in order after it has been used. **make up a bed** (*a*) put bedclothes on a bed; (*b*) prepare an extemporized resting-place for the night. MIXED *bed*. **out of bed** from between the lower and upper bedclothes, up and about away from one's bed. **put to bed** prepare (a person) for rest in bed; send (a newspaper) to press. *Reading beds*: see READING *a.*[2] I. *red beds*: see RED *a.* **take to (one's) bed** retire to bed because of illness, often for a prolonged period of time. *test bed*: see TEST *n.*[1]

Comb.: **bed-bottle** a bottle for urination for the use of male invalids in bed; **bedbug** a bloodsucking hemipteran insect of the genus *Cimex* (esp. *C. lectularius*), which infests beds; **bedchamber** a bedroom (*arch.* exc. in the titles of attendants of the monarch, as *lady, lord, gentleman of the bedchamber*, etc.); **bedclothes** the sheets, blankets, covers, etc., which are put on a bed; *bed-cover*: see COVER *n.*[1] 2b; **bedfast** *Sc.* & *north.* confined to bed; **bedfellow** a person who shares a bed with another; a companion, an associate (*lit.* & *fig.*); **bedgown** *arch.* (*a*) a nightgown, a nightdress; (*b*) *north.* a kind of jacket formerly worn (usu. over a petticoat) by working women; **bed-head** the upper end of a bed; **bed-hop** *v.i.* (*colloq.*) engage in successive casual sexual affairs; **bedjacket** a short jacket worn, esp. by women, when sitting up in bed; **bedlinen** sheets and pillowcases; **bedload** the sediment transported by a river in the form of particles too heavy to be in suspension; **bedmaker** a person who puts beds in order after use; *spec.* a person who attends to the bedrooms and other living accommodation in a college, hotel, etc.; **bed-moulding** *Archit.*: under a projection, as a cornice; **bedpan** †(*a*) a warming-pan; (*b*) an invalid's utensil for urination or defecation when in bed; **bedplate** a metal plate forming the base of a machine; **bedpost** one of the upright supports of the framework of a bed (*between you and me and the bedpost*: see BETWEEN *prep.* 3); **bedrest** (*a*) a support for a person in bed; (*b*) the confinement of a sick person to bed; **bedrock** solid rock underlying alluvial deposits etc.; *fig.* the ultimate facts or principles of a belief, character, etc.; **bedroll** *N. Amer.* & *NZ* bedding rolled into a bundle for carrying; **bed-settee** a settee that can be converted into a bed; **bedsitting room**, (*colloq.*) **bedsitter, -sit** a room serving as both a bedroom and a sitting-room; **bedsock** a warm sock worn in bed; **bedsore** an ulceration of the buttocks, heels, etc., developed by the constant pressure of the mattress on an invalid's skin; **bedspread** (orig. *US*) a cloth or sheet to cover a bed when not in use; †**bedstaff** a staff from a bed, used as a cudgel; **bedstead** †(*a*) the place occupied by a bed; (*b*) the framework of a bed (*French bedstead*: see FRENCH *a.*); **bedstock** (*obs.* exc. *dial.*) one of the upright parts of the framework of a bed; a bedstead; **bedtable** a small tray or table for the use of a person sitting up in bed; **bedtick** a flat four-sided case or cover filled with feathers, straw, or other material to form a bed; **bed-warmer** a device for warming a bed; **bedwetter** a person, esp. a child, given to bedwetting; **bedwetting** urinary incontinence while in bed.

beddy *a.* (of stone) having natural cleavages, with a tendency to split E18. **beddy-bye(s)** /ˈbɛdɪbʌɪ(z)/ *n.* (*nursery* & *joc.*) bed, sleep E20. **bedward(s)** *adv.* [orig. *to bedward*] †(*a*) towards bedtime; (*b*) towards bed: LME. **bed-worthy** *a.* (*colloq.*) sexually attractive E20.

bed /bɛd/ *v.* Infl. **-dd-**. [OE *beddian*, f. as prec.] **I** Uses conn. w. a bed for sleeping. †**1** *v.i.* & *t.* w. cognate obj. Prepare (a bed). OE–LME. **2** *v.t.* Put to bed; put (an animal) to rest for the night; provide with a bed or bedding. Also foll. by *down*. Freq. as *bedded* pa. pple. ME. **3** *v.i.* Go to bed (*with*). Now usu. foll. by *down*. ME. **4** *v.t.* Take (a woman) to bed; have sexual intercourse with. M16.

2 W. WHATELEY To see a stranger bedded with him instead of his owne Spouse. J. WESLEY See . . that your horse be rubbed, fed, and bedded. DYLAN THOMAS Young girls lie bedded soft. 3 H. CAREY O then we'll wed, and then we'll bed. N. MARSH She meant to come back and bed down with Garcia. T. STURGE MOORE They bedded on the downs. 4 SHAKES. *Tam. Shr.* Him . . that would thoroughly woo her, wed her, and bed her. P. COHEN Rodolphe, her previous lover who was only interested in bedding her.

II Other uses. **5** *v.t.* Plant (*out*) in or as in a garden bed. LME. **6** *v.t.* Lay (bricks, stones, etc.) in position in cement or mortar. LME. **7** *v.t.* Embed. M16. **8** *v.t.* Lay or strew in a layer; stratify in beds. Chiefly as *bedded* ppl a. E17. **9** *v.i.* Form a compact layer. E17. **10** *v.i.* Rest *on*, lie *on* for support. M19.

7 R. HOOKER A place where the ships lie bedded. I. WALTON Many of them [eels] together bed themselves, and live without feeding on anything. MRS H. WOOD The bullet . . must have bedded itself in the wall.

beddable *a.* sexually attractive M20.

bedabble /bɪˈdab(ə)l/ *v.t. arch.* L16. [f. BE- 1 + DABBLE *v.*] Sprinkle over or stain with dirty liquid. Chiefly as *bedabbled* ppl a.

bedad /bɪˈdad/ *int. Anglo-Ir. arch.* E18. [Alt. of *by God!*: cf. BEGAD etc.] Expr. amazement or emphasis.

bedaff /bɪˈdaf/ *v.t.* Long *obs.* exc. *dial.* LME. [f. BE- 3 + DAFF *n.*[1]] Make a fool of, bewilder.

bedangled /bɪˈdaŋg(ə)ld/ *a. rare.* E17. [f. BE- 1 + DANGLE *v.* + -ED[1].] Adorned or hung about with dangling objects.

bedark /bɪˈdɑːk/ *v.t. rare.* LME. [f. BE- 1 + DARK *v.*] Cover with darkness.

bedarken /bɪˈdɑːk(ə)n/ *v.t.* L16. [f. BE- 1 + DARKEN *v.*] Make dark; overshadow; obscure.

bedash /bɪˈdaʃ/ *v.t.* LME. [f. BE- 1 + DASH *v.*[1]] **1** Beat about; dash down. LME. **2** Cover with dashes of colour etc. L15.

bedaub /bɪˈdɔːb/ *v.t.* M16. [f. BE- 1 + DAUB *v.*] **1** Besmear; *fig.* vilify. M16. **2** Overload with ornamentation; bedizen. L16.

1 T. OTWAY The names of Honest Men bedawb'd. P. H. GOSSE With a painter's brush had bedaubed the trunks of several large trees. 2 MARVELL Set off, and bedawb'd with Rhetorick. M. W. MONTAGU All bedaubed with diamonds.

bedaze /bɪˈdeɪz/ *v.t.* LME. [f. BE- 1 + DAZE *v.*] Daze; bewilder; stupefy. Chiefly as *bedazed* ppl a.

bedazement *n.* L19.

bedazzle /bɪˈdaz(ə)l/ *v.t.* L16. [f. BE- 1 + DAZZLE *v.*] Dazzle completely or thoroughly; confuse by excess of brilliance.

bedazzlement *n.* E19.

bedder /ˈbɛdə/ *n.*[1] LME. [f. BED *n.* + -ER[1].] **I 1** A manufacturer of beds; an upholsterer. *obs.* exc. *dial.* LME. **2** A college bedmaker. *colloq.* L19. **3** *early, late*, etc., (*go-to-*)*bedder*, a person who habitually goes to bed early etc. E20. **II 4** A bedding-out plant. M19.

bedder /ˈbɛdə/ *n.*[2] *slang.* L19. [f. BED *n.* + -ER[6].] A bedroom.

bedding /ˈbɛdɪŋ/ *n.* OE. [f. BED *n.* or *v.* + -ING[1].] **1** *collect. sing.* or †*pl.* The articles which compose a bed, as mattress, bedclothes, etc.; materials provided for sleeping or resting on. OE. †**b** Sleeping accommodation. LME–L17. **2** A putting to bed, esp. of a bride; (an act of) sexual intercourse. L16. **3** A bottom layer, a foundation. E17. **4** *Geol.* Layering or stratification of rocks. M19. **5** The process of planting flowers (*out*) in beds. M19.

1 JONSON He hath sold my hangings, and my beddings! DRYDEN Spread with Straw, the bedding of thy Fold. C. V. WEDGWOOD Fairfax . . ordered the citizens to provide bedding so that every two soldiers could share a mattress, a bolster and a pair of sheets and blankets. b SPENSER The ground . . which useth to be his bedding. 2 SIR W. SCOTT A . . description of the wedding, bedding, and throwing the stocking. V. S. PRITCHETT Their private sexual comedy, in momentary beddings in the backs of cars.

Comb.: **bedding(-out) plant** a plant suitable for setting out in a garden bed; **bedding plane** a plane forming the junction between two layers or strata of rock.

bedeck /bɪˈdɛk/ *v.t.* M16. [f. BE- 1 + DECK *v.*] Deck round, adorn, (*with*).

bedeguar /ˈbɛdɪgɑː/ *n.* LME. [Fr. *bédégar* f. Pers. *bād-āwar(d* lit. 'wind-brought'.] A mosslike gall on a rose bush caused by the gall-wasp *Diplolepis rosae*.

bedel(l) *ns.* see BEADLE.

bedene /bɪˈdiːn/ *adv. obs.* exc. *dial.* ME. [f. unkn. 1st elem. + OE *ǣne* once, at once, in one, together.] = ANON *adv.*; occas. a mere expletive or rhyme word.

bedesman *n.* see BEADSMAN.

bedevil /bɪˈdɛv(ə)l/ *v.t.* Infl. **-ll-**, ***-l-**. L16. [f. BE- 3, 4 + DEVIL *n.*] **1** Possess (*as*) with a devil. Chiefly as *bedevilled* ppl a. L16. **2** Transform mischievously; corrupt, spoil. L17. **3** Treat with diabolical violence or abuse; drive frantic; plague, afflict. M18.

1 CARLYLE One age, he is hagridden, bewitched; the next, priestridden, befooled; in all ages, bedevilled. 2 DISRAELI So bedevil a bottle of Geisenheim . . you wouldn't know it from the greenest Tokay. 3 BYRON My poor . . Muse . . they have . . so be-deviled with their . . ribaldry. S. RUSHDIE Confused thinking was to bedevil much of his career.

bedevilment *n.* E19.

bedew /bɪˈdjuː/ *v.t.* ME. [f. BE- 4 + DEW *n.*] Cover or soak with dew or drops of moisture; bathe, suffuse.

Bedford cord /ˌbɛdfəd ˈkɔːd/ *n. phr.* L19. [*Bedford*, a town in central England + CORD *n.*[1]] A woven fabric with prominent cords running in the direction of the warp. In *pl.*, trousers made of this.

Bedfordshire /ˈbɛdfədʃə/ *n. joc.* or *nursery.* M17. [An English county.] = BED *n.* 1 in prep. phrases.

bediasite /bɪˈdʌɪəsʌɪt/ *n.* M20. [f. *Bedias* a locality in Texas + -ITE[1].] *Geol.* A tektite from the strewn field in Texas.

bedight /bɪˈdʌɪt/ *v.t. arch.* Pa. t. **bedight**; pa. pple **bedight(ed)**. LME. [f. BE- 1 + DIGHT *v.*] Equip, apparel, bedeck.

bedim /bɪˈdɪm/ *v.t. arch.* Infl. **-mm-**. M16. [f. BE- 1 + DIM *v.*] Make dim, cloud, obscure.

bedip /bɪˈdɪp/ *v.t. arch.* Infl. **-pp-**. [OE *bedyppan*: see BE- 1, DIP *v.*] Dip, immerse.

†**bedirt** *v.t.* E16–E18. [f. BE- 4 + DIRT *n.*] Make dirty, throw filth at, defile.

bedizen /bɪˈdʌɪz(ə)n, -ˈdɪz-/ *v.t.* M17. [f. BE- 1 + DIZEN *v.*] Deck or ornament, esp. overlavishly; trick out.

bedizenment *n.* M19.

bedlam /ˈbɛdləm/ *a.* & *n.* In senses A.1, 2, & occas. others **B-**. LME. [Form of *Bethlehem* (see below).] **A** *n.* †**1** The town of Bethlehem in Judaea. LME–E17. **2** The Hospital of St Mary of Bethlehem (Bethlem Royal Hospital in London), used as an asylum for the insane. *arch.* LME. †**3** A person who was mentally ill; *spec.* a discharged but not fully cured patient of the Hospital of St Mary of Bethlehem, licensed to beg. E16–E18. **4** A lunatic asylum; a madhouse. *arch.* M17. **5** (A scene of) mad confusion; a wild uproar. M17.

2 **Tom** or **Jack o' Bedlam** *arch.* a person who is mentally ill. 3 SWIFT She roar'd like a Bedlam. 4 R. GRAVES Declared him a lunatic and shut him up in a Bedlam. 5 QUILLER-COUCH Hearkenin' to the bedlam outside: for 'twas the big storm in 'Seventy. M. MITCHELL Amid a bedlam of hounds barking and small black children shouting. J. P. DONLEAVY I'm a man for bedlam . . Did you ever relish the broken dish or twisted chandelier?

B *adj.* Belonging to or fit for a madhouse; lunatic; foolish. L16.

MILTON This which followes is plaine bedlam stuff.

Bedlamite *n.* an inmate of Bedlam or a madhouse, a mentally ill person L16.

bedlar /ˈbɛdlə/ *a.* & *n. obs.* exc. *Sc.* LME. [f. BED *n.* + ON *lag* lying + -ER[1].] (A person who is) bedridden.

Bedlington /ˈbɛdlɪŋt(ə)n/ *n.* M19. [A village in Northumberland, N. England.] In full *Bedlington terrier*. A narrow-headed sporting terrier with fairly long legs and curly grey hair.

Bedouin /ˈbɛdʊɪn/ *n.* & *a.* Also **Beduin**, **b-**. LME. [OFr. *beduin* (mod. *bédouin*) ult. (through med.L *beduini* pl.) f. Arab. *badawī*, pl. *badawīn* (f. *badw* desert, nomadic desert tribes): see -INE[1]. Cf. BEDU.] **A** *n.* **1** An Arab of the desert. LME. **2** A person living a nomadic life; a Gypsy. M19. **B** *adj.* Of the desert or Bedouins; nomadic, wandering. M19.

bedrabble /bɪˈdrab(ə)l/ *v.t. arch.* LME. [f. BE- 1 + DRABBLE *v.*] Make wet or dirty with rain or mud. Chiefly as *bedrabbled* ppl a.

bedraggle /bɪˈdrag(ə)l/ *v.t.* E18. [f. BE- 1 + DRAGGLE *v.*] Wet (an article of clothing etc.) so that it hangs limp; make (a person) wet and untidy or dishevelled (chiefly as *bedraggled* ppl a.).

bedral /ˈbɛdr(ə)l/ *n.*[1] *Sc.* E16. [App. alt. of BEADLE, perh. under infl. of next.] A minor church officer, often acting as clerk, sexton, and bell-ringer. Also, a gravedigger.

bedral /ˈbɛdr(ə)l/ *a.* & *n.*[2] *Sc.* Also **-rel**. E16. [Prob. metath. alt. of BEDLAR.] †**A** *adj.*

Bedridden. E16–E17. **B** *n.* A bedridden person. E16.

bedrench /bɪˈdrɛn(t)ʃ/ *v.t.* LME. [f. BE- 1 + DRENCH *v.*] Drench completely; soak.

bedrid /ˈbɛdrɪd/ *n.* & *a. arch.* [OE *bedreda*, *-rida*, f. as BED *n.* + short base of RIDE *v.*] †**A** *n.* A bedridden person. OE–ME. **B** *adj.* = BEDRIDDEN. OE.

bedridden /ˈbɛdrɪd(ə)n/ *a.* ME. [Irreg. f. prec. + -EN[4].] Confined to bed through sickness or infirmity; *fig.* worn-out, decrepit.

bedroom /ˈbɛdruːm, -rʊm/ *n.* L15. [f. BED *n.*[1] + ROOM *n.*[1]] **1** Space in a bed. *rare.* L15. **2** A room intended to house a bed; a sleeping apartment. E17.

1 SHAKES. *Mids. N. D.* Then by your side, no bedroom me deny.

Comb.: **bedroom eyes** eyes holding an expression of sensual invitation; **bedroom farce** a play depicting an absurd situation deriving from one or more (esp. extramarital) sexual adventures; **bedroom slipper** a soft indoor shoe intended to be worn when one is not fully dressed.

bedrop /bɪˈdrɒp/ *v.t. arch.* Infl. as DROP *v.* LME. [f. BE- 2, 4 + DROP *v.*, *n.*] Drop upon; sprinkle with or (chiefly as *pa. ppl a.*) as with drops.

bedside /ˈbɛdsʌɪd/ *n.* ME. [Contr. of *bed's side*: see BED *n.*, -'S[1], SIDE *n.*] The place or position at the side of a bed.

bedside lamp, *bedside table*, etc.

Comb.: **bedside book** a book for reading in bed; **bedside manner** the manner of a doctor when attending a patient (freq. w. specifying adj., as *good*).

bedstraw /ˈbɛdstrɔː/ *n.* LME. [f. BED *n.* + STRAW *n.*] †**1** Straw used for bedding. LME–M17. **2** Any of numerous straggling plants of the genus *Galium*, belonging to the madder family and bearing many tiny flowers; *esp.* (in full *lady's bedstraw*) a yellow-flowered European plant, *Galium verum*, of dry grassland. E16.

bedtime /ˈbɛdtʌɪm/ *n.* ME. [f. BED *n.* + TIME *n.*] The hour at which a person habitually goes to bed.

bedtime story a story told to a child at bedtime.

Bedu /ˈbɛduː/ *n.* & *a.* Pl. of n. same. E20. [Arab. *badw*: see BEDOUIN.] (Of) a Bedouin; *collect.* (of) Bedouins.

Beduin *n.* & *a.* var. of BEDOUIN.

bedull /bɪˈdʌl/ *v.t.* L16. [f. BE- 1 + DULL *v.*] Make dull.

bedust /bɪˈdʌst/ *v.t. arch.* LME. [f. BE- 4 + DUST *n.*] Cover with dust. Chiefly as *bedusted* ppl a.

bedye /bɪˈdʌɪ/ *v.t.* E16. [f. BE- 1 + DYE *v.*] Stain (as) with dye. Chiefly as *bedyed* ppl a.

bee /biː/ *n.*[1] [OE *bēo* = OFris. *bē*, MLG, MDu. *bīe* (Du. *bij*), OHG *bīa* (G dial. *Beie*), ON *bý*, f. Gmc.] **1** A stinging hymenopterous social insect of the genus *Apis*, which collects nectar and pollen and produces wax and honey: a colony consists of one perfect female or 'queen', several males or 'drones', and very many sterile females or 'workers'. OE. **b** Any of numerous other insects, including both social and solitary species, constituting the superfamily Apoidea. Freq. w. specifying wd. OE. **2** A busy worker. Also (now *rare* or *obs.*), a pleasing writer. M18. **3** A gathering for combined work or amusement. Usu. w. wd specifying its purpose. Orig. *US.* M18. **4** A lump of yeast which rises and falls in a brew as bubbles of carbon dioxide are produced. E20.

1b *bumble-bee*, *carpenter bee*, *mason bee*, *mining bee*, etc. 3 W. IRVING Now were instituted quilting bees and husking bees and other rural assemblages. J. GALT I made a bee; that is, I collected . . the settlers to assist at the raising. SPELLING *bee*.

Phrases: **as busy as a bee** very busy or industrious. **bees and honey** *rhyming slang* money. *goat and bee jug*: see GOAT. **have a bee in one's bonnet** be obsessed on some point. **put the bee on** (*slang*, chiefly *US*) (*a*) put an end to; beat; (*b*) ask for a loan, borrow money, from (cf. STING *v.*). **the bee's knees** *slang* something or someone outstandingly good.

Comb.: **bee-balm** the plant Oswego tea, *Monarda didyma*; **bee-bird** any of various birds, *esp.* a spotted flycatcher; **bee-biter** *dial.* the great tit; **bee-bread** †(*a*) a honey-containing honeycomb; (*b*) (honey and) pollen used as food by bees; **bee-eater** a brightly coloured insectivorous bird of the family Meropidae; esp. *Merops apiaster*, a rare visitor to Britain (*wattled bee-eater*: see WATTLED 2); **bee-fly** a parasitic fly of the family Bombylliidae, resembling a bee; **bee-glue** propolis; **bee-gum** *US* a hollow gum tree acting as or fashioned into a beehive; **bee-keeper** a person who keeps bees; **beeline** a straight line or course between two places (*make a beeline for*, hurry towards, go straight up to); **bee man**, **-master** a man who keeps bees; **bee martin** *US* a kingbird (*Tyrannus*); **bee-moth** = *wax moth* s.v. WAX *n.*[1]; **bee orchid** an orchid, *Ophrys apifera*, with a flower in part resembling a bee; **bee plant** any plant visited by bees for nectar; *esp.* (more fully *Rocky Mountain bee plant*) a N. American cleome, *Cleome serrulata*, formerly grown by bee-keepers.

bee /biː/ *n.*[2] [OE *bēag*, *bēah* = ON *baugr*, OHG *bouc*, f. Gmc; rel. to BOW *v.*[1]] **1** A ring or torque of metal, usu. for the arm or neck. Long *obs.* exc. *Sc.* OE. **2** In full *bee block.* A wooden block bolted to the side of a bowsprit, occas. with metal sheaves to reeve the fore-topmast stays through. L15.

Beeb /biːb/ *n. colloq.* M20. [Abbrev.] *The* BBC.

beebee *n.* var. of BIBI.

beech /biːtʃ/ *n.* [OE *bēce* = MLG *bōke*, *bȫke* (wk fem.) f. Gmc base rel. to that of OE *bōc* (see BUCKWHEAT): cogn. w. L *fagus* beech, Gk *phagos*, *phēgos* edible oak.] **1** A forest tree of the genus *Fagus*, having thin, smooth bark and glossy oval leaves, and bearing nuts; *esp.* the European *F. sylvatica*. Also (usu. w. specifying wd), any of various similar trees, esp. (in the southern hemisphere) of the genus *Nothofagus*. Also *beech tree*. OE. **2** The wood of this tree. ME.

1 *copper beech*: see COPPER *n.*[1] *red beech*: see RED *a.* *silver beech*: see SILVER *n.* & *a.* **southern beech** = NOTHOFAGUS.

Comb.: **beech-drops** *N. Amer.* a broomrape, *Epifagus virginiana*, parasitic on beech roots; **beech-fern** a fern of damp rocky woods, *Phegopteris connectilis*; **beech marten** the stone marten, *Martes foina*; **beechmast** the fruit of the beech; **beech-oil** an oil extracted from beechmast; **beech tree** = sense 1 above; **beechwood** (*a*) = sense 2 above. (*b*) a wood of beech trees.

beechen *a.* (*arch.* & *poet.*) (*a*) of, pertaining to, or derived from the beech; (*b*) made of the wood of the beech: OE. **beechy** *a.* of, characterized by, or having many beeches E17.

beedi *n.* var. of BIDI.

beef /biːf/ *n.* Pl. **beefs**, in sense 2 also **beeves** /biːvz/. ME. [AN, OFr. *boef*, *buef* (mod. *bœuf*) f. L *bov-*, *bos* ox: cf. COW *n.*[1]] **1** The flesh of an ox, bull, or cow, used as food. ME. **b** *fig.* Muscle, flesh; strength, size, power. M19. **2** An ox or similar beast, *esp.* a fattened one or its carcass. Exc. *US* usu. in *pl.* ME. **b** *collect.* Cattle. *US.* E18. **3** A complaint, a grievance. *slang* (orig. *US*). L19.

1 *beef olive*, *beef stew*, etc. *baby beef*: see BABY *a.* *beef* STROGANOFF. *corned beef*: see CORNED *a.*[2] 2. *sour beef*: see SOUR *a.* **b** P. V. WHITE As from his cattle, the beef had dwindled from the man, but he was still large. R. M. PATTERSON We . . were . . putting all the beef we could behind it. **beef to the heel**(**s**) *slang* (of a person) massive, brawny. 2 CLARENDON One half in Money, and the other half in good Beefs. **b** S. E. WHITE Drivin' some beef up to the troops. 3 D. RUNYON A beef from her over keeping the baby out in the night air.

Comb.: **beefburger** a hamburger; **beefcake** *slang* (the display of) sturdy masculine physique; **beef cattle**: raised for beef; **beefeater** (*a*) an eater of beef; †(*b*) *colloq.* a well-fed menial; (*c*) *colloq.* a Yeoman of the Guard, a Yeoman Warder in the Tower of London; **beefsteak** a thick slice of beef, usu. cut from the hindquarters, for frying or grilling (*beefsteak fungus*, a red bracket fungus, *Fistulina hepatica*, resembling raw meat in appearance); **beef tea** stewed-beef juice used as food for invalids; **beef tomato** an exceptionally large and firm variety of tomato; **beef-witted** stupid; **beef-wood** (the timber of) any of various Australian and W. Indian trees with red wood, esp. (*Austral.*) casuarina.

beefer *n.* an animal bred for beef M17.

beef /biːf/ *v.* M19. [f. the n.] **1** *v.t.* Slaughter for beef; *fig.* (*US slang*) knock down. M19. **2** *v.t.* Put muscle into, strengthen, reinforce; add power or importance to. Usu. foll. by *up. slang* (orig. *US*). M19. **3** *v.i.* Complain, grumble, protest. *slang* (orig. *US*). L19.

2 D. ACHESON The Defense Department required no persuasion that the defense of Europe needed, in their phrase, 'beefing up'. 3 STEVIE SMITH Not beefing about being solitary Or the sparseness of the fare.

beefalo /ˈbiːfələʊ/ *n.* Pl. **-oes**, same. L20. [f. BEEF *n.* + BUFFALO.] (An animal of) a breed of bovine that is 5/8 buffalo and 3/8 domestic cow.

beefing *n.* see BIFFIN.

beefy /ˈbiːfi/ *a.* M18. [f. BEEF *n.* + -Y[1].] Resembling beef; containing much beef; muscular, solid.

beefiness *n.* M19.

beehive /ˈbiːhʌɪv/ *n.* ME. [f. BEE *n.*[1] + HIVE *n.*] **1** An artificial habitation for bees, traditionally of thick straw work in the shape of a dome, but now usu. a wooden box containing the combs on wooden slides. ME. **b** *fig.* A busy place etc. E17. **2** *the Beehive*, (the name of) a star-cluster in the constellation Cancer. Also called *Praesepe*. M19. **3** A hat or hairstyle having the shape of a traditional beehive. E20.

Comb.: **beehive-hat** a hat shaped like a traditional beehive; **beehive tomb** a dome-shaped tomb cut into a hillside, distinctive of Mycenaean Greece.

Beelzebub /bɪˈɛlzɪbʌb/ *n.* OE. [Late L *Beëlzebub* (Vulgate), tr. (i) Heb. *baʿal zĕḇūḇ* Lord of Flies, a Philistine god (*2 Kings* 1:2) and (ii) Gk *Beelzeboul* (*Matt.* 12:24).] The Devil; a devil.

been *v.* pa. pple of BE *v.*

been-to /ˈbiːntuː/ *n. Afr.* & *Asia.* M20. [f. prec. + TO *prep.*] A person who has been to Britain, esp. for education.

beep /biːp/ *n.* & *v.* E20. [Imit.] **A** *n.* The sound of a motor-car horn; a short high-pitched sound emitted by any device (e.g. an echo-sounder). E20. **B** *v.t.* & *i.* (Cause to) emit a beep or beeps. M20.

beeper *n.* a device that emits beeps M20.

beer /bɪə/ *n.*[1] [OE *bēor* = OFris. *biār*, *bier*, MLG, MDu. *bēr* (Du. *bier*), OHG *bior* (G *Bier*), f. a WGmc wd f. monastic L *biber* drink, f. *bibere* to drink.] **1** Alcoholic liquor produced by fermentation of malt etc. and flavoured with hops or other bitters, *esp.* the lighter kind of liquor so produced; a type of this; a drink of this. Cf. ALE, PORTER *n.*[2] OE. **2** A similar drink made from other ingredients. Usu. w. specifying wd. OE.

1 *bitter beer*, *keg beer*, *lager beer*, *mild beer*, etc. (*not*) *all beer and skittles*: see SKITTLE *n.* **on the beer** on a bout of drinking. *porter's beer*: see PORTER *n.*[2] 3. *single beer*: see SINGLE *a.* & *adv.* **small beer** weak beer, or a small measure of beer (usu. half a pint); *fig.* small matters, something of little importance (*think no small beer of*, have a high opinion of). 2 *birch beer*, *ginger beer*, *nettle beer*, *root beer*, *spruce beer*, etc.

Comb.: **beer belly** *slang* = *beer gut* below; **beer-boy** (now *arch.* or *Hist.*) a pot-boy; **beer-cellar** a cellar for storing beer; a bar etc. selling beer in a cellar or basement; **beer-engine** = *beer pump* below; **beer garden** a garden where beer is served; **beer glass** a glass for beer or similar long drinks; **beer gut** *slang* a protruding abdomen (regarded as) due to drinking large quantities of beer; **beer hall** a hall where beer is served; **beerhouse** a public house licensed for the sale of beer, but not spirits; **beer-mat** a small table-mat for a beer glass; **beer money** (*a*) *Hist.* an allowance of money to servants, instead of beer; (*b*) a small amount of money allowed or earned; **beer-off** *slang* an off-licence; **beer-parlo(u)r** *Canad.* a room in a hotel or tavern where beer is served; **beer pump** a machine for drawing beer up from barrels in the cellar to the bar; **beer-swilling** *a.* (*derog.*) that drinks a lot of beer; disreputable, rowdy; **beer-up** a drinking-bout or party.

beerage *n.* (*slang*) brewers collectively, *esp.* those who have been created peers; *derog.* the British peerage: L19. **beerless** *a.* M19.

beer /ˈbiːə/ *n.*[2] *rare.* Also **be-er**. LME. [f. BE *v.* + -ER[1].] Someone who is or exists, esp. *the* Self-existent, God.

beer /bɪə/ *n.*[3] E18. [Alt. of BIER.] In weaving, a (variable) number of ends in a warp.

beer *n.*[4] var. of BERE *n.*[2]

beeregar /ˈbɪərɪgə/ *n.* L15. [f. BEER *n.*[1] after VINEGAR.] = ALEGAR.

Beerenauslese /ˈbeːrən,aʊsleːzə/ *n.* Also **b-**. Pl. ***-sen*** /-zən/, ***-ses***. E20. [G, f. *Beeren* berries, grapes + as AUSLESE.] A white wine made (esp.

in Germany) from selected individual grapes picked later than the general harvest.

Beersheba *n.* see DAN *n.*[3]

beery /ˈbɪəri/ *a.* M19. [f. BEER *n.*[1] + -Y[1].] Pertaining to or containing beer; resembling beer; showing the influence of beer.

beeriness *n.* L19.

†**beest** *n.* OE–L18. [OE *bēost* = NFris. *bjast*, *bjüst*, (M)Du. *biest*, OHG *biost* (G *Biest*, as in *Biestmilch*), f. WGmc: ult. origin unkn.] = BEESTINGS.

†**beest** *v.* see BE *v.*

beestings /ˈbiːstɪŋz/ *n.pl.* Also **beast-**. OE. [Rel. to BEEST *n.*] The first milk drawn, esp. from a cow, after parturition.

beesty *n.* var. of BHISTI.

beeswax /ˈbiːzwaks/ *n.* & *v.* L17. [f. BEE *n.*[1] + -'S[1] + WAX *n.*[1]] A *n.* Wax secreted by bees as material for their combs, used as a polish etc. L17. B *v.t.* Rub or polish with beeswax. M19.

beeswing /ˈbiːzwɪŋ/ *n.* E19. [f. BEE *n.*[1] + -'S[1] + WING *n.*] A filmy second crust of tartar formed in port and other wines after long keeping; an old wine.

beet /biːt/ *n.*[1] [OE *bēte* = MLG *bēte* (LG *beete*, whence G *Bete*), MDu. *bēte* (Du. *beet*), OHG *bieza*, f. early WGmc f. L *beta*, perh. of Celt. origin.] A plant, *Beta vulgaris*, of the goosefoot family, having a red or white succulent root; numerous varieties are cultivated as garden vegetables, as cattle food, and as a source of sugar. Also = BEETROOT *n.*

seakale beet, silver beet, spinach beet, sugar beet, etc.
Comb.: BEETROOT *n.*; **beet sugar** sugar from beets.

beet *n.*[2] var. of BEAT *n.*[2]

beet /biːt/ *v.t. obs.* exc. *dial.* [OE *bētan*, older *bœtan* = OS *bōtian* (MLG *bōten*, MDu. *boeten*), OHG *buozen* (G *büßen*), ON *bœta*, Goth. *botjan* f. Gmc, f. base of BOOT *n.*[1]] 1 Make good; mend or repair; relieve or supply (a want). OE. 2 Make, kindle, mend, or feed (a fire). OE.

Beethovenian /beɪthəʊˈviːnɪən/ *a.* & *n.* L19. [f. *Beethoven* (see below) + -IAN.] A *adj.* Of or pertaining to the German composer Ludwig van Beethoven (1770–1827), his music, or his theories of musical composition. L19. B *n.* An interpreter, student, or admirer of Beethoven or his music. M20.

ˈ**Beethovenish** *a.* resembling or suggestive of Beethoven or his music, characteristic of Beethoven L19.

beetle /ˈbiːt(ə)l/ *n.*[1] [OE *bētel*, (WS) *bīetel* f. Gmc, f. base of BEAT *v.*[1]: see -LE[1].] 1 A tool with heavy head and handle for ramming, crushing, driving wedges, etc. OE. 2 A machine for beetling cloth. L19.

1 **deaf** or **dumb as a beetle** *arch.* insensitive, dumb.
Comb.: **beetle-brain** = *beetle-head* (a) below; **beetle-head** (*a*) a blockhead; (*b*) the monkey of a pile-driving engine.

beetle /ˈbiːt(ə)l/ *n.*[2] [OE *bitula*, *bitela*, f. short base of *bītan* BITE *v.*: see -LE[1].] 1 An insect of the order Coleoptera, having the forewings converted to hard, opaque wing-cases closing over the hindwings; in pop. use extended to other (esp. black) insects of similar appearance, such as the cockroach. OE. 2 *fig.* A person who is (esp. intellectually) short-sighted. L16. 3 A dice game with the object of drawing or assembling a figure resembling a beetle. M20.

1 *black beetle, diving beetle, shard-born beetle, skipjack beetle*, etc. **blind as a beetle** short-sighted; devoid of moral etc. sense. 2 A. TUCKER A blockhead, yea a numbskull, not to say a beetle.
Comb.: **beetle-back** a back shaped like the closed wing-cases on the back of a beetle; **beetle-backed** *a.* having a beetle-back; **beetle-crusher** *colloq.* a heavy boot or foot; **beetle drive** a social gathering at which beetle is played.

beetle /ˈbiːt(ə)l/ *a.* LME. [Origin unkn.] 1 *beetle-browed*, having prominent or bushy eyebrows; scowling. LME. 2 *beetle brow(s)*, prominent or bushy eyebrows; a scowling expression. M16.

1 R. H. BARHAM A beetle-browed hag. 2 *fig.*: P. SIDNEY A pleasant valley of either side of which high hills lifted up their beetle-browis.
beetled *a.* = *beetle-browed* above E16.

beetle /ˈbiːt(ə)l/ *v.*[1]*i.* E17. [f. prec.] Project, overhang; *fig.* hang threateningly. Of eyebrows (also): lour.

SHAKES. *Haml.* The dreadful summit of the cliff That beetles o'er his base into the sea. DICKENS His beetling brow almost obscured his eyes. R. W. EMERSON The justice of states, which we could well enough see beetling over his head. K. CROSSLEY-HOLLAND Thor's eyebrows beetled and the farmers . . cowered.
¶ First recorded in Shakes.

beetle /ˈbiːt(ə)l/ *v.*[2]*t.* E17. [f. BEETLE *n.*[1]] Beat with a beetle in order to crush, flatten, etc.; emboss or heighten the lustre of (cloth) by pressure from rollers.

beetle /ˈbiːt(ə)l/ *v.*[3]*i. colloq.* E20. [f. BEETLE *n.*[2]] Move or fly (like a beetle), make one's way; go, take oneself *off*.

P. G. WODEHOUSE 'What are you doing about two weeks from now?' . . 'Nothing in particular. Just beetling around.' N. COWARD There was . . a terrible scene . . and Freda beetled off to America.

beetroot /ˈbiːtruːt/ *n.* & *a.* L16. [f. BEET *n.*[1] + ROOT *n.*[1]] A *n.* A root of beet, *esp.* the deep crimson form eaten as a vegetable. L16. B *attrib.* or as *adj.* Deep red, crimson; red-faced esp. from embarrassment. *colloq.* E20.

beetster *n.* var. of BEATSTER *n.*[1]

beeve /biːv/ *n.* M19. [Back-form. f. next.] An ox; = BEEF *n.* 2.

beeves *n.* see BEEF *n.*

beezer /ˈbiːzə/ *n. slang.* E20. [Origin unkn.: senses perh. different wds.] 1 A (smart) person; a chap, a fellow. Orig. *Sc.* E20. 2 The nose. E20.

Befa /biːˈfɑː/ *n. obs.* exc. *Hist.* Also **B fa**. LME. [f. *B* as a pitch letter + *fa* designating a tone in the solmization of Guido d'Arezzo (*c* 990–1050).] *Medieval Mus.* The note B flat in Guido d'Arezzo's 3rd and 6th hexachords, where it was sung to the syllable *fa*. Cf. ALAMIRE, BEMI, CEFAUT, etc.

befall /bɪˈfɔːl/ *v.* Pa. t. **befell** /bɪˈfɛl/; pa. pple **befallen** /bɪˈfɔːl(ə)n/. [OE *befeallan* = OFris. *befalla*, OS, OHG *bifallan*: see BE-, FALL *v.*] †1 *v.i.* Fall. Chiefly *fig.* OE–M17. 2 *v.i.* Fall *to*; pertain, belong, be fitting. *arch.* ME. 3a *v.i.* Take place, happen; *arch.* foll. by (*un*)*to*, *upon* (a person etc.). ME. b *v.t.* (orig. w. dat. obj.). Happen to. ME. †4 *v.i.* Become *of*. LME–L16.

2 J. M. NEALE Giving to the dearer ones What to each befalleth. 3a THACKERAY Ethel's birthday befel in the Spring. C. KINGSLEY And so it befell that they often quarrelled. b MILTON Thus it shall befall Him who . . Lets her Will rule. C. CHAPLIN Only when ill-fortune befell her did she seek relief. D. JACOBSON The most significant events that befell the kingdom and its people during David's reign. 4 SHAKES. *Com. Err.* Do me the favour to dilate at full What have befall'n of them and thee till now.
befalling *n.* (*a*) the action of the vb; (*b*) an occurrence, an event: LME.

befile /bɪˈfʌɪl/ *v.t.* Long *rare*. OE. [f. BE- 1 + FILE *v.*[1]] Befoul, defile.

befit /bɪˈfɪt/ *v.t.* Infl. **-tt-**. L16. [f. BE- 1 + FIT *v.*[1]] 1 Be fitted or appropriate for, suit. L16. b Be morally right for. E17. †2 Equip *with*. L16–M18.

1 SHAKES. *Temp.* Any business that We say befits the hour. E. L. DOCTOROW His son now had a desk, as befitted all young students. B. TRAPIDO We're giving you the guest room, as befits your station as . . senior guest. b SHAKES. *Haml.* It us befitted To bear our hearts in grief. 2 L. STERNE He had . . befitted him with just such a bridle and saddle.
befitting *a.* suitable, fitting, appropriate, due M16. **befittingly** *adv.* M17.

beflower /bɪˈflaʊə/ *v.t.* L16. [f. BE- 4 + FLOWER *n.*] Cover or deck (as) with flowers.

befoam /bɪˈfəʊm/ *v.t.* E17. [f. BE- 4 + FOAM *n.*] Cover (as) with foam.

befog /bɪˈfɒg/ *v.t.* Infl. **-gg-**. E17. [f. BE- 4 + FOG *n.*[2]] Envelop in fog; obscure, confuse.

befool /bɪˈfuːl/ *v.t.* LME. [f. BE- 3, 4 + FOOL *n.*[1]] Make a fool of, dupe, delude; treat as or call a fool.

before /bɪˈfɔː/ *adv.*, *prep.*, & *conj.* [OE *beforan* = OFris. *befora*, OS *biforan*, OHG *bifora* (G *bevor*), f. Gmc: see BY *adv.* & *prep.*, FORE *adv.* & *prep.*] A *adv.* 1 In front in place or order; ahead, at or on the front. OE. 2 Earlier in time; previously, beforehand, in the past. ME. b *spec.* Contrasted w. *after* (see AFTER *adv.* 2b): preceding an event or (esp.) the use of a remedy, cosmetic, or other product. M18.

1 SHAKES. *Mids. N. D.* I am sent with broom before, To sweep the dust behind the door. *Macb.* Had he his hurts before? . . Ay, on the front. S. BARING-GOULD Onward, Christian soldiers, Marching as to war, With the Cross of Jesus Going on before. 2 LD MACAULAY Charles the First, eighteen years before, withdrew from his capital. ARNOLD BENNETT He had never spoken to Tom Orgreave before. C. CAUSLEY He felt younger than he had for some time before. D. BOGARDE He would come back one day and it would all be as before. *have been* THERE *before*. *have seen it all before*: see SEE *v.* *the mixture as before*: see MIXTURE 2. b *Puck* A 'before and after' racket for a hair-renewer advertisement.

B *prep.* I Of motion or position. 1 Of motion: ahead of, in advance of. OE. b Driven in front of, under the impulse of. M16. 2 Of position or direction: in front of. OE. 3 In the sight or presence of; under the notice of. OE. 4 In the view or opinion of. *arch.* OE. 5 Open to the knowledge of; claiming the attention of. LME. 6 In prospect for, open to; awaiting. (Merging with branch II, of time.) LME.

1 LD MACAULAY Behind him march the halbardiers; before him sound the drums. b SHAKES. *2 Hen. VI* Our enemies shall fall before us. A. SILLITOE Running before the wrath of cop or farmer. A. J. P. TAYLOR The anti-waste campaign . . swept all before it. 2 TENNYSON Once more before my face I see the moulder'd Abbey-walls. T. S. ELIOT Each man fixed his eyes before his feet. A. SILLITOE Emerging to scrub himself dry . . before the fire. M. BRAGG His back to the fells, before him the plain and the sea. 3 STEELE As ill an Action as any that comes before the Magistrate. J. M. BARRIE Is it to be before the ladies, Mr. Ernest, or in the privacy of the wood? TOLKIEN The song of Lúthien before Mandos was the song most fair that ever in words was woven. 4 P. STUBBES Though this be not theft before the world. 5 H. T. BUCKLE The accusations . . are before the world. T. HARDY Such was the argument that Oak set outwardly before him. 6 MILTON The World was all before them, where to choose, Their place of rest. B. WEBB Sidney and I have plenty of work before us—Sidney in the Labour Party and I on Government Committees.

II Of time. 7 Preceding in order of time. OE. 8 Previous to, earlier than (an event, point of time, etc.). ME. b Earlier than the end of (a future period of time). M19.

7 BYRON Brave men were living before Agamemnon. J. D. WATSON With luck, Francis's coiled coils would get into print as soon as if not before Pauling's. 8 S. JOHNSON It was written before the Conquest of Granada. A. J. P. TAYLOR Singapore had been neglected before the war and still more during it. b A. TROLLOPE This grief . . may be cured some day before long.

III Of order or rank. 9 In advance of in development; further on than. ME. 10 In preference to, rather than. ME. 11 In comparison with. E18.

9 HOBBES Atrides is before you in command. LD MACAULAY The nation which was so far before its neighbours in science. 10 AV *2 Sam.* 6:21 The Lord . . chose me before thy father, & before all his house. D. H. LAWRENCE I was a good animal before everything. 11 ADDISON The Women were of such an enormous Stature, that we appeared as Grashoppers before them.
Phrases: **before Christ** (of a date) reckoned backwards from the birth of Jesus. **before God** as God sees me (usu. as solemn asseveration). *before one's time*: see TIME *n.* *before the beam*: see BEAM *n.* *before the mast*: see MAST *n.*[1] 1. *before the secular worlds*: see SECULAR *a.* 5. **before the wind** helped or driven on by the force of the wind. *leg before wicket*: see LEG *n.* *not before time*: see TIME *n.* *walk before one can run*: see WALK *v.*[1]

C *conj.* 1 Previous to the time when. Also (arch.) *before that*. ME. 2 Of preference: sooner than that, rather than that. L16.

1 AV *John* 1:48 Before that Philip called thee . . I saw thee. E. HEMINGWAY I woke for good long before it was light. D. LODGE His hair is the texture and colour of Brillo pads before they've been used. 2 SHAKES. *Merch. V.* Treble that, Before a friend . . Shall lose a hair through Bassanio's fault. OED I will die before I submit.

beforehand /bɪˈfɔːhand/ *adv.* & *pred. a.* Orig. two wds. ME. [f. BEFORE *prep.* + HAND *n.*:

cf. AN, OFr. *avant main*.] In advance; in anticipation; in readiness, esp. (*arch.*) financially.

AV *Mark* 13:11 Take no thought before hand what ye shall speake. STEELE Having little or nothing beforehand, and living from Hand to Mouth. K. AMIS Do you write all this stuff out beforehand and learn it off, or . . [do] you make it up as you go along? **be beforehand with** anticipate, forestall.

†beforesaid *a.* Orig. two wds. ME–M18. [f. BEFORE *adv.* + SAID *ppl a.*] Previously mentioned, aforesaid.

beforetime /bɪˈfɔːtʌɪm/ *adv.* Orig. two wds. ME. [f. BEFORE *prep.* + TIME *n.*] Formerly, previously.

befortune /bɪˈfɔːtʃuːn/ *v.t.* & *i. rare.* L16. [f. BE- 1 + FORTUNE *v.*] Befall.

befoul /bɪˈfaʊl/ *v.t.* ME. [f. BE- 1 + FOUL *v.*] Make foul (*lit.* & *fig.*), cover with filth.

befoulment *n.* M19.

befriend /bɪˈfrɛnd/ *v.t.* M16. [f. BE- 3 + FRIEND *n.*] Act as a friend to; help, favour.

befriender *n.* M19.

befringe /bɪˈfrɪndʒ/ *v.t.* E17. [f. BE- 1 + FRINGE *v.*] Border, provide, or adorn (as) with a fringe.

befrog /bɪˈfrɒg/ *v.t.* Infl. **-gg-**. M19. [f. BE- 4 + FROG *n.*[3]] Decorate with frogging.

befuddle /bɪˈfʌd(ə)l/ *v.t.* L19. [f. BE- 1 + FUDDLE *v.*] Make stupid through drink etc.; confuse, bewilder.

befuddlement *n.* E20.

befur /bɪˈfɜː/ *v.t.* Infl. **-rr-**. L15. [f. BE- 1, 4 + FUR *v.*[1], *n.*[1]] Cover (as) with a fur or furs; deck out with furs. Chiefly as *befurred* ppl a.

beg /bɛg/ *n.*[1] L16. [Turk.: cf. BEGUM, BEY.] *Hist.* = BEY.

beg /bɛg/ *v.* & *n.*[2] ME. [Prob. f. OE *bedecian*, f. Gmc base of BID *v.*: cf. Goth. *bidagwa* beggar.] A *v.* Infl. **-gg-**. **1 a** *v.t.* Ask for (food, money, etc.) as a charitable gift. ME. **b** *v.i.* Ask for (or *for*) a charitable gift of food, money, etc.; live by asking for such gifts. (Foll. by *of*, *from*, †*at* a person.) ME. **2** *v.t.* & *i.* Ask someone earnestly or humbly for a thing desired. As obj. the person asked, the thing asked (which may take the form of a n. or pron., a cl. introduced by *that*, or an inf. phr.), or both. (Also foll. by †*at*, *of*, *from* the person asked, *for* the thing desired.) E16. **3** *v.t.* Ask (pardon, leave, etc.) formally or politely. L16. **b** *ellipt.* Ask or take leave *to do* something. M18. **c** *ellipt.* As an epistolary formula: offer, wish to send (compliments etc.). *arch.* M18. **4** *v.t.* Take (a disputed matter) for granted without warrant. Chiefly in *beg the question* below. L16. **5** *v.t.* & *i.* Foll. by *off*: get (a person) excused a penalty etc.; decline to take part etc. M18. **6** *v.t.* & *i. Cards.* Of the elder hand in all fours (seven-up): ask for (a point, or three additional cards and a new trump). L18. **7** *v.i.* Of a (trained) dog: sit up with forepaws raised expectantly. Freq. in *imper.* as a command. E19.

1 C. S. LEWIS Father's ruin was approaching, that we should all soon beg our bread in the streets. S. BECKETT I went to the house and begged a glass of milk and a slice of bread and butter. **beg, borrow, or steal** acquire by any means at all. b G. ORWELL A fat man eating quails while children are begging for bread is a disgusting sight. P. S. BUCK Holding up a bowl and begging of any one who passed. C. HAMPTON A hunchback . . who used to sit on the pavement and beg. P. SCOTT If the hippie was there, and came begging at the coffee shop, Ibrahim threw him a few paise. **go (a-)begging** *fig.* (of an opportunity etc.) find no taker; (of a thing) be unwanted. 2 TINDALE *Matt.* 27:58 Ioseph . . went to Pilate and begged the body of Iesus. SHAKES. *L.L.L.* How I would make him fawn, and beg, and seek. EVELYN Our prisoners . . beg at us, as a mercy, to knock them on the head. HOR. WALPOLE I have three favours to beg of you. TENNYSON I will beg of him to take thee back. LD MACAULAY Shrewsbury begged that . . he might be appointed. C. STEAD She also begged them for money so that she could take home presents to all the children. A. KOESTLER I beg you to take note that I am not moralising. J. BALDWIN Of them all she would have begged forgiveness, had they come with ears to hear. D. LODGE He turned up again yesterday evening to beg a rather odd favour. J. UPDIKE Did they die ignobly, begging and cackling for mercy? 3 ADDISON I must however beg Leave to dissent from so great an Authority. *beg (someone's) pardon*: see PARDON *n.* 2. b OED I beg to enclose my price list. D. L. SAYERS Here Sir Impey Biggs interposed and begged with submission to suggest that his lordship should remind the jury of the evidence given by Mr. Challoner. c DICKENS Begging my best remembrances to Mrs. Thomson. 4 H. ROGERS Many say it is begging the point in dispute. **beg the question** assume the truth of a thing to be proved or a thing equivalent to it; *pop.* evade a difficulty. 5 S. RICHARDSON Is the Creature begging me off from Insult? J. RATHBONE I was a little drunk and very tired and begged off.

Comb.: **begging letter**: asking for a charitable gift to be sent; **beg-pardon** (*Austral.* & *NZ colloq.*) an apology.

B *n.* An act of begging. E19.

beggingly *adv.* in the manner of a person who begs. L16.

begad /bɪˈgad/ *int.* L16. [Alt. of *by God!*: cf. EGAD etc.] Expr. amazement or emphasis.

begah *n.* var. of BIGHA.

began *v.* pa. t. of BEGIN.

begat *v.* see BEGET.

begem /bɪˈdʒɛm/ *v.t.* Infl. **-mm-**. M18. [f. BE- 4 + GEM *n.*] Set about or stud with gems.

beget /bɪˈgɛt/ *v.t.* Pa. t. **begot** /bɪˈgɒt/, (*arch.*) **begat** /bɪˈgat/; pres. pple **begetting**; pa. pple **begotten** /bɪˈgɒt(ə)n/. [OE *beġietan*, corresp. to OS *bigetan* seize, OHG *bigezzan* receive = Goth. *bigetan* find: see BE-, GET *v.*] **†1** Get, acquire, esp. by effort. OE–E17. **2** Procreate (usu. said of the father, occas. of both parents). ME. **†b** Get *with child*. LME–E17. **3** *fig.* Call into being, occasion; give rise to. L16.

2 SHAKES. *1 Hen. VI* Richard, Edward's son, The first-begotten and the lawful heir. V. WOOLF Begetting one son . . by Lady Bradshaw. A. STORR It is unproven that the strongest males necessarily beget the strongest offspring. *fig.*: *Book of Common Prayer* The Son is of the Father alone: not made, nor created, but begotten. 3 CONAN DOYLE As usual, familiarity begat contempt.

begetter *n.* a person who begets; a procreator, an originator: LME.

beggar /ˈbɛgə/ *n.* ME. [f. BEG *v.* + -AR[3].] **1** A person who begs; *esp.* a person who lives by begging. ME. **2** A person in needy circumstances; a poor person. ME. **3** A mean or low fellow; *joc.* a person, a chap. Now also *euphem.* for BUGGER *n.*[1] 3. ME. **†4** A person who begs a favour; a suppliant. LME–E17. **†5** A person who begs the question. L16–E19.

1 *Proverb*: Beggars cannot be choosers. *sturdy beggar*: see STURDY *a. valiant beggar*: see VALIANT *a.* 1. 2 COVERDALE *Ecclus* 37:30 Some man . . can geve . . prudent councell . . and contynueth a begger. 3 E. LANGLEY At last, the poor little beggars did their dialogue to a thunder of well-fed applause. *Fortune* The plane starts taxiing in from the runway, and look: the beggars are already standing up, ready to jump off.

Comb.: **beggar-ticks** (the prickly fruits of) any of several N. American bur-marigolds, esp. *Bidens frondosa*.

beggarhood *n.* (people in) the condition of a beggar ME. **beggarism** *n.* (now *rare*) practice characteristic of a beggar, beggary M17.

beggar /ˈbɛgə/ *v.t.* LME. [f. the n.] **1** Make a beggar of; impoverish. LME. **2** Exhaust the resources of; go beyond, outdo. E17.

1 M. MITCHELL The Cause which had taken their friends, lovers, husbands and beggared their families. M. NA GOPALEEN He also beggared nine weak-minded relatives. **beggar-my-neighbour** a card-game in which one seeks to capture one's opponent's cards; *fig.* a policy of advancement at the expense of one's neighbours. 2 SHAKES. *Ant. & Cl.* For her own person, It beggar'd all description. C. PRIEST It beggared belief that she should twice interrupt me at precisely the same place.

beggarly /ˈbɛgəli/ *a.* E16. [f. BEGGAR *n.* + -LY[1].] **1** In the condition of or befitting a beggar; poverty-stricken; *fig.* intellectually poor, valueless. E16. **2** Mean, sordid. L16.

beggarliness *n.* M16.

beggarly /ˈbɛgəli/ *adv. arch.* LME. [f. BEGGAR *n.* + -LY[2].] As a beggar; indigently, humbly.

beggary /ˈbɛgəri/ *n.* LME. [f. BEGGAR *n.* + -Y[3].] **1** The condition of a beggar; extreme poverty. LME. **2** The action or habit of begging. LME. **†3** Contemptible stuff, rubbish. M16–M17. **4** Beggars collectively. *arch.* M16. **†5** Contemptible meanness. Only in E17.

1 SWIFT This coin . . will reduce the kingdom to beggary. 2 X. HERBERT Perhaps he would abandon beggary when there was no poor fool about to beg from. 3 J. FOXE Your Ceremonies in the Church be beggary and poyson. 5 SHAKES. *Cymb.* Not I . . pronounce the beggary of his change.

beghard /ˈbɛgəd/ *n.* M16. [med.L *Beghardus* f. OFr. *Bégard*, *-art*, MDu. *Beggaert*, MHG *Beghart*, f. stem of *Beguīna* etc.: see BEGUINE *n.*[1], -ARD.] *Hist.* A member of one of the lay brotherhoods which arose in the Low Countries in the 13th cent. in imitation of the female beguines.

begift /bɪˈgɪft/ *v.t.* LME. [f. BE- 4 + GIFT *n.*] **†1** Entrust. Only in LME. **2** Present with gifts. L16.

begild /bɪˈgɪld/ *v.t.* Pa. pple **begilded, begilt** /bɪˈgɪlt/. L16. [f. BE- 1 + GILD *v.*[1]] Cover with, or as with, gold.

begin /bɪˈgɪn/ *v.* Pa. t. **began** /bɪˈgan/, **†begun**. Pres. pple **beginning** /bɪˈgɪnɪŋ/. Pa. pple **begun** /bɪˈgʌn/. [OE *beġinnan* = OFris. *biginna*, OS, OHG *biginnan* (Du., G *beginnen*), f. WGmc, f. as BE- + Gmc base of unkn. origin, found in various compounds meaning 'begin'.] **1** *v.i.* Take the first step in some action or process; commence, start. (Foll. by inf.) OE. **2** *v.i.* Come into being, start occurring, arise; have its commencement or nearest boundary (at some place or time). OE. **3** *v.t.* Set about doing, start upon; perform the first part of. OE. **4** *v.t.* Start (a thing) on its course, bring into being, initiate; be the first to do. ME. **5** *v.i.* & *t.* Start speaking (with the words). LME. **6** *v.i.* (Usu. w. preceding neg.) Come anywhere near, show any attempt or likelihood *to do* something; *ellipt.* (*US*) compare in any degree (*with*). *colloq.* M19.

1 AV *Gen.* 4:26 Then began men to call upon the Name of the Lord. BYRON My way is to begin with the beginning. E. O'NEILL During dinner I began to get a headache. DAY LEWIS The night I began to be born. G. VIDAL He paused and then he began to speak carefully but casually. 2 AV *Num.* 16:46 There is wrath gone out from the Lord; the plague is begun. J. BRYCE The greatness of the Prussian monarchy begins with Frederick II. OED The paragraph begins about the middle of the page. L. DURRELL He had already given the signal for dinner to begin. 3 CHESTERFIELD The Spaniards began their conquests . . by the islands of St. Domingo and Cuba. EARL OF CHATHAM I rejoice to hear you have begun Homer's Iliad. J. B. PRIESTLEY They begin work at half-past seven and end at five. R. GRAVES The senior Consul called for order and began reading the letter. 4 POPE Proud Nimrod first the savage chace began. J. M. BARRIE Watch whether Crichton begins any of his answers to my questions with 'The fact is'. R. H. TAWNEY The events which seemed to aristocratic Parliamentarians to close the revolution seemed to the left wing of the victorious army only to begin it. 5 MILTON To whom th' Arch-Enemy . . Breaking the horrid silence, thus began: [etc.]. SCOTT FITZGERALD 'You ought to live in California—' began Miss Baker, but Tom interrupted her. 6 M. TWAIN There ain't a book that begins with it. N. MAILER The American hipsters' writings cannot begin to compare with the work of the arch-hipsters of modern European literature, Celine and Genet. LADY BIRD JOHNSON I cannot begin to say how impressed I am with Mrs. Rose Kennedy.

Phrases, & with preps. in specialized senses: **begin at** start from. *begin on*: see *begin upon* below. **begin school** attend school for the first time. *begin the dance*: see DANCE *n.* **begin the world** start in life. **begin (up)on** set to work at. **begin with** take first or as one's starting-point. **to begin with** at the outset; as a first point.

beginning *a.* that begins; *Educ.* (*N. Amer.*) elementary: L16.

beginner /bɪˈgɪnə/ *n.* LME. [f. prec. + -ER[1].] **1** A person who begins; an originator. LME. **2** A person just beginning to learn a skill etc.; a novice, an inexperienced person. LME.

2 **beginner's luck** good luck supposed to attend a beginner at games etc.

beginning /bɪˈgɪnɪŋ/ *n.* ME. [f. as prec. + -ING[1].] **1** Entering upon existence or action; bringing into existence; commencing, origination. ME. **2** The point at which anything begins; *spec.* the time when the universe began to be. ME. **3** An origin or source. ME. **†b** A first cause, a first principle. LME–L16. **4** The first part (of a period of time, of a book, journey, etc.); the earliest stage of development (freq. in *pl.*). ME.

2 COVERDALE *Hab.* 1:12 Thou o Lorde . . art from the begynnynge. B. SPOCK If you miss, you must penalize yourself, go back to the beginning, and start again. P. DAVIES The vexed question of whether it is possible . . for time to have a beginning or ending has been debated by philosophers for over two thousand years. 3 CARLYLE Thy true . . Beginning and Father is in Heaven. 4 *Book of Common Prayer* Who hast safely brought us to the beginning of this day. ADAM SMITH Great fortunes acquired from small beginnings. J. R. GREEN The beginnings of physical science were more slow and timid there. G. B. SHAW You have made a slip at the very beginning of your fairy tale. ISAIAH BERLIN All movements have origins, forerunners, imperceptible beginnings. DAY LEWIS Looking at that photograph of our house in the Queen's County, and blindly reaching out across fifty-four years to my beginnings. **the beginning of the end** the first clear sign of the end of something.

beginningless *a.* without a beginning, uncreated L16.

begird /bɪˈɡəːd/ *v.t.* Now *literary*. Pa. t. & pple **begirt** /bɪˈɡəːt/. [OE *begyrdan*: see BE- 1, GIRD *v.*[1]] 1 Gird about or around. OE. 2 Encompass, encircle *with*. OE. †3 Besiege. L16–L18.

begirdle /bɪˈɡəːd(ə)l/ *v.t.* M19. [f. BE- 1 + GIRDLE *v.*] Encompass like a girdle.

begirt /bɪˈɡəːt/ *v.*[1]*t.* Pa. t. & pple same. E17. [f. BE- 1 + GIRT *v.*[1]] Surround, encircle.

begirt *v.*[2] pa. t. & pple of BEGIRD.

beglamour /bɪˈɡlamə/ *v.t.* Also ***-or**. M19. [f. BE- 4 + GLAMOUR *n.*] Glamorize; invest with (deceptive) glamour.

beglerbeg /ˈbɛɡləbɛɡ/ *n.* Also **-bey** /-beɪ/. M16. [Turk. = bey of beys, f. BEG *n.*[1], pl. *begler*.] *Hist.* The governor of a province of the Ottoman Empire, in rank next to the grand vizier.

begloom /bɪˈɡluːm/ *v.t.* L18. [f. BE- 4 + GLOOM *n.*[1]] Render gloomy.

begnaw /bɪˈnɔː/ *v.t.* Pa. pple **-ed, begnawn** /bɪˈnɔːn/. [OE *begnagan*: see BE- 1, GNAW *v.*] Gnaw at, nibble, corrode.

bego /bɪˈɡəʊ/ *v.t.* Long *obs.* exc. as pa. pple **begone** /bɪˈɡɒn/, now only in WOEBEGONE. [OE *begān*, OS *bigangan*, OHG *bigān*, Goth. *bigaggan*: see BE- 2, GO *v.*] Go round or about; surround, overrun; beset, afflict; adorn, clothe.

begob /bɪˈɡɒb/ *int. Anglo-Ir.* L19. [Alt. of *by God!*: cf. BEGAD etc.] Expr. amazement or emphasis.

begone /bɪˈɡɒn/ *v.*[1]*i.* Only in *imper.* & *inf.* LME. [Imper. & inf. *be gone* (see GO *v.* 30) treated as one wd; cf. BEWARE.] Go away immediately.

CARLYLE Kaiser's Ambassador . . is angrily ordered to begone. W. DE LA MARE Sweet sounds, begone.

begone *v.*[2] see BEGO.

begonia /bɪˈɡəʊnɪə/ *n.* M18. [mod.L (see below), f. Michel *Bégon* (1638–1710), Fr. patron of science: see -IA[1].] A plant of the genus *Begonia*, having a coloured perianth but no petals, and often brilliant foliage.

begorra /bɪˈɡɒrə/ *int. Anglo-Ir.* Also **-ah**. M19. [Alt. of *by God!*: cf. BEGAD etc.] Expr. amazement or emphasis.

begot, begotten *vs.* see BEGET.

begrace /bɪˈɡreɪs/ *v.t.* E16. [f. BE- 3 + GRACE *n.*] Address as 'your grace'.

begrease /bɪˈɡriːs/ *v.t.* M16. [f. BE- 1 + GREASE *v.*] Besmear with grease.

begrime /bɪˈɡrʌɪm/ *v.t.* M16. [f. BE- 4 + GRIME *n.*] Blacken with grime; make grimy.

begrudge /bɪˈɡrʌdʒ/ *v.t.* LME. [f. BE- 1 + GRUDGE *v.*] Feel or show dissatisfaction at (a thing); resentfully envy (a person) the possession of; give reluctantly.

SHAFTESBURY They will . . begrudg the pains of attending. S. UNWIN No time spent by parents on their children during that period should be begrudged. A. SILLITOE He begrudged big talkers their unearned glory. D. LODGE I didn't really begrudge him the food, since he was obviously starved of decent home cooking.

begrudgingly *adv.* in a grudging manner or spirit M19.

begrutten /bɪˈɡrʌt(ə)n/ *a. Sc.* E17. [f. BE- + *grutten* pa. pple of GREET *v.*[2]] Swollen in the face with much weeping.

beguile /bɪˈɡʌɪl/ *n. arch.* Long *obs.* exc. *Sc.* LME. [f. the vb.] Deception.

beguile /bɪˈɡʌɪl/ *v.t.* ME. [f. BE- 1 + GUILE *v.*: cf. MDu. *begīlen*, AN *degiler*.] 1 Deceive, delude. ME. 2 Deprive *of* by fraud; cheat (*out*) *of* (something) or *into* (doing). ME. †3 Cheat (hopes etc., or a person in them); disappoint, foil. L15–M17. 4 Divert, distract (a person, his or her attention); charm, amuse. L16. 5 Divert one's attention pleasantly from (time passing, something tedious or unpleasant); while away (time). L16.

beguilement *n.* E19. **beguiler** *n.* LME. **beguiling** *ppl a.* that beguiles; *esp.* charming, fascinating: L16. **beguilingly** *adv.* M19.

béguin /beɡɛ̃/ *n.* Pl. pronounced same. E20. [Colloq. Fr.] An infatuation, a fancy.

beguine /beɪˈɡiːn/ *n.*[1] Also **bé-**. LME. [(O)Fr. *béguine* (MDu., MHG *begīne*), med.L *Beguina*, perh. ult. f. MDu. vb = mutter (prayers): see -INE[3].] A member of a lay sisterhood in the Low Countries, formed in the 12th cent. and not bound by vows.

beguinage /ˈbeɪɡɪnɪdʒ, -nɑːʒ/ *n.* an establishment of, or house for, beguines L17.

beguine /bɪˈɡiːn/ *n.*[2] E20. [Amer. Fr. f. Fr. BÉGUIN.] (The distinctive rhythm of) a dance of W. Indian origin.

begum /ˈbeɪɡəm/ *n.* M17. [Urdu *begam* f. E. Turkic *begim*, f. as BEG *n.*[1] + *-im* 1st person sing. possess. suff.] In the Indian subcontinent: a Muslim noblewoman or lady of high rank. Also (**B-**), a title given to a married Muslim woman (= Mrs).

begun *v.* see BEGIN.

begunk /bɪˈɡʌŋk/ *n.* & *v. Sc.* E18. [Origin unkn.] A *n.* A piece of deception, a trick. E18. B *v.t.* Play a trick on, take in. E19.

behalf /bɪˈhɑːf/ *n.* ME. [f. combination of earlier phrs. *on his halve* and *bi halve him*, both meaning 'on his side': see BY *prep.*, HALF *n.*] 1 *on* or (now chiefly N. Amer.) *in behalf of*: a As the agent or representative of (another); in the name of. ME. b On the part of, proceeding from. (Long *rare* or *obs.* but revived L20.) LME. c In the interest or for the benefit of (another person, a cause, etc.); for the sake of. L16. 2 *in* (or †*on*) *this* (or *that*) *behalf*, in respect of or concerning a particular matter. *arch.* LME.

behang /bɪˈhaŋ/ *v.t. obs.* exc. as pa. pple **behung** /bɪˈhʊŋ/. [OE *behōn*: see BE- 1, HANG *v.*] Drape or hang (a thing) about *with*.

†**behappen** *v.t.* & *i.* LME–M17. [f. BE- 1, 2 + HAPPEN *v.*] Befall.

Behari *a.* & *n.* var. of BIHARI.

behave /bɪˈheɪv/ *v.* LME. [f. BE- 1 + HAVE *v.* (w. early stressed pronunc.).] 1 *v.refl.* & (now usu.) *i.* Conduct or bear oneself in a specified manner. LME. †2 *v.t.* Handle, manage, regulate. E16–M17. 3 *v.refl.* & *i.* Esp. to or of a child: conduct oneself well or with propriety; show good manners. L17. 4 *v.i.* Of a thing: function, act, or react in a specified manner. M19.

1 **behave to** or **towards** deal with or treat (someone) in a specified way. *ill-behaved*: see ILL *adv.* *well-behaved*: see WELL *adv.*

behavior *n.* **-ioral** *a.*, **-iorism** *n.* see BEHAVIOUR etc.

behaviour /bɪˈheɪvjə/ *n.* Also ***-or**. LME. [f. prec. after HAVIOUR.] 1 Manner of bearing oneself; demeanour, manners; observable actions; treatment shown *to* or *towards* another or others. LME. †b *spec.* Good manners, elegant deportment. L16–E18. 2 (As a count n.) An instance or way of behaving. Now usu. of animals or people as objects of study: an observable pattern of actions, a response to a stimulus. M16. 3 The way in which an object, device, substance, etc., acts or works. L17.

1 **be on one's best** (or **good**) **behaviour** take care to behave well (when being observed or tested).

Comb.: **behaviour pattern** a set of actions which occur characteristically in a given situation and are regarded as a unified whole; **behaviour therapy** treatment of a psychological disorder by gradual training of the patient to react normally.

behavioural /bɪˈheɪvjər(ə)l/ *a.* Also ***-ior-**. E20. [f. prec. + -AL[1].] Of, pertaining to, or forming part of behaviour.

behavioural science the science of animal (and human) behaviour.

behaviouralism *n.* behavioural science esp. as applied to politics M20. **behaviouralist** *n.* & *a.* (*a*) *n.* a practitioner of behaviouralism; (*b*) *adj.* of or pertaining to behaviouralism or behaviouralists: M20. **behaviourally** *adv.* as regards behaviour M20.

behaviourism /bɪˈheɪvjərɪz(ə)m/ *n.* Also ***-ior-**. E20. [f. as prec. + -ISM.] *Psychol.* The doctrine that objective investigation of stimuli and responses is the only valid psychological method; psychological analysis in terms of stimulus and response.

behaviourist *n.* an adherent or practitioner of behaviourism E20. **behaviouˈristic** *a.* E20. **behaviouˈristically** *adv.* E20.

behead /bɪˈhɛd/ *v.t.* [OE *behēafdian*: see BE- 4, HEAD *n.*] Cut off the head or top part of; kill in this way.

beheadal *n.* M19.

beheld *v.* pa. t. & pple of BEHOLD.

behemoth /bɪˈhiːmɒθ, ˈbiːhɪməʊθ/ *n.* LME. [Heb. *bĕhēmōṯ* intensive pl. of *bĕhēmāh* beast.] An enormous creature (in *Job* 40:15 prob. a hippopotamus or a crocodile); *fig.* something vast.

S. B. FLEXNER The *Great Eastern* . . , an iron behemoth designed for the England-to-India run.

behemothian /biːhɪˈməʊθɪən/ *a.* (*literary*) of a behemoth; monstrously huge: E20.

behest /bɪˈhɛst/ *n.* [OE *behǣs* (+ parasitic *t*) f. Gmc base meaning 'bid, call': see BE-, HEST, HIGHT *v.*] †1 A vow, a promise. OE–L16. 2 A command; bidding, instigation. Now chiefly in *at the behest of*. ME.

behight /bɪˈhʌɪt/ *v.t.* Long *obs.* exc. *dial.* (*rare*). Pa. t. & pple **behight**, (later) **-ed**. [OE *behātan*, *bi-* = OHG *biheizzan*: see BE-, HIGHT *v.*] I Proper uses. 1 Vow, promise; hold out hope of; warrant. OE. II Improper uses introduced by Spenser. †2 Grant, deliver; command, ordain. Only in L16. 3 Call, name. L16.

behind /bɪˈhʌɪnd/ *adv.*, *prep.*, & *n.* [OE *behindan*, *bi-* = OS *bihindan*, f. *bi* BY *prep.* + *hindan* from behind (= OHG *hintana* (G *hinten*) behind, Goth. *hindana* beyond, etc.: cf. HIND *a.*] A *adv.* 1 Remaining after the departure of oneself or others; in a place, position, state, etc., from which others or other things have gone or been removed. OE. b In reserve, still to come. *arch.* ME. c In the past. LME. 2 At the back of something stationary, in the rear; on the far side of something, hidden. OE. b *spec.* Behind the scenes in a theatre. E19. 3 In the rear of something moving; following, trailing; at a less advanced stage of progress, rank, attainment, etc. ME. b Less advanced than one should be; in arrears (*with* payments etc.). LME. 4 Late; slow in coming forward. Long *obs.* exc. *dial.* ME. 5 Towards or into the rear; backwards. LME.

1 DONNE To leave this world behinde, is death. T. H. HUXLEY The salt is left entirely behind, and nothing but pure water evaporated. A. J. P. TAYLOR Conditions for those who remained behind were also bad. P. JAY I left the table behind In the attic. b LD MACAULAY But stronger evidence is behind. c SHAKES. *Sonn.* My grief lies onward and my joy behind. 2 SHAKES. *Jul. Caes.* Damned Casca, like a cur, behind Struck Cæsar on the neck. T. S. ELIOT Shall I part my hair behind? J. SQUIRE A place Of dingy yards with towering buildings behind. *Daily Telegraph* To be caught behind off the last ball of an over. *stop behind*: see STOP *v.* 22c. 3 JAS. MILL The opponents were not behind in violence. W. S. CHURCHILL In a poll of about 23,000 votes . . I was 1,300 behind and Mr. Mawdsley about 30 lower. B. ENGLAND Now Lt Truly hobbles on from the right, far behind, limping. **come from behind** win after lagging. b W. MAXWELL His father gets behind in his spring plowing because of the rains. E. FIGES A bit rushed, having somehow got behind with everything. 5 WORDSWORTH O'er rough and smooth she trips along, And never looks behind.

B *prep.* (in OE also w. dat. obj.). 1 In a place, position, state, etc. left by (a person who or thing which has gone); existing from or belonging to the earlier life of (a person still alive or now dead). (Usu. w. pronoun.) OE. 2 At the rear or back of (someone or something stationary); on the further side of (esp. so as to be concealed), beyond. OE. b *fig.* At the back of as a supporter or as a cause or instigator. M19. 3 Towards the back or further side of; backwards from; into a position at the rear of. ME. b *fig.* Out of one's attention or thought. M19. 4 In the rear of; after, following; inferior to in progress, rank, attainment, etc. LME. 5 Later than (a set time). L16.

1 SHAKES. *Twel. N.* He left behind him myself and a sister. G. B. SHAW I had left the follies . . of the old days behind me for ever. K. AMIS The last two and a half years freelancing . . , with even a book behind him. S. HILL The gate clicked shut behind Doctor Sparrow. 2 S. JOHNSON They wondered how a youth of spirit could spend the prime of life behind a counter. G. EWART I know that behind her spectacles she / has the most beautiful eyes. J. LE CARRÉ He lives in Chelsea, just behind Sloane Square. *behind bars*: see BAR *n.*[1] 2a. *behind* CLOSED *doors. behind one's back*: see BACK *n.*[1] *behind the curtain*: see CURTAIN *n.* 4. *behind the scenes*: see SCENE. *behind the veil*: see VEIL *n.* 3. *hide behind a person's skirts*: see SKIRT *n.* 1. b J. MARTINEAU Behind every phenomenon we must assume a power. S. HILL She liked flowers, liked even more the thought behind them. B. ENGLAND At least it would have the sanction of proper authority behind it. 3 AV *Matt.* 26:23 Get thee behind mee, Satan. S. JOHNSON Venturing to look behind him. OED The sun has sunk behind the mountains. L. URIS She walked up behind him and touched his shoulder. b **put behind one** refuse to consider. 4 R. HOOKER Beasts, though otherwise behind men, may . . in actions of sense and fancy go beyond them. SIR W. SCOTT Behind him rode two gallant squires. E. WAUGH Of the University he said: 'No, I was never here. It just means you start life three years behind the other fellow'. J. LE CARRÉ Peters was three or four behind him in the queue. *behind the times*: see TIME *n.* 5 SHAKES. *A.Y.L.* If you . . come one minute behind your hour, I will think you the most pathetical break-promise. **behind schedule** or **time** unpunctual, late.

Other phrases: **†behind the hand** = BEHINDHAND.

C *n.* 1 The buttocks. *colloq.* L18. 2 *Austral. Rules Football.* A kick etc. scoring one point. L19.

behindhand /bɪˈhʌɪndhand/ *adv.* & *pred. a.* M16. [f. BEHIND *prep.* + HAND *n.*, after BEFOREHAND.] 1 In arrears with regard to payments or other obligations. M16. 2 Less advanced than others or than one should be; lacking *in* (a quality etc.). M16. 3 Behind time, late; out of date. E18.

behither /bɪˈhɪðə/ *prep.* & *adv. obs.* exc. *dial.* E16. [f. BE- + HITHER: cf. BEHIND etc.] On this side (of).

Behmenism *n.* var. of BOEHMENISM.

behold /bɪˈhəʊld/ *v. literary* or *arch.* Pa. t. **beheld** /-ˈhɛld/; pa. pple **beheld, †beholden** (cf. next). [OE *bihaldan* = OFris. *bihalda*, OS *bihaldan*, (Du. *behouden*), OHG *bihaltan* (G *behalten*): see BE-, HOLD *v.*] †1 *v.t.* Hold, retain. OE–E16. †2 *v.t.* & *i.* Concern, relate to; pertain *to*. OE–LME. †3 *v.t.* & *i.* Regard, consider; have regard *(un)to*. OE–LME. 4 *v.t.* See, become aware of by sight; hold in view, watch. OE. 5 *v.i.* Look. *obs.* exc. as in sense 7. ME. †6 *v.t.* Of buildings, land, etc.: look towards, face. LME–L17. 7 In *imper.* as *int.*, used to call or direct attention: Look! Lo! M16.

7 *lo and behold*: see LO *int.*[1]

beholder *n.* a person who beholds, a watcher: LME. **beholding** *n.* seeing, sight; a thing beheld, a vision: ME. **beholding** *a.* (*a*) looking, watching; (*b*) (*obs.* exc. *dial.*: orig. an error for *beholden*) under an obligation, dependent: L15.

beholden /bɪˈhəʊld(ə)n/ *pred. a.* LME. [Orig. pa. pple of prec., which is not otherwise attested in these senses.] 1 Under an obligation (*to*); indebted. LME. 2 Duty-bound. Now *rare* or *obs.* LME.

behoof /bɪˈhuːf/ *n. arch.* [OE *behōf* = OFris. *bihōf*, (M)Du. *behoef*, MHG *behuof* (G *behuf*), f. WGmc, f. as BE- + var. of base of HEAVE *v.*] Benefit, advantage. Chiefly in *for, on,* or *to (the) behoof of.*

behove /bɪˈhəʊv/ *v.* Also ***behoove** /bɪˈhuːv/. [OE *behōfian* = OFris. *bihōvia*, MLG *behōven*, MDu. *behoeven*, f. prec.] †1 *v.t.* Have need of, require. OE–M17. †2 *v.t.* & *i.* Be physically of use or needful (to). OE–M17. 3 *v.t.* Be morally required of (a person), be incumbent upon; befit. Now usu. *impers.* in *behoves*, (usu.) *it behoves* etc. *to do*. OE. 4 *v.i.* Be proper or due, be suited. Now usu. *impers.* in (*it*) *behoves* etc. (Foll. by *to*; impers. *to do, that*.) *arch.* OE. 5 *v.i.* (w. pers. subj.) Be under obligation *to do*. Long *obs.* exc. *Sc.* LME.

behovely *a.* (long *rare*) = BEHOVEFUL OE.

behoveful /bɪˈhəʊvfʊl, -f(ə)l/ *a. arch.* LME. [f. BEHOOF + -FUL.] Advantageous, expedient; necessary, fitting.

behung *v.* pa. t. & pple of BEHANG.

beige /beɪʒ, beɪdʒ/ *n.* & *a.* M19. [Fr.] A *n.* 1 A fine woollen fabric, usu. undyed and unbleached. M19. 2 A yellowish-grey colour like that of undyed and unbleached wool. L19. B *adj.* Esp. of fabrics: of a yellowish-grey colour. L19.

beigel *n.* var. of BAGEL.

beignet /ˈbɛnjeɪ, bɛnˈjɛ; *foreign* bɛɲɛ (*pl. same*)/ *n.* M19. [Fr.] A fritter; *spec.* (*US*) a square of fried dough eaten hot sprinkled with icing sugar. Usu. in *pl.*

bein /biːn/ *a.* & *adv.* Long *obs.* exc. *dial.* (chiefly *Sc.*). Also **bien**. ME. [Origin unkn.] A *adj.* 1 Pleasant, kindly; nice, good. ME. 2 Comfortable, well-furnished. M16. 3 Comfortably off, well-to-do. M16. B *adv.* Pleasantly, nicely. LME.

being /ˈbiːɪŋ/ *n.* ME. [f. BE + -ING[1].] 1 Existence, material or immaterial; life. ME. b Existence in some specified condition, circumstance, etc. E16. †2 Condition; standing, position; livelihood. ME–E19. 3 Substance, constitution; nature, essence; person. ME. 4 That which exists or is conceived as existing; *esp.* a person or other intelligent creature. LME.

1 TINDALE *Acts* 17:28 In him we lyve, move & have oure beynge. S. JOHNSON Good humour . . is the balm of being. E. A. FREEMAN The house had no corporate being. TOLKIEN The Light of the Trees I brought into being. **being-for-itself** *Philos.* conscious being, being as actuality. **being-in-itself** *Philos.* being that lacks conscious awareness, being as potentiality. *call into being*: see CALL *v. fleet in being*: see FLEET *n.*[1] **in being** existing, in existence. b COVERDALE *Luke* 9:33 Master here is good beynge for vs. G. BURNET What he has acquired during his being a Bishop. W. FAULKNER Evil is a part of man, . . the same as repentance and being brave. 2 STEELE Such . . as want help towards getting into some being in the world. 3 TREVISA The comparyson bitwene a poynte and a lyne in beynge. M. DE LA ROCHE He awoke with a start, excited in all his being. B. BETTELHEIM Man's innermost being . . —man's soul. 4 BARONESS ORCZY A surging, seething, murmuring crowd, of beings that are human only in name. I. MURDOCH A separate being with troubles and desires of her own. C. SAGAN The probability that we are frequently visited by extraterrestrial beings. *human being*: see HUMAN *a.* **the Supreme Being** God.

beingness *n.* M17.

being *v.* pres. pple of BE.

beisa /ˈbeɪsə/ *n.* M19. [Amharic.] A gemsbok of the E. African race, *Oryx gazella beisa*. Also *beisa oryx*.

Beja /ˈbɛdʒə/ *n.* & *a.* E19. [Afr. name] A *n.* Pl. same. A member of a nomadic Cushitic people living between the Nile and the Red Sea; the Cushitic language of this people. E19. B *adj.* Of or pertaining to the Beja. M20.

bejabers /bɪˈdʒeɪbəz/ *int. Anglo-Ir.* Also **-jabb-** /-ˈdʒab-/, **†-jap(p)-**. E19. [Alt. of *by Jesus!*: cf. BEJESUS.] Expr. amazement or emphasis.

bejant /ˈbiːdʒ(ə)nt/ *n. Sc.* Also **†-jan.** M17. [Fr. *béjaune*, f. *bec jaune* yellow beak, i.e. fledgling, w. parasitic *t*.] A first-year undergraduate, orig. at any Scottish university but now only at St Andrews.

†bejap(p)ers *int.* vars. of BEJABERS.

bejasus *int.* var. of BEJESUS.

bejel /ˈbeɪdʒ(ə)l, ˈbɛdʒ-/ *n.* E20. [Iraqi Arab.] *Med.* A non-venereal form of syphilis formerly endemic in N. Africa and the Middle East.

bejesuit /bɪˈdʒɛzjʊɪt/ *v.t.* M17. [f. BE- 3, 4 + JESUIT.] Initiate into Jesuitism; subject to the influence of Jesuits.

bejesus /bɪˈdʒiːzəs/ *int.* Also (esp. *Anglo-Ir.*) **bejasus** /bɪˈdjeɪzəs/. E20. [Alt. of *by Jesus!*: cf. BEJABERS.] Expr. amazement or emphasis.

bejewel /bɪˈdʒuːəl/ *v.t.* Infl. **-ll-**, ***-l-**. M16. [f. BE- 4 + JEWEL *n.*] Deck or adorn (as) with jewels; spangle.

bekiss /bɪˈkɪs/ *v.t.* L16. [f. BE- 1 + KISS *v.*] Kiss excessively; cover with kisses.

beknave /bɪˈneɪv/ *v.t.* E16. [f. BE- 3 + KNAVE *n.*] Treat as or call a knave.

beknow /bɪˈnəʊ/ *v.t.* Long *arch.* & *dial.* Pa. t. **beknew** /bɪˈnjuː/; pa. pple **beknown** /bɪˈnəʊn/. ME. [f. BE- 1 + KNOW *v.*] Be or become acquainted with; recognize, acknowledge, know.

be beknown of be aware of, avow, acknowledge.

bel /bɛl/ *n.*[1] E20. [f. Alexander Graham *Bell* (1847–1922), inventor of the telephone.] A logarithmic unit used in comparing electrical power levels, intensities of sounds, etc., corresponding to a power ratio of 10 to 1. Cf. DECIBEL.

bel *n.*[2] var. of BAEL.

†bel *a.* ME–L17. [OFr. (fem. *bele*) f. L *bellus*, fem. *bella*.] Fair, fine, beautiful.

belabour /bɪˈleɪbə/ *v.t.* Also ***-or**. LME. [f. BE- 1, 2 + LABOUR *v.*] †1 Cultivate, till. Only in LME. 2 Buffet, thrash, assail. LME. †3 Labour at, ply. Only in 17. 4 Labour (a point etc.); treat at excessive length, overuse. E20.

†bel-accoil *n.* ME–L16. [OFr. *bel acoil* fair welcome.] Kindly greeting, welcome.

belah /ˈbiːlə/ *n. Austral.* Also **-ar**. M19. [Aborig.] (The timber of) any of various trees of the genus *Casuarina*.

†belamour *n.* L16–E17. [Fr., f. as BEL *a.* + AMOUR.] A loved one, a sweetheart.

†belamy *n.* ME–L17. [OFr. *bel ami*.] Fair friend (esp. as a form of address).

belap /bɪˈlap/ *v.t.* Long *rare*. Infl. **-pp-**. ME. [f. BE- 1 + LAP *v.*[2]] Lap about, enfold, surround.

belar *n.* var. of BELAH.

belate /bɪˈleɪt/ *v.t.* Earliest & now only as next. E17. [f. BE- 3 + LATE *a.*] Make late, delay.

belated /bɪˈleɪtɪd/ *a.* E17. [f. prec. + -ED[1].] 1 Overtaken by darkness. *arch.* E17. 2 Delayed; tardy; coming (too) late. M17.

1 G. WHITE Belated shepherd swains See the cowl'd spectre. 2 S. T. WARNER I have been shamelessly belated in writing to thank you. D. BAGLEY He . . realized with belated terror that he had nearly been shot.

belatedly *adv.* L19. **belatedness** *n.* M17.

Belauan *n.* & *a.* var. of PALAUAN.

belaud /bɪˈlɔːd/ *v.t.* M19. [f. BE- 1 + LAUD *v.*] Load with praise.

belay /bɪˈleɪ, *in Mountaineering also* ˈbiːleɪ/ *v.* & *n.* [OE *beleċgan* = OFris *bilega*, Du. *beleggen*, OHG *bileggen* (G *belegen*); branch II is app. a re-formation on the Du.: see BE-, LAY *v.*[1]] A *v.* †I 1 *v.t.* Surround, enclose, adorn, etc., *with*; beset, beleaguer; waylay. OE–M18.

1 SPENSER A woodmans iacket . . Of Lincolne greene, belayd with silver lace. DRYDEN The speedy Horse all passages belay.

II 2 *v.t.* & *i. Naut.* Fix (a rope) round a cleat, pin, etc., to secure it; secure (something) thus. M16. b In *imper.*, freq. foll. by *there*: stop! enough! no more of (something)! *slang.* E19. 3 *transf.* a *v.t. gen.* Make fast, tie, secure. M18. b *v.t.* & *i. Mountaineering.* Fix (a rope) round a rock, piton, etc.; secure (a climber, oneself) thus. E20.

2 **belaying pin** a heavy wooden or iron pin which can be fixed in position for belaying on.

B *n. Mountaineering.* An act of belaying; the point where this is done. E20.

running belay, thread belay, etc.

bel canto /bɛl ˈkantəʊ/ *n. phr.* L19. [It. = fine song.] (A style of) singing characterized by full rich broad tone, legato phrasing, and accomplished technique.

belch /bɛltʃ/ *v.* & *n.* Also (long *obs.* exc. *dial.*) **belk** /bɛlk/. See also BOLK. [OE: forms in /k/

repr. *bælcan*, forms in /tʃ/ repr. either a related form or a shortening of *belċettan, beal-*.] A *v.* 1 *v.i.* Emit wind noisily from the stomach through the mouth. OE. 2 *v.t.* Emit by belching; utter forcibly, give vent to. Usu. foll. by *out*. OE. 3 *v.t.* †a *lit.* Vomit. M16–L18. b Eject, send *forth* or *out*; expel violently. L16. 4 *v.i.* Gush out; flow in gulps. L16. B *n.* 1 An act of belching. E16. 2 Poor beer; malt liquor. *arch. slang.* L17.

belcher /ˈbɛltʃə/ *n. arch.* E19. [Jem *Belcher* (d. 1811), Eng. pugilist.] A neckerchief with white spots on a blue ground.

beldam /ˈbɛldəm/ *n. arch.* Also **-dame**. LME. [f. BEL *a.* + DAM *n.*[2]] †1 A grandmother; any remote ancestress. LME–M19. 2 An old woman; a hag, a virago. L16.

beleaguer /bɪˈliːɡə/ *v.t.* L16. [Du. *belegeren*, f. as BE- + LEAGUER *n.*[1] or *v.*] Besiege (*lit.* or *fig.*).

beleaguerer *n.* (*rare*) E17.

belee /bɪˈliː/ *v.t. rare.* Pa. t. & pple **beleed**. E17. [f. BE- 4 + LEE *n.*[1]] Cut off from the wind, becalm.

belemnite /ˈbɛləmnʌɪt/ *n.* E17. [mod.L *belemnites*, f. Gk *belemnon* dart: see -ITE[1].] *Palaeont.* A tapering sharp-pointed fossil from the internal shell of an extinct cephalopod of the order Belemnoidea, most abundant in Jurassic and Cretaceous deposits; the animal itself.

belemnitic /-ˈnɪtɪk/ *a.* pertaining to or yielding belemnites M19. **belemnoid** *a.* & *n.* (a cephalopod) belonging to Belemnoidea; pertaining to or resembling an animal of this order: L19.

bel esprit /bɛl ɛspri/ *n. phr.* Pl. ***beaux esprits*** /boz ɛspri/. M17. [Fr. = fine mind.] A brilliant or witty person.

belfry /ˈbɛlfri/ *n.* ME. [OFr. *berfrei*, later *belfrei*, *be(l)froi* (mod. *beffroi*), in med.L *bel-*, *berfridus*, etc., f. Frank. (= MHG *ber(c)vrit*), prob. f. vb meaning 'protect' + base of FRITH *n.*[1]: forms w. *l* reinforced by assoc. w. *bell*.] 1 A (movable) wooden tower employed as a siege engine. Long *obs.* exc. *Hist.* ME. 2 A bell tower, usu. attached to a church etc., but sometimes standing separate. ME. b A chamber or storey in which bells are hung. M16. c A chamber or space where bell-ringers stand. M16. 3 A shed for cattle, carts, etc. *dial.* M16. 4 A housing or canopy for a ship's bell, often highly decorated. M18. 5 The head. *slang.* E20.

2b *have bats in the belfry*: see BAT *n.*[3]

Belgae /ˈbɛldʒiː/ *n.pl.* E17. [L.] An ancient people of N. Gaul and S. Britain.

†**belgard** *n.* L16–E19. [It. *bel guardo*.] A kind or loving look.

Belgian /ˈbɛldʒ(ə)n/ *n.* & *a.* E17. [f. *Belgium* (see below) + -AN.] (A native or inhabitant) of Belgium, orig. the whole Continental territory of the Belgae or the Low Countries generally, since 1830 an independent country on the south shore of the North Sea and English Channel.

Special collocations: **Belgian block** *US* a type of stone paving block; **Belgian hare** a dark-red slender long-eared breed of domestic rabbit.

Belgic /ˈbɛldʒɪk/ *a.* L16. [f. L *Belgicus*, f. BELGAE: see -IC.] 1 Of or pertaining to the Belgae. L16. 2 Of the Low Countries. E17.

Belgie /ˈbɛldʒi/ *n.* Now *derog.* E17. [f. BELGIAN + -IE.] A Belgian.

Belgravian /bɛlˈɡreɪvɪən/ *n.* & *a.* M19. [f. *Belgravia* (see below), f. *Belgrave* Square in this district: see -IA[1], -AN.] (A resident) of Belgravia, a fashionable part of London S. of Knightsbridge.

Belial /ˈbiːlɪəl/ *n.* ME. [Heb. *bĕlîyyaʻal* worthlessness.] The Devil, Satan.

belibel /bɪˈlʌɪb(ə)l/ *v.t.* Infl. **-ll-**, ***-l-**. E17. [f. BE- 1 + LIBEL *v.*] Assail with libels; traduce, slander.

belie /bɪˈlʌɪ/ *v.t.* Pa. t. **belied** /bɪˈlʌɪd/; pres. pple **belying** /bɪˈlʌɪɪŋ/. [OE *belēogan* = OFris. *biliuga*, OHG *biliugan* (G *belügen*): see BE-, LIE *v.*[2]] I †1 Deceive by lying. Only in OE. 2 Tell lies about (someone); slander. ME. †b Tell lies about (*the truth*, something). LME–M17. †3 Give the lie to, contradict; reject as false L16–M17. 4 Misrepresent; give a false notion of. E17. b Disguise, mask. E18. 5 Act or speak at variance with, be false or faithless to; show to be false, fail to corroborate or justify. L17.

2 D. HUME It was rendered criminal to belie the subjects of the king. 3 AV *Jer.* 5:12 They haue belyed the Lord, and said; It is not he. 4 MILTON He a declar'd Papist, If his own letter to the Pope belye him not. G. GREENE Her face didn't belie her nature, for she was the kindest woman I knew. b L. DEIGHTON The grimy condition of the coasters was belied by the fresh rain that had glossed their decks and given their hulls the polish of old jackboots. 5 W. COWPER Novels . . Belie their name, and offer nothing new. M. BEERBOHM Only in that he forgot there was nothing to pay did he belie his calm. M. BRAGG There was a silence after he stepped into the cottage, one so marked that it belied the existence of the querulous voice which had bidden him in. H. CLURMAN The actor who merely 'imitates' the surface impression that we might gather from a perusal of the play's text . . belies the art of the theatre. J. C. OATES That Veronica had a dainty appetite was bluntly belied by her full, comfortable figure.

†II 6 Fill with lies. *rare* (Shakes.). Only in E17.

belier *n.* a person who belies M16.

belief /bɪˈliːf/ *n.* ME. [Alt. of OE *ġelēafa*: cf. next.] 1 Trust, confidence; faith. (Foll. by *in*, †*of* a person or thing.) ME. b *spec.* Trust in God; religious faith; acceptance of any received theology (passing into sense 2). ME. 2 Mental acceptance of a statement, fact, doctrine, thing, etc., as true or existing. (Foll. by *in* a thing, *in* or *of* a statement etc., *that* something is the case.) ME. 3 The thing believed; a proposition or set of propositions held to be true; a religion; an opinion or persuasion. ME. 4 *the* (or †*one's*) *Belief*, the Apostles' Creed. *arch.* ME.

1 TENNYSON Beyond mine old belief in womanhood. A. J. P. TAYLOR He had no belief in the administrative capacity of the Unionists. b CARLYLE That war of the Puritans . . the war of Belief against Unbelief. C. P. SNOW He went to church out of propriety more than belief. 2 P. SIDNEY My only defence shal be beleefe of nothing. OED His statements are unworthy of belief. ARNOLD BENNETT He had been brought up in the belief that the Dragon was a place of sin. R. D. LAING Many people are prepared to have faith in the sense of scientifically indefensible belief in an untested hypothesis. *beyond belief*: see BEYOND *prep.* 6. *to the best of one's belief*: see BEST *a.* etc. 3 M. W. MONTAGU It is my belief you will not be at all the richer. J. GALSWORTHY If he had a political belief, it was a tax on wheat. C. S. FORESTER Some of his beliefs and convictions had been almost shaken lately.

believe /bɪˈliːv/ *v.* [Late OE *belȳfan*, *belēfan*, replacing, by prefix-substitution, earlier *ġelēfan*, (WS) *ġelīefan* = OFris. *gelēva*, OS *gilōbian* (Du. *gelooven*), OHG *gilouben* (G *glauben*), Goth. *galaubjan*, f. Gmc, f. as Y- + LIEF.] I *v.i.* 1 Have confidence or faith *in* or (*arch.*) *on* (a person, God, etc.). LOE. 2 Put one's trust or have confidence *in* (or †*on*) the truth of (a proposition, doctrine, etc.), the efficacy or advisability of (a principle, institution, practice, etc.), the existence of (a person or thing), the occurrence of (an event). LOE. 3 *absol.* Exercise (esp. religious) faith; *gen.* hold an opinion, think. LME. †4 Give credence *to* (a person, statement, etc.). LME–M17.

1 AV *John* 3:16 For God . . gave his only begotten Sonne: that whosoever beleeveth in him, should not perish, but have eternall life. G. B. SHAW I am going to be frank with you, I don't believe in doctors. G. BOYCOTT Be positive and believe in yourself, otherwise you will start to doubt your own ability. 2 M. W. MONTAGU I find that I have . . a strong disposition to believe in miracles. J. B. PRIESTLEY It is only up here that you can believe in such people as Heathcliffe. G. VIDAL Sullivan believed in exercise. A. J. P. TAYLOR Protection was carried by the Conservatives who claimed to believe in free enterprise. 3 H. FIELDING I will not believe so meanly of you. G. B. SHAW The right to think and believe according to our conscience. B. RUBENS How long ago, Norman thought, had he truly believed, and when and at what precise moment, had he lost his faith.

II *v.t.* 5 Accept the truth or reality of (a proposition etc.). ME. 6 Hold as true, be of the opinion, *that*; (w. advb. obj.) think *so* etc.; *ellipt.* (passing into *v.i.*, parenthetically) think that it is, was, etc. ME. 7 Give credence to (someone making statements etc.). LME. †8 Hold as true the existence of. L15–M18. 9 Think or suppose (someone or something) to be or *to be*. E16.

5 J. TYNDALL The Guide Chef evidently did not believe a word of it. E. O'NEILL The bartender cannot believe his luck for a moment. 6 DEFOE He believed there were more wolves a coming. B. JOWETT Some one—Critias, I believe—went on to say [etc.]. E. WAUGH There's another sister too, I believe, in the schoolroom. G. ORWELL How easy it was, thought Winston, . . to believe that the physical type set up by the Party as an ideal . . existed and even predominated. 7 SHAKES. *Sonn.* When my love swears that she is made of truth, I do believe her. 8 G. BERKELEY Shall we believe a God? 9 MILTON Our Conqu'ror whom I now Of force believe Almighty. B. LOVELL Anaximander believed our world to be only one of many.

Phrases: **believe it or not** *colloq.* it is surprising though true. *believe me*: see *believe you me* below. **believe one's ear**(**s**), **eyes**, etc., accept that what one apparently perceives is true (usu. in neg. contexts). **believe** (**you**) **me** *colloq.* it really is so. *make believe*: see MAKE *v.* **would you believe it?** *colloq.*: emphasizing the truth of a surprising fact etc. *you'd better believe* (*it*): see BETTER *a.* etc.

believaˈbility *n.* ability to be believed; credibility: M19. **believable** *a.* able to be believed; credible: LME. **believer** *n.* a person who believes, *esp.* in a particular religion (*Old Believer*: see OLD *a.*) LME. **believingly** *adv.* with belief or faith M17.

belike /bɪˈlʌɪk/ *adv.* & *a. arch.* M16. [f. BY *prep.* + LIKE *a.* or *n.*[2]] A *adv.* Probably; perhaps. Freq. *iron.* M16. †B *adj.* Like, likely (*to do* something). M16–E19.

Belisha beacon /bɪˈliːʃə ˈbiːk(ə)n/ *n. phr.* M20. [Leslie Hore-*Belisha* (1893–1957), Brit. politician, Minister of Transport 1931–7.] A black and white post topped by an amber-coloured globe (now usu. containing a flashing light), erected on the pavement at each end of a pedestrian crossing.

belittle /bɪˈlɪt(ə)l/ *v.t.* Orig. *US.* L18. [f. BE- 3 + LITTLE *a.*] 1 Make small; diminish in size. L18. 2 Depreciate, decry. L18. 3 Cause to appear small; dwarf. M19.

belittlement *n.* L19. **belittlingly** *adv.* in a belittling manner, depreciatingly L20.

belive /bɪˈlʌɪv/ *adv. obs.* exc. *Sc.* ME. [f. BY *prep.* + obl. form of LIFE *n.*: cf. ALIVE.] Quickly, speedily; before long, soon.

Belizean /bɛˈliːzɪən/ *n.* & *a.* Also **-ian**. M20. [f. *Belize* (see below) + -AN, -IAN.] (A native or inhabitant) of Belize, a country on the Caribbean coast of Central America, formerly British Honduras.

belk *v.* & *n.* see BELCH.

bell /bɛl/ *n.*[1] [OE *belle* = MLG, MDu. *belle* (Du. *bel*): perh. rel. to BELL *v.*[1]] 1 A hollow body formed to emit a sound when struck, typically of cast metal in a deep cup shape widening at the lip, and emitting a clear musical note when struck by a clapper or hammer usu. suspended within it; any instrument or device designed to emit a similar sound for calling attention etc. Also, the sounding of such an instrument or device for a particular purpose (identified contextually or specified), as summoning worshippers to church, schoolchildren to classes, etc., signalling the start of the final lap of a track race, warning of a fire or other hazard, (of church bells) celebrating a wedding or a happy event of national importance, etc. (see also sense 2 below). OE. 2 *spec.* a A bell rung to tell the hours; the bell of a clock. LME. b *Naut.* The bell which is struck on board ship every half-hour, indicating by the number of strokes the number of half-hours elapsed in a watch; a period thus indicated. E19. c In boxing etc., the bell rung to mark the start or end of a round. M20. d A telephone call. *colloq.* L20. 3 Any object or part shaped like a bell; *spec.*: a A bell-shaped corolla of a flower; the female flowering cone of the hop. Also in the names of plants with bell-shaped flowers. L16. b A bell-shaped vessel. M17. c *Archit.* The part of a Corinthian or composite capital around which the foliage and volutes are arranged. M17. d *Mus.* The flared open end of a wind instrument. E19.

1 *alarm-bell, church bell, dinner bell, doorbell, electric bell, fire bell, handbell, school bell, sleigh-bell, vesper bell,*

wedding bells, etc. **2b** R. H. DANA At seven bells in the morning all hands were called aft. **3** *bluebell*, *Canterbury bells*, *Coventry bells*, *harebell*, etc.

Phrases: **bear (away) the bell** take first place, win. **bell, book, and candle**: a formula for cursing (alluding to the rite of excommunication). **bells and whistles** *Computing* (*colloq.*) speciously attractive but superfluous facilities. **bells of Ireland** the shell-flower, *Moluccella laevis*. *cap and bells*: see CAP *n.*[1] *(as) clear as a bell*: see CLEAR *a*. *diving-bell*: see DIVING *vbl n*. *hell's bells*: see HELL *n*. **ring a bell** *colloq.* awaken a memory. **ring the bell** *colloq.* be the best of the lot (in allusion to a fairground strength-testing machine). *ring the bells backward(s)*: see BACKWARD *adv.* 8. **saved by the bell** in boxing, saved by the end of a round from being counted out; *fig.* saved (from an unpleasant occurrence) in the nick of time. *slow bell*: see SLOW *a.* & *adv.* **sound as a bell** very sound, in good order or health. *tubular bells*: see TUBULAR *a.* I. *warm the bell*: see WARM *v.*

Comb.: **bell-animal(cule)** = VORTICELLA; **bellbird** any of various S. American or Australasian birds with a clear ringing call, *esp.* a cotinga of the genus *Procnias*; **bell-bottomed** *a.* (of trousers) flared below the knee; **bell-bottoms** bell-bottomed trousers; **bell-boy** *N. Amer.* a page-boy in a hotel or club; **bell-buoy** a buoy with a warning bell rung by wave motion; **bell captain** *N. Amer.* a supervisor of a group of bell-boys; **bell-cord** a cord that is pulled to ring a bell; **bell-cot(e)** a shelter protecting a bell; **bell-crater** *Gk Antiq.* a large wine-mixing bowl shaped like an inverted bell; **bell curve** a graph of a normal (Gaussian) distribution; **bellflower** a campanula (*ivy-leaved bellflower*: see IVY *n.*); **bell-founder, -founding, -foundry** a caster, the casting, a manufactory, of large bells; **bell-glass** a bell-shaped glass cover for plants; **bell-hanger** a person who installs bells; **bell-heather** *Erica cinerea*, a common heath with bell-shaped flowers; also called *fine-leaved heath*; **bell-hop** *N. Amer.* = *bell-boy* above; **bellhouse** *arch.* a belfry; **bell-jar** a bell-shaped glass esp. for covering instruments or containing gas in a laboratory; **bell lyra** = *lyra glockenspiel* s.v. GLOCKENSPIEL 2; **bellman** *Hist.* a town crier; **bell-metal** an alloy of copper and tin (with more tin than in bronze), used for casting bells; **bell-miner** an Australian honeyeater, *Manorina melanophrys*, noted for its bell-like call; **bell-pepper** a large bell-shaped variety of capsicum; **bell-pull** a cord or handle attached to a bell-wire, by which a bell is rung; **bell-punch** a punch which perforates a ticket and rings a bell at the same time; **bell-push** a button that is pushed to ring an electric bell; **bell-ringer** a practitioner of bell-ringing; **bell-ringing** the ringing of church etc. bells with changes, freq. as a hobby; **bell-rope** a rope by which a bell is rung, esp. in a church; **bell-shaped** *a.* shaped like a bell, *esp.* having the shape of an inverted cup widening at the lip; **bell-skirt** a skirt flared widely from a narrow waist; **bell-sleeve** a long sleeve flared at the lower edge; **bell-string** = *bell-rope* above; **bell-tent** a conical tent with a central pole; **bell-topper** a top-hat, esp. one with a bell-shaped crown. **bell-wether** (*a*) the leading sheep of a flock, on whose neck a bell is hung; (*b*) a ringleader; (*c*) a clamorous person; **bell-wire** a wire pulled to ring a bell, esp. at a door; **bellwort** *N. Amer.* a plant of the genus *Uvularia* of the lily family, bearing yellow bell-like flowers.

bell-like *a.* resembling (that of) a bell, bell-shaped, having a clear musical note M18.

bell /bɛl/ *n.*[2] Now chiefly *Sc.* L15. [Origin unkn.: cf. synon. Du. *bel*, MDu. *bellen* bubble up; corresp. to BELL *v.*[4]] A bubble.

bell /bɛl/ *n.*[3] E16. [f. BELL *v.*[1]] The cry of a stag or buck at rutting time.

bell /bɛl/ *v.*[1] [OE *bellan*, corresp. to OHG *bellan* (G *bellen*) bark, bray: cf. ON *belja* and BELLOW *v.*] **1** *v.i.* Bellow, roar (*spec.* of a stag or buck at rutting time). OE. **2** *v.t.* Shout, bellow forth. L16.

bell /bɛl/ *v.*[2]*i.* *obs.* exc. *Sc.* Pa. pple **bollen** /ˈbɒlən/. ME. [Perh. f. OE *belgan*, pa. pple *bolgen* swell.] Swell up, be puffed out.

bell /bɛl/ *v.*[3] LME. [f. BELL *n.*[1]] **1** *v.t.* Provide or equip with a bell. LME. **2** *v.i.* Of hops: be or begin to be in flower (the female flowers being in bell-shaped cones). L16. **3** *v.t.* & *i.* (Cause to) spread or flare *out* like the lip of a bell. L19.

1 bell the cat take the danger of a shared enterprise upon oneself (in allusion to the fable in which mice proposed hanging a bell around a cat's neck so as to be warned of its approach).

bell /bɛl/ *v.*[4]*i.* *obs.* exc. *dial.* L16. [f. BELL *n.*[2]] Bubble.

belladonna /bɛləˈdɒnə/ *n.* M18. [mod.L f. It. *bella donna* lit. 'fair lady'.] **1** *belladonna lily*, a southern African amaryllis, *Amaryllis belladonna*, with red or white flowers. M18. **2a** A therapeutic preparation of the leaves and root of deadly nightshade, of which the active principle is atropine. L18. **b** Deadly nightshade, *Atropa belladonna*. M19.

bellarmine /ˈbɛləmiːn/ *n.* M17. [St Robert F. R. *Bellarmine* (1542–1621), Jesuit cardinal and theologian.] *Hist.* A large glazed drinking-jug in the form of a pot-bellied burlesque likeness of Cardinal Bellarmine.

belle /bɛl/ *n.* E17. [Fr., fem. of *bel*, BEAU, f. L *bella* fem. of *bellus* pretty.] A beautiful woman; *the* reigning beauty *of* a place etc.

J. GRENFELL I'd like a great big . . party And the belle of the ball is me. E. McBAIN A Southern belle waiting to be asked for a dance. *bathing belle*: see BATHE *v.* 5. *yellow belle*: see YELLOW *a.*

belled /bɛld/ *a.* M18. [f. BELL *n.*[1], *v.*[3]: see -ED[2], -ED[1].] **1** (With flowers) shaped like a bell. M18. **2** Furnished with a bell or bells. M19.

Belleek /bɛˈliːk/ *n.* M19. [A town in Fermanagh, N. Ireland.] In full *Belleek ware* etc. A light, fragile kind of porcelain pottery produced in Belleek.

belle époque /bɛl eɪˈpɒk/ *n. phr.* Pl. **belles époques** /bɛlz eɪˈpɒk/. M20. [Fr. = fine period.] A period of settled comfort and prosperity, spec. *the* period in France from the late 19th cent. to the war of 1914–18.

belle laide /bɛl lɛd/ *n. phr.* Pl. **-s -s** (pronounced same). E20. [Fr., f. *belle* beautiful + *laide* ugly (fem. adjs.).] An attractive though ugly woman.

belleric /bɪˈlɛrɪk/ *n.* Now *rare* or *obs.* M17. [Fr. *belléric* ult. f. med. Arab. *balīlaj* f. Pers. *balīla*.] The fruit of the Indian tree *Terminalia bellirica*, a source of tannin. Also *belleric myrobalan*.

belles laides *n. phr.* pl. of BELLE LAIDE.

belles-lettres /bɛlɛtr/ *n.pl.* (occas. treated as *sing.*). M17. [Fr., lit. 'fine letters'.] Studies or writings of a purely literary character, *esp.* essays, criticism, etc. Orig. more widely, literature generally, the humanities.

belletrist /bɛlˈlɛtrɪst/ *n.* Also **†belles-lettreist**. E19. [f. prec. + -IST.] A devotee or practitioner of *belles-lettres*.

belletrism *n.* the study or composition of *belles-lettres* M20. **belleˈtristic** *a.* of or pertaining to *belles-lettres* E19. **belleˈtristical** *a.* = BELLETRISTIC L18.

bellicose /ˈbɛlɪkəʊs/ *a.* LME. [L *bellicosus*, f. *bellicus* warlike, f. *bellum* war: see -IC, -OSE[1].] Inclined to war or fighting; warlike.

bellicosity /bɛlɪˈkɒsɪti/ *n.* warlike inclination M19.

bellied /ˈbɛlɪd/ *a.* L15. [f. BELLY *n.*, *v.*: see -ED[2], -ED[1].] **1** Having a belly (usu. of a specified size or form). L15. **b** Big-bellied, corpulent; *fig.* bombastic. M16. **2** Made large and full; blown or puffed out. L16.

belligerence /bɪˈlɪdʒ(ə)r(ə)ns/ *n.* E19. [f. next + -ENCE.] The carrying on of hostilities; pugnacious behaviour; the position or status of a belligerent.

belligerency *n.* = BELLIGERENCE M19.

belligerent /bɪˈlɪdʒ(ə)r(ə)nt/ *a.* & *n.* Also **†-ant**. L16. [L *belligerant-* pres. ppl stem of *belligerare* wage war, f. *belliger* waging war, f. *bellum* war: later irreg. assim. to *gerent-* pres. ppl stem of *gerere* bear, carry, carry on; see -GEROUS, -ENT.] **A** *adj.* **1** Waging regular war as recognized by the law of nations; pugnacious, aggressively hostile. L16. **2** Of or pertaining to a belligerent. M19. **B** *n.* A nation, party, or person engaged in conflict. E19.

belligerently *adv.* M19.

†belligerous *a.* M16–L18. [f. L *belliger*: see prec., -GEROUS.] Waging war, belligerent.

bellipotent /bɪˈlɪpət(ə)nt/ *a.* Now *rare* or *obs.* M17. [L *bellipotent-*, *-ens*, f. *bellum* war + *potens* mighty, POTENT *a.*[2]] Mighty or powerful in war.

Bellona /bɛˈləʊnə/ *n.* L16. [L *Bellona* Roman goddess of war, f. *bellum* war.] A war-goddess; a spirited woman of commanding presence.

bellow /ˈbɛləʊ/ *v.* & *n.* ME. [Perh. f. late OE *bylgan* rel. to BELL *v.*[1]] **A** *v.* **1** *v.i.* Of a bull or excited cow: roar. Of another animal or a human: roar like a bull; cry in a loud deep voice, shout; roar with pain. Of a thing: make a loud roaring noise. ME. **2** *v.t.* Utter or proclaim loudly and usu. angrily; give forth with loud noise. Freq. foll. by *out*, *forth*. L16.

1 MILTON Not fit for that liberty which they . . bellowed for. WORDSWORTH And Ocean bellow from his rocky shore. **2** A. RANSOME He put his hand like a trumpet to his mouth and bellowed one word. K. VONNEGUT Everything that any one of us said . . was bellowed out at the crowd through . . horns.

B *n.* A bellowing sound; a roar. L18.

bellower *n.* a person who or thing which bellows M17.

bellows /ˈbɛləʊz/ *n.pl.* (occas. treated as *sing.*). ME. [Prob. repr. OE *belga*, *belgum* pl. of *bel(i)ġ*, *bæl(i)ġ* BELLY *n.*, abbrev. of *blǣstbel(i)ġ* 'blowing-bag' = ON *blástrbelgr*: cf. G *Blasebalg*.] **1** A portable or fixed contrivance for producing a blast of air, esp. for fanning a fire or for supplying an organ, harmonium, etc. (The simplest form consists of two boards connected by flexible sides and enclosing a cavity of alterable volume so that air may be drawn in and then expelled through an attached nozzle.) ME. **b** *fig.* That which blows up or fans the fires of passion etc. LME. **c** *fig.* The lungs. E17. **2** An expansible, light-tight, flexible sleeve connecting the lens to the body of a camera. L19.

1 pair of bellows a two-handled bellows used to blow a fire. **b** KEATS My voice is not a bellows unto ire. **c bellows to mend** *colloq.* short wind.

Comb.: **bellows-blower** a person who works the bellows of an organ etc.; **bellows-fish** the snipe fish, *Macrorhamphosus scolopax*; **bellows pocket** a patch pocket with side folds allowing it to expand or lie flat.

†bellows *v.t.* E17–M18. [f. prec.] Blow (with bellows); gather *up* (wind).

Bell's inequality /bɛlz ɪnɪˈkwɒlɪti/ *n. phr.* L20. [John S. *Bell* (1928–90), Brit. physicist.] The statement (serving as a test of the validity of quantum theory) that the number of pairs of particles measured as having positive spin in one pair out of three directions is less than the total number of pairs measured as having positive spin in the other two pairs of directions.

Bell's palsy /bɛlz ˈpɔːlzi/ *n. phr.* M19. [Sir Charles *Bell* (1774–1842), Sc. anatomist.] *Med.* Paralysis of the facial nerve causing muscular weakness in one side of the face with drooping of the corner of the mouth and inability to close the eye.

†belluine *a.* E17–M18. [L *belluinus*, f. *bellua* beast: see -INE[1].] Pertaining to or characteristic of beasts; brutal.

bellum /ˈbɛləm/ *n.* E20. [Iraqi Arab. *belem*.] A small wooden boat used to carry passengers for short distances along the coasts of the Persian Gulf.

belly /ˈbɛli/ *n.* [OE *beliġ*, var. of *bæl(i)ġ* (WS) *biel(i)ġ*, *byl(i)ġ* = MDu. *balch*, OHG *balg*, ON *belgr*, Goth. *balgs* f. Gmc (= bag), f. a base meaning 'be inflated, swell'.] **†I1** A bag, a purse. Only in OE.

II Of humans (increasingly regarded as colloq. or coarse) and animals. **2** The cavity of the human body from the diaphragm to the groin, containing the stomach, bowels, etc.; the abdomen; the front surface of the body from waist to groin. ME. **b** The part of a garment covering the belly. L16. **3** The corresponding part or surface of the body of an animal. LME. **b** In full *belly-wool*. The inferior wool from a sheep's belly. *Austral.* & *NZ.* M19. **c** In full *belly of pork*. A cut of pork from the underside between the legs. L19. **4** The stomach; the body as needing food; appetite; gluttony. LME. **†b** The bowels. LME–L17. **5** The womb. LME. **†6** The internal cavity of the body. L15–M17.

3 MILTON A monstrous Serpent on his Belly prone. C. A. JOHNS The Common Curlew . . belly white, with longitudinal dusky spots. **4** S. JOHNSON He who does not mind his belly, will hardly mind any thing else. **5** SHAKES. *L.L.L.* She's quick; the child brags in her belly already. **6** R. BERNARD It made my heart cold in my belly.

III Of things. 7 The internal cavity or interior of anything, whether material or immaterial. M16. 8 The bulging part of anything, e.g. of a pot or bottle, a vein of ore, etc.; a concave surface; the front, inner, or lower surface of anything. L16. 9 *spec.* a The surface of a violin etc. across which the strings pass. L16. b The thicker part of a muscle. E17. c The soundboard of a piano. M19. d The under part of the fuselage of an aircraft. E20.

7 J. POTTER Ships of Burden . . having large and capacious Bellies. J. A. FROUDE A . . candle lighted in the belly of a dark dead past. 8 SPENSER Leaning on the belly of a pot. R. H. DANA To fall from aloft and be caught in the belly of a sail. G. JONES Put the belly of your hand here on my heart and swear it.

Comb.: **bellyache** *n.* & *v.* (*a*) *n.* pain or discomfort in the abdomen, colic; *slang* a querulous complaint; (*b*) *v.i.* (*slang*) complain whiningly, grumble; **bellyband** a band around a horse's belly for holding carriage shafts etc. in place; *slang* a wide belt or corset; **belly button** *colloq.* the navel; **belly-dance** an oriental solo dance by a woman, involving the rippling of her abdominal muscles; **belly-dancer** a woman who performs belly-dances; **belly-flop** *n.* & *v.* (*colloq.*) (make) a dive landing flat on the belly; **belly-god** (*arch.* exc. *Jamaican*) a glutton; **belly-landing** the crash-landing of an aircraft on its belly without the use of the undercarriage; **belly-laugh** *colloq.* a deep unrestrained laugh; **belly-timber** (*obs.* exc. *dial.*) food, provisions; *belly-wool*: see sense 3b above.

belly /ˈbɛli/ *v.* E17. [f. the n.] 1 *v.t.* & *i.* (Cause to) swell out (usu. of sails). E17. †2 *v.i.* Become corpulent. M17–L18.

bellyful /ˈbɛlɪfʊl, -f(ə)l/ *n.* M16. [f. BELLY *n.* + -FUL.] As much as the belly will hold; a sufficiency of food; *slang* as much as or more than one wants of anything.

SMOLLETT I never once had my belly-full, even of dry bread. S. BECKETT Will you stop whining! I've had about my bellyful of your lamentations.

†belock *v.t. rare* (Shakes.). Only in E17. [f. BE- 1 + LOCK *v.*[1]] Lock firmly, clasp.

belomancy /ˈbɛləʊmansi/ *n.* M17. [f. Gk *belos* dart + -MANCY.] Divination by means of arrows.

belong /bɪˈlɒŋ/ *v.i.* ME. [Prob. intensive of LONG *v.*[2]: see BE- 1.] I Foll. by *to*, *†unto*. 1 Be rightly assigned or appropriate to as an adjunct, function, duty, etc. ME. 2 Pertain or relate to. *arch.* ME. 3 Be the property or rightful possession of. LME. b Be a property or an attribute of. M17. 4 Be connected with as a member, part, inhabitant, dependency, etc. LME.

1 AV *Dan.* 9:9 To the Lord our God belong mercies. GEO. ELIOT He . . works with all the zest that belongs to fresh ideas. 2 AV *1 Cor.* 7:22 He that is unmarried careth for the things that belong to the Lord. 3 M. MCCARTHY Around one tan wrist was a gold bracelet that had belonged to her grandmother. b J. LOCKE This way of containing all things can by no means belong to God. 4 ADDISON The great Yard that belongs to my Friend's Country-House. O. SITWELL Its flat spread dome belongs to an exceedingly primitive type. L. HELLMAN I belonged, on my mother's side, to a banking, storekeeping family from Alabama. JAN MORRIS Every undergraduate [in Oxford] belongs to a college.

II *absol.* & w. other consts. 5 Be right or appropriate *to do*, *be*. Usu. *impers.* in (*it*) *belongs* etc. *arch.* M17. 6 (W. other preps. and w. advs.) Be related or connected; be naturally or rightly placed; be classified. Orig. *US.* E19. 7 *absol.* Be a member; fit a specified environment, not be out of place. E20.

5 KEATS Here . . it doth not well belong To speak. C. CAUSLEY And a Cornish man with a Cornish maid is how it belongs to be. 6 W. WHITMAN He was not a closet man, belonged out-of-doors. P. G. WODEHOUSE I looked as if I belonged in Whipsnade. J. AGEE He had lost their contempt and could belong among them if he wanted to. J. HELLER A woman belongs with her husband always. 7 D. H. LAWRENCE He belonged [to the choir] just because he had a tenor voice, and enjoyed singing. M. MCCARTHY It was the Moscow trials that made him know . . that he did not really 'belong'.

belonging /bɪˈlɒŋɪŋ/ *n.* E17. [f. prec. + -ING[1]; pl. perh. f. pres. pple, = 'things belonging'.] I In *pl.* (*sing.* rare). 1 Circumstances or relations connected with a person or thing. *arch.* E17. 2 Possessions, goods, effects. E19. 3 One's family or relatives. *colloq.* M19.

1 BROWNING All my belongings, what is summed in life, I have submitted wholly . . to your rule. 2 W. S. CHURCHILL It struck me as rather grim to see the intimate belongings of one's comrade of the day before . . thus unceremoniously distributed among strangers. 3 DICKENS I have been trouble enough to my belongings in my day.

II 4 The fact of appertaining or being a part; relationship; *esp.* an individual's membership of, and acceptance by, a group or society. L19.

4 W. PLOMER He had little sense of belonging.

belongingness *n.* †(*a*) the state of having properties appropriate to something; (*b*) the state or condition of belonging: M17.

belord /bɪˈlɔːd/ *v.t.* L16. [f. BE- 3 + LORD *n.*] Call 'lord', address as 'lord'.

Belorussian /bɛləʊˈrʌʃ(ə)n/ *a.* & *n.* Also **Byelo-** /bjɛləʊ-/. M20. [f. *Belorussia* (see below) f. Russ. *Belorossiya*, f. *belyĭ* white + *Rossiya* Russia, + -AN.] A *adj.* Of or pertaining to Belorussia (now Belarus), a country west of Russia and north of Ukraine (formerly a republic of the USSR), its people, or their East Slavonic language. M20. B *n.* A native or inhabitant of Belorussia; the language of the people of Belorussia. M20.

¶Also called WHITE RUSSIAN.

belote /bəˈlɒt/ *n.*[1] Also **belotte**. M20. [Fr., perh. f. F. *Belot*, a Frenchman said to have developed the game.] A card-game like pinochle, played with a 32-card pack, popular in France; the combination of king and queen of trumps in this game.

belove /bɪˈlʌv/ *v.* ME. [f. BE- 1 + LOVE *v.*] †1 *v.i.* Please, be pleasing. Only in ME. 2 *v.t.* Love. Now only in *pass.* (foll. by *by*, *of*). LME.

2 SHAKES. *Mids. N. D.* I am belov'd of beauteous Hermia. BYRON I loved, and was beloved again. G. B. SHAW The master beloved by masters, Mozart.

beloved /bɪˈlʌvɪd, *less usu.* -ˈlʌvd/ *ppl a.* & *n.* LME. [f. prec. + -ED[1].] A *ppl a.* Dearly loved. LME.

SHAKES. *Lear* Sorrow would be a rarity most beloved If all could so become it. LD MACAULAY Impatient to be once more in his beloved country.

B *n.* A beloved person, a sweetheart. LME.

below /bɪˈləʊ/ *adv.* & *prep.* LME. [f. *be* BY *prep.* + LOW *a.*] A *adv.* 1 *gen.* At or to a lower position relative to another; lower down. LME. b Lower down a slope or the course of a river, downstream. M17. c Lower on a sheet or page; at the foot of the page; later in a book or article. L17. 2 a Under heaven; on earth (often preceded by *here*). *arch.* or *poet.* L16. b Under the earth; *rhet.* in hell. E17. 3 On or to a lower floor; downstairs; *esp.* (*Naut.*) below deck. L16. 4 *fig.* In or to a lower rank, position, station, etc. E17. 5 Lower than the zero of a temperature scale. L18.

1 GOLDSMITH The child . . leaped from her arms into the flood below. TENNYSON From below Sweet gales, as from deep gardens, blow. K. AMIS The slamming of the car doors below made them both jump. 2a KEATS Finer spirits cannot breathe below In human climes. b SHAKES. *Temp.* Night kept chain'd below. SOUTHEY The fiends below were ringing his knell. 3 SHAKES. *Merry W.* There's one Master Brook below would fain speak with you. R. H. DANA It being the turn of our watch to go below. 4 D. M. WALKER The result of an appeal may be to affirm, modify, or reverse the decision of the court below. 5 P. THEROUX This is the worst winter I've ever seen. Ten below in Chicago.

B *prep.* 1 *gen.* Lower in position than, at less elevation than. L16. b Lower down a slope than; downstream from; further south than. E17. c Lower down a page than; later in a work than. M18. 2 Directly beneath; covered by, underneath; deeper than. E17. 3 Lower in rank, position, etc., than. E17. b Lower in some quality than; inferior to. E18. c Lower in amount, value, weight, temperature, etc., than. E18. 4 Unworthy of, unbefitting to, lowering to (more freq. expressed by *beneath*). M17.

1 SIR W. SCOTT He never counted him a man Would strike below the knee. T. S. ELIOT At dawn we came down to a temperate valley, Wet, below the snowline. b SHAKES. *Meas. for M.* Meet me at the consecrated fount, A league below the city. *Publishers Weekly* In the desperately poor South, the country below Naples. 2 TENNYSON Some dolorous message knit below The wild pulsation of her wings. LD KELVIN The necessity for study below the surface seems to have been earliest recognised in anatomy. A. S. J. TESSIMOND The still green light below tall trees. 3 STEELE He . . gives his orders . . to the Servants below him. J. HELLER In marrying your father, I married very far below my station. b LD MACAULAY How far my performance is below excellence. 4 STEELE It was below a Gentlewoman to wrangle. R. A. PROCTOR Too far below contempt to be worth castigating.

Phrases (of adv. & prep.): *below deck(s)*: see DECK *n.*[1] 2. *below ground*: see GROUND *n.* *below one's breath*: see BREATH *n.* *below par*: see PAR *n.*[1] *below stairs*: see STAIR 1. *below the belt*: see BELT *n.* *below the gangway*: see GANGWAY *n.* 3b. **below there!**: warning to beware of a falling object. *below the salt*: see SALT *n.*[1] **from below** from a lower place. *watch below*: see WATCH *n.*

Bel Paese /bɛl pɑːˈeɪzi, *foreign* bɛl paˈeːze/ *n. phr.* E20. [It., lit. 'beautiful country'.] (Proprietary name for) a rich, white, creamy cheese of mild flavour orig. made in Italy.

Belshazzar *n.* see BALTHAZAR.

†belswagger *n.* L16–L18. [Perh. a contr. of *belly-swagger* 'one who swags his belly': see SWAG *v.*, -ER[1].] A swaggering bully; a pimp.

¶In 18 only in Dicts.

belt /bɛlt/ *n.* [OE *belt*, corresp. to OHG *balz*, ON *belti* (Sw. *bälte*, Da. *bælte*), f. Gmc f. L *balteus* girdle, of Etruscan origin. In branch II f. the vb.] I 1 A flat encircling strip of cloth, leather, etc., worn around the waist or from the shoulder to the opposite hip to support clothes, weapons, etc., or as a decorative accessory. OE. b *spec.* Such a belt worn as a mark of rank or distinction by an earl, knight, boxing champion, etc. LME. c *spec.* Such a belt used to support the figure; a suspender belt; a corset. L19. d (W. specifying colour.) Such a belt indicating by its colour the wearer's level of proficiency in judo or karate; a person entitled to wear this. E20. 2 A broad strip or stripe of any kind, or a continuous series of objects, encircling something. M17. 3 A broad flexible strap. L17. b A flexible strip for feeding a machine-gun with ammunition. L19. 4 An endless strap passing around wheels, rollers, etc., for communicating motion or for conveying articles or material. L18. 5 A broad band or stripe crossing a surface (esp. that of the earth) from which it is differentiated in some way; a zone or region of distinct character or occupancy. E19.

1 C. BOUTELL The sword . . hung from a belt that passed over the shoulder. A. POWELL He wore a loosely made camel's-hair overcoat, the unfastened belt of which trailed behind him. J. STEINBECK His jeans were held up by a wide harness-leather belt with a big square brass buckle. *chastity belt*, *suspender belt*, etc. *fig.*: SHAKES. *Macb.* He cannot buckle his distemper'd cause Within the belt of rule. b THACKERAY They fight each other for the champion's belt and two hundred pounds a side. c R. LEHMANN Etty wears . . just her belt and knickers. d *black belt*, *red belt*, *white belt*, etc. 2 SOUTHEY A level belt of ice which bound . . The waters of the sleeping Ocean round. R. W. EMERSON A belt of mirrors round a taper's flame. P. MOORE Through a small telescope Jupiter shows as a yellowish, flattened disk, crossed by the streaks which we term belts. 3 *conveyor belt*, *safety-belt*, *seat-belt*, etc. 4 C. S. FORESTER The belt bore the peas steadily along to the farther drum. *Reader's Digest* Automobiles leaving the belt as finished products. 5 A. B. HART Illinois is divided into a wheat belt, a corn belt, and the city of Chicago. TOLKIEN A belt of tall and very ancient oaks. U. LE GUIN The Green Mountains where it rained up to forty inches a year, the rain belt. BIBLE *Belt*. *green belt*: see GREEN *a.*

II 6 The wool sheared from the hindquarters of a sheep. Now *rare* or *obs.* M17. 7 A heavy blow or stroke. L19.

Phrases: **belt and braces** *fig.* a policy of twofold security. *hit below the belt*: see HIT *v.* SAM BROWNE *belt*. **tighten one's belt** *fig.* (*a*) bear hunger philosophically; (*b*) introduce rigorous economies. **under one's belt** eaten or otherwise absorbed. VAN ALLEN (*radiation*) *belt*.

Comb.: **belt conveyor** a conveyor belt; **belt drive** a driving mechanism powered by a flexible endless belt; **belt line** *US* a railway or tramline that encircles a city or metropolitan area; **belt-tightening** *fig.* the introduction of rigorous economies; **beltway** *N. Amer.* a highway that encircles a city or metropolitan area.

beltless *a.* LME.

belt /bɛlt/ *v.* ME. [f. the n.] **1** *v.t.* Put a belt on or around; invest with a distinctive belt (esp. of knighthood). ME. **b** Fasten on with a belt. E16. **2** *v.t.* Thrash with a belt. L15. **b** Hit; attack; give a thrashing to. M19. **3** *v.t.* Shear the hindquarters of (a sheep). Now *rare* or *obs.* E16. **4** *v.t.* Encircle with a band of colour etc.; surround; mark with bands or stripes. M16. **5** *v.i.* Hurry, rush. *colloq.* L19.

1 SIR W. SCOTT Allen-a-Dale was ne'er belted a knight. b T. PENNANT An enormous shield . . is belted to his body. 2b J. GALSWORTHY Megan'll get his mates to belt him. **belt the bottle** *slang* drink heavily. 4 WORDSWORTH They belt him round with hearts undaunted. J. N. LOCKYER The meteors belted the sky like the meridians on a terrestrial globe. 5 T. MANGOLD There can be no errors when the equivalent of five million tons of TNT is belting towards Washington at 18,000 miles an hour.

With advs. in specialized senses: **belt down** *colloq.* of the sun's rays etc.: beat down (see BEAT *v.*[1] 4b). **belt out** *v.phr.t.* (*colloq.*) sing, play, utter, etc., vigorously. **belt up** *colloq.* (*a*) be quiet, shut up; (*b*) fasten a seat belt, wear a seat belt.

Beltane /ˈbɛlteɪn/ *n.* LME. [Gael. *bealltainn, -tuin* (= OIr. *bel(l)taine*, Manx *boaltinn, boaldyn*).] **1** The first day of May, Old Style, one of the ancient Scottish quarter days. LME. **2** An ancient Scottish and Irish festival celebrated on May Day, at which great bonfires were lit. M18.

belted /ˈbɛltɪd/ *a.* L15. [f. BELT *n.*, *v.*: see -ED[2], -ED[1].] **1** Wearing or fastened by a belt; *esp.* (usu. *rhet.*) wearing the distinctive cincture of an earl etc. L15. **2** Marked by a band or bands of colour etc. L16.

2 *belted* GALLOWAY.

belter /ˈbɛltə/ *n.* E19. [f. BELT *n.* or *v.* + -ER[1].] **1** A heavy blow; a beating. *Sc. & north.* E19. **2** An impressive performer; an outstanding person or thing; a person who sings or speaks loudly and forcibly. *slang.* L20.

belting /ˈbɛltɪŋ/ *n.* M16. [f. BELT *n.* or *v.* + -ING[1].] **1** Belts collectively, material for belts; a belt. M16. **2** The action of BELT *v.*; *esp.* a beating, a thrashing. M19.

beluga /bɪˈluːgə/ *n.* L16. [Russ. (sense 1) *beluga*, (sense 2) *belukha*, f. *belyĭ* white + *-uga, -ukha* formative suffixes.] **1** (Caviar from) the great sturgeon or hausen, *Huso huso*, of the Caspian and Black Seas. L16. **2** The white whale, *Delphinapterus leucas*, of the Arctic Ocean. L18.

belvedere /ˈbɛlvɪdɪə/ *n.* L16. [It. = fair sight, f. *bel, bello* beautiful + *vedere* see.] **1** A raised turret or summer-house commanding a fine view. L16. **2** The summer cypress, *Bassia scoparia.* L16.

belying *v.* pres. pple of BELIE.

bema /ˈbiːmə/ *n.* Pl. **-mas, -mata** /-mətə/. L17. [Gk *bēma* a step, a raised place to speak from.] **1** *Chr. Ch.* The altar part or sanctuary in ancient and Orthodox churches; the chancel. L17. **2** *Gk Antiq.* The platform from which Athenian orators spoke. E19.

bemad /bɪˈmad/ *v.t.* Infl. **-dd-**. E17. [f. BE- 1 + MAD *v.*] Make mad.

SHAKES. *Lear* Unnatural and bemadding sorrow.

bemata *n.pl.* see BEMA.

bemaul /bɪˈmɔːl/ *v.t.* E17. [f. BE- 1 + MAUL *v.*] Maul thoroughly.

bemazed /bɪˈmeɪzd/ *a. arch.* ME. [f. BE- + *mazed* pa. pple of MAZE *v.*] Stupefied, bewildered.

Bemba /ˈbɛmbə/ *n.* Pl. same. M20. [Bantu.] A member of a people in Zambia and Zaire; the Bantu language of this people.

Bembo /ˈbɛmbəʊ/ *n.* M20. [Pietro *Bembo* (1470–1547), It. cardinal and scholar.] A typeface modelled on that used in the Aldine edition of Bembo's tract *De Aetna*.

bemean /bɪˈmiːn/ *v.t.* M17. [f. BE- 3 + MEAN *a.*[1], prob. after DEMEAN *v.*[2]] Render mean, abase.

†**bemeet** *v.t.* & *i.* Infl. as MEET *v.* E–M17. [f. BE- 1 + MEET *v.*] Meet (*with*).

SHAKES. *Lear* Our very loving sister, well bemet.

†**bemete** *v.t. rare* (Shakes.). Only in L16. [f. BE- 1 + METE *v.* 1.] Measure.

Bemi /biːˈmiː/ *n. obs.* exc. *Hist.* Also **B mi**. LME. [f. *B* as a pitch letter + *mi* designating a tone in the solmization of Guido d'Arezzo (*c* 990–1050).] *Medieval Mus.* The note B in Guido d'Arezzo's 1st, 4th, and 7th hexachords, where it was sung to the syllable *mi*. Cf. ALAMIRE, BEFA, CEFAUT, etc.

bemire /bɪˈmaɪə/ *v.t.* M16. [f. BE- 4 + MIRE *n.*[1]] Befoul with or plunge in mire; (in *pass.*) sink in the mire, be stuck in mud.

SWIFT I was filthily bemired. *fig.*: J. WESLEY Doubt . . bemires the soul.

bemist /bɪˈmɪst/ *v.t.* L16. [f. BE- 4 + MIST *n.*[1]] Cover or surround (as) with mist; confuse, obscure.

bemoan /bɪˈməʊn/ *v.t.* & *i.* [OE *bemǣnan*, f. as BE- + MEAN *v.*[2], alt. (16) after MOAN *v.*] Lament; weep or express sorrow (for or over); *refl.* bewail one's lot.

AV *Job* 42:11 They bemoned him, and comforted him. BACON Politique persons . . are euer bemoaning themselves, what a Life they lead. C. LAMB I do not know whether I ought to bemoan or rejoice that my old friend is departed. J. M. BARRIE Foreign words in the text annoyed her and made her bemoan her want of a classical education.

bemock /bɪˈmɒk/ *v.t.* E17. [f. BE- 1 + MOCK *v.*] Flout; delude mockingly.

SHAKES. *Coriol.* Nay, but his taunts! . . Bemock the modest moon.

bemoil /bɪˈmɔɪl/ *v.t. obs.* exc. *dial.* L16. [f. BE- 1 + MOIL *v.*] Bemire.

bemoisten /bɪˈmɔɪs(ə)n/ *v.t.* L16. [f. BE- 1 + MOISTEN *v.*] Make moist.

bemonster /bɪˈmɒnstə/ *v.t.* E17. [f. BE- 3 + MONSTER *n.*] **1** Make monstrous, deform. E17. **2** Regard as or call a monster. L17.

bemuse /bɪˈmjuːz/ *v.t.* M18. [f. BE- 2 + MUSE *v.*[2]] Make utterly muddled, as with drink; stupefy. Chiefly as **bemused** ppl a.

bemusedly /-zɪdli/ *adv.* L19.

ben /bɛn/ *n.*[1] M16. [Repr. N. Afr. pronunc. of Arab. *bān* ben tree.] The seeds of Asian and N. African trees of the genus *Moringa* (family Moringaceae), esp. *M. oleifera*, which yield a valuable oil. Usu. in *comb.*, as *ben nut, oil, tree.*

ben /bɛn/ *n.*[2] L18. [Gael., Ir. *beann* = OIr. *benn*, Welsh *ban* prominence, peak, height.] A Scottish or Irish mountain peak. Chiefly in names, as *Ben Nevis, Ben Bulben.*

ben /bɛn/ *adv., prep., a.,* & *n.*[3] *Sc. & north.* LME. [Repr. OE *binnan* (= OFris. *binna*, (M)LG, (M)Du., (M)HG *binnen*), f. as BY *prep.* etc. + IN *adv.*] **A** *adv.* Within, towards the inner part; *spec.* in or into the inner part of a house (orig. the parlour of a two-roomed house with only one outer door, opening into the kitchen). Cf. BUT *adv.* 1. LME. **B** *prep.* In or into the inner part of (a house). L17. **C** *adj.* Inner, interior. L18. **D** *n.* The inner room of a two-roomed house. Cf. BUT *n.* 2. L18.

Phrases: but and ben: see BUT *n.* 2.

benab /ˈbɛnab/ *n.* M19. [Arawak (*u*)*bannabuhu*.] In Guyana: a shelter made of a framework of poles, covered with branches and leaves.

†**bename** *v.t.* Pa. t. & pple **benamed, benempt(ed)**. [OE *benemnan*, f. as BE- + NAME *v.*] **1** Declare solemnly or on oath. OE–E17. **2** Name; describe as. L16–M19.

bench /bɛn(t)ʃ/ *n.* See also BINK. [OE *benč* = OFris. *benk*, OS *banc* (Du. *bank*), OHG *bank* (G *Bank*), (cf. also ON *bekkr*, Icel. *bekkur*), f. Gmc: rel. to BANK *n.*[1], *n.*[2]] **1** A long seat, usually of wood or stone, with or without a back. OE. **b** A seat or thwart in a boat. M16. **2** A bank or shelf of ground; a level ledge in earthwork, masonry, etc.; an outcropping level stratum; *US* a river terrace. ME. **3** The seat on which the judge or judges sit in court; the office or status of a judge. ME. **b** A place where justice is administered; a court of law. ME. **c** The judge or magistrate; the judges or magistrates collectively. L16. **4** A seat where a number of people sit side by side in some official capacity; *esp.* one occupied by a group in the British Parliament. ME. **b** The people collectively who occupy such a seat; their status or dignity. E17. **5** Formerly, a merchant's table; a banker's counter. Now, a worktop used by a carpenter etc., or in a laboratory. LME. **6** *Law* (now *Hist.*). *free bench* [AL *bancus francus*], a widow's dower out of copyholds to which she was entitled by the customs of some manors. L17. **7** A ledge or floor upon which retorts stand; a set of retorts. M19. **8** A collection of dogs as exhibited at a show on benches or platforms. L19. **9** A seat used by officials and players when not participating in a game; the persons collectively who occupy such a seat. E20.

1 COVERDALE *Esther* 1:6 The benches were of golde and siluer. M. SPARK The small girls took their lessons seated on three benches arranged about the elm. 3 D. JACOBSON He was in due course promoted to the bench, on which he served to the end of his days. **on the bench** serving as a judge or magistrate. b **King's** or **Queen's Bench** a division of the High Court (formerly a court at which the monarch presided). c DISRAELI Now, prisoner, the bench is ready to hear your confession. 4 W. SHENSTONE A little bench of heedless bishops And there a chancellor in embryo. W. S. CHURCHILL I invite former colleagues on the opposite Bench to share the credit. *back bench, cross-bench, front bench, Treasury bench*, etc. 5 J. S. HUXLEY Between days of hard work at my bench I explored the exciting neighbourhood. *optical bench*: see OPTICAL *a.*

Comb.: **bench-end** the end of a seat in a church, freq. ornamented; †**bench-hole** a privy, a lavatory; **bench-hook** a board with stops fitted at each end on opposite faces, used on a carpenter's bench to secure a workpiece; **bench press** a body-building and weightlifting exercise in which a lifter lies on a bench with feet on the floor and raises a weight with both arms; **bench-press** *v.t.* & *i.* raise (a weight) in a bench press; **bench-screw** a vice attached to a carpenter's bench; **bench seat** a seat across the whole width of a car etc.; **bench-stop, -strip** a pillar or strip which projects above the surface of a carpenter's bench, used to secure a workpiece; **bench-table** (*a*) a low stone seat on the inside of walls or round the bases of pillars, in churches, cloisters, etc.; (*b*) *Hist.* an official body of benchers at the Inner Temple; **bench test** a test of a motor engine carried out in a workshop before it is fitted to a motor body; **bench-test** *v.t.* subject to a bench test, test in conditions simulating real use; **bench-warmer** *N. Amer. Sports slang* a player who does not get selected to play, a substitute; **bench-warrant** a warrant issued by a judge in court for the arrest of a person who fails to appear, as opp. to a justice's or magistrate's warrant.

benchlet *n.* a little bench; a stool: M19.

bench /bɛn(t)ʃ/ *v.* LME. [f. the n.] **1** *v.t.* Equip with benches. LME. **2** *v.t.* & *i.* Seat (oneself) on a bench. L16. **b** *v.t.* Put (a dog) on a show-bench for exhibition; exhibit at a dog-show. L19. **3** *v.t.* Remove or retire (a player) to the bench for non-participants. *N. Amer.* E20.

bencher /ˈbɛn(t)ʃə/ *n.* ME. [f. as prec. + -ER[1].] **1** A person who sits on a bench, *esp.* a magistrate, judge, etc. ME. **2** Each of the senior members of an Inn of Court. L16.

1 *back-bencher*: see BACK-. CROSS-BENCHER. *front-bencher*: see FRONT *n.* & *a.*

benchership *n.* the position of a bencher in an Inn of Court E19.

benchmark /ˈbɛn(t)ʃmɑːk/ *n., a.,* & *v.* M19. [f. BENCH *n.* + MARK *n.*[1]] **A** *n.* **1** A surveyor's mark consisting of a broad arrow with a horizontal bar through its apex, cut in rock etc. to indicate a point whose position and height have been surveyed. M19. **2** *fig.* A point of reference, a criterion. L19.

B *attrib.* or as *adj.* Serving or used as a benchmark. M20.

Intercity Magazine Bass Draught is a benchmark bitter, with an excellent balance of ingredients.

C *v.t.* Test or check by comparison with a benchmark. (Foll. by *to*.) L20.

bend /bɛnd/ *n.*[1] [OE *bend* = Goth. *bandi*, f. Gmc, f. base of BIND *v.*: later infl. by OFr. *bende* BAND *n.*[2] Replaced by *band* or *bond* exc. in Naut. use.] †**1** A band, a fetter; in *pl.*, bonds, imprisonment. OE–LME. †**2** A clamp; a connecting piece. ME–L16. **3** *Naut.* Any of various kinds of knot, as *cable bend, fisherman's bend*, etc. E18.

bend /bɛnd/ *n.*[2] OE. [App. orig. a sense of prec. Later identified w. OFr. *bende* (mod. *bande*): see

BAND *n.*[2]] **1** A thin flat strip used to bind round; a ribbon, fillet, etc.; a scroll etc. in decorative work. *obs.* exc. *dial.* OE. **2** *Her.* An ordinary drawn from the dexter chief to the sinister base of the shield, with breadth one fifth or, if charged, one third part of the field. LME. **3** A shape or size in which hides are tanned into leather, forming half of a butt (BUTT *n.*[4] 4). L16.

2 bend sinister a bend drawn from sinister chief to dexter base (a supposed mark of bastardy). **in bend** placed in a diagonal line. **party per bend** divided diagonally. **sinister bend** = *bend sinister* above.

Comb.: **bend-leather** the leather of a bend, i.e. the stoutest kind; sole leather.

bendlet *n.* (*Her.*) a bend with half the normal width L16. **bendwise** *adv.* (*Her.*) at the angle of a bend E17.

bend /bɛnd/ *n.*[3] LME. [f. BEND *v.*] **1** The action or an act of bending. LME. **†2** Inclination of the eye in any direction; glance. *rare* (Shakes.). Only in L16. **†3** Turn of mind, inclination, bent. L16–E19. **4** A thing of bent shape; a curved part of a thing; a curve of a road, river, etc. L16. **5** *Naut.* A ship's wale. Usu. in *pl.* E17. **6** In *pl.*, usu. with *the*. Pain (esp. in the joints) which is a symptom of decompression sickness. Also, the illness itself. *colloq.* L19.

1 N. HAWTHORNE A wave just on the bend, and about to break over. K. VONNEGUT He . . did a deep-knee bend. **3** H. FUSELI The prevalent bend of the reigning taste. **4** R. MACAULAY Aunt Dot was a clever, impetuous driver, taking the sharpest bends with the greatest intrepidity. P. MATTHIESSEN The river curves in a broad bend of . . gravel bars. *U-bend, Z-bend*, etc.

Phrases: **above one's bend** *US* beyond one's powers. *Grecian bend*: see GRECIAN *a.* **on the** (or **a**) **bend** *slang* on a spree (cf. BENDER). **round the bend** *colloq.* crazy, insane.

bend /bɛnd/ *v.* Pa. t. & pple **bended** (*arch.* exc. in *bended knee(s)*: see below), **bent** /bɛnt/. [OE *bendan* = ON *benda*, f. Gmc, f. base of BAND *n.*[1]] **I** Constrain; bow, curve. **†1** *v.t.* Put in bonds. Only in OE. **2** *v.t.* Bring (a bow etc.) into tension by a string; *fig.* tighten, wind up, brace. Freq. foll. by *up*. OE. **b** *Naut.* Tie, fasten on, make fast. LME. **3** *v.t.* Force (a thing having some rigidity) out of straightness or normal form; bow, curve, crook, inflect. ME. **4** *v.i.* Assume or receive a curved or angled form; curve over from an erect position. LME. **5** *v.i. spec.* Of a person: incline the body, stoop; bow, esp. in submission; *fig.* yield (*to*), be pliant or subservient. LME. **6** *v.t.* Cause (a person, the will, etc.) to bow, stoop, incline, or relent. LME. **7** *v.t.* Turn away from the straight line; deflect, turn. E16. **8** *v.t.* Pervert, make illicit or dishonest (now *slang*); modify or interpret (rules etc.) to suit oneself. (*rare* bef. M19.) M16. **†9** *v.t.* & *i.* Incline in mind. M16–M18. **10** *v.i.* Have a direction away from the straight line; incline, trend. L16.

2 SHAKES. *Hen. V* Hold hard the breath, and bend up every spirit To his full height. SIR W. SCOTT Her whole mind apparently bent up to the solemn interview. **b** R. L. STEVENSON He had with his own hand bent and run up the colours. **3** J. GERARD Branches . . so easie to be bent or bowed, that hereof they make Hoops. DICKENS His form is bent by age. A. RANSOME He stooped and bent his long legs and worked his way through the tunnel. HARPER LEE Mrs Crenshaw took some chicken wire and bent it into the shape of a cured ham. T. E. HULME To bend the steel out of its own curve and into the exact curve you want. **4** DRYDEN The waving Harvest bends beneath his blast. F. O'BRIEN He . . roosted on its slender perch till it bowed beneath him and bent till it slammed him to the ground. **5** MILTON Who hate the Lord should then be fain To bow to him and bend. LYTTON He bent down and kissed her cheek. C. MACKENZIE His thin body bending over the table like a tall black note of interrogation. C. FREEMAN She missed Jacob terribly and berated herself for not being able to bend to his will. **6** LD MACAULAY The spirit of the rustic gentry was not to be bent. J. W. KRUTCH He has learned her [Nature's] laws and can bend her to his will, making her serve *his* purposes, not hers. **7** J. BRONOWSKI Blue [light] is bent or refracted more than red. **8** *Observer* There are honest landladies . . who let a flat to someone they think is an ordinary girl, who then proceeds to 'bend' it: uses it for prostitution. *Times* Trying to get other members of the European Community to 'bend the rules' so that exports can be resumed. **10** LONGFELLOW And now the land . . Bent southward suddenly.

II Direct, aim. **11** *v.i.* (*arch.*) & *t.* Direct or turn (one's way, steps, etc.). LME. **12** *v.t.* Apply or bring to bear (one's mind, energies, etc.) *on* or *upon*. E16. **b** *v.refl.* & *i.* Apply oneself *to* or *to do*. *arch.* L16. **†13** *v.t.* Aim or level (weapons, forces, etc.; *against* or *at*). M16–E19. **14** *v.t.* Direct or turn (one's eyes, *on* something seen; one's ears, *to* something heard). L16. **15** *v.t. fig.* & *gen.* Direct or turn (*against, on, to(wards)*, etc.). L16.

11 SHAKES. *All's Well* For thence we came And . . Thither we bend again. MILTON Thither his course he bends Through the calm Firmament. **12** A. J. CRONIN Immobilized suddenly, his attention bent upon the sheet before him. D. J. ENRIGHT He bends his strength against the flood. H. J. LASKI Yet it was a great work to which they bent their effort. **b** BUNYAN If any shall . . bend themselves to disappoint the designs of the Eternal God. E. K. KANE Bending to our oars. **13** SPENSER So bent his speare and spurd his horse. O. CROMWELL They bent their guns at the frigate. **14** MILTON And to my cries . . Thine ear with favor bend. SOUTHEY Every eye on her was bent. **15** WILLIAM COLLINS To Britain bend his iron Car. E. WELTY [He] bent on her his benign smile.

Phrases: **bend one's elbow** *slang* = *crook one's elbow* s.v. CROOK *v.* 1. **bend over** put oneself into position to be thrashed on the buttocks. *bend over backward(s)*: see BACKWARD *adv.* 1. **bend someone's ear** importune someone with persistent talk; have a word with someone. **bend the brow(s)** †(*a*) arch the eyebrows; (*b*) knit the brow; scowl. **bend the head**, **†the face** bow the head. *bend the rules*; see RULE *n.* **catch a person bending** *colloq.* catch a person at a disadvantage. **on bended knee(s)** kneeling, esp. in reverence, supplication, or submission.

bendable *a.* E17.

benday process /ˈbɛndeɪ ˌprəʊsɛs/ *n. phr. obs.* exc. *Hist.* Also **Ben Day process**. E20. [*Benjamin Day* (1838–1916), US printer.] A method of tint production in lithography and photo-engraving by transferring lines or dots from gelatin sheets.

bender /ˈbɛndə/ *n.* L15. [f. BEND *v.* + -ER[1].] **1** An instrument for bending; a pair of pliers. L15. **2** A person who bends. L16. **b** A homosexual. *slang. derog.* L20. **†3a** A hard drinker. *Sc.* E18–E19. **b** A bout of drinking; a riotous party. M19. **4** A sixpence. Cf. CRIPPLE *n.* 2a. *slang.* E19. **5** A leg, a knee. *slang.* Orig. *US.* M19.

bendy /ˈbɛndi/ *a.* L15. [OFr. *bendé* (mod. *bandé*): see BEND *n.*[2], -Y[5].] *Her.* Of a field: divided into an even number of bends, coloured alternately.

bene /biːn/ *n.* Long *arch.* [OE *bēn* = ON *bœn* f. Gmc base of BOON *n.*[1]] Prayer, petition.

beneaped /bɪˈniːpt/ *a.* L17. [f. BE- 5 + NEAP *v.* + -ED[2].] Left aground by a neaping spring tide.

beneath /bɪˈniːθ/ *adv.*, *prep.*, & *a.* [OE *biniþan*, *bineoþan*, f. *bi* BY *prep.* etc. + *niþan*, *neoþan* below, down, (orig.) from below, f. Gmc base of NETHER.] **A** *adv.* **1** *gen.* In a lower position; = BELOW *adv.* 1. OE. **b** *fig.* Lower in rank, position, quality, etc. *arch.* OE. **2a** Under heaven; on earth. *arch.* ME. **b** Under the earth; in hell. *arch.* ME. **3** Directly below; underneath. ME.

1 SOUTHEY Pure water in a font beneath reflects The many-colour'd rays. **3** DRYDEN Spread with Straw, the bedding of thy Fold; With Fern beneath. D. DU MAURIER It was a gold chain for my keys, with a disk upon it bearing our initials, . . and the date beneath.

B *prep.* **1** *gen.* In a position lower than (= BELOW *prep.* 1); downhill or downstream from. Now *rare* or *obs.* OE. **2** *fig.* Lower than in rank, position, quality, etc. OE. **3** Unbefitting the dignity of; unworthy of. OE. **4** Directly down from; overhung by; at the foot of. ME. **5** Under, as overwhelmed by pressure; under the weight of. Often *fig.* ME. **6** Immediately under; covered or concealed by. E17.

2 ADDISON Beings above and beneath us have probably no Opinions at all. J. MCCOSH The copies ever fall beneath the original. **3** SHAKES. *Twel. N.* So far beneath your soft and tender breeding. S. BELLOW I shut the door with a crash, already aware, under my anger, that this was beneath me and altogether out of proportion to the provocation. **4** DRYDEN Lands that lye beneath another Sun. W. H. AUDEN We see you sitting / in a wide-brimmed hat beneath a monkey-puzzle. W. TREVOR In the far distance, a speck on the beach beneath the cliffs, Commander Abigail ran towards the sea. **5** SHAKES. *Macb.* Our country sinks beneath the yoke. R. BLOOMFIELD Brisk goes the work beneath each busy hand. **6** DAY LEWIS A scoop of sandy earth beneath a boulder. B. BAINBRIDGE The underground spring that ran beneath the sloping street overflowed from time to time. *fig.*: A. HAILEY Beneath his outward reaction, Nim was startled and shocked.

Phrases: **beneath contempt** not worth despising. *beneath one's dignity*: see DIGNITY 2. *beneath the sun*: see SUN *n.*[1]

†C *adj.* Lower. *rare* (Shakes.). Only in E17.

benedicite /bɛnɪˈdʌɪsɪti/ *int.* & *n.* ME. [L, 2nd person pl. imper. of *benedicere* wish well to, bless, f. *bene* well + *dicere* say.] **A** *int.* **1** Expr. a wish: God bless you! ME. **2** Expr. astonishment: Good gracious! ME. **B** *n.* **1** An invocation of a blessing; *esp.* a grace at table. ME. **2** Chr. Ch. *the Benedicite*, the canticle beginning *Benedicite, omnia opera* 'O all ye works [of the Lord], bless ye [the Lord]', known also as 'The Song of the Three Children', which is an alternative to the *Te Deum* at matins in the *Book of Common Prayer*. M17.

Benedick /ˈbɛnɪdɪk/ *n.* Also **-dict** /-dɪkt/. E19. [A character in Shakespeare's *Much Ado.*] A newly married man; *esp.* an apparently confirmed bachelor who marries.

Benedictine /bɛnɪˈdɪktɪn/ *n.*[1] & *a.* E17. [Fr. *bénédictin* or mod.L *benedictinus*, f. *Benedictus* of Nursia (St Benedict), *c*480–*c*550, abbot of Monte Cassino: see -INE[1].] **A** *n.* A member of a community of monks (also known, from their dress, as 'Black Monks'), following the rule established by St Benedict *c*529. E17. **B** *adj.* Of or belonging to St Benedict or the order following his rule. M17.

Benedictine /bɛnɪˈdɪktiːn/ *n.*[2] Also **b-**. L19. [Fr. *Bénédictine*, fem. of *bénédictin* (see prec.).] (Proprietary name for) a liqueur of brandy and herbs, made orig. by Benedictine monks.

benediction /bɛnɪˈdɪkʃ(ə)n/ *n.* LME. [((O)Fr. *bénédiction* f.) L *benedictio(n-)*, f. *benedict-* pa. ppl stem of *benedicere*: see BENEDICITE, -ION.] **1** The utterance of a blessing; devout or formal invocation of blessedness, prosperity, etc., esp. at the conclusion of a church service, at the consecration of an abbot, or as a grace at table. LME. **b** A chiefly Roman Catholic service in which the congregation is blessed with the Blessed Sacrament. E19. **2** Blessedness, favour. L15.

1 J. A. FROUDE Amidst the benedictions of tens of thousands of people. **2** SHAKES. *Wint. T.* As if my trinkets . . brought a benediction to the buyer. F. NORRIS A sense of benediction brooded low—a divine kindliness manifesting itself in beauty, in peace, in absolute repose.

benedictional *n.* a book of forms of benediction M18. **benedictionary** *n.* = BENEDICTIONAL L18. **benedictory** *a.* of or pertaining to the utterance of benediction E18.

benedictive /bɛnɪˈdɪktɪv/ *a.* M17. [f. L *benedict-* (see prec.) + -IVE.] Tending to bless.

Benedictus /bɛnɪˈdɪktəs/ *n.* M16. [L, pa. pple of *benedicere* bless: see BENEDICITE.] **1** The canticle beginning *Benedictus Dominus Deus* 'Blessed be the Lord God' from the hymn of Zacharias (*Luke* 1:68). M16. **2** The fifth section of the ordinary of the Mass, beginning *Benedictus qui venit* 'Blessed is he who comes'; a musical setting of this. L19.

benedight /bɛnɪˈdʌɪt/ *a.* Long *arch.* ME. [f. L *benedictus* (see prec.), w. assim. to DIGHT.] Blessed.

bene esse /ˈbɛnɪ ɛsi/ *n. phr.* E17. [mod.L.] Well-being, welfare, esp. opp. ESSE.

benefact /ˈbɛnɪfakt/ *v.* L16. [Back-form. f. BENEFACTOR.] **†1** *v.i.* Act as a benefactor. *rare.* Only in L16. **2** *v.t.* Help or endow as a benefactor. L19.

benefaction /bɛnɪˈfakʃ(ə)n/ *n.* M17. [Late L *benefactio(n-)*, f. *bene facere* do good (to), pa. ppl stem *fact-*: see -FACTION.] **1** A doing good, beneficence; a benefit or blessing. M17. **2** *esp.*

The bestowal of money for a charitable purpose; a gift, an endowment. L17.

benefactive /bɛnɪˈfaktɪv/ *a.* & *n.* M20. [f. L *benefactus* capable of giving (f. as prec.) + -IVE.] *Gram.* (An affix, phrase, or verbal aspect) indicating that someone is benefited.

benefactor /ˈbɛnɪfaktə/ *n.* LME. [L, f. *bene facere*: see BENEFACTION, -OR.] 1 A person who gives friendly aid; a patron of or donor to a cause or charitable institution. LME. 2 A person who does good. *rare.* E17.

1 J. LE CARRÉ You cannot imagine that some kindly benefactor . . would ever concern himself with putting you on your feet. K. M. E. MURRAY As a benefactor of Keble College he was influential in Oxford circles. 2 SHAKES. *Meas. for M.* Well—what benefactors are they? Are they not malefactors?

benefactory *a.* of or pertaining to a benefactor; beneficial: M18. **benefactress** *n.* a female benefactor E18. †**benefactrice** *n.* = BENEFACTRESS LME–E18. **benefactrix** *n.* = BENEFACTRESS E17.

benefic /bɪˈnɛfɪk/ *a.* E17. [L *beneficus* f. as prec.: see -FIC.] 1 *Astrol.* Of favourable influence. E17. 2 *gen.* Beneficent, kindly. M17.

benefice /ˈbɛnɪfɪs/ *n.* & *v.* ME. [OFr. (mod. *bénéfice* profit, perquisite) f. L *beneficium* favour, support, f. (after *beneficus* BENEFIC) *bene* well + *fic-* var. of *fac-* in *facere* do, make. In sense A.2 tr. L.] A *n.* I 1 An ecclesiastical living; property held by a rector, vicar, or other church officer. ME. 2 *Hist.* Land granted in feudal tenure, a fief. L15. II †3 A kindness or favour; an indulgence. LME–L17. 4 Favourable influence or operation; advantage, protection. *obs.* exc. *Hist.* LME. †5 Beneficial property or action (as of natural causes). LME–M17. B *v.t.* Endow or invest with a church living. Chiefly as *beneficed* ppl a. LME.

beneficence /bɪˈnɛfɪs(ə)ns/ *n.* LME. [L *beneficentia*, f. *beneficus*: see BENEFIC, -ENCE.] 1 Doing good, active kindness. LME. 2 A benefaction; a gift; a good deed. M17.

1 A. S. NEILL A child is born neither good nor bad, but with tendencies toward both beneficence and criminality. 2 CARLYLE Sterling now . . zealously forwarded schools and beneficences. R. NIEBUHR The universal beneficences of nature.

beneficency *n.* (now *rare*) = BENEFICENCE I L16.

beneficent /bɪˈnɛfɪs(ə)nt/ *a.* E17. [L *beneficent-* stem of *beneficentior* compar. of *beneficus* BENEFIC: cf. MAGNIFICENT.] Doing good; actively kind; showing or expressive of active kindness; beneficial (*to*).

POPE Gentle of speech, beneficent of mind. H. J. LASKI A revolution which, beneficent to the masses, would be fatal to themselves. W. STYRON His face is illumined by a beneficent smile.

beneficential /-ˈsɛnʃ(ə)l/ *a.* of or pertaining to beneficence M19. **beneficently** *adv.* E18.

beneficiaire /ˌbɛnɪfɪʃɪˈɛː/ *n.* M19. [Fr. *bénéficiaire*, f. *bénéfice* BENEFICE + *-aire* -AR[2].] The recipient of the proceeds from a benefit performance etc.

beneficial /bɛnɪˈfɪʃ(ə)l/ *a.* LME. [(O)Fr. *bénéficial* or late L *beneficialis*, f. *beneficium*: see BENEFICE, -AL[1].] 1 Of benefit, advantageous, (*to*). LME. †b Lucrative, bringing pecuniary profit. E16–M19. †2 Actively kind. E16–M17. †3 Of or pertaining to a church benefice; beneficed. M16–M19. 4 *Law.* Of, pertaining to, or having the use or benefit of property etc. M19.

beneficially *adv.* M16. **beneficialness** *n.* E16.

beneficiary /bɛnɪˈfɪʃ(ə)ri/ *a.* & *n.* E17. [L *beneficiarius*, f. *beneficium*: see BENEFICE, -ARY[1].] A *adj.* Holding, held as, or pertaining to the holding of, a benefice; *spec.* (*Hist.*) feudatory. E17. B *n.* 1 *Hist.* The holder of a fief; a feudatory. E17. 2 The holder of a church living. M17. 3 A person who receives or is entitled to receive a favour or benefit, esp. under a trust or will or life insurance policy. M17.

beneficiate /bɛnɪˈfɪʃɪeɪt/ *v.t.* L19. [f. Sp. *beneficiar*, f. *beneficio* benefit: see -ATE[3].] Treat (ore, raw material, etc.) to improve its properties.

benefici'ation *n.* L19.

benefit /ˈbɛnɪfɪt/ *n.* LME. [AN *benfet*, OFr. *bienfet*, *-fait* ult. f. L *benefactum* good deed, f. *bene facere*: see BENEFACTION.] †1 A thing well done; a good deed. LME–E19. 2 A kind deed; a favour, gift; a benefaction. *arch.* LME. 3 *Law* (now *Hist.*). The advantage of belonging to a privileged order exempted from the jurisdiction or sentence of ordinary courts of law. L15. 4 *gen.* (An) advantage, (a) good. E16. †b A natural advantage or gift. *rare* (Shakes.). L16–E17. c Pecuniary profit. L16. 5 = BENEFICE *n.* 1. *obs.* exc. *dial.* M16. 6 A theatrical performance, concert, sporting event, etc., the proceeds of which go to a player or other particular person or group; also, the proceeds from such a performance etc. E18. 7 The allowance to which a person is entitled under a social security or insurance scheme or as the member of a benefit-club or benefit society. L19.

2 SHAKES. *A.Y.L.* [Fortune's] benefits are mightily misplaced. 4 S. JOHNSON Having long laboured for the benefit of mankind. J. F. KENNEDY We have, however, one great advantage over the English. We have the benefit of their experience. B. PLAIN The . . fancy decorated birthday cake was for the children's benefit. B. BETTELHEIM Whatever practical benefits may be derived from psychoanalysis, they are only incidental to its cultural achievements. b SHAKES. *A.Y.L.* Disable all the benefits of your own country. c STEELE My Estate is seven hundred Pounds a Year, besides the Benefit of Tin-Mines. 6 C. CHAPLIN Three months before I left the troupe we appeared at a benefit for my father. R. K. NARAYAN It was a benefit show for building a maternity home. *benefit match, performance,* etc. 7 *maternity benefit, retirement benefit, sickness benefit, supplementary benefit, unemployment benefit,* etc.

Phrases: *benefit of* CLERGY. **benefit of the doubt** assumption of a person's innocence, rightness, etc., rather than the contrary in the absence of proof. *fringe benefit*: see FRINGE *n.* & *a.* **on benefit** supported by social security etc. payments. *social benefit*: see SOCIAL *a.*

Comb.: **benefit-club**, **benefit society**: whose members, by the regular payment of small sums, are entitled to pecuniary help in time of distress.

benefit /ˈbɛnɪfɪt/ *v.* Infl. **-t-**, also ***-tt-**. L15. [f. the n.] 1 *v.t.* Do good to, be of advantage to; improve. L15. 2 *v.i.* Receive benefit; profit. (Foll. by *by*, *from*.) E17.

1 J. GALSWORTHY It had long been her pet plan that her uncles should benefit themselves and Bosinney by building country homes. H. KISSINGER The lessons we learned benefited our handling of later crises. 2 N. MITFORD The younger ones were now benefiting from the fact that Louisa and Linda were married women. E. LONGFORD Lord Castlereagh was no financial wizard and it was through Wellington's labours that the world at large benefited.

Benelux /ˈbɛnɪlʌks/ *n.* M20. [Acronym, f. *Be*lgium, *Ne*therlands, *Lux*emburg.] Belgium, the Netherlands, and Luxembourg collectively; *esp.* these countries in association as a regional economic group.

benempt(ed) *v.* see BENAME.

benet /ˈbɛnɪt/ *n.* LME. [AN *benet*, OFr. *beneëit* f. L *benedictus* blessed: see BENEDICTUS.] *Eccl. Hist.* = EXORCIST 1b.

benet /bɪˈnɛt/ *v.t.* Infl. **-tt-**. ME. [f. BE- 1, 4 + NET *v.*[1] or *n.*[1]] Cover as with, or catch in, a net. Chiefly *fig.*

Beneventan /bɛnɪˈvɛnt(ə)n/ *a.* E20. [It. *beneventano* f. med.L *Beneventanus*, f. *Beneventum* Benevento, a province of Italy + -AN.] Designating or pertaining to a medieval script principally of southern Italy.

Also **Beneventine** *a.* (now *rare* or *obs.*) L19.

benevolence /bɪˈnɛvəl(ə)ns/ *n.* ME. [(O)Fr. *bénévolence* (OFr. also *beni-*) f. L *benevolentia*, f. *benevolent-*: see BENEVOLENT, -ENCE.] 1 Disposition to do good; kindness, generosity, charitable feeling (towards humankind at large). ME. †2 Affection, goodwill (towards a particular person or on a particular occasion). LME–E19. 3 An act of kindness; a gift of money, a charitable contribution. LME. 4 *Hist.* A forced loan or contribution levied by certain English monarchs without the consent of Parliament (first demanded by Edward IV in 1473 as a token of goodwill). L15.

2 **do one's benevolence** lend one's friendly offices.

†**benevolency** *n.* M16–M18. [f. as prec.: see -ENCY.] The quality of being benevolent; a gift of money.

benevolent /bɪˈnɛv(ə)l(ə)nt/ *a.* LME. [OFr. *benivolent* f. L *benevolent-* pres. ppl stem of *bene velle* wish well: see -ENT.] 1 Desirous of the good of others; of a kindly disposition; charitable. LME. 2 Well-disposed (*to* another). L15.

1 POPE Beloved old man! benevolent as wise. J. GALSWORTHY Her plan met with more opposition from Providence than so benevolent a scheme deserved. 2 MILTON Raphael now . . Benevolent and facil thus repli'd.

benevolently *adv.* M16.

Bengal /bɛŋˈɡɔːl/ *n.* & *a.* L17. [A former Indian province: see BENGALI.] A *n.* †1 In *pl.* Fabrics or clothing, esp. silks, imported from Bengal. L17–M19. 2 *royal Bengal*, = (*royal*) *Bengal tiger* below. L19.

B *attrib.* or as *adj.* Of or pertaining to Bengal. E18.

Bengal light a firework producing a steady and vivid blue light. **Bengal quince** = BAEL. (**royal**) **Bengal tiger** a tiger of a variety found in the Indian subcontinent, distinguished by unbroken stripes.

Bengalese /bɛŋɡəˈliːz/ *a.* & *n.* Pl. of n. same. L18. [f. prec. + -ESE.] = next.

Bengali /bɛŋˈɡɔːli/ *a.* & *n.* Also †**-lee**. L18. [f. Hind. *baṅgālī*.] A *adj.* Of or pertaining to Bengal, a former Indian province, now constituting Bangladesh and the Indian State of West Bengal, its people, or their language. L18. B *n.* A native or inhabitant of Bengal, or of Bangladesh or West Bengal; the Indo-Aryan language of Bengal, the national language of Bangladesh and the official language of West Bengal. E19.

benight /bɪˈnʌɪt/ *v.t.* LME. [f. BE- 4 + NIGHT *n.*] 1 Cover, hide, or involve in the darkness of night. Usu. (and *arch.* exc.) in *pass.* LME. 2 *fig.* Involve in intellectual or moral darkness; darken, cloud. Freq. in *pass.* E17.

1 DE QUINCEY The tourists were benighted in a forest. 2 W. DAVENANT Now jealousie no more benights her face. J. WILSON What men . . call Religion, now benighting half the earth. ISAIAH BERLIN The mass of the proletarians themselves were too benighted to grasp the role which history had called on them to play.

benightedness *n.* the state of being benighted M19. **benightment** *n.* (*rare*) M17.

benign /bɪˈnʌɪn/ *a.* ME. [(O)Fr. *bénigne* f. L *benignus* prob. for *benigenus*, f. *bene* well + *-genus* born; for the formation cf. MALIGN *a.*, for the sense L *gentilis* GENTLE *a.*] 1 Of a kindly disposition, gracious. ME. 2 Manifesting kindly feeling; bland, gentle, mild. LME. 3 Of a thing: favourable, propitious, salutary. LME. 4 *Med.* †a Of a medicine: mild in action. M17–M18. b Of a disease or tumour: not malignant. M18.

1 R. D. LAING Assurance that during sleep he is being watched over by benign presences (parents, good fairies, angels). 2 R. MACAULAY He nodded and was benign, but anyone could see he did not agree. J. HELLER Sid was regarding the assault upon Gold with a smiling and benign countenance. **benign neglect** lack of attention reflecting confidence in or a favourable disposition towards a person or thing; well-intentioned or beneficial neglect. 3 C. BRONTË On whose birth benign planets have certainly smiled. A. J. P. TAYLOR The weather was uniformly benign. E. F. SCHUMACHER We were very rapidly using up a certain kind of irreplaceable capital asset, namely the *tolerance margins* which benign nature always provides.

benignly *adv.* LME.

benignant /bɪˈnɪɡnənt/ *a.* L18. [f. prec. or L *benignus*, after *malignant*: see -ANT[1].] 1 Kind or gracious to inferiors or dependants; (esp. condescendingly) benevolent. L18. 2 Of things: favourable, beneficial. L18. 3 *Med.* = BENIGN 4b. L19.

benignancy *n.* L19. **benignantly** *adv.* L18.

benignity /bɪˈnɪɡnɪti/ *n.* LME. [(O)Fr. *bénignité* or L *benignitas*, f. *benignus*: see BENIGN, -ITY.] 1 Kindly feeling; kindness of disposition or of manner (esp. towards inferiors or juniors). LME. b A kindly or generous deed. M16. 2 Of things: benign quality. *arch.* E17.

Benin /bɛˈniːn/ *n.* & *a.* L19. [Origin unkn.] (Of or pertaining to) a people of southern Nigeria, noted for their production of fine bronzes and carved ivories.

Benioff /ˈbɛnɪɒf/ *n.* M20. [V. Hugo *Benioff* (1899–1968), US seismologist.] *Geol.* **1** *Benioff seismograph, seismometer*, an instrument of a kind invented by Benioff in which movement of a horizontal rod induces an electrical voltage. M20. **2** *Benioff zone*, an inclined zone of high seismicity underlying island-arc systems at the overlap of oceanic and continental crust. M20.

benison /ˈbɛnɪz(ə)n, -s-/ *n.* ME. [OFr. *beneiçon*, (later) *benisson* f. L *benedictio(n-)* BENEDICTION.] A blessing, benediction; blessedness, beatitude.
JER. TAYLOR The most glorious issues of Divine Benison upon this Kingdome. SIR W. SCOTT I have slept sound under such a benison. P. NORMAN The benison of that smile, bestowed on well-eaten dinner or an unusual Dinky car.

bénitier /benitje/ *n.* Pl. pronounced same. M19. [Fr., f. *bénit(e* blessed + *-ier* -ER².] A vessel for holy water.

benitoite /bəˈniːtəʊʌɪt/ *n.* E20. [f. San *Benito* County, California + -ITE¹.] *Min.* A sapphire-blue hexagonal barium titanium silicate, sometimes of gem quality.

benjamin /ˈbɛndʒəmɪn/ *n.*¹ M16. [Alt. of *benjoin* var. of BENZOIN, by assoc. with male forename *Benjamin*.] = BENZOIN I.
Comb.: **benjamin bush** = *benjamin-tree* (b) below; **benjamin-tree** (*a*) a tree yielding benzoin; (*b*) a spicebush.

benjamin /ˈbɛndʒəmɪn/ *n.*² *arch.* E19. [Perh. the name of a tailor.] A type of overcoat for men.

Benjamin /ˈbɛndʒəmɪn/ *n.*³ M19. [The youngest son of the patriarch Jacob (*Gen.* 43 etc.).] The youngest (and favourite) child.
Benjamin's portion the largest share.

†benjoin *n.* var. of BENZOIN.

benne *n.* var. of BENNI.

bennet /ˈbɛnɪt/ *n.*¹ LME. [OFr. *herbe beneïte*, med.L *herba benedicta* 'blessed plant' (said to put the devil to flight).] Usu. (now only) in full *herb bennet*. Wood avens, *Geum urbanum*. Formerly also, any of several other plants, *esp.* hemlock.

bennet *n.*² see BENT *n.*¹

benni /ˈbɛni/ *n.* Also **benne**. M18. [Mande.] The sesame plant, *Sesamum orientale*. Usu. in *comb.*, as *benniseed*.

benny /ˈbɛni/ *n.*¹ *US slang*. E20. [App. abbrev. of BENJAMIN *n.*²: see -Y⁶.] A sack coat; an overcoat.

benny /ˈbɛni/ *n.*² *slang* (orig. *US*). M20. [f. BEN(ZEDRINE + -Y⁶.] (A tablet of) Benzedrine.

benomyl /ˈbɛnəmɪl/ *n.* M20. [f. BEN(Z)O- + M(ETH)YL.] An imidazole derivative used as a systemic fungicide on fruit and vegetable crops.

benorth /bɪˈnɔːθ/ *adv.* & *prep.* Long *obs.* exc. *Sc.* [OE *be norþan*, f. BY *prep.* + *norþan* (adv.) from the north: cf. BEFORE.] To the north (of).

Bensonian /bɛnˈsəʊnɪən/ *a.* & *n.* E20. [f. *Benson* (see below) + -IAN.] *Hist.* **A** *adj.* Of or pertaining to the actor-manager Sir F. R. Benson (1858–1939) or his Shakespearian company. E20. **B** *n.* A member of this company. E20.

bent /bɛnt/ *n.*¹ Also (now *dial.*) **bennet** /ˈbɛnɪt/. ME. [Repr. OE *beonet* in place-names, e.g. *Beonetlēah* (Bentley), perh. 'meadow of stiff grass': corresp. to OS *binet*, OHG *binuz* (G *Binse*), f. WGmc, of unkn. origin.] **1** A place covered with grass, an open field; unenclosed pasture, heath; *arch.* a field of battle. ME. **2** A stiff-stemmed reedy or rushlike grass; such grass collectively; *Bot.* any grass of the genus *Agrostis*. Also *bent-grass*. LME. **3** The stiff flower-stalk of grasses. L16.
1 take the bent escape to open country. **2** R. HERRICK Sweet bents wode bow, to give my love the day. **creeping bent** = FIORIN.
benting *n.* (now *dial.*) feeding on bents (by birds) L17. **benty** *a.* of the nature of or pertaining to bent; covered with bent: M16.

bent /bɛnt/ *n.*² LME. [Prob. f. BEND *v.* on the analogy of pairs like *descend* and *descent*, *extend* and *extent*.] **1** The condition of being deflected in some direction; a twist, inclination, cast; chiefly *fig.*, mental inclination, disposition, bias, tendency. LME. **2** A curved position, form, or piece; curvature. Now *rare*. M16. **†3** An act of bending, bowing, or stooping. M16–E18. **†4** Aim, purpose. L16–L18. **†5** Impetus, *élan*. L16–M18. **6** Degree of tension (of a bow etc.); degree of endurance; limit of capacity. Now only in *to the top of one's bent* (after Shakes. *Haml.*), to one's heart's content. L16. **7** A section of a framework or framed building. E19.
1 SHAKES. *Tr. & Cr.* But gives all gaze and bent of amorous view On the fair Cressid. MILTON The whole bent of their actions was against the King. SHELLEY I sit—and smile or sigh as is my bent. J. GROSS If he showed a special bent, it was towards mathematics. **2** T. ELYOT In the fourme of a bowe, that hath a great bente. I. WALTON Make these fast at the bent of the hook. **4** T. R. MALTHUS The principal bent of this work. **5** E. YOUNG False joys, indeed, are born from want of thought; From thought's full bent, and energy, the true. **6** M. DRAYTON Beyond the bent of his unknowing Sight.

bent /bɛnt/ *a.* ME. [pa. pple of BEND *v.*] **†1** Wound up or braced for action; levelled as a weapon. ME–L17. **2** Constrained into a curve, bowed, crooked; deflected from a straight line. LME. **3** Determined, resolved, set. Now only *pred.* Foll. by *on*, *upon*, (arch.) *to do*. LME. **4** *fig.* Dishonest, criminal; illicit, stolen; perverted, homosexual. Cf. CROOKED *a.* 3, 4. *slang*. E20.
2 J. G. COZZENS A man in a worn grey felt hat and a shabby brown suit stepped, bent, into the rain. P. DAVIES In a bent spacetime, it is no surprise if the paths of light rays are bent. **bent brow** *arch.* a wrinkled or knit brow. **bentwood** wood artificially curved for making furniture. **3** R. ASCHAM The bent enemie against God and good order. W. MORRIS Like my fathers, bent to gather fame. L. M. MONTGOMERY As you're evidently bent on talking you might as well talk to some purpose. G. CHARLES I was still bent . . on a career in journalism. **4** P. LAURIE They could go bent on us—I hope most policemen would laugh at £500, but they might not. G. F. NEWMAN The two rooms held nothing bent. Q. CRISP I used to tell the audience that I was about to deliver a straight talk from a bent speaker.

bent *v.* pa. t. & pple: see BEND *v.*

Benthamism /ˈbɛntəmɪz(ə)m, ˈbɛnθ-/ *n.* L18. [f. *Bentham* (see below) + -ISM.] **1** An act characteristic of Bentham (see sense 2). *rare*. L18. **2** The utilitarian philosophical system of Jeremy Bentham (1748–1832), Eng. jurist and writer, in which the pursuit of the greatest happiness of the greatest number is the highest moral goal. E19.
Benthamic /-ˈtamɪk, -θ-/ *a.* = BENTHAMITE *a.* M19. **Benthamite** *n.* & *a.* (*a*) *n.* an adherent of Benthamism; (*b*) *adj.* of or pertaining to Bentham or Benthamism: E19.

benthos /ˈbɛnθɒs/ *n.* L19. [Gk = depth of the sea.] The flora and fauna of the bottom of the sea (or a lake).
benthic *a.* of or pertaining to the benthos E20. **ben'thonic** *a.* = BENTHIC L19.

bentincks /ˈbɛntɪŋks/ *n.pl.* M19. [Capt. J. A. *Bentinck* (1737–75), their inventor.] *Naut.* (now *Hist.*). Triangular sails for use on the lowest yards of square-rigged vessels.

bentonite /ˈbɛntənʌɪt/ *n.* L19. [f. Fort *Benton*, Montana, US + -ITE¹.] A highly colloidal, plastic, absorbent kind of clay having numerous uses esp. as an absorbent or filler.
bentonitic /-ˈnɪtɪk/ *a.* M20.

ben trovato /bɛn trɔˈvaːto/ *a. phr.* L19. [It., lit. 'well found'.] Of a story etc.: happily invented; appropriate though untrue.

benumb /bɪˈnʌm/ *v.t.* L15. [f. strong pa. pple of OE *beniman* deprive, f. as BE- I + NIM *v.*: cf. NUMB *a.*] Make insensible, torpid, or powerless (esp. of cold); deaden, stupefy; paralyse (the mind or will, action, etc.).

benz- /bɛnz/ *comb. form* of BENZENE or BENZOIC. Cf. BENZO-.
ben'zaldehyde *n.* a colourless liquid aromatic aldehyde, C_6H_5CHO, which has the odour of bitter almonds and is used esp. in the manufacture of dyes and perfumes M19. **benz'hydrol** *n.* diphenyl carbinol, $(C_6H_5)_2CHOH$, forming colourless crystals M20. **benzidine** *n.* biphenyl-4,4′-diamine $(C_6H_4NH_2)_2$, a colourless basic solid used in dye manufacture L19. **benzil** *n.* the compound 1,2-diphenylethanedione, $C_6H_5{\cdot}CO{\cdot}CO{\cdot}C_6H_5$, a yellow crystalline diketone formed by oxidation of benzoin with nitric acid M19. **benzilic** /-ˈzɪlɪk/ *a.*: *benzilic acid*, a colourless solid, $(C_6H_5)_2C(OH)COOH$, formed when benzil rearranges in the presence of alkali M19. **benz'pyrene** *n.* a polycyclic aromatic hydrocarbon, $C_{20}H_{12}$, found in coal tar and considered to be the major carcinogen of tobacco smoke E20. **benzyl** *n.* the radical $C_6H_5CH_2{\cdot}$, also called *phenylmethyl* M19. **ben'zylic** *a.* of, pertaining to, or of the nature of benzyl M19.

Benzedrine /ˈbɛnzɪdriːn/ *n.* M20. [f. prec. + EPH)EDRINE.] (Proprietary name for) amphetamine; a tablet of this.

benzene /ˈbɛnziːn/ *n.* M19. [f. BENZOIC + -ENE.] *Chem.* A colourless liquid cyclic hydrocarbon, C_6H_6, obtained from coal and petroleum and used esp. as a solvent, as a fuel, and in chemical manufacture.
Comb.: **benzene ring** the conjugated ring of six carbon atoms present in benzene and most aromatic compounds.
benzenoid *a.* derived from, related to, or pertaining to benzene L19.

benzine /ˈbɛnziːn/ *n.* Also **†-in**. M19. [f. as prec. + -INE⁵.] **1** = prec. Now *rare* or *obs.* M19. **2** A mixture of paraffins distilled from petroleum, used as a solvent and fuel. L19.

benzo- /ˈbɛnzəʊ/ *comb. form* of BENZENE or BENZOIC: see -O-. Cf. BENZ-.
benzodiazepine /ˌbɛnzəʊdʌɪˈeɪzɪpiːn, -ˈazəpiːn/ *n.* [DIAZO- + -EPINE] any of a class of heterocyclic compounds used as tranquillizers, including Librium and Valium M20. **benzo'quinone** *n.* the simplest quinone, $C_6H_4O_2$ M20. **benzoyl** /-zəʊʌɪl, -zəʊɪl/ *n.* the radical $C_6H_5COO{\cdot}$, benzenecarbonyl M19.

benzoic /bɛnˈzəʊɪk/ *a.* L18. [f. next + -IC.] Chem. *benzoic acid*, a colourless crystalline aromatic acid, C_6H_5COOH, present in gum benzoin and many other resins.
'benzoate *n.* a salt or ester of benzoic acid L18.

benzoin /ˈbɛnzəʊɪn/ *n.* Also **†benjoin**. M16. [Fr. *benjoin* = Sp. *benjuí*, Port. *benjoim*, It. *benzoi*, f. Proto-Romance f. Arab. *lubānjāwī* incense from Sumatra (the Proto-Romance reflex of *lu-* being taken for the def. article).] **1** A fragrant aromatic resin obtained from eastern Asian trees of the genus *Styrax*. Also *gum benzoin*. Cf. BENJAMIN *n.*¹ M16. **2** The spicebush, *Lindera benzoin*. (Formerly a genus name.) M18. **3** *Chem.* A colourless crystalline ketone present in gum benzoin; 2-hydroxy-1,2-diphenylethanone, $C_6H_5{\cdot}CHOH{\cdot}CO{\cdot}C_6H_5$. M19.

benzol /ˈbɛnzɒl/ *n.* Also **-ole** /-əʊl/. M19. [f. BENZOIC *a.* + -OL.] Benzene, esp. in impure commercial forms used as fuel.

Beothuk /bɪˈəʊθək/ *n.* & *a.* Pl. **-s**, same. E19. [Prob. Beothuk.] A member of, of or pertaining to, an extinct Indian people of Newfoundland; (of) the language of this people.

bepaint /bɪˈpeɪnt/ *v.t.* L15. [f. BE- I + PAINT *v.*] Paint over; paint obtrusively; colour.

bepatched /bɪˈpatʃt/ *a.* E17. [f. BE- + PATCH *v.* + -ED¹.] Mended with patches; wearing patches.

bepearled /bɪˈpəːld/ *a.* M17. [f. BE- 5 + PEARL *n.*¹ + -ED².] Covered (as) with pearls.

bepelt /bɪˈpɛlt/ *v.t.* E17. [f. BE- I + PELT *v.*¹] Pelt thoroughly (with missiles etc.).

bepity /bɪˈpɪti/ *v.t. arch.* L16. [f. BE- I + PITY *v.*] Pity exceedingly.

beplaster /bɪˈplɑːstə/ *v.t.* E17. [f. BE- I + PLASTER *v.*] Plaster over or about; smear thickly (*with*).

beplumed /bɪˈpluːmd/ *a.* L16. [f. BE- 5 + PLUME *n.* + -ED².] Furnished with feathers.

bepommel /bɪˈpɒm(ə)l/ *v.t.* Infl. **-ll-**, ***-l-**. L16. [f. BE- I + POMMEL *v.*] Pommel soundly, drub.

bepowder /bɪˈpaʊdə/ *v.t.* L16. [f. BE- I + POWDER *v.*¹] Powder over.

bepraise /bɪˈpreɪz/ *v.t.* M17. [f. BE- I + PRAISE *v.*] Praise greatly or to excess.

bepuff /bɪˈpʌf/ *v.t.* M19. [f. BE- I + PUFF *v.*] Puff out; *fig.* puff up, praise greatly.

bepuzzle /bɪˈpʌz(ə)l/ *v.t.* L16. [f. BE- I + PUZZLE *v.*] Puzzle utterly.
bepuzzlement *n.* E19.

bequeath /bɪˈkwiːð/ *v.t.* OE. [f. BE- + QUETHE.] †1 Say, declare; express, mean. OE–ME. 2 Leave (an estate or piece of property) *to* a person by will. Also w. the inheritor as indirect obj. Cf. DEVISE *v.* 7. OE. †b Transfer (property) *to* a person with immediate effect. ME–E17. c *fig.* Transmit (an example, quality, etc.) to posterity. E17. †3 Commit *to, unto*; entrust, bestow, yield. ME–E19.

2b SHAKES. *John* Wilt thou forsake thy fortune, Bequeath thy land to him and follow me? c S. JOHNSON This narrative he has bequeathed to future generations. A. SCHLEE Her beautiful hair was scarcely faded from the deep coppery colour she had bequeathed to her daughter. 3 EVELYN Gentlemen.. who generally so bequeath themselves to this service. N. FAIRFAX That which bequeaths it this slow pace. POPE We to flames our slaughtered friends bequeath.

bequeathable *a.* M17. **bequeathal** *n.* the action of bequeathing M17. **bequeather** *n.* E16. **bequeathment** *n.* the action of bequeathing, a bequest E17.

bequest /bɪˈkwɛst/ *n.* ME. [f. (after prec.) BE- + ME †*quiste* repr. OE *-cwiss* (in comb.), repl. *cwide* saying, testament: for the parasitic *t* cf. BEHEST.] 1 The action of bequeathing; gift by will. Cf. DEVISE *n.* 2. ME. 2 A thing bequeathed; a legacy. LME.

ber /bɛː/ *n.* M19. [Hind.] In the Indian subcontinent: a jujube tree, *Ziziphus jujuba*; its edible fruit.

berate /bɪˈreɪt/ *v.t.* M16. [f. BE- 1 + RATE *v.*[2]] Scold, rebuke.

berattle /bɪˈrat(ə)l/ *v.t. rare* (usu. after Shakes.). M16. [f. BE- 1 + RATTLE *v.*[1]] Rattle away upon or at; fill with din.

SHAKES. *Haml.* These.. so berattle the common stages.. that many wearing rapiers.. dare scarce come thither.

beray /bɪˈreɪ/ *v.t.* Now *rare* or *obs.* Also **bewray**. M16. [f. BE- 1 + RAY *v.*[1]] Disfigure, defile, befoul; *fig.* besmirch, slander.

Berber /ˈbəːbə/ *n.* & *a.* M18. [f. Arab. *barbar*: cf. BARBARY.] A *n.* Pl. **-s**, same. A member of any of the indigenous Caucasian peoples of N. Africa; their Hamito-Semitic language (of which there are several local forms). M18. B *attrib.* or as *adj.* Of or pertaining to the Berbers or their language. E19.

Berberine /bəːbəˈriːn/ *n.*[1] Also †**Barbarin**. E19. [f. prec., perh. after ALGERINE, TANGERINE.] A Berber.

berberine /ˈbəːbəriːn/ *n.*[2] M19. [f. next + -INE[5].] A bitter yellow alkaloid obtained from barberry and other plants.

berberis /ˈbəːbərɪs/ *n.* L16. [mod.L or OFr. f. med.L *barbaris*.] Any shrub of the genus *Berberis* (see BARBERRY); *esp.* one grown for ornament.

berberry *n.* var. of BARBERRY.

berceau /bɛrso/ *n.* Pl. **-eaux** /-o/. L17. [Fr., lit. 'cradle'.] An arbour, a bower; a shaded or leafy walk.

berceuse /bɛrsøːz, bɛːˈsəːz/ *n.* Pl. pronounced same. L19. [Fr., f. *bercer* to rock + fem. agent-suff. *-euse*.] *Mus.* A lullaby; an instrumental piece with a gently rocking rhythm.

berdache /bəˈdaʃ/ *n.* Also **-dash**. E19. [Fr. *bardache* BARDASH.] Among N. American Indians: a transvestite.

bere /bɪə/ *n.*[1] Chiefly *Sc.* Also †**bear**. [OE: see BARLEY *n.*] Barley; *spec.* six-rowed barley, *Hordeum vulgare*, or its reputedly hardier four-rowed variety (cf. BIG *n.*[2]).

bere /bɪə/ *n.*[2] *obs.* exc. *dial.* Also **bear, beer**. LME. [Origin uncertain: connection with LG *büre* (G *Bühre*) has been proposed.] A pillowcase. Usu. more fully *pillow-bere*.

bereave /bɪˈriːv/ *v.t.* Pa. t. & pple **-d, bereft** /bɪˈrɛft/, (*arch.*) **bereaven** /-v(ə)n/. [OE *berēafian* = OFris. *birāvia*, OS *birōbon* (Du. *beroven*), OHG *biroubōn* (G *berauben*), Goth. *biraubōn* f. Gmc: see BE-, REAVE *v.*[1]] 1 Deprive, dispossess *of* a possession (now usu. immaterial) or (by death) *of* a relative or loved one. OE. b With double obj.: deprive of. *arch.* ME. 2 Plunder, despoil; leave desolate, orphaned, or widowed. ME. †3 Remove by violence. ME–E18.

1 SHAKES. *Merch. V.* Madam, you have bereft me of all words. L. P. HARTLEY His hands dropped to his sides, and he looked as bereft of dignity as any human being could. J. R. ACKERLEY He was lately bereaved of his wife, a Swiss girl who had died only a few months previously. b MILTON Bereaue me not.. thy gentle looks, thy aid. 2 G. MACDONALD I cry to thee.. Because I am bereft. *fig.*: P. USTINOV Laughter would be bereaved if snobbery died. 3 SHAKES. *Lucr.* If.. thine honour lay in me, From me by strong assault it is bereft.

¶The more usual form of ppl a. is *bereaved* in the case of loss by death, and *bereft* w. ref. to the loss of things.

bereavement *n.* the state or an instance of being bereaved (now only of a relative etc. by death) M18.

bereft *v.* pa. t. & pple of prec.

Berenice's Hair /bɛrɪˈnʌɪsɪz hɛː/ *n. phr.* M16. [tr. L COMA BERENICES.] = COMA BERENICES.

beret /ˈbɛreɪ, -ri/ *n.* E19. [Fr. *béret* f. SW Fr. dial. & OProv. *berret*: see BIRETTA.] A round felt or cloth cap that lies flat on the head, covering it closely (as traditionally worn by Basque peasantry); such a cap forming part of military uniform.

Basque beret: see BASQUE *a.* *Green Beret*: see GREEN *a.*

beretta *n.* var. of BIRETTA.

berg /bəːg/ *n.*[1] E19. [Abbrev. of ICEBERG.] A very large floating mass (of ice); an iceberg.

tabular berg: see TABULAR 1.

bergy *a.* having many icebergs; of the nature of an iceberg: M19.

berg /bəːg, *foreign* bɛrx/ *n.*[2] *S. Afr.* E19. [Afk. f. Du. = OE *beorg* etc. BARROW *n.*[1]] A mountain.

Comb.: **berg adder** an adder, *Bitis atropos*, found in highland areas of southern Africa; *Berg* DAMARA; **berg wind** a hot dry northerly wind blowing in the coastal regions of the Cape Province and Natal.

Bergamasque /ˈbəːgəmɑːsk/ *a.* & *n.* Also †**-mask**; in sense B.1 **b-**. L16. [(Fr. f.) It. *Bergamasco* of Bergamo (see below).] A *adj.* Of or pertaining to the northern Italian city and province of Bergamo. L16. B *n.* 1 A dance resembling a tarantella. L16. 2 A native or inhabitant of Bergamo. E17.

bergamot /ˈbəːgəmɒt/ *n.*[1] E17. [Fr. *bergamotte* f. It. *bergamotta* f. Turk. *begarmudu*, f. *beg* prince, BEG *n.*[1] + *armud* pear + *-u* possess. suff.] A variety of fine pear.

bergamot /ˈbəːgəmɒt/ *n.*[2] L17. [f. *Bergamo*, a city & province in N. Italy.] 1 A citrus tree, *Citrus aurantium* subsp. *bergamia*, bearing fruit similar to an orange, from the rind of which a fragrant essence is prepared. L17. 2†a Snuff scented with this essence. Only in 18. b The essence itself. M18. 3 Any of several labiate plants smelling like bergamot, *esp.* (*a*) (more fully *bergamot mint*) a mint, *Mentha* × *piperita* var. *citrata*, grown for its fragrance; (*b*) *N. Amer.* (more fully *wild bergamot*) = MONARDA. M19.

1 *bergamot-orange, bergamot tree.*

Bergan *n.* var. of BERGEN.

bergander /bəˈgandə/ *n. dial.* Also **bar-** /bɑː-/. M16. [Perh. f. ON *ber* berry (from the red horn on the beak of the male) + GANDER *n.*] A shelduck.

Bergen /ˈbəːgən/ *n.* Also **-gan, b-**. E20. [Origin unkn.] In full *Bergen pack, rucksack*, etc. A type of rucksack supported by a frame.

bergenia /bəˈgiːnɪə/ *n.* M19. [mod.L, f. K. A. von *Bergen* (1704–60), Ger. physician & botanist: see -IA[1].] Any of various perennial plants of the genus *Bergenia*, of the saxifrage family, having large, thick leaves and usu. pink, red, or purple flowers.

bergère /bɛrʒɛːr/ *n.* Pl. pronounced same. M18. [Fr. = shepherdess.] A long-seated upholstered armchair fashionable in the 18th cent. Also, a chair with canework seat, back, and sides.

bergerette /bəːʒəˈrɛt/ *n.* Also †**bargeret**. LME. [Fr., f. *berger* shepherd: see -ETTE.] A pastoral or rustic song about shepherds, for dancing to.

berghaan /ˈbəːghɑːn, *foreign* ˈbɛrx-/ *n. S. Afr.* M19. [Afk., f. BERG *n.*[2] + *haan* cock.] An eagle, *esp.* a bateleur.

bergschrund /ˈbəːgʃrʊnd, *foreign* ˈbɛrkʃrʊnt/ *n.* Pl. **-ds** /-dz/, **-de** /-də/. M19. [G, f. *Berg* mountain (see BARROW *n.*[1]) + SCHRUND.] A crevasse or gap at the junction of a glacier or snowfield with a steep upper slope.

Bergsonian /bəːgˈsəʊnɪən/ *a.* & *n.* E20. [f. *Bergson* (see below) + -IAN.] A *adj.* Of, pertaining to, or characteristic of the French philosopher Henri Bergson (1859–1941). E20. B *n.* A follower or adherent of Bergson. E20.

bergylt /ˈbəːgɪlt/ *n.* L18. [f. ON *berg* rock + *gyltr* sow, GILT *n.*[1]] 1 The ballan wrasse. *Shetland dial.* L18. 2 The Norway haddock. M19.

berhyme /bɪˈrʌɪm/ *v.t.* Also **berime**. L16. [f. BE- 2, 4 + RHYME *v.* or *n.*] Compose rhymes about; lampoon in rhyme.

beriberi /bɛrɪˈbɛri/ *n.* E18. [Sinhalese = weakness.] A disease due to vitamin B_1 deficiency, which is characterized by polyneuritis and freq. oedema and cardiac disorder, and is mainly associated with rice-based diets.

berime *v.* var. of BERHYME.

berk /bəːk/ *n. slang.* Also **birk, burk**(**e**). M20. [Abbrev. of BERKELEY HUNT.] A fool.

Berkeleian /bɑːˈkliːən/ *n.* & *a.* E19. [f. *Berkeley* (see below) + -AN.] (A follower or adherent) of the Irish philosopher Bishop George Berkeley (1685–1753) or of his philosophy, in which the objective existence of matter was denied.

Berkeleianism *n.* the philosophical opinions held by Berkeley and his followers E19. ˈ**Berkeleyism** *n.* = BERKELEIANISM M19.

Berkeley hunt /ˈbəːkli hʌnt, ˈbɑː-/ *n. phr. rhyming slang.* M20. [A hunt in Gloucestershire.] = CUNT (esp. sense 2).

berkelium /bəːˈkiːlɪəm, ˈbəːklɪəm/ *n.* M20. [f. *Berkeley*, California, where first made + -IUM.] A radioactive metallic chemical element of the actinide series, atomic no. 97, which is produced artificially. (Symbol Bk.)

Berkshire /ˈbɑːkʃə/ *n.* E19. [A county in England.] In full *Berkshire pig* etc. (An animal of) a breed of black pig.

Berlin /bəːˈlɪn/ *n.*[1] In sense 1 usu. **b-**, & also (after Fr.) **-line** /-ˈliːn/. L17. [A city in N. Germany.] 1 Chiefly *Hist.* A four-wheeled covered carriage with a hooded seat behind. L17. 2 *attrib.* Designating things associated with Berlin. L18.

2 **Berlin black** a black varnish used on metal ware. **Berlin blue** Prussian blue. **Berlin glove** a strong glove of washable cotton. **Berlin pattern** a pattern in Berlin work. **Berlin wool** a fine dyed merino wool used for knitting or embroidery. **Berlin work** worsted embroidery on canvas.

Berliner *n.* a native or inhabitant of Berlin M19.

berlin *n.*[2], **berling** *n.* vars. of BIRLING.

Berliozian /bɛːlɪˈəʊzɪən/ *a.* & *n.* E20. [f. *Berlioz* (see below) + -IAN.] A *adj.* Of, pertaining to, resembling, or characteristic of the French composer Hector Berlioz (1803–69) or his music. E20. B *n.* An interpreter, student, or admirer of Berlioz or his music. M20.

berm /bəːm/ *n.* E18. [Fr. *berme* f. Du. *berm*, prob. rel. to ON *barmr* brim.] 1 A narrow space or ledge; *esp.* in fortification, the space between a ditch and the base of a parapet. E18. 2 A flat strip of land, raised bank, or terrace bordering a river etc.; a path or grass strip beside a road. L19.

Bermuda /bəˈmjuːdə/ *n.* M17. [A group of islands in the W. Atlantic.] I 1 A variety of cigar or rolled tobacco. Now *rare* or *obs.* M17. 2 In *pl.* Bermuda shorts. M20.

II 3 *attrib.* Also (earlier) †**-as**. Designating things from or associated with Bermuda. M18.

3 **Bermuda buttercup** a bulbous yellow-flowered southern African oxalis, *Oxalis pes-caprae*, widespread as a weed in warmer parts of the world. **Bermuda cedar**, †**Bermudas cedar** a juniper, *Juniperus bermudiana*, native to Bermuda. **Bermuda grass** *N. Amer.* = DOG'S TOOTH 2. **Bermuda rig** a yachting rig with a high tapering mainsail. **Bermuda shorts** knee-length shorts. **Bermuda Triangle** an area of the W. Atlantic Ocean where a disproportionately large number of ships and aeroplanes are said to have been mysteriously lost.

Bermudan *a.* = BERMUDIAN *a.* L19.

Bermudian /bəˈmjuːdɪən/ *n.* & *a.* L18. [f. prec. + -IAN.] A *n.* A native or inhabitant of

Bermuda; a vessel from Bermuda; a ship with a Bermuda rig. L18. **B** *adj.* Of or pertaining to Bermuda or its inhabitants. E19.

Bermudian mainsail a high tapering mainsail. **Bermudian rig** = BERMUDA *rig*.

Bernardine /ˈbəːnədɪn/ *n.* & *a.* M16. [mod.L *Bernardinus*, f. St *Bernard* (1091–1153), abbot of Clairvaux in France and a pioneer of the Cistercian order: see -INE[1].] = CISTERCIAN.

Bernese /bəːˈniːz/ *n.* & *a.* L17. [f. *Bern(e)* (see below) + -ESE.] **A** *n.* Pl. same. A native or inhabitant of Berne (Bern), a city and canton of Switzerland. L17. **B** *adj.* Of or pertaining to Berne. E19.

Also †**Bernois** *n.* L17–M19.

Bernician /bəːˈnɪʃ(ə)n/ *n.* & *a.* E19. [f. med.L *Bernicia* (see below) + -AN: cf. OE *Beornice* inhabitants of Bernicia.] **A** *n.* A native or inhabitant of Bernicia, an Anglian kingdom founded in the 6th cent., later forming part of Northumbria. E19. **B** *adj.* Of or pertaining to Bernicia or its inhabitants; *Geol.* designating the Lower Carboniferous rocks of Northumberland and its borders. M19.

Bernoulli /bəːˈnuːi, -ˈnuːli/ *n.* M18. [Name of a Swiss family: sense 1 f. Jacques (1654–1705), sense 2 f. Daniel (1700–82), mathematicians.] **1 a** *Bernoulli('s) numbers, series*, a series of rational numbers arising in formulae for the sums of powers of integers. M18. **b** *Bernoulli Law*, = *law of large numbers* s.v. LARGE *a.* M19. **2** *Bernoulli's theorem* or *principle*, a statement of the inverse relation between pressure and the square of velocity in a steadily-moving incompressible fluid. M19.

Bernoullian *a.* (esp. w. ref. to Bernoulli numbers): L19.

berob /bɪˈrɒb/ *v.t.* Infl. **-bb-**. ME. [f. BE- 1 + ROB *v.*] Rob.

beroe /ˈbɛrəʊi/ *n.* M18. [L *Beroë* f. Gk *Beroē* a daughter of Oceanus.] A bell-shaped ctenophore of the genus *Beroe*, lacking tentacles. Now only as mod.L genus name.

berry /ˈbɛri/ *n.*[1] [OE *beri(ġ)e*, cogn. w. OS *beri*, MDu. *bēre*, (M)Du. *bezie* (Du. *bes*), OHG *beri* (G *Beere*), ON *ber*, Goth. *basi*, f. Gmc.] **1** Any small globular or ovate juicy fruit, not having a stone. In early use *esp.* a grape. OE. **b** *Bot.* A fruit with seeds enclosed in pulp, as grape, gooseberry, tomato, etc. E19. **2** An egg of a fish or lobster. M18. **3** A dollar; a pound. Usu. in *pl. slang.* E20. **4** *the berries*, an outstandingly good person or thing. *slang.* E20.

berried *a.* (*a*) = BACCATE *a.*; (*b*) bearing eggs: M18. **berry-like** *a.* resembling a berry, esp. in size and shape M19.

berry /ˈbɛri/ *n.*[2] Long *obs.* exc. *dial.* ME. [Repr. OE *beorġe* dat. of *beorg* hill: see BARROW *n.*[1]] A mound, hillock, or barrow.

berry /ˈbɛri/ *n.*[3] Long *obs.* exc. *dial.* LME. [Var. of BURROW *n.*[2]] A (rabbit's) burrow.

berry /ˈbɛri/ *v.i.* M19. [f. BERRY *n.*[1]] **1** Come into berry. M19. **2** Go gathering berries. M19.

bersaglieri /bersaʎˈʎɛːri, ˌbɛːsɑːlɪˈɛːriː/ *n.pl.* M19. [It., f. *bersaglio* target.] Highly trained Italian infantry, orig. riflemen or sharpshooters.

berserk /bəˈsəːk, -z-/ *n.* & *a.* Also (*arch.*) **baresark** /ˈbɛːsɑːk/, **bersark** /bəˈsɑːk/; (chiefly as n.) **berserker**, **-kar** /bəˈsəːkə/. E19. [ON *berserkr*, accus. *berserk* (Icel. *berserkur*), prob. f. *birn-*, *bjǫrn* BEAR *n.*[1] + *serkr* coat, SARK *n.*, but also explained as f. BARE *a.*] **A** *n.* A wild Norse warrior who fought with frenzied fury. E19. **B** *adj.* Wild, frenzied. Esp. in *go berserk*. M19.

berserkly *adv.* M20.

berth /bəːθ/ *n.* & *v.*[1] Orig. *Naut.* Also †**birth**. E17. [f. BEAR *v.*[1] (sense 17) + -TH[1].] **A** *n.* **1** *Naut.* **a** Sea room (to avoid hazards, swing at anchor, etc.). Usu. w. specifying adj. etc.; *simply*, adequate sea room. E17. **b** A place where a ship lies at anchor; a ship's place at a wharf. M18. **2 a** *Naut.* The space allotted to a ship's company for storage of belongings, eating, sleeping, etc. E18. **b** *transf.* The proper place for something; an allotted place in a barracks, conveyance, etc. M18. **3 a** *Naut.* A situation or office on board ship or elsewhere. E18. **b** *transf.* A paid position of employment; a situation, an appointment, esp. a comfortable or easy one. M18. **4 a** *Naut.* A sleeping-place in a ship; a long box or shelf on the side of the cabin for sleeping. L18. **b** *transf.* A similar sleeping-place or bunk in a railway carriage, caravan, etc. E19.

1a J. SMEATON Giving the Lighthouse a clear birth of 50 fathoms to the southward. **give a wide berth to** *Naut.* & *gen.* not go too near, steer clear of, avoid. **b** N. SHUTE Peter Holmes walked down to the berth occupied by H.M.A.S. Sydney. **2a** F. MARRYAT The first day in which he had entered the midshipmen's berth, and was made acquainted with his messmates. **b** SIR W. SCOTT The first comer hastens to secure the best berth in the coach. **3a** J. DOS PASSOS He had taken a berth as donkey-engineman on a freighter bound for South America. **b** M. MCCARTHY Her background was perfect for a berth in publishing. *Sunday Telegraph* In ministerial quarters there are plenty of plushy berths to be filled. **4a** BYRON Passengers their berths are clapt in. **b** Z. M. PIKE We returned to the chief's lodge, and found a birth provided for each of us. J. DOS PASSOS He lay awake all night in the upper berth in the sleeper for Pittsburgh.

B *v.* **1** *v.t.* Moor (a ship) in a suitable place. M17. **2** *v.i.* Of a ship: come to mooring. M19. **3** *v.t.* Provide (a person) with a berth. M19. **4** *v.i.* Of a person: occupy a berth or berths. L19.

1 B. ENGLAND A small jetty . . where a boat sat sluggishly berthed. **2** J. B. MORTON She will not berth like other liners, but will turn round outside the harbour. **4** H. WOUK He was berthing below with the refugees.

berthage *n.* position in a berth; accommodation for mooring vessels; the dues payable for such accommodation: M19. **berthing** *n.*[1] (*a*) the action of the vb; (*b*) mooring position; accommodation in berths: E19.

berth /bəːθ/ *v.*[2]*t.* & *i.* L16. [Perh. f. Icel. *byrða*, f. ON *byrði* board (side) of a ship.] *Shipbuilding.* Construct or cover (the side etc. of a ship) with planks. Also foll. by *up*.

berthing *n.*[2] (*a*) the action of the vb; (*b*) the upright planking of the sides etc. of a ship, *esp.* that above the sheer strake: E18.

bertha /ˈbəːθə/ *n.*[1] Also **berthe** /bəːθ/. M19. [*Bertha* (Fr. *Berthe*) female forename.] A deep falling collar or small cape on a dress.

Bertha /ˈbəːθə/ *n.*[2] *Soldiers' slang.* E20. [Frau *Bertha* Krupp von Bohlen und Halbach, owner of the Krupp steel works in Germany 1903–43.] A German gun or mortar of large bore, used in the 1914–18 war. Freq. *Big Bertha*.

bertillonage /bɛrtijɔnaʒ/ *n.* L19. [Fr. *bertillonnage*, f. *Bertillon* (see below) + -AGE.] The system of identification of criminals by anthropometric measurements, fingerprints, etc., invented by the French criminologist Alphonse Bertillon (1853–1914).

bertrandite /ˈbəːtrəndʌɪt/ *n.* L19. [f. Émile *Bertrand*, 19th-cent. Fr. mineralogist + -ITE[1].] *Min.* An orthorhombic basic silicate of beryllium, occurring as small tabular colourless or pale yellow crystals.

beryl /ˈbɛrɪl/ *n.* & *a.* ME. [OFr. *beril* (mod. *béryl*) f. L *beryllus* f. Gk *bērullos*, prob. of foreign origin.] **A** *n.* **1** A transparent precious stone of a pale green colour passing into light blue, yellow, and white, distinguished only by colour from emerald and including aquamarine. Also *beryl-stone*. ME. †**2** Crystal; a piece of cut crystal. LME–E17. **3** *Min.* A hexagonal silicate of beryllium and aluminium of which beryl (sense 1), emerald, morganite, etc., are varieties. M19. **4** The colour of beryl (sense 1). M19. **B** *attrib.* or as *adj.* Of beryl; composed of or resembling beryl. L15.

beryllium /bəˈrɪlɪəm/ *n.* M19. [f. prec. + -IUM.] A chemical element, atomic no. 4, which is the lightest of the alkaline earth metals and of which the mineral beryl is the major source (symbol Be). Orig. called *glucinum*.

beryllia *n.* beryllium oxide, BeO, a white refractory solid L19. **berylli'osis** *n.*, pl. **-oses** /-ˈəʊsiːz/, *Med.* poisoning caused by exposure to beryllium compounds, *esp.* a severe pneumoconiosis due to their inhalation M20.

beryllonite /bəˈrɪlənʌɪt/ *n.* L19. [f. prec. + *-on* + -ITE[1].] *Min.* A monoclinic phosphate of beryllium and sodium, occurring as colourless or pale yellow prisms.

besaiel /bɪˈseɪ(ə)l/ *n.* Long *obs.* exc. *Hist.* Also **-aile**, **-ayle**. LME. [OFr. *besaiuel*, *besaiol* (mod. *bisaïeul*), f. *bes* f. L *bis* twice + as AIEL.] *Law.* A great-grandfather.

writ of besaiel *Law* an action by a party based on the seisin of a great-grandfather for the recovery of land of which that party had been dispossessed.

besaint /bɪˈseɪnt/ *v.t.* *arch.* E17. [f. BE- 3 + SAINT *n.*] Make a saint of, canonize.

besayle *n.* var. of BESAIEL.

bescatter /bɪˈskatə/ *v.t.* L16. [f. BE- 1 + SCATTER *v.*] Sprinkle (*with*); scatter about.

bescratch /bɪˈskratʃ/ *v.t.* M16. [f. BE- 1 + SCRATCH *v.*] Cover with scratches.

bescrawl /bɪˈskrɔːl/ *v.t.* M16. [f. BE- 1 + SCRAWL *v.*[2]] Scribble over; cover with scrawl.

bescreen /bɪˈskriːn/ *v.t.* L16. [f. BE- 1 + SCREEN *v.*] Screen from view; obscure, overshadow.

bescribble /bɪˈskrɪb(ə)l/ *v.t.* L16. [f. BE- 1 + SCRIBBLE *v.*[1]] Write scrawlingly; scribble about; scribble on.

besee /bɪˈsiː/ *v.* Long *arch.* Infl. as SEE *v.* [OE *besēon*, *bi-* = OS, OHG *bisehan*, Goth. *bisaihwan*, f. as BE- + SEE *v.*] †**I 1** *v.i.* Look; see *to*, attend *to*. OE–ME. **2** *v.t.* Look at; see to, attend to; ordain, determine. OE–L16.

II 3 As pa. pple *beseen*. Seen or viewed, having an appearance; provided or furnished with, appointed. LME.

3 SPENSER I late was wont to . . maske in mirth with Graces well beseene. W. MORRIS The dukes . . well beseen in purple dye and gold.

†**beseech** *n.* Only in E17. [f. the vb.] (An) entreaty.

SHAKES. *Tr. & Cr.* Therefore this maxim out of love I teach: Achievement is command; ungain'd, beseech.

beseech /bɪˈsiːtʃ/ *v.* Pa. t. & pple **-ed, besought** /bɪˈsɔːt/. ME. [f. as BE- + SEEK *v.*: *seech* would be the normal reflex of OE *sēċan*.] †**1** *v.t.* Search for, try to obtain. Only in ME. **2** *v.t.* Ask earnestly for (a thing; also foll. by *that*, †*to do*). ME. **3** *v.t.* Entreat, implore, (a person; a person *to do*, *for* or †*of* a thing, *that* (arch.), †a thing). ME. **4** *v.i.* Make an earnest request (*for* or †*of* a thing; †*(un)to* a person). *arch.* ME.

beseecher *n.* LME. **beseeching** *n.* (*a*) the action of the vb; (*b*) an earnest request, an entreaty: ME. **beseechingly** *adv.* M19. **beseechment** *n.* (*rare*) L17.

beseem /bɪˈsiːm/ *v.* *arch.* ME. [f. BE- 1 + SEEM *v.*] †**1** *v.i.* Seem, look. ME–L19. **2** *v.t.* & *i.* (now usu. *impers.* in (*it*) *beseems* etc.). **a** With qualification: appear or look *well*, *ill*, etc., for (a person) to wear, have, do, etc. ME. **b** Without qualification: be fitting (for), be creditable (to). LME.

beseemingly *adv.* E17. **beseemingness** *n.* M17. **beseemliness** *n.* the quality of being beseemly M17. **beseemly** *a.* becoming, befitting M18.

beseen *v.* pa. pple of BESEE.

beset /bɪˈsɛt/ *v.t.* Infl. **-tt-**. Pa. t. & pple **beset**. [OE *besettan* = OFris. *bisetta*, OS *bisettian* (Du. *bezetten*), OHG *bisezzan* (G *besetzen*), Goth. *bisatjan*, f. Gmc, f. as BE- + SET *v.*[1]] **I 1** Set about or surround *with* (esp. appendages or accessories). Now only as pa. pple. *arch.* OE. **2** Surround with hostile intent, besiege, assail on all sides. Freq. *fig.* of temptations, doubts, difficulties, etc. OE. **3** Occupy and make impassable (a gate, road, etc.). ME. **4** *gen.* Close round, hem in. M16.

1 DE QUINCEY A tiara beset with pearls. **2** POPE The lioness . . beset by men and hounds. H. KELLER As I began to teach her, I was beset by difficulties. W. S. CHURCHILL There were no more half-rations . . to give to the soldiers, and they were beset on three sides. A. MOOREHEAD They were so beset by flies and dust they wore goggles and veils. C. CHAPLIN A spell of melancholy beset me. **besetting sin** a temptation to which a person is especially subject; a characteristic weakness. **3** J. R. MCCULLOCH The mob . . beset all the avenues to the House of Commons. **4** N. HAWTHORNE The mountains which beset it round.

†**II 5** Place, set, bestow. OE–E17. **6** Arrange, ordain. LME–L15.

besetment *n.* the act of besetting; the condition of being beset; a besetting sin etc.: E19.

beshade /bɪˈʃeɪd/ *v.t.* [OE *besċeadian*, f. as BE- 1 + SHADE *v.*[1]] Cover with shade, obscure.

beshadow /bɪˈʃadəʊ/ *v.t.* ME. [f. BE- 1 + SHADOW *v.*] Cast a shadow on; screen from light.

beshine /bɪˈʃʌɪn/ *v.t. arch.* Infl. as SHINE *v.* [OE *besċīnan*, *bi-* = OFris. *bischīna*, OS, OHG *biscīnan*, Goth. *biskeinan*, f. Gmc, f. as BE- 1 + SHINE *v.*] Illumine; shine about or upon.

¶Long obs. but revived by Carlyle.

beshrew /bɪˈʃruː/ *v.t. arch.* ME. [f. BE- 1 + SHREW *v.*] †1 Make wicked; deprave. ME–M16. 2 Invoke evil upon; curse; blame for a misfortune. Now chiefly in imprecations: the Devil take —, curse —. LME.

2 SHAKES. *Oth.* Beshrew me, if I would do such a wrong for the whole world. G. SWIFT We agreed with her, beshrewed 'other people', and enjoyed ourselves in our own way.

beside /bɪˈsʌɪd/ *adv.* & *prep.* [OE *be sīdan*, f. as BY *prep.* etc. + SIDE *n.* First found as one wd in ME.] A *adv.* (*arch.*: largely superseded by BESIDES.) 1 By the side, by one's side; close by, near. OE. 2 = BESIDES *adv.* 2. ME. †3 = ASIDE *adv.* 1. LME–E17. †4 By the side so as to miss, past. LME–L16. 5 = BESIDES *adv.* 3. L16.

1 SOUTHEY Mervyn beside, Hangs over his dear mistress. J. P. DONLEAVY Massive horses galloping beside. 2 CARLYLE It was by stealth if he read or wrote any thing beside. BROWNING Beside, when he found speech, you guess the speech. 4 SHAKES. *Ven. & Ad.* Yet sometimes falls an orient drop beside Which her cheek melts. 5 J. WILSON We talk'd Of thee and none beside.

B *prep.* 1 By the side of, close by, next to. ME. b Compared with; on a level with. E16. 2 = BESIDES *prep.* 3. ME. 3 Outside of, out of, wide of, away from. Now only *fig.* LME. 4 = BESIDES *prep.* 2. LME.

1 AV *S. of S.* 1:8 Feede thy kiddes beside the shepheards tent. DAY LEWIS I stood beside her, manipulating the stops of the harmonium. b J. RUSKIN Gainsborough's power of colour . . is capable of taking rank beside that of Rubens. 2 G. H. LEWES Other men beside ourselves. 3 S. BUTLER Vagabonds . . are ne'er beside their way. M. W. MONTAGU This question almost put him beside his gravity. S. JOHNSON At Durham, beside all expectation, I met an old friend. J. A. FROUDE The point on which the battle was being fought lay beside the real issue. *beside the mark, point, question*, etc. **beside oneself** distraught (*with* or *for* an emotion). *beside the saddle*: see SADDLE *n.* 4 R. DAHL The only one beside myself who had come alone.

besides /bɪˈsʌɪdz/ *adv.* & *prep.* ME. [f. prec. + -S[3].] A *adv.* †1 = BESIDE *adv.* 1. Only in ME. 2 In addition, as well; moreover. M16. 3 Other than that mentioned, else. L16. †4 = BESIDE *adv.* 4. E–M17.

2 ARNOLD BENNETT Besides, the letter would be more effective. V. S. NAIPAUL Ramlogan had . . come to regard Ganesh as a total loss and a crook besides. 3 I. ASIMOV Military potential, standard of living, happiness, and all besides.

B *prep.* †1 = BESIDE *prep.* 1. ME–L17. 2 Other than, else than, except, excluding. LME. 3 Over and above, in addition to, as well as. E16. †4 = BESIDE *prep.* 3. E16–E18.

2 ADDISON No living Creature ever walks in it besides the Chaplain. 3 R. FRY Mankind is so constituted as to desire much besides pleasure.

besiege /bɪˈsiːdʒ/ *v.t.* ME. [f. ASSIEGE by substitution of BE-.] 1 Place armed forces before or around (a town etc.) in order to capture it; lay siege to. ME. 2 *transf.* & *fig.* Assail, crowd round, beset. E17.

2 SHAKES. *Sonn.* When forty winters shall besiege thy brow. W. GERHARDIE He was besieged with notes requesting private interviews.

besieger *n.* M16.

besilver /bɪˈsɪlvə/ *v.t.* E17. [f. BE- 1 + SILVER *v.*] Cover over or adorn with silver.

besing /bɪˈsɪŋ/ *v.t. arch.* Infl. as SING *v.*[1] M16. [f. BE- 2 + SING *v.*[1]] Sing to or about; celebrate in song.

beslave /bɪˈsleɪv/ *v.t.* E17. [f. BE- 3 + SLAVE *n.*] Make a slave of, enslave; treat or address as a slave.

beslaver /bɪˈslavə, -ˈsleɪv-/ *v.t.* L16. [f. BE- 2 + SLAVER *v.*] Slaver or dribble over.

beslobber /bɪˈslɒbə/ *v.t.* LME. [f. BE- 1, 2 + SLOBBER *v.*] Slaver or slobber over.

beslubber /bɪˈslʌbə/ *v.t.* LME. [f. BE- 1 + SLUBBER *v.*] Smear or daub over with liquid or sticky matter.

besmear /bɪˈsmɪə/ *v.t.* [OE *bismierwan*, f. as BE- + SMEAR *v.*] Smear over; cover or soil with a greasy or sticky substance; *fig.* sully (reputation etc.), defame.

besmirch /bɪˈsməːtʃ/ *v.t.* L16. [f. BE- 1 + SMIRCH *v.*] Dull or discolour, as with smoke or mud; dim the brightness of; *fig.* sully (reputation etc.).

besmoke /bɪˈsməʊk/ *v.t.* LME. [f. BE- 2 + SMOKE *v.*] Subject to or suffuse with smoke; fumigate; make smoky.

besmut /bɪˈsmʌt/ *v.t.* Infl. **-tt-**. E17. [f. BE- 1 + SMUT *v.*] Blacken (as) with soot; *fig.* defame.

besmutch /bɪˈsmʌtʃ/ *v.t.* M19. [f. BE- 1 + SMUTCH *v.*] = BESMIRCH.

besnow /bɪˈsnəʊ/ *v.t.* [OE *bisnīwian*, f. as BE- + SNOW *v.*] Cover (as) with snow.

†**besognio** *n.* Also **besonio**, **bisogn(i)o**. L16–E19. [It. *bisogno* lit. 'need, want'.] A raw recruit, esp. one poorly equipped. Also, a needy or worthless fellow. Cf. BEZONIAN.

besoil /bɪˈsɔɪl/ *v.t.* ME. [f. BE- 1 + SOIL *v.*[1]] Soil, sully; defile.

besom /ˈbiːz(ə)m, ˈbɪz-/ *n.* & *v.* [OE *bes(e)ma* = OFris. *besma*, OS *besmo* (Du. *bezem*), OHG *besamo* (G *Besen*), f. WGmc.] A *n.* †1 A bundle of rods or twigs used for flogging. OE–ME. 2 An implement for sweeping; *spec.* a brush consisting of a bunch of birch or other twigs tied to one end of a stick. OE. 3 A woman or girl. *joc.* or *derog.* Chiefly *Sc.* & *dial.* L18.

2 *fig.*: T. FULLER The riuer Kishon, God's besom to sweep away Sisera's great army. 3 J. AGATE In comparison with Rosalind's pure flame Juliet is a man-struck little besom.

B *v.* †1 *v.i.* Sweep with force. Only in LME. 2 *v.t.* Sweep (*away, out*, etc.). L18.

†**besonio** *n.* var. of BESOGNIO.

†**besort** *v.* & *n. rare* (Shakes.). Only in E17. [f. BE- 2 + SORT *v.*] A *v.t.* Befit, match. E17. B *n.* Suitable company. E17.

besot /bɪˈsɒt/ *v.t.* Infl. **-tt-**. L16. [f. BE- 1, 3 + SOT *v.* or *n.*, after ASSOT.] 1 Make foolishly affectionate; infatuate *with*. Now chiefly as *besotted* ppl a. L16. 2 Stupefy mentally or morally; intoxicate. L16.

besottedly *adv.* E17. **besottedness** *n.* E17.

besought *v.* pa. t. & pple of BESEECH *v.*

besouth /bɪˈsaʊθ/ *prep.* Long *obs.* exc. *Sc.* LME. [f. BE- + SOUTH.] On the south side of; to the south of.

bespake *v.* see BESPEAK *v.*

bespangle /bɪˈspaŋg(ə)l/ *v.t.* L16. [f. BE- 4 + SPANGLE *n.*] Decorate or adorn (as) with spangles.

bespatter /bɪˈspatə/ *v.t.* M17. [f. BE- 1 + SPATTER *v.*] Spatter (liquid etc.) over or about; asperse *with* abuse, flattery, etc.; vilify, defame.

bespeak /bɪˈspiːk/ *n.* L18. [f. the vb.] *Theatr.* A benefit night with a specially chosen play.

bespeak /bɪˈspiːk/ *v.* Pa. t. **bespoke** /bɪˈspəʊk/, (*arch.*) **bespake** /bɪˈspeɪk/. Pa. pple **bespoken** /bɪˈspəʊk(ə)n/, (less commonly) **bespoke**. Pa. ppl a. BESPOKE *a.*, (less commonly) **bespoken**. [OE *bisprecan* = OFris. *bispreka*, OS *besprekan* (Du. *bespreken*), OHG *bisprehhan* (G *besprechen*): see BE-, SPEAK *v.*] †1 *v.i.* & *t.* Speak up or out; exclaim (*that*); (later simply) speak. OE–L18. †2 *v.t.* Speak against, oppose. OE–ME. †3 *v.t.* Speak about; discuss; determine upon or *to do*. ME–M17. 4 *v.t.* Arrange for, engage beforehand; order (goods), commission to be made; ask for (a favour etc.). L16. †b Request or engage (a person) *to do*. L16–M18. 5 *v.t.* Speak to (a person); address. Chiefly *poet.* L16. 6 *v.t.* Indicate; give evidence of; augur. E17.

1 MILTON Until their Lord himself bespake, and bid them go. 4 STEELE She bespoke the Play of Alexander the Great, to be acted by the Company of Strollers. E. BOWEN The taxi bespoken by Cousin Francis to drive him back. L. GARFIELD The good offices of a certain gentleman were not yet bespoke. 5 POPE Medon first th' assembled chiefs bespoke. b N. HAWTHORNE Circumstances that bespeak war and danger. D. LODGE His handsomely bound old missal bespeaks wealth and taste.

bespeck /bɪˈspɛk/ *v.t.* M16. [f. BE- 1 + SPECK *v.*] Mark with spots or specks. Usu. in *pass.*

bespeckle /bɪˈspɛk(ə)l/ *v.t.* E17. [f. BE- 1 + SPECKLE *v.*] Speckle over; cover with dots or flecks.

bespectacled /bɪˈspɛktək(ə)ld/ *a.* M18. [f. BE- 5 + SPECTACLE *n.*[1] + -ED[2].] Wearing spectacles.

bespell /bɪˈspɛl/ *v.t.* L19. [f. BE- 4 + SPELL *n.*[1]] Cast a spell on; bewitch, enchant.

bespoke /bɪˈspəʊk/ *a.* & *n.* M18. [See BESPEAK *v.*] A *adj.* That has been bespoken; *spec.* of goods: commissioned, made to order, (opp. *ready-made*); of a person: making or selling such goods. M18. B *n.* A bespoke article. E20.

bespoke *v.* see BESPEAK *v.*

bespoken *v.* see BESPEAK *v.*

besport /bɪˈspɔːt/ *v.t.* & *i.* M19. [Alt. of DISPORT *v.* by substitution of BE-.] Disport (*oneself*).

bespot /bɪˈspɒt/ *v.t.* Infl. **-tt-**. ME. [f. BE- 1 + SPOT *v.*] Mark or cover with spots or with blemishes.

bespout /bɪˈspaʊt/ *v.t.* L16. [f. BE- 1 + SPOUT *v.*] Spout out or over; utter or address in a declamatory manner.

bespread /bɪˈsprɛd/ *v.t.* Pa. t. & pple **bespread**. ME. [f. BE- 1, 2 + SPREAD *v.*] 1 Spread *with*. ME. 2 Cover by spreading over. M16. 3 Spread out. M16.

besprenge /bɪˈsprɛndʒ/ *v.t.* Long *obs.* exc. as pa. pple & ppl a. (*arch.*) **besprent** /bɪˈsprɛnt/. [OE *besprengan*, f. as BE- + SPRENGE *v.*] 1 Sprinkle all over *with* (pa. ppl a. also in *comb.*). OE. 2 Sprinkle about, strew. E16.

1 MILTON Knot-grass dew-besprent. 2 W. MORRIS The flowers besprent about.

besprent *v.* & *ppl a.* see prec.

besprinkle /bɪˈsprɪŋk(ə)l/ *v.t.* M16. [f. BE- 1, 2 + SPRINKLE *v.*] 1 Sprinkle all over *with*; dot *with*; sprinkle (liquid etc.) *over*. M16. 2 Of a liquid etc.: be sprinkled on. M18.

1 GIBBON The walls were besprinkled with holy water. DICKENS Sloping banks besprinkled with pretty villas.

Bessarabian /bɛsəˈreɪbɪən/ *a.* & *n.* M19. [f. *Bessarabia* (see below) + -AN.] (A native or inhabitant) of Bessarabia, a region in eastern Europe, now divided between Moldova and Ukraine.

Bessel function /ˈbɛs(ə)l ˌfʌŋ(k)ʃ(ə)n/ *n. phr.* L19. [Friedrich W. *Bessel* (1784–1846), Ger. astronomer.] A solution of a certain differential equation, which occurs in many problems in mathematical physics.

Bessemer /ˈbɛsɪmə/ *n.* M19. [Sir Henry *Bessemer* (1813–98), Eng. engineer.] *Bessemer process*, a steel-making process (now obsolete) in which carbon, silicon, etc. are removed from molten pig-iron by an air blast in a special retort; *Bessemer converter*, such a retort; *Bessemer steel, iron*, etc., the products of this process.

bessemerize *v.t.* treat by the Bessemer process L19.

best /bɛst/ *a.*, *n.*, & *adv.* [OE *betest*, adv. *betost*, *betst* = OFris., OS (Du.) *best*, OHG *bezzist-o* (G *best*), ON *beztr*, *baztr*, Goth. *batist-s*, f. Gmc superl.: cf. BET *adv.* & *pred. a.*, BETTER *a.* etc., & see -EST[1].] A *adj.* Superl. of GOOD *a.* 1 Excelling all others in quality (inherently or relative to some standard); outstanding. OE. 2 Most appropriate, advantageous, or desirable; of a person also: kindest. OE. 3 Greatest in size or quantity; largest, most. M16.

1 H. FIELDING I will fight the best man of you all for twenty pound. J. AUSTEN The little Table . . has most conveniently taken itself off into the best bedroom. LD MACAULAY The best Roman Catholic families in England. 2 SHAKES. *Macb.* In best time We will require her welcome. J. N. LOCKYER The best way to obtain a knowledge of the various constellations. S. BEDFORD It would be best if we had something from old Felden himself. 3 M. MEYER He was to continue his voluntary exile for the best part of two decades.

B *absol.* or as *n.* I *absol.* 1 pl. *The* best people, things, circumstances, etc. OE. 2 *The* chief advantage, merit, etc. ME. 3 *One's* best (possible) achievement, condition, clothes, etc. ME.

II Individualized, as a count n. 4 That which is best; *esp.* in *Sport*, a best performance recorded to date. L16.

4 SHAKES. *Sonn.* These particulars are not my measure: All these I better in one general best.

C *adv.* (Superl. of WELL *adv.*) In the best manner; to the greatest degree; most usefully. (With (ppl) adjs. & in *comb.* freq. written w. hyphen.) OE.

R. BURNS The best-laid schemes o' mice an' men Gang aft agley. COLERIDGE He prayeth best, who loveth best All things both great and small. ARNOLD BENNETT The best-dressed woman in the place.

Special collocations, phrases, & comb.: **all the best**: an expression of goodwill, used as a toast or a valediction. **as best one can** or **may** as well as one is able to do under the circumstances. **at best** on the most hopeful view. **at its** or **one's best** in the best state or condition possible. **at the best of times** even in the most favourable circumstances. *be on one's best* BEHAVIOUR. **best before date**: marked on food to show the date after which it can be expected to deteriorate. *best bib and tucker*: see BIB *n. best bower*: see BOWER *n.*[3] **best boy** the assistant to the chief electrician of a film crew. *best buy*: see BUY *n.* **best end** the rib end of a neck of lamb etc. for cooking. **best friend** one's favourite friend (*best friends* (colloq.) mutually favourite friends (*with*)). **best girl** (orig. *US*) a man's favourite female companion. **best man** *spec.* a bridegroom's chief attendant at a wedding. **best-seller** (orig. *US*) (the author of) a book having a large sale. **best-selling** *a.* that is a best-seller. *do one's best*: see DO *v.* **for the best** aiming at or tending to the best result. **get** or **have the best of it** win a fight, argument, etc.; come out on top. **give** (a person or thing) **best** admit the superiority of, give way to. *have the best of it*: see *get the best of it* above. **make the best of a bad bargain, job,** etc., achieve the best available resolution of difficult circumstances. **make the best of it, things** accept adverse conditions with equanimity. **make the best of one's way** *arch.* go by the quickest route, go with the greatest possible speed. *make the best of things*: see *make the best of it* above. **one had best do** (earlier †**were best (to) do**), orig. *impers.* w. obl. case (= for one), later *pers.* (w. nom.) one would find it most advisable or advantageous to do. **one of the best** an excellent person. **one's Sunday best** one's smartest or most formal clothes. **put one's best foot forward** make the greatest effort of which one is capable. **six of the best** a caning, a beating, (also with other specified numbers of strokes). *the best club in London*: see CLUB *n.* **the best of** (an odd number): one more than half of. *the best of both worlds*: see WORLD *n. the best of British (luck)*: see BRITISH *a.* 2. *the best thing since sliced bread*: see SLICED 1b. **to the best of one's ability, belief, knowledge, power,** etc., to the furthest extent of one's ability etc.; so far as one can do, judge, etc. **with the best (of them)** as well as anyone.

bestest *a., n., & adv.* (*dial. & joc.*) very best M19. **bestness** *n.* M16.

best /bɛst/ *v.t. colloq.* M19. [f. prec.: cf. WORST *v.*] Get the better of; take advantage of; defeat, outwit.

bester *n.* a person who gets the better of another; a cheat: M19.

†**bestad** *pa. pple & ppl a.* var. of BESTED.

bestain /bɪˈsteɪn/ *v.t.* M16. [f. BE- 1 + STAIN *v.*] Mark with stains.

bestar /bɪˈstɑː/ *v.t.* Infl. **-rr-**. E17. [f. BE- 4 + STAR *n.*[1]] Spangle or decorate (as) with stars. Chiefly as *bestarred* ppl a.

bestead *pa. pple & ppl a.* var. of BESTED.

bestead /bɪˈstɛd/ *v.t.* & *i. arch.* Pa. t. **besteaded**; pa. pple **bestead**. L16. [f. BE- 1 + STEAD *v.*] Help; avail.

bested /bɪˈstɛd/ *pa. pple & ppl a. arch.* Also **bestead,** †**bestad**. ME. [f. BE- 1 + ON *staddr* pa. pple of *steðja* to place, w. later assim. to native *ste(a)d.*] 1 With advs., esp. *ill, hard, sore,* etc.: circumstanced, situated. ME. †b Without adv.: badly circumstanced. LME–L16. 2 Beset *by* or †*with* enemies, *with* dangers etc. ME. †3 Located; settled. Only in ME.

¶ Spenser also uses *bestad* as a pa. t.

bestial /ˈbɛstɪəl/ *n.* Long *obs.* exc. *Sc.* ME. [Partly f. OFr. *bestial* f. med.L *bestiale* use as n. of neut. sing. of late L *bestialis* (see next); partly (ME forms) f. OFr. *bestaille* f. med.L *bestialia* neut. pl. of *bestialis.*] 1 *collect.* Farm and domestic animals; cattle. ME. 2 A single beast. LME.

bestial /ˈbɛstɪəl/ *a.* LME. [OFr. f. late L *bestialis*, f. L *bestia* BEAST *n.*: see -IAL.] 1 Of or pertaining to the lower animals, esp. quadrupeds. LME. 2 Like a beast or beasts; brutish, irrational; cruel, savage; depraved, lustful, obscene. LME.

bestialize *v.t.* change into the form or nature of a beast; debase: L17. **bestially** *adv.* LME.

bestiality /bɛstɪˈalɪti/ *n.* LME. [(O)Fr. *bestialité*, f. as prec.: see -ITY.] 1 The state or quality of being bestial. LME. 2 Copulation between a person and an animal. E17. 3 A disgusting vice, a beastly practice. Now *rare.* M17.

bestiary /ˈbɛstɪəri/ *n.* M19. [med.L *bestiarium*, f. L *bestia* BEAST *v.*: see -ARY[1].] A medieval moralizing treatise on beasts.

bestick /bɪˈstɪk/ *v.t.* Pa. t. & pple **bestuck** /bɪˈstʌk/. E17. [f. BE- 1, 2 + STICK *v.*[1]] Stick all over, bedeck; *arch.* pierce through, transfix. Usu. in *pass.*

bestill /bɪˈstɪl/ *v.t.* L18. [f. BE- 1 + STILL *v.*[1]] Make still or quiet.

bestir /bɪˈstəː/ *v.* Infl. **-rr-**. ME. [f. BE- 1 + STIR *v.*] 1 *v.t.* Stir up; exert or busy *oneself*; rouse to action. ME. 2 *v.i.* Exert oneself, move quickly. *rare* (Shakes.). E17.

bestorm /bɪˈstɔːm/ *v.t.* M17. [f. BE- 1 + STORM *v.*] Storm; assail on all sides.

bestow /bɪˈstəʊ/ *v.t.* ME. [f. BE- 4 + STOW *v.*[1]] 1 Apply, employ (time, effort, etc., *in* an occupation). *arch.* ME. †b *spec.* Spend, lay out, (money). LME–M17. †c *refl.* Acquit oneself. L16–E17. 2 Place, locate, put; store, stow away; lodge, put up. *arch.* LME. 3 Settle or give in marriage. *arch.* LME. 4 Confer as a gift (*on, upon,* †*of* a person; †*to* a purpose). M16.

1 I. WALTON Bestow one day with me and my friends in hunting the otter. 2 TINDALE *Luke* 12:17 I have noo roume where to bestowe my frutes. BYRON See that the women are bestow'd in safety In the remote apartments. V. SACKVILLE-WEST Stooping . . to bestow the presents into eager hands. L. A. G. STRONG She received his hat and his Malacca cane, and bestowed them safely. 3 H. ALLEN A widower . . anxious to see his only child well and securely bestowed. 4 L. EDEL The hope that ultimately she will bestow upon him more than sweet words and a smile. F. TUOHY The Rudowskis had . . bestowed on him a name that could not be anglicized. E. REVELEY The impulse to bestow trinkets.

bestowal *n.* the action of bestowing L18. **bestower** *n.* M16. **bestowment** *n.* (*a*) bestowal; (*b*) *rare* a gift: M18.

†**bestraught** *a.* M16–M18. [f. DISTRAUGHT *a.* by substitution of BE-.] Distracted, distraught.

bestreak /bɪˈstriːk/ *v.t.* L16. [f. BE- 1 + STREAK *v.*[2]] Mark or decorate with streaks.

bestrew /bɪˈstruː/ *v.t.* Also **bestrow** /bɪˈstrəʊ/. Pa. pple **bestrewed, bestrewn** /bɪˈstruːn/; **bestrown** /bɪˈstrəʊn/. [OE *bestrēowian*, f. as BE- + STREW *v.*] 1 Strew (a surface) *with*. OE. 2 Scatter (things) about. M17. 3 Lie scattered over. E18.

bestride /bɪˈstrʌɪd/ *v.t.* Pa. t. **bestrode** /bɪˈstrəʊd/, †**bestrid**; pa. pple **bestridden** /bɪˈstrɪd(ə)n/, **bestrode,** †**bestrid**. [OE *bestrīdan*, f. as BE- + STRIDE *v.*] 1 Get or sit upon (orig. and esp. a horse) with legs astride. OE. 2 Stand astride over (a place, person, etc.), esp. as a victor over the fallen or to defend a fallen man; straddle; span. E16. 3 Step or stride across. E17.

1 SHAKES. *Rich. II* That horse that thou so often hast bestrid. T. GRAY Sisters, hence with spurs of speed, . . Each bestride her sable steed. *fig.*: W. COWPER Through the pressed nostrils, spectacle-bestrid. 2 SHAKES. *Ant. & Cl.* He doth bestride the narrow world Like a Colossus. E. YOUNG How I bestride your prostrate conqueror! TENNYSON As he bestrode my Grandsire, when he fell, And all else fled. 3 SHAKES. *Coriol.* When I first my wedded mistress saw Bestride my threshold.

†**bestrip** *v.t.* OE–E17. [OE *bestrȳpan*, f. as BE- + STRIP *v.*[1]: cf. MHG *bestroufen*.] Despoil (*of*).

bestrode *v.* pa. t.: see BESTRIDE.

bestrow(n) *v.* see BESTREW.

bestuck *v.* pa. t. & pple of BESTICK.

bestud /bɪˈstʌd/ *v.t.* Infl. **-dd-**. E17. [f. BE- 1 + STUD *v.*] Decorate (as) with studs.

bet /bɛt/ *n.* L16. [Origin uncertain: perh. aphet. f. ABET *n.*, but see next.] 1 The staking of money etc. on the outcome of a doubtful issue; a wager; the sum of money etc. staked. L16. b *fig.* *One's* guess or opinion. *colloq.* M20. 2 With qualifying adj., esp. *good* or *best*: a person, event, etc., on which to bet, a choice, a course of action. *colloq.* E20.

1 A. SILLITOE A bet on Fair Glory in the two-thirty won him twelve pounds. b J. B. PRIESTLEY My bet is there's been a fair amount of swift dirty work round here. 2 P. G. WODEHOUSE Thinks I'm not a good bet? L. A. G. STRONG Keep that up. . . It's our best bet.

Phrases: *safe bet*: see SAFE *a. Yankee bet*: see YANKEE *a.*

bet /bɛt/ *v.t.* & *i.* Infl. **-tt-**. Pa. t. & pple **bet, betted**. L16. [Perh. f. the n., but the vb & n. are contemporaneous.] 1 Stake (an amount of money etc.) against another's in support of an affirmation or on the outcome of a doubtful event; risk an amount of money etc. against (a person) by agreeing to forfeit it if the truth or outcome is not as specified. (Foll. by *on* or *against* an outcome or competitor, *that* something is or will be so, *against* a person who disagrees.) L16. 2 In hyperbolical asseverations & absol.: (be able to) feel sure (*that*). *colloq.* M19.

1 SHAKES. *2 Hen. IV* 'A [he] shot a fine shoot. John a Gaunt . . betted much money on his head. THACKERAY I don't bet on horses I don't know. J. GALSWORTHY Offering to bet the driver half a crown he didn't do it in the three-quarters of an hour. C. P. SNOW Humphrey would have betted that . . Briers would take on more drink that evening. C. ISHERWOOD You could bet thousands of dollars against this happening. 2 J. K. JEROME If Harris's eyes fill with tears, you can bet it is because Harris has been eating raw onions. J. GRENFELL And I bet I look a million years old and he won't even recognise me. I. SHAW 'You're ruining my sex life,' he said. 'I bet,' she said.

Phrases: *bet like the Watsons*: see WATSON *n.*[2] *bet one's bottom dollar*: see BOTTOM *a. bet one's shirt*: see SHIRT *n.* **you bet (you), you bet your boots** or **life** you can be certain (*that*) (cf. BETCHER).

†**bet** *adv. & pred. a.* OE–M17. [OE *bet* = OFris. *bet*, OS *bat, bet*, OHG *baz* (G *bass*), ON *betr*, f. Gmc adv.: cf. BEST *a.* etc., BETTER *a.* etc.] Better.

beta /ˈbiːtə/ *n.* ME. [L f. Gk.] 1 The second letter (*Β, β*) of the Greek alphabet. ME. 2 Denoting the second in a numerical sequence: a *attrib. Sci.* Freq. written *β*: (*a*) *Astron.* (preceding the genitive of the L name of the constellation) designating the second brightest star in a constellation; (*b*) *Chem.* designating the second of a number of isomeric forms of a compound, or of allotropes of an element, etc.; (*c*) *Physics* designating a negatively-charged particle now known to be an electron, which is one of the three main types of decay product emitted by radioactive substances; also designating decay, emission, radiation, etc., associated with such a particle; (*d*) *beta rhythm, waves,* rapid low-amplitude electrical activity of the conscious brain, consisting of oscillations with a frequency of 18 to 25 hertz; (*e*) Med. *beta receptor*, one of two kinds of adrenergic receptor in the sympathetic nervous system, stimulation of which results esp. in increased cardiac activity; *beta-adrenergic* adj., pertaining to or involving beta receptors; *beta blocker*, a drug preventing stimulation of beta receptors; (*f*) *beta test*, a test of machinery, software, etc., in the final stages of development, carried out by a party unconnected with its development; *beta-test* v.t., perform a beta test on. L17. b A second-class mark in an examination etc. E20.

2a *beta* GLOBULIN. b **beta plus, minus** rather better, worse, than the average second class.

betaine /ˈbiːtəiːn, ˈbiːteɪn/ *n.* M19. [Irreg. f. L *beta* BEET *n.*[1] + -INE[5]: the first was isolated from sugar beet.] *Chem.* A zwitterionic *N*-trialkyl derivative of an amino acid; *spec.* that derived from glycine, $(CH_3)_3N^+{\cdot}CH_2CO_2^-$, a crystalline base found in many plant juices.

betake /bɪˈteɪk/ *v.* Pa. t. **betook** /bɪˈtʊk/; pa. pple **betaken** /bɪˈteɪk(ə)n/. ME. [f. BE- 1 + TAKE *v.*] †1 *v.t.* = BETEACH. Long *dial.* ME–L19. 2a *v.refl.* & (long *rare*) *i.* Have recourse *to*; go (*to*). L16. **b** *v.t.* w. (part of) the body as obj. = sense 2a above. M19.

1 EVELYN To God Almighty I betake it for support and speedy good success. 2a SPENSER Then to her yron wagon she betakes. BUNYAN They betook themselves to a short debate. G. F. KENNAN Ambassador Francis.. betook himself.. to the provincial town of Vologda. b J. AGATE The kind of place to which.. Evelyn Waugh's characters would have betaken their vile bodies.

betatron /ˈbiːtətrɒn/ *n.* M20. [f. BETA + -TRON.] *Physics.* An apparatus for accelerating electrons electromagnetically in a circular path.

betcher /ˈbɛtʃə/ *v. pres. colloq.* Also **betcha**. E20. [Repr. an informal pronunc.] Bet you, bet your (life): see BET *v.* 2.

†beteach *v.t.* Infl. as TEACH *v.* OE–M18. [OE *betǣcan*, f. as BE- + TEACH *v.*] Hand over; entrust *to*; commit or commend *to*.

betel /ˈbiːt(ə)l/ *n.* M16. [Port. f. Malayalam *verrila*.] The leaf of a climbing evergreen shrub, *Piper betle*, of the pepper family, which is chewed in the East with areca-nut parings and a little lime. Also (more fully *betel pepper*), the plant itself.

Comb.: **betel-nut** the nut of the areca palm; **betel-palm, -tree** the areca palm, *Areca catechu*.

bête noire /beɪt ˈnwɑː, *foreign* bɛt nwaːr/ *n. phr.* Pl. **-s -s** (pronounced same). M19. [Fr., lit. 'black beast'.] The bane of someone's life; an insufferable person or thing; an object of aversion.

Beth Din /beɪt ˈdiːn/ *n. phr.* L18. [Heb. *bēṯ dīn* house of judgement.] A Jewish court of law composed of three rabbinic judges, responsible for matters of Jewish religious law and the settlement of civil disputes between Jews.

bethel /ˈbɛθ(ə)l/ *n.* E17. [Heb. *bēṯ-ʾēl*, f. *bēṯ* house of + *ʾēl* god.] 1 A place where God is worshipped (see *Gen.* 28:17–19). E17. 2 *transf.* A Nonconformist chapel; a seamen's church. E19.

Bethesda /bɛˈθɛzdə/ *n. arch.* M19. [A place mentioned in *John* 5:2–4: given as a name to some Nonconformist chapels etc.] A Nonconformist chapel.

Beth Hamidrash /beɪt hamiˈdrɑːʃ, beɪt haˈmɪdrɑːʃ/ *n. phr.* L19. [Heb. *bēṯ ham-midrāš* lit. 'the house of study'.] A place where Jews gather to study and pray.

bethink /bɪˈθɪŋk/ *v.* Pa. t. & pple **bethought** /bɪˈθɔːt/. [OE *biþenćan* = OFris. *bithanka*, *bithenzia*, OS *biþenkian*, OHG *bidenken* (Du., G *bedenken*), Goth. *biþagkjan*, f. Gmc, f. as BE- + THINK *v.*[2]] I *v.t.* 1 Bear in mind; recall, recollect. Now only (*arch.*) w. obj. cl. OE. †2 Think over; plan, arrange. ME–M17. †3 *be bethought* = branch II. ME–E17.

II *v.refl.* †4 Collect one's thoughts; take thought. OE–M17. 5 Reflect, stop to think, remind oneself. (Foll. by obj. cl. (esp. indirect interrog.), as *how*; *of*, †(*up*)*on*, †*to do*.) ME. 6 Resolve. (Foll. by *of*, *that*, †*to do*.) *arch.* LME.

5 W. IRVING Rip bethought himself a moment. A. HELPS To bethink themselves how little they may owe to their own merit. L. P. HARTLEY She bethought her of her duties as a hostess. 6 SHAKES. *Jul. Caes.* It may be I shall otherwise bethink me. J. GALSWORTHY He bethought him that he would go to the opera.

III *v.i.* 7 Consider, think. (Formerly foll. by *of*, (*up*)*on*.) *arch.* ME.

7 BYRON Bethink ere thou dismiss us, ask again.

†bethrall *v.t. rare* (Spenser). Only in L16. [f. BE- 3 + THRALL *n.*] Enthrall, enslave.

bethumb /bɪˈθʌm/ *v.t.* M17. [f. BE- 1 + THUMB *v.*] Take hold of or mark with the thumb.

bethump /bɪˈθʌmp/ *v.t.* L16. [f. BE- 1 + THUMP *v.*] Thump soundly.

bethwack /bɪˈθwak/ *v.t.* M16. [f. BE- 1 + THWACK *v.*] Thrash or cudgel soundly.

bethwine /ˈbɛθwʌɪn/ *n. dial.* E17. [Origin unkn.] Any of various twining plants, e.g. bindweed, traveller's joy.

betide /bɪˈtʌɪd/ *v.* ME. [f. BE- 1 + TIDE *v.*[1]] 1 *v.i.* & *t.* (orig. w. dat. obj.). Happen (to or (*un*)*to*), befall. Only in inf. & 3rd person (now pres. subjunct.). ME. 2 *v.t.* Bode, betoken. *rare.* L18.

1 SHELLEY Took that child so fair From his weak arms, that ill might not betide him Or her. E. DICKINSON I hope I'm ready for 'the worst'—Whatever prank betides! **woe betide** (a person): orig. a curse, now usu. a warning. 2 W. COWPER Awaking, how could I but muse At what such a dream should betide?

†betime *adv.* ME–M17. [f. as BY *prep.* + TIME *n.*] In good time; early; at an early hour.

SHAKES. *Ant. & Cl.* To business that we love we rise betime.

betimes /bɪˈtʌɪmz/ *adv.* ME. [f. prec. + -S[3].] 1 At an early time, period, or season. ME. 2 *spec.* Early in the morning. LME. 3 In good time; before it is too late. LME. 4 Soon; speedily. LME.

bêtise /beɪˈtiːz, bɛˈtiːz/ *n.* Pl. pronounced same. E19. [Fr. = stupidity, f. *bête* foolish f. OFr. *beste* BEAST *n.*] A foolish, ill-timed remark or action; a piece of folly.

betitle /bɪˈtʌɪt(ə)l/ *v.t.* M17. [f. BE- 3 + TITLE *n.*] Give a name or title to; entitle.

†betoil *v.t.* M17–M19. [f. BE- 2, 4 + TOIL *v.*[1] or *n.*[1]] Worry or preoccupy with toil.

betoken /bɪˈtəʊk(ə)n/ *v.t.* [OE *betācnian* = OFris. *bitēknia*, Du. *betekenen*, OHG *bizzeihhanōn* (G *bezeichnen*): see BE-, TOKEN *v.*] †1 Signify; express in words. OE–E17. †2 Typify; symbolize. ME–M17. 3 Be a sign or omen of; augur, presage. ME. 4 Give evidence of, indicate, suggest. L15.

2 MILTON In the Cloud a Bow.. Betok'ning peace from God and Cov'nant new. 3 SHAKES. *Ven. & Ad.* Like a red morn, that ever yet betoken'd Wreck to the seaman, tempest to the field. 4 L. M. MONTGOMERY He had the buggy and the sorrel mare, which betokened that he was going a considerable distance. I. COLEGATE That rather ironical, rather penetrating look which not everyone knew betokened affection.

betony /ˈbɛtəni/ *n.* ME. [(O)Fr. *bétoine* f. pop.L var. of L *betonica* f. *Vettonica* (Pliny), perh. f. name of an Iberian tribe.] 1 A purple-flowered labiate plant, *Stachys officinalis*. ME. 2 Any of various similar plants. ME.

2 *Paul's betony*, *water betony*, etc.

betook *v.* pa. t. of BETAKE.

†betorn *ppl a.* ME–L18. [f. BE- 1 + *torn* pa. pple of TEAR *v.*[1]] Torn, tattered.

betrap /bɪˈtrap/ *v.t. arch.* Infl. **-pp-**. [OE *betreppan*, *-træppan*: see BE-, TRAP *v.*[2]] Entrap, enclose.

betray /bɪˈtreɪ/ *v.* ME. [f. BE- 1 + TRAY *v.*] I *v.t.* 1 Give up treacherously (a person or thing, *to* an enemy, †*to* punishment). ME. 2 Be or prove false to; be disloyal to; disappoint the expectations of. ME. 3 Lead astray, deceive. ME. 4 Reveal treacherously or involuntarily. L16. 5 Show incidentally; constitute evidence or a symptom of. L17.

2 E. M. FORSTER I will never forgive Eleanor. She has betrayed my confidence. R. MACAULAY I had betrayed David, broken my promise. 3 E. B. PUSEY Pride and self-confidence betray man to his fall. C. ISHERWOOD The poor betrayed girl who gets abandoned by her lover. 4 A. RANSOME Looking for a hat, a hand, a leg, no matter what, that betray their hiding place. J. C. RANSOM This speech may have betrayed a fluttery private apprehension which should not have been made public. S. BRETT A tremble of her features betrayed the truth. 5 H. ADAMS A figure also called a king, but so charmingly delicate in expression that the robes alone betray his sex.

II *v.i.* 6 Act treacherously; deceive. E17.

6 GOLDSMITH When lovely Woman stoops to folly, And finds too late that men betray.

betrayal *n.* the act of betraying; a treacherous or disloyal act; a disclosure: E19. **betrayer** *n.* L15. **betrayment** *n.* (*rare*) M16.

betrim /bɪˈtrɪm/ *v.t.* Infl. **-mm-**. E17. [f. BE- 1 + TRIM *v.*] Trim, decorate.

betroth /bɪˈtrəʊð, -θ/ *v.t.* ME. [f. as BE- + TRUTH *n.*, later assim. to TROTH.] 1 Enter into an engagement to marry (a woman). *arch.* ME. 2 Bind (two people; one person, esp. a woman, *to* another) in an engagement to marry. Usu. in *pass.* M16. †3 *gen.* Engage; pledge (oneself) *to*; pledge oneself to. M16–L17.

betrothal *n.* the act of betrothing; the fact of being betrothed; an engagement to marry: M19. **betrothed** *n.* the person to whom one is betrothed, one's fiancé(e) L16. **betrothment** *n.* = BETROTHAL M16.

†betrust *v.t.* LME–M18. [f. BE- 1 + TRUST *v.*] Trust; entrust.

Betsy /ˈbɛtsi/ *n. slang* & *dial.* (chiefly *US*). Also **b-**. M19. [Female forename, a familiar abbrev. of *Elizabeth*: cf. BETTY.] (A name given to) a gun or pistol, *esp.* a favourite one. Also *old Betsy*.

¶See also *heavens to Betsy!* s.v. HEAVEN *n.*

better /ˈbɛtə/ *n.*[1] E17. [f. BET *v.* + -ER[1].] A person who bets; = BETTOR.

better /ˈbɛtə/ *a.*, *n.*[2], & *adv.* [OE *betera* (masc. adj.) = OFris. *betera*, OS *betiro* (Du. *beter*), OHG *bezziro* (G *besser*), ON *betri*, Goth. *batiza*, f. Gmc compar.: cf. BEST *a.* etc., BET *adv.* & *pred. a.*, & see -ER[3].] A *adj.* Compar. of GOOD *a.* (In pred. & ellipt. uses merging w. the adv.) 1 Of superior quality; more outstanding. OE. 2 More appropriate, advantageous, or desirable; of a person also: kinder. ME. 3 Greater in size or quantity; larger; more. ME. 4 Improved in health; partly or fully recovered from illness. LME.

1 G. B. SHAW The grey mare is the better horse here. V. WOOLF Andrew would be a better man than he had been. ALDOUS HUXLEY Better planes, better explosives, better guns and gases—every improvement increases the sum of fear and hatred. 2 MILTON Better to reign in Hell than serve in Heav'n. L. STERNE I can give no better advice. W. STEVENS It would have been better for his hands To be convulsed. A. BEVAN There are other and better ways of dealing with alleged abuses than by throwing in the sponge. 3 WORDSWORTH For the better part Of two delightful hours we strolled along. 4 S. JOHNSON Dr. Taylor is better, and is gone out in the chaise.

B *absol.* or as *n.* 1 *One's* superior in some personal quality or attainment or (now only in *pl.*) in social status. OE. 2 Something better. OE. 3 More. ME. 4 *The* superiority or mastery. Now chiefly in *get the better of*, defeat, outwit. LME.

1 SHAKES. *2 Hen. VI* Ambitious Warwick, let thy betters speak. 2 J. USSHER The Iberians had the better of it. G. B. SHAW The change from burning to hanging or shooting may strike us as a change for the better. 3 *New Yorker* Since the members of the select Committee.. voted by better than two to one to release the report.

C *adv.* [Superseding earlier BET *adv.*] (Compar. of WELL *adv.* In pred. uses after *be* & ellipt. merging w. the adj.) In a better manner; to a greater degree; more usefully. (With (ppl) adjs. & in *comb.* freq. written w. hyphen.) ME.

L. STERNE The dirtier the fellow is, the better generally he succeeds in it. SYD. SMITH His awe of better-dressed men and better-taught men. V. WOOLF Without knowing why she felt that he liked her better than he had ever done before. F. SWINNERTON I could run any paper in England.. better than it's ever been run before.

Phrases, special collocations, & comb.: *against one's better* JUDGEMENT. *be better than one's word*: see WORD *n.* *better days*: see DAY *n.* **better feelings** conscience. *better late than never*: see LATE *adv.* **better off** better situated as regards money or other personal circumstances; *the better off* (absol.), those so situated. **better-to-do** above the well-to-do in social condition and material wealth; *the better-to-do*, those above the well-to-do. **for better (or) for worse** whatever changes may take place, whatever happens. *get better*: see GET *v.* **go one better (than)**, (*N. Amer.*) **go (a person) one better** outbid etc. by one unit, outdo. *got to a better place* or *world*: see GO *v.* *have seen better days*: see SEE *v.* **know better (than that, than to do)** be too wise or well-informed (to believe that), be too experienced or well-mannered (to do), etc. **no better than** practically, merely. **no better than one should** or **ought to be** of doubtful moral character, (usu.) of easy virtue. **one had better do** (earlier †**were better (to) do**, orig. impers. w. obl. case (= for one), later pers. (w. nom.)) one would find it more advisable or advantageous to do; (also *colloq.* w. ellipsis of *had*). **one's better half** (now chiefly *joc.*) a person very close to one; one's husband or (*esp.*) one's wife. *one's better nature*: see NATURE *n.* *one's better self*: see SELF *n.* 3a. *streets better (than)*: see STREET *n.* *think (all) the better of*, *think better of*: see THINK *v.*[2] **you'd better believe (it)** *colloq.* you may be assured.

betterness *n.* the quality of being better; *spec.* fineness of precious metals above the standard: LME.

better /ˈbɛtə/ *v.* LME. [f. BETTER *a.* etc.] **1** *v.t.* Amend; improve; *refl.* improve one's financial or social condition. LME. **2** *v.t.* Surpass. M16. **3** *v.i.* Grow better, improve. M17.

1 F. MARRYAT She left to better herself, and obtained the situation of nurse. W. C. WILLIAMS Their speech and dress were bettered while she kept them in her charge. L. DURRELL I lack the will-power to do anything with my life, to better my position by hard work. 2 L. DEIGHTON His Hamlet had been compared with Gielgud's, and his Othello bettered only by Olivier. 3 CARLYLE The general condition of the poor must be bettering instead of worsening.

betterment /ˈbɛtəm(ə)nt/ *n.* L16. [f. prec. + -MENT.] **1** Improvement, amendment. L16. **2** A local improvement to property; an improved property. *US.* L18. **3** Enhanced value (of real property) through local improvements. Orig. *US.* L19.

betting /ˈbɛtɪŋ/ *n.* L16. [f. BET *v.* + -ING[1].] **1** The action of BET *v.* L16. **2** The odds offered. E20.

Comb.: **betting office**, *colloq.* **shop** an establishment licensed to handle bets (on horse-races, dog-races, etc.); **betting slip** a slip of paper on which a bet is entered.

bettong /ˈbɛtɒŋ/ *n. Austral.* E19. [Aborig.] A short-nosed rat-kangaroo of the genus *Bettongia*.

bettor /ˈbɛtə/ *n.* M17. [f. BET *v.* + -OR.] A person who bets; = BETTER *n.*[1]

Betty /ˈbɛti/ *n.* Also **b-**. M17. [Female forename, a familiar abbrev. of *Elizabeth*: cf. BETSY.] **1** A crowbar used by burglars. *slang.* Long *arch.* M17. **2** Hist. *Betty lamp*, a type of hanging lamp used in America. L19.

¶See also *(all) my eye (and) Betty Martin* s.v. EYE *n.*, *Brown Betty* s.v. BROWN *a.*, *Cousin Betty* s.v. COUSIN *n.* 6.

betulin /ˈbɛtjʊlɪn/ *n.* M19. [f. L *betula* birch + -IN[1].] *Chem.* A solid terpenoid alcohol, $C_{30}H_{50}O_2$, present in birch-bark.

†betumble *v.t. rare* (Shakes.). Only in L16. [f. BE- 1 + TUMBLE *v.*] Disorder.

between /bɪˈtwiːn/ *prep.*, *adv.*, & *n.* [OE *betwēonum* (beside *betwēon* and *betwēonan*), f. as BY *prep.* etc. + Gmc formation with *-n*-suff. (cf. OFris. *twīne*, Goth. *tweihnai* two each) f. base of OE *twēo*, OS *tweho*, OHG *zweho* doubt, difference, ult. rel. to TWO.] **A** *prep.* **1** Expr. reciprocal action or relation involving two or more agents individually; reciprocally on the part of. OE. **2** Expr. motion or communication from each of two or more bodies, places, etc., to the other or others; to and from. OE. **3** Expr. confinement or restriction to two or more parties. OE. **4** In the interval separating (two points of time, events, etc.); intermediate to (two quantities etc.); partaking of the nature of (two qualities etc.). (The separate times, quantities, etc., joined by *and* or (colloq.) *to*.) OE. **5** In or through the space, line, or route (*lit.* & *fig.*) separating (two points, objects, etc.) or bounded by (more than two points etc. considered individually). OE. **6** Occupying the space bounded by (two points etc.); dividing, separating; connecting, uniting. ME. **7** By the joint action of; (to be) shared by (collectively or distributively); in portions to each of. ME. **8** So as to separate, select from, or discriminate one from another of; in or involving selection from (alternatives). ME. **9** In alternation of; by the combined effect of. E17.

1 W. CATHER I thought that day there was some kind of feeling, something unusual, between them. A. BEVAN The unbridgeable antagonism between private wealth, poverty and political democracy. M. AMIS A brilliant argument was taking place between Sir Herbert and Willie, all about youth. 2 STEELE Two Letters which passed between a Mother and Son lately. A. RANSOME Titty and Dorothea raced backwards and forwards between the camp and the well. 3 **between ourselves, between you and me** (**and the bedpost** or **gatepost** or **lamppost**) in confidence. 4 K. MANSFIELD She looked fascinating in her black suit, something between a Bishop and a Fly. C. MORGAN When he was between boy and man, he had often driven these waggons himself. J. BETJEMAN To travel by the Underground all day Between the rush hours. *Listener* Panels can be built up . . to form screen sizes of between 5.3 to 17.6 feet. 5 MILTON Jehovah . . thron'd Between the Cherubim. HOR. WALPOLE To hold the balance between liberty and prerogative. TENNYSON By thirty hills I hurry down Or slip between the ridges. S. HEANEY Between my finger and my thumb The squat pen rests. F. SWINNERTON Anna . . had been delayed by traffic between Broadcasting House and the River. *be torn between*: see TEAR *v.*[1] *between a rock and a hard place*: see ROCK *n.*[1] *between cup and lip*: see CUP *n.* 1. *between the devil and the deep (blue) sea*: see DEVIL *n.* *between wind and water*: see WIND *n.*[1] **come** or **stand between**: *esp.* as a mediator, as a protector, or to keep from or destroy union. *fall between two stools*: see STOOL *n.* 2b. *stand between*: see *come between* above. 6 R. BURNS The lang Scots miles That lie between us and our hame. W. PALEY There is no comparison between a fortune which a man acquires by well-applied industry, and one . . received from another. DICKENS The lines of demarcation between the two colours. LD MACAULAY A coalition was formed between the Royalists and a large body of Presbyterians. J. FRAME The unmade road between Maheno and Waipori. 7 OED They had it between them. G. B. SHAW Our Prime Ministers . . divide their time between the golf course and the Treasury Bench. R. DAVIES I think between us we'll do something extraordinary with this film. 8 R. HOOKER To judge rightly between truth and error. LD MACAULAY A complete separation between the naval and military services. OED The choice lies between the two last-named applicants. 9 ROBERT BURTON Thus between hope and fear, suspicions, angers . . we bangle away our best days. S. JOHNSON I . . hope, that, between publick business, improving studies, and domestick pleasures, neither melancholy nor caprice will find any place for entrance.

B *adv.* (mostly the prep. w. obj. understood). **1** In or into an intermediate position or course (*lit.* & *fig.*); intermediately in amount, order, etc.; occupying intermediate space, intervening. OE. **2** In the interval; at intervals. ME. **3** To and fro as a mediator. Long *obs.* exc. in GO-BETWEEN. ME.

1 POPE He hangs between, in doubt to act or rest. SOUTHEY The man . . That instant rush'd between. T. HARDY And I am here, and you are there, And a hundred miles between! BETWIXT *and between*. *far between*: see FAR *adv.* FEW *and far between*. *in between*: see IN *adv.* 2 TENNYSON They would pelt me with starry spangles and shells, Laughing and clapping their hands between. 3 SHAKES. *Tr. & Cr.* I have . . gone between and between, but small thanks for my labour.

Comb. (of prep. & adv.): **between-decks** *adv.* & *n.* (in) the space(s) between the decks of a ship; **between-lens shutter** *Photogr.* a type of shutter fitted between the components of a compound lens close to the diaphragm; **between-maid** a servant assisting two others, as the cook and the housemaid; **between-time** an intervening time, an interval; **between times, -whiles** *advs.* in the interval between other actions, occasionally.

C *n.* An interval (also *in between* s.v. IN *adv.*); something intermediate. *rare.* E17.

betweenity *n.* [after *extremity* etc.] intermediateness of kind, quality, or condition; anything intermediate: M18. **betweenness** /-n-n-/ *n.* the condition or fact of being between L19.

betwixt /bɪˈtwɪkst/ *prep.* & *adv.* Now *poet.*, *arch.*, & *dial.* [OE *betwēohs*, *betweox*, *betwyx* corresp. to OFris. *bituischa*, *bituiskum*, f. as BY *prep.* etc. + Gmc base repr. also by OFris. *twiska*, OS *twisc*, OHG *zwiski* two each, twofold, f. as TWO + -ISH[1].] = BETWEEN *prep.* & *adv.*

betwixt and between *colloq.* intermediate(ly), neither one thing nor the other. *betwixt cup and lip*: see CUP *n.* 1.

beudantite /ˈbjuːdəntʌɪt/ *n.* E19. [f. François *Beudant* (1787–1850), Fr. mineralogist + -ITE[1].] *Min.* A hexagonal basic sulphate of lead and ferric iron, occurring as black, dark green, or brown rhombohedra.

beurre /bœːr/ *n.* M19. [Fr. = butter.] **1** *beurre noir* /nwaːr/ [= black], a sauce made by heating butter until it is brown, usu. mixing it with vinegar. M19. **2** *beurre manié* /manje/ [= handled], a mixture of flour and butter used for thickening sauces or soups. M20.

beurré /ˈbjʊəri, *foreign* bœːre/ *n.* E18. [Fr, lit. 'buttered, buttery'.] A mellow variety of pear.

bevel /ˈbɛv(ə)l/ *a.* & *n.* Also (now *rare*) **bevil**. L16. [f. OFr. dim. of *baïf* open-mouthed (mod. *béveau*), f. *baer* to gape: see BAY *n.*[4]: cf. OFr. *bever* give bias to. Cf. earlier BEVILLY.] **A** *adj.* Oblique; at more than a right angle; sloping. L16.

L. MACNEICE The blue and bevel hills of Uig.

B *n.* **1** A joiner's and mason's tool consisting of a flat rule with a movable tongue stiffly jointed to one end, for adjusting angles. E17. **2** An obtuse angle; a slope from the horizontal or vertical; a sloping surface. L17.

Comb.: **bevel gear** a gear working one shaft from another at an angle to it by bevel wheels; **bevel wheel** a toothed wheel whose working face is oblique to the axis.

bevel /bɛv(ə)l/ *v.* Also **bevil**. Infl. **-ll-**, ***-l-**. L17. [f. the n.] **1** *v.t.* Impart a bevel to; cut away (a square edge) to a more obtuse angle. L17. **2** *v.i.* Slope, slant. L17.

bevelled *a.* (*a*) made with a bevel; (*b*) *Her.* = BEVILLY: M18. **beveller** *n.* L19. **bevelment** *n.* the process of bevelling E19.

bever /ˈbiːvə/ *n.* Also **beaver**. LME. [AN *bever*, OFr. *beivre*, (later *boivre*) drinking, drink, use as n. of vb *beivre* (mod. *boire*) f. L *bibere* to drink.] **†1** A drink, potation; a time for drinking. LME–E17. **2** Light refreshment between meals; a snack. Now chiefly *colloq.* & *dial.* E16.

beverage /ˈbɛv(ə)rɪdʒ/ *n.* ME. [OFr. *be(u)vrage* (mod. *breuvage*) f. Proto-Romance, f. L *bibere* to drink: see prec., -AGE.] **1** A liquid for drinking; drink. In early use also *spec.* a drink to seal a bargain, *transf.* a bargain sealed by a drink. Now *formal* or *joc.* ME. **b** A specific drink, as lemonade, cider, etc., according to locality. *dial.* E17. **†2** Drinking; a draught of liquid; *fig.* suffering, a bitter experience. ME–L17.

bevil *a.* & *n.*, *v.* see BEVEL *a.* & *n.*, *v.*

bevilly /ˈbɛvɪli/ *a.* M16. [f. as BEVEL *a.*] *Her.* Of a line: having a break formed from alternate right and left turns at equal acute angles (and resembling a bevel).

Bevin boy /ˈbɛvɪn bɔɪ/ *n. phr.* M20. [Ernest *Bevin* (1881–1951), Minister of Labour and National Service 1940–5.] During the war of 1939–45, a young man of age for National Service selected by lot to work as a miner.

bevue /bevy/ *n.* Pl. pronounced same. L17. [Fr., f. *bé-*, *bes-* pejorative + *vue* VIEW *n.*] An error of inadvertence; a blunder.

bevvy /ˈbɛvi/ *n.* & *v.i. slang.* Also **bevy**. L19. [f. BEV(ERAGE + -Y[6].] **A** *n.* (A) drink, esp. (of) beer or other alcoholic liquor. L19. **B** *v.* **1** *v.i.* Drink, esp. beer or other alcoholic liquor. M20. **2** *v.t.* Make drunk. Chiefly as *bevvied* ppl a. M20.

bevy /ˈbɛvi/ *n.*[1] LME. [Origin unkn.] **1** A company of ladies, roes, quails, or larks. LME. **2** A group or company of any kind. E17.

bevy *n.*[2] & *v.* var. of BEVVY.

bewail /bɪˈweɪl/ *v.* ME. [f. BE- 2 + WAIL *v.*] **1** *v.t.* Wail over (esp. the dead). ME. **2** *v.t.* Express great sorrow or regret for; mourn. LME. **3** *v.i.* Lament, mourn. LME.

bewailable *a.* E17. **bewailer** *n.* E17. **bewailment** *n.* (*rare*) E17.

beware /bɪˈwɛː/ *v.* Orig. & now again only in *imper.* & *inf.* ME. [Imper. & inf. *be ware* treated as one wd: cf. BEGONE *v.*[1]] **1** *v.i.* & *t.* Be cautious; take heed (of or *of* a danger etc.; *lest*, *how*, *that* . . *not*). ME. **†2** *v.i.* & *t.* Take care (of or *of*, *that*, *to do*); take notice *of*. LME–M19. **†3** *v.i.* Take warning *by*. E16–E17. **†4** *v.t.* Make cautious. L16–E18.

1 SHAKES. *Macb.* Macbeth! Macbeth! Beware Macduff. MILTON I had bewar'd if I had foreseen. W. MORRIS Beware lest . . Thou tell'st the story of thy love unseen. H. ALLEN Someone who . . he felt was an enemy; a being to beware of. 2 SHAKES. *1 Hen. VI* Priest, beware your beard; I mean to tug it. AV *Exod.* 23:21 Behold, I send an Angel before thee. . . Beware of him, and obey his voice. R. W. EMERSON We beware to ask only for high things. 3 W. CAMDEN It is good to beware by other mens harmes. 4 DRYDEN Once warn'd is well bewar'd.

†bewed *v.t.* Infl. **-dd-**. Pa. t. & pple **bewedded, bewed**. OE–E18. [OE *beweddian*, f. as BE- + WED *v.*] Marry; unite closely *to*.

beweep /bɪˈwiːp/ *v. arch.* Pa. t. & pple **bewept** /bɪˈwɛpt/. [OE *bewēpan*, f. as BE- + WEEP *v.*] **1** *v.t.* Weep for or over; deplore; lament. OE. **2**

v.t. Wet or moisten (as) with tears. LME. †3 *v.i.* Weep. Only in LME.

bewest /bɪˈwɛst/ *adv.* & *prep.* Long *obs.* exc. *Sc.* [OE *be westan*, f. as BE- + *westan* (adv.) from the west.] †A *adv.* On or to the west. OE–L15. B *prep.* To the west of. OE.

bewet /ˈbjuːɪt/ *n.* Also **bewit**. L15. [App. f. an unrecorded AN or OFr. dim. of OFr. *buie* collar, bond, fetter, f. pop.L var. of L *boiae* (pl.) collar for the neck.] *Falconry.* A ring or slip of leather for attaching a bell to a hawk's leg.

†**bewet** *v.t.* Infl. **-tt-**. LME–L18. [BE- 1 + WET *v.*] Wet profusely.

†**bewhore** *v.t.* E–M17. [f. BE- 3 + WHORE *n.*] Call whore; make a whore of.
SHAKES. *Oth.* My lord hath so bewhor'd her, Thrown such . . heavy terms upon her.

Bewick /ˈbjuːɪk/ *n.* M19. [Thomas *Bewick* (1753–1828), Eng. engraver and naturalist.] *Bewick('s) swan*, a Eurasian race of the tundra swan, *Cygnus columbianus*, which breeds in Arctic regions of Siberia and winters in northern Europe and central Asia.

bewig /bɪˈwɪg/ *v.t.* Infl. **-gg-**. L18. [f. BE- 4 + WIG *n.*[3]] Provide or cover with a wig. Chiefly as *bewigged* ppl a.

bewilder /bɪˈwɪldə/ *v.t.* L17. [f. BE- 1 + WILDER *v.*] Lead astray, cause to lose the way; perplex; confuse; puzzle.
bewildered *a.* (*a*) led astray, perplexed, puzzled; (*b*) *transf.* pathless, confusingly tangled: L17. **bewilderingly** *adv.* in a bewildering manner, so as to bewilder M19. **bewilderment** *n.* (*a*) the condition of being led astray, perplexity, puzzlement; (*b*) *rare* a tangled confusion, an inextricable medley: E19.

bewit *n.* var. of BEWET *n.*

bewitch /bɪˈwɪtʃ/ *v.t.* ME. [f. BE- 1 + WITCH *v.*[1]] Subject to the (esp. malefic) influence of magic or witchcraft; cast a spell over; enchant, fascinate; charm.
bewitcher *n.* M16. **bewitchery** *n.* (*arch.*) bewitching influence or charm; bewitchment: M17. **bewitchingly** *adv.* charmingly, in a bewitching manner L17. **bewitchment** *n.* the act of bewitching; the ability to charm; the state of being bewitched: E17.

bewrap /bɪˈrap/ *v.t.* Long *rare*. Infl. **-pp-**. ME. [f. BE- 1 + WRAP *v.*] Wrap up, envelop, conceal.

bewray /bɪˈreɪ/ *v.*[1]*t.* Long *arch.* ME. [f. BE- 1 + WRAY *v.*] †1 Accuse, malign. Only in ME. †2 Expose (a person) by divulging his or her secrets etc.; reveal as the unknown doer of an act. ME–E17. 3 Divulge or reveal (a secret) prejudicially. LME. †4 *gen.* Make known, show, reveal. LME–E17. †5 Expose or betray (a fugitive *to* enemies or justice). M16–E17. 6 Reveal unintentionally, esp. the existence, presence, or true character of (a person or thing). M16. †7 = BETRAY 5. L16–M18.
bewrayer *n.* LME.

bewray *v.*[2] see BERAY.

bewritten /bɪˈrɪt(ə)n/ *ppl a.* L19. [Orig. pa. pple: see BE-, WRITE *v.*] Written about.

bey /beɪ/ *n.* L16. [Turk., mod. form of BEG *n.*[1]] The governor of a district or province in the Ottoman Empire. Also formerly used in Turkey and Egypt as a courtesy title.
beylik, **-lic** /ˈbeɪlɪk/ *n.* [Turk. *beylik*] the (area of) jurisdiction of a bey M18.

beyond /bɪˈjɒnd/ *adv.*, *prep.*, & *n.* [OE *beġ(e)ondan*, f. *be* BY *prep.* etc. + *ġ(e)ondan* f. Gmc base of YOND *prep.* & *adv.*] A *adv.* At or to the further side; further away. OE.

B *prep.* 1 At or on the further side of, at a more distant point than. OE. 2 To the further side of, so as to leave behind, further than. OE. 3 In addition to, besides, over and above; (in neg. contexts) apart from. LME. 4 Later than, past. LME. 5 Surpassing or exceeding in quality or quantity; superior to; more than. L15. 6 Outside the limit of; out of the reach, comprehension, or range of; not subject to. E16.

1 MILTON Both here and beyond the seas. J. RUSKIN Out of which rise the soft rounded slopes of mightier mountains, surge beyond surge. 2 KEATS His spirit pass'd beyond its golden bourn Into the noisy world. G. GREENE The water rose beyond my waist. M. FRAYN He felt unable to look beyond the prospect of small pleasures in the immediate future. 3 W. H. DIXON Beyond his labours as a preacher, he composed . . twenty-six books of controversy. S. RAVEN Beyond writing to his uncle about money he had made no effort to communicate with Baron's Lodge. 4 C. BRONTË We arrived . . about an hour and a half beyond our time. 5 MILTON Beyond the bliss of dreams. JOYCE The meal was prolonged beyond an hour and still my uncle did not come. 6 GOLDSMITH It was beyond one man's strength to remove it. E. O'NEILL Why Gordon should take such a fancy to that old sissy is beyond me. M. KEANE Complicated conversations requiring answers far beyond Mrs. Brock's limited knowledge of the language. W. BRONK Beyond the slightest doubt I find you right.

Phrases: **beyond a joke** outside the limits of what can be considered funny; serious. **beyond belief** unbelievable, incredible. *beyond measure*: see MEASURE *n.* *beyond one's grasp*: see GRASP *n.* *beyond price*: see PRICE *n.* *beyond question*: see QUESTION *n.* *beyond reproach*: see REPROACH *n.* *beyond sea(s)*: see SEA *n.* *beyond the black stump*: see STUMP *n.*[1] *beyond the sea(s)*: see SEA *n.* *beyond the veil*: see VEIL *n.* 3. **beyond words** (modifying an adj.) to an inexpressible degree, in the extreme. †**go beyond** *fig.* circumvent. †**look beyond** *fig.* (*rare*, Shakes.) misconstrue, misunderstand.

C *n.* Anywhere distant, distant places; a remote place or experience; *the* future life, *the* unknown. L16.
the back of beyond a very remote or out-of-the-way place.

bezant /ˈbɛz(ə)nt/ *n.* Also **byzant** /bɪˈzant/. ME. [OFr. *besant*, nom. *besanz*, f. L *Byzantius* (sc. *nummus* coin) adj.: see BYZANTIAN.] 1 *Hist.* A gold or silver coin, orig. minted at Byzantium (later Constantinople, the modern Istanbul), widely used in the currency of medieval Europe. ME. 2 *Her.* A gold roundel representing such a coin. L15.

bezantee *a.* var. of BEZANTY.

bez-antler /ˈbeɪantlə, ˈbeɪz-/ *n.* L16. [OFr. *besantoillier*, f. *bes-* twice + *antoillier* ANTLER.] = BAY *n.*[8]
Also **bez tine** *n.* M19.

bezanty /bɪˈzanti/ *a.* Also **bezantee**. E17. [OFr. *besanté*: see BEZANT, -Y[5].] *Her.* Charged with bezants.

bezel /ˈbɛz(ə)l/ *n.* & *v.* Also (esp. in sense A.1) **basil** /ˈbaz(ə)l, -zɪl/. L16. [OFr. (mod. *biseau*, *béseau*), of unkn. origin.] A *n.* 1 The groove and projecting lip holding a gem, watch-glass, etc.; the rim holding a cover of glass etc. L16. 2 The sloped edge of a chisel or other cutting tool. E17. 3 The oblique sides or faces of a cut gem. E19. B *v.* Infl. **-ll-**, ***-l-**. Grind or cut to a sloping edge; bevel. Now *rare*. L17.

bezesteen /ˈbɛzɪstiːn/ *n.* M17. [(Ult., perh. through Fr. or It., f.) Turk. *bezesten* (now *bedesten*) covered market for fine cloth and valuables, f. Pers. *bazistān*, f. *baz* (Turk. *bez*) f. Arab. *bazz* cloth + *-istān* suff. of place.] An exchange, bazaar, or market-place in the Middle East.

bezique /bɪˈziːk/ *n.* M19. [Fr. *bésigue*, also *bésy*, perh. f. Pers. *bāzīgar* acrobat, *bāzī* game.] A card-game for two like pinochle, played usu. with a double pack of sixty-four cards (from seven up to ace only); the combination in this game of queen of spades and jack of diamonds.

bezoar /ˈbiːzɔː, ˈbɛzəʊɑː/ *n.* L15. [Fr. *bézoard* (earlier *bezar*, *bezahar(d)*), Sp. *bezar*, mod.L *beza(h)ar*, ult. f. Arab. *bādizahr*, *bāzahr* f. Pers. *pādzahr* antidote, f. *pād* protecting (from) + *zahr* poison.] †1 A stone, a concretion. L15–M17. 2 A concretion with a hard nucleus found in the stomach or intestines of certain animals (chiefly ruminants), formerly believed to be antidotal. L16. †3 An antidote. Passing into fig. use of sense 2. L16–M18. †4 More fully *bezoar goat, antelope*. The wild goat of Persia (the best-known source of the concretion of sense 2). E17–L18.
bezoardic /bɛzəʊˈɑːdɪk/, †**-tic** *a.* & *n.* (*arch.*) [mod.L *bezoardicus*, *-ticus*] (*a*) *adj.* of or pertaining to a bezoar, antidotal; (*b*) an antidote: E17.

†**bezonian** *n.* L16–M19. [It. *bisogno*, Sp. *bisoño* need + -AN, -IAN: see BESOGNIO.] = BESOGNIO.

bezzle /ˈbɛz(ə)l/ *v.* Long *obs.* exc. *dial.* LME. [AN *besiler*, *beseler*, OFr. *besillier*, Prov. *besillar* maltreat, ravage, of unkn. origin: see EMBEZZLE.] †1 *v.t.* Plunder or spoil; make away with (the property of another). LME–E18. 2 *v.i.* & *t.* Consume (drink) to excess; guzzle; 'booze'. E17.

bhajan /ˈbʌdʒ(ə)n/ *n.* E20. [Skt *bhajana*.] *Hinduism.* A devotional song.

bhakta /ˈbʌktə/ *n.* E19. [Skt.] *Hinduism.* A religious devotee; a worshipper, a believer.

bhakti /ˈbʌkti/ *n.* M19. [Skt.] *Hinduism.* Religious devotion or piety as a means of salvation.
bhakti-marga /-mɑːgə/ [*mārga* path] the way to salvation through religious devotion or faith.

bhang /baŋ/ *n.* Also †**bang**. L16. [(Port. *bangue* f.) Pers. & Urdu *bang*, later assim. to Hind. *bhāṅ* f. Skt *bhaṅgā*.] = CANNABIS 2. Also (now *rare*) = CANNABIS 1, *Indian hemp* (a) s.v. INDIAN *a.*

bhangra /ˈbɑːŋgrə/ *n.* M20. [Panjabi *bhāṅgrā*.] 1 A type of Punjabi folk-dance for men. M20. 2 A style of popular (esp. dance) music combining Punjabi folk music with rock and roll or disco music. L20.

bharal /ˈbʌr(ə)l/ *n.* Also **burhel**. M19. [Hind.] The wild or blue sheep of the Himalayas and Tibet, *Pseudois nayaur*.

Bheel *n.* var. of BHIL.

bheesty *n.* var. of BHISTI.

bhikkhu /ˈbɪkuː/ *n.* Also ***bhikku***. M19. [Pali *bhikkhu* f. as next.] A Buddhist mendicant or religious devotee. Cf. next.

bhikshu /ˈbɪkʃuː/ *n.* Pl. *-s*, same. E19. [Skt *bhikṣu* beggar, f. *bhikṣ* beg.] A brahminical or Buddhist mendicant or religious devotee. Cf. prec.

Bhil /biːl/ *n.* & *a.* Also **Bheel**. E19. [Hind. *Bhīl* f. Skt *Bhilla*.] A member of, of or pertaining to, a central Indian people.

bhisti /ˈbiːsti/ *n.* Also **b(h)eesty**. L18. [Urdu *bhīštī* f. Pers. *bihištī* a person of paradise.] In the Indian subcontinent: a servant who supplies an establishment with water.

bhoodan /buːˈdɑːn/ *n.* M20. [Skt *bhūdana*, f. *bhū* earth, land + *dāna* gift.] In India, the giving by landowners of land to the poor.

bhoosa /ˈbuːsə/ *n.* Also **bhoos**, **bhusa**. E19. [Hind. *bhūs*, *bhūsā*.] In the Indian subcontinent: husks and broken straw, used as food for cattle.

Bhora *n.* var. of BORA *n.*[1]

†**Bhotanese** *n.* & *a.* var. of BHUTANESE.

Bhotia /ˈbəʊtɪə/ *n.* & *a.* Also **Bhutia** /ˈbuːtɪə/ & other vars. E19. [Skt *Bhoṭīya* Tibetan, f. *Bhoṭa* Tibet.] (A native or inhabitant) of the region including Tibet and Bhutan; (of) the language of this region.

bhoy /bəˈhɔɪ/ *n.* *colloq.* Also **b'hoy**. M19. [Repr. a supposed Ir. pronunc. of BOY *n.*] A lively or spirited fellow.

bhusa *n.* var. of BHOOSA.

bhut /buːt/ *n.* Also ***bhuta*** /ˈbuːtə/. L18. [Skt *bhūt(a)* lit. 'a being'.] In the Indian subcontinent: a spirit; a demon, a goblin.

Bhutanese /buːtəˈniːz/ *n.* & *a.* Also †**Bhot-**. Pl. of n. same. M19. [f. *Bhutan* (see below) + -ESE.] (A native or inhabitant) of Bhutan, a country in the SE Himalayas.

Bhutia *n.* & *a.* var. of BHOTIA.

bi /bʌɪ/ *a.* & *n.* *slang.* M20. [Abbrev.] = BISEXUAL.

bi- /bʌɪ/ *pref.* Often **bin-** /bɪn/ bef. a vowel (cf. BIS-). [L (earlier *dui-*, cogn. w. Gk DI-[2], Skt *dvi-*) = twice, doubly, having two, two-.] Used in wds adopted f. L and in Eng. formations modelled on these, and as a productive pref., forming (*a*) adjs. (and corresp. advs. etc.) f. adjs. or advs., w. the senses 'having or involving two', as *bicoloured*, *bilateral*, *bimanual*, *binaural*, 'doubly, in two ways', as *biconcave*, *bipyramidal*, (*Bot.* & *Zool.*) 'twice over, divided into similarly divided parts', as *bipinnate*, 'lasting for two, appearing every two', or (w. resulting ambiguity) 'appearing twice in', as *biannual*, *biennial*, *bimonthly*, and 'joining two', as *biparietal*; (*b*) ns. f. ns. w. the sense 'double, thing having two', as *bilayer*, *biplane*; in *Chem.* forming names of salts having a doubled proportion of acid to base radicals, as *bicarbonate*, *binoxalate*, *bisulphate*, or of molecules formed from two identical radicals, as *biphenyl*.

Biafran /bɪ'afrən, bʌɪ-/ *a.* & *n.* M20. [f. *Biafra* (see below) + -AN.] (A native or inhabitant) of Biafra, an ancient region of W. Africa, which seceded from federal Nigeria from 1967 to 1970.

bianco sopra bianco /'bjaŋko ˌsopra 'bjaŋko/ *n. phr.* L19. [It., lit. 'white upon white'.] A form of white decoration upon white porcelain. Cf. earlier SOPRA BIANCO.

biannual /bʌɪ'anjʊəl/ *a.* & *n.* L19. [f. BI- + ANNUAL.] A *adj.* Appearing, occurring, etc., twice a year. L19. B *n.* = BIENNIAL. L19.

biannually *adv.* L19.

bias /'bʌɪəs/ *a.*, *n.*, & *adv.* M16. [(O)Fr. *biais* f. Prov., perh. irreg. f. Gk *epikarsios* oblique, athwart.] A *adj.* †1 a Slanting, oblique. M16–L17. b *Dressmaking* etc. Cut obliquely across the warp. E19. †2 Bulging like the bias fashioned into a bowl. *rare* (Shakes.). Only in E17.

B *n.* 1 An oblique or slanting line. *obs.* exc. *Dressmaking* etc., an edge cut obliquely across the warp. M16. 2 *Bowls*. The eccentric form given to a bowl; the swerving course in which this makes it run; the type of impetus effecting such a course. L16. 3 An inclination, a propensity, a predisposition, (*towards*); prejudice. L16. †4 A set course. L16–L18. 5 A directing influence. L16. †6 *Cricket*. The turning of the course of a ball from leg to off side after pitching. M19–E20. 7 *Statistics*. (A) systematic distortion of a result, arising from a neglected factor. E20. 8 A steady voltage, magnetic field, etc., applied to an electronic system or device to establish its operation over a particular range, esp. used for minimizing distortion in tape recording. E20.

1 **cut on the bias** cut obliquely across the warp. 2 SHAKES. *Tam. Shr.* Well, forward, forward! thus the bowl should run, And not unluckily against the bias. HAZLITT The skittle-player bends his body to give a bias to the bowl he has already delivered from his hand. A. W. HARE Just as a bowl with a bias, if you try to send it straight, the longer it rolls, the further it will swerve. 3 C. S. FORESTER Choosing his words with the greatest possible care, . . so that they could be read . . without conveying an impression of bias. W. J. ONG Made up . . of images (with a bias towards visual images). J. BARTH Republicans with a pronounced anti-liberal bias. 4 D. HUME Superstition, which throws the Government off its bias. 5 GLADSTONE He could not possibly be under any bias.

C *adv.* 1 Obliquely. *obs.* exc. *Dressmaking* etc., obliquely across the warp. L16. †2 *fig.* Off the straight, awry. E–M17.

Comb.: **bias binding** *Dressmaking* etc., a narrow strip of cloth cut on the bias and used for binding.

biaswise *adv.* (now *rare*) obliquely M16.

bias /'bʌɪəs/ *v.* Infl. **-s-**, **-ss-**. E17. [f. prec.] 1 *v.t.* Give a bias to (a bowl etc.); cause to swerve from a course (*lit.* & *fig.*); influence (usu. unfairly), inspire with prejudice. E17. †2 *v.i.* Incline to one side, swerve from the right course. Only in 17. 3 *v.t.* Apply a steady voltage, magnetic field, etc., to: see BIAS *n.* 8. E20.

bias(s)ed *ppl a.* having a bias; influenced, prejudiced: E17.

biathlon /bʌɪ'aθlɒn, -lən/ *n.* M20. [f. BI- + Gk *athlon* contest, after PENTATHLON.] An athletic or sporting contest in which competitors engage in two events, skiing and shooting.

biathlete *n.* a competitor in a biathlon L20.

biauricular /bʌɪɔː'rɪkjʊlə/ *a.* M19. [f. BI- + AURICULAR *a.*] Having two auricles; pertaining to both auricles (of the ears).

biaxial /bʌɪ'aksɪəl/ *a.* M19. [f. BI- + AXIAL.] Having or pertaining to two axes; *esp.* of crystals: having two optic axes.

biaxially *adv.* L19.

bib /bɪb/ *n.* L16. [Prob. f. the vb.] 1 A cloth etc. placed under a child's chin to keep his or her dress-front clean; the top front part of an apron, overall, etc. L16. b A patch resembling a bib under the bill of a bird. M19. 2 An edible marine fish, *Trisopterus luscus*, of the cod family, having a distensible membrane able to cover its head. Also called *pout(ing)*. L17.

1 **best bib and tucker** best clothes.

bib /bɪb/ *v.t.* & *i. arch.* Infl. **-bb-**. LME. [Prob. f. L *bibere* to drink.] Drink much or often; tipple.

bi'bation *n.* tippling M19. **bibber** *n.* a tippler (freq. as 2nd elem. of comb., as *wine-bibber*) M16.

bibacious /bɪ'beɪʃəs/ *a.* L17. [f. L *bibax*, *-acis* + -OUS: see -ACIOUS.] Given to drinking, bibulous.

bibacity /bɪ'basɪti/ *n.* addiction to drinking, tippling L16.

bibasic /bʌɪ'beɪsɪk/ *a.* M19. [f. BI- + BASIC *a.*] *Chem.* Dibasic.

bibb /bɪb/ *n.* L18. [Var. of BIB *n.*] *Naut.* A bracket under the trestle-tree of a mast.

bibble /'bɪb(ə)l/ *v.* E16. [f. BIB *v.* + -LE[3].] 1 *v.i.* & *t.* Keep drinking; drink, tipple. E16. 2 *v.i.* Dabble with the bill as a duck. M16.

bibbler *n.* a tippler M16.

bibble-babble /'bɪb(ə)lbab(ə)l/ *n.* M16. [Redupl. of BABBLE *n.*: cf. *tittle-tattle* etc.] Idle talk, prating.

bib-cock /'bɪbkɒk/ *n.* L18. [Perh. f. BIB *n.* + COCK *n.*[1]] A tap with a bent nozzle fixed at the end of a pipe.

bibelot /'bɪbələʊ; *foreign* biblo (*pl. same*)/ *n.* L19. [Fr., f. redupl. of *bel* beautiful: cf. BAUBLE.] A small curio or artistic trinket.

biberon /bibrɔ̃/ *n.* Pl. pronounced same. M19. [Fr.] A drinking-vessel with elongated spout, formerly used by travellers, invalids, and children.

bibi /'biːbiː/ *n.* Also **beebee**. E19. [Urdu *bībī* f. Pers.] In the Indian subcontinent: a mistress of a household; a non-European female consort.

bibira *n.* var. of BEBEERU.

bibition /bɪ'bɪʃ(ə)n/ *n.* L15. [Late L *bibitio(n-)*, f. *bibere* to drink: see -ITION.] (A bout of) drinking.

Bible /'bʌɪb(ə)l/ *n.* Also **b-**. ME. [(O)Fr. *bible* = Prov. *bibla*, Sp. *biblia*, It. *bibbia*, f. eccl.L *biblia* neut. pl. (taken as fem. sing.), f. Gk (*ta*) *biblia* 'the books'. The Gk sing. *biblion*, dim. of *biblos*, *bublos* papyrus, scroll, etc. (of Semitic origin) lost its dim. sense and became the ordinary wd for 'book' before its application to the Judaeo-Christian sacred writings.] 1 *The* Scriptures; *spec.* (*a*) *the* Christian sacred writings collected as the Old and New Testaments (formerly & *dial.* also occas. the Old Testament alone); a copy of these; (with specifying wd or contextually) (a copy of) a particular edition of these; (*b*) the Hebrew Scriptures; a copy of these. ME. 2 The sacred writings of some other religion. LME. 3 A large or lengthy book; a tome. Now *rare*. LME. 4 *gen.* An authoritative textbook or indispensable work. E19.

1 *Bishops' Bible*: see BISHOP *n.* *Breeches Bible*: see BREECH *n.* *Great Bible*: see GREAT *a.* *Printers' Bible*: see PRINTER. *Vinegar Bible*: see VINEGAR. *Wicked Bible*: see WICKED *a.*[1] I.

Comb.: **Bible-banger**, **-basher**, **-pounder**, **-puncher**, **-thumper** *slang* a person who expounds or follows the Bible in an aggressive way, *esp.* an evangelical member of the clergy; **Bible-banging**, **-bashing**, **-pounding**, **-punching**, **-thumping** *vbl ns.* & *ppl adjs.* (*slang*) aggressively expounding or following the Bible; **Bible Belt** an area of the central and southern US noted for its puritanical and fundamentalist Christian beliefs; **Bible-box** a large flat-lidded box, esp. of the 17th cent., able to hold a family Bible; **Bible class** a class for the study of the Bible; **Bible clerk** a student of the Bible; *spec.* a student at some of the colleges at Oxford having the duty of reading the lessons in chapel and saying grace in Hall; **Bible Christian** (*a*) a Christian according to scriptural standard; (*b*) *Hist.* a member of a 19th-cent. Methodist sect founded in SW England by William O. Bryan; **Bible oath** a solemn oath taken on the Bible; *Bible-pounder*, *-ing*, etc.: see *Bible-banger*, *-banging* above.

biblist /'bɪblɪst/ *n.* a person who makes the Bible the sole rule of faith; a biblical student: M16.

biblical /'bɪblɪk(ə)l/ *a.* L18. [f. med.L *biblicus*, f. *biblia* (see prec.) + -AL[1].] Of, pertaining to, or contained in the Bible; resembling the language of the Bible.

biblic *a.* (now *rare*) = BIBLICAL L17. **biblically** *adv.* M19.

biblio- /'bɪblɪəʊ/ *comb. form.* [Gk stem & comb. form of *biblion* book: see -O-.] Used in wds adopted f. Gk and in Eng. formations modelled on these, w. the sense 'of or relating to books or a book'.

biblioklept /-klɛpt/ *n.* [Gk *kleptēs* thief] a book-thief L19. **bibli'olatry** *n.* extravagant admiration of a book or for books M18. **bibli'ology** *n.* the branch of knowledge that deals with books, book-lore; bibliography: E19. **bibliomancy** *n.* divination by books; *spec.* divination by verses of the Bible: M18. **bibliomane** *n.* = BIBLIOMANIAC *n.* E19. **biblio'mania** *n.* a passion for the collecting and possessing of books M18. **biblio'maniac** *n.* & *a.* (a person) affected with or given to bibliomania E19. **biblioma'niacal** *a.* (of a) bibliomaniac E19. **biblio'metric** *a.* of or pertaining to bibliometrics L20. **biblio'metrics** *n.* statistics as applied in bibliography; statistical analysis of books, articles, or other publications: M20. **bibliopegy** /-'ɒpədʒi/ *n.* [Gk *-pēgia*, f. *pēgnunai* fix] bookbinding as a fine art L19. **biblio'therapy** *n.* the use of reading matter for therapeutic purposes E20. **biblio'thetic** *a.* relating to the placing and arrangement of books on the shelves of a library L19.

bibliograph /'bɪblɪəgrɑːf/ *n. rare.* E19. [Prob. f. Fr. *bibliographe*, f. Gk *bibliographos*: see BIBLIOGRAPHER.] A bibliographer.

bibliograph /'bɪblɪəgrɑːf/ *v.t.* M20. [Back-form. f. BIBLIOGRAPHY.] Compile a bibliography of; provide (a scholarly work) with a bibliography.

bibliographer /bɪblɪ'ɒgrəfə/ *n.* M17. [f. Gk *bibliographos* (f. as BIBLIO- + -GRAPH) + -ER[1].] †1 A writer of books; a copyist. M17–M18. 2 A practitioner of bibliography. L18.

bibliography /bɪblɪ'ɒgrəfi/ *n.* L17. [Fr. *bibliographie* or mod.L *bibliographia* f. Gk: see BIBLIO-, -GRAPHY.] †1 The writing of books. Only in L17. 2 The history or systematic description of books, their authorship, printing, publication, editions, etc. E19. b A book containing such details, esp. of the books on a particular subject. E19. 3 A list of books of a particular author, printer, country, etc.; a list of works consulted in a scholarly work; a reading list. E19.

biblio'graphic *a.* of or pertaining to bibliography E19. **biblio'graphical** *a.* = BIBLIOGRAPHIC L17. **biblio'graphically** *adv.* E19. **bibliographize** *v.t.* compile a bibliography of E19.

bibliophile /'bɪblɪəfʌɪl/ *n.* Also **-phil** /-fɪl/. E19. [Fr.: see BIBLIO-, -PHILE.] A lover of books; a book-collector.

bibliophilic /-'fɪlɪk/ *a.* of or pertaining to bibliophiles or bibliophily L19. **bibli'ophily** *n.* love of books L19.

bibliopole /'bɪblɪəpəʊl/ *n.* L18. [L *bibliopola* f. Gk *bibliopōlēs*, f. *biblion* book + *pōlēs* seller.] A dealer in (esp. rare) books.

biblio'polic *a.* E19. **bibli'opolist** *n.* = BIBLIOPOLE M16. **bibli'opoly** *n.* bookselling M19.

bibliotheca /bɪblɪə'θiːkə/ *n.* OE. [L f. Gk *bibliothēkē* library, f. *biblion* book + *thēkē* repository.] †1 The Bible. Only in OE. 2 A collection of books or treatises; a library; a bibliographer's catalogue. E19.

bibli'othec *n.* & *a.* (*a*) *n.* a librarian; (*b*) *adj.* belonging to a library or librarian: M17. **biblio'thecal** *a.* belonging to a library E19.

bibliothecary /bɪblɪ'ɒθɪk(ə)ri/ *n.* & *a.* L16. [L *bibliothecarius*, *-um*, f. as prec. + -ARY[1].] A *n.* †1 A library. Only in L16. 2 A librarian. E17. B *adj.* Of or belonging to a library or librarian. E19.

bibliothe'carial *a.* = BIBLIOTHECARY *a.* L19. **bibliothe'carian** *a.* & *n.* = BIBLIOTHECARY L17.

bibliothèque /bibliɔtɛk/ *n.* Pl. pronounced same. M16. [Fr. f. as BIBLIOTHECA.] A library.

¶Formerly naturalized, but now treated as French.

biblus /'bɪbləs/ *n.* Also **-os**. M17. [(L f.) Gk *biblos*.] (The inner bark of) the papyrus.

bibulous /'bɪbjʊləs/ *a.* L17. [f. L *bibulus* freely or readily drinking, f. *bibere* to drink: see -ULOUS.] 1 Absorbent of moisture. L17. 2 Relating to drink. E19. 3 Given to drinking alcoholic liquors. M19.

bibu'losity *n.* (fondness for) tippling E20. **bibulously** *adv.* M19. **bibulousness** *n.* M19.

bicameral /bʌɪ'kam(ə)r(ə)l/ *a.* M19. [f. BI- + L CAMERA chamber + -AL[1].] Having two (legislative) chambers; having two compartments.

bicameralism *n.* advocacy or adoption of a bicameral system M20.

bicarb /bʌɪˈkɑːb/ *n. colloq.* E20. [Abbrev. of next.] Sodium bicarbonate (see next).

bicarbonate /bʌɪˈkɑːbəneɪt/ *n.* E19. [f. BI- + CARBONATE *n.*] *Chem.* A salt containing the anion HCO_3^-, i.e. containing double the proportion of carbon dioxide present in a carbonate. Pop. *spec.* (in full *sodium bicarbonate, bicarbonate of soda*) the sodium salt $NaHCO_3$, used as an antacid and in baking powder.

bice /bʌɪs/ *a.* & *n.* ME. [(O)Fr. *bis* dark grey = Prov. *bis*, It. *bigio*, of unkn. origin.] †**A** *adj.* Brownish grey, dark grey. Only in ME. **B** *n.* **1** More fully *blue bice*. A shade of blue duller than ultramarine or azure. LME. **2** A pigment of this colour made from basic copper carbonate or smalt; (more fully *green bice*) a green pigment similarly made. M16.

¶From the Fr. *azur bis* 'dark blue' and *vert bis* 'dark green' the sense of *bice* was transferred in Eng. to the pigments and colours they represented.

bicentenary /bʌɪsɛnˈtiːnəri, -ˈtɛn-, bʌɪˈsɛntɪn-/ *a.* & *n.* M19. [f. BI- + CENTENARY.] (The occasion or a celebration) of a two-hundredth anniversary.

bicentennial /bʌɪsɛnˈtɛnɪəl/ *a.* & *n.* L19. [f. BI- + CENTENNIAL.] **A** *adj.* Lasting or occurring every two hundred years; of or pertaining to a two-hundredth anniversary. L19. **B** *n.* = BICENTENARY *n.* L19.

bicephalous /bʌɪˈsɛf(ə)ləs, -ˈkɛf-/ *a.* E19. [f. BI- + Gk *kephalē* head + -OUS.] Two-headed.

biceps /ˈbʌɪsɛps/ *a.* & *n.* M17. [L, f. BI- + *-ceps*, *caput* head.] **A** *adj.* Having two heads or summits. Now only *spec.* of a muscle: having two heads or points of attachments at one end. M17. **B** *n.* Pl. same. A biceps muscle; *esp.* a flexor muscle of the front of the upper arm (often taken as the type of physical strength) or of the thigh. M17.

bicep *n.* (*non-standard*) = BICEPS *n.* M20.

bichromate /bʌɪˈkrəʊmeɪt/ *n.* M19. [f. BI- + CHROMATE.] *Chem.* = DICHROMATE *n.*[1]

bichrome /ˈbʌɪkrəʊm/ *n.* & *a.* E20. [f. BI- + Gk *khrōma* colour.] (A design etc.) having two colours.

bicipital /bʌɪˈsɪpɪt(ə)l/ *a.* M17. [f. L *bicipit-*, BICEPS + -AL[1].] **1** = BICEPS *a.* M17. **2** Of or pertaining to a biceps muscle. M19.

bick /bɪk/ *n.* L19. [Abbrev. of BICKERN or its var. *bick-iron*.] = BICKERN.

bicker /ˈbɪkə/ *n.*[1] ME. [Origin unkn.: cf. BICKER *v.*] **1** Skirmishing; a skirmish; an encounter with missiles. *obs.* exc. *Sc.*, a street or school fight with stones etc. ME. **2** A quarrel; an angry altercation. ME. **3** A short rapid run (cf. BICKER *v.* 5b). *Sc.* L18. **4** Noise as of contention. L19.

bicker /bɪkə/ *n.*[2] *Sc.* LME. [Var. of BEAKER.] A (wooden) bowl or dish for containing liquor; formerly a drinking cup.

bicker /ˈbɪkə/ *v.* ME. [Origin unkn.: cf. BICKER *n.*[1]] **1** *v.i.* Skirmish, fight. ME. **2** *v.t.* Attack with repeated strokes. Long *obs.* exc. *dial.* ME. **3** *v.i.* Quarrel, wrangle, squabble. L15. **4** *v.i.* Flash, gleam, quiver, glisten. *poet.* M17. **5** *v.i.* Make any repeated noisy action, as the showering of blows, the flowing of a stream over a stony channel, the pattering of rain, etc. M18. **b** Make a short rapid run (describing the pounding of the feet). *Sc.* L18.

1 C. KINGSLEY Slaughtered bickering for some petty town. 3 E. M. FORSTER He had .. squabbled with his sister, and bickered with his mother. 4 SHELLEY The restless wheels .. Whose flashing spokes Bicker and burn. 5 COLERIDGE Against the glass The rain did beat and bicker. TENNYSON And sparkle out among the fern, To bicker down a valley.

bickering *n.* the action of the vb; a skirmish; a quarrel, a squabble: ME. **bickerment** *n.* bickering L16.

bickern /ˈbɪkən/ *n.* Also (by false etym.) **beak-iron** /ˈbiːkʌɪən/, **bick-iron** /ˈbɪkʌɪən/. M17. [Alt. of BICORN *n.* 1, or f. its source Fr. *bigorne.*] An anvil with two projecting taper ends; one such taper end of an anvil.

bicky /ˈbɪki/ *n. nursery* or *joc.* Also **bikky**. E20. [Dim. of BISCUIT: see -Y[6].] A biscuit.

bicolour /ˈbʌɪkʌlə/ *a.* & *n.* Also ***-color.** L19. [L *bicolor* or Fr. *bicolore* adj.: see BI-, COLOUR *n.*] (A blossom or animal) of two colours.

bicoloured /ˈbʌɪkʌləd/ *a.* Also ***-color-.** M19. [f. BI- + COLOURED *a.*] Of two colours.

biconcave /bʌɪˈkɒnkeɪv/ *a.* M19. [f. BI- + CONCAVE *a.*] Concave on both sides.

biconditional /bʌɪkənˈdɪʃ(ə)n(ə)l/ *n.* M20. [f. BI- + CONDITIONAL *a.*] *Logic.* The relation between two propositions when one is true only if the other is true, and false if the other is false, represented by the logical operator 'if and only if'.

bicone /ˈbʌɪkəʊn/ *n.* E20. [f. BI- + CONE *n.*] An object, esp. a bead, of the form of two cones placed base to base.

biconical /bʌɪˈkɒnɪk(ə)l/ *a.* L19. [f. BI- + CONICAL.] Of the shape of a bicone.

biconvex /bʌɪˈkɒnvɛks/ *a.* M19. [f. BI- + CONVEX *a.*] Convex on both sides.

bicorn /ˈbʌɪkɔːn/ *n.* & *a.* LME. [(Fr. *bigorne* (in sense A.1) f. Prov. *bigorna* f.) L *bicornis* two-horned, two-pronged, f. BI- + *cornu* horn.] **A** *n.* †**1** = BICKERN. LME–M18. **2** An animal with two horns. LME. **B** *adj.* Having two horns or hornlike processes. M19.

bicorned *a.* = BICORN *a.* E17. **bi'cornous** *a.* = BICORN *a.* M17.

bicultural /bʌɪˈkʌltʃ(ə)r(ə)l/ *a.* M20. [f. BI- + CULTURAL.] Having or combining two cultures.

biculturalism *n.* M20.

bicuspid /bʌɪˈkʌspɪd/ *a.* & *n.* M19. [f. BI- + L *cuspid-*, *-is* CUSP: see -ID[2].] **A** *adj.* Having two cusps or points. M19.

bicuspid valve the mitral valve of the heart.

B *n.* A human premolar tooth. M19.

bicycle /ˈbʌɪsɪk(ə)l/ *n.* & *v.* M19. [f. BI- + Gk *kuklos* circle, wheel, CYCLE *n.*] **A** *n.* A vehicle having two wheels turned by pedalling, typically with handlebars at the front and a seat or saddle for the rider. M19.

exercise bicycle: see EXERCISE *n.* *motor bicycle*: see MOTOR *n.* & *a.* *safety bicycle*: see SAFETY *n.* & *a.* *stationary bicycle*: see STATIONARY *a.*

Comb.: **bicycle chain** a chain which transmits the driving power from the pedals of a bicycle to its rear wheel (also used as a weapon in street fighting); **bicycle clip** a clip used to confine a cyclist's trouser-leg at the ankle; **bicycle lizard** = RACEHORSE *lizard*; **bicycle moto-cross** bicycle racing on a dirt track (abbrev. *BMX*); **bicycle pump** a portable pump for inflating the tyres of bicycles; **bicycle-rickshaw** a rickshaw pulled by a person on a bicycle.

B *v.i.* Ride on a bicycle. M19.

bicycler *n.* = BICYCLIST M19. **bicyclist** *n.* a person who rides a bicycle, a cyclist L19.

bicyclic /bʌɪˈsʌɪklɪk, -ˈsɪk-/ *a.* L19. [f. BI- + Gk *kuklos* circle + -IC.] Having two circles or rings; *esp.* in *Chem.*, (composed of molecules) with two usu. fused rings of atoms.

bid /bɪd/ *n.* L18. [f. the vb.] **1** The offer of a price, esp. at an auction; an offer made at a stated price, a tender. L18. **2** *Cards.* A proposal to win a specified minimum number of tricks (in Bridge, the number in excess of six) or points, usu. with a specified trump-suit or in no-trumps; a player's turn to bid. L19. **3** *fig.* An attempt to obtain something; a try, an effort. L19.

3 *Punch* Britain's Bid for War-Plane Supremacy. J. VAN DRUTEN That's not a bid for pity, it's just telling you why I feel this way. **make a bid for** try to secure.

Comb.: **bid price** the price at which a market-maker or institution, esp. a unit trust, will buy back shares or units (cf. *offer price* s.v. OFFER *n.*).

bid /bɪd/ *v.* Pa. t. & pple **bid**; pres. pple **bidding**; alternative forms (*obs.* in sense 7, not used in sense 8): pa. t. **bade** /bad, beɪd/, †**bad**; pa. pple **bidden** /ˈbɪd(ə)n/. OE. [Combining two vbs: (i) OE *biddan* (pa. t. *bæd*, *bǣdon*, pa. pple *beden*) ask, entreat, demand = OFris. *bidda*, *bidia*, OS *biddian*, MDu. *bidden*, OHG, G *bitten*, ON *biðja*, Goth. *bidjan* f. Gmc, f. base repr. by OE *ġebed* prayer, BEAD *n.*; (ii) OE *bēodan* (pa. t. *bēad*, *budon*, pa. pple *boden*) offer, proclaim, announce, command, decree = OFris. *biada*, OS *biodan*, (M)Du. *bieden*, OHG *biotan* (G *bieten*), ON *bjóða*, Goth. *biudan* f. IE.] **I** Senses chiefly from OE *biddan*. **1** *v.t.* & *i.* Ask pressingly, beg, entreat, pray. Long *obs.* exc. in *bid a bead* (see BEAD *n.* 1), *bidding-prayer* (see BIDDING *n.*), etc. (which are now usu. understood in other senses of the vb). OE. **2** *v.t.* Command, enjoin, order, tell. (Foll. by inf., †cl.) Now *literary* or *dial.* OE. **3** *v.t.* Ask to come, invite. *arch.* & *dial.* ME. **4** *v.t.* Say, express, *welcome*, *farewell*, *good morning*, etc., (to). (Orig. w. some sense of invocation or wishing.) ME.

2 E. A. FREEMAN The two Earls were .. bidden to be diligent. L. M. MONTGOMERY Just you go and do as I bid you. W. H. AUDEN Good Captain, bid the drums be silent. 3 J. BARET I was bidde to an other place to dinner. AV *Zeph.* 1:7 He hath bid his ghests. TENNYSON I made a feast; I bad him come.

II Senses chiefly from OE *bēodan*. **5** *v.t.* Proclaim, declare, announce. *arch.* OE. **6** *v.t.* Offer (esp. as a challenge). *obs.* exc. in *bid defiance* and in spec. senses. OE. **b** *v.i. bid fair*, offer a reasonable prospect (*for*), seem likely (*to do*). M17. **7** *v.t.* Offer (a certain price, *for*). ME. **b** *v.i.* Offer a price (*for*); make an offer at a stated price, make a tender; *fig.* try (*for*, *to do*). E17. **8** *Cards.* **a** *v.i.* Make a bid. L19. **b** *v.t.* Make a bid of (a specified number), in (a specified suit), or as the holder of (a given hand). L19.

5 POPE The herald .. To bid the banquet interrupts their play. SOUTHEY At this late hour, When even I shall bid a truce to thought. 6 T. FULLER Whom he bade battle, and got the day. *bid base*: see BASE *n.*[2] 7 S. JOHNSON [They] bade her half the price she asked. OED Who bids five shillings for this lot? **b** R. B. SHERIDAN I stood a chance of .. being knocked down without being bid for. G. B. SHAW We all bid for admiration without the least intention of earning it. E. HUXLEY A paunchy Jew tries to auction sheets and bedspreads; no one bids. **bid against** compete with in bidding. **bid up** raise in price by successive bids. **8** R. DAHL The girl badly overestimated her partner's hand and bid six spades. *fig.*: A. J. P. TAYLOR In trying to remain a World Power in all spheres, the British people .. were bidding above their strength.

Comb.: †**bid-ale** an entertainment or celebration to which a general invitation was given; †**bidstand** a highwayman.

bidarka /bʌɪˈdɑːkə/ *n.* E19. [Russ. *baĭdarka*, pl. *-ki*, dim. of *baĭdara* an umiak.] In Alaska and adjacent regions: a portable canoe for one or more persons; a kayak.

biddable /ˈbɪdəb(ə)l/ *a.* L18. [f. BID *v.* + -ABLE.] **1** Ready to do what is bidden; obedient, docile. L18. **2** *Cards.* Of a hand: strong enough to warrant a bid. Of (cards held in) a suit: strong enough to warrant a bid in that suit. Of a contract: that can be the result of normal bidding. L19.

bidda'bility *n.* obedience M20.

biddance /ˈbɪd(ə)ns/ *n.* E19. [f. BID *v.* + -ANCE.] Bidding, invitation.

bidden *v.* see BID *v.*

bidder /ˈbɪdə/ *n.* ME. [f. BID *v.* + -ER[1].] A person who bids, esp. at an auction or at cards.

biddery *n.* var. of BIDRI.

bidding /ˈbɪdɪŋ/ *n.* ME. [f. BID *v.* + -ING[1].] **1** *gen.* The action of BID *v.* ME. **2** The offering or an offer of a price for an article; *collect.* the offers at an auction. ME. **3** A command, an order. Usu. *the bidding of* or *someone's bidding*. ME. **4** An invitation, a summons. E19. **5** *Cards.* The act or process of making a bid or bids; the bid or bids made. L19.

Phrases: †**bidding of prayers** praying of prayers; (later understood as) directing or enjoining of prayers. *force the bidding*: see FORCE *v.*[1]

Comb.: **bidding-prayer** a prayer inviting the congregation to join in, now usu. a group of intercessionary prayers.

biddy /ˈbɪdi/ *n.*[1] E17. [Origin unkn.: cf. CHICKABIDDY. Sense 2 prob. infl. by next; sense 3 perh. a different wd.] **1** A chicken; a fowl. *obs.* exc. *dial.* E17. **2** A woman. Usu. somewhat *derog.* L18. **3** In full *red biddy*. A drink consisting of methylated spirits and cheap red wine; inferior red wine. E20.

biddy /ˈbɪdi/ *n.*[2] Chiefly *US.* M19. [f. *Biddy*

familiar form of female forename *Bridget*.] An Irish maidservant.

biddy-bid /ˈbɪdɪbɪd/ *n. NZ.* Also **biddy-biddy, bidibidi**, /-bɪdi/. M19. [Alt. of Maori PIRIPIRI.] (The bur of) the piripiri.

bide /bʌɪd/ *v.* Exc. as in sense 5 now *arch.* & *dial.* [OE *bīdan* = OS *bīdan*, OHG *bītan*, ON *bíða*, Goth. *beidan*, f. Gmc.] **I** *v.i.* **1** Remain in expectation; wait. OE. **2** Remain or continue *in* some state or action. OE. **3** Stay, esp. when others go. Of a thing: remain, be left. OE. **4** Remain in residence; dwell. ME.
2 bide by stand firm by, adhere to.
II *v.t.* **5** Wait for, await. *obs.* exc. in *bide one's time*, await one's opportunity. OE. **6** Await in resistance, face, encounter; = ABIDE 6. ME. †**7** Endure, suffer, bear; = ABIDE 7. ME–E19. **8** Tolerate, put up with; = ABIDE 9. ME.

bident /ˈbʌɪd(ə)nt/ *n.* L17. [L *bident-*, *-dens* having two teeth, two-pronged, f. as BI- + *dent-*, *dens* tooth.] **1** An instrument or weapon with two prongs. L17. **2** A two-year-old sheep. *rare.* M19.

bidental /bʌɪˈdɛnt(ə)l/ *n.* E17. [f. L *bident-*: see prec., -AL¹.] *Rom. Antiq.* A place struck by lightning, consecrated, and enclosed.

bidentate /bʌɪˈdɛnteɪt/ *a.* E19. [f. BI- + -DENTATE.] **1** *Zool.* Having two teeth or toothlike projections. E19. **2** *Chem.* Of a ligand: forming two bonds, usu. with the same central atom. Of a molecule or complex: formed by such a ligand. M20.

bidet /ˈbiːdeɪ/ *n.* M17. [Fr. = pony, ass, f. *bider* to trot, of unkn. origin.] **1** A small horse. M17. **2** A shallow oval basin used for washing esp. the genital and anal regions. L18.

bidi /ˈbiːdi/ *n.* Also **beedi, biri** /ˈbiːri/. L19. [Hindi *bīṛī* betel plug, cigar, f. Skt *vīṭikā*.] In the Indian subcontinent: a cigarette or cigar of unprocessed tobacco rolled in leaves.

bidialectal /ˌbʌɪdʌɪəˈlɛkt(ə)l/ *a.* M20. [f. BI- + DIALECTAL.] Fluent in the use of two dialects of the same language, involving the use of two dialects, esp. a standard and a non-standard variety.
bidialectalism, bidialectism *ns.* facility in using two dialects of the same language, the use of two dialects, esp. a standard and a non-standard variety M20.

bidibidi *n.* var. of BIDDY-BID.

bidimensional /bʌɪdɪˈmɛnʃ(ə)n(ə)l, -dʌɪ-/ *a.* E20. [f. BI- + DIMENSIONAL.] Having, or perceived in, two dimensions.

biding /ˈbʌɪdɪŋ/ *n.* ME. [f. BIDE + -ING¹.] **1** The action of BIDE *v.*; awaiting, remaining, dwelling. ME. †**2** A dwelling, an abode. Only in 17.
2b SHAKES. *Lear* I'll lead you to some biding.
Comb.: **biding-place** place of abode.

bidirectional /bʌɪdɪˈrɛkʃ(ə)n(ə)l, -dʌɪ-/ *a.* M20. [f. BI- + DIRECTIONAL.] Functioning in two directions.
bidirectionally *adv.* M20.

bidon /bidɔ̃/ *n.* Pl. pronounced same. M19. [Fr.] A container for liquids; a canteen for water etc.; an oil drum or petrol tin.

bidonville /ˈbɪd(ə)nvɪl; *foreign* bidɔ̃vil (*pl. same*)/ *n.* M20. [Fr., f. prec. + *ville* town.] A shanty-town built of oil drums etc., esp. on the outskirts of a French or N. African city.

bidri /ˈbɪdri/ *n.* Also **biddery** /ˈbɪd(ə)ri/, **bidry**. L18. [Urdu *bidrī*, f. *Bidar* or *Bedar* a town in India.] An alloy of copper, lead, tin and zinc, used as a ground for inlaying with gold and silver, in *bidri-ware*.

Biedermeier /ˈbiːdəmʌɪə/ *a.* (*attrib.*). *derog.* Also **-maier, -meyer**. E20. [Gottlieb *Biedermaier*, fictitious G poet created by L. Eichrodt in 1854.] Designating, pertaining to, or characteristic of the styles of interior decoration, esp. of furniture, fashionable in Germany in the period 1815–48; *transf.* conventional, bourgeois.

bield /biːld/ *n. obs.* exc. *dial.* [OE *beldu*, (WS) *bieldu* = OHG *baldī*, Goth. *balþei* boldness, f. Gmc, f. as BOLD *a.*: cf. next.] †**1** Boldness. OE–L15. †**2** (A means or provider of) help or succour. ME–E19. **3** (A place of) refuge or shelter. *Sc.* & *north.* LME.
bieldy *a.* (*Sc.*) affording shelter M18.

bield /biːld/ *v. obs.* exc. *dial.* Pa. t. **bield(ed)**; pa. pple **bield**. [OE *beldan*, (WS) *bieldan* = OS *beldian*, OHG *belden*, Goth. *balþjan*, f. Gmc, f. as BOLD *a.*] †**1** *v.t.* & *i.* Make, grow or be, bold. OE–L15. **2** *v.t.* Defend, protect, shelter. *Sc.* & *north.* ME. †**b** *v.i.* Find protection or shelter. Only in LME.

Bielid /ˈbiːlɪd/ *n.* L19. [f. Wilhelm von *Biela* (1782–1856), Austrian astronomer, discoverer of a comet of which the Andromedid meteor swarm is believed to be the remnant, + -ID³.] *Astron.* = ANDROMEDID.

bien *a.* & *adv.* var. of BEIN.

bien entendu /bjɛ̃n ɑ̃tɑ̃dy/ *adv. phr.* M19. [Fr., f. *bien* well + *entendu* pa. pple of *entendre* hear, understand.] Of course; that goes without saying.

bien-être /bjɛ̃nɛːtr/ *n.* M19. [Fr., f. *bien* well + *être* be.] A state of well-being.

biennale /biːɛˈnɑːli/ *n.* M20. [It., f. as BIENNIAL.] A large (esp. biennial) art exhibition or music festival, orig. *spec.* (**B-**) that held biennially in Venice, Italy.

biennia *n.pl.* see BIENNIUM.

biennial /bʌɪˈɛnɪəl/ *a.* & *n.* E17. [f. L *biennis* of two years, or BIENNIUM: see BI-, -AL¹, and cf. ANNUAL.] **A** *adj.* **1** Existing or lasting for two years; *esp.* (*Bot.*) that is a biennial. E17. **2** Occurring every two years. M18. **B** *n.* **1** *Bot.* A plant which springs from seed and vegetates one year, and flowers, fructifies, and perishes the next. L18. **2** An event taking place biennially. Chiefly *US.* M19.
biennially *adv.* every two years L18.

biennium /bʌɪˈɛnɪəm/ *n.* Pl. **-iums, -ia** /-ɪə/. E20. [L, f. as BI- + *annus* year.] A period of two years.

bien pensant /bjɛ̃ pɑ̃sɑ̃/ *a.* & *n. phr.* As n. ***bien-pensant*** (pl. pronounced same). E20. [Fr., *bien* well, *pensant* pres. pple of *penser* think.] (A person who is) right-thinking, orthodox, conservative.

bienséance /bjɛ̃seɑ̃ːs/ *n.* L17. [Fr., f. *bien* well + *séant*, f. *seoir* befit.] Decorum.

†**bienvenue** *n.* LME. [Fr., f. *bien* well + *venue* coming.] **1** Welcome. LME–M17. **2** A fee exacted from a new workman. L17–L18.

bier /bɪə/ *n.* [OE *bēr*, (WS) *bǣr* = OFris. *bēre*, OS, OHG *bāra* (G *Bahre*), f. WGmc, f. Gmc base of BEAR *v.*¹] **1** A framework for carrying; a handbarrow; a litter. Long *obs.* exc. *Hist.* OE. **2** A movable frame on which a coffin or corpse is placed before burial or cremation; a support on which a coffin or corpse is carried to the grave. OE. **3** *transf.* A tomb; a sepulchre. LME.
Comb.: †**bier-balk** a balk in a field where there is a right of way for funerals; †**bier-right** an ordeal in which those accused of murder were required to approach the corpse and clear themselves on oath.

bierhaus /ˈbiːrhaʊs/ *n.* Pl. ***-häuser*** /-hɔyzər/. M20. [G, f. *Bier* beer + *Haus* house.] A public house or alehouse in a German-speaking country.

Bierstube /ˈbiːrʃtuːbə, -st-/ *n.* Pl. ***-ben*** /-bən/, ***-bes***. E20. [G, f. *Bier* beer + *Stube* room.] A German tavern, taproom, or bar. Cf. WEINSTUBE.

biface /ˈbʌɪfeɪs/ *n.* M20. [BI- + FACE *n.*] *Archaeol.* A type of prehistoric stone implement flaked on both faces.

bifacial /bʌɪˈfeɪʃ(ə)l/ *a.* L19. [f. BI- + FACIAL *a.*] Having two faces; *spec.* (*a*) *Bot.* having distinct dorsal and ventral surfaces; (*b*) *Archaeol.* (of a flint etc.) worked on both faces.
bifacially *adv.* M20.

bifarious /bʌɪˈfɛːrɪəs/ *a.* M17. [f. L *bifarius* twofold, double (f. as BI-) + -OUS.] †**1** Twofold; ambiguous. M17–L18. **2** *Bot.* Ranged in two rows. L18.
bifariously *adv.* M17.

biff /bɪf/ *int.*, *v.*, & *n. colloq.* (orig. *US*). As int. also **bif**. M19. [Imit.] **A** *int.* Repr. the sound of a smart blow. M19.
B *v. slang.* **1** *v.t.* Hit, strike. L19. **2** *v.i.* Go; proceed. E20. **3** *v.t.* & *i.* Throw. *Austral.* & *NZ.* M20.
1 E. WAUGH I'd like to hear less about denying things to the enemy and more about biffing him. *Club Tennis* She was not put on this earth to biff balls over nets. **2** P. G. WODEHOUSE To biff down to Twing and rally round young Bingo.
C *n.* A blow; a whack. L19.

biffin /ˈbɪfɪn/ *n.* Also **beefing** /ˈbiːfɪŋ/, (by false etym.) **beaufin** /ˈbəʊfɪn/. L18. [Repr. dial. pronunc. of *beefing*, f. BEEF *n.* (w. ref. to the colour) + -ING³.] **1** A deep-red cooking apple cultivated esp. in Norfolk. L18. **2** A baked apple flattened in the form of a cake. E19.

bifid /ˈbʌɪfɪd/ *a.* M17. [L *bifidus*, f. as BI- + base of *findere* split. Cf. *trifid*.] Divided into two parts by a deep cleft or notch.
biˈfidity *n.* L19. **bifidly** *adv.* M19.

bifilar /bʌɪˈfʌɪlə/ *a.* M19. [f. BI- + L *filum* thread + -AR¹.] Consisting of or involving two threads or wires.
bifilarly *adv.* L19.

bifocal /bʌɪˈfəʊk(ə)l/ *a.* & *n.* E19. [f. BI- + FOCAL.] **A** *adj.* Having two foci; *esp.* of spectacles: having lenses combining distant- and near-vision sections. E19. **B** *n.* In *pl.* Bifocal spectacles. L19.
bifocalled *a.* wearing bifocals M20.

bifold /ˈbʌɪfəʊld/ *a.* E17. [f. BI- + -FOLD.] Double, twofold.

bifolium /bʌɪˈfəʊlɪəm/ *n.* Pl. **-ia** /-ɪə/. M20. [f. BI- + L *folium* leaf.] *Palaeogr.* A pair of conjoint leaves.

biforked /ˈbʌɪfɔːkt/ *a.* L16. [f. BI- + FORKED.] Having two forks, branches, or peaks.

biform /ˈbʌɪfɔːm/ *a.* E19. [L *biformis* f. BI- + *forma* shape, FORM *n.*] Having or partaking of two forms.
biformed *a.* = BIFORM L16. **biˈformity** *n.* E17.

bifront /ˈbʌɪfrʌnt/ *a.* L16. [L *bifrons*, *-front-*, f. BI- + *frons* forehead, face.] Having two faces or aspects; double.
biˈfrontal *a.* = BIFRONT M19. **biˈfronted** *a.* = BIFRONT L16.

biftek /biftɛk/ *n.* Pl. pronounced same. M19. [Fr., f. *beefsteak* (see BEEF *n.*).] (A) beefsteak.

bifurcate /bʌɪˈfəːkət/ *a.* M19. [med.L *bifurcatus*, f. as next: see -ATE².] Having two forks, branches, or peaks.

bifurcate /ˈbʌɪfəkeɪt/ *v.t.* & *i.* E17. [med.L *bifurcat-* pa. ppl stem of *bifurcare*, f. L *bifurcus* two-forked, f. BI- + *furca* FORK *n.*: see -ATE³.] Divide into two forks, branches, or peaks.
bifurˈcation *n.* division into two forks or branches; the point of such division; each or both of two such forks or branches: E17.

big /bɪg/ *n.*¹ *obs.* exc. *dial.* Also **bigg**. LME. [Origin unkn.] A teat.

big /bɪg/ *n.*² *Sc.* & *dial.* Also **bigg**. LME. [ON *bygg* barley (Da. *byg*, Sw. *bjug*), corresp. to OE *bēow* grain, OS *beo*, *bewod* harvest.] The four-rowed barley, an inferior but hardy variety of six-rowed or winter barley.

big /bɪg/ *a.* & *adv.* Compar. & superl. **-gg-**. ME. [Origin unkn.] **A** *adj.* †**1** Of a living being: great in strength; mighty. ME–L16. **2** Of a thing: strong; stiff; violent; vehement. Long *obs.* exc. *dial.* LME. **3** Of considerable size, amount, extent, intensity, etc. (less formal than *large* and usu. without the emotional implications of *great*). (In comparisons, neutral as to absolute size.) LME. **b** *esp.* Grown large(r) or tall(er); (more) grown up; elder. LME. **c** Of a letter: capital, upper-case. L19. **4** Far advanced in pregnancy; filled to bursting, distended. Usu. foll. by *with*. M16. **5** Full in voice, loud. L16. **6** Of a high position; important; influential; momentous. L16. **7** Haughty; pretentious; boastful. L16. **8** Generous, magnanimous. Usu. *iron. colloq.* (orig. *US*). M20. **9** Keen *on*. *colloq.* M20.
2 SHAKES. *Oth.* Farewell the plumed troops, and the big wars That makes ambition virtue. **3** MILTON Seeming bigger than they are through the mist and vapour. TENNYSON Apt at arms and big of bone. I. MURDOCH How very big Peter was, plump and burly,

broad-shouldered. A. BURGESS It's all big words nowadays in whatever you read. J. HERRIOT He wasn't a big eater but he did love his breakfast. b ARNOLD BENNETT Your big sister isn't out of school yet? c *Times* An attempt to impose Culture, with a big 'C', on the . . people. 4 BURKE The mind of this political preacher . . big with some extraordinary design. A. HALEY One man's wife, big with child, had died on the road. 6 C. ISHERWOOD James L. Schraube, he explained, was a very big man in Chicago. A. HALEY Virgil sent L'il Kizzy racing from the field to tell . . that something big must have happened. 8 N. COWARD That's big of her I must say.

Phrases: **be a big boy** or **girl (now)** be old enough to take responsibility for one's own actions, no longer need protection or supervision. *go big*: see GO *v. go for the big spit*: see SPIT *n.*[2] *great big*: see GREAT *a. heap big*: see HEAP *n.* **in a big way** on a large scale; *colloq.* with great enthusiasm or display. *the Big Apple*: see APPLE *n. the big bird*: see BIRD *n.* **the big C** *colloq.* cancer. *the Big Drink*: see DRINK *n. the big* IDEA. *the big pond*: see POND *n.* 2. *the big screen*: see SCREEN *n.*[1] *the big smoke*: see SMOKE *n.* **the Big Three, Four,** etc. the dominant group of three etc. **too big for one's boots** or **breeches** *colloq.* conceited.

Special collocations & comb.: **big band** a large band of musicians playing jazz, dance-music, etc. **big bang** (*a*) (*Astron.*) *the* violent expansion of all matter from a state of high density and temperature, postulated as the origin of the universe; (*b*) (*Stock Exch., colloq.*) *the* deregulation of the London Stock Exchange in 1986. **Big Ben**, the great bell, or *loosely* the clock or tower, of the Palace of Westminster in London. *Big Bertha*: see BERTHA *n.*[2] **Big Board** *US colloq. the* New York Stock Exchange. **big bore** *US* a rifle of large calibre. **Big Brother** [from the head of State in George Orwell's novel *Nineteen Eighty-Four*] an apparently benevolent but ruthlessly omnipotent dictator. **big bud** a plant disease caused by gall-mites. **big bug** *colloq.* an important person. **big business** (orig. *US*) (those involved in) large mercantile organizations or transactions (freq. with sinister implications). *big cheese*: see CHEESE *n.*[2] 2. *big chief*: see CHIEF *n.* **Big Daddy** a paternal, dominating, or influential person. **big deal** *colloq.* a cause of concern or excitement (chiefly in neg. contexts). *big dipper, Big Dipper*: see DIPPER 5. **big end** the end of the connecting-rod that encircles the crankpin. **big game** large animals as lions, elephants, etc., hunted as game. **big gun** *colloq.* an important person. **big-head** (*a*) a disease of sheep or other livestock in which there is swelling of the head; (*b*) *US* & *Austral.*, any of various large-headed fishes; (*c*) *colloq.* conceit, arrogance; a conceited or arrogant person. **big-headed** *a.* (*a*) large-headed; (*b*) *colloq.* conceited, arrogant. **big-headedness** *colloq.* conceit, arrogance. **big-hearted** *a.* generous. **big-heartedness** generosity. **bighorn** the Rocky Mountain sheep, *Ovis canadensis*. **big house** (*a*) the principal house of an estate, village, etc.; (*b*) *slang* a prison. **big league** a major baseball league; *transf.* a top group. **big-league** *attrib. a.* top-class. **big-leaguer** a player in or member of a big league. **big money** (orig. *US*) much money, esp. as pay or profit. **big mouth** (orig. *US*) a very talkative or boastful person; loquacity, boastfulness. **big-mouthed** *a.* loquacious, boastful. **big name** (orig. *US*) a famous person, esp. in the field of entertainment. **big noise, pot, shot** *colloq.* an important person. *big show*: see SHOW *n.*[1] **big stick** (orig. *US*) (a display of) force or power. *big stiff*: see STIFF *n. big talk*: see TALK *n.*[1] **big-ticket** *attrib. a.* constituting a major expense. **big time** *slang* (orig. *US*) *the* highest rank (among entertainers etc.). **big-timer** a top-ranker. **big toe** either of the innermost and largest toes. **big top** (the main tent of) a circus. **big tree** *US* the wellingtonia, *Sequoiadendron giganteum*. **big wheel** (*a*) a Ferris wheel; (*b*) *colloq.* an important person. *big white chief*: see CHIEF *n.* **bigwig** *colloq.* [w. allus. to the large wigs formerly worn by men of importance] an important person.

B *adv.* In a big manner. Esp. as below. M16.

come, or **go, over big**: with great effect, successfully. **look big**: haughtily. **talk big**: boastfully, confidently. **think big**: ambitiously.

biggie *n.* (*a*) *slang* someone or something big, an important person or event; (*b*) in *pl.* (*nursery* or *euphem.*), excrement: M20. **biggish** *a.* rather big E17. **biggity** /ˈbɪgɪti/ *a.* (chiefly *US dial.*) [perh. after *bigoted* or *uppity*] conceited, boastful, assertive: L19. **bigly** *adv.* †(*a*) violently, firmly; (*b*) loudly, boastfully, haughtily: LME. **bigness** *n.* large size; (in comparisons) size; pompousness: L15.

big /bɪg/ *v. obs.* exc. *Sc.* & *north.* Infl. **-gg-**. ME. [ON *byggja*.] †**1** *v.i.* & *t.* Dwell (in); place *oneself.* ME–L15. **2** *v.t.* Build; erect, pile up. ME.

bigging *n.* (*a*) the action of the vb; †(*b*) a dwelling-place; (*c*) a building, an outbuilding: ME. **bigly** *a.* habitable, pleasant LME.

biga /ˈbʌɪgə/ *n.* Pl. **-gae** /-giː/. E17. [L.] *Rom. Antiq.* A two-horsed chariot.

bigamy /ˈbɪgəmi/ *n.* ME. [(O)Fr. *bigamie*, f. *bigame* f. late L *bigamus*, f. L BI- + Gk *-gamos* married.] **1** The crime of going through a form of marriage while a previous marriage is still in existence; having two wives or husbands at once. ME. **2** *Eccl. Law.* Remarriage after the death of a spouse; marriage with a widow or widower. *obs.* exc. *Hist.* LME.

bigamist *n.* a person who commits or lives in bigamy M17. **bigamous** *a.* living in or involving bigamy M19. **bigamously** *adv.* L19.

bigarade /bɪgəˈrɑːd; *foreign* bigarad (*pl. same*)/ *n.* E18. [Fr. f. Prov. *bigarrado*.] The Spanish bitter orange.

bigarreau /ˈbɪgərəʊ/ *n.* Pl. **-s, -x** (pronounced same). E17. [Fr., f. *bigarré* variegated.] In full *bigarreau cherry*. A variety of sweet cherry, usu. heart-shaped and with firm flesh.

bigeminal /bʌɪˈdʒɛmɪn(ə)l/ *a.* M19. [f. BI- + L *geminus* twin + -AL[1].] Existing or arranged in pairs.

bigeminy *n.* (*Med.*) the occurrence of double pulse-beats E20.

bigeminate /bʌɪˈdʒɛmɪnət/ *a.* M18. [f. BI- + GEMINATE *a.*] = prec.

bigener /ˈbʌɪdʒɪnə/ *n.* M19. [L, f. BI- + *gener-*, GENUS.] *Bot.* A hybrid between two genera.

bigeˈneric *a.* L19.

bigg *n.* var. of BIG *n.*[1], *n.*[2]

biggen /ˈbɪgən/ *v.t.* & *i. obs.* exc. *dial.* M17. [f. BIG *a.* + -EN[5].] Make or become big; increase.

biggin /ˈbɪgɪn/ *n.*[1] Now *arch.* or *Hist.* L15. [Fr. *béguin*, f. as BEGUINE *n.*[1]] **1** A child's cap; *the biggin* (fig.), infancy. L15. **2** A hood for the head; the coif of a serjeant-at-law. L15.

biggin /ˈbɪgɪn/ *n.*[2] L18. [App. f. a Mr *Biggin* of Manchester (fl. late 18c.), its inventor.] *Hist.* A type of coffee-pot containing a strainer preventing the grounds from mixing with the infusion.

biggonet /ˈbɪgənɪt/ *n. Sc.* Now *arch.* or *Hist.* M17. [Dim. of BIGGIN *n.*[1]; cf. OFr. *beguinet*.] A woman's cap or head-dress.

bigha /ˈbiːgə/ *n.* Also **begah** & other vars. M18. [Hind. *bīghā*.] In the Indian subcontinent: a measure of land area varying locally from ⅓ to 1 acre (⅛ to ⅖ hectare).

bight /bʌɪt/ *n.* [OE *byht* f. Gmc: cf. MLG *bucht* (whence Du. *bocht*, G *Bucht*, Sw., Da. *bugt*); rel. to BOW *v.*[1]] **1** A bending, a bend; an angle, a hollow, a fork. Now *rare* in *gen.* sense. OE. **2** A bend or curve as a geographical feature; an indentation in a coastline, body of ice, etc.; a bend in a river; *spec.* a bay, esp. in names as *Bight of Benin, Australian Bight.* L15. **3** The loop of a rope (as distinct from its ends). E17.

bignonia /bɪgˈnəʊnɪə/ *n.* L18. [mod.L, f. Abbé J. P. *Bignon* (1662–1743), librarian to Louis XIV: see -IA[1].] A plant of the chiefly tropical genus *Bignonia*, with showy trumpet-shaped flowers.

bigot /ˈbɪgət/ *n.* L16. [Fr., of unkn. origin.] †**1** A hypocritical or superstitious adherent of religion. L16–M17. **2** An obstinate and unreasonable adherent of a religious or other opinion; an intolerant and narrow-minded person. M17.

bigoted *a.* unreasonably intolerant M17.

bigotry /ˈbɪgətri/ *n.* L17. [f. prec. + -RY; partly through Fr. *bigoterie*.] Obstinate and unreasonable adherence to a religious or other opinion; narrow-minded intolerance.

biguanide /bʌɪˈgwɑːnʌɪd/ *n.* L19. [f. BI- + GUANIDINE + -IDE.] *Chem.* A crystalline base, $NH(C(NH)(NH_2))_2$, formed by condensation of two guanidine molecules; any substituted derivative of this.

Bihari /bɪˈhɑːri/ *a.* & *n.* Also **Be-**. L19. [Hind. *bihārī*, f. *Bihār* (see below).] (A native or inhabitant) of Bihar, a State of NE India; (of) a group of Indo-Aryan dialects of NE India.

bijection /bʌɪˈdʒɛkʃ(ə)n/ *n.* M20. [f. BI- after *injection*.] *Math.* A mapping that is both one-to-one and onto.

bijective *a.* of the nature of or pertaining to a bijection M20.

bijou /ˈbiːʒuː, *foreign* biʒu/ *n.* & *a.* M17. [Fr. f. Breton *bizoù* finger-ring, f. *biz* finger.] **A** *n.* Pl. **-oux** /-uː(z), *foreign* -u/. A jewel, a trinket. M17. **B** *adj.* Small and elegant. M19.

bijouterie /biʒutri/ *n.* [Fr.: see -ERY] jewellery, trinkets, etc. E19.

bijugate /bʌɪˈdʒuːgət/ *a.* E18. [f. BI- + L *jugatus* pa. pple of *jugare* join together: see -ATE[2].] **1** Of a coin: bearing two overlapping side-facing heads. E18. **2** *Bot.* Having two pairs of leaflets. M19.

bike /bʌɪk/ *n.*[1] *Sc.* & *north.* ME. [Origin unkn.] **1** A nest of wasps, hornets, or wild bees; a swarm. ME. **2** *fig.* A well-provisioned storehouse or dwelling. L15. **3** *fig.* A swarm of people, a crowd. M16.

bike /bʌɪk/ *n.*[2] & *v. colloq.* L19. [Abbrev. of BICYCLE.] **A** *n.* A bicycle; a motorcycle. L19.

exercise bike: see EXERCISE *n.* **get off one's bike** *Austral.* & *NZ colloq.* become annoyed. **(get) on your bike** *slang* go away (and do something useful). *motor bike*: see MOTOR *n.* & *a. push-bike*: see PUSH-. *scrambler bike*: see SCRAMBLER 2. *stationary bike*: see STATIONARY *a.*

Comb.: **bike boy** *colloq.* a disreputable young motorcyclist; **bike chain, clip, pump** = *bicycle chain, clip, pump* s.v. BICYCLE *n.*; **bikeway** a path or lane for the (usu. exclusive) use of bicycles.

B *v.i.* Ride on a bike. L19.

biker *n.* a cyclist; a motorcyclist, *esp.* = *bike boy* above: L19. **bikie** *n.* (*Austral.* & *NZ colloq.*) = *bike boy* above: M20.

bikini /bɪˈkiːni/ *n.* M20. [*Bikini*, an atoll in the Marshall Islands, where an atomic bomb test was carried out in 1946.] A scanty two-piece beach garment worn by women and girls.

Comb.: **bikini briefs** women's briefs resembling those of a bikini.

bikky *n.* var. of BICKY.

bilabial /bʌɪˈleɪbɪəl/ *a.* & *n.* M19. [f. BI- + LABIAL *a.*] **A** *adj.* **1** = next. *rare.* M19. **2** *Phonet.* Of certain consonants (e.g. /p/, /b/, /m/, /w/): produced by the juncture or apposition of the lips. L19. **B** *n. Phonet.* A bilabial consonant. L19.

bilabiate /bʌɪˈleɪbɪət/ *a.* M18. [f. BI- + LABIATE *a.*] Chiefly *Bot.* = *two-lipped* s.v. TWO *a.*

bilander /ˈbɪləndə, ˈbʌɪ-/ *n.* Also **-ll-, by-**. M17. [Du. *bijlander* (Flem. *billander*), f. *bij* BY *prep.* + *land* LAND *n.*[1]: see -ER[1].] *Hist.* A small Dutch or Flemish merchant ship with a lateen mainsail and square foresail, used esp. for coastal traffic.

bilateral /bʌɪˈlat(ə)r(ə)l/ *a.* L18. [f. BI- + LATERAL *a.*] **1** Of, on, or with, two sides. L18. **2** Orig. (*Law*), made or entered on by two parties. Later more widely, involving two States as parties to an agreement, esp. in respect of trade and finance. E19.

1 bilateral symmetry symmetry about a plane.

bilateralism *n.* = BILATERALITY M19. **bilateˈrality** *n.* bilateral nature or condition L19. **bilaterally** *adv.* M19.

bilayer /ˈbʌɪleɪə/ *n.* M20. [f. BI- + LAYER *n.*] *Biochem.* A film two molecules thick (formed e.g. by lipids), in which each molecule is arranged with its hydrophobic end directed inwards towards the opposite side of the film and its hydrophilic end directed outwards.

bilbergia *n.* var. of BILLBERGIA.

bilberry /ˈbɪlb(ə)ri/ *n.* Also †**bill-**. L16. [Prob. of Norse origin: cf. Da. *böllebær*, f. *bölle* bilberry + *bær* BERRY *n.*[1]] **1** (The small blue-black fruit of) a dwarf hardy northern European shrub, *Vaccinium myrtillus*, growing on heaths, moors, and in mountain woods. Also called *whortleberry, blaeberry.* L16. **2** Any of certain related plants or their fruit. M17.

bilberrying *vbl n.* collecting bilberries M19.

bilbo /ˈbɪlbəʊ/ *n.* Pl. **-o(e)s.** M16. [f. *Bilboa* = Bilbao in Spain.] *Hist.* A slender sword having a blade of notable temper and elasticity.

†**bilbocatch** *n.* see BILBOQUET.

bilboes /ˈbɪlbəʊz/ *n.pl.* M16. [Origin unkn.]

Hist. An iron bar with sliding shackles for confining the ankles of prisoners.

bilboquet /bɪlbəʊˈkɛt/ *n.* In sense 2 also **†-catch**. E17. [Fr. (*bille boucquet* in Rabelais), of uncertain origin.] †1 A cord with sticks fastened to it, for measuring or laying out garden beds. Only in 17. 2 (The game and plaything) cup-and-ball. M18.

bilby /ˈbɪlbi/ *n. Austral.* L19. [Prob. Aborig.] The rabbit-bandicoot.

Bildungsroman /ˈbɪldʊŋzro,maːn/ *n.* Pl. **-e** /-ə/. E20. [G, f. *Bildung* education + *Roman* novel.] A novel dealing with one person's formative years or spiritual education.

bile /bʌɪl/ *n.*[1] M16. [Fr. f. L *bilis*.] **1a** A bitter yellow, brown, or green fluid secreted by the liver, stored in the gall bladder, and passed into the duodenum to assist in the digestion of fats; formerly regarded as one of the four humours of the body (cf. CHOLER). M16. **b** Excess or derangement of the bile. E19. **2** *fig.* Anger, peevishness. M19.

1a **black bile** = *choler adust* s.v. CHOLER.

Comb.: **bile duct** a duct conveying bile from the liver to the intestine; **bile pigment** any of a number of coloured compounds formed by the breakdown of haemoglobin and excreted in the bile.

†bile *n.*[2] var. of BOIL *n.*[1]

bilge /bɪldʒ/ *n.* & *v.* Also **†billage**. L15. [Prob. var. of BULGE *n.*] **A** *n.* **1** The nearly horizontal part of a ship's bottom; the lowest internal portion of the hull. L15. **2** The belly or widest part of the circumference of a barrel or similar vessel. E16. **3** In full *bilge-water*. The filth, stale water, etc., which collects inside the bilge of a ship. E17. **b** Nonsense, rubbish, rot. *slang.* L19.

1 *round bilge*: see ROUND *a.*

Comb.: **bilge-keel** a timber or plate fastened under the bilge of a ship to prevent rolling or to support the ship's weight in dry dock; **bilge-pump** a pump to draw off bilge-water; *bilge-water*: see sense 3 above.

B *v.* **1** *v.t.* Stave in the bilge of (a ship). M16. **2** *v.i.* Spring a leak in the bilge. E18. **3** *v.i.* Bulge, swell out. E19.

bilgy *a.* L19.

bilharzia /bɪlˈhaːtsɪə/ *n.* M19. [mod.L, former name of the genus *Schistosoma*, f. Theodor *Bilharz* (1825–62), Ger. physician: see -IA[1].] *Med.* A schistosome; also, schistosomiasis.

bilharzial *a.* L19. **bilharˈziasis** *n.*, pl. **-ases** /-əsiːz/, schistosomiasis E20. **bilharziˈosis** *n.*, pl. **-oses** /-ˈəʊsiːz/, schistosomiasis E20.

bili- /ˈbɪli/ *comb. form* of L *bilis* BILE *n.*[1]: see -I-.

bilifiˈcation *n.* the production of bile; making into bile: L17. **biliˈrubin** *n.* [L *ruber* red] one of the two major bile pigments, an orange compound containing four pyrrole nuclei M19. **bilirubiˈnaemia** *n.* (*Med.*) the presence of excess bilirubin in the blood, causing jaundice if sufficiently great E20. **biliˈverdin** *n.* [Fr. *vert* green] one of the two major bile pigments, a green oxidized precursor of bilirubin M19.

biliary /ˈbɪlɪəri/ *a.* M18. [Fr. *biliaire*, f. as BILE *n.*[1] + *-aire* -ARY[2].] **1** Of or pertaining to the bile. M18. **2** Bilious. Now *rare* or *obs.* M19.

bilimbi /bɪˈlɪmbi/ *n.* Also **blimbing** /ˈblɪmbɪŋ/. L18. [Malay *bilimbing*.] (The edible astringent fruit of) a tropical Asian evergreen tree, *Averrhoa bilimbi*, of the oxalis family. Also called *cucumber tree*.

biliment /ˈbɪlɪm(ə)nt/ *n. obs.* exc. *Hist.* Also **-ll-**. M16. [Aphet. f. HABILIMENT.] An ornamental article of women's dress, esp. for the head or head-dress.

bilinear /bʌɪˈlɪnɪə/ *a.* M19. [f. BI- + LINEAR.] *Math.* **1** Of, pertaining to, or contained by two straight lines. M19. **2** Linear and homogeneous in two (sets of) variables. L19.

bilineˈarity *n.* (in sense 2) M20.

bilingual /bʌɪˈlɪŋgw(ə)l/ *a.* & *n.* M19. [f. L *bilinguis*, f. BI- + *lingua* tongue, + -AL[1].] **A** *adj.* **1** Having two languages; speaking two languages fluently; *loosely* bidialectal. M19. **2** Of an inscription etc.: written or inscribed in two languages. M19. **B** *n.* **1** A bilingual inscription. L19. **2** A bilingual person. M20.

bilingualism *n.* facility in using two languages or (*loosely*) dialects L19. **bilinguˈality** *n.* = BILINGUALISM M20.

bilious /ˈbɪlɪəs/ *a.* M16. [L *biliosus*, f. *bilis* BILE *n.*[1]: see -OUS.] †**1** = BILIARY I. M16–L17. **2** *fig.* Choleric, peevish, ill-tempered. M16. **3** Affected by, liable to, or arising from excess or derangement of the bile; *loosely* nauseated, nauseous. M17.

biliously *adv.* M19. **biliousness** *n.* E19.

biliteral /bʌɪˈlɪt(ə)r(ə)l/ *a.* L18. [f. BI- + LITERAL *a.*] Consisting of two letters.

-bility /ˈbɪlɪti/ *suff.* [Fr. *-bilité*, L *-bilitatem*.] Forming abstract ns. from adjs. in -BLE.

bilk /bɪlk/ *n.* & *v.* M17. [Origin uncertain: perh. alt. of BAULK *n.*, *v.*] **A** *n.* †**1** A meaningless or worthless statement. M17–M18. **2** A hoax, a deception; also, a person who cheats or bilks. *arch.* M17. †**3** *Cribbage.* A balking or spoiling of the opponent's score in his or her crib. L18–E19. **B** *v.t.* †**1** *Cribbage.* Balk or spoil the score of (an opponent, an opponent's crib). M17–M19. **2** Balk (expectation etc.); cheat (*of*); evade payment of (a creditor, a bill); give the slip to. L17.

bilker *n.* E18.

bill /bɪl/ *n.*[1] [OE *bil* = OS *bil*, OHG *bill* (MHG *bil*, G *Bille* axe), f. WGmc.] **1** *Hist.* Any of various bladed or pointed hand weapons, as a kind of broadsword mentioned in OE poetry, a weapon like a halberd with a hook instead of a blade, a similar long-handled weapon carried by constables of the watch. OE. **2** An implement with a long concave-edged blade often (in this form also called *billhook*) ending in a sharp hook, used for pruning, lopping trees, etc. OE. **3** *Hist.* More fully *bill-man*. A soldier, watchman, etc., armed with a bill. L15.

bill /bɪl/ *n.*[2] [OE *bile*, of unkn. origin.] **1** A bird's beak, esp. when slender, flattened or weak, and in pigeons and web-footed birds. OE. **b** The muzzle of a platypus M19. **2** A beaklike projection; *spec.* a narrow promontory, as in *Portland Bill*. LME. **3** *Naut.* The point of an anchor-fluke. M18.

Comb.: **billfish** (*a*) any of various large marine game-fishes of the family Istiophoridae, with long spearlike upper jaws, comprising the sailfish, marlins, and spearfishes; (*b*) = GARFISH; (*c*) = SAURY.

billed *a.* having a bill (usu. as 2nd elem. of combs., as *broad-*, *soft-billed*, etc.) LME.

bill /bɪl/ *n.*[3] ME. [AN *bille* or AL *billa*, prob. alt. of OFr. *bulle*, med.L *bulla* BULL *n.*[2]] **1** A written list or catalogue; an inventory. Long *obs.* exc. w. specifying wd or phr. & in some techn. & spec. uses, as: (*a*) at certain public schools, a list of pupils; hence, roll-call; (*b*) *Naut.* a list of people appointed to duties; (*c*) *Printing* a list of the quantities of each letter required for a font. ME. †**b** *Med.* A prescription. E16–M18. **2** A document (orig. sealed); a formal statement in writing, a memorandum. *obs.* exc. w. specifying phr. in legal and commercial use (see below). LME. †**b** A lampoon. LME–L16. †**3** A written supplication; a petition. LME–E18. **4** A draft of proposed legislation. LME **5** *Law.* A written statement of a case, esp. that of a plaintiff. *obs.* exc. in *true bill* below. LME. **6** A note of charges for goods supplied or services rendered; the amount thus owed. LME. †**7** A label. *rare.* L15–E17. **8** A written or printed advertisement, a poster, a placard, an announcement. L15. **b** (A list of) the items of entertainment on a theatre etc. programme. M19. **9** More fully *bill of exchange*. A written order to pay a specified sum of money on a certain date to a drawer or to a named payee; a promissory note. L16. **b** A banknote. Chiefly *N. Amer.* L17.

Phrases: ACCOMMODATION *bill*. **bill of costs** a solicitor's account of charges and expenses incurred on a client's business. *bill of exchange*: see sense 9 above. **bill of fare** a menu; *fig.* a programme. **bill of goods** (chiefly *N. Amer.*) a consignment of merchandise (*sell a bill of goods*, persuade (a person) to accept something undesirable, swindle). **bill of health** a certificate relating to the incidence of infectious disease on ship or in port at time of sailing; *clean bill of health*, certification of freedom from such infection, freq. *fig.* of a person or thing examined and found in good condition. *bill of* INDICTMENT. **bill of lading** a shipmaster's detailed receipt to a consignor of goods for carriage by sea. **bill of mortality** *Hist.* a weekly statement of deaths in and near London. *bill of privilege*: see PRIVILEGE *n.* **bill of quantities** a detailed statement of work, prices, dimensions, etc., for the erection of a building by contract. *Bill of Rights*: see RIGHT *n.*[1] **bill of sale** a certificate of transfer of personal property, *esp.* a borrower's certificate that a chattel is pledged as security. *bill of sufferance*: see SUFFERANCE 5b. *butcher's bill*: see BUTCHER *n.* *double bill*: see DOUBLE *a.* & *adv.* **fill** or **fit the bill** fulfil the necessary requirements; come up to the requisite standard. *public bill*: see PUBLIC *a.* & *n.* *send a bill upstairs*: see UPSTAIRS *adv.* 2a. *short bill*: see SHORT *a.* *treasury bill*: see TREASURY 5. *true bill*: see TRUE *a.*

Comb.: **billboard** a large outdoor board or hoarding for advertisements; **bill-clerk** *US* a clerk who deals with bills at a hotel; **billfold** *US* a wallet for banknotes; **billhead** a printed account form with the issuer's name etc. at the head; **billposter, billsticker** a person who pastes up placards.

Bill /bɪl/ *n.*[4] *slang.* M20. [Dim. of male forename *William*.] The police; a police officer. Also *Old Bill*.

bill /bɪl/ *v.*[1]*i.* ME. [f. BILL *n.*[2]] †**1** Peck. ME–L17. **2** Of doves: stroke bill with bill. L16. **b** *transf.* Exchange caresses. Esp. in *bill and coo*. E17.

bill /bɪl/ *v.*[2]*t.* ME. [f. BILL *n.*[3]] †**1** Enter in a catalogue, book, account, etc. ME–M17. **2** Enter the name of in a list, enroll, enlist. *arch.* LME. **3** Announce by bill; place in a programme; advertise *as*. L17. **4** Plaster over with bills. E19. **5** Send a bill or account to; charge. M19. **6** Book as passenger or freight. *US.* M19.

2 J. MASEFIELD Send out your press. Bill every able-bodied man. Bill the women if the men won't come. 3 A. E. STEVENSON The conference had been billed as an effort to define the relationship of the federal government to education. A. S. BYATT The Father was billed to speak on Openings for the Ambitious. *fig.*: E. BOWEN She was billed, it appeared, for yet another confession. 5 N. SHUTE If there's a scratch on it, I'll bill you for it.

billable *a.* †(*a*) indictable; (*b*) liable to be charged for: L16.

bill /bɪl/ *v.*[3]*t.* LME. [f. BILL *n.*[1]] Hack, lop, or chop (as) with a bill.

billabong /ˈbɪləbɒŋ/ *n. Austral.* M19. [Aborig. *Billibang* Bell River, f. *billa* water, *bang* channel dry except after rain.] A branch of a river, forming a blind channel, backwater, or stagnant pool.

†billage *n.* & *v.* var. of BILGE.

billander *n.* var. of BILANDER.

billard /ˈbɪləd/ *n. obs.* exc. *dial.* Also **billet** /ˈbɪlɪt/. M17. [Origin unkn.] A saithe, *esp.* a young one.

billbergia /bɪlˈbəːgɪə/ *n.* Also **bilb-**. E19. [mod.L, f. Gustaf *Billberg* (1772–1844), Swed. botanist: see -IA[1].] A tropical American epiphyte of the genus *Billbergia*, which belongs to the bromelia family and includes several ornamental species.

†billberry *n.* var. of BILBERRY.

billet /ˈbɪlɪt/ *n.*[1] LME. [AN *billette* or AL *billetta* dim. of *billa* BILL *n.*[3]: see -ET[1].] **1** A short written document, a small notice. Long *obs.* in *gen.* sense. LME. **2** A short informal letter, a note. *arch.* L16. †**3** A ballot-paper. E17–L18. **4** An order requisitioning lodging for military personnel, civilian evacuees, etc.; a lodging for troops etc.; a place to stay; a destination; an appointment, a situation. M17. **5** An admission ticket, a pass. *arch.* L17.

2 LD MACAULAY Carrying billets backward and forward between his patron and the ugliest maids of honour. 4 J. WESLEY He never received one wound. So true is the odd saying of King William, that 'every bullet has its billet'. E. W. HORNUNG If ever she went back to Australia, she'd remember my young man, and get him a good billet. P. G. WODEHOUSE So George took up his abode . . in the plainly-furnished but not uncomfortable cottage. . . He might have found a worse billet. E. WAUGH Getting harder to find billets, particularly since the anti-aircraft battery had come to South Grappling. A. SILLITOE We were allotted to four different houses, and taken by car to our separate billets. 5 E. DOWSON Tell me whether you will come, as otherwise I will give Johnson your billet.

billet /ˈbɪlɪt/ *n.*[2] LME. [OFr. *billette* and *billot*, dims. of *bille* tree-trunk, length of round timber,

f. med.L *billa*, *billus* branch, trunk, prob. of Celt. origin (cf. (O)Ir. *bile* sacred tree, large tree): see -ET[1].] **I 1** A thick length of wood, *esp.* one cut for firewood. LME. †**b** Firewood. LME–M17. **2** A small bar of metal. E17. **3** *Archit.* A decorative short cylindrical piece inserted at intervals in a moulding. M19.

1 G. ANSON Some of our men . . were employed in cutting down trees, and splitting them into billets. F. RAPHAEL A bomb had fallen almost next door and the shop was crutched with wooden billets. 2 A. G. GARDINER Billets of steel that scorch you as they pass from the furnace to the steam-press.

II Senses perh. f. prec. **4** *Her.* A charge in the form of an upright rectangle. LME. **5** *Saddlery.* A strap which enters a buckle; a loop which receives a buckled strap. L15.

billet *n.*[3] var. of BILLARD.

billet /ˈbɪlɪt/ *v.* L16. [f. BILLET *n.*[1]] **1** *v.t.* Quarter (troops etc., *on* or *with* a person, *on*, *in*, or *at* a place); assign accommodation to, place. L16. **b** Of a householder etc.: provide (a soldier etc.) with board and lodging, lodge. M17. **2** *v.i.* Have quarters. *rare.* E17. †**3** *v.t.* Enter in a list, enrol. Only in E17.

bille'tee *n.* a person who is billeted M20. **billeter** *n.* one who billets M17.

billet-doux /bɪlɪˈduː/ *n.* Now chiefly *joc.* Pl. **billets-doux** /bɪlɪˈduːz/. L17. [Fr., lit. 'sweet note'.] A love-letter.

billeté /ˈbɪləti/ *a.* Also **-etté**, **-etty**. L16. [Fr. *billeté* f. *billette*: see BILLET *n.*[2] 4, -Y[2].] *Her.* Charged with billets.

billiards /ˈbɪljədz/ *n.* (orig. *pl.*, but soon treated as *sing.*). Sing. form used only in comb. L16. [Fr. *billard* the game and the cue, f. *bille*: see BILLET *n.*[2], -ARD.] A game played with cues and balls on an oblong smooth cloth-covered table: in the standard form played with three balls on a table with six pockets at the corners and sides into which the balls are struck.

bar billiards: see BAR *n.*[1] *pocket billiards*: see POCKET *n.* & *a.*

Comb.: *billiard-ball*, *-cloth*, *-cue*, *-hall*, *player*, *-room*, *-table*, etc.; **billiard-marker** a person or apparatus whose function is to record the score in billiards.

¶ Cf. POOL *n.*[2], SNOOKER *n.*[2].

billiardist *n.* a person who plays billiards M19.

billie *n.* var. of BILLY *n.*[1]

billiken /ˈbɪlɪkɪn/ *n.* Also **-kin**. E20. [Prob. f. BILLY *n.*[2] + -KIN.] A small, squat, smiling figure used as a mascot.

billiment *n.* var. of BILIMENT.

billingsgate /ˈbɪlɪŋzgeɪt/ *n.* Also **B-**. M17. [*Billingsgate* market, a fish-market in London noted for vituperative language.] **1** Scurrilous abuse, violent invective. M17. †**2** A foul-mouthed person, a scold. M17–L18.

billion /ˈbɪljən/ *n.* & *a.* L17. [Fr., f. as MILLION by substitution of BI-.] **A** *n.* Pl. same w. specified number, **-s** when indefinite. **1** A million million, 10^{12}. Cf. TRILLION. (Now only in British pop. use.) L17. **2** A thousand million, 10^9; in *pl.* (without specifying wd), several billions, very large numbers. M19. **B** *adj.* After an article, possessive, etc.: a million times a million (now only in British pop. use); a thousand times a million; *hyperbol.* a very great many. After a numeral or quantifier: multiples of a billion. M20.

billio'naire *n.* [after MILLIONAIRE] a person possessing a thousand million dollars etc. M19. **billionth** *a.* & *n.* (*a*) *adj.* one thousand (or million) millionth; (*b*) *n.* a billionth part; the billionth person or thing: L18.

billitonite /ˈbɪlɪtənaɪt/ *n.* E20. [f. *Billiton* (see below) + -ITE[1].] *Geol.* A tektite from Belitung (formerly Billiton) Island, Indonesia.

billon /ˈbɪlən/ *n.* E18. [(O)Fr., (orig.) ingot, (now) bronze or copper money, f. *bille*: see BILLET *n.*[2], -OON.] An alloy of gold or silver with a predominating amount of base metal.

billow /ˈbɪləʊ/ *n.* & *v.* M16. [ON *bylgja* (Sw. *bölja*, Da. *bølge*), f. Gmc base rel. to that of BELLY *n.*] **A** *n.* **1** A great wave (of a stretch of water, esp. the sea, or *transf.* of flame, smoke, sound, moving bodies, etc.); *poet.* (*sing.* & in *pl.*) *the* sea. M16. †**2** A swell on the sea. M16–E17.

B *v.i.* Rise in billows; surge, swell; undulate. L16.

H. VAUGHAN When his waters billow thus, Dark storms and wind Incite them. T. ROETHKE Their skirts billowing out wide into tents. A. MACLEAN Black smoke billowing into the night sky.

billowy *a.* of, pertaining to, characterized by, or of the nature of billows E17.

billy /ˈbɪli/ *n.*[1] *Sc.* & *north.* Also **billie**. E16. [Origin unkn.] A comrade or close friend; a companion; a brother.

billy /ˈbɪli/ *n.*[2] L18. [f. *Billy*, pet-form of male forename *William*.] **1** A slubbing machine. L18. **2** A bludgeon; *spec.* (*US*, more fully *billy club*) a police officer's truncheon. M19. **3** More fully *billy-goat*. A male goat. M19.

¶ See also *silly billy* s.v. SILLY *a.*

billy /ˈbɪli/ *n.*[3] *Austral.* & *NZ.* M19. [Origin uncertain: perh. f. Aborig. *billa* water.] A cylindrical tin etc. or enamelled container used as kettle, cooking-pot, food-carrier, etc. Also *billycan*.

boil the billy: see BOIL *v.*

billycock /ˈbɪlɪkɒk/ *n.* M19. [Said to be f. the name of *William Coke*, nephew of Thomas William Coke, Earl of Leicester (1752–1842).] *Hist.* A kind of bowler hat.

billy-o /ˈbɪlɪəʊ/ *n. colloq.* Also **-oh**. L19. [Origin unkn.] *like billy-o*, intensely, vigorously, etc.

fight, *rain*, *run*, etc. *like billy-o*.

bilobate /baɪˈləʊbeɪt/ *a.* L18. [f. BI- + LOBATE.] Having two lobes.

bilobed /baɪˈləʊbd/ *a.* M18. [f. BI- + LOBED *a.*] = prec.

bilocation /baɪləˈkeɪʃ(ə)n/ *n.* M17. [f. BI- + LOCATION.] The fact or power of being in two places simultaneously.

bilocular /baɪˈlɒkjʊlə/ *a.* L18. [f. as BI- + LOCULAR.] Having or divided into two cavities or compartments.

bilophodont /baɪˈlɒfədɒnt/ *a.* M19. [f. BI- + LOPHO- + -ODONT.] *Zool.* Of molar teeth: having two transverse ridges on the grinding surface.

biltong /ˈbɪltɒŋ/ *n. S. Afr.* E19. [Afk., f. Du. *bil* buttock + *tong* tongue.] Lean meat cut into strips and dried.

Bim /bɪm/ *n.*[1] *colloq.* M19. [Origin unkn.] A native or inhabitant of Barbados in the W. Indies.

bim /bɪm/ *n.*[2] *N. Amer. slang.* E20. [Abbrev.] = BIMBO 2.

bimanous /ˈbaɪmənəs/ *a.* M19. [f. mod.L *bimana* neut. pl., two-handed animals (in Cuvier's obsolete classification), f. L BI- + *manus* hand, + -OUS.] Having two hands.

Also **bimanal** *a.* M19.

bimanual /baɪˈmanjʊəl/ *a.* L19. [f. BI- + MANUAL *a.*] Performed with both hands.

bimanually *adv.* L19.

bimbashi /bɪmˈbɑːʃi/ *n.* E19. [Turk. *binbaşı* = 'a person who is head of a thousand', f. *bin* thousand + *baş* head + *-ı* possess. suff. Cf. YUZBASHI.] A Turkish major, naval commander, or squadron-leader. Also formerly in Egypt, a British officer in the service of the Khedive.

bimbo /ˈbɪmbəʊ/ *n. slang* (usu. *derog.*). Pl. **-o(e)s**. E20. [It. = little child, baby.] **1** A fellow, a chap. E20. **2** A woman, *esp.* a sexually attractive or provocative but empty-headed or unintelligent one. E20.

bim'bette *n.* a young (female) bimbo L19.

bimeby /ˈbaɪmbaɪ/ *adv. dial.* E18. [Reduced form.] By and by.

bimestrial /baɪˈmestrɪəl/ *a.* M19. [f. L *bimestris*, f. BI- + *mensis* month, + -AL[1].] Lasting two months; occurring every two months.

bimetallic /baɪmɪˈtalɪk/ *a.* L19. [Fr. *bimétallique*, f. BI- + *métallique* METALLIC *a.*] **1** Using gold and silver as legal tender to any amount at a fixed ratio to each other. L19. **2** *gen.* Made of or using two metals. E20.

2 **bimetallic strip** a temperature-sensitive device (used in thermostats etc.), made of two bands of different metals, one of which expands more than the other on heating, causing the strip to bend.

'bimetal *n.* & *a.* (*a*) *n.* a bimetallic object or material; (*b*) *adj.* bimetallic: M20. **bi'metallism** *n.* the system of bimetallic currency L19. **bi'metallist** *n.* an advocate of bimetallism L19.

bimillenary /baɪmɪˈlenəri, -ˈliːn-; baɪˈmɪlənəri/ *a.* & *n.* M19. [f. BI- + MILLENARY.] (A period) of two thousand years; (a celebration) of the two thousandth anniversary.

bimodal /baɪˈməʊd(ə)l/ *a.* E20. [f. BI- + MODAL *a.*] Chiefly *Statistics.* Having two modes.

bimo'dality *n.* E20.

bimolecular /baɪməˈlekjʊlə/ *a.* L19. [f. BI- + MOLECULAR.] *Chem.* Involving two molecules; of a reaction: having a molecularity of two.

bimonthly /baɪˈmʌnθli/ *adv.*, *a.*, & *n.* M19. [f. BI- + MONTHLY *adv.*, *a.* & *n.*] **A** *adv.* Every two months or twice a month. M19. **B** *adj.* & *n.* (A periodical) appearing or occurring bimonthly. M19.

bimorphemic /baɪmɔːˈfiːmɪk/ *a.* M20. [f. BI- + MORPHEMIC.] *Ling.* Consisting of or pertaining to two morphemes.

bin /bɪn/ *n.* & *v.* [OE *bin(n)*, *binne* f. Brittonic base of Welsh *ben* cart or f. Gaulish (recorded in med.L as *benna*) whence Fr. *banne*, It. dial. *benna* hamper, Du. *ben*, G *Benne* body of a cart.] **A** *n.* **I 1** *gen.* A receptacle (orig. of wicker- or basketwork). OE. **II** *spec.* **2** A receptacle for provender in a stable; a manger. Long *obs.* exc. *dial.* OE. **3** (Freq. w. specifying wd.) a A receptacle for storing grain, bread, or other foodstuffs. OE. **b** A receptacle for storing coal etc. M19. **c** A receptacle for litter, household rubbish, etc. M19. **4** A canvas receptacle used in hop-picking. M18. **5** A partitioned stand for storing wine in bottle; *transf.* wine from a particular bin. M18. **6** Any of a number of open compartments in a woolshed where wool is stowed by classes after sorting. *Austral.* & *NZ.* M19. **7** In full *loony bin*. A mental home or hospital. *colloq.* E20. **8** Each of a series of ranges of numerical value into which data are sorted in statistical analysis. M20.

Comb.: **bin-bag** a (usu. plastic) bag for holding rubbish; **bin-end** one of the last bottles of wine from a particular bin; **bin-liner** a strong bag put inside a litter or rubbish bin and removed along with the contents when the bin is full; **binman** (*a*) a man in charge of a bin during hop-picking; (*b*) *Sc.*, *Ir.*, & *north.* a dustman.

B *v.t.* Infl. **-nn-**. **1** Place in a bin; throw away, discard. M19. **2** Group together (data) in bins. L20.

bin- *pref.* see BI-.

binal /ˈbaɪn(ə)l/ *a.* M17. [med.L *binalis* twin, f. L *bini* two together: see -AL[1].] Twin, double, twofold.

binant /ˈbaɪnənt/ *n.* E20. [f. BIN- after QUADRANT *n.*[1]] A half of a circle or circular body.

binary /ˈbaɪnəri/ *n.* & *a.* LME. [Late L *binarius*, f. *bini* two together: see -ARY[1].] **A** *n.* **1** A combination of two things; a pair; a duality. LME. **2** *Astron.* A binary star. M19. **3** *Math.* The binary scale; binary arithmetic. M20. **4** A binary weapon. L20.

2 *visual binary*: see VISUAL *a.*

B *adj.* Of, pertaining to, characterized by, or compounded of, two; of or involving pairs; dual. L16.

binary arithmetic: employing the binary scale. **binary coded decimal** (designating) a number in which each digit of a decimal number is represented by its binary equivalent. **binary compound** *Chem.* a compound of two elements or radicals. **binary digit** either of two digits (usu. 0 and 1) used to express numbers in the binary scale. **binary fission** *Biol.* the division of a cell or organism into two parts. **binary form** *Mus.*: of a movement in two complementary sections. **binary measure** *Mus.*: of two beats in a bar. **binary scale** a scale of numerical notation in which the base is two (successive places denoting units, twos, fours, etc.). **binary star** a system of two stars revolving round each other. **binary tree** *Computing* a tree in which each node has no more than two subtrees or pointers. **binary weapon** a poison gas which is stored and handled in the form of two separate harmless precursors.

binate /ˈbaɪneɪt/ *a.* E19. [mod.L *binatus*, f. L *bini* two together: see -ATE[2].] *Bot.* Composed of two equal parts; growing in pairs.

binational /bʌɪˈnaʃ(ə)n(ə)l/ *a.* L19. [f. BI- + NATIONAL *a.*] Concerning or consisting of two nations.

binaural /bɪˈnɔːr(ə)l, bʌɪ-/ *a.* M19. [f. BIN- + AURAL *a.*[1]] 1 Of, pertaining to, or used with both ears. M19. 2 Of sound reproduction: employing two separate microphones, with the recordings usu. transmitted separately to the two ears of the hearer; of, pertaining to, or produced by such a system. M20.
binaurally *adv.* M20.

bind /bʌɪnd/ *n.* See also BINE. OE. [f. the vb.] 1 Something used to bind; a band, a tie. OE. b *Mus.* A (usu. curved) line above or below notes of the same pitch indicating that they are to be joined as a continuous sound; a tie. L19. 2a = BINE. LME. b = BINDWEED (now only sense 1). LME. 3 A quantitative measure of salmons and eels. *obs.* exc. *dial.* L15. 4 Capacity, limit. *Sc.* E16. 5 Indurated clay. L18. 6 A bore, a nuisance. *slang.* M20. 7 A position that prevents free action. *colloq.* M20.
7 *double bind*: see DOUBLE *a.* & *adv.* **in a bind** *N. Amer.* in difficulty.

bind /bʌɪnd/ *v.* Pa. t. **bound** /baʊnd/; pa. pple **bound,** (*arch.*) **bounden** /ˈbaʊnd(ə)n/. See also BOUND *a.*[2], BOUNDED *a.*[2], BOUNDEN, YBOUND. [OE *bindan* str. = OFris. *binda*, OS *bindan*, (M)Du. *binden*, OHG *bintan* (G *binden*), ON *binda*, Goth. *bindan*, f. IE base repr. also by Skt *bandh-*.] I *v.t.* 1 Tie, fasten, attach, (*lit.* & *fig.*). (Foll. by *to*, (*up*)*on*, *together*.) OE. 2 Put in bonds; restrain; confine; obstruct (esp. in pass. combs. as *fogbound*, *snowbound*, etc.). OE. 3 Fasten round, encircle, (something); bandage (the body, a part of it). (Foll. by *with*.) OE. b Put dressings and bandages on (a wound). Usu. foll. by *up*. ME. c Fasten, wreathe, (something) *about*, (*a*)*round*, *on*. LME. 4 Fasten or hold together; unite in marriage. OE. 5 *v.t.* (Now esp. in *Cookery*.) Cause to cohere. OE. b Hold by chemical bonding; combine with. E20. 6 Edge with a strengthening material, as a garment with braid, a box or jewel with metal, etc. ME. 7 Conclude (a bargain, an agreement; †a story); ratify, secure (a contract). ME. 8 Oblige by covenant, promise, etc., or by legal authority, (*to* or *from* an action, *to do*, *that*); (freq. foll. by *over*) subject to a legal obligation (*to*, *to do*; absol. *spec.* to keep the peace). ME. b In *pass.* Be compelled or obliged (*to do*); be certain (*to be*, *do*) (also *impers.* in *there is* or *was bound* etc., there is or was certain *to be* etc.); *N. Amer.* be resolved. ME. 9 Make constipated. LME. 10 Fasten together the sheets of (a book), fasten (the sheets of a book, issues of a periodical, etc.), into a (usu. stiff) cover. LME. 11 Indenture as an apprentice (or *apprentice*). (Foll. by *out*, *over*.) E16. 12 Bore, weary. *slang.* E20.
1 AV *Deut.* 6:8 Thou shalt bind them for a seal upon thine hand. BURKE The way in which you take up my affairs binds me to you. N. MITFORD A community of .. people, bound together by shared intellectual tastes. R. BRADBURY The pair of .. bicycle clips that bound his thin pants to his bony ankles. 2 B. JOWETT My father bound him hand and foot and threw him into a ditch. J. JOSEPH I knew That grief has uses—that a father dead Could bind the bully's fist a week or two. 3 POPE A belt her waist, a fillet binds her hair. A. WILSON The icy tightness of the bandage as she began to bind his ankle. c TENNYSON I, maiden, round thee, maiden, bind my belt. 4 MILTON Her bow'r she leaves, With Thestylis to bind the sheaves. G. CRABBE To bind in law, the couple bound by love. **bound up** closely associated *with*; concerned *in* to a degree that excludes other considerations. 5 SMOLLETT When Lybian sands are bound in frost. W. STYRON The blood, which we saved to bind stews. 8 DICKENS The Mayor .. declared he would .. bind them over to keep the peace. F. O'BRIEN I bind you that .. you will come to me each evening. K. AMIS Whether he was going to bind them to silence. b BACON Princes are not bound to communicate all matters. J. CARY After a really serious crisis .. there is bound to be an enquiry. HARPER LEE He was bound and determined they wouldn't get away with it. **I'll be bound** I guarantee the truth of (a statement), I feel certain. *in honour bound*: see HONOUR *n.* 11 THACKERAY Rebecca .. was bound-over as an articled-pupil. J. DOS PASSOS His mother bound him out to a farmer. J. MORTIMER They sent me away when I was your age... Bound as a stable lad.
II *v.i.* 13 Of a hawk or hawks: grapple (*with* or with each other). L16. 14 Cohere in a mass. L17. 15 Form a chemical bond *to* a substance; combine chemically *with*. M20. 16 Complain. *slang.* M20.

binder /ˈbʌɪndə/ *n.* OE. [f. prec. + -ER[1].] 1 *gen.* A person who binds. OE. 2 *spec.* a A bookbinder. LME. b A person who binds sheaves. M16. †3 A substance that causes constipation. E16–L17. 4 A bandage, a band; a headband. E17. 5 A connecting-piece, as a tie-beam, a bondstone in a wall, etc. M17. 6 A cementing substance. L17. 7 A machine for (reaping and) binding grain into sheaves. M19. 8 A detachable cover for unbound magazines, papers, etc. M19. 9 A large quantity, esp. of food; a satisfying meal. *dial.* & *NZ colloq.* L19. 10 A last (alcoholic) drink. *slang.* L19.
bindery *n.* a bookbinder's workshop E19.

bindi-eye /ˈbɪndiʌɪ/ *n. Austral.* E20. [Aborig.] A small plant, *Calotis cuneifolia*, with fruits resembling burs.

binding /ˈbʌɪndɪŋ/ *n.* ME. [f. BIND *v.* + -ING[1].] 1 The action of BIND *v.*; the state of being bound. ME. 2 Something with which a thing is bound; a fastening. ME. 3 *spec.* a (A) tape, braid, etc., for protecting raw edges. L16. b A band of masonry and brickwork; a connecting timber etc. E17. c The strong covering of a book holding the sheets together. M17.
3c *perfect binding*, *unsewn binding*, etc.

binding /ˈbʌɪndɪŋ/ *ppl a.* LME. [f. as prec. + -ING[2].] 1 That binds physically; causing or tending to cohere; astringent, styptic. LME. 2 *fig.* Obligatory (*on*), coercive. E17.
1 **binding energy** *Physics* the mass defect (see MASS *n.*[2]) of a nucleus, expressed as energy; also, the energy required to remove a given particle from a nucleus.

bindle /ˈbɪnd(ə)l/ *n. N. Amer. slang.* E20. [Prob. alt. of BUNDLE *n.*] A bundle or package; *esp.* a tramp's bundle of bedding etc.
Comb.: **bindle-stiff** a tramp carrying a bundle of bedding etc.

bindweed /ˈbʌɪndwiːd/ *n.* M16. [f. BIND *v.* + WEED *n.*[1]] 1 Any of various twining plants of the family Convolvulaceae, with funnel-shaped corollas; *esp.* (*a*) (more fully *hedge bindweed*) *Calystegia sepium*, a hedge plant with large white flowers; (*b*) (more fully *field bindweed*) *Convolvulus arvensis*, a cornfield weed with smaller white or pink flowers. M16. 2 Any of various other climbing plants, e.g. honeysuckle. L16.
1 *sea bindweed*: see SEA *n.* 2 **black bindweed** a twining weed of the knotgrass family, *Fallopia convolvulus*, with heart-shaped leaves and small white flowers.

bine /bʌɪn/ *n.* E19. [Var. of BIND *n.*] A flexible shoot; a stem of a climbing plant, esp. of the hop.

Binet /ˈbiːneɪ/ *n.* Also **Binet-Simon** /-ˌsiːmɔ̃/. E20. [Alfred *Binet* (1857–1911) & Théodore *Simon* (1873–1961), Fr. psychologists.] *Binet scale, test*, (a scale of intelligence associated with) a form of intelligence test developed by Binet and Simon.

bing /bɪŋ/ *n.*[1] ME. [With sense 1 cf. Da. *bing* bin; sense 2 f. ON *bingr* heap (Sw. *binge*).] 1 = BIN *n.* Now *dial.* ME. 2 A heap or pile, esp. of metallic ore or of waste from a mine. Now chiefly *Sc.* E16.

bing /bɪŋ/ *n.*[2] & *int.* L19. [Imit.] A *n.* A sudden bang; a thump. *dial.* L19. B *int.* Indicating a sudden action or event. E20.

binge /bɪn(d)ʒ/ *n.*[1] *Sc.* L15. [f. BINGE *v.*[1]] A servile bow.

binge /bɪn(d)ʒ/ *n.*[2] M19. [f. BINGE *v.*[2]] 1 A soaking. *dial.* M19. 2 A bout of heavy drinking etc.; a spree. *slang.* M19.

binge /bɪn(d)ʒ/ *v.*[1]*i.* *Sc.* L15. [App. after *bow*, *bend*, etc., and *cringe* etc.] Make a servile bow; curtsy; fawn.

binge /bɪn(d)ʒ/ *v.*[2] Pres. pple **bingeing, binging.** E19. [Origin unkn.] 1 *v.t.* Soak. *dial.* E19. 2 *v.refl.* & *i.* Have a bout of heavy drinking etc.; go on a spree. *slang.* M19. 3 *v.t.* Liven *up*, ginger *up*. *slang.* L19.

bingee *n.* var. of BINGY.

binghi /ˈbɪŋʌɪ/ *n. Austral. slang* (usu. *derog.*). M19. [Aborig.] An Aborigine.

bingle /ˈbɪŋg(ə)l/ *n.* & *v.* E20. [f. BOB *n.*[1] + SHINGLE *n.*[1]] A *n.* A short hairstyle for women, between a bob and a shingle. E20. B *v.t.* Cut (hair) in this style. E20.

bingo /ˈbɪŋgəʊ/ *n.*[1] *arch. slang.* L17. [Prob. f. initial *b-* of *brandy* + ST)INGO.] Brandy.

bingo /ˈbɪŋgəʊ/ *n.*[2] M20. [Perh. f. the winner's exclamation: cf. next.] A popular gambling game like lotto, played esp. in public halls, with cards divided into numbered squares, in which the first player to cover all or a specified set of numbers on the card wins a prize.

bingo /ˈbɪŋgəʊ/ *int.* E20. [Imit.: cf. BING *int.*] Indicating a sudden action or event (= BING *int.*), esp. the winning of a game of bingo.

bingy /ˈbɪn(d)ʒi/ *n. Austral. slang.* Also **bingee**. L18. [Aborig.] The stomach, the belly.

biniou /ˈbɪnɪuː/ *n.* M19. [Breton *bin(r)iou*, pl. of *benveg* tool, (musical) instrument.] A Breton bagpipe.

binit /ˈbɪnɪt/ *n.* M20. [Abbrev.] A binary digit.

Binitarian /bʌɪnɪˈtɛːrɪən/ *n.* & *a.* Also **b-**. E20. [f. L *bini* two together, after TRINITARIAN.] A believer in, of or pertaining to, the doctrine of a Godhead of two persons only.
Binitarianism *n.* E20.

bink /bɪŋk/ *n. Sc.* & *north.* LME. [Var. of BENCH *n.*] A bench; a shelf; a plate-rack, a dresser.

binnacle /ˈbɪnək(ə)l/ *n.* Orig. **†bittacle** & similar forms. L15. [Sp. *bitácula*, *bitácora* or Port. *bitacola*, corresp. to Prov. *abitacle*, It. *abitacolo*, Fr. *habitacle*, f. L *habitaculum* HABITACLE.] A receptacle for a ship's compass, usu. on the navigation bridge or, in small sailing vessels, a box on the deck near the helm.
¶Forms w. /n/ recorded from M18.

binocle /ˈbɪnək(ə)l/ *n. arch.* L17. [Fr., f. as next.] = BINOCULAR *n.*

binocular /bɪˈnɒkjʊlə/ *a.* & *n.* E18. [f. L *bini* two together + *oculus* eye + -AR[1], after OCULAR.] A *adj.* †1 Having two eyes. *rare.* Only in E18. 2 Adapted to or using two eyes; also, stereoscopic. M18. B *n. sing.* & (usu.) in *pl.* A field-glass or opera-glass for use with both eyes. L19.
binocuˈlarity *n.* binocular quality; simultaneous employment of both eyes: M19.

binomial /bʌɪˈnəʊmɪəl/ *n.* & *a.* M16. [f. Fr. *binôme* or mod.L *binomium*, f. BI- + Gk *nomos* part, portion + -AL[1].] A *n.* 1 *Math.* An expression which contains the sum or difference of two terms. M16. 2 A name having two parts, esp. of a plant or animal (cf. sense B.2 below). E20.
B *adj.* 1 *Math.* Consisting of two terms; of or pertaining to a binomial or the binomial theorem (see below). L16. 2 Having or using two names, esp. those of genus and species in scientific nomenclature of living organisms. M17.
1 **binomial theorem** a formula for the expansion of any power of a binomial.
binomially *adv.* L19.

binominal /bʌɪˈnɒmɪn(ə)l/ *a.* L19. [f. L *binominis*, f. BI- + *nomin-*, *nomen* name, + -AL[1].] = BINOMIAL *a.* 2.

binoxalate /bɪˈnɒksəleɪt/ *n.* E19. [f. BIN- + OXALATE.] *Chem.* An acid salt of oxalic acid.

bint /bɪnt/ *n. colloq.* (usu. *derog.*). M19. [Arab. = daughter, girl.] A girl, a woman.
¶Orig. *Army slang.*

binturong /ˈbɪntjʊrɒŋ/ *n.* E19. [Malay.] A large prehensile-tailed civet, *Arctictis binturong*, of southern Asia.

binucleate /bʌɪˈnjuːklɪət/ *a.* L19. [f. BI- + NUCLEATE *a.*] *Biol.* Having two nuclei.

bio /ˈbʌɪəʊ/ *n. colloq.* Pl. **-os.** M20. [Abbrev.] A biography.

bio- /ˈbʌɪəʊ/ *comb. form* of Gk *bios* life, course or way of living (opp. *zōē* animal life, organic life) in scientific wds usu. with the senses 'of living organisms', 'biological': see -O-.

bio-a'ssay *n.* measurement of the concentration or strength of a substance by means of its effect on a living organism E20. **bioavaila'bility** *n.* the rate at which a drug etc. is absorbed by the body or exerts an effect after absorption L20. **biobiblio'graphical** *a.* of or pertaining to biobibliography E19. **biobibli'ography** *n.* a bibliography containing biographical information about the author(s) E20. **bio'centric** *a.* centring in life; regarding or treating life as a central fact: L19. **bio'centrism** *n.* the view or belief that all life is important L20. **biochip** *n.* a device analogous to a conventional chip but made of proteins or other organic material L20. **bio'cidal** *a.* that acts as a biocide M20. **biocide** *n.* (*a*) the destruction of life; (*b*) a poisonous substance, *esp.* a pesticide: M20. **biocli'matic** *a.* of or pertaining to the interrelation of climate and the activities and distribution of living organisms E20. **bioclima'tology** *n.* biology in relation to climate E20. **biocompati'bility** *n.* the property of being biocompatible L20. **biocom'patible** *a.* not harmful or toxic to living tissue L20. **biodata** *n.sing.* & *pl.* (esp. in the Indian subcontinent) a curriculum vitae, biographical details M20. **biodi'versity** *n.* diversity of plant and animal life L20. **bio-ener'getic** *a.* of or pertaining to bio-energetics M20. **bio-ener'getics** *n.* (the branch of science that deals with) the transformation of energy in living organisms M20. **bio-engi'neer** *n.* a person engaged in bio-engineering M20. **bio-engi'neering** *n.* the application of engineering and the physical sciences to biological processes; the industrial use of biological processes: M20. **bio'feedback** *n.* the use of electronic monitoring of a normally automatic bodily function in order to train a person to acquire voluntary control of that function L20. **bio'flavonoid** *n.* any of the citrin flavonoids (see CITRIN) M20. **biofouler** *n.* an organism that causes biofouling L20. **biofouling** *n.* the fouling of underwater pipes and other surfaces by organisms such as barnacles and algae L20. **biogas** *n.* gaseous fuel (usu. methane) produced by fermentation of organic matter, esp. in apparatus designed for this purpose L20. **biogeo'chemical** *a.* of or pertaining to biogeochemistry M20. **biogeo'chemistry** *n.* the science of the interaction of living organisms with the chemistry of the environment M20. **biohazard** *n.* a risk to man or the environment associated with biological work, *esp.* with harmful micro-organisms; something constituting such a risk: M20. **bio'hazardous** *a.* of the nature of a biohazard L20. **bioherm** *n.* [Gk *herma* sunken rock, reef] *Geol.* a circumscribed body of sedimentary rock consisting of the remains of living organisms E20. **bio'hermal** *a.* (of the nature) of a bioherm M20. **biolumi'nescence** *n.* the biochemical production of light; light so emitted: E20. **biolumi'nescent** *a.* exhibiting bioluminescence E20. **biomass** *n.* (*a*) the total weight of living organisms in a given area or of a given species; (*b*) organic matter consisting of or recently derived from living organisms (esp. regarded as fuel): M20. **biomathe'matics** *n.* the science of the application of mathematics to biology E20. **biome** *n.* [-OME] *Ecol.* (the distinct major habitat occupied by) a community of plants and animals, e.g. in a prehistoric period E20. **bio'medical** *a.* of or pertaining to both biology and medicine M20. **biomedicine** *n.* biology and medicine considered together E20. **biomi'metic** *a.* (of the synthesis of a naturally-occurring substance) mimicking a biochemical process L20. **biomorph** *n.* a decorative form representing a living object L19. **bio'morphic** *a.* of the nature of a biomorph L19. **bio-or'ganic** *a.* pertaining to or designating the organic chemistry of living organisms M20. **biopoesis** /-pəʊ'iːsɪs/ *n.* [Gk *poiēsis* making] the hypothetical origination of life from replicating inanimate matter M20. **bio'polymer** *n.* a polymeric biochemical M20. **bioscience** *n.* (any of) the life sciences M20. **bioscientist** *n.* a life scientist M20. **bioscope** *n.* †(*a*) a view or survey of life; (*b*) an early form of cinematograph; (*c*) *S. Afr.* a cinema, a moving picture: E19. **biosensor** *n.* a thing for detecting chemicals by the use of a living organism or a product of one; an organism used for this purpose: L20. **bio'social** *a.* of or pertaining to the interaction of biological and social factors E20. **biosocio'logical** *a.* of or pertaining to biology and sociology E20. **biosphere** *n.* the regions of the earth's crust and atmosphere occupied by living organisms L19. **bio'spheric** *a.* of or pertaining to the biosphere E20. **biostrome** /-strəʊm/ *n.* [Gk *strōma* mattress, bed] *Geol.* a bedded stratum of sedimentary rock consisting of the remains of living organisms M20. **biotope** *n.* (*Ecol.*) the region of a habitat associated with a particular ecological community E20. **biotur'bated** *a.* (*Geol.*) affected by bioturbation M20. **biotur'bation** *n.* (*Geol.*) the disturbance of sedimentary deposits by living organisms M20. **biotype** *n.* a group of organisms having an identical genetic constitution E20.

biocenosis *n.* see BIOCOENOSIS.

biochemical /bʌɪə(ʊ)'kɛmɪk(ə)l/ *a.* & *n.* M19. [f. BIO- + CHEMICAL *a.*] **A** *adj.* Of or pertaining to biochemistry. M19. **B** *n.* A substance involved in biochemical processes. M20.

bio'chemic *a.* biochemical L19. **biochemically** *adv.* L19.

biochemistry /bʌɪə(ʊ)'kɛmɪstri/ *n.* L19. [f. BIO- + CHEMISTRY.] (The branch of science that deals with) the chemical and physico-chemical processes which occur in living organisms.

biochemist *n.* an expert in or student of biochemistry L19.

biocoenosis /ˌbʌɪə(ʊ)sɪ'nəʊsɪs/ *n.* Also ***-cen-**. Pl. **-noses** /-'nəʊsiːz/. L19. [mod.L, f. BIO- + Gk *koinōsis* sharing, f. *koinos* common.] *Ecol.* An association of organisms forming a closely integrated community; the relationship existing between these organisms.

biocoenology *n.* the branch of science that deals with biocoenoses M20. **biocoenotic** /-'nɒtɪk/*a.* of, pertaining to, or of the nature of a biocoenosis E20.

biodegradable /ˌbʌɪə(ʊ)dɪ'greɪdəb(ə)l/ *a.* M20. [f. BIO- + DEGRADE *v.* + -ABLE.] Able to be decomposed by bacteria or other organisms.

biodegrada'bility *n.* M20. **biodegra'dation** *n.* decomposition brought about by living organisms M20. **biodegrade** *v.i.* & *t.* (cause to) undergo biodegradation L20.

biodynamic /ˌbʌɪə(ʊ)dʌɪ'namɪk/ *a.* L19. [f. BIO- + DYNAMIC *a.*] Of or pertaining to dynamic effects brought about or experienced by living organisms; (of farming) using only organic fertilizers etc.

biodynamics /ˌbʌɪə(ʊ)dʌɪ'namɪks/ *n.* M20. [f. BIO- + DYNAMICS.] (The study or application of) biodynamic effects collectively.

bio-electricity /ˌbʌɪəʊɪlɛk'trɪsɪti/ *n.* M20. [f. BIO- + ELECTRICITY.] Electricity or electrical phenomena produced within living organisms.

bio-e'lectric *a.* E20. **bio-e'lectrical** *a.* M20.

bioethics /bʌɪəʊ'ɛθɪks/ *n.* L20. [f. BIO- + *ethics*: see ETHIC *n.* 4.] The ethics of biological research, esp. of medical techniques such as organ transplantation.

bioethical *a.* L20. **bioethicist** /-sɪst/ *n.* an expert in or student of bioethics L20.

biog /'bʌɪɒg/ *n. colloq.* M20. [Abbrev.] A biography.

biogenesis /bʌɪə(ʊ)'dʒɛnɪsɪs/ *n.* L19. [f. BIO- + -GENESIS.] **1** The hypothesis that living matter arises only from other living matter. L19. **2** The synthesis of a substance by living organisms. M20. **3** The hypothetical development of living matter from complex inanimate substances. M20.

biogenesist *n.* (*Hist.*) an advocate of the hypothesis of biogenesis (sense 1) L19. **biogenetic** /-dʒɪ'nɛtɪk/ *a.* of, pertaining to, or produced by biogenesis, in any sense L19. **biogenetically** /-dʒɪ'nɛtɪk(ə)li/ *adv.* M20.

biogenic /bʌɪə(ʊ)'dʒɛnɪk/ *a.* E20. [f. BIO- + -GENIC.] **1** = BIOGENETIC *a.* E20. **2** Produced or brought about by living organisms. (The predominant sense.) E20.

biogenically *adv.* M20.

biogenous /bʌɪ'ɒdʒɪnəs/ *a.* M20. [f. BIO- + -GENESIS + -OUS.] = prec.

biogeography /ˌbʌɪəʊdʒɪ'ɒgrəfi, -'dʒɒg-/ *n.* L19. [f. BIO- + GEOGRAPHY.] The science of the geographical distribution of living organisms.

biogeographer *n.* E20. **biogeo'graphic** *a.* L19. **biogeo'graphical** *a.* E20. **biogeo'graphically** *adv.* E20.

biography /bʌɪ'ɒgrəfi/ *n.* & *v.* L17. [Fr. *biographie* or mod.L *biographia*, med.Gk *biographia*: see BIO-, -GRAPHY.] **A** *n.* **1** The history of the lives of individuals, as a branch of literature. L17. **2** A written life of a person. L18. **3** The life-course of a living (esp. human) being. M19. **B** *v.t.* Write the life of; make the subject of a biography. M19.

biogra'phee *n.* a person who is the subject of a biography M19. **biographer** *n.* a writer of biographies or the life of a person E18. **bio'graphic** *a.* of or pertaining to (a) biography L18. **bio'graphical** *a.* = BIOGRAPHIC *a.* M18. **bio'graphically** *adv.* M18. **biographist** *n.* = BIOGRAPHER M17. **biographize** *v.t.* & *i.* write a biography (of) E19.

biological /bʌɪə(ʊ)'lɒdʒɪk(ə)l/ *a.* & *n.* M19. [f. BIOLOGY *n.* + -ICAL.] **A** *adj.* Of, pertaining to, or of the nature of biology or the phenomena of living organisms. M19.

biological clock an innate mechanism controlling rhythmic activity of an organism. **biological control** the control of a pest by the introduction of a natural enemy of it. **biological science** = *life science* s.v. LIFE *n.* **biological mother, father, parent**: who procreated the child in question (esp. as opp. to the one(s) who nursed or brought up the child). **biological warfare** the use of harmful micro-organisms or biological products as weapons.

B *n.* A biological product, esp. one used therapeutically. E20.

biologic *a.* = BIOLOGICAL *a.* M19. **biologically** *adv.* L19.

biologise *v.* var. of BIOLOGIZE.

biologism /bʌɪ'ɒlədʒɪz(ə)m/ *n.* M19. [f. BIOLOGY *n.* + -ISM.] †**1** = ELECTROBIOLOGY (b). *rare.* Only in M19. **2** The interpretation of human life from a strictly biological point of view. E20.

biolo'gistic *a.* M20.

biologist /bʌɪ'ɒlədʒɪst/ *n.* E19. [f. BIOLOGY *n.* + -IST.] A person who studies biology.

biologize /bʌɪ'ɒlədʒʌɪz/ *v.* Also **-ise**. M19. [f. BIOLOGY + -IZE.] †**1** *v.t.* Mesmerize. M–L19. **2** *v.i.* & *t.* Practise biology or biologism; treat or interpret biologically. L19.

biology /bʌɪ'ɒlədʒi/ *n.* E19. [Fr. *biologie* f. G (as BIO-, -LOGY).] The science of life, dealing with the morphology, physiology, anatomy, behaviour, origin, and distribution of living organisms; occas. = PHYSIOLOGY. Also, life processes and phenomena collectively.

MOLECULAR *biology*.

biomagnetism /bʌɪə(ʊ)'magnɪtɪz(ə)m/ *n.* L19. [f. BIO- + MAGNETISM.] †**1** Animal magnetism. Only in L19. **2** The interaction of living organisms with magnetic fields. M20.

biomag'netic *a.* L19.

biomechanics /ˌbʌɪə(ʊ)mə'kanɪks/ *n.pl.* (usu. treated as *sing.*). E20. [f. BIO- + MECHANICS.] The mechanics of the structures and movements of living organisms.

biomechanical *a.* M20. **biomechanically** *adv.* M20.

biometric /bʌɪə(ʊ)'mɛtrɪk/ *a.* E20. [f. BIO- + -METRIC.] Of or pertaining to biometry.

biometrical *a.* E20. **biometrically** *adv.* E20.

biometrics /bʌɪə(ʊ)'mɛtrɪks/ *n.* E20. [f. prec.: see -ICS.] = BIOMETRY *n.* 2.

biome'trician *n.* E20.

biometry /bʌɪ'ɒmɪtri/ *n.* M19. [f. BIO- + -METRY.] †**1** The measurement and study of the duration of human life. M–L19. **2** The application of statistical methods to biological investigation. E20.

bionic /bʌɪ'ɒnɪk/ *a.* E20. [f. BIO- + ELECTRONIC.] Of or relating to bionics; having mechanical body parts, or superhuman powers resulting from these. Also in trivial use: powerful, energetic.

bionics /bʌɪ'ɒnɪks/ *n.* M20. [f. prec.: see -ICS.] The study and construction of mechanical systems that function like (parts of) living beings.

bionomic /bʌɪə(ʊ)'nɒmɪk/ *a.* L19. [f. BIO- + ECONOMIC.] Of or pertaining to bionomics; ecological.

Also **bionomical** *a.* E20.

bionomics /bʌɪə(ʊ)'nɒmɪks/ *n.* L19. [f. BIO- + ECONOMICS.] The branch of biology that deals with organisms' behaviour and modes of life in their natural environment; ecology.

-biont /'bʌɪɒnt/ *suff.* [Extracted f. SYMBIONT.] *Biol.* Forming ns. denoting kinds of living organism, esp. w. ref. to particular modes of life, as *halobiont*, *parabiont*, *trophobiont*, freq. after adjs. in *-biotic*.

biophysics /bʌɪə(ʊ)'fɪzɪks/ *n.* L19. [f. BIO- + PHYSICS.] The science of the application of the laws of physics to biological phenomena.

biophysical *a.* E20. **biophysically** *adv.* L20. **biophysicist** *n.* an expert in or student of biophysics E20.

biopic /ˈbʌɪəʊpɪk/ *n. colloq.* M20. [f. BIO(GRAPHICAL + PIC *n.*[3]] A biographical film.

biopsy /ˈbʌɪɒpsi/ *n.* & *v.* L19. [f. BIO- + Gk *opsis* sight, after *necropsy*.] A *n.* Examination of tissue taken from the human body for diagnostic purposes; the removal of such tissue. L19. B *v.t.* Subject to biopsy. M20.

biorhythm /ˈbʌɪə(ʊ)rɪð(ə)m/ *n.* M20. [f. BIO- + RHYTHM *n.*] Any recurring cycle in the physiology of an organism; *spec.* a cyclic pattern of physical, emotional, or mental activity said to occur in the life of a person.

bioˈrhythmic *a.* pertaining to or of the nature of biorhythm M20. **bioˈrhythmically** *adv.* with regard to biorhythms or biorhythmics L20. **bioˈrhythmicist** *n.* an advocate or student of biorhythmics L20. **bioˈrhythmics** *n.* the branch of science that deals with biorhythms, esp. one's own M20.

biospeleology /ˌbʌɪə(ʊ)spiːlɪˈɒlədʒi/ *n.* Also **-laeo-**. M20. [Fr. *biospéléologie*: see BIO-, SPELEOLOGY.] The branch of science that deals with the fauna and flora of caves.

biospeleoˈlogical *a.* M20. **biospeleologist** *n.* M20.

biostatistics /ˌbʌɪə(ʊ)stəˈtɪstɪks/ *n.* Orig. *US.* L19. [f. BIO- + STATISTICS.] The branch of statistics that deals with data relating to life; vital statistics.

biostatistical *a.* M20. **biostatiˈstician** *n.* M20.

biostratigraphy /ˌbʌɪə(ʊ)strəˈtɪɡrəfi/ *n.* E20. [f. BIO- + STRATIGRAPHY.] The branch of stratigraphy that deals with life in the geological past; stratigraphy based on fossils.

biostratigrapher *n.* M20. **biostratiˈgraphic** *a.* E20. **biostratiˈgraphical** *a.* M20. **biostratiˈgraphically** *adv.* M20.

biosynthesis /bʌɪə(ʊ)ˈsɪnθɪsɪs/ *n.* M20. [f. BIO- + SYNTHESIS.] Synthesis (of a chemical substance) by a living organism.

biosynthesize *v.t.* produce by biosynthesis M20. **biosynˈthetic** *a.* of, pertaining to or produced by biosynthesis M20. **biosynˈthetically** *adv.* M20.

biosystematics /ˌbəɪə(ʊ)sɪstəˈmatɪks/ *n.* M20. [f. BIO- + *systematics*: see SYSTEMATIC *n.* 2.] Taxonomy based on the study of the genetic evolution of plant and animal populations.

biosystematic *a.* of or pertaining to biosystematics M20. **biosystematically** *adv.* M20. **biosyˈstematist** *n.* M20.

biota /bʌɪˈəʊtə/ *n.* E20. [mod.L f. Gk *biotē* life.] The animal and plant life of a region.

biotech /ˈbʌɪəʊtɛk/ *n. colloq.* L20. [Abbrev.] = next.

biotechnology /ˌbʌɪə(ʊ)tɛkˈnɒlədʒi/ *n.* M20. [f. BIO- + TECHNOLOGY.] Orig., the branch of technology that dealt with the actions and requirements of human beings. Now, the industrial application of biological processes.

biotechnoˈlogical *a.* M20. **biotechnologist** *n.* L20.

biotic /bʌɪˈɒtɪk/ *a.* E17. [Late L *bioticus* f. Gk *biōtikos*, f. *bios* life: see -IC. In mod. use f. Fr. *biotique*.] †1 Of or pertaining to (secular) life. *rare*. Only in E17. 2 Of, pertaining to, or resulting from living organisms, esp. in their ecological relations. L19.

biotical *a.* (*rare*) = BIOTIC 2 M19. **biotically** *adv.* M20.

biotin /ˈbʌɪətɪn/ *n.* M20. [f. Gk *biotos* life + -IN[1].] *Biochem.* A vitamin of the B complex which is found widely in nature, esp. in yeast, liver, and egg-yolk, and is essential for the metabolism of fats in particular. Also (chiefly *US*) called *vitamin H*.

biotite /ˈbʌɪətʌɪt/ *n.* M19. [f. J.-B. *Biot* (1774–1862), Fr. physicist + -ITE[1].] *Min.* A dark brown, green, or black ferromagnesian mica which is a constituent of many igneous and metamorphic rocks.

biparental /bʌɪpəˈrɛnt(ə)l/ *a.* E20. [f. BI- + PARENTAL.] *Biol.* Of, pertaining to, or derived from, two parents.

biparietal /bʌɪpəˈrʌɪɪt(ə)l/ *a.* M19. [f. BI- + PARIETAL *a.*] *Anat.* Joining or involving the two parietal bones of the skull.

biparous /ˈbɪpərəs/ *a.* M18. [f. BI- + -PAROUS.] 1 Producing two offspring at once. M18. 2 *Bot.* Of a cyme: having two branches at every node; forming a dichasium. L19.

biparted /bʌɪˈpɑːtɪd/ *a.* L16. [f. BI- + PARTED *a.*[1]] = BIPARTITE.

bipartisan /ˌbʌɪpɑːtɪˈzan/ *a.* E20. [f. BI- + PARTISAN *a.*] Of, representing, or composed of members of two (political etc.) parties.

bipartite /bʌɪˈpɑːtʌɪt/ *a.* LME. [L *bipartitus* pa. pple of *bipartire*, f. as BI- + PARTITE.] 1 Divided into or consisting of two parts. LME. 2 Of a treaty, contract, etc.: drawn up in two corresponding parts. E16. 3 Shared by or involving two parties. E17. 4 *Math.* Of a curve, graph, etc.: consisting of two distinct sets of points. M19.

bipartitely *adv.* M17. **biparˈtition** *n.* M17.

biped /ˈbʌɪpɛd/ *n.* & *a.* M17. [L *biped-*, *-pes*, f. BI- + *ped-*, *pes* foot.] A *n.* A two-footed animal. M17. B *adj.* Having two feet. L18.

bipedal /bʌɪˈpiːd(ə)l/ *a.* LME. [L *bipedalis*, f. as prec. + -AL[1]; in mod. use f. prec. + -AL[1].] †1 Two feet long. Only in LME. 2 Having two feet; *spec.* using the hind limbs for locomotion. E17. 3 Of, pertaining to, or caused by a biped. E19.

bipedalism *n.* E20. **bipeˈdality** *n.* M19. **bipedally** *adv.* L19.

biphasic /bʌɪˈfeɪzɪk/ *a.* E20. [f. BI- + PHASE *n.* + -IC.] Having two phases.

biphenyl /bʌɪˈfiːnʌɪl, -ˈfɛnɪl/ *n.* L19. [f. BI- + PHENYL.] *Chem.* A crystalline aromatic hydrocarbon, $(C_6H_5)_2$, formed by pyrolysis of benzene and containing two benzene rings; any substituted derivative of this.

POLYBROMINATED *biphenyl*. POLYCHLORINATED *biphenyl*.

bipinnate /bʌɪˈpɪneɪt/ *a.* M18. [f. BI- + PINNATE.] 1 *Bot.* Of a compound leaf: pinnately divided, with the leaflets themselves pinnate. M18. 2 *Zool.* Having feathery appendages in opposed pairs. M19.

bipinnatifid /bʌɪpɪˈnatɪfɪd/ *a.* E19. [f. BI- + PINNATIFID.] *Bot.* Of leaves: pinnatifid, with the pinnae themselves similarly divided.

Also **bipinnatisect** *a.* L19.

biplane /ˈbʌɪpleɪn/ *n.* L19. [f. BI- + PLANE *n.*[3], *n.*[4]] †1 *Math.* Either of two planes tangential to a surface at the same point. L19–E20. 2 An aeroplane having two sets of wings, one above the other. L19.

biˈplanar *a.* (Math.) situated in two tangent planes M19.

bipolar /bʌɪˈpəʊlə/ *a.* E19. [f. BI- + POLAR *a.*] 1 Having two poles or opposite extremities. E19. 2 *spec.* a Of a nerve cell: having two axons, one either side of the cell body. M19. b Of psychiatric illness: characterized by both manic and depressive episodes, or manic ones only (in individual or family history). M20. 3 Of or occurring in both polar regions. L19.

bipoˈlarity *n.* (*a*) the state of having two poles; (*b*) the occurrence of the same species in each of the polar regions: M19.

biprism /ˈbʌɪprɪz(ə)m/ *n.* L19. [f. BI- + PRISM.] *Physics.* A combination of two long narrow prisms joined by the base, or an equivalent single prism, used to produce interference effects. Also *Fresnel biprism*.

bipyramidal /bʌɪpɪˈramɪd(ə)l/ *a.* M19. [f. BI- + PYRAMIDAL.] Having the form of two like pyramids joined base to base.

biˈpyramid *n.* a bipyramidal object or structure E20.

biquadratic /bʌɪkwɒˈdratɪk/ *a.* & *n.* M17. [f. BI- + QUADRATIC.] *Math.* A *adj.* Of, pertaining to, or containing the fourth power (or root) of a number. M17. B *n.* A biquadratic equation. Formerly also, the fourth power of a number. M17.

Also †**biquadrate** *a.* & *n.* L17–E19.

†**biquaternion** *n.* M19–E20. [f. BI- + QUATERNION.] *Math.* A quaternion with complex coefficients. Also, a combination of two quaternions obeying certain conditions.

bi-racial /bʌɪˈreɪʃ(ə)l/ *a.* E20. [f. BI- + RACIAL.] Concerning or containing (members of) two racial groups.

biramous /bʌɪˈreɪməs/ *a.* L19. [f. BI- + RAMUS + -OUS.] *Zool.* Distally forked (esp. of crustacean limbs and antennae).

Also **biramose** *a.* L19.

birational /bʌɪˈraʃ(ə)n(ə)l/ *a.* L19. [f. BI- + RATIONAL *a.*] *Math.* Of a transformation: relating two sets of variables of which each set is expressed rationally in terms of the other.

birationally *adv.* E20.

birch /bəːtʃ/ *n.* Also (*north.*) **birk** /bəːk/. [OE *birċe*, *bierċe* = MLG *berke*, OHG *birihha*, *birka* (G *Birke*) f. Gmc.] 1 Any of various hardy northern trees or shrubs of the genus *Betula* (family Betulaceae), having smooth, tough bark and slender branches; *esp.* (in Europe) *B. pendula* (more fully *silver birch*) and *B. pubescens* (more fully *downy birch*), and (in N. America) *B. papyrifera* (more fully *paper birch*). Also *birch tree*. OE. 2 The wood of the birch. LME. 3 A bundle of birch twigs used for flogging. M17. 4 In *pl.* in form *birks*. A grove of birches. *north.* E18. 5 A canoe made of the bark of *Betula papyrifera*. *N. Amer.* M19.

1 *black birch*, *canoe birch*, *river birch*, etc.

Comb.: **birch-bark** *N. Amer.* (a canoe made of) the bark of *Betula papyrifera*; **birch beer** *N. Amer.* a fermented beverage flavoured with oil extracted from the birch; a soft drink resembling this; **birch partridge** *N. Amer.* the ruffed grouse, *Bonasa umbellus*; **birch-rod** = sense 3 above; *birch tree*: see sense 1 above; **birch-water** the sap obtained from the birch in spring; **birch-wine** wine prepared from birch-water; **birchwood** (*a*) a wood of birch trees; (*b*) = sense 2 above.

birchen *a.* of or pertaining to (the) birch; composed of birch: ME.

birch /bəːtʃ/ *v.t.* M19. [f. the n.] Flog with a birch.

birching *n.* the action of the vb; a flogging with a birch: M19.

bircher /ˈbəːtʃə/ *n.*[1] L19. [f. prec. + -ER[1].] A person who flogs somebody with a birch; an advocate of birching.

Bircher /ˈbəːtʃə/ *n.*[2] M20. [John *Birch*, a USAF officer killed by Chinese Communists in 1945, 'the first casualty of the Cold War' + -ER[1].] A member or supporter of the John Birch Society, an extreme right-wing and anti-Communist American organization founded in 1958.

bird /bəːd/ *n.* [OE *brid*, (late Northumb.) *bird*, of unkn. origin and without cognates.] 1 A nestling, a fledgling; a chick. Long *obs.* exc. *north.* OE. 2 A feathered, warm-blooded, amniote animal of the vertebrate class Aves, characterized by modification of the forelimbs as wings for flight, oviparous reproduction, and care for the young. ME. b *Sport.* A game-bird; *spec.* a partridge; *fig.* prey. LME. 3 A maiden, a girl; a young woman. (Orig. a var. of BURD, later taken as *fig.* use of sense 1 or 2.) Now *slang* (freq. *derog.*). ME. 4 A person (freq. w. specifying adj.). *colloq.* M19. 5 A first-rate person, animal, or thing. *US slang.* M19. 6 [Abbrev. of BIRDLIME *n.* 2.] A prison sentence; prison. *slang.* E20. 7 An aeroplane; a missile, rocket, satellite, spacecraft, etc. *slang.* M20. 8 In badminton: a shuttlecock. L20.

2 *game-bird*: see GAME *n.*

Phrases: **a bird in the hand** something certain. **a little bird** an unnamed informant. ARABIAN *bird*. **Bird of Freedom** *US* the emblematic bald eagle of the US. **bird of Jove** the eagle. **bird of Juno** the peacock. **bird of paradise** (*a*) any of the family Paradisaeidae of passerine birds, mostly native to New Guinea, which are remarkable for the beauty and brilliance of their plumage; (*b*) (*the Bird of Paradise*) = APUS; (*c*) *bird-of-paradise flower* = STRELITZIA. *bird of passage*: see PASSAGE *n.* **bird of prey** a bird that kills and feeds on the flesh of other animals; *spec.* one belonging to the orders Cathartiformes, Accipitiformes, or Falconiformes (or sometimes Strigiformes). **birds of a feather** those of like character. *box of birds*: see BOX *n.*[2] *for the birds*: see *strictly for the birds* etc. below. *hear a bird sing*: see SING *v.*[1] **kill two birds with one stone** achieve two aims at once. **like a bird** swiftly; easily; without resistance or hesitation. *old bird*: see OLD *a.* *rare bird*: see RARE *a.*[1] *singing bird*: see SINGING *ppl a.* *soldier bird*: see SOLDIER *n.* *stinking bird*: see STINKING *a.* (**strictly**) **for the birds** trivial; appealing only to the gullible. **the (big) bird** *slang* (orig. *Theatr.*) hissing and booing; dismissal, the sack; (esp. in *get* or *give the* (*big*) *bird*). **the bird has flown** the prisoner etc. has escaped. †**the bird in the bosom** one's own secret or pledge, one's conscience. **the birds and the bees** *colloq. euphem.* details of human sexual functions. **the early bird** one who rises early or acts promptly.

Comb.: **bird-banding** = *bird-ringing* below; **bird-bath** a basin in a garden etc. with water for birds to bathe in; †**bird-bolt** a blunt-headed arrow used for shooting birds; **birdbrain** *colloq.* a birdbrained person; **birdbrained** *a.* (*colloq.*) stupid, flighty; **birdcage** a (usu. wire) cage for a bird or birds; an object of similar design; *Sporting slang* a paddock at a racecourse; **bird-call** the natural call of a bird; an instrument imitating this; **bird cherry** a Eurasian wild cherry, *Prunus padus* (in Britain mostly northern), which bears its flowers in long racemes; **bird dog** *N. Amer.* a gun dog trained to retrieve birds; also, a tout; **bird-eating spider** any of various large tropical spiders which occasionally trap small birds; **bird-fancier** a person who knows about, collects, breeds, or deals in, birds; **bird-life** = AVIFAUNA; **birdman** (*a*) a man who catches, sells, etc. birds; *colloq.* an ornithologist; (*b*) *colloq.* an airman; †**bird-mouthed** *a.* unwilling to speak out; **bird-ringing** the fixing of an identifying band to a bird's leg; **bird sanctuary** an area where birds are protected and encouraged to breed; **bird's-beak moulding** a moulding which in cross-section forms an ovolo or ogee with or without a fillet under it, followed by a hollow; **birdseed** special seeds given as food to caged birds; **bird's-eye** (*a*) any of various plants with small round bright flowers, *esp.* a primrose, *Primula farinosa* (usu. *bird's-eye primrose*), having yellow-centred purple flowers, and germander speedwell, *Veronica chamaedrys*; (*b*) manufactured tobacco with the ribs of the leaves cut along with the fibre; (*c*) (a fabric woven in) a design consisting in a small diamond with a centre dot; (*d*) *attrib.* of or pertaining to a bird's eye; marked as with bird's eyes, spotted; *bird's eye view*, a view from overhead *of* a landscape etc., such as a bird might have, *fig.* a résumé or overview *of* a subject; **bird's-foot** (*a*) any of various objects, esp. plants, resembling a bird's foot; *spec.* a vetch, *Ornithopus perpusillus*, having claw-shaped seed-pods; (*b*) *attrib.*: *bird's-foot delta*, a delta built out from a coastline by deposition along a number of channels; *bird's-foot fenugreek*, a small white-flowered clover, *Trifolium ornithopodioides*, sometimes classified with the fenugreeks (*Trigonella*); *bird's-foot fern*, a small fern, *Pellaea mucronata*, native to the south-western US; *bird's-foot trefoil*, a superficially trifoliate leguminous plant of the genus *Lotus*, esp. *L. corniculatus*, with yellow flowers streaked with red and pods that spread like a bird's claw; *bird's-foot violet*, a violet, *Viola pedata*, of the eastern US; **bird shot** the smallest size of shot (for sporting-rifles etc.); **bird's nest** (*a*) the nest of a bird; *bird's-nest soup*, soup made from the edible nests of SE Asian swifts of the genus *Aerodramus*; (*b*) (usu. w. hyphen) any of various plants, *esp.*. the wild carrot and either of two saprophytic plants, *Neottia nidus-avis* (usu. called *bird's-nest orchid*) and *Monotropa hypopitys* (usu. called *yellow bird's-nest*); **bird's-nest** *v.i.* search for birds' nests, usu. to take the eggs; **bird's-nesting** (*a*) the action or occupation of searching for birds' nests; (*b*) the furring of a passage, *spec.* of a boiler tube; **birdsong** the musical call or sound made by a bird or birds; **bird-strike** a collision between an aircraft and a bird or birds; **bird table** a raised platform on which food for birds is placed; **bird-watch** *v.i.* engage in bird-watching; **bird-watcher** one who observes birds in their natural surroundings; **bird-watching** the occupation of a bird-watcher; **bird-witted** *a.* (*colloq.*) lacking the faculty of attention.

birdless *a.* having no birds, unfrequented by birds E16. **birdlike** *a.* resembling (that of) a bird L16.

bird /bəːd/ *v.i.* M16. [f. the n.] Engage in fowling or in bird-watching. Freq. as *birding* vbl n.

birder /ˈbəːdə/ *n.* ME. [f. BIRD *n.* + -ER[1].] †1 A fowler. ME–M17. †2 A wild cat. *dial.* E18–M19. 3 A breeder of birds. E19. 4 A bird-watcher. M20.

birdie /ˈbəːdi/ *n.* & *v.* L18. [f. BIRD *n.* + -IE.] A *n.* 1 A small bird. Also, a little girl, a young woman. (Used affectionately.) L18. 2 *Golf.* A hole played in one stroke under par or bogey. E20. B *v.t. Golf.* Play (a hole) in one stroke under par or bogey. M20.

birdlime /ˈbəːdlʌɪm/ *n.* & *v.* LME. [f. BIRD *n.* + LIME *n.*[1]] A *n.* 1 A glutinous substance spread on twigs to catch birds. LME. 2 Time; *spec.* a term of imprisonment. *rhyming slang.* M19. B *v.t.* Smear or catch (as) with birdlime. L16.

birefringence /bʌɪrɪˈfrɪndʒ(ə)ns/ *n.* L19. [f. BI- + REFRINGENT *a.* + -ENCE.] Double refraction.

birefringent *a.* having double refraction L19.

bireme /ˈbʌɪriːm/ *n.* & *a.* L16. [L *biremis*, f. BI- + *remus* oar.] *Hist.* (A galley) having two banks of oars.

biretta /bɪˈrɛtə/ *n.* Also **ber-**, **birr-**. L16. [It. *berretta* or Sp. *birreta*, fem. dims. corresp. to OProv. *berret* BERET, based on late L *birrus*, *-um* hooded cape or cloak, perh. of Celt. origin.] A square cap worn by Roman Catholic ecclesiastics (black by priests, purple by bishops, red by cardinals) or by other clergymen.

biri *n.* var. of BIDI.

biriani *n.* var. of BIRYANI.

birk *n.*[1] var. of BERK.

birk *n.*[2] see BIRCH *n.*

birkie /ˈbəːki/ *n.* & *a. Sc.* Also **-k(e)y**. E18. [Origin unkn.] A *n.* 1 A fellow; a man who forms his own opinions; a swaggering fellow. E18. 2 The card-game beggar-my-neighbour (see BEGGAR *v.* 1). L18. B *adj.* Mettlesome. E19.

birl /bəːl/ *n.* In sense 3 also **burl** /bəːl/. M19. [Imit.: cf. next.] 1 A twist, a spin, a whirl. *Sc.* & *north.* M19. 2 A rattling or whirring sound. *Sc.* & *north.* L19. 3 A try, an attempt. Esp. in *give it a birl*. *Austral.* & *NZ colloq.* E20.

birl /bəːl/ *v.* Orig. & chiefly *Sc.* E18. [Imit.: cf. prec.] 1 *v.t.* Cause to rotate rapidly; spin (a coin); toss (a coin) on the table as one's contribution to a joint fund, contribute. E18. 2 *v.i.* Revolve or rotate rapidly (often with a rattling or whirring sound). L18.

birle /bəːl/ *v.* Long *obs.* exc. *dial.* [OE *byrelian*, ON *byrla* f. *byrele* cup-bearer, perh. rel. to BEAR *v.*[1]] 1 *v.t.* Draw or pour out (drink, *to* or *for* a person). OE. 2 *v.t.* Supply or ply *with* drink. ME. 3 *v.i.* & *t.* Carouse; drink and pass (the cup). L16.

birley, -lie *ns.* see BYRLAW.

birling /ˈbəːlɪŋ, ˈbɪə-/ *n.* Also **berlin(g)**, **birlinn**. L16. [Gael. *birlinn*, *beirlinn*.] A large rowing boat or barge, formerly used in the Western Islands of Scotland.

Birmingham /ˈbəːmɪŋəm/ *n.* & *a.* Also †**Brummagem** & other local vars. L17. [A town (now a city) in central England, w. ref. to the counterfeit coins etc. once made there.] *Eng. Hist.* (Designating) a supporter of the 1680 Exclusion Bill, (a) Whig. Cf. ANTI-BIRMINGHAM.

Biro /ˈbʌɪrəʊ/ *n.* Also **b-**. Pl. **-os**. M20. [László József *Biró* (1899–1985), Hungarian inventor.] (Proprietary name for) a ball-point pen.

birr /bəː/ *n.*[1] ME. [Branch I f. ON *byrr* favouring wind; branch II prob. imit.] I Long chiefly *Sc.* & *north.* 1 A strong wind. ME. 2 Momentum, impetus; might; also, a thrust. ME. b Force of enunciation. E19. II 3 An energetic whirring sound. M19.

birr /bəː/ *n.*[2] Pl. same, **-s**. L20. [Amharic.] The basic monetary unit of Ethiopia, equal to 100 cents.

birr /bəː/ *v.i.* Chiefly *Sc.* E16. [f. BIRR *n.*[1]] Emit a whirring noise; move with a whirring noise.

birretta *n.* var. of BIRETTA.

birse /bəːs/ *n.* Long only *Sc.* [OE *byrst* = OS *brusta*, OHG *burst* (G *Borste*) ON *burst*(*i*).] = BRISTLE *n.*

birsle /ˈbəːs(ə)l/ *v.t. Sc.* & *north.* LME. [Origin unkn.: cf. BRISTLE *v.*[2]] Scorch, parch, toast hard.

birth /bəːθ/ *n.*[1] ME. [ON *byrð* = Goth. *gabaurþs* f. EGmc (corresp. to OE *ġebyrd*, OS *giburd*, OHG *giburt* (G *Geburt*) f. WGmc), f. base of BEAR *v.*[1]: see -TH[1].] 1 The emergence of young from the body of the mother (viewed as an act of the mother or as a fact pertaining to the offspring). ME. 2 Of things: †a Rising of the sun or a star. Only in ME. b Coming into existence; origin, beginning. E17. 3†a That which is borne in the womb. ME–M17. b That which is born into the world; offspring; product, creation. *arch.* LME. 4 Parentage, descent, inherited position; conditions or relations involved in birth; *spec.* noble lineage. ME. †5 Natural character; kind. ME–L16. †6 Fortune as influenced by the planets at the moment of birth. Only in L16.

1 H. FIELDING The birth of an heir by his beloved sister. TENNYSON Mine by right, from birth till death. **give birth to** bring (offspring) into the world (*lit.* & *fig.*). **new birth** *Theol.* spiritual regeneration. *virgin birth*: see VIRGIN *a.* 2b J. BENTHAM Offences which owe their birth to the joint influence of indolence and pecuniary interest. 3b ADDISON Others hatch their Eggs and tend the Birth, 'till it is able to shift for it self. 4 D. HUME Birth, titles, & place, must be honoured above industry & riches. J. GALSWORTHY Political by birth rather than by nature. J. DOS PASSOS My own sister by birth and blood. P. WARNER The arrow took no account of rank or birth. 5 SHAKES. *Rom. & Jul.* Nor aught so good but, strain'd from that fair use, Revolts from true birth. 6 SHAKES. *2 Hen. VI* A cunning man did calculate my birth And told me that by water I should die.

Comb.: **birth certificate** an official document giving the date and place of a person's birth; **birth control** (the practice of) methods of preventing unwanted pregnancy; **birth father** a biological (as opp. to an adoptive etc.) father; **birthmark** an unusual mark, esp. a blotch of brown or dark red skin, on the body at or from birth; **birth mother** a biological (as opp. to an adoptive etc.) mother; **birthnight** (the anniversary of) the night of one's birth; **birth parent** a biological (as opp. to an adoptive etc.) parent; **birth pill** a contraceptive pill; **birthplace** place of birth, origin, or commencement; **birth rate** the ratio of the number of births to the population, usu. calculated per thousand of population per year; **birthright** the rights, privileges, or possessions belonging to one by birth, as an eldest son, as being born in a certain status or country, or as a human being; **birth-root** *N. Amer.* trillium, *esp.* the purple *T. erectum*; **birth-sign** the astrological sign under which one is born; **birthstone** a gemstone associated with the month of one's birth; **birthweight** weight at birth; **birthwort** = ARISTOLOCHIA.

†**birth** *n.*[2] var. of BERTH *n.*

birth /bəːθ/ *v.*[1] ME. [f. BIRTH *n.*[1]] 1 *v.i.* Have birth, be born. *rare.* ME. 2 *v.i.* Give birth. Chiefly as *birthing* vbl n. E20. 3 *v.t.* Give birth to. *dial.* (esp. *US*). E20.

Comb.: **birthing pool** a large bath for women to give birth in.

†**birth** *v.*[2] var. of BERTH *v.*[1]

birthday /ˈbəːθdeɪ/ *n.* ME. [f. BIRTH *n.*[1] + DAY *n.*] (The anniversary of) the day of one's birth; the day of origin or commencement.

official birthday: see OFFICIAL *a.*

Comb.: **birthday book** a book in diary form for recording birthdays; **birthday boy**, **girl** *colloq.* the person present or otherwise known whose birthday it is; **birthday card** a greetings card marking the anniversary of a person's birthday; *birthday girl*: see *birthday boy* above; **birthday honours** the titles of honour conferred by the British monarch on each anniversary of his or her official birthday; **birthday party**, **present**: given to mark the anniversary of a person's birthday; **birthday suit** (*a*) *Hist.* a dress worn on the monarch's birthday; (*b*) *joc.* the bare skin.

biryani /bɪrˈjɑːni, bɪrɪˈɑːni/ *n.* Also **biriani** & other vars. M20. [Urdu f. Pers. *biryānī*, f. *biriyān* fried, grilled.] A dish of the Indian subcontinent consisting of spiced meat or vegetables and cooked rice.

bis /bɪs/ *adv.* E17. [Fr. & It., f. L *bis* twice.] Encore; again; twice; *spec.* as a direction in a musical score indicating that a passage is to be repeated.

bis- /bɪs/ *pref.* Var. of BI- used occas. bef. *s*, *c*, or a vowel, and in *Chem.* to form the names of compounds containing two groups identically substituted or coordinated, as *bis*(*2-chloroethyl*) *ether* (cf. TETRAKIS-, TRIS-).

biscacha *n.* var. of VISCACHA.

Biscayan /ˈbɪskeɪən/ *n.* & *a.* Now *arch.* or *Hist.* L16. [f. *Biscay* in NW Spain (Sp. *Vizcaya*, now a province of the region of Vascongadas y Navarra) + -AN: cf. BASQUE.] (A native or inhabitant) of Biscay or the Basque country.

†**biscotin** *n.* E18–E19. [Fr. f. It. *biscottino* dim. of *biscotto* corresp. to Fr. BISCUIT.] A kind of sweet biscuit.

biscuit /ˈbɪskɪt/ *n.* & *a.* Also †**bisket**. ME. [OFr. *bescuit*, *besquit* (mod. *biscuit*), ult. f. L *bis* twice + *coctus* pa. pple of *coquere* to cook.] A *n.* 1 A piece of usu. unleavened cake or bread of various ingredients, usu. crisp, dry, and hard, and in a small flat thin shape. ME. b A small round cake like a scone. *N. Amer.* E19. 2 Porcelain or other ware which has undergone firing but no further treatment. L18. 3 A light-brown colour regarded as characteristic of biscuits. L19. 4 Each of the three square sections of a soldier's mattress. E20.

1 *Bourbon biscuit, dog-biscuit, garibaldi biscuit, pilot biscuit, rich tea biscuit, Savoy biscuit*, etc. *take the biscuit*: see TAKE *v.*

Comb.: **biscuit barrel** a barrel or barrel-shaped container for biscuits.

B *attrib.* or as *adj.* Of the colour of biscuit, light-brown. L19.

biscuit-like *a.* resembling a biscuit M19. **biscuity** *a.* resembling a biscuit in texture, flavour, colour, etc. L19.

bise /biːz/ *n.* ME. [Fr., of unkn. origin.] A keen dry north wind prevalent in Switzerland, southern France, etc.

bisect /bʌɪˈsɛkt/ *v.t.* M17. [f. BI- + L *sect-* pa. ppl stem of *secare* to cut.] Cut or divide into two (orig. equal) parts.

bisection *n.* division into two (equal) parts M17.

bisexual /bʌɪˈsɛksjʊəl, -ʃʊəl/ *a.* & *n.* E19. [f. BI- + SEXUAL.] A *adj.* Of two sexes; having both sexes in one individual; (of a person) sexually attracted to individuals of both sexes. E19. B *n.* A bisexual person. E20.

bisexuˈality *n.* M19.

bish /bɪʃ/ *n.*[1] *joc.* E20. [Abbrev.] = BISHOP *n.*

bish /bɪʃ/ *n.*[2] *slang.* M20. [Origin unkn.] A mistake, a blunder.

bish /bɪʃ/ *v.*[1]*t. arch. joc.* L19. [Abbrev.] = BISHOP *v.*[1]

bish /bɪʃ/ *v.*[2]*t. Austral.* & *NZ slang.* M20. [Imit.] Throw.

bishop /ˈbɪʃəp/ *n.* Also (esp. in titles) **B-**. [OE *biscop* = OFris., OS *biskop*, (M)Du. *bisschop*, OHG *biscof* (G *Bischof*), ON *biskop* f. pop. var. of eccl.L *episcopus* f. Gk *episkopos* overseer, f. EPI- + *-skopos* looking (see -SCOPE).] 1 *Chr. Ch.* a In episcopal Churches, a member of the clergy consecrated as the governor of a diocese, possessing the powers to confirm, institute, and ordain, ranking next below an archbishop (where these exist) and above priests, deacons, etc. OE. b In some versions of the New Testament, an officer or overseer of the early Church (tr. Gk *episkopos*, used both as a descriptive term and as a title). Also (as a descriptive term only) a pastor or chief elder of a non-episcopal Church. LME. 2 A chief priest of any religion. Now *rare* or *obs.* OE. 3 *Chess.* Each of the four pieces that move diagonally and have the upper part shaped like a mitre. Cf. ARCHER 3, ALFIN. E16. 4a A ladybird; a moth. *dial.* L16. b Any of several African weaver-birds of the genus *Euplectes*. Also *bishop-bird*. L19. 5 Mulled and spiced wine (esp. port). M18. 6 Any of various articles of clothing; *spec.* (*a*) *US* (*Hist.*) a bustle; (*b*) *dial.* a smock or all-round pinafore. L18.

1a *cardinal bishop, metropolitan bishop, suffragan bishop, titular bishop*, etc. *Lord Bishop*: see LORD *n.* 4b *red bishop*: see RED *a.*

Comb.: *bishop-bird*: see sense 4b above; **Bishops' Bible** a version of the Bible published in 1568; **bishop's cap** mitrewort; **bishop sleeve** a full sleeve gathered at the wrist; **bishopstool** (now *arch.* or *Hist.*) the throne or see of a bishop; *bishop suffragan*: see SUFFRAGAN *n.* 1; **bishop's weed** ground elder, *Aegopodium podagraria*; **bishop's wort** betony.

bishopdom *n.* †(*a*) = BISHOPHOOD; (*b*) episcopal order, bishops collectively: OE. **bishopess** *n.* (chiefly *joc.*) (*a*) the wife of a bishop; (*b*) a female bishop: L17. **bishophood** *n.* the rank or office of a bishop OE. **bishoplike** *a.* & *adv.* (*a*) *adj.* resembling a bishop; formerly also, episcopal; (*b*) *adv.* in the manner of a bishop: M16. **bishoply** *a.* (now *rare*) episcopal OE. **bishopric** *n.* [OE *rīce* realm, rule] the diocese or jurisdiction of a bishop; the rank or office of a bishop: OE.

bishop /ˈbɪʃəp/ *v.*[1]*t. arch.* [OE *biscēopian*, f. prec.] 1 Administer the rite of confirmation to; confirm. Now *rare* or *obs.* OE. 2 Appoint to the office of bishop. M16.

bishop /ˈbɪʃəp/ *v.*[2]*t.* E18. [f. *Bishop*, a surname.] File and tamper with the teeth of (a horse) to deceive as to age.

bisk *n.* var. of BISQUE *n.*[3]

bisket *n.* obs. var. of BISCUIT.

Bislama /ˈbɪʃləmɑː/ *n.* L20. [Alt. of BEACH-LA-MAR.] An English-based pidgin used as a lingua franca in Fiji and esp. in Vanuatu (formerly New Hebrides).

Bismarck /ˈbɪzmɑːk/ *n.* Also **b-**; (in sense 4) **-mark**. L19. [f. as next; sense 4 perh. a different wd.] 1 In full *Bismarck brown*. = VESUVIN. L19. 2 A drink consisting of a mixture of champagne and stout. Cf. *black velvet* s.v. BLACK *a.* E20. 3 In full *Bismarck herring*. A marinaded herring served cold. M20. 4 A jam-filled doughnut. *US.* M20.

Bismarckian /bɪzˈmɑːkɪən/ *a.* L19. [f. *Bismarck* (see below) + -IAN.] Of, pertaining to, or characteristic of the German statesman Prince Otto von Bismarck (1815–98) or his policies.

Bismarckianism *n.* L19.

Bismark *n.* see BISMARCK.

bismillah /bɪsˈmɪlə/ *int.* & *n.* L18. [Arab. *bi-smi-llāh(i)*, the first word of the Koran.] (The exclamation) in the name of God: used by Muslims at the beginning of any undertaking.

bismite /ˈbɪzmʌɪt/ *n.* M19. [f. next + -ITE[1].] *Min.* Monoclinic bismuth trioxide, occurring usu. as greyish-green to yellow granular or earthy masses.

bismuth /ˈbɪzməθ/ *n.* Also **†wismuth**. M17. [mod.L *bisemutum* f. G *Wismut*, of unkn. origin.] A reddish-white easily fusible metallic chemical element, atomic no. 83 (symbol Bi). Also, a compound of this used medicinally.

Comb.: **bismuth glance** = BISMUTHINITE; **bismuth ochre** =BISMITE.

bismuthate *n.* a salt formed (as) by reaction of bismuth trioxide with an alkali M19. **bismuthic** /-ˈmjuː-/ *a.* of or containing bismuth L18. **bismuthyl** *n.* the radical ·BiO; the cation BiO^+: L19.

bismuthine /ˈbɪzm(j)ʊθiːn/ *n.* M19. [f. prec. + -INE[5].] 1 *Min.* = next. Now *rare* or *obs.* M19. 2 *Chem.* A very unstable gas, BiH_3. Also, any substituted derivative of this. L19.

bismuthinite /bɪzˈm(j)ʊθɪnʌɪt/ *n.* M19. [f. prec. + -ITE[1].] *Min.* Orthorhombic bismuth trisulphide occurring usu. as grey or white metallic needles or foliated masses.

bismutite /ˈbɪzm(j)ʊtʌɪt/ *n.* Also **-thite** /-θʌɪt/. M19. [G *Bismutit*, f. mod.L *bisemutum* BISMUTH: see -ITE[1].] *Min.* A tetragonal bismuthyl carbonate, which usu. occurs as dull yellow or grey earthy masses.

†bisogn(i)o *ns.* vars. of BESOGNIO.

bison /ˈbʌɪs(ə)n/ *n.* Pl. same. LME. [L, ult. f. Gmc base also of WISENT.] 1 Either of two heavily-built wild oxen of the genus *Bison*, with a high shoulder hump, long shaggy hair on the shoulders and forequarters, and a large head with short horns: (*a*) (more fully *European bison*) *B. bonasus*, exterminated in the wild but re-established in Poland and the Caucasus (also called *wisent*), (*b*) (more fully *American bison*) *B. bison*, surviving in small numbers on the N. American plains (also called *buffalo*). LME. 2 More fully *Indian bison* = GAUR. L19.

biˈsontine *a.* [L *bisont-*] pertaining to or resembling the bison L19.

bisque /bɪsk/ *n.*[1] M17. [Fr., of unkn. origin.] In various games, esp. tennis, croquet, and golf, (the allowing of) a point or stroke to be scored or taken when desired as a handicapping advantage.

bisque /bɪsk/ *n.*[2] M17. [f. BISCUIT.] A variety of unglazed white porcelain used for statuettes etc. Also = BISCUIT 2.

bisque /bɪsk, biːsk/ *n.*[3] Also **bisk** /bɪsk/. M17. [Fr = crayfish soup.] A rich soup usu. made from shellfish but also from birds etc.

bissextile /bɪˈsɛkstʌɪl/ *a.* & *n.* L16. [Late L *bi(s)sextilis* (*annus*) (year) containing the *bis sextus dies*, the doubled sixth day before the calends of March, i.e. 24 February] A *adj.* Containing the extra day the Julian calendar inserts in a leap year. L16. B *n.* A leap year. L16.

†bisson *a.* [OE (late Northumb.) *bisene* of unkn. origin.] 1 Blind; purblind. OE–L19. 2 Blinding. *rare* (Shakes.). Only in E17.

2 SHAKES. *Haml.* Threat'ning the flames With bisson rheum.

bistable /bʌɪˈsteɪb(ə)l/ *a.* M20. [f. BI- + STABLE *a.*] Having two stable states.

bister *n.* var. of BISTRE.

bistort /ˈbɪstɔːt/ *n.* E16. [Fr. *bistorte* or med.L *bistorta*, f. *bis* twice + *torta* fem. pa. pple of *torquere* twist.] Any of certain polygonums with twisted roots; *spec.* the species *Persicaria bistorta*, which bears cylindrical spikes of pink flowers and has an astringent root.

bistoury /ˈbɪstʊri/ *n.* M18. [Fr. *bistouri*, earlier *bistorie* dagger, of unkn. origin.] A surgeon's knife with a straight or curved narrow blade.

bistre /ˈbɪstə/ *n.* Also **bister**. E18. [Fr., of unkn. origin.] (The colour of) a brown pigment prepared from soot.

bistred *a.* stained with bistre L19.

bistro /ˈbiːstrəʊ, ˈbɪs-/ *n.* Pl. **-os**. Also **-ot**. E20. [Fr.] A small bar or restaurant.

bisulphate /bʌɪˈsʌlfeɪt/ *n.* Also ***-sulf-**. E19. [f. BI- + SULPHATE *n.*] *Chem.* A salt of the anion HSO_4^-, i.e. containing double the proportion of the acid radical present in a sulphate.

bit /bɪt/ *n.*[1] [OE *bite* = OFris. *bit(e)*, OS *biti* (MDu. *bēte*, Du. *beet*), OHG *biz* (G *Biss*), ON *bit* (Sw. *bett*, Da. *bid*), f. Gmc, f. base also of BITE *v.*] I Biting; what one bites. †1 The act or action of biting; = BITE *n.* 1. OE–M17. 2 Food to bite; victuals. Chiefly *dial.* E18.

II The biting or gripping part of something. †3a The cutting blade or edge of an edged tool, axe, etc. ME–M18. b The biting or cutting end or part of a tool, as the movable boring-piece of a drill, the cutting head of a (machine) lathe, the nipping-part of pincers, etc. L16. 4 The part of a key that engages with the lock-lever. M17. 5 The metal head of a soldering iron. L19.

III 6 The mouthpiece of a horse's bridle. LME.

6 *bridle-bit, snaffle-bit, tongue-bit*, etc. *champing at the bit*: see CHAMP *v.* 1. **off the bit** on a loose rein. **on the bit** on a tight rein. **take the bit between** (or **†in**) **one's teeth** escape from control. **up to the bit** to the highest speed allowed by the restraint applied.

bitless *a.* not having a bridle-bit E17.

bit /bɪt/ *n.*[2] & *a.* [OE *bita* = OFris. *bita*, OHG *bizzo* (MHG *bizze*, G *Bissen*), ON *biti*, f. Gmc, f. base of BITE *v.*] A *n.* †1 A bite or mouthful. OE–M17. 2 A morsel or small piece of food. ME. 3 A small piece, a fragment (of something); a small portion or quantity, a little. Freq. foll. by *of.* L16. b A small item in a popular periodical. *arch.* L19. c More fully *bit part*. A small acting role in a play or film. E20. 4a *A* sum of money. *arch. slang.* E17. b An obsolete silver coin of the southern States of America, the W. Indies, etc., having a value equal to some fraction of the Spanish dollar; the value of this coin. Still *US*, a unit of value equivalent to one-eighth of a dollar, the amount of 12½ cents, (used almost exclusively in even multiples). L17. c A small coin. *colloq.* E19. 5a *A* moment; *a* short time. *colloq.* M17. b *The* nick of time. *Sc.* L18. c A prison sentence. *slang.* M19. 6 In full *bit of fluff, goods*, (arch.) *muslin, skirt, stuff*, etc. A (young) woman. *slang* (usu. *derog.*). E19. 7 An action or display of attitude, an adopted role. Esp. in *the* or *one's — bit* (the specified action etc. being well known or characteristic). *slang* (orig. *US*). M20.

3 SHAKES. *Tr. & Cr.* The fragments, scraps, the bits, and greasy relics Of her o'er-eaten faith. J. HAWTHORNE I can take a bit draw of the pipe. B. STOKER A most noble ruin . . full of beautiful and romantic bits. D. H. LAWRENCE He's lost every bit of shame—every bit—if ever he had any—which I doubt very much. L. URIS By 1900 there were fifty thousand Jews in Palestine and a bit more social life for Jossi. 4b J. W. SCHULTZ Whisky dropped to the price of 'two bits' per drink. J. A. MICHENER Each item was priced in bits—Spanish silver dollars sawed into eight parts so that twenty-five cents was equal to two bits. c *threepenny bit* etc. 5a K. AMIS He couldn't be expected to get on with his play for a bit. c E. R. HAGEMANN Forgery, second degree, was his next quick conviction, and away he went to the Minnesota big house for a

ten-year bit. 6 M. GEE Mr. Tatlock . . went and married some young bit half his age. 7 F. ASTAIRE We were in Detroit—stranded—and that is where Mother did the pawning-of-the-jewels bit.

Phrases: **a bit —** *colloq.* somewhat —. **a bit much** rather excessive, annoying. **a bit of** *colloq.* (*a*) rather; (*b*) a small quantity of; (*c*) a fair quantity of. **a bit of a** a small or unimportant. *a bit of all right*: see ALL RIGHT *n. phr. a bit of crumpet*: see CRUMPET 5. *a bit of no good*: see GOOD *n. a bit thick*: see THICK *a.* **bit by bit** gradually. *bit of fluff, goods, muslin*: see sense 6 above. *bit of rough*: see ROUGH *n. bit of skirt*: see sense 6 above. *bit of spare*: see SPARE *n.*[1] 3. *bit of stuff*: see sense 6 above. **bits and bats, bobs, pieces** *colloq.* odds and ends. **do one's bit** *colloq.* contribute service or money to a cause. **every bit as** *colloq.* quite as. *give a bit of one's mind*: see MIND *n.*[1] **go to bits** *colloq.* go to pieces. **not a bit (of it)** *colloq.* not at all. *one's — bit*: see sense 7 above. **take a bit of doing** *colloq.* require all one's efforts, be difficult to do. *tear off a bit*: see TEAR *v.*[1] *the — bit*: see sense 7 above. **to bits** *colloq.* into small fragments. TWIDDLY *bit*.

Comb.: *bit part*: see sense 3c above; **bit-player** an actor of bit parts.

B *attrib.* or as *adj.* Little, small. *Sc.* L18.

bit /bɪt/ *n.*[3] M20. [Abbrev. of *binary digit* (see BINARY *a.*), after prec.] Chiefly *Computing*. A unit of information expressed as a choice between two equally probable alternatives (represented by the values 0 and 1).

parity bit: see PARITY *n.*[1] 3c.

Comb.: **bitmap** *n.* & *v.* (*a*) *n.* a representation in which each item is shown by one or more bits of information; *esp.* a display of the contents of a memory store; (*b*) *v.t.* provide with or represent by a bitmap; **bit string** a sequence of bits representing a character.

bitwise *a.* designating an operator in a programming language which manipulates the individual bits in a byte or word L20.

bit /bɪt/ *v.*[1]*t.* Infl. **-tt-**. L16. [f. BIT *n.*[1]] Provide with or accustom to a bit; *fig.* curb, restrain.

bit *v.*[2] var. of BUDE.

bit *v.*[3] pa. t. & pple of BITE *v.*

bitch /bɪtʃ/ *n.* & *a.* [OE *biċċe* rel. to ON *bikkja*.] **A** *n.* **1** A female dog. OE. **b** A female fox, otter, wolf, or (occas.) similar animal. LME. **2a** A man. Latterly *derog.* Now *rare*. ME. **b** A woman, esp. a lewd, malicious, or treacherous one. *derog.* LME. **c** Something difficult or unpleasant. *colloq.* E19. **3** A simple lamp made by placing a wick in some bacon fat. *Alaska* & *Canada*. E20.

2b *son of a bitch*: see SON *n.*[1]

B *attrib.* or as *adj.* (Of an animal) female; like a bitch. LME.

bitch goddess (material or worldly) success.

bitchery *n.* bitchy behaviour M16.

bitch /bɪtʃ/ *v.* L17. [f. the n.] †**1** *v.i.* Frequent the company of whores; call someone 'bitch'. L17–E18. **2** *v.t.* Spoil, botch. Freq. foll. by *up*. *colloq.* E19. **3** *v.t.* Behave bitchily towards; be spiteful, malicious, or unfair to. *colloq.* M20. **4** *v.i.* Complain, grumble. *colloq.* M20.

bitchy /ˈbɪtʃi/ *a.* E20. [f. BITCH *n.* + -Y[1].] **1** Sexually provocative; malicious, catty. E20. **2** Of a male dog: resembling a bitch. M20.

bitchily *adv.* M20. **bitchiness** *n.* M20.

bite /bʌɪt/ *n.* L15. [f. the vb.] **1** The action or an act of biting. L15. **b** The bringing together of the teeth in occlusion; the imprint of this in a plastic material. M19. **c** The corrosive action of acid on a metal in etching. L19. **d** The action of a machine indenting metal etc. L19. **e** The keen cutting effect of a harsh wind. L19. **f** *fig.* Incisiveness; point or cogency of style, language, etc. L19. **2a** A piece bitten off; a mouthful; a morsel of food; a small meal, a snack. Now freq. explicitly *a bite to eat*. M16. **b** Food to eat. *arch.* M16. **3** *Angling*. The seizure of bait by a fish. L16. **4** A wound inflicted by biting. E17. **5** *Printing* (now *Hist.*). A blank due to the accidental covering of part of the forme by the frisket. L17. †**6** An imposition, a deception; a person who or thing which swindles or deceives. *slang*. E18–M19. **7** Grip, hold, (*lit.* & *fig.*). M19. **8** A share of profits etc. *N. Amer. slang*. E20.

2a TOLKIEN I haven't had a bite since breakfast. C. ISHERWOOD Taking a huge bite out of his sandwich. T. SHARPE He'd . . have a bite to eat in a pub. M. GEE Grandpa never ate more than a bite and the rest sat on his plate. b M. E. BRADDON He had lain . . for fourteen days without either bite or sup. 3 W. S. MAUGHAM Occasionally he got a bite, now and then a fish. 4 R. LEHMANN Rat bites can be very poisonous. W. BOYD The tiny black flies that raised florin sized bites.

Phrases: (*a*) *bite and* (*a*) *sup*: see SUP *n.*[1] *bite(s) at the cherry*: see CHERRY *n.* **one's bite** (opp. *one's bark*) one's actions as opp. to one's words. *open bite*: see OPEN *a.* **put the bite on** *slang* (orig. *US*) ask for a loan, extort money from, threaten, blackmail.

Comb.: **bite-size(d)** *adjs.* small enough to be eaten in one bite; very small or short.

bite /bʌɪt/ *v.* Pa. t. **bit** /bɪt/; pa. pple **bitten** /ˈbɪt(ə)n/, chiefly *arch.* **bit**. [OE *bītan* = OFris. *bīta*, OS *bītan* (Du. *bijten*), OHG *bīzan* (G *beissen*), ON *bíta*, Goth. *beitan*, f. Gmc.] **1** *v.t.* & *i.* Cut (into), pierce, nip, or wound with the teeth (*v.i.* habitually); take a bite (from); (w. advb. compl.) remove or sever by biting. OE. **2** *v.t.* & *i.* Of something sharp or with a sharp edge: cut (into), penetrate. OE. **3** *v.t.* & *i.* Wound with mouthparts, the jaw, pincers, etc.; *loosely* (of a living creature) sting. ME. †**4** *v.t.* & *i.* Nibble, eat. ME–M17. **5** *v.t.* & *i.* Cause a sharp (esp. smarting) pain (to). ME. †**6** *v.t.* & *i.* Speak sharply or deprecatingly (against); carp (at). ME–L17. **7** *v.t.* & *i.* Engage (sympathy, interest, etc.); impress. *arch.* LME. **8** *v.t.* & *i.* Of an implement, part of a mechanism, etc.: grip or take hold of (a surface etc.). E16. **b** *v.i. spec.* in *Cricket*. Of the ball: get a grip of the surface of the ground on pitching. M19. **9** *v.t.* & *i.* Affect painfully or injuriously with intense cold. Cf. *frost-bitten*. M16. **10** *v.t.* & *i.* Corrode, as an acid or alkali; act as a mordant (upon). E17. **11** *v.i.* Of a fish & *fig.*: take or be caught by bait; snap *at* bait. M17. **12** *v.t.* Deceive, swindle. Now only in *pass. colloq.* E18. **13** *v.i.* Have an (esp. adverse) effect; make an impression. E20. **14** *v.t.* Borrow from (a person), esp. without intention or likelihood of repayment. (Foll. by *for* the thing borrowed.) *Austral. slang*. E20. **15** *v.t.* Excite; worry, perturb. Esp. in *what's biting you? colloq.* (orig. *US*). E20.

1 I. WATTS Let dogs delight to bark and bite. DAY LEWIS I bite into my chocolate. S. BECKETT Takes carrot from coat pocket, bites off a piece. W. MAXWELL My grandfather . . was bitten on the ear by a rat or a ferret and died . . of blood poisoning. D. M. THOMAS She was . . nibbling a cucumber sandwich (he glimpsed her small, pearly, even teeth as she bit). 2 TENNYSON Who heaved his blade aloft, And crack'd the helmet thro', and bit the bone. B. ENGLAND The razor bit deeply in and the blood spouted startlingly. P. MATTHIESSEN The thin straps bite at my shoulders. 3 AV *Prov.* 23:32 At the last it biteth like a serpent. G. B. SHAW He put his handkerchief round my neck because a gnat bit me. 5 J. LYLY These medecines bite hot. 10 J. BETJEMAN The chemicals from various factories Have bitten deep into the Portland stone. 11 I. WALTON He thought that Trout bit not for hunger but wantonness. T. JEFFERSON Do not bite at the bait of pleasure till you know there is no hook beneath it. M. PUZO 'It's a good story, you'll like it.' And she saw me bite.

Phrases: **bite a person's head** (or †**nose**) **off** respond curtly or angrily. **bite back** restrain (speech) by an effort. *bite by the nose*: see NOSE *n.* **bite off more than one can chew** (orig. *US*) undertake too much, be too ambitious. *bite one's lip*: see LIP *n. bite one's nails*: see NAIL *n. bite on granite*: see GRANITE *n.* **bite (on) the bullet** behave stoically, avoid showing fear or distress. **bite the dust** (or **ground**) *joc.* & *rhet.* fall and die. **bite the hand that feeds one** injure a benefactor, act ungratefully. *bite the thumb at*: see THUMB *n.* **bitten with** infected by (enthusiasm etc.). **something to bite on** *fig.* a problem to work on or think seriously about. **the biter bit** the deceiver deceived in turn.

biter /ˈbʌɪtə/ *n.* ME. [f. prec. + -ER[1].] **1** *gen.* A person who or thing which bites. ME. **2** *spec.* A deceiver, a swindler. *obs.* exc. in *the biter bit* (cf. BITE *v.*). L17.

biternate /bʌɪˈtəːneɪt/ *a.* L18. [f. BI- + TERNATE.] *Bot.* Of a compound leaf: ternate with the primary divisions themselves being ternate.

biting /ˈbʌɪtɪŋ/ *a.* ME. [f. BITE *v.* + -ING[2].] **1** That bites. ME. **2** *spec.* That causes sharp physical or mental pain; pungent, stinging; sarcastic. ME.

Special collocations: *biting lice*: see LOUSE *n.* 1. *biting* MIDGE. *biting stonecrop*: see STONE *n., a., & adv.*

bitingly *adv.* LME.

bitonality /bʌɪtəʊˈnalɪti/ *n.* E20. [f. BI- + TONALITY.] *Mus.* The simultaneous use of two keys in a composition.

biˈtonal *a.* characterized by bitonality M20.

bitsy /ˈbɪtsi/ *a. colloq.* E20. [f. BIT *n.*[2] or BITTY *a.* + -SY.] Tiny, (charmingly) small. Cf. ITSY-BITSY.

bitt /bɪt/ *n.* & *v.* ME. [Prob. orig. a LG sea term: cf. LG, Du. *beting*.] **A** *n.* Any of the posts fixed in pairs on the deck of a ship, for fastening cables, belaying ropes, etc. Usu. in *pl.* ME. **B** *v.t.* Coil or fasten upon the bitts. M18.

†**bittacle** *n.* see BINNACLE.

bitten *v.* pa. pple of BITE *v.*

bitter /ˈbɪtə/ *n.*[1] OE. [f. the adj.] **1** That which is bitter; bitterness. OE. **2** A bitter medicinal substance; now *esp.* a liquor flavoured with gentian, wormwood, orange peel, etc., used to promote appetite or digestion or as a flavouring. Now usu. in *pl.* E18. **3** (A drink of) bitter beer. M19.

1 TENNYSON All words . . Failing to give the bitter of the sweet. E. JONG Woman is a Mixture of Sweets and Bitters. 2 J. DOS PASSOS Gin with a dash of bitters in it . . helped her over the last few days of the crossing. 3 *Westminster Gazette* A bitter having been bought, he quaffed it to his second's health. D. L. SAYERS He ordered a tankard of bitter.

bitter /ˈbɪtə/ *n.*[2] E17. [f. BITT *n.* + -ER[1].] *Naut.* A turn of the anchor cable around the bitts.

Comb.: **bitter end** (*a*) a part of the anchor cable attached to the bitts, remaining on board when the ship is at anchor; (*b*) (see BITTER *a.*).

†**bitter** *n.*[3] see BITTERN *n.*[1]

bitter /ˈbɪtə/ *a.* & *adv.* [OE *biter* = OS, OHG *bittar* (Du., G *bitter*), ON *bitr*, Goth. *baitrs*, prob. f. Gmc base of BITE *v.*] **A** *adj.* **1** Having a sharp pungent taste, as of wormwood, quinine, etc. Opp. *sweet*. OE. **b** *fig.* Unpalatable; unpleasant; hard to swallow or admit. E19. **2** Attended by severe pain or suffering; grievous; full of affliction. OE. †**3** Causing pain or suffering; cruel, injurious, severe. OE–M17. **4** Characterized by intense animosity; virulent. OE. **5** Of words or their utterer: stinging, cutting, harsh, cruelly reproachful. ME. **6** Of wind: sharp, keen, severe. Of weather: bitingly cold. ME. **7** Expressing or betokening intense grief or affliction of spirit. ME. **8** Mournful; full of affliction L15.

1 BURKE All men are agreed to call vinegar sour, honey sweet, and aloes bitter. M. MITCHELL Without sugar or cream it was bitter as gall. ANTHONY HUXLEY Bitter and very toxic leaves which even goats will not sample. *a bitter taste in the mouth*: see TASTE *n.*[1] b COLERIDGE Some bitter truths, respecting our military arrangements. 2 W. S. CHURCHILL The same bitter struggle with nature. E. M. FORSTER I know by bitter experience. 3 SHAKES. *1 Hen. IV* Those blessed feet Which fourteen hundred years ago were nail'd For our advantage on the bitter cross. 4 DAY LEWIS She was . . capable of bitter resistance against domestic bullying. C. HILL Renegades against whom Cromwell was particularly bitter. 5 P. G. WODEHOUSE It was a good exit speech—mordant—bitter, satirical. 6 J. C. POWYS The bitter east wind made the girl pull her black woollen scarf tightly round her neck. J. CARY It had been a bitter winter—Fred and I came into the . . kitchen quite perished. 7 C. KINGSLEY Bursting into bitter tears. 8 WORDSWORTH Concealing In solitude her bitter feeling.

Comb. & *special collocations*: **bitter-apple** = COLOCYNTH; **bitter bark** any of various shrubs and trees yielding a bitter principle from the bark; **bitter beer**: much flavoured with hops (opp. *mild*); *bitter cassava*: see CASSAVA 1; **bitter-cress** any cruciferous plant of the genus *Cardamine*; **bitter-cucumber** = *bitter-gourd* below; **bitter end** *the* last extremity [but perh. f. *bitter end* (a) s.v. BITTER *n.*[2]]; **bitter-ender** *colloq.* one who fights or holds out to the bitter end, one who refuses to yield or compromise; **bitter-gourd** (*a*) = COLOCYNTH; (*b*) = KARELA; **bitter-nut** *N. Amer.* swamp hickory, *Carya amara*; **bitter orange** the Seville orange; *bitter* PECAN; **bitter pill** *fig.* a hard thing to take, an unpalatable truth etc.; **bitter pit** a disease of apples, characterized by sunken brown spots; **bitter-root** any of various plants with bitter roots; esp. (*N. Amer.*) *Lewisia rediviva*, of the purslane family, with edible roots and red or white flowers; **bitter sage** = *wood sage* s.v. WOOD *n.*[1] & *a.*[1] **bitter-**

vetch any of certain vetches and vetchlings, esp. *Lathyrus linifolius* and *Vicia orobus*; **bitter-weed** any of various bitter plants, esp. (*N. Amer.*) of the family Compositae; **bitter-wood** (the wood of) a W. Indian tree, *Picrasmia excelsa*. See also BITTER-SWEET.

B *adv.* Bitterly. *arch.*, *poet.*, & *dial.* OE.

T. CAMPBELL How bitter she wept o'er the victim of war! S. BEDFORD It was bitter cold.

bitterish *a.* L16. **bitterly** *adv.* in a bitter manner, with bitterness OE. **bitterness** *n.* the quality or state of being bitter; bitter taste; grievousness to the mind; acrimony, animosity; intensity of frost or cold: OE.

bitter /ˈbɪtə/ *v.* [OE *biterian*, f. as BITTER *a.*] †**1** *v.i.* Be or become bitter. Only in OE. **2** *v.t.* Make bitter. ME.

bitterling /ˈbɪtəlɪŋ/ *n.* L19. [G, f. as BITTER *a.* (tr. L *amarus*) + -LING[1].] A small central European freshwater fish, *Rhodeus amarus*, of the carp family.

bittern /ˈbɪtən/ *n.*[1] Orig. †**-r**. See also BLITTER. LME. [OFr. *butor* f. Proto-Romance, f. L *butio* bittern + *taurus* bull. Forms with *-n* (16) are perh. due to assoc. w. *hern* HERON.] Any of several marsh birds of the heron family, generally smaller than herons; *esp.* the European *Botaurus stellaris* and the American *B. lentiginosus*, which have brown and buff striated plumage and are noted for the deep booming call of the male in the breeding season.

little bittern a small bittern of the genus *Ixobrychus*, esp. *I. minutus*, a vagrant to Britain. *sun bittern*: see SUN *n.*[1]

bittern /ˈbɪtən/ *n.*[2] L17. [Obscurely f. BITTER *a.*] **1** The lye which remains after the crystallization of salt from seawater etc. L17. **2** A mixture of quassia and other bitter substances formerly used in adulterating beer. L18.

bitter-sweet /ˈbɪtəswiːt/ *n.* & *a.* In senses 3, 4 usu. **bittersweet**. LME. [f. BITTER *a.* + SWEET *n.*, *a.*] **A** *n.* **1** A bitter-sweet thing; sweetness or pleasure alloyed with bitterness. LME. **2** A variety of apple with a bitter-sweet taste. LME. **3** = *woody* NIGHTSHADE. M16. **4** Any of several climbing shrubs of the genus *Celastrus* (family Celastraceae), *esp.* (more fully *climbing*, *false*, or *American bitter-sweet*) *C. scandens* of N. America (also called *staff vine*). E19. **B** *adj.* Sweet with an admixture or aftertaste of bitterness; *fig.* agreeable or pleasant with an alloy of pain or bitterness. E17.

†**bitter-sweeting** *n.* (*rare*, Shakes.) = BITTER-SWEET *n.* 2: only in L16.

bittock /ˈbɪtək/ *n. Sc.* & *north.* E19. [f. BIT *n.*[2] + -OCK.] A small piece or portion.

bitty /ˈbɪti/ *a.* L19. [f. BIT *n.*[2] + -Y[1].] **1** Made up of unrelated bits, scrappy. L19. **2** Covered with bits of some material. E20. **3** = BITSY. *N. Amer. colloq.* E20.

bittiness *n.* M20.

Bitumastic /bɪtjʊˈmastɪk/ *n.* L19. [f. BITUMEN + MASTIC *n.*] (Proprietary name for) any of various asphaltic compositions used as protective coatings etc.

†**bitume** *n.* & *v.* E17. [Fr. & It., f. as next.] **A** *n.* = next. E–M17. **B** *v.t.* Smear or spread with bitumen. *rare* (Shakes.). Only in E17.

bitumen /ˈbɪtjʊmən/ *n.* LME. [L *bitumen*, *-min-*.] **1** Naturally-occurring asphalt from the Middle East, used as mortar etc. LME. **2** Any natural or artificial black or brown solid or viscous liquid consisting largely of hydrocarbons. E17. **3** A pigment made from asphalt. M19. **4** *The* tarred road. *Austral. colloq.* M20.

†**bituminate** *v.t.* cement with bitumen; convert into or impregnate with bitumen: E17–L18. **bitumiˈniferous** *a.* yielding bitumen L18.

bituminize /bɪˈtjuːmɪnʌɪz/ *v.t.* Also **-ise**. M18. [f. as prec. + -IZE.] Convert into bitumen; impregnate or cover with bitumen.

bituminiˈzation *n.* E19.

bituminous /bɪˈtjuːmɪnəs/ *a.* M16. [Fr. *bitumineux* f. L *bituminosus*, f. as BITUMEN: see -OUS.] Of or containing bitumen; of the nature of bitumen.

bituminous coal black coal which has a relatively high volatile content and burns with a bright smoky flame.

biunique /bʌɪjuːˈniːk/ *a.* M20. [f. BI- + UNIQUE.] Designating or having a one-to-one correspondence between members of two sets.

biuniqueness *n.* M20.

biuret /ˈbʌɪjʊrɛt/ *n.* M19. [G, f. as BI-, UREA, -URET.] *Chem.* A crystalline compound, $NH_2CONHCONH_2$, formed when urea is heated.

Comb.: **biuret reaction** the formation of a violet colour when compounds containing the group ·CONH· are treated with copper sulphate solution in the presence of alkali; **biuret test** this reaction used as a test esp. for proteins.

bivalence /*esp. Chem.* bʌɪˈveɪl(ə)ns, *esp. Cytol.* ˈbɪv(ə)l(ə)ns/ *n.* L19. [f. BI- + VALENCE *n.*[1]] **1** *Chem.* & *Cytol.* The quality of being divalent. L19. **2** *Logic.* The existence of only two truth values; *spec.* in *principle of bivalence*: that every proposition is either true or false. M20.

bivalency *n.* L19.

bivalent /*esp. Chem.* bʌɪˈveɪl(ə)nt, *esp. Cytol.* ˈbɪv(ə)l(ə)nt/ *a.* & *n.* M19. [f. BI- + -VALENT.] **A** *adj.* **1** *Chem.* Having a valency of two; divalent. M19. **2** *Cytol.* Of, pertaining to, or forming a bivalent (see below). L19. **B** *n. Cytol.* A pair of homologous or partly homologous chromosomes united during meiosis. M20.

bivallate /bʌɪˈvalət/ *a.* M20. [f. BI- + VALLATE *a.*] Having two encircling ramparts.

bivalve /ˈbʌɪvalv/ *a.* & *n.* M17. [f. BI- + VALVE *n.*] **A** *adj.* **1** Chiefly *Zool.* Having two folding parts; *spec.* (of a mollusc) having a shell of two parts hinged together by a ligament. M17. **2** *Bot.* Of a seed capsule: having two valves. M18. **B** *n. Zool.* A member of the class Bivalvia; a bivalve mollusc. L17.

bivariate /bʌɪˈvɛːrɪət/ *a.* E20. [f. BI- + VARIATE *n.*] *Statistics.* Involving or depending on two variates.

biventral /bʌɪˈvɛntr(ə)l/ *a.* E18. [f. BI- + VENTRAL *a.*] *Anat.* = DIGASTRIC *a.*

†**biventer** *n.* = DIGASTRIC *n.* E18–M19.

bivious /ˈbɪvɪəs/ *a.* M17. [f. L *bivius*, f. BI- + *via* way, + -OUS.] Having or offering two ways.

bivium /ˈbɪvɪəm/ *n.* L19. [L = place where two ways meet, f. as BI- + *via* way: see -IUM.] *Zool.* The two posterior ambulacra of an echinoderm (dorsal in a holothurian). Cf. TRIVIUM 2.

bivoltine /bʌɪˈvɒltʌɪn/ *a.* L19. [Fr. *bivoltin*, f. It. *volta* time: see BI-, -INE[1].] Of an insect (esp. a silkworm moth): producing two broods in a year.

bivouac /ˈbɪvʊak, ˈbɪvwak/ *n.* & *v.* E18. [Fr., prob. f. Swiss G *Bīwacht* lit. 'extra watch' (see BY *a.*, WATCH *n.*), said to have been used in Aargau and Zürich to denote a patrol of citizens to assist the ordinary town watch.] **A** *n.* Orig., a night-watch by a whole army. Later, a temporary encampment, usu. for the night, without tents; the place of such an encampment. E18. **B** *v.i.* & *t.* in *pass.* Infl. **-ck-**. Remain in the open air (esp. during the night) without tents etc. E19.

bivvy /ˈbɪvi/ *n. slang.* E20. [Abbrev. of BIVOUAC *n.*] A shelter; a small tent.

biweekly /bʌɪˈwiːkli/ *adv.*, *a.*, & *n.* M19. [f. BI- + WEEKLY *adv.*, *a.* & *n.*] **A** *adv.* Every two weeks or twice a week. M19. **B** *a.* & *n.* (A periodical) appearing or occurring biweekly. L19.

bixbyite /ˈbɪksbɪʌɪt/ *n.* L19. [f. Maynard *Bixby*, late 19th-cent. US mineralogist + -ITE[1].] *Min.* A rare mixed oxide of manganese and ferric iron occurring as black metallic cubic crystals.

bixin /ˈbɪksɪn/ *n.* M19. [f. mod.L *Bixa* (*orellana*), the tree yielding annatto (f. Carib *bija* red) + -IN[1].] *Chem.* A carotenoid which is the principal pigment of annatto.

biyearly /bʌɪˈjɪəli, -ˈjəː-/ *a.* & *adv.* L19. [f. BI- + YEARLY *a.*] (Appearing or occurring) every two years or twice a year.

biz /bɪz/ *n. colloq.* (orig. *US*). M19. [Abbrev.] Business. Freq. in *showbiz* s.v. SHOW *n.*[1]

bizarre /bɪˈzɑː/ *a.* & *n.* M17. [Fr. f. It. *bizzarro* angry, of unkn. origin. Cf. Sp. & Port. *bizarro* handsome, brave.] **A** *adj.* **1** Eccentric, fantastic, grotesque. M17. **2** Designating variegated forms of garden flowers, as carnations, tulips, etc. M18. **B** *n.* **1** A bizarre carnation, tulip, etc. L18. **2** *absol.* *The* bizarre quality of things; bizarre things. M19.

bizarrely *adv.* L19. **bizarreness** *n.* E20. **bizarrerie** /bɪˈzɑːrəriː/ *n.* [Fr.: see -ERY] (a) bizarre quality M18.

†**bizcacha** *n.* var. of VISCACHA.

blab /blab/ *n.*[1] ME. [Prob. ult. f. imit. Gmc base: cf. OHG *blabbizōn* (MHG *blepzen*), Icel. *blabbra* (Da. *blabbre*).] **1** A person who gossips or chatters; a babbler; a tell-tale. ME. **2** Loose talk or chatter; gossip. LME.

blab /blab/ *n.*[2] Long *obs.* exc. *dial.* M17. [Var. of BLEB *n.*, BLOB *n.*] A bubble; a blister.

blab /blab/ *v.*[1] Infl. **-bb-**. LME. [f. BLAB *n.*[1]] **1** *v.i.* Chatter, babble. Now *spec.* talk foolishly or indiscreetly, reveal secrets. LME. **2** *v.t.* Babble. Now *spec.* tell foolishly or indiscreetly, reveal (a secret). Freq. foll. by *out*. M16.

1 C. MORGAN An honest blackmailer who never blabbed without reason. **2** W. H. DIXON He blabbed out the secret to his priest. T. E. LAWRENCE I begin to blab . . what I feel, just like any other chap. *transf.*: SHAKES. *2 Hen. VI* Beaufort's red sparkling eyes blab his heart's malice.

Comb.: **blab-mouth** *slang* = BLAB *n.*[1] I.

blab /blab/ *v.*[2] *t. obs.* exc. *Sc.* Infl. **-bb-**. E17. [Cf. BLAB *n.*[2]] Make swollen (the cheeks) with weeping etc.; bedaub.

blabber /ˈblabə/ *n.* ME. [f. BLAB *v.*[1] + -ER[1].] = BLAB *n.*[1] I.

†**blabber** *a.* see BLUBBER *a.*

blabber /ˈblabə/ *v.* Now *Sc.* & *N. Amer.* LME. [f. as BLAB *n.*[1]: see -ER[5].] †**1** *v.i.* Speak inarticulately, mumble, babble. LME–L18. **2** *v.i.* Chatter, blab. LME. †**3** *v.t.* = BLAB *v.*[1] 2. E16–E17. †**4** *v.i.* Move the tongue between the lips in mockery. M16–E17.

2 A. J. CRONIN Get ahead wi' it now and don't blabber so much.

Comb.: **blabbermouth** *slang* = BLAB *n.*[1] I.

black /blak/ *n.* OE. [The adj. used ellipt. or absol.] **1** Black substance; *spec.* †(*a*) ink; (*b*) black pigment, dye, or varnish (freq. w. specifying wd); (*c*) *dial.* soot. OE. **b** *The* credit side of an account. Cf. RED *n.* 1d. E20. **2** Black colour; a shade of this; blackness, darkness. ME. **3** A black speck or particle; *spec.* (*a*) in *pl.*, fungus or smut attacking wheat etc.; (*b*) a flake of soot, a smut. ME. †**4** *The* pupil of the eye. LME–M17. **5** Black clothing or fabric, in *pl.* black clothes or (*arch.*) hangings, esp. as a sign of mourning. LME. **6** (Also **B-**.) A Negro, a Negroid; a member of a dark-skinned people; *Austral.* an Aborigine. E17. **7** Esp. *Italian Hist.* A member of a party, faction, etc., adopting black as its colour. Cf. WHITE *n.* 14. L17. **8** *ellipt.* Anything distinguished by black colour, as the black divisions in roulette and rouge-et-noir, the black ball in snooker, a black postage stamp, a black horse, a black pigeon or duck, etc.; (usu. **B-**) the player of the black pieces in chess or draughts. M19. **9** = BLACKMAIL *n.* 1b. *slang.* E20. **10** A serious mistake or blunder (cf. *black mark* s.v. BLACK *a.*). *slang.* M20.

1 *carbon-black*, *ivory black*, *lampblack*, etc. **b in the black** solvent, in credit. **2** W. M. CRAIG We must take black and white into our list, as colours with the painter though not with the optician. J. CHEEVER The cold black of 6 A.M. **in black and white** (*a*) recorded in writing or print, (*b*) in monochrome film. †**under black and white** = *in black and white* (a) above. **5** L. STRACHEY The widowed lady, in her voluminous blacks. DYLAN THOMAS The Reverend Eli Jenkins . . gropes out of bed into his preacher's black. *All Black*: see ALL *adv.* 1. **8** *Egyptian black*: see EGYPTIAN *a.* *Welsh Black*: see WELSH *a.* **9 put the black on** blackmail (a person). **10 put up a black** make a serious error.

Comb.: **black spot** the spot on which the black ball is placed in snooker.

black /blak/ *a.* [OE *blæc*, *blac-* corresp. to OS *blac* ink, OHG *blah-*, *blach-*; cf. ON *blakkr* dusky, black, dun: ult. origin unkn.] **I** *lit.* **1** Opposite to white; colourless from the absence or complete absorption of light. Also, so near this as to have no distinguishable colour, very dark. OE. **b** *Cards.* Belonging to spades or clubs. L17. **c** Of coffee or (occas.) tea: served without milk, cream, etc. L18. **2** **a** Dark-skinned or dark-haired; swarthy. *obs.* in *gen.* sense. OE. **b** (Also **B-**.) Negro, Negroid; Australian Aboriginal; of a dark-skinned people; of or pertaining to such persons; restricted to such persons. LME. **3** Wearing black clothing. ME. **4** Deeply stained with dirt, soiled, filthy. ME. **5** Characterized by the absence of light; dusky, gloomy; overcast. LME.

1 AV *Matt.* 5:36 Thou canst not make one haire white or blacke. POPE The priest himself.. Pours the black wine. J. RHYS Her eyes.. were the blackest I had ever seen. 2b T. KENEALLY 'Are there even any black ministers of religion?' 'The Benedictine priests.. did—I believe—ordain three aboriginal priests.' N. GORDIMER Whites are not allowed to go into black townships without a permit. *New Statesman* A black section.. as an internal training-ground and pressure group. 4 M. DRABBLE It was vaulted and filthy, black with the grime of decades. 5 BYRON The blackest sky Foretells the heaviest tempest. D. BAGLEY The sun had set and it was pitchy black.

II *fig.* **6** Foreboding or threatening; angry, sulky; dismal; melancholy. LME. **7** Foul, atrocious; wicked; hateful. M16. **8** **a** Malignant, deadly; sinister. L16. **b** Macabre; presenting tragedy or bitter reality in comic terms. M20. **9** Disgraceful, deserving censure, illegal. E17. **10** **a** Of work, goods, etc.: not (to be) undertaken or handled, because of an industrial dispute. E20. **b** Of or performed by blacklegs during a strike. M20. **11** Contravening economic regulations. M20.

6 V. BRITTAIN The black apprehension of the previous year, with its fear of bread riots and revolutions. S. KING The depression had lifted.., but he remembered how black it had been. 7 P. J. BAILEY Die with the black lie flapping on your lips. 8 HOR. WALPOLE The throne.. usurped by the Queen's black enemy, Philip. b *Listener* His recent group of Swiftean black comedies.

Phrases: **black and blue** discoloured with bruises. **black and tan** (*a*) (a terrier) with a black back and tan markings on face, flanks, and legs; (*b*) a drink composed of porter (or stout) and ale. **Black and Tans** *colloq.* an irregular force recruited in 1920 to fight Irish nationalist forces, so-called from their wearing a mixture of black constabulary and khaki military uniforms. **black and white** (*a*) written, printed, etc., in black ink on white paper; (*b*) of a building: painted white with black timbers; (*c*) of film: not colour, monochrome; (*d*) *fig.* comprising only opposite extremes. **black in the face** purple in the face through strangulation, passion, or exertion. *little black dress*: see LITTLE *a.* **not so black as one is painted** better than one's reputation. *paint a person black*: see PAINT *v.*

Special collocations & comb.: **Black Africa** Africa south of the Sahara inhabited predominantly by Blacks (as opp. to Arabs) or governed by Blacks (as opp. to Whites). *black alder*: see ALDER *n.* 1b. **black ant** any of various ants which are black in colour; *esp.* the small *Lasius niger*, which is abundant in Eurasia and N. America. *black* ANTIMONY. **black arches** = NUN *n.*[1] 3. **black art** [prob. after LG *swarte kunst*, G *schwarze Kunst*; cf. L *niger* black, (fig.) wicked, and med.L var. *nigromantia* of *necromantia* NECROMANCY] magic, necromancy. **black ash** (the wood of) a N. American ash, *Fraxinus nigra*. **blackback** = *black-backed gull* below. **black-backed** *a.* having a black back; *black-backed gull*, any of several gulls with black backs and wings, *esp.* (more fully *greater black-backed gull*) *Larus marinus* and (more fully *lesser black-backed gull*) *L. fuscus*, both of the N. Atlantic. **black ball** (*a*) (also **blackball**) a ball placed in a ballot-box etc. to record an adverse vote; (*b*) (also **blackball**) a hard black or black and white sweet; (*c*) *black ball game*, a game of snooker the outcome of which depends on the final potting of the black ball. **blackball** *v.t.* record an adverse vote against (a candidate) by placing a black ball in a ballot-box etc.; *loosely* reject, ostracize. **black-band** (a deposit of) an earthy ironstone or siderite containing carbonaceous matter. **black bass** either of two freshwater fishes of the percoid family Centrarchidae, native to N. America and widely introduced elsewhere, the large-mouth *Micropterus salmoides* and the small-mouth *M. dolomieui*. **black bean** (*a*) (the black seed of) any of certain plants of the genus *Phaseolus*; (*b*) (the timber of) an Australian hardwood tree, *Castanospermum australe*. *black bear*: see BEAR *n.*[1] 1. **black beetle** the cockroach. **black belt** (*a*) a region of the southern US in which Blacks predominate; (*b*) (the holder of) a belt marking the attainment of a certain high degree of proficiency in judo or karate. **black bent** a bent-grass, *Agrostis gigantea*. *black bindweed*: see BINDWEED 2. **black birch** (the wood of) either of two N. American birches, *Betula lenta* and *B. nigra*. **blackboard** a board with a dark (usu. black) surface used in schools etc. for writing or drawing on with chalk. **black body** *Physics* a hypothetical perfect absorber and radiator of electromagnetic radiation. **black book** (*a*) *Hist.* the distinctive name of various official books (usu. bound in black) of public significance; (*b*) (a book containing) a record of the names of people liable to censure or punishment (*in someone's black books*: see BOOK *n.*). **black bottom** (*a*) *US* a low-lying area inhabited by a Black population; (*b*) a popular dance of the 1920s. **black box** any apparatus of unspecified or unknown internal design, *esp.* a flight-recorder in an aircraft (not black in colour). **blackboy** (*a*) a young Black man, a Black manservant (now usu. considered *offensive*); (*b*) an Australian grass-tree of the genus *Xanthorrhoea*, esp. *X. preissii*. **black bread** coarse rye bread. **black-browed** *a.* dark-browed, dark-faced; frowning; scowling. *black bryony*: see BRYONY 2. **blackbuck** an Indian gazelle, *Antilope cervicapra*. **black bun** (a) rich fruit cake in a pastry case, traditionally eaten in Scotland at New Year. **blackbutt** (the timber of) an Australian eucalyptus, *Eucalyptus pilularis*. **black butter** = BEURRE *noir*. **black cap**, **blackcap** (*a*) (*black cap*) *Hist.* a cap worn by a judge when passing a sentence of death; (*b*) (*blackcap*) any of various birds having the top of the head black; *spec.* a warbler, *Sylvia atricapilla*; (*c*) a halved apple baked with the flat side downwards and topped with (caramelized) sugar; (*d*) *N. Amer.* = *black* RASPBERRY. *black* CATTLE. *black chameleon*: see CHAMELEON *n.* 2. *black cherry*: see CHERRY *n.* **black coal** †(*a*) charcoal; (*b*) coal of a black colour, *esp.* bituminous coal. **black-coat** (**worker**) one in a clerical or professional as distinguished from an industrial or commercial occupation. **blackcock** the male of the black grouse, *Tetrao tetrix*. *black coffee*: see COFFEE *n.* *black* COHOSH. **Black Country** areas of the West Midlands of England supposedly blackened by the coal and iron trades. *black cumin*: see CUMIN 2. *black* CURASSOW. **black damp** = *choke-damp* s.v. CHOKE *v.* **Black Death** the great epidemic of plague in Europe in the 14th cent. *black diamond*: see DIAMOND *n.* **black disc** a black vinyl gramophone record (opp. *compact disc*). **black disease** (of sheep) necrotic hepatitis accompanying liver-fluke infestation. **black dog** †(*a*) *slang* a base silver coin; (*b*) melancholy or depression; *have the black dog on one's back*, be in the sulks. *black draught*: see DRAUGHT *n.* 3c. **black drop** †(*a*) a dark-coloured preparation containing opium; (*b*) a drop-shaped appearance of the disc of a planet (esp. Venus) at the beginning and end of solar transit. **black earth** dark soil, *spec.* = CHERNOZEM. **black economy** financial transactions etc. not officially declared or recorded. **Black English** the form(s) of English used by Blacks, esp. in the US. **black eye** (*a*) an eye with a very dark-coloured iris; (*b*) an eye around which the skin is bruised and discoloured; (*c*) *fig.* a severe rebuff; a snub; (*d*) *black-eye pea*, = *black-eyed pea* below. **black-eyed** *a.* having black eyes; *black-eyed Susan*, any of various plants having light-coloured flowers with dark centres, *esp.* the yellow *Rudbeckia hirta* of N. America; *black-eyed bean*, *pea*, a kind of cowpea having white seeds with a black hilum; the (freq. dried) seed of this plant, eaten as a pulse. **blackface** (*a*) an animal, esp. a sheep, with a dark face (*Scottish blackface*: see SCOTTISH *a.*); (*b*) make-up for the role of a Black; *blackface minstrel* (chiefly *Hist.*), a member of a troupe of entertainers, usu. White men who blacken their faces, performing songs and dances associated with plantation life in the southern US (also called *nigger minstrel*). **black-faced** *a.* having a dark face; *fig.* threatening, foreboding. **blackfellow** *Austral.* (*arch.* or *Hist.*) an Aborigine. **black-figure** *a.* (*Archaeol.*) designating a type of Greek pottery ornamented with figures in black silhouette. **blackfish** (*a*) a salmon just after spawning; (*b*) a small whale, *esp.* a pilot whale; also, a killer whale; (*c*) any of several dark-coloured fishes, e.g. the marine fish *Centrolophus niger*, the tautog (*N. Amer.*), and the Australian freshwater fish *Gadopsis marmoratus*. *black flag*: see FLAG *n.*[4] **blackfly** any of various dark-coloured insects, *esp.* (*a*) certain thrips and aphids infesting plants; (*b*) a biting fly of the family Simuliidae; = SIMULIUM. **blackfoot** *Sc.* (pl. **-feet**) a lovers' go-between. **Blackfoot** *n.* & *a.* (*a*) *n.* (pl. **-feet**, same) a member of a N. American Indian confederacy comprising the Siksika, the Bloods, and the Piegan; the Algonquian language of these people; (*b*) *adj.* of or pertaining to these people or their language. **Black Forest cake**, **gâteau** [tr. G *Schwarzwald*, a forest area in SW Germany] a rich chocolate cake or gâteau with black cherries. **black fox** a dark colour phase of the N. American red fox. **Black Friar** [f. the colour of the order's habit] a Dominican friar. *black frost*: see FROST *n.* **black game** the black grouse. **black gold** (*colloq.*, chiefly *N. Amer.*) oil. **black grape**: that is purple or blue-black when ripe. **black grouse** a large Eurasian grouse, *Tetrao tetrix*, the male of which has glossy blue-black plumage and a lyre-shaped tail (cf. *blackcock* above, *greyhen* s.v. GREY *a.*); also called *black game*. **black gum** *N. Amer.* (the wood of) a deciduous tree of the south-east US, *Nyssa sylvatica*; also called *sour gum*. **blackhead** (*a*) any of various black-headed birds, *esp.* the scaup, *Aythya marila*, or the black-headed gull, *Larus ridibundus*; (*b*) a black-tipped plug of sebaceous matter in a hair follicle; (*c*) an infectious disease of turkeys producing discoloration of the head, caused by a protozoon. **black-headed** *a.* having a black head; *black-headed gull*, any of several gulls with black heads, esp. *Larus ridibundus*, common in many parts of the Old World. **black-heart** (*a*) a dark reddish-black variety of sweet cherry; (*b*) malleable cast iron with a core of graphite. **black heat** a temperature just below visible red. **black hole** (*a*) *Mil. Hist.* the punishment cell of a barracks; *loosely* any place of confinement; (*b*) *Astron.* a region where gravitation is so powerful that no matter or electromagnetic radiation can escape (*Schwarzschild black hole*: see SCHWARZSCHILD 2). *black* HOREHOUND. **black house** *Sc.* (*a*) a turf house; (*b*) a house built of unmortared stone, found esp. in NW Scotland and the Hebrides. **black ice** a thin, hard, transparent ice, esp. as forming on roads. **black Irish** Irish people of Mediterranean appearance. **black Italian poplar** a commonly planted hybrid poplar that resembles the black poplar but has upcurved branches. *black ivory*: see IVORY *n.* **black jack**, **blackjack** †(*a*) *Sc.* a black leather jerkin; (*b*) *Hist.* a large tar-coated leather jug for beer; (*c*) zinc blende; (*d*) *N. Amer.* (the wood of) a shrubby oak, *Quercus marilandica*; also *blackjack oak*; (*e*) a small black beetle or caterpillar; *esp.* the larva of the turnip sawfly, *Athalia spinarum*; (*f*) *Hist.* a pirate's black ensign; (*g*) (chiefly *S. Afr.*) a S. American bur-marigold, *Bidens pilosa*, introduced elsewhere; the hooked seed of this plant; (*h*) a flexible loaded bludgeon; (*i*) = VINGT-ET-UN. *Black Jew*: see JEW *n.* **black kite** a dark brown kite, *Milvus migrans*, of southern Europe, Africa, Asia, and Australia. **blacklead** *n.* & *v.* (*a*) *n.* graphite, esp. as used in pencils or as a domestic polish; (*b*) *v.t.* polish with graphite. *black* LEOPARD. **black letter** (printing in) a heavy early style of type. **black level** *Television* the level of the picture signal that corresponds to black in the transmitted image. **black light** invisible ultraviolet or infrared radiation. **blacklist** *n.* & *v.* (*a*) *n.* a list of the names of those who have incurred suspicion, censure, or punishment; (*b*) *v.t.* enter the name of (a person) on a blacklist. *black locust*: see LOCUST *n.* 3(c). **black lung** (chiefly *US*) = ANTHRACOSIS. *black magic*: see MAGIC *n.* *black* MAMBA. **black man** (*a*) a man having a black or very dark skin; (*b*) *colloq.* & *dial.* an evil spirit, devil, or bogey man. *black* MANGROVE. **Black Maria** (*a*) *colloq.* a van for the conveyance of prisoners; (*b*) a card-game having) the queen of spades as a penalty card. **black mark** a mark of discredit against a person's name (*lit.* & *fig.*). **black market** (a place of) illegitimate traffic in officially controlled goods or currencies or in commodities in short supply. **black marketeer** a person engaged in dealing in the black market. **black marketeering** dealing in the black market. **Black Mass** (*a*) a mass for the dead at which vestments and drapings are black; a requiem mass; (*b*) a travesty of the Mass said to be used in the cult of Satanism. *Black* MONDAY. **black money** †(*a*) copper coins; (*b*) money not declared for tax. **Black Monk** [f. the colour of the order's habit] a Benedictine monk. *black Moor*: see BLACKAMOOR. **black-mouth** †(*a*) one having a black mouth; *fig.* a slanderer; (*b*) *dial.* a saithe. **Black Muslim** a member of a sect of Black US Muslims, formerly advocating separation of Blacks and Whites. *black mustard*: see MUSTARD *n.* **black neb** (*a*) a crow or other black-billed bird; (*b*) *Sc. Hist.* a sympathizer with the French Revolution. *black* NIGHTSHADE. **black oak** (the wood of) any of various trees with dark bark or foliage; *spec.* the quercitron, *Quercus velutina*. **black oil** any of various dark-coloured oils; *spec.* heavy crude oil used for lubrication. *black olive*: see OLIVE *n.*[1] 1b. **black panther** (*a*) = *black* LEOPARD; (*b*) (with cap. initials) a member of an extremist organization in the US fighting for Blacks' rights. *black pepper*: see PEPPER *n.* **black pine** any of several conifers, *esp.* the Austrian pine, the matai, and the matsu. **black plate** thin sheets of iron not coated with tin. **blackpoll** (**warbler**) an American warbler, *Dendroica striata*, streaked grey and white with a black crown. *Black Pope*: see POPE *n.*[1] **black poplar** a Eurasian poplar, *Populus nigra*, with a blackish-brown trunk and arching lower branches; also = *black Italian poplar* above. **black-pot** a beer-mug; a toper. **black powder** gunpowder. **Black Power** (a slogan used by) a movement in support of Black civil rights. **Black Prince** (a name given to) the eldest son of Edward III of England. **black pudding** a sausage-shaped pudding made with blood and suet. **black quarter** = BLACKLEG *n.* 1a. *black* RASPBERRY. *black rat*: see RAT *n.*[1] *black* REDSTART. *black* RHINOCEROS. **blackrobe** *Canad. Hist.* (an Indians' name for) a Christian priest. **Black Rod** (the office of) the chief gentleman usher to the Lord Chamberlain's department, usher to the House of Lords, etc. **black rubric** (an inaccurate term for) the declaration explanatory of the rubric concerning kneeling at the reception of Holy Communion, first inserted at the end of the Communion service in the *Book of Common Prayer* of 1552. **black rust** = *stem rust* s.v. STEM *n.*[1] *black sage*: see SAGE *n.*[1] 1b. *black* SALSIFY. *black* SALTWORT. **black sand** an alluvial or beach sand, esp. in Australia and New Zealand, consisting predominantly of grains of heavy dark minerals or rocks. **black scoter** a scoter, *Melanitta nigra*, of Arctic and north temperate regions. **black sheep** a scoundrel, an unsatisfactory member (*of* a family etc.). **blackshirt** a member of the Italian Fascist Party, *gen.* a Fascist. **black-shouldered kite** either of two small Old World kites of the genus *Elanus*, with pale grey and white plumage and black shoulder patches. **black-snake** (*a*) any of various dark-coloured snakes; *esp.* an Australian cobra, *Pseudeschis porphyriacus*, and a N. American racer, *Coluber constrictor*; (*b*) *US* (more fully *black-snake whip*) a long whiplash. **blacksnake** *v.t.* flog with a black-snake whip. *black snakeroot*: see SNAKE *n.* **black soil** = *black earth* above. *black* SPAULD. **black spleenwort** a small fern of rocks and walls, *Asplenium adiantum-nigrum*, with a triangular frond. **black spot, blackspot** (*a*) any of various diseases of plants, esp. of roses, producing black spots; (*b*) a place of anxiety or danger, *esp.* a section of a road noted for accidents. *black squall*: see SQUALL *n.*[1] 1. *black stinkwood*: see STINK *n.* **Black Stone** the sacred reddish-black stone built into the outside wall of the Kaaba. *black stump*: see STUMP *n.*[1] *black swallower*: see SWALLOWER (b). *black swallowwort*: see SWALLOWWORT 1. **black swan** (*a*) an Australian and New Zealand swan, *Cygnus atratus*, having all black plumage with a red beak; (*b*) an extremely rare thing. **blacktail** (*a*) any of various fishes, *esp.* (*S. Afr.*) = DASSIE 2; (*b*) the mule deer, *Odocoileus hemionus*, of western N. America. *black tang*: see TANG *n.*[2] *black tar*: see TAR *n.*[1] 1d. **black tea** tea fully fermented before drying (cf. *green tea* s.v. GREEN *a.*); (see also sense 1c above). **black tern** an Old World migratory tern, *Chlidonias niger*, with a dark head and underparts. **black tie** *spec.* a man's black bow-tie worn with a dinner jacket; *ellipt.* evening dress including a black tie. *black* TIL. *black tin*: see TIN *n.* 1. *black titi*: see TITI *n.*[2] **blacktop** *US* a type of blackish road surfacing, asphalt, tarmacadam; a road etc. surfaced with this. **black tracker** *Austral.* an Aborigine employed by the police to track down fugitives or persons lost in the bush. *black treacle*: see TREACLE *n.* 4. **black tripe** unbleached tripe. *black truffle*: see TRUFFLE *n.* 1. *black* TURNSTONE. **black velvet** (*a*) a drink consisting of a mixture of champagne and stout (cf. BISMARCK 2); (*b*) *Austral.* & *NZ slang* (*derog.*) an Aboriginal woman; Aboriginal women collectively. **black vomit** yellow fever; dark material (containing blood) vomited during this. **black vulture** (*a*) a vulture, *Aegypius monachus*, found from Spain to central Asia; (*b*) a vulture, *Coragyps atratus*, of N. and S. America. *black walnut*: see WALNUT 3. *black wash*: see WASH *n.* **Black Watch** the Royal Highland Regiment (distinguished by their dark-coloured tartan). **black water, blackwater** (*a*) a stream stained brown by peat; (*b*) a disease of animals, esp. a form of babesiasis, in which dark urine is passed; (*c*) (a term used by Indians, esp. Hindus, for) the sea; (*d*) *blackwater fever*, a form of malignant tertian malaria in which haemoglobin is present in the urine owing to massive red-cell destruction. **black widow** a venomous black N. American spider of the genus *Latrodectus*, esp. *L. mactans*, the female of which usu. devours its mate. **blackwood** (the dark timber of) any of various hardwood trees, esp. of the tropical genus *Dalbergia*, and *Acacia melanoxylon* of Australia and South Africa.

blackish *a.* tending to black L15. **blackly** *adv.* in a black or gloomy manner M16. **blackness** *n.* ME. **blacky** *a.* somewhat black, blackish L16. **blacky** *n.* (*a*) *colloq.* (freq. *derog.* & usu. considered *racially offensive*) a Black; (*b*) *dial.* & *colloq.* a blackbird: E19.

black /blak/ *v.* ME. [f. the adj.] †1 *v.i.* Be or become black. Long *dial. rare.* ME–M19. 2 *v.t.* Make black; put black colour on. ME. b *spec.* Polish with blacking. M16. c *spec.* Bruise or discolour (a person's eye). E20. 3 *v.t.* Defame, speak evil of. LME. 4 *v.t.* Blackmail. *slang.* E20. 5 *v.t.* Declare (goods etc.) black in an industrial dispute. M20.

With advs. in specialized senses: **black out** (*a*) *v.phr.t.* obliterate or obscure (as) with black; extinguish all lights in, extinguish or obscure (lights), esp. during a stage performance or in anticipation of air raids; (*b*) *v.phr.i.* be obscured or extinguished, undergo a blackout of lighting; (*c*) *v.phr.i.* suffer temporary loss of consciousness, loss of memory, or blindness. **black up** *v.refl.* & *i.* (*Theatr.*) colour one's face to play the role of a Black.

blacker *n.* M17.

blackamoor /ˈblakəmʊə, -mɔː/ *n. arch.* Also **†black Moor**. E16. [f. BLACK *a.* + MOOR *n.*[2]: connecting *-a-* unexpl.] A Black African; a very dark-skinned person.

blackavised /ˈblakəvʌɪzd, -st/ *a. arch.* (chiefly *north.*). M18. [f. BLACK *a.* + Fr. *vis* face (perh. orig. *black-à-vis* or *black o'vis*) + -ED[2].] Dark-complexioned.

blackberry /ˈblakb(ə)ri/ *n.* OE. [f. BLACK *a.* + BERRY *n.*[1]] 1a The fruit of the bramble shrub. OE. b The shrub itself. L16. 2 The blackcurrant; the bilberry. *north.* M16.

1a **as plentiful as blackberries** as plentiful as can be.

blackberrying *n.* gathering blackberries L18.

blackbird /ˈblakbəːd/ *n.* ME. [f. BLACK *a.* + BIRD *n.*] 1 A common European thrush, *Turdus merula*, the male of which is black with an orange beak, and the female brown. ME. 2 Any of various N. American birds, esp. grackles, with black plumage. E17. 3 *Hist.* A kidnapped Black or Polynesian on a slave ship. L19.

blackbirder *n.* (*Hist.*) a man or a vessel engaged in blackbirding L19. **blackbirding** *n.* (*Hist.*) the capture and transportation of Black or Polynesian slaves L19.

Blackburnian /blakˈbəːnɪən/ *n. N. Amer.* L18. [f. Mrs Hugh *Blackburn* (fl. 18th cent.) + -IAN.] More fully *Blackburnian warbler*. A N. American warbler, *Dendroica fusca*, distinguished by orange or yellow throat markings.

blackcurrant /blakˈkʌr(ə)nt/ *n.* Also **black currant**. E17. [f. BLACK *a.* + CURRANT.] The small round edible black berry of the shrub *Ribes nigrum*, of the gooseberry family, borne in loose hanging clusters; this shrub, much grown for its fruit.

attrib.: *blackcurrant jam, jelly*, etc.

blacken /ˈblak(ə)n/ *v.* ME. [f. BLACK *a.* + -EN[5].] 1 *v.i.* Become or grow black(er); darken. ME. 2 *v.t.* Make black(er) or dark(er); defame, speak evil of. LME.

blackener *n.* M17.

blackguard /ˈblagɑːd, -gəd/ *n.* & *a.* Orig. two wds. E16. [f. BLACK *a.* + GUARD *n.*: orig. significance unkn.] A *n.* I A body of people. †1 A guard or group of attendants black in person, dress, or character. E16–E18. †2 *the blackguard*: a The lowest menials of a household; the scullions; an army's camp-followers. M16–E18. b Vagabonds, criminals, or vagrant children, as a group or class. L17–M18. II An individual. †3 A guard or attendant black in person, dress, or character. M16–M18. †4 A vagrant child, a shoeblack, etc. Only in 18. 5 A scoundrel, a villain; a foul-mouthed person. M18. †III 6 More fully *Irish blackguard*. A kind of snuff. L18–L19. B *adj.* †1 Of the vagrant children, shoeblacks, etc. L17–E19. 2 Scoundrelly, villainous; scurrilous. L18.

blackguardism *n.* blackguardly language or behaviour L18. **blackguardly** *adv.* & *a.* (*a*) *adv.* (*rare*) in the manner of a blackguard; (*b*) *adj.* characteristic of a blackguard, scoundrelly, scurrilous: E19.

blackguard /ˈblagɑːd, -gəd/ *v.* L18. [f. the n.] †1 *v.i.* Behave like a blackguard. *rare.* Only in L18. 2 *v.t.* Treat as a blackguard; abuse scurrilously, revile. E19.

blacking /ˈblakɪŋ/ *n.* L16. [f. BLACK *v.* + -ING[1].] 1 A preparation for making something black; *spec.* a paste or liquid for blacking or polishing boots etc. L16. 2 The action of BLACK *v.* E17.

blackleg /ˈblaklɛg/ *n.* & *a.* E18. [f. BLACK *a.* + LEG *n.*] A *n.* 1 *sing.* or in *pl.* a An acute infectious bacterial disease of cattle and sheep, causing necrosis in one or more legs. E18. b Any of various diseases of vegetables. L19. 2 A swindler, *esp.* a swindling bookmaker. L18. 3 A person who continues to work despite a ban or strike by a trade union etc.; a person who takes a striker's place. M19. B *attrib.* or as *adj.* That is a blackleg during a strike etc.; of or pertaining to blacklegs. L19.

blackleg /ˈblaklɛg/ *v.* Infl. **-gg-**. L18. [f. the n.] 1 *v.i.* Act as a blackleg. L18. 2 *v.t.* Replace, injure, or betray as a blackleg. L19.

blackmail /ˈblakmeɪl/ *n.* & *v.* Orig. two wds. M16. [f. BLACK *a.* + MAIL *n.*[1]] A *n.* 1a *Hist.* A tribute levied by freebooting Scottish chiefs in return for protection or immunity from plunder. M16. b *transf.* Any payment or other benefit extorted by threats or pressure, esp. by threatening to reveal a discreditable secret; the criminal action of seeking to extort such a payment or benefit; the use of threats or moral pressure. E19. 2 *Law* (now *Hist.*). Rent payable in cattle, labour, or coin other than silver. E17. B *v.t.* Extort money from by blackmail, use threats or moral pressure against. L19.

blackmailer *n.* M19.

†black Moor *n.* var. of BLACKAMOOR.

blackout /ˈblakaʊt/ *n.* E20. [f. *black out* s.v. BLACK *v.*] 1 An act of blacking out or the state of being blacked out; *spec.* (*a*) the darkening of a theatre stage for a performance; (*b*) the extinguishing or obscuring of lights in anticipation of air raids; (*c*) a temporary complete failure of memory or loss of consciousness; an aviator's temporary blindness etc. resulting esp. from centrifugal force when a sudden turn is made; (*d*) the loss of radio reception through fading or jamming; (*e*) the suppression of information or news. E20. 2 A period during which lights must be extinguished or obscured. M20.

blacksmith /ˈblaksmɪθ/ *n.* L15. [f. BLACK *a.* + SMITH *n.*] A smith who works in iron.

black'smithery *n.* (*a*) *US* a smithy; (*b*) (orig. *US*) blacksmith's work: M19. **blacksmithing** *n.* performing blacksmith's work M19.

blackthorn /ˈblakθɔːn/ *n.* ME. [f. BLACK *a.* + THORN *n.*] 1a A thorny European shrub, *Prunus spinosa*, of the rose family, bearing white flowers before the leaves and fruit (sloes) like small dark plums. ME. b A stick or cudgel of the wood of this shrub. M19. 2 Any of certain other shrubs; *esp.* a N. American hawthorn, *Crataegus calpodendron*. M18.

Comb.: **blackthorn winter** a period of cold weather with north-east winds at the time of the blackthorn's flowering in early spring.

Blackwood /ˈblakwʊd/ *n.* M20. [E. F. *Blackwood* (1903–92), Amer. bridge player, inventor of the system.] *Bridge.* A system of bidding four no-trumps so that the partner's response can show the number of aces held.

blad /blad/ *v.* & *n. Sc.* Also **blaud** /blɔːd/. E16. [Prob. imit.: the senses of the n. perh. not all the same wd.] A *v.t.* Infl. **bladd-**. Slap heavily. E16. B *n.* 1 A fragment, a large portion; a selection, a specimen. E16. †2 A bodily injury; an illness. Usu. in *pl.* M16–M19. 3 A heavy slap; a stroke, a blow. E18. 4 A blast (of wind); a downpour. E19.

bladder /ˈbladə/ *n.* [OE *blǣdre*, later *blæddre* = OS *blādara*, MLG, MDu. *blāder* (Du. *blaar*), OHG *blātara* (G *Blatter*), ON *blāðra*, f. Gmc, f. base of BLOW *v.*[1] + instr. suff. corresp. to L *-trum*, Gk. *-tra*, *-tron*, Skt *-tram*.] 1a The muscular membranous bag in the human or other animal body which serves as the receptacle for urine from the kidneys. Also *urinary bladder*. OE. b Any of various similar organs. Usu. w. specifying wd. ME. 2 A morbid vesicle containing fluid; a boil, blister. OE. 3 The prepared bladder of an animal used for various purposes, as a container, inflated as a float, etc. ME. 4 A bubble. L15. 5 *fig.* Anything inflated and hollow; a pompous person, a windbag; *slang* a newspaper, esp. a poor one. L16. 6 *Bot.* An inflated pericarp; a hollow vesicle, as in many seaweeds. L16.

1b *gall-bladder*: see GALL *n.*[1] *swim-bladder*: see SWIM *n.* 3 **bladder of lard** *slang* a bald-headed or fat person.

Comb.: **bladder-campion** a common white campion, *Silene vulgaris*, with an inflated calyx; **bladder-fern** a fern of the genus *Cystopteris*, having bladder-like indusia; **bladder nut** any of various north temperate shrubs and small trees of the genus *Staphylea* (family Staphyleaceae) with white flowers and inflated capsules; *esp.* the central European *S. pinnata*; **bladder senna** a leguminous shrub, *Colutea arborescens*, with inflated pods; **bladder worm** a tapeworm larva in its encysted state, or in the intermediate or first host; **bladderwort** any of various chiefly aquatic plants constituting the genus *Utricularia* (family Lentibulariaceae), which have capillary leaves bearing bladders in which insects are trapped; **bladderwrack** a seaweed with air vesicles in its fronds, esp. *Fucus vesiculosus*.

bladder-like *a.* resembling (that of) a bladder: E17.

blade /bleɪd/ *n.* & *v.* [OE *blæd*, pl. *bladu*, = OFris. *bled*, OS (Du.) *blad*, OHG *blat* (G *Blatt*), ON *blað* leaf, blade of rudder, knife, etc., f. Gmc, perh. pa. ppl formation on the base of BLOW *v.*[2]] **A** *n.* **1 a** The leaf of a herb or plant. Now *dial.* & *poet.* in *gen.* sense. OE. **b** *spec.* A flat spear-shaped leaf, esp. of grass or a cereal crop; the whole of such plants before the ear appears. LME. **2** The broad, flattened part of any instrument or utensil, as an oar, spade, bat, paddle-wheel, turbine, propeller, etc. OE. **3** A broad flat bone; *esp.* that of the shoulder of man or other large animals (of some also as a joint of meat). ME. **4 a** The thin cutting part of a sword, chisel, knife, etc. ME. **b** An edged weapon; a sword. Chiefly *literary*. LME. **c** In full *razor-blade*. A flat piece of metal with usu. two sharp edges, used in a safety razor. M19. **d** In *pl.* Hand shears. *Austral.* & *NZ*. E20. **5** A dashing, pleasure-seeking fellow. L16. **6** A thin piece *of* something (esp. mace). M17. **7** *Bot.* The broad, thin part of a leaf or petal, excluding the petiole. E19. **8** Esp. *Phonet.* The flat part of the tongue behind the tip. L19. **9** *Archaeol.* A long narrow flake. E20.

1b in the blade with only the blade (not yet the ear) showing; *fig.* in the early stage, immature. **3** *shoulder-blade*: see SHOULDER *n.* **4** *switch-blade*: see SWITCH *n.* **5** S. PEPYS The present fashion among the blades. S. JOHNSON When we meet we will be jolly blades. G. CLARE Father was neither a young blade nor a rake.

Comb.: **blade-bone** = sense 3 above; **blade-consonant** *Phonet.* a consonant (e.g. /s/, /n/) formed with the blade of the tongue; **blade-work** control of the blade of an oar in rowing.

B *v.* **1** *v.t.* Remove the (esp. outside) leaves from. *dial.* LME. **2** *v.t.* Provide with a (cutting) blade. LME. **3** *v.i.* Put out blades or leaves, sprout. M16.

bladed *a.* (*a*) having blades or a blade (freq. as 2nd elem. of comb., of a specified kind); (*b*) having been bladed; †(*c*) having put out leaves: L16. **bladeless** *a.* M19. **bladelike** *a.* resembling a blade M19.

blady /ˈbleɪdi/ *a.* E17. [f. BLADE *n.* + -Y[1].] Like a blade; characterized by blades.

blady grass a coarse grass, *Imperata arundinacea*, of Australia and the E. Indies.

blae /bleɪ/ *a.* & *n. Sc.* & *north.* ME. [ON *blár* (whence also BLO): see BLUE *a.*] **A** *adj.* **1** Blackish-blue; livid; lead-coloured. ME. **2** Bleak, sunless. E16. **B** *n.* A kind of bluish-grey soft slate. M17.

blaeberry /ˈbleɪb(ə)ri/ *n. Sc.* & *north.* ME. [f. BLAE *a.* + BERRY *n.*[1]] = BILBERRY.

blag /blag/ *n.* & *v. slang.* L19. [Origin unkn.] **A** *n.* A (violent) robbery. L19. **B** *v.i.* & *t.* Infl. **-gg-**. Rob, esp. with violence; steal. M20.

blagger *n.* M20.

blague /blag/ *n.* M19. [Fr.] Humbug, claptrap.

sans blague: see SANS *prep.*

blagueur /blagœːr/ *n.* Pl. pronounced same. L19. [Fr., f. as prec. + *-eur* -OR.] A pretentious talker; a joker, a teller of tall stories.

blah /blɑː/ *n.*, *v.*, & *a. colloq.* Also redupl. **blah-blah**. E20. [Imit.] **A** *n.* Meaningless, nonsensical, insincere, or pretentious talk or writing. E20. **B** *v.i.* Utter or write nonsense; be insincere or pretentious. E20. **C** *adj.* **1** Mad. E20. **2** Dull, unexciting; pretentious. M20.

blahs /blɑːz/ *n.pl. colloq.* (orig. *US*). M20. [Repr. a dial. pronunc. of *blues*.] *The* blues (see BLUES), depression.

blain /bleɪn/ *n.* & *v.* [OE *bleġen* = MDu. *bleine* (Du. *blein*), LG *bleien*, f. WGmc.] **A** *n.* An inflamed swelling or sore on the skin. OE.

CHILBLAIN.

B *v.t.* Affect with blains. LME.

Blakeian /ˈbleɪkɪən/ *a.* E20. [f. *Blake* (see below) + -IAN.] Of, pertaining to, or characteristic of the poet and painter William Blake (1757–1827) or his work, esp. in its visionary aspects.

blamable *a.* var. of BLAMEABLE.

blame /bleɪm/ *n.* ME. [OFr., f. as next.] **1** The action of blaming, censure. ME. **2** Responsibility for a bad result or something wrong. ME. †**3** An accusation. ME–L16. **4** Blameworthiness; fault. *arch.* ME.

1 G. GREENE No one can please me much with praise or hurt me with blame. W. TREVOR The poor nurse will get the blame for negligence. **2** Esp. in *bear the blame* (*for*); *lay*, *put*, etc. *the blame on*. **4** SHAKES. *1 Hen. VI* And shall my youth be guilty of such blame?

blameful *a.* (*a*) imputing or conveying blame; (*b*) deserving blame: LME. **blameless** *a.* †(*a*) exempt from blame; (*b*) guiltless: LME. **blamelessly** *adv.* E17. **blamelessness** *n.* L17. **blameworthiness** *n.* the quality or state of being blameworthy L16. **blameworthy** *a.* deserving blame LME.

blame /bleɪm/ *v.*, *adv.*, & *a.* ME. [OFr. *bla(s)mer* (mod. *blâmer*) f. pop.L *blastemare* for eccl.L *blasphemare* revile, reproach, f. Gk *blasphēmein* (dial. *blast-*) BLASPHEME.] **A** *v.t.* **1** Find fault with (*for* an offence etc.). ME. †**2** Rebuke, scold. ME–M16. †**3** Accuse (*of*). ME–M17. **4 a** Fix the responsibility on, hold answerable. ME. **b** Fix the responsibility for (a bad result etc.) *on*. *colloq.* M19. †**5** Bring into disrepute. L16–E17. **6** *imper.* & in *pass.* = DAMN *v.* 3. *dial.* & *N. Amer.* M19.

6 M. TWAIN Blame it, I ain't going to stir him much. R. KIPLING Blame that boy! H. R. MARTIN I'm blamed if I dare adwise you.

Phrases: **be to blame** deserve censure, be responsible, (*for*).

B *adv.* & *adj.* = BLAMED. *dial.* & *N. Amer.* M19.

blamed *a.* & *adv.* (*dial.* & *N. Amer.*) confounded(ly), damned M19. **blamer** *n.* LME.

blameable /ˈbleɪməb(ə)l/ *a.* Also **blamable**. LME. [f. BLAME *v.* + -ABLE.] Deserving blame, culpable.

blameably *adv.* (earlier in UNBLAMEABLY) E18.

blanc /blɑ̃/ *n.* Pl. pronounced same. M18. [Fr. = white: see BLANK *a.*] **I** Used without qualification. **1** White paint, esp. for the face. Now *arch.* or *Hist.* M18. **2** A type of light-coloured stock or gravy. M19. **II** In phrases. **3** *blanc fixe* /fiks/, barium sulphate, esp. as used in paints. M19. **4** *blanc de chine* /də ʃin/, a white glazed Chinese porcelain, esp. of the Ming period, = DEHUA. L19. **5** *blanc de perle* /də pɛrl/, pearl-white. L19. **6** *blanc de blanc(s)* /də blɑ̃/, a (usu. sparkling) white wine made from white grapes only. M20.

blancbec /blɑ̃bɛk/ *n.* Pl. pronounced same. M19. [Fr., lit. 'white beak'.] A raw youngster, a greenhorn.

blanch /blɑːn(t)ʃ/ *a.*, *n.*, & *adv.* Now *arch.* or *Hist.* Also (*Sc.*) **blench** /blɛn(t)ʃ/. ME. [(O)Fr. *blanche* fem. of *blanc* white: see BLANK *a.*] **A** *adj.* **1** White, pale. Long *arch.* ME. **2** *Hist.* = BLANCHFARM *a.* M16. **B** *n. Hist.* = BLANCHFARM *n.* M16. **C** *adv. Hist.* = BLANCHFARM *adv.* M16.

blanch /blɑːn(t)ʃ/ *v.*[1] Also (by assoc. w. BLENCH *v.*[1]) **blench** /blɛn(t)ʃ/. ME. [(O)Fr. *blanchir*, f. as prec.] **1** *v.t.* Make white, esp. by withdrawing colour; bleach. ME. **2** *v.t.* Peel (almonds etc.), esp. by scalding. Now also, cook (vegetables or meat) lightly in boiling water. LME. **3** *v.t.* Palliate by misrepresentation. (Foll. by *over*.) Long *rare*. M16. **4** *v.t.* Make pale with cold, fear, hunger, etc. E17. **5** *v.t.* Whiten (plants) by depriving them of light. M17. **6** *v.i.* Turn white; bleach; pale. M18.

1 KEATS Blanched linen, smooth and lavendered. T. S. ELIOT The hedgerow Is blanched . . with transitory blossom Of snow. **3** MILTON To blanch and varnish her deformities.

blanch *v.*[2] see BLENCH *v.*[1]

blanchfarm /ˈblɑːn(t)ʃfɑːm/ *n.*, *adv.*, & *a. obs.* exc. *Hist.* Chiefly *Sc.* Also **blench-** /ˈblɛnt(t)ʃ-/. LME. [OFr. *blanche ferme* white rent.] **A** *n.* Rent paid in silver; any nominal quitrent. LME.

in blanchfarm as one's property for payment of a blanchfarm.

B *adv.* = *in blanchfarm* above. L15.

C *adj.* Held in or paid as blanchfarm. L15.

blancmange /bləˈmɒnʒ, -ˈmɑːnʒ/ *n.* Also (earlier) †**-manger**. LME. [OFr. *blanc mangier* (mod. *blancmanger*), f. *blanc* white + *mang(i)er* food, use as n. of *mang(i)er* eat. Shortened in 18.] †**1** A dish of white meat or fish in a cream sauce. LME–L15. **2** An opaque jelly made with isinglass or gelatin and milk or (now usu.) cornflour and milk, often flavoured and sweetened. M16.

blanco /ˈblaŋkəʊ/ *n.* & *v.t.* L19. [f. Fr. *blanc* white (see BLANK *a.*) + -O.] *Mil.* (Treat with) a white preparation for whitening belts etc., or a similar coloured substance.

bland /bland/ *n.* E17. [ON *blanda* mixture of fluids: see BLEND *v.*[2]] In Orkney and Shetland: a drink made of buttermilk and water.

bland /bland/ *a.* LME. [f. L *blandus* soft, smooth.] **1** Gentle or suave in manner. LME. **2** Of things: mild, soothing; not irritating, not stimulating. M17.

blandly *adv.* E19. **blandness** *n.* M19.

blandander /blanˈdandə/ *v.t. colloq.* L19. [Cf. Ir. *blanndar* dissimulation, flattery.] Tempt by blandishment (*into*); cajole.

blandish /ˈblandɪʃ/ *v.* ME. [f. OFr. *blandiss-* lengthened stem of *blandir* f. L *blandiri*, f. as BLAND *a.*: see -ISH[2].] **1** *v.t.* Flatter gently, coax; cajole. ME. **2** *v.i.* Use blandishments. ME.

blandishment *n.* (usu. in *pl.*) flattery, cajolery, *fig.* (an) allurement L16.

blank /blaŋk/ *n.* LME. [The adj. used absol. or ellipt.] †**1** A small French coin, orig. of silver, later of copper. Also, a silver coin of Henry V's reign, current in the parts of France then held by the English. LME–M19. **2** The 1/230400 part of a grain weight. M16. **3 a** A blank space left to be filled up in a document. M16. **b** A document with a blank space or blank spaces to be filled up. M16. **4** A lottery ticket which does not gain a prize. M16. **5** The white spot in the centre of a target; *fig.* something aimed at. Also, the range of an aim (*lit.* & *fig.*), esp. point-blank range. L16. **6** Blank verse. L16. **7** A piece of metal, wood, glass, wax, etc., intended for further fabrication; *esp.* in coinage, the disc of metal before stamping. L16. **8** A vacant space, place, or period. E17. **9** Anything insignificant; nothing at all. L17. **10** Used as a substitute for an omitted letter, name, or (esp. abusive or profane) noun or in reading a printed or written dash so used. L18. **11** A domino without pips on one or (also *double blank*) both of its halves. E19. **12** A zero score in a game. *N. Amer.* M19. **13** A blank cartridge. L19. **14** (A substance employed in) a control test done without a specimen. E20. **15** A blank leaf in a printed book or a manuscript. M20.

3 in blank [after Fr. *en blanc*] with blank spaces for the filling in of details. **4** *draw a blank*: see DRAW *v.* **8**. **8** SLOAN WILSON He had . . tried hard to think of nothing, to make his mind a complete blank. D. PIPER Those two years before he entered the Inns of Court in 1592 are virtually a blank. **9** SIR W. SCOTT His debts amount to blank—his losses to blank—his funds to blank—leaving a balance of blank in his favour. **10** B. HARTE What in blank are you waiting for? *Listener* Anecdotes . . about Lord Blank's personality and foolish views.

blank /blaŋk/ *a.* & *adv.* ME. [(O)Fr. *blanc* white f. Proto-Romance f. Gmc base of OHG *blanc* white, shining, OE *blanca* white steed, ON *blakkr* pale (horse).] **A** *adj.* †**1** White; pale, colourless. ME–E19. **2** Of paper, (a part of) a piece of paper, etc.: left white, not written or printed on, to be filled in. Of a document: with a space or spaces left for a signature or details. LME. **3** Void of interest, incident, result, or expression. M16. **b** Disconcerted, nonplussed, puzzled. M16. **4** Of emotions: stark, unrelieved; *gen.* pure, sheer, absolute (with negative or privative force). M17. 5 *gen.* Empty, without contents. M18. 6 Used as a substitute for an (esp. abusive or profane) adjective or in reading a printed or written dash so used. M19. 7 *Cards.* Lacking in support from other cards of the same suit. L19.

1 MILTON The blanc Moone. 2 SHAKES. *Merry W.* I warrant he hath a thousand of these letters, writ with blank space for different names. LD MACAULAY A blank safe conduct in the largest terms. J. G. COZZENS Each article and report began with a big inset blank square which was to be filled by an illuminated initial. 3 D. LESSING Molly's voice had gone blank, empty even of condemnation. J. RHYS Trying to protect herself with silence and a blank face. A. GRAY Every life has its blank moments when . . there's nothing to do but think. b MILTON Adam . . amaz'd, Astonied stood and Blank. 4 W. DE LA MARE His deadliest danger now was blank despair. T. BENN Pressure for full disclosure is likely to be met by a blank refusal. 5 W. OWEN The stark, blank sky. L. WOOLF One of those people whose minds go blank the moment they are faced by the slightest crisis. 6 M. DIVER Colonel Stanham Buckley . . inquired . . when . . this blankety blank train was supposed to start.

Special collocations & combs.: **blank-book** a book of clean writing-paper; **blank cartridge**: without a bullet, to make a sound only; **blank charter** a document given to the agents of the crown in Richard II's reign, with power to fill it up as they pleased; *transf.* & *fig.* = CARTE BLANCHE; **blank cheque** a cheque which is not made out; a cheque which is made out except for the amount, which the payee is to decide and fill in; *transf.* & *fig.* = CARTE BLANCHE; **blank flange** a disk used to block off the end of a pipe; **blank test** a control test done without a specimen; **blank verse** verse without rhyme; *esp.* the iambic pentameter or unrhymed heroic; **blank wall** (*a*) a wall without an opening in it; (*b*) an apparently impenetrable obstacle; **blank window** an imitation window.

B *adv.* Used as a substitute for an (esp. abusive or profane) adverb or in reading a printed or written dash so used. L19.

blankety, blanky *adjs.* & *advs.* = BLANK *a.* 6, *adv.* L19. **blankly** *adv.* E19. **blankness** *n.* M19.

blank /blaŋk/ *v.* L15. [f. the n.] †1 = BLANCH *v.*[1] I. L15–M17. 2 *v.t.* Put out of countenance; disconcert. *arch.* M16. 3 *v.t.* Frustrate; make void; invalidate. *arch.* M16. 4 *v.t.* Veil from sight; make invisible or undetectable. Also foll. by *out.* M18. 5a *v.t.* Substitute a dash for, indicate by a dash. *rare.* L18. b *v.t.* & *i.* Used as a substitute for an (esp. abusive or profane) verb or in reading a printed or written dash so used. L19. 6 *v.t. Cards.* Leave (a card) unsupported by another card of the same suit. L19. 7 *v.t.* Dismiss (a sports team) without a score; prevent from scoring. *N. Amer.* L19. 8 *v.t.* Seal, render inoperative. Foll. by *off, up.* E20. 9 *v.t.* & *i.* Cut or prepare (as) a blank for fabrication. Freq. foll. by *out.* E20. 10 *v.i.* Become blank or empty. Also foll. by *out.* M20. 11 *v.t.* Cold-shoulder, ignore (a person). *slang.* L20.

5b C. READE Blank him! that is just like him. 10 R. LOWELL My mind always blanked . . when Mother asked prying questions.

blanked *ppl a.* & *adv.* (*a*) *adj.* that has been blanked; (*b*) *adj.* & *adv.* = DAMNED *a.* 4, *adv.*: E16.

blanket /ˈblaŋkɪt/ *n.* & *a.* ME. [ONFr. *blanquet*, *blanket*, OFr. *blanchet* (AL *blanchettum*, *-ketum*, *-chetta*), f. *blanc*, *blanche* white: see BLANK *a.*, BLANCH *a.*, -ET[1].] A *n.* †1 An undyed woollen stuff used for clothing. Only in ME. 2 A large piece of woollen etc. material used for warmth, esp. as a bed-covering, horse-cloth, primitive garment, etc. ME. 3 *fig.* A thick covering mass or layer (*of*). E17. 4 *Printing.* A woollen etc. cloth used to equalize the impression of the platen or cylinder or intaglio plate; in offset printing, a rubber-surfaced sheet transferring the impression from plate to paper etc. L17. 5 In full *blanket-piece.* A layer of blubber in whales. M19.

3 A. E. STEVENSON America was covered with a blanket of trees. A. SILLITOE A blanket of dark cloud lay low over the city as if, were God to pull a lever, it would release a six-foot blanket of snow.

Phrases: **born on the wrong side of the blanket** illegitimate. **electric blanket** a blanket that can be connected to the mains and heated by means of internal wiring. *pig in a blanket*: see PIG *n.*[1] *receiving blanket*: see RECEIVING *a.* *stroud blanket*: see STROUD I. WAGGA *blanket. wet blanket*: see WET *a.*

Comb.: **blanket bath** the washing of a patient in bed; **blanket bog** an extensive peat bog existing as a consequence of high rainfall or humidity rather than of local water sources; **blanket coat** *N. Amer.* a coat made from a blanket; **blanket finish** a very close finish in a race (such that the contestants could be covered with a blanket); **blanket flower** = GAILLARDIA; *blanket-piece*: see sense 5 above; **blanket roll** *US* a soldier's blanket and kit made into a roll for use on active service; **blanket stiff** *slang* a tramp; **blanket stitch** a buttonhole stitch worked on the edge of blankets or other material too thick to be hemmed.

B *adj.* Covering all or many cases or classes, inclusive, general rather than individual, indiscriminate. L19.

T. HEGGEN The blanket prescription of aspirin tablets for all complaints. J. GLASSCO His blanket condemnation of almost everything.

blanke'teer *n.* (*obs.* exc. *Hist.*) a person who uses a blanket; *spec.* in *pl.*, a body of hand-loom weavers who met at Manchester in 1817, provided with blankets etc., in order to march to London and call attention to their grievances: M18.

blanket /ˈblaŋkɪt/ *v.t.* E17. [f. the n.] 1 Cover (as) with a blanket; stifle, keep quiet, (a scandal, question, etc.). E17. 2 Toss in a blanket (as a punishment). *obs.* exc. *Hist.* E17. 3 Supply with blankets. L19. 4 *Sailing.* Take the wind from the sails of (another craft) by passing to windward. L19. 5 Exclude (a radio signal) from reception by the use of a stronger signal. (Foll. by *out.*) M20.

blanketing /ˈblaŋkɪtɪŋ/ *n.* L16. [f. BLANKET *v.* or *n.* + -ING[1].] 1 The action or an instance of tossing a person in a blanket (as a punishment). *obs.* exc. *Hist.* L16. 2 Material for blankets; supply of blankets. L17. 3 The action of covering (as) with a blanket. L19.

blanquette /blɑ̃kɛt/ *n.* Pl. pronounced same. M18. [Fr., f. as BLANKET *n.*] A dish of light meat, esp. veal, cooked in a white sauce.

Blanquism /ˈblɑ̃ːkɪz(ə)m/ *n.* E20. [f. *Blanqui* (see below) + -ISM.] The doctrine that socialist revolution must be initiated by a small conspiratorial group, advocated by the French revolutionary communist Louis Auguste Blanqui (1805–81).

Blanquist *n.* L19.

blare /blɛː/ *n.* E19. [f. the vb.] 1 A strident sound; the sound of a trumpet etc.; *dial.* the sound of weeping, bellowing, etc. E19. 2 Brightness and conspicuousness of colour; a bright conspicuous colour. L19.

blare /blɛː/ *v.* LME. [(M)Du. *bleren*, MLG, MDu. *blaren*: of imit. origin.] 1 *v.i.* Roar with prolonged sound in weeping, as a child; bellow, as a calf. Now chiefly *dial.* LME. 2 *v.i.* Of a trumpet etc.: sound out. Of a broadcasting apparatus etc.: sound stridently. L18. 3 *v.t.* Utter or sound stridently. Also foll. by *out.* M19.

1 W. GOLDING The shattering call of a rutting stag blared just under the tree. 3 TENNYSON A tongue To blare its own interpretation. E. HUXLEY A radio blares out pop music at full blast. B. PLAIN Traffic . . blared furious horns.

blarney /ˈblɑːni/ *n.* & *v.* L18. [*Blarney*, a village and castle near Cork in the Republic of Ireland, with a stone said to confer a cajoling tongue on whoever kisses it.] A *n.* Smoothly flattering or cajoling talk; nonsense. L18. B *v.* 1 *v.i.* Use blarney. E19. 2 *v.t.* Subject to blarney. M19.

blart /blɑːt/ *v.i. dial.* E19. [Prob. a form of BLEAT *v.*] 1 Bleat, low. E19. 2 Cry, howl, whimper. L19.

blasé /ˈblɑːzeɪ/ *a.* E19. [Fr.] Cloyed with or tired of pleasure; bored or unimpressed by things from having seen or experienced them too often.

blaspheme /blasˈfiːm/ *v.* ME. [OFr. *blasfemer* (mod. *blasphémer*) f. eccl.L *blasphemare* revile, reproach f. Gk *blasphēmein*, f. *blasphēmos*: see next. Cf. BLAME *v.*] 1 *v.i.* Talk profanely. ME. 2 *v.t.* Speak irreverently of (something supposed to be sacred). LME. 3 *v.t.* Speak evil of; calumniate; abuse. LME.

blasphemer *n.* LME.

blasphemous /ˈblasfəməs/ *a.* LME. [f. eccl.L *blasphemus* (f. Gk *blasphēmos* evil-speaking) + -OUS.] 1 Uttering profanity; impiously irreverent. LME. †2 Abusive; slanderous; defamatory. Only in E17.

blasphemously *adv.* M16. **blasphemousness** *n.* M19.

blasphemy /ˈblasfəmi/ *n.* ME. [OFr. *blasfemie* f. eccl.L *blasphemia* f. Gk *blasphēmia* slander, blasphemy: see -Y[3].] Profane talk of something supposed to be sacred; impious irreverence.

blast /blɑːst/ *n.*[1] [OE *blǣst* = OHG *blāst*, ON *blástr* (perh. the immediate source in ME) f. Gmc, f. base also of BLAZE *v.*[2]] 1 A blowing or strong gust of air or wind. OE. 2 A puff of air through the mouth or nostrils; a breath. *arch.* ME. 3 A blow on a trumpet or other wind instrument or on a whistle; a sounding of a car horn, siren, etc.; the sound of a trumpet, whistle, car horn, etc. ME. 4 A sudden infection destructive to vegetable or animal life; blight; a blasting, withering, or pernicious influence; a curse. *arch.* M16. 5 A strong current of air produced artificially, *spec.* one used in smelting etc. E17. b A severe reprimand, a violent outburst. *colloq.* L19. †6 A stroke of lightning; a thunderbolt. M17–M18. 7 An explosion. M17. b A destructive wave of highly compressed air spreading outwards from an explosion. M19. c The quantity of explosive used in a blasting operation. L19. 8 A party; a good time; an enjoyable experience. *slang.* M20.

Phrases: (**at** or †**in**) **full blast** at maximum speed or capacity, at full pitch, very loudly. †**at one blast** [L *uno flatu*] at the same time. **out of blast** not at work; stopped.

Comb.: **blast bomb**: depending for its effect on the blast of air spreading outwards from the explosion (see sense 7b above); **blast-freezing** refrigeration (of meat etc.) in rapidly circulating cold air; **blast-furnace** a smelting furnace in which a blast of air is used, *esp.* one for iron-smelting using a compressed hot air blast; **blast-hole** a hole for an explosive charge in blasting; **blast-pipe** (*a*) a pipe through which air is passed into a blast-furnace; (*b*) in a steam locomotive, a pipe conveying the steam from the cylinders into the funnel and so increasing the draught.

blasty *a.* characterized by gusts of wind L15.

blast /blast/ *n.*[2] E20. [Gk *blastos*: see -BLAST.] *Biol.* An immature proliferative differentiated cell of an organism. Also *blast cell.*

blast /blɑːst/ *v.* ME. [f. BLAST *n.*[1]] I *gen.* 1 *v.i.* Blow; puff violently, pant. Long *obs.* exc. *Sc.* ME. †2a *v.i.* & *t.* Blow (a trumpet etc.). LME–M16. b *v.t.* Assail with trumpeting etc. E17–M19. 3 *v.t.* Fill (*up*) with air etc., swell (*up*). Long *dial.* L16. 4 *v.t.* Blow up (rocks etc.) by explosion; create *out of* or *from* rocks etc. by explosion. M18. 5 *v.i.* Of a rocket, spacecraft, etc.: take *off* from the launching site. M20.

4 *blasting* GELATIN. **blasting powder** a mixture like gunpowder but with sodium nitrate instead of potassium nitrate, used for blasting.

II To ill effect. 6 *v.t.* Of a wind etc.: blow or breathe balefully or perniciously on; wither, shrivel, (a plant, limb, etc.). M16. 7 *v.t. transf.* & *fig.* a Blight, ruin, (plans, prosperity, etc.); bring infamy upon (character, reputation, etc.). L16. b Strike (the eyes or vision) with dimness or horror. *arch.* L18. †8 *v.i.* Wither or fall under a blight. L16–M19. 9 *v.t.* Curse, strike with the wrath of heaven. Freq. in imprecations in imper. or optative form (for *God* etc. *blast* —). M17. b *v.i.* Curse, use profane language. M18. c *v.i.* as *int.* = DAMN *v.* 3b. E20.

9 LD MACAULAY Calling on their Maker to curse them . . blast them, and damn them. W. OWEN O blast this pencil. 'Ere, Bill, lend's a knife. b B. BEHAN He . . never damned or blasted. c E. F. BENSON 'There's an extra confirmation class this evening.' . . 'Oh, blast!'

blaster *n.* a person who or thing which blasts; *fig.* a heavy lofted golf club for playing from bunkers: L16.

-blast /blast/ *suff.* [Gk *blastos* sprout, germ.] Forming ns. denoting embryonic cells (as *erythroblast*: cf. -CYTE) or germ tissue (*epiblast*).

blasted /ˈblɑːstɪd/ *a.* & *adv.* M16. [f. BLAST *v.* + -ED[1].] A *adj.* 1 *gen.* That has been blasted. M16. 2 Cursed, damnable, bloody. *colloq.* L17. 3 Intoxicated. *slang.* L20. B *adv.* Cursedly, damnably, bloody. *colloq.* M19.

blastema /bla'stiːmə/ *n.* Pl. **-mas, -mata** /-mətə/. M19. [Gk *blastēma* sprout.] *Biol.* A mass of undifferentiated cells from which a part develops or is regenerated.
blastemal *a.* M19. **blaste'matic** *a.* M19.

blasto- /'blastəʊ/ *comb. form* of Gk *blastos* sprout, germ: see -O-. Used chiefly in *Biol.* w. the sense 'germ', 'bud'.
blastocoel(e) /'blastə(ʊ)siːl/ *n.* [Gk *koilos* hollow] the central cavity of a blastula L19. **blasto'coelic** *a.* of or pertaining to a blastocoele L19. **blastocyst** *n.* a mammalian blastula in which some differentiation of cells has occurred L19. **blastoderm** *n.* a blastula having the form of a disc of cells on top of the yolk M19. **blastodisc** *n.* = BLASTODERM L19. **blasto'genesis** *n.* reproduction by budding or gemmation L19. **blasto'genic** *a.* of, pertaining to, or formed by blastogenesis L19. **blastomere** *n.* each of the cells formed by cleavage of a fertilized ovum L19. **blastomy'cosis** *n.* a disease caused by infection with parasitic fungi of the genus *Blastomyces*, affecting the skin or the internal organs E20. **blasto'mylonite** *n.* (*Petrogr.*) recrystallized mylonite retaining traces of cataclastic structure M20. **blasto'poral** *a.* of or pertaining to a blastopore L19. **blastopore** *n.* an opening formed by invagination of the surface of a blastula L19. **blastospore** *n.* a fungal spore formed by budding M20.

blast-off /'blɑːstɒf/ *n.* M20. [f. *blast off*: see BLAST *v.* 5.] (The initial thrust for) the launching of a rocket, spacecraft, etc.

blastoid /'blastɔɪd/ *n.* & *a.* L19. [f. mod.L *Blastoidea* (see below): see BLASTO-, -OID.] *Palaeont.* A *n.* An extinct echinoderm of the class Blastoidea. L19. B *adj.* Of or pertaining to this class. L19.

blastula /'blastjʊlə/ *n.* Pl. **-lae** /-liː/, **-las.** L19. [mod.L, f. Gk *blastos*: see BLASTO-, -ULE.] *Biol.* A structure, freq. a hollow sphere, formed by the cells of an embryo after cleavage of the ovum and before gastrulation. Cf. BLASTOCYST.
blastular *a.* E20. **blastu'lation** *n.* formation of a blastula L19.

blat /blat/ *n.*[1] *slang.* Also **-tt.** M20. [G *Blatt.*] A newspaper.

blat /blat/ *v.* & *n.*[2] Chiefly *US.* M19. [Imit.] A *v.* Infl. **-tt-**. 1 *v.i.* Bleat, make a sound like a bleat; make a loud harsh noise; talk garrulously or impulsively. M19. 2 *v.t.* Blurt *out*; blast out. L19. B *n.* A bleat or similar cry; a loud harsh noise. E20.

blatant /'bleɪt(ə)nt/ *a.* Also **†-tt-**. L16. [Perh. alt. of Sc. *blatand* bleating, assoc. w. BLATTER.] 1 *the blatant beast*, the thousand-tongued monster produced by Cerberus and Chimaera, symbolizing calumny. L16. 2 Noisy, vulgarly clamorous, noticeably loud. M17. 3 Bleating. *poet.* L18. 4 Obtrusive to the eye; conspicuous, palpable; unashamed. L19.
¶First recorded in Spenser.
blatancy *n.* blatant quality E17. **blatantly** *adv.* M19.

blate /bleɪt/ *a. Sc.* & *north.* LME. [Origin uncertain: corresp. phonet. but not in sense to OE *blāt* pale, ghastly.] 1 Spiritless, timid, bashful. LME. 2 Dull, stupid. E16.

blateration /blatə'reɪʃ(ə)n/ *n. rare.* M17. [Late L *blateratio(n-)*, f. *blaterat-* pa. ppl stem of *blaterare*: see BLATTER, -ATION.] Babbling chatter.

blather /'blaðə/ *v.* & *n.* Orig. *Sc.* & *north.* Also **blether** /'blɛðə/. See also BLITHER. LME. [ON *blaðra*, f. *blaðr* nonsense.] A *v.* 1 *v.i.* Talk loquacious nonsense. LME. 2 *v.t.* Utter loquaciously. E19. 3 *v.i.* Cry loudly, blubber. *dial.* M19. B *n.* 1 Loquacious nonsense. E18. 2 An idle chatterer. E19.

blatherskite /'blaðəskʌɪt/ *n. dial.* & *US colloq.* Also **bletherskate** /'blɛðəskeɪt/. M17. [f. prec. + SKATE *n.*[3]] A foolish and voluble talker, a blathering person. Also, foolish talk, nonsense.
¶Popularized in the US during the War of Independence through the Sc. song *Maggie Lauder* by F. Sempill.

blatt *n.* var. of BLAT *n.*[1]

blatta /'blatə/ *n.* Pl. **-ttae** /-tiː/. E17. [L.] A nocturnal insect; *spec.* a cockroach. Now only as mod.L genus name.

†blattant *a.* var. of BLATANT.

blatter /'blatə/ *v.* & *n.* M16. [Partly f. L *blaterare* babble, partly imit.] A *v.* 1 *v.i.* & *t.* Prate volubly. M16. 2 *v.i.* Move with a clatter; strike repeatedly. Chiefly *Sc.* E18. B *n.* A volley of clattering words; a sound of rapid motion. Chiefly *Sc.* E19.
blatterer *n.* a voluble prater E17.

blaud *v.* & *n.* var. of BLAD.

blawort /'blɑːwət/ *n. Sc.* E18. [f. BLAE + WORT *n.*[1]] A harebell; a cornflower.

blaxploitation /ˌblaksplɔɪ'teɪʃ(ə)n/ *n. US colloq.* L20. [Blend of *Blacks* pl. (see BLACK *n.* 6) and EXPLOITATION.] The exploitation of Blacks, esp. in films.

blay /bleɪ/ *n.* Also **bley.** [OE *blǣġe* = MLG, MDu. *bleie* (Du *blei*), G *Blei(h)e*, f. WGmc, of unkn. origin.] = BLEAK *n.*

blaze /bleɪz/ *n.*[1] [OE *blæse*, *blase* f. Gmc; cf. MHG *blas* torch, rel., through the gen. sense 'shining', to next.] †1 A torch. OE–M16. 2 A bright flame or fire. OE. b In *pl.* Hell. *slang.* E19. 3 A brilliant display; a glow of bright colour; brilliancy; clear or full light (*lit.* & *fig.*). LME. 4 A violent outburst (*of* passion etc.). L16. 5 *Poker.* A hand containing court-cards only. L19.
2 **in a blaze** in flames, on fire. b DICKENS How the blazes you can stand the head-work you do, is a mystery to me. DAY LEWIS What the blue blazes is all this? *ballyhoo of blazes*: see BALLYHOO *n.*[1] **go to blazes** be ruined or destroyed; (as *int.*) go away. **like blazes** furiously, with great energy. 3 MILTON O dark, dark, dark, amid the blaze of noon. LD MACAULAY The theatres were . . one blaze of orange ribands. W. E. H. LECKY The blaze of publicity. J. B. PRIESTLEY The hall was now a blaze of light.

blaze /bleɪz/ *n.*[2] M17. [Origin uncertain. Identical in meaning with ON *blesi*, MDu. *blesse* (Du. *bles*), G *Blässe*, *Blesse*: cf. synon. OHG *blassa* (MHG *blasse*) and OHG *blas/ros*, MLG *blasenhengst* horse with a blaze; also MHG *blas* bald, G *blass* pale, and parallel formations with *r*, as MLG *blare*, Du. *blaar* cow with a blaze, MDu. *blaer* bald.] 1 A white spot or streak on the face of a horse, ox, etc. M17. 2 A mark made on a tree by chipping off bark, to indicate a route. M18.
blazed *a.* having a blaze L17.

blaze /bleɪz/ *v.*[1] ME. [f. BLAZE *n.*[1]: no corresp. vb in other Gmc langs.] 1 *v.i.* Burn with a bright flame. ME. b Be lit by a blaze. L19. 2 *v.i.* Show intense passion, anger, excitement, etc. ME. 3 *v.i.* Shine like fire; show bright colours; emit bright light; be conspicuously brilliant (*lit.* & *fig.*). LME. 4 *v.t.* Cause to burn with a flame. L15.
3 ALDOUS HUXLEY Masses of mesembryanthemums blazed with an intense magenta glare. G. ORWELL The sun blazed on them. J. UPDIKE The white woman's eyes blazed.
With advs. in specialized senses: **blaze away** fire continuously with a rifle etc. (*at*), work enthusiastically at anything. **blaze out** *arch.* exhaust in passion or excess. **blaze up** burst into flame, burst out in anger.

blaze /bleɪz/ *v.*[2] LME. [MLG, MDu. *blāzen* blow = OHG *blāsen* (G *blasen*), ON *blása*, Goth. *uf/blesan* puff up, f. Gmc extension (whence also BLAST *n.*[1]) of base of BLOW *v.*[1]] †1 *v.t.* Blow *out* on a trumpet etc. Only in LME. †2 *v.t.* Adorn with heraldic devices etc.; emblazon. *rare.* LME–E19. †3 *v.t.* = BLAZON *v.* 1. LME–E17. †4 *v.i.* Blow, puff. L15–M16. 5 *v.t.* Proclaim (as with a trumpet), make known. Freq. foll. by *abroad.* M16. †6 *v.t.* = BLAZON *v.* 2. M16–M17.

blaze /bleɪz/ *v.*[3] M18. [f. BLAZE *n.*[2]] Mark (a tree, a path, etc.) by chipping off bark.
blaze the trail, **way**, etc., show the way for others to follow (*lit.* & *fig.*).

blazer /'bleɪzə/ *n.*[1] Now *rare* or *obs.* LME. [f. BLAZE *v.*[2] + -ER[1].] = BLAZONER.

blazer /'bleɪzə/ *n.*[2] M17. [f. BLAZE *v.*[1] + -ER[1].] 1 A thing which blazes or shines. *rare* in *gen.* sense. M17. 2 A person who or thing which attracts attention. Chiefly *US.* M19. 3 A small cooking apparatus. L19. 4 A lightweight unlined jacket worn by schoolchildren, sportsmen, etc.; a man's plain or striped jacket not worn with matching trousers. L19.
blazered *a.* wearing a blazer M20.

blazing /'bleɪzɪŋ/ *a.* LME. [f. BLAZE *v.*[1] + -ING[2].] 1 That blazes. LME. 2 Used as a substitute for an abusive or profane adjective. L19.
1 **blazing star** †(*a*) a comet; (*b*) *arch.* a centre of attraction or admiration; (*c*) *N. Amer.* any of various plants with star-shaped flowers; spec. *Aletris farinosa*, a member of the lily family, with yellow or white flowers; also = *devil's bit* (b) s.v. DEVIL *n.*; also = LIATRIS.
blazingly *adv.* M19.

blazon /'bleɪz(ə)n/ *n.* ME. [(O)Fr. *blason* (orig.) shield (whence Sp. *blasón*, Port. *brasão*, It. *blasone*) = Prov. *blezon*, *blizon*; of unkn. origin.] 1 A shield, orig. as armour, long *spec.* as bearing a heraldic device; a coat of arms; armorial bearings; a banner bearing arms. ME. 2 A correct description of armorial bearings etc.; a record or description, esp. of virtues etc. L16. 3 Divulgation, publication. *rare.* E17.

blazon /'bleɪz(ə)n/ *v.t.* LME. [f. prec. and BLAZE *v.*[2]] 1 Describe heraldically in a correct manner. LME. 2 Describe fitly or vividly; depict; celebrate. L15. 3 Announce boastfully. M16. 4 Proclaim; = BLAZE *v.*[2] 5. Also foll. by *out.* Freq. *derog.* L16. 5 Depict or paint heraldically. L16. 6 Paint or depict in colours; illuminate. L17. 7 Inscribe with (or *with*) arms, names, etc., in colours or ornamentally. E19.
blazoner *n.* (*a*) a person who blazons arms, a herald; (*b*) a recorder or proclaimer (*of*): L16. **blazonment** *n.* proclamation, making known L19.

blazonry /'bleɪz(ə)nri/ *n.* E17. [f. BLAZON *v.* + -RY.] 1 (The correct description or depicting of) heraldic devices or armorial bearings. E17. 2 Brightly coloured display. E19.

-ble /b(ə)l/ *suff.* [(O)Fr. f. L *-bilem*, nom. *-bilis* forming act. or pass. vbl adjs. f. vbs or pa. ppl stems.] See -ABLE, -IBLE, -UBLE.

bleach /bliːtʃ/ *n.* [OE *blǣċe*, f. *blǣċ* pale. Branch II f. BLEACH *v.*] I 1 Whiteness, paleness. Long *rare.* OE. †2 Leprosy; a skin disease. OE–E17. II 3a *attrib.* [partly repr. the vb.] Designating locations of industrial bleaching, as *bleachfield*, *bleachworks*, etc. E18. b An act of bleaching; a bleaching process, a bleached condition. L19. 4 (A) bleaching substance. L19.

bleach /bliːtʃ/ *v.* [OE *blǣċan* = ON *bleikja* f. Gmc, f. a base meaning 'shining, white, pale' (whence also BLEAK *a.*).] 1 *v.t.* Blanch, make white; deprive of colour; *spec.* whiten (linen etc.) by washing and exposure to sunlight or by a chemical process. OE. b *Photogr.* Remove the silver image from (a negative or print) after development. L19. 2 *v.i.* Become white, pale, or colourless; whiten. Also foll. by *out.* E17.
1 W. HOLTBY Hair . . bleached flax-white by sun and weather. J. RABAN The wood . . had been bleached to a pale whisky colour. 2 SHAKES. *Wint. T.* The white sheet bleaching on the hedge. A. BRINK Where one could shrivel up and bleach out like a dried bone in the sun.
bleachery *n.* a place where bleaching is carried out. E18.

bleacher /'bliːtʃə/ *n.* ME. [f. prec. + -ER[1].] 1 A person who bleaches (esp. textiles). ME. 2 A vessel or chemical used in bleaching. L19. 3 An outdoor uncovered bench for spectators at a sports ground. Usu. in *pl.* exc. *attrib.* Chiefly *N. Amer.* L19.

bleak /bliːk/ *n.* L15. [Prob. f. ON *bleikja* = OHG *bleicha*, f. Gmc, f. as next.] A small silvery river-fish, *Alburnus alburnus*, of the carp family. Also, any of certain related fishes.
¶The earlier term was BLAY.

bleak /bliːk/ *a.* [OE *blāc* = ON *bleikr* shining, white, f. Gmc, f. base also of BLEACH *v.*; later directly f. ON.] †1 Shining, white. OE–L15. 2 Pale, pallid, wan; of a sickly hue; drained of colour. Long *obs.* exc. *dial.* OE. b Yellow. *north.* L16. 3 Bare of vegetation; exposed. M16. 4 Cold, chilly. L16. 5 *fig.* Cheerless, dreary; unpromising; inhospitable. E18.
3 R. L. STEVENSON Toano, a little station on a bleak, high-lying plateau in Nevada. 4 WORDSWORTH In bleak December, I retraced this way. 5 P. G. WODEHOUSE He looked into the future. It had a grey and bleak aspect. A. MACLEAN The room was bleak, monastic, linoleum-covered.

bleakish *a.* L16. **bleakly** *adv.* M16. **bleakness** *n.* E17. **bleaky** *a.* (*poet.*) tending to bleakness, somewhat bleak L17.

blear /blɪə/ *v.*, *a.*, & *n.* ME. [Origin unkn.: cf. MHG *blerre* blurred vision, LG *blarroged*, *blerr-* bleary-eyed.] **A** *v.* **1** *v.i.* Have watery or inflamed eyes, be bleary-eyed. Long *rare*. ME. **2** *v.t.* Dim (the eyes) with tears, rheum, sleep, etc. ME. **3** *v.t.* Blur (the face etc.) with tears, rheum, etc.; make bleary-eyed. LME.

2 blear the eye(s) of *arch.* hoodwink, deceive.

B *adj.* **1** Of the eyes: bleary. Chiefly in *blear-eyed* below. LME. **2** *gen.* Dim, misty, indistinct. M17.

Comb.: **blear-eyed** *a.* = BLEARY-*eyed*; **blear-eyedness** = BLEARY-*eyedness*.

C *n.* †**1** In *pl.* Bleary eyes. *rare*. Only in E17. **2** The state or condition of being bleared. *rare*. M19.

blearedness *n.* LME. **blearness** *n.* M16.

bleary /ˈblɪəri/ *a.* LME. [f. BLEAR *a.* + -Y[1].] (Of the eyes) dim, dull, filmy, full of sleep; *gen.* dim, misty, indistinct.

Comb.: **bleary-eyed** *a.* having bleary eyes; half asleep; *fig.* dull of perception, short-sighted; **bleary-eyedness** the state or condition of being bleary-eyed.

blearily *adv.* E20. **bleariness** *n.* LME.

bleat /bliːt/ *v.* & *n.* [OE *blǣtan* = OHG *blāzen*, Du. *blaten*, of imit. origin.] **A** *v.* **1** *v.i.* Of a sheep, goat, or calf: give its natural tremulous cry. OE. **2** *v.i.* Speak, cry, etc., in a feeble manner, foolishly, or plaintively M16. **3** *v.t.* Say, cry, etc., (as) with a bleat. Also foll. by *out*. L17. **B** *n.* †**1** = BLEATER. Only in LME. **2** The natural tremulous cry of a sheep, goat, or calf; any similar cry, *esp.* a querulous or feeble one. E16. **3** A feebly expressed complaint or grievance. *colloq.* E20.

bleater *n.* an animal that bleats M16. **bleatingly** *adv.* in a bleating manner, plaintively M20.

bleb /blɛb/ *n.* & *v.* E17. [Var. of earlier BLOB *n.*] **A** *n.* **1** A small swelling on the skin; a similar swelling on plants. E17. **2** A bubble in water, glass, or other substances previously fluid. M17. **3** A vesicular body. L18. **4** *Cytol.* A swelling due to injury on the surface of a cell. M20. **B** *v.* Infl. **-bb-**. **1** *v.t.* Provide with blebs. *rare*. E19. **2** *v.i.* Form or develop a bleb or blebs. M20.

blebby *a.* full of blebs M18.

bleck /blɛk/ *n.* & *v.* *obs.* exc. *dial.* & *Sc.* ME. [ON *blek* (Sw. *bläck*, Da. *blæck*) ink, f. base of BLACK *a.*] **A** *n.* **1** A black fluid substance; *spec.* (*a*) ink; (*b*) a preparation used for blacking leather; (*c*) black grease for axles etc. ME. **2** Soot; a particle of soot. L16. **B** *v.t.* **1** Make black; blacken with ink etc. LME. **2** *fig.* Blacken morally; defile. LME. **3** Enter with ink; write. LME.

bled /bled/ *n.* M20. [Fr. f. colloq. (Algerian) Arab., corresp. to classical Arab. *balad* vast stretch of country, *bilād* land, country.] In NW Africa: uncultivated land behind a fertile populated area.

bled *v.* pa. t. & pple of BLEED *v.*

blee /bliː/ *n.* Long *arch.* [OE *blēo(h)*, *blīo(h)* = OFris., OS *blī*, N. Fris. *bläy*.] **1** Colour. OE. **2** Complexion; visage. ME.

bleed /bliːd/ *n.* L16. [f. the vb.] **1** The action or an instance of bleeding. L16. **2** A page printed or trimmed so as to leave no margin (cf. BLEED *v.* 8, 14). M20.

1 *nosebleed*: see NOSE *n.*

bleed /bliːd/ *v.* Pa. t. & pple **bled** /blɛd/. [OE *blēdan* = OFris. *blēda*, MLG *blōden*, ON *bloeða*, f. Gmc, f. base of BLOOD *n.*] **I** *v.i.* **1** Emit, discharge, or lose blood. OE. **2** Lose blood from severe wounds; be severely wounded; die by bloodshed. ME. **3** Drop, flow, ooze. ME. **4** *bleed well*, (of corn etc.) give a large yield. *north.* M17. **5** Part with money; pay lavishly (*for*); have money extorted. *colloq.* M17. **6** Of a plant: emit sap. L17. **7** Of a dye: come out in water. M19. **8** *Typogr.* Be cut into when pages are trimmed. M19. **9** Be as red as blood. M19.

1 one's or **the heart bleeds** (freq. *iron.*) one feels sorry (*for*). **2** SHAKES. *Jul. Caes.* O that we then could come by Caesar's spirit, And not dismember Caesar! But, alas, Caesar must bleed for it! **3** SHAKES. *John* But a quantity of life, Which bleeds away. POPE For me the balm shall bleed, and amber flow. **9** D. WEVILL I watch the blue-veined snowfields bleed with sunrise.

II *v.t.* **10** Emit (blood or any other fluid) as from a wound. ME. **11** Draw or let blood from, *spec.* (chiefly *Hist.*) as a method of treatment in medicine. LME. **12** Draw or extort money from. *colloq.* L17. **13** Allow (a fluid) to drain or escape from a closed system through a valve etc.; treat (a system) thus. L19. **14** *Typogr.* Extend (usu. an illustration) to the edge of a page when trimming; cut into the printed area of (a book etc.) when trimming. E20.

10 DRYDEN Roapy Gore, he from his Nostrils bleeds. B. TAYLOR Thy tawny hills shall bleed their purple wine. **12** D. STOREY It bled us, you know, educating you. **bleed white** drain completely of resources.

bleeder /ˈbliːdə/ *n.* ME. [f. prec. + -ER[1].] **1** Chiefly *Hist.* A person who draws blood, esp. surgically; a phlebotomist. ME. **2** A person who loses or sheds blood; *spec.* one inclined to bleed excessively from a slight wound, a haemophiliac. LME. **3** A stupid, unpleasant, or contemptible person or thing. *slang.* L19.

bleeding /ˈbliːdɪŋ/ *a.* & *adv.* ME. [f. prec. + -ING[2].] **A** *adj.* **1** Losing or emitting blood; losing any other fluid (such as sap in plants) as from a wound. ME. **2** Running or suffused with blood. *rare*. ME. **3** Full of anguish from suffering, compassion, etc. L16. **4** Of a nation etc.: devastated by war or other catastrophe. L17. **5** Cursed, damnable, bloody. *colloq.* M19.

Phrases: **bleeding heart** (*a*) any of various plants; *esp.* a member of the genus *Dicentra*, of the fumitory family, with arching stems of red flowers; (*b*) *colloq.* a person who is too soft-hearted or sentimental.

B *adv.* †**1** Conspicuously, completely. *rare* (Shakes., modifying *new*). Only in E17. **2** Cursedly, damnably, bloody. *colloq.* L19.

bleep /bliːp/ *n.* & *v.* M20. [Imit.: cf. BLIP.] **A** *n.* An intermittent high-pitched sound, esp. as a radio signal or to replace censored words in broadcasting. Also (the word itself), used as a substitute for a censored word or phrase in reading aloud. M20. **B** *v.* **1** *v.i.* Emit a bleep or bleeps. M20. **2** *v.t.* Substitute a bleep or bleeps for. Also foll. by *out*. L20. **3** *v.t.* Alert or summon by a bleep or bleeps. L20.

bleeper *n.* a miniature radio receiver that emits bleeps M20. **bleeping** *a.* (*a*) that bleeps; (*b*) *slang* = BLEEDING *a.* 5: M20.

blellum /ˈblɛləm/ *n.* *Sc.* L18. [Perh. blend of BLAB *n.*[1], BLABBER *n.* and *skellum* var. of SKELM.] A blab, an idle chatterer.

blemish /ˈblɛmɪʃ/ *n.* E16. [f. the vb.] A physical or moral defect; a stain; a flaw.

blemishless *a.* L16.

blemish /ˈblɛmɪʃ/ *v.t.* LME. [OFr. *ble(s)miss-* lengthened stem of *ble(s)mir* render pale, injure, prob. of Gmc origin: see -ISH[2].] †**1** Hurt, damage, deface. LME–E17. **2** Injure the working of. LME. **3** Impair the beauty, brightness, or perfection of; sully, stain. LME. †**b** Defame. LME–M18.

blemisher *n.* LME. **blemishment** *n.* L16.

†**blench** *n.*[1] Also (*Sc.* & *north.*) **blenk**. ME. [f. BLENCH *v.*[1]; later infl. by BLINK *n.*] **1** (As *blench.*) A trick. Only in ME. **2** (As *blenk.*) A sudden gleam of light. ME–E16. **3** (Both forms.) A (usu. bright or cheerful) glance; a side glance. LME–L16.

blench *a.*, *n.*[2], & *adv.* see BLANCH *a.*, *n.*, & *adv.*

blench /blɛn(t)ʃ/ *v.*[1] Also (by assoc. w. BLANCH *v.*[1]) **blanch** /blɑːn(t)ʃ/; (chiefly *Sc.* & *north.*) †**blenk**. [OE *blenċan* = ON *blekkja* impose upon, f. Gmc; later infl. by BLINK *v.*] **I** All forms. †**1** *v.t.* Deceive, cheat. OE–E17. **2** *v.i.* Start aside, shy, flinch, shrink; of the eyes: lose firmness of glance, quail. ME. **3** *v.t.* Elude, avoid; flinch from; ignore. ME. **4** *v.t.* Turn (esp. deer) aside; *fig.* disconcert. L15. †**II** Chiefly *Sc.* & *north.*, as *blenk*. **5** *v.i.* Glitter, gleam. ME–E17. **6** *v.i.* Glance. LME–E17.

blencher *n.* †(*a*) a person who or thing which frightens away or turns (esp. deer) aside; (*b*) one who flinches (*at*): M16.

blench *v.*[2] see BLANCH *v.*[1]

blenchfarm *n.* var. of BLANCHFARM.

blend /blɛnd/ *n.* L19. [f. BLEND *v.*[2]] **1** A blending; a mixture formed by blending various sorts or grades (of spirits, tea, tobacco, wool, etc.) or personal or abstract qualities. L19. **2** A portmanteau word. E20.

1 DAY LEWIS That strange Anglo-Irish blend of reticence and emotionalism.

†**blend** *v.*[1]*t.* [OE *blendan* = OFris. *blenda*, MLG *blenden*, OHG *blenten* (G *blenden*), f. Gmc causative f. as BLIND *a.*] **1** = BLIND *v.* 1. OE–E17. **2** *fig.* Blind the understanding, judgement, or moral sense of. ME–L16.

blend /blɛnd/ *v.*[2] Pa. t. & pple **blended**, (*poet.* & *rhet.*) **blent** /blɛnt/. ME. [Prob. of Scand. origin, f. *blend-* pres. stem, *blĕnd-* pa. stem of ON *blanda* mix = OE, OS, Goth. *blandan*, OHG *blantan* mix: cf. BLAND *n.*] **I** *v.t.* **1 a** Mix or mingle together. *obs.* in *gen.* sense. ME. **b** Mix (sorts or grades of spirits, tea, tobacco, etc.) so as to produce a certain quality; produce by so mixing. LME. **c** Mix (components) intimately or harmoniously so that they are inseparable and their individuality is obscured; produce by so mixing. E17. †**2** Stir up; trouble, agitate, disturb. ME–L16. **3** Mix or mingle intimately or closely *with*; mix thoroughly *in* (*with*) or *into*. L16.

1b blended whisky: *spec.* made of blended malt and grain whiskies. **c** CONAN DOYLE A cry in which joy and surprise seemed to be blended. TOLKIEN Evil dreams and evil waking were blended into a long tunnel of misery. D. LESSING Ant-heap earth . . has . . been blended by the jaws of a myriad workers. **2** SPENSER These stormes, which now his beauty blend, Shall turn to calmes. **3** WORDSWORTH Never to blend our pleasure or our pride With sorrow of the meanest thing that feels. R. CARRIER Blend in egg yolks until the mixture is a smooth homogeneous mass.

II *v.i.* **4** Mix or mingle together; unite intimately so as to form a uniform or harmonious mixture; (esp. of colours) pass imperceptibly into each other. LME. **5** Mix or mingle intimately or closely *with*; mix harmoniously or thoroughly *in* (*with*); pass imperceptibly *into*. LME.

4 B. PLAIN The air was full of sounds, blending into one long hum of afternoon. M. MOORCOCK The town and country met and blended in almost perfect harmony. **5** P. G. WODEHOUSE Pleasant Spring scents . . to blend with the robuster aroma of coffee and fried bacon. J. MCPHEE His fur blends so well into the tundra colors that sometimes it is hard to see him.

blender *n.* a person who blends (esp. spirits, tea, tobacco, etc.); an implement for blending, *esp.* a (usu. electric) device for blending foods (*Waring blender*: see WARING *n.*[2]): M19.

blende /blɛnd/ *n.* L17. [G, f. *blenden* deceive (see BLEND *v.*[1]): so called from its resembling galena but yielding no lead.] Native zinc sulphide, sphalerite.

Blenheim /ˈblɛnɪm/ *n.* M19. [*Blenheim* Palace, the name of the Duke of Marlborough's seat, at Woodstock, Oxfordshire, named after his victory (1704) at Blenheim in Bavaria.] **1** In full *Blenheim spaniel*. A white variety of spaniel with chestnut markings. M19. **2** A golden-coloured late-ripening variety of apple. Also more fully *Blenheim Orange*, *Pippin*. M19.

†**blenk** *n.*, *v.* see BLENCH *n.*[1], *v.*[1]

blenniid /ˈblɛnɪɪd/ *a.* & *n.* L19. [f. BLENNY + -ID[3].] (A blenny) of the family Blenniidae.

blenno- /ˈblɛnəʊ/ *comb. form* of Gk *blennos*, *blenna* mucus: see -O-.

blenno'rrhagia, **-'rrhoea** *ns.* a copious discharge of mucus, esp. from the urethra in gonorrhoea E19.

blenny /ˈblɛni/ *n.* M18. [f. L *blennius* f. Gk *blennos* slime (with ref. to the mucous coating of the scales).] Any of various small spiny-finned marine fishes belonging to the Blenniidae or a related family, most of which are bottom-dwelling fishes of intertidal and shallow inshore waters.

BUTTERFLY *blenny*. *smooth blenny*: see SMOOTH *a.* & *adv.* *viviparous blenny*: see VIVIPAROUS 1.

blent *v.* see BLEND *v.*[2]

blepharitis /blɛfəˈrʌɪtɪs/ *n.* M19. [f. as next + -ITIS.] *Med.* Inflammation of an eyelid.

blepharo- /ˈblɛf(ə)rəʊ/ *comb. form* of Gk *blepharon* eyelid: see -O-.

blepharoconjuncti'vitis *n.* inflammation of the eyelid and conjunctiva L19. **blepharoplast** *n.* (*Biol.*) an organelle from which a flagellum or cilium develops L19. **blepharo'plastic** *a.* of or pertaining to blepharoplasty M19. **blepharoplasty** *n.* (an instance of) the surgical repair or reconstruction of an eyelid M19. **blepharospasm** *n.* involuntary tight closure of the eyelids L19.

blerry /'blɛri/ *a.* & *adv. S. Afr. slang.* Also **blirry** /'blɪri/. E20. [Alt. of BLOODY *a.* & *adv.*] Bloody, damn, cursed(ly).

blesbok /'blɛsbɒk/ *n.* Also **-buck** /-bʌk/. E19. [Afk., f. Du. *bles* BLAZE *n.*[2] + *bok* BUCK *n.*[1]] A white-faced southern African antelope, *Damaliscus dorcas*.

bless /blɛs/ *v.*[1]*t.* Pa. t. & pple **blessed** /blɛst, *arch.* & *poet.* 'blɛsɪd/, (*arch.*) **blest** /blɛst/. See also BLESSED. [OE *blētsian, blēdsian, blœdsian*, f. as BLOOD *n.* No corresp. vb in other Gmc langs.] 1 Consecrate by a religious rite, a spoken formula, a prayer, etc.; invoke divine favour upon. OE. b *spec.* Sanctify by the sign of the cross. *arch.* OE. 2 Call holy, adore, praise, (God); give thanks to for especial goodness or beneficence; attribute one's good fortune to (esp. one's stars). OE. 3 Pronounce words to confer or invoke divine favour upon; load with devout good wishes. OE. 4 Confer well-being upon, make happy, cause to prosper; endow *with.* OE. †5 Protect, guard, (another, oneself, a thing) *from* evil or danger. ME-M19. 6 *refl.* Account oneself supremely happy or fortunate (*in, that, with*). *arch.* E17. 7 *iron.* Pronounce an imprecation upon; curse; damn. *colloq.* E19.

1 SOUTHEY The bishop had blest the meat. b M. W. MONTAGU I fancy I see you bless yourself at this terrible relation. 2 SHAKES. *Tam. Shr.* Then, God be bless'd, it is the blessed sun. 3 STEELE The Fatherless . . and the Stranger bless his unseen Hand in their Prayers. 4 BYRON I have possess'd, And come what may, I have been blest. 5 MILTON The bellmans drowsy charm To bless the doors from nightly harm. SMOLLETT He blessed himself from such customers. 6 AV *Jer.* 4:2 The Lord liveth . . ; and the nations shall bless themselves in him. 7 DICKENS Blessed if I don't think he's got a main in his head as is always turned on.

Phrases: **bless his, her**, etc., **heart**: expr. pleasure in a person. **bless my heart**: expr. surprise. **(God) bless me, my soul**: exclams. expr. surprise, pleasure, or indignation. **(God) bless you**: expr. surprise, pleasure, or indignation, or well-wishing, or to a person who has sneezed. **God bless** (*sc.* you): expr. well-wishing. *Lord bless me, my soul, you*, etc.: see LORD *n.* **not have a penny to bless oneself with** be impoverished (w. ref. to the cross on the silver penny).

¶'Mark or consecrate with blood' was prob. the original meaning (for this type of rite cf. *Exod.* 12:23). During the Christianizing of Britain, however, the wd was used to render L *benedicere* 'praise, (from Heb.) bend the knee, worship'. Later also assoc. w. BLISS *n.*

blesser *n.* L16.

†**bless** *v.*[2]*t.* & *i.* ME. [AN *blechier*, OFr. *blecier* (mod. *blesser*) injure, wound; sense 2 perh. a different wd.] 1 Inflict injury or damage (on); thrash. ME-E17. 2 Wave about, brandish; make a flourish round (*with*). L16-E17.

blessed /'blɛsɪd, *esp. pred.* blɛst/ *a., n.,* & *adv.* Also (now chiefly *poet.*) **blest** /blɛst/. ME. [f. BLESS *v.*[1] + -ED[1].] A *adj.* 1 Enjoying supreme felicity; fortunate; happily endowed *with*; *RC Ch.* beatified. ME. 2 Consecrated, made holy. ME. 3 Worthy to be reverenced; adorable. ME. 4 Pleasurable; bringing happiness; blissful. LME. b Of plants and herbs: endowed with healing virtues. Now chiefly in plant-names. M16. 5 *iron.* Wretched; cursed, damnable, bloody. *colloq.* M18.

1 R. BURNS Kings may be blest, but Tam was glorious. C. CHAPLIN Mrs Jackson was not blessed with abundant good looks. 2 *the Blessed Sacrament*: see SACRAMENT *n.* 3 *Blessed Virgin* (*Mary*): see VIRGIN *n. the Blessed Holy Virgin*: see VIRGIN *n.* 4 F. A. KEMBLE The blessed unconsciousness and ignorance of childhood. b *blessed thistle*: see CARDUUS. 5 W. WINDHAM One of the happy consequences of our blessed system of printing debates. S. O'CASEY A letter that I got today . . I'm blessed if I know where I put it.

B *absol.* as *n. The* souls in paradise; (*RC Ch.*) *the* beatified saints. ME.

C *adv.* Blessedly; *esp.* cursedly, extremely. E17.

blessedly, (*arch.*) **blestly** *adv.* in a blessed manner; *colloq.* cursedly, extremely: LME. **blessedness** *n.* the state of being blessed, esp. with divine favour (*single blessedness*, orig. (Shakes. *Mids. N. D.*) the state of a life consecrated to chastity, now *joc.* the state of being unmarried) ME.

blessing /'blɛsɪŋ/ *n.* OE. [f. BLESS *v.*[1] + -ING[1].] 1 The bestowal, declaration, or invocation of (esp. divine) favour and prospering influence; a benediction. OE. †2 Consecration, hallowing; *spec.* making the sign of the cross. OE-M16. 3 A gift of God, nature, etc.; anything of which one is glad. ME. †b A favour, a present. LME-E17.

1 SHAKES. *Temp.* All the blessings Of a glad father compass thee about. J. M. SYNGE The blessing of God and the holy angels on your head, young fellow. M. RICHLER In the synagogue, Joshua stumbled through the blessings he was obliged to pronounce. **ask a blessing** say grace before or after food. *second blessing*: see SECOND *a.* 3 SHAKES. *Hen. VIII* Eminence, wealth, sovereignty . . are blessings. K. AMIS What a blessing to be in such good hands. **blessing in disguise** an apparent misfortune that eventually does good, an unwelcome but salutary experience. **count one's blessings** not forget the things one should be glad of. MIXED *blessing*. UNMIXED *blessing*.

blest *v., a., n.,* & *adv.*: see BLESS *v.*[1], BLESSED.

blether *v.* & *n.*, **bletherskate** *n.* vars. of BLATHER, BLATHERSKITE.

bleu /blɜː, *foreign* blø (*pl. same*)/ *n.* & *a. Canad.* L19. [Fr. = blue.] In French-Canadian politics: (a) conservative.

bleu celeste /blɜː sɪ'lɛst/ *n.* & *a. phr.* L20. [Fr. = celestial blue.] *Her.* (Of) the tincture sky-blue.

bleu-du-roi /blødyrwa/ *n.* & *a.* Also **-de-** /-də-/. M19. [Fr. = king's blue.] (Of) the ultramarine blue of Sèvres porcelain.

†**blew** *n., a., v.*[1] see BLUE *n., a., v.*[1]

blew *v.*[2], *v.*[3] pa. t. of BLOW *v.*[1], *v.*[2]

†**blewish** *a.* var. of BLUISH.

blewits /'bluːɪts/ *n.* E19. [Prob. f. BLUE *a.*] A late edible mushroom of the genus *Lepista*, with a lilac stem.

bley *n.* var. of BLAY.

blight /blʌɪt/ *n.* M16. [Origin uncertain: perh. ult. rel. to BLEACH *n.*] 1 (An) inflammation or eruption of the skin. M16. 2 (The state resulting from) an atmospheric or other influence that suddenly blasts, nips, withers, or destroys plants or affects them with disease; *spec.* a plant disease caused by fungoid parasites, as mildew, rust, smut, etc. L16. b *collect.* Destructive aphids. L19. 3 Any (esp. obscure) malignant influence or effect. M17. b *spec.* More fully *urban blight* (The development or existence of) derelict or unsightly areas in a town or city. M20.

2 *late blight*: see LATE *a. ray blight*: see RAY *n.*[1] 3 S. BELLOW The insidious blight of nostalgia. C. MCCULLOUGH The rabbits were as much of a blight as ever.

Comb.: **blight-bird** *Austral.* & *NZ* the white-eye (noted for feeding on insect pests).

blight /blʌɪt/ *v.t.* M17. [f. the n.] Affect with blight; exert a malignant influence on; frustrate; wither, mar.

blighted *ppl a.* (*a*) that has been blighted; (*b*) *slang* = BLASTED 2: M17. **blighter** *n.* (*a*) a blighting agent or influence; (*b*) *slang* a (usu. contemptible or annoying) person: E19.

Blighty /'blʌɪti/ *n.* & *a. Army slang.* Also **b-**. E20. [Urdu *b'lāytī*, colloq. form of *bilāyatī*, *wilāyatī* foreign, (esp.) European, f. Arab. *wilāya(t)* dominion, district. Cf. VILAYET.] A *n.* 1 England, home, after foreign service. E20. 2 A wound securing return to England or home. E20. B *attrib.* or as *adj.* Of or pertaining to England or home; securing return to England or home. E20.

blik /blɪk/ *n.* M20. [Arbitrary.] *Philos.* A personal slant on something; a conviction, *esp.* a religious one.

blimbing *n.* var. of BILIMBI.

blimey /'blʌɪmi/ *int. coarse slang.* L19. [Alt. of *blind me!* or *blame me!*: see BLIND *v.*, BLAME *v.* 6.] Expr. surprise, contempt, etc. Freq. in *cor blimey!* (see COR *int.* and cf. GORBLIMEY).

blimp /blɪmp/ *n.* E20. [Origin unkn.] 1 A small non-rigid airship; a barrage balloon. E20. 2 A soundproof cover for a cine-camera. E20. 3 (Also **B-**.) More fully *Colonel Blimp* [f. a character invented by the cartoonist David Low (1891-1963).] (A name given to the type of) an obese reactionary ex-officer, a pompous elderly die-hard. M20.

blimpery *n.* behaviour or speech characteristic of a blimp M20. **blimpish** *a.* typical of a blimp M20.

blin /blɪn/ *n.* Pl. **blini, -y** /'blɪni/, **blinis** /'blɪnɪz/. L19. [Russ.] A kind of pancake, freq. stuffed. Cf. BLINTZE.

†**blin** *v.i.* & *t.* OE-M18. [OE *blinnan*, f. as BE- + LIN *v.*] Leave off, stop, cease (from).

blind /blʌɪnd/ *n.* OE. [f. BLIND *a.* or *v.*] I The adj. used *absol.* 1 A blind person. Long only *collect. pl., the* class of blind people. OE. 2 A blind baggage car. *US.* L19.

1 AV *Matt.* 15:14 If the blind lead the blind, both shall fall into the ditch. 2 *ride the blind(s)*: see RIDE *v.*

II 3 A screen or other protective structure in fortification etc. E17. 4 A place of concealment; *spec.* (*US*) a hide or screen for a hunter or naturalist. M17. 5 *fig.* A thing or action intended to conceal one's real design; a pretence, a pretext; a legitimate business concealing an illegitimate one. M17. 6 A thing which obstructs the light or sight; *spec.* (*a*) a screen for a window, *esp.* one mounted on a roller; an awning over a shop window; (*b*) *US* a blinker for a horse etc. E18. 7 *Poker.* A stake put up by a player before seeing his or her cards. M19. 8 A drunken bout or orgy. *slang.* E20.

5 SWIFT These verses were only a blind to conceal the most dangerous designs of the party. *double-blind*: see DOUBLE *a.* & *adv.* 6 *Venetian blind*: see VENETIAN *a.*

blindage *n.* = BLIND *n.* 3 E19. **blindless** *a.* M19.

blind /blʌɪnd/ *a.* & *adv.* [OE *blind* = OFris., OS *blind*, OHG *blint* (G *blind*), ON *blindr*, Goth. *blinds*, f. Gmc.] A *adj.* 1 Without the sense of sight. OE. b *Aeronaut.* Without direct observation, using instruments only. E20. 2 Enveloped in darkness. *arch.* OE. †b Having its light extinguished. LME-E18. 3 Lacking discernment or foresight; deficient in intellectual or moral perception. OE. 4 Reckless, heedless; not ruled by purpose. ME. 5 Covered or concealed from sight; out of the way; secret, obscure; (of a way or path) confusing, intricate, uncertain. ME. b Of a corner or other feature of a road: round or to the other side of which one cannot see. E20. 6 Dim, indistinct; faintly marked. *arch.* LME. †7 False, deceitful. LME-M16. 8 Having no openings for light or passage; walled or boarded up; that cannot be seen through. E16. 9 Closed at one end; (of a geographical feature) terminating abruptly. M17. 10 Drunk, thoroughly intoxicated. *colloq.* M17. 11 Of a plant: without buds or eyes, or without a terminal flower. M19. 12 Without complete information; (of a test or experiment) in which information which might bias results is withheld from the tester or the subject or both. M20. 13 *attrib.* Slight(est), single. Esp. in *a blind bit of*, the slightest, the least. Usu. in neg. contexts. *colloq.* M20.

1 *blind as a bat, beetle*, etc. *colour-blind, green-blind*, etc. 2 S. PEPYS The little blind bed-chamber. 3 H. ROBBINS Men were sometimes such blind fools. 4 HARPER LEE He just broke into a blind raving charge at the fence. 5 MILTON In the blind mazes of this tangled wood. S. PEPYS A blind place where Mr. Goldsborough was to meet me. J. MORSE Blind rocks, sunk a few feet below the water. 6 N. HAWTHORNE Written in such a queer, blind . . hand. 8 POPE Some huntsman . . From the blind thicket wounds a stately deer. J. H. PARKER The clerestory window has a smaller blind arch on each side of it. 12 *double-blind*: see DOUBLE *a.* & *adv.* 13 C. CAUSLEY Maloney never said a blind word to contradict him.

Phrases: **blind to** incapable of appreciating or recognizing. *steal (a person) blind*: see STEAL *v. strike me blind*: see STRIKE *v.* **turn a blind eye (to)** pretend not to notice.

Special collocations & comb.: **blind alley** †(*a*) an out-of-the-way or secret alley; (*b*) a cul-de-sac; *fig.* an unprofitable or useless course of action; also *attrib.* designating a job etc. with no prospect of advancement. **blind baggage car** *US* a railroad car without end doors, for baggage. **blind coal** anthracite (from its burning without a bright flame). **blind date** *colloq.* a social engagement with a view to a personal relationship between two people (usu. of the opposite sex) who have not met before; a person with whom such a date is arranged. **blind fish** any of various fishes with eyes vestigial or absent, living in subterranean waters. **blind god** Eros or Cupid (associated with love). **blind gut** the caecum. *blind* HOOKEY. **blind man's buff**, *N. Amer.* **bluff** a game in which a blindfold player tries to catch other players, who push him or her about. **blind-man's holiday** the time just before lamps are lit. **blind nettle** a dead-nettle or similar plant. **blind pig** *N. Amer. colloq.* a place where liquor is illicitly sold. **blind side** (*a*) the unguarded, weak, or assailable side of a person or thing; †(*b*) the unsightly or unpresentable side. **blind-side** *v.t.* (*N. Amer.*) attack on the blind side, take advantage of, take unawares. **blind snake** any of various small burrowing snakes of the infraorder Scolecophidia, with reduced eyes, esp. of the family Typhlopidae. **blind spot** (*a*) a part of the retina insensitive to light, at the point of entry of the optic nerve; (*b*) *Cricket* that spot of ground in front of the batsman where a ball pitched by the bowler leaves the batsman in doubt whether to play forward or back; (*c*) *Radio* a point of unusually weak reception; (*d*) *transf.* & *fig.* an area where vision or understanding is lacking. **blind-stitch** *n.* & *v.* (*a*) *n.* a sewing stitch visible on one side only; (*b*) *v.t.* & *i.* sew thus. **blind stamping, tooling** *Bookbinding* ornamentation by impression without the use of colour or gold leaf. **blind tiger** *US colloq.* = *blind pig* above. **blind trust** a trust independently administering the private business interests of a person in public office to prevent conflict of interest. **blindworm** (*a*) the slow-worm (from its small eyes); (*b*) any of various legless skinks of the genus *Typhlosaurus*.

B *adv.* Blindly. L18.

bake blind bake (a pastry or flan case etc.) without a filling. **blind drunk** insensible through drink. **go blind** *Poker* put up a stake before seeing one's cards. **go it blind** *colloq.* act recklessly or without proper consideration. **swear blind** swear vehemently (*that*).

blindish *a.* E17. **blindling** *n.* (long *rare*) a blind person M16. **blindling(s)** *adv.* (*Sc.* & *north.*) blindly, recklessly ME. **blindly** *adv.* OE. **blindness** *n.* (*a*) the state or condition of being blind; †(*b*) (*rare*, Shakes.) concealment: OE.

blind /blʌɪnd/ *v.* ME. [f. prec., repl. BLEND *v.*[1]] I *v.t.* 1 Make unable to see, permanently or temporarily. ME. 2 Rob of understanding, judgement, or moral sense, deceive, (with regard *to*). ME. 3 Conceal, obscure. *arch.* ME. 4 Deprive of light, darken; eclipse. *arch.* L15. 5 [f. BLIND *n.*] a Draw a blind over (a window etc.). E18. b Provide with protective structures. M19.

1 **blind me!, him!**, etc.: used as an imprecation. *eff and blind*: see EFF 2. 2 R. B. SHERIDAN How jealousy blinds people! W. S. MAUGHAM The glamour of their resounding titles blinded him to their faults. *blind with* SCIENCE. 3 KEATS Wherefore did you blind Yourself from his quick eyes. 4 DRYDEN Such darkness blinds the sky. TENNYSON [Aurora's] sweet eyes . . blind the stars.

II *v.i.* 6 Become blind. *rare.* ME. 7 Go blindly or heedlessly, esp. in a motor vehicle. *slang.* E20.

blindingly *adv.* in a blinding manner M19.

blinder /ˈblʌɪndə/ *n.* L16. [f. BLIND *v.* + -ER[1].] 1 *gen.* A person who or thing which blinds. L16. 2 A blinker for a horse etc.; a shade for a person's eye. Chiefly *US.* E19. 3 An excellent performance in a game; something very good. *colloq.* M20.

†**blindfell** *v.t.* OE–M16. [OE *geblindfellian*, f. as BLIND *a.* & *adv.* + FELL *v.*[1]] Strike blind; blindfold.

†**blindfeld** *a.* & *adv.* blindfold LME–L16.

blindfold /ˈblʌɪn(d)fəʊld/ *n.* M17. [f. next.] †1 Blindfolding. *rare.* Only in M17. 2 A bandage to prevent a person from seeing; *fig.* an obstruction to perception or judgement. L19.

blindfold /ˈblʌɪn(d)fəʊld/ *a.* & *adv.* M16. [f. BLINDFELD, as next.] With eyes bandaged to prevent vision; *Chess* without sight of board or pieces; *fig.* without circumspection, heedless(ly).

blindfold /ˈblʌɪn(d)fəʊld/ *v.t.* E16. [f. pa. t. & pple of BLINDFELL, by assoc. w. FOLD *v.*[1]] 1 Deprive (the eyes, a person) of sight with a bandage. E16. 2 *fig.* Obscure the understanding or judgement of. L16.

blindfolder *n.* M17.

blini(s) *n.pl.* see BLIN *n.*

blink /blɪŋk/ *n.* ME. [f. BLINK *v.*: cf. BLENCH *n.*[1]] †1 A trick; in *pl.* boughs thrown to turn aside deer. ME–E17. 2 A glimmer, a spark, a sudden brief gleam of light, (*lit.* & *fig.*). ME. 3 A (usu. bright or cheerful) glance; a brief glimpse. Chiefly *Sc.* L16. 4 In *pl.* A fleshy plant of the purslane family, *Montia fontana*, with tiny white flowers, of damp and wet habitats in temperate regions worldwide. Also *water-blinks.* L17. 5a More fully *iceblink*. A luminous appearance on the horizon, caused by the reflection from ice. L18. b *loosely.* A large mass or pack of ice. M19. 6 An instant. Chiefly *Sc.* E19. 7 The action or an act of blinking. E20.

2 **on the blink** *slang* in a bad state, going wrong.

¶Rare bef. L16.

blink /blɪŋk/ *a.* E19. [Afk. = shining.] Bright. Only in *blink klip* s.v. KLIP I, 3.

blink /blɪŋk/ *v.* ME. [Partly f. †*blenk* var. of BLENCH *v.*[1], partly f. (M)Du. *blinken* shine, glitter: cf. Da. *blinke*, Sw. *blinka* wink, twinkle.] 1 *v.t.* Deceive, cheat. *dial.* (now *Sc.*). ME. †2 *v.i.* = BLENCH *v.*[1] 2. *rare.* Only in ME. †3 *v.i.* Open the eyes from sleep. *rare.* Only in ME. 4 *v.i.* Glance, (now) look with the eyes opening and shutting; move the eyelids up and down; shut the eyes for a moment, esp. involuntarily. M16. †5 *v.t.* & *i.* Turn sour. E17–M18. 6 *v.t.* Shut the eyes to; ignore; avoid consideration of. M18. 7 *v.i.* Cast a sudden gleam of light; shine intermittently or fitfully. L18. 8 *v.t.* Cause (the eyes) to shut momentarily; shut (one's eyes) momentarily. M19. 9 *v.t.* Look on with the evil eye, bewitch. *Sc.* & *Ir.* L19. 10 *v.t.* Send (tears) *away*, *back*, by blinking. E20.

4 SHAKES. *Mids. N. D.* Show me thy chink, to blink through with mine eyne. S. J. PERELMAN A fat orange tabby blinks before the fire. P. LIVELY Other eyes have blinked in the light from that window. 6 A. TATE There is no use blinking these facts. 7 G. SWIFT The lighthouse beacon blinking in the dusk.

Comb.: **blink-eyed** *a.* given to blinking.

¶Rare bef. L16.

blinking *a.* & *adv.* (*a*) *adj.* that blinks; (*b*) *adj.* & *adv.* (*colloq.*) cursed(ly), bloody: M16.

blinkard /ˈblɪŋkəd/ *n.* & *a.* *arch.* E16. [f. BLINK *n.* + -ARD.] A *n.* 1 A person who blinks or has imperfect sight. E16. 2 A person who lacks intellectual perception. E16. B *adj.* Of or pertaining to a blinkard; dull; heedless. E16.

blinker /ˈblɪŋkə/ *n.* & *v.* E17. [f. as prec. + -ER[1].] A *n.* 1 A person who blinks; a purblind person. E17. 2 In *pl.* Corrective or protective spectacles; goggles. Now *rare* or *obs.* E18. 3 Either of a pair of usu. leather screens fitted to a bridle to prevent a horse etc. from seeing sideways. Usu. in *pl.* L18. 4 A sporting dog that refuses to see and mark the position of the game. E19. 5 More fully *blinker-light*. An intermittent flashlight. E20. B *v.t.* Put blinkers on; *fig.* hoodwink, deceive. M19.

blinkered *ppl a.* provided with blinkers; *fig.* having a limited range of outlook: M19.

blintze /blɪn(t)s/ *n.* E20. [Yiddish *blintse* f. Russ. *blinets* dim. of BLIN *n.*] = BLIN *n.*

bliny *n.pl.* see BLIN *n.*

blip /blɪp/ *n.* & *v.* L19. [Imit.: cf. BLEEP.] A *n.* 1 A sudden rap or tap; a twitch. L19. 2 A quick popping sound; a short bleep. M20. 3 A small image of an object on a radar screen etc. M20. 4 A temporary and insignificant movement or fluctuation; a sudden small change, esp. for the worse. L20. B *v.* Infl. **-pp-**. 1 *v.t.* Rap or tap suddenly; press (an accelerator etc.) briefly; open (the throttle of a motor vehicle) momentarily. E20. 2 *v.i.* Switch an engine on and off in rapid succession; of an engine: switch on and off. E20. 3a *v.i.* Make a quick popping sound or short bleep. M20. b *v.t.* Substitute a short bleep for (words) in broadcasting. M20. 4 *v.i.* Of a figure, price, etc.: rise, esp. in short sporadic bursts. Also foll. by *up*. L20.

blirry *a.* & *adv.* var. of BLERRY.

blirt /bləːt/ *n.* & *v.* *Sc.* & *north.* E17. [Imit.: cf. BLURT.] A *n.* †1 = BLURT *n.* 1. Only in E17. 2 An outburst of tears, a sudden fit of weeping. L18. 3 A gust of wind and rain; a squall. E19. B *v.i.* Burst into tears, weep violently. E18.

blirty, -ie *a.* squally E19.

bliss /blɪs/ *n.* [OE *bliss*, *blīþs* = OS *blīzza*, *blīdsea*, *blīzzea*, f. Gmc, f. base of BLITHE.] †1 Blitheness of aspect, kindness of manner. Only in OE. 2 Gladness, enjoyment, perfect joy or happiness; blessedness; the state of being in heaven; paradise. OE. 3 A cause of perfect joy or happiness. Now *poet.* OE.

blissful *a.* (*a*) full of bliss; perfectly joyous or happy; happily oblivious; †(*b*) beatified, sacred: ME. **blissfully** *adv.* ME. **blissfulness** *n.* LME. **blissless** *a.* L16.

bliss /blɪs/ *v.* [OE *blissian*, *blīþsian* = OS *blidsean*, *blizzen*, f. as prec.] †1 *v.i.* Be glad, rejoice. OE–LME. †2 *v.t.* Give joy to, gladden. OE–M17. 3 *v.t.* Foll. by *out*: cause to reach ecstasy. Freq. as *blissed-out* ppl a. *N. Amer. slang.* L20.

Comb.: **blissout** *N. Amer. slang* a state of ecstasy.

blister /ˈblɪstə/ *n.* ME. [Perh. f. OFr. *blest(r)e*, *blo(u)stre* swelling, pimple.] 1 A thin vesicle on the skin filled with serum, caused by friction, a burn, other injury, or disease. ME. 2 *Med.* An application to raise a blister. Now chiefly *Hist.* M16. 3 A swelling (filled with air or fluid) on the surface of a plant, cloth, cooled metal, painted wood, etc. L16. 4 An offensive or troublesome person; a worthless fellow. *slang.* E19. 5 A disease of peach trees caused by the fungus *Taphrina deformans*, which produces a distortion of the leaves. M19. 6 *Naut.* An underwater outer covering fitted to a vessel. E20. 7 A summons. *slang.* E20. 8 A rounded compartment protruding from the body of an aeroplane. M20.

Comb.: **blister-beetle, -fly** any of various beetles of the family Meloidae, exuding a vesicant when disturbed, esp. *Lytta vesicatoria* (also called *Spanish fly*); **blister blight** a fungal disease of tea plants, producing blistered leaves; **blister copper** impure copper with a blistered appearance, obtained during smelting; *blister-fly*: see *blister-beetle* above; **blister gas** poison gas causing blisters on the skin; **blister pack, packaging**: consisting of a transparent moulded cover sealed to a card etc.; **blister pearl** an irregular pearly excrescence on an oyster shell; **blister steel** carbon steel made by cementation, freq. with a blistered surface.

blistery *a.* characterized by blisters LME.

blister /ˈblɪstə/ *v.* LME. [f. the n.] 1 *v.i.* Be or become covered with blisters. LME. 2 *v.t.* Cover with blisters; raise blisters on. LME. 3 *v.i.* Cause blisters. LME.

blistering *a.* that causes blisters; *colloq.* (contextually) extremely hot, fast, severe, etc.: LME. **blisteringly** *adv.* L19.

blite /blʌɪt/ *n.* LME. [L *blitum* f. Gk *bliton*.] Any of various plants of the goosefoot family formerly eaten as vegetables; *esp.* Good King Henry, *Chenopodium bonus-henricus*.

sea-blite: see SEA *n.* STRAWBERRY *blite*.

blithe /blʌɪð/ *a.* & *adv.* [OE *blīþe* = OFris. *blī(d-)*, OS *blīþi* (Du. *blijde*, *blij*), OHG *blīdi* cheerful, friendly, ON *blíðr*, Goth. *bleiþs*: f. Gmc. Cf. BLISS *n.*] A *adj.* 1 Kindly, clement, gentle. Long *obs.* exc. *Sc. dial.* OE. 2 Joyous, merry; glad, happy, well pleased. Now chiefly *poet.* OE. 3 Heedless, careless. E20.

2 MILTON A daughter fair, So buxom, blithe, and debonair. SIR W. SCOTT A blithe salute The minstrels well might sound. 3 A. MCCOWEN Their complacency, and their blithe intolerance of most of the outside world.

B *adv.* In a blithe manner. Now chiefly *poet.* OE.

blitheful *a.* †(*a*) kindly, friendly; (*b*) joyous, merry: OE. **blithefully** *adv.* M19. **blithely** *adv.* in a blithe manner; heedlessly, carelessly: OE. **blitheness** *n.* OE. **blithesome** *a.* cheerful E18. **blithesomely** *adv.* M19.

blither /ˈblɪðə/ *v.* & *n.* *colloq.* M19. [Var. of BLATHER.] A *v.i.* & *t.* = BLATHER *v.* 1, 2. M19. B *n.* = BLATHER *n.* 1. M19.

blithering *a.* senselessly discursive or talkative; (as an intensive) consummate, utter, hopeless; contemptible: L19.

blitter /ˈblɪtə/ *n.* *dial.* L18. [Var.] = BITTERN *n.*[1]

bog-blitter: see BOG *n.*[1]

blitz /blɪts/ *n.* & *v.* M20. [Abbrev. of next.] A *n.* 1 A sudden or intensive (esp. aerial) attack with the object of immediate destruction or reduction of defences; spec. *the* air raids on London in 1940. M20. 2 *transf.* & *fig.* a *gen.* A period of sudden or intense activity. M20. b *N. Amer. Football.* A charge by one or more defensive backs into the offensive backfield to anticipate a pass. M20.

2a *Guardian* The women did only the bare essentials of housework during the week, with a 'blitz' at weekends.

B *v.* 1 *v.i.* Make a sudden or intensive (esp. aerial) attack. M20. 2 *v.t.* Attack, damage, or destroy by a blitz. M20. 3 *v.i. N. Amer. Football.* Charge into the offensive backfield. M20.

blitzkrieg /ˈblɪtskriːg/ *n.* Also **B-**. M20. [G, f. *Blitz* lightning + *Krieg* war.] A violent campaign intended to bring about speedy victory.

blivit /ˈblɪvɪt/ *n. US slang.* Also **-et**. M20. [Origin unkn.] Something pointless, useless, or impossible; a nuisance. Also, a gadget.

blizzard /ˈblɪzəd/ *n.* Orig. *US.* E19. [Origin uncertain: perh. imit.] 1 A sharp blow or knock; a shot. *US.* E19. 2 A severe snowstorm. L19.

blizzardy *a.* L19.

†**blo** *a. dial.* ME–L18. [f. as BLAE.] = BLAE *a.* 1.

bloat /bləʊt/ *n.* M19. [f. BLOAT *a.*[2]] 1 A conceited or contemptible person. *US slang.* M19. 2a A disease of livestock characterized by an accumulation of gas in the stomach. L19. b *gen.* Bloatedness. E20.

†**bloat** *a.*[1] ME. [Perh. f. an ON wd parallel to *blautr* soaked: w. sense 2 cf. ON *blautr fiskr* soft fish. Relation to next obscure.] 1 Soft and wet. *rare.* Only in ME. 2 *bloat herring*, a bloater. L16–M17.

bloat /bləʊt/ *a.*[2] *arch.* ME. [ON *blautr* soft, infl. by prec. The spelling *bloat* is recorded f. M17 although it is not the regular representative of ME *blout*, and has been used for the *blowt* of quartos of Shakes. *Haml.* III. iv. 182 f. M18.] †1 Soft, pliable. Only in ME. 2 Swollen, puffy, esp. with overindulgence. E17.

¶Now only in echoes of Shakes.

bloat /bləʊt/ *v.*[1]*t.* L16. [App. f. BLOAT *a.*[1]] Cure (herring etc.) by salting and smoking slightly.

OED *Bloated* herrings are opposed to *dried* or *red* herrings.

bloat /bləʊt/ *v.*[2] L17. [App. f. BLOAT *a.*[2]] 1 *v.t.* Blow out, inflate, make turgid. L17. 2 *v.i.* Swell, become turgid. M18.

bloated *a.* swollen, puffy, esp. through overindulgence; of excessive size; swollen with pride, pampered: M17. **bloatedness** *n.* M17.

bloater /ˈbləʊtə/ *n.* M19. [f. BLOAT *v.*[1] + -ER[1].] A herring cured by bloating.

YARMOUTH *bloater.*

blob /blɒb/ *n.* & *v.* See also BLEB. LME. [Imit.: cf. BLUBBER *n.*, *v.*, BUBBLE *n.*, *v.*] A *n.* 1 A bubble. *obs.* exc. *north.* LME. †2 A pimple, a pustule. *Sc.* & *north.* LME–E17. 3 A drop or globule of liquid or viscous substance. E18. 4 A small roundish mass, esp. of colour. M19. 5 A batsman's score of no runs (0) at cricket. *slang.* L19. 6 A blunder, a senseless error; a fool, an idiot, a useless person. *slang.* E20. B *v.t.* Infl. **-bb-**. Mark with a blob of ink, colour, etc.; blot. LME.

blobby *a.* LME.

†**blobber** *a.* see BLUBBER *a.*

bloc /blɒk/ *n.* E20. [Fr. = next.] A combination of States, parties, groups, or people, formed to promote a particular interest.

Comb.: **bloc vote** = *block vote* s.v. BLOCK *n.*

block /blɒk/ *n.* ME. [(O)Fr. *bloc* f. MDu. *blok*, (M)LG *block*, of unkn. origin.] I A solid piece or mass. 1 A log; a tree stump. ME. 2 A large piece of wood on which chopping, hammering, etc., is done. LME. b *spec. Hist.* The piece of wood on which the condemned were beheaded. L15. c A piece of wood on which something can be moulded or shaped; *esp.* a mould for a hat; *fig.* (*arch.*) a style or fashion of hat. L16. d A stump etc. from which to mount a horse. E17. e In full *starting-block*. A shaped rigid piece for bracing the foot of a runner at the start of a race. M20. 3 A pulley or system of pulleys mounted in a case, used to direct or increase the lifting power of the rope(s) running through it. LME. 4 *gen.* Any bulky or massive piece of matter; a large amount or body of anything treated as a whole. LME. b *spec.* An unhewn lump of rock; a piece of stone or other material prepared for building; one of a set of wooden or plastic cubes etc. that fit together, as a child's toy. M19. c A compact set of sheets of drawing-paper etc. fastened together at one edge. M19. d A body of rock (often of large extent) bounded by faults. L19. e = BLOC. E20. f A square unit in a patchwork design. E20. 5 A lump of stone, wood, or other material that bars one's way; an obstacle. Now chiefly in *stumbling-block* s.v. STUMBLE *v.* L15. b A chock. M20. 6 *fig.* a A stupid person, a blockhead; a stolid or hard-hearted person. M16. b The head. *slang.* E17. 7 A piece of wood or metal engraved for printing on paper or fabric. M18. 8a A compact mass of buildings bounded by (usu. four) streets; (chiefly *N. Amer.*) any urban or suburban area so bounded, the length of such an area. L18. b A large area of land or seabed sold or allocated to one person or organization for settlement, development, etc. M19. c A large single building, *esp.* one divided into offices or flats. M19.

1 **chip off** (or **of**) **the old block** a child resembling a parent or ancestor, esp. in character. **on the block** *N. Amer.* for sale at auction. 2 *Chinese block*: see CHINESE *a.* 3 *block and tackle*: see TACKLE *n.* 5a. 4 J. TYNDALL The more solid blocks of ice shoot forward in advance of the lighter debris. J. G. HOLLAND The combination began by selling large blocks of the Stock for future delivery. O. DOPPING The information on the tape is concentrated into blocks, separated by empty gaps. b *erratic block*: see ERRATIC *a.* 6b **do** or **lose one's block** (chiefly *Austral.* & *NZ*) become angry or agitated. **knock** (**someone's**) **block off** *slang* strike (someone) about the head, thrash (someone). **off one's block** *slang* crazy, angry. 8a A. MILLER There's not a person on the block who doesn't know the truth. S. KAUFFMANN He had walked six blocks to the nearest subway station. J. T. STORY She cruised round the block twice. b *backblocks*: see BACK-. c *tower block*: see TOWER *n.*[1] 3h.

II Senses f. the vb. †9 A bargain, an exchange; a scheme. *Sc.* E16–L18. 10 An act or instance of blocking; a stoppage, an obstruction. E19. b An interruption of physiological function, esp. in the passage of nerve impulses. L19. c *Psychol.* A sudden and temporary inability to continue a thought process or mental link. In *pop.* use usu. more fully *mental* or *psychological block*. M20. d *Amer. Football.* Obstruction of an opponent with the body, as a legal move. M20. 11 *Cricket.* The spot on which the batsman rests the toe of the bat when facing the bowling. M19. 12 *Chess.* A problem position in which Black is not under threat but must become exposed to a threat if obliged to move. E20.

10 J. GALSWORTHY Swithin was so long over this course . . that he caused a block in the progress of the dinner. P. G. WODEHOUSE One of those blocks in the traffic which are inevitable in so congested a system as that of London. J. T. STORY We were stopped by a two-car police block at the junction with the Huntingdon Road. *roadblock*: see ROAD *n.* b *heart-block*: see HEART *n.* *spinal block*: see SPINAL *a.* c M. STEWART He's been going through a bad period, a more or less complete block since he got *Tiger Tiger* off his desk.

Comb.: **block-board** a plywood board with a core of thin wooden strips; **block-book**: printed from woodcut blocks; **block booking** the booking of a large number of seats etc. as a unit; **blockbuster** *slang* (*a*) a heavy aerial bomb; (*b*) a thing of great power or size, *esp.* an epic best-selling book or successful film; **block capitals** capital block letters; **block delete** *Computing* the deletion of a block of text or data in a single operation; **block diagram**: in which squares and other conventional symbols show the general arrangement of parts of an apparatus; **block-faulting** *Geol.* faulting which divides a region into blocks having different elevations; **block grant** an inclusive grant made for a particular purpose; **blockhead** †(*a*) a wooden block for hats or wigs; a wooden head (*lit.* & *fig.*); (*b*) *colloq.* a stupid person; **blockheaded, -ish** *adjs.* (*colloq.*) stupid, dull, obtuse; **blockheadism** *colloq.* blockheaded behaviour, stupidity; **block heater** a storage heater; **blockhole** *Cricket* (*a*) = sense II above; (*b*) an indentation marking this; **blockhouse** [(M)Du. *blokhuis*] (*a*) a detached fortified defensive building with loopholes, usu. of timber or concrete; (*b*) a house of squared logs; (*c*) a concrete shelter; **block letters** (esp. capital) letters written without serifs and separate from each other; **block mountain** a mountain formed by block-faulting; **block move** *Computing* the process or an act of moving a block of text or data as a whole; **block party** *US* a (usu. outdoor) party for all the residents of a block or neighbourhood; **block plane** a plane with a blade set at an acute angle, used esp. for planing end-grain; **block release** release of a person from his employment for the whole of a stated period to attend a course of study; **block-ship** a ship moored or grounded in order to block a channel; **block signalling, system** a system of railway signalling which divides the track into sections and allows no train to enter a section that is not wholly clear; **block tin** refined tin cast in ingots; **block vote** (a vote by) a method of voting whereby a delegate's vote has influence according to the number of members he or she represents.

blockish *a.* of the nature of a block; like a block in form or character; obtuse, stupid, clumsy: M16. **blockishly** *adv.* M16. **blockishness** *n.* M16. **blocky** *a.* of the nature of or resembling a block or blocks L19.

block /blɒk/ *v.* LME. [f. the n. or f. Fr. *bloquer*, f. as BLOC.] I Obstruct, hinder. 1 *v.t.* Obstruct, close, seal, or confine with obstacles; put obstacles in the way of, hinder the progress of, prevent. Freq. foll. by *up*, *in*, or *off*. LME. 2 *v.t. spec.* Blockade, besiege. L16. 3 *v.t.* & *i. Cricket.* Stop (a ball) with the bat, with no attempt to score runs. L18. 4 *v.t.* Obstruct or prevent (a physiological or mental function or effect, esp. the passage of nerve impulses); interrupt the action of (a nerve, organ, etc.). L19. 5 *v.t. Cards.* Prevent (cards, esp. in a particular suit) from being played as winners. L19. 6 *v.t.* & *i. N. Amer. Football.* Obstruct (an opponent) with the body, as a legal move. L19. 7 *v.t.* Restrict the use or conversion of (currency or other assets). M20.

1 W. PRYNNE Blocking vp their hearts against the Lord. E. K. KANE Our little harbor was completely blocked in by heavy masses [of ice]. T. WILLIAMS Mitch has started towards the bedroom. Stanley crosses to block him. G. GREENE The passage was nearly blocked by dustbins. E. J. HOWARD Cressy had tried to talk to him, but he had courteously blocked conversation.

II In constructive senses. 8 *v.i.* Make a bargain or an exchange. *Sc.* L16. 9 *v.t.* Shape, mould, or smooth on a block. L16. b Emboss or impress a design on (a book-cover) by means of a block. M19. 10 *v.t.* Sketch or mark *out* or *in* roughly; lay out, plan. L16. 11 *v.t.* Make into blocks; provide or support with blocks. M19.

10 J. G. LOCKHART The latter Cantos having . . been merely blocked out when the first went to press. P. MCGERR Wednesday Warren finished blocking the first act. 11 **blocked letters**: designed so as to appear three-dimensional.

blockage *n.* a blocked(-up) state; an obstruction: L19. **blocking** *n.* (*a*) the action of the vb; (*b*) railway signalling by the block system; (*c*) a wooden block; blocks collectively: L16.

blockade /blɒˈkeɪd/ *n.* & *v.* L17. [f. prec. + -ADE, prob. after *ambuscade*.] A *n.* 1 The surrounding of a place, blocking of a harbour, patrolling of a coast, etc., by hostile forces in order to prevent supplies or forces from entering or leaving it. L17. 2 *fig.* & *transf.* A stoppage or obstruction, esp. (*N. Amer.*) of a road or railway by snow etc. M18. b Obstruction or prevention of a physiological or mental function. M20.

1 **raise a** (or **the**) **blockade** (compel to) withdraw the blockading forces. **run a** (or **the**) **blockade** (attempt to) evade the blockading force.

Comb.: **blockade-man** *Hist.* a coastguard active against smuggling; **blockade-runner** a ship or a person attempting to run a blockade.

B *v.t.* Subject to blockade; block up, obstruct. L17.

blockader *n.* a person or a ship engaged in a blockade M19.

blocker /ˈblɒkə/ *n.* ME. [f. BLOCK *n.* or *v.* + -ER[1].] 1 A person who uses a block (in various trades). ME. 2 A person or thing which blocks or obstructs; *spec.* (*a*) *Cricket* a habitually defensive batsman; (*b*) *N. Amer. Football* a player whose task is to block opponents; (*c*) a substance which prevents or inhibits a given physiological function. M19. 3 A person who occupies or farms a block of land. Chiefly in *backblocker* s.v. BACK-. L19. 4 A bowler hat. *slang.* M20.

2 *beta blocker*: see BETA 2a(e).

blodge /blɒdʒ/ *n.* M20. [Imit.: cf. *blotch, splodge, splotch*, etc.] A splotch, a blotch.

bloke /bləʊk/ *n. colloq.* M19. [Shelta.] A man, a fellow.

blond /blɒnd/ *a.* & *n.* Also (fem., but often used indiscriminately) **blonde.** L15. [(O)Fr. f. med.L *blundus, blondus* yellow, perh. of Gmc origin: fem. form introduced from Fr. in 17.] A *adj.* (Esp. of the hair) of a light golden-brown colour, flaxen, fair; (of the complexion) light-coloured with fair hair. L15.

blond beast [tr. G *blonde Bestie*] a man of the Nordic type. *blond(e) bombshell*: see *bombshell* s.v. BOMB *n.* **blonde lace** silk lace (orig. unbleached) of two threads, twisted and formed in hexagonal meshes. **blonde ray**, a pale brown ray, *Raja brachyura*, of SW European coastal waters. *silver blond*: see SILVER *n.* & *a.*

B *n.* 1 A person (esp. a woman) with blond hair and complexion. M18. 2 = *blonde lace* above. M18.

blondish *a.* somewhat blond or light-coloured M20. **blond(e)ness** *n.* L19.

Blondin /ˈblɒndɪn/ *n.* Also **b-.** M19. [Professional name of J. F. Gravelet (1824–97), Fr. tightrope-walker.] A tightrope-walker; a tightrope, a cableway.

blondine /blɒnˈdiːn/ *n.* & *v. US.* L19. [f. BLOND *a.* + -INE[4].] A *n.* A bleach for the hair. L19. B *v.t.* Bleach with blondine. L19.

blood /blʌd/ *n.* [OE *blōd* = OFris., OS *blōd* (Du. *bloed*), OHG *bluot* (G *Blut*), ON *blóð*, Goth. *blōþ* (Crimean Goth. *plut*), f. Gmc, of unkn. origin.] 1 A complex fluid, red when oxygenated and containing various suspended cells, circulating in the arteries and veins of the higher animals; the corresponding fluid in other multicellular organisms. OE. b A liquid or juice resembling blood (always w. conscious ref. to the primary sense). LME. 2a Blood that is shed, in theological writings esp. in sacrifice, as that of Christ; the taking of life. OE. b The guilt of bloodshed. OE. c A blood-and-thunder story. Freq. in *penny blood*. Usu. in *pl. arch.* L19. †3 Vital fluid; the vital principle; life. ME–M18. 4a The blood as the supposed seat of emotion; passion, temperament, mettle. ME. b The blood as the supposed seat of animal or sensual appetite; sexual desire. ME. 5a The blood as the vehicle of hereditary characteristics or relationship; consanguinity; parentage, lineage; family, race, nationality. ME. b Persons of any specified blood or family collectively; kindred. ME. c Good parentage or stock. LME. d One's offspring; a near relative. *arch.* LME. †6 A living being. Only in ME. †7 A disease in sheep or swine. E16–L18. 8a A rowdy, a roisterer; a dandy; a rake. Now *arch.* or *Hist.* M16. b A leader of fashion, esp. at a public school or university. *slang.* L19. 9 (**B-.**) Pl. **-s**, same. A member of a N. American Indian people belonging to the Blackfoot confederacy. Pl. same. L18.

1b SHAKES. *Timon* Go, suck the subtle blood o' th' grape. 2a R. HOOKER Either my blood or banishment shall sign it. ADDISON An Affront that nothing but Blood can expiate. b C. V. WEDGWOOD The blood of Strafford lay heavy on his conscience because he had consented to his death in the knowledge that he was innocent. 4a SHAKES. *Merch. V.* The brain may devise laws for the blood, but a hot temper leaps o'er a cold decree. 5a POPE Your antient but ignoble blood Has crept thro' Scoundrels ever since the Flood. L. VAN DER POST They had clear traces of Bushman blood. *Proverb*: Blood is thicker than water. b SHAKES. *John* Father, to arms! . . Against the blood that thou hast married? c R. W. EMERSON The obstinate prejudice in favour of blood, which lies at the base of the feudal and monarchical fabrics of the old world. d DRYDEN Thou art my blood where Jonson has no part. HOR. WALPOLE So many cousins, and uncles, and aunts and bloods.

Phrases: **bad blood** ill feeling. **blood and iron** [tr. G *Blut und Eisen*] military force as distinguished from diplomacy, esp. as associated with Bismarck (see BISMARCKIAN). *blue blood*: see BLUE *a.* CORRUPTION *of blood.* **first blood** the first shedding of blood (in *Boxing* or *fig.*). *flesh and blood*: see FLESH *n. freeze someone's blood*: see FREEZE *v.* **fresh blood** = *new blood* below. *full-blood*: see FULL *a.* **get blood out of** or **from a stone** or **turnip** achieve the impossible, *esp.* obtain pity from the hard-hearted or money from the impecunious or avaricious. †**God's blood!** an oath or forcible exclamation; abbrev. 'SBLOOD. *half-blood*: see HALF-. **ill blood** = *bad blood* above. **in blood** *Hunting* (of an animal) full of life, vigorous. **in cold blood** without passion, deliberately. **in one's blood** characteristic of one's family etc., fundamental in one's character. **let (a person) blood** (now *arch.* or *Hist.*) bleed (a person) as medical treatment, *transf.* shed the blood of, kill, (a person) (freq. in indirect pass. as *be let blood*). MIXED *blood.* **new blood** a new member or new members admitted to a family, society, etc. *one's blood boils*: see BOIL *v.* **one's blood is up** one is in fighting mood. **one's blood runs cold** one is horrified. **out for a person's blood** determined to defeat him or her. **out of blood** *Hunting* (of an animal) lifeless, not vigorous. **restore in** or **to blood** *Hist.* re-admit (a person under sentence of 'corruption of blood') to forfeited privileges. *seal one's testimony with blood*: see TESTIMONY *n.* 3. *spit blood*: see SPIT *v.*[2] *suck the blood of*: see SUCK *v. sweat blood*: see SWEAT *v.* 2b. **taste blood** *fig.* be stimulated by early success. **the blood (royal)** the royal lineage or family (*of the blood*, royal). **young blood** (*a*) *arch.* a young rowdy or dandy; (*b*) a young member of a party etc.

Comb.: **blood-ally** a white playing-marble marked with red spiral lines; **blood-and-soil** *a.* [f. Nazi catch-phrase *Blut und Boden*] of or pertaining to Nazism; **blood-and-thunder** *a.* designating a book etc. describing bloodshed and violence; **blood bank** a place where a supply of blood for transfusion is stored; **blood-bath** a massacre; †**blood-boltered** *a.* (esp. of hair) clotted with blood; **blood-brother** (*a*) a brother by birth; (*b*) a person who has been bound to another in solemn friendship by a ceremonial mingling of blood; **blood cell, corpuscle** any of the kinds of cell normally circulating in the blood; **blood count** (a determination of) the number of corpuscles in a definite volume of blood; **blood-curdling** *a.* so horrific as to seem to curdle the blood; **blood donor** a person who gives blood for transfusion; **blood eagle** [ON *blóð-ǫrn*] *Hist.* a Viking method of killing someone, usu. the slayer of a man's father, by cutting out the ribs in the shape of an eagle; **blood feud** a feud between families of which one has killed or injured a member or members of the other; **blood-flower** (*a*) = *blood-lily* below; (*b*) a tropical American plant, *Asclepias curassavica*, with deep red flowers; **blood group** any of the types into which human blood may be divided according to its compatibility in transfusion; *esp.* each of the four types based on the A and B antigens; **blood-grouping** the determination of the blood group of a person or sample of blood; **blood-guilt, -guiltiness** responsibility for bloodshed; **blood-guilty** *a.* responsible for bloodshed; **blood-heat** the ordinary temperature of human blood in health, approx. 37°C (98°F); **blood horse** (chiefly *N. Amer.*) a thoroughbred horse; **bloodhound** a large keen-scented dog, formerly used to track cattle, criminals, etc.; *fig.* a detective; **blood-knot** a knot tied in a rope used as a whip, in order to draw blood; **blood-letter** a person who or thing which lets blood; **blood-letting** surgical removal of some of a patient's blood; *joc.* bloodshed; **blood-lily** a haemanthus, *esp.* one grown for ornament; **blood-line** descent, pedigree, esp. as transmitting characteristics in an animal; **blood-lust** lust for the shedding of blood; **blood meal** [G *Blutmehl*] dried blood used for feeding animals and as a fertilizer; **blood-money** (*a*) a reward for bringing about the death of another, as a reward paid to a witness for securing a capital sentence; (*b*) a fine paid to the next of kin for the slaughter of a relative; **blood orange** a variety of orange with red-streaked pulp; **blood plasma** the straw-coloured liquid fraction of the blood, in which the cells and platelets are suspended; *blood* PLATELET; **blood-poisoning** the presence of pathogenic bacteria or bacterial toxins in the blood; **blood pressure** the pressure of circulating blood on the walls of the arteries; *colloq.* hypertension; **blood pudding** (a) black pudding; **blood-red** red as blood; **blood relation, relative** a person related to another or others by blood, not marriage; **bloodroot** any of various plants; esp. a N. American plant, *Sanguinaria canadensis*, of the poppy family, with white flowers and red sap; **blood sausage** (a) black pudding; **bloodshedder** a slaughterer, a murderer; **bloodshedding** (*a*) = BLOODSHED *n.* 1; †(*b*) = BLOODSHED *n.* 2; *blood spavin*: see SPAVIN *n.*[1]; **blood sports** sports involving the killing of animals, *esp.* hunting; **bloodstain** a stain made by blood; **bloodstained** *a.* stained with blood, *fig.* disgraced by bloodshed; **bloodstock** thoroughbred or pedigree horses collectively; **bloodstone** a precious stone, esp. a green chalcedony, that is streaked or spotted with red; †**blood-strange** [origin unkn.] the plant mousetail, *Myosurus minimus*; **bloodstream** the circulating blood; **blood-sugar** (the concentration of) glucose contained in the blood; **blood-test** a test performed on a sample of blood esp. for diagnosis; **blood-test** *v.t.* test the blood of (a person or animal); **bloodthirst** eagerness for bloodshed; *blood transfusion*: see TRANSFUSION 2; **blood-tub** *slang* a theatre presenting lurid melodrama; **blood-vein (moth)** a geometrid moth, *Timandra griseata*, with a red line across its wings; **blood-vessel** a vein, artery, or capillary, conveying blood; **blood wagon** *slang* an ambulance; **bloodwite, -wit** [WITE *n.*[2]] (*a*) *Hist.* in Anglo-Saxon England, a fine for shedding blood paid to an alderman or king (cf. WERGELD); (*b*) *gen.* a penalty for murder; **bloodwood** (the red wood of) any of various trees, esp. certain Australian eucalypts; **bloodworm** a bright red worm or wormlike creature, *esp.* (*a*) a worm of the genus *Arenicola* or *Tubifex*; (*b*) the aquatic larva of a midge of the genus *Chironomus*; **blood-wort** a plant with red roots or leaves, *esp.* red-veined dock, *Rumex sanguineus*.

†**blooding** *n.* a black pudding LME–L18. **bloodlike** *a.* resembling blood LME.

blood /blʌd/ *v.t.* M16. [f. the n.] 1 Bleed, esp. surgically. M16. 2 Wet or smear with blood. Now *rare* in *gen.* sense. L16. †3 Arouse the hostile feelings of (esp. soldiers) *against* an enemy. Only in 17. 4 Give a first taste of blood to (a hound); smear the face of (a novice at hunting) with the blood of the kill; initiate. L18.

blooded /ˈblʌdɪd/ *a.* ME. [f. BLOOD *n., v.*: see -ED[2], -ED[1].] †1 Stained with blood. ME–M17. 2 As 2nd elem. of comb.: having blood of the specified kind. L16. 3 Of a horse: of good breed, thoroughbred. L18.

2 *cold-blooded, full-blooded, warm-blooded*, etc.

bloodless /ˈblʌdlɪs/ *a.* ME. [f. BLOOD *n.* + -LESS.] 1 Without blood, lifeless; pale, pallid; unemotional. ME. 2 Without bloodshed. E17.

bloodlessly *adv.* E19. **bloodlessness** *n.* L19.

bloodshed /ˈblʌdʃɛd/ *n.* & *a.* LME. [f. *shed blood.*] A *n.* 1 The spilling of the blood of another or others; slaughter. LME. †2 The shedding of one's own blood (orig. & chiefly w. ref. to Jesus). L15–M19. †3 An act of spilling blood. L16–L17. †4 = BLOODSHOT *n.* L17–M18. B *adj.* = BLOODSHOT *a.* 2. Long *obs.* exc. *Sc.* E17.

bloodshot /ˈblʌdʃɒt/ *a.* & *n.* M16. [f. BLOOD *n.* + SHOT *ppl a.*] A *adj.* †1 Of a person: with eyeballs tinged with blood. Only in M16. 2 Of the eyeball: tinged with blood. E17. †B *n.* An effusion of blood affecting the eyeball. L16–L17.

Also **bloodshotten** *a.* (*arch.*) LME.

bloodsucker /ˈblʌdsʌkə/ *n.* LME. [f. BLOOD *n.* + SUCKER *n.*] 1 An animal which sucks blood; *esp.* (*a*) the leech; (*b*) any of various Asian and Australian lizards, *esp.* an Australian crested lizard of the genus *Amphibolurus*. LME. †2 A bloodthirsty or blood-guilty person. M16–M17. 3 An extortioner; a sponger. E17.

bloodsucking *a.* & *n.* L16.

bloodthirsty /ˈblʌdθəːsti/ *a.* M16. [f. BLOOD *n.* + THIRSTY, after Luther's *blutdürstig*.] Eager for bloodshed.

¶First recorded in Coverdale.

bloodthirstily *adv.* L19. **bloodthirstiness** *n.* M17.

bloody /ˈblʌdi/ *a.* & *adv.* [OE *blōdiġ* = OFris. *blōdich*, OS *blōdig* (Du. *bloedig*), OHG *bluotag* (G *blutig*), ON *blóðigr* f. Gmc: see BLOOD *n.*, -Y[1].] A *adj.* 1 Of the nature of, composed of, resembling, or pertaining to blood. OE. 2 Covered, smeared, or stained with blood. OE. 3 Accompanied by or involving bloodshed. ME. 4 Of thoughts, words, etc.: concerned with, portending, or decreeing bloodshed. ME. †5 Of animal bodies: containing blood. LME–E19. 6 Bloodthirsty, blood-guilty. M16. 7 Blood-red. L16. 8 (See comment at sense B.2.) a Used vaguely as a strong imprecation or intensive; confounded, damnable, cursed. M17. b Unpleasant, deplorable; perverse. M20.

2 YEATS Their throats torn and bloody. 3 D. BAGLEY Serrurier . . took power in bloody revolution and kept it by equally bloody government. 5 E. TOPSELL A Serpent [is] . . a Bloody Beast without feet. 6 AV *Ps.* 5:6 The Lord will abhorre the bloodie and deceitfull man. 7 G. M. HOPKINS Tender pinks with bloody

Tyrian dye. 8 OED Not a bloody *one*. S. L. ELLIOTT The Army must be payin' you more than the bloody Colonel. E. BLISHEN That bloody boy! Wait till I get you home. *call a spade a bloody shovel*: see SPADE *n.*[1] b C. CONNOLLY Oxford is just bloody. R. LEHMANN He made me so mean and bloody.

B *adv.* †**1** Bloodily. Only in ME. **2** Used vaguely as a strong imprecation or intensive; exceedingly, very; confoundedly, damnably. Also inserted within words (tmesis). (In general colloq. use until M18; later regarded as on a par with obscene or profane language, hence numerous euphemistic alternatives as *blasted*, *blinking*, *blooming*, etc.; now usu. regarded as strong but not deeply offensive.) L17.

2 DRYDEN The doughty Bullies enter bloody drunk. H. FIELDING This is a bloody positive old fellow. G. B. SHAW Walk! Not bloody likely. L. W. MEYNELL Remember the *News Chronicle*? . . On sale one day. Amalga-bloody-mated the next. R. RENDELL The furthest bloody abroad I'm going ever again will be the Isle of Wight.

Comb. & *special collocations*: **bloody flux**, †**flix** dysentery; **bloody grave** the grave of one who has been murdered; **bloody hand**: the armorial device of some baronets; **Bloody Mary** (*a*) Mary Tudor; (*b*) a mixed drink of vodka and tomato juice; **bloody-minded** *a.* (*a*) inclined to bloodshed, bloodthirsty, cruel; (*b*) perverse, cantankerous, stubbornly intransigent; **bloody-mindedly** *adv.* in a bloody-minded manner; **bloody-mindedness** the state or quality of being bloody-minded; *Bloody Monday*: see MONDAY *n.*; **bloody-nosed beetle** a large black beetle, *Timarcha tenebricosa*, which exudes a red liquid from its mouth when handled; *bloody shirt*: see SHIRT *n.*; **bloody sweat** an exudation of blood mixed with sweat; *bloody warrior*: see WARRIOR *n.* 2; *raw head and bloody bones*: see RAW *a.*

bloodily *adv.* in a bloody manner; with blood, with bloodshed: M16. **bloodiness** *n.* L16.

bloody /ˈblʌdi/ *v.t.* E16. [f. the adj.] Make bloody; stain with blood.

blooey /ˈbluːɪ/ *a.* & *adv.* *US slang.* E20. [Origin unkn.] (Gone) awry, amiss.

bloom /bluːm/ *n.*[1] ME. [ON *blóm* flower, blossom; *blómi* prosperity, pl. flowers, = OS *blōmo*, MDu. *bloeme* (Du. *bloem*), OHG *bluomo*, *-ma* (G *Blume*), Goth. *blōma* f. Gmc, f. base of BLOW *v.*[2]] **1** A blossom or flower of a plant, *esp.* one which is grown or admired chiefly for this; *collect.* blossom, flowers. ME. **2** Flowering; *fig.* the state or season of greatest beauty; prime; perfection. ME. **3** The delicate powdery deposit on grapes, plums, etc.; a similar deposit or appearance; a cloudiness on a shiny surface. M17. **b** Freshness; delicate beauty. L18. **c** In full *water-bloom* (A scum formed by) the rapid proliferation of microscopic algae on water. E20. **4** The crimson tint of the cheek; flush; glow. M18.

1 MILTON Sight of vernal bloom. L. M. MONTGOMERY 'June bells', those shyest and sweetest of woodland blooms. *fig.*: R. ELLIS A chosen array, rare bloom of valorous Argos. 2 ADDISON While her Beauty was yet in all its Height and Bloom. 3 H. E. BATES Covered with a white bloom of chalk dust. N. GORDIMER The blur of frost: a cold bloom formed on the outside of a glass. 4 H. FIELDING Miss Bath had not only recovered her health but her bloom.

Phrases: **in bloom** in flower, flowering. **take the bloom off** deprive (a thing) of its first freshness or beauty.

bloomless *a.* L16. **bloomy** *a.* (chiefly *poet.*) (*a*) full of blooms, flowery; (*b*) in the bloom of youth; (*c*) covered with or resembling a powdery bloom: L16.

bloom /bluːm/ *n.*[2] [OE *blōma*, identical in form w. prec., but prob. a different wd.] A mass of iron, steel, or other metal rolled or hammered into a thick bar for further working. Also *loosely*, an unworked mass of puddled iron.

bloomery, **-ary** *n.* a forge or mill where blooms (esp. of wrought iron) are rolled or hammered L16.

bloom /bluːm/ *v.*[1] ME. [f. BLOOM *n.*[1]] **I** *v.i.* **1** Bear flowers, come into flower. ME. **2** Come into or be in full beauty or vigour; flourish; culminate. ME. **3** Glow with warm colour. M19.

2 B. JOWETT Your beauty is fading away, just as your true self is beginning to bloom. 3 J. TYNDALL Heaps of snow . . bloomed with a rosy light.

II *v.t.* **4** Bring into bloom; cause to flourish. *arch.* L16. **5** Colour with a soft warm tint. E19. **6** Cloud (a shiny surface). M19. **7** *Photogr.* Coat (a lens) so as to reduce reflection from its surfaces. M20.

4 R. GREENE Each fair thing that summer bloomed. 5 KEATS While barred clouds bloom the soft-dying day.

blooming *a.* & *adv.* (*a*) *adj.* that blooms; (*b*) *adj.* & *adv.* (*colloq.*) cursed(ly), bloody: LME. **bloomingly** *adv.* M19.

bloom /bluːm/ *v.*[2]*t.* E19. [f. BLOOM *n.*[2]] Make (iron etc.) into blooms. Chiefly as *blooming* vbl n.

bloomed /bluːmd, *poet.* ˈbluːmɪd/ *a.* E16. [f. BLOOM *n.*[1], *v.*[1]: see -ED[2], -ED[1].] **1** In bloom; bearing blooms. Chiefly *poet.* E16. **2** That has been bloomed (esp. in sense 7 of BLOOM *v.*[1]). M20.

bloomer /ˈbluːmə/ *n.*[1] M18. [f. BLOOM *v.*[1] + -ER[1].] **1** A plant that blooms (esp. in a specified manner). M18. **2** A floriated letter. L19. **3** [= *blooming error*.] A great mistake, a blunder. *slang.* L19.

bloomer /ˈbluːmə/ *n.*[2] M19. [Amelia Jenks *Bloomer* (1818–94) of New York, who advocated such dress.] **I** *sing. Hist.* **1** In full *bloomer costume, dress*, = sense 4 below. M19. **2** *bloomer trousers*, = sense 5 below. M19. **3** A woman who wears a bloomer costume. M19. **II** In *pl.* **4** *Hist.* A woman's costume with loose trousers gathered at the ankle or knee. M19. **5** *Hist.* Knee-length trousers or knickerbockers, esp. as worn by women for active pursuits as cycling etc. L19. **6** A woman's or girl's loose knee-length knickers; *colloq.* knickers of any style. E20.

bloomered *a.* wearing bloomers L19. **bloomerism** *n.* (*Hist.*) the principles of A. J. Bloomer as to female dress M19.

bloomer /ˈbluːmə/ *n.*[3] M20. [Origin unkn.] A large loaf with a rounded diagonally slashed top.

Bloomfieldian /bluːmˈfiːldɪən/ *n.* & *a.* M20. [f. *Bloomfield* (see below) + -IAN.] **A** *n.* An adherent or student of the (largely structuralist) linguistic theories of the American scholar Leonard Bloomfield (1887–1949). M20. **B** *adj.* Of, pertaining to, or characteristic of Bloomfield or his theories or adherents. M20.

Bloomsbury /ˈbluːmzb(ə)ri/ *a.* & *n.* E20. [A district in west central London.] **A** *adj.* Designating, characteristic of, or pertaining to a group of writers and aesthetes living in or associated with Bloomsbury in the early 20th cent.; intellectual, highbrow. E20. **B** *n.* The Bloomsbury group; (also *joc.* **Bloomsberry**) a member of this. E20.

Bloomsburyite *n.* a member of the Bloomsbury group M20.

bloop /bluːp/ *v.*, *n.*, & *a.* E20. [Imit.] **A** *v.* **1** *v.i.* (Cause a radio set to) emit a howling noise. E20. **2** *v.t.* Patch or treat (a splice on a soundtrack) so as to prevent an intrusive noise during projection. M20. **3** *v.t. Baseball.* Score (a run) by hitting a ball high beyond the reach of the infielders. L20. **B** *n.* A howling or popping sound. M20. **C** *adj. Baseball.* Of a run: scored by hitting a ball high beyond the reach of the infielders. M20.

blooper *n.* (*colloq.*) (*a*) a radio set that causes others to bloop; (*b*) an embarrassing error, a blunder (*c*) *Baseball* a ball hit high beyond the reach of the infielders, or thrown high by the pitcher: E20.

blooth *n.* see BLOWTH.

blore /blɔː/ *n.* Long *arch.* LME. [Prob. imit.: cf. *blow*, *blast*.] A violent blowing.

blossom /ˈblɒs(ə)m/ *n.* [OE *blōstm*, *blōs(t)ma* = WFris. *blossum*, (M)Du. *bloesem*, MLG *blōs(s)em* (cf. also ON *blómstr*), gen. referred to the same base as BLOOM *n.*[1]] **1** A flower, esp. as promising fruit; *collect.* the mass of flowers on a fruit tree etc. OE. **2** The state or season of blossoming (*lit.* & *fig.*); an early stage of growth; promise. ME. **3** A person who is lovely and full of promise. LME. **4** (Minerals forming) the decomposed outcrop of an ore or coal deposit. E19.

1 DAY LEWIS The white blossom streaming away on a gale. W. BRONK Tulips or other big blossoms. *fig.*: W. H. PRESCOTT The first blossoms of that literature which was to ripen into so rich a harvest. 2 SHAKES. *Haml.* Thus was I . . cut off even in the blossoms of my sin. 3 SHAKES. *1 Hen. VI* And there died, my Icarus, my blossom, in his pride.

Phrases: **in blossom** in flower, blossoming.

blossomed *a.* covered with blossoms; in blossom: LME. **blossomless** *a.* M19. **blossomy** *a.* covered or adorned with blossoms LME.

blossom /ˈblɒs(ə)m/ *v.i.* [OE *blōstmian*, f. as prec.] Bear blossom; open into flower (*lit.* & *fig.*); develop desirably or advantageously (*into*).

POPE Now hawthorns blossom. M. L. KING [Neither] expected this quiet beginning to blossom into a large-scale operation. D. STOREY Mrs. Reagan, in adversity, appeared to blossom. S. KING This thought suddenly blossomed in his mind.

blot /blɒt/ *n.*[1] LME. [Prob. of Scand. origin; cf. ON *blettr* (Icel. *blettur*) blot, stain, Da. dial. *blat* spot, blot.] **1** A spot or stain of ink, mud, etc.; any black or dark patch; a blemish, a disfigurement. LME. **b** *spec.* An obliteration by way of correction. E18. **2a** A moral stain; a disgraceful act or quality in a good character; a defect. LME. **b** Imputation of disgrace; defamation. L16. **c** A person who is in disgrace. *colloq.* E20. **3** *Biol.* & *Med.* The distribution of proteins etc. on a medium on to which they have been blotted. L20.

1 N. MITFORD It looked . . like an ordinary ink blot. *Listener* Charabancs and monstrous hordes of hikers are blots upon the landscape. *a blot on one's* ESCUTCHEON. 2 J. R. GREEN The execution of Wallace was the one blot on Edward's clemency. 3 *Northern blot*: see NORTHERN *a.* SOUTHERN BLOT. *Western blot*: see WESTERN *a.*

blotless *a.* LME. **blotty** *a.* M19.

blot /blɒt/ *n.*[2] L16. [Prob. Du. *bloot* naked, exposed, but as n. only in Eng.] **1** *Backgammon.* An exposed piece liable to be taken; the action of exposing a piece. L16. **2** An exposed point in one's procedure; a mark, a butt. M17.

blot /blɒt/ *v.* Infl. **-tt-**. LME. [f. BLOT *n.*[1]] **I** *v.t.* **1** Spot or stain with ink, tears, etc.; blur, smudge. LME. †**2** Cover (paper) with worthless writing. LME–M17. **3** Disgrace; tarnish, sully, (good qualities or reputation). *arch.* LME. †**b** Stigmatize, calumniate. LME–E17. **4** Obliterate (writing); efface; obscure (a view etc.); exterminate, destroy. Usu. foll. by *out*. LME. **5** Dry with blotting-paper. M19. **6** *Biol.* & *Med.* Transfer from a medium used for electrophoretic or chromatographic separation to an immobilizing medium where the constituents can be identified. L20.

1 **blot one's copybook** *colloq.* spoil one's character or record, commit an indiscretion. 3 N. ROWE Blot not thy innocence with guiltless blood. 4 SHAKES. *Rich. II* My name be blotted from the book of life. C. S. FORESTER The German trenches were blotted out by the smoke and debris. E. FIGES My arrival has been blotted out: I cannot remember it. A. PRICE Any chance of a reply . . was blotted out by the roar of another big jet.

II *v.i.* **7** Of a pen, ink, etc.: make blots. LME. †**8** Sully a reputation etc. *rare* (Shakes.). Only in L16. **9** Become blotted, smudge. M19.

blotch /blɒtʃ/ *n.* M17. [Partly alt. of PLOTCH *n.* after BLOT *n.*[1], partly blend of BLOT *n.*[1] and BOTCH *n.*[1]] **1** A discoloured patch on the skin; a pustule, a boil. M17. **b** A plant disease characterized by areas of discoloration. E20. **2** A large irregular spot or blot of ink, colour, etc. M18.

1b *leaf blotch*: see LEAF *n.*[1] *sooty blotch*: see SOOTY *a.*

blotchy *a.* E19.

blotch /blɒtʃ/ *v.t.* E17. [f. the n.] Mark with a blotch or blotches.

blotter /ˈblɒtə/ *n.* L16. [f. BLOT *v.* + -ER[1].] **1** A person who or thing which blots or blots out (or *out*); *spec.* (*a*) an inferior writer, a scribbler; (*b*) something used for drying ink-marks, as a blotting-pad. L16. **2** A temporary recording-book, as a police charge-sheet. *N. Amer.* L17.

blottesque /blɒˈtɛsk/ *a.* M19. [f. BLOT *v.* + -ESQUE, after *grotesque* etc.] Of painting: characterized by blotted touches heavily laid on.

blotting /ˈblɒtɪŋ/ *n.* LME. [f. BLOT *v.* + -ING[1].] **1** The action of BLOT *v.*; an instance of this; a blot, smear, obliteration. Also foll. by *out*. LME. **2** (Material for) blotting-paper. L19.

Comb.: **blotting-pad** a pad of blotting-paper; **blotting-paper** absorbent unsized paper for drying wet ink.

blotto /ˈblɒtəʊ/ *a. slang.* E20. [f. BLOT *n.*[1] or *v.* + -O.] Very drunk, intoxicated.

blouse /blaʊz/ *n.* & *v.* E19. [Fr., of unkn. origin.] A *n.* 1 A loose linen or cotton garment resembling a shirt, usu. belted at the waist, worn by workmen or peasants, esp. in France. E19. b *transf.* A French workman. M19. 2 A jacket as part of US military uniform; the upper part of a soldier's or airman's battledress. M19. 3 A woman's loose upper garment usu. worn tucked into a skirt or trousers at the waist. L19. B *v.* 1 *v.i.* Swell out or hang loosely like a blouse. E20. 2 *v.t.* Make (a bodice etc.) loose like a blouse. M20.

blouson /ˈbluːzɒn; *foreign* bluzɔ̃ (*pl. same*)/ *n.* E20. [Fr.] A short jacket shaped like a blouse.

blow /bləʊ/ *n.*[1] LME. [Origin unkn.] 1 A (usu. hard) stroke with the fist, an implement, etc. LME. b A stroke of the shears in shearing sheep. *Austral.* & *NZ.* L19. c An outcrop of mineral. *Austral.* & *NZ.* L19. 2 *fig.* A sudden disaster, a shock, a setback. L17.

1 D. H. LAWRENCE Catching him a light blow . . with the back of her hand. R. DAHL It was too late to check the blow and the axe blade struck the tree. *fig.*: SHAKES. *Lear* A most poor man, made tame to fortune's blows. **at one blow** at a single stroke, in one operation. *a word and a blow*: see WORD *n.* *break a blow*: see BREAK *v.* **come,** (*arch.*) **fall, to blows** begin fighting. **exchange blows** fight. **strike a blow** (**for, against**) take action (on behalf of, in opposition to). **strike the first blow** take the first action, begin a process. **without striking a blow** without a struggle, putting up no opposition. b *long blow*: see LONG *a.*[1] 2 C. CHAPLIN Dicky died at the age of nineteen, a sad and terrible blow from which she never recovered.

Comb.: **blow-by-blow** *a.* (of a description etc.) giving all details in sequence.

blow /bləʊ/ *n.*[2] L15. [f. BLOW *v.*[1]] 1 A blowing; a blast of air; a gust of wind; *colloq.* a breath of fresh air; a blowing of one's nose; a blowing of a wind instrument; *slang* a jazz session. L15. b (The quantity of metal dealt with in) a single operation of a steel-making retort using an oxygen or air blast. L19. 2 A fly's egg deposited in meat etc. (Earlier in FLY-BLOW *n.*) E17. 3 A boast; boastfulness; a boaster. Chiefly *US.* L17.

blow /bləʊ/ *n.*[3] *arch.* E18. [f. BLOW *v.*[2]] 1 A display of blossoms; a brilliant display. E18. 2 Blossoming; bloom. M18. 3 (A) blossom. L18.

blow /bləʊ/ *v.*[1] Pa. t. **blew** /bluː/; pa. pple **blown** /bləʊn/, (senses 12d, 19, & *non-standard*) **blowed.** [OE *blāwan*, pa. t. *blēow*, pa. pple *blāwen* = OHG *blā(h)an*, repl. by wk OHG *blājan* (G *blähen* blow up, swell), f. IE base repr. also by L *flare*.] I Senses conn. w. the production of an air current. 1 *v.i.* Of wind, air, etc., or *impers.* w. *it*: move along, act as an air current. Freq. w. the type or strength of wind as compl. OE. 2 *v.i.* Send a directed air current from the mouth; (of a bellows etc.) produce an air current. OE. †b Hiss; whistle. ME–M16. c Of a whale: eject water and air, spout. L17. 3 *v.t.* Send out by breathing; emit or pass (air); drive, carry, or move by an air current; *fig.* proclaim, publish. Usu. w. advs. & preps. of direction. ME. 4 *v.i.* Breathe hard, puff, pant; *dial.* (simply) breathe. LME. 5 *v.i.* Bluster; boast, brag. Chiefly *dial.* or *US* & *Austral. colloq.* LME. †b *v.t.* Utter, esp. boastfully, angrily, or maliciously. Also foll. by *out.* LME–L19. 6 *v.t.* Work (bellows); work the bellows of (an organ etc.). LME. 7 *v.t.* Cause to pant, exhaust of breath. Usu. in *pass.* M17. 8 *v.i.* Be driven, carried, or moved by the wind or other air current. Freq. w. advs. & preps. of direction. M17. b *v.i.* & *t.* Depart suddenly (from). *slang.* E20.

1 I. WALTON Heark how it rains and blows. OED It blew a gale. J. STEINBECK The wind blew fierce and strong. 3 DRYDEN Winnow'd Chaff by Western Winds is blown. SIR W. SCOTT As soon as Richard's return is blown abroad. P. SAVAGE The winds . . blow the dead leaves down. J. HERRIOT He blew smoke pleasurably from his nostrils. A. PRICE He . . blew the dust from it. 4 POPE Each spent courser at the chariot blow. 7 *Blackwood's Magazine* The Russians . . were . . pretty well blown in the pursuit. 8 TENNYSON Her cap blew off, her gown blew up. W. CATHER Her skirts blowing in the wind. b E. LINKLATER He's blown. He's gone up north. R. MACDONALD I'm blowing this town tonight.

II Senses conn. w. the application of an air current. 9 *v.t.* Make (a wind instrument) sound; *slang* play jazz on (any instrument). Also, sound (a note, a signal) on (or *on, upon, with*) a wind instrument. Of a wind instrument: sound (a note, a signal). OE. 10 *v.i.* Of a wind instrument, its blower, or the note etc. produced: sound. Also (*slang*) play jazz (on any instrument). ME. 11 *v.t.* Direct an air current at so as to cool, warm, dry, etc. (also w. the effect as compl.) or (w. a fire as obj.) to make burn more brightly (also foll. by *up*). ME. †b *fig.* Inflame, arouse, (feeling). Usu. foll. by *up.* ME–L18. 12 *v.t.* Swell by an air current; make or shape (a bubble, glass, etc.) by blowing into it. (Foll. by *up, out.*) LME. †b Inflate (a person) with pride or vanity. Usu. foll. by *up.* LME–E18. c Enlarge, magnify; exaggerate. Usu. & now only foll. by *up.* M16. d Cause (the stomach of an animal) to swell. L18. e In *pass.* Of a food-tin etc.: be swollen by internal gas pressure. L19. 13 *v.t.* Clear (the nose, a pipe, an egg, etc.) by an air current. M16. 14 *v.t.* Scatter, destroy, or send flying by an explosion etc. (freq. w. advs., esp. *up*, or w. the result as compl.); break into (a safe etc.) with explosives; *fig.* (*colloq.*) bungle. Foll. by *up* also †(*a*) destroy, ruin; (*b*) *colloq.* reprove, scold. L16. b *v.i.* Be shattered etc. by an explosion, explode, (usu. foll. by *up*); *fig.* foll. by *up*, lose one's temper. L17. c *v.t.* Produce (a hole etc.) by an explosion etc. L19. 15 *v.t.* Expose, reveal; inform on. (Foll. by †*up.*) Now *slang.* L16. b *v.i.* Act as an informer, reveal a secret. *slang.* M19. 16 *v.i.* & *t.* Of an electric filament or fuse: melt when overloaded. Also, cause (an electric filament etc.) to melt on overload. Also foll. by *out.* L19. 17 *v.t.* Fellate. *coarse slang.* M20.

9 TENNYSON The belted hunter blew His wreathed bugle-horn. N. SHUTE The siren blew five blasts. 10 TENNYSON Let the mournful martial music blow. R. KIPLING The bugles blew for dinner. J. KEROUAC Everybody in Frisco blew. R. BOLT A pilot's whistle, upon which he will blow. 11 SHAKES. *Ven. & Ad.* To . . blow them dry again. F. MARRYAT The winter was cold . . and he blew his fingers. 12 J. DICKEY I blew up the air mattresses with a hand pump. c *Punch* I blew up the two faces on an epidiascope. 14 STEELE One of our Bombs fell into a Magazine . . and blew it up. R. CONQUEST The bridge attributed to Belisarius Is blown. J. BETJEMAN When mankind Has blown himself to pieces. b C. KINGSLEY The mountain had blown up like a barrel of gunpowder. J. CLAVELL When the magazine blew. 16 J. RABAN Every light bulb blows when you switch it on.

III Other senses. 18 *v.t.* Of a fly etc.: deposit eggs on or in; = FLY-BLOW *v.* 1. L16. †b *v.t.* & *i.* Deposit (eggs). E17–L18. 19 *v.t.* Curse, confound, damn, (freq. in *pass.*). Foll. by *if* with 1st person expr. surprise or as a disclaimer (also foll. by †*up*). *slang.* L18. b *v.i.* in *imper.* Damn! E20. 20 *v.t.* Squander, spend (money) recklessly. Also (chiefly *US*) foll. by *in.* (Cf. BLUE *v.*[2]) *slang.* L19. 21 *v.t.* Treat (a person *to*). *US slang.* L19.

18 A. BURGESS The flies blew the cold beef on the kitchen table. 19 P. EGAN Blow me tight if ever I saw such a thing in my life before. DICKENS One blowed thing and another.

Phrases: **blow a cloud** *colloq.* smoke a pipe. *blow a fuse*: see FUSE *n.*[2] *blow a gasket*: see GASKET *n.* **blow a kiss** kiss one's fingers and wave or pretend to blow something from them to a (distant) person. **blow a person's brains out** shoot a person through the head. **blow a person's mind** *slang* cause a person to have drug-induced hallucinations or a similar experience. **blow great guns** (of wind) blow violently. **blow high, blow low** *US* whatever may happen. **blow hot and cold** vacillate, be inconsistent. **blow one's cool** *slang* lose one's composure, become angry or agitated. **blow one's own trumpet** praise oneself. **blow one's top,** (*N. Amer.*) **stack** *colloq.* show great anger. *blow sky-high*: see SKY *n.* *blow (something) for a game of soldiers*: see SOLDIER *n.* *blow the gaff*: see GAFF *n.*[3] **blow the whistle on** draw attention to (something illicit or undesirable), bring to a sharp conclusion, inform on. *blow trade*: see TRADE *n.*

With advs. & preps. in specialized senses: **blow away** *slang* kill, destroy, defeat. **blow in** (*a*) *v.phr.t.* (*Metall.*) set (a blast-furnace) in operation; (*b*) *v.phr.i.* (*colloq.*) come in unexpectedly; (see also sense 20 above). **blow off** *v.phr.t.* allow (steam etc.) to escape forcibly; *fig.* get rid of (superfluous energy etc.) in a noisy way. **blow on** or **upon** — discredit, defame, make stale; (see also sense 9 above). **blow out** (*a*) *v.phr.t.* & *i.* extinguish or be extinguished by blowing; (*b*) *v.phr.t.* (*Metall.*) take (a blast-furnace) out of operation; (*c*) *v.phr.i.* (of a pneumatic tyre) burst; (see also senses 5b, 12, 16 above). **blow over** pass off without threatened consequences. **blow up** *v.phr.i.* (of a wind) increase in force; arise, come to notice; (see also senses 11, 12, 14, 15, 19 above). *blow upon*: see *blow on* above.

Comb.: **blow-away** *a.* likely to be blown away by the wind etc.; **blow-back** the action or process of blowing back, esp. (*a*) of pressure in a boiler or internal-combustion engine; (*b*) of gunpowder that has not burned completely; (*c*) of the slide or breech-block of some firearms; **blow-ball** the globular seed-head of a dandelion etc.; **blow-drier** a blower used in blow-drying; **blow-dry** *v.* & *n.* (*a*) *v.t.* arrange (hair) while drying it with a hand-held blower; (*b*) *n.* an act or instance of blow-drying hair; **blowfish** (a pop. name for) any of several fishes which inflate their bodies when frightened etc.; **blowfly** any of various flies of the family Calliphoridae, which deposit their eggs on meat and carcasses; a bluebottle, a meat-fly; **blowhard** *a.* & *n.* (*colloq.*) (a person who is) boastful; **blow-hole** (*a*) a hole for breathing through; the nostril of a whale etc.; (*b*) a hole formed by escaping air, steam, etc.; (*c*) a vent in a tunnel etc. for the escape of steam, gas, etc.; **blow-job** *coarse slang* an act or instance of fellatio or cunnilingus; **blowlamp** a lamp or torch for directing a very hot flame on a selected spot; **blow-off** *a.* & *n.* (of or pertaining to) the removal of water or sediment from a boiler by the force of steam; *fig.* an outburst; **blow-out** (*a*) *colloq.* a large meal; (*b*) *dial.* & *US* an outbreak of anger, a row; (*c*) (orig. *US*) an isolated hill with a crater-like top created by the wind; a hollow eroded by the wind; (*d*) a bursting of a pneumatic tyre; (*e*) a rapid uncontrolled uprush of fluid from an oil well; *blow-out preventer*: see PREVENTER 3; **blowpipe** (*a*) a tube for heating flame by blowing air or other gas into it; (*b*) a tube used in glass-blowing; (*c*) a tube for propelling arrows or darts by blowing; **blowtorch** = *blowlamp* above; **blow-up** (*a*) an explosion; *fig.* an outburst of anger, a row; (*b*) the vessel in which raw sugar is dissolved; (*c*) *colloq.* a photographic enlargement.

blow /bləʊ/ *v.*[2] *arch.* Pa. t. **blew** /bluː/; pa. pple **blown** /bləʊn/. [OE *blōwan* str., corresp. to wk vbs OFris. *blōia*, OS *blōjan* ((M)Du. *bloeien*), OHG *bluojan, bluoen* (G *blühen*), f. Gmc base also of BLOOM *n.*[1], BLOSSOM *n.* & perh. BLADE.] 1 *v.i.* Blossom, flower; *fig.* flourish, bloom. OE. †2 *v.t.* Cause to bloom. M17–E19.

blowed *v.* see BLOW *v.*[1]

blowen /ˈbləʊən/ *n. arch. slang.* Also **blowing** /ˈbləʊɪŋ/. L17. [Origin unkn.] A prostitute, a wench.

blower /ˈbləʊə/ *n.*[1] OE. [f. BLOW *v.*[1] + -ER[1].] 1 *gen.* A person or thing which blows. (Foll. by *of.*) OE. 2 A boaster, a blusterer. Chiefly *dial.* or *US* & *Austral. colloq.* L16. 3 An apparatus that produces or increases an air current, as a sheet of iron across a fireplace to increase a fire's draught, a fan heater, etc. L18. 4 An escape of gas through a fissure in a coalmine etc.; a fissure through which gas escapes. E19. 5 A telephone; a speaking-tube. *colloq.* E20.

blower /ˈbləʊə/ *n.*[2] *rare.* M18. [f. BLOW *v.*[2] + -ER[1].] A plant that blooms *early, late*, etc.

blowing *n.* var. of BLOWEN.

blown *v.*[1], *v.*[2] pa. pple of BLOW *v.*[1], *v.*[2]

blowse *n.* & *v.*, **blowsy** *a.* vars. of BLOWZE, BLOWZY.

blowth /bləʊθ/ *n.* Long *obs.* exc. *dial.* Also *dial.* **blooth** /bluːθ/. E17. [f. BLOW *v.*[2] + -TH[1].] Blossoming; bloom.

blowy /ˈbləʊɪ/ *a.* E19. [f. BLOW *v.*[1] + -Y[1].] Windy.

blowze /blaʊz/ *n.* & *v.* Also **blowse.** L16. [Origin unkn.] A *n.* †1 A (beggar's) wench. L16–E18. 2 A coarse red-faced woman; a slattern. Long *obs.* exc. *dial.* L16. B *v.* 1 *v.t.* Make red-faced; dishevel. Chiefly as *blowzed* ppl

a. M18. †2 *v.i.* Tend to be blowzy. Chiefly as *blowzing* ppl a. M18–M19.

blowzy /ˈblaʊzi/ *a.* Also **blowsy**. E17. [f. prec. + -Y[1].] Coarse and red-faced; slatternly; unkempt, dishevelled.

blowzily *adv.* E20. **blowziness** *n.* M19.

blub /blʌb/ *v.* & *n. colloq.* E19. [Abbrev. of BLUBBER *v.*] **A** *v.* Infl. **-bb-**. **1** *v.t.* Wet or disfigure with weeping. E19. **2** *v.i.* Shed tears, weep. M19. **B** *n.* A fit or spell of weeping. L19.

blubber /ˈblʌbə/ *n.* LME. [Prob. imit.: cf. LG *blubbern* bubble, G *blubbern* bubble, splutter.] †**1** The foaming of the sea. Only in LME. **2** A bubble on water. *obs.* exc. *dial.* LME. **3** The fat of whales, seals, etc. LME. **4** More fully *sea blubber*. A jellyfish. E17. **5** The action of blubbering. M17.

blubbery *a.* L18.

blubber /ˈblʌbə/ *a.* Also (the earliest form) †**blab-**; †**blob-**. L15. [Prob. imit.: cf. BLEB, BLOB, BUBBLE *n.* & *a.*] Esp. of the lips or cheeks: swollen, protruding.

¶ First recorded in comb. *blubber-lipped* adj.

blubber /ˈblʌbə/ *v.* LME. [f. BLUBBER *n.*] **1** *v.i.* Bubble (up); make a bubbling sound. LME. **2** *v.i.* Weep noisily; weep and sob unrestrainedly. LME. **3** *v.t.* Utter with crying and sobbing. (Foll. by *out*, arch. *forth*.) L16. **4** *v.t.* Wet, disfigure, or swell (the face) with weeping. L16.

blubberer *n.* L18. **blubberingly** *adv.* with noisy weeping M19.

blucher /ˈbluːkə, *foreign* ˈblyçər/ *n.* Also **B-**. E19. [G. L. von *Blücher* (1742–1819), Prussian general.] *Hist.* **1** A kind of horse-drawn cart or coach. Also more fully *Blucher coach*. E19. **2** A strong laced leather half-boot or high shoe. Also *blucher boot*. Usu. in *pl.* M19.

bludge /blʌdʒ/ *v.* & *n. slang* (chiefly *Austral.* & *NZ*). E20. [Back-form. f. BLUDGER.] **A** *v.* **1** *v.i.* a Impose *on*. E20. **b** Shirk responsibility or hard work. M20. **c** Pimp. M20. **2** *v.t.* Cadge, scrounge. M20. **B** *n.* An easy job or assignment. M20.

bludgeon /ˈblʌdʒ(ə)n/ *n.* & *v.* M18. [Origin unkn.] **A** *n.* A heavy-headed stick or club. M18.

B *v.t.* Strike repeatedly or fell with a bludgeon; coerce. M19.

A. BURGESS I did not wish to give up my freedom. I was bludgeoned into marriage.

bludgeoner *n.* a person who is armed with or uses a bludgeon M19.

bludger /ˈblʌdʒə/ *n. slang.* M19. [Abbrev. of BLUDGEONER.] **1** A man who works with prostitutes to rob their clients; a pimp. M19. **2** A loafer, a shirker, a hanger-on. *Austral.* & *NZ.* M20.

blue /bluː/ *n.* Also †**blew**. ME. [The adj. used ellipt. or absol.] **1** Blue colour; a shade of this. ME. **b** A pigment of a blue colour (freq. w. specifying wd); a blue substance; *spec.* a blue powder used as a whitener in laundering. L15. **2** Blue clothing, dress, or uniform; blue fabric. ME. **b** *spec.* The uniform of the Union troops in the American Civil War. *US.* M19. **3** *ellipt.* Anything distinguished by blue colour, as the blue ball in snooker, a blue butterfly (*spec.* one of the family Lycaenidae), etc. L16. **4** The clear sky; the sea; the desert; the indefinite distance, the unknown. M17. **5** As the colour adopted by a party, faction, etc. (cf. BLUE *a.* 5); *transf.* a member of such a group. M17. **b** = BLUESTOCKING *n. arch.* L18. **c** (Also **B-**.) A person who has represented his or her university (esp. Oxford or Cambridge) or school in athletics, a sport, etc.; such a distinction. L19. **6** A soldier, police officer, etc., in blue uniform. Usu. in *pl.* M18. **7** An argument, a fight or brawl; a mistake, a blunder. *Austral.* & *NZ slang.* M20.

1 J. RUSKIN The blue of distance, however intense, is not the blue of a bright blue flower. *Alice blue, cobalt blue, electric blue, Eton blue, navy blue, Prussian blue, royal blue, soluble blue, violet-blue*, etc. **b** S. ROWLANDS Set her to starch a band . . She euer spoyles the same with too much blew. *French blue*: see FRENCH *a. scratch blue*: see SCRATCH *v.* SCRATCHED *blue*. VERDIGRIS *blue*. **2** **men, boys** etc., **in blue** policemen; the Royal Navy; US Federal troops. **3** **Admiral of the Blue** *Hist.*: of the Blue squadron (one of three divisions of the Royal Navy made between the 17th and 19th cents.). *Danish blue*: see DANISH *a.* RUSSIAN *Blue* See also BLUES. **4** GEO. ELIOT Where one may float between blue and blue. J. T. STORY I am not . . one of those people who can vanish into the blue never to be heard of again. N. MACCAIG The weather doodles a faint cloud / on the blue / then pensively washes it out. *bolt from* (or *out of*) *the blue*: see BOLT *n.*[1] **out of the blue** without warning, unexpectedly. **5** **dark, light blue**: adopted by the Universities of Oxford and Cambridge respectively. **c** **get, win**, etc., **one's blue** represent one's university etc. in a sporting contest. **6** R. KIPLING Next time you see the 'blue' ashore you do not stare unintelligently. **the Blues** (in the British army) the Royal Horse Guards, later merged with the 1st Dragoons as *the Blues and Royals*. **7** K. TENNANT Every time Rene comes round there's some kind of a blue. N. SHUTE I put up a blue right away by ordering a pink gin.

Comb.: **blue bag** a bag containing laundry blue, used also in the treatment of insect bites and stings; **blue spot** the spot on which the blue ball is placed in snooker.

¶ The usual spelling until 18 was *blew*.

blue /bluː/ *a.* Also †**blew**. ME. [(O)Fr. *bleu* f. Proto-Romance f. Gmc (whence also OE *blǣhǣwen, blǣwen* blue, ON *blár* dark-blue, livid, BLAE).] **1** Of the colour of the sky and the deep sea, between green and violet in the spectrum; of a hue resembling this. ME. **b** Livid, leaden-coloured (esp. of the skin as a result of cold, fear, etc.). ME. **c** Of a flame or flash: without red glare. L16. **2a** Taken as the colour of constancy. LME. **b** Taken as the colour of sorrow or anguish (see also sense 3). LME. **c** Taken as the colour of plagues and things hurtful. E16. **3** *fig.* Depressed, low-spirited; dismayed, downcast; (of circumstances) dismal, unpromising. M16. **b** Intoxicated. *slang* (chiefly *US*). E19. **c** *Mus.* Pertaining to or characteristic of the blues. E20. **4** Dressed in blue; wearing blue. L16. **5** Belonging to a party etc. that has chosen blue for its colour; *spec.* (*a*) (*Hist.*) *true-blue*, of the Scottish Presbyterian or Whig party in the 17th cent.; (*b*) of the Conservative Party in the UK. M17. **6** Of a woman: learned, pedantic (cf. BLUESTOCKING). *arch. derog.* L18. **7** Obscene, indecent; profane. *colloq.* M19.

1 SHAKES. *Ant. & Cl.* My bluest veins to kiss. SCOTT FITZGERALD The blue smoke of brittle leaves. C. MACKENZIE Eyes as blue as the kingfisher's wing. L. VAN DER POST A great plain between blue hills. I. MCEWAN 'Can I borrow a blue pencil?' 'Blue for the sea or blue for the sky?' **b** MILTON Blue meagre hag. T. C. WOLFE His lips chattered and turned blue. *black and blue*: see BLACK *a.* **blue in the face** livid with effort, excitement, etc. (used *hyperbol.*). **c** DEFOE When the candles burn blue the Devil is in the room. **2a** **true blue** faithful, unwavering, genuine (see also sense 5 above). **b** V. NABOKOV A combination of blue sulks and rosy mirth, Lolita. **c** E. YOUNG Riot, pride, perfidy, blue vapours breathe. **3** R. BOLDREWOOD It seemed a rather blue look-out. G. STEIN She wondered . . how she could go on living when she was so blue. **4** *thin blue line*: see THIN *a.* **5** G. B. SHAW The bluest of Tories. **6** M. EDGEWORTH They are all so wise, and so learned, so blue. **7** P. G. WODEHOUSE A jocund little tale, slightly blue in spots. R. LOWELL What blue movie is worth a seat at the keyhole.

Special collocations & comb.: **blue asbestos** crocidolite. **blue baby** a baby with congenital cyanosis. **blueback** (chiefly *N. Amer.*) a bird or fish, esp. a trout or a sockeye salmon, having a bluish back. **blue bag** a barrister's (orig. a solicitor's) brief-bag of blue material; (see also BLUE *n.*). **blue beat (music)** = SKA. **blueberry** any of certain N. American shrubs of the genus *Vaccinium*, of the heath family, allied to the bilberry but bearing their fruits in clusters; the sweet edible blue or blackish fruit of such a plant. **blue-bill** *N. Amer.* & *dial.* = SCAUP. **bluebird** (*a*) a small N. American bird of the genus *Sialia*, related to the thrushes, and having sky-blue upperparts; *esp.* the eastern bluebird, *S. sialis*; (*b*) *fig.* happiness. **blue-black** *a.* & *n.* (of) a black colour with a tinge of blue. **blue blood** [tr. Sp. *sangre azul*, claimed by certain families of Castile, as having no Moorish, Jewish, or other admixture] a sign of high birth. **blue-blooded** *a.* aristocratic. **blue-bonnet** (*a*) a peasant or soldier wearing a broad round flat woollen cap, formerly in general use in Scotland; (*b*) any of various blue flowers and blue-headed birds; *esp.* (*N. Amer.*) either of two lupins, *Lupinus subcarnosus* and *L. texensis*, native to Texas. **blue book** a book bound in blue, *spec.* (*a*) a parliamentary or Privy-Council report, issued in a blue cover; (*b*) *US* a printed book giving personal details of government officials. **bluebottle** (*a*) a cornflower or occas. another blue-flowered plant; (*b*) a nickname for a beadle (*arch.*) or a police officer; (*c*) a large dark-blue fly of the genus *Calliphora*; (*d*) *Austral.*, *NZ*, & *S. Afr.*, a Portuguese man-of-war. *bluebunch wheat-grass*: see WHEAT *n.* **blue-bush** any of various shrubs with bluish foliage or blue flowers, *esp.* (*Austral.*) a bluish-leaved shrub of the genus *Bassia*. **bluecap** † (*a*) a Scotsman; (*b*) *dial.* a salmon in its first year (so called because of a blue spot on its head); a cornflower; a blue tit. **blue-cheeked** *a.* having blue cheeks; *blue-cheeked bee-eater*, an African and Asian bee-eater, *Merops superciliosus*, which has mainly green plumage with a black eyestripe bordered by pale blue. **blue cheese** cheese marked with veins of blue mould (*Danish blue cheese*: see DANISH *a.*). **blue chip** (orig. *US*) a high-value poker counter; *transf.* a stock exchange investment considered to be fairly reliable, though not entirely without risk. **blue-chip** *a.* of the highest quality; (of an investment) fairly reliable. **blue-coat** a person who wears a blue coat, e.g. a police officer, a sailor, a scholar at a charity school (esp. Christ's Hospital), (formerly) an almsman, a beadle. *blue* COHOSH. **blue-collar** *a.* designating a manual or industrial worker, as opp. to a 'white-collar' (office) worker. *blue* COPPERAS. **blue crab** a large edible crab, *Callinectes sapidus*, of the N. American Atlantic coast. *blue crane*: see CRANE *n.*[1] 1b. **blue dahlia** something rare or unheard of. **blue devil** (*a*) a baleful demon; (*b*) in *pl.* depression of spirits; delirium tremens (cf. BLUES 1). **blue-domer** *colloq.* one who does not go to church, preferring to worship beneath the 'blue dome' of heaven. **blue duck** a grey-blue duck, *Hymenolaimus malacorhynchos*, of mountain streams in New Zealand; also called *mountain duck, whio*. *blue ensign*: see ENSIGN *n.* **blue eye** (*a*) an eye of which the iris is blue; † (*b*) = *black eye* (b) s.v. BLACK *a.*; (*c*) a blueness round the eye from weeping etc. **blue-eyed** *a.* having a blue eye or blue eyes; *blue-eyed boy* (colloq.) a favourite, a pet; *blue-eyed grass*, any of several plants of the genus *Sisyrinchium*, bearing blue flowers; *blue-eyed Mary*, a blue-flowered ornamental plant, *Omphalodes verna*, of the borage family. **bluefin (tuna)** *N. Amer.* the common tuna, *Thunnus thynnus*. **bluefish** any of various fishes of a blue colour; *esp.* (*a*) (chiefly *N. Amer.*) *Pomatomus saltatrix* (family Pomatomidae), a large edible blue-backed percoid marine fish; (*b*) (*Austral.* & *NZ*) *Girella cyanea* (family Kyphosidae), a bright blue edible percoid marine fish. **blue fly** a bluebottle. **blue funk** *slang* a state of extreme nervousness. **bluegill (sunfish)** a small fish, *Lepomis macrochirus*, of lakes and ponds in central and south-eastern US. **blue gown** *Hist.* in Scotland, (the dress of) a king's bedesman or licensed beggar. **bluegrass** (*a*) any of various grasses with bluish flowers; spec. *Poa pratensis*, characteristic of Kentucky and Virginia, or other grasses of the same genus; (*b*) the State of Kentucky; (*c*) a type of folk music associated with Kentucky and Virginia. **blue-green (alga)** a primitive prokaryotic alga containing blue and green photosynthetic pigments. **blue-grey** a breed of cattle, a cross between Aberdeen Angus and shorthorn. *blue groper*: see GROPER *n.*[2] 2. **blue ground** dark greyish-blue brecciated kimberlite in which diamonds may be found. **bluegum** any of several Australian eucalypts with bluish bark or leaves. **blue hare** = MOUNTAIN *hare*. **blue hawk** any of various bluish-grey birds of prey; *esp.* the male hen-harrier. **blue heeler** *Austral.* & *NZ* a cattle-dog with a dark speckled body. **bluejacket** a sailor, esp. as opp. to a marine. **blue jay** (*a*) a crested jay, *Cyanocitta cristata*, largely blue with white underparts, native to eastern N. America; (*b*) = ROLLER *n.*[2] **Blue John** (*a*) a blue or purple variety of fluorite found in Derbyshire, England; † (*b*) = *after-wort* s.v. AFTER-. **blue-joint** *US* a grass of the genus *Calamagrostis* or a related genus, with bluish stems. **blue laws** *US* severe puritanical laws, orig. those alleged to have been in force among early colonists of New England. **blue line**: *spec.* marking off an area of play in a game, as in *Ice Hockey* either of the two lines midway between the centre of the rink and each goal. **blue ling** either of two small lings, *Molva macrophthalma* and *M. dypterygia*. *blue* MARGUERITE. **Bluemantle** one of four pursuivants of the English College of Arms. **blue metal** bluish argillaceous shale, used in road-making. **blue monkey** the samango monkey, *Cercopithecus mitis*. **blue moon** *colloq.* a rarely recurring period (esp. in *once in a blue moon*). **blue mould** a fungus in food, esp. in certain cheeses when mature. **Blue Mountain (coffee)** a type of Jamaican coffee. **blue-mouth** *Austral.* a spiny deep-water scorpaenid fish of the N. Atlantic, *Helicolenus dactylopterus*, with a reddish body and a blue mouth; also called *red bream*. **blue murder** *slang* an extravagant outcry, a loud or alarming noise. **blue-nose** (chiefly *N. Amer.*) (*a*) (**B-**) a person or thing from Nova Scotia; (*b*) a priggish or puritanical person.

blue-nosed *a.* (chiefly *N. Amer. colloq.*) priggish, puritanical; contemptible. **blue note** *Mus.* a minor interval where a major would be expected; an off-pitch note. *blue* PEAFOWL. **blue pencil** a pencil with a blue lead, used in marking corrections, etc. **blue-pencil** *v.t.* score through or obliterate with a blue pencil, make cuts in, censor. **Blue Peter** a blue flag with a white square in the centre, hoisted by a ship as a signal of immediate sailing. **blue pill** (chiefly *Hist.*) a mercurial antibilious pill. *blue* PINCUSHION. **blue-plate** *a.* (*N. Amer.*) designating a restaurant meal in which the main course is served as a single menu item. *blue* POINTER. **blueprint** *n.* & *v.* (*a*) *n.* a photographic print composed of white lines on a blue ground or vice versa, used for making copies of plans and designs; *fig.* a plan, scheme; (*b*) *v.t.* plan, project. **blue riband, ribbon** (*a*) a ribbon of blue silk, worn as a badge of honour; *esp.* that of the Order of the Garter; (*b*) the greatest distinction, the first place or prize; *attrib.* of first quality, carefully chosen; (*c*) a small strip of blue ribbon worn as a sign of teetotalism. **blue rinse** (an elderly woman with) a bluish tint for grey or white hair. **blue-rinsed** *a.* having a blue rinse. *blue roan*: see ROAN *a.* & *n.*[2] *blue rock*: see ROCK *n.*[1] **blue rod** an official of the order of St Michael and St George. **blue ruin** *slang* gin, esp. of poor quality. *blue runner*: see RUNNER 5c. **blue shark** a large shark, *Prionace glauca*, having a dark-blue back. **blue shift** displacement of spectral lines towards shorter wavelengths or the blue end of the spectrum (opp. REDSHIFT *n.*). **blue-sky** *a.* (*a*) *N. Amer.*, designating dealing in worthless securities or legislation to prevent their sale; (*b*) hypothetical; not yet practicable or profitable. *blue sowthistle*: see *sowthistle* s.v. SOW *n.*[1] **blue stone** (*a*) copper sulphate; (*b*) a bluish-grey stone used for building, esp. *US* a sandstone from near the Hudson River, *Austral.* & *NZ* a basalt; (*c*) any of the dolerite stones forming the inner parts of Stonehenge, believed to be from the Preseli Hills, S. Wales. **blue streak** *colloq.* (chiefly *N. Amer.*) a fast-moving thing or person; a constant stream of words. *blue tangle*: see TANGLE *n.*[2] 3. **bluethroat** a Eurasian bird, *Luscinia svecica*, related to the robin, having a blue throat with a chestnut or white spot. **blue tit** a common European tit, *Parus caeruleus*, having blue upperparts. **bluetongue** (*a*) (orig. *S. Afr.*) an insect-borne viral disease of sheep (transmissible with less serious effects to cattle and goats), characterized by fever, lameness, and a blue, swollen mouth and tongue; also occas. a comparable disease of horses; (*b*) *Austral.* a lizard of the genus *Tiliqua*. *blue* TULP. **blue vinn(e)y (cheese)** a blue-mould skimmed-milk cheese; also called *Dorset cheese*. *blue* VITRIOL. **blue water** the open sea. **blue whale** a baleen whale, *Balaenoptera musculus*, the largest of all animals. **blue whiting** a small blue-backed oceanic whiting, *Micromesistius poutassou*, common in the eastern Atlantic. **blue-wing** the blue-winged teal, *Anas discors*, of N. America.

¶The usual spelling until 18 was *blew*.

bluely *adv.* (*a*) with a blue colour or tinge; †(*b*) badly (only in *come off bluely*): M17. **blueness** *n.* L15.

blue /bluː/ *v.*[1]*t.* Also †**blew** (cf. BLUE *a.*). Pres. pple **blueing, bluing.** E17. [f. the adj.] 1 Make blue. E17. 2 Treat (laundry) with blue. L18.

blu(e)ing *n.* (*a*) the action of the vb; (*b*) laundry blue: M17.

blue /bluː/ *v.*[2]*t.* *slang.* Pres. pple & vbl n. **blueing, bluing.** M19. [Perh. f. past tense of BLOW *v.*[1] 20.] Spend extravagantly, squander.

Bluebeard /ˈbluːbɪəd/ *n.* E19. [A character in a fairy tale told in Fr. (*Barbe-bleue*) by Perrault.] A man who has murdered several wives and concealed their bodies, or has other mysterious or horrible things to conceal.

bluebell /ˈbluːbɛl/ *n.* L16. [f. BLUE *a.* + BELL *n.*[1]] 1 The harebell, *Campanula rotundifolia*. Chiefly *Sc.* & *north.* L16. 2 A bulbous-rooted woodland plant, *Hyacinthoides non-scripta*, bearing racemes of narrow bell-like blue flowers in spring; a flowering stem of this plant. L18.

2 *Spanish bluebell*: see SPANISH *a.* *Virginia bluebell*: see VIRGINIA I.

blueish *a.* var. of BLUISH.

blueism /ˈbluːɪz(ə)m/ *n.* *arch.* Also **bluism.** L18. [f. BLUE *a.* + -ISM.] The characteristics or behaviour of a bluestocking; feminine learning.

blues /bluːz/ *n.* M18. [Ellipt. for *blue devils*: see BLUE *a.*] 1 *pl.* *the blues*, depression of spirits, melancholy. M18. 2 *pl.* & (sometimes) *sing.* A (type of) haunting melody or melancholy song, freq. in a twelve-bar sequence using blue notes, originating among southern American Blacks. E20.

1 S. BELLOW He realized he had not spoken three words to a living soul and the blues descended on him. 2 J. BALDWIN Frank sang the blues. R. D. LAING Martyn's electronic version of the Skip James blues 'I'd Rather Be The Devil'. RHYTHM *and blues*.

bluesy *a.* of, pertaining to, or characteristic of blues music M20.

bluestocking /ˈbluːstɒkɪŋ/ *a.* & *n.* *derog.* L17. [f. BLUE *a.* + STOCKING *n.*[2]] A *adj.* 1 Wearing blue worsted stockings; in homely dress. *arch.* L17. 2 Designating or pertaining to (those frequenting) assemblies for literary conversation etc. held at Montagu House in London about 1750 (where some of the men wore the blue stockings of ordinary daytime dress). L18. 3 Of a woman: having or affecting literary tastes, learned. E19. B *n.* A female supporter of bluestocking assemblies; a learned woman. L18.

bluestockingism *n.* E19.

bluet /ˈbluːɪt/ *n.* Chiefly *US.* E18. [Fr. *bl(e)uet* dim. of *bleu* BLUE *a.*: see -ET[1].] Any of various blue-flowered plants; *esp.* (*a*) the cornflower, *Centaurea cyanus*; (*b*) the plant *Hedyotis caerulea*, of the madder family. Also called *innocence*, *quaker-lady*. Freq. in *pl.*

bluey /ˈbluːi/ *a.*, *adv.*, & *n.* E19. [f. BLUE *a.* + -Y[1].] A *adj.* & *adv.* More or less blue; with a blue tinge. E19.

B *n.* I 1 Lead. *slang.* Now *rare* or *obs.* M19. II *Austral.* & *NZ colloq.* 2a A bushman's bundle (often wrapped in a blue blanket); a swag. L19. b A rough outer garment; the material from which such garments are made. L19. 3 A summons (on blue paper) to appear in court. E20. 4 A blue cattle-dog. M20.

2 **hump bluey** travel with a swag, hit the trail.

bluff /blʌf/ *n.*[1] Orig. *N. Amer.* M17. [f. the adj.] 1 A cliff or headland with a broad precipitous face; a high steep bank, esp. by a river or shore. M17. 2 A grove or clump of trees. *Canad.* M18.

bluff /blʌf/ *n.*[2] L18. [Prob. f. the vb, to which it is certainly related, but perh. earlier.] 1 A blinker for a horse. Now *obs.* or *dial.* L18. 2 The game of poker; the action or an act of bluffing, orig. in poker; threatening or confident language or behaviour adopted without basis, in order to intimidate or mislead an opponent. Orig. *US.* M19.

2 C. CONNOLLY I learnt that sulking, crying, moping, and malingering were bluffs that paid. A. WILSON There's a lot of bluff goes with this act; he knows nothing about brandy. **call someone's bluff** challenge or invite a showdown with someone believed to be bluffing. *double bluff*: see DOUBLE *a.* & *adv.*

bluff /blʌf/ *a.* E17. [Orig. naut., perh. of LDu. origin.] 1 Presenting a broad, flattened front; (of a ship's bows) broad and with little or no rake. E17. 2 *fig.* a Rough or surly in manner; abrupt, curt. E18. b Good-naturedly blunt; frank, hearty. E19.

2a SWIFT I maul'd you when you look'd so bluff. LYTTON Finally wound up with a bluff 'Go, or let alone'. B. PLAIN You're so blunt and bluff lately, so outspoken! b R. L. STEVENSON He had a bluff, rough-and-ready face. W. FAULKNER He would correct them . . with a bluff, hearty amiability, making a joke of it.

bluffly *adv.* L18. **bluffness** *n.* M19.

bluff /blʌf/ *v.* L17. [Du. *bluffen* brag, boast, or *bluf* bragging, boasting.] 1 *v.t.* Blindfold, hoodwink. Now *obs.* or *dial.* L17. 2 *v.t.* & *i.* (Attempt to) deceive or intimidate by a pretence of strength (orig. in the game of poker). Orig. *US.* M19.

2 CONAN DOYLE I bluffed him by giving him the impression that I was absolutely certain. J. F. KENNEDY There was considerable feeling . . that Hitler and Mussolini were just bluffing. Show strength and they will back down. **bluff it out** seek to avoid trouble by bluffing. **bluff off** frighten off by bluffing.

bluffer *n.* L19.

bluggy /ˈblʌgi/ *a.* L19. [Repr. a supposed infantile pronunc. of BLOODY *a.*] Bloody; *spec.* bloodthirsty, blood-and-thunder.

bluing *v.* & *n.* see BLUE *v.*[1], *v.*[2]

bluish /ˈbluːɪʃ/ *a.* Also **blueish,** †**blewish.** LME. [f. BLUE *a.* + -ISH[1].] Somewhat blue; with a blue tinge.

bluishness *n.* E17.

bluism *n.* var. of BLUEISM.

blunder /ˈblʌndə/ *n.* LME. [App. f. the vb.] †1 Confusion; clamour. LME–L18. 2 A stupid or careless mistake. E18.

blunder /ˈblʌndə/ *v.* ME. [Prob. of Scand. origin: cf. MSw. *blundra*, Norw. *blundre* shut the eyes, frequent. of ON, Sw. *blunda*, ODa. *blunde*, rel. to BLIND *a.*] 1 *v.i.* Move blindly; flounder, stumble. ME. 2 *v.t.* Orig., treat clumsily, damage. Later, mingle; make turbid; mix up (*lit.* & *fig.*). *arch.* & *dial.* ME. 3 *v.t.* Utter thoughtlessly; blurt *out*. L15. 4 *v.i.* Make a stupid or careless mistake. E18. 5 *v.t.* Mismanage, make a blunder in. E19.

1 J. B. PRIESTLEY He felt as if he had blundered into a party given by a complete stranger. B. BAINBRIDGE Someone behind him, blundering through the undergrowth. **blunder upon** find through a stupid or careless mistake. 4 TENNYSON The soldier knew Someone had blunder'd. 5 SIR W. SCOTT The banker's clerk, who was directed to sum my cash-account, blundered it three times. **blunder away** waste or lose by mismanagement.

blunderer *n.* LME. **blunderingly** *adv.* in a blundering manner E19.

blunderbuss /ˈblʌndəbʌs/ *n.* M17. [Alt. (by assoc. with *blunder*) of Du. *donderbus*, f. *donder* thunder + *bus* gun (orig. box, tube; cf. G *Büchse*).] 1 *Hist.* A short gun with a large bore, firing many balls or slugs at once. M17. 2 A talkative or blundering person. L17.

blunderhead /ˈblʌndəhɛd/ *n.* L17. [Prob. alt. of DUNDERHEAD.] A blundering dunderheaded person.

blunderheaded *a.* M18.

blunge /blʌn(d)ʒ/ *v.t.* E19. [Combining *plunge* w. wds in *bl-* as *blend*.] *Pottery.* Mix (clay, bone, flint-powder, etc.) with water in a revolving apparatus.

blunger *n.* an apparatus for blunging E19.

†**blunket** *a.* & *n.* LME–L18. [Origin unkn.: unlikely to be rel. to BLANKET *n.* & *a.*] (Fabric of) greyish blue.

blunt /blʌnt/ *a.* & *n.* ME. [Perh. f. Scand. neut. formation (cf. *scant*, *thwart*) on base of ON *blundr* dozing, sleep, *blunda* shut the eyes (Norw. *blunde* doze): cf. BLUNDER *v.*] A *adj.* 1 Of sight, the perceptions generally, the intellect: dull, insensitive. ME. 2 Without a sharp edge or point; (of an angle, point, etc.) not sharp, obtuse. LME. 3 Rude, unpolished, without refinement. Now *rare* or *obs.* LME. †4 Barren, bare. M–L16. 5 Abrupt in speech or manner; unceremonious; outspoken; uncompromising. L16.

2 AV *Eccles.* 10:10 If the yron be blunt, and he does not whet the edge, then must he put to more strength. G. GREENE The man's moving fingers . . were short, blunt and thick. **blunt instrument** *fig.* a crude means to an end. 3 POPE Tho' not in phrase refin'd; Tho' blunt my tale. 5 A. RADCLIFFE Be pretty blunt with them if they want to come in here. W. S. CHURCHILL In his blunt way he declared . . that the militia was useless. K. CROSSLEY-HOLLAND Good, blunt words with Anglo-Saxon roots.

B *n.* †1 A blunt sword for fencing. E17–E19. 2 Ready money. *arch. slang.* E19. 3 A type of needle used for heavy stitching work. M19.

bluntish *a.* M16. **bluntly** *adv.* LME. **bluntness** *n.* LME.

blunt /blʌnt/ *v.* LME. [f. the adj.] I *v.t.* 1 Dull or make less sharp (an edge, point, etc.). LME. 2 Make dull (the feelings or faculties). L16. 3 Weaken the sharpness of (anything acid etc.); neutralize partly; dilute. M18.

1 C. MCCULLOUGH Eucalyptus wood blunted the sharpest axe in no time at all. *fig.*: H. ARENDT It blunts the impact of one of the basic totalitarian tenets. 2 I. MURDOCH My appetite for Hugo's conversation was not blunted. J. HELLER Twenty-nine months in the service had not blunted his genius for ineptitude.

II *v.i.* 4 Become dull or less sharp. L17.

4 M. MITCHELL Her weapons of scorn, coldness and abuse blunted in her hands.

blur /bləː/ *n.* M16. [Perh. rel. to BLEAR.] 1 A smear which partially obscures; *fig.* a moral stain or blemish. M16. 2 An indistinct, unfocused, or dim image, sound, or apprehension; confused dimness. M19.

1 F. QUARLES He that clenses a blot with blotted fingers makes a greater blurre. MILTON These blurs

are too apparent in his life. 2 S. GIBBONS A confused blur of voices and boots in the yard outside. I. MURDOCH The farther roses merged into a multi-coloured blur.

blurriness *n.* blurry condition M20. **blurry** *a.* full of blurs, indistinct L19.

blur /blɜː/ *v.* Infl. **-rr-**. M16. [f. as prec.] **I** *v.t.* **1** Smear (clear writing etc.) with ink etc. M16. **2** *fig.* Sully, disfigure, defile. L16. **3** Make indistinct. E17. **4** Dim or make undiscriminating (the senses, judgement, etc.). E17.

2 SHAKES. *Haml.* Such an act That blurs the grace and blush of modesty. 3 TENNYSON One low light.. Blurr'd by the creeping mist. N. GORDIMER Reception was blurred by static interference. R. HAYMAN A narrative style which helps to blur distinctions between mental events and external reality. 4 H. WOUK The alcohol hadn't blurred his brain.

II *v.i.* **5** Become smeared or indistinct. E17. **6** Make blurs in writing. E17.

With advs. in specialized senses: **blur out** efface, blot out. **blur over** obscure by a blur, make indistinct.

blurb /blɜːb/ *n. slang* (orig. *US*). E20. [Fanciful form by US humorist Gelett Burgess.] A publisher's brief, usu. eulogistic, description of a book, printed on its jacket or in advertisements; descriptive or commendatory matter.

blurt /blɜːt/ *v.* & *n.* L16. [Prob. imit.: cf. BLIRT.] **A** *v.* **1** *v.t.* Utter abruptly or injudiciously; burst *out* with. L16. †**2** *v.i.* Make a contemptuous puffing gesture with the lips. L16–M17.

1 Q. BELL She told secrets, not realising they would be blurted out in company. W. STYRON 'I'm going to miss you, Sophie,' I blurted.

B *n.* †**1** An (esp. contemptuous) eruptive emission of breath. L16–E17. **2** An abrupt or injudicious utterance. *rare.* M19.

blush /blʌʃ/ *n.* & *a.* LME. [f. the vb.] **A** *n.* **1** A gleam; a blink; a glance, glimpse. *obs.* exc. as below. LME. **2** A reddening, redness, of the face caused by embarrassment, shame, modesty, etc. L16. **3** A flush of light or colour; *spec.* a rosy colour or glow as of dawn. L16.

1 **at, on, (the) first blush** on the first glance or impression. 2 WORDSWORTH Her blushes are joy-flushes. W. BOYD The hot blush had left his face but he felt his ears were still glowing. **put to the blush** put to shame. **spare a person's blushes** not embarrass a person by praise.

B *adj.* Delicate pink; of the colour of a blush. L16.

blushful *a.* given to blushing; rosy, ruddy: E17. **blushless** *a.* M16. **blushy** *a.* E17.

blush /blʌʃ/ *v.* Pa. t. & pple **-ed**, (*arch.*) **-t**. [OE *blyscan* corresp. to MLG *bloschen*, LG *blüsken*; rel. to MDu. *blōzen*, *blōzen* (Du. *blozen*) blush. Cf. OE *āblysian* blush, etc.] **1** *v.i.* Glow red; be or become roseate. OE. †**2** *v.i.* Shine forth; glance. Only in LME. **3** *v.i.* Become red in the face because of embarrassment, shame, modesty, etc. LME. **4** *v.i.* Be ashamed *at, for, to do.* M16. **5** *v.t.* Make red or roseate. L16.

1 SHAKES. *Rich. II* The blushing discontented sun. 3 J. BRAINE She blushed and turned away. D. M. THOMAS She blushed scarlet and was full of apologies. 5 SHAKES. *2 Hen. VI* To blush and beautify the cheek.

blushingly *adv.* with blushing, as if ashamed L16.

blusher /ˈblʌʃə/ *n.* M17. [f. prec. + -ER¹.] **1** Something red or roseate. *rare.* M17. **2** A person who blushes with embarrassment etc. L19. **3** The edible mushroom *Amanita rubescens*, the flesh of which reddens when bruised. L19. **4** A cosmetic used to give colour to the face. M20.

blusht *v.* see BLUSH *v.*

bluster /ˈblʌstə/ *n.* L16. [f. the vb.] **1** Boisterous blowing; a rough and stormy blast; *fig.* the storm or tempest of the passions; a noisy commotion. L16. **2** (A sound like) the blast of a wind instrument. *rare.* E18. **3** Noisy, inflated talk; violent but empty self-assertion, menace, etc. E18.

blusterous *a.* rough, stormy; truculent, given to blustering: M16. **blusterously** *adv.* M16. **blustery** *a.* stormy, windy; noisily self-assertive: M18.

bluster /ˈblʌstə/ *v.* LME. [Ult. imit.: cf. LG *blustern*, *blistern* flutter. Sense 1 may be another wd.] †**1** *v.i.* Wander or stray blindly. Only in LME. **2** *v.i.* Of the wind, waves, or other elements: blow or beat violently. LME. **3** *v.i.* Of a person: storm or rage boisterously; talk with exaggerated violence; utter loud empty menaces, protests, etc. LME. **4** *v.t.* Utter with stormy violence. Usu. foll. by *out.* LME. **5** *v.t.* Force *into* (an action) by violent or hectoring talk. M17.

2 J. K. BAXTER Waves bluster up the bay. J. T. STORY The rain.. was blustering against the window. 3 A. WILSON Ron began to bluster and expostulate.

blusterer *n.* L16. **blustering** *ppl a.* stormy, tempestuous; noisily self-assertive: E16. **blusteringly** *adv.* M16.

blutwurst /ˈbluːtvəːst/ *n.* M19. [G, f. *Blut* blood + *Wurst* sausage.] (A) black pudding.

B mi *n.* var. of BEMI *n.*

bo /bəʊ/ *n.*¹ *slang* (chiefly *US*). E19. [Perh. a shortening of *boy*.] (As a form of address) mate, old chap.

bo /bəʊ/ *int.* & *n.*². Now *rare* or *obs.* Also **boh**. LME. [Imit.: cf. BOO *int.*, *n.*²] An exclamation intended to startle.

boa /ˈbəʊə/ *n.* LME. [L (Pliny), of unkn. origin.] **1** Any of numerous constricting snakes of the family Boidae, *esp.* any of the larger New World examples; *loosely* any constricting snake, a python. LME. **2** A long coil of fur or feathers worn around a woman's neck. M19.

1 *rainbow boa, sand boa, tree boa, yellow boa*, etc.

Comb.: **boa constrictor** a very large boa, *Constrictor constrictor*, of South and Central America; *loosely* = sense 1 above.

Boal *n.* var. of BUAL.

Boanerges /bəʊəˈnəːdʒiːz/ *n.pl.* (also used as *sing.*). E17. [Gk, prob. ult. f. Aram. (= sons of thunder), repr. the name given by Jesus to the two sons of Zebedee (*Mark* 3:17).] Loud vociferous speakers or preachers; (as *sing.*) one such person.

boar /bɔː/ *n.* [OE *bār* = OS *bēr-swīn*, (M)Du. *beer*, OHG *bēr* (G *Bär*), f. WGmc.] **1** An uncastrated male pig. Also, the (full-grown) male of certain other animals, esp. the badger, guinea-pig, and hedgehog. OE. **b** *wild boar*, the wild pig, *Sus scrofa*, of Europe, Asia, and Africa. ME. **2** The flesh of the animal. ME.

Comb.: **boar-fish** a marine fish, *Capros aper*, related to the dory.

boarish *a.* pertaining to or resembling a boar; sensual, cruel; (cf. BOORISH): M16.

board /bɔːd/ *n.* See also BORD. [OE *bord*, combining two Gmc wds w. meanings 'board, plank' and 'border, ship's side': reinforced in ME by cognate OFr. *bort*, Fr. *bord*, edge, rim, ship's side, and ON *borð* board, table.] **I** A piece of wood etc. **1** A long thin usu. narrow piece of sawn timber, a thin plank, often *spec.* as used for floors or other purposes in building; such timber collectively. OE. **2** A thin rigid usu. rectangular piece of any substance, used esp. for display or support; *spec.* a blackboard; a notice-board; a scoreboard. Also, a surface or structure likened to this. ME. **b** *spec.* The surface or frame on which some games are played, as chess, backgammon, Monopoly, etc. Also, the target in darts. LME. **c** A surfboard. L18. **3** In *pl.* Rectangular pieces of strong card etc. used for the cover of a hardback book. L15. **4** Material of various kinds, esp. compressed wood fibres, made into stiff sheets. M17.

1 SOUTHEY They carried her upon a board In the clothes in which she died. TENNYSON Pattering over the boards, she comes and goes at her will. J. STEINBECK Grass grew up through the porch boards. W. VAN T. CLARK The buildings were log or unpainted board. *floorboard, skirting board, tread board*, etc. 2 *Times* They had 84 on the board for eight wickets. A. BRINK When I come into my classroom, I find insults scrawled all over the board. *billboard, blackboard, circuit board, clapperboard, dashboard, diving-board, drawing-board, emery-board, finger-board, footboard, headboard, ironing-board, keyboard, mortar-board, notice-board, pegboard, running-board, sandwich-board, scoreboard, skateboard, soundboard, splash-board, springboard, surfboard, switchboard, weatherboard*, etc. **b** C. S. LEWIS All over the board my pieces were in the most disadvantageous positions. *chessboard, dartboard, draughtboard, shovelboard*, etc. 4 *cardboard, chipboard, hardboard, pasteboard, strawboard*, etc.

II A table. **5** *gen.* A table. *obs.* exc. as below. OE. **b** A piece of furniture like a table. Now chiefly in *sideboard*. LME. **6** A table used for meals or spread for a meal. ME. **b** Food served at a table; the provision of daily meals (and often also lodging), esp. at an agreed price or in return for services. ME. **c** The condition of boarding at a house etc. LME. **7** A table at which meetings are held; the meeting of a council etc. round a table; a committee, a body of examiners, interviewers, etc.; *spec.* the body of directors of a company. M16.

5 *stall-board*. ABOVE-BOARD. 6 G. M. TREVELYAN The labourer.. ate at the board of the farmer. **b** J. HEATH-STUBBS He'd be glad of a share of your board, Or a place by the fire. J. C. OATES To work at the castle for no salary, only for room and board? **c** J. CLEVELAND An expensive Lord, That.. lives at board. 7 LD MACAULAY How little he was pleased with what had passed at the board. A. J. P. TAYLOR The poor law was administered by local boards of guardians. H. FAST The second vice president of the Seldon Bank.. delivered the formal sentiments of the board. *Board of Customs and Excise, Board of Inland Revenue, Federal Reserve Board, medical board*, etc.

†**III** **8** A shield. OE–M16.

IV A side, an edge. **9** A border, an edge; a coast. Long *obs.* exc. in SEABOARD. OE. **10** The side of a ship. Now only in distinct phrases and combs. (often used in non-naut. contexts). OE. **11** *Naut.* A distance covered in one tack. M16. **12** *Mining.* = BORD. E18.

10 *larboard, overboard, starboard*, etc. 11 CAPT. COOK We passed the night in making short boards.

Phrases: **across the board** all-embracing(ly), general(ly). *bed and board*: see BED *n.* **board and board** (*a*) (of ships) close alongside, side by side; (*b*) (sailing) by a succession of short tacks. **board and lodging** provision of accommodation and meals. **board of control**, a supervisory body; *spec.* (*Hist.*) a board of six members established by Pitt in 1784 to govern British India. **board of trade** (*a*) *US* a Chamber of Commerce; (*b*) (*B- T-*) a (now nominal) British government department concerned with commerce and industry (*Board of Trade Unit* (Hist.), a kilowatt-hour). *full board*: see FULL *a.* **go by the board** (of a mast etc.) fall overboard; *fig.* be entirely neglected, go for good and all. *half-board*: see HALF-. **on board** = ABOARD *adv.* & *prep.* *red board*: see RED *a.* *sweep the board*: see SWEEP *v.* **take on board** *fig.* (*a*) drink, consume, swallow; (*b*) accept (an idea etc.), come to terms with. **the board** *Austral.* & *NZ* the part of the floor of a shearing-shed where the shearers work, the shearers working there. **the boards** *spec.* those forming the stage of a theatre or music hall; *fig.* the actor's profession. *tread the boards*: see TREAD *v.* **within** (or **without**) **board** *Naut.* within (or outside of) the ship.

Comb.: **board foot** a unit of volume (for timber) equal to 144 cu. in.; **board game** a game played on a special board; **boardroom** (the meeting place of) the directors of a company; **boardsailing** windsurfing; **board school** *Hist.* an elementary school under the management of a School Board, established in Britain by the Education Act of 1870; **board-wages** *arch.* wages allowed to servants for food; **boardwalk** (chiefly *N. Amer.*) a footway (of a type originally) made of boards; **board-work** wig-making.

board /bɔːd/ *v.* LME. [f. the n.: cf. ABORD *v.*, Fr. *border*.] **I** Rel. to *board* = side. **1** *v.t.* & *i.* Orig., come close up to or alongside (a ship), usu. for the purpose of attacking (†*v.i.* foll. by *with* the ship). Now, force one's way on board (a ship). LME. **2** *v.t. fig.* Approach, assail; make advances to. *arch.* M16. **3** *v.t.* & *i.* Go on board of, embark on (a ship); enter (a train, vehicle, aircraft, etc.). L16. †**4** *v.t.* & *i.* Border (*on*); approach; lie close *by*. L16–M17. **5** *v.i.* & *t.* (with *it*). Of a ship: tack. E17.

1 M. ARNOLD To decide the battle by boarding. 2 J. VANBRUGH What.. do you expect from boarding a woman.. engag'd to another?

II Rel. to *board* = thin plank, table. **6** *v.t.* Cover or provide with boards; close *up* with boards. LME. **7** *v.t.* Provide with daily meals and usu. also lodging, esp. at a fixed rate. M16. **b** Put up and feed (an animal). L19. **8** *v.i.* Receive daily meals and usu. also lodging; live *with* for an agreed price. M16. **9** *v.t.* Place in lodgings etc. Freq. foll. by *out.* M17. **10** *v.t.* Bring (a candidate) before a board of interviewers. E20.

6 W. D. HOWELLS The floors were roughly boarded over. W. HAVIGHURST Many people boarded their houses tight. L. HELLMAN I went down to the corner store. It was boarded up and nobody answered the

bell. 7 SHAKES. *Hen. V* We cannot lodge and board a dozen or fourteen gentlewomen. 8 W. IRVING He had engaged to board with the family. C. MCCULLOUGH They were sent to the convent . . to board, for there was no school closer. 9 E. FIGES My brother . . had been boarded out with the family of a schoolfriend. 10 *New Society* Of the 715 candidates boarded, 104 were selected.

boarder *n.* (*a*) a person who boards at a house etc.; *spec.* a pupil who boards at a school; (*b*) a sailor who boards an enemy ship: M16. **boarding** *n.* (*a*) the action of the vb; *boarding-house* a house offering board and lodging for paying guests; *boarding-school* a school at which most or all pupils board; (*b*) material for boards, boards collectively: L15.

boardly *a.* var. of BUIRDLY.

boart *n.* var. of BORT.

boast /bəʊst/ *n.*[1] ME. [Origin unkn.: cf. BOAST *v.*[1]] 1 Loud speech, outcry, clamour; menacing speech, threats. Long *obs.* exc. *dial.* ME. 2 Proud or vainglorious speech, bragging; an excessively proud statement. ME. 3 An occasion or cause of pride. L16.

2 SHAKES. *Cymb.* The swell'd boast Of him that best could speak. E. A. FREEMAN They soon found such a boast was vain indeed. 3 T. E. LAWRENCE Some make a boast of vice, to cover innocence. M. SPARK One of Joyce Emily's boasts was that her brother . . had gone to fight in the Spanish Civil War.

boastful *a.* full of or given to boasting ME. **boastfully** *adv.* LME. **boastfulness** *n.* E19.

boast /bəʊst/ *n.*[2] L19. [Perh. f. Fr. *bosse* a projection of the wall in a French tennis-court.] *Real Tennis & Rackets.* A stroke which causes the ball to strike either of the side-walls before hitting the end wall.

boast /bəʊst/ *v.*[1] LME. [Origin unkn.: cf. BOAST *n.*[1]] 1 *v.t.* & *i.* Threaten, speak menacingly (to). Long *obs.* exc. *dial.* LME. 2 *v.i.* & †*refl.* Praise oneself, make boasts; brag *of*, *about*. LME. 3 *v.t.* Speak of with (excessive) pride, claim proudly (*that*). Chiefly w. obj. cl. LME. 4 *v.t.* Display ostentatiously, show off. L16. 5 *v.t.* Possess as a source of pride, have to show. L17.

boaster *n.*[1] a person who boasts ME. **boastingly** *adv.* in a boasting manner LME.

boast /bəʊst/ *v.*[2]*t.* E19. [Origin unkn.] Shape or model (stone, wood, etc., or a design in these) roughly with a chisel.

boaster *n.*[2] a heavy chisel used on masonry etc. (cf. BOLSTER *n.*[2]) L19.

boast /bəʊst/ *v.*[3]*t.* & *i.* L19. [Cf. BOAST *n.*[2]] *Real Tennis & Rackets.* Play a boast; make (a stroke) into a boast.

boat /bəʊt/ *n.* [OE *bāt* rel. to ON *beit*, f. Gmc: Du. *boot*, G *Boot*, Fr. *bateau*, have come from Eng. or Scand.] 1 A small open vessel propelled by oars, engine, or sail. Also (*colloq.*, esp. among submariners) a submarine. OE. b Any small or distinctive kind of vessel, *esp.* a fishing-vessel, mail packet, ferry, or small steamer. Also (chiefly *US*) a large seagoing vessel. L16. 2 A boat-shaped utensil for holding gravy, sauce, incense, etc. L17.

1 *cockboat, ferryboat, gunboat, houseboat, lifeboat, longboat, motor boat, narrow boat, rowing boat, showboat, speedboat, stake-boat, steamboat, tugboat, U-boat, whaleboat,* etc. *bridge of boats*: see BRIDGE *n.*[1] 1. *burn one's boats*: see BURN *v.* 8. *dreamboat*: see DREAM *n.*[2] **in the same boat** *fig.* in the same predicament, facing like risks etc. *miss the boat*: see MISS *v.*[1] **push the boat out** *colloq.* celebrate. *rock the boat*: see ROCK *v.*[1] **ship's boat** a small boat carried on board a ship. *swing-boat*: see SWING *v.* **take boat** embark in a boat. **take to the boats** escape from a sinking ship using the ship's boats; *fig.* abandon an undertaking precipitously. *the man in the boat*: see MAN *n.* 2 *gravy-boat, sauce-boat,* etc.

Comb.: **boat-axe** *Archaeol.* [Sw. *båtyx*] a boat-shaped battleaxe of the neolithic period in northern Europe; **boat-bill** a neotropical heron, *Cochlearius cochlearius*, with a broad, flat bill; **boat-cloak**: orig. for use by officers on duty at sea, now worn mainly on social occasions; **boat-deck** the deck from which a ship's boats are launched; **boat-drill** exercise in the launching and manning of a ship's boats; **boat-fly** a water-boatman; **boat-hook** a long pole bearing a hook and spike, for fending off or pulling a boat; **boat-house** a shed at the water's edge for keeping a boat or boats; **boatlift** [after *airlift* s.v. AIR *n.*[1]] the transportation of people by boat; **boatload** as many or as much as a boat will hold; **boatman** (*a*) a man who hires out a boat or boats, or who provides transport by boat; (*b*) (in full *water-boatman*) an aquatic bug of the family Notonectidae, which swims on its back; **boatmanship** (skill in) managing a boat; **boat neck(line)** a wide neckline passing below the collar-bone; **boat people** (*a*) people who live on boats; (*b*) refugees fleeing a country by boat; **boat race** (*a*) a race between rowing crews; *spec.* that between Oxford and Cambridge Universities, held annually on the River Thames from Putney to Mortlake; (*b*) *rhyming slang* the face; **boat-shaped** *a.* resembling a boat in shape; *spec.* shaped like the outline of the hull of a boat; **boat-tail** a N. American grackle, *Quiscalus major*, with a boat-shaped tail; **boat-train** a train scheduled to connect with the arrival or departure of a boat; **boatwoman** a woman who rows or manages a boat; **boat-yard**: in which boats are built and stored.

boatful *n.*, pl. **boatfuls**, †**boatsful**, as much or as many as a boat will hold LME. **boatie** *n.* (*colloq.*, chiefly *Austral.* & *NZ*) a person who goes boating, an owner of a small boat L20.

boat /bəʊt/ *v.* E16. [f. the n.] 1 *v.t.* Place or carry in a boat. E16. 2 *v.i.* Take boat, embark. *Sc.* M16. 3 *v.i.* & *t.* (w. *it*). Go in a boat; row, sail, esp. for pleasure. Chiefly as *boating* vbl n. L17. 4 *v.t.* Go in boats upon or across, navigate. L17.

1 **boat the oars** lift the oars out of the rowlocks and lay them inside the boat.

boatable *a.* navigable by boat L17. **boatage** *n.* (a charge paid for) carriage by boat E17.

boatel *n.* var. of BOTEL.

boater /ˈbəʊtə/ *n.* ME. [f. BOAT *n.* or *v.* + -ER[1].] 1 A person who rows or manages a boat; a person who goes boating. *rare.* ME. 2 A hard flat straw hat (orig. assoc. w. boating). L19.

boatswain /ˈbəʊs(ə)n/ *n.* Also BOSUN. [Late OE *bātswegen*, f. as BOAT *n.* + SWAIN.] 1 A ship's petty officer or warrant officer who has charge of sails, rigging, etc., and is responsible for summoning men to duty. LOE. 2 The Arctic skua, *Stercorarius parasiticus*. L18.

Comb.: **boatswain bird** a tropic bird; **boatswain's chair** a wooden seat suspended from ropes for work on the side of a ship or building; **boatswain's mate** a boatswain's deputy or assistant.

bob /bɒb/ *n.*[1] LME. [Origin unkn.: cf. BOB *v.*[4]] I 1 A bunch, a cluster. *north.* & *Sc.* LME. †2 The grub of a beetle used as a bait for fish. Also, a beetle (usu. in *comb.*). L16–L18. 3 A rounded mass at the end of a rod etc.; a knob. L16. b *spec.* The weight on a pendulum, a plumb-line, etc. L17. 4 An ornamental pendant; a pendent earring. M17. 5 A bunch of lobworms threaded together as bait for eels. M17. 6 A knot or bunch of hair; a short bunch, a curl resembling a tassel. L17. b In full *bob-periwig, -peruke, -wig.* A wig having the bottom locks turned up into bobs or short curls. L17. 7 A horse's tail docked short; a short knoblike tail. E18. b A style of cutting the hair short and even all round; hair cut in this way. E20. 8 A knob, knot, or bunch of coloured ribbons; a weight on the tail of a kite. M18. 9 A short sleigh-runner. *N. Amer.* M19. b In full *bob-sled, -sleigh.* Either of two types of sledge, (*a*) *US* (either of) two short sledges coupled and used for tobogganing and drawing logs; (*b*) a mechanically braked and steered sledge used in Alpine sport. M19.

II 10 The refrain or burden of a song. *arch.* E17. b The short line at the end of the stanza in some old forms of versification. Cf. WHEEL *n.* M19.

Phrases: **bear a bob** *arch.* join in a chorus. *bits and bobs*: see BIT *n.*[2] *odds and bobs*: see ODDS *n.pl.*

Comb.: **bobcat** a short-tailed N. American lynx, *Felis rufus*; *bob-periwig, -peruke*: see sense 6b above; **bobskate** *Canad.* an adjustable skate for a child's foot, consisting of two sections of double runners; *bob-sled*: see sense 9b above; **bob-sledding** riding in a bob-sled, esp. as a sport; *bob-sleigh*: see sense 9b above; **bob-sleighing** = *bob-sledding* above; *bob-wig*: see sense 6b above.

boblet *n.* a bob-sled for two people E20.

bob /bɒb/ *n.*[2] M16. [f. BOB *v.*[3]] 1 An act of bobbing or suddenly jerking up and down; *Sc.* any of various dances. M16. 2 A curtsy. E19.

bob /bɒb/ *n.*[3] *obs.* exc. *dial.* L16. [f. BOB *v.*[2]] 1 A blow with the fist. L16. 2 A sharp rebuke; a taunt, a bitter gibe. L16.

bob /bɒb/ *n.*[4] L17. [Perh. conn. w. BOB *n.*[3]] *Campanol.* One of several kinds of change in long peals.

plain bob: see PLAIN *a.*[1] & *adv.*

bob /bɒb/ *n.*[5] E18. [Pet-form of male forename *Robert.*] 1 W. certain specifying adjs. (see below): a man, a boy. E18. 2 = BOBWHITE. L19.

1 **dry-bob, wet-bob** (at Eton College) a boy who is involved in land or water sports respectively, esp. in the summer term. **light-bob** a soldier of the light infantry.

Other phrases & comb.: *Bob's-a-dying*: see BOBSY-DIE. **Bob's** (or **bob's**) **your uncle** *slang* everything is all right, the thing needed is done.

bob /bɒb/ *n.*[6] *slang.* Pl. same. L18. [Origin unkn.] A shilling (now *Hist.*); five decimal pence, a five pence piece.

bob a job: the former slogan of the Scout Association's annual fund-raising effort during which odd jobs are done for a nominal charge (orig. a shilling). **bob a nob** a payment of a shilling a head.

bob /bɒb/ *a.* M17. [Sense 1 *bob* in BOBTAIL used as a separate wd; sense 2 perh. f. BOB *v.*[3]] 1 Cut short (as a horse's tail). M17. 2 Lively; agreeable. *arch. slang.* E18.

bob /bɒb/ *v.*[1]*t. obs.* exc. *dial.* Infl. **-bb-**. ME. [OFr. *bober* befool (cf. *bobu* stupid, and Sp. *bobo* fool): see BOOBY *n.*[1]] 1 Make a fool of; deceive; cheat. ME. †2 Take by deception; filch. *rare* (Shakes.). Only in E17.

1 **bob (out) of** cheat (out) of.

bob /bɒb/ *v.*[2]*t.* Infl. **-bb-**. ME. [Prob. imit.] †1 Strike with the fist; buffet. ME–E17. 2 Cause to rap or bounce *against*, *at*, etc. (Merging into BOB *v.*[3] 2.) E17. 3 Rap, tap. M18.

bob /bɒb/ *v.*[3] Infl. **-bb-**. LME. [Prob. same wd as prec.] 1 *v.i.* Make a quick short movement up and down; rebound; dance; curtsy; come or go *in*, *into*, *up*, etc., quickly or briefly. LME. 2 *v.t.* Move (a thing) up and down with a slight jerk. (Merging into BOB *v.*[2] 2.) L17. 3 *v.t.* Move up and down quickly or briefly in (a curtsy). L19.

1 **bob and weave** make quick bodily movements up and down and from side to side (as a boxer evading punches, etc.). **bob for** try to catch (floating or hanging fruit) with the mouth, as a game.

Comb.: **bob-apple, -cherry** a game in which the players bob for apples or cherries respectively; **bob-fly** *Angling* a dry fly that bobs on the water, to indicate the position of the tail-fly.

bob /bɒb/ *v.*[4] Infl. **-bb-**. E17. [Origin unkn.: cf. BOB *n.*[1] Prob. earlier in BOBTAIL.] 1 *v.i.* Fish with a bob (*for* eels). E17. 2 *v.t.* Provide with a bob; *esp.* dock, cut short, (a horse's tail etc.). M17. b Cut (a person's hair) short and even all round. E20. 3 *v.i.* Ride on a bob-sleigh. Chiefly as *bobbing* vbl n. L19.

bobac /ˈbəʊbak/ *n.* Also **-ak**. L17. [Pol. *bobak.*] A marmot, *Marmota bobak*, of the east European and Asian steppes.

bobachee /ˈbɒbatʃiː/ *n. arch.* Also **-archee**; **-jee** /-dʒiː/. E19. [Urdu *bābarchī* f. Pers. *bāwarch.*] In the Indian subcontinent: a male cook.

Bobadil /ˈbɒbədɪl/ *n.* L18. [A character in Jonson's *Every Man in His Humour.*] A braggart who pretends to prowess.

bobajee *n.* var. of BOBACHEE.

bobak *n.* var. of BOBAC.

bobance /ˈbɒb(ə)ns/ *n.* Long *arch.* or *Hist.* ME. [OFr.] Boasting; pomp.

bobarchee *n.* var. of BOBACHEE.

bobber /ˈbɒbə/ *n.*[1] L18. [f. BOB *v.*[3] + -ER[1].] A person who or thing which bobs up and down; *spec.* in *Angling* (*a*) a type of float; (*b*) a bob-fly.

bobber /ˈbɒbə/ *n.*[2] L19. [f. BOB *v.*[4] + -ER[1].] 1 A person who bobs for eels. L19. 2 A bob-sleigh rider. E20.

bobber /ˈbɒbə/ *n.*[3] E20. [Perh. f. BOB *n.*[6], as an hourly rate of pay.] A workman who unloads fish from trawlers and drifters.

bobbery /ˈbɒb(ə)ri/ *n.* & *a.* Chiefly *Anglo-Ind.* E19. [Alt. of Hind. *Bāp re* O father! an exclam. of surprise or grief.] A *n.* A noisy disturbance; a row. E19. B *adj.* (Of a pack of hounds) miscellaneous in breed or quality; *loosely* poor in quality, made from what is available. L19.

bobbin /ˈbɒbɪn/ *n.* M16. [Fr. *bobine*, †*bobin*, of unkn. origin.] 1 A small cylinder or similar article round which thread or yarn is wound, in order to be wound off again easily and as required, for use in weaving, sewing, etc.; a reel round which wire etc. is coiled; a spool. M16. 2 A fine cord or narrow braid in haberdashery. L16. 3 A rounded piece of wood attached to a string for raising a door-latch. E18.

Comb.: **bobbin-lace** lace made by hand with threads wound on bobbins and worked over a pillow; *bobbin-net*: see next.

bobbinet /ˈbɒbɪnɛt/ *n.* Also **bobbin-net**. M19. [f. prec. + NET *n.*[1]] A machine-made cotton or silk net, orig. imitating bobbin-lace.

bobbish /ˈbɒbɪʃ/ *a. dial.* & *slang.* L18. [f. BOB *a.* or *v.*[3] + -ISH[1].] Well; in good spirits.

bobbishly *adv.* E19.

bobble /ˈbɒb(ə)l/ *n.*[1] E20. [f. BOB *n.*[1] + -LE[1].] A small woolly ball used as an ornament or trimming.

bobbled *a.* ornamented with bobbles M20.

bobble /ˈbɒb(ə)l/ *v.* & *n.*[2] *colloq.* E19. [f. BOB *v.*[3] + -LE[3].] A *v.* 1 *v.i.* & *refl.* Move with continual bobbing. E19. 2 *v.i.* & *t. Sport.* Fumble (a catch), mishandle (a ball). *US.* M20. B *n.* 1 Bobbling motion; choppiness of water. L19. 2 *Sport.* A fumbling of a catch, a mishandling of a ball. *US.* E20.

bobbly *a.* uneven, knobbly E20.

bobby /ˈbɒbi/ *n.*[1] *colloq.* Also **B-**. M19. [Pet-form of male forename *Robert*, after Sir Robert Peel (1788–1850), who founded the Irish constabulary and introduced the new Police Act in Britain in 1828. Cf. PEELER *n.*[2]] A (British) policeman.

bobby /ˈbɒbi/ *attrib. a.* & *n.*[2] L19. [Prob. f. BOB *n.*[1] + -Y[1].] A *adj.* In various collocations (see below), usu. w. the sense 'small, short'. L19.

bobby calf an unweaned calf slaughtered soon after birth. **bobby-pin** *N. Amer.* a kind of sprung hairpin or small clip, orig. for use with bobbed hair. **bobby socks**, **sox** (orig. *US*) socks reaching just above the ankle, *esp.* those worn by girls. **bobby-soxer** (usu. *derog.*) an adolescent girl wearing bobby socks. **bobby wren** *dial.* the wren.

B *n.* = *bobby calf* above. E20.

bobby-dazzler /bɒbɪˈdazlə/ *n. dial.* & *slang.* M19. [f. obscure 1st elem. + DAZZLER.] A remarkable or excellent thing or person; a strikingly-dressed person.

bobolink /ˈbɒbəlɪŋk/ *n.* Also (earlier) **bob(-o')-lincoln** /bɒb(ə)ˈlɪŋkən/ & other vars. L18. [App. imit. of the bird's call.] A N. American songbird, *Dolichonyx oryzivorus* (family Icteridae), the male of which is black with yellow and white markings, and the female yellowish buff. Also called *meadow bird*.

bobotie /bəˈbʊəti/ *n. S. Afr.* L19. [Afk., prob. of Malay or Jav. origin.] A dish of curried minced meat with a variety of additional ingredients.

bobstay /ˈbɒbsteɪ/ *n.* M18. [f. BOB (uncertain in what sense) + STAY *n.*[1]] *Naut.* A rope used to hold down the bowsprit of a ship and keep it steady.

bobsy-die /bɒbzɪˈdʌɪ/ *n. dial.*, *Austral.*, & *NZ.* Also (earlier) **Bob's-a-dying** /bɒbzəˈdʌɪɪŋ/. E19. [See BOB *n.*[5]] A great fuss, pandemonium.

bobtail /ˈbɒbteɪl/ *n.* & *v.* M16. [Prob. f. BOB *v.*[4] (though recorded earlier) + TAIL *n.*[1]] A *n.* †1 A broad-headed arrow. Only in M16. 2 (A horse or dog with) a docked tail. E17. 3†a A contemptible person. Only in E17. b *collect.* in *ragtag* (or *rag, tag*) *and bobtail*, earlier *tagrag* (or *tag, rag*) *and bobtail*. The rabble, the common herd. M17. 4 In full *bobtail discharge*. A dishonourable discharge. *US.* L19. 5 In full *bobtail flush, straight*. A hand needing one card to make a flush or a straight in draw poker. *US.* L19. B *v.t.* Dock the tail of; *fig.* curtail. L16.

bobtailed *a.* with tail cut short, short-tailed M17.

bobwhite /ˈbɒbwʌɪt/ *n.* E19. [Imit. of the bird's call.] Any of several quails constituting the American genus *Colinus*, esp. *C. virginianus*. Also *bobwhite quail*.

bob-wire /ˈbɒbwʌɪə/ *n. N. Amer. colloq.* E20. [Alt. of *barb wire*.] Barbed wire.

bocage /bəˈkɑːʒ, *foreign* bɔkaːʒ (*pl. same*)/ *n.* L16. [Fr.: see BOSCAGE.] 1 Wooded country interspersed with pasture (in France); a thicket, a wood. L16. 2 (A, the) representation of silvan scenery in ceramics. Freq. *attrib.* E20.

Bocardo /bəˈkɑːdəʊ/ *n.* E16. [A mnemonic of scholastic philosophers first used in med.L, O indicating a particular negative proposition and A a universal affirmative proposition.] 1 *Logic.* The fifth mood of the third syllogistic figure, in which a particular negative conclusion is drawn from a particular negative major premiss and a universal affirmative minor. E16. 2a *Hist.* The prison in the old North Gate of the city of Oxford, pulled down in 1771. M16. †b (**b-**.) Pl. **-os**. A prison, a dungeon. M16–E18.

bocasin /ˈbɒkəsɪn/ *n.* LME. [Sp. *bocací(n)* cotton stuff used for lining (so Fr. *boucassin*, †*boccasin*) f. Turk. *boğası*.] A fine buckram.

bocca /ˈbɒkə/ *n.* L18. [It. = mouth.] 1 A circular opening in a glass-furnace through which the pots can be inserted and withdrawn. L18. 2 A volcanic vent from which lava emerges. L19.

boccaro /ˈbɒkərəʊ/ *n.* Also **bucc-** /ˈbʌk-/. Pl. **-os**. L19. [Prob. f. Sp. *búcaro* f. Port. *púcaro* clay cup, ult. f. L *poculum* cup.] A scented red unglazed earthenware of a type orig. made by the Portuguese.

bocconia /bəˈkəʊnɪə/ *n.* E19. [mod.L, f. Paolo *Boccone* (1633–1704), Sicilian botanist: see -IA[1].] A plant or shrub of the genus *Bocconia*, of the poppy family, or one formerly included in this genus; esp. *Macleaya cordata*, which bears cream-coloured flowers.

Boche /bɒʃ/ *n.* & *a. slang. derog.* E20. [Fr. slang, = rascal, (from the war of 1914–18) German.] A *n.* A German (soldier); *the* Germans collectively. E20. B *adj.* German. E20.

bock /bɒk/ *n.* M19. [Fr. f. G, abbrev. of (*Eim*)*bockbier* = *Einbecker bier*, f. *Einbeck*, a town in Lower Saxony.] A strong dark variety of German beer; a glass or drink of this or other beer.

bocking /ˈbɒkɪŋ/ *n.* M18. [*Bocking*, a village in Essex, England.] A coarse woollen drugget or baize made in or near Bocking.

bod /bɒd/ *n. slang.* Orig. *Sc.* L18. [Abbrev. of BODY *n.*; in Sc. use perh. f. next.] A body; *esp.* a person.

odd bod: see ODD *a.*

¶Not recorded outside Scotland bef. M20.

bodach /ˈbɒdɑːx/ *n. Sc.* & *Anglo-Ir.* E19. [Gael. & Ir.] A male peasant. Also (*Sc.*), a spectre.

bodacious /bəˈdeɪʃəs/ *a.* & *adv. US dial.* M19. [Perh. var. of BOLDACIOUS.] Complete(ly), utter(ly), downright.

bodaciously *adv.* M19.

bode /bəʊd/ *n.*[1] Long *obs.* exc. *Hist.* [OE *boda* = OFris. *boda*, OS *bodo*, OHG *boto* (G *Bote*), ON *boði*, f. Gmc, f. weak grade of base of BID *v.*] A herald, a messenger.

bode /bəʊd/ *n.*[2] *arch.* & *dial.* [OE *bod* (chiefly north. for *gebod*) = OFris. *bod*, OS *gibod*, OHG *gibot* (G *Gebot*), ON *boð*, f. Gmc, f. base also of prec.] †1 A command; behest. OE–ME. †2 A message, tidings. ME–M17. 3 A bid. Long *obs.* exc *Sc.* & *north. dial.* ME. 4 A premonition, an omen; a foreboding. *arch.* LME.

Comb.: **bodeword** (*Sc.* & *north. dial.*) †(*a*) a command; †(*b*) a message; (*c*) a premonition.

bode /bəʊd/ *v.*[1] [OE *bodian* = OFris. *bodia*, f. as BODE *n.*[1]] †1 *v.t.* Announce, proclaim. OE–ME. b *v.i.* Preach the gospel. OE–ME. 2 *v.t.* Of a person: foretell, presage, have a presentiment of (esp. evil). OE. 3 *v.t.*, & *i.* w. *well, ill.* Of a thing: betoken, portend, promise. ME. †4 *v.t.* Command (a person) *that*. Only in ME.

2 B. FRANKLIN There are croakers in every country, always boding its ruin. 3 J. TYNDALL That lingering rosy hue which bodes good weather. A. SILLITOE Winnie laughed, an expression of mirth that boded no good for her husband.

bodement *n.* an augury, omen; a presentiment; a prophecy, a prediction: E17. **boder** *n.* OE. **boding** *n.* (*a*) the action of the vb; (*b*) = BODEMENT: OE. **bodingly** *adv.* ominously; with a presentiment: E19.

bode *v.*[2] var. of BUDE.

bodeful /ˈbəʊdfʊl, -f(ə)l/ *a.* E19. [f. BODE *n.*[2] + -FUL.] Ominous, presageful.

bodega /bəˈdiːɡə, *foreign* boˈdega/ *n.* M19. [Sp. f. L *apotheca*: see BOUTIQUE.] (Orig. in Spain) a shop selling wine.

bodegón /bodeˈɡɒn/ *n.* Pl. ***bodegones*** /bodeˈɡɒnes/. M19. [Sp., f. prec., as orig. representing a bodega scene.] A Spanish picture representing still life or a genre subject.

boden /ˈbəʊdɪn, ˈbɒd-/ *a. Sc. arch.* Also **-in**. LME. [Origin unkn.] †1 Accoutred, armed. LME–E19. 2 (Esp. *well, ill*) provided, prepared, dressed. LME.

Bode's law /ˈbəʊdz lɔː, ˈbəʊdəz/ *n. phr.* M19. [Johann E. *Bode* (1747–1826), Ger. astronomer, who drew attention to the law; it had been discovered earlier by another German, Johann D. Titius (1729–96).] *Astron.* An empirical formula giving the approximate distances of several planets from the sun as a geometric progression in powers of 2, starting at the orbit of Mercury.

bodge /bɒdʒ/ *v.* & *n.* M16. [Alt. of BOTCH *v.* (cf. *grudge* f. *grutch*).] A *v.t.* = BOTCH *v.* M16. B *n.* = BOTCH *n.*[2] L16.

bodger /ˈbɒdʒə/ *n.*[1] Now *dial.* M16. [f. BODGE *v.* + -ER[1].] = BOTCHER *n.*[1]

bodger /ˈbɒdʒə/ *n.*[2] *dial.* M18. [Perh. var. of BADGER *n.*[1]] A pedlar, a dealer.

bodger /bɒdʒə/ *a. Austral. slang.* M20. [Prob. f. BODGE *v.*] Inferior, worthless; (of a name) false, assumed.

bodgie /ˈbɒdʒi/ *n. Austral.* & *NZ.* Now *Hist.* M20. [Perh. f. prec. + -IE.] A young lout, a larrikin; a Teddy boy.

Bodhisattva /bɒdɪˈsɑːtvə/ *n.* E19. [Skt = a person whose essence is perfect knowledge, f. *bodhi* perfect knowledge (f. *budh-* know: see BUDDHA) + *sattva* being, reality.] *Buddhism.* In Mahayana Buddhism, a person who is near to attaining nirvana but delays doing so because of compassion for human suffering. In Theravada Buddhism, the future Buddha.

bodice /ˈbɒdɪs/ *n.* Orig. †**bodies** pl. M16. [Pl. of BODY *n.*, retaining earlier unvoiced sound of -S[1] (cf. DICE *n.*).] 1 The upper part of a woman's or girl's dress down to the waist; *spec.* the part covering the upper body (excluding sleeves); a (usu. sleeveless) undergarment for the upper body. M16. 2 *Hist. pl.* More fully *pair of bodice*. A whalebone corset for the upper body. E17.

1 *liberty bodice, petticoat bodice, Watteau bodice, Zouave bodice*, etc.

Comb.: **bodice-ripper** *colloq.* a sexually explicit romantic (esp. historical) novel or film with seduction of the heroine.

bodied /ˈbɒdɪd/ *a.* LME. [f. BODY *n.* + -ED[2]: cf. BODY *v.*] 1 As 2nd elem. of comb.: having a body of the specified kind. LME. 2 Having material form, corporeal, embodied. *rare.* M17.

1 SHAKES. *Com. Err.* Ill-fac'd, worse bodied, shapeless everywhere. *able-bodied, big-bodied, full-bodied, wide-bodied*, etc. 2 BROWNING Like the bodied heaven in clearness Shone the stone.

bodikin /ˈbɒdɪkɪn/ *n. arch.* L16. [Dim. of BODY *n.*: see -KIN.] 1 (*God's, ods*) *bodikins!* God's dear body!: an oath. L16. †2 A small body, a corpuscle. M17–L18.

bodiless /ˈbɒdɪlɪs/ *a.* LME. [f. BODY *n.* + -LESS.] Having no body; incorporeal; insubstantial.

bodily /ˈbɒdɪli/ *a.* ME. [f. BODY *n.* + -LY[1].] 1 Corporeal, physical, (opp. spiritual); real, actual. Now *rare.* ME. 2 Of, belonging to, or affecting the human body or physical nature. LME. †3 Solid; of or pertaining to a solid. M16–E17.

1 R. G. COLLINGWOOD Something bodily and perceptible, a painted canvass, a carved stone, . . and so forth. 2 T. REID My memory is not limited by any bodily organ. F. SWINNERTON A return of bodily discomforts and melancholy thoughts. *grievous bodily harm*: see GRIEVOUS *a.*

bodiliness *n.* (*rare*) corporeality, substance L16.

bodily /ˈbɒdɪli/ *adv.* ME. [f. prec.: see -LY[2].] †1 Corporeally, unspiritually. ME–L17. 2 In body, in person. LME. 3 With the whole bulk or body; as a whole, completely. L18.

2 SOUTHEY This is our father Francisco, Among us bodily. 3 E. B. BROWNING As if that . . Bodily the wind did carry The great altar. J. CONRAD To hurl himself bodily against the panels.

bodin *a.* var. of BODEN.

bodkin /ˈbɒdkɪn/ *n.* ME. [Origin uncertain; perh. dim. f. Celt. (cf. Ir. *bod*, Welsh *bidog*, Gael. *biodag* dagger).] †1 A dagger, a stiletto. ME–M17. 2 A small pointed instrument for piercing cloth etc. LME. 3 A long pin used to fasten up the hair. L16. 4 A person squeezed between two others. *arch.* M17. 5 *Printing.* An instrument for removing pieces of type for correction etc. L17. 6 A blunt thick needle with a large eye for drawing tape etc. through material. E18.

4 **ride** (**sit** etc.) **bodkin** ride etc. squeezed between two others.

bodle /ˈbɒd(ə)l/ *n.* M17. [Perh. f. a mint-master named *Bothwell*: cf. BAWBEE.] *Hist.* A Scottish copper coin equivalent to one-sixth of an English (old) penny; the smallest coin. Also called *turner*.

SIR W. SCOTT Not that I cared a brass bodle for his benison.

Bodleian /ˈbɒdlɪən, *esp. as adj.* bɒdˈliːən/ *n.* & *a.* M17. [f. Sir Thomas *Bodley* (1545–1613), Eng. diplomat, who re-founded the library in 1603, + -AN.] (Designating, of, or pertaining to) *the* Library of Oxford University.

Also **Bodley** *n.* (*colloq.*) M17.

Bodoni /bəˈdəʊni/ *n.* & *a.* L19. [See below.] (A book or edition) printed by the Italian printer Giambattista Bodoni (1740–1813); (in) a typeface based on that of Bodoni.

†**bodrag** *n.* M–L16. [Prob. f. Ir.: cf. *buaidhreadh* molestation, disturbance, tumult, OIr. *búdraise* excitement.] A hostile incursion, a raid.

Also †**bodraging** *n.*: only in L16.

body /ˈbɒdi/ *n.* [OE *bodiġ* corresp. to OHG *botah* corpse (MHG *botich*, mod. Bavarian dial. *Bottech* body of a chemise), ult. origin unkn.] I The material frame of people or animals. 1 The physical frame of a human or an animal; the whole material organism. OE. b The corporeal nature of a human; flesh as opp. to soul or spirit. ME. 2 A corpse. ME. 3 *Chr. Ch.* The consecrated bread used in the Eucharist. ME. 4 An individual, a person. Now chiefly *colloq.* ME. 5 The material being of a human; the person. LME.

1 J. STEINBECK Then down from the car the weary people climbed, and stretched stiff bodies. D. ATTENBOROUGH Elongated animals with segmented bodies. b POPE All are but parts of one stupendous whole, Whose body Nature is, and God the soul. SIR W. SCOTT While we are yet in the body. 2 SHAKES. *John* At Worcester must his body be interr'd. TENNYSON In the ghastly pit . . a body was found. 4 SHAKES. *Merry W.* 'Tis a great charge to come under one body's hand. F. WELDON She was a plump, busy little body, with a husband two years dead. *anybody, everybody, nobody, somebody.* 5 *Book of Common Prayer* With this Ring I thee wed . . with my body I thee worship.

II The main portion. 6 The main part of the human or animal frame, apart from the head and limbs; the trunk. OE. b The main stem of a tree, plant, etc. ME. 7 The main portion of something as distinct from subordinate parts or appendages, as the nave of a church, hull of a ship, load-bearing part of a vehicle, central text of a document, etc. (Foll. by *of*.) OE. 8 The majority, the larger part of anything. (Foll. by *of*.) LME. 9a The part of a dress down to the waist, or the portion of the dress that covers the body as distinct from the arms. See also BODICE. *arch.* M16. b A woman's usu. close-fitting stretch garment for the upper body, fastening at the crotch. L20. †10 A chemical retort. M16–E19. 11 *Typogr.* (The breadth of) a shank of metal type from head to tail; the nominal depth of photocomposed type. L17.

6 SHAKES. *3 Hen. VI* But when the fox hath once got in his nose, He'll soon find means to make the body follow. 7 C. COTTON The body of the Emblem was a figure of the Duke himself. A. TROLLOPE The body of the will was in the handwriting of the widow, as was also the codicil. E. BLISHEN Once inside we hurled ourselves into the body of the cinema. 8 LD MACAULAY The great body of the people leaned to the royalists. 9 A. UTTLEY Becky went upstairs to change to her blue silk body and her black skirt.

III An aggregate of individuals. 12 An artificial person created by legal authority; a corporation; an officially constituted organization, an assembly, an institution, a society. ME. 13 A force of fighting men; *gen.* an assemblage of persons or things characterized by a common purpose or attribute; a collective mass. L16. 14 A collection of the details of any subject; a collection of information; *arch.* a textbook. M17.

12 B. T. WASHINGTON The Alabama Legislature was in session. . . This body passed a resolution to adjourn. JAN MORRIS The Thames Water Authority, the managing body of the river. 13 W. ROBERTSON Escorted by a body of horse. J. P. MAHAFFY This large and respectable body of opinion. H. J. LASKI The State must live with other States, both as regards its individual members, and as a collective body. 14 ADDISON I could wish our Royal Society would compile a Body of Natural History.

IV A portion of matter; substance. 15 A separate piece of matter, a material thing. LME. b *Geom.* A figure of three dimensions, a solid. *arch.* M16. c *Anat.* & *Med.* With specifying wd: a distinguishable component of structure. M19. 16 Substance as opp. to representation; reality. LME. 17 A distinct form or kind of matter: †a Each of the seven metals, gold, silver, iron, mercury, lead, tin, and copper, answering to the seven heavenly bodies (see below). Only in LME. b *Chem.* & *Min.* Any kind of (solid, liquid, or gaseous) substance. *arch.* M16. c Paste or clay (of a particular kind) used in porcelain manufacture. L18. 18 *Metaphysics* etc. A thing which has existence and occupies space; that which is perceptible to the senses, matter. L16. 19 A compact quantity, an amount, a bulk; *spec.* a deposit of metalliferous ore. M17. 20 Comparative solidity or fullness; substantial character or flavour in a material, wine, colour, etc. M17.

15 S. JOHNSON All attraction is increased by the approach of the attracting body. F. HOYLE All bodies collapse in one way or another when the forces inside them become large enough. 16 W. VAN T. CLARK Sparks had given a kind of body . . to an ideal. 17b D. BREWSTER Crystallised bodies, such as nitre and arragonite. 18 J. S. MILL A body . . may be defined, the external cause to which we ascribe our sensations. F. BOWEN We cannot think of body without extension. 19 R. I. MURCHISON Another body of igneous rock lies subjacent. C. FRANCIS The oceans and seas of the world form one continuous body of salt water. 20 R. DAHL It [a wine] is far too light in the body to be from either St Emilion or Graves. J. C. OATES Her hair . . was dull and lusterless, and lacked body.

Phrases: *astral body*: see ASTRAL *a.* 3. *black body*: see BLACK *a.* **body corporate** a corporation. **body of Christ** (*a*) the community of the Christian Church, of which Christ is held to be the head; (*b*) = sense 3 above. **body politic** the State; organized society. **celestial body** the sun, the moon, a planet, a star, etc. **dead body** a corpse. (*over my* etc. *dead body* (hyperbol.), entirely without my etc. consent, with the strongest opposition from me etc.). *fruiting body*: see FRUIT *v. governing body*: see GOVERN *v.* **heavenly body** the sun, the moon, a planet, a star, etc. (*the seven heavenly bodies*, (in medieval astrology etc.) the sun, the moon, Mars, Mercury, Saturn, Jupiter, and Venus). *heir of one's* or *the body*: see HEIR *n.* **in a body** all together, as one. **keep body and soul together** manage to remain alive. PITUITARY *body*. *Platonic body*: see PLATONIC *a.* 1. *polar body*: see POLAR *a. soul and body lashing*: see SOUL *n. squire of the body*: see SQUIRE *n.*[1] 1c.

Comb.: **body bag** (*a*) a sleeping-bag; (*b*) a bag for carrying a corpse from the scene of warfare, an accident, a crime, etc.; **body-blow** a blow to the body in boxing etc.; *fig.* a crushing setback; **body-builder** (*a*) a person who builds vehicle bodies; (*b*) a person who develops the muscles of the body by systematic exercise; **body-building** (*a*) the building of vehicle bodies; (*b*) development of the muscles of the body by systematic exercise; **body-centred** *a.* (of a crystal structure) in which an atom or ion occurs at each vertex and at the centre of the unit cell; **body-check** *n.* & *v.* (*a*) *n.* (in various sports) the placing of one's body in the way of an opponent in order to impede him; (*b*) *v.t.* impede thus; **body clock** the biological clock of the human body; **body-colour** an opaque pigment; **body count** *colloq.* a list or total of casualties; **bodyguard** (a member of) an escort or personal guard of a dignitary etc.; **body language** gestures and movements by which a person unconsciously conveys meaning; **body-line** (**bowling**) *Cricket* fast short-pitched bowling on the leg side, threatening the batsman's body; **body louse** a human louse infesting the body rather than the head; **body odour** the (esp. unpleasant) smell of the body; **body-popping** (orig. *US*) a kind of dancing with jerky movements of the joints; **body scanner** a scanner designed to screen the whole body for the presence of cancer etc.; **body search** a search of a person's body and clothing for a hidden weapon, concealed drugs, etc.; **body-servant** a valet; **body shop** a workshop where vehicle bodies are repaired; **body-snatcher** *Hist.* an illicit exhumer of corpses for dissection; **body-snatching** *Hist.* illicit exhumation of corpses for dissection; **body-stocking** a (woman's) one-piece undergarment covering the trunk and legs; **bodysuit** a close-fitting one-piece stretch garment, esp. worn by women for sporting activities; **body type**: used for printing the main text of a book; **body wave** an artificial wave in the hair to give it fullness; **body-whorl** *Conchol.* the last-formed and usu. largest whorl of a spiral shell, containing the animal itself when alive; **bodywork** the structure of a vehicle body.

bodyhood *n.* (*rare*) the quality of having or being a body L17.

body /ˈbɒdi/ *v.t.* LME. [f. the n.] 1 Provide with a body; embody; give substance to; reinforce. *arch.* LME. 2 Foll. by *forth*: give mental shape to; exhibit in outward form; typify. L16.

Boehm /bəːm, *foreign* bøːm/ *n.* M19. [Theobald *Böhm* (1794–1881), Ger. musician.] Applied *attrib.* to a system of keys and fingering which Böhm invented, and to woodwind instruments (esp. flutes) which use this system.

Boehmenism /ˈbəːmənɪz(ə)m/ *n.* Also **Beh-** /ˈbeɪ-/. M17. [f. Jacob *Böhme* or *Boehme* (see below), known in Britain also as *Behmen*, + -ISM.] The mystical and theosophical doctrines of the German mystic Böhme, (1575–1624).

Boehmenist *n.* & *a.* M17. **Boehmist** *n.* & *a.* M18.

boehmite /ˈbəːmʌɪt/ *n.* E20. [f. Johann *Böhm* (1895–1952), Ger. chemist + -ITE[1].] *Min.* An orthorhombic basic aluminium oxide occurring esp. as a major constituent of bauxite.

Boeotarch /bɪˈəʊtɑːk/ *n.* E19. [Gk *Boiōtarkhēs*, f. *Boiōtia* Boeotia (see next) + *-arkhēs* -ARCH.] *Ancient Hist.* A chief magistrate of the Boeotian league.

Boeotian /bɪˈəʊʃ(ə)n/ *n.* & *a.* L15. [f. *Boeotia* (see below) + -AN.] A *n.* A native of Boeotia, a district of ancient Greece proverbial for the stupidity of its inhabitants; a stupid person. L15. B *adj.* Of Boeotia; dull, stupid. L16.

Boeotic /bɪˈɒtɪk/ *a.* = BOEOTIAN *a.* M17.

Boer /bɔː, ˈbəʊə, bʊə/ *n.* & *a.* M19. [Du. *boer* farmer: cf. BOOR.] A *n.* A South African of Dutch descent, an Afrikaner; *Hist.* an early Dutch inhabitant of the Cape. Cf. BOOR 1b. M19.

B *attrib.* or as *adj.* Of, made by, or typical of Boers. L19.

Boer War: between Britain and the Boer Republics in South Africa 1880–1 and (esp.) 1899–1902.

bœuf /bœf/ *n.* E20. [Fr. = beef.] *Cookery.* Used in the names of various beef dishes.

bœuf bourguignon /burgiɲɔ̃/ [= of Burgundy] beef stewed in red wine. *bœuf* STROGANOFF.

boff /bɒf/ *n. US slang.* M20. [Perh. f. *box office.*] 1 A resoundingly successful theatrical production, song, etc., a hit. M20. 2 A joke, line, etc., intended to produce a belly-laugh. M20.

boffin /ˈbɒfɪn/ *n. slang.* M20. [Origin unkn.] 1 An elderly naval officer. M20. 2 A person engaged in backroom (esp. scientific or technical) research. M20.

boffin(e)ry *n.* boffins (sense 2) collectively; the activity of a boffin: M20.

boffo /ˈbɒfəʊ/ *a. N. Amer. slang.* M20. [Abbrev. of next.] 1 (Of a review of a theatrical production etc.) wholeheartedly commendatory; resoundingly successful; extraordinarily good.

M20. **2** (Of a laugh) deep and unrestrained, loud, raucous; boisterously funny. M20.

boffola /bɒˈfəʊlə/ *n. US slang.* M20. [Extension of BOFF: cf. -OLA.] = BOFF.

Bofors /ˈbəʊfəz/ *n.* M20. [Site of a munition works in Sweden.] In full *Bofors gun* etc. A type of light anti-aircraft gun with single or twin 40-mm (approx. 1.6-inch) barrels.

bog /bɒg/ *n.*[1] ME. [Gael. (& Ir.) *bogach*, f. *bog* soft.] (A tract of) wet, spongy ground too soft to support any heavy body; *Ecol.* wet land with acid, peaty soil (cf. *fen*).

RAISED *bog*. SERBONIAN *bog*.

Comb.: *bog asphodel*: see ASPHODEL 2; **bog-bean** = BUCKBEAN; **bog berry** cranberry; **bog-blitter, -bumper** *dial.* the bittern; **bog-butter** butter of medieval or earlier origin found buried in peat-bogs; **bog fir, oak, pine**: preserved as ancient timber in a blackened state in peat-bogs; **bog-garden** a piece of land laid out and irrigated to grow plants which prefer a damp habitat; **bog-hole** a natural hole in the ground with a swampy bottom; **bog iron (ore)** soft, spongy limonite deposited in bogs; **bog-land** marshy land; *joc.* Ireland; *bog* LEMMING; **bog moss** sphagnum; **bog myrtle** a fragrant shrub, *Myrica gale*, which grows in moist ground; = GALE *n.*[1]; *bog oak*: see *bog fir* above; *bog onion*: see ONION *n.* 1b; **bog orchid** a small orchid, *Hammarbya paludosa*, with tiny yellow-green flowers; **bog ore** = *bog iron ore* above; *bog* PIMPERNEL; *bog pine*: see *bog fir* above; **bog rosemary** = ANDROMEDA 2; **bog-rush** (*a*) a densely tufted sedge of the genus *Schoenus*; esp. *S. nigricans* of Eurasia and N. Africa; (*b*) *N. Amer.* a rush of the genus *Juncus*; *bog-spavin*: see SPAVIN *n.*[1]; **bog-trot** *v.i.* trot over, live among, bogs; **bog-trotter** *derog.* an Irishman; **bog violet** (*a*) butterwort; (*b*) a violet of wet acid peaty places, *Viola palustris* (also called *marsh violet*).

bogginess *n.* boggy quality M17. **boggy** *a.* of the nature of, or characterized by, bog L16.

bog /bɒg/ *n.*[2] *colloq.* M17. [Origin uncertain: perh. same wd as prec.] A privy, a lavatory. Orig. as *bog-house* (now *arch.*).

bog /bɒg/ *v.t.* & *i.* Infl. **-gg-**. E17. [f. BOG *n.*[1]] Sink or submerge in a bog (*lit.* & *fig.*). Freq. in *pass.* and foll. by *down*.

P. V. WHITE He would proceed awkwardly across the mud, but soon became bogged. A. MOOREHEAD They . . bogged most fearfully in the waterholes. A. POWELL He gets bogged down in self-pity about the difficulties of a writer's life. **bog off** *slang* go away (usu. in *imper.*).

bogey /ˈbəʊgi/ *n.*[1] Also **bogy**. M19. [Prob. rel. to BOGLE etc., BUG *n.*[1]] **1** (As a proper name, **B-**.) The Devil. M19. **2** An evil spirit, a goblin; a bogle. Also *bogey man*. M19. **3** *fig.* A bugbear. M19. **4** A detective, a police officer. *slang.* E20. **5** A piece of nasal mucus. *colloq.* M20. **6** An unidentified enemy aircraft. *slang.* L20.

bogey /ˈbəʊgi/ *n.*[2] *Austral. colloq.* Also **bogie, bogy**. M19. [f. BOGEY *v.*[1]] A swim, a bathe; a bath.

bogey /ˈbəʊgi/ *n.*[3] L19. [Prob. f. BOGEY *n.*[1] as an imaginary opponent.] *Golf.* Orig., the number of strokes a scratch player should need for the course or for a hole. Now, a score of one over par for a hole.

double bogey: see DOUBLE *a.* & *adv.*

bogey /ˈbəʊgi/ *v.*[1]*i. Austral. colloq.* Also **bogie, bogy**. M19. [Aborig. *bu-gi*.] Swim, bathe.

bogey /ˈbəʊgi/ *v.*[2]*t.* & *i.* M20. [f. BOGEY *n.*[3]] *Golf.* Complete (a hole) in one stroke over par.

boggard /ˈbɒgəd/ *n. dial.* Also **-art** /-ət/. L16. [Rel. to BOGGLE *v.* & *n.*[2], BOGLE, etc.] **1** = BOGLE. L16. †**2** An object at which a horse boggles. E17–E18.

boggle *n.*[1] var. of BOGLE.

boggle /ˈbɒg(ə)l/ *v.* & *n.*[2] L16. [Prob. of dial. origin & rel. to BOGLE, BOGGARD, etc.] **A** *v.* **1** *v.i.* Start with fright, shy as a startled horse. L16. **2** *v.i.* Equivocate, quibble. E17. **3** *v.i.* Hesitate, demur *at, about*, etc.; (of the mind) be overwhelmed or baffled. M17. **4** *v.t.* Cause to hesitate or demur; baffle, overwhelm mentally. (*rare* bef. M20.) M17.

4 *mind-boggling*: see MIND *n.*[1]

B *n.* **1** The act of shying or taking alarm. *dial.* M17. **2** Scruple, demur. Chiefly in *make a boggle*. M17. **3** A bungle. M19.

boggler *n.* a person who boggles or hesitates E17.

bogie /ˈbəʊgi/ *n.*[1] E19. [Origin unkn.] **1** A low truck on four small wheels; a trolley. *north.* E19. **2** An undercarriage with two or more wheel-pairs, pivoted below the end of a railway locomotive, carriage, etc. M19.

bogie *n.*[2], *v.* var. of BOGEY *n.*[2], *v.*[1]

bogle /ˈbəʊg(ə)l/ *n. Sc.* & *north. dial.* Also (*north.*) **boggle** /ˈbɒg(ə)l/. E16. [Prob. rel. to BOGY.] **1** A phantom; a goblin; an undefined creature conjured up by superstitious dread. E16. **2** A bugbear; a scarecrow. M17.

Bogomil /ˈbəʊgəmɪl, ˈbɒg-/ *n.* Also **-mile** /-mʌɪl/. M19. [med.Gk *Bogomilos* f. *Bogomil*, the first propagator of the heresy, lit. 'beloved of God', f. Old Ch. Slav. *Bogŭ* god + *milŭ* dear.] *Eccl. Hist.* A member of a heretical medieval Balkan sect professing a modified Manichaeism.

Bogo'milian *a.* & *n.* M19. **Bogomilism** *n.* L19.

bogong /ˈbəʊgɒŋ/ *n. Austral.* Also **bug-** /ˈbuːg-/. M19. [Aborig.] A large dark noctuid moth, *Agrotis infusa*, prized as food by Aborigines.

bogue /bəʊg/ *n.* M19. [Fr. f. OProv. *boga* f. med.L *boca*, L, Gk *bōx*, f. *boax* a grunting fish.] A sea bream, *Boops boops*, found mainly in the Mediterranean.

bogus /ˈbəʊgəs/ *n.* & *a.* Orig. *US.* L18. [Origin unkn.] †**A** *n.* An apparatus for making counterfeit coins; a counterfeit coin. L18–M19. **B** *adj.* Spurious, sham, fictitious. M19.

bogusly *adv.* M19. **bogusness** *n.* E20.

bogy *n.*[1], *n.*[2], *v.* vars. of BOGEY *n.*[1], *n.*[2], *v.*[1]

boh *int.* & *n.* var. of BO *int.* & *n.*[2]

Bohairic /bəˈhʌɪrɪk/ *n.* & *a.* Also **Bahiric**. M19. [f. *Bohairah* etc., a province of Lower Egypt, f. Arab. *buḥayra* lake: see -IC.] (Of) the standard form of Coptic formerly spoken in Alexandria and the NW Nile Delta, and used in the Bible of the Coptic Church.

bohea /bəʊˈhiː/ *a.* & *n.* E18. [Chin. dial. *Bu-yi* var. of *Wu-yi* (see below).] **A** *adj.* Of the Wuyi hills in Fukien province, SE China, whence black tea first came to Britain; applied also to black tea grown elsewhere. E18. **B** *n.* (An infusion of) black tea, orig. of the finest, now of the lowest, quality. E18.

Bohemia /bəʊˈhiːmɪə/ *n.* M19. [f. as next in transf. uses.] The world of social Bohemians.

Bohemian /bəʊˈhiːmɪən/ *n.* & *a.* In senses A.3, B.3 also **b-**. LME. [f. *Bohemia* (see below) + -AN; senses A.2, 3, B.2, 3 f. Fr. *bohémien*.] **A** *n.* **1** A native or inhabitant of Bohemia, formerly a central European kingdom, now forming the western part of the Czech Republic. LME. **2** A Gypsy. L17. **3** A socially unconventional person, esp. an artist or writer, of free-and-easy habits, manners, and sometimes morals. M19.

B *adj.* **1** Of or pertaining to Bohemia; *loosely* Czech. E17. **2** Of or pertaining to Gypsies. M18. **3** Of, or characteristic of, social Bohemians. M19.

1 *Bohemian* WAXWING.

Bohemianism *n.* the conduct and manners of a social Bohemian M19.

bohereen *n.* var. of BOREEN.

Bohora *n.* var. of BORA *n.*[1]

Bohr /bɔː/ *n.* E20. [Niels *Bohr* (1885–1962), Da. physicist.] *Physics.* Used *attrib.* with ref. to a simple theory of atomic structure in which the nucleus is surrounded by planetary electrons in quantized orbits.

bohunk /ˈbəʊhʌŋk/ *n. N. Amer. slang.* (*derog.*) E20. [App. f. BOHEMIAN + *-hunk* alt. of HUNG(ARIAN. Cf. HUNK *n.*[3]] An immigrant from central or SE Europe; a rough fellow, a lout.

boier *n.* var. of BOYER.

boil /bɔɪl/ *n.*[1] Also †**bile**. [OE *bȳl*, *bȳle* = OFris. *bēle*, *beil*, OS *būla* (Du. *buil*), OHG *bûlla* bladder (G *Beule*), f. WGmc (cf. Goth. *uf*)*bauljan* puff up, ON *beyla* hump).] An inflamed suppurating swelling of the skin, caused usu. by infection of a hair follicle.

boil /bɔɪl/ *n.*[2] LME. [f. BOIL *v.*] **1** An act of boiling. LME. **b** *spec.* An act of making tea, esp. outdoors. M20. **2** Something boiled, a boiling preparation. M18. **3** (The state of being at) the boiling point. E19. **4** A swirling upheaval of water in a river etc.; a whirlpool. *N. Amer.* E19. **5** *Angling.* A sudden rise of a fish at a fly. L19.

1 *rolling boil*: see ROLLING *a.* 3 **off the boil** *fig.* no longer at its most active or urgent. **on** (or **at**) or **to the boil** at or to boiling point (*lit.* & *fig.*).

Comb.: **boil-off** the evaporative loss from liquefied gases; **boil-up** an act of boiling, esp. of water for making tea.

boil /bɔɪl/ *v.* ME. [OFr. *boillir* (earlier *bolir*, mod. *bouillir*) f. L *bullire* bubble, boil, f. *bulla* a bubble.] **I** *v.i.* **1** Of liquid: be at or reach the temperature at which it becomes a vapour; bubble up, undulate. Also predicated of the containing vessel or of any substance in the heated liquid (for cooking etc.). ME. **2** Move with agitation like boiling water; seethe. ME. **3** *fig.* Of passions, persons, etc.: be stirred up or inflamed. LME.

1 P. FLETCHER Boyling in sulphur, and hot-bubbling pitch. E. SMITH [Pierce] the oranges as they are boiling. B. JOWETT Putting in anything that we like while the pot is boiling. J. CHEEVER He puts some water on to boil. 2 POPE The storm thickens, and the billows boil. G. SANTAYANA A torrent romantically boiled among the wildest of rocks and bushes. 3 D. HUME Resentment was boiling in his sullen, unsociable mind. C. S. FORESTER Curzon boiled with contempt for Phelps at that moment.

II *v.t.* **4** Subject to the heat of boiling liquid; *esp.* cook in boiling water. ME. **b** *Hist.* Execute (a person) by boiling. M16. **5** Bring (liquid, the vessel containing it, a substance in it) to or keep at the boiling point; cause to bubble with heat; manufacture (soap etc.) by boiling. LME. †**b** *fig.* Agitate or inflame (a person, feelings, etc.); make fervent. LME–E18.

4 AV *Ezek.* 46:20 The place where the Priests shall boyle the trespasse offring. 5 H. GLASSE When you boil a leg of pork . . save the liquor. A. SIMON Add cream, but do not boil mixture again. B. PYM She never really used the kitchen except to boil a kettle or make a piece of toast.

Phrases: *boil a wallop*: see WALLOP *n.* 2. **boil the kettle**, (*Austral.* & *NZ*) **billy** *colloq.* make tea. *boil the pot, keep the pot boiling*: see POT *n.*[1] **one's blood boils** one is in a state of extreme anger or indignation.

With advs. in specialized senses: **boil away** *v.phr.i.* & *t.* (cause to) evaporate in boiling. **boil down** (*a*) *v.phr.t.* reduce by boiling; *fig.* condense, epitomize; (*b*) *v.phr.i.* w. *to* (*fig.*) amount to, signify basically. **boil off** *v.phr.t.* cause to evaporate in boiling. **boil over** *v.phr.i.* overflow by boiling; *fig.* (of passions etc.) get out of control, (of a person) lose one's temper. **boil up** *v.phr.i.* (*a*) reach boiling point; (*b*) *colloq.* boil water, make tea.

boiled /bɔɪld/ *a.* & *n.* LME. [f. BOIL *v.* + -ED[1].] **A** *adj.* **1** Brought to the boiling point; subjected to boiling. LME. **2** Intoxicated. *slang.* L19.

1 : *boiled lobster*: see LOBSTER *n.*[1] 2. **boiled oil** a preparation of linseed oil used as a drying-oil. **boiled shirt** a dress-shirt with a starched front. **boiled sweet** a sweet made of boiled sugar. *hard-boiled*: see HARD *a., adv.,* & *n. soft-boiled*: see SOFT *a.*

B *n.* Boiled beef, mutton, etc. *arch. colloq.* E19.

boiler /ˈbɔɪlə/ *n.* ME. [f. BOIL *v.* + -ER[1].] **1** A person who or thing which boils something. ME. **2** A vessel in which water or other liquid is boiled; *esp.* a strong vessel for generating steam under pressure in a locomotive, ship, etc.; a tank in which water is heated for central heating etc.; a metal tub for boiling laundry. E18. **3** An article of food best cooked by boiling. E19.

1 *pot-boiler*: see POT *n.*[1] 2 *Cornish boiler, double boiler, Lancashire boiler, Scotch boiler*, etc.

Comb.: **boilermaker** a person who makes boilers, a metalworker in heavy industry; **boiler-plate** (a piece of) rolled steel for making boilers; *fig.* (*US*) stereotyped writing esp. as syndicated for newspapers; *Mountaineering* (in *pl.*) smooth, overlapping, and undercut slabs of rock; **boiler suit** a one-piece garment combining overalls and shirt; **boiler-tube** each of the tubes by which heat is diffused through the water in a boiler.

boilery /ˈbɔɪləri/ *n.* E17. [Fr. *bouillerie* distillery, f. *bouillir* BOIL *v.*: see -ERY.] A place where boiling (of salt, sugar, etc.) is carried on. Freq. in *comb.*

sugar-boilery etc.

boiling /ˈbɔɪlɪŋ/ *n.* LME. [f. BOIL *v.* + -ING[1].] **1** The action of bubbling up under the influence of heat; the action of bringing to or keeping at the boiling point. LME. 2 *fig.* Violent agitation; raging. LME. 3 A substance or quantity of liquid subjected to boiling; a decoction. L17.

3 **the whole boiling** *slang* the whole lot.

Comb.: **boiling point** the temperature at which a liquid (esp. water) boils; *fig.* a state of high excitement or extreme agitation.

boiling /'bɔılıŋ/ *a.* & *adv.* ME. [f. BOIL *v.* + -ING².] A *adj.* 1 (Bubbling up) at the boiling point. ME. 2 Violently agitated; raging. LME. 3 Very hot. *colloq.* M20. B *adv. boiling hot*, very hot. *colloq.* E17.

boilingly *adv.* (*rare*) E19.

boina /bo'ina/ *n.* E20. [Sp. f. Basque.] A flat cap worn in northern Spain.

boing /bɔıŋ/ *int.* Also redupl. **boing boing**. M20. [Imit.] Repr. the noise of a compressed spring suddenly released, or a reverberating sound.

bois brûlé /bwɑ bryle/ *n. phr. N. Amer.* Pl. ***bois brûlés*** (pronounced same). E19. [Fr. = burnt wood.] An American Indian half-breed, *esp.* one of French and Indian descent.

bois d'arc /bwɑ dark/ *n. phr. N. Amer.* E19. [Fr. = bow-wood.] The wood of the maclura (Osage orange), used by American Indians for making bows.

boiserie /bwazri/ *n.* M19. [Fr.] Wainscoting, wooden panelling.

boist /bɔıst/ *n. obs.* or *dial.* ME. [OFr. *boiste* (mod. *boîte*) f. med.L *buxida* f. late Gk *puxid-*, *-is* box.] †1 A box, a casket. ME–M17. 2 A temporary bed or lodging-place. *dial.* M19.

†**boisteous** *a.* var. of BOISTOUS.

boisterous /'bɔıst(ə)rəs/ *a.* LME. [Alt. of next, through var. of *-eous*.] †1 Coarse in texture; rank; stiff, unyielding. LME–E18. †2 Of a thing: violent in action or properties. M16–L17. 3 Of a person or action: rough and turbulent in behaviour and speech; (now *esp.*) exuberant, noisily cheerful. M16. †b Savage, truculent. L16–L18. †4 Rough in effect or operation. L16–E17. 5 Of wind, weather, etc.: rough, stormy, wild. L16. †6 Massive, bulky, cumbrous. L16–M17.

boisterously *adv.* LME. **boisterousness** *n.* LME.

boistous /'bɔıstəs/ *a.* Long *obs.* exc. *dial.* Also **bustious** /'bʌstıəs/; †**-eous**, †**-uous**. ME. [Origin unkn.] †1 Of a person: rustic, coarse, unpolished. ME–M16. 2 Massive, bulky. Now only of a person: corpulent. ME. †3 Fierce, powerful, rough. LME–E19. b = BOISTEROUS 5. L15–L16. †4 = BOISTEROUS I. LME–L16.

†**boistously** *adv.* LME–L16. †**boistousness** *n.* LME–L16.

boîte /bwat/ *n.* Pl. pronounced same. E20. [Fr. = box.] A small (French) restaurant or nightclub.

bokay /bəʊ'keı/ *n. non-standard.* M19. [Repr. a pronunc.] = BOUQUET.

†**boke** *n.*¹ var. of BOKO.

boke /bəʊk/ *v.*¹*t. obs.* exc. *dial.* M16. [App. var. of POKE *v.*¹] Prod, butt.

boke *v.*² & *n.*² var. of BOLK.

Bokhara /bə'kɑːrə/ *n.* E20. [*Bukhara*, a town and district in Uzbekistan, central Asia.] A Turkoman rug or carpet (most commonly having red as the main colour).

Bokmaal *n.* var. of BOKMÅL.

bokmakierie /bɒkmə'kıəri/ *n. S. Afr.* M19. [Afk., imit. of the bird's call.] A yellow, green, and black shrike, *Telophorus zeylonus*, of southern Africa.

Bokmål /'boːkmɔːl/ *n.* Also ***Bokmaal***. M20. [Norw., f. *bok* BOOK *n.* + *mål* language.] The Danish language as modified and used in Norway after its separation from Denmark. Cf. LANDSMÅL, RIKSMÅL.

boko /'bəʊkəʊ/ *n. slang.* Pl. **-os**. Also †**boke**. M19. [Origin unkn.] The nose.

bola *n.* see BOLAS.

bolar /'bəʊlə/ *a.* L17. [f. BOLE *n.*² + -AR¹.] Consisting or of the nature of bole clay.

Also †**bolary** *a.* (*rare*): only in M17.

bolas /'bəʊləs/ *n.sing.* (w. pl. **bolases**) or *pl.* Also (*sing.*) **bola** /'bəʊlə/. E19. [Sp., Port., pl. of *bola* ball.] A missile (chiefly S. American) consisting of balls connected by a strong cord, which is thrown to entangle the legs of a quarry.

bold /bəʊld/ *a.*, *adv.*, & *n.* [OE *bald*, (WS) *beald* = OS *bald* (Du. *boud*), OHG *bald* (MHG *balt*, surviving in G adv. *bald* soon), ON *ballr* dangerous, fatal, f. Gmc.] A *adj.* 1 Courageous, enterprising, confident, stout-hearted; daring, brave. OE. 2 Presumptious, forward, immodest. ME. 3 Strong, big. Now *dial.* or *obs.* ME. †4 Certain, sure (*of*), trusting (*in*). ME–E17. 5 Of a cliff, coast, etc.: steep, projecting, bluff. Also (*Naut.*), used of water close to a steeply-shelved shore. E17. 6 Striking, well marked, clear; free or vigorous in conception etc. M17. b *Typogr.* Of type: having a heavy and conspicuous appearance. L19.

1 MILTON The bold design Pleas'd highly those infernal States. R. GRAVES Nobody could be found bold enough to take their places. W. S. MAUGHAM Though shattered, he put on a bold front. 2 K. A. PORTER The girl .. had fine eyes, but her bold, airy manner spoiled her looks. 3 A. RAMSAY Boreas with his blasts sae bauld. 4 SHAKES. *Cymb.* I would I were so sure To win the King as I am bold her honour Will remain hers. 6 S. JOHNSON I do not think Gray a first-rate poet. He has not a bold imagination.

Phrases: *as bold as brass*: see BRASS *n.* **make** or **be** (**so**) **bold** (**as**) venture, presume, (*to do*). †**make bold with** take liberties with.

Comb.: **bold-face** *n.* & *a.* (*a*) (a person who is) impudent; (*b*) *Typogr.* bold (type); **bold-faced** *a.* (*a*) that looks bold, impudent; (*b*) *Typogr.* = sense 6b above.

B *adv.* In a bold manner. Now *rare.* ME.

C *absol.* as *n.* 1 A bold person. Now only as pl. *the bold.* ME. 2 *Typogr.* Bold type. L19.

boldly *adv.* OE. **boldness** *n.* ME.

bold /bəʊld/ *v.* Long *obs.* exc. *Sc.* & *north.* [OE *baldian* = OHG *baldēn*, f. prec.] †1 *v.i.* Be or appear bold; grow strong. OE–E18. †2 *v.t.* Embolden, encourage. ME–E17. 3 *v.t.* Kindle (glowing coals); blow up (a fire). LME.

boldacious /bəʊl'deıʃəs/ *a. SW dial.* L19. [f. BOLD *a.* + AUDACIOUS.] Impudent, brazen.

bolden /'bəʊld(ə)n/ *v.t. obs.* exc. *dial.* E16. [f. BOLD *a.* + -EN⁵.] Embolden.

boldo /'bɒldəʊ/ *n.* Pl. **-os**. E18. [Amer. Sp. f. Araucanian *voldo*.] A Chilean evergreen tree, *Peumus boldus*. Also, a medicinal preparation of its leaves, formerly used as a tonic.

bole /bəʊl/ *n.*¹ ME. [ON *bolr*: cf. MHG *bole* (G *Bohle*) plank. Perh. rel. to BAULK *n.*] The stem or trunk of a tree.

bole /bəʊl/ *n.*² ME. [Late L BOLUS.] 1 Any of various kinds of fine, compact, earthy clay, usu. coloured by the presence of iron oxide. ME. †2 = BOLUS *n.* Ia. E17–E18.

1 **Armenian bole** (also †**bole Armeniac**) an astringent earth from Armenia, formerly used as an antidote and styptic.

bole /bəʊl/ *n.*³ *Sc.* Also (earlier) †**bowall**, **-ell**. E16. [Origin unkn.] 1 A small recess in a wall for holding articles; a small cupboard. E16. 2 An unglazed (usu. shuttered) aperture in a wall for admitting air or light. E19.

†**bole** *n.*⁴ L17–M19. [AL *bola*, of unkn. origin.] A place or furnace where lead ores were anciently smelted.

bolection /bə'lɛkʃ(ə)n/ *a.* & *n.* Also **ba-**. M17. [Origin unkn.] (Designating) a decorative moulding above or around a panel etc.

bolero /bə'lɛːrəʊ, *in sense 2 also* 'bɒlərəʊ/ *n.* Pl. **-os**. L18. [Sp.] 1 A lively Spanish dance; a piece of music for this dance. L18. 2 A short jacket just reaching the waist, worn by men in Spain; a woman's short open jacket, with or without sleeves. L19.

boletus /bə'liːtəs/ *n.* Also Anglicized as **bolet** /bə'lɛt/, **-lete** /-'liːt/. E16. [L *boletus* f. Gk *bōlitēs*, perh. f. *bōlos* lump.] A mushroom or toadstool of the large genus *Boletus*, having the undersurface of the cap full of pores.

bolide /'bəʊlʌıd/ *n.* E19. [Fr. f. L *bolid-*, *bolis*, f. Gk *bolis* missile.] A large meteor, a fire-ball.

bolivar /bɒlı'vɑː, bɒ'liːvɑː/ *n.* L19. [f. *Bolivar*: see next.] The basic monetary unit of Venezuela, equal to 100 centimos.

Bolivian /bə'lıvıən/ *a.* & *n.* M19. [f. *Bolivia* (see below), f. Simón *Bolívar* (1783–1830), S. Amer. soldier and statesman: see -AN.] (A native or inhabitant) of Bolivia, a republic in S. America.

boliviano /bəlıvı'ɑːnəʊ/ *n.* Pl. **-os**. L19. [Sp., f. as prec.] The basic monetary unit of Bolivia (1863–1962 and since 1987), equal to 100 centavos or cents.

bolk /bəʊk/ *v.* & *n. dial.* Also **boke**. ME. [Var. of BELCH *v.*] A *v.i.* & *t.* Belch, vomit, retch. ME. B *n.* A belch, a vomiting. LME.

boll /bəʊl/ *n.*¹ ME. [MDu. *bolle*, Du. *bol* round object: corresp. to OE *bolla* BOWL *n.*¹] †1 A bubble. Only in ME. 2 A rounded seed-vessel or pod, esp. of flax or cotton. LME.

Comb.: **boll-weevil** a weevil, *Anthonomus grandis*, which is a pest of cotton plants in N. America; **bollworm** (chiefly *US*) an insect pest of cotton, *esp.* (*a*) the boll-weevil or its larva; (*b*) = *corn ear worm* s.v. CORN *n.*¹; (*c*) = *pink bollworm* s.v. PINK *a.*²

†**bolled** *a.* having bolls. M16–M17.

boll /bəʊl/ *n.*² ME. [ON *bolli* (cf. *blótbolli* sacrificial bowl) = OE *bolla* BOWL *n.*¹: cf. prec.] A dry measure for grain etc., most commonly equivalent to six bushels.

†**boll** *n.*³ var. of BOWL *n.*¹

Bollandist /'bɒləndıst/ *n.* M18. [f. *Bolland* (see below) + -IST.] Any of the Jesuit writers who continued *Acta Sanctorum*, first published by the Flemish Jesuit John Bolland (1595–1665).

bollard /'bɒlɑːd, -ləd/ *n.* ME. [Perh. f. ON *bolr* BOLE *n.*¹ + -ARD.] 1 A post on a ship, quay, etc., for securing ropes to. ME. 2 A post on a traffic island. M20.

¶ After an isolated ME use not recorded again until 19.

bollen *v.* pa. pple of BELL *v.*²

bollix /'bɒlıks/ *v.* & *n.pl. coarse slang.* Also **-lux** /-ləks/. M20. [Alt. of *bollocks*, pl. of next.] A *v.t.* Bungle, confuse; mess *up.* M20. B *n.pl.* = BOLLOCK *n.* 2. M20.

bollock /'bɒlək/ *n. coarse slang.* Pl. **-s**, BOLLIX. M18. [Var. of BALLOCK *n.*] 1 A testicle. Usu. in *pl.* M18. 2 *fig.* In *pl.* (treated as *sing.*). Nonsense; a mess, a muddle. Also as *int.* E20.

bollock *v.* var. of BALLOCK *v.*

bollux *v.* & *n.pl.* var. of BOLLIX.

bolo /'bəʊləʊ/ *n.*¹ Also **B-**. Pl. **-os**. E20. [Paul *Bolo*, a Frenchman executed in 1918 for pro-German activities: later reinforced by association with BOLSHEVIK.] A Bolshevik, a Communist.

bolo /'bəʊləʊ/ *n.*² *US.* Pl. **-os**. M20. [Origin unkn.] *Boxing.* An upper-cut.

Bologna /bə'ləʊnjə, -'lɒn-/ *n.* M19. [A city in Italy.] 1 (Also **b-**.) In full *Bologna sausage.* A large sausage made of bacon, veal, pork-suet, etc. and usu. sold ready for eating cold. M19. 2 *Bologna spar, stone*, native barium sulphate from near Bologna, exhibiting phosphorescence when calcined. L19.

Bolognian *a.* of or pertaining to Bologna L16.

Bolognese /bɒlə'n(j)eız, *foreign* bolo'ɲeːze/ *n.* & *a.* M18. [It.: see prec., -ESE.] A *n.* Pl. same. 1 *Hist. The* territory of Bologna, in Italy. M18. 2 A native or inhabitant of Bologna. E19. 3 The Italian dialect of Bologna. M19.

B *adj.* Of or pertaining to Bologna. E19.

SPAGHETTI *Bolognese.*

bolometer /bə'lɒmıtə/ *n.* L19. [f. Gk. *bolē* ray of light + -OMETER.] *Physics.* An instrument for measuring the intensity of electromagnetic radiation (esp. infrared and microwaves) electrically.

bolo'metric *a.* of, pertaining to, employing, or measured by a bolometer; *bolometric magnitude* (Astron.), a measure of the total energy emitted (e.g. by a star) over all wavelengths: L19. **bolo'metrically** *adv.* M20. **bolometry** *n.* E20.

boloney /bə'ləʊni/ *n. slang.* Also **ba-**. E20. [f. BOLOGNA.] 1 A Bologna sausage. *N. Amer.* E20. 2 Humbug; nonsense. Also as *int.* E20.

Bolshevik /'bɒlʃıvık/ *n.* & *a.* E20. [Russ. *bol'shevik* = member of the majority, f. *bol'she* greater f. *bol'shoĭ* big.] A *n.* 1 *Hist.* A member of the majority faction of the Russian Social-Democratic Party, which in 1903 favoured extreme measures; an advocate of proletarian dictatorship in Russia by soviets; a Russian Communist. Cf. MENSHEVIK *n.* E20. 2 *gen.* A socialist revolutionary. E20. B *adj.* Of or pertaining to Bolsheviks or Bolshevism. E20.

Bolshevism *n.* the doctrine and practices of the Bolsheviks; revolutionary communism: E20. **Bolshevist** *n.* & *a.* = BOLSHEVIK E20. **Bolshevize** *v.t.* make Bolshevik; convert (a country etc.) to Bolshevik government: E20.

Bolshie /ˈbɒlʃi/ *n.* & *a. slang.* Also **-shy, b-**. E20. [f. prec. + -Y⁶.] A *n.* = BOLSHEVIK *n.* E20. B *adj.* = BOLSHEVIK *a.*; left-wing; uncooperative, recalcitrant. E20.

bolshiness *n.* L20.

bolson /ˈbəʊls(ə)n/ *n.* Orig. *US.* M19. [Sp. *bolsón* augm. of *bolsa* purse.] A basin-shaped depression surrounded by mountains, esp. in the southern US and Mexico.

bolster /ˈbəʊlstə/ *n.*[1] [OE = cushion = (M)Du. *bolster*, OHG *bolstar* (G *Polster*), ON *bolstr*, f. Gmc, perh. f. base meaning 'swell': cf. BELLY *n.*] 1 A long firm (esp. under-)pillow across a bed or couch. OE. 2 Any of various kinds of padding or support, esp. in a machine or instrument; *Naut.* a piece of wood fitted to prevent chafing. E16. †b A surgical compress. M16–E19.

bolster /ˈbəʊlstə/ *n.*[2] E20. [Prob. alt. of BOASTER *n.*[2]] A heavy chisel used to cut bricks etc.

bolster /ˈbəʊlstə/ *v.* E16. [f. BOLSTER *n.*[1]] 1 *v.t.* Support with a bolster; *fig.* prop up, aid, strengthen; uphold, aid and abet (evil, wrongdoers, etc.). Freq. foll. by *up.* E16. 2 *v.t.* Pad; stuff out with padding. M16. †b Equip with a surgical compress. E17–M19. †3 *v.i.* Share the same pillow. *rare* (Shakes.). Only in E17. 4 *v.t.* Belabour with bolsters. M19.

1 WELLINGTON I have done every thing in my power to bolster up the credit of the government. M. DRABBLE Inseparable friends, who bolstered each other by their mutual devotion. *Daedalus* The Inquisitors had bolstered their principal accusation with . . vague secondary charges.

bolstering *n.* (*a*) the action of the vb; (*b*) padding, support: M16.

bolt /bəʊlt/ *n.*[1] [OE *bolt* = MLG *bolte(n)* bolt, fetter, (M)Du. *bout*, OHG *bolz* (G *Bolzen*) arrow, bolt for a door: of unkn. origin.] I A projectile. 1 An arrow, *esp.* a short heavy one for a cross-bow. OE. 2 A discharge of lightning with a clap of thunder. (Earlier in THUNDERBOLT.) L16.

1 **have shot one's bolt** *fig.* have done all one can. 2 **a bolt from the blue** *fig.* something completely unexpected.

II 3 A stout pin for fastening; a door-fastening comprising a sliding bar and a socket on a jamb, lintel, or threshold; a metal pin with a head for holding things together, usu. secured with a nut or riveted. ME. †4 A fetter. L15–L17. 5 The sliding piece of the breech mechanism of a rifle. M19.

3 *expansion bolt, joint bolt, safety-bolt, screw-bolt, toggle-bolt*, etc. *nuts and bolts*: see NUT *n.*

III 6 A measure of rolled fabric. ME. 7 A bundle of osiers etc. of a certain size. ME.

Comb.: **bolt-head** (*a*) the head of a bolt; (*b*) *arch.* a long-necked globular flask used in distillation; **bolt-rope** a rope sewn round the edge of a sail to prevent tearing.

boltless *a.* M19.

bolt /bəʊlt/ *n.*[2] Also **boult**. LME. [f. BOLT *v.*[1]] 1 A flour-sieve. Long *dial.* LME. 2 *Hist.* A hypothetical law case privately propounded and argued for practice by students of the Inns of Court. M16.

bolt /bəʊlt/ *n.*[3] M16. [f. BOLT *v.*[2]] 1 A sudden start. M16. 2 An act of breaking away or fleeing. Freq. in *make a bolt.* M19.

bolt /bəʊlt/ *v.*[1]*t.* Also **boult**. ME. [OFr. *bulter* (mod. *bluter*), earlier *buleter* = It. *burattare*, ult. origin unkn.: the spelling *bolt* has arisen by assoc. w. BOLT *n.*[1]] Sift, pass through a sieve; *fig.* investigate, find out.

bolter *n.*[1] (*a*) a person who sifts flour etc.; (*b*) a sieve, a piece of cloth, etc., for sifting: LME. **bolting** *n.*[1] (*a*) the action of the vb; (*b*) in *pl.*, coarse matter separated by sifting: ME.

bolt /bəʊlt/ *v.*[2] ME. [f. BOLT *n.*[1]] I Move suddenly. †1 *v.i.* Spring or start (*up, upright*); fall back, recoil. ME–E19. 2 *v.t.* Discharge like a bolt; shoot, expel. LME. b Cause (an animal) to leave its hole or burrow. L16. 3 *v.i.* Move suddenly, dart, rush, (*away, forth, off*); flee, escape; spring, bound, (*into,* †*upon*). E16. b Of a rabbit, fox, etc.: escape from its burrow or earth. Of a horse: escape from control. L16. 4 *v.t.* Ejaculate, blurt (*out, forth*). L16. 5 *v.t.* Gulp down or *down* hastily without chewing. *colloq.* L18. 6 *v.t.* & *i.* Break away from, refuse to support further, (a political party etc.). *US colloq.* E19. 7 *v.i.* Of a plant: run to seed. L19.

1 SIR W. SCOTT Screaming with agony and fright, He bolted twenty feet upright. 3 N. HAWTHORNE The landlord . . keeping his eye on a man who he suspected of an intention to bolt. D. LODGE They seemed to avoid him, bolting into their offices just as he emerged from his own. 5 L. LEE I sprinkled some sugar on a slice of bread and bolted it down.

II Make fast. †8 *v.t.* Fetter, shackle. LME–E17. 9 *v.t.* Secure (a door etc.) with a bolt; shut *in, out, up*, etc., thus. L16. 10 *v.t.* Fasten (together) with bolts. E18. 11 *v.i.* Of a door etc.: be secured with a bolt (in a particular manner). E20.

9 R. HAYMAN It is useless to bolt the door against him: he breaks it down with an axe. 10 J. BRAINE My feet seemed bolted to the floor.

Comb.: **bolt-hole** a hole by which to escape; **bolt-on** *a.* (of car parts etc.) able to be fixed by bolts; *fig.* able to be added when required.

bolter *n.*[2] a person who or thing which bolts, *esp.* (*a*) a horse etc. liable to bolt; (*b*) *Austral. Hist.* a fugitive: L17. **bolting** *n.*[2] (*a*) the action of the vb (*bolting-hole* = *bolt-hole* above); (*b*) a sudden flight etc.: L17.

bolt /bəʊlt/ *adv.* ME. [f. BOLT *n.*[1], *v.*[2]] 1 *bolt upright* (or †*up*), rigidly erect (like a bolt). ME. 2 With sudden rapid motion. E19.

2 T. HOOD Bolt up the stairs they ran.

bolt-ˈuprightness *n.* E18.

boltel /ˈbəʊlt(ə)l/ *n.* Also **bowtell** /ˈbəʊt(ə)l/. LME. [Origin unkn.] *Archit.* A plain round moulding; a shaft of a clustered pillar.

bolter *n.*[1], *n.*[2] see BOLT *v.*[1], *v.*[2]

bolter *n.*[3] var. of BOULTER.

bolter *v.* var. of BALTER *v.*[2]

Boltzmann /ˈbəʊltsmən/ *n.* L19. [Ludwig *Boltzmann* (1844–1906), Austrian physicist.] *Physics.* Used *attrib.* and in *possess.* to designate various concepts, esp. relating to the statistical description of large systems of molecules obeying classical mechanics.

Boltzmann constant: see *Boltzmann('s) constant* below. **Boltzmann distribution** (a formula describing) the statistical distribution of particles in a system among different energy levels, proportional to $\exp(-E/kT)$, where E is the level energy, k is Boltzmann's constant, and T is the absolute temperature. **Boltzmann('s) constant** the gas constant per molecule, equal to 1.381×10^{-23} joule per kelvin. STEFAN-BOLTZMANN.

bolus /ˈbəʊləs/ *n.* & *v.* M16. [Late L f. Gk *bōlos* clod, lump of earth.] A *n.* 1 a A large pill of medicine. Often *contempt. arch.* exc. *Vet. Med.* (cf. sense 1c below). M16. b A small rounded mass of anything, esp. of masticated food at the moment of swallowing. L18. c *Med.* A single dose of a pharmaceutical preparation given intravenously. M20. 2 = BOLE *n.*[2] 1. Now *rare* or *obs.* L16. B *v.t.* Dose with a bolus or boluses. M18.

boma /ˈbəʊmə/ *n. E. Afr.* L19. [Kiswahili.] A defensible enclosure, esp. for animals; a police or military post; a magistrate's office.

bomb /bɒm/ *n.* L16. [Fr. *bombe* f. It. *bomba* prob. f. L *bombus* f. Gk *bombos* booming, humming, of imit. origin.] †1 *bomb of fire* [tr. Sp. *bomba de fuego*], a fire-ball (weapon). Only in L16. 2 Orig., an explosive projectile fired from a mortar. Now, a container filled with high explosive or incendiary material, smoke, poison gas, etc., or a body of high explosive etc., which may be dropped from an aircraft, fired from a gun, thrown, or deposited manually, and is exploded in various ways. L17. 3 *Hist.* In full *bomb-ketch, -vessel*, etc. A small naval vessel equipped with one or more mortars for throwing bombs. L17. 4 In full *volcanic bomb.* A rounded mass of lava thrown out of a volcano. Also *lava bomb.* L18. 5 An airtight vessel used to conduct scientific experiments under pressure. E20. 6 A large sum of money. *slang.* M20. 7 An old road vehicle. *Austral.* & *NZ slang.* M20. 8 A marijuana cigarette. *slang.* M20. 9 *N. Amer. Football.* A long pass or kick. M20.

2 *atomic bomb, buzz-bomb, hydrogen bomb, incendiary bomb, Mills bomb, nuclear bomb, plastic bomb, smoke bomb, Stokes bomb, time bomb*, etc.

Phrases: **go down a bomb** *colloq.* be a great success. **like a bomb** *colloq.* at great speed; very successfully. **the bomb** the atomic or hydrogen bomb as the supreme weapon.

Comb.: **bomb bay** a compartment in an aircraft for holding bombs; **bomb disposal** the defusing, or removal and detonation, of unexploded and delayed-action bombs; **bomb factory** a factory or other place where bombs are made, esp. illegally by terrorists; **bomb-happy** *a.* (*colloq.*) shell-shocked; *bomb-ketch*: see sense 3 above; **bombproof** *a.* & *n.* (*a*) *adj.* able to resist attack by bombs; *US* not exposed to the dangers of war; (*b*) *n.* a bombproof shelter; *US* = *bombproofer* below; **bombproofer** *US* a person who avoids exposure to the dangers of war; **bombshell** an artillery shell; *fig.* a devastating or shattering act, event, etc. (*blonde bombshell*, a fair-haired person, esp. a woman, regarded as having a startling physique or good looks); **bomb-sight** a device used in an aircraft for aiming bombs; **bomb-site** an area where buildings have been destroyed by bombing; **bomb squad** a division of a police force appointed to investigate the planting and exploding of terrorist bombs; *bomb-vessel*: see sense 3 above.

bomblet *n.* a small bomb M20.

bomb /bɒm/ *v.* L17. [f. the n.] 1 *v.t.* & *i.* Attack with a bomb or bombs; throw or drop a bomb or bombs (on). L17. b *v.t.* Drive *out* of a building etc. by bombing. E20. 2 *v.t.* Foll. by *up*: load (an aircraft etc.) with bombs. M20. 3 *v.i.* Fail, flop. *slang* (orig. *US*). M20. 4 *v.i.* Move or travel quickly. Usu. w. adv. or adv. phr. *slang.* M20.

bombed *a.* (*a*) subjected to bombing (*bombed-out*, driven out by bombing, rendered uninhabitable by bombing); (*b*) *slang* (also *bombed-out*) intoxicated by drink or drugs: M20. **bombing** *vbl n.* the action of attacking with bombs, the throwing or dropping of bombs (*bombing run*, the flight of a bombing aircraft over its target); the loading *up* of aircraft etc. with bombs: L17.

†**bombace** *n.* See also BOMBAST *n.* M16–M17. [OFr. f. med.L *bombax, -acis*, alt. of BOMBYX. Cf. BOMBAZINE.] Raw cotton; cotton fibre for padding etc.

bombachas /bɒmˈbatʃəz/ *n.pl.* M20. [S. Amer. Sp., f. *bombacho* loose-fitting, wide.] Baggy trousers worn in some S. American countries.

bombard /ˈbɒmbɑːd/ *n.* In sense 2 also **-de**. LME. [(O)Fr. *bombarde*, med.L *bombarda*, prob. f. L *bombus*: see BOMB *n.*] 1 *Hist.* A cannon of the earliest type, usu. firing stone cannon-balls. LME. 2 *Mus.* A low-pitched shawm. LME. b A bombardon stop in an organ. L19. 3 A leather jug or bottle for liquor. *obs.* exc. *Hist.* L16. †4 = BOMB *n.* 3. L18–M19.

bombard /bɒmˈbɑːd/ *v.* L16. [Fr. *bombarder*, f. as prec.] 1 *v.t.* & †*i.* Fire heavy guns at, batter with shot and shell, assault with artillery. L16. 2 *v.t. transf.* & *fig.* Assail forcefully (*with* arguments, questions, abuse, etc.); subject to a hail of missiles. M18. b *Physics.* Subject (a substance) to a stream of high-energy particles. E20. 3 *v.t.* Stuff (a fillet of veal). Now *rare* or *obs.* M18.

bombarder *n.* L16. **bombardment** *n.* E18.

bombardier /bɒmbəˈdɪə/ *n.* M16. [Fr.: see BOMBARD *n.*, -IER.] 1 A soldier in charge of a bombard, an artilleryman; a master-gunner's man employed with mortars and howitzers. Now *arch.* or *Hist.* M16. 2 In the British army, a non-commissioned officer in the artillery. M19. 3 An aimer and releaser of bombs from an aircraft. *N. Amer.* M20.

Comb.: **bombardier beetle** any of various carabid beetles able to eject audibly an irritant vapour when alarmed; spec. *Brachinus crepitans*, found in Britain.

bombardon /ˈbɒmbɑːd(ə)n/ *n.* Also **-done** /-ˈdəʊni/. M19. [It. *bombardone* augm. of *bombardo* BOMBARD *n.*] *Mus.* A low-pitched brass instrument of the tuba family; an organ reed-stop imitating this.

†bombase *v.t.* See also BOMBAST *a.* M–L16. [f. BOMBACE.] Stuff (with cotton wool), pad.

bombasine *n.* var. of BOMBAZINE.

bombast /ˈbɒmbast/ *n.* M16. [Var. of BOMBACE.] **1** Raw cotton; cotton wool, esp. as padding. *obs.* exc. *Hist.* M16. **2** *fig.* Inflated, turgid, or high-sounding language; empty rhetoric. L16.

bomˈbastic *a.* of the nature of bombast; given to inflated language: E18. **bomˈbastical** *a.* (*arch.*) = BOMBASTIC M17. **bomˈbastically** *adv.* E19.

bombast /ˈbɒmbast/ *a.* M16. [Orig. pa. pple of BOMBASE *v.*; later = the n. used attrib.] **†1** Stuffed, padded. M16–M17. **2** *fig.* Puffed, empty, inflated; grandiloquent, bombastic. E17.

bombast /bɒmˈbast, ˈbɒmbast/ *v.t. arch.* M16. [f. the n.] **†1** Stuff or pad with cotton wool or the like. M16–E19. **2** *fig.* Stuff, swell out, inflate. M16.

bombax /ˈbɒmbaks/ *n.*[1] M19. [mod.L f. L BOMBYX.] Any deciduous tropical tree of the genus *Bombax*, bearing fruit containing seeds surrounded by a silky fibre; *esp.* the Indian silk-cotton tree, *B. ceiba*.

†bombax *n.*[2] var. of BOMBYX.

Bombay duck /ˌbɒmbeɪ ˈdʌk, bɒmˌbeɪ/ *n. phr.* M19. [Alt. of *bombil* (see BUMMALO), infl. by *Bombay* (now Mumbai), a city in India.] Bummalo, esp. dried as a relish.

bombazine /ˈbɒmbəziːn/ *n.* Also **-sine**. M16. [(O)Fr. *bombasin* f. med.L *bombacinum* f. *bombycinum* neut. of *bombycinus* silken, f. BOMBYX: see -INE[1].] **†1** = BOMBACE. M–L16. **2** A twilled dress-material of worsted with or without silk or cotton; *esp.* a black kind formerly much used in mourning. L16.

bombe /bɒmb, *foreign* bɔ̃ːb (*pl. same*)/ *n.* L19. [Fr. = BOMB *n.*] A conical or cup-shaped confection, freq. frozen.

bombé /bɔ̃be/ *a.* E20. [Fr., pa. pple of *bomber* swell out: cf. next.] Esp. of furniture: rounded, convex.

bombed /bɒmd, *poet.* ˈbɒmbɪd/ *a.*[1] *rare.* L19. [f. as prec. + -ED[1].] Rounded, convex.

bombed *a.*[2] see BOMB *v.*

bomber /ˈbɒmə/ *n.* E20. [f. BOMB *v.* + -ER[1].] **1** A person who throws, plants, activates, or is otherwise involved in the use of, bombs, esp. as a terrorist. E20. **2** An aircraft used for dropping bombs. E20. **3** A large rolled cigarette containing marijuana, cannabis resin, etc. Also, a barbiturate drug. *slang.* M20.

Comb.: **bomber jacket** a jacket tightly gathered at the waist and cuffs.

bombilate /ˈbɒmbɪleɪt/ *v.i. literary.* L19. [med.L *bombilat-* pa. ppl stem of *bombilare* buzz, f. L *bombus*: see BOMB *n.*, -ATE[3]. Cf. BOMBINATE.] Buzz, hum.

bombiˈlation *n.* M17.

bombilla /bɒmˈbɪljə/ *n.* M19. [Amer. Sp., dim. of Sp. *bomba* strainer.] A tube with a strainer at the end, from which maté is drunk in S. America.

bombinate /ˈbɒmbɪneɪt/ *v.i. literary.* L19. [med.L *bombinat-* pa. ppl stem of *bombinare* buzz, f. L *bombus*: see BOMB *n.*, -ATE[3]. Cf. BOMBILATE.] Buzz, hum.

bombiˈnation *n.* E19.

bombora /bɒmˈbɔːrə/ *n. Austral.* M20. [Aborig.] A dangerous stretch of water where waves break over a submerged reef.

bombyx /ˈbɒmbɪks/ *n.* Also **†-ax**. LME. [L f. Gk *bombux*.] A silkworm or silkworm moth.

bombykol *n.* a pheromone secreted by the female of the silkworm moth *Bombyx mori* M20.

bon /bɔ̃/ *a.* [Fr.: see BOON *a.*] The Fr. (masc.) for 'good', occurring in various phrases used in Eng.

bon appétit /bɔn apeti/ [lit. 'good appetite']: used as a salutation to a person about to eat M19. ***bon chrétien*** /kretjɛ̃/, pl. ***-s -s*** (pronounced same), [lit. 'good Christian'] any of several varieties of pear L16. ***bon enfant*** /bɔn ɑ̃fɑ̃/ [lit. 'good child'] good company M19. ***bon gré mal gré*** /gre mal gre/ [lit. 'good will, ill will'] (whether) willingly or unwillingly E19. ***bon jour*** /ʒuːr/, ***bonjour*** *int.* good day, hello L16. ***bon mot*** /mo/, pl. ***-s -s*** (pronounced same), [lit. 'good word'] a clever or witty remark, a witticism M18. ***bon ton*** /tɔ̃/ [lit. 'good tone'] the fashionable world, *arch.* good breeding M18. ***bon vivant*** /vivɑ̃/, pl. ***-s -s*** (pronounced same), [lit. 'who lives well'] a gourmand, an epicure L17. ***bon viveur*** /vivœːr/, pl. ***-s -s*** (pronounced same), [pseudo-Fr. after *bon vivant*, f. *viveur* a living person] a person who lives luxuriously M19. ***bon voyage*** /vwajaːʒ/ [lit. 'pleasant journey']: used as a salutation to a person about to travel L17. (See also *no bon* s.v. NO *a.*)

bona fide /ˌbəʊnə ˈfʌɪdi/ *adv.* & *a. phr.* M16. [L = with good faith (abl. of next).] (Acting or done) in good faith; sincere(ly), genuine(ly).

bona fides /ˌbəʊnə ˈfʌɪdiːz/ *n. phr.* L18. [L = good faith.] **1** Good faith, freedom from intent to deceive. L18. **2** (Erron. treated as pl.) Guarantees of good faith, credentials. M20.

bonaght /bəˈnɔːt/ *n.* M16. [Ir.] *Ir. Hist.* A tax or tribute levied by Irish chiefs for the maintenance of soldiers.

bonallie /bɒˈnali/ *n. arch. Sc.* Also **bonnail(lie)** /bɒˈneɪl(ɪ)/. L15. [f. (O)Fr. BON + *aller* go.] (A wish for) a good journey, farewell.

Esp. in *drink a person's bonallie*.

bonanza /bəˈnanzə/ *n.* & *a.* Orig. *US.* E19. [Sp. = fair weather, prosperity, f. L *bonus* good.] **A** *n.* A run of good luck, an unexpected success (orig. esp. in mining); prosperity; a source of great wealth or good fortune. E19. **B** *adj.* Greatly prospering or productive. L19.

Bonapartist /ˈbəʊnəpɑːtɪst/ *n.* & *a.* Also **Buon-**. E19. [f. *Bonaparte* (see below) + -IST.] *Hist.* **A** *n.* An adherent of the government and dynasty of Napoleon Bonaparte (1769–1821), Emperor of France. E19. **B** *adj.* Of or adhering to Bonaparte or Bonapartism. E19.

Bonapartism *n.* attachment to or advocacy of the government and dynasty of Napoleon E19.

bona-roba /bəʊnəˈrəʊbə/ *n.* Now *rare* or *obs.* L16. [It. *buonaroba*, f. *buona* good + *roba* dress.] A wench; a prostitute.

bonasus /bəˈnasəs/ *n.* Now *rare* or *obs.* Pl. **-nasi** /-ˈnasʌɪ, -ˈnasiː/. L16. [L f. Gk *bonasos*.] The European bison.

bona vacantia /ˌbəʊnə vəˈkantɪə/ *n. phr.* M18. [L = ownerless goods (*vacare* be ownerless).] *Law.* Goods without any apparent owner, and to which the Crown has right.

bonaventure /bɒnəˈvɛntʃə/ *n. obs.* exc. *Hist.* L15. [It. *bonaventura* lit. 'good fortune', f. †*bona* (now *buona*) good + *ventura* fortune.] *Naut.* A lateen sail carried on an extra mizen mast; the mast itself. Freq. as *bonaventure mast* or *mizen*.

¶Commonly found as a ship's name, with its It. signification.

bonavist /ˈbɒnəvɪst/ *n.* M17. [Perh. f. *Bona Vista* var. of Boa Vista, Cape Verde islands.] = LABLAB. Also *bonavist bean*.

bon-bon /ˈbɒnbɒn/ *n.* L18. [Fr., lit. 'good-good': see BON.] A piece of confectionery, a sweet.

bonbonnière /bɔ̃bɔnjɛːr (*pl. same*)/ *n.* a fancy box for holding sweets E19.

bonce /bɒns/ *n.* M19. [Origin unkn.] **1** (A game played with) a large marble. M19. **2** The head. *slang.* L19.

bond /bɒnd/ *n.*[1] & *a.* LOE. [ON *bóndi* occupier and tiller of the soil (cf. HUSBAND *n.*) f. *bóandi* use as n. of pres. pple of *bóa* var. of *búa* dwell, f. Gmc base also of BOOTH.] **A** *n.* **†1** A householder, a husband. Only in LOE. **†2** A peasant. Only in ME. **3** A serf, a base vassal; a slave. *obs.* exc. *Hist.* ME. **B** *adj.* **1** In a state of slavery; in bondage; tied *to*. *arch.* ME. **†2** Servile, slavish. LME–M16.

Comb.: **bond-land** *Hist.* land held by bondage; **bondmaid(en)** a slave girl; **bondman** (now *arch.* or *Hist.*) a peasant; a serf, a slave; a villein; **bondmanship** the state or condition of a bondman; **bondservice** slavery; **bondslave** a slave; a person in a state of utter servitude; **bondwoman** a slave-woman.

bond /bɒnd/ *n.*[2] ME. [Alt. of BAND *n.*[1], preserving more the connection with *bind*, *bound*.] **I** *lit.* **1** Something with which a person is bound; a shackle; a fetter; confinement, imprisonment, custody. Now usu. in *pl.* ME. **2** Something with which a thing is tied, fastened to another, or made to cohere. ME. **†3** A bandage. LME–L17.

1 MILTON To endure Exile, or ignominy, or bonds, or pain. **2** L. T. C. ROLT Bags of clay laced with hazel rods to form a bond.

II *fig.* **4** A restricting or imprisoning circumstance; a constraining force, a tie. ME. **†b** Obligation, duty. LME–M17. **5** A binding engagement, an agreement. ME. **6** A uniting or cementing force or influence; adhesion, union. LME.

4 F. M. FORD To enjoy a woman's favours made him feel that she had a bond on him for life. D. H. LAWRENCE Breaking the bonds of authority. **5** R. C. SHERRIFF An honourable man whose word was his bond. **6** J. LOCKE Speech being the great Bond that holds Society together. J. GALSWORTHY Attached to the dead by the bond of kinship. W. H. AUDEN Siblings can live in a bond / as close as wedlock.

III Legal & techn. uses. **7** A deed by which one person binds himself or herself to pay another; a (government's) documentary promise to repay borrowed money, usu. with interest; a debenture; an insurance policy; a financial guarantee against the collapse of a company, esp. a tour operator etc. L16. **8** Surety; *spec.* security for a released prisoner's return for trial, bail. Now *arch.* & *US.* M17. **9** The jointing or fastening of masonry, timber, etc.; *esp.* any of various methods of holding a wall together by making bricks overlap. L17. **10** Storage of goods in special warehouses under the charge of Customs pending the payment of duty by the importer. Chiefly in *in bond*, *out of bond*, etc. M19. **11** *Chem.* A linkage between atoms in a molecule; *esp.* = *covalent bond* s.v. COVALENT *a.* M19. **12** *Electr.* A conductor connecting metal parts, esp. for the purpose of earthing. M19. **13** In full *bond paper*. Writing-paper of high quality suitable for bonds etc. L19.

9 **English bond** *Bricklaying*: with alternate courses of headers and stretchers. **Flemish bond** *Bricklaying*: with courses of alternate headers and stretchers. **monk bond** *Bricklaying*: with courses alternating with pairs of stretchers. **11** *double bond*: see DOUBLE *a.* & *adv.* *metallic bond*: see METALLIC *a.* *sigma-bond*: see SIGMA 2a.

Comb.: **bondholder** a person holding a bond granted by a private person or company; *bond paper*: see sense 13 above. **bondstone** a stone or brick running through a wall to bind or strengthen it; **bond-washing** dividend-stripping.

bond /bɔ̃nt/ *n.*[3] *S. Afr.* Also ***B-***. L19. [Afk. f. Du. (= G *Bund*), f. *binden* bind.] An Afrikaner league or association.

bond /bɒnd/ *v.* L16. [f. BOND *n.*[2]] **I** *v.t.* **1** Pledge or confirm by a bond. L16. **b** In *pass.* Of a travel agency, tour operator, etc.: be bound by an agreement limiting loss and inconvenience to customers if the company should cease trading. L20. **2** Reinforce or make solid by a bond or bonds; bind (bricks etc.) together by making them overlap; cement or clamp together; hold together by embedding in a solid. L16. **3** Connect by overlapping or by a bond *to*. L18. **4** Put (goods) into bond. E19. **5** Subject to bondage. M19. **6** Connect by means of an electrical bond. L19. **7** *Chem.* Join or hold by a chemical bond. Freq. in *pass.* E20. **8** Join or hold by an emotional or psychological bond. M20.

4 **bonded warehouse**: where goods are kept in bond.

II *v.i.* **9** Hold together; adhere. M19. **10** Form an emotional or psychological bond (*with*). L20.

10 A. TYLER She and her husband need to bond with the baby.

bonding *n.* (*a*) the action of the vb; (*b*) the manner in which bricks, atoms, etc., are bonded, bonds collectively: L17.

bondage /ˈbɒndɪdʒ/ *n.* & *v.* ME. [AL *bondagium*, f. BOND *n.*[1]: see -AGE. Infl. in sense by BOND *n.*[2]] **A** *n.* **1** Serfdom, slavery; *Hist.* tenure in villeinage, services due from a tenant to a proprietor. ME. **2** The condition of being bound or tied; *fig.* subjection to authority, constraining force, or obligation. LME. **b** *spec.* Sado-masochism involving binding, handcuffing, etc. M20. **3** That which binds; obligation. *rare.* E17. **B** *v.t.* Reduce to bondage, enslave. *arch.* E17.

bondager *n.* (*Hist.*) a person who performs services as a condition of feudal tenure; in S. Scotland and NE England, a female outworker supplied to a proprietor by a tenant: M19.

bonder /ˈbɒndə/ *n.*[1] *rare.* M19. [f. BOND *v.* + -ER[1].] **1** *Building.* A binding stone or brick. M19. **2** A person who puts goods into bond or owns goods in bond. L19.

bonder /ˈbɒndə/ *n.*[2] M19. [Erron. f. Norw. *bonde*, pl. *bönder*.] *Hist.* A Norwegian peasant farmer or petty freeholder.

bondieuserie /bɔ̃djøzri/ *n.* Pl. pronounced same. M20. [Fr., f. *bon* good + *Dieu* God.] A church ornament or devotional object, *esp.* one of little artistic merit; such objects collectively.

bondsman /ˈbɒn(d)zmən/ *n.* Pl. **-men.** E18. [f. BOND *n.*[1], *n.*[2] + -'S[1] + MAN *n.*] **1** A person who stands surety for a bond. E18. **2** A person in bondage, a slave; = *bondman* s.v. BOND *n.*[1] M18.

bonduc /ˈbɒndʌk/ *n.* L17. [Fr. f. Arab. *bunduk* hazelnuts, ult. f. Gk *pontikon* marine (*karuon* nut).] = *nicker-tree* s.v. NICKER *n.*[4]

bone /bəʊn/ *n.* [OE *bān* = OFris., OS *bēn* (MDu., LG *been*), OHG, G *bein*, ON *bein*, f. Gmc.] **1** Any of the pieces of hard tissue that make up the skeleton of a vertebrate animal, and consist largely of calcium phosphate or carbonate in a matrix of collagen fibres. OE. **b** (Part of) a bone to which some meat adheres, providing possible sustenance. LME. **c** *spec.* A bone used by Australian Aborigines in spells to cause death or sickness. E20. **2** In *pl.* The skeleton; the body; the mortal remains; *fig.* the essential framework of anything. OE. **3** The bony structure of the body; the body's hard, solid, or essential part. OE. **4** The material or tissue of the bones; any similar animal substance, as ivory, dentine, etc. OE. **5** An article orig. or usu. made from bone or ivory, *esp.* a domino, (in *pl.*) dice, castanets. LME. **b** *spec.* A strip of whalebone or other stiffening material in a corset etc. L16. **6** A dollar. *US slang.* L19.

1 *backbone, breastbone, cheek-bone, collar-bone, frontal bone, funny-bone, jawbone, knuckle-bone, marrowbone, shin-bone, thigh-bone, wishbone*, etc. **2** P. LARKIN The plain bones of the matter is just this: if you're prepared to work . . we shall get on splendidly. W. GOLDING Here the bones of the land showed, lumps of smooth grey rock. **3** DICKENS An immense brown horse displaying great symmetry of bone. **4** *whalebone* etc.

Phrases: **a bone in her mouth** *Naut.* (*arch.*) water foaming before a ship's bows. **a bone in one's leg** (or **head**) *colloq.* a (feigned) reason for idleness. **a bone to pick with someone** a dispute or problem to resolve with someone. *bag of bones*: see BAG *n.* **bare bones** the mere essentials. *be skin and bone*: see SKIN *n.* **bone of contention** a subject of dispute. *bred in the bone*: see BRED *ppl a.* **close to the bone** = *near the bone* below. *dog and bone*: see DOG *n.* **feel, know,** etc., **in one's bones**: instinctively, in one's innermost being. *lay one's bones*: see LAY *v.*[1] *long bone*: see LONG *a.*[1] **make no bones about** not hesitate or scruple about. **make old bones** live to an old age. NAPIER'S BONES; **near the bone** (*a*) destitute; (*b*) near the permitted limit (esp. of decency). **point the bone**: in an Australian Aboriginal ritual intended to bring about a person's death or sickness. *rack of bones*: see RACK *n.*[4] *roll the bones*: see ROLL *v.* *skin and bone*: see SKIN *n.* **to the bone** *fig.* to the bare minimum; penetratingly. **work one's fingers to the bone** work very hard.

Comb.: **bone-ache** *arch.* pain in the bones, *spec.* as a symptom of venereal disease; **bone-ash** the mineral residue of calcined bones; **bone-black** a mixture of bone-ash and charcoal obtained by carbonizing bones; **bone breccia** breccia containing fossil bones; **bone-charcoal** = *bone-black* above; **bone china** chinaware made of clay mixed with bone-ash; **bone-dry** *a.* completely dry; **bone-earth** = *bone-ash* above; *bonefire*: see BONFIRE; **bonefish** (chiefly *N. Amer.*) a fish with many small bones, spec. *Albula vulpes*, a silvery marine game-fish; **bonehead** *slang* a stupid person; **boneheaded** *a.* (*slang*) thick-headed, stupid; **bone idle** *a.* utterly idle; **bone-lace** bobbin-lace of a type orig. made with bone bobbins; **bone lazy** *a.* utterly lazy; *bone marrow*: see MARROW *n.*[1] 1; **bone-meal** crushed or ground bones used esp. as fertilizer; **bone-oil** dark, fetid oil obtained in the carbonizing of bones; **bone-seed** a chiefly southern African plant of the genus *Osteospermum*, of the composite family; **bone-seeking** *a.* (of a substance) tending to be deposited in the bones; **bone-setter** a person who sets broken or dislocated bones, esp. without being a qualified surgeon; **boneshaker** *colloq.* a jolting vehicle; *Hist.* a bicycle without rubber tyres; *bone spavin*: see SPAVIN *n.*[1]; **bone-tired** *a.* utterly tired; *bone turquoise*: see TURQUOISE *n.* 2; **bone weary** *a.* utterly weary; †**bone-wort** any of various plants held to be of use in healing bone, e.g. the daisy and the violet; **bone-yard** a place where the bones of dead animals are deposited; *slang* a cemetery.

boned *a.* having bones (of a specified kind) ME. **boneless** *a.* without bones; *fig.* wanting backbone or will-power; *boneless wonder*: see WONDER *n.*: OE. **boner** *n.* (*slang*, orig. *US*) a stupid mistake E20.

bone /bəʊn/ *v.*[1] L15. [f. the n.: sense 3 is perh. a different wd.] **1** *v.t.* Remove the bones from (meat, fish, etc.). L15. **2** *v.t.* Treat or equip with bone, esp. as stiffening or strengthening. L17. **3** *v.i.* Apply oneself diligently; study intensively. Usu. foll. by *up*, study hurriedly. (Foll. by *on* the object of study etc.). *slang* (orig. *US*). M19. **4** *v.t.* Point a bone at (a person) as part of an Australian Aboriginal ritual intended to bring about death or sickness. E20.

bone /bəʊn/ *v.*[2]*t.* *slang.* L18. [Origin unkn.] Seize; snatch, steal.

boneen /bəˈniːn/ *n.* *Anglo-Ir.* Pl. **-s**, same. M19. [Ir. *bainbhín*, f. *banbh* sucking-pig + *-in* dim. suff.] A young pig.

†**bonefire** *n.* & *v.* var. of BONFIRE.

boneset /ˈbəʊnsɛt/ *n.* L17. [Prob. f. BONE *n.* + SET *v.*[1], on account of medicinal use.] †**1** Comfrey. Only in L17. **2** A plant of the composite family, *Eupatorium perfoliatum*, bearing white flowers; = THOROUGHWORT 2. *N. Amer.* E19.

boneta *n.* var. of BONITO.

bonfire /ˈbɒnfʌɪə/ *n.* & *v.* Also †**bonefire.** LME. [f. BONE *n.* + FIRE *n.*] **A** *n.* Orig., a large open-air fire in which bones were burnt; also, a fire in which heretics, proscribed books, etc., were burnt. Now, any large open-air fire kindled for the disposal of waste material, brushwood, garden refuse, etc., or in celebration of some event or occasion (as was often the case with 'bone-fires'), or for other purposes. LME.

W. RALEIGH Celebrate the victorie with bonefiers in euerie town. **make a bonfire of** destroy.

Comb.: **Bonfire Night** 5 November, the anniversary of the Gunpowder Plot (1605), on which large fires are built and effigies of the conspirator Guy Fawkes are burnt.

B *v.t.* & *i.* Light bonfires (in). E17.

bong /bɒŋ/ *n.*[1] & *v.i.* Orig. *US.* E20. [Imit.] (Emit) a low-pitched sound as of a bell.

bong /bɒŋ/ *n.*[2] M20. [Prob. imit.] *Mountaineering.* A large piton.

bongo /ˈbɒŋgəʊ/ *n.*[1] Pl. same, **-s.** M19. [Kikongo.] A large striped antelope, *Tragelaphus euryceros*, of central Africa.

bongo /ˈbɒŋgəʊ/ *n.*[2] Pl. **-o(e)s.** E20. [Amer. Sp. *bongó*.] Either of a pair of small drums, usu. held between the knees and played with the fingers.

bongrace /ˈbɒngreɪs/ *n.* M16. [Fr. *bonnegrace* lit. 'good grace': see BON, GRACE *n.*] **1** A shade worn on the front of a woman's bonnet to protect the complexion. *obs.* exc. *Hist.* M16. **2** A broad-brimmed hat. *arch.* & *dial.* L16.

bonham /ˈbɒnəm/ *n.* *Anglo-Ir.* L19. [Ir. *banbh*.] A sucking-pig.

bonheur du jour /bɒnœːr dy ʒuːr/ *n. phr.* Pl. ***bonheurs du jour*** (pronounced same). L19. [Fr., lit. 'happiness of the day'.] A small writing-table, usu. fitted to hold toilet accessories, popular in 18th-cent. France.

bonhomie /ˈbɒnəmiː/ *n.* Also †**-hommie.** L18. [Fr., f. next + *-ie* -Y[3].] Good-natured friendliness, geniality.

bonhomous *a.* showing bonhomie E20.

bonhomme /ˈbɒnɒm, *foreign* bɔnɔm (*pl. same*)/ *n.* E16. [Fr., lit. 'good man, good fellow': in med.L *bonus homo*.] *Hist.* A member of an order of medicant friars who arrived in England in the 13th cent.

†**bonhommie** *n.* var. of BONHOMIE.

Boniface /ˈbɒnɪfeɪs/ *n.* *arch.* E19. [A character in G. Farquhar's *Beaux' Stratagem*.] (A name for) an innkeeper.

boniform /ˈbɒnɪfɔːm/ *a.* L17. [mod.L *boniformis* (Henry More) tr. Gk *agathoeidēs* (Plato): see -FORM.] Cognizant of moral goodness; having the form of good.

bonify /ˈbɒnɪfʌɪ/ *v.t.* E17. [Fr. *bonifier* improve, f. as BON + *-fier* -FY.] †**1** Benefit. Only in E17. **2** Make good; turn into good. L17.

boning /ˈbəʊnɪŋ/ *n.* L18. [Origin unkn.] *Surveying* etc. The process of judging the straightness of a surface or line by eye, as by looking along the tops of two straight edges, or along a line of poles. Freq. *attrib.*

bonism /ˈbɒnɪz(ə)m/ *n.* L19. [f. L *bonus* good + -ISM.] The doctrine that the world is good, but not the best possible.

bonist *n.* L19.

bonitary /ˈbɒnɪt(ə)ri/ *a.* M19. [f. late L *bonitarius* f. L *bonitas* goodness + *-arius* -ARY[1].] *Rom. Law.* Beneficial; having beneficial possession without formal legal title.

Also **boni'tarian** *a.* M19.

bonito /bəˈniːtəʊ/ *n.* Pl. **-os.** Also **boneta** /bəˈniːtə/. L16. [Sp.] Any of various striped tuna, esp. *Sarda sarda* of the Atlantic and Mediterranean.

†**bonity** *n.* L16–L18. [L *bonitas* goodness, BOUNTY: see -ITY.] Goodness.

bonjour *int.* see BON.

bonk /bɒŋk/ *n.* *slang.* M20. [Imit.] **1** An abrupt heavy sound of impact; a bump. M20. **2** An act of sexual intercourse. L20.

bonk /bɒŋk/ *v.t.* & *i.* *slang.* E20. [Imit.] **1** Hit resoundingly; bang, bump. E20. **2** Have sexual intercourse (with). L20.

bonkers /ˈbɒŋkəz/ *a.* *slang.* M20. [Origin unkn.: see -ER[6].] Crazy; insane.

bonnail, bonnaillie *ns.* vars. of BONALLIE.

bonne /bɒn/ *a.* & *n.* E16. [Fr., fem. of BON.] **A** *adj.* Good. Long restricted to certain phrs. adopted from Fr. (see below). E16.

(*à la*) ***bonne femme*** /(a la) bɒn fam/ [lit. 'in the manner of a good housewife'] applied esp. postpositively to designate particular dishes of food. ***bonne bouche*** /buʃ/, pl. ***-s -s*** (pronounced same), [Fr. = mouth] a dainty morsel, a titbit, esp. to end a meal. ***bonne fortune*** /bɒn fɔrtyn/, pl. ***-s -s*** (pronounced same), a lady's favours, as a source of pride for the recipient.

B *n.* Pl. pronounced same. †**1** A good girl. Only in E16. **2** A (French) nursemaid. L18.

bonnet /ˈbɒnɪt/ *n.* LME. [OFr. *bonet* f. med.L *abonnis* headgear.] **1a** A head-dress of men and boys, usu. soft and brimless; a round brimless Scotch cap. LME. **b** An outdoor head-dress of women or children, usu. with no brim at the back, and tied with strings. L15. **c** The ceremonial head-dress of an American Indian. Usu. more fully *war-bonnet.* M19. **d** *Her.* The velvet cap within a coronet. L19. **2** *Naut.* An additional strip of canvas laced to the foot of a sail to catch more wind. LME. **3** A raised portion of a fortification at a salient angle, serving to protect from enfilade fire etc. L17. **4** The reticulum or second stomach of a ruminant. L18. **5** A thing or person used to put a good face on underhand proceedings. *arch. slang.* E19. **6** A protective cover or cap, *esp.* a hood over the engine of a motor car, a cowl on a chimney, etc. M19.

1a fill a person's bonnet fill a person's place. *have a bee in one's bonnet*: see BEE *n.*[1] *poke-bonnet*: see POKE *n.*[3] *Scotch bonnets*: see SCOTCH *a.* *vail* (*the* or *one's*) *bonnet*: see VAIL *v.*[2] 2.

Comb.: **bonnethead** a hammerhead shark, *Sphyrna tiburo*, with a relatively narrow head; **bonnet laird** *arch.* a petty Scottish landowner wearing a bonnet like the humbler classes; **bonnet monkey** an Indian macaque, *Macaca radiata*, having a tuft of hair on top of the head; **bonnet-piece** a gold coin of James V of Scotland, on which the king is represented wearing a bonnet; ***bonnet rouge*** /bɒnɛ ruːʒ/, pl. ***-s -s*** (pronounced same), [Fr. = red] the red cap of the

French sansculottes of 1793, taken as a symbol of the revolutionary spirit.

bonnet /ˈbɒnɪt/ *v.* E17. [f. the n.] †1 *v.i.* Take off the bonnet in token of respect. *rare* (Shakes.). Only in E17. 2 *v.t.* Put a bonnet on. E19. 3 *v.t.* Crush down the hat of (a person) over the eyes. M19.

bonnibel /ˈbɒnɪbɛl/ *n. arch.* L16. [Perh. f. Fr. *bonne et belle* 'good and fair'.] A fair maid.

bonny /ˈbɒni/ *a. dial.* & *colloq.* L15. [Origin uncertain: perh. to be referred to OFr. BON (fem. *bone*) good.] 1 Pleasing to the sight; comely; expressing homely beauty. *Sc.* & *north.* L15. 2 Nice, good, fine. Often *iron. Sc.* & *north.* M16. †3 Smiling; bright. L16–E19. 4 Of fine size, big. Now usu. (healthily) plump, looking well. L16.

bonnily *adv.* L16. **bonniness** *n.* E17.

bonny-clabber /ˈbɒnɪklabə/ *n. Anglo-Ir.* E17. [Ir. *bainne clabair* thick milk for churning, f. *bainne* milk, *clabar* dasher of a churn.] Milk naturally clotted on souring.

bonobo /ˈbɒnəbəʊ/ *n.* Pl. **-os.** M20. [Afr. name.] The pygmy chimpanzee, *Pan paniscus*, of Zaire.

bonsai /ˈbɒnsʌɪ/ *n.* Pl. same. E20. [Jap., f. *bon* tray + *sai* planting.] The (Japanese) practice of cultivating artificially dwarfed potted plants or small trees; a plant or tree cultivated by this method.

bonsense /ˈbɒns(ə)ns/ *n.* L17. [f. Fr. BON good, after *nonsense*.] Good sense.

bonspiel /ˈbɒnspiːl/ *n. Sc.* M16. [Prob. of LG origin: cf. WFlem. *bonespel* a children's game.] A sporting contest, a match. Now *spec.* a major curling-match.

bontebok /ˈbɒntəbɒk/ *n.* Also **-tb-** /-tb-/. Pl. same. L18. [Afk., f. Du. *bont* pied + *bok* BUCK *n.*[1]] A reddish white-faced southern African antelope (usu. regarded as conspecific with the blesbok *Damaliscus dorcas*).

bonus /ˈbəʊnəs/ *n.* L18. [Prob. joc. or ignorant use of L *bonus* (masc.) for *bonum* (neut.) good thing: prob. orig. Stock Exch. slang.] 1 Something, esp. money, over and above that which is normally expected; something to the good or into the bargain. Occas., a douceur, a bribe. L18. 2 *spec.* An extra dividend paid to shareholders of a company; a portion of profits allowed to the holder of an insurance policy; a gratuity to employees beyond their normal pay. E19.

2 *no-claim(s) bonus*: see NO *a.*

Comb.: **bonus issue** = *scrip issue* s.v. SCRIP *n.*[3]

bonxie /ˈbɒŋksi/ *n.* Orig. *Shetland.* L18. [Norw. *bunksi*, f. *bunke* dumpy body f. ON *bunki* heap (cf. Norw. *bunke* fat woman).] The great skua.

bony /ˈbəʊni/ *a.* LME. [f. BONE *n.* + -Y[1].] 1 Of, pertaining to, or of the nature of bone or bones; consisting or made of bone or bones. LME. 2 Having many bones; having large or prominent bones, esp. with little flesh. LME.

Special collocations: **bony fish** (*a*) a fish with bones rather than a cartilaginous skeleton, i.e. a member of the class Pisces (or Osteichthyes), to which the majority of living fishes belong; (*b*) *N. Amer.* the menhaden, *Brevoortia tyrannus*. **bony labyrinth** *Anat.* the system of bony canals and chambers surrounding the membranous labyrinth of the inner ear.

boniness *n.* L19.

bonze /bɒnz/ *n.* L16. [Fr. *bonze* or Port. *bonzo* (prob. f. Jap. *bonzō*, *bonsō* priest.] A Japanese or Chinese Buddhist religious teacher.

bon'zess *n.* (*rare*) a female bonze M19.

bonzer /ˈbɒnzə/ *a. Austral.* & *NZ slang.* E20. [Perh. alt. of BONANZA.] Excellent, first-rate.

boo /buː/ *n.*[1] *slang.* M20. [Origin unkn.] Marijuana.

boo /buː/ *int.*, *n.*[2], & *v.* E19. [Imit.: cf. BO *int.* & *n.*[2]] A *int.* & *n.* A prolonged sound expressing derision or disapproval, or an exclamation intended to startle. Occas., a sound (as) of cattle lowing. E19.

can't say boo to a goose is very timid or shy.

B *v.t.* & *i.* Make such a sound (at); jeer (a person, an action, etc.). E19.

booer *n.* E20.

booay /ˈbuːʌɪ/ *n. NZ colloq.* Also **boo(h)ai.** M20. [Perh. f. place-name *Puhoi*, N. Auckland, NZ.] *The* remote rural districts.

up the booay completely wrong or astray.

boob /buːb/ *n.*[1] & *v. slang* (orig. *US*). E20. [Abbrev. of BOOBY *n.*[1]] A *n.* 1 = BOOBY *n.*[1] 1. E20. 2 A lock-up, a cell. E20. 3 A foolish mistake. M20.

Comb.: **boob tube** *n.*[1] *the* or a television.

B *v.i.* Make a foolish mistake. M20.

boob /buːb/ *n.*[2] *slang* (orig. *US*). M20. [f. BUB *n.*[3] or abbrev. of BOOBY *n.*[2]] A woman's breast. Usu. in *pl.*

Comb.: **boob tube** *n.*[2] a woman's low-cut close-fitting usu. strapless top.

boobialla *n.* var. of BOOBYALLA.

booboisie /buːbwɑːˈziː/ *n. US slang.* E20. [Joc. f. BOOB *n.*[1] after *bourgeoisie*.] Boobs as a class, stupid people.

boo-boo /ˈbuːbuː/ *n. slang* (orig. *US*). E20. [Prob. redupl. of BOOB *n.*[1]] 1 A prank, a trick. E20. 2 = BOOB *n.*[1] 3. E20.

boobook /ˈbuːbʊk/ *n.* E19. [Aborig., imit. of the bird's call.] In full *boobook owl*. A small brown spotted owl, *Ninox novaeseelandiae*, native to Australasia. Also called *mopoke*, *morepork*.

booby /ˈbuːbi/ *n.*[1] E17. [Prob. f. Sp. *bobo* (in both senses), f. L *balbus* stammering, stuttering: see -Y[6].] 1 A silly, stupid, or childish person. E17. 2 Any of various sea birds of the genus *Sula*, closely related to the gannet. M17.

Comb.: **booby-hatch** (*a*) *Naut.* a small companion or hatch-cover; (*b*) *US slang* a lock-up, a cell; an asylum; **booby prize**: awarded in fun or ridicule to the last competitor, lowest scorer, etc.; **booby trap** (*a*) something designed as a practical joke to catch the unwary, *esp.* an object placed on top of a door so as to fall on the first opener; (*b*) an apparently harmless device concealing an explosive charge designed to go off when tampered with; **booby-trap** *v.t.* place one or more booby traps in or on.

boobyish *a.* awkward and silly L18.

booby /ˈbuːbi/ *n.*[2] *slang* (orig. *US*). M20. [Alt. of BUBBY *n.*[1]] = BOOB *n.*[2] Usu. in *pl.*

boobyalla /buːbɪˈalə/ *n. Austral.* Also **boobi-.** M19. [Aborig.] Any of various coastal trees and shrubs, *esp.* a wattle, *Acacia longifolia*, or a shrub of the genus *Myoporum*.

boodie /ˈbuːdi/ *n. Austral.* M19. [Aborig.] A rat-kangaroo, *Bettongia lesueuri*. Also *boodie-rat*.

boodle /ˈbuːd(ə)l/ *n.* & *v. slang* (chiefly *US*). E17. [Du. *boedel*, *boel* possessions, disorderly mass, = OFris. *bōdel* movable goods, LG *bödel*.] A *n.* 1 Crowd, pack, lot; = CABOODLE. E17. 2 Money; *spec.* money acquired or spent illegally or improperly; proceeds of corruption. M19. B *v.t.* & *i.* Bribe; give or take bribes. L19.

¶ Rare bef. 19.

boodler *n.* a person who gives or takes bribes L19.

boogaloo /buːgəˈluː/ *n.* & *v.i.* Chiefly *US.* M20. [Perh. alt. of BOOGIE-WOOGIE after *hullabaloo* etc.] (Perform) a dance with swivelling and shuffling movements.

boogie /ˈbuːgi/ *n.*[1] *US slang. derog.* E20. [Perh. alt. of BOGEY *n.*[1]] A Black.

boogie /ˈbuːgi/ *n.*[2] & *v.* E20. [Origin unkn.] A *n.* 1 A party, *esp.* a rent party. *US slang.* E20. 2 = BOOGIE-WOOGIE. M20. B *v.i.* Dance (orig. to boogie-woogie music). M20.

boogie-woogie /buːgɪˈwuːgi/ *n.* E20. [Prob. redupl. of BOOGIE *n.*[2]] A percussive style of playing blues, esp. on piano, with a repetitive bass figure.

boohai *n.* var. of BOOAY.

boohoo /buːˈhuː/ *int.*, *n.*, & *v.i.* M19. [Imit.] (Make) a sound of loud esp. childish weeping, or occas. laughter or derision.

boojum /ˈbuːdʒəm/ *n.* L19. [Nonsense wd invented by Lewis Carroll.] An imaginary dangerous animal.

book /bʊk/ *n.* [OE *bōc* = OFris., OS *bōk* (Du. *boek*), OHG *buoh* (G *Buch*), ON *bók* (cf. Goth. *bōka* letter of the alphabet), f. a Gmc base usu. taken to be rel. to BEECH, as the wood of rune-tablets.] 1 A writing, a written document; a charter, a deed. Long *obs.* exc. *Hist.* OE. †2 A narrative, a record, a list. OE–L17. 3 A collection of sheets of paper or other material, blank, written, or printed, fastened together so as to form a material whole; *esp.* one with sheets pasted or sewn together at the edge, with protective covers; a literary composition of any kind long enough to fill one or more such volumes. OE. 4 *spec.* a *The* Bible. Formerly also, a copy of the Bible. ME. b A volume of blank sheets in which financial transactions, minutes, notes, etc., are entered; in *pl.*, accounts, annals, records. LME. c The script of a play, film, etc.; the libretto of an opera, oratorio, etc. L16. d A magazine. Now *colloq.* E19. e A record of bets made with several different people on a particular race etc. E19. f *The* telephone directory. E20. 5 A main subdivision of a literary composition; any of the component works forming the Bible. ME. 6 Book learning, study, scholarship. Now only in *pl.*, passing into sense 3. ME. †b Benefit of clergy. E17–E18. 7 *fig.* Anything from which one may learn or be instructed; an imaginary narrative, record, etc. LME. 8 A set of things bound or collected together to resemble a book, e.g. sheets of gold leaf, tickets, matches, stamps, six tricks at cards, etc.; an aggregate of laminar crystals. L15.

1 AV *Jer.* 32:12 The witnesses, that subscribed the booke of the purchase. 2 AV *Gen.* 5:1 The booke of the generations of Adam. 3 G. GISSING She must read the best books that had been written on the training of children's minds. ALDOUS HUXLEY Life became safe, things assumed meaning, only when they had been translated into words and confined between the covers of a book. R. HOGGART Of another author's books more than six million copies are said to have been sold in three years. K. A. PORTER She sits in her deep chair with an open book on her knees. *commonplace-book*, *daybook*, *guidebook*, *handbook*, *hymn-book*, *log-book*, *notebook*, *picture-book*, *prompt-book*, *scrapbook*, *service-book*, *textbook*, *wordbook*, etc. 4b J. MORLEY The books show that the nett profits . . had exceeded £23,000 for the year. B. HINES Just tell him to put it in t' book and I'll pay him at t' week-end. e P. G. WODEHOUSE I am still willing to make a little book from time to time to entertain sportsmen and gentlemen. 5 SHAKES. *Hen. V* In the book of Numbers is it writ. J. GROSS As a child, Mill [had] . . an entire book of *The Faerie Queene* read aloud to him. 6 SHAKES. *Merry W.* My son profits nothing in the world at his book. 7 SHAKES. *Wint. T.* My name put in the book of virtue! J. G. STRUTT That great poet to whom the book of Nature . . seemed . . laid open.

Phrases: *bell, book, and candle*: see BELL *n.*[1] *black book*: see BLACK *a.* *blue book*: see BLUE *a.* **book of fate** the future as being predetermined. **book of life** *Theol.* the record of those achieving salvation. *book of reference*: see REFERENCE *n.* 7. **book of words** a libretto; a set of rules etc. **bring to book** call to account. **by the book** according to the rules; in set phrases. **closed book** a thing of which one has no understanding. **close the books** make no further entries, cease business etc. *comic book*: see COMIC *a.* **good book** *the* Bible. *have one's nose in a book*: see NOSE *n.* **in someone's bad** (or **black**), **good, books**: in disfavour, favour, with someone. **in my book** as I see the matter. **know someone like a book** have a thorough knowledge of someone's character. *make a book*: see MAKE *v.* **not in the book** not allowed, irregular. *one for the book*: see ONE *a.*, *n.*, & *pron.* **on** (or **upon**) **the books** listed as a member etc., on the staff. *open book*: see OPEN *a.* **people of the Book** the Jews and Christians as regarded by Muslims. **read someone like a book** understand someone's motives or intentions fully. *red book*: see RED *a.* SEALED *book*. *Sibylline books*: see SIBYLLINE *a.* **speak** etc. **like a book**: with full or correct information. **suit one's book** be convenient to one. *symbolical books*: see SYMBOLICAL 4. *take a leaf out of a person's book*: see LEAF *n.*[1] *talking book*: see TALKING *ppl a.* **throw the book at** make all possible charges against. *upon the books*: see *on the books* above. **without book** from memory; without authority.

Comb.: **bookbinder** a person whose trade is bookbinding; **bookbindery** a bookbinding establishment; **bookbinding** the binding of books; **bookcase** a case containing shelves for books; **book club** a society whose members can buy selected books on special terms; **book-craft** *arch.* scholarship; authorship; **book-end** either of a pair of often ornamental props for keeping a row of books upright; **book-fell** *Hist.* a skin prepared for writing on; a vellum or parchment manuscript; **book-hand** *Hist.* a formal style of handwriting used by professional transcribers of books before the invention of printing; **bookkeep** *v.i.* [back-form.] do bookkeeping;

bookkeeper a person responsible for keeping the accounts of a trader, public office, etc.; **bookkeeping** (the art of) keeping accounts; **bookland** *Hist.* land granted by charter into private ownership; **book-Latin** Latin; scholarly language; **book-learned** *a.* knowing books (but lacking practical experience); **book learning, -lore** knowledge gained from books, mere theory; **book-louse** a minute insect of the order Psocoptera, injurious to old books; **book-lung** a lamellate respiratory organ of an arachnid; **bookmaker** (*a*) a professional betting person; a person who manages a betting-shop; (*b*) (usu. *derog.*) a compiler of books; †(*c*) a printer and bookbinder; **bookmaking** the trade or action of a bookmaker; **bookman** (*a*) a scholar; (*b*) an author or publisher, a literary man; **bookmark(er)** a strip of leather, paper, etc., for marking one's place in a book; **bookmobile** *N. Amer.* a mobile library; **book-muslin** fine muslin (folded like a book when sold in the piece); **book name** a name for a plant or animal (other than its scientific name) not widely used except in books; **book page** (*a*) a page of a book; (*b*) a page of a newspaper etc. devoted to reviews of books; **book-plate** a label affixed to a book as a mark of ownership; **book-post** the transmission of books by post at special lower rates; **book-rest** an adjustable support for an open book on a table etc.; **book-scorpion** a small pseudoscorpion, *Chelifer caucroides*, found in houses; **bookseller** a dealer in books; **bookselling** the selling of books, esp. as a trade; **bookshop** a shop where books are sold; **book-shy** *a.* reluctant or unwilling to read books; *bookstack*: see STACK *n.* 1c; **bookstall** a stall for the sale of books out of doors or in a station etc.; **bookstore** *N. Amer.* a bookshop; **book token** a voucher exchangeable for books costing up to a specified amount of money; **book-trough** a V-shaped rack for displaying books on a table etc. to show their titles; **book value** value as entered in a book, as opp. to market value; **book-wise** *a.* = *book-learned* above; **bookwork** the studying of textbooks, as opp. to practical work; **bookworm** (*a*) a beetle- or moth-larva destructive to books; (*b*) *fig.* a person devoted to reading.

bookful *n.* the entire contents of a book; as much as fills a book: L16. **bookless** *a.* destitute of books; *poet.* unscholarly, uneducated: L16. **booklet** *n.* a small book, esp. if paper-covered M19. **booklike** *adv.* & *a.* (*a*) *adv.* in the manner of a book; (*b*) *adj.* resembling (that of) a book: M19. **bookling** *n.* (now *rare*) a tiny book E19. **booky** *a.* (*colloq.*) bookish M19.

book /bʊk/ *v.* OE. [f. the n.] **1** *v.t.* Grant or assign (land) by charter. *obs.* exc. *Hist.* OE. **2** *v.t.* Enter in a book or list; record, register, enrol. ME. **b** *spec.* Of a police officer, referee, etc.: make an entry of or against the name of (a person) for an (alleged) offence; *slang* apprehend, catch. M19. **c** *v.t.* & *i.* Register the arrival or departure of (a guest at a hotel, an employee, etc.), or of oneself. Usu. foll. by *in*, *out*, or *off*. E20. **3** *v.t.* & *i.* Engage (one or more seats, tickets, etc.) for oneself or others, usu. in advance; reserve. E19. **b** *v.t.* Engage seats, rooms, transport, etc., for; issue a travel ticket to. E19. **4** *v.t.* Engage (a person) as a guest, performer, etc. L19.

bookable *a.* E20.

booker /ˈbʊkə/ *n.* OE. [f. BOOK *n.* + -ER[1]: later re-formed on BOOK *v.*] †**1** A writer of books. OE–ME. **2** A person who makes entries in a book etc., a bookkeeper. M19.

bookie /ˈbʊki/ *n. colloq.* L19. [Abbrev.: see -IE.] = *bookmaker* (a) s.v. BOOK *n.*

booking /ˈbʊkɪŋ/ *n.* L16. [f. BOOK *v.* + -ING[1].] **1** The action of BOOK *v.*; an instance of this. L16. **2** *spec.* **a** A reservation of a seat, room, ticket, etc. L19. **b** The issue of a ticket for travel. L19. **c** The recording of a person's name for an (alleged) offence. M20.

2b *booking-clerk, -hall, -office*, etc.

bookish /ˈbʊkɪʃ/ *a.* M16. [f. BOOK *n.* + -ISH[1].] **1** Of or pertaining to a book or books; (of language) literary rather than colloquial. M16. **2** Studious, addicted to reading books; getting knowledge only from books. L16.

bookishly *adv.* M17. **bookishness** *n.* L16.

booksy /ˈbʊksi/ *a. colloq.* M20. [f. BOOK *n.* + -SY.] Having literary or bookish pretensions.

bool *n.* var. of BOUL.

Boolean /ˈbuːlɪən/ *a.* Also **-ian**. M19. [f. George *Boole* (1815–64), Eng. mathematician + -AN.] Of, pertaining to, or described by an abstract system of postulates and symbols applicable to logical problems.

boom /buːm/ *n.*[1] L15. [f. BOOM *v.*[1]] A loud deep resonant sound as of a distant explosion, breaking surf, a bass drum, etc.; a hum or buzz; the cry of the bittern.

sonic boom: see SONIC 2.

Comb.: **boom box** *slang* a portable radio and cassette recorder.

boomy *a.*[1] having a loud, deep, resonant sound E19.

boom /buːm/ *n.*[2] M16. [Du. = BEAM *n.*, tree, pole.] †**1** *gen.* A beam, a pole. Only in M16. †**2** A pole set up to mark a channel etc. in water. L16–M18. **3** A bar or barrier stretched across a river etc. to obstruct navigation. E17. **b** A line of floating timber stretched across a river etc. to retain or guide floating logs. *N. Amer.* L17. **4** A long spar or pole hinged at one end, securing the bottom of a ship's sail. E17. **b** In *pl.* Part of a sailing ship's deck where the spare spars are stowed. M18. **5** A movable arm supporting a camera, microphone, etc. M20.

Phrases: *lower the boom*: see LOWER *v.*[1]

boom /buːm/ *n.*[3] Orig. *US*. L19. [Prob. f. BOOM *v.*[1]] A sudden increase or development esp. in business or economic activity; a rapid rise in the price of a commodity, in profits, etc.

attrib.: R. LOWELL The risk—a small one in those boom years—of resigning from the Navy. **boom and bust** (a cycle of) great prosperity followed by economic slump.

Comb.: **boom town** a town owing its origin, growth, or prosperity to a boom in some commodity or activity.

boomlet *n.* a small boom, esp. on a stock exchange L19. **boomy** *a.*[2] of or pertaining to a boom in business etc. L19.

boom /buːm/ *v.*[1] LME. [Ult. imit.: perh. f. Du. *bommen* hum, buzz.] **1** *v.i.* Make a loud, deep, resonant sound; hum or buzz like a bee etc.; speak loudly and with deep resonance. Of the (male) bittern: utter its characteristic resonant call. LME. **2** *v.i.* Rush violently along. M16. **3** *v.t.* Give forth or utter with a booming sound. Usu. foll. by *out*. M19.

booming *n.* (*a*) the action of the vb; (*b*) a deep resonant sound: M16. **boomingly** *adv.* with a booming sound M19.

boom /buːm/ *v.*[2]*t.* E17. [f. BOOM *n.*[2]] Provide with a boom or booms; extend (a sail) with a boom (usu. foll. by *out*).

boom /buːm/ *v.*[3] Orig. *US*. L19. [f. BOOM *n.*[3]] **1** *v.i.* Burst into sudden economic activity; prosper. L19. **2** *v.t.* Force upon the attention of the public, promote. L19.

1 K. M. E. MURRAY Trade for him never boomed and he earned only about twelve shillings a week. 2 S. LEACOCK We're doing all we can . . to boom Toronto as a Whisky Centre.

boomer /ˈbuːmə/ *n.* M19. [Prob. f. BOOM *v.*[1] + -ER[1]. In branch II ellipt.] **I1** A large male kangaroo. *Austral.* M19. **2** Something large or notable of its kind. *Austral. slang.* L19. **II3** = *baby boomer* s.v. BABY *n.* M19. *colloq.* (chiefly *N. Amer.*). L20.

boomerang /ˈbuːməraŋ/ *n.* & *v.* L18. [Aborig., perh. modified: cf. Kamilaroi *būmarin*.] **A** *n.* **1** A thin curved hardwood missile (of a kind) used by Australian Aborigines as a hunting weapon, *esp.* one that can be thrown so as to return to the thrower. L18. **2** *fig.* A scheme etc. that recoils on its originator. M19. **B** *v.i.* Act as a boomerang; *fig.* recoil on the originator. L19.

boomslang /ˈbuːmslaŋ/ *n.* L18. [Afk., f. Du. *boom* tree + *slang* snake.] A highly venomous southern African tree-snake, *Dispholidus typus*.

boon /buːn/ *n.*[1] ME. [ON *bón* (Sw., Da. *bön*) f. Gmc base also of BENE.] †**1** A prayer, a petition; the asking of a favour. ME–E17. †**2** A request made with authority; a command couched as a request. ME–L16. **3** The matter prayed for or asked; a thing asked as a favour. *arch.* ME. **4** Something, now esp. an immaterial thing, freely given whether in response to asking or not; a gift, a gratuity. *arch.* LME. **5** *Hist.* An unpaid service due by a tenant to the landlord. L16. **6** A gift considered with reference to its value to the recipient; a blessing, an advantage. M18.

3 J. MASEFIELD You in my life for always is the boon I ask from life. 4 R. C. TRENCH The gods had no better boon for him than an early death. F. HOYLE Our expected lifetime (granted the boon of indefinite good health) would be a few thousand years. 6 H. KELLER It is an unspeakable boon to me to be able to speak in winged words that need no interpretation. B. RUSSELL Enjoying more of what makes life a boon and not a curse.

Comb.: **boon service, work** *Hist.* unpaid service due by a tenant to the landlord.

boon /buːn/ *n.*[2] LME. [Origin unkn.: cf. BUN *n.*[1]] The stalk of flax or hemp after the fibre has been removed.

boon /buːn/ *a.* LME. [(O)Fr. *bon* f. L *bonus* good.] †**1** Good, goodly. LME–L17. †**2** Advantageous, fortunate, favourable. LME–M17. **3** Convivial, jolly, genial. Orig. & chiefly in *boon companion*. M16. **4** Gracious, bounteous, benign. *poet.* E17.

boon /buːn/ *v.* ME. [f. BOON *n.*[1]] †**1** *v.t.* Pray for, ask as a boon. Only in ME. **2** *v.i. Hist.* Do boon service. *rare.* L17. **3** *v.t.* Repair (public roads). *obs.* exc. *dial.* L18.

boondock /ˈbuːndɒk/ *n. N. Amer. slang.* M20. [Tagalog *bundok* mountain.] *sing.* & (usu.) in *pl.* Rough or isolated country; remote parts.

boondoggle /ˈbuːndɒg(ə)l/ *n.* & *v. N. Amer. slang.* M20. [Origin unkn.] **A** *n.* A trivial, useless, or unnecessary undertaking. Also, a dishonest undertaking, a fraud. M20. **B** *v.i.* Engage in such an undertaking. M20.

boong /buːŋ/ *n. Austral. slang. derog.* M20. [Aborig.] An Aborigine; a native of New Guinea; any non-White person.

boongary /buːnˈgɛːri/ *n. Austral.* L19. [Aborig.] A tree-kangaroo, *Dendrolagus lumholtzi*, of northern Queensland.

boor /bʊə/ *n.* M16. [LG *būr* or Du. *boer*: repr. earlier by OE *ġebūr*. Cf. BOER, NEIGHBOUR *n.*] **1** A husbandman, a peasant; *esp.* a Dutch, German, or other foreign peasant. Now *rare* or *obs.* M16. †**b** *spec.* (**B-**.) = BOER *n.* L18–M19. **2** A rustic, a yokel; a clumsy or unrefined person; a rude, ill-mannered, inconsiderate person. L16.

1 **boor's mustard** [rendering G *Baurensenfe* 'peasant's mustard'] field penny cress, *Thlaspi arvense*.

boorish *a.* of, pertaining to, or characteristic of boors; rude, ill-mannered; coarse, uncultured: M16. **boorishly** *adv.* E17. **boorishness** *n.* L18.

boosa *n.* var. of BOZA.

boost /buːst/ *n.* & *v.*[1] Orig. *US*. E19. [Origin unkn.] **A** *n.* **1** A push from below, a lift; a help; a scheme of advertisement, a promotion; an increase (in value, reputation, etc.); a reinforcement of self-confidence or morale; encouragement, assistance, increase. *colloq.* E19. **2** (The action of) a booster; a supercharger, supercharging. M20.

1 SEBA SMITH I got a pretty good boost in Boston, by the editors giving me recommendations. *Listener* The recording needs treble boost, but is otherwise excellent. A. STORR The patient's dependency on him is providing him with a boost to his own self-esteem.

B *v.* **1** *v.t.* Push from below; assist; raise; increase the reputation, value, etc., of by praise, advertising, etc. *colloq.* E19. **2** *v.t.* Amplify (an electrical signal); raise (voltage etc.); *gen.* equip or augment with a booster. E20. **3** *v.i.* & *t.* Steal, shoplift; rob. *US slang.* E20.

boost /buːst/ *v.*[2] (orig. 3 *sing. pres. indic.*). *Sc.* & †*north.* Also **buist** /byst/, †**bus**, & other vars. ME. [Contr. of *behoves*: -*t* perh. by assoc. w. *must*. Cf. BUDE.] †**1** *impers.* in (*it*) *boosts* etc., (it) behoves. ME–L15. **2** Must, ought. L18.

booster /ˈbuːstə/ *n.* Orig. *US*. L19. [f. BOOST *v.*[1] + -ER[1].] **1** A person who boosts. *colloq.* L19. **b** A shoplifter, a thief. *US slang.* E20. **2** An apparatus for providing an increase or temporary assistance; *esp.* (*a*) a device for increasing electrical voltage, signal strength, etc., an amplifier; (*b*) an auxiliary engine or rocket for giving an initial acceleration. Freq. *attrib.* L19. **3** *Med.* A dose of a vaccine etc. increasing or renewing the effect of an earlier one. M20.

2 *booster rocket, seat*, etc.

boosterism *n.* (*colloq.*) the tendency to praise,

advertise, or promote oneself or one's own (town, country, product, etc.) E20.

boosy /'bu:zi/ *n. dial.* [OE *bōsiġ*.] A stall for an ox or cow; a manger.

boot /bu:t/ *n.*[1] In *Hist.* use chiefly **bot(e)** /bəʊt/. [OE *bōt* = OFris. *bōte*, OS *bōta*, (M)Du. *boete*, OHG *buoza* (G *Busse*), ON *bót*, Goth. *bōta*, f. Gmc, f. base also of BETTER, BEST *adjs.* etc.] I Good, advantage. 1 *to boot*, besides, as well, additionally. OE. †2 Advantage, profit, use. ME–L17. 3 A premium, compensation. *obs.* exc. *Sc. dial.* L15.
II Making good or mending; amends. 4 (A contribution levied for) the repair of decaying structures. Long *obs.* exc. *Hist.* OE. **b** The right of a tenant to take timber etc. for necessary purposes such as repair. Usu. w. specifying wd. E16. †5 A medicinal cure or remedy. OE–M16. 6 Help or deliverance from evil or peril; relief, rescue. *arch.* OE. †**b** A way of mending matters, a better alternative. ME–L16. 7 A payment or compensation for injury etc. Usu. w. specifying wd. Long *obs.* exc. *Hist.* OE. 8 Expiation of sin, an offering by way of atonement. Long *obs.* exc. *Hist.* OE.

4b *fire-boot, housebote*, etc. 7 *manbote* etc.

boot /bu:t/ *n.*[2] See also BOOTS. ME. [ON *bóti* or its source OFr. *bote* (mod. *botte*), prob. rel. to *bot* blunt, stumpy, & ult. to BUTT *n.*[1]] 1 An outer foot-covering, usu. of leather, extending above the ankle. ME. †**b** A greave. LME–E17. **c** A covering for the lower part of a horse's leg. E19. 2 *Hist.* A former instrument of torture in Scotland, which encased the foot while wedges were driven between it and the foot. M16. 3 A cover of leather, rubber, etc., which fits over an object in the manner of a boot on the foot. L16. †4**a** An uncovered space on or by the step on a coach where attendants sat; the step itself; a low outside compartment before or behind the body of the vehicle. L16–E19. **b** A receptacle for luggage etc. in a coach under the seat of the guard or coachman (chiefly *Hist.*); the luggage compartment of a motor vehicle, usu. situated at the rear. L18. 5 The feathered leg of a bird; *Ornith.* an undivided tarsal envelope characteristic of the legs of some birds. M19. 6 *US slang.* **a** A navy or marines recruit under basic training. E20. **b** A person; *spec.* (*a*) a Black person; (*b*) a woman, *esp.* an unattractive one (see also *old boot* s.v. OLD *a.*). *derog.* M20. 7 A (heavy) kick. *slang.* E20.

1 *Chelsea boot, Cossack boot, cowboy boot, hiking-boot, riding-boot*, etc.

Phrases: **boot and saddle** [alt. of Fr. *boute-selle* place saddle]: a cavalry signal to mount. **boots and all** *Austral.* & *NZ colloq.* with no holds barred, wholeheartedly. **get, give (the order of) the boot** be dismissed, dismiss, from employment. *hang up one's boots*: see HANG *v. have one's heart in one's boots*: see HEART *n. lick a person's boots*: see LICK *v.* **like old boots** *slang* vigorously, tremendously. *old boot*: see OLD *a.* **put the boot in** kick brutally, take decisive action. *seven-league boots*: see SEVEN *n.* **the boot is on the other foot** or **leg** the position is reversed, the advantage etc. is the other way round. *too big for one's boots*: see BIG *a. tough as old boots*: see TOUGH *a. you bet your boots*: see BET *v.* 2.

Comb.: **bootblack** *N. Amer.* a person who blacks boots and shoes; **bootblacking** (blacking for) polishing shoes etc.; **bootboy** (*a*) a boy employed to clean shoes etc.; (*b*) *slang* a hooligan (wearing heavy boots); **boot camp** *N. Amer. slang* a centre for the initial training of marine or naval recruits; **boot-faced** *a.* grim, expressionless; **Boot Hill** *US* (*joc.*) the cemetery in a frontier town; **boot-hose** = *boot-stocking* below; **bootjack** an appliance for pulling boots off; **bootlace** a cord or leather strip for lacing boots; a thin strip of anything resembling this; **bootlick** *v.* & *n.* (*a*) *v.t.* & *i.* curry favour (with), toady (to); (*b*) *n.* = *bootlicker* below; **bootlicker** a toady, a sycophant; **bootmaker** a maker or manufacturer of boots; **boot-stocking** a stocking which covers the leg like a jackboot; BOOTSTRAP; **boot-top** *n.* & *v.* (*a*) *n.* the upper part of a boot; *Naut.* = *boot-topping* below; (*b*) *v.t.* apply protective boot-topping to; **boot-topping** *Naut.* part of the hull of a vessel between the light and load lines; any protective film or treatment applied to this; **boot-tree** a mould for keeping a boot in shape.

bootery *n.* (*US*) a shop selling boots and shoes E20.

boot /bu:t/ *n.*[3] *arch.* L16. [App. f. BOOT *n.*[1], infl. by BOOTY.] Booty, spoil, plunder.

Esp. in *make boot of*.

boot /bu:t/ *n.*[4] L20. [f. as BOOT *v.*[3]] *Computing.* The operation or procedure of booting a computer or an operating system; a bootstrapping routine.

warm boot: see WARM *a.*

boot /bu:t/ *v.*[1] ME. [f. BOOT *n.*[1]: repl. BEET *v.*] †1 *v.t.* Make better; make good (a deficiency etc.). ME–M16. 2 *v.t.* & *i. impers.*, usu. w. subj. *it*. Profit, avail; matter to or *to*. Usu. in neg. & interrog. contexts. *arch.* LME. †3 *v.t.* Benefit, enrich. *rare* (Shakes.). Only in E17.

2 A. COWLEY With Fate what boots it to contend? BROWNING Little boots Our sympathy with fiction!

boot /bu:t/ *v.*[2] LME. [f. BOOT *n.*[2]] 1 *v.t.* & *i.* Put boots on (oneself or another); put on one's boots. LME. 2 *v.t. Hist.* Torture with the boot. L16. 3 *v.t.* Kick (hard). *colloq.* L19. 4 *v.t.* Eject, dismiss (a person). Freq. foll. by *out* (*of* one's house, job, etc.). *colloq.* L19.

boot /bu:t/ *v.*[3] L20. [Abbrev. of BOOTSTRAP.] *Computing.* 1 *v.t.* Prepare (a computer) for operation by causing an operating system to be loaded into its memory; cause (an ·operating system) to be loaded in this way; load a routine on (a disc) into a computer's memory. Freq. foll. by *up*. L20. 2 *v.i.* Undergo booting; (of an operating system) be loaded into a computer's memory; (of a computer) have an operating system loaded into it. L20.

boota'bility *n.* the facility or property of being bootable L20. **bootable** *a.* able to be booted; containing the software required for booting a computer: L20.

bootakin *n.* var. of BOOTIKIN.

booted /'bu:tɪd/ *a.* M16. [f. BOOT *n.*[2], *v.*[2]: see -ED[2], -ED[1].] 1 Having boots on, equipped with boots. M16. 2 Of a bird: having feathered legs; having an undivided tarsal envelope. L18.

bootee /bu:'ti:/ *n.* L18. [f. BOOT *n.*[2] + -EE[2].] A woman's short lined boot; an infant's boot of wool etc.

Boötes /bəʊ'əʊti:z/ *n.* M16. [L f. Gk *boōtēs* ploughman, Boötes, f. *bous* ox + *ōthein* to push.] (The name of) a constellation of the northern hemisphere between Draco and Virgo; the Herdsman.

booth /bu:ð, bu:θ/ *n.* ME. [ON var. of *buð* (Sw., Da. *bod* stall, shop), f. *bóa*: see BOND *n.*[1]] 1 A temporary dwelling or shelter of branches, canvas, etc. ME. 2 A covered place where business is transacted, as (*a*) a market stall; (*b*) a refreshment tent at a fair; (*c*) a boxlike office at which tickets etc. are sold. ME. 3 A partly or completely enclosed area for voting, telephoning, sitting in a restaurant, etc. M19.

2 *ticket booth, token booth, tollbooth*, etc. 3 *polling-booth, telephone booth*, etc.

bootikin /'bu:tɪkɪn/ *n.* Also **-tak-** /-tək-/. E18. [Dim. of BOOT *n.*[2]: cf. MANNIKIN.] 1 *Hist.* = BOOT *n.*[2] 2. E18. 2†**a** A soft boot or mitten worn as a cure for gout. M–L18. **b** = BOOTEE. M19.

bootleg /'bu:tlɛg/ *a.*, *n.*, & *v.* Orig. *US.* E20. [f. BOOT *n.*[2] + LEG *n.*] **A** *adj.* 1 (Of goods, esp. liquor) smuggled, sold illicitly; (of musical recordings) pirated. E20. 2 *N. Amer. Football.* Designating or pertaining to a play in which a player carrying the ball feigns a pass to another then continues with the ball concealed near his hip. M20. **B** *n.* 1 Smuggled or illicit liquor. E20. 2 *N. Amer. Football.* A bootleg play. M20. **C** *v.* Infl. **-gg-**. 1 *v.t.* & *i.* Smuggle, sell (esp. liquor) illicitly; pirate (musical recordings). E20. 2 *v.i. N. Amer. Football.* Make a bootleg play. M20.

bootlegger *n.* a smuggler of liquor, a trafficker in illicit goods or pirated recordings L19.

bootless /'bu:tlɪs/ *a.*[1] & *adv.* OE. [f. BOOT *n.*[1] + -LESS.] **A** *adj.* 1 Of an injury: unable to be compensated by payment etc. Long *obs.* exc. *Hist.* OE. †2 Incurable, remediless. ME–M17. 3 Unavailing, to no purpose. LME. **B** *adv.* Bootlessly. Chiefly *poet.* LME.

bootlessly *adv.* unavailingly, unsuccessfully E17.

bootless /'bu:tlɪs/ *a.*[2] LME. [f. BOOT *n.*[2] + -LESS.] Without boots.

boots /bu:ts/ *n.* E17. [Pl. of BOOT *n.*[2], used as sing.] 1 As 2nd elem. of combs. w. the sense 'person, fellow', in familiar or joc. appellations, as *bossyboots, slyboots*, etc. E17. 2 (A name for) a hotel servant who cleans boots and shoes, carries luggage, etc. L18.

bootstrap /'bu:tstrap/ *n.* & *v.* L19. [f. BOOT *n.*[2] + STRAP *n.*] **A** *n.* 1 A strap attached to a boot for pulling it on, or for holding down a woman's riding habit; a bootlace. L19. 2 Chiefly *Computing.* The action of bootstrapping; a bootstrapping procedure or routine. Usu. *attrib.* M20.

1 **pull** (or **lift** etc.) **oneself up by one's own bootstraps**: by one's own unaided efforts.

B *v.t.* Infl. **-pp-**. 1 Make (one's way) or get (oneself) *into* a new state using existing resources; modify or improve by making use of what is already present. Usu. *refl.* M20. 2 *Computing.* = BOOT *v.*[3] 1. Freq. as *bootstrapping* vbl n. M20.

1 R. M. PIRSIG Some valuable Aristotelian technique of bootstrapping oneself into new areas of knowledge. 2 D. R. HOFSTADTER Once a certain minimal core of compiler had been written, then that . . could translate bigger compilers into machine language—which in turn could translate yet bigger compilers. . . This process is affectionately known as 'bootstrapping'.

booty /'bu:ti/ *n.* LME. [MLG *būte*, *buite* exchange, distribution (whence G *Beute*) rel. to ON *býta* deal out, exchange, of unkn. origin.] 1 Orig., plunder, spoil, etc., acquired in common and destined to be divided. Now, anything gained by plunder etc. whether common property or not; spoil. LME. 2 A thing taken by force, a prize. Usu. in *pl.* Now *rare* or *obs.* M16.

Phrases: **play booty** *arch.* (in games) combine against another player; play or act falsely for gain, lose intentionally.

booza *n.* var. of BOZA.

booze /bu:z/ *v.* & *n. colloq.* Also **bouse, bowse** /baʊz/. ME. [MDu. *būsen* (Du. *buizen*) drink to excess.] **A** *v.i.* & (now *rare*) *t.* Drink for company and enjoyment; drink (alcoholic liquor) habitually or excessively. ME.

B *n.* 1 Drink, *esp.* alcoholic drink. ME. 2 A drinking-bout. L18.

1 *hit the booze*: see HIT *v.* 2 **on the booze** on a heavy drinking session.

Comb.: **booze-up** a drinking-bout.

¶The spelling *booze* is not recorded until 18.

boozed *a.* intoxicated, drunk, (also foll. by *up*) M19. **boozer** *n.* (*a*) a person who boozes; (*b*) *slang* a public house: E17. **booze'roo** *n.* (*NZ slang*) a drinking-spree M20. **boozily** *adv.* in a boozy manner L19. **booziness** *n.* the quality of being boozy M19. **boozy** *a.* showing the effects of alcoholic drink; characterized by or given up to boozing: E16.

bop /bɒp/ *n.*[1] *colloq.* M20. [Imit.] A popping sound. Also, a blow with a fist, club, etc.

bop /bɒp/ *n.*[2] *colloq.* M20. [Abbrev.] 1 = BEBOP. Orig. *US.* M20. 2 A dance to pop music; a social occasion for such dancing. M20.

bopster *n.* = BEBOPPER M20.

bop /bɒp/ *v.*[1] Infl. **-pp-**. L19. [Imit.] 1 *v.t.* **a** Throw down with a resounding noise. *dial. rare.* L19. **b** Hit, strike, punch. *colloq.* (orig. *US*). M20. 2 *v.i.* Fight. *US colloq.* M20.

bop /bɒp/ *v.*[2]*i. colloq.* (orig. *US*). Infl. **-pp-**. M20. [f. BOP *n.*[2]] Play or sing bebop; dance, jive.

bopper *n.* = BEBOPPER (see also TEENY-BOPPER) M20.

bo-peep /bəʊ'pi:p/ *n.* E16. [f. BO *int.* + PEEP *v.*[2]] 1 = PEEKABOO *n.* E16. 2 A peep, a look. *Austral.* & *NZ colloq.* M20.

Bora /bɒ'rɑ:, 'bɔ:rə/ *n.*[1] Also **Bhora, Borah, Bohora** /bɒ'hɔ:rə/. L17. [Hind. *bohrā*.] A member of a Shiite Muslim sect found mainly in western India. Formerly also, a Muslim Indian trader.

bora /'bɔ:rə/ *n.*[2] M19. [Dial. var. of It. *borea* f. L *boreas* north wind.] A strong northerly squally wind which blows in the northern Adriatic.

bora /'bɔ:rə/ *n.*[3] Also **borah**. M19. [Kamilaroi *buuru*.] A rite among the Aborigines of eastern Australia signifying admission to manhood.

†**borachio** *n.* L16. [Sp. *borracha* leather bag for wine, *borracho* drunkard.] 1 In Spain: a goatskin

bag used for wine or other liquors. L16–L18. 2 A drunkard. E17–E18.

boracic /bəˈrasɪk/ *a.* L18. [f. med.L *borac-*, BORAX *n.*[1] + -IC.] Of, containing, or derived from borax.

boracic acid = BORIC *acid.*

boracite /ˈbɔːrəsʌɪt/ *n.* L18. [f. as prec. + -ITE[1].] *Min.* A chloroborate of magnesium usu. occurring as greyish-white cubic crystals.

borage /ˈbɒrɪdʒ/ *n.* ME. [(O)Fr. *bourrache* f. med.L *bor(r)ago, -agin-*, perh. f. Arab. *'abū huraš* father of roughness, w. ref. to the leaves.] A plant of the genus *Borago* (family Boraginaceae); *esp.* the plant *B. officinalis*, which has hairy leaves and bright blue flowers, and is sometimes used in salads, cordials, etc.

boragi'naceous *a.* (*Bot.*) of or pertaining to the family Boraginaceae M19.

Borah, borah *ns.* vars. of BORA *n.*[1], BORA *n.*[3]

borak /ˈbɔːrak/ *n. Austral.* & *NZ colloq.* Also **borax** /-ks/. M19. [Aborig.] Nonsense; banter. Freq. in *poke borak*, poke fun (*at*).

borane /ˈbɔːreɪn/ *n.* E20. [f. BORON + -ANE.] *Chem.* Any of the series of binary compounds of boron and hydrogen, or a substituted derivative of such a compound.

†boras *n.* var. of BORAX *n.*[1]

borasco /bəˈraskəʊ/ *n.* Now *rare*. Pl. **-os**. Also **-ca** /-kə/, **-asque** /-ask/. E17. [Fr. *bourrasque*, It. *burrasca*, Sp. *borrasca*, f. L *boreas*: see BORA *n.*[2]] A violent squall of wind.

borassus /bəˈrasəs/ *n.* L18. [mod.L f. Gk *borassos* palm tree fruit.] A palm of the genus *Borassus*; *esp.* the palmyra, *B. flabellifer*. Also *borassus palm*.

borate /ˈbɔːreɪt/ *n.* L18. [f. BORAX *n.*[1] + -ATE[1].] *Chem.* A salt or ester of boric acid; any salt with an oxyanion containing boron.

borax /ˈbɔːraks/ *n.*[1] Also **†boras**. LME. [med.L f. colloq. Arab. *būrāk* f. Pahlavi *būrak* (Pers. *būra*).] 1 A hydrated sodium borate, $Na_2B_4O_7{\cdot}10H_2O$, which is a white efflorescent crystalline solid found as a native deposit or prepared from other minerals. LME. 2 Cheap, inferior, or ostentatious goods, esp. furniture; inferior and tasteless design (after a borax soap producer who gave away cheap furniture as a premium). Freq. *attrib.* Orig. *US.* M20.

borax *n.*[2] var. of BORAK.

Borazon /ˈbɔːrəzɒn/ *n.* M20. [f. BORON with insertion of AZO-.] (Proprietary name for) a form of boron nitride, used as an abrasive.

borborygm /ˈbɔːbərɪgəm/ *n.* Also in mod.L form **borborygmus** /bɔːbəˈrɪgməs/, pl. **-mi** /-mʌɪ/. E18. [Gk *borborugmos*.] A rumbling in the bowels.

borbo'rygmic *a.* characterized by borborygms or rumblings E20.

bord /bɔːd/ *n.* M19. [Var. of BOARD *n.*] Any of a series of parallel workings in a coal seam.

bord and pillar a system of working with pillars of coal left at intervals.

bordage /ˈbɔːdɪdʒ/ *n.* ME. [(O)Fr. (= med.L *bordagium*), f. *borde* small farm, cottage, f. Proto-Gallo-Romance f. Frank. (= BOARD *n.*): see -AGE.] *Hist.* 1 More fully *bordage tenure*. The tenure of a bordar. ME. 2 The services due from a bordar. ME.

bordar /ˈbɔːdə/ *n.* ME. [AL *bordarius* (= (O)Fr. *bordier*), f. *borda* f. (O)Fr. *borde*: see prec., -ER[2].] *Hist.* A villein of the lowest rank, who rendered menial service for a cottage held at the will of his lord.

Bordeaux /bɔːˈdəʊ/ *n.* Pl. same /-z/. M16. [A city in SW France.] 1 (A) red (claret) or white wine from the district of Bordeaux. M16. 2 *Bordeaux mixture*, copper sulphate and lime used as a fungicide. L19.

bordel /bɔːˈdɛl/ *n.* Now chiefly *US.* ME. [(O)Fr. (= med.L *bordellum, -us*) dim. of *borde*: see BORDAGE, -EL[2].] = next.

bordello /bɔːˈdɛləʊ/ *n.* Now chiefly *N. Amer.* Pl. **-os.** L16. [It., f. as prec.] A brothel.

border /ˈbɔːdə/ *n.* Also (*arch. rare* exc. in branch II, where now usual) **-ure** /-jʊə/. LME. [OFr. *bordeüre* (mod. *bordure*) f. Proto-Romance, ult. f. one of the Gmc bases of BOARD *n.*: see -ER[2].] I Mod. *border.* 1 A side, an edge, a brink, a margin; a limit, a boundary (*lit.* & *fig.*); the part lying along the boundary or outline. LME. 2a *sing.* & (now usu.) in *pl.* A frontier district of a country or territory. LME. b The frontier line which separates one country from another. M16. 3 A continuous bed which forms a fringe round a garden area. LME. 4 A distinct edging for strength, ornament, or definition round anything. LME. †5 A plait or braid of hair worn round the forehead or temples. E17–M19. 6 *sing.* & (usu.) in *pl.* A strip of cloth masking the top of a theatre stage as seen from the auditorium. E19.

1 HOR. WALPOLE He affected an impartiality that by turns led him to the borders of insincerity and contradiction. 2a **the Border** (*a*) *sing.* & (freq.) in *pl.*, the boundary and adjoining districts between England and Scotland; (*b*) the boundary between Northern Ireland and the Republic of Ireland, or between the US and Mexico. 3 MIXED *border.* 4 OED The newspapers appeared with black borders in sign of mourning. L. M. MONTGOMERY It was an old-fashioned oval . . surrounded by a border of very fine amethysts. J. MASTERS Har Singh stitched a border on to one of the plain white saris. TRAC *border.*

II Mod. *bordure.* 7 *Her.* A bearing of uniform width around the edge of a shield. LME.

Comb.: **Border ballad**: celebrating a raid in the Borders; **border collie** a medium-sized sheepdog of a breed originating near the border between England and Scotland; **borderland** land or district on or near a border; *fig.* an intermediate condition, debatable ground; **Border Leicester** (an animal of) a breed of sheep originating as a cross between the Cheviot and the Leicester; **borderline** *n.* & *a.* (*a*) *n.* a strip of land forming a boundary; a line of demarcation; (*b*) *adj.* on the borderline, marginal; **border print** printed cotton fabric with a design running parallel to the edge; **Border terrier** (an animal of) a breed of small rough-haired terrier originating in the Cheviot Hills.

border /ˈbɔːdə/ *v.* Also **†-ure.** LME. [f. the n.] I *v.t.* 1 Put or form a border, edging, or boundary to. LME. †b Keep within bounds; confine. *rare* (Shakes.). Only in E17. †2 Cut up (a pasty). E16–M19. 3 Lie on the borders of; adjoin. M17.

1 SWIFT His night-cap border'd round with lace. H. WILLIAMSON Trimmed quickthorn hedges bordering the road. *bordered pit*: see PIT *n.*[1] 3 C. LYELL Lands bordering the Mediterranean.

II *v.i.* 4 Foll. by *on, upon*: lie on the border of, be contiguous to; *fig.* approach in character, verge on. M16.

4 M. ELPHINSTONE Hill tribes, bordering on cultivated countries. B. MAGEE A sense of persecution which bordered on paranoia.

bordereau /bɔːdəˈrəʊ, *foreign* bɔrdəro/ *n.* Pl. **-eaux** /-əʊz, *foreign* -o/. L19. [Fr., dim. of *bord* BOARD *n.*] A memorandum of contents, a schedule, a docket.

borderer /ˈbɔːdərə/ *n.* LME. [f. BORDER *v.* or *n.* + -ER[1].] 1 A person who lives near a border, esp. that of England and Scotland. Also (**B-**), a member of a regiment from the Welsh or Scottish borders. LME. 2 A person who or (*rare*) thing which borders (*on, upon*); a nearest neighbour. M16.

bord-land /ˈbɔːdland/ *n.* ME. [f. as BORDAGE or BORDAR + LAND *n.*[1]] *Hist.* Land held in bordage tenure.

bordure *n., v.* see BORDER *n., v.*

bore /bɔː/ *n.*[1] ME. [Partly f. BORE *v.*[1], partly f. ON *bora* borehole = OHG *boro* auger: cf. OE *bor* gimlet, ON *borr* borer, f. Gmc base also of BORE *v.*[1]] 1 A hole made by boring, a perforation, an aperture. *obs.* or *arch.* exc. as below. ME. 2 The hollow of a gun barrel, tube, cylinder, etc. L16. b The internal diameter of this; calibre. L16. 3 A deep narrow hole made in the earth, esp. to find water, oil, etc. Also (*Austral.*), an artificial water-hole for animals. L17.

1 R. BURNS Frighted rattons . . seek the benmost bore. 2 H. WILLIAMSON Owing to the cordite in the cartridges . . remaining in the bore, flashes occurred during re-loading.

Comb.: **borehole** = sense 3 above.

bore /bɔː/ *n.*[2] ME. [Perh. f. ON *bára* wave.] †1 A wave, a billow. Only in ME. 2 More fully *tidal bore.* A steep-fronted wave caused by the meeting of two tides or by the constriction of a spring tide as it passes up a narrowing estuary. E17.

bore /bɔː/ *n.*[3] M18. [Origin unkn.: early sources suggest Fr. derivation.] †1 Boredom, ennui; a dull time. M18–M19. 2 A thing which bores; a tedious nuisance or annoyance. L18. 3 A tiresome or tediously dull person. L18.

boredom *n.* (*a*) the state of being bored; tedium, ennui; (*b*) (now *rare*) the behaviour of a bore, bores collectively: M19. **boresome** *a.* tending to be a bore, boring L19. **boresomeness** *n.* M19.

bore /bɔː/ *v.*[1] [OE *borian* = MLG, MDu. *boren*, OHG *borōn* (G *bohren*), ON *bora* f. Gmc base also of BORE *n.*[1]; sense 4 may be a different wd.] 1 *v.t.* Pierce, make a hole in or through, esp. (as) with an auger etc. OE. b Pierce with a cylindrical cavity; hollow out (a gun barrel, tube, etc.). M18. 2 *v.i.* Make a hole or perforation (*in, into, through*); sink a borehole. ME. 3 *v.t.* Make (a hole, tunnel, one's way, etc.) by boring, excavation, pressure, etc. E16. b *v.t.* & *i.* Of a horse: push (another horse etc.) out of the way; thrust the head straight forward. L17. †4 *v.t.* Trick, cheat. Only in E17.

borer *n.* (*a*) a person who bores; a horse which bores; (*b*) any of various worms, molluscs, insects, or other creatures which bore holes; (*c*) an instrument for boring: L15. **boring** *n.* (*a*) the action of the vb; (*b*) a borehole: LME.

bore /bɔː/ *v.*[2]*t.* M18. [f. (as) BORE *n.*[3]] Weary by tedious talk, dullness, or monotony.

G. A. BIRMINGHAM The Major yawned without an attempt to hide the fact that he was bored. E. M. FORSTER Perhaps Italy bores him; you ought to try the Alps or the Lakes. D. RUSK We were prepared to consult with de Gaulle's government until it bored them to tears. *bore stiff*: see STIFF *a.*

boring *a.* tediously dull, wearisome: M19. **boringly** *adv.* M19. **boringness** *n.* L19. **borish** *a.* (now *rare*) boring M18.

bore *v.*[3] pa. t. of BEAR *v.*[1]

boreal /ˈbɔːrɪəl/ *a.* & *n.* LME. [(O)Fr. *boréal* or late L *borealis*, f. as next: see -AL[1].] **A** *adj.* 1 Northern; of the North or the Arctic; of the north wind. LME. 2a Designating or characteristic of a biogeographical zone south of the Arctic, esp. the cold temperate region dominated by taiga and forests of birch, poplar, and conifers. M19. b (**B-**.) Designating or pertaining to a relatively warm dry climatic period in post-glacial northern Europe between the Preboreal and Atlantic periods, marked by the spread of hardwood forests. L19. **B** *n. The* Boreal period. M20.

Boreas /ˈbɔːrɪəs/ *n. literary.* LME. [L f. Gk.] The north wind, esp. personified; the god of the north wind.

borean *a.* (*rare*) = BOREAL 1 M17.

borecole /ˈbɔːkəʊl/ *n.* E18. [Du. *boerenkool* lit. 'peasant's cabbage', f. *boer* BOOR + *kool* COLE *n.*[1]] = KALE 1.

boree /ˈbɔːriː/ *n.*[1] *Austral.* L19. [Kamilaroi.] The weeping myall, *Acacia pendula.*

†boree *n.*[2] var. of BOURRÉE.

boreen /bɔːˈriːn/ *n. Anglo-Ir.* Also **bohereen.** M19. [Ir. *bóithrín* dim. of *bóthar* road: see -EEN[2].] A narrow country road, a lane.

borel *a.* var. of BORREL.

boric /ˈbɔːrɪk/ *a.* M19. [f. BORON + -IC.] *Chem.* Of boron; *boric acid*, a weakly acidic crystalline solid, $B(OH)_3$, which is derived from borax and is used as an antiseptic.

boride /ˈbɔːrʌɪd/ *n.* M19. [f. BORON + -IDE.] *Chem.* A binary compound of boron with a metallic element.

born /bɔːn/ *ppl a.* (orig. *pple*). [OE *boren* pa. pple of BEAR *v.*[1]: long distinct from *borne.*] I *pred.* 1 Brought forth by birth as offspring; *fig.* brought into existence, started in life; destined; innately suited. OE.

1 SHAKES. *Temp.* If he be not born to be hang'd, our case is miserable. TENNYSON Some sudden turn of anger born Of your misfaith. N. MITFORD She was born a Miss Perrotte. M. H. ABRAMS Poets who are

born and poets who are made. L. HELLMAN An old, very black lady who had been born into slavery. J. G. FARRELL The other infant, a girl born to Mrs Wright . ., survived. D. FRASER His eldest child . . had just been born. *first-born, free-born, high-born, low-born*, etc.

II *attrib.* 2 That has been born; of (specified) birth; *fig.* destined by birth or inherent qualities; naturally gifted; (in unfavourable sense) utter, hopeless. ME. 3 Of a quality: innate, inherited. M18.

2 DRYDEN Authors nobly born will bear their part. S. RICHARDSON I, a poor helpless Girl . . shall put on Lady-airs to a Gentlewoman born. E. A. FREEMAN The Danish-born Bernard. G. B. SHAW An ignorant dupe and a born fool into the bargain. K. M. E. MURRAY He was himself a born teacher, never . . able to resist passing on information.

Phrases & comb.: **born-again** *a.* (*a*) regenerate, revitalized, *esp.* claiming spiritual rebirth as a Christian; (*b*) full of enthusiastic zeal for a cause. *born and bred*: see BRED *ppl a.* *born in the purple*: see PURPLE *a.* & *n.* *born with a silver spoon in one's mouth*: see SPOON *n.* *not born* YESTERDAY. **one's born days** one's life hitherto. *to the manner born*: see MANNER *n.*[1]

born /bɔːn/ *v. US.* M20. [Irreg. f. prec.] 1 *v.t.* Cause to be born; bring into the world. *rare.* M20. 2 *v.i.* Be born; come to birth or into existence. Chiefly as *borning* ppl a. & vbl n. (cf. ABORNING). M20.

borne *v.* pa. pple & ppl a. of BEAR *v.*[1]

borné /bɔrne/ *a.* L18. [Fr., pa. pple of *borner* limit.] Limited in scope, intellect, outlook, etc.

Bornean /ˈbɔːnɪən/ *a.* & *n.* E19. [f. *Borneo* (see below) + -AN.] A *adj.* Of or pertaining to the E. Indian island of Borneo. E19. B *n.* A native or inhabitant of Borneo. M19.

borneol /ˈbɔːnɪɒl/ *n.* M19. [f. as prec. + -OL.] *Chem.* A crystalline terpenoid alcohol, $C_{10}H_{18}O$, present in many essential oils; *esp.* that of the Borneo camphor tree *Dryobalanops aromatica*.

Bornholm disease /ˈbɔːnhəʊm dɪˌziːz/ *n. phr.* M20. [*Bornholm*, a Danish island in the Baltic.] An epidemic viral disease causing severe pain in the intercostal muscles and the diaphragm.

bornite /ˈbɔːnʌɪt/ *n.* E19. [f. Ignatius von *Born* (1742–91), Austrian mineralogist + -ITE[1].] *Min.* A brittle reddish-brown sulphide of copper and iron, occurring usu. as cubic or dodecahedral crystals.

boro- /ˈbɔːrəʊ/ *comb. form* of next: see -O-.

boroˈhydride *n.* a compound of the anion BH_4^- M20. **boroˈsilicate** *n.* a substance derived from or containing both silica and boric oxide (B_2O_3), *esp.* a kind of glass E19.

boron /ˈbɔːrɒn/ *n.* E19. [f. BORAX *n.*[1] after *carbon*, which it resembles in certain respects.] A relatively inert non-metallic chemical element, atomic no. 5, occurring as a dark brown amorphous powder and as black crystals. (Symbol B.)

boronia /bəˈrəʊnɪə/ *n.* L18. [mod.L, f. Francesco *Borone* (1769–94), It. botanist: see -IA[1].] A fragrant Australian shrub of the genus *Boronia*, of the rue family.

borough /ˈbʌrə/ *n.* Sense 1 *Hist.* also **burh**. See also BURGH, BURROW *n.*[2] [OE *burg, burh* = OFris. *burch*, OS *burg* (MDu. *burch*, Du. *burg*), OHG *burug* (G *Burg*), ON *borg*, Goth. *baurgs*, f. Gmc; rel. to OE *beorgan*: see BORROW *v.*[1]] 1 A fortress, a castle, a citadel; a court, a manor-house. Long *obs.* exc. *Hist.* as *burh*. OE. 2 Orig., a fortified town. Later, a town, district, large village, etc., with some form of municipal organization. In Britain, long *obs.* or *Hist.* exc. as below. OE. b *spec.* An administrative division of London or of New York City. L19. c *spec.* In Alaska, a territorial division corresponding to a county. M20. 3 A town (as distinct from a city) with a corporation and privileges granted by royal charter; *Hist.* a town sending representatives to Parliament. LME. 4 *Hist.* A property held by burgage tenure. E18.

3 **close borough**, **pocket borough** *Hist.* a borough where elections were controlled by a wealthy private person or family. **rotten borough** *Hist.* a borough represented in Parliament although no longer having a real constituency. **the Borough**: *esp.* that of Southwark, London.

Comb.: **borough council** a council which conducts the affairs of a borough; **borough-English** *Hist.* tenure whereby the youngest son inherited all lands and tenements; †**borough-master** = BURGOMASTER; **boroughmonger** *Hist.* a person who traded in parliamentary seats for boroughs; **boroughmongering** *ppl a.* & *vbl n.* (*Hist.*) (involved in) trading in parliamentary seats for boroughs; **boroughmongery** *Hist.* the practice of boroughmongering; **borough-reeve** †(*a*) the governor of a town or city; (*b*) *Hist.* the chief municipal officer of certain English towns; **borough-town** *arch.* a town which is a borough.

borrel /ˈbɒr(ə)l/ *a. arch.* Also **borel**. LME. [Perh. orig. an attrib. use of BUREL w. ref. to coarse clothing.] 1 Belonging to the laity. LME. 2 Unlearned, rude; rough. L15.

Borrovian /bɒˈrəʊvɪən/ *n.* & *a.* L19. [f. *Borrow* (see below) + -IAN, after *Harrovian* etc.] A *n.* An admirer or student of the English writer George Borrow (1803–81) or his work; the diction characteristic of Borrow's writing. L19. B *adj.* Of, pertaining to, or characteristic of Borrow or his writing. E20.

borrow /ˈbɒrəʊ/ *n.* [OE *borg* = OFris. *borg*, MHG *borc* pledge, f. Gmc; rel. to OE *beorgan* (see next). Sense 4 f. next.] 1 A pledge; a guarantee, bail; a ransom. Long *arch.* exc. *Sc. Law.* OE. 2 A surety; a person who stands bail. Long *arch.* OE. 3 *Hist.* A frank-pledge, a tithing. L16. 4 A borrowing. *rare* in *gen.* sense. E17. b *Golf.* A borrowing to allow for the slope of the green etc.; the amount borrowed. M19.

1 *law-borrow(s)*: see LAW *n.*[1]

Comb.: **borrow-head** *Hist.* = BORSHOLDER; **borrow-hole**, **-pit**: made by removing material for use in embanking etc.

borrow /ˈbɒrəʊ/ *v.*[1] [OE *borgian* = OFris. *borgia*, MLG, MDu. *borgen*, OHG *borgēn* (G *borgen*), f. Gmc, rel. to OE *beorgan* = OS, OHG *bergan* (Du., G *bergen*), ON *bjarga*, Goth. *bairgan*, f. Gmc base meaning 'protect, shelter', whence also BURY *v.*] 1 *v.t.* & *i.* Orig., take (a thing) on security given for its safe return. Now, get temporary use of (money or property to be returned later); take on loan. (Foll. by *from, of* a person etc.) OE. b *Math.* In subtraction, transfer (a unit of the next higher denomination) in the number being subtracted from, compensating for this at the next step L16. 2 *v.t. fig.* Adopt, use without being the true owner or inventor; derive from another; import from an alien source. ME. 3 *v.t.* Be surety for; ransom. Long *arch.* ME. 4 *v.t. Mus.* Derive (an organ-stop) from the pipe of another stop; equip (an organ) with such stops. Chiefly as *borrowed* ppl a. M19. 5 *v.t.* & *i. Golf.* Allow (a certain distance) for sideways motion due to wind or slope, when putting. L19.

1 COVERDALE *2 Esd.* 5:3 Let vs borowe money of the kinge vpon vsury. G. B. SHAW I will not borrow from my friends. W. STYRON He had managed once again to borrow Larry's car for the weekend. 2 SHAKES. *John* Inferior eyes, That borrow their behaviours from the great. B. JOWETT No man can be happy who, to borrow Plato's illustration, is leading the life of an oyster.

Phrases: *beg, borrow, or steal*: see BEG *v.* **borrowed days** *Sc. Folklore* the last three days of March (Old Style), said to have been borrowed from April and to be particularly stormy. **borrowed light** (*a*) reflected light; (*b*) a window in an internal wall designed to admit light. **borrowed plumage, plumes** a pretentious display not of one's own making. **borrowed time** an unexpected extension of time, esp. of life (chiefly in *living on borrowed time*). **borrow trouble** *N. Amer. colloq.* go out of one's way to find trouble.

borrower *n.* LME. **borrowing** *n.* (*a*) the action of the vb (*borrowing days* = *borrowed days* above); (*b*) that which is borrowed: LME.

borrow /ˈbɒrəʊ/ *v.*[2]*i.* L16. [Perh. var. of BURROW *v.*] *Naut.* Approach closely to land or wind.

Borsalino /bɔːsəˈliːnəʊ/ *n.* Also **b-**. Pl. **-os**. E20. [Name of the manufacturer.] (Proprietary name for) a man's wide-brimmed felt hat.

borsch *n.* var. of BORTSCH.

borsholder /ˈbɔːshəʊldə/ *n.* ME. [AL *borgesalder* (AN *burghaldre*), f. ME *borȝes* genit. sing. of BORROW *n.* + *alder*, OE *aldor* chief (see ALDERMAN).] *Hist.* The chief of a frank-pledge. Later; a petty constable.

Borstal /ˈbɔːst(ə)l/ *n.* Also **b-**. E20. [A village in Kent, England, site of the first such institution.] In full *Borstal institution*. A custodial institution to which young offenders may be sent for reformative training.

borstch *n.* var. of BORTSCH.

bort /bɔːt/ *n.* Also **boart**. E17. [Du. *boort*.] Coarse diamonds of poor quality; diamond fragments esp. used as an abrasive.

bortsch /bɔːtʃ/ *n.* Also **borsch** /bɔːʃ/, **borstch** /bɔːstʃ/. E19. [Russ. *borshch*.] A Russian or Polish soup of various ingredients including beetroot and cabbage.

Borussian /bəʊˈrʌʃ(ə)n/ *a.* & *n. arch.* E17. [f. med.L *Borussi* pl., *Borussia*, alt. of *Prussi*, *Prussia* as if f. Slav. *po* by, alongside, + *Russi*, *Russia*: see PRUSSIAN, RUSSIAN, -IAN.] (A) Prussian.

borzoi /ˈbɔːzɔɪ/ *n.* L19. [Russ. *borzoĭ* adj., *borzaya* n., f. *borzyĭ* swift.] (An animal of) a Russian breed of large wolfhound, with a usu. white silky coat.

bosa *n.* var. of BOZA.

bosbok /ˈbɒsbɒk/ *n. S. Afr.* Also †**bosch-**. L18. [Afk., f. Du. *bosch* BUSH *n.*[1] + *bok* BUCK *n.*[1]] = *bushbuck* s.v. BUSH *n.*[1]

boscage /ˈbɒskɪdʒ/ *n.* Also **-sk-**. LME. [OFr. (mod. BOCAGE) f. Proto-Gallo-Romance, ult. f. base of BUSH *n.*[1]: see -AGE.] 1 A mass of trees or shrubs, a thicket; wooded scenery. LME. †2 A representation of wooded landscape, foliage, etc. Only in 17.

†**boschbok** *n.* var. of BOSBOK.

bose /bəʊs/ *v.t.* E20. [Perh. alt. of BOSS *v.*[1]] Test (ground) for the presence of buried structures by noting the sound of percussion from a weighted object. Chiefly as *bosing* vbl n.

boser *n.* an instrument used for bosing ground M20.

Bose–Einstein statistics /bəʊzˈʌɪnstʌɪn stəˌtɪstɪks/ *n. phr.* E20. [S. N. *Bose* (see BOSON) + A. *Einstein* (see EINSTEINIAN).] *Physics.* A type of quantum statistics used to describe systems of identical particles to which the exclusion principle does not apply.

bosey *n.* var. of BOSIE.

bosh /bɒʃ/ *n.*[1] L17. [Origin unkn.] 1 In *pl.*, the inwardly sloping sides of a blast-furnace, extending downwards from the belly to the hearth. Later also *sing.*, this lower part of the furnace. L17. 2 A trough or sink, esp. for cooling metal in water. *dial.* L19.

bosh /bɒʃ/ *n.*[2] *slang.* M19. [Turk. *boş* empty, worthless.] Nonsense, foolish talk. Also as *int.*

bosher *n.* a person who talks bosh E20. **boshy** *a.* worthless; nonsensical: M19.

bosie /ˈbəʊzi/ *n. Austral.* Also **-sey**. E20. [f. B. J. T. *Bos(anquet* (1877–1936), Eng. cricketer + -IE.] = GOOGLY *n.*

bosk /bɒsk/ *n.* ME. [Var. of BUSH *n.*[1]: in mod. literary use back-form. f. BOSKY.] 1 A bush. Long *obs.* exc. *dial.* ME. 2 A thicket of bushes etc.; a small wood. E19.

boskage *n.* var. of BOSCAGE.

bosker /ˈbɒskə/ *a. Austral.* & *NZ slang.* E20. [Origin unkn.] Good, excellent, first-rate.

bosket /ˈbɒskɪt/ *n.* Also **-squ-**. M18. [Fr. *bosquet* f. It. *boschetto* dim. of *bosco* wood. Cf. BOUQUET.] A plantation of small trees in a garden, park, etc.; a thicket.

bosky /ˈbɒski/ *a.* L16. [f. BOSK + -Y[1]: sense 2 may be a different wd.] 1 Full of bushes or thickets; bushy. L16. 2 Fuddled by drink, tipsy. *dial.* & *slang.* M18.

bo's'n *n.* var. of BOSUN.

Bosnian /ˈbɒznɪən/ *n.* & *a.* L18. [f. *Bosnia* (see below) + -IAN.] A *n.* A native or inhabitant of Bosnia, a region in the Balkans now a part of Bosnia-Herzegovina. L18. B *adj.* Of or pertaining to Bosnia. M19.

Also **Bosniac** *n.* M19.

bosom /ˈbʊz(ə)m/ *n.* & *a.* [OE *bōsm* = OFris. *bōsm*, OS *bōsom* (Du. *boezem*), OHG *buosam* (G *Busen*), f. WGmc, perh. ult. f. base of BOUGH.]

A *n.* 1 The breast of a human being, esp. of a woman; *poet.* the breast of a bird etc. Also (*colloq.*, chiefly *US*) in *pl.*, a woman's breasts. OE. 2 *fig.* The surface *of* the sea, a river, the ground, etc. OE. 3 The part of the dress which covers the breast; the space between the dress and the breast, esp. considered as a receptacle for money, letters, etc. OE. b A shirt-front. *US.* M19. 4 A concavity, a recess, a hollow interior. OE. 5 The enclosure formed by the breast and the arms. ME. 6 The breast considered as the seat of emotions, desires, secret thoughts, etc. ME. 7 *fig.* The interior, the midst; the enfolding relationship *of* one's family, the Church, etc. LME. †8 *transf.* A person. Cf. *hand, head,* etc. L16–M18. 9 = *bosom friend* below. *colloq.* E20.

6 SHAKES. *Oth.* I will bestow you where you shall have time To speak your bosom freely. *friend* or *wife of one's bosom* (with rhet. emphasis). 7 GEO. ELIOT Deep in the bosom of the hills.

Phrases: Abraham's bosom: see ABRAHAM *n.* I. **take to one's bosom** *arch.* marry. *the bird in the bosom*: see BIRD *n.*

B *attrib.* or as *adj.* Intimate, confidential. Chiefly in *bosom friend* below. L16.

bosom friend [cf. G *Busenfreund*] a specially intimate or dear friend.

bosomy *a.* (*a*) full of sheltered hollows; (*b*) (of a woman) with a prominent bosom: E17.

bosom /ˈbʊz(ə)m/ *v.* LME. [f. the n.] 1 *v.i.* Swell out. Now *rare* or *obs.* LME. 2 *v.t.* Put into or carry in the bosom; embrace, take to the bosom; *fig.* receive into intimate companionship; keep in mind (a secret thought etc.). *arch.* L16.

bosomed /ˈbʊz(ə)md/ *a.* E17. [f. BOSOM *n.*, *v.*: see -ED[2], -ED[1].] 1 Having a bosom (of a specified kind); shaped like a bosom, swelled out. E17. 2 Confined in the bosom; enclosed, hidden, (of the breath) bated. M17.

boson /ˈbəʊzɒn/ *n.* M20. [f. S. N. *Bose* (1894–1974), Indian physicist, who with Einstein stated the statistical relations describing the behaviour of such particles: see -ON.] *Physics.* A particle that has a symmetric wave function, and hence integral spin, and can be described by Bose–Einstein statistics. Cf. FERMION.

bosquet *n.* var. of BOSKET.

boss /bɒs/ *n.*[1] ME. [OFr. *boce* (mod. *bosse*) f. Proto-Romance, of unkn. origin.] 1 A protuberance on the body of an animal or plant; a convex or knoblike excrescent portion of an organ or structure. ME. 2 A round knob in sculptured or carved work; an ornamental projection at an intersection in vaulting; a metal stud on a book, bridle, shield, etc. LME. b An enlarged or projecting mechanical part, e.g. of a shaft, stern-post, etc.; the central part of a propeller. M19. 3 A rocky outcrop or knoll; *Geol.* a mass of rock protruding through other strata, *esp.* an igneous intrusion of rounded form. L15. 4 A soft pad used in ceramics and glass manufacture for smoothing colours and for cleaning. M19.

1 S. BECKETT Cascades of light . . fell on the hairless domes and bosses of his skull. P. V. WHITE He stood in the entrance to the cave . . resting his forehead against a boss of cold rock.

bosset *n.* a small protuberance or knob M19.

boss /bɒs/ *n.*[2] M16. [Perh. f. MDu. *bosse, busse,* Du. *bos, bus* box.] A plasterer's tray; a hod.

boss /bɒs/ *n.*[3] Now *dial.* L17. [Perh alt. of BASS *n.*[3], but cf. Du. *bos* bundle of straw.] A seat of straw; a hassock.

boss /bɒs/ *n.*[4] & *a. colloq.* (orig. *US*). E19. [Du. *baas* master.] A *n.* 1 The master; a person in authority, an overseer, a business manager. Freq. as a form of address. E19. 2 A manager of a political organization. *US.* M19. B *attrib.* or as *adj.* (Of a person) master, chief; (of a thing) most excellent; *US slang* excellent, wonderful. M19.

Special collocations & comb.: **boss cocky** *Austral. slang* a farmer who shares the work with employees; a person in authority. **boss-man** a man in charge, the master.

bossism *n.* (*US*) the system in which political parties are controlled by bosses L19. **boss-ship** *n.* the rule or position of a boss or bosses, esp. in politics L19.

boss /bɒs/ *n.*[5] *dial.* & *US.* E19. [Origin unkn.] A cow; a bovine animal. Chiefly as a form of address.

bossy *n.* a cow, a calf M19.

boss /bɒs/ *n.*[6] *dial.* & *slang.* L19. [Rel. to BOSS *v.*[3]] In full *boss shot.* A bad shot or aim; an unsuccessful attempt.

boss /bɒs/ *v.*[1] LME. [f. BOSS *n.*[1]] †1 *v.t.* & *i.* (Cause to) project; swell or round out. LME–M17. 2 *v.t.* Shape in relief; beat or press *out* into a raised ornament; emboss. LME. 3 *v.t.* Provide or ornament with bosses. M16. 4 *v.t.* Smooth (a ceramic surface) by means of a boss. M19. 5 *v.t.* & *i.* Bang. *dial.* L19.

boss /bɒs/ *v.*[2]*t. colloq.* (orig. *US*). M19. [f. BOSS *n.*[4]] Be the master or manager of; give orders to, direct.

boss about continually give peremptory orders to.

boss /bɒs/ *v.*[3]*t.* & *i. dial.* & *slang.* L19. [Rel. to BOSS-EYED.] Miss or bungle (a shot); make a mess (of).

bossage /ˈbɒsɪdʒ/ *n.* E18. [Fr., f. *bosse* BOSS *n.*[1]: see -AGE.] *Archit.* Projecting stonework, bosses; *esp.* a type of rustic work.

bossa nova /bɒsə ˈnəʊvə/ *n. phr.* M20. [Port. *bossa* tendency, *nova* fem. sing. of *novo* new.] A style of Brazilian music related to the samba; a dance to this music.

bosselated /ˈbɒsɪleɪtɪd/ *a.* M19. [Fr. *bosselé* pa. pple of *bosseler*, f. *bosse* BOSS *n.*[1]: see -ATE[3], -ED[1].] Formed into small protuberances.

boss-eyed /ˈbɒsʌɪd/ *a. colloq.* M19. [Origin unkn.: cf. BOSS *n.*[6], *v.*[3]] Having only one good eye; squint-eyed, cross-eyed; *fig.* crooked.

bossy /ˈbɒsi/ *a.*[1] M16. [f. BOSS *n.*[1] + -Y[1].] Swelling in or projecting like a boss; having bosses.

bossiness *n.*[1] L19.

bossy /ˈbɒsi/ *a.*[2] *colloq.* (orig. *US*). L19. [f. BOSS *n.*[4] + -Y[1].] Given to acting like a boss; domineering.

Comb.: **bossyboots** an unwarrantedly bossy person.

bossiness *n.*[2] E20.

bostangi /bɒsˈtandʒi/ *n. obs.* exc. *Hist.* L17. [Turk. *bostancı* lit. 'gardener'.] A soldier of the Turkish palace guard.

bosthoon /bɒsˈtuːn/ *n. Anglo-Ir.* M19. [Ir. *bastún*] An ignorant lout; a tactless, insensitive person.

Boston /ˈbɒst(ə)n/ *n.* & *v.* E19. [A city in Massachusetts, USA: sense A.1 is through Fr.] A *n.* 1 A card-game resembling solo whist. E19. 2 *Boston baked beans*, a dish of baked beans with salt pork and molasses. M19. 3 A variation of the waltz or of the two-step. L19. 4 In full *Boston* (*bull*) *terrier.* (A dog of) a breed of small smooth-coated terrier originating in Massachusetts from a crossing of the bulldog and terrier. L19. 5 *Boston ivy*, a Virginia creeper, *Parthenocissus tricuspidata.* L19. 6 *Boston crab*, a wrestling hold in which a wrestler sits astride a prone opponent and pulls upwards on the opponent's legs. M20. B *v.i.* Dance the Boston. E20.

Bostoˈnese *n.* (*a*) *collect.* Bostonians; (*b*) the method of speech or the manners said to be affected by Bostonians: L18. **Bosˈtonian** *n.* & *a.* (*a*) *n.* a native or inhabitant of Boston; (*b*) *adj.* belonging or native to Boston: L17.

bostryx /ˈbɒstrɪks/ *n.* L19. [Gk *bostrux* curl of hair.] *Bot.* A helicoid cyme.

bosun /ˈbəʊs(ə)n/ *n.* Also **bo's'n, bo'sun.** M17. [Repr. pronunc. of BOATSWAIN.] = BOATSWAIN.

Boswell /ˈbɒzwɛl/ *n.* M19. [James *Boswell* (1740–95), companion and biographer of Samuel Johnson.] A person who, as a constant companion or attendant, witnesses and records the life of another.

Bosˈwellian, -ean *a.* & *n.* (*a*) *adj.* resembling Boswell as a biographer; (*b*) an admirer or student of Boswell or his writing: M19. **Boswellism** *n.* the manner or style of Boswell as a biographer E19. **Boswellize** *v.t.* & *i.* write (of) in the manner of Boswell M19.

bot /bɒt/ *n.*[1] Also **-tt.** E16. [Prob. of LDu. origin: cf. Du. *bot*, WFris. *botten* (pl.), WFlem. *botse*, NFris. *galboten* liver-worm, WFris. *botgalle* disease caused by bots.] 1 A parasitic worm or maggot infesting livestock; *spec.* the larva of a fly (called *bot-fly*) of the genus *Oestrus*, which affects esp. the digestive organs; *the bots* (as *sing.*), the disease caused by these parasites. E16. 2 A cadger; a useless person; a hanger-on. *Austral.* & *NZ slang.* E20.

bot /bɒt/ *n.*[2] *nursery* or *slang.* Also **-tt.** E20. [Abbrev. of BOTTOM *n.*: cf. BOTTY.] The buttocks.

bot *n.*[3] see BOOT *n.*[1]

bot /bɒt/ *v.i. Austral.* & *NZ slang.* Infl. **-tt-.** M20. [f. BOT *n.*[1]] Foll. by *on*: impose on, cadge from.

botanic /bəˈtanɪk/ *a.* & *n.* M17. [Fr. *botanique* or its source late L *botanicus* f. Gk *botanikos*, f. *botanē* plant: see -IC.] A *adj.* Of or pertaining to botany; *arch.* exc. in names of institutions etc., as *botanic gardens.* M17. B *n.* †1 A botanist. M17–E18. 2 In *pl.* Botany. Now *rare.* L17.

botanical /bəˈtanɪk(ə)l/ *a.* M17. [f. as prec. + -AL[1].] Of, pertaining to, or concerned with botany.

botanically *adv.* M18.

botanise *v.* var. of BOTANIZE.

botanist /ˈbɒt(ə)nɪst/ *n.* M17. [Fr. *botaniste*, f. as BOTANIC + *-iste* -IST.] An expert in or student of botany.

botanize /ˈbɒt(ə)nʌɪz/ *v.* Also **-ise.** M18. [mod.L *botanizare* f. Gk *botanizein* gather plants, f. *botanē* plant: see -IZE.] 1 *v.i.* Seek plants for botanical purposes; study plants, esp. where they are growing. M18. 2 *v.t.* Explore or examine botanically. M19.

botanizer *n.* E19.

botano- /ˈbɒt(ə)nəʊ/ *comb. form* of Gk *botanē* plant: see -O-.

botaˈnographer *n.* (*rare*) a person who describes plants L17. †**botanographist** *n.* = BOTANOGRAPHER M17–E18. †**botanology** *n.* botany M17–E18. **botanomancy** *n.* (*rare*) divination by means of plants E17.

botany /ˈbɒt(ə)ni/ *n.* L17. [f. BOTANIC + -Y[3].] 1 The science of the structure, physiology, classification, and distribution of plants. L17. 2 a *Botany Bay* (Hist.) [in New South Wales, Australia, named from its varied flora and formerly the site of a convict settlement], the destination of a transported convict, transportation. E19. b In full *Botany wool.* Merino wool, esp. from Australia. L19.

botargo /bəˈtɑːgəʊ/ *n.* Pl. **-o(e)s.** L16. [It. f. (med.) Gk *arghotarakho*, perh. through Pontic dial. *ovotarakho.*] A relish made of the roe of the mullet or tuna.

botch /bɒtʃ/ *n.*[1] LME. [ONFr. *boche* var. of OFr. *boce* BOSS *n.*[1]] †1 A hump, a swelling, a tumour. LME–E16. 2 A boil, an ulcer, a pimple. Now *dial.* LME. †3 An eruptive disease or plague. Chiefly in *botch of Egypt.* LME–M19.

†**botchy** *a.*[1] pertaining to, or of the nature of, a botch; covered with botches: LME–M18.

botch /bɒtʃ/ *n.*[2] E17. [f. BOTCH *v.*] 1 A botched place or part; a blemish arising from unskilful workmanship, a clumsy patch. E17. 2 A bungled piece of work. M17. 3 = BOTCHER *n.*[1] *dial.* & *colloq.* E19.

botchy *a.*[2] full of bungling work L19.

botch /bɒtʃ/ *v.* LME. [Origin uncertain: perh. transf. use of BOTCH *n.*[1] Cf. BODGE *v.*] 1 *v.t.* (freq. foll. by *up*) & *i.* Patch, mend, repair (now only clumsily or imperfectly). LME. 2 *v.t.* Spoil by unskilful work; bungle. M16. 3 *v.t.* Put or stitch together clumsily; construct or compose in a bungling manner. Freq. foll. by *up, together.* M16.

botcher /ˈbɒtʃə/ *n.*[1] LME. [f. prec. + -ER[1].] 1 An unskilful worker; a bungler. LME. 2 A mender, a patcher; *esp.* a cobbler or tailor who does repairs. L15.

botchery *n.* a botcher's work E17.

botcher /ˈbɒtʃə/ *n.*[2] E17. [Origin unkn.] A young salmon; a grilse.

bote *n.* see BOOT *n.*[1]

botel /bəʊˈtɛl/ *n.* Orig. *US.* Also **boatel.** M20. [Blend of BOAT *n.* and HOTEL.] 1 A hotel catering for boat-owners. M20. 2 A ship with the facilities of a hotel. M20.

boteroll /ˈbəʊtərɒl/ *n.* M19. [Fr. *bouterolle* tip of a scabbard etc.] *Her.* A charge resembling the tip of a scabbard.

both /bəʊθ/ *a.* & *pron.* (in mod. usage also classed as a *determiner*), *pron.*, & *adv.* ME. [ON *báðir* masc., *báðar* fem., *báði*, *bæði* neut. = OFris. *be(i)the*, *be(i)de*, OS *bēþia*, OHG *bēde* (G *beide*): extended form of the base found in OE *bēgen* masc., *bā*, *bū* fem. and neut., Goth. *bai* masc., *bā* neut., and in L *ambo*.] **A** *adj.* The one and the other; the two (and not just one). (Within the n. phr.: preceding a pl. n. and any determiners (demonstratives, possessives, etc.); †between a determiner and a pl. n.; following a pl. pron. or (with emphasis, esp. w. the subject of a sentence) n. Outside the n. phr.: following *be* or (*rare*) *become*, *seem*, etc., or an auxiliary vb.) ME.

G. CHAPMAN To plate the both horns round about with gold. TENNYSON Both thy brethren are in Arthur's hall. DICKENS We are both men of the world. OED The brothers might both have come. E. HEMINGWAY I held on to the timber with both hands. R. MACAULAY We both keep a kind of daily journal. J. JOHNSTON One heart seemed to beat in both their bodies. **both ways** *Racing* = EACH *way*. *cut both ways*: see CUT *v.* *have it both ways*: see HAVE *v.* *play both sides of the street*: see STREET *n.* *swing both ways*: see SWING *v.* *the best of both worlds*: see WORLD *n.*

B *pron.* **1** The one and the other (and not just one). ME. **2** Each, the two, *of* (two persons, things, etc.). Also (*colloq.*) *the both of*. Usu. followed by a pron. L16.

1 S. JOHNSON The old gentlewoman considered herself wiser than both. LD MACAULAY Both were Tories: both were men of hot temper and strong prejudices. **2** AV *Gen.* 22:8 They went both of them together. B. JOWETT Both of us often talk to the lads. J. P. DONLEAVY I'll make a nice pot of tea for the both of us.

C *adv.* With equal truth in either of two (or *arch.* more) cases. (Preceding (or, for reasons of style or emphasis, following) two wds or phrs. of the same kind coupled by *and*, *both* adds emphasis by means of an implied contrast.) ME.

SHAKES. *1 Hen. VI* I will rule both her, the King, and realm. GOLDSMITH A masterpiece both for argument and style. R. HODGSON See an old unhappy bull, Sick in soul and body both. J. IRVING There were a million images from the film on his mind, both real and imagined. A. MCCOWEN The actor is both pimp and prostitute.

bother /ˈbɒðə/ *n.* & *v.* L17. [Of Anglo-Ir. origin: prob. rel. to Ir. *bodhaire* deafness, noise, *bodhraim* deafen, annoy.] **A** *n.* **1** Noise; prating, chatter. *dial.* L17. **2** (A cause of) worry, fuss, minor trouble; a worried state. L18.

2 J. GALSWORTHY One had better save oneself the bother of thinking too. G. GREENE It's no bother It's the 'short times' that are the bother. B. PYM It was a bother to cook anything.

B *v.* **1** *v.t.* Bewilder with noise; confuse, fluster. *dial.* E18. **2** *v.t.* Give trouble to; pester, annoy, worry. M18. **b** *v.t.* & *i.* In *imper.* (expr. impatience). Curse, confound, damn. M19. **3** *v.i.* Worry or trouble oneself, make a fuss; make the required effort; be concerned (*with*, *about*). L18.

2 J. DOS PASSOS All the boys bothered their parents to buy them Rough Rider suits. E. ALBEE Why don't you go back to your necking and stop bothering me? I want to read. M. DRABBLE Oh, I'm not bothered, it's all the same to me. M. MOORCOCK I had begun to develop one of the headaches which have since bothered me all my life. **can't be bothered** will not make the required effort. *hot and bothered*: see HOT *a.* **b** DICKENS To this amorous address Miss Brass briefly responded 'Bother!' L. O'FLAHERTY Bother the mugs. We can drink outa the neck. **3** CARLYLE Make money; and don't bother about the Universe. L. M. MONTGOMERY I'd always be too tired at night to bother saying prayers. E. M. FORSTER You despise my mother . . because she's conventional and bothers over puddings. J. CHEEVER It was quite dark, but no one had bothered to turn on a light.

botheˈration *n.* the act of bothering; freq. as *int.*, bother!: L18. **bothersome** *a.* causing bother, mildly troublesome or annoying M20.

bothy /ˈbɒθi/ *n.* *Sc.* Also **-ie**. L18. [Obscurely rel. to Ir., Gael. *both*, *bothán*, perh. cogn. w. BOOTH.] A hut, a cottage; a one-roomed building in which labourers are lodged.

botling /ˈbɒtlɪŋ/ *n.* Now *rare* or *obs.* E17. [Perh. rel. to Du. *bot* stumpy.] The chub.

botony /ˈbɒtəni/ *a.* Also **bott-**. L16. [OFr. *botoné* (mod. *boutonné* covered with buds): see BUTTON *n.*, -Y⁵.] *Her.* Of a cross: having the end of each limb ornamented with three projections like buds.

bo-tree /ˈbəʊtriː/ *n.* M19. [Repr. Sinhalese *bōgaha*, f. *bō* (f. Pali and Skt *bodhi* perfect knowledge) + *gaha* tree.] A fig tree, *Ficus religiosa*, of India and SE Asia, regarded as sacred by Buddhists (because the Buddha received enlightenment under one). Also called *peepul*, *pipal*.

botryoidal /ˈbɒtrɪɔɪd(ə)l/ *a.* L18. [f. Gk *botruoeidēs*, f. *botrus*: see next, -OID, -AL[1].] Chiefly *Min.* Resembling a cluster of grapes in shape.

Also **botryoid** *a.* M18.

botrytis /bəˈtrʌɪtɪs/ *n.* L19. [mod.L, f. Gk *botrus* cluster of grapes.] A fungus of the genus *Botrytis*; plant disease caused by such a fungus.

Botswanan /bɒtˈswɑːnən/ *n.* & *a.* M20. [f. *Botswana* (see below) + -AN.] A native or inhabitant of, of or pertaining to, Botswana, an inland country of southern Africa (formerly Bechuanaland).

bott *n.* var. of BOT *n.*[1], *n.*[2]

Botticellian /bɒtɪˈtʃɛlɪən/ *a.* L19. [f. *Botticelli* (see below) + -AN.] Characteristic of or resembling the work of the Florentine painter Sandro Botticelli (1444–1510).

bottine /ˈbɒtiːn/ *n.* Now *rare* or *obs.* E16. [Fr., dim. of *botte* BOOT *n.*[2]: see -INE⁴.] A buskin or half-boot.

bottle /ˈbɒt(ə)l/ *n.*[1] LME. [OFr. *boteille* (mod. *bouteille*) f. med.L *butticula* dim. of late L *buttis* BUTT *n.*[3]] **1** A narrow-necked vessel, orig. of leather, now usu. of glass or plastic, for storing liquids. LME. **b** *spec.* An infant's feeding-bottle. M19. **c** A hot-water bottle. M19. **d** A metal cylinder for liquefied or compressed gas. E20. **2** The quantity (esp. of liquor) held by a bottle. L17. **3** The act or habit of drinking alcoholic liquor. E18. **4** A collection or share of money. *slang.* L19. **5a** In full *bottle and glass*. = ARSE *n.* *rhyming slang.* M20. **b** Courage, nerve, guts. *slang.* M20.

1 *beer bottle*, *feeding-bottle*, *hot-water bottle*, *ink bottle*, *milk bottle*, *water-bottle*, *wine bottle*, etc.

Phrases: *hit the bottle*: see HIT *v.* **lose one's bottle** *slang* lose one's nerve. *magnetic bottle*: see MAGNETIC *a.* **no** (or **not much**) **bottle** *slang* no good, useless. **on the bottle** drinking heavily, addicted to alcohol. **over a bottle** while drinking. *ship in a bottle*: see SHIP *n.* 1.

Comb.: **bottle-age** time spent by a wine etc. maturing in the bottle; **bottle-arsed** *a.* (of type) wider at one end than the other; **bottle bank** a receptacle for used bottles to be left for recycling of glass; **bottle-brush** (*a*) a cylindrical brush for cleaning the insides of bottles; (*b*) a plant suggestive of this, *esp.* an Australian shrub (e.g. banksia or callistemon) with brushlike flowers; **bottle-fed** *a.*, **-feed** *v.t.* & *i.*, **-feeding**: with milk from a feeding-bottle rather than from a woman's breast; **bottle-glass** coarse dark-green glass; *bottle-gourd*: see GOURD 1; **bottle-green** dark green; **bottle-head** (now *rare* or *obs.*) (*a*) a stupid person; (*b*) = *bottlenose* (c) below; **bottle-holder** a person who holds a bottle, *esp.* (*arch.*) a pugilist's second; **bottleneck** (*a*) the neck of a bottle; *spec.* one used over a guitarist's finger to produce sliding effects on the strings; any implement so used; guitar-playing with sliding effects; (*b*) a narrow place where road traffic etc. readily becomes congested; an obstruction to the even flow of production etc.; **bottlenose** (*a*) a swollen nose or snout; (*b*) *dial.* a puffin; (*c*) (more fully *bottlenose whale*) a whale of the genus *Hyperoodon*, or a dolphin of the genus *Tursiops*, with a long snout; **bottle-nosed** *a.* having a swollen nose or snout; **bottle-opener** a device for removing the caps from bottles of beer etc.; **bottle party** a drinking-party; a party to which each guest brings a bottle of wine etc.; **bottle-tit** *dial.* the long-tailed tit, *Aegithalos caudatus* (so called from the form of its nest); **bottle tree** an Australian tree of the genus *Brachychiton*, of the sterculia family, with a swollen bottle-shaped trunk; **bottle-washer** *colloq.* a menial, a factotum, an underling.

bottle-o(h) *n.* (*Austral.* & *NZ colloq.*) a collector of empty bottles E20.

bottle /ˈbɒt(ə)l/ *n.*[2] Now *dial.* or *obs.* exc. in phr. below. LME. [OFr. *botel* dim. of *botte* bundle, f. MLG, MDu. *bōte* bundle of flax, prob. f. Gmc base of BUTT *v.*[1]] A bundle of hay or straw.

look for a needle in a bottle of hay: see NEEDLE *n.*

bottle /ˈbɒt(ə)l/ *n.*[3] M16. [Alt. of BUDDLE *n.*[1]: infl. by BOTTLE *n.*[1]] A flower or insect, usu. of a distinctive colour. Now only as 2nd elem. of comb. forming distinct names, as *bluebottle*, *greenbottle*, etc.

bottle /ˈbɒt(ə)l/ *v.* E17. [f. BOTTLE *n.*[1]] **1** *v.t.* Put into a bottle or bottles for keeping; preserve (fruit etc.) in bottles; *fig.* (usu. foll. by *up*) conceal, restrain (feelings etc.) for a time; entrap or keep entrapped. E17. **2** *v.i.* Foll. by *out*: fail to act, back out through cowardice etc., = CHICKEN *v. slang.* L20.

bottled /ˈbɒt(ə)ld/ *a.* L16. [f. BOTTLE *n.*[1], *v.*: see -ED², -ED¹.] **1** Bottle-shaped; protuberant, swollen. Now *rare.* L16. **2** Stored or kept in a bottle or bottles; *fig.* (usu. foll. by *up*) pent up, kept under restraint. M17. **3** Drunk. *slang.* E20.

2 bottled gas liquefied butane.

bottler /ˈbɒtlə/ *n.* LME. [f. as prec. + -ER¹.] †**1** A bottle-maker. LME–L15. **2** A person who bottles liquor. L19. **3** Someone or something excellent. *Austral.* & *NZ slang.* L19.

bottom /ˈbɒtəm/ *n.* & *a.* [OE *botm* (*boþm*) = OS *bodom* (Du. *bodem*), corresp. w. variation of suff. (cf. OE *bytme*, *byþme*, *byþne* bottom, keel) to ON *botn*, and parallel to OE *bodan*, corresp. to OHG *Bodam* (G *Boden* ground, earth), f. Gmc, rel. to L *fundus*: sense 2 is infl. by Du.] **A** *n.* **I** The lowest part or surface. **1** The lowest part of a material thing; the surface of an object upon which the object rests; the undersurface, the base. OE. **b** The buttocks. Also, the seat of a chair. L18. **2** The keel or (horizontal part of) the hull of a ship; a ship or other vessel, esp. considered as a cargo-carrier. OE. **3** The ground under the water of the sea, a lake, a river, etc. OE. †**4** A deep place, an abyss. OE–M18. **5** The lowest part of a valley; a low-lying alluvial plain; a dell, a hollow. ME. **6** The lowest part of anything considered as a position in space, as the foot of a hill or slope, etc. ME. **b** The last place in a list etc.; the lowest place in point of honour, rank, etc.; the person occupying such a place. M17. **c** *sing.* & (freq.) in *pl.* The lowest workings in a mine. L18. **7** The furthest, most remote, or inmost part. E17. **8** *sing.* & (usu.) in *pl.* Matter remaining at the bottom of a liquid; dregs, sediment. M17.

1 LD MACAULAY Barrels with the bottoms knocked out served the purpose of chimneys. J. STEINBECK His stiff jeans, with the bottoms turned up eight inches to show his heeled boots. **b** D. DU MAURIER He sent my nurse packing . . because she smacked my bottom with a hair-brush. **2** BYRON He transferr'd his lading . . to another bottom. **3** G. BENNETT Two salvoes sent the *Cöln* to the bottom, with Admiral Maass . . and all but one of her crew. **4** AV *Wisd.* 17:14 The same sleepe . . came vpon them out of the bottomes of ineuitable hell. **6** C. KINGSLEY At the bottom of a hill they came to a spring. S. BECKETT In the other direction, I mean from top to bottom, it was the same. J. LE CARRÉ It was his signature all right . . . She'd seen it at the bottom of roneoed notices masses of times. **b** M. MCCARTHY That was like starting from the bottom in a factory. E. BLISHEN You came bottom in geography, didn't you, Hutchings? **7** DAY LEWIS At the bottom of the garden lay the lily ponds. P. O'BRIAN At the bottom of the bay [lay] the village of Trégonnec.

II Something which underlies or supports. **9** A thing upon which something is built or rests. Now only *fig.*, foundation, basis, footing. LME. **b** A core on which to wind thread; a skein or ball of thread. Long *dial.* LME. **10** The fundamental character, essence, reality. L16. **11** Physical resources, staying power; substance, stability. L18. **12** *Particle Physics.* = BEAUTY *n.* 5. L20.

9 HENRY MORE All the stately works and monuments Built on this bottome. W. PENN If we could not all meet upon a Religious Bottom, at least we might upon a Civil One. **10** G. ANSON If this matter was examined to the bottom. **11** A. BOYLE I personally prefer Trevor-Roper's thesis to Angleton's; it has more 'bottom' and better perspective. S. CRAIG

Whatever his faults, C. P. Snow possesses .. that old-fashioned English upper-class quality *bottom*.

Phrases: **at bottom** in reality, essentially, basically. **be at the bottom of** cause, underlie. *black bottom*: see BLACK *a*. *bottom of the heap*: see HEAP *n*. **bottoms up!**: a call to drain one's glass. **bottom up** upside down. *from the bottom of one's heart*: see HEART *n*. *from top to bottom*: see TOP *n*.[1] **get to the bottom of** fully investigate and explain, find out the truth about. *knock the bottom out of*: see KNOCK *v*. *second bottom*: see SECOND *a*. **stand on one's own bottom** *arch*. be independent, act for oneself. **the bottom drops** (or **falls**) **out of** there is a collapse of. **touch bottom** (*a*) reach the bottom of the water (esp. with the feet); reach the lowest or worst point; (*b*) be in possession of the full facts.

B *adj*. 1 Lowest, last; at or forming the bottom. M16. 2 *Particle Physics*. Designating a *b* quark. L20.

1 I. FLEMING The captain was sitting at the wheel, a light aluminum affair consisting only of the bottom half of a circle. S. HILL He put his foot on the bottom rung of the loft ladder. O. SCHELL Golden carp and common carp .. are bottom fish.

Special collocations & comb.: **bottom dog** = UNDERDOG. **bottom dollar** (one's) last dollar (*bet one's bottom dollar*, stake all, be very confident). **bottom drawer** *fig*. a woman's store of clothes etc. kept in preparation for marriage. **bottom-dwelling** *a*. (of an aquatic organism) dwelling on or near the bed of the sea, a lake, etc. *bottom edge*: see EDGE *n*. 4. **bottom fermentation** *Brewing* a process in which the yeast falls to the bottom during fermentation, as in the making of lager beers. **bottom-fermented** *a*. (*Brewing*) (of beer) made by bottom fermentation. **bottom gear** a vehicle's lowest gear. **bottom-land** *US* low-lying land, esp. by a river. **bottom line** the final total of an account, balance sheet, etc.; *fig*. the underlying reality, the final position. **bottom yeast** a yeast that falls to the bottom during fermentation.

bottomless *a*. without bottom; baseless; inexhaustible; immeasurably deep (*the bottomless pit*, hell): LME. **bottommost** *a*. at the very bottom, lowest M19.

bottom /ˈbɒtəm/ *v*. E16. [f. the n.] 1 *v.t*. Put a bottom to, provide with a bottom; *fig*. base, ground, (*up*)*on*. E16. †2 *v.t*. Wind (as a skein). L16–E17. †3 *v.i*. Be based or grounded. M17–L18. 4 *v.t*. Reach or touch the bottom of; find the extent or real nature of; drain, empty (a glass etc.). L18. 5 *v.i*. Reach or touch bottom; reach its lowest level (freq. foll. by *out*). L19. b *spec*. Strike gold etc. Also foll. by *on* (gold etc.). *Austral*. & *NZ*. L19.

1 OED Send this saucepan to be new bottomed. 4 COLERIDGE Openly declaiming on subjects .. which they had never bottomed. 5 *Glasgow Herald* Others with shallower purses are content to wait until prices have bottomed.

bottomer *n*. a person who provides or fits bottoms (esp. for chairs) E18.

bottomed /ˈbɒtəmd/ *a*. M16. [f. BOTTOM *n*., *v*.: see -ED[2], -ED[1].] Having a bottom, provided with a bottom or foundation (of specified form or nature).

bottomry /ˈbɒtəmri/ *n*. & *v*. L16. [f. BOTTOM *n*. + -RY, after Du. *bodemerij*.] A *n*. The system of lending money to the owner or master of a ship on the security of the ship for the purpose of completing a voyage, the lender losing the money if the ship is lost. L16. B *v.t*. Pledge (a ship) thus. M18.

bottony *a*. var. of BOTONY.

botty /ˈbɒti/ *n*. *nursery* or *slang*. L19. [f. BOTTOM *n*. + -Y[6]: cf. BOT *n*.[2]] The buttocks.

botulism /ˈbɒtjʊlɪz(ə)m/ *n*. L19. [G *Botulismus* orig. 'sausage-poisoning', f. L *botulus* sausage: see -ISM.] Food poisoning due to the bacillus *Clostridium botulinum*, found esp. in improperly sterilized tinned meats and other preserved foods.

botulin *n*. the bacterial toxin involved in botulism E20. **botulinum toxin** /bɒtjʊˈlʌɪnəm ˈtɒksɪn/, **botulinus toxin** /-əs/ *n*. *phrs*. = BOTULIN E20.

boucan /ˈbuːk(ə)n/ *n*. Also **buccan** /ˈbʌk(ə)n/. E17. [Fr. f. Tupi *mukem*, *mocaém*.] 1 In S. America: a wooden frame for cooking, smoking, or drying meat over an open fire. Cf. BARBECUE *n*. 4. E17. 2 Meat cooked or cured on such a frame. Cf. BARBECUE *n*. 2. M19. 3 = BARBECUE *n*. 5. M19.

boucan /ˈbuːk(ə)n/ *v.t*. Also **buccan** /ˈbʌk(ə)n/. E17. [Fr. *boucaner*, f. as prec.] Cook, smoke, or dry (meat etc.) on a boucan. Cf. BARBECUE *v*.

bouchée /buʃe/ *n*. Pl. pronounced same. M19. [Fr. = mouthful, f. *bouche* mouth.] A small baked confection. Usu. in *pl*.

bouclé /ˈbuːkleɪ/ *a*. & *n*. L19. [Fr. = buckled, curled.] (Fabric) woven with a knotted and curled appearance; (yarn) of looped or curled ply.

boudin /*in sense 2 only* ˈbuːdɪn; *foreign* budɛ̃ (*pl*. *same*)/ *n*. M19. [Fr.] 1 (Not naturalized.) A black pudding; forcemeat shaped like a sausage. M19. 2 *Geol*. Any of a number of roughly parallel elongated sections resulting from the fracturing of a rock stratum during folding. E20.

boudinage /buːdɪˈnɑːʒ/ *n*. (*Geol*.) (the formation of) a structure containing a number of boudins E20.

boudoir /ˈbuːdwɑː/ *n*. L18. [Fr., lit. 'place to sulk in', f. *bouder* pout, sulk.] A (woman's) small private room.

bouffant /ˈbuːfɑ̃/ *n*. & *a*. E19. [Fr., pres. pple of *bouffer* swell: see -ANT[1].] A *n*. A puffed-out part of a dress etc.; a puffed-out hairstyle. E19. B *adj*. Of a dress, hairstyle, etc.: puffed out. L19.

bougainvillea /buːg(ə)nˈvɪlɪə/ *n*. Also **-llaea**, **-llia**. M19. [mod.L, f. L. A. de *Bougainville* (1729–1811), Fr. navigator: see -A[1], -IA[1].] A tropical S. American plant of the genus *Bougainvillea*, with large brightly coloured bracts almost concealing the flowers.

bouge /buːdʒ/ *n*. & *v*. *obs*. exc. *dial*. See also BUDGE *n*.[2] LME. [(O)Fr.: see BUDGET *n*., BULGE *n*. & *v*.] A *n*. †1 = BULGE *n*. 1. LME–E17. †2 A swelling, a hump. LME–L15. 3 The bilge of a cask. M18. B *v*. 1 *v.i*. Swell out, bulge. LME. †2 *v.t*. Stave in (a ship's bottom, etc.), bilge. L15–E17.

bouget /ˈbuːdʒɪt/ *n*. L16. [Var. of BUDGET *n*.] *Her*. An ancient water vessel consisting of a yoke with two leather pouches or skins attached.

bough /baʊ/ *n*. & *v*. [OE *bōg*, *bōh* = MLG *boch*, *būch* (LG *boog*), MDu. *boech* (Du. *boeg* shoulders, chest of a horse, bows of a ship), OHG *buog* shoulder, forearm (G *Bug* horse's hock or point of shoulder, bow of a ship), ON *bógr* shoulder, f. Gmc, rel. to Gk *pēkhus* forearm, cubit.] A *n*. †1 The shoulder of an animal. OE–LME. 2 Any of the larger limbs or offshoots of a tree; a (main) branch. OE. 3 A limb, a leg. *Sc*. M16. 4 The gallows. *arch*. L16.

Comb.: **bough-house** (*a*) *US* a temporary structure made of boughs; (*b*) *dial*. (now *Hist*.) a house opened only at fair-time for the sale of liquor; **bough-pot** (*arch*. & *dial*.) = BEAU-POT.

B *v.t*. Strip of boughs. *rare*. E16.

boughed /baʊd/ *a*. having boughs; stripped of boughs: LME.

bought /baʊt/ *n*.[1] & *v*.[1] Long *arch*. & *dial*. LME. [Prob. LG *bucht* (see BIGHT): cf. BOUT *n*.] A *n*. 1 A bend, a curve. LME. 2 A loop or turn of a rope etc.; a coil. LME. B *v.t*. & *i*. Bend, wind, fold. LME.

bought /baʊxt, bʌxt/ *n*.[2] & *v*.[2] *Sc*. Also **bught**. LME. [Origin unkn.] A *n*. A sheepfold. LME. B *v.t*. Pen or fold (sheep); fence in. E18.

bought *v*. pa. t. & pple of BUY *v*.

boughten /ˈbɔːt(ə)n/ *ppl a*. *N. Amer*., *dial*., & *poet*. L18. [f. next: see prec., -EN[6].] Bought; purchased at a shop as opp. to home-made.

boughten *v*. pa. pple: see BUY *v*.

bougie /ˈbuːʒi/ *n*. M18. [Fr. f. *Bougie* (Arab. *Bijāya*) a town in Algeria which carried on a trade in wax.] 1 A wax candle. M18. 2 *Med*. A rod or tube for exploring or dilating the passages of the body. M18.

bougienage /buːdʒɪˈnɑːʒ/ *n*. (*Med*.) dilatation by means of a bougie E20.

bouillabaisse /buːjəˈbeɪs, *foreign* bujabɛs/ *n*. M19. [Fr. f. mod.Prov. *bouiabaisso*.] A Provençal dish of fish stewed in water or white wine.

bouilli /ˈbuːji, *foreign* buji/ *n*. E17. [Fr., use as n. of pa. pple of *bouillir* BOIL *v*.: cf. BULLY *n*.[2]] Boiled or stewed meat, esp. beef.

bouillon /ˈbuːjɔ̃, *foreign* bujɔ̃/ *n*. M17. [Fr., f. *bouillir* BOIL *v*.] Broth, thin soup. See also COURT BOUILLON.

Comb.: **bouillon cube** a stock cube.

bouk /buːk/ *n*. Now *Sc*. & *dial*. [OE *būc* = OFris., MLG *būk*, OHG *būh* (G *Bauch*), ON *búkr*, f. Gmc.] †1 The belly. OE–L15. 2 The trunk; the body of a person or animal. ME. 3 Bulk, volume, size. L17.

boul /buːl/ *n*. *obs*. exc. *Sc*. & *north*. Also **bool**. L15. [Perh. f. MDu. *böghel* (Du. *beugel*, G *Bügel*) rel. to Gmc base of BOW *v*.[1]: see -EL[1].] Something bent into a curve; *esp*. the curved handle of a pail, kettle, etc.

boulangerite /bʊˈlandʒərʌɪt/ *n*. M19. [f. C. L. *Boulanger* (1810–49), Fr. mining engineer + -ITE[1].] *Min*. A monoclinic sulphide of antimony and lead, usu. occurring as elongated or fibrous grey metallic crystals.

Boulangist /buːˈlandʒɪst/ *n*. & *a*. L19. [f. *Boulanger* (see below) + -IST.] *Hist*. (A member) of a French political party formed by General Georges E. J. M. Boulanger (1837–91), advocating a policy of anti-German militarism.

Boulangism *n*. L19.

boulder /ˈbəʊldə/ *n*. & *v*. Also ***bowlder**. LME. [Shortened f. next.] A *n*. A large water- or weather-worn stone. LME.

Comb.: **boulder-clay** *Geol*. clay containing many large stones and boulders, formed by deposition from melting glaciers and ice sheets.

B *v*. 1 *v.t*. Make into boulders. *rare*. M19. 2 *v.i*. Climb large boulders. Chiefly as *bouldering* vbl n. E20.

bouldery *a*. characterized by the presence of boulders M19.

boulderstone /ˈbəʊldəstəʊn/ *n*. ME. [Of Scand. origin: cf. Sw. dial. *bullersten*, *buldurstajn*, perh. rel. to Sw. *bullra* rumble.] A boulder.

boule /ˈbuːli/ *n*.[1] M19. [Gk *boulē* senate.] A legislative body of ancient or modern Greece.

boule /buːl, *foreign* bul/ *n*.[2] Pl. **boules** /*in sense 2* buːl, *in sense 3* buːlz, *foreign* bul/. E20. [Fr. = BOWL *n*.[2]] 1 A form of roulette. E20. 2 *sing*. & in *pl*. A French form of bowls played on rough ground, usu. with metal bowls. E20. 3 A small pear-shaped mass of synthetic sapphire, ruby, etc., made by fusing suitably tinted alumina. M20.

boule *n*.[3] var. of BUHL.

boulevard /ˈbuːləvɑːd, *foreign* bulvaːr (*pl*. *same*)/ *n*. M18. [Fr. f. as BULWARK: in Fr. orig. = rampart, (later) a promenade on the site of this.] A broad street (esp. in France) with rows of trees planted along it; *US* a broad main urban road.

boulevarded *a*. provided with boulevards L19.

boulevardier /bulvardje/ *n*. Pl. pronounced same. L19. [Fr., f. as prec. + *-ier* -ER[1].] A person who frequents (French) boulevards.

bouleverse /buːlˈvəːs/ *v.t*. L17. [Fr. *bouleverser* turn as a ball, f. as BOULE *n*.[2] + *verser* turn.] Overturn, upset.

bouleversement /bulvɛrsəmɑ̃/ *n*. Pl. pronounced same. L18. [Fr., f. as prec.: see -MENT.] An inversion, *esp*. a violent one; an upset, an upheaval.

boulle *n*. var. of BUHL.

boult *n*., *v*. vars. of BOLT *n*.[2], *v*.[1]

boulter /ˈbəʊltə/ *n*. Also **bolter**. L16. [Origin unkn.] A long fishing-line with many hooks.

†**boun** *a*. var. of BOUND *a*.[1]

boun /baʊn/ *v*. Long *arch*. & *dial*. ME. [f. †*boun* var. of BOUND *ppl a*.[1]] 1 *v.t*. (usu. *refl*.) & *i*. Prepare (oneself); make ready; dress. ME. 2 *v.i*. Set out, go *to*. ME.

bounce /baʊns/ *n*.[1] E16. [f. the vb.] 1 A resounding knock; a heavy blow, a thump; an explosion, the report of a gun. Now *rare* or *obs*. E16. 2 A leap, a bound; *esp*. the rebound of a ball etc. from a hard surface. E16. 3 Orig., a swaggering boast, a boastful falsehood. Now, swagger, exaggeration; rebounding power, vitality, exuberance. E18. b A buoyant musical rhythm. *colloq*. (orig. *US*). M20. 4 An act of ejection or dismissal. *slang* (orig. *US*). L19.

2 **on the bounce** (*a*) in continual spasmodic motion; (*b*) in the act of rebounding. 3 DE QUINCEY The whole story is a bounce of his own. L. P. HARTLEY All the glow and bounce and boyishness had gone out of him.

Comb.: **bounce-flash** (a device for giving) reflected photographic flashlight.

bouncy *a.* that bounces, boisterous, buoyant; resilient, springy (*bouncy castle*: see CASTLE *n.*[1] 1b): E20.

bounce /baʊns/ *n.*[2] E18. [Origin unkn.] The nurse hound, *Scyliorhinus stellaris*.

bounce /baʊns/ *v.* ME. [Origin uncertain: perh. f. LDu. (cf. LG *bunsen* beat, thump, Du. *bons* a thump), or of independent imit. origin.] I †1 *v.t.* Beat, thump; slam (a door etc.). ME–E19. †2 *v.i.* Make an explosive or banging noise; knock loudly at a door etc. (Cf. earlier BOUNCE *int.* 1.) M16–E18. 3 *v.t.* & *i.* Talk big, bluster (at); hector; swagger; hustle by bluff etc. *into* or *out of* something. E17. b Blurt *out*; come *out with*. M17. II Of movement. 4a *v.i.* & †*t.* w. *it.* Move boundingly; rebound (as a ball). E16. b *v.i.* Come or go *in, into, out*, etc., energetically or noisily; move *about* vigorously or unceremoniously; jump *up*. L17. c *v.i.* Of a cheque: be returned by a bank when there are no funds to meet it. E20. 5 *v.t.* Cause to rebound (as a ball); present (a cheque) which has to be returned by the bank (see sense 4c above). L19. b *Cricket*. Bowl a bouncer or bouncers at (a batsman). M20. 6 *v.t.* Eject summarily; dismiss, sack. *colloq.* (orig. *US*). L19.

bouncing *a.* that bounces; boisterous; big of its kind, (of a baby) big and healthy; *bouncing Bet*, the soapwort (*Saponaria officinalis*); *bouncing castle*: see CASTLE *n.*[1] 1b: E16. **bouncingly** *adv.* E16.

bounce /baʊns/ *int.* & *adv.* E16. [Imit. or f. the vb.] A *int.* †1 Repr. the sound of a gun or a heavy blow: bang! E16–E17. 2 Repr. a bouncing movement. M19. B *adv.* With a bounce. E17.

bouncer /ˈbaʊnsə/ *n.* L16. [f. BOUNCE *v.* + -ER[1].] 1 A large specimen of its kind; *spec.* a gross or flagrant lie. *arch.* L16. 2 A person who blusters or talks big; a boaster, a liar. *arch.* M18. 3 A person employed to eject troublesome persons from a dancehall, nightclub, etc. *colloq.* M19. 4 *Cricket*. A fast short-pitched ball that rises sharply. E20.

bound /baʊnd/ *n.*[1] ME. [AN *bounde*, OFr. *bodne*, later *bo(u)sne*, *bo(u)ne*, *bonde*, etc. (mod. *borne*), f. med.L *bodina*, earlier *butina*, of unkn. origin: cf. BOURN *n.*[2]] †1a A landmark. Only in ME. b A territorial limit, a boundary line. Usu. in *pl.* LME. 2 *sing.* & (usu.) in *pl.* Territory situated near a boundary; borderland; land within set limits. ME. b A tract of ground taken in by a tin-miner. L17. 3 *fig.* A limitation or restriction upon feeling, action, duration, etc. Usu. in *pl.* LME. b A limiting value. Chiefly in *upper, lower bound*. E20.

1 *beat the bounds*: see BEAT *v.*[1] 15. **out of bounds** beyond set limits, esp. those set by the rules of a school, military regulations, etc.; forbidden, inaccessible.

bound /baʊnd/ *n.*[2] E16. [(O)Fr. *bond*, f. as BOUND *v.*[2]] A springy movement upward or forward, a leap; a bounce or recoil (of a ball etc.).

by leaps and bounds: see LEAP *n.*[1]

bound /baʊnd/ *a.*[1] Orig. †**boun**. ME. [ON *búinn* pa. pple of *búa* prepare, *-d* partly euphonic, partly infl. by next: cf. BOUN *v.*] †1 Ready, prepared; attired. ME–M19. 2 Ready to start or having set out (*for, on*, †*to*); moving in a specified direction. LME. 3 About *to do*, going *to do*. *north*. M19.

1 SIR W. SCOTT A band of war Has for two days been ready boune. 2 J. F. W. HERSCHEL Bound on we know not what errand. C. A. LINDBERGH My grandfather . . embarked on a ship bound for America. *homeward-bound, northbound, outward-bound, southbound*, etc.

bound /baʊnd/ *a.*[2] LME. [pa. pple of BIND *v.*, abbrev. of BOUNDEN *a.*] 1 That has been bound: see BIND *v.* I. LME. 2 *Ling.* Of a grammatical element: occurring only in combination with another form. E20.

¶ Earlier in UNBOUND *a.*[1]

bound /baʊnd/ *v.*[1] LME. [f. BOUND *n.*[1]] 1 *v.t.* Set bounds to, limit, restrict. Now only *fig.* LME. 2 *v.i.* Abut *on* a territory etc.; share a boundary (*with*). *arch.* M16. 3 *v.t.* Form the boundary of; enclose. L16.

1 MILTON He shall . . bound his Reign With earth's wide bounds. A. B. JAMESON His views were not bounded by any narrow ideas of expediency. 3 H. BELLOC Some wood which bounded our horizon.

bounding *n.*[1] (*a*) the action of the vb; †(*b*) a boundary: M16.

bound /baʊnd/ *v.*[2] L16. [(O)Fr. *bondir* resound, (later) rebound, f. Proto-Romance var. of late L *bombitare* var. of *bombilare*: see BOMBILATE.] 1 *v.i.* Spring, leap; advance lightly and buoyantly. L16. 2 *v.i.* Recoil, rebound; bounce. L16. †3 *v.t.* Cause (a horse) to leap. Only in L16.

bounding *vbl n.*[2] (*a*) the action of the vb; (*b*) a leap, a bound: E17.

bound /baʊnd/ *v.*[3]*i.* & *refl.* *rare*. L16. [Var. of BOUN *v.*] Direct one's course, go.

bound *v.*[4] pa. t. & pple of BIND *v.*

boundary /ˈbaʊnd(ə)ri/ *n.* E17. [Alt. of BOUNDER *n.*[1], perh. after *limitary*.] 1 A thing which serves to mark the limits of something; the limit itself, a dividing line. E17. 2 *spec.* The limit of a cricket field; a hit to this, scoring four or six runs. M19.

Comb.: **boundary condition** *Math.* a condition that is required to be satisfied at all or part of the boundary of a region in which a set of differential conditions is to be solved; **boundary layer** the layer of a fluid adjacent to a body in it when the two are in relative motion; **boundary-rider** *Austral.* & *NZ* a stockman employed to ride round a sheep or cattle station mending fences etc; **boundary value** *Math.* a value specified by a boundary condition.

bounded /ˈbaʊndɪd/ *a.*[1] L16. [f. BOUND *v.*[1] + -ED[1].] Subject to bounds or limits; *fig.* circumscribed, restricted.

boundedness *n.* bounded quality; limited range: L17.

†**bounded** *a.*[2] L16–E19. [f. BOUND *a.*[2] + -ED[1].] = BOUND *a.*[2] 1.

bounden /ˈbaʊnd(ə)n/ *a.* ME. [pa. pple of BIND *v.*] 1 = BOUND *a.*[2] 1. *arch.* ME. 2 Of duty etc.: obligatory. M16.

bounden *v.* pa. pple: see BIND *v.*

bounder /ˈbaʊndə/ *n.*[1] E16. [f. BOUND *v.*[1] + -ER[1].] 1 A limit, a boundary; a landmark. Long *arch.* & *dial.* E16. 2 A person who occupies a boundary area; *spec.* the holder of a bound of tin-ore ground. Now *rare*. M16. 3 A person who sets or marks bounds or limits. L16.

bounder /ˈbaʊndə/ *n.*[2] *slang*. M19. [f. BOUND *v.*[2] + -ER[1].] †1 A four-wheeled cab or trap. Only in M19. 2 An ill-bred person, a cad. L19.

boundless /ˈbaʊndlɪs/ *a.* L16. [f. BOUND *n.*[1] + -LESS.] Without bounds or limits; unrestricted, infinite.

boundlessly *adv.* E17. **boundlessness** *n.* E17.

bounteous /ˈbaʊntɪəs/ *a.* Now chiefly *rhet.* LME. [f. OFr. *bontif*, *-ive* benevolent (f. *bonté* BOUNTY) after PLENTEOUS.] 1 Full of goodness (to others); generous, munificent. LME. 2 Of things: generously bestowed; ample, abundant. M16.

bounteously *adv.* M16. **bounteousness** *n.* liberality, munificence LME.

bountiful /ˈbaʊntɪfʊl, -f(ə)l/ *a.* E16. [f. BOUNTY + -FUL.] = prec.

Lady Bountiful: see LADY *a.* & *n.*

bountifully *adv.* L16. **bountifulness** *n.* L15.

bountihead /ˈbaʊntɪhɛd/ *n.* *arch.* *rare*. L16. [f. BOUNTY + -HEAD.] Bounteousness.

¶ First recorded in Spenser.

bountith /ˈbaʊntɪθ, ˈbʌn-/ *n.* *arch.* *Sc.* & *north.* LME. [App. f. OFr. *bontet*, *buntet* earlier form of *bonté*: see next.] A gratuity; a reward.

bounty /ˈbaʊnti/ *n.* ME. [(O)Fr. *bonté* f. L *bonitas*, f. *bonus* good: see -TY[1].] †1 Goodness in general, worth, excellence; high estate; in *pl.*, virtues. ME–E17. †b Valour, prowess. ME–M16. †2 (An act of) kindness. ME–M17. 3 Goodness shown in giving, munificence, liberality. ME. 4 An act of generosity; a gift, a gratuity. ME. b *spec.* A monetary reward or premium paid by the State, Crown, etc., e.g. (*a*) to recruits on enlistment, (*b*) for promoting trade in particular ways, (*c*) for the killing of dangerous animals etc. E18.

4 **king's** or **queen's bounty** *Hist.* a grant paid to the mother of three or more children born at once. **Queen Anne's bounty** *Hist.* a fund for augmenting poor benefices.

Comb.: **bounty-hunter** a person who tracks and captures outlaws or kills dangerous animals etc. for the reward offered; **bounty-jumper** *US Hist.* a recruit who enlisted for the bounty and promptly deserted (to enlist again).

bouquet /bʊˈkeɪ, bəʊˈkeɪ, ˈbʊkeɪ/ *n.* See also BOKAY. E18. [Fr. (earlier = clump of trees), f. dial. var. of OFr. *bos*, *bois* wood. Cf. BUSH *n.*[1], -ET[1].] 1 A bunch of flowers, *esp.* a large attractive one for use at a ceremony. E18. b *fig.* A compliment. E20. 2 The perfume of wine etc. M19. 3 *bouquet garni* /ˈgɑːni/ [Fr., lit. 'garnished bouquet'], a bunch of herbs for flavouring. M19. 4 A number of rockets etc. fired together. L19.

bouquetier /bʊkəˈtɪə, *foreign* buktje (*pl. same*)/ *n.* a small holder for a bunch of flowers L18.

bouquetin /ˈbuːkətɪn/ *n.* L18. [Fr. f. OFr. *boc estaign*, f. MHG STEINBOCK.] The Alpine ibex.

Bourbon /ˈbʊəbən/ *n.*[1] & *a.* M18. [Fr. (see below), f. *Bourbon* (*l'Archambault*), a town in central France.] A *n.* 1 *Hist.* A member of the House of Bourbon, a former royal dynasty holding sovereignty in France, Naples, and Spain. M18. 2 [f. the former name (Isle de *Bourbon*) of the island of Réunion.] A hybrid rose, *Rosa* × *borboniana*, of a group descended from *Rosa chinensis* and *R. damascena*. Also *Bourbon rose*. E19. 3 A political reactionary. *US*. M19.

B *attrib.* or as *adj.* Of or pertaining to the House of Bourbon; *US* reactionary in politics. M18.

Bourbon biscuit a chocolate-flavoured biscuit with a chocolate-cream filling.

Bourbonism *n.* adherence to the Bourbon dynasty or (*US*) to reactionary policies L19. **Bourbonist** *n.* a supporter of the Bourbon dynasty E19.

bourbon /ˈbəːbən, ˈbʊə-/ *n.*[2] Also **B-**. M19. [*Bourbon* County, Kentucky.] (A drink of) an American whiskey distilled from maize and rye.

bourd /bʊəd/ *n.* & *v.* *obs.* exc. *Sc.* ME. [(O)Fr. *bourde* lie, cheating = Prov. *borda*, of unkn. origin.] A *n.* An amusing tale, a jest; joking, banter, fun. ME. B *v.* 1 *v.i.* & *t.* Say things in jest; make fun (of), mock. ME. †2 *v.i.* Play games. LME–M16.

bourder *n.* (*obs.* exc. *Hist.*) a jester; a mocker: ME.

bourdon /ˈbʊəd(ə)n/ *n.* Also **burdoun**. ME. [(O)Fr. = drone, f. Proto-Romance, of imit. origin.] 1 = BURDEN *n.* 6 (with which early merged). Now *rare* or *obs.* ME. 2 A low-pitched stop in an organ or harmonium; the drone pipe of a bagpipe. M19. 3 The lowest-pitched in a peal of bells. E20.

bourdonné /bʊəˈdɒneɪ, *foreign* burdɔne/ *a.* E17. [Fr., f. *bourdon* (pilgrim's knobbed) staff.] *Her.* Terminating in knobs or balls.

bourg /bʊəg/ *n.* LME. [(O)Fr. f. med.L *burgus* BOROUGH.] A town or village under the shadow of a castle (*Hist.*); a Continental town.

bourgade /burgad/ *n.* Pl. pronounced same. E17. [Fr., f. as prec. + -ADE.] A (continental) large village or straggling unwalled town.

bourgeois /bəːˈdʒɔɪs/ *n.*[1] E19. [Conjectured to be f. the name of a printer; but perh. referring to its intermediate size.] A former size of type between long primer and brevier.

bourgeois /ˈbʊəʒwɑː, *foreign* burʒwa/ *a.* & *n.*[2] M16. [Fr.: see BURGESS.] A *adj.* 1 Of, pertaining to, characteristic of, or resembling, the bourgeois (see sense B. below); middle-class; conventionally respectable and unimaginative, humdrum; selfishly materialistic; capitalistic, reactionary. M16. 2 Of French wine: next in quality to wines classified as the best. E20. B *n.* Pl. same. 1 Orig., a (French) citizen or freeman of a city or burgh, as distinct from a peasant or a gentleman. Now, any member of the middle class. L17. 2 In Communist or socialist writing: a capitalist, an exploiter of the proletariat. *derog.*

L19. 3 A socially or aesthetically conventional person, a philistine. *derog.* M20.

¶See also PETIT BOURGEOIS, *petty bourgeois* s.v. PETTY *a.*, ÉPATER *le(s) bourgeois*.

bourgeoisdom *n.* (the political ascendancy of) the bourgeoisie L19. **bourgeoisification** /bʊəˌʒwɑːzɪfɪˈkeɪʃ(ə)n/ *n.* the action of bourgeoisifying a community etc. M20. **bourgeoisify** /bʊəˈʒwɑːzɪfʌɪ/ *v.t.* convert to a bourgeois outlook or way of life M20.

bourgeoise /ˈbʊəʒwɑːz, burʒwaz/ *n.* & *a. fem.* Pl. of n. pronounced same. L18. [Fr., fem. of prec.] A *n.* A female bourgeois. L18. B *adj.* Of a female: bourgeois. M20.

bourgeoisie /bʊəʒwɑːˈziː, *foreign* burʒwazi/ *n.* E18. [Fr., f. BOURGEOIS *a.* & *n.*[2]: see -Y[3].] The bourgeois collectively; the middle class.

HAUTE BOURGEOISIE. PETITE BOURGEOISIE. *petty bourgeoisie*: see PETTY *a.*

bourn /bɔːn, bʊən/ *n.*[1] Also **bourne**. ME. [S. Eng. var. of BURN *n.*[1]] A small stream, a brook.

bourn /bɔːn, bʊən/ *n.*[2] Also **bourne**. E16. [Fr. *borne*: see BOUND *n.*[1]] †1 A boundary between fields etc.; a frontier. E16–L18. 2 A bound, a limit. *arch.* E17. 3 Destination; a goal. *arch.* E19. 4 Realm, domain. *poet. rare.* E19.

2 J. THOMSON From the far bourne Of utmost Saturn. 3 WORDSWORTH The selected bourne Was now an Island. 4 KEATS In water, fiery realm, and airy bourne.

¶Senses 3 & 4 both arise from interpretations of Shakes. *Haml.* ('Something after death—The undiscover'd country, from whose bourn No traveller returns'), which prob. belongs w. sense 1.

bourne *n.* var. of BOURN *n.*[1], *n.*[2]

bournonite /ˈbʊənənʌɪt/ *n.* E19. [f. Count J. L. de *Bournon* (1751–1825), Fr. mineralogist + -ITE[1].] *Min.* An orthorhombic sulphide of lead, copper, and antimony, usu. occurring as steel-grey prisms.

bourock /ˈbuːrək/ *n. Sc.* M18. [Perh. rel. to BOWER *n.*[1] or to BOROUGH: see -OCK.] 1 A mound; a heap; a mass. M18. 2 A little cot or hut. L18. 3 A group; a crowd. E19.

bourrée /ˈbʊəreɪ; *foreign* bure (*pl. same*)/ *n.* Also †**boree**. L17. [Fr.] A lively dance of French origin, resembling the gavotte; a piece of music for this dance or in its rhythm, *esp.* one which forms a movement of a suite.

Comb.: **bourrée step** a sideways step in dancing in which one foot crosses behind or in front of the other.

bourse /bʊəs/ *n.* L16. [Fr.: see BURSE.] A money market; an exchange; *esp.* (**B-**) the Paris stock exchange. Cf. BURSE 2.

¶Rare bef. M19 (*burse* being usual) when readopted f. mod.Fr.

bourtree /ˈbʊətriː/ *n. Sc.* & *north.* LME. [Origin unkn.] The elder, *Sambucus nigra*.

bouse *n.* & *v.*[1] var. of BOOZE.

bouse /baʊz/ *v.*[2]*t.* Also **bowse**. L16. [Origin unkn.] Chiefly *Naut.* Haul with tackle.

boustrophedon /baʊstrəˈfiːd(ə)n, buː-/ *adv.* & *a.* E17. [Gk = as the ox turns in ploughing, f. *bous* ox + *-strophos* STROPHE + *-don* advb. suff.] (Written) from right to left and from left to right in alternate lines.

boustrophe'donic *a.* E19.

bout /baʊt/ *n.* & *v.* M16. [var. of BOUGHT *n.*[1]: assoc. w. next.] A *n.* 1 A bending, a curve; = BOUGHT *n.*[1] 1; *esp.* a curve of the side of a violin etc. M16. 2†a A circuit, a roundabout way. M16–M17. b The going of a plough along two adjacent furrows. E17. 3 A spell of or a turn at work or exercise. L16. b A spell of drinking. L17. 4 A boxing- or wrestling-match; a fight, a contest of strength. L16. 5 An attack of illness etc. L19.

3 **this** (or **that**) **bout** (now *dial.*) this (or that) occasion or time.

B *v.t.* Plough in bouts. M18.

bout /baʊt/ *prep.* & (*rare*) *adv. colloq.* & *dial.* ME. [Aphet.] = ABOUT.

boutade /buːˈtɑːd/ *n.* E17. [Fr., f. *bouter* thrust: see -ADE.] A sudden outburst or outbreak.

†**boutefeu** *n.* L16–M19. [Fr., f. *bouter* put + *feu* fire.] A person who kindles strife, a firebrand.

boutique /buːˈtiːk/ *n.* M18. [Fr. f. OProv. *botica* (It. *bottega*) f. L *apotheca* f. Gk *apothēkē* storehouse: cf. BODEGA.] A small shop. Now usu. a shop, or department in a store, selling (esp. fashionable) clothes or accessories.

bouton /ˈbuːtɒn/ *n.* M19. [Fr. = button.] 1 In full *bouton pearl*. A round pearl with a flat back. M19. 2 *Anat.* An enlarged part of a nerve fibre or cell, esp. an axon, where it forms a synapse. M20.

boutonnière /buːtɒnˈjɛː; *foreign* butɔnjɛːr (*pl. same*)/ *n.* L19. [Fr.] = BUTTONHOLE *n.* 3.

bouts rimés /buː riːˈmeɪ/ *n. phr. pl.* E18. [Fr. = rhymed endings.] Rhyming words upon which verses are (to be) composed.

bouvardia /bʊˈvɑːdɪə/ *n.* L18. [mod.L, f. Charles *Bouvard* (1572–1658), superintendent of the Jardin du Roi, Paris: see -IA[1].] A Central American plant of the genus *Bouvardia*, of the madder family, bearing handsome red, yellow, or white flowers.

bouzouki /bʊˈzuːki/ *n.* M20. [Gk. *mpouzouki*: cf. Turk. *bozuk* spoilt, w. ref. to roughly made instruments.] A Greek form of long-necked lute.

bovarism /ˈbəʊvərɪz(ə)m/ *n.* E20. [Fr. *bovarysme*, f. the principal character in Flaubert's novel *Madame Bovary*: see -ISM.] (Domination by) a romantic or unreal conception of oneself.

bovarize *v.i.* & *refl.* view oneself in a romantic or unreal light E20.

bovate /ˈbəʊveɪt/ *n.* L17. [med.L *bovata*, f. L *bov-*, *bos* ox: see -ATE[1].] *Hist.* An oxgang of land.

bove /bʌv/ *adv.* & *prep.* Now *poet.* Now also **'b-**. [OE *bufan*, f. *bi* BY *prep.* + *ufan* above (ult. f. as UP *adv.*[1] etc.); later aphet. f. ABOVE.] = ABOVE.

Bovey coal /ˈbʌvi kəʊl/ *n. phr.* M18. [f. *Bovey*, a parish in Devonshire.] A form of lignite found in SW England.

bovid /ˈbəʊvɪd/ *a.* & *n.* L19. [f. L *bov-*, *bos* ox + -ID[3].] *Zool.* A *adj.* Of, pertaining to, or designating the family Bovidae of ruminants, including cattle, antelope, sheep, and goats. L19. B *n.* An animal of this family. L19.

bovine /ˈbəʊvʌɪn/ *a.* & *n.* E19. [Late L *bovinus*, f. as prec.: see -INE[1].] A *adj.* 1 Pertaining to or characteristic of an ox or similar animal; belonging to the ox tribe. E19. 2 *fig.* Sluggish; stupid. M19.

1 **bovine somatotrophin** a growth hormone occurring naturally in cows that has been added to cattle feed to increase milk production; abbrev. *BST*. **bovine spongiform encephalopathy** a usually fatal virus disease of cattle involving the central nervous system and causing extreme agitation; abbrev. *BSE*.

B *n.* A bovine animal. M19.

bovinely *adv.* E20.

Bovril /ˈbɒvrɪl/ *n.* Also **b-**. L19. [f. L *bov-*, *bos* ox; perh. based on VRIL.] (Proprietary name for) a concentrated essence of beef; a drink of this.

bovrilize *v.t.* (*arch. colloq.*) condense, epitomize E20.

bovver /ˈbɒvə/ *n. slang.* M20. [Repr. a cockney pronunc. of BOTHER *n.*] Deliberate trouble-making.

Comb.: **bovver boot** a heavy boot; **bovver boy** a violent hooligan.

bow /bəʊ/ *n.*[1] [OE *boga* = OFris. *boga*, OS *bogo* (Du. *boog*), OHG *bogo* (G *Bogen*), ON *bogi*, f. Gmc: cf. BOW *v.*[1]] 1 A thing bent or curved; a bend, a bent line; *esp.* (chiefly *poet.*) a rainbow. OE. †b An arc of a circle. M16–L17. 2 An arch (of masonry). *obs.* exc. *dial.* OE. 3 A weapon for shooting arrows, consisting of a cord joining the ends of a curved piece of elastic wood etc. OE. b In *pl.* Archers. L15. 4 A yoke for oxen. Cf. OXBOW. LME. 5 A knot with a single or double loop; a necktie, ribbon, etc., so tied. M16. 6 *Mus.* A rod with horsehair etc. stretched along it for playing a stringed instrument; a single passage of this across the strings. L16. 7 A ring or hoop forming a handle; = BAIL *n.*[4] E17. b A side-piece or lens-frame of a pair of spectacles. Chiefly *US.* E18. 8 *Archit.* A curved part of a building projecting from a straight wall; *esp.* = *bow-window* (a) below. E18. 9 *Calligraphy.* A curved stroke forming part of a letter. E20.

1 MILTON A dewie Cloud, and in the Cloud a bow. P. GALLICO The grim line of her mouth unfroze and altered, down-drawn into a bow of pain. *bow of promise*: see PROMISE *n. saddle-bow*: see SADDLE *n. secondary bow*: see SECONDARY *a.* 3 *Cupid's bow*: see CUPID. *have two, many*, etc., *strings to one's bow*: see STRING *n. second string to one's bow*: see STRING *n.* See also CROSSBOW, *longbow* s.v. LONG *a.*[1] 6 *musical bow*: see MUSICAL *a. Tourte bow*: see TOURTE *n.*[2]

Comb.: **bow-arm**, **-hand**: holding the bow (in archery or music); **bow-backed** *a.* (*arch.*) [perh. partly f. BOW *v.*[1]] hunchbacked, having an arched back; **bow-bearer** a person who carries a bow; *esp.* (*Hist.*) a forester who dealt with trespasses affecting vert and venison; **bow-compass(es)** a pair of compasses with jointed legs; †**bow-draught** = *bowshot* below; **bowfin** a large voracious holostean fish, *Amia calva*, of still fresh waters in eastern N. America; *bow-hand*: see *bow-arm* above; **bowhead (whale)** the Greenland right whale, *Balaena mysticetus*; **bowhunt** *v.t.* & *i.* hunt (animals) with a bow rather than a firearm; **bowhunter** a person who bowhunts; **bow-legged** having outwardly bent legs, bandy-legged; **bow-legs** bandy legs; **bowman** *n.*[1] an archer; **bow-net** a cylinder of wickerwork closed at one end and having a narrow funnel-shaped entrance at the other, used to trap lobsters etc.; **bow-saw**: having a narrow blade stretched like a bowstring on a light frame. **bowshot** the distance an arrow can be shot from a bow; †**bowstaff**, pl. **-staves**, a stick to be made into a bow; **bow-tie** a necktie (to be) tied in the manner of a bow; **bow-window** (*a*) a curved bay window; (*b*) *slang* a big belly.

bowless *a.* M19.

bow /buː, bəʊ/ *n.*[2] Long *obs.* exc. *Sc. dial.* & *Hist.* ME. [ON *bú* farming, farm, farm stock, corresp. to OE, OS *bū* dwelling, habitation, OHG *bū* dwelling, building, tillage (MHG *bū*, *bou*, G *Bau*, Du. *bouw* tillage, building), f. Gmc wd rel. to L *colere* cultivate.] The stock of cattle on a farm; a herd.

bow /baʊ/ *n.*[3] LME. [LG *boog*, Du. *boeg* (whence Sw. *bog*, Da. *boug*): see BOUGH. Pronunc. infl. by pop. assoc. w. BOW *v.*[1]] 1 *sing.* & (freq.) in *pl.* The fore-end of a boat or ship from where it begins to curve inwards to the stem. LME. 2 = *bowman* below. M19.

1 **bow(s)-on** with the bow turned towards the object considered. **on the bow** within 45° of the point right ahead. **shot across the bows** a warning salvo (freq. *fig.*).

Comb.: **bow-chaser** a forward-firing gun in the bow of a ship; **bow-fast** a mooring rope etc. at the bow; **bow line** the line of a ship's forebody in vertical section (see also BOWLINE); **bowman** *n.*[2] the oarsman who sits nearest to the bow of a boat; **bow oar** (the rower of) the oar nearest the bow; **bow wave** a wave set up at the bow of a vessel under way or in front of any object moving through a fluid.

bow /baʊ/ *n.*[4] M17. [f. BOW *v.*[1]] A forward bending of the head or upper body in salutation, assent, etc.

make one's bow make a formal entrance or exit. **take a bow** acknowledge applause.

Bow /bəʊ/ *n.*[5] M18. [Stratford-le-*Bow*, a village in Essex (now a district in London).] In full *Bow china, porcelain*. Fine porcelain of a kind orig. manufactured at Stratford-le-Bow.

bow /baʊ/ *v.*[1] [OE *būgan* corresp. to MLG *būgen*, MDu. *būghen*, OHG *biogan* (G *biegen*), Goth. *biugan*, f. Gmc: cf. BOW *n.*[1]] I *v.i.* & †*refl.* 1 Assume a bent or crooked shape or attitude; bend; stoop. *arch.* & *dial.* OE. †2 Turn aside, off, or away; swerve; make one's way, go. OE–L16. †3 Have a curved direction, be bent; tend. OE–M18. 4 Bend the neck (as if) beneath a yoke. Now chiefly *fig.*, be subject (*to*), submit, yield. OE. 5 Bend or kneel (*down*) in token of reverence, respect, or submission. (Foll. by *to*, *before*.) OE. 6 Incline the head or body (*to*) in recognition or assent; make a bow. E17.

1 SHAKES. *Meas. for M.* Like an ass whose back with ingots bows. AV *Eccles.* 12:3 When . . the strong men shall bowe themselves. TENNYSON She bow'd down And wept in secret. 4 DRYDEN Under Iron Yokes make Indians Bow. A. P. STANLEY He at last bows to the inevitable course of events. 5 GIBBON An hundred princes bowed before his throne. *bow in the house of Rimmon*: see HOUSE *n.*[1] 6 **bow and scrape** behave obsequiously. **bowing acquaintance** a slight degree of acquaintance.

II *v.t.* 7 Cause to bend, curve; cause to stoop, crush (as) with a load. ME. †8 Turn, direct. ME–E18. 9 Bend downwards, lower, incline.

ME. †10 Obey. Only in ME. 11 Express with a bow; usher *in* or *out* by bowing. E17.

7 SHAKES. *Hen. VIII* A threepence bow'd would hire me. MILTON With sickness and disease thou bow'st them down. F. ORMSBY This late guest bowed with winter offerings. 9 E. A. FREEMAN Lanfranc refused to bow his shoulders to such a burden. DAY LEWIS The worshippers bowed their heads to the gale. *bow the knee*: see KNEE *n.*

With advs. in specialized senses: **bow out** take one's leave, esp. with formality; retreat, withdraw.

bowing *n.*[1] (*a*) the action of the vb; (*b*) (*obs.* exc. *dial.*) a curved or bent part: LME.

bow /bəʊ/ *v.*[2]*i.* & *t.* M19. [f. BOW *n.*[1]] Use the bow on (a violin etc.); play with the bow.

bowing *n.*[2] (the manner of) playing a violin etc. with a bow M19.

†bowall *n.* var. of BOLE *n.*[3]

bowdlerize /ˈbaʊdləraɪz/ *v.t.* Also **B-**, **-ise**. M19. [f. Thomas *Bowdler* (1754–1825), Eng. editor, who published an expurgated edition of Shakespeare: see -IZE.] Expurgate (a book etc.) by removing or altering material considered improper or offensive; emasculate.

bowdlerism *n.* textual expurgation M19. **bowdleri'zation** *n.* the act of bowdlerizing L19.

bowel /ˈbaʊəl/ *n.* & *v.* ME. [AN *buel*, OFr. *boël*, *bouel* (mod. *boyau*), f. L *botellus* pudding, sausage (Martial), small intestine, dim. of *botulus* sausage: see -EL[2] I.] A *n.* 1 The part of the alimentary canal below the stomach; the intestine; the gut. Exc. in medical use now usu. in *pl.*, the intestines, the entrails. ME. †b Any internal organ of the body. LME–L18. 2 In *pl.* The interior of the body. Chiefly *fig.*, (the innermost source of) pity or sympathetic feeling. *arch.* LME. 3 In *pl.* The innermost parts *of* anything. E16. †4 In *pl.* Offspring. E16–L17.

2 CARLYLE Had idle readers any bowels for him. *bowels of compassion, mercy*, etc. 3 S. RUSHDIE He lived somewhere in the insanitary bowels of the old wooden-house quarter. **bowels of the earth** the depths of the earth. 4 SHAKES. *Meas. for M.* Thine own bowels which do call thee sire.

B *v.t.* Infl. **-ll-**, ***-l-**. Disembowel. *arch.* ME.

bowelled *a.* (*a*) having bowels or recesses; (*b*) disembowelled: L16. **bowelless** /-l-l-/ *a.* (*arch.*) without mercy, pitiless M17.

†bowell *n.* var. of BOLE *n.*[3]

bowenite /ˈbəʊənaɪt/ *n.* M19. [f. George T. *Bowen* (1803–28), US mineralogist + -ITE[1].] *Min.* A hard, compact, translucent form of serpentine, resembling nephrite.

bower /ˈbaʊə/ *n.*[1] [OE *būr* corresp. to OS *būr* (LG *buur*), OHG *būr* (G *Bauer* birdcage), ON *bur*, f. Gmc, f. base meaning 'dwell' (also of BUILD *v.*): for mod. sp. cf. FLOWER *n.*, TOWER *n.*[1]] 1 A dwelling, a habitation; *esp.* an ideal abode. Now chiefly *poet.* OE. 2 An inner apartment; a bedroom. *arch.* & *dial.* OE. b A lady's private apartment; a boudoir. Now *poet.* OE. 3 A place closed in with foliage; an arbour; a summer-house. L15. 4 A structure raised by a bowerbird. M19.

Comb. & *phrases*: **bowerbird** (*a*) any of various passerine birds of the family Ptilonorhynchidae, native to Australia and New Guinea, which construct elaborate runs adorned with feathers, shells, etc., during courtship; (*b*) *Austral. slang* a collector of trivia or odds and ends; **bower-maiden**, **-woman** *arch.* a lady-in-waiting, a chambermaid; *virgin's bower*: see VIRGIN *n.*

bower /ˈbaʊə/ *n.*[2] ME. [f. BOW *n.*[1] + -ER[1].] †1 = BOWYER I. ME–M18. 2 A person who plays with a bow on a violin etc. *rare.* L17.

bower /ˈbaʊə/ *n.*[3] L15. [f. BOW *n.*[3] + -ER[1].] Either of two anchors carried at a ship's bow (more fully *bower anchor*). Also (usu. more fully *bower cable*), the cable of such an anchor.

best, **small**, **bower** the starboard, port, bower anchor (or cable).

bower /ˈbaʊə/ *n.*[4] L16. [f. BOW *v.*[1] + -ER[1].] A person who bows or bends; a thing which causes bending.

bower /ˈbaʊə/ *n.*[5] L19. [G *Bauer* lit. 'husbandman, peasant, rustic': see BOOR.] Either of the two highest cards in euchre, the jack of trumps (*right bower*) and the jack of the same colour (*left bower*).

bower /ˈbaʊə/ *v.* L16. [f. BOWER *n.*[1]] 1 *v.t.* Embower, shade, enclose (*lit.* & *fig.*). L16. †2 *v.i.* Lodge, shelter. *rare* (Spenser). Only in L16.

bowery /ˈbaʊəri/ *n.* & *a.* *US.* M17. [Du. *bouwerij* husbandry, farm, f. *bouwen* cultivate: cf. BOOR & see -ERY.] A *n.* A (former) farm or plantation in Dutch colonial America; *spec.* (*the Bowery*) a street in New York City (on the site of a former governor's bowery) notorious as a resort of prostitutes, drunks, derelicts, etc. M17. B *attrib.* or as *adj.* (**B-**.) Of, pertaining to, or characteristic of the Bowery in New York City; disreputable, rough, rowdy. M19.

bowery /ˈbaʊəri/ *a.* E18. [f. BOWER *n.*[1] + -Y[1].] Embowering; leafy, shady.

bowet /ˈbaʊɪt, ˈbuːɪt/ *n.* *Sc. obs.* exc. *Hist.* LME. [App. f. med.L *boeta* box or pyx as housing for a candle: cf. BOIST.] A small lantern.

bowie /ˈbaʊɪ, ˈbəʊɪ/ *n.*[1] *Sc.* M16. [Perh. dim. of Sc. form of BOLL *n.*[1]: see -Y[6].] A shallow tub; a wooden milk-bowl.

Bowie /ˈbəʊɪ/ *n.*[2] Also **b-**. M19. [James *Bowie* (1799–1836), Amer. soldier.] More fully *Bowie-knife*. A long knife with a blade double-edged at the point, used as a weapon by American pioneers.

bowl /bəʊl/ *n.*[1] Also (earlier) **†boll**. [OE *bolla*, *bolle* corresp. to OS *bollo* cup (Du. *bol* round object, BOLL *n.*[1]), OHG *bolla* bud, round pod, globular vessel, f. Gmc base meaning 'swell'.] 1 A vessel, usu. hemispherical or nearly so, to hold liquids or food; a basin. OE. b *esp.* Such a vessel for holding drink. *arch.* OE. c The contents of a bowl; a bowlful. M16. 2 A more or less bowl-shaped part, as of a cup, tobacco-pipe, spoon, balance, etc. OE. †3 *Naut.* A round space at the masthead for men to stand in. E17–E19. 4 A bowl-shaped natural basin; a (bowl-shaped) stadium (freq. in the names of American football stadiums), an amphitheatre. M19. b A sporting occasion held in a football stadium, featuring a football game; *spec.* = *bowl game* below. *US.* M20.

1 *finger-bowl, goldfish bowl, punch-bowl, salad bowl, soup bowl, sugar-bowl, wash-bowl*, etc. b *hanging bowl*: see HANGING *a.* **the bowl** drinking; conviviality. 4 P. THEROUX San Salvador . . lies in a bowl, surrounded by mountains. *dust bowl*: see DUST *n.*

Comb.: **bowl-barrow** a prehistoric grave-mound in the shape of an inverted bowl; **bowl game** *US* an established American football fixture after the main season, usu. at a stadium with 'bowl' in its name.

bowlful *n.* the contents of a bowl, the quantity held by a bowl E17.

bowl /bəʊl/ *n.*[2] LME. [(O)Fr. *boule* f. L BULLA.] 1 A sphere, a globe, a ball. Long *obs.* exc. *dial.* in *gen.* sense. LME. 2 *spec.* A ball of wood, hard rubber, etc., rolled in various games; in the game of bowls itself (see sense 3 below) now made slightly out of spherical shape to make it run in a curved course; in skittles, ninepins, etc., made either flattened or spherical. LME. 3 In *pl.* (usu. treated as *sing.*). A game played with bowls, on a green or in an alley; *spec.* a game in which players aim bowls at a target ball (the jack). L15. 4a A delivery of the ball in cricket (now usu. *ball*); a spell of bowling. M19. b A turn in bowls, skittles, etc.; a delivery of the ball in bowls etc. L19. 5 A roller or antifriction wheel, esp. for moving or pressing fabrics. L19.

bowl /bəʊl/ *v.* LME. [f. BOWL *n.*[2]] 1 *v.i.* Play at bowls or skittles etc.; roll a bowl, hoop, etc., along the ground. LME. 2 *v.t.* Cause to roll; send rolling. L16. b Convey on wheels (in a carriage etc.). E19. 3 *v.i.* Move by revolution; move on wheels. E17. 4 *v.i.* & *t.* *Cricket.* Propel towards the batsman (the ball, an over, etc.), orig. underarm; dismiss (a batsman) by the ball thus propelled breaking the wicket; get (a side) *out*. M18. b *v.t.* Use (a player) to bowl. M19.

2 M. HARRIS Some of the boys had large iron hoops . . ; for miles and miles they bowled them. 3 S. JOHNSON A fashionable lady . . bowling about in her own coach. 4 E. BLISHEN He took the ball and prepared to bowl the first over. N. CARDUS I have . . not been able to find out if Trumble bowled over or round the wicket. b A. ROSS Hutton bowled Tyson and Statham for an hour.

With advs. in specialized senses: **bowl along** go fast and smoothly. **bowl over** knock down; *fig.* disconcert, render helpless, impress greatly.

bowlder *n.* & *v.* var. of BOULDER.

bowler /ˈbəʊlə/ *n.*[1] E16. [f. BOWL *v.* + -ER[1].] 1 A person who plays at bowls. E16. 2 A player who bowls at cricket. E18.

2 *fast bowler, medium(-pace) bowler, slow bowler*, etc. **bowler's wicket** a cricket pitch favouring bowlers.

bowler /ˈbəʊlə/ *n.*[2] M19. [William *Bowler*, Eng. hatter who designed it in 1850.] In full *bowler hat*. A hard felt hat with a rounded crown and a narrow curled brim.

be given, **get**, etc., **one's bowler (hat)** *slang* be retired to civilian life, be demobilized.

Comb.: **bowler-hatted** *a.* (*a*) wearing a bowler; (*b*) *slang* civilian, retired from the forces.

bowline /ˈbəʊlɪn/ *n.* ME. [MLG *bōlīne*, MDu. *boechlijne* f. *boeg* BOW *n.*[3] + *lijne* LINE *n.*[2]] 1 A rope passing from the weather edge of a square sail to the port or starboard bow, for the purpose of holding the sail closer to the wind. ME. 2 In full *bowline knot*. A simple knot for forming a non-slipping loop at the end of a rope. E17.

1 **on a bowline** close-hauled. See also *bow line* s.v. BOW *n.*[3] 2 *running bowline*: see RUNNING *a.* *Spanish bowline*: see SPANISH *a.*

bowling /ˈbəʊlɪŋ/ *n.* E16. [f. BOWL *v.* + -ING[1].] 1 Playing at bowls; the action of rolling a ball etc. E16. 2 *Cricket.* The action of delivering the ball. M18. b The strength or resources of the bowlers in a cricket team. M19.

1 *tenpin bowling*: see *tenpin* s.v. TEN *n.* 2 *fast bowling, medium(-pace) bowling, slow bowling*, etc.

Comb.: **bowling-alley** (a building containing) an alley for playing at bowls or skittles; *bowling analysis*: see ANALYSIS 2; **bowling-crease** in cricket, the line from behind which the bowler delivers the ball; **bowling-green** a smooth green upon which to play bowls.

Bowman's capsule /bəʊmənz ˈkapsjuːl, -jʊl/ *n. phr.* L19. [Sir William *Bowman* (1816–92), Eng. surgeon.] *Anat.* & *Zool.* A cup-shaped dilatation of the end of a uriniferous tubule, surrounding each glomerulus in the vertebrate kidney.

bowse *v.*[1] & *n.* var. of BOOZE.

bowse *v.*[2] var. of BOUSE *v.*[2]

bowser /ˈbaʊzə/ *n.* Also **B-**. E20. [Origin unkn.] A tanker used for fuelling aircraft, tanks, etc., or for supplying water; (chiefly *Austral.* & *NZ*, proprietary name for) a petrol pump.

bowsprit /ˈbəʊsprɪt/ *n.* ME. [(M)LG *bōgsprēt*, MDu. *boechspriet*, f. as BOW *n.*[3], SPRIT *n.*[1]] A large spar or boom running out from the stem of a vessel, to which the forestays are fastened.

Bow Street /bəʊ striːt/ *n. phr.* E19. [Site of the principal metropolitan magistrates' court in London.] Hist. *Bow Street officer, runner*, a (London) detective, *spec.* of the early 19th cent.

bowstring /ˈbəʊstrɪŋ/ *n.* & *v.* OE. [f. BOW *n.*[1] + STRING *n.*] A *n.* The cord of a bow; *spec.* (*Hist.*) this used in Turkey for strangling offenders. OE.

Comb.: **bowstring-bridge** a girder bridge consisting of an arch and a horizontal tie; **bowstring hemp** = SANSEVIERIA.

B *v.t.* Pa. t. & pple **-stringed**, **-strung**. Chiefly *Hist.* Strangle with a bowstring. E19.

bowtell *n.* var. of BOLTEL.

bow-wow /*int.* & *v.* baʊˈwaʊ; *n.* ˈbaʊwaʊ/ *int.*, *n.*, & *v.* L16. [Imit.] A *int.* Repr. the sound of a dog barking, or a similar sound. L16. B *n.* 1 The bark of a dog. L18. 2 A dog. *joc.* & *nursery.* L18. C *v.i.* Bark. M19.

bowyang /ˈbəʊjaŋ/ *n.* *Austral.* & *NZ* & (sense 1) *dial.* Sense 1 **bow-yanky** /ˈbəʊjaŋki/ & other vars. M19. [Origin unkn.] 1 In *pl.* Leather leggings. M19. 2 A band or strap worn over the trousers below the knee, esp. by labourers. L19.

bowyer /ˈbəʊjə/ *n.* ME. [f. BOW *n.*[1] + -YER: cf. BOWER *n.*[2]] 1 A person who makes or trades in bows. ME. 2 An archer. LME.

box /bɒks/ *n.*[1] OE. [L *buxus* f. Gk *puxos.*] 1 More fully *box tree*. A small evergreen tree or shrub of the genus *Buxus* (family Buxaceae); esp. *Buxus sempervirens*, with dark leathery leaves, often planted in garden borders. OE. b

Any of various Australasian eucalypts and other trees with wood like that of *Buxus*. E19. **2** The hard, heavy, close-grained wood of the box, or of certain other trees, much used by turners and engravers. LME.

1b *grey box, white box*, etc.

Comb.: **box elder** a pinnate-leaved N. American elder, *Acer negundo*; **box-gum** = sense 1b above; **box-thorn** a shrub of the genus *Lycium*, of the nightshade family, bearing red berries, some species of which are used for hedging; esp. *L. barbarum*, naturalized in Britain; *box tree*: see sense 1 above; **boxwood** = sense 2 above; also, the tree itself.

boxen *a.* (*arch.*) of or pertaining to box; made of or like boxwood: M16.

box /bɒks/ *n.*[2] LOE. [Prob. f. late L *buxis*, *-id-* var. of L PYXIS box of boxwood.] **1** A case or receptacle, usu. rectangular or cylindrical and with a lid, of wood, metal, card, etc. (Freq. w. function, type, etc., specified or understood contextually.) LOE. **b** A numbered receptacle at a post office in which letters for a subscriber are kept until called for, or at a newspaper office for replies to an advertisement. M19. **c** A coffin. *slang*. E20. **d** *the box*, television. *slang*. M20. **e** The female genitals. *N. Amer. slang*. M20. **2** A box and its contents; the quantity contained in a box, a boxful. ME. **b** *spec.* A money box and its contents; a fund. LME. **c** A Christmas-box. L16. **3** A protective case or covering for a piece of mechanism, such as a compass; a cylinder in which the journal of an axle etc. revolves. L15. **b** *Cricket*. A light protective shield worn over the genitals. M20. **4** (A box under) the coachman's seat on a carriage. E17. **5** A separate compartment, esp. in court for a witness or jury or one with seats at a theatre, restaurant, stadium, etc. E17. **b** *transf.* In *pl. The* occupants of the boxes at a theatre etc. (orig. for ladies). L17. **c** A separate stall for a horse in a stable or vehicle; a closed vehicle for transporting one or more horses. M19. **d** The confessional. E20. **6** A simple shelter or building; *esp.* one for a sentry, railway signals, or a telephone. E18. **7** A small country house, *esp.* one for temporary use while hunting etc. E18. **8** An excavation in the trunk of a tree for sap to collect. E18. **9** A confined area; a space enclosed by (esp. printed) lines; the area occupied by the batter or pitcher in baseball; (*Football colloq.*) *the* penalty area. L19. **10** A mixing up of different flocks of sheep. *Austral.* & *NZ*. L19. **11** A close formation of aircraft, pattern of bombs, etc. M20.

1 S. JOHNSON My landlady . . took the opportunity of my absence to search my boxes. E. BOWEN Who, seeing the house shuttered, would have dropped a letter in at the box? *ballot-box, Christmas-box, dispatch-box, juke-box, letter-box, mailbox, matchbox, money box, music(al) box, pillar-box, pillbox, postbox, snuffbox, soapbox, soundbox, strongbox, tuck box, window-box*, etc. *chatterbox*: see CHATTER *n.* **b** P. G. WODEHOUSE My address will be Box 341, *London Morning News*. **2** B. JOWETT He who is to be a workman should have his box of tools when he is a child. R. MAUGHAM Munching her way through a large box of chocolates. **b** SHAKES. *Timon* Nothing but an empty box . . which . . I come to entreat your honour to supply. **3** *gearbox* etc. **5** *jury-box, witness-box*, etc. **6** T. HOOD The Watchman in his box was dosing. *call-box, prompt-box, sentry-box, signal-box, telephone box*, etc. **9** A. S. BYATT He filled the little boxes, date of birth, places of education, parentage, nationality.

Phrases: **a box of birds** *Austral.* & *NZ colloq.* excellent, very well, fine. *black box*: see BLACK *a. Chinese box*: see CHINESE *a.* **in the same box** in a similar predicament. **in the wrong box** unsuitably or awkwardly placed; in a difficulty, at a disadvantage. *loose box*: see LOOSE *a.* **one out of the box** *Austral.* & *NZ colloq.* an excellent person or thing. *red box*: see RED *a. Skinner box*: see SKINNER *n.*[2] SOLANDER box

Comb.: **box barrage**: directed to all sides of an area, to prevent escape; **box camera** a simple box-shaped hand camera; **box canyon** a narrow canyon with a flat bottom and vertical walls; **boxcar** *N. Amer.* an enclosed railway goods wagon; **box-cloth** thick coarse cloth used esp. for riding garments; **box coat** a heavy caped overcoat for a coachman etc.; **box-fish** = *trunkfish* s.v. TRUNK *n.*; **box girder**: made of plates fastened in the shape of a box; **box junction** a road junction with a central yellow-striped area which a vehicle must not enter unless it can leave immediately, except when turning right with only oncoming traffic preventing exit; **box kite** a tailless kite with a light rectangular frame at each end; **box number**: identifying a box in a post office or newspaper office (sense 1b above); **box office** an office for booking seats at a theatre etc.; *fig.* entertainment etc. likely to attract audiences; **box pew**: enclosed like a box; **box pleat**: with two parallel contrary pleats forming a raised band; **boxroom** a room in which boxes, trunks, etc., are stored; **box score** the tabulated results of a baseball game etc.; **box-seat** the driver's seat on a carriage; **box spanner** a cylindrical spanner with a socket head fitting over the nut; **box spring** each of a set of vertical springs in a mattress; **box-tortoise, -turtle** a N. American land turtle of the genus *Terrapene*, able by means of a hinged lower carapace to close itself up completely; **box-wallah** (in the Indian subcontinent) a dealer, a pedlar.

boxful *n.* as much or as many as a box will hold E18. **boxlike** *a.* resembling (that of) a box M19. **boxy** *a.* resembling, comparable to, or suggesting a box; (of recorded sound) restricted in tone: M19.

box /bɒks/ *n.*[3] LME. [Origin unkn.] **1** A blow. *obs.* in *gen.* sense. LME. **2** *spec.* A slap on the ear or the side of the head. LME.

box /bɒks/ *v.*[1]*t.* LME. [f. BOX *n.*[2]] **1** Provide or fit with a box; put into a box, enclose in a box or casing; fit compactly as in a box; *fig.* confine and restrict the movement of, confine uncomfortably. Freq. foll. by *in, up*. LME. **b** Print within a border of rules. E20. †**2** Bleed by cupping. LME–E17. **3** Make an excavation in the trunk of (a tree) for sap to collect. E18. **4** Mix *up*, muddle, (esp. different flocks of sheep). Chiefly *Austral.* & *NZ*. M19.

box /bɒks/ *v.*[2] E16. [f. BOX *n.*[3]] **1** *v.t.* Beat, strike. Now *spec.* slap (the ear or the side of the head), cuff. E16. **2** *v.t.* & *i.* Fight (a person) with the fists, now usu. in padded gloves as a sport, with set rules. M16.

1 N. MITFORD She was so furious she . . rushed at Polly and boxed her ears. **2** C. MCCULLOUGH A lightweight under orders to keep Frank at a distance and find out if he could box as well as he could punch. **box clever** *slang* use one's wits.

box /bɒks/ *v.*[3] M18. [Perh. f. Sp. *bojar* (*boxar*) sail round, f. MLG *bōgen* bend, bow, f. base of BOW *n.*[1], *v.*[1]] *Naut.* **1** *v.t. box the compass*, (be able to) recite the compass points in correct order; *fig.* make a complete turn, go round and end where one began. M18. **2** *v.t.* & *i.* Turn (a ship), *spec.* by hauling the head-sheets to windward and laying the head-yards aback. Also = BOX-HAUL. Usu. foll. by *off*. M18.

Box and Cox /bɒks (ə)nd ˈkɒks/ *n. phr.* L19. [Title of a play by J. M. Morton (1811–91), in which two people unknowingly become tenants of the same room.] Two people who are never together or never at home at the same time; two people who take turns in a part etc. Chiefly in *play Box and Cox*.

boxcalf /ˈbɒkskɑːf/ *n.* E20. [f. Joseph *Box*, late-19th-cent. London bootmaker + CALF *n.*[1]] Chrome-tanned calfskin with a hatched grain.

boxer /ˈbɒksə/ *n.*[1] *rare*. M16. [f. BOX *v.*[1] + -ER[1].] A person who puts things in boxes.

boxer /ˈbɒksə/ *n.*[2] L17. [f. BOX *v.*[2] + -ER[1].] **1** A person who boxes; a pugilist. L17. **2** *Hist.* (**B-**.) [Repr. Chin. *yì hé quán* lit. 'righteous harmonious fists'.] A member of a Chinese nationalist secret society responsible for a rising in 1900. E20. **3** A dog of a smooth-coated square-built breed of the bulldog type, originating in Germany. E20.

Comb.: **boxer shorts** men's loose shorts or underpants.

box-haul /ˈbɒkshɔːl/ *v.t.* M18. [f. BOX *v.*[3] + HAUL *v.*] *Naut.* Veer (a ship) round on its stern.

boxiana /bɒksɪˈɑːnə/ *n.pl.* E19. [f. BOXING *n.*[2] + -IANA.] Publications or other items concerning or associated with boxing and boxers.

boxing /ˈbɒksɪŋ/ *n.*[1] E16. [f. BOX *v.*[1] + -ING[1].] The action of BOX *v.*[1] Also, boxes, casing.

Boxing Day the first day (strictly, the first weekday) after Christmas Day (on which Christmas-boxes were traditionally given).

boxing /ˈbɒksɪŋ/ *n.*[2] E18. [f. BOX *v.*[2] + -ING[1].] The action of fighting with fists, *spec.* as a sport, using padded gloves.

Comb.: **boxing glove** a thick padded glove used in boxing; **boxing ring** an enclosure, now usu. a raised square with surrounding ropes, for boxing; **boxing weight** any of a series of weight ranges at which boxers are officially matched (as *bantamweight, flyweight, heavyweight*, etc.).

boy /bɔɪ/ *n.* ME. [Perh. rel. to OE *Bōia, Bōja*, OHG *Buobo* male pers. names, MHG *buobe* boy; cf. also Fris. *boi* boy.] **1** A male servant, an underling, *esp.* a young one; a helper, a messenger. *obs.* exc. as in sense 1b or when a boy in sense 4. ME. **b** A native servant or labourer. Now freq. considered *offensive*. E17. †**2** A male person of lowly status, a common fellow; a worthless fellow, a knave. ME–E17. **3** (Affectionately, playfully, or slightingly.) A young man, a fellow; a man belonging to some specified or understood group (as one's habitual companions, a team, a gang, the army, etc.). Freq. as a familiar form of address. LME. **b** A familiar form of address to a male dog, horse, or other animal. LME. **c** A man of any age. *dial.* (esp. *Anglo-Ir.*). M18. **4** A male child; a youth. Also, a grown-up son. LME. **5** As *int.* An exclamation of surprise, excitement, relief, etc. Freq. *oh boy!* Orig. *US*. E20.

1 COVERDALE *1 Sam.* 2:13 The prestes boye came, whyle the flesh was seething. P. LOVESEY Newspaper-boys . . bawled their wares. *button-boy, page-boy, shop-boy*, etc. **2** SHAKES. *Coriol.* Name not the god, thou boy of tears . . no more. **3** SHAKES. *Much Ado* If thou kill'st me, boy, thou shalt kill a man. *Spectator* The public relations boys could really go to town. J. LE CARRÉ It was just like old times . . in Berlin: the boys together and the night their oyster. I. F. ELIS 'That's all right, my boy', said the officer, forgetting . . that Wil was several years his senior. G. CHARLES 'You boys can take me in the van', Polly said to the two sound men and his own assistant. **4** BYRON Ah! happy years! once more who would not be a boy? ARNOLD BENNETT Edwin had left school; and, if he was not a man, he was certainly not a boy. E. WAUGH That . . was Lord Sebastian Flyte. . . The Marquis of Marchmain's second boy. P. G. WODEHOUSE I tried to tell him that boys will be boys and you're only young once. **6** M. HODGE Boy! They don't wear a damned thing! N. SHUTE I slithered in over the fence and put her down and boy! was I glad to be on the ground!

Phrases: *backroom boy*: see BACK-. *be a big boy* (*now*): see BIG *a.* 3b. *best boy*: see BEST *a.* etc. **Boys' Brigade** a boys' organization resembling the Scouts, connected with Presbyterian and Nonconformist churches. *boys in blue*: see BLUE *n.* 2. BROTH *of a boy*. *home boy*: see HOME *a.* **jobs for the boys** preferment for one's supporters or favourites. *man and boy*: see MAN *n. mother's boy*: see MOTHER *n.*[1] *naked boys*: see NAKED *a. old boy*: see OLD *a.* **one of the boys** a man who conforms to the behaviour of his companions, a good fellow. *principal boy*: see PRINCIPAL *a.* SKOLLY boy *sort out the men from the boys*: see MAN *n.* **the boy** *arch. slang* champagne. *the boy next door*: see NEXT *a. white-headed boy*: see WHITE *a. wide boy*: see WIDE *a.*

Comb.: **boyfriend** a girl's or woman's, or a homosexual man's, usual or preferred male companion; **boy-meets-girl** a conventional or ideal romance (freq. *attrib.*); *Boy Scout*: see SCOUT *n.*[3] 2c; **boy's-love** southernwood, *Artemisia abrotanum*; **boys' play** *arch.* amusement for boys, child's play; **boy wonder** an exceptionally talented young man or boy.

¶It is not clear which is the earliest Eng. meaning. However, sense 4, 'male child', is predominant and colours all other senses.

boyhood *n.* (*a*) the state of being a boy; the time when one is a boy; (*b*) boys collectively: M18. **boyish** *a.* of or pertaining to boys or boyhood; boylike, high-spirited: M16. **boyishly** *adv.* L16. **boyishness** *n.* M16. **boyism** *n.* (now *rare*) a boyish characteristic; boyish character: E18. **boykin(s)** *n.* (*arch.*) a small boy (esp. as an affectionate form of address) M16. **boylike** *adv.* & *a.* characteristic(ally) of a boy or boys M19.

boy /bɔɪ/ *v. rare*. M16. [f. the n.] **1** *v.i.* Act like a boy. M16. **2** *v.t.* Represent on stage by a boy actor; call 'boy'. L16.

boyar /bəʊˈjɑː/ *n.* Also †**-ard**. L16. [Russ. *boyarin* grandee.] *Hist.* A member of an order of Russian aristocracy (abolished by Peter the Great), next in rank to a prince.

boycott /ˈbɔɪkɒt/ *v.* & *n.* Also †**B-**. L19. [Capt. C. C. *Boycott* (1832–97), land-agent in Ireland who was so treated in 1880.] **A** *v.t.* Combine to coerce or punish (a person, group, nation, etc.) by a systematic refusal of normal commercial or social relations; refuse to handle or buy (goods), refuse to attend (a meeting, lecture, etc.), with this aim. L19. B *n.* Such a course of action. L19.

boycotter *n.* L19.

boyer /ˈbɔɪə/ *n.* Also **boier**. M16. [Du. *boeier* smack.] A single-masted Dutch vessel, orig. a seagoing sloop but now a bluff-ended craft used on inland waterways.

Boyle's law /ˈbɔɪlz lɔː/ *n. phr.* M19. [Robert *Boyle* (1627–91), Eng. scientist.] *Chem.* A law stating that the pressure and volume of a gas are in inverse proportion to each other at constant temperature.

boyo /ˈbɔɪəʊ/ *n. Welsh* & *Anglo-Ir. colloq.* Pl. **-os**. L19. [f. BOY *n.* + -O.] Boy, lad, fellow. Chiefly as a familiar form of address.

boysenberry /ˈbɔɪz(ə)nbɛri, -s-/ *n.* M20. [f. Rudolph *Boysen*, 20th-cent. US horticulturist + BERRY *n.*[1]] A cultivar of the loganberry, with larger fruit; the fruit of this plant.

boza /ˈbəʊzə/ *n.* Also **bosa**, **boo-** /ˈbuː-/. M17. [Turk. f. Pers.] A fermented drink made in Turkey and the Middle East; *spec.* an infusion of millet-seed.

bozo /ˈbəʊzəʊ/ *n. slang* (chiefly *N. Amer.*). Pl. **-os**. E20. [Origin unkn.] A stupid, despised, or insignificant person.

bra /brɑː/ *n.*[1] M20. [Abbrev.] A brassière.

braless *a.* M20. **bralessness** *n.* L20.

bra /brɑː/ *n.*[2] M20. [f. BRA(CKET *n.*: cf. KET *n.*[2]] *Quantum Mech.* A vector in Hilbert space that is the complex conjugate of a ket and is symbolized by <|. Freq. *bra vector*.

braai /ˈbrɑːɪ/ *n.* & *v. S. Afr.* M20. [Abbrev. of next.] A *n.* = next. M20. B *v.t.* & *i.* Grill (meat) over an open fire. M20.

braaivleis /ˈbrɑːɪfleɪs/ *n. S. Afr.* M20. [Afk. = grilled meat, f. *braai* to grill + *vleis* meat.] Meat grilled over an open fire; a picnic, barbecue, etc., at which meat is cooked in this way.

brab /brab/ *n.* L17. [Port. (*palmeira*) *braba* wild (palm tree).] The palmyra, *Borassus flabellifer*.

brabble /ˈbrab(ə)l/ *v.* & *n.* Now *arch.* & *dial.* E16. [Prob. ult. imit., but perh. f. (M)Du. *brabbelen* jabber, or a blend of BRAWL *v.* and BABBLE *v.*] A *v.i.* †1 Dispute obstinately. E16–E17. 2 Quarrel about trifles; quarrel noisily, squabble. M16. B *n.* 1 A paltry altercation, a noisy quarrel. M16. †b A brawl, a skirmish. L16–E17. †2 A quibble; *spec.* a frivolous legal action. L16–L17. 3 Discordant babble. M19.

brabblement *n.* altercation, contentious uproar M16. **brabbler** *n.* †(*a*) a quibbler; (*b*) a brawler: M16.

braccio /ˈbratʃəʊ/ *n.* Pl. **-ccia** /-tʃə/. M18. [It. = arm.] A former Italian measure of length, about 60 centimetres.

brace /breɪs/ *n.*[1] LME. [OFr. = two arms, the distance between the fingertips with arms extended (mod. *brasse* fathom) f. L *bracchia* pl. of *bracchium* arm (whence Fr. *bras*) f. Gk *brakhiōn*. Some senses f. BRACE *v.*[1]] I A pair of arms. †1 A portion of a suit of armour covering the arms. LME–E17. †b A suit of armour; armed state. *rare* (Shakes.). Only in E17. †2 A measure of length, orig. the distance between fingertips with arms extended. LME–M18. 3 A tool in carpentry having a crank handle and a socket etc. to hold a bit for boring. M16.

II A thing which clasps. 4 A clasp, buckle, or other fastener. LME. b *Dentistry.* A wire device for straightening the teeth. M20. 5 A leather thong which slides up and down the cord of a drum, regulating the tension of the skins, and hence the pitch of any note produced. L16. 6 The sign } (or {) used in printing etc. for the purpose of uniting two or more lines, words, staves of music, etc. or in pairs as a form of brackets; *loosely* in *pl.*, square brackets [ ]. M17. 7 Either of a pair of straps of elastic, leather, etc., used to support trousers etc. Usu. in *pl.* L18. 8 *Naut.* A metal strap secured to the stern-post and bottom planks for supporting the rudder. M19.

4 *French brace*: see FRENCH *a.* 7 *belt and braces*: see BELT *n.*

III Pl. usu. same (preceded by a numeral or quantifier). 9 A pair, a couple, esp. of dogs, game, pistols, *derog.* persons, *Cricket* ducks. LME.

9 *in a brace of shakes*: see SHAKE *n.*

IV A thing which imparts rigidity. 10 A strengthening piece of metal or timber in a building. LME. b *Theatr.* A rod or length of timber used to brace a flat. M19. 11 A metal band used as a support, e.g. in mounting church bells. M18.

10 *main brace*: see MAIN *a.*

brace /breɪs/ *n.*[2] LME. [Fr. *bras* (*de vergue*) lit. '(yard-)arm', assim. to prec.] *Naut.* A rope attached to the yard of a square-rigged vessel for the purpose of trimming the sail.

main brace: see MAIN *a.*

brace /breɪs/ *v.*[1] ME. [OFr. *bracier* embrace, f. as BRACE *n.*[1]: later senses directly f. BRACE *n.*[1]] I *v.t.* 1 Clasp, fasten up tight. ME. †2 Embrace. LME–L16. 3 Encompass, surround, encircle. LME. 4 Make tight or tense. LME. 5 Tense or give firmness or tone to (nerves, sinews, oneself, etc.); invigorate; *fig.* prepare mentally for a task, unwelcome intelligence, etc. (Foll. by *up.*) L15. 6 Fix, render firm, steady, set rigidly or firmly down (esp. by tightly binding); support. L18.

1 POPE The adverse winds in leathern bags he brac'd. 3 T. AIRD A flowing wood the middle mountain braced. 4 SHAKES. *John* Even at hand a drum is ready brac'd That shall reverberate all as loud as thine. 5 C. THIRLWALL Nothing now remained but to brace every nerve for the battle. W. GOLDING He braced his hands, stiffening the muscles of his arms. D. LODGE Mentally, you brace yourself for the ending of a novel. K. M. E. MURRAY A few days change . . would brace him up. 6 G. J. WHYTE-MELVILLE He braced his foot in the stirrup to afford a purchase for her ascent.

II *v.i.* 7 Foll. by *up*: brace oneself; pull oneself together for an effort; take a drink for this purpose. Orig. *US*. E19.

bracing *n.* (*a*) the action of the vb; (*b*) an appliance or arrangement that braces: LME. **bracing** *ppl a.* that braces; *esp.* (of air, climate, etc.) invigorating: M18.

brace /breɪs/ *v.*[2]*t.* & *i.* M17. [f. BRACE *n.*[2]: cf. Fr. *brasser.*] *Naut.* Swing (a yard) round by means of braces. Freq. w. advs., as *aback*, *about*, *in*, *to*, etc.

bracelet /ˈbreɪslɪt/ *n.* LME. [(O)Fr., f. *bras* arm: see -EL[2], -ET[1].] 1 An ornamental ring or band worn on the arm or wrist. LME. 2 *Hist.* A piece of armour covering the arm. L16. 3 A fetter for the wrists; *slang* a handcuff. Usu. in *pl.* E17.

braceleted *a.* M17.

bracer /ˈbreɪsə/ *n.*[1] LME. [OFr. *braciere*, f. *bras* arm.] A portion of a suit of armour covering the arm (now *Hist.*); a sort of wristguard used in archery etc.

bracer /ˈbreɪsə/ *n.*[2] M16. [f. BRACE *v.*[1] + -ER[1].] 1 A thing which clamps or binds, a brace. M16. 2 A tonic or medicine for bracing the nerves. Now chiefly (*colloq.*) a drink taken to brace one up, a pick-me-up. M18.

brach /bratʃ/ *n. arch.* LME. [Orig. in pl. f. OFr. *brachez* pl. of *brachet* dim. of Prov. *brac* f. Proto-Romance f. Frank. (whence also OHG *brakko*, G *Bracke*).] A kind of hound which hunts by scent. In later use *gen.* and always fem.: a bitch hound.

Also **brachet** *n.* LME.

brachial /ˈbreɪkɪəl/ *n.* & *a.* LME. [L *brachialis* adj., f. *brachium* arm: see -AL[1].] A *n.* †1 A vestment or a piece of armour for the arm. LME–M16. 2 *ellipt.* A brachial vein, bone, etc. M19. B *adj.* Chiefly *Anat.* & *Zool.* 1 Of the arm. L16. 2 Of the nature of or resembling an arm. M19.

brachialis /-ˈeɪlɪs/ *n.* (*Anat.*) a muscle in the upper arm, serving to flex the forearm L19.

brachiate /ˈbrakɪət, ˈbreɪk-/ *a.* Now *rare* or *obs.* M18. [L *brachiatus* with boughs or branches, f. as prec.: see -ATE[2].] *Bot.* Having long decussate branches.

brachiate /ˈbrakɪeɪt/ *v.i.* M20. [Back-form. f. next: see -ATE[3].] Move as a brachiator does.

brachiˈation *n.* L19.

brachiator /ˈbrakɪeɪtə/ *n.* M19. [f. L *brachium* arm + -ATOR.] *Zool.* An ape which moves by using the arms to swing from branch to branch.

brachiocephalic /ˌbrakɪəsɪˈfalɪk, -kɛˈfalɪk/ *a.* M19. [mod.L *brachiocephalicus*, f. Gk *brakhiōn* arm: see -CEPHALIC.] *Anat.* Pertaining to both arm and head; *esp.* designating the innominate veins and artery.

brachiopod /ˈbrakɪəpɒd/ *n.* M19. [mod.L *brachiopoda* pl., f. Gk *brakhiōn* arm + -POD.] *Zool.* A marine invertebrate of the phylum Brachiopoda (esp. a fossil one), with a two-valved chalky shell and a ciliated feeding arm (lophophore); a lamp-shell.

brachiosaurus /brakɪəˈsɔːrəs/ *n.* Pl. **-ruses**, **-ri** /-rʌɪ/. E20. [mod.L, f. Gk *brakhiōn* arm + *sauros* -SAUR.] A huge sauropod dinosaur of the genus *Brachiosaurus*, with the forelegs longer than the hind legs, found fossilized in Jurassic strata.

brachistochrone /brəˈkɪstəkrəʊn/ *n.* L18. [f. Gk *brakhistos* superl. of *brakhus* short (see -O-) + *khronos* time.] A curve joining two points such that a body travelling along it (e.g. under gravity) takes a shorter time than is possible along any other curve between the points.

brachium /ˈbreɪkɪəm, ˈbrak-/ *n.* M18. [L.] *Anat.* & *Zool.* The arm; *spec.* the upper arm from shoulder to elbow.

brachy- /ˈbraki/ *comb. form* of Gk *brakhus* short. (Cf. DOLICHO-, PLATY-.)

brachycataˈlectic *a.* & *n.* (*Pros.*) (a verse) lacking one foot or two syllables E17. **brachyˈdactylous** *a.* having abnormally short fingers and toes L19. **brachyˈdactyly** *n.* brachydactylous condition L19. **brachyodont** *a.* characterized by or designating teeth with low crowns and well-developed roots L19. **brachyˈpellic** *a.* [Gk *pella* bowl] having or designating a pelvis whose anteroposterior diameter is much greater than its transverse diameter M20. **braˈchypterous** *a.* short-winged M19.

brachycephalic /ˌbrakɪsɪˈfalɪk, -kɛˈfalɪk/ *a.* Also †**-keph-**. M19. [f. prec. + -CEPHALIC.] Short-headed; *spec.* having a cranial index between 80 and 85.

brachycephal /brakɪˈsɛf(ə)l, ˈbrakɪsɛf(ə)l; -kɛf-/ *n.* [back-form. f. mod.L *brachycephales* pl.] a brachycephalic person E20. **brachycephales** /-liːz/, **-cephali** /-lʌɪ, -liː/ *ns.pl.* (now *rare* or *obs.*) [mod.L] brachycephals M19. **brachyˈcephalism** *n.* brachycephalic condition M19. **brachyˈcephalous** *a.* brachycephalic L19. **brachyˈcephaly** *n.* brachycephalism M19.

brachygraphy /brəˈkɪɡrəfi/ *n. obs.* exc. *Hist.* L16. [Fr. *brachygraphie*: see BRACHY-, -GRAPHY.] = STENOGRAPHY.

brachylogy /brəˈkɪlədʒi/ *n.* Also (earlier) in L form †**-logia**. M16. [Late L *brachylogia* f. Gk *brakhulogia*: see BRACHY-, -LOGY.] Concise speech; a concise expression.

brachyurous /brakɪˈjʊərəs/ *a.* E19. [f. BRACHY- + Gk *oura* tail + -OUS.] *Zool.* Of a decapod crustacean: having a relatively short abdomen.

brachyuran *n.* & *a.* (*a*) *n.* a crustacean (e.g. many crabs) belonging to the section Brachyura which includes most brachyurous kinds; (*b*) *adj.* of or pertaining to the Brachyura: L19.

brack /brak/ *n.*[1] ME. [In branch I f. ON *brak* = OE *ġebræc*, OS *gibrak* creaking noise, f. Gmc base of BREAK *v.* In branch II parallel to BREAK *n.*[1]] †I1 Noise, outcry. ME–E16. II†2 A breach, rupture; a quarrel; a broken piece, a fragment. M16–E19. 3 A flaw (in cloth). Now chiefly *dial.* M16.

brack /brak/ *n.*[2] & *v.t.* Now *rare* or *obs.* M18. [G *Bracke* n., *bracken* vb.] (Sort or examine by) a system of inspection at Baltic ports.

bracker *n.* an official carrying out this system M18.

brack /brak/ *n.*[3] *Anglo-Ir.* M19. [f. (as) BARNBRACK.] = BARNBRACK.

brack /brak/ *a.* & *n.*[4] *obs.* exc. *dial.* E16. [MLG, MDu. *brac* (LG, Du. *brak*), of unkn. origin.] A *adj.* Salt, brackish. E16. B *n.* Salt water, the sea. L16.

bracky *a.* brackish L16.

bracken /ˈbrak(ə)n/ *n.*[1] ME. [ON (Sw. *bräken*, Da. *bregne*).] 1 A large fern, *Pteridium aquilinum*, common on hillsides, heaths, etc.; any of various other ferns of the genus *Pteridium*: *collect.* a mass of such ferns. ME. 2 A shade of brown. E20.

Comb.: **bracken-clock** a common chafer (beetle), *Phyllopertha horticola*.

brackened *a.* overgrown with bracken L19. **brackeny** *a.* = BRACKENED M19.

†bracken *n.*[2] Also **brochan**. M16–L19. [Gael. *breacan*, Ir. *breacán* f. *breac* chequered.] A tartan plaid.

bracket /ˈbrakɪt/ *n.* Orig. **†-g(g)-**. L16. [Fr. *braguette* codpiece, or Sp. *bragueta* codpiece, bracket, corbel, dim. of Fr. *brague* mortise, (in pl.) breeches, lashing, f. Prov. *braga* (pl.) breeches, ult. f. L *braca*, pl. *bracae* breeches.] **1** A flat-topped, usu. decorated, projection from a wall, serving as a support to a statue, arch, etc. L16. **b** A small (ornamental) shelf with a slanting underprop for fixing to a wall. M17. **2** A wooden or metal angular support; a support for a lamp, projecting from a wall. E17. **3** Either of the two side-pieces of a gun-carriage. M18. **4** A mark used, usu. in pairs ( ), [ ], { }, < >, for enclosing a word or words, figures, etc., so as to separate them from the context; *spec.* (*Typogr.*) a square bracket. M18. **5** *Mil.* (The distance between) shots fired short of and over the target in rangefinding. L19. **6** A group (of people) classed together as similar or as falling between certain limits (of income etc.). L19. **7** *Skating.* A series of turns resembling a bracket { L19.

4 *angle bracket, round bracket, square bracket*, etc. 6 M. INNES They were both from the same social bracket. J. K. GALBRAITH Tax reductions affecting the upper surtax brackets.

Comb.: **bracket clock**: designed to stand on a wall-bracket; **bracket fungus**: forming shelflike projections on tree-trunks etc.

bracket /ˈbrakɪt/ *v.* M19. [f. the n.] **1** *v.t.* Link or couple (lines, names, etc.) by means of a brace; *fig.* imply connection or equality of. (Foll. by *together*, *with* another.) M19. **2** *v.t.* Provide with brackets; enclose in brackets as parenthetic, spurious, etc., or (*Math.*) to indicate some special relation to what precedes or follows. M19. **3** *v.i.* & *t.* *Mil.* Find the range for artillery by means of a bracket; fire or land short of and over (the target). E20.

bracketing *n.* (*a*) framework etc. used as a support for moulding etc. on a wall; (*b*) the action of the vb: E19.

Brackett series /ˈbrakɪt sɪəriːz/ *n. phr.* M20. [Frederick Sumner *Brackett* (b. 1896), US physicist.] A series of lines in the infrared spectrum of atomic hydrogen, between 4.04 and 1.46 micrometres.

brackish /ˈbrakɪʃ/ *a.* M16. [f. BRACK *a.* + -ISH[1].] **1** Of water: slightly salt. M16. **2** Spoilt by mixture. E17.

brackishness *n.* L16.

brackmard /ˈbrakmɑːd/ *n. obs.* exc. *Hist.* E16. [Fr. *braquemart*.] A short broad-bladed sword, a cutlass.

braconid /ˈbrakənɪd/ *n.* & *a.* L19. [mod.L *Braconidae* (see below), f. *Bracon* genus name (irreg. f. Gk *brakhus* short) + -ID[3].] **A** *n.* Any insect of the family Braconidae of hymenopterous insects similar to ichneumon flies. L19. **B** *adj.* Of, pertaining to, or designating this family. L19.

bract /brakt/ *n.* Orig. also in L form **†bractea**, pl. **-eae**. L18. [L *bractea* var. of *brattea* thin plate of metal, gold leaf.] *Bot.* A leaf or scale, usu. small, growing below the calyx of a plant.

bractlet *n.* = BRACTEOLE M19.

bracteate /ˈbraktɪət/ *a.* & *n.* E19. [L *bracteatus*, f. as prec.: see -ATE[2].] **A** *adj.* **1** *Bot.* Having or bearing bracts. E19. **2** Made of metal beaten thin. M19. **B** *n.* A coin or ornament of thinly beaten metal. M19.

bracteated *a.* = BRACTEATE *a.* I E19.

bracteole /ˈbraktɪəʊl/ *n.* E19. [L *bracteola* dim. of *bractea* BRACT: see -OLE[1].] *Bot.* A small bract.

bracteolate *a.* having bracteoles E19.

brad /brad/ *n.* LME. [Var. of BROD *n.*] A thin, flat, small-headed nail.

bradawl /ˈbradɔːl/ *n.* E19. [f. prec. + AWL.] A small boring-tool with a non-spiral blade.

Bradbury /ˈbradb(ə)ri/ *n. colloq.* (now *Hist.*). E20. [John S. *Bradbury*, Brit. Secretary to the Treasury 1913–19.] A one-pound note.

bradoon *n.* var. of BRIDOON.

Bradshaw /ˈbradʃɔː/ *n.* M19. [George *Bradshaw* (1801–53), Brit. printer.] *Hist.* (Colloq. name for) *Bradshaw's Railway Guide*, a timetable of (esp. British) passenger trains, published 1839–1961.

brady- /ˈbradi/ *comb. form* of Gk *bradus* slow.

brady'cardia *n.* abnormal slowness of heart action L19. **bradymeta'bolic** *a.* (*Zool.*) pertaining to or characterized by bradymetabolism L20. **bradyme'tabolism** *n.* (*Zool.*) the low level of metabolism characteristic of cold-blooded vertebrates; poikilothermy: L20. **bradypepsy** *n.* (now *rare* or *obs.*) [Gk *bradupepsia*] slowness of digestion L16.

bradykinin /bradɪˈkʌɪnɪn/ *n.* M20. [f. prec. + Gk *kinēsis* motion + -IN[1].] *Biochem.* Any of a class of naturally-occurring peptides which cause contraction of smooth muscle. Cf. KININ.

bradyseism /ˈbradɪsʌɪz(ə)m/ *n.* L19. [f. BRADY- + Gk *seismos* earthquake.] A slow rise or fall of the earth's crust.

brady'seismic *a.* L19.

brae /breɪ/ *n.* *Sc.* & *north.* ME. [ON *brá* eyelash = OE *brǣw* eyelid, OFris. *brē*, OS, OHG *brāwa* (G *Braue*) eyebrow: the sense-development is parallel to that of BROW *n.*[1]] A steep bank beside a river valley; a hillside, a slope.

brag /brag/ *n.* LME. [Origin unkn.: cf. next, BRAG *v.*] **1** Arrogant or boastful language; boasting; a boast. LME. **†2** Show; pompous demeanour. LME–M17. **†3** The bray of a trumpet. L15–E16. **4** A braggart. L17. **5** A card-game resembling poker. M18.

1 SHAKES. *A.Y.L.* Caesar's thrasonical brag of 'I came, saw, and overcame'. MILTON Beauty is nature's brag.

brag /brag/ *a.* & *adv.* ME. [Origin unkn.: cf. prec., next.] **A** *adj.* **†1** Mettlesome, spirited, lively. ME–E17. **†2** Boastful (*of*). ME–M17. **3** First-rate, surpassingly good. *US.* M19. **†B** *adv.* Boastfully. LME–L16.

†bragly *adv.* M16–E18.

brag /brag/ *v.* Infl. **-gg-**. LME. [Origin unkn.: cf. prec., BRAG *n.*] **†1** *v.i.* & *t.* Sound (a trumpet) loudly. Only in LME. **2** *v.i.* & *t.* Boast (of). LME. **†b** *v.i.* Swagger, show off. M–L16. **3** *v.t.* Challenge; bully, overawe by boasting. Chiefly *dial.* M16.

bragger *n.* a boaster, a braggart LME. **braggery** *n.* (*a*) bragging; †(*b*) *the* rabble: M16.

†braget *n.* var. of BRACKET *n.*

Bragg /brag/ *n.* E20. [Sir William Henry (1862–1942) and his son Sir William Lawrence (1890–1971) *Bragg*, Eng. physicists.] Physics. *Bragg('s) law*, a relation giving the conditions for maximum reflection of electromagnetic waves (esp. X-rays) or particles by planes of atoms in a crystal. Hence *Bragg angle*, an angle of incidence at which maximum reflection occurs for a given wavelength.

braggadocio /bragəˈdəʊtʃɪəʊ/ *n.* Pl. **-os**. L16. [Pseudo-It. pers. name (Spenser), f. *brag* or *braggart* + *-occio* It. augm. suff.] **1** An empty idle boaster. L16. **2** Empty boasting, bluster. M18.

†braggadocian *a.* L16–E18.

braggart /ˈbragət, -ɑːt/ *n.* & *a.* L16. [Fr. †*bragard*, f. †*braguer* vaunt: see -ART.] **A** *n.* A person given to bragging, a boaster. L16. **B** *adj.* Given to bragging, boastful. E17.

braggartism *n.* L16.

bragget /ˈbragət/ *n.*[1] LME. [Early Welsh *brac(h)aut* (mod. *bragod*) = Ir. *brogóid*, f. Celt., f. base repr. by L *brace*, Gaulish *bracis* kind of grain.] A drink made of honey, or (latterly) sugar and spices, and ale fermented together.

†bragget *n.*[2] var. of BRACKET *n.*

†brahm *n.* var. of BRAHMAN *n.*[1]

Brahma /ˈbrɑːmə/ *n.*[1] Also **Brahman**. L17. [Skt *brahmā* (nom. of *brahmán*) priest.] In Hinduism: the creator, one of the three supreme personal deities. In Hindu and Buddhist thought: the highest god.

Brahma /ˈbrɑːmə/ *n.*[2] L19. [Abbrev.] = BRAHMAPUTRA.

brahma *n.*[3] var. of BRAHMAN *n.*[1]

brahmacharya /brɑːməˈtʃɑːrɪə/ *n.* E20. [Skt *brahmacarya*, f. *brahman* prayer, worship + *carya* conduct.] Purity of life, esp. regarding sexual matters (freq. used with reference to the life and teachings of M. K. Gandhi).

brahmachari *n.* a person who practises brahmacharya L18.

brahman /ˈbrɑːmən/ *n.*[1] Also **brahma** /ˈbrɑːmə/, **†brahm**, **B-**. L18. [Skt *brahman* sacred utterance.] In Hindu philosophy: the ultimate reality underlying all phenomena.

Brahman *n.*[2] var. of BRAHMA *n.*[1]

brahman *n.*[3] var. of BRAHMIN.

Brahmaputra /brɑːməˈpuːtrə/ *n.* Also **b-**, **†-pootra**. M19. [*Brahmaputra*, a river in Bangladesh and West Bengal.] A variety of domestic fowl originating in the Indian subcontinent.

Brahmi /ˈbrɑːmi/ *n.* L19. [Skt *brāhmī*.] One of the two oldest alphabets of the Indian subcontinent, of Semitic origin. Cf. KHAROSHTI.

brahmic /ˈbrɑːmɪk/ *a.* M19. [f. Skt *brāhma* (see BRAHMO) + -IC.] Pertaining to the Hindu movement Brahmo Sabha or Samaj (cf. BRAHMO).

brahmin /ˈbrɑːmɪn/ *n.* Also **-man** /-mən/, **B-**. ME. [Skt *brāhmaṇa* one of the brahmin caste, f. *brahman* (nom. *brahmā*) priest.] **1** A member of the highest or priestly Hindu caste. ME. **2** *transf.* (Usu. **B-**.) A highly cultured or intellectually aloof person; *spec.* a member of the upper classes of Boston, Massachusetts, USA. M19. **3** (Usu. **B-**.) In full *Brahmin bull, ox*, etc. A zebu ox, or an animal of a breed of beef cattle developed from this. M19.

brah'minic, **-'manic** /-ˈman-/ *a.* of or pertaining to the brahmins M19. **brah'minical**, **-'manical** /-ˈman-/ *a.* = BRAHMINIC L16. **brahminism**, **-manism** *n.* the principles and practice of brahmins E19.

brahminy /ˈbrɑːmɪni/ *a.* Also *arch.* **-nee**, **B-**. E19. [f. prec. on the analogy of native Indian wds like BENGALI.] Pertaining to the brahmin caste; appropriated to the brahmins. Now chiefly as below.

Brahminy bull = BRAHMIN 3. **Brahminy duck** the ruddy shelduck, *Tadorna ferruginea*. **Brahminy kite** a white-headed kite of southern Asia and Australia, *Haliastur indus*.

Brahmo /ˈbrɑːməʊ/ *n.* & *a.* Pl. of n. **-os**. L19. [Bengali f. Skt *brāhma* a person who knows brahman.] (An adherent) of the Hindu reform movement Brahmo Sabha (or Brahmo Samaj) 'society of worshippers of Brahma'.

Brahmoism, **†Brahmism** *n.* the doctrines of the Brahmo movement M19.

Brahmsian /ˈbrɑːmzɪən/ *a.* & *n.* L19. [f. *Brahms* (see below) + -IAN.] **A** *adj.* Of, pertaining to, or characteristic of the German composer Johannes Brahms (1833–97) or his music. L19. **B** *n.* An interpreter, student, or admirer of Brahms or his music. E20.

Brahui /brəˈhuːi/ *n.* & *a.* E19. [Brahui.] **A** *n.* Pl. **-s**, same. A member of a pastoral people of Baluchistan; their Dravidian language. E19. **B** *attrib.* or as *adj.* Of or pertaining to the Brahuis or their language. M19.

braid /breɪd/ *n.* See also BREDE *n.*[2] OE. [f. BRAID *v.*[1]] **†1** An adroit turn; a trick, a subtlety. OE–L16. **†2** A sudden or brisk movement. ME–E19. **3** A blow, an attack, an outburst. Long *obs.* exc. *dial.* ME. **4** A thing plaited or interwoven, *esp.* a plait of hair. M16. **b** A string or band confining or entwined in the hair. L16. **5** A woven band made of thread of silk, gold, silver, etc., used for trimming or binding garments. L16.

5 *Hercules braid, military braid, soutache braid*, etc.

†braid *a.*[1] *rare* (Shakes.). Only in E17. [Of uncertain meaning and origin: cf. BRAID *n.* I.] Deceitful.

braid *a.*[2], *adv.* see BROAD *a.*, *adv.*

braid /breɪd/ *v.*[1] Pa. pple & ppl a. **braided**, BROWDEN. See also BREDE *v.*[2] [OE *bregdan* = OFris. *breida*, *brīda*, OS *bregdan* (Du. *breien*), OHG *brettan*, ON *bregða*, f. Gmc, of unkn. origin. In senses 5, 6 f. BRAID *n.*] **I** **†1** *v.t.* Make a sudden movement with (the hand, foot, etc.); brandish (a spear), draw (a sword etc.); jerk, fling, etc., with a sudden effort. OE–E17. †2 *v.i.* Change suddenly or abruptly. OE–LME. 3 *v.i.* Start, usu. out of sleep; burst into motion, speech, etc. *arch.* ME. II 4 *v.t.* Twist in and out, interweave; embroider; make (a cord, garment, etc.) by plaiting; arrange (the hair) in braids. OE. 5 *v.t.* Bind (the hair) with a braid, ribbon, etc. L18. 6 *v.t.* Ornament or trim with braid; outline (a design for point-lace work) by means of braid. M19.

With preps. in specialized senses: **braid of** *dial.* take after, resemble.

braider *n.* a person who or thing which makes or applies braids M19. **braiding** *n.* (*a*) the action of the vb; (*b*) braids collectively; braided work: LME.

†braid *v.*²*t.* LME–E17. [Aphet. f. UPBRAID *v.*] Upbraid; reproach.

brail /breɪl/ *n.* & *v.* LME. [OFr. *braiel*, *braël* f. med.L *bracale* waist-belt, f. *braca*: see BRACKET *n.*] A *n.* 1 In *pl.* Small ropes fastened to the leech of fore-and-aft sails to truss them up before furling. LME. 2 In *pl.* The rump of an animal; *spec.* the feathers about a hawk's rump. Now *rare* or *obs.* LME. 3 A girdle used to confine a hawk's wings. E19. B *v.t.* 1 Haul *up* (sails) by means of brails. E17. 2 Confine (a hawk's wings) with a girdle. M17.

Braille /breɪl/ *n.* & *v.* M19. [f. Louis *Braille* (1809–52), Fr. teacher of the blind, who invented the system.] A *n.* A system of printing or writing for the blind, in which the characters are represented by arrangements of raised points. M19. B *v.t.* Print or transcribe in Braille characters. M20.

brain /breɪn/ *n.* [OE *brægen* = MLG *bragen*, *bregen*, (M)Du. *brein* f. WGmc.] 1 The mass of substance contained in the skull of humans and other vertebrates; *sing.* & (usu.) in *pl.* cerebral substance. Orig. *spec.* the cerebrum, now the entire organ; *transf.* an analogous organ of an invertebrate. OE. 2 This organ as the seat of sensation, motion, or human speech, the organ of thought, memory, or imagination; *sing.* & (freq.) in *pl.* intellectual power, intellect; thought, sense, imagination. ME. b *sing.* & (freq.) in *pl.* A clever person; *the* cleverest person in a group etc., *the* mastermind. *colloq.* M19. 3 An electronic device comparable in function to a brain; a computer. Usu. more fully *electronic brain*. M20.

2 W. STUBBS Was that plan the conception of any one brain? V. BRITTAIN Men of all ages who .. hadn't the brains of an earwig. b C. KINGSLEY The accomplished Mysseri .. was in fact the brain of our corps. *Times* Admiral .. Wynter, 'the brains' of the victory.

Phrases: **beat, (cudgel, rack,** etc.) **one's brains** search for ideas, think very hard. *blow a person's brains out*: see BLOW *v.*¹ *cells of the brain*: see CELL *n.*¹ 7b. *cudgel one's brains*: see *beat one's brains* above. **get** or **have on the brain** be constantly thinking of, be obsessed by. *pick a person's brains*: see PICK *v.*¹ *rack one's brains*: see *beat one's brains* above. SOFTENING *of the brain*. *turn a person's brain*: see TURN *v.* VISCERAL *brain*. *wash one's brain*: see WASH *v.* *water on the brain*: see WATER *n.*

Comb.: **brain-box** (*a*) the cranium; (*b*) *colloq.* the mind, the intellect; a clever person; **brain-case** *colloq.* the cranium; **brain-cell** any of the cells forming the brain tissue; **brainchild** *colloq.* the product of thought; an invention; **brain-coral** coral forming a compact mass with a surface resembling the convolutions of the brain; **brain-damage** injury to the brain (permanently) impairing its functions; **brain-damaged** *a.* having suffered brain-damage; **brain-dead** *a.* having suffered brain death; **brain death** permanent cessation of the functions of the brainstem that control respiration etc.; **brain drain** *colloq.* the loss of highly trained or qualified people by emigration; **brain-fag** *colloq.* mental exhaustion; **brain fever** inflammation or other malaise affecting the brain; *brain-fever bird*, an Indian hawk-cuckoo, *Cuculus varius*, having a maddeningly persistent call; **brain-pan** *colloq.* the cranium; **brainpower** mental ability or intelligence; **brain-sand** minute calcareous particles deposited in the pineal gland; **brain scan** a diagnostic radiographic scan of the brain; **brain scanner** an apparatus for performing a brain scan; **brainsick** *a.* diseased in the mind, mad; proceeding from a diseased mind; **brainsickly** *adv.* (*rare*) in a brainsick manner; **brainstem** the medulla oblongata, pons, and midbrain; **brain-stone** = *brain-coral* above; **brainstorm** (*a*) a succession of sudden and severe phenomena, due to some cerebral disturbance; (*b*) = *brainwave* (c) below; (*c*) (orig. *US*) a brainstorming session; **brainstorming** (orig. *US*) attack on a problem by spontaneous discussion in search of new ideas; **brain-teaser** a difficult problem or puzzle; **brain** (or **brains) trust** (*a*) (usu. *brains trust*) a group of people assembled to give impromptu views on topics of interest; (*b*) a group of experts appointed to give advice or guidance to a government etc.; **brain-twister** = *brain-teaser* above; **brainwash** *v.t.* systematically and often forcibly replace established ideas in the mind of (a person) by new (usu. political) ideas; **brainwave** (*a*) a hypothetical telepathic vibration; (*b*) *sing.* & (usu.) in *pl.*, a measurable electrical impulse in the brain; (*c*) *colloq.* a sudden inspiration or bright idea; **brainwork** mental activity.

brained *a.* having a brain or brains (of a specified kind) LME. **brainish** *a.* (*arch.*) passionate, headstrong M16. **brainless** *a.* (*a*) devoid of brain; (*b*) foolish; wanting intelligence: LME. **brainlessly** *adv.* E17. **brainlessness** *n.* L19.

brain /breɪn/ *v.t.* LME. [f. the n.] 1 Dash out the brains of; kill with a heavy blow to the head. LME. †2 Conceive in the brain. *rare* (Shakes.). Only in E17.

brainy /ˈbreɪni/ *a.* M19. [f. BRAIN *n.* + -Y¹.] Having plenty of brains; acute, clever.

brainily *adv.* E20. **braininess** *n.* E20.

braird /brɛːd/ *n.* & *v.* Orig. & chiefly *Sc.* L15. [Alt. of BRERD.] A *n.* The first shoots of grass, corn, or other crop. L15. B *v.i.* Sprout; appear above the ground. L15.

braise /breɪz/ *v.* & *n.* M18. [Fr. *braiser*, f. *braise* live coals: cf. BRAZIER *n.*²] A *v.t.* Cook slowly with a little liquid in a tightly closed vessel. M18. B *n.* Braised meat; the materials for braising meat etc. with. M18.

brak /brak/ *a.* & *n.* *S. Afr.* L18. [Afk. f. Du.: see BRACK *a.* & *n.*⁴] A *adj.* Brackish; alkaline. L18. B *n.* Brackishness; alkalinity of soil or water. L19.

brake /breɪk/ *n.*¹ [OE *bracu* (recorded in genit. pl. *fearnbraca* beds of fern), corresp. to MLG *brake* branch, twig, tree stump; perh. reinforced in ME f. LG.] 1 *Fernbrake*, a bed or thicket of ferns. OE. 2 *gen.* A clump of bushes, brushwood, or briers; a thicket. LME.

brake /breɪk/ *n.*² ME. [Perh. shortening of BRACKEN *n.*¹, the latter being interpreted as pl.] A fern; bracken.

brake /breɪk/ *n.*³ LME. [Corresp. to MLG *brake* or ODu. *braeke*, Du. *braak* flax-brake, f. Du. *breken* BREAK *v.*] 1 A toothed instrument for braking flax or hemp. LME. 2 A baker's kneading-machine. LME. 3 In full *brake-harrow*. A heavy harrow for crushing clods. M17. 4 An instrument for peeling the bark from willows for basket-making. E19.

brake /breɪk/ *n.*⁴ LME. [Origin uncertain: perh. rel. to Fr. *braquer* point (a cannon), turn (the rudder).] †1 The winch of a crossbow; a crossbow, ballista, or similar engine. LME–M19. 2 The handle of a pump. E17.

†brake *n.*⁵ LME–M18. [Perh. f. ODu. *braeke* (see BRAKE *n.*³) in sense 'a nose-ring for a draught-ox'.] A bridle, a curb.

brake /breɪk/ *n.*⁶ In branch II also **break**. E16. [Origin unkn.: the two branches may represent different wds.] I †1 A cage, a trap; a snare, a difficulty. E16–M17. †2 An instrument of torture; a rack. M16–M19. 3 A framework intended to hold something steady; a frame in which a horse's foot is placed when being shod. E17.

II 4 A carriage-frame without a body, for breaking-in young horses. M19. 5 A large wagonette; an estate car. M19.

5 **shooting brake** an estate car.

brake /breɪk/ *n.*⁷ Also **break**. L18. [Prob. f. BRAKE *n.*⁴ or *n.*⁵] An apparatus for checking (usu. rotary) motion; *fig.* a retarding agency.

apply, put on, the brakes *fig.* moderate one's enthusiasm.

Comb.: **brake block** (*a*) the block which holds a brake shoe; (*b*) a block (usu. made of hardened rubber) which is applied to a bicycle wheel as a brake; **brake-cylinder** the cylinder in which the piston of an air or hydraulic brake works; **brake drum** a cylinder attached to a wheel or hub, upon which the brake shoe presses; **brake fluid** specially formulated liquid for use in hydraulic brakes; **brake horsepower** the power available at the shaft of an engine, measurable by means of a brake; **brake lining** a layer of material attached to the face of a brake shoe to increase friction and provide a renewable surface; **brakeman** a man in charge of a brake or brakes, esp. on a train; **brake parachute** a parachute attached to the tail of an aeroplane and opened to serve as a brake; **brake-pipe** the pipe of an air-, vacuum-, or hydraulic brake, conveying the working medium to the brakes of a train, motor vehicle, etc.; **brake shoe** that part of a brake which comes in contact with the object whose motion is to be checked; **brakesman** = *brakeman* above; **brake van** a compartment, carriage, or wagon in a train which contains braking apparatus operated by the guard.

brake /breɪk/ *v.*¹*t.* LME. [f. BRAKE *n.*³] 1 Beat and crush (flax, hemp, etc.). LME. 2 Break (clods) with a harrow. E19. 3 Knead (dough). M19.

†brake *v.*²*t.* & *i.* LME–M18. [Perh. rel. to OE *bræc* phlegm, mucus, saliva, = MLG *brēke*: cf. ODu. *bracken*, MLG, Du. *braken* vomit, rel. to BREAK *v.*] Spew, vomit.

brake /breɪk/ *v.*³ M19. [f. BRAKE *n.*⁷] 1 *v.t.* Apply a brake to; retard or stop by means of a brake or brakes. M19. 2 *v.i.* Apply or be checked by the brake(s). L19.

Comb.: **braking distance** the distance covered by a vehicle etc. before coming to rest following application of the brakes (usu. in specified conditions).

brake *v.*⁴ see BREAK *v.*

braky /ˈbreɪki/ *a.* M17. [f. BRAKE *n.*¹ or *n.*² + -Y¹.] Overgrown with brushwood or fern.

Bramantip /ˈbram(ə)ntɪp/ *n.* M19. [A mnemonic of scholastic philosophers, A indicating a universal affirmative proposition, I a particular affirmative proposition.] *Logic.* The first mood of the fourth syllogistic figure, in which two universal affirmative premisses yield a particular affirmative conclusion.

bramble /ˈbramb(ə)l/ *n.* [OE *bræmbel*, earlier *brǣmel*, *brēmel*, f. Gmc base also of BROOM: see -LE¹.] 1 A rough prickly shrub of the genus *Rubus*, with long trailing shoots; *esp.* any member of the aggregate species *R. fruticosus*, with purplish-black fruit; a blackberry-bush. OE. 2 A blackberry. Chiefly *Sc.* & *north.* E19.

Comb.: **bramble-berry** the fruit of the bramble; a blackberry; **bramble-rose** a white trailing dogrose.

brambly *a.* covered or overgrown with brambles L16.

bramble /ˈbramb(ə)l/ *v.* E17. [f. the n.] 1 *v.t.* Cover or make overgrown with brambles. Chiefly as *brambled* ppl a. E17. 2 *v.i.* Gather blackberries. Chiefly as *brambling* vbl n. Chiefly *Sc.* & *north.* M19.

brambling /ˈbramblɪŋ/ *n.* M16. [Origin uncertain: cf. BRANDLING 2, G †*Brämling*.] A brightly coloured finch, *Fringilla montifringilla*, which is a winter visitor to Britain.

†brame *n.* *rare* (Spenser). Only in L16. [Prob. f. It. *brama* strong desire.] Longing.

Bramley /ˈbramli/ *n.* E20. [f. Matthew *Bramley*, a Nottinghamshire butcher, in whose garden it is said to have been first grown *c* 1850.] In full *Bramley('s) seedling*. A large green variety of cooking apple.

bran /bran/ *n.* ME. [(O)Fr. *bran*, †*bren* (formerly) bran, (now) excrement, muck, filth, = Prov., OSp., It. dial. *bren*, of unkn. origin (adopted in Celt. langs. from Fr. and Eng.).] 1 Husks of grain separated from flour after grinding. ME. †2 Dandruff. LME–L16.

Comb.: **bran-pie, -tub** a tub filled with bran or other material in which prizes are hidden, to be drawn out at random by children.

branlike *a.* resembling that or those of bran; resembling bran, esp. in consistency: L19. **branny** *a.* consisting of, containing, or resembling bran LME.

branch /brɑːn(t)ʃ/ *n.* ME. [(O)Fr. *branche* = Prov., Sp. *branca* claw, It. *branca* claw, paw, Romanian *brîncă* hand, paw, f. late L *branca* (in *branca ursina* bear's foot, acanthus), of unkn. origin.] 1 A limb of a tree or shrub springing from the trunk or stem, or from a bough. ME. 2 A lateral extension or subdivision of a main body, e.g. of a mountain range, river, railway, road, artery, deer's horn, candelabrum, etc. ME. †**b** A candelabrum or chandelier, esp. in a church. LME–L18. †**c** A human arm (or hand). *rare* (Shakes.). Only in L16. **d** A small stream. *US.* M17. 3 (Conn. w. *family tree.*) A division of a family or race according to the differing lines of descent from the common ancestor. ME. **b** A descendant, a child. Now only *joc.* ME. 4 A (sub)division of a subject, pursuit, philosophy, detailed proposition, etc. E16. 5 A component part of an organization or system such as a government, police force, church, etc. L17. 6 A subordinate establishment of a library, bank, or other business, serving a particular area. E19. 7 The nozzle of a fire-hose. L19.

1 OLIVE BRANCH. *root and branch*: see ROOT *n.*[1] 2 W. WHISTON A Branch or Bay of the Great Ocean. J. BARNES The Metropolitan Line (by which the purist naturally meant the Watford, Chesham and Amersham branches). *private branch exchange*: see PRIVATE *a.* 3 *Red Branch*: see RED *a.* 4 W. CRUISE The express declaration of the testator in almost every branch of his will. R. MACAULAY May one ask what branch of art you have been practising this evening? Drawing in charcoal? A. J. P. TAYLOR Coal entered into every branch of industrial life. 5 J. REED Others were dispatched to provincial cities, to form branches of the Committee for Salvation. E. CRISPIN Graveney was the Inspector in charge of Glazebridge's uniform branch. I. HAMILTON The army medical corps or some similar noncombatant branch of the forces. *Special Branch*: see SPECIAL *a.*

Comb.: **branch library** a library other than the main one in an area; **branch-line** a secondary railway line running from a main line to a terminus; **branch officer** the equivalent, in the Royal Navy, of a warrant officer; **branch-work** ornamental figured patterns.

branchery *n.* (*a*) branches in the mass; †(*b*) the ramifications of the endocarp in a fruit: L17. **branchless** *a.* E17. **branchlet** *n.* a little branch M18.

branch /brɑːn(t)ʃ/ *v.* LME. [f. the n.] 1 *v.i.* Bear branches; put branches *forth, out.* LME. 2 *v.i.* Spring or spread out in the manner of branches from a tree; deviate, diverge, divide. Chiefly w. advs. LME. 3 *v.t.* Adorn or embroider with work representing flowers and foliage. E16. 4 *v.t.* Divide into or spread out as branches; arrange in branches. *arch.* E17.

2 MAX-MÜLLER Speech from which these dialects branched off. E. A. FREEMAN The Foss Way.. branched off from the Eastern gate. L. MACNEICE In one chapter of this book.. he branches out into a very much wider field. T. COLLINS The track branches there. 4 J. BENTHAM The whole system of offences.. is branched out into five classes. TENNYSON Gold that branch'd itself Fine as ice-ferns.

branching *a.* (*a*) that branches; (*b*) *poet.* antlered: LME.

branched /brɑːn(t)ʃt/ *a.* LME. [f. BRANCH *n.*, *v.*: see -ED[2], -ED[1].] 1 Having branches (of a specified kind or number). LME. 2 Embroidered, chased, etc., with figured work. E16.

brancher /ˈbrɑːn(t)ʃə/ *n.* LME. [AN var. of (O)Fr. *branchier* (orig. adj.), f. as BRANCH *n.* + -ER[2].] A young hawk etc. when it first leaves the nest and takes to the branches.

branchia /ˈbraŋkɪə/ *n.* Pl. **-iae** /-ɪiː/, same. L17. [L, pl. *-iae*, f. Gk *bragkhia* pl.: see -A[3], -AE.] A respiratory organ of fishes etc.; a gill. Also, a vestigial gill cleft present in mammalian embryos. Usu. in *pl.*

branchiate *a.* having gills L19. **branchiated** *a.* = BRANCHIATE M19.

branchial /ˈbraŋkɪəl/ *a.* L18. [f. as prec. + -AL[1].] Of or pertaining to branchiae; of the nature of or resembling gills.

branchial arch = *gill arch* s.v. GILL *n.*[1] **branchial cleft** = *gill slit* s.v. GILL *n.*[1] *branchial tuft*: see TUFT *n.* 1a.

branchio- /ˈbraŋkɪəʊ/ *comb. form* of Gk *bragkhia* gills: see -O-.

branchiobdellid /ˌbraŋkɪə(ʊ)ˈdɛlɪd/ *n.* & *a.* [Gk *bdella* leech] (*a*) *n.* an oligochaete worm of the family Branchiobdellidae, members of which resemble leeches and commonly live among the gills of crayfish; (*b*) *adj.* of or pertaining to the Branchiobdellidae: M20. **branchioˈmeric** *a.* (esp. of the visceral muscles of fishes) displaying branchiomerism E20. **branchiˈomerism** *n.* arrangement into a number of segments each containing a gill arch or cleft L19. **branchiˈostegal** *a.* [Gk *stegein* to cover] pertaining to the protection of the gills; covering or protecting the gills: M18. **branchiˈostegite** *n.* a membrane covering the gills (of crustaceans) L19. **branchiˈostegous** *a.* (*a*) having gill-covers; (*b*) = BRANCHIOSTEGAL: M18.

branchiopod /ˈbraŋkɪə(ʊ)pɒd/ *a.* & *n.* E19. [f. mod.L *Branchiopoda* (see below), f. as prec. + -POD + -A[3].] *Zool.* Of or pertaining to, a crustacean of, the subclass Branchiopoda, having gills upon the feet.

branchy /ˈbrɑːn(t)ʃi/ *a.* LME. [f. BRANCH *n.* + -Y[1].] Bearing or consisting of branches; putting forth offshoots, ramifying; antlered.

branchiness *n.* E17.

brand /brand/ *n.* [OE *brand* = OFris., (M)Du. *brand*, OHG *brant* (G *Brand*), ON *brandr*, f. Gmc, f. base also of BURN *v.*] †1 Burning. OE–ME. 2 A burning or charred log or stick; *poet.* a torch. OE. 3 A sword, a blade. *poet.* or *arch.* OE. 4 A permanent mark made by burning with a hot iron, usu. deliberately. M16. **b** *fig.* A mark, usu. of infamy; a stigma. L16. **c** *spec.* A mark of ownership impressed on cattle, horses, etc., by branding. M17. 5 A kind of blight in which leaves etc. look burnt. M17. 6 An iron stamp for burning-in a mark. E19. 7 (A make or kind of goods bearing) a trade mark; *fig.* a kind, a sort. E19.

2 **brand from the burning** *fig.* a rescued person, a convert. 4 DEFOE My comrade, having the brand of an old offender, was executed. **b** R. HOOKER To mark that age with the brand of error and superstition. **brand of Cain** blood-guilt. 7 D. LESSING A brand of Marxist Socialism peculiar to himself.

Comb.: **brand-image** the assumed impression of a product in the minds of potential consumers; *fig.* the general or popular conception of some person or thing; BRANDIRON; **brand-leader** the best-selling or best-known product of its type; **brand-mark** (*a*) the mark left by a hot iron stamp; (*b*) a trade mark; BRAND-NEW; **brand-name** a trade or proprietary name.

brand /brand/ *v.t.* LME. [f. the n.] 1 Burn and mark permanently with a hot iron, usu. a sign of ownership (of cattle etc.) or to distinguish criminals, slaves, etc.; *gen.* mark indelibly for such purpose. LME. 2 Stigmatize. E17. 3 Apply as a brand, denote by means of a brand; *fig.* impress indelibly on the memory etc. L17. 4 Label with a trade mark. L19.

3 C. KINGSLEY To brand upon your thoughts How she was once a woman. E. F. BENSON It was an evening branded into her memory.

brandade /brɑ̃dad/ *n.* E19. [Fr. f. mod.Prov. *brandado* lit. 'thing which has been moved or shaken'.] A Provençal dish made from salt cod.

branded /ˈbrandɪd/ *a. obs.* exc. *dial.* LME. [North. var. of BRINDED.] Brindled.

brandenburgs /ˈbrand(ə)nbəːgz/ *n.pl.* M18. [f. *Brandenburg*, town and former principality in NE Germany, prob. because worn in the Elector's army.] Ornamental facings to the breast of an officer's coat. Also, froggings on a woman's coat etc.

brander /ˈbrandə/ *n.* & *v. Sc.* & *north. dial.* LME. [Alt. of next.] **A** *n.* A gridiron. LME. **B** *v.t.* & *i.* Cook on a gridiron; grill. L18.

brandering *n.* the covering of joists with battens for plastering M19.

brandiron /ˈbrandʌɪən/ *n. obs.* exc. *dial.* LME. [f. BRAND *n.* + IRON *n.* See also BRANDER.] 1 A gridiron; a trivet. LME. †2 A sword. L16–E17.

brandise /ˈbrandɪs/ *n. dial.* [OE *brandīsen*, f. BRAND *n.* + *īsen* IRON *n.*: cf. prec.] A gridiron; a trivet; (= BRANDIRON 1).

¶Not recorded between OE and 19: intervening history uncertain.

brandish /ˈbrandɪʃ/ *v.* & *n.* ME. [(O)Fr. *brandiss-* lengthened stem (see -ISH[2]) of *brandir* f. Proto-Romance, f. Gmc base of BRAND *n.*: see -ISH[2].] **A** *v.* 1 *v.t.* Flourish (a weapon) by way of threat or display; wave or flaunt as if a weapon. ME. †2 *v.i.* & *t.* Scatter (rays of light), glitter, flash. M16–M17. 3 *v.i.* Of a sword etc.: be flourished. *rare.* M17.

1 MILTON Lawes which they so impotently brandish against others. A. HALEY Flailing their arms, brandishing their fists. P. ACKROYD His wife brandished a copy of a women's magazine.

B *n.* An act of brandishing. L16.

brandisher *n.* E17.

brandling /ˈbrandlɪŋ/ *n. dial.* M17. [f. BRAND *n.* + -LING[1].] 1 A red worm with rings of brighter colour, used as bait by anglers. Also *brandling worm.* M17. 2 = BRAMBLING. *rare.* L17. 3 A salmon parr. E18.

brand-new /bran(d)ˈnjuː/ *a.* Also **bran-new** /branˈnjuː/. L16. [f. BRAND *n.* + NEW *a.* (as if glowing from the furnace).] Conspicuously or completely new.

brandreth /ˈbrandrɪθ/ *n. dial.* LME. [ON *brandreið* grate, f. *brandr* BRAND *n.* + *reið* carriage, vehicle.] 1 A gridiron; a trivet. LME. 2 A wooden framework as a container, support, etc. LME.

brandy /ˈbrandi/ *n.* & *v.* E17. [Du. *brandewijn* (G *Branntwein*), f. *branden* burn, distil + *wijn* WINE *n.*] **A** *n.* Earlier †*brandy-wine.* 1 A strong spirit distilled from wine, or from fermented fruit-juice (as *apple, cherry, peach,* etc., *brandy*). E17. 2 A drink of this. L19.

Comb.: **brandy-ball** a kind of sweet flavoured with brandy; **brandy-bottle** (*a*) a bottle (for) containing brandy; (*b*) *dial.* the yellow water lily, *Nuphar luteum*; *brandy butter*: see BUTTER *n.*[1] 1; **brandy-cherry** (*a*) a cherry preserved in brandy; †(*b*) cherry brandy; **brandy-pawnee** /-pɔːni/ [Hind. *pānī* water] *Anglo-Ind.* brandy and water; **brandy-snap** a rolled gingerbread wafer; *brandy-wine*: see above.

B *v.t.* †1 *brandy it*, drink brandy in excess. *rare.* Only in E19. 2 Mix or treat with brandy; refresh with brandy. M19.

brangle /ˈbraŋg(ə)l/ *v.* & *n. obs.* exc. *dial.* E16. [Fr. *branler* shake: infl. by WRANGLE *v.*] **A** *v.* 1 *v.t.* & *i.* Shake, (cause to) totter, (*lit.* & *fig.*). E16. 2 *v.i.* Wrangle, squabble. E16. **B** *n.* A brawl, a wrangle. M16.

branglement *n.* disorderly dispute E17. **brangler** *n.* a brawler, a wrangler E17.

brank /braŋk/ *n.*[1] *obs.* exc. *dial.* L16. [Origin unkn.] Buckwheat.

brank *n.*[2] see BRANKS.

brank /braŋk/ *v.*[1]*i. dial.* & *Sc.* LME. [Origin unkn.] Of a horse: prance. Of a person: strut, prance.

brank /braŋk/ *v.*[2]*t. Sc.* M16. [App. f. sing. of next.] Bridle, restrain.

branks /braŋks/ *n.pl.* Chiefly *Sc.* Also (*rare*) in sing. **brank**. M16. [Origin uncertain: cf. BARNACLE *n.*[2], G *Pranger* the pillory, a barnacle for a horse, Du. *prang* a fetter.] 1 *Hist.* An instrument of punishment for a scolding woman, consisting of an iron framework for the head and a sharp metal gag for restraining the tongue. M16. 2 A type of wooden muzzle used as a bridle. M16. 3 The mumps. L18.

brank-ursine /braŋkˈəːsɪn/ *n.* LME. [Fr. *branche* (dial. *branque*) *ursine* or med.L *branca ursina*, lit. 'bear's claw': see BRANCH *n.*, URSINE *a.*] Bear's breech, acanthus.

branle /ˈbran(ə)l/ *n.* Also †**bransle**. L16. [Fr., f. *branler* shake.] †1 Wavering, agitation. Only in L16. 2 Chiefly *Hist.* A rustic ring dance of French origin. Cf. BRAWL *n.*[2] 2. L16.

bran-new *a.* var. of BRAND-NEW.

†**bransle** *n.* var. of BRANLE.

brant *n.* var. of BRENT *n.*

brant /brant/ *a.* & *adv. Sc.* & *north.* Also **brent** /brɛnt/. [OE *brant* corresp. to ON *brattr* (Sw. *brant*, Da. *brat*).] **A** *adj.* Lofty, steep, sheer. OE. **B** *adv.* Straight (up); steeply. LME.

†**brantle** *n.* M17–M19. [f. as BRANLE: cf. OFr. *brandeler* shake.] = BRANLE 2.

brasero /braˈsero/ *n.* Pl. **-os** /-ɒs/. M17. [Sp.] = BRAZIER *n.*[2]

brash /braʃ/ *n.*[1] Chiefly *dial.* & *Sc.* LME. [Perh. imit.] 1 Orig., a crash, a blow. Later, an assault, an attack, a bout. LME. 2 A slight attack of illness. E17. 3 An eruption of fluid; a shower. E19.

3 **water-brash** a painful regurgitation of acid gastric juice.

brashy *a.*[1] (*Sc.*) showery E19.

brash /braʃ/ *n.*[2] L18. [Origin unkn.] Loose broken rock or ice, rubble; hedge refuse, clippings, twigs.

brashy *a.*[2] of the nature of brash; broken, crumbly: E18.

brash /braʃ/ *a.*[1] Now chiefly *US.* M16. [Perh. imit.] Fragile, brittle.

brash /braʃ/ *a.*[2] Orig. *dial.* E19. [Perh. expressive form of *rash.*] 1 Rash, impetuous; cheeky; vulgarly self-assertive. E19. 2 Rough, harsh; active, lively. *US.* M19.

1 A. S. BYATT Orange had never been a colour he liked, seeming brash and violent. D. HALBERSTAM He was cocky and brash and self-mocking.

brashly *adv.* M19. **brashness** *n.* M19.

brash /braʃ/ *v.*[1]*t. Sc.* L16. [f. BRASH *n.*[1]] Assault, batter, breach.

brash /braʃ/ *v.*[2]*t.* M20. [f. BRASH *n.*[2]] Remove the lower branches from (a tree, plantation, etc.).

†**Brasil** *n.* var. of BRAZIL *n.*[1]

†**Brasilian** *a.* & *n.* var. of BRAZILIAN.

brasque /brɑːsk/ *n.* & *v.* Now *rare* or *obs.* M19. [Fr. f. It. dial. *brasca* coal-ash.] A *n.* An inert lining material for furnaces and crucibles, consisting of clay and charcoal. M19. B *v.t.* Line with brasque. L19.

brass /brɑːs/ *n.* & *a.* [OE *bræs* = OFris. *bres*, MLG *bras* metal, of unkn. origin.] A *n.* 1 Orig., any alloy of copper with tin or zinc or occas. other metals. Now, a yellow alloy of copper and zinc only (cf. BRONZE *n.*). OE. b Brass taken as a type of hardness or insensitivity; impudence, effrontery, nerve. LME. 2 A brass object; such objects collectively, brassware; *spec.* wind instruments of brass, the section of an orchestra or band comprising these. LME. b A monumental or sepulchral tablet of brass, bearing figures, inscriptions, etc., laid in the floor or set into the wall of a church. M16. c A bearing or block for a shaft. M16. d In full *horse-brass.* A brass ornament worn by a draught horse. E20. e A brass block or die used to impress a design etc. on a book-cover. M20. 3 Orig., copper or bronze coin. Now (*colloq.*), money generally, cash. LME. 4 High-ranking officers in the armed forces (cf. *brass hat* below); *gen.* leaders, bosses. Also *top brass. slang* (orig. *US*). L19. 5 *ellipt.* = *brass nail* below. *slang.* M20.

1 *Corinthian brass*: see CORINTHIAN *a.* 1. NAVAL *brass. white brass*: see WHITE *a.* b SHAKES. *Hen. VIII* Men's evil manners live in brass: their virtues We write in water. T. T. LYNCH An empty, vaunting person, who has brass enough to face the world. **as bold as brass** very bold(ly), impudent(ly); brazen-faced(ly). 2 D. L. SAYERS Her manner is unpolished, but I have observed that her brass is not.

Comb.: **brass-rubbing** the process of reproducing the design on a monumental brass by rubbing paper laid upon it with heelball etc.; an impression so produced.

B *attrib.* or as *adj.* (Made) of brass, brazen. LME.

brass band a group of musicians with brass (and percussion) instruments. **brass farthing** the least possible amount (usu. in neg. contexts). **brass hat** *slang* an officer of high rank (having gold braid on the cap). **brass-monkey**(s) [cf. MONKEY *n.*] *slang* (of weather etc.) bitterly cold. **brass nail** [rhyming slang for *tail*] *slang* a prostitute. **brass plate** an engraved plate with the name, trade, etc., of its owner displayed outside the owner's home or place of business. **brass rags** sailors' cleaning cloths; *part brass rags* cease friendship (*with*). *brass rule*: see RULE *n.* **brass tacks** *slang* actual details, real business (chiefly in *get down to brass tacks*). **brassware** utensils etc. made of brass.

brass /brɑːs/ *v.* M19. [f. prec.] 1 *v.t.* Coat with brass; *fig.* cover with effrontery. M19. 2 *v.i.* Pay *up.* L19. 3 *v.t.* & *i.* Foll. by *off*: grumble; tell off. *slang.* E20.

brassage /ˈbrasɪdʒ/ *n.* L18. [Fr., f. *brasser* to mix, brew, f. pop.L, f. L *brace*: see BRAGGET *n.*[1], -AGE.] A mint-charge to cover the cost of coining money.

brassard /ˈbrasɑːd/ *n.* L16. [Fr., f. *bras* arm: see -ARD.] 1 *Hist.* A piece of armour for the upper arm. L16. 2 A badge worn on the arm; an armlet. L19.

brassed /brɑːst/ *a.* ME. [f. BRASS *n.*, *v.*: see -ED[2], -ED[1].] 1 Made of or overlaid with brass. ME. 2 *brassed off,* fed up, disgruntled. *slang.* M20.

brasserie /ˈbrasəri/ *n.* M19. [Fr. (orig. = brewery), f. *brasser* to brew.] A (French) saloon selling beer and usu. food; *gen.* an informal restaurant.

brassey *n.* var. of BRASSIE.

brassica /ˈbrasɪkə/ *n.* Pl. **-cas, -cae** /-kiː/. E19. [L = cabbage.] A cruciferous plant of the genus *Brassica* (family Brassicaceae or Cruciferae), which includes cabbage, turnip, rape, etc.

brassiˈcaceous *a.* of or pertaining to the family Brassicaceae (Cruciferae), cruciferous M19.

brassie /ˈbrasi, ˈbrɑːsi/ *n.* Now *rare.* Also **brass(e)y.** L19. [f. BRASS *n.* + -IE.] A wooden golf club shod with brass; a shot played with such a club.

brassière /ˈbrasɪə, -z-/ *n.* Also **-iere.** E20. [Fr. = child's reins, camisole, etc.] A woman's undergarment worn to support the breasts.

brassil *n.* var. of BRAZIL *n.*[2]

brassy *n.* var. of BRASSIE.

brassy /ˈbrɑːsi/ *a.* L16. [f. BRASS *n.* + -Y[1].] 1 Consisting of or covered in brass. L16. 2 *fig.* a Pitiless, unfeeling. L16. b Impudently confident. L16. c Pretentious. L16. 3a Tasting like brass. L18. b Looking like brass. E19. c Sounding like brass instruments, harsh-toned. M19.

brassily *adv.* L19. **brassiness** *n.* M18.

brast *v.* see BURST *v.*

brastle *v.* var. of BRUSTLE *v.*[1]

brat /brat/ *n.*[1] Now *dial.* [OE (late Northumb.) *bratt* f. OIr. *bratt* (Ir., Gael. *brat*) mantle.] 1 Orig., a cloak. In later *dial.* use, a pinafore, an apron; *contempt.* a rag, a scrap (of clothing). OE. 2 The tough skin which forms on porridge etc. *Sc.* L17.

brat /brat/ *n.*[2] Usu. *derog.* M16. [Perh. abbrev. of BRATCHET, or same wd as prec.] A child. Now *esp.* an ill-behaved child.

O. CROMWELL I should be glad to hear how the little brat doth. I. MURDOCH Your loathsome idle spineless ill-mannered brat of an offspring.

bratling *n.* a little brat M17. **brattery** *n.* a nursery, a collection of brats L18. **bratty** *a.* of, pertaining to, or characteristic of a brat M20.

brat /brat/ *n.*[3] M18. [Var. of BRET.] The turbot.

bratchet /ˈbratʃɪt/ *n. Sc.* Usu. *derog.* L16. [App. same wd as BRACHET.] A little brat, an infant.

brattice /ˈbratɪs/ *n.* & *v.* Also (*dial.*) **-ish** /-ɪʃ/. ME. [AN, OFr. *bretesche* (mod.Fr. *bretèche*) f. med.L *brittisca* f. OE *brittisc* BRITISH.] A *n.* 1 A temporary breastwork, parapet, or gallery of wood, for use during a siege. *obs.* exc. *Hist.* ME. 2 A wooden partition or shaft-lining in a mine. M19. B *v.t.* †1 Fortify with a brattice. Only in LME. 2 Foll. by *up*: line (a shaft etc.) with a brattice. M19.

bratticing /ˈbratɪsɪŋ/ *n.* Also (*dial.* in branch I, the usual sp. in branch II) **-ishing** /-ɪʃɪŋ/. See also BARTIZAN. LME. [f. prec. + -ING[1].] I†1 (The erection of) a temporary breastwork, parapet, etc.: see BRATTICE *n.* 1. LME–M17. 2 Partitioning or shaft-lining in a mine. M19. II 3 *Archit.* A cresting of open carved work on a screen or shrine. M16.

brattish *n.* & *v.* see BRATTICE.

brattishing *n.* see BRATTICING.

brattle /ˈbrat(ə)l/ *n.* & *v.* Chiefly *Sc.* E16. [Prob. imit., by assoc. with *break, rattle.*] A *n.* A sharp rattling sound, esp. of something breaking, of blows, of scampering feet, etc. E16. B *v.i.* Produce a rattling noise; rush with a rattling noise; scamper. E16.

bratwurst /ˈbratvəːst, *foreign* ˈbratvʊrst/ *n.* Pl. **-wursts, -würste** /-vyrstə/. E20. [G, f. *Brat* a spit (*braten* roast etc.) + *Wurst* sausage.] (A) mild-flavoured German pork sausage.

braunite /ˈbraʊnʌɪt/ *n.* E19. [f. A.E. *Braun,* 19th-cent. Ger. treasury official and mineralogist + -ITE[1].] *Min.* A tetragonal oxide and silicate of manganese, usu. with some iron, which occurs as dark brownish-black pyramidal crystals or granular masses.

brava /ˈbrɑːvə/ *n.* & *int.* E19. [It., fem. of *bravo*: see BRAVO *int.* & *n.*[2]] (A cry addressed to a woman or girl meaning) excellent, well done!

†**bravade** *n.* & *v.* L16. [Fr. f. It. *bravata,* f. *bravo*: see BRAVE *a.* etc., -ADE.] A *n.* = BRAVADO *n.* 1. L16–M19. B *v.i.* & *t.* Assume a bold or brazen manner (towards); swagger; defy. L16–E19.

bravado /brəˈvɑːdəʊ/ *n.* & *v.* L16. [Sp. *bravada,* f. *bravo* BRAVO *n.*[1] w. alt. of suff.: see -ADO.] A *n.* Pl. **-o(e)s.** 1 Boastful or threatening behaviour (freq. to conceal timidity etc.); ostentatious boldness or defiance; (now *rare*) an instance of this, a show of daring. L16. †2 A swaggering fellow; a bravo. M17–M19. B *v.i.* Show bravado. Now *rare* or *obs.* L16.

Bravais lattice /ˈbraveɪ ˈlatɪs/ *n. phr.* M20. [Auguste *Bravais* (1811–63), Fr. physicist.] *Cryst.* A lattice in which every point has exactly the same environment (as regards the distances and directions of other points of the lattice); *spec.* any of the fourteen different lattices of this kind in three dimensions.

brave /breɪv/ *a., int., adv.,* & *n.* See also BRAW. L15. [Fr. f. It. *bravo* bold or Sp. *bravo* courageous, savage, f. Proto-Romance f. L *barbarus* BARBAROUS.] A *adj.* 1 Courageous, daring; intrepid; able to face and withstand danger or pain. L15. 2 Splendid; spectacular; showy; handsome. Now *literary.* M16. 3 Of excellent quality, admirable; fine, capital. *arch.* & *dial.* L16.

1 MILTON High hopes of living to be brave men, and worthy Patriots. S. HILL It is a brave act of valour to condemn death. 2 SIR W. SCOTT Now might you see the tartans brave. 3 W. PENN Many brave Families have been ruin'd by a Gamester. **brave new world** [title of a satirical novel by Aldous Huxley (1932), after Shakes. *Temp.*] a utopia produced by technological and social advance (usu. *iron.*).

B *int.* Capital! excellent! Now *arch.* & *dial.* L16.

C *adv.* Bravely. *poet.* L16.

D *n.* 1 A boast, a threat; a bravado. Now *rare* or *obs.* L16. †2 A bravo, a hired bully. L16–M19. 3 *absol.* Now only as *pl. The* brave men; *the* brave people. L17. 4 A fighting man; *esp.* an American Indian warrior. M18.

3 W. COWPER Toll for the brave! The brave that are no more.

bravely *adv.* E16. **braveness** *n.* (now *rare*) M16.

brave /breɪv/ *v.* M16. [Fr. *braver,* f. as prec., after It. *bravare.*] 1 *v.t.* Treat with bravado; challenge; dare. *arch.* M16. †2 *v.i.* Boast, vaunt. M16–E19. †3 *v.t.* Deck out, adorn. L16–E17. †4 *v.i.* Dress splendidly. Only in L16. †5 *v.t.* w. *it.* Swagger; make a splendid show. L16–E18. 6 *v.t.* Meet (danger) with courage; defy; encounter with bravery. L18.

6 **brave it out** defy suspicion or blame.

braver *n.* L16.

bravery /ˈbreɪv(ə)ri/ *n.* M16. [Fr. *braverie* or It. *braveria,* f. as BRAVE *a.* etc. + -ERY.] †1 (An act of) bravado; ostentatious defiance, swaggering. M16–E19. 2 Display; show, ostentation; splendour. Now *literary.* M16. b Finery; an embellishment; an ornament. *arch.* M16. †c A thing to exhibit; a thing to be proud of. L16–M17. 3 Brave conduct or nature; daring; fortitude, valour. L16. †4 A gallant, a beau; gallants etc. collectively. E–M17.

bravo /ˈbrɑːvəʊ/ *n.*[1] Pl. **-o(e)s.** L16. [It.: see BRAVE *a.* etc.] 1 A hired ruffian; a desperado. L16. †2 = BRAVADO *n.* 1. *rare.* E17–E18.

bravo /brɑːˈvəʊ, ˈbrɑːvəʊ/ *int.* & *n.*[2] M18. [Fr. f. as prec.: cf. BRAVA.] A *int.* Excellent, well done! M18. B *n.* Pl. **-os.** A cry of 'bravo!', a cheer. M19.

bravura /brəˈv(j)ʊərə/ *n.* & *a.* M18. [It., f. *bravo* BRAVE *a.*: see -URE.] 1 (A passage or style of music, esp. singing) requiring exceptional powers of execution. M18. 2 (A performance that is) brilliant or ambitious; (a display that is) daring, dash(ing). E19.

braw /brɔː/ *a.* & *n. Sc.* L16. [Var. of BRAVE *a.* etc.] A *adj.* 1 Worthy; capital; fine, good. L16. 2 Handsome; splendid, showy. E18. B *n.* In *pl.* Fine clothes, adornments. E18.

brawly *adv.* well, excellently M17.

brawl /brɔːl/ *n.*[1] LME. [f. BRAWL *v.*] 1 A noisy quarrel; a rowdy fight. LME. †2 A noisy exclamation; a clamour. M16–E17.

†**brawl** *n.*[2] E16. [Fr. BRANLE.] 1 A certain pace or movement in dancing. E–M16. 2 A French dance resembling a cotillion; a piece of music for this dance. M16–M19.

brawl /brɔːl/ *v.* LME. [Perh. ult. imit. Cf. Du. & LG *brallen* brag; OProv. *braul(h)ar*, *bralhar*, etc. ((O)Fr. *brailler*) rel. to BRAY *v.*[1]] 1 *v.i.* Quarrel or fight noisily; wrangle. LME. 2 *v.i.* a Make a clamour or disturbance. Now *rare* or *obs.* LME. b Of a stream: run noisily. L16. 3 *v.t.* Revile, scold. *obs.* exc. *dial.* L15. 4 *v.t.* Drive or force *down*, *out*, etc., by clamouring, quarrelling, etc. L16.

brawler *n.* a quarrelsome or blustering person LME.

brawn /brɔːn/ *n.* & *v.* ME. [AN *braun*, OFr. *braon* fleshy part esp. of the hind leg, f. Gmc (OHG *brāto*, G *Braten* roast flesh; cf. synon. OE *brǣde*, and *brǣdan* to roast).] A *n.* 1 Muscle, lean flesh, esp. of the arm, leg, or thumb; *loosely* muscularity, physical strength. ME. †b The arm, calf, or buttock. LME–M19. 2 Boar's flesh as food. Now usu. *spec.*, pig's head etc. boiled, chopped, and moulded. LME. †3 The flesh of other animals as food. LME–M17. 4 A boar fattened for the table. *obs.* exc. *dial.* LME. †5 Calloused skin. M16–M17.

2 *shield of brawn*: see SHIELD *n.*[1] 4a.

B *v.* †1 *v.t.* Harden, make callous. L16–M17. 2 *v.t.* & *i.* Fatten (a boar), (of a boar) grow fat, for the table. Now *rare* or *obs.* L16.

brawner *n.* (*obs.* exc. *dial.*) a boar fattened for the table M17.

brawny /ˈbrɔːni/ *a.* LME. [f. BRAWN *n.* + -Y[1].] 1 Characterized by brawn; strong, muscular. LME. 2 Calloused, hardened. Now *rare* or *obs.* L16.

brawniness *n.* M17.

Braxton Hicks /ˈbrakstən ˌhɪks/ *n.* E20. [John *Braxton Hicks* (1823–97), Eng. gynaecologist.] Med. *Braxton Hicks' contractions* or *sign*, intermittent weak contractions of the uterus occurring during pregnancy.

braxy /ˈbraksi/ *n.* & *a.* Orig. *Sc.* L18. [Origin uncertain: perh. f. BRACK *n.*[1]] A *n.* 1 A fatal clostridial infection of sheep, esp. in upland areas; *spec.* infection by *Clostridium septicum*. L18. 2 Meat from a diseased or otherwise naturally dead sheep. L18. B *attrib.* or as *adj.* Of meat: from a diseased or otherwise naturally dead sheep. E19.

bray /breɪ/ *n.* ME. [f. next or OFr. *brai(t)* a cry, f. as next.] †1 Outcry; a yell, a shriek. ME–L16. 2 (A sound like) the sound of a harshly-played trumpet. L16. 3 (A sound like) the cry of an ass; a harsh whine. M17.

bray /breɪ/ *v.*[1] ME. [(O)Fr. *braire* to cry, f. Proto-Romance, perh. of Celt. origin.] †1 *v.i.* Cry out, shriek. ME–E17. 2 *v.i.* Of wind, a wind instrument (esp. a trumpet), etc.: produce a harsh jarring sound. ME. 3 *v.i.* Of an animal (now chiefly of an ass): utter a harsh cry. LME. b Of a person or voice: speak loudly without thought or meaninglessly. M17. 4 *v.t.* Utter (a harsh cry etc.); utter with a bray. (Foll. by *out.*) LME.

brayer *n.*[1] a person who or thing which brays, esp. an ass L16.

bray /breɪ/ *v.*[2]*t.* LME. [AN *braier*, OFr. *breier* (mod. *broyer*), f. Gmc base of BREAK *v.*] 1 Pound or crush into small pieces, esp. with a pestle and mortar. LME. 2 Beat, thrash. *dial.* E19.

brayer *n.*[2] (*Printing*, now *Hist.*) a wooden pestle employed to rub out ink L17.

bray /breɪ/ *v.*[3]*t. S. Afr.* Also **brei, brey.** M19. [Afk. *brei*, f. Du. *breien* BRAID *v.*[1]] Prepare for use, dress, (the skin of an animal).

braze /breɪz/ *v.*[1]*t.* Now *rare.* [OE *brasian*, f. BRASS *n.*: reinforced by anal. of GLASS *n.*, GLAZE *v.*[1]] Make of or like brass; ornament with brass; *fig.* harden, inure.

braze /breɪz/ *v.*[2] & *n.* M16. [Partly f. OFr. *braser* burn, partly f. Fr. *braser* solder, ult. f. Gmc.] A *v.t.* †1 Expose to the action of fire. M–L16. 2 Solder with an alloy of copper and zinc. L17. B *n.* The process of brazing; a brazed joint. M20.

brazeless *a.* made without or not involving brazing L19.

brazen /ˈbreɪz(ə)n/ *a.* [OE *bræ sen*, f. BRASS *n.* & *a.*: see -EN[4].] 1 Made of brass; strong as brass. OE. 2 Hardened in effrontery; shameless; impudent. L16. 3 Of a brassy colour or sound; burnished; strident; harsh. L16.

1 **brazen age** a mythological age of humankind, said to come between the silver and the iron age. 2 J. BALDWIN She offended him because she was so brazen in her sins. 3 P. S. BUCK This brazen, glittering sunshine.

Comb.: **brazen-face** *arch.* an impudent or shameless person; **brazen-faced** *a.* impudent, shameless; **brazen-facedly** *adv.* in a brazen-faced manner.

brazenly *adv.* E18. **brazenness** /-n-n-/ *n.* M18.

brazen /ˈbreɪz(ə)n/ *v.t.* M16. [f. the adj.] 1 Foll. by *out*: face or undergo without shame or impudently. M16. 2 Harden; render brazen in appearance; make uncaring or careless. E19.

1 R. B. SHERIDAN I am resolved to brazen the brunt of the business out. **brazen it out** act as if unashamed of one's (mis)behaviour, show no remorse. 2 HUGH WALPOLE Do not believe novelists are pleased with their efforts. They only brazen their faces before the world.

brazier /ˈbreɪzjə, -ʒə/ *n.*[1] *arch.* ME. [Prob. f. BRASS *n.* + -IER, on the analogy of GLASS *n.*, GLAZIER.] A worker in brass.

braziery *n.* a brazier's work L18.

brazier /ˈbreɪzjə, -ʒə/ *n.*[2] L17. [Fr. *brasier*, f. *braise* live coals: cf. BRAISE.] A pan or stand for holding lighted coals as a portable heater.

Brazil /brəˈzɪl/ *n.*[1] Also **b-, †-s-.** ME. [f. med.L *brasilium*, of uncertain origin; in sense 3, name of the S. Amer. country (Port. *Brasil*), which derived its name from the wood.] 1 The hard red wood of various tropical trees, esp. of the genus *Caesalpinia*. Now usu. *Brazil-wood*. ME. †2 A red dye obtained from this wood. LME–E19. 3 In full *Brazil nut*. The large three-sided nut of the S. American tree *Bertholletia excelsa*. M19.

¶In sense 1 formerly taken as a type of hardness, and as such often confused w. BRAZIL *n.*[2], with corresp. pronunc.

brazil /ˈbraz(ə)l/ *n.*[2] *dial.* Also **brassil.** E18. [Prob. f. BRASS *n.*] Iron pyrites; coal containing this.

¶See note s.v. BRAZIL *n.*[1]

braziletto /braziˈlɛtəʊ/ *n.* M17. [Sp., Port. *brasilete*, Port. *brasileto*, dim. of *brasil* Brazil-wood.] Any of various mainly W. Indian dyewoods, related (but inferior) to Brazil-wood.

Brazilian /brəˈzɪlɪən/ *a.* & *n.* Also **†-s-.** E17. [f. *Brazil* the country (see BRAZIL *n.*[1]) + -IAN.] A *adj.* Of or pertaining to the S. American country of Brazil. E17.

Brazilian nutmeg: see NUTMEG *n.* **Brazilian rosewood** = PALISANDER. **Brazilian tapir** a dark brown tapir, *Tapirus terrestris*, found widely in tropical S. America east of the Andes.

B *n.* A native or inhabitant of Brazil. Also, Brazilian coffee. E17.

brazilin /ˈbrazɪlɪn/ *n.* M19. [f. BRAZIL *n.*[1] + -IN[1].] *Chem.* A yellow crystalline polycyclic alcohol, $C_{16}H_{14}O_5$, which is isolated from Brazil-wood and is a reduced form of the red colouring-matter of the wood.

breach /briːtʃ/ *n.* & *v.* ME. [(O)Fr. *brèche* = Prov. *breca* f. Proto-Gallo-Romance f. Frank. f. Gmc base of BREAK *v.* Superseded OE *bryće* (ult. related), with which there is no continuity.] A *n.* I The action of breaking. †1 The physical act of breaking; fracture; breakage. ME–L17. 2 The breaking or neglect of (or *of*) a legal or moral bond or obligation; the infraction of (or *of*) someone's privileged rights. LME. †3 An inroad *into*, an infringement *upon*. L16–M18. 4 A breaking of relations of (or *of*) union, continuity, etc.; *esp.* a separation, an estrangement, a quarrel. L16. 5 The breaking of waves over a vessel or on a coast. E17. 6 The leaping of a whale clear out of the water. M19.

2 SHAKES. *L.L.L.* Receive such welcome . . As honour, without breach of honour, may Make tender of to thy true worthiness. C. S. FORESTER To call out in that fashion was a grave breach of discipline. F. RAPHAEL His manager's breach of the rationing laws. *breach of confidence, contract, trust*, etc. *breach of faith*: see FAITH *n.* **breach of promise** the breaking of one's word, esp. of a promise to marry **breach of the peace** public disturbance, or conduct likely to provoke one. **in breach of** so as to infringe or contravene. 4 SHAKES. *Oth.* There's fall'n between him and my lord An unkind breach. W. BLACKSTONE By the breach and dissolution of . . the relation itself.

II The product of breaking. 7 A portion of land broken up by the plough. *obs.* exc. *dial.* ME. 8 A break or fissure; *esp.* a gap in a fortification made by artillery. LME. †9 Surf; a breaker. Usu. in *pl.* E16–E18. †10 An interval; a division marked by breaks or intervals. Only in L16. †11 A bay, a harbour. *rare.* Only in E17. 12 A state of severed relations or disagreement. L17.

8 S. JOHNSON The crew implore the liberty of repairing their breaches. M. RENAULT A great breach blasted in the walls of heaven. **stand in the breach** bear the brunt of an attack. **step into the breach** fill someone's place or give help, esp. in a crisis. 12 R. GRAVES The breach with the Pope had been healed.

B *v.* 1 *v.t.* Break through, make a gap in; *fig.* contravene, violate. M16. †2 *v.i.* Cause or make a breach; separate. L16–M17. 3 *v.i.* Of a whale: leap clear out of the water. M19.

1 W. S. CHURCHILL He breached the ramparts with his cannon. I. WALLACE I should not have breached security by leaving my briefcase unlocked.

breachy *a.* (chiefly *US*) (of cattle) apt to break fences and get out of enclosures L18.

bread /brɛd/ *n.*[1] [OE *brēad* = OFris. *brād*, OS, (M)LG *brōd*, OHG *brōt* (G *Brot*), ON *brauð*, f. Gmc, of unkn. origin.] †1 A piece or morsel of food. Only in OE. 2 Flour moistened, kneaded, and baked, usu. with leaven. OE. b A loaf, a roll; a piece of bread. Now *rare.* LME. c *Hist.* Ship's biscuit. M17. 3 Essential food. ME. 4 The means of subsistence; one's livelihood. E18. 5 Money. *slang.* M20.

3 K. SMITH The field is clear, its straw / lined and ordered: it will be bread and bedding for safe cattle. 4 C. ISHERWOOD I wish to leave school and begin to learn something useful, that I can win my bread.

Phrases etc.: *baker's bread*: see BAKER. *bee-bread*: see BEE *n.*[1] *black bread*: see BLACK *a.* **bread and butter** (*a*) slices of bread spread with butter; necessary food; (*b*) *fig.* one's livelihood, routine work to provide an income (*quarrel with one's bread and butter*: see QUARREL *v.*). **bread-and-butter** *a.* (*a*) *arch.*, of an age when bread and butter is staple fare, boyish or girlish; (*b*) commonplace, humdrum; (*c*) *bread-and-butter letter*, a guest's written thanks for hospitality. *bread and circuses*: see CIRCUS 7. **bread and milk** pieces of bread in hot boiled milk. **bread and scrape** bread scantily buttered. **bread and water**: the plainest possible diet. **bread and wine** *Chr. Ch.* the Eucharist. **bread of idleness** food not worked for. *bread of trete*: see TREAT *n.*[1] I. **break bread** *arch.* take food, share a meal *with* someone. **breaking of bread** *Chr. Ch.* the Eucharist. *brown bread*: see BROWN *a. cast one's bread upon the waters*: see WATER *n.* **daily bread** a livelihood. **eat the bread of** be subjected to (affliction etc.). *French bread*: see FRENCH *a.* **have, want,** etc., **one's bread buttered on both sides** have etc. a state of easy prosperity. **know which side one's bread is buttered** know where one's advantage lies. *light bread*: see LIGHT *a.*[1] *loaf of* or *o' bread*: see LOAF *n.*[1] *quick bread*: see QUICK *a.* & *adv. sour bread*: see SOUR *a. sourdough bread* see SOURDOUGH 1b. *sweet bread*: see SWEET *a.* & *adv.* **take the bread out of a person's mouth** deprive a person of his or her living, esp. by competition. *the best, greatest,* etc., *thing since sliced bread*: see SLICED 1b. *wastel-bread*: see WASTEL 1. *white bread*: see WHITE *a.*

Comb.: **bread basket** (*a*) a basket for bread; (*b*) *slang* the stomach; (*c*) (a region etc. which is) a producer of cereals for bread, a source of staple food; **bread bin** a container for loaves; **breadboard** a strong flat board for cutting bread on; *colloq.* a board on which an electric circuit etc. can be set out; **bread-corn** grain for making bread; **breadcrumb** *n.* & *v.* (*a*) *n.* a crumb of bread, *esp.* (in *pl.*) such crumbs used in cooking, e.g. as a coating for fried or grilled food; the soft inner part of bread; (*b*) *v.t.* coat with breadcrumbs; **breadfruit** any of various tropical fruits with edible breadlike pulp; *spec.* that of the tree *Artocarpus altilis* of the Pacific islands; **bread-kind** *W. Indies* food like bread, e.g. yams, sweet potatoes; **bread-knife** a long knife, usu. with a serrated edge, for slicing bread; **breadline** (orig. *US*) a queue of poor people waiting to receive food; (fig.) *the* subsistence level; *bread roll*: see ROLL *n.*[1]; **bread-root** (the edible root of) a N. American leguminous plant, *Psoralea esculenta*; also called *prairie turnip*; **bread sauce** a milk sauce thickened with breadcrumbs; **bread-stick** a long thin roll of crisp bread; **breadstuffs** (*a*) grain flour; (*b*) articles of bread; **bread-tree** a tree yielding breadfruit or other breadlike food; *bread wheat*: see WHEAT *n.* I; **breadwinner** the person whose work supports a family.

breaden *a.* (*arch.*) made of bread L16. **breadless** *a.* without bread; without food: LME. **breadlike** *a.* L17.

†**bread** *n.*[2] var. of BREDE *n.*[2]

bread /brɛd/ *v.*[1]*t.* E17. [f. BREAD *n.*[1]] Dress with breadcrumbs; treat or provide with bread. Chiefly as *breaded* ppl a.

†**bread** *v.*[2] var. of BREDE *v.*[2]

breadth /brɛdθ, -t-/. *n.* E16. [f. BREDE *n.*[1] + -TH[1], after LENGTH.] **1** Measure or distance from side to side; broadness, width. E16. **2** A piece (of cloth etc.) of full breadth, a width. L16. **3** Extent, distance, room. L16. **4** *Art.* A broad effect; unity achieved by disregarding unnecessary detail. L18. **5** *fig.* Largeness, freedom from limitations (esp. *of* mind or view); liberality, catholicity; toleration. M19.

1 *hair's breadth*: see HAIR *n. thumb's breadth*: see THUMB *n.* 2.

breadthen *v.i.* (*rare*) increase in breadth E19. **breadthless** *a.* M17. **breadthways** *adv.* in the direction of the breadth L17. **breadthwise** *adv.* = BREADTHWAYS M18.

break /breɪk/ *n.*[1] ME. [f. the vb.] **1** An act of breaking or separation; fracture, breakage, severance. ME. **b** The act of breaking electrical contact; the position or condition in which contact is broken. L19. **2** A broken place, a gap, an opening. ME. **3** An interruption of continuity or uniformity; a change of direction etc. L15. **b** A mark indicating an abrupt pause in print or writing. E18. **c** A short spell of recreation or refreshment in a period of work etc. M19. **d** A sudden or sharp fall in share prices etc. L19. **e** A short solo or instrumental passage in jazz or popular music. E20. **4** The first appearance of light, onset. Chiefly in *break of day*, dawn. L16. **5** A tract of ground of distinct appearance, *esp.* an area broken up for cultivation, or (*US*) an area of rough broken country. L17. **6** A surplus piece of metal remaining on the shank of a newly cast type. L17. **7** A quantity or amount; a large number. Chiefly *dial.* L18. **8** An act of breaking out or away; a sudden dash; an escape from prison etc. M19. **b** A bud or shoot sprouting from a stem. M20. **9** *Cricket* etc. The deviation of a ball on pitching. M19. **10** *Billiards, Snooker*, etc. (The points scored in) a consecutive series of successful shots. M19. **11a** A mistake, a blunder. *colloq.* L19. **b** An opportunity, a (fair) chance; a piece of (good) luck. *colloq.* E20.

1 *tie-break*: see TIE-. **2** E. HEMINGWAY The last of the sun came through in the breaks between the strips of matting. D. ATTENBOROUGH We cannot hear a break between sounds of less than one tenth of a second. J. CHEEVER He noticed . . a break in the wall of buildings. **3** R. H. DANA Foster went as far as the break of the deck. S. HILL We were strafed for about three hours without a break. *clean break*: see CLEAN *a.* **c** S. UNWIN A short break for a sandwich lunch. F. RAPHAEL The children spilled out for their break like mice. S. RAVEN Perhaps Georgy and Bessie would like a little trip abroad. We all need a bit of a break. *coffee-break, tea break*, etc. **8** T. ROOSEVELT The slightest attempt at a break would result in their being shot down. **9** *leg break*: see LEG *n. off break*: see OFF-. **11a** P. G. WODEHOUSE Fear he was going to make a break of some kind. **b** G. GREENE We had a lucky break. B. SCHULBERG Learn to give the other fellow a break and we'll *all* live longer. **bad break** (*a*) an unfortunate remark or ill-judged action; (*b*) a piece of bad luck. **even break** a fair chance.

break *n.*[2] see BRAKE *n.*[6]

break *n.*[3] var. of BRAKE *n.*[7]

break /breɪk/ *v.* Pa. t. **broke** /brəʊk/, (*arch.*) **brake** /breɪk/. Pa. pple **broken** /ˈbrəʊkən/, (chiefly *arch.*) **broke** /brəʊk/ (see also BROKE, BROKEN *adjs.*). [OE *brecan* = OFris. *breka*, OS *brekan* (Du. *breken*), OHG *brehhan* (G *brechen*), Goth. *brikan* f. Gmc, f. IE base also of L *frangere* break.] **I** Sever, fracture, part; shatter, crush, destroy. **1** *v.t.* Divide into distinct parts by force (by accident or design), other than by cutting or tearing; part by violence, fracture; shatter, smash. OE. **b** Rend, tear, (cloth etc.). *obs.* exc. *dial.* OE. **c** Cut up, tear in pieces, (an animal's body). ME. †**d** Wreck (a ship). ME–E17. **e** Make (a whole) incomplete; divide, take away a part from; spend partially, change (a banknote etc.) for currency of smaller denominations. M18. **f** *Phonol.* Subject (a vowel) to breaking. M19. **g** Open (a gun) at the hinge between the stock and the barrel. L19. **2** *v.t.* Fracture, undergo fracture of, the bones of (a limb etc., a person's body); dislocate the bones of (the back, the neck). OE. **3** *v.t.* Lay open the surface of; rupture, burst, crack; graze. ME. **4** *v.t.* Destroy, make useless, ruin; defeat, foil. ME. †**b** Disband; dissolve. L16–L18. **c** Nullify (a will) by legal process. *arch.* L19. **d** Better (a record, score, etc.). L19. **e** Defeat the object of (a strike), esp. by engaging other workers. E20. **f** *Tennis.* Win a game against (an opponent's service, the server). M20. **g** Disprove (an alibi). M20. **5a** *v.t.* Cause (a formation of troops etc.) to part or disperse in confusion. ME. **b** *v.i.* Of a formation of troops etc.: be parted, disperse in confusion. L16. **c** *v.i.* Of clouds etc.: show a gap, disperse. E19. **d** *v.t.* & *i. Billiards, Snooker*, etc. Of a player: aim to strike (the ball(s)) with the cue-ball, *spec.* as the first stroke of a game. Of the balls: separate on being struck. M19. **6** *v.t.* Separate or remove by parting or snapping. ME. **7** *v.t.* Disrupt, loosen, (a tie or band, a confining or restricting force); disconnect (electrical contact etc.), opp. *make*. ME. **8** *v.i.* Undergo fracture, severance by force, shattering, rupture, etc.; part, dissolve, fail. ME. **b** Of waves etc.: curl over and disintegrate in foam, beat as surf. LME. **c** Of the voice: change tone with emotion or at (male) puberty. M17. **d** Of a lake etc.: display water-bloom. L19. **e** Of boxers etc.: separate after a clinch, esp. on the order of the referee. E20. **f** *Bridge.* Of a suit: be distributed between two hands (in a specified way or *absol.* evenly). M20. **9** *v.t.* Crush in strength, spirit, or resistance; weary, exhaust; discourage, intimidate. L15. **b** Reduce to obedience or discipline, tame; subject or habituate *to*. L15. **10a** *v.i.* Become bankrupt, fail financially. Now *rare*. L16. **b** *v.t.* Ruin financially, make bankrupt. E17. **c** *v.t.* Wreck the career of; cashier, strip of rank. L17.

1 STEELE A natural Inclination to break Windows. SIR W. SCOTT I've broke my trusty battle-axe. N. COWARD Once I broke four gramophone records over his head. *Daily Telegraph* Break the three eggs into a mixing bowl. **c** SIR W. SCOTT Raven . . watching while the deer is broke. **2** R. L. STEVENSON Anderson's ball . . had broken his shoulder-blade and touched the lung. B. JAMES Caldow broke a leg. **3** SHAKES. *Com. Err.* Back, slave, or I will break thy pate across. A. PRICE He couldn't break the skin on a rice pudding. **4** HENRY MORE Each laboureth to breake that the other maketh. E. A. FREEMAN Their moral force was utterly broken. **5** TENNYSON The foeman's line is broke. **6** AV *Gen.* 27:40 Thou shalt breake his yoke from off thy necke. OED Great boughs broken from the trees. **7** LD MACAULAY The spell which bound his followers to him was not altogether broken. E. F. BENSON Real friendships . . must not be lightly broken. **8** SHAKES. *Ven. & Ad.* The berry breaks before it staineth. G. O. TREVELYAN His health was breaking fast. J. TYNDALL The glacier was evidently breaking beneath our feet. I. MURDOCH The clasp had broken and Tallis had said he'd mend it. **9** MILTON An Iron Rod to bruise and breake Thy disobedience. D. HUME A person . . easily broken by affliction. N. MONSARRAT No desperate assault ever broke their spirit.

II Violate, transgress; disrupt or be disrupted in continuance or uniformity. **11** *v.t.* Fail to keep (a law, promise, treaty, etc.), act contrary to. OE. **12** *v.t.* Cut short, stop; suspend, interrupt; add variation to; become no longer subject to (a habit). ME. **13** *v.i.* Interrupt or pause in one's activities; be interrupted or stopped; *esp.* (of weather) change suddenly after a long settled period. LME. **b** Of prices etc.: fall suddenly or sharply. L19. **14** *v.i.* & *t.* (Cause to) change direction or course; change *into* a different way of proceeding. LME. **b** *v.t.* & *i.* *Hort.* (Cause to) become striped or variegated under cultivation. E18. **c** *v.i.* & *t. Cricket* etc. Of a ball: change direction on pitching. Of a bowler: cause (a ball) to do this. M19. **d** *v.i.* Of a horse: change gait. M19.

11 COVERDALE *Luke* 16:18 Who so ever putteth awaye his wife and marieth another breaketh matrimony. G. K. CHESTERTON There is something wrong with a man if he does not want to break the Ten Commandments. J. BARTH I was breaking a thirteen-year-old habit of not seeing doctors. **12** G. K. CHESTERTON His meditations were broken by a sudden and jarring stoppage. H. HENDERSON Breaking a jeep journey at Capuzzo. H. KISSINGER Once the deadlock was broken, the tension all but vanished. I. MCEWAN High, dark walls, broken at irregular intervals by deeply recessed doorways. **13** G. VIDAL Ice clattered and the silence broke. C. PRIEST The drought had at last broken, and it had been raining . . for the past week. E. FIGES It would soon be time to break for a bite to eat.

III Penetrate, enter or leave forcibly; issue, escape, begin, release. **15** *v.t.* Burst (a barrier) so as to force a way through. Usu. w. advs. OE. **b** Make (a hole, a passage, a trail, a way, etc.) by force, by separating obstacles, etc. ME. **c** Solve (a code etc.). E20. **16** *v.t.* Enter (a house etc.) by force or illegally. Now chiefly in *break and enter*, *housebreaking*, and related phrs. OE. **17** *v.t.* & *i.* Escape (from) or leave by force or without permission; escape from restraint; emerge from hiding etc. suddenly, flee. OE. **b** *v.i.* Of an athlete: get off the mark prematurely. L19. **18** *v.i.* Issue forth, emerge; come suddenly to notice; (of a storm etc.) begin violently; (of news etc.) be made known. ME. **b** Of plants, buds, etc.: sprout into bloom. ME. **c** Begin to give light, emerge out of darkness. M16. **d** Happen, occur, turn out (favourably). *slang.* E20. **19** *v.t.* Deliver, reveal, publish, disclose, (news, thoughts, etc.). LME. †**b** *v.i.* Speak *with* (or *to*) someone concerning news etc. LME–E17. **c** *v.t.* Utter, display; crack (a joke etc.). L16. **d** *v.t.* Free and shake out (a flag, sail, etc.). Freq. foll. by *out*. L19. **20** *v.t.* Impinge upon, penetrate; relieve (a state, mood, etc.). L16.

15 SHAKES. *Coriol.* They . . sigh'd forth proverbs —That hunger broke stone walls. GIBBON The doors were instantly broke open. **17** BURKE Am I to congratulate an highwayman . . who has broke prison, upon the recovery of his natural rights? OED Scholars gated for a week for breaking bounds. DAY LEWIS My struggle to break free. B. MALAMUD He wanted to break and run but didn't dare. **18** J. AGATE A terrific thunderstorm broke. Great crashes and a lot of lightning. E. WAUGH A big story is going to break. O. MANNING At that moment a voice broke shrilly from the loud-speaker. F. TUOHY Tears of laughter broke from his eyes. I. WALLACE Dilman's immediate reaction of concern broke across his features. **19** M. M. ATWATER Are you breaking the story in the morning papers? A. BRINK Will you please tell Dad? But break it gently. **b** SHAKES. *Two Gent.* I am to break with thee of some affairs That touch me near. **c** SOUTHEY He brake a sullen smile. H. MACDIARMID The hawthorn tree Which in early Spring breaks Fresh emerald. **20** C. THIRLWALL Only one ray of hope broke the gloom of her prospects. W. SANSOM Only the trotting jingle of our sleigh-bell broke the air.

IV 21 *v.i.* Perform break-dancing. L20.

Phrases: **break a blow, a fall**: weaken its effect. *break a* BUTTERFLY *on a wheel. break a close*: see CLOSE *n.*[1] I. *break a fall*: see *break a blow* above. **break a horse (to the rein)** accustom a horse to being controlled by reins. **break a lance** enter into competition (*with*). **break a leg** *imper.* (*Theatr. slang*) do well, good luck, (as it is considered unlucky to wish good luck directly). **break and enter** force one's way into (a house etc.) illegally, commit burglary. **break a set** sell the parts of a set separately. *break bread*: see BREAD *n.*[1] *break bulk*: see BULK *n.*[1] **break cover** (of game etc.) emerge into the open. **break even** have balancing gains and losses, make no net profit or loss. *break for (the) tall timber*: see TALL *a.* **break ground** = *break the ground* below. *break in(to) shivers*: see SHIVER *n.*[1] I. **break new ground** do pioneering work. **break of**: make (someone) no longer have (a habit etc.) **break one's duck** *Cricket* score one's first run. *break one's fast*: see FAST *n.*[1] **break one's head**: graze or bruise it. *break one's heart*: see HEART *n. break one's silence*: see SILENCE *n.* †**break one's wind** exhaust oneself. *break one's word*: see WORD *n.* **break on the wheel** fracture the bones of or dislocate on a wheel as a form of punishment or torture. *break rank(s)*: see RANK *n. break shins*: see SHIN *n.*[1] **break ship** fail to rejoin a ship after absence on leave. *break short (off)*: see SHORT *adv. break silence*: see SILENCE *n. break someone's heart*: see HEART *n. break step*: see STEP *n.*[1] *break the back of*: see BACK *n.*[1] **break the bank** (in gaming) exhaust the bank's resources or limit of payment, win spectacularly. **break the ground** begin digging, plough for the first time; do pioneering or preparatory work (*for*). *break the habit*: see HABIT *n. break the ice*: see ICE *n. break the mould*: see MOULD *n.*[3] **break the pack** *Snooker* disturb the triangle of red balls. *break the record*: see RECORD *n. break the sound barrier*: see SOUND *n.*[2] **break the wicket** *Cricket* dislodge the bails in stumping or running out a batsman. †**break time** *Mus.* fail to keep time. **break water** (*a*) appear at the surface; (*b*) *Hunting* (of a stag etc.) wade a river etc. **break wind** void wind from the stomach or bowels. *make or break*: see MAKE *v. one's heart breaks*: see HEART *n. the last straw that breaks the camel's back*: see STRAW *n.*

With advs. & preps. in specialized senses: **break away** make or become separate or free, secede. **break down** (*a*) *v.phr.i.* collapse, fail, cease to function, be decomposed, lose self-control; (*b*) *v.phr.t.* demolish, decompose, analyse (*into* components), overcome (resistance etc.). **break forth** burst out, suddenly emerge. **break in** (*a*) *v.phr.i.* intrude forcibly, esp. as a thief; interrupt (foll. by (*up*)*on* a person or action interrupted); (*b*) *v.phr.t.* tame, subject (an animal) to discipline, accustom to habit or use etc., wear until comfortable; *Austral.* & *NZ* bring (land) under cultivation. **break into** enter forcibly, begin to utter (laughter etc.), *colloq.* manage to become involved in (an activity or occupation); (see also sense 14 above). **break off** (*a*) *v.phr.i.* become detached, detach oneself, cease; (*b*) *v.phr.t.* detach by breaking, discontinue, bring to an end; (*c*) *v.phr.i.* play the first stroke in billiards, snooker, etc. **break out** (*a*) *v.phr.i.* begin suddenly or violently, burst from restraint or concealment, exclaim, become covered *in* (a rash etc.); *Austral.* & *NZ* (of a gold-field) come into operation; (*b*) *v.phr.t.* open up (a container) and begin to remove its contents, get from out of storage; (see also sense 19d above). **break through** *v.phr.t.* & *i.* penetrate, force one's way through, make sudden rapid progress. **break up** (*a*) *v.phr.t.* & *i.* break into small pieces, disintegrate; (esp. of school at end of term) disband, disperse; stop; disconcert; terminate a personal, esp. sexual, relationship (*with*); (*b*) *v.phr.i.* become feeble or convulsed (*with* laughter etc.), (of weather) = sense 13 above. **break with** quarrel or cease relations with; (see also sense 19b above).

breakable *a.* & *n.* (*a*) *adj.* able to be broken; (*b*) *n.* in *pl.*, breakable things: L16. **breakage** *n.* the action or fact or an instance of breaking; loss or damage caused by breaking: L18.

break- /breɪk/ *comb. form.* ME. [Repr. BREAK *v.* or (occas.) *n.*[1]] Prefixed esp. to ns. and advs. to form ns. and adjs. usu. w. the sense (a thing) which breaks, an act or state of breaking'.

break-back *a.* & *n.* (*a*) *adj.* that breaks the back, crushing, very heavy; (*b*) *n.* (*Cricket*) a ball which turns sharply from the off side on pitching. **break-bone (fever)** dengue. **break-crop**: grown to avoid the repeated growing of cereals. **break-dance** *v.i.* perform break-dancing. **break-dancer** a person who performs break-dancing. **break-dancing** (orig. *US*) an energetic kind of (usu. solo) dancing, freq. involving spinning on the floor on the back or head. **break-even** *a.* & *n.* (designating or pertaining to) the point or state at which one breaks even. **break-front** *a.* & *n.* (a piece of furniture) having the line of its front broken by a curve or angle. **break-line** *Typogr.* the last line of a paragraph (usu. not of full length). **breakneck** *a.* & *n.* (*a*) *adj.* endangering the neck, headlong, dangerously fast; †(*b*) *n.* a headlong fall, destruction. **break-point** (*a*) a point at which an interruption or change is made; a turning-point; (*b*) = BREAKING-*point*; (*c*) *Tennis* a situation in which the receiving player(s) can break the opponent's service at the next point; a point at which the service is or can be broken. **breakstone** (now *rare* or *obs.*) a saxifrage; also, parsley-piert. **breakwater** a structure which provides protection against the force of sea-waves, *esp.* a mole or groyne. **breakwind** (chiefly *Austral.*) a wind-break.

breakaway /ˈbreɪkəweɪ/ *n.* & *a.* L19. [f. BREAK- + AWAY *adv.*] A *n.* 1 The action of breaking away; severance, secession. L19. 2 *Sport.* A sudden attack or forward movement; a false start to a race. L19. 3 A stampede. *Austral.* L19. 4 A person who or thing which breaks away. L19. b *Rugby Football.* An outside second-row forward. M20. B *attrib.* or as *adj.* That breaks away or has broken away. E20.

breakdown /ˈbreɪkdaʊn/ *n.* E19. [f. BREAK- + DOWN *adv.*] 1 A boisterous country dance. *US.* E19. 2 Collapse, failure; (a stoppage due to) mechanical malfunction; failure of health or (esp.) mental powers. M19. b Failure of electrical insulation; the sudden passage of current through an insulator. E20. c Chemical or physical decomposition. E20. 3 An analysis or classification (of statistics etc.). M20.

2 NERVOUS *breakdown*.

breaker /ˈbreɪkə/ *n.*[1] ME. [f. BREAK *v.* + -ER[1].] 1 A person who or thing which breaks (in any sense), crushes, or destroys. ME. 2 *spec.* A person who violates or transgresses a law, oath, promise, etc. LME. 3 A person who subdues, tames, or trains (horses etc.). Also *breaker-in.* M16. 4 A heavy ocean wave breaking on the coast or on a reef etc. L17. 5 A person who interrupts the conversation of others on citizens' band radio; any user of citizens' band radio. *slang.* M20. 6 A break-dancer. L20.

1 *circuit-breaker, housebreaker, record-breaker, ship-breaker*, etc.

breaker /ˈbreɪkə/ *n.*[2] M19. [f. Sp. *bareca, barrica*: see BARRICO.] *Naut.* A small keg, esp. for drinking-water.

breakfast /ˈbrɛkfəst/ *n.* & *v.* LME. [f. BREAK- + FAST *n.*[1]] A *n.* The first meal of the day. Occas., any meal. LME.

SHAKES. *Two Gent.* I would have been a breakfast to the beast Rather than have false Proteus rescue me. *bed and breakfast*: see BED *n. Continental breakfast*: see CONTINENTAL *a. dog's breakfast*: see DOG *n. English breakfast*: see ENGLISH *a.* **have for breakfast** *fig.* (*slang*) easily defeat (a person). *second breakfast*: see SECOND *a.* WEDDING *breakfast*.

Comb.: **breakfast-service** a matching set of cups, saucers, plates, etc., for serving breakfast.

B *v.* 1 *v.i.* Have breakfast. M17. 2 *v.t.* Provide with breakfast. M17.

breakfasting *vbl n.* (*a*) the action of the vb; (*b*) *arch.* a taking of breakfast: M18. **breakfastless** *a.* L18.

break-in /ˈbreɪkɪn/ *n.* M19. [f. BREAK- + IN *adv.*] 1 An interruption. *rare.* M19. 2 A collapse inwards. *rare.* E20. 3 A forcible entry; an incursion; *spec.* an illegal entry into a house etc., a burglary. M20.

breaking /ˈbreɪkɪŋ/ *n.* OE. [f. BREAK *v.* + -ING[1].] 1 The action of BREAK *v.* OE. b *Phonol.* The development of a diphthong from a simple vowel owing to the influence of an adjacent sound, esp. a following consonant; a diphthong so formed. L19. c Break-dancing. L20. 2 A piece of land newly ploughed for the first time. *US.* M19.

1 *breaking of bread*: see BREAD *n.*[1]

Comb.: **breaking-point** the point at which a thing or person gives way under stress; **breaking-strength** the maximum stress that a thing can withstand without breaking.

break-off /ˈbreɪkɒf/ *n.* E19. [f. BREAK- + OFF *adv.*] 1 A part of the stock of a musket or rifle into which the barrel fits. E19. 2 Discontinuance; a severing of relations. M19.

break-out /ˈbreɪkaʊt/ *n.* E19. [f. BREAK- + OUT *adv.*] 1 A bursting from confinement etc.; an escape, esp. of several people. E19. 2 An outbreak. L19.

breakthrough /ˈbreɪkθruː/ *n.* E20. [f. BREAK- + THROUGH *adv.*] An act of breaking through an obstacle, barrier, etc.; a major advance in knowledge etc.

Comb.: **breakthrough bleeding** bleeding from the uterus occurring between menstrual periods (a side-effect of some oral contraceptives).

breakup /ˈbreɪkʌp/ *n.* L18. [f. BREAK *v.* + UP *adv.*[1]] The action of breaking up; an act or instance of breaking up; *esp.* (*a*) a dissolution or disruption of a meeting, government, etc.; (*b*) the end of term at a school etc.; (*c*) a termination of a personal, esp. sexual, relationship; (*d*) a winding up and dispersal of the assets of a company etc.; (*e*) *Canad.* the breaking up of thawing ice, or the melting of snow and unfreezing of the ground, in spirng.

bream /briːm/ *n.* Pl. same. Also (*N. Amer.* & *Austral.*) **brim** /brɪm/. LME. [OFr. *bre(s)me* (mod. *brème*) f. Frank. (= OS *bressemo*, OHG *brahsema* (G *Brachsen, Brassen*)).] 1 A deep-bodied freshwater fish of the carp family, *Abramis brama*, of northern Europe and parts of Asia. Also, any of certain related fishes, *esp.* (more fully *silver bream, white bream*), a European freshwater fish, *Blicca bjoerkna*, similar to *Abramis brama.* LME. 2 Any of various similar percoid marine fishes, *esp.* (*a*) = SEA *bream*; (*b*) = POMFRET 2. LME. 3 A freshwater sunfish of the genus *Lepomis* (family Centrarchidae). *N. Amer.* M17.

2 RAY'S BREAM. *red bream*: see RED *a.*

bream /briːm/ *v.t.* L15. [Prob. of LG origin and rel. to BROOM *n.* (cf. Du. *brem* broom, furze).] *Hist.* Clear (a ship's bottom, or the vessel itself) of accumulated weed, shells, etc., by burning and scraping.

breast /brɛst/ *n.* [OE *brēost* = OFris. *briast*, OS *briost*, ON *brjóst*, f. Gmc.] 1 Either of two soft protuberant organs situated on the front of a woman's thorax, secreting milk for a period after parturition; the analogous rudimentary organ in men; *the* organs as a source of milk; *fig.* a source of nourishment. OE. 2 The front of the human thorax, the chest. OE. b Part of a garment, piece of armour, etc., covering this. LME. 3 The seat of the affections, emotions, etc.; the heart; one's private thoughts or feelings. OE. 4 The thorax of an animal. ME. b A joint of meat or portion of poultry cut from the breast. LME. †5 The whole of the upper torso. LME–M18. †6 Breath, voice in singing. LME–E18. †7 A broad even front of a moving company. Cf. ABREAST. LME–E19. 8 Any surface, part of a thing, etc., analogous in shape or position to the human breast; a broad or bulging forward part. M16.

1 SHAKES. *Macb.* Come to my woman's breasts, And take my milk for gall, you murd'ring ministers. STEELE One Country Milch-Wench, to whom I was . . put to the Breast. 2 F. NORRIS A gray flannel shirt, open at the throat, showed his breast. *beat one's breast*: see BEAT *v.*[1] 1. 3 C. CAUSLEY She destroys hope In the breasts of the sick. **make a clean breast of** confess fully. 4 O. WILDE The Nightingale flew to the Rose-tree, and set her breast against the thorn. 6 J. FLETCHER Let's hear him sing, he has a fine breast. 8 G. E. EVANS The kids had been up on the breast of Gilfach-y-Rhyd, playing Indians among the rocks. **chimney-breast** the projecting wall enclosing the flues of a chimney within a room.

Comb.: **breast-board** the mould-board of a plough; **breastbone** = STERNUM; **breast collar** a part of harness across a draught animal's breast through which the power of drawing is directly exerted; **breast-drill** a drill on which pressure is brought to bear by the operator's breast; **breast-fed** *a.*, **-feed** *v.t.* & *i.*, **-feeding**: with milk from a woman's breasts rather than from a feeding-bottle; **breast-high** *a.* & *adv.* high as the breast; (submerged) to the breast; **breast-pin** a jewelled or other ornamental pin worn in the tie; **breastplate** a vestment or piece of armour worn over the chest; the lower shell of a tortoise, turtle, etc.; an inscription plate on a coffin; **breast-plough** a type of plough pushed by the breast; **breast-pocket** a pocket over the breast of a garment; **breast-pump** an instrument for drawing milk from the breasts by suction; **breast shell** a shallow receptacle that fits over the nipple of a lactating woman to catch any milk that flows; **breast-stroke** a stroke made while swimming on the breast by extending the arms in front and sweeping them back; BREASTSUMMER; **breast-wall** a retaining wall, *esp.* one supporting a bank of earth; **breast-wheel** a water-wheel in which the water is admitted near the axle; **breastwork** a breast-high fieldwork thrown up for defence; a parapet.

breasted *a.* having a breast (of specified form) ME. **breastwise** *adv.* side by side, abreast E17. **breasty** *a.* (*colloq.*) (of a woman) with prominent breasts M20.

breast /brɛst/ *v.* M16. [f. the n.] 1 *v.t.* Protect with a breastwork. Now *rare* or *obs.* M16. 2 *v.t.* Apply or oppose the breast to, push with the breast; meet in full opposition, contend with, face. L16. 3 *v.i.* Press forward, climb; leap forward. *Sc.* L18.

2 KEATS As swift As bird on wing to breast its eggs again. J. BUCHAN A baker's van breasted the hill. B. BAINBRIDGE Like a swimmer breasting a wave. *breast the tape*: see TAPE *n.* 1c.

breasting *n.* (*a*) the action of the vb; (*b*) a breastplate; a breastwork: L16.

breastsummer /ˈbrɛstsʌmə/ *n.* Also **bressumer** /ˈbrɛsʌmə/. E17. [f. BREAST *n.* + SUMMER *n.*[2]] A beam spanning a wide opening and supporting a superstructure.

breath /brɛθ/ *n.* [OE *brǣþ* f. Gmc f. IE, f. base meaning 'burn, heat'. In sense 3 etc. replaced OE *æþm*, *anda*.] 1 An odour, a smell, a scent. Long *obs.* exc. *dial.* OE. 2†a A vapour given off by heated objects etc.; reek; steam. ME–M17. b Air exhaled from anything, or impregnated with its exhalations (cf. sense 7 below). E17. 3 Air exhaled from the lungs (as made manifest by smell or sight); *gen.* air inspired or expired in respiration. ME. b The air blown into or out of a musical instrument. *poet.* E17. c *Phonet.* Voiceless expiration of air. M19. 4 The faculty or action of breathing; existence, spirit, life. ME. 5 An act of breathing, a single inspiration. ME. 6 A whisper; an utterance, a speech; spoken judgement or will. ME. 7 A gentle blowing (*of* wind etc.), a puff; *fig.* the enlivening or favourable influence (*of*); (passing into sense 2b), a whiff, a trace. LME. 8 The power of breathing; free or easy breathing. L16. 9 An opportunity or time for breathing. Cf. BREATHER 4. L16.

2b R. KIPLING A land-breeze.. Milk-warm wi' breath of spice an' bloom. G. ORWELL The heat rolled from the earth like the breath of an oven. 3 G. B. SHAW Mrs Dudgeon, greatly relieved, exhales the pent up breath and sits at her ease again. W. TREVOR He could see her breath on the icy air. b DRYDEN Before the Breath Of brazen Trumpets rung the Peals of Death. 4 T. HOOD I often wish the night Had borne my breath away. TENNYSON And so the Word had breath. 5 SIR W. SCOTT To cry for assistance and almost in the same breath to whimper for mercy. W. S. MAUGHAM Almost in a breath they touched upon the latest play, the latest dressmaker, the latest portrait painter. M. M. KAYE His first breath had been a lungful of the cold air that blew down from the far rampart of the mountains. 6 I. MCEWAN The faintest sound, barely more than a breath, left her lips. *fig.*: J. GALSWORTHY Every breath of the old scandal had been carefully kept from her. 7 H. R. REYNOLDS Forced into new attitudes by the changing breath of human appreciation. J. RHYS There was no breeze, not a breath of air. J. CLAVELL A few days here, half a year there, like a butterfly on the summer's breath. 8 SIR W. SCOTT Two dogs.. Unmatched for courage, breath, and speed. 9 SHAKES. *Rich. III* Give me some little breath, some pause, dear lord, Before I positively speak in this.

Phrases: *bate one's breath*: see BATE *v.*[2] 2. **below** or **under one's breath** in a whisper. **breath of fresh air** *fig.* someone or something refreshing, a pleasant change. **catch one's breath** stop breathing for a moment in fear, anticipation, etc. **draw breath** breathe, live. **hold one's breath** stop breathing for a short time. **keep one's breath to cool one's porridge** abstain from useless talk. **out of breath** unable to breathe quickly enough after exertion. **save one's breath (to cool one's porridge)** = *keep one's breath to cool one's porridge* above. SHORTNESS *of breath*. *stop the breath of*: see STOP *v.* **take breath** pause to recover free or easy breathing. **take a person's breath away** make a person breathless with delight, surprise, etc. **the breath of life** *fig.* a necessity. *under one's breath*: see *below one's breath* above. **waste breath** talk in vain. *yield (up) one's breath*: see YIELD *v.*

Comb.: **breath consonant** *Phonet.* a voiceless (esp. continuant) consonant; **breathtaking** *a.* that takes one's breath away, surprising, astonishing; **breathtakingly** *adv.* in a breathtaking manner, to a breathtaking extent; **breath test** a test administered to determine the level of alcohol in the breath; **breath-test** *v.t.* administer a breath test to.

breathed *a.* having breath (of a specified kind); *long-breathed*, long-winded, long-lived: M16. **breathful** *a.* (now *rare* or *obs.*) full of breath; having breath, alive; redolent: L16.

breathalyser /ˈbrɛθəlʌɪzə/ *n.* Also ***-zer**, (proprietary) **Breathalyzer.** M20. [f. BREATH *n.* + ANALYSER.] An instrument for determining the level of alcohol in the breath. Cf. DRUNKOMETER.

breathalyse *v.t.* carry out a test on (a person) using a breathalyser M20.

breathe /briːð/ *v.* ME. [f. BREATH.] I *v.i.* †1 Exhale, steam, evaporate. ME–L17. 2 Emit odour, smell. Now only *fig.*, be redolent *of.* LME. 3a Exhale air from the lungs. LME. b Exhale and inhale, respire. LME. 4 Live, exist. LME. 5 Take breath; *fig.* pause, take rest. L16. 6 Give forth audible breath; speak, sing, be sounded. L16. 7 Of wind etc.: blow softly. E17. 8 Of wine, the skin, etc.: have or be affected by contact with air. Of material: admit air or moisture. M20.

1 SHAKES. *Per.* A warmth Breathes out of her. 2 TENNYSON Francis just alighted from the boat, And breathing of the sea. 3a YEATS Breathe on the burnished mirror of the world. b TENNYSON And answer made King Arthur, breathing hard. *Scientific American* An ostrich breathes about six times a minute. 4 SHAKES. *Rich. III* Clarence still breathes; Edward still lives and reigns. DISRAELI Within five minutes you will breathe a beggar and an outcast. 5 J. OZELL Orders to give Antony no Time to Breathe, but to pursue him forthwith. TENNYSON Twice they fought, and twice they breathed. 6 MILTON As I wake, sweet music breathes. 7 POPE Where cooling vapours breathe along the mead. 8 A. E. LINDOP I opened a bottle of wine and left it to 'breathe'. N. GOULD Rubber soles.. do not 'breathe'. *Daily Telegraph* We go jogging in trainers which don't allow the feet to breathe.

II *v.t.* 9 Exhale; send *out* as breath; (of a thing) emit; *fig.* infuse *into*, communicate. LME. 10 Exercise briskly. Now *spec.* put out of breath, tire. LME. 11a Utter passionately or vehemently. Also, utter quietly; whisper. M16. b Display, evince. M17. 12 Allow to breathe, rest. L16. 13 Respire; *esp.* inhale. L16. 14 Let blood from (a vein). *obs.* exc. *Hist.* M17. 15 Give breath to, blow (a wind instrument). E18.

9 W. COWPER Place me where Winter breathes his keenest air. J. MORLEY He breathed new life into them. I. MCEWAN He inhaled.. and breathed smoke across the pots of geraniums. 10 J. F. COOPER The warriors who had breathed themselves so freely in the preceding struggle. 11a SPENSER Two knights.. breathing vengeaunce. J. CONRAD Those red lips that almost without moving could breathe enchanting sounds into the world. R. DAVIES 'Looking so alive it is,' Ivor breathed in admiration. b A. P. STANLEY The whole period breathes a primitive simplicity. 12 W. S. CHURCHILL Having breathed my horse, for I did not wish to arrive in a flurry. 13 L. DEIGHTON Breathing long grassy lungfuls of the wet night air.

Phrases, & with advs. & preps. in specialized senses: **breathe again** *fig.* recover from fear etc., be at ease after a crisis. **breathe down a person's neck** be close behind a person, esp. in mistrust or pursuit. **breathe freely** *fig.* be at ease. **breathe in** inhale. **breathe one's last** die. **breathe out** exhale. *breathe short*: see SHORT *adv.* †**breathe to** aspire to. **breathe upon** *fig.* infect, contaminate, tarnish. **not breathe a word of** keep quite secret.

breathable *a.* fit or agreeable to breathe M18.

breather /ˈbriːðə/ *n.* LME. [f. BREATHE + -ER[1].] 1 A person who breathes, a living being; a person who speaks or utters. LME. †2 A person who or thing which supplies breath; an inspirer. E17–E18. 3 A spell of exercise. Now *rare.* M19. 4 A short rest, a break from exercise etc. E20. 5 More fully *breather-pipe* etc. A vent allowing release of pressure e.g. from the crankcase of an internal-combustion engine. E20.

breathing /ˈbriːðɪŋ/ *n.* LME. [f. BREATHE + -ING[1].] 1 The action of BREATHE; an instance of this; respiration; a breath. LME. †2 Ventilation; a vent. LME–L17. †3 Time to rest; respite. L16–L17. 4 = BREATHER 3. Now *rare.* M18. 5 An aspiration, an aspirate; *spec.* (Gk Gram.) *rough*, *smooth breathing*, the signs ʽ and ʼ respectively indicating the presence or absence of aspiration on an initial vowel, diphthong, or rho. M18.

1 *deep breathing*: see DEEP *a.*

Comb.: **breathing-room, -space** time or space to breathe, a rest, a period of inactivity.

breathless /ˈbrɛθlɪs/ *a.* LME. [f. BREATH + -LESS.] 1 Not breathing; lifeless, dead. LME. 2 Out of breath, panting, breathing with difficulty. (The usual sense.) LME. 3 Holding the breath through excitement etc. E19. 4 Unstirred by wind. E19.

breathlessly *adv.* M19. **breathlessness** *n.* E17.

breathy /ˈbrɛθi/ *a.* E16. [f. BREATH + -Y[1].] 1 Of, pertaining to, or of the nature of breath. E16. 2 Of the (singing-)voice: having an admixture of the sound of breathing. L19.

breathiness *n.* L19.

breccia /ˈbrɛtʃə, -tʃɪə/ *n.* L18. [It. = gravel, rubble, cogn. w. (O)Fr. *brèche*, f. Gmc base of BREAK *v.*] *Geol.* Rock consisting of angular fragments cemented together e.g. by lime.

brecciate /ˈbrɛtʃɪeɪt/ *v.t.* L18. [f. prec. + -ATE[3].] Form into breccia. Chiefly as *brecciated* ppl a.

brecciˈation *n.* L19.

brecham /ˈbrɛxəm/ *n.* *Sc.* E16. [Metath. f. as BARFAM.] A collar for a draught horse.

Brechtian /ˈbrɛxtɪən, -kt-/ *a.* & *n.* M20. [f. *Brecht* (see below) + -IAN.] A *adj.* Of, pertaining to, or characteristic of, the German playwright and poet Bertolt Brecht (1898–1956) or his plays or dramatic technique. M20. B *n.* An admirer or student of Brecht or his writing. M20.

breck /brɛk/ *n.* ME. [Parallel to BREAK *n.*[1] or directly f. BREAK *v.*] 1 A breach, a tear, a fracture; a blemish. Long *dial.* ME. 2 = BREAK *n.*[1] 5; *spec.* (in *pl.* or as *Breckland*) the region of heathland around Thetford in Norfolk, England. L18.

bred /brɛd/ *n.* Long *dial.* [OE *bred* = OHG *bret* (G *Brett*) f. Gmc var. of BOARD *n.*] A board; a tablet.

bred /brɛd/ *a.* ME. [pa. pple of BREED *v.*] 1 That has been bred; reared, brought up, trained, esp. in a specified way. ME. 2 Esp. of an animal: of good breed, of (specified) purity of breed. E18.

1 W. GURNALL Paul was a bred scholar. **born and bred**, (less commonly) **bred and born**, by birth and upbringing. **bred in the bone** hereditary. *country-bred*, *ill-bred*, *well-bred*, etc. 2 *half-bred*, *thoroughbred*, etc.

bred *v.* pa. t. & pple of BREED *v.*

brede /briːd/ *n.*[1] Now *north.* [OE *brǣdu* = OFris. *brēde*, OHG *breitī* (G *Breite*), ON *breidd*, Goth. *braidei* f. Gmc base of BROAD *a.*] 1 Breadth, width. OE. 2 A standard width of fabric; a piece of stuff of the full breadth. LME.

brede /briːd/ *n.*[2] *arch.* Also †**bread.** M17. [Var. of BRAID *n.*] = BRAID *n.* 4.

brede /briːd/ *v.*[1]*t.* & *i.* Long *dial.* [OE *brǣdan* = OS *brēdian*, OHG, G *breiten*, ON *breiða*, Goth. *braidjan*, f. Gmc (as BREDE *n.*[1]).] Broaden; spread out, extend.

†**brede** *v.*[2]*t.* Also **bread.** LME–L17. [Var. of BRAID *v.*[1]] Intertwine, plait, wreathe, twist.

bree /briː/ *n.*[1] Long *obs.* exc. *Sc.* & *north.* [OE *brǣw* eyelid, OFris. *brē*, OS, OHG *brāwa* (G *Braue*) eyebrow, ON *brá* eyelash: cf. BRAE. Not allied to BROW *n.*[1]] †1 The eyelid. OE–ME. 2 The eyebrow. ME. †3 An eyelash. LME–M17.

bree /briː/ *n.*[2] Long *obs.* exc. *Sc.* [OE *brīw*, *brīġ* = MLG, MDu. *brī* (Du. *brij*), OHG *brīo* (G *Brei*) f. Gmc.] †1 A thick pottage made of meal etc. OE–ME. 2 Liquor in which anything has been steeped or boiled, or which flows from it; broth, juice. LME.

breech /briːtʃ/ *n.* In sense 2c also **britch** /ˈbrɪtʃ/. In sense 1b pl. also pronounced /ˈbrɪtʃɪz/. See also BREEK. [OE *brōc*, pl. *brēċ*, corresp. to OFris. *brōk*, pl. *brēk*, OS *brōk* (Du. *broek*), OHG *bruoh* (G †*Bruch*), ON *brók*, pl. *brœkr*, f. Gmc.] 1†a A garment covering the loins and thighs. OE–M17. b In *pl.* & †*sing.* Short trousers, *esp.* those fastened below the knee, now used esp. for riding or in court costume etc.; knickerbockers; *dial.* & *colloq.* trousers. Also *pair of breeches*. ME. 2 The buttocks. *arch.* in *gen.* sense. M16. b *spec.* The buttocks of a baby at or before birth. Also, a breech presentation or birth. L17. c The hindquarters of an animal or its skin or fleece. E18. 3 The hinder part of anything; *spec.* the back part of a rifle or gun barrel, the part of a cannon behind the bore. L16. 4 The roe of the cod. Long *dial.* L17. 5 *Naut.* The external angle of a ship's knee-timber etc. M19.

1b *leather breeches*: see LEATHER *n.* & *a.* *too big for one's breeches*: see BIG *a.* 3. *wear the breeches*: see WEAR *v.*[1]

Comb.: **breech action** the mechanism at the breech of a gun; **breech baby** a baby born in a breech presentation; **breech birth, delivery, presentation,** etc.: in which the baby is so positioned in the uterus that its buttocks (or feet) are delivered first; **breech-**

a cat, ɑː arm, ɛ bed, əː her, ɪ sit, i cosy, iː see, ɒ hot, ɔː saw, ʌ run, ʊ put, uː too, ə ago, ʌɪ my, aʊ how, eɪ day, əʊ no, ɛː hair, ɪə near, ɔɪ boy, ʊə poor, ʌɪə tire, aʊə sour

block the block in a breech-loading firearm which closes the rear of the bore against the force of the charge; *breech delivery*: see *breech birth* above; **Breeches Bible** the Geneva bible of 1560 (so named on account of the rendering of *Gen.* 3:7 with *breeches* for *aprons*, although this occurred already in Wyclif); **breeches buoy** a lifebuoy on a rope with a canvas support resembling breeches; **breeches part** a theatrical role in which a woman dresses as a man; **breech-loader, -loading** *a.* (a firearm) that is loaded at the breech and not through the muzzle; *breech presentation*: see *breech birth* above.

breechless *a.* without breeches, having bare buttocks LME.

breech /briːtʃ, brɪtʃ/ *v.t.* LME. [f. the n.] 1 Cover or clothe with, or as with, breeches; *arch.* put (a boy) into breeches instead of petticoats. LME. †2 Flog. L16–E19. 3 *Naut.* Secure (a cannon etc.) by a breeching. L16.

1 R. L. STEVENSON Before he was breeched, he might have clambered on the boxes. *fig.*: SHAKES. *Macb.* Their daggers Unmannerly breech'd with gore.

breeching /ˈbriːtʃɪŋ, ˈbrɪtʃ-/ *n.* E16. [f. BREECH *n.*, *v.* + -ING[1].] 1 A strong leather strap passing round the hindquarters of a shaft-horse, enabling the horse to push backwards. E16. †2 A flogging. E16–E17. 3 *Naut.* A thick rope used to secure the carriages of cannon etc. and to absorb the force of the recoil. E17. 4 = *breech action* s.v. BREECH *n.* E19.

Comb.: †**breeching-boy, scholar** a young scholar still subject to the birch.

breed /briːd/ *n.* LME. [f. the vb.] †1 Growth. Only in LME. 2 Breeding, birth; lineage; extraction. L15. 3 A stock, a strain, a race; a line of descendants perpetuating particular hereditary qualities, *esp.* a stock of animals of a particular species, developed by deliberate selection. M16. b *gen.* A kind, a species, a set. L16. 4 Offspring; a litter, a brood. Now *dial.* L16. 5 A person of mixed descent, a half-breed. Chiefly *N. Amer.* L19.

2 G. HERBERT Nothing useth fire, But man alone, to show his heavenly breed. CONAN DOYLE He has breed in him, a real aristocrat of crime. 3 SIR W. SCOTT Two dogs of black Saint Hubert's breed. JOHN BROOKE The Hanoverians were a tough breed. *lesser breed*: see LESSER *a.* b D. HALBERSTAM He was of the old breed of reporters, he liked action stories. 4 SHAKES. *Sonn.* Nothing 'gainst Time's scythe can make defence Save breed.

breed /briːd/ *v.* Pa. t. & pple **bred** /brɛd/. [OE *brēdan* = OHG *bruotan* (G *brüten*), f. WGmc, f. Gmc base of BROOD *n.*] 1 *v.t.* Bring (offspring) forward from conception to birth; hatch (young) from the egg; bear, generate, (offspring). OE. 2 *v.i.* a Of an animal species: produce young, reproduce. ME. b Of a woman: be pregnant. E17. 3 *v.t.* Give rise to; be the source of; engender, develop; produce. ME. b Produce (fissile material) within a nuclear reactor. Cf. BREEDER 2. M20. 4 *v.i.* Come into being or existence; be produced; arise, originate. ME. 5 *v.t.* Promote or control the propagation of, raise, (animals, plants, etc.); develop (a particular breed or kind of animal or plant). LME. b Put (an animal) *to* another for mating. L19. 6 *v.t.* Bring up from childhood, raise (as); bring up *in* a faith etc., train up *to* a profession, status, etc.; (now *arch. rare*) train, educate (as). Also foll. by *up*. LME. †7 *v.t.* Begin to exhibit naturally (teeth, wings, etc.). M16–M18.

3 J. BARET Rotten timber breedeth wormes. J. BUCHAN I couldn't leave any clues to breed suspicions. T. S. ELIOT April is the cruellest month, breeding Lilacs out of the dead land. M. L. KING Poverty and ignorance breed crime. 4 BACON Fleas breed principally of Straw or Mats, where there hath been a little moisture. JAS. MILL [He] allowed .. discontents & jealousies to breed in the army. 5 J. RAY The manner of breeding Canary-birds. ANTHONY HUXLEY Breeding short-stemmed cereals for ease of combine harvesting. 6 T. FULLER Sir John Mason was .. bred in All Souls in Oxford. DEFOE Thou talkest as if thou hadst been bred a heathen. SOUTHEY He did not determine upon breeding him either to the Church or the Law. H. T. BUCKLE The old traditions in which they had been bred. D. H. LAWRENCE She was demeaning herself shamefully... After all, she had been bred up differently from that.

With advs. & preps. in specialized senses: **breed in** (usually) mate with or marry near relatives. **breed in and in**: within a limited stock. **breed out** eliminate (a characteristic) by (controlled) breeding.

Comb.: †**breed-bate** a mischief-maker.

breedy *a.* breeding readily, prolific M18.

breeder /ˈbriːdə/ *n.* M16. [f. prec. + -ER[1].] 1 A thing which or person who breeds or produces; a person who rears animals etc. M16. 2 A nuclear reactor which can create more fissile material than it uses in the chain reaction. Also *breeder reactor*. M20.

2 *fast-breeder (reactor)*: see FAST *a.*

breeding /ˈbriːdɪŋ/ *n.* ME. [f. as prec. + -ING[1].] 1 Bringing to birth; hatching; the production of young, reproduction. ME. †b Extraction; parentage. L16–E17. 2 Origination; production; development. M16. b *spec.* The production of fissile material. M20. 3 The rearing and training of the young (formerly *spec.*, education). L16. 4 The results of training as shown in (good) manners and behaviour. L16.

1 attrib.: *breeding plumage, season*, etc. 3 S. LEWIS He knew himself to be of a breeding altogether more esthetic and sensitive than Thompson's. 4 DISRAELI Her ignorance of all breeding is amusing. C. BLACKWOOD A couple of rough young men with no breeding at all. *good breeding*: see GOOD *a.* *ill breeding*: see ILL *a.* & *adv.*

Comb.: **breeding ground** (*a*) an area of land where an animal, esp. a bird, habitually breeds; (*b*) a thing that favours the development or occurrence of something, esp. something unpleasant (foll. by *for*).

breek /briːk/ *n. dial.* ME. [Var. of BREECH *n.*] Usu. in *pl.* (*sing.* long *rare*). Trousers, breeches.

breeze /briːz/ *n.*[1] [OE *briosa*, of unkn. origin.] A gadfly or similar insect. Also *breeze-fly*.

breeze /briːz/ *n.*[2] M16. [Prob. f. OSp., Port. *briza* (Sp. *brisa*) north-east wind (cf. It. *brezza*, dial. *brisa* cold wind).] †1 A north or north-east wind. M16–E18. 2 The cool onshore wind that blows by day on warm coasts. Also, the offshore wind that blows by night. Now chiefly as *sea breeze, land breeze* respectively. E17. 3 Any gentle or light wind; on the Beaufort scale, a wind of 6–50 k.p.h.; *Naut.* any wind. E17. 4 *fig. slang.* a A disturbance; a row. L18. b A breath of news; a whisper, a rumour. L19. c Something that is easy to achieve, handle, etc. Orig. *US.* E20.

Phrases: **get, have the breeze up** *colloq.* = *get, have the wind up* s.v. WIND *n.*[1] **hit the breeze** *slang* depart. **put the breeze up** *colloq.* = *put the wind up* s.v. WIND *n.*[1] *shoot the breeze*: see SHOOT *v.* **split** or **take the breeze** *slang* = *hit the breeze* above.

Comb.: **breezeway** (chiefly *N. Amer.*) a roofed outdoor passage.

breezeless *a.* M18.

breeze /briːz/ *n.*[3] L16. [Fr. *braise*, earlier *brese*, burning charcoal, hot embers, etc.] Small cinders, coke dust, etc., often used with sand and cement to make lightweight building blocks (*breeze-blocks*).

breeze /briːz/ *v.i.* L17. [f. BREEZE *n.*[2]] 1 Blow gently, as a breeze. *rare.* L17. 2 Move *along*, come *in*, etc., in a lively or offhand manner. *colloq.* (orig. *US*). E20.

With advs. in specialized senses: **breeze up** (*a*) *Naut.* (of a wind) freshen; (*b*) (of a noise) rise on the breeze.

breezy /ˈbriːzi/ *a.* E18. [f. BREEZE *n.*[2] + -Y[1].] 1 Exposed to breezes, windswept. E18. 2 Attended by breezes; (pleasantly) windy. Also *fig.*, fresh, airy, spirited, jovial; careless. M18.

breezily *adv.* M19. **breeziness** *n.* M19.

bregma /ˈbrɛgmə/ *n.* Pl. **-mas, -mata** /-mətə/. L16. [Gk = front of the head.] *Anat.* The region of the skull where the frontal and the two parietal bones join.

bregmatic /brɛgˈmatɪk/ *a.* M19.

Breguet /ˈbrʌgeɪ/ *n.* & *a.* E19. [A. L. *Breguet* (1747–1823), Fr. watchmaker.] (Designating, a timepiece with) a hairspring ending in an overcoil.

Brehon /ˈbriːhən/ *n.* M16. [Ir. *breitheamhan* genit. pl. of *breitheamh* (in OIr. *brithem*), f. *breith* judgement.] *Hist.* A judge in ancient Ireland.

Comb.: **Brehon law** the code of law which prevailed in Ireland before its occupation by the English.

brei /brʌɪ/ *n.* M20. [G = pulp, mush, jelly.] *Biol.* A homogenized pulp of organic tissue prepared for experimental work.

brei *v.* var. of BRAY *v.*[3]

breithauptite /ˈbrʌɪthaʊptʌɪt/ *n.* M19. [f. Johann F. A. *Breithaupt* (1791–1873), Ger. mineralogist + -ITE[1].] *Min.* Nickel antimonide, a hexagonal copper-red mineral with a metallic appearance, usu. occurring in massive form in veins.

breitschwanz /ˈbrʌɪtʃvaːnts/ *n.* E20. [G = broad tail.] The lustrous pelt of a young karakul lamb.

brekekekex /brɛkəkəˈkɛks/ *n.* & *int.* E17. [Gk, imit., used by Aristophanes.] (Repr.) the croaking of frogs (usu. w. *coax coax* /kəʊˈaks/).

brekker /ˈbrɛkə/ *n. slang* (orig. *Univ.*). L19. [f. BREAK(FAST *n.* + -ER[6].] Breakfast.

brekkie /ˈbrɛki/ *n. slang.* Also **-y.** E20. [f. BREAK(FAST *n.* + -Y[6].] Breakfast.

breloque /brəˈləʊk/ *n.* M19. [Fr.] A small ornament fastened to a watch-chain; a trinket.

breme /briːm/ *a.* Now *arch.* & *dial.* Also **brim** /brɪm/. ME. [Origin unkn.] 1 Fierce, stern, raging, furious. Long *obs.* in *gen.* sense. ME. 2 *spec.* Of the sea, wind, etc.: rough, stormy, raging, severe. ME.

bremsstrahlung /ˈbrɛmzʃtraːlʊŋ/ *n.* M20. [G, f. *bremsen* to brake + *Strahlung* radiation.] *Physics.* Electromagnetic radiation emitted by a charged particle upon retardation by an electric field (esp. by that of a nucleus).

thermal bremsstrahlung: see THERMAL *a.*

bren /brɛn/ *n.* Also **B-.** M20. [f. *Br*no in Moravia (where orig. made) + *En*field (see ENFIELD where later made).] In full *bren-gun*. A kind of light quick-firing machine-gun.

brennage /ˈbrɛnɪdʒ/ *n.* M18. [OFr. *brenage*, f. *bren* BRAN + -AGE, or med.L *brennagium*.] *Hist.* A payment in, or in lieu of, bran, made by tenants to feed their lord's hounds.

brent /brɛnt/ *n.* Also ***brant** /brant/. LME. [Origin unkn.] In full *brent-goose*. A small black, grey, and white goose, *Branta bernicla*, which breeds in the Arctic and visits Britain in winter.

¶By early writers often confused with the barnacle goose.

brent *a.* & *adv.* var. of BRANT *a.* & *adv.*

brent *v.* pa. t. & pple: see BURN *v.*

brer /brɛː, brəː/ *n. colloq.* (orig. *US*). L19. [Repr. a Black or southern US pronunc. of BROTHER *n.*] Brother.

brerd /brəːd/ *n.* Long *obs.* exc. *dial.* See also BRAIRD. [OE *brerd*: cf. OHG *brort*, *brord* prow, margin, lip.] The topmost surface or edge; the brim.

bressumer *n.* var. of BREASTSUMMER.

bret /brɛt/ *n.* See also BRAT *n.*[3] LME. [Origin unkn.] †1 A brill, a turbot. LME–M19. 2 = BRIT *n.*[2] E18.

bretelle /brəˈtɛl/ *n.* M19. [Fr. = strap, sling, (in pl.) trouser-braces.] Each of a pair of ornamental straps extending over the shoulders from the belt on the front of a dress to the belt on the back. Usu. in *pl.*

bretessy /ˈbrɛtəsi/ *a.* L16. [Fr. *bretessé* bratticed: see -Y[5].] *Her.* Embattled on both sides with the battlements at the same points on each edge. Cf. COUNTER-EMBATTLED.

Also **bretessed** *a.* E19.

brethren *n.pl.* see BROTHER *n.*

Breton /ˈbrɛt(ə)n/ *n.* & *a.* LME. [OFr.: see BRITON.] A *n.* A native or inhabitant of Brittany in NW France; the Celtic language of Brittany. LME.

B *attrib.* or as *adj.* Belonging to, or characteristic of Brittany, its inhabitants, or their language. L15.

Breton hat a type of hat with a round crown and an upward-curved brim. *Breton lai*: see LAI *n.*[1] †**Breton tackle** = BURTON *n.*[1] 1.

Brett *n.* var. of BRIT *n.*[1] & *a.*[1]

Bretwalda /brɛtˈwɔːldə/ *n.* [OE *Bretwalda*, varying w. *Brytenwalda*, f. *Brettas* (see BRIT *n.*[1] & *a.*[1]), *Bryten* (see BRITAIN *n.*[1]) + Gmc base of WIELD *v.*] *Hist.* Lord of the Britons, lord of Britain: a title given in the Anglo-Saxon

Chronicle to King Egbert, and (retrospectively) to some earlier Anglo-Saxon kings, and occas. assumed by later ones.

bretzel *n.* see PRETZEL.

breve /briːv/ *n.* ME. [Var. of BRIEF *n.*[1]] 1 *Hist.* An authoritative letter, esp. from a pope or monarch. ME. 2 *Mus.* A note of the value of two semibreves (now rarely used). LME. †3 *Gram.* A short syllable. *rare.* M16–M18. 4 The mark ˘ written or printed over a short or unstressed vowel, or as a diacritic over various letters in certain languages. L19.

brevet /ˈbrɛvɪt/ *n.* & *v.* LME. [(O)Fr., f. as BRIEF *n.*[1] + -ET[1].] A *n.* †1 An official letter; *esp.* a papal indulgence. LME–M18. 2 A document from a monarch or government conferring privileges; *spec.* one conferring nominal military rank without corresponding pay. Freq. *attrib.* L17.

Comb.: **brevet captain, colonel**, etc., **brevet rank** a nominal rank (of captain, colonel, etc.) conferred by a brevet.

B *v.t.* Confer a brevet rank on. M19.

breviary /ˈbriːvɪəri/ *n.* LME. [L *breviarium* summary, abridgement, f. *breviare*: see ABBREVIATE *v.*, -ARY[1].] 1 *Chr. Ch.* A book containing the service for each day, to be recited by those in orders. In early use also, an abridged version of the psalms. LME. †2 *gen.* A brief statement, a summary. M16–E19.

1 **matter of breviary** an accepted truth.

†breviate *n.* & *ppl a.* LME. [L *breviatus* pa. pple of *breviare*: see ABBREVIATE *v.*, -ATE[2].] A *n.* 1 A letter, a short note. LME–M18. 2 A summary, an abridgement. E16–M19. 3 A lawyer's brief. L16–M18. B *ppl a.* Shortened, abbreviated. E16–M17.

†breviator *n.* M16–M18. [L *breviator*, f. *breviare*: see ABBREVIATE *v.*, -ATOR.] = ABBREVIATOR.

brevier /brɪˈvɪə/ *n.* L16. [Du. or G, f. med.L use of L *breviarium* BREVIARY (perh. from its use in the printing of breviaries).] A former size of type between bourgeois and minion.

breviloquence /brɪˈvɪləkw(ə)ns/ *n. rare.* M17. [L *breviloquentia*, f. *brevis* BRIEF *a.*, short, + *loquentia* speaking.] Brevity of speech.

†brevi manu *adv. phr.* E19–E20. [L, lit. 'with short hand'.] *Law.* Summarily; without due process.

brevit /ˈbrɛvɪt/ *v.i.* Long *obs.* exc. *dial.* E17. [Origin unkn.] Forage; beat about for game; hunt; search.

brevity /ˈbrɛvɪti/ *n.* L15. [OFr. *br(i)eveté* (earlier *br(i)eté*) f. L *brevitat-*, f. *brevis* (forms w. *-i-* after OFr. *brief*): see BRIEF *a.* & *adv.*, -ITY.] 1 Compact written or spoken expression; conciseness. L15. 2 Short span, esp. of time, life, etc. M16.

brew /bruː/ *n.*[1] E16. [f. the vb.] The process or result of brewing; the amount brewed at one time; (the quality of) what is brewed; an infusion, a concoction.

brew *n.*[2] var. of BUROO.

brew /bruː/ *v.* [OE *brēowan* = OS *breuwan* (Du. *brouwen*), OHG *briuwan*, *brūwan* (G *brauen*, *bräuen*), ON *brugga*, f. Gmc.] 1 *v.t.* a Make (beer etc., a quantity of beer etc.) by infusion, boiling, and fermentation. OE. b Make (tea etc., a quantity of tea etc.) by infusion or mixture. Also foll. by *up*. E17. 2 *v.i.* a Make beer etc. ME. b Foll. by *up*: make tea. *colloq.* E20. 3 *v.t.* Concoct, contrive, bring about, set in train, (usu. evil or mischief). ME. 4 *v.i.* Undergo infusion, fermentation, etc.; be in the course of preparation; (esp. of evil or mischief) mature, fester, gather force. ME. 5 *v.t.* Convert (malt etc., a quantity of malt etc.) into fermented liquor. Now *arch.* & *dial.* LME. †6 *v.t.* Mix (liquors); dilute. E16–M17.

3 TOLKIEN We saw a cloud of smoke and steam... We feared that Saruman was brewing some new devilry for us. 4 A. UTTLEY He knew when a storm was brewing. J. MASTERS So this strike is brewing, and I'm trying to find out what is known about it here.

Comb.: **brewhouse** a brewery; **brew-up** *colloq.* (a pause for) the making of tea.

brewing *n.* (*a*) the action of the vb; (*b*) the amount of liquor brewed at one time: ME.

brewage /ˈbruːɪdʒ/ *n.* M16. [f. prec. + -AGE, prob. after Fr. *breuvage* BEVERAGE.] The process of brewing; a brew, a decoction; a concocted beverage.

brewer /ˈbruːə/ *n.* ME. [f. BREW *v.* + -ER[1].] 1 A person who brews; *spec.* a person whose trade is the brewing of beer etc. ME. 2 *fig.* A concocter or contriver *of*. M16.

brewery /ˈbrʊəri/ *n.* M17. [f. as prec. + -ERY, prob. after Du. *brouwerij*.] 1 A place or establishment for brewing. M17. †2 The process or trade of brewing. Only in 18.

brewis /ˈbruːɪs/ *n. obs.* exc. *dial.* Also **browis** /ˈbraʊɪs/. See also BROSE. ME. [OFr. *bro(u)ez*, *-ets* pl., *bro(u)et* sing. (mod. *brouet*), f. *breu* = Prov. *bro*, f. Proto-Romance f. Gmc (= BROTH).] 1 Bread soaked in fat or dripping. ME. 2 A kind of broth, freq. thickened with bread or meal. E16. 3 = BROSE. *rare.* M19.

brewster /ˈbruːstə/ *n.*[1] Chiefly *Sc.* & *north.* Also **†browster**. ME. [f. BREW *v.* + -STER: cf. BAXTER.] A brewer, orig. *spec.* a female brewer.

Comb.: **Brewster Sessions** magistrates' sessions for the issue of licences to permit trade in alcoholic liquors.

Brewster /ˈbruːstə/ *n.*[2] L19. [Sir David *Brewster* (1781–1868), Sc. physicist.] Used *attrib.* and in *possess.* with ref. to Brewster's discoveries in optics.

Brewster('s) angle the angle of incidence at the surface of a dielectric for which a wave polarized in the plane of incidence is not reflected at all, and an unpolarized wave is reflected as a plane-polarized wave. **Brewster's law**: that the tangent of the Brewster angle for a given medium is equal to the refractive index of that medium, or (at any interface) equals the ratio of the refractive indices of the media on either side.

brewsterite /ˈbruːstərʌɪt/ *n.* M19. [f. as prec. + -ITE[1].] *Min.* A naturally-occurring zeolite which is a hydrated silicate of aluminium, barium, and strontium.

brey *v.* var. of BRAY *v.*[3]

briar *n.*[1], *n.*[2] vars. of BRIER *n.*[1], *n.*[2]

Briard /brɪˈɑːd, *foreign* briaːr (*pl. same*)/ *n.* M20. [Fr. (adj.), f. BRIE: see -ARD.] A sheepdog of a French breed.

Briareus /brʌɪˈɛːrɪəs/ *n. literary.* E17. [Gk *Briareōs*, one of three mythological giants who aided Zeus against the Titans.] A hundred-armed giant.

Briarean *a.* & *n.* (belonging to or characteristic of) a Briareus: L16.

bribable /ˈbrʌɪbəb(ə)l/ *a.* Also **bribeable**. E19. [f. BRIBE *v.* + -ABLE.] Able to be bribed, corrupt.

¶ Earlier in UNBRIBABLE.

bribaˈbility *n.* M19.

bribe /brʌɪb/ *n.* LME. [f. the vb.] †1 A stolen article; theft; plunder. LME–E16. 2 A sum of money or another reward offered or demanded in order to procure an (often illegal or dishonest) action or decision in favour of the giver. LME.

bribe /brʌɪb/ *v.* LME. [OFr. *briber*, *brimber* beg, of unkn. origin.] I *v.t.* †1 Take dishonestly; purloin; rob; extort. LME–M17. 2 Offer or give a bribe to; persuade by means of a bribe (*to do something*); win over by some inducement. E16. 3 Purchase or obtain by bribery. *arch.* E18.

2 B. MALAMUD He had money, bribed the guards for favours. C. ISHERWOOD I am bribed with fruit not to be tiresome about the English language. 3 SWIFT To bribe the judge's vote.

II *v.i.* †4 Steal; extort. LME–M16. 5 Practise bribery. M17.

5 LD MACAULAY He fawned, bullied, and bribed indefatigably.

briˈbee *n.* the recipient of a bribe M19.

bribeable *a.* var. of BRIBABLE.

briber /ˈbrʌɪbə/ *n.* LME. [Partly f. AN *bribour*, OFr. *bribeur*, *brimbeur* beggar, vagabond, f. as BRIBE *v.*; partly f. BRIBE *v.*: see -ER[1].] †1 A thief; an extortioner; a person who takes or exacts bribes. LME–E17. †2 A beggar, a vagabond; a wretch, a rascal. LME–L16. 3 A person who offers or gives a bribe. L16. †4 A bribe, a price paid. *rare* (Shakes.). Only in E17.

bribery /ˈbrʌɪb(ə)ri/ *n.* LME. [OFr. *briberie*, *brimberie* mendicancy, f. as BRIBE *v.*: see -ERY.] †1 Theft, robbery; taking by force, extortion. LME–L16. 2 The exaction or acceptance of a bribe. *arch.* M16. 3 The giving or offering of a bribe. L16.

bric-à-brac /ˈbrɪkəbrak/ *n.* Also **bric-a-brac**, **bricabrac**. M19. [Fr., f. †*à bric et à brac* at random.] Miscellaneous old ornaments, trinkets, small pieces of furniture, etc; antiquarian knick-knacks.

brick /brɪk/ *n.* & *a.* LME. [MLG, MDu. *bricke*, *brike*, Du. dial. *brik*, WFlem. *brijke*; prob. reinforced by (O)Fr. *brique*, f. same source: ult. origin unkn.] A *n.* 1 Clay kneaded, moulded, and baked or sun-dried, used as a building material. LME. 2 A small usu. rectangular block of this substance. Also, a similarly-shaped block of concrete or other building material. E16. b A child's toy building block. M19. 3 A loaf, block of tea, or other food item formed like a brick. Now *esp.* an ice-cream block. M18. 4 A stalwart, loyal, or generous person. *colloq.* M19. 5 A dull orange-red colour characteristic of brick. L19.

1 GIBBON He had found his capital of brick, and.. left it of marble. 2 P. S. BUCK The kitchen was made of earthen bricks.., great squares of earth dug from their own fields. 4 W. H. AUDEN When he is well She gives him hell, But she's a brick When he is sick.

Phrases etc.: **bricks and mortar** *fig.* buildings, a house as property. *bricks without straw*: see STRAW *n.* **drop a brick** *slang* say something indiscreet. *gold brick*: see GOLD *n.*[1] & *a.* *hit the bricks*: see HIT *v.* *like a cat on hot bricks*: see HOT *a.* **like a load** or **ton of bricks** *slang* with crushing weight or force. *make bricks without straw*: see STRAW *n.* *red-brick*: see RED *n.* *shit a brick* (or *bricks*): see SHIT *v.*

Comb.: **brickbat** a piece of brick, *esp.* one used as a missile; *fig.* an uncomplimentary remark; **brick-dust** (the colour of) powdered brick; **brick-earth** clay used for making bricks; **brick-field** a piece of ground in which bricks are made; **brickfielder** *Austral.* a hot dry northerly wind (orig. as raising dust); **brick-kiln**: for baking bricks; **bricklayer** a worker building with bricks; **bricklaying** the craft or occupation of building with bricks; **brickmaker** a person whose trade is the making of bricks; *brick-nogging* see NOGGING 1; **brick-red** *a.* & *n.* (of) a dull orange-red colour; **brick-stitch** *Embroidery* couching in which the laid threads are secured by cross-stitches arranged like the vertical joints of brickwork; **brickwork** (*a*) builder's work in brick; (*b*) in *pl.*, a factory making bricks; **brickyard** a place where bricks are made.

B *attrib.* or as *adj.* Built of brick. Also, brick-red. LME.

bang, knock or *run one's head against a brick wall*, *see through a brick wall*, *talk to a brick wall*: see WALL *n.*[1]

brickish *a.* resembling a brick in appearance or colour, bricky; *colloq.* stalwart, loyal, generous: M19.

brick /brɪk/ *v.* L16. [f. the n.] 1 *v.t.* Cover or seal (a window, opening, etc.) *up* or *over* with bricks; close *in* with bricks. L16. 2 *v.t.* Make, line, or face with brick; give the appearance of brickwork to. L17. 3 *v.i.* Work with or make bricks. L18.

brickie /ˈbrɪki/ *n. colloq.* Also **bricky**. L19. [f. BRICK *n.* + -IE, -Y[6].] A bricklayer.

brickle *a.* see BRUCKLE.

bricky *n.* var. of BRICKIE.

bricky /ˈbrɪki/ *a.* L16. [f. BRICK *n.* + -Y[1].] Made of or having many bricks. Also, brick-red.

bricolage /brɪkəˈlɑːʒ; *foreign* brikɔlaːʒ (*pl. same*)/ *n.* M20. [Fr., f. *bricoler* do odd jobs, repair, f. as next: see -AGE.] Construction or creation from whatever is immediately available for use; something constructed or created in this way, an assemblage of haphazard or incongruous elements.

bricole /ˈbrɪk(ə)l, brɪˈkəʊl/ *n.* E16. [(O)Fr. f. Prov. *bricola* or It. *briccola*, of unkn. origin.] 1 An engine or catapult for discharging stones or bolts. *obs.* exc. *Hist.* E16. 2 A rebound of the ball from a side-wall or cushion in real tennis, billiards, etc. L16.

bricoleur /brɪkəˈləː; *foreign* brikɔlœːr (*pl. same*)/ *n.* M20. [Fr. = handyman, f. *bricoler* (see BRICOLAGE) + *-eur* -OR.] A person who engages in bricolage; a constructor or creator of bricolages.

bridal /ˈbrʌɪd(ə)l/ *n.* & *a.* [OE *brȳd-ealu*, f. as BRIDE *n.*[1] + ALE: use and pronunc. strongly infl. by assoc. w. adjs. in -AL[1].] A *n.sing.* & in *pl.* A wedding; a nuptial feast. *arch.* OE.

B *adj.* Of, pertaining to, or appropriate to a wedding or a bride. LME.

bridal suite in a hotel, a suite of rooms esp. for the use of a newly married couple. **bridal wreath** any of certain white-flowered ornamental plants; *esp.* a Chilean shrub, *Francoa sonchifolia*, of the saxifrage family.

bridally *adv.* M19. **bridalty** *n.* (*rare*) a wedding M17.

bride /brʌɪd/ *n.*[1] [OE *brȳd* = OFris. *brēd*, *breid*, OS *brūd* (Du. *bruid*), OHG *brūt* (G *Braut*), ON *brúðr*, Goth. *brūþs*, f. Gmc, of unkn. origin.] 1 A woman about to be married or very recently married. OE. 2 A bridegroom. Long *obs.* exc. *Jamaican.* LME.

1 *mourning bride*: see MOURNING *a.*

Comb. (orig. w. the sense 'wedding'): **bride-ale** [the analytical form of BRIDAL *n.*] *Hist.* a wedding celebration with drinking of ale, a wedding-feast; **bride-bed** *arch.* the marriage bed; **bride-cake** (a) wedding cake; **bride-chamber** *arch.* the room in which a wedding is celebrated; **bride-cup** (*a*) a bowl or cup handed round at a wedding; (*b*) a spiced drink prepared at night for a newly wedded pair; **bride-lace** (*obs.* exc. *Hist.*) a coloured ribbon worn as a wedding-favour; **bridemaid** (now *rare* or *obs.*) = BRIDESMAID; **brideman** † (*a*) = BRIDEGROOM; (*b*) (*obs.* exc. *dial.*) = BRIDESMAN; **bride-price** *Anthropol.* a payment of money or goods made to a bride or her parents by the bridegroom or his parents.

bride /brʌɪd/ *n.*[2] ME. [(O)Fr. = bridle, bonnet-string, ult. f. Gmc base also of BRIDLE *n.*] †1 A bridle, a rein. Only in ME. 2 A link in the network which connects the patterns in lace. Also, a bonnet-string. Usu. in *pl.* M19.

bride /brʌɪd/ *v.* M16. [f. BRIDE *n.*[1]] †1 *v.i.* & *t.* (w. *it*). Act the bride. M16–M17. 2 *v.t.* Wed, marry. *obs.* exc. *dial.* L16.

bridegroom /ˈbrʌɪdgruːm/ *n.* [OE *brȳdguma* = OS *brudigomo* (Du. *bruidegom*), OHG *brūtigomo* (G *Bräutigam*), ON *brúðgumi*: the 2nd elem. OE *guma* man, assim. to GROOM *n.*[1]] A man about to be married or very recently married.

bridesmaid /ˈbrʌɪdzmeɪd/ *n.* L18. [Alt. of earlier *bridemaid* s.v. BRIDE *n.*[1]] A girl or unmarried woman (usu. one of several) attending the bride at a wedding.

bridesman /ˈbrʌɪdzmən/ *n.* Pl. **-men.** E19. [Alt. of earlier *brideman* s.v. BRIDE *n.*[1]] The best man (the usual term) at a wedding, a groomsman.

bridewell /ˈbrʌɪdw(ə)l/ *n. arch.* Also **B-.** M16. [f. (St) *Bride's Well* in the City of London, near which such a building stood.] A prison, a reformatory.

bridge /brɪdʒ/ *n.*[1] Also (*Sc.* & *north.*) **brig** /brɪg/. [OE *brycg* = OFris. *brigge*, *bregge*, OS *bruggia*, MDu. *brugghe* (Du. *brug*), OHG *brucca* (G *Brücke*), ON *bryggja* (whence north. dial. *brig*), f. Gmc.] 1 A structure carrying a road, path, railway, etc., across a stream, river, ravine, road, railway, etc. OE. 2 A gangway for a boat; a landing-stage, a jetty, a pier. *obs.* exc. *dial.* ME. 3 The upper bony part of the nose; the central part of a pair of spectacles, fitting over this. LME. 4 The upright piece over which the strings of a violin etc. are stretched. LME. 5 A ridge of rock, sand, or shingle, projecting into or crossing a body of water. (See also *land-bridge* s.v. LAND *n.*[1]) Chiefly *dial.* or in names, as *Filey Brig.* E19. 6 The raised platform or compartment, usu. amidships, from which a ship is directed. M19. 7 *Billiards, Snooker*, etc. The support for the cue formed by the hand or at the end of a rest; occas., a rest. L19. 8 An electric circuit for measuring resistance or another property by equalizing the potential at two points. L19. 9 *Dentistry.* A partial denture supported by natural teeth on either side. L19.

1 *Bailey bridge, bascule bridge, cantilever bridge, drawbridge, floating bridge, foot-bridge, hump(back) bridge, overbridge, packhorse bridge, skew bridge, suspension bridge, swing-bridge, swinging-bridge, toll-bridge, transporter bridge, underbridge*, etc. *asses' bridge*: see ASS *n.*[1] 2. **bridge of boats**: formed by boats moored abreast over a body of water. *burn one's bridges*: see BURN *v.* 8. **cross a bridge when one comes to it** deal with a problem when and if it arises. **gold** (or **silver**) **bridge** an easy and attractive escape route for an enemy. *much water has flowed* etc. *under the bridge*: see WATER *n.* *water under the bridge*: see WATER *n.* *weighbridge*: see WEIGH *v.* 8 *post-office bridge, Wheatstone bridge*, etc.

Comb.: **bridge-bote** *Hist.* a tax for the repair of bridges; **bridge-building** *fig.* the promotion of friendly relations, esp. between countries; **bridge circuit** = sense 8 above; **bridge-deck** = sense 6 above; **bridgehead** a position held on the opposite side of a river etc. in advance of one's main forces; *fig.* an initial position established beyond some dividing feature, as a basis for further advance. **bridge-house** *Hist.* a house connected with a bridge; *spec.* the establishment formerly concerned with the care and repair of London Bridge; **bridge-man, bridgemaster** an officer having control of a bridge (formerly, in some boroughs, a member of the corporation); **bridge passage** a transitional passage in a musical or literary composition; **bridgeward** *Hist.* the keeper or warden of a bridge; **bridgework** (the insertion of) a dental bridge.

bridgeless *a.* E19.

bridge /brɪdʒ/ *n.*[2] L19. [Prob. of eastern Mediterranean origin.] A card-game derived from whist, in which one player's cards are exposed at a certain point and are thereafter played by his or her partner; now usu. = *contract bridge* below.

auction bridge: in which the players bid for the right to name trumps, and all tricks won count towards game whether contracted for or not. **contract bridge**: in which the players bid for the right to name trumps, and tricks won count towards game only if contracted for. *duplicate bridge*: see DUPLICATE *a.*

Comb.: **bridge-roll** a small soft bread roll.

bridge /brɪdʒ/ *v.t.* [OE *brycgian*, f. BRIDGE *n.*[1]] 1 Be or make a bridge over. OE. b Span as with a bridge. M19. 2 Form (a way) by means of a bridge. *rare.* M17.

1 P. MATTHIESSEN A canal bridged here and there by ten-foot granite slabs. b M. TWAIN A speculator bridged a couple of barrels with a board. *fig.*: B. C. BRODIE To bridge over the space which separates the known from the unknown. *bridge a gap*: see GAP *n.*

bridgeable *a.* M19. **bridging** *vbl n.* (*a*) the action of the vb; (*b*) *Mountaineering* a method of climbing chimneys etc. with legs astride: LME. **bridging** *ppl a.* that bridges something; *bridging loan*, a loan made to cover the short interval between buying a house etc. and selling another: E19.

Bridgettine /ˈbrɪdʒətɪn/ *n.* & *a.* M16. [med.L *Brigittinus* adj., f. *Brigitta* of Sweden (St Bridget), 1303–73: see -INE[1].] (A member, usu. a nun) of a religious order founded by St Bridget.

bridle /ˈbrʌɪd(ə)l/ *n.* [OE *bridel* = OFris. *brīdel*, (M)Du. *breidel*, OHG *brittil*, f. WGmc, f. Gmc base of BRAID *v.*[1]: see -LE[1].] 1 The gear by which a horse etc. is controlled and guided, comprising headstall, bit, and rein. OE. 2 *fig.* A restraint, a curb. ME. 3 A securing rope or cord etc. Chiefly *Naut.*: (*a*) a loop of rope etc. attached to a spar etc., by which a line can be attached; (*b*) the end part of a fixed mooring, which can be secured to a vessel. ME. 4 = BRANKS 1. Also *scold's bridle.* E17. 5 A ligament or membrane restricting the motion of a bodily part. L17. 6 The action or gesture of bridling (BRIDLE *v.* 2). M18.

1 *double bridle, draw bridle, snaffle-bridle*, etc. *turn bridle*: see TURN *v.* 2 BACON The reverence of a mans self is, next religion, the chiefest Bridle of all Vices. J. A. FROUDE He kept his tongue under a bridle.

Comb.: **bridle-hand** the hand which holds the bridle in riding; **bridle-path, -road, -way**: a thoroughfare fit for riders but not vehicles; **bridle-rein** a rein attached to the bit of a bridle; *bridle-road, -way*: see *bridle-path* above; **bridle-wise** *a.* (*US*) (of a horse) readily guided by a touch of the bridle.

bridleless /-l-l-/ *a.* LME.

bridle /ˈbrʌɪd(ə)l/ *v.* [OE *brīdlian*, f. prec.] 1 *v.t.* Put a bridle on, equip with a bridle; *fig.* curb, check, restrain, hold *in.* OE. 2a *v.i.* Express offence, wounded pride, etc., by throwing up the head and drawing in the chin; assume a dignified or offended manner. Also foll. by *up.* LME. †b *v.t.* Move (the head etc., oneself) thus. L15–M19.

1 D. HUME Forts were erected in order to bridle Rochelle. F. M. FORD A sudden explosion of the passion that had been bridled all his life. 2a DICKENS Everybody bridled up at this remark. B. CHATWIN If she saw him bridling with annoyance, she would change the subject.

bridler *n.* L16.

bridoon /brɪˈduːn/ *n.* Also **bradoon** /brəˈduːn/. M18. [Fr. *bridon*, f. as BRIDE *n.*[2]: see -OON.] The snaffle in a double bridle.

Brie /briː/ *n.* Also **b-.** M19. [An agricultural district in northern France.] A soft creamy cheese with a white mould skin, orig. and esp. made in Brie.

brief /briːf/ *n.*[1] See also BREVE, BRIEVE. ME. [AN *bref*, OFr. *brief*, f. late L *breve* dispatch, note, use as n. of neut. of L *brevis*: see BRIEF *a.* & *adv.*] 1 *Hist.* An official or legal letter of authority; a royal mandate; a writ, a summons. ME. b Letters patent issued by the British monarch as Governor of the Church of England, licensing a collection in churches for a specific object of charity. L16. 2 A disciplinary letter from the Pope to an individual or community (less formal than a *bull*). LME. †3 *gen.* A letter, a dispatch, a note; writing, something written. LME–L18. †4 *Mus.* A short note; a breve. LME–M17. 5 A short account or summary, a synopsis. Now *US* (exc. as below). M16. 6 A list, a catalogue, etc. *arch.* L16. 7 *Law.* A summary of the facts and legal points in a case, drawn up for counsel; a piece of work for a barrister; *US Law* a written statement of the arguments for a case. M17. b *gen.* A set or summary of instructions etc.; an appointed task; *esp.* a set of instructions for carrying out a military operation. M19.

7 *dock brief*: see DOCK *n.*[4] **hold a brief for** be retained as counsel for; *fig.* wish or be obliged to argue in favour of (usu. in neg. contexts). **take a brief** accept the conduct of a case. *watching brief*: see WATCH *v.* b D. JACOBSON My special brief was to take care of the political prisoners. *Times* [He] rounds on the .. Authority for exceeding its brief. JO GRIMOND A minister opening a debate must speak from a prepared brief.

Comb.: **brief-bag** a bag in which a barrister carries briefs; **briefcase** a rectangular case for carrying papers, documents, etc.

briefless *a.* without a brief, (of a barrister etc.) unemployed E19.

brief /briːf/ *n.*[2] LME. [f. the adj.] 1 *in brief*, in short, briefly. LME. †2 *The* little that need be said etc. L16–E17. 3 In *pl.* Short underpants or knickers. M20.

brief /briːf/ *a.* & *adv.* ME. [AN *bref*, OFr. *brief* (mod. *bref*), f. L *brevis* short, brief. The origin of sense A.4 is obscure.] **A** *adj.* 1 Of short duration, quickly passing. ME. †b Hasty, expeditious. LME–E17. 2 Short in (spatial) extent; curtailed, limited. ME. 3 Consisting of or employing few words; concise in expression. LME. 4 Rife, prevalent, epidemic. *dial.* E18.

1 TOLKIEN In his living face they caught a brief vision of the power and majesty of the kings of stone. W. S. CHURCHILL Their freedom was brief The British refused to recognise the republic. 2 SIR W. SCOTT Wearing the briefest petticoat of any nymph of St. Ronan's. 3 S. KAUFFMANN A brief note simply to say that they had arrived safely. J. D. SALINGER As brief as a gatekeeper at a Trappist monastery. **be brief** speak in few words.

B *adv.* Briefly; in brief. Now *rare.* M16.

briefly *adv.* shortly, in a few words LME. **briefness** *n.* (*a*) brevity, conciseness; †(*b*) quickness: LME.

brief /briːf/ *v.t.* M19. [f. BRIEF *n.*[1]] 1 Reduce to the form of a legal brief; put into a brief. M19. 2 Give a brief to (a barrister), instruct by brief; retain as counsel in a suit. M19. 3 Instruct or inform thoroughly; give precise instructions to, esp. with regard to a military operation etc. M19.

briefing *n.* (*a*) the action of the vb; (*b*) a meeting for this: M19.

brier /ˈbrʌɪə/ *n.*[1] Also **briar.** [OE (Anglian) *brēr*, (WS) *brǣr*, of unkn. origin.] 1 A prickly bush, esp. of a wild rose. OE. 2 A branch or twig of a wild rose etc. ME. 3 Prickly bushes collectively. LME. 4 *fig.* In *pl.* Troubles, vexations. *arch.* E16.

1 **Austrian brier** an orange-yellow rose, *Rosa foetida*, with an unpleasant scent. **green brier** a vine of the genus *Smilax* of the lily family, esp. *S.*

rotundifolia. **sensitive brier** an ornamental leguminous plant of the genus *Schrankia*, with pink or purple flowers and sensitive leaves. **sweet-brier** any of several roses with fragrant-smelling leaves; esp. *Rosa rubiginosa*, a rose with deep pink flowers that is often cultivated; also called *eglantine*.

Comb.: **brier-rose** a dogrose.

briered *a.* covered or overgrown with briers; entangled in briers: M16. **briery** *a.* full of or consisting of thorns or briers; thorny; vexatious: ME.

brier /ˈbrʌɪə/ *n.*[2] Also **briar**. M19. [Fr. *bruyère* heath, ult. f. Gaulish: assim. to prec.] **1** A southern European shrub or small tree, *Erica arborea*, whose root is used for making tobacco-pipes. Also called *tree heath*. M19. **2** A pipe made of the wood of the brier. L19.

brieve /briːv/ *n.* E17. [Var. of BRIEF *n.*[1]] *Sc. Law* (now *Hist.*). A Chancery writ directing trial by jury of a specified question.

brig /brɪɡ/ *n.*[1] E18. [Shortened f. BRIGANTINE *n.*[1]] **1** Orig., = BRIGANTINE *n.*[1] 1. Now, a two-masted square-rigged vessel with an additional lower fore-and-aft sail on a gaff and boom to the mainmast. E18. **2** A place of detention, orig. on board a ship; a naval or military prison. *slang* (orig. *US*). M19.

1 hermaphrodite brig = BRIGANTINE *n.*[1] 3.

brig *n.*[2] see BRIDGE *n.*[1]

brigade /brɪˈɡeɪd/ *n.* & *v.* M17. [Fr. f. It. *brigata* troop, company, f. *brigare* contend, be busy with, f. *briga* strife, contention: see -ADE.] **A** *n.* †**1** A company or set of people. Only in M17. **2** A large body of troops; *spec.* a subdivision of an army. In the British army: an infantry unit consisting of usu. three battalions and forming part of a division; a corresponding armoured unit. M17. **3** A uniformed or organized band of workers etc. E19.

Phrases: *Boys' Brigade*: see BOY *n. fire brigade*: see FIRE *n. International Brigade*: see INTERNATIONAL *a.* NAVAL *brigade. Red Brigade(s)*: see RED *a.*

Comb.: **brigade-major** a staff officer attached to a brigade to assist the brigadier in command.

B *v.t.* Form into a brigade. E19.

brigadier /brɪɡəˈdɪə/ *n.* Also (esp. in titles) **B-**. L17. [Fr., f. as prec. + -IER.] An officer commanding a brigade; (a titular rank granted to) a staff officer of similar standing, above colonel and below major-general. Formerly also *brigadier general*.

Comb.: **brigadier general** (*a*) *Hist.* see above; (*b*) an officer ranking above a colonel and below a major-general in the US Army, Air Force, and Marine Corps; **brigadier wig** *Hist.* a full wig tied back in two curls.

brigalow /ˈbrɪɡələʊ/ *n. Austral.* M19. [Perh. f. Kamilaroi *burigal*.] Any of various acacias forming thick scrub.

brigand /ˈbrɪɡ(ə)nd/ *n.* & *v.* LME. [Fr. f. It. *brigante*, orig. = foot-soldier, use as n. of pres. pple of *brigare*: see BRIGADE.] **A** *n.* †**1** A lightly armed irregular foot-soldier. LME–L18. **2** A bandit or robber, *esp.* one of a band living by pillage and ransom. LME. **B** *v.t.* In *pass.* Be attacked by brigands. *rare*. L19.

brigandage *n.* the practice of brigands, banditry, pillage; brigands collectively: E17. **brigandish** *a.* L19. **brigandism** *n.* the life of brigands, brigandage M19. **brigandry** *n.* = BRIGANDISM E20.

brigandine /ˈbrɪɡ(ə)ndiːn/ *n.* Also **-tine** /-tiːn/. LME. [Fr., or its source It. *brigantina*, f. as prec.: see -INE[4].] A coat of mail, esp. one made of iron rings or plates attached to canvas etc.

brigantine /ˈbrɪɡ(ə)ntiːn/ *n.*[1] E16. [OFr. *brigandine* (mod. *brigantin*) or its source It. *brigantino*, f. *brigante*: see BRIGAND, -INE[4].] **1** A small vessel equipped for both sailing and rowing, employed for espionage, piracy, etc. *obs.* exc. *Hist.* E16. **2** *loosely*. A foreign vessel, as a galleon etc. M16. **3** A two-masted vessel with a square-rigged foremast and fore-and-aft rigged mainmast. L16.

brigantine *n.*[2] var. of BRIGANDINE.

bright /brʌɪt/ *a.* & *n.* [OE *beorht*, (Anglian) *berht*, (Northumb.) *breht* = OS *ber(a)ht*, OHG *beraht*, *-eht*, ON *bjartr*, Goth. *bairhts*, f. Gmc.] **A** *adj.* **1** Emitting or reflecting much light, shining; pervaded by light, sunlit; (of wine etc.) clear, translucent. OE. **b** *fig.* Lit up with happiness, gladness, hope, etc.; hopeful, encouraging, cheering. M18. †**2** Clear or luminous to mental perception. OE–M18. **3** Of sound: clear; shrill, giving (undue) prominence to high frequencies. OE. **4** Illustrious, glorious, splendid. OE. **5** Of a person: beautiful, handsome. *arch.* ME. **6** Vividly or brilliantly coloured. Of a colour: intense, vivid. ME. **b** Of tobacco: having a light shade or colour. Orig. *US*. M18. **7** Of a person, a face etc.: cheerful, animated, vivacious. E17. **8** Of thought, conversation, writing, etc.: witty, clever, imaginative, sparkling. E18. **9** Displaying great intelligence; quick-witted; talented. M18.

1 TINDALE *Rev.* 22:16 The bright mornynge starre. J. BETJEMAN The church is bright with candlelight. E. BIRNEY Dusty September orchards . . bright with apples. B. PLAIN Even on the brightest afternoon, the bulb . . had to be lit. **bright lights** urban places of entertainment. **brightwork** polished metalwork on ships etc. **b** I. MURDOCH A sad eclipse of all their bright hopes. *bright-eyed and bushy-tailed*: see BUSHY *a. honour bright*: see HONOUR *n.* **look on the bright side** *colloq.* be optimistic or cheerful. 4 SHAKES. *Lucr.* Troy had been bright with fame, and not with fire. 5 COLERIDGE A bright lady, surpassingly fair. 6 HUGH WALPOLE Light grey flannel trousers . . showing bright purple socks. J. RHYS She had a bright patchwork counterpane. **bright-line brown-eye** = *tomato moth* s.v. TOMATO *n. paint in bright colours*: see COLOUR *n.* 7 SHAKES. *Macb.* Be bright and jovial among your guests to-night. S. LEACOCK The bright smiling faces of working people. **bright young thing** a fashionable member of the younger generation (esp. in the 1920s and 1930s) noted for exuberant and outrageous behaviour. 8 A. G. GARDINER I thought of a bright thing to say now and then. 9 JILLY COOPER They're also quite bright: you can't get in unless you have five O's and three A-levels. G. F. NEWMAN It wasn't very bright threatening to break Evans's arms. *iron.*: J. M. KEYNES The bright idea of reducing Economics to a mathematical application of the hedonistic calculus of Bentham!

B *n.* Brightness, light. *arch.* ME.

brightish *a.* L16. **brightly** *adv.* in a bright manner, with brightness OE. **brightness** *n.* OE. **brightsome** *a.* (*arch.*) showing brightness, brightish M16. **brightsomeness** *n.* (*arch.*) M16.

bright /brʌɪt/ *v. arch.* [OE *beorhtian*, f. BRIGHT *a.*] †**1** *v.i.* Be bright, shine. OE–ME. **2** *v.t.* Make bright. OE.

bright /brʌɪt/ *adv.* [OE *beorhte*, f. the adj.] Brightly.

bright and early very early in the morning.

brighten /ˈbrʌɪt(ə)n/ *v.t.* & *i.* [OE *ġe)beorhtnan* v.i., *-ian* v.t., f. as BRIGHT *a.* Later f. BRIGHT *a.*: see -EN[5].] Make or become bright(er). Often *fig.*, make or become more cheerful, lively, hopeful, etc. Freq. foll. by *up*.

brightener *n.* L18.

Bright's disease /ˈbrʌɪts dɪˌziːz/ *n. phr.* M19. [Richard *Bright* (1789–1858), Eng. physician.] *Med.* Kidney disease associated with albuminuria; *esp.* glomerulonephritis.

brigue /briːɡ/ *n.* LME. [(O)Fr. f. It. *briga*: see BRIGADE.] †**1** Strife, contention. LME–L17. **2** Intrigue, faction. Now *rare* or *obs.* M17.

†**brigue** *v.* LME. [f. prec. or Fr. *briguer*: sense 1 may repr. a different wd.] **1** *v.t.* Ensnare. Only in LME. **2** *v.i.* Intrigue; solicit. Chiefly *Sc.* L16–M19.

brill /brɪl/ *n.* Pl. same. L15. [Origin unkn.] A flatfish, *Scophthalmus rhombus*, resembling the turbot.

brill /brɪl/ *a. slang.* L20. [Abbrev. of BRILLIANT *a.*] Excellent, outstanding.

†**brillant** *n.*, *a.* var. of BRILLIANT *n.*, *a.*

brillante /brɪˈlɑːnteɪ/ *adv.* & *a.* M18. [It.] *Mus.* (A direction:) in a showy or sparkling style.

brilliance /ˈbrɪlj(ə)ns/ *n.* M18. [f. BRILLIANT *a.*: see -ANCE.] Brilliant quality; intense or sparkling brightness, radiance, or splendour. Freq. *fig.*

Also **brilliancy** *n.* M18.

brilliant /ˈbrɪlj(ə)nt/ *n.* Also †**brillant**. L17. [Fr. *brillant*, f. as next.] †**1** Brilliance. Only in L17. **2** A diamond of the finest cut and brilliance; *spec.* one cut with horizontal upper and lower faces joined by facets. L17. **3** A former very small size of type equal to about 3½ points. L19.

brilliant /ˈbrɪlj(ə)nt/ *a.* Also †**brillant**. L17. [Fr. *brillant* pres. pple of *briller* shine, f. It. *brillare*, prob. ult. f. L *beryllus* BERYL.] **1** Brightly shining; glittering, sparkling, lustrous. L17. **2** *fig.* Splendid, celebrated; *spec.* distinguished by cleverness, talent, etc. M18. **b** Excellent. *colloq.* L20.

2 ARNOLD BENNETT Edwin's own suggestions never seemed very brilliant, . . but they were never silly. C. POTOK This boy . . was brilliant, literally a genius. **b** S. TOWNSEND I allowed Pandora to visit me in my darkened bedroom. We had a brilliant kissing session.

brilliantly *adv.* E19.

brilliant /ˈbrɪlj(ə)nt/ *v.t. rare.* M18. [f. the n.] Cut (a diamond) as a brilliant.

brilliantine /ˈbrɪlj(ə)ntiːn/ *n.* L19. [Fr. *brillantine*, f. *brillant* BRILLIANT *a.*] **1** A cosmetic for imparting a gloss to the hair. L19. **2** A shiny fabric for dresses etc. *N. Amer.* L19.

brilliantined *a.* made glossy with brilliantine E20.

brim /brɪm/ *n.*[1] ME. [Origin uncertain: corresp. in sense to MHG *brem* (G *Bräme*, *Brähme*), ON *barmr* edge.] **1** The border, margin, edge, brink, etc., of the sea or any piece of water, or *gen.* of other things. Now *obs.* or *dial.* exc. as transf. use of sense 2. ME. **2** The edge, margin, or lip of a cup, bowl, basin, or anything of similar shape, artificial or natural. LME. **3** The upper surface of water. *arch.* M16. **4** The projecting edge of a hat. L16.

1 SPENSER Upon the brim of his brode-plated shield. JER. TAYLOR He . . is at the margin and brim of that state of finall reprobation. 2 AV *2 Chron.* 4:2 He made a molten Sea of ten cubites, from brim to brim. *fig.*: SHAKES. *Ant. & Cl.* He will fill thy wishes to the brim With principalities. **pelvic brim** the rim between the upper and lower parts of the pelvis. 3 SIR W. SCOTT Not lighter does the swallow skim Along the smooth lake's level brim.

Comb.: **brim-full**, (*arch.*) **brimful** *a.* full to the brim, on the point of overflowing.

brimless *a.* E17. **brimmed** *a.* (of a hat etc.) having a brim (of a specified kind) E17. **brimmy** *a.* (of a hat) having a wide brim; broad-brimmed: L19.

brim *n.*[2] see BREAM *n.*

brim *a.* var. of BREME.

brim /brɪm/ *v.* Infl. **-mm-**. E17. [f. BRIM *n.*[1]] **1** *v.t.* Fill to the brim. E17. **2** *v.i.* Be or become full to the brim (*with*). E19.

2 brim over overflow.

brimming *ppl a.* (*a*) that rises to the brim of its vessel, basin, bed, etc.; (*b*) (of a container) full to overflowing: M17.

brimborion /brɪmˈbɔːrɪən/ *n.* Also **-rium** /-rɪəm/. M17. [Fr., earlier *breborion*, alt. of med.L *breviarium* BREVIARY.] A thing without use or value; trash, nonsense.

brimmer /ˈbrɪmə/ *n.* Now *arch.* & *dial.* M17. [f. BRIM *n.*[1], *v.* + -ER[1].] **1** A brimming cup or goblet. M17. **2** A hat (*spec.* a straw hat) with a brim. M17.

brimstone /ˈbrɪmst(ə)n, -stəʊn/ *n.* [Late OE *brynstān*, prob. f. *bryne* (= ON *bruni*) burning (f. as BURN *v.*) + STONE *n.*] **1** Sulphur; *esp.* (otherwise *arch.*) burning sulphur, (the fuel of) hell-fire. LOE. **b** *fig.* Fire, passion. E17. †**2** A virago, a spitfire; a promiscuous woman. L17–E19. **3** In full *brimstone butterfly*. A pierid butterfly, *Gonepteryx rhamni*, with sulphur-yellow wings. E18.

Comb.: *brimstone butterfly*: see sense 3 above; **brimstone moth** a geometrid moth, *Opisthograptis luteolata*, with yellow wings; **brimstone-wort** a yellow-flowered umbellifer of the genus *Peucedanum*, sulphur-wort.

brimstony *a.* of, pertaining to, or resembling brimstone; sulphureous, fiery: LME.

brinded /ˈbrɪndɪd/ *a. arch.* See also BRANDED. ME. [Prob. of Scand. origin: cf. ON *brǫndóttr* brindled, f. *brandr* burning, and *brandkrossóttr* brindled, having a white cross on the forehead.] = BRINDLED.

brindle /ˈbrɪnd(ə)l/ *a.* & *n.* L17. [Back-form. f. next.] **A** *adj.* = BRINDLED. L17. **B** *n.* (A dog etc. of) brindled colour. L17.

brindled /ˈbrɪnd(ə)ld/ *a.* L17. [Alt. of BRINDED, prob. by assoc. w. *grizzled*, *speckled*, etc.] Of a tawny or brownish colour with (esp. indistinct) streaks or spots of a different hue; *gen.* streaked, spotted, (*with*).

brindled beauty a European geometrid moth, *Lycia hirtaria*, with grey-brown banded wings.

brine /brʌɪn/ *n.* & *v.* [OE *brīne* = MDu. *brīne* (Du. *brijn*), of unkn. origin.] A *n.* 1 Water saturated or strongly impregnated with salt; salt water. OE. 2 (The water of) the sea. Usu. *poet.* L16. 3 (Salty) tears. *poet.* L16.

Comb.: **brine-pan** (*a*) a shallow iron vessel in which salt is evaporated; (*b*) a salt-pan; **brine-shrimp** any of various branchiopods of the genus *Artemia*, inhabiting salt lakes, brine-pans, etc.

B *v.t.* Steep in or saturate with brine. M16.

brinish *a.* of or like brine, briny L16.

Brinell /brɪˈnɛl/ *n.* E20. [J. A. *Brinell* (1849–1925), Swed. engineer.] Used *attrib.* with ref. to a test for hardness in which a steel ball is pressed into the material and the diameter of the indentation measured.

bring /brɪŋ/ *v.t.* Pa. t. & pple **brought** /brɔːt/, (*dial.*) **brung** /brʌŋ/. [OE *bringan* (pa. t. *brōhte*, pple *brōht*) = OFris. *bringa*, OS, OHG *bringan* (Du. *brengen*, G *bringen*), Goth. *briggan*, f. Gmc.] 1 Cause to come, come with, or convey, by carrying, leading, impelling, attracting, etc. OE. b Escort, accompany on his or her way. *obs.* exc. *dial.* LME. 2 Prefer (a charge); initiate (legal action); advance (an argument etc.). OE. 3 Produce as a consequence, cause to have, result in; be sold for (a price). OE. 4 Bear (young, fruit, etc.), yield, produce; = *bring forth* below. ME. 5 Cause to come *from*, *into*, *out of*, *to*, etc., a state or condition, *to* an action; cause to become; cause, induce, persuade (usu. a reluctant person) *to be* or *to do*. ME. †6 Deduce, infer, derive. L16–E18. 7 *Naut.* Cause to come or go into a certain position or direction. L17.

1 DRYDEN I . . shall in Triumph come From conquer'd Greece, and bring her Trophies home. THACKERAY Those lines . . brought tears into the Duchess's eyes. TENNYSON She brought strange news. J. T. STORY Finally I brought both fists down together and he fell like an axed pig. I. MCEWAN The narrow passage-way had brought them on to a large . . square. **bring-and-buy sale, stall**, etc.: at which customers bring things for sale and buy what others have brought. *bring home the bacon*: see BACON *n.* 1. *bring into line*: see LINE *n.*[2] *bring to bay*: see BAY *n.*[1] 2. *bring to light*: see LIGHT *n.* **bring to mind** (cause oneself to) remember. *brought to bed*: see BED *n.* 2 M. EDGEWORTH Arguments . . brought by his companions in their . . master's justification. 3 TENNYSON The loss that brought us pain. J. UPDIKE Gifts bring men, men bring bullets, bullets bring oppression. 4 COVERDALE *Hab.* 3:17 The londe shall bringe no corne. 5 COVERDALE *Judg.* 3:30 Thus were the Moabites broughte vnder the hande of the children of Israel. J. BUTLER Persons . . by a course of vice, bring themselves into new difficulties. C. THIRLWALL The prosecutors brought Demosthenes to trial first. D. W. JERROLD A woman may be brought to forgive bigamy, but not a joke. D. LODGE Some kind of physical malformation which the man could not even bring himself to describe. *bring a person to his or her senses*: see SENSE *n.* *bring home to*: see HOME *adv.* **bring into being** cause to exist. *bring into play*: see PLAY *n.* **bring into the world** give birth to, (of a midwife etc.) deliver. *bring to a head*: see HEAD *n.* 28. *bring to bear*: see BEAR *v.*[1] *bring to book*: see BOOK *n.* *bring to* GRIEF. *bring to life*: see LIFE *n.* *bring to pass*: see PASS *n.*[2] *bring to utterance*: see UTTERANCE *n.*[2] 6 SHAKES. *1 Hen. VI* He From John of Gaunt doth bring his pedigree. 7 DEFOE Her main-mast and fore-mast were brought by the board. *bring the starboard* (or *port*) *tacks aboard*: see TACK *n.*[1] *bring the tacks aboard*: see TACK *n.*[1]

With advs. in specialized senses: **bring about** (*a*) cause to happen, accomplish; †(*b*) complete by a revolving; (*c*) turn round; reverse (a ship); convert. **bring back** cause to return, recall, bring to mind. **bring down** (*a*) cause to fall or collapse (*bring down the house*, *bring the house down* (Theatr.), get loud applause); (*b*) cause (a flying bird, an aircraft, etc.) to fall to the ground; cause (a penalty etc.) to fall *on*; kill, wound; overthrow; abase; (*c*) lower (a price etc.); (*d*) continue (a record etc.) *to* a point in time. **bring forth** (*a*) produce, yield, give birth to, cause; †(*b*) utter; advance as an argument etc.; †(*c*) bring to light, expose to public view. **bring forward** (*a*) draw attention to; (*b*) move to an earlier date or time, transfer from a previous page or account. **bring in** (*a*) introduce (a custom, fashion, topic, legislation, etc., †a person), adduce; produce as profit or increase; (*b*) pronounce (a verdict; a person *guilty* etc.). **bring off** (*a*) rescue (*arch.* in *gen.* sense), *spec.* conduct away from a ship, wreck, etc.; (*b*) conduct successfully, succeed in, achieve. **bring on** (*a*) introduce (a topic for discussion, etc.), cause, bring into action; (*b*) advance the progress of. **bring out** †(*a*) produce, yield; (*b*) express, publish, make known, exhibit clearly, make prominent; (*c*) introduce (a girl) to society. **bring over** win over, convert; **bring round** (*a*) restore to consciousness; (*b*) win over. **bring through** treat or tend successfully through illness etc. **bring to** (*a*) *v.phr.t.* & *i.* check the motion of; come to a stop; (*b*) *v.phr.t.* restore to consciousness. **bring under** subdue. **bring up** (*a*) *v.phr.t.* supervise the training of (a child) in habits, manners, etc.; be responsible for or care for to the point of maturity; in *pass.* also, grow up, esp. in a particular place or manner; (*b*) *v.phr.t.* call attention to; (re)introduce (a topic etc.); cause to appear in court etc.; (*c*) *v.phr.t.* vomit; (*d*) *v.phr.t.* & *i.* (orig. *Naut.*) (cause to) come to a stop, pull up; (*e*) *bring up short*: see SHORT *adv.*; (*f*) *bring up the rear*: see REAR *n.*; (*g*) *bring up with a round turn*: see ROUND *a.* **bring up to date** provide with what is needed to cover the most recent developments.

bringer *n.* ME.

†**brinie** *n.* var. of BYRNIE.

brinjal /ˈbrɪndʒɔːl/ *n.* E17. [Ult. f. Port. *berinjela*, f. as AUBERGINE.] Esp. in the Indian subcontinent: an aubergine.

brinjarry /brɪnˈdʒɑːri/ *n.* *arch.* Also **bunjara** /bʌnˈdʒɑːrə/. M17. [Alt. of Deccan Urdu *banjāra* f. Hind., ult. f. Skt *vaṇijā* trade.] A travelling grain and salt merchant of the Deccan in southern India.

brink /brɪŋk/ *n.* ME. [ON *brekka* slope corresp. to MLG *brink* edge of a field, (brow of) a hill (whence G dial. *Brink* hill), MDu. *brinc* (Du. *brink* grassland), of unkn. origin.] 1 The margin or bank of a body of water; *gen.* an edge, a margin, a border. (Now usu. only when steep, passing into sense 3.) ME. 2 *fig.* The verge *of* some state, event, action, time, etc.; the point *of being*, *doing*, etc. ME. 3 The edge, margin, or border of a steep place, such as a precipice, chasm, etc. LME. 4 The brim of a vessel. *obs.* exc. *dial.* LME.

1 BYRON All these are coop'd within one Quarto's brink. J. MASEFIELD To halt at the chattering brook, in the tall green fern at the brink. 2 DICKENS She is on the brink of being sold into wretchedness for life. W. CATHER Hard times that brought everyone . . to the brink of despair. D. ACHESON The United States hesitated on the brink of action. *teeter on the brink*: see TEETER *v.* 1b. **the brink** the verge of (esp. nuclear) war. 3 MILTON The warie fiend Stood on the brink of Hell and look'd a while. T. H. HUXLEY The church . . is now on the very brink of the cliff. TOLKIEN The places behind where there was a black brink and an empty fall into nothingness.

brinkmanship *n.* [-MANSHIP] a policy or the art of advancing to the very brink of some action (esp. war) but not engaging in it M20.

briny /ˈbrʌɪni/ *a.* & *n.* L16. [f. BRINE *n.* + -Y[1].] A *adj.* Of or pertaining to brine or the sea; saturated with salt. L16. B *n.* *The* sea, *the* ocean. *slang.* M19.

brio /ˈbriːəʊ/ *n.* M18. [It.] Vivacity, liveliness, verve.

See also CON BRIO.

brioche /briːˈɒʃ, ˈbriːɒʃ/ *n.* E19. [Fr.] A small usu. round sweet cake made with light yeast dough.

briony *n.* var. of BRYONY.

briquet /brike/ *n.*[1] Pl. pronounced same. E19. [Fr.] A steel for striking light from a flint; a representation of this, esp. as a heraldic ornament.

briquet *n.*[2] var. of next.

briquette /brɪˈkɛt/ *n.* & *v.* Also **-et**. L19. [Fr., dim. of *brique* BRICK *n.*: see -ETTE.] A *n.* A small block or slab, esp. of compressed coal-dust for use as fuel. L19. B *v.t.* Form into briquettes. L19.

brisé /brize/ *n.* Pl. pronounced same. L18. [Fr., pa. pple of *briser* break.] *Ballet.* A movement in which the feet or legs are lightly beaten together in the air.

brise-soleil /brizsɔlɛːj, briːzsɒˈleɪ/ *n.* Pl. pronounced same. M20. [Fr., lit. 'sun-breaker'.] A device (as a perforated screen, louvre, etc.) for shutting out direct or excessive sunlight.

brish /brɪʃ/ *v.t.* & *i.* *dial.* M17. [Var. of BRUSH *v.*[2]] = BRUSH *v.*[2] 3. Chiefly as *brishing* vbl n.

brisk /brɪsk/ *a.* & *v.* L16. [Prob. f. Fr. BRUSQUE.] A *adj.* 1 Quick, smart, or efficient in movement or action; lively, rapid, active. L16. b In an unfavourable sense: curt, brusque, peremptory. Also (now *rare* or *obs.*) transient; fast-living; hasty. E17. 2 Agreeably sharp to the taste, effervescent. Also, (of the air etc.) fresh, keen. L16. †3 Spruce, smartly dressed. L16–E17.

1 P. KAVANAGH Demand for all sorts of cattle was brisk. D. DU MAURIER He whipped the horses to a brisker pace. P. H. JOHNSON This brisk and officer-like behaviour. W. TREVOR She wished she was grown-up, brisk and able to cope. b SHAKES. *Twel. N.* These most brisk and giddy-paced times. C. CIBBER The briskest loose Liver or intemperate Man. C. ISHERWOOD Her tone was peremptory and brisk. 2 SHAKES. *2 Hen. IV* A cup of wine that's brisk and fine. L. DURRELL It is brisk weather, clear as waterglass.

B *v.t.* & *i.* †1 Smarten (*up*), dress smartly. L16–M19. 2 Make or become (more) brisk or lively; quicken, enliven; move or behave briskly. Freq. foll. by *up*. E17.

2 R. L. STEVENSON Modestine brisked up her pace. H. L. WILSON As I brisked out of bed the following morning. T. ROETHKE A flicker of fire brisked by a dusty wind.

brisken *v.i.* & *t.* become or make brisk (also foll. by *up*), = BRISK *v.* 2 M18. **briskly** *adv.* L16. **briskness** *n.* M17. **brisky** *a.* brisk, lively, smart L16.

brisket /ˈbrɪskɪt/ *n.* ME. [Perh. f. ON *brjósk* (Norw., Da. *brusk*) cartilage, gristle + -ET[1].] 1 The breast of an animal, esp. as a joint of meat. ME. 2 The human breast. *Sc. colloq.* L18.

brisling /ˈbrɪslɪŋ, ˈbrɪz-/ *n.* Also **bristling**. Pl. same, **-s**. E20. [Norw., Da.] The sprat, *Sprattus sprattus*.

bristle /ˈbrɪs(ə)l/ *n.* ME. [f. as BIRSE + -EL[1]. Prob. in OE: cf. (M)Du. *borstel.*] 1 Any of the stiff hairs that grow on the back and sides of the pig, esp. as used in brushes etc. ME. 2 *gen.* Any short stiff hair or filament, e.g. of a man's short-cropped beard; a filament of a brush, of whatever material; a seta; bristles collectively. ME.

2 R. CHANDLER A black brush with a few blond hairs in its black bristles. J. FULLER Patches of unshaven bristle on his jowls.

Comb.: **bristle-bird** an Australian reed-warbler of the genus *Dasyornis*; **bristlecone pine** a very slow-growing, shrubby pine, *Pinus aristata*, of western N. America, important for dendrochronology; **bristle-fern** any of various chiefly tropical ferns of the genus *Trichomanes*, with a hairlike receptacle protruding from the indusium; **bristle-grass** a grass of the genus *Setaria*; **bristletail** an apterygote insect of the orders Thysanura (including the silverfish and firebrat, more fully *three-pronged bristletail*) or Diplura (more fully *two-pronged bristletail*); **bristle-worm** a polychaete.

bristle-like *a.* resembling (that of) a bristle or bristles M19. **bristly** *a.* covered or set with bristles; of the nature of or like bristles: LME.

bristle /ˈbrɪs(ə)l/ *v.*[1] See also BRUSTLE *v.*[2] ME. [f. the n.] I *v.t.* 1 Cover, set, or tip with bristles; make prickly or bristly; *fig.* set thickly as with bristles. ME. 2 Erect (hair etc.) stiffly like bristles; *fig.* cause to show anger or hostility. Also foll. by *up*. L16.

1 HOBBES The brissled Ranks Of th' armed Greeks. LYTTON He would bristle all the land with castles. K. KESEY His arms . . are sunburned and bristled with curly orange hairs. 2 SHAKES. *John* Now . . Doth dogged war bristle his angry crest. C. KINGSLEY He would . . bristle up his feathers, just as a cock-robin would.

II *v.i.* 3 Become or stand stiff like bristles. L15. 4 Raise the bristles as a sign of anger or excitement; *fig.* be roused to temper or hostility. Also foll. by *up*. M16. 5 Be or become bristly; be thickly set (as) with bristles; chiefly *fig.*, be covered, teem, abound *with*. E17.

3 G. ORWELL White moustaches that bristled forward like those of a prawn. W. S. CHURCHILL Solid squares with eighteen foot pikes bristling in every direction. J. BRAINE There was something about its tone which . . made the hairs on the nape of my neck

bristle. 4 THOMAS HUGHES There now! don't bristle up like a hedgehog. J. FENTON My dog had halted, Its skin bristling. 5 CARLYLE All France to the utmost borders bristles with bayonets. C. I. LEWIS Treatises . . bristling with . . difficulties. K. A. PORTER Faded dry hair bristling with wire hairpins. U. LE GUIN He had left the chin bristling to match his short, iron-grey head hair.

bristle /ˈbrɪs(ə)l/ *v.*[2]*t.* & *i. obs.* exc. *dial.* L15. [Origin unkn.: cf. BIRSLE.] Make or become crisp with heat.

bristling *n.* var. of BRISLING.

Bristol /ˈbrɪst(ə)l/ *n.* In sense 2 usu. **b-**. M16. [A city and port in the west of England.] **I 1** Used *attrib.* to designate things from or associated with Bristol. M16.

Bristol board a kind of fine pasteboard with a smooth surface. **Bristol cream** (proprietary name for) a kind of sweet sherry. **(shipshape and) Bristol fashion** (orig. *Naut.*) with all in good order. **Bristol glass** opaque (esp. blue) glass manufactured in Bristol. *Bristol milk*: see MILK *n.* **Bristol porcelain** a kind of porcelain resembling delftware, manufactured in Bristol. **Bristol stone** etc., rock-crystal from the Bristol area.

II 2 In *pl.*, or in full *Bristol cities* (= titties). The breasts. *rhyming slang.* M20.

brisure /ˈbriːʒə/ *n.* E17. [Fr. = fracture.] *Her.* A variation of or addition to a coat of arms serving as a distinguishing mark.

Brit /brɪt/ *n.*[1] & *a.*[1] Long *obs.* exc. *Hist.* Also **Brett** /brɛt/. [OE *Bret* (pl. *Brettas*), based on L *Britto* (pl. *Brittones*) or its Celt. equiv. Cf. BRIT *n.*[3] & *a.*[2]] **A** *n.* An ancient Briton (the ordinary name in the Anglo-Saxon Chronicle). OE. **B** *adj.* British. *rare.* M16.

brit /brɪt/ *n.*[2] *dial.* Also **-tt.** E17. [Origin unkn.] A young herring or sprat; *gen.* small fry.

Brit /brɪt/ *n.*[3] & *a.*[2] *colloq.* Often *derog.* E20. [Abbrev. of BRITON, BRITISH, or BRITISHER. Cf. BRIT *n.*[1] & *a.*[1]] **A** *n.* A British person. E20. **B** *adj.* British. M20.

Britain /ˈbrɪt(ə)n/ *n.*[1] [OE *Breoten*, *Breten*, *Bryten* f. L *Brittones* (see BRITON); later forms f. OFr. *Bretaigne* (mod. *-agne*), f. L *Brittan(n)ia* f. *Brit(t)anni*, corresp. to Gk *Bret(t)anoi*, *Pret(t)anoi*.] More fully (esp. as a political term) *Great Britain.* As a geographical and political term: (the main island and smaller offshore islands making up) England, Scotland, and Wales, sometimes with the Isle of Man. Also (as a political term) the United Kingdom, Britain and its dependencies, (formerly) the British Empire.

Middle Britain: see MIDDLE *a. North Britain*: see NORTH *a.*

¶*Britain*, after the OE period, was for long used only as a historical term, but in 1604 James I & VI was proclaimed 'King of Great Britain' and this name was adopted for the then United Kingdom at the Union in 1707.

†**Britainer** *n.* = BRITON *n.* L16–E19.

Britain /ˈbrɪt(ə)n/ *n.*[2] & *a.* M16. [L *Brit(t)annus*, *Brittanus* Briton, British: cf. prec.] †**A** *n.* An ancient Briton. M16–M18. **B** *adj.* †**1** = BRITISH *a.* 1. L16–M17. **2** = BRITISH *a.* 2. Now only in *Britain crown*, a gold coin struck in the reign of James I & VI, orig. valued at 5*s.*, afterwards at 5*s.* 6*d.* E17.

Britannia /brɪˈtanjə/ *n.* OE. [L *Brit(t)annia*, *Brittania* (Bede), corresp. to Gk *Brettania* (Diodorus Siculus): see BRITAIN *n.*[1]] **1** The Latin name of Britain; Britain personified as a female; the figure emblematic of Britain, a woman with a shield, helmet, and trident, shown on coins etc. OE. **2** In full *Britannia metal.* An alloy of tin with small proportions of antimony and copper, resembling silver. E19.

Comb.: *Britannia metal*: see sense 2 above. **Britannia silver** hallmarked silver of at least 95.8 per cent purity.

Britannian *a.* (now *rare*) = BRITISH *a.* 2 L16. †**Britany** *n.* Britain LME–M17.

Britannic /brɪˈtanɪk/ *a.* M17. [L *Britannicus*, f. as prec.: see -IC.] Of Britain; British. Chiefly in *Her* or *His Britannic Majesty.*

Britannically *adv.* (now *rare*) in British fashion; in reference to Great Britain: E18. **Britannicize** *v.t.* make British in form or character L19.

britch *n.* see BREECH *n.*

britchel *a.* see BRUCKLE.

Briticisation *n.* var. of BRITICIZATION.

Briticism /ˈbrɪtɪsɪz(ə)m/ *n.* Also **-tt-.** M19. [f. BRITISH after *Gallicism*, *Scotticism*, etc.] A word, phrase, or idiom characteristic of the English of Great Britain as opp. to the US etc.

Briticization /ˌbrɪtɪsʌɪˈzeɪʃ(ə)n/ *n.* Also **Britt-**, **-isation.** M20. [f. as prec. + -IZATION, after *Anglicization* etc.] The process of making British (esp. by the ancient Britons); the result of this.

British /ˈbrɪtɪʃ/ *a.* & *n.* [OE *Brettisć*, *Brittisć*, *Bryttisć*, f. as BRIT *n.*[1] & *a.*[1] + -ISH[1].] **A** *adj.* **1** Of or pertaining to the ancient Britons or their Celtic language (cf. BRITTONIC *a.*); *loosely* Welsh, (occas.) Cornish. OE. **2** Of or pertaining to Great Britain or its inhabitants. LME.

2 *British Commonwealth*: see COMMONWEALTH. **British crown** a gold crown (coin) struck in the reign of Charles I. **British disease** a problem or failing supposed to be characteristically British, *esp.* proneness to industrial unrest. **British Empire** *Hist.* the empire consisting of Great Britain and the other British possessions, dominions, and dependencies. **British English** the English language as spoken or written in the British Isles, esp. as contrasted with those forms of English characteristic of the US or other English-speaking countries. **British Isles** Britain, Ireland, and the Isle of Man, and sometimes also the Channel Islands. *British Lion*: see LION *n.* 3b, c. *British* RAJ. **British Restaurant** *Hist.* a government-subsidized restaurant opened in Britain during and after the war of 1939–45. *British Service warm*: see WARM *n.* **British Standard** (a document containing) the specification of recommended procedure, terminology, etc., in a particular field, drawn up and published by the British Standards Institution. **British Standard Time** *Hist.* the time system used in Britain from 1968 to 1971, which was the same as Central European Time and was equivalent to the extension of British Summer Time throughout the year. *British Summer Time*: see SUMMERTIME 2. *British storm petrel*: see STORM PETREL 1. **British thermal unit** the quantity of heat necessary to heat one pound of water at its maximum density by one degree Fahrenheit; = 1055 joule. *British warm*: see WARM *n. Great British Public*: see GREAT *a.* **the best of British (luck)**: an expression of encouragement, often with the iron. implication that good luck will not be forthcoming.

B *n.* **1** The Celtic language of the ancient Britons (formerly also *Old British*; cf. BRITTONIC *n.*); *loosely* Welsh, (occas.) Cornish. M16. **2** *collect. pl. The* British people; British soldiers etc. M17.

Britisher *n.* a British subject (usu. as distinct from an American) E19. **Britishism** *n.* (any of) the characteristic qualities of the British; a British peculiarity, a Briticism: L19. **Britishly** *adv.* †(*a*) *rare* in the British language; (*b*) after the manner of the British; in British fashion: M17. **Britishness** *n.* †(*a*) *rare* the conditions of life of the ancient Britons; (*b*) the quality or character of the British: L17.

Brito- /ˈbrɪtəʊ/ *comb. form.* [L, f. *Brit(t)o* BRITON.] Forming adjs. & ns. w. the sense 'British (or ancient British) and', as *Brito-Roman.*

Brito'centric *a.* having Britain as the centre E20.

Briton /ˈbrɪt(ə)n/ *n.* & *a.* ME. [(O)Fr. *Breton* f. L *Britto*, *-on-* or its Celt. equiv. (whence Welsh *Brython*).] **A** *n.* **1** A native or inhabitant of (Great) Britain; (now *rare* exc. *Hist.* of the British Empire) a British subject. ME. **2** *spec.* (Now more fully *ancient Briton*) A member of the (Celtic) people living in S. Britain at the time of the Roman conquest. ME.

1 *North Briton*: see NORTH *a.*

†**B** *adj.* = BRITISH *a.* M16–E17.

Britoness *n.* (*rare*) a female Briton L16.

Britonic *a.* & *n.* var. of BRITTONIC.

britt *n.* var. of BRIT *n.*[2]

Britticisation, -icism, -icization *ns.* vars. of BRITICIZATION, -ICISM.

brittle /ˈbrɪt(ə)l/ *a.* LME. [f. base of OE *ġebryttan* break in pieces, ult. f. Gmc base also of OE *brēotan* break up = ON *brjóta*: see -LE[1].] **1** Liable to break; easily broken, fragile; *fig.* frail, weak; insecure, unstable, transitory. LME. †**2** Liable to destruction; perishable, mortal. LME–L18.

1 **brittle fracture**: occurring in a metal without appreciable prior plastic deformation. **brittle-star** a starfish-like echinoderm of the class Ophiuroidea, with long thin brittle arms.

brittlely *adv.* L16. **brittleness** *n.* L15. **brittly** *adv.* L17.

Brittonic /brɪˈtɒnɪk/ *a.* & *n.* Also **Britonic.** E20. [f. L *Britto*, *-on-* BRITON + -IC.] **A** *adj.* Of or pertaining to the ancient Britons; *spec.* designating or pertaining to Brittonic (see sense B. below). E20. **B** *n.* The language group comprising Welsh, Cornish, and Breton; = *P-Celtic* s.v. CELTIC *n.* Cf. BRITISH *n.* 1, BRYTHONIC *n.* M20.

britzka /ˈbrɪtskə/ *n.* Also **britzska** & other vars. E19. [Pol. *bryczka.*] Chiefly *Hist.* An open carriage with calash top and space for reclining.

bro /brəʊ/ *n. colloq.* & as a written abbrev. Pl. **bros, Bros.** /brɒs, brʌz/. M17. [Abbrev. of BROTHER *n.*] A brother. In pl. (*Bros.*) freq. in names of firms.

broach /brəʊtʃ/ *n.*[1] Also †**broche**, BROOCH. ME. [Branch I f. (O)Fr. *broche* spit, f. Proto-Romance use as n. of fem. of L *brocc(h)us* in *brocci dentes* projecting teeth; branch II f. BROACH *v.*[1]] **I 1** A pointed rod; a lance; a bodkin, an awl, a skewer, etc.; *esp.* a roasting-spit. *arch.* & *dial.* ME. **2a** A spindle. *obs.* exc. *Sc.* LME. **b** A shuttle used in weaving tapestry. L18. **3** A pointed, pliant rod of wood, used in thatching to fix work. LME. **4** A (church) spire; now *spec.* the base of an octagonal spire rising from a square tower without a parapet. E16. **5** The sharply pointed growth of a young stag's first antlers. L16. **6** A tapered boring-bit used for smoothing or enlarging holes. M18.

II 7 An incision made by piercing or boring; a perforation. E16.

7 **on broach** (now *rare*) = ABROACH.

Comb.: **broach spire** etc.: supported by a broach.

broach /brəʊtʃ/ *n.*[2] E17. [*Broach* (now *Bharuch*), a city and district of Gujarat State, India.] Surat cotton from the Bharuch district.

broach /brəʊtʃ/ *v.*[1]*t.* Also †**broche.** ME. [(O)Fr. *brochier* (now *brocher*), f. Proto-Romance deriv. of base of BROACH *n.*[1]] †**1** Spur, prick with spurs. ME–M16. **2** Stab, pierce through; pin. LME. **b** Incise (stone) with a narrow-pointed chisel. M16. †**3** Transfix (meat etc.) with a spit; stick *on* a spit or pointed weapon. LME–E18. **4** Pierce (a cask) to draw off liquor, tap; release (liquid) by this means; *loosely* open and begin to use the contents of (a box etc.); make a start on, set in train. LME. **5** Begin a discussion of (a subject); make public; air; raise. L16. **6** Enlarge or finish (a drilled hole) with a boring-bit. Freq. foll. by *out.* M19.

4 R. L. STEVENSON A barrel of apples standing broached . . , for any one to help himself. R. HUGHES They ransacked the vessel . . broaching rum-casks and breaking the necks off wine-bottles. 5 E. F. BENSON It was the fulfilment of . . ideas which he had broached to her before marriage. E. HEATH Rather tentatively over coffee and cognac I broached the question.

broacher *n.* (*a*) a person who broaches something; †(*b*) a spit: L16.

broach /brəʊtʃ/ *v.*[2]*i.* & *t.* E18. [Origin unkn.] Veer or cause (a ship) to veer and present a side to wind and waves. Usu. w. *to.*

R. H. DANA They hove the wheel up just in time to save her from broaching to. *fig.*: T. H. WHITE Its lovely ruined walls . . standing broached to the sun and wind.

broad /brɔːd/ *n.* ME. [f. the adj.] †**1** *on broad*, = ABROAD *adv.* Only in ME. **2** (Usu. **B-**.) A large extent of fresh water formed by the widening of a river, *spec.* (usu. **B-**) any of several in East Anglia. M17. **3** *Hist.* = *broad-piece* s.v. BROAD *a.* E18. **4** The broad part (*of* the back etc.). M18. **5** In *pl.* Playing-cards. *slang.* L18. **6** A woman (usu. *derog.*); a prostitute. *slang* (orig. & chiefly *N. Amer.*). E20.

broad /brɔːd/ *a.* Also (*Sc.* & *north.*) **braid** /breɪd/. [OE *brād* = OFris., OS *brēd* (Du. *breed*), OHG, G *breit*, ON *breiðr*, Goth. *braiþs*, f. Gmc.] **1** Extended in direction from side to side, large across, wide, not narrow; (a specified extent) in breadth. OE. **b** Designating or pertaining to certain fabrics (orig.) distinguished by their width, esp. *broadcloth* below. LME. **2**

Less definitely: of great extent, spacious, ample. OE. †3 Large in amount. OE–LME. 4 Wide open; fully developed or expanded. OE. 5 Plain, clear, explicit; most apparent, main. LME. 6 Of language, a speaker, etc.: outspoken, unreserved, trenchant; vulgar, somewhat coarse or indecent. L15. 7 Of speech, pronunciation, etc.: markedly dialectal, distinctive of a region or class. Cf. BROAD *adv.* 3. L16. 8 Unrestrained, going to full lengths. E17. 9 Tolerant, liberal, catholic, widely inclusive. M19. 10 Bold in effect or style; *Mus.* slow and expressive. M19. 11 Widely applicable, far-ranging; inclusive; general. L19. 12 Designating a phonetic transcription that distinguishes phonemes but not allophones. L19.

1 EVELYN A Leaf no broader than a Three-pence. C. DAY A bed . . so broad that it could have easily held several guests. D. MURPHY Shoulders too broad for feminine grace. **as broad as it is long** *fig.* (*colloq.*) the same either way. 2 MILTON In ample space under the broadest shade. (**land of) the broad acres** Yorkshire. 4 C. ACHEBE He broke into a broad smile showing smoke- and kola-stained teeth. A. BRINK When I woke up it was broad daylight and the birds were singing. 5 R. BENTLEY Surely this is a hint broad enough. 6 H. HALLAM The broadest and most repulsive declaration of all the Calvinistic tenets. S. MIDDLETON Hollies dropped no sexual hint; the broad tongue of the dining room he'd discarded for a politer approach. 7 T. GUNN One of my contemporaries arrived at Cambridge with a broad Yorkshire accent. 8 W. IRVING She was the picture of broad, honest, vulgar enjoyment. 9 *New Society* The Broad Left—ie, Labour plus Communists. 10 G. GROTE A portrait . . drawn in colours broad and glaring. 11 J. MORLEY Intellectual education in the broadest sense. N. CHOMSKY The effects of the American invasion were far broader. *Times* In broad outline, the bill disolves all registered trade unions.

Special collocations & comb.: **broad arrow** a mark resembling a broad arrowhead, distinguishing British government stores, esp. (formerly) prison clothing. **broad-axe** an axe with a broad head. *broad bean*: see BEAN *n.* 1a. **broad-bill** any of certain birds with broad bills; *esp.* (*a*) a shoveler, a scaup; (*b*) a tropical passerine of the Old World family Eurylaimidae. **broad-brim** a hat with a broad brim; *arch.* a member of the Society of Friends (wearing such a hat). **broad-brow** *colloq.* a person with broad interests. **broad-brush** *a.* general, generalized, incomplete, lacking detail. **Broad Church** Anglican clergy favouring comprehensiveness over an exclusivity of doctrine; *transf.* any group allowing its members a wide range of opinion. **broadcloth** [phr. in Act of Parliament of 1482 specifying width retained, as designation of high quality] cloth of fine twilled woollen or worsted, or of plain-woven cotton. **broad gauge** a railway gauge wider than the standard one (in Great Britain 1.435 metres); *spec.* (*Hist.*) the 7-foot (2.1 m) gauge of the Great Western Railway, abolished in 1892. **broad-jump** (now *N. Amer.*) = *long jump* s.v. LONG *a.*[1] **broad-leaf** (*a*) any of certain trees or other plants with broad leaves, *esp.* a Jamaican tree, *Terminalia latifolia*, or (*NZ*) the papauma, *Griselinia littoralis*; (*b*) a non-coniferous tree. **broad-leaved** *a.* having broad leaves; *spec.* (of trees) having relatively broad flat leaves rather than needles, i.e. non-coniferous; (of woodland) composed of such trees; *broad-leaved* ENDIVE. **broad ligament** *Anat.* either of the folds of peritoneal tissue that support the uterus, ovaries, and fallopian tubes. **broadloom** (a carpet) woven in broad width. *broad pennant*: see PENNANT *n.*[1] **broad-piece** *Hist.* a twenty-shilling piece of the reigns of James I and Charles I (broader and thinner than succeeding coinage). **broadscale** *a.* on a broad scale, extensive. **broad seal** (chiefly *Hist.*) the Great Seal of England. **broadsheet** (*a*) a large sheet of paper carrying information etc. printed on one side only; (*b*) a newspaper with a large format. **broad-spectrum** *a.* (of a drug) effective against a wide range of pathogens. **broadsword** a cutting-sword with a broad blade. **broadtail** = BREITSCHWANZ. **broadwalk** a broad street or footpath. **broadway** (*a*) a wide road; (*b*) (**B-**) [a street in New York City famous for its theatres] the main commercial part of New York theatre life.

broaden *v.t.* & *i.* make or become broader; widen (*out*), dilate. E18. **broadish** *a.* LME. †**broadling(s)** *adv.* = BROADWAYS ME–E18. **broadly** *adv.* in a broad manner; widely, generally, fully: L16. **broadness** *n.* (*a*) (now *rare*) breadth; (*b*) coarseness, indelicacy: LME. **broadways**, †**-way** *adv.* in the direction of the breadth, laterally L16. **broadwise** *adv.* = BROADWAYS L17.

broad /brɔːd/ *adv.* Also (*Sc.* & *north.*) **braid** /breɪd/. [OE *brāde*, f. as prec.] 1 Broadly, in an extensive way; widely; fully. OE. 2 Outspokenly, plainly. LME. 3 With a broad pronunciation etc. M16. 4 *Naut.* At a distance to one side. Foll. by *on* the bow etc. M19.

1 J. WESLEY Being in bed, but broad awake.

broadcast /ˈbrɔːdkɑːst/ *a.*, *n.*, & *adv.* M18. [f. prec. + pa. pple of CAST *v.*] A *adj.* 1 Of seed, sowing, etc.: sown or performed by scattering widely rather than by placing in drills or rows. Also *gen.* (chiefly *fig.*), widely disseminated or scattered abroad. M18. 2 Disseminated by means of radio or television. E20. B *n.* 1 Broadcast sowing of seed. M18. 2 (An act of) broadcasting by radio or television; a radio or television transmission or programme. E20.

2 *outside broadcast*: see OUTSIDE *a.*

C *adv.* (Sown etc.) in a broadcast manner. M19.

broadcast /ˈbrɔːdkɑːst/ *v.* Pa. t. & pple **-cast**, (occas.) **-casted**. L18. [f. BROAD *adv.* + CAST *v.*] 1 *v.t.* Sow (seed) in a broadcast manner; *gen.* (chiefly *fig.*) spread widely. L18. 2a *v.t.* Disseminate (news, music, etc.) by radio or television. E20. b *v.i.* Speak, sing, play, etc., for radio or television transmission; put out a radio or television transmission. E20.

broadcaster *n.* (*a*) a person whose speech, performance, etc., is (esp. habitually) broadcast on radio or television; a person, company, etc., that puts out broadcasts; (*b*) an instrument for broadcasting seed etc.: E20.

broad-minded /brɔːdˈmaɪndɪd/ *a.* L19. [f. BROAD *a.* + MINDED.] Tolerant or liberal in thought or opinion.

broad-mindedness *n.* L19.

broadside /ˈbrɔːdsaɪd/ *n.*, *adv.*, & *v.* Orig. two wds. E16. [f. BROAD *a.* + SIDE *n.*] A *n.* 1 The part of a ship's side above the water between the bow and the quarter. E16. 2 (A discharge of) all the guns situated or able to fire on one side of a ship; *fig.* a verbal onslaught. L16. 3 A broadsheet. L16.

B *adv.* With the side turned to or *to* a given point or object; *loosely* set sideways. L19.

broadside on with the side turned towards a given object etc.

C *v.i.* Of a motorcycle, motorcyclist, etc.: perform a controlled skid as part of a deliberate manoeuvre. M20.

Brobdingnagian /brɒbdɪŋˈnagɪən/ *n.* & *a.* E18. [f. *Brobdingnag*, a land in Swift's *Gulliver's Travels* where everything is on a gigantic scale, + -IAN.] A *n.* An inhabitant of Brobdingnag; a giant, a huge person. E18. B *adj.* Gigantic, colossal. E18.

Also **Brobdingnag** *a.* E19.

Broca /ˈbrəʊkə/ *n.* L19. [P. Paul *Broca* (1824–80), Fr. surgeon and anthropologist.] Used in *possess.* to denote things studied by Broca.

Broca's aphasia aphasia with severe impairment or loss of speech. **Broca's area** the region of the frontal cortex of the brain concerned with the production of speech.

brocade /brəˈkeɪd/ *n.* & *v.* Orig. †**-a(r)do**. L16. [Sp., Port. *brocado*, with blending of Fr. *brocart* f. It. *broccato* = embossed fabric, f. *brocco* twisted thread: see -ADE.] A *n.* A rich fabric woven with raised patterns, orig. with added gold or silver threads. L16. B *v.t.* Work with a raised pattern. Chiefly as *brocaded* ppl a. M17.

†**brocage** *n.* var. of BROKAGE.

brocard /ˈbrəʊkəd, *foreign* brɔkaːr (*pl. same*)/ *n.* M16. [Fr., or med.L *brocardus*, appellative use of the Latinized form of *Burchart*, 11th-cent. bishop of Worms and compiler of volumes of ecclesiastical rules.] 1 A cutting speech, a gibe. *rare.* M16. 2 An elementary legal principle or maxim. E17.

†**brocardo** *n.* see BROCADE *n.*

brocatelle /brɒkəˈtɛl/ *n.* M17. [Fr. (earlier *brocatel*) f. It. *broccatello* gold tinsel, dim. of *broccato*: see BROCADE.] An inferior type of brocade, usu. of silk or wool.

brocatello /brɒkəˈtɛləʊ/ *n.* M18. [It. *brocatello di Siena*, so called from its colouring: see prec.] A kind of variegated marble, clouded and veined chiefly with yellow.

broccoli /ˈbrɒkəli/ *n.* Also †**brocoli**. M17. [It. pl. of *broccolo* cabbage sprout or head, dim. of *brocco* shoot, BROACH *n.*[1]] A hardy variety of cauliflower; *esp.* (often more fully *sprouting broccoli*) a form of this producing many small heads.

broch /brɒk, brɒx/ *n.* In senses 1 & 2 *Sc.* & *north.* Also **brough**, **brugh**, /brʌx, brʌf/. L15. [Metath. alt. of BURGH: cf. ON *borg* enclosure, castle.] 1 = BURGH. L15. 2 A luminous ring round the moon etc.; a halo. L15. 3 (In *Archaeol.* usu. *broch.*) A prehistoric round stone tower in N. Scotland and adjacent islands. M17.

brochan /ˈbrɒxən/ *n.*[1] *Sc.* E18. [Gael.] Gruel; thin porridge.

†**brochan** *n.*[2] var. of BRACKEN *n.*[2]

brochantite /ˈbrɒʃ(ə)ntaɪt/ *n.* E19. [f. A.J.M. *Brochant* de Villiers (1772–1840), Fr. geologist + -ITE[1].] *Min.* A bluish-green monoclinic basic copper sulphate usu. occurring as prismatic or elongated crystals or as crystal aggregates.

†**broche** *n.*, *v.*[1] see BROACH *n.*[1], *v.*[1], BROOCH.

†**broche** *v.*[2]*t.* L15–M19. [f. Fr. *brocher* to stitch, brocade: see BROACH *v.*[1]] Stitch or work with raised figures.

broché /ˈbrəʊʃeɪ, *foreign* brɔʃe/ *a.* & *n.* L19. [Fr., pa. pple of *brocher*: see prec.] (A material, esp. silk) woven with a pattern on the surface.

brochette /brɒˈʃɛt/ *n.* L15. [Fr. dim. of *broche* BROACH *n.*[1]] 1 A small broach, skewer, or spit; *spec.* a skewer on which chunks of meat are cooked. L15. 2 A pin or bar used to fasten medals, orders, etc., to clothing; a set of decorations worn in this way. M19.

brochure /ˈbrəʊʃə, brɒˈʃʊə/ *n.* M18. [Fr., lit. 'stitching, stitched work', f. as BROCHE *v.*[1] + -URE.] A booklet or pamphlet, esp. giving information about the amenities of a place etc.

brock /brɒk/ *n.*[1] [OE *broc(c)* f. Celt. base of Welsh, Corn. *broch*, Breton *broc'h*, Ir., Gael. *broc*, OIr. *brocc*.] 1 A badger (often qualified as *stinking*). OE. 2 A stinking or dirty fellow; a rotter. E17.

brock /brɒk/ *n.*[2] Now *rare* or *obs.* E16. [Abbrev.] = BROCKET 1.

brock *n.*[3] see BROKE *n.*

brocked *a.* var. of BROCKIT.

Brocken /ˈbrɒk(ə)n/ *n.* E19. [The highest of the Harz Mountains in Germany, where particularly observed.] *Brocken spectre*, *spectre of the Brocken*, a magnified shadow on a bank of cloud in high mountains, often with a coloured halo.

brocket /ˈbrɒkɪt/ *n.* LME. [AN *broquet* dim. (see -ET[1]) of *broque* dial. var. of *broche* BROACH *n.*[1]: cf. Fr. *brocard* young roe, brocket.] 1 A red deer stag in its second year, with straight horns. LME. 2 A small Central or S. American deer of the genus *Mazama*. M19.

brockit /ˈbrɒkɪt/ *a.* *Sc.* Also **brocked**. L16. [Perh. f. BROCK *n.*[1] + -ED[2], but cf. Norw. *broket*, Da. *broget*.] Of mixed colour, esp. black and white; with black and white spots or stripes.

Brock's benefit /brɒks ˈbɛnɪfɪt/ *n. phr.* E20. [Name of the public fireworks display held annually at the Crystal Palace, London, from 1865 to 1936, f. C. T. *Brock*, firework manufacturer.] A spectacular display of pyrotechnics. Freq. *fig.*

†**brocoli** *n.* var. of BROCCOLI.

brod /brɒd/ *n.* & *v.* Long *obs.* exc. *dial.* See also BRAD. ME. [App. f. ON *broddr* = OE *brord* spike: cf. BROG *n.*, PROD *n.*[1]] A *n.* †1 A shoot. Only in ME. 2 = BRAD. ME. 3 (A prick from) a goad. LME. B *v.* Infl. **-dd-**. †1 *v.i.* Sprout. Only in ME. 2 *v.t.* Goad, prod. *Sc.* & *north.* LME.

brodder *n.* (*Sc.* & *north.*) a person who uses a brod L19.

brodekin /ˈbrɒdɪkɪn/ *n.* Also **-quin**, **brodkin** /ˈbrɒdkɪn/. L15. [Fr. *brodequin*: see BUSKIN.] *Hist.* A buskin.

broderer /ˈbrəʊdərə/ *n. arch.* LME. [Var. of BROIDERER.] An embroiderer. (Now only used as a guild-name.)

broderie anglaise /ˌbrəʊd(ə)rɪ ɒŋˈgleɪz/ *n. phr.* M19. [Fr. = English embroidery.] Open embroidery on linen, cambric, etc.; fabric so embroidered.

brodkin *n.* var. of BRODEKIN.

Broeder /ˈbruːdə, *foreign* ˈbrudər/ *n. S. Afr.* M20. [Afk. f. Du.: see BROTHER *n.*] A member of the Broederbond, a largely secret society open only to male Protestant Afrikaners.

brog /brɒg/ *n.* & *v. Sc.* & *north.* L15. [Origin unkn.: cf. BROD.] A *n.* 1 A pricking or boring instrument, a bradawl. Also, a prick with this. L15. 2 A short stick, esp. to stand in the ground. L18. B *v.* Infl. **-gg-**. 1 *v.i.* = BROGGLE. L17. 2 *v.t.* Prick, prod; pierce with a brog. L18.

brogan /ˈbrəʊg(ə)n/ *n.* M19. [Ir. *brógán*, Gael. *brógan* dim. of *bróg* BROGUE *n.*[2]] A coarse stout leather shoe reaching to the ankle.

†**brogger** *n.* LME–E18. [Var. of BROKER: thus AN *brogour* beside *brocour*.] A broker; *esp.* a corrupt jobber of offices.

broggle /ˈbrɒg(ə)l/ *v.i. north.* M17. [Frequent. of BROG *v.*: see -LE[3].] Fish for eels with a baited stick, sniggle.

brogue /brəʊg/ *n.*[1] Long *obs.* exc. *Sc.* M16. [Origin unkn.] An escheat; a fraud, a trick.

brogue /brəʊg/ *n.*[2] L16. [Ir., Gael. *bróg* (OIr. *bróc*) f. ON *brók*: see BREECH *n.*] 1a A rough shoe of untanned hide worn (esp. formerly) in the wilder parts of Ireland and the Scottish Highlands. L16. b A strong outdoor shoe with ornamental perforated bands. E20. †2 In *pl.* Hose, trousers; waterproof leggings with feet, used in angling. E17–L19.

brogued *a.* (*a*) made with a strong vamp like a brogue; (*b*) *rare* wearing brogues: E19.

brogue /brəʊg/ *n.*[3] & *v.* E18. [Perh. same wd as prec.] A *n.* A strongly-marked dialectal (esp. Irish) accent. E18. B *v.t.* & *i.* Speak or utter with a brogue. *rare.* E19.

†**broid** *v.t.* ME–E17. [Alt. of BRAID *v.*[1] after pa. pple *broiden*: see BROWDEN.] Plait, interweave.

†**broiden** *ppl a.* var. of BROWDEN.

broider /ˈbrɔɪdə/ *v.t.* & *i. arch.* LME. [OFr. *brosder*, *brou(s)der* (mod. *broder*) w. inf. ending retained; alt. by assoc. w. BROID.] Embroider; adorn (as) with embroidery.

broiderer *n.* (*arch.*) an embroiderer LME. **broidery** *n.* (*poet.*) embroidery LME.

broil /brɔɪl/ *n.*[1] E16. [f. BROIL *v.*[2]] A tumult; a quarrel.

broil /brɔɪl/ *n.*[2] L16. [f. BROIL *v.*[1]] 1 A broiling; great heat. L16. 2 (A piece of) broiled meat. E19.

2 LONDON *broil*.

broil /brɔɪl/ *v.*[1] LME. [OFr. *bruler*, *bruller*, earlier *brusler* (mod. *brûler*) burn, f. Proto-Romance, perh. f. Gmc base of BURN *v.* + L *ustulare* burn up.] †1 *v.t.* Burn; char. LME–M16. 2 *v.t.* Cook (meat) by placing it over a fire on a gridiron etc.; grill. LME. 3 *v.i.* Be subjected to heat; become very hot, esp. *fig.* with excitement, anger, etc. M16. 4 *v.t.* Scorch, make very hot. M17.

broil /brɔɪl/ *v.*[2] LME. [AN *broiller*, OFr. *bröoillier* (mod. *brouiller*), f. Proto-Romance, f. base of OFr. *breu*: see BREWIS.] †1 *v.t.* Mix confusedly. LME–M17. 2 *v.i.* Engage in a broil, wrangle. LME. 3 *v.t.* Involve in confusion, discompose; embroil. Now *rare* or *obs.* E16.

broiler /ˈbrɔɪlə/ *n.*[1] ME. [f. BROIL *v.*[1] + -ER[1].] 1 A person or thing which broils meat etc. ME. b *spec.* A gridiron or other apparatus used in broiling. LME. c A very hot day. *colloq.* E19. 2 A chicken reared for broiling. M19.

Comb.: **broiler chicken**, **fowl** = sense 2 above; **broiler house** a building for rearing broiler chickens in close confinement.

broiler /ˈbrɔɪlə/ *n.*[2] *rare.* M17. [f. BROIL *v.*[2] + -ER[1].] A person who stirs up or engages in broils.

†**brokage** *n.* Also **brocage**. LME–M18. [AN *brocage*, AL *brocagium*: see BROKER, -AGE.] Brokerage; usu. in an unfavourable sense: corrupt dealing, bribery, pimping, etc.

broke /brəʊk/ *n.* Also (now *dial.*) **brock** /brɒk/. [OE *broc* (sense 1), *gebroc* (sense 2), f. as BREAK *v.*] †1 Affliction, misery. Only in OE. 2 A fragment. Long *obs.* exc. *dial.* OE. †3 A wound, a rupture. LME–M16. 4 In *pl.* Short pieces of wool esp. from the edge of a fleece. L19.

broke /brəʊk/ *a.* ME. [pa. pple (now arch.) of BREAK *v.*] 1 = BROKEN. Long *arch.* in *gen.* sense. ME. 2 *pred.* Without money, penniless; ruined, bankrupt. *colloq.* E18. 3 Of a horse: broken to harness. Chiefly *US.* E19.

2 With intensive: *dead*, *flat*, *stony broke*, *broke to the wide*, etc. **go broke** go bankrupt. **go for broke** (orig. *US*) give one's all, make strenuous efforts.

broke /brəʊk/ *v.*[1]*i.* & (*rare*) *t.* LME. [Back-form. f. BROKER.] Bargain, negotiate; traffic (in). Now *spec.* in commercial matters: act as a broker or agent (*in*, *for*).

broke *v.*[2] pa. t. of BREAK *v.*

broken /ˈbrəʊk(ə)n/ *a.* ME. [pa. pple of BREAK *v.*] I *gen.* 1 In the senses of BREAK *v.*: separated forcibly into parts, in fragments, fractured, shattered, burst, split, not intact or in working order, damaged; produced by breaking, fragmentary. ME.

1 AV *Ps.* 31:12 I am like a broken vessell. J. TYNDALL Broken fragments of rock. T. PYNCHON The table littered with broken-spined books.

II *spec.* 2 Of a limb etc.: having the bone fractured. Of the back or neck: suffering fracture or dislocation of bones. Of the head: grazed, laid open. LME. 3 Not continuous or uniform; uneven, interrupted, disjointed, disconnected. LME. b Of language: imperfectly spoken, with incomplete syntax. L16. 4 Crushed in health, strength, feelings, etc.; exhausted, enfeebled; subdued, humbled. L15. b Chiefly of animals: trained to obedience or discipline; tamed. Freq. foll. by *in*. E19. 5 Financially ruined, bankrupt. L16. 6 Violated, transgressed, not kept. E17. 7 Of water: foaming, turbulent; choppy, rough. L18. 8 Dispersed in confusion, routed. E19. 9 *Mus.* Of an octave or other chord: of which the notes are played in succession rather than together. L19.

3 LD MACAULAY His rest that night was broken. BOSW. SMITH The Carthaginian cavalry and elephants extricated themselves . . from the broken ground. J. MCPHEE The skies are broken, and around the gray clouds are wide bays of blue. b A. POWELL A Viennese . . who talked Comic Opera broken English. 6 A. LEWIS A mirror cracked by broken vows. 8 SIR W. SCOTT Now leader of a broken host.

Special collocations & comb.: **broken-backed** *a.* †(*a*) hunch-backed; (*b*) having a broken back; *Naut.* (of a ship) drooping at both ends through damage to the frame. **broken colour**: mixed or juxtaposed closely with another. **broken-down** worn out, dilapidated, decayed, ruined, having ceased to function. **broken field** *N. Amer. Football* the area beyond the line of scrimmage where the defenders are relatively scattered (giving opportunities for the opposing players to run with the ball). **broken-field** *adv.* (*N. Amer. colloq.*) in the manner of a footballer running in the broken field. **broken heart** a spirit crushed by grief etc. **broken home**: that of a family lacking one parent, usu. through divorce or separation. **broken line**: made up of dashes. **broken man** (*a*) a man reduced to despair; (*b*) *Sc. Hist.* an outlaw. *broken reed*: see REED *n.*[1] **broken tea** tea-siftings. **broken time** (working) time reduced by interruptions. **broken wind** a chronic disabling condition of horses due to rupture of air-cells in the lungs. **broken-winded** *a.* suffering from broken wind (often *fig.*).

brokenly *adv.* L16. **brokenness** /-n-n-/ *n.* E17.

broken-hearted /brəʊk(ə)nˈhɑːtɪd/ *a.* E16. [f. prec. + HEARTED.] Having a broken heart; crushed by grief etc.

broken-heartedly *adv.* L17. **broken-heartedness** *n.* L18.

broker /ˈbrəʊkə/ *n.* & *v.* ME. [AN *brocour*, *brogour* = AL *brocator*, Prov. *abrocador*, of unkn. origin.] A *n.* †1a A retailer; *derog.* a pedlar, a petty dealer. ME–M18. b A dealer in second-hand furniture, clothing, etc.; a pawnbroker. L16. 2 A middleman in business, *esp.* a stockbroker; an agent, a commissioner; *gen.* an intermediary. ME. †3 A go-between in love affairs, a matchmaker; a pimp, a bawd. LME–L17. 4 A person licensed to sell or appraise distrained goods. E19.

2 *honest broker*: see HONEST *a.*

Comb.: **broker-dealer** a person combining the former functions of a broker and jobber on the Stock Exchange.

B *v.* 1 *v.i.* Act as a broker. Chiefly as *brokering* vbl n. & ppl a. *rare.* M17. 2 *v.t.* Act as a broker with respect to, arrange as a broker. M20.

brokerage *n.* (*a*) = BROKING 1; (*b*) a broker's fee or commission: LME. **brokeress** *n.* (now *rare* or *obs.*) a female broker L16. †**brokery** *n.* (*a*) = BROKING 1; (*b*) a broker's wares: L16–M18.

broking /ˈbrəʊkɪŋ/ *n.* M16. [f. BROKE *v.*[1] + -ING[1].] 1 The trade of a broker, acting as a broker. M16. †2 Dishonest or disreputable dealing. L16–E17.

brolga /ˈbrɒlgə/ *n.* L19. [Kamilaroi *buralga*.] An Australian crane, *Grus rubicunda*. Also called *native companion*.

brolly /ˈbrɒli/ *n.* L19. [Alt. of UMBRELLA.] 1 An umbrella. *colloq.* L19. 2 A parachute. *slang.* M20.

brom- *comb. form* see BROMO-.

bromate /ˈbrəʊmeɪt/ *n.* M19. [f. BROMIC + -ATE[1].] *Chem.* A salt or ester of bromic acid.

bromatology /brəʊməˈtɒlədʒi/ *n. rare.* E19. [f. Gk *brōmat-*, *brōma* food + -OLOGY.] The science of food; a treatise on this.

brome /brəʊm/ *n.* M18. [mod.L *Bromus* (see below) f. L *bromos*, f. Gk *bromos*, *brōmos* oats.] Any of several grasses of the genus *Bromus* and related genera, usu. having spikelets in loose panicles and with long-awned lemmas. Also *brome-grass*.

false brome any of several grasses resembling bromes, of the genus *Brachypodium*, esp. *B. sylvaticum*, common in woods and hedges. *soft brome*: see SOFT *a.*

bromelia /brəˈmiːlɪə/ *n.* E19. [mod.L, f. Olaf *Bromel* (1639–1705), Swed. botanist: see -IA[1].] A plant of the New World family Bromeliaceae (and esp. of the genus *Bromelia*), having short stems and lance-shaped spiny leaves, e.g. pineapple.

bromeli'aceous *a.* of or pertaining to the family Bromeliaceae L19. **bromeliad** *n.* a plant of the family Bromeliaceae M19.

bromelin /ˈbrəʊməlɪn/ *n.* L19. [f. prec. + -IN[1].] A proteolytic enzyme present in the juice of the pineapple.

bromic /ˈbrəʊmɪk/ *a.* E19. [f. BROMINE + -IC.] *Chem.* Of or containing bromine; *bromic acid*, a strongly oxidizing acid, $HBrO_3$, known only as an aqueous solution.

bromide /ˈbrəʊmʌɪd/ *n.* M19. [f. BROMINE + -IDE.] 1 *Chem.* A compound of bromine with a less electronegative element or radical; a salt or ester of hydrobromic acid. M19. 2a (A dose of) potassium or sodium bromide taken as a sedative. L19. b *fig.* Something or someone boring, commonplace, or conventional; *esp.* a soothing platitude or trite remark. Orig. *US.* E20. 3 A reproduction on bromide paper. L20.

Comb.: **bromide paper** photographic printing paper coated with silver bromide emulsion.

bromidic /brə(ʊ)ˈmɪdɪk/ *a.* of the nature of a bromide; commonplace, trite: E20.

bromidrosis /brəʊmɪˈdrəʊsɪs/ *n.* M19. [f. Gk *brōmos* stink + *hidrōs* sweat + -OSIS.] *Med.* Offensively odorous perspiration due to bacterial breakdown of sweat.

brominate /ˈbrəʊmɪneɪt/ *v.t.* M19. [f. next + -ATE[3].] Treat with bromine; *Chem.* introduce one or more bromine atoms into (a compound or molecule) usu. in place of hydrogen. Freq. as *brominated* ppl a.

bromi'nation *n.* M19.

bromine /ˈbrəʊmiːn/ *n.* E19. [f. Fr. *brome* bromine, f. Gk *brōmos* stink: see -INE[5].] A rank-smelling, highly toxic, dark red volatile liquid which is a chemical element of the halogen group, atomic no. 35. (Symbol Br.)

bromize *v.t.* (now *rare* or *obs.*) treat, compound, or impregnate with bromine or its compounds M19.

bromism /ˈbrəʊmɪz(ə)m/ *n.* M19. [f. prec. + -ISM.] *Med.* A condition of torpor and weakness caused by excessive intake of bromides.

bromo /ˈbrəʊməʊ/ *n. colloq.* Pl. **-os**. E20. [f. BROMIDE + -O.] A bromide (BROMIDE 2a, b), bromides. Also, toilet paper.

bromo- /ˈbrəʊməʊ/ *comb. form* of BROMINE: see -O-. Bef. a vowel also **brom-** /brəʊm/.

bromargyrite /brəˈmɑːdʒɪrʌɪt/ *n.* (*Min.*) native silver bromide, a mineral crystallizing in the cubic system and usu. occurring as colourless, grey, pale yellow, or green crystals M19. **bromoform** *n.* (*Chem.*) a colourless liquid, $CHBr_3$, analogous to chloroform and formerly having some germicidal use M19. **Bromo-'Seltzer** *n.* (proprietary name for) an analgesic preparation containing sodium bromide L19. †**bromuret** *n.* = BROMIDE I M-L19. **bromyrite** /ˈbrəʊmɪrʌɪt/ *n.* = BROMARGYRITE M19.

Brompton /ˈbrɒm(p)t(ə)n/ *n.* E18. [*Brompton* Park Nursery, London.] *Hort.* In full *Brompton stock*. A biennial variety of stock.

bronc /brɒŋk/ *n. colloq.* L19. [Abbrev.] A bronco.

bronchi *n.* pl. of BRONCHUS.

bronchia /ˈbrɒŋkɪə/ *n.pl.* Now *rare* or *obs.* Formerly also treated as *sing.* with pl. **-chiae** /-kiiː/. L17. [Late L f. Gk *brogkhia*, f. *brogkhos* windpipe.] The ramifications of the two main bronchi in the lungs. Cf. BRONCHUS.

bronchial /ˈbrɒŋkɪəl/ *a.* L17. [f. prec. + -AL[1].] Of or pertaining to the bronchi or their branches.

bronchially *adv.* L19.

bronchiectasis /brɒŋkɪˈɛktəsɪs/ *n.* L19. [f. BRONCHIA + Gk *ektasis* dilatation.] *Med.* Widening of the bronchi or their branches.

bronchio- *comb. form* see BRONCHO-.

bronchiole /ˈbrɒŋkɪəʊl/ *n.* M19. [mod.L *bronchiolus*, *-um* dims. of BRONCHIA: see -OLE[1].] *Anat.* Any of the smallest branches of a bronchus, without mucous glands or cartilage.

bronchiolar /brɒŋkɪˈəʊlə/ *a.* E20. **bronchiolitis** /ˌbrɒŋkɪəˈlʌɪtɪs/ *n.* inflammation of the bronchioles L19.

bronchitic /brɒŋˈkɪtɪk/ *a.* & *n.* M19. [f. next + -IC.] A *adj.* Of, or pertaining to bronchitis; suffering from bronchitis. M19. B *n.* A sufferer from bronchitis. L19.

bronchitis /brɒŋˈkʌɪtɪs/ *n.* E19. [f. BRONCHUS + -ITIS.] Inflammation of the mucous membranes of the bronchi.

verminous bronchitis: see VERMINOUS 3a.

broncho *n.* & *a.* var. of BRONCO.

broncho- /ˈbrɒŋkəʊ/ *comb. form.* Also (occas.) **bronchio-** /ˈbrɒŋkɪəʊ/. [Gk *brogkho-*, f. *brogkhos* BRONCHUS; forms w. *-io-* f. BRONCHIA: see -O-.] Forming ns. and adjs. w. the sense 'of the bronchi, windpipe, or lungs'.

bronchocele *n.* [Gk *brogkhokēlē*: see -CELE] (*a*) localized widening of a bronchus; (*b*) (now *rare* or *obs.*) goitre: M17. **bronchocon'striction** *n.* narrowing of the bronchi E20. **bronchocon'strictor** *n.* a substance which causes bronchoconstriction E20. **bronchodi'lator** *n.* a substance which causes widening of the bronchi E20. **bronchogenic** /-ˈdʒɛnɪk/ *a.* of bronchial origin E20. **bronchogram** *n.* an X-ray image of the bronchi produced by partially filling them with a radio-opaque material M20. **bronchography** /brɒŋˈkɒɡrəfi/ *n.* X-ray examination of the bronchi M20. **bronchophonic** /-ˈfɒnɪk/ *a.* of or pertaining to bronchophony M19. **bronchophony** /brɒŋˈkɒfəni/ *n.* abnormally loud vocal resonance audible stethoscopically in consolidating lung disease M19. **bronchopneu'monia** *n.* infection of the pulmonary alveoli spreading by the bronchi and bronchioles M19. **broncho'pulmonary** *a.* pertaining to or affecting the bronchi and lungs M19. **broncho'rrhoea** *n.* persistently excessive bronchial secretion of mucus M19. **bronchoscope** *n.* an instrument for internal inspection of the bronchi L19. **bronchoscopic** /-ˈskɒpɪk/ *a.* of or pertaining to the bronchoscope or bronchoscopy E20. **bronchoscopy** /brɒŋˈkɒskəpi/ *n.* the use of a bronchoscope E20. **bronchospasm** *n.* spasm of bronchial smooth muscle producing narrowing of the bronchi E20. **bronchotomy** /brɒŋˈkɒtəmi/ *n.* (now *rare* or *obs.*) tracheotomy E18.

bronchus /ˈbrɒŋkəs/ *n.* Usu. in pl. **bronchi** /ˈbrɒŋkʌɪ/. L17. [Late L f. Gk *brogkhos* windpipe.] *Anat.* Orig., either of the two branches into which the windpipe divides. Now also, any of the ramifying system of cartilage-lined passages between the windpipe and the bronchioles. Cf. BRONCHIA, BRONCHIOLE.

bronco /ˈbrɒŋkəʊ/ *n.* & *a.* Also **-cho.** M19. [Sp. = rough, rude.] A *n.* Pl. **-os.** A wild or half-tamed horse, esp. of the western US. M19.

Comb.: **bronco-buster** *slang* a breaker-in of broncos.

B *adj.* Wild, uncontrollable, rough. *US colloq.* M19.

bronto- /ˈbrɒntəʊ/ *comb. form* of Gk *brontē* thunder: see -O-.

brontology /brɒnˈtɒlədʒi/ *n.* (*rare*) the branch of knowledge that deals with thunder M18. **bronto'phobia** *n.* irrational fear of thunderstorms E20. **brontothere** *n.* a titanothere, esp. of the genus *Brontotherium* L19.

brontosaurus /brɒntəˈsɔːrəs/ *n.* Pl. **-ruses, -ri** /-rʌɪ/. L19. [mod.L, f. as prec. + Gk *sauros* -SAUR.] A large herbivorous sauropod dinosaur of the genus *Brontosaurus* (or *Apatosaurus*), known as fossils of the Jurassic and Cretaceous periods.

'brontosaur *n.* a large dinosaur of the group which includes the brontosaurus; *spec.* = BRONTOSAURUS: L19. **brontosaurian** *a.* of or like a brontosaurus; chiefly *fig.*, ponderous, clumsy: E20.

Bronx /brɒŋks/ *n. US.* E20. [A borough of New York City.] 1 In full *Bronx cocktail*. A cocktail of gin, vermouth, and orange juice. E20. 2 *Bronx cheer*, a sound of derision or contempt made by blowing through closed lips with the tongue between; = RASPBERRY 3a. E20.

bronze /brɒnz/ *n.* & *a.* E18. [Fr. f. It. *bronzo*, prob. f. Pers. *birinj* brass.] A *n.* 1 A brown alloy of copper with up to one-third tin, often with small amounts of other metals; (w. specifying wd) such an alloy with a particular composition or constituent. Cf. BRASS *n.* E18. b Bronze taken as a type of hardness or insensitivity; impudence, effrontery, nerve. Now *rare*. E18. c = *bronze medal* below. M20. 2 A statue or other work of art made of bronze. E18. 3 A brown metallic powder used in painting etc. M18. 4 The colour of bronze. E19.

1 ALUMINIUM *bronze*. *Corinthian bronze*: see CORINTHIAN *a.* I. MANGANESE *bronze*. PHOSPHOR *bronze*. *plastic bronze*: see PLASTIC *a.* & *n.*[3] *white bronze*: see WHITE *a.*

B *attrib.* or as *adj.* Made of bronze; of the colour of bronze. M19.

Special collocations & comb.: **Bronze Age** the period when weapons and tools were predominantly made of copper and its alloys. **bronze diabetes** = HAEMOCHROMATOSIS. **bronze medal**: awarded for a third place in the modern Olympic Games etc. **bronze powder** = sense A.3 above. **bronzewing** any of a number of Australasian pigeons, esp. *Phaps chalcoptera*.

bronzy *a.* tinged with bronze colour; like bronze: M19.

bronze /brɒnz/ *v.* M17. [f. the n. or Fr. *bronzer*.] 1 *v.t.* Give a surface of bronze or resembling bronze to. M17. b *fig.* Make unfeeling or shameless, harden. Now *rare* or *obs.* E18. 2 *v.t.* & *i.* Make or become like bronze in colour; brown, suntan. L18.

2 **bronzed diabetes** = HAEMOCHROMATOSIS.

bronzite /ˈbrɒnzʌɪt/ *n.* E19. [f. BRONZE *n.* + -ITE[1].] *Min.* A bronze-coloured iron-containing variety of enstatite.

broo /bruː/ *n.*[1] *Sc.* LME. [OFr. *breu*: see BREWIS.] = BREE *n.*[2] 2.

broo *n.*[2] var. of BUROO.

brooch /brəʊtʃ/ *n.* & *v.* Also †**broche**. ME. [Var. of BROACH *n.*[1]] A *n.* 1 An ornament with a hinged pin and catch, usu. worn fastened to a woman's clothing or as a badge etc. ME. †2 Any jewelled ornament; a trinket. ME-L17.

1 *spray brooch*: see SPRAY *n.*[1] 2c. *stomacher brooch*: see STOMACHER *n.*[1] 2.

B *v.t.* Adorn as with a brooch. *rare.* E17.

brood /bruːd/ *n.* [OE *brōd*, corresp. to MDu. *broet* (Du. *broed*), OHG *bruot* (G *Brut*), f. Gmc, f. base meaning 'warm, heat'.] 1 Progeny or offspring of animals that lay eggs; a family of young from one hatching; *spec.* (*a*) bee or wasp larvae; (*b*) the spat of oysters in its second year. OE. b Of human beings: a family, children. Now *derog.* or *joc.* ME. c *fig.* The products or results of circumstances, actions, etc. L16. 2 The fostering of the foetus in egg or womb; hatching, breeding. *arch.* exc. in *comb.* below. ME. †b Parentage, descent. ME-L16. 3 A race, a kind; a group of men, things, etc., having common qualities. Usu. *derog.* LME. 4 A state or period of contemplative brooding. L19.

1 AV *Luke* 13:34 As a henne doeth gather her brood vnder her wings. b SHAKES. *Temp.* She will become thy bed . . And bring thee forth brave brood. c MILTON The brood of Folly without father bred. GEO. ELIOT A brood of guilty wishes. 2 **sit on brood** sit as a hen on her eggs, sit brooding (cf. ABROOD). b SPENSER The virgin borne of heauenly brood. 3 ADDISON Its tainted air and all its broods of poisons. E. A. FREEMAN A brood of petty despots. 4 W. GOLDING I drifted off into a dreary brood.

Comb.: **brood cell, comb** a cell in, the part of, a comb used for the rearing of bee larvae; **brood-hen, mare,** etc.: kept for breeding; **brood patch** a denuded area of a bird's ventral surface, facilitating the transfer of heat from the parent to the egg(s); **brood queen** = QUEEN *n.* 6.

brood /bruːd/ *v.* LME. [f. the n.] I *v.t.* 1 Sit on (eggs) so as to hatch them, incubate. LME. b *fig.* Breed, hatch, (products, projects). E17. 2 Cherish (young) under the wings, as a hen. L16. b *fig.* Cherish in the mind etc.; contemplate, nurse (wrath etc.). Now *rare* (cf. sense 5 below). L16.

1b SOUTHEY There brood the pestilence and let The earthquake loose. 2b DRYDEN You'll sit and brood your Sorrows on a throne.

II *v.i.* 3 Incubate eggs; sit as a hen on eggs. L16. 4 *fig.* Of night, silence, etc.: hang or hover close *over*, (*up*)*on*, etc. M17. 5 Meditate (*on*, *upon*, *over*, *about*), esp. moodily or resentfully. L17. 6 Lie as a cherished nestling, thought, etc. L17.

4 DRYDEN Perpetual Night . . In silence brooding on th' unhappy ground. LD MACAULAY Mists and storms brood over it [Glencoe] through the greater part of the finest Summer. 5 R. MACAULAY She brooded darkly for a while. A. BRINK Ben was in no mood to talk, brooding over his own thoughts. 6 N. HAWTHORNE The themes that were brooding deepest in their hearts.

brooder *n.* (*a*) a hen etc. that broods or hatches eggs; (*b*) a person who broods over things; (*c*) a heated house or a device providing heat for chicks, piglets, etc.: L16. **broodingly** *adv.* in a brooding manner M19.

broody /ˈbruːdi/ *a.* & *n.* E16. [f. BROOD *n.* + -Y[1].] A *adj.* 1 Apt or inclined to breed; prolific. *obs.* exc. *dial.* E16. 2 Of a hen: wishing or inclined to incubate eggs. Of a woman (*joc.*): wishing to be pregnant. E16. 3 Inclined to meditate resentfully; feeling depressed. M19. B *n.* A broody hen. E20.

broodiness *n.* L19.

brook /brʊk/ *n.* [OE *brōc*, corresp. to LG & HG wds meaning 'marsh, bog', MLG *brōk*, (M)Du. *brock*, OHG *bruoh* (G *Bruch*): of unkn. origin.] A small stream; orig., a torrent.

babbling brook: see BABBLE *v.* 2.

Comb.: **brook char** = *brook trout* (b) below; **brooklime** [OE *hleomoce*, name of the plant] a speedwell common in wet places, esp. *Veronica beccabunga*; **brook trout** †(*a*) the brown trout, *Salmo trutta*; (*b*) a migratory char, *Salvelinus fontinalis*, native to north-eastern N. America; also called *brown char*; **brookweed** a small white-flowered plant, *Samolus valerandi*, of the primrose family, found in wet places; also called *water pimpernel*.

brooklet *n.* a little brook E19.

brook /brʊk/ *v.t.* [OE *brūcan* = OFris. *brūka*, OS *brūkan* (Du. *bruiken*), OHG *brūhhan* (G *brauchen*), Goth. *brūkjan*, f. Gmc base meaning 'to use', f. IE (whence L *frui* enjoy).] 1 Enjoy the use of, profit by; possess, hold. *arch.* exc. *Sc.* OE. †2 Make use of (food); digest. OE-L16. 3 Put up with, tolerate; admit of. Usu. w. neg. Now *literary*. M16.

3 M. MUGGERIDGE A son-in-law who was an elementary school supply teacher was not to be brooked. E. REVELEY Her mother's frenzy brooked no delay.

brookable *a.* (chiefly *Sc.*) endurable, tolerable (earlier in UNBROOKABLE) E19.

brookite /ˈbrʊkʌɪt/ *n.* E19. [f. Henry J. *Brooke* (1771–1857), Eng. mineralogist + -ITE[1].] *Min.* The orthorhombic form of titanium dioxide, usu. occurring as dark brown or black prisms.

Brooklynese /brʊklɪˈniːz/ *n.* E20. [f. *Brooklyn* (see below) + -ESE.] An uncultivated form of

New York speech associated esp. with the borough of Brooklyn.

brool /bruːl/ *n.* M19. [G *Brüll* (poet. for *Gebrüll*), f. *brüllen* to roar.] A low humming sound; a murmur.

broom /bruːm/ *n.* & *v.* [OE *brōm*, corresp. to MLG *brām*, MDu. *brāme* (Du. *braam*), OHG *brāmo*, *brāma*, f. Gmc base also of BRAMBLE *n.*] **A** *n.* **1** Any of various chiefly yellow-flowered leguminous shrubs of the genera *Cytisus* and *Genista*, esp. the common species *C. scoparius* of western Eurasia. Also (w. specifying wd), any of certain other plants similar to these in use or appearance. OE. **2** A sweeping-implement, usu. on a long handle, orig. one made of twigs of broom, heather, etc. ME.

1 *butcher's broom*, *Spanish broom*, *spart-broom*, *sweet broom*, etc. 2 **new broom** *fig.* a newly appointed person eager to make changes. *shovel and broom*: see SHOVEL *n.* 1.

Comb.: **broom-corn** *N. Amer.* a variety of sorghum whose dried inflorescences are used for brooms; **broom-grass** *N. Amer.* = *broom-sedge* below; **broomrape** [L *rapum* tuber] a brown leafless plant belonging to the genus *Orobanche* or a related genus, and growing on the roots of other plants; **broom-sedge** *N. Amer.* any of various coarse grasses, esp. of the genus *Andropogon*, occas. used for brooms or thatch; **broomstaff**, pl. **-staffs**, **-staves**, a broomstick; **broomstick** the handle of a broom (allegedly ridden through the air by witches); *marry over the broomstick*, go through a sham marriage ceremony in which the parties jump over a broom.

B *v.t.* **1** = BREAM *v.* Only in Dicts. E17. **2** Sweep with a broom. E19.

broomie *n.* (*Austral.* & *NZ colloq.*) a person who sweeps the floor in a shearing-shed M20. **broomy** *a.* covered with or having much broom M17.

broose /bruːz/ *n.* *Sc.* M17. [Origin unkn.] A traditional race by young men present at country weddings in Scotland, the course being from the bride's former home to the bridegroom's house.

Bros. *n.pl.* see BRO.

brose /brəʊz/ *n.* Chiefly *Sc.* M17. [Var. of BREWIS.] A dish of oatmeal with boiling water or milk poured on it.

ATHOLE BROSE. PEASE-*brose*.

broth /brɒθ/ *n.* [OE *broþ* = OHG *brod*, ON *broð*, f. Gmc, f. base of BREW *v.*] **1** Unclarified meat or fish stock; a thin soup made from this and vegetables. OE. **2** Stock etc. used as a culture medium for bacteria. L19.

1 **broth of a boy** (chiefly *Anglo-Ir.*) a good fellow. *Scotch broth*: see SCOTCH *a.*

brothy *a.* (*rare*) of, or of the nature of, broth M17.

brothel /ˈbrɒθ(ə)l/ *n.* LME. [Ult. f. OE *brēoþan* deteriorate, degenerate, of unkn. origin. In sense 3 abbrev. of *brothel-house*, infl. by and superseding BORDEL.] †**1** A worthless wretch, a good-for-nothing. LME–L16. †**2** A prostitute. LME–E17. **3** A house where prostitutes work. L16.

Comb.: **brothel-creepers** *slang* soft-soled (usu. suede) shoes; **brothel-house** *arch.* = sense 3 above.

†**brotheller** *n.* a whoremonger E17–E19. **brothelly** *a.* (*rare*) whorish E17. **brothelry** *n.* (*a*) *arch.* lewdness; †(*b*) a brothel: M16.

brother /ˈbrʌðə/ *n.* & *a.* Pl. **brothers,** (chiefly in senses 2b & 3) **brethren** /ˈbrɛðr(ə)n/. [OE *brōþor* = OFris. *brōther*, *brōder*, OS *brōþar*, (M)Du. *broeder*, (M)LG *brōder*, OHG *bruodar* (G *Bruder*), ON *bróðir*, Goth. *brōþar*, f. Gmc f. IE, whence L *frater*, Gk *phratēr*, Skt *bhrātṛ*.] **A** *n.* **1** A male related to one or more other persons (male or female) by having the same parents or by having one parent in common. OE. **b** Chiefly in biblical translations (a Hebraism): a kinsman, as uncle, nephew, or cousin. ME. **2** (With possible inclusion of a minority of females in pl., if not considered significant. Also used before a name and as a form of address or reference.) **a** A man who is a close friend; a (male) fellow citizen or fellow countryman; an associate, an equal; a person of the same race, colour, or class; a fellow creature. OE. **b** A (male) fellow Christian, a co-religionist, a (male) fellow member of a religious society or sect. In *pl.* (**Brethren**) *spec.* members of the Plymouth Brethren (see below). OE. **c** *RC Ch.* A member of a men's religious congregation or order. ME. **d** A (male) fellow member of a guild, trade union, society, regiment, profession, etc.; an official of certain companies etc. LME. **e** Used as a familiar form of address to a man. Also as *int.* expr. surprise, annoyance, etc. Chiefly *N. Amer.* E20. **3** *fig.* An identical or similar thing, a counterpart. LME.

1 AV *Prov.* 18:24 A friend that sticketh closer than a brother. TENNYSON Here two brothers .. had met And fought. *adoptive brother*, *foster-brother*, *full brother*, *half-brother*, *stepbrother*, etc. 2a TENNYSON My friend, the brother of my love, My Arthur! C. G. SELIGMAN The extinct Guanches of the Canary Islands showed as least as much racial mixture as their brethren of the mainland. *Black Scholar* This Black Studies Class will help open the eyes of our so many sleeping brothers. A. STORR Faced with a common enemy .. we become brothers in a way which never obtains in ordinary life. **b** J. MORLEY The Protestants .. found warm hospitality among their northern brethren. W. G. SIMMS Call me not Mr., I pray thee. .. If thou wilt call me Brother Cross, my heart shall acknowledge the bonds between us. **c** B. MOORE Behind Brother Martin, gazing at the shiny tonsure. **d** A. H. QUINN He was a member of Kappa Phi, and .. he had a right to anything his brothers could give him. 4 POPE Grove nods at grove, each Alley has a brother.

Phrases: *a man and a brother*: see MAN *n.* *Big Brother*: see BIG *a.* **brother consanguineous, consanguineous brother** (esp. *Rom. Law*): having the same father only. **brother german**: having the same parents. **brother uterine, uterine brother**: having the same mother only. *consanguineous brother*: see *brother consanguineous* above. *Elder Brother*: see ELDER *a.* *lay brother*: see LAY *a.* **the Brethren** (*a*) in the New Testament, the members of the early Christian Churches; (*b*) the Plymouth Brethren. **(the) Christian Brethren** (members of) the Plymouth Brethren. **(the) Exclusive Brethren** (members of) the more exclusive section of the Plymouth Brethren. **(the) Open Brethren** (members of) the less exclusive section of the Plymouth Brethren. **(the) Plymouth Brethren** a Calvinistic religious body formed at Plymouth *c* 1830 with no formal creed and no official order of ministers. *United Brethren*: see UNITED *a.* *uterine brother*: see *brother uterine* above.

B *attrib.* or as *adj.* (Freq. w. hyphen.) That is a brother; belonging to the same group; close as a brother; fellow-. LME.

POPE Two brother-heroes shall from thee be born. R. BURNS Land o' Cakes and brither Scots. J. RABAN One of his brother officers wandered into the mess.

Special collocations & *comb.*: **brother-in-arms** a fighter in the same cause. **brother-in-law**, pl. **brothers-in-law**, the brother of one's husband or wife, or the husband of one's sister(-in-law). *Brother* JONATHAN.

brothership *n.* (a) brotherhood OE.

brother /ˈbrʌðə/ *v.t.* LME. [f. the n.] Make a brother of; admit to brotherhood; treat or address as brother.

brotherhood /ˈbrʌðəhʊd/ *n.* Also †**-head**. ME. [Prob. f. BROTHERRED w. assim. to -HEAD, -HOOD.] **1** The (freq. spiritual) relation of a brother or of brothers mutually. ME. **2** Brotherliness, companionship, friendly alliance. ME. **3** Orig., Christian fellowship. Now *gen.*, community of feeling, fellowship, unity. LME. **4** The members of a fellowship etc. collectively; an association of equals for mutual help; a fraternity, a guild, etc. LME. **b** *spec.* (*a*) A trade union, esp. of railwaymen; (*b*) a profession. *N. Amer.* L19. †**5** The rank of brother in a corporation etc. M16–E17. **6** *fig.* A group of related or similar things. E18.

2 N. HAWTHORNE We live in great harmony and brotherhood. 3 R. W. DALE There is a brotherhood between Christ and all believers. JOYCE Three cheers for universal brotherhood! G. MURRAY A scholar .. draws the strength that comes from communion or brotherhood. 4 SOUTHEY The grey brotherhood Chaunted the solemn mass. SHELLEY And make the earth One brotherhood. P. H. GIBBS A new brotherhood of peoples turning their backs on blood and ruin.

brotherly /ˈbrʌðəli/ *a.* & (less usually) *adv.* [OE *brōþorlić* adj., f. as BROTHER *n.* + -LY[1].] (In a manner) of or befitting a brother; kind(ly), affectionate(ly).

brotherliness *n.* the quality of being brotherly, brotherly feeling. M16.

†**brotherred** *n.* OE–M16. [f. BROTHER *n.* + -RED.] A brotherhood.

brotulid /ˈbrɒtjʊlɪd/ *n.* & *a.* L19. [f. mod.L *Brotula* genus name, prob. f. Amer. Sp. *brótula*, + -ID[3].] (A fish) of a numerous group of predominantly deep-sea or cave-dwelling fishes belonging to the cusk-eel family Ophidiidae.

brough *n.* var. of BROCH.

brougham /ˈbruː(ə)m/ *n.* M19. [Henry Peter, Lord *Brougham* (1778–1868).] Chiefly *Hist.* A one-horse closed carriage. Also, a similar electric vehicle, or a motor car with the driver's seat outside.

brought *v.* pa. t. & pple of BRING *v.*

brouhaha /ˈbruːhɑːhɑː/ *n.* L19. [Fr.] A commotion, a sensation; uproar, hubbub.

brouillon /brujɔ̃/ *n.* Pl. pronounced same. L17. [Fr.] A rough draft.

brow /braʊ/ *n.*[1] [OE *brū* f. Gmc f. IE, whence Gk *ophrus*, Skt *bhrū*.] †**1** In *pl.* The eyelashes. Only in OE. **2** An arch of hair growing in a ridge over the eye; an eyebrow. Usu. in *pl.* OE. **b** In *pl.* The prominences of the forehead above the eyes. Now *poet.* = sense 3. L16. **3** The whole part of the face above the eyes, the forehead, *poet.* esp. as expressing emotion; hence (*arch.*) expression of countenance, confronting aspect. ME. †**b** Composure, confidence, effrontery. M17–E18. **c** [f. *highbrow* etc.] Level of intellectual attainment or interest. *colloq.* E20. **4** The top or projecting edge of a cliff, hill, etc., standing over a precipice or slope; the top of a hill in a road. LME.

2 **knit one's brows** frown. **b** SHAKES. *Jul. Caes.* Did not they Put on my brows this wreath of victory? 3 SIR W. SCOTT The old man, who had .. resisted the brow of military and civil tyranny. LD MACAULAY That brow of hate, that mouth of scorn. SIAN EVANS His hair .. hung in tags over a flat red brow. *by the sweat of one's brow*: see SWEAT *n.* **have no brow of** *Sc.* not be impressed by.

Comb.: **brow antler** = *brow tine* below; **brow-band** a band worn across the brow; *spec.* the band of a bridle etc. which passes in front of a horse's forehead; **brow ridge** a superciliary ridge; **brow tine** the lowest tine of a stag's horn.

browed *a.* having a brow or brows (of a specified kind) LME. **browless** *a.* †(*a*) without shame, unabashed; (*b*) without eyebrows: E17.

brow /braʊ/ *n.*[2] M19. [Prob. f. Norw. *bru*, ON *brú* bridge.] *Naut.* A gangway from ship to shore. Also, the hinged part of the bow or stern of a landing-craft or ferry, which is lowered to form a landing platform or ramp.

brow /braʊ/ *v.t.* *rare.* M17. [f. BROW *n.*[1]] Form a brow to; be on the brow of.

browallia /brəʊˈwɔːlɪə/ *n.* L18. [mod.L, f. Johann *Browall* (1707–55), Swed. botanist: see -IA[1].] A tropical American plant of the genus *Browallia*, of the nightshade family, with violet, blue, or white flowers.

browbeat /ˈbraʊbiːt/ *v.t.* & *i.* Infl. as BEAT *v.*[1] L16. [f. BROW *n.*[1] + BEAT *v.*[1]] Intimidate or discourage with stern, arrogant, or insolent looks or words; bully.

browbeater *n.* L17.

browden /ˈbraʊd(ə)n/ *a.* Long *obs.* exc. *Sc.* Also †**broiden**. [OE (*ġe*)*broġden* pa. pple of *breġdan* BRAID *v.*[1]] †**1** Plaited, interwoven. OE–LME. †**2** Embroidered; adorned. LME–M19. **3** Enamoured, fond. L16. **4** Impudent, bold. M19.

browis *n.* var. of BREWIS.

brown /braʊn/ *n.* ME. [The adj. used ellipt. or absol.] **1** Brown colour; a shade of this; a pigment of a brown colour. ME. **2** A thing distinguished by brown colour, as the brown ball in snooker, a brown butterfly (*spec.* one of the family Satyridae), brown ale, brown clothing, etc. ME. **b** A copper coin. *slang.* E19. **c** A mulatto. M19.

1 *chocolate-brown*, *clove-brown*, *nigger brown*, *saddle brown*, *Spanish brown*, *toffee-brown*, *Vandyke brown*, etc. **fire into the brown (of them)** fire into the brown mass of a flock of game-birds instead of singling out one; *transf.* let fly at random into a mass. 2 *wall brown*: see WALL *n.*[1]

Comb.: **brown spot** the spot on which the brown ball is placed in snooker.

brown /braʊn/ *a.* [OE *brūn* = OFris., OS *brūn* (Du. *bruin*), OHG *brūn* (G *braun*), ON *brúnn*, f. Gmc (whence Fr., Prov. *brun*, It. *bruno*). Reinforced in ME by (O)Fr. *brun*.] 1 Dusky, dark. Now only *poet.* OE. 2 Of a person: having the skin of a dark or dusky colour as a racial characteristic; also, dark-complexioned, tanned. OE. 3 Of or denoting a composite colour produced by a mixture of red, yellow, and black, or as the result of toasting bread etc. ME. †4 Of steel etc.: burnished. ME–L18.

Phrases: *bright-line brown-eye*: see BRIGHT *a.* 6. **do brown** *slang* deceive, cheat.

Special collocations & comb.: **brown alga** an alga of the division Phaeophyta, members of which contain xanthophyll in addition to chlorophyll and include many seaweeds. *brown argus*: see ARGUS 2. **brown bag** (chiefly *N. Amer.*) a plain paper bag, esp. for carrying food and drink, often used to conceal the nature of its contents. **brown-bag** *v.t.* (chiefly *N. Amer.*) carry (esp. food and drink) in a plain paper bag, esp. to conceal the contents. **brown-bagger** (chiefly *N. Amer.*) a person who carries a brown bag, esp. containing food or drink. *brown bear*: see BEAR *n.*[1] 1. **brown belt** (the holder of) a belt marking the attainment of a certain degree of proficiency in judo or karate. **Brown Bess** *colloq.* (*Hist.*) the old British army flintlock musket, with brown walnut stock. **Brown Betty** (chiefly *N. Amer.*) a baked pudding containing apples and breadcrumbs. **brown-bill** *Hist.* a kind of halberd used by foot-soldiers and watchmen. **brown bread** any bread of a darker colour than white bread; *spec.* bread made of unbolted flour or whole meal. **brown coal** lignite. **brown creeper** (chiefly *N. Amer.*) the common treecreeper, *Certhia familiaris*. **brown earth** a type of soil having a brown humus-rich surface layer. **brown eye**: with a brown iris. **brown-eyed** *a.* having brown eyes. *brown* GEORGE. **brown goods** household furniture such as television sets and audio equipment (opp. *white goods*). **brown hare** a common Eurasian hare, *Lepus europaeus* (esp. as distinct from the blue or Arctic hare). *brown* HAEMATITE. **brown holland** an unbleached linen fabric. *brown* HYENA. **brown job** *slang* a soldier; *collect.* the Army. *brown loaf*: see LOAF *n.*[1] **brown malt**: roasted to a dark brown colour. *brown mustard*: see MUSTARD *n.* 2. **brown-nose(r)** *slang* (chiefly *N. Amer.*) a sycophant. **brown owl** (*a*) the tawny owl; (*b*) (with cap. initials) the adult leader of a Brownie pack. **brown paper** a coarse stout kind of paper made of unbleached materials, used chiefly for wrapping. *brown rat*: see RAT *n.*[1] 1a. **brown rice** unpolished rice with only the husk of the grain removed. **brown rot (disease)** a fungal disease of various plants, esp. of the rose family, causing mummification of the fruit. **brown sauce** a savoury sauce made with browned fat or gravy; any brown-coloured savoury sauce. **Brown-shirt** *Hist.* a Nazi; *spec.* a member of the *Sturmabteilung* (SA) in Nazi Germany. **brown snake** a poisonous Australian snake of the genus *Pseudonaja*. **brown spar** any hexagonal carbonate mineral coloured brown by the presence of iron, e.g. siderite, ankerite. **brownstone** *n.* & *a.* (*US*) (*a*) *n.* a kind of reddish-brown sandstone used for building (esp. in front elevation); a house faced with this; (*b*) *adj.* affluent, well-to-do. **brown study** a state of mental abstraction or musing; *esp.* an idle reverie. **brown sugar** unrefined or partially refined sugar. **brown-tail** a white European moth, *Euproctis chrysorrhoea* (family Lymantriidae), which has a brown tip to the abdomen and the larvae of which have irritating hairs. *brown thrasher*: see THRASHER *n.*[2] **brown top** any of various pasture grasses of Australia or New Zealand. **brown trout** the trout, *Salmo trutta*; *spec.* a small dark non-migratory form occurring in smaller rivers and pools. **brownwort** water figwort, *Scrophularia auriculata*.

brownish *a.* LME. **brownly** *adv.* with a brown colour E19. **brownness** /-n-n-/ *n.* LME. **browny** *a.* inclining to brown L16.

brown /braʊn/ *v.* ME. [f. the adj. or (sense 3) n.] 1 *v.i.* Become brown. ME. 2 *v.t.* Make brown; roast brown; give a dull brown lustre to (gun barrels etc.). L16. 3 *v.t.* Fire indiscriminately at (a covey of birds, a mass of men, etc.) L19.

2 **browned off** *slang* bored, fed up, discontented.

Comb.: **brown-out** (chiefly *Austral.* & *N. Amer.*) a partial blackout.

Brownian /ˈbraʊnɪən/ *a.* L19. [f. Robert *Brown* (1773–1858), Eng. botanist + -IAN.] *Brownian motion, movement*, the irregular oscillations of microscopic particles suspended in a fluid.

brownie /ˈbraʊni/ *n.* In sense 4 also **B-**. E16. [f. BROWN *a.* + -IE.] 1 A benevolent goblin, supposed to haunt old houses (esp. farmhouses in Scotland) and occas. to do household work secretly. E16. 2a A sweet currant-bread. *Austral.* & *NZ.* L19. b A small square of rich (usu. chocolate) cake containing nuts. *N. Amer.* L19. 3 (An angler's name for) a trout. E20. 4 A member of the junior branch of the Guides. E20.

Comb.: **brownie point** a credit for an achievement.

browning /ˈbraʊnɪŋ/ *n.*[1] M18. [f. BROWN *v.* + -ING[1].] 1 A preparation for giving a brown colour to gravy etc. M18. 2 The action of BROWN *v.* L18.

Browning /ˈbraʊnɪŋ/ *n.*[2] E20. [John M. *Browning* (1855–1926), US designer.] A type of esp. automatic firearm.

Browningesque /braʊnɪŋˈɛsk/ *a.* L19. [f. *Browning* (see below) + -ESQUE.] Of, pertaining to, or characteristic of the English poet Robert Browning (1812–89) or his style.

Brownism /ˈbraʊnɪz(ə)m/ *n.* E17. [f. *Brown* (see below) + -ISM.] *Hist.* The system of church government advocated by the Puritan Robert Brown (*c*1550–*c*1633), and adopted by the Independents.

Brownist *n.* an adherent or student of the ecclesiastical principles of Robert Brown L16. **Brow'nistical** *a.* M17.

browse /braʊz/ *n.*[1] Also †**-ze**. E16. [OFr. *brost*, later *broust* (mod. *brout*) bud, young shoot, prob. of Gmc origin.] 1 Young shoots and twigs of shrubs, trees, etc., used as food by animals; something that is or can be browsed. E16. 2 The action of browsing. E19.

browse /braʊz/ *n.*[2] M19. [Origin unkn.] A mixture of partly-reduced ore and fuel, produced during smelting of lead.

browse /braʊz/ *v.* Also †**-ze**. LME. [OFr. *broster* (mod. *brouter*) to crop, f. as BROWSE *n.*[1]] 1 *v.i.* Of an animal: feed on or *on* the leaves and shoots of trees and bushes. LME. 2 *v.t.* Crop and eat (leaves, twigs, etc.). LME. 3 *v.t.* Feed (an animal) *on* twigs etc. M16. 4 *v.i.* & *t. fig.* Look through (books etc.) casually; read desultorily. L19.

browser *n.* †(*a*) a person who feeds deer (in wintertime); (*b*) an animal which browses; a person who browses among books etc.: M16. **browsing** *n.* (*a*) the action of the vb; (*b*) shoots and leaves; browsing ground: LME. **browsy** *a.* †(*a*) (of vegetation) scanty, twiggy; (*b*) characterized by or suitable for browsing or casual reading: M18.

browst /braʊst/ *n. Sc.* E16. [f. base of BREW *v.*] A brewing; a brew.

†**browster** *n.* var. of BREWSTER *n.*[1]

†**browze** *n*, *v.* var. of BROWSE *n.*[1], *v.*

brrr /br-r-r/ *int.* L19. [Imit.] Expr. shivering.

brucellosis /bruːsəˈləʊsɪs/ *n.* Pl. **-loses** /-ˈləʊsiːz/. M20. [f. mod.L *Brucella* (see below), f. Sir David *Bruce* (1855–1931), Sc. physician + -ELLA: see -OSIS.] Infection with bacteria of the genus *Brucella*, which produces contagious abortion in cattle and other livestock, and undulant fever in man.

bruchid /ˈbruːkɪd/ *n.* & *a.* L19. [mod.L *Bruchidae* (see below), f. *Bruchus* genus name f. L *bruchus* f. Gk *broukhos* wingless locust: see -ID[3].] A *n.* Any beetle of the family Bruchidae, which includes many species resembling weevils and destructive to leguminous crops. L19. B *adj.* Of, pertaining to, or designating this family. L19.

brucine /ˈbruːsiːn/ *n.* E19. [f. mod.L *Brucea* genus name of a tree formerly thought to be the source of false angostura bark, f. James *Bruce* (1730–94), Sc. traveller: see -INE[5].] *Chem.* A highly toxic alkaloid present in false angostura bark and nux vomica.

brucia *n.* (now *rare* or *obs.*) = BRUCINE E19.

brucite /ˈbruːsʌɪt/ *n.* E19. [f. Archibald *Bruce* (1777–1818), US mineralogist + -ITE[1].] *Min.* Native magnesium hydroxide, which usu. occurs as white, grey, or light green hexagonal tabular crystals or in massive form.

bruckle /ˈbrʌk(ə)l/ *a.* Long *dial.* Also **brickle** /ˈbrɪk(ə)l/, **britchel** /ˈbrɪtʃ(ə)l/. [OE *-brucol*, *-bryċel* ult. f. Gmc base of BREAK *v.* For vars. cf. *mickle*, *muckle*, *much*.] †1 As 2nd elem. of comb. Liable to cause breakage of, that breaks. Only in OE. 2 Liable to break; fragile, brittle; frail, delicate, uncertain. ME.

brugh *n.* var. of BROCH.

bruilzie *n.* var. of BRULZIE.

Bruin /ˈbruːɪn/ *n.* Also **b-**. L15. [Du. = brown, a name for the bear in *Reynard the Fox*.] (A personal name for) a bear.

bruise /bruːz/ *n.* LME. [f. the vb.] †1 A breaking, a breach. LME–M16. 2 A hurt or injury to the body manifested as a discoloration of the skin, caused by an impact or blow. M16. b A discoloration of the surface of a plant, fruit, etc. L17.

¶Perh. earlier in BRUISEWORT.

bruise /bruːz/ *v.* [OE *brȳsan* reinforced in ME by AN *bruser*, OFr. *bruisier* (mod. *briser*) break, smash, of unkn. origin.] 1 *v.t.* Injure or damage with a heavy blow or weight. Now usu. *spec.*, injure by a blow which discolours the skin but does not lacerate it or break any bones. OE. b Produce a similar lesion in (a plant, fruit, etc.). LME. †2 *v.t.* [after Fr.] Break, smash. ME–E17. 3 *v.t. fig.* Crush, wound, disable; hurt (pride etc.). ME. 4 *v.t.* Beat small, crush, grind down. LME. 5 *v.t.* Crush by pressure, jam, squeeze. *obs.* exc. *Sc.* E17. 6 *v.i.* Esp. of fruit: become bruised. E20.

3 MILTON An Iron Rod to bruise and breake Thy disobedience. J. HELLER She was bruising his most vulnerable feelings. 4 DRYDEN Some scatt'ring Pot-herbs . . bruis'd with Vervain.

bruiser *n.* (*a*) a person who bruises; (*b*) a prizefighter, a brawny muscular man; (*c*) a machine or implement for crushing or grinding: L16. **bruising** *n.* (*a*) the action of the vb; (*b*) injury so caused; (*c*) prizefighting: LME.

bruisewort /ˈbruːzwɔːt/ *n.* OE. [f. BRUISE *n.* or *v.* + WORT *n.*[1]] Any of various plants supposed to heal bruises, *esp.* the daisy.

bruit /bruːt; *in sense 4 foreign* brɥi (*pl. same*)/ *n. arch.* LME. [(O)Fr., use as n. of pa. pple of *bruire* roar f. Proto-Romance alt. of L *rugire* roar by assoc. w. source of BRAY *v.*[1]] 1 Noise, clamour. LME. 2 Rumour, report. LME. †3 Fame, reputation. L15–E17. 4 *Med.* Any sound (esp. an abnormal one) heard in auscultation. M19.

bruit /bruːt/ *v. arch.* exc. *US.* L15. [f. the n.] 1 *v.t.* Spread (a report etc.) *abroad* or *about*, rumour. L15. 2 *v.t.* Speak of, make famous. E16. 3 *v.i.* Make noise. *rare.* E19.

1 SHAKES. *1 Hen. VI* I find thou art no less than fame hath bruited. LYTTON They do bruit it that he sees visions. J. I. M. STEWART For a fortnight . . nothing about it could be bruited abroad. 2 MILTON A man so much bruited for learning. 3 KEATS Bronze clarions . . faintly bruit, Where long ago a giant battle was.

brulzie /ˈbruːli, -lji/ *n. Sc.* Also **bruil-**. M16. [f. as BROIL *n.*[1]] A disturbance, a squabble.

Brum /brʌm/ *n. slang.* M19. [Shortened f. BRUMMAGEM.] (A nickname for) the town (now a city) of Birmingham, England.

Brumaire /bruːˈmɛː, *foreign* brymɛːr/ *n.* E19. [Fr., f. as BRUME + *-aire* -ARY[1].] *Hist.* The second month of the French Republican calendar (introduced 1793), extending from 22 October to 20 November.

brumal /ˈbruːm(ə)l/ *a. literary.* E16. [L *brumalis*, f. *bruma* winter: see -AL[1].] Like winter, wintry.

brumby /ˈbrʌmbi/ *n.* & *a. Austral.* L19. [Origin unkn.] (Designating) a wild or unbroken horse.

brume /bruːm/ *n. literary.* E18. [Fr. = fog, f. L *bruma* winter.] Fog, mist, vapour.

Brummagem /ˈbrʌmədʒ(ə)m/ *a.* & *n. arch.* M17. [Dial. form of BIRMINGHAM.] A *adj.* 1 Of the quality of coins and some other goods made in Birmingham, England; counterfeit, sham, tawdry. M17. †2 See BIRMINGHAM. B *n.* †1 See BIRMINGHAM. 2 (An article of) counterfeit or cheap and showy ware. M19.

Brummie /ˈbrʌmi/ *n.* & *a. colloq.* Also **-y**. M20. [f. as prec.: see -IE.] (A native or inhabitant) of Birmingham, England.

brumous /ˈbruːməs/ *a. literary.* M19. [Fr. *brumeux* f. late L *brumosus*, f. *bruma* winter: see -OUS.] Foggy; wintry.

brunch /brʌn(t)ʃ/ *n.* & *v. colloq.* L19. [Blend of BREAKFAST *n.* and LUNCH *n.*] A *n.* A single meal intended to combine breakfast and lunch. L19.

Comb.: **brunch coat** *Austral.* & *NZ* a woman's short housecoat.

B *v.i.* Eat brunch. M20.

bruncher *n.* L20.

brunet /bruːˈnɛt, ˌbrʊ-/ *n.* & *a.* Also (fem.) **brunette**. M16. [Fr. *brunet* masc., *-ette* fem., dim. of *brun* brown: see -ET[1], -ETTE.] (A White person, in form *-ette* esp. a woman or girl) with a dark complexion or (now usu.) brown hair. Of the complexion: dark.

brung *v.* see BRING.

Brünnich's guillemot /ˈbruːnɪtʃɪz ˈɡɪlɪmɒt/ *n. phr.* L19. [M. T. *Brünnich* (1737–1827), Da. naturalist.] A guillemot, *Uria lomvia*, with a shorter beak than the common guillemot and restricted to latitudes north of the British Isles.

Brunswick /ˈbrʌnzwɪk/ *n.* L15. [In branch I f. *Brunswick*, a city and province of northern Germany, LG *Brunswīk*, G *Braunschweig*; in branch II, f. a county named after this in Virginia, US.] I 1 A fabric or garment from Brunswick; *esp.* (in full *Brunswick gown*) a long-sleeved gown with a train from the shoulders. *obs.* exc. *Hist.* L15. 2 *Brunswick green*, a dark green pigment orig. made of a basic chloride of copper; this shade of green. E19. II 3 *Brunswick stew*, a stew of squirrel, now also of game or chicken, with onions and sometimes other vegetables. *US.* M19.

brunt /brʌnt/ *n.* LME. [Origin unkn.] †1 A blow. LME–E17. †2 A sudden movement or effort. LME–L17. †3 An assault, an attack, (*lit.* of an army etc. or *fig.* of sickness, temptation, etc.). LME–E19. 4 Shock, violence, force, (*of* an attack etc.). Now *rare* in *gen.* sense. LME. 5 The chief stress, violence, or burden (*of*). Chiefly in *bear the brunt of.* M18.

brunt /brʌnt/ *v. rare.* LME. [f. the n.] †1 *v.i.* Make an assault or attack. LME–L17. 2 *v.t.* Bear the brunt of. LME.

brush /brʌʃ/ *n.*[1] ME. [AN *bruce*, OFr *broce* (mod. *brousse*), perh. ult. f. L *bruscum* excrescence on the maple.] 1 Loppings of trees or hedges; *US* cut brushwood; a faggot of this. ME. 2 Undergrowth, thicket, small trees and shrubs; land covered in such growth; *Austral.* forest. Now chiefly *N. Amer., Austral.,* & *NZ.* ME. 3 Stubble. *obs.* exc. *dial.* L17.

Comb.: **brushfire** *n.* & *a.* (*a*) *n.* a fire in brush or scrub; (*b*) *adj.* (of a war etc.) small-scale, localized; **brush kangaroo** = *brush wallaby* below; **brush-turkey** any of several Australasian megapodes which build mounds for incubating their eggs, esp. *Alectura lathami* of E. Australia; **brush wallaby** any of various wallabies found esp. in coastal brush; **brushwood** undergrowth, thicket; cut or broken twigs etc.

brushed *a.* covered or overgrown with brush M17.

brush /brʌʃ/ *n.*[2] ME. [OFr. *broisse*, (also mod.) *brosse*, perh. ult. = prec. Branch III & perh. branch I f. BRUSH *v.*[1] Branch IV perh. a different wd.] I 1 A hostile collision or encounter. Now usu. a short, sharp encounter, a skirmish (*with*). ME. 2 A rapid race; a contest of speed. Chiefly *US.* M19.

1 SHAKES. *Tr. & Cr.* Tempt not yet the brushes of the war. J. A. MICHENER Three ugly brushes with the law over charges he could not understand. **at** (or **after**) **first brush** at (or after) the first meeting.

II 3 An implement consisting of bristles of hair, wire, plastic, or similar material, set in wood etc. and used for scrubbing, sweeping, etc. LME. 4 An instrument consisting of a bunch of hairs etc. attached to a straight handle, quill, etc., for applying paint, ink, glue, etc. L15. b The painter's art or skill. L17. 5 Any brushlike tuft or bunch; *esp.* the bushy tail of a fox. L16. b A brushlike organ on the leg of a bee, used to carry pollen. E19. 6a More fully *brush discharge.* A brushlike electrical discharge of sparks. L18. b A brushlike figure seen when crystals etc. are examined with polarized light. E19. 7 A piece of carbon or metal, ending in wires or strips, securing electrical contact between a fixed and a moving part; a movable strip of conducting material for making and breaking connection. L19. 8 Either of a pair of thin sticks with long wire bristles for striking a drum, cymbal, etc. E20.

3 *bottle-brush, clothes-brush, hairbrush, nail-brush, scrubbing-brush, toothbrush, wire brush,* etc. **daft** or **soft as a brush** *colloq.* (of a person or animal) very daft or soft-hearted. **live over the brush** *colloq.* (of a man and a woman) live together unmarried. 4 *paintbrush, paste-brush, shaving-brush,* etc. *airbrush*: see AIR *n.*[1] *painter's brush*: see PAINTER *n.*[1] b BYRON A young American brother of the brush. 5 G. DURRELL A Brush-tailed Porcupine . . about the size of a cat. K. A. PORTER White-blond hair clipped in a brush over his . . forehead.

III 9 An application of a brush; a brushing. Also, a graze. E18.

9 C. CAUSLEY Tenderly kisses his wife's cheek—The brush of a child's lips. J. OSBORNE His hair is . . thick and silky from its vigorous daily brush. *wash and brush-up*: see WASH *n.* 1.

IV 10 A girl, a young woman; *collect.* girls, young women. *Austral.* & *NZ slang.* M20.

Comb.: *brush discharge*: see sense 6a above; **brushtail** (**possum**) any of several Australian possums of the genus *Trichosurus*, having a bushy tail, pointed snout, and prominent ears; *esp.* the common *T. vulpecula*, which has a commercially valuable pelt; **brushware** brushes of various kinds; **brushwork** a painter's (style of) manipulation of the brush.

brushless *a.* (*a*) without a brush; (*b*) (of shaving-cream etc.) made for use without a brush: M19. **brushlike** *a.* resembling (that of) a brush M19.

brush /brʌʃ/ *v.*[1] LME. [Perh. (O)Fr. *brosser* sweep f. *brosse* BRUSH *n.*[2] In mod. use infl. by next.] †1 *v.i.* Rush with force or speed, usu. into a collision. LME–M17. 2 *v.t.* Force on, drive with a rush; drive hard. *obs.* exc. *US.* L15. 3 *v.i.* Burst away with a rush, move off abruptly, make off. *arch.* L17. 4 *v.i.* Move *by, through, against,* etc., so as to make brief contact in passing. Cf. BRUSH *v.*[2] 5. L17.

4 J. CLARE Often brushing through the dripping grass. V. WOOLF The friction of people brushing past her was evidently painful. F. HERBERT Do not brush against a bush lest you leave a thread to show our passage.

brush /brʌʃ/ *v.*[2] See also BRISH. LME. [f. BRUSH *n.*[2]] 1 *v.t.* Pass a brush across (a surface); sweep or scrub clean, put in order, with a brush; treat (a surface) with a brush to change its nature or appearance. LME. b *v.i.* Use a brush. E19. 2 *v.t.* Remove with a brush; sweep away (as) with a brush. L15. 3 *v.t.* Trim (a hedge). Cf. BRISH. E16. 4 *v.t.* Rub or touch lightly in passing. M17. 5 *v.i.* Come lightly *against*, pass lightly *over*, as with a brush. Cf. BRUSH *v.*[1] 4. M17. 6 *v.t.* Injure (a horse etc.) by a grazing blow. L17. 7 *v.t.* Paint or put in, apply with the brush. Freq. foll. by *in.* L19.

2 J. B. PRIESTLEY The other [hand] trying to brush the cigar ash off his lapels. 4 J. HEATH-STUBBS Hope, the butterfly, but seldom brushes my page With her mazarine wing. G. BOYCOTT The ball brushed his thigh-pad just hard enough to take the pace off it. 5 J. SELDEN His Feathers brushed against the Kings Crown. M. SHADBOLT Pale green tree ferns . . brushed lightly over his face.

With advs. in specialized senses: **brush aside** push out of the way in passing; *fig.* dismiss or dispose of curtly or lightly. **brush off** remove by brushing; *fig.* dismiss, rebuff. **brush over** paint lightly with a brush; (see also sense 5 above). **brush up** (*a*) refurbish by brushing; (*b*) *fig.* refresh one's acquaintance with (a subject etc.); also foll. by *on* the subject etc.

Comb.: **brushback** *a.* & *n.* (*Baseball*) (designating) a pitch thrown close to the batter's body in an attempt to force him to step back from the plate; **brush-off** a dismissal, a rebuff; **brush-up** the action of brushing up; an instance of this.

brushed *ppl a.* (*a*) swept or smoothed with a brush; (*b*) (of fabric) having a raised nap; (*c*) *brushed aluminium*: treated so as to be lustreless: L15. **brusher** *n.* a person who uses a brush L16.

brushite /ˈbrʌʃʌɪt/ *n.* M19. [f. George J. *Brush* (1831–1912), US mineralogist + -ITE[1].] *Min.* A monoclinic acid phosphate of calcium, usu. occurring on phosphate deposits as efflorescences and crusts of minute colourless crystals.

brushy /ˈbrʌʃi/ *a.* L16. [f. BRUSH *n.*[1] or *n.*[2] + -Y[1].] 1 Bushy, shaggy. L16. 2 Covered with brushwood. M17.

brusk /brʊsk/ *n.* & *a.*[1] *arch.* L15. [Origin unkn.] *Her.* (Of) the colour tenné.

†**brusk** *a.*[2] var. of next.

brusque /brʊsk, bruːsk/ *a.* & *v.* Also †**brusk**. E17. [Fr. = lively, fierce, harsh, f. It. *brusco* sour, tart, use as adj. of n. = Sp., Port. *brusco* butcher's broom (a spiny bush) f. Proto-Romance.] A *adj.* †1 Tart. Only in E17. 2 Rough or rude in manner or speech; blunt, off-hand, abrupt. M17. B *v.t.* Treat in an offhand manner. Now *rare.* L18.

brusquely *adv.* L17. **brusqueness** *n.* M19. **brusquerie** /ˈbrʊsk(ə)riː, bruː-; *foreign* bryskəri/ *n.* [Fr.: see -ERY] bluntness or abruptness of manner M18.

Brussels /ˈbrʌs(ə)lz/ *n.* Also (in sense 3) **Brussel**. M18. [A city in the Low Countries, now the capital of Belgium.] 1 *Brussels lace*, a rich type of pillow-lace or needle-lace. M18. 2 In full *Brussels carpet.* A kind of carpet with a woollen pile and a stout linen back. L18. 3 In full *Brussels sprout.* A variety of cabbage producing many small cabbage-like buds; one of these buds eaten as a vegetable. Usu. in *pl.* L18. 4 The Commission of the European Community, with headquarters in Brussels. M20.

brustle /ˈbrʌs(ə)l/ *v.*[1]*i.* Also **brastle** /ˈbras(ə)l/. [OE *brastlian*, of imit. origin.] †1 Crackle, rustle. OE–M18. 2 Bustle, go hastily. *obs.* exc. *Sc.* M17.

†**brustle** *v.*[2]*i.* E17–E18. [Var. of BRISTLE *v.*[1]] = BRISTLE *v.*[1] 4.

Brut /bruːt/ *n. obs.* exc. *Hist.* ME. [Welsh = chronicle, transf. use of *Brut* = *Brutus* (see below).] A chronicle of British history from the time of Brutus, the legendary founder of the British race.

brut /bruːt, *foreign* bryt/ *a.* L19. [Fr.] Of wine: unsweetened, very dry.

brut /brʌt/ *v.i.* & *t. obs.* exc. *dial.* Infl. **-tt-**. L16. [Perh. f. Fr. *brouter* (see BROWSE *v.*) or f. OE *brēotan* (see BRITTLE).] Browse upon trees etc.; break *off* (by browsing).

bruta fulmina *n. phr.* pl. of BRUTUM FULMEN.

brutal /ˈbruːt(ə)l/ *a.* L15. [(O)Fr., or med.L *brutalis*, f. as BRUTE + -AL[1].] †1 = BRUTE *a.* 1. Also, belonging to the (lower) animals. L15–M19. 2 = BRUTISH 3. Now *rare.* E16. 3 Inhuman, savagely cruel; merciless. M17. 4 Crude, coarse; unrefined. E18.

1 G. S. FABER The angel . . daily infuses them into human and brutal bodies. 2 SMOLLETT The slaves of brutal appetite. DISRAELI The students affected a sort of brutal surprise. 3 G. K. CHESTERTON Our ordinary treatment of the poor criminal was a pretty brutal business. A. N. WILSON Able to admit the brutal truth to herself. 4 LD MACAULAY His brutal manners made him unfit to represent the . . crown. J. CHEEVER The forthright and sometimes brutal language that came from the loudspeaker.

brutalism *n.* brutal state, brutality; *spec.* a style of art, architecture, etc., characterized by a deliberate crudity of design: E19. **brutalist** *n.* & *a.* (*a*) *n.* an exponent of brutalism, esp. in art, architecture, or literature; (*b*) *adj.* pertaining to or marked by brutalism: M20. **brutally** *adv.* M18.

brutalise *v.* var. of BRUTALIZE.

brutality /bruːˈtalɪti/ *n.* M16. [f. prec. + -ITY: cf. Fr. *brutalité.*] †1 A state of brutish ignorance. Only in M16. 2 Brutal quality or condition, inhumanity, savage cruelty; sensuality. M17. 3 A brutal action. L19.

brutaliˈtarian *n.* & *a.* [after *humanitarian*] (*a*) *n.* a person who practises or advocates brutality; (*b*) *adj.* pertaining to or characteristic of brutalitarians: E20.

brutalize /ˈbruːt(ə)lʌɪz/ *v.* Also **-ise**. E18. [f. as prec. + -IZE: cf. Fr. *brutaliser.*] 1 *v.t.* Render brutal or inhuman. E18. 2 *v.i.* Live in the fashion of a brute; become brutal. E18. 3 *v.t.* Treat (a person) as a brute; treat brutally. L19.

brutaliˈzation *n.* L18.

brute /bruːt/ *a.* & *n.* LME. [Fr. *brut, brute* = Sp., It. *bruto*, f. L *brutus* heavy, stupid, dull.] A *adj.* 1 Of animals: not possessing the capacity of reason or understanding. LME. 2 Of people or their actions etc.: unthinking, unreasoning; senseless, stupid; bestial, cruel; sensual, passionate. M16. b Crude, unrefined; = BRUTAL 4. Now *rare*. M16. 3 Of things: unconscious, impersonal, merely material. M16. 4 Of surfaces etc.: rugged, unpolished. *rare*. E17.

1 G. BERKELEY To degrade human-kind to a level with brute beasts. 2 J. SYLVESTER Man (alas!) is bruter than a Brute. Y. MENUHIN Imposing the only order the Soviets know, which is brute order. 3 M. FRAYN The brute glare of the noonday sun. 4 SOUTHEY The value of the brute diamond.

Special collocations: **brute creation** *the* animals (as opp. to humans). **brute fact** a simple inescapable or unexplained fact; *loosely* (often in *pl.*) the plain truth. **brute force** irrational force; the simple or unthinking exertion of strength.

B *n.* 1 Any of the lower animals, as distinguished from humans; a large or powerful animal. E17. 2 A person of brutish or animal tendencies; a person lacking in sensibility; (*colloq.*) a disliked or despised person. L17. b *transf.* A large, awkward, or unpleasant thing. *colloq.* L19.

1 POPE Man . . the middle Link between Angels and Brutes. W. HOLTBY The big black brute that Carne rode. **the brute** animal nature in man. 2 G. STEIN What could you expect when Melanctha had such a brute of a . . father. E. LANGLEY She's often asked him to bring us down to see her; but the brute wouldn't. b GEO. ELIOT The brute of a cigar required relighting.

brutedom *n.* brutish nature L19. **brutehood** *n.* M19. **brutely** *adv.* (now *rare*) in a brutal or brutish manner L16. **bruteness** *n.* M16.

brutify /ˈbruːtɪfʌɪ/ *v.t.* & *i.* L16. [f. BRUTE + -FY.] Make or become brutish; brutalize.

brutifiˈcation *n.* L17.

brutish /ˈbruːtɪʃ/ *a.* L15. [f. BRUTE *n.* + -ISH[1].] †1 Rough; savage, brutal. L15–L18. 2 Of or pertaining to the lower animals, as opp. to humans. M16. 3 Resembling or characteristic of an animal, esp. in unreasoning or sensual nature; irrational; stupid. M16. †4 *spec.* Of a thunderbolt: striking blindly (cf. BRUTUM FULMEN). Also *transf.*, random. L16–L19.

brutishly *adv.* L16. **brutishness** *n.* M16.

brutism /ˈbruːtɪz(ə)m/ *n.* L17. [f. BRUTE *n.* + -ISM.] The behaviour or condition of a brute.

brutum fulmen /ˌbruːtəm ˈfʌlmən/ *n. phr.* Pl. ***bruta fulmina*** /ˌbruːtə ˈfʌlmɪnə/. E17. [L, lit. 'unfeeling thunderbolt' (Pliny).] A mere noise; an ineffective act, an empty threat.

Brutus /ˈbruːtəs/ *a.* & *n.* L18. [Marcus Junius *Brutus* (85–42 BC).] *Hist.* (Designating) a head or wig of short roughly cropped hair, fashionable in the 18th cent.

bruvver /ˈbrʌvə/ *n. dial.* & *slang.* L19. [Repr. a Cockney pronunc.] = BROTHER *n.*

bruxism /ˈbrʌksɪz(ə)m/ *n.* M20. [f. Gk *brukhein* gnash the teeth + -ISM.] *Med.* Involuntary or habitual grinding or clenching of the teeth.

bryology /brʌɪˈɒlədʒi/ *n.* M19. [f. Gk *bruon* moss + -OLOGY.] The branch of botany that deals with mosses and liverworts.

bryoˈlogical *a.* L19. **bryoˈlogically** *adv.* L19. **bryologist** *n.* M19.

bryony /ˈbrʌɪəni/ *n.* Also **bri-** & (in medicinal contexts) in L form **bryonia** /brʌɪˈəʊnɪə/. OE. [L *bryonia* f. Gk *bruōnia*.] 1 A climbing plant of the genus *Bryonia*, of the gourd family; *esp.* (more fully *white bryony*) *Bryonia dioica*, which bears greenish-white flowers and red berries. OE. 2 More fully *black bryony* (from the colour of its tubers). A similar but unrelated plant, *Tamus communis*, of the yam family. L16.

bryophyte /ˈbrʌɪəfʌɪt/ *n.* L19. [mod.L *Bryophyta* pl., f. Gk *bruon* moss: see -PHYTE.] Any plant of the group Bryophyta of small primitive cryptogams, comprising the liverworts and mosses.

bryophytic /-ˈfɪtɪk/ *a.* E20.

bryozoan /brʌɪəˈzəʊən/ *n.* & *a.* L19. [f. mod.L *Bryozoa* (see below), f. Gk *bruon* moss + *zōia* pl. of *zōion* animal: see -AN.] *Zool.* A *n.* A member of the group Bryozoa (now regarded as comprising the phyla Ectoprocta and Entoprocta) of lophophorates, which form colonies often suggesting mossy growths. Also *spec.* = ECTOPROCTAN *n.* L19. B *adj.* Of or pertaining to the group Bryozoa. L19.

bryozoˈologist *n.* an expert in or student of bryozoology M20. **bryozoˈology** *n.* the branch of zoology that deals with bryozoans M20. **bryozoon** *n.*, pl. **-zoa**, = BRYOZOAN *n.* (usu. in *pl.*) M19.

Brythonic /brɪˈθɒnɪk/ *a.* & *n. arch.* L19. [f. Welsh *Brython* (see BRITON) + -IC.] = BRITTONIC.

B-tree /ˈbiːtriː/ *n.* M20. [f. *B* repr. *balanced* or *binary* + TREE *n.*] *Computing.* A tree in which all the terminal nodes are at the same distance from the root and all the non-terminal nodes have between *n* and *2n* subtrees or pointers, where *n* is a positive integer.

Bual /ˈbuːal/ *n.* Also **Boal, b-.** L19. [Port. *boal.*] A variety of wine-making grape grown esp. in Madeira; (a drink of) medium sweet Madeira made from this.

bub /bʌb/ *n.*[1] L17. [Perh. imit.] 1 Alcoholic liquor; *esp.* strong beer. *arch. slang.* L17. 2 A mixture of meal and yeast with warm wort and water, used to promote fermentation. M19.

bub /bʌb/ *n.*[2] *N. Amer. colloq.* M19. [Abbrev. of BUBBY *n.*[2]] Boy, man, brother: used chiefly as a familiar form of address.

bub /bʌb/ *n.*[3] *colloq.* M19. [Abbrev. of BUBBY *n.*[1]] A woman's breast. Usu. in *pl.*

bubal /ˈbjuːb(ə)l/ *n.* Also **-ale.** L18. [Fr. *bubale* f. L *bubalus*: see BUFFALO.] A hartebeest; *spec.* one of the N. African race, now extinct. Also *bubal hartebeest.*

bubaline /ˈbjuːbəlʌɪn/ *a.* E19. [f. mod.L *Bubalus* genus name f. L *bubalus* BUFFALO: see -INE[1].] Of or pertaining to buffaloes.

bubble /ˈbʌb(ə)l/ *n.* & *a.* ME. [Partly imit. (as Du. *bobbel*, G dial. *Bobbel, Bubbel*), partly alt. of BURBLE *n.*] A *n.* 1 A gas-filled cavity in liquid or in solidified liquid (as glass, amber, paint etc.); a spherical envelope of liquid enclosing air etc. ME. 2 *fig.* An unsubstantial or visionary (esp. commercial or financial) project, enterprise, etc. L16. †3 A person who is cheated or duped. M17–E19. 4 The process, sound, or appearance of bubbling; an agitated or bubbling motion. M19. 5 A motor car. Also *ellipt.*, a bubble car. *colloq.* E20. 6 A transparent domed canopy covering the cockpit of an aeroplane. *slang.* M20. 7 A small mobile domain of reverse magnetization in a crystalline material, *esp.* one forming a unit of stored information in a computer memory. Also *magnetic bubble.* M20.

2 *South Sea bubble*: see SOUTH *adv.*, *a.*, etc. 4 **bubble and squeak** (*a*) cold meat or (now. usu.) potatoes fried with cabbage or other vegetables; (*b*) *rhyming slang* (a) Greek.

Comb.: **bubble bath** (a bath in water to which has been added) a usu. perfumed toilet preparation which causes water to foam; **bubble car** a small usu. three-wheeled motor car with a transparent dome; **bubble chamber** *Physics* a container of superheated liquid used to detect charged particles by the trails of bubbles which they produce; **bubble gum** (*a*) chewing-gum that can be blown into bubbles; (*b*) (in full *bubble-gum music*) pop music with simple trivial words; **bubblehead** *slang* a foolish, unintelligent, or empty-headed person; **bubble memory** *Computing* a type of memory which stores data as a pattern of magnetic bubbles in a thin layer of magnetic material; **bubble pack** a small package enclosing goods in a transparent case on a flat backing; **bubble-shell** any of various opisthobranchs with thin, more or less cylindrical, external shells.

B *attrib.* or as *adj.* Of a project, enterprise, etc.: unsubstantial, delusive, fraudulent. Now *arch.* or *Hist.* M17.

E. LINKLATER In 1837 he lost some money by speculating in one of the many bubble companies of that year.

bubble /ˈbʌb(ə)l/ *v.* LME. [Partly imit. (as Du. *bobbelen*, G dial. *bobbeln, bubbeln*, Sw. *bubla*, Da. *boble*), partly alt. of BURBLE *v.*] 1 *v.i.* Form or rise in or like bubbles; well *up*, *out*, etc., in or like bubbles; boil or brim *over* (lit.) in bubbles or (fig.) *with* merriment, anger, excitement, etc.; make the sound of bubbles. LME. 2 *v.t.* Send out in or like bubbles. E17. 3 *v.t.* Delude, dupe, cheat, esp. in a commercial or financial enterprise. Now *rare.* L17. 4 *v.i.* Weep, lament. *Sc.* & *north.* E18. 5 *v.t.* Cause (a baby) to bring up wind. *US colloq.* M20.

1 TENNYSON Yon swoll'n brook that bubbles fast. C. KINGSLEY Wild thoughts bubbled within her. P. G. WODEHOUSE The silver bubbling of a thrush. J. MASEFIELD A spring comes bubbling up there.

bubblement *n.* (now *rare*) effervescence L19. **bubbler** *n.* a person who or thing which bubbles; *esp.* (*arch.*) a swindler, a cheat: E18.

bubbly /ˈbʌbli/ *a.* & *n.* M16. [f. BUBBLE *n.* + -Y[1].] A *adj.* Full of bubbles, frothy. Of a person: vivacious; full of high spirits. M16. B *n.* Champagne. *slang.* E20.

bubbly-jock /ˈbʌblɪdʒɒk/ *n. Sc.* E19. [f. *bubbly* imit. of the bird's call + male forename *Jock.*] A turkey-cock.

bubby /ˈbʌbi/ *n.*[1] Now *dial.* L17. [Cf. G dial. *Bübbi* teat.] A woman's breast. Usu. in *pl.*

bubby /ˈbʌbi/ *n.*[2] *US colloq.* M19. [Childish form of BROTHER *n.* or f. G *Bube* boy.] = BUB *n.*[2]

bubo /ˈbjuːbəʊ/ *n.* Pl. **-oes.** LME. [L f. Gk *boubōn* groin, swelling in the groin.] A swollen inflamed lymph node esp. in the groin or armpit.

bubonic /bjuːˈbɒnɪk/ *a.* L19. [f. L *bubon-*, BUBO + -IC.] Characterized by the presence of buboes.

bubonic plague a highly contagious bacterial disease in which buboes appear.

bubonocele /bjuːˈbɒnəsiːl/ *n.* Now *rare* or *obs.* E17. [mod.L f. Gk *boubōnokēlē*, f. as BUBO: see -CELE.] *Med.* Hernia of the groin.

buccal /ˈbʌk(ə)l/ *a.* E19. [f. L *bucca* cheek + -AL[1].] Of the cheek; of or in the mouth.

buccally *adv.* towards the cheek M20.

buccan *n.*, *v.* var. of BOUCAN *n.*, *v.*

buccaneer /bʌkəˈnɪə/ *n.* & *v.* M17. [Fr. *boucanier*, f. as BOUCAN *v.*: see -EER.] A *adj.* †1 A person, esp. a hunter, who cooks or cures meat on a boucan. M17–M18. 2 A pirate, orig. of the Spanish-American coasts; an unscrupulous adventurer. L17. B *v.* 1 *v.i.* Be or act as a pirate or adventurer. E18. 2 *v.t.* = BOUCAN *v.* Now *rare.* L18.

buccaneerish *a.* E19.

buccaro *n.* var. of BOCCARO.

buccinator /ˈbʌksɪneɪtə/ *n.* L17. [L, f. *buccinare* blow the trumpet, f. *buccina* kind of trumpet: see -ATOR.] *Anat.* A flat thin muscle in the wall of the cheek.

buccinatory *a.* of or pertaining to a trumpet or trumpeter (*buccinatory muscle* = BUCCINATOR) M18.

buccinum /ˈbʌksɪnəm/ *n.* E17. [L, f. *buccina*: see prec.] A whelk; *spec.* one of the genus *Buccinum.*

buccinoid *a.* resembling a buccinum M19.

bucco- /ˈbʌkəʊ/ *comb. form* of L *bucca* cheek: see -O-.

buccoˈlingual *a.* of or pertaining to the cheeks and tongue; (of direction) passing through both tongue and cheek: E20. **buccoˈlingually** *adv.* in the buccolingual direction E20.

buccra *n.* var. of BUCKRA.

bucellas /bjuːˈsɛləs/ *n.* E19. [A village near Lisbon.] A Portuguese white wine; a drink of this.

Bucentaur /bjuːˈsɛntɔː/ *n.* Also †**Bucentoro.** M16. [Fr. *bucentaure* f. (after *centaure* CENTAUR) It. *bucentoro*, perh. f. Venetian, lit. 'barge in gold'.] *Hist.* The state barge used by the Doge of Venice for the Ascension Day festival of marrying the Adriatic.

Bucephalus /bjuːˈsɛfələs/ *n.* Chiefly *joc.* M17. [L f. Gk *Boukefalos*, Alexander the Great's charger, f. *bous* ox + *kephalē* head.] A horse for riding, a mount.

Buchmanism /ˈbʊkmənɪz(ə)m, ˈbuːk-/ *n.* Usu. *derog.* E20. [f. Frank *Buchman* (1878–1961) Amer. evangelist + -ISM.] The theories or practice of the Oxford Group Movement.

Buchmanite *n.* & *a.* (*a*) *n.* an adherent of Buchmanism; (*b*) *adj.* of or pertaining to Buchmanites or Buchmanism: E20.

buchu /ˈbʌkuː, ˈbʊxʊ/ *n.* M18. [Afk. f. Nama.] Any of various South African shrubs of the rue family (esp. *Agathosma betulina* and *A. crenulata*) whose leaves yield a diuretic drug; the powdered dried leaves of such a shrub.

buck /bʌk/ *n.*[1] & *a.* OE. [Partly OE *buc* male deer = MDu. *boc* (Du. *bok*), OHG *boc* (G *Bock*), ON *bukkr*, *bokkr*, partly OE *bucca* he-goat = ON *bokki* my good fellow, old buck, both f. Gmc.] A *n.* I The male of various animals. (The corresponding female animal is usu. called *doe*.) †1 A male goat (cf. GOAT 1). OE–M16. 2 The male of British deer, *spec.* the fallow deer and roe-deer. OE. 3 The male of certain other kinds of deer, as the reindeer; the male of certain other horned mammals, as the antelope; *US* a ram. L17. 4 A male hare, rabbit, ferret, or rat. M18. 5 An adult male kangaroo. *Austral.* M19. II *transf.* 6 A man. *rare* exc. as below. ME. 7 A dashing fellow; a dandy. *arch.* E18. 8 A male American Indian; a male Black; a male Australian Aborigine. Usu. *derog.* Chiefly *US* & *Austral.* E19.

Comb.: **buck-brush** *N. Amer.* brush on which deer browse; any of various shrubs of this sort; **buck-bush** buck-brush; also, any of various Australian shrubs; **buck fever** *US* nervousness when called on to take action; **buckhorn** (*a*) (the material of) a male deer's horn; (*b*) *dial.* dried whiting or other fish; **buck-hound** a small variety of staghound; **buck-jump** *n.*, *v.i.* = BUCK *n.*[4] 2, BUCK *v.*[2] 2a; **buck-jumper** (*a*) a horse that bucks; (*b*) one who rides bucking horses in rodeos etc.; **buck rarebit** Welsh rarebit with poached egg; **buck's horn** any of various plants resembling a male deer's horn, esp. a plantain, *Plantago coronopus* (usu. more fully *buck's horn plantain*); **buckshot** coarse lead shot used in shotgun shells; **buckskin** (*a*) (leather of) the skin of a male deer or similar skin; in *pl.*, breeches made of this; (*b*) a strong smooth cotton, woollen, or twilled cloth; **buckstall** *Hist.* a large net for catching deer; **buck-tooth** a tooth that projects.

B *attrib.* or as *adj.* 1 Of an animal or *derog.* a Black etc.: male. E17. 2 Of the lowest grade of a specific military rank. *US slang.* E20.

buckish *a.* LME. †**buckism** *n.* foppish behaviour M18–E19.

buck /bʌk/ *n.*[2] *obs.* exc. *Hist.* M16. [f. BUCK *v.*[1]] 1 Alkaline lye in which linen, yarn, etc., was steeped or boiled in buck-washing (see below) or bleaching. M16. 2 A quantity of clothes etc. (to be) steeped or boiled in buck. M16.

Comb.: **buck-washing** washing very dirty linen by boiling it in an alkaline lye and afterwards beating and rinsing it in clear water.

†**buck** *n.*[3] L16–E19. [Abbrev.] = BUCKWHEAT.

buck /bʌk/ *n.*[4] L16. [f. BUCK *v.*[2]] †1 An act of copulation by a male rabbit, hare, etc. L16–E17. 2 A vertical jump by a horse etc. with the back arched and feet drawn together. L19. 3 A try, an attempt. *Austral.* & *NZ slang.* E20.

Comb.: **buck-and-wing** *n.* & *a.* (*US*) (designating) a lively solo dance usu. performed in wooden-soled shoes; **buck dance** *US* a buck-and-wing dance.

buck /bʌk/ *n.*[5] L17. [Perh. var. of BOUK.] The body of a cart.

Comb.: **buckboard** *US* (a vehicle with) a body formed by a plank on wheels.

buck /bʌk/ *n.*[6] L17. [Origin unkn.] (Esp. on the River Thames) a wooden framework at a weir supporting baskets for trapping eels; a basket for trapping eels.

buck /bʌk/ *n.*[7] E19. [Du. (*zaag-*)*bok* (G (*Säge*)*bock*), f. as SAW *n.*[1] + BUCK *n.*[1]: cf. Fr. *chèvre*.] 1 A frame supporting wood for sawing. *N. Amer.* E19. 2 A short vaulting-horse. M20.

Comb.: **buck-saw** *N. Amer.* a heavy frame-saw used with a buck.

buck /bʌk/ *n.*[8] *N. Amer.* & *Austral. slang.* M19. [Origin unkn.] A dollar.

a fast (or **quick**) **buck** easy money.

buck /bʌk/ *n.*[9] M19. [Origin unkn.] An article placed as a reminder before a player whose turn it is to deal at poker.

fig.: H. S. TRUMAN On my desk I have a motto which says 'The buck stops here.' **pass the buck** *fig.* (*slang*) shift responsibility (*to* another).

Comb.: **buck-passing** *slang* shifting of responsibility to another.

buck /bʌk/ *n.*[10] *slang.* L19. [Hind. *bak.*] Conversation; boastful talk.

buck /bʌk/ *v.*[1]*t.* *obs.* exc. *Hist.* LME. [Corresp. to MHG *büchen* (G *beuchen*), LG *büken*, Sw. *byka*, Da. *byge*, f. Gmc: prob. in OE.] 1 Steep or boil in an alkaline lye in buck-washing or bleaching. LME. †2 Drench, soak. L15–E17.

bucking *n.* (*a*) the action of the vb; (*b*) = BUCK *n.*[2]: L15.

buck /bʌk/ *v.*[2] M16. [f. BUCK *n.*[1]] †1 *v.i.* & *t.* Of a male rabbit, hare, etc.: copulate (with). M16–M18. 2a *v.i.* Of a horse etc.: jump vertically with the back arched and feet drawn together. M19. b *v.t.* Throw (a rider or burden) by so jumping. Also foll. by *off.* L19. 3 *v.i.* & *t.* Foll. by *up*: a Dress up. *arch.* & *dial.* M19. b Cheer up; become or make more vigorous or lively; hurry up, make an effort. *colloq.* M19.

bucked *a.* (*colloq.*) encouraged, elated E20. **bucker** *n.*[1] a horse etc. that bucks M19.

buck /bʌk/ *v.*[3]*t.* L17. [Cf. Du. *boken*, *boocken* beat or strike.] *Mining.* Break (ore) into small pieces with a special hammer.

bucker *n.*[2] (*Mining*) a hammer for bucking ore M17.

buck /bʌk/ *v.*[4] M18. [Perh. alt. of BUTT *v.*[1] by assoc. w. BUCK *n.*[1]] 1 *v.t.* Push with the head; butt into or against; *fig.* come up against, oppose, resist, get the better of, (cf. BUCK *v.*[2] 2b). Chiefly *dial.* (in *lit.* sense) & *N. Amer.* M18. 2 *v.i.* Foll. by *against*, *at*: oppose, resist. Chiefly *N. Amer.* M19.

1 F. CHICHESTER I.. kept swimming, not trying to buck the flood. K. KESEY Some mornings.. I hide and try to buck the schedule. *buck the tiger*: see TIGER *n.* 2 G. BONNER There's no good bucking against bad luck.

buck /bʌk/ *v.*[5]*t.* *N. Amer.* L19. [f. BUCK *n.*[7]] Cut (wood) with a buck-saw.

bucker *n.*[3] a person who saws trees into logs E20.

buck /bʌk/ *v.*[6]*i.* *slang.* L19. [Cf. BUCK *n.*[10]] Swagger, brag.

buckaroo /bʌkəˈruː/ *n.* *US.* *arch.* E19. [Alt. of VAQUERO.] A cowboy.

buckbean /ˈbʌkbiːn/ *n.* L16. [Flem. *bocks boonen* goat's beans.] A common marsh plant, *Menyanthes trifoliata*, bearing racemes of white or pinkish flowers. Also called *marsh trefoil.*

buckeen /bʌˈkiːn/ *n.* *Anglo-Ir.* L18. [f. BUCK *n.*[1] + -EEN[2].] *Hist.* A young (impecunious) man from inferior Irish gentry.

bucket /ˈbʌkɪt/ *n.*[1] ME. [AN *buket*, *buquet* tub, pail (AL *bokettum*, *bu-*), perh. f. OE *būc* belly, pitcher: see -ET[1].] 1 A (usu. round) open vessel with a handle, for use when drawing water etc. or for holding or carrying liquids or other substances or objects (orig. of leather or wood, now also of metal, plastic, and other materials). Also, a bucketful. ME. 2 The piston of a lift-pump. M17. 3 Each of the compartments on the circumference of a water-wheel; each of the scoops of a dredger, grain-elevator, etc. M18. 4 A (usu. leather) socket or rest for a whip, carbine, or lance. M19. 5 *Rowing.* A hurried or jerky forward movement of the body. L19.

1 *a drop in the bucket*: see DROP *n.* 3.

Comb.: **bucket seat** a seat with a rounded back to fit one person; **bucket-shop** an unauthorized office for gambling in stocks, speculating on markets, dealing in discounted airline tickets, etc.; **bucket-wheel** a contrivance for raising water, comprising buckets fixed round the rim of a wheel, which fill at the bottom and empty themselves at the top.

bucketful *n.* the amount contained in a bucket; in *pl.*, large quantities of rain, tears, etc.: M16.

bucket /ˈbʌkɪt/ *n.*[2] Long *obs.* exc. as below. L16. [Perh. f. OFr. *buquet* balance.] A beam or yoke on which anything may be hung.

kick the bucket [perh., & now usu. interpreted as, BUCKET *n.*[1]] *slang* die.

bucket /ˈbʌkɪt/ *v.* L16. [f. BUCKET *n.*[1]] 1 *v.i.* Use a bucket (of water). Chiefly as *bucketing* vbl n. L16. 2 *v.t.* Pour buckets of water over. E17. 3 *v.t.* Lift or carry in buckets. M17. 4a *v.t.* Ride (a horse) hard; drive or move (a vehicle etc.) jerkily or bumpily. M19. b *v.i.* Of a vehicle etc.: jerk or bounce up and down, move roughly. E20. 5 *v.i.* & *t.* *Rowing.* Hurry the forward swing of (the body); hurry (recovery of position). L19. 6 *v.i.* & *t.* with *it.* Of rain etc.: pour down (or *down*) heavily. *colloq.* E20.

bucketing *ppl a.* (*Rowing*) hurried, jerky M19.

buckeye /ˈbʌkʌɪ/ *n.* & *a.* Exc. sense A.1 *US.* M18. [f. BUCK *n.*[1] + EYE *n.*] A *n.* 1 (The nut or fruit of) a tree or shrub of the genus *Aesculus*; an American horse chestnut. M18. 2 A backwoodsman; a native of Ohio. E19. 3 An inferior person or thing; a shop selling inferior goods. M19.

Comb.: **Buckeye State** Ohio, where buckeye trees are abundant.

B *attrib.* or as *adj.* 1 Of Ohio. M19. 2 Inferior; showy but not impressive. E20.

buckie /ˈbʌki/ *n.* *Sc.* E16. [Sense 1 of unkn. origin (cf. BUCCINUM); sense 2 app. f. BUCK *n.*[1] + -IE.] 1 A whorled mollusc's shell. E16. 2 A perverse or refractory person. E18.

buckle /ˈbʌk(ə)l/ *n.* ME. [AN *bucle*, OFr. *bocle* (mod. *boucle*) f. L *buccula* cheek-strap of a helmet, dim. of *bucca* cheek.] 1 A flat frame with a hinged pin, for securing a strap, belt, etc.; a similarly shaped ornament on a shoe etc. ME. †2 The state of hair when crisped and curled; a kink or curl in hair. E18–E19.

buckle /ˈbʌk(ə)l/ *v.* LME. [Branch I f. the n.; branch II f. Fr. *boucler* bulge.] I 1 *v.t.* Fasten with a buckle. (Foll. by *up*, *on*, etc.) LME. b *v.i.* Foll. by *up*: fasten a seat belt, wear a seat belt. *N. Amer.* L20. 2 *v.i.* Grapple, engage, *with.* Now *dial.* M16. 3 *v.i.* & †*refl.* Equip oneself, prepare, for battle, an expedition, etc. Now only *fig.* foll. by *to* (prep. & adv.), *down* (*to*): prepare for or set about (work etc.), apply oneself vigorously (to). M16. 4 *v.i.* & *t.* Marry. *joc.* & *dial.* L17. †5 *v.t.* Fix (hair) in curl. E18–M19.

2 SIR W. SCOTT Would.. interrupt you just when you were buckling with your labours. 3 BURKE I have shook off idleness, and begun to buckle to. T. F. DIBDIN Now buckles himself to the uninterrupted perusal of the.. text. B. HARTE Chiquita Buckled right down to her work. E. REVELEY You'll really have to buckle down and cram for those exams.

II 6 *v.t.* & *i.* (Cause to) give way or crumple up, esp. under longitudinal pressure. E16. 7 *v.i.* *fig.* Submit, cringe. *obs.* exc. *dial.* M17.

6 A. POWELL One of the legs buckled, but the chair did not break. D. ATTENBOROUGH The.. rocks.. are twisted and buckled. T. BERGER Her knees threatened to buckle.

Comb.: †**buckle-beggar** *Sc.* a clergyman who performed irregular marriages.

buckler /ˈbʌklə/ *n.* & *v.* ME. [AN *bucler*, OFr. *bocler* (mod. *bouclier*), orig. adj. in *escu bocler* shield having a boss, f. *bocle* boss, BUCKLE *n.*: see -ER[2].] A *n.* 1 *Hist.* A small round shield usu. held by a handle. ME. 2 *fig.* A means of defence. LME. 3 A shieldlike part of the protective covering of an animal. E19.

Comb.: **buckler-fern** any of certain ferns of the genus *Dryopteris*, with kidney-shaped indusia.

B *v.t.* 1 Act as a buckler to, shield. L16. †2 Ward or catch (blows). *rare* (Shakes.). Only in L16.

bucklered *a.* armed with a buckler, furnished with bucklers M19.

Buckley's /ˈbʌklɪz/ *n.* *Austral.* & *NZ colloq.* L19. [Origin unkn.] In full *Buckley's chance.* Little or no chance.

buckling /ˈbʌklɪŋ/ *n.* E20. [G *Bückling* bloater.] A smoked herring.

buckminsterfullerene /ˌbʌkmɪnstəˈfʊləriːn/ *n.* L20. [f. R. *Buckminster Fuller* (1895–1983), US engineer and architect who invented the geodesic dome + -ENE.] *Chem.* A form of carbon in which 60 carbon atoms are joined together as a hollow polyhedron of 12 pentagons and 20 hexagons.

bucko /ˈbʌkəʊ/ *a.* & *n.* *Naut. slang.* Pl. of n. **-o(e)s**. L19. [f. BUCK *n.*[1] + -O.] (A person who is) swaggering or domineering.

Comb.: **bucko mate** an officer who drives the crew by bullying methods.

buckra /ˈbʌkrə/ *n.* *W. Indies* & *Southern US.* Freq. *derog.* Also **buccra** & other vars. M18. [Ibibio & Efik (*m*)*bakara* European, master.] (A Blacks' name for) a White man, a master.

buckram /ˈbʌkrəm/ *n.*, *a.*, & *v.* ME. [AN *bukeran*, OFr. *boquerant* (mod. *bougran*), corresp. to Prov. *bocaran*, Sp. *bucaran*, It. *bucherame*, perh. obscurely f. *Bukhara*, a town in central Asia, west of Samarkand: for the change of final *n* to *m* cf. *grogram*, *megrim*, *vellum*.] A *n.* 1 A kind of fine linen or cotton fabric. Long *obs.* exc. *Hist.* ME. 2 A coarse linen or other cloth stiffened with gum or paste. LME. 3 *fig.* Stiffness of manner. L17.

2 **men in buckram** non-existent persons, figments (in allusion to SHAKES. *1 Hen. IV*).

B *attrib.* or as *adj.* Of or like buckram; *fig.* stiff in manner. M16.

C *v.t.* Pad or stiffen with buckram; *fig.* give a starched pomposity or illusory strength to. L18.

Buck's Fizz /bʌks 'fɪz/ *n. phr.* M20. [f. *Buck's* Club, London + FIZZ *n.*] Champagne or sparkling white wine mixed with orange juice; a drink of this.

buckshee /bʌk'ʃiː, *esp. attrib. adj.* 'bʌkʃiː/ *n.*[1], *a.*, & *adv. slang.* E20. [Alt. of BAKSHEESH.] A *n.* Something in addition to the usual allowance; something extra or free. E20. B *adj.* & *adv.* Free of charge, gratuitous(ly). E20.

buckshee *n.*[2] var. of BUKSHI.

buckthorn /'bʌkθɔːn/ *n.* L16. [f. BUCK *n.*[1] + THORN *n.*, tr. mod.L *cervi spina* stag's thorn.] A shrub or small tree of the genus *Rhamnus* (family Rhamnaceae); *esp.* (more fully *purging buckthorn*) the shrub *R. cathartica*, whose berries yield sap-green and are strongly cathartic.

ALDER *buckthorn.* SEA *buckthorn.*

buckwheat /'bʌkwiːt/ *n.* M16. [MDu. *boecweite* or MLG *bōkwēte* lit. 'beech wheat', its grains resembling beechmast.] 1 A cereal plant of the genus *Fagopyrum* (family Polygonaceae), esp. *F. esculentum*, the seed of which is used for horse and poultry food, and in N. America is milled for making breakfast pancakes. M16. 2 A buckwheat cake. *N. Amer.* M19.

buckyball /'bʌkɪbɔːl/ *n. informal.* L20. [f. BUCK(MINSTERFULLERENE + -Y[6] + BALL *n.*[1]] *Chem.* A fullerene molecule.

bucolic /bjuː'kɒlɪk/ *n.* E16. [L *bucolica*, Gk *boukolika* (both pl.), f. as next.] 1 A pastoral poem, e.g. Virgil's eclogues. Usu. in *pl.* E16. 2 A pastoral poet; *joc.* a rustic. *rare.* L18.

bucolic /bjuː'kɒlɪk/ *a.* E17. [L *bucolicus* f. Gk *boukolikos*, f. *boukolos* herdsman, f. *bous* ox: see -IC.] Of shepherds, pastoral; rustic, rural.

bucolical *a.* (now *rare*) bucolic E16. **bucolically** *adv.* L19.

bud /bʌd/ *n.*[1] LME. [Origin unkn.] 1a A rudiment of a shoot, flower, or foliage; a leaf or flower not yet fully open. LME. b *Zool.* A growth which later separates to form a new individual asexually. M19. 2 Anything resembling a bud, esp. in respect of shape or of immature state of development; *spec.* (*a*) a child, a youngster; (*b*) *dial.* a yearling calf; (*c*) *colloq.* (chiefly *US*) a débutante; (*d*) the rudiment of a horn or of an insect's leg or other appendage when it begins to sprout; (*e*) a small wad of cotton wool etc. on a stick. L16.

1a **in bud** putting forth buds. **nip in the bud** *fig.* destroy at an early stage of development. *red bud*: see RED *a.*

Comb.: **budworm** a grub or caterpillar destructive to buds.

budless *a.* M19. **budlet** *n.* a small or secondary bud M19.

bud /bʌd/ *n.*[2] *N. Amer. colloq.* M19. [Abbrev.] = BUDDY *n.*

bud /bʌd/ *v.* Infl. **-dd-**. LME. [f. BUD *n.*[1]] 1 *v.i.* Send out buds, sprout; come or push *out* as a bud. LME. 2 *v.i. fig.* Begin to grow or develop. M16. 3 *v.t.* & *i. Zool.* Form (as) a bud. L16. 4 *v.t.* Bring into bud, cause to bud. E17. 5 *v.t. Hort.* Graft a bud of (a plant) on to another plant. M17.

2 E. WAUGH Two daughters just budding into womanhood. 3 D. MORRIS It must divide and bud off a lower, second cell. D. ATTENBOROUGH The polyps bud in a different way and produce miniature medusae which detach themselves and wriggle away.

budda /'bʌdə/ *n. Austral.* Also **-ah**. L19. [Aborig. *budaa.*] An E. Australian tree, *Eremophila mitchelli*, with aromatic timber resembling sandalwood.

Buddha /'bʊdə/ *n.* L17. [Skt = enlightened, pa. pple of *budh-* awake, know, perceive.] The title of the successive teachers, past and future, of Buddhism (see next), esp. of its founder, the Indian religious teacher Gautama (fl. 5th cent. BC); any of the numerous and often massive carved figures of the Buddha.

Buddhahood *n.* the condition of a Buddha M19.

Buddhism /'bʊdɪz(ə)m/ *n.* E19. [f. prec. + -ISM.] The religious and philosophical system founded by the Buddha Gautama (see prec.), teaching that all human sorrows arise from desire and can be eradicated by following the disciplines of his eightfold path.

Buddhist *a.* & *n.* (*a*) *adj.* relating to or connected with Buddhism; (*b*) *n.* an adherent of Buddhism: E19. **Bu'ddhistic(al)** *adjs.* = BUDDHIST *a.* M19.

budding /'bʌdɪŋ/ *a.* L16. [f. BUD *v.* + -ING[2].] 1 That forms buds. L16. 2 *fig.* Beginning to develop to maturity. L16.

2 G. MACDONALD This gave a great help to his budding confidence. L. T. C. ROLT Budding engineers who bombarded the Company with impracticable schemes.

buddle /'bʌd(ə)l/ *n.*[1] *dial.* LME. [Origin unkn.] The corn marigold.

buddle /'bʌd(ə)l/ *n.*[2] & *v.* M16. [Origin unkn.] *Mining.* A *n.* A shallow inclined vat in which ore is washed. M16. B *v.t.* Wash (ore) in a buddle. L17.

buddleia /'bʌdlɪə/ *n.* Also **-lea**. L18. [mod.L, f. Adam *Buddle* (d. 1715), Eng. botanist: see -IA[1].] A shrub or tree of the genus *Buddleja*, native to America, Asia, and southern Africa; esp. *B. davidii*, a large ornamental shrub bearing panicles of fragrant lilac flowers which attract butterflies. Also called *butterfly bush.*

buddy /'bʌdi/ *n.* & *v. colloq.* (orig. *US*). M19. [Alt. of BROTHER *n.* or var. of BUTTY *n.*[1]] A *n.* 1 Occas. also redupl. **buddy-buddy**. Brother, companion, friend (freq. as a familiar form of address). M19. 2 *spec.* a A working companion (assigned or chosen) with whom close cooperation is required. E20. b A person who befriends and gives special help to another with an incapacitating disease, esp. Aids. L20.

Comb.: **buddy film, buddy movie** a film featuring friendship between two individuals, esp. men; **buddy system** (*a*) organized cooperation of individuals for mutual help or safety; (*b*) the practice of appointing friends or allies to positions of influence.

B *v.i.* Become friendly. Usu. foll. by *up.* M20.

buddy /'bʌdi/ *a. rare.* L16. [f. BUD *n.*[1] + -Y[1].] Full of buds; like a bud.

bude /buːd, byd/ *v.* (orig. 3rd person sing. pa. indic., later other persons, pres., pa. pple, & inf.). *Sc.* & †*north.* Also **bit** /bɪt/, **bode** /bəʊd/, **buit** /byt/, & other vars. ME. [Contr. of *behoved*: cf. BOOST *v.*[2]] Behoved, behoves, behove (see above); must, ought.

budge /bʌdʒ/ *n.*[1] & *a. obs.* exc. *Hist.* LME. [Origin unkn. (orig. disyllabic, = AL *buggetum*).] A *n.* A fur of lamb's skin with the wool dressed outwards. LME. †B *attrib.* or as *adj.* Made of budge; wearing budge. Hence, solemn in demeanour, pompous, formal. LME–L18.

budge /bʌdʒ/ *n.*[2] *rare* exc. as below. E17. [Var. of BOUGE *n.*] = BOUGE *n.* 1.

Comb.: **budge-barrel** *Hist.* a small powder barrel having a leather cover with a long neck.

†**budge** *n.*[3] *slang.* L17–M18. [Origin unkn.] A sneak-thief.

budge /bʌdʒ/ *v.* L16. [Fr. *bouger* = Prov. *bolegar* disturb oneself, It. *bulicare* bubble up, f. Proto-Romance frequent. of L *bullire*, f. BULLA.] 1 *v.i.* Stir, move from one's or its place; change opinion. (Almost always in neg. contexts.) L16. †b Wince, flinch, shirk. L16–M17. 2 *v.t.* Stir or move (a heavy thing). L16.

1 R. L. STEVENSON We'll have to budge, mates. A. CARTER The old car stuck fast in a rut, wouldn't budge an inch. S. BRETT I've argued with him about this, but he won't budge.

budger *n.* (*rare*) E17.

budgeree /'bʌdʒəri/ *a. Austral. colloq.* L18. [Aborig. *bujari.*] Good, excellent.

budgerigar /'bʌdʒ(ə)rɪgɑː/ *n.* M19. [Aborig., f. as prec. + *gar* cockatoo.] A small Australian parakeet, *Melopsittacus undulatus*, a popular cage-bird, green in the wild state, although captive birds are bred in a variety of colours.

budgerow /'bʌdʒərəʊ/ *n. Anglo-Ind. obs.* exc. *Hist.* E18. [Hind., Bengali *bajrā.*] A type of barge formerly much used on the Ganges.

budget /'bʌdʒɪt/ *n.* & *a.* See also BOUGET. LME. [OFr. *bougette* dim. of *bouge* leather bag f. L *bulga*: see BULGE, -ET[1].] A *n.* 1 A pouch or wallet. *obs.* exc. *dial.* LME. †b *spec.* A leather container, *esp.* a leather or skin bottle. L16–M19. 2 The contents of a bag or wallet; a bundle, a collection, a stock. *arch.* L16. b *spec.* A long letter full of news. E19. 3 A periodic (esp. annual) estimate of the revenue and expenditure of a country or organization; an account or statement of this, *esp.* one made by the Chancellor of the Exchequer in the House of Commons; a similar estimate for a private individual or family. Also, the amount of money needed or available for spending. M18.

1 **open one's budget** speak one's mind. 2 SWIFT I read . . the whole budget of papers you sent. *fig.*: HAZLITT His budget of general knowledge. b DAY LEWIS I had a budget from her last week. 3 J. K. GALBRAITH The balanced budget . . has been the *sine qua non* of sound and sensible management of the public purse. B. CASTLE The Chancellor must be free to have a later budget next year. P. DAVIES Most 'pure' scientists work in large laboratory teams . . and annual budgets run into hundreds of millions of dollars. **on a budget** with a restricted amount of money.

Comb.: **budget buster** (chiefly *US*) a person, policy, or measure proposing or effecting expenditure in excess of an agreed budget.

B *attrib.* or as *adj.* Designed or suitable for someone of limited means; cheap. M20.

Woman's Own Budget meals for the family. *budget account*: see ACCOUNT *n.*

budgetary *a.* of or pertaining to a budget L19. **budge'teer** *n.* a person who makes up or supports a budget M19.

budget /'bʌdʒɪt/ *v.* E17. [f. the n.] †1 *v.t.* Put in a budget or wallet; store *up.* Only in E17. 2 *v.i.* Draw up or prepare a budget, esp. *for* a certain supply, establishment, or a particular financial result. L19. b *v.t.* Arrange (for) in a budget. L19.

budgie /'bʌdʒi/ *n. colloq.* E20. [Abbrev.: see -IE.] A budgerigar.

buer /'bjʊə/ *n. north.* & *slang.* Usu. *derog.* (or so interpreted). E19. [Origin unkn.] A sexually attractive or available woman.

buff /bʌf/ *n.*[1] LME. [OFr. *bufe* BUFFET *n.*[1]] A blow, a stroke, a buffet. Now chiefly in *blind man's buff* s.v. BLIND *a.*

stand buff *arch.* stand firm, not flinch.

buff /bʌf/ *n.*[2] & *a.* M16. [Prob. f. as BUFFLE. In recent use in sense A.1 repr. an abbrev. of BUFFALO.] A *n.* 1 A buffalo. Now *colloq.* M16. 2 Stout dressed ox-leather of a dull-yellow colour and velvety surface. L16. b Military attire (for which buff was formerly much used). *arch.* L16. 3 *The* bare skin, *the* nude. *colloq.* E17. 4 *Med.* = *buffy coat* s.v. BUFFY *a.*[1] M18. 5 Hist. *the* (*Old*) *Buffs*, the 3rd regiment of the line, later the East Kent Regiment (so called from their buff facings). M18. 6 The colour of buff; pale dull yellow. L18. 7 A stick or wheel covered with buff or a similar material, used for polishing. M19. 8 Orig., an enthusiast for watching fires (so called from the buff uniforms of volunteer firemen in New York City). Now, an enthusiast or expert in any (specified) subject or activity: *colloq.* (orig. *US*). E20.

2b SIR W. SCOTT In buff and bandoleer for King Charles. 3 G. MCINNES Undressing down to the buff. 5 *steady the Buffs*: see STEADY *a.*, *adv.*, & *int.* 8 E. REVELEY Though no wine buff, even he could tell that this must have been one of Felix's finest hocks.

B *attrib.* or as *adj.* Made of buff; like buff; of the colour of buff, pale dull yellow. L16.

buff arches: see ARCH *n.*[1] 6. **buff coat** a coat of buff; *transf.* (*arch.*) a soldier. **buff leather** = sense A.2 above. **buff-stick, -wheel** = sense A.7 above.

buffed *a.* clad in or covered with buff M17. **buffish** *a.* E19.

†**buff** *n.*[3] *colloq.* E–M18. [Cf. BUFFER *n.*[13]] = BUFFER *n.*[1] 2.

buff /bʌf/ *v.*[1] *obs.* exc. *dial.* ME. [Prob. imit.: cf. *puff*, BUFF *n.*[1]] 1 *v.i.* Stutter, splutter; burst *out* into laughter etc. ME. 2 *v.i.* & *t.* Make a sound as a soft inflated object does when struck; strike so as to cause such a sound. M16.

buff /bʌf/ *v.*²*t.* M19. [f. BUFF *n.*²] **1** Polish, *spec.* with a buff. M19. **2** Impart a velvety surface to (leather). L19.

1 K. KESEY Get them to work buffing the floor. F. KING Fingernails buffed to an opalescent pink.

buffalo /ˈbʌfələʊ/ *n.* & *v.* M16. [Prob. immed. f. Port. *bufalo* (now *bufaro*) = It. *bufalo*, Sp. *búbalo*, *búfalo*, f. late L *bufalus* f. L *bubalus* f. Gk *boubalos* wild ox, antelope. Cf. BUFF *n.*², BUFFLE.] **A** *n.* Pl. **-oes**, same. **1** **a** Any of several wild Asiatic oxen of the genus *Bubalus*, with long curved horns, esp. *B. arnee* (more fully *water-buffalo*), which has been domesticated. M16. **b** A similar wild African ox, *Syncerus caffer* (more fully *Cape buffalo*). L17. **2** = *American bison* s.v. BISON I. Chiefly *N. Amer.* M17. **3** A large river-fish of the genus *Ictiobus*, of the sucker family. *N. Amer.* L18. **4** In full *buffalo robe*. A rug or cloak made of lined trimmed buffalo hide. *N. Amer.* E19. **5** (**B-**.) A member of the Royal Antediluvian Order of Buffaloes, a social club and benevolent society. M19. **6** An amphibious tank. M20.

Comb.: **buffalo berry** (the edible fruit of) a tree or shrub of the N. American genus *Shepherdia*, of the oleaster family, esp. *S. canadensis* and *S. argentea*; **buffalo bird** (*a*) an oxpecker; (*b*) a cowbird; **buffalo chips** dried buffalo dung used as fuel; **buffalo clover** a native N. American clover, *Trifolium stoloniferum*, found on the prairies; **buffalo fish** *N. Amer.* = sense 2 above; **buffalo fly, gnat** = *blackfly* (b) s.v. BLACK *a.*; **buffalo grass** any of various grasses, esp. (N. Amer.) *Buchloe dactyloides*, (Austral. & NZ) *Stenotaphrum secundatum*; **buffalo-nut** (the oily nut of) a parasitic N. American shrub, *Pyrularia pubera*, of the sandalwood family; *buffalo robe*: see sense 3 above; **buffalo runner** *N. Amer. Hist.* a swift horse for hunting buffalo.

B *v.t.* Overawe, bemuse, baffle, outwit. *N. Amer. slang.* E20.

M. PUZO He could still command a hefty advance for a book, he still had critics buffaloed.

buffe /bʊf/ *n.* L16. [It. *buffa*.] †**1** A breathing-hole of a helmet. Only in L16. **2** *Hist.* A piece of armour for the chin, pierced with breathing-holes. E17.

buffel *n.* var. of BUFFLE.

buffer /ˈbʌfə/ *n.*¹ & *v.* LME. [Prob. f. BUFF *v.*¹ + -ER¹.] **A** *n.* **I** †**1** A stammerer. Only in LME. **2** A fellow; *esp.* an old-fashioned or incompetent fellow. Freq. in *old buffer. slang.* M18. **b** *Naut.* A boatswain's mate; a petty officer. M19. **II** **3** An apparatus for deadening impact; *spec.* either of a pair of projecting shock absorbers fitted to a cross-beam at the end of a railway vehicle or on a fixed mounting across the end of a railway line (usu. in *pl.*). Also *fig.*, a protective intermediary. M19. **4** *Chem.* A substance or mixture of substances (usu. a weak acid or base with one of its salts) which tends to stabilize the pH of a solution; a solution containing this. E20. **5** *Computing.* An intermediate memory for the temporary storage of information during data transfers, *esp.* one that accepts data at one rate and delivers them at another. M20.

3 B. TRAPIDO She has a tendency to answer questions for him as if he needed her as a buffer between himself and a hostile world.

Comb.: **buffer area** (*lit.* & *fig.*): separating potential belligerents; **buffer solution** *Chem.* a solution containing a buffer; **buffer State** a small country lying between two possible belligerents, diminishing the chance of hostilities; **buffer stock** a stock of a commodity held in reserve so as to offset price fluctuations; **buffer stop** a pair of buffers fixed at the end of a railway line; **buffer zone**: separating potential belligerents.

B *v.t.* **1** Act as a buffer to (chiefly *fig.*); lessen the impact of. L19. **2** *Chem.* Treat with a buffer; stabilize by means of a buffer. E20.

buffer /ˈbʌfə/ *n.*² *arch.* E19. [Prob. imit.] A dog.

buffer /ˈbʌfə/ *n.*³ M19. [f. BUFF *v.*² + -ER¹.] A person who polishes with a buff; a device for buffing.

buffet /ˈbʌfɪt/ *n.*¹ ME. [OFr. *buf(f)et* dim. of *bufe* BUFF *n.*¹: see -ET¹.] **1** A blow, esp. with the hand; a knock, an impact. ME. **2** *Aeronaut.* = BUFFETING (c). M20.

1 A. P. HERBERT Mr. Walker gave him a buffet in the ribs with his fist. S. T. WARNER Calamities go on having a buffet at us.

buffet /ˈbʌfɪt/ *n.*² Now *dial.* LME. [OFr. *buf(f)et*, of unkn. origin.] **1** A low stool; a footstool. Also *buffet-stool*. LME. **2** A hassock. L19.

buffet /ˈbʊfeɪ; *in sense 1 also* ˈbʌfɪt/ *n.*³ E18. [Fr., f. as prec.] **1** A sideboard or recessed cupboard for china, plate, etc. E18. **2** (A place offering) a service of food from a sideboard or counter where guests or customers can help themselves; *esp.* (*a*) a refreshment room in a station or other public building; (*b*) (in full *buffet car*) a railway carriage serving light refreshments. L18.

Comb.: *buffet car*: see sense 2 above. **buffet meal, party**, etc.: at which food is served from a sideboard etc.

buffet /ˈbʌfɪt/ *v.* ME. [(O)Fr. *buffeter*, f. as BUFFET *n.*¹] **1** *v.t.* Beat, strike, thump, knock about, (*lit.* & *fig.*). ME. **b** Beat back, contend with (waves, wind, etc.). L16. **2** *v.i.* Deal blows, fight, struggle. L16. **3** *v.t.* Drive, force, or produce by buffeting. L17.

1 O. MANNING As the crowd pressed past him, he was buffeted mercilessly from side to side. B. BAINBRIDGE The train, buffeted by wind, was swaying over the steel lattice of a bridge. b SHAKES. *Jul. Caes.* The torrent roar'd, and we did buffet it With lusty sinews. 2 *fig.*: TENNYSON I heard . . the great echo flap And buffet round the hills. 3 F. PARKMAN He buffeted his way to riches and fame.

buffeting *n.* (*a*) the action of the vb; (*b*) a beating, a thumping; (*c*) *Aeronaut.* irregular oscillation of a part of an aircraft owing to turbulence, esp. near sonic speed: ME.

†**buffin** *n.* L16–E18. [Origin unkn.] (A gown of) a kind of a coarse cloth.

buffle /ˈbʌf(ə)l/ *n.* Long *obs.* exc. in comb. Also **-el**. E16. [(O)Fr. f. It. *bufalo*: see BUFFALO.] **1** A buffalo. E16. **2** A fool, a fat-head. M17.

Comb.: **bufflehead** (*a*) = sense 2 above; (*b*) a black and white N. American diving duck, *Bucephala albeola*, with a relatively large head; **buffle-headed** *a.* †(*a*) having a head like a buffalo's; (*b*) large-headed; fat-headed, foolish, stupid.

buffo /ˈbʊfəʊ/ *n.* & *a.* M18. [It. = puff of wind, buffoon, f. *buffare*: see next.] **A** *n.* Pl. **-os**. A comic actor, a singer in comic opera. M18.

primo buffo: see PRIMO *a.*

B *adj.* Comic, burlesque. L18.

BASSO *buffo*.

buffoon /bəˈfuːn/ *n.*, *a.*, & *v.* M16. [Fr. *bouffon* f. It. *buffone*, f. med.L *buffo* clown, f. Proto-Romance vb meaning 'puff', of imit. origin: see -OON.] **A** *n.* †**1** A pantomine dance. *Sc. rare.* Only in M16. **2** A (professional) jester, a clown. *arch.* L16. **3** A (vulgar or ludicrous) joker, a wag, a mocker. Usu. *derog.* L16. **B** *attrib.* or as *adj.* Belonging to or characteristic of a buffoon; vulgarly jocular. *arch.* E17. **C** *v.* **1** *v.t.* Ridicule, burlesque. *arch.* M17. **2** *v.i.* Play the buffoon. L17.

buffoonery *n.* the actions or an act of a buffoon; silliness, farce: E17. **buffoonish** *a.* like or characteristic of a buffoon; silly, ridiculous: L17.

buffy /ˈbʌfi/ *a.*¹ L18. [f. BUFF *n.*² or *a.* + -Y¹.] Resembling buff in colour or appearance.

buffy coat *Med.* a thin pale layer of white cells which forms on clotted blood, or between the red cells and plasma when blood is centrifuged.

buffy /ˈbʌfi/ *a.*² *slang.* M19. [Origin unkn.] Tipsy, moderately drunk.

†**bufonite** *n.* M17–M19. [f. L *bufon-*, *bufo* toad + -ITE¹.] = TOADSTONE *n.*¹

bufotenine /bjʊfəˈtɛniːn/ *n.* E20. [Fr. *bufoténine*, f. L *bufo* toad + (prob.) *tenere* hold (because of an ability to cause paralysis): see -INE⁵.] *Chem.* An alkaloid which occurs in various amphibian secretions, mushrooms, and tropical plants, and has hallucinogenic, hypertensive, and vasoconstrictive actions.

†**bug** *n.*¹ LME–L19. [Rel. to BOGGARD, BOGLE, etc. Connection w. Welsh *bwg*, *bwgan* (ghost, hobgoblin), *bygwl* (fear, threat) uncertain. Cf. BUGBEAR.] An (imaginary) object of terror; a bugbear, a bogey; a scarecrow.

Comb.: **bug-word** a word meant to frighten.

bug /bʌg/ *n.*² E17. [Origin uncertain. Perh. f. OE *-budda*, as in *sćearnbudda* dung-beetle, or rel. to prec.] **1** **a** A hemipteran insect; orig. *spec.* the bedbug (see BED *n.*). E17. **b** *gen.* Any insect, *esp.* a small beetle or grub. Freq. w. specifying wd, as *harvest bug*, *June bug*, *ladybug*, *red bug*, etc. (absol. chiefly *N. Amer.*). *colloq.* M17. **2** A person obsessed by an idea; an enthusiast. Also, an obsession, a craze. *slang.* M19. **3** A defect or fault in a machine, plan, etc.; *spec.* a mistake or malfunction in a computer program or system. *colloq.* L19. **4** A (school)boy, usu. of specified status etc. *slang.* E20. **5** A micro-organism, *esp.* a virus; a disease caused by this. *colloq.* E20. **6** A burglar-alarm system. *US slang.* E20. **7** A concealed microphone. M20.

1 *big bug*: see BIG *a.* 2 *Plain Dealer* (*Cleveland, Ohio*) Cusick is a bug on weight-lifting. *fire-bug*, *jitterbug*, etc. 4 *new bug*: see NEW *a.*

Comb.: **bugbane** any of various tall plants of the genus *Cimicifuga* of the buttercup family, bearing small white flowers (*C. foetida* was formerly used to drive away bedbugs); **bug-hunter** *slang* an entomologist; a naturalist; **bugwort** = *bugbane* above.

bug /bʌg/ *a.* Long *obs.* exc. *dial.* M16. [Origin unkn.] Pompous; conceited; fine.

bug /bʌg/ *v.*¹*t.* Infl. **-gg-**. M19. [f. BUG *n.*²] **1** Clear (plants etc.) of insects. M19. **2** Equip with an alarm system or a concealed microphone; listen to by means of a concealed microphone. E20. **3** Annoy, bother. *colloq.* M20.

bug /bʌg/ *v.*²*i.* *N. Amer. colloq.* Infl. **-gg-**. L19. [Origin unkn.] Of the eyes: bulge *out*.

Comb.: **bug-eyed** *a.* having bulging eyes (*bug-eyed monster*, an extraterrestrial monster (with bulging eyes)).

bug /bʌg/ *v.*³*i.* *slang* (chiefly *US*). Infl. **-gg-**. M20. [Origin of sense 1 uncertain. In sense 2 abbrev. of BUGGER *v.*] **1** Get *out*, leave quickly. M20. **2** Foll. by *off*: go away. L20.

bugaboo /ˈbʌgəbuː/ *n.* M18. [Cf. Welsh *bwci bo* bogey, Corn. *bucca*.] **1** A bogey; a bugbear. M18. **2** Loud or empty talk; nonsense, rubbish. L19.

bugaku /ˈbʊgakuː/ *n.* L19. [Jap., f. *bu* dancing + *gaku* music.] A Japanese classical dance in which pure dance form and symmetry are emphasized, and masks are used.

bugbear /ˈbʌgbɛː/ *n.* & *a.* L16. [Prob. f. BUG *n.*¹ + BEAR *n.*¹] **A** *n.* **1** A sort of hobgoblin (perhaps in the shape of a bear) supposed to devour naughty children; *gen.* any imaginary being invoked to frighten children. L16. **2** *transf.* An object of (needless) dread; an imaginary terror; an annoyance. L16. **B** *attrib.* or as *adj.* Needlessly alarming or annoying. E17.

bugger /ˈbʌgə/ *n.*¹ ME. [(MDu. f.) (O)Fr. *bougre* †heretic, sodomite (arch.), person (colloq.), f. med.L *Bulgarus* Bulgarian (esp. as adhering to the Orthodox Church), heretic, Albigensian: see BULGAR.] **I** †**1** (**B-**.) A heretic; *spec.* an Albigensian. ME–M18. **2** A person who commits buggery. *coarse slang* exc. *Law.* M16.

II Extended uses: all *coarse slang.* **3** An unpleasant or undesirable person or thing; (in weakened sense) a person, a chap. Cf. BEGGAR *n.* 3. E18. **4** A negligible amount. E20.

3 F. MANNING There are two poor buggers dead. G. ORWELL This business of class-breaking is a bugger. **play silly buggers** fool about, mess around. 4 *not care* or *give a bugger. bugger all*: see ALL *pron.* & *n.* 3.

bugger /ˈbʌgə/ *n.*² M20. [f. BUG *v.*¹ + -ER¹.] A person who instals a concealed microphone.

bugger /ˈbʌgə/ *v.* L16. [f. BUGGER *n.*¹] **I** **1** *v.t.* & *i.* Commit buggery (with). L16.

II Extended uses: all *coarse slang.* **2** *v.t.* Curse, damn. Freq. in imprecations in imper. or in optative form (for *God* etc. *bugger* —). L18. **b** *v.i.* Curse. As *int.*: damn! M19. **3** **a** *v.t.* Ruin, spoil; mess *up*; mess *about* or *around* (with); tire, exhaust, (chiefly as *buggered* ppl a.). E20. **b** *v.i.* Mess or potter *about*, *around*. M20. **4** *v.i.* Foll. by *off*: go away. E20.

2 S. BECKETT Bugger these buttons! C. P. SNOW I'm buggered if I vote for Crawford.

buggery /ˈbʌgəri/ *n.* ME. [MDu. *buggerie*, OFr. *bougrerie*, *bouguerie*, f. as BUGGER *n.*¹: see -Y³.] †**1** Abominable heresy. Only in ME. **2** Sodomy.

Also = BESTIALITY 2. E16. 3 *to buggery*, to hell, to the devil, to damnation. *coarse slang*. E20.

3 E. LINDALL 'Go to buggery,' Minogue snarled.

†**Buggess** *n*. L17–E19. [f. as BUGIS.] A SE Asian soldier in European service.

Buggins' turn /ˈbʌgɪnz tɜːn/ *n. phr.* E20. [f. *Buggins*, a 'typical' surname used generically + TURN *n*.] Appointment in rotation rather than by merit.

buggy /ˈbʌgi/ *n*. M18. [Origin unkn.] 1 A light horse-drawn vehicle for one or two people, with two or (in N. America) four wheels. M18. 2 *transf.* a A pram. More fully *baby buggy*. *N. Amer.* L19. b A motor vehicle; *esp.* a small sturdy vehicle (freq. w. specified use). E20.

1 *horse-and-buggy*: see HORSE *n*. 2b *beach buggy*, *dune buggy*, etc.

Comb.: **buggy-ride** (chiefly *N. Amer.*) a ride in a buggy (*thanks for the buggy-ride* (colloq.): an expression of thanks for help given).

buggy /ˈbʌgi/ *a*. E18. [f. BUG *n*.[2] + -Y[1].] Infested with bugs; like a bug.

bughouse /ˈbʌghaʊs/ *a*. & *n*. *slang*. L19. [f. BUG *n*.[2] + HOUSE *n*.[1]] A *adj*. Crazy; very eccentric. Chiefly *US*. L19. B *n*. 1 A mental hospital. Orig. *US*. E20. 2 A theatre or cinema. *derog*. M20.

bught *n*. & *v*. var. of BOUGHT *n*.[2] & *v*.[2]

Bugis /ˈbuːgɪs/ *n*. & *a*. Also **Bugi** /ˈbuːgi/. E18. [Malay.] A *n*. Pl. **-i(s)**. A member of a people of southern Sulawesi (Celebes), Indonesia; the language of this people. E18. B *attrib*. or as *adj*. Of or pertaining to the Bugis or their language. E19.

Also **Bugi'nese** *n*. & *a*. (pl. of n. same) E20.

bugle /ˈbjuːg(ə)l/ *n*.[1] ME. [OFr. f. L *buculus* dim. of *bos* ox.] †1a A buffalo or wild ox. ME–L17. b A young bull. *dial*. L19. 2 In full *bugle-horn*. Orig., a horn of a wild ox etc. used to give signals in hunting. Now, a brass instrument like a small trumpet similarly used or for giving military signals, or (*US*) in marching bands. ME.

2 *key-bugle*: see KEY *n*.[1]

bugler *n*. a person who plays a bugle; *spec*. a soldier who signals orders on a bugle: M19. **buglet** *n*. a small bugle E19.

bugle /ˈbjuːg(ə)l/ *n*.[2] ME. [Late L *bugula*.] A creeping plant of the genus *Ajuga*, of the mint family; esp. *A. reptans*, which bears blue flowers.

Comb.: **bugleweed** *N. Amer.* (*a*) = sense above; (*b*) a related plant, *Lycopus virginicus*, found in wet soil.

bugle /ˈbjuːg(ə)l/ *n*.[3] L16. [Origin unkn.] A tube-shaped bead, usu. black, sewn on a dress etc. as ornament.

attrib.: SHAKES. *A.Y.L.* Your inky brows, your black silk hair, your bugle eyeballs.

bugle /ˈbjuːg(ə)l/ *v*. M19. [f. BUGLE *n*.[1]] 1 *v.t.* Give forth (a sound) like a bugle; sound (a call) on a bugle. M19. 2 *v.i.* Sound a bugle; make a sound like a bugle. L19.

bugloss /ˈbjuːglɒs/ *n*. LME. [(O)Fr. *buglosse* or L *buglossus* f. Gk *bouglōssos* 'ox-tongued', f. *bous* ox + *glōssa* tongue.] Any of various plants of the borage family, *esp.* (*a*) a Eurasian weed of arable land, *Anchusa arvensis*, bearing blue flowers; (*b*) *US* a kind of alkanet, *Anchusa officinalis*.

viper's bugloss: see VIPER *n*.

bugology /bʌˈgɒlədʒi/ *n*. *joc*. Chiefly *US*. M19. [f. BUG *n*.[2] + -OLOGY.] Entomology.

bugologist *n*. L19.

bugong *n*. var. of BOGONG.

buhl /buːl/ *n*. & *a*. Also **boul(l)e**, **B-**. E19. [G *buhl*, Fr. *boule*, f. André Charles *Boulle* (1642–1732), Fr. cabinet-maker.] (Of) brass, tortoise-shell, etc., worked into ornamental patterns for inlaying; (work) inlaid thus.

buhr *n*. see BURR *n*.[4]

build /bɪld/ *n*. LME. [f. the vb: cf BUILT *n*.] †1 A building. Only in LME. 2 Style of construction, make; proportions of the human body, physique. M17.

2 S. PEPYS The difference in the build of ships now and heretofore. M. MUGGERIDGE A tall man, rather the build of Bernard Shaw.

build /bɪld/ *v*. Pa. t. & pple **built** /bɪlt/, (*poet*. & *arch*.) **builded**. See also BUILT *ppl a*. [OE *byldan* (cf. *bylda* builder), f. *bold*, *botl* dwelling, house = OFris. *bōdel*, OS *bodl*, ON *ból*, f. Gmc, f. base meaning 'dwell' (also of BOWER *n*.[1]).] 1 *v.t.* Construct (a house, nest, etc.) as a dwelling; construct (a school, factory, stable, church, etc.) for occupation; construct (a ship, vehicle, fire, road, or other structure large relative to the user or requiring much time or effort in the construction) by putting parts or material together. OE. b *v.i.* Be built. Only in *be building*. L17. 2 *v.t.* Give form to, create; establish or accumulate gradually; improve; benefit spiritually, edify. ME. 3 *v.i.* Erect a building or buildings; engage in building; construct a nest etc. ME. 4 *v.t.* Put together (parts, material) *into* a structure; join *together* to form a structure; lay, insert, or incorporate *in* (adv.) or *into* as an integral part of a larger unit. LME. 5 *v.t.* & *i.* Found (an argument, hope, confidence, progress, etc.) *on* a basis; rely *on*. E16.

Phrases: *build a sconce*: see SCONCE *n*.[2] 2. *build (castles) in the air*: see AIR *n*.[1] 3.

With advs. in specialized senses: **build down** reduce or destroy gradually or in a planned way. **build in** surround with houses etc., block up, enclose by building; (see also sense 4 above). **build round** surround with houses etc. **build up** (*a*) *v.phr.t.* & *i.* increase in size, mass, or strength; accumulate; establish (itself) gradually; (*b*) *v.phr.t.* surround with houses etc., block up; (*c*) *v.phr.t.* boost, praise.

Comb.: **build-down** a systematic reduction or destruction. **build-up** a favourable description in advance; preparation for or a gradual approach to a climax or maximum; an accumulation.

buildable *a*. able to be built (on) E20.

builder /ˈbɪldə/ *n*. ME. [f. prec. + -ER[1].] 1 A person who builds; *esp*. a contractor for building houses. ME. 2 A substance added to soap or to a detergent to increase its efficiency. M20.

1 **builders' merchant** a supplier of materials to builders. *speculative builder*: see SPECULATIVE 4.

building /ˈbɪldɪŋ/ *n*. ME. [f. as prec. + -ING[1].] 1 A thing which is built; a structure, an edifice; a permanent fixed thing built for occupation, as a house, school, factory, stable, church, etc. ME. 2 The action of BUILD *v*. LME. 3 A company (of rooks); a rookery. *rare*. LME.

Comb.: **building-block** (*a*) = BLOCK *n*. 4b; (*b*) one of the temporary supports for a ship's keel while the ship is being built; **building-brick** = BRICK *n*. 2, 2b; **building-lease** a lease of land upon which to build; **building line** a prescribed limit beyond which a building must not extend; **building society**: accepting investments at interest, and lending to persons building or buying houses etc.; **building-term** the duration of a building-lease.

†**built** *n*. E17–L18. [f. BUILD *v*.] Style of construction; build.

built /bɪlt/ *ppl a*. L16. [pa. pple of BUILD *v*.] Constructed or constituted, esp. in a specified way; having a specified build; *spec*. composed of separately prepared parts (= *built-up* (b) below).

M. PRIOR With well-built Verse to keep his Fame alive. J. RUSKIN The built and tower-like shaft. L. URIS Ari Ben Canaan was . . built like his father. **built-in** (esp. of the fittings of a house) constructed to form an integral part of a larger unit; *fig*. inherent, integral, innate. *built on sand*: see SAND *n*. **built-up** (*a*) increased in height etc. by addition of parts; (*b*) composed of separately prepared parts; (*c*) (of a locality) fully occupied by houses etc. *clinker-built*: see CLINKER *n*.[1]

built *v*. pa. t. & pple of BUILD *v*.

buirdly /ˈbyrdli/ *a*. *Sc*. Also **boardly** /ˈbɔːdli/. L18. [Var. of BURLY *a*. w. *-d-* perh. after forms of BOARD *n*.] Large and well made, stately; sturdy.

buist *v*. var. of BOOST *v*.[2]

buit *v*. var. of BUDE.

bukshi /ˈbʌkʃiː/ *n*. *Anglo-Ind*. *obs*. exc. *Hist*. Also **bu(c)kshee**. E17. [Pers. *bakšī* giver, f. *bakšīdan* give: cf. BAKSHEESH.] A paymaster-general; an army paymaster.

bulb /bʌlb/ *n*. & *v*. LME. [L *bulbus* f. Gk *bolbos* onion, bulbous root.] A *n*. 1 The globular underground organ of an onion, lily, or similar plant, which contains the following year's bud and scale leaves that serve as food reserves. Also, a plant growing from a bulb. LME. †b *spec*. An onion. M16–E18. 2 *Anat*. A spheroidal dilatation of the end of an organ or other structure, e.g. of the spinal cord (the medulla oblongata) or of a hair-root. E18. 3a A dilated part of a glass tube, e.g. forming the reservoir of a thermometer. E19. b (The glass envelope of) an electric lamp. M19. c A compressible rubber device for the pneumatic operation of a syringe etc. L19. B *v.i.* Form a root shaped like a bulb; swell into a form like a bulb or rounded. L17.

bulbed *a*. shaped like a bulb; having a bulb or bulbs: L16. **bulbiferous** /bʌlˈbɪf(ə)rəs/ *a*. bearing a bulb, producing bulbs L17. **bulbiform** *a*. shaped like a bulb M19. **bulblet** *n*. a bulbil M19. **bulblike** *a*. resembling (that of) a bulb M19.

bulbar /ˈbʌlbə/ *a*. L19. [f. BULB *n*. + -AR[1].] Chiefly *Anat*. Of or pertaining to a bulb, esp. to the medulla oblongata (see BULB *n*. 2).

†**bulbel** *n*. var. of BULBIL.

bulberry *n*. see BULL *n*.[1]

bulbil /ˈbʌlbɪl/ *n*. Also †**-el**. M19. [mod.L *bulbillus* dim. of *bulbus* BULB.] A small aerial bulb borne in a leaf axil or an inflorescence, which can develop into an independent plant when detached. Also, a small bulb formed at the side of an ordinary bulb.

bulbo- /ˈbʌlbəʊ/ *comb. form* of L *bulbus* BULB *n*., used chiefly in *Anat*.: see -O-.

bulbo-u'rethral *a*. of or pertaining to the urethra and the bulb (proximal region) of the penis; *bulbo-urethral gland*, either of a pair of small glands which open into the urethra at the base of the penis and secrete a constituent of seminal fluid (also called *Cowper's gland*): M19.

bulbous /ˈbʌlbəs/ *a*. L16. [f. L *bulbosus* or directly f. BULB *n*. + -OUS.] 1 Of, pertaining to, or of the nature of a bulb. L16. 2 Growing from a bulb; having roots like bulbs. L16. 3 Shaped like a bulb; rounded, swollen. L18.

3 W. GOLDING The bulbous legs of a grand piano. R. GRAVES The bulbous nose, the sunken chin.

bulbose *a*. (*rare*) bulbous L16. **bulbosity** /bʌlˈbɒsɪti/ *n*. bulbous condition or quality E20.

bulbul /ˈbʊlbʊl/ *n*. M17. [Pers., of imit. origin.] Any of various Asian or African songbirds of the large family Pycnonotidae; *spec*. an Iranian bird admired for its song. Also *fig*., a singer, a poet.

†**bulchin** *n*. var. of BULKIN.

bulfinch *n*. see BULLFINCH.

Bulgar /ˈbʌlgɑː/ *n*. LME. [med.L *Bulgarus* f. Old Ch. Slav. *Blŭgary* pl. Bulgarian *Bălgari* pl.).] A member of an ancient Turkic people who settled in the region of Bulgaria in the 7th cent. Also, a native or inhabitant of Bulgaria (see next).

¶Rare bef. M18.

Bulgarize *v.t.* make Bulgarian in character M19.

Bulgarian /bʌlˈgɛːrɪən/ *n*. & *a*. M16. [f. (med.L) *Bulgaria* (see below), f. as prec., + -AN.] A *n*. A native or inhabitant of Bulgaria, a country in the Eastern Balkans. Also, the Slavonic language of Bulgaria. M16. B *adj*. Of or pertaining to Bulgaria, its people, or their language. L18.

bulge /bʌldʒ/ *n*. & *v*. ME. [OFr. *bou(l)ge* f. L *bulga* leather sack, bag, of Gaulish origin.] A *n*. †1 A wallet or bag, esp. of hide. ME–E17. 2 = BILGE *n*. 1. Now *rare* or *obs*. E17. 3 A convex part or irregular swelling on an otherwise flat(ter) surface or line. M18. b *spec*. A protuberance added to a ship's hull for protection or increased stability. E20. c *Mil*. A salient. E20. 4 *fig*. a An advantage, a lead. Chiefly in *have* or *get the bulge on*, get an advantage over (a person). *slang* (chiefly *N. Amer.*). M19. b A temporary increase or rise in volume, numbers, etc. *colloq*. L19.

3 L. DEIGHTON He didn't want to . . stuff it into his pocket for it would make bulges in his newly pressed uniform jacket. W. BOYD His palm cautiously inched up the slack bulge of her breast. 4b *Lancet* The number of births will increase . . when the people born in the 'bulge' of the 1950's start to reproduce.

B *v*. †1 *v.t.* = BILGE *v*. 1. LME–E19. †2 *v.i.* = BILGE *v*. 2. Also, strike (*on*, *against*) so as to damage the bilge. E17–E19. 3 *v.i.* Protrude, swell out; be swollen, esp. by being full. L17. 4 *v.t.* Make protuberant, cause to swell, esp. by filling. M19. 5 *v.i.* Rush *in*; make a dash *for*. *US colloq*. M19.

3 E. NESBIT Boxes . . with more Indian things bulging out of them. I. FLEMING The muscles bulged

under the exquisitely cut shark-skin jacket. A. C. BOULT His pockets bulging with £20 notes. 4 S. PLATH A snug corset affair that curved her in at the middle and bulged her out again spectacularly above and below. J. HERRIOT Her plump figure bulged her uniform tightly.

bulgy *a.* swollen, that bulges M19.

bulghur *n.* var. of BULGUR.

bulgur /ˈbʌlgə/ *n.* Also **-gh-**. M20. [Turk. = Pers. *bulġūr* bruised grain.] = BURGHUL.

bulimarexia /bjʊˌlɪməˈrɛksɪə, ˌbʊ-/ *n.* L20. [f. next + ANOREXIA.] *Med.* Bulimia nervosa (see next).

bulimarexic *a.* & *n.* L20.

bulimia /bjʊˈlɪmɪə, ˌbʊ-/ *n.* Also (earlier) Anglicized as †**bulimy**. LME. [med.L *bolismus* or mod.L *bulimia* f. Gk *boulimia* ravenous hunger, f. *bou-* huge (f. *bous* ox) + *limos* hunger: see -IA[1].] *Med.* Abnormal craving for food; *esp.* (in full *bulimia nervosa* /nəːˈvəʊsə/) gross overeating alternating with self-induced vomiting or evacuation of the food eaten.

bulimic *a.* & *n.* (*a*) *adj.* of, pertaining to, or exhibiting bulimia; (*b*) *n.* a person with bulimia (nervosa): M19.

bulk /bʌlk/ *n.*[1] & *a.* ME. [Senses 1, 2 f. ON *búlki* cargo; other senses perh. alt. of BOUK.] A *n.* 1 A ship's cargo, esp. as a whole; the whole amount (of a commodity). ME. 2 A heap, a pile (now *rare* in *lit.* use); a large quantity. LME. 3 The hull or hold of a ship. Long *obs.* exc. *dial.* LME. 4 The body, the trunk; now *spec.* a bodily frame of large proportions. LME. 5 Bodily magnitude; volume, size, weight. LME. b *spec.* Considerable volume etc. E17. c Roughage in food. M20. 6 A (large) mass or shape. L16. 7 *The* greater part or number *of*. E18.

1 OED The bulk is not equal to sample. **break bulk** begin unloading. 2 **in bulk** loose, not packaged; in large quantities. 4 F. NORRIS His arms moved, and his head, but the great bulk of the man remained immobile in its place. E. FIGES He shifted his bulk in the creaking chair. 5 T. H. HUXLEY Sea water is denser.., bulk for bulk, than fresh water. J. A. MICHENER Those [bones] that were higher in her body were of successively lighter bulk. b LD MACAULAY The facility and assiduity with which he wrote are proved by the bulk..of his works. 6 TENNYSON A Tudor-chimnied bulk Of mellow brickwork. 7 R. L. STEVENSON The bulk of the time I spent in repeating as much French poetry as I could remember.

B *attrib.* or as *adj.* In bulk. L17.

Comb.: **bulk-buying** (*a*) buying in large amounts at a discount; (*b*) the purchase by one buyer of all or most of a producer's output; **bulk carrier** a ship that carries cargo in bulk; **bulk modulus** the relative change in volume of a body produced by unit compressive or tensile stress acting uniformly over its surface.

bulked *a.* having bulk, bulky LME. **bulker** *n.* a bulk carrier L20.

bulk /bʌlk/ *n.*[2] M16. [Prob. f. BAULK *n.* or (its source) ON *bálkr*.] A framework projecting from the front of a shop; a stall.

bulk /bʌlk/ *v.* M16. [f. BULK *n.*[1]] 1 *v.i.* Be of bulk; appear large or weighty; seem *large* etc. in respect of size or importance. M16. 2 *v.t.* Pile in heaps. E17. 3 *v.t.* Combine (consignments of a commodity) together. L19. 4 *v.t.* Make (paper, yarn, etc.) appear thicker by suitable treatment. M20.

1 G. GORER Some qualities which bulk very high for one sex, drop to practical insignificance for the other. **bulk up** swell, rise in bulk or mass.

bulkhead /ˈbʌlkhɛd/ *n.* L15. [f. as BULK *n.*[2] + HEAD *n.*] 1 A (substantial) upright partition separating compartments in a ship, aircraft, etc. L15. 2 (The roof of) a projecting stall. E18.

bulkheaded *a.* E19.

bulkin /ˈbʊlkɪn/ *n. obs.* exc. *Jamaican*. Also †**bulchin**. ME. [MDu. *bul(le)tjen*, *bul(le)kīn* bull-calf & *boeletjen*, *boelekijn* darling: see BULL *n.*[1], BULLY *n.*[1], -KIN.] A bull-calf. Also used as a term of endearment, or of contempt.

bulky /ˈbʌlki/ *a.* LME. [f. BULK *n.*[1] + -Y[1].] Of large bulk, voluminous, massive; of too great size, unwieldy.

bulkily *adv.* L19. **bulkiness** *n.* L17.

bull /bʊl/ *n.*[1] & *a.* [Late OE *bula* (only in place-names) f. ON *boli*, corresp. to MLG *bulle*, MDu. *bulle*, *bolle* (Du. *bul*).] A *n.* 1 The uncastrated male of the ox or other bovine animal. LOE. 2 The male of various other large animals, e.g. the elephant, rhinoceros, whale, and seal. LME. 3 (Usu. **B-**.) *The* constellation and zodiacal sign Taurus. LME. 4 *Stock Exch.* etc. Orig., stock bought in the hope of selling for a higher price later. Now, a person who buys such stock, a speculator for a rise. Cf. BEAR *n.*[1] 4. E18. 5 A police officer. *US slang.* L19.

1 **bull in a china shop** a reckless or clumsy destroyer. *cock-and-bull story*: see COCK *n.*[1] *full as a bull*: see FULL *a.* **like a bull at a gate** with direct or impetuous attack. *red rag to a bull*: see RED RAG 3. **take the bull by the horns** meet a difficulty boldly.

B *attrib.* or as *adj.* Like a bull; like that of a bull; large, coarse; (esp. of an animal) male. ME.

J. T. FARRELL 'Pipe down!' a bull voice called out. W. P. KELLER A mature bull elk bugling his mating call. R. WEST A bull neck almost the same size round as his head.

Comb. & *special collocations*: **bull-and-cow** *rhyming slang* = ROW *n.*[3]; **bull ant** *Austral.* = BULLDOG *n.* 4b; **bull-at-a-gate** *a.* directly or impetuously attacking; **bull-baiting** *Hist.* baiting a captive bull with dogs, for sport; **bull-bat** *US* the common night-hawk, *Chordeiles minor*; †**bull-beggar** [perh. f. a different wd] a scarecrow; a bogey, a bugbear; **bul(l)berry** = *buffalo berry* s.v. BUFFALO *n.*; **bull-dust** *Austral.* (*a*) coarse dust; (*b*) *slang* rubbish, nonsense; **bull-fiddle** *US colloq.* a double-bass; **bullfight**, **bullfighter**, **bullfighting** (an event, a participant, in) a chiefly Spanish sport in which a bull is first baited by armed fighters on horseback and on foot, and finally killed by a matador; BULLFINCH; **bullfrog** any of several large frogs with bellowing calls; *esp.* the largest N. American frog, *Rana catesbiana*; **bullhead** (*a*) any of certain small freshwater fishes with large heads; *spec.* the miller's thumb, *Cottus gobio*, or (*N. Amer.*) a catfish of the genus *Ictalurus* (esp. the horned pout, *I. nebulosus*); (*b*) *dial.* a tadpole; (*c*) a blockhead; **bull-headed** *a.* obstinate, impetuous, blundering; **bull-headedly** *adv.* in a bull-headed manner, obstinately; **bull-headedness** the quality or condition of being bull-headed, obstinacy; **bull-horn** a megaphone; *bull huss*: see HUSS *n.*; **bull-kelp** a large kelp found in Pacific and Antarctic waters; **bull market** (*Stock Exch.* etc.): with rising prices; **bull-mastiff** (a dog of) a crossbreed of bulldog and mastiff; **bull-neck** a short thick neck; **bull-necked** *a.* having a bull-neck; **bull-nose** *n.* & *a.* (having) a nose or other projection with a rounded end; **bull-nosed** *a.* having a bull-nose; **bull-of-the-bog** the bittern; **bullpen** (chiefly *N. Amer.*) (*a*) a pen or enclosure for bulls; *transf.* any enclosure, a lock-up; (*b*) an exercise area for baseball pitchers, esp. relief pitchers; *transf.* the relief pitchers; **bull-pine** *N. Amer.* the ponderosa pine; **bull point** *colloq.* a point of superiority; **bull-puncher** *Austral.* a bullock-driver; **bull-pup** a bulldog pup; **bullring** (*a*) an arena for bullfighting; (*b*) *Hist.* a place where bulls were baited; **bullroarer** a flat strip of wood tied to a string, making a roaring sound when whirled round, esp. as used in religious rites by Australian Aborigines; **bullrout** *Austral.* an E. Australian estuarine and freshwater fish, *Notesthes robusta*, with poisonous spines; **bullshit** *n.* & *v.* (*coarse slang*) (*a*) *n.* = BULL *n.*[4] 3, 4; (*b*) *v.t.* & *i.* talk nonsense (to), mislead, bluff; **bullshitter** *coarse slang* a person who talks nonsense, a boaster, a pretentious person; **bull-snake** a large N. American constricting snake of the genus *Pituophis*; **bull's wool** *Austral.* & *NZ* (*a*) the inner bark of the stringy-bark tree; (*b*) *slang* rubbish, nonsense; **bull-terrier** a (breed of) stocky short-haired dog that is a cross between bulldog and terrier (*pit bull-terrier*, *Staffordshire bull-terrier*, etc.); *bull thatch*: see THATCH *n.* 2b; **bull trout** any of various large migratory trout, *esp.* the sea trout and lake trout; *US* the trout *Salvelinus confluentus* of the west coast of the US; **bull-weed** [perh. f. BOLL *n.*[1]] knapweed; **bull-whacker** *US* a cattle-driver; **bull-whip** *n.* & *v.* (chiefly *N. Amer.*) (*a*) *n.* a whip with a long heavy lash; (*b*) *v.t.* thrash with such a whip; **bullwort** a large European umbelliferous plant, *Ammi majus*.

¶Cf. cow *n.*[1] & *a.*

bull /bʊl/ *n.*[2] ME. [(O)Fr. *bulle* f. L BULLA (in med.L) seal, sealed document.] †1 A seal attached to an official document, *esp.* the leaden seal of a papal edict. ME–M18. 2 An edict or mandate; *spec.* a papal edict. ME.

bull /bʊl/ *n.*[3] E16. [Origin unkn.] Each of the main bars of a harrow.

bull /bʊl/ *n.*[4] E17. [Origin unkn. In senses 3, 4 usu. assoc. w. synonymous *bullshit* s.v. BULL *n.*[1]: cf. BULL *v.*[3]] 1 An expression containing a contradiction in terms or implying a ludicrous inconsistency. Often more fully *Irish bull*. E17. 2 A bad blunder. *US slang.* M19. 3 Trivial, insincere, or worthless talk or writing; nonsense. *slang.* E20. 4 Unnecessary routine tasks or ceremonial; pointlessly excessive discipline; red tape. *slang* (orig. *Mil.*). M20.

1 R. L. STEVENSON The only weak brother I am willing to consider is (to make a bull for once), my wife. 3 P. G. WODEHOUSE You threw a lot of bull about being the brains of the concern. 4 A. BARON Them turning out the guard for us, us marching past eyes right, all that sort of bull.

Comb.: **bull session** *N. Amer.* an informal group discussion.

bull /bʊl/ *n.*[5] E19. [Abbrev.] = BULLDOG *n.* 1.

bull /bʊl/ *n.*[6] M19. [Origin unkn.] A drink made of water flavoured by being put in an empty spirits cask.

bull /bʊl/ *n.*[7] M19. [Origin unkn.] A deck-game in which small flat sandbags are thrown on an inclined board marked with numbered squares.

bull /bʊl/ *n.*[8] E20. [Abbrev.] = BULL'S-EYE 6.

bull /bʊl/ *v.*[1]*t.* & *i.* ME. [f. BULL *n.*[1]] 1 Serve (a cow) with the bull. Of a cow: take or seek the bull. ME. 2 *Stock Exch.* etc. Speculate for a rise; produce a rise in the price of (stocks etc.). M19. 3 Behave or move like a bull; act or treat violently. M19.

bull /bʊl/ *v.*[2]*t.* Now *rare* or *obs.* ME. [f. BULL *n.*[2]] Publish as a (papal) bull; deal with in a papal bull.

bull /bʊl/ *v.*[3] M16. [OFr. *boler*, *bouler* deceive: later assoc. with BULL *n.*[4]] 1 *v.t.* Make a fool of; cheat, deceive. Now *slang.* M16. 2 *v.i.* Talk emptily or boastfully. *slang.* M19. 3 *v.t.* Polish (equipment etc.) in order to meet excessive standards of neatness. *Mil. slang.* M20.

bulla /ˈbʊlə/ *n.* Pl. **bullae** /ˈbʊliː/. E19. [L = bubble.] 1 *Med.* A large blister on the skin containing watery fluid. Also, a thin-walled air cavity in the lung due to emphysema or of congenital origin. E19. 2 *Zool.* An opisthobranch of the genus *Bulla*. M19. 3 *Anat.* A rounded bony prominence, *esp.* that of the ethmoid bone. L19.

bullace /ˈbʊlɪs/ *n.* ME. [OFr. *buloce*, *beloce* sloe, f. Proto-Romance, perh. of Gaulish origin.] A wild or semi-cultivated plum from the tree *Prunus domestica* subsp. *insititia*; the tree itself (also *bullace-tree*).

bullamacow /ˈbʊləməkaʊ/ *n.* L19. [Fijian Eng., comb. of BULL *n.*[1] and COW *n.*[1]] In Polynesia etc.: cattle; corned beef.

bullary /ˈbʊləri/ *n.* Also in L form **bullarium** /bʊˈlɛːrɪəm/. L17. [med.L *bullarium*, f. *bulla* BULL *n.*[2]: see -ARY[1].] A collection of papal bulls.

bullate /ˈbʊleɪt/ *a.* M18. [med.L *bullatus*, f. as BULLA + -ATE[2].] Chiefly *Bot.* Having blisters or swellings resembling blisters.

bullated *a.* blistered, bullate L17.

bull-dike /ˈbʊldʌɪk/ *n. slang. derog.* M20. [f. BULL *n.*[1] + *dike* var. of DYKE *n.*[2]] A particularly masculine lesbian.

Also **bull-diker** *n.* E20.

bulldog /ˈbʊldɒg/ *n.* & *v.* E16. [f. BULL *n.*[1] + DOG *n.*] A *n.* 1 (An animal of) a thickset, large-headed, and smooth-haired breed of dog, renowned for power and boldness. E16. b *fig.* A tenacious and courageous person. M19. 2 Orig., a sheriff's officer. Now, a proctor's attendant at Oxford and Cambridge Universities. *colloq.* L17. 3 A gun; a cannon; a revolver. *colloq.* (now *rare* or *obs.*). E18. 4a A large biting fly of the genus *Tabanus*. *N. Amer.* L18. b A large ant with a vicious sting. *Austral.* M19. 5 A short brier pipe. L19.

Comb.: **bulldog ant** = sense 4b above; **bulldog bond** a sterling bond issued by an overseas borrower; **bulldog breed** Englishmen regarded as archetypes of dogged courage; **bulldog clip** a clip with a powerful closure; **bulldog issue**: of bulldog bonds.

B *v.t.* Infl. **-gg-**. Attack like a bulldog, wrestle with; treat roughly. Chiefly *US*. M19.

bulldoze /ˈbʊldəʊz/ *v.t. colloq.* (orig. *US*). L19. [Perh. f. BULL *n.*[1] + alt. of DOSE *n.*] 1 Coerce by violence or threats; intimidate, force. (Increasingly infl. by sense 2.) L19. 2 Clear, level, move, etc., with a bulldozer; force (one's way) thus. M20.

1 C. P. SNOW She was not going to be bulldozed into a conviction she did not feel. 2 ANTHONY HUXLEY This vigorous growth has been bulldozed . . to make room for the replanting of coconuts. *fig.*: B. CASTLE He and Harold have got the whole government machine with which to bulldoze their views through.

bulldozer /ˈbʊldəʊzə/ *n.* L19. [f. prec. + -ER[1].] 1 A person who bulldozes (BULLDOZE *v.* 1). Chiefly *US.* L19. 2 A powerful tractor with a broad upright blade at the front, used for clearing or levelling ground. M20.

bullen-bullen *n.* var. of BULN-BULN.

buller /ˈbʊlə/ *n.*[1] *Sc.* L15. [Prob. imit.: cf. Sw. *buller* noise, roar, Da. *bulder* tumbling noise, MHG, G *bollern* make a noise.] A roaring noise of waves etc.; a boiling up or tumult of water.

buller /ˈbʊlə/ *n.*[2] *slang.* E20. [f. BULLDOG + -ER[6].] A proctor's attendant at Oxford and Cambridge Universities.

bullet /ˈbʊlɪt/ *n.* E16. [Fr. *boulet*, *-ette* dim. of *boule* BALL *n.*[1]: see -ET[1].] 1 A ball for a cannon or other piece of ordnance. *obs.* exc. *Hist.* E16. 2 A projectile of lead etc. for a rifle, revolver, machine-gun, etc. (orig. round but now usu. cylindrical and pointed). M16. b *fig.* Notice to quit, *the* sack. *slang.* M19. †3 A missile from a sling. L16–M19. 4 A small ball of any material. L16. b In *pl.* Peas or beans. *slang.* E20. 5 An ace in poker etc. *US slang.* E19. 6 *Printing.* A small circle used to identify items in a list, draw attention to a line, etc. M20.

2 *bite (on) the bullet*: see BITE *v.* *magic bullet*: see MAGIC *a.* *plastic bullet*: see PLASTIC *a.* & *n.*[3]

Comb.: **bullet-head** a round head; **bullet-headed** *a.* round-headed; *fig.* (*US*) obstinate; **bulletproof** impenetrable by bullets; **bullet train** a high-speed passenger train, *esp.* a Shinkansen (in Japan).

bulletin /ˈbʊlɪtɪn/ *n.* & *v.* M17. [Fr., f. It. *bullettino*, *boll-*, f. *bulletta* passport, dim. of *bulla* BULL *n.*[2]: sense 1 directly f. It.] A *n.* 1 In Italy, France, etc.: an official warrant or certificate. Now *rare.* M17. 2 A short official account, statement, or broadcast report of a public event, news, weather conditions, a prominent invalid's health, etc. M18.

Comb.: **bulletin-board** (*a*) *N. Amer.* a notice-board; (*b*) a system for storing information in a computer so that any authorized user can access and add to it from a remote terminal or personal computer.

B *v.t.* Make known by or describe in a bulletin. E19.

bullet-tree *n.* var. of BULLY-TREE.

bullfinch /ˈbʊlfɪn(t)ʃ/ *n.* In sense 1 also **bulfinch**. L16. [f. BULL *n.*[1] + FINCH *n.* In sense 2 perh. alt. of *bull fence*.] 1 Any of a number of Eurasian finches of the genus *Pyrrhula*; spec. *P. pyrrhula*, a sturdy grey, black, and white finch the male of which has a rose-pink throat and breast. L16. 2 A quickset hedge with a ditch. M19.

bullgine /ˈbʊldʒʌɪn/ *n.* *colloq.* (chiefly *N. Amer.*). M19. [f. BULL *n.*[1] after ENGINE *n.*] A locomotive or steam engine.

Bulli /ˈbʊli/ *n.* *Austral.* E20. [A town in New South Wales, Australia.] In full *Bulli earth, soil.* A kind of soil used esp. for cricket pitches.

bullimong /ˈbʊlɪmʌŋ/ *n.* ME. [Perh. f. BULL *n.*[1] + *-imong* f. OE *ġemang*, *ġemong* mixture.] A mixture of grains sown together for feeding cattle.

bullion /ˈbʊlj(ə)n/ *n.*[1] ME. [AN, app. = mint, var. of (O)Fr. *bouillon* f. Proto-Romance, f. L *bullire* to boil: see -ION.] †1 A melting-house, a mint; a place of exchange. ME–E18. 2 Metal, esp. gold or silver, in lump form before coining or manufacture, or valued simply as raw metal. LME. b Solid gold or silver as opp. to superficial imitations. L16. †3 Impure gold or silver; base metal. L16–E19.

bullionist *n.* (*Hist.*) an advocate of a currency based on gold or silver E19.

bullion /ˈbʊlj(ə)n/ *n.*[2] LME. [App. f. Fr. *boulon* (spelt *bouillon* in Cotgrave), f. as BOULE *n.*[2]: see -OON.] †1 A knob or boss, usu. of metal; a convex ornament on a book, harness, etc. LME–M19. 2 = BULL'S-EYE 5. M19. 3 A small round pane of glass. L19.

bullion /ˈbʊlj(ə)n/ *n.*[3] M16. [Fr. *bouillon*: see BULLION *n.*[1] (with which the wd is now often associated).] †1 Trunk-hose, puffed out at the upper part in several folds. M16–M17. 2 An ornamental fringe made of twists of gold or silver thread; material for this. M17.

bullish /ˈbʊlɪʃ/ *a.* M16. [f. BULL *n.*[1] + -ISH[1].] 1 Like a bull, esp. in nature; impetuous, aggressive. M16. 2 *Stock Exch.* etc. Pertaining to, showing, or tending to produce a rise in prices; *gen.* optimistic. L19.

bullishly *adv.* E19. **bullishness** *n.* L19.

†bullition *n.* E17–L18. [Late L *bullitio(n-)*, f. *bullit-* pa. ppl stem of *bullire* to boil: see -ION.] Bubbling, boiling.

bullock /ˈbʊlək/ *n.* [Late OE *bulluc* dim. of BULL *n.*[1]: see -OCK.] Orig., a young bull. Now, a bull after castration. Also *loosely*, any bovine animal, an ox.

Comb.: **bullock-cart** a cart drawn by one or more bullocks; **bullock-puncher** *Austral.* & *NZ* a cattle-driver; **bullock's heart** (the fruit of) a W. Indian custard-apple, *Annona reticulata*; **†bullock's lungwort** great mullein, *Verbascum thapsus.*

bullocky *a.* & *n.* (*a*) *adj.* like a bullock; having to do with bullocks; (*b*) *n.* (*Austral.* & *NZ*) a cattle-driver: L19.

bullock /ˈbʊlək/ *v.* E18. [f. the n., or alt. of BULLY *v.*[1]] 1 *v.t.* & *i.* = BULLY *v.*[1] *obs.* exc. *dial.* E18. 2 *v.i.* Work strenuously without intermission. *Austral.* & *NZ colloq.* L19. 3 *v.t.* Force (one's way) heavily. E20.

bullous /ˈbʊləs/ *a.* M19. [f. BULLA + -OUS.] *Med.* Characterized by bullae of the skin; resembling a bulla.

bullrush *n.* var. of BULRUSH.

bull's-eye /ˈbʊlzʌɪ/ *n.* *transf.* & *fig.* M18. [f. BULL *n.*[1] + -'S[1] + EYE *n.*] 1 *Naut.* A block of wood with a central hole for a rope to pass through, and a groove around the rim for a second rope. M18. 2 A large round peppermint sweet. E19. 3 A hemispherical piece or thick disc of glass used as a light esp. in a ship's deck or side. Also, any small circular window or opening. E19. 4 (A lantern with) a hemispherical lens. M19. 5 A boss of glass formed at the centre of a blown glass sheet. M19. 6 (A shot, dart, etc., that hits) the centre of a target; *fig.* an accurate remark or guess. M19. 7 Any of various large-eyed Australian fishes; *esp.* the edible red *Priacanthus macracanthus.* L19.

bullsh /bʊlʃ/ *n.* *coarse slang.* E20. [Abbrev.] = *bullshit* n. s.v. BULL *n.*[1] & *a.*

bully /ˈbʊli/ *n.*[1] M16. [Prob. f. MDu. *boele* lover (MHG *buole*, G *Buhle*): cf. BULCHIN.] 1 Orig. sweetheart, darling. Later only of a man: good friend, mate. (Usu. as a term of endearment or familiarity.) Now *arch.* & *dial.* M16. 2 A person who uses strength or power to coerce or intimidate weaker persons. L17. b A hired ruffian. Now usu. more fully *bully-boy.* M18. 3 A pimp. *arch.* E18.

Comb.: **bully-boy** (*a*) a young bully, *spec.* a hired ruffian; (*b*) *arch.* a fine fellow, a gallant; **†bully-rock, -rook** [origin unkn.] = senses 1, 2 above.

bully /ˈbʊli/ *n.*[2] M18. [Alt. of BOUILLI.] In full *bully beef.* Boiled or (usu.) corned beef, esp. as part of army rations etc.

bully /ˈbʊli/ *n.*[3] M19. [Perh. f. BULLY *n.*[1]] 1 A scrimmage in the Eton College wall game. M19. 2 *Hockey.* A procedure for putting the ball in play, beginning with the threefold striking of two opposing players' sticks. Also *bully-off.* L19.

bully /ˈbʊli/ *n.*[4] M19. [Perh. f. *bullhead* s.v. BULL *n.*[1]] A small fish; *esp.* (*NZ*) = COCKABULLY.

bully /ˈbʊli/ *a.* & *int.* L16. [Attrib. use of BULLY *n.*[1]] A *adj.* 1 Of a person: worthy, gallant, fine, jolly. *arch.* L16. 2 Resembling or characteristic of a bully or ruffian. Now *rare.* E18. 3 Very good, capital, first-rate. *slang* (chiefly *N. Amer.*). M19.

1 SHAKES. *Mids. N. D.* What sayest thou, bully Bottom? 2 SWIFT Those bully Greeks, who . . Instead of paying chairmen, run them through. 3 H. L. WILSON It sounded just the thing to call him. It sounded bully.

B *int.* Bravo! Chiefly in *bully for you!, them!,* etc. Freq. *iron.* M19.

bully /ˈbʊli/ *v.*[1] E18. [f. BULLY *n.*[1]] 1 *v.t.* & *i.* Act the bully (towards); persecute, intimidate, oppress (physically or morally) by threats or superior force. E18. 2 *v.t.* Drive or force by threats or superior force *into*, *out of*, etc. E18.

1 DICKENS Mr. Bumble . . had a decided propensity for bullying . . and, consequently, was (it is needless to say) a coward. W. PLOMER He bullies her dreadfully, keeps her in her place, orders her about. 2 DEFOE What ails you, to bully away our customers so? J. BRIGHT I have no belief that Russia . . would have been bullied into any change of policy. R. HAYMAN Kafka needed a friend who would bully him to write, and to publish.

bully /ˈbʊli/ *v.*[2] L19. [f. BULLY *n.*[3]] *Hockey.* 1 *v.t.* Put (the ball) into play with a bully. *rare.* L19. 2 *v.i.* Start play with a bully. Usu. foll. by *off.* E20.

bullyrag *v.* var. of BALLYRAG.

bully-tree /ˈbʊlɪtriː/ *n.* Also **bullet-tree** /ˈbʊlɪtˌtriː/. M17. [Alt. of BALATA.] = BALATA.

buln-buln /ˈbʊlnbʊln/ *n.* Also **bullen-bullen** /ˈbʊlənbʊlən/. *Austral.* M19. [Aborig., of imit. origin.] The lyre-bird.

bulrush /ˈbʊlrʌʃ/ *n.* Also **bull-**. LME. [Prob. f. BULL *n.*[1] & *a.*, w. the sense 'large, coarse' (cf. *bullfrog*, *bullfinch*), + RUSH *n.*[1]] Any of various tall water-plants resembling rushes, *esp.* (*a*) the club-rush *Schoenoplectus lacustris*; (*b*) a reed-mace of the genus *Typha*; (*c*) (in the Bible) a papyrus plant.

AV *Exod.* 2:3 She tooke for him an arke of bulrushes. M. WEBB Tall bulrushes with their stout heads of brown plush. *seek a knot in a bulrush*: see KNOT *n.*[1]

Comb.: **bulrush millet** a millet, *Pennisetum americanum*, with a long spike of flowers.

†bulse *n.* E18–M19. [Port. *bolsa* f. med.L *bursa* BURSE.] A package of diamonds, gold-dust, etc.

bult /bʌlt, *foreign* bœlt/ *n.* *S. Afr.* M19. [Afk. f. Du. = hump, unch.] A ridge, a rise.

bulwark /ˈbʊlwək/ *n.* & *v.* LME. [MLG, MDu. *bolwerk* (= MHG *bol(e)werk*, G *Bollwerk*), ult. f. as BOLE *n.*[1] + WORK *n.*] A *n.* 1 A substantial defensive work; a rampart, a fortification. LME. b A mole, a breakwater. E16. 2 *fig.* A person or principle etc. that acts as a defence or shelter. LME. 3 The part of a ship's side above the level of the deck. Usu. in *pl.* E19.

2 POPE He stood, the bulwark of the Grecian band. H. HALLAM Preserving human learning as a bulwark to theology. I. MURDOCH Rupert's strong, full reassuring presence, a completely effective bulwark against anxiety of any kind.

B *v.t.* Provide with bulwarks; serve as a bulwark to, defend, protect, shelter. LME.

bum /bʌm/ *n.*[1] LME. [Origin unkn.] 1 (The region of) the buttocks. LME. 2 A lazy or worthless person. Now identified w. BUM *n.*[2] M16. 3 *Hist.* In full *bum-bailiff.* [So called as approaching from behind.] A bailiff employed in arrests. E17.

1 *tit(s) and bums*: see TIT *n.*[1]

Comb.: **bumbag** a small bag or pouch worn on a belt around the waist; *bum-bailiff*: see sense 3 above; **bumbaste** *v.t.* (*obs.* exc. *dial.*) beat on the buttocks, flog; **bum-boat** †(*a*) a scavenger's boat removing refuse and filth from ships moored in the River Thames (and also bearing provisions); (*b*) a boat bearing fresh provisions etc. to ships; **bumboy** *slang* a young male homosexual, *esp.* a prostitute; a catamite; **bum-fodder** *slang* = BUMF; **bum-freezer, -perisher, -shaver** *slang* a short jacket, coat, etc.; **bum-suck** *v.i.* (*slang*) toady, suck up; **bum-sucker** (*slang*) a sycophant.

bum /bʌm/ *n.*[2] & *a.* *slang* (orig. & chiefly *N. Amer.*). M19. [Prob. f. BUMMER: cf. BUM *n.*[1] 2.] A *n.* 1 A habitual loafer or tramp; a lazy dissolute person. M19. 2 *on the bum*, vagrant, begging; also, in a disordered state. L19.

1 **the bum's rush** forcible ejection.

B *adj.* Of poor quality, worthless, useless. M19. **bum rap** imprisonment on a false charge. *bum steer*: see STEER *n.*[3]

bum /bʌm/ *v.*[1]*i.* *obs.* exc. *dial.* Infl. **-mm-**. LME. [Var. of BOOM *v.*[1]] Hum loudly; boom.

Comb.: **bum-bee** *Sc.* a bumble-bee; **bum-clock** *Sc.* & *north.* a cockchafer or similar beetle.

bum /bʌm/ *v.*²*t.* Long *rare.* Infl. **-mm-**. L16. [Perh. f. BUM *n.*¹] Strike, beat, thump.

bum /bʌm/ *v.*³ *slang* (orig. *US*). Infl. **-mm-**. M19. [Perh. f. G *bummeln*: see BUMMER and cf. BUM *n.*²] 1 *v.i.* Wander aimlessly *around*, travel *around* as a tramp; loaf, be lazy and dissolute. M19. 2 *v.t.* Cadge, scrounge. M19.

bumbaze /bʌm'beɪz/ *v.t.* Chiefly *Sc.* M17. [App. f. BAZE w. *bum-* as a meaningless intensive or redupl. pref.] Confound, bamboozle.

†bumbelo *n.* see BUMMALO.

bumble /'bʌmb(ə)l/ *n.* M17. [Imit.: in sense 3 f. the name of the beadle in Dickens's *Oliver Twist.*] 1 A confusion, a jumble. M17. 2 A blunderer; an idler. L18. 3 A self-important official. M19.

bumbledom *n.* stupid officiousness and pomposity, esp. by petty officials M19.

bumble /'bʌmb(ə)l/ *v.* LME. [Partly f. BOOM *v.*¹, BUM *v.*¹ + -LE³; partly f. prec.] 1 *v.i.* Hum, buzz, drone; ramble *on* in speaking; move or act ineptly or flounderingly. LME. †2 *v.t.* Grumble at, blame, take to task. L17–L18.

bumbler *n.* (*a*) a blunderer; (*b*) a bumble-bee: L16.

bumble-bee /'bʌmb(ə)lbiː/ *n.* M16. [f. prec. + BEE *n.*¹] A large loud-humming bee of the genus *Bombus*; a humble-bee.

bumble-puppy /'bʌmb(ə)lpʌpi/ *n.* E19. [Origin unkn.] 1 = *nine-holes* (a) s.v. NINE *a.* & *n. obs.* exc. *Hist.* E19. 2 Whist, bridge, etc., played disregarding or reversing rules. M19. 3 A game in which a tennis-ball attached by string to a post is struck with a racket by each player with the object of winding the string entirely around the post. E20.

bumbo /'bʌmbəʊ/ *n.* Now *arch.* or *Hist.* M18. [Perh. f. It. *bombo* child's word for a drink.] A drink composed of rum, sugar, water, and nutmeg; any similar drink.

bumf /bʌmf/ *n. slang.* Also **bumph**. L19. [Abbrev. of *bum-fodder* s.v. BUM *n.*¹] Toilet paper; worthless literature; (usu. *derog.*) documents, official papers.

bumiputra /buːmɪ'puːtrə/ *n.* & *a.* M20. [Malay from Skt, lit. 'son of the soil'.] A *n.* Pl. **-s**, same. A Malaysian of indigenous Malay origin. M20. B *attrib.* or as *adj.* Of or pertaining to the bumiputras; indigenous Malay. L20.

bumiputrai'zation *n.* the policy or practice of giving precedence to indigenous Malays (rather than Chinese) in business, education, etc. L20.

bumkin /'bʌmkɪn/ *n.* Also **bump-** /'bʌmp-/. M17. [Du. *boomken* (also *boompje*), f. *boom* tree, boom + *-ken* -KIN.] *Naut.* A short boom, esp. on the stern to sheet the mizen-sail.

bummalo /'bʌmələʊ/ *n.* Also (earlier) **†bumbelo**. Pl. same. L17. [Perh. f. Marathi *bombīl.*] A small edible fish, *Harpodon nehereus*, of southern Asian coasts. Also called *Bombay duck*.

bummaree /bʌmə'riː/ *n.* L18. [Origin unkn.] 1 *Hist.* A middleman at Billingsgate fish-market, London. L18. 2 A self-employed licensed porter at Smithfield meat-market, London. M20.

bummel /'bʊm(ə)l, 'bʊm-/ *n.* & *v.* E20. [G *Bummel* a stroll, *bummeln* to stroll, loaf about. Cf. next.] A *n.* A leisurely stroll or journey. E20. B *v.i.* Stroll or wander in a leisurely fashion. E20.

bummer /'bʌmə/ *n.* Orig. & chiefly *N. Amer. slang.* M19. [Perh. f. G *bummler*, f. *bummeln*: see prec.] 1 An idler, a loafer. M19. 2 An unpleasant occurrence or experience; a mistake; a failure. M20.

†bummery *n.* M17–M19. [Du. *bommerye*, *bodmerij*: see BOTTOMRY.] = BOTTOMRY *n.*

bump /bʌmp/ *n.*¹ L16. [Imit., perh. of Scand. origin: cf. MDa. *bumpe* strike with the fist.] 1a A swelling caused by a blow or collision; an irregular prominence on a road, cricket pitch, etc. L16. b *Phrenol.* One of the prominences of the cranium associated with various mental capacities; a faculty indicated by such a prominence. E19. c The protruding abdomen of a pregnant woman. *colloq.* L20. 2 A dull-sounding blow, knock, or collision. E17. b In a race where boats start at fixed intervals (chiefly at the Universities of Oxford and Cambridge): an overtaking (and touching) of a boat by the next in line, entitling the latter to start before the former in the next race. M19. 3 A sudden (esp. upwards) movement (whether or not accompanied by noise); *spec.* (*a*) (a rising air current causing) an irregularity in an aircraft's motion; (*b*) *slang* a dancer's forward thrust of the abdomen. L19.

Phrases: **bump of locality** (a phrenological bump indicating) a supposed faculty of recognizing places and finding one's way. *musical bumps*: see MUSICAL *a.* **with a bump** *fig.* abruptly, with a shock.

Comb.: **bump-ball** *Cricket* a ball hit hard on to the ground close to the bat and coming to a fielder like a possible catch; **bump supper** (chiefly in the Universities of Oxford and Cambridge) a dinner held to celebrate a college's achievements in the bumping-races.

bump /bʌmp/ *n.*² E16. [f. BUMP *v.*²] The cry of the bittern.

bump /bʌmp/ *v.*¹ & *adv.* M16. [f. as BUMP *n.*¹] A *v.* †1a *v.i.* Bulge out; be big. M16–E18. b *v.t.* Cause to swell *up*. M17–E18. 2 *v.t.* Push, thump, knock heavily, (usu. *against*, *on*); hurt (one's head etc.) by striking it (*against*, *on*). E17. 3 *v.t.* & *i.* Overtake and touch (the next boat) in a bumping-race (see BUMPING *vbl n.* below). E19. 4 *v.i.* Strike solidly (*against*, *into*); come with a bump or jolt *against*; go (*along*) with repeated bumps. M19. b *Cricket.* Of a ball: rise abruptly to an unusual height. M19. c Boil explosively. L19. 5 *v.t.* Displace; move from position by a bump; oust, dismiss; *spec.* transfer to another airline flight because of overbooking etc.; *slang* murder. Chiefly *N. Amer.* E20.

2 J. HILTON Bumping his head against the roof. J. L. WATEN Arms folded, each endeavoured to bump the other to the ground. 4 J. D. SALINGER Careful not to bump into anything and make a racket. C. ISHERWOOD Jostling, bumping against each other's bodies. **bump into** *fig.* (*colloq.*) meet by chance.

Phrases: **bump and run** *Amer. Football* (of a cornerback) deliberately bump into the receiver and run with him to block a pass.

With advs. in specialized senses: **bump off** *slang* (orig. *US*) kill, murder. **bump up** *colloq.* increase or raise suddenly.

B *adv.* With a bump; suddenly, violently. E19.

bumpety, **-ity** *adv.* with a bump (usu. redupl. *bumpety-bump*) M19. **bumping** *n.* the action of the vb; a bump; *bumping-race*, a boat race in which places are determined by bumps (see BUMP *n.*¹ 2b): M19. **bumping** *ppl a.* (*a*) *arch. colloq.* huge, great; (*b*) that bumps: M16.

bump /bʌmp/ *v.*² M17. [Imit.] Of the bittern: make its characteristic cry.

bumper /'bʌmpə/ *n.*¹ L17. [f. BUMP *v.*¹ (branch I as BUMPING *ppl a.* (a)) + -ER¹.] I 1 A cup or glass of wine etc. filled to the brim, esp. for a toast. L17. 2 Anything unusually large, abundant, or excellent. Usu. *attrib.* M18. 3 *spec.* A crowded house at the theatre. *slang.* L18.

2 LYNDON B. JOHNSON A bumper crop, the largest in India's history.

II 4 A railway buffer. *US.* M19. 5 A shock-absorbing attachment on a ship, vehicle, etc.; *spec.* a metal, rubber, or plastic bar attached to (usu. the front or back) of a motor vehicle etc. to reduce damage in collisions or as a trim. M19. 6 *Cricket.* A short-pitched ball that rises high after pitching. M19. 7 *gen.* A person who or thing which bumps. L19.

Comb.: **bumper car** = DODGEM; **bumper sticker** a sticker with a slogan, advertisement, etc., to be displayed on a vehicle's bumper; **bumper-to-bumper** (travelling) very close together.

bumper /'bʌmpə/ *n.*² *Austral.* & *NZ slang.* E20. [Blend of BUTT *n.*⁴ and STUMP *n.*¹ + -ER¹.] A cigarette-end.

bumper /'bʌmpə/ *v. arch.* L17. [f. BUMPER *n.*¹] 1 *v.t.* w. *it* & *i.* Drink bumpers. L17. 2 *v.t.* Fill to the brim. L18. 3 *v.t.* Toast in a bumper. E19.

bumph *n.* var. of BUMF.

bumpkin /'bʌm(p)kɪn/ *n.*¹ L16. [Perh. f. Du. *boomken* little tree, or MDu. *bommekijn* little barrel, used fig. for 'squat figure'.] A rustic or awkward person.

bumpkinet *n.* (*rare*) a little bumpkin L18. **bumpkinish** *a.* L18. **bumpkinly** *a.* (*rare*) L17.

bumpkin *n.*² var. of BUMKIN.

bumpology /bʌm'pɒlədʒi/ *n. joc.* E19. [f. BUMP *n.*¹ + -OLOGY.] Phrenology.

bumpologist *n.* a phrenologist E19.

bumptious /'bʌm(p)ʃəs/ *a.* E19. [Joc. f. BUMP *v.*¹ after FRACTIOUS.] Self-assertive, offensively conceited.

bumptiously *adv.* L19. **bumptiousness** *n.* M19.

bumpy /'bʌmpi/ *a.* M19. [f. BUMP *n.*¹ or *v.*¹ + -Y¹.] Full of bumps; causing bumps, uneven.

bumpiness *n.* E19.

bun /bʌn/ *n.*¹ Long *obs.* exc. *dial.* [OE *bune*, of unkn. origin.] 1 A hollow stem, esp. of an umbelliferous plant. OE. 2 The stalk or stalky part of flax or hemp. LME.

bun /bʌn/ *n.*² LME. [Origin unkn.] 1 A small soft round sweet bread or cake with currants etc.; *Sc.* a rich fruit cake or currant bread. LME. 2 (A hairstyle with) hair in a coil at the back of the head. L19.

1 *black bun*: see BLACK *a.* *bun in the oven*: see OVEN *n.* (*hot*) *cross bun*: see CROSS-. *Kitchener bun*: see KITCHENER *n.*² & *a.* *saffron bun*: see SAFFRON *a.* *take the bun*: see TAKE *v.*

Comb.: **bun fight** *slang* a tea party.

bun /bʌn/ *n.*³ E16. [Origin unkn.] 1 *sing.* & (*N. Amer.*) in *pl.* The buttocks. *Sc.* & *N. Amer. slang.* E16. 2 A hare's or rabbit's tail. *Sc.* & *north.* E18.

bun /bʌn/ *n.*⁴ Chiefly *dial.* L16. [Origin unkn. Cf. BUNNY *n.*²] A squirrel; a rabbit. Also used as a term of endearment to a person.

Buna /'bjuːnə/ *n.* Also **b-**. M20. [G, f. as BUTADIENE + *Natrium* sodium.] Synthetic rubber made by polymerization of butadiene.

Buna N *Hist.* = PERBUNAN.

Bunbury /'bʌnb(ə)ri/ *n.* L19. [An imaginary person (so used) in O. Wilde's *The Importance of Being Earnest*).] A fictitious excuse for making a visit or avoiding an obligation.

bunce /bʌns/ *n. slang.* E18. [Origin unkn.] Money; profit.

bunch /bʌn(t)ʃ/ *n.* LME. [Origin unkn.] 1 A protuberance, a hump; a goitre. Now *rare.* LME. 2 A cluster of things growing or fastened together; (less commonly) a quantity of a substance brought together; a collection, the lot; *slang* a gang, a group. LME.

2 TENNYSON Grapes with bunches red as blood. A. G. GARDINER A bunch of wood to boil our kettle. V. BRITTAIN A large bunch of the year's first Parma violets. E. F. BENSON The younger son of an impecunious baronet . . was the best of the bunch. G. ORWELL A bunch of nerves at the back of the neck. R. LARDNER I'm not going to have a bunch of cheap reporters make a fool of me. *bunch of fives*: see FIVE *n.* MIXED *bunch*.

Comb.: **bunch-berry** *N. Amer.* (the fruit of) a dwarf cornel, *Cornus canadensis*; **bunch-flower** *N. Amer.* a plant of the lily family, *Melanthium virginicum*, with greenish-yellow flowers; **bunch-grass** *N. Amer.* any of various kinds of grass growing in clumps.

bunch /bʌn(t)ʃ/ *v.*¹*t.* Long *obs.* exc. *dial.* ME. [Origin unkn.: perh. imit.] Strike, thump; bruise; kick.

bunch /bʌn(t)ʃ/ *v.*² LME. [f. BUNCH *n.*] †1 *v.i.* Bulge, protrude, stick *out*. LME–E18. 2 *v.i.* Form a bunch or bunches; crowd together in a body. E17. 3 *v.t.* Make into a bunch or bunches; gather (material) into close folds. L19. 4 *v.t.* Present (a person) with a bunch of flowers. E20.

buncher /'bʌn(t)ʃə/ *n.* L19. [f. BUNCH *n.* or *v.*² + -ER¹.] 1 A person who or thing which bunches; *spec.* a machine for forming bunches or collecting things in bunches. L19. 2 *Physics.* A device that modulates a beam of charged particles and causes them to collect in groups. M20.

bunchy /'bʌn(t)ʃi/ *a.* LME. [f. BUNCH *n.* + -Y¹.] 1 Bulging, protuberant; full of protuberances or swellings. LME. 2 Like a bunch; having bunches; gathered into close folds. E19.

2 **bunchy top** a viral disease of plants (esp. bananas), causing crowded growth of leaves at the tip of the stem.

bunco /'bʌŋkəʊ/ *n.* & *v. US slang.* Also **bunko**. L19. [Perh. f. Sp. *banca* a card-game.] A *n.* Pl.

-os. A swindle, esp. by card-sharping or a confidence trick. L19.

Comb.: **bunco-steerer** a swindler.

B *v.t.* Swindle. L19.

buncombe *n.* var. of BUNKUM.

bund /bʌnd/ *n.*[1] & *v.* Chiefly *techn.* & *Indian subcontinent.* E19. [Urdu *band* f. Pers.] A *n.* An embankment, a causeway, a quay. E19. **B** *v.t.* Embank. L19.

bund /bʊnd, *foreign* bʊnt/ *n.*[2] Also **B-**. Pl. **bunds, *bunde*** /ˈbʊndə/. M19. [G: rel. to BAND *n.*[2], BIND *v.*] A German league, confederacy, or association.

bunder /ˈbʌndə/ *n.* E17. [Urdu *bandar* f. Pers.] In the Indian subcontinent: a landing-place, a quay, a harbour.

Comb.: **bunder-boat**: used for coastal and harbour work.

Bundesrat /ˈbʊndəzrɑːt/ *n.* Also †**-rath**. L19. [G, f. genit. of BUND *n.*[2] + *Rat(h)* council.] A federal council in Germany and German-speaking countries; *spec.* the Upper House of Parliament in Germany and in Austria.

Bundestag /ˈbʊndəztɑːg/ *n.* L19. [G, f. as prec. + *tagen* confer.] A representative assembly in Germany and German-speaking countries; *spec.* the Lower House of Parliament in Germany.

bundle /ˈbʌnd(ə)l/ *n.* ME. [Orig. perh. repr. OE *byndelle* binding, taken in concr. sense, = OS *bundilin* (Du. *bundel* bundle), OHG *gibuntili* (G *Bündel*), but reinforced later by (if not wholly due to) LG, Du. *bundel*.] **1** A collection of things fastened together, esp. loosely (now esp. clothes, papers, or odds and ends in a large handkerchief or paper); (freq. *contempt.*) a collection, a lot. ME. **2** A collection of fibres (esp. nerves), vessels, or the like, running parallel in an animal body or plant. M18. **3** A woman, *esp.* a fat woman. *dial.* & *slang. derog.* M19. **4** A large amount of money. *slang* (orig. *US*). E20. **5** A fight, a scrap. *slang.* M20.

Phrases: *bundle of nerves*: see NERVE *n.* CONCENTRIC *bundle*. **drop one's bundle** *Austral.* & *NZ slang* give up hope, surrender. **go a bundle on** *slang* (orig. *US*) (*a*) bet much money on; (*b*) *fig.* be very fond of. VASCULAR *bundle*.

Comb.: **bundle-sheath** the layer of cells surrounding the vascular bundle of a leaf.

bundly *a.* (*rare*) like a bundle L19.

bundle /ˈbʌnd(ə)l/ *v.* L16. [f. the n.] **1** *v.t.* Tie in a bundle; make *up* into a bundle; wrap (*up*) warmly or cumbersomely (usu. in *pass.*). L16. **b** *fig.* Collect or group *together* without distinction. E17. **2** *v.i.* Pack for a journey; leave with one's luggage etc.; move or go hurriedly or unceremoniously. (Foll. by *in, off, out.*) L18. **3** *v.i.* Sleep in one's clothes *with* another person (esp. as a former local custom during courtship). Also foll. by *up.* L18. **4** *v.t.* Put or send (esp. a person) hurriedly or unceremoniously *out, off, away*, etc.; throw confusedly *into* a receptacle. E19.

1 C. M. YONGE She . . bundled up her hair as best she might. W. STYRON Men and women bundled against the cold. b A. STORR Are dreams, day-dreams and works of art all to be bundled together in the same category? 2 R. BURNS Bundle and go! D. ABSE Leo bundled out of the train. C. CHAPLIN We bundled into Mr Sennett's . . racing car. 4 D. WELCH I tried . . to bundle my guest through the dining-room. W. S. MAUGHAM I . . bundled my things into my rucksack. W. TREVOR They came briefly, as moments rapidly hurrying, one bundled away by the next.

bundobust /ˈbʌndəbʌst/ *n.* Also **bandobast**. L18. [Urdu f. Pers. *band-o-bast* tying and binding.] In the Indian subcontinent: arrangements, organization.

bundook /ˈbʌnduːk/ *n.* L19. [Urdu *bandūk* f. Pers. *bundūk* firearm; rel. to BONDUC.] In the Indian subcontinent: a musket or similar firearm.

bundu /ˈbʊnduː/ *n. S. Afr.* M20. [Prob. f. Shona *bundo* grasslands.] An uncivilized rural region; *the* wilds.

bung /bʌŋ/ *n.*[1] LME. [MDu. *bonghe*, of unkn. origin.] **1** A stopper, *esp.* a large cork for stopping the hole in a cask. LME. **2** *transf.* = *bung-hole* below. *obs.* exc. *dial.* L16. **3** A brewer; a publican. M19.

Comb.: **bung-ho** *int.* an exclamation at parting or as a toast; **bung-hole** a hole in a cask for filling and emptying it.

†**bung** *n.*[2] *slang.* M16. [Origin unkn.] **1** A purse. M16–E18. **2** A pickpocket. *rare* (Shakes.). Only in L16.

bung /bʌŋ/ *n.*[3] *slang.* M20. [Origin unkn.: cf. BUNG *v.*[3]] A bribe; a tip.

bung /bʌŋ/ *a. Austral.* & *NZ slang.* L19. [Aborig.] Ruined, useless, broken; bankrupt. Formerly also, dead.

bung /bʌŋ/ *v.*[1]*t.* M16. [f. BUNG *n.*[1]] Stop (with a bung); shut *up*, block, close.

bung /bʌŋ/ *v.*[2] & *adv. dial.* & *slang.* E19. [Imit.] **A** *v.t.* Throw, toss; put forcibly or unceremoniously. E19.

C. MACKENZIE Let's bung these sticks into the sea. B. TRAPIDO We're giving you the guest room . . and bunging Katherine in with the children.

B *adv.* Abruptly, unceremoniously; exactly. Cf. BANG *adv.* L19.

bung /bʌŋ/ *v.*[3]*t. slang.* M20. [Origin unkn.: cf. BUNG *n.*[3]] Bribe; tip.

bungalow /ˈbʌŋgələʊ/ *n.* L17. [Hind. *baṅglā* belonging to Bengal.] A one-storeyed house.

bungaloid *a.* (usu. *derog.*) resembling a bungalow, consisting of bungalows E20.

bungarotoxin /bʌŋgərə(ʊ)ˈtɒksɪn/ *n.* M20. [f. mod.L *Bungarus*, genus name (perh. f. Skt *bhaṅgura* bent) + -O- + TOXIN.] *Biochem.* Each of three neurotoxins from the venom of a krait, *Bungarus multicinctus*, which bind to acetylcholine receptors with a high degree of specificity.

bungarra /ˈbʌŋgarə/ *n.* L19. [Aborig.] = *sand goanna* s.v. SAND *n.*

bungee /ˈbʌndʒi/ *n.* Also **bungie, bungy**. E20. [Origin unkn.] **1** A rubber, an eraser. *slang.* E20. **2** Strong elasticated cord or cable; a piece of this, usu. with a hook at each end and used esp. for securing baggage in transit. Also *bungee cord, rope.* M20.

Comb.: *bungee cord*: see sense 2 above; **bungee jumping** jumping from a height, as from a bridge, while attached to an elasticated rope, as a sport or recreation.

bungle /ˈbʌŋg(ə)l/ *n.* M17. [f. the vb.] A botch, a blunder; muddle, failure.

E. LONGFORD Through some bungle the courier . . had missed them on the road. N. GORDIMER Care to avoid bungle by haste and lack of strategy.

bungle /ˈbʌŋg(ə)l/ *v.* M16. [Imit.: cf. BUMBLE *v.*] **1** *v.t.* Do or make clumsily or unskilfully; spoil by clumsiness or lack of skill; fail to accomplish (a task). M16. **2** *v.i.* Be or act clumsily or unskilfully, blunder. M16.

bunglesome *a.* (*US*) bungling and troublesome L19. **bungler** *n.* M16. **bungling** *ppl a.* (*a*) that bungles; (*b*) showing clumsiness or lack of skill: L16. **bunglingly** *adv.* E17.

bungy *n.* var. of BUNGEE.

bunion /ˈbʌnj(ə)n/ *n.* E18. [Perh. extension of BUNNY *n.*[1], or ult. f. OFr. *buignon*, f. *buigne* (mod. *bigne*) bump on the head, perh. of Gmc origin (cf. MHG *bunge* lump): see -OON.] An inflamed swelling on the foot, esp. of the bursa of the first joint of the big toe.

bunjara *n.* var. of BRINJARRY.

bunk /bʌŋk/ *n.*[1] M18. [Origin uncertain: perh. rel. to BUNKER.] A sleeping-berth, *esp.* one of two or more arranged one on top of the other.

Comb.: **bunk-bed** (a bunk in) a piece of furniture comprising two bunks; **bunk-house** a house where workmen etc. are lodged.

bunkie *n.* (*US colloq.*) a person who shares a bunk with another M19.

bunk /bʌŋk/ *n.*[2] *slang.* L19. [Origin unkn.: cf. BUNK *v.*[2]] *do a bunk*, make off, vanish.

bunk /bʌŋk/ *n.*[3] *slang.* E20. [Abbrev. of BUNKUM.] Nonsense, humbug.

bunk /bʌŋk/ *v.*[1]*i.* M19. [f. BUNK *n.*[1]] Sleep in or lie *down* on a bunk or improvised bed.

bunk /bʌŋk/ *v.*[2] *slang.* M19. [Origin unkn.: cf. BUNK *n.*[2]] **1** *v.i.* Be off, vanish. Also foll. by *off.* M19. **2** *v.t.* Expel from school. L19.

bunker /ˈbʌŋkə/ *n.* & *v.* M16. [Origin unkn.] **A** *n.* **1** A seat or bench. *Sc.* M16. **2** An earthen seat or bank in the fields. *dial.* E19. **3** *Golf.* A pit containing sand etc. and constituting a hazard. E19. **4** A (large) container for fuel. M19. **5** A reinforced underground shelter. M20. **B** *v.* **1 a** *v.t.* Fill the bunkers of (a ship etc.). L19. **b** *v.i.* Of a ship: take in a supply of coal or oil. L19. **2** *v.t. Golf.* Trap (a ball, *transf.* a player, a shot) in a bunker. Usu. in *pass.* L19. **b** *fig.* Bring into difficulties. L19.

bunko *n.* & *v.* var. of BUNCO.

bunkum /ˈbʌŋkəm/ *n.* Also **buncombe**. M19. [f. *Buncombe* County, N. Carolina, USA, whose member made an irrelevant speech in Congress *c*1820 simply to impress his constituents.] Nonsense; ostentatious talking.

bunk-up /ˈbʌŋkʌp/ *n. dial.* & *slang.* E20. [Origin unkn.] A push or pull up.

†**bunny** *n.*[1] LME–L19. [OFr. *buigne*: see BUNION.] A swelling, esp. on an animal's joint.

bunny /ˈbʌni/ *n.*[2] E17. [f. BUN *n.*[4] + -Y[6].] †**1** Used as a term of endearment to a person. Only in 17. **2** (A pet name for) a rabbit. L17. **b** More fully *bunny girl*. A club hostess wearing a brief costume suggestive of a rabbit. M20.

Comb.: *bunny girl*: see sense 2b above; **bunny-hug** a dance in ragtime rhythm with close contact between partners.

bunodont /ˈbjuːnədɒnt/ *a.* L19. [f. Gk *bounos* mound + -ODONT.] Characterized by molar teeth whose crowns have a number of rounded cusps. Of molar teeth: having this form.

Bunraku /ˈbʊnrakʊ, *foreign* ˈbunraku/ *n.* & *a.* E20. [Jap.] (Of, pertaining to, or characteristic of) Japanese puppet drama, *spec.* as practised by the Bunraku-za company.

Bunsen /ˈbʌns(ə)n/ *n.* L19. [Robert W. *Bunsen* (1811–99), Ger. chemist.] In full *Bunsen burner*. A small gas and air burner used esp. in chemical laboratories to heat substances.

bunt /bʌnt/ *n.*[1] L16. [Origin unkn.] **1** *Naut.* The middle part of a sail. L16. **2** The cavity or baggy part of a fishing net etc. E17.

Comb.: **buntline** a rope confining the bunt of a sail and preventing it from bellying when being furled.

bunt /bʌnt/ *n.*[2] E17. [Origin unkn.] **1** A puffball fungus. Now *rare* or *obs.* E17. **2** A smut fungus of the genus *Tilletia*, attacking wheat; disease caused by this. L18.

bunty *a.* infested with bunt M19.

bunt /bʌnt/ *n.*[3] M18. [Cf. BUTT *v.*[1], *n.*[9], BUNT *v.*[2]] **1** A push with the head or horns, a butt. Chiefly *N. Amer.* & *dial.* M18. **2** *Baseball.* An act of letting the ball rebound from the bat without swinging. L19.

bunt /bʌnt/ *v.*[1] *Naut.* E17. [f. BUNT *n.*[1]] **1** *v.t.* Haul up the middle part of (a sail) in furling. E17. **2** *v.i.* Of a sail: belly. L17.

bunt /bʌnt/ *v.*[2]*t.* & *i. US* & *dial.* E19. [f. (as) BUNT *n.*[3]] **1** Push with the head or horns, butt. E19. **2** *Baseball.* Let (the ball) rebound from the bat without swinging. L19.

buntal /ˈbʌnt(ə)l/ *n.* E20. [Tagalog.] Straw made from the talipot palm. Cf. BALIBUNTAL.

bunter /ˈbʌntə/ *n.*[1] *obs.* exc. *dial.* E18. [Origin unkn.] A woman who gathers rags and bones in the streets; a disreputable woman.

Bunter /ˈbʌntə/ *n.*[2] & *a.* Also **b-**. M19. [G *bunter* (*Sandstein* sandstone), f. *bunt* variegated.] *Geol.* (Designating or pertaining to, the sandstones and conglomerates of) the Lower Triassic in Europe, esp. Germany.

bunting /ˈbʌntɪŋ/ *n.*[1] ME. [Origin unkn.] **1** Any of numerous mainly seed-eating birds of the subfamily Emberizinae, related to the finches. ME. **2** Used as a term of endearment (infl. by BUNTING *a.*). M16. **3** A kind of shrimp or prawn. *dial.* Now *rare* or *obs.* M18.

1 *cirl bunting, corn bunting, reed bunting, snow bunting, yellow bunting*, etc. **2** *Nursery rhyme*: Bye baby bunting, Daddy's gone a hunting.

bunting /ˈbʌntɪŋ/ *n.*[2] E18. [Origin unkn.] (A loosely woven fabric used for) flags and festive decorations.

bunting /ˈbʌntɪŋ/ *a. dial.* L16. [f. BUNT *v.*[1] + -ING[2].] Swelling; plump.

bunton /ˈbʌntən/ *n.* M17. [Origin unkn.] 1 A piece of squared timber. Long *obs.* in *gen.* sense. M17. 2 Any of a series of strong balks of timber placed crosswise in a mine shaft. Usu. in *pl.* M19.

bunya-bunya /ˈbʌnjəbʌnjə/ *n. Austral.* Also **bunya**. M19. [Aborig.] A tall Australian tree, *Araucaria bidwillii*, bearing large cones with an edible pulp.

Bunyanesque /bʌnjəˈnɛsk/ *a.* L19. [f. *Bunyan* (see below) + -ESQUE.] 1 Of, pertaining to, or characteristic of the English author John Bunyan (1628–88). L19. 2 Of, pertaining to, or characteristic of the legendary American hero Paul Bunyan. M20.

bunyip /ˈbʌnjɪp/ *n. Austral.* M19. [Aborig.] A fabulous monster of swamps and lagoons.

Buonapartist *n.* & *a.* var. of BONAPARTIST.

buoy /bɔɪ/ *n.* ME. [Prob. f. MDu. *bo(e)ye, boeie* (Du. *boei*) f. Gmc base meaning 'signal', whence also Fr. *bouée*, Sp. *boya*.] 1 A floating object fastened in a particular place to point out the position of shoals, rocks, anchors, etc. under the water, or the course for ships etc., or to float a cable in a rocky anchorage. ME. b In full *lifebuoy*. A device, usu. a ring, used to keep a person afloat. E19. 2 *fig.* Something which marks out a course, indicates danger, or keeps one afloat. E17.

1 *stream the buoy*: see STREAM *v.*

buoyage *n.* providing of or with buoys; buoys collectively; a series of buoys which mark out a channel: E19.

buoy /bɔɪ/ *v.* L16. [Branch I f. Sp. *boyar* (see BUOYANT); branch II f. prec.] I†1 *v.i.* Rise to or float on the surface of a liquid; rise, swell (as the sea) L16–L17. 2a Foll. by *up*: raise to the surface of a liquid; bring afloat (a sunken ship etc.). E17. b Keep from sinking, keep afloat. Usu. foll. by *up*. M17. 3 *v.t. fig.* Sustain (a person, courage, etc.); raise (the spirits etc.), uplift, encourage. Usu. foll. by *up*. M17.

1 SHAKES. *Lear* The sea . . would have buoy'd up and quench'd the stelled fires. 3 D. CECIL Belonging to a famous and venerated institution, and buoyed up by its confident corporate spirit.

II 4 *v.t.* Provide or mark (as) with a buoy or buoys. L16.

buoyancy /ˈbɔɪənsi/ *n.* E18. [f. next: see -ANCY.] 1 Power of floating on liquid or in air; tendency to float; power of supporting a floating body. E18. b The vertical upward force of a fluid on a floating or immersed body, which is equal to the weight of fluid displaced by the body. L18. 2 *fig.* Elasticity of spirit, resilience, recuperative power; cheerfulness. Also, tendency to rise (in stock market prices, revenue, etc.). E19.

2 DAY LEWIS Children . . can ride such disasters with extraordinary buoyancy. *Observer* On the strength of this buoyancy, the group launched a . . £55 million rights issue.

Comb.: **buoyancy aid** a jerkin of a buoyant material, worn for sailing and other water sports.

buoyant /ˈbɔɪənt/ *a.* L16. [OFr. *bouyant* or Sp. *boyante* light-sailing, pres. pple of *boyar* float, f. *boya* BUOY *n.*: see -ANT[1].] 1 Able to float; tending to float or rise; floating; lightly elastic; resilient, able to recover, light-hearted. L16. 2 Able to keep things up or afloat. L17.

1 A. BRIGGS Trade remained buoyant and agriculture improved. X. J. KENNEDY The springer spaniel and the buoyant hare Seem half at home reclining in mid-air. U. BENTLEY He was buoyant, childishly happy.

buoyantly *adv.* M19. **buoyantness** *n.* (*rare*) M17.

buphthalmos /bʊfˈθalmɒs/ *n.* E19. [Gk *bouphthalmon* ox-eye, f. *bous* ox + *ophthalmos* eye.] *Ophthalm.* Gross enlargement of the eyeball owing to increased intra-ocular pressure; now *spec.* (as a sign of) congenital glaucoma.

buphthalmic *a.* characterized by or displaying buphthalmos L19.

buppie /ˈbʌpi/ *n. colloq.* (chiefly *US*). L20. [Blend of BLACK *a.* and YUPPIE *n.*, or acronym f. *B*lack *u*rban *p*rofessional + -IE.] A young Black professional working in a city, a Black yuppie.

bur /bəː/ *n.*[1] Also **burr** (for other senses see BURR *n.*[4]). ME. [Branch I perh. of Scand. origin: cf. Da. *burre* bur, burdock, Sw. *kard-borre* burdock. Branch II perh. f. Fr.: cf. BURL *n.*[1], *bourre* vine-bud.] I 1 A rough or prickly seed-vessel or flower-head of a plant, *esp.* the flower-head of the burdock; also, the husk of the chestnut. ME. 2 A plant which produces burs. L15. 3 *fig.* Something which clings like a bur; a person who is hard to shake off. L16.

1 **bur in the throat** a thing that appears to stick in the throat.

II 4 The rounded knob forming the base of a deer's horn. L16. 5a A knob or knot in a tree. E18. b An ornamental (esp. walnut) veneer, containing knots. L19. 6 The female catkin of the hop before fertilization. E19.

Comb.: **bur-marigold** any of several plants constituting the genus *Bidens*, of the composite family, with flat yellow flower-heads; **bur-oak** (the wood of) a N. American oak, *Quercus macrocarpa*, with large fringed acorn-cups; **bur-parsley** either of two umbelliferous plants, *Caucalis platycarpos* and *Turgenia latifolia*, with bristly fruits; **bur-reed** any of several aquatic plants constituting the genus *Sparganium*, with globose flower-heads; **bur walnut** walnut wood containing knots, used as a veneer; **bur-weed** = *cocklebur* s.v. COCKLE *n.*[1]

bur *n.*[2] var. of BURR *n.*[1]

bur *n.*[3] var. of BURR *n.*[4]

buran /ˈbuːrɑːn/ *n.* M19. [Russ. f. Turkic *boran*.] In the steppes, a snowstorm, *esp.* one accompanied by high winds; a blizzard.

burble /ˈbəːb(ə)l/ *n.* ME. [f. the vb.] 1 A bubble; bubbling. Long *obs.* exc. *Sc.* ME. 2 A pimple, a boil. Long *obs.* exc. *dial.* LME. 3 A murmurous flow of words. L19.

burble /ˈbəːb(ə)l/ *v.* ME. [Imit.: cf. Sp. *borbollar* bubble, gush, *barbullar* talk loud and fast, It. *borbugliare*.] 1 *v.i.* Bubble. Long *obs.* exc. *Sc.* ME. 2 *v.i.* & *t.* Speak or say murmurously or in a rambling manner; make a murmuring noise. L19. 3 *v.i. Aeronaut.* Of an airflow: break up into turbulence. Chiefly as *burbling* vbl n. E20.

Comb.: **burble point**: at which the smooth flow of air over an aerofoil is broken up.

burbot /ˈbəːbət/ *n.* ME. [OFr. *borbete* (mod. *bourbotte*), prob. f. OFr. *borbe* mud, slime.] A freshwater fish, *Lota lota*, of the cod family, with a broad head and barbels.

Burchell's zebra /bəːtʃ(ə)lz ˈziːbrə, ˈzɛbrə/ *n. phr.* M20. [f. William John *Burchell* (1782–1863), Eng. naturalist.] The common zebra, *Equus burchellii*, which has broad stripes and a striped belly, and is abundant on the E. African savannah.

burd /bəːd/ *n.* Long *obs.* exc. *poet.* ME. [Origin unkn.] A woman, a lady, a maiden.

burden /ˈbəːd(ə)n/ *n.* Also (*arch.*) **burthen** /ˈbəːð(ə)n/. [OE *byrþen* = OS *burþinnia*, f. WGmc, f. base of BIRTH *n.*[1]: see -EN[2]. In senses 6–8 conf. w. BOURDON.] 1 That which is borne; a load (*lit.*, or *fig.* of labour, duty, sorrow, etc.). OE. b An obligatory expense. M17. 2 The bearing of loads. Chiefly in phrs. below. ME. 3 A load, as a measure of quantity. Now only the carrying capacity of a ship, as a measure of weight; tonnage. LME. 4 In biblical translations tr. Heb. *maśśā'* (*Zech.* 12:1 etc.): an oracle, an oracular judgement. (Understood as) a burdensome or heavy lot or fate. *arch.* LME. †5a That which is borne in the womb; a child. L15–M17. b That which is borne by the soil; produce, crop. E16–M19. 6 The bass or undersong of a melody; the drone of a bagpipe. Now *rare* or *obs.* L16. 7 The refrain or chorus of a song. L16. 8 *fig.* The chief theme or gist of a poem, book, speech, etc. M17.

1 E. M. FORSTER Carrying a burden of acorns. E. GLASGOW I'd rather die . . than be a burden. E. ROOSEVELT The burden of training a family. **burden of proof** the obligation to prove a controversial assertion, falling upon the person who makes it; *Law* onus probandi. *the white man's burden*: see WHITE *a.* 2 *beast of burden*: see BEAST *n.* **ship of burden** a merchant ship.

†**burdened** *a.* (*rare*, Shakes.) imposed as a burden: only in L16. †**burdenous** *a.* (*a*) burdensome; (*b*) oppressed: E16–E19. **burdensome** *a.* (*a*) of the nature of a burden, oppressive, wearisome; †(*b*) *US* capable of carrying a good burden: M16. **burdensomely** *adv.* (*rare*) E17. **burdensomeness** *n.* L16.

burden /ˈbəːd(ə)n/ *v.t.* Also (*arch.*) **burthen** /ˈbəːð(ə)n/. M16. [f. the n.] 1 Lay a burden on, load, (*lit.* & *fig.*); encumber, oppress. M16. †2 Charge (a person) *with* (an accusation); lay as a charge *upon* M16–L18.

burdock /ˈbəːdɒk/ *n.* L16. [f. BUR *n.*[1] + DOCK *n.*[1]] Any of several coarse plants constituting the genus *Arctium*, of the composite family, with purplish-red flower-heads, prickly fruits, and large leaves like those of the dock.

burdoun *n.* var. of BOURDON.

bure /bjʊə/ *n.* L16. [Fr.: see next.] A coarse woollen stuff.

bureau /ˈbjʊərəʊ/ *n.* Pl. **-x** /-z/, **-s**. L17. [Fr. (OFr. *burel*), orig. = woollen stuff, baize (used for covering writing-desks), prob. f. *bure* var. of *buire* dark brown f. Proto-Romance alt. of L *burrus* fiery red f. Gk *purros* red.] 1 A writing-desk with drawers for papers etc. L17. b A chest of drawers. *N. Amer.* E19. 2 An office, esp. for the transaction of public business; a department of public administration. L17. b An office or business with a specified function; an agency for the coordination of related activities, the distribution of information, etc. E20.

2b *information bureau, marriage bureau*, etc.

bureaucracy /bjʊ(ə)ˈrɒkrəsi/ *n.* Also †**-cratie**. E19. [Fr. *bureaucratie*: see prec., -CRACY.] (Government by) a central administrative group, esp. one not accountable to the public etc.; officials of such a group collectively; excessive official routine.

bureaucrat /ˈbjʊərəkrat/ *n.* M19. [Fr. *bureaucrate*: see BUREAU, -CRAT.] An official, esp. an unimaginative or doctrinaire one, in a bureaucracy; a person who endeavours to centralize administrative power.

bureauˈcratic *a.* of or pertaining to bureaucracy; excessively concerned with official routine: M19. **bureauˈcratically** *adv.* M19. **buˌreaucratiˈzation** *n.* transformation into a bureaucracy; making bureaucratic: E20. **bureaucratize** *v.t.* transform into a bureaucracy; make bureaucratic: L19.

†**bureaucratie** *n.* var. of BUREAUCRACY.

†**burel** *n.* ME–E18. [OFr.: see BUREAU.] A coarse woollen cloth, frieze; a garment of this; plain clothing.

burette /bjʊˈrɛt/ *n.* Also ***-et**. M19. [Fr.] A graduated glass tube with tap, used for measuring small quantities of liquid in chemical analysis.

burg /bəːg/ *n.* M18. [Sense 1 f. late L *burgus* (see BURGESS); sense 2 f. G *Burg* (see BOROUGH).] 1 *Hist.* An ancient or medieval fortress or walled town. M18. 2 A town, a city. *N. Amer. colloq.* M19.

burgage /ˈbəːgɪdʒ/ *n. obs.* exc. *Hist.* LME. [med.L *burgagium*, f. *burgus*: see BURGESS, -AGE.] 1 *Law.* More fully *burgage tenure*. A tenure by which lands, tenements, etc., in towns or cities were held from the lord for an annual rent or service. LME. 2 A freehold property in a borough; a house etc. held by burgage tenure. LME.

burgee /bəːˈdʒiː/ *n.* M18. [Origin uncertain: perh. f. Fr. *bourgeois* (see BURGESS) = master, owner.] A triangular or swallow-tailed flag flown by yachts etc., usu. bearing distinguishing colours or the emblem of a yacht club or sailing club.

burgeon /ˈbəːdʒ(ə)n/ *n.* Now *literary.* ME. [OFr. *borjon, bur-* (mod. *bourgeon*), f. Proto-Romance f. late L *burra* wool.] A young shoot or bud; a new growth.

burgeon /ˈbəːdʒ(ə)n/ *v.* Now *literary.* ME. [(O)Fr. *bourgeonner*, f. *bourgeon*: see prec.] 1 *v.i.* Put out shoots or buds; spring forth as a young shoot or shoots; *fig.* begin to develop rapidly. ME. 2 *v.t.* Put out as a young shoot or shoots; develop rapidly. Long *rare.* LME.

1 G. PEELE The watery flowers burgen all in ranks. SIR W. SCOTT A hydra whose heads burgeoned . . as fast as they were cut off. P. USTINOV A burgeoning country, in the grip of an industrial revolution.

burger /ˈbəːɡə/ *n. colloq.* (orig. *US*). M20. [Abbrev.] A hamburger. Also as 2nd elem. of combs. w. specification of ingredients, as *beefburger*, *cheeseburger*, *nutburger*, etc.

burgess /ˈbəːdʒɪs/ *n.* ME. [AN *burgeis*, OFr. *borjois* (mod. *bourgeois*) f. Proto-Romance, f. late L *burgus* castle, fort (in med.L fortified town, BOROUGH) + *-ensis* (see -ESE).] 1 An inhabitant of a borough having full municipal rights; a citizen. ME. b *Hist.* A member of Parliament for a borough, corporate town, or university. L15. 2 A magistrate or member of the governing body of a town. *Hist.* exc. *US.* ME.
Comb.: **burgess oath** *Hist.*: taken by a burgess, swearing acceptance of the authorized religion of the realm.
burgessdom *n.* (*rare*) the body of burgesses M17. **burgess-ship** *n.* the status and privileges of a burgess LME.

burggrave *n.* var. of BURGRAVE.

burgh /ˈbʌrə/ *n. Sc.* or *Hist.* See also BROCH. LME. [Var. of BOROUGH.] A borough, a chartered town.
royal burgh: see ROYAL *a.*
Comb.: **burgh-bote** *Hist.* a tax for the repair of fortifications; **burghmote** *Hist.* the judicial assembly of a borough.
burghal /ˈbəːɡ(ə)l/ *a.* of or pertaining to a burgh L16.

burgher /ˈbəːɡə/ *n.* ME. [f. BURGH + -ER[1], partly f. G or Du. *burger*, f. *burg* BOROUGH.] 1 An inhabitant of a borough or chartered town (now *arch.* or *joc.*); a freeman or citizen of a foreign town. ME. 2 *Hist.* (B-.) A member of the section of the Secession Church in Scotland which upheld the legality of the burgess oath. Cf. ANTIBURGHER. M18. 3 *S. Afr. Hist.* A citizen of the Cape not employed by the Dutch East India Company; a citizen of a Boer republic. M18. 4 In Sri Lanka (Ceylon): a descendant of a Dutch or Portuguese colonist. E19.
Comb.: **burghermaster** (*rare*) = BURGOMASTER.
burgherly *a.* of or characteristic of a burgher M18. **burghership** *n.* the rights and privileges of a burgher M16.

burghul /bəːˈɡuːl/ *n.* Also **-gul**. E20. [Arab. *burġul* f. Pers. *burġūl* var. of *bulġūr*: see BULGUR.] Wholewheat partially boiled and then dried; a dish made from this.

burglar /ˈbəːɡlə/ *n.* & *v.* M16. [Law Fr. †*burgler* (cf. AN *burgur*), AL *burg(u)lator*, app. f. base meaning 'pillage'.] A *n.* A person who is guilty of burglary. M16.
cat-burglar: see CAT *n.*[1]
Comb.: **burglar alarm** (a device with) an alarm that sounds if a house etc. is broken into.
B *v.t.* & *i.* = BURGLE *v.* Now *rare.* L19.
burglarize *v.t.* & *i.* = BURGLE *v.* L19.

burglarious /bəːˈɡlɛːrɪəs/ *a.* M18. [f. next + -OUS: cf. *felonious*.] Of or pertaining to burglary; like a burglar.
burglariously *adv.* E19.

burglary /ˈbəːɡləri/ *n.* E16. [Law Fr. †*burglarie* (cf. AN *b(o)urgerie*, AL *burgaria*), f. as BURGLAR: see -Y[3].] 1 The crime of entering a building (in English law formerly by night only) with intent to commit an arrestable offence. E16. 2 An act of so entering a building. E17.
¶The legal definition has varied in different jurisdictions and periods.

burgle /ˈbəːɡ(ə)l/ *v.* & *n.* Orig. *colloq.* & *joc.* L19. [Back-form. f. BURGLAR.] A *v.* 1 *v.i.* Commit burglary. L19. 2 *v.t.* Rob (a place or person) by burglary; steal (goods) by burglary. L19. B *n.* A burglary. *rare.* L19.

burgomaster /ˈbəːɡəmɑːstə/ *n.* L16. [Du. *burgemeester* (both senses), f. *burg* (see BOROUGH) + *meester*, assim. to MASTER *n.*[1]] 1 The mayor of a Dutch or Flemish town. L16. 2 The glaucous gull, *Larus hyperboreus*. L17.

burgonet /ˈbəːɡənɛt/ *n.* L16. [Fr. *bourguignotte*, perh. fem. of *bourgignot* Burgundian, w. assim. to -ET[1].] *Hist.* A visored helmet that can be fitted or attached to the gorget or neck-piece. Also, a pikeman's light steel cap.

†**Burgonian** *n.* & *a.* M16–E17. [f. Fr. *Bourgogne* (see BURGUNDY) + -IAN.] = BURGUNDIAN *n.* & *a.*

burgoo /bəːˈɡuː/ *n.* L17. [f. as BURGHUL.] 1 A thick porridge. *Naut. slang.* L17. 2 Soup or stew for an outdoor meal. *N. Amer.* M18.

burgrave /ˈbəːɡreɪv/ *n.* Also **-gg-**. M16. [G *Burggraf*, f. *Burg* BOROUGH + *Graf* GRAVE *n.*[2]] *Hist.* The governor or (*esp.*) hereditary ruler of a German town or castle.

burgul *n.* var. of BURGHUL.

Burgund /ˈbəːɡʌnd/ *n.* [OE *Burgendan*, *-as* pl. f. late L *Burgundii*, *-iones* pl.: ult. origin unkn.] *Hist.* A member of the Germanic Burgundians. Usu. in *pl.*

Burgundian /bəːˈɡʌndɪən/ *n.* & *a.* E17. [f. *Burgundy* (see next) + -AN; partly f. late L *Burgundii* (see prec.). Cf. earlier BURGONIAN.] A *n.* A native or inhabitant of Burgundy, France. Also *Hist.*, a member of a Germanic people who inhabited a region from the Main to the Vistula and who entered Gaul and established the kingdom of Burgundy in the 5th cent. AD. E17. B *adj.* Of or pertaining to Burgundy or the Burgundians. M17.

burgundy /ˈbəːɡəndi/ *n.* & *a.* In sense A.1 also **B-**. L17. [*Burgundy* (Fr. *Bourgogne*) a region of eastern France (formerly a duchy, earlier a kingdom) f. med.L *Burgundia*, f. late L *Burgundii*: see BURGUND.] A *n.* 1 (A) wine made in Burgundy (without specification usu. (a) red wine). Also, (a) similar wine from other countries. L17. 2 The red colour of this wine. L19.
Comb.: **Burgundy pitch** resin from the Norway spruce.
B *adj.* Of the red colour of burgundy. L19.

burh *n.* see BOROUGH.

burhel *n.* var. of BHARAL.

buriable /ˈbɛrɪəb(ə)l/ *a.* L16. [f. BURY + -ABLE.] Able to be buried.

burial /ˈbɛrɪəl/ *n.* Also (earlier) †**buriels**. [OE *byrġels* = OS *burgisli* f. Gmc, f. as BURY: see -LE[1]. Early (ME) taken erron. as pl.] 1 A burying-place, a grave, a tomb. *obs.* exc. *Archaeol.* OE. 2 The action of burying something, esp. a dead body; an interment; a funeral. ME.
2 BURKE Every Minister shall keep a register of births, burials and marriages.
Phrases: *crouched burial*: see CROUCH *v.* 1. *secondary burial*: see SECONDARY *a.*
Comb.: **burial ground** a cemetery; **burial service** a religious service held at a funeral.

Buriat /ˈbuːrɪət/ *n.* & *a.* Also **Buryat**. M19. [Mongolian *Buriyad*.] A *n.* 1 A member of a Mongolian people inhabiting the borders of Lake Baikal, Siberia. M19. 2 The Mongolic language of this people. L19. B *attrib.* or as *adj.* Of or pertaining to the Buriats or their language; designating or pertaining to the territory of the Buriats. E20.

†**buriels** *n.* see BURIAL.

burier /ˈbɛrɪə/ *n.* OE. [f. BURY + -ER[1].] A person who or thing which buries something or someone. Formerly also, a gravedigger.

burin /ˈbjʊərɪn/ *n.* M17. [Fr., rel. to It. *burino* (*bulino*), perh. conn. w. OHG *bora* boring-tool: see BORE *v.*[1]] A tool for engraving on copper or wood.

burk *n.* var. of BERK.

burka /ˈbʊəkə/ *n.*[1] M19. [Urdu (Pers.) *burka'* f. Arab. *burku'*.] A Muslim woman's long enveloping garment worn in public. Also, a yashmak.

burka /ˈbʊəkə/ *n.*[2] L19. [Russ.] A long Caucasian cloak of felt or goat's hair.

burke *n.* var. of BERK.

burke /bəːk/ *v.t.* E19. [William *Burke*, executed at Edinburgh in 1829 for murdering by suffocation or strangulation to sell bodies for dissection.] 1 Kill (a person) to sell the body for dissection; suffocate or strangle secretly. *arch.* E19. 2 *fig.* Stifle, smother (publicity or inquiry); hush up, suppress (rumour); avoid (a problem). M19.

Burkinan /bəːˈkiːnən/ *a.* & *n.* L20. [f. *Burkina* (see below) + -AN.] (A native or inhabitant) of Burkina Faso, an inland country of W. Africa. Cf. UPPER VOLTAN.

Burkitt /ˈbəːkɪt/ *n.* M20. [D. P. *Burkitt* (1911–93), Brit. surgeon.] Med. *Burkitt's lymphoma*, *Burkitt tumour*, a malignant tumour of the lymphatic system occurring esp. in the jaw and viscera, and mostly affecting young children in tropical Africa.

burkundaz /bəːk(ə)nˈdɑːz/ *n.* L18. [Urdu *barkandāz* musketeer, f. Pers., f. Arab. *barḳ* lightning + Pers. *andāz* thrower.] *Hist.* In the Indian subcontinent: an armed guard, a constable.

burl /bəːl/ *n.*[1] & *v.* LME. [OFr. *bourle* tuft of wool, dim. of (O)Fr. *bourre*, Sp., Port. *borra* coarse wool, f. late L *burra* wool: cf. BUR *n.*[1]] A *n.* 1 A knot in wool or cloth. LME. †2 A pimple. E–M17. 3 A knot or excrescence in wood. *N. Amer.* L19. B *v.t.* & *i.* Dress (cloth), esp. by removing knots or lumps. Now *rare.* L15.
burler *n.* ME.

burl *n.*[2] see BIRL *n.*

burlap /ˈbəːlap/ *n.* Orig. †**-ps**. L17. [Origin unkn.] A coarse canvas esp. of jute for sacking etc.; a similar (finer) material for dress or furnishing.

burlesque /bəːˈlɛsk/ *a.*, *n.*, & *v.* M17. [Fr. f. It. *burlesco*, f. *burla* ridicule, joke, fun, of unkn. origin: see -ESQUE.] A *adj.* †1 Jocular, odd, grotesque. M17–M19. 2 Derisively or amusingly imitative; mock-heroic or mock-pathetic; bombastic. (Now chiefly of literary composition or dramatic representation.) M17. B *n.* 1 Derisively or amusingly imitative literary or dramatic composition, bombast; mock-seriousness; an instance or example of this; (a) parody; (a) caricature. M17. 2a *Hist.* The concluding portion of a blackface minstrel entertainment, containing dialogue and sketches. *US.* M19. b A variety show, freq. featuring striptease. Orig. & chiefly *US.* L19. C *v.t.* Imitate to deride or amuse; parody; caricature. L17.
burlesquely *adv.* E19. **burlesquer** *n.* (*a*) a person who burlesques; (*b*) an actor in burlesque drama: M17.

burletta /bəːˈlɛtə/ *n. obs.* exc. *Hist.* M18. [It., dim. of *burla*: see prec., cf. -ETTE.] A musical farce.

Burley /ˈbəːli/ *n.*[1] Also **b-**. L19. [Origin unkn.] A variety of tobacco, pale or dark, grown mainly in Kentucky, USA.

burley *n.*[2], **burlie** *n.* see BYRLAW.

burly /ˈbəːli/ *a.* ME. [Prob. f. as BOWER *n.*[1] + -LY[1]; perh. already in OE: cf. OHG *burlīh* exalted, stately.] †1 Stately, dignified, imposing. ME–M17. b Of a thing: goodly, excellent. LME–L19. 2 Sturdy; big and strong; massively built. LME. 3 Domineering; forceful; bluff, forthright. L16.
2 E. B. BROWNING Burly oaks projecting from the line. R. HAYMAN The big, burly, bull-necked, .. successful business man. 3 J. H. NEWMAN As generous as they are hasty and burly. GEOFFREY HILL Against the burly air I strode.
burlily *adv.* M19. **burliness** *n.* E17.

Burman /ˈbəːmən/ *n.* & *a.* E19. [f. as next + -AN.] = next.

Burmese /bəːˈmiːz/ *a.* & *n.* E19. [f. *Burma* (see below) + -ESE.] A *adj.* Of or pertaining to Burma (Myanmar), a country in SE Asia, its inhabitants, or their language. E19.
Burmese cat a breed of short-coated domestic cat. *Burmese* ROSEWOOD.
B *n.* Pl. same. 1 A native or inhabitant of Burma; *spec.* a member of the majority ethnic group of Burma. E19. 2 The Sino-Tibetan language of the Burmese people. M19. 3 = *Burmese cat* above. M20.

burn /bəːn/ *n.*[1] Now *Sc.* & *north.* [OE *burna*, *burne*, *burn*, corresp. to OFris. *burna*, MLG *borne*, *born*, MDu. *borne* (LG, Du. *born*), repr. a metathetic var. of Gmc base of OS, OHG *brunno* (Du. *bron*, G *Brunnen*), ON *brunnr*, Goth. *brunna*: cf. BOURN *n.*[1]] A stream, a brook, a spring.

burn /bəːn/ *n.*[2] E16. [f. the vb.] 1 The act or effect of burning; a mark or injury made by burning. E16. 2 The clearing of vegetation by burning; an area so cleared. *N. Amer.*, *Austral.*, & *NZ.* L18. 3 A smoke, a cigarette. *slang.* M20. 4

A spell of operation by a spacecraft's engine. M20. 5 A car race, a fast drive. *slang*. M20.

1 **slow burn** *colloq*. (a state of) slowly mounting annoyance or anger.

Comb.: **burn-bag, -basket** *US*: for classified (esp. incriminating) material which is to be destroyed by burning.

burn /bəːn/ *v*. Pa. t. **burned, burnt** /bəːnt/, †**brent**; pa. pple **burned, burnt,** (*dial.*) **brent** /brɛnt/. See also BURNT *ppl a.*, YBRENT. [OE *birnan* var. of *brinnan* (branch I) = OS, OHG, Goth. *brinnan*; OE *bærnan* (branch II) = OS, OHG *brennan* (G *brennen*), ON *brenna*, Goth. *brannjan*: both f. same Gmc base.] I *v.i.* 1 Of fire, a furnace, etc.: be in the state of activity characteristic of fire, be in combustion. OE. b Of a spacecraft's engine: provide thrust. M20. 2 Be on fire, be consumed by flames; undergo combustion; undergo oxidation with evolution of heat. OE. b Undergo nuclear reactions producing energy. M20. 3 *fig.* Be passionate, rage; be consumed with emotion, longing, etc. OE. 4 Be or become very hot; feel a sensation of heat, be inflamed. OE. b *fig.* Be very close to the object sought (in games etc.). Cf. HOT *a.* 8b. E19. 5 Give light by combustion or heat; glow, shine, appear as if on fire. OE. 6 Suffer the effects of combustion, heat, the sun's rays, acid, extreme cold, etc.; be scorched, blackened, parched, or tanned; be charred by overcooking. ME. b Cause injury or pain by the action of fire, heat, extreme cold, etc.; (of acid etc.) eat its way *into* by burning. M17. 7 Suffer death by fire. *arch.* ME.

1 A. SILLITOE A bright fire burned in the modernised grate. J. RHYS The flames burned straight. 2 SHAKES. *Rich. II* That hand shall burn in never-quenching fire That staggers thus my person. A. J. P. TAYLOR They were medieval towns, full of wooden houses, and burnt well. F. HOYLE All the oxygen would have been quickly consumed, since biomaterial burns very easily. 3 AV *Gen.* 44:18 Let not thine anger burne against thy seruant. R. L. STEVENSON I burn to see you on the gallows. G. EWART I burned with desire to distress you. 4 **one's ears burn** one feels (rightly or wrongly) that one is being talked about. 5 SHAKES. *Jul. Caes.* How ill this taper burns! E. O'NEILL One bulb burning doesn't cost much. B. SPENCER Snow on pine gorges can burn blue like Persian cats. 6 V. WOOLF Bones bleach and burn far away in Indian sands. T. FRISBY Would you like to make sure that nothing burns in the kitchen? b J. H. NEWMAN Ice which blisters may be said to burn. 7 T. FORREST Here.. women often.. burn with their deceased husbands.

II *v.t.* 8 Of fire: consume, destroy. Of a person etc.: cause to be alight, or to be destroyed or consumed by fire. OE. b Make a burnt offering of; sacrifice or execute by burning. ME. c Consume as fuel for heat or light; oxidize with evolution of heat; use the nuclear energy of. L16. d *fig.* Spend or use freely. *slang.* L19. e Smoke (tobacco). *slang.* E20. 9 Produce the effects of fire or heat upon, expose to fire or heat; scorch, blacken; char or cause to adhere by overcooking; calcine, bake. OE. b Make by burning. ME. 10 Injure or cause pain to by the action of fire or heat. ME. b Cauterize; brand. ME. †c Infect with (esp. venereal) sores. E16–M18. d *fig.* Swindle, cheat. *slang.* M17. 11 *fig.* Inflame or consume with emotion etc.; *slang* annoy, rile. ME. 12 Produce an effect on like that of fire or heat, e.g. by corrosive substances, extreme cold, sunlight, etc.; injure or hurt thus; corrode, wither, parch, tan. ME.

8 SPENSER The fire which them to ashes brent. P. SHAFFER It's fantastically dangerous to burn a naked flame in this room! A. S. BYATT The pierced dustbin in which he burned garden rubbish. **burn alive** kill by burning. **burn one's boats** or **bridges** or **ships** commit oneself irrevocably to a course of action. **have to burn** have (money etc.) in great abundance. *pare and burn*: see PARE *v.* b SHAKES. *1 Hen. VI* O, burn her, burn her! Hanging is too good. MILTON One [altar] of Syrian mode whereon to burn His odious offerings. **burn daylight** *arch.* use artificial light in daytime; waste day(light). c O. LODGE Burning 1,000 tons of coal. *Lancet* The thesis.. that muscles could burn sugar only. *burn the candle at both ends*: see CANDLE *n.* *burn (the) midnight oil*: see OIL *n.* 9 T. D'URFEY 'Till Pudding and Dumpling are burnt to Pot. M. DRABBLE It was burned black on the outside and raw in the middle. J. G. FARRELL No clay or shale that you can burn into bricks. *burn to a chip, a cinder, a crisp, a frazzle*, etc. b DEFOE These [earthen vessels] I burnt in the fire. **burn a hole in one's pocket** (esp. of money) make one wish to spend or dispose of it. 10 S. HILL You cannot manage it without burning your mouth. B. ENGLAND MacConnachie's wrist, where the rope had burned it, was suppurating a little. **burn one's fingers** *fig.* suffer, esp. financially, for meddling or rashness. 11 DRYDEN With two fair Eyes his Mistress burns his Breast. 12 DRYDEN Goats.. graze the Field, and burn it bare. W. S. MAUGHAM His face and neck burnt brown by the hot sun.

With advs. in specialized senses: **burn away** diminish to nothing by burning. **burn down** (*a*) burn less vigorously as fuel fails; (*b*) destroy (a building etc.) by burning. **burn in** imprint by burning (*lit.* & *fig.*). **burn low** nearly go out. **burn off** (*a*) (cause to) evaporate, disappear, etc., under the action of heat; (*b*) *N. Amer., Austral.*, & *NZ* clear (land) for cultivation by burning vegetation; burn (vegetation) to clear land. **burn out** (*a*) burn away, (make) fail by burning; consume the contents of by burning, *fig.* exhaust the powers of; (*b*) make homeless by burning a dwelling, drive out *of* by burning a place. **burn up** (*a*) get rid of, consume completely, by fire; (*b*) flash into a blaze; (*c*) *N. Amer. slang* be or make furious; (*d*) *colloq.* traverse at high speed.

Comb.: *burning-glass*: see GLASS *n.*; **burn-off** *N. Amer., Austral.*, & *NZ* the clearing of land for cultivation by burning vegetation; **burn-out** destruction by fire; failure of an electrical component etc. through overheating; exhaustion, disillusion, or depression associated with occupational stress; **burn-up** (*a*) consumption of fuel; (*b*) *slang* a very fast drive or motorcycle ride etc.

burnable *a.* able to be burnt or consumed by fire E17.

burned *ppl a.* var. of BURNT.

burner /ˈbəːnə/ *n.* LME. [f. prec. + -ER[1].] 1 A person who burns or consumes with fire. LME. b With specifying adj.: a substance, esp. a fuel, that burns in the specified manner. L20. 2 A person who produces charcoal etc. by burning. LME. 3 An appliance which provides a flame for heating, lighting, etc., usu. using gas or liquid fuel; the part of a lamp, cooker, etc., which is the site of and shapes the flame. L18.

3 *Argand burner*, *Bunsen burner*, *fishtail burner*, *oil burner*, etc. **on the back** (or **front**) **burner** *slang* receiving little (or much) attention, having a low (or high) priority.

burnet /ˈbəːnɪt/ *a.* & *n.* ME. [OFr. *brunet* adj. (see BRUNET) & *brunete*, *burnete* ns. = brown cloth, brown-flowered plant, dims. of *brun* BROWN *a.*: see -ET[1].] †A *adj.* Of a dark brown colour. ME–E17. B *n.* †1 A superior wool cloth, orig. of dark brown colour. Only in ME. 2 A plant of the genus *Sanguisorba*, of the rose family, with pinnate leaves and globular heads of apetalous flowers; *esp.* either of two Eurasian plants, *S. officinalis* (more fully *great burnet*) of damp meadows, with ovate leaflets, and *S. minor* (more fully *salad burnet*) of calcareous grassland, with roundish leaflets tasting of cucumber. LME. 3 A day-flying moth of the genus *Zygaena*, typically dark green with crimson-spotted wings. Also *burnet-moth*. L18.

Comb.: *burnet-moth*: see sense B.3 above; **burnet rose** a small wild rose, *Rosa pimpinellifolia*, with white flowers and leaves like those of salad burnet; **burnet saxifrage** an umbellifer of the genus *Pimpinella*; *esp.* the Eurasian species *P. saxifraga* of dry grassland, with rosette leaves freq. like those of salad burnet.

Burnham /ˈbəːnəm/ *n.* E20. [Viscount *Burnham* (1862–1933), first chairman of the committee.] *Burnham scale*, a national salary scale for teachers in maintained schools in England and Wales, recommended by a standing committee (*Burnham committee*) of Local Education Authorities' and teachers' representatives (established 1919).

burning /ˈbəːnɪŋ/ *a.* OE. [f. BURN *v.* + -ING[2].] 1 *lit.* That burns; that is on fire or very hot. OE. 2 *fig.* Ardent, passionate; flagrant; exciting, hotly discussed, controversial. ME.

1 **burning bush** [w. allus. to *Exod.* 3] (*a*) any of various shrubs with red fruits or red autumn foliage; (*b*) = FRAXINELLA (because of its production of flammable volatile essences). **burning mountain** *arch.* a volcano. 2 STEELE It is really a burning shame this Man should be tolerated. SOUTHEY With copious tears Of burning anger. A. J. P. TAYLOR There was no burning question to excite the passions of the electors. M. GEE Moira Penny had one burning ambition.

burningly *adv.* ME.

burnish /ˈbəːnɪʃ/ *v.*[1] & *n.* ME. [OFr. *burniss-* lengthened stem of *burnir* var. of *brunir* make brown, f. *brun* BROWN *a.*: see -ISH[2].] A *v.* 1 *v.t.* Polish (esp. metal) by rubbing. ME. b Of a stag: rub the dead velvet from (the antlers or head). LME. 2 *v.t.* Make bright or glossy in any way; spread with lustre. LME. 3 *v.i.* Become bright or glossy; shine, gleam. E17.

1 WORDSWORTH The whole wide lake.. like a burnished mirror glows. 2 MILTON Fruit burnisht with Golden Rind, Hung amiable. D. LESSING The autumn green of the trees was gilded and burnished with the low sunlight. 3 SWIFT I've seen a snake.. Burnish, and make a gaudy show.

B *n.* A polish by rubbing; burnished appearance, lustre. *rare.* M17.

burnisher *n.* a person who or thing which burnishes something; a tool for burnishing: ME.

burnish /ˈbəːnɪʃ/ *v.*[2]*i.* *obs.* exc. *dial.* LME. [Origin unkn.] Grow plump or stout; increase in girth.

burnous /bəːˈnuːs/ *n.* Also **-oose** & other vars. L16. [Fr. f. Arab. *burnus*, *-ūs*.] An Arab or Moorish hooded cloak; a fashion garment resembling this.

Burnsian /ˈbəːnzɪən/ *a.* & *n.* E20. [f. *Burns* (see below) + -IAN.] A *adj.* Of or pertaining to the Scottish poet Robert Burns (1759–96); characteristic of Burns or his style. E20. B *n.* An admirer or student of Burns or his works. E20.

Burnsi'ana *n.pl.* [-ANA] publications or other items concerning or associated with Burns L19.

burnside /ˈbəːnsʌɪd/ *n.* *US.* *arch.* L19. [General Ambrose *Burnside* (1824–81), US army officer.] *sing.* & (freq.) in *pl.* Moustache and whiskers with no beard on the chin.

burnt /bəːnt/ *ppl a.* Also **burned** /bəːnt, bəːnd/. ME. [pa. pple of BURN *v.*] Consumed by fire; affected, damaged, or injured by fire or extreme heat; charred, scorched.

burnt almond an almond enclosed in caramelized sugar. **burnt cork** charred cork used esp. to blacken the face, hands, etc. **burnt cream** = *crème brûlée* s.v. CRÈME 1. **burnt ochre, sienna, umber**, etc.: having a deeper colour obtained by calcination. **burnt offering** a religious sacrifice offered by burning. **burnt-out** *a.* (*a*) gutted or driven out by fire; exhausted, spent; (*b*) cured of leprosy (esp. in *burnt-out case*); also *fig.* passing into sense (a). *burnt sienna*: see *burnt ochre* above. **burnt taste**: like that of food that has been charred. *burnt umber*: see *burnt ochre* above.

buroo /bəˈruː/ *n.* *colloq.* (orig. & chiefly *Sc.*). Also **brew, broo,** /bruː/. M20. [Alt. of BUREAU.] A social security office, a labour exchange.

on the buroo receiving unemployment benefit.

burp /bəːp/ *n.* & *v.* *colloq.* (orig. *US*). M20. [Imit.] A *n.* A belch. M20.

Comb.: **burp gun** *US* an automatic pistol.

B *v.i.* & *t.* (Cause to) belch. M20.

burpee /ˈbəːpiː/ *n.* Also **-ie** /-ɪ/. M20. [Royal H. *Burpee* (b. 1897), Amer. psychologist.] A physical exercise with a squat thrust between standing positions.

burr /bəː/ *n.*[1] Also **bur**. LME. [Abbrev. of as BOROUGH: cf. BROCH.] 1 A circle. *rare* in *gen.* sense. LME. †2 A broad iron ring on a tilting spear. L15–E17. 3 A washer placed on the small end of a rivet before the end is swaged down. E17. 4 A luminous ring round the moon etc., a halo. M17.

Comb.: **burr-pump** *Naut.* a bilge-pump with the piston so made as not to require a valve.

burr /bəː/ *n.*[2] L16. [Origin unkn.] A sweetbread.

burr /bəː/ *n.*[3] L16. [Origin unkn.] The external meatus of the ear; the opening leading to the tympanum.

burr /bəː/ *n.*[4] Also **bur** (for other senses see BUR *n.*[1]). In branch II also **buhr**. E17. [Var. of BUR *n.*[1]] I 1 A rough edge left on cut or punched metal, paper, etc. E17. 2 In full *burr-drill*. A dentist's or surgeon's tool for producing a smooth cavity. M19. II More fully (esp. in sense 3) *burr-stone*. 3 A hard siliceous rock used for millstones, whetstones, etc.; a piece of this; a millstone or whetstone of this. M17. 4 A kind of limestone used for building, containing hard siliceous inclusions. *dial.* E19. 5 A mass of vitrified brick; a clinker. E19.

burr /bəː/ *n.*^{5} & *v.* M18. [Prob. imit., but perh. transf. use of prec.] A *n.* 1 A rough sounding of the phoneme /r/ (repr. by the letter r); *spec.* the uvular trill characteristic of Northumberland. M18. b *loosely.* A rough or dialectal pronunciation. M19. 2 A whirr; a vibratory, buzzing, or rushing noise. E19. B *v.* 1 *v.i.* Make a buzzing or whirring noise. L18. 2 *v.i.* Use a uvular trill; use a rough or dialectal pronunciation; speak indistinctly. E19. 3 *v.t.* Pronounce with a burr. M19.

burr *n.*^{6} var. of BUR *n.*^{1}

burra /ˈbʌrə/ *a.* E19. [Hind. *baṛā*, *barā* great, greatest.] In the Indian subcontinent: prominent, high-ranking, great. Only in *burra sahib*, *memsahib*, and similar phrases used as modes of reference to important people.

burras *n.* var. of BARRAS.

burrawang /ˈbʌrəwaŋ/ *n.* Also **-wong** /-wɒŋ/. *Austral.* E19. [Aborig.] A cycad of the genus *Macrozamia*; a seed of such a tree.

burrel-fly /ˈbʌrəlflʌɪ/ *n.* M17. [Origin unkn.] The gadfly.

burrito /bʌˈriːtəʊ/ *n.* Pl. **-os.** M20. [Amer. Sp., dim. of next.] A tortilla rolled round a filling of spiced beef and other ingredients.

burro /ˈbʌrəʊ/ *n.* Chiefly *N. Amer.* Pl. **-os.** E19. [Sp.] A small donkey used as a pack-animal.

burrow /ˈbʌrəʊ/ *n.*^{1} Long *obs.* exc. *dial.* [OE *beorg*, *beorh*, f. *beorgan*: see BORROW *v.*^{1}] (A) shelter.

burrow /ˈbʌrəʊ/ *n.*^{2} ME. [Var. of BOROUGH.] I See also BERRY *n.*^{3} 1 A hole or excavation in earth made by a rabbit, a fox, etc., as a place of shelter. ME. 2 *transf.* & *fig.* Any secluded or small dwelling-place or retreat. M17.

1 *village burrow*: see VILLAGE 3.

II 3 In *pl.* exc. *attrib.* Boroughs, towns; burgesses collectively. *Sc. arch.* LME. †III 4 = BROCH 2. L15–M17.

Comb.: **burrow-duck** *dial.* the shelduck; **burrows-town** *Sc. arch.* = BOROUGH-*town*.

burrow /ˈbʌrəʊ/ *n.*^{3} *dial.* & *techn.* L15. [Var. of BARROW *n.*^{1}] A heap or mound, esp. of mining refuse.

burrow /ˈbʌrəʊ/ *v.* E17. [f. BURROW *n.*^{2}] 1 *v.i.* Make a burrow; live in a burrow; hide oneself in or as in a burrow. E17. 2 *v.t.* Hide in or as in a burrow (usu. in *pass.* of oneself); push *in* or *into* as in(to) a burrow. E17. 3 *v.i.* Bore or make one's way under the surface. E19. 4 *v.t.* Make (a hole etc., one's way) by excavating. M19.

1 **burrowing owl** a small American owl, *Speotyto cunicularia*, nesting in burrows. 2 G. CRABBE An infant .. Left by neglect, and burrowed in that bed. J. BUCHAN He .. burrowed a drowsy head into the cushions. 3 N. HAWTHORNE We were burrowing through its bewildering passages. B. ENGLAND He .. burrowed deep into the thick scrub. **burrow into** *fig.* investigate the mysteries etc. of.

burrower *n.* M19.

burru /ˈbʌruː/ *n.* Also **buru.** E20. [Perh. f. Twi *búru* filthiness, sluttishness or Yoruba *buru* wicked.] A Jamaican dance with provocative posturing; music or drumming to accompany this.

burry /ˈbəːri/ *a.* LME. [f. BUR *n.*^{1} + -Y^{1}.] Full of burs; rough, prickly.

bursa /ˈbəːsə/ *n.* Pl. **-sae** /-siː/. E19. [med.L = bag, PURSE *n.*] *Anat.* A fluid-filled sac of fibrous tissue, *esp.* one serving to lessen friction between moving parts, e.g. at a joint, or formed in response to unusual friction. Also, a pouch of the peritoneum.

bursa of Fabricius /fəˈbrɪʃəs/ [Latinized form of the name of Girolamo *Fabrici* (1533–1619), It. anatomist] *Ornith.* a glandular sac which opens into a bird's cloaca and is involved in the development of the bird's immune system.

bursal *a.* of, pertaining to, or of the nature of a bursa M18.

bursar /ˈbəːsə/ *n.* LME. [Sense 1 f. (O)Fr. *boursier* or med.L *bursarius*: see BURSARY, -AR^{2}, -ER^{2}. Sense 2 f. Fr. *boursier.*] 1 A treasurer; a person in charge of the funds or other property of a college etc. LME. 2 A student who holds a bursary. Orig. *Sc.* M16.

1 *domestic bursar*: see DOMESTIC *a.* 1. *estates bursar*: see ESTATE *n.*

bursarship *n.* (*a*) the position of a bursar; (*b*) a bursary for a student: E17.

bursarial /bəːˈsɛːrɪəl/ *a.* M19. [f. prec. + -IAL or next + -AL^{1}.] Of or pertaining to a bursar or bursary.

bursary /ˈbəːsəri/ *n.* LME. [Sense 1 f. med.L *bursarius*, senses 2 & 3 f. med.L *bursaria* bursar's office (cf. OFr. *bourserie* money coffer): see BURSA, -ARY^{1}.] †1 = BURSAR 1. LME–M16. 2 A treasury; the bursar's room at a college etc. L17. 3 An endowment given to a student. Orig. *Sc.* M18.

burse /bəːs/ *n.* LME. [(O)Fr *bourse* or med.L BURSA; in sense 2 cf. BOURSE.] 1 A purse, *esp.* as the designation of one of the official insignia of the Lord Chancellor. LME. 2 A money market, an exchange, (= BOURSE). *obs.* exc. *Hist.* as below. M16. 3 = BURSARY 3. M16. †b A fund to provide bursaries. L17–M18. 4 A German college or academic hall. L16.

2 **the Burse** *Hist.* the Royal Exchange in Cornhill, London.

bursectomy /bəːˈsɛktəmi/ *n.* E20. [f. BURSA: see -ECTOMY.] Surgical removal or (hormonal) destruction of a bird's bursa of Fabricius, esp. in immunological research; an instance of this.

burˈsectomize *v.t.* perform bursectomy on E20.

bursiform /ˈbəːsɪfɔːm/ *a.* M19. [f. BURSA + -I- + -FORM.] Purse-shaped.

bursitis /bəːˈsʌɪtɪs/ *n.* M19. [f. BURSA + -ITIS.] Inflammation of a bursa.

burst /bəːst/ *n.* See also BUST *n.*^{2} [OE *byrst* = OHG *brust* f. Gmc base of BURST *v.*; branch II directly f. the vb.] †I 1 Damage, injury, harm. OE–LME.

II 2 An act or the result of bursting open or splitting. ME. 3 A sudden and violent issuing out (of flame, light, gunfire, etc.); a vehement outbreak (of emotion, laughter, etc.); an explosion, an eruption; a pulse (of radiation etc.). LME. b A sudden opening on the view. L18. 4 A spell of increased activity; a display of energy, a spurt; a hard gallop. L18. 5 A spree, a drinking-bout; a large meal. *colloq.* M19.

2 G. MEREDITH When beech-buds were near the burst. 3 SOUTHEY Burst after burst the innocuous thunders brake. P. G. WODEHOUSE She flung her arms round his neck in a burst of remorseful affection. W. BOYD A loud and prolonged burst of applause. b J. AUSTEN Here is a fine burst of country. 4 THACKERAY A burst over the Downs after a hare. M. ARNOLD The burst of creative activity in our literature. I. HAY They .. proceeded to row courses, half courses .. and short bursts.

burst /bəːst/ *v.* Pa. t. & pple **burst**; (*dial.*) **-ed, -en** /-(ə)n/. Also (*arch.* & *dial.*) **brast** /brast/. See also BUST *v.* [OE *berstan* = OFris. *bersta*, OS, OHG *brestan* (Du. *bersten*, *barsten*), ON *bresta*, f. Gmc.] I *v.i.* †1 Break suddenly, snap, crack. OE–E19. 2 Fly apart or into pieces or break open with expansion of contents or release of pressure; split; explode; (of a cloud etc.) release rain with sudden force; (of a door) fly *open* suddenly. OE. 3 Issue suddenly (as if) by breaking restraint or overcoming resistance; break out suddenly or forcibly. OE. b Of thoughts, emotions, etc.: find (sudden) utterance or manifestation. M16. 4 Force one's way *through, out, into*, etc., come or appear suddenly, intrude. ME. 5 Be full to overflowing (*with*); be unable to contain oneself; have an overwhelming desire or urgent need *to do* something; (of the heart) break. ME. 6 Break out into sudden activity or expression of feelings; exclaim, begin suddenly. Usu. w. *into*, *out*. LME.

2 SPENSER Poyson .. Made him to swell, that nigh his bowells brust. S. SASSOON A bomb burst in the water. DAY LEWIS A gigantic wave had just burst on the fo'c'sle. J. BOWEN Bubbles on a tarred roof, which grew, and burst, and grew again. P. F. BOLLER There was a loud ripping sound; the seam of his trousers had burst. *bursting at the seams*: see SEAM *n.*^{1} **bursting point** the internal pressure at which a container will burst (usu. *transf.*). *burst in(to) shivers*: see SHIVER *n.*^{1} 1. 3 BUNYAN What sighs and groans brast from Christians heart. TENNYSON A river .. Ready to burst and fill the world with foam. 4 S. O'FAOLÁIN The weeds bursting through the gravel. V. BRITTAIN Winifred Holtby burst suddenly in upon this morose atmosphere of ruminant lethargy. 5 AV *Prov.* 3:10 Thy presses shall burst out with new wine. G. B. SHAW It was something that was just bursting to be said. DAY LEWIS Plums bursting with ripeness. S. HILL She was bursting .. to talk now. 6 SPENSER The wisard .. brusting forth in laughter, to her sayd. B. JOWETT The crew of his own trireme also burst out laughing. T. H. HUXLEY The taper will burst again into full flame. J. CARY She burst into tears and called for her mama. K. AMIS Bowen burst into song.

II *v.t.* 7 Cause to fly apart or into pieces, disrupt with internal pressure, rupture, cause to split; suffer rupture of. ME. b *spec.* Separate (esp. computer printout paper) along perforated edges, esp. automatically. M20. 8 Open (a door etc.) forcibly, force one's way through, break free from (bonds etc.). LME. 9 *gen.* Break suddenly, snap, shatter; interrupt. Now *rare* or *obs.* LME. 10 Cause (the body) to swell to bursting point (usu. *hyperbol.*, as an imagined result of overeating or exertion); fill to overflowing; break (the heart). LME.

7 C. KINGSLEY He .. played leap-frog .. till he burst his buttons. G. B. SHAW Morell bursts open the cover of a copy of The Church Reformer. *Daily Express* The force of the explosion burst the water tanks. C. FRY One day I shall burst my bud Of calm, and blossom into hysteria. *burst one's sides*: see SIDE *n.* 8 SHAKES. *1 Hen. VI* Open the gates unto the Lord Protector, Or we'll burst them open. A. F. DOUGLAS-HOME A .. crowd .. burst the barriers and swarmed across the route. **burst its banks** (of a river etc.) break through or overflow its banks and cause flooding. 9 C. MARLOWE Whose chariot-wheels have burst the Assyrians' bones. TENNYSON Many a .. heel against the pavement echoing burst their drowse. 10 MILTON Cramm'd and gorged, right burst With suck'd and glutted offal. DRYDEN That Crop .. bursts the crowded Barns. DEFOE Water, with which .. he would have burst himself.

burster /ˈbəːstə/ *n.* E17. [f. prec. + -ER^{1}.] 1 A person who or thing which bursts. E17. b *spec.* A machine for separating continuous stationery into its constituent sheets. M20. 2 = BUSTER 3. *Austral.* & *NZ.* M19. 3 *Astron.* A cosmic source of powerful short-lived bursts of X-rays or other radiation. L20.

burthen *n.*, *v.* see BURDEN *n.*, *v.*

burton /ˈbəːt(ə)n/ *n.*^{1} E18. [Alt. of BRETON (*tackle*).] *Naut.* 1 More fully *burton-tackle*. A light handy two-block tackle. E18. 2 Athwartship stowage of casks etc. Also *a-burton* adv. [A-^{2}]. M19.

1 *Spanish burton*: see SPANISH *a.*

burton /ˈbəːt(ə)n/ *n.*^{2} *slang* (orig. *RAF*). Also **B-.** M20. [Origin uncertain: perh. f. *Burton* ale f. *Burton*-on-Trent, a town in Staffordshire, England.] *go for a burton*, be killed, destroyed, ruined, or lost.

buru *n.* var. of BURRU.

bury /ˈbɛri/ *v.t.* [OE *byrgan* f. WGmc, f. base also of OE *beorgan*: see BORROW *v.*^{1}] 1 Deposit (a corpse, human remains) in the earth, in a tomb, in the ocean, etc., with funeral rites; lose (a relative etc.) by death. OE. b Put under the ground in sign of final abandonment or abrogation; dispose of thus. M16. 2 *fig.* Consign to oblivion, abandon and forget; renounce; consign to obscurity or inaccessibility. ME. 3 *gen.* Cover up with earth; conceal in the ground. ME. 4 Plunge deeply *in(to)* so as to remove from sight; immerse, hide; *fig.* profoundly absorb or engross (oneself) *in* (freq. in *pass.*). LME. 5 Of inanimate agents: cover up or over with material, submerge. M18.

1 STEELE My elder Sister buried her Husband about Six Months ago. B. CHATWIN There were snowdrops in the graveyard when they buried her. *dead and buried*: see DEAD *a.* b SHAKES. *Temp.* I'll break my staff, Bury it certain fathoms in the earth. *bury the hatchet*: see HATCHET *n.* *bury the tomahawk*: see TOMAHAWK *n.* 2 SIR W. SCOTT To retire from the world and bury herself in the recesses of the cloister. A. B. ELLIS The natives .. had buried their own differences and united

to repel the invaders. 3 E. W. LANE I.. buried 3000 pieces of gold. T. A. COWARD One habit [of the jay].. is that of burying nuts, acorns, or even inedible objects. **burying beetle** = SEXTON *beetle. bury one's head in the sand*: see SAND *n.* 4 BYRON Bury your steel in the bosoms of Gath. S. LEACOCK So buried in his own thoughts that he was oblivious of our approach. J. CHEEVER He buried his nose in the paper. 5 O. SITWELL Vesuvius has doubtless in its time buried town after town. R. P. JHABVALA Some of the older houses would collapse and bury the people inside.

burying *vbl n.* (*a*) the action of the vb (*burying-ground, -place*, a cemetery); (*b*) (now *dial.*) a burial, a funeral: ME.

Buryat *n.* var. of BURIAT.

bus /bʌs/ *n.* Also (now *rare*) **'bus**; (sense 4) **buss.** Pl. **buses, *busses.** E19. [Abbrev. of OMNIBUS.] 1 A large passenger road vehicle running on a fixed route. E19. 2 Any conveyance, as a motor car, aeroplane, etc. *colloq.* L19. 3 A hand-pushed trolley used esp. for carrying dishes etc. in a cafeteria. *N. Amer.* M20. 4 *Computing.* = HIGHWAY 1C. M20.

1 *miss the bus*: see MISS *v.*[1]

Comb.: **busbar** an electrical conductor serving as a common connection between several circuits, esp. in a generating station; **busboy** *N. Amer.* a waiter's assistant who clears tables etc.; a person who pushes a trolley carrying dishes etc. in a cafeteria; **bus-conductor** (*a*) the conductor of a bus; (*b*) = *busbar* above; **bus-conductress** a female bus-conductor; **bus lane** a traffic-lane mainly for the use of buses; **busman** a driver of a bus (*busman's holiday*, a period of leisure time spent in the same kind of occupation as one's regular work); **bus shelter** a roadside shelter affording protection from the weather to passengers awaiting buses; *bus station*: see STATION *n.*; **bus-stop** a place at which a bus regularly stops; **busway** a bus lane, *spec.* one with means to guide the movement of buses.

bus /bʌs/ *v.*[1] Infl. **-s-, *-ss-.** M19. [f. the n.] 1 *v.i.* & *t.* with *it.* Go by bus. M19. 2 *v.t.* Transport by bus, *spec.* (*US*) to a school in a different area in order to counteract racial segregation. Chiefly *N. Amer.* M20. b Carry or remove (dishes etc.) in a cafeteria etc., clear from tables; clear (a table in a cafeteria etc.) of dishes etc. *US.* M20.

†bus *v.*[2] var. of BOOST *v.*[2]

busby /ˈbʌzbi/ *n.* M18. [Origin unkn.] †1 A large bushy wig. M18–L19. 2 A tall fur hat forming part of the dress uniform of hussars, artillerymen, and guardsmen. E19.

busbied *a.* wearing a busby E20.

buscarl /ˈbʌskɑːl/ *n.* Long *obs.* exc. *Hist.* Also **butsecarl** /ˈbʌtsɪkɑːl/. OE. [ON *búzukarl.*] A seaman, a sailor.

bush /bʊʃ/ *n.*[1] Also (*dial.*) **busk** /bʌsk/. See also BOSK. ME. [Partly f. OFr. *bos, bosc* vars. of *bois* wood, partly f. ON *buski*, f. Gmc base repr. also by OS *busc* (Du. *bos, bosch*), OHG *busc* (G *Busch*) (corresp. form prob. in OE but not recorded). Sense 7 prob. directly f. Du. *bosch.*] 1 A shrub or clump of shrubs with stems of moderate length. ME. b A subshrub; a clump of dwarf shrubs or herbaceous plants. *Sc.* & *north.* E16. 2 Thicket; bushy ground. *obs.* exc. as coinciding w. sense 7. ME. 3 A bunch of ivy anciently used as a vintner's sign. LME. 4 A luxuriant growth of hair. E16. b Pubic hair, esp. of a woman. *slang.* E20. †5 A bushy mass of foliage, feathers, etc. E16–M17. †6 A bushy tail; a fox's brush. L16–E17. 7 (An area of) woodland, forest, uncultivated land, *the* remote rural areas, esp. in Australia, New Zealand, or Africa. M17.

1 *beat about the bush*: see BEAT *v.*[1] 15. *burning bush*: see BURNING 1. *caustic bush*: see CAUSTIC *a.* 1. *stag bush*: see STAG *n. take the rag off the bush*: see RAG *n.*[1] 3 *Proverb*: Good wine needs no bush. 7 **go bush** *Austral.* leave one's usual surroundings (for the country), run wild. *native bush*: see NATIVE *a. Sydney or the bush*: see SYDNEY 2.

Comb.: **bushbaby** a small tree-dwelling African primate of the subfamily Galaginae (family Lorisidae); *bush basil*: see BASIL *n.*[1] 1; **bush-bean** *N. Amer.* the kidney bean; **bushbuck** a small African antelope, *Tragelaphus scriptus*, red-brown with white chest-band and spots; **bush burn** *NZ* the burning of bush on cultivable land, land so cleared; **bush canary** *Austral.* & *NZ* any of various songbirds; **bush carpenter** *Austral.* & *NZ* an untrained or unskilled carpenter; **bush-cat** the serval; **bush clover** = LESPEDEZA; **bush cow** (*a*) a wild cow of the bush; (*b*) a tapir; **bushcraft** skill in living in the bush; *bush cranberry*: see CRANBERRY 2; *bush-cricket*: see CRICKET *n.*[1]; **bush-eel** *dial.* a snake, esp. as food; **bush-fighting** fighting in the bush, guerrilla warfare; **bushfire** a fire in the bush (sense 7); **bush-fly** a pestiferous Australian fly, esp. *Musca vestusissima*; **bush-harrow** *n.* & *v.t.* (*Hist.*) (harrow etc. with) an agricultural implement underneath which bushes are interwoven, for harrowing grassland or covering in seed; **bush hen** *NZ* the weka; **bush jacket** a belted cotton jacket; **bush lawyer** *NZ* & *Austral.* (*a*) the New Zealand bramble, *Rubus australis*; (*b*) a layman pretending to legal knowledge; an argumentative person; **bush league** *N. Amer.* a minor league of a professional sport, orig. *spec.* baseball; **bush-league** *a.* (*N. Amer. colloq.*) inferior, minor, unsophisticated; **bush-leaguer** *N. Amer.* a player in a bush league; **bushline** the altitude above which bush does not grow; **bushmaster** a large venomous viper, *Lachesis muta*, of tropical America; also called *surucucu*; **bush-pig** (*a*) a long-haired southern African wild hog, *Potamochoerus porcus*; (*b*) *NZ* a wild pig; **bush poppy** *N. Amer.* a yellow-flowered shrub of the poppy family, *Dendromecon rigida*, native to California and NW Mexico; **bush-ranger** *Hist.* an Australian brigand living in the bush; **bush-ranging** *Hist.* living as a bush-ranger; **bush-rat** any of various small rodents; **bush-rope** a tropical vine or creeper; **bush shrike** any African shrike of the subfamily Malaconotinae; **bush shirt** = *bush jacket* above; **bush-sick** *a.* (chiefly *NZ*) suffering from bush-sickness; **bush-sickness** (chiefly *NZ*) disease of animals due to cobalt deficiency in soil; **bush tea**: made from the dried leaves of certain shrubs and used medicinally in southern Africa; **bush telegraph** a rapid informal spreading of information, rumour, etc.; **bush-tit** a N. American tit of the genus *Psaltriparus*; **bushveld** veld composed largely of bush; a wooded region in Transvaal; **bush vetch** a climbing purple-flowered vetch, *Vicia sepium*; **bush walk** *Austral.* & *NZ* a tramp or camping expedition in the bush; **bush-walk** *v.i.* (*Austral.* & *NZ*) go tramping or camping in the bush; **bushwhack** *v.t.* & *i.* deal with or act in the manner of a bushwhacker; **bushwhacker** (*a*) a backwoodsman; (*b*) *US Hist.* a deserter, a guerrilla; (*c*) *Austral.* & *NZ* a person who clears land of bush, a timber-worker.

busher *n.* (*N. Amer. colloq.*) = *bush-leaguer* above E20. **bushless** *a.* M19.

bush /bʊʃ/ *n.*[2] L15. [MDu. *busse* (Du. *bus*). Cf. G *Büchse.*] A metal lining for an axle-hole or other circular orifice; a perforated plug; a box or bearing in which a shaft revolves; *Electr.* an insulating sleeve.

bushing *n.* a bush, esp. of an electrically insulating material L19.

bush /bʊʃ/ *v.*[1] ME. [f. BUSH *n.*[1]] †1 *v.t.* Conceal in a bush. Usu. in *pass.* (of oneself). ME–E17. 2 *v.t.* & *i.* (Cause to) grow thick like a bush; (cause to) grow or stick *out* like a bush. L15. 3 *v.t.* Protect or support with bushes. E17. 4 *v.t.* w. *it* & *i.* Camp in the bush. *Austral.* & *NZ.* E19.

bush /bʊʃ/ *v.*[2]*i. obs.* exc. *dial.* LME. [Perh. f. OFr. *buschier* knock, beat or f. MDu. *buuschen* (= MHG *biuschen*) in same sense.] Butt, push.

bush /bʊʃ/ *v.*[3]*t.* M16. [f. BUSH *n.*[2]] Provide with a bush.

bushed /bʊʃt/ *a. colloq.* L19. [f. BUSH *n.*[1] + -ED[2].] 1 Lost in the bush; bewildered. *Austral.* & *NZ.* L19. 2 Tired, exhausted. Chiefly *N. Amer.* L19.

bushel /ˈbʊʃ(ə)l/ *n.* & *v.*[1] ME. [OFr. *boisell* (mod. *boisseau*) = Prov. *boissel*, perh. of Gaulish origin.] A *n.* 1 A British unit of dry and liquid measure equal to 8 gallons or 32 quarts (approx. 36.4 litres); a US unit of dry measure equal to 4 pecks or 32 quarts (approx. 35.2 litres). ME. 2 *loosely.* A very large number or quantity. LME. 3 A vessel used as a measure of a bushel. *arch.* exc. as below. LME.

1 *Winchester bushel*: see WINCHESTER 1. 3 **hide one's light under a bushel** conceal one's merits.

B *v.t.* Hide (a light etc.) under a bushel (*fig.*): see sense A.3 above. *rare.* M17.

bushelful *n.* as much as a bushel will hold; a large quantity: LME.

bushel /ˈbʊʃ(ə)l/ *v.*[2]*t.* & *i. US.* M19. [Perh. f. G *bosseln* do odd jobs.] Mend or alter (clothes).

Comb.: **bushelman, -woman**: employed to mend or alter clothes.

bushido /ˈbuːʃɪdəʊ, bʊˈʃiːdəʊ/ *n.* L19. [Jap. = military knight's way.] The code of honour and morals evolved by the samurai.

bushie *n.* var. of BUSHY *n.*

Bushman /ˈbʊʃmən/ *n.* & *a.* Also (esp. in sense A.2) **b-.** L18. [f. BUSH *n.*[1] + MAN *n.*; sense A.1 after Du. *boschjesman.*] A *n.* Pl. **-men.** 1a A member of any of various aboriginal southern African peoples. L18. b (Any of) the group of languages of these peoples, = SAN *n.*[2] 2. M19. 2 A dweller, farmer, or traveller in the bush of Australia or New Zealand. In NZ also, a person who fells timber. M19.

B *attrib.* or as *adj.* Of or pertaining to the Bushmen or their language. M19.

bushman grass *S. Afr.* = TWAA-GRASS.

Bushmanoid *a.* (*Anthropol.*) resembling Bushmen in physical type M20. **bushmanship** *n.* bushcraft L19.

bushment /ˈbʊʃm(ə)nt/ *n. arch.* LME. [Sense 1 aphet. f. AMBUSHMENT; sense 2 app. f. BUSH *n.*[1] + -MENT.] 1 = AMBUSHMENT. LME. 2 A mass of bushes. L16.

bushwa /ˈbʊʃwɑː/ *n. N. Amer. slang.* Also **-wah.** E20. [App. euphem. for *bullshit* n. s.v. BULL *n.*[1] & *a.*] Rubbish, nonsense.

bushy /ˈbʊʃi/ *n. Austral.* & *NZ.* Also **bushie.** L19. [f. BUSH *n.*[1] + -Y[6].] A dweller in the bush.

bushy /ˈbʊʃi/ *a.* LME. [f. BUSH *n.*[1] + -Y[1].] 1 Having many bushes; covered with bush. LME. 2 Growing thickly; like a bush. M16.

Comb.: **bushy-tailed** *a.* with a bushy tail; *fig.* alert, lively (freq. in *bright-eyed and bushy-tailed*).

busily /ˈbɪzɪli/ *adv.* ME. [f. BUSY *a.* + -LY[2].] In a busy manner.

business /ˈbɪznɪs/ *n.* [OE *bisignis*, f. as BUSY *a.* + -NESS.] †I The state of being busy (cf. BUSYNESS). 1 Anxiety; distress, uneasiness. OE–L16. 2 The state of being busily engaged; activity; application, industry; diligent labour. ME–E18. 3 Eagerness; importunity; officiousness. LME–L16. 4 Attention, care; observance. LME–M16. 5 Trouble, difficulty; ado; commotion. LME–L17.

II The object of concern or activity. †6 The object of serious effort; an aim. LME–M16. 7 An appointed task; a duty, a province; *spec.* a particular errand, a cause of coming. LME. 8 Action demanding time and labour; serious work. LME. 9 A habitual occupation, a profession, a trade. L15. 10 A thing that concerns one; a matter in which one may take part. E16. 11 A particular matter requiring attention; a piece of work; a job; an agenda. M16. †b A topic, a subject. Only in 17. c A difficult matter. *colloq.* M19. 12 *gen.* An affair; a concern, a process; a matter; a structure; *slang* all that is available. Usu. *derog.* E17. 13 Dealings, intercourse, (*with*). E17. 14 *Theatr.* Action on stage (as opp. to dialogue). L17. 15 Trade; commercial transactions or engagements; total bookings, receipts, etc. E18. 16 A commercial house, a firm. L19.

7 BUNYAN What is your business here so late to Night? W. S. CHURCHILL The Prime Minister.. believed that the primary business of government was to administer the existing order. 8 *Proverb*: Business comes before pleasure. 9 CARLYLE I wished to be a fisherman, and tried that business for a time. 10 M. LEITCH What went on in between was their business, none of hers. 11 POPE What I act, survey, And learn from thence the business of the day. c CARLYLE If he had known what a business it was to govern the Abbey. 12 C. STEAD The difficult.. and dangerous business of climbing on the roof. D. CUSACK That nasty business in Second Year... They lampooned the Staff in their class paper.

Phrases etc.: **any other business** matters not specifically listed on the agenda for a meeting. *bad business*: see BAD *a. big business*: see BIG *a.* **business as usual** normal trading, proceedings, etc., despite disturbances. **do one's business** *colloq.* urinate or (*esp.*) defecate. **do the business** *colloq.* do what is required or expected, achieve the desired result. *funny business*: see FUNNY *a.* **get down to business** begin serious work, begin in earnest. **go about one's business** stop interfering in another's affairs, go away, (freq. in *imper.*). **in business** habitually occupied in trade or commerce; *fig.* able to begin operations, operational. **in the business of** engaged or involved in, concerned with, (usu. in neg. contexts). *line of* business: see LINE *n.*[2] **make it one's business to** make a particular effort to, undertake to. **mean business** be in earnest. **mind one's own business** refrain from interfering in another's affairs (freq. in *imper.*). *mind-your-own-business*: see MIND *v. monkey business*: see MONKEY *n.* **nobody's business** *colloq.* something extraordinary (*like nobody's business*, to an extraordinary degree). **on business** with a definite purpose, esp. one relating to one's trade or profession. **send** (a person) **about his** or **her business** send packing, dismiss. *way of business*: see WAY *n.*

Comb.: **business card**: with one's name and information about one's firm etc.; **business cycle** the trade cycle; **business end** *colloq.* the working end of a tool etc.; **business hours**: in which business is regularly transacted, during which shops or offices are open; **business lunch**: at which commercial transactions are discussed; **businessman**: engaged in trade or commerce (*the* TIRED *businessman*); **business studies** the analysis of commercial activities as an academic subject; **business suit** a lounge suit; **businesswoman**: engaged in trade or commerce.

¶Orig. trisyllabic (cf. BUSYNESS). The disyllabic pronunc. has been promoted through loss of direct assoc. w. BUSY *a.*

businesslike *a.* efficient, practical, systematic L18.

busk /bʌsk/ *n.*[1] L16. [Fr. *busc* f. It. *busco* splinter, rel. to OFr. *busche* (mod. *bûche*) log, f. Gmc.] *Hist.* A strip of wood, whalebone, steel, etc. used for stiffening the front of a corset; a corset.

busk *n.*[2] see BUSH *n.*[1]

busk /bʌsk/ *v.*[1] Now *Sc.* & *north.* ME. [ON *búask* refl. of *búa* prepare: cf. BOUND *a.*[1]] 1 *v.i.* & *refl.* Get oneself ready; get dressed. ME. 2 *v.t.* Prepare, fit out; adorn, attire. Also foll. by *up.* ME. 3 *v.i.* & *t.* Hurry, hasten; betake *oneself.* ME.

busker *n.*[1] M16.

busk /bʌsk/ *v.*[2]*i. obs.* exc. *dial.* M16. [Origin unkn.] Of a bird: move or shift about; nestle.

busk /bʌsk/ *v.*[3] M17. [Fr. †*busquer* seek, hunt for, f. It. *buscare* or Sp. *buscar*, f. Gmc.] 1 *v.i. Naut.* Cruise about, tack. Now *rare* or *obs.* M17. 2 *v.i.* Look *for*, seek *after*. *rare.* M18. 3 *v.i.* Play music, or otherwise entertain, for money in public places. Formerly also, peddle goods. Chiefly as *busking* vbl n. M19. 4 *v.t.* & *i.* Improvise. *slang.* M20.

busker *n.*[2] an itinerant musician or actor, *esp.* one performing in the street M19.

buskin /ˈbʌskɪn/ *n.* & *a.* Now *Hist.* or *arch.* E16. [Prob. f. OFr. *bousequin* var. of *brousequin* (mod. *brodequin*) prob. f. MDu. *broseken*, corresp. to Catal., Sp. *borcegui*, Prov. *borzeguim*, It. *borzacchino*, of unkn. origin.] A *n.* 1 A half-boot. E16. 2 A kind of thick-soled boot worn by tragic actors in the ancient Athenian theatre; *fig.* tragic drama, tragedy. L16.

2 BYRON He was a critic upon operas, too, And knew all niceties of the sock and buskin. **put on the buskin(s)** assume a tragic style, write tragedy. *sock and buskin*: see SOCK *n.*[1]

B *attrib.* or as *adj.* Of or pertaining to tragic drama. E17.

buskined *a.* shod with buskins; *fig.* concerned with tragedy, elevated, lofty: L16.

†**buskle** *v.i.* & *t.* M16–M17. [f. BUSK *v.*[1] + -LE[3].] = BUSK *v.*[1]

busky /ˈbʌski/ *a.* Now *arch.* & *dial.* L16. [f. BUSK *n.*[2] + -Y[1].] Full of bushes or thickets, bushy, (= BOSKY 1).

buss /bʌs/ *n.*[1] ME. [OFr. *buce*, (later) *busse*, infl. by MDu. *buisse* (mod. *buis*): ult. origin unkn.] *Hist.* 1 A ship for carrying loads. ME. 2 A two- or three-masted vessel of various sizes, used esp. in the North Sea herring-fishery. L15.

buss /bʌs/ *n.*[2] & *v.t.* & *i.* Now *arch.*, *dial.*, & *N. Amer. colloq.* L16. [Prob. alt. of BASS *n.*[3], *v.*[1]] (A) kiss.

buss *n.*[3] see BUS *n.*

bussu /bəˈsuː/ *n.* M19. [Port. f. Tupi *ubu-ussu*, f. *ubu* leaf + *ussu* big.] A palm of tidal swamps in Central and S. America, *Manicaria saccifera*, with immense leaves that are used for thatching.

bust /bʌst/ *n.*[1] M17. [(Fr. *buste* f.) It. *busto* f. L *bustum* funeral pyre, tomb, sepulchral monument.] †1 The upper part or torso of a larger sculpture. *rare.* Only in M17. 2 A piece of sculpture representing a person's head, shoulders, and chest. L17. b (Such a piece as) a sepulchral monument. *poet.* M18. 3 The upper front of the body; the bosom, esp. of a woman. E18. b The circumference of a woman's body at the level of her bust. L19.

busty *a.* (*colloq.*) (of a woman) having a prominent bust M20.

bust /bʌst/ *n.*[2] *colloq.* (orig. *US*). M18. [Var. of BURST *n.*] 1 = BURST *n.* 2. *rare.* M18. 2 A spree, a drinking-bout, (= BURST *n.* 5). M19. 3 A sudden failure or collapse of trade etc. M19. 4 A burglary. M19. 5 A worthless thing or person; *spec.* a bad hand at cards. E20. 6 A blow with the fist. E20. 7 A police raid, an arrest. M20.

2 A. POWELL He.. would celebrate with some sort of bust in the way of food and drink. 3 H. A. WALLACE We cannot afford either a speculative boom or its inevitable bust. 5 P. G. WODEHOUSE At the age of ten I was a social bust. 6 J. F. POWERS How'd you like a bust in the nose?

bust /bʌst/ *v. colloq.* (orig. *US*). Pa. t. & pple **bust, busted.** E19. [Var. of BURST *v.*] I *v.t.* 1 Burst; break; beat or smash *up.* E19. 2 Reduce to insolvency. E19. 3 Break into (a house etc.). M19. 4 Break in (a horse). L19. 5 Dismiss; demote; arrest; catch in possession of illegal drugs; jail. Usu. in *pass.* E20. 6 Strike with the fist etc. E20.

1 *bust a gut*: see GUT *n.* 2. 2 **go bust** become bankrupt.

II *v.i.* 7 Burst, explode. M19. 8 Go bankrupt. M19.

Comb.: **bust-up** an explosion (*lit.* & *fig.*); a violent severance; a quarrel.

bustard /ˈbʌstəd/ *n.* L15. [Perh. f. AN blending of OFr. *bistarde*, *oustarde*, both f. L *avis tarda* 'slow bird', the inappropriate adj. being unexpl.] 1 Any of various large swift-running birds of the family Otididae, allied to the cranes and rails. L15. 2 = BUZZARD *n.*[2] *dial.* M19.

1 RUFFED *bustard.* STANLEY *bustard.*

bustee /ˈbʌstiː/ *n.* L19. [Hind. *bastī* dwelling, settlement.] A group of huts in a shanty town or slum in the Indian subcontinent.

busteous *a.* see BOISTOUS.

buster /ˈbʌstə/ *n.* Chiefly *colloq.* M19. [Var. of BURSTER or f. BUST *v.* + -ER[1].] 1 = BURSTER 1. Chiefly as 2nd elem. of comb.: a person who or thing which breaks, beats, masters, prevents, or eliminates (the 1st elem.). M19. 2a An impressive or startling person or event; a person who or thing which provokes admiration. M19. b A mate, a fellow, a chap. Usu. as a familiar or disrespectful form of address. E20. 3 A violent gale. M19. 4 A horse-breaker. *N. Amer.* L19. 5 A heavy fall. *Austral.* & *NZ.* E20.

1 *ball-buster, chart-buster, crime-buster, dam buster*, etc. 3 *Barcoo buster.* 4 *bronco-buster.*

†**bustian** *n.* LME–E18. [Perh. alt. of OFr. *bustan(n)e* kind of fabric made at Valenciennes, after FUSTIAN.] A cotton fabric of foreign manufacture.

bustier /ˈbʌstɪeɪ, ˈbʊst-; *foreign* bystje (*pl. same*)/ *n.* L20. [Fr., f. *buste*: see BUST *n.*[1]] A close-fitting usu. strapless bodice or top worn by women.

bustious *a.* see BOISTOUS.

bustle /ˈbʌs(ə)l/ *n.*[1] E17. [f. the vb.] 1 Conflict; a struggle; a scuffle. *arch.* E17. 2 Excited activity; fuss; a state of busy haste. M17. b Movement during fermentation. *arch.* L17. 3 Money. *Criminals' slang.* Now *rare* or *obs.* M18.

bustle /ˈbʌs(ə)l/ *n.*[2] L18. [Origin unkn.] *Hist.* A pad or frame worn to puff out the top of a woman's skirt at the back.

bustle /ˈbʌs(ə)l/ *v.* LME. [Perh. var. of BUSKLE.] 1 *v.i.* Be fussily or noisily active; bestir oneself energetically; make a show of activity; hurry *about.* LME. b Of a place: be teeming *with.* L19. 2 *v.t.* Bestir, rouse, (oneself or another); hurry in a fussy manner. Also foll. by *up.* Now *rare.* M16. †3 *v.i.* Struggle, scuffle; contend. E17–E18.

bustler *n.* L17. **bustlingly** *adv.* in a bustling manner E19.

†**busto** *n.* Pl. **-o(e)s.** E17–M19. [It.: see BUST *n.*[1]] = BUST *n.*[1] 2.

bustuous *a.* see BOISTOUS.

busy /ˈbɪzi/ *n. slang.* E20. [f. the adj.] A detective; a police officer.

busy /ˈbɪzi/ *a.* [OE *bisiġ* = MLG, MDu. *besich* (Du. *bezig*), of unkn. origin.] 1 Occupied, actively engaged or employed, with attention concentrated. (Foll. by *in*, *with*, *at*, *doing*, (arch.) *about.*) OE. b Of a telephone line: engaged. L19. 2 Constantly active or in motion; unresting; habitually employed. ME. †3 Solicitous, careful. Only in ME. 4 Fussy, meddlesome; prying; officious, importunate. LME. †5 Of a thing: involving much work; elaborate; intricate. LME–E17. 6 Of an action, employment, etc.: requiring or carried on with energy; keenly pursued. M16. 7 Indicating activity or business. M17. 8 Of a time or place: full of business and stir; bustling. L17. 9 Full of detail. E20.

1 OED Don't interrupt me, I'm busy. D. H. LAWRENCE She was busy washing a garment in the bowl. J. B. PRIESTLEY Their fingers would be busy with the sewing machines or irons, but their minds could be far away. C. PRIEST The other people seemed unaware of me, busy in their own lives. 2 S. HILL Miss Cress is a busy woman, I am astonished she would waste a whole afternoon in such a way. 4 COLERIDGE A busy and inquisitorial tyranny. 6 POPE On every side the busy combat grows. 7 M. W. MONTAGU People, with.. busy faces. 8 E. HEMINGWAY The hospital was quite busy.. and that kept her occupied.

Phrases & comb.: *as busy as a bee*: see BEE *n.*[1] *busy Lizzie*: see LIZZIE 4. **busywork** work that keeps a person busy but has little value in itself.

busyness *n.* the state of being busy (cf. BUSINESS I) E19.

busy /ˈbɪzi/ *v.* [OE *bisġian*, *bysġian*, f. prec.] 1 *v.t.* Occupy (esp. oneself, one's hands etc.); keep busy. (Foll. by *with*, *in*, *at*, *about*, *doing.*) OE. †2 *v.t.* Trouble; afflict; disturb. OE–L16. 3 *v.i.* Be busy; occupy oneself; take trouble. (Foll. by *with*, *about*, etc.) Now *rare.* LME. 4 *v.t.* Occupy (time) fully. *rare.* E17.

busybody /ˈbɪzɪbɒdi/ *n.* & *v.* E16. [f. BUSY *a.* + BODY *n.*] A *n.* 1 A meddlesome, prying person; a mischief-maker. E16. 2 A mirror set at the side of a building to reflect a view of the street etc. *US.* L19. B *v.i.* Meddle; pry; interfere; behave as a busybody. M19.

busybodied *a.* (now *rare*) meddlesome, prying L18. **busybodyness** *n.* (*rare*) meddlesomeness, desire to interfere M17.

but /bʌt/ *n.* L16. [f. as next.] 1 The conjunction 'but'; a statement beginning with 'but', an objection. L16. 2 The outer room of a two-roomed house. Cf. BEN *n.*[3] *Sc.* & *north.* E18.

1 *but me no buts*: see BUT *v.* 2. **ifs and buts** uncertainties, doubtful factors, qualifications. 2 **but and ben** a two-roomed cottage, a small or humble home.

but /bʌt/ *v.* Infl. **-tt-.** M16. [f. next.] 1 *v.i.* Make a statement beginning with 'but'; raise an objection. *rare.* M16. 2 *v.t. but me no buts*, do not raise objections. E18.

but /bʌt/ *prep.*, *adv.*, *conj.*, & *rel. pron.* [OE *būtan* (*beūtan*, *būton*, *būta*) = OS *biūtan*, *būtan*, OHG *biūzan* (MHG *būzen*), f. WGmc, f. as BY *prep.* & *adv.* + OUT *adv.*] A *prep.* 1 Outside of; without, lacking. Long *obs.* exc. *Sc.* & *north.* OE. 2 Leaving out, barring, with the exception of. (No longer clearly distinguishable from the conj.: see below.) OE.

1 OED Gang but the house and see who is there.

B *adv.* (Not always distinguishable from the conj.) 1 Without, outside; *spec.* in or into the outer part of a house (orig. the kitchen of a two-roomed house, into which the only outer door opened). Cf. BEN *adv.* Long *obs.* exc. *Sc.* & *north.* OE. 2 Only, no more than. ME.

2 F. NORRIS They agreed to charge but two-fifty, and they've got to stick to it. L. LERNER Those airs But fascinate the sight; No true delight is hers. P. REDGROVE Is there but one spider in all this spacious room?

C *conj.* & *neg. rel. pron.* 1 In a simple sentence, introducing a wd, phr., or (rarely) cl.: without, with the exception of, except, save; if not, unless; *ellipt.* anything else than, other(wise) than. OE. 2 In a complex sentence, introducing a subord. cl. (also (arch.) *but that*): a Except that, if it were not that, short of the condition that. OE. b If not, unless, except; rather than..

shall prove untrue; even though the preceding were necessary. OE. c (With neg. & interrog.) That . . not; *ellipt.* not to say that . . not; without; *arch.* that, before, than. Also (colloq.) *but what.* LME. 3 In a compound sentence, connecting the two parts (the second of which may be greatly contracted), or introducing a separate but related sentence: a On the contrary. OE. b Nevertheless, yet, however; on the other hand, despite this; moreover. ME. c As an intensive, freq. after an exclamation, or introducing an emphatic repetition. M19.

1 SHAKES. *Temp.* I should sin To think but nobly of my grandmother. STEELE There needed no more but to advance one step. M. EDGEWORTH He wants nothing but a little common sense. T. JEFFERSON I cannot but be gratified by the assurance. F. D. HEMANS The boy stood on the burning deck, Whence all but he had fled. W. C. SMITH You have no choice but marry Doris now. OED Why have they come but to annoy us? WILL ROGERS I got all my feet through but one. R. LOWELL Who but my girl-friend set the town on fire? 2a SOUTHEY I too should be content to dwell in peace . . But that my country calls. H. MATTHEWS Nothing would please him but I must try on his mitres. b DEFOE I'd burn the house down but I'd find it. C. M. YONGE Ten to one but the police have got them. c ROBERT BURTON How is it possible but that we should be discontent? H. FIELDING No sooner acquainted my brother, but he immediately wanted to propose it. A. TROLLOPE Nor am I yet so old but what I can rough it still. J. RUSKIN I do not doubt but that you are surprised. OED Not but that I should have gone if I had had the chance. J. FREEMAN There's not a bird singing upon this bough But sings the sweeter in our English ears. *Proverb*: It never rains but it pours. 3a J. HEALEY Monkeyes, and Babiounes, were not men but beasts. M. HAMBURGER He must not sleep, but leans against the boards. D. ATTENBOROUGH You might be excused for thinking . . that the lamprey is a true fish. But it is not. b G. PUTTENHAM It is not only allowable, but also necessary. J. WILSON Fare ye well. But list! sweet youths . . beware. B. JOWETT They not only tell lies but bad lies. N. COWARD Had she my talent for organisation? . . No, but she hadn't your mother either. H. NEMEROV He cries a little but is brave. A. PRICE 'Did you have a brilliant idea?' . . 'Not exactly brilliant, but an idea.' c OED Excuse me! but your coat is dusty. M. CORELLI 'I believe you would do it if I asked you!' . . 'But, of course!' D. H. LAWRENCE And about *everything* I talked to her: but everything. I. FLEMING I'm goin' fix that man, but good.

Phrases: *anything but*: see ANYTHING *pron.* **but and** (*obs.* exc. *Sc.*) and also. **but for** except for, were it not for. **but one, two,** etc., if one, two, etc., were excluded from the count (with ordinals etc.). *but that, but what*: see sense C.2 above. *but then*: see THEN *adv.* etc. **but too** — only too —.

butadiene /bju:tə'dʌɪi:n/ *n.* E20. [f. next + DI-² + -ENE.] *Chem.* A gaseous unsaturated hydrocarbon, C_4H_6, of which there are two isomers; *esp.* the isomer $CH_2{:}CH{\cdot}CH{:}CH_2$ (*buta-1,3-diene*), used in making synthetic rubber.

butane /'bju:teɪn/ *n.* L19. [f. BUTYL + -ANE.] *Chem.* A gaseous alkane, C_4H_{10} (of which there are two isomers), used esp. in liquefied form as a fuel.

buta'noic *a.* = BUTYRIC M20. **butanol** *n.* each of four isomeric liquid alcohols, C_4H_9OH; butyl alcohol: L19. **butanone** *n.* a liquid ketone, $C_2H_5COCH_3$; methyl ethyl ketone: E20.

Butazolidin /bju:tə'zɒlɪdɪn/ *n.* Also **b-, -ine.** M20. [f. BUTYL + PYRAZOLE + -IDINE.] *Pharm.* (Proprietary name for) the drug phenylbutazone.

butch /bʊtʃ/ *n.*¹ *colloq.* (chiefly *N. Amer.*). E20. [Abbrev.] A butcher; *esp.* = BUTCHER *n.* 4.

news butch: see NEWS *n.*

butch /bʊtʃ/ *n.*² & *a.* *slang.* M20. [Origin uncertain.: perh. f. BUTCHER *n.*] A *n.* A tough youth or man; a mannish woman; a homosexual (esp. female) of masculine behaviour or appearance. M20.

B *adj.* Toughly masculine, mannish (freq. of homosexuals). M20.

butch haircut *N. Amer.* a crew cut.

butch /bʊtʃ/ *v.t.* & *i.* *dial.* L18. [Back-form. f. next.] Follow the trade of a butcher; cut up, hack.

butcher /'bʊtʃə/ *n.* ME. [AN var. of OFr. *bo(u)chier* (mod. *boucher*), f. OFr. *boc* he-goat (mod. *bouc*), prob. f. Celt. f. as BUCK *n.*¹: see -ER².] 1 A person whose trade is to slaughter animals for food, or simply (now the predominant sense) to sell the flesh of animals for food; a trader in meat. ME. 2 *fig.* A person responsible directly or indirectly for the slaughter of people; a person who kills needlessly or wantonly; a brutal murderer. ME. 3 A kind of artificial angling-fly. M19. 4 A seller of refreshments, newspapers, etc. in a train, theatre, etc. *N. Amer. colloq.* L19. 5 *butcher(')s*, = *butcher's hook* below. M20.

1 FAMILY *butcher*. 4 *news butcher*: see NEWS *n.*

Phrases & comb.: **butcher-bird** a shrike of the family Laniidae or (*Austral.*) Cracticidae. **butcher blue** a dark blue like that often used for butchers' aprons. **butcher-boots** high boots without tops. **butcher's bill** *colloq.* the list of casualties in a battle. **butcher's broom** a low evergreen shrub of the chiefly Mediterranean genus *Ruscus*, of the lily family; esp. *R. aculeatus*, which has stiff flat spine-tipped leaflike shoots. **butcher's hook** *n.* & *a.* (*rhyming slang*) (*a*) *n.* a look; (*b*) *adj.* (*Austral.* & *NZ*) [f. CROOK *a.* 3] angry. **butcher's knife** a meat-knife; any large strong-bladed knife. **butcher-meat, butcher's meat**: excluding poultry, fish, game, and cured meats. **the butcher, the baker, the candlestick-maker** people of all trades.

butcherly *a.* like a butcher; brutal: E16.

butcher /'bʊtʃə/ *v.* M16. [f. the n.] 1 *v.t.* Slaughter in the manner of a butcher; kill needlessly, wantonly, or brutally. M16. b *fig.* Ruin by clumsiness or ineptitude. M17. 2 *v.t.* & *i.* Cut up and divide (meat) as a butcher does; carry on the trade of a butcher. L18.

butcherer *n.* M17.

butchery /'bʊtʃəri/ *n.* ME. [(O)Fr. *boucherie* f. as BUTCHER *n.* + -Y³.] 1 A butcher's establishment (usu. public), a slaughterhouse, a meat-market. ME. 2 The trade of a butcher. Now usu. *attrib.* LME. 3 Cruel or wanton slaughter, carnage. M16.

butea /'bju:tɪə/ *n.* L18. [mod.L, f. John Stuart, Earl of *Bute* (1713–92): see -A¹.] A leguminous tree or climbing plant of the genus *Butea*, native to tropical Asia; *esp.* the dhak tree, *B. monosperma*.

butene /'bju:ti:n/ *n.* L19. [f. BUTYL + -ENE.] *Chem.* A gaseous alkene, C_4H_8, of which there are three isomers. Also called *butylene*.

butenyl *n.* a radical, $C_4H_7{\cdot}$, derived from any of these isomers L19.

buteonine /bjʊ'ti:ənʌɪn/ *a.* M19. [f. L *buteo(n-)* hawk, buzzard + -INE¹: see BUZZARD *n.*¹] Of the nature of or resembling a buzzard.

†**butine** *n.* var. of BUTYNE.

butler /'bʌtlə/ *n.* & *v.* ME. [AN *buteler*, (O)Fr. *bouteillier* cup-bearer, f. *bouteille* BOTTLE *n.*¹: see -ER².] A *n.* 1 A servant who has charge of a household's or other establishment's wine cellar and plate etc.; a principal manservant. ME. 2 *Hist.* An officer of high rank (nominally) in charge of wine for the royal table. ME. B *v.t.* & *i.* Act as a butler (to); deal with as a butler. M18.

butlerage *n.* (*a*) *Hist.* a duty on imported wine payable to the king's butler; (*b*) the office of butler, a butler's department: L15. **butleress** *n.* (*rare*) a female butler E17. **butlership** *n.* the office of butler M16. **butlery** *n.* a butler's room or pantry; a buttery: ME.

butment /'bʌtm(ə)nt/ *n.* E17. [f. BUTT *v.*² + -MENT.] An abutment; an abutting piece of ground etc.

butobarbitone /bju:təʊ'bɑ:bɪtəʊn/ *n.* M20. [f. BUT(YL + -O- + BARBIT(URIC + -ONE.] *Pharm.* A sedative and hypnotic drug, 5-butyl-5-ethylbarbituric acid, $C_{10}H_{16}N_2O_3$.

¶A proprietary name for this drug is SONERYL.

butoxide /bju:'tɒksʌɪd/ *n.* M20. [f. BUTYL + OXIDE.] *Chem.* A compound of the radical $C_4H_9O{\cdot}$.

butsecarl *n.* var. of BUSCARL.

Butskellism /'bʌtskəlɪz(ə)m/ *n.* M20. [Blend of R. A. *Butler* (Conservative Chancellor of the Exchequer 1951–5) and H. T. N. *Gaitskell* (Labour Chancellor of the Exchequer 1950–1 and subsequently Shadow Chancellor) + -ISM.] *Brit. Polit.* The adoption of economic policies broadly acceptable to both main political parties.

Butskellite *a.* & *n.* (an adherent) of Butskellism M20.

butt /bʌt/ *n.*¹ Long *dial.* ME. [MLG *but*, MDu. *but(te)*, *bot(te)*, prob. rel. to LG *but*, MDu. *bot* stumpy: cf. BUTT *n.*⁴] A flatfish, *esp.* a sole, plaice, or turbot. Cf. HALIBUT.

butt /bʌt/ *n.*² ME. [(O)Fr. *but*, of unkn. origin: perh. infl. by Fr. *butte* rising ground, knoll, (also) target (cf. BUTT *n.*¹⁰).] 1 A mound upon which a target is set up for archery or shooting practice; a target; in *pl.*, a range for target practice. ME. b The length of a shooting-range. Now *rare* or *obs.* M16. c A concealed stand for grouse-shooting, screened by a low wall of turf or stone. L19. 2 A terminal point, a boundary mark. Now *dial.* & *N. Amer.* LME. 3 A thing towards which one's efforts are directed; an end, an aim, a goal. L16. 4 An object of (or *of*) teasing, ridicule, abuse, etc. E17.

3 SHAKES. *Hen. V* To which is fixed as an aim or butt Obedience. 4 P. MORTIMER Poor man, the butt of everyone's anger. K. M. E. MURRAY He was the butt of the bigger boys because of his inability to pronounce 'ch'. P. F. BOLLER As Truman's popularity . . dropped . . he became the butt of bad jokes and nasty quips.

butt /bʌt/ *n.*³ LME. [AN *but*, OFr. *bot*, *bout* (mod. *botte*), f. late L *buttis*. In AL *butta*, *bota*.] A cask or barrel, esp. for wine or ale; this as a former measure of capacity, usu. equal to two hogsheads.

SIR T. MORE Hastely drouned in a Butte of Malmesey. J. MASEFIELD Only the water . . gurgled through the rain-pipe to the butt. SCUTTLEBUTT. SCUTTLED *butt*.

butt /bʌt/ *n.*⁴ LME. [App. rel. to (M)Du. *bot* stumpy (cf. BUTT *n.*¹) and to base of BUTTOCK (cf. BUTT *n.*⁵).] 1 The thicker end of anything, esp. of a tool or weapon, or of the handle of a gun, fishing-rod, etc. LME. 2 The end of a plank (in a ship's side) which meets a similar plank end-on. LME. 3 The buttocks. *dial.* & *N. Amer.* LME. 4 (Leather made from) the thicker or hinder end of a hide. M16. 5 The trunk of a tree, *esp.* the part just above the ground. E17. b The foot of a branch or leaf-stalk. L17. 6 The stub of a cigarette or cigar. M19.

Comb.: **butt-end** a butt (chiefly senses 2 and 6 above); **butt-head** = sense 2 above; **butt joint, weld**: in which pieces are joined end-to-end.

butt /bʌt/ *n.*⁵ LME. [Prob. f. base of BUTTOCK; rel. to LG *butt*, MDu. *botte*, MHG *butze*, ON *butr*, OE *bytt* small piece of land. Perh. already in OE (cf. AL *butta*, *buttes*).] A ridge of ploughed land, esp. a short one at the edge of a field; *sing.* & (usu.) in *pl.*, a small piece of land.

butt /bʌt/ *n.*⁶ LME. [Fr. *botte* f. MLG *bōte*: cf. BOTTLE *n.*²] A bundle (of cloth etc.); *dial.* a hassock.

butt /bʌt/ *n.*⁷ *dial.* M16. [Origin unkn.] A basket used for catching fish.

butt /bʌt/ *n.*⁸ L16. [Perh. f. BUTT *v.*¹] A promontory, a headland. *obs.* exc. in proper names, as *Butt of Lewis*.

butt /bʌt/ *n.*⁹ M17. [f. BUTT *v.*¹] A push or thrust with the head or horns.

full butt with violent collision, head-on, full tilt.

butt /bʌt/ *n.*¹⁰ *obs.* exc. *dial.* L17. [(O)Fr. BUTTE.] A hillock, a mound.

butt /bʌt/ *v.*¹ ME. [AN *buter*, OFr. *bo(u)ter* f. Gmc (repr. by MDu. *botten* strike, sprout).] 1 *v.t.* & *i.* Strike, thrust, shove, usu. with the head or horns; thrust (the head) forward thus; drive or push thus. ME. 2 *v.i.* Project, jut (*out*). LME.

1 J. DORAN A couple of rams butting at each other. J. B. MORTON The ridiculous speed with which big boats butt through the waves. A. HIGGINS A heifer was butting its skull against the bars of a gate. P. ROTH With a sharp upward snap of the skull, she butted me on the underside of the jaw. P. THEROUX Most people merely put their heads down and butted their way into the next car. **butt in** intrude; intervene, meddle. **butt out** *slang* stop intruding, intervening, or meddling. 2 T. CORYAT A little square gallery butting out from the Tower.

butt /bʌt/ *v.*² ME. [Partly f. BUTT *n.*²; partly aphet. f. ABUT.] 1 *v.i.* & *t.* (Cause to) touch with an end, abut, or adjoin; *spec.* lie or place with one end flat *against*, *on*, etc., meet or join end to end. ME. 2 *v.t.* Fix or mark (*out*) the limits of lengthwise; terminate, limit, bound. Usu. in *pass.* Now *rare* or *obs.* E16.

butte /bjuːt/ *n.* M19. [Fr.: see BUTT *n.*^{2}] *Physical Geogr.* & *N. Amer.* An isolated hill with steep sides and a flat top, similar to but narrower than a mesa.

butter /ˈbʌtə/ *n.*^{1} [OE *butere*, corresp. to OFris., OHG *butera* (Du. *boter*, G *Butter*), f. WGmc f. L *butyrum* f. Gk *bouturon*.] 1 The fatty substance obtained from cream by churning, used to spread on bread etc., and in cookery. OE. b *fig.* Unctuous flattery. *colloq.* E19. 2 *transf.* Any substance resembling butter in appearance or consistency. LME. b *Chem.* The anhydrous chloride *of* antimony, arsenic, etc. *arch.* M17.

1 *black butter*: see BLACK *a.* **brandy**, **rum**, etc., **butter** a hard sauce containing brandy, rum, etc., and butter. *bread and butter*: see BREAD *n.*^{1} **look as if butter would not melt in one's mouth** seem demure. **melted butter** (*a*) butter that has been melted; (*b*) a sauce of butter, flour, etc. 2 **butter of almonds** a preparation of cream, whites of eggs, and blanched almonds. *cocoa butter*: see COCOA *n.*^{1} PEANUT *butter*. SHEA *butter*. **vegetable butter** any edible fatty substance similar to butter, obtained from plants.

Comb.: **butter-and-egg man** *US slang* a wealthy but unsophisticated man who spends money freely; **butter-and-eggs** a plant whose flower has two shades of yellow, esp. toadflax; **butterball** (*a*) a piece of butter moulded into a ball; (*b*) *N. Amer.* [because very fat in autumn] = *bufflehead* (b) s.v. BUFFLE; **butter-bean** (*a*) a variety of French bean with yellow pods; (*b*) a dried white Lima bean; **butter-box** (*a*) a box for holding butter; a vessel or vehicle resembling this; (*b*) *derog.* a Dutchman; a Dutch ship; (*c*) *US* = *butterball* (b) above; **butterbur** a streamside plant of the composite family, *Petasites hybridus*, bearing spikes of pale purple flowers and with large soft leaves formerly used for wrapping butter; also (w. specifying wd), any of several related plants; **butter-bush** *Austral.* a small tree, *Pittosporum phylliraeoides*, of which the wood is used for turnery and the leaves for fodder; **butter cloth** a thin loosely woven cloth with a fine mesh, orig. used primarily as a wrapping for butter; **butter-cooler** a vessel for keeping butter cool when on the table; **butter-cream** a mixture of butter, sugar, etc., as a filling or a topping for a cake; **butterfat** the essential fats of pure butter; **butter-fingered** *a.* apt to let things fall or slip; **butter-fingers** a butter-fingered person; *esp.* one who fails to hold a catch; **butterfish** any of various slippery mucus-coated fishes, *esp.* the gunnel, or (*N. Amer.*) an edible marine fish of the family Stromateidae; **butter-knife** a blunt knife for cutting butter at table; **buttermilk** the acidulous milk which remains after the butter has been churned out; **butter muslin** = *butter cloth* above; **butter-nut** (*a*) any of certain trees or bushes yielding oily nuts; *esp.* the N. American white walnut, *Juglans cinerea*; also, its timber or fruit; (*b*) *N. Amer.* a brownish-grey colour (usu. *attrib.*); **butter-pat** (*a*) a pat of butter; (*b*) a wooden implement for working butter into shape; **butter-print** a stamp for marking butter-pats; an impression from this; **butterscotch** a kind of toffee made chiefly with butter and sugar; **butter-tree** an African or Indian tree yielding vegetable butter, *esp.* the shea; †**butter-weight** 18 or more ounces to the pound; good measure; **butterwort** any of various insectivorous plants of peat bogs, of the genus *Pinguicula* of the bladderwort family, with purple flowers and yellowish-green greasy leaves.

butterless *a.* M19.

†**butter** *n.*^{2} L15–E17. [(O)Fr. *boutoir*, f. *bo(u)ter* BUTT *v.*^{1}] = BUTTERIS.

butter /ˈbʌtə/ *n.*^{3} E17. [f. BUTT *v.*^{1} + -ER^{1}.] An animal that butts.

butter /ˈbʌtə/ *v.t.* LME. [f. BUTTER *n.*^{1}] 1 Spread with butter; cook or dish up with butter. LME. 2 *fig.* Flatter lavishly. Now usu. foll. by *up*. E18.

1 *Proverb*: Fine words butter no parsnips. *have* etc. *one's bread buttered on both sides* and similar phrs.: see BREAD *n.*^{1} 2 M. MITCHELL Buttering them up with smiles and kind words was the surest way to get their business for her mill.

butter-bump /ˈbʌtəbʌmp/ *n. dial.* L17. [f. var. of BITTERN *n.*^{1} + BUMP *v.*^{2}] The bittern.

buttercup /ˈbʌtəkʌp/ *n.* In sense 2 orig. †**-cups**. E16. [f. BUTTER *n.*^{1} + CUP *n.*] †1 A cup for holding butter. E–M16. 2 Any of various plants of the genus *Ranunculus* (family Ranunculaceae), bearing bright yellow cup-shaped flowers; a flowering stem of such a plant. L18.

2 *creeping buttercup*, *meadow buttercup*, *turban buttercup*, etc.

Phrases: *Bermuda buttercup*: see BERMUDA 3.

buttercupped, **-cuppy** *adjs.* having many buttercups, covered with buttercups L19.

butterfly /ˈbʌtəflʌɪ/ *n.* OE. [f. BUTTER *n.*^{1} + FLY *n.*^{1}, perh. w. ref. to the yellow or creamy-white colour of familiar species such as the brimstone.] 1 Any of a large group of insects which together with moths constitute the order Lepidoptera and are distinguished from moths (in most instances) by diurnal activity, clubbed or dilated antennae, thin bodies, the usu. erect position of the wings when at rest, and brighter colouring. OE. 2 *fig.* a A showy or frivolous person. L16. b A person whose period of work or occupation of a place is transitory or seasonal. L19. 3 Usu. in *pl.* Fluttering sensations felt before any formidable venture. Esp. in *butterflies in the stomach* etc. E20. 4 In full *butterfly stroke*. A swimming stroke in which both arms are lifted out of the water at the same time. M20.

1 **break a butterfly on a wheel** use unnecessary force in destroying something fragile. *brimstone butterfly*, *comma butterfly*, *monarch butterfly*, *peacock butterfly*, *tortoiseshell butterfly*, etc. 2a *social butterfly*: see SOCIAL *a.* 3 *Sunday Times* I always have butterflies when I open Parliament.

Comb.: **butterfly blenny** a blenny, *Blennius ocellaris*, having a broad, ocellated dorsal fin; **butterfly bow** a bow made up or tied with the loop and end on each side spread apart like the expanded wings of a butterfly; **butterfly bush** a buddleia, *esp.* the species *Buddleja davidii*; **butterfly-fish** any of various fishes suggesting a butterfly in shape or coloration, esp. (*a*) = *butterfly blenny* above; (*b*) = CHAETODON; **butterfly flower** (*a*) a papilionaceous flower; (*b*) = SCHIZANTHUS; **butterfly kiss** a fluttering of the eyelashes against the cheek; **butterfly net**: for catching butterflies; **butterfly nose** a dog's nose when spotted or mottled; **butterfly nut** a wing-nut; **butterfly orchid** any of various orchids with flowers resembling a butterfly in shape; *esp.* either of two widely distributed European orchids, *Platanthera chlorantha* and *P. bifolia*, with whitish or greenish-white flowers; **butterfly pea** a S. American leguminous plant (esp. of the genus *Clitoria*), with papilionaceous flowers; *butterfly stroke*: see sense 4 above; **butterfly valve** a valve with hinged semicircular plates; **butterfly weed** *N. Amer.* a milkweed, esp. the orange-flowered *Asclepias tuberosa*.

butteris /ˈbʌt(ə)rɪs/ *n.* L16. [Unexpl. alt. of BUTTER *n.*^{2}] A farrier's tool for paring a horse's hoof.

buttery /ˈbʌt(ə)ri/ *n.* ME. [AN *boterie*, perh. f. *but* BUTT *n.*^{3} or rel. to OFr. *botelerie* BUTLERY: see -ERY.] A place where provisions (orig. liquor) are kept and supplied, *esp.* one in a college or other establishment.

Comb.: **buttery-bar** a board or ledge on a buttery-hatch, on which to rest tankards etc.; **buttery-book**: in which are kept college members' accounts with the buttery; **buttery-hatch** a half-door over which provisions from a buttery are served.

buttery /ˈbʌt(ə)ri/ *a.* LME. [f. BUTTER *n.*^{1} + -Y^{1}.] 1 Of the nature of or containing butter; smeared with butter. LME. 2 Like butter in consistency. LME.

butteriness *n.* E16.

buttinsky /bʌˈtɪnski/ *n. slang* (orig. *US*). E20. [f. *butt in* (see BUTT *v.*^{1}) + *-sky* final elem. in many Slavonic names.] A person who (habitually) butts in; an intruder, a meddler.

buttle /ˈbʌt(ə)l/ *v.t.* & *i. joc.* M19. [Back-form. f. BUTLER.] Serve out (drink); do a butler's work.

buttock /ˈbʌtək/ *n.* & *v.* [OE *buttuc*: see BUTT *n.*^{5}, -OCK.] A *n.* †1 = BUTT *n.*^{5} Only in OE. 2 Either of the two fleshy protuberances on the lower rear part of the human body; a corresponding part of an animal. Usu. in *pl.* ME. 3 *Naut.* The breadth of a ship where the hull rounds down to the stern. E17. 4 *Wrestling.* A throw using the buttocks or hip. L17. 5 *Coalmining.* A break in the line of a face, from which coal is being broken out. L19.

2 T. HARDY Sheep . . stood with their buttocks to the winds. M. BRADBURY Plastic chairs, their seats moulded to the shape of some average universal buttock.

B *v.t.* †1 Overtake (a horse) in a race. Only in E17. 2 *Wrestling.* Throw by a manoeuvre using the buttocks or hip. L19.

buttocked *a.* having buttocks (of a specified kind) LME.

button /ˈbʌt(ə)n/ *n.* ME. [(O)Fr. *bouton* f. Proto-Romance f. Gmc (rel. to BUTT *v.*^{1}).] 1 A small knob, stud, or disc attached to any object; *esp.* one sewn to a garment to fasten it by passing through an opening (a buttonhole), or for ornament, or attached as a badge. ME. b A button as a type of anything of little value. ME. c In *pl.* (treated as *sing.*). (A name for) a boy servant in livery, a page. *colloq.* M19. 2 A bud, or other similarly shaped part of a plant; *esp.* = *button mushroom* below. ME. b In names of plants: having button-like flowers, seed-vessels, etc. Usu. in *pl.* M16. 3 A small rounded lesion, esp. of leishmaniasis. L16. 4 Any small rounded body, as a knob fixed on the point of a fencing foil (to make it harmless), a globule of metal remaining in a crucible after fusion, etc. E17. b The point of the chin. *US slang.* E20. 5 A knob etc. which is pressed or turned to fasten a door, operate a mechanism, complete an electric circuit, etc. E17.

1 F. RAPHAEL His privilege was to wear the top two buttons of his jacket undone. b J. CLAVELL Cheap . . they hardly cost a button a week. 4 *belly button*: see BELLY *n.* 5 A. MACLEAN Schaffer pressed the 'start' button and a generator whined into life.

Phrases: **a button short** *colloq.* of low intelligence, not very bright. *bachelor's button(s)*: see BACHELOR. *olive button*: see OLIVE *n.*^{1} & *a.* **on the button** (chiefly *N. Amer.*) on the point of the chin; exactly on the target; precise(ly), on the dot. *pink button*: see PINK *a.*^{2} **press the button** *fig.* initiate an action or train of events, esp. nuclear war. **take by the button** = BUTTONHOLE *v.* 2.

Comb.: **buttonball** = *button-wood* (a) below; **button-boy** a page; **button-bush** *N. Amer.* a shrub of the madder family, *Cephalanthus occidentalis*, with globular flower-heads; **button chrysanthemum** *US* a variety of chrysanthemum with many small round flower-heads; **button day** *Austral.* a day on which money is raised for a cause by the sale of badges which are worn as evidence of support; **button ear** a dog's ear which laps over and hides the inside; **button-grass** *Austral.* any of various sedges and grasses with rounded or compact inflorescences; †**button-hold** *v.t.* [back-form. f. *button-holder*] = BUTTONHOLE *v.* 2; **button-holder** †(*a*) a person who buttonholes another; (*b*) a case for holding buttons; **buttonhook** (*a*) a hook for drawing small buttons into place; (*b*) *Amer. Football* a type of pass for the receiver running straight downfield and then doubling back a few steps to receive it; **button-mould** a disc of wood etc. to be covered with cloth to form a button; **button mushroom** a young unopened mushroom; **button-nosed** *a.* having a small roundish nose; **button-quail** a bird of the family Turnicidae, resembling a quail but related to the crakes and rails; **button-stick** an appliance used to protect the cloth around a button during polishing; **button-tree** a tropical tree or shrub of the genus *Conocarpus*, found in mangrove swamps; **button-wood** (*a*) the N. American plane, *Platanus occidentalis*; (*b*) its timber; (*c*) = *button-tree* above.

buttonless *a.* M17. **button-like** *a.* resembling a button, small and round M19. **buttony** *a.* L16.

button /ˈbʌt(ə)n/ *v.* LME. [f. the n.] I Corresp. to BUTTON *n.* I. 1 *v.t.* Provide or adorn with a button or buttons. LME. 2 *v.t.* Fasten or secure with buttons; fasten the clothing of (a person, esp. oneself) with buttons. Freq. foll. by *up*. LME. b *v.t. fig.* Close (*up*) tightly, fasten, confine. L16. c *v.i.* Fasten one's buttons *up*. M19. 3 *v.i.* Of a garment: be (able to be) fastened (*up*) with buttons. L18.

2 R. L. STEVENSON I buttoned myself into my coat. b CARLYLE Thoughts—which he must button close up. **button one's lip**, **face** *slang* be silent, stop talking.

II Corresp. to BUTTON *n.* 2. 4 *v.i.* Of (a part of) a plant: bud; assume a globular shape. LME.

Comb.: **button-down** *a.* (orig. *US*) (of a collar) having the points buttoned to the shirt; **button-through** *a.* (of a dress etc.) fastening by buttons over its whole length; **button-up** *a.* that buttons up.

¶Earlier in UNBUTTON.

buttoning *n.* (*a*) the action of the vb; †(*b*) a fastening, a button: L16.

buttoned /ˈbʌt(ə)nd/ *a.* M16. [f. BUTTON *n.*, *v.*: see -ED[2], -ED[1].] 1 Having buttons (of specified kind or number); adorned with buttons. M16. 2 Fastened with buttons; with one's clothes fastened with buttons. E19.

2 **buttoned up** *fig.* (*a*) (of a person) reserved, uncommunicative; (*b*) *slang* (of a plan etc.) successfully arranged.

buttonhole /ˈbʌt(ə)nhəʊl/ *n.* & *v.* M16. [f. BUTTON *n.* + HOLE *n.*[1] In sense B.2 app. alt. of †*button-hold* s.v. BUTTON *n.*] A *n.* 1 An opening made in a garment in order to receive a button for fastening; a similar opening made for ornamentation in the lapel of a coat etc. M16. 2 *transf.* A slit or other opening resembling a buttonhole. L16. 3 A flower or bouquet worn in a lapel buttonhole. L19.

1 **take a buttonhole lower, take down a buttonhole** humiliate.

Comb.: **buttonhole stitch** a looped stitch used for edging buttonholes.

B *v.* 1 *v.i.* Sew buttonholes. E19. b *v.t.* Make buttonhole openings in; sew with buttonhole stitch. E20. 2 *v.t.* Take hold of (as) by a coat or waistcoat button; detain (a listener) willy-nilly. M19.

2 J. GALSWORTHY It was his salutary custom to buttonhole a director afterwards, and ask him whether he thought the coming year would be good or bad.

buttonholer *n.* (*a*) a person who makes buttonholes; (*b*) an appliance for making buttonholes; (*c*) a person who buttonholes another: L19.

buttress /ˈbʌtrɪs/ *n.* & *v.* ME. [OFr. (*ars*) *bo*(*u*)*terez* thrusting arch, f. *bo*(*u*)*ter* BUTT *v.*[1]] A *n.* 1 A structure of wood, stone, or brick built against a wall to strengthen or support it. ME. 2 *loosely.* A prop, a pier, an abutment. LME. 3 A similarly projecting portion of a hill or mountain. L17.

1 H. ADAMS At this corner the architect had to provide a heavy buttress against a double strain. *fig.*: T. FULLER His title . . had strong buttresses. *flying buttress*: see FLYING *ppl a.* 2 W. H. PRESCOTT An aqueduct . . carried . . on huge buttresses of masonry. 3 P. MATTHIESSEN A series of ridges that terminate in buttresses . . where the mountain falls away into Black River.

Comb.: **buttress-root** a tree-root whose upper parts project from the trunk like a buttress.

B *v.t.* Provide, sustain, or strengthen with a buttress (freq. *fig.*). Occas. foll. by *up*. LME.

E. LINKLATER Their tenuous blood-relationship was buttressed firmly by friendship. L. VAN DER POST Traps . . woven out of reeds and buttressed with young karee wood.

butty /ˈbʌti/ *n.*[1] *dial.* L18. [Prob. f. *play* BOOTY.] 1 A confederate; a mate. L18. 2 *Mining.* A middleman who contracts to raise coal or ore. *obs.* exc. *Hist.* M19. 3 In full *butty-boat*. A second barge or freight-boat in tow by a first. E20.

Comb.: **butty-gang** a gang of men jointly undertaking a large job and sharing the profits equally.

butty /ˈbʌti/ *n.*[2] *north.* M19. [f. BUTTER *n.*[1] + -Y[6].] A slice of bread and butter; a sandwich.

butut /ˈbuːtuːt/ *n.* Pl. **-s**, same. L20. [W. Afr.] A monetary unit of Gambia, equal to one-hundredth of a dalasi.

butyl /ˈbjuːtʌɪl, -tɪl/ *n.* M19. [f. BUTYRIC + -YL.] *Chem.* 1 A radical, C_4H_9·, derived from a butane. Usu. in *comb.* Also called *tetryl.* M19. 2 In full *butyl rubber*. Synthetic rubber made by polymerizing isobutylene (2-methylpropene). M20.

butylate *v.t.* introduce a butyl substituent into (a compound) M20. **butylene** *n.* = BUTENE M19.

butyne /ˈbjuːtʌɪn/ *n.* Orig. †**-ine**. L19. [f. prec. + -YNE.] *Chem.* A gaseous alkyne, C_4H_6, of which there are two isomers.

butyraceous /bjuːtɪˈreɪʃəs/ *a.* M17. [f. as next + -ACEOUS.] 1 Of the nature of butter; buttery. M17. 2 Producing or containing butter. M19.

butyrate /ˈbjuːtɪreɪt/ *n.* M19. [f. next + -ATE[1].] *Chem.* A salt or ester of butyric acid.

butyric /bjuːˈtɪrɪk/ *a.* E19. [f. L *butyrum* BUTTER *n.*[1] + -IC.] Of or pertaining to butter (*rare* in *gen.* sense); *butyric acid* (Chem.), a syrupy fatty acid, C_3H_7COOH, present in rancid butter (also called *butanoic acid*).

butyrometer /bjuːtɪˈrɒmɪtə/ *n.* L19. [f. as prec. + -OMETER.] A refractometer used for measuring the amount of butter-fat in milk.

butyrophenone /ˌbjuːtɪrəʊfɪˈnəʊn, -ˈfɛnəʊn/ *n.* E20. [f. as BUTYRIC + -PHENONE.] *Chem.* & *Pharm.* A liquid ketone, $C_6H_5{\cdot}CO{\cdot}(CH_2)_2CH_3$, *n*-propyl phenyl ketone. Also, any of a class of piperidine derivatives of this used as antipsychotic drugs.

butyrous /ˈbjuːtɪrəs/ *a.* Now *rare* or *obs.* M17. [f. as BUTYRIC + -OUS.] = BUTYRACEOUS.

buvette /bjuːˈvɛt, *foreign* byvɛt (*pl. same*)/ *n.* M18. [Fr.] A tavern; a small inn; a refreshment bar or room.

buxarry /ˈbʌksəri/ *n. obs.* exc. *Hist.* M18. [Hind. *baksārī* native of *Baksar* (Buxar), a town in Bihar, India.] In the Indian subcontinent: a soldier with a matchlock.

buxom /ˈbʌksəm/ *a.* ME. [f. stem of OE (*ġe*)*būgan* bend, BOW *v.*[1] + -SOME[1].] †1 Compliant (*to*); meek; gracious, obliging, kindly; easily moved, prone (*to do*). ME–M19. †2 Physically pliable, flexible, unresisting. L16–L17. 3 Blithe, bright, lively, gay. *arch.* L16. 4 Chiefly of a woman: full of health, vigour, and good temper; plump and comely. L16.

2 MILTON Wing silently the buxom air. 3 R. HEBER Freedom's buxom blast. 4 CONAN DOYLE An elderly, motherly woman of the buxom landlady type. *Economist* Her jolly, kindly personality and her buxom charm.

buxomness *n.* ME.

buy /bʌɪ/ *n.* Orig. *US.* L19. [f. the vb.] A purchase; a thing bought or considered for buying.

best buy: that giving the best value for money. **good buy** a favourable bargain, a thing cheaply bought.

buy /bʌɪ/ *v.* Pa. t. **bought** /bɔːt/; pa. pple **bought**, (*dial.*) **boughten** /ˈbɔːt(ə)n/. [OE *byċġan* = OS *buggian*, ON *byggja* let out, lend, Goth. *bugjan*, f. Gmc.] I *v.t.* 1 Get possession of by giving an equivalent, usu. in money; obtain by paying a price; purchase. Also w. indirect obj., obtain for (oneself, another) thus. OE. b Of things: be an equivalent price for; be the means of procuring, be the payment for. L16. 2 *fig.* Obtain in exchange for something else, or by making some sacrifice; *arch.* redeem, ransom. ME. †3 = ABY *v.* 2. ME–E17. 4 Win over, hire, engage. Usu. in a bad sense: win the favour of by money, influence, etc., bribe. M17. 5 Suffer (some mishap); *esp.* (w. *it*) be wounded, killed, or destroyed. *slang.* E19. 6 Believe; accept; approve. *slang.* E20.

1 SHAKES. *2 Hen. IV* He's gone into Smithfield to buy your worship a horse. J. STEINBECK Water grew scarce, water was to be bought, five cents, ten cents, fifteen cents a gallon. **bought and sold** *fig.* (*arch.*) betrayed for a bribe. **bought deal**: in which a securities firm buys a complete issue of shares and then resells them at a prearranged price. *buy a pig in a poke*: see PIG *n.*[1] *buy a pup*: see PUP *n. buy* GAPE-SEED. **buy money** *slang* bet heavily on a favourite at short odds. *buy the rabbit*: see RABBIT *n.* 2 MILTON Oh dearly bought revenge, yet glorious! *Times* The preservation of Jordan last month has bought time. I. WATTS God the Son . . who bought us with his blood. C. V. WEDGWOOD He had been expected . . to buy his life by incriminating the King. 3 G. CHAPMAN Not long . . Before thou buy this curious skill with tears. 4 DRYDEN Nor is [he] with Pray'rs, or Bribes, or Flatt'ry bought. 5 R. LEHMANN The whole street . . had bought it in the blitz. 6 I. WALLACE Part of a conspiracy to overthrow the government—I don't think anyone will buy that. **I'll buy it** I do not know the answer to your question.

II *v.i.* 7 Make a purchase or purchases. OE.

7 R. P. JHABVALA People are buying from the hawkers. *bring-and-buy sale, stall*, etc.: see BRING *v.* I. **buy into** purchase a commission in; obtain a share in by payment; subscribe to (an idea, proposal, etc.).

With advs. in specialized senses: **buy in** (*a*) *v.phr.t.* & *i.* collect a stock of (commodities) by purchase; (*b*) *v.phr.t.* buy back for the owner, e.g. at an auction when the bids are too low; (*c*) *v.phr.t.* & *i.* obtain (entry, a share, etc.) by purchase; purchase (a commission etc.). **buy off** pay to get rid of; induce (a person) to forgo a claim, opposition, etc., by a payment of money. **buy out** (*a*) pay (a person) to give up property, a share, a post, etc.; (*b*) obtain release for (oneself) by payment; (*c*) get rid of (liability) by payment; †(*d*) ransom, redeem. **buy over** win over by a payment, bribe. **buy up** purchase (a stock or the whole of any commodity) with a view to controlling the supply; buy as much as possible of; absorb (a firm etc.) by purchase.

Comb.: **buy-back** buying a thing after having sold it; **buy-in** (*a*) *US Stock Exch.* a procedure whereby a broker buys replacement stock for stock not received as contracted, losses being chargeable to the party failing to deliver; (*b*) a buying back of a company's own shares; **buyout** the purchase of the controlling share in a company.

buyable *a.* L15.

buyer /ˈbʌɪə/ *n.* ME. [f. prec. + -ER[1].] 1 A person who buys. ME. 2 *spec.* An agent who selects and buys stock for a large shop etc. L19.

1 **buyer's** or **buyers' market** conditions in which goods are plentiful and cheap. FIRST-*time buyer. special buyer*: see SPECIAL *a.*

†**buz** *n.*, *v.* vars. of BUZZ *n.*[1], *v.*[1]

buzz /bʌz/ *n.*[1] Also †**buz.** E17. [f. BUZZ *v.*[1]] 1 A sibilant hum, as that of bees, flies, and other insects. E17. b The buzzing sound made by a telephone, electric bell, etc.; *slang* a telephone call. E20. 2 A confused sound made by many people talking or busily occupied; a stir, a ferment; general movement. E17. †3 A groundless fancy; a whim. E–M17. 4 A busy rumour, news. L18. 5 A feeling of excitement or euphoria, *esp.* one induced by narcotic drugs. *slang.* M20.

2 ADDISON I found the whole . . Room in a Buz of Politicks. C. MACKENZIE There was a buzz of agreement.

Comb.: **buzz-bomb** *colloq.* a flying bomb esp. in the war of 1939–45; **buzz-saw** (orig. *US*) a circular saw; **buzz-word** a catchword, a slogan, a pretentious word of little exact meaning.

buzzy *a.*[1] making a buzz; full of buzzing: L19.

buzz /bʌz/ *n.*[2] E17. [Perh. imit.: cf. FUZZ *n.*[1]] 1 A bur. E17. 2 A chafer or similar beetle used as bait; an imitation of this. M18.

Comb.: **buzzwig** [perh. rel. to BUSBY] a large bushy wig; a person wearing such a wig, a bigwig.

buzzy *a.*[2] hairy, fuzzy M19.

buzz /bʌz/ *v.*[1] Also †**buz** (infl. **-zz-**). LME. [Imit.] 1 *v.i.* Make a humming sibilant sound like that of bees etc.; fly *in*, *out*, etc., with such a sound. LME. b *fig.* Flutter or hover (*about*, *over*, etc.) like a buzzing insect; move about busily. M17. c Go (quickly). Chiefly in *buzz off. slang.* E20. 2 *v.i.* a Mutter; murmur busily. Usu. *derog. arch.* M16. b Make the hum produced by many people talking; be filled with (or *with*) activity. M19. 3 *v.t.* Tell in a low murmur; whisper busily. *arch.* L16. 4 *v.t.* Spread as a rumour with whispering or busy talk. E17. 5 *v.t.* Assail by buzzing. Now *spec.* fly an aircraft fast and close to (another etc.). L17. 6 *v.t.* Utter with, or express by, buzzing. M18. 7 *v.t.* Cause to make a buzz. E19. 8 *v.t.* Throw swiftly or forcibly. *colloq.* L19. 9 *v.t.* Signal or telephone by a buzzer; telephone. E20.

1b SWIFT Boys and wenches buzzing about the cake-shops like flies. 2b Q. BELL Cambridge was . . a place buzzing with ideas. 3 F. W. FARRAR Buzzing their envenomed slanders into the ears of these country people. 4 GEO. ELIOT Stories . . beginning to be buzzed about. 6 THACKERAY The professional gentlemen hummed and buzzed a sincere applause.

buzz /bʌz/ *v.*[2]*t. colloq.* L18. [Origin unkn.] Finish to the last drop in the bottle.

†**buzz** *int.* E17. [Origin unkn.] 1 Expr. impatience. Only in E17. 2 (Used by conjurors and jugglers.) Expr. command. M17–M19.

buzzard /ˈbʌzəd/ *n.*[1] LME. [OFr. *busard*, *buson* f. L *buteo*(*n*-) falcon: see -ARD.] 1 A bird of prey of the genus *Buteo* (family Accipitridae), with broad wings and rounded tail; *esp.* one of the common Eurasian species *Buteo buteo*. Also used (esp. formerly) in names of other raptors regarded as unsuitable for falconry. LME. b A New World vulture, a condor; *esp.* (also *turkey buzzard*) the turkey vulture. *N. Amer.* E19. 2 An ignorant or stupid person. Now usu. with weakened sense, fellow, chap, (esp. in *old buzzard*). *colloq.* LME.

1 **between hawk and buzzard** *arch.* between good and bad of the same kind. *honey buzzard*: see HONEY *n.* *rough-legged buzzard*: see ROUGH *a.*

buzzard /'bʌzəd/ *n.*² *dial.* M17. [f. BUZZ *v.*¹ + -ARD.] A moth, cockchafer, or other insect flying at night.

buzzer /'bʌzə/ *n.* E17. [f. BUZZ *v.*¹ + -ER¹.] **1** An insect that buzzes. E17. †**2** A person who whispers tales. *rare* (Shakes.). Only in E17. **3** An apparatus for making a buzzing noise as a signal; a whistle, a hooter; an electric bell. L19.

bwana /'bwɑːnə/ *n.* L19. [Kiswahili.] In Africa: master, sir. Freq. (formerly) as a term of respectful address.

by /bʌɪ/ *n.*¹ OE. [ON *bœr*, *býr* (Sw., Da. *by*), f. *búa* dwell: a common elem. in place-names, as *Grimsby*.] *Hist.* A place of habitation, village, or town (of orig. Scandinavian settlement); *gen.* a place whose name ends in *-by*.

by *n.*², *a.* vars. of BYE *n.*, *a.*

by /bʌɪ, *unstressed prep.* bɪ/ *prep.* & *adv.* [OE *bī*, unstressed *bi*, *be* = OFris., OS, OHG *bī*, *bi* (Du. *bij*, G *bei*), Goth. *bi*, f. Gmc, prob. identical with the 2nd syll. of Gk *amphi-*, L *ambi-*, OE *ymb(e)-* around.] **A** *prep.* **1** Of position in space. **a** At the side or edge of; near, close to, beside; in the company of; about the person or in the possession of. OE. **b** In the region or general direction of, towards; slightly inclining to. OE. **c** In the domain of, (vaguely) on, in. Chiefly in *by land*, etc. (passing into sense 5). ME. **d** In addition to, beside. *Sc.* & *north.* ME. **e** Beyond; against, in spite of. *obs.* exc. *Sc.* LME. **2** Of motion. **a** Alongside of, along; in passing along; through, via (passing into sense 5); so as to pass, past; outstripping; avoiding. OE. **b** Near to, into the presence of. ME. **c** At, to, or within the distance of; *gen.* expr. the amount of excess or increase, inferiority or diminution. ME. **3** Of time. **a** In the course of, at, in, on; during, for. Now only in *by day*, *by night*. OE. **b** On or before, not later than. ME. **4** Of relationship. **a** In forms of swearing or adjuration: as surely as one believes in, in the name of; (app. orig. w. some sense of touching or presence). OE. **b** With respect to, as regards, concerning. Now chiefly w. ref. to actions or (*colloq.*) indicating agreement or acquiescence. OE. **c** In accordance or conformity with. OE. **d** According to (a quantity or rate). OE. **e** Indicating succession of groups, quantities, etc., of the same kind, multiplication (esp. as expressing area), or division. ME. **5** Indicating agency, means, cause, attendant circumstance, conditions, manner, effects. OE. **b** *spec.* Indicating the partner in begetting offspring or the sire of a colt, filly, etc. OE. **c** *spec.* (In accounts etc.) indicating means or amount of payment. L17.

1a COVERDALE *Acts* 9:43 He taried .. at Joppa by one Simon. DICKENS Down by the Docks they 'board seamen' at the eating houses. R. JARRELL A cat sits on the pavement by the house. **b** J. STALLWORTHY Greatcoats, lined By the right, marched from their pegs. **c** C. KINGSLEY I never saw one yet, by flood or field. **d** SIR W. SCOTT Few folks ken o' this place .. there's just twa living by mysell. **e** OED That's by belief. **2a** LD BERNERS To goo by the stretes as vacabundes. R. BURNS They gang as saucy by poor folk, As I wad by a stinking brock. E. BOWEN The ducks went .. out by the window again. M. INNES The best connexion was by Leeds. H. MACDIARMID The ladder he has come up by. C. SAGAN *Pioneer 10* passed by Jupiter in early December, 1973. **b** OED Come close by me, and tell me what is the matter. **c** CAXTON There is nother castell nor towne by xx myles nyghe aboute it. JONSON He is taller than either of you by the head. G. GREEN Blackpool were in the lead by two goals to one. **3a** AV *Acts* 20:31 By the space of three yeeres, I ceased not to warne euery one. **b** MILTON Had Judah that day joined .. They had by this possessed the towers of Gath. D. ABSE He'll be back by now. I. MURDOCH Pinn .. was usually home by five. **4a** R. W. EMERSON By God, it is in me, and must go forth of me. L. URIS He swore by the beard of Allah that the Jews would be thrown into the sea. **b** H. FIELDING I always love to speak by people as I find. GOLDSMITH He murdered Hiempsal .. and attempted the same by Adherbal. J. AUSTEN He will consider it a right thing by Mrs. Grant, as well as by Fanny. N. SHUTE If it pleases you to think like that, it's O.K. by me. G. CHARLES A musician by profession. **c** LD MACAULAY The right by which freeholders chose knights of the shire. C. KINGSLEY They had timed their journey by the tides. R. HARDY The families of settlers met by arrangement. **d** J. P. DONLEAVY We sell butter usually by the weight—half pound or a pound. **e** E. A. FREEMAN By twenties, by hundreds, by thousands, the force gathered. I. C. SMITH Stone by stone the castles crumble. W. BRONK The garden grew more tangled year by year. **5** H. LATIMER Christe .. draweth soules unto hym by his bloudy sacrifice. SHAKES. *3 Hen. VI* Warwick's brother, and by that our foe. AV *Matt.* 4:4 Man shall not live by bread alone. C. THIRLWALL He began by banishing 700 families. J. B. YEATS By ambition the rebel angels fell. M. TWAIN No gas to read by. W. OWEN By his dead smile I knew we stood in Hell. DAY LEWIS A brisk walk, which by a tremendous effort I prevent from degenerating into a trot. D. J. ENRIGHT How did he get there .. ? By lift? By helicopter? A. WHITE I like being admired, flattered, .. and listened to by men. J. BRONOWSKI Spiritual and carnal love are inseparable. A poem by John Donne says that. A. MCCOWEN We were joined by Lapkah and the bearers. **b** J. AUSTEN By a former marriage, Dashwood had one son. W. HOLTBY A grand animal, by Albert the Good out of Sweet Sophia. **c** *Which?* You are protected if you pay by credit card.

Phrases: (Of the many phrs. in which *by* governs a n. or forms an elem. in a phrasal vb, few are listed here: see the ns. and vbs.) **by oneself** etc., alone, unaided, without prompting. *by seeming*: see SEEMING *n. by the bye*: see BYE *n.* **by the head, stern** *Naut.*: deeper in the water there. *by* THEMSELVES. *by then* (*that*): see THEN *adv.* etc. *by the way*: see WAY *n. by the yard*: see YARD *n.*² *by turns*, *by turn*: see TURN *n. by water*: see WATER *n. by your leave*: see LEAVE *n.*¹ **north by east** etc., one point east of north, i.e. between N and NNE, etc. *two by two*: see TWO *n.* 1.

B *adv.* (Earlier as BY-.) **1** Near, close at hand, in another's presence or vicinity. ME. **2** Aside, out of the way; out of use or consideration; in reserve. LME. **3** Past a certain point or time, beyond. LME. †**4** In addition, besides, also. LME–E19. **5** Over, finished, past; done for, dead. *Sc.* & *north.* L18.

1 P. MASSINGER My brother being not by now to protect her. D. IGNATOW To forgo love .. is to set bread upon the table and a knife discreetly by. **2** GOLDSMITH Vile things that nature designed should be thrown by into her lumber room. W. WINDHAM Laying something by for a rainy day. **3** JONSON They marched by in pairs. DISRAELI The days are gone by for senates to have their beards plucked in the forum. **5** R. L. STEVENSON You're by with it, James More. You can never show your face again.

Phrases: (For *by* adv. as an element in phrasal vbs see the vbs.) BY AND BY. **by and large** (*a*) *Naut.* to the wind and off it; (*b*) on the whole, everything considered. **full and by** *Naut.* close-hauled to the wind.

by- /bʌɪ/ *comb. form.* Also **bye-**. OE. [Repr. BY *adv.* See also BYE *a.*] Forming combs. (chiefly w. ns.) in advb. or adj. relation, w. the senses 'beside, past' (*bygone*, *bypass*, *bystander*), 'at or to one side, aside' (*by-blow*, *by-room*), 'subsidiary, subordinate' (*byname*, *byplay*), 'unfrequented, devious' (*byroad*, *byway*), 'incidental, casual, extra' (*by-election*, *by-product*), 'underhand, private' (*by-end*).

-by /bi/ *suff. arch.* [After place-names and surnames in *-by*: see BY *n.*¹] Forming (joc. or derog.) descriptive ns., as *rudesby*, *sneaksby*, *wigsby*, etc.

by and by /bʌɪ (ə)nd 'bʌɪ/ *adv.* & *n. phr.* ME. [See BY *adv.*, AND *conj.*¹] **A** *adv. phr.* †**1** One by one, successively. Only in ME. †**2** Continuously. ME–E17. **3** Before long; presently; soon; shortly. E16. †**4** Therefore, as a consequence. M16–E17. †**5** Directly; immediately. L16–L17. **B** *n. phr.* Procrastination; a delay; the (or *the*) future. L16.

by-blow /'bʌɪbləʊ/ *n.* L16. [f. BY- + BLOW *n.*¹] **1** A blow aimed at a person who is not a main opponent; a side-stroke. L16. **2** An illegitimate child. L16.

bycoket /bɪ'kɒkɪt/ *n.* Long *obs.* exc. *Hist.* LME. [OFr. *bicoquet* ornate military head-dress etc., of unkn. origin.] A kind of medieval cap or head-dress, peaked at front and back.

by-corner /'bʌɪkɔːnə/ *n. arch.* M16. [f. BY- + CORNER *n.*] An out-of-the-way corner; a nook.

bye /bʌɪ/ *n.* Also (in sense 1) **by**. M16. [Ellipt. use of BY- or BYE *a.*] **1** A secondary object or undertaking, a side issue, an incidental matter. Now chiefly in *by the bye*, parenthetically, incidentally. M16. **2** A (sporting) match not listed in the programme; a side event. E18. **3** *Cricket.* A run made from a ball that passes the batsman without being struck. M18. **4** *Golf.* A hole or holes remaining to be played when a match is decided. L19. **5** (The position of) a competitor against whom no opponent has been drawn, and who proceeds to the next round of a sporting competition without a contest. L19.

1 the Bye *Hist.* = *the Bye Plot* s.v. BYE *a.* **3 leg-bye** a bye from a ball that touches the batsman.

bye /bʌɪ/ *a.* Also **by**. M17. [Independent use of BY-: see below.] Situated to one side, out of the way; *fig.* subsidiary, incidental, secondary; clandestine.

S. RICHARDSON Nothing can be more bye and unfrequented. **the Bye Plot** *Hist.* the less important of two plots against the government of James I (opp. *the Main Plot*).

¶Not always distinguishable from BY- in adj. relation. The date represents earliest use w. separation from the n.

bye /bʌɪ/ *int. colloq.* E18. [Abbrev.] Goodbye.

bye- *comb. form* var. of BY-.

bye-bye /'bʌɪbʌɪ/ *n.* Also **-byes** /-bʌɪz/. M19. [f. a refrain or sound used in lullabies.] (A child's word for) sleep, bed.

bye-bye /bʌɪ'bʌɪ/ *int. colloq.* E18. [Child's or nursery var. of GOODBYE.] Goodbye.

bye-byes *n.* var. of BYE-BYE *n.*

by-effect /'bʌɪɪfɛkt/ *n.* E19. [f. BY- + EFFECT *n.*] A side-effect.

bye-law *n.* var. of BY-LAW.

by-election /'bʌɪɪlɛkʃ(ə)n/ *n.* L19. [f. BY- + ELECTION.] The election of a Member of Parliament etc. held at a time other than that of a general election.

bye-line *n.* see BYLINE.

Byelorussian *a.* & *n.* var. of BELORUSSIAN.

by-end /'bʌɪɛnd/ *n.* E17. [f. BY- + END *n.*] A secondary or subordinate aim or object, *esp.* one with a covert purpose of personal advantage.

by-form /'bʌɪfɔːm/ *n.* L19. [f. BY- + FORM *n.*] A secondary form of a word etc.

bygoing /'bʌɪgəʊɪŋ/ *vbl n.* Chiefly *Sc.* Also (*Sc.*) **byganging** /'bʌɪgaŋɪŋ/. E17. [f. BY- + GOING *n.*] The action of passing by.

in the bygoing by the way, incidentally.

bygone /'bʌɪgɒn/ *a.* & *n.* LME. [f. BY- + GONE *a.*] **A** *adj.* **1** That has gone by in time, past, former. LME. **2** No longer living. E16. **3** Antiquated. M19.

B *n.* **1** In *pl.* Past events; *esp.* past offences. Now chiefly as below. M16. **2** In *pl.* Overdue payments, arrears. Chiefly *Sc.* L16. **3** A person or thing of the past; *spec.* an obsolete domestic object or other artefact (usu. in *pl.*). M19.

1 let bygones be bygones forgive and forget.

bylander *n.* var. of BILANDER.

by-lane /'bʌɪleɪn/ *n.* L16. [f. BY- + LANE *n.*¹] A side lane; a side passage in a mine.

by-law /'bʌɪlɔː/ *n.* Also **bye-**. ME. [Prob. f. BYRLAW, but assoc. w. BY-, LAW *n.*¹] **1** = BYRLAW; *spec.* an ordinance made by common consent in a court leet or court baron. Long *obs.* exc. *Hist.* ME. **2** A regulation made by a local authority or corporation; a regulation of a company etc. LME. **3** A secondary, subordinate, or accessory law. M16.

Comb.: **bylawman** *Hist.* = BYRLAW*man*.

bylina /bə'liːnə/ *n.* Pl. **-ny** /-ni/, **-nas**. L19. [Russ.] A Russian traditional heroic poem.

byline /'bʌɪlʌɪn/ *n.* & *v.* In sense A.2 also **bye-**. E20. [f. BY *prep.*, BY- + LINE *n.*²] **A** *n.* **1** A line in a newspaper etc. naming the writer of an article. E20. **2** The goal-line in soccer etc. M20. **B** *v.t.* Print with a byline. M20.

byliner *n.* a journalist etc. whose work is bylined M20.

byliny *n.* pl. of BYLINA.

byname /'bʌɪneɪm/ *n.* & *v.* L16. [f. BY- + NAME *n.*] **A** *n.* A subsidiary name; a sobriquet; a nickname. L16. **B** *v.t.* Give a specified name to; nickname. Long *rare.* L16.

bypass /ˈbʌɪpɑːs/ *n.* & *v.* M19. [f. BY- + PASS *n.*[1]] A *n.* 1 A secondary channel permitting the free flow of gas, electricity, blood, etc., when a main passage is blocked. M19. 2 A road passing round (the centre of) a town, providing an alternative route for through traffic. E20. 3 *transf.* & *fig.* An alternative route or means. E20.
B *v.t.* 1 Provide with a bypass. L19. 2 Take an indirect route around; avoid. E20. 3 Conduct (gas, liquid, etc.) by means of a bypass. E20.
1 *Times* A By-passed village in Kent. 2 LYNDON B. JOHNSON A President must be willing to bypass the Congress to take the issue to the people. F. WELDON Pulling out the gas cooker to adjust the pipe so that the supply would bypass the meter.

by-passer /ˈbʌɪpɑːsə/ *n.* *arch.* M16. [f. BY- + PASSER.] A passer-by.

bypast /ˈbʌɪpɑːst/ *a.* *arch.* LME. [f. BY- + PAST *a.*] Bygone.

bypath /ˈbʌɪpɑːθ/ *n.*[1] LME. [f. BY- + PATH *n.*[1]] A side-path; a secluded way; *fig.* a minor branch of a subject etc.

by-place /ˈbʌɪpleɪs/ *n.* *arch.* L16. [f. BY- + PLACE *n.*[1]] An out-of-the-way place; an odd corner.

byplay /ˈbʌɪpleɪ/ *n.* E19. [f. BY- + PLAY *n.*] Subsidiary action, esp. on stage; incidental play.

by-product /ˈbʌɪprɒdʌkt, -dʌkt/ *n.* M19. [f. BY- + PRODUCT *n.*] An incidental or secondary product of manufacture etc.; a side-effect.

byre /ˈbʌɪə/ *n.* [OE *bȳre*, perh. cogn. w. BOWER *n.*[1]] A cow-shed.

byrlaw /ˈbəːlɔː/ *n.* *obs.* exc. *Hist.* In comb. also **birley, burley, -ie,** /ˈbəːli/. See also BY-LAW. ME. [f. ON *býjar* genit. sing. of *býr* (see BY *n.*[1]) + *lagu* LAW *n.*[1]] The local custom or law of a manor, district, etc., whereby disputes over boundaries, trespass, etc., were settled without recourse to the public courts of law.
Comb.: **byrlaw-court**: to settle local disputes etc.; **byrlawman** an officer appointed to administer the byrlaw.

byrnie /ˈbəːni/ *n.* *obs.* exc. *Hist.* Also (earlier) †**brinie**. ME. [ON *brynja*. Metathetic var. orig. Sc.] A coat of mail.

byroad /ˈbʌɪrəʊd/ *n.* M16. [f. BY- + ROAD *n.*] A side or minor road; a little-frequented road.

Byronic /bʌɪˈrɒnɪk/ *a.* & *n.* E19. [f. *Byron* (see below) + -IC.] A *adj.* Of, pertaining to, or characteristic of the poet George Gordon, Lord Byron (1788–1824) or his writings. E19. B *n.* In *pl.* Byronic utterances or behaviour. M19.
Byronically *adv.* in a Byronic manner M19.

Byronism /ˈbʌɪrənɪz(ə)m/ *n.* E19. [f. as prec. + -ISM.] The characteristics of Byron or his poetry; imitation of Byron.

by-room /ˈbʌɪruːm, -rʊm/ *n.* Now *rare.* L16. [f. BY- + ROOM *n.*[1]] A side-room; a small or private room.

byssi *n.* pl. of BYSSUS.

byssine /ˈbɪsɪn/ *n.* & *a.* LME. [L *byssinus* (*byssinum* n.) f. Gk *bussinos*, f. *bussos*: see BYSSUS, -INE[1].] *Hist.* (Made of) byssus or fine linen.

byssinosis /bɪsɪˈnəʊsɪs/ *n.* Pl. **-noses** /-ˈnəʊsiːz/. L19. [f. as prec. + -OSIS.] *Med.* Chronic lung disease due to inhalation of fine particles of textile fibres.
byssinotic /-ˈnɒtɪk/ *a.* M20.

byssus /ˈbɪsəs/ *n.* Pl. (*rare*) **byssi** /ˈbɪsʌɪ/, **byssuses**. LME. [L f. Gk *bussos*, of Semitic origin.] 1 *Hist.* A fine textile fibre and fabric, orig. of flax. LME. †2 (A) filamentous fungoid growth. M18–M19. 3 *Zool.* A tuft of fine filaments by which some bivalve molluscs adhere to rocks. M19.
byssal *a.* (*Zool.*) of, pertaining to, or of the nature of a byssus L19.

bystander /ˈbʌɪstandə/ *n.* M16. [f. BY- + STANDER.] A person who is standing by; a passive witness; a spectator.

bystanding /ˈbʌɪstandɪŋ/ *a.* E17. [f. BY- + STANDING *a.*] Standing by or near.

by-street /ˈbʌɪstriːt/ *n.* L17. [f. BY- + STREET *n.*] A side-street; a little-used street.

by-talk /ˈbʌɪtɔːk/ *n.* *arch.* M16. [f. BY- + TALK *n.*[1]] Incidental talk; small talk; gossip.

byte /bʌɪt/ *n.* M20. [Arbitrary, based on BIT *n.*[3] and BITE *n.*] *Computing.* A group of binary digits (usu. eight) operated on as a unit.

by-thing /ˈbʌɪθɪŋ/ *n.* *arch.* E18. [f. BY- + THING *n.*[1]] A minor matter; a side issue.

by-time /ˈbʌɪtʌɪm/ *n.* E17. [f. BY- + TIME *n.*] Time not occupied by one's main work or pursuits; spare time; odd hours.

bytownite /ˈbʌɪtaʊnʌɪt/ *n.* M19. [f. *Bytown*, former name of Ottawa, Canada + -ITE[1].] *Min.* A calcic plagioclase feldspar occurring in many basic igneous rocks.

†**by-view** *n.* M18–E19. [f. BY- + VIEW *n.*] An unavowed or self-interested aim.

by-walk /ˈbʌɪwɔːk/ *n.* M16. [f. BY- + WALK *n.*] A private or secluded walk; a by-path (*lit.* & *fig.*).

bywater /ˈbʌɪwɔːtə/ *n.* L19. [f. BY- + WATER *n.*] A diamond of inferior water, *esp.* one that is yellowish.

byway /ˈbʌɪweɪ/ *n.* ME. [f. BY- + WAY *n.*] A byroad, a bypath.

bywoner /ˈbʌɪwəʊnə, ˈbeɪvəʊnə/ *n.* *S. Afr.* L19. [Afk., f. *by* with + *woon* live + *-er* -ER[1].] A farmer holding land under a *métayage* system.

byword /ˈbʌɪwəːd/ *n.* [OE *bīwyrde* = OHG *bīwurti*, rendering L *proverbium* PROVERB: see BY-, WORD *n.*] 1 A proverb; a proverbial saying. OE. 2 A person etc. taken as typical of a (usu. bad) quality; a quality in a person etc. that is widely recognized. M16. b A (usu. scornful or mocking) nickname. Now *rare.* L16. †3 A casual word; a hint; an aside. M16–M17. †4 A word or phrase frequently used, esp. by an individual. M16–E18.
2 J. A. FROUDE The Church courts were a byword for iniquity. L. DEIGHTON Blessing's efficiency was a byword. P. ACKROYD I would rather be a byword of infamy . . than an object of gross ridicule. b R. L. STEVENSON They are . . known by a generic byword, as Poor Whites.

by-work /ˈbʌɪwəːk/ *n.* L16. [f. BY- + WORK *n.*] Incidental work; work performed in spare time or odd hours. Also, work with an unavowed or self-interested aim.

byzant *n.* var. of BEZANT.

Byzantian /bɪˈzantɪən, bʌɪ-, -ʃ(ə)n/ *n.* & *a.* E17. [f. L *Byzantius*, f. *Byzantium* (see next), + -AN.] = BYZANTINE *n.* 2, *a.* 1.

Byzantine /bɪˈzantʌɪn, bʌɪ-/ *n.* & *a.* L16. [Fr. *byzantin* or L *Byzantinus*, f. *Byzantium* f. Gk *Buzantion* Byzantium, the city later called Constantinople, now Istanbul: see -INE[1].] A *n.* 1 (**b-**.) *Hist.* = BEZANT. L16. 2 A native or inhabitant of Byzantium or the Eastern Roman Empire. M17. B *adj.* 1 Of or pertaining to Byzantium, the Eastern Roman Empire, or the Orthodox Church. L18. 2 *spec.* Characteristic of the artistic (esp. architectural) style developed in the Eastern Roman Empire. M19. 3 Like Byzantine politics; complicated; inflexible; underhand. M20.
Byzantinism /-tɪn-/ *n.* the style and methods of architecture etc. developed in the Eastern Roman Empire M19. **Byzantinist** /-tɪn-/ *n.* an expert in or student of Byzantine matters L19.

C

C, c /siː/, the third letter of the modern Eng. alphabet and of the ancient Roman one, orig. corresp. to Gk *gamma*, Semitic *gimel*. In early L the letter represented both the voiced /g/ and voiceless /k/ velar plosive consonants; subsequently it stood only for the latter. When the Roman alphabet was introduced into Britain, C had only the /k/ sound, and this remains the case in the Celtic langs. As a result of developments both in Britain and in Continental Europe in the OE and ME periods, C in mod. Eng. has a number of values according to the following general rules. (i) C has the 'hard' sound /k/ bef. *a, o, u*, bef. a consonant exc. *h*, and when final. Final *c* is largely avoided exc. in mod. wds adopted from or modelled on L or Gk (*disc, sac, italic*), the /k/ sound being usu. expressed by *k* or *ck*. When hard *c* is followed in inflection by *e* or *i*, it is usu. changed to *ck* (*frolicking, picnicker*). (ii) C has the 'soft' sound /s/ bef. *e, i, y*. Where the /s/ sound is final, it is written *ce*, and this *e* is retained in composition bef. *a, o, u*. (iii) *ci* (rarely *ce*) preceding another vowel has freq. the sound /ʃ/, esp. in the endings *-cious, -cial, -cion* (cf. T, T). (iv) *ch* is in effect a separate consonant: see bef. the beginning of the *ch-* wds. (v) In adoptions from other langs. C may retain the foreign pronunciation (*ceilidh, cello*). Pl. **cees, C's, Cs.**

I 1 The letter and its sound. **2** The shape of the letter.

2 C-shaped *a.* having a shape or cross-section like the letter C. **C-spring** a C-shaped spring, used to support the body of a carriage.

II Symbolical uses. **3** Used to denote serial order; applied e.g. to the third group or section, sheet of a book, etc. **4** *Mus.* (Cap. C.) The first note of the natural major scale (C major), often defined as having a frequency of 256 Hz. Also, the scale of a composition with C as its keynote. **5** The third hypothetical person or example. **6** *Math.* (Usu. italic *c*.) The third known quantity; a constant; *spec.* (*Physics*) denoting the velocity of light in a vacuum. **7** (Usu. cap. C.) Designating the third-highest class (of academic marks, population as regards affluence, etc.). **8** The roman numeral for 100. **9** (Cap. C.) Designating a range of international standard paper sizes with a fixed shape and twice the area of the next size, as *C0, C1, C2, C3, C4*, etc.

3 C-DNA *Biochem.* a form of double-stranded DNA adopted in the presence of certain solvents, more tightly coiled than B-DNA. **4 C clef** the soprano, alto, or tenor clef. *middle C*: see MIDDLE *a.* **7 C Special** *Hist.* a member of an unpaid occasional police force in Northern Ireland. **C3** /siː 'θriː/ the lowest grade of medical fitness in the war of 1914–18; *colloq.* unfit, worthless.

III 10 Abbrevs.: (A small selection only is given here. Those all in caps. or small caps. also occur with a full stop after each letter; some of those all in caps. also occur (i) with initial cap. only, (ii) in small caps.) **C.** = Cape; Catholic; Command Paper (second series, 1870–99); Conservative. **C** = cancer (in *the big C* s.v. BIG *a.*); (*Electr.*) capacitance; (*Chem.*) carbon; Celsius, centigrade; Channel (as in *C4*, a television channel); (*Particle Physics*) charge conjugation; cocaine; (*Mus.*) common time; (*Physics*) coulomb(s). **c.** = (*Cricket*) caught by; cent(s); centuries; century; chapter; (*Meteorol.*) cloudy; cold; colt; cubic. **c.** = [L] *circa* about (also **ca.**). **c** = (as *pref.*) centi-; (*Particle Physics*) = CHARM *n.*[1] 4. **c/-** (*Austral.* & *NZ*) = care of. **©** = copyright. **CA** = California; (*Sc.* & *Canad.*) chartered accountant. **Ca** (*Chem.*) = calcium. **ca.** = [L] *circa* about (also **c.**). **CAA** = Civil Aviation Authority. **CAB** = Citizens' Advice Bureau; (*US*) Civil Aeronautics Board. **CAD** = computer-aided (or -assisted) design. **CAF** (*US*) = cost and freight. **CAI** = computer-aided (or -assisted) instruction. **CAL** = computer-aided (or -assisted) learning. **Cal** = (large) calorie. **cal** = (small) calorie. **Cal., Calif.** = California. **Camb.** = Cambridge. **Cambs.** = Cambridgeshire. **CAMRA** /'kamrə/ = Campaign for Real Ale. **Can.** = Canada; Canadian. **c & b** (*Cricket*) = caught and bowled by. **C & W** = country and western. **Cant.** = Canticles (in the Bible). **CAP** = Common Agricultural Policy (of the European Community). **Capt.** = Captain. **Card.** = Cardinal. **Carms.** = Carmarthenshire (former Welsh county). **CAS** = Chief of the Air (Force) Staff. **CAT** /kat/ = (chiefly *Hist.*) College of Advanced Technology; (*Med.*) computed (or computerized) axial (or computer-assisted) tomography (cf. *CT* below). **Cath.** = cathedral; catholic. **CB** = citizens' band (radio); Companion (of the Order) of the Bath; confined, confinement, to barracks. **Cb** (*Chem.*, now *Hist.*) = columbium. **CBC** = Canadian Broadcasting Corporation. **CBD** (*US*) = cash before delivery. **CBE** = Commander of (the Order of) the British Empire. **CBI** = Confederation of British Industry. **CBS** = Columbia Broadcasting System. **CBW** = chemical and biological warfare, weapons. **CC** = City Council; Companion of (the Order of) Canada; County Council(lor); Cricket Club. **cc** = carbon copy; cubic centimetre(s). **CD** = Civil Defence; compact disc, compact disc player (*CD-video*, a system of simultaneously reproducing sound and video pictures from a compact disc); [Fr.] *corps diplomatique* diplomatic corps. **Cd.** = Command Paper (third series, 1900–18). **Cd** (*Chem.*) = cadmium. **cd** = candela. **CD-I** = compact disc (interactive). **Cdr.** (*Mil.*) = Commander. **Cdre.** = Commodore. **CD-ROM** /siːdiː'rɒm/ = compact disc (with) read-only memory. **CDT** (*N. Amer.*) = Central Daylight Time. **CDTV** = compact disc television. **CDV** = CD-video. **CE** = Church of England; Civil Engineer. **CE** = Common (or Christian) Era. **Ce** (*Chem.*) = cerium. **CEGB** = Central Electricity Generating Board. **C.Eng.** = chartered engineer. **CERN** /səːn/ = [Fr.] *Conseil Européen pour la Recherche Nucléaire* European Organization for Nuclear Research (later European Laboratory for Particle Physics). **cert.** = certificate; certified. **Cert. Ed.** /*freq.* səːt'ɛd/ = Certificate in Education. **CET** = Central European Time. **CF** = Chaplain to the Forces; cystic fibrosis. **Cf** (*Chem.*) = californium. **cf.** = [L] *confer* compare. **c.f.** = carried forward. **CFC** = chlorofluorocarbon. **CFE** = College of Further Education. **cg** = centigram(s). **CGA** (*Computing*) = colour graphics adapter. **CGM** = Conspicuous Gallantry Medal. **CGS** = centimetre-gram-second (system); Chief of the General Staff. **cgs** = centimetre-gram-second (system). **CH** = Companion of Honour. **Ch.** = Church. **ch.** = chapter; chestnut. **Chas.** = Charles. **Ch. B** = [L] *Chirurgiae Baccalaureus* Bachelor of Surgery. **Ches.** = Cheshire. **Ch. M.** = [L] *Chirurgiae Magister* Master of Surgery. **CHP** = combined heat and power. **Chr., Chron.** = Chronicles (in the Bible). **CI** = Channel Islands; (*Hist.*) Order of the Crown of India. **Ci** = curie. **CIA** (*US*) = Central Intelligence Agency. **CID** = Criminal Investigation Department; (*Hist.*) Committee of Imperial Defence. **CIE** = Companion of (the Order of) the Indian Empire. **c.i.f.** = cost, insurance, freight (as being included in a price). **CIGS** (*Hist.*) = Chief of the Imperial General Staff. **C.-in-C.** = commander-in-chief. **CIS** = Commonwealth of Independent States. **CJ** = Chief Justice. **Cl** (*Chem.*) = chlorine. **cl.** = class; clause. **cl** = centilitre(s). **C.Lit.** = Companion of Literature. **Cllr.** = Councillor. **CM** = Member of the Order of Canada. **Cm** (*Chem.*) = curium. **Cm.** = Command Paper (sixth series, 1986–). **cm** = centimetre(s). **Cmd.** = Command Paper (fourth series, 1918–56). **Cmdr.** = Commander. **Cmdre.** = Commodore. **CMG** = Companion of (the Order of) St Michael and St George. **Cmnd.** = Command Paper (fifth series 1956–86). **CMV** (*Med.*) = cytomegalovirus. **CNAA** = Council for National Academic Awards. **CND** = Campaign for Nuclear Disarmament (*CNDer*, a member or supporter of CND). **CNG** = compressed natural gas. **cnr.** = corner. **CNS** = central nervous system; Chief of the Naval Staff. **CO** = Colorado; Commanding Officer; conscientious objector. **Co** (*Chem.*) = cobalt. **Co.** = Company (*and Co.* /kəʊ/ (*colloq.*), and the rest of them, and similar things, etcetera); County. **c/o** = care of. **COD** = cash (or (*US*) collect) on delivery; Concise Oxford Dictionary. **C. of E.** = Church of England. **COHSE** /'kəʊzi/ = Confederation of Health Service Employees. **COI** = Central Office of Information. **Col.** = Colonel; Colorado; Colossians (New Testament). **col.** = column. **COM** = computer output on microfilm or microfiche. **Comp[a], Compa** = Company (esp. on banknotes). **Conn.** = Connecticut. **Cons.** = Conservative. **Cor.** = Corinthians (New Testament); (*US*) corner. **CORE** (*US*) = Congress of Racial Equality. **Corp.** = Corporal; (*N. Amer.*) Corporation. **COS** = Chief of Staff. **COSPAR** /'kəʊspɑː/ = Committee on Space Research. **Coy.** (esp. *Mil.*) = Company. **CP** = Cape Province; (*Particle Physics*) charge conjugation and parity; Communist Party; (*Austral.*) Country Party. **cp.** = [L] *compara* compare. **c.p.** = candlepower. **CPA** (*US*) = certified public accountant. **Cpl.** = Corporal. **CPO** = Chief Petty Officer. **CPR** = Canadian Pacific Railway. **CPRE** = Council for the Protection of Rural England. **cps.** = (*Computing*) characters per second; cycles per second. **CPSA** = Civil and Public Services Association. **CPT** (*Particle Physics*) = charge conjugation, parity, and time reversal. **CPU** = central processing unit. **CR** (*Chr. Ch.*) = Community of the Resurrection. **Cr.** = Councillor; creditor. **Cr** (*Chem.*) = chromium. **CRC** = camera-ready copy. **Cres.** = Crescent. **cres., cresc.** (*Mus.*) = crescendo. **CRT** = cathode-ray tube. **CS** = chartered surveyor; Civil Service; (also *CS gas*) Corson Stoughton (gas) [B. B. *C*orson (1896–) & R. W. *S*toughton (1906–57), US chemists], (name of) an irritant compound used in finely-divided form for riot control etc.; Court of Session. **Cs** (*Chem.*) = caesium. **c/s** = cycles per second. **CSC** = Civil Service Commission; Conspicuous Service Cross. **CSE** (*Hist.*) = Certificate of Secondary Education. **CSI** = Companion of (the Order of) the Star of India. **CSIRO** = Commonwealth Scientific and Industrial Research Organization. **CSM** = Company Sergeant-Major. **CST** (*N. Amer.*) = Central Standard Time. **CSU** = Civil Service Union. **CT** = (*Med.*) computed (or computerized) tomography (cf. *CAT* above); Connecticut. **Ct.** = Count; Court. **ct.** = carat; cent. **CTC** = City Technology College;

Cyclists' Touring Club. **CU** = Cambridge University. **Cu** (*Chem.*) = [L] *cuprum* copper. **cu.** = cubic. **Cumb.** = Cumberland (former English county). **CUP** = Cambridge University Press. **c.v.** = curriculum vitae. **CVO** = Commander of the Royal Victorian Order. **CVS** (*Med.*) = chorionic villus sampling. **CW** = chemical warfare, weapons; continuous wave. **Cwlth.** = Commonwealth. **c.w.o.** = cash with order. **CWS** = Cooperative Wholesale Society. **cwt** [L *centum* hundred] = hundredweight.

ca' *n.*, *v.* see CALL *n.*, *v.*

Caaba *n.* var. of KAABA.

caa'ing whale *n. phr.* var. of CA'ING WHALE.

caatinga /'kɑːtɪŋgə/ *n.* M19. [Port. f. Tupi, f. *caá* natural vegetation, forest + *tinga* white.] In Brazil, a forest consisting of thorny shrubs and stunted trees.

cab /kab/ *n.*[1] E19. [Abbrev. of CABRIOLET] **1** a *Hist.* A hackney carriage. E19. **b** A taxi. Also *taxi-cab*. L19. **2** A driver of a cab. M19. **3** A shelter or compartment for the driver of a train, lorry, crane, etc. M19.

Phrases & comb.: **cabman** a man who drives a cab. **cab-rank, -stand** a place where cabs are authorized to wait. *spy in the cab*: see SPY *n*.

†**cab** *n.*[2] see KAB.

cab /kab/ *v.i.* & *t.* (w. *it*). Infl. **-bb-**. M19. [f. CAB *n.*[1]] Travel in or drive a cab.

caba /kə'bɑː/ *n.* Chiefly *US*. Also **cabas** /kə'bɑːs/. M19. [Fr. *cabas* basket, pannier.] A small satchel or handbag.

†**cabaia** *n.* see KEBAYA.

cabal /kə'bal/ *n.* & *v.* L16. [Fr. *cabale* f. med.L *cab(b)ala* (It., Sp. *cabala*): see CABBALA.] **A** *n.* †**1** = CABBALA. L16–M18. **2** A secret intrigue, a conspiracy; petty plotting. *arch.* E17. **3** A secret meeting (of intriguers). *arch.* M17. **4** A political clique, a faction; *spec.* (**C-**) a committee of five ministers under Charles II whose surnames happened to begin with C, A, B, A, and L (Clifford, Arlington, Buckingham, Ashley, and Lauderdale). M17.

2 BURKE Centres of cabal. W. IRVING Cabals breaking out in the company. 3 MARVELL Is he in caball in his cabinett sett. 4 G. B. SHAW The radical cabal in the cabinet which pursues my family with rancorous class hatred.

B *v.i.* Infl. **-ll-**. Combine (*together*) for some private end (usu. *derog.*); intrigue (*against*). L17.

caballer *n.* a person who cabals, an intriguer L17.

cabala *n.* var. of CABBALA.

cabaletta /kabə'lɛtə/ *n.* M19. [It., var. of *coboletta* dim. of *cob(b)ola* stanza, couplet f. OProv. *cobla* f. L COPULA.] *Mus.* A simple aria with a repetitive rhythm; the uniformly quick final section of an aria.

caballada /kabə'ljɑːdə/ *n.* *US*. See also CAVAYARD. M19. [Sp., f. *caballo* horse.] A drove of horses or mules.

caballero /kabə'ljɛːrəʊ/ *n.* Pl. **-os**. M19. [Sp. = Fr. *chevalier*, It. *cavaliere*: see CAVALIER *n.*] A Spanish gentleman.

caballine /'kabəlʌɪn/ *a.* LME. [L *caballinus*, f. *caballus* horse: see -INE[1].] Equine.

caballine fountain [L *fons caballinus*] the fountain Hippocrene (see HIPPOCRENE).

caban /kə'bɑːn/ *n.* L17. [(Pers. f.) Arab. *ḳabā'*.] A type of coat or tunic worn esp. by Arab men.

cabana /kə'bɑːnə/ *n.* Chiefly *US*. Also **-ñ-** /-nj-/. L19. [Sp. *cabaña* f. late L *capanna*, *cav-* CABIN.] A cabin; *spec.* a shelter at a beach or swimming pool.

cabane /kə'bɑːn/ *n.* M19. [Fr.: see CABIN.] **1** A hut, a cabin. *Fr. Canad.* M19. **2** A pyramidal structure supporting the wings of an aircraft. E20.

cabaret /'kabəreɪ; *in sense 1 also foreign* kabarɛ (*pl. same*)/ *n.* M17. [(O)Fr., orig. Walloon & Picard, f. MDu. var. of *camaret*, *cambret* f. OPicard *camberet* little room.] **1** A public house in France etc. M17. **2** An entertainment provided in a restaurant etc. while customers are at table; a restaurant, nightclub, etc., providing such entertainment. E20.

cabas *n.* var. of CABA.

cabbage /'kabɪdʒ/ *n.*[1] LME. [OFr. (Picard) *caboche* head, var. of OFr. *caboce*, of unkn. origin.] **1** The compact round head or heart formed by the leaves of a cultivated variety of the cruciferous plant *Brassica oleracea*, used as a green culinary vegetable; a plant of this species. Also (w. specifying wd), any of various related or otherwise similar plants. LME. **2** The edible terminal bud of a cabbage palm or other palm. M17. **3** A brainless person; someone utterly lacking interests or ambition, or reduced by illness to inactivity, a 'vegetable'. *colloq.* L19. **4** Money. *slang* (chiefly *N. Amer.*). E20.

1 *Chinese cabbage, Kerguelen cabbage, red cabbage, Savoy cabbage*, etc. **my cabbage** [tr. Fr. *mon chou*] my dear, my darling. 3 *Guardian* I stayed at home for nearly a year. It was awful. I became a cabbage.

Comb.: **cabbage-bark** (the bark or timber of) the angelin, *Andira inermis*; **cabbage butterfly** = *cabbage white* below; **cabbage-head** *fig.* a stupid person; *cabbage-looking*: see *be not so green as one is cabbage-looking* s.v. GREEN *a.*; **cabbage lettuce** a variety of lettuce with broad rounded leaves forming a more or less globular head close to the ground; **cabbage moth** a noctuid moth, *Mamestra brassicae*, whose larvae are pests of cabbages; **cabbage palm** any of various palms having edible terminal buds or other similarities to the cabbage, *esp.* (*a*) either of two tall W. Indian palms, *Roystonea oleracea* and *Sabal palmetto*, with edible buds; (*b*) an Australian palm, *Livistona australis*, with large leaves used to make hats, etc.; **cabbage rose** an old double garden rose, *Rosa centifolia*, with a large round compact flower; **cabbage tree** any of various tropical trees suggesting cabbages, *esp.* = *cabbage palm* above, or (*NZ*) a tree of the agave family, *Cordyline australis*, with narrow leaves crowded at the top of the stem; **cabbage white** a white pierid butterfly whose larvae feed on cabbage-leaves, esp. the large white, *Pieris brassicae*.

cabbage-like *a.* resembling (that of) a cabbage M19. **cabbagy** *a.* M19.

cabbage /'kabɪdʒ/ *n.*[2] M17. [Origin unkn.] **1** Shreds (or larger pieces) of cloth appropriated by tailors in cutting out clothes. M17. †**2** A tailor. *slang.* L17–E18.

cabbage /'kabɪdʒ/ *v.*[1] Sense 1 also †**caboche**. LME. [Fr. *cabocher*, f. *caboche* (see CABBAGE *n.*[1]) or directly f. CABBAGE *n.*[1]] **1** *v.t.* Cut off (a deer's head) close behind the horns; cut off the head of (a deer) so. LME. †**2** *v.i.* Of the horns of a deer: grow to a head. Only in E16. **3** *v.t.* In *pass.* Be formed into a head like a cabbage. L16. **4** *v.i.* Of a cabbage, lettuce, etc.: form a head. E17.

cabbage /'kabɪdʒ/ *v.*[2] *t.* & *i.* E18. [f. CABBAGE *n.*[2]: cf. OFr. *cabas* deceit, theft, Du. *kabassen* pilfer.] Pilfer (orig. pieces of cloth), appropriate surreptitiously.

H. L. MENCKEN The quacks .. in all probability cabbaged most of their victims' property.

cabbala /kə'bɑːlə, 'kabələ/ *n.* Also **cabala, kabbala**, & (in sense 1) w. cap. initial. E16. [med.L *cab(b)ala* f. rabbinical Heb. *qabbālāh* tradition, f. *qibbēl* receive, accept.] **1** The esoteric and mystical Jewish tradition, first transmitted orally, of which the Zohar (13th cent.) is the basic text. E16. **2** *gen.* †**a** (An) oral tradition. M–L17. **b** (An) esoteric doctrine; (a) mystic interpretation; occult lore. M17.

cabbalism *n.* the system of the Jewish cabbala; (an) esoteric doctrine, occult lore: L16. **cabbalist** *n.* one versed in the Jewish cabbala or in mystic arts M16. **cabba'listic** *a.* pertaining to or of the nature of the cabbala or cabbalists; having a private or mystic sense: E17. **cabba'listical** *a.* L16. **cabba'listically** *adv.* M17.

cabby /'kabi/ *n. colloq.* M19. [f. CAB *n.*[1] + -Y[6].] A driver of a cab.

caber /'keɪbə/ *n.* *Sc.* E16. [Gael., Ir. *cabar.*] A roughly trimmed tree-trunk, *esp.* one with a slightly tapered end used in Highland Games.

tossing the caber the sport of throwing such a tree-trunk.

Cabernet /'kabəneɪ, *foreign* kabɛrnɛ/ *n.* M19. [Fr.] (Any of several vines yielding) a black grape used in wine-making; red wine made from these grapes.

Cabernet Franc /frɑ̃, frɒ̃/, **Cabernet Sauvignon** /'səʊvɪnjɒn, *foreign* soviɲɔ̃/: two of the chief varieties.

cabildo /ka'bildo, kə'bɪldəʊ/ *n.* Pl. ***-os*** /-ɔs, -əʊz/. E19. [Sp. f. late L *capitulum* chapter-house: see CHAPTER *n.*] A town hall or town council in Spain and Spanish-speaking countries.

cabin /'kabɪn/ *n.* & *v.* ME. [(O)Fr. *cabane* f. Prov. *cabana* = It. *capanna* f. late L *capanna*, *cavanna*.] **A** *n.* **1** A room or compartment in a ship, aircraft, spacecraft, etc., for housing passengers, crew (in an aircraft), or cargo. ME. †**b** A berth in a ship. L16–M18. †**2** A temporary shelter; a booth. LME–M19. **3** A permanent habitation of rough or rudimentary construction; a poor dwelling. LME. †**4** A small room; a cell. LME–E17. †**5** A natural cave or grotto; an animal's den. LME–L18. †**6** A litter for carrying a person. L16–M17. †**7** A political cabinet. Usu. *attrib.* M–L17. **8** A driver's cab; the enclosed compartment of a crane, lorry, etc. M20.

1 *ladies' cabin*: see LADY *n.* & *a.* *outside cabin*: see OUTSIDE *a.* *pressure cabin*: see PRESSURE *n.*

Comb.: **cabin-boy**: attending to officers or passengers on a ship; **cabin class** an intermediate class of accommodation on a passenger ship; **cabin crew**: attending to passengers and cargo on an aircraft; **cabin cruiser** a power-driven vessel equipped with a cabin and living accommodation; **cabin fever** *N. Amer. colloq.* lassitude, irritability, etc., resulting from long confinement or isolation in one's home etc. during the winter.

B *v.* **1** *v.i.* & *t.* Dwell or lodge (as) in a cabin; take or give shelter (as) in a cabin. L16. **2** *v.t.* Confine in a small space; cramp. Chiefly as *cabined* ppl a. E17.

cabinet /'kabɪnɪt/ *n.* & *v.* M16. [f. prec. + -ET[1], infl. by Fr. *cabinet* f. It. *gabinetto* closet, press, chest of drawers.] **A** *n.* **I** *gen.* †**1** A secret receptacle, a repository. Chiefly *fig.* M16–L17. **2** A case or cupboard with drawers, shelves, etc., for storing or displaying objects. M16. **b** A piece of furniture containing a radio or television receiver etc. M20. **3** A small chamber; a private room. *arch.* M16. †**4** A small cabin; a tent; a rustic lodging; an animal's den. L16–M17. †**5** A summer-house; a bower. L16–M18. †**6** A room devoted to the display of works of art; a gallery. L17–L18.

II *Polit.* (f. sense 3). (Usu. **C-**.) **7** *The* council-chamber in which the inner circle of a Government meet; *the* world of politics. *arch.* E17. **8** A committee of senior ministers responsible for determining Government policy. M17. †**9** A meeting of a Cabinet. E18–E19.

8 *inner cabinet*: see INNER *a*.

Comb.: **Cabinet Council** *arch.* = senses 8, 9 above; **cabinet-maker** a person who makes cabinets, a skilled joiner; **cabinet-making** the activity or occupation of a cabinet-maker; **Cabinet Minister** a member of the Cabinet; **cabinet organ** (*a*) a reed-organ in a case resembling that of an upright piano; (*b*) a chamber or portative organ; **cabinet photograph**: measuring approximately six by four inches; **cabinet piano** a small upright piano; **cabinet pudding** a steamed pudding made with dried fruit; *cabinet scraper*: see SCRAPER 3; **cabinet-work** fine furniture, skilled joinery.

B *v.t.* Infl. **-t-**, ***-tt-**. Enclose (as) in a cabinet. M17.

Cabistan *n.* & *a.* var. of KABISTAN.

cable /'keɪb(ə)l/ *n.* ME. [AN, ONFr. var. of OFr. *chable* (mod. *câble* f. Prov. *cable*) f. late L *cap(u)lum* halter, assoc. w. L *capere* seize, hold; reinforced by (M)LG, (M)Du. *kabel* f. Proto-Romance.] **1** A strong thick rope of hemp or wire. ME. **2** *Naut.* A strong rope or studded link chain attached to an anchor. LME. **b** More fully *cable length*. A unit of length of 200 yards. M16. **3** (A length of) material in the form of an insulated wire or wires sheathed in a protective casing (orig. of wire strands, now also of plastic etc.), and used for carrying electric signals and electric power. M19. **b** A cablegram. L19. **c** In full *cable television*, *TV*. The system of transmitting television signals by cable, usu. to the receiving sets of individual subscribers. M20. **4** *Archit.* More fully *cable moulding*. An ornamental moulding that looks like rope. M19. **5** In full *cable pattern*, *stitch*. A pattern or stitching in knitting or embroidery that looks like twisted rope. L19.

2 *slip one's cable*: see SLIP *v.*[1] 3 *cable's end*: see END *n.* 7b. COAXIAL *cable*. CONCENTRIC *cable*. *jumper cable*: see JUMPER *n.*[1] *paper cable*: see PAPER *n.* & *a.* *pilot cable*: see PILOT *n.* 5. *standard cable*: see STANDARD *a.*

Comb.: **cable-car**: moved by an endless cable; **cable-laid** *a.* (of rope) having three triple strands; *cable length*: see sense 2b above; *cable moulding*: see sense 4 above; *cable pattern*: see sense 5 above; **cable railway**: with cars or carriages drawn along an endless cable moved by a fixed engine; *cable stitch*: see sense 5 above; *cable television, TV*: see sense 3c above; **cablevision** cable television (see sense 3c above); **cableway** a transporting-system with a (usu. elevated) cable.

cablegram *n.* a message by telegraphic cable M19. **cable-'ese, cab'lese** *n.* the contracted or cryptic style of expression used in cablegrams M20. **cablet** /'keɪblɪt/ *n.* a small cable or cable-laid rope, *spec.* one of less than ten inches in circumference L15.

cable /'keɪb(ə)l/ *v.* E16. [f. the n.] **1** *v.t.* Provide or equip with a cable or cables; fasten (as) with a cable, tie *up*. E16. **2** *v.t. Archit.* Ornament with cable moulding. M17. **3** *v.t.* & *i.* Transmit (a message) or transmit a message to (a person) by telegraphic cable. L19. **4** *v.t.* Provide with or equip for cable television. L20.

cabler *n.* L19.

cabob *n.* see KEBAB.

caboceer /kabə'sɪə/ *n.* E18. [Port. *caboceiro*, f. *cabo* head: cf. -EER.] A headman of a W. African village or tribe.

†caboche *v.* see CABBAGE *v.*[1]

caboched *a.* var. of CABOSHED.

cabochon /'kabəʃɒn/ *a.* & *n.* M16. [(O)Fr., dim. of *caboche*: see CABBAGE *n.*[1], -OON.] (A gem) polished but not faceted.

See also EN CABOCHON.

Caboclo /kə'bəʊkləʊ/ *n.* Pl. **-os**. E19. [Brazilian Port., perh. f. Tupi *Kaa-boc* one who has the colour of copper.] An American Indian descended from the aboriginals of Brazil. Also, a Brazilian of mixed White and Indian or Indian and Black ancestry.

caboodle /kə'buːd(ə)l/ *n. slang* (orig. *US*). M19. [Perh. f. *kit and boodle*: see KIT *n.*[1], BOODLE *n.* 1.] *the whole (kit and) caboodle*, the lot, everyone, the whole number or quantity.

caboose /kə'buːs/ *n.* Also (now *rare*) **camb-** /kam'buːs/. M18. [Du. *cabuse*, *combuse*, now *kabuis*, *kombuis*, = (M)LG *kabūse*, of unkn. origin.] **1** A small kitchen on the deck of a ship. M18. **b** An oven or fireplace erected on land. E19. **2** A hut, a cabin; a poor dwelling. Chiefly *N. Amer.* E19. **3** A guard's van on a train; a car for workmen etc. on a goods train. *N. Amer.* M19. **4** = CALABOOSE. *slang* (orig. *US*). M19. **5** A mobile hut or bunk-house. *Canad.* E20.

caboshed /kə'bɒʃt/ *a.* Also **caboched**, **cabossed** /kə'bɒst/. L16. [f. Fr. *caboché* pa. pple of *cabocher*: see CABBAGE *v.*[1], -ED[1].] *Her.* Of the head of a stag, bull, etc.: shown full-faced and cut off close behind the ears.

cabotage /'kabətɑːʒ, -ɪdʒ/ *n.* M19. [Fr., f. *caboter* coast along (a place), perh. ult. f. Sp. *cabo* CAPE *n.*[1]: see -AGE.] **1** Coastal trade. M19. **2** The reservation to a country of (esp. air) traffic operation within its territory. M20.

cabotin /kabɔtɛ̃/ *n.* Fem. ***-tine*** /-tin/. Pl. pronounced same. E20. [Fr. = strolling player, perh. f. as prec. from resemblance to vessels travelling from port to port.] A third-rate or low-class actor.

cabotinage /kabɔtinɑːʒ/ *n.* the life and behaviour supposedly characteristic of third-rate actors. L19.

cabri /'kabri, kə'briː/ *n. Canad.* L18. [Prob. Fr. = kid f. L *capra* goat, but perh. repr. an Indian wd.] = *pronghorn* s.v. PRONG *n.*

cabriole /kabrɪ'əʊl; *foreign* kabri(j)ɔl (*pl. same*)/ *n.* L18. [Fr., f. *cabrioler*, earlier *caprioler*, f. It. *capriolare*: see CAPRIOLE.] **1** A springing dance step in which one leg is extended and the other brought up to it. L18. **2** *Hist.* More fully *cabriole chair*. A kind of small armchair. L18. **3** Chiefly *Hist.* = CABRIOLET 1. L18. **4** A kind of curved leg characteristic of Chippendale and Queen Anne furniture. L19.

cabriolet /'kabrɪəleɪ/ *n.* M18. [Fr., f. as prec. + -ET[1].] **1** Chiefly *Hist.* A light two-wheeled hooded one-horse chaise. M18. **2** A bonnet or hat shaped like a cabriolet. L18. **3** A motor car with a folding top. E20.

†Cabuli *a.* & *n.* var. of KABULI.

cac- *comb. form* see CACO-.

ca'canny /kɑː'kani, *Sc.* -'kɒni/ *n.* L19. [f. *ca'* var. of CALL *v.* (sense 9) + CANNY *adv.*] Moderation, caution; the policy of going slow or limiting output at work.

cacao /kə'kɑːəʊ, -'keɪəʊ/ *n.* Pl. **-os**. See also COCOA *n.*[1] M16. [Sp. f. Nahuatl *cacauatl*, f. *uatl* tree.] **1** The seed of the tree *Theobroma cacao*, native to tropical America, from which cocoa and chocolate are made. M16. **†2** = COCOA *n.*[1] 2. Only in M17. **3** The tree itself. M18.

Comb.: **cacao bean** = sense 1 above; **cacao butter** fat extracted from the seeds of cacao or related trees, used esp. in confectionery manufacture; **cacao tree** = sense 2 above.

†cacaroch *n.* var. of COCKROACH.

cachalot /'kaʃəlɒt/ *n.* M18. [Fr., f. Sp., Port. *cachalote*, f. *cachola* big head.] = SPERM WHALE 1.

cache /kaʃ/ *n.* & *v.* L18. [Fr., f. *cacher* to hide.] **A** *n.* **1** A hiding place for goods, provisions, ammunition, treasure, etc. L18: **2** A hidden store of provisions etc. M19. **3** An auxiliary computer memory from which high-speed retrieval is possible. Also *cache memory*. M20. **B** *v.t.* Place or store in a cache. E19.

cachectic /kə'kɛktɪk/ *a.* E17. [Fr. *cachectique* or L *cachecticus*, f. Gk *kakhektikos*: see CACHEXIA, -IC.] Of or pertaining to cachexia; characterized by or affected with cachexia.

Also **cachectical** *a.* (now *rare* or *obs.*) E17.

cache-peigne /kaʃpɛɲ/ *n.* Pl. pronounced same. L19. [Fr., f. *cacher* to hide + *peigne* comb.] A bow or other trimming for a hat, usu. worn at the back.

cache-pot /kaʃpo (*pl. same*), 'kaʃpɒt/ *n.* L19. [Fr., f. as prec. + *pot* POT *n.*[1]] An ornamental holder for a flowerpot.

cache-sexe /kaʃsɛks (*pl. same*), 'kaʃsɛks/ *n.* E20. [Fr., f. as prec. + *sexe* SEX *n.*] A covering for the genitals.

cachet /'kaʃeɪ/ *n.* E17. [Fr., f. *cacher* (in sense 'press', repr. now in *écacher* crush) f. Proto-Romance alt. of L *coactare* constrain.] **1** A seal for letters, documents, etc. Now *rare* or *obs.* E17. **2** A characteristic or distinguishing mark; a characteristic feature or quality conferring prestige or distinction; high status. M19. **3** A small digestible case enclosing a dose of medicine. L19.

1 LETTRE *de cachet*.

cachexia /kə'kɛksɪə/ *n.* Also Anglicized as **cachexy** /-'kɛksi/. M16. [Fr. *cachexie* or late L *cachexia* f. Gk *kakhexia*, f. *kakos* bad + *hexis* habit: see -IA[1].] **1** *Med.* A condition of weakness and wasting due to severe chronic illness. M16. **2** A bad mental condition; a state of depravity. M17.

cachinnate /'kakɪneɪt/ *v.i.* E19. [L *cachinnat-* pa. ppl stem of *cachinnare*, of imit. origin: see -ATE[3].] Laugh loudly or immoderately.

cachin'natory *a.* of or connected with loud laughter E19.

cachinnation /kakɪ'neɪʃ(ə)n/ *n.* E17. [L *cachinnatio(n-)*, f. as prec.: see -ATION.] Loud or immoderate laughter.

cacholong /'kaʃəlɒŋ/ *n.* L18. [Fr. f. Mongolian *kas chilagun* precious stone.] An opaque variety of opal.

cachou /'kaʃuː, kə'ʃuː/ *n.* L16. [Fr. f. Port. *cachu* f. Malay *kacu*.] **1** = CATECHU. L16. **2** A lozenge taken to sweeten the breath. E18.

cachucha /kə'tʃuːtʃə/ *n.* M19. [Sp.] A lively Spanish solo dance with castanets.

cacique /kə'siːk/ *n.* M16. [Sp. or Fr., f. Taino.] **1** A W. Indian or S. American Indian native chief. M16. **2** A political boss in Spain or Latin America. L19.

caciquism *n.* government by caciques E20.

cack /kak/ *n.* Now *dial.* [OE *cac-* in *cachūs* (*hūs* house), rel. to next.] **1** Excrement, dung. OE. **2** Soft or flabby substance. L19.

cacky *a.* L19.

cack /kak/ *v.* Now *dial.* LME. [MLG, MDu. *cacken* (Du. *kakken*) f. L *cacare*.] **1** *v.i.* Defecate. LME. **2** *v.t.* Void as excrement. L15.

cack-handed /kak'handɪd/ *a. colloq.* M19. [f. CACK *n.* + HAND *n.* + -ED[2].] Left-handed; clumsy.

cackle /'kak(ə)l/ *v.* & *n.* ME. [Prob. f. (M)LG, MDu. *kākelen*, partly of imit. origin, partly f. *kāke* jaw, cheek.] **A** *v.* **1** *v.i.* Of a hen: make the clucking noise characteristically made after laying an egg. Of a goose: make its similar characteristic noise, gaggle. ME. **†b** Of a jackdaw, magpie, starling, etc.: chatter. ME–L17. **2** *v.i.* Of a person: be full of noisy chatter; laugh spasmodically or in a loud and silly manner. ME. **3** *v.t.* Utter with or express by cackling. ME.

B *n.* **1** The cackling of a hen or goose. ME. **2** Idle chattering; noisy inconsequential talk. L17. **3** A spasmodic or loud and silly laugh. M19.

2 **cut the cackle** *colloq.* (stop talking and) come to the point.

cackler *n.* LME.

caco- /'kakəʊ/ *comb. form.* Bef. a vowel also **cac-**. [Repr. Gk *kako-*, f. *kakos* bad: see -O-.] In wds f. Gk and in Eng. wds modelled on these, w. the sense 'bad, evil'.

†cacochymic *a.* pertaining to or suffering from an unhealthy state of the bodily humours LME–M19. **†cacochymical** *a.* = CACOCHYMIC E17–M19. **†cacochymy** *n.* [Gk *kakokhumia*] an unhealthy state of the bodily humours LME–M19. **ca'codorous** *a.* ill-smelling, malodorous M19. **caco'doxical** *a.* (*rare*) of or pertaining to wrong opinion, heterodox L17. **cacodoxy** *n.* (*rare*) [Gk *kakodoxia*] a wrong doctrine, heterodoxy M19. **caco-magician** *n.* an evil sorcerer M17. **caconym** *n.* an example of bad (scientific) nomenclature or terminology L19.

cacodemon /kakə'diːmən/ *n.* Also **-daemon**. L16. [Gk *kakodaimōn* evil genius, f. as CACO- + *daimōn*: see DEMON *n.*[1]] **1** An evil spirit. L16. **2** A malignant or deprecated person. E18.

cacodyl /'kakədʌɪl, -dɪl/ *n.* M19. [f. Gk *kakōdēs* stinking + -YL.] *Chem.* A malodorous, toxic, spontaneously flammable liquid, tetramethyl-diarsine, $((CH_3)_2As)_2$. Also, the radical $(CH_3)_2As\cdot$, dimethylarsenic (freq. *comb.*).

caco'dylic *a.* of cacodyl; *cacodylic acid*, dimethylarsinic acid, $(CH_3)_2AsO(OH)$: M19. **caco'dylate** *n.* a salt or ester of cacodylic acid M19.

cacoepy /kə'kəʊɪpi, 'kakəʊ-/ *n.* L19. [Gk *kak(o)epia*, f. as CACO- + *epos* word: see -Y[3].] Bad pronunciation (opp. *orthoepy*).

cacoethes /kakəʊ'iːθiːz/ *n.* M16. [L f. Gk *kakoēthes* use as n. of adj. *kakoēthes* ill-disposed, f. as CACO- + ETHOS.] An evil habit; a passion or 'itch' for doing something inadvisable.

cacoethes scribendi /skrɪ'bɛndiː/ an irresistible desire to write.

cacography /kə'kɒgrəfi/ *n.* L16. [f. CACO- + -GRAPHY, after *orthography*.] **1** Incorrect spelling; a bad system of spelling. L16. **2** Bad handwriting; bad writing. M17.

cacographer *n.* L19. **caco'graphical** *a.* M19.

cacology /kə'kɒlədʒi/ *n.* E17. [Gk *kakologia* vituperation, f. as CACO- + -LOGY.] **†1** Evil report. Only in Dicts. Only in 17. **2** Bad choice of words; bad pronunciation. L18.

cacomistle /'kakəmɪs(ə)l/ *n.* M19. [Amer. Sp. *cacomixtle* f. Nahuatl *tlacomiztli*.] A small racoon of Central America, Mexico, and the south-western US, belonging to the genus *Bassariscus*.

cacophonous /kə'kɒf(ə)nəs/ *a.* L18. [f. Gk *kakophōnos* ill-sounding, f. as CACO- + *phōnē* sound: see -OUS.] Discordant in sound; ill-sounding.

cacophonously *adv.* M19.

cacophony /kə'kɒf(ə)ni/ *n.* M17. [Fr. *cacophonie* f. Gk *kakophōnia*, f. as prec.: see -PHONY.] Discordant sound.

caco'phonic(al) *adjs.* = CACOPHONOUS M19.

cactus /'kaktəs/ *n.* Pl. **cacti** /'kaktʌɪ/, **-uses**. E17. [L f. Gk *kaktos* cardoon.] **†1** = CARDOON. E17–E19. **2** A succulent plant of the family Cactaceae, with thick fleshy stems, usu. spiny and without leaves, and often brilliantly coloured flowers. M18.

Comb.: **cactus dahlia** a variety of dahlia with rolled-back flower-rays resembling a cactus flower.

cactaceous /kakˈteɪʃəs/ *a.* of or pertaining to the family Cactaceae M19.

cacuminal /kəˈkjuːmɪn(ə)l/ *a.* M19. [f. L *cacuminare* make pointed (f. *cacumin-*, *-men* top, summit) + -AL[1].] *Phonet.* Pronounced with the tongue-tip curled up towards the hard palate.

cad /kad/ *n.* L18. [Abbrev. of CADDIE *n.* or CADET *n.*[1]] †1 An unbooked passenger taken up by a coach-driver for his own profit. Only in L18. 2 One who takes the fare of or attends to the passengers of a coach; a conductor of a coach or omnibus. *obs.* exc. *Hist.* E19. 3 = CADDIE *n.* 2. *arch.* M19. 4 A vulgar ill-bred person; a person guilty or capable of ungentlemanly behaviour, a blackguard. M19.

cadastral /kəˈdastr(ə)l/ *a.* M19. [Fr., f. as next + -AL[1].] Of or according to a cadastre; having reference to the extent, value, and ownership of land, *spec.* for taxation; *loosely*, showing the extent and measurement of every plot of land.

cadastre /kəˈdastə/ *n.* L18. [Fr. f. mod.Prov. *cadastro* f. It. *catast(r)o* earlier *catastico* f. late Gk *katastikhon* list, register, f. *kata stikhon* line by line.] A register of property showing the extent, value, and ownership, of land for taxation.

cadaver /kəˈdɑːvə, -ˈdeɪ-/ *n.* LME. [L *cadaver*, f. *cadere* to fall.] Chiefly *Med.* A corpse.

cadaveric /kəˈdav(ə)rɪk/ *a.* M19. [Fr. *cadavérique* or f. prec. + -IC.] Of, pertaining to, or characteristic of a corpse.

cadaverine /kəˈdav(ə)riːn/ *n.* L19. [f. as CADAVER + -INE[5].] *Chem.* A toxic liquid base, 1,5-diaminopentane, $H_2N(CH_2)_5NH_2$, formed by the putrefaction of proteins.

cadaverous /kəˈdav(ə)rəs/ *a.* LME. [L *cadaverosus*, f. as CADAVER: see -OUS.] Of, pertaining to, or resembling a corpse; *esp.* deathly pale.

cadaverously *adv.* M19. **cadaverousness** *n.* M17.

cad-bait /ˈkadbeɪt/ *n.* Now *dial.* Also (earlier) **cod-**. E17. [f. as CAD-WORM: see BAIT *n.*[1]] = CADDIS *n.*[2] 1.

caddice *n.* var. of CADDIS *n.*[2]

caddie /ˈkadi/ *n.* Orig. *Sc.* Also **caddy**, **CADEE**, †**cadie**. M17. [Fr. CADET *n.*[1]] †1 = CADET *n.*[1] 2. M17–E19. 2 A boy or man on the lookout for odd jobs. M18. 3 A young fellow, a lad. *Sc. joc.* L18. 4 A golfer's assistant for carrying clubs etc. L18.

Comb.: **caddie-car**, **-cart** a light two-wheeled trolley for transporting golf clubs during a game.

caddie /ˈkadi/ *v.i.* Also **caddy**. E20. [f. the n.] Act as caddie (*for* a golfer).

caddis /ˈkadɪs/ *n.*[1] *obs.* exc. *Sc.* ME. [Sense 1 f. OFr. *cadas*, *-z*, sense 2 f. (O)Fr. *cadis* f. Prov., both of unkn. origin.] 1 Cotton wool; floss silk; fluff; surgical lint. ME. †2 (A tape or binding of) worsted yarn, crewel; worsted material; coarse serge. M16–L19.

caddis /ˈkadɪs/ *n.*[2] Also **-ice**. E17. [Origin unkn.: cf. CAD-BAIT, CADEW, CAD-WORM.] 1 More fully *caddis-bait*, *worm*. The aquatic larva of a caddis-fly (see sense 2 below), which often makes cylindrical protective cases of debris and is commonly used as fishing-bait. E17. 2 *caddis-fly*, a feeble-flying usu. nocturnal insect of the order Trichoptera, living near water. M17.

caddish /ˈkadɪʃ/ *a.* M19. [f. CAD *n.* + -ISH[1].] Of the nature of or characteristic of a cad; ungentlemanly; blackguardly.

caddishly *adv.* L19. **caddishness** *n.* M19.

caddle /ˈkad(ə)l/ *v.* & *n. dial.* L18. [Origin unkn.] A *v.t.* Trouble, disturb. L18. B *n.* Disorder, confusion; trouble. E19.

caddow /ˈkadəʊ/ *n.*[1] *obs.* exc. *dial.* LME. [Prob. f. as CAW + DAW *n.*: cf. KAE *n.*] A jackdaw.

caddow /ˈkadəʊ/ *n.*[2] Long *obs.* exc. *dial.* L16. [Cf. CADDIS *n.*[1] 2.] A rough woollen covering.

caddy /ˈkadi/ *n.*[1] L18. [Alt. of CATTY *n.*] 1 More fully *tea caddy*. A small box for holding tea. L18. 2 A container, sometimes with divisions, for other substances or small objects ready for use. L19.

caddy *n.*[2], *v.* var. of CADDIE *n.*, *v.*

†**cade** *n.*[1] ME–L19. [L *cadus* wine-jar, measure for liquids f. Gk *kados* cask, jar, of Semitic origin (cf. Heb. *kad* pitcher).] A cask, a barrel, *esp.* of herrings.

cade /keɪd/ *n.*[2] & *a.* LME. [Origin unkn.] (A lamb, foal, etc.) brought up by hand as a pet.

cade /keɪd/ *n.*[3] L16. [Fr. f. Prov. f. med.L *catanus*, perh. f. Gaulish.] *cade oil*, *oil of cade*, a bitter dark oil, having some medicinal use, distilled from the wood of a juniper, *Juniperus oxycedrus*.

cadeau /kado/ *n.* Pl. ***-eaux*** /-o/. L18. [Fr.] A gift.

†**cadee** *n.* M17–L18. [Fr. CADET *n.*[1]: cf. CADDIE *n.*] = CADET *n.*[1] 2.

cadence /ˈkeɪd(ə)ns/ *n.* & *v.* LME. [OFr. f. It. *cadenza* f. pop.L, f. L *cadent-* pres. ppl stem of *cadere* fall: see -ENCE.] A *n.* 1 (A) rhythm; (a) metrical or musical beat; (a) measured movement, esp. of sounds. LME. 2a (A pattern of) falling intonation or pitch of voice, esp. at the end of a sentence etc. L16. b *gen.* Intonation; an intonation pattern; (a) modulation of the voice; (a) national or local accent. E18. 3 The close of a musical phrase; a sequence of notes resolving discord or establishing arrival in a key. Also, a flourish at the close of a movement, a cadenza. L16. †4 Sinking or falling down. E–M17. 5 The sound of the rising and (esp.) falling of a storm, the sea, etc. *arch.* M17.

1 SHAKES. *L.L.L.* The elegancy, facility, and golden cadence of poesy. F. NORRIS Listening to the one-two-three, one-two-three cadence of the musicians. *Scientific American* A bicyclist confronting a head wind . . tries to maintain his customary . . pedaling cadence by shifting gears. 2a L. STERNE A low voice, with a . . sweet cadence at the end of it. b G. MURRAY The accent, the cadences, the expression, with which the words were originally spoken. J. BERGER The cadence of their voices is like that of a couple talking in bed. 3 *imperfect cadence*: see IMPERFECT *a. medial cadence*: see MEDIAL *a. perfect cadence*: see PERFECT *a.* PLAGAL *cadence*. 4 MILTON Now was the Sun in Western cadence low.

Comb.: **cadence braking** repeated rhythmic application of the brakes of a motor vehicle.

B *v.* 1 *v.t.* Compose metrically. *rare.* M18. 2 *v.i.* Flow in rhythm; resolve discord or establish a key with a cadence. E20.

cadenced *a.* characterized by cadence, rhythmical, measured L18.

cadency /ˈkeɪd(ə)nsi/ *n.* E17. [f. as prec.: see -ENCY.] 1 = CADENCE *n.* 1. Now *rare.* E17. 2 The status of a younger branch of a family. E18.

cadent /ˈkeɪd(ə)nt/ *a.* & *n.* L16. [L *cadent-*: see CADENCE.] A *adj.* 1 *Astrol.* Designating or pertaining to each of the four mundane houses (the 3rd, 6th, 9th, and 12th of the twelve divisions of the heavens) next clockwise from the angles (ANGLE *n.*[3] 3). Cf. SUCCEDENT *a.* 2. L16. 2 Falling in intonation or pitch; rhythmical; modulated. *arch.* E17. 3 *gen.* Falling. Long *arch.* E17. B *n. Astrol.* A cadent house (see A.1 above). *obs.* exc. *Hist.* L16.

cadential /kəˈdɛnʃ(ə)l/ *a.* M19. [f. CADENCE, after *essence*, *essential*, etc.: see -IAL.] Of or pertaining to a cadence or cadenza.

cadenza /kəˈdɛnzə/ *n.* M18. [It.: see CADENCE.] *Mus.* A (sometimes improvised) flourish or passage for a solo instrument or voice, usu. near the close or between the divisions of a movement; *spec.* such a passage in a concerto in which the main themes of the movement (usu. the first or last) are developed.

cadet /kəˈdɛt/ *n.*[1] E17. [Fr., earlier *capdet* f. Gascon dial. (= Prov. *capdel*) f. Proto-Romance dim. of L *caput*, *-it-* head: see -ET[1].] 1 A younger son or brother; also occas. (a member of) a younger branch of a family. E17. b *The* youngest son or brother. M17. 2 *Hist.* A gentleman who entered the army without a commission, to learn the profession. M17. 3 A student in a naval, military, or air force college. L18. 4 A young man learning sheep-farming. *NZ.* M19. 5 A member of a corps receiving elementary military or police training. L19.

cadetship *n.* a place as a cadet; the status of a cadet: E19.

Cadet /kəˈdɛt/ *n.*[2] Also **K-**. E20. [Russ. *Kadet*, f. *Ka de*, pronunc. of the initials of *Konstitutsionnyĭ demokrat* Constitutional Democrat, with ending assimilated to that of CADET *n.*[1]] *Russ. Hist.* A member of the Constitutional Democratic Party.

cadew /ˈkadjuː/ *n.* Now *rare* or *obs.* M17. [Rel. to CAD-BAIT, CADDIS *n.*[2], CAD-WORM.] = CADDIS *n.*[2] 1.

cadge /kadʒ/ *n.*[1] E17. [App. alt. of CAGE *n.*, perh. conf. w. CADGE *v.* 2.] *Falconry.* A (usu. wooden) framework on which hawks are carried.

cadge /kadʒ/ *v.* & *n.*[2] LME. [Origin unkn. Exc. in sense A.1 (which may be a different wd) perh. back-form. f. next.] A *v.* 1 *v.t.* Fasten, tie, bind, knot. *obs.* exc. *dial.* LME. 2 *v.t.* Carry about. *obs.* exc. *dial.* E17. 3 *v.t.* Load, stuff, (the stomach). *dial.* L17. 4 *v.t.* Hawk, peddle (*Sc.*); get by begging or scrounging. E18. 5 *v.i.* Go about begging or scrounging. E19.

1 T. ROETHKE So caged and cadged. 4 R. HOGGART Those who can cadge a few coppers from their mothers. E. REVELEY I'm cadging a lift home with you people. 5 J. BUCHAN I cadged . . for invitations to tea.

B *n.* †1 A circuit for begging. *Sc.* Only in L17. 2 *The* action of cadging. *colloq.* E19.

cadger /ˈkadʒə/ *n.*[1] L15. [Origin unkn.: cf. prec.] 1 A carrier; an itinerant dealer, esp. travelling between town and country; a hawker. *arch.* Chiefly *Sc.* & *north.* L15. 2 A person who scrounges or begs habitually; a sponger. M19.

cadger /ˈkadʒə/ *n.*[2] M19. [Prob. f. CADGE *n.*[1] + -ER[1]: cf. OFr. *cagier*.] *Falconry.* A man who carries hawks.

cadgy /ˈkadʒi/ *a. Sc.* & *north.* E18. [Origin unkn.] 1 Amorous; wanton. E18. 2 Cheerful, merry. E18.

cadgily *adv.* E18. **cadginess** *n.* L19.

cadi /ˈkɑːdi, ˈkeɪdi/ *n.* Also **k-**, **q-**. L16. [Arab. *(al-)ḳāḍī*. See also KAZI.] A civil judge in a Muslim country.

†**cadie** *n.* var. of CADDIE *n.*

cadilesker /kɑːdɪˈlɛskə/ *n.* L16. [Turk. *cadilaskar* f. Arab. *ḳāḍī (a)l-ʿaskar* judge of the army.] *Hist.* A chief judge in the Ottoman Empire, whose jurisdiction originally included the army.

†**cadjan** *n.* & *a.* see KAJANG.

Cadmean /kadˈmiːən/ *a.* Also **-aean**. E17. [f. L *Cadmeus* f. Gk *Kadmeios*, f. *Kadmos* Cadmus (see below) + -AN.] Pertaining to Cadmus, the legendary founder of Thebes; Theban; *spec.* designating a victory gained at too great a cost.

cadmium /ˈkadmɪəm/ *n.* E19. [f. L *cadmia* (see CALAMINE) + -IUM.] A bluish-white metallic chemical element, atomic no. 48, which occurs in small amounts in zinc ores and resembles zinc chemically. (Symbol Cd.)

Comb.: **cadmium cell** a voltaic cell with cadmium amalgam and mercury electrodes and saturated cadmium sulphate electrolyte, used as a standard of electromotive force; **cadmium yellow** an intense yellow pigment containing cadmium sulphide.

cadˈmiferous *a.* yielding cadmium E19.

†**cadouk** *a.* & *n.* Chiefly *Sc.* As n. also **caduac**. LME. [Fr. *caduc*: see CADUCITY.] A *adj.* Liable to fall; perishable; transitory; frail. LME–L17. B *n.* An incidental payment; a windfall. M17–E19.

cadre /ˈkɑːdə, ˈkɑːdr(ə), ˈkadri/ *n.* M19. [Fr. f. It. *quadro* f. L *quadrus* square.] 1 A frame, a framework; a plan. *rare.* M19. 2 *Mil.* a A permanent establishment of trained personnel forming a nucleus for expansion at need. M19. b (A list of) the complement of the officers of a regiment etc. M19. 3 (A member of) a group of workers acting to promote the aims and interests of the Communist Party. M20. b In the People's Republic of China, an office-holder in a Party, governmental, or military organization. M20.

†**caduac** *n.* var. of CADOUK *n.*

caduceus /kəˈdjuːsɪəs/ *n.* Pl. **-cei** /-sɪʌɪ/. L16. [L *caduceus*, *-um* f. Doric Gk *karuk(e)ion* = Attic *kērukeion* neut. adj. used as n., f. *kērux*, *-uk-* herald.] In *Class. Hist.*, a Greek or Roman herald's wand; *spec.* (also **C-**) the wand carried by the messenger-god Hermes or Mercury, usu. represented with two serpents twined round it.

caducean *a.* M17.

caduciary /kəˈdjuːsjəri/ *a.* Now *rare.* M18. [Late L *caducarius*, f. *caducus* (in *bona caduca* lapsed possessions): see next, -ARY[1].] *Law.* (Of a bequest, esp. of an estate) subject to reversion; pertaining to reversion of a bequest.

caducity /kəˈdjuːsɪti/ *n.* M18. [Fr. *caducité*, f. *caduc* f. L *caducus* liable to fall, perishable, f. *cadere* to fall: see -ITY.] 1 The infirmity of old age, senility. M18. 2 *gen.* Tendency to fall; transitoriness; frailty. L18. 3 *Law.* The lapse of a testamentary gift. L19.

caducous /kəˈdjuːkəs/ *a.* L17. [f. L *caducus* (see prec.) + -OUS.] †1 Epileptic. Only in L17. 2 *Bot.* & *Zool.* Of an organ or part: that falls off naturally after serving its purpose. Opp. PERSISTENT I. M18. 3 *Law.* Of a bequest: subject to reversion. L19.

cad-worm /ˈkadwəːm/ *n.* Now *dial.* Also (earlier) †**cod-**. LME. [Origin of 1st elem. unkn.: cf. CAD-BAIT, CADDIS *n.*[2], CADEW. See WORM *n.*] = CADDIS *n.*[2] I.

cady /ˈkeɪdi/ *n. dial.* & *slang.* M19. [Origin unkn.] A hat, a cap.

Caecias /ˈsiːsɪəs/ *n. literary.* E17. [L f. Gk *kaikios.*] The north-east wind, esp. personified.

caecilian /sɪˈsɪlɪən/ *n.* Also **coe-**. L19. [f. mod.L *Caecilia* genus name f. L *caecilia* slow-worm: see -AN.] A legless, superficially snakelike, burrowing amphibian of the order Gymnophiona, with poorly-developed eyes; = APODAN.

caecum /ˈsiːkəm/ *n.* Also ***cecum**. Pl. **-ca** /-kə/. LME. [L (*intestinum*) *caecum* blind gut, tr. Gk *tuphlon enteron.*] *Anat.* 1 The blind prolongation of the large intestine beyond the junction with the small intestine, bearing the vermiform appendix; the blind gut. LME. 2 Any blind-ended tube or vessel. M18.

caecal *a.* of, pertaining to, or resembling the caecum E19. **caecitis** /siːˈsaɪtɪs/ *n.* inflammation of the caecum M19. **caecostomy** /siːˈkɒstəmi/ *n.* (an instance of) the surgical formation of an opening in the caecum through which intestinal contents may be removed L19.

Caelum /ˈsiːləm/ *n.* M19. [L *caelum* chisel.] A minor constellation of the southern hemisphere, next to Eridanus; the Chisel.

caenogenesis /siːnəˈdʒɛnɪsɪs/ *n.* Also **keno-** /ˈkiːnə/, ***ceno-**; **caino-**, **kaino-** /ˈkeɪnə-/. L19. [f. Gk *kainos* new, recent + -GENESIS.] *Biol.* Orig., the development of features in ontogenesis which are the result of environmental adaptation (opp. *palingenesis* or *recapitulation*). Now *spec.*, the development in embryonic or larval forms of functional adaptations not present in the adult.

caenogeˈnetic *a.* L19.

Caenozoic *a.* & *n.* var. of CENOZOIC.

Caen stone /ˈkeɪn stəʊn/ *n. phr.* LME. [f. *Caen*, a town in Normandy.] A lightish-yellow building stone found near Caen.

Caerphilly /kɛːˈfɪli, kɑː-, kə-/ *n.* E20. [A town in S. Wales.] More fully *Caerphilly cheese.* A kind of mild white cheese, orig. marketed in Caerphilly.

caerulean *a.* & *n.* var. of CERULEAN.

Caesar /ˈsiːzə/ *n.* [OE *cāsere*, OFris. *kaiser*, *keiser*, OS *kēsar*, OHG *keisar*, ON *keisari*, Goth. *kaisar*, f. Gmc f. L family name of Gaius Julius *Caesar*, Roman statesman d. 44 BC: cf. KAISER, TSAR.] 1 A Roman emperor, *esp.* one of those from Augustus to Hadrian. OE. †**b** (The heir of) the Emperor of the Holy Roman Empire. M16–E18. 2 *transf.* & *fig.* **a** An absolute monarch; an autocrat. ME. **b** A temporal ruler; the civil power. E17. 3 *Med.* (A case of or baby delivered by) Caesarean section. Now *slang.* M16.

1 **appeal to Caesar**: to the highest possible authority. **Caesar's wife** a person required to be above suspicion.

Comb.: **Caesar baby** *Med. slang*: delivered by Caesarean section.

Caesarism *n.* the principle of absolute government; imperialism: M19. **Caesarist** *n.* †(*a*) *rare* a monarch, an emperor; (*b*) an adherent of Caesarism: L16. **Caesaro-ˈpapism** *n.* the supremacy of the civil power in ecclesiastical affairs L19.

Caesarean /sɪˈzɛːrɪən/ *n.* & *a.* Also ***Ces-**, **-ian**. E16. [f. L *Caesarianus* or *Caesareus*, f. *Caesar*: see prec., -EAN, -IAN.] **A** *n.* 1 A follower or adherent of Caesar; a person in favour of autocracy or imperialism. E16. 2 *ellipt.* (A) Caesarean section; a Caesarean birth. E20. **B** *adj.* 1 [From the story that Julius Caesar was so delivered.] *Caesarean section, operation*, the surgical operation of cutting the walls of the abdomen to deliver a child. Hence *Caesarean birth, delivery*, etc. E17. 2 Of or pertaining to Caesar or the Caesars; imperial. M17.

caesious /ˈsiːzɪəs/ *a.* E19. [f. L *caesius* + -OUS.] Greyish-blue or -green.

caesium /ˈsiːzɪəm/ *n.* Also ***ces-**. M19. [f. as prec. + -IUM: named from having characteristic lines in the blue part of the spectrum.] A soft highly reactive chemical element of the alkali metal group, atomic no. 55. (Symbol Cs.)

caespititious /sɛspɪˈtɪʃəs/ *a.* Also ***ces-**. L18. [L *caespiticius*, f. as next: see -ITIOUS[2].] Made of turf.

caespitose /ˈsɛspɪtəʊs/ *a.* Also ***ces-**. M18. [f. L *caespit-*, *-es* sod, turf + -OSE[1].] Chiefly *Bot.* Growing in tufts or clumps.

caesura /sɪˈzjʊərə/ *n.* M16. [L *caesura*, f. *caespa.* ppl stem of *caedere* cut: see -URE.] 1 *Pros.* A break or pause between words within a metrical foot in classical prosody or near the middle of a line in English etc. prosody. M16. 2 *gen.* A break, a stop, an interruption. L16.

caesural *a.* M18.

caf *n.* var. of CAFF.

cafard /kaˈfɑː, *foreign* kafaːr/ *n.* M16. [Fr. = cockroach, hypocrite, prob. f. late L *caphardum*: see CAFFA.] †1 A hypocrite. M16–M17. 2 Melancholia. E20.

café /ˈkafeɪ, -fi; *joc. or slang* kaf, keɪf/ *n.*[1] Also **cafe**, **CAFF**. E19. [Fr. = coffee(-house).] A coffee-house; a teashop; an informal restaurant; *US* a bar.

Comb.: **café society** regular patrons of fashionable cafés and nightspots.

café /kafe/ *n.*[2] Pl. pronounced same. [See prec.] The Fr. for 'coffee' or 'coffee-house', occurring in various phrases used in Eng.

café au lait /o lɛ/ coffee with milk; (of) the light brown colour of this: M18. ***café chantant*** /ʃɑ̃tɑ̃/ [lit. 'singing café'], pl. **-s -s** (pronounced same), a café with live musical entertainment M19. ***café noir*** /nwaːr/ black coffee M19.

cafeteria /kafɪˈtɪərɪə/ *n.* Orig. *US.* M19. [Amer. Sp. *cafeteria*, f. *café* coffee.] A coffee-house; a restaurant; now *esp.* a self-service restaurant.

cafetière /kaftjɛːr/ *n.* Pl. pronounced same. M19. [Fr., f. as CAFÉ *n.*[1]] A coffee-pot; a coffee-making machine; a coffee-percolator.

caff /kaf/ *n. slang.* Also **caf**. M20. [Abbrev.] = CAFÉ *n.*[1], CAFETERIA.

†**caffa** *n.* L15. [OFr. f. late L *caphardum* university gown, of unkn. origin.] 1 A rich silk cloth. L15–M17. 2 A kind of painted cotton cloth made in India. M18–E19.

caffeine /ˈkafiːn/ *n.* M19. [Fr. *caféine*, f. as CAFÉ *n.*[1] + -INE[5].] *Chem.* A crystalline alkaloid, $C_8H_{10}N_4O_2$, which is found esp. in tea and coffee plants and is a central nervous system stimulant; 1,3,7-trimethylxanthine.

caffeinism *n.* headache, sleeplessness, and palpitations caused by excessive intake of caffeine L19.

caffle /ˈkaf(ə)l/ *v.i. dial.* M19. [Var. of CAVIL *v.*] Argue; prevaricate.

Caffrarian *a.* see KAFFRARIAN.

Caffre *n.* see KAFFIR.

cafila /ˈkɑːfɪlə/ *n.* L16. [Arab. *kāfila*: cf. COFFLE.] A company of travellers in the Middle East, a caravan.

caftan /ˈkaftan, kafˈtɑːn/ *n.* Also **k-**. L16. [Turk. *kaftan* f. Pers. *kaftān*, partly through Fr. *cafetan.*] 1 An Eastern man's long tunic with a waist girdle. L16. 2 A long loose dress; a loose-fitting shirt. M20.

cafuffle *n.* var. of KERFUFFLE.

cag /kag/ *n. obs.* exc. *Sc.* & *US dial.* See also KEG. LME. [ON *kaggi.*] A small cask, a keg.

cage /keɪdʒ/ *n.* & *v.* ME. [(O)Fr. f. L *cavea* stall, cage, coop, etc.] **A** *n.* 1 A box or place of confinement for birds, animals, etc., made wholly or partly of wire, or bars of metal, wood, etc., so as to admit air and light. ME. 2 A prison, a lock-up. ME. **b** An enclosure for prisoners of war. E20. 3 *fig.* That which confines or imprisons. ME. 4 A structure resembling a cage for birds etc.; an open framework of various kinds; *spec.* (*a*) a frame for hoisting men, wagons, etc., in a mine; (*b*) a compartment for passengers etc. in a lift. LME.

1 GILDED *cage.* 3 W. BEVERIDGE The Cage of Flesh, Wherein the Soul is penned. 4 RIBCAGE. THORACIC *cage.*

Comb.: **cage-bird**: (of a kind customarily) kept in a cage; **cage-work** (*a*) openwork like the bars of a cage; †(*b*) the upper works of a ship.

B *v.t.* Confine in or as in a cage. L16.

cageling *n.* a bird kept in a cage M19.

cagey /ˈkeɪdʒi/ *a. colloq.* (orig. *US*). Also **cagy**. E20. [Origin unkn.] Shrewd; wary; secretive; uncommunicative.

cageyness, **caginess** *n.* M20. **cagily** *adv.* E20.

cagmag /ˈkagmag/ *n.* & *v. dial.* M18. [Origin unkn.] **A** *n.* A tough old goose; unwholesome meat; offal. M18. **B** *v.i.* & *t.* Quarrel; nag. L19.

cagnotte /kaɲɔt/ *n.* L19. [Fr.] Money reserved from the stakes for the bank at certain gambling games.

cagot /kago/ *n.* Pl. pronounced same. M16. [Fr.] †1 An affectedly pious person. *Sc.* Only in M16. 2 A member of an outcast group in southern France (*Hist.*); an outcast, a pariah. E19.

cagoulard /kagulaːr/ *n.* Pl. pronounced same. M20. [Fr., f. as next: see -ARD.] *Hist.* A member of a secret French right-wing organization in the 1930s.

cagoule /kəˈguːl/ *n.* Also **k-**. M20. [Fr., lit. 'cowl'.] A hooded thin waterproof garment pulled on over the head.

cagy *a.* var. of CAGEY.

cahier /kaje/ *n.* Pl. pronounced same. L18. [Fr.: see QUIRE *n.*[1]] 1 *Hist.* In *pl.* The instructions prepared by each of the three representative bodies as a guide for their policy at the French National Assembly of 1789. L18. 2 An exercise-book; a pamphlet, a fascicle. M19.

cahoot /kəˈhuːt/ *n. slang* (orig. *US*). E19. [Origin unkn.] *sing.* & (now usu.) in *pl.* Company, partnership; collusion. Chiefly in *in cahoots with.*

cahoun *n.* var. of COHUNE.

cahow /kəˈhaʊ/ *n.* E17. [Imit.] A large rare petrel, *Pterodroma cahow*, which breeds in Bermuda.

caid *n.* see KAID.

cailleach /ˈkɛljʌx/ *n. Sc.* Also **-iach**. E19. [Gael. = old woman.] An old (Highland) woman, a crone.

†**caimacam** *n.* var. of KAIMAKAM.

caiman *n.* var. of CAYMAN.

cain /keɪn/ *n.*[1] *Sc.* & *Anglo-Ir.* Also **k-**. ME. [Ir. & Gael. *cáin.*] A rent paid in kind.

Cain /keɪn/ *n.*[2] ME. [The eldest son of Adam, who murdered his brother Abel (*Gen.* 4).] 1 A murderer, a fratricide. ME. 2 *raise Cain*, make a disturbance, create trouble. *colloq.* M19.

Cainite *n.* (*Eccl. Hist.*) a member of a gnostic sect which exalted everyone and everything reviled by God in the Old Testament M17.

-caine /keɪn/ *suff.* Also **-cain**. [f. COCAINE.] *Pharm.* Forming ns. denoting drugs, esp. ones with anaesthetic properties, as *lignocaine*, *Novocain.*

ca'ing whale /ˈkɑːɪŋ weɪl/ *n. phr.* Also **caa'ing**. M20. [Sc. *ca'ing* calling (see CALL *v.* 9).] The pilot whale, *Globicephala melaena.*

cainogenesis *n.* var. of CAENOGENESIS.

Cainozoic *a.* & *n.* var. of CENOZOIC.

caique /kaɪˈiːk, kə-/ *n.*[1] E17. [Fr. *caïque* f. It. *caicco* f. Turk. *kayık.*] 1 A light rowing boat or skiff used on the Bosporus. E17. 2 An eastern Mediterranean sailing vessel. M17.

caique /kʌɪˈiːkə, -keɪ/ *n.*[2] M20. [Sp. or Port.] Either of two small tropical S. American parrots of the genus *Pionites*, mainly green, yellow, and black in colour. Cf. SACKIE.

caird /kɛːd/ *n. Sc.* LME. [Gael. *ceard* artificer in metal = Ir. *ceard*, OIr. *cerd* craftsman.] A travelling tinker; a Gypsy.

Cairene /ˈkʌɪriːn, kʌɪˈriːn/ *n.* & *a.* M19. [f. *Cairo* (see below) + *-ene*, after *Nazarene* etc.] **A** *n.* A native or inhabitant of the Egyptian city of Cairo. M19. **B** *adj.* Of or pertaining to Cairo or its inhabitants. M19.

cairn /kɛːn/ *n.* & *v.* LME. [Gael. *carn* corresp. to OIr., Welsh *carn*.] **A** *n.* **1** A pyramid of rough stones raised as a memorial or to mark a path etc. LME. **2** In full *cairn terrier*. A small terrier with short legs, a longish body, and a shaggy coat. E20.

1 *horned cairn*: see HORNED *a.* *stalled cairn*: see STALL *v.*[1]

B *v.t.* Provide or mark with a cairn or cairns; pile as a cairn. Chiefly as *cairned* ppl a. M16.

cairngorm /ˈkɛːngɔːm/ *n.* L18. [A mountain in Grampian, Scotland, = Gael. *carn gorm* blue cairn.] (A piece of) smoky quartz, esp. as found in parts of Scotland. Also *cairngorm stone*.

caisson /ˈkeɪs(ə)n, kəˈsuːn/ *n.* L17. [Fr. = large chest, f. It. *cassone* w. assim. to *caisse* CASE *n.*[2]: see -OON.] **1** A large watertight chamber open at the bottom, from which the water is kept out by air pressure, used in laying foundations under water. L17. **b** A floating vessel used as a dock gate. M19. **2** An ammunition chest; an ammunition wagon. E18.

Comb.: **caisson disease** illness of workers in compressed air, resulting from too rapid decompression; the 'bends'.

caitiff /ˈkeɪtɪf/ *n.* & *a. arch.* ME. [OFr. *caitif* captive, var. of *chaitif* (mod. *chétif* wretched) f. Proto-Romance alt. of L *captivus* CAPTIVE *a.*] **A** *n.* †**1 a** A captive, a prisoner. ME–E17. **b** A wretched or miserable person, a poor wretch. LME–L17. **2** A base, despicable wretch; a villain; a coward. ME. **B** *adj.* †**1** Wretched, miserable. ME–L16. **2** Vile, base, wicked; worthless; cowardly. ME.

cajan /ˈkeɪdʒ(ə)n, ˈkɑː-/ *n.* L17. [Malay *kacang*.] A tropical leguminous shrub of the genus *Cajanus*, esp. *C. cajan*, cultivated for its edible pulses.

cajang *n.* & *a.* see KAJANG.

cajeput *n.* var. of CAJUPUT.

cajole /kəˈdʒəʊl/ *v.* M17. [Fr. *cajoler*.] **1** *v.t.* Persuade or prevail upon (a person) by delusive flattery, specious promises, etc. (Foll. by *into*, *out of*, *to do*.) M17. **b** Coax (something) *out of* a person. M18. **2** *v.i.* Use cajolery. M17.

1 W. IRVING The populace.. are not to be cajoled out of a ghost story by any of these plausible explanations. V. WOOLF We tried to cajole him to write with £10 p. 1,000 for bait. T. DREISER She cajoled him into getting things for her and then would not even let him kiss her. 2 S. KING Herb talked to her, then cajoled, finally demanded.

cajolement *n.* E19. **cajoler** *n.* L17.

cajolery /kəˈdʒəʊləri/ *n.* M17. [Fr. *cajolerie*, f. as prec.: see -ERY.] The action or an instance of cajoling; persuasion by flattery, deceit, etc.

Cajun /ˈkeɪdʒ(ə)n/ *n.* & *a. N. Amer. colloq.* M19. [Alt. of ACADIAN.] **A** *n.* A French-speaking descendant of early settlers in Acadia, living esp. in Louisiana and Maine; *gen.* an Acadian. M19. **B** *adj.* Of or pertaining to the Cajuns; *gen.* Acadian. L19.

cajuput /ˈkadʒəpʌt/ *n.* Also **caje-**. L18. [Malay *kayuputih*, name of the tree, f. *kayu* tree + *puteh* white.] More fully *cajuput oil*, *oil of cajuput*. An aromatic medicinal oil obtained from certain E. Indian trees of the genus *Melaleuca*, of the myrtle family.

cake /keɪk/ *n.* ME. [Of Scand. origin: cf. Icel., Sw. *kaka*, Da. *kage*, rel. to G *Kuchen*.] **1** (A quantity of) bread baked in smallish flattened rounds or other regular shapes, usu. turned in baking and so hard on both sides. Now chiefly *Hist.* ME. **2** (A quantity of) thin oaten bread. (Cf. *oatcake* s.v. OAT *n.*) *Sc.* & *north.* LME. **3** (A quantity of) sweet usu. unleavened bread with other ingredients besides flour, e.g. currants, spice, butter, eggs, sugar, usu. baked in a round or other ornamental shape. LME. **4** A flattish compact mass of other food or of any compressed substance. LME.

3 *birthday cake, chocolate cake, cup-cake, seed-cake, shortcake, sponge-cake, teacake, upside-down cake*, etc. *cheesecake*: see CHEESE *n.*[1] *wastel cake*: see WASTEL 1. 4 *cake of soap*, etc. *cattle-cake, cotton-cake, fish cake, linseed cake, mint-cake, oilcake, potato cake*, etc. *beefcake*: see BEEF *n.*

Phrases: **cakes and ale** merrymaking, good things. *hot cake*: see HOT *a.* **have one's cake and eat it, eat one's cake and have it** enjoy both alternatives. **land of cakes** (sense 2) Scotland. **piece of cake** *colloq.* something easy or pleasant. **the cake** *fig.* assets etc. to be shared out (*slice of the cake*, a share in benefits etc.). *take the cake*: see TAKE *v.*

Comb.: **cake-bread** (now *rare*) (*a*) bread of the fine texture of cake; (*b*) bread made in flattened cakes; †**cake-house**: where cakes are sold; **cake-hole** *slang* a person's mouth; **cake-mix** the prepared ingredients of a cake sold ready for cooking.

cakelet *n.* a small cake M19. **caky** *a.* like (a) cake M16.

cake /keɪk/ *v.* E17. [f. the n.] **1** *v.t.* & *i.* Form into a compact mass. E17. **2** *v.t.* Cover *with* a hardened mass. M20.

1 SHAKES. *Timon* Their blood is cak'd, 'tis cold, it seldom flows. H. G. WELLS Black mud.. had caked in hard ridges. 2 P. L. FERMOR Hair caked with snow.

cakewalk /ˈkeɪkwɔːk/ *n.* & *v.* Orig. *US.* M19. [f. CAKE *n.* + WALK *n.*] **A** *n.* **1** (A dance developed from) a Blacks' contest in graceful walking with a cake as the prize. M19. **2** A moving platform on which people walk, as a fairground entertainment. E20. **3** An easy task. E20. **B** *v.i.* Walk as in a cakewalk; dance the cakewalk. L19.

calabar *n.* var. of CALABER.

Calabar bean /ˈkaləbɑː biːn/ *n. phr.* L19. [f. *Calabar* a town and province in Nigeria + BEAN *n.*] The poisonous seed of a leguminous climbing plant, *Physostigma venenosum*, which contains physostigmine and is used in W. Africa in trials of witchcraft; = ORDEAL *bean*.

calabash /ˈkaləbaʃ/ *n.* M17. [Fr. *calebasse* f. as next.] **1 a** A gourd or similar large fruit that can be used as a container for liquid; *esp.* the fruit of the bottle-gourd or (*N. Amer.*) that of the tree *Bignonia cujete*. M17. **b** A tree yielding such a fruit, *esp.* (*a*) a bignonia; (*b*) the baobab. Also *calabash tree*. M17. **2** A vessel or other utensil (as a pipe) made from or having a resemblance to such a fruit; such a vessel full *of* a substance. M17. †**3** The head. *US slang.* E18–M19.

Comb.: *calabash nutmeg*: see NUTMEG *n.* 1; *calabash tree*: see sense 1b above.

calabaza /kaləˈbɑːzə/ *n.* L16. [Sp., perh. ult. f. Pers. *ḵarbuz* melon.] = CALABASH 1.

calaber /ˈkaləbə/ *n.* Also **-bar**. LME. [med.L *calabris*, *-ebrum*, app. f. *Calabria*: see CALABRIAN.] Squirrel fur; now *spec.* the fur of grey varieties of the common Eurasian squirrel *Sciurus vulgaris*.

calaboose /kaləˈbuːs/ *n. US.* L18. [Southern US Blacks' Fr. *calabouse* f. Sp. *calabozo* dungeon.] A prison, a lock-up.

calabrese /ˈkaləbriːs, kaləˈbriːs, kaləˈbreɪsi/ *n.* M20. [It. = Calabrian.] A variety of sprouting broccoli.

Calabrian /kəˈlabrɪən/ *a.* & *n.* L16. [f. *Calabria* (see below) + -AN.] (A native or inhabitant) of Calabria, a region of S. Italy.

caladium /kəˈleɪdɪəm/ *n.* M19. [mod.L, f. Malay *keladi*: see -IUM.] A plant of the tropical American genus *Caladium*, of the arum family, with starchy tubers.

calalu /kaləˈluː/ *n.* Also **callaloo**. M18. [Amer. Sp. *calalú*.] Any of various tropical American plants, esp. of the aroid genus *Xanthosoma*, cultivated for their edible leaves; soup or stew made with these.

calamanco /kaləˈmaŋkəʊ/ *n.* & *a.* Pl. of n. **-oes**. L16. [Origin unkn.: cf. Du. *kal(a)mink*, G *kalmank*, Fr. *calmande*.] *Hist.* (Of) a glossy worsted material.

calamander /ˈkaləmandə/ *n.* E19. [Sinhalese *kaḷumädiriya*, perh. f. Eng. COROMANDEL *ebony*, assim. to Sinhalese *kaḷu* black.] A fine-grained red-brown ebony, streaked with black, from the southern Asian tree *Diospyros quaesita*. Also, the tree itself.

calamary /ˈkaləməri/ *n.* M16. [med.L *calamarium* pen-case, use as n. of neut. of L *calamarius* adj., f. *calamus* f. Gk *kalamos* pen: see -ARY[1].] A squid with a long, tapering, horny, internal shell, esp. one of the common genus *Loligo*.

calambac /ˈkal(ə)mbak/ *n.* L16. [Fr., Sp., or Port., f. Malay *kelembak*.] = *aloes wood* s.v. ALOE.

calamine /ˈkaləmʌɪn/ *n.* LME. [(O)Fr. f. med.L *calamina* alt. of L *cadmia* f. Gk *kadm(e)ia* (*gē*) Cadmean (earth), f. *Kadmos*: see CADMEAN.] An ore of zinc, *spec.* the carbonate (smithsonite), or less commonly the basic silicate (hemimorphite). Also, a pink preparation of powdered zinc carbonate or oxide used in lotions, ointments, etc.

calamint /ˈkaləmɪnt/ *n.* ME. [OFr. *calament* f. med.L *calamentum* f. late L *calaminthe* f. Gk *kalaminthē*.] An aromatic herb or shrub of the genus *Clinopodium* (formerly *Calamintha*), of the mint family.

calamistrum /kaləˈmɪstrəm/ *n.* Pl. **-stra** /-strə/. [L = curling-iron.] *Zool.* A comblike structure on the fourth pair of legs of certain spiders, serving to 'card' the silk as it is secreted.

calamite /ˈkaləmʌɪt/ *n.* M19. [mod.L *Calamites* genus name, f. as CALAMUS: see -ITE[1].] *Palaeont.* A reedlike plant of an extinct group related to the horsetails, found as fossils chiefly of Carboniferous age.

calaˈmitean *a.* L19.

calamitous /kəˈlamɪtəs/ *a.* M16. [Fr. *calamiteux* or L *calamitosus*, f. as next: see -OUS.] **1** Disastrous, deeply distressing. M16. †**2** In deep distress; grievously afflicted. M17–M18.

calamitously *adv.* L18. **calamitousness** *n.* (*rare*) M17.

calamity /kəˈlamɪti/ *n.* LME. [(O)Fr. *calamité* f. L *calamitas*: see -ITY.] **1** Adversity; deep distress. LME. **2** A grievous disaster. M16.

1 S. JOHNSON So full is the world of calamity, that every source of pleasure is polluted. 2 E. WILSON And all the kinds of calamities befell them: fires and typhoid epidemics.

Comb.: **calamity-howler**, **Calamity Jane** *N. Amer.* a prophet of disaster.

calamus /ˈkaləməs/ *n.* LME. [L f. Gk *kalamos*.] †**1** A reed; a cane. LME–E18. **2** More fully *sweet calamus*: a An Eastern aromatic plant mentioned in the Bible (e.g. *Ex.* 30:23). LME. **b** The sweet flag, *Acorus calamus*. M17. **3** A rattan palm of the genus *Calamus*. M19. **4** The hollow lower part of the shaft of a feather, which lacks barbs. L19.

†**calander** *n.* see CALANDRA.

calando /kəˈlandəʊ, *foreign* kaˈlando/ *adv.* E19. [It. = slackening.] *Mus.* Gradually decreasing in speed and volume.

calandra /kəˈlandrə/ *n.* Orig. †**-der**. L16. [(O)Fr. *calandre* f. med.L *calandrus* f. Gk *kalandros*.] More fully *calandra lark*. A lark, *Melanocorypha calandra*, native to southern Europe, N. Africa, and the Middle East.

calandria /kəˈlandrɪə/ *n.* E20. [Sp., f. Gk *kylindros* CYLINDER.] A closed cylindrical vessel with a number of tubes passing through it, serving as a heat-exchanger etc.

calanoid /ˈkalənɔɪd/ *n.* & *a.* M20. [f. mod.L *Calanus* genus name + -OID.] *Zool.* (Designating or pertaining to) a planktonic copepod of the order Calanoida.

calash /kəˈlaʃ/ *n.* Also **calèche**, **-eche**, /kəˈlɛʃ/, †**galeche**. M17. [Fr. *calèche*, †*g-* f. G *Kalesche* f. Pol. *kołasa* (or Czech *kolesa*), f. *koło* (*kolo*) wheel.] Chiefly *Hist.* **1** A light low-wheeled carriage with a removable folding hood. M17. **2** In Canada, a two-wheeled one-horse vehicle with a seat for the driver on the splashboard.

M18. 3 A woman's large and folding hooped hood. L18. 4 A folding hood on a vehicle. M19.

calathus /ˈkaləθəs/ *n.* Pl. **-thi** /-θʌɪ/. M18. [L f. Gk *kalathos*.] *Class. Antiq.* A basket, as depicted in sculpture etc.

calavance /ˈkaləvans/ *n. obs.* exc. *Canad. dial.* Earlier †**cara-**. E17. [Ult. f. Sp. *garbanzo* chick-pea.] Any of certain kinds of pulse; a small bean.

calaverite /kaləˈvɛːrʌɪt/ *n.* M19. [f. *Calaveras* County, California + -ITE[1].] *Min.* A monoclinic gold telluride, usu. occurring as elongated bronze-yellow or silvery-white metallic crystals, or as granular or massive deposits.

calc- /kalk/ *comb. form.* [G *kalk* lime, alt. after L *calc-* CALX: cf. CALCI-.] Forming wds chiefly *Geol.* & *Min.* w. the sense 'lime'.

cal'calkaline *a.* (*Petrogr.*) relatively rich in both calcium and alkali metals E20. **calc-sinter** *n.* a crystalline calcareous deposit from mineral springs; travertine: E19. **calc-spar** *n.* calcite E19. **calc-tuff** *n.* a porous calcareous deposit from mineral springs E19.

calcanea *n.* pl. of CALCANEUM.

calcaneo- /kalˈkeɪnɪəʊ/ *comb. form* of next: see -O-.

calcaneo'cuboid *a.* of or pertaining to both calcaneum and cuboid bone M19.

calcaneum /kalˈkeɪnɪəm/ *n.* Pl. **-ea** /-ɪə/. Also **-eus** /-ɪəs/, pl. **-ei** /-ɪʌɪ/. M18. [L.] *Anat.* The large bone of the heel.

calcaneal *a.* M19. **calcanean** *a.* L19. †**calcany** *n.* (*rare*) = CALCANEUM: only in L16.

calcar /ˈkalkɑː/ *n.*[1] Now *rare* or *obs.* M17. [It. *calcara*: cf. late L *calcaria* limekiln.] A small calcining furnace used in glass-making.

calcar /ˈkalkɑː/ *n.*[2] M18. [L = spur.] *Bot.* & *Zool.* A spurlike projection on a petal, bone, etc.

calcarate *a.* having a calcar or spur E19.

calcarenite /kalkəˈriːnʌɪt/ *n.* E20. [f. CALC- + L (*h*)*arena* sand + -ITE[1].] *Geol.* A limestone built up from particles similar in size to sand grains.

calcareous /kalˈkɛːrɪəs/ *a.* Also **-ious**. L17. [f. L *calcarius* of lime (see CALX, -ARY[1]) + -OUS.] Of or containing calcium carbonate or other, usu. insoluble, calcium salt; of the nature of calcium carbonate.

calcarine /ˈkalkərʌɪn/ *a.* L19. [f. L CALCAR *n.*[2] + -INE[1].] *Anat.* Spurlike: esp. designating a small fissure of the occipital lobes of the cerebrum.

calcarious *a.* var. of CALCAREOUS.

calcedony *n.* var. of CHALCEDONY.

calceolaria /kalsɪəˈlɛːrɪə/ *n.* L18. [mod.L, f. L *calceolus* dim. of *calceus* shoe + *-aria*: see -ARY[1].] A S. American plant of the genus *Calceolaria*, of the figwort family, bearing slipper-shaped flowers.

calceolate /ˈkalsɪəleɪt/ *a.* M19. [f. L *calceolus* (see prec.) + -ATE[2].] *Bot.* Shaped like a slipper.

calces *n.pl.* see CALX.

calci- /ˈkalsi/ *comb. form* of L *calc-*, CALX lime, usu. w. the sense 'calcium carbonate': see -I-. Cf. CALC-.

calcicole *a.* & *n.* [L *colere* inhabit] *Bot.* (a plant) growing best in calcareous soil L19. **cal'cicolous** *a.* = CALCICOLE *a.* L19. **cal'cigerous** *a.* containing lime M19. **calcifuge** *a.* & *n.* (*Bot.*) (a plant) not suited by calcareous soil M19. **calci'tonin** *n.* a polypeptide hormone secreted by the thyroid, having the effect of lowering blood calcium; also called *thyrocalcitonin*: M20.

calcic /ˈkalsɪk/ *a.* M19. [f. CALCIUM + -IC.] Of or containing calcium; relatively rich in calcium.

calciferol /kalˈsɪfərɒl/ *n.* M20. [f. next + -OL: so called because of its activity in promoting bone calcification.] *Biochem.* A sterol which is formed when its isomer ergosterol is exposed to ultraviolet light, and is essential for the deposition of calcium in bones and the prevention of rickets and osteomalacia. Also called *vitamin* D_2, *ergocalciferol*.

calciferous /kalˈsɪf(ə)rəs/ *a.* L18. [f. CALCI- + -FEROUS.] Yielding calcium carbonate.

calcify /ˈkalsɪfʌɪ/ *v.* M19. [f. CALCI- + -FY.] 1 *v.t.* Convert into calcium carbonate or other insoluble calcium compounds; harden by deposition of such compounds; petrify. Freq. as *calcified* ppl a. M19. 2 *v.i.* Undergo or become hardened by such deposition. M19.

1 *fig.*: P. GALLICO The humanity in her had been calcified by the pursuit of money.

cal'cific *a.* of or pertaining to calcification M19. **calcifi'cation** *n.* the process of becoming calcified; a calcified structure: M19.

calcimine /ˈkalsɪmʌɪn/ *n.* & *v.* M19. [Alt., after L *calc-*, CALX lime.] = KALSOMINE.

calcination /kalsɪˈneɪʃ(ə)n/ *n.* LME. [(O)Fr., or med.L *calcinatio(n-)*, f. *calcinat-* pa. ppl stem of *calcinare*: see next, -ATION.] 1 The action or process of reducing to a friable substance by heat; calcining. LME. †b Oxidation. E17–E19. 2 *gen.* Burning to ashes, roasting; complete combustion. E17.

calcine /ˈkalsʌɪn, -sɪn/ *v.* LME. [OFr. *calciner* or med.L *calcinare*, f. late L *calcina* lime, f. L *calc-*, CALX.] 1 *v.t.* a Reduce by roasting or burning to quicklime or a similar friable substance or powder. LME. b *gen.* Burn to ashes, consume by fire; roast. E17. †c *fig.* Consume or purify as if by fire. M17–E18. 2 *v.i.* Undergo any of these processes. E18.

2 V. S. NAIPAUL In the dry season the earth baked, cracked, and calcined.

cal'cinable *a.* M17. **cal'ciner** *n.* (*a*) *rare* a person who calcines; (*b*) a kiln or other apparatus for calcining: M17.

calcio- /ˈkalsɪəʊ/ *comb. form.* [f. CALCIUM + -O-] Used esp. to form mineral names.

calcite /ˈkalsʌɪt/ *n.* M19. [f. L *calc-*, CALX + -ITE[1].] *Min.* Trigonal calcium carbonate, which occurs widely in a variety of forms, e.g. as prismatic crystals of Iceland spar etc., or in limestone, marble, and other rocks, and is colourless or white when pure.

calcitic /kalˈsɪtɪk/ *a.* of, pertaining to, or of the nature of calcite L19.

calcitrate /ˈkalsɪtreɪt/ *v.t.* & *i.* E17. [L *calcitrat-* pa. ppl stem of *calcitrare* kick out with the heels, f. *calx* heel: see -ATE[3].] Kick.

calci'tration *n.* M17.

calcium /ˈkalsɪəm/ *n.* E19. [f. L *calc-*, CALX + -IUM.] A greyish-white chemical element, atomic no. 20, which is one of the alkaline earth metals and occurs abundantly in nature, esp. as its carbonate (limestone etc.). (Symbol Ca.)

calcrete /ˈkalkriːt/ *n.* E20. [f. CALC- + CON)CRETE *n.*] A breccia or conglomerate cemented together by calcareous material; a calcareous duricrust.

calculable /ˈkalkjʊləb(ə)l/ *a.* M18. [f. next + -ABLE.] Able to be calculated. Of a person: predictable.

calcula'bility *n.* L19.

calculate /ˈkalkjʊleɪt/ *v.* LME. [Late L *calculat-* pa. ppl stem of *calculare*, f. as CALCULUS: see -ATE[3].] 1 *v.t.* Estimate or determine by arithmetical or mathematical reckoning; estimate or determine by practical judgement or on the basis of experience. LME. 2 *v.t.* Ascertain esp. beforehand the time or circumstances of (an event etc.) by exact reckoning. LME. 3 *v.i.* Perform a calculation or calculations; make an estimate; form a judgement about the future. E17. 4 *v.t.* Plan deliberately; think out, frame. M17. 5 *v.t.* Arrange, design, adjust, adapt; be intended. Foll. by *for* a purpose, *to do*. Now always pass. in meaning and usu. in form (see CALCULATED 1). M17. 6 *v.i.* Rely, reckon, count, *on*, *upon*. E19. 7 *v.t.* Suppose, believe, (*that*); intend (*that*, *to do*). *US colloq.* E19.

1 S. BELLOW He could calculate percentages mentally at high speed. I. MURDOCH She was now calculating how soon she could decently rise to go. 2 SHAKES. *2 Hen. VI* A cunning man did calculate my birth And told me that by water I should die. 4 R. W. EMERSON The English did not calculate the conquest of the Indies. 5 T. S. ELIOT His manners and appearance did not calculate to please. 6 H. B. TRISTRAM We had calculated on a quiet Sunday.

calculative *a.* of or pertaining to calculation; given to calculating: M18. **calculatory** *a.* (now *rare*) of or pertaining to calculation E17.

calculated /ˈkalkjʊleɪtɪd/ *ppl a.* E18. [f. prec. + -ED[1].] 1 Intended *to do*; fitted, suited, apt, *to do*. E18. 2 Reckoned, estimated; considered; with consequences etc. known. M19.

1 S. J. PERELMAN A scene of activity calculated to inspire even the most torpid. 2 GEO. ELIOT When he did speak it was with a calculated caution. *Listener* Obviously, the Soviet Union is taking a calculated risk.

calculatedly *adv.* L19.

calculating /ˈkalkjʊleɪtɪŋ/ *ppl a.* E19. [f. as prec. + -ING[2].] That calculates; *esp.* shrewdly or selfishly reckoning the chances of gain or advantage, acting self-interestedly.

calculatingly *adv.* M19.

calculation /kalkjʊˈleɪʃ(ə)n/ *n.* LME. [(O)Fr. f. late L *calculatio(n-)*, f. as CALCULATE: see -ATION.] 1 Arithmetical or mathematical reckoning; computation; estimation of outcome or probability; shrewd or selfish reckoning of the chances of gain or advantage. LME. b An act or instance of so reckoning or estimating. LME. 2 A form in which reckoning is made; a product or result of calculating; a forecast. LME.

1 M. KLINE Calculation was done on various forms of the abacus. J. GROSS The impression which remains longest is one of artfulness and calculation. b E. J. HOWARD She did some . . calculations then, and said thirty-eight. 2 J. AUSTEN If the first calculation is wrong, we make a second better.

calculational *a.* L19.

calculator /ˈkalkjʊleɪtə/ *n.* LME. [L *calculator*, f. as CALCULATE: see -OR. In mod. use f. CALCULATE + -OR.] 1 A person who calculates; a reckoner. LME. 2 A set of tables to facilitate calculations; a machine to carry out calculations. L18. b A programmed electronic device for carrying out calculations, *esp.* (also *pocket calculator*) a small flat one with a keyboard and visual display. M20.

†**calcule** *n.* L16–M18. [Fr. *calcul* f. L CALCULUS.] = CALCULATION.

calculiform /ˈkalkjʊlɪfɔːm/ *a.* E20. [f. L CALCULUS + -I- + -FORM.] Pebble-shaped.

calculous /ˈkalkjʊləs/ *a.* E17. [f. L *calculosus*, f. as next: see -ULOUS.] *Med.* Of, pertaining to, or of the nature of a calculus; affected with calculi.

calculus /ˈkalkjʊləs/ *n.* Pl. **-li** /-lʌɪ, -liː/, **-luses**. M17. [L = small stone (used in reckoning with an abacus).] 1 a A particular method or system of calculation or reasoning; *esp.* (*Math.*) infinitesimal calculus (see below). M17. †b *gen.* Computation; calculation. L17–E19. 2 *Med.* A stone. M18.

1 *calculus of variations*: see VARIATION. **differential calculus** the part of infinitesimal calculus that deals with derivatives and differentiation. **infinitesimal calculus** the branch of mathematics that deals with the finding and properties of derivatives and integrals of functions, by methods orig. based on the summation of infinitesimal differences. **integral calculus** the part of infinitesimal calculus that deals with integrals and integration. *predicate calculus*: see PREDICATE *n.* PROPOSITIONAL *calculus*.

caldarium /kalˈdɛːrɪum/ *n.* Pl. ***-ria*** /-rɪə/. M18. [L.] *Hist.* A (Roman) hot bath or bathroom.

caldera /kɒlˈdɛːrə, -ˈdɪərə/ *n.* L17. [Sp. f. late L *caldaria* pot for boiling.] A volcanic crater of great size; *spec.* one whose breadth greatly exceeds that of the vent(s) within it.

caldron *n.* var. of CAULDRON.

calean /ˈkalɪɑːn/ *n.* M18. [Pers. *ġilyān*, *kalyān* f. Arab. *ġilyān* for *ġalayān* bubbling up, boiling: cf. KALIAN.] A hookah.

calèche, -eche *n.* vars. of CALASH.

Caledonian /kalɪˈdəʊnɪən/ *a.* & *n.* E17. [f. L *Caledonia* Caledonia, Roman name of part of northern Britain, later applied to Scotland or the Scottish Highlands, + -AN.] A *adj.* 1 Of or pertaining to ancient Caledonia; Scottish, of the Scottish Highlands, (now *joc.* or *literary* exc. in names of existing institutions etc.). E17. 2 *Geol.* Designating or pertaining to an episode of mountain-building in NW Europe in the Palaeozoic era. E20. B *n.* A native or inhabitant of ancient Caledonia; a Scotsman, a Scottish Highlander, (now *joc.* or *literary*). M18.

¶ See also *New Caledonian* s.v. NEW *a.*

caledonite /ˈkalɪdənʌɪt/ *n.* M19. [f. as prec. + -ITE[1].] *Min.* An orthorhombic basic sulphate and carbonate of copper and lead, usu. occurring as blue or blue-green prisms.

calefacient /kalɪˈfeɪʃ(ə)nt/ *n.* & *a.* M17. [L, pres. ppl stem of *calefacere*, f. *calere* be warm: see -FACIENT.] *Med.* (A substance) producing a sense of warmth.

calefaction /kalɪˈfakʃ(ə)n/ *n.* Now *rare.* LME. [(O)Fr. *caléfaction* or late L *calefactio(n-)*, f. *calefact-* pa. ppl stem of *calefacere*: see prec., -FACTION.] 1 (A) heated condition of the body. LME. 2 The action of making something warm (*lit.* & *fig.*); heating. E16.

calefactive /kalɪˈfaktɪv/ *a.* Now *rare.* LME. [f. L *calefact-* (see prec.) + -IVE.] Having the tendency to warm; warming.

calefactory /kalɪˈfakt(ə)ri/ *n.* & *a.* LME. [Late L *calefactorius* adj., med.L *-torium* n., f. as prec.: see -ORY[1].] A *n.* †1 *Med.* = CALEFACIENT *n.* LME-M17. 2 *Hist.* A vessel providing heat; *spec.* a metal ball containing hot water on which a priest could warm his hands before administering the Eucharist. M16. 3 A warm room in a monastery. L17. B *adj.* Adapted to warming; producing warmth. E18.

calembour /kalɑ̃buːr/ *n.* Also ***-bourg*** /-buːr/. Pl. pronounced same. E19. [Fr.] A pun.

calendar /ˈkalɪndə/ *n.* Also (now *rare*) **k-**. ME. [AN *calender*, OFr. *calendier* (mod. *calendrier*) f. L *kalendarium*, *c-* account-book, f. *kalendae* (the day on which accounts were due): see CALENDS, -AR[2].] 1 The system by which the beginning, duration, and subdivisions of a year are fixed. ME. 2 A table or set of tables displaying the months, weeks, festivals, etc., of a given year, or with dates important to a particular pursuit or occupation. LME. b A contrivance for reckoning days, months, etc.; an adjustable device showing the day's date etc. E18. †3 *fig.* A guide; an example; a model. LME-E17. 4 A list, a register, *spec.* (*a*) of canonized saints, (*b*) of cases for trial, (*c*) of documents arranged chronologically with summaries, (*d*) *US* of matters for debate. LME.

1 *Gregorian calendar*: see GREGORIAN *a.* *Julian calendar*: see JULIAN *a.* *Liberian calendar*: see LIBERIAN *a.*[1] 2 *gardener's calendar*, *racing calendar*, etc. *perpetual calendar*: see PERPETUAL *a.* 4 *Newgate Calendar*: see NEWGATE *n.*

Comb.: **calendar month** any of the (usu. twelve) portions into which a year is divided; the period between the same dates in successive months; *calendar year*: see YEAR *n.*[1] 2.

calenˈdarial *a.* of, pertaining to, or according to a calendar E19. **calendary** *n.* & *a.* †(*a*) *n.* = CALENDAR *n.*; (*b*) *adj.* = CALENDARIAL: LME. **caˈlendric** *a.* of the nature of a calendar L19. **caˈlendrical** *a.* = CALENDRIC *a.* M19.

calendar /ˈkalɪndə/ *v.t.* L15. [f. the n.] 1 Register or enter in a calendar, esp. of saints or saints' days. L15. 2 Arrange, analyse, and index (documents). M19.

calendarer *n.* M19.

calender /ˈkalɪndə/ *n.*[1] E16. [(O)Fr. *calandre*, f. as CALENDER *v.*] †1 = CALENDERER. E16-L18. 2 A machine in which cloth, paper, etc. is pressed by rollers to glaze or smooth it. E17.

calender /ˈkalɪndə/ *n.*[2] L16. [Pers. *ḳalandar*.] A mendicant dervish.

calender /ˈkalɪndə/ *v.t.* L15. [(O)Fr. *calandrer*, of unkn. origin.] Press (cloth, paper, etc.) in a calender.

calenderer *n.* a person who calenders cloth etc. L15.

calends /ˈkalɪndz/ *n.pl.* Also **k-** & †in *sing.* OE. [(O)Fr. *calendes* f.) L *kalendae*, *c-* (pl.) first day of the month, when the order of days was proclaimed, f. base of L *calare*, Gk *kalein* call, proclaim.] †1 In *sing.* A month; an appointed time. Only in OE. †2 The Jewish festival of the new moon. LME-E17. 3 The first day of the month in the ancient-Roman calendar. LME. †4 A prelude, a beginning. LME-E17. 5 A calendar, a record. *rare.* LME.

3 **on** or **at, till the Greek Calends** never, for ever.

calendula /kəˈlendjʊlə/ *n.* L16. [mod.L, dim. of *calendae* (see prec.), perh. because it flowers for most of the year.] A marigold of the genus *Calendula*, with large yellow or orange flowers.

calenture /ˈkal(ə)ntjʊə/ *n.* L16. [Fr. f. Sp. *calentura*, f. *calentar* be hot f. Proto-Romance f. L *calere* be warm.] 1 A form of delirium formerly supposed to afflict sailors in the tropics, in which the sea is mistaken for green fields; a fever, sunstroke. L16. 2 *fig.* A burning passion, ardour, zeal. L16.

calescence /kəˈlɛs(ə)ns/ *n.* *rare.* M19. [f. L *calescent-* pres. ppl stem of *calescere* grow warm, f. *calere* be warm: see -ESCENCE.] Increasing warmth or heat.

calescent *a.* E19.

calf /kɑːf/ *n.*[1] Pl. **calves** /kɑːvz/. [OE *cælf*, *ċealf* = OS *calf* (Du. *kalf*), OHG *kalb* neut. (G *kalb*), *kalba* fem., ON *kálfr*, Goth. *kalbō*, f. Gmc. In sense 4 f. ON.] 1 A young bovine animal, esp. the domestic cow, *spec.* in its first year. OE. b A stupid or inoffensive person. M16. 2 The young of some other large mammals, as the elephant, deer, whale, etc. LME. 3 *sea-calf*, the common seal. LME. 4 A small island lying close to a larger one. *rare* exc. in *the Calf of Man* (off the Isle of Man). L17. 5 Leather made from the hide or skin of a calf, used esp. in shoemaking and bookbinding. E18. 6 A floating piece of ice detached from an iceberg. E19.

5 MOTTLED *calf*. *rough calf*: see ROUGH *a.*

Phrases: GOLDEN *calf*. **in, with, calf** (of a cow etc.) pregnant. *kill the fatted calf*: see FAT *v.*

Comb.: **calf-love** romantic affection felt by a young person; **calf's foot** (*a*) the foot of a calf, esp. as food; †(*b*) wild arum, cuckoo-pint; **calfskin** = sense 5 above; **calf's snout** the plant weasel's snout, *Misopates orontium*.

calfhood *n.* L19. **calfless** *a.*[1] LME.

calf /kɑːf/ *n.*[2] Pl. **calves** /kɑːvz/. ME. [ON *kálfi*, of unkn. origin.] The fleshy hinder part of the leg below the knee; *transf.* the corresponding part of a stocking, trouser-leg, etc.

Comb.: **calf-length** *a.* (of a garment, boots, etc.) reaching to the calf.

calfless *a.*[2] E16.

calfish /ˈkɑːfɪʃ/ *a.* Also **calvish** /ˈkɑːvɪʃ/. L16. [f. CALF *n.*[1] + -ISH[1].] Like a calf; stupid; untrained, immature.

Caliban /ˈkalɪban, -bən/ *n.* L17. [A character in Shakes. *Temp.*] A man of a degraded bestial nature.

caliber *n.* see CALIBRE.

calibogus /kalɪˈbəʊgəs/ *n.* *US.* M18. [Origin unkn.] A mixture of rum and spruce beer.

calibrate /ˈkalɪbreɪt/ *v.t.* M19. [f. CALIBRE + -ATE[3].] Measure the calibre of; measure the irregularities of (a tube, gauge, etc.) before graduating it; graduate (a tube, etc.) with allowance for irregularities; determine the correct value, position, capacity, etc. of; correlate the readings of (an instrument) with a standard.

calibrator *n.* an instrument or device used in calibrating E20.

calibration /kalɪˈbreɪʃ(ə)n/ *n.* L19. [f. prec.: see -ATION.] The action or process of calibrating an instrument, gauge, etc. Also, (one of) a set of graduations on an instrument, etc.

calibre /ˈkalɪbə, kəˈliːbə/ *n.* Also ***-ber**. M16. [(O)Fr. f. It. *calibro* or Sp. *calibre*, perh. f. Arab. *ḳālib* mould f. *ḳālab* ult. f. Gk *kalapous* shoemaker's last.] 1 (Orig. social) standing, rank, importance; ability, personal capacity, weight of character; worth. M16. 2 The diameter of a projectile; the bore or internal diameter of a gun. L16. b *transf.* The diameter of any body of circular section, esp. a tube, as an artery etc. E18.

1 B. MAGEE Works of this calibre, complexity and depth take a lot of getting to know. D. PIPER Two of the three most impressive sculptors who flourished in England in his lifetime were of considerable calibre. 2b H. ALLEN The gross calibre of the white linen socks ending in small, black, varnished shoes.

calibred *a.* having a calibre (of a specified kind) L19.

calice *n.* var. of CALIX.

caliche /kəˈliːtʃi/ *n.* M19. [Amer. Sp.] A mineral deposit found in arid areas of N. or S. America, *esp.* Chile nitre.

caliciform /ˈkalɪsɪfɔːm/ *a.* M19. [f. L CALIX, *-ic-* + -I- + -FORM.] Cup-shaped; resembling a calyx.

calicle /ˈkalɪk(ə)l/ *n.* M19. [L *caliculus* dim. of CALIX, *-ic-*: see -CLE.] *Zool.* A small cup-shaped structure.

calicular /kəˈlɪkjʊlə/ *a.* of or pertaining to a calicle, cuplike M19.

calico /ˈkalɪkəʊ/ *n.* & *a.* Orig. also †**-cut**. M16. [Alt. of *Calicut*, a town in India.] A *n.* Pl. **-oes**, ***-os**. 1 a Orig. *calico cloth.* Cotton cloth, orig. as imported from the East; fabric resembling this. Now *esp.* (*a*) plain white unprinted bleached or unbleached cotton cloth; (*b*) *N. Amer.* printed cotton cloth. M16. b A piece or example of such cloth. L16. 2 A piebald horse. *US.* M19.

Comb.: **calico-bush** *N. Amer.* the mountain laurel, *Kalmia latifolia*; **calico-printer**, **-printing** (one engaged in) the production of printed patterns on calico.

B *adj.* 1 Of calico. L16. 2 Suggestive of printed calico; multicoloured; piebald. *N. Amer.* E19.

2 **calico cat** a cat with black, ginger, and white patches.

calid /ˈkalɪd/ *a.* *arch.* LME. [L *calidus.*] Warm, tepid; hot.

caliduct /ˈkalɪdʌkt/ *n.* M17. [f. as prec., after *aqueduct.*] A pipe for conveying heat.

calif, califate *ns.* vars. of CALIPH, CALIPHATE.

Californian /kalɪˈfɔːnɪən/ *a.* & *n.* E18. [f. *California* (see below) + -AN.] A *adj.* Of or belonging to, native or peculiar to, California, a state on the Pacific coast of N. America. E18.

Californian CONDOR. **Californian holly** the toyon, *Heteromeles arbutifolia*. *Californian jack*: see JACK *n.*[1] **Californian poppy** a plant of the poppy family, *Eschscholtzia californica* (see ESCHSCHOLTZIA). *Californian sea lion*: see SEA LION 3.

B *n.* A native or inhabitant of California. L18.

californite /kalɪˈfɔːnʌɪt/ *n.* E20. [f. as prec. + -ITE[1].] *Min.* A green variety of vesuvianite resembling jade.

californium /kalɪˈfɔːnɪəm/ *n.* M20. [f. *California* University, where first made + -IUM.] A radioactive metallic chemical element of the actinide series, atomic no. 98, which is produced artificially. (Symbol Cf.)

caliginous /kəˈlɪdʒɪnəs/ *a.* *arch.* M16. [L *caliginosus*, f. *caligo*, *-in-* mistiness: see -OUS.] Misty, dim; obscure, dark.

caligiˈnosity *n.* (*arch.*) dimness of sight M17.

calinda /kəˈlɪndə/ *n.* M18. [Amer. Sp.] A Black American dance found in Latin America and the southern US.

calipash /ˈkalɪpaʃ/ *n.* L17. [Perh. W. Indian or alt. of Sp. *carapacho* CARAPACE.] Orig. the upper shell or carapace of the turtle. Now, that part next to this, containing a dull green gelatinous substance; also, this substance, which is regarded as a delicacy. Cf. next.

calipee /ˈkalɪpiː/ *n.* M17. [Perh. W. Indian: cf. prec.] Orig., the lower shell or plastron of the turtle. Now, that part next to this, containing a light yellowish gelatinous substance; also, this substance, which is regarded as a delicacy. Cf. prec.

caliper *n.* & *v.* var. of CALLIPER.

caliph /ˈkeɪlɪf, ˈka-/ *n.* Also **calif, khalif**. LME. [(O)Fr. *caliphe* (med.L *calipha*, *-es*) f. Arab. *ḵalīfa* deputy (of God), f. title *ḵalīfat Allāh*, or successor (of Muhammad), f. title *ḵalīfat rasūl Allāh* of the Messenger of God, f. *ḵalafa* succeed. See also KHALIFA.] Chiefly *Hist.* The chief civil and religious ruler of the Muslim community.

caliphal *a.* L19.

caliphate /ˈkalɪfeɪt/ *n.* Also **-f-, khalif-**. E17. [f. prec. + -ATE[1]: cf. Fr. *caliphat.*] Chiefly *Hist.* 1 A country governed by a caliph. E17. 2 The reign or term of office of a caliph. M18. 3 The rank or dignity of a caliph. M18.

Callippic *a.* var. of CALLIPPIC.

calisthenic *a.* & *n.* var. of CALLISTHENIC.

caliver /ˈkalɪvə/ *n.* *obs.* exc. *Hist.* M16. [Var. of CALIBRE, prob. first in Fr. *arquebuse*, *pièce de calibre.*] A light kind of harquebus fired without a rest.

calix /ˈkeɪlɪks/ *n.* Also **-ice** /-ɪs/. Pl. **-ices** /-ɪsiːz/. E18. [L *calix*, *-ic-* cup: cf. CALYX.] Chiefly *Anat.* A cuplike cavity or structure; *esp.* one of the divisions of the renal pelvis.

Calixtine /ˈkalɪkstɪn/ *n.* E18. [med.L *Calixtini* pl., f. as prec. Cf. Fr. *calixtin.*] *Eccl. Hist.* A member of a section of the Hussites who maintained that both the cup and the bread should be administered to the laity during the Eucharist.

calk /kɔːk/ *n.* Also ***cork**. L16. [App. ult. f. L *calc-*, *calcaneum* heel, or *calcar* spur: see CALKIN.] 1 = CALKIN. L16. 2 A piece of iron projecting from the heel of a boot etc. to prevent slipping. *US.* E19.

calk /kɔːk/ *v.*[1]*t.* Also ***cork**. E17. [f. the n.] Provide (a horseshoe, a boot, etc.) with a calk or calkin.

calker *n.* (chiefly *Sc.*) = CALKIN L18.

calk /kɔːk/ *v.*[2]*t.* M17. [Fr. *calquer* to copy, trace f. It. *calcare* f. L *calcare* to tread.] Copy (a design etc.) by colouring the back and following its lines so as to trace them on to a surface placed beneath.

calk *v.*[3] see CAULK *v.*[1]

calkin /ˈkɔːkɪn, ˈkalkɪn/ *n.* LME. [MDu. *kalkoen* or its source OFr. *calcain*, f. L *calcaneum* heel, f. *calx*, *calc-* heel.] 1 The turned-down ends of a horseshoe; a turned edge under the front of a horseshoe. LME. 2 The irons nailed on the heels and soles of shoes or clogs to make them last. M19.

call /kɔːl/ *n.* Also (*Sc.*) **ca'** /kɑː/ (the usual form in sense 10). ME. [f. the vb.] **I** 1 A loud vocal utterance; a cry, a shout. ME. **b** The reading aloud of a list of names; a roll-call. E17. 2 The cry of an animal, esp. a bird. Also, an imitation of this, or an instrument imitating this, esp. as used to attract birds. M16. †**b** A decoy bird. L16–E18. 3 A signal, summons, or short theme sounded on an instrument; a whistle etc. used for this. L16.

1 BUNYAN They gave but a call, and in came their Master. *roll-call*: see ROLL *n.*[1] 2 J. STEINBECK The twittering call of a raccoon. 3 J. MASTERS Two buglers . . blew a short loud call.

II With less emphasis on the actual sound. 4 A summons, an invitation; exhortation, bidding. ME. **b** *spec.* An invitation or summons to undertake the office of pastor, from God, one's conscience, or a congregation. M17. **c** A summons for an actor etc. to appear on stage to receive applause, begin a performance, etc. L18. **d** *Cards.* A bid, pass, double, or redouble; a player's right or turn to bid. M19. **e** *Cricket.* A shouted direction by a batsman to his or her partner to run or to remain in the crease; the responsibility to do this in a particular case. M19. **f** A direction in a square dance given by the caller. M19. **g** A shout or call by an umpire or referee indicating that the ball has gone out of play or that a fault or foul has been committed; the decision or ruling indicated. L19. 5 A demand, a requisition, a claim. ME. **b** Chiefly *Stock Exch.* A demand for the payment of lent or unpaid capital. Also, an option of buying stock at a fixed price at a given date. E18. 6 Divine, spiritual, or inner prompting; a vocation, calling. M16. 7 Requirement, need; occasion. L17. 8 A short visit; a stop en route. L18. 9 A communication by telephone, radio, etc.; a telephone conversation. L19.

4 P. BROOK Alienation is a call to halt: alienation is . . holding something up to the light, making us look again. E. LONGFORD The call had come. He was to be Prime Minister. *Times* An official TUC call not to take part in the protest. **c** *curtain-call*: see CURTAIN *n.* 5a. **g** *bad call, late call*, etc. 5 S. JOHNSON The call for novelty is never satisfied. CONAN DOYLE The busy medical man, with calls on him every hour. 7 K. AMIS A girl like you's got no call to be depressed about anything. L. GARFIELD He was inclined to show courage when there was no call for it. 8 A. TROLLOPE She had . . made a morning call on Martha Biggs. 9 L. DEIGHTON I heard the operator asking Charlie if he'd accept a reversed charge call.

III 10 Driving; a place where cattle etc. are driven; exertion, hard breathing. *Sc.* M18.

Phrases: **at** or **on call** ready or available when wanted; (of money lent) repayable on demand; *at the beck and call of*: see BECK *n.*[3] 2. *call of nature*: see NATURE *n. call to the bar*: see BAR *n.*[1] 16. *close call*: see CLOSE *a.* & *adv.* **get one's** (or **the**) **call** *dial.* die, be about to die. *house of call*: see HOUSE *n.*[1] *hurry call*: see HURRY *n. local call*: see LOCAL *a. moderate* (*in*) *a call*: see MODERATE *v.* **pay a call** make a visit (*pay a call on a person, pay a person a call*); *colloq.* go to the lavatory. **port of call** a place at which a ship etc. calls. *sick call*: see SICK *a.* **within call** near enough to be summoned by calling.

Comb.: **call-box** a public telephone kiosk; **call-boy** (*a*) a messenger boy; *spec.* a prompter's attendant employed to summon the actors; (*b*) a male prostitute accepting appointments by telephone; **call changes** *Campanol.* changes rung in response to oral instructions; **call-day, -night**: on which law students are called to the bar; **call-girl** a prostitute accepting appointments by telephone; **call note** a bird's characteristic call; **call-sign(al)** a conventional signal indicating the identity of a radio transmitter.

call /kɔːl/ *v.* Also (*Sc.*) **ca'** /kɑː/ (the usual form in sense 9). LOE. [ON *kalla* cry, summon loudly = MLG, (M)Du. *kallen*, OHG *kallōn* talk, chatter, f. Gmc.] **I** Shout, utter loudly; summon. 1 *v.i.* Cry, shout, (*out*); speak loudly or distinctly, in order to engage attention. (Foll. by *after*, *to* a person.) LOE. **b** Of an animal: make its characteristic note. L15. **c** Rhythmically shout or chant (the steps or figures) to people performing a barn dance. M19. 2 *v.t.* Utter loudly or distinctly, shout (*out*), proclaim; read out (a list of names, etc.). ME. **b** *v.t.* & *i. Cards.* Make a demand for (a card, show of hands, etc.); name (a suit, contract) in bidding. L17. **c** *v.t.* & *i.* Name (heads or tails) in the tossing of a coin. E19. **d** *v.t. Cricket.* Of an umpire: declare (a bowler) to have bowled a no-ball; declare (a delivery) illegal. M19. 3 *v.t.* Summon by calling; demand the presence or attention of. ME. **b** *v.t. spec.* Summon to another world; take by death. E16. **c** *v.t.* Rouse from sleep, summon to get up. E17. **d** *v.t.* & *i.* Make a telephone call (to); communicate (with) by radio. L19. **e** *Computing.* Cause the execution of (a subroutine, procedure, etc.); invoke (a program). M20. 4 *v.t.* Convene, fix a time for, (a meeting etc.); announce as ensuing. ME. 5 *v.t.* Nominate by a personal summons, inspire with a vocation; of duty, God, etc.: bid, enjoin, urge, *to do* something. ME. **b** Invite formally to a pastorate. M16. 6 *v.i.* Make or pay a visit (orig. w. the notion of a summons at the door); of a vessel, train, etc.: make a brief visit. (Foll. by *on*, *upon* someone, *at* a place). L16.

1 SHAKES. *Tam. Shr.* Sometimes you would call out for Cicely Hacket. T. ELLWOOD He calling earnestly after me. S. T. WARNER He called softly. *fig.*: TENNYSON To the billow the fountain calls. **b** J. GRENFELL The little owls that call by night. 2 THACKERAY The word we used at school when names were called. LD MACAULAY His duties were to call the odds when the Court played at hazard. R. GRAVES Gratus called out, 'Hey, Sergeant! Look whom we have here!' J. L. WATEN I continued to call my wares as though at the market. 3 COVERDALE *Mark* 15:16 The soudyers . . called the whole multitude together. P. MORTIMER My mother called the doctor in. C. ISHERWOOD George calls the bartender—very loudly, so he can't pretend not to have heard. T. STOPPARD What witnesses do you want to call? B. MASON A long blast on a whistle called her home. 4 LD MACAULAY It might be necessary to call a Parliament. *Daily Telegraph* The strike was called because we want to ensure that any future owners . . will take notice of what we say. 5 SHAKES. *1 Hen. VI* Is my Lord of Winchester . . call'd unto a cardinal's degree? AV *Acts* 13:7 Separate me Barnabas and Saul for the work whereunto I have called them. J. WESLEY I am called to preach the Gospel both by God and man. 6 W. COWPER A young gentleman called here yesterday who came six miles out of his way to see me. G. F. FIENNES The Fishguard boat train called at Challow to pick up commuters. I. COLEGATE Her friend . . simply detested being called on before 4 o'clock in the afternoon.

II Name, describe as. 7 *v.t.* Give as name or title to; name; style, designate, or address as; reckon, consider. ME. 8 *v.t.* Apply rude or abusive names to, vilify. *dial.* E19.

7 COVERDALE *Matt.* 1:25 He . . called his name Iesus. DONNE You can cal it pleasure to be beguil'd in troubles. G. BERKELEY To call things by their right names. SOUTHEY Her parents mock at her and call her crazed. TOLKIEN Nobody else calls us hobbits; we call ourselves that. H. WILLIAMSON A shame, I calls it, Mr. Maddyzun. C. HILL His mother, his wife and his favourite daughter were all called Elizabeth. ANNE STEVENSON The aunts . . called everybody 'sugar'.

III 9 *v.t.* & *i.* Drive, urge forward; be driven. *Sc.* LME.

R. BURNS Ca' the yowes to the knowes.

Phrases, & with advs. & preps. in specialized senses: *be called to the bar, within the bar*: see BAR *n.*[1] 16. *ca' canny*: see CANNY *adv.* **call a halt** (**to**) demand or order a stop (to). *call all to naught*: see NAUGHT *pron.* & *n.* 1. **call a person names** abuse someone in speech. *call a spade a* (*bloody*) *shovel*: see SPADE *n.*[1] *call a spade a spade*: see SPADE *n.*[1] *call a truce*: see TRUCE *n.* **call attention to** direct notice to, point out. **call away** divert, distract. **call back** (*a*) *v.phr.t.* summon to return, recall, retract; (*b*) *v.phr.i.* & *t.* return to pay a short visit; repeat or return a telephone call or radio communication (to). **call cousin(s)** *arch.* address each other as cousin, claim kinship *with*. **call down** (*a*) invoke from above; (*b*) *colloq.* reprimand, reprove. **call for** (*a*) ask for, order, demand; need, require; (*b*) go to or stop briefly at a place in order to get. **call forth** elicit, summon up. *call home*: see HOME *adv.* **call in** (*a*) *v.phr.t.* withdraw from circulation, recall to oneself, require repayment of; seek advice or help from; (*b*) *v.phr.i.* pay a short visit, esp. in passing. *call in evidence*: see EVIDENCE *n.* **calling hare** a pika. **call in** or **into question** cast doubt on, dispute. **call into being** or **existence** create. *call into play*: see PLAY *n. call into question*: see *call in question* above. *call it a day*: see DAY *n. call it quits*: see QUITS *a.* **call off** (*a*) cancel (an engagement etc.); (*b*) order (a pursuer etc.) to desist, divert. **call on** or **upon** (*a*) invoke, appeal to; request or require *to do* etc.; †(*b*) impeach, challenge; (*c*) pay a short visit to (someone). **call one's own** claim ownership of, possess. *call one's shot*: see SHOT *n.*[1] *call one's soul one's own*: see SOUL *n.* **call out** summon out esp. to active service (as troops to aid civil authorities); elicit; challenge to a duel; summon (workers) to strike; (see also senses 1, 2 above). **call out of one's name** *arch.* address by a name other than the true one. **call over** (*a*) read aloud (a list etc.); (*b*) *call over the coals*: see COAL *n. call quits*: see QUITS *a. call someone's bluff*: see BLUFF *n.*[2] 2. *call the roll*: see ROLL *n.*[1] *call the shots*: see SHOT *n.*[1] *call the tune*: see TUNE *n. call the turn*: see TURN *n.* **call to account** summon to answer for his or her conduct, bring to justice. **call to mind** recollect. **call to order** request to be orderly, declare (a meeting) open. *call truce*: see TRUCE *n.* **call up** (*a*) summon from below, summon up; recollect; (*b*) call to action; conscript for military service; (*c*) call on the telephone. *pay the piper and call the tune*: see PAY *v.*[1]

Comb.: **call-down** *N. Amer.* a rebuke, an abusive tirade; **call-over** a roll-call; the reading aloud of a list of betting prices; **call-up** a summons to action or service; *spec.* conscription.

callable *a.* E19. **callee** *n.* a person who is called or called on L19.

calla /ˈkalə/ *n.* E19. [mod.L: cf. It. *calla* arum lily.] An aquatic plant of the arum family, *Calla palustris.* Also, an arum lily (*Zantedeschia*) or similar plant. Also *calla lily*.

callaloo *n.* var. of CALALU.

Callanetics /kaləˈnɛtɪks/ *n.* Also **c-**. L20. [f. *Callan* Pinckney (b. 1939), US deviser of the system, perh. after *athletics*.] (Proprietary name for) a system of physical exercises based on small repeated movements.

callant /ˈkɑːl(ə)nt/ *n. Sc.* & *north.* E16. [Flem. *kalant* f. NFr. dial. *caland*, earlier *calland*, var. of *chaland* customer, chap, f. *chaloir* be warm f. L *calere.*] †1 A customer. E16–M17. 2 A boy, a youth; a (young) fellow. L16.

caller /ˈkɔːlə/ *n.* LME. [f. CALL *v.* + -ER[1].] 1 One who or that which calls aloud. LME. **b** *spec.* One who announces the directions in a square dance, or calls out the numbers in bingo etc. L19. **c** One who makes a telephone call. L19. **d** One employed to knock up workers for duty. L19. 2 A driver. *Sc.* LME. 3 One who pays a (short) visit. L18.

caller /ˈkɑːlə/ *a. Sc.* & *north.* LME. [Alt. of CALVER *a.*: cf. *siller*, *silver*.] 1 Esp. of fish: fresh, not decaying. LME. 2 Of air etc.: fresh and cool. E16.

callet /ˈkalɪt/ *n.* & *v. obs.* exc. *dial.* LME. [(O)Fr. *caillette* dim. of *caille* QUAIL *n.*: see -ET[1].]

A *n.* A lewd woman, a prostitute; a hag, a scold. LME. B *v.i.* Scold, rail. L17.

calliard /ˈkalɪɑːd/ *n. dial.* L18. [Origin unkn.] A hard smooth flinty gritstone.

callidity /kəˈlɪdɪti/ *n.* Now *rare* or *obs.* LME. [Fr. *callidité* or L *calliditas*, f. *callidus* skilful, cunning: see -ITY.] Craftiness, cunning.

calligraph /ˈkalɪgrɑːf/ *n.* & *v.* M19. [Fr. *calligraphe* f. med.L *calligraphus* f. Gk *kalligraphos*: see CALLIGRAPHY. Sense A.2 and vb after *autograph* etc.] A *n.* 1 One who writes beautifully, a calligrapher. M19. 2 An example of calligraphy. L19. B *v.t.* Write beautifully or ornamentally. L19.

calligrapher /kəˈlɪgrəfə/ *n.* M18. [f. as next + -ER[1].] A person who writes beautifully; *spec.* a professional transcriber of manuscripts.

calligraphy /kəˈlɪgrəfi/ *n.* E17. [Gk *kalligraphia*, f. *kalligraphos* fair writer, f. *kalli-*, *kallos* beauty: see -GRAPHY.] 1 Beautiful handwriting; elegant penmanship. E17. 2 Style of handwriting, penmanship generally. M17. 3 In painting etc.: beauty of line; (elegant) brushwork. E20.

calliˈgraphic *a.* of or pertaining to calligraphers or calligraphy; having beauty of style or line: L18. †**calligraphical** *a.* = CALLIGRAPHIC: only in M17. **calliˈgraphically** *adv.* L19. **calligraphist** *n.* = CALLIGRAPHER E19.

calling /ˈkɔːlɪŋ/ *n.* ME. [f. CALL *v.* + -ING[1].] I 1 The action of CALL *v.* ME.

II 2 (An inward conviction of) divine prompting to salvation or to serve God (w. ref. to the Christian ministry w. mixture of sense 4); a strong impulse towards a course of action as the right thing to do; (a) vocation. ME. †3 Station in life; rank. M16–L17. 4 An occupation, a profession, a trade. M16.

2 F. NIGHTINGALE What is it to feel a calling for any thing? M. L. KING I am a preacher by calling. 4 J. BUCHAN Business is now accepted as a calling for those who have received a liberal education. M. HARRIS Men who were known by their calling—Carter Temple, Shepherd Spindlow, .. Cowman Godfrey.

Comb.: **calling-card** (chiefly *N. Amer.*) a visiting-card; *esp.* (*fig.*) a distinctive mark left behind by someone.

calliope /kəˈlʌɪəpi/ *n. N. Amer.* M19. [Gk *Kalliopē* (lit. 'beautiful-voiced') the Muse of epic poetry.] A set of steam-whistles producing musical notes, played by a keyboard like that of an organ. Also *steam calliope*.

calliper /ˈkalɪpə/ *n.* & *v.* Also **cali-**. L16. [App. alt. of CALIBRE.] A *n.* 1 *calliper compasses*, (*pair of*) *callipers*, compasses with bowed legs for measuring the diameter of convex bodies, or with out-turned points for measuring cavities. L16. 2 A metal support for the leg. Also *calliper splint*. L19. B *v.t.* Measure with callipers. L19.

Callippic /kəˈlɪpɪk/ *a.* Also **Calippic**. L17. [f. *Callippus* Gk astronomer of the 4th cent. BC + -IC.] *Astron.* (*Hist.*) Designating a period of 76 years, equal to four Metonic cycles, at the end of which, by omission of one day, the phases of the moon recur at the same day and hour.

callipygian /kalɪˈpɪdʒɪən/ *a.* L18. [f. Gk *kallipūgos* (epithet of a statue of Venus), f. *kalli-*, *kallos* beauty + *pūgē* buttocks: see -IAN.] Pertaining to or having well-shaped buttocks.

Also **callipygous** /-ˈpɪdʒəs, -ˈpʌɪgəs/ *a.* E20.

callistemon /kalɪˈstiːmən/ *n.* M19. [mod.L, f. Gk *kalli-*, *kallos* beauty + *stēmōn* thread, STAMEN.] An evergreen myrtaceous shrub or small tree of the Australian genus *Callistemon*, bearing flowers (resembling a bottle-brush) with many long red or yellow stamens.

callisthenic /kalɪsˈθɛnɪk/ *a.* & *n.* Also **cali-**. E19. [f. Gk *kalli-*, *kallos* beauty + *sthenos* strength + -IC.] A *adj.* Suitable for producing strength and grace; of or pertaining to callisthenics. E19. B *n.* In *pl.* gymnastic exercises designed to promote bodily health and grace of movement. E19.

callithrix /ˈkalɪθrɪks/ *n.* Also **-trix** /-trɪks/. E17. [mod.L f. L = a kind of Ethiopian monkey, f. Gk *kallitrikhos* beautiful-haired.] A marmoset. Now only as mod.L genus name.

callithumpian /kalɪˈθʌmpɪən/ *n.* & *a.* *US colloq.* M19. [Fanciful: cf. GALLITHUMPIAN.] A *n.* A member of a band of discordant instruments. M19. B *adj.* Designating, pertaining to, or resembling such a band. M19.

callitriche /kəˈlɪtrɪki/ *n.* L18. [mod.L genus name f. Gk *kallitrikhos*: see CALLITHRIX.] A water starwort (see STARWORT 1).

callitrix *n.* var. of CALLITHRIX.

calloo /kəˈluː/ *n. Sc.* L18. [Imit. of the duck's call.] The long-tailed duck, *Clangula hyemalis*.

callop /ˈkaləp/ *n. Austral.* E20. [Aborig.] = *golden perch* s.v. GOLDEN *a.*

callosal /kəˈləʊs(ə)l/ *a.* M19. [f. as next + -AL[1].] *Anat.* Of or pertaining to the corpus callosum of the brain.

callose /kəˈləʊs/ *a.* M19. [L *callosus*: see CALLOUS, -OSE[1].] *Bot.* Having callosities.

callosity /kəˈlɒsɪti/ *n.* LME. [Fr. *callosité* or L *callositas*, f. as prec.: see -ITY.] 1 Abnormal hardness and thickness of the skin or other tissue. LME. 2 A callus; a hardened insensitive part of the skin etc. LME. 3 *fig.* A hardened state of mind; callousness. M17.

callous /ˈkaləs/ *a.*, *n.*, & *v.* LME. [(Fr. *calleux* f.) L *callosus*, f. *callum*, *-us* hardened skin: see -OUS.] A *adj.* 1 Chiefly of the skin or other tissue: hardened, indurated, esp. by continual friction; naturally hard. LME. 2 *fig.* Hardened in feeling etc.; insensitive, unfeeling. L17.

1 W. CONGREVE With labouring callous hands. 2 ARNOLD BENNETT He had shown a singular, callous disregard for the progress of the rest of the house. H. T. LANE Hardened in wrongdoing and callous to all good influence.

B *n.* = CALLUS 1. M17.

C *v.t.* Make callous, harden. Chiefly *calloused* ppl a. Cf. CALLUS *v.* M19.

callously *adv.* L19. **callousness** *n.* (*a*) callous quality or condition; *esp.* callous behaviour, insensitivity; (*b*) a callosity: M17.

callow /ˈkaləʊ/ *a.* & *n.* [OE *calu* = MLG *kale*, MDu. *kale* (Du. *kaal*), OHG *kalo* (G *kahl*) f. WGmc, prob. f. L *calvus* bald.] A *adj.* †1 Bald. OE–LME. 2 Unfledged; downy, downlike; chiefly *fig.*: inexperienced, raw, youthful. L16. 3 Of land: bare; *Anglo-Ir.* low-lying and liable to flooding. L17.

2 DRYDEN The callow Down began to cloath my Chin. C. LAMB The first callow flights in authorship. N. MITFORD The callow young world of my acquaintance.

B *n.* †1 A bald person. Only in ME. †2 A callow nestling; a raw youth. M–L17. 3 Topsoil, overburden. *dial.* M19. 4 A low-lying meadow liable to flooding. *Anglo-Ir.* M19.

callowly *adv.* L20. **callowness** *n.* M19.

calluna /kəˈluːnə/ *n.* E19. [mod.L, f. Gk *kallunein* beautify, sweep clean, f. *kallos* beauty.] Common heather or ling, *Calluna vulgaris*.

callus /ˈkaləs/ *n.* & *v.* M16. [L (more commonly *callum*).] A *n.* 1 A thickened and hardened part of the skin or soft tissue, a callosity. M16. 2 *Med.* The bony healing tissue which forms around the ends of broken bone. L17. 3 *Bot.* A hard formation of tissue; new tissue formed over a wound. L19.

1 E. LINKLATER Their noses were unremarkable, being small and without sufficient callus to give them a definite shape. *fig.*: O. W. HOLMES Editors have .. to develop enormous calluses at every point of contact with authorship.

B *v.i.* Form a callus, become hardened (*over*). Cf. CALLOUS *v.* M19.

Also †**callum** *n.* LME–L18.

calm /kɑːm/ *n.*[1] LME. [Perh. f. pop.L alt. (cf. med.L *calmus* adj., *calmacio(n-)*) of late L *cauma* f. Gk *kauma* heat (of the day or sun), by assoc. w. L *calere* be warm.] 1 Stillness, tranquillity, quiet, serenity, (of the weather, air, or sea, of (esp. social or political) conditions or circumstances, of the mind or behaviour). LME. 2 An absence of wind; a period of stillness or tranquillity. E16.

calm /kɑːm, kɔːm, *in sense 2 also* keɪm/ *n.*[2] Sense 2 also **came** /keɪm/. E16. [Origin unkn.] 1 A mould in which metal objects are cast. *Sc.* E16. 2 An enclosing frame for a pane of glass etc.; *spec.* a grooved slip of lead used for framing the glass in lattice windows (usu. in *pl.*). L16.

calm /kɑːm/ *a.* LME. [med.L *calmus*, f. as CALM *n.*[1]] 1 Of the weather, air, or sea, of the mind or behaviour, of conditions or circumstances: still, tranquil, quiet, serene. LME. 2 Self-confident; impudent. *colloq.* M20.

Phrases: *keep a calm sough*: see SOUGH *n.*[1]

calmly *adv.* L16. **calmness** *n.* E16. **calmy** *a.* (*literary*, now *rare*) tranquil, peaceful L16.

calm /kɑːm/ *v.* LME. [f. the adj.] 1 *v.i.* Become calm. Now only foll. by *down*. LME. 2 *v.t.* Make calm. Also foll. by *down*. M16. †3 *v.t.* Becalm (a ship). L16–M18.

1 L. URIS Let's stop yelling at each other... Let's calm down. 2 G. GREENE It calms the nerves and soothes the emotions.

calmant /ˈkɑːm(ə)nt, ˈkal-/ *n.* [Fr.] a calmative, a sedative E19. **calmer** *n.* a person who or thing which calms M17. **calmingly** *adv.* in a calming manner E20.

calmative /ˈkɑːmətɪv, ˈkal-/ *a.* & *n.* L19. [f. prec. + -ATIVE.] *Med.* (An agent) that has a calming effect, (a) sedative.

calmodulin /kalˈmɒdjʊlɪn/ *n.* L20. [f. CAL(CIUM + MODUL(ATE + -IN[1].] *Biochem.* A calcium-binding protein in eukaryotic cells which is involved in regulating a variety of cellular activities.

†**calmstone** *n.* see CAMSTONE.

calomel /ˈkaləmɛl/ *n.* L17. [mod.L, perh. f. Gk *kalos* beautiful + *melas* black.] Mercury(I) chloride, Hg_2Cl_2, a white powder formerly much used as a purgative.

Calor /ˈkalə/ *n.* M20. [L *calor* heat.] In full *Calor gas*. Proprietary name for liquefied gas (chiefly butane) supplied under pressure in containers for use as domestic fuel.

caloric /kəˈlɒrɪk, ˈkalərɪk/ *n.* & *a.* L18. [Fr. *calorique*, f. L *calor* heat: see -IC.] A *n.* 1 *Hist.* A hypothetical fluid formerly thought to be responsible for the phenomena of heat. L18. 2 Heat. *arch.* L18. B *adj.* Of or pertaining to heat; expressed in calories. M19.

calorically /kəˈlɒrɪk(ə)li/ *adv.* as or in the manner of heat; as regards heat: M19.

calorie /ˈkaləri/ *n.* Also **calory**. M19. [Fr., f. L *calor* heat + Fr. *-ie* -Y[3].] A unit of heat or energy; *spec.* (*a*) the quantity of heat required to raise the temperature of one kilogram of water by one degree centigrade (also called *kilocalorie*, *large* or *great calorie*), freq. used as a measure of the energy value of foods (abbrev. *Cal*); (*b*) the quantity of heat required to raise the temperature of one gram of water by one degree centigrade, equal to approximately 4.19 joule (also called *small calorie*, abbrev. *cal*).

empty calories: see EMPTY *a.*

calorific /kaləˈrɪfɪk/ *a.* L17. [L *calorificus*, f. *calori-*, *calor* heat: see -FIC.] Producing heat; *loosely* of or pertaining to heat.

Comb.: **calorific value** the quantity of heat obtainable from a given quantity (of a fuel).

calorimeter /kaləˈrɪmɪtə/ *n.* L18. [f. L *calori-*, *calor* heat + -METER.] An apparatus for measuring the amount of heat involved in a chemical reaction or other process.

calorimetric /kalərɪˈmɛtrɪk/ *a.* of, pertaining to, or by means of calorimeters or calorimetry M19. **caloriˈmetrical** *a.* = CALORIMETRIC L19. **caloriˈmetrically** *adv.* L19. **calorimetry** *n.* the measurement of quantities of heat M19.

calory *n.* var. of CALORIE.

calotte /kəˈlɒt/ *n.* M17. [Fr., perh. rel. to *cale* CAUL *n.*[1]] 1 A skullcap, esp. as worn by Roman Catholic priests. M17. 2 A snowcap, an ice-cap. L19.

calotype /ˈkalətʌɪp/ *n.* & *v.* M19. [f. Gk *kalos* beautiful + -TYPE.] *Hist.* A *n.* A photographic process in which negatives were made using paper coated with silver iodide. M19. B *v.t.* Photograph by this process. M19.

caloyer /ˈkalɔɪə, *foreign* kaloje (*pl. same*)/ *n.* L16. [Fr. f. It. *caloiero* f. eccl.Gk *kalogēros*, f. *kalos* beautiful + *gērōs*, *-as* old age.] A Greek monk, esp. of the order of St Basil.

calpac /ˈkalpak/ *n.* Also **-pack, kalpa(c)k**. L16. [Turk. *kalpak*.] An oriental cap; *spec.* a tall felt or sheepskin cap worn in east central Asia.

calque /kalk/ *n.* & *v.* M20. [Fr. = copy, tracing, f. as CALK *v.*²] **A** *n.* A loan-translation (*of, on*). M20. **B** *v.t.* Form as a calque. Usu. in *pass.* (foll. by *on*). M20.

caltha /ˈkalθə/ *n.* L16. [mod.L *Caltha* genus name f. L.] A marsh marigold.

caltrop /ˈkaltrəp/ *n.* Also **-trap**. [OE *calcatrippe* f. med.L *calcatrippa, -trappa*; senses 2 & 3 f. (ult. identical) OFr. *kauketrape* dial. var. of *cauchetrape, chauche-* (mod. *chaussetrape*), f. *chauchier* tread + *trappe* trap.] **1** Orig., a plant which tended to catch or entangle the feet. Later, a plant with a flower-head suggestive of the military instrument (sense 3 below); *spec.* (*a*) a water chestnut, *Trapa natans* (also *water caltrop(s)*); (*b*) a member of the genus *Tribulus*. OE. †**2** A trap or snare for the feet. ME–M19. **3** *Hist.* An iron ball with four spikes placed so that one is always projecting upwards, thrown on the ground to impede cavalry horses. Also, a heraldic representation of this. LME.

calumba /kəˈlʌmbə/ *n.* E19. [Perh. f. *Colombo*, Sri Lanka (Ceylon), erron. regarded as the source.] The dried root of the tree *Jateorhiza palmata*, native to E. Africa and Madagascar, used as a bitter tonic. Also *calumba root*.

calumet /ˈkaljʊmɛt/ *n.* L17. [Fr., dial. var. of *chalumeau* f. late L *calamellus* dim. of CALAMUS reed.] An American Indian tobacco-pipe with a clay bowl and reed stem, smoked esp. as a sign of peace; *transf.* & *fig.* a symbol of peace.

calumniate /kəˈlʌmnɪeɪt/ *v.* M16. [L *calumniat-* pa. ppl stem of *calumniari*, f. as CALUMNY *n.*: see -ATE³.] **1** *v.t.* Slander, defame, make false charges against. M16. †**2** *v.i.* Utter calumnies. E17–E18.

calumniˈation *n.* (*a*) the action of calumniating; (*b*) a calumny: M16. **calumniator** *n.* a slanderer, a false accuser M16. **calumniatory** *a.* slanderous E17.

calumnious /kəˈlʌmnɪəs/ *a.* L15. [(O)Fr. *calomnieux* or L *calumniosus*, f. as next: see -OUS.] Of the nature of a calumny; slanderous; defamatory.

calumniously *adv.* M16.

calumny /ˈkaləmni/ *n.* LME. [L *calumnia*.] Malicious misrepresentation, slander, libel; a false charge, a slanderous statement or report.

calumny /ˈkaləmni/ *v.* M16. [(Fr. *calomnier* f.) late L *calumniare* for *calumniari* (see CALUMNIATE). In mod. use f. the n.] †**1** *v.t.* Utter calumnies. Only in M16. †**2** *v.t.* Declare calumniously. Only in M16. **3** *v.t.* Calumniate, slander. E19.

†**calumnize** *v.t.* calumniate E17–E18.

calvados /ˈkalvədɒs/ *n.* E20. [*Calvados*, a department in Normandy, France.] Apple brandy, traditionally made in the Calvados region; a drink of this.

calvaria /kalˈvɛːrɪə/ *n.* Pl. **-iae** /-ɪiː/. Also **-ium** /-ɪəm/, pl. **-ia** /-ɪə/. LME. [L *calvaria*: see next.] *Anat.* The vault of the skull.

Calvary /ˈkalv(ə)ri/ *n.* Also **c-**. L17. [The site of the Crucifixion of Jesus, f. L *calvaria* skull (f. *calva* scalp, *calvus* bald), tr. Gk GOLGOTHA.] **1** Her. *Calvary cross, cross Calvary*: with the upper and side limbs of equal length and the lower limb considerably longer, mounted on a pyramid of three grises or steps. L17. **2** *RC Ch.* A sculptured or pictorial representation of the Crucifixion. E18. **3** A place of crucifixion (*lit.* & *fig.*). L19.

calve /kɑːv/ *v.*¹ [OE *calfian, ċealfian*, f. CALF *n.*¹] **1** *v.i.* Give birth to a calf. OE. **2** *v.t.* Give birth to (a calf). Usu. in *pass.* LME. **3** *v.t.* & *i.* Of an iceberg etc.: split to produce (a detached part). E19.

calver *n.* a cow that calves L18.

calve *v.*² see CAVE *v.*³

calved /kɑːvd/ *a.* L16. [f. CALF *n.*²: see -ED².] Having calves (of a given description etc.).

calver /ˈkɑːvə/ *a.* & *v.* Long *obs.* exc. *Hist.* ME. [Perh. rel. to MLG *keller* & *F.* Gmc base meaning 'be cold'.] **A** *adj.* Of fish, esp. salmon: fresh; prepared in a now unknown way while alive or newly dead. Cf. CALLER *a.* ME. **B** *v.* **1** *v.t.* Prepare (fish) when fresh in a now unknown way. Chiefly as *calvered* ppl a. E17. †**2** *v.i.* Behave as a 'calver' fish when cooked. M17–M18.

calves *n.* pl. of CALF *n.*¹

Calvinian /kalˈvɪnɪən/ *a.* & *n.* M16. [f. *Calvin* (see next) + -IAN.] **A** *adj.* Of or pertaining to Calvin; Calvinistic. M16. †**B** *n.* A Calvinist. M16–M18.

Calvinise *v.* var. of CALVINIZE.

Calvinism /ˈkalvɪnɪz(ə)m/ *n.* L16. [Fr. *calvinisme* or mod.L *calvinismus*, f. *Calvin* (see below): see -ISM.] The doctrines of the French Protestant reformer Jean Calvin (1509–64) and his followers, *esp.* those relating to grace and election to salvation; adherence to these doctrines.

Calvinist /ˈkalvɪnɪst/ *n.* & *a.* M16. [f. as prec. + -IST.] **A** *n.* An adherent of Calvinism. M16. **B** *adj.* Of or pertaining to Calvinists or Calvinism. M16.

Calviˈnistic *a.* of, pertaining to, or following the doctrines of Calvinism M18. **Calviˈnistical** *a.* = CALVINISTIC L16. **Calviˈnistically** *adv.* L17.

Calvinize /ˈkalvɪnʌɪz/ *v.* Also **-ise**. M17. [f. *Calvin* (see CALVINISM) + -IZE.] **1** *v.i.* Follow Calvin; teach Calvinism. M17. **2** *v.t.* Imbue with Calvinism. E19.

calvish *a.* var. of CALFISH.

calvity /ˈkalvɪti/ *n. rare.* E17. [L *calvitium*, f. *calvus* bald.] Baldness.

calx /kalks/ *n.* Pl. **calces** /ˈkalsiːz/, †**calxes**. LME. [L *calx, calc-* lime, prob. f. Gk *khalix* pebble, limestone.] **1** A powder or friable substance produced by roasting or burning a mineral or metal, formerly taken as the essence of the mineral. *arch.* LME. **2** Orig. more fully †*calx vive*. Quicklime. *arch.* LME. **3** The area behind goal-line in the Eton College wall game. M19.

calycanthus /kalɪˈkanθəs/ *n.* L18. [mod.L, f. as CALYX + Gk *anthos* flower.] A shrub of the N. American genus *Calycanthus*; *esp.* Carolina allspice (ALLSPICE 2).

calyces *n.pl.* see CALYX.

calycine /ˈkalɪsʌɪn/ *a.* M18. [f. L *calyci-*, CALYX + -INE¹.] Of or pertaining to the calyx; resembling a calyx.

calycle /ˈkalɪk(ə)l, ˈkeɪ-/ *n.* Also in L form **calyculus** /kəˈlɪkjʊləs/, pl. **-li** /-lʌɪ, -liː/. M18. [L *calyculus* dim. of CALYX, *-yc-*: see -CLE.] *Bot.* A small calyx or calycine structure, esp. of bracts.

calycled *a.* = CALYCULATED L18. **calycular** /kəˈlɪkjʊlə/ *a.* of or pertaining to a calycle, calycine M17. **calyculate** /kəˈlɪkjʊlət/ *a.* = CALYCULATED M19. **calyculated** /kəˈlɪkjʊleɪtɪd/ *a.* enclosed in or furnished with a calycle L17.

calypso /kəˈlɪpsəʊ/ *n.* Pl. **-os**. E20. [Origin unkn.] A type of W. Indian (orig. Trinidadian) ballad or song, usu. with a topical theme; the kind of music to which this is sung.

calypˈsonian *n.* a composer and singer of calypsos M20.

calyptra /kəˈlɪptrə/ *n.* M18. [mod.L f. Gk *kaluptra* covering, veil.] *Bot.* A hood, a protective cover; *spec.* (*a*) a layer of parenchymatous cells protecting the tip of a growing root (also called *root-cap*); (*b*) a structure over the capsule of a moss.

calyx /ˈkalɪks, ˈkeɪ-/ *n.* Pl. **-yces** /-ɪsiːz/, **-yxes**. L17. [L *calyx, -yc-* f. Gk *kalux* shell, husk, pod, f. base of *kaluptein* to hide.] **1** *Bot.* A whorl of leaves (sepals), forming the outer case of a bud or the envelope of a flower. L17. **2** = CALIX. M19.

Comb.: *calyx-tube*: see TUBE *n.* 10.

cam /kam/ *n.* L18. [Du. *kam* comb, as in *kamrad* toothed wheel, cog-wheel.] A projecting part of a wheel etc. in machinery, used to impart reciprocal or variable motion to another part with which it makes sliding contact as it rotates.

Comb.: **camshaft** a shaft carrying a cam or cams, esp. (in an internal-combustion engine) for operating the cylinder valves (*overhead cam*: see OVERHEAD *a.* 1).

cam /kam/ *a.* & *adv.* Long *obs.* exc. *dial.* Also †**k-**. M16. [Welsh (also Ir., Gael., Manx) f. Celt.] Crooked(ly), perverse(ly); awry, askew.

camaieu /kamajø/ *n.* Pl. pronounced same. L16. [Fr.: see CAMEO.] †**1** A cameo. L16–L18. **2** A method of monochrome painting. E18.

camail /ˈkameɪl/ *n.* L17. [(O)Fr. f. Prov. *capmalh*, f. *cap* head + *malh, malhar* MAIL *n.*¹] *Hist.* **1** A hood worn by the Roman Catholic clergy. Also, a blue or purple ornament worn by a bishop over his rochet. L17. **2** A piece of chain-mail attached to the headpiece and protecting the neck and shoulders. E19.

Camaldolese /kəˈmaldəliːz/ *a.* & *n.* E19. [f. *Camaldoli* (see below) + -ESE.] **A** *adj.* Designating or belonging to a religious order founded by St Romuald at Camaldoli, Italy, in the 11th cent. E19. **B** *n.* Pl. same. A member of this order. E19.

Camaldolite *n.* = CAMALDOLESE *n.* E18.

camalote /kaməˈləʊti/ *n.* Also **camel-**. L19. [Amer. Sp.] A floating island of vegetation in N. or S. America; a blue-flowered aquatic plant of the genus *Pontederia*, which forms such islands.

caman /ˈkamən/ *n.* L19. [Ir. *camán*, OIr. *cammán*, f. *cam* bent, crooked.] The stick used in shinty.

camaraderie /kaməˈrɑːd(ə)ri, -riː/ *n.* M19. [Fr., f. *camarade* COMRADE: see -ERY.] The mutual trust and sociability of comrades.

camarilla /kaməˈrɪlə, -ljə/ *n.* M19. [Sp., dim. of *camara* CHAMBER.] A cabal, a clique.

camaron /kaməˈrəʊn, ˈkamər(ə)n/ *n.* L19. [Sp. *camarón* shrimp.] A freshwater shrimp or prawn resembling a crayfish.

camas, camass *n.* vars. of QUAMASH.

camber /ˈkambə/ *n.* LME. [OFr. *cambre*, f. dial. var. of *chambre* arched f. L *camurus* curved inwards.] **1** A harbour, a dock; a dockyard where cambering is performed. *rare.* LME. **2** A slight convexity above, an arched form, esp. of a road surface in cross-section, a beam, deck, aircraft wing, etc. E17. **b** Sideways inclination of a motor vehicle's wheel. M20.

camber /ˈkambə/ *v.* LME. [Fr. *cambrer*, f. as prec.] **1** *v.i.* Be or become slightly convex so that the centre is higher than the ends. LME. **2** *v.t.* Cause (a beam etc.) to arch upwards slightly in the middle; give camber to (a road surface, wing, etc.). E17.

Camberwell beauty /ˈkambəwɛl ˈbjuːti/ *n. phr.* M18. [*Camberwell*, a village, now a district of SE London.] A holarctic nymphalid butterfly, *Nymphalis antiopa*, with dark brown cream-bordered wings, which is a rare migrant to Britain from Continental Europe. Cf. *mourning cloak* (b) s.v. MOURNING *n.*¹

cambia *n.* pl. of CAMBIUM.

†**cambio** *n.* Pl. **-os**. M16–L18. [It. f. med.L CAMBIUM.] (A place, a bill, of) exchange.

cambist /ˈkambɪst/ *n.* Now *rare* or *obs.* E19. [Fr. *cambiste* f. It. *cambista*, f. as prec.: see -IST.] An expert in or a manual of financial exchange; a dealer in bills of exchange, a speculator.

cambium /ˈkambɪəm/ *n.* Pl. **-ia** /-ɪə/. L16. [med.L = (ex)change.] **1** One of the alimentary humours formerly supposed to nourish the body. *obs.* exc. *Hist.* L16. **2** *Bot.* (A layer of) cellular tissue from which phloem, xylem, or cork grows by division. L17. **3** (A place of) exchange or barter. *rare.* E18.

cambial *a.* (*a*) *Bot.* of, pertaining to, or of the nature of cambium; †(*b*) relating to financial exchange: M19.

†**camblet** *n.* & *v.* var. of CAMLET.

†**cambock** *n.* var. of CAMMOCK *n.*²

Cambodian /kamˈbəʊdɪən/ *n.* & *a.* L18. [f. *Cambodia* (see below) + -AN.] **A** *n.* **1** A native or inhabitant of Cambodia (Kampuchea), a country in SE Asia. L18. **2** The language of Cambodia, Khmer. M19. **B** *adj.* Of or pertaining to Cambodia, its people, or its language. M19.

camboose *n.* var. of CABOOSE.

cambré /kɑ̃bre/ *a.* E20. [Fr., pa. pple of *cambrer* CAMBER *v.*] Curved, arched; *Ballet* (of the body) bent from the waist sideways or backwards.

cambrel /ˈkambr(ə)l/ *n. obs.* exc. *dial.* In sense 2 also †**ch-**. LME. [Sense 1 perh. f. AN var. of OFr. *chambril* lath; sense 3 prob. rel. to Welsh *cambren* crooked tree, bent stick, swingletree, butcher's cambrel, etc., f. *cam* crooked (see CAM *a.* & *adv.*) + *pren* wood, stick. Cf. GAMBREL.] †**1** A spatula. Only in LME. **2** The hock of a horse's hind leg. E17. **3** A bent piece of wood or iron used by butchers to hang carcasses on. M17.

Cambrian /ˈkambrɪən/ *a.* & *n.* M17. [f. med.L *Cambria* Wales, var. (with differentiation of sense) of *Cumbria* (see CUMBRIAN), + -AN.] **A** *adj.* **1** Of or pertaining to Wales, Welsh; a Welsh person. M17. **2** *Geol.* Designating or pertaining to the earliest period of the Palaeozoic era, preceding the Ordovician. M19. **B** *n. Geol.* The Cambrian period; the system of rocks dating from this time. M19.

cambric /ˈkambrɪk, ˈkeɪm-/ *n.* & *a.* LME. [Flem. *Kamerijk* Cambrai, a town in northern France, where orig. made.] (Of) a fine white linen; (of) a similar cotton fabric.

Comb.: **cambric tea** *US* a drink mainly of hot milk and water given esp. to children.

Cambridge /ˈkeɪmbrɪdʒ/ *n.* M19. [A university city and the county town of Cambridgeshire, a county in eastern England.] **1** *Cambridge sausage*, a variety of pork sausage. M19. **2** *Cambridge blue*, a light blue (adopted by Cambridge University). L19.

Cambridgeshire nightingale /ˈkeɪmbrɪdʒʃə ˈnʌɪtɪŋgeɪl/ *n. phr.* M19. [f. *Cambridgeshire* (see prec.) + NIGHTINGALE *n.*[1]: they were introduced into East Anglia in the 17th cent.] = *edible frog* s.v. EDIBLE *a.*

Cambro- /ˈkambrəʊ/ *comb. form.* E17. [mod.L, f. *Cambria* (see CAMBRIAN), or f. CAMBRIAN: see -O-.] Welsh (as *Cambro-Briton*); Cambrian (as *Cambro-Ordovician*).

camcorder /ˈkamkɔːdə/ *n.* L20. [f. CAMERA + RECORDER *n.*[1]] A portable video camera incorporating a built-in video recorder.

came *n.* see CALM *n.*[2]

came *v.* pa. t. of COME *v.*

camel /ˈkam(ə)l/ *n.* OE. [L *camelus* f. Gk *kamēlos* f. Semitic (cf. Heb. *gāmāl*): in ME reinforced by OFr. *c(h)amel, -eil*.] **1** Either of two large hornless long-necked domesticated ruminants of the genus *Camelus*, (more fully *Arabian camel*) the dromedary, *C. dromedarius*, with one hump, and (more fully *Bactrian camel*) *C. ferus*, with two humps. OE. **2** An apparatus consisting of one or more watertight chests, used to provide buoyancy for a sunken ship etc. E18. **3** A shade of fawn colour. L19.

1 swallow a camel (w. allusion to *Matt.* 23:24) make no difficulty about something incredible or unreasonable. *the last straw that breaks the camel's back*: see STRAW *n.*

Comb.: **camel-back** a kind of rubber used esp. to retread tyres; **camel('s)-hair** the hair of the camel, or (in paintbrushes) of a squirrel's tail; **camel-spider** = SOLIFUGID; **camel-thorn** (*a*) a Middle Eastern leguminous shrub, *Alhagi camelorum*; (*b*) a southern African shrub, *Acacia giraffae*.

cameˈleer *n.* a camel-driver E19. **camel-like** *a.* resembling (that of) a camel M18. **cameloid** *a.* & *n.* (an animal) belonging to the family Camelidae, which includes the camels and llamas; camel-like: L19. **camelry** *n.* troops mounted on camels M19.

†**cameleon** *n.* var. of CHAMELEON.

cameline /ˈkam(ə)lɪn/ *n.*[1] Now *rare* or *obs.* ME. [OFr. *camelin* f. med.L *camelinum*, use as n. of neut. of adj. *camelinus* of a camel: see CAMEL, -INE[1].] A kind of fabric made from or supposedly made from camel's hair; a garment made of this. Cf. CAMLET.

cameline /ˈkamɪlʌɪn/ *n.*[2] L16. [Fr., earlier *camamine*, f. late L *chamaemelinus* resembling camomile.] A cruciferous plant of the genus *Camelina*; *esp.* gold of pleasure, *C. sativa*.

camellia /kəˈmiːlɪə, -ˈmɛlɪə/ *n.* M18. [mod.L, f. Joseph Kamel or *Camellus* (1661–1706), Moravian Jesuit and botanist: see -IA[1].] An evergreen shrub of the Far Eastern genus *Camellia*, of the tea family; esp. *C. japonica*, bearing showy red, pink, or white flowers.

camelopard /ˈkamɪlə(ʊ)pɑːd, kəˈmɛləpɑːd/ *n.* Also (now only in sense 2) in L forms **-pardalis** /kəmɛləˈpɑːd(ə)lɪs/, **-pardus** /kəmɛləˈpɑːdəs/. LME. [L *camelopardus*, *-pardalis* f. Gk *kamēlopardalis*, f. *kamēlos* (see CAMEL) + *pardalis* (see PARD *n.*[1]).] **1** A giraffe. *arch.* LME. **2** (**C-**.) A constellation of the northern hemisphere between the polestar and Perseus; the Giraffe. M18.

camelote *n.* var. of CAMALOTE.

Camembert /ˈkamɑ̃bɛː, ˈkaməmbɛː/ *n.* L19. [A village in Normandy, France.] A rich soft cheese orig. made near Camembert.

Camenes /ˈkam(ə)niːz/ *n.* M19. [A mnemonic of scholastic philosophers, A indicating a universal affirmative proposition, E a universal negative proposition.] *Logic.* The second mood of the fourth syllogistic figure, in which a universal affirmative major premiss and a universal negative minor premiss yield a universal negative conclusion.

cameo /ˈkamɪəʊ/ *n.* Pl. **-os**. LME. [OFr. *came(h)u*, *camahieu* (mod. CAMAÏEU): cf. med.L *camahutus* etc. Later infl. by It. *cam(m)eo*, corresp. to med.L *cammaeus*.] **1** A small piece of relief-carving in onyx, agate, etc., usu. with colour-layers, the lower of which serves as ground; a relief design of similar form. LME. **2** A short literary sketch or acted scene; (more fully *cameo part*) a small character part in a play, film, etc. M19.

Comb.: **cameo glass** a decorative glass consisting of layers of different colours, the outermost being cut away to leave a design in relief; *cameo part*: see sense 2 above.

camera /ˈkam(ə)rə/ *n.* L17. [L = vault, arched chamber, f. Gk *kamara* object with arched cover: cf. CHAMBER *n.*] **1** In Italy, Spain, etc. a (council or legislative) chamber; the treasury department of the papal curia. L17. **2** An arched or vaulted roof or chamber. Chiefly in the names of (parts of) buildings. See also IN CAMERA. E18. **3** *ellipt.* = CAMERA OBSCURA. M18. **4** Any apparatus used for taking photographs or television pictures. M19.

4 *cine camera, movie camera, monorail camera, television camera, video camera, X-ray camera*, etc. *candid camera*: see CANDID *a.* 6. **off camera** while not being filmed. **on camera** while being filmed.

Comb.: **camera-eye** an eye that records detailed impressions; a person capable of unusually detailed or detached observation or memory; **cameraman**: operating a camera professionally, esp. in cinema or television; **camera-ready** *a.* (*Printing*) (of copy) in a form suitable for photographing or electronic scanning; **camera shake** (blurring due to) unintentional movement of the camera during photography or filming; **camera-shy** *a.* not liking to be photographed or filmed; **camerawoman**: operating a camera professionally esp. in cinema or television; **camera-work** the manner or technique of positioning and using cameras in films, television, etc.

camerist *n.* (chiefly *US arch.*) a person who uses a camera M19.

†**camerade** *n.* see COMRADE.

cameral /ˈkam(ə)r(ə)l/ *a.* M18. [G *kameral* f. med.L *cameralis*, f. L CAMERA (in med.L sense 'treasury'): see -AL[1].] *Hist.* Of or pertaining to the management of State finance in Germany.

cameralism /ˈkam(ə)r(ə)lɪz(ə)m/ *n.* E20. [f. prec. + -ISM.] *Hist.* The theory that economic management should be directed primarily at benefiting the treasury (prevalent in 18th-cent. Germany); advocacy of this theory.

cameralist *n.* an advocate of cameralism E20.

cameralistic /ˌkam(ə)r(ə)ˈlɪstɪk/ *a.* L19. [f. CAMERAL or CAMERALIST: see -ISTIC.] Characteristic of cameralism or cameralists; *gen.* pertaining to or characterized by emphasis on political factors in economic management.

camera lucida /ˌkam(ə)rə ˈluːsɪdə/ *n. phr.* Pl. **camera lucidas**. M18. [L = bright chamber.] An instrument by which the rays of light from an object are reflected by a prism and produce an image on paper placed beneath the instrument, traceable with a pencil.

camera obscura /ˌkam(ə)rə ɒbsˈkjʊərə/ *n. phr.* Pl. **camera obscuras**. E18. [L = dark chamber.] A darkened box or enclosure with an aperture for projecting an image of external objects on a screen placed at the focus of the lens; a building containing such a box or enclosure.

camerate /ˈkam(ə)rət/ *a.* M16. [L *cameratus* pa. pple, f. as next: see -ATE[2].] Divided into chambers.

camerate /ˈkam(ə)reɪt/ *v.t.* Now *rare* or *obs.* E17. [L *camerat-* pa. ppl stem of *camerare* vault or arch over, f. as CAMERA: see -ATE[3].] Chiefly as *camerated* ppl a. **1** *Archit.* Vault, arch over. E17. **2** Divide into chambers. M19.

camerlingo /kaməˈlɪŋgəʊ/ *n.* Also **-lengo** /-ˈlɛŋgəʊ/. Pl. **-os**. E17. [It. f. Frank.: see CHAMBERLAIN.] A chamberlain or treasurer; *spec.* (*a*) the Pope's chamberlain and financial secretary; (*b*) the treasurer of the Sacred College of cardinals.

Cameronian /kaməˈrəʊnɪən/ *n.* & *a.* L17. [f. *Cameron* (see below) + -IAN.] *Hist.* **A** *n.* A follower of Richard Cameron (1648–80), a Scottish Covenanter; a member of the Reformed Presbyterian Church. Also, a member of the Cameronian regiment (see below). L17.

B *adj.* Of or pertaining to Richard Cameron, his tenets, or his followers. L17.

Cameronian regiment a former infantry regiment of the British army orig. raised from Cameron's followers and other Presbyterians.

Cameroonian /kaməˈruːnɪən/ *n.* & *a.* Also **-oun-**. M20. [f. *Cameroon* (see below) + -IAN.] A native or inhabitant of, of or pertaining to, Cameroon, a country on the west coast of Africa between Nigeria and Gabon.

Camestres /kəˈmɛstriːz/ *n.* M16. [A mnemonic of scholastic philosophers first used in med.L, A indicating a universal affirmative proposition, E a universal negative proposition.] *Logic.* The second mood of the second syllogistic figure, in which the major premiss is a universal affirmative, the minor premiss and the conclusion universal negatives.

Camford /ˈkamfəd/ *n.* M19. [f. CAMBRIDGE + OXFORD.] = OXBRIDGE.

camiknickers /ˈkamɪnɪkəz/ *n. pl.* E20. [f. CAMISOLE + KNICKERS.] A woman's one-piece undergarment which combines camisole and knickers.

camion /ˈkamɪən/ *n.* L19. [Fr.] A large dray; a lorry; a bus.

†**camis** *n. rare* (Spenser). Also **camus**. Only in L16. [Prob. Sp., Port. *camisa* f. late L *camisia*: see CHEMISE.] A light loose dress of silk or linen.

camisado /kamɪˈsɑːdəʊ/ *n.* Now *arch.* or *Hist.* Pl. **-oes**. M16. [Sp. *camisada*, f. *camisa*: see prec., -ADO.] A night attack; orig. one in which the attackers wore shirts over their armour as a means of mutual recognition.

Camisard /ˈkamɪsɑː, kamɪˈsɑː/ *n.* E18. [Fr. f. Prov. *camisa* f. late L *camisia* (see CHEMISE): see -ARD.] *Hist.* Any of the French Protestant insurgents of the Cévennes who rebelled against the persecution following the revocation of the Edict of Nantes (1685).

camise *n.* see KAMEEZ.

camisole /ˈkamɪsəʊl/ *n.* E19. [Fr. f. It. *camiciola* or Sp. *camisola*, dim. of (respectively) *camicia*, *camisa* f. late L *camisia*: see CHEMISE, -OLE[1].] **1** *Hist.* A type of sleeved short jacket worn by men. E19. **2** *Hist.* A short loose jacket worn by women when dressed in négligé. M19. **3** A woman's underbodice, usu. straight with shoulder-straps and embroidered or otherwise ornamentally trimmed. M19.

camlet /ˈkamlɪt/ *n.* & *v. arch.* Also †**cham-** (earlier), †**-blet**. LME. [OFr. *chamelot*, *c-*, ult. f. Arab. *ḵamla(t)* nap, pile of velvet: pop. assoc. with CAMEL.] **A** *n.* Orig., a costly eastern fabric. Later, a light cloth used for cloaks etc., made of various materials. Also, a garment of such a fabric. LME.

†**watered camlet**: having a wavy appearance.

†**B** *v.t.* Mark or variegate as (watered) camlet. E17–E18.

camleteen *n.* an imitation or inferior camlet M18.

cammock /ˈkamək/ *n.*[1] *obs.* exc. *dial.* [OE *cammoc*, of unkn. origin.] Rest-harrow. Also, any of various other weeds of pasture.

cammock /ˈkamək/ *n.*[2] *obs.* exc. *Sc.* Also †**-bock**. LME. [App. f. med.L *cambuca*, *-buta* curved stick, crosier, app. of Gaulish origin and rel. to CAM *a.* & *adv.*, CAMAN.] **1** A crooked staff; *esp.* a hockey-stick etc.; a game in which this is used. LME. **2** A crooked piece of wood; a cambrel. LME.

camois *a.* & *n.* var. of CAMUS *a.* & *n.*[2]

camomile /ˈkaməmʌɪl/ *n.* Also **ch-**. ME. [(O)Fr. *camomille* f. late L *c(h)amomilla* alt. of *chamaemelon* f. Gk *khamaimēlon* lit. 'earth apple': so called from the smell of the flowers.] A creeping aromatic plant of the composite family, *Chamaemelum nobile*, with yellow-centred white-rayed flowers, formerly much grown for its fragrance. Also (w. specifying wd), any of various plants (mostly weeds) of the related genera *Anthemis*, *Chamomilla*, and *Matricaria*.

stinking camomile: see STINKING *a.*

Comb.: **camomile tea**: an infusion of the flowers of *Chamaemelum nobile*, taken as a tonic.

camoodi *n.* var. of CAMOUDIE.

Camorra /kəˈmɔːrə, -ˈmɒrə/ *n.* Also **c-**. M19. [It., perh. f. Sp. *camorra* dispute, quarrel.] A secret society akin to the Mafia operating in the Neapolitan district; *gen.* any organized body engaged in extortion or other dishonest activities.

camoudie /kəˈmuːdi/ *n.* Also **-oodi** & other vars. E19. [Arawak *kamudu*.] A boa constrictor.

camouflage /ˈkaməflɑːʒ, -mʊf-/ *n.* & *v.* E20. [Fr., f. *camoufler* vb (thieves' slang) f. It. *camuffare* disguise, deceive, perh. assoc. w. Fr. *camouflet* whiff of smoke in the face: see -AGE.] **A** *n.* The disguising or concealment of guns, ships, aircraft, etc., by obscuring with splashes of various colours, foliage, netting, smokescreens, etc.; the disguise so used; *gen.* any means of disguise or evasion. E20.

J. K. GALBRAITH An extraordinarily elaborate exercise in social camouflage has kept us from seeing what has been happening. *attrib.*: N. TINBERGEN Developed dark cross-bars (the stickleback's disruptive camouflage pattern).

B *v.t.* Conceal by camouflage. E20.

F. TUOHY A scarlet wool dress designed to celebrate rather than camouflage her pregnancy. ANTHONY HUXLEY Unripe fruits are green to camouflage them.

camp /kamp/ *n.*[1] Long *obs.* exc. *Hist.* [OE *camp*, *comp* = OFris. *camp*, *comp*, MDu. *camp* (Du. *kamp*), OHG *champf* (G *kampf*), ON *kapp*, f. Gmc f. L *campus* CAMP *n.*[2] (in med.L sense 'combat, battle').] †**1** Combat, battle, war. OE–LME. **2** In full *camp-ball*. An ancient form of football in which large numbers engaged on each side. E17.

camp /kamp/ *n.*[2] E16. [(O)Fr. (alongside *champ*) f. It. *campo* f. L *campus* level field, place for games or military exercises.] **1** A place where troops are lodged or trained; (the remains of) an ancient fortified site. E16. **b** (The scene of) military service; military life in general. E18. **2** An encampment; the temporary quarters, often in tents or cabins, of nomads, Gypsies, detainees, travellers, holiday-makers, Scouts, Guides, etc. M16. **b** An assembly place for sheep or cattle. *Austral.* & *NZ.* L19. **3** A body of troops etc. encamping and moving together; an army on campaign; *fig.* a host. *arch.* M16. **4** A body of travellers, Scouts, etc., encamped together; a camping-out, a period spent encamped. M18. **5** *fig.* A body of adherents of a particular doctrine, theory, or party. L19. **6** [Afk. *kamp*.] A portion of veld fenced off for pasture. *S. Afr.* L19.

1 DRYDEN The Youth of Rome . . pitch their sudden Camp before the Foe. *armed camp*: see ARMED *a.*[1] 1. *causewayed camp*: see CAUSEWAY. **b** J. KEBLE Through court and camp. **2** AV *Exod.* 16:13 At even the Quailes came vp, and couered the campe. J. STEINBECK There was no order in the camp; little gray tents, shacks, cars were scattered about at random. *concentration camp*, *holiday camp*, *motor camp*, *summer camp*, etc. *Siwash camp*: see SIWASH *a.* **3** S. JOHNSON Multitudes follow the camp only for want of employment. **5** JOHN BROOKE Europe was divided into two great camps: Catholic and Protestant. M. J. LASKY One of Milton's traditionalist contemporaries in the moderate camp. **a foot in both camps** connection or sympathy with two opposite groups, factions, etc.

Comb.: **camp-bed**, **-chair**, etc.: folding and portable; **campcraft** skill at living in camp; **camp-fever** typhus; **camp-fire** an open-air fire in a camp etc.; *camp fire girl* (US), a member of a training and recreational organization; **camp-follower** (now usu. *derog.*) (*a*) a non-military worker or hanger-on in a camp etc.; (*b*) a disciple of a group or theory; **camp-meeting** *US* a religious open-air or tent meeting often lasting several days; **camp oven** *Austral.* & *NZ* a three-legged iron cooking-pot with a flat top; **camp-site** a place for camping; **camp-stool** a light stool with collapsible legs.

camp /kamp/ *a.* & *n.*[3] E20. [Origin unkn.] **A** *adj.* Ostentatious, exaggerated, affected, theatrical; effeminate, homosexual. E20.

B *n.* Camp behaviour, mannerisms, etc. E20.

high camp: see HIGH *a.*

campy *a.* (*colloq.*) = CAMP *a.* M20.

camp /kamp/ *v.*[1]*i.* *obs.* exc. *dial.* or *Hist.* [OE *campian*, f. CAMP *n.*[1]] Contend, esp. at camp-ball.

camp /kamp/ *v.*[2] M16. [Fr. *camper*, f. as CAMP *n.*[2]] **1** *v.i.* Live or stay in a camp or tent; form or pitch one's camp; encamp; *gen.* take up residence, lodge. M16. **2** *v.t.* Establish or place in a camp. Now usu. in *pass.* M16. **3** *v.i.* Of sheep or cattle: flock together, usu. for rest or at night. *Austral.* & *NZ.* M19. **4** *v.t.* & *i.* *Teleph.* Reserve (a call) for connection on to or *on to* an engaged telephone as soon as it becomes free. L20.

1 camp out lodge in the open in a camp. **2** OED The troops would be camped along the river side.

Comb.: **camp-on** (**busy**) *Teleph.* a facility allowing a call to be camped on to an engaged telephone.

camp /kamp/ *v.*[3]*t.* & *i.* M20. [f. CAMP *a.* & *n.*[3]] Do or behave in a camp manner.

camp it up behave affectedly or with exaggeration, overact.

campagna /kamˈpɑːnjə, *foreign* kamˈpaɲɲa/ *n.* Also †**-a(g)nia**. L16. [It. f. late L *campania*: see CHAMPAIGN. Cf. next.] **1** Open country; champaign. Now *rare* exc. w. ref. to the Campagna di Roma. L16. †**2** A military campaign. M–L17.

campaign /kamˈpeɪn/ *n.* & *v.* E17. [Fr. *campagne* (alongside (O)Fr. *champagne*) f. late L *campania*: see CHAMPAIGN. Cf. prec.] **A** *n.* **1** (A tract of) open country, as opp. to hills, woods, etc.; champaign. Now *rare* or *obs.* E17. **2** A series of military operations in a definite area or with one objective or forming the whole or a distinct part of a war. M17. †**3** An expedition, an excursion; a tour. Only in 18. **4** Any organized course of action analogous to a military campaign; *esp.* one designed to arouse public support for a party in an election, a cause, etc. L18.

2 on campaign on military service in the field. **4** DICKENS I am now preparing for a final reading campaign. E. ROOSEVELT President Wilson . . started out on a campaign to take the cause of the League of Nations to the American people. *plan of campaign*: see PLAN *n.*

Comb.: **campaign trail** a route taken in the course of a political campaign, with stops for canvassing etc. (chiefly in *on the campaign trail*); **campaign wig** *Hist.* a close-fitting wig with a curled forehead, worn for travelling.

B *v.i.* Serve on or conduct a campaign. E18.

campaigner *n.* a person who serves in a campaign; *esp.* one who has served in many campaigns (*old campaigner*, a veteran, a person skilled in adapting to circumstances): L17.

campana /kamˈpɑːnə/ *n.* E17. [Late L *campana* bell.] **1** A bell; a bell-shaped flower. Now *rare* or *obs.* E17. **2** A bell-shaped vase. E19.

campanero /kampəˈnɛːrəʊ/ *n.* Pl. **-os**. E19. [Sp., f. *campana* bell.] The S. American bellbird.

†**campania** *n.* var. of CAMPAGNA.

campaniform /kamˈpanɪfɔːm/ *a.* M18. [f. as CAMPANA + -I- + -FORM.] Bell-shaped.

campanile /kampəˈniːli/ *n.* M17. [It., f. *campana* bell + *-ile* -IL, -ILE.] A (usu. lofty and detached) bell-tower, esp. in Italy.

campanist /ˈkampənɪst/ *n.* L19. [med.L *campanista*, f. as CAMPANA: see -IST.] A person versed in the subject of bells, a campanologist.

campanology /kampəˈnɒlədʒi/ *n.* M19. [mod.L *campanologia*, f. as CAMPANA + -OLOGY.] The subject of bells, their founding, ringing, etc.

campanologer *n.* = CAMPANOLOGIST E19. **campanoˈlogical** *a.* M19. **campanoˈlogically** *adv.* L19. **campanologist** *n.* an expert in campanology, a student of bells M19.

campanula /kamˈpanjʊlə/ *n.* E17. [mod.L, f. as CAMPANA: see -ULE.] A plant of the genus *Campanula*, with usu. blue, pink, or white bell-shaped flowers; a bellflower.

campanularian /ˌkampanjʊˈlɛːrɪən/ *a.* & *n.* M19. [f. mod.L *Campanularia* genus name, f. as prec. + *-aria*: see -ARY[1], -AN.] *Zool.* **A** *adj.* Of, pertaining to, or characteristic of the order Calyptoblastea of hydrozoans possessing bell-shaped hydrothecae. M19. **B** *n.* A member of this order. L19.

campanulate /kamˈpanjʊlət/ *a.* M17. [f. as CAMPANULA + -ATE[2].] Chiefly *Bot.* & *Zool.* Bell-shaped.

Also **campanulated** *a.* M18.

Campari /kamˈpɑːri/ *n.* E20. [The It. manufacturer.] (Proprietary name for) an aperitif flavoured with bitters; a drink of this.

Campeachy /kəmˈpiːtʃi/ *n.* Also **Campeche**. E17. [*Campeche*, port and State of Mexico.] In full *Campeachy wood*. = LOGWOOD.

camper /ˈkampə/ *n.* M17. [f. CAMP *n.*[2], *v.*[2] + -ER[1].] †**1** A military man, a soldier; a camp-follower. M–L17. **2** A person who takes part in a camp-meeting. *US.* E19. **3** A person who lives or lodges in a camp or tent; a resident in a holiday camp, summer camp, etc. M19. **4** A trailer or (more fully *camper van*) motor vehicle furnished with beds and other equipment for camping. Orig. *US.* M20.

campesino /kampeˈsino, kampəˈsiːnəʊ/ *n.* Pl. ***-os*** /-ɒs, -əʊz/. M20. [Sp.] In Spain and Spanish-speaking countries: a peasant farmer.

campestral /kamˈpɛstr(ə)l/ *a.* E18. [f. L *campester*, *-tr-*, f. *campus*: see CAMP *n.*[2], -AL[1].] Pertaining to fields or open country; growing or living in fields.

Also †**campestrial** *a.*: only in 17.

camph- /kamf/ *comb. form* of CAMPHOR *n.*

camphene *n.* (*Chem.*) a crystalline bicyclic terpene, $C_{10}H_{16}$, present in many essential oils. M19. **camphine** *n.* (*Hist.*) an oil for lamps, distilled from turpentine M19.

camphor /ˈkamfə/ *n.* ME. [OFr. *camphore* or med.L *camphora* f. Arab. *kāfūr* f. Malay *kapur* ult. f. Skt *karpūra*.] **1** A colourless crystalline terpenoid ketone, $C_{10}H_{17}O$, with an aromatic smell and bitter taste, which occurs in certain essential oils and is used esp. in pharmacy and as an insect repellent. ME. **b** *Borneo camphor*, †*camphor of Borneo*, an essential oil consisting chiefly of borneol, obtained from the tree *Dryobalanops aromatica*. L17. †**2** A tree yielding camphor (cf. *camphor tree* below). L16–L17.

Comb.: **camphor laurel** *Austral.* any of various trees of the genus *Cinnamomum*; **camphor tree** a tree of the laurel family, *Cinnamomum camphora*, which is native to the Far East and is the major natural source of camphor; **camphor-wood** (the timber of) any of various trees with fragrant wood.

camphorate *n.* a salt or ester of camphoric acid L18. †**camphorate** *a.* camphorated LME–E18. **camphorate** *v.t.* impregnate or treat with camphor M17. **camphoric** /kamˈfɒrɪk/ *a.* of or pertaining to camphor (*camphoric acid*, a crystalline dibasic acid, $C_{10}H_{16}O_4$, obtained by the oxidation of camphor) L18.

camphor /ˈkamfə/ *v.t.* M16. [f. the n.] Camphorate.

campimeter /kamˈpɪmɪtə/ *n.* L19. [f. L *campus* field (see CAMP *n.*[2]) + -IMETER.] An apparatus for measuring or mapping the field of vision of the eye.

campimetry *n.* E20.

campion /ˈkampɪən/ *n.* M16. [Perh. rel. to CHAMPION *n.*[1] Orig. used for L *lychnis coronaria*, Gk *lukhnis stephanōmatikē* rose campion 'used for garlands'.] Any of various plants of the genera *Silene* and *Lychnis* of the pink family, bearing red or white flowers with notched petals. Cf. LYCHNIS, SILENE.

bladder campion, moss campion, red campion, white campion, etc.

cample /ˈkamp(ə)l/ *v.i. obs.* exc. *dial.* L15. [App. f. CAMP *v.*[1] + -LE[3].] Quarrel, dispute, wrangle.

campo /ˈkampəʊ/ *n.* Pl. **-os.** M19. [(Amer.) Sp. or Port. = field, open country, f. L *campus*: see CAMP *n.*[2]] In S. America (esp. Brazil), a grass plain with occasional stunted trees; a savannah. Freq. in *pl.*

campong *n.* see KAMPONG.

campoo /kamˈpuː/ *n.* E19. [Hind. *kampū* f. Port. *campo* camp.] *Hist.* A brigade of Maratha troops, led by a European mercenary.

campshed /ˈkampʃɛd/ *n.* Also **-shot** /-ʃɒt/ & other vars. L15. [Prob. f. CANT *n.*[1] + SHIDE.] A facing of piles and boarding along the bank of a river etc. or at the side of an embankment.

campshedding (also **-sheeting** & other vars.) *n.* a campshed; campsheds collectively: E19.

campus /ˈkampəs/ *n.* Orig. *US.* L18. [L: see CAMP *n.*[2]] The grounds and buildings of a college, university, etc., esp. where forming a distinct area; a separate part of a university; university or college life.

campylite /ˈkampɪlʌɪt/ *n.* M19. [f. as next + -ITE[1].] *Min.* A variety of mimetite, occurring as small rounded orange-yellow crystals.

campylobacter /ˈkampɪləʊˌbaktə, ˌkampɪləʊˈbaktə/ *n.* L20. [mod.L (see below), f. as next + BACTER(IUM.] A bacterium of the genus *Campylobacter*, which includes curved and spiral forms causing food poisoning in humans and abortion in some farm animals.

campylotropous /kampɪˈlɒtrəpəs/ *a.* M19. [f. Gk *kampulos* bent + *-tropos* turning + -OUS.] *Bot.* Of an ovule: bent transversely across its funicle.

camstone /ˈkamstəʊn/ *n. Sc.* Also (earlier) †**calm-**. E16. [f. unidentified 1st elem. + STONE *n.*] A white limestone; pipeclay used to whiten doorsteps etc.

†**camus** *n.*[1] var. of CAMIS.

camus /ˈkaməs/ *a.* & *n.*[2] Now *rare* or *obs.* Also **-mois.** LME. [(O)Fr., of unkn. origin.] A *adj.* Of the nose: low and concave. Of a person: snub-nosed. LME. †**B** *n.* A person or animal with a low concave nose. L15–M18.

camwood /ˈkamwʊd/ *n.* L17. [Prob. f. Temne *k'am* + WOOD *n.*[1]] = BARWOOD.

can /kan/ *n.* [OE *canne*, corresp. to MDu. *kanne* (Du. *kan*), OHG *channa* (G *kanne*), ON *kanna*, ult. Gmc or f. late L *canna*.] **1** A vessel for holding liquids, now *spec.* one of metal, and usu. cylindrical with a handle over the top. Also (chiefly *N. Amer.*), any large cylindrical metal container, a bin. OE. **b** A measure of capacity; about a gallon. *Sc.* E19. **2** A (usu. cylindrical) container of tin plate or aluminium in which food, drink, etc., can be hermetically sealed; (such a container and) its contents. Cf. TIN *n.* 2. M19. **3a** A chimney pot. Chiefly *Sc.* M19. **b** A lavatory. *N. Amer. slang.* E20. **c** *the can*, jail. *slang* (chiefly *US*). E20. **d** The buttocks. *N. Amer. slang.* M20. **e** A protective jacket for a nuclear fuel rod. M20. **f** In *pl.* Headphones. *slang.* L20.

1 WORDSWORTH I have brought thee in this can fresh water from the brook. *ashcan, jerrycan, oil can, watering-can*, etc. **2** J. B. PRIESTLEY We sat in the office, with a can of beer each.

Phrases: *can of worms*: see WORM *n.* **carry the can (back)** *slang* bear the responsibility or blame. **in the can** safely recorded on film, tape, etc., completed. **take the can (back)** *slang* = *carry the can (back)* above. *tie a can on* or *to*: see TIE *v.*[1]

Comb.: **can bank** a collection point to which empty cans may be taken for recycling; **can-buoy** a large cone-shaped marker buoy; **can-dock** a water lily, esp. of the yellow-flowered species; **can-opener** a tool for opening cans of food etc.

canful *n.* as much or as many as a can will hold, the contents of a can E18.

can /kan, *unstressed* k(ə)n/ *v.*[1] Pres.: **can**; 2 sing. (*arch.*) **canst** /kanst, k(ə)nst/. Pa.: **could** /kʊd, *unstressed* kəd/; 2 sing. (*arch.*) **couldst** /kʊdst, kədst/, **couldest** /ˈkʊdɪst/. Neg. **can not, cannot** /ˈkanət/, (*informal*) **can't** /kɑːnt/; **could not,** (*informal*) **couldn't** /ˈkʊd(ə)nt/. No other parts used. See also CON *v.*[1] [OE *cunnan* = OFris. *kunna*, OS *cunnan* (Du. *kunnen*), OHG *kunnan* (G *können*), ON *kunna*, Goth. *kunnan*, ult. f. IE base found also in L *gnoscere*, Gk *gignōskein* know: a Gmc preterite-present vb w. primary meaning 'have learned, come to know'.] **I** As full vb. †**1** *v.t.* Know; be acquainted with; have learned. OE–M19. **2** *v.i.* Have knowledge, know *of. arch.* ME.

1 J. FOXE Unlearned men that can no letters. JONSON She could the Bible in the holy tongue. **2** S. ROWLANDS I never was there (that I can of). SIR W. SCOTT Thou canst well of wood-craft.

II As auxiliary vb (often *ellipt.* with vb understood or supplied from the context). **3** Know how to, have learned to. Now absorbed in sense 4. ME. **4** Have the power or capacity to; be able to. ME. **5** May possibly; be enabled by circumstances etc. to. ME. **b** Be allowed or given permission to; may. *colloq.* L19. **6** In pa. form (*could* etc.). Feel inclined to, would like to. M17.

3 SPENSER Well couth hee tune his pipe. **4** AV *Exod.* 7:21 The Egyptians could not drinke of the water. DEFOE I will do all I can with them. OED Such language can do no good to the cause. DAY LEWIS I can remember no pain, no perturbation, no sense of parting. **5** STEELE The best Sort of Companion that can be. LD MACAULAY Even if it could be believed that the court was sincere. ANTHONY SMITH Other kinds of brain-dead patients could, or should, be regarded as potential donors. **b** T. B. REED Father says you can come. **6** ADDISON I could wish our Royal Society would compile a Body of Natural History. J. P. DONLEAVY 'Take that ten shilling note, Mr Dangerfield, and get some eggs.' 'No, I couldn't.' 'Do. Please. I insist.'

Phrases: *as far as I can see*: see SEE *v. as far as one can tell*: see TELL *v. can do*: see *no can do* below. *cannot for the life of me*: see LIFE *n. cannot, could not resist*: see RESIST *v.* 2. *can skill*: see SKILL *n. can you tie that*: see TIE *v.*[1] **(no) can do** *colloq.* it is (not) possible, I am (not) able or willing to do it. *walk before one can run*: see WALK *v.*[1] †*who cannot want the thought?*: see WANT *v. you can say that again*: see SAY *v.*[1] *you can* or *can't talk*: see TALK *v. you* etc. *can't lose*: see LOSE *v. you can't take it with you*: see TAKE *v.*

can /kan/ *v.*[2]*t.* Infl. **-nn-**. M19. [f. CAN *n.*] **1** Put into a can; preserve (meat, fruit, etc.) by sealing in cans. Cf. TIN *v.* 2. M19. **b** *fig.* & *transf.* Confine; preserve, esp. by recording on film, tape, etc. M19. **c** Cover (a nuclear fuel rod) with a protective jacket. M20. **2a** Expel, suspend, dismiss. *N. Amer. slang.* E20. **b** Desist from, leave off, cut out. *slang* (orig. *US*). E20.

†**can** *v.*[3] see GIN *v.*[1]

can *v.*[4] var. of CON *v.*[2]

Canaan /ˈkeɪnən/ *n.* E17. [eccl.L *Chanaan* f. eccl.Gk *Khanaan* f. Heb. *kĕnaʿan* ancient name of western Palestine, promised in the Old Testament and Hebrew Scriptures to the children of Israel (*Exod.* 3:17 etc.).] A land of promise; heaven.

Canaanite /ˈkeɪnənʌɪt/ *n.* M16. [f. prec. + -ITE[1]. In sense 2 tr. Gk *Kananitēs*, f. Heb. *qannaʾ* zealous.] **1** A native or inhabitant of Canaan; *fig.* a heathen. M16. **2** A zealot. Now *rare* or *obs.* E17.

Canaanitic /-ˈnɪtɪk/ *a.* of Canaan; of or like a Canaanite: L19. **Canaanitish** *a.* = CANAANITIC M16.

Canada /ˈkanədə/ *n.* L17. [A Federal State (formerly a British territory) in N. America.] **I** *attrib.* **1** Used *attrib.* to designate things found in or associated with Canada. L17.

1 Canada balsam a resin exuded from the N. American balsam fir, *Abies balsamea*, and used esp. for mounting microscope specimens. **Canada bird** *Canad.* = PEABODY. **Canada Day** 1 July, observed as a public holiday in Canada to observe the day in 1867 when four of the former colonial provinces were united under one government as the Dominion of Canada (formerly called *Dominion Day*). **Canada goose** a large grey-brown, black, and white goose, *Branta canadensis*, native to N. America and widely introduced elsewhere. **Canada jay** the N. American grey jay, *Perisoreus canadensis*. **Canada thistle** *N. Amer.* a naturalized European thistle, *Cirsium arvense*, with spreading roots.

II *ellipt.* **2** A Canada goose. L19.

Canadian /kəˈneɪdɪən/ *n.* & *a.* M16. [f. prec. + -IAN.] **A** *n.* A native or inhabitant of Canada. M16. **B** *adj.* Of or pertaining to Canada or its people. L17.

Phrases & special collocations: **Canadian pondweed** = *Canadian waterweed* s.v. WATER *n. Canadian waterweed*: see *waterweed* (b) s.v. WATER *n. French Canadian*: see FRENCH *a.*

Canadiˈana *n.pl.* [-ANA] publications or other items concerning or associated with Canada M19. **Canadianism** *n.* (*a*) Canadian character or spirit; (*b*) a Canadian idiom or word: L19. **Canadianize** *v.t.* render Canadian in character E19.

Canadien /kanadjɛ̃/ *n.* & *a.* Fem. ***-ienne*** /-jɛn/. Pl. pronounced same. M19. [Fr. = prec.] (A) French Canadian.

†**canaglia** *n.* E17–E19. [It.: see next.] = next.

canaille /kanaːj/ *n.* L16. [Fr. f. It *canaglia* lit. 'pack of dogs', f. *cane* dog.] *The* rabble, *the* populace.

canakin *n.* var. of CANNIKIN.

canal /kəˈnal/ *n.* LME. [(O)Fr. refash. of *chanel* CHANNEL *n.*[1] after L *canalis* or It. *canale*. Cf. CANNEL *n.*[1], KENNEL *n.*[2]] **1** *gen.* A pipe or tube for conveying fluid; a faucet; a tubular cavity. Now *rare* or *obs.* LME. **2** A tubular duct or passage in a plant or animal body. LME. **b** A groove in a mollusc's shell for protrusion of a breathing tube. M19. **3** A watercourse, a channel; a strait. *obs.* exc. as in sense 4 or (*N. Amer.*) in proper names. M16. †**b** An ornamental strip of water in a garden etc. M17–E19. **4** An artificial watercourse constructed for the purpose of inland navigation or to convey water for irrigation etc. (Now the predominant sense.) L17. **5** *Astron.* [tr. It. *canali* channels.] Any of a network of dubious linear markings on Mars reported by telescopic observers. L19.

2 ALIMENTARY *canal.* SEMICIRCULAR *canal. spinal canal*: see SPINAL *a.* STENSEN'*s canal.* VALLECULAR *canal.* **4** *junction canal*: see JUNCTION *n.* 2.

Comb.: **canal boat** a long narrow boat designed for use on canals; **canal rays** [tr. G *Kanalstrahlen* 'channel rays'] *Physics* streams of positive ions which move towards the cathode in a high-vacuum discharge tube.

canal /kəˈnal/ *v. rare.* Infl. **-ll-**. E19. [f. the n.] **1** *v.t.* = CANALIZE *v.* 1. E19. **2** *v.i.* Construct a canal or canals; travel by canal. Chiefly as *canalling* vbl n. M19.

canaliculus /kanəˈlɪkjʊləs/ *n.* Pl. **-li** /-lʌɪ, -liː/. M16. [L *canaliculus* dim. of *canalis*: see CANAL *n.*, -CULE.] Chiefly *Anat.* A small channel or duct.

canalicular *a.* of or pertaining to a canaliculus; minutely tubular: L19. **canaliculate** *a.* minutely channelled or grooved M18. **canaliculated** *a.* = CANALICULATE M18. **caˈnalicule** *n.* = CANALICULUS M19.

canalize /ˈkan(ə)lʌɪz/ *v.t.* Also **-ise.** M19. [Fr. *canaliser*: see CANAL *n.*, -IZE.] **1** Make a canal through, provide with canals; provide with locks etc. like a canal, make into a canal. M19. **2** Provide with or convey through ducts or channels. L19. **3** *fig.* Give a specific direction etc. to. E20.

3 J. M. KEYNES Dangerous human proclivities can be canalised into comparatively harmless channels. A. WILSON She must not allow middle-aged rancour to canalize her happiness.

canaliˈzation *n.* M19.

canapé /ˈkanəpeɪ, -pi/ *n.* L19. [Fr.] **1** A piece of bread, toast, etc., with a small savoury on top. L19. **2** A sofa. L19.

canard /kəˈnɑːd, ˈkanɑːd/ *n.* M19. [Fr., lit. 'duck'.] **1** A false report, a hoax. M19. **2** An extra surface attached to an aircraft, hydrofoil, etc., for stability or control. Also, an aircraft fitted with this. E20.

Canarese *a.* & *n.* var. of KANARESE.

Canarian /kəˈnɛːrɪən/ *n.* & *a.* M17. [f. as next + -IAN.] **A** *n.* A native or inhabitant of the Canary Islands. M17. **B** *adj.* Of or pertaining to the Canary Islands off the west coast of Africa. L18.

canary /kəˈnɛːri/ *n.* Also (esp. in senses 1 & 2) **C-**. L16. [f. *Canary* Islands off the west coast of Africa, f. Fr. *Canarie* f. Sp. *Canāria* f. L *Canaria* (*insula* island), f. *canis* dog: one of the islands was noted in Roman times for large dogs. In sense 3 f. Fr. *canari*, †*-ie* f. Sp. *canario*.] 1 *Hist. sing.* & †in *pl.* A lively dance similar to the jig (perh. orig. from the Canary Islands). L16. 2 *Hist. sing.* & †in *pl.* Sweet wine from the Canary Islands. L16. 3 A songbird of the finch family, *Serinus canaria*, native to the Canary Islands, Madeira, and the Azores, of which wild individuals are green and the numerous cage varieties usu. yellow. Also, any of certain other birds of this genus. Also more fully *canary-bird*. L16. b A jailbird, a convict. *slang.* L17. c A gold coin (from its colour). L18. 4 A bright yellow. Freq. *attrib.* M19.

Comb.: *canary-bird*: see sense 3 above; **canary-coloured** *a.* canary yellow; **canary creeper** a yellow-flowered climbing nasturtium, *Tropaeolum peregrinum*; **canary-grass** a grass, *Phalaris canariensis*, grown as a source of birdseed; also, with specifying wd, any other plant of this genus (*reed canary-grass*: see REED *n.*[1]); **canary-seed** seed used to feed canaries, *esp.* that of canary-grass; **canary yellow** *n.* & *a.* (of) a bright yellow.

†canary *v.i.* L16–E19. [f. the n.] Perform the canary or other lively dance.

canasta /kəˈnastə/ *n.* M20. [Sp. = basket, ult. f. L *canistrum* CANISTER.] A two-pack card-game of the rummy family and of Uruguayan origin, usu. played by four in two partnerships; a meld of seven or more cards in this game.

canaster /kəˈnastə/ *n.* E19. [Sp. *canastro* basket (used to pack tobacco) f. med.L: see CANISTER.] A kind of tobacco made of coarsely-broken dried leaves.

canaut /kəˈnɔːt/ *n.* Now *rare.* E17. [Urdu f. Pers. f. Turk. *kanāt*.] In the Indian subcontinent: the side-wall of a tent; a canvas enclosure.

cancan /ˈkankan/ *n.* M19. [Fr., redupl. of *canard* duck.] A lively dance of French origin, orig. a form of quadrille, now performed by a woman and involving high kicks, usu. while holding up the front of the skirts.

cancel /ˈkans(ə)l/ *n.* E19. [f. the vb.] 1 *Printing.* The suppression of text by excision (of a leaf, fold, or sheet) or by pasting over it. Also (*a*) (also *cancel leaf*) a leaf so cancelled; (*b*) the new leaf substituted. Cf. CANCELLANDUM, CANCELLANS *n.* E19. 2 *gen.* An act of cancelling; a countermand. L19. 3 *Mus.* A natural-sign cancelling a preceding sharp or flat. *US.* E20.

cancel /ˈkans(ə)l/ *v.* Infl. **-ll-**, ***-l-**. LME. [(O)Fr. *canceller* f. L *cancellare* make lattice-wise, cross out (a writing), f. *cancellus*, pl. *-li* crossbars: see CANCELLI, CHANCEL.] I *v.t.* 1 Deface or obliterate (writing), by drawing or stamping lines across it, or by puncturing or tearing what it is written on; annul (a deed, a stamp, etc.) by so marking. LME. b *Printing.* Suppress (text, a page, leaf, etc.) after it has been set up or printed off. M18. 2 *fig.* Render void (an obligation, promise, etc.). Also foll. by *out.* LME. 3 *gen.* Obliterate, abolish; countermand, revoke an order or arrangements for; put an end to. Also (*rare*) with *off.* M16. 4 *Math.* Strike out (the same factor) from the numerator and denominator, from both sides of an equation, etc. L16. 5 Neutralize, counterbalance, make up for. Freq. with *out.* M17. 6 *Mus.* Mark a return to natural pitch after (a sharp or flat). *US.* M19.

1 T. ARNOLD In my Catholic Pamphlet . . there is one paragraph which I should now cancel. R. GRAVES A postage-stamp . . issued and cancelled by the postmaster of . . Antigua. 2 C. THIRLWALL All debts were to be cancelled. 3 MILTON Canceld from Heav'n and sacred memorie, Nameless in dark oblivion let them dwell. J. GALSWORTHY He had just cancelled their trusteeships of his will. E. HEMINGWAY It would be too wet and . . the bull-baiting . . would be cancelled. 5 DRYDEN With publick Zeal to cancel private Crimes. J. STALLWORTHY Credit And debit columns cancelled themselves out.

II *v.i.* †7 Become void or null. *rare.* Only in M17. 8 Neutralize or counterbalance each other; be equal and opposite. Freq. with *out.* E20.

8 *Listener* The personal preferences of your contributors are . . likely to cancel out.

cancellable *a.* (earlier in UNCANCELLABLE) L17. **canceller** *n.* E17. **cancelment** *n.* (*rare*) = CANCELLATION E17.

canceleer /kansəˈlɪə/ *n.* & *v.* L16. [ONFr. *canceler* to swerve (mod. *chanceler*), used as n.: cf. -ER[4].] A *n.* The action of a hawk in canceleering. L16. B *v.i.* Of a hawk: turn once or twice on the wing, in order to recover before striking. M17.

cancellandum /kansəˈlandəm/ *n.* Pl. **-da** /-də/. E20. [L, neut. gerundive of *cancellare* CANCEL *v.*] *Printing.* In full *cancellandum leaf.* A leaf for which another is substituted. Cf. next, CANCEL *n.* 1.

cancellans /ˈkans(ə)lanz/ *n.* & *a.* E20. [L, pres. pple of *cancellare* CANCEL *v.*] *Printing.* A *n.* A leaf which replaces another. Cf. prec., CANCEL *n.* 1. E20. B *adj.* Designating a leaf, sheet, fold, etc., which replaces another, or a slip which cancels text. M20.

cancellarian /kansəˈlɛːrɪən/ *a. rare.* M19. [f. med.L *cancellarius* CHANCELLOR + -AN.] Of, or of the nature of, a chancellor.

cancellate /ˈkans(ə)lət/ *a.* M17. [f. as next + -ATE[2].] Chiefly *Biol.* Marked or divided (as) with cross lines; (of bone) cancellous.

Also **cancellated** *a.* L17.

cancellation /kansəˈleɪʃ(ə)n/ *n.* M16. [f. L *cancellat-* pa. ppl stem of *cancellare* CANCEL *v.* + -ION: cf. med.L *cancellatio(n-)*.] 1 The action of or an instance of cancelling; a cancelling mark etc. M16. 2 *spec.* The action or an instance of cancelling the reservation of a seat, room, etc.; a seat, room, etc., reservation of which has been cancelled. M20.

cancelli /kanˈsɛlʌɪ/ *n.pl.* M17. [L, dim. of *cancer*, pl. *cancri* crossing bars, grating.] †1 Bars of lattice-work; *spec.* the latticed screen between the choir and body of a church. *rare.* M17–E18. 2 *Anat.* The lattice-work of spongy bone tissue; the mesh of spaces within this. E19.

cancellous *a.* (of bone) containing cancelli, having a spongy appearance, porous M19.

cancer /ˈkansə/ *n.* OE. [L = crab, creeping ulcer, after Gk *karkinos*: cf. CANKER *n.*, CARCINOMA.] 1 (**C-**.) (The name of) an inconspicuous constellation of the northern hemisphere, on the ecliptic between Gemini and Leo; *Astrol.* (the name of) the fourth zodiacal sign, usu. associated with the period 22 June to 22 July (see note s.v. ZODIAC); the Crab. OE. b A person born under the sign Cancer. M20. 2 A malignant tumour or growth of body tissue that tends to spread and may recur if removed; disease in which such a growth occurs. Cf. CANKER *n.* 1 (the usual form until 17). OE. b *fig.* An evil spreading in the manner of a cancer. M17. †3 A crab. E17–L18.

1 *attrib.*: E. KIRK The Cancer men are far more constant than the Cancer women. *tropic of Cancer*: see TROPIC *n.* & *a.* 2 *soft cancer*: see SOFT *a.* b M. L. KING A dangerous cancer of hatred and racism in our society.

Comb.: **cancer bush** *S. Afr.* a leguminous shrub, *Sutherlandia frutescens*, cultivated for its red flowers; **cancer-root** broomrape; **cancer stick** *slang* a cigarette; †**cancer-wort** fluellen.

Cancerian /kanˈsɪərɪən/ *n.* & *a.* (*a*) *n.* a person born under the sign Cancer; (*b*) *adj.* of or pertaining to the sign Cancer; (characteristic of one) born under Cancer: E20. **canceriˈcidal**, **canceroˈcidal** *adjs.* tending to destroy cancer cells M20.

cancer /ˈkansə/ *v.t.* L18. [f. the n.] Affect with or as with cancer; eat into in the manner of a cancer.

GOLDSMITH The application of toads to a cancered breast. M. BRAGG This strident fanaticism which had . . cancered him with revolt.

cancerate /ˈkansəreɪt/ *v.t.* & *i.* L17. [Late L *cancerat-* pa. ppl stem of *cancerare*, f. as CANCER *n.*: see -ATE[3].] Make or become cancerous. Chiefly as *cancerated* ppl a.

cancerous /ˈkans(ə)rəs/ *a.* M16. [f. CANCER *n.* + -OUS.] Of the nature of or affected with cancer.

fig.: K. TYNAN This fantasy, once mild, has grown cancerous and now infects his whole world.

cancerously *adv.* M18. **cancerousness** *n.* M18.

cancrine /ˈkaŋkrʌɪn/ *a. rare.* M18. [f. L *cancr-* CANCER *n.* + -INE[1].] 1 Like or suggestive of a crab. M18. 2 *spec.* Of Latin verse: palindromic. M19.

cancrinite /ˈkaŋkrɪnʌɪt/ *n.* M19. [f. Georg *Cancrin* (1774–1845), Russ. statesman + -ITE[1].] *Min.* A hexagonal aluminosilicate and carbonate of sodium and calcium which belongs to the feldspathoid group and usu. occurs as masses of yellow-brown crystals.

cancrizans /ˈkaŋkrɪzanz/ *a.*, *adv.*, & *n.* L18. [med.L pres. pple of *cancrizare* walk backwards, f. as next: see -IZE.] *Mus.* (Designating, pertaining to, in the manner of) a canon in which the theme or subject is repeated backwards in the second part.

cancroid /ˈkaŋkrɔɪd/ *a.* & *n.* E19. [f. L *cancr-*, CANCER *n.* + -OID.] A *adj.* 1 Like a crab, esp. in structure. E19. 2 Resembling cancer. M19. B *n.* 1 A crab or related crustacean. *rare.* M19. 2 A disease resembling cancer; a mild form of cancer. M19.

candareen /kandəˈriːn/ *n.* E17. [Malay *kenderi*.] A former Chinese monetary unit equal to ten cash; a former Chinese unit of weight equal to about 0.4 gram (six grains).

candela /kanˈdɛlə, -ˈdiːlə, ˈkandɪlə/ *n.* M20. [L *candela*: see CANDLE *n.*] *Physics.* A unit of luminous intensity, equal to $1/60$ of the luminous intensity per square centimetre of the surface of a black body at the temperature of solidification of platinum.

candelabrum /kandɪˈlɑːbrəm, -ˈleɪ-/ *n.* Pl. **-bra** /-brə/, ***-brums**. Also **-bra**, pl. same, **-as**. E19. [L, f. *candela* CANDLE *n.*] A large usu. branched ornamental candlestick or lamp-holder carrying several lights.

Comb.: **candelabrum tree** a tropical African tree of the genus *Euphorbia*, with foliage shaped like a candelabrum.

candelilla /kandəˈliːljə/ *n.* E20. [Sp. = little candle.] A southern N. American shrub of the genus *Euphorbia*, yielding a hard wax (*candelilla wax*).

candent /ˈkand(ə)nt/ *a.* Now *rare.* L15. [L *candent-* pres. ppl stem of *candere* be white, glow: see -ENT.] At a white heat; glowing with heat.

candescent /kanˈdɛs(ə)nt/ *a. rare.* E19. [f. L *candere*: see prec., -ESCENT.] Glowing (as) with heat.

candescence *n.* L19.

candid /ˈkandɪd/ *a.* & *n.* M17. [Fr. *candide* or L *candidus*, f. *candere* be white, glisten: see -ID[1].] A *adj.* †1 White. M17–E19. †2 Illustrious, fortunate. M17–E18. 3 Pure, clear, innocent. *arch.* M17. 4 Unbiased, impartial; just, fair. *arch.* M17. †5 Free from malice; kindly; favourably disposed. M17–E19. 6 Frank, open; ingenuous; outspoken. L17. b Of a photograph or photography: unposed, informal. E20.

1 DRYDEN The stones came candid forth, the hue of innocence. 3 BROWNING Where does the figment touch her candid fame? 4 EARL OF CHATHAM Keep your mind in a candid state of suspense. 5 POPE Laugh where we must, be candid where we can. 6 J. A. FROUDE A . . very candid account of Henry's feelings. J. BARNES Previously I had . . been honest just for effect, comparatively candid. 6 **candid camera** a small camera for taking informal pictures of people, freq. without their knowledge.

B *n.* An informal or unposed photograph. *colloq.* M20.

candidly *adv.* M17. **candidness** *n.* E17.

candida /ˈkandɪdə/ *n.* M20. [mod.L (see below), fem. of L *candidus*: see prec.] 1 A yeastlike fungus of the genus *Candida*, esp. *C. albicans.* M20. 2 = CANDIDIASIS. L20.

candidacy /ˈkandɪdəsi/ *n.* M19. [f. next: see -ACY.] The position or status of a candidate; candidature.

candidate /ˈkandɪdeɪt, -dət/ *n.* & *v.* E17. [(O)Fr. *candidat* or L *candidatus* clothed in white, a candidate for office (who appeared in a white toga), f. *candidus*: see CANDID, -ATE[1].] A *n.* I 1 A person who seeks or is nominated for (election to) an office, honour, position, etc.; *spec.* an examinee; more *gen.*, an aspirant, one who seeks something. (Foll. by *for*, †*of*.) E17. 2 A person or thing thought likely or worthy to gain a particular position. M18.

1 S. JOHNSON A candidate for literary fame. J. BUCHAN I became the Conservative candidate for the counties of Peebles and Selkirk. DAY LEWIS The 'infant' candidate for baptism turned out to be a strapping boy of nine or ten. 2 GOLDSMITH If ever there was a candidate for Tyburn, this is one. J. NARLIKAR The X-ray source Cygnus X-1 is perhaps the most promising candidate for the location of a black hole so far known.

II 3 *Rom. Hist.* A member of one of four companies into which the imperial guard was divided. M17.

B *v.i.* Stand as a candidate. Chiefly *US.* M19.

candidateship *n.* = CANDIDACY L18.

candidature /ˈkandɪdətʃə, -tʃʊə/ *n.* M19. [f. prec. + -URE, prob. after Fr.] The action of standing for election; the fact or status of being a candidate.

candidiasis /kandɪˈdʌɪəsɪs/ *n.* Pl. **-ases** /-əsiːz/. M20. [f. CANDIDA + -IASIS.] *Med.* & *Vet. Med.* Infection with candida, esp. causing oral or vaginal thrush.

candied /ˈkandɪd/ *ppl a.* E17. [f. CANDY *v.* + -ED¹.] 1 Preserved or encrusted (as) with sugar; crystallized. E17. 2 *fig.* Specious, flattering. E17.

1 **candied peel**: of citrous fruits, preserved with sugar and used in cookery.

candiru /kandɪˈruː/ *n.* M19. [Port. f. Tupi *candirú.*] A tiny bloodsucking catfish, *Vandellia cirrhosa*, of the Amazon river system.

candle /ˈkand(ə)l/ *n.* OE. [L *candella*, earlier *candela*, f. *candere* be white, glisten. In ME f. AN & OFr., also f. L.] 1 A (usu. cylindrical) body of wax, tallow, etc., enclosing a wick, for giving light by burning. OE. b *fig.* A source of light, or of mental or spiritual illumination; the 'light' of life. Now *rare* or *obs.* OE. 2 A preparation containing aromatic etc. substances for diffusion during burning; a pastille. *obs.* exc. *Hist.* LME. 3 *Physics.* A unit of luminous intensity, superseded by the candela. Also *international candle.* Cf. *candlepower* below. L19. 4 The flower of a horse chestnut tree. E20.

1 *bell, book, and candle*: see BELL *n.*¹ **burn the candle at both ends** exhaust one's strength or resources through undertaking too much. *mould-candle*: see MOULD *n.*³ 14. *mutton candle*: see MUTTON 4. **not able** or **fit to hold a candle to** not to be compared with, inferior to. **not worth the candle** not worth the cost or effort (esp. in *the game is not worth the candle*). *paschal candle*: see PASCHAL *a.* *Roman candle*: see ROMAN *a.* **sell** etc. **by the candle** (or **by inch of candle**) *arch.*: by auction at which the time allowed for bids is set by the burning of a candle, the last bid received during this time securing the article. *smell of the candle*: see SMELL *v.* 8a. *tallow candle*: see TALLOW *n.* 3. 3 *standard candle*: see STANDARD *a.* 4 **in candle** (of a horse-chestnut tree) in flower.

Comb.: **candle-beam** a rood-beam; **candleberry** (the fruit of) any of various trees or shrubs whose fruit yields a wax or oil used for candles; *esp.* (*a*) (also *candleberry myrtle*) a bayberry or related shrub; (*b*) (also *candleberry tree*) the kukui tree; **candle-end** the burnt-down end of a candle; *fig.* (*arch.*) a trifle, a scrap; **candle-fish** *N. Amer.* = EULACHON; **candlelight** (*a*) the light given by a candle or candles; (*b*) dusk, twilight; **candlelit** *a.* lit by a candle or candles; **candle-nut** = KUKUI; also, its fruit; **candlepower** illuminating power expressed in candles (sense 3); *candle-snuffer*: see SNUFFER *n.*¹; **candlestick** a holder for a candle or (less commonly) candles (*the butcher, the baker, the candlestick-maker*: see BUTCHER *n.*); **candle-tree** (*a*) = *candleberry* (a) above; (*b*) the Central American tree *Parmentiera cerifera*, with very long cylindrical fruit; **candle-waster** *arch.* a person who studies or revels late into the night; **candlewick** (*a*) the wick of a candle; (*b*) (material with a raised usu. tufted pattern in) a thick soft cotton yarn; **candle-wood** resinous wood burning with a bright flame; a tree yielding this, esp. (*N. Amer.*) of the genus *Fouquieria.*

candle /ˈkand(ə)l/ *v.t.* L17. [f. the n.] †1 Cover over or rub with candle-grease. *rare.* L17–E19. 2 Examine the contents of (an egg etc.) by holding it between the eye and a source of light. L19.

candler *n.* E20.

Candlemas /ˈkand(ə)lmas, -məs/ *n.* [OE *candelmæsse*, f. CANDLE *n.* + MASS *n.*¹] (The date, 2 February, of the celebration of) the feast of the Purification of the Virgin Mary and the presentation of Jesus in the Temple, when candles are blessed.

candour /ˈkandə/ *n.* Also ***-or.** LME. [L *candor*, f. base of *candidus*, *candere*: see CANDID, -OUR. Cf. Fr. *candeur.*] 1 Whiteness; brilliancy. Long *rare.* LME. †2 Stainless character; purity, innocence. L15–E18. 3 Freedom from bias, impartiality, fairness. Now *rare* or *obs.* M17. †4 A favourable disposition; good nature; kindness. M17–E19. 5 Frankness, openness; ingenuousness; outspokenness. M18.

candy /ˈkandi/ *n.*¹ E17. [Marathi *khaṇḍī.*] A weight formerly used in the Indian subcontinent, generally equal to 230 or 250 kg.

candy /ˈkandi/ *n.*² M17. [f. SUGAR-CANDY.] 1 Crystallized sugar, made by repeated boiling and slow evaporation. M17. 2 A sweet confection; sweets collectively. Chiefly *N. Amer.* E19. 3 Drugs, narcotics. *N. Amer. slang.* M20.

2 *cotton candy, cough candy*, etc.

Comb.: **candy ass** *N. Amer. slang* a timid or cowardly person, a despicable person; **candy-assed** *a.* (*N. Amer. slang*) timid, cowardly, despicable; **candy bar** *N. Amer.* a bar of toffee or other sweet substance, a bar of chocolate; **candy cane** *N. Amer.* a stick of striped rock with a curved end, resembling a walking-stick; *candyfloss*: see FLOSS *n.*² 4; **candy-man** (*a*) (chiefly *Hist.*) an itinerant seller of sweets etc.; (*b*) *N. Amer. slang* a pedlar or pusher of drugs; **candy-store** *N. Amer.* a sweetshop; **candystripe** a pattern, in alternate stripes of white and colour (esp. pink); **candystriped** *a.* having candystripes; **candystriper** *N. Amer.* a (usu. teenage) volunteer assistant nurse in a hospital (from the striped uniform worn); **candy-sugar** = SUGAR-CANDY.

candy /ˈkandi/ *v.* M16. [f. prec., after Fr. *candir*, f. *candi* taken as pa. pple: see SUGAR-CANDY.] 1 *v.t.* Preserve by coating and impregnating with crystallized sugar; *fig.* sweeten, render more acceptable in form or appearance. M16. 2 *v.t.* Crystallize (sugar) by boiling; *gen.* make into crystals. L16. 3 *v.t.* Cover or coat with a crystalline substance. E17. 4 *v.i.* Crystallize; become encrusted (as) with sugar. M17.

candytuft /ˈkandɪtʌft/ *n.* E17. [f. *Candy* obs. form of *Candia* the island of Crete + TUFT *n.*] Any of various cruciferous plants of the genus *Iberis*, with white, pink, or purple flowers in flat tufts; = IBERIS.

cane /keɪn/ *n.*¹ & *v.* LME. [OFr. *can(n)e* f. L *canna* reed, cane, tube, pipe, f. Gk *kanna, kannē* f. Semitic (cf. Assyr. *qanū*, Heb. *qāneh* reed).] A *n.* 1 The hollow jointed woody stem of certain reeds and grasses, as bamboo and sugar cane; the solid stem of slender palms, as the rattan, Malacca, etc. Also, the stem of the raspberry and its congeners. LME. †2a A pipe, a tube. LME–E18. b A solid stick or rod of various substances, esp. glass. E17. 3 A length of cane used as an instrument of punishment, as a walking-stick, as a support for a plant, etc.; any slender walking-stick. L16. †b A dart or lance made of a cane. L16–L17. 4 Canes collectively, esp. as material for wickerwork. L18.

1 *sugar cane*: see SUGAR *n.* 3 MALACCA *cane.* WHANGEE *cane.*

Comb.: **cane-brake** *N. Amer.* (*a*) a tract of land overgrown with canes; (*b*) a tall woody grass, *Arundinaria gigantea*, forming brakes; **cane chair** a chair with a seat of woven strips of cane; **cane-coloured** *a.* (esp. of pottery) of the colour of cane, buff, yellowish; **cane-grass** (*a*) = *cane-brake* (b) above; (*b*) a tall Australian grass, *Glyceria ramigera*; **cane-juice** the juice of the sugar cane; **cane-rat** an African rodent of the genus *Thryonomys*; **cane sugar** sugar obtained from the sugar cane; sucrose; **cane-syrup** syrup obtained from the sugar cane; **cane toad** a very large brown toad, *Bufo marinus*, which is native to tropical and subtropical America and has been introduced elsewhere for purposes of pest control; also called *giant toad, marine toad*; **cane-trash** bagasse from sugar cane; **cane-work** strips of cane interwoven and used to form the backs and seats of chairs and other articles of furniture; **cane-worker** a person who makes articles of cane.

B *v.t.* 1 Beat with a cane. M17. b Beat (a lesson) *into* a person with a cane. M19. 2 Weave cane into (a chair etc.). L17.

caning *vbl n.* (*a*) the action of the vb; (*b*) a beating with a cane. E18.

†**cane** *n.*² var. of KHAN *n.*²

†**canel** *n.*¹ Also **-nn-**. ME–M18. [OFr. *canele* (mod. *cannelle*) f. Prov. *canela* dim. of *cana* CANE *n.*¹ Cf. med.L CANELLA.] Cinnamon.

†**canel** *n.*² var. of CANNEL *n.*¹

canella /kəˈnɛlə/ *n.* Also **-nn-**. L17. [med.L = CANEL *n.*¹] †1 *gen.* Cinnamon. L17–L19. 2 = *wild cinnamon* s.v. CINNAMON. M18.

canephora /kəˈnɛf(ə)rə, -ˈniː-/ *n.* Pl. **-rae** /-riː/. E17. [L *canephora* fem., f. Gk *kanēphoros* adj., f. *kaneon* basket + *-phoros* carrying.] In ancient Greece, each of the maidens who carried on their heads baskets bearing sacred things used at certain feasts; *Archit.* a caryatid representing or resembling such a maiden.

Canes Venatici /ˌkeɪniːz viːˈnatɪsʌɪ/ *n. phr.* E18. [L *canes venatici*, f. *canis* dog + *venaticus* used for hunting.] (The name of) an inconspicuous constellation of the northern hemisphere near Ursa Major; the Hunting Dogs.

canezou /ˈkɑːnzuː/ *n.* E19. [Fr., of unkn. origin.] *Hist.* A woman's garment like a blouse of muslin or cambric.

Canfield /ˈkanfiːld/ *n.* E20. [R. A. *Canfield* (1855–1914), Amer. gambler.] A card-game of patience for one player, in N. America the same as British demon, in Britain the same as N. American Klondike.

cang *v.* & *n.* var. of CANGUE *v.* & *n.*

cangia /ˈkandʒə/ *n.* E18. [It. f. Turk. *kanca* hook (in *kancabaş* boat with recurved bows) f. Venetian It. *ganzo* f. Sp. *gancho* ult. f. Celt.: cf. Fr. *cange.*] A light boat used on the Nile.

cangue /kaŋ/ *v.t.* & *n.* Also **cang**, (earliest) †**congo**. L17. [Fr. f. Port. *canga* yoke f. Annamese *gong.*] Chiefly *Hist.* (Cause to wear) a heavy wooden board hung round the neck as punishment in China.

can-hooks /ˈkanhʊks/ *n. pl.* L15. [f. obscure 1st elem. + HOOK *n.* + -S¹.] Chiefly *Naut.* (Tackle consisting of) two hooks joined by a short length of chain or rope, used for hoisting casks etc.

canicular /kəˈnɪkjʊlə/ *a.* ME. [Late L *canicularis*, f. *canicula* dog-star, dim. of *canis* dog.] 1 Of or pertaining to the dog-star (Sirius); of or pertaining to the dog-days. ME. 2 Pertaining to a dog. *joc.* L16.

1 E. POUND The dry earth pants against the canicular heat. **canicular days** the dog-days. **canicular year** the ancient Egyptian year computed from one heliacal rising of Sirius to the next.

canicule *n.* (*rare*) [Fr.] the dog-days E18.

canid /ˈkanɪd/ *n.* L19. [mod.L *Canidae* (see below), f. L *canis* dog: see -ID³.] *Zool.* An animal of the family Canidae, which includes dogs, wolves, and foxes.

canine /ˈkeɪnʌɪn, ˈka-/ *n.* & *a.* LME. [Fr. *canin(e* or L *caninus*, *-ina*, f. *canis* dog: see -INE¹.] A *n.* 1 A canine tooth (see below). (*rare* bef. M19.) LME. 2 A dog (chiefly *joc.*); *gen.* any canid. M19.

B *adj.* 1 Of, pertaining to, or characteristic of a dog or dogs; having the nature or qualities of a dog; (of appetite etc.) voracious, bulimic. E17. 2 *canine tooth*, a strong pointed tooth situated between the incisors and premolars (one of four in a complete human dentition). E17.

1 **canine madness** *arch.* rabies. *canine* PARVOVIRUS.

ca'niniform *a.* (of teeth) having a shape like that of a canine tooth L19. **caninity** /kəˈnɪnɪti/ *n.* doglike nature, canine quality L18.

canions /ˈkanɪənz/ *n.pl.* L16. [f. as CANYON. Cf. CANNON *n.* 2c.] *Hist.* Ornamental rolls on the ends of the legs of breeches.

Canis /ˈkeɪnɪs/ *n.* LME. [L *canis* dog, dog-star, Canis Major.] 1 *Canis Major*: (the name of) a constellation of the southern hemisphere on the edge of the Milky Way, near Puppis; the Great Dog; (formerly) Sirius, its brightest star. LME. 2 *Canis Minor*: (the name of) a constellation of the northern hemisphere on the edge of the Milky Way, near Gemini; the Little Dog; (formerly) Procyon, its brightest star. LME.

canister /ˈkanɪstə/ *n.* & *v.* L15. [L *canistrum* f. Gk *kanastron* wicker basket, f. *kanna* reed: see

CANE *n.*[1]] A *n.* 1 A basket (for bread, flowers, etc.). *literary.* L15. 2 A small container, usu. of metal, used for tea, shot, etc. E18. 3 *Hist.* In full *canister-shot.* Small bullets packed in cases that fit the bore of a gun. E19. B *v.t.* 1 Fasten a canister to. Now *rare* or *obs.* E19. 2 Put in a canister. M19.

canities /kə'nɪʃiːz/ *n.* E19. [L, f. *canus* white.] *Med.* Whitening or greying of the hair.

canker /'kaŋkə/ *n.* ME. [ONFr. *cancre* (OFr. CHANCRE) f. L *cancr-*, CANCER *n.*] 1 Orig. = CANCER *n.* 2. Later, a sore, an ulcer, ulcerous disease, (esp. of animals). ME. 2a A caterpillar or grub that destroys buds or leaves. Cf. *canker-worm* below. LME. b Necrotic disease of plants, esp. fruit trees. M16. 3 Rust. *obs.* exc. *dial.* LME. 4 *fig.* A corrupting or corrosive influence. M16. 5 In full *canker-rose.* A dogrose. *dial.* L16.

Comb.: †**canker-bloom** the flower of the dogrose; †**canker-blossom** = sense 2a above; *canker-rose*: see sense 5 above; **canker-worm** = sense 2a above; *spec.* (*N. Amer.*) a geometrid moth larva which destroys the foliage of trees.

cankerous *a.* of the nature of a canker; corroding, infectious: LME. **cankery** *a.* (*a*) cankerous; cankered; (*b*) *Sc.* cantankerous, ill-natured: LME.

canker /'kaŋkə/ *v.* LME. [f. the n.] 1 *v.t.* Consume (as) with canker; infect, corrupt. LME. b Rust, corrode, tarnish. *obs.* exc. *dial.* LME. 2 *v.i.* Become consumed or infected (as) with canker; rot, fester, decay. E16.

cankered *a.* affected with canker; *fig.* corrupt, soured, malignant, crabbed: LME.

†**cann** *v.* var. of CON *v.*[2]

canna /'kanə/ *n.*[1] M18. [mod.L *Canna* (see below) f. L *canna* CANE *n.*[1]] A plant of the genus *Canna*, native to tropical and subtropical America, with bright yellow, red, or orange flowers and ornamental leaves. Also *canna lily.*

canna *n.*[2] var. of CANNACH.

cannabinoid /'kanəbɪnɔɪd/ *n.* M20. [f. as next + -OID.] *Chem.* Any of a group of closely related compounds which includes cannabinol and the active constituents of cannabis.

cannabinol /'kanəbɪnɒl, kə'nab-/ *n.* L19. [f. next + -OL.] *Chem.* A crystalline tricyclic phenol, $C_{21}H_{26}O_2$, derivatives of which (notably a tetrahydro-derivative) are the physiologically active constituents of cannabis.

cannabis /'kanəbɪs/ *n.* E18. [L f. Gk *kannabis.*] 1 = *Indian hemp* (a) s.v. INDIAN *a.* E18. 2 A preparation of any part of this plant used as an intoxicating or hallucinogenic drug, or medicinally. M19.

Comb.: **cannabis resin** a sticky substance containing the active principles of cannabis, prepared esp. from the flowering tops of the female plant.

¶Cf. BHANG, CHARAS, GANJA, HASHISH, MARIJUANA, etc. As an intoxicating or hallucinogenic drug the substance has many slang names as *grass, pot,* etc.

cannach /'kaːnəx/ *n. Sc.* Also **canna** /'kanə/. E19. [Gael., Ir. *canach.*] Cotton-grass.

canned /kand/ *a.* M19. [f. CAN *v.*[2] + -ED[1].] 1 Preserved or contained in a can; tinned. M19. 2 *fig.* Of music etc.: artificially produced; *esp.* recorded, not live. E20. 3 Intoxicated, drunk. *slang.* E20.

†**cannel** *n.*[1] Also **canel**. ME–M18. [ONFr. *canel* = OFr. *chanel*: see CHANNEL *n.*[1] Cf. CANAL *n.*, KENNEL *n.*[2]] A channel, a watercourse; a gutter; a pipe, a tube, a faucet.

Comb.: **cannel-bone** (*a*) the collar-bone; (*b*) the cervical vertebrae.

cannel /'kan(ə)l/ *n.*[2] Orig. *north.* M16. [Origin unkn.] In full *cannel coal.* A bituminous coal which burns with a bright flame.

†**cannel** *n.*[3] var. of CANEL *n.*[1]

cannella *n.* var. of CANELLA.

cannelloni /kanə'ləʊni/ *n.pl.* M20. [It., augm. pl. of *cannello* stalk: see -OON.] Rolls of pasta filled with meat or cheese and seasonings; an Italian dish consisting largely of this and usu. a sauce.

cannelon /'kan(ə)lɒn/ *n.* M19. [Prob. f. as prec.] A roll of pastry with a filling.

cannelure /'kan(ə)ljʊə/ *n.* M18. [Fr., f. *canneler* to groove, flute, f. *canne* reed: see CANE *n.*[1], -URE.] A groove or fluting, esp. around a bullet etc.

canner /'kanə/ *n.* L19. [f. CAN *v.*[2] + -ER[1].] 1 A person who cans food; a machine for canning food. L19. 2 An animal whose flesh is suitable only for canned foods. Also, a fruit or vegetable suitable for canning. Chiefly *N. Amer.* L19.

cannery /'kanəri/ *n.* L19. [f. CAN *v.*[2] + -ERY.] A factory where foodstuffs are canned.

cannibal /'kanɪb(ə)l/ *n.* & *a.* M16. [Sp. *Canibales* (pl.), a form (recorded by Columbus) of the name *Caribes* a people of the W. Indies: see CARIB.] A *n.* 1 A person who eats human flesh; *fig.* a bloodthirsty savage. M16. 2 An animal that eats members of its own species. L18. B *attrib.* or as *adj.* Cannibalistic, bloodthirsty. L16.

canniba'lean *a.* (*rare*) = CANNIBALISTIC E17. **canni'balic** *a.* = CANNIBALISTIC E19. **cannibalism** *n.* the practice of eating (the flesh of) members of one's own species L18. **canniba'listic** *a.* of, pertaining to, or characteristic of cannibals; practising cannibalism: M19. **canniba'listically** *adv.* in the manner of a cannibal M19. **cannibally** *adv.* (*rare*) cannibalistically E17.

cannibalize /'kanɪb(ə)lʌɪz/ *v.t.* Also **-ise**. M17. [f. prec. + -IZE.] †1 In *pass.* Be eaten by cannibals. *rare.* Only in M17. 2 Use (a machine etc.) as a source of spare parts for another, take (a part of a machine etc.) for use in another. M20.

cannibali'zation *n.* M20.

cannikin /'kanɪkɪn/ *n.* Also **cana-** /'kanə-/ L16. [Du. *kanneken*: see CAN *n.*, -KIN.] A small can or drinking-vessel.

cannon /'kanən/ *n.* LME. [(O)Fr. *canon* f. It. *cannone* augm. of *canna* tube f. L: see CANE *n.*[1], -OON. In sense 3 alt. of CAROM.] 1a *Hist.* (Pl. usu. same.) A piece of ordnance; a gun of a size requiring it to be mounted for firing. LME. b An automatic shell-firing gun in an aircraft. E20. †2a A tube; a cylindrical bore. L16–E18. b In full *cannon-bit.* A smooth round bit for a horse. L16. c *Hist.* In *pl.* = CANIONS. L16. d In full *cannon curl.* A cylindrical curl in the hair, worn horizontally. E19. e *Mech.* A hollow cylinder moving independently on a shaft. L19. 3 A stroke in billiards in which the player's cue-ball is made to hit both other balls; *transf.* a rebounding collision. E19. 4 A pickpocket. *US slang.* E20.

3 *nursery cannon*: see NURSERY 6.

Phrases: *loose cannon*: see LOOSE *a.*

Comb.: **cannon-ball** *Hist.* a solid spherical projectile fired by a cannon; *cannon-ball tree* a S. American tree, *Couroupita guianensis*, bearing globular woody fruit; *cannon-bit*: see sense 2b above; **cannon-bone** a tube-shaped bone between a horse's hock and fetlock; **cannon-fodder** [tr. G *Kanonenfutter*] men regarded merely as material to be consumed in war; **cannon-shot** (*a*) the shooting of a cannon; (*b*) ammunition fired from a cannon, cannon-balls; (*c*) the range of a cannon.

cannonry *n.* the use or discharge of cannon; artillery: L16.

cannon /'kanən/ *v.* L16. [f. the n.] 1 *v.t.* & *i.* = CANNONADE *v.* L16. 2 *v.i.* Strike a cannon in billiards. M19. 3a *v.t.* Come into collision with. *rare.* M19. b *v.i.* Come into collision, strike obliquely, *against, into.* L19.

cannonade /kanə'neɪd/ *n.* & *v.* M16. [Fr. f. It. *cannonata*, f. *cannone*: see CANNON *n.*, -ADE.] A *n.* A continued discharge of cannon, continuous gunfire; an attack with cannon. M16. B *v.t.* & *i.* Attack with cannon; discharge cannon (against). M17.

cannoneer /kanə'nɪə/ *n.* M16. [Fr. *canonnier* f. It. *cannoniere*, f. *cannone*: see CANNON *n.*, -EER.] *Hist.* An artilleryman who lays and fires cannon.

cannot *v.* see CAN *v.*[1]

cannula /'kanjʊlə/ *n.* L17. [L, dim. of *canna* CANE *n.*[1]] *Surg.* A small tube which can be inserted into a body cavity or vessel to allow the entry or escape of fluid.

cannulate *v.t.* introduce a cannula into E20. **cannu'lation** *n.* M20.

canny /'kani/ *a.* & *adv.* Orig. *Sc.* L16. [f. CAN *v.*[1] + -Y[1].] A *adj.* 1 Prudent, knowing; worldly-wise, shrewd; wary, circumspect, cautious. L16. 2 Safe to meddle with; lucky, propitious, fortunate. L16. 3 Clever, skilful; cunning, wily; endowed with occult power. Now *arch. rare.* M17. 4 Careful with money, thrifty, frugal. E18. 5 Agreeable, comely, nice, tidy, good. *north.* E18. 6 Careful in action, gentle, quiet; snug, comfortable; (of humour etc.) sly, pawky. M18. B *adv.* Cautiously, warily, quietly. Esp. in *ca' canny*, go or act thus (see also CA'CANNY). *Sc.* E18.

cannily *adv.* L16. **canniness** *n.* M17.

canoe /kə'nuː/ *n.* Also (earlier) †**canow** & other vars. M16. [Sp. *canoa* f. Arawak f. Carib *canaoua*. Present sp. due to Fr. *canoë*.] A narrow keelless boat propelled by paddling; *spec.* (*a*) one simply constructed from a hollowed-out tree-trunk or of a wooden frame covered with skins, bark, etc.; (*b*) a lightweight recreational craft resembling an Eskimo kayak, made from fibreglass or wood etc.

dugout canoe, log canoe, woodskin canoe, etc. *north canoe*: see NORTH *adv., a., n.,* & *v.* **paddle one's own canoe** *fig.* depend on oneself alone.

Comb.: **canoe birch** *N. Amer.* the white or paper birch, *Betula papyrifera*; **canoe wood** *N. Amer.* (the timber of) the tulip tree, *Liriodendron tulipifera*.

canoeist *n.* a person who paddles a canoe M19. **canoe-like** *a.* resembling (that of) a canoe M19.

canoe /kə'nuː/ *v.i.* M18. [f. the n.] Travel by or paddle a canoe.

canola /kə'nəʊlə/ *n.* L20. [f. CAN(ADA + -OLA (w. ref. to L *oleum* oil).] Any of several varieties of oil-seed rape developed in Canada; (more fully *canola oil*) the vegetable oil obtained from these.

canon /'kanən/ *n.*[1] OE [L f. Gk *kanōn* rule: reinforced in ME by AN *canun*, (O)Fr. *canon*.] 1 An ecclesiastical law or decree; *esp.* a rule laid down by an ecclesiastical council; *sing.* & (usu.) in *pl.*, canon law. OE. 2 The part of the Mass containing the words of consecration. ME. 3 A general law, rule, or edict; a fundamental principle. LME. †b *Math.* A general rule, formula, or table. LME–L18. c A standard of judgement; a criterion. E17. 4 (The set of) those biblical books officially accepted by any of the Christian Churches as genuinely inspired; any collection or list of sacred works accepted as genuine. LME. b A list or catalogue of recognized saints. E18. c (A list of) the recognized genuine works of a particular author, composer, etc. L19. 5 *Mus.* (The style of) a composition in which different parts take up the same subject successively in strict imitation. L16. 6 *Law.* A customary payment made to the Church; a quit-rent. Now *rare* or *obs.* M17. 7 A former size of type equal to four-line pica. L17. 8 [Prob. a different wd: cf. CANNON *n.* 2.] A metal loop at the top of a bell, by which it is hung. Usu. in *pl.*, of crossed loops. L17. 9 (A period or era serving as) a basis for chronology. M19.

1 SHAKES. *All's Well* Self-love . . the most inhibited sin in the canon. 3 D. CARNEGIE I violated all the canons of courtesy, ignored everyone else. J. K. GALBRAITH The balanced budget, so long a canon of the conventional wisdom. c G. MURRAY We are establishing a new conventional canon of what is poetical and what not. 4c D. LODGE A series of commentaries on Jane Austen which would work through the whole canon, one novel at a time.

Phrases: MURATORIAN *canon.*

Comb.: **canon law** ecclesiastical law, esp. as laid down by papal and council pronouncements.

canon /'kanən/ *n.*[2] ME. [OFr. *canonie* f. eccl.L *canonicus* use as n. of adj. (see CANONIC), assim. to prec.] *Eccl.* 1 A member of an order of clergy living near or within the precincts of a cathedral etc. in accordance with the canons of the church. ME. 2 Each of the resident ecclesiastics responsible, under the dean, for a cathedral. M16.

1 **canon regular**, **regular canon** a canon living according to a rule and so renouncing private property. **secular canon** a canon not living according to a rule. 2 **honorary canon** a titular non-residential non-stipendiary member of a cathedral chapter. **minor canon**, †**petty canon** a member of the clergy who assists in the daily service of a cathedral but is not a member of the chapter.

canoness *n.* (*a*) a member of a community of women living according to an ecclesiastical rule as opp. to having taken perpetual vows; (*b*) a woman holding a prebend or canonry: L17. **canonship** *n.* = CANONRY I M16.

cañon *n.* & *v.* var. of CANYON.

canonic /kəˈnɒnɪk/ *n.* & *a.* OE. [(O)Fr. *canonique* or L *canonicus* f. Gk *kanonikos*, f. as CANON *n.*[1]: see -IC.] **A** *n.* **1** = CANON *n.*[2] *rare.* OE. **2** A system of logical rules or dialectic. M17. **B** *adj.* = CANONICAL *a.* L15.

canonical /kəˈnɒnɪk(ə)l/ *a.* & *n.* LME. [med.L *canonicalis* f. L *canonicus*: see prec., -AL[1].] **A** *adj.* **1** Prescribed by, in conformity with, or relating to canon law. LME. **2** Of the nature of a canon or rule; authoritative; standard; accepted. M16. **b** *Math.* Of the nature of a general rule or standard formula; relating to or according to such an expression. M18. **3** Included in the scriptural canon; relating to any (sets of) sacred books regarded as authentic. M16. **4** Of or belonging to (any member of) an ecclesiastical chapter. L16. **5** *Mus.* According to the rules of canon; in canon form. *rare.* E17.

1 canonical hour *Eccl.* (usu. in *pl.*) (*a*) each of the times of daily prayer appointed in the breviary; each of seven offices (matins with lauds, prime, terce, sext, nones, vespers, and compline) appointed for these times; (*b*) in the Church of England, the time (now usu. between 8 a.m. and 6 p.m.) during which a marriage may lawfully be celebrated. **canonical obedience**: owed by a member of the clergy to a bishop or other clerical superior according to canon law. **2 canonical epistles** (*rare*) = *Catholic Epistles* s.v. CATHOLIC *a.*

B *n.* **1** A canonical epistle. *rare.* M16. **2** In *pl.* The prescribed canonical dress of the clergy. M18.

canonically *adv.* E16. **canonicalness** *n.* M17.

canonicate /kəˈnɒnɪkət/ *n.* M17. [Fr. *canonicat* or med.L *canonicatus*, f. L *canonicus*: see CANONIC, -ATE[1].] The office or dignity of a canon; a canonry.

canonicity /kanəˈnɪsɪti/ *n.* L18. [f. CANONIC + -ITY.] Canonical status; *esp.* inclusion within the scriptural canon.

canonisation *n.*, **-ise** *v.* vars. of CANONIZATION, -IZE.

canonist /ˈkanənɪst/ *n.* M16. [(O)Fr. *canoniste* or med.L *canonista*, f. as CANON *n.*[1]: see -IST.] An expert in canon law.

cano'nistic *a.* pertaining to a canonist; relating to the exposition of canon law: M17.

canonization /ˌkanənʌɪˈzeɪʃ(ə)n/ *n.* Also **-isa-**. LME. [med.L *canonizatio(n-)*, f. *canonizat-* pa. ppl stem of *canonizare*: see next, -ATION. Cf. (O)Fr. *canonisation*.] The action of canonizing; *esp.* formal admission to the canon of saints.

canonize /ˈkanənʌɪz/ *v.t.* Also **-ise**. LME. [Late L *canonizare* admit as authoritative, (in med.L) admit to the canon of saints, f. as CANON *n.*[1] + -IZE.] **1** Admit formally to the canon of saints; regard as a saint; *fig.* idolize, glorify. LME. **†b** Deify; apotheosize. M16–L18. **2** Admit to a canon of sacred writings, esp. that of any of the Christian Churches. LME. **3** Sanction by church authority. LME.

canonizer *n.* L16.

canonry /ˈkanənri/ *n.* LME. [f. CANON *n.*[2] + -RY.] **1** The benefice, office, or status of a canon. LME. **2** An establishment of canons or canonesses. L19.

canoodle /kəˈnuːd(ə)l/ *v.i.* & *t.* *slang* (orig. *US*). M19. [Origin unkn.] Cuddle amorously; fondle, pet.

canophilist /kəˈnɒfɪlɪst/ *n.* Chiefly *joc.* L19. [Irreg. f. L *canis* dog + -PHIL + -IST.] A lover of dogs.

cano'philia *n.* affection for dogs M20.

Canopic /kəˈnəʊpɪk/ *a.* Also **c-**. L19. [L *Canopicus*, f. *Canopus* a town in ancient Egypt: see next, -IC.] Designating (in *Canopic vase, jar*) a covered urn used in ancient Egyptian burials to hold the entrails and other visceral organs from an embalmed body.

Canopus /kəˈnəʊpəs/ *n.* Sense 2 usu. **c-**. M16. [L *Canopus* f. Gk *Kanōpos*, (i) a star (see below), (ii) a town in ancient Egypt.] **1** The brightest star in the constellation Carina. M16. **2** A Canopic vase. E18.

canopy /ˈkanəpi/ *n.* & *v.* LME. [med.L *canopeum* baldachin, alt. of L *conopeum*, *-ium* net over a bed, pavilion f. Gk *kōnōpeion* Egyptian bed with mosquito curtains, f. *kōnōps* mosquito.] **A** *n.* **1** A covering suspended or held over a throne, bed, person, etc.; an awning. LME. **2** *gen.* A covering, an overhanging shade or shelter, (often applied *fig.* to the sky). E17. **b** The upper branches of the trees in a forest, as forming a more or less continuous layer. E20. **3** *Archit.* A rooflike ornamental projection over a niche, door, tomb, etc. L17. **4** An overhead covering forming part of the upper structure of a vehicle etc.; *esp.* the cover of the cockpit of an aircraft. L19. **5** The expanding part of a parachute. M20.

1 HOBBES The Popes are carried by Switzers under a Canopie. 2 M. F. MAURY A canopy of perpetual clouds. J. MASTERS The part of the platform sheltered by the canopy was crowded with would-be passengers. C. SAGAN Thousands of stars . . peppered across the canopy of night.

B *v.t.* Cover (as) with a canopy. Freq. as *canopied* ppl a. L16.

canorous /kəˈnɔːrəs/ *a.* M17. [f. L *canorus*, f. *canere* sing: see -OUS.] Melodious, resonant.

canst *v.* see CAN *v.*[1]

canstick /ˈkanstɪk/ *n.* Long *obs.* exc. *dial.* LME. [Contr.] A candlestick.

cant /kant/ *n.*[1] ME. [In branch I f. MLG *kant* point, creek, border, *kante* side, edge, (M)Du. *cant* border, side, corner, f. Proto-Romance var. (repr. by OFr. *cant*, Fr. *chant*, *champ*, Sp., It. *canto* edge, corner, side) of L *cant(h)us* iron tyre. In branch II f. CANT *v.*[2]] **I** **†1** An edge, brink, side. Only in ME. **2** A corner, an angle; a corner piece; a triangular piece. *obs.* exc. *dial.* E17. **3** Each of the side-pieces in the head of a cask. E17. **4** *Naut.* Each of the timbers of a ship etc. towards the bow and the stern which are sharply angled from the keel. Also, a supporting timber. L18. **5** The oblique line or surface which cuts off the corner of a square, cube, etc.; an oblique, inclined, or slanting face. M19. **II** **6** A sudden movement, esp. a toss, pitch, etc., which overturns. E18. **7** A slope, a tilt; a deflection from the perpendicular or horizontal. M19.

Comb.: **cant-line** the space between two strands on the outside of a rope, or between the bilges of two barrels side by side; **cantrail** a timber or stay supporting the roof of a railway wagon etc.

cant /kant/ *n.*[2] Long *obs.* exc. *dial.* LME. [Origin uncertain: perh. rel. to CANT *v.*[1], CANTLE.] A portion, a share, a division.

cant /kant/ *n.*[3] E16. [In branch I sporadic uses f. L CANTUS. In branch II f. CANT *v.*[3]] **†I** **1** Singing: musical sound. E16–E18. **2** Accent; intonation. M17–M18.

II **3** A whining manner of speaking; a whine. Now *rare* or *obs.* M17. **4** The special phraseology of a class, sect, profession, etc.; jargon, slang. Usu. *derog.* L17. **5** A set form of words repeated mechanically; *esp.* a stock phrase or word temporarily in fashion. *arch.* L17. **6** Ephemeral catchwords; affected or insincere phraseology; *esp.* language (or occas. action) implying piety which does not exist; hypocrisy. E18. **†7** A person who uses such language. E18–L19.

6 G. SANTAYANA The talk about a nasty world and living pure in a nunnery was just the cant of those days. A. S. NEILL To condemn an interest in sex is sheer hypocrisy and cant.

cant /kant/ *n.*[4] Chiefly *Anglo-Ir.* Now *rare* or *obs.* L16. [f. CANT *v.*[4] or aphet. f. Fr. *encant* (mod. *encan*). Cf. Ir. *ceant*.] Sale by auction.

cant /kant/ *a.*[1] *Sc.* (formerly) & *north.* ME. [App. same wd as mod.Du. *kant* neat, clever, perh. f. *kant* CANT *n.*[1] Cf. CANTY.] Bold, brisk, lively, hearty.

cant /kant/ *a.*[2] Usu. *derog.* E18. [f. CANT *n.*[3]] Of words, phrases, speech, etc.: of the nature of cant; jargonistic; ephemerally fashionable; uttered mechanically.

cantly *adv.* in canting phraseology; in slang: E19.

†cant *v.*[1]*t.* LME–M16. [Origin uncertain: perh. rel. to CANTLE.] Divide, apportion, share out.

cant /kant/ *v.*[2] M16. [f. CANT *n.*[1]] **1** *v.t.* Give an oblique or slanting edge to; bevel (*off*). M16. **2** *v.t.* Throw off or empty out by tilting. M17. **3** *v.t.* Pitch as by the sudden lurching of a ship; toss; push or pitch sideways. L17. **4** *v.i.* & *t.* Slope, slant, tilt; turn upside down or *over.* E18. **5** *v.i.* *Naut.* Of a ship etc.: change course, swing round. L18.

2 **cant off** decant. 3 J. SMEATON The boat took a sudden yaw . . which canted me overboard. 4 S. SMILES A loose plank, which canted over. T. COLLINS The black collie was sitting . . with his head slightly canted to one side. L. DURRELL The telescope barrel had been canted downwards so that it no longer pointed at the sky. 5 R. D. BLACKMORE The boat canted round towards the entrance of the creek.

Comb.: **cant-dog** (*a*) a handspike with a hook; (*b*) = *cant-hook* below; **cant-hook** (an implement consisting of) an iron hook at the end of a long handle, used for rolling logs.

cant /kant/ *v.*[3] M16. [Prob. f. L *cantare*: see CHANT *v.*] **†1** *v.i.* Whine; beg. M16–M19. **†2** *v.i.* & *t.* Speak; talk; say. *slang* & *dial.* M16–L18. **3** *v.i.* Use cant or jargon; affect fashionable or pietistic phraseology. M16. **4** *v.t.* Utter with cant phraseology. Now *rare.* M17. **†5** *v.t.* & *i.* Chant; sing. M17–E19.

canting *a.* (*a*) that cants, using cant; (*b*) *arch.* of the nature of cant; (*c*) *Her.* containing an allusion to the name of the bearer: L16. **cantingly** *adv.* L17.

cant /kant/ *v.*[4]*t.* Chiefly *north.* & *Anglo-Ir.* Now *rare* or *obs.* L16. [Origin uncertain: cf. CANT *n.*[4], L *incantare*, *accantare* proclaim, put up to auction.] Dispose of by auction.

can't *v.* see CAN *v.*[1]

Cantab /ˈkantab/ *n.* & *a.* M18. [Abbrev. of CANTABRIGIAN or (adj.) mod.L *Cantabrigiensis.*] **A** *n.* A Cantabrigian. *colloq.* M18. **B** *adj.* (Also **Cantab.** (point).) Of Cambridge University. L19.

cantabile /kanˈtɑːbɪli/ *adv.*, *a.*, & *n.* E18. [It. = that can be sung.] *Mus.* **A** *adv.* & *adj.* In a smooth flowing style, as if singing. E18. **B** *n.* Cantabile style; a piece or movement in this style. M18.

Cantabrian /kanˈteɪbrɪən/ *n.* & *a.* M16. [f. L *Cantabri* pl. (the people) or *Cantabria* (see below) + -AN.] **A** *n.* *Hist.* A member of an ancient warlike people inhabiting Cantabria, a region of northern Spain. M16. **B** *adj.* **1** *Hist.* Of or pertaining to the Cantabrians. M17. **2** Of or pertaining to Cantabria. M18.

Cantabrigian /kantəˈbrɪdʒɪən/ *a.* & *n.* M16. [f. L *Cantabrigia* Cambridge (England) + -AN.] **1** (A native or inhabitant) of Cambridge, England; (a member) of Cambridge University. M16. **2** (A native or inhabitant) of Cambridge, Massachusetts; (a member) of Harvard University in Cambridge, Massachusetts. L19.

Cantal /ˈkantɑːl/ *n.* L19. [A department of the Auvergne, France.] In full *Cantal cheese.* A hard strong cheese made chiefly in the Auvergne.

cantaloup /ˈkantəluːp/ *n.* Also **-loupe**. L18. [Fr. f. It. *Cantaluppi*, near Rome, where, on its introduction from Armenia, it was first grown.] A small round ribbed variety of melon, with orange flesh. Also called *rock melon.*

cantankerous /kanˈtaŋk(ə)rəs/ *a.* M18. [Prob. blend of RANCOROUS and uncertain elem.] Quarrelsome; perverse; bad-tempered.

cantankerously *adv.* M19. **cantankerousness** *n.* L19.

cantar *n.* var. of KANTAR.

cantarist /ˈkantərɪst/ *n.* E19. [med.L *cantarista*, f. *cantaria* CHANTRY: see -IST.] *Hist.* A chantry priest.

cantata /kanˈtɑːtə/ *n.* E18. [It. (sc. *aria* air), fem. pa. pple of *cantare* sing.] *Mus.* An extended composition for one or more voices with instrumental accompaniment; orig., a narrative recitative or sequence of recitatives and ariettas, for solo voice; later, a choral work resembling a short oratorio.

Cantate /kanˈtɑːteɪ, -ti/ *n.* M16. [L = sing ye, the first wd of the psalm (see below).] Psalm 98 (97 in the Vulgate) used as a canticle.

cantation /kan'teɪʃ(ə)n/ *n. rare.* E17. [L *cantatio(n-)* song, (in late L) spell, incantation, f. *cantat-* pa. ppl stem of *cantare*: see CHANT *v.*, -ION.] †1 Singing. E–M17. 2 Incantation. M19.

cantator /kan'teɪtə, -'tɑːtə/ *n. rare.* M19. [L *cantator*, f. *cantat-*: see prec., -OR.] A (male) singer.

cantatrice /'kantətriːs/ *n.* E19. [Fr. & It., f. L *cantatrix*: see -TRICE and cf. prec.] A female professional singer.

canteen /kan'tiːn/ *n.* M18. [Fr. *cantine* f. It. *cantina* cellar, perh. f. *canto*: see CANT *n.*[1]] 1 A provision or liquor shop in a military camp or barracks; a bar, refreshment-counter, etc., at a place of public resort or at a (large) factory, school, or other institution. M18. 2 A set of cooking, eating, or drinking utensils, or a water-flask, for soldiers, travellers, etc. M18. b A case or chest of plate or cutlery for domestic use. L19.

1 **dry canteen**: without liquor. **wet canteen**: chiefly for liquor. 2b Esp. in *canteen of cutlery*.

cante hondo /'kante 'xondo, ˌkɑːnteɪ 'hɒndəʊ/ *n. phr.* Also ***cante jondo***. M20. [Sp. = deep song.] Flamenco singing, songs, of a predominantly mournful or tragic character.

canter /'kantə/ *n.*[1] E17. [f. CANT *v.*[2] + -ER[1].] 1 A person who uses the cant of thieves; a rogue. Now *rare* or *obs.* E17. 2 A person who uses professional or religious cant. M17.

canter /'kantə/ *n.*[2] M18. [Short for *Canterbury gallop* s.v. CANTERBURY *n.*[1] I.] A gait between trot and gallop; an easy gallop.

win in a canter: easily.

canter /'kantə/ *v.* E18. [f. as prec.] 1 *v.i.* Of a horse etc. or rider: move at a canter. Also *transf.*, move briskly or easily. E18. 2 *v.t.* Make (a horse etc.) go at a canter. M19.

Canterbury /'kantəb(ə)ri/ *n.*[1] M16. [A city in Kent, famous as the seat of the Primate of all England, and the site of the shrine of Thomas à Becket (St Thomas of Canterbury).] I 1 Used *attrib.* to designate things associated with Canterbury, Kent, esp. as a former object of pilgrimage. M16.

1 **Canterbury bell(s)** [with ref. to the bells on pilgrims' horses], a southern European bellflower, *Campanula medium*, grown for ornament; any of several native British bellflowers. **Canterbury gallop, pace, trot**, etc., the pace of mounted pilgrims; a slow easy gallop (cf. CANTER *n.*[2]), trot. **Canterbury hoe**: with three prongs attached to the handle at right angles. **Canterbury tale** a story told on pilgrimage (orig. one of those in Chaucer's *Canterbury Tales*); a long tedious story.

†II 2 An easy gallop; a canter. M17–E18. 3 A stand with partitions to hold music etc. E19.

Canterbury /'kantəb(ə)ri/ *n.*[2] Now *rare.* L19. [A province in South Island, NZ.] In full *Canterbury lamb*. In Great Britain, formerly: lamb or mutton imported from New Zealand. In New Zealand: certain grades of lamb or mutton.

cantharides *n.pl.* see next.

cantharis /kan'θarɪs/ *n.* Pl. **-rides** /-rɪdiːz/. LME. [L f. Gk *kantharis*.] 1 The Spanish fly, *Lytta vesicatoria*. Now *rare* or *obs.* LME. 2 In *pl.* A preparation of the dried beetles, having toxic and vesicant properties, and sometimes taken as an aphrodisiac. LME.

cantha'ridean *a.* of the nature of or containing cantharides L18. **cantharidin** *n.* a lactone, $C_{10}H_{12}O_4$, obtained from the elytra of the insect, which is the active principle of cantharides: E19. **cantharidize** *v.t.* (now *rare*) affect or treat with cantharides L18.

cantharus /'kanθ(ə)rəs/ *n.* Pl. **-ri** /-rʌɪ/. Also **kantharos, c-**, pl. **-roi** /-rɔɪ/. M19. [L f. Gk *kantharos*.] 1 *Class. Antiq.* A large two-handled drinking-cup. M19. 2 A fountain or laver placed in the courtyard of an ancient church for the use of worshippers. M19.

canthus /kanθəs/ *n.* Pl. **-thi** /-θʌɪ/. M17. [L f. Gk *kanthos*.] *Anat.* The outer or inner corner of the eye, where the lids meet.

canticle /'kantɪk(ə)l/ *n.* ME. [L *canticulum* dim. of *canticum* song.] 1 A (little) song; a hymn, *spec.* one of those used in the liturgy of the Christian Church. ME. 2 *the Canticles*, the Song of Solomon. LME. †3 A canto of a poem. L16–M17.

canti fermi *n. phr.* pl. of CANTO FERMO.

cantikoy *n.* var. of KANTIKOY.

cantilena /kantɪ'leɪnə, -'liːnə/ *n.* M18. [It., or L *cantilena*.] *Mus.* A simple or sustained vocal melody, or an instrumental passage performed in a smooth lyrical style. Also, the (highest) melodic part in a composition.

cantilever /'kantɪliːvə/ *n.* M17. [Origin unkn.] 1 A long projecting bracket supporting a balcony, cornice, etc. M17. 2 A long projecting beam or girder fixed at only one end, esp. in bridge-construction. M19.

Comb.: **cantilever bridge**: with piers each of which has two cantilevers, and long girders connecting the cantilevers of adjacent piers.

cantilevered *a.* projecting like or supported by a cantilever E20.

cantillate /'kantɪleɪt/ *v.t.* & *i.* M19. [L *cantillat-* pa. ppl stem of *cantillare* sing low, hum, f. *cantare*: see CHANT *v.*, -ATE[3].] Chant, recite musically; *spec.* intone as in a Jewish synagogue.

canti'llation *n.* E19.

cantina /kan'tiːnə/ *n.* L19. [Sp. & It.] (In Spain, Spanish-speaking countries, and the south-western US) a bar-room, a saloon; (in Italy) a wine-shop.

cantle /'kant(ə)l/ *n.* & *v.* ME. [AN *cantel* = OFr. *chantel* (mod. *chanteau*) f. med.L *cantellus* dim. of L *cant(h)us*: see CANT *n.*[1], -EL[2].] A *n.* 1 A nook, a corner; a projecting corner or angle of land. Long *rare.* ME. †b A corner or other portion that has been cut off; a sliver. LME–E17. 2 A section or segment cut out of anything; a thick slice or cut of bread, cheese, etc. *arch.* ME. b A segment of a circle or sphere. M16. 3 A (separate or distinct) part or portion. *arch.* ME. 4 The protuberant part at the back of a saddle. L16. 5 The crown of the head. *Sc.* E19. †B *v.t.* 1 Piece together (cloth). Only in M16. 2 Cut into segments, divide; portion *out.* L16–L17.

cantlet *n.* (*arch.*) a small part or portion L17. †**cantling** *n.* = CANTLET L17–E19.

canto /'kantəʊ/ *n.* Pl. **-os.** L16. [It., lit. 'song', f. L CANTUS.] 1 Each of the divisions of a long poem. L16. †2 A song, a ballad. E17–E18. 3 *Mus.* The upper part or melody in a composition. E18.

canto fermo /kantəʊ 'fəːməʊ/ *n. phr.* Pl. **canti fermi** /-ti -mi/. L16. [It., tr. med.L CANTUS FIRMUS.] *Mus.* Orig., an unadorned melody, plainsong; later *spec.* a melody used as a basis for counterpoint. Now also, an existing melody taken as a basis for a new polyphonic composition.

canton /'kantən; *in sense 1 also* kan'tɒn/ *n.*[1] E16. [(O)Fr. f. Prov. f. obl. case of Proto-Romance var. of L *cant(h)us*: see CANT *n.*[1]] 1 A subdivision of a country; a small district; *spec.* one of the several States which form the Swiss confederation. E16. b A division of a French *arrondissement*, containing several communes. E17. 2 A corner, an angle; a nook. Now *rare* or *obs.* M16. 3 *Her.* A square division, less than a quarter, orig. occupying one-ninth part and the upper (usu. dexter) corner of a shield. L16. †4 A quarter; a division of anything, a part. Only in 17.

cantonal *a.* of, pertaining to, or of the nature of a canton M19. **cantoni'zation** *n.* division into cantons; making cantonal: M20. **cantonize** *v.t.* & *i.* (now *rare*) divide into parts; form (into) cantons; separate: E17.

†**canton** *n.*[2] L16–E17. [Alt. of CANTO, perh. by assoc. w. CANZON, CANZONE.] = CANTO 1, 2.

canton /'kantən *in sense 5 also* kan'tuːn/ *v.* L16. [Partly f. CANTON *n.*[1], partly f. Fr. *cantonner* to quarter, It. *cantonnare* to canton, quarter.] 1 *v.t.* Quarter, divide; share *out*; subdivide (into cantons). L16. 2 *v.t.* Divide *from* or cut *out* of a whole. Now *rare* or *obs.* M17. 3 *v.t. Her.* Provide with a canton or cantons; place in a canton. L17. 4 *v.i.* Take up quarters. L17. 5 *v.t.* Quarter (soldiers); provide with quarters. E18.

1 DEFOE He Canton'd out the Country to his Men. C. THIRLWALL They cantoned their great dioceses into Archdeaconries. 2 J. LOCKE They canton out to themselves a little Goshen in the intellectual world.

cantoned *ppl a.* (*a*) formed or divided into cantons; (*b*) quartered in cantonments; (*c*) *Archit.* having decorated angles: E17.

Cantonese /kantə'niːz/ *a.* & *n.* L18. [f. *Canton* Eng. name of the city Guangzhou + -ESE.] A *n.* Pl. same. A native or inhabitant of Canton in SE China; the dialect of Chinese commonly used in Canton. L18. B *adj.* Of or pertaining to Canton, its inhabitants, their dialect, cuisine, etc. M19.

cantonment /kan'tɒnm(ə)nt, -'tuːn-/ *n.* M18. [Fr. *cantonnement*, f. *cantonner*: see CANTON *v.*, -MENT.] 1 The quartering of troops. M18. 2 A military encampment; quarters. In India, (the former site of) a permanent military station. M18.

cantor /'kantɔː, -ə/ *n.* M16. [L = singer, f. *canere*: see CHANT *v.*, -OR.] 1 a A precentor in a church. M16. b An official who sings liturgical music and leads prayer in a synagogue, = HAZZAN. L19. †2 *gen.* A singer. E–M17.

cantorial /kan'tɔːrɪəl/ *a.* L18. [f. prec. + -IAL.] Of the precentor; *spec.* designating or pertaining to the north side of the choir of a church, on which the precentor usually sits (cf. DECANAL 2).

cantoris /kan'tɔːrɪs/ *a.* M17. [L, genit. of CANTOR.] Of or belonging to the cantor or precentor; cantorial; to be sung by the cantorial side in antiphonal singing (cf. DECANI).

cantred /'kantrəd/ *n.* Also in Welsh form **-ef** /-əv/. ME. [App. f. Welsh *cantref*, (f. *cant* hundred + *tref* town, settlement, farmstead) w. assim. to HUNDRED.] *Hist.* A district of (approximately) one hundred townships, a hundred; an area consisting of two or more commots.

cantrip /'kantrɪp/ *n. Sc.* L16. [Origin unkn.] A spell, a charm; a witch's trick; a playful or extravagant act.

cantus /'kantəs/ *n.* Pl. ***cantus*** /'kantuːs, -təs/. L16. [L = song. Cf. CANT *n.*[3], CANTO, CHANT *n.*] *Early Mus.* A song, a melody, esp. in church music. Also, the highest voice in a polyphonic song.

cantus firmus /ˌkantəs 'fəːməs/ *n. phr.* Pl. **cantus firmi** /'fəːmʌɪ/. M19. [med.L = firm song.] *Mus.* = CANTO FERMO.

canty /'kanti/ *a. Sc.* & *north.* E18. [f. CANT *a.*[1] + -Y[1].] Cheerful, lively, brisk.

Canuck /kə'nʌk/ *n.* & *a. N. Amer. colloq.* M19. [App. f. CANADA.] A *n.* 1 A Canadian, orig. *esp.* a French Canadian; a Canadian horse or pony. M19. 2 Canadian French. E20. B *adj.* Canadian, orig. *esp.* French Canadian. M19.

canvas /'kanvəs/ *n.*[1] & *a.* Also **canvass**. LME. [ONFr. *canevas* var. of OFr. *chanevaz* f. Proto-Romance, ult. f. L CANNABIS.] A *n.* I As a non-count n. 1 A strong unbleached cloth of hemp, flax, or other coarse yarn, used for sails, tents, painting on, etc.; hence, sails collectively. LME. 2 A type of this cloth woven in regular meshes and used as a basis for tapestry and embroidery. E17.

1 **under canvas** (*a*) in a tent or tents; (*b*) with sails spread. VITRY *canvas*. 2 JAVA *canvas*. *Penelope canvas*: see PENELOPE 3.

II As a count n. 3 A piece of canvas. *obs.* exc. as below. LME. 4 A piece of canvas primed for painting; a painting, esp. in oils. E18. 5 A covering over the ends of a racing-boat (orig. made of canvas); *transf.* the length between the bow and the first oarsman. L19. 6 *The* floor of a boxing, wrestling, etc., ring, with a canvas covering. E20.

5 **win, lose**, etc., **by a canvas** (in boat-racing): by a narrow margin.

B *attrib.* or as *adj.* Made of canvas. LME.

Comb.: **canvas-back** (*a*) a back of a garment made of canvas; (*b*) a N. American diving duck, *Aythya valisineria*, so called from the white back of the male.

canvas *n.*[2] var. of CANVASS *n.*[1]

canvas /'kanvəs/ *v.t.* Infl. **-s-**, **-ss-**. Also **canvass.** M16. [f. CANVAS *n.*[1]] I †1 *Falconry.* Entangle or catch in a net. M16–M17. 2 Cover, line, or provide with canvas. M16.

2 *sand and canvas*: see SAND *v.*

II See CANVASS *v.*

canvass /ˈkanvəs/ *n.*[1] Also **canvas.** E17. [f. CANVASS *v.*] †1 A shaking up; a shock, an attack; a repulse. E–M17. †2 An examination of pros and cons. Only in 17. 3 The action or process of personally soliciting votes before an election, or of ascertaining the amount of support a candidate may count on. L17. b A scrutiny of votes in an election. *US.* L18. 4 A solicitation of support, custom, etc. L18.

canvass *n.*[2] & *a.* var. of CANVAS *n.*[1] & *a.*

canvass /ˈkanvəs/ *v.* Also **canvas.** E16. [f. CANVAS *n.*[1]: the sense-development is unexpl.] I†1 *v.t.* Toss in a canvas sheet as a sport or punishment; knock about, batter. E16–M17. 2 *v.t.* Discuss, criticize, examine fully; seek to ascertain; discuss with a view to adoption, propose (a plan etc.). M16. b *v.i.* Engage in debate or discussion. M17. c *v.t.* Scrutinize (votes). *obs.* exc. *US.* E18. 3 *v.i.* Solicit votes, support, goods, etc. M16. 4 *v.t.* Solicit votes, support, custom, etc., from; seek to ascertain the sentiments or intentions of. L17.

2 DISRAELI It was canvassed and criticised sentence by sentence. J. K. GALBRAITH We canvass our public wants to see where happiness can be improved. P. G. WODEHOUSE His first act . . had been to canvass Ed. Robinson's views. b F. MARRYAT We sat there canvassing over the affair. 3 T. DREISER His father canvassed for a washing machine and wringer company. 4 J. L. MOTLEY His most trustworthy agent . . was now actively canvassing the governments and peoples of Germany. JOYCE Mr O'Connor had been engaged by Tierney's agents to canvass one part of the ward.

II See CANVAS *v.*

canvasser *n.* L16.

cany /ˈkeɪni/ *a.* M17. [f. CANE *n.*[1] + -Y[1].] Of cane; like cane.

canyon /ˈkanjən/ *n.* & *v.* Also **cañon.** M19. [Sp. *cañón* tube, pipe, gun barrel, etc., augm. of *caña* f. L *canna*: see CANE *n.*[1], -OON.] A *n.* A deep gorge (esp. in the US or Mexico), frequently with a stream at its bottom. M19. B *v.* 1 *v.i.* Flow in or into a canyon. M19. 2 *v.t.* Cut into canyons. L19.

canzona /kanˈtsəʊnə, -z-/ *n.* L19. [It. f. next.] (A musical setting of the words of) a canzone; an instrumental piece resembling a madrigal in character.

canzone /kanˈtsəʊni, -z-/ *n.* Pl. **-ni** /-ni/. L16. [It. = song (corresp. to (O)Fr. *chanson*) f. L *cantio(n-)* singing, f. *cant-* pa. pple of *canere* sing.] An Italian or Provençal song or ballad; a style of lyric resembling a madrigal.

Also **canzon** /ˈkants(ə)n, -z-/ *n.* (long *arch. rare*) L16.

canzonet /kantsəˈnɛt, -z-/ *n.* L16. [It. *canzonetta*, dim. of prec.] A short light song; a short canzone.

Also **canzonetta** *n.* E18.

Caodaism /kaʊˈdʌɪɪz(ə)m/ *n.* M20. [f. Vietnamese *Cao Dai*, name of the sect, lit. 'great palace' + -ISM.] A syncretistic religion of SE Asia.

Caodaist *n.* an adherent of Caodaism M20.

caoine /ˈkiːnə/ *n.* E18. [Ir., f. as KEEN *v.*[2]] = KEEN *n.*

caoutchouc /ˈkaʊtʃʊk/ *n.* & *a.* L18. [Fr. f. obs. Sp. *cauchuc* f. Quechua *kauchuk.*] (Of) unvulcanized natural rubber.

cap /kap/ *n.*[1] OE. [Late L *cappa*, perh. f *caput* head.] I A covering for the head. †1 A hood. Only in OE. 2 A head-dress for women; latterly usu. a light one of muslin etc. for indoor use, worn by a nurse, woman servant, etc. ME. 3 Any of various kinds of brimless head-dress, usu. soft and often with a peak, to be worn outdoors or for a special purpose (e.g. as part of academic or Highland dress), orig. only by men or boys. LME. b *spec.* A helmet, a headpiece of mail. LME. c A cardinal's biretta. L16. d A special cap awarded as a sign of membership of a sporting team, esp. a national team in international competition; *transf.* a person awarded such a cap. L19. 4 In full *cap-paper*: a A kind of wrapping paper. L16. b A size or kind of writing-paper. Cf. FOOLSCAP. M19. 5 A sum of money collected in a cap, esp. at a fox-hunt etc. from those who are not subscribing members. M19.

2 *mob-cap*: see MOB *n.*[2] 3. 3 *Basque cap, cloth-cap, dunce's cap, jockey cap, nightcap, skullcap, swimming cap, trencher cap*, etc.

II Something resembling this in shape, position, or use. 6 A caplike natural covering or topmost part. LME. b *spec.* The top of a bird's head, when distinctively coloured. Also in names, as *blackcap.* L17. c The pileus of a mushroom or toadstool. Also in names, as *death cap.* M18. 7 A caplike part fitting over or forming the top or end of an object; a caplike cover or case; a device sealing the opening of a bottle etc., or protecting the lens of a camera etc. or the nib of a fountain pen. LME. 8 *Naut.* A wooden collar used to hold two masts together. E17. 9 A part laid horizontally along the top of various structures. L17. 10 In full *percussion cap.* A metal or paper device (orig. cap-shaped) used with (real or toy) firearms and containing explosive powder which is exploded by the fall of a hammer. E19. 11 A contraceptive diaphragm. Cf. *Dutch cap* s.v. DUTCH *a.* E20.

6 W. WHITMAN The tossing waves, . . the snowy, curling caps. F. O'CONNOR Her face, reddish under a cap of fox-colored hair. *ice-cap, kneecap, snowcap*, etc. WHITECAP. 7 J. RAY The refining Furnace is covered with a thick cap of stone. J. STEINBECK Tom . . loosened the oil cap with a pair of pliers. *toecap*: see TOE *n.* 9 R. HOLME A Wall with a Cap or Head over the Door.

III Partly f. the vb. 12 An imposed upper limit; an act of imposing an upper limit. L20.

Phrases: **cap and bells**: the insignia of the professional jester. **cap in hand** *fig.* humbly. **cap of liberty** a conical cap given to Roman slaves on emancipation, often used as a Republican symbol. **cap of maintenance** a cap or hat worn as a symbol of official dignity, or carried before a monarch etc. on ceremonial occasions. *Hungarian cap*: see HUNGARIAN *a.* *Kilmarnock cap*: see KILMARNOCK I. *Polar cap*: see POLAR *a.* *pull caps*: see PULL *v.* *put on one's thinking cap*: see THINKING *n.* 1a. *saffron milk-cap*: see SAFFRON *a.* **set one's cap at** seek to attract as a suitor. SHAGGY *cap.* **the cap fits** *fig.* a general remark is true of the person in question. *throw one's cap over the windmill*: see WINDMILL *n.* I.

Comb.: **cap-money** = sense 5 above; *cap-paper*: see sense 4 above; **cap rock** an overlying stratum of (esp. resistant) rock; **cap sleeve**: extending only a short distance from the shoulder; **capstone** a stone which caps or crowns, a coping stone.

capful *n.* the amount that a cap will contain M17. **capless** *a.* M19. **caplike** *a.* resembling a cap in appearance, position, or use M19.

cap /kap/ *n.*[2] *Sc.* L16. [App. var. of COP *n.*[1]] 1 A wooden bowl used as a drinking-vessel. L16. 2 A measure of quantity: a quarter of a Scots peck. E17.

cap /kap/ *n.*[3] *colloq.* Also **cap'.** M18. [Abbrev.] = CAPTAIN *n.*

cap /kap/ *n.*[4] *colloq.* (chiefly *N. Amer.*). M20. [Abbrev.] A capsule, esp. of a drug.

cap *n.*[5] var. of CAP. *n.*

cap /kap/ *v.*[1] Infl. **-pp-.** LME. [f. CAP *n.*[1]] 1 *v.t.* Provide (a person, head) with a cap, put a cap on; award a cap to for membership of a team etc., select as a member of a national team; *Sc.* & *NZ* confer a university degree on. LME. 2 *v.t.* & *i.* Take off one's cap in token of respect (to). M16. 3 *v.t.* Cover or protect as with a cap; cover at the top or end; seal with a cap. L16. b Seal (a well) to prevent or control the loss of gas or oil. L20. c *fig.* Impose an upper limit on; limit the expenditure of. L20. 4 *v.t. fig.* a Serve as a climax or culmination to; overtop, outdo, beat; follow (an anecdote, witticism, etc.) with a better or more apposite one. L16. b Pass the comprehension of, puzzle. *dial.* M18. 5 *v.t.* Form a cap or upper part to; overlie. E17. 6 *v.t.* & *i.* Give cap-money to; take cap-money. M19.

1 J. SKELTON With her clothes on her hed . . like an Egyptian capped about. *Times* Baker, capped five times for England in 1959–60. 2 THACKERAY He and the Proctor capped each other as they met. G. A. SALA Soon I was well known and Capped to. 3 P. NICHOLSON The extremities of beams, etc., have sometimes been capped with pitch. J. CARY Sphinx-like tors with their crowns of granite capped with ermine. B. PLAIN Jessie put the remainder of the lunch into a bag and capped the Thermos. 4a SHAKES. *Hen. V* I will cap that proverb with 'There is flattery in friendship'. M. BEERBOHM Katie . . uttered a loud sob. Mrs Batch capped this with a much louder one. S. UNWIN There was a Municipal Reception, a Foreign Office Reception . . a luncheon . . and finally to cap it all the members . . were invited to lunch . . with the President. *Times* The announcement . . capped a day of speculation. **cap verses** reply with a verse beginning with the last letter of the previous one. 5 C. LYELL The basalts . . capping the hills. B. TAYLOR One block Shall cap the pediment.

capped, †**capt** *ppl a.* (*a*) wearing or having a (specified) cap or covering; (*b*) *dial.* puzzled, astonished: LME. **capping** *n.* (*a*) the action of the vb; (*b*) that with which anything is capped, covered, or overlaid: LME.

cap /kap/ *v.*[2]*t.* Infl. **-pp-.** L16. [OFr. *caper* seize.] 1 Arrest. *obs.* exc. *Sc.* L16. 2 Appropriate by violence, seize. *Sc.* E19.

cap. /kap/ *n.* Also **cap** (no point). M19. [Abbrev.] A capital letter.

small cap: see SMALL *a.*

capa /ˈkapa/ *n.* L18. [Sp. f. late L *cappa*: see CAP *n.*[1]] In Spain and Spanish-speaking countries: a cape, a cloak.

capability /keɪpəˈbɪlɪti/ *n.* L16. [f. next + -ITY.] 1 The quality of being capable; power *of* (action, *doing*); capacity *for.* L16. 2 An undeveloped or unused faculty. Freq. in *pl.* L18.

1 B. C. BRODIE The capability of fixing the attention. H. KISSINGER Had Hanoi possessed the capability it could have inflicted . . higher casualties. *negative capability*: see NEGATIVE *a.* 2 A. W. WARD He recognised the capabilities of the character.

capable /ˈkeɪpəb(ə)l/ *a.* M16. [Fr. f. late L *capabilis*, f. *capere* take: see -ABLE.] †1a Able to take in (*lit.* & *fig.*); having sufficient room or capacity. Foll. by *of*, *to do.* (= CAPACIOUS I.) M16–L18. b = CAPACIOUS 2. L16–M17. 2 Foll. by *of*: open to, admitting of, susceptible to. L16. 3 Having the ability, power, or fitness for some specified purpose or activity; wicked or impudent enough. (Foll. by *of*, †*to do.*) L16. 4 *Law.* Qualified or entitled to inherit, possess, etc. (Foll. by *of.*) L16. 5 Having general capacity, intelligence, or ability; competent; gifted. E17.

1a MILTON Not capable her eare Of what was high. b T. FULLER That capable vessell of brass. 2 SHAKES. *2 Hen. IV* You were advis'd his flesh was capable Of wounds and scars. R. BOLT Some men think the Earth is round, others think it flat; it is a matter capable of question. 3 O. MANNING As soon as he is capable, he will be ordered to leave. S. THEMERSON He wouldn't be capable of committing such a crime! 4 D. M. WALKER A person may be capable of marriage at a different age from that at which he acquires capacity to vote. 5 J. S. BLACKIE A more capable . . witness could not be desired. B. TARKINGTON Lucy is so capable; she keeps house exquisitely.

capableness *n.* L16. **capably** *adv.* L19.

capable de tout /kapabl də tu/ *a. phr.* L19. [Fr.] Capable of anything; without scruple or restraint.

capacious /kəˈpeɪʃəs/ *a.* E17. [f. L *capac-*, *capax*, f. *capere* take: see -ACIOUS.] †1 = CAPABLE 1a. E17–L18. 2 Able to hold much; roomy, spacious, wide; comprehensive. E17. 3 Disposed or adapted for the reception *of. arch.* L17.

1 W. BRERETON A spacious harbour capacious of many thousand sail. 2 HAZLITT The capacious soul of Shakspeare. A. N. WILSON It was a large, comfortable, reassuring brick house, with capacious bow windows on three floors. 3 M. BEERBOHM Women of her own age and kind, capacious of tragedy.

capaciously *adv.* E19. **capaciousness** *n.* M17.

capacitance /kəˈpasɪt(ə)ns/ *n.* L19. [f. CAPACITY + -ANCE.] Ability to store electrical charge; the ratio of the change in the electrostatic charge of a body to the corresponding change in its potential.

capacitate /kəˈpasɪteɪt/ *v.t.* M17. [f. CAPACITY + -ATE[3].] Endow with capacity (*for*, *to do*), make capable; make legally competent; *Biol.* cause (a spermatozoon) to undergo changes in the female reproductive tract that enable it to penetrate and fertilize an ovum (usu. in *pass.*).

capaciˈtation *n.* M19.

capacitive /kəˈpasɪtɪv/ *a.* E20. [f. CAPACITY + -IVE.] Of or pertaining to electrical capacitance.

capacitative *a.* = CAPACITIVE M20. **capacitatively, -tively** *advs.* through the medium of, as regards, capacitance M20.

capacitor /kəˈpasɪtə/ *n.* E20. [f. next + -OR.] An electric circuit component which provides capacitance, usu. consisting of conducting plates separated by an insulating material; a condenser.
padder capacitor: see PADDER *n.*[2] 3.

capacity /kəˈpasɪti/ *n.* & *a.* LME. [Fr. *capacité* f. L *capacitas*, f. as CAPACIOUS: see -ACITY.] **A** *n.* **1** Ability to receive, contain, hold, produce, or carry; cubic content, volume (formerly also surface area, width). LME. **b** = CAPACITANCE. L18. **c** The maximum amount or number that can be contained, produced, etc. E20. **d** The total cylinder volume that is swept by the pistons in an internal-combustion engine. M20. **2** Mental or intellectual power, as an inherent faculty or as developed; (a) talent; a mental faculty. LME. **3** Legal competency or qualification. LME. †**4** A containing space or area; a void; a cavity. M16–M18. **5** An ability, power, or propensity for some specified purpose, activity, or experience; a susceptibility, a possibility. (Foll. by *of, for, to do*.) M17. **6** A position, a condition, a relative character. M17.
1 SHAKES. *Ant. & Cl.* Had our great palace the capacity To camp this host, we would all sup together. A. MACLEAN His capacity for brandy was phenomenal. F. HOYLE The cranial capacity eventually grew to about 1600 cubic centimetres. **measure of capacity** a measure of volume used for vessels and liquids, grain, etc. *specific heat capacity*: see SPECIFIC *a.* *specific inductive capacity*: see SPECIFIC *a.* *thermal capacity*: see THERMAL *a.* *vital capacity*: see VITAL *a.* **c** J. K. GALBRAITH Production is at or near capacity. **to capacity** fully, completely. **2** G. BERKELEY He wants capacity to relish what true piety is. ISAIAH BERLIN The more mysterious capacities called 'insight' and 'intuition'. **3** *legal capacity*: see LEGAL *a.* **5** DEFOE To deprive them of the capacity of ever returning. S. BUTLER We are endued with Capacities of action, of happiness and misery. H. L. MENCKEN There was grave uneasiness about his physical capacity for the job. N. SHUTE It was within the capacity of his ship to execute. E. REVELEY It was not that Erv had ever laid a hand on her but the capacity was there. **6** G. K. CHESTERTON The King . . reviewed it in his capacity as literary critic. G. GREENE I was working for him . . in a secretarial capacity.
B *attrib.* or as *adj.* That reaches or fills maximum capacity; fully occupying. M20.
Times Lit. Suppl. Both the play and film are now drawing capacity houses in London. F. ASTAIRE Business was capacity wherever we went.

cap-à-pie /kapəˈpiː/ *adv. arch.* E16. [OFr. *cap a pie* (mod. *de pied en cap*).] From head to foot, fully (armed, ready, etc.).

caparison /kəˈparɪs(ə)n/ *n.* Now *arch.* or *Hist.* E16. [Fr. †*caparasson* (mod. *caparaçon*) f. Sp. *caparazón* saddle-cloth, perh. f. CAPA.] **1** An ornamented covering spread over a horse's saddle or harness; (usu. in *pl.*) a horse's trappings. E16. **2** *transf.* A set of clothes or ornaments, an outfit. L16.

caparison /kəˈparɪs(ə)n/ *v.t.* L16. [Fr. *caparassoner*, f. as prec.] Put trappings or hangings on; deck.

capataz /kapaˈtaθ/ *n.* Pl. **-taces** /-ˈtaθes/. E19. [Sp., irreg. f. L *caput* head.] In Spain or Spanish-speaking America: an overseer, a superintendent, a boss.

cape /keɪp/ *n.*[1] LME. [(O)Fr. *cap* f. Prov. (= Sp. *cabo*) f. Proto-Romance f. L *caput* head.] **I** *gen.* **1** A headland, a promontory. LME. **II** *spec.* **2** *the Cape*, some familiar headland, *esp.* (the province containing) the Cape of Good Hope at the southern tip of Africa. M17. **3** More fully *capeskin*. A soft leather made from South African sheepskin. E20.
Comb.: **Cape Barren goose** [*Cape Barren*, an island in Bass Strait, Australia] a large Australian goose, *Cereopsis novaehollandiae*, which has a short black bill that is almost covered by a swollen waxy yellow cere; also called *cereopsis (goose)*; **Cape brandy** *S. Afr.* brandy made from vines in the Cape Province; crude brandy; *Cape buffalo*: see BUFFALO *n.* 1b; **Cape cart** *S. Afr.* a two-wheeled horse-drawn cart; **Cape chestnut** a southern African evergreen tree, *Calodendrum capense*, of the rue family; **Cape Cod** *N. Amer.* (designating) a type of rectangular house with a steeply-gabled roof, characteristic of Cape Cod, Massachusetts; **Cape Coloured** (a member) of the Coloured population of the Cape Province; **Cape cowslip** = LACHENALIA; **Cape daisy** a yellow-flowered plant of the composite family, *Arctotis fastuosa*, native to southern Africa and widely introduced as an ornamental; **Cape doctor** *S. Afr.* a strong south-east wind; **Cape Dutch** *n.* & *a.* (*a*) *n.* the early Dutch settlers at the Cape of Good Hope; *arch.* Afrikaans (regarded as a dialect of Dutch); (*b*) *adj.* of or pertaining to the Cape Dutch; *spec.* designating a style of architecture characterized by gables and whitewashed walls; **Cape fox** a fox, *Vulpes chama*, with a silvery-grey back, occurring in the drier areas of southern Africa; *Cape* GANNET; **Cape gooseberry** a S. American physalis or ground cherry, *Physalis peruviana*; the edible round yellow berry of this plant; *Cape* HARTEBEEST; **Cape hunting dog** = *hunting dog* (b) s.v. HUNTING *n.*; *Cape* HYACINTH; **Cape jasmine, Cape jessamine** gardenia; esp. *Gardenia jasminioides*, native to China; *Cape leaping hare*: see LEAPING *ppl a.*; *Cape Malay*: see MALAY 1b; **Cape marigold** = DIMORPHOTHECA; *Cape pigeon*: see PIGEON *n.*[1] 1; **Cape pondweed** a southern African aquatic plant, *Aponogeton distachyos*, with two spikes of fragrant white flowers; **Cape primrose** = STREPTOCARPUS; **Cape salmon** *S. Afr.* any of various fishes; *esp.* = GEELBEK; *capeskin*: see sense 3 above; *Cape smoke*: see SMOKE *n.* 7a; **Cape sparrow** a dark-coloured sparrow of southern Africa, *Passer melanurus*; **Cape-weed** any of various plants; *esp.* (*Austral.* & *NZ*) = *Cape daisy* above.

cape /keɪp/ *n.*[2] M16. [Fr. f. Prov. *capa* (= (O)Fr. CHAPE) f. late L *cappa*: see CAP *n.*[1]] **1** A short (formerly also a long) sleeveless cloak; a fixed or detachable part of a longer cloak, coat, etc., falling loosely over the shoulders from the neckband; *spec.* the red cloak used by a bullfighter. M16. **2** *transf.* A growth of feathers or hair suggesting a cape. L19.
1 *Inverness cape*: see INVERNESS 1.
caped *a.* having a cape, wearing a cape M16. **capelet** *n.* a small cape E20.

†**cape** *v.i.* E16–M19. [Origin uncertain: perh. ult. rel. to Fr. *cap* head of the ship.] *Naut.* Of a vessel or its crew: head, bear.

capeador /kapɪəˈdɔː/ *n.* E20. [Sp., f. *capear* trick a bull with a cape, f. CAPA.] A person who aids a bullfighter by distracting the bull with his cloak.

capelin /ˈkeɪplɪn, ˈkap-/ *n.* Also **caplin**. E17. [Fr. f. Prov. *capelan* CHAPLAIN.] A smelt, *Mallotus villosus*, of northern oceans.

capeline /ˈkap(ə)lɪn/ *n.* LME. [(O)Fr. f. Prov. *capelina*, f. *capel* hat (= mod.Fr. *chapeau*).] **1** *Hist.* An iron skullcap worn by medieval archers. LME. **2** A woman's hat, *esp.* one with a wide brim trimmed with feathers. Also, a light hood with an attached cape. L18.

capellane /ˈkap(ə)leɪn/ *n.* Long *obs.* exc. *Hist.* OE. [med.L *cappellanus*: see CHAPLAIN.] A chaplain; a keeper of sacred relics.

caper /ˈkeɪpə/ *n.*[1] LME. [Fr. *câpres* or L *capparis* f. Gk *kapparis*: treated as pl.] **1** A trailing shrub, *Capparis spinosa*, of southern Europe. LME. **2** Usu. in *pl.* **a** The flower-buds of this shrub, used for pickling and served esp. in a sauce. L15. **b** The seed-pods of other plants, e.g. nasturtium, used similarly; any such plant. Cf. *bean caper* s.v. BEAN *n.* L16. **3** A kind of scented tea. L18.
Comb.: **caper spurge** an ornamental poisonous spurge, *Euphorbia lathyris*.

caper /ˈkeɪpə/ *n.*[2] L16. [Abbrev. of CAPRIOLE *n.*] **1** A frisky movement, a leap, a spring; *fig.* a fantastic proceeding. L16. **2** An activity or occupation, esp. a risky or questionable venture; a 'dodge'. *slang.* M19.
1 cut a caper, capers move friskily, *arch.* dance.

caper /ˈkeɪpə/ *n.*[3] *obs.* exc. *Hist.* M17. [Du. *kaper*, f. *kapen* take away, rob, plunder.] (The captain of) a privateer; a corsair.

caper /ˈkapə/ *n.*[4] *colloq.* E20. [Abbrev.] = CAPERCAILLIE.

caper /ˈkeɪpə/ *v.i.* L16. [f. as CAPER *n.*[2]] Move friskily, skip, dance, (*about*).
caperer *n.* L17.

capercaillie /kapəˈkeɪli/ *n.* Also **-lzie** /-lji, -lzi/. M16. [Gael. *capull coille* lit. 'horse of the wood': the spelling *-lz-* derives from ME *-lʒ-*.] A large grouse, *Tetrao urogallus*, formerly native to and now re-established in the Scottish Highlands.

Capernaite /kəˈpəːnɪʌɪt/ *n. arch. derog.* M16. [f. *Capernaum* in Galilee (*John* 6:26–59) + -ITE[1].] A believer in transubstantiation.
¶Used esp. in theological controversy in 16 & 17.
Caperna'itic *a.* L19. **Caperna'itical** *a.* L16.

capernoited /kapəˈnɔɪtɪd/ *a. Sc. arch.* E18. [Origin unkn.] Irritable; peevish; muddle-headed; affected by drink.

Capetian /kəˈpiːʃ(ə)n/ *a.* & *n.* M19. [Fr. *Capétien*.] (A member) of the dynasty of French kings founded by Hugh Capet in 987.

Caphtor /ˈkaftə/ *n.* Pl. **-rim** /-rɪm/. LOE. [Heb. *Kaptōr*, f. place-name = *Caphtor*: see below. Cf. KEFTIU.] *Ancient Hist.* A native or inhabitant of Caphtor, a region of the eastern Mediterranean mentioned in the Bible but not firmly located. Usu. in *pl.*

capias /ˈkeɪpɪəs, ˈkap-/ *n.* LME. [L = you are to seize, 2nd person sing. pres. subjunct. of *capere* take.] *Law.* A writ or process commanding the arrest of the person named.
capias ad satisfaciendum /ad ˌsatɪsfasɪˈɛndəm/: after judgement, directing the imprisonment of the defendant until the plaintiff's claim is satisfied (abbrev. CA. SA.). *capias in* WITHERNAM. PLURIES *capias*.

capillaceous /kapɪˈleɪʃəs/ *a.* E18. [L *capillaceus*, f. *capillus* hair: see -ACEOUS.] Hairlike, threadlike.

capillaire /kapɪˈlɛː/ *n.* M18. [Fr. f L *capillaris*, late L *capillaris herba* maidenhair fern: see CAPILLARY.] A syrup of maidenhair fern; a syrup flavoured with orange-flower water.

†**capillament** *n.* L17–M19. [L *capillamentum* the hair collectively, f. *capillus* hair.] A hairlike fibre, a filament.

capillarity /kapɪˈlarɪti/ *n.* M19. [Fr. *capillarité*, f. as next + -ITY.] Capillary attraction or repulsion; the property of exerting this.

capillary /kəˈpɪləri/ *a.* & *n.* M17. [L *capillaris*, f. *capillus* hair, after (O)Fr. *capillaire*: see -ARY[2].] **A** *adj.* **1** Of or pertaining to hair; hairlike, esp. in tenuity. M17. **2** Of a tube etc.: having a hairlike bore. M17. **3** Of, pertaining to, or occurring in capillaries. E19.
3 capillary attraction, repulsion the tendency of liquid in a capillary tube to rise, recede, as a result of surface forces.
B *n.* **1** A capillary vessel; *esp.* any of the extremely narrow blood-vessels which form a network between the arterioles and venules. M17. †**2** A fern, esp. the maidenhair. M17–M18.
Also †**capillar** *a.* LME–L17.

capillitium /kapɪˈlɪʃɪəm/ *n.* M19. [L = hair collectively, f. *capillus* hair.] *Mycol.* Spore-containing fibrous tissue in the sporangia of certain fungi.

capital /ˈkapɪt(ə)l/ *n.*[1] ME. [OFr. *capitel* (mod. *chapiteau*) f. late L *capitellum* dim. of *caput, capit-* head: mod. sp. *-al* through assoc. w. next.] **1** The head or cornice of a pillar or column. ME. **2** The cap of a chimney, crucible, etc. E18.

capital /ˈkapɪt(ə)l/ *a.* & *n.*[2] ME. [(O)Fr. f. L *capitalis*, f. *caput, capit-* head: see -AL[1].] **A** *adj.* **I** Relating to the head. †**1** Of or pertaining to the head or top. ME–L17. **2** Involving loss of the head or life; vitally injurious, fatal. LME. †**b** Of an enemy, enmity: deadly, mortal. LME–M18. **c** Of a crime etc.: punishable by death. E16.
2 CAXTON To have capytal sentence & be beheded. *fig.*: W. H. PRESCOTT In the outset, he seems to have fallen into a capital error.
II Standing at the head (*lit.* & *fig.*). **3** Chief, principal; important, leading. LME. **4** Orig. (of a letter or word), standing at the head of a page, passage, etc. Now (of a letter), having the form and size used to begin a sentence, proper name, etc. LME. **5** Of funds, stock, etc.: original, serving as a basis for commercial or financial operations. E18. **6** Excellent, first-rate. Freq. as an exclam. of approval. *colloq.* M18.
3 W. BLACKSTONE The eldest son had the capital fee . . of his father's possessions. T. WARTON The cloister . . of some capital monastery. R. W. DALE The old traditions . . made Obedience the capital virtue of childhood. **4** W. VAN T. CLARK When Joyce spoke about Davies he said 'he' as if it had a capital H. **a — with a capital A** (or similar phr.) emphatically a —,

the real or quintessential a —. 5 ADAM SMITH The capital stock of Great Britain was not diminished even by the enormous expense of the late war. 6 B. JOWETT Capital, Socrates; by the gods, that is truly good. A. MOOREHEAD He is a capital officer, zealous and untiring in the performance of his duties.

B *n.* 1 A capital letter. LME. 2 The stock with which a company or person enters into business; the total sum of shareholders' contributions in a joint-stock company; accumulated wealth, *esp.* as used in further production. M16. b The holders of wealth as a class; capitalists, employers of labour. M19. 3 A capital town or city. M17.

1 *small capitals*: see SMALL *a.* 2 BURKE You began ill .. You set up your trade without a capital. F. RAPHAEL Lack of capital prevented Nat's buying a practice. H. MACMILLAN A widespread desire that .. economic development should be .. supported by British capital. **fixed capital**: invested in permanent assets such as land, buildings, machinery, etc. **make capital out of** *fig.* turn to account, turn to one's own advantage. *organic composition of capital*: see ORGANIC *a. refugee capital*: see REFUGEE *a.* **working capital**: available for the actual carrying-on of business. b W. HOLTBY Here gallant Labour, with nothing to lose but its chains, would fight entrenched and armoured Capital.

Special collocations & comb.: **capital gain** profit from the sale of investments or property. **capital goods** goods (to be) used in producing commodities, as opp. to consumer goods. **capital-intensive** *a.* requiring much use of capital. **capital levy** the appropriation by the State of a proportion of a nation's private wealth. **capital punishment** infliction of death by an authorized public authority as punishment for a crime. **capital ship** a battleship or other large warship. **capital sum** a lump sum of money, *esp.* one payable to an insured person. **capital territory**: containing the capital city of a country. **capital transfer tax**: levied on the transfer of capital by gift, bequest, etc. (in Britain 1975–86).

capitalling *n.* the furnishing of a word with a capital letter L17. **capitally** *adv.* in a capital manner E17.

capitalise *v.* var. of CAPITALIZE.

capitalism /ˈkapɪt(ə)lɪz(ə)m/ *n.* M19. [f. CAPITAL *n.*[2] + -ISM.] The possession of capital or wealth; a system in which private capital or wealth is used in the production or distribution of goods; the dominance of private owners of capital and of production for profit.

popular capitalism: see POPULAR *a.*

capitalist /ˈkapɪt(ə)lɪst/ *n.* & *a.* Freq. *derog.* L18. [f. as prec. + -IST.] A *n.* A person who has capital, esp. one who uses it in (large-scale) business enterprises. L18.

B *adj.* Of or pertaining to capitalists or capitalism. M19.

capitalist road: see ROAD *n. capitalist roader*: see ROADER *n.*[1] 2.

capitaˈlistic *a.* of or pertaining to capitalists; characterized by capitalism: L19. **capitaˈlistically** *adv.* L19.

capitalize /ˈkapɪt(ə)lʌɪz/ *v.* Also **-ise**. M18. [f. CAPITAL *n.*[2] + -IZE. Cf. Fr. *capitaliser.*] 1 *v.t.* Write or print (a letter) as a capital; begin (a word) with a capital letter; write or print in capitals. M18. 2 *v.t.* Convert into a capital sum; compute or realize the current value of; reckon the value of by setting future benefits against the cost of maintenance. M19. 3 *v.t.* & *i.* (foll. by *on*). Make capital out of, use to one's advantage, turn to account. M19. 4 *v.t.* Provide with capital. Orig. *US.* L19.

3 *Publishers Weekly* The publishers .. do not intend to capitalize the publicity. N. CHOMSKY The Cambodian left is now in a position to mobilize the peasantry, capitalizing on Sihanouk's personal prestige. 4 *Observer* At the current price of 213p, Burmah is capitalised at a little over £300 million.

capitaliˈzation *n.* M19.

capitan /ˈkapɪt(ə)n, kapɪˈtɑːn/ *n.* M18. [Sp. *capitán* CAPTAIN *n.*] Chiefly *Hist.* A captain, a naval commander.

Capitan Pasha *Hist.* the chief admiral of the Turkish fleet.

capitana /kapɪˈtɑːnə/ *n.* L17. [It., Sp., & Port.] The ship of the admiral of an Italian, Spanish, etc., fleet.

capitano /kapɪˈtɑːnəʊ/ *n.* Pl. **-os**. L16. [It. = CAPTAIN *n.*] In Italy or among Italian-speakers: a captain, a headman, a chief.

capitao /kapɪˈtaʊ/ *n.* L19. [Port. *capitão* = CAPTAIN *n.*] A headman, leader of a gang, etc., in E. Africa.

capita succedanea *n. phr.* pl. of CAPUT SUCCEDANEUM.

capitate /ˈkapɪteɪt/ *a.* M17. [L *capitatus*, f. *caput, capit-* head: see -ATE[2].] 1 Chiefly *Anat.* Having a distinct head, knob-headed; *spec.* denoting the largest bone of the wrist. M17. 2 *Bot.* Having the inflorescence in a close terminal cluster. L17.

Also **capitated** *a.* (now *rare* or *obs.*) L17.

capitation /kapɪˈteɪʃ(ə)n/ *n.* E17. [Fr., or late L *capitatio(n-)*, f. as prec.: see -ATION.] 1 The counting of heads or persons. E17. 2 (The levying of) a tax or fee of so much a head; a payment of so much a head. M17.

Comb.: **capitation fee**, **grant**, etc.: of so much per head subject to certain conditions.

capite /ˈkapɪti/ *n.* E17. [L, abl. of *caput* head.] *Hist.* In full *tenure in capite*. Tenure by which land was held immediately of the Crown.

capitellum /kapɪˈtɛləm/ *n.* Pl. **-lla** /-lə/. E17. [Late L, dim. of L *capit-, caput* head: see -ELLUM.] †1 = CAPITAL *n.*[1] I. Only in E17. 2 *Anat.* The capitulum of the humerus. L19.

Capitol /ˈkapɪt(ə)l/ *n.* LME. [OFr. *capitolie, -oile*, later assim. to the source, L *Capitolium*, f. *caput, capit-* head.] 1 A citadel on top of a hill; esp. *the* temple of Jupiter Optimus Maximus, on the Saturnian or Tarpeian (later called Capitoline) Hill at Rome. LME. 2 *The* building occupied by the US Congress in Washington DC; in some other cities, the State legislature building. L17.

Capitolian /kapɪˈtəʊlɪən/ *a.* = CAPITOLINE E17. **Capitoline** /kəˈpɪtəlʌɪn/ *a.* designating or pertaining to the hill at Rome on which the Capitol stood; of or pertaining to the Capitol. E17.

capitonné /kapɪtɒne/ *a.* L19. [Fr., pa. pple of *capitonner* upholster, quilt.] Designating or characterized by a style of upholstery or embroidery in which the material is drawn in at intervals to present a quilted appearance.

capitular /kəˈpɪtjʊlə/ *a.* & *n.* E16. [Late L *capitularis*, f. L *capitulum*: see CHAPTER *n.*, -AR[1].] A *adj.* 1 Of, pertaining to, or governed by a cathedral chapter. E16. 2 Chiefly *Anat.* Pertaining to or of the nature of a capitulum. M19. B *n.* = CAPITULARY *n.* M17.

†**capitularly** *adv.* as a chapter E–M18.

capitulary /kəˈpɪtjʊləri/ *n.* & *a.* M17. [Late L *capitularius*, f. as prec.: see -ARY[1].] A *n.* 1 *Hist.* A collection of ordinances, esp. of Frankish kings. M17. 2 A member of a chapter. Now *rare* or *obs.* L17. 3 A heading, a title. *rare.* E19. B *adj.* = CAPITULAR *a.* I. L18.

capitulate /kəˈpɪtjʊleɪt/ *v.* M16. [med.L *capitulat-*, pa. ppl stem of *capitulare* draw up under distinct heads, f. late L *capitulum* head of a discourse: see CHAPTER *n.*, -ATE[3]. In sense 3 through Fr. *capituler.*] †1 *v.i.* Draw up articles of agreement; treat, parley; make conditions. M16–E19. b *v.t.* Make terms about, negotiate. L16–M17. †2 *v.t.* Draw up in chapters or under heads; enumerate. L16–L17. 3 *v.i.* & (less usually) *t.* Surrender, esp. on stated conditions. L17.

3 W. ROBERTSON Want of provisions quickly obliged Trevulci to capitulate. W. STYRON I knew that I was on the verge of capitulating to him, backing down.

capitulator *n.* E17. **capitulatory** *a.* E19.

capitulation /kəpɪtjʊˈleɪʃ(ə)n/ *n.* M16. [Late L *capitulatio(n-)*, f. as prec.: see -ATION. In sense 3 through Fr. *capitulation.*] †1 a The making of terms; a covenant, treaty. M16–M19. b In *pl.* Articles of agreement, terms, conditions; *spec.* articles giving special immunities and privileges within a State to subjects of another State. Now *Hist.* L16. 2 A statement of the main divisions of a subject. Cf. RECAPITULATION. L16. 3 The action of surrendering, esp. on stated conditions; an instrument containing terms of surrender. M17.

capitulum /kəˈpɪtjʊləm/ *n.* Pl. **-la** /-lə/. E18. [L, dim. of *caput, capit-* head: see -ULE.] A small rounded head or knob; *esp.* (*a*) *Anat.* a bony protuberance articulating with another bone, *esp.* the prominence at the end of the humerus which articulates with the radius; (*b*) *Bot.* a dense flat terminal cluster of sessile flowers or florets on a common receptacle, as in the composite family.

caple /ˈkeɪp(ə)l/ *n.* Long *obs.* exc. *dial.* Also **capul**. ME. [ON *kapall* f. L *caballus.*] A horse.

Caplet /ˈkaplɪt/ *n.* Also **c-**. M20. [f. CAP(SULE *n.* & *a.* + TAB)LET *n.*] *Pharm.* (Proprietary name for) a coated capsule or tablet.

caplin *n.* var. of CAPELIN.

cap'n /ˈkapm/ *n. colloq.* Chiefly *N. Amer.* E19. [Abbrev.] = CAPTAIN *n.*

capnomancy /ˈkapnəmansi/ *n. rare.* E17. [f. Gk *kapnos* smoke + -MANCY, perh. through Fr. *capnomancie.*] Divination by smoke.

capo /ˈkapəʊ/ *n.*[1] Pl. **-os**. M20. [Abbrev.] = CAPOTASTO.

capo /ˈkapəʊ/ *n.*[2] Chiefly *US.* Pl. **-os**. M20. [It. f. L *caput* head.] The head of a crime syndicate or one of its branches.

capon /ˈkeɪp(ə)n/ *n.* & *v.* LOE. [AN *capun* var. of (O)Fr. *capon*, f. Proto-Romance f. L *capo, -onis.*] A *n.* 1 A castrated domestic cock (usu. one fattened for eating). Cf. POULARD. LOE. †2 A eunuch. ME–L17. 3 A dull-witted person. *obs.* exc. *dial.* M16. †4 A billet-doux. Cf. POULET. *rare* (Shakes.). Only in L16. 5 A kind of fish, *esp.* a red herring. *dial.* M17.

5 *Norfolk capon*: see NORFOLK I.

B *v.t.* Make a capon of; castrate. L16.

†**caponet** *n.* a small capon L16–E18. **caponize** *v.t.* = CAPON *v.* M17.

caponier /kapəˈnɪə/ *n.* L17. [Sp. *caponera* (whence Fr. *caponnière*) lit. 'capon-pen'.] *Fortif.* A covered passage across a ditch.

capot /kəˈpɒt/ *n.*[1] & *v.* M17. [Fr., perh. f. *capoter* dial. var. of *chapoter* castrate.] *Piquet.* A *n.* The winning of all the tricks by one player; a score awarded for this. M17. B *v.t.* Infl. **-tt-**. Win all the tricks from. M17.

¶Formerly stressed on 1st syll.

capot /ˈkapəʊ, kəˈpɒt; *foreign* kapo (*pl. same*)/ *n.*[2] L17. [Fr., masc. form of CAPOTE.] = CAPOTE 1a.

capotasto /kapəʊˈtastəʊ/ *n.* Pl. **-os**. Also **capo tasto**. L19. [It., lit. 'head stop': cf. TASTO.] *Mus.* A movable bar attached to the finger-board of a stringed instrument to make possible the simultaneous adjustment of the pitch of all the strings.

capote /kəˈpəʊt/ *n.* E19. [Fr., dim. of *cape* CAPE *n.*[2]] 1 a A long hooded cloak worn by soldiers, travellers, etc. E19. b A long mantle worn by women. M19. 2 A bonnet with a soft crown and stiff projecting brim. E19.

capouch *n.* var. of CAPUCHE.

cappa /ˈkapə/ *n.* M19. [It. = CAPE *n.*[2]] A cloak forming part of a religious habit; a cope.

Cappadocian /kapəˈdəʊʃ(ə)n/ *a.* & *n.* E17. [f. *Cappadocia* (see below) + -AN.] (A native or inhabitant) of Cappadocia, an ancient kingdom of Asia Minor, now part of Turkey.

capper /ˈkapə/ *n.* ME. [f. CAP *n.*[1] or *v.*[1] + -ER[1].] 1 A cap-maker. *obs.* exc. *Hist.* ME. 2 A person who or thing which provides or forms a cap. L16. 3 An accomplice, *esp.* a confederate in a gambling game. *slang* (chiefly *US*). M18. 4 A person or thing that outdoes all rivals; something surprising or puzzling. *dial.* L18.

cappuccino /kapʊˈtʃiːnəʊ/ *n.* Pl. **-os**. M20. [It.: see CAPUCHIN.] (A cup of) coffee with milk, esp. made with espresso coffee and topped with white foam.

Capri /ˈkapriː, kəˈpriː/ *n.* L19. [An island in the Bay of Naples.] 1 A wine from Capri. L19. 2 In *pl.*, or as *Capri pants*. Women's close-fitting tapered trousers. M20.

capric /ˈkaprɪk/ *a.* M19. [f. L *caper, capr-* goat + -IC.] 1 Chem. *capric acid*, a crystalline fatty acid present in butter, coconut oil, etc.; *n*-decanoic acid, $CH_3(CH_2)_8COOH$. M19. 2 Of a goat; goatlike. L19.

caprate *n.* a salt or ester of capric acid M19.

capriccio /kəˈprɪtʃɪəʊ/ *n.* Pl. **-os**. E17. [It.: see CAPRICE.] †1 = CAPRICE I. E17–E19. †2 A sudden movement; a trick, a prank, a caper.

M17–M19. 3 A thing or work of lively fancy in art etc.; *esp.* a lively usu. short musical composition, more or less free in form. L17.

capriccioso /kəprɪtʃɪ'əʊzəʊ/ *adv.* M18. [It.: see CAPRICIOUS.] *Mus.* A direction: in a free and impulsive style.

caprice /kə'priːs/ *n.* M17. [Fr. f. It. *capriccio* (lit.) head with the hair standing on end, (hence) horror, (later, by assoc. w. *capra* goat) sudden start, f. *capo* head (see CAPO *n.*[2]) + *riccio* hedgehog (ult. f. L (*h*)*ericius* URCHIN).] 1 An unaccountable change of mind or conduct; a whim; a freakish fancy. M17. b Inclination or disposition to such changes etc.; capriciousness. M17. 2 = CAPRICCIO 3. E18.

capricious /kə'prɪʃəs/ *a.* E17. [Fr. *capricieux* f. It. *capriccioso*, f. *capriccio* (see prec.) + *-oso* -OUS.] †1 Humorous; fantastic; characterized by far-fetched comparisons etc. E17–E18. 2 Guided by caprice; readily swayed by whim or fancy; inconstant. Of a thing: subject to sudden change, irregular, unpredictable. E17.

2 J. CHEEVER They cultivated tropical plants in a capricious climate.

capriciously *adv.* E17. **capriciousness** *n.* L16.

Capricorn /'kaprɪkɔːn/ *n.* In sense 1 also in L form **Capricornus** /kaprɪ'kɔːnəs/. OE. [L *capricornus*, f. *caper-*, *capr-* goat + *cornu* horn, after Gk *aigokerōs* goat-horned, (as n.) Capricorn.] 1 (The name of) a constellation of the southern hemisphere, on the ecliptic between Sagittarius and Aquarius; *Astrol.* (the name of) the tenth zodiacal sign, usu. associated with the period 22 December to 19 January (see note s.v. ZODIAC); the Goat. OE. b A person born under the sign Capricorn. M20. †2 An ibex; a chamois. M17–M19.

1 *attrib.*: E. KIRK Capricorn people resent all interference. *tropic of Capricorn*: see TROPIC *n.* & *a.*

Comb.: **Capricorn beetle** a longhorn beetle of the genus *Cerambyx*.

Capri'cornian *n.* & *a.* (*a*) *n.* a person born under the sign Capricorn; (*b*) *adj.* of or pertaining to Capricorn; (characteristic of one) born under Capricorn: E20.

caprid /'kaprɪd/ *a.* & *n.* M19. [f. L *caper*, *capr-* goat + -ID[3].] A *adj.* Of or pertaining to the tribe of ruminants including the goats and sheep. M19. B *n.* A caprid animal. L20.

caprification /kaprɪfɪ'keɪʃ(ə)n/ *n.* E17. [L *caprificatio(n-)*, f. *caprificat-* pa. ppl stem of *caprificare*, f. *caprificus* wild fig tree: see -ATION.] 1 A process of ripening figs by means of punctures produced on the fruit by the action of insects or artificially. E17. 2 Artificial fertilization. M19.

caprifoil /'kaprɪfɔɪl/ *n.* Now *rare* or *obs.* LME. [med.L *caprifolium* 'goat-leaf', with spelling assim. to *trefoil* etc.] Honeysuckle.

caprine /'kaprʌɪn/ *a.* LME. [L *caprinus*, f. *caper*, *capr-* goat: see -INE[1]. Cf. (O)Fr. *caprin*.] Of or pertaining to a goat or goats; goatlike.

capriole /'kaprɪəʊl/ *n.* & *v.* L16. [Fr. (now *cabriole*), f. It. *capriola*, f. *capriolare* to leap, f. *capriolo* roebuck f. L *capreolus* dim. of *caper*, *capr-* goat: see -OLE[1].] A *n.* 1 A leap or caper, esp. as made in dancing (cf. CABRIOLE 1). L16. 2 A trained horse's horizontal leap with the hind legs kicking vigorously. L16. B *v.i.* Perform a capriole; skip, leap, caper. L16.

capriped /'kaprɪpɛd/ *a.* & *n. rare.* Also **-pede** /-piːd/. M18. [L *capripes*, *-ped-*, f. *caper*, *capr-* goat + *pes*, *ped-* foot.] (A person) having feet like those of a goat.

caproic /kə'prəʊɪk/ *a.* M19. [f. L *capr-*, *caper* goat + -OIC.] Chem. *caproic acid*, = HEXANOIC *acid*.

'caproate *n.* a salt or ester of this acid M19. **capro'lactam** *n.* a crystalline lactam, $C_6H_{11}NO$, which is an intermediate in nylon manufacture M20. **caproyl** /'kaprəʊʌɪl, -əʊɪl/ *n.* the radical $C_5H_{11}CO\cdot$ M19.

capryl /'kaprʌɪl, -prɪl/ *n.* M19. [f. CAPRIC + -YL.] *Chem.* The radical $C_9H_{19}CO\cdot$; *n*-decanoyl. Usu. in *comb.* Occas. confused w. CAPRYLYL.

caprylic /ka'prɪlɪk/ *a.* M19. [f. L *capr-*, *caper*, goat + -YL + -IC.] Chem. *caprylic acid*, a liquid fatty acid present in butter and other fats; *n*-octanoic acid, $CH_3(CH_2)_6COH$.

'caprylate *n.* a salt or ester of this acid M19. **'caprylyl** *n.* the radical $CH_3(CH_2)_6\cdot$; *n*-octanoyl; (cf. CAPRYL): E20.

capsa /'kapsə/ *n.* Pl. **capsae** /'kapsiː/, **capsas**. M20. [L: see CASE *n.*[2]] *Rom. Antiq.* A cylindrical box for holding upright rolls of documents.

capsaicin /kap'seɪɪsɪn/ *n.* L19. [Alt. of CAPSICINE: see -IN[1].] *Chem.* A cyclic amide, $C_{18}H_{27}NO_3$, responsible for the pungency of capsicums.

Capsian /'kapsɪən/ *a.* & *n.* E20. [Fr. *capsien*, f. L *Capsa* for Gafsa, central Tunisia: see -IAN.] *Archaeol.* (Designating or pertaining to) a late palaeolithic culture of N. Africa.

capsicum /'kapsɪkəm/ *n.* L16. [mod.L, perh. f. L *capsa* CASE *n.*[2]] Any plant of the tropical genus *Capsicum*, of the nightshade family, esp. *C. annuum*, different forms of which bear chilli peppers and sweet peppers; the fruit of such a plant, *esp.* one of the more pungent varieties.

capsicine /-siːn/ *n.* (now *rare* or *obs.*) (*Chem.*) a substance formerly regarded as an alkaloid responsible for the pungency of capsicums M19.

capsid /'kapsɪd/ *n.*[1] & *a.* L19. [mod.L *Capsidae* (see MIRID), f. *Capsus* genus name: see -ID[3].] *Entomol.* = MIRID.

capsid /'kapsɪd/ *n.*[2] M20. [f. L *capsa* CASE *n.*[2] + -ID[2].] *Microbiol.* The protein coat or shell of certain viruses.

capsize /kap'sʌɪz/ *v.* & *n.* L18. [Perh. ult. f. Sp. *capuzar* sink (a ship) by the head, f. *cabo* head + *chapuzar* to dive, duck.] A *v.* 1 *v.t.* Overturn, upset, (esp. a boat, people in boat). L18. 2 *v.i.* Of a boat etc.: be overturned or upset. E19. B *n.* An act or instance of capsizing. E19.

capsizal *n.* = CAPSIZE *n.* L19.

capsomere /'kapsəʊmɪə/ *n.* M20. [Fr. *capsomère*: see CAPSID *n.*[2], -MER.] *Microbiol.* Each of a number of protein subunits from which the capsid of a virus is built up.

capstan /'kapst(ə)n/ *n.* Also †**capstern** & other vars. LME. [Prov. *cabestan* (earlier *cabestran*), f. *cabestre* halter f. L *capistrum*, f. *capere* seize.] 1 A revolving barrel on a vertical axis for winding cable etc., esp. on board ship: worked by persons walking round pushing bars fitting into the barrel, or by electricity, steam, etc. LME. 2 A revolving spindle on a tape recorder etc. M20.

Comb.: **capstan lathe**: with a revolving tool-holder.

capsulate /'kapsjʊlət/ *a.* M17. [f. next + -ATE[2].] Chiefly *Bot.* Enclosed in, formed into, or furnished with a capsule.

Also **capsulated** *a.* M17.

capsule /'kapsjuːl, -sjʊl/ *n.* & *a.* Formerly also in L form †**-ula**, pl. **-lae**. LME. [Fr. f. L *capsula* dim. of *capsa* CASE *n.*[2]; see -ULE.] A *n.* 1 *gen.* A small case or container; an envelope, a sheath. LME. 2 *Anat.* A membranous or fibrous envelope around an organ, joint, etc.; a sac. L17. 3 *Bot.* A dry seed-case which opens when ripe by the parting of valves. L17. †4 *Chem.* A shallow vessel for roasting or evaporating. E18–L19. 5 A top or cover for a bottle. M19. 6 A small case of gelatin etc. enclosing a dose of medicine. L19. 7 A detachable nose-cone of a rocket, compartment of a spacecraft, etc., containing instruments or crew. M20.

1 *fig.*: N. MAILER This is all very sketchy, but I'm trying to put seven years into a capsule. *time-capsule*: see TIME *n.* 2 *Tenon's capsule*: see TENON *n.*[2]

B *attrib.* or as *adj.* Brief, condensed; small and compact. Chiefly *US.* M20.

capsular *a.* of, pertaining to, or of the nature of a capsule M18. **capsulitis** /-'lʌɪtɪs/ *n.* (*Med.*) inflammation of a capsule, esp. of a joint M19.

capsule /'kapsjuːl, -sjʊl/ *v.t.* M19. [f. the n.] Enclose in or provide with a capsule.

capsulize /'kapsjʊlʌɪz/ *v.t.* Orig. *US.* Also **-ise**. M20. [f. CAPSULE *n.* + -IZE.] Compress (information etc.) into a brief and compact form.

capsulo- /'kapsjʊləʊ/ *comb. form* of L *capsula* CAPSULE *n.*: see -O-.

capsulotomy /-'lɒtəmi/ *n.* (an instance of) surgical incision into the capsule of the lens of the eye L19.

captain /'kaptɪn/ *n.* & *v.* LME. [Late OFr. *capitain* (mod. *capitaine*), superseding earlier *chevetaigne* CHIEFTAIN and *chataigne*, *catanie*, f. late L *capitaneus* chief, f. *caput*, *capit-* head.] A *n.* 1 A chief or leader, esp. a military leader or commander. LME. 2 A military officer holding subordinate command. LME. b *spec.* An officer in the army or (US etc.) air force, ranking below a major and above a lieutenant. M16. c An officer in the Salvation Army, ranking below a major and above a lieutenant. L19. 3 A naval officer commanding a warship; an officer in the navy or marines, ranking below a rear admiral and above a commander or lieutenant. Also (as a courtesy title), a commander. M16. b The master or commander of a merchant ship, passenger vessel, etc. M17. c The chief sailor of a group having specific duties. E19. 4 A great soldier; an experienced commander; a strategist. L16. 5 The head boy or girl of a school or class. L16. 6 The superintendent of a mine; a foreman; (chiefly *N. Amer.*) a supervisor of a group of waiters, bellboys, etc. E17. 7 As *voc.*: sir. *arch. slang.* E17. 8 The leader of a sports team, sports club, etc. E19. 9 The pilot of a civil aircraft. E20. 10 In the US and elsewhere: a police officer ranking next below a chief officer. E20.

1 H. A. L. FISHER The illustrious Emperor . . the captain of Roman Christianity in the western world. **captain of industry** an industrial magnate. 2b *group captain*: see GROUP *n.* 3 **Captain of the Fleet** the officer on an admiral's staff in charge of maintenance. **captain's biscuit** a hard fancy biscuit. *post captain*: see POST *n.*[4] c *captain of the foretop, hold*, etc. 4 E. A. FREEMAN How great a captain England had in her future king. 7 SHAKES. *Timon* Why, how now, Captain? What do you in this wise company?

Comb.: **captain-general** (*a*) *Hist.* a commander-in-chief, a military governor; (*b*) an honorary rank esp. in the British artillery or Royal Marines; **captain-generalcy** *Hist.* the office or province of a captain-general; **captain-lieutenant** *Hist.* a military officer commanding a company or troop, with a captain's rank and lieutenant's pay.

B *v.t.* Be captain of, lead. L16.

captainess *n.* (now *rare*) a female captain LME. **captainless** *a.* L16. †**captainry** *n.* captaincy; a district under a captain: LME–L18.

Captain Cooker /ˌkaptɪn 'kʊkə/ *n. phr. NZ.* Also (earlier) **Captain Cook**. L19. [f. Capt. James *Cook* (1728–79), navigator and explorer + -ER[1].] A wild boar.

captaincy /'kaptɪnsi/ *n.* E19. [f. CAPTAIN *n.* + -CY.] 1 The position, rank, office, or authority of a captain. E19. 2 A captain's skill, the ability to lead. M19.

captainship /'kaptɪnʃɪp/ *n.* LME. [f. as prec. + -SHIP. Sense 4 tr. Sp. *capitania*.] 1 = CAPTAINCY 1. LME. 2 = CAPTAINCY 2. E17. 3 With possess. adj. (as *your* etc. *captainship*): a mock title of respect given to a captain. Now *rare.* E17. 4 *Hist.* A district in S. America etc. under the rule of a captain. L17.

captation /kap'teɪʃ(ə)n/ *n.* E16. [Fr., or L *captatio(n-)*, *captat-* pa. ppl stem of *captare* frequent. of *capere* seize: see -ATION.] An attempt to acquire something, esp. dexterously; the making of an *ad captandum* appeal.

caption /'kapʃ(ə)n/ *n.* & *v.* LME. [L *captio(n-)*, f. *capt-* pa. ppl stem of *capere* seize: see -ION.] A *n.* 1 a Seizure, capture, taking. Now *rare* or *obs.* in *gen.* sense. LME. b *Law* (orig. *Sc.*, now *Hist.*). Arrest or seizure under civil process; a warrant for the civil arrest of a debtor. L15. 2 A captious argument; a cavil. Now *rare.* L16. 3 *Law.* A certificate attached to or written on a legal instrument detailing before whom it was made. L17. 4 A heading of a chapter, article, etc.; wording appended to an illustration, cartoon, etc.; a (cinema or television) subtitle. Orig. *US.* L18. B *v.t.* Provide with (as) a caption; entitle. E20.

captious /'kapʃəs/ *a.* LME. [(O)Fr. *captieux* or L *captiosus*, f. *captio(n-)*: see prec., -OUS.] 1 Fond of taking exception or raising objections; carping. LME. 2 Apt or intended to deceive; fallacious, misleading. *arch.* LME. †3 Capacious. *rare* (Shakes.). Only in E17.

captiously *adv.* M16. **captiousness** *n.* M16.

†**captivance** *n. rare* (Spenser). Only in L16. [f. CAPTIVE *v.* + -ANCE.] Captivity.

captivate /ˈkaptɪveɪt/ *v.t.* E16. [Late L *captivat-* pa. ppl stem of *captivare*: see CAPTIVE *v.*, -ATE[3].] †1 Subjugate (the mind, reason, etc.) *to*. E16–M19. 2 Enthrall, fascinate, charm. M16. 3 Make or hold captive, capture. Now *rare* or *obs.* M16. b *spec.* = CAPTURE *v.* 2. L18.

†**captivate** *ppl a.* captivated M16–L17. **captivater** *n.* (now *rare*) M17. **captivatingly** *adv.* in a captivating manner M19. **captivator** *n.* M19.

captivation /kaptɪˈveɪʃ(ə)n/ *n.* E17. [Late L *captivatio(n-)*, f. as prec.: see -ATION.] The action of taking or holding captive; the state of being held captive. Now only *fig.*: fascination, enthralment.

captive /ˈkaptɪv/ *a.* & *n.* LME. [L *captivus*, f. *capt-* pa. ppl stem of *capere* seize: see -IVE. Cf. CAITIFF.] A *adj.* 1 Taken prisoner; kept in confinement or under restraint; unable to escape. LME. 2 Of or like a prisoner. L16.

1 R. GRAVES He would bring back the whole Spartan force captive within twenty days. *fig.*: SHAKES. *All's Well* A wife . . whose words all ears took captive. **captive audience**: unable to avoid being addressed etc. **captive balloon**: held by a rope from the ground. *lead captive*: see LEAD *v.*[1] 2 MILTON I sorrowed at his captive state.

B *n.* A person or animal captured, held in confinement, or under restraint. LME.

lead captive: see LEAD *v.*[1]

captive /ˈkaptɪv, *poet. also* kapˈtʌɪv/ *v.t. arch.* L15. [(O)Fr. *captiver* f. late L *captivare*, f. *captivus*: see prec.] Take captive; captivate.

captivity /kapˈtɪvɪti/ *n.* LME. [L *captivitas*, f. as CAPTIVE *a.* & *n.*: see -ITY.] 1 The condition of a captive; the state of being held captive. LME. b *fig.* The subjugation of the mind, reason, etc.; captivation. *arch.* M16. 2 Captives collectively. Chiefly in or after biblical translations. Long *arch.* LME.

1 **the Captivity**: of the Jews in Babylon, 6th cent. BC.

captor /ˈkaptə/ *n.* M16. [L, f. *capt-*: see CAPTIVE *a.* & *n.*, -OR.] A person who takes by force a captive or a prize.

capture /ˈkaptʃə/ *n.* M16. [Fr., f. L *captura*, f. *capt-*: see CAPTIVE *a.* & *n.*, -URE.] I 1 The act of seizing or taking as a prisoner or prize; gaining possession of by force, surprise, stratagem, etc. M16. 2 The capturing of a piece in chess etc. M19. 3 *Physical Geogr.* The diversion of the waters of a stream into the channel of another, due to erosional encroachment by the second stream. L19. 4 *Astron.* The process whereby a less massive body becomes permanently linked gravitationally to a star, planet, etc. E20. 5 *Physics.* The absorption of an atomic or subatomic particle. E20. 6 In full *data capture*. The action or process of entering data into a computer, esp. as an accompaniment to a related operation. M20.

5 *M-capture*: see M, M 6. RADIATIVE *capture*.

II 7 A thing or person captured. E18.

Comb.: **capture myopathy** *Vet. Med.* a condition involving muscular wasting and partial paralysis which affects some wild animals when captured; also called *overstraining disease*.

capture /ˈkaptʃə/ *v.t.* L18. [f. the n.] 1 Effect the capture of; take prisoner; seize or gain as a prize. L18. 2 In *Chess* etc., remove (an opponent's piece) from the board as the rules of the game allow when particular relative positions are taken up or particular moves are made. Cf. earlier CAPTIVATE 3b. E19. 3 *Physical Geogr.* Of a stream etc.: divert the upper course of (another) by encroaching on its basin. E20. 4 *Astron.* Of a star, planet, etc.: bring (a less massive body) permanently within its gravitational influence. E20. 5 *Physics.* Absorb (an atomic or subatomic particle). E20. 6 Put in a relatively permanently accessible form, e.g. by portraiture or photography. M20. b Cause (data) to be entered into a computer. L20.

1 *fig.*: J. BUCHAN A book of Norse mythology which strongly captured my fancy.

capturable *a.* M19. **capturer** *n.* a person who or thing which captures E19.

capuche /kəˈpuːʃ/ *n.* Also **capouch**. L16. [Fr. (now *capuce*), f. It. *cappuccio*: see next.] The hood of a cloak, *esp.* that of a Capuchin.

capuchin /ˈkap(j)ʊtʃɪn/ *n.* In sense 1 **C-**. L16. [Fr. (now *capucin*) f. It. *cappuccino*, f. *cappuccio* hood, cowl, augm. of *cappa* CAPE *n.*[2]] 1 More fully *Capuchin Friar* etc. A Franciscan friar of the new rule of 1528 (so called from the sharp-pointed capuche adopted by the order). L16. 2 *Hist.* A woman's cloak and hood resembling the dress of a Capuchin. M18. 3 In full *capuchin pigeon*. A variety of jacobin. M18. 4 In full *capuchin monkey*. Any of various monkeys of the genus *Cebus*, of Central and S. America, with head hair suggestive of a cowl. L18.

capul *n.* var. of CAPLE.

caput /ˈkapət/ *n. obs.* exc. *Hist.* E18. [L = head.] The former ruling body of Cambridge University; *occas.* a member of this.

caput mortuum /ˌkapət ˈmɔːtuːəm/ *n. phr.* M17. [L = dead head.] †1 A death's head, a skull. Only in M17. 2 *Alch.* The residue remaining after distillation or sublimation. M17. 3 Worthless residue. E18.

caput succedaneum /ˌkapət sʌksɪˈdeɪnɪəm/ *n. phr.* Pl. **capita succedanea** /ˌkapɪtə sʌksɪˈdeɪnɪə/. M19. [mod.L, lit. 'substitute head'.] *Med.* A temporary swelling of the head of an infant during childbirth resulting from compression by the birth canal.

capybara /kapɪˈbɑːrə/ *n.* E17. [Sp. *capibara* or Port. *capivara*, f. Tupi *capiuára*, f. *capĩ* grass + *uára* eater.] A large tailless river-dwelling rodent, *Hydrochoerus hydrochaeris*, of Central and S. America, resembling a guinea-pig.

car /kɑː/ *n.* LME. [AN, ONFr. *carre* f. Proto-Romance var. of L *carrum* neut., *carrus* masc., f. Celt. base repr. by (O)Ir. *carr*, Welsh *car*.] 1 *gen.* A wheeled conveyance, a carriage. Without specification of type now *rare*. LME. 2 A sledge, a sleigh. Long *obs.* exc. *Sc.* & *Canad. dial.* LME. 3 A chariot, esp. of war, triumph, or pageantry. *literary*. L16. 4 The passenger compartment of a balloon, airship, cableway, etc. L18. b The cage of a lift. Chiefly *US*. L19. 5 A railway carriage or van; a tramway vehicle. Chiefly *N. Amer.* exc. as 2nd elem. of comb. E19. b As many or as much as a railway car will hold; a carload. *N. Amer.* M19. 6 A usu. four-wheeled motorized vehicle for use on roads, able to carry a small number of people; an automobile. L19.

1 *jaunting car*: see JAUNT *v. side-car*: see SIDE *n.* 3 TENNYSON A reverent people behold The towering car, the sable steeds. 5 *boxcar, buffet car, dining-car, freight car, observation car, railcar, sleeping-car, streetcar*, etc. 6 *bubble car, estate car, racing car, rally car, sports car*, etc.

Comb.: **car bomb** a bomb concealed by terrorists under or in a (usu. parked) car; **car-boot sale** an outdoor sale at which people sell unwanted possessions from the boots of their cars; **car coat** a short coat designed esp. for motorists; **carfare** *N. Amer.* a passenger's fare to travel by streetcar, bus, etc.; **carhop** *US colloq.* a waiter at a drive-in restaurant etc.; **carload** (*a*) as many or as much as can be carried in a car; (*b*) *US* a minimum quantity of goods for which a lower rate is charged for transport; **carman** a driver of a van etc., a carrier; **car park** a space or building for parking cars; **car-phone** a radio telephone for use in a car; **car pool** *N. Amer.* an arrangement for sharing a car for regular travelling, a group of people with such an arrangement; **car-pool** *v.i.* (*N. Amer.*) form or join a car pool, share a car for regular travelling; **car pooler** *N. Amer.* a member of a car pool; **carport** a roofed open-sided shelter for a car; **carsick** *a.* affected with carsickness; **carsickness** nausea caused by the motion of a motor car; **car wash** (an establishment with) a piece of equipment for washing cars automatically.

carabid /ˈkarəbɪd/ *n.* & *a.* L19. [mod.L *Carabidae* (see below), f. L *carabus* a kind of crab: see -ID[3].] (A large carnivorous beetle) of the family Carabidae.

caˈrabidan *n.* (now *rare* or *obs.*) = CARABID *n.* M19. **caraˈbideous** *a.* = CARABID *a.* M19.

†**carabine** *n.* var. of CARBINE.

carabineer /karəbɪˈnɪə/ *n.* Also **-ier**. M17. [Fr. *carabinier*, f. as CARBINE: see -EER.] A cavalry soldier armed with a carbine.

the Carabiniers a former regiment of Dragoon Guards, now incorporated in the Royal Scots Dragoon Guards.

carabinero /karabiˈnero, karəbɪˈnɛːrəʊ/ *n.* Pl. **-os** /-ɔs, -əʊz/. M19. [Sp., lit. = CARABINEER.] A (Spanish) customs or revenue officer; a (Spanish) frontier guard.

carabinier *n.* var. of CARABINEER.

carabiniere /karabiˈnjere, karəbɪˈnjɛːri/ *n.* Pl. **-ri** /-ri/. M19. [It., lit. = CARABINEER.] An Italian soldier in a corps serving as a police force.

caracal /ˈkarəkal/ *n.* M18. [Fr. or Sp., f. Turk. *karakulak*, f. *kara* black + *kulak* ear.] A lynxlike feline, *Felis caracal*, of Africa and SW Asia.

caracara /karəˈkɑːrə/ *n.* M19. [Sp. or Port. *caracará*, f. Tupi-Guarani, of imit. origin.] Any of several mainly neotropical raptors of the family Falconidae that are related to the falcons but somewhat resemble vultures.

common caracara a caracara, *Polyborus plancus*, of S. America and southern N. America.

caracole /ˈkarəkəʊl/ *n.* Also **-ol** /-ɒl/. E17. [Sense 1 f. Fr. *caracol(e)* snail's shell, spiral; sense 2 f. as next.] †1 a A spiral shell. Only in E17. b *Archit.* A helical staircase. *rare.* E18. 2 A half-turn or wheel to the right or left by a horse or rider. Formerly also, a series of such turns alternately to right and left. E17.

caracole /ˈkarəkəʊl/ *v.* Also **-ol** /-ɒl/. M17. [Fr. *caracoler*, f. *caracol(e)*: see prec.] 1 *v.i.* Of a horse or rider: execute a caracole; *loosely* prance about. M17. 2 *v.t.* Make (a horse) caracole. M19.

†**caract** *n.*[1] var. of CARAT.

†**caract** *n.*[2] var. of CHARACT.

caracul *n.* & *a.* var. of KARAKUL.

carafe /kəˈraf, -ˈrɑːf/ *n.* L18. [Fr. f. It. *caraffa*, of unkn. origin.] A glass bottle for water or wine at a table, in a bedroom, etc.

caragana /karəˈgɑːnə/ *n.* M19. [mod.L (see below), of Turkic origin.] Any of various leguminous shrubs and trees of the genus *Caragana*, native to central Asia and Siberia and widely planted in N. America; *esp.* the Siberian pea-tree, *C. arborescens*.

†**Caraite** *n.* & *a.* see KARAITE.

carama *n.* var. of SERIEMA.

caramba /kəˈrambə, *foreign* kaˈramba/ *int.* M19. [Sp.] Expr. surprise or dismay.

carambola /kar(ə)mˈbəʊlə/ *n.* L16. [Port., prob. f. Marathi *karambal*.] A SE Asian tree, *Averrhoa carambola*, of the oxalis family; its astringent yellow fruit (also called *star fruit*).

carambole /ˈkar(ə)mbəʊl/ *n.* & *v.i.* L18. [Sp. *carambola* (whence Fr. *carambole* red ball in billiards), app. f. *bola* ball.] (Make) a cannon in billiards.

caramel /ˈkarəmɛl, -m(ə)l/ *n.* & *v.* E18. [Fr. f. Sp. *caramelo*.] A *n.* 1 Burnt sugar or syrup used for colouring spirits etc.; (a) toffee made with sugar that has been melted and heated further. E18. 2 A light-brown colour. Freq. *attrib.* E20.

See also *crème caramel* s.v. CRÈME 1.

B *v.t.* & *i.* = next. E18.

caramelize /ˈkar(ə)məlʌɪz/ *v.t.* & *i.* Also **-ise**. M19. [Fr. *caraméliser*, f. as prec.: see -IZE.] Turn into caramel.

carameliˈzation *n.* L19.

Carancahua *n.* & *a.* var. of KARANKAWA.

carangid /kəˈrandʒɪd/ *n.* & *a.* L19. [mod.L *Carangidae* (see below), f. *Caranx* genus name: see -ID[3].] (A percoid fish) of the large family Carangidae, which includes the scads and pompanos.

Also **carangoid** *n.* & *a.* M19.

carap(a) *n.* see CRAB *n.*[3]

carapace /ˈkarəpeɪs/ *n.* Also †**-pax**. M19. [Fr. f. Sp. *carapacho*, of unkn. origin.] The upper shell of a tortoise, crustacean, etc.

fig.: N. BAWDEN I wanted to hurt you. Get through that carapace of self-regard somehow.

carapaced *a.* having a carapace L19.

cara sposa /ˈkaːra ˈspoːza/ *n. phr.* Pl. **care spose** /ˈkaːre ˈspoːze/. L18. [It.] (One's) dear wife; a devoted wife. Cf. CARO SPOSO.

carat /ˈkarət/ *n.* Also †**-act**, ***k-**. LME. [Fr. f. It. *carato* f. Arab. *ḳīrāṭ* weight equal to one twenty-fourth of a *miskal*, f. Gk *keration* fruit of the carob, dim. of *keras* horn.] **1** A proportional measure of one twenty-fourth used in stating the purity of gold (pure gold being 24 carats). LME. **2** A unit of weight used for precious stones, equal to 200 milligrams. M16. †**3** *fig.* Worth, value. L16–L17.

1 *twenty-four carat*: see TWENTY *n.* 3 SHAKES. *2 Hen. IV* Therefore thou best of gold art worst of gold. Other, less fine in carat, is more precious.

caratch /kəˈratʃ, -ɑːtʃ/ *n. obs.* exc. *Hist.* Also **ha-**. L17. [Turk. f. Arab. *ḵarāj* land tax, tax.] A tribute levied by the Ottoman Turks on their Christian subjects.

caravan /ˈkarəvan, karəˈvan/ *n.* & *v.* L15. [Fr. *caravane* f. Pers. *kārwān*. Cf. VAN *n.*[3]] **A** *n.* **1** A company of merchants, pilgrims, etc., travelling together, esp. across the desert in Asia or N. Africa. L15. †**2** A fleet of Turkish or Russian (merchant) ships. L16–M18. **3** *gen.* A travelling company of people. M17. **4** A covered carriage or cart (cf. VAN *n.*[3]). Now usu. a dwelling on wheels, able to be towed by a horse or a motor vehicle. L17.

4 *motor caravan*: see MOTOR *n.* & *a.*

Comb.: **caravan park, site** a place where caravans may be parked as holiday accommodation or as more permanent dwellings.

B *v.i.* Infl. **-nn-**. Travel or live in a caravan; spend a holiday in a caravan. L19.

caravaˈneer *n.* = CARAVANNER M18. **caravaˈnette** *n.* a motor vehicle furnished with beds and other domestic equipment M20. **caravanner** *n.* (*a*) a person who lives, travels, or spends holidays in a caravan; (*b*) a leader of a (travelling) caravan: E20. **caraˈvette** *n.* = CARAVANETTE M20.

†**caravance** *n.* see CALAVANCE.

caravanserai /karəˈvansərʌɪ, -ri/ *n.* Also **-sary, -sery**, & other vars. L16. [Pers. *kārwānsarāy*, f. *kārwān* (see CARAVAN) + as SERAI *n.*[1]] An Eastern inn with a large inner court where caravans rest.

caravel /ˈkarəvɛl/ *n.* E16. [Fr. *caravelle*: see CARVEL.] *Hist.* A small light fast ship, chiefly Spanish or Portuguese, of the 15th to the 17th cents.

caraway /ˈkarəweɪ/ *n.* ME. [med.L *carui* or allied Romance form f. Arab. *karawiyā*, prob. ult. f. Gk *karon* cumin.] An umbelliferous European plant, *Carum carvi*; (in full *caraway seed*) the small aromatic fruit of this, used in cakes etc. and as a source of oil.

carb /kɑːb/ *n.* *colloq.* M20. [Abbrev.] = CARBURETTOR.

carb- *comb. form* see CARBO-.

carbamic /kɑːˈbamɪk/ *a.* M19. [f. as next + -IC.] Chem. *carbamic acid*, the hypothetical compound NH_2COOH, of which many salts and esters are known.

ˈcarbamate *n.* a salt or ester of carbamic acid (cf. URETHANE 1) M19.

carbamide /ˈkɑːbəmʌɪd/ *n.* M19. [f. CARBO- + AMIDE.] *Chem.* = UREA 1.

carbamyl *n.* the radical $NH_2CO\cdot$ E20.

carbide /ˈkɑːbʌɪd/ *n.* M19. [f. CARBON *n.* + -IDE.] **1** *Chem.* A binary compound of carbon with an element of lower or comparable electronegativity. M19. **2** *spec.* Calcium carbide, CaC_2, used to generate acetylene by reaction with water. L19.

1 SILICON *carbide*. *sintered carbide*: see SINTER *v.* TUNGSTEN *carbide*.

carbine /ˈkɑːbʌɪn/ *n.* Also †**carabine**. E17. [Fr. *carabine*, f. *carabin* mounted musketeer, of uncertain origin.] A short rifle or smooth-bored gun orig. for use by cavalry.

Spencer carbine: see SPENCER *n.*[1] 4.

carbinol /ˈkɑːbɪnɒl/ *n.* M19. [f. CARBON *n.* + -INE[5] + -OL.] *Chem.* A monohydric alcohol; *spec.* methanol. Usu. in *comb.*

¶ Chiefly in names of more complex alcohols w. preceding radical name.

carbo- /ˈkɑːbəʊ/ *comb. form.* Bef. a vowel **carb-**. [f. CARBON *n.*: see -O-.] *Chem.* Of or containing carbon.

carbanion /kɑːˈbanʌɪən/ *n.* an organic anion in which a carbon atom bears the negative charge M20. **carbazole** *n.* a crystalline tricyclic heteroaromatic compound, $C_{12}H_9N$, present in coal tar L19. **carbene** *n.* a compound of divalent carbon, examples of which occur as intermediates in some organic reactions M20. **carboˈcyclic** *a.* containing a ring or rings of carbon atoms only L19.

carbohydrate /kɑːbəˈhʌɪdreɪt/ *n.* M19. [f. prec. + HYDRATE *n.*] *Chem.* Any of a class of organic compounds that contain hydrogen and oxygen in the same ratio as water (2:1), and can be broken down to release energy in the animal body, e.g. sugars, starch, and other polysaccharides.

carbolic /kɑːˈbɒlɪk/ *a.* & *n.* M19. [f. CARBO- + -OL + -IC.] **A** *adj.* *carbolic acid*, = PHENOL 1; *carbolic soap*, soap containing phenol as a disinfectant. M19. **B** *n.* Carbolic acid or soap. L19.

ˈcarbolate *v.t.* treat or impregnate with phenol (chiefly as *carbolated* ppl a.) L19. **ˈcarbolize** *v.t.* = CARBOLATE L19.

carbon /ˈkɑːb(ə)n/ *n.* L18. [Fr. *carbone* f. L *carbon-*, *carbo* coal.] **1** A non-metallic chemical element, atomic no. 6, which occurs in crystalline form as diamond and graphite, in amorphous form as coal and charcoal, and is the basis of all organic compounds. (Symbol C.) L18. **2** An electrode made of carbon, esp. in an arc lamp. M19. **3** A piece of carbon paper; a carbon copy. L19.

1 *activated, active, carbon*: see ACTIVATE *v.* 1, ACTIVE *a.* 5. PYROLYTIC *carbon*. RADIOCARBON.

Comb.: **carbon-black** an amorphous form of carbon suitable for use as a pigment, e.g. lampblack; **carbon copy** a copy made with carbon paper; *fig.* an exact copy; **carbon cycle** (*a*) *Biol.* the continuous transfer of carbon in various forms from the atmosphere to living organisms by plant photosynthesis, and back to the atmosphere by respiration and decay; (*b*) *Astron.* a thermonuclear chain reaction postulated to occur within stars, in which carbon nuclei act as catalysts in the fusion of hydrogen to form helium; **carbon dating** = *radiocarbon dating* s.v. RADIOCARBON; **carbon dioxide** a colourless odourless unreactive gas, CO_2, formed by combustion of carbon and in breathing; **carbon disulphide** a colourless toxic liquid, CS_2, used as a solvent for rubber; **carbon fibre** a thin strong polycrystalline filament of carbon, freq. incorporated in plastic etc. as a strengthening material; **carbon-14** a radioactive carbon isotope of mass number 14, used in isotopic dating (cf. RADIOCARBON); **carbon microphone** a microphone depending for its action on the varying electrical resistance of carbon granules; **carbon monoxide** a poisonous, colourless, odourless gas, CO, formed by the incomplete combustion of carbon; **carbon paper** thin paper coated with carbon or another pigmented material, used to make copies of anything written or typed upon it; **carbon steel** any steel whose properties are mainly determined by its carbon content; **carbon tetrachloride** a colourless toxic liquid, CCl_4, used as a solvent in dry cleaning etc.

carbonless *a.* M19.

carbon /ˈkɑːb(ə)n/ *v.* E20. [f. the n.] **1** *v.t.* (usu. in *pass.*) & *i.* Coat or become coated with carbon. E20. **2** *v.t.* Make a carbon copy of. M20.

carbonaceous /kɑːbəˈneɪʃəs/ *a.* L18. [f. CARBON *n.* + -ACEOUS.] Of the nature of or like coal or charcoal; consisting of or containing carbon.

carbonade /kɑːbəˈnɑːd, -ˈneɪd/ *n.* In sense 2 also **-nn-**. M17. [Fr., f. as CARBON *n.*: see -ADE.] **1** = CARBONADO *n.*[1] *rare.* M17. **2** A rich beef stew made with onions and beer. L19.

†**carbonade** *v.t.* L16–M18. [f. as prec.] = CARBONADO *v.*

carbonado /kɑːbəˈneɪdəʊ/ *n.*[1] & *v.* L16. [Sp. *carbonada*, f. *carbon* coal ult. f. L *carbon-*: see CARBON *n.*, -ADO.] **A** *n.* Pl. **-os**. A piece of meat or fish which is scored across and broiled on coals. Long *arch.* L16. **B** *v.t.* Score across and broil (meat or fish); *transf.* cut, slash, hack. L16.

carbonado /kɑːbəˈneɪdəʊ/ *n.*[2] Pl. **-os**. M19. [Port.] A dark opaque kind of diamond used as an abrasive etc.

Carbonari /kɑːbəˈnɑːri/ *n.pl.* Also (*rare*) in sing. **-naro** /-ˈnɑːrəʊ/. E19. [It. pl. of *carbonaro* collier, charcoal-burner, f. *carbone* coal ult. f. L *carbon-* CARBON *n.*] *Hist.* The members of a secret republican association in the kingdom of Naples in the early 19th cent.

Carbonarism *n.* the political principles of the Carbonari or similar revolutionaries M19.

carbonate /ˈkɑːbəneɪt/ *n.* L18. [f. CARBON *n.* + -ATE[1].] *Chem.* A salt or ester of carbonic acid.

carbonate of lime: see LIME *n.*[1]

carbonate /ˈkɑːbəneɪt/ *v.t.* L18. [In sense 1, f. CARBON *n.* + -ATE[3]; in sense 2 f. the n.] †**1** Carbonize; combine with carbon. Freq. as *carbonated* ppl a. L18–M19. **2** Convert into carbonate; impregnate with carbon dioxide, aerate. Freq. as *carbonated* ppl a. E19.

carboˈnation *n.* L19. **carbonator** *n.* a person who or thing which carbonates L19.

carbonatite /kɑːˈbɒnətʌɪt/ *n.* E20. [f. CARBONATE *n.* + -ITE[1].] *Geol.* Any igneous rock composed chiefly of carbonates rather than silicates.

carbonic /kɑːˈbɒnɪk/ *a.* L18. [f. CARBON *n.* + -IC.] *Chem.* Of or pertaining to carbon; *carbonic acid*, a weak dibasic acid, H_2CO_3, formed in aqueous solutions of carbon dioxide.

carbonic acid gas *arch.* carbon dioxide. †**carbonic paper** carbon paper.

carboniferous /kɑːbəˈnɪf(ə)rəs/ *a.* & *n.* In *Geol.* usu. **C-**. L18. [f. as prec. + -I- + -FEROUS.] **A** *adj.* **1** Producing or yielding coal. *rare.* L18. **2** *Geol.* Designating or pertaining to the fifth period of the Palaeozoic era, following the Devonian and preceding the Permian, in which many coal deposits were formed. E19. **B** *n.* *Geol.* The Carboniferous period; the system of rocks dating from this time. L19.

carbonise *v.* var. of CARBONIZE.

carbonium /kɑːˈbəʊnɪəm/ *n.* E20. [f. CARBO- after *ammonium*.] *Chem.* In full *carbonium ion*. An organic cation in which the positive charge is borne by a carbon atom.

carbonize /ˈkɑːbənʌɪz/ *v.t.* Also **-ise**. E19. [f. CARBON *n.* + -IZE.] **1** Convert into carbon; reduce to charcoal or coke; char. E19. †**2** Carburize. Only in 19. **3** Coat (paper) with carbon for use in copying. L19.

carboniˈzation *n.* E19. **carbonizer** *n.* a person who or thing which carbonizes E20.

carbonnade *n.* see CARBONADE *n.*

carbonyl /ˈkɑːbənʌɪl, -nɪl/ *n.* M19. [f. CARBON *n.* + -YL.] *Chem.* The divalent group :CO, present in ketones, aldehydes, etc.; usu. in *comb.* Also, (a complex containing) carbon monoxide bonded to a metal atom as a neutral ligand.

carbonyˈlation *n.* the introduction of a carbonyl group into a compound M20.

carborundum /kɑːbəˈrʌndəm/ *n.* Also (US proprietary name) **C-**. L19. [f. as prec. + CORUNDUM.] = SILICON *carbide*.

carboxy- /kɑːˈbɒksi/ *comb. form.* [f. CARBO- + OXY-.] *Chem.* Usu. denoting the presence of the carboxyl group.

carboxyhaemoˈglobin *n.* a compound of haemoglobin and carbon monoxide, formed in the blood when carbon monoxide is inhaled L19.

carboxyl /kɑːˈbɒksʌɪl, -sɪl/ *n.* M19. [f. as prec. + -YL.] *Chem.* The acidic radical $\cdot COOH$, present in most organic acids. Usu. in *comb.*

carboxylate *n.* & *v.* (*a*) a salt or ester of a carboxylic acid; (*b*) *v.t.* introduce a carboxyl group into (a compound etc.): L19. **carboxyˈlation** *n.* the introduction of a carboxyl group into a compound E20. **carboxylic** /kɑːbɒkˈsɪlɪk/ *a.* containing the carboxyl group L19.

carboy /ˈkɑːbɔɪ/ *n.* M18. [Ult. f. Pers. *ḳarāba* large glass flagon.] A large globular bottle, usu. of coloured glass and protected by a frame, used chiefly for holding acids and other corrosive liquids.

carbuncle /ˈkɑːbʌŋk(ə)l/ *n.* ME. [OFr. *charbu(n)cle* etc. f. L *carbunculus* small coal: see CARBON *n.*, -UNCLE.] **1** A red precious stone; *spec.* a garnet cut in a boss shape. ME. **2** *Her.* = ESCARBUNCLE. LME. **3** A severe abscess, esp. on the neck; a multiple boil; a red facial spot or pimple. M16.

carbuncled *a.* †(*a*) adorned with carbuncles (sense 1); (*b*) affected with carbuncles (sense 3); †(*c*) (of earth) parched by the sun: L16. **carbuncly** *a.* of or like a carbuncle; bearing carbuncles: L19. **car'buncular** *a.* of the nature of or resembling a carbuncle (sense 3); affected with carbuncles: M18. **car'bunculous** *a.* = CARBUNCULAR E17.

carburation /kɑːbjʊˈreɪʃ(ə)n/ *n.* Also ***-retion** /-ˈrɛʃ(ə)n/. L19. [f. CARBURET *v.* + -ATION.] The action of a carburettor.

†carburator *n.* var. of CARBURETTOR.

carburet /ˈkɑːbjʊrɛt/ *n. arch.* L18. [f. CARBO- + -URET.] *Chem.* = CARBIDE 1.

carburet /kɑːbjʊˈrɛt/ *v.t.* Infl. **-tt-, -t-.** E19. [f. the n.] Charge with hydrocarbons; provide with a carburettor; *arch.* combine or charge with carbon. Chiefly as *carburetted* ppl a.

carburetion *n.* see CARBURATION.

carburettor /kɑːbjʊˈrɛtə, -bə-/ *n.* Also **-etter, *-etor, †-ator.** M19. [f. prec. + -OR.] An apparatus for charging air with a fine spray of liquid fuel for combustion, esp. in a petrol engine.

twin carburettor: see TWIN *a.* & *n.*

carburize /ˈkɑːbjʊrʌɪz/ *v.t.* Also **-ise.** M19. [f. as prec. + -IZE.] Chiefly *Metall.* Combine with carbon; add carbon to (iron).

carburi'zation *n.* M19.

carbylamine /kɑːˈbʌɪləmiːn/ *n.* M19. [f. CARBO- + -YL + AMINE.] *Chem.* An isocyanide; *obs.* exc. w. ref. to a test for amines (the *carbylamine test*) depending on the generation of an isocyanide.

carcajou /ˈkɑːkədʒuː, -əʒuː/ *n. N. Amer.* E18. [Canad. Fr., f. Montagnais *kwa:hkwa:če:w.*] = WOLVERINE 1.

carcake /ˈkɑːkeɪk/ *n. Sc.* E19. [f. CARE *n.* 1 + CAKE *n.*] A small cake baked with eggs, eaten on Shrove Tuesday in parts of Scotland.

†carcan *n.* M16. [Fr. = Prov. *carcan*, med.L *carcannum*, It. *carcome*, ult. f. Gmc.] 1 An iron collar used for punishment. M16–L18. 2 = next. M16–L17.

carcanet /ˈkɑːkənɛt/ *n. arch.* M16. [f. prec. + -ET[1].] A collar or necklace, usu. of gold or jewelled.

carcass /ˈkɑːkəs/ *n.* In branch I also **-ase.** ME. [AN *carcois* (= OFr. *charcois*) & Fr. *carcasse*; in AL *carcasium, -osium, -oisum*: ult. origin unkn.] **I 1** A human corpse (now *derog.*); the dead body of an animal; *spec.* the trunk of a slaughtered animal, without the hide, head, or offal. ME. 2 Orig., the living body of a person or animal considered in its material nature. Now only *joc.* or *derog.*, the human body. LME. 3 *fig.* A shell or husk; the decaying skeleton *of* a building, ship, etc. L16. 4 The skeleton or framework upon which a building, ship, piece of furniture, etc., is built up; the foundation of a motor-vehicle tyre. M17. 5 The bones of a cooked bird. L19.

2 W. RALEIGH His Trances proceeded through the weakness of his earthly Carcase. R. L. STEVENSON For what would they risk their carcasses but money? 3 S. O'FAOLÁIN The carcase of the abandoned car lay damming the . . stream. A. THWAITE The carcasses of marriages of friends. 4 R. V. JONES The extremely light carcase of the rocket was . . based on Zeppelin-type construction.

II 6 *Hist.* A spherical projectile filled with combustible material to ignite buildings etc. L17.

Comb.: **carcass meat** raw meat as distinct from corned or tinned meat.

carcass /ˈkɑːkəs/ *v.t.* E17. [f. the n.] 1 Make a carcass of (an animal, *rarely* a person). E17. 2 Put up the carcass of (a building). L19.

¶Rare bef. L19.

carcel lamp /ˈkɑːs(ə)l lamp/ *n. phr.* M19. [f. *Carcel*, its Fr. inventor.] *Hist.* A lamp in which oil is pumped up to the wick by clockwork.

carceral /ˈkɑːs(ə)r(ə)l/ *a.* L16. [Late L *carceralis*, f. *carcer* prison: see -AL[1].] Of or belonging to a prison.

carcinogen /kɑːˈsɪnədʒ(ə)n/ *n.* M19. [f. CARCINOMA + -GEN.] A substance which is able to cause cancer (strictly, carcinoma).

¶Rare bef. M20.

carcinogenic /ˌkɑːs(ɪ)nəˈdʒɛnɪk/ *a.* E20. [f. as prec. + -GENIC.] Able to cause cancer (strictly, carcinoma); cancer-producing.

carcinogenesis *n.* the production or origin of cancer E20. **carcinogenicity** /-ˈnɪsɪti/ *n.* M20.

carcinoid /ˈkɑːsɪnɔɪd/ *a.* & *n.* L19. [f. CARCINOMA + -OID.] *Med.* **A** *adj.* †1 = CANCROID *a.* 2. Only in L19. 2 Of, pertaining to or of the nature of a carcinoid; associated with carcinoids. E20. **B** *n.* = ARGENTAFFINOMA. E20.

carcinology /kɑːsɪˈnɒlədʒi/ *n.* M19. [f. Gk *karkinos* crab + -OLOGY.] The zoological study of crabs and other crustaceans.

carcino'logical *a.* M19. **carcinologist** *n.* L19.

carcinoma /kɑːsɪˈnəʊmə/ *n.* Pl. **-mas, -mata** /-mətə/. E18. [L f. Gk *karkinōma, -mat-*, f. as prec. + -OMA.] *Med.* A cancer; now *spec.* a malignant tumour of epithelial origin.

ˌcarcinoma'tosis *n.* widespread dissemination of carcinoma in the body E20. **carcinomatous** *a.* of the nature of or characterized by carcinoma E18.

carcoon /kɑːˈkuːn/ *n.* Also **karkun.** E19. [Hind. *kārkun* f. Pers. = manager.] In the Indian subcontinent: a clerk.

card /kɑːd/ *n.*[1] LME. [(O)Fr. *carde* f. Prov. *carda*, f. *cardar* tease, comb, f. pop.L f. L *carere* to card.] A toothed instrument, wire brush, etc., for raising the nap on cloth or for disentangling the fibres of wool, hemp, etc., before spinning.

card /kɑːd/ *n.*[2] LME. [(O)Fr. *carte* f. L *charta* papyrus-leaf, paper f. Gk *khartēs* papyrus-leaf. Cf. CHART *n.*] 1 A flat object, typically oblong and made from layers of pasteboard pressed together, used with similar objects in a pack for playing various games, such objects being uniquely identifiable and distinguishable from one another by markings on the face (according to rank, suit, etc., in a conventional pack (see PLAYING-*card*)) but not from the back. LME. b In *pl.* A game or games played with cards; card-playing. LME. c *fig.* A plan or expedient of specified likelihood of success. M16. 2a A map, a plan; a chart. *obs.* exc. *dial.* E16. b A circular piece of stiff paper etc. bearing the thirty-two points of the compass. Also *compass card.* L16. 3 A flat (usu. rectangular) piece of thick paper, thin pasteboard, etc., or now (esp. where durability is required) of plastic, blank or bearing writing, print, a picture, etc., and of various kinds for particular purposes (identified contextually or specified), as conveying an invitation, greeting, or message, displaying rules, information, etc., identifying the bearer or owner, recording membership, registration, or admission, etc. L16. b *spec.* A programme of events at a race meeting etc. Also, a score-card. M19. c In full *punched card.* A piece of stiff paper etc. punched with holes in a certain pattern to represent specific information. M19. d In *pl.* An employee's documents held by an employer. *colloq.* E20. 4 A published advertisement, notice, etc. *US.* M18. 5 A backing of pasteboard etc. to which several small objects, or samples of a commercial product, are fastened. M18. 6 A person with a specified quality or specified qualities; an eccentric person, a character. *colloq.* E19. 7 Pasteboard, cardboard. M20. 8 *Electronics.* A printed circuit board. L20.

1 *court-card, high card, picture card, tarot card, trump card*, etc. **a card up one's sleeve** a plan in reserve, a hidden advantage. *force a card*: see FORCE *v.*[1] *house of cards*: see HOUSE *n.*[1] **lay, put,** etc. **(all) one's cards on the table** disclose (all) one's plans or resources. **on,** (*N. Amer.*) **in, the cards** likely, possible. *pair of cards*: see PAIR *n.*[1] 1. **play one's cards right, well,** etc., carry out a scheme successfully, act cleverly. **play the — card** introduce a specified (advantageous) usu. political factor. *show one's cards*: see SHOW *v.* *stack the cards (against a person)*: see STACK *v.* 3. *wild card*: see WILD *a., n.,* & *adv.* b *short cards*: see SHORT *a.* c *doubtful card, safe card, sure card*, etc. 2b *fig.*: R. HOOKER That Law . . is the Card to guide the World by. **speak by the card** *arch.* express oneself carefully, be precise. 3 *bank card, birthday card, business card, cheque card, Christmas card, cigarette card, credit card, identity card, index card, invitation card, membership card, party card, phone card, postcard, score-card, show-card, time-card, valentine card, visiting-card, wedding-card*, etc. *green card*: see GREEN *a.* *leave a card on a person*: see LEAVE *v.*[1] *red card*: see RED *a.* *yellow card*: see YELLOW *a.* b **mark a person's card** tip possible winners at a race meeting; *fig.* give prior information or advice. *race card*: see RACE *n.*[1] d **ask for, get, one's cards** resign, be dismissed from employment. 5 R. RENDELL Handkerchiefs, a box of tissues, a card of hairclips. 6 DICKENS Potter whose great aim it was to be considered as a 'knowing card'. ARNOLD BENNETT It would be . . a topic for years, the crown of his reputation as a card.

Comb.: **card-carrying** *a.* having a valid (and usu. publicly-known) membership of a political party or other organization; **card case** a case for visiting-cards; **card-game**: using playing-cards; **card index**: in which each item is entered on a separate card; **card-index** *v.t.* make a card index of; **cardmember** a holder of a particular credit or charge card; **cardphone** a public telephone operated by means of a prepaid card; **card player, -playing** a person who plays, the playing of, card-games; **card-room** a room for playing cards; **card-sharp, -sharper** a swindler at card-games; **card-swipe** an electronic reader through which a credit or charge card etc. is passed to record its number etc.; **card-table** a table, usu. one which folds, designed for card-playing; **card trick** a conjuring trick using playing-cards; **card vote** = *block vote* s.v. BLOCK *n.*

card /kɑːd/ *v.*[1]*t.* LME. [f. CARD *n.*[1]] 1 Prepare, cleanse, or comb (wool etc.) with a card; raise the nap on (cloth) with a card. LME. 2 Lacerate (as) with a card. M16. †3 Stir and mix (as if) with a card. L16–M17.

1 **carding-wool** short-stapled wool.

carder *n.*[1] a person who or thing which cards wool etc.; *carder bee*, any of various bumble-bees which make a nest of moss or grass shreds above ground: LME.

card /kɑːd/ *v.*[2] L15. [f. CARD *n.*[2]] 1 *v.i.* Play cards. Now *rare.* L15. 2 *v.t.* Write or print on a card; enter in a card index. M19. 3 *v.t.* Communicate (with) by card. L19. 4 *v.t.* Affix to a card. L19.

carder *n.*[2] (*obs.* exc. *dial.*) a card-player LME.

cardamom /ˈkɑːdəməm/ *n.* Also **-mum.** LME. [(O)Fr. *cardamome* or L *cardamomum* f. Gk *kardamōmon*, f. *kardamon* cress + *amōmon* AMOMUM.] A spice consisting of or made from the seed capsules of various Indo-Malayan plants, esp. *Elettaria cardamomum*; a plant yielding this.

cardan /ˈkɑːd(ə)n/ *n.* Also **C-.** M18. [f. *Cardan* (Gerolamo Cardano (1501–76), It. mathematician).] Used *attrib.* and in *possess.* to designate things associated with Cardan.

cardan joint a universal joint. **Cardan's formula** *Math.* a formula for finding the roots of a cubic equation after it has been reduced to a form without a quadratic term. **Cardan's rule** = *Cardan's formula* above. **cardan shaft** a shaft with a universal joint at one or both ends.

cardboard /ˈkɑːdbɔːd/ *n.* & *a.* M19. [f. CARD *n.*[2] + BOARD *n.*] **A** *n.* 1 A pasteboard used esp. for cutting cards from or for making boxes etc. M19. 2 *fig.* Something insubstantial. L19. **B** *adj.* 1 Made of cardboard. M19. 2 *fig.* Insubstantial, artificial. L19.

Comb.: **cardboard city** an area where homeless people make shelters from cardboard packing cases.

cardboardy *a.* = CARDBOARD *a.* E20.

cardecu /ˈkɑːdɪkjuː/ *n.* E17. [Fr. *quart d'écu* quarter of an ÉCU.] *Hist.* An old French silver coin worth a quarter of the gold *écu.*

cardi *n.* var. of CARDIE.

cardia /ˈkɑːdɪə/ *n.* L18. [Gk *kardia* (also = heart).] *Anat.* The upper opening of the stomach, where the oesophagus enters.

cardiac /ˈkɑːdɪak/ *n.* & *a.* LME. [Fr. *cardiaque* or L *cardiacus* adjs., f. Gk *kardiakos*, f. *kardia*: see prec., -AC.] **A** *n.* †1 A pain or ailment referred to the heart. LME–L15. 2 A medicine etc. affecting the heart; a cordial. Now *rare* or *obs.* M18. 3 A person with heart disease. *colloq.* M20.

B *adj.* 1 Of or pertaining to the heart. E17. 2 Of medicines etc.: stimulating the heart; formerly, invigorating, cordial. M17. 3 Pertaining to or affected with heart disease. M18. 4 *Anat.* Of or pertaining to the cardia of the stomach. M19.

1 *cardiac arrest*: see ARREST *n.* 2b. †**cardiac passion** palpitation of the heart, heartburn. *cardiac tamponade*: see TAMPONADE 2. 2 **cardiac glycoside** any of a class of steroid glycosides which occur in plants and are heart stimulants, e.g. those present in digitalis.

cardiacal /kɑːˈdʌɪək(ə)l/ *a.* (now *rare*) = CARDIAC *a.* LME.

cardial /ˈkɑːdɪəl/ *a.* M19. [Sense 1 f. as CARDIA + -AL[1]; sense 2 f. mod.L *Cardium* genus name of the common cockle.] 1 = CARDIAC *a.* 1. *rare.* M19. 2 *Archaeol.* Of neolithic pottery: decorated with impressions made using cockle-shells. M20.

cardialgy /ˈkɑːdɪaldʒi/ *n.* Now *rare* or *obs.* Also in L form **-algia** /-ˈaldʒə/. M17. [mod.L *cardialgia* f. Gk *kardialgia*, f. *kardia*: see CARDIA, -ALGIA, -Y[3].] *Med.* Heartburn.

cardie /ˈkɑːdi/ *n. colloq.* Also **-di**, **-dy**. M20. [Abbrev.] = next.

cardigan /ˈkɑːdɪg(ə)n/ *n.* M19. [James Thomas Brudenell, seventh Earl of *Cardigan* (1797–1868), leader of the charge of the Light Brigade in the Crimean War.] A knitted woollen etc. jacket with or without sleeves.

cardinal /ˈkɑːd(ɪ)n(ə)l/ *n.* OE. [(O)Fr. f. med.L *cardinalis*: see next. Branch II f. next.] **I** 1 Any of the leading dignitaries of the Roman Catholic Church who together form the sacred college which elects the Pope. OE. **b** Either of two minor canons of St Paul's Cathedral, London. M18. 2 Any of a number of songbirds of the American subfamily Cardinalinae (family Emberizidae), related to the buntings; esp. the common N. American *Cardinalis cardinalis*, the male of which has scarlet plumage. E18. 3 *Hist.* A woman's cloak, orig. of scarlet cloth with a hood. M18. **II** 4 In *pl.* The cardinal numerals, points, virtues, etc. LME.

Comb.: **cardinal-flower** a scarlet-flowered lobelia, *Lobelia cardinalis*, native to N. America; **cardinal-grosbeak** = sense 2 above; **cardinal's hat** the red hat worn by a cardinal; *fig.* the dignity or office of a cardinal; **cardinal spider** a very large spider, spec. *Tegenaria parietina*.

cardinalate *n.* the office, dignity, or rank of a cardinal M17. **cardinaˈlatial** *a.* = CARDINALITIAL L19. **cardinalism** *n.* (*rare*) the institution or system of cardinals L17. **cardinalist** *n.* (*rare*) a supporter of a cardinal or cardinalism M17. **cardinalitial** /kɑːd(ɪ)nəˈlɪʃ(ə)l/ *a.* pertaining to cardinals as a group L17. **cardinalize** *v.t.* raise to the rank of cardinal E17. **cardinalship** *n.* the state or (tenure of) office of a cardinal LME.

cardinal /ˈkɑːd(ɪ)n(ə)l/ *a.* LME. [(O)Fr., or L *cardinalis*, f. *cardo*, *cardin-* hinge: see -AL[1]. Branch II f. prec.] **I** 1 On which something hinges; fundamental, crucial; important; pre-eminent. LME. 2 *Zool.* Of or pertaining to the hinge of a bivalve. M19.

1 A. BURGESS It was a cardinal rule in the East not to show one's true feelings. *cardinal humour*: see HUMOUR *n.* **cardinal number**, **cardinal numeral** any of the positive whole numbers, one, two, three, etc., showing how many elements there are in a certain set (cf. *ordinal number*, *numeral* s.v. ORDINAL *a.* 2); any of a series of analogous transfinite numbers. **cardinal point** any of the four main points of the compass, north, south, east, and west. **cardinal vein** any of a number of veins which drain the head and trunk in an embryo. **cardinal virtue** each of the four chief moral virtues (orig. of scholastic philosophy), justice, prudence, temperance, and fortitude (also called *natural virtue*); more widely, each of seven chief virtues comprising these with the three theological virtues; *gen.* an outstanding quality, a particular excellence. **cardinal vowel** each of a series of vowel sounds established by the British phonetician Daniel Jones (1881–1967), used as a standard of reference to assist in the description and classification of vowel sounds in any language. **cardinal wind**: blowing from a cardinal point.

II Corresp. to CARDINAL *n.* 1 (merging w. *attrib.* uses). 3 Belonging to the sacred college; appointed to the Roman diocese. With a title: that is also a cardinal. M17. 4 Of deep scarlet (as a cardinal's robe). L19.

3 **cardinal vicar** the Pope's delegate acting as bishop for the diocese of Rome.

cardinally *adv.* E17.

cardinality /kɑːdɪˈnalɪti/ *n.* E16. [f. CARDINAL *n.*, *a.* + -ITY.] †1 = CARDINALATE. E16–E17. 2 *Math.* The number of elements in a set or other grouping, as a property of the set etc. M20.

cardines *n.* pl. of CARDO.

cardio- /ˈkɑːdɪəʊ/ *comb. form* of Gk *kardia* heart: see -O-.

Cardiofunk *n.* (proprietary name for) a system of physical exercises combining aerobic methods with dance movements L20. **cardiogram** *n.* a record of heart action produced by a cardiograph L19. **cardiomyˈopathy** *n.* (a) chronic disease of heart muscle, *esp.* one of uncertain cause M20. **cardioˈpulmonary** *a.* pertaining to or involving the heart and the lungs E20. ˌ**cardioreˈspiratory** *a.* relating to the action of both heart and lungs L19. **cardiospasm** *n.* = ACHALASIA E20. **cardioˈvascular** *a.* pertaining to or involving the heart and blood-vessels L19.

cardiograph /ˈkɑːdɪəgrɑːf/ *n.* L19. [f. prec. + -GRAPH.] An instrument which records the action of the heart.

BALLISTOCARDIOGRAPH, ELECTROCARDIOGRAPH, MAGNETOCARDIOGRAPH, etc.

cardiˈographer *n.* a person who uses a cardiograph M20. **cardioˈgraphic** *a.* L19. **cardioˈgraphically** *adv.* E20. **cardiˈography** *n.* L19.

cardioid /ˈkɑːdɪɔɪd/ *n.* & *a.* M18. [f. Gk *kardioeidēs* heart-shaped, f. as CARDIA: see -OID.] **A** *n.* 1 *Math.* A heart-shaped curve traced by a point on the circumference of a circle as it rolls round another, identical, circle, and represented by the equation $r = a(1 + \cos\theta)$. Cf. LIMAÇON 2. M18. 2 A cardioid microphone. M20. **B** *adj.* Of the form of a heart-shaped curve; *esp.* (of a microphone) having a pattern of sensitivity of this form. M20.

cardiology /kɑːdɪˈɒlədʒi/ *n.* M19. [f. CARDIO- + -LOGY.] The branch of knowledge that deals with the structure, action, and diseases of the heart.

cardioˈlogical *a.* E20. **cardiologist** *n.* L19.

carditis /kɑːˈdʌɪtɪs/ *n.* L18. [f. as CARDIA + -ITIS.] Inflammation of the heart.

cardo /ˈkɑːdəʊ/ *n.* Pl. **-dines** /-dɪniːz/. L16. [L: see CARDINAL *a.*] †1 *Astrol.* In *pl.* The cardinal points. L16–M17. †2 *fig.* A turning point. Only in M17. 3 The hinge of a bivalve. M18.

cardoon /kɑːˈduːn/ *n.* E17. [Fr. *cardon*, f. *carde* edible part of the artichoke, f. mod.Prov. *cardo* f. Proto-Romance f. L *cardu(u)s* thistle, artichoke: see -OON.] A plant of the composite family, *Cynara cardunculus*, resembling a thistle and related to the globe artichoke; the fleshy inner leaf-stalks of this plant, eaten as a vegetable.

carduus /ˈkɑːdjʊəs/ *n.*LME. [L: see prec.] A thistle; *esp.* the blessed thistle, *Cnicus* (formerly *Carduus*) *benedictus*, from which a tonic was prepared. Now only as mod.L genus name.

cardy *n.* var. of CARDIE.

care /kɛː/ *n.* [OE *caru* = OS *kara*, OHG *chara* grief, lament, ON *kǫr* (genit. *karar*) bed of sickness, Goth. *kara*, f. Gmc.] 1 Mental suffering; sorrow, grief. *obs.* exc. in CARCAKE, *Care Sunday* below. OE. 2 A troubled state of mind arising from fear, doubt, etc; trouble, anxiety, solicitude; an occasion for this. OE. 3 Serious attention, heed; caution, pains; regard, inclination, (*to*, *for*). OE. 4 Charge, protective oversight, guardianship. LME. 5 An object or matter of concern; a thing to be done or seen to. L16.

1 POPE His words infix'd unutterable care Deep in great Hector's soul. 2 TENNYSON Cast all your cares on God. E. MUIR Public trouble and private care Faith and hope and love can sever. 3 GEO. ELIOT Public spirit . . its essence is care for a common good. E. WAUGH She arranged her paints and bottles with habitual care. 4 J. MARQUAND It was given into my care by a friend who wishes it to be in safe hands. S. BELLOW Elena was burdened with the care of the children. 5 B. JOWETT He could not himself spare the time from cares of state. S. LEACOCK My first care was to make a fire.

Phrases: **care and maintenance** the keeping of a building, ship, etc., in good condition although not in present use (freq. *attrib.*). **care of X** at X's address. **have a care** be cautious, not neglect or fail. **have the care of** be responsible for. **in care** under official guardianship. **in care of** *US* = *care of* above. **in need of care** (**and protection**) (of a destitute or dangerously circumstanced child etc.) qualifying for official guardianship. *intensive care*: see INTENSIVE *a.* 2. **take care** = *have a care* above. **take care of** look after, deal with, provide for, dispose of. *tender loving care*: see TENDER *a.*

Comb.: **care label**: giving advice on the cleaning of a garment or fabric; **care-laden** *a.* laden with anxieties; **Care Sunday** the fifth Sunday in Lent; **caretake** *v.t.* & *i.* [back-form.] act as caretaker (of); **caretaker** *n.* & *a.* (*a*) *n.* a person hired to take charge, esp. of a house in its owner's absence; a person looking after a public building; (*b*) *adj.* exercising temporary control; **care-worn** *a.* wearied by anxieties.

care /kɛː/ *v.* [OE *carian* = OS *karon*, OHG *charōn*, *-ēn*, Goth. *karōn*, f. Gmc; in later senses f. the n.] †1 *v.i.* Sorrow, grieve. OE–M16. 2 *v.i.* Feel concern or interest (*about*, *for*, *if*, *though*, *whether*; *whom*, *what*, etc.); feel deference, fondness, affection, etc. (*about*, *for*). Freq. w. advs. of degree or expletives. OE. 3 *v.i.* Foll. by *for*: provide for, look after, take care of. ME. 4 *v.t.* Take care of, look after, regard. Long *obs.* exc. *dial.* LME. 5 *v.i.* Have an inclination *for*; be inclined or disposed *to*, *to do*; be agreeable or willing *to do*. M16.

2 J. GALSWORTHY I don't . . care a fig for his opinion. DYLAN THOMAS I don't care a bugger whether you won't or will. J. BRAINE I don't mean that one has to love people, but simply that one ought to care. STEVIE SMITH What care I if good God be If he be not good to me? B. TARKINGTON Don't you care enough about me to marry me? **for all I care** *colloq.* as a matter of complete indifference to me. *know little* (or *nothing*) *and care less*: see KNOW *v.* *not care a cent*, *a chip*, *a hang*, *a snap*, *a tinker's curse*, etc. 3 R. MACAULAY A cared-for looking white skin. 5 A. FRASER His sister . . did not care to study the art of how to please. J. FENTON Would you care for a boiled sweet?

carer *n.* a person who cares or (now esp.) takes care of another or others L17.

care-cloth /ˈkɛːklɒθ/ *n. obs.* exc. *Hist.* M16. [Origin unkn.] A cloth held over or placed upon the heads of bride and bridegroom while they knelt during the marriage service.

careen /kəˈriːn/ *n.* & *v.* L16. [Fr. *carène*, †*carine*, f. It. dial. *carena* f. L *carina* keel.] **A** *n.* The position of a ship laid or heeled over on one side; an instance of careening. L16. **B** *v.* 1 *v.t.* & *i.* Turn (a ship) over on one side for cleaning. E17. 2 *v.i.* Of a ship: incline to one side or lie over when sailing on a wind. M18. **b** *transf.* Lean over, tilt. L19. 3 *v.t.* Cause (a ship) to heel over. M19. 4 *v.i.* (Infl. by CAREER *v.*) Rush headlong, hurtle unsteadily. *N. Amer.* E20.

careenage *n.* (the place for) the careening of a ship; the cost of this: L18.

career /kəˈrɪə/ *n.* & *a.* M16. [Fr. *carrière* f. It. *carriera* f. Prov. *carreira* f. Proto-Romance, f. L *carrus* CAR.] **A** *n.* †1 A racecourse; the enclosure at a tournament etc.; course, road. M16–M18. †2 A short gallop of a horse at full speed; a charge, an encounter on horseback. M16–M18. 3 A (swift) running course; an act of careering; full speed, impetus. M16. 4 A course or progress through life or history; an occupation or profession engaged in as a life-work, a way of making a livelihood and advancing oneself. E19.

3 MILTON The Sun . . was hasting now with prone carreer To th' Ocean Iles. C. S. FORESTER Mr. Graham put out a huge hand that stopped a taxi in full career. Y. MENUHIN A dizzy career by jeep through the empty streets. 4 W. A. PERCY To the grown-ups turtle soup was simply the predestined last act of a soft-shell turtle's career. T. CAPOTE He had attempted several careers, as soldier, ranch hand, mechanic, thief. JO GRIMOND The law . . seemed a suitable career for an aspiring politician.

Comb.: **careers master**, **mistress**, **teacher**: responsible for advising pupils on a choice of career; **career structure** the structure of an organization or profession as providing opportunities for advancement and a developing career.

B *attrib.* or as *adj.* Permanently employed in a particular profession; (esp. of a woman) devoted to the pursuit of a profession. E20.

F. J. STIMSON The career professors look somewhat askance at one who comes in from the outside world. B. FRIEDAN They are not career women . .; they are women whose greatest ambition has been marriage and children.

careerism *n.* the practice or policy of a careerist M20. **careerist** *n.* & *a.* (a person) mainly intent on furthering his or her own career, esp. unscrupulously E20.

career /kəˈrɪə/ *v.i.* L16. [f. the n.] †1 Take a short gallop; charge; (of a horse) weave from side to side while running. L16–L17. 2 Go swiftly or wildly, rush headlong, hurtle. M17.

2 L. A. G. STRONG A young man on a bicycle . . careered out into the main street.

carefree /ˈkɛːfriː/ *a.* L18. [f. CARE *n.* + -FREE.] Free from anxiety or responsibility.

carefreeness *n.* E20.

careful /ˈkɛːfʊl, -f(ə)l/ *a.* OE. [f. CARE *n.* + -FUL.] †1 Full of grief, sorrowful. OE–E18. 2 Full of trouble; anxious, concerned. *arch.* OE. 3 Full of care or concern *for*; attentive to the interests *of*; taking good care *of*. OE. 4 Applying care or attention; painstaking, circumspect. (Foll. by *to do*, *that*, *what*, etc.) OE. 5 Fraught with trouble or anxiety. ME. †6 On one's guard, wary. L16–E18. 7 Done with or showing care. M17.

carefully *adv.* OE. **carefulness** *n.* OE.

careless /ˈkɛːlɪs/ *a.* OE. [f. CARE *n.* + -LESS.] 1 Free from care, apprehension, or anxiety. Now *arch.* or *poet.* OE. 2 Unconcerned, taking no heed *of*; light-hearted. OE. 3 Inattentive, negligent (*of*), thoughtless; inaccurate. L16. 4 Done, caused, or said heedlessly, thoughtlessly, effortlessly, or negligently; artless, unstudied. Formerly also, uncared-for, untended. L16.

4 SHAKES. *Macb.* To throw away the dearest thing he ow'd As 'twere a careless trifle. J. OSBORNE She still looks quite smart, but in an unpremeditated, careless way. J. LE CARRÉ Careless lines of mortar hastily put on.

carelessly *adv.* M16. **carelessness** *n.* OE.

Carelian *n.* & *a.* var. of KARELIAN.

care spose *n. phr.* pl. of CARA SPOSA.

caress /kəˈrɛs/ *n.* M17. [Fr. *caresse* f. It. *carezza* f. Proto-Romance, f. L *carus* dear: see -ESS².] An action of endearment, a fondling touch, a kiss; a blandishment.

caress /kəˈrɛs/ *v.t.* M17. [f. prec. or Fr. *caresser*.] Bestow a caress on; stroke or pat tenderly; fondle; treat kindly or affectionately.

fig.: J. L. WATEN The warm sun caressed our faces. H. L. MENCKEN It caresses my ego today to think of men reading me half a century after I am gone.

caressable *a.* M17. **caressingly** *adv.* M19. **caressive** *a.* that caresses; of the nature of a caress: E19. **caressively** *adv.* E20.

caret /ˈkarət/ *n.* L17. [L, 3rd person sing. pres. indic. of *carere* be without, lack.] A mark (strictly ^) placed below a line of writing or printing, in a margin, etc., to show the place of an omission.

carex /ˈkɛːrɛks/ *n.* Pl. **-rices** /-rɪsiːz/. LME. [L *carex*.] A sedge; a plant of the genus *Carex*.

carezza *n.* var. of KAREZZA.

carf /kɑːf/ *n. obs.* exc. *dial.* LME. [Var. of KERF, infl. by CARVE. See also CURF.] A cut, esp. in timber; a notch, a slit, an incision.

carfax /ˈkɑːfaks/ *n.* Also (now *rare*) **-fox** /-fɒks/. ME. [AN *carfuks* = OFr. *carrefurcs* (mod. *carrefour*) f. pop.L, f. L QUADRI- + *furca* FORK *n.*] A place where (usu. four) roads or streets meet. Now chiefly in proper names.

†**carfour** *n.* var. of CARREFOUR.

carfox *n.* see CARFAX.

carga /ˈkɑːgə/ *n.* E17. [Sp.: see CARGO *n.*] In Spain and Spanish-speaking countries: a load as a measure of weight.

cargador /kɑːgəˈdɔː/ *n.* Pl. **-dores** /-ˈdɔːriːz/. E19. [Sp., f. as prec.] In Spanish-speaking parts of America: a porter.

†**cargason** *n.* Also **-z-**. L16–L19. [Sp. *cargazon* double augm. of *carga*.] A (ship's) cargo.

cargo /ˈkɑːgəʊ/ *n.* Pl. **-oes**, ***-os**. M17. [Sp. (also *carga*), corresp. to (O)Fr. *charge* load: see CHARGE *n.*] The goods carried by a ship, aircraft, lorry, etc.; a load.

Comb.: **cargo boat**, **ship**, etc.: carrying only or chiefly freight; **cargo cult** (orig. in Pacific islands) a belief in the forthcoming arrival of supernatural benefactors.

cargo /ˈkɑːgəʊ/ *v.t.* L19. [f. the n.] Load (*with* cargo); carry as cargo.

cargoose /ˈkɑːguːs/ *n.* Now *rare* or *obs.* Pl. **-geese** /-giːs/. L17. [App. f. CARR *n.*² + GOOSE *n.*] The great crested grebe.

cariama *n.* var. of SERIEMA.

Carian /ˈkɛːrɪən/ *n.*¹ & *a.* E17. [f. L *Caria* (see below) f. Gk *Karia*: see -AN.] A *n.* A native or inhabitant, or the language, of Caria (SW Anatolia), an ancient province of Asia Minor. E17. B *adj.* Of or pertaining to Caria or its language. E17.

†**Carian** *n.*² see KAREN.

†**Carianer** *n.* see KAREN.

Carib /ˈkarɪb/ *n.* & *a.* M16. [Sp. *caribe* f. Haitian creole: cf. CANNIBAL.] A *n.* Pl. **-s**, same. 1 Any of the aboriginal inhabitants of the southern W. Indian islands and adjacent coasts. M16. 2 The American Indian language of these people. L19. B *attrib.* or as *adj.* Of or pertaining to these people or their language. M19.

Also **Cariˈbee** *n.* (now *rare* or *obs.*) a Carib E18.

Caribbean /karɪˈbiːən, kəˈrɪbɪən/ *n.* & *a.* E18. [f. prec. + -EAN.] A *n.* 1 A Carib. *rare.* E18. 2 The region of the Atlantic between the southern W. Indian islands and Central America. L19. B *adj.* 1 Of or pertaining to the Caribs. L18. 2 Designating or pertaining to the Caribbean; West Indian. L19.

caribe /kəˈriːbeɪ, ˈkarɪbeɪ/ *n.* M19. [Sp.: see CARIB.] = PIRANHA.

caribou /ˈkarɪbuː/ *n.* Also **-oo**. Pl. same. M17. [Canad. Fr. f. Micmac *γalipu* lit. 'snow-shoveller'.] A N. American reindeer.

Comb.: **caribou moss** reindeer moss.

†**caricatura** *n.* L17–E19. [It.: see next.] = CARICATURE *n.*

caricature /ˈkarɪkətjʊə/ *n.* & *v.* M18. [Fr. f. It. *caricatura*, f. *caricare* to load, exaggerate, f. late L *car(ri)care*: see CHARGE *v.*, -URE.] A *n.* 1 Grotesque or ludicrous representation by exaggeration of characteristic traits, in drawing, writing, mime, etc.; a portrait or other representation displaying this. M18. 2 An exaggerated or debased imitation or version (*of*), naturally or unintentionally ludicrous. M18.

1 E. A. FREEMAN Stories . . which . . illustrate, if only by caricature, some real feature in his character. E. WAUGH One man drew an offensive caricature of me. 2 G. SAINTSBURY *The Wanderer* is a caricature of all the very worst faults of eighteenth-century poetic diction. S. NAIPAUL He glanced at me out of the corner of his eyes, a caricature of petty crookedness.

B *v.t.* Portray or imitate by a grotesque or ludicrous exaggeration of characteristic traits; burlesque. M18.

caricaˈtural *a.* of the nature of a caricature L19. **caricaturist** *n.* a person who practises caricature L18.

carices *n.* pl. of CAREX.

caries /ˈkɛːriːz/ *n.* Pl. same. L16. [L.] Decay of a tooth or bone.

carillon /ˈkarɪljən, -lɒn, kəˈrɪljən/ *n.* L18. [Fr., alt. of OFr. *car(e)ignon*, *quarregnon*, f. Proto-Romance = peal of four bells.] 1 A set of bells sounded either from a keyboard or mechanically. L18. 2 A tune played on such bells. L18. 3 A musical instrument or part of an organ designed to imitate a peal of bells. E19.

2 *fig.*: H. ACTON Nancy's laughter rose above theirs in a carillon that was almost operatic.

carilloˈnneur *n.* [Fr.] a person who plays a carillon L18.

carina /kəˈrʌɪnə, -ˈriː-/ *n.* Pl. **-nas**, **-nae** /-niː/. E18. [L = keel.] 1 *Biol.* A keel-like structure, a ridge; *esp.* (*a*) the keel of a bird's breastbone; (*b*) the cartilage at the bifurcation of the trachea to form the bronchi; (*c*) = KEEL *n.*¹ 3c. E18. 2 (**C-**.) (The name of) a constellation of the southern hemisphere between Volans and the Milky Way, orig. part of Argo; the Keel. M19.

carinal *a.* pertaining to or of the nature of a carina L19.

carinate /ˈkarɪneɪt, -ət/ *a.* L18. [L *carinatus*, f. as next: see -ATE².] Chiefly *Biol.* Having a ridge, keel, or carina; (of birds) having a keeled breastbone (opp. *ratite*).

carinate /ˈkarɪneɪt/ *v.t.* L17. [L *carinat-* pa. ppl stem of *carinare* supply with a keel or shell, f. as CARINA: see -ATE³.] Chiefly *Biol.* Provide with a ridge, keel, or carina. Chiefly as *carinated* ppl a.

cariˈnation *n.* L19.

caring /ˈkɛːrɪŋ/ *a.* M20. [f. CARE *v.* + -ING².] Compassionate, concerned; involved in caring for others.

¶ Earlier (L18) in UNCARING.

carioca /karɪˈəʊkə/ *n.* M19. [Port.] 1 A native of Rio de Janeiro, Brazil. M19. 2 A Brazilian dance resembling a samba; a piece of music for this dance. M20.

cariogenic /kɛːrɪəˈdʒɛnɪk, kar-/ *a.* M20. [f. CARIES + -O- + -GENIC.] Causing or promoting tooth decay.

cariogenicity /-ˈnɪsɪti/ *n.* M20.

cariole *n.* var. of CARRIOLE.

cariosity /kɛːrɪˈɒsɪti/ *n.* Now *rare* or *obs.* M17. [f. as next + -ITY.] Carious condition; a carious formation.

carious /ˈkɛːrɪəs/ *a.* M16. [f. L *cariosus*, f. CARIES: see -OUS.] Decayed, rotten; *spec.* affected with caries.

cari sposi *n. phr.* pl. of CARO SPOSO.

carissima /kaˈrissima/ *a.* M19. [It., superl. of *cara* dear.] A term of endearment to a woman: dearest, darling.

caritas /ˈkarɪtɑːs/ *n.* M19. [L: see CHARITY.] = CHARITY I.

caritive /ˈkarɪtɪv/ *a.* & *n.* M19. [f. L *carit-* ppl stem of *carere* lack: see -IVE.] *Gram.* A *adj.* Designating, being in, or pertaining to a case in Caucasian and other languages expressing the lack of something. M19. B *n.* *The* caritive case; a word, form, etc., in the caritive case. M20.

cark /kɑːk/ *n.* Long *arch.* or *Sc.* ME. [AN *karke* repr. north. var. of OFr. *c(h)arche*, f. *c(h)archier*, f. late L *car(ri)care*: see CHARGE *v.*] †1 A load, a weight. ME–M16. †2 A charge, a burden. ME–L16. 3 Trouble, anxiety; labour; toil. ME. †4 Care, pains; heed. LME–E17.

3 LONGFELLOW The swart mechanic comes to drown his cark and care.

cark /kɑːk/ *v.* Long *arch.* or *Sc.* ME. [ONFr. *carkier* f. OFr. *c(h)archier*: see prec.] †1 *v.t.* Load, burden; impose as a charge on. Only in ME. 2 *v.t.* Worry, harass, vex, trouble. ME. 3 *v.i.* Be anxious, be concerned; fret oneself; toil. ME. †4 *v.i.* Care *for*, take thought. LME–E17.

carking *vbl n.* grieving, solicitude, anxiety ME. **carking** *ppl a.* burdensome, wearying; toiling, anxious, niggardly: M16.

carl /kɑːl/ *n.* Long *arch.* & *dial.* Also **carle**. OE. [ON *karl* man, male, freeman = OHG *kar(a)l*, *charlo*, f. Gmc: rel. to CHURL.] 1 A man of low rank; a countryman; a peasant; a bondman; a villein. OE. 2 A low-born fellow; a churl; a boor; a mean, niggardly, or grudging person. ME. 3 In full *carl hemp*. The more robust kind of hemp plant (orig. considered male but later found to be the female plant). E16. 4 A (usu. strong or sturdy) man; a fellow. M16.

carlish *a.* of or pertaining to a carl; churlish, coarse, vulgar, mean: ME. †**carlot** *n.* (*rare*, Shakes.) a peasant, a churl: only in L16.

carl /kɑːl/ *v.*¹*i.* *obs.* exc. *dial.* E17. [Perh. f. CARL *n.*] Speak gruffly, snarl; behave churlishly.

carl /kɑːl/ *v.*²*t.* *obs.* exc. *dial.* E17. [Perh. back-form. f. CARLING *n.*¹ taken as a ppl form.] Prepare as carlings; parch (peas etc.).

carle *n.* var. of CARL *n.*

Carley /ˈkɑːli/ *n.* E20. [Horace S. *Carley* (fl. 1900), US inventor.] More fully *Carley float*, *raft*. A large emergency raft carried on board ship.

carline /ˈkɑːlɪn/ *n.*¹ Also **-ling** /-lɪŋ/. ME. [ON *karling* fem. of *karl* CARL *n.*] 1 An (old) woman; *esp.* a witch. Chiefly *Sc.* ME. 2 *Naut.* Any of the squared timbers fitted fore and aft between the deck beams of a wooden ship to support the deck planking. LME.

carline /ˈkɑːlɪn/ *n.*² L16. [Fr. f. med.L *carlina* perh. f. *cardina* (f. *cardo* thistle) by assoc. with *Carolus* Magnus (Charlemagne), to whom its medicinal qualities were reputedly revealed.] In full *carline thistle*. A spiny plant of the genus *Carlina* of the composite family.

†carline *n.*[3] E18–M19. [(O)Fr. *carlin* f. It. *carlino*, f. *Carlo*, name of several kings of Naples: cf. CAROLINE *n.*] A small silver coin formerly current in Naples and Sicily.

carling /ˈkɑːlɪŋ/ *n.*[1] *obs.* exc. *dial.* M16. [Perh. f. CARE *n.* in *Care Sunday*.] Usu. in *pl.* Parched peas, traditionally eaten on *Carling Sunday*, Care Sunday (see CARE *n.*).

carling *n.*[2] var. of CARLINE *n.*[1]

Carlism /ˈkɑːlɪz(ə)m/ *n.* M19. [Fr. *carlisme* f. Sp. *carlismo*, f. Don *Carlos* (1788–1855), brother of King Fernando VII of Spain: see below, -ISM.] A Spanish counter-revolutionary movement originating in support for Don Carlos and his heirs as the legitimate successors of Fernando VII, as opp. to the line of Fernando's daughter Isabella II.

Carlist *n.* & *a.* (*a*) *n.* a supporter of Carlism; (*b*) *adj.* of or pertaining to Carlism or Carlists: M19.

Carlovingian /kɑːləˈvɪndʒɪən/ *a.* & *n.* M18. [Fr. *carlovingien*, f. *Karl* Charles after *mérovingien* MEROVINGIAN *a.*] = CAROLINGIAN.

Carlsbad plum /ˈkɑːlzbad ˈplʌm/ *n. phr.* L19. [*Carlsbad*, a spa town formerly in Germany, now (renamed *Karlovy Vary*) in Bohemia.] A blue-black usu. crystallized dessert plum.

Carlylism /kɑːˈlʌɪlɪz(ə)m/ *n.* M19. [f. *Carlyle* (see below) + -ISM.] The teachings or literary style of the Scottish-born essayist and historian Thomas Carlyle (1795–1881); a literary mannerism of Carlyle.

Carlylean *a.* of, pertaining to, or characteristic of Carlyle or his works E19. **Carlyˈlese** *n.* the language or style of Carlyle M19.

carmagnole /karmaɲɔl/ *n.* Pl. pronounced same. L18. [Fr., orig. a style of jacket popular during the French Revolution, prob. ult. f. *Carmagnola*, a town in Piedmont.] 1 A popular song and round dance of the French Revolutionary period. L18. 2 A French revolutionary soldier; *transf.* an author of mischief. L18.

Carmathian *n.* & *a.* var. of KARMATHIAN.

Carmelite /ˈkɑːmɪlʌɪt/ *n.* & *a.* LME. [Fr. *carmélite* or med.L *Carmelita* (cf. late L *carmelites* inhabitant of Mount *Carmel*, Palestine): see -ITE[1].] A *n.* 1 A member of an order of mendicant friars (also known as the White Friars), founded at Mount Carmel in the 12th cent. Also, a nun of an order modelled on the White Friars. LME. 2 (Also **c-**.) A fine usu. grey woollen material. E19. B *adj.* Of or pertaining to the Carmelites. E16.

Also **†Carme** *n.* & *a.* LME–L18. **†Carmelitan** *n.* & *a.* L16–M18.

carminative /ˈkɑːmɪnətɪv, kɑːˈmɪnətɪv/ *a.* & *n.* LME. [(O)Fr. *carminatif*, *-ive* or med.L *carminat-* pa. ppl stem of *carminare* heal by incantation, f. L *carmen*, *-min-*: see CHARM *n.*[1], -ATIVE.] *Med.* (A medicine) having the property of relieving flatulence.

carmine /ˈkɑːmʌɪn, -mɪn/ *n.* & *a.* E18. [(O)Fr. *carmin* ult. f. Arab. *ḳirmiz*: see CRIMSON.] A *n.* 1 A crimson pigment obtained from cochineal; = *carminic acid* below. E18. 2 The colour of this. L18. B *adj.* Of the colour of carmine; deep crimson. M18.

carmined *a.* reddened with carmine L19. **carˈminic** *a.* (*Chem.*): *carminic acid*, a phenolic anthraquinone derivative which is the colouring matter of cochineal M19.

Carnaby Street /ˈkɑːnəbi striːt/ *n. phr.* M20. [A street in central London.] Used (freq. *attrib.*) as the type of the fashionable in dress for young people, *spec.* in London in the 1960s.

carnac /ˈkɑːnak/ *n. rare.* E18. [Fr. *cornac*, Port. *cornaca*, perh. f. Skt *kari-nāyaka* person in charge of elephants.] A mahout.

carnage /ˈkɑːnɪdʒ/ *n.* E17. [Fr. f. It. *carnaggio* f. med.L *carnaticum*, f. L *caro*, *carn-* flesh: see -AGE.] 1 The slaughter of a great number, esp. of men in battle; butchery, massacre. E17. 2 Carcasses collectively. Now *rare* or *obs.* M17.

carnal /ˈkɑːn(ə)l/ *a.* LME. [Chr.L *carnalis*, f. L *caro*, *carn-* flesh: see -AL[1].] 1 Bodily, corporeal; of flesh. LME. †b Related by blood. LME–L16. 2 Pertaining to the body as the seat of passions or appetites; fleshly, sensual; sexual. LME. 3 Not spiritual; material, temporal, secular; worldly. LME. †4 Bloody, murderous. *rare* (Shakes.). Only in L16.

2 **carnal knowledge (of)** (chiefly *Law*) full or partial sexual intercourse (with). *carnal members*: see MEMBER *n.*

carnality /kɑːˈnalɪti/ *n.* the state of being carnal; fleshliness; sensuality; worldliness; sexual intercourse: LME. **carnalize** *v.t.* make carnal L17. **carnally** *adv.* LME.

carnallite /ˈkɑːn(ə)lʌɪt/ *n.* M19. [f. Rudolf von *Carnall* (1804–74), Ger. mining engineer + -ITE[1].] *Min.* An orthorhombic hydrated chloride of potassium and magnesium, usu. occurring as white or reddish massive deposits.

carnaptious /kəˈnapʃəs/ *a. Sc.* & *Anglo-Ir. dial.* M19. [Origin unkn.] Bad-tempered, quarrelsome.

carnassial /kɑːˈnasɪəl/ *a.* & *n.* M19. [f. Fr. *carnassier* carnivorous + -AL[1].] *Zool.* (A carnivore's premolar tooth) adapted for tearing.

Carnata *a.* & *n.* see KARNATA.

Carnatic /kɑːˈnatɪk/ *n.* & *a.* L18. [Anglicization of *Karnataka* in SW India: see -IC.] A *n. the Carnatic*, the region of Karnataka in SW India when under British rule. *obs.* exc. *Hist.* L18. B *adj.* Of or pertaining to the Carnatic (*obs.* exc. *Hist.*) or to the State of Karnataka; *spec.* designating or pertaining to the traditional music of southern India. E19.

†carnation *n.*[1] ME–E18. [OFr. *carnacion*, *-tion*, app. aphet. f. as INCARNATION.] Incarnation.

carnation /kɑːˈneɪʃ(ə)n/ *n.*[2] & *a.* M16. [Fr. f. It. *carnagione* f. late L *carnatio(n-)* fleshiness, f. L *caro*, *carn-* flesh: see -ATION.] A *n.* 1 Flesh-colour; a light rosy pink; sometimes a darker crimson as in the carnation flower. M16. 2 In *pl.* Flesh tints; those parts of a painting representing naked skin. E18. B *adj.* Flesh-coloured. M16.

carnationed *a.* (*a*) reddened; †(*b*) flesh-coloured: M17.

carnation /kɑːˈneɪʃ(ə)n/ *n.*[3] L16. [Perh. ult. f. misreading of Arab. *ḳaranful* clove, clove pink, f. Gk *karyophyllon*.] A clove pink of a cultivated variety; a flower or flowering stem of this plant.

MALMAISON *carnation*. *perpetual-flowering carnation*: see PERPETUAL *a.*

carnauba /kɑːˈnɔːbə, -ˈnaʊbə/ *n.* M19. [Port. f. Tupi.] A Brazilian palm, *Copernicia prunifera*, whose leaves exude a yellowish wax (*carnauba wax*) used as a polish etc.

†carnel *n.* & *v.* var. of KERNEL *n.*[2] & *v.*[2]

carnelian *n.* var. of CORNELIAN *n.*[1]

carneous /ˈkɑːnɪəs/ *a.* L16. [f. late L *carneus*, f. L *caro*, *carn-* flesh: see -OUS.] 1 Consisting of flesh, fleshy. L16. 2 Flesh-coloured. Now *rare* or *obs.* L17.

carnet /ˈkɑːneɪ, *foreign* karnɛ (*pl. same*)/ *n.* E19. [Fr.] 1 A notebook. *rare.* E19. 2 A permit; *spec.* (*a*) one allowing a motorist to drive across a frontier; (*b*) one allowing use of some camp-sites. E20.

carney /ˈkɑːni/ *n.*[1] *rare.* L17. [Origin unkn.] A disease of horses in which the mouth becomes furred so that they cannot eat.

carney /ˈkɑːni/ *n.*[2], *v.*, & *a. dial.* & *slang.* Also **-ny.** E19. [Origin unkn.] A *n.* Hypocritical or wheedling language; a smooth talker, a flatterer. E19. B *v.t.* & *i.* Wheedle, cajole; use flattery or persuasion. E19. C *adj.* Artful, sly. L19.

carney *n.*[3] var. of CARNY *n.*[1]

Carnian /ˈkɑːnɪən/ *a.* E19. [f. as prec. + -IAN.] 1 = CARNIC 1. *rare.* E19. 2 *Geol.* Designating or pertaining to the lowest division of the Upper Triassic in Europe. M20.

Carnic /ˈkɑːnɪk/ *a.* E17. [L *Carnicus*, f. *Carni* a Celtic people of northern Italy: see -IC.] 1 *Carnic Alps*, a range of mountains along the border of Austria and Italy. E17. 2 *Geol.* = CARNIAN 2. Now *rare.* L19.

carnie *n.* var. of CARNY *n.*[1]

carnifex /ˈkɑːnɪfɛks/ *n. obs.* exc. *Hist.* M16. [L = executioner, (in med.L also) butcher.] An executioner.

carnification /kɑːnɪfɪˈkeɪʃ(ə)n/ *n.* M18. [f. CARNIFY: see -FICATION.] *Med.* Alteration of tissue into a fleshy fibrous form, esp. in the lungs in some forms of pneumonia.

carnificial /kɑːnɪˈfɪʃ(ə)l/ *a.* M17. [f. L *carnifex*, *-fic-* + -IAL.] Of an executioner or butcher; butcherly.

carnify /ˈkɑːnɪfʌɪ/ *v.* M17. [f. L *caro*, *carn-* flesh + -FY.] 1 *v.t.* Make or convert into flesh. Usu. in *pass.* M17. †2 *v.i.* Generate flesh. M17–E19. 3 *Med.* a *v.t.* Bring about carnification of. M18. b *v.i.* Undergo carnification. M19.

carnival /ˈkɑːnɪv(ə)l/ *n.* & *a.* M16. [It. *carne-*, *carnovale* (whence Fr. *carnaval*) f. med.L *carnelevamen*, *-varium* Shrovetide, f. L *caro*, *carn-* flesh + *levare* put away.] A *n.* 1 In Roman Catholic countries, the week (orig. the day) before Lent, devoted to festivities; Shrovetide; the festivity of this season. M16. 2 Any period or occasion of riotous revelry or feasting; a festival (esp. at a regular date) usu. involving a procession. L16. 3 A travelling funfair; a circus. *N. Amer.* M20. B *attrib.* or as *adj.* Of or pertaining to a carnival; resembling or characteristic of a carnival. E17.

carnivaˈlesque *a.* characteristic or of the style of a carnival M18. **carnivalite** *n.* a reveller at a carnival L19.

carnivore /ˈkɑːnɪvɔː/ *n.* M19. [Fr., f. L *carnivorus*: see next.] A carnivorous animal; a member of the order Carnivora of mainly carnivorous mammals (including dogs, cats, bears, seals, etc.). Also, a carnivorous plant.

carnivorous /kɑːˈnɪv(ə)rəs/ *a.* L16. [L *carnivorus* f. *caro*, *carn-* flesh: see -VOROUS.] 1 Feeding on flesh; preying on other animals; *Zool.* belonging to the order Carnivora (see prec.). L16. 2 Of plants: able to absorb and digest animal substances. M19.

carnivorously *adv.* M19. **carˈnivory** *n.* carnivorous behaviour E20.

carnose /ˈkɑːnəʊs/ *a.* LME. [L *carnosus*, f. *caro*, *carn-* flesh: see -OSE[1].] Consisting of flesh; fleshy.

carnosity /kɑːˈnɒsɪti/ *n.* LME. [(O)Fr. *carnosité* or med.L *carnositas*, f. as prec.: see -ITY.] †1 Fleshiness; pulpiness. LME–M17. 2 A morbid fleshy growth. LME.

Carnot /ˈkɑːnəʊ/ *n.* M19. [Sadi *Carnot* (1796–1832), Fr. scientist.] *Physics.* Used *attrib.* and in *possess.* with ref. to a particular thermodynamic cycle describing the operation of an ideal heat engine.

Carnot('s) cycle, *Carnot('s) theorem*, etc.

carnotite /ˈkɑːnətʌɪt/ *n.* L19. [f. M. A. *Carnot* (1839–1920), Fr. inspector of mines + -ITE[1].] *Min.* A monoclinic hydrated vanadate of uranium and potassium, usu. occurring as lemon-yellow microcrystalline aggregates.

carnous /ˈkɑːnəs/ *a.* Now *rare* or *obs.* LME. [f. as CARNOSE + -OUS.] Pulpy, fleshy.

carny /ˈkɑːni/ *n.*[1] *N. Amer. slang.* Also **carney, carnie.** M20. [f. CARNIVAL + -Y[6].] A carnival; a person who works at a carnival.

carny *n.*[2], *v.*, & *a.* var. of CARNEY *n.*[2], *v.*, & *a.*

carob /ˈkarəb/ *n.* Also (after Arab.) **carouba** /kəˈrəʊbə/. LME. [Fr. †*car(r)obe* (mod. *caroube*) f. med.L *carrubia*, *-ium*, etc., f. Arab. *ḳarrūb(a)*. Cf. ALGARROBA.] 1 The edible horn-shaped fleshy seed-pod of an evergreen leguminous tree, *Ceratonia siliqua*, native to the Mediterranean region. Also *carob-bean*, *-pod*. LME. 2 In full *carob tree*. The tree itself. M16.

caroche /kəˈrɒʃ/ *n. obs.* exc. *Hist.* L16. [Fr. †*carroche* f. It. *carraccio*, *-ia*, augm. of *carro* chariot, CAR: cf. CAROSSE.] A stately or luxurious carriage.

carol /ˈkar(ə)l/ *n.* ME. [OFr. (now dial.) *carole* = Prov. *carola*, *corola* (whence It. *carola*), of unkn. origin.] I 1 A ring-dance accompanied by song. *obs.* exc. *Hist.* ME. †2 A revel. ME–L15. 3 A (joyful) song; *transf.* the song of a bird. ME. 4 A joyful hymn; *esp.* (in full *Christmas carol*) one sung at Christmas. LME. †II 5 A ring, esp. of standing stones. Cf. CARREL. Only in ME.

Comb.: **carol service** a religious service largely devoted to the singing of Christmas carols; **carol-singer** a person who takes part in carol-singing; **carol-singing** the singing of carols, *spec.* by groups who go from door to door at Christmas with the object of raising money.

carol /ˈkar(ə)l/ *v.* Infl. **-ll-**, ***-l-**. ME. [OFr. *caroler*, f. as prec.] †1 *v.i.* Sing and dance in a ring. Also, make merry, revel. ME–M16. 2 *v.t.* & *i.* Sing (as) a carol; sing joyously; celebrate in song. LME.

Carolean /karəˈliən/ *a.* & *n.* E20. [f. med.L CAROLUS + -EAN.] *Hist.* A *adj.* Of or pertaining to Charles I (reigned 1625–49) or Charles II (reigned 1660–85), Kings of Great Britain; (characteristic) of their period. E20. B *n.* A supporter or contemporary of either King Charles. E20.

caroler *n.* var. of CAROLLER.

Carolin *n.* var. of CAROLINE *n.*

Carolina /karəˈlʌɪnə/ *n.* L17. [A former British colony named after Charles II (see CAROLINE *a.*), now (as *North & South Carolina*) forming two States of the USA.] Used *attrib.* to designate things from or associated with Carolina.

Carolina allspice: see ALLSPICE 2. *Carolina* JASMINE. **Carolina pink** pinkroot, *Spigelia marilandica*. **Carolina rice** a variety of rice with a yellowish husk.

Caroline /ˈkarəlʌɪn/ *n. obs.* exc. *Hist.* Also **-lin** /-lɪn/. M16. [med. or mod.L *Carolinus* (see next), used as n.] Any of various coins of different countries and values, depicting the head of a King Charles (or Karl, Carlo, etc.); *spec.* (*a*) = CARLINE *n.*[3]; (*b*) a gold coin of Bavaria and Württemburg. Cf. CAROLUS.

Caroline /ˈkarəlʌɪn/ *a.* E17. [med. or mod.L *Carolinus*, f. med.L CAROLUS: see -INE[1].] Of, pertaining to, or of the period of, a (King) Charles; *spec.* (*a*) = CAROLINGIAN *a.*; (*b*) = CAROLEAN *a.*

Carolingian /karəˈlɪndʒɪən/ *a.* & *n.* L19. [Refash. of CARLOVINGIAN after med.L CAROLUS.] A *adj.* 1 Of, relating, or belonging to the dynasty of Frankish kings founded by Charlemagne (d. 814). L19. 2 Designating or displaying a style of minuscule handwriting developed in France at the time of Charlemagne. L19. B *n.* A member or supporter of the Carolingian dynasty. Also, Carolingian script. L19.

Carolinian /karəˈlɪnɪən/ *a.* & *n.* E18. [f. CAROLINA + -IAN.] (A native or inhabitant) of (N. or S.) Carolina.

carolitic /karəˈlɪtɪk/ *a.* Also **-lytic**. E19. [Alt. of Fr. *corollitique*, f. L COROLLA: see -IC.] *Archit.* Of a column: having a foliated shaft.

caroller /ˈkarələ/ *n.* Also **caroler**. L16. [f. CAROL *v.* + -ER[1].] †1 A reveller. Only in L16. 2 A person who carols; a carol-singer. E19.

Carolus /ˈkarələs/ *n.* & *a.* E16. [med.L = Charles, Karl.] *Hist.* (Designating) a coin bearing 'Carolus' as the name of the monarch, *spec.* a gold piece of the reign of Charles I of Great Britain.

carolytic *a.* var. of CAROLITIC.

carom /ˈkarəm/ *n.* & *v.* Also **-rr-**. L18. [Abbrev. of CARAMBOLE.] A *n.* 1 A cannon in billiards. Now chiefly *N. Amer.* L18. 2 More fully *carom billiards*. A game resembling billiards but played on a table without pockets and depending on cannons for scoring. L19. B *v.i.* Make a carom; strike and rebound (*off*). Now chiefly *N. Amer.* M19.

caroon /kəˈruːn/ *n. obs.* exc. *Hist.* Also **-rr-**, **-m** /-m/. M17. [Origin unkn.] A licence from the Lord Mayor of London for keeping a cart.

caro sposo /ˈkaːro ˈspoːzo/ *n. phr.* Pl. ***cari sposi*** /ˈkaːri ˈspoːzi/. L18. [It.] (One's) dear husband; a devoted husband. Cf. CARA SPOSA.

carosse /kəˈrɒs/ *n.* L16. [Obs. Fr. (now *-rr-*) f. It. *carrozza* augm. of *carro* chariot, CAR: cf. CAROCHE.] Chiefly *Hist.* A (horse-drawn) carriage, a coach.

carotene /ˈkarətiːn/ *n.* Also **-tin** /-tɪn/. M19. [f. L *carota* carrot + -ENE.] *Chem.* An orange or red hydrocarbon, $C_{40}H_{56}$, of which there are several isomers, which occurs in carrots and many other plants and is a precursor of vitamin A.

carotenoid *n.* & *a.* (*a*) *n.* any of a class of mainly yellow or red pigments of wide natural occurrence having the conjugated molecular structure typified by carotene; (*b*) *adj.* of, pertaining to, or characteristic of such a compound: E20.

carotic /kəˈrɒtɪk/ *a.* Now *rare* or *obs.* M17. [Gk *karōtikos* stupefying: see next, -IC.] 1 = CAROTID *a.* M17. 2 Of the nature of stupor; in a state of stupor. L17.

carotid /kəˈrɒtɪd/ *a.* & *n.* E17. [Fr. *carotide* or mod.L *carotides* f. Gk *karōtides* pl. of *karōtis* drowsiness f. *karoun* stupefy: so named because compression of the arteries was thought to cause stupor.] *Anat.* A *adj.* 1 *carotid artery*, either of the two main arteries (or their major branches) which supply blood to the head and neck. E17. 2 Of, pertaining to, or adjoining a carotid artery. M19.

2 **carotid body** a small mass of receptors in the carotid artery sensitive to chemical change in the blood.

B *n.* A carotid artery. E18.

carotin *n.* var. of CAROTENE.

carouba *n.* var. of CAROB.

carousal /kəˈraʊz(ə)l/ *n.* E18. [f. CAROUSE *v.* + -AL[1].] A bout of carousing; a drunken revel. Formerly also identified w. CAROUSEL 1.

carouse /kəˈraʊz/ *adv.*, *n.*, & *v.* M16. [G *gar aus* (*trinken*) (drink) right out, completely; as n. f. the adv. taken as obj. of a vb.] †A *adv.* (*Drink*, *quaff*, etc.) to the bottom of the glass etc. M16–M17. B *n.* †1 The act or fashion of drinking all up; a cupful drunk all up; a whole cupful, a full draught. M16–E19. 2 A drinking-bout; carousing. L17. C *v.* 1 *v.i.* Have or engage in a drinking-bout; drink heavily. M16. b Drink health, success, etc., *to*. Now *rare* or *obs.* L16. †2 *v.t.* Drink up, drain; drink (a health). L16–E19.

carouser *n.* L16.

carousel /karəˈsɛl, -ˈzɛl/ *n.* Also ***-rr-**. M17. [Fr. *carrousel* f. It. *carosello*, *ga-*.] 1 *Hist.* A kind of tournament in which variously dressed companies of knights engaged in plays, chariot races, exercises, etc. M17. 2 A merry-go-round; a roundabout. Chiefly *N. Amer.* L17. 3 A rotating delivery or conveyor system, *esp.* one in an airport for the delivery of passengers' luggage. M20.

carozzi *n.* see KARROZZIN.

carp /kaːp/ *n.*[1] ME. [f. CARP *v.*] †1 Discourse. Only in ME. 2 A carping speech, remark, etc. E17.

carp /kaːp/ *n.*[2] Pl. usu. same. LME. [(O)Fr. *carpe* f. Prov. *carpa*, or the common source, late L *carpa*.] A freshwater fish of the genus *Cyprinus*, esp. *C. carpio*, freq. kept in ponds. Also, any of various related fishes belonging to the family Cyprinidae.

crucian carp, *leather carp*, *mirror carp*, etc. KOI *carp*. *looking-glass carp*: see LOOKING-GLASS. *mirror carp*: see MIRROR *n.* *Prussian carp*: see PRUSSIAN *a.*

carplike *a.* resembling a carp L19.

carp /kaːp/ *v.* ME. [Senses 1–3 f. ON *karpa* brag; later senses infl. by or f. L *carpere* pluck, slander, calumniate.] †1 *v.i.* & *t.* Speak, talk; say, tell. ME–E17. 2 *v.i.* Sing, recite. *obs.* exc. *dial.* LME. †3 *v.i.* Prate, chatter. LME–M16. 4 *v.i.* Talk querulously; find fault, cavil. (Foll. by *at*.) LME. †5 *v.t.* Find fault with, take exception to. M16–L17.

carper *n.* LME. **carping** *ppl a.* that carps; captious: L16.

carpal /ˈkaːp(ə)l/ *a.* & *n.* M18. [f. CARPUS + -AL[1].] *Anat.* & *Zool.* A *adj.* Of or pertaining to the wrist or carpus. M18. B *n.* Any of the bones of the wrist. M19.

Carpathian /kaːˈpeɪθɪən/ *a.*[1] E17. [f. *Carpathos* (see below) + -IAN.] Of or pertaining to Carpathos (Karpathos), an island in the Aegean Sea.

Carpathian /kaˈpeɪθɪən/ *a.*[2] & *n.* L17. [Prob. f. G *Karpathen* f. L *Carpatus* f. Gk *Karpatos*, + -IAN.] A *adj.* Designating or pertaining to a range of mountains in central and eastern Europe. L17. B *n.* In *pl.* & †*sing.* *The* Carpathian mountains. L17.

carpel /ˈkaːp(ə)l/ *n.* M19. [Fr. *carpelle* or mod.L *carpellum*, f. Gk *karpos* fruit: see -EL[2].] *Bot.* The basic unit of the female reproductive part of a flower (gynoecium), consisting of ovary, stigma, and (usually) style, which occurs either singly or as one of a group.

carpellary *a.* of, pertaining to, or of the nature of a carpel M19.

carpent /ˈkaːp(ə)nt/ *v.t.* *rare.* E17. [med.L *carpentare*.] Make by carpentry; construct, put together.

carpenter /ˈkaːp(ə)ntə/ *n.* & *v.* ME. [AN, & OFr. *carpentier*, (also mod.) *charpentier*, f. late L *carpentarius* (*artifex*) carriage(-maker), f. *carpentum* two-wheeled carriage, of Gaulish origin, rel. to CAR: see -ER[2].] A *n.* A craftsman in woodwork esp. of rough solid kinds as in house or shipbuilding (cf. JOINER). ME.

Comb.: **carpenter ant**, **bee**: of a kind which bores into trees (*violet carpenter bee*: see VIOLET *a.*); **carpenter-work** = CARPENTRY.

B *v.* 1 *v.i.* Do carpenter's work. LME. 2 *v.t.* Make by carpentry; put together mechanically, construct (*lit.* & *fig.*) LME.

carpentry /ˈkaːp(ə)ntri/ *n.* LME. [AN *carpentrie* = (O)Fr. *charpenterie*, f. *charpentier*: see prec., -RY.] 1 The work, trade, or skill of a carpenter; woodworking. LME. 2 Woodwork made by a carpenter. LME.

carpet /ˈkaːpɪt/ *n.* ME. [OFr. *carpite* or med.L *carpita* f. It. †*carpita* woollen counterpane, corresp. to Fr. *charpie* lint, use as n. of pa. pple of *charpir* f. Proto-Romance var. of L *carpere* pluck, pull to pieces.] 1 A thick usu. woollen fabric used as a cover for beds, tables, etc.; a piece of this; a tablecloth. *obs.* exc. in *on the carpet* (a) below. ME. 2 A piece of thick fabric, made in one piece or of lengths joined together, often woven in a pattern of colours, used for covering a floor, stairway, etc.; material for this, carpeting. Also, w. specifying wd, a rug, *esp.* a large oriental rug. LME. 3 *fig.* A smooth, soft, or bright covering or expanse, as of grass or flowers, resembling a carpet. L16. b The ground. *slang.* L19. 4 In full *carpet-moth*. Any of various geometrid moths with variegated colouring. M19.

2 *Axminster carpet*, *Brussels carpet*, *Exeter carpet*, *Kilim carpet*, *oriental carpet*, *Persian carpet*, *Turkey carpet*, *Turkish carpet*, *Turkoman carpet*, *velvet carpet*, *Venetian carpet*, etc.

Phrases: *magic carpet*: see MAGIC *a.* **on the carpet** *fig.* (*a*) under discussion; (*b*) *colloq.* being reprimanded. *red carpet*: see RED *a.* *sweep a thing under the carpet*: see SWEEP *v.*

Comb.: **carpet-bag** *n.* & *v.* (*a*) *n.* a travel bag, orig. made of carpet; (*b*) *v.i.* (*derog.*, chiefly *US*) travel lightly, be a carpet-bagger; **carpet-bagger** (*derog.*, chiefly *US*) a person seeking to achieve political success or private gain in a place with which he is unconnected (orig. *spec.* a northerner in the southern US after the Civil War); **carpet-bed** a garden bed with dwarf plants arranged densely in a pattern; **carpet beetle** any of various dermestid beetles of the genus *Anthrenus*, whose larvae are destructive to carpets etc.; **carpet bombing** the dropping of a large number of bombs uniformly over an area; **carpet dance** an informal dance for which the carpet is not taken up; **carpet knight** *arch.* an idler, a philanderer, a ladies' man; *carpet-moth*: see sense 4 above; **carpet-rod** a stair-rod; **carpet-shark** any of several sharks with irregular markings on the back, esp. of the genus *Orectolobus*; **carpet shell** (the shell of) any of various bivalve molluscs of the genus Venerupis (family Veneridae), with irregular coloured markings resembling tapestry; **carpet slipper** a slipper, orig. with upper made of thick material like carpet; **carpet-snake** (*a*) a large variegated specimen of the Australian python *Python spilotes*; (*b*) (in the Indian subcontinent) a harmless snake which enters houses, *esp.* a wolf snake, *Lycodon aulicus*; **carpet square** a more or less small square of carpet intended to fit together with others as a floor-covering; **carpet sweeper** a household implement with a revolving brush or brushes for sweeping carpets.

carpet /ˈkaːpɪt/ *v.t.* LME. [f. the n.] 1 Cover

(as) with a carpet. LME. 2 Reprimand, reprove. *colloq.* M19.

carpeting *n.* (*a*) the action of the vb; *esp.* a telling-off; (*b*) material for carpets, carpets collectively: L16.

carphology /kɑːˈfɒlədʒi/ *n.* M19. [Gk *karphologia*, f. *karphos* straw + *legein* collect: see -Y[1].] *Med.* Plucking at the bedclothes by a delirious patient.

carpincho /kɑːˈpɪntʃəʊ/ *n.* Pl. **-os**. M19. [Amer. Sp., prob. f. Tupi.] = CAPYBARA.

carpo- /ˈkɑːpəʊ/ *comb. form*[1] of CARPUS: see -O-.

carpoˈpedal *a.* relating to or involving the hands and the feet L19.

carpo- /ˈkɑːpəʊ/ *comb. form*[2] of Gk *karpos* fruit: see -O-.

carpophore *n.* (*Bot.*) a prolongation of the axis of a flower, raising the pistil above the stamens L19. **carpospore** *n.* (*Bot.*) a diploid spore produced by a carpogonium L19.

Carpocratian /kɑːpəʊˈkreɪʃ(ə)n/ *n.* L16. [f. *Carpocrates* (see below) + -IAN.] *Hist.* A follower of Carpocrates of Alexandria, 2nd-cent. AD Gnostic philosopher, who asserted the mortality of Christ's body and the creation of the world by angels.

carpogonium /kɑːpə(ʊ)ˈgəʊnɪəm/ *n.* Pl. **-nia** /-nɪə/. L19. [f. CARPO-[2] + Gk *gonos* race + -IUM.] *Bot.* The non-motile female reproductive organ of a red alga.

carpogonial *a.* L19.

carpology /kɑːˈpɒlədʒi/ *n.* E19. [f. CARPO-[2] + -LOGY.] The biology of fruits and seeds.

carpoˈlogical *a.* E19.

carpus /ˈkɑːpəs/ *n.* Pl. **-pi** /-pʌɪ/. LME. [mod.L f. Gk *karpos* wrist.] The part of the human skeleton between the forearm and the metacarpus, consisting of eight small bones and forming the wrist; *Zool.* the corresponding part in other tetrapods (e.g. the knee of a horse).

carr /kɑː/ *n.*[1] *north.* & *Sc.* OE. [Origin unkn.] A rock; *esp.* a rocky islet off the (Northumbrian or Scottish) coast.

carr /kɑː/ *n.*[2] ME. [ON *kjarr* brushwood in *kjarr-mýrr* marsh grown with brushwood (cf. Da. *kær*, *kjær*, Sw. *kärr*, Norw. *kjær*, *kjerr*).] 1 A marsh, a fen; wet boggy ground; meadowland reclaimed from bog or marsh. ME. 2 A marshy copse, esp. of alders; boggy ground overgrown with shrubs. LME.

carrack /ˈkarək/ *n. obs.* exc. *Hist.* LME. [(O)Fr. *caraque*, perh. (corresp. to It. *caracca*) f. Sp. *carraca* f. Arab., perh. f. *karākir* pl. of *ḳurḳūra* a type of (sometimes very large) merchant vessel.] A large merchant-ship equipped for warfare, *esp.* a Portuguese Indiaman; a galleon.

carrageen /ˈkarəgiːn/ *n.* Also **-gheen**. E19. [Ir. *carraigín*.] In full *carrageen moss*. An edible purple seaweed, *Chondrus crispus*, found on the coasts of northern Europe and N. America. Also called *Irish moss*.

carraˈgeenan *n.* a mixture of polysaccharides (galactans) extracted from various red and purple seaweeds and used as a gelling, thickening, and emulsifying agent in food products M20.

carrefour /karfuːr/ *n.* Pl. pronounced same. Also †***carfour***. L15. [Fr.: see CARFAX.] A crossroads, a carfax (now only in France).

¶Formerly naturalized.

carrel /ˈkar(ə)l/ *n.* Also **-ll**. L16. [App. rel. to CAROL *n.* in sense 'ring'.] 1 *Hist.* A small enclosure or study in a cloister. L16. 2 A cubicle for a reader in a library. E20.

carretera /kareˈtera, kɑːrəˈtɛːrə/ *n.* M19. [Sp.] In Spain and Spanish-speaking countries: a main road.

carriage /ˈkarɪdʒ/ *n.* LME. [ONFr. *cariage*, f. *carier* CARRY *v.*: see -AGE.] I The action of carrying. 1 Conveying, transport, esp. of merchandise. LME. †2 A toll or duty payable on the transport of goods. LME–L18. 3 (Payment in lieu of) carrying performed by a tenant as feudal service. *obs.* exc. *Hist.* LME. 4 The cost of conveying goods etc.; charge so incurred. LME. †5 Ability to carry. *rare.* L16–M18. 6 The action of carrying out, execution; conduct, management; administration. E17. 7 The carrying of a motion. L19.

4 **carriage forward** with carriage to be paid by the receiver of a parcel etc. **carriage paid** with carriage paid by the sender of a parcel etc.

II A thing carried; a manner of carrying. †8 Baggage; movable property. LME–M18. 9 A load, a quantity carried, a burden; *fig.* import, meaning. *obs.* exc. *dial.* LME. 10 Manner of carrying, esp. of the head, body, etc.; deportment; bearing. L16. 11 Demeanour; behaviour; habitual conduct. *arch.* L16. †b A piece of conduct, an action. Only in 17.

10 J. CARY The girl was walking with her usual self-contained air..; the proper carriage of a school prefect and débutante. R. GITTINGS He seemed taller, partly because of the erect carriage of his limbs and head. 11 DEFOE The affectionate carriage of this poor woman to her infant.

III Means of carrying. 12 A means of conveyance; *esp.* a wheeled vehicle for conveying people. LME. b *spec.* A four-wheeled private vehicle drawn by two or more horses. M18. c A railway passenger vehicle. M19. 13 A wheeled framework or support, esp. (in full *gun-carriage*) for a gun. See also UNDERCARRIAGE. M16. 14 A sliding or other moving part of a mechanism, whose function is to carry and move other parts, esp. in a typewriter. L17.

12 *baby carriage*, *hackney carriage*, *invalid carriage*, *railway carriage*, etc. b **carriage and pair** (**four**, **six**, etc.): with number of horses specified. LANDAU *carriage*. c *ladies' carriage*, *saloon carriage*, *smoking carriage*, etc. *train of carriages*: see TRAIN *n.*[1] 13.

Comb.: **carriage clock** a portable clock in a rectangular case with a handle; **carriage-dog** a dalmatian; **carriage release** the operation of allowing a typewriter to move freely, independently of the keys; a lever which makes this possible; *carriage return*: see RETURN *n.* 9b; **carriage trade** (now *arch.* or *joc.*) (trade with) those of sufficient wealth or social standing to maintain a private carriage; **carriageway** the part of a road intended for vehicular traffic (*dual carriageway*: see DUAL *a.*; *single carriageway*: see SINGLE *a.*).

carriageable *a.* (*a*) *rare* portable; (*b*) (of a road) passable by wheeled vehicles: L16. **carriaged** *a.* having a carriage or carriages (of a specified kind or number) M17.

carrick bend /ˈkarɪk bɛnd/ *n. phr.* E19. [Perh. f. alt. of CARRACK + BEND *n.*[1]] *Naut.* A round knot to join ropes required to go round a capstan.

carrier /ˈkarɪə/ *n.* LME. [f. CARRY *v.* + -ER[1].] I 1 *gen.* A person who or thing which carries; a bearer, a conveyor, a porter. LME. 2 A person or company undertaking for hire the conveyance of goods or passengers. LME. 3 In full *carrier pigeon*. A homing pigeon (employed to carry messages tied to its leg). M17. 4 A conduit or drainage channel for water. L18. 5 A part of a machine designed to bear or carry; *esp.* a basket, rack, etc., fixed to a bicycle for carrying luggage etc. M19. 6 A vessel intended or used to carry a particular kind of cargo or load; freq. *ellipt.* = AIRCRAFT *carrier*. L19. 7 An insoluble or inert substance used to support a pigment, catalyst, etc., or to convey a radioisotope, chromatographic sample, etc. L19. 8 A substance which effects a transference of an atom or other species, esp. in a biochemical process. L19. 9 A particle carrying an electric charge; a mobile electron or hole in a semiconductor. E20. 10 More fully *carrier wave* etc. A wave or current on which a signal can be superimposed by modulation, esp. in telecommunications. E20. 11 A person or animal that can transmit a disease, or an organism that can pass on a genetic characteristic to its offspring, without showing its effects. E20. 12 In full *carrier bag*. A strong paper or plastic bag with handles, used for shopping. E20.

2 *common carrier*: see COMMON *a. fig.*: ADAM SMITH The Dutch were the great carriers of Europe. 6 *bulk carrier*, *ore-carrier*, *troop-carrier*, etc.

II 13 (C-.) [So called from their custom of a widow's carrying (for a period) the cremated remains of her husband in a leather bag.] A member of an Athapaskan Indian people inhabiting British Columbia; the language of this people. Also *Carrier Indian*. L18.

carriole /ˈkarɪəʊl/ *n.* Also **cariole**. M18. [Fr. f. It. *carriuola* dim. of *carro* CAR: see -OLE[1].] 1 Chiefly *Hist.* A small open carriage for one; a covered light cart. M18. 2 A kind of sledge used in Canada. E19.

carrion /ˈkarɪən/ *n.* & *a.* ME. [AN, ONFr. *caroi(g)ne*, OFr. *charoigne* (mod. *charogne*) f. Proto-Romance, f. L *caro* flesh.] A *n.* †1 A dead body; a carcass. ME–M18. 2 Dead putrefying flesh. ME. 3a Human or animal flesh regarded as no better than the dead. *obs.* exc. as passing into sense 4. ME. b A worthless or noxious person or beast. *obs.* exc. *dial.* L15. 4 *fig.* Corruption, garbage, filth; something vile. LME.

2 D. ATTENBOROUGH The nautilus feeds not only on carrion but on living creatures such as crabs. 4 J. A. FROUDE Roman fashionable society hated Cæsar, and any carrion was welcome to them which would taint his reputation.

B *attrib.* or as *adj.* Of or pertaining to rotting flesh or putrefaction; rotten, loathsome. LME.

G. M. HOPKINS Not, I'll not, carrion comfort, Despair, not feast on thee.

Comb.: **carrion-beetle** a beetle of the family Silphidae, feeding on carrion; *carrion crow*: see CROW *n.*[1] 1; **carrion-flower** (*a*) a plant of the African genus *Stapelia* of the milkweed family Asclepiadaceae; (*b*) a N. American plant of the lily family, *Smilax herbacea*, having fetid flowers.

Carrion's disease /karɪˈɒnz dɪˌziːz/ *n. phr.* E20. [f. Daniel *Carrión* (*c*1850–86), Peruvian medical student, who died from the disease after voluntarily contracting it.] *Med.* Bartonellosis; *esp.* the acute form of this (= OROYA FEVER).

carritch /ˈkarɪtʃ/ *n. Sc.* M18. [Alt. of CATECHISE *n.*] *sing.* & in *pl.* = CATECHISM.

carriwitchet /karɪˈwɪtʃɪt/ *n. obs.* exc. *Sc.* Also **carwitchet** /kɑːˈwɪtʃɪt/. E17. [Origin unkn.] A pun; a conundrum.

carrom *n.* & *v.* var. of CAROM.

carronade /karəˈneɪd/ *n.* L18. [f. *Carron*, near Falkirk in Scotland, where orig. made + -ADE.] *Hist.* A (chiefly naval) short large-calibred gun.

carroon *n.* var. of CAROON.

carrot /ˈkarət/ *n.* L15. [(O)Fr. *carotte* f. L *carota* f. Gk *karōton*.] 1 An umbelliferous plant, *Daucus carota*, having a large tapering root which in cultivated forms is orange-coloured and edible; a root of this, eaten as a vegetable. L15. b *fig.* (w. allus. to the traditional use of a carrot to induce a donkey to move, freq. opp. *stick*). An enticement; a promised reward. L19. 2 Something carrot-shaped, esp. (*N. Amer.*) a plug of tobacco. M17. 3 In *pl.* Red hair; (a name for) a red-haired person. *slang.* L17.

1b J. K. GALBRAITH Along with the carrot of pecuniary reward must go the stick of personal economic disaster.

carroty *a.* like carrots; orange-red; red-haired: L17.

carrousel *n.* see CAROUSEL.

†**carrow** *n. Anglo-Ir.* L16–E19. [OIr. *cerrbach* (mod. *cearrbhach*).] An itinerant gambler.

carrozzi *n.* see KARROZZIN.

carry /ˈkari/ *n.* E17. [f. the vb.] 1 A vehicle, a cart, a barrow. *Sc.* & *north.* E17. 2 The drift of the clouds in the wind; the clouds collectively, the sky. *Sc.* L18. 3 The range of a gun; the distance traversed by a golf ball etc. before pitching; a trajectory. M19. 4a The action or an act of carrying a boat, supplies, etc., between rivers etc. or around an obstacle to navigation. *N. Amer.* M19. b *gen.* The action or an act of carrying; a manner of carrying. L19. c *Amer. Football.* The action or an act of running or rushing with the ball. M20. 5 A place or route between navigable points, over which boats, supplies, etc., have to be carried. *N. Amer.* M19.

carry /ˈkari/ *v.* LME. [AN, ONFr. *carier* var. of *charier* (mod. *charrier* cart, drag) corresp. to Prov. *carrejar*, f. *car* CAR.] I *v.t.* 1 Bear from one place to another, convey, transport, (by vehicle, ship, aircraft, etc.; on horseback; on a river, the wind, etc., by its own motion; on the person, in the hand, or *fig.* in the mind). LME. b Escort, lead, conduct, (a person, animal, etc.); take with one, esp. by force. Now *arch.* & *dial.* E16. c Of a road, pipe, wire, etc.: conduct, convey, be traversed by (traffic, liquid, electric current, etc.). E17. **d** *fig.* Continue to have with or beside one as one moves. L18. **2** Cause to move or go, impel, drive; cause or enable to proceed; (of a journey etc.) lead, bring, *to* etc. LME. **b** Urge, influence; deprive of self-control. *arch.* (now usu. *carry away*). M16. **3** Propel (a missile, ball, etc.) to a specified distance or on a specified course. LME. **b** Propel a golf ball, cricket ball, etc., beyond (a point). L19. **4** Hold up, while in motion; have on one's person, possess; bear with or within one; keep in mind. LME. **b** Have as an attribute, property, meaning, consequence, etc.; display, exhibit; involve, imply. L16. †**c** Wield (power, influence). L16–M17. **d** Be pregnant with. L18. **e** *Mil.* Hold (a weapon) in the position for saluting. L18. **f** Keep on hand; stock. M19. **g** Of a newspaper etc.: print (an article) in its pages, publish. Of a broadcasting station: put out (a programme). E20. **5** Extend, prolong, or continue (a line, process, etc.) in a specified direction or way, or to a specified point. Chiefly *fig.* LME. **6** Bear the weight of; sustain, support, (*lit.* & *fig.*). LME. †**b** Tolerate, endure. L16–L17. **c** Support with financial or other assistance; help or compensate for (a team-member etc. who does not pull his or her weight); be the major cause of the effectiveness of. L19. **7** Bear (the body, head, etc., oneself) in a specified way. L16. **8** Conduct, manage (a matter, affair, etc.). (Now usu. *carry on.*) *arch.* L16. **9** Obtain as the result of effort, win; take by assault, capture. L16. **b** Gain victory or acceptance for; *esp.* get (a measure) passed or adopted in a vote. E17. **c** Gain (a district etc.) in an election. Chiefly *US.* M19. **10** Transfer (a figure etc.) to a new page or account (now usu. *carry forward*); transfer (a figure) to the next column in an arithmetical operation. M18.

1 SHAKES. *Temp.* I'll bear your logs . . I'll carry it to the pile. G. BERKELEY If we carry our thoughts from the corporeal to the moral world. LD MACAULAY The news . . had been carried to the Earl of Pembroke. E. HEMINGWAY He wore his overcoat and carried his wet hat. R. MACAULAY Carried out to sea by the tide. P. V. WHITE The master of the Osprey will carry you to Newcastle. R. DAVIES I went back . . as fast as my artificial leg would carry me. J. D. MACDONALD Offshore islands . . composed of the materials the rivers had carried down to the sea and deposited. **b** S. JOHNSON The lady carried her horse a thousand miles. J. GALSWORTHY After three days at Robin Hill she carried her father back with her to Town. **c** G. M. TREVELYAN The improved roads carried visitors . . far afield. **2** LD MACAULAY A scanty stock of silver, which . . was to carry the nation through the summer. E. A. FREEMAN The great march which carried Harold . . to Stamford Bridge. J. R. GREEN A mission carried him in early life to Italy. A. SCHLEE More and more people entered behind her and she was carried inevitably forward . . by their pressure. **3b** B. LOCKE It is important . . to be able to hit very high iron shots to carry formidable obstacles, such as big bunkers. **4** J. CONRAD A prisoner being partly carried, partly dragged along the hall. W. CATHER He can't carry a drink or two as he used. B. SPOCK This is a special memory problem (just the way some children can't carry a tune). M. PUZO He had a license to carry a gun. J. G. FARRELL Young men carrying Sinn Fein flags. **b** SHAKES. *Hen. VIII* Words cannot carry Authority so weighty. MILTON His habit carries peace, his brow defiance. E. R. CONDER A positive judgment carrying immense consequences. B. TRAPIDO He has about him the same confident ease but carries it with greater subtlety. **f** E. REVELEY Some sort of special medicine—I'm not even sure the chemists here carry it. **g** V. S. NAIPAUL Next morning the *Trinidad Sentinel* carried this story on page five. **5** E. A. FREEMAN He did not tarry long in carrying his purpose into effect. C. P. SNOW The bedrooms . . carried comfort to such a point that it was difficult to sleep at all. C. HILL Laud's religious policy carried the re-catholicizing tendencies . . to their logical conclusion. **6** J. RUSKIN Main arches . . carried by . . pillars. H. G. WELLS A red wooden curtain pole . . carried green and dust-coloured curtains. *Conservation News* The Zambesi region . . carries a very rich vegetation. **b** SHAKES. *Lear* Man's nature cannot carry Th' affliction nor the fear. **9** C. MERIVALE He strove to carry with his own hand the victory. D. L. SAYERS Better use shock tactics and carry the place by assault. **b** P. H. STANHOPE They carried their candidates in the centres of popular election. A. BRIGGS The bill . . was finally carried by 263 votes to 46. B. CASTLE We carried the vote in committee by nine votes to six. **10** W. COBBETT You are to put down the 4 and carry 2.

II *v.i.* †**11** Ride, move with speed or energy. LME–M16. **12** Bear loads; act as a carrier. L16. **13** *Falconry.* Fly away with the quarry. E17. **14** Propel a missile. M17. **15** Of a missile, sound, etc.: travel or be propelled for a specified distance or in a specified manner (*absol.* far, well). M17. †**16** Behave. M17–E18.

14 JOHN PHILLIPS About as high as a crossbow can carry. **15** W. MAXWELL A man cursing . . can be heard a long way. All sounds carry. G. M. FRASER Their rank stench carried a good half-mile.

Phrases: **carry all before one** overcome all opposition, succeed. *carry an M under one's girdle*: see M, M 7. *carry a torch for*: see TORCH *n. carry coals to Newcastle*: see COAL *n.* **carry conviction** be convincing. **carry it** (*a*) have the advantage, win the day; †(*b*) act, behave, in a specified way. *carry one's bat*: see BAT *n.*[1] 2. **carry sail** have sails set. *carry the bat*: see BAT *n.*[1] 2. *carry the can (back)*: see CAN *n.* 1. **carry the day** win, succeed. *carry the world before one*: see WORLD *n.* **carry weight** (*a*) be influential or important; (*b*) *Horse-racing* carry weight as a handicap. **carry with one** persuade, convince (one's hearer etc.). *cash and carry*: see CASH *n.*[1] *fetch and carry*: see FETCH *v.*

With advs. in specialized senses: **carry away** (*a*) *v.phr.t.* transport, remove, inspire, fire with (excessive) enthusiasm, deprive of self-control; (*b*) *v.phr.t.* & *i.* (*Naut.*) break off and remove (a ship's mast etc.) forcibly; be lost thus; †(*c*) *carry it away*, have the advantage, win the day. **carry back** take (a person) back in thought to a past time. **carry forward** transfer (a figure etc.) to a new page or account. **carry off** (*a*) remove by force, abduct; be the cause of death of; (*b*) win, achieve; render (one's action, condition, etc.) acceptable or passable by one's manner; *carry it off (well)*, do well under difficulties. **carry on** (*a*) *v.phr.t.* continue, keep up, conduct (a conversation, a business, etc.), advance (a process etc.); (*b*) *v.phr.i.* go on with what one is doing, continue one's course, be continued; *colloq.* behave strangely or excitedly, speak angrily, flirt or have an affair (*with*). **carry out** perform, conduct to completion, put into practice. **carry over** transfer, esp. = *carry forward* above; postpone to a later time. **carry through** bring safely out of difficulties, perform to completion. **carry up** (*a*) continue (building etc.) to a given point; (*b*) trace back in time; †(*c*) bear, hold up.

Comb.: **carry-all** a carriole; *N. Amer.* a car with sideways seats; **carry-cot** a portable cot for a baby; **carry-forward** a balance of money carried forward; CARRY-ON; **carry-out** *n.* & *a.* (a quantity of prepared food, drink, etc.) bought for consumption off the premises; a take-away meal, restaurant, etc.; **carry-over** (*a*) *Stock Exch.* postponement of payment to next settling day; (*b*) a sum held over or transferred; a transference; †**carry-tale** a tell-tale.

carrying /ˈkarɪɪŋ/ *vbl n.* LME. [f. prec. + -ING[1].] **1** The action of CARRY *v.* LME. **2** *carrying(s)-on*, excitement, commotion, questionable behaviour, flirtation. *colloq.* M17.

Comb.: **carrying-place** *N. Amer.* = CARRY *n.* 5; **carrying-trade** the transportation of goods from one country to another by water or air as a business.

carry-on /ˈkarɪɒn; *in sense A.1 also* karɪˈɒn/ *n.* & *a.* L19. [f. CARRY *v.* + ON *adv.*] **A** *n.* **1** A fuss, a to-do; excitement, carryings-on. *colloq.* L19. **2** A bag or suitcase suitable for carrying on to an aircraft as hand luggage. M20. **B** *adj.* That may be carried on; suitable for carrying on to an aircraft. M20.

carse /kɑːs/ *n. Sc.* ME. [Perh. pl. of CARR *n.*[2]] (A stretch of) alluvial lowland beside a river.

carsey *n.* var. of KARZY.

Carshuni *n.* var. of GARSHUNI.

carstone /ˈkɑːstəʊn/ *n.* E19. [Prob. dial. var. of *quern-stone* s.v. QUERN *n.*] *Geol.* Hard ferruginous sandstone of Lower Cretaceous age.

carsy *n.* var. of KARZY.

cart /kɑːt/ *n.* & *v.* ME. [ON *kartr* (= OE *cræt*), prob. infl. by AN, ONFr. *carete* (mod. *charette*) dim. of *carre* CAR.] **A** *n.* †**1** A chariot, a carriage. ME–E17. **2** A strong two-wheeled or four-wheeled conveyance usu. with a low-sided rectangular body, used esp. in farming and for carrying heavy goods, and formerly for conveying convicts to the gallows and for the public exposure of offenders: without contrary specification usu. understood as horse-drawn. ME. **3** A light two-wheeled one-horse vehicle for driving in. E19.

1 SHAKES. *Haml.* Full thirty times hath Phoebus' cart gone round Neptune's salt wash and Tellus' orbed ground. **2** ROBERT BURTON As good horses draw in carts as coaches. A. E. HOUSMAN Here the hangman stops his cart: Now the best of friends must part. DAY LEWIS The rest of the flat cart was filled with hens for the market. *bullock-cart*, *handcart*, etc. *dustcart*, *hay-cart*, etc. **3** *dogcart* etc.

Phrases: **in the cart** *slang* in an awkward or losing position; in trouble. **put the cart before the horse** reverse the proper order of things; take an effect for a cause.

Comb.: **cart-body** the part of a cart in which the load is placed; **cart-horse** (orig.) a horse used to draw a cart; (now) a strong thickset horse fit for heavy work; **cart-load** a cartful; a large quantity of something (*a cart-load of monkeys*: see MONKEY *n.*); **cartman** a man who drives a cart; **cart-road** a rough road suitable only for carts and other farm vehicles; **cart-rut** a deep rut cut in soft ground by the wheels of a cart; **cart-track** (*a*) a rough track suitable only for carts and other farm vehicles; (*b*) a cart-rut; **cart('s) tail** the rear of a cart, to which formerly offenders were tied to be dragged through the streets or flogged; **cart-way** a rough way suitable only for carts and other farm vehicles; CARTWHEEL; **cart-whip** a long heavy horse-whip; **cart-wright** a maker of carts.

B *v.* **1** *v.i.* Work with or use a cart. *rare.* LME. **2** *v.t.* Convey or transport (as) in a cart; *colloq.* carry (esp. something cumbersome or heavy) over an unduly long distance, carry or take unceremoniously. LME. **b** Convey publicly in a cart as a means of punishment. *obs.* exc. *Hist.* M16. **3** *v.t.* Get (someone) into trouble; betray the hopes of, let down. Chiefly as *carted* ppl a. *slang.* L19. **4** *v.t. Cricket.* Hit hard. E20.

2 DE QUINCEY We were all carted to the little town. J. K. JEROME Harris and I . . carted out our luggage on to the doorstep. F. ASTAIRE She took on the challenging job of carting her two brats to New York in search of a career. **cart off** remove, esp. by force. **b** G. CRABBE Suspected, tried, condemned, and carted in a day.

cartage *n.* (the cost of) conveyance by cart LME. **carter** *n.* †(*a*) a charioteer; (*b*) a person who drives a cart (formerly as a type of low birth or boorish manners): ME. **cartful** *n.* as much or as many as a cart will hold LME.

carte /kɑːt/ *n.*[1] LME. [Fr. f. L *c(h)arta*: see CARD *n.*[2], CHART *n.*] †**1** A charter, a document; an exposition; a chart, a diagram. LME–M18. **2** A playing-card; in *pl.*, a game of cards. *Sc.* L15. **3** A bill of fare. Cf À LA CARTE. E19. **4** = CARTE-DE-VISITE. M19.

carte *n.*[2] see QUART *n.*[2]

carte blanche /kɑːt ˈblɑːnʃ, *foreign* kart(ə) ˈblɑ̃ːʃ/ *n. phr.* Pl. **cartes blanches** /kɑːts ˈblɑːnʃ, *foreign* kart(ə) blɑ̃ːʃ/. L17. [Fr. = blank paper.] **1** A blank sheet of paper to be filled in as a person wishes; *fig.* full discretionary power granted (now the usual sense). L17. **2** *Cards.* In piquet and bezique, a hand containing no court-cards as dealt, and attracting a compensatory score. E19.

carte-de-visite /ˌkɑːtdəvɪˈziːt/ *n.* Now *arch.* or *Hist.* Pl. **cartes-de-visite** (pronounced same). M19. [Fr. = visiting-card.] A small photographic portrait mounted on a card.

carte d'identité /kart didɑ̃tite/ *n. phr.* Pl. ***cartes d'identité*** (pronounced same). E20. [Fr.] An identity card.

carte du pays /kart dy pe(j)i/ *n. phr.* Pl. ***cartes du pays*** (pronounced same). M18. [Fr., lit. 'map of the country'.] (A statement of) the state of affairs.

cartel /*branch I* ˈkɑːt(ə)l, *branch II* kɑːˈtɛl/ *n.* Branch I also †**ch-**. M16. [Fr. f. It. *cartello* placard, challenge, dim. of *carta* f. L *c(h)arta* (see CARD *n.*[2], CHART *n.*). Branch II f. G *Kartell* f. Fr.] **I 1** In full *cartel of defiance.* A written challenge. Now *arch.* or *Hist.* M16. **2** *Hist.* A written agreement relating to the exchange or ransom of prisoners; an exchange or ransom of prisoners; (in full *cartel ship*) a ship commissioned for the exchange of prisoners. L17. **3** *gen.* A paper or card bearing writing or printing. L17. **II 4** A combination between political parties to promote a mutual interest.

L19. 5 A manufacturers' agreement or association formed to control marketing arrangements, regulate prices, etc. E20.

cartel(l)i'zation *n.* formation of or into cartels E20. **cartel(l)ize** *v.t.* & *i.* form (into) a business etc. cartel E20.

cartes blanches *n. phr.* pl. of CARTE BLANCHE.

cartes d'identité, du pays *n. phrs.* pls. of CARTE D'IDENTITÉ, DU PAYS.

Cartesian /kɑːˈtiːzjən, -ʒ(ə)n/ *a.* & *n.* M17. [mod.L *Cartesianus*, f. *Cartesius* Latinized form of the name of René *Descartes* (1596–1650), Fr. philosopher and scientist: see -IAN.] **A** *adj.* Pertaining to or characteristic of Descartes, his philosophy, or his mathematical methods. M17.

H. HALLAM *Cogito; Ergo sum*, this famous enthymem of the Cartesian philosophy. **Cartesian coordinate** each of a set of coordinates describing the position of a point in relation to a set of intersecting straight axes (usu. in *pl.*). **Cartesian devil, diver** a toy that rises and falls in a liquid when the vessel containing it is subjected to varying pressure.

B *n.* A follower of Descartes. M17.

Cartesianism *n.* the philosophy of Descartes M17.

Carthaginian /kɑːθəˈdʒɪnɪən/ *n.* & *a.* M16. [f. L *Carthago*, *-ginis* Carthage (see below) + -IAN.] (A native or inhabitant) of Carthage, a powerful ancient city of N. Africa near Tunis, defeated and destroyed by Rome in 146 BC, but later recolonized.

Carthaginian peace a peace settlement which imposes very severe terms on the defeated side.

carthamus /ˈkɑːθəməs/ *n.* M16. [mod.L f. Arab. *ḳirṭim*, *ḳurṭum* safflower.] Any plant of the genus *Carthamus* of the composite family, *esp.* safflower, *C. tinctorius*.

carthamin *n.* (*Chem.*) a red quinonoid glycoside which is the colouring matter of safflower M19.

Carthusian /kɑːˈθjuːzɪən/ *n.* & *a.* M16. [med.L *Carthusianus*, f. *Cart(h)usia* La Grande Chartreuse, a monastery near Grenoble, France: see -IAN. Cf. CHARTERHOUSE, CHARTREUSE, CHARTREUX.] **1** (A member) of the austere order of monks founded by St Bruno in 1084. M16. **2** (A past or present member) of Charterhouse School (see CHARTERHOUSE 2). M19.

cartilage /ˈkɑːt(ɪ)lɪdʒ/ *n.* LME. [Fr. f. L *cartilago*, *-agin-*.] A firm, elastic, semi-opaque connective tissue of the vertebrate body; gristle. Also, a structure made of this.

hyaline cartilage, *Meckel's cartilage*, *nasal cartilage*, *thyroid cartilage*, etc. **temporary cartilage** that cartilage in the young which later ossifies.

cartilaginifi'cation *n.* formation of or conversion into cartilage M19. **carti'laginoid** *a.* of the form or nature of cartilage M19.

cartilaginous /kɑːtɪˈladʒɪnəs/ *a.* LME. [OFr (also *-eus*), or L *cartilaginosus*, f. as prec.: see -OUS.] **1** Of, or of the nature of, cartilage. LME. **2** *Bot.* Of the texture of cartilage. L17.

1 cartilaginous fish a fish with a skeleton of cartilage, i.e. a member of the class Selachii (or Chondrichthyes), which includes the sharks and rays.

cartle *n.* see KATEL.

cartogram /ˈkɑːtəgram/ *n.* L19. [Fr. *cartogramme*, f. *carte* map: see CARD *n.*[2], -GRAM.] A map with diagrammatic statistical information.

cartographer /kɑːˈtɒgrəfə/ *n.* Also (now *rare*) **ch-**. M19. [f. next or after Fr. *cartographe*: see -GRAPHER, -ER[1]. W. *ch-* after L *charta*.] A person who draws maps; an expert in or practitioner of cartography.

cartography /kɑːˈtɒgrəfi/ *n.* Also (now *rare*) **ch-**. M19. [Fr. *cartographie*, f. *carte* map: see CARD *n.*[2], -OGRAPHY. W. *ch-* after L *charta*.] The drawing of maps or charts.

carto'graphic *a.* M19.

cartomancy /ˈkɑːtəmansi/ *n.* L19. [Fr. *cartomancie*, f. *carte* CARD *n.*[2]: see -MANCY.] Fortune-telling by playing-cards.

carton /ˈkɑːt(ə)n/ *n.* & *v.* E19. [Fr. f. as CARTOON.] **A** *n.* **1a** A light cardboard or pasteboard box; a light container of waxed cardboard, plastic, etc., in which drinks and other foodstuffs are packaged. E19. **b** Cardboard, pasteboard; papier mâché. L19. **2** The disc within the bull's-eye of a target; a shot that hits this. M19.

1a J. THURBER Fifteen large cartons filled with old Christmas cards. R. LOWELL Milk cartons, .. Two plates sheathed with silver foil.

B *v.t.* Pack in a carton. Chiefly as *cartoned* ppl a. E19.

cartonnage /ˈkɑːt(ə)nɪdʒ/ *n.* Also **cartonage**. M19. [Fr., f. as prec.: see -AGE.] *Egyptol.* A mummy-case made of tightly fitting layers of linen or papyrus glued together.

carton-pierre /kartɔ̃pjɛr/ *n.* M19. [Fr., lit. 'cardboard (of) stone'.] Papier mâché made to resemble stone or bronze.

cartoon /kɑːˈtuːn/ *n.* & *v.* L16. [It. *cartone* augm. of *carta*: see CARTEL, -OON.] **A** *n.* **1** A full-size drawing made on stout paper as a design for a painting, tapestry, mosaic, etc. L16. **2** An illustrative drawing (orig. full-page or large) in a newspaper or magazine, esp. as a vehicle for political satire or humour; an amusing drawing with or without a caption; a sequence of these in a strip. M19. **b** A film made by animating a series of drawings. E20.

2 *strip cartoon*: see STRIP *n.*[1] 3b.

B *v.* **1** *v.i.* Draw a cartoon or cartoons. Chiefly as *cartooning* vbl n. M19. **2** *v.t.* Represent in a cartoon; caricature in a cartoon. L19.

cartoonery *n.* cartoons collectively; the making of cartoons: M19. **cartoonish** *a.* resembling (the style of) a cartoon (sense 2); showing simplification or exaggeration of some features: L20. **cartoonishly** *adv.* L20. **cartoonishness** *n.* L20. **cartoonist** *n.* a person who draws cartoons L19.

cartophily /kɑːˈtɒfɪli/ *n.* M20. [f. Fr. CARTE *n.*[1] or It. *carta* (see CARTEL) + -O- + -PHILY.] The collection of picture cards, as cigarette cards etc., as a pursuit or hobby.

carto'philic *a.* & *n.* (*rare*) L19. **cartophilist** *n.* a collector of cigarette cards etc. M20.

cartouche /kɑːˈtuːʃ/ *n.* E17. [Fr. f. It. *cartoccio*, f. *carta*: see CARTEL.] **I 1** = CARTRIDGE 1. *obs.* exc. *Hist.* E17. **†b** A case of wood, pasteboard, etc., for cannon-balls. E17–M18. **II 2a** *Archit.* A scroll-shaped ornament; a scroll-shaped corbel, mutule, or modillion; a tablet representing a scroll with rolled-up ends or edges, with or without an inscription. E17. **b** A painting or drawing of a scroll with rolled-up ends, with or without a text; an ornate frame in the shape of such a scroll. L18. **3** *Egyptol.* An elongated oval with a straight bar at the end containing the hieroglyphic names and titles of kings. M19.

Comb.: **cartouche-box** (*obs.* exc. *Hist.*) a cartridge-box.

cartridge /ˈkɑːtrɪdʒ/ *n.* L16. [Alt. of prec.] **I 1** A paper, metal, etc. case containing a charge of propellent explosive for firearms or blasting, with a bullet or shot if intended for small arms. L16. **2** A case and its contents prepared for more or less direct insertion into a particular mechanism, as a spool of photographic film or magnetic tape in a container, an ink-container for a pen, etc. E20. **3** A removable pick-up head of a record-player. M20.

1 *blank cartridge*: see BLANK *a.* 3 *turnover cartridge*: see TURNOVER *a.*

†II 4 = CARTOUCHE 2. E17–M18.

Comb.: **cartridge-belt** a belt fitted with sockets for cartridges; **cartridge-box** a box for storing or carrying cartridges; **cartridge-case** (*a*) = *cartridge-box* above; (*b*) the paper, metal, etc. shell of a cartridge; **cartridge paper** a thick, rough paper used for cartridges, drawing, and for making strong envelopes.

cartulary /ˈkɑːtjʊləri/ *n.* Also **ch-**. LME. [med.L *c(h)artularium*, f. *c(h)artula* dim. of *c(h)arta*: see CHARTA, CARD *n.*[2], -ULE, -ARY[1].] **†1** A collection of medical recipes. Only in LME. **2** A place where charters or records are kept; a collection of charters or records. M16.

cartwheel /ˈkɑːtwiːl/ *n.* & *v.* Also **cart-wheel**. LME. [f. CART *n.* + WHEEL *n.*] **A** *n.* **1** A wheel of a cart. LME. **2** A lateral handspring with the arms and legs extended. M19. **3** A large coin. M19. **4** In full *cartwheel hat*. A hat with a wide circular brim. L19.

2 turn a cartwheel, cartwheels execute one of, a succession of, these movements.

B *v.i.* Move like a rotating wheel; turn a cartwheel or cartwheels; revolve. E20.

carucage /ˈkarjʊkɪdʒ/ *n.* L16. [med.L *car(r)ucagium*, f. *car(r)uca*: see next, -AGE.] *Hist.* A feudal tax levied on each carucate of land.

carucate /ˈkarjʊkeɪt/ *n.* LME. [med.L *car(r)ucata*, f. *car(r)uca* (orig.) coach, chariot, in Gaul early applied to the wheel-plough, rel. to L *carrus* CAR *n.*: see -ATE[1].] *Hist.* A measure of land equivalent to the area that could be ploughed in a year by one plough and eight oxen; a plough-land.

caruncle /ˈkarəŋk(ə)l, kəˈrʌŋ-/ *n.* L16. [Obs. Fr. f. L *caruncula* dim. of *caro* flesh: see -UNCLE.] A fleshy excrescence or swelling, such as that at the inner corner of the eye (the *lacrimal caruncle*), or the wattles of a turkey, etc., or (*Bot.*) adjoining the micropyle of certain seeds.

ca'runcular *a.* of the nature of or resembling a caruncle M19. **ca'runculate** *a.* having a caruncle or caruncles E19. **ca'runculated** *a.* (now *rare*) = CARUNCULATE E19.

carvacrol /ˈkɑːvəkrɒl/ *n.* M19. [f. mod.L (*Carum*) *carvi* caraway + L *acris* ACRID *a.* + -OL.] *Chem.* A fungicidal liquid phenol, $C_{10}H_{14}O$, present in many essential oils.

carval /ˈkɑːv(ə)l/ *n.* L19. [Manx.] A Manx carol or ballad on a sacred subject.

carve /kɑːv/ *v.* Pa. pple **carved**, (*arch.* & *poet.*) **carven** /ˈkɑːv(ə)n/. [OE *ċeorfan* = OFris. *kerva*, (M)Du. *kerven*, MHG *kerben*, f. WGmc.] **1** *v.t.* & *i.* Cut. Long *obs.* in *gen.* sense. OE. **2** *v.t.* Produce or shape by cutting, chiselling, or sculpturing, (a statue, portrait, representation in relief or intaglio, an inscription, a design, *out of*, *in*, or *on* a material). OE. **b** *v.t.* Fashion (a material, *into* something) by cutting, chiselling, or sculpturing; cover or adorn with (or *with*) figures cut out, cut designs, etc. ME. **c** *v.i.* Cut figures, designs, etc.; practise sculpture, engraving, etc. M16. **3** *v.i.* & *t.* Cut up (meat etc.) into portions for serving; cut *into* (meat etc.) to produce servings. ME. **†b** *v.i.* Of a woman: be hospitable, be affable. *rare* (Shakes.). Only in L16. **c** *v.t.* Slash or cut with a knife or razor. Also foll. by *up*. *slang.* E20. **†4** *v.t.* Divide or part by cutting, cleave. LME–E17. **5** *v.t.* & *i.* Cut (a way, passage, etc.). LME. **†6** *v.t.* & *i.* Apportion; reserve, take, (*for*); minister *to*. L16–M18. **7** *v.t.* Divide into several pieces or portions; subdivide. E18.

2 TENNYSON An angel .. carved in stone. R. KIPLING I carved on the stone: '*After me cometh a Builder.*' b J. MARQUAND Sandal-wood, carved into a design of herons and lotus flowers. R. LEHMANN A crook-handled Alpenstock carved with edelweiss. K. CLARK He carved marble faster than any mason. 3 J. WYNDHAM Over at a side-table three girls were .. carving chickens. J. GRIGSON As you carve into the chicken, sprinkle it lightly with salt. 5 W. OWEN Swimmers carving thro' the sparkling cold. **6 carve for oneself** take at one's pleasure; indulge oneself.

With advs. in specialized senses: **carve out** (*a*) take from a larger whole (*Law* esp. a smaller estate from a larger one); (*b*) cut out (a way, passage, etc.); create or bring about by much effort (a career, name, etc., *for* oneself or oneself and others). **carve up** (*a*) cut up into several pieces (see also sense 3c above); divide into several portions; (*b*) *slang* cheat, swindle.

Comb.: **carve-up** *slang* (the result of) a sharing-out, esp. of dishonest gains.

carvel /ˈkɑːv(ə)l/ *n.* LME. [OFr. *carvelle* (mod. *caravelle*) f. Port. *caravela* dim. of *caravo* f. late L *carabus* f. Gk *karabos* horned beetle, crayfish, light ship.] = CARAVEL.

Comb.: **carvel-built, -planked** *adjs.* (of a boat etc.) with planks that are set flush (opp. *clinker-built*).

carver /ˈkɑːvə/ *n.*[1] LME. [f. CARVE + -ER[1].] **1** A person who carves. LME. **2** A carving-knife; (in *pl.*) a carving-knife and -fork. M19. **3** An armchair in a set of dining-room chairs. E20.

Carver /ˈkɑːvə/ *n.*[2] *US.* E20. [John *Carver* (1576–1621), first governor of Plymouth Colony.] In full *Carver chair*. A chair with a rush seat, arms, and a back having horizontal and vertical spindles.

carvery /ˈkɑːvəri/ *n.* M19. [f. CARVE + -ERY.] **1** Meat for carving. *rare.* M19. **2** Carved work. *rare.*

M19. 3 A buffet or restaurant where meat is carved from a joint as required. M20.

carving /ˈkɑːvɪŋ/ *n.* ME. [f. CARVE + -ING[1].] 1 The action of CARVE. ME. 2 Carved work; a carved figure, design, etc. LME.

Comb.: **carving-fork**: long-tined, used to steady a joint etc. and serve portions; **carving-knife**: long-bladed, used for cutting portions of meat for serving.

carvone /ˈkɑːvəʊn/ *n.* L19. [f. as CARVACROL + -ONE.] *Chem.* A liquid cyclic ketone, $C_{10}H_{14}O$, with a characteristic odour, present in caraway and dill oils.

carwitchet *n.* var. of. CARRIWITCHET.

caryatid /karɪˈatɪd/ *n.* Pl. **-ides** /-ɪdiːz/, **-ids** M16. [(Fr. *caryatide* f. It. *cariatide* f.) L *caryatides* f. Gk. *karuatides* (pl.) priestesses of Artemis at *Karuai* (Caryae) in Laconia.] *Archit.* A female figure used as a pillar to support an entablature. Cf. TELAMON.

caryophyllaceous /ˌkarɪəʊfɪˈleɪʃəs/ *a.* M19. [f. mod.L *Caryophyllaceae* (see below), f. *caryophyllus* clove-pink f. Gk *karuophullon*: see -ACEOUS.] *Bot.* Of or pertaining to the family Caryophyllaceae, including the pinks, campions, and stitchworts.

caryopsis /karɪˈɒpsɪs/ *n.* Pl. **-opses** /-ˈɒpsiːz/. E19. [mod.L, f. Gk *karuon* nut + *opsis* appearance.] *Bot.* A one-seeded indehiscent fruit having the pericarp fused to the seed-coat, as in wheat and maize.

carz(e)y *ns.* vars. of KARZY.

ca. sa. /keɪ ˈseɪ, kɑː ˈsɑː/ *n. phr.* L18. [Abbrev.] *Law.* = CAPIAS *ad satisfaciendum.*

casale /kaˈsaːle/ *n.* Also *-sal* /-ˈsɑːl/. E16. [It., f. *casa* house.] In Italy, Malta, etc.: a hamlet.

†casamat *n.* see CASEMATE.

Casanova /kasəˈnəʊvə, -z-/ *n.* E20. [Giovanni Jacopo *Casanova* de Seingalt (1725–98), It. adventurer.] A man who engages in promiscuous love affairs.

casbah *n.* var. of KASBAH.

cascabel /ˈkaskəb(ə)l/ *n.* Also **-able**. M17. [Sp. *cascabel*, f. Catal. (Prov.) *cascavel* f. med.L *cascabellus* little bell.] The knob at the rear end of a cannon; also, the whole section of a cannon behind the ring bolted to the emplacement.

cascade /kasˈkeɪd/ *n.* & *v.* M17. [Fr. f. It. *cascata*, f. *cascare* fall f. Proto-Romance, f. L *casus* fall: see CASE *n.*[1], -ADE.] **A** *n.* 1 A waterfall, esp. a small one; a section of a large broken (esp. artificial) waterfall; a falling body of water. M17. **b** *transf.* & *fig.* A quantity of material etc. falling; a falling stream *of*. M19. 2 A pyrotechnic device imitating a waterfall. M18. 3 A succession of electrical devices or stages in a process. M19. 4 A wavy arrangement of hanging lace etc. L19.

1 F. TUOHY The rain . . fell in a solid cascade. **b** R. KIPLING A cascade of Survey-instruments, books, diaries, [etc.]. C. S. FORESTER The battle had begun in a muddle amid a cascade of vague orders.

B *v.* 1 *v.i.* Fall in or like a cascade. E18. 2 *v.i.* Vomit. *arch. colloq.* L18. 3 *v.t.* Connect (electrical devices) in a cascade. E20.

1 R. CHANDLER From his outer breast pocket cascaded a show handkerchief. D. WELCH Short, sneering Chinese words cascaded out of his mouth. G. HUNTINGTON Down a little ravine a stream cascaded.

cascara /kaˈskɑːrə/ *n.* L19. [Sp. *cáscara* (*sagrada*) lit. '(sacred) bark'.] In full *cascara sagrada* /səˈgrɑːdə/. The bark of a Californian buckthorn, *Rhamnus purshiana*; an extract of this, used as a purgative.

cascarilla /kaskəˈrɪlə/ *n.* L17. [Sp., dim. of prec.] The aromatic bark of the W. Indian plant *Croton eluteria*. Also *cascarilla bark*.

case /keɪs/ *n.*[1] ME. [(O)Fr. *cas* f. L *casus*, f. base of *cadere* to fall. In branch II directly f. L, tr. Gk *ptōsis* lit. 'fall'.] **I †1** A thing that befalls or happens, an event, occurrence; chance, hazard. ME–L16. 2 An instance of a thing's occurrence, a circumstance, a fact, etc. ME. **b** A person (of a specified sort); an eccentric or comical person. *slang.* M19. **c** An infatuation, an instance of falling in love. *slang.* M19. 3 Condition, state, plight; (good) physical condition. *arch.* exc. in certain phrs. (see below). ME. 4 The state of matters relating to a given person or thing, one's circumstances or position; *the* actual state of affairs, *the* fact. LME. 5 The condition of disease or injury of a person etc.; an instance of disease or injury; *colloq.* a patient, a person in need of (specified) treatment. LME. 6 A legal action or suit, *esp.* one brought to trial; a statement of the facts in an adjudicated case, drawn up for a higher court's consideration; an action or suit that has been decided and may be cited. E16. 7 The sum of arguments on one side of a legal cause or *transf.* of any matter of debate or controversy; a valid set of arguments. L16. 8 An incident or set of circumstances for investigation by police, a detective agency, a social worker, etc. M19.

1 CAXTON By caase of fortune. SPENSER I you recount a ruefull cace. 2 R. DAVIES You get used to vanity, but Andro was a very special case. A. HAILEY A clear case of the women versus the men. **b** K. WATERHOUSE They laughed . . , shaking their heads. 'He's a case, i'n't he?' 3 AV *Exod.* 5:19 They were in euill case. SWIFT Their Horses large, but extreamly out of Case. R. BOLT I have . . been several times in such a case that I thought to die within the hour. 4 JER. TAYLOR He hath no need to use them, as the case now stands. LD MACAULAY The case with me is the reverse. J. F. KENNEDY In Germany's case . . the old ideas and beliefs were completely destroyed. L. EDEL As has often been the case, changes in philosophical thought heralded technical innovations in the arts. 5 W. H. DIXON At Deal they shipped a case of small-pox. N. MITFORD Not . . able to leave the Treatment Room . . except to carry 'cases' upstairs to the Hospital. W. C. WILLIAMS My first case was one of dandruff which I treated with some simple remedy. H. ROBBINS She's a mental case. T. S. ELIOT I will not discuss my case before another patient. 6 SHAKES. *Haml.* Why may that not be the skull of a lawyer? Where be his quiddities now, . . his cases, his tenures, and his tricks? F. RAPHAEL It was six months before the case came up. 7 M. DRAYTON My doubtfull Case to plead. R. A. KNOX In arguing, never disguise from yourself the strength of the other man's case. T. BENN Let me try and make the case for fundamental changes to the way our economy is organised. 8 L. LEE The police left . . with the case unsolved.

II 9 *Gram.* Any of the inflected forms of noun, adjective, or pronoun which express the varied relation in which the word may stand to other words in the sentence; this relation itself whether indicated by inflection or not. LME.

Phrases: **as the case may be** according to the situation. *by the (very) nature of the case*: see NATURE *n.* *case in point*: see POINT *n.*[1] *case of* CONSCIENCE. *from the (very) nature of the case*: see NATURE *n.* *hard case*: see HARD *a.* **have a case on** *slang* be infatuated or in love with. **†if case** = *in case* below. *in any case*: see ANY *a.* 1a. **in case** if, in the event that, lest. **in case of** in the event of. **in good, bad,** etc., **case** *arch.* in good, bad, etc., condition, well, badly, etc., off. **in no case** under no circumstances. **in that case** if that is true, should that happen. **in the case of** as regards. *in the (very) nature of the case*: see NATURE *n.* **(just) in case** (as a precaution) against some possible occurrence. **leading case** *Law* a case serving as a precedent for deciding others. **make out a case (for)** put forward valid arguments (for). *meet the case*: see MEET *v.* **on the case** *Hist.* (of a common-law action) based on a writ setting out fully details of a personal wrong not involving force. *special case*: see SPECIAL *a.* *state a case*: see STATE *v.* STATED *case*. *subjective case*: see SUBJECTIVE *a.* 5. *test case*: see TEST *n.*[1] *the state of the case*: see STATE *n.* *trespass on the case*: see TRESPASS *n.* 3.

Comb.: **casebook** a book containing records of legal, medical, or other cases; **case conference** a meeting of professionals (as doctors, teachers, social workers, etc.) to discuss a particular case; **case grammar** *Ling.* a form of transformational grammar in which the deep structure of sentences is analysed in terms of semantic case relationships; **case history** a record of a person's origins, personal history, and other information, for use in determining (esp. medical) treatment or other course of action; **case-law** law as settled by decided cases; **case-load** the cases with which a doctor etc. is concerned at any one time; **case-study** (a record of) an attempt to understand a person, matter, etc., from collected information about his, her, or its development; **casework** social work concerned with individual persons or small groups (also more fully *social casework*); **caseworker** a social worker involved in casework (also more fully *social caseworker*).

case /keɪs/ *n.*[2] LME. [OFr. *casse* dial. var. of *chasse* (mod. *châsse* reliquary, frame) f. L *capsa* box, bookcase, f. base of *capere* to hold: in sense 5 perh. infl. by It. *casa* house.] 1 A thing fitted to contain something else; a box, receptacle, bag, sheath, etc.; a glass box for displaying specimens, curiosities, etc. LME. 2 The outer protective or covering part of a natural or manufactured object, as a seed-vessel, chrysalis, sausage, watch, book, etc. LME. 3 The frame in which a door, stair, window, etc., is set. E16. 4 A box with its appropriate contents; hence, a brace (of pistols etc.), *gen.* a set. M16. 5 The shell or carcass of a building; a house, esp. (*slang*) a brothel. M16. 6 *Printing* (now chiefly *Hist.*). A receptacle divided into compartments for type. L16. 7 In full *case-shot*. Bullets in an iron case fired from a cannon; shrapnel. E17. 8 In faro, the fourth card of a denomination, remaining in the box when the other three have been dealt. M19.

1 *attaché case, bookcase, brief-case, card case, cigarette-case, crankcase, dressing-case, notecase, packing-case, pillowcase, showcase, spectacle-case, suitcase,* etc. WARDIAN *case.* 2 SHAKES. *Wint. T.* They seem'd almost, with staring on one another, to tear the cases of their eyes. OED Cloth cases . . for binding the volume will be issued with the December number. 4 C. MARLOWE This case of rapiers. SIR W. SCOTT Cicely . . displayed a case of teeth which might have rivalled ivory. R. BRAUTIGAN A couple of cases of sweet wine.

Phrases: **come, get,** etc., **down to cases** *US colloq.* come to the point. **keep cases** *US colloq.* note cards as they are dealt, keep a close watch. **lower case** (*a*) (chiefly *Hist.*) a receptacle for type for small letters; (*b*) the small letters used in printing or (*loosely*) in writing, typing, etc. **upper case** (*a*) (chiefly *Hist.*) a receptacle for type for capital letters; (*b*) the capital letters used in printing or (*loosely*) in writing, typing, etc.

Comb.: **case-bottle** (*a*) a bottle that fits in a case with others; (*b*) a bottle with a protective case; **case-harden** *v.t.* harden on the surface; *spec.* give a steel surface to (iron) by carburizing; *fig.* make callous; **case-knife** a knife carried in a sheath; **case-oil** oil etc. transported in containers packed in wooden cases; *case-shot*: see sense 7 above; **case-weed** *dial.* shepherd's purse; **case-worm** a caddis-worm.

case /keɪs/ *v.t.* LME. [f. CASE *n.*[2]] 1 Provide with a case; enclose in or as in a case; encase, surround *with*. LME. 2 Strip of its case; skin. Now *dial.* & *N. Amer.* L16. 3 Examine beforehand, size up, spy out, esp. in preparation for robbery. *slang.* E20.

1 POPE They case their limbs in brass; to arms they run. E. K. KANE Bones of seals, walrus, and whales—all now cased in ice. J. GWILT A brick wall . . cased with stone. 3 J. STEINBECK He was casing the field for a career.

casing *n.* (*a*) the action of the vb; (*b*) material or a structure that encases (*surface casing*: see SURFACE *n.* & *a.*): L16.

caseation /keɪsɪˈeɪʃ(ə)n/ *n.* LME. [med.L *caseatio(n-)*, f. L *caseus* cheese: see -ATION.] 1 The coagulation of milk; conversion into cheese. Long *rare* or *obs.* LME. 2 *Med.* A form of necrosis characteristic of tuberculosis, in which diseased tissue forms a firm and dry mass like cheese in appearance. M19.

ˈcaseate *v.i.* [back-form.] undergo caseation (sense 2) L19.

casein /ˈkeɪsiːn, -sɪɪn/ *n.* M19. [f. L *caseus* cheese + -IN[1].] The chief protein of milk; *esp.* this in coagulated form, as in cheese.

caseinogen /-ˈsiːn-, -sɪˈɪn-/ *n.* the soluble form in which casein occurs in milk L19.

casemate /ˈkeɪsmeɪt/ *n.* Also (earlier) **†casamat**. M16. [(Fr. f.) It. *casamatta*, earlier *camata*, perh. f. Gk *khasma*, pl. *-mata*, CHASM.] A chamber in the thickness of a wall of a fortress, provided with embrasures for defence. Also, an armoured enclosure protecting guns in a warship.

casemated *a.* provided with casemates M18.

casement /ˈkeɪsm(ə)nt/ *n.* LME. [AL *cassimentum*, f. *cassa* (L *capsa* CASE *n.*[2]): see -MENT.] 1 *Archit.* A hollow moulding, *esp.* a cavetto. Also, a matrix made to receive a monumental brass. LME. 2 A vertically-hinged frame with glass forming (part of) a window (the usual sense); *literary* a window. M16.

Comb.: **casement cloth** plain fabric used chiefly for curtains; **casement window**: with a vertically-hinged frame.

caseous /ˈkeɪsɪəs/ *a.* M17. [f. L *caseus* cheese + -OUS.] **1** Of or like cheese, cheesy. M17. **2** *Med.* Like cheese in appearance; characterized by caseation. M18.

caser /ˈkeɪsə/ *n. slang.* M19. [Prob. f. Yiddish *keser* f. Heb. *keṯer* crown.] A crown, five shillings or (now) 25 pence; *US* a dollar.

casern /kəˈzəːn/ *n.* Also **-z-**, **-ne**. L17. [Fr. *caserne* f. Prov. *cazerna* f. Proto-Romance f. L *quaterna* (hut) for four.] A barrack; *esp.* one erected temporarily in a garrison town.

casevac /ˈkasɪvak/ *n. slang.* M20. [f. CASUALTY + EVACUATION. Cf. TACEVAL.] The evacuation of casualties of battle by air.

cash /kaʃ/ *n.*[1] L16. [Fr. *casse* or its source It. *cassa* f. L *capsa* CASE *n.*[2]] †**1 a** A box for money; a cash-box. L16–M18. **b** A sum of money. L17–M18. **2** Ready money, actual coins, notes, etc., (opp. *credit*); (in banking and commerce) coins, or coins and banknotes, as opp. to cheques and orders; *gen.* (*colloq.*) money, wealth. L16.

2 **cash and carry** (designating) a system whereby the purchaser pays cash for (bulk orders of) goods and takes them away personally; (a store) trading thus. *cash down*: see DOWN *adv.* **cash on delivery** the forwarding of goods against cash to be paid to the postman or carrier; abbrev. *COD.* **hard cash** (*a*) coins as opp. to paper money; (*b*) money as opp. to cheques etc. *petty cash*: see PETTY *a.*

Comb.: **cash-account**: to which nothing is carried but cash received and cash paid; **cash-book**: in which is entered a record of all cash paid and received; **cash-box** a box where cash is kept; **cashcard** a coded card inserted into a cash-dispenser to make a withdrawal; **cash crop** (orig. *US*): cultivated primarily for its commercial value (as opp. to subsistence); **cash desk** a desk where cash is taken in a shop etc.; *cash dispenser*: see DISPENSER 3; **cash flow** the movement of money as affecting liquidity, or as a measure of profitability; **cash nexus** *the* relationship constituted by monetary transactions; **cash payment**: in ready money; **cashpoint** (a location of) a cash-dispenser; **cash price**: for payment in ready money (the lowest); **cash register** a till which visibly records the amount of each purchase, totals receipts, etc.; **cash-sale**: for ready money; **cash surrender value** the value of an insurance policy etc. cashed before it matures; **cash value** (*a*) the value in cash, *spec.* = *cash surrender value* above; (*b*) *Philos.* the empirical content of a concept, word, or proposition.

cashless *a.* M18.

cash /kaʃ/ *n.*[2] Pl. same. L16. [Port. †*caxa*, *caixa* f. Tamil *kācu*, infl. by prec.] *Hist.* Any of various southern Indian, SE Asian, and Chinese coins of low value.

†**cash** *v.*[1]*t.* M16–E19. [Var. of CASS *v.*] = CASHIER *v.* 1, 2.

cash /kaʃ/ *v.*[2] E19. [f. CASH *n.*[1]] **1** *v.t.* Give or obtain cash for (a note, cheque, etc.) E19. **b** *Bridge.* Lead (a winning card); win (a trick) by leading a winning card. M20. **2** *cash up*: a *v.i.* Pay the full amount of arrears, pay up. Now chiefly *US.* E19. **b** *v.t.* & *i.* Add up (takings etc.). M20. **3** *cash in*: a *v.t.* Exchange for cash. L19. **b** *v.i.* Settle accounts (orig. at the end of a poker game); *fig.* die. L19. **c** Foll. by *on*: realize profit on; *fig.* get advantage from. E20.

3a **cash in one's chips, checks**, etc., exchange counters for money on leaving the gaming-table; settle accounts; *fig.* die.

cashable *a.* able to be cashed L19.

†**casha** *n.* see KASHA *n.*[1]

cashel /ˈkaʃ(ə)l/ *n.* M19. [Ir. *caiseal* f. L *castellum* fortlet.] In Ireland, an ancient circular wall enclosing a group of ecclesiastical buildings.

cashew /ˈkaʃuː, kəˈʃuː/ *n.* L16. [Port. f. Tupi (*a*)*cajú*.] (More fully *cashew tree*) a large tree, *Anacardium occidentale*, native to tropical America and cultivated for its edible kidney-shaped nuts; (more fully *cashew-nut*) a nut of this tree; the fleshy receptacle bearing several such nuts.

cashier /kaˈʃɪə/ *n.* L16. [Du. *cassier* or its source Fr. *caissier*, f. *caisse* CASH *n.*[1]: see -IER.] A person in charge of a bank's or business's cash; a person who handles customer payments in a shop etc.

cashier /kəˈʃɪə, ka-/ *v.t.* L16. [Early Flem. *kasseren* disband (soldiers), revoke (a will), f. Fr. *casser* break, dismiss, rescind = It. *cassare* cancel, f. L *quassare* QUASH *v.*] †**1** Discharge or disband (troops). L16–M18. **2** Dismiss from a position of command or authority, esp. with disgrace; depose. L16. **3** *gen.* Dismiss. *obs.* exc. as *fig.* use of sense 2. L16. **4** Discard; get rid of. *arch.* L16.

2 W. S. MAUGHAM He'd been kicked out of the Officers' Club at Warsaw and cashiered because he'd been caught cheating at cards. 3 ADDISON The Ladies .. have already cashiered several of their Followers.

cashierment *n.* M17.

cashmere /kaʃˈmɪə, *esp. adj.* ˈkaʃmɪə/ *n.* & *a.* L17. [Early spelling of *Kashmir* in Asia (see KASHMIRI): cf. CASSIMERE.] **A** *n.* **1** (Material made from) the fine soft wool of the Kashmir goat or the wild goat of Tibet; woollen fabric imitating this. L17. **2** A cashmere shawl etc. E19. **B** *adj.* Made of cashmere. E19.

¶Rare bef. 19.

casino /kəˈsiːnəʊ/ *n.* Pl. **-os**. See also CASSINO. M18. [It., dim. of *casa* house f. L *casa* cottage.] **1** Orig., a public room used for social meetings; *esp.* a public music or dancing saloon. Now, a building for gambling, often with other amenities. M18. **2** A summer-house (*spec.* in Italy). M18.

cask /kɑːsk/ *n.* & *v.* E16. [Fr. *casque* or Sp. *casco* helmet, CASQUE. In sense 1 only in Eng.] **A** *n.* **1** A wooden vessel of cylindrical form, usu. bulging in the middle, made of curved staves bound together by hoops, with flat ends, used esp. for alcoholic drinks; a similar vessel of metal, plastic, etc.; a barrel. E16. **b** Such a vessel and its contents; the capacity of such a vessel as a measure for wine, spirits, etc. E18. †**2 a** = CASKET *n.* 1. *rare* (Shakes.). Only in L16. **b** A case; a shell. M17–E18. †**3** = CASQUE 1. L16–L18.

3 *fig.*: SHAKES. *Coriol.* Not moving From th' cask to th' cushion, but commanding peace .. As he controll'd the war.

Comb.: **cask-conditioned** *a.* (of beer) matured naturally in a cask, without chemical processing.

B *v.t.* Put into a cask. M16.

casket /ˈkɑːskɪt/ *n.* & *v.* LME. [Perh. AN alt. of synon. (O)Fr. CASSETTE.] **A** *n.* **1** A small box or chest for jewels, letters, cremated ashes, or other things of value, itself often of value and richly ornamented. LME. **2** A (rectangular) coffin. Orig. *US.* M19.

1 *fig.*: SHAKES. *John* They found him dead, .. An empty casket, where the jewel of life .. was .. ta'en away.

B *v.t.* Enclose or store in a casket. E17.

†**Casleu** *n.* see KISLEV.

Caslon /ˈkazlən/ *n.* M19. [William *Caslon*, father (1692–1766) and son (1720–78), Eng. typefounders.] More fully *Caslon font, type*, etc. A style of type cut by the Caslons or imitated from theirs.

Caspian /ˈkaspɪən/ *a.* & *n.* M16. [f. L *Caspius* (Gk *Kaspios*) + -AN.] **A** *adj.* Designating, of, or pertaining to an inland sea of central Asia. M16. **B** *n.* *The* Caspian Sea. L16.

casque /kɑːsk/ *n.* L17. [Fr. f. Sp. *casco*: cf. CASK.] **1** A piece of armour to cover the head; a helmet. Now *Hist.* or *poet.* L17. **2** *Zool.* A helmet-like structure, as in the cassowaries and hornbills. L18.

casquet /ˈkɑːskɪt; *foreign* kaske (*pl. same*)/ *n.* E17. [Fr., dim. of CASQUE: see -ET[1].] *Hist.* A light and open helmet.

cass /kas/ *v.t. obs.* exc. *Sc.* LME. [Fr. *casser* f. L *quassare* QUASH *v.*, the sense later infl. by *cassare* annul.] **1** Make void, annul, quash. LME. **2** Discharge; cashier. M16.

cassab /kəˈsɑːb/ *n.* L19. [Urdu f. Arab. *ḳaṣṣāb* player of a flute or pipe.] An Asian merchant seaman.

cassada *n.* var. of. CASSAVA.

Cassandra /kəˈsandrə/ *n.* E17. [L f. Gk *Kas*(*s*)*andra*, daughter of Priam king of Troy, condemned by Apollo to prophesy correctly but never to be believed.] A prophet of disaster, *esp.* one who is disbelieved.

cassareep /ˈkasəriːp/ *n.* M19. [Carib.] A thick brown syrup prepared by boiling down the juice of the cassava with sugar, spices, etc.

cassata /kəˈsɑːtə/ *n.* E20. [It.] A Neapolitan ice-cream containing fruit and nuts.

†**cassate** *v.t.* L15–M18. [L *cassat-* pa. ppl stem of *cassare*: see CASS *v.*, -ATE[3].] = CASS *v.*

cassation /kəˈseɪʃ(ə)n/ *n.*[1] LME. [f. as prec.: see -ATION.] Annulment, cancellation.

Court of Cassation a court of appeal in France etc.

cassation /kaˈseɪʃ(ə)n/ *n.*[2] L19. [G *Kassation* serenade f. It. *cassazione*.] *Mus.* An eighteenth-century orchestral composition resembling a serenade.

cassava /kəˈsɑːvə/ *n.* Also **-da** /-də/. M16. [Taino *casávi*, *cazábbi*, infl. by Fr. *cassave*, Sp. *cassava*.] **1** A plant of the spurge family, *Manihot esculenta* (manioc), grown in the tropics for its tuberous roots and having two groups of cultivars (called more fully *bitter* and *sweet cassava* according to the amount of cyanide in their untreated roots). M16. **2** Starch or flour obtained from its roots; bread made from this. L16.

casse /kɑːs/ *n.*[1] L19. [Fr., f. *casser* to break.] Souring of certain wines, accompanied by the loss of colour and the throwing of a sediment.

casse *n.*[2] var. of CASSIE *n.*[1]

Cassegrain /kasɪˈgreɪn/ *n.* L19. [f. Giovanni *Cassegrain* (1625–1712), Fr. astronomer.] *Astron.* **1** Used *attrib.* with ref. to a kind of reflecting telescope having a convex secondary mirror which produces a focus at an aperture in the centre of the primary mirror, as *Cassegrain focus, telescope*, etc. L19. **2** A Cassegrain telescope. L19.

Cassegrainian *a.* pertaining to or designating a telescope of this kind E19.

Casseiver /kəˈsiːvə/ *n.* Also **c-**. L20. [f. CASSETTE + RECEIVER.] (Proprietary name for) a combined cassette recorder and radio receiver.

casserole /ˈkasərəʊl/ *n.* & *v.* E18. [Fr., extension of *cassole* dim. of *casse* f. Prov. *casa* f. late L *cattia* ladle, pan f. Gk *kuathion*, *-eion* dim. of *kuathos* cup: see -OLE[1].] **A** *n.* **1** A covered heatproof vessel in which food is cooked and served (now also *casserole dish, pan*, etc.); (a dish of) food cooked in this. E18. **2** The edging or outer portion of certain dressed dishes. Now *rare*. E18. **B** *v.t.* Cook in a casserole. M20.

cassette /kəˈsɛt/ *n.* L18. [Fr., dim. of *casse*, *caisse* CASE *n.*[2]: see -ETTE.] **1** A casket. Now *rare*. L18. **2** A container for transporting photographic plates; a frame or holder for an X-ray plate or film. L19. **3** A container for a spool of magnetic tape, photographic film, etc., fashioned so as to be immediately usable on insertion into equipment designed for it; (now usu.) such a container together with its tape, film, etc.; a video or audio magnetic recording on such a tape etc. M20. **4** *Genetics.* A block of genetic material which can be inserted or moved as a unit, *esp.* one which is expressed only at one location. L20.

Comb.: **cassette deck, player, (tape-)recorder**: designed to (record and) play back magnetic tapes.

cassia /ˈkasɪə/ *n.* OE. [L *cas*(*s*)*ia* f. Gk *kasia* f. Heb. *qĕṣīʿāh*.] **1** An inferior kind of cinnamon; *esp.* the bark of the Far Eastern tree *Cinnamomum cassia*, of the bay family. Also *cassia bark*. OE. **b** The tree yielding this. Also *cassia tree*. LME. **c** A fragrant tree or shrub (cf. *Ps.* 45:8). *poet.* L16. **2** Any leguminous plant of the genus *Cassia*, *esp.* one yielding senna. Also called *shower tree*. LME. **b** Any medicinal product obtained from this. M16.

†**cassidony** *n.*[1] ME–M18. [OFr. *cassidoine* pop. var. of *calcidoine* f. as CHALCEDONY.] = CHALCEDONY.

†**cassidony** *n.*[2] L16–M18. [Origin unkn.] French lavender, *Lavandula stoechas*.

cassie /ˈkasi/ *n.*[1] Also **casse** /kas/. L17. [Fr. (*papier*) *cassé* broken (paper).] In full *cassie paper*. The paper of the two outside quires of a ream.

cassie /ˈkasi/ *n.*[2] *N. Amer.* L19. [Fr. f. Prov. *cacio* acacia.] The opopanax tree, *Acacia farnesiana*.

cassimere /ˈkasɪmɪə/ *n.* M18. [Var. of

CASHMERE.] A medium-weight twilled woollen cloth of soft texture. Cf. KERSEYMERE.

Cassinese /kasɪˈniːz/ *a.* & *n.* Pl. of n. same. L19. [It., f. Monte *Cassino* where the earliest Benedictine monastery was founded: see -ESE.] (A monk) of the Benedictine order of Monte Cassino.

cassinette /kasɪˈnɛt/ *n.* E19. [Perh. alt. of CASSIMERE: see -ETTE.] A thin fine twilled cloth with a cotton warp and a weft of wool or wool and silk.

Cassinian /kəˈsɪnɪən/ *a.* E18. [f. *Cassini* (see below) + -AN.] *Math.* Of or pertaining to the French astronomer G. D. Cassini (1625–1712) or other astronomers descended from him, or their work. Chiefly in *Cassinian oval* below.

Cassinian oval an oval with two foci such that the product of the focal distances of any point on the curve is a constant (instead of their sum being constant, as in an ellipse); any closed curve defined in this way.

cassino /kəˈsiːnəʊ/ *n.* L18. [Var. of CASINO.] A two-handed card-game in which players match or combine cards exposed on the table with cards from their hands. Also, either of two high-scoring cards in this game, (*a*) *big cassino*, (now *rare*) *great cassino*, the ten of diamonds, (*b*) *little cassino*, the two of spades.

Cassiopeia /ˌkasɪəʊˈpiːə, kasɪˈəʊpɪə/ *n.* M16. [Mother of Andromeda in Gk mythol.] (The name of) a conspicuous constellation of the northern hemisphere, between the polestar and Andromeda.

cassiri /kaˈsɪəri/ *n.* L18. [Carib: cf. CASSAREEP.] An intoxicating liquor made in Guyana from sweet potatoes.

cassis /kaˈsiːs, ˈkasɪs/ *n.* L19. [Fr. = blackcurrant, app. f. L CASSIA.] A (freq. alcoholic) syrup made from blackcurrants and used to flavour drinks etc.

cassiterite /kəˈsɪtərʌɪt/ *n.* M19. [f. Gk *kassiteros* tin + -ITE[1].] *Min.* Native tin dioxide, SnO_2, which is the major ore of tin and is a tetragonal mineral usu. occurring as yellow, brown, or reddish prisms.

Cassius /ˈkasɪəs/ *n.* M19. [Andreas *Cassius* (*c* 1605–73), Ger. physician and chemist.] *purple of Cassius*, a purple pigment consisting of a colloidal mixture of metallic gold and tin(IV) dioxide.

cassock /ˈkasək/ *n.* & *v.* M16. [Fr. *casaque* long coat f. It. *casacca* riding-coat, prob. f. Turkic *kazak*: see COSSACK.] A *n.* I 1 A long coat or cloak worn by soldiers. Long *obs.* exc. *Hist.* M16. 2 A kind of long loose coat or gown worn by men or women. Long *obs.* exc. *Hist.* M16. 3 A close-fitting garment with sleeves, fastened at the neck and reaching to the heels, worn under surplice, alb, or gown by clerics, choristers, etc., or as ordinary clerical costume. M17.

3 **the cassock** *fig.* the position or office of being a member of the clergy.

II 4 A wearer of a cassock; *esp.* a member of the clergy. E17.

B *v.t.* Dress in or provide with a cassock. Chiefly as *cassocked* ppl a. L18.

cassolette /kasəˈlɛt/ *n.* Also **-et**. M17. [Fr. f. Prov. *casoleta* dim. of *casola*, f. *casa*: see CASSEROLE, -ETTE.] 1 A vessel in which perfumes are burned. M17. 2 A box with a perforated cover for diffusing the odour of perfume in it. E19. 3 A small casserole dish; (a dish of) food cooked in this. E19.

†cassonade *n.* L16–E19. [Fr., f. *casson* broken sugar, f. *casser* break: see -ADE.] Unrefined cane-sugar (imported in casks).

cassone /kaˈsəʊni, *foreign* kasˈsoːne/ *n.* Pl. **-nes** /-nɪz/, **-ni** /-ni/. L19. [It., augm. of *cassa* chest.] A large Italian coffer, esp. to hold a bride's trousseau.

cassoulet /ˈkasʊleɪ/ *n.* M20. [Fr., dim. of dial. *cassolo* stew-pan, tureen.] A ragout of meat and beans.

cassowary /ˈkasəwəri, -wɛːri/ *n.* E17. [Malay *kesuari*.] Any of the large flightless birds of the genus *Casuarius*, related to the emu and native to New Guinea, neighbouring islands, and Queensland.

Cassubian *n.* & *a.* see KASHUBIAN.

cassumunar /kasəˈmjuːnə/ *n.* Now *rare* or *obs.* Also **†-iar**. L17. [App. of Eastern origin.] The aromatic root of a plant of the ginger family used medicinally in the Indian subcontinent and eastern Asia, and probably a form of zedoary.

cast /kɑːst/ *n.*[1] ME. [f. CAST *v.*] I Senses conn. w. throwing or movement. 1 An act of casting, a throw of a missile, fishing-line, net, sounding-line, etc.; the distance thrown; *spec.* a throw of dice, the number thrown. ME. b *Angling.* That which is cast; (formerly) a length of gut with hook and fly, (now) a leader (usu. of nylon monofilament). Also (now *rare*), a place suited for casting. E19. 2 A throw or stroke of fortune; chance, lot, fate. *obs.* exc. *dial.* ME. 3 A turn of the eye in any direction; a look, a glance. ME. 4 A throw in wrestling; a fall, an overthrow. Now *rare* or *obs.* LME. 5 That which is thrown, thrown out, or (chiefly *dial.*) produced; a quantity or amount thrown etc. at one time. LME. b *spec.* A number of hawks flown off at a time (usu. a couple). LME. c A warp (of herring). L15. d A second swarm thrown off by a beehive in a season. M17. e A (convoluted) mass of earth, mud, or sand thrown out from its hole by a worm etc. E18. f A pellet regurgitated by a bird of prey. M19. 6 *fig.* A stroke, a touch; a sample. M16. 7 A lift in a vehicle. *obs.* exc. *dial.* M17. 8 A spreading out (as) of hunting hounds in search of a scent. M19. b The sweep of a trained dog in sheep-mustering. *Austral.* & *NZ.* M20.

1 AV *Luke* 22:41 He was withdrawn from them about a stones cast. W. ROBERTSON Their clothes, their arms, are staked .. upon a single cast. R. GRAVES As the hare doubled the leader killed it with a javelin cast. *measuring cast*: see MEASURING *n.* 3 O. JOHNSON His big blue eyes had an upward cast toward the angels. 5 MALORY Two cast of bread, with fat venison baked. DRYDEN A cast of scatter'd dust. 6 W. WYCHERLEY If you hate Verses, I'll give you a cast of my Politics in Prose. 7 S. RICHARDSON If .. you are for the Village, I'll give you a Cast. 8 R. SUTCLIFF To work their way north in a series of casts .. in the manner of a hound cutting across a scent.

II Senses conn. w. arrangement, shaping, or appearance. 9 †a The plan or conformation of a building etc. ME–L16. b The way in which something is laid out or drawn up; disposition, arrangement; *spec.* the assignment of parts in a play etc. to the various actors; the actors themselves; formerly also the part assigned to one actor. L16. †10 Purpose, aim; a contrivance, a trick. LME–E17. 11 Calculation, reckoning; *esp.* the addition of columns of an account. L15. 12 A model made by casting in a mould; a moulded mass of solidified material, esp. of plaster enclosing a fractured limb etc.; a negative impression of an object made in plaster, wax, etc. E16. †b Casting, founding. *rare* (Shakes.). Only in E17. c *Med.* A mass of dead cells and other matter formed in a diseased kidney and passed in the urine. M19. d A fossil impression of the inside of a hollow structure. L19. 13 A permanent twist or inclination, *esp.* a squint (*in* an eye). E16. 14 *fig.* Form, shape, appearance, (esp. of facial features); inclination; stamp, mould; nature, kind, style, quality. M16. 15 A dash of some colour; a tinge, a shade. E17.

9b M. ARNOLD The happy cast and flow of the sentence. J. AGATE A .. musical comedy played by a sixteen-year-old cast. 11 OED If the account does not balance now, there must be an error in the cast. 12 W. SHENSTONE A most excellent figure, and I shall wish much to get a good cast of it. D. L. SAYERS When he makes a new key, he keeps a cast of it. E. BIRNEY The up-patients had gone about autographing all the casts with indelible pencils. b SHAKES. *Haml.* Why such daily cast of brazen cannon. 13 R. HOGGART Her left eye had a violent cast. 14 I. WALTON This fish is of a fine cast and handsome shape. ADDISON The Mind that hath any Cast towards Devotion. S. JOHNSON A cast of talk, peculiar to their own fraternity. GIBBON Heroines of such a cast may claim our admiration. R. CHURCH A sallow skin that gave him a Spanish cast. S. KING His cast of mind makes it impossible for him to think otherwise. 15 SHAKES. *Haml.* Sicklied o'er with the pale cast of thought. J. GARDNER His blue eyes had a pink cast, as they always did when the light was strong.

Comb.: **cast-net** a fishing net which is cast and drawn immediately, rather than set and left.

†cast *n.*[2] var. of CASTE.

cast /kɑːst/ *ppl a.* LME. [pa. pple of next.] That has been cast.

Special collocations & comb.: **cast-for-age** *a.* (*Austral.* & *NZ*) (of a sheep) disposed of because too old. **cast iron** a hard alloy of iron, carbon (in greater proportion than in steel), and silicon, cast in a mould (*malleable cast iron*: see MALLEABLE 1). **cast-iron** *a.* made of cast iron; *fig.* hard, unchangeable, impregnable. **cast steel** steel made by melting and casting blister steel. See also CASTAWAY, CAST-OFF.

cast /kɑːst/ *v.* Pa. t. & pple **cast**. See also KEST. ME. [ON *kasta*.] I Throw; throw down, defeat; put forcibly: generally replaced by THROW *v.* 1 *v.t.* Throw, move (as) by throwing, fling, hurl, toss. ME. b *v.i.* Aim, throw; *esp.* †(*a*) shoot projectiles; (*b*) throw dice. ME. 2 *v.refl.* Throw or project oneself. ME. 3 *v.t.* Throw forth (a net, fishing-line, sounding-lead, etc.). ME. b Throw a fishing-line over (a piece of water). L19. 4 *v.t.* Direct (one's eyes, a glance, etc.). ME. 5 *v.t.* Cause (light, a shadow, etc.) to fall (*on*, *over*, etc.). ME. †6 *v.t.* Emit, give out (heat, odour, etc.). ME–M18. 7 *v.t.* Toss (the head). Long *obs.* exc. *Sc.* ME. 8 *v.t.* Place or apply hastily, forcefully, or decisively; place or cause to fall (doubt, blame, a spell, etc.) (*up*)*on*. ME. †b Cover by applying mortar etc.; plaster, daub. Cf. ROUGHCAST. L16–E19. 9 *v.t.* Put, cause to be put, *into* prison etc., or (*arch.*) *into* a rage, sleep, etc. ME. †b Set (a person) *upon doing*, *to do*. LME–M18. 10 *v.t.* Throw to the ground; overthrow, defeat. *arch.* & *dial.* ME. b Throw (an animal) on its back or side. Usu. in *pass.* L16. †11 *v.t.* Find guilty, convict; condemn. LME–M19. 12 *v.t.* Add, throw in *to*; bestow, confer, allot. Now *rare* or *obs.* LME. 13 *v.t.* Give or deposit (one's vote) in a vote or election. L19.

1 AV *John* 8:7 Hee that is without sinne among you, let him first cast a stone at her. T. HERBERT The wind blowing strongly, we were cast upon the shoales .. of Mozambique. EVELYN Never cast Water on things newly planted. C. S. FORESTER Tomorrow or the next day would see fate cast the dice—liberty or prison. b R. GRAVES He cast, and the javelin came darting surely down. 3 *fig.*: K. TYNAN The lady might .. cast her net wider than her special talents would permit. 4 DRYDEN Th' unwary Lover cast his Eyes behind. E. F. BENSON Lucia cast him a quick glance. 5 TENNYSON There is no bright form Doth not cast a shade. C. ODETS A traffic light .. casts its colours on the faces of the boy and girl. 8 W. RALEIGH Casting ungratefully on Moses all their misadventures. MILTON His ponderous shield behind him cast. S. WILBERFORCE My guide cast on my shoulders a beautiful mantle. A. MASON A spell to cast harm on a neighbour. M. EDWARDES The Committee also cast doubt on the value of the Ryder Report. 9 W. DAMPIER Our continuing wet .. cast us all into Fevers. B. JOWETT They were being taken away to be cast into hell. 10 SHAKES. *Macb.* Though he took up my legs sometime, yet I made a shift to cast him. THACKERAY Low he lies .. who was cast lower than the poorest. b J. HERRIOT A horse which had got cast in its stall. 11 T. STANLEY Socrates was cast by 281 voices. H. MACKENZIE I was tried for the crime, & was cast for transportation. 13 H. WILSON Twelve members elected .. by 280-odd MPs each with twelve votes to cast.

II Throw off, out, or up: except in sense 14b, now generally expressed with the use of advs. (see below). 14 *v.t.* Throw off, shed, slough, esp. in the process of growth; cease to wear (clothes). ME. b Esp. of a tree, an animal, etc.: drop or shed out of due season; give birth to prematurely. LME. 15 *v.t.* & *i.* Throw up from within, vomit. Now chiefly *dial.* ME. †b *v.t.* Utter forcibly, ejaculate (words etc.). ME–E18. c *v.t.* & *i.* Of a bird of prey: regurgitate. L15. 16 *v.t.* Throw aside, reject, discard; dismiss, expel. ME. 17 *v.t.* Throw up with a spade etc., dig up or out. Now chiefly *Sc.* LME. †b Raise by digging, throw up (a mound etc.). L16–M17.

14 J. SELDEN The Eagle had cast its feathers, and could towre no more. THACKERAY The horse had cast a shoe. b AV *Rev.* 6:13 As a figge tree casteth her vntimely figs when she is shaken of a mighty winde. 15b POPE Not louder shouts to pitying Heav'n are

cast. 16 SHAKES. *Oth.* The state.. Cannot with safety cast him. 17 W. RALEIGH A newe ditch lately cast by Perseus. b MILTON Pioneers.. to trench a field Or cast a rampart.

III Calculate, devise, design. 18 *v.t.* & *i.* Reckon, calculate, sum up (accounts etc.); calculate and record the details of (a horoscope). ME. †b Forecast, speculate. LME-M17. 19 *v.t.* & †*i.* (w. inf.). Contrive, devise, scheme. ME. †20 *v.t.* & *i.* Revolve in the mind, deliberate, ponder. LME-E18. †21 *v.i.* Intend, determine *to do*. LME-E19.

18 D. BREWSTER Drawing an income from casting nativities. TENNYSON Who would cast and balance at a desk? 19 I. WALTON Before you begin to angle, cast to have the wind on your back. E. B. BROWNING Do not cast Ambiguous paths.. for my feet. 20 CAXTON They caste.. how they myght breng hym out of prison. ADDISON Casting in my thoughts the several unhappinesses of life. 21 SIR W. SCOTT The marshall and myself had cast To stop him.

IV Arrange, shape; found. 22 *v.t.* Put into shape, arrange, dispose, lay out; put *into* a particular form. Now only of immaterial things, and passing into *fig.* use of sense 23. ME. 23 *v.t.* Form (a plastic or liquid substance, esp. molten metal) into a shape by pouring it into a mould; form (an object) of metal etc. in this way; found. L15. †24 *v.t.* Arrange or dispose (colours) in painting. M16-M17. 25 *v.t.* Allocate (the roles in a play, film, etc.) to the actors; appoint (an actor) *in* or *for* a role, *as* a character. E18.

22 AV They did not cast the streets, nor proportion the houses in such comely fashion. ADDISON Casting into an Opera the Story of Whittington and his Cat. P. G. WODEHOUSE The thing was cast in narrative form. 23 R. EDEN They.. melte it & caste it fyrste into masses or wedges. W. HOGARTH A figure cast in soft wax. *fig.*: R. GRAVES These lieutenants.. were all cast in the same mould. 24 J. LYLY Cunning Painters who for the whitest worke, cast the blackest ground. 25 P. G. WODEHOUSE Cast for the part of Macbeth. L. HELLMAN I.. cast the play with a kind of abandoned belief that good actors can play anything.

V Turn, twist; incline. 26 *v.i.* & *t.* Turn, veer; bring (a ship) round. Now only *Naut.* LME. 27 *v.t.* (in *pass.*) & *i.* Of timber: be warped, warp. M16. 28 *v.t.* Turn (the scale or balance). Now only *fig.* Cf. *casting vote* s.v. CASTING *ppl a.* L16. †29 *v.i.* Incline, slant. L16-L18. 30 *v.i.* Of hunters, hounds, etc.: go searching, spread out and search (in a given general direction). (Cf. *cast about* below.) L16.

26 F. MARRYAT Her foresail is loose, all ready to cast her. W. C. RUSSELL The wind has so got hold of her that she won't cast one way or the other. 29 T. BEST Which way the ground casts. 30 G. J. WHYTE-MELVILLE Like a hound.. casting forward upon a vague speculation.

VI 31 *v.t.* & *i.* Tie (a knot), make (a loop); entangle, catch. L16.

31 R. PRICE Struggling.. to hold off the snake from casting again. Two coils—you're lost.

Phrases, & with advs. in specialized senses: **cast about** (*a*) go this way and that in search, seek to discover or devise means, (*for, to do, how*); (*b*) *arch.* change course or direction. *cast accounts*: see ACCOUNT *n.* *cast a clout*: see CLOUT *n.*[1] 4. **cast adrift** leave to drift. *cast anchor*: see ANCHOR *n.*[1] **cast an eye** glance, have a quick look. **cast around** = *cast about* above. **cast ashore** (of waves etc.) deposit on the shore. **cast aside** discard, abandon. *cast a slur (up)on*: see SLUR *n.*[3] 1. **cast aspersions (on)** utter aspersions (regarding), slander. *cast a stone* or *stones (at)*: see STONE *n.* **cast away** (*a*) throw away, squander, reject; (*b*) cast ashore, strand (cf. CASTAWAY); (in *pass.*, of a ship) be wrecked. †**cast by** discard. **cast down** (*a*) throw down, destroy, demolish, overthrow; (*b*) bend or turn downward; dispirit, depress, (usu. in *pass.*; cf. DOWNCAST *a.*). **cast forth** throw out, expel, eject. *cast in a heroic* etc. *mould*: see MOULD *n.*[3] *cast in a person's teeth*: see TOOTH *n.* *cast in one's lot with*: see LOT *n.* *cast light on*: see LIGHT *n.* **cast loose** unfasten, set adrift, detach (oneself). *cast lots*: see LOT *n.* **cast off** (*a*) throw off, abandon, discard; (*b*) *Knitting* take (a stitch) off a needle by looping it over the next; take off all stitches in this way to finish an edge; (*c*) *v.phr.t.* & *i.* loosen and throw off (a mooring rope etc.); (*d*) *Typogr.* calculate the space required in print by (copy). **cast on** *Knitting* make (a stitch) on a needle; make the first row of stitches on a needle. *cast one's bread upon the waters*: see WATER *n.* *cast one's mind back*: see MIND *n.*[1] **cast out** (*a*) expel, eject; (*b*) *dial.* disagree, quarrel. *cast pearls before swine*: see PEARL *n.*[1] 2. **cast round** = *cast about* above. *cast stones (at)*: see STONE *n.* *cast the first stone*: see STONE *n.* *cast the glove*: see GLOVE *n.* *cast the gorge (at)*: see GORGE *n.*[1] *cast the lead*: see LEAD *n.*[1] **cast up** (*a*) throw up; (of the sea etc.) deposit on shore; raise up by digging etc.; (*dial.* or *obs.*) vomit; *cast up the gorge*: see GORGE *n.*[1]; (*b*) add (a column of figures etc.), count; (*c*) *dial.* utter as a reproach. †**cast water** diagnose disease by the inspection of urine. *the die is cast*: see DIE *n.*[1]

Castalian /ka'steɪlɪən/ *a.* L16. [f. L *Castalia* (see below) f. Gk *Kastalia*.] Of or pertaining to Castalia, the fountain sacred to the Muses on Mount Parnassus; of or pertaining to the Muses.

Castalie /'kastəli/ *n.* *arch.* or *poet.* Also **-ly.** E17. [Alt. of *Castalia*: see prec.] A spring of pure water; a source of inspiration.

castaneous /ka'steɪnɪəs/ *a.* *rare.* L17. [f. L *castanea* chestnut (see CHESTEN) + -OUS: see -EOUS.] Chestnut-coloured.

castanet /kastə'nɛt/ *n.* E17. [Sp. *castañeta* (w. later assim. to Fr. *castagnette*) dim. of *castaña* f. L *castanea* chestnut: see CHESTEN, -ET[1].] A small concave piece of hardwood, ivory, etc., clicked or rattled in pairs as a rhythmic accompaniment to a Spanish dance etc. Usu. in *pl.*

castaway /'kɑːstəweɪ/ *n.* & *a.* E16. [f. CAST *ppl a.* + AWAY *adv.*] A *n.* 1 A reprobate. *arch.* E16. 2 A shipwrecked person. L18. 3 An outcast; a drifter. M19. B *adj.* Rejected, abandoned; shipwrecked, stranded; (*arch.*) reprobate. M16.

caste /kɑːst/ *n.* Also †**cast**. M16. [Sp. & Port. *casta* use as n. (sc. *raza*, *raça* race) of fem. of *casto* pure, unmixed f. L *castus*: cf. CHASTE *a.*] 1 A race, a stock, a breed. *obs.* in *gen.* sense. M16. 2 A Hindu hereditary class of socially equal persons, united in religion and usu. following similar occupations, distinguished from other castes in the hierarchy by its relative degree of purity or pollution. E17. b Any more or less exclusive social class. E19. 3 The position conferred by membership of a caste. L18. 4 The system of division of society into castes. M19. 5 The form of a social insect having a particular function. M19.

1 *half-caste*: see HALF-. 2 *Scheduled Caste*: see SCHEDULED. b R. G. COLLINGWOOD The view that artists can or should form a special order or caste. B. ANDERSON Elimination of the samurai as a legal caste. 3 **lose caste** be deprived of membership of one's caste; descend in the social scale. 4 MAX-MÜLLER In India caste.. has existed from the earliest times.

Comb.: **caste-mark**: on the forehead, denoting membership of a particular Hindu caste; **caste-system** a system of division of society into castes.

¶The four original Hindu castes, later greatly augmented, were priests, warriors, merchants, and artisans (see BRAHMIN, KSHATRIYA, VAISYA, SUDRA).

casteless *a.* L19.

casteism /'kɑːstɪz(ə)m/ *n.* Also **castism**. L19. [f. prec. + -ISM.] (Belief in or advocacy of) the system of division of society into castes.

casteist *n.* & *a.* (*a*) *n.* a believer in or advocate of casteism; (*b*) *adj.* of or pertaining to casteism or casteists: M20.

castelet /'kastəlɪt/ *n.* Also **-ll-**. ME. [ONFr. (mod. *châtelet*) dim. of *castel*: see CASTLE *n.*[1], -ET[1]. Cf. CASTLET, CHATELET.] A small castle.

castellan /'kastələn/ *n.* Also †**-ane**. See also CASTILIAN *n.*[2] LME. [ONFr. *castelain* (mod. *châtelain*) f. med.L *castellanus* use as n. of L adj., f. *castellum* fortified place: see CASTLE *n.*[1], -AN, and cf. CHATELAIN. In sense 2 f. med.L.] 1 *Hist.* The governor of a castle. LME. †2 = CASTILIAN *n.*[2] *Sc.* E16-E17.

castellany *n.* the office or jurisdiction of a castellan; the territory subject to a castellan: LME.

castellar /ka'stɛlə/ *a.* L18. [f. L *castellum* (see CASTLE *n.*[1]) + -AR[1].] Pertaining to or of the nature of a castle.

castellate /'kastəleɪt/ *v.* *rare.* M19. [Back-form. f. next.] 1 *v.i.* Take the form of a castle. M19. 2 *v.t.* Build like a castle; build with battlements. M19.

castellated /'kastəleɪtɪd/ *a.* L17. [f. med.L *castellatus*, f. *castellum*: see CASTLE *n.*[1], -ATE[2], -ED[1].] 1 Built like a castle; battlemented; resembling a castle. L17. 2 Furnished or dotted with castles. E19.

Also **castellate** *a.* (*rare*) M19.

castellation /kastə'leɪʃ(ə)n/ *n.* E19. [f. med.L *castellat-* pa. ppl stem of *castellare* build castles, f. *castellum*: see CASTLE *n.*[1], -ATION.] The building of castles or battlements; a castellated structure, a battlement.

castellet *n.* var. of CASTELET.

castelry /'kast(ə)lri/ *n.* *obs.* exc. *Hist.* L17. [OFr. *castelerie* f. med.L *castellaria*, f. *castellum*: see CASTLE *n.*[1], -RY.] (The territory subject to) the jurisdiction of a castle.

caster /'kɑːstə/ *n.* In branch II also (& more usual in sense 4) **-or.** LME. [f. CAST *v.* + -ER[1].] I 1 A person who casts something. LME. 2 A Monotype machine for casting type. E20. II 3 A small bottle, jar, etc., with a perforated top, used for sprinkling pepper, sugar, etc., on food (in *pl.* sometimes including cruets for vinegar, oil, etc.). L17. 4 A small swivel wheel on the leg of a chair, table, etc. M18.

Comb.: **castor action** the swivelling of vehicle wheels to ensure stability; **caster sugar** finely granulated white sugar.

castigate /'kastɪgeɪt/ *v.t.* E17. [L *castigat-* pa. ppl stem of *castigare*, f. *castus* pure: see -ATE[3].] 1 Inflict suffering on to punish or subdue; chastise; rebuke severely. E17. †2 Reduce in intensity, moderate. M17-L18. 3 Correct, revise, and emend (a literary work etc.). *arch.* M17.

1 A. BRINK Castigating my body like some mediaeval nun. H. KISSINGER An editorial castigating the Nixon Administration for misleading the American people. 2 R. BURNS When your castigated pulse Gies now and then a wallop. 3 EVELYN Seneca's tragedies.. have.. been castigated abroad by several learned hands.

castigator *n.* E17. **castigatory** *a.* & *n.* (*a*) *adj.* corrective, punitive; †(*b*) *n.* an instrument of chastisement: E17.

castigation /kastɪ'geɪʃ(ə)n/ *n.* LME. [L *castigatio(n-)*, f. as prec.: see -ATION.] The action or an act of castigating; chastisement; a rebuke; *arch.* (a) revision, (an) emendation.

Castile /ka'stiːl/ *n.* Also †**castle**. LME. [*Castile* (see next) in Spain, where orig. made.] In full *Castile soap*. A fine hard white or mottled soap made with olive oil and soda.

Castilian /ka'stɪlɪən/ *n.*[1] & *a.* L15. [Sp. *Castellano*, f. *Castella* Castile (see below); later f. *Castile*: see -AN, -IAN.] A *n.* 1 A particular Spanish gold coin. Long *obs.* exc. *Hist.* L15. 2 The form of Spanish spoken in the province (earlier the kingdom) of Castile; standard literary Spanish. M16. 3 A native or inhabitant of Castile. L16. B *adj.* Of or pertaining to Castile, Castilian, or Castilians. M16.

castilian /ka'stɪlɪən/ *n.*[2] *obs.* exc. *Hist.* L16. [Alt. of CASTELLAN.] A member of the garrison of a castle; a person living in a castle.

casting /'kɑːstɪŋ/ *n.* ME. [f. CAST *v.* + -ING[1].] 1 The action of CAST *v.* ME. 2a That which is cast up; a worm-cast etc.; a pellet disgorged by a hawk etc. LME. b An object cast in metal. L18.

Comb.: **casting-bottle** *Hist.* a vinaigrette; **casting-couch** *joc.*: on which actresses are said to be seduced in return for being awarded parts in films etc.; **casting-director** one responsible for assigning roles in a film, play, etc.; **casting-net** = *cast-net* s.v. CAST *n.*[1]

casting /'kɑːstɪŋ/ *ppl a.* ME. [f. as prec. + -ING[2].] 1 That casts. ME. 2 Deciding, decisive. E17.

2 **casting vote** a vote that decides between two equal parties, esp. when (entitled to be) used by a chairman etc.

castle /'kɑːs(ə)l/ *n.*[1] LOE. [AN, ONFr. *castel* var. of *chastel* (mod. *château*) f. L *castellum* dim. of *castrum* fortified place: see -LE[2]. In branch II rendering late L (Vulgate) *castellum* village, L *castra* camp.] I 1 A (usu. large) fortified building or set of buildings; a stronghold (*lit.* & *fig.*); (esp. in proper names) a mansion that was once such. Also (in proper names), a site of ancient earthworks. LOE. b A model or representation of such a building or buildings. LME. 2 A tower mounted on an elephant's back; a movable tower formerly used in warfare. ME. 3 An elevated structure on the deck of a ship. *obs.* exc.

in FORECASTLE. ME. 4 A large ship, esp. of war. *literary*. L16. 5 *Chess* = ROOK *n.*[2] M17.

1 *Proverb*: An Englishman's house is his castle. **castle in the air, in Spain** a visionary project, a daydream unlikely to be realized (see also *build castles in the air* s.v. AIR *n.*[1] 3). **the Castle** *Ir. Hist.* the viceregal government and administration, of which Dublin Castle was the seat. b **bouncing** or **bouncy castle** a large inflatable in the form of a castle for people to throw themselves around in. *sandcastle*: see SAND *n.*

†II 6 In biblical translations and allusions: a village. LOE–M16. †7 *sing.* & (usu.) in *pl.* A camp. ME–L15.

Comb.: **castle-builder** *fig.* a person who builds castles in the air, a daydreamer; **castle-building** *fig.* the building of castles in the air, daydreaming; **castle-guard** *Hist.* a form of feudal service by which a tenant was bound to defend his lord's castle; the tenure of such service; a tax orig. paid in commutation of this service; **castle-nut** *Mech.* a nut with a notched extension for a locking-pin; **castle pudding**: steamed or baked in a small mould; **castleward** *Hist.* = *castle-guard* above.

†castle *n.*[2] var. of CASTILE.

castle /ˈkɑːs(ə)l/ *v.* LME. [f. CASTLE *n.*[1]] 1 *v.t.* Provide or equip with castles or battlements. Chiefly as *castled* ppl a. LME. 2 *v.t.* Enclose (as) in a castle. L16. 3 *v.i. Chess.* Move the king two squares towards a rook and the rook to the square which the king has crossed; (of the king) move thus in relation to a rook. M17. b *v.t.* Move (the king) thus in relation to a rook. M18.

castlet /ˈkɑːslɪt/ *n.* M16. [Var. of CASTELET assim. to CASTLE *n.*[1], or f. CASTLE *n.*[1] + -LET.] A small castle.

castling /ˈkɑːstlɪŋ/ *n.* Long *obs.* exc. *dial.* L16. [f. CAST *ppl a.* or *n.*[1] + -LING[1].] 1 An aborted offspring. L16. †2 = CAST *n.*[1] 5d. E–M17.

castock /ˈkastɒk/ *n. Sc.* & *north.* Also **cust-** /ˈkʌst-/. L15. [Phonet. devel. of *kale-stock* s.v. KALE.] A cabbage stalk or stem.

cast-off /ˈkɑːstɒf/ *ppl a.* & *n.* E18. [f. CAST *ppl a.* + OFF *adv.*] A *ppl a.* Thrown away, abandoned, rejected, discarded. E18. B *n.* 1 A person who or thing which is cast off, *esp.* an unwanted garment. E18. 2 *Typogr.* A calculation of the space required for a given amount of copy in a particular typographic form. L19.

castor /ˈkɑːstə/ *n.*[1] LME. [(O)Fr. or L f. Gk *kastōr*.] 1 The beaver; its pelt. Now *rare*. LME. 2 A pungent, bitter-tasting, reddish-brown substance obtained from two perineal sacs of the beaver, used in medicine and perfumery. E17. 3 A hat, orig. of (beaver's) fur. *arch. slang.* M17.

castor /ˈkɑːstə/ *n.*[2] M18. [Origin uncertain: perh. = CASTOR *n.*[1] 2, as having succeeded it in medical use.] *castor oil*, a pale yellow oil from the seeds of a tropical or subtropical shrub or tree, *Ricinus communis*, used as a purgative and lubricant.

Comb.: **castor (oil) bean** (a seed of) the castor oil plant; **castor oil plant** the plant that yields castor oil, esp. as grown as a pot plant.

castor *n.*[3] see CASTER.

castoreum /kaˈstɔːrɪəm/ *n.* Also **†-ry**. ME. [L, f. as CASTOR *n.*[1]] = CASTOR *n.*[1] 2.

castral /ˈkastr(ə)l/ *a. rare.* M16. [f. L *castra* camp + -AL[1].] Of or pertaining to a camp.

castrametation /ˌkastrəmɪˈteɪʃ(ə)n/ *n.* L17. [Fr. *castramétation*, f. L *castra metari* measure or mark out a camp.] The designing or laying out of military camps.

castrate /ˈkastreɪt/ *n.* & *a.* LME. [L *castratus* pa. pple, f. as next: see -ATE[1], -ATE[2].] A *n.* A castrated man or animal. LME. B *adj.* Castrated. Now *rare* or *obs.* E18.

castrate /kaˈstreɪt, ˈkastreɪt/ *v.t.* M16. [L *castrat-* pa. ppl stem of *castrare*: see -ATE[3].] 1 Remove the testicles of; geld; *fig.* deprive of potency, vigour, or force. M16. 2 Expurgate (a text). *obs.* exc. as passing into fig. use of sense 1. E17.

caˈstrative *a.* of or pertaining to castration, tending to deprive of potency M20. **caˈstrator** *n.* E19.

castration /kaˈstreɪʃ(ə)n/ *n.* LME. [Fr., or L *castratio(n-)*, f. as prec.: see -ATION.] The action of castrating someone or something; the fact of being castrated.

Comb.: **castration complex** *Psychoanalysis* (*a*) a man's neurotic and unconscious fear of castration resulting from childhood fears of his father; (*b*) a woman's neurotic anxiety caused by her unconsciously feeling that she has been castrated.

castrato /kaˈstrɑːtəʊ/ *n.* Pl. **-ti** /-ti/. M18. [It., use as n. of pa. pple of *castrare* castrate.] *Hist.* An adult male singer castrated in boyhood so as to retain a soprano or alto voice.

castrensian /kaˈstrɛnsɪən/ *a.* M17. [f. L *castrensis* adj., f. *castra* camp, + -AN.] Of or pertaining to a military camp.

Castroism /ˈkastrəʊɪz(ə)m/ *n.* M20. [f. Fidel *Castro* Ruz (1927–), Cuban statesman + -ISM.] The political principles or actions of Fidel Castro or his adherents or imitators. Cf. FIDELISM.

castrum /ˈkastrəm/ *n.* Pl. **castra** /ˈkastrə/. M19. [L.] A Roman encampment or fortress.

casual /ˈkaʒjʊəl, -zj-/ *a.* & *n.* LME. [(O)Fr. *casuel* and L *casualis* (in its late and med. uses), f. *casus* CASE *n.*[1]: see -AL[1].] A *adj.* 1 Due to, characterized by, or subject to chance; accidental, fortuitous. LME. †b Non-essential. LME–M17. 2 Occurring unpredictably; irregular; occasional. LME. †3 Frail, precarious, unreliable. E16–E18. 4 Occurring or brought about without design or premeditation; having no specific plan, method, motivation, or interest; performed or entered into casually; *spec.* designating or pertaining to sex between individuals who are not regular or established sexual partners. M17. 5 Of a person, action, etc.: unmethodical, careless; unconcerned, uninterested; informal, unceremonious. L19. b Of an item of clothing: suitable for informal wear. M20.

1 W. RALEIGH That which seemeth most casual and subject to fortune, is yet disposed by the ordinance of God. MILTON Where casual fire had wasted woods. 2 CLARENDON Both the known and casual Revenue. J. CARY The few shillings a week earned . . at casual and temporary jobs. 3 J. WORLIDGE In case . . the weather prove casual. 4 D. G. MITCHELL I made some casual remark about the weather. J. CONRAD A casual stroll or a casual spree on shore. CONAN DOYLE A problem without a solution may interest the student, but can hardly fail to annoy the casual reader. 5 G. GREENE It needed only a casual inspection to realise how badly the office had been kept. A. LURIE We were both very strained, though we pretended to be casual. J. IRVING He puts up a casual hand to catch it.

Special collocations: **casual acquaintance**: whom one met incidentally or whom one meets only occasionally. **casual labourer**: without permanent employment, working when the chance comes. **casual pauper, poor** (now *arch.* or *Hist.*): receiving occasional relief, admitted temporarily to a workhouse, casual ward, etc. **casual ward** a place for the temporary accommodation of vagrants. **casual water** *Golf* a temporary accumulation of water not constituting one of the recognized hazards of the course.

B *n.* †1 A chance. Usu. in *pl.* LME–M17. 2 A casual item of income. *rare.* E19. 3 A casual labourer. M19. 4 A casual pauper. Now *arch.* or *Hist.* M19. 5 A introduced plant, animal, etc., which fails to establish itself. L19. 6 An item of casual clothing; *spec.* a low-heeled slip-on shoe. Usu. in *pl.* M20. 7 A hooligan who dresses conventionally in casual clothing. *slang.* L20.

casualism *n.* the doctrine that all things exist or happen by chance L19. **casually** *adv.* LME. **casualness** *n.* L19.

casuality /kaʒjʊˈalɪti, -zj-/ *n.* Now *rare.* E16. [Fr. *casualité* f. med.L *casualitas*, f. *casualis*: see CASUAL, -ITY.] †1 A casual item of income. E16–L17. †2 (A) chance; *esp.* an unfortunate accident. M16–L18. 3 The quality or state of being casual, casualness. L19.

casualty /ˈkaʒjʊəlti, -zj-/ *n.* LME. [Alt. of med.L *casualitas* (see prec.) after *penalty, royalty*, etc.: see -TY[1].] 1 Chance. Now *rare.* LME. 2 A chance occurrence; an accident, a mishap, a disaster. LME. b A person killed or injured in war or an accident; a thing lost or destroyed. M19. 3 An incidental charge or payment; *spec.* (*Sc. Law*, now *Hist.*) a payment due from a vassal in certain contingencies. LME. †4 Subjection to chance, uncertainty. E16–E19. 5 In full *casualty department, ward*. The part of a hospital where casualties are attended to. M19.

1 S. JOHNSON Combinations of skilful genius with happy casualty. 2 SHAKES. *Per.* Time hath rooted out my parentage, And to the world and awkward casualties Bound me in servitude. SWIFT Several casualties have happened this week, and the bill of mortality is very much increased. b S. SASSOON About 40 casualties; only 4 killed. J. T. STORY His own father's wool business was a casualty of the war years.

casuarina /kasjʊəˈriːnə/ *n.* L18. [mod.L, f. *casuarius* cassowary (from resemblance of the branches to the bird's feathers).] A tree of the genus *Casuarina* (family Casuarinaceae), native to Australia and parts of SE Asia, with jointed branches resembling gigantic horsetail plants.

casuist /ˈkazjʊɪst, -ʒj-/ *n.* E17. [Fr. *casuiste* f. Sp. *casuista* f. mod.L, f. L *casus* CASE *n.*[1]: see -IST.] A person, esp. a theologian, who resolves cases of conscience, duty, etc.; a sophist, a quibbler.

casuˈistic(al) *adjs.* of or pertaining to casuists or casuistry M17. **casuˈistically** *adv.* L17. **casuistry** *n.* the reasoning of the casuist; the resolution of cases of conscience by the application of general rules to particular instances, freq. disclosing a conflict of duties; sophistry: E18.

†casule *n.* OE–E19. [(OFr. f.) late L *casula* hooded cloak: see CHASUBLE.] = CHASUBLE.

casus belli /ˌkɑːsʊs ˈbɛliː, ˌkeɪsəs ˈbɛlaɪ/ *n. phr.* Pl. same. M19. [f. L *casus* CASE *n.*[1] + *belli* genit. of *bellum* war.] An act or situation justifying or precipitating war.

casus foederis /ˌkɑːsʊs ˈfɔɪdərɪs, ˌkeɪsəs ˈfiːdərɪs/ *n. phr.* Pl. same. L18. [f. L *casus* CASE *n.*[1] + *foederis* genit. of *foedus* treaty.] An event which under the terms of a treaty of alliance, entitles one of the allies to help from the other(s).

cat /kat/ *n.*[1] [OE *catt* masc. (= ON *kǫttr*), *catte* fem. (= OFris., MDu. *katte*, Du. *kat*, OHG *kazza*, G *katze*), reinforced in ME by AN, ONFr. *cat* var. of (O)Fr. *chat* f. late L *cattus*.] 1 An agile, partly nocturnal, quadrupedal carnivorous mammal, *Felis catus*, with smooth fur and retractile claws, long domesticated as a pet. OE. b Any of numerous related animals constituting the family Felidae, including the lion, tiger, leopard, lynx, etc. Also, any of various catlike animals of other taxa. M16. c In full *catfish*: (*a*) any of various mainly freshwater fishes of the order Siluriformes, having several sensory barbels and scaleless bodies; (*b*) = *wolf-fish* s.v. WOLF *n.*; (*c*) a cuttlefish or other cephalopod. L16. 2 *fig.* A spiteful person, *esp.* (*derog.*) a spiteful or malicious woman; a prostitute (*obs.* exc. in *cat-house* (a) below). ME. b A person, a fellow (usu. of a specified kind); a jazz enthusiast. *slang.* E20. 3 A small piece of wood tapering at each end, used in the game of tipcat; the game itself. LME. 4 *Hist.* A movable penthouse used by besiegers for protection. L15. 5 *Naut.* (In full *cathead*, †*cat's-head*) a horizontal beam extending from each side of a ship's bow for raising and carrying an anchor; (in full *cat-purchase, -tackle*) a tackle used in hoisting an anchor to the cathead. L15. 6 *Hist.* In full *cat-o'-nine-tails*. A rope whip with nine knotted lashes for flogging sailors, soldiers, or criminals. L17. 7 A double tripod with six legs so placed that it always rests on three legs. E19.

1 *Maltese cat, Manx cat, Persian cat, Siamese cat, tortoiseshell cat, tabby cat*, etc. b *big cat, bobcat, civet-cat, native cat, polecat, sea-cat, tiger-cat, wild cat*, etc. 2b C. MACINNES The coloured cats saw I had an ally, and melted. *hep-cat*: see HEP *a. hip-cat*: see HIP *a.*

Phrases: *bell the cat*: see BELL *v.*[3] **enough to make a cat laugh** extremely amusing. *fat cat*: see FAT *a. grin like a Cheshire cat*: see CHESHIRE 2. KILKENNY *cat.* **let the cat out of the bag** reveal a secret, esp. involuntarily. **like a cat on hot bricks** & vars., (moving) quickly and uneasily. *like a scalded cat*: see SCALDED *a.*[1] **like something the cat brought in** bedraggled, unkempt. *no room to swing a cat in*: see ROOM *n.*[1] **not a cat in hell's chance** no chance whatever. *not room to swing a cat in*: see ROOM *n.*[1] **play cat and mouse** toy *with* a weaker party; engage in prolonged wary manoeuvres. **put** *a* or **the cat among the pigeons** create a violent intrusion, cause a severe upset. *queen cat*: see QUEEN *n.* 6. **rain cats and dogs** rain very hard. **see which way the cat jumps** wait for an opinion or result to declare itself. *shoot the cat*: see SHOOT *v. singed cat*: see SINGE *v.*

I. *skin the cat*: see SKIN *v.* *suffering cats!*: see SUFFERING *ppl a.* 3. *tame cat*: see TAME *a.* I. *tear a* or *the cat*: see TEAR *v.*[1] **turn cat in pan, turn the cat in the pan** †(*a*) reverse the order or nature of things, make black seem white; (*b*) change sides, be a turncoat. *whip the cat*: see WHIP *v.*

Comb.: **cat-and-dog** *a.* quarrelsome, inharmonious; **cat-and-mouse** *a.* involving playing cat and mouse (see above); **catbird** any of various birds with mewing cries; *esp.* a N. American mockingbird, *Dumetella carolinensis*, with slaty-black plumage; (*Austral.*) any of a number of bowerbirds; **cat-burglar**: who climbs a wall to enter an upper storey; **cat-door** a small door which can be pushed open by a cat, enabling its entrances and exits; *catfish*: see sense 1c above (*walking catfish*: see WALKING *ppl a.*); **cat-flap** = *cat-door* above; **cat foot** a dog's compact round foot, with the toes well knuckled up; **cat-foot** *v.t.* w. *it* (chiefly *N. Amer.*) walk stealthily or noiselessly; **cat-footed** *a.* stealthy in movement; **cat-haul** *n.* & *v.* (*US*) (*a*) *n.* a punishment in which a cat is caused to maul the victim; (*b*) *v.t.* subject to this punishment; *fig.* examine stringently; *cathead*: see sense 5 above. **cat-hole** (*a*) a hole large enough to let a cat through; (*b*) *Naut.* a hole at the stern of a ship, through which a cable or hawser can be passed; **cat-house** (*a*) a brothel; (*b*) a house for felines in a zoo; **cat-ice** thin ice unsupported by water; **cat-lap** *slang* slops, weak tea, etc.; **catlick** *colloq.* a perfunctory wash; *cat litter*: see LITTER *n.* 3. **catmint** [after med.L *herba catti* or *cattaria*] an aromatic plant of the large genus *Nepeta*, of the mint family, esp. *N. cataria*, whose smell is irresistible to cats; **catnap** *n.* & *v.i.* (have) a brief sleep in a chair etc.; **catnip** [*nip*, var. of NEP *n.*[1]] catmint; *cat-o'-nine-tails*: see sense 6 above; *cat-purchase*: see sense 5 above; **cat's cradle** (a children's game with) string forming patterns held between the fingers and passed between players; **cat's-ear** any of several composite plants constituting the genus *Hypochaeris*, with heads of yellow ligulate flowers and leaves in rosettes; esp. *H. radicata*, a common plant of grassland; **cat's-foot** *fig.* †(*a*) = CAT'S-PAW 2; (*b*) ground ivy, *Glechoma hederacea*; (*c*) a hill plant, *Antennaria dioica*, of the composite family, with heads of inconspicuous white flowers; **cat's-head** *fig.* †(*a*) see sense 5 above; †(*b*) a variety of apple; (*c*) (now *rare*) = *beak-head* (c) s.v. BEAK *n.*[1]; †**cat-silver** mica; **cat's-meat** horseflesh or other meat prepared and sold as food for cats; **cat's pyjamas** *slang* (orig. *US*) *the* acme of excellence, the cat's whiskers (see below); **catstick** a stick used in tipcat and trap-ball; **catsuit** an all-in-one, usu. close-fitting, garment with trouser legs; **cat's whisker** (*a*) (in *pl.*) *slang* (orig. *US*) *the* acme of excellence (cf. *cat's pyjamas* above); (*b*) a fine adjustable wire in a crystal wireless receiver; *cat-tackle*: see sense 5 above; *cat-tail*: see CAT'S-TAIL; **catwalk** a narrow footway or platform; **cat-witted** *a.* (*arch.*) petty-minded and spiteful.

catlike *a.* resembling (that of) a cat; stealthy; agile: L16.

cat /kat/ *n.*[2] *obs.* exc. (perh.) in CATBOAT L17. [Perh. same wd as prec.: cf. med.L *catta* a kind of ship, OFr. *chat* etc. merchant ship.] A strong merchant sailing vessel with a narrow stern, projecting quarters, and a deep waist, formerly used esp. in the coal and timber trade on the north-east coast of England.

cat /kat/ *a.* & *n.*[3] *colloq.* M20. [Abbrev. of CATALYTIC *a.*] A *adj. cat cracker, cracking*, (an installation for) the catalytic cracking of hydrocarbons. M20. B *n.* = CATALYTIC *converter.* L20.

cat /kat/ *v.t.* Infl. **-tt-**. L16. [f. CAT *n.*[1]] 1 *Naut.* Raise (the anchor) from the surface of the water to the cathead. L16. 2 Flog with a cat-o'-nine-tails. M19.

cata- /ˈkatə/ *pref.* Bef. a vowel or *h* usu. **cat-**. Also **k-**. [Gk *kata.*] Used in wds adopted f. Gk and in Eng. wds modelled on these, in senses (*a*) down, in position or in quantity or degree, as *catadromous, catalysis, catastrophe*; (*b*) amiss, mis-, as *catachresis, catatonia*; (*c*) against, alongside, as *catadioptric, catechize*; (*d*) thoroughly, entirely, as *catalepsy, catalogue.*

catabaptist /katəˈbaptɪst/ *n.* M16. [med.Gk *katabaptistēs* administrator of irregular or schismatic baptism, f. *katabaptizein*, f. as CATA-, BAPTIZE.] *Hist.* (A 16th- and 17th-cent. nickname for) an opponent of the orthodox view of baptism.

catabatic *a.* see KATABATIC.

catabolic /katəˈbɒlɪk/ *a.* Also **k-**. L19. [f. as next + -IC.] *Biol.* Pertaining to, involved in, or characterized by catabolism. Opp. ANABOLIC.

catabolism /kəˈtabəlɪz(ə)m/ *n.* Also **k-**. L19. [f. Gk *katabolē* throwing down, ult. f. as CATA- + *ballein* throw: see -ISM.] *Biol.* Destructive metabolism with the release of energy; the breakdown of complex substances within the body. Opp. ANABOLISM.

catabolite *n.* a product of catabolism M20. **catabolize** *v.t.* break down by catabolism M20.

catabothron *n.* var. of KATAVOTHRON.

catacaustic /katəˈkɔːstɪk/ *a.* & *n.* E18. [f. CATA- + CAUSTIC.] *Physics.* A *adj.* Of a curve or surface: formed by the intersection of rays of light reflected from a curved surface. E18. B *n.* A catacaustic curve or surface. Cf. DIACAUSTIC. E18.

catachresis /katəˈkriːsɪs/ *n.* Pl. **-chreses** /-ˈkriːsiːz/. M16. [L *catachresis* f. Gk *katakhrēsis*, f. *katakhrēsthai* to misuse, f. as CATA- + *khrēsthai* use.] (An instance of) the incorrect use of words.

catachrestic /-ˈkrɛst-, -ˈkriː-/ *a.* (of a word etc.) misused, misapplied; of the nature of catachresis: M17. **catachrestical** /-ˈkrɛst-, -ˈkriː-/ *a.* E17. **catachrestically** /-ˈkrɛst-, -ˈkriː-/ *adv.* E17.

cataclasis /katəˈkleɪsɪs/ *n.* Pl. **-clases** /-ˈkleɪsiːz/. M20. [f. CATA- + Gk *klasis* breaking.] *Geol.* (A) crushing of rock.

cataclasm /ˈkatəklaz(ə)m/ *n.* E19. [Gk *kataklasma*, f. *kataklan* break down, f. as CATA- + *klan* break.] A violent break or disruption.

cataclastic /katəˈklastɪk/ *a.* L19. [f. CATA- + CLASTIC.] *Geol.* Pertaining to, involving, or formed by crushing of rock.

cataclysm /ˈkatəklɪz(ə)m/ *n.* E17. [Fr. *cataclysme* f. L *cataclysmos* f. Gk *kataklusmos* deluge, f. as CATA- + *kluzein* to wash.] A violent geological or meteorological event; *the* Flood (in Genesis); *fig.* a political or social upheaval.

cataˈclysmal *a.* M19. **cataˈclysmic** *a.* M19. **cataˈclysmically** *adv.* L19.

catacomb /ˈkatəkuːm, -kəʊm/ *n.* OE. [(O)Fr. *catacombes* f. late L *catacumbas* = sense 1 below (so named in 5th cent. AD): ult. origin unkn.] 1 In *pl.* & †*sing.* The subterranean cemetery of St Sebastian near Rome, consisting of galleries or passages with recesses excavated in the sides for tombs. OE. 2 In *pl.* The many other Roman subterranean galleries; similar works elsewhere. M17. 3 *sing.* A single crypt or gallery in such works. *rare.* E18. 4 *transf.* A (wine) cellar. L18.

catacoustics /katəˈkuːstɪks/ *n.* Now *rare* or *obs.* L17. [f. CATA- + ACOUSTICS.] The science of reflected sound. Cf. DIACOUSTICS.

catadioptric /ˌkatədʌɪˈɒptrɪk/ *a.* E18. [f. CATA- + DIOPTRIC *a.*] Pertaining to or involving both the reflection and the refraction of light.

catadioptrical *a.* L17.

catadromous /katəˈdrəʊməs/ *a.* L19. [f. CATA- after ANADROMOUS *a.*] Of fish: that descend rivers to lower reaches or to the sea to spawn.

†**catadupe** *n.* L16–M18. [Fr. *catad(o)upe* f. L *catadupa* (pl.) f. Gk *katadoupoi* (pl.), f. as CATA- + *doupos* thud.] A cataract, a waterfall, orig. of the Nile.

catafalque /ˈkatəfalk/ *n.* Also (now *rare*) **catafalco** /katəˈfalkəʊ/, pl. **-o(e)s**. M17. [Fr. f. It. *catafalco* of unkn. origin: cf. SCAFFOLD *n.*] 1 A decorated structure fashioned so as to carry the coffin or effigy of a distinguished person during a funeral service or for a lying in state. M17. 2 A structure on which a coffin is drawn in procession. M19.

catagmatic /katəgˈmatɪk/ *n.* & *a.* Now *rare* or *obs.* M17. [Fr. †*catagmatique* f. Gk *katagmatikos*, f. *katagma* fracture: see -IC.] *Med.* A *n.* A medicine used in healing fractures. M17. B *adj.* Of or pertaining to fractures or their treatment. L17.

†**Cataian** *n.* L16–M17. [Var. of CATHAYAN *n.*] A sharper, a thief, a scoundrel.

Catalan /ˈkatəlan/ *n.* & *a.* LME. [Fr. f. Prov. & Sp., f. Sp. *Cataluña*, Catalan *Catalunya* Catalonia (see below): see -AN.] A *n.* 1 A native or inhabitant of Catalonia, a province of NE Spain, once an independent principality. LME. 2 The Romance language of Catalonia. L18. B *attrib.* or as *adj.* Of or pertaining to Catalonia, its people, or their language. M19.

Catalanist *a.* & *n.* (a person) favouring the independence of Catalonia E20.

catalase /ˈkatəleɪz/ *n.* E20. [f. CATALYSIS *n.* + -ASE.] *Biochem.* An enzyme which catalyses the reduction of hydrogen peroxide.

catalectic /katəˈlɛktɪk/ *a.* & *n.* L16. [Late L *catalecticus* f. Gk *katalēktikos*, f. *katalēgein* leave off, f. as CATA- + *lēgein* cease: see -IC.] *Pros.* (A line or verse) lacking one syllable in the last foot.

catalepsy /ˈkat(ə)lɛpsi/ *n.* LME. [Fr. *catalepsie* or late L *catalepsia*, f. Gk *katalēpsis*, f. *katalambanein* seize upon: see CATA-, -Y[3].] 1 *Med.* A condition of trance or seizure with loss of sensation or consciousness and abnormal maintenance of posture. LME. †2 *Philos.* Comprehension, apprehension. M17–M19.

cataˈleptic *a.* & *n.* (*a*) *adj.* pertaining to, affected by, or of the nature of catalepsy; (*b*) *n.* a person suffering from catalepsy: L17.

catalexis /katəˈlɛksɪs/ *n.* M19. [Gk *katalēxis* termination, f. *katalēgein*: see CATALECTIC.] *Pros.* Absence of a syllable in the last foot of a line or verse.

catallactic /katəˈlaktɪk/ *a.* & *n.* M19. [Gk *katallaktikos* (not in this sense), f. *katallassein*, f. as CATA- + *allassein* change, exchange: see -IC.] A *adj.* Pertaining to exchange of money etc. M19. B *n.* In *pl.* (treated as *sing.*). Economics as the science of exchange. M19.

catalo *n.* var. of CATTALO.

catalogue /ˈkat(ə)lɒg/ *n.* & *v.* Also ***-log**. LME. [(O)Fr. f. late L *catalogus* f. Gk *katalogos*, f. *katalegein* pick out, enrol, f. as CATA- + *legein* choose.] A *n.* 1 A list, register, or complete enumeration; now *spec.* one systematically or methodically arranged, often with brief particulars or descriptions aiding identification etc. LME. 2 *fig.* An enumeration, series, etc. L16.

1 *Liberian catalogue*: see LIBERIAN *a.*[1] *thematic catalogue*: see THEMATIC *a.* 2. 2 D. LODGE Mrs Zapp .. recited a catalogue of her husband's sins to me.

B *v.t.* 1 Make a catalogue or list of. L16. 2 Inscribe or insert in a catalogue. M17.

1 J. STEINBECK His mind was cataloguing weak points and suspicious things about the car. 2 HOR. WALPOLE If religion is thrown into the quarrel, the most innocent acts are catalogued with sins.

cataloguer *n.* M19. **cataloguist** *n.* L18. **cataloguize** *v.t.* = CATALOGUE *v.* E17.

catalogue raisonné /katalɔg rɛzɔne/ *n. phr.* Pl. ***-s -s*** (pronounced same). L18. [Fr. = reasoned catalogue.] A descriptive catalogue with explanations or comments.

Catalonian /katəˈləʊnɪən/ *a.* & *n.* L16. [f. *Catalonia* (see CATALAN) + -AN.] = CATALAN.

catalpa /kəˈtalpə/ *n.* M18. [Creek.] An American or Asian tree of the genus *Catalpa*, of the bignonia family, with heart-shaped leaves, trumpet-shaped flowers, and long pods.

catalyse /ˈkat(ə)lʌɪz/ *v.t.* Also ***-lyze**. L19. [f. next after *analyse.*] *Chem.* Accelerate or promote (a reaction or process) by catalysis.

fig.: *Nature* The technology bred of science has catalysed stupendous economic growth.

catalysed *a.* (*a*) that has been catalysed; (*b*) (of a motor vehicle) having a catalytic converter: M20. **catalyser** *n.* a catalyst E20.

catalysis /kəˈtalɪsɪs/ *n.* Pl. **-lyses** /-lɪsiːz/. M17. [mod.L f. Gk *katalusis*, f. *kataluein* dissolve, f. as CATA- + *luein* set free.] †1 Dissolution, destruction. M–L17. 2 *Chem.* The action or effect of a substance in increasing the rate of a reaction without itself being consumed; an instance of this. M19.

2 **negative catalysis** an analogous slowing of a reaction.

catalyst /ˈkat(ə)lɪst/ *n.* E20. [f. prec. after *analyst.*] *Chem.* A substance which brings about catalysis. Also *fig.*, an agent that facilitates a change.

catalytic /katəˈlɪtɪk/ *a.* M19. [f. CATALYSIS after *analysis*, *analytic* etc.] Of the nature of, involving, or pertaining to catalysis; acting as a catalyst.

catalytic converter a device fitted in the exhaust system of some motor vehicles which converts pollutant gases into less harmful ones by catalytic action. **catalytic cracker** a device for cracking petroleum oils by catalysis.

catalytically *adv.* M19.

catamaran /katəmə'ran/ *n.* E17. [Tamil *kaṭṭu-maram* lit. 'tied wood'.] 1 A raft or float of logs tied side by side with the longest in the middle; a raft of two boats fastened side by side; a sailing boat with two hulls side by side. E17. 2 *Hist.* A naval weapon consisting of a floating chest packed with gunpowder. E19. 3 A quarrelsome woman. *colloq.* M19.

catamenia /katə'mi:nɪə/ *n.pl.* Now *rare* or *obs.* M18. [Gk, neut. pl. of *katamēnios* monthly, f. as CATA- + *mēn* month.] The menstrual discharge.

catamenial *a.* M19.

catamite /'katəmʌɪt/ *n.* L16. [L *catamitus* (through Etruscan *catmite*) f. Gk *Ganumēdēs* GANYMEDE.] A boy kept for homosexual practices; the passive partner in anal intercourse.

catamount /'katəmaʊnt/ *n.* M17. [Abbrev. of next.] †1 = CATAMOUNTAIN I. M17–M18. 2 The puma. *N. Amer.* L18.

catamountain /katə'maʊntɪn/ *n.* Also **cat o' mountain**. Orig. †**cat of the mountain**. LME. [Rendering L *pardus*, Gk *pardos* PARD *n.*[1]] 1 A leopard, puma, or similar cat. LME. 2 *fig.* A wild aggressive person. E17.

catananche /katə'naŋki/ *n.* E19. [mod.L f. L *catanance* plant used in love-potions, f. Gk *katanagkē*, f. as CATA- + *anagkē* compulsion.] A plant of the genus *Catananche*, of the composite family, with blue or yellow flowers, native to the Mediterranean region.

catapan /'katəpan/ *n.* E18. [med.L *catapanus*, *cate-* f. Gk *katepanō tōn axiōmatōn* (he who is) placed over the dignities.] *Hist.* The governor of Calabria and Apulia under the Byzantine emperors.

cataphatic /katə'fatɪk/ *a.* M19. [Gk *kataphatikos* affirmative, f. *kataphasis* affirmation, f. as CATA- + *phanai* speak: see -IC.] *Theol.* Of knowledge of God: obtained through affirmation. Opp. APOPHATIC.

cataphora /kə'taf(ə)rə/ *n.* M16. [In sense 1 f. Gk *kataphora*, f. as CATA- + *pherein* carry; in sense 2 f. CATA- after ANAPHORA.] 1 *Med.* (An attack of) pathological sleepiness. Now *rare*. M16. 2 *Ling.* The use of an expression which refers to or stands for a later word or group of words. L20.

cataphoresis /katəfə'ri:sɪs/ *n.* L19. [f. CATA- + Gk *phorēsis* being carried.] 1 *Med.* The use of electricity to enable medicinal substances to pass through the skin. L19. 2 = ELECTROPHORESIS I. M20.

cataphoretic /-'rɛt-/ *a.* L19.

cataphoric /katə'fɒrɪk/ *a.* L19. [Gk *kataphorikos*, f. as prec.: see -IC.] 1 Of or pertaining to cataphoresis. L19. 2 *Ling.* Referring to or standing for a later word or group of words. L20.

cataphract /'katəfrakt/ *n.* L16. [L *cataphractes* (sense 1), *-tus* (sense 2) f. Gk *kataphraktēs*, *-tos*, f. *kataphrassein* clothe in mail.] 1 *Hist.* An ancient coat of mail. L16. 2 A soldier in full armour. L17.

cataplasm /'katəplaz(ə)m/ *n.* LME. [(O)Fr. *cataplasme* or late L *cataplasma* f. Gk *kataplasma*, f. *kataplassein* plaster over, f. as CATA- + *plassein* to plaster.] A plaster; a poultice.

cataplexy /'katəplɛksi/ *n.* L19. [f. Gk *kataplēxis* stupefaction, f. *kataplēssein*, f. as CATA- + *plēssein* to strike.] A sudden temporary paralysis due to fright or other strong emotion.

cata'plectic *a.* L19.

catapult /'katəpʌlt/ *n.* & *v.* L16. [(O)Fr. *catapulte* or L *catapulta* = Gk *katapeltēs*, f. as CATA- + var. of base of *pallein* hurl.] A *n.* 1 *Hist.* A military engine worked by levers and twisted rope for discharging darts, stones, etc. L16. 2 A contrivance of a forked stick and elastic for shooting small stones etc. M19. 3 A mechanical contrivance for launching a glider or other aircraft, esp. from the deck of a ship. E20. B *v.* 1 *v.t.* Launch with a catapult; hurl (as) from a catapult; fling forcibly (*lit.* & *fig.*). M19. 2 *v.i.* Move (as if) from a catapult. E20.

cataract /'katərakt/ *n.* & *v.* LME. [L *cataracta* waterfall, floodgate, portcullis, f. Gk *kataraktēs*, *-rrh-* down-rushing (water etc.), prob. f. *katarassein*, f. as CATA- + *arassein* strike, smash. In sense 2 app. fig. use of sense 'portcullis'.] A *n.* †1 In *pl.* Floodgates, *spec.* of heaven (*Gen.* 7:11, 8:2). LME–L17. b *transf.* A waterspout. M16–M17. 2 *Med.* (A condition of) partial or complete opacity of the lens of the eye. LME. 3 A waterfall, *spec.* a large and sheer one; a torrent. L16. †4 A portcullis; the grating of a window. *rare.* M17–M19. B *v.* 1 *v.t.* Pour in a torrent. *rare.* L18. 2 *v.i.* Fall in or like a cataract. M19.

cataractal *a.* of the nature of a cataract L19. †**cataractic** *a.* (*rare*) cataractal L17–E19. **cataractous** /'katəraktəs, katə'raktəs/ *a.* of or affected by cataract of the eye E19.

catarrh /kə'tɑ:/ *n.* E16. [Fr. *catarrhe* f. late L *catarrhus* f. Gk *katarrhous*, f. *katarrhein* run down, f. as CATA- + *rhein* flow.] 1 Excessive discharge of mucus from inflamed membranes, esp. in the nose and throat; inflammation producing this. E16. †2 Cerebral effusion or haemorrhage; apoplexy. M16–E18.

catarrhal *a.* of the nature of, involving, pertaining to, or affected with catarrh M17. **catarrhous** *a.* = CATARRHAL. L16.

catarrhine /'katərʌɪn/ *n.* & *a.* M19. [f. CATA- + Gk *rhinos*, *rhis* nose.] *Zool.* A *n.* A catarrhine primate. M19. B *adj.* Pertaining to or designating a primate having nostrils close together and directed downwards (as in all the apes and Old World monkeys). M19.

catasetum /katə'si:təm/ *n.* E19. [mod.L, f. as CATA- + L *seta* bristle (on account of the form of the rostellum).] An epiphytic orchid of the genus *Catasetum*, native to tropical America.

catasta /kə'tastə/ *n.* Pl. **-stae** /-sti:/. M17. [L = scaffold, stage.] *Hist.* A block on which slaves were exposed for sale.

catastasis /kə'tastəsɪs/ *n.* Pl. **-ases** /-əsi:z/. M16. [Gk *katastasis* settling, appointment, f. as CATA- + STASIS.] The third part of the ancient drama, in which the action is heightened for the catastrophe.

catastrophe /kə'tastrəfi/ *n.* M16. [L *catastropha* f. Gk *katastrophē* overturning, sudden turn, f. *katastrephein*, f. as CATA- + *strephein* turn.] 1 The dénouement of a play, esp. a tragedy; the final resolution of a novel etc. M16. 2 A disastrous conclusion; overthrow, ruin, calamitous fate. L16. †b The buttocks. *joc. rare* (Shakes.). Only in L16. 3 A revolutionary event. L17. b *Geol.* (An event causing) a sudden upheaval or discontinuity in the stratigraphic record. M19. 4 A sudden or widespread or noteworthy disaster; an extreme misfortune. M18.

Phrases: *ultraviolet catastrophe*: see ULTRAVIOLET *a.* 2.

Comb.: **catastrophe theory** *Math.* the topological description of systems which display abrupt discontinuous change.

catastrophic /-'strɒfɪk/ *a.* of or pertaining to a catastrophe; disastrous, dreadful: M19. **cata'strophical** *a.* = CATASTROPHIC E19. **cata'strophically** *adv.* L19.

catastrophism /kə'tastrəfɪz(ə)m/ *n.* M19. [f. CATASTROPHE *n.* + -ISM.] Belief in the occurrence of catastrophes; *esp.* the theory that geological or biological changes have occurred in sudden violent and unusual events (cf. UNIFORMITARIANISM).

catastrophist *n.* & *a.* (*a*) *n.* a person who holds such a belief or theory; (*b*) *adj.* of or pertaining to catastrophism or catastrophists: M19.

catatonia /katə'təʊnɪə/ *n.* Also †**k-**. L19. [f. CATA- + Gk *tonos* TONE *n.* + -IA[1].] *Med.* Abnormal motor behaviour (esp. episodes of catalepsy or overactivity), associated esp. with a form of schizophrenia; catalepsy.

catatoniac *n.* a person affected with catatonia L19. **catatonic** /-'tɒnɪk/ *a.* & *n.* pertaining to or characterized by catatonia; (a person) affected with catatonia: E20.

catavothron *n.* etc.: see KATAVOTHRON.

catawampus /katə'wɒmpəs/ *a.* & *n.* *dial.* & *slang* (chiefly *N. Amer.*). As adj. also **-ous**. M19. [Origin unkn.] A *adj.* Fierce, destructive; askew, awry. M19. B *n.* A fierce imaginary animal. M19.

catawba /kə'tɔ:bə/ *n.* E19. [f. the *Catawba*, a river in the Carolinas, USA.] (White wine from) a N. American variety of grape.

catboat /'katbəʊt/ *n.* L19. [Perh. f. CAT *n.*[2] + BOAT *n.*] A sailing boat with a single mast placed well forward and carrying only one sail.

catcall /'katkɔ:l/ *n.* & *v.* M17. [f. CAT *n.*[1] + CALL *n.*] A *n.* 1 *Hist.* A squeaking instrument or kind of whistle used esp. at a theatre to express impatience or disapproval. M17. 2 A shrill whistle (now usu. with the lips, formerly on the instrument) expressing impatience or disapproval at a theatre, public meeting, etc. M18. B *v.* 1 *v.t.* Subject to catcalls. L17. 2 *v.i.* Sound or make a catcall. M18.

catch /katʃ/ *n.*[1] LME. [f. the vb.] 1 The amount of fish etc. caught at one time. LME. 2 That by which anything is caught and held, *esp.* a contrivance for checking the motion of a door. LME. †3 Real tennis. *Sc.* L15–L16. 4 The act or fact of catching. L16. 5 A thing or person caught or worth catching, esp. in matrimony by virtue of wealth, social position, etc. L16. 6 *Mus.* A round for three or more equal voices, occas. so devised as to produce punning or other humorous verbal combinations. L16. †7 A fragment or scrap of anything caught up; a snatch of song etc. Also, a short sight, a glimpse, a view. E17–M19. 8 A cunning question, esp. containing an element of deception or surprise; a concealed difficulty or drawback in a proposal or course of action; a snag. L17. 9 In cricket, baseball, etc., a chance of or success in catching the ball, esp. (in cricket) so as to dismiss the batsman. Also w. qualifying adj.: a player who is *good* etc. at catching the ball. L18. 10 A check or impediment in the voice, breath, throat, etc. L19.

4 †**on the catch** in wait, on the lookout. 7 J. GLANVILL We retain a catch of these pretty stories. S. JOHNSON Such houses as had any catch of the river. 8 W. FREKE Most of their arguments . . are nothing but a few empty Catches in mere words. A. NIN I thought . . there must be a catch in it. **catch-22** [f. a novel (1961) by J. Heller] a condition or consequence that precludes success, a dilemma where the victim cannot win. 10 A. HAILEY A catch in his voice, with tears not far away. *Scotch catch*: see SCOTCH *a.*

catch /katʃ/ *n.*[2] *obs.* exc. *dial.* LME. [Prob. f. CATCH *v.* or *n.*[1]: cf. KETCH *n.*] A small boat; a ketch.

catch /katʃ/ *v.* Pa. t. & pple **caught** /kɔ:t/, (now *dial.* & *non-standard*) **catched**. Also (*dial.*) **ketch** /kɛtʃ/. ME. [AN, OFr. *cachier* var. of OFr. *chacier* (mod. *chasser*): see CHASE *v.*[1] Infl. in sense 'seize' and in conjugational forms by LATCH *v.*[1]] †I 1 *v.t.* & *i.* Chase. ME–M16.

II Capture; reach. 2 *v.t.* Capture (a person or animal that tries or would try to escape); ensnare, entrap; deceive, 'take in'. ME. †3 *v.t.* Obtain by exertion; attain. ME–E17. 4 *v.t.* Hit (a person, usu. *on* a part of the body); land (a blow etc.) on. ME. 5 *v.t.* Overtake, reach (an agent in motion; freq. foll. by *up*: see below); be in time to get to or reach (a thing, as a train etc., or person about to depart); in extended use, (be in time to) see or hear (a television or radio programme, etc.). E17. 6 *v.t.* Come upon (a person) unexpectedly; surprise, detect, (a person, *in* or *at* some activity, *doing*). In *pass.* also (*colloq.*) become pregnant. E17.

2 R. CAMPBELL We used to catch snakes for the Zoo. E. LONGFORD Lady Georgina Fane, unmarried daughter of Lord Westmorland, . . never gave up hope of catching him. 3 SHAKES. *3 Hen. VI* I . . Torment myself to catch the English crown. *Macb.* If th' assassination Could . . catch . . success. 4 OED She caught him a sounding box on the ear. W. GASS His arm . . caught me on the side of the neck. 5 ADDISON Caught in a shower. D. HAMMETT Not expecting to catch him in his office, but hoping to learn how to reach him at his home. R. MACAULAY She . . probably

caught the night train. N. MAILER He . . kept racing back to his room to catch the news. 6 STEELE I catched her once . . at Chuck-Farthing among the Boys. E. O'NEILL He was caught red-handed and thrown off the force. D. HAMMETT When you catch her in a lie, she admits it. SLOAN WILSON Do you catch yourself wishing for her when you're making love to me?

III Seize, take, grasp, snatch. 7 *v.t.* Take hold of suddenly or forcibly; seize; (of fire) set alight; (of other natural agency) affect. ME. 8 *v.t.* Take hold of suddenly or forcibly and remove. Now usu. foll. by *up*: see below. ME. 9 *v.t.* Entangle and hold; check suddenly; interrupt or intercept the motion of and hold; *spec.* in cricket, baseball, etc., prevent (the ball) from touching the ground after striking the bat. ME. b In cricket, baseball, etc., dismiss (a batsman) by catching the ball after it has struck the bat and before it touches the ground. Also foll. by *out*. E18. 10 *v.t.* Take, get, (rest, sleep, etc., now only for a brief period). ME. †11 *v.t. gen.* Take. ME–M17. 12 *v.t.* Take advantage of (opportunity etc.) as it occurs. LME. 13 *v.t.* Arrest the attention of; arrest (the attention etc., a faculty or organ of sense); captivate. LME. 14 *v.i.* Of fire or something combustible: start to burn, take hold. Of an engine etc.: ignite, start up. M16. 15 *v.t.* Grasp with the senses or mind; see, hear, etc., esp. by an effort; perceive; reveal to perception; apprehend and reproduce a likeness of. L16. 16 *v.i.* Snatch or grasp *at* (†*after*, †absol.). L16. 17 *v.i.* Become entangled or fixed (*in*, *on*, etc.); be impeded or checked. L18.

7 SHAKES. *Oth.* Perdition catch my soul But I do love thee. J. CONRAD Catching me round the neck as any child almost will do. G. L. MALLORY The wind and sun . . have fairly caught us all. M. M. KAYE He watched the grass flare up and catch the sticks of wood. 8 AV *Acts* 8:39 The Spirit of the Lord caught away Philip, that the eunuch saw him no more. TENNYSON He . . hastily caught His bundle . . and went his way. 9 G. MACDONALD Find a basin or plate . . and put it to catch the drop here. R. KIPLING A grain-cart's axle caught them by the horns. I. MURDOCH Felix . . caught the falling Miranda in his arms. C. POTOK The ball was coming back to me, and I caught it neatly. b R. A. FITZGERALD Gilbert . . was also caught and bowled by Eastwood. 10 R. WILBUR He'll catch a little nap. 11 CHAUCER Pryvely she kaughte forth a knyf. W. CAMDEN So they called parchment which wee have catcht from the Latine *Pergamentum*. 13 DRYDEN The soothing arts that catch the fair. H. MARTINEAU A rustle . . caught her excited ear. 14 V. WOOLF The flames had fairly caught. L. WOOLF Lizzy had put a large piece of newspaper 'to draw up the fire', the newspaper had 'caught'. J. GARDNER George . . ground on the starter a minute before the truck motor caught and roared. 15 TOLKIEN They caught faintly the fragrance of woodland flowers. S. BECKETT I could not catch the words. J. T. STORY My headlights had caught what seemed to be spots of blood on the road. B. TRAPIDO Jonathan enacted the episode . ., catching his grandmother's speech and gesture. 16 T. FULLER Mercy is a Grace which they hold the fastest, that most catch after it. W. COWPER Catching at his rein. 17 S. BELLOW His arm caught in the sleeve. T. WILLIAMS Her voice catches.

IV Get or take passively. 18 *v.t.* Receive, incur; be exposed to. Now esp. in phrases: see below. ME. 19 *v.t.* Become affected or inspired by (an emotion etc.). *obs.* exc. as passing into fig. uses of sense 20. LME. 20 *v.t.* Take (as) by infection; contract (disease etc.); acquire by sympathy or imitation. LME.

18 SHAKES. *3 Hen. VI* Fight closer or . . you'll catch a blow. GOLDSMITH Ye lakes, whose vessels catch the busy gale. I. COLEGATE The study caught the early morning sunshine. 19 POPE Presumptuous Troy . . catch'd new fury at the voice divine. 20 G. GREENE He has caught mumps from the ambassador's son. E. O'NEILL They catch his excitement.

Phrases: *a sprat to catch a herring, mackerel, whale*: see SPRAT *n.*[1] *be caught short*: see SHORT *adv. be caught with chaff*: see CHAFF *n.*[1] **catch (a) cold** contract a cold in the head; *fig.* encounter trouble or difficulties. *catch a crab*: see CRAB *n.*[1] **catch a glimpse of** see for a moment. **catch a likeness** reproduce a characteristic look in a picture etc. *catch a packet*: see PACKET *n.* 3. *catch a Tartar*: see TARTAR *n.*[2] *catch at a straw* or *straws*: see STRAW *n. catch bending*: see BEND *v. catch cold*: see *catch a cold* above. **catch fire** ignite, begin to burn, *fig.* be inflamed with passion, excitement, etc. **catch hold of** grasp, clutch at and seize. **catch it** *colloq.* incur a severe punishment. **catch me, him,** etc., **at, doing, something!** *colloq.* there is no possibility of my etc. doing that thing. *catch napping*: see NAP *v.*[1] *catch one's* BREATH. *catch one's* DEATH (*of cold* etc.). *catch on the hop*: see HOP *n.*[2] 1. *catch sight of*: see SIGHT *n.* **catch the eye of** meet the glance of (another person) with one's own, either by chance or design; *fig.* bring oneself to a person's notice, be noticed by. *catch unawares*: see UNAWARES *adv.*

With advs. in specialized senses: **catch on** (*a*) become popular or fashionable; (*b*) understand what is meant or what is happening (also foll. by *to*). **catch out** detect in a mistake etc., take unawares; (see also sense 9b above). **catch up** (*a*) *v.phr.t.* raise suddenly aloft; pick up; raise and fasten up; (*b*) *v.phr.t.* & *i.* w. *with* overtake, reach (an agent in motion); (*c*) *v.phr.i.* make up arrears (*on*). **caught up** entangled or unwillingly involved *in*; completely absorbed *in*.

catchable *a.* L17. **catcher** *n.* a person who or thing which catches; *spec.* the fielder in baseball who stands behind the batter; (*torpedo-boat catcher*: see TORPEDO *n.*): LME. **catching** *ppl a.* that catches; *spec.* infectious (*lit.* & *fig.*): LME. **catchingness** *n.* (*rare*) M17. **catchy** *a.* that catches; *esp.* attractive; (of a tune etc.) readily learned and remembered: E19.

catch- /katʃ/ *comb. form.* [f. CATCH *v.* or *n.*[1]] Mainly the vb in phraseological combs. as: (*a*) with ns., in sense 'a person who or thing which catches (the object)', also in sense 'to catch, the catching of (the object)'; (*b*) in attrib. relation to ns. in sense 'that catches or for catching'.

catch-all *n.* & *a.* (something) designed to catch or include various items, a general receptacle M19. **catch-as-catch-can** *n.* & *a.* (designating or pertaining to) a wrestling style in which all holds are permissible L19. **catch-crop** *n.* a crop grown between two staple crops (in position or time) L19. **catchfly** *n.* any of certain campions with sticky stems, chiefly of the genera *Silene* and *Lychnis* (NOTTINGHAM *catchfly*, *sweet-william catchfly*: see SWEET *a.* & *adv.*) L16. **catch-line** *n.* a short eye-catching line of type, esp. one inserted by the compositor for identification M19. **catchpenny** *a.* & *n.* (*a*) *adj.* intended merely to sell readily, superficially attractive but of little intrinsic worth; †(*b*) *n.* a publication etc. of this kind: M18. **catch-phrase** *n.* a phrase in frequent current use M19. **catch-points** *n.pl.* points to derail a train etc., e.g. when running away down a slope L19. **catch-question** *n.* a question with a deliberate hidden difficulty, a trick question M19. **catch-stitch** *n.* (*a*) *Bookbinding* kettle-stitch; (*b*) a cross-stitch used for hems etc.: M19. **catch-title** *n.* an abbreviated title at the foot of a page sufficient to identify the work to which it belongs L19. **catch-water** *n.* (*a*) a drain or ditch for collecting surface or surplus water; also *catch-water course, drain*; (*b*) a vessel designed to catch water: L18. **catchweed** *n.* (now *rare* or *obs.*) cleavers L18. **catch-weight** *n.* & *a.* (*Sport*) (*a*) *n.* unrestricted weight; (*b*) *adj.* unrestricted as regards weight: E19. **catchword** *n.* (*a*) the first word of a page given at the foot of the previous one; (*b*) a word so placed as to draw attention, as the first or last headword repeated at the top of a dictionary etc. page, the rhyming word in a verse, the last word of an actor's speech which forms the cue, etc.; (*c*) a word or phrase caught up and repeated, esp. in connection with party politics, a slogan: E18.

catched *v.* see CATCH *v.*

catchment /ˈkatʃm(ə)nt/ *n.* M19. [f. CATCH *v.* + -MENT.] *catchment area*, the area from which rainfall flows into a river, reservoir, etc., *fig.* from which a hospital's patients, a school's pupils, etc. are drawn.

catchpole /ˈkatʃpəʊl/ *n.* Also **-poll.** LOE. [AN, OFr. var. of OFr. *chacepol*, or f. AL *cacepollus*, f. Proto-Romance var. of L *captare* (see CHASE *v.*[1]) + L *pullus* fowl.] †1 A tax-gatherer; a Roman publican. LOE–M17. 2 *Hist.* A sheriff's officer, esp. one who arrests for debt. LME.

catchup *n.* var. of KETCHUP.

cate /keɪt/ *n. arch.* LME. [Aphet. f. ACATE.] †1 An act of selling something, a bargain. *rare.* Only in LME. †2 In *pl.* Provisions bought, victuals, (= ACATE 2). L15–M19. 3 A choice article of food; a dainty, a delicacy. Usu. in *pl.* M16.

catechesis /katɪˈkiːsɪs/ *n.* Pl. **-eses** /-iːsiːz/. M18. [eccl.L *catechesis* f. Gk *katēkhēsis* instruction by word of mouth, f. *katēkhein*: see CATECHIZE.] 1 Oral instruction given to catechumens; catechizing. M18. 2 A book for the instruction of catechumens. M18.

catechetic /katɪˈkɛtɪk/ *a.* & *n.* M17. [eccl.Gk *katēkhētikos*, f. *katēkhētēs* catechist, f. *katēkhein*: see CATECHIZE, -IC.] A *adj.* Of or pertaining to catechesis; according to a catechism, esp. that of a Christian Church. M17. B *n.* In *pl.* (treated as *sing.*). Christian theology as it deals with catechesis. M19.

catechetical /katɪˈkɛtɪk(ə)l/ *a.* E17. [f. as prec.: see -ICAL.] 1 = CATECHETIC *a.* E17. 2 Consisting of questions and answers; proceeding by question and answer. L17.

catechetically *adv.* M18.

catechin /ˈkatɪtʃɪn/ *n.* M19. [f. CATECHU + -IN[1].] *Chem.* The major constituent of catechu, a crystalline phenolic compound, $C_{15}H_{14}O_6$, of which there are several isomers.

catechise /ˈkatɪkiːz/ *n. obs.* exc. *dial.* M16. [App. f. Fr. *catéchèse* CATECHESIS, conf. w. CATECHIZE (Fr. *catéchiser*).] = CATECHESIS, CATECHISM.

catechise *v.* var. of CATECHIZE.

catechism /ˈkatɪkɪz(ə)m/ *n.* E16. [eccl.L *catechismus* f. eccl.Gk, f. *katēkhizein*: see CATECHIZE, -ISM.] †1 Catechetical instruction; catechesis. E16–E17. 2 A treatise for instruction in the principles of the Christian religion, in the form of question and answer. E16. 3 *transf.* & *fig.* a A course of question and answer; a series of questions put to anyone. L16. b A book of instruction by question and answer. M17.

2 **Church Catechism**: of the Anglican Church. **Longer Catechism, Shorter Catechism**: of Presbyterian Churches.

cateˈchismal *a.* E19.

catechist /ˈkatɪkɪst/ *n.* M16. [eccl.L *catechista* f eccl.Gk *katēkhistēs*, f. *katēkhizein*: see CATECHIZE.] A teacher giving oral instruction in Christianity by means of a catechism. Also, a teacher of native origin in a mission church.

cateˈchistic *a.* = CATECHISTICAL L17. **cateˈchistical** *a.* of or pertaining to the office, teaching, or mode of instruction of a catechist; catechetical: L16. **cateˈchistically** *adv.* M17.

catechize /ˈkatɪkʌɪz/ *v.t.* Also **-ise.** LME. [eccl.L *catechizare* f. eccl.Gk *katēkhizein*, f. *katēkhein* sound through, instruct orally, f. as CATA- + *ēkhein* to sound, f. *ēkhē*: see ECHO *n.*, -IZE.] 1 Instruct orally in the elements of the Christian religion by repetition (formerly) or by question and answer, esp. using a catechism; *transf.* instruct by question and answer. LME. 2 Question systematically or at length; interrogate; examine (as) with a catechism. E17.

catechizer *n.* LME.

catechol /ˈkatɪtʃɒl/ *n.* L19. [f. next + -OL.] *Chem.* A crystalline dihydric phenol first obtained by distilling catechu; benzene-1,2-diol, $C_6H_4(OH)_2$.

cateˈcholamine /katɪˈkəʊləmiːn/ *n.* any of various catechol derivatives which have amine substituents and possess neurotransmitter and hormonal activity, e.g. dopamine, adrenalin M20. **catecholaminergic** /-ˌkəʊləmɪˈnəːdʒɪk/ *a.* (*Physiol.*) releasing or involving a catecholamine as a neurotransmitter L20.

catechu /ˈkatɪtʃuː/ *n.* L17. [mod.L, unexpl. deriv. of Malay *kacu*: cf. CACHOU.] Any of various astringent tannin-rich vegetable extracts used esp. in tanning, e.g. gambier.

catechumen /katɪˈkjuːmɛn/ *n.* LME. [(O)Fr. *catéchumène* or eccl.L *catechumenus* f. Gk *katēkhoumenos* being instructed, pres. pple pass. of *katēkhein*: see CATECHIZE.] A Christian convert under instruction before baptism. Also, a young Christian preparing for confirmation.

catechumenate *n.* the position or condition of a catechumen L17. **catechuˈmenical** *a.* L18.

categorem /ˈkatɪɡərɛm/ *n.* Now *rare.* L16. [Gk *katēgorēma*, *-mat-*, accusation, predicate, f. *katēgorein* accuse.] *Logic.* †1 A predicate. L16–M17. 2 A categorematic word. M19.

categorematic /ˌkatɪɡ(ə)rɪˈmatɪk/ *a.* E19. [f. as prec. + -IC.] *Logic* & *Ling.* Of a word: able to be used by itself as a term. Opp. *syncategorematic*.

categorematical *a.* (*rare*) M17. **categorematically** *adv.* (*rare*) M17.

categorial /katɪˈgɔːrɪəl/ *a.* E20. [f. CATEGORY + -AL[1], after G *kategorial*.] Chiefly *Logic* & *Ling.* Relating to or involving categories.

categoric /katɪˈgɒrɪk/ *a.* & *n.* L17. [Fr. *catégorique* or late L *categoricus*, f. Gk *katēgorikos* accusatory, affirmative, (later) categorical, f. *katēgoria*: see CATEGORY, -IC.] **A** *adj.* = CATEGORICAL. L17. †**B** *n.* A categorical statement or proposition. L17–M19.

categorical /katɪˈgɒrɪk(ə)l/ *a.* & *n.* L16. [f. as prec. + -AL[1].] **A** *adj.* Unconditional, absolute; explicit, direct, plain-speaking. L16.

categorical imperative *Ethics* an unconditional moral obligation derived from pure reason.

B *n.* A categorical proposition or statement. L17.

categorically *adv.* E17.

category /ˈkatɪg(ə)ri/ *n.* LME. [Fr. *catégorie* or its source late L *categoria* f. Gk *katēgoria* statement, accusation, f. *katēgorein* speak against, f. as CATA- + *agoreuein* speak in the assembly, f. as AGORA *n.*[1]] **I** *Philos.* **1** Any of a possibly exhaustive set of basic classes among which all things might be distributed (orig. each of ten classes postulated by Aristotle: cf. PREDICAMENT 1). LME. **2** Any of the a priori conceptions applied by the mind to sense-impressions. (After Kant.) E19. **3** Any relatively fundamental philosophical concept. E20.

II *gen.* **4** A class, a division. M17. **5** *Math.* An entity consisting of a class of abstract objects sharing a particular property together with a class of mappings which preserve that property. M20.

4 N. CHOMSKY The notion 'Subject' . . designates a grammatical function rather than a grammatical category. G. BOYCOTT Play . . only safety shots—and the hook and the hit over the top certainly do not come into that category.

categoriˈzation *n.* the action or an act of placing something in a category, classification L19. **categorize** *v.t.* place in a category, classify E18.

catena /kəˈtiːnə/ *n.* Pl. **-nae** /-niː/, **-s**. M17. [L *catena* chain, as in eccl.L *catena patrum* chain of the fathers (of the Church).] A chain or connected series of things, esp. of the patristic comments on Scripture.

catenary /kəˈtiːnəri/ *n.* & *a.* M18. [mod.L *catenaria* use as n. of fem. of L *catenarius* adj., f. as prec.: see -ARY[1].] **A** *n.* A curve of the kind formed by a uniform chain hanging freely from two points not in the same vertical line. M18. **B** *adj.* **1** Relating to a catena or series. M19. **2** Having the form of a catenary; pertaining to or characterized by a catenary. L19.

catenary bridge a suspension bridge hung by uniform chains from two points not in the same vertical line.

cateˈnarian *a.* (now *rare* or *obs.*) = CATENARY *a.* M18. **ˈcatenoid** *n.* a surface generated by rotation of a catenary about an axis L19.

catenate /ˈkatɪneɪt/ *v.t.* E17. [L *catenat-* pa. ppl stem of *catenare*, f. *catena*: see CATENA, -ATE[3].] Connect like the links of a chain.

cateˈnation *n.* M17.

catenulate /kəˈtiːnjʊlət/ *a.* E19. [f. L *catena* CATENA + -ULE + -ATE[2].] *Bot.* & *Zool.* Resembling a chain; having a chainlike series of projections.

†**cater** *n.*[1] ME–M17. [Aphet. f. *acater* var. of ACATOUR.] A buyer of provisions; a caterer.

cater /ˈkeɪtə/ *n.*[2] LME. [(O)Fr. *quatre* four.] **1** The four on a die or (*arch.*) in a pack of cards; a throw of four at dice. LME. **2** *Campanol.* In *pl.* Changes on nine bells in which four couples of bells change places in the order of ringing. E19.

cater /ˈkeɪtə/ *v.*[1]*t.* & *adv. dial.* L16. [f. (as) prec.] (Place, set) rhomboidally; (cut, move, etc.) diagonally.

cater /ˈkeɪtə/ *v.*[2] L16. [f. CATER *n.*[1]] **1** *v.i.* Act as a caterer (*for*). L16. **2** *v.t.* Provide or purvey as food. M17. **3** *v.i. gen.* Provide amusements, requisites, etc., *for, to*; make allowances *for*. M17. **b** Pander *to* (evil inclinations etc.). M19.

catering *vbl n.* the action of the vb; the trade or work of a caterer: E19.

cateran /ˈkat(ə)r(ə)n/ *n.* ME. [med.L *cateranus*, *kethernus* or its source Gael. *ceathairne* peasantry (= Ir. *ceithearn* KERN *n.*[1]).] **1** *Hist.* An irregular fighting-man of the Scottish Highlands. (Orig. in *pl.* & as *collect. sing.*) ME. **2** *transf.* A raider, a marauder. L19.

catercorner /ˈkeɪtəkɔːnə/ *adv.* & *a. N. Amer.* & *dial.* Also **catty-** /ˈkatɪ-/, **-cornered** /-kɔːnəd/, & other vars. M19. [f. CATER *adv.* + CORNER *n.* (+ -ED[2]).] (Placed or situated) diagonally.

cater-cousin /ˈkeɪtəkʌz(ə)n/ *n. arch.* E16. [Origin of 1st elem. uncertain: perh. f. CATER *n.*[1] w. ref. to boarding together.] An intimate friend.

caterer /ˈkeɪt(ə)rə/ *n.* ME. [f. CATER *n.*[1] or *v.*[2] + -ER[1].] **1** A person who caters or provides provisions for a household, club, etc.; *esp.* a person whose trade is to supply, cook, serve, etc., food at a social function. ME. **2** *gen.* A person who provides amusements, requisites, etc. E18.

cateress /ˈkeɪt(ə)rɪs/ *n.* M17. [f. CATER *n.*[1] or *v.*[2] + -ESS[1].] A female caterer.

caterpillar /ˈkatəpɪlə/ *n.* LME. [Perh. f. AN var. of OFr. *chatepelose* lit. 'hairy cat', infl. by PILLAR.] **1** The larva of a butterfly or moth; *loosely* any of the similar larvae of various insects. LME. **2** *fig.* A rapacious person; one who preys on society. Now *rare* or *obs.* M16. **3** *sing.* & (usu.) in *pl.* Any of several Mediterranean plants of the leguminous genus *Scorpiurus*, with spirally curved pods. Also *caterpillar plant*. L16. **4** (Also **C-**.) (Proprietary name for) a vehicle with an endless articulated steel band (*Caterpillar track*, *tread*, etc.) passing round and worked by two wheels, for travelling on rough ground. E20.

1 *lobster caterpillar*: see LOBSTER *n.*[1] 3. *nigger caterpillar*: see NIGGER *n.* 3. *saddleback caterpillar*: see SADDLEBACK *n.* 2. **vegetable caterpillar** = AWHETO.

caterwaul /ˈkatəwɔːl/ *v.* & *n.* LME. [f. CAT *n.*[1] + *-er-* connective + imit. final elem.] **A** *v.i.* **1** Of a cat: make the screaming noise characteristic of a cat on heat. LME. **b** *transf.* Make a discordant screaming noise. L16. **2** Be in heat; behave lasciviously; pursue the opposite sex. *derog. arch.* M16. **B** *n.* A screaming noise (as) of a cat during the mating season. E18.

caterwauler *n.* (*rare*) E17.

catery /ˈkeɪt(ə)ri/ *n.* Long *obs.* exc. *Hist.* LME. [Aphet. f. ACATERY.] The office concerned with the provisioning of the royal household.

catgut /ˈkatgʌt/ *n.* L16. [App. f. CAT *n.*[1] (use unexpl.) + GUT *n.*] **1** The dried and twisted intestines of the sheep, horse, or ass, used for the stringing of musical instruments, rackets, etc., and for surgical sutures. L16. **2** A violin; stringed instruments collectively. E18. †**3** A coarse cloth of thick cord, used as a stiffening. M18–E19.

Cathar /ˈkaθɑː/ *n.* Pl. **Cathars**, **Cathari** /ˈkaθɑːrʌɪ/. M17. [med.L *Cathari* (pl.) f. Gk *katharoi* the pure.] *Eccl. Hist.* A member of a sect seeking to achieve purity; *spec.* an Albigensian.

Catharist *n.* E17. **Catharism** *n.* L16.

Catharine *n.* var. of CATHERINE.

catharsis /kəˈθɑːsɪs/ *n.* In sense 2 also **k-**. Pl. **-tharses** /-ˈθɑːsiːz/. E19. [mod.L f. Gk *katharsis*, f. *kathairein* cleanse, f. *katharos* pure. In sense 2 f. Aristotle's *Poetics*.] **1** *Med.* Purgation. E19. **2** (A) purification of the emotions by vicarious experience, esp. through drama, or, in psychotherapy, by abreaction. M19.

cathartic /kəˈθɑːtɪk/ *a.* & *n.* In sense 2 also **k-**. E17. [Late L *catharticus* f. Gk *kathartikos*, f. *kathairein*: see prec., -IC.] **A** *adj.* **1** *Med.* Purgative. E17. **2** *gen.* Purifying; effecting catharsis. M17. **B** *n.* A purgative. M17.

cathartical *a.* (now *rare*) M17. **cathartically** *adv.* E19.

Cathay /kaˈθeɪ/ *n. arch.* & *poet.* M16. [med.L *Cat(h)aya* f. Turkic *Khitāy*.] The country of China.

Cathayan *a.* & *n.* L16.

cathectic /kaˈθɛktɪk/ *a.* E20. [Gk *kathektikos* capable of holding.] *Psychol.* Of or relating to cathexis.

cathect *v.t.* [back-form.] charge (an idea, impulse, etc.) with mental energy or emotion M20.

cathedra /kəˈθiːdrə/ *n.* LME. [L f. Gk *kathedra* chair.] A seat; *spec.* the chair of a bishop in his church; the episcopal see.

See also EX CATHEDRA.

cathedral /kəˈθiːdr(ə)l/ *a.* & *n.* ME. [(O)Fr. *cathédral* f. late L *cathedralis*, f. L CATHEDRA: see -AL[1]. As n. short for *cathedral church*.] **A** *adj.* **1** Of or pertaining to a bishop's throne or see. (Not always distinguishable from the n. used attrib.) ME. **2** Of or pertaining to a chair of office or authority; *ex cathedra*. E17.

2 T. B. SHAW The style is too uniformly didactic, cathedral, and declamatory.

B *n.* **1** The principal church of a diocese, containing the bishop's throne. L16. **2** A principal Presbyterian church; any important, large, or imposing church. E19.

Special collocations & *comb.*: **cathedral church** a cathedral. **cathedral city**: in which there is a cathedral. **cathedral glass**: coloured and leaded like that of churches, for domestic etc. use.

catheˈdratic *a.* (now *rare*) = CATHEDRAL *a.* M17.

catheretic /kaθəˈrɛtɪk/ *a.* & *n.* Now *rare* or *obs.* M17. [Gk *kathairetikos* destructive, f. *kathairein* destroy.] *Med.* (An agent) having power to destroy, reduce, or consume.

Catherine /ˈkaθ(ə)rɪn/ *n.* Also (less commonly) **-ar-**, **K-**. L16. [Female forename, f. mod.L *Catharina*, earlier *Katerina* repr. Gk *Aikaterina*, assim. to *katharos* pure. In sense 1 a legendary saint of Alexandria martyred on a spiked wheel.] **1** *Catherine wheel*: **a** Esp. *Her.* The figure of a wheel with curved spikes projecting from its circumference. L16. **b** A firework which rotates in the manner of a wheel. M18. **c** *Archit.* In full *Catherine wheel window*. A circular window with radiating spokes. E19. **d** A lateral handspring with the arms and legs extended. L19. **2** *Catherine pear*, a small and early variety of pear. E17.

catheter /ˈkaθɪtə/ *n.* Also **k-**. E17. [Late L *catheter* f. Gk *kathetēr*, f. *kathienai* send or let down.] *Med.* A tube which can be passed into the bladder or other body cavity or canal to allow the draining of fluid.

catheteriˈzation *n.* the use of a catheter M19. **catheterize** *v.t.* employ a catheter on (a patient); introduce a catheter into: L19. **catheterism** *n.* (now *rare* or *obs.*) = CATHETERIZATION E18.

cathetometer /kaθɪˈtɒmɪtə/ *n.* Also **k-**. M19. [f. next + -OMETER.] An instrument for measuring vertical distances, esp. small differences of level of liquid columns in tubes.

cathetus /ˈkaθɪtəs/ *n.* Now *rare* or *obs.* Pl. **-ti** /-tʌɪ/. L16. [L f. Gk *kathetos* (*grammē*) perpendicular line, f. *kathienai*: see CATHETER.] A straight line falling perpendicularly on another straight line or surface.

cathexis /kəˈθɛksɪs/ *n.* E20. [Gk *kathexis* holding, retention, a rendering of G (*Libido*)*besetzung* (Freud).] *Psychoanalysis.* The concentration or accumulation of libidinal energy on a particular object.

cathode /ˈkaθəʊd/ *n.* Also †**k-**. M19. [Gk *kathodos* way down, f. *kata* CATA- + *hodos* way.] A negative electrode or terminal. Opp. ANODE.

cold cathode: see COLD *a. hot cathode*: see HOT *a.* VIRTUAL *cathode*.

Comb.: **cathode ray** a beam of electrons emitted from the cathode of a vacuum tube (*cathode-ray oscilloscope*: see OSCILLOSCOPE 2; *cathode-ray tube*, a vacuum tube in which cathode rays produce a luminous image on a fluorescent screen).

cathodal *a.* of or pertaining to a cathode L19.

cathodic /kəˈθɒdɪk/ *a.* Also †**k-**. M19. [f. prec. + -IC.] Of or pertaining to a cathode.

cathodic protection prevention of corrosion of a metal structure by making it act as the cathode of an electrolytic cell.

cathodically *adv.* M20.

cathodo- /ˈkaθədəʊ/ *comb. form* of CATHODE: see -O-. Also †**k-**.

cathodolumiˈnescence *n.* luminescence excited by the impact of an electron beam E20.

Catholic /ˈkaθ(ə)lɪk/ *a.* & *n.* In branch II of the adj. **c-**. LME. [(O)Fr. *catholique* or its source Chr.L *catholicus* f. Gk *katholikos* general, universal, f. *katholou* (*kath' holou*) in general, generally, f. *kata* in respect of, *holos* whole.] **A**

adj. I *Chr. Ch.* 1 Of, belonging to, or designating the ancient Church before the great schism between East and West, or to any Church standing in historical continuity with it, as (*a*) the Western or Latin Church after the schism (distinguished from *Eastern*, *Orthodox*), (*b*) the Latin Church that remained under the Roman obedience after the Reformation (= ROMAN CATHOLIC *a. phr.*, opp. *Protestant* etc.), (*c*) the Anglican Church regarded as a continuation of both the Ancient and Latin Churches (= ANGLO-CATHOLIC *a.*). LME. 2 Of, belonging to, or designating the Christian Church as a whole. M16. 3 Recognizing or having sympathies with all Christians. M17.

3 R. BAXTER The Lord Protector is noted as a man of a catholic spirit, desirous of the unity and peace of all the servants of Christ.

II 4 *gen.* Universal; of interest or use to everyone. M16. †b Of a medicine, remedy, etc.: universally applicable. E17–M18. †c Common, prevalent. Only in 17. 5 Having sympathies with all; all-embracing; broad-minded, tolerant. L16.

4 J. A. FROUDE What was of catholic rather than national interest. 5 A. BURGESS I've got catholic tastes. Catholic with a small 'c', of course.

B *n.* 1 A member of a Catholic Church; *esp.* = ROMAN CATHOLIC *n. phr.* LME. †2 = CATHOLICOS. E17–M18.

Phrases & comb.: ANGLO-CATHOLIC. **Catholic (and) Apostolic Church** a religious body founded about 1835 according to the teachings of Edward Irving. *Catholic Emancipation*: see EMANCIPATION. **Catholic Epistles**: those of James, Peter, and Jude, and the first of John, as not being addressed to particular Churches or persons. **Catholic King** *Hist.* the King of Spain. **German Catholic** (*a*) *n.* a member of either of two religious parties who separated from the Roman Catholic communion in 19th-cent. Germany (usu. in *pl.*); (*b*) *adj.* of or pertaining to the German Catholics. **his Catholic Majesty** = *Catholic King* above. **Old Catholic** (*a*) *n.* a member of any of various religious parties who separated from the Roman Catholic communion, esp. the Church of Utrecht in the 18th cent. and the German Catholics (usu. in *pl.*); a member of a Roman Catholic family in England since the Reformation; (*b*) *adj.* of or pertaining to Old Catholics. ROMAN CATHOLIC. ROMISH *Catholic.*

Catholically *adv.* E16. **Catholicism** /kəˈθɒlɪsɪz(ə)m/ *n.* (adherence to) the system, faith, and practice of a Catholic (esp. the Roman Catholic) Church L16. **Catholicization** /kəˌθɒlɪsʌɪˈzeɪʃ(ə)n/ *n.* the action of making Catholic E20. **Catholicize** /kəˈθɒlɪsʌɪz/ *v.t.* & *i.* make Catholic or catholic; become (a) Catholic: E17. **Catholicly** *adv.* in accordance with the faith or teaching of the Catholic Church M16.

catholicate /kəˈθɒlɪkeɪt/ *n.* M19. [med.L *catholicatus*, f. *catholicus* CATHOLIC: cf. CATHOLICOS & see -ATE[1].] The jurisdiction of a Catholicos.

catholicity /kaθəˈlɪsɪti/ *n.* In sense 3 C-. E19. [f. CATHOLIC + -ITY: cf. Fr. *catholicité*.] 1 The quality of having sympathies with all or being all-embracing; broad-mindedness, tolerance. E19. 2 Universality; universal prevalence or recognition. E19. 3 The character of belonging to or being in accordance with a Catholic Church; *spec.* Roman Catholicism. E19.

1 H. REED It is important to cultivate a true catholicity of taste. 3 E. B. PUSEY They wish to claim for the English Church the character of Catholicity.

catholicon /kəˈθɒlɪkɒn/ *n.* LME. [Fr. *catholicon*, *-cum* f. mod.L *catholicum* use as n. (sc. *remedium* remedy) of *catholicus*: see CATHOLIC. In sense 1 cf. med.L *catholicon* dictionary.] 1 A comprehensive treatise. LME. 2 A universal remedy; a panacea. LME.

Catholicos /kəˈθɒlɪkɒs/ *n.* E17. [med.Gk *katholikos*: see CATHOLIC.] *Chr. Ch.* The Patriarch of the Armenian or the Nestorian Church.

Comb.: **Catholicos-Patriarch** the head of the Georgian Church.

Catiline /ˈkatɪlʌɪn/ *n.* L16. [L *Catilina*, cognomen of a Roman who conspired against the Roman republic in 63 BC: see -INE[1].] A conspirator, esp. against government.

Catilinarian /ˌkatɪlɪˈnɛːrɪən/ *a.* & *n.* (a person) resembling Catiline; conspiring, a conspirator, esp. against government: E19.

cation /ˈkatʌɪən/ *n.* M19. [f. CAT(HODE or CATA- + ION.] A positively-charged ion, i.e. one which would be attracted to a cathode. Opp. ANION.

catiˈonic *a.* of or pertaining to cations; of the nature of a cation: E20.

catkin /ˈkatkɪn/ *n.* L16. [Du. †*katteken* lit. 'kitten': see CAT *n.*[1], -KIN.] A cylindrical unisexual inflorescence, usu. pendent and downy or silky, borne by various trees.

catling /ˈkatlɪŋ/ *n.* In sense 2 also **-in** /-ɪn/. E17. [f. CAT *n.*[1] + -LING[1].] 1 Catgut. E17. 2 *Surg.* A long, narrow, double-edged, straight knife for amputations. E17. 3 A kitten; a little cat. M17.

catlinite /ˈkatlɪnʌɪt/ *n.* M19. [f. George *Catlin* (1796–1872), US artist + -ITE[1].] The sacred pipe-stone of the American Indians, a red clay of the Upper Missouri region.

catocalid /katə(ʊ)ˈkeɪlɪd/ *a.* & *n.* L19. [f. mod.L *Catocala* (see below), f. Gk *katō* below + *kalos* beautiful: see -ID[3].] (A moth) belonging to the noctuid genus *Catocala*, which includes the red underwing.

cat o' mountain *n. phr.* var. of CATAMOUNTAIN.

Catonian /keɪˈtəʊnɪən/ *n.* & *a.* M16. [L *Catonianus*, f. *Cato*, cognomen of Cato the Censor (234–149 BC and Cato of Utica (95–46 BC), both noted for the severity of their manners: see -IAN.] †A *n.* A follower of either Cato. Only in M16. B *adj.* Severe in manner, stern, austere. L17.

catoptric /kaˈtɒptrɪk/ *n.* & *a.* M16. [Gk *katoptrikos* adj., f. *katoptron* mirror: see -IC.] A *n.sing.* & (now) usu. in *pl.* (treated as *sing.*). The branch of optics that deals with reflection. M16. B *adj.* Of or relating to mirrors or reflection. E18.

catoptrical *a.* (now *rare* or *obs.*) L17.

catoptromancy /kəˈtɒptrəmansi/ *n.* E17. [f. Gk *katoptron* (see prec.) + -MANCY.] Divination by means of a mirror or mirrors.

catostomid /kəˈtɒstəmɪd/ *n.* & *a.* L19. [mod.L *Catostomidae* (see below), f. *Catostomus* genus name, f. Gk *katō* down + *stoma* mouth: see -ID[3].] (A freshwater fish) of the chiefly N. American family Catostomidae, which includes the suckers and buffaloes.

cat's-eye /ˈkatsʌɪ/ *n. fig.* M16. [f. CAT *n.*[1] + -'S[1] + EYE *n.*] 1 A gemstone, esp. a variety of chalcedony, which displays a lustre resembling the contracted pupil of a cat's eye. Also called *sunstone*. M16. 2 A speedwell, forget-me-not, or similar bright flower. E19. 3 The operculum of a turban shell. L19. 4 Also C-. (Proprietary name for) a light-reflecting stud set into the surface of a road to demarcate traffic lanes etc. at night. M20.

†**catso** *n.* & *int. slang.* See also GADSO. E17. [It. *cazzo* lit. 'penis'.] A *n.* A rogue. Only in 17. B *int.* = GADZOOKS. Only in E18.

cat's-paw /ˈkatspɔː/ *n. fig.* M18. [f. CAT *n.*[1] + -'S[1] + PAW *n.*[1]] 1 A light breeze that ripples the surface of water in places. M18. 2 A person used as a tool by another. Cf. *cat's-foot* (a) s.v. CAT *n.*[1] L18. 3 *Naut.* A twisting hitch made in the bight of a rope to form two bights, to hook a tackle on. L18.

cat's-tail /ˈkatsteɪl/ *n. fig.* Also **cat-tail**. ME. [f. CAT *n.*[1] + -'S[1] + TAIL *n.*[1]] 1 Any of various plants with long thin parts suggestive of cats' tails, esp. (*a*) the reed-mace; (*b*) a horsetail; (*c*) (more fully *cat's-tail grass*) a grass of the genus *Phleum*. ME. 2 A catkin. L16.

catsup *n.* var. of KETCHUP.

cattalo /ˈkatələʊ/ *n. N. Amer.* Also **catalo**. Pl. **-o(e)s**. L19. [f. CATTLE + BUFFALO.] A cross between a male buffalo and a domesticated cow.

†**cattan** *n.* see KATANA.

Cattern *n.* & *v.* var. of KATTERN.

cattery /ˈkatəri/ *n.* L18. [f. CAT *n.*[1] + -ERY.] A colony of cats; a place where cats are bred or looked after.

cattish /ˈkatɪʃ/ *a.* L16. [f. CAT *n.*[1] + -ISH[1].] 1 Of or like a cat. L16. 2 *spec.* Sly and spiteful; catty. L19.

cattishly *adv.* E20. **cattishness** *n.* L19.

cattle /ˈkat(ə)l/ *n.* ME. [f. AN, ONFr. *catel* var. of OFr. *chatel* CHATTEL.] I Property. †1 (Personal) property; wealth, goods. ME–L15. †2 A chattel. L15–E18. II Treated as *pl.* Livestock. 3 Animals of the genus *Bos*, oxen; (now *arch.* & *dial.*) livestock, (in stables) horses. ME. 4 *contempt.* People (likened to cattle). *arch.* L16. †5 Vermin; insects. Only in 17.

3 **black cattle** oxen of Scottish and Welsh highland breeds, orig. black.

Comb.: **cattle-cake** concentrated food for cattle, in cake form; **cattle-dog** *Austral.* & *NZ* a dog bred or trained to work cattle; **cattle-egret** a small white heron, *Bubulais ibis*, often associated with grazing cattle; **cattle-grid**, (*US*) **-guard** a ditch covered by spaced bars to allow the passage of vehicles and pedestrians but not cattle etc.; **cattle-lifter** a cattle-thief; **cattleman** *N. Amer.* a person who tends or rears cattle; **cattle-plague** rinderpest; **cattle-rustler** a cattle-thief; **cattle-stop** *NZ* = *cattle-grid* above; **cattle-truck** a truck for the transport of cattle; *fig.* a crowded uncomfortable vehicle.

cattleya /ˈkatlɪə/ *n.* E19. [mod.L, f. William *Cattley* (d. 1832), Eng. patron of botany: see -A[1].] An epiphytic neotropical orchid of the genus *Cattleya*, with handsome violet, pink, or yellow flowers.

catty /ˈkati/ *n.* L16. [Malay, Jav. *kati*. Cf. CADDY *n.*[1], KATI.] Any of various weights of around 600 grams or 1⅓ lb, used in China and SE Asia.

catty /ˈkati/ *a.* L19. [f. CAT *n.*[1] + -Y[1].] 1 Sly and spiteful. L19. 2 Of or pertaining to cats. E20.

cattily *adv.* E20. **cattiness** *n.* E20.

cattycorner(ed) *advs.* & *adjs.* see CATER-CORNER.

Catullian /kəˈtʌlɪən/ *a.* M19. [f. *Catullus* (see below) + -IAN.] Of, pertaining to, or characteristic of the Latin lyric poet Catullus (*c* 84–*c* 54 BC) or his writing.

Also **Catullan** *a.* M20.

catydid *n.* var. of KATYDID.

caubeen /kɔːˈbiːn/ *n. Anglo-Ir.* & *Canad. dial.* E19. [Ir. = old hat, old cap, f. *cáibín* dim. of *cába* cape: see -EEN[2].] A hat, a cap.

Caucasian /kɔːˈkeɪzjən, -ʒ(ə)n/ *a.* & *n.* E17. [f. *Caucasus* (see below), *Caucasia*: see -IAN, -AN.] A *adj.* 1 Of, pertaining to, or inhabiting the Caucasus, a mountainous region between the Black and Caspian Seas; of or pertaining to the non-Indo-European languages of this region, including Circassian and Georgian. E17. 2 Of, relating to, or designating the White or light-skinned division of humankind, formerly supposed to have originated in the Caucasus. E19. B *n.* A White or light-skinned person. Also, a native or inhabitant of the Caucasus; the Caucasian languages collectively. M19.

Caucasic /kɔːˈkasɪk/ *a.* = CAUCASIAN *a.* 2 L19. **ˈCaucasoid** *a.* & *n.* (*a*) *adj.* of, pertaining to, or resembling the Caucasian division of humankind; (*b*) *n.* a Caucasoid person E20.

Cauchy /ˈkəʊʃi/ *n.* L19. [A.-L. *Cauchy* (1789–1857), Fr. mathematician.] *Math.* 1 Used *attrib.* and in *possess.* to designate concepts introduced by Cauchy or arising out of his work. L19. 2 *Cauchy–Riemann equation* [RIEMANN], each of two partial differential equations which must be satisfied if a function of two variables is to be separable into a real part and an imaginary part. E20. 3 *Cauchy–Schwarz inequality*, = SCHWARZ *inequality*. M20.

1 **Cauchy sequence** any sequence of numbers a_n which satisifes the condition that, for any positive number ϵ, a value of n can be chosen so that any two members of the sequence after a_n differ by a quantity less than ϵ. **Cauchy('s) integral (formula)** a formula expressing the value of a function at a point in terms of an integral round a closed curve enclosing the point. **Cauchy's theorem** *spec.* the theorem that the integral of an analytic function of a complex variable round a closed curve which encloses no singularities is zero.

caucus /ˈkɔːkəs/ *n.* & *v.* Orig. *US.* M18. [Perh. f. Algonquian *cau'-cau'-as'u* adviser.] A *n.* A committee of members of a political party, esp. elected representatives, meeting regularly to determine policy, select candidates, etc.; a group or bloc of such members; the systematic exercise of political control through such committees. Also (freq. *derog.*), a usu. secret meeting of a group active within a larger organization or party; a group of this kind. M18.

J. R. LOWELL In the Greek epic, the gods are partisans, they hold caucuses, they lobby and log-roll for their candidates. G. B. SHAW Mere politicians, the drudges of the caucus and the polling booth.

B *v.i.* Hold or form a caucus. L18.

cauda /ˈkɔːdə/ *n.* Pl. **-dae** /-diː/. L17. [L = tail.] *Anat.* & *Zool.* A structure resembling a tail. Chiefly in *cauda equina* /ɪkˈwʌɪnə/, the bundle of nerves descending from the lower end of the spinal cord.

caudal /ˈkɔːd(ə)l/ *a.* & *n.* M17. [mod.L *caudalis*, f. as prec.: see -AL[1].] *Anat.* & *Zool.* **A** *adj.* Of, pertaining to, or of the nature of a tail; situated in or near the tail or posterior part of the body. M17. **B** *n.* A caudal fin, vertebra, etc. M19.

caudally *adv.* L19.

caudate /ˈkɔːdeɪt/ *a.* E17. [med.L *caudatus*, f. as CAUDA: see -ATE[2].] Having a tail or an appendage resembling a tail; tailed.

caudate nucleus *Anat.* the upper of the two grey nuclei of the corpus striatum.

Also **cauˈdated** *a.* E19.

caudex /ˈkɔːdɛks/ *n.* Pl. **-dices** /-dɪsiːz/. L18. [L, earlier form of CODEX.] *Bot.* The axis of a plant (esp. a palm or fern) consisting of stem and root.

caudicle /ˈkɔːdɪk(ə)l/ *n.* M19. [f. L CAUDEX, *-dic-* after *caulicle* etc.: see -CULE.] *Bot.* A small stalklike appendage to the pollinium of an orchid.

caudillo /kaʊˈdiːljəʊ/ *n.* Pl. **-os.** M19. [Sp. f. late L *capitellum* dim. of *caput* head.] In Spain and Spanish-speaking countries: a head of State, a military or political leader.

the Caudillo the title assumed by General Francisco Franco, ruler of Spain 1938–75.

caudle /ˈkɔːd(ə)l/ *n.* & *v. arch.* ME. [ONFr. *caudel*, OFr. *chaudel* (mod. *chaudeau*) f. med.L dim. of L *caldum* hot drink, f. *cal(i)dus* warm.] **A** *n.* A drink of warm gruel containing spice, sugar, and wine, for invalids. ME. **B** *v.t.* **1** Administer a caudle to. Cf. CODDLE *v.*[2] E17. **2** Mix as in a caudle. L18.

caught *v.* pa. t. & pple of CATCH *v.*

cauk /kɔːk/ *n. obs.* exc. *dial.* Also (esp. in sense 2) **cawk**. LME. [Perh. north. var. of CHALK *n.*, or f. MDu. *calc* CHALK *n.*] **1** Chalk. Also, lime, calcite, etc. LME. **2** Barytes. M17.

cauk *v.*[1] var. of COCK *v.*[4]

†**cauk** *v.*[2] see CAULK *v.*[1]

caul /kɔːl/ *n.*[1] See also KELL. ME. [Origin uncertain: perh. f. (O)Fr. *cale* head-covering, but recorded earlier.] **1** A close-fitting netted head-dress, esp. of a type worn by women indoors. Also, the plain back part of a woman's head-dress. *obs.* exc. *Hist.* ME. †**b** The netted substructure of a wig. L17–L18. †**2** A spider's web. LME–M17. **3a** An enveloping membrane. Long *obs.* in *gen.* sense. LME. **b** The omentum. LME. **c** The amnion or inner membrane enclosing the foetus before birth; a portion of this occas. found on a child's head at birth, thought to be lucky, and supposed to be a preservative against drowning. M16. †**4** *gen.* A net. L15–L17.

caul /kɔːl/ *n.*[2] *Sc.* Also **cauld** /kɔːld/. M16. [Origin unkn.] A weir or dam for diverting river-water.

†**caul** *n.*[3] var. of COLE *n.*[1]

cauld *n.*, *a.* & *adv.* see COLD *n.* etc.

cauldrife /ˈkɔːldrɪf/ *a. Sc.* M17. [f. prec. + RIFE. Cf. WASTRIFE.] Causing cold, chilling; susceptible to cold.

cauldron /ˈkɔːldr(ə)n, ˈkɒl-/ *n.* Also **cald-**. ME. [AN, ONFr. *caudron* (mod. *chaudron*) augm. of Proto-Romance var. of late L *cal(i)darium* cooking-pot, f. *cal(i)dus* hot. The spelling with *l* after L appeared in 15 and later infl. the pronunc., as in *fault*.] A large cooking-pot, usu. of a deep basin shape with a hoop handle and removable lid.

fig.: W. SHENSTONE Vesuvio's horrid cauldrons roar. N. MONSARRAT The harbour . . became a cauldron of smoke and flame and columns of erupting water.

Comb.: **cauldron subsidence**: of a roughly cylindrical or conical mass of rock into a magma chamber.

caules *n.* pl. of CAULIS.

caulescent /kɔːˈlɛs(ə)nt/ *a.* M18. [f. L CAULIS + -ESCENT.] *Bot.* Having an obvious stem.

caulicle /ˈkɔːlɪk(ə)l/ *n.* M17. [L *cauliculus*, f. as CAULIS: see -CULE.] *Bot.* A little stalk, esp. a radicle.

caulicole /ˈkɔːlɪkəʊl/ *n.* E19. [Fr., or its source It. *colicolo* f. L *cauliculus*: see prec., -OLE[1].] *Archit.* Any of the fluted stalks arising from the larger stalks of a Corinthian capital and bearing leaves or volutes.

cauliflory /ˈkɔːlɪflɔːri/ *n.* E20. [f. L CAULIS + *flos*, *floris* flower + -Y[3].] *Bot.* The production of flowers directly from the main stem or branches.

cauliflower /ˈkɒlɪflaʊə/ *n.* & *v.* L16. [Alt. (by assim. to COLE *n.*[1], FLOWER *n.*) of Fr. †*chou fleuri* (*flori*), prob. f. It. *cavolfiore*, pl. *cavoli fiori* or mod.L *cauliflora* 'flowered cabbage'.] **A** *n.* **1** A cultivated variety of cabbage with a large, dense, white flower-head; the flower-heads eaten as a vegetable. L16. **2** Something resembling a cauliflower in shape. M18.

Comb.: **cauliflower cheese** a savoury dish made of cauliflower and cheese sauce; **cauliflower ear** an ear (esp. of a boxer) thickened and disfigured by repeated blows.

B *v.t.* **1** Powder (a wig). *rare.* L18. **2** Thicken or disfigure (an ear) by repeated blows, esp. in boxing. Chiefly as *cauliflowered* ppl a. M20.

cauline /ˈkɔːlʌɪn/ *a.* M18. [f. L CAULIS + -INE[1].] *Bot.* Of or belonging to the stem; *esp.* (of a leaf) borne on the stem (opp. *radical*).

caulis /ˈkɔːlɪs/ *n.* Pl. **caules** /ˈkɔːliːz/. M16. [L = stem, stalk.] *Archit.* Each of the four principal stalks in a Corinthian capital.

caulk /kɔːk/ *n. Naut. slang.* M19. [Perh. f. the vb.] **1** A small drink of liquor, a dram. M19. **2** A short sleep, a nap. E20.

caulk /kɔːk/ *v.*[1] Also ***calk**. In branch I **cauk**, **cawk**. LME. [ONFr. *cauquer*, *caukier* var. of *cauchier* tread, press with force (mod. *côcher*) f. L *calcare* tread, press, f. *calx*, *calc-* heel.] †**I1** Of birds: copulate. LME–E18.

II2 *v.t.* Stop up the seams of (a ship etc.) with oakum etc. and waterproofing material or by driving the plate-junctions together; stop up (seams) thus. L15. **3** *v.t.* Stop up or seal the crevices of (windows etc.); seal (crevices). E17. **4** *v.i.* Sleep, take a nap. *Naut. slang.* E19.

2 caulking iron a tool for driving oakum etc. into the seams of a ship.

caulker *n.* (*a*) a person who caulks ships; (*b*) an implement for caulking; (*c*) *Naut. slang* = CAULK *n.* 1: L15.

caulk *v.*[2] var. of COCK *v.*[4]

†**cauponate** *v.t.* M17–E18. [L *cauponat-* pa. ppl stem of *cauponari*, f. *caupo*, *-on-* huckster, innkeeper: see -ATE[3].] Deal like a huckster with; traffic in (dishonestly) for gain.

†**cauponation** *n.* petty or unfair dealing; adulteration M16–E18.

†**cauponize** *v.t.* Also **-ise**. M17–L18. [f. L *caupo*, *-on-*: see prec., -IZE.] = prec. Also, mix and adulterate for gain.

Caurus /ˈkɔːrəs/ *n. arch.* LME. [L.] The stormy north-west wind, esp. personified.

causal /ˈkɔːz(ə)l/ *n.* & *a.* LME. [Late L *causalis* adj., f. *causa*: see CAUSE *n.*, -AL[1].] **A** *n.* A causal conjunction or particle. LME.

B *adj.* **1** *Gram.* & *Logic.* Introducing or expressing a cause. M16. **2** Of or relating to a cause or causes; acting as a cause; of the nature of cause and effect. L16.

2 HENRY MORE As being a means to this end, and, therefore, Causal thereto. R. BLACKMORE The links of all the causal chain. P. DAVIES No signal could travel faster than light without producing causal chaos.

causally *adv.* in the manner of, or as being, the cause; by way of cause and effect: LME.

causalgia /kɔːˈzaldʒə/ *n.* M19. [f. Gk *kausos* heat, fever + -ALGIA.] *Med.* A severe burning pain in a limb caused by injury to a peripheral nerve.

causality /kɔːˈzalɪti/ *n.* L15. [Fr. *causalité* or med.L *causalitas*, f. as CAUSAL: see -ITY.] **1** Causal quality; the fact or state of acting as a cause. L15. **2** The operation or relation of cause and effect. M17. **3** *Phrenol.* A mental faculty of tracing effects to causes. L19.

causation /kɔːˈzeɪʃ(ə)n/ *n.* L15. [(O)Fr., or L *causatio(n-)* pretext etc., (in med.L) action of causing, f. *causat-* pa. ppl stem of *causari*, *-are*: see CAUSE *v.*, -ATION.] The causing or producing of an effect; the relation of cause and effect.

social causation: see SOCIAL *a.*

causational *a.* E20.

causative /ˈkɔːzətɪv/ *a.* & *n.* LME. [(O)Fr. *causatif*, *-ive* or late L *causativus*, f. *causat-*: see prec., CAUSE *v.*, -ATIVE.] **A** *adj.* **1** Effective as a cause, productive *of*. LME. **2** *Gram.* Expressing a cause or causation. E17. **B** *n.* A causative agency; a causative word. L15.

causatively *adv.* M17. **causaˈtivity** *n.* = CAUSALITY 1 M19.

cause /kɔːz/ *n.* ME. [(O)Fr. f. L *causa* reason, motive, lawsuit.] **1** *gen.* That which produces an effect or consequence; an antecedent or antecedents followed by a certain phenomenon. ME. **b** A person or other agent who occasions something, with or without intent. LME. **2** A fact, circumstance, or consideration which moves a person to action; ground for action, reason, motive; *esp.* adequate motive or justification. ME. **3** A matter about which a person goes to law, a subject of litigation; a legal case, (the case of one party in) a lawsuit. ME. **b** *gen.* A matter of concern; the case as it concerns anyone, the situation. *obs.* exc. *dial.* LME. **4** That side of any question or controversy espoused by a person or party; a movement which inspires the efforts of its supporters. ME. †**5** Sickness, disease. LME–E17.

1 S. JOHNSON The greatest events may be often traced to slender causes. G. B. SHAW Bruno is buried, and his death from natural causes duly certified. H. INNES The sound of it falling must have been the cause of my waking. b G. BERKELEY God is the supreme and universal Cause of all things. TENNYSON Am I the cause . . that men Reproach you? 2 AV To amend it where he saw cause. J. R. GREEN The causes which drew students and teachers within the walls of Oxford. B. ENGLAND He was a hard man. But never without cause. 3 GOLDSMITH He that has most opinions is most likely to carry his cause. W. B. CARPENTER Further proceedings . . in a cause which he had heard some years previously. b SHAKES. *Lucr.* The cause craves haste. 4 SHAKES. *John* Such temperate order in so fierce a cause. W. S. CHURCHILL The greatest of the European movements in these years was the cause of Italian unity. L. AUCHINCLOSS She had many causes, but currently she was absorbed in the fight against the Vietnamese war. H. CARPENTER A political rebel leaves his lover to fight for the cause. 5 SHAKES. *Coriol.* Leave us to cure this cause.

Phrases: **cause and effect** (the operation or relation of) a cause and the effect it produces; the doctrine of causation. **efficient cause** *Philos.* that which produces or occasions the thing caused. **final cause** *Philos.* the purpose or end of the thing caused. **First Cause** the Creator of the universe. **formal cause** *Philos.* that which defines the thing caused. †**for someone's cause** on someone's account, for the sake of someone. **good cause** (*a*) adequate justification; (*b*) a movement deserving support, esp. a charity. **in the cause of** to defend or support. **lost cause** a hopeless undertaking. **make common cause with** join forces with, ally oneself with. **material cause** *Philos.* the matter that constitutes the thing caused. *meritorious cause*: see MERITORIOUS *a.* *occasional cause*: see OCCASIONAL *a.* 4. *primary cause*: see PRIMARY *a.* *probable cause*: see PROBABLE *a.* *secondary cause*: see SECONDARY *a.* **second cause** a cause which is itself caused.

Comb.: **cause list** a list of cases awaiting trial.

causeful *a.* (*rare*) (*a*) having (good) cause, well founded; (*b*) that is a cause *of*: LME. **causeless** *a.* (*a*) having no antecedent cause; (*b*) *arch.* having no (legal) cause or reason; groundless, unjustifiable: LME. **causelessly** *adv.* M16.

cause /kɔːz/ *v.* LME. [(O)Fr. *causer* or L *causari* give as a pretext etc., med.L *-ari*, *-are* be the cause of, f. *causa*: see CAUSE *n.*] **1** *v.t.* Be the cause of, effect, bring about; occasion, produce;

induce, make, (a person or thing *to do*, †*do*, a thing *to be done*, †*be done*); (arch.) bring it about *that*. LME. †**2** *v.i.* Give reasons or excuses. *rare* (Spenser). Only in L16.

1 SPENSER She caused them be led.. Into a bowre. AV *John* 11:37 Could not this man.. have caused that even this man should not have died? DRYDEN A Drench of Wine.. the Patient's Death did cause. C. BEATON The visitor pressed an electric button that caused a glass wall to roll back. L. DURRELL A cruel satirical short story, which.. caused me great pain. *cause havoc*: see HAVOC *n.* 2.

causable *a.* (*rare*) that can be caused M17. **causer** *n.* a person or thing which causes something LME.

'cause /kɒz, kəz/ *adv.* & *conj. colloq.* & *dial.* See also COS *adv.* & *conj.* LME. [Abbrev.] = BECAUSE.

cause célèbre /koːz selɛbr/ *n. phr.* Pl. **-s -s** (pronounced same). M18. [Fr.] A notorious legal case; a lawsuit that attracts much attention.

causerie /kozri/ *n.* Pl. pronounced same. E19. [Fr., f. *causer* to talk.] Informal (esp. literary) talk; a chatty article.

causes célèbres *n. phr.* pl. of CAUSE CÉLÈBRE.

causeuse /kozøːz/ *n.* Pl. pronounced same. M19. [Fr., f. *causer*: see prec.] A small sofa for two people.

causeway /ˈkɔːzweɪ/ *n.* & *v.* LME. [f. next + WAY *n.*] **A** *n.* **1** A raised way, path, or road across a low or wet place or stretch of water; a raised footway beside a road. Formerly also, a mole or pier running into the sea or a river. LME. **2** A (paved) highway (*obs.* exc. *Hist.* & in proper names); a paved (part of a) path or road (now *dial.*). L16. **b** *spec.* = CAUSEY *n.* 3b. *Sc.* E19.

B *v.t.* **1** Cross with a causeway; provide with a causeway. Freq. as *causewayed* ppl a. E18. **2** = CAUSEY *v.* M18.

1 **causewayed camp** a type of neolithic settlement in southern Britain, characterized by a series of concentric ditches crossed by one or more causeways.

causey /ˈkɔːzi, -si/ *n.* & *v.* ME. [AN var. of ONFr. *cauciée* (mod. *chaussée*) f. Proto-Romance fem. pa. pple (sc. *via* way, road) f. L CALX, *calc-* lime.] **A** *n.* †**1** A mound, embankment, or dam to retain the water of a river or pond. ME–L18. **2** = CAUSEWAY *n.* 1. ME. **3** = CAUSEWAY *n.* 2. Now *dial.* or *Hist.* LME. **b** *spec.* A cobbled (part of a) street or pavement; a paved area. Chiefly *Sc.* L15. **B** *v.t.* Pave with small stones. Chiefly *Sc.* & *dial.* M16.

causidical /kɔːˈzɪdɪk(ə)l/ *a.* L18. [f. L *causidicus* pleader + -AL[1].] Of or pertaining to a pleader of legal causes.

caustic /ˈkɔːstɪk, ˈkɒst-/ *a.* & *n.* LME. [L *causticus* f. Gk *kaustikos*, f. *kaustos* combustible, f. *kaiein* to burn: see -IC.] **A** *adj.* **1** That burns or corrodes organic tissue. LME. **b** *fig.* Sarcastic, sharp, biting. L18. **2** *Physics.* Of a curve or surface: formed by the intersection of rays of light reflected or refracted from a curved surface. E18.

1 **caustic bush** *Austral.* a trailing succulent, *Sarcostemma australe*, containing milky juice toxic to livestock; also called *milk-bush*. **caustic creeper** *Austral.* a spurge, *Euphorbia drummondii*, containing a milky juice poisonous to sheep. **caustic plant** = *caustic bush* above. *caustic potash*: see POTASH 2. **caustic soda** sodium hydroxide, NaOH. **caustic vine** = *caustic bush* above. **caustic weed** = *caustic creeper* above.

B *n.* **1** A caustic substance. LME. **2** *Physics.* A caustic curve or surface. E18.

1 *lunar caustic*: see LUNAR *a.*

caustically *adv.* M19. **causticity** /-ˈstɪsɪti/ *n.* L18.

cautel /ˈkɔːt(ə)l/ *n.* LME. [(O)Fr. *cautèle* or L *cautela*, f. *caut-* pa. ppl stem of *cavere* take heed.] †**1** Cunning, trickery; a trick, a stratagem. LME–E17. †**2** Caution, wariness. LME–M17. **3** A precautionary instruction or provision; *spec.* (*Chr. Ch.*) a rubrical direction for the proper administration of the sacraments. LME.

cautelous *a.* (*arch.*) crafty, deceitful, wily; cautious, wary, circumspect: LME.

cauter /ˈkɔːtə/ *n.* M16. [(O)Fr. *cautère* f. L *cauterium*: see CAUTERY.] = CAUTERY 1.

cauterize /ˈkɔːtəraɪz/ *v.t.* Also **-ise**. LME. [(O)Fr. *cautériser* f. late L *cauterizare* f. Gk *kautēriazein*, f. *kautērion*: see next, -IZE.] **1** Burn or sear with heat or a caustic substance, esp. in surgical operations. LME. **2** *fig.* Deaden, make insensible or callous. L16.

2 SOUTHEY Custom soon cauterizes human sympathy.

cauteriˈzation *n.* LME.

cautery /ˈkɔːt(ə)ri/ *n.* LME. [L *cauterium* f. Gk *kautērion* branding-iron, f. *kaiein* to burn.] **1** A metal instrument or caustic substance for searing tissue. LME. **2** The action of cauterizing. LME.

1 **actual cautery** *arch.* a hot iron for cauterizing. **potential cautery** *arch.* a caustic substance used for cauterizing. **2** *fig.*: W. OWEN Their senses in some scorching cautery of battle Now long since ironed.

caution /ˈkɔːʃ(ə)n/ *n.* & *v.* ME. [(O)Fr. f. L *cautio(n-)*, f. *caut-* pa. ppl stem of *cavere* take heed: see -ION.] **A** *n.* **1** Security given, bail; a guarantee. Now chiefly *Sc.* & *US.* ME. **b** A person who stands surety, a guarantor. L16. †**2** A proviso. L16–L17. **3** A word of warning; a fact etc. that acts as a warning; an official reprimand and warning regarding a person's future conduct. L16. †**4** A precaution, a taking of heed. E17–E19. **5** Prudence, taking care; attention to safety, avoidance of rashness. M17. **6** A surprising or amusing person or thing. *colloq.* (orig. *US*). M19.

2 MILTON What meant that caution joind, *if ye be found Obedient*? **3** SHAKES. *Macb.* Whate'er thou art, for thy good caution, thanks. R. GRAVES The accused was at once dismissed with a caution. **5** H. H. MILMAN Godfrey.. had learned caution by his eventful life; it had degenerated into craft. SLOAN WILSON He had almost gone charging.. to berate her, but an innate caution had stopped him. A. MACLEAN With infinite caution, a fraction of an inch at a time. *sound a note of caution*: see NOTE *n.*[2] **6** D. H. LAWRENCE Oh, he's a caution, that lad—but not bad, you know.

Comb.: **caution-money** money deposited as security for good conduct.

B *v.t.* & (*rare*) *i.* Warn (*against*; *to do*, *not to do*), advise; warn and reprove, esp. officially. E17.

cautioner *n.* (*Sc. Law*) a person who stands surety for another E16.

cautionary /ˈkɔːʃ(ə)n(ə)ri/ *a.* & *n.* L16. [med.L *cautionarius*, f. L *cautio(n-)*: see prec., -ARY[1].] **A** *adj.* **1** Of, pertaining to, or of the nature of a pledge or security; held as a pledge or security. *obs.* exc. *Hist.* & *Sc. Law.* L16. †**2** Marked by caution; cautious. E17–M19. **3** Conveying a warning, admonitory. M17. †**4** Of the nature of a provision against danger; precautionary. L17–E19. **B** *n.* A security, guarantee, bail; a surety. Now only in *Sc. Law*, an obligation undertaken to guarantee against or answer for the default of another. L16.

cautious /ˈkɔːʃəs/ *a.* M17. [f. CAUTION *n.* on the model of *ambition*, *ambitious*, etc.: see -TIOUS.] Characterized by caution; wary, careful, circumspect.

T. FORREST I was very cautious of touching upon what had happened that morning. D. L. SAYERS Inclined to take a cautious view of rumours and suspicions. C. MILNE Let us buy not just our usual cautious one or two copies; let us take a dozen. †**cautious to do** careful not to do.

cautiously *adv.* M17. **cautiousness** *n.* M17.

cava /ˈkeɪvə/ *n.* Pl. **cavae** /ˈkeɪviː/. E19. [Abbrev.] *Med.* = VENA *cava*.

caval *a.* of or pertaining to one or both of the venae cavae L19.

cavalcade /kav(ə)lˈkeɪd, ˈkav(ə)lkeɪd/ *n.* & *v.* L16. [Fr. f. It. *cavalcata*, f. *cavalcare* to ride etc. f. Proto-Romance, f. L *caballus* horse.] **A** *n.* †**1** A ride or raid on horseback. L16–L17. **2** A company or procession of riders, carriages, motor vehicles, etc., esp. on a festive or solemn occasion. M17. **B** *v.i.* Ride in a cavalcade. E18.

cavalier /kavəˈlɪə/ *n.* & *a.* M16. [Fr., or its source It. *cavaliere* deriv. of L *caballus* horse: see -IER. Cf. CHEVALIER.] **A** *n.* **1** *Fortif.* A raised defence work on the level ground of a bastion, constructed to command the surrounding work and beyond. M16. **2** A horseman; *esp.* a cavalryman. *arch.* L16. **3** A lively military man; a courtly or fashionable gentleman, a gallant, esp. as an escort to a lady. L16. **4** *Hist.* (Usu. **C-**.) A supporter of Charles I in the Civil War of 1642–9, a 17th-century Royalist. M17.

B *adj.* †**1** Gallant. *rare.* Only in M17. **2** Offhand; (esp. haughtily) careless in manner; curt; supercilious. M17. **3** *Hist.* (Usu. **C-**.) Supporting Charles I in the Civil War of 1642–9, Royalist; pertaining to or characteristic of the Cavaliers. E18.

2 CARLYLE This cavalier tone from an unknown person.. did not please me. H. ACTON Nancy's amiability with the French differed from her cavalier treatment of the American soldiers. **3** **cavalier cuff** a cuff of gauntlet shape.

cavalierish *a.* M17. **cavalierism** *n.* M17. **cavalierly** *a.* characteristic of a cavalier, knightly M19. **cavalierly** *adv.* in a cavalier manner L17.

cavalier /kavəˈlɪə/ *v.i.* & *t.* (w. *it*). L16. [f. prec.] Play the cavalier; pay court to women.

cavaliere servente /kavaˈljeːre serˈvɛnte/ *n. phr.* M18. [It., lit. 'gentleman-in-waiting'.] A (married) woman's lover or solicitous admirer.

cavallard *n.* var. of CAVAYARD.

cavally /kəˈvali/ *n. arch.* Also **-llo** /-ləʊ/. E17. [Sp. *caballo* lit. 'horse', perh. infl. by It. *cavalli* pl. of *cavallo* mackerel.] A horse-mackerel or related marine fish.

cavalry /ˈkav(ə)lri/ *n.* M16. [Fr. *cavallerie* f. It. *cavalleria*, f. *cavallo* horse f. L *caballus*: see -ERY, -RY.] **1** *collect.* (usu. treated as *pl.*). Soldiers on horseback; that part of a military force which consists of mounted troops. Now also, soldiers in motor vehicles. M16. **b** A force or troop of cavalry. E17. **c** *transf.* Horse-riders; horses for riding. L17. †**2** Horsemanship. L16–L17.

Comb.: **cavalryman** a soldier of a regiment of cavalry; **cavalry sword** a sword used by cavalry, *esp.* a sabre; **cavalry twill** a strong fabric woven in a double twill.

cavass *n.* see KAVASS.

cavatina /kavəˈtiːnə/ *n.* E19. [It.] *Mus.* A short simple song; a songlike piece of instrumental music, usu. slow and emotional.

cavayard /ˈkavɪjɑːd/ *n. US.* Also **cavallard** /ˈkav(ə)ljɑːd/, **cavy-yard**, & other vars. E19. [Alt. of Sp. CABALLADA.] A drove of horses or mules; = CABALLADA.

cave /keɪv/ *n.*[1] ME. [(O)Fr. f. L *cava* use as n. of fem. sing. or neut. pl. of *cavus* hollow.] **1** A large natural underground hollow, usu. with a horizontal opening. ME. **2** *Polit.* A dissident group (cf. ADULLAMITE 2). M19.

1 *idols of the cave*: see IDOL *n.*

Comb.: **cave art**, **-painting**: primitive or prehistoric, on the interiors of caves, esp. depicting animals; **cave-bear**: of an extinct species known from remains found in caves; **cave-dweller**, **caveman**, **cavewoman**: prehistoric, living in a cave or caves; *fig.* of primitive or violent passions, instincts, and behaviour; **cave-fish** = *blind fish* s.v. BLIND *a.*

cave /ˈkeɪvi/ *n.*[2] & *int.* LME. [L, imper. sing. of *cavere* beware.] **A** *n.* †**1** A warning; an injunction. LME–L15. **2** *keep cave*, act as a lookout. *School slang.* E20. **B** *int.* As a warning cry: look out! *School slang.* M19.

cave /keɪv/ *v.*[1] LME. [f. CAVE *n.*[1]] **1** *v.t.* Hollow out, excavate. LME. **2** *v.i.* Lodge or lurk in a cave. E17. **3** *v.i.* Explore caves. Chiefly as *caving* vbl n. M20.

cave /keɪv/ *v.*[2]*i.* & *t. dial.* (chiefly *Sc.* & *north.*). E16. [Origin(s) unkn.] **1** Cause to fall clumsily or helplessly; tip over; topple. E16. **2** Toss (the head or other part of the body). L17.

cave /keɪv/ *v.*[3] Also (*dial.*) **calve** /kɑːv/. E18. [Perh. of LG origin: cf. WFlem. *inkalven* fall in, Du. *afkalven* fall away, *uitkalven* fall out. Infl. by CAVE *v.*[1], *v.*[2]] Usu. foll. by *in* (without *in* chiefly *US*). **1** *v.i.* Fall in over a hollow, subside; give way, yield to pressure, (*lit.* & *fig.*); submit, withdraw opposition. E18. **2** *v.t.* Cause to subside or yield to pressure; smash, bash, or beat in. E19.

1 W. IRVING The earth caved in, so as to leave a vacant space. L. STEFFENS Men caved all around, but the women were firm. D. BAGLEY The front of the building caved in.., seeming to collapse in slow motion. **2** B. HARTE Reckons she's caved in his head.

Comb.: **cave-in** a fall of earth, an inward collapse under pressure.

†cave *v.*[4] var. of CHAVE.

cavea /ˈkeɪvɪə/ *n.* Pl. **-eae** /-iiː/. E17. [L = a hollow.] *Rom. Antiq.* The (concave) auditorium of a theatre; a theatre.

caveat /ˈkavɪat, ˈkeɪ-/ *n.* & *v.* M16. [L, 3rd person sing. pres. subjunct. of *cavere* beware.] **A** *n.* **1** A warning, a proviso; *spec.* in *Law* (*a*) a process in an ecclesiastical court to suspend proceedings; (*b*) a notice to a court (esp. *Sc. Law*) or an entry in a register preventing a proceeding (as granting of a probate) until the objector's arguments have been heard. M16. **†2** A precaution. L16–L17.

1 Esp. in *enter, put in, a caveat.*

B *v.* **1** *v.t.* Enter a caveat against. *rare.* M17. **2** *v.i. Fencing.* Disengage. Now *rare* or *obs.* M17.

cavea'tee *n.* (*Law*) a person against whose interests a caveat is entered E20. **caveator** *n.* (*Law*) a person who enters a caveat L19.

†caveer *n.* var. of CAVIAR.

cavel /ˈkav(ə)l/ *n.* & *v. Sc.* & *north.* ME. [Corresp. to Du. *kavel* lot, parcel (*kavelen* cast lots), MDu. *cavele* lot: cf. MLG *kavele* little stick (with runes) for casting lots.] **A** *n.* **1** A lot (that is cast). ME. **2** A division made by lot. LME. **B** *v.i.* & *t.* Apportion (by lot). LME.

cavendish /ˈkav(ə)ndɪʃ/ *n.* M19. [Prob. f. surname *Cavendish.*] Tobacco softened, sweetened, and pressed into cakes.

caver /ˈkeɪvə/ *n.* M17. [f. CAVE *n.*[1] or *v.*[1] + -ER[1].] **†1** A person who frequents mines to take ore that has been left etc. M17–M19. **2** An explorer of caves. M20.

cavern /ˈkav(ə)n/ *n.* & *v.* LME. [(O)Fr. *caverne* or L *caverna*, f. *cavus* hollow: cf. CAVE *n.*[1]] **A** *n.* An underground hollow, a (vast) cave; a dark cavity. LME.

COLERIDGE Where Alph, the sacred river, ran Through caverns measureless to man. L. P. HARTLEY Her eye sockets were caverns which revealed the skull.

B *v.t.* **1** Enclose (as) in a cavern. M17. **2** Hollow out into a cavern or caverns. M19.

caverned *a.* (*a*) having caverns; hollowed out into caverns; (*b*) enclosed in a cavern: E18.

cavernicolous /kavəˈnɪkələs/ *a.* L19. [f. L *caverna* CAVERN *n.* + -I- + -COLOUS.] *Biol.* Inhabiting caves.

cavernicole /kəˈvəːnɪkəʊl/ *n.* a cavernicolous animal M20.

cavernous /ˈkav(ə)nəs/ *a.* LME. [(O)Fr. *caverneux* or L *cavernosus*, f. *caverna* CAVERN *n.*: see -OUS.] **1** Having many caverns. LME. **2** Full of cavities or interstices. LME. **3** Of or resembling a cavern; suggestive of a cavern. M19. **4** *Med.* Of respiration: marked by a prolonged hollow resonance. M19.

cavernously *adv.* M19.

cavernulous /kavəˈnjʊləs/ *a.* M18. [f. L *cavernula* dim. of *caverna*: see -ULOUS.] Full of minute cavities; porous.

cavesson /ˈkavɪs(ə)n/ *n.* L16. [Fr. *caveçon*, It. *cavezzone* augm. of *cavezza* halter, f. Proto-Romance, f. med.L *capitium* head-covering, f. L *caput, capit-* head.] A noseband fitted with rings to which a lunge or reins may be attached, used in training young horses. In early use also, a similar noseband designed to bring a horse under control by inflicting pain on it.

cavetto /kəˈvɛtəʊ/ *n.* Pl. **-tti** /-ti/. M17. [It., dim. of *cavo* hollow f. L *cavus* hollow: cf. CAVE *n.*[1]] *Archit.* A hollow moulding with a quadrantal cross-section.

caviar /ˈkavɪɑː, kavɪˈɑː/ *n.* Also **-iare**, **†-iary**, **†-eer**, & other vars. M16. [It. *caviale* (earlier & dial. *caviaro*, pl. *-ri*), Fr. *caviar*, prob. f. med.Gk *khaviari* (whence also perh. Turk. *havyar*).] The pickled roe of the sturgeon or other large fish, eaten as a delicacy.

caviar to the general [Shakes. *Haml.* II. ii] a good thing unappreciated by the ignorant. *red caviar*: see RED *a.*

cavie /ˈkeɪvi/ *n. Sc.* E16. [App. f. MDu. *kēvie*, Du. or Flem. *kevie*, ult. f. L *cavea*: see CAGE *n.*] A hen-coop.

cavil /ˈkav(ə)l/ *v.* & *n.* M16. [(O)Fr. *caviller* f. L *cavillari*, f. *cavilla* scoffing, mockery.] **A** *v.* Infl. **-ll-**, ***-l-**. **1** *v.i.* Raise a captious or frivolous objection (*at, about*). M16. **2** *v.t.* Object to captiously. L16. **B** *n.* A captious or frivolous objection. L16.

caviller *n.* L16. **†cavillous** *a.* full of cavils or cavilling; apt to cavil: L16–M19.

cavillation /kavɪˈleɪʃ(ə)n/ *n.* LME. [(O)Fr. f. L *cavillatio(n-)*, f. *cavillat-* pa. ppl stem of *cavillari*: see prec., -ATION.] **†1** The use of legal quibbles; a legal quibble; chicanery, overreaching sophistry. LME–M17. **2** *gen.* The action of cavilling; a cavil. M16.

cavitary /ˈkavɪt(ə)ri/ *a.* M19. [Fr. *cavitaire*, f. *cavité*: see CAVITY, -ARY[1].] Of the nature of or pertaining to a cavity.

cavitation /kavɪˈteɪʃ(ə)n/ *n.* L19. [f. next + -ATION.] **1** The formation of bubbles or cavities in a liquid caused by the rapid movement of a propeller etc. through it. L19. **2** *Med.* The formation of cavities in diseased tissue. E20.

'cavitate *v.i.* [back-form.] induce or undergo cavitation E20.

cavity /ˈkavɪti/ *n.* M16. [(O)Fr. *cavité* or late L *cavitas*, f. *cavus* hollow: see -ITY.] A hollow place; a hollow; an empty space in a solid body, *spec.* in a decayed tooth.

COTYLOID *cavity. pit cavity*: see PIT *n.*[1] *resonant cavity*: see RESONANT *a.* THORACIC *cavity. tympanic cavity*: see TYMPANIC *a.* I. VISCERAL *cavity.*

Comb.: *cavity resonator*: see RESONATOR 3b; **cavity wall** a double wall with an internal cavity.

cavort /kəˈvɔːt/ *v.i. colloq.* (orig. *US*). L18. [Perh. alt. of CURVET *v.*] Prance, caper about.

†cavous *a.* LME–M18. [L *cavosus*, f. *cavus* hollow: see -OUS.] Having a cavity; hollow; concave.

cavy /ˈkeɪvi/ *n.* L18. [mod.L *cavia* f. Galibi *cabiai.*] A rodent of the family Caviidae, native to S. America; *esp.* a guinea-pig.

Patagonian cavy: see PATAGONIAN *a.*

cavy-yard *n.* var. of CAVAYARD.

caw /kɔː/ *v., n.,* & *int.* L16. [Imit.] **A** *v.i.* Of a rook, crow, raven, etc.: make its harsh natural cry. Of a person: make a sound contemptuously likened to this. L16. **B** *n.* & *int.* (Repr.) the cry of a rook, crow, raven, etc. M17.

cawk *n.*[1] var. of CAUK *n.*

cawk /kɔːk/ *v.*[1]*i.* & *n.*[2] M18. [Imit.] Caw; (utter) a harsh cry.

†cawk *v.*[2] see CAULK *v.*[1]

cawl /kɔːl/ *n.* Long *obs.* exc. *dial.* [OE *cawl, ceawl.*] A basket; a Cornish creel.

†caxon *n.* M18–M19. [Perh. f. the surname *Caxon.*] A kind of wig.

cay /keɪ, kiː/ *n.* L17. [Sp. *cayo* f. Fr. *quai*, †*cay* QUAY *n.* Cf. KEY *n.*[2]] An insular bank or reef of coral, sand, etc.

cayenne /keɪˈɛn, *attrib.* ˈkeɪɛn/ *n.* E18. [Orig. f. Tupi *kyynha, quiynha*, later assim. to *Cayenne*, chief town of French Guiana.] In full *cayenne pepper.* A pungent red powder prepared from ground dried chillies, used as a seasoning.

cayenned *a.* seasoned with cayenne E19.

cayman /ˈkeɪmən/ *n.* Also **cai-**. L16. [Sp. *caimán*, Port. *caimão*, f. Carib *acayuman.*] Any of a number of crocodilians closely related to the alligator and native to S. and Central America; *loosely* any New World crocodilian.

spectacled cayman: see SPECTACLED 2.

Cayuga /keɪˈjuːgə, ˈkʌɪ-/ *n.* & *a.* Pl. of n. **-s**, same. M18. [Iroquoian place-name.] A member of, of or pertaining to, an Iroquois Indian people, one of the five of the original Iroquois confederation, formerly inhabiting part of New York State; (of) the language of this people.

Cayuse /ˈkʌɪjuːs/ *n.* & *a.* In sense A.2 **c-**. E19. [Penutian.] **A** *n.* **1** Pl. same, **-s**. A member of a Penutian Indian people of Washington and Oregon; the language of this people. E19. **2** Pl. **-s**. An Indian pony; *colloq.* any horse. *N. Amer.* M19. **B** *attrib.* or as *adj.* Of or pertaining to the Cayuse or their language. M19.

caza *n.* var. of KAZA.

cazern(e) *n.* vars. of CASERN.

ceanothus /siːəˈnəʊθəs/ *n.* L18. [mod.L f. Gk *keanōthos* a kind of thistle.] Any of various N. American shrubs, freq. grown for ornament, that constitute the genus *Ceanothus*, of the buckthorn family, and bear clusters of small starry blue or white flowers.

cease /siːs/ *n.* Now *literary.* ME. [OFr. *ces*, f. as next.] Stopping, ending. Now only in *without cease.*

cease /siːs/ *v.* See also CESS *v.*[2] ME. [(O)Fr. *cesser* f. L *cessare* stop, f. *cess-* pa. ppl stem of *cedere* CEDE.] **I** *v.i.* **1** Of people and other agents: stop, leave off, desist, discontinue. (Foll. by *from,* †*of, to do.*) ME. **†b** (Take) rest, be or remain at rest. LME–M17. **2** Of actions, feelings, phenomena, etc.: come to or be at an end. ME. **3** No longer exist, become extinct; die. *literary.* LME.

1 SHELLEY Oh, cease! must hate and death return? Cease! Must men kill and die? TENNYSON Fold our wings, And cease from wanderings. G. VIDAL At five-thirty the world ceased to be official and became private. 2 QUILLER-COUCH Presently the turf ceased. Dismounting, I ran to the edge. J. STEINBECK When hostilities ceased everyone had his wounds. 3 V. WOOLF Did it matter that she must inevitably cease completely; all this must go on without her?

II *v.t.* **†4** Cause to leave off (*of* an action); appease, bring to rest. ME–L16. **†5** Put a stop to (the action of others, a state or condition of things). LME–L17. **6** Leave off, discontinue (one's own action, feeling, etc.; *doing*). LME. **b** *Campanol.* Bring (a peal) to an end; let (a bell) down. L17.

4 TINDALE *Acts* 19:35 When the toune clarcke had ceased the people. 5 MILTON He, her fears to cease, Sent down the meek-eyed Peace. 6 J. GALSWORTHY He did not believe her excuse, but ceased his opposition. J. UPDIKE Ezana would not cease his flirting with . . Mrs. Gibbs. **cease fire** discontinue firing.

Comb.: **cease-fire** a signal for the ceasing of active hostilities; an armistice, a period when hostilities are suspended.

ceaseless /ˈsiːslɪs/ *a.* L16. [f. CEASE *n.* + -LESS.] Not ceasing, incessant, uninterrupted.

ceaselessly *adv.* L16. **ceaselessness** *n.* L19.

cebid /ˈsiːbɪd/ *n.* & *a.* L19. [mod.L *Cebidae* (see below), f. *Cebus* genus name: see -ID[3].] *Zool.* **A** *n.* A monkey of the family Cebidae, which includes most of the New World monkeys. L19. **B** *adj.* Of, pertaining to, or designating this family. E20.

ceboid *a.* & *n.* = CEBID E20.

cecidium /sɪˈsɪdɪəm/ *n.* Pl. **-dia** /-dɪə/. E20. [f. Gk *kēkis* a gall + -IDIUM.] = GALL *n.*[3]

cecidi'ology *n.* the scientific study of galls and their formation E20.

cecity /ˈsiːsɪti/ *n. literary.* L15. [L *caecitas*, f. *caecus* blind: see -ITY. Cf. (O)Fr. *cécité.*] Blindness (chiefly *fig.*).

cecropia /sɪˈkrəʊpɪə/ *n.* E19. [mod.L (see sense 1), f. *Cecrops* a king of Attica: see -IA[1].] **1** A tree of the tropical American genus *Cecropia*, which belongs to the mulberry family and includes some species yielding rubber. E19. **2** In full *cecropia moth.* A N. American saturniid silk moth, *Platysamia cecropia.* M19.

cecum *n.* see CAECUM.

cedar /ˈsiːdə/ *n.* OE. [(OFr. *cedre* f.) L *cedrus* f. Gk *kedros.*] **1** An evergreen conifer of the genus *Cedrus*; esp. *Cedrus libani* (more fully *cedar of Lebanon*), native to Asia Minor. Also *cedar tree.* OE. **b** The fragrant durable wood of such a tree. ME. **2** Any of various trees more or less similar to this; the wood of these trees; *esp.* = *red cedar* (a) s.v. RED *a.* LME.

1 **Indian cedar** = DEODAR. 2 *Bermuda cedar, Japanese cedar, sharp cedar, stinking cedar, white cedar,* etc.

Comb.: **cedar-bird** a N. American waxwing, *Bombycilla cedrorum*; *cedar tree*: see sense 1 above; **cedar waxwing** = *cedar-bird* above.

cedared *a.* (*poet.*) marked by the presence of cedars E19. **cedarn** *a.* (*poet.*) of cedars or cedar wood M17. **†cedrine** *a.* of or pertaining to cedar M–L18.

cede /siːd/ *v.* E16. [Fr. *céder* or L *cedere* give way, yield, retreat.] **1** *v.t.* Give up, surrender, yield (*to*); *esp.* grant (territory, *to*) by treaty etc. E16. **†2** *v.i.* Give way, give place *to.* E17–M18.

cedent *n.* (*Sc. Law*) a person who assigns property to another L16.

cedi /ˈsiːdi/ *n.* M20. [Ghanaian, perh. f. alt. of SHILLING.] The basic monetary unit of Ghana, equal to 100 pesewas.

cedilla /sɪˈdɪlə/ *n.* L16. [Sp. (now *zedilla*), dim. of *zeda* letter Z. Cf. CERILLA.] The diacritic mark ¸ written under *c* to show that it is sibilant /s/ or /ts/, as before *a, o, u* in French and Portuguese and (formerly) Spanish; a similar mark under *c* and *s* indicating a manner of articulation in various other contexts, as distinguishing the voiceless from the voiced consonants in modern Turkish.

cedrat /ˈsiːdrət/ *n.* Also **-ate**. E18. [Fr. *cédrat* f. It. *cedrato*, f. *cedro* citron, f. L CITRUS.] A variety of citron or lemon.

cedrela /sɪˈdriːlə/ *n.* M19. [mod.L f. Sp., dim. of *cedro, cedra* cedar.] (The soft timber of) a tropical tree of the genus *Cedrela*, of the mahogany family.

cedula /ˈθedulə, s-/ *n.* E18. [Sp. *cédula* schedule.] In Spain and some Spanish-speaking countries: an official permit or order; a government security.

Ceefax /ˈsiːfaks/ *n.* L20. [Repr. initial syllables of *seeing* + *facs*imile.] (Proprietary name for) a teletext system developed and operated by the BBC.

Cefaut /siːfɑːˈʊt/ *n. obs.* exc. *Hist.* Also **C fa ut**. LME. [f. *C* as a pitch letter + *fa* and *ut* designating tones in the solmization of Guido d'Arezzo (*c*990–1050).] *Medieval Mus.* The note C in Guido d'Arezzo's 1st and 2nd hexachords, where it was sung to the syllables *fa* and *ut* respectively. Cf. ALAMIRE, BEMI, CESOLFA, etc.

ceiba /ˈsʌɪbə/ *n.* E17. [Sp. f. Taino = giant tree.] The kapok tree, *Ceiba pentandra*.

ceil /siːl/ *v.* & *n.* Also **ciel**. LME. [Origin uncertain: perh. rel. to L *celare*, Fr. *celer*, hide, conceal.] A *v.t.* †1 Cover with a lining of woodwork, plaster, etc. LME–E17. 2 Line or plaster the roof of; construct an inner roof for. *arch.* E16. B *n.* A ceiling. *poet. rare.* M19.

ceilidh /ˈkeɪli/ *n.* L19. [Ir. *céilidhe* (now *céilí*), Gael. *cèilidh*, f. OIr. *céilide* visit, act of visiting, f. *céile* companion.] An informal gathering for (esp. Scottish or Irish) folk music, dancing, song, etc.

ceiling /ˈsiːlɪŋ/ *n.* Also **ciel-**. ME. [f. CEIL *v.* + -ING[1].] 1 The action of CEIL *v. arch.* ME. 2 The wooden lining of a room; panelling; wainscoting. Long *obs.* exc. *dial.* LME. b *Naut.* The inside planking or lining of a ship's bottom and sides. LME. †3 A screen of tapestry; a curtain. LME–M17. 4 The undercovering of the roof of a room, concealing timbers etc.; the top of a room or other compartment. M16. 5 *transf.* & *fig.* a *Aeronaut.* The maximum altitude which a given aircraft can attain under specified conditions. E20. b *Meteorol.* (The altitude of) the base of a cloud layer. M20. c *gen.* An upper limit (to quantity, prices, etc.); a maximum. M20.

4 **hit the ceiling** *colloq.* become very angry. *suspended ceiling*: see SUSPENDED *ppl a.*

ceinture /sɛ̃tyːr/ *n.* Pl. pronounced same. LME. [Fr. f. as CINCTURE.] = CINCTURE *n.*

¶Fell into disuse after LME; reintroduced E19.

cel *n.* var. of CELL *n.*[2]

celadon /ˈsɛlədɒn/ *n.* & *a.* M18. [Fr. *céladon*, f. the name of a character in D'Urfé's *L'Astrée*.] A *n.* 1 A pale greyish shade of green. M18. 2 A glaze of this colour used on (esp. Chinese) pottery or porcelain; ceramic ware thus glazed. M19. B *attrib.* or as *adj.* Of this colour; covered with this glaze. L19.

celandine /ˈsɛləndʌɪn/ *n.* Orig. †**celidony** & other vars.; also (long *obs.* exc. *dial.*) **saladine**. OE. [OFr. *celidoine*, f. med.L *celidonia* adj., ult. f. Gk *khelidōn* the swallow: for the inserted *-n-* (LME) cf. *passenger*.] 1 In full *greater celandine*. A yellow-flowered plant of the poppy family, *Chelidonium majus*; a flowering stem of this plant. OE. 2 In full *lesser celandine*. A common plant of the buttercup family, *Ranunculus ficaria*, bearing bright yellow flowers in early spring; a flowering stem of this plant. LME.

Celarent /sɪˈlɛːrənt/ *n.* M16. [L = they might hide, used as a mnemonic of scholastic philosophers, E indicating a universal negative proposition and A a universal affirmative proposition.] *Logic.* The second mood of the first syllogistic figure, in which a universal negative major premiss and a universal affirmative minor give a universal negative conclusion.

celature /ˈsiːlətjʊə/ *n.* Now *rare* or *obs.* LME. [L *caelatura*, f. *caelare* emboss, engrave.] Embossing; embossed work.

†**cele** *n.* L16–M18. [f. as next.] *Med.* A swelling, *esp.* one in the groin.

-cele /siːl/ *suff.* Also **-coele**. [Gk *kēlē* tumour.] Forming ns. denoting swellings, hernias, etc., as *gastrocele*, *mucocele*, *urocele*, etc.

celeb /sɪˈlɛb/ *n. colloq.* (orig. *US*). E20. [Abbrev.] A celebrity.

celebrant /ˈsɛlɪbr(ə)nt/ *n.* M19. [Fr. *célébrant*, or L *celebrant-* pres. ppl stem of *celebrare*: see next, -ANT[1].] A person who celebrates; *esp.* the priest who officiates at the Eucharist.

celebrate /ˈsɛlɪbreɪt/ *v.* LME. [L *celebrat-* pa. ppl stem of *celebrare*, f. *celeber, -bris* frequented, renowned: see -ATE[3].] I *v.t.* 1 Perform (a religious ceremony) publicly and in due form; solemnize; officiate at (the Eucharist). LME. 2 Observe (a festival etc.) with due rites; honour or commemorate with ceremonies, festivities, etc. E16. 3 Make publicly known, proclaim; extol, praise widely. L16.

2 J. GALSWORTHY We must organize a little dinner to celebrate the event. A. C. BOULT Three concerts to celebrate Elgar's seventy-fifth birthday. 3 MILTON To celebrate his Throne With warbl'd Hymns. E. WILSON A succession of books . . that celebrate lyrically the marvels of nature.

II *v.i.* 4 Officiate at the Eucharist. M16. 5 Engage in festivities; carouse. E20.

celebrated *a.* (*a*) famous, renowned; †(*b*) performed with due rites: L16. **celebrative** *a.* pertaining to or characterized by celebration M19. **celebrator**, †**-ter** *n.* a person who celebrates E17. **celebratory** *a.* serving to celebrate, used in celebration E20.

celebration /sɛlɪˈbreɪʃ(ə)n/ *n.* E16. [(O)Fr. *célébration* or L *celebratio(n-)*, f. *celebrat-*: see prec., -ATION.] 1 The observing of a feast etc.; the commemoration of an event etc. with ceremonies or festivities. E16. 2 The performance of a solemn ceremony; *spec.* the action of celebrating the Eucharist. M16. 3 Making publicly known, proclamation; extolling. M17. †4 Renown, fame. Only in 18.

celebrational *a.* E20.

celebret /ˈsɛlɪbrɛt/ *n.* M19. [L = let him celebrate, 3rd person sing. pres. subjunct. of *celebrare* CELEBRATE.] *RC Ch.* A document granting permission by a bishop to a priest to celebrate mass in a particular parish.

celebrious /sɪˈlɛbrɪəs/ *a.* M16. [f. L *celeber, -bris* (see CELEBRATE) + -OUS.] †1 Frequented, crowded, festive. M16–L17. 2 Renowned, famous. Now *arch.* & *dial.* E17.

celebrity /sɪˈlɛbrɪti/ *n.* LME. [(O)Fr. *célébrité* or L *celebritas*, f. *celeber, -bris*: see CELEBRATE, -ITY.] †1 A solemn ceremony; a celebration; due observance of ceremonies; pomp, solemnity. LME–L18. 2 The condition of being widely known or esteemed; fame, renown. LME. 3 A celebrated person; a (popular) public figure. M19.

celeriac /sɪˈlɛrɪak/ *n.* M18. [f. CELERY, w. arbitrary use of -AC.] A variety of celery with a root like a turnip.

celerity /sɪˈlɛrɪti/ *n. arch.* or *literary.* L15. [(O)Fr. *célérité* f. L *celeritas*, f. *celer* swift: see -ITY.] 1 Swiftness, speed. (Now chiefly of the actions of living beings.) L15. †2 A particular speed. M–L18.

celery /ˈsɛləri/ *n.* M17. [Fr. *céleri* f. It. dial. *selleri* ult. f. Gk *selinon* parsley.] An umbelliferous plant, *Apium graveolens*, grown for its crisp blanched leaf-stalks which are eaten raw in salads or cooked as a vegetable. Also (more fully *wild celery*), the wild form of this, a Eurasian plant found chiefly in brackish ditches.

Comb.: **celery salt** a mixture of salt and ground celery seed used for seasoning; **celery top** = *celery-top(ped) pine* below; **celery-top(ped) pine** an Australasian conifer of the genus *Phyllocladus*, with branchlets producing foliage like that of celery.

celesta /sɪˈlɛstə/ *n.* L19. [App. pseudo-Latinization of Fr. *céleste*: see next.] A small keyboard instrument in which hammers strike on steel plates, producing an ethereal bell-like sound.

celeste /sɪˈlɛst/ *n.* L19. [Fr. *céleste* f. L *caelestis*: see next.] 1 A stop on the organ and harmonium with a soft tremulous tone (Fr. *voix céleste*). Also, a form of soft pedal on a piano. L19. 2 = CELESTA. M20.

celestial /sɪˈlɛstɪəl/ *a.* & *n.* LME. [OFr. *celestial*, *-el* f. med.L *caelestialis*, f. L *caelestis*, f. *caelum* heaven: see -IAL.] A *adj.* 1 Of or pertaining to heaven, as the abode of God, angels, spirits, etc. LME. 2 Of or pertaining to the sky or material heavens. LME. 3 Divine, heavenly; divinely beautiful, excellent. LME. 4 *Hist.* Chinese. Chiefly in *Celestial Empire*. E19.

1 C. CULLEN She thinks that even up in Heaven Her class lies late and snores, While poor black cherubs rise at seven To do celestial chores. 2 *celestial body*: see BODY *n. celestial equator*: see EQUATOR *n.* 1. *celestial globe*: see GLOBE *n.* 3. *celestial latitude*: see LATITUDE 5a. **celestial mechanics** the branch of theoretical astronomy that deals with the calculation of the motions of celestial objects. **celestial navigation**: using the observed positions of celestial objects. *celestial pole*: see POLE *n.*[2] 1. *celestial sphere*: see SPHERE *n.* 2. 3 W. STYRON A phrase of music, celestial and tender.

B *n.* 1 An inhabitant of heaven. L16. †2 In *pl.* Heavenly objects, bodies, or attributes. L16–M18. 3 *Hist.* A subject of the Celestial Empire; a Chinese. M19.

celestiˈality *n.* E19. **celestially** *adv.* LME.

†**celestify** *v.t. rare.* M17–M18. [f. L *caelestis* CELESTIAL + -FY: cf. OFr. *celestifier*.] Make heavenly.

Celestine /ˈsɛlɪstʌɪn, sɪˈlɛstʌɪn; -tɪn/ *n.*[1] L15. [med.L *Caelestinus*, f. name *Caelistinus* Celestine: see -INE[4].] *Hist.* A member of a reformed branch of the Benedictine Order, founded by Pope Celestine V in the 13th cent.

celestine /sɪˈlɛstiːn, ˈsɛlɪstiːn; -tʌɪn/ *n.*[2] E19. [f. L *caelestis* CELESTIAL (on account of the colour) + -INE[5].] *Min.* Anhydrous strontium sulphate, occurring as colourless or sky-blue tabular orthorhombic crystals.

Also **celestite** *n.* M19.

celiac *a.* see COELIAC.

celibacy /ˈsɛlɪbəsi/ *n.* M17. [f. L *caelibatus*, f. *caelebs, -ib-* unmarried, bachelor: see -ACY.] The state of living unmarried, abstention from sexual intercourse, esp. by resolve or as an obligation.

celibatarian /ˌsɛlɪbəˈtɛːrɪən/ *a.* & *n.* M19. [f. Fr. *célibataire*, f. *célibat*: see next, -ARIAN.] A *adj.* Of or pertaining to celibacy; favouring celibacy. M19. B *n.* A person who lives in or advocates celibacy. M19.

celibate /ˈsɛlɪbət/ *n.*[1] *arch.* E17. [Fr. *célibat* or L *caelibatus* CELIBACY: see -ATE[1].] The state of celibacy; an order of celibates.

celibate /ˈsɛlɪbət/ *a.* & *n.*[2] E19. [f. CELIBACY, after *magistracy, magistrate*, etc.: see -ATE[1], -ATE[2].] A *adj.* Unmarried, single; abstaining from sexual intercourse; bound or resolved not to marry or have sexual intercourse. E19. B *n.* A person who is celibate, esp. by resolve or as an obligation. M19.

†**celidony** *n.* see CELANDINE.

celio- *comb. form* see COELIO-.

cell /sɛl/ *n.*[1] OE. [OFr. *celle*, or its source L *cella* storeroom, chamber, small apartment, 'chapel' in a temple.] I A small room or dwelling. 1 A (small) monastery or nunnery, dependent on some larger house. OE. †2 A store-closet. ME–L16. 3 A single-chambered dwelling inhabited by a hermit etc. ME. 4 Any of a number of small chambers in a building; *spec.* a room for one person in a monastery etc.; a room for one or more prisoners. ME. 5 A humble dwelling; a lonely nook; an isolated retreat. Also, the grave. *poet.* L16.

1 E. A. FREEMAN A priory of Lapley, which was a cell to Saint Remigius. 3 SHAKES. *Rom. & Jul.* There she shall at Friar Lawrence' cell Be shriv'd and married. 4 R. KIPLING You 'ave been absent without leave an' you'll go into cells for that. E. WAUGH Left to herself in a concrete cell which she called her apartment. **condemned cell, death cell**: occupied by a prisoner condemned to death. *padded cell*: see PAD *v.*[2] 1. 5 T. GRAY Each in his narrow cell for ever laid. SIR W. SCOTT Like hunted stag, in mountain cell.

II *transf.* 6 A compartment in a cabinet, dovecote, bees' honeycomb, etc. LME. 7 An enclosed or circumscribed space, cavity, or volume, in an organism, mineral, fluid, etc., usu. distinguished by some property. LME. b In *pl.* More fully *cells of the brain*. The imaginary cavities of the brain, formerly or fancifully identified with particular faculties. LME. 8 *Biol.* The basic structural and functional unit of which living organisms and tissues are composed, usu. microscopic and consisting of cytoplasm bounded by a membrane, with genetic material (DNA) contained in a nucleus; a similar entity living independently, with or (in the case of bacteria) without a distinct nucleus. L17. 9 A vessel containing electrodes for electricity generation or electrolysis. Also, a unit in a device for converting chemical or radiant energy into electrical energy. E19. 10 Any of the spaces into which a surface is divided by lines or a volume by surfaces; *spec.* a space between the ribs of a vaulted roof, or between the veins of an insect's wing. M19. b A position or element in an arrangement in two or more dimensions. M20. c The local area covered by one of the short-range radio stations in a cellular telephone system. L20. 11 A container for a specimen or sample in microscopy, spectroscopy, etc. L19. 12 A small group of people (occas. one person) working, often clandestinely, as a nucleus of political (esp. revolutionary) activity; the headquarters of such a group. E20. 13 *Computing.* A unit of data storage. M20.

7 LANGMUIR *cell.* b W. COWPER The cells Where Mem'ry slept. 8 R. DAWKINS As an adult, you consist of a thousand million million cells. D. LESSING To breed like cells under a microscope. *germ-cell, nerve cell, red cell, sickle-cell, vegetative cell, white cell*, etc. *wandering cell*: see WANDERING *ppl a.* 9 *fuel cell, photocell, photoelectric cell, solar cell, voltaic cell*, etc. 10 *Scientific American* Nine kings, eight bishops or eight rooks are needed to attack all vacant cells on a standard chessboard. *primitive cell, unit cell*, etc.

Comb.: *cell membrane*: see MEMBRANE 1C; **cellphone** a telephone giving access to a cellular radio system.

celled *a.* provided with cells, arranged or constructed in the form of cells (usu. of a specified kind or number) L18.

cell /sɛl/ *n.*[2] Also **cel**. M20. [Abbrev. of CELLULOID.] A transparent sheet of celluloid or similar film material, which can be drawn on and used in combination with others in the production of cartoons etc.

cell /sɛl/ *v.* LME. [f. CELL *n.*[1]] 1 *v.t.* Shut up (as) in a cell. LME. 2 *v.i.* Live in a cell; *esp.* share a prison cell *with* another person. L16. 3 *v.t.* Store in cells. E19.

cella /ˈkɛlə/ *n.* Pl. **cellae** /ˈkɛliː/. L17. [L: see CELL *n.*[1]] The internal section of a Greek or Roman temple housing the hidden cult image; a similar part of other ancient temples.

cellar /ˈsɛlə/ *n.* & *v.* ME. [AN *celer* = OFr. *celier* (mod. *cellier*) f. late L *cellarium* set of cells, storehouse for food, f. *cella* CELL *n.*[1]: see -AR[2].] A *n.* 1 A storehouse or storeroom. *obs.* in *gen.* sense. ME. 2 An underground room or vault, esp. for storage. ME. 3 In full *wine cellar.* A place in which wine is kept; *transf.* the contents of this, a person's stock of wines. LME. †4 A box, a case, esp. of bottles. (See also SALT-CELLAR.) Only in M17.

2 *beer-cellar, coal-cellar*, etc.

Comb.: **cellar beetle** any of several large slow-moving tenebrionid beetles of the genus *Blaps*; esp. *B. mucronata*, which frequents cellars etc.; **cellar-book**: for keeping a record of the stock of wines etc. in a cellar; **cellarman**: in charge of a cellar; **cellarway** a passage through cellars.

B *v.t.* Put into a cellar; store (as) in a cellar. E16.

cellarage *n.* (*a*) cellar accommodation, cellars; (*b*) *Hist.* a feudal duty on wine in a cellar; (*c*) a charge for the use of a cellar: E16. **cellared** *a.* (*a*) provided with a cellar or cellars; (*b*) stored or housed in a cellar: M17. **cellarer** *n.* (*Hist.*) an officer in a monastery etc. in charge of food and drink ME. **cellaress** *n.* (*Hist.*) a female cellarer LME. **cella'ret** *n.* a case or sideboard for holding wine bottles in a dining-room E19. **cellaring** *n.* (*a*) = CELLARAGE (a); (*b*) placing in a cellar or cellars: LME.

cellated /səˈleɪtɪd/ *a.* M19. [f. L *cellatus*, f. *cella* CELL *n.*[1]: see -ATE[2], -ED[1].] Divided into or furnished with cells.

Cellnet /ˈsɛlnɛt/ *n.* Also **c-**. L20. [f. CELL *n.*[1] or CELLULAR + NET *n.*[1]] (Proprietary name for) a cellular telephone service. Occas. also, a cellular telephone.

cello /ˈtʃɛləʊ/ *n.* Also **'cello**. Pl. **cellos, celli** /ˈtʃɛli/. L19. [Abbrev. of VIOLONCELLO.] A four-stringed bass instrument like a large violin, held resting on the floor by a seated player; a player on this in an orchestra etc.

cellist *n.* a player of the cello L19.

cellobiose /sɛləʊˈbʌɪəʊz, -s/ *n.* E20. [f. CELLULOSE *n.* + -O- + BI- + -OSE[2].] *Chem.* A synthetic disaccharide which is a dimer of glucose and is obtained by partial hydrolysis of cellulose.

celloidin /sɛˈlɔɪdɪn/ *n.* L19. [f. CELLULOSE *n.* + -OID + -IN[1].] A pure form of pyroxylin used in microscopy to embed tissue specimens for sectioning.

Cellophane /ˈsɛləfeɪn/ *n.* Also **c-**. E20. [f. CELLULOSE *n.* + -O- + *-phane* after DIAPHANE.] (Proprietary name for) a glossy transparent material made from viscose, used chiefly for wrapping goods, food, etc.

cellotape *n.* & *v.* see SELLOTAPE.

cellular /ˈsɛljʊlə/ *a.* M18. [Fr. *cellulaire* f. mod.L *cellularis*, f. L *cellula*: see next, -AR[1].] 1 Of, pertaining to, characterized by, or consisting of biological cells; (of a plant) lacking a distinct stem, leaves, etc. (opp. *vascular*). M18. 2 Of or pertaining to the cells of a monastery, prison, etc. E19. 3 Of or having small compartments, cavities, or divisions of area; porous; (of a fabric or garment) having an open texture. E19. b Designating or pertaining to a mobile telephone system that uses a number of short-range radio stations to cover the area it serves, the signal being automatically switched from one station to another as the user travels about. L20.

cellu'larity *n.* M19.

cellule /ˈsɛljuːl/ *n.* LME. [Fr., or L *cellula* dim. of *cella* CELL *n.*[1]: see -ULE.] †1 A small compartment, a pigeon-hole; a 'cell of the brain'. LME–E19. 2 *Biol.* A minute cell, cavity, or pore. Now *rare.* M19.

cellulate *a.* composed of or containing cells LME. **cellulated** *a.* = CELLULATE L17.

cellulite /sɛljʊˈlʌɪt/ *n.* M20. [Fr. = next.] Fatty tissue regarded as causing a dimpled or lumpy texture of (esp. a woman's) skin.

cellulitis /sɛljʊˈlʌɪtɪs/ *n.* M19. [f. as CELLULE + -ITIS.] *Med.* Inflammation of loose subcutaneous connective tissue.

cellulitic /-ˈlɪtɪk/ *a.* pertaining to or characterized by cellulitis E20.

celluloid /ˈsɛljʊlɔɪd/ *n.* & *a.* M19. [f. CELLULOSE *n.* + -OID. Cf. LOID.] A *n.* A plastic made from camphor and nitrocellulose; a piece of this; *transf.* photographic film, the cinema. M19. B *adj.* Made of celluloid; *fig.* of, pertaining to, or appearing in films; synthetic, unreal. M19.

cellulose /ˈsɛljʊləʊz, -s/ *n.* & *v.* M19. [Fr., f. as CELLULE + -OSE[2].] A *n.* 1 A polymeric carbohydrate which forms the main constituent of the cell walls of plants. M19. 2 A compound of this; *esp.* the soluble thermoplastic acetate or nitrate used as the basis of paints, lacquers, etc. L19. B *v.t.* Treat or coat with a cellulose-based material. M20.

cellu'losic *a.* & *n.* (*a*) *adj.* of the nature of or derived from (a compound of) cellulose; (*b*) *n.* a cellulosic compound or material: L19.

†**cellulose** *a.* M18–M19. [mod.L *cellulosus*, f. as CELLULE + -OSE[1].] = next.

cellulous /ˈsɛljʊləs/ *a.* E19. [f. CELLULE + -OUS.] Consisting of cells; full of minute cavities.

celom *n.*, **celomate** *a.* & *n.* see COELOM etc.

celosia /sɪˈləʊsɪə, -ʃə/ *n.* E19. [mod.L, f. Gk *kēlos* burnt, dry (from the appearance of the flowers of some species): see -IA[1].] A plant of the genus *Celosia*, of the amaranth family; *esp.* cockscomb, *C. cristata*.

celsian /ˈsɛlsɪən/ *n.* L19. [f. CELSIUS + -AN.] *Min.* A barium aluminosilicate belonging to the feldspar group and occurring as colourless monoclinic crystals.

celsitude /ˈsɛlsɪtjuːd/ *n.* Now *literary.* LME. [L *celsitudo*, f. *celsus* lofty: see -TUDE.] Lofty position, eminence; loftiness; height.

Celsius /ˈsɛlsɪəs/ *a.* & *n.* M19. [Anders *Celsius* (1701–44), Swed. astronomer.] A *adj.* Designating or pertaining to the centigrade scale of temperature on which water freezes at 0° and boils at 100° under standard conditions; *postpositive* (with a specified temperature) on this scale. M19. B *n.* The Celsius scale; a Celsius thermometer. E20.

Celt /kɛlt, s-/ *n.*[1] Also **K-** /k-/. M16. [L *Celtae* pl. f. Gk *Keltoi* (later *Keltai*, perh. f. L); later f. Fr. *Celte* Breton (as representative of the ancient Gauls).] 1 *Hist.* A member of any of a group of ancient peoples of western Europe that included the Gauls and Britons. M16. 2 *gen.* A member of any of the peoples descended from the ancient Celts or speaking a Celtic language, as the Irish, Gaels, Manx, Welsh, Cornish, and Bretons. L18.

celt /sɛlt/ *n.*[2] E18. [med.L *celtis* chisel.] A stone or metal chisel-edged prehistoric implement; *loosely* any prehistoric stone axe.

Celtiberian /kɛltɪˈbɪərɪən/ *n.* & *a.* E17. [f. L *Celtiberia* (see below), f. as CELT *n.*[1], -I-, IBERIAN.] *Hist.* (A native or inhabitant) of Celtiberia, an ancient province of Iberia lying between the Tagus and Ebro rivers.

Celtic /ˈkɛltɪk, ˈs-/ *a.* & *n.* Also **K-** /ˈk-/. L16. [L *Celticus* (f. *Celtae*) or Fr. *Celtique* (f. *Celte*): see CELT *n.*[1], -IC.] A *adj.* Of or pertaining to the Celts and related peoples, or (with specification as for the n., a stage or division of) their language group. L16.

Celtic cross a Latin cross with a circle around the centre. **Celtic fringe** (the land of) the Highland Scots, Irish, Welsh, and Cornish in relation to the rest of Britain. *Celtic nard*: see NARD *n.* 2. **Celtic Sea** the area of sea south of Ireland and west of Cornwall. *Celtic spikenard*: see SPIKENARD 2. **Celtic twilight** [the title of an anthology collected by W. B. Yeats] the romantic fairy tale atmosphere of Irish folklore; literature etc. conveying this. *spike Celtic*: see SPIKE *n.*[2] 3.

B *n.* A branch of the Indo-European language family including Irish, Gaelic, Manx, Welsh, Cornish, and Breton, and the languages from which they have developed. E17.

Common Celtic, (*arch.*) **Old Celtic**: the undifferentiated Indo-European language branch. **P-Celtic** the group of Celtic languages (represented by Welsh, Cornish, and Breton) in which Common Celtic **q*ᵘ developed to *p*; Brittonic. **Q-Celtic** the group of Celtic languages (represented by Irish, Gaelic, and Manx) in which Common Celtic **q*ᵘ was retained; Goidelic.

Celticism /-sɪz(ə)m/ *n.* a Celtic custom or expression; devotion to Celtic customs; the branch of knowledge that deals with Celtic languages etc.: M19. **Celticist** /-sɪst/ *n.* a student of Celtic languages or other Celtic matters E20. **Celticize** /-sʌɪz/ *v.t.* make Celtic in form, language, culture, etc. L19.

cembalo /ˈtʃɛmbələʊ/ *n.* Pl. **-os**. M19. [It., abbrev. of CLAVICEMBALO.] A harpsichord.

cembra /ˈsɛmbrə/ *n.* Also †**-bro**. M18. [mod.L f. G dial. *zember*, *zimber* TIMBER *n.*[1]] In full *cembra pine*. The Swiss stone pine, *Pinus cembra*.

cement /sɪˈmɛnt/ *n.* ME. [(O)Fr. *ciment* f. L *caementum* quarry stone, (in pl.) chips of stone, f. *caedere* hew: see -MENT. Cf. SIMMON.] 1 A powdered substance mixed with water and applied as a paste which hardens into a stony consistency for binding together stones or bricks and for forming floors, walls, etc.; *esp.* a strong mortar of calcined lime and clay. ME. 2 Any substance applied in a soft form that later hardens, used for sticking things firmly together, filling cavities, etc.; *fig.* a principle, quality, etc., that unites. LME. 3 = CEMENTUM 2. M19. 4 *Metall.* A powdered metal or other substance, esp. a precipitated metal. Usu. *attrib.*, as *cement copper, gold, steel*, etc. L19.

1 *hydraulic cement, Keene's cement, Parian cement, Portland cement, Roman cement*, etc. 2 E. IRVING Faith is the cement of all domestic and social union. *rubber cement*: see RUBBER *n.*[1]

Comb.: **cement-mixer** a machine (usu. with a revolving drum) for mixing cement (and freq. also sand, gravel, etc.) with water.

cement /sɪˈmɛnt/ *v.* ME. [(O)Fr. *cimenter*, f. as prec.] 1 *v.t.* Unite (as) with cement (*lit.* & *fig.*). ME. 2 *v.i.* Cohere firmly (as) by the application of cement; stick. L17. 3 *v.t.* Apply cement to; line or cover (as) with cement. L19.

1 SHAKES. *Ant. & Cl.* The fear of us May cement their divisions. N. GORDIMER The dented silver stopper . . was cemented to the glass neck by . . dried Silvo polish.

cementer *n.* a person who or thing which cements M18. **cementing** *vbl n.* (*a*) the action of the vb; †(*b*) *Alch.* the process of cementation: LME.

cementation /siːmɛnˈteɪʃ(ə)n/ *n.* L16. [f. prec. + -ATION.] 1 The process by which one solid is made to combine with another by heating, without liquefaction; *spec.* the making of steel by heating iron with carbon. L16. 2 The action or process of cementing; the state thus produced. M17.

cementite /sɪˈmɛntʌɪt/ *n.* L19. [f. CEMENT *n.* + -ITE[1].] *Metall.* A hard, brittle iron carbide, Fe_3C, present in cast iron and most steels.

cementitious /siːmɛnˈtɪʃəs/ *a.* E19. [f. as prec. + -ITIOUS[1].] Of the nature of cement.

cementum /sɪˈmɛntəm/ *n.* E17. [L form of CEMENT *n.*] †1 *gen.* Cement. Only in E17. 2 *Anat.* The hard bony tissue forming the outer layer of the root of a tooth. M19.

cemetery /ˈsɛmɪtri/ *n.* LME. [Late L *coemeterium* f. Gk *koimētērion* dormitory, f. *koiman* put to sleep.] 1 A place used for burials; *esp.* a usu. large area of public ground belonging to a town, city, etc., and laid out for the interment of the dead. LME. †2 A churchyard. L15–E19.

1 *fig.*: SWIFT It is with libraries as with other cœmeteries.

ceme'terial *a.* relating to a cemetery; used for burial: E17.

cenacle /ˈsɛnək(ə)l/ *n.* LME. [(O)Fr. *cénacle* f. L *cenaculum*, f. *cena* dinner: see -CULE.] 1 A dining-room; *spec.* the room in which the Last Supper was held. LME. 2 A place where a discussion group, literary clique, etc., meets; the group itself. L19.

Cencibel /θɛnθɪˈbɛl, sɛnsɪˈbɛl/ *n.* M20. [Sp., of unkn. origin.] In the Valdepeñas region of Spain: the Tempranillo grape.

ceneme /ˈkɛniːm/ *n.* Also **k-**. M20. [f. Gk *kenos* empty + -EME.] *Ling.* A minimal unit of expression without content; a meaningless unit of sound. Opp. PLEREME.

cene'matic *a.* of or pertaining to cenemes M20. **cene'matics** *n.* the branch of glossematics that deals with cenemes M20.

cenobite, cenobium, cenoby *ns.* see COENOBITE etc.

cenogenesis *n.* see CAENOGENESIS.

cenotaph /ˈsɛnətɑːf, -taf/ *n.* & *v.* E17. [Fr. *cénotaphe* f. late L *cenotaphium* f. Gk *kenotaphion*, f. *kenos* empty + *taphos* tomb.] A *n.* An empty tomb; a sepulchral monument to honour someone whose body is elsewhere. E17.

the Cenotaph *spec.* that in Whitehall, London, commemorating the dead of the wars of 1914–18 and 1939–45.

B *v.t.* Honour or commemorate with a cenotaph. M19.

cenote /seˈnote/ *n.* M19. [Yucatan Sp. f. Maya *tzonot*.] A natural underground reservoir of water, such as occurs in the limestone of Yucatan, Mexico.

Cenozoic /siːnəˈzəʊɪk/ *a.* & *n.* Also **Caen-**, **Cain-** /kʌɪn-/. M19. [f. Gk *kainos* new, recent + -ZOIC.] *Geol.* A *adj.* Designating or pertaining to the latest era of geological time, following the Mesozoic and comprising the Tertiary and Quaternary periods (formerly, the Tertiary only). M19. B *n.* The Cenozoic era; the rocks collectively dating from this time. L19.

cense /sɛns/ *n.* ME. [OFr. f med.L *censa* for L CENSUS (whence mod.Fr. *cens*).] †1 = CENSUS *n.* 1. ME–M18. 2 = CENSUS *n.* 3. M16. 3 Income, taken as determining position or rank; rating. E17.

cense /sɛns/ *v.*[1] LME. [Aphet. f. (O)Fr. *encenser* INCENSE *v.*[1]] 1 *v.t.* Perfume with the odour of burning incense; worship or honour with burning incense. LME. 2 *v.i.* Burn or offer incense. LME.

cense /sɛns/ *v.*[2]*t.* Now *rare.* E17. [L *censere* assess.] Estimate, assess, judge.

censer /ˈsɛnsə/ *n.* ME. [AN (also *senser*), OFr. *censier*, aphet. of *encensier*, f. *encens* INCENSE *n.*] 1 A vessel in which incense is burnt, esp. one that is swung during a religious ceremony. ME. †2 A cassolette; a perfume burner or diffuser. *rare* (Shakes.). Only in L16.

censor /ˈsɛnsə/ *n.* & *v.* M16. [L, f. *censere* pronounce as an opinion, rate, assess: see -OR.] A *n.* 1 *Hist.* Either of two magistrates in ancient Rome who compiled censuses of its citizens, etc., and supervised public morals. M16. 2 A person who exercises supervision or judgement over the conduct or morals of others. L16. 3 An adverse critic; a person who censures or finds fault. Now *rare.* L16. 4 An official with the power to suppress the whole or parts of books, plays, films, etc., on the grounds of obscenity, seditiousness, etc. M17. b An official who, esp. in times of war, is empowered to censor private letters, news reports, etc. E20. 5 *Psychol.* [mistr. G *Zensur* censorship (Freud).] A mental power by which certain anxiety-provoking unconscious ideas and memories are prevented from emerging into consciousness. E20. B *v.t.* Act as censor of; officially inspect and make deletions or changes in (a book, film, article, letter, etc.). L19.

censorable *a.* subject to censorship; in need of censorship: E20.

censorial /sɛnˈsɔːrɪəl/ *a.* L16. [f. as next + -AL[1].] 1 = CENSORIOUS 1. *rare.* L16. 2 Of, pertaining to, or characteristic of an official censor. L18.

Also **censorian** *a.* L16.

censorious /sɛnˈsɔːrɪəs/ *a.* M16. [f. L *censorius* (f. as CENSOR) + -OUS.] 1 Fault-finding, severely critical; inclined to disapproval. M16. 2 Befitting a censor; grave, severe. Now *rare.* M17.

1 C. ANSTEY Bath is a very censorious Place. E. WAUGH He felt these prejudices to be peculiar to himself; none of them made him at all censorious of anyone else. 2 JONSON His [Bacon's] language . . was nobly censorious.

censoriously *adv.* L17. **censoriousness** *n.* M17.

censorship /ˈsɛnsəʃɪp/ *n.* L16. [f. CENSOR *n.* + -SHIP.] 1 The action or function of a censor, esp. in controlling newspapers, films, letters, etc. L16. 2 *Hist.* The office or function of a Roman censor. E17. 3 *Psychol.* The function of a subconscious mental censor. E20.

censual /ˈsɛnsjʊəl/ *a.* E17. [Late L *censualis*, f. as CENSUS: see -AL[1]. Cf. (O)Fr. *censuel*.] Of or relating to a census.

censure /ˈsɛnʃə/ *n.* LME. [(O)Fr. f. L *censura* CENSUS: see -URE.] †1 A judicial (esp. ecclesiastical) sentence; a condemnatory judgement. LME–M19. 2 The position or action of an official censor; censorship. Formerly also, a censor. M16. 3 Judgement, opinion; critical assessment. Now *rare.* L16. 4 Correction, esp. critical recension or revision. Now *rare.* L16. 5 (An) adverse judgement; (a) hostile criticism; an expression of disapproval or reprimand. E17.

1 SWIFT The council thought the loss of your eyes too easy a censure. 3 W. RALEIGH To write my censure of this booke. W. H. AUDEN Greeks, in your censure, were rogues, / all teenagers delinquent. 4 H. HALLAM So arduous a task as the thorough censure of the Vulgate text. 5 SHAKES. *Meas. for M.* No might nor greatness in mortality Can censure scape. CONAN DOYLE Beyond a mild censure for the delay . . the lucky owner got away scatheless. SLOAN WILSON Misinterpreting his silence as censure. *vote of censure*: see VOTE *n.*

censureship *n.* (*rare*) = CENSORSHIP E17.

censure /ˈsɛnʃə/ *v.* L16. [Fr. *censurer*, f. as prec.] 1 *v.t.* & *i.* Form or give an opinion (of); estimate, assess critically, judge. *obs.* exc. *dial.* L16. 2 *v.t.* & *i.* Criticize unfavourably; find fault (with), reprove, blame. L16. †3 *v.t.* Pronounce judicial sentence on; sentence (*to*). Only in 17.

1 SHAKES. *Jul. Caes.* Censure me in your wisdom, and awake your senses, that you may the better judge. S. LATHAM Censure better of me. T. FULLER Eli . . censured Hannah . . to be drunk with wine. 2 M. DRAYTON Duke Robert iustly censured stood, For Disobedience and unnaturall Pride. J. CHAMBERLAYNE They . . proceed accordingly to censure or commend, as they find cause. E. M. FORSTER Laura censured his immoral marriage. 3 CAPT. J. SMITH Some were censured to the whipping post.

censurable *a.* M17. **censurableness** *n.* (*rare*) M17. **censurer** *n.* (*a*) a person who finds fault or blames; †(*b*) a censor, a judge: L16.

census /ˈsɛnsəs/ *n.* & *v.* E17. [L, f. *censere* assess: cf. CENSE *n.*] A *n.* †1 A tax, a tribute; *esp.* a poll tax. E17–M19. 2 *Hist.* The registration of citizens and their property in ancient Rome, usu. for taxation purposes. M17. 3 An official enumeration of the population of a country etc., or of a class of things, usu. with statistics relating to them. M18. B *v.t.* Conduct a census of; count, enumerate. L19.

cent /sɛnt/ *n.*[1] LME. [Fr., or It. *cento*, L *centum*. Cf. SEN *n.*[2]] 1 A hundred. Now only in PER CENT. LME. 2 *gen.* A hundredth part. *rare.* L17. 3 A monetary unit equal to one-hundredth of a dollar in the US, Canada, Australia, New Zealand, and numerous other countries, as Barbados, Jamaica, Liberia, Singapore, Tivalu, and Zimbabwe; one-hundredth of the basic monetary unit in certain other countries, as one-hundredth of a shilling in Kenya, Somalia, Tanzania, and Uganda, of a guilder in the Netherlands and Suriname, of a rand in Namibia and South Africa, of a rupee in Mauritius and Sri Lanka, etc.; a coin of this value; *loosely* a small coin, the smallest sum possible. L18.

1 *cent per cent*: see PER CENT. 3 K. TENNANT If you marry that Alec, you don't get a cent. *like thirty cents*: see THIRTY *a.* **not care a cent** not care at all. *red cent*: see RED *a.*

centage *n.* (now *rare*) = PERCENTAGE L18.

cent /sɛnt/ *n.*[2] *obs.* exc. *Hist.* M16. [Origin uncertain: perh. same as prec.] 1 A card-game said to have resembled piquet, with a winning score of 100. M16. 2 A counter used in playing ombre. M18.

cental /ˈsɛnt(ə)l/ *n.* L19. [f. L *centum* a hundred + -AL[1], perh. after *quintal*.] A weight of one hundred pounds, used esp. for corn etc.

centaur /ˈsɛntɔː/ *n.* LME. [L *centaurus* f. Gk *kentauros*, of unkn. origin.] 1 *Gk Mythol.* A fabulous creature with the form of a horse, having a human body, arms, and head, in place of its neck and head. LME. 2 (Usu. **C-**.) (The name of) *the* constellation Centaurus. LME.

1 *fig.*: BYRON That moral centaur, man and wife.

centaurea /sɛnˈtɔːrɪə, sɛntəˈriːə/ *n.* E19. [mod.L, f. as CENTAURY.] Any plant of the genus *Centaurea*, of the composite family, which includes the cornflower and knapweed.

Centaurus /sɛnˈtɔːrəs/ *n.* L17. [L: see CENTAUR.] (The name of) a constellation of the southern hemisphere partly in the Milky Way and enclosing Crux; the Centaur.

centaury /ˈsɛntɔːri/ *n.* LME. [Late L *centauria*, *-ea*, ult. f. Gk *kentauros* CENTAUR: the plant's medicinal properties were said to have been discovered by the centaur Chiron.] 1 A plant of the genus *Centaurium*, of the gentian family, usu. with pink flowers; esp. *Centaurium erythraea* (more fully *common centaury*). Also (w.

specifying wd), any of several plants of allied genera. LME. 2 = CENTAUREA. Now *rare* or *obs.* LME.

1 *yellow centaury*: see YELLOW *a.*

centavo /sɛnˈtɑːvəʊ/ *n.* Pl. **-os**. L19. [Sp. & Port., f. L *centum* a hundred.] A monetary unit equal to one-hundredth of the basic monetary unit in Portugal and other (chiefly Latin American) countries, as one-hundredth of an escudo in Portugal and the Cape Verde Islands, of a peso in Chile, Colombia, Cuba, Mexico, etc., of a sucre in Equador, of a colón in El Salvador, of a metical in Mozambique, and (formerly) of a cruzeiro in Brazil.

centenarian /sɛntɪˈnɛːrɪən/ *n.* & *a.* M19. [f. as next + -AN.] (A person) a hundred or more years old.

centenarianism *n.* the state or fact of being a centenarian L19.

centenary /sɛnˈtiːnəri, -ˈtɛn-; ˈsɛntɪnəri/ *n.* & *a.* E17. [L *centenarius* containing a hundred, f. *centeni* a hundred each, f. *centum* a hundred: see -ARY[1]. Cf. next.] A *n.* I1 A space or duration of a hundred years; a century. E17. 2 A centennial anniversary; a celebration or festival in honour of this. (The usual sense.) L18. †II3 A hundredweight. M17–L18. B *adj.* 1 Of or pertaining to the period of one hundred years; *esp.* of or pertaining to (the celebration of) a hundredth anniversary. M17. 2 *gen.* Of or belonging to a hundred. *rare.* M18.

centenier /ˈsɛntənɪə/ *n.* Also (earlier) †**-ner**. ME. [AN *centener*, (O)Fr. *centenier*, f. late L *centenarius* (f. as prec.) for L CENTURION: see -IER. In branch II f. OFr. *centenaire* f. L *centenarium.*] I†1 A centurion. ME–E17. 2 A police officer on the island of Jersey. M19. †II3 A hundredweight. LME–L16.

centennial /sɛnˈtɛnɪəl/ *a.* & *n.* L18. [f. L *centum* a hundred, after *biennial.*] A *adj.* Of or relating to (the completion of) a period of one hundred years; occurring every hundred years; relating to a centenary or its celebration. L18.

Centennial State *US* Colorado, admitted as a State in 1876, the centennial year of the United States.

B *n.* A hundredth anniversary or its celebration; a centenary. L19.

center *n.* & *a.*, *v.* see CENTRE *n.* & *a.*, *v.*

centering *vbl n.* see CENTRING.

centesimal /sɛnˈtɛsɪm(ə)l/ *a.* & *n.* L17. [f. L *centesimus* hundredth, f. *centum* a hundred: see -AL[1].] A *adj.* †1 Hundredfold. Only in L17. 2 Reckoning or reckoned by hundredths. E19. B *n.* A hundredth part. Now *rare* or *obs.* L17.

centesimally *adv.* E18. **centesimate** *v.t.* select every hundredth person in (a group) for punishment M18. **centesiˈmation** *n.* execution etc. of every hundredth person M17.

centesimo /tʃɛnˈteɪzɪməʊ/ *n.* Pl. **-mi** /-mi/. M19. [It.] A monetary unit of Italy, equal to one-hundredth of a lira.

centésimo /sɛnˈteɪzɪməʊ/ *n.* Pl. **-os**. E20. [Sp.] A monetary unit of Uruguay, equal to one-hundredth of a peso; a monetary unit of Panama, equal to one-hundredth of a balboa.

†**centesm** *n.* L15–E19. [OFr. *cent(i)esme*, *-isme* (mod. *centième*), f. L *centesimus*: see CENTESIMAL.] A hundredth part.

centi- /ˈsɛnti/ *comb. form.* [L, f. *centum* a hundred: see -I-.] Used in names of units of measurement to denote a factor of one-hundredth, as *centigram*, *centilitre*, *centipoise*. Abbrev. *c.*

centigrade /ˈsɛntɪgreɪd/ *a.* & *n.* E19. [Fr., f. as CENTI- + L *gradus* step, GRADE *n.*] A *adj.* Having a hundred divisions; *spec.* designating or pertaining to the Celsius scale of temperature, *postpositive* (with a specified temperature) on this scale. E19. B *n.* A centigrade scale or thermometer. M20.

centile /ˈsɛntʌɪl/ *n.* & *a.* E20. [Abbrev.] = PERCENTILE.

centillion /sɛnˈtɪljən/ *n.* *rare.* L19. [f. CENTI- after *million*, *billion*, etc.] Orig. (esp. in the UK), the hundredth power of a million (10^{600}). Now usu. (orig. *US*), the 101st power of a thousand (10^{303}). Also *loosely*, an enormous number.

centillionth *n.* & *a.* M19.

centime /ˈsɒntiːm; *foreign* sɑ̃tim (*pl. same*)/ *n.* E19. [Fr., f. as CENTESM.] A monetary unit equal to one-hundredth of a franc in France, Belgium, Liechtenstein, Luxembourg, Monaco, and Switzerland; a coin of this value. Also, a monetary unit equal to one-hundredth of a gourde in Haiti or of a dirham in Morocco.

centimetre /ˈsɛntɪmiːtə/ *n.* Also ***-meter**. L18. [f. CENTI- + METRE *n.*[2]] One-hundredth of a metre, equal to 0.3937 inch.

Comb.: **centimetre-gram-second** *a.* designating or pertaining to a system of measurement in which these form the basic units of length, mass, and time respectively.

centimetric /sɛntɪˈmɛtrɪk/ *a.* of the order of one centimetre in (wave-)length; pertaining to or involving electromagnetic radiation having a wavelength of 1 to 10 centimetres: M20.

céntimo /ˈsɛntɪməʊ, *foreign* ˈθentimo/ *n.* Also **ce-**. Pl. **-os** /-əʊz, *foreign* -ɔs/. L19. [Sp.] A monetary unit of Spain (also used in Andorra), equal to one-hundredth of a peseta; a coin of this value. Also, a monetary unit equal to one-hundredth of the basic monetary unit in some Latin American countries, as one-hundredth of a colón in Costa Rica, of a guarani in Paraguay, or of a bolivar in Venezuela.

†**centinel** *n.*, *v.* var. of SENTINEL *n.*, *v.*

centipedal /sɛnˈtɪpɪd(ə)l/ *a.* L19. [f. L CENTI- + *ped-*, *pes* foot + -AL[1].] *Pros.* Of one hundred metrical feet.

centipede /ˈsɛntɪpiːd/ *n.* Also †**-pee**. M17. [Fr. *centipède* or L *centipeda*, f. as CENTI- + *ped-*, *pes* foot.] Any of numerous predatory terrestrial arthropods belonging to the class Chilopoda, having an elongated body with many segments most of which bear a pair of legs.

centner /ˈsɛntnə/ *n.* M16. [G (now *Zentner*) f. L *centenarius* CENTENARY.] A German unit of weight usu. equal to 50 kg; a metric hundredweight.

cento /ˈsɛntəʊ/ *n.* Pl. **-os**, †**-ones**. E17. [L, lit. 'patchwork garment'.] †1 A piece of patchwork; a patchwork garment. E–M17. 2 A hotchpotch, a medley; *spec.* a composition made up of quotations from other authors. E17.

centra *n.pl.* see CENTRUM.

central /ˈsɛntr(ə)l/ *a.* & *n.* M17. [Fr., or L *centralis*, f. *centrum* CENTRE *n.*: see -AL[1].] A *adj.* 1 Of or pertaining to the centre or middle; situated in, proceeding from, containing or constituting the centre of anything. M17. 2 *fig.* Most important or significant; chief, leading, dominant; essential or fundamental *to*. M17. b Of a body, office, association, etc.: controlling all branches of an organization etc. from a common centre. E19. 3 *Biol.* & *Med.* Involving or affecting the central nervous system (see below). M19. 4 *Phonet.* Of a vowel: formed with the centre of the tongue raised (towards the juncture of the soft and hard palates). M20.

1 J. HUGHES Around the central sun in circling eddies roll'd. R. SWINHOE The island . . from its central position would form a good depôt. 2 E. B. BROWNING The central truth. B. JOWETT Odysseus is the central figure of the one poem. N. FRYE Literature seems . . to be central to the arts. b GLADSTONE Commence not with local but central institutions. U. BENTLEY There's no central authority in this school.

Special collocations: **Central America** the isthmus joining N. and S. America, extending from Mexico to Colombia. **Central American** (a native or inhabitant) of Central America. *central bank*: see BANK *n.*[3] 3. **central force** a force attracting or repelling from a centre. **central heating** (the apparatus for) warming a building by hot water or hot air or steam conveyed by pipes from a central source, or by a general system of radiators etc. *central lobby*: see LOBBY *n.* 3a. **central nervous system** the brain and spinal cord considered together. **Central Powers** Germany and Austria-Hungary before and during the war of 1914–18. **central processing unit** the part of a computer in which the control and execution of operations occur. *central reservation*: see RESERVATION 7b. *central reserve*: see RESERVE *n.* 4c. **Central Time** standard time used in central Canada and the US.

B *n.* Something central; *esp.* (*US*) a telephone exchange. L19.

centralism *n.* a centralizing system; (support for) centralization: M19. **centralist** *n.* & *a.* (*a*) *n.* an advocate of centralism; (*b*) *adj.* pertaining to or advocating centralism: E19. **centrally** *adv.* in a central manner or position; with regard to the centre; *centrally-heated*, equipped with central heating: LME. **centralness** *n.* L19.

centrale /sɛnˈtreɪli/ *n.* Pl. **-lia** /-lɪə/. L19. [Short for L *os centrale* central bone.] *Anat.* A central carpal bone which is possessed by many animals but is not usu. present in humans.

Centralia /sɛnˈtreɪlɪə/ *n.*[1] L19. [f. CENTRAL *a.* + *Australia.*] Orig., a name proposed for the central strip of Australia comprising the present State of South Australia and the Northern Territory. Now, the remote central regions of Australia.

centralia *n.*[2] pl. of CENTRALE.

centralisation *n.*, **centralise** *v.* vars. of CENTRALIZATION, -IZE.

centrality /sɛnˈtralәti/ *n.* M17. [f. CENTRAL *a.* + -ITY.] The quality or fact of being central (*lit.* & *fig.*); central nature or position.

F. W. FARRAR The centrality of its position . . made it a great commercial emporium. *Word* The centrality of languages to political life in Belgium.

centralization /sɛntrəlʌɪˈzeɪʃ(ə)n/ *n.* Also **-isation**. E19. [f. next + -ATION, or Fr. *centralisation.*] The fact or action of centralizing; *esp.* the concentration of administrative power in a central authority.

centralize /ˈsɛntrəlʌɪz/ *v.* Also **-ise**. E19. [f. CENTRAL *a.* + -IZE, or Fr. *centraliser.*] 1 *v.i.* Come together at a centre; form a centre; be concentrated. E19. 2 *v.t.* Bring to or locate in a centre; make central; concentrate (administrative powers etc.) in a single place. E19. b *Phonet.* Make (a vowel) central, shift towards a central position. Chiefly as *centralized* ppl a. M20.

2 A. HELPS Business always tends to centralize itself. H. E. BATES One of those centralized courtyards . . enclosed on three sides by the house and on the fourth by a balustrade.

centralizer *n.* a person who centralizes or promotes centralization M19.

centre /ˈsɛntə/ *n.* & *a.* Also ***center**. LME. [(O)Fr., or directly f. L *centrum* f. Gk *kentron* goad, peg, stationary point of a pair of compasses, f. base of *kentein* to prick.] A *n.* I1 The middle point equidistant from all points on the circumference of an arc, circle, or sphere. LME. b *ellipt.* The centre of the earth; the earth itself considered as the centre of the universe. *arch.* LME. 2 The point, pivot, or axis around which a body revolves. LME. 3 A point around which things group themselves; a focus of concentration or attraction; a point of dispersion, a nucleus, a source. E17. b A building or group of buildings forming a central point, or constituting a main site for a particular activity; an installation etc. devoted to a particular activity. M19. c *spec.* A location in the brain or nervous system responsible for a particular faculty etc. M19. 4 In a lathe etc., a conical adjustable support for a workpiece. L18. 5 The area of a target located between the bull's eye and the outer; the hitting of this part. L19.

1 *fig.*: DONNE This bed thy center is, these wals thy spheare. b C. LAMB The feeling . . that all betwixt sky and centre was my own. 2 MILTON As a rock Of adamant, and as a centre, firm. *fig.*: CARLYLE Even an anarchy . . must have a centre to revolve around. 3 JOYCE Hell is the centre of evils. M. KLINE Great banking houses made Italy the financial center. R. L. FOX Pella . . was the centre of a tribal aristocracy. b *attendance centre*, *civic centre*, *detention centre*, *health centre*, *information centre*, *jobcentre*, *music centre*, *shopping centre*, *youth centre*, etc. c P. PARISH The centres in the brain which control movement.

II6 The middle point or point of equilibrium of a body or figure of any shape; the point equidistant or at a median distance from the extremities of a body or figure; the midpoint of a line; *gen.* the middle part or portion, the midst.

LME. **b** *spec.* The main body of troops occupying the space between the wings of an army; the middle division of a fleet. L16. **c** (**C-**.) *The* remote central regions of Australia. Also *Red Centre.* E20. **7** *Archit.* A temporary framework supporting a superstructure; *esp.* = CENTRING 2. E16. **8** *Sport.* **a** A player whose position is in the middle of a line or field of players. M19. **b** *Soccer, Hockey*, etc. A kick or pass from either of the wings towards the middle of the pitch, esp. in the vicinity of the opponent's goal area. E20. **9** Orig., those deputies of moderate political opinions in the French Chamber who sit on central benches in front of the President. Now, (the views and aims of) any party or group holding moderate political views. M19.

6 J. HOWELL They dwelt in the center of Spain not far from Toledo. D. WELCH The chocolate had a cream centre. J. JOHNSTON Steam . . hid the centre of the bridge. *fig.* R. W. EMERSON If the man is off his centre, the eyes show it. 9 *Listener* All three parties . . are now parties of the centre.

Phrases: **centre of attraction** (*a*) a point to which bodies tend by gravity; (*b*) a person or thing drawing general attention. **centre of buoyancy** the centroid of the volume of fluid displaced by a floating body. *centre of curvature*: see CURVATURE 1b. **centre of flotation** (*a*) the centre of gravity of the water plane of a floating body; (*b*) = *centre of buoyancy* above. **centre of gravity** (*a*) = *centre of mass* below; (*b*) *fig.* the point or object of greatest importance or interest. **centre of inertia, centre of mass** the point representing the mean position of the matter in an object or system. *centre of ossification*: see OSSIFICATION 1. **centre of pressure** a point on a surface through which the resultant force due to pressure passes. *dead centre*: see DEAD *a.* etc. *left centre*: see LEFT *a. left, right, and centre*: see LEFT *adv. optical centre*: see OPTICAL *a. right centre*: see RIGHT *a. right, left, and centre*: see LEFT *adv. shifting centre*: see SHIFTING *a.* 1. *stage centre*: see STAGE *n.* 4.

B *attrib.* or as *adj.* Situated in or forming the centre; of or pertaining to the centre; central. L18.

J. BENTHAM The center one of the 5 uppermost Cells. R. K. DOUGLAS The centre figures of his philosophy.

Comb. & *special collocations*: **centre-back** in *Football, Hockey*, etc., (the position of) a back who plays primarily in the centre of the pitch; **centre-bit** a boring tool with a centre point and side cutters; **centreboard** a board for lowering through the keel of a sailing boat to prevent leeway; **centre field** *Baseball* (a fielder in) the central part of the outfield; **centre fielder** *Baseball* a fielder in the centre field; **centrefold** a centre spread that folds out; a (usu. naked or scantily clad) model pictured on such a spread in a magazine; **centre forward** in *Football, Hockey*, etc., (the position of) the middle player in a forward line; **centre half** in *Football, Hockey*, etc., (the position of) the middle player in a half-back line; *loosely* = *centre-back* above; **centre-line** a real or imaginary line through the centre of something; **centrepiece** the principal item on display (*lit.* & *fig.*); *spec.* a glass or china ornament designed for the centre of a table; **centre-second** (a clock or watch with) a seconds hand mounted on the centre arbor; **centre spread** (the illustration, text, etc., occupying) the two facing middle pages of a newspaper etc.; **centre three-quarter** *Rugby Football* either of two middle players in the line of three-quarters.

centremost *a.* most central, midmost M19.

centre /ˈsɛntə/ *v.* Also ***center**. Pres. pple **centring, -treing, *-tering**. L16. [f. the n.] **1** *v.t.* Place in the centre or a central position; make exactly central; concentrate or focus *in*, (*up*)*on*, (*a*)*round*; mark with a centre, constitute the centre of. Freq. in *pass.* L16. **b** *v.t.* & *i. Soccer, Hockey*, etc. Kick or hit (the ball) from the wing to the centre of the pitch, esp. in the vicinity of the opponent's goal area. L19. **2** *v.i.* Be situated (as) on a fixed centre; have its centre or be concentrated *in*, (*up*)*on*, (*a*)*round*; move (as) round a focal point. E17.

1 GOLDSMITH In reverie centred. C. HUTTON The necessity of well centring the object glass of a large telescope. K. LITTLE A plot of . . grass centred by a basin. R. CHURCH My universe was still centred in my mother's fragrant person. 2 BUNYAN Here centreth Luke the Evangelist. W. SANSOM That strange figure around whom this account properly centres. B. BAINBRIDGE Tedious conversations centred on food.

centreing *vbl n.* var. of CENTRING.

centric /ˈsɛntrɪk/ *a.* L16. [Gk *kentrikos*, f. *kentron*: see CENTRE *n.* & *a.*, -IC.] **1** That is in or at the centre, central. L16. **2** Of, pertaining to, or characterized by a centre. E18. **3** *Cytol.* = CENTROMERIC. M20.

1 C. MARLOWE This centric earth. 2 R. BLACKMORE Orbs centric and excentrick.

centrical *a.* = CENTRIC M17. **centrically** *adv.* L18. **centricity** /sɛnˈtrɪsɪti/ *n.* centric quality or position; relation to a centre: E19.

-centric /ˈsɛntrɪk/ *suff.* [After CONCENTRIC, ECCENTRIC, etc., f. Gk *kentrikos*: see prec.] Forming adjs. w. the senses 'having a (specified) centre', 'having as its centre', as: *anthropocentric, heliocentric, polycentric, theocentric*, etc.

centrifugal /sɛnˈtrɪfjʊɡ(ə)l, ˈsɛntrɪfjuːɡ(ə)l, sɛntrɪˈfjuːɡ(ə)l/ *a.* & *n.* E18. [f. mod.L *centrifugus*, f. *centrum* CENTRE *n.* + *-fugus* fleeing, f. *fugere* flee: see -AL[1].] **A** *adj.* **1** Moving or tending to move away from a centre (*lit.* & *fig.*; opp. *centripetal*); *centrifugal force*, (the inertial force causing) the tendency of a body rotating about a centre to move outwards from that centre. E18. **2** Of a machine, process, etc.: employing centrifugal force or motion. Of a product: obtained by the use of such a machine. M18. **3** Chiefly *Bot.* Developing or progressing from the centre outwards. M19. **B** *n.* A centrifugal machine; a centrifuge. M19.

centrifuˈgality *n.* M20. **centrifugaliˈzation** *n.* the process of centrifugalizing E20. **centrifugalize** *v.t.* subject to a centrifugal force or process L19. **centrifugally** *adv.* E19.

centrifugate /sɛnˈtrɪfjʊɡeɪt/ *v.t.* M19. [f. as prec. + -ATE[3].] = CENTRIFUGE *v.*

centrifuˈgation *n.* E19.

centrifuge /ˈsɛntrɪfjuːdʒ/ *a.*, *n.*, & *v.* E18. [Fr., f. mod.L *centrifugus* CENTRIFUGAL.] †**A** *adj.* = CENTRIFUGAL *a.* 1. E18–E19. **B** *n.* A centrifugal machine; *esp.* a device for effecting separation, usu. of one liquid from another or of a solid from a liquid, by rapid rotation. L19. **C** *v.t.* Subject to centrifugal motion; separate by means of a centrifuge. E20.

cenˈtrifugate *n.* material separated using a centrifuge E20.

†**centrinel** *n.* var. of SENTINEL *n.*

centring /ˈsɛntrɪŋ/ *vbl n.* Also **centering** (the usual form in sense 2), **centreing**, /-t(ə)rɪŋ/. M17. [f. CENTRE *v.* + -ING[1].] **1** The action of CENTRE *v.*; placing in the centre; making central; bringing centres into alignment. M17. **2** *Archit.* The temporary framework used to support an arch, dome, etc., while under construction. M18.

centriole /ˈsɛntrɪəʊl/ *n.* L19. [mod.L *centriolum* dim. of *centrum* centre: see -OLE[1].] *Cytol.* A cylindrical organelle in the centrosome of a cell, involved esp. in the development of microtubular structures such as spindles and cilia.

centriˈolar *a.* M20.

centripetal /sɛnˈtrɪpɪt(ə)l, ˈsɛntrɪpiːt(ə)l, sɛntrɪˈpiːt(ə)l/ *a.* E18. [f. mod.L *centripetus*, f. *centrum* CENTRE *n.* + *-petus* seeking, f. *petere* seek: see -AL[1].] **1** Moving or tending to move towards a centre (*lit.* & *fig.*; opp. *centrifugal*); *centripetal force*, the force directed towards the centre of rotation which acts upon a body in circular motion. E18. **2** Chiefly *Bot.* Developing or progressing from the periphery inwards. M19.

centripetally *adv.* M19.

centrist /ˈsɛntrɪst/ *n.* & *a.* L19. [Fr. *centriste*, f. as CENTRE *n.* & *a.* + -IST.] **A** *n.* Orig., a member of the French political centre (see CENTRE *n.* 9). Now, any holder of moderate (political) views. L19. **B** *adj.* Of or pertaining to centrists; characterized by centrism. E20.

centrism *n.* (the policy of adopting) a middle position between extreme views M20.

centro- /ˈsɛntrəʊ/ *comb. form* of L *centrum* CENTRE *n.*: see -O-.

centroˈbaric *a.* (now *rare* or *obs.*) relating to or possessing a centre of gravity E18. **centroˈlecithal** *a.* (of an egg or egg cell) having a centrally-placed yolk L19. **centromere** *n.* [Gk *meros* part] *Cytol.* the part of a chromosome with which the spindle fibres become associated in cell division E20. **centroˈmeric** *a.* pertaining to or associated with a centromere; having or involving a centromere: M20. **centrosome** *n.* (*Cytol.*) a region of cytoplasm which is adjacent to the nucleus during interphase and forms the centre of an aster during division L19. **centrosphere** *n.* (*Cytol.*) a centrosome; *spec.* the central part of an aster during division: L19.

centrode /ˈsɛntrəʊd/ *n. rare.* L19. [f. prec. + -ODE[2].] *Math.* The path traced by the instantaneous centre of rotation of a moving plane figure.

centroid /ˈsɛntrɔɪd/ *n.* L19. [f. as prec. + -OID.] *Math.* A point defined in relation to a given figure in a manner analogous to the centre of mass of a corresponding body. Orig. also = prec.

†**centronel** *n.* var. of SENTINEL *n.*

centrum /ˈsɛntrəm/ *n.* Pl. **-trums, -tra** /-trə/. M19. [L.] A centre; *spec.* (*Anat.*) the solid central part of a vertebra, to which the arches and processes are attached.

†**centry** *n.*[1] E16. [Origin uncertain: cf. AL *centrie, -ii* (pl.).] **1** In *pl.* The centering of a bridge etc. E16–M19. **2** The centre, midst. Only in L16.

†**centry** *n.*[2] var. of SENTRY *n.*[1]

centum /ˈsɛntəm/ *n.* M17. [L.] = CENT *n.*[1] 1. Chiefly in *per centum*.

centum /ˈkɛntəm/ *a.* E20. [L (see prec.): this wd and SATEM exemplifying this distinction between the two groups.] *Philol.* Designating or pertaining to a chiefly western group of Indo-European languages having (voiceless) velar plosives where cognate words in the eastern group have sibilants.

centumvir /sɛnˈtʌmvəː, k-/ *n.* Pl. **-viri** /-vəri/, **-virs**. E17. [L, f. *centum* a hundred + *viri* men.] *Rom. Hist.* Any of a body of (orig. 105) judges appointed to decide common causes among the Roman people.

centumviral *a.* L17. **centumvirate** *n.* the position of being centumviri, the centumviri collectively; *transf.* any body of 100 men: M18.

centuple /ˈsɛntjʊp(ə)l/ *a.*, *n.*, & *v.* E17. [Fr., or eccl.L *centuplus* var. of *centuplex*, f. *centum* hundred.] **A** *adj.* & *n.* A hundredfold (amount). E17. **B** *v.t.* Multiply by a hundred. E17.

centuplicate *v.*, *a.*, & *n.* = CENTUPLE M17. **centupliˈcation** *n.* L19.

centurial /sɛnˈtjʊərɪəl/ *a.* E17. [L *centurialis*, f. *centuria* CENTURY: see -AL[1].] Of or pertaining to a century.

centuriate /sɛnˈtjʊərɪət/ *a.* E17. [L *centuriatus* pa. pple, f. as next: see -ATE[2].] *Rom. Hist.* Of, pertaining to, or divided into units of a hundred; *spec.* designating an assembly (L *comitia centuriata*) in which the people voted by units of a hundred.

centuriate /sɛnˈtjʊərɪeɪt/ *v.t.* E18. [L *centuriat-* pa. ppl stem of *centuriare* divide into centuries, f. *centuria* CENTURY: see -ATE[3].] *Rom. Hist.* Divide into hundreds; *spec.* divide (land) into units of a hundred or so estates for assigning to colonists.

centuriˈation [L *centuriatio(n-)*] *n.* M19.

Centuriator /sɛnˈtjʊərɪeɪtə/ *n.* M17. [mod.L, f. as prec.: see -OR.] *Hist.* Any of a number of 16th-cent. Protestant divines who compiled a thirteen-volume Church History of which each volume embraced a century. More fully *Centuriator of Magdeburg*. Usu. in *pl.*

centurion /sɛnˈtjʊərɪən/ *n.* ME. [L *centurio(n-)*, f. *centuria* CENTURY: see -ION.] **1** *Hist.* A commander of a century in the ancient Roman army; an officer in command of 100 men. ME. **2** A person who has achieved a sporting century; *spec.* the scorer of a century in cricket. *colloq.* L19.

century /ˈsɛntʃʊri/ *n.* LME. [L *centuria*, f. *centum* a hundred: see -Y[3].] **1** *Hist.* A company in the ancient Roman army, consisting nominally of a hundred men. LME. **2** A group of a hundred things; a hundred. *arch.* exc. as below. L16. **b** A sum of a hundred dollars, pounds, etc. *slang.* M19. **c** A score of a hundred made in a sport or game; *esp.* a hundred or more runs made in one batsman's innings at cricket. L19. **3** *Hist.* Each of the 193 divisions by which the Roman people voted in the centuriate assembly. E17. 4 Orig. more fully *century of years*. A period of 100 years. E17. 5 Each of the hundred-year periods reckoned successively from an accepted epoch, esp. from the date assumed for the birth of Jesus. M17.

1 *transf.*: DE QUINCEY Centuries of armed men.. firing from windows. 2 SHAKES. *Cymb.* A century of prayers. *double century*: see DOUBLE *a.* & *adv.* *triple century*: see TRIPLE *a.* & *adv.* 4 A. ALISON Not years, but centuries must elapse. 5 **first century** AD 1–100; **twentieth century** 1901–2000, *pop.* 1900–1999; **second century** BC 200–101 BC; (etc.).

Comb.: **century plant** = *American aloe* s.v. ALOE 4.

centuried *a.* established for centuries; centuries old E19.

ceorl *n.* see CHURL.

cep /sɛp/ *n.* Also **cèpe** /sɛp (*pl. same*)/. M19. [Fr. *cèpe* f. Gascon *cep* tree-trunk, mushroom, f. L *cippus* stake.] An edible boletus.

'cep *prep.* & *conj.* var. of 'CEPT.

cèpe *n.* var. of CEP.

cephal- *comb. form* see CEPHALO-.

cephalalgy /ˈsɛfəlaldʒi/ *n.* Now *rare*. Also in L form **-algia** /sɛfəˈlaldʒə/. M16. [L *cephalalgia* f. Gk *kephalalgia*, f. *kephalē* head: see -ALGIA, -Y³. Cf. (O)Fr. *céphalalgie*.] Headache.

cephalic /sɪˈfalɪk, kɛˈfalɪk/ *a.* & *n.* LME. [(O)Fr. *céphalique* f. L *cephalicus* f. Gk *kephalikos*, f. *kephalē* head: see -IC.] A *adj.* 1 Of, relating, or pertaining to the head; situated in the head; of the nature of a head. LME. 2 Curing or relieving disorders of the head. Now *rare* or *obs.* M17.

1 **cephalic index** the ratio of the maximum breadth of a skull (multiplied by 100) to its maximum length. **cephalic presentation** the presentation of a foetus such that it is delivered head first. **cephalic vein** a major vein of the arm (so called because opening it was anciently supposed to relieve disorders of the head).

†B *n.* A medicine for ailments of the head. LME–M18.

-cephalic /sɪˈfalɪk, kɛ-/ *suff.* [f. Gk *kephalē* head + -IC.] = -CEPHALOUS.

cephalin /ˈsɛfəlɪn, ˈkɛ-/ *n.* L19. [f. CEPHALO- + -IN¹.] *Biochem.* Any of a class of phospholipids present in cell membranes, esp. in the brain.

cephalization /sɛfəlʌɪˈzeɪʃ(ə)n, kɛ-/ *n.* Also **-isa-**. M19. [f. CEPHALO- + -IZATION.] A greater development of the head in relation to the rest of the body (as in an embryo); the extent of this.

cephalo- /ˈsɛfələʊ, ˈkɛ-/ *comb. form*. Also (*rare*) **k-** /k-/. Bef. a vowel or *h* also **cephal-**. [f. Gk *kephalē* head: see -O-.] 1 Forming ns. and adjs. w. the sense 'head, skull'. 2 *Pharm.* Forming names of drugs related to cephalosporin.

cephalhaema'toma *n.*, pl. **-mas**, **-mata** /-mətə/, *Med.* a swelling caused by a collection of blood between the skull and pericranium E20. **cepha'litis** *n.* (now *rare* or *obs.*) = ENCEPHALITIS E19. **cephalocele** *n.* (*Med.*, now *rare*) = ENCEPHALOCELE L19. **cephalo'chordate** *a.* & *n.* (*Zool.*) (of, pertaining to, or designating) a protochordate animal of the subphylum Cephalochordata, a lancelet M20. **cephalo'metric** *a.* (*Med.*) pertaining to or involving cephalometry L19. **cepha'lometry** *n.* (*Med.*) measurement of the head, esp. that of a foetus L19. **cephalo'pelvic** *a.* (*Med.*) of the relation between the maternal pelvis and the foetal head M20. **cephalothin** *n.* [THIO-] *Pharm.* an antibiotic related to cephalosporin, used to treat bacterial infections M20. **cephalotho'racic** *a.* of or pertaining to a cephalothorax M19. **cephalo'thorax** *n.* (*Zool.*) the fused head and thorax possessed by chelicerate arthropods and some crustaceans M19.

cephalon /ˈsɛfəlɒn/ *n.* L19. [f. Gk *kephalē* head.] *Zool.* The region of the head in some arthropods, esp. trilobites.

cephalopod /ˈsɛf(ə)ləpɒd, ˈkɛ-/ *n.* & *a.* E19. [f. mod.L *Cephalopoda* (see below), f. as CEPHALO- + -POD.] (A mollusc) of the class Cephalopoda, members of which have a well-developed head surrounded by tentacles, and include the cuttlefish, octopus, nautilus, and extinct forms such as ammonites.

cepha'lopodal *a.* L19. **cepha'lopodous** *a.* (now *rare* or *obs.*) M19.

cephalosporin /sɛfələ(ʊ)ˈspɔːrɪn, kɛ-/ *n.* M20. [f. mod.L *Cephalosporium* (see below) + -IN¹.] Any of a class of semisynthetic antibiotics derived from a mould of the genus *Cephalosporium*.

-cephalous /ˈsɛf(ə)ləs, ˈkɛf-/ *suff.* [f. Gk *kephalē* head + -OUS.] Forming adjs. (chiefly *Anthropol.*) in sense '-headed, having a head of a specified kind', as *brachycephalous*, *dolichocephalous*, etc.

cepheid /ˈsiːfiɪd, ˈsɛ-/ *a.* & *n.* Also **C-**. E20. [f. next + -ID³.] *Astron.* A *adj.* Belonging or pertaining to a class of variable stars, typified by δ Cephei, which have regular cycles of brightness which can be used to deduce their distances. E20. B *n.* A star of this type. E20.

Cepheus /ˈsiːfjuːs, -fɪəs/ *n.* M16. [L *Cepheus*, Gk *Kēpheus*, father of Andromeda in Gk mythol.] (The name of) a constellation of the northern hemisphere on the edge of the Milky Way, near the polestar.

'cept /sɛpt/ *prep.* & *conj. colloq.* Also **'cep**. M19. [Abbrev.] = EXCEPT *prep.*, *conj.*

ceraceous /sɪˈreɪʃəs/ *a.* Now *rare*. M18. [f. L *cera* wax + -ACEOUS.] Of the nature of wax, waxy.

ceral /ˈsɪər(ə)l/ *a.* L19. [Sense 1 f. CERE *n.*; sense 2 f. L *cera* wax: see -AL¹.] 1 Of or pertaining to the cere of a bird's bill. L19. 2 Of or relating to wax. L19.

cerambycid /sɛrəmˈbʌɪsɪd/ *n.* & *a.* L19. [f. mod.L *Cerambycidae* (see below), f. *Cerambyx* genus name, f. Gk *kerambux* a kind of beetle: see -ID³.] *Entomol.* A *n.* A beetle of the family Cerambycidae, which comprises the longhorn beetles. L19. B *adj.* Of, pertaining to, or designating this family. E20.

ceramic /sɪˈramɪk/ *a.* & *n.* E19. [Gk *keramikos*, f. *keramos* potter's earth, pottery: see -IC.] A *adj.* Of or relating to (the art of) pottery; designating or pertaining to hard brittle substances produced by the process of strong heating of clay etc. E19. B *n.* An article made of pottery. In *pl.* also, pottery, the art of making pottery. M19.

ceramicist /-ɪsɪst/ *n.* = CERAMIST M20. **'ceramist** *n.* a person skilled in the art of pottery M19.

cerargyrite /sɪˈrɑːdʒɪrʌɪt/ *n.* M19. [Irreg. f. Gk *keras* horn + *arguros* silver + -ITE¹.] *Min.* A waxy mineral consisting of silver halides, esp. the chloride, and crystallizing in the cubic system; horn silver.

cerastes /sɪˈrastiːz/ *n.* LME. [L *cerastes* f. Gk *kerastēs*, f. *keras* horn.] A viper of the genus *Cerastes*, of N. Africa; *esp.* the horned viper, *C. cornuta*.

cerastium /sɪˈrastɪəm/ *n.* L18. [mod.L, f. Gk *kerastēs* horned (from the shape of the capsule in many species): see -IUM.] A white-flowered plant of the genus *Cerastium*, which belongs to the pink family and includes mouse-ear chickweed.

cerate /ˈsɪərət/ *n.* Now *rare* or *obs.* LME. [L *ceratum* = Gk *kerōton* neut. of adj. *kerōtos*, covered with wax. Cf. Fr. *cérat*.] *Med.* A stiff ointment composed of wax, lard, or oil, and other ingredients.

ceration /sɪˈreɪʃ(ə)n/ *n. obs.* exc. *Hist.* E17. [med.L *ceratio(n-)*, f. *cerat-* pa. ppl stem of *cerare*, f. *cera* wax: see -ION.] *Alch.* The process of softening a hard substance.

ceratite /ˈsɛrətʌɪt, ˈsɪər-/ *n.* M19. [f. mod.L *ceratites* (see below), f. Gk *keras*, *kerat-* horn: see -ITE¹.] *Palaeont.* An ammonoid fossil of the genus *Ceratites* or a related genus, common in Permo-Triassic rocks, and having usu. partly frilled, partly lobed suture lines. Cf. AMMONITE, GONIATITE.

ceratitic /-ˈtɪtɪk/ *a.* pertaining to or characteristic of a ceratite E20.

cerato- /ˈsɛrətəʊ, k-/ *comb. form* of Gk *keras*, *kerat-* horn, occas. as var. of KERATO-: see -O-.

cerato'branchial *a.* & *n.* (of, pertaining to, or designating) any of the paired cartilaginous sections of the branchial arch (e.g. in fishes) M19. **cerato'hyal** *a.* & *n.* (of, pertaining to, or designating) any of the paired sections of the hyoid arch of the vertebrate skeleton M19.

Cerberus /ˈsəːb(ə)rəs/ *n.* M17. [L f. Gk *Kerberos* the three-headed watchdog which guarded the entrance of Hades.] A watchdog.

a sop to Cerberus something to propitiate a guard, official, etc.

cercaria /səːˈkɛːrɪə/ *n.* Pl. **-iae** /-ɪiː/. M19. [mod.L, irreg. f. Gk *kerkos* tail: see -ARY¹.] *Zool.* A digenean trematode (fluke) in the free-swimming larval stage developed from the redia, in which form it passes from the intermediate to the definitive host. Cf. MIRACIDIUM.

cercarial *a.* L19. **cercarian** *a.* M19.

cerclage /səːˈklɑːʒ/ *n.* Also **cir-**. M20. [Fr., lit. 'encirclement'.] *Med.* The use of a ring or loop to bind together the ends of an obliquely fractured bone or encircle the os of an incompetent cervix.

cercopithecoid /səːkəˈpɪθɪkɔɪd/ *a.* & *n.* L19. [f. L *cercopithecus* f. Gk *kerkopithēkos* a long-tailed monkey, f. *kerkos* tail + *pithēkos* ape: see -OID.] *Zool.* A *adj.* Of, pertaining to or characteristic of the superfamily Cercopithecoidea, which comprises the Old World monkeys. L19. B *n.* A cercopithecoid monkey. M20.

cercus /ˈsəːkəs/ *n.* Pl. **cerci** /ˈsəːkʌɪ/. E19. [mod.L f. Gk *kerkos* tail.] *Zool.* Either of a pair of small appendages at the end of the abdomen of certain insects and other arthropods.

cercal *a.* L19.

cere /sɪə/ *n.* Also **†s-**. L15. [L *cera* wax.] The soft waxlike covering of the base of the beak in certain birds (esp. birds of prey), in which the nostrils are pierced.

cere /sɪə/ *v.t.* LME. [L *cerare* to wax, f. *cera* wax.] 1 Wrap in a cerecloth. LME. †b Anoint with spices etc., embalm. L15–L16. †2 Smear, cover, or impregnate with wax. LME–M17.

cereal /ˈsɪərɪəl/ *a.* & *n.* E19. [L *cerealis* pertaining to the cultivation of grain, f. *Ceres* Roman goddess of agriculture: see -AL¹.] A *adj.* Of, pertaining to, or of the nature of edible grain. E19. B *n.* 1 Any of the plants of the grass family Gramineae which are cultivated for their edible seeds; a grain used for human food. Usu. in *pl.* M19. 2 Food made from wheat, maize, or another grain (usu. as a breakfast dish). L19.

cerebellum /sɛrɪˈbɛləm/ *n.* M16. [L, dim. of CEREBRUM: see -ELLUM.] *Anat.* The larger part of the hindbrain, responsible for the control of muscle tone and balance.

†cerebel *n.* = CEREBELLUM E17–M19. **cerebellar** *a.* of or pertaining to the cerebellum E19.

cerebral /ˈsɛrɪbr(ə)l/ *a.* & *n.* E19. [f. L CEREBRUM + -AL¹: cf. Fr. *cérébral*.] A *adj.* 1 Of or pertaining to the brain. E19. b Appealing to the intellect rather than to the emotions; clever; intellectual. E20. 2 *Phonet.* = CACUMINAL *a.* E19.

1 **cerebral palsy** a disorder chiefly characterized by spastic paralysis due to brain damage before or at birth.

B *n. Phonet.* A cerebral consonant. E19.

cerebralism *n.* (*a*) intellectualism; (*b*) (now *rare*) the theory that mental processes arise from the action of the brain: L19. **cerebralist** *n.* (*a*) an intellectualist, an intellectual; (*b*) (now *rare*) a supporter of the theory of cerebralism: L19. **cerebrally** *adv.* L19.

cerebrate /ˈsɛrɪbreɪt/ *v.* L19. [f. as next + -ATE³.] 1 *v.t.* Subject to or produced by brain action. L19. 2 *v.i.* Cogitate. E20.

cerebration /sɛrɪˈbreɪʃ(ə)n/ *n.* M19. [f. L CEREBRUM + -ATION.] The working of the brain; *esp.* (in full *unconscious cerebration*) the action of the brain in producing results without conscious thought.

cerebro- /ˈsɛrɪbrəʊ/ *comb. form* of L CEREBRUM: see -O-.

cerebro'centric *a.* centring on the brain M20. **cerebroside** *n.* [-OSE² + -IDE] *Biochem.* any of a group of glycolipids present in the sheaths of nerve fibres (cf. GANGLIOSIDE) L19. **cerebro'spinal** *a.* of, pertaining to, or involving the brain and spinal cord (*cerebrospinal fluid*, the clear watery fluid occupying the space between the arachnoid membrane and the pia mater) E19. **cerebro'tonic** *a.* & *n.* (*a*) *adj.* temperamentally resembling or characteristic of an ectomorph, with predominantly intellectual interests; (*b*) *n.* a cerebrotonic person: M20. **cerebro'vascular** *a.* of or pertaining to the brain and the blood-vessels which supply it M20.

cerebrum /ˈsɛrɪbrəm/ *n.* E17. [L = brain.] *Anat.* The larger, anterior part of the brain, responsible for voluntary activity and mental processes.

cerecloth /ˈsɪəklɒθ/ *n.* & *v.* LME. [f. *cered cloth*: see CERE *v.*, CLOTH.] **A** *n.* (A piece of) cloth made waterproof by smearing or impregnation with wax; *spec.* (*a*) one used for wrapping a corpse, a winding-sheet; †(*b*) one used as a plaster. LME. †**B** *v.t.* Wrap in or cover with a cerecloth. E–M17.

cerement /ˈsɪəm(ə)nt/ *n.* *literary.* E17. [App. f. CERE *v.* + -MENT.] **1** In *pl.* (Waxed) wrappings for the dead; grave-clothes. E17. **2** A cerecloth. *rare.* E19.

1 SHAKES. *Haml.* Tell Why thy canoniz'd bones . . Have burst their cerements.

¶First recorded in Shakes.

ceremonial /sɛrɪˈməʊnɪəl/ *a.* & *n.* LME. [Late L *caerimonialis*, f. *caerimonia* CEREMONY: see -AL[1]. Cf. (O)Fr. *cérémonial.*] **A** *adj.* **1** Relating to or consisting of ceremonies or rites; ritual; formal. LME. **2** Relating to or involving social formalities. M16. †**3** = CEREMONIOUS 2. L16–M17.

1 A. J. P. TAYLOR The upper-class uniform of top hat and tail coat was worn only on ceremonial occasions, such as weddings and race-meetings. E. H. PINTO Ceremonial tools of considerable elaboration were made for presentation to the notabilities invited to lay foundation stones. **2 ceremonial law**: enforced by custom.

B *n.* †**1** A ceremonial commandment. LME–E17. **2** A system of rites; a rite or ceremony; the formalities proper to an occasion. LME. **3** *RC Ch.* A book containing the order of ritual. E17. **4** The observance of ritual or convention; ceremonial display. M19.

2 H. FIELDING The two ladies . . after very short previous ceremonials, fell to business. I. D'ISRAELI The ceremonial prescribed in the Anglican service. J. BRONOWSKI A precise ceremonial which fixes the sequence of operations so that they are exact and memorable.

ceremonialism *n.* addiction to or fondness for ceremonies; ritualism: M19. **ceremonialist** *n.* a ritualist, one given to ceremonies L17. **ceremonialize** *v.* (*a*) *v.t.* render ceremonial or ritualistic; (*b*) *v.i.* carry out a ceremony: M19. **ceremonially** *adv.* M17.

ceremonious /sɛrɪˈməʊnɪəs/ *a.* M16. [Fr. *cérémonieux* or late L *caerimoniosus*, f. *caerimonia*: see next, -OUS.] **1** = CEREMONIAL *a.* 1. M16. **2** Addicted or given to ceremony; punctilious. M16. **3** According to prescribed or customary formalities. L16. **4** Full of ceremony; accompanied by rites. E17.

ceremoniously *adv.* L16. **ceremoniousness** *n.* L16.

ceremony /ˈsɛrɪməni/ *n.* LME. [L *caerimonia* religious worship, (in pl.) ritual observances, perh. through (O)Fr. *cérémonie*: see -MONY.] **1** An outward rite or observance; the performance of some solemn act according to a prescribed form. LME. **b** (A rite regarded as) an empty form; a mere formality. M16. **2** A formal act of politeness, courtesy, civility, etc. LME. †**3** An object or symbolic attribute of worship, state, or pomp. L16–E18. †**4** A portent, an omen. *rare* (Shakes.). Only in L16. **5** (Non-count.) Performance of (religious) rites; ceremonial display; pomp, state; precise observance of conventional forms; punctilious behaviour. L16.

1 R. W. EMERSON They repeated the ceremonies of the eleventh century in the coronation of the present Queen. A. N. WILSON It was not until she herself married that she became aware . . that this was a ceremony which her parents had never actually undergone. **b** ROBERT BURTON It is . . a meer flash, a ceremony, a toy, a thing of nought. **2** H. JAMES She went and knocked at his door—a ceremony without which she never crossed the threshold. **5** SHAKES. *Hen. V* What have kings that privates have not too, Save ceremony. G. MACDONALD I was shown with much ceremony . . into the presence of two ladies.

Phrases: **Master of Ceremonies** a person in charge of ceremonies observed on state or public occasions; a person introducing speakers at a banquet, entertainers in a variety show, etc. *sans cérémonie*: see SANS *prep.* **stand on ceremony** insist on the observance of formalities. **without ceremony** informally, casually.

Cerenkov radiation /tʃəˈrɛŋkɒf reɪdɪˈeɪʃ(ə)n/ *n. phr.* Also **Cherenkov.** M20. [Pavel A. Cherenkov (b. 1904), Soviet physicist.] *Physics.* Light emitted by a charged particle moving in a medium at a speed greater than that of light in the same medium.

cereologist /sɪərɪˈɒlədʒɪst/ *n.* L20. [f. *Ceres* (see CEREAL) + -OLOGIST.] A student or investigator of crop circles.

cereology *n.* L20.

cereopsis /sɛrɪˈɒpsɪs/ *n.* M20. [mod.L *Cereopsis* genus name, f. Gk *kerinos* waxen (f. *keros* wax) + *opsis* face, with ref. to the swollen waxy cere.] In full *cereopsis goose*. = *Cape Barren goose* s.v. CAPE *n.*[1]

cereous /ˈsɪərɪəs/ *a.* E17. [f. L *cereus* waxen, f. *cera* wax: see -OUS.] Of the nature of wax; waxen, waxy.

†**Ceres** *n.* & *a.* see SERI.

ceresin /ˈsɛrɪsɪn/ *n.* L19. [f. mod.L *ceres* f. L *cera* wax + -IN[1].] A hard whitish paraffin wax used with or instead of beeswax.

cereus /ˈsɪərɪəs/ *n.* L17. [L: see CEREOUS.] Any of numerous neotropical cacti now or formerly included in the genus *Cereus*.

night-blooming cereus: see NIGHT *n.*

¶Many species, esp. those designated 'night-blooming', are now placed in other genera.

ceric /ˈsɪərɪk/ *a.* M19. [f. CERIUM + -IC.] *Chem.* Of cerium in its higher valency (4). Cf. CEROUS.

†**cerilla** *n.* L16–M19. [Sp., var. of CEDILLA.] = CEDILLA.

cerin /ˈsɪərɪn/ *n.* E19. [f. L *cera* wax + -IN[1].] *Chem.* **1** A terpenoid ketone extracted from cork. E19. **2** The alcohol-soluble part of beeswax. E19.

Cerinthian /sɪˈrɪnθɪən/ *n.* & *a.* LME. [f. *Cerinthus* (see below) + -IAN.] *Eccl. Hist.* **A** *n.* An adherent of Cerinthus, a Gnostic of the 1st cent. AD who is usu. presented as antagonistic to the Apostle John. LME. **B** *adj.* Of or pertaining to Cerinthus or his teaching. L16.

ceriph *n.* see SERIF.

†**Ceris** *n.* & *a.* see SERI.

cerise /səˈriːz, -s/ *a.* & *n.* M19. [Fr. = cherry.] (Of) a light clear red.

cerite /ˈsɪəraɪt/ *n.* E19. [f. next + -ITE[1].] *Min.* An orthorhombic hydrated silicate of cerium and other lanthanides, occurring as brown granular masses.

cerium /ˈsɪərɪəm/ *n.* E19. [f. *Ceres*, an asteroid discovered shortly before this element + -IUM.] A metallic chemical element, atomic no. 58, which is the most abundant of the lanthanide series. (Symbol Ce.)

cermet /ˈsəːmɛt/ *n.* M20. [f. CERAMIC + METAL *n.*] A heat-resistant material made by sintering an intimate mixture of ceramic and metallic powders.

†**cern** *v.t.* *rare* (Shakes.). Only in L16. [Abbrev.] = CONCERN *v.*

cernuous /ˈsəːnjʊəs/ *a.* M17. [f. L *cernuus* inclined forwards + -OUS.] (Chiefly *Bot.*, of flowers) bowing downwards, drooping.

cero /ˈsɪərəʊ/ *n.* Pl. **-os**, same. L19. [Sp. *sierra* saw, sawfish.] A mackerel, *Scomberomorus regalis*, found in warm parts of the western Atlantic. Also called *sierra*.

cero- /ˈsɪərəʊ/ *comb. form* of L *cera* or Gk *kēros* wax: see -O-.

ceˈrography *n.* writing, engraving, designing, or painting on or in wax L16. **ceroˈplastic** *a.* of or relating to modelling in wax E19.

ceroon *n.* var. of SERON.

†**cerote** *n.* M16–M18. [L *cerotum* f. Gk *kērōton*: see CERATE.] = CERATE.

cerotic /sɪˈrɒtɪk/ *a.* M19. [f. as prec. + -IC.] Chem. *cerotic acid*, a fatty acid, $C_{26}H_{53}COOH$, present in insect waxes, usu. as the ceryl ester.

ˈ**cerotate** *n.* a salt or ester of cerotic acid L19. ˈ**cerotin** *n.* ceryl alcohol, $C_{27}H_{55}OH$, obtained from insect waxes M19.

cerous /ˈsɪərəs/ *a.* M19. [f. CERIUM + -OUS.] *Chem.* Of cerium in its lower valency (3). Cf. CERIC.

cert /səːt/ *n.* *slang.* L19. [Abbrev. of CERTAIN or CERTAINTY.] A certainty, a sure thing; something bound to happen; a racehorse etc. regarded as certain to win. Freq. in *dead cert*

for cert = *for certain* (see next).

certain /ˈsəːt(ə)n, -tɪn/ *a.*, *n.*, *pron.*, & *adv.* ME. [(O)Fr. f. Proto-Romance extension of L *certus* settled, sure.] **A** *adj.* **I 1** Determined, fixed; not variable. Occas. *postpositive.* ME. **b** Definite, precise, exact. *arch.* LME. **2** Sure; inevitable; unfailing; wholly reliable. ME. **3** Established as a truth or fact; not to be doubted. LME. **4** Of a person: having no doubt, assured, convinced. LME. **b** Destined, undoubtedly going *to do*. M17.

1 H. J. STEPHEN Payment of money on a day certain. J. ARLOTT The fixed and certain oak. **b** MARVELL The answer is now much shorter and certainer. **2** SPENSER Fearfull more of shame Then of the certeine perill he stood in. M. SOMERVILLE A certain indication of a coming tempest. H. CECIL An absolutely certain thing for the four o'clock had come in second. **3** B. RUSSELL Is there any knowledge in the world which is so certain that no reasonable man could doubt it? J. STEINBECK Putting his certain ignorance against this man's possible knowledge. **make certain** make sure. **4** C. ISHERWOOD He can't be certain if Kenny answered his question or not. W. TREVOR One of the daily women was only a little sceptical, while the other was certain and adamant. I. MURDOCH He was quite certain that he was acting rightly. **morally certain** so sure that one is justified in acting upon the conviction. **b** OED We are certain to meet him in the course of our rambles.

II 5 Known and particularized but not explicitly identified: (with sing. n.) a particular, (with pl. n.) some particular, some definite. ME. **b** Of some extent at least; some though not much. M16. **c** *euphem.* Which it is not polite or necessary to define further. M18. **d** Of a person: unknown except by name; existing, but probably unknown to the reader or hearer. L18.

5 L. M. MONTGOMERY If it isn't carried in just a certain way the handle pulls out. M. FRAYN I shall want him to bring certain designated books and documents. *up to a certain point*: see POINT *n.*[1] **b** J. TYNDALL The ice is disintegrated to a certain depth. **c a certain age** an age when one is no longer young (usu. of a woman). **a certain disease** venereal disease. *in a certain condition*: see CONDITION *n.* 8. **of a certain description** (of a woman) of the demi-monde. **d** SOUTHEY A certain Benjamin Franklin French writes to me from New Orleans.

B *ellipt.* as *n.* or *pl. pron.* **1** What is certain, certainty. *obs.* exc. in *for certain* below. ME. †**2** A particular quantity, amount, number, etc., *of*; *ellipt.* a particular sum of money. ME–E17. **3** Some but not all (*of*). LME.

1 SHAKES. *Hen. V* I will live so long as I may, that's the certain of it. **for certain**, (*dial.*) **for a certain**, (*arch.*) **of (a) certain** as a certainty, assuredly.

C *adv.* Certainly; assuredly. Now *dial.* or *arch.* ME.

certain sure very certain.

certainly /ˈsəːt(ə)nli, -tɪn-/ *adv.* ME. [f. prec. + -LY[2].] **1** In a manner that is certain; in a way that may be surely depended on. ME. †**b** Exactly. LME–E17. **2** With certainty; unfailingly; indubitably, assuredly, admittedly; (in answers) without doubt, undeniably, yes (*certainly not*, (emphatically) no). ME. **b** Fixedly. Now *rare.* L16.

certainty /ˈsəːt(ə)nti, -tɪn-/ *n.* ME. [AN *certainté*, OFr. *certaineté*: see CERTAIN, -TY[1].] **1** The quality or fact of being objectively certain. ME. **2** The quality or state of being subjectively certain; assurance, confidence; certitude. ME. **3** A definite number or quantity. *obs.* exc. *Theatr.*, a flat rate. LME. **4** An undoubted fact; an indubitable prospect; a thing or person which may be relied on (*to do*). E17.

1 J. KEILL Geometry, which truly boasts the Beauty of Certainty. **2** BACON If a man will begin with certainties, hee shall end in doubts. R. P. WARREN He was filled with certainty, a . . conviction that engulfed him. **4** M. W. MONTAGU I would not advise you to neglect a certainty for an uncertainty. G. B. SHAW Though these are only risks to the individual, to the community they are certainties.

Phrases: **for a certainty** beyond possibility of doubt. *moral certainty*: see MORAL *a.*

certes /ˈsəːtɪz/ *adv. arch.* ME. [(O)Fr., prob. f. Proto-Romance f. L *certus*: see CERTAIN.] Of a truth; assuredly, I assure you.

certie /ˈsəːti/ *n. Sc.* Also **-y.** E19. [Perh. back-form. f. prec., taken as pl.] *my certie* (advb. phr.), in good faith, on my word.

certifiable /ˈsəːtɪfʌɪəb(ə)l/ *a.* M19. [f. CERTIFY + -ABLE.] 1 Able to be certified; *spec.* (of a person) so deranged as to be certifiably insane; (of mental illness) of such a type as to warrant certification. M19. 2 Of infectious disease: notifiable. *US.* E20.

certifiably *adv.* in a manner or degree warranting certification L19.

certificate /səˈtɪfɪkət/ *n.* LME. [Fr. *certificat* or med.L *certificatum* use as n. of neut. pa. pple of *certificare*: see CERTIFY, -ATE[1].] †1 The action or fact of certifying or giving assurance; certification, attestation. LME–M17. 2 A document in which a fact is formally certified or attested; *esp.* one formally attesting status, medical condition, abilities, fulfilment of requirements, ownership of shares, etc.; a licence. M16. 3 *Law.* A writing made in one court, by which notice of its proceedings is given to another. Now *rare.* E17.

2 *birth certificate, marriage certificate, medical certificate, X-certificate,* etc. *certificate of origin*: see ORIGIN 1. **Certificate of Secondary Education** *Hist.* (the certificate gained by passing) an examination for secondary-school pupils in England and Wales, usu. set and marked by individual schools; abbrev. *CSE.* **General Certificate of Education** *Hist.* (the certificate gained by passing) an examination esp. for secondary-school pupils in England and Wales, set and marked by an independent examination board; abbrev. *GCE.* **General Certificate of Secondary Education** (the certificate gained by passing) an examination for secondary-school pupils in England and Wales, including course-work assessment by individual schools; abbrev. *GCSE. silver certificate*: see SILVER *n.* & *a.*

†**certificate** *pa. pple* & *ppl a.* E–M16. [med.L *certificatus* pa. pple of *certificare*: see CERTIFY, -ATE[2]. Cf. next.] Certified; assured.

certificate /səˈtɪfɪkeɪt/ *v.t.* M18. [f. the n.: see -ATE[3]. Cf. prec.] 1 Provide with a certificate; license or authorize by certificate. M18. 2 Attest by a certificate. L19.

certification /ˌsəːtɪfɪˈkeɪʃ(ə)n/ *n.* LME. [(O)Fr., or med.L *certificatio(n-)*, f. L *certificat-* pa. ppl stem of *certificare*: see CERTIFY, -ATION.] I 1 Sure information; assurance. Now *rare.* LME. 2 *Sc. Law.* Notice or a warning to a party of the consequences of a failure to obey the summons or other writ. L15. 3 The action or an instance of certifying the truth of something. M16. 4 Provision of a formal or legal certificate, esp. of insanity. L19. †II 5 A certificate. M16–L18.

certificatory /səˈtɪfɪkət(ə)ri/ *a.* LME. [med.L *certificatorius*, f. L *certificat-*: see prec., -ORY[2].] Serving to certify; of the nature of a certificate.

letter certificatory a written testimonial.

certified /ˈsəːtɪfʌɪd/ *a.* E17. [f. next + -ED[1].] That has been certified; having a certificate, attested by certificate; *arch.* certain.

certified cheque: whose value is guaranteed by a bank. **certified mail** *US*: whose delivery is recorded. **certified milk**: guaranteed free from tuberculosis bacillus. **certified (public) accountant** *US*: holding a certificate of professional competence. **certified transfer** *Stock Exch.*: for which the shares are guaranteed to be available.

certify /ˈsəːtɪfʌɪ/ *v.* ME. [(O)Fr. *certifier* f. late L *certificare*, f. *certus*: see CERTAIN, -FY.] 1 *v.t.* Make (a thing) certain; guarantee as certain; give certain information of. ME. 2 *v.t.* Declare or attest by a formal or legal certificate. ME. b *spec.* Declare (a person) officially insane. L19. 3 *v.t.* Make (a person) certain (*of*); assure; give (a person) formal or legal attestation (*of*). *arch.* ME. 4 *v.i.* Testify *to*; vouch *for*. ME. b *Law.* Give a certificate for costs on a certain scale. Now *rare.* L19.

certifier *n.* L16.

certiorari /səːtɪəˈrɛːrʌɪ, -ˈrɑːri/ *n.* LME. [Late law L, pass. of L *certiorare* inform, f. *certior* compar. of *certus* CERTAIN. Cf. SISERARY.] *Law.* An order or (formerly) writ issuing from a superior court (in England the High Court) to an inferior court or tribunal and calling up the records and proceedings in some cause for review or a speedier judgement.

certiorate /ˈsəːtɪəreɪt, ˈsəːʃ-/ *v.t.* Now *rare* or *obs.* M16. [Late L *certiorat-* pa. ppl stem of *certiorare*: see prec., -ATE[3].] Inform authoritatively.

certitude /ˈsəːtɪtjuːd/ *n.* LME. [Late L *certitudo*, f. *certus*: see CERTAIN, -TUDE.] 1 Subjective certainty; assurance, confidence. LME. b A feeling of certainty. Now *rare.* E17. 2a Objective certainty. Now *rare* or *obs.* in *gen.* sense. M16. b Sureness of action, unfailing quality. L16.

certy *n.* var. of CERTIE.

cerulean /sɪˈruːlɪən/ *a.* & *n.* Chiefly *poet.* Also **cae-.** M17. [f. L *caeruleus* sky-blue, sea-blue (or -green), f. *caelum* sky, heaven: see -EAN.] (Of) the colour of the cloudless sky; deep blue, azure.

Also **cerule** *a.* & *n.* (*poet.*) L16.

cerumen /sɪˈruːmən/ *n.* L17. [mod.L, f. L *cera* wax.] The yellow waxlike substance secreted in the outer ear.

ceruminous *a.* E19.

ceruse /ˈsɪəruːs, sɪˈruːs/ *n.* LME. [(O)Fr. *céruse* f. L *cerussa*, perh. ult. f. Gk *kēros* wax.] White lead (basic lead carbonate), esp. as a cosmetic.

cerussite /ˈsɪərəsʌɪt/ *n.* M19. [f. L *cerussa* (see prec.) + -ITE[1].] *Min.* Orthorhombic lead carbonate, most commonly occurring as white, grey, or yellowish crystals. Also called *lead-spar.*

Cervantic /səːˈvantɪk/ *a.* M18. [f. *Cervantes* (see below) + -IC.] Of, pertaining to, or characteristic of the Spanish novelist and dramatist Miguel de Cervantes Saavedra (1547–1616).

cervantite /səːˈvantʌɪt/ *n.* M19. [f. *Cervantes*, a locality in Galicia, Spain + -ITE[1].] *Min.* Orthorhombic antimony tetroxide, usu. occurring as yellow or reddish needles.

cervelat /ˈsəːvəlɑː/ *n.* E17. [Fr. (now *cervelas*), f. It. *cervellata* Milanese sausage.] A kind of smoked pork sausage.

cervical /ˈsəːvɪk(ə)l, səːˈvʌɪk(ə)l/ *a.* & *n.* L17. [Fr., or mod.L *cervicalis*, f. L *cervicis*, CERVIX: see -AL[1].] *Anat.* A *adj.* 1 Of or pertaining to the neck. L17. 2 Of or pertaining to a cervix, *spec.* that of the womb. M19.

2 *cervical smear*: see SMEAR *n.* 2b.

B *n.* A cervical nerve, vertebra, etc. M18.

cervicitis /səːvɪˈsʌɪtɪs/ *n.* L19. [f. L *cervic-*, CERVIX + -ITIS.] *Med.* Inflammation of the neck of the womb.

cervico- /səːˈvʌɪkəʊ/ *comb. form* of L *cervicis*, CERVIX: see -O-.

cervicoˈfacial *a.* pertaining to the neck and face. M19.

cervid /ˈsəːvɪd/ *n.* & *a.* L19. [mod.L *Cervidae* (see below), f. L *cervus* deer: see -ID[3].] (A ruminant) of the family Cervidae, to which most deer belong.

cervine /ˈsəːvʌɪn/ *a.* & *n.* M19. [L *cervinus*, f. *cervus* deer: see -INE[1].] Of or like a deer; (an animal) of the deer family.

cervisial /səːˈvɪzɪəl/ *a. joc.* L18. [f. L *cervisia* beer + -AL[1].] Of or pertaining to beer.

cervix /ˈsəːvɪks/ *n.* Pl. **-vices** /-vɪsiːz/. M18. [L.] *Anat.* The neck; a part of an organ resembling or forming a neck; *spec.* the narrow passage forming the lower end of the womb adjacent to the vagina.

ceryl /ˈsɪərʌɪl, -rɪl/ *n.* L19. [f. L *cera* wax + -YL.] *Chem.* The straight-chain radical $C_{27}H_{55}$, present in cerotin. Usu. in *comb.*

Cesare /ˈsiːzəri/ *n.* M16. [A mnemonic of scholastic philosophers first used in med.L, E indicating a universal negative proposition and A a universal affirmative proposition.] *Logic.* The first mood of the second syllogistic figure, in which a universal negative major premiss and a universal affirmative minor yield a universal negative conclusion.

Cesarean, -ian *n.* & *a.* see CAESAREAN.

Cesarewitch /sɪˈzarəwɪtʃ/ *n.* In sense 1 also **-vitch** /-vɪtʃ/, **c-.** M19. [Russ. *tsesarevich*, f. *tsesar'* emperor (f. L *Caesar*) + patronymic *-evich*. Cf. TSAREVICH.] 1 *Hist.* = TSAREVICH. M19. 2 A long-distance handicap horse-race run annually at Newmarket, England. M19.

cesium *n.* see CAESIUM.

Cesolfa /siːsɒlˈfɑː/ *n. obs.* exc. *Hist.* Also **C sol fa.** ME. [f. *C* as a pitch letter + *sol* and *fa* designating tones in the solmization of Guido d'Arezzo (*c* 990–1050).] *Medieval Mus.* The note C in Guido d'Arezzo's 3rd and 4th hexachords, where it was sung to the syllables *sol* and *fa* respectively. Cf. ALAMIRE, BEFA, CEFAUT, next, etc.

Cesolfaut /siːsɒlfɑːˈʊt/ *n. obs.* exc. *Hist.* Also **C sol fa ut.** LME. [f. *C* as a pitch letter + *sol*, *fa* and *ut* designating tones in the solmization of Guido d'Arezzo (*c* 990–1050).] *Medieval Mus.* The note C in Guido d'Arezzo's 3rd, 4th, and 5th hexachords, where it was sung to the syllables *sol*, *fa*, and *ut* respectively. Cf. ALAMIRE, BEFA, prec., etc.

cespititious *a.* see CAESPITITIOUS.

cespitose *a.* see CAESPITOSE.

cess /sɛs/ *n.*[1] Also †**s-.** L15. [f. CESS *v.*[1] or aphet. f. ASSESS *n.*] 1 *Ir. Hist.* The obligation to supply the Lord Deputy's household and soldiers with provisions at prices fixed by government. L15. 2 A local tax or rate; *Sc.* land tax. *obs.* exc. *dial.* M16. †3 Assessment, estimation. Only in L16.

3 SHAKES. *1 Hen. IV* Poor jade is wrung in the withers out of all cess.

cess /sɛs/ *n.*[2] *Anglo-Ir.* M19. [Perh. w. ref. to CESS *n.*[1] 2.] *bad cess to*, may evil befall.

cess /sɛs/ *v.*[1]*t.* Also †**s-.** LME. [Aphet. f. ASSESS *v.*] †1 = ASSESS *v.* 1. LME–M18. 2 = ASSESS *v.* 2. *obs.* exc. *dial.* L15. 3 *v.t. Ir. Hist.* Impose (soldiers etc.) on the community (see CESS *n.*[1] 2). E17.

†**cess** *v.*[2]*i.* LME–M18. [Var. of CEASE *v.*] Cease to perform a legal duty. Cf. CESSAVIT.

cessation /sɛˈseɪʃ(ə)n/ *n.* LME. [L *cessatio(n-)*, f. *cessat-* pa. ppl stem of *cessare*: see CEASE *v.*, -ATION.] 1 Ceasing; a pause, stoppage. LME. †b *ellipt.* An armistice, a truce. M17–M18. †2 Inactivity. E17–E19.

cessavit /sɛˈseɪvɪt/ *n.* E16. [L, 3rd person sing. preterite of *cessare*: see CEASE *v.*] *Hist.* A writ to recover lands, which lay when a tenant ceased to pay rent or perform legal duties for the space of two years.

cesser /ˈsɛsə/ *n.* M16. [Use as n. of AN, (O)Fr. *cesser* CEASE *v.*: see -ER[4].] *Law.* 1 *Hist.* Ceasing of a tenant to pay rent or perform legal duties for the space of two years (cf. prec.). M16. 2 Cessation, termination (of a term, liability, etc.). E19.

cessile /ˈsɛsʌɪl/ *a. rare.* L16. [f. L *cess-* (see CESSION) + -ILE.] Of the air: yielding.

cession /ˈsɛʃ(ə)n/ *n.* LME. [(O)Fr., or its source L *cessio(n-)*, f. *cess-* pa. ppl stem of *cedere* CEDE: see -ION.] †1a The relinquishing of title or office. LME–M18. b *Eccl. Law.* The vacating of a benefice by taking another without dispensation. L16. 2 Ceding, giving up (*of* rights, property, etc., esp. *of* territory by a State). LME. b *Law.* The voluntary surrender by a debtor of all his or her effects to creditors. L16. †3 *gen.* Giving way, yielding. Only in 17.

cessionary /ˈsɛʃ(ə)n(ə)ri/ *n.* L15. [med.L *cessionarius* n., f. *cessio(n-)*: see prec., -ARY[1].] 1 An assignee. L15. †2 A bankrupt who makes cession. Only in 17.

†**cessment** *n.* var. of SESSMENT.

†**cessor** *n.* var. of SESSOR.

cesspipe /ˈsɛspʌɪp/ *n.* L19. [f. the imagined base of CESSPOOL, w. implied sense 'sewage, liquid waste', + PIPE *n.*[1]] A pipe leading to or from a cesspool.

cesspit /ˈsɛspɪt/ *n.* M19. [f. as prec. + PIT *n.*[1]] A pit for the disposal of sewage.

cesspool /ˈsɛspuːl/ *n.* L17. [Prob. alt. of SUSPIRAL, w. assim. to POOL *n.*[1]] 1 A trap made under a drain etc. to retain solid matter. Also, a rainwater head in guttering. L17. 2 An underground chamber for the temporary storage or disposal of foul water or sewage. L18.

2 *fig.* (*attrib.*): MALCOLM X I got my first schooling about the cesspool morals of the white man from the best source, from his own women. **cesspool of iniquity** etc., a place of rampant vice.

cest /sɛst/ *n. poet.* L16. [Fr. *ceste* or L CESTUS *n.*[1]] = CESTUS *n.*[1]

cestode /'sɛstəʊd/ *n.* & *a.* M19. [f. mod.L *Cestoda* (see below), f. L CESTUS *n.*[1]: see -ODE[1].] A *n.* A parasitic flatworm of the class Cestoda; a tapeworm. M19. B *adj.* Of, pertaining to, or designating this class. M19.

Also **cestoid** *n.* & *a.* (now *rare*) M19.

Cestrian /'sɛstrɪən/ *a.* M17. [f. *Cester*, OE form of *Chester* + -IAN.] Of or pertaining to the city of Chester or the county of Cheshire, in England.

cestui /'sɛti/ *n.* M16. [AN & OFr., f. Proto-Romance, f. L *ecce* lo! + *iste* that (one), w. element *-ui* as in *cui* dat. of *quis* who.] *Law.* The person (who), he (who). Only in phrases.

cestui que trust /kɪ trʌst/, ***cestui que use*** /kɪ juːs/ the person for whose benefit anything is given in trust to another. ***cestui que vie*** /kɪ viː/ a person for whose life an estate or interest in property is held by another.

cestus /'sɛstəs/ *n.*[1] Pl. **-ti** /-tʌɪ/. M16. [L f. Gk *kestos* use as n. of ppl a. = stitched.] A (bridal) belt or girdle for the waist, *esp.* that of Aphrodite or Venus.

cestus /'sɛstəs/ *n.*[2] Pl. **-ti** /-tʌɪ/. L17. [L *caestus*, f. *caedere* to strike.] *Hist.* A covering for the hand made of thongs of bull-hide loaded with metallic strips, used by boxers in ancient Rome.

cetacean /sɪ'teɪʃ(ə)n/ *n.* & *a.* M19. [f. mod.L *Cetacea* (see below), f. L *cetus* f. Gk *kētos* whale: see -ACEAN.] A *n.* A mammal of the order Cetacea, which includes the whales, dolphins, and porpoises. M19. B *adj.* Of, pertaining to, or characteristic of cetacea. M19.

cetaceous /sɪ'teɪʃəs/ *a.* M17. [f. L *cetus* (see prec.) + -ACEOUS.] Of the nature of a whale; cetacean.

cetane /'siːteɪn/ *n.* L19. [f. CETYL + -ANE.] *Chem.* The liquid straight-chain isomer of hexadecane, used as a solvent and ignition standard.

Comb.: **cetane number** a measure of the ignition properties of a diesel fuel.

cete /siːt/ *n.*[1] *arch.* ME. [OFr. f. L *cete* neut. pl. f. Gk *kētē* (sing. *kēteos*) whales.] A whale, a sea-monster.

cete /siːt/ *n.*[2] LME. [Perh. f. L *coetus* assembly, company.] A group *of* badgers.

ceterach /'sɛtərak/ *n.* LME. [med.L, of unkn. origin.] A fern of the genus *Ceterach*, of the spleenwort family, with scaly undersides to its fronds; *esp.* the rustyback fern, *C. officinarum*.

ceteris paribus /ˌkeɪtərɪs 'parɪbəs, ˌsɛt-, ˌsiːt-/ *adv. phr.* E17. [mod.L.] Other things being equal or unchanged.

cetology /siː'tɒlədʒi/ *n.* M19. [f. L *cetus* whale (see CETACEAN) + -OLOGY.] The branch of zoology that deals with whales, dolphins, and porpoises.

ceto'logical *a.* M19. **cetologist** *n.* M20.

Cetti's warbler /'tʃɛtɪz 'wɔːblə/ *n. phr.* L19. [Francesco *Cetti*, 18th-cent. It. ornithologist.] A chestnut-brown warbler, *Cettia cetti*, resident in Britain since the 1970s, and noted for its strikingly loud and abrupt song.

Cetus /'siːtəs/ *n.* L17. [L *cetus* whale: see CETACEAN.] (The name of) a constellation on the celestial equator, between Taurus and Aquarius; the Whale.

cetyl /'siːtʌɪl, -tɪl/ *n.* M19. [f. L *cetus* whale + -YL: the first compounds were isolated from spermaceti.] *Chem.* The straight-chain radical $C_{16}H_{33}$·, *n*-hexadecyl. Usu. in *comb.*

Comb.: **cetyl alcohol** a waxy alcohol, $CH_3(CH_2)_{15}OH$, occurring in faeces and (esterified) in spermaceti and wool wax, and used in cosmetics and as an emulsifier.

ceviche *n.* var. of SEVICHE.

ceylanite *n.* var. of CEYLONITE.

Ceylon /sɪ'lɒn/ *n.* M19. [Former name of Sri Lanka: see SRI LANKAN.] 1 *Ceylon moss*, a red seaweed of the Indian subcontinent, *Gracilaria lichenoides*, which is the major source of agar-agar. M19. 2 In full *Ceylon tea*. A Pekoe tea produced in Sri Lanka. L19.

Ceylonese /sɪlə'niːz/ *a.* & *n.* Pl. of n. same. L18. [f. prec. + -ESE.] = SRI LANKAN. Also *spec.*, = SINHALESE.

ceylonite /'siːlənʌɪt/ *n.* Also **ceylanite**. E19. [Fr. *ceylanite* f. *Ceylan* CEYLON: see -ITE[1].] *Min.* A dark iron-rich variety of spinel.

ch. A consonantal digraph introduced in early ME, at first used in adoptions of OFr. wds in *ch-*, and for OE wds in *c(e)-*, *c(i)-*. *ch* has the following principal values: /tʃ/ in all native Germanic wds; /k/ in wds taken from Gk (or Hebrew through Gk); /ʃ/ in wds from mod.Fr.; /x/ (for which /k/ is often substituted) in Scottish, Welsh, Irish, German, and some other foreign wds.

cha /tʃɑː/ *n.* Now *slang*. Also **chah**, **char**. L16. [Chin. (Mandarin) *chá*.] Tea.

¶Rare (and not naturalized) bef. E20.

chabazite /'kabəzʌɪt/ *n.* Also **-site**, **†-sie**, **†-zie**. E19. [Fr. *chabazie*, f. Gk *khabazie* erron. reading for *khalazie*, voc. of *khalazios* hailstone, f. *khalaza* hail: see -ITE[1].] *Min.* A colourless, pink, or yellow zeolite which usu. occurs as rhombohedral crystals.

Chablis /'ʃabliː/ *n.* M17. [Fr. (see below).] A white burgundy wine, made at Chablis (Yonne), in central France.

chabootra *n.* var. of CHABUTRA.

†chabuk *n.* var. of CHAWBUCK *n.*

chabutra /tʃə'buːtrə/ *n.* Also **-boot-**. E19. [Hind. *cabūtrā*, *-tarā*.] In the Indian subcontinent: a platform or terrace, often adjoining a house or in a garden.

chace *n.*, *v.* see CHASE *n.*[1], *v.*[1]

cha-cha /'tʃɑːtʃɑː/ *n.* & *v.* Also **cha-cha-cha** /tʃɑːtʃɑː'tʃɑː/. M20. [Amer. Sp.] A *n.* A type of ballroom dance to a Latin American rhythm; a piece of music for this dance. M20. B *v.i.* Perform this dance. M20.

chacham *n.* var. of HAHAM.

chack /tʃak/ *v.* & *n.* Also **chak**. E16. [Imit.] A *v.i.* 1 Snap or chatter with the teeth; suddenly shut the jaws or a door, window, drawer, etc. *Sc.* E16. 2 Of a bird: make a harsh call. E20. B *n.* 1 A harsh note or call of a bird. L18. b *dial.* A wheatear. E19. 2 A light meal, a snack. E19.

chacma /'tʃakmə/ *n.* M19. [Nama.] A dark-furred baboon, *Papio ursinus*, of southern Africa. Also *chacma baboon*. Also called *ursine baboon*.

chaco *n.* see SHAKO.

chaconne /ʃə'kɒn/ *n.* L17. [Fr. f. Sp. *chacona*.] A moderately slow musical composition on a ground bass, usu. in triple time; a dance to this music.

Chad /tʃad/ *n.*[1] M20. [Origin unkn.] In full *Mr Chad*. The figure of a human head looking over a wall, with a caption protesting against shortages etc. that usu. begins 'Wot, no —?'.

chad /tʃad/ *n.*[2] M20. [Origin unkn.] *Computing*. (A piece of) the waste material removed from punched cards or tape by punching.

chadless *a.* not producing chads M20.

chad *n.*[3] var. of SHAD.

chadar /'tʃɑːdə/ *n.* Also **chaddar**, **chador**, **chuddar** /'tʃʌdə/, & other vars. E17. [(Urdu *chādar*, *chaddar* f.) Pers. *čādar* sheet, veil.] A large piece of material worn as a long shawl or cloak by Muslim women, and sometimes by Hindu or other women, esp. in the Indian subcontinent and Iran. Also, any of various similar garments worn by men in the Indian subcontinent.

Chadian /'tʃadɪən/ *a.* & *n.* M20. [f. *Chad* (see below) + -IAN.] (A native or inhabitant) of the Republic of Chad, a State in north central Africa, formerly part of French Equatorial Africa.

Chadic /'tʃadɪk/ *a.* & *n.* L20. [f. as prec. + -IC.] (Designating, of, or pertaining to) an Afro-Asiatic language group of western and central Africa.

chador *n.* var. of CHADAR.

chaeta /'kiːtə/ *n.* Pl. **-tae** /-tiː/. M19. [mod.L f. Gk *khaitē* long hair.] A chitinous bristle; a seta.

chae'tigerous *a.* = SETIGEROUS L19.

chaetodon /'kiːtədɒn/ *n.* M18. [mod.L, f. as prec. + -ODON.] A brightly coloured marine fish of the family Chaetodontidae, with a deep, flattened body and bristle-like teeth. Also called *butterfly-fish*.

chaetodont *n.* & *a.* (a fish) of the family Chaetodontidae M19.

chaetognath /'kiːtənaθ/ *n.* L19. [f. mod.L *Chaetognatha* (see below), f. as CHAETA + Gk *gnathos* jaw.] A small marine planktonic worm of the phylum Chaetognatha, with numerous spines on its head for seizing prey. Also called *arrow worm*, *sea-arrow*.

chafe /tʃeɪf/ *n.* Also **†chaff**. M16. [f. the vb.] 1 A state of vexation or irritation; a rage, a temper. M16. 2 (An injury caused by) rubbing. M19.

chafe /tʃeɪf/ *v.* Also **†chaff**. LME. [(O)Fr. *chauffer* f. Proto-Romance var. of L *cal(e)facere* make warm, f. *calere* be warm + *facere* make.] I *lit.* 1 *v.t.* & *i.* Make or become warm. Long *obs.* exc. in CHAFING-*dish*. LME. 2 *v.t.* a Rub with the hand, esp. to restore warmth or sensation. LME. b Abrade or injure by rubbing. E16. 3 *v.i.* Rub (*against*, *on*, etc.). E17.

2a T. WILSON Waxe chaufed with the handes is made softer. D. LODGE Chafing his chilled limbs . . to keep the circulation going. b B. MALAMUD The legholes were tight and chafed his flesh if he tried to turn. 3 A. SCHLEE A rash on his neck where the stiff uniform had chafed.

II *fig.* †4 *v.t.* Inflame (feelings); excite. LME–E18. 5 *v.t.* & *i.* Make or become vexed or irritated; fret. LME. †6 *v.t.* Scold. LME–L17.

5 DICKENS Chafing like an angry sea, the crowd pressed after them. V. WOOLF Visitors do tend to chafe one, though impeccable as friends. K. M. E. MURRAY Furnivall appreciated the standard of James' work . . although he might chafe at his slowness. I. COLEGATE The . . horse and rider chafed to leave.

Comb.: **chafe-wax** *Hist.* an officer in Chancery who prepared the wax for sealing documents.

chafer /'tʃeɪfə/ *n.*[1] Also **†-ff-**. [OE *ċeafor*, *ċefer* = OS, (M)Du. *kever*, OHG *chevar*, *-iro*, f. Gmc: rel. to CHAFF *n.*[1], JOWL *n.*[1]] A large beetle destructive to plants; *spec.* any of a group of scarabaeid beetles including the cockchafer and the rose-chafer.

chafer /'tʃeɪfə/ *n.*[2] See also CHAUFFER. LME. [f. CHAFE *v.* + -ER[1].] 1 A vessel for heating water etc.; a portable grate or chafing-dish. LME. 2 *Hist.* = *chafe-wax* s.v. CHAFE *v.* L15.

chafery /'tʃeɪf(ə)ri/ *n.* Now *rare* or *obs.* E17. [(O)Fr. *chaufferie*, f. as CHAFE *v.*: see -ERY.] *Metall.* A small hearth or furnace for reheating and reworking wrought iron.

chafeweed *n.* var. of CHAFFWEED.

chaff /tʃɑːf, tʃaf/ *n.*[1] & *v.*[1] [OE *ċæf*, *ċeaf* = MLG, (M)Du., MHG *kaf* (G dial. *kaff*), corresp. to OHG *keva* husk, prob. f. Gmc base w. the sense 'gnaw, chew': rel. to CHAFER *n.*[1]] A *n.* 1 The husks of corn etc. separated from the grain by threshing or winnowing. OE. 2 Cut hay (and straw) used for feeding cattle. OE. 3 *transf.* Refuse, worthless stuff or residue. LME. 4 *Bot.* Thin dry bracts or scales, esp. the bracts at the base of the florets in plants of the composite family. L18. 5 Strips of metal foil released in the air to obstruct radar detection. M20.

Phrases: **be caught with chaff** be easily deceived or trapped. **separate the wheat from the chaff** *fig.* distinguish good from bad.

Comb.: **chaff-cutter** a machine for cutting hay and straw.

B *v.t.* Cut (hay etc.) for fodder. L19.

†chaff *n.*[2], *v.*[2] vars. of CHAFE *n.*, *v.*

chaff /tʃɑːf, tʃaf/ *v.*[3] & *n.*[3] E19. [Perh. var. of CHAFE *v.*] A *v.t.* Banter or rail at, usu. in a light-hearted manner. E19. B *n.* Banter, good-humoured raillery or repartee. M19.

chaffingly *adv.* L19.

chaffer /'tʃafə/ *n.*[1] ME. [f. as CHEAP *n.* + FARE *n.*[1], prob. after ON *kaupfǫr* trading-journey. In mod. use f. the vb.] 1 Orig., trade, trading. Now *spec.* haggling, bargaining, barter. ME. †2 Goods, wares. ME–L17.

†chaffer *n.*[2] var. of CHAFER *n.*[1]

chaffer /'tʃafə/ *v.* ME. [f. CHAFFER *n.*[1]] **1** *v.i.* Orig., traffic, deal, trade. Now *spec.* bargain, haggle about terms or price. ME. **b** *fig.* Bandy words, discuss terms, dispute. LME. **2** *v.t.* Orig., traffic, deal, or trade in. Now *spec.* haggle over, barter. ME.

2 †**chaffer words** bandy words.

chafferer *n.* LME.

chaffinch /'tʃafɪn(t)ʃ/ *n.* OE. [f. CHAFF *n.*[1] + FINCH.] A common European finch, *Fringilla coelebs*.

chaffron *n.* var. of CHAMFRAIN.

chaffweed /'tʃafwiːd/ *n.* In sense 1 also **chafe-** /'tʃeɪf-/. M16. [Prob. f. CHAFE *v.* + WEED *n.*[1]] †**1** Cudweed. M16–L19. **2** A pimpernel, *Anagallis minima*, with very small white or pink flowers. L18.

chaffy /'tʃɑːfi, 'tʃafi/ *a.* M16. [f. CHAFF *n.*[1] + -Y[1].] **1** Of, pertaining to, resembling, or of the nature of chaff; *spec.* (*Bot.*) paleaceous. M16. **2** *fig.* Light, empty, worthless. L16.

chafing /'tʃeɪfɪŋ/ *vbl n.* LME. [f. CHAFE *v.* + -ING[1].] The action of CHAFE *v.*

Comb.: **chafing-dish** a vessel with an outer pan of hot water for keeping warm anything placed on top of it; a dish with a spirit-lamp etc. for cooking at table.

chaft /tʃaft/ *n.* Long *obs.* exc. *Sc.* & *north.* ME. [ON (Sw. *käft*, Da. *kieft*, etc.), rel. to JOWL *n.*[1]] Jaw. Usu. in *pl.*

Chaga *n.* & *a.* var. of CHAGGA.

chagal /'tʃɑːg(ə)l/ *n.* E20. [Skt *chāgala* coming from a goat.] In the Indian subcontinent: a water-bottle, usu. of canvas or leather.

chagan /kə'gɑːn/ *n.* L18. [med.L *c(h)aganus*, in Byzantine Gk *khaganos* f. OTurk. *kağan* king, monarch: cf. CHAM *n.*, KHAN *n.*[1]] *Hist.* = KHAN *n.*[1]; *spec.* the monarch of the Avars in the 6th and 7th cents.

Chagas' disease /'tʃɑːgəs dɪˌziːz/ *n. phr.* Also **Chagas's** /'tʃɑːgəsɪz/. E20. [f. Carlos *Chagas* (1879–1934), Brazilian physician.] *Med.* A progressive form of trypanosomiasis endemic in S. and Central America, transmitted by reduviid bugs.

Chagatai /dʒagə'tʌɪ/ *n.* & *a.* Also (earlier) **J-**. M19. [Name of a dynasty founded by Chaghatai a son of Genghis Khan, which reigned in Transoxiana 1227–1358.] (Designating or pertaining to) the literary Turkic language of central Asia between the 15th and 19th cents.

Chagataian *a.* M19. **Chagataic** *a.* & *n.* M19.

Chagga /tʃagə/ *n.* & *a.* Also **Chaga**. M19. [Bantu.] **A** *n.* Pl. same, **-s**, WACHAGGA. **1** A member of a Bantu-speaking people of northern Tanzania. M19. **2** The Bantu language of this people, Kichaga. L19. **3** Coffee grown by the Wachagga; *loosely* Tanzanian coffee. M20. **B** *attrib.* or as *adj.* Of or pertaining to the Wachagga or their language. L19.

chagigah *n.pl.* see HAGIGAH.

chagrin /'ʃagrɪn/ *n.* See also SHAGREEN. M17. [Fr. lit. 'rough skin', of unkn. origin.] **I** †**1** Worry, anxiety; melancholy. M17–M19. **2** Mortification arising from disappointment or failure; acute vexation or annoyance. E18. **3** In *pl.* Troubles, vexations. M18. †**II 4** = SHAGREEN. L17–M19.

†**chagrin** *a.* M17–E18. [Fr., f. as prec.] Worried; melancholy; chagrined.

chagrin /'ʃagrɪn, ʃə'griːn/ *v.t.* M17. [Fr. *chagriner*, f. as CHAGRIN *n.*] Affect with chagrin. Usu. in *pass.*

chah *n.* var. of CHA.

chain /tʃeɪn/ *n.* ME. [OFr. *chaine*, (earlier) *chaeine* (mod. *chaîne*) f. L *catena*.] **1** A series of links (usu. metal) passing through each other, or otherwise jointed together, so as to form a strong but flexible means of connection. (Of various kinds for particular purposes etc., identified contextually or specified.) ME. **2** (A chain as) a bond or fetter; in *pl.*, fetters, bonds, confinement, captivity. ME. **b** *fig.* A thing which prevents freedom of action. LME. **3** (A chain as) a barrier obstructing the entrance to a street, harbour, etc. ME. **4** A personal ornament in the form of a chain worn around the neck; such a chain worn as a badge of office. ME. **5** *fig.* A connected series, a sequence, a set, (of material or immaterial things). LME. **b** *spec.* A sequence of geographical features (as mountains, lakes, etc.) disposed in a linear series with actual or imagined connections. L17. **c** A figure in a quadrille. M19. **d** A group of associated shops, hotels, newspapers, etc. Orig. *US.* M19. **e** *Computing.* A set of files, data, program instructions, etc., related by chaining. M20. **6** A measuring-line in land-surveying, consisting of one hundred jointed metal rods. E17. **b** A length equal to this (66 feet, approx. 20.12 m.). M17. **7** *Naut.* = *chain-plate* below. In *pl.* also, a small platform on either side of a ship from which the leadsman heaves the lead when sounding. E17. **8** The warp in weaving. E18. **9** *Hist.* In full *chain-shot*. Two half or whole cannon-balls joined by a chain, for cutting masts etc. E19. **10** A chain for fastening a door to its jamb as a security device. M19. **11** *Chem.* A number of similar atoms, usu. carbon, joined in series in a molecule. L19.

1 *albert chain, bicycle-chain, daisy-chain, guard-chain, night chain, paper chain, safety-chain, tyre-chain*, etc. *drag the chain*: see DRAG *v.* 1. 2 MILTON To bottomless perdition, there to dwell In Adamantine Chains and penal Fire. P. HENRY Is life so dear . . as to be purchased at the price of chains and slavery? *ball and chain*: see BALL *n.*[1] 3. b HAZLITT The chain of habit. 5 C. M. YONGE I tried to get them to form a chain and drench the warehouses. E. MANNIN How far back could you go in the chain of causality? *food-chain* etc. MARKOV *chain*. 11 *long chain, open chain*, etc.

Comb.: **chain-armour**: made of interlaced rings; **chain bridge** a suspension bridge on chains; **chain drive**: with transmission by endless chains; **chain-gang**: of convicts, chained together, or forced to work in chains; **chain-gear**: transmitting motion by an endless chain; **chain-letter**: of which the recipient is asked to make copies to be sent to a (named) number of others (those being asked to do the like); **chain-link** *a.* made of wire in a diamond-shaped mesh; **chain-mail** = *chain-armour* above; **chain-plate** *Naut.* a strong link or plate on a ship's side, to which the shrouds are secured; **chain printer** a line printer in which the printing types are carried on a moving endless chain; **chain-pump**: to raise water, with a series of buckets etc. usu. passing through a tube on an endless chain; **chain reaction** a series of chemical or nuclear reactions each initiated by a product of the previous reaction; *fig.* a series of events each due to the previous one; **chain-saw**: with teeth on an endless chain; *chain-shot*: see sense 9 above; **chain-smoke** *v.t.* & *i.* smoke (cigarettes etc.) continuously, esp. by lighting the next cigarette etc. from the one last smoked; **chain-smoker** a person who chain-smokes; **chain snake** a king-snake with chainlike markings; **chain-stitch** an ornamental crochet or embroidery stitch like a chain (*magic chain-stitch*: see MAGIC *a.* 3); **chain store** any of a series of shops owned by one firm and selling the same type of goods; **chain-wale** = CHANNEL *n.*[2]; **chain-wheel**: transmitting power by a chain fitted to its edges; **chain-work** (*a*) chainlike ornamental work in sculpture etc.; (*b*) interlinked metal rings in a network; (*c*) a texture formed by knitting with a single thread.

chainless *a.* E19. **chainlet** *n.* a little chain E19. **chainlike** *a.* resembling a chain in appearance or structure L18.

chain /tʃeɪn/ *v.* LME. [f. the n.] **1** *v.t.* Secure or confine with a chain (*lit.* & *fig.*). Also foll. by *up*. LME. **2** *v.t.* Obstruct or close with a chain. LME. **3** *v.t.* Measure with a (surveyor's) chain. E17. **4** *v.t.* & *i. Computing.* Link (a file etc.), be linked, with another by the inclusion in each item of an address by which a successor may be located. Chiefly as *chaining* vbl n. M20.

chaîné /ʃɛne/ *n.* M20. [Fr. = linked.] *Ballet.* A quick step or turn from one foot to another, or a series of these, performed in a line.

chained /tʃeɪnd/ *a.* M16. [f. CHAIN *n.*, *v.*: see -ED[2], -ED[1].] **1** Provided or adorned with a chain or chains. M16. **2** That has been chained. E17. **3** Of lightning: having the form of a long zigzag line. M19.

chair /tʃɛː/ *n.*[1] ME. [AN *chaere*, OFr. *chaiere* (mod. *chaire* bishop's throne etc.) f. L CATHEDRA.] **1** A separate seat for one person, of various forms, usu. with a rest for the back and more or less comfortable. ME. **b** *The* electric chair. *US.* E20. **2** A seat of authority, state, or dignity; *fig.* a place or situation of authority etc. ME. **b** The seat from which a professor etc. delivers lectures. Now chiefly *fig.*, a professorship. LME. **c** The seat of a bishop in his church; *fig.* episcopal dignity or authority. Now *arch.* or *Hist.* L15. **d** The seat of a person presiding at a meeting, public dinner, etc.; *fig.* the office of such a person; a chairman or chairwoman. M17. **e** The seat of the chief elected official of a corporate town; *fig.* the office of such an official, a mayoralty. L17. **f** A seat occupied by a Welsh bard at an Eisteddfod, *esp.* one awarded as a trophy; *fig.* a convention, now each of four, connected with the Eisteddfod. E19. **3** = SEDAN 1. *obs.* exc. *Hist.* LME. †**4** A pulpit. M17–L19. **5** Chiefly *Hist.* A kind of light chaise. M18. **6** An iron or steel socket fixed to a railway sleeper, securing a rail in place. E19.

1 *armchair, Bath chair, deck-chair, dining-chair, easy chair, elbow-chair, folding chair, garden chair, Glastonbury chair, high chair, pushchair, rocking-chair, wheelchair*, etc. *boatswain's chair*: see BOATSWAIN. *chair of estate*: see ESTATE *n.* 4. *electric chair*: see ELECTRIC *a.* *musical chairs*: see MUSICAL *a.* **take a chair** sit down. *wainscot chair*: see WAINSCOT *n.* 1. **3d be in the chair**, **take the chair** be chairman. **e past** or **above the chair**, **below the chair** (of an alderman etc.) who has, has not, been mayor.

Comb.: **chair-bed** a chair that unfolds into a bed; **chair-borne** *a.* (*colloq.*) administrative rather than active; **chair-car** a railway carriage with chairs instead of long seats, a parlour car; **chairlady** a chairwoman; **chair-lift** a series of chairs on an endless cable for carrying passengers up a mountain etc.; **chairoplane** a fairground roundabout with seats suspended on chains flung in a wide circle by the revolution of the machinery; **chair organ** = *choir organ* s.v. CHOIR *n.*; **chairperson** a chairman (of either sex) of a meeting etc.; **chairwoman** a female chairman of a meeting etc.

chair /tʃɛː/ *n.*[2] *obs.* exc. *Hist.* Also (earlier) †**char**. ME. [(O)Fr. *char*, ONFr. *charre*: see CHARIOT. Assim. to prec.] A chariot; a cart.

chair /tʃɛː/ *v.t.* M16. [f. CHAIR *n.*[1]] **1** Install in a chair, esp. one of authority. M16. **2** Place (as if) in a chair and carry aloft (the winner of a contest etc.). M18. **3** Provide with a chair or chairs. M19. **4** Act as the chairman of, preside over (a meeting). E20.

chairman /'tʃɛːmən/ *n.* Pl. **-men**. M17. [f. CHAIR *n.*[1] + MAN *n.*] **1** A person chosen to preside over a meeting; a permanent president of a committee, board of directors, firm, country, etc.; the master of ceremonies at an entertainment. M17. **2** *Hist.* **a** Either of the two sedan-bearers. L17. **b** A person who wheels a Bath chair. M18.

chairmanship *n.* the office of chairman; the action of presiding as chairman: M19.

chaise /ʃeɪz/ *n.* Pl. pronounced same. M17. [Fr., var. of *chaire* CHAIR *n.*[1]] **1** Chiefly *Hist.* A pleasure or travelling carriage, esp. a light open one for one or two people. See also POST-CHAISE. M17. **2** = CHAISE LONGUE. M20.

¶ Sense 1 sometimes taken as pl., whence sing. *chay*, SHAY *n.*[1]

chaise longue /ʃeɪz 'lɒŋ, *foreign* ʃɛːz lɔ̃ːg/ *n. phr.* Pl. **chaise longues** /ʃeɪz 'lɒŋgz/, **chaises longues** /ʃeɪz 'lɒŋ(z), *foreign* ʃɛz lɔ̃ːg/. E19. [Fr. = long chair.] A kind of sofa with a backrest at only one end.

chaise percée /ʃɛːz pɛrse/ *n. phr.* Pl. **-s -s** (pronounced same). M20. [Fr. = pierced chair.] A chair incorporating a chamber-pot.

chaises longues *n. phr.* pl. see CHAISE LONGUE.

chaises percées *n. phr.* pl. of CHAISE PERCÉE.

chaitya /'tʃʌɪtjə/ *n.* L19. [Skt *caitya* (resembling) a funeral pile, mound, etc., f. *citā* funeral mound.] A Buddhist place or object of reverence.

chak *v.* & *n.* var. of CHACK.

chakra /'tʃʌkrə/ *n.* L18. [Skt *cakra* (cogn. w. WHEEL *n.*).] **1** A thin knife-edged disc of steel formerly used as a weapon by Sikhs. L18. **2** A discus or mystic circle depicted in the hands of Hindu deities. L19. **3** *Yoga.* Each of the centres of spiritual power in the human body. L19. **4**

The circular emblem on the flag of the Indian Union. M20.

chal /tʃal/ *n.* M19. [Romany = person, fellow.] A male Gypsy. Also *Romany chal.*

chalan /tʃə'lɑːn/ *n.* M19. [Urdu *chalān, chālan* f. Pers. *čalān.*] In the Indian subcontinent: a waybill, a voucher; a draft of prisoners.

chalaza /kə'leɪzə/ *n.* Pl. **-zae** /-ziː/. E18. [mod.L f. Gk *khalaza* small knot.] **1** *Zool.* Either of two twisted membranous strands which join the yolk to the ends of an egg. E18. **2** *Bot.* The region of the ovule where the nucellus joins the integuments. M19.

chalazal *a.* (chiefly *Bot.*) M19.

chalazion /kə'leɪzɪən/ *n.* Pl / **-zia** /-zɪə/. E18. [Gk *khalazion* dim. of *khalaza*: see prec.] *Med.* A swollen, inflamed sebaceous gland in the eyelid. Also called *meibomian cyst.*

chalcanthite /kal'kanθʌɪt/ *n.* M19. [f. L *chalcanthum* f. Gk *khalkanthon*, f. *khalkos* copper + *anthos* flower: see -ITE[1].] *Min.* Native hydrated copper(II) sulphate, a blue triclinic mineral usu. occurring as tabular crystals.

Chalcedonian /kalsɪ'dəʊnɪən/ *n.* & *a.* M18. [f. *Chalcedon*, a city of ancient Bithynia, + -IAN.] **A** *n.* A person upholding the canons etc. of the ecumenical council of Chalcedon (AD 451), which were eventually accepted by all except the Monophysite Churches. M18.

B *adj.* Of or pertaining to the council of Chalcedon, its canons, etc. L18.

Chalcedonian definition the declaration that there are two natures, divine and human, in the one person of Jesus Christ.

chalcedony /kal'sɛdəni/ *n.* Also †**cal-**. LME. [L *c(h)alcedonius* f. Gk *khalkēdōn*. Cf. CASSIDONY *n.*[1]] *Min.* A fine-grained fibrous variety of quartz having many precious or semiprecious forms such as agate, onyx, cornelian, and chrysoprase.

chalce'donic *a.* E19.

chalcenterous /kal'sɛnt(ə)rəs/ *a.* M20. [f. Gk *khalkenteros*, f. *khalkos* copper, brass + *enteron* intestine: see -OUS.] With bowels of bronze; tough.

Also **chalcenteric** *a.* M20.

chalcid /'kalsɪd/ *a.* & *n.* L19. [f. mod.L *Chalcis* genus name f. Gk *khalkos* copper, brass: see -ID[3].] **A** *adj.* Of, pertaining to, or designating the superfamily Chalcidoidea of mostly parasitic hymenopterous insects, many of which have a metallic sheen. L19.

chalcid fly, wasp = sense B below.

B *n.* An insect of this superfamily. L19.

chalcidid *a.* & *n.* = CHALCID; *spec.* (an insect) of the included family Chalcididae: L19.

Chalcidian /kal'sɪdɪən/ *n.* & *a.*[1] M17. [f. L *Chalcis, Chalcid-* (see below) f. Gk *Khalkis, Khalkid-*: see -IAN.] (A native or inhabitant) of Chalcis, chief city of the Greek island of Euboea.

chalco- /'kalkəʊ/ *comb. form* of Gk *khalkos* copper, brass: see -O-.

chalcocite *n.* (*Min.*) orthorhombic copper(I) sulphide, usu. occurring as black, fine-grained masses M19. **chalco'lithic** *a.* & *n.* (*Archaeol.*) (designating or pertaining to) a brief period following the end of the Stone Age in some areas, during which copper implements were used as well as stone ones, before bronze technology was introduced E20. **chal'cophanite** *n.* [Gk *phan-* showing] *Min.* a hydrated oxide of zinc and manganese, sometimes with a bronze lustre L19. **chalcophile, -phil** *a.* & *n.* (*Geol.* & *Chem.*) (designating) an element which commonly occurs as a sulphide and is supposed to have become concentrated in the mantle E20.

chalcogen /'tʃalkədʒ(ə)n/ *n.* M20. [G *Chalkogen*, f. Gk *khalkos* in supposed sense 'ore', after *halogen*.] *Chem.* Any of the elements of group VIA of the periodic table (oxygen, sulphur, selenium, tellurium, and polonium).

chal'cogenide *n.* a binary compound of a chalcogen M20.

chalcography /kal'kɒgrəfi/ *n.* M17. [f. Gk *khalkos* copper, brass + -GRAPHY: cf. Fr. *chalcographie*.] The art of engraving on copper.

chalcographer *n.* M17. **chalco'graphic** *a.* of or pertaining to chalcography L18.

chalcopyrite /kalkə'pʌɪrʌɪt/ *n.* M19. [mod.L *chalcopyrites*, f. as CHALCO- + PYRITE.] *Min.* A tetragonal sulphide of copper and iron which is the principal ore of copper and usu. occurs as metallic brass-yellow masses. Also called *copper pyrites*.

Chaldean /kal'diːən/ *n.* & *a.* M16. [f. L *Chaldaeus* f. Gk *Khaldaios* masc., *Khaldaia* fem. (also as n. (sc. *gē* earth) Chaldea), f. Assyr. *kaldū*: see -AN.] **A** *n.* **1** A native or inhabitant of ancient Chaldea or Babylonia; *transf.* a person skilled in occult matters, an astrologer. M16. **2** The language of the Chaldeans. L17. **B** *adj.* Of or pertaining to Chaldea, its inhabitants or their language; occult. E17.

Also **Chaldaic** /kal'deɪɪk/ *a.* M17.

Chaldee /kal'diː, 'kaldiː/ *n.* & *a.* LME. [L *Chaldaei* (pl.) Chaldeans, (sing.) Chaldea, f. as prec.] **A** *n.* **1** = CHALDEAN *n.* 1. LME. **2** = CHALDEAN *n.* 2. Also, Aramaic as used in books of the Bible. LME. **B** *adj.* = CHALDEAN *a.* L17.

chalder /'tʃɔːldə/ *n.* Chiefly *Sc.* & *north.* Now *arch.* or *Hist.* ME. [(O)Fr. *chaudière*: see next.] A dry measure of capacity (of variable magnitude) for various materials, esp. coal, lime, grain, etc. Cf. CHALDRON *n.*[1] 2.

chaldron /'tʃɔːldrən/ *n.*[1] M16. [OFr. *chauderon* (mod. *chaudron*) augm. of *chaud(i)ère* f. late L *cal(i)darium* cooking-pot: see -OON. Cf. CAULDRON.] †**1** = CAULDRON. M16–M18. **2** A dry measure of capacity (cf. prec.). Now only *spec.* a measure for coals of approximately 36 bushels. E17.

†**chaldron** *n.*[2] var. of CHAWDRON.

chalet /'ʃaleɪ/ *n.* L18. [Swiss Fr., dim. of OFr. *chasel* farmstead f. Proto-Romance deriv. of L *casa* hut, cottage.] A Swiss mountain cowherd's hut; a Swiss peasant's wooden cottage; a house with a widely overhanging roof; a small villa; a small house in a holiday camp etc.

chalice /'tʃalɪs/ *n.* OE. [OFr., or its source L CALIX, *-ic-*.] **1** A drinking-cup, a goblet; the contents of this. Now *poet.* OE. **2** *spec.* The cup used in the administration of the Eucharist. OE. **3** The calyx of a flower. M17.

1 *poisoned chalice*: see POISON *v.* 2.

Comb.: **chalice vine** a solandra, *Solandra maxima*, grown for ornament in the tropics.

chaliced *a.* having cuplike blossom; contained in a chalice: E17.

chalicothere /'kalɪkəθɪə/ *n.* E20. [f. mod.L *Chalicotherium* genus name, f. Gk *khalik-, khalix* gravel + *thērion* wild animal.] *Palaeont.* A perissodactyl of the extinct family Chalicotheriidae, similar to a horse but with clawed feet.

chalifa *n.* see KHALIFA.

chalk /tʃɔːk/ *n.* [OE *ċealc* = OS *calc* (Du. *kalk*), OHG *kalk* (G *kalk*), f. WGmc f. L CALX, *calc-*.] †**1** Lime. (*rare* after OE.) OE–L16. **2** A white soft earthy limestone consisting almost wholly of calcite. OE. **3** This or a substance of like texture or properties in prepared form, as for use in crayons for drawing, for writing on a blackboard, for rubbing on the tip of a billiards-cue, etc. L15. **b** A piece or crayon of chalk. E19. **4** A mark, line, or score made with chalk; *spec.* (*a*) such a mark formerly used to record credit in a public house etc.; *arch.* a running account, credit; (*b*) (such a mark recording) a point scored in a game. E16. **5** Any of various earths resembling chalk (sense 2). Usu. w. specifying wd. E17. **6** *Geol.* A deposit or stratum composed mainly of chalk; *spec.* (**C-**) (the deposits of) the Upper Cretaceous system of western Europe. E19.

Phrases: **as different as chalk and** (or **from**) **cheese** unlike in the essentials. **by a long chalk, by long chalks** by far, by a long way. **chalk and talk** teaching by traditional methods (employing blackboard, chalk, and dialogue). *French chalk*: see FRENCH *a. red chalk*: see RED *a. Venetian chalk*: see VENETIAN *a. walk the chalk*: see WALK *v.*[1]

Attrib. & *comb.*: In the sense 'made up or consisting (largely) of chalk', as *chalk cliff, down*, etc. In the sense 'drawn with chalk, executed in chalk', as *chalk drawing, head*, etc. Special combs., as **chalkboard** *N. Amer.* a blackboard; **chalkhill blue** a lycaenid butterfly of chalk grassland, *Lysandra coridon*; **chalk-line** a line drawn in chalk; *walk a chalk-line* (fig.), behave with propriety, keep to a course of action or set of rules; **chalk-pit** a quarry in which chalk is dug; **chalk-stone** a concretion of urates like chalk found in tissues and joints, esp. those of the hands and feet; **chalk-stripe, -striped** *a.* (having) a pattern of thin white stripes on a dark background; **chalk talk** *US* a talk, lecture, etc. in which the speaker uses blackboard and chalk.

chalk /tʃɔːk/ *v.t.* L15. [f. the n.] **1** Rub, mark, or inscribe (a surface) with chalk. L15. **2** Mix or treat with chalk. L16. **3** Write, draw, or record with chalk. (Foll. by *down, out, up*, etc.) L16.

With advs. in specialized senses: **chalk out** sketch, plan as a thing to be accomplished; (see also sense 3 above). **chalk up** charge, attribute, (*to* a person, account, experience, etc.); register (a success etc.); (see also sense 3 above).

chalky /'tʃɔːki/ *a.* LME. [f. CHALK *n.* + -Y[1].] Having much chalk; resembling chalk, esp. in whiteness; like or containing chalk-stones.

chalkiness *n.* E19.

challenge /'tʃalɪn(d)ʒ/ *n.* ME. [OFr. *c(h)alenge* f. L *calumnia* CALUMNY *n.*] †**1** An accusation, a reproach, an objection. ME–L17. †**2** A (false) claim; the act of demanding as a right. ME–M18. **3** An invitation or summons to take part in a trial or contest, *spec.* (*a*) to a duel, (*b*) to a sporting contest, esp. one issued to the reigning champion; a test of one's abilities, a demanding or difficult task. ME. **4** A call to respond; *esp.* a sentry's demand for a password etc. LME. **5** *Law.* An exception taken, to a person or thing; *spec.* an objection made to a juror. LME. **6** A calling in question; the state of being called in question. E19. **7** *Immunol.* A dose of antigen given to a previously exposed person or animal in order to detect immunity or hypersensitivity. M20.

3 R. LYND My challenge to any of the great leaders of the Christian churches . . to come and debate the question of religion and free thought. D. ACHESON The tremendous challenge of his post, and the problems he faced. E. LONGFORD The Martyrs' Memorial . . an occasional challenge to the climbing skills of students. 4 E. BLUNDEN I heard the challenge 'Who goes there?' 5 *peremptory challenge*: see PEREMPTORY *a.* 1. *principal challenge*: see PRINCIPAL *a.* 6 SIR W. SCOTT Schemes . . for bringing her title into challenge.

challenge /'tʃalɪn(d)ʒ/ *v.* ME. [OFr. *c(h)alengier* f. L *calumniari*: see CALUMNIATE *v.*] **I** *v.t.* †**1** Accuse, bring a charge against; bring as a charge. ME–L17. **2a** Reprove; call to account. *obs.* exc. *Sc.* ME. **b** (Of a sentry etc.) ask (a person) for a password etc.; call to respond (*lit.* & *fig.*). L18. **3a** Lay claim to, demand as a right. (Foll. by †*that*, †*to do*.) *arch.* ME. **b** Have a natural right or claim to, call for, (now *spec.* a responsive action or recognition, as attention, admiration, etc.). LME. **4** Invite or summon to take part in a trial, contest, duel, discussion, etc.; dare, defy; present a challenge to; stimulate. (Foll. by *to, to do*.) LME. **b** Invite (emulous, hostile, or critical action of any kind). E17. **5** Call into question; dispute, deny. LME. **6** *Law.* Take exception or object to (a juror, evidence, etc.). L16. **7** *Immunol.* Give a dose that constitutes a challenge to (a person, an animal). M20.

1 P. SIDNEY To be challenged of unkindness. 2a OED I have never been challenged for crossing these fields. b E. HEMINGWAY Orders to challenge all travellers and ask to see their papers. 3a T. HERBERT I challenge no thanks for what I publish. b T. BROWN Horace and Juvenal . . challenge a superiority above all the rest. 4 MILTON I . . challenge Dagon to the test. C. KINGSLEY He challenges all comers to wrestle with him. J. DICKEY A bad road always challenged him. J. ARCHER Inside the two-furlong marker—Highclere and Rosalie move up to challenge Buoy. b J. H. BLUNT Challenging controversy in every possible way. 5 T. H. HUXLEY I do not presume to challenge its wisdom.

II *v.i.* **8** Issue a challenge to a duel etc. (*arch.*); present a challenge, offer interesting difficulties. LME. †**9** Make or have a claim. *rare* (Shakes.). Only in E17. **10** *Hunting.* Of a hound: give tongue on finding a scent. L17. **11** *Law.* Take exception, object. L19.

challengeable *a.* LME. **challenger** *n.* LME.

challenging /ˈtʃalɪn(d)ʒɪŋ/ *ppl a.* M19. [f. CHALLENGE *v.* + -ING².] That challenges; *spec.* that presents a test of one's abilities.

challengingly *adv.* E20.

challis /ˈʃalɪs, ˈʃali/ *n.* M19. [Perh. f. the surname *Challis*.] A lightweight soft clothing fabric of silk and worsted.

chalon /ˈʃalən/ *n.* Long *obs.* exc. *Hist.* ME. [App. f. *Châlons*-sur-Marne in NE France: cf. SHALLOON.] A blanket or coverlet for a bed.

chaloner *n.* a maker of chalons ME.

chalone /ˈkaləʊn, ˈkeɪ-/ *n.* E20. [f. Gk *khalōn* pres. pple of *khalaō* slacken, after HORMONE.] *Physiol.* A substance secreted like a hormone but having the effect of inhibiting a bodily process; *spec.* an inhibitor of mitosis in particular tissues.

chaˈlonic *a.* E20.

chaloupe *n.* var. of SHALLOP.

chalumeau /ʃalymo/ *n.* Pl. ***-eaux*** /-o/. E18. [Fr. f. late L *calamellus* dim. of *calamus* reed.] A musical pipe of reed or straw; an instrument having a reed mouthpiece, *esp.* the forerunner of the clarinet. Also (in full *chalumeau register*), the lowest register of the clarinet.

Chalybean /kalɪˈbiːən, *in Milton* kəˈlɪbɪən/ *a.* *rare.* L17. [f. L *chalybeius* of steel, of the Chalybes (see below), f. *chalybs*: see next, -AN.] Pertaining to the Chalybes, an ancient people of Asia Minor famous for their skill in working iron.

¶First recorded in Milton.

chalybeate /kəˈlɪbɪət/ *a.* & *n.* M17. [mod.L *chalybeatus*, f. L *chalybs* f. Gk *khalub-*, *khalups* steel: see -ATE².] (A mineral water, a spring, etc.) impregnated with iron salts.

†chalybeate *v.t.* L16–E18. [f. as prec. + -ATE³.] Impregnate with iron salts.

chalybite /ˈkalɪbʌɪt/ *n.* M19. [f. Gk *khalub-*, *khalups* steel + -ITE¹.] *Min.* Siderite (native ferrous carbonate).

cham /kam/ *n.* LME. [Fr. *cham*, *chan* f. Turkic *kān* KHAN *n.*¹ Cf. CHAGAN, KHAN *n.*¹] = KHAN *n.*¹ Now only *transf.* & *fig.*, an autocrat, a dominant critic etc. (applied esp. to Samuel Johnson).

SMOLLETT That great Cham of literature, Samuel Johnson.

cham /tʃam/ *v.* Long *obs.* exc. *dial.* Infl. **-mm-**. LME. [Prob. imit.: cf. CHAMP *v.*] 1 *v.i.* & *t.* = CHAMP *v.* 1, 2. LME. 2 *v.t.* = CHAMP *v.* 3. Chiefly *Sc.* E16.

chama /ˈkeɪmə/ *n.* M18. [L f. Gk *khēmē* cockle.] A sessile bivalve mollusc of the genus *Chama*, with rough, irregular valves, found in warm or tropical seas.

chamade /ʃəˈmɑːd/ *n.* L17. [Fr. f. Port. *chamada*, f. *chamar* f. L *clamare*: see CLAIM *v.*, -ADE 1.] *Mil. Hist.* A signal by beat of drum or sound of trumpet inviting to a parley.

Chamaeleon *n.* see CHAMELEON.

chamaephyte /ˈkamɪfʌɪt/ *n.* E20. [f. Gk *khamai* low, on the ground + -PHYTE.] *Bot.* A plant which bears buds on or near the ground.

chamar /tʃəˈmɑː/ *n.* Also **chu-**. M19. [Hind. *camār*.] A member of a low Hindu caste whose traditional occupation is leather-working; a tanner, a shoemaker.

chamber /ˈtʃeɪmbə/ *n.* & *v.* ME. [(O)Fr. *chambre* f. L CAMERA.] A *n.* 1 An apartment in a house or other place of residence, a private room, *esp.* a bedroom. Now *arch.* or *poet.* exc. in *comb.* & as in sense b below. ME. b In *pl.* A set of rooms in a larger building, esp. in the Inns of Court, let separately. Also, a judge's room for hearing cases, or for other official proceedings, out of court. M17. 2 (A hall used by) a deliberative or judicial body; *esp.* each of the houses of a parliament. LME. 3 The hangings or furniture of a chamber. Now *rare* or *obs.* LME. 4 The treasury of a government, corporation, etc. Now *arch.* or *Hist.* LME. 5 A cavity in the body of an animal or plant. LME. †6a A detached charge piece put into the breech of a gun. LME–M19. b A piece of ordnance standing on its breech, used to fire salutes etc. M16–M18. †7 A kingdom's chief city etc.; a royal residence; a royal port. M16–L17. 8 A relatively spacious underground hollow or section of such a hollow (dug out by an animal etc. or as a natural formation). L16. b *Mining.* A large well-defined deposit of ore. L19. 9 A part of a firearm in which a charge is placed, as a space in the bore of old ordnance, each of the bores of an early revolver, (each section of) the cartridge compartment of a modern revolver, etc. L16. 10 *gen.* A space, cavity, or room constructed for various purposes (specified or identified contextually); an enclosed space or compartment in a structure, mechanism, etc. M18. 11 A chamber-pot. L19.

1 *audience-chamber*, *bedchamber*, *guest-chamber*, *presence chamber*, etc. **†chamber of dais, deas** *Sc.* a parlour, a best bedroom. *robe de chambre*: see ROBE *n.*¹ 2 *council-chamber*, *Star Chamber*, etc. **Chamber of Commerce** an association to promote and protect the interests of local commerce. *Lower Chamber*: see LOWER *a.* *privy chamber*: see PRIVY *a.* *Red Chamber*: see RED *a.* *second chamber*: see SECOND *a.* SYNDICAL *chamber*. 5 P. PARISH The volume of blood in the heart chambers. 8 F. HOYLE Although the cave is nearly 300 metres long, most of the paintings are in a chamber 18 by 9 metres. 10 *bubble chamber*, *cloud chamber*, *decompression chamber*, *fume-chamber*, *gas chamber*, *spark chamber*, etc. *Chamber of Horrors*: see HORROR *n.* *lethal chamber*: see LETHAL *a.* *torture chamber*: see TORTURE *n.*

Comb.: **chamber concert** a concert of chamber music; **†chamber-council** a private concern; **chamber-deacon** *Hist.* a poor clerk, esp. from Ireland, frequenting an English university in the 15th cent. and not belonging to any college or hall; **chamber-fellow** *arch.* one who shares a room or rooms with another; **chamber-lye** (*obs.* exc. *dial.*) urine, esp. as formerly used for washing; **chambermaid** (*a*) a housemaid, esp. one in a hotel etc. who attends to the bedrooms; †(*b*) a lady's maid; **chamber music** music for a small group of instruments, particularly fitted for performance in a private room or a small hall; **chamber orchestra** a small orchestra; **chamber organ** a positive organ; an organ for domestic use, developed from the positive organ; **chamber-pot** a receptacle for urine etc., for use in a bedroom or by a young child; **chamber-tomb** *Archaeol.* a chambered tomb.

B *v.* I *v.t.* 1 Place or shut (*up*) in or as in a chamber; *fig.* (*arch.*) restrain (one's words etc.). LME. 2 Provide with a chamber or chambers; form into a chamber or chambers. E17. 3 Hold in or as in a chamber. M19. II *v.i.* 4 Behave wantonly or lewdly. Long *arch.* E16.

chambered *a.* furnished with, formed into, or confined within a chamber or chambers; *Archaeol.* (of a tomb) containing one or more burial chambers: LME. **chamberlet** *n.* a small chamber M19.

chamberer /ˈtʃeɪmb(ə)rə/ *n.* *arch.* ME. [AN *chamb(e)rer(e* = OFr. *chamb(e)rier*, *-ière* (mod. *chambrier*, *-ière* chambermaid), f. as prec.: see -ER².] †1 A chambermaid; a personal attendant, a valet. ME–E18. 2 A person who frequents ladies' chambers; a gallant. E17.

chamberlain /ˈtʃeɪmbəlɪn/ *n.* ME. [OFr. *chamberlain*, *-lenc* (mod. *chambellan*) f. Frank. (whence med.L *camerlingus*), f. OS *kamera* f. L CAMERA: see -LING¹.] 1 A personal attendant of a king or nobleman in his bedroom (now *arch.* or *Hist.*). Also, an officer managing the private chambers or household of a monarch, noble, etc. ME. 2 A steward; an officer appointed to receive revenue etc.; *esp.* the treasurer of a corporation etc. LME. †3 An attendant at an inn, in charge of the bedrooms. M16–E19.

1 **Lord Chamberlain (of the Household)** the head of management of the royal household, formerly the licenser of plays for performance. **Lord Great Chamberlain (of England)** the hereditary holder of a ceremonial office, whose responsibilities include attendance on the monarch at a coronation.

chamberlainship *n.* the position or office of chamberlain LME.

Chambertin /ˈʃɒbətã, *foreign* ʃɑ̃bɛrtɛ̃/ *n.* L18. [The vineyard of origin, in the Côte de Nuits, eastern France.] A fine French red burgundy wine; a drink of this.

Chambéry /ˈʃɒ̃bəriː, *foreign* ʃɑ̃beri/ *n.* M20. [The town of origin, in SE France.] A dry French vermouth; a drink of this.

†chamblet *n.* & *v.* var. of CAMLET.

chambranle /ʃɑ̃brɑ̃ːl/ *n.* Pl. pronounced same. E18. [Fr.] *Archit.* An ornamental bordering around a door, window, or fireplace.

chambray /ˈʃambreɪ/ *n.* & *a.* Orig. *US.* E19. [Irreg. f. *Cambrai* (see CAMBRIC).] (Made of) a type of gingham with white weft and coloured warp.

chambré /ˈʃɒmbreɪ, *foreign* ʃɑ̃bre/ *a.* M20. [Fr., pa. pple of *chambrer*, f. as CHAMBER.] Of wine: at room temperature. Usu. *pred.*

†chambrel *n.* see CAMBREL.

chameleon /kəˈmiːlɪən/ *n.* & *a.* Also **†cam-**, (in sense 4) **-mael-**. ME. [L *chamaeleon* f. Gk *khamaileōn*, f. *khamai* on the ground + *leōn* lion.] A *n.* 1 Any of numerous small lizards of the Old World family Chamaeleontidae, with prehensile tails and the ability to change colour according to their surroundings. ME. b An anole or other lizard able to change colour. *N. Amer.* L18. †2 *Bot.* Either of two plants of the composite family native to southern Europe, *Atractylis gummifera* (more fully *white chameleon*) and *Cardopatium corymbosum* (more fully *black chameleon*). E16–E18. 3 *fig.* Someone or something inconstant or variable. L16. 4 (Usu. **C-**.) (The name of) an inconspicuous circumpolar constellation of the southern hemisphere. Also *the Chameleon*. L17. †5 *Chem.* Potassium manganate, K_2MnO_4 (so called from the gradual change in colour of a solution from green to purple on exposure to air). Also *mineral chameleon*. Only in 19. B *attrib.* or as *adj.* = CHAMELEONIC. L16.

chameleˈonic *a.* chameleon-like E19. **chameleon-like** *a.* resembling a chameleon; inconstant: L16.

chametz *n.* var. of HAMETZ.

chamfer /ˈtʃamfə/ *v.* & *n.* M16. [Back-form. f. next.] A *v.t.* 1 Cut a channel or groove in; flute; furrow. *arch.* M16. 2 Bevel (a right-angled edge or corner) symmetrically. L17. B *n.* †1 A small groove, channel, etc. E17–E18. 2 A surface produced by bevelling a right-angled edge or corner symmetrically. M19.

chamfering /ˈtʃamf(ə)rɪŋ/ *n.* M16. [f. Fr. *chamfrain*, f. *chant* edge (see CANT *n.*¹) + *fraint* pa. pple of *fraindre* f. L *frangere* break: assim. to -ING¹.] †1 Grooving, a groove, in wood, stone, etc. M16–E18. 2 The bevelling of a right-angled edge or corner symmetrically; a surface so produced. M18.

chamfrain /ˈtʃamfreɪn/ *n.* *arch.* Also **chaffron** /ˈtʃafrən/, **chamfron** /ˈtʃamfrən/. LME. [(O)Fr. *chamfrein*, perh. f. OFr. *chafresner* (= Prov. *capfrenar*) put on a bridle, f. *chef* head (see CHIEF *n.*) + *frein* f. L *frenum* bridle, bit.] The frontlet of a barded horse. Also, a piece of armour for a horse's face.

chamiso /tʃəˈmiːsəʊ/ *n.* Pl. **-os**. M19. [Mex. Sp.] An evergreen shrub of the rose family, *Adenostoma fasciculatum*, native to California.

†chamlet *n.* & *v.* see CAMLET.

chamois /ˈʃamwɑː; *in sense 2 of n., adj., usu.* ˈʃami/ *n.* & *a.* Pl. of n. same /ˈʃamwɑːz, ˈʃamɪz/. Sense 2 of n., adj., also **shammy** /ˈʃami/, (now *rare*) **shamoy** /ˈʃamɔɪ, ˈʃami/. M16. [(O)Fr., prob. ult. f. Swiss Proto-Romance Cf. Gallo-L *camox*.] A *n.* 1 A goatlike antelope, *Rupicapra rupicapra*, found in the mountains of Europe and Asia Minor. M16. 2 More fully *chamois leather*. Soft pliable leather from the chamois or (now more usu.) from sheep, goats, deer, etc.; a piece of this for polishing etc. L16. B *attrib.* or as *adj.* 1 Made of chamois leather. E17. 2 Of the colour of chamois leather; yellowish brown. M17.

chamois /ˈʃamwɑː, ˈʃami/ *v.* Also (esp. sense 3) **shammy** /ˈʃami/, (esp. sense 2) **shamoy** /ˈʃamɔɪ, ˈʃami/. E17. [Fr. *chamoiser*, f. as prec.] †1 *v.t.* Make out of chamois leather. *rare.* Only in E17. 2 *v.i.* & *t.* Prepare (leather, a skin) in imitation of true chamois leather. M18. 3 *v.t.* Polish etc. with a chamois leather. M20.

†chamoisite *n.* see CHAMOSITE.

chamomile *n.* var. of CAMOMILE.

chamosite /ˈʃaməzʌɪt/ *n.* Orig. **†chamois-**. M19. [f. *Chamo(i)son*, a locality in Switzerland + -ITE¹.] *Min.* A greenish-grey or black clay mineral that is a monoclinic aluminosilicate of iron and occurs in oolitic and other bedded iron ores.

chamo'sitic *a.* M20.

†champ *n.*[1] ME. [(O)Fr. f. L *campus*: see CAMP *n.*[2]] 1 A field, esp. of battle. ME–E19. 2 A ground in embroidery, painting, etc. ME–L16.

1 **champ clos** an enclosure for a judicial duel or tourney.

champ /tʃamp/ *n.*[2] E17. [f. CHAMP *v.*] A champing action or noise.

champ /tʃamp/ *n.*[3] M19. [Hind. *cāp̃* CHAMPAC.] The timber of the champac.

champ /tʃamp/ *n.*[4] *colloq.* M19. [Abbrev.] = CHAMPION *n.*[1] 3.

champ /tʃamp/ *v.* LME. [Prob. imit.: cf. CHAM *v.*, CHOMP.] 1 *v.i.* Make a noisy biting or chewing action (esp., of a horse etc., *at*, *on* the bit). LME. 2 *v.t.* a Munch (fodder etc.) noisily. M16. b Bite noisily on (something hard); *esp.* (of a horse etc.) work (the bit) noisily in the teeth. L16. 3 *v.t.* Mash, pound; crush under foot. *Sc.* L18.

1 **champing at the bit** *fig.* restlessly impatient to begin.

champer *n.* L16.

champac /'tʃʌmpək, 'tʃam-/ *n.* Also **chempaka** /'tʃɛmpəkə/ & other vars. L18. [Skt *campaka*, Malay *cempaka*.] A southern Asian evergreen tree, *Michelia champaca*, of the magnolia family, which bears fragrant orange-coloured flowers and is sacred to Hindus and Buddhists. Also occas. applied to other trees with fragrant flowers.

champagne /ʃam'peɪn, *attrib.* 'ʃampeɪn/ *n.* M17. [*Champagne* (see below) f. as next.] 1 (A) wine from Champagne, a region (formerly a province) of NE France; *esp.* (a) naturally sparkling white wine from Champagne or elsewhere; *loosely* (a) sparkling white wine; a drink of any of these. M17. 2 *fig.* Something exhilarating or excellent. L19. 3 A pale straw colour. L19.

1 *oeil-de-perdrix champagne*: see OEIL-DE-PERDRIX 2. *pink champagne*: see PINK *a.*[2] 2 C. FRANCIS Its delicate flavour has earned it the description 'the champagne of teas'.

Comb.: **champagne breakfast**, **supper**, etc.: at which champagne is served; **Champagne Charley**, **Charlie** any noted (male) champagne-drinker.

cham'pagn(e)y *a.* resembling champagne or its exhilarating qualities M19.

champaign /'tʃampeɪn/ *n.* & *a.* Now chiefly *literary*. Also **-ain**, **†-ian**, **†-ion**. LME. [(O)Fr. *champagne* f. late L *campania* use as n. of fem. sing. & neut. pl. of *campanius* adj., f. L *campus*: see CAMP *n.*[2] Cf. CAMPAGNA, CAMPAIGN.] A *n.* 1 (An expanse of) level open country. LME. †2 The field of battle; a battlefield. LME–M19. †3 Unenclosed or common land. M16–M17. 4 *fig.* A field of enquiry, observation, etc.; a sphere of operation. L16. B *attrib.* or as *adj.* †1 Of, pertaining to, or designating unenclosed or common land. LME–E18. 2 Of, pertaining to, or designating level open country. E16.

†champain *n.*[1] M16–E18. [Cf. Fr. *champagne* lower third of the shield.] *Her.* An embattled line but with the top and bottom of each division pointed instead of square.

champain *n.*[2] var. of CHAMPAIGN.

champers /'ʃampəz/ *n. slang.* M20. [f. CHAMPAGNE: see -ER[6].] Champagne.

champerty /'tʃampəːti/ *n.* LME. [AN *champartie*, f. (O)Fr. *champart* the feudal lord's share of the produce, f. L *campus* (see CAMP *n.*[2]) + *pars* PART *n.*] †1 Partnership in power. LME–M16. 2 *Law.* The action of assisting a party in a suit in which one is not naturally interested, with a view to receiving a share of the disputed property (an offence in the US and formerly in Britain). LME. b An act or (now *US*) case of champerty. LME. 3 *fig.* A combination for an evil purpose. Now *rare.* E17.

champertor *n.* (now *rare*) a person engaged in champerty E16. **champertous** *a.* (*rare*) of the nature of champerty M17.

†champian *n.* & *a.* var. of CHAMPAIGN.

champignon /tʃam'pɪnjən, 'ʃampɪnjɒ̃; *foreign* ʃɑ̃piɲɔ̃ (*pl. same*)/ *n.* Also **†-inion**. L16. [Fr. (earlier *champaignon*), dim. of *champagne*: see CHAMPAIGN.] A mushroom; a toadstool. Now *spec.* (*a*) the edible field mushroom *Agaricus campestris*; (*b*) an agaric, *Marismius oreades*, which often forms fairy-rings.

champion /'tʃampɪən/ *n.*[1], *a.*[1], & *adv.* ME. [(O)Fr. f. med.L *campio(n-)*, f. L *campus* CAMP *n.*[2] Cf. CAMP *n.*[1]] A *n.* 1 A fighting man; a stout fighter. *arch.* ME. 2 A person who fights, argues, etc., on behalf of another or for a cause. ME. 3 An athlete, boxer, etc., who has defeated all competitors; an overall winner of a series of competitions; an animal, a plant, etc., adjudged to be superior to all others in a show. E18.

2 J. R. ACKERLEY A formidable champion of the rights of her own sex. 3 G. GREEN West Germany became the world champions against all the odds.

Phrases: **King's Champion, Queen's Champion, champion of England** a hereditary official who offers to defend a new monarch's title to the crown at his or her coronation. *seven champions*: see SEVEN *a.*

B *adj.* That is a champion (esp. sense 3); that has been adjudged to be superior in competition; *colloq.* first-rate, splendid. E19.

J. M. SYNGE They're cheering a young lad, the champion playboy of the Western World. K. A. PORTER An English bulldog of champion stock.

C *adv.* Splendidly. *colloq.* & *dial.* E20.

W. DEEPING We get on champion.

championess *n.* (now *rare*) a female champion L16. **championship** *n.* (*a*) the position or title of champion in a competition; a competition for this; (*b*) advocacy, defence: E19.

†champion *n.*[2] & *a.*[2] var. of CHAMPAIGN.

champion /'tʃampɪən/ *v.t.* E17. [f. CHAMPION *n.*[1]] †1 Challenge to a contest. *rare.* E17–E19. 2 Support the cause of; argue in favour of; defend. E19.

champlevé /'ʃampləveɪ, *foreign* ʃɑ̃ləve/ *a.* & *n.* M19. [Fr., f. *champ* field + *levé* raised.] (Enamel-work) in which hollows made in the surface are filled with enamel colours.

chance /tʃɑːns/ *n.*, *adv.*, & *a.* ME. [AN *ch(e)aunce*, OFr. *chëance*, (mod. *chance*), f. *chëoir* fall, befall, f. Proto-Romance var. of L *cadere* fall.] A *n.* 1 The way things happen of themselves; the absence of design or discoverable cause; the course of events regarded as a power; fortune, fate. ME. †b *One's* fortune or lot. ME–E18. 2 An event that is without apparent cause or unexpected; a casual circumstance; an accident. ME. 3 An opportunity, as of escape, of dismissing a batsman in cricket, of scoring a goal in football, etc. ME. 4 A possibility, a probability. Freq. in *pl.* L18.

1 W. C. BRYANT The chance of war Is equal, and the slayer oft is slain. W. PLOMER It was pure chance that was now to bring us together. 2 A. MCCOWEN By a happy chance [I] got a job almost immediately. D. ADAMS He hadn't done it deliberately, it was just a random chance. 3 BURKE A change of climate is his only chance. L. URIS I didn't even get a chance to tell you that your brother forgives you. 4 E. HEMINGWAY The train was full and I knew there was no chance of a place. S. SASSOON The chances are about five to one against my ever using it.

Phrases: **by any chance** (in interrog. contexts) as is (just) possible. **by chance** as it happens or happened; without design or discoverable cause. **game of chance**: decided by luck not skill. *leave nothing to chance*: see LEAVE *v.*[1] *long chance*: see LONG *a.*[1] *main chance*: see MAIN *a.* *not a chance in hell*: see HELL *n.* *not a snowball's chance (in hell)*: see SNOWBALL *n.* 1. *off chance*: see OFF *prep.* & *adv.* **on the chance** in view of the possibility (*of*, *that*). *sporting chance*: see SPORTING *ppl a.* 3. *stand a chance*: see STAND *v.* **take a, one's, chance (on, with)** let things go as they may, consent to take what comes (as regards). **take a chance, take chances** behave riskily. *the chance of a lifetime*: see LIFETIME 1. **(the) chances are that** *colloq.* the likelihood is that. *the main chance*: see MAIN *a.* *treble chance*: see TREBLE *a.*

B *adv.* By chance. *arch.* M16.

C *adj.* That occurs or is by chance; casual, incidental. L17.

G. GREENE I had spoilt the occasion suddenly by a chance word. L. DURRELL I was something more than a chance traveller, . . I planned to stay in the island.

chanceful *a.* (*arch.*) (*a*) casual, accidental; (*b*) unpredictable, eventful: L16. **chancefully** *adv.* (*arch. rare*) †(*a*) unfortunately; (*b*) in a chanceful manner: ME.

chance /tʃɑːns/ *v.* LME. [f. the n.] 1 *v.i.* Happen without design or discoverable cause. (With the event as subj. (†& the person or thing affected as indirect obj.); impers. subj. (esp. *it*) & *that* the event; the person or thing affected as subj. (†or indirect obj. w. impers. subj.) & *to do* the event.) LME. b Come *on*, *upon*, *across*, etc., by chance. M16. †2 *v.i.* Fare, have luck (of a specified kind). LME–M16. 3 *v.t.* Risk. *colloq.* M19.

1 SPENSER Him chaunst to meete . . A faithlesse Sarazin. M. TWAIN If it so chance that we be separated, let each make for London Bridge. H. JAMES An occasion chanced to present itself. TOLKIEN They fell silent, wondering what would chance. D. MURPHY My mother chanced to be passing. **†how chance . . ?** how is (or was) it that . . ? b SAKI The first crossing-sweeper . . she chanced across. J. G. COZZENS Mr. Hurst's librarian chanced on it in a completely forgotten portfolio. 3 R. RENDELL Occupants . . could come and go without . . chancing an encounter with porters. **chance one's arm** take one's (possibly slight) chance of doing something successfully.

chanceable *a.* (long *arch.*) happening by or subject to chance M16. **chancer** *n.* (*slang*) a person who takes chances or does risky things L19.

chancel /'tʃɑːns(ə)l/ *n.* ME. [OFr. (mod. *cancel*) f. L *cancelli* (pl.) dim. of *cancer* lattice, perh. dissimilated form of *carcer* barrier, prison.] A part of a church near the altar, reserved for the clergy, choir, etc., and usu. enclosed.

chancellery /'tʃɑːns(ə)l(ə)ri, -slɘri/ *n.* Also **-ory**; **-elry** /-(ə)lri/. ME. [(O)Fr. *chancellerie*, f. *chancelier*: see next, -ERY.] 1 The position of a chancellor. ME. 2 The department, staff, or office of a chancellor. L17. 3 An office attached to an embassy or consulate. M19.

chancellor /'tʃɑːns(ə)lə/ *n.* LOE. [AN *c(h)anceler*, OFr. *c(h)ancelier*, f. late L *cancellarius* porter, secretary, f. *cancelli* (see CHANCEL) + *-arius* -ER[2].] 1 *gen.* A secretary (of a king, foreign ruler, etc.). *obs.* exc. *Hist.* LOE. 2 A high-ranking State or law official of various kinds (specified by title or contextually identified). LOE. 3 A titular head of a university, now usu. an honorary office, the actual duties being performed by a vice-chancellor. ME. 4 A foreman of a Scottish jury. Now *rare.* L15. 5 One of the four chief dignitaries in cathedrals of old foundation; a bishop's law officer. L16. 6 An officer of an order of knighthood who seals commissions etc. L16. 7 A chief minister of a European State, now only of the Federal Republic of Germany and of Austria. E17. 8 The president of a chancery court. *US.* M18.

2 **Chancellor of England** *Hist.* = *Lord Chancellor* below, before the Union with Scotland. **Chancellor of the Duchy of Lancaster** the representative of the Crown as Duke of Lancaster, now a member of the British (earlier English) government, often a Cabinet Minister employed on non-departmental work. **Chancellor of the Exchequer** the finance minister of the United Kingdom (earlier of England or Great Britain), orig. an official with custody of the seal of the exchequer. **Lord (High) Chancellor** the highest judicial officer of the United Kingdom (earlier of England or Great Britain), keeper of the great seal, now presiding over the House of Lords, the Chancery Division, and the Court of Appeal. 6 *Chancellor of (the Order of) the Garter* etc. 7 *Iron Chancellor*: see IRON *n.* & *a.*

chancellorship *n.* the position of a chancellor L15.

chancelry *n.* var. of CHANCELLERY.

chance-medley /tʃɑːns'mɛdli/ *n.* L15. [AN *chance medlee*, f. as CHANCE *n.* + *medlee* fem. pa. pple of *medler* mix: see MEDDLE *v.*] 1 *Law* (now *Hist.*). An action, esp. homicide, mainly but not entirely unintentional; a casual affray in which a person kills in self-defence after being assaulted and refusing to fight further (formerly regarded as excusable). L15. 2 *transf.* Inadvertency, haphazard or random action. L16.

chancery /'tʃɑːns(ə)ri/ *n.* In sense 2 also **C-**. LME. [Contr. of CHANCELLERY.] †1 = CHANCELLERY 1. LME–M17. 2 The court of the Lord Chancellor of the United Kingdom (earlier of England or Great Britain), now a division of the High Court of Justice. Also (*High*) *Court of Chancery*. LME. **b** More fully *chancery court, court of chancery*. A similar court elsewhere; *US* a court of equity. M16. **3** An office for public records. E16. **4** = CHANCELLERY 2. M16. **5** = CHANCELLERY 3. (Now the official term in Brit. diplomatic use.) E20.

Phrases: **in chancery** (of the head of a boxer or wrestler) held under the opponent's arm and being pummelled. *Inns of Chancery*: see INN *n.* *Master in Chancery*: see MASTER *n.*[1] 4c. **ward in Chancery** a ward of court under the protection of the Court of Chancery.

chancre /ˈʃaŋkə/ *n.* L16. [Fr., f. L CANCER *n.*: cf. CANKER *n.*] *Med.* A painless ulcer, *esp.* one occurring on the genitals and resulting from syphilis.

soft chancre = CHANCROID *n.*

chancroid *n.* & *a.* (of) a venereal infection with the bacterium *Haemophilus ducreyi* causing enlarged, ulcerated lymph nodes of the groin (also called *soft sore*) M19. **chancrous** *a.* (now *rare* or *obs.*) M18.

chancy /ˈtʃɑːnsi/ *a.* E16. [f. CHANCE *n.* + -Y[1].] **1** Lucky; safe to meddle with, 'canny'. *Sc.* E16. **2** Uncertain, risky. M19.

chancily *adv.* M20. **chanciness** *n.* L19.

chandelier /ʃandəˈlɪə/ *n.* M17. [Fr., f. *chandelle*: see next, -IER.] **1** *Mil.* A wooden frame filled with fascines to form a traverse in sapping. M17. **2** A branched hanging support for several lights, orig. candles. M18.

chandler /ˈtʃɑːndlə/ *n.* ME. [AN *chaundeler*, OFr. *chandelier* candle-maker, -seller, f. *c(h)andeile*, *c(h)andelle* (mod. *chandelle*) f. L *candela*: see CANDLE *n.*, -ELLA, -ER[2].] **I 1** A person who makes or sells candles. ME. **2** An officer responsible for the supply of candles to a household. Long *obs.* exc. *Hist.* LME. **3** A retailer of provisions and items of equipment for a particular purpose, without specification (now *arch.* or *Hist.*) usu. of candles, oil, soap, paint, groceries, etc., for households. L16.

1 *tallow-chandler, wax-chandler*. **3** *corn chandler, ship('s) chandler*, etc.

†**II 4** A stand or support for a candle. LME–L18.

chandlery *n.* (*a*) (now chiefly *Hist.*) a place where candles etc. are kept; (*b*) the goods produced or sold by a chandler: E17.

Chandler wobble /ˈtʃɑːndlə ˈwɒb(ə)l/ *n. phr.* M20. [Seth C. *Chandler* (1846–1913), US astronomer.] A nutation of the earth's principal axis of inertia about its axis of rotation (with a period of approx. 14 months), manifested as a small oscillation in the latitude of points on the earth's surface.

chang /tʃaŋ/ *n.* E19. [Tib. *chaṅ*.] A Tibetan beer or wine made chiefly from barley or rice.

change /tʃeɪndʒ/ *n.* ME. [AN *chaunge*, (O)Fr. *change*, f. as next.] **1** (An instance of) making or becoming different; the substitution of one thing or set of conditions for another; the following of one thing or set of conditions on another; (an) alteration in state or quality; variety; variation, mutation. ME. **b** More fully *change of the moon*. The arrival of the moon at a fresh phase, esp. at a new moon. LME. **c** A round or sequence of steps within a dance. L16. **d** *Mus.* Modulation. Now *rare* or *obs.* L16. **e** One's death. *arch.* E17. †**f** Changefulness; (a) caprice. Only in 17. **g** *Cricket.* The substitution of one bowler or type of bowling for another during the course of a match. E19. **h** A gear-change in a vehicle. M20. **2** A person or thing which is or may be substituted for another of the same kind. ME. **b** *Cricket.* A change-bowler. M19. **3** Money given in exchange for notes, coins, etc., of a higher denomination or of a different currency; the balance returned when anything is paid for by an amount of money greater than its price. Hence, coins, esp. of low denominations. ME. †**4** Exchange. ME–E17. **5** (Also **C-**.) A place where merchants meet for the transaction of business; an exchange. (From E19 also written *'change* as if for *exchange*.) ME. **6** *Campanol.* In *pl.* The different permutations in which a peal of bells may be rung. M17.

1 R. B. SHERIDAN Do you really see any change in me? J. RHYS Her health was not good and she needed a change. A. TOFFLER He thrives on change, enjoys travel, new foods, [etc.]. *change of address, key, pace*, etc. *social change, sound-change*, etc. *change of air*: see AIR *n.*[1] 2. *change of front*: see FRONT *n.* 5b. *change of gear, gear-change*: see GEAR *n.* *change of heart*: see HEART *n.* *change of mind*: see MIND *n.*[1] *change of* SCENE. *change of the monsoon*: see MONSOON 1. *chop and change*: see CHOP *n.*[5] **for a change** *colloq.* for variety, as an exception to usual practice. *grammatical change*: see GRAMMATICAL *a.* †**put the change upon** deceive (a person). SEA *change*. **the change (of life)** the menopause. **f** SHAKES. *Lear* You see how full of changes his age is. **2** R. GREENE Mistresse Lamilia, like a cunning Angler made readie her chaunge of baytes. A. HAILEY He would pause occasionally to pencil in a change. **change of clothes** a second outfit in reserve. **3** B. ALLWOOD The pub . . has change for a pound. E. BOWEN Shovelling into his pocket the change from a pound note. J. WAIN They jingle the hopeful change in their pockets. **get no change out of** *slang* get no return, result, or satisfaction from; fail to get the better of (a person). **give change**, *N. Amer.* **make change** give money in exchange for notes, coins, etc., of a higher denomination, or in adjustment of a payment. *loose change*: see LOOSE *a.* **small change** coins of low denominations; *fig.* trivial remarks. **5 on change** at the exchange. **6 ring the changes** (*a*) go through all the changes in ringing a peal of bells; (*b*) go through all the possible variations of any process (foll. by *on*); (*c*) *slang* substitute bad money for good.

Comb.: **change-bowler** *Cricket* a bowler who relieves the regular bowlers in a match; **change-house** *Sc.* (now *rare* or *obs.*) a small inn or alehouse; **change-ringer, -ringing** *Campanol.* (a person who engages in) the ringing of a set of bells in a constantly varying order.

changeful *a.* full of change; variable, inconstant: L16. **changefulness** *n.* L18. **changeless** *a.* without change, unchanging, immutable L16. **changelessly** *adv.* E20. **changelessness** *n.* E19.

change /tʃeɪndʒ/ *v.* ME. [(O)Fr. *changer* f. late L *cambiare* f. L *cambire* exchange, barter, prob. of Celt. origin.] **1** *v.t.* Put, take, or use another or others instead of; give up, get rid of, *for*. ME. **b** *spec.* Give or obtain money of smaller denomination or different currency in exchange for (money of a defined kind or amount). LME. **2** *v.t.* Substitute one for another of (things of the same kind); go from one to another of (things of the same kind). ME. **b** *v.i.* Change trains, boats, etc. L19. **3** *v.t.* Give and receive reciprocally (things of the same kind); exchange (*with*). Now *rare* exc. in *change places* (*with*). ME. †**b** *v.i.* Make an exchange (*for, with*). M16–M17. †**c** *v.t.* Exchange (a thing) *with* (a person). L16–M17. **4** *v.t.* Make different, alter; turn or convert *into, to*, (*from*). ME. **5** *v.i.* Become different; turn *into, to*, (*from*). ME. **b** Of the moon: pass through phases; arrive at a fresh phase, esp. at a new moon. LME. †**c** Change countenance; turn pale, blush, etc. L16–E17. **6** *v.i.* & (*rare*) *t.* Shift, transfer, (usu. *from* one place *to* another); remove to another place or into other circumstances. LME. **7 a** *v.i.* & (now *Sc.*) *refl.* change one's clothes; *spec.* change into evening dress. L15. **b** *v.t.* Put fresh clothes on (another person); put fresh coverings on (a bed); *spec.* change the nappy of (a baby). E20.

1 G. GREENE You changed your newspaper once and you soon got used to it. I. MURDOCH She had not changed her clothes. J. HERRIOT Stewie had changed his . . Austin Seven for a . . Ford V Eight. **b** E. NESBIT We would bring his share as soon as we could get the half-crown changed. **2** T. STOPPARD The dancing farmhands changing partners. **b** OED Passengers for Cambridge change at Bletchley. **3** SIR W. SCOTT Her attendants changed expressive looks with each other. TENNYSON If you . . change a word with her he calls his wife. **4** V. WOOLF Experiences . . such as change a face . . from a pink innocent oval to a face lean, contracted, hostile. J. STEINBECK All night they walked and never changed their pace. **5** R. P. WARREN He watched the expression of her face change from pleasure to surprise. E. WAUGH Alastair . . had changed little since he joined the army. G. CHARLES He waited at the crossing for the traffic lights to change. **6** D. H. LAWRENCE He changed his hat to his left hand. W. TREVOR Mrs Rush changed from second to third gear.

Phrases, & with advs. in specialized senses: *change colour*: see COLOUR *n.* **change down** engage a lower gear in a vehicle. *change ends*: see END *n.* *change eyes*: see EYE *n.* **change gear** engage a different gear in a vehicle. *change hands*: see HAND *n.* *change horses in midstream*: see HORSE *n.* *change leg*: see LEG *n.* *change note*: see NOTE *n.*[2] *change one's condition*: see CONDITION *n.* 8. **change one's feet** *colloq.* put on other shoes etc. *change one's mind*: see MIND *n.*[1] *change one's mood*: see MOOD *n.*[1] *change one's note*: see NOTE *n.*[2] *change one's skin*: see SKIN *n.* *change one's tune*: see TUNE *n.* **change over** change from one system or situation to another (also foll. by *from, to*). *change step*: see STEP *n.*[1] *change the subject*: see SUBJECT *n.* **change up** engage a higher gear in a vehicle. **changing room** a room where one can change one's clothes, esp. at a sports ground. *chop and change*: see CHOP *v.*[2] 2.

Comb.: **change-over** a change from one system or situation to another; *spec.* the action of handing over the baton to the next runner in a relay race; **change-up** *Baseball* an unexpectedly slow pitch designed to deceive the batter's expectations.

changeable /ˈtʃeɪndʒəb(ə)l/ *a.* & *n.* ME. [(O)Fr., f. as CHANGE *v.* + -ABLE.] **A** *adj.* **1** That may change or be changed (by others); subject to change; mutable, variable, inconstant. ME. **2** Showing different colours under different aspects; shot. LME.

2 H. MCCLOY A ball dress of changeable silk, pale blue and rose.

B *n.* A changeable thing or person. Now *rare* or *obs.* E18.

changeaˈbility, changeableness *ns.* the quality of being changeable; mutability; inconstancy: LME.

changeling /ˈtʃeɪndʒlɪŋ/ *n.* & *a.* M16. [f. CHANGE *v.* + -LING[1].] **A** *n.* **1** A person given to change; a waverer, a turncoat. *arch.* M16. **2** A person or thing (surreptitiously) put in exchange for another; *spec.* a child secretly substituted for another in infancy. M16. **3** A halfwitted person. *arch.* E17. †**B** *adj.* Changeable, variable, inconstant. M17–E18.

changement /ˈtʃeɪndʒm(ə)nt/ *n.*[1] *rare.* LME. [(O)Fr., f. as CHANGE *v.* + -MENT.] Change, alteration, variation.

changement /ʃɑ̃ʒmɑ̃/ *n.*[2] Pl. pronounced same. M19. [Fr. = prec.] *Ballet.* In full *changement de pieds* /də pje/ [= of feet]. A jump during which the dancer changes the position of the feet.

changer /ˈtʃeɪndʒə/ *n.* ME. [AN *changëour*, OFr *changëor* (mod. *changeur*), in med.L *cambiator*, f. as CHANGE *v.* + -ER[2]. Also immed. f. CHANGE *v.* + -ER[1].] **1** A person who or thing which changes something (identified contextually or specified); *spec.* (the earliest use, now *rare*) one who exchanges money. ME. **2** A person who changes. *rare.* E17.

chank /tʃaŋk, tʃʌŋk/ *n.* L17. [Skt *śaṅkha*, partly through Port. *chanco, chanquo*.] The spiral shell of a gastropod, *Xancus pyrum*, used by Hindus for libation vessels and ornaments.

chank /tʃaŋk/ *v.t.* Now *US* & *dial.* M16. [Imit.: cf. CHAMP *v.*] = CHAMP *v.* 2.

channel /ˈtʃan(ə)l/ *n.*[1] ME. [OFr. *chanel* partially Latinized var. of *chenel* f. L *canalis* pipe, groove, channel, f. *canna* CANE *n.*[1]: see -EL[2]. Cf. CANAL *n.*, CANNEL *n.*[1], KENNEL *n.*[2]] **I** Of water etc. **1** The hollow bed of running water (formerly also, of the sea). ME. **2** A gutter in a street etc. *obs.* exc. *dial.* LME. **3** A natural or artificial tubular passage, esp. for liquids or fluids. LME. †**4** A stream, a rivulet. L15–E18. **5** A navigable passage between shallows in an estuary or other waterway. E16. **6** A piece of water, wider than a strait, joining two larger pieces, usu. seas. M16. †**7** = CANAL *n.* 4. Only in 17.

6 the (English) Channel: between England and France (*Chops of the Channel*: see CHOP *n.*[2] 3).

II *transf.* & *fig.* †**8** The neck, the throat. ME–L16. **9** That through which information, news, trade, etc., passes; a medium of communication; an agency. M16. **10** Gravel. *Sc.* & *north.* L16. **11** The course in which anything moves; a direction, a line. M17. **12** A groove, a furrow; *spec.* in *Archit.*, a fluting of a column. L17. **13** An electric circuit, band of radio frequencies, etc., used as a means of conveying or transmitting a signal in telecommunications, broadcasting, sound reproduction, etc.; a broadcasting service using a particular frequency band. M19.

9 J. S. MILL No new . . channel for investment has been opened. T. STOPPARD The newspapers . . are the channel of the government's answerability to the governed. **the usual channels** the approved or traditional modes of approach etc. 11 SWIFT The world went on in the old channel. M. MCCARTHY She managed to steer the conversation into safer channels. *green channel*: see GREEN *a. red channel*: see RED *a.* 13 *second channel*: see SECOND *a.*

Comb.: †**channel-bone** the collar-bone; **channel-cat(fish)** *N. Amer.* a freshwater catfish, esp. *Ictalurus punctatus*; **Channel Fleet** *Hist.* the portion of the British fleet detailed for service in the English Channel; **Channel Islander** a native or inhabitant of the Channel Islands; **Channel Islands** British Crown dependencies in the English Channel off the north-west coast of France, including Jersey, Guernsey, Alderney, and Sark; **channel-stone** a stone used in paving gutters; **Channel Tunnel** a tunnel under the English Channel linking England and France (cf. CHUNNEL).

channelly *a.* (*Sc.* & *north.*) gravelly E17.

channel /'tʃan(ə)l/ *n.*[2] M18. [Alt. of *chain-wale* s.v. CHAIN *n.*: see WALE *n.*[1] Cf. *gunnel*, *gunwale*.] *Naut.* A broad thick plank projecting horizontally from a ship's side abreast of the mast, to widen the basis of support for the shrouds.

channel /'tʃan(ə)l/ *v.t.* Infl. **-ll-**, ***-l-**. LME. [f. CHANNEL *n.*[1]] 1 Form channels in; groove. LME. 2 Convey (as if) in a channel; guide, direct. M17. 3 Excavate or cut out as a channel. E19. 4 Provide (a street) with gutters. L19.

1 SHAKES. *1 Hen. IV* No more shall trenching war channel her fields. 2 R. SCRUTON In so far as religious feeling exists, it is . . better that it be channelled towards its proper object.

channelize /'tʃan(ə)lʌɪz/ *v.t.* Chiefly *US.* Also **-ise**. E17. [f. CHANNEL *n.*[1] + -IZE.] = CHANNEL *v.* 2.

¶In isolated use bef. M20.

channeli'zation *n.* E20.

channer /'tʃanə/ *v.i. Sc.* LME. [Prob. imit.: cf. CHUNNER, CHUNTER.] Mutter, grumble, murmur querulously.

chanson /ʃɑ̃sɔ̃/ *n.* Pl. pronounced same. L15. [(O)Fr. f. L *cantio(n-)*: see CANZONE.] A French song.

chanson de geste /də ʒɛst/ [= of heroic deeds] any of a group of medieval French epic poems.

chansonette /ʃɑ̃sɔnɛt (*pl. same*)/ *n.* a short song E19. ***chansonnier*** /ʃɑ̃sɔnje (*pl. same*)/ *n.* (*a*) a writer or performer of esp. satirical songs (in France); (*b*) a collection of (French) songs: L19.

chant /tʃɑːnt/ *n.* Also (now *Sc.*) **chaunt** /tʃɔːnt/. L17. [f. the vb: cf. (O)Fr. *chant* f. L CANTUS.] 1 A song; singing. L17. 2 *Mus.* A short musical passage in two or more phrases each with a reciting note to which any number of syllables may be sung, for singing unmetrical words; a psalm, canticle, etc., so sung. L18. 3 A measured monotonous song, a musical recitation of words; a singsong intonation in talk. E19.

1 MILTON Chant of tuneful birds. 2 *Ambrosian chant*, *Gregorian chant*, etc. 3 GEO. ELIOT The clear-cut, emphatic chant which makes a truth doubly telling in Scottish utterance. R. HOGGART Rhyming chants survive, to accompany the games.

chant /tʃɑːnt/ *v.* Also (now *Sc.*) **chaunt** /tʃɔːnt/. LME. [(O)Fr. *chanter* f. L *cantare* frequent. of *canere* sing.] 1 *v.i.* & *t. gen.* Sing. Chiefly *arch.* or *poet.* LME. b *v.t.* Sing of, celebrate in song. *poet.* L16. 2 *v.i.* & *t.* Recite musically or rhythmically; intone; sing (to) a chant. LME. 3 *v.i.* & *t.* Talk or repeat (a statement) monotonously. L16. 4 *v.t.* Praise (a horse) fraudulently to sell it. *arch. slang.* E19.

1 R. BURNS How can ye chant, ye little birds. TENNYSON He . . chanted a melody. *chanting* GOSHAWK. 2 SIR W. SCOTT With pious fools go chant and pray. B. CHATWIN He would . . chant the lines his mother taught him. 3 MILTON Let them chaunt while they will of prerogatives.

chantable *a.* (*rare*) LME.

chantage /ʃɑ̃taːʒ, 'tʃɑːntɪdʒ/ *n.* L19. [Fr.] Extortion of money by blackmail.

chantarelle *n.* var. of CHANTERELLE *n.*[2]

chanter /'tʃɑːntə/ *n.* Also (now *Sc.*) **chaunter** /'tʃɔːntə/. LME. [AN *chauntour*, OFr. *chantëor* (mod. *chanteur*), f. L *cantator* singer, f. *cantare*: see CHANT *v.*, -ER[2].] 1 A person who chants or sings; *spec.* (*a*) a chorister; (*b*) a precentor, a cantor; (*c*) a priest who sings masses in a chantry. LME. 2 The melody-pipe, with finger-holes, of a bagpipe. M17. 3 A person who fraudulently praises horses to sell them. *arch. slang.* M19.

chantership *n.* the office of a chanter or precentor E16.

chanterelle /'tʃɑːntərɛl, tʃɑːntə'rɛl/ *n.*[1] E17. [Fr., f. as CHANT *v.*: see -EL[2].] †1 A decoy-bird. Only in E17. 2 The highest-pitched string of a plucked or bowed musical instrument. L18.

chanterelle /'tʃɑːntərɛl/ *n.*[2] Also **-tar-**. L18. [Fr., f. mod.L *cantharellus* dim. of *cantharus* f. Gk *kantharos* drinking-vessel: see -EL[2].] A yellow funnel-shaped edible fungus, *Cantharellus cibarius*.

false chanterelle a fungus, *Hygrophoropsis aurantiaca*, resembling the chanterelle but inedible.

chanteuse /ʃɑ̃tøːz/ *n.* Pl. pronounced same. M19. [Fr.] A female singer of popular songs, esp. in France.

chantey *n.* var. of SHANTY *n.*[2]

chanticleer /'tʃɑːntɪklɪə/ *n.* Also **C-**. ME. [OFr. *chantecler* (mod. *chanteclair*), the cock in *Reynard the Fox* and Chaucer's *Nun's Priest's Tale*. Cf. PARTLET *n.*[1]] (A personal name for) a domestic cock.

Chantilly /ʃan'tɪli; *foreign* ʃɑ̃tiji/ *n.* & *a.* L18. [A town near Paris, France.] 1 (Designating) a soft-paste porcelain made at Chantilly in the 18th cent. L18. 2 (Designating) a delicate kind of bobbin-lace, orig. made near Chantilly. M19. 3 (Designating a dish made with) sweetened whipped cream. M19.

3 *crème Chantilly*: see CRÈME 1. *meringue* (*à la*) *Chantilly*: see MERINGUE *n.*[1]

chantress /'tʃɑːntrɪs/ *n. arch.* LME. [OFr. *chanteresse*, f. as CHANTER: see -ESS[1].] A female chanter or singer.

chantry /'tʃɑːntri/ *n.* LME. [AN *chaunterie*, OFr. *chanterie*, f. *chanter*: see CHANT *v.*, -ERY, -RY.] †1 Singing or chanting of the Mass etc. LME–L16. 2 An endowment for a priest or priests to sing Masses for the soul of the founder etc.; the priests, altar, chapel, etc., so endowed. LME.

chanty *n.* var. of SHANTY *n.*[2]

Chanuk(k)ah *ns.* vars. of HANUKKAH.

chaos /'keɪɒs/ *n.* L15. [Fr. or L, f. Gk *khaos* vast chasm, void.] †1 A gaping void, yawning gulf, chasm, abyss. L15–M17. 2 Formless primordial matter. Now *Hist.* or *literary.* M16. 3 (A state of) utter confusion and disorder; *arch.* a confused mass or mixture. M16. b *Sci.* Behaviour of a system which is governed by deterministic laws but is so unpredictable as to appear random, owing to its extreme sensitivity to initial conditions. L20. †4 An amorphous lump. M–L16.

3 A. MILLER The very impulse to write . . springs from an inner chaos crying for order. K. CROSSLEY-HOLLAND The giants . . represent the forces of chaos. B. CASTLE Industrial action which can cause chaos in hospitals. b attrib.: *Discover* Mathematical techniques often associated with chaos theory.

cha'ologist *n.* an expert in or student of chaology L20. **cha'ology** *n.* the branch of science that deals with chaos L20.

chaotic /keɪ'ɒtɪk/ *a.* E18. [f. prec. after *erotic*, *hypnotic*, etc.] 1 Of or pertaining to primordial chaos. Now *Hist.* or *literary.* E18. 2 Utterly confused and disordered; *Sci.* exhibiting or characterized by chaos. M18.

2 **chaotic attractor** = *strange attractor* s.v. STRANGE *a.*

chaotical *a.* (*rare*) L17. **chaotically** *adv.* E19.

chap /tʃap/ *n.*[1] LME. [Origin unkn.: rel. to CHAP *v.*[2] Cf. CHOP *n.*[1]] 1 A crack, an open seam, esp. in the skin or in dry ground. Usu. in *pl.* LME. 2 A stroke, a knock, a rap. *Sc.* & *north.* E16.

Comb.: **Chap Stick** *US* (proprietary name for) a stick of lipsalve.

chap /tʃap/ *n.*[2] M16. [Origin unkn.: cf. CHOP *n.*[2]] 1 Either of the jaws of an animal or (*joc.* or *derog.*) a human, as forming part of the mouth. Usu. in *pl.* M16. b Either half of the bill of a bird. M17. †c In *pl.* The jaws of a vice etc. L17–M19. 2 Either side of the external jaw, a cheek. Usu. in *pl.* E18. 3 The lower jaw. M19. 4 The lower half of the cheek of a pig etc., as food. L19.

4 *Bath chap*: see BATH *n.*[1]

Comb.: **chap-fallen** with the jaw hanging down; dispirited, dejected.

chapless *a.* without the lower jaw L16.

chap /tʃap/ *n.*[3] L16. [Abbrev. of CHAPMAN.] 1 A buyer, a customer. Now *dial.* L16. 2 A man, a boy, a fellow; in *pl.* also, people. *colloq.* E18.

2 THACKERAY What sad wild fellows some of the chaps were. E. C. BENTLEY Geography is about Maps But Biography is about Chaps.

chap /tʃap/ *v.*[1]*t.* & *i. obs.* exc. *dial.* Infl. **-pp-**. ME. [In early use, var. of CHEAP *v.* Later, back-form. f. CHAPMAN.] Buy and sell, barter.

chap /tʃap/ *v.*[2] Infl. **-pp-**. LME. [Origin unkn.: rel. to CHAP *n.*[1] Cf. CHOP *v.*[1]] I 1 *v.i.* & *t.* (Cause to) crack or open in chaps; crack in fissures. LME. 2 *v.t.* Chop. Long *obs.* exc. *Sc.* LME. II Strike. *Sc.* & *north.* 3 *v.t.* Strike. M16. 4 *v.i.* Of a clock, the hour: strike. L16. 5 *v.i.* Knock, rap, at a door etc. L18. III 6 *v.i.* & *t.* Choose. *Sc.* E18.

chaparejos /ʃapə'reɪhəʊs, tʃ-/ *n.pl. US.* Also **-rreras** /-'rɛːrəs/. M19. [Mex. Sp. *chaparreras*, f. *chaparra*, *-o*: see next. Later form *-ejos* prob. infl. by Sp. *aparejo* equipment.] = CHAPS.

chaparral /ʃapə'ral, tʃ-/ *n. US.* M19. [Sp., f. *chaparra*, *-o* dwarf evergreen oak.] Thicket of dwarf evergreen oaks; dense tangled brushwood.

Comb.: **chaparral cock** the roadrunner, *Geococcyx californianus*.

chaparreras *n.pl.* see CHAPAREJOS.

chapatti /tʃə'pɑːti, -'pati/ *n.* Also **chapati**, **chupatti**, & other vars. E19. [Hind. *capātī*, f. *capānā* flatten, roll out, ult. f. Dravidian.] In Indian cookery, a small flat thin cake of coarse unleavened bread.

chap-book /'tʃapbʊk/ *n.* E19. [f. CHAP(MAN + BOOK *n.*] *Hist.* A small pamphlet of tales, ballads, tracts, etc., hawked by chapmen.

chape /tʃeɪp/ *n.* & *v.* ME. [(O)Fr. = cape, hood (whence Sp., Port. *chapa*) in techn. uses: see CAPE *n.*[1]] A *n.* †1 A plate of metal with which anything is overlaid or trimmed. Only in ME. 2 The metal plate of a scabbard, *esp.* that which covers the point. LME. 3 The tip of a fox's tail. L17. 4 The part of a buckle by which it is fastened to a strap. L17. B *v.t.* Equip (a scabbard etc.) with a chape. LME.

chapeless *a.* (*rare*) L16.

chapeau /'ʃapəʊ/ *n.* Pl. **-eaux** /-əʊ/. L15. [Fr., in OFr. *c(h)apel*, f. L *cappellum* dim. of *cappa* CAP *n.*[1]] Now chiefly *Her.* A cap, a hat; now *esp.* a cap of maintenance, usu. of red velvet turned up ermine.

chapeau-bras /ʃapobra/ *n.* Pl. ***chapeaux-bras*** (pronounced same). M18. [Fr., f. prec. + *bras* arm.] A three-cornered flat silk hat able to be carried under the arm.

chapeaux *n.* pl. of CHAPEAU.

chapeaux-bras *n.* pl. of CHAPEAU-BRAS.

chapel /'tʃap(ə)l/ *n.* & *a.* ME. [OFr. *chapele* f. med.L *cappella* dim. of *cappa* cape, cloak: see CAP *n.*[1], -EL[2] 1. Orig. the sanctuary in which the cloak of St Martin was kept.] A *n.* 1 *gen.* A place of Christian worship other than a parish or cathedral church, *esp.* one attached to a private house or institution. ME. 2 A place for private worship in a larger building, with an altar; *esp.* such a part of a cathedral etc., separately dedicated. ME. 3 A place of public worship of the national episcopal Church subordinate to a parish church. LME. 4 *transf.* A lesser temple, fane, or sanctuary, with an altar to a god. Now *rare.* LME. 5 A choir attached to a chapel (usu. of a monarch or noble); hence, any group of singers or musicians attached to a church or institution. LME. 6 A non-Anglican, esp. Protestant Nonconformist, place of Christian worship. M17. 7 A chapel service; attendance at chapel. M17. 8a A printing works. Now *rare.* L17. b A meeting or association of the journeymen in a printing works; the smallest organized union group in a printing works, publishing house, etc. M18.

7 J. AUSTEN Without danger of reprobation because chapel was missed.

Phrases: **chapel of ease**: for the convenience of remote parishioners. **chapel of rest** an undertaker's mortuary. **chapel royal**: attached to a royal palace. **father of (the) chapel** the spokesman or shop steward of a printers' chapel. *Lady chapel*: see LADY *n.* *Sistine Chapel*: see SISTINE *a.*

Comb.: **chapel-master** the director of music at a royal etc. chapel; **chapelwarden** (now *rare*) a churchwarden at a chapel.

B *adj.* Belonging to or regularly attending a Nonconformist chapel. *colloq.* M20.

J. CARY Mrs. Wilmot was chapel I'm sure she never went to a play.

chapelle ardente /ʃapɛl ardɑ̃t/ *n. phr.* Pl. **-s -s** (pronounced same). E19. [Fr. = burning chapel.] A chamber prepared for the lying-in-state of a distinguished person, and lit up with candles, torches, etc.

chapelry /ˈtʃap(ə)lri/ *n.* ME. [OFr. *chapelerie* (in med.L *cappellaria*), f. as CHAPEL: see -ERY, -RY.] **1** A division of a parish, having its own chapel. ME. **2** A chapel with its precinct and accessory buildings. E19.

chaperon /ˈʃapərəʊn/ *n.* & *v.* Also **-one**. LME. [(O)Fr., f. as CHAPE.] **A** *n.* **1** A hood, a cap. *obs.* exc. *Hist.* LME. †**2** A small escutcheon placed esp. on the forehead of a horse drawing a hearse. L17–L18. **3** A person who ensures propriety, *esp.* a married or older woman accompanying a young unmarried woman on social occasions. E18. **B** *v.t.* Act as a chaperon to. L18.

chaperonage *n.* attendance as a chaperon. E19. **chaperonless** *a.* without a chaperon M19.

chaperonin /ʃapəˈrəʊnɪn/ *n.* L20. [f. prec. + -IN[1].] *Biochem.* A protein that aids the assembly and folding of other protein molecules.

chapiter /ˈtʃapɪtə/ *n.* See also CHAPTER *n.* ME. [(O)Fr. *chapitre*: see CHAPTER *n.*] †**1** Early form of CHAPTER *n.* ME–M17. **2** *Archit.* The capital of a column. LME.

†**chapiter** *v.* see CHAPTER *v.*

chaplain /ˈtʃaplɪn/ *n.* ME. [AN, OFr. *chapelain* f. med.L *cappellanus* (whence earlier CAPELLANE) orig. custodian of the cloak of St Martin, f. *cappella*: see CHAPEL, -AN.] **1** The member of clergy attached to a chapel; *spec.* a member of the clergy officiating in the private chapel of a household or institution, on board ship, or for a regiment, school, etc. ME. **2** A nun who recites the inferior services in the chapel of a nunnery. LME.

chaplaincy *n.* the office or position of a chaplain M18. **chaplainry** *n.* (*obs.* exc. *Sc. Hist.*) = CHAPLAINCY LME. **chaplainship** *n.* = CHAPLAINCY M16.

chaplet /ˈtʃaplɪt/ *n.* LME [(O)Fr. *chapelet* dim. of *chapel* (mod. *chapeau* hat) f. Proto-Romance dim. of *cappa* CAPE *n.*[2]: see -LET.] **1** A wreath of flowers, leaves, gold, gems, etc., for the head; a coronal. LME. **b** *Her.* A charge representing a garland of leaves with four flowers at equal distances. L17. **2** *Archit.* A bead-moulding. E17. **3a** A string of beads for counting prayers, of five decades. M17. **b** A necklace. M19. **4** *Founding.* A metal support of the core of a hollow moulding, as a cylindrical pipe. L19.

Chaplinesque /tʃaplɪnˈɛsk/ *a.* E20. [f. *Chaplin* (see below) + -ESQUE.] Resembling or characteristic of the comedy and pathos of the English-born film actor Charles Spencer ('Charlie') Chaplin (1889–1977).

chapman /ˈtʃapmən/ *n.* Now *arch.* or *Hist.* Pl. **-men**. [OE *ċēapman*, f. as CHEAP *n.* + MAN *n.*] **1** A man who buys and sells; a merchant, a dealer. OE. **2** *spec.* A pedlar. ME. †**3** A customer. ME–E19. †**4** A broker. LME–M17.

chapmanship *n.* the occupation or activities of a chapman M16.

chappal /ˈtʃap(ə)l/ *n.* Also **chappli** /ˈtʃapli/. L19. [Hind. *cappal*, *caplī*.] In the Indian subcontinent: a sandal, esp. of leather.

chappie /ˈtʃapi/ *n. colloq.* (orig. *Sc.*). Also **-y**. E18. [f. CHAP *n.*[3] + -IE, -Y[6].] A (little) chap or fellow.

chappli *n.* var. of CHAPPAL.

chappow /tʃaˈpaʊ/ *n. Anglo-Ind.* E19. [Pashto.] A plundering expedition; a raid.

chappy *n.* var. of CHAPPIE.

chappy /ˈtʃapi/ *a.* E17. [f. CHAP *n.*[1] + -Y[1].] Full of chaps or clefts.

chaprassi /tʃəˈprasi/ *n.* Pl. **-i(e)s**. Also **chuprassy**. E19. [Urdu *caprāsī*, f. *caprās* official badge, f. Pers. *čaprāst*.] In the Indian subcontinent: an attendant, a messenger, a household official.

chaps /ʃaps, tʃ-/ *n.pl. N. Amer.* L19. [Abbrev. of CHAPAREJOS.] Stout protective trousers for cowboys etc.

chaptalization /tʃaptəlʌɪˈzeɪʃ(ə)n/ *n.* Also **-isation**. L19. [f. J. A. *Chaptal* (1756–1832), Fr. chemist who invented the process + -IZATION.] In wine-making, the correction or improvement of must by the addition of calcium carbonate to neutralize acid or of sugar to increase alcoholic strength.

chaptalize *v.t.* correct or improve thus E20.

chapter /ˈtʃaptə/ *n.* Also (earlier) †**chapiter** & other vars. ME. [(O)Fr. *chapitre*, earlier *chapitle*, f. L *capitulum* dim. of *caput* head.] **I 1** A main division of a book. ME. **b** *RC Ch.* A short scriptural passage or lesson read at certain services. LME. **c** An Act of Parliament numbered as part of a session's proceedings. M16. **2** *fig.* A category, a heading, a subject. *arch.* LME. **3** *transf.* & *fig.* A part, section, or period. E17.

2 HOR. WALPOLE There are some chapters on which I still fear we shall not agree. 3 R. W. EMERSON 'Tis a curious chapter in modern history, the growth of the machine-shop.

II 4 An assembly or the totality of the canons of a collegiate or cathedral church, or of the members of a monastic or knightly order. ME. **5** A local branch of a society. *N. Amer.* E19.

Phrases: **chapter and verse** *fig.* exact reference or authority. *the chapter of accidents*: see ACCIDENT 1b. **to the end of the chapter** *fig.* always, throughout.

Comb.: **chapter house** a building where a chapter meets; **chapterman** a member of the chapter of a monastic order.

chapter /ˈtʃaptə/ *v.t.* Earlier †**chapiter** etc. L15. [Sense 1 f. the n.; sense 2 f. Fr. *chapitrer*, f. as prec.] **1** Divide into chapters. L15. **2** Reprimand, take to task. *rare*. M16.

†**chapwoman** *n.* Pl. **-women**. LME–E19. [f. CHAP(MAN + WOMAN *n.*] A female pedlar or dealer.

char /tʃɑː/ *n.*[1] Also (now *rare*) **chare** /tʃɛː/. See also CHORE *n.*[2], JAR *n.*[3] [OE *ċerr*, (WS) *ċierr*, late *ċyrr* rel. to CHAR *v.*[1]] †**1** A return; a turn; an occasion, a time. Long only in *a-char* AJAR *adv.*[1] & *pred. a.*[1] OE–L18. †**2** A turn of work; a deed; a piece of business. OE–L17. **3** An odd job, esp. of domestic work; in *pl.*, the housework of a domestic servant. Now only in *comb.* ME. **4** A charwoman. *colloq.* E20.

Comb.: **charlady, charwoman** a woman hired by the hour or day or week to clean rooms in offices or houses.

char /tʃɑː/ *n.*[2] Also **charr**. Pl. same. M17. [Origin uncertain: perh. f. Celt.] A small trout of the genus *Salvelinus*; esp. *S. alpinus* (also *Arctic char*), of Arctic waters and northern lakes. Also (*N. Amer.*), the brook trout, *S. fontinalis*.

char /tʃɑː/ *n.*[3] L19. [f. CHAR *v.*[2]] A charred substance; *esp.* the residue resulting from the removal of volatile materials from coal.

†**char** *n.*[4] see CHAIR *n.*[2]

char *n.*[5] var. of CHA.

char /tʃɑː/ *v.*[1] Infl. **-rr-**. Also (now *rare*) **chare** /tʃɛː/. See also CHORE *v.* [OE *ċierran* rel. to CHAR *n.*[1]] †**1** *v.t.* & *i.* Turn; *esp.* turn away or aside. OE–L17. †**2** *v.t.* Do (a turn of work). L16–E19. **3** *v.i.* Do odd jobs, esp. of domestic work; work as a charwoman. E18.

char /tʃɑː/ *v.*[2] Infl. **-rr-**. L17. [App. back-form. f. CHARCOAL: cf. CHARK *v.*[2]] **1** *v.t.* Burn to charcoal; scorch, blacken with fire. L17. **2** *v.i.* Become reduced to charcoal. E18.

chara /ˈkɛːrə/ *n.*[1] M18. [L, name of an unkn. plant.] A charophyte of the genus *Chara* (family Characeae), the members of which characteristically are encrusted with lime and have a fetid smell.

chaˈraceous *a.* resembling a chara; of or pertaining to the family Characeae (the stoneworts): M19.

chara /ˈʃarə/ *n.*[2] *colloq.* E20. [Abbrev. of next.] A motor coach.

charabanc /ˈʃarəbaŋ/ *n. arch.* Also **char-à-banc**. E19. [Fr. *char-à-bancs* lit. 'carriage with seats'.] A long and light vehicle with transverse seats looking forward; a motor coach.

characin /ˈkarəsɪn/ *n.* L19. [mod.L *Characinus* genus name, f. Gk *kharax* a kind of fish, lit. a pointed stake.] A freshwater fish of the large family Characidae, most members of which (e.g. the piranhas, tetras) occur in S. and Central America.

charact /ˈkarakt/ *n. arch.* Also †**car-**. LME. [OFr. *c(h)aract* masc., *c(h)aracte* fem., perh. ult. f. Gk *kharaktos* given or impressed as a mark, taken as n.] †**1** A mark, a sign; an engraved or impressed character. LME–M17. **2** A magical or cabbalistic sign or emblem. LME.

character /ˈkarəktə/ *n.* ME. [(O)Fr. *caractère* f. L *character* f. Gk *kharaktēr* instrument for marking, f. *kharassein* engrave; assim. to L in 16.] **1** A distinctive mark impressed, engraved, or otherwise formed. *arch.* in *gen.* sense. ME. **2** = CHARACT 2. *arch.* LME. †**b** *gen.* A symbol, an emblem; a representation. E17–E18. **3** A graphic symbol, *esp.* one denoting a sound or idea. Usu. in *pl.* L15. **b** A writing-system, a set of letters etc.; writing, printing; a style of writing or printing. *arch.* L16. †**c** In *pl.* Shorthand. M17–E18. †**d** A cipher for secret correspondence etc. M17–M18. **e** *Computing.* A letter, digit, or other symbol which can be read, stored, and output by a computer; a representation of such a symbol. M20. **4** *fig.* A token; a feature, trait, characteristic. *arch.* in *gen.* sense. E16. **b** *Biol.* A distinguishing characteristic of a species etc. E18. **5** A description; *spec.* a description or detailed report of a person's qualities, a testimonial. M16. **6** The estimate formed of a person's qualities; reputation; good repute. E17. †**7** Personal appearance. E17–M18. **8** Collective peculiarities; nature, sort, style; the distinctive mental or moral qualities of an individual, a people, etc.; distinction, individuality. E17. **9** Recognized official rank; status, position; role. M17. **10a** A person regarded as the possessor of specified qualities; a personage, a personality. M17. **b** A person portrayed in a novel, a drama, etc; a part played by an actor or (*arch.*) a dissembler. M17. **c** An eccentric or noticeable person. L18. **11** Moral strength, esp. if highly developed or evident. M18.

3 F. KING Some in Western letters and some in Japanese characters. D. WALCOTT An old lady writes me in a spidery style, Each character trembling. **b** SPENSER The Saxons Character is the same with the Irish. SHAKES. *Meas. for M.* Here is the hand and seal of the Duke. You know the character, I doubt not. 4 BURKE Tell me, what one character of liberty the Americans have. 5 A. WILSON If you land back in the approved school don't come to me for a good character. 6 E. A. FREEMAN His character for sanctity. 8 A. CRUMP The amount and character of the deposits of English banks. M. INNES Inquiries on the character and habits of the missing girl. C. G. SELIGMAN In character the Tuareg are independent, brave, impulsive, and mendacious. 9 G. BURNET He had the appointments of an ambassador, but would not take the character. **10a** L. P. HARTLEY Both were exceedingly strong characters. J. CANNAN The character who owns *Mab* . . leaves his gear out in her. **b** G. GREENE A story with a senior civil servant as the main character. 11 DAY LEWIS A delicate vivid face, giving an impression of character beyond her years.

Phrases: **in, out of, character** in, not in, accord with a person's nature and reputation. *optical character reader, recognition*: see OPTICAL *a. social character*: see SOCIAL *a. specific character*: see SPECIFIC *a. titular character*: see TITULAR *a.* 3. *unit character*: see UNIT *n.*[1] & *a.*

Comb.: **character actor, actress**: specializing in character parts; **character assassination** deliberate destruction of a person's reputation; **character part** an acting part requiring strong delineation of individual, esp. eccentric or unusual, character; **character reference** a testimonial to a person's qualities; **character sketch** a brief (written) description of a person's qualities; **character string** a linear sequence of characters, esp. stored in or processed by a computer; **character witness** a person who attests to another person's good reputation.

characterful *a.* full of character, individual E20. **characterless** *a.* without character or individuality E17. **characterlessness** *n.* M19. **charactery, -try** *n.* (now *poet.*) expression of thought by symbols or characters; the symbols or characters collectively: L16.

character /ˈkarəktə/ *v.t. arch.* L16. [f. the n.] 1 Engrave; inscribe. L16. 2 Represent, portray. L16. 3 Describe. (Foll. by †*as*, †*to be*.) Cf. CHARACTERIZE 2. E17. 4 = CHARACTERIZE 4. M17. 5 = CHARACTERIZE 5. M17.

†**characterical** *a.* E17. [f. Gk *kharaktērikos*, f. *kharaktēr*: see CHARACTER *n.*, -ICAL.] 1 Characteristic, distinctive. E17–M18. 2 Of or pertaining to symbolic characters, magical symbols, or charms. M–L17.

characterisation *n.*, **-ise** *v.* vars. of CHARACTERIZATION, -IZE.

†**characterism** *n.* Also (earlier) in L form **-ismus**. M16. [Late L *characterismus* f. Gk *kharaktērismos*, f. *kharaktēr*: see CHARACTER *n.*, -ISM.] 1 Characterization, description of character. M16–E19. 2 Characteristic quality; a characteristic. M17–L19.

characteristic /karəktəˈrɪstɪk/ *a.* & *n.* M17. [Fr. *caractéristique* or med.L *characteristicus* f. late Gk *kharaktēristikos*, f. Gk *kharaktēr*: see CHARACTER *n.*, -ISTIC.] A *adj.* Indicative of character; typical; distinctive. (Foll. by *of*.) M17.

characteristic curve: showing the relation between two interdependent quantities (esp. properties of a device). STATIC *characteristic curve*.

B *n.* 1 A distinctive mark; a distinguishing trait, peculiarity, or quality. M17. 2 *Math.* The integral part of a logarithm. M17. 3 A characteristic curve. E20.

3 *mutual characteristic*: see MUTUAL *a.* STATIC *characteristic*.

characteristical *a.* & *n.* (*a*) *adj.* (*arch.*) = CHARACTERISTIC *a.*; †(*b*) *n.* = CHARACTERISTIC *n.* 1: E17. **characteristically** *adv.* M17. **characteristicalness** *n.* (*arch.*) L18. **characteristicness** *n.* E19.

characterization /karəkt(ə)rʌɪˈzeɪʃ(ə)n/ *n.* Also **-isation**. L16. [f. next + -ATION.] The action or result of characterizing; *esp.* (*a*) portrayal in words etc., description; (*b*) the (effective) creation of a fictitious character or fictitious characters.

characterize /ˈkarəktərʌɪz/ *v.* Also **-ise**. L16. [Fr. *caractériser* or med.L *characterizare*, f. Gk *kharaktērizein*, f. *kharaktēr*: see CHARACTER *n.*, -IZE.] †1 *v.t.* Engrave, inscribe; = CHARACTER *v.* 1. L16–E19. 2 *v.t.* Describe the character or peculiar qualities of; describe *as* (also †*to be*). E17. †3 Represent, portray; = CHARACTER *v.* 2. M17–E18. 4 *v.t.* Mark or distinguish as a character does; be a characteristic of. M18. 5 *v.i.* & *t.* Impart character (to). E19.

characterizer *n.* M18.

characterology /karəktəˈrɒlədʒi/ *n.* E20. [f. CHARACTER *n.* + -OLOGY, tr. G *Charakterologie*.] The branch of psychology that deals with character, esp. its development and variation between individuals.

characteroˈlogical *a.* E20. **characterologist** *n.* E20.

charade /ʃəˈrɑːd/ *n.* L18. [Fr. f. mod.Prov. *charrado* conversation, f. *charra* chatter, perh. of imit. origin.] 1 A written or (now usu.) acted clue from which a syllable of a word or a complete word is to be guessed. L18. b (In *pl.* usu. treated as *sing.*) A game of guessing words from such clues. M19. 2 *fig.* An absurd pretence. L19.

charas /ˈtʃɑːrəs/ *n.* Also **churrus** /ˈtʃʌrəs/. M19. [Hind. *caras*.] A narcotic resin from the flower-heads of hemp; cannabis resin.

charbroil /ˈtʃɑːbrɔɪl/ *v.t.* Orig. *US.* M20. [f. CHARCOAL *n.* + BROIL *v.*[1]] Grill (meat etc.) on a rack over charcoal.

charchaf *n.* var. of CHARSHAF.

charcoal /ˈtʃɑːkəʊl/ *n.* & *v.* LME. [Origin uncertain: conn. w. COAL *n.* in sense 'charcoal'.] A *n.* 1 *sing.* & †in *pl.* The black porous residue of partly burnt wood, bones, etc., a form of carbon. LME. 2 A charcoal pencil or crayon; a drawing in this medium. L17. 3 In full *charcoal grey*. A dark grey. E20.

1 *activated charcoal*: see ACTIVATE *v.* 1. *active charcoal*: see ACTIVE *a.* 5. *mineral charcoal*: see MINERAL *a.*

Comb.: **charcoal biscuit**: containing wood-charcoal as an aid to digestion; **charcoal-burner** a maker of charcoal; **charcoal filter**: using charcoal to absorb impurities; *charcoal grey*: see sense 3 above.

B *v.t.* 1 Mark, write, or blacken with charcoal. M19. 2 Suffocate with the fumes of charcoal. M19.

charcuterie /ʃarkytri (*pl. same*); ʃɑːˈkuːt(ə)riː/ *n.* M19. [Fr., f. †*char* (mod. *chair*) *cuite* cooked flesh: see -ERY.] Cold cooked meats; a shop selling these; a (French) pork-butcher's shop.

charcutier /ʃarkytje (*pl. same*); ʃɑːˈkuːtɪeɪ/ *n.* a (French) pork-butcher; a person who prepares or sells *charcuterie*: L19.

chard /tʃɑːd/ *n.* Also **sh-** /ʃ-/. M17. [Fr. *carde*, perh. alt. by assoc. w. *chardon* thistle: see CARDOON.] The blanched shoots of globe artichoke or salsify. Also (more fully *Swiss chard*), (the edible leaves and stalks of) seakale beet.

Chardonnay /ˈʃɑːdəneɪ/ *n.* E20. [Fr.] (The vine bearing) a white grape used in wine-making; (a drink of) dry white wine made from these grapes. Also *Pinot Chardonnay*.

chare /tʃɛː/ *n.*[1] *north.* ME. [Perh. same wd as CHARE *n.*[2], CHAR *n.*[1]] A narrow lane; an alley.

chare *n.*[2], *v.* see CHAR *n.*[1], *v.*[1]

†**charet** *n.* Also **-ette**. LME–E19. [(O)Fr. *charrette*, f. as CHAIR *n.*[2]: see -ET[1], -ETTE.] A cart; a chariot.

charge /tʃɑːdʒ/ *n.* ME. [(O)Fr. f. Proto-Romance, f. late L *car(ri)care*: see CHARGE *v.*] I†1 A (material) load, burden, or weight. ME–E18. 2 *fig.* A load (of trouble, inconvenience, etc.); a source of trouble or inconvenience. ME. 3 A task or duty laid upon one; commission, responsibility. ME. 4 The duty or responsibility of taking care *of* (a person or thing); care, custody, control, superintendence. LME. b A thing or person entrusted to the care of someone; *spec.* the people or district committed to the care of a member of the clergy. M16. †5 Importance, moment. LME–L16. 6a Pecuniary burden, cost. *arch.* LME. b *sing.* & in *pl.* Expense. *arch.* E16. c *Comm.* In *pl.* Incidental expenses. M16. d A price required or demanded for service rendered or goods supplied. E19. 7 A liability to pay money laid on a person or estate. LME. 8 A precept, an order, *spec.* an official instruction or admonition given by a judge to a jury, by a bishop to his clergy, etc. LME. 9 An accusation; *spec.* that upon which a prisoner is brought up for trial. L15. 10 *Her.* A device or bearing placed on a shield, crest, or supporter. L16. 11 *Farriery.* A thick adhesive plaster; a protective pad for the foot. E17. 12 The quantity of something which a receptacle, mechanism, etc., is designed to bear or receive at one time; *esp.* the appropriate quantity of explosive for a gun. M17. b A quantity of explosive; an explosive device. L19. 13a An accumulation of electricity on or in a body, or of chemical energy in a battery that is available for conversion to electricity; the amount of this, = *electric charge* s.v. ELECTRIC *a.* Also, the process of charging a battery. M18. b *fig.* A concentration of emotion etc. M19. c A quantity of electricity borne by an atom, molecule, or subatomic particle. L19. 14 *slang.* a A dose or injection of a drug. E20. b A thrill; a sharp stimulant effect; a feeling of excitement or satisfaction. M20. c Marijuana. M20.

2 A. FRASER The village was selfishly concerned that the baby should not be abandoned there, as a charge on the parish. 3 W. S. CHURCHILL I have therefore laid down the charge which was placed upon me. 4b J. FOWLES That sustained .. attention to her charges that a governess's duties require. 5 SHAKES. *Rom. & Jul.* The letter was not nice, but full of charge Of dear import. 6b THACKERAY A .. cathedral built by the present bishop at his own charges. LD MACAULAY Well armed and mounted at their own charge. d A. C. BOULT The charge for admission .. was always one penny. 8 H. JAMES The very words of the lady of Woollett ..; her parting charge to her child. 9 R. TRAVERS His warrant for the arrest of one Frank Harwood .. on the charge of wilful murder. *bring, lay, prefer*, etc., *a charge* (*against*). 12 POPE A charge of snuff the wily virgin threw. S. SASSOON The trigger .. had come loose .. and wouldn't fire the charge. b F. FITZGERALD The Viet Cong had set off plastic charges in the midst of the crowd. 13b P. BROOK A verse play is half way between prose and the opera, .. yet with a higher charge than prose. 14b J. RABAN It gives one a charge as strong as a snift of cocaine. c *Melody Maker* Smoking charge on the premises.

II 15 A rushing attack by soldiers, police, members of a team, an animal, etc.; an attack made by throwing oneself against an opponent in football etc. M16. b *Mil.* A signal for attack sounded on a trumpet or other instrument. M17. †16 The position of a weapon ready for action. L16–M17.

15 P. G. WODEHOUSE The Old Guard made their last desperate charge up the blood-soaked slopes of Waterloo. b C. S. FORESTER He yelled to his bugler to sound the charge.

Phrases: **free of charge** without payment. **give in charge** hand over (a person) to the custody of the police. **in charge** in control, with overall responsibility. **in charge of** (*a*) under the supervision or control of; (*b*) having supervision or control of. **lay to someone's charge** impute to someone as a fault; charge someone with. **on a charge** accused of a particular offence under (esp. military) law. **on charge** (of a battery) being charged. *prior charge*: see PRIOR *a.* **put in charge** cause (a person) to have supervision or control. **put on a charge** accuse of a particular offence under (esp. military) law. **return to the charge** *fig.* begin again, esp. in argument. *reverse the charges*: see REVERSE *v.* 7. *shaped charge*: see SHAPED 1. *specific charge*: see SPECIFIC *a.* STRATIFIED *charge*. **take charge** assume control or direction (*of*); *colloq.* (of things) get out of control, esp. with disastrous results.

Comb.: **charge account** a credit account at a shop etc.; **charge-book**: in which are recorded cases and charges at a police court; **charge cap** an imposed upper limit on the amount that can be charged; **charge-cap** *v.t.* subject to charge-capping; **charge-capping** imposition of an upper limit on the amount that can be charged, esp. by a local authority for public services; **charge card** a credit card, esp. for use at a particular store or chain of stores or for an account which must be cleared in full on receipt of a statement; **charge carrier** = CARRIER *n.* 9; **charge-hand** a worker who is in charge of others; **charge-house** †(*a*) a (boarding-)school; (*b*) a workshop in which explosive is loaded into shells etc.; **charge-nurse**: in charge of a ward etc.; **charge-sheet**: on which are recorded cases and charges made at a police station.

†**chargeful** *a.* burdensome; costly; full of responsibility: LME–E17. **chargeless** *a.* (now *rare*) L16.

charge /tʃɑːdʒ/ *v.* ME. [(O)Fr. *charger* f. late L *car(ri)care* to load, f. L *carrus* CAR.] I 1 *v.t.* Place a load on or in. *obs.* exc. as passing into other senses. ME. †b Overload. LME–L18. 2 *v.t.* Load or fill (a thing) to the full or proper extent; *spec.* load (a gun) with explosive and shot. ME. b Load, fill, saturate, *with* (*lit.* & *fig.*); imbue *with*. L16. c Give an electric charge to (a body); store a charge in (a battery etc.). Also foll. by *up*. M18. †3 *v.t.* Burden *with* sin, guilt, sickness, etc. ME–M17. †4 *v.t.* Burden with or put to expense etc. ME–M17. 5 *v.t.* Entrust or commission *with* as a duty, task, or responsibility. ME. 6 *v.t.* Command, order, *to do*, *that* (w. subjunct.). ME. b Deliver an official or formal instruction or exhortation to. E17. 7 *v.t.* Blame, censure; accuse, *spec.* of a particular offence under law. (Foll. by *with* an offence.) ME. b Lay as a charge *against*, *on*, *upon*; state or assert in an indictment; make the charge *that*. E17. †8 *v.t.* Attach weight or importance to; regard. ME–M16. 9a *v.t.* Subject or make liable (a person, estate, etc.) to a pecuniary obligation or liability. (Foll. by *with* the liability.) ME. b *v.t.* Require or demand (a price, *for* service rendered or goods supplied); impose as a liability or pecuniary charge (*on* a person, estate, etc.); put as a charge (*up*) *to*, *against*, *on*, an account; debit to an account. L18. c *v.t.* w. double obj. Require or demand (a price) from (a person etc.). (Foll. by *for*.) M19. **d** *v.i.* Make a pecuniary charge. M19. **10** *Her.* Place a bearing on (an escutcheon or another bearing). L16.

2 J. HERRIOT A bottle of Glenlivet Malt to charge Granville's glass. **b** E. A. PARKES Water highly charged with calcium carbonate. H. JAMES A table charged with purchases. T. COLLINS The air was still charged with dust. W. C. WILLIAMS Poetry is language charged with emotion. F. HERBERT Starlight displaced just enough of the night to charge each shadow with menace. **5** J. C. RANSOM The department of English is charged with . . the communication of literature. **6** SIR W. SCOTT He charged, That his array Should southward march. R. V. JONES Stafford Cripps was charged by Churchill to conduct an enquiry. **7** F. RAPHAEL Cricklewood Police Station where his father had been charged. H. KISSINGER He had charged his predecessors with weakness. **b** DRYDEN Charge the crime, On native sloth. L. A. FIEDLER It has been charged against vulgar art that it is sadistic. S. KINGSLEY Mr. Reynolds charges you gave him money from the public treasuries. **9a** W. CRUISE: H. Lawson . . charged all his personal estate, with the payment of his debts. **b** A. LOOS They would charge up all the bills to Lady Francis Beekman. W. FAULKNER Have you been charging things at stores again? T. S. ELIOT The villages dirty and charging high prices. E. WAUGH This is the first time I've charged anything on expenses. G. M. FRASER Fifteen dollars a bottle they were charging for claret. **c** OED They were charged five shillings a head for dinner. **d** MRS H. WOOD I could not charge . . please say no more about payment. **10 charged with** bearing.

II 11 *v.t.* & *i.* Make a rushing attack (on); rush or throw oneself (against or upon) with all one's force. LME. **12** *v.t.* Place (a weapon) in position for action. E16.

11 M. MITCHELL Charging up the hill at his usual breakneck speed. M. ROBERTS I thought I was going to be killed when those police horses charged us.

chargeable *a.* †(*a*) of the nature of a charge or burden; responsible; burdensome; costly; (*b*) able or liable to be charged: LME. **charged** *ppl a.* that has been charged, now *spec.* with electricity or (*fig.*) emotion etc. LME.

chargé /'ʃɑːʒeɪ; *foreign* ʃarʒe (*pl. same*)/ *n.* M19. [Abbrev.] = CHARGÉ D'AFFAIRES.

chargé d'affaires /ˌʃɑːʒeɪ da'fɛː; *foreign* ʃarʒe dafɛːr/ *n. phr.* Pl. **chargés d'affaires** (pronounced same). Also †**chargé des affaires**. M18. [Fr. = (a person) in charge of affairs.] **1** A minister who transacts diplomatic business during the temporary absence of an ambassador; a State's representative at a minor foreign court or government. M18. **2** *gen.* A person temporarily in charge. L18.

chargee /tʃɑː'dʒiː/ *n.* Now *rare.* L19. [f. CHARGE *v.* or *n.* + -EE[1].] *Law.* The person to whom a charge on an estate etc. is due.

charger /'tʃɑːdʒə/ *n.*[1] ME. [AN *chargeour* (cf. OFr. *chargeoir* basket strapped on the back, *chargeoire* device for loading guns): see CHARGE *v.*, -OUR, -ER[2].] A large plate or flat dish.

charger /'tʃɑːdʒə/ *n.*[2] L15. [f. CHARGE *v.* + -ER[1].] **1** An appliance for charging a gun, rifle, electric battery, etc. L15. **2** A person who makes a charge, an accuser. *rare.* L16. **3** A cavalry horse; *poet.* any horse. M18. **4** *Law.* A person who must pay a charge on an estate etc. Now *rare.* M19.

chariot /'tʃarɪət/ *n.* & *v.* LME. [(O)Fr., augm. of *char* ult. f. L *carrum*, *-us*: see CAR. Cf. CHAIR *n.*[2], CHARET.] **A** *n.* A wheeled conveyance, usu. horse-drawn, *spec.* †(*a*) a cart, a wagon; (*b*) *poet.* a stately or triumphal carriage; (*c*) a two-wheeled vehicle used in ancient warfare and racing; (*d*) (chiefly *Hist.*) a light four-wheeled carriage with back seats only. LME. **B** *v.* **1** *v.i.* Drive or ride in a chariot. M16. **2** *v.t.* Carry or convey in or as a chariot. M17.

chario'tee *n.* (*US*, *Hist.*) a light four-wheeled pleasure carriage with two seats E19. **chariotry** *n.* †(*a*) *rare* the art of driving a chariot; (*b*) the body of soldiers who fought from chariots: L17.

charioteer /tʃarɪə'tɪə/ *n.* & *v.* ME. [OFr. *charieter*, *charioteur*, f. as prec.; later directly f. prec.: see -EER.] **A** *n.* **1** The driver of a chariot. ME. **2** (Usu. **C-**.) *The* constellation Auriga. E20. **B** *v.* **1** *v.i.* & *t.* Drive (a chariot). E19. **2** *v.t.* Drive (a person) in a chariot. M19.

charioteership *n.* performance as a charioteer M19.

charism /'karɪz(ə)m/ *n.* L15. [f. as next.] *Chr. Theol.* = CHARISMA 1.

charisma /kə'rɪzmə/ *n.* Pl. **-mata** /-mətə/. M17. [eccl.L f. Gk *kharisma*, *-mat-*, f. *kharis* favour, grace.] **1** *Chr. Theol.* A divinely conferred power or talent. M17. **2** A capacity to inspire devotion and enthusiasm; aura. M20.

charismatic /karɪz'matɪk/ *a.* & *n.* L19. [f. Gk *kharismat-* (see prec.) + -IC.] **A** *adj.* **1** *Chr. Theol.* Of or pertaining to a charisma; divinely conferred. L19. **b** Designating, of, or pertaining to Christian worship marked by enthusiasm, spontaneity, ecstatic utterance, etc.; Pentecostal. M20. **2** Having charisma. M20. **B** *n.* A person who claims divine inspiration; an adherent of charismatic worship. M20.

charismatically *adv.* M20.

charitable /'tʃarɪtəb(ə)l/ *a.* ME. [(O)Fr., f. as CHARITY: see -ABLE.] †**1** Showing Christian charity or the love of God and man. ME–M17. †**2** Tender-hearted; loving; benevolent. LME–M17. **3** Full of active charity to others; *esp.* generous in giving to the poor. LME. **4** Connected with or devoted to a recognized object of charity; of the nature of a charity. L16. **5** Apt to judge favourably of persons, acts, motives, etc. E17.

4 I. MURDOCH A charitable organization supported mainly by American contributions. **5** BACON By a charitable construction it may be a sermon. A. F. DOUGLAS-HOME The most even-tempered and charitable of persons.

charitableness *n.* LME. **charitably** *adv.* LME.

charitarian /tʃarɪ'tɛːrɪən/ *n.* M19. [f. CHARITY + -ARIAN.] A supporter of charities; a do-gooder.

charitative /'tʃarɪtətɪv/ *a.* Now *rare.* LME. [OFr. *charitatif* f. med.L *caritativus*, f. L *caritat-*: see next, -IVE.] **1** Of the nature of or pertaining to charity. LME. †**2** Of the nature of a charitable gift or donation. L16–E18.

charity /'tʃarɪti/ *n.* LOE. [(O)Fr. *charité* f. L *caritas*, f. *carus* dear: see -ITY. Cf. CARITAS.] **1** Christian love; *esp.* Christian love of one's fellow-men. LOE. **2** *gen.* Love, kindness, natural affection; spontaneous goodness. ME. †**b** Fairness, equity. LME–M17. **c** A disposition to think favourably of others, their actions, etc., and to make allowance for their shortcomings. L15. **d** In *pl.* Feelings or acts of affection. M17. **3** Beneficence; liberality to or provision for those in need or distress; alms-giving. ME. **b** Money, a gift, or other assistance to relieve need or distress. ME. **c** A trust, foundation, organization, etc., for the benefit of others, esp. of those in need or distress. L16. **d** In *pl.* Acts or works of liberality. E17.

3 R. H. TAWNEY Each town must organize charity for the support of the honest poor. *Proverb*: Charity begins at home. *charity ball, concert*, etc. *cold as charity* (w. allus. to the unsympathetic administration of charity). **Brother, Sister, of Charity** a male, female, member of a religious order devoted to charity. *legal charity*: see LEGAL *a.*

Comb.: **Charity Commission(ers)** a board established to control charitable trusts; **charity school**: supported by charitable contributions; **charity walk** a sponsored walk to raise money for a charity; **charity walker** a participant in a charity walk.

charivari /ʃɑːrɪ'vɑːri/ *n.* & *v.* See also SHIVAREE. M17. [Fr., of unkn. origin.] **A** *n.* A cacophonous mock serenade in derision of an unpopular person, marriage, etc.; a discordant medley of sounds, a hubbub. M17. **B** *v.t.* Greet or serenade with a charivari. E19.

chark /tʃɑːk/ *n. obs.* exc. *dial.* E18. [App. f. CHARK *v.*[2]] Charred wood or coal; charcoal.

chark /tʃɑːk/ *v.*[1]*i. obs.* exc. *dial.* [OE *ċearcian*: cf. CHIRK *v.*] **1** Grind one's teeth; (of teeth) grind. OE. †**2** Creak. Only in LME. **3** Complain querulously. *Sc.* E19.

chark /tʃɑːk/ *v.*[2]*t.* M17. [f. CHARCOAL analysed as *chark coal*: cf. CHAR *v.*[2]] Burn to charcoal or coke; char.

charka /'tʃɜːkə/ *n.* Also **-kha**. L19. [Urdu *charka*, *-kā* spinning-wheel f. Pers. *čark(a)* rel. to Skt *cakra* wheel.] In the Indian subcontinent: a domestic spinning-wheel, used chiefly for cotton.

charlatan /'ʃɑːlət(ə)n/ *n.* & *a.* E17. [Fr. f. It. *ciarlatano*, f. *ciarlare* to babble, patter, of imit. origin.] **A** *n.* **1** A mountebank; *esp.* an itinerant vendor of medicines. *obs.* exc. as passing into sense 2. E17. **2** A false pretender to knowledge or skill, orig. and esp. in medicine; a quack; a pretentious impostor. L17. **B** *adj.* Of, pertaining to, or characteristic of a charlatan. L17.

charlatanic /ʃɑːlə'tanɪk/ *a.* M19. **charlatanical** /ʃɑːlə'tanɪk(ə)l/ *a.* M17. **charlatanism** *n.* the practice or method of a charlatan; the condition of being a charlatan: E19. **charlatanry** *n.* quackery, imposture M17.

Charles' law /'tʃɑːlz lɔː/ *n. phr.* Also **Charles's law** /'tʃɑːlzɪz lɔː/. L19. [J. A. C. *Charles* (1746–1823), Fr. physicist.] *Chem.* A law stating that the volume of an ideal gas at constant pressure is directly proportional to the absolute temperature.

Charles's Wain /tʃɑːlzɪz 'weɪn/ *n. phr.* [OE *Carles wæġn* the wain of Carl or Charles (Charlemagne), perh. by assoc. of the star Arcturus with King Arthur, himself assoc. w. Charlemagne.] *The* Plough (PLOUGH *n.* 4).

Charleston /'tʃɑːlst(ə)n, -lz-/ *n.* & *v.* Also **c-**. E20. [A city and county in S. Carolina, USA.] **A** *n.* A dance characterized by side-kicks from the knee. E20. **B** *v.i.* Dance the Charleston; kick sideways from the knee. E20.

Charley *n.* var. of CHARLIE.

charley horse /'tʃɑːli hɔːs/ *n. phr. N. Amer. slang.* L19. [Origin unkn.] Stiffness or cramp in an arm or a leg.

Charlie /'tʃɑːli/ *n.* Also **-ley**, **c-**. E19. [Dim. of male forename *Charles*: see -IE, -Y[6].] †**1** A night-watchman. E–M19. **2** A small triangular beard, as worn by King Charles I. E19. **3** A name for the fox. M19. **4** In *pl.* A woman's breasts. *slang.* L19. **5** A fool, an idiot. *slang.* M20. **6** A native or inhabitant, esp. a soldier, of (North) Vietnam. *US* & *Austral. slang.* M20.

Phrases: *tail-end Charlie*: see TAIL-END 1b.

charlock /'tʃɑːlɒk/ *n.* [OE *ċerlic*, *ċyrlic*, of unkn. origin.] Wild mustard, *Sinapis arvensis*, a yellow-flowered cruciferous weed of cultivated land. Formerly also, any of several other similar plants.

charlotte /'ʃɑːlət/ *n.* L18. [Fr.] A pudding made of stewed fruit with a casing or covering of bread, biscuits, sponge cake, or breadcrumbs.

charlotte russe /ruːs/ [Fr. *russe* Russian.] a custard etc. enclosed in a sponge cake or sponge biscuits.

charm /tʃɑːm/ *n.*[1] ME. [(O)Fr. *charme* f. L *carmen* song, verse, oracular response, incantation.] **1** The chanting of a verse supposedly having magic power; an incantation; any action, process, verse, etc., credited with such properties; a magic spell, a talisman. ME. **2** A quality or feature exciting love or admiration; attractiveness; the indefinable power of delighting; in *pl.*, sexual attractiveness. L16. **3** A thing worn to avert evil etc.; an amulet; a trinket on a bracelet etc. L16. **4** *Particle Physics.* A quark flavour associated with a charge of +⅔. (Symbol c.) M20.

Phrases: **work like a charm** work perfectly.

Comb.: **charm-bracelet**: hung with charms; **charm school**: at which the social graces are taught.

charmful *a.* full of charms or spells; charming: M17. **charmless** *a.* E18. **charmlessly** *adv.* L19. **charmlessness** *n.* E20.

charm *n.*[2] see CHIRM *n.*

charm /tʃɑːm/ *v.*[1] ME. [(O)Fr. *charmer*, f. as CHARM *n.*[1] Sense 7 prob. infl. by prec.] **1** *v.i.* Work charms, use spells, practise magic. Now *rare.* ME. **2** *v.t.* Act upon (as) with a charm or magic; put a spell on; bewitch. LME. **b** Bring *from* or *out* (*of*), send *away*, etc., by a charm or charms. M16. **3** *v.t.* Give (seemingly) magical powers or virtues to; give special good fortune or protection to. LME. **4** *v.t.* Enthral, captivate, delight; give pleasure to. LME. **b** *v.i.* Be enthralling; give pleasure. *poet.* E18. **5** *v.t.* Subdue as if by magic power; soothe, allay. M16.

†6 *v.t.* Invoke; entreat in the name of a power. L16–M18. †7 *v.t.* Temper, tune, play, (an instrument or melody). L16–E17.

1 SHAKES. *Haml.* No fairy takes, nor witch hath power to charm. 2 E. K. KANE They wanted me to charm or cure him. 4 ADDISON He every where charms and pleases us by the Force of his own Genius. P. G. WODEHOUSE 'Like you.. to meet my friends. Lady Underhill. Mr. Devereux.' 'Charmed,' said Ronnie affably. 5 POPE Music the fiercest grief can charm.

charmer *n.* a person who charms; *spec.* (*a*) an enchanter; (*b*) a particularly attractive or delightful person; (*c*) a person who subdues or controls as if by magic power (*snake-charmer*: see SNAKE *n.*): ME. **charming** *ppl a.* that charms; *spec.* (*a*) (now *rare*) using charms, exercising magic power; (*b*) particularly attractive, delightful (freq. *iron.*) (*Prince Charming*: see PRINCE *n.*): LME. **charmingly** *adv.* E17. **charmingness** *n.* M18.

charm *v.*[2] see CHIRM *v.*

charmed /tʃɑːmd/ *a.* LME. [f. CHARM *v.*[1], *n.*[1]: see -ED[1], -ED[2].] 1 That has been charmed; enchanted; protected by a charm. LME. 2 *Particle Physics.* Designating a *c* quark; having the property charm. M20.

1 E. P. THOMPSON Binns, who bore a charmed life, was acquitted of high treason.

charmeuse /ʃɑːˈməːz, *foreign* ʃarmøːz/ *n.* E20. [Fr., fem. of *charmeur* charmer, f. as CHARM *v.*[1]] A soft smooth silky dress-fabric.

charmonium /tʃɑːˈməʊnɪəm/ *n.* L20. [f. CHARM *n.*[1] + -ONIUM.] *Physics.* A combination of a charmed quark and antiquark.

†**charneco** *n.* L16–M17. [Said to be f. the name of a village near Lisbon, Portugal] A Portuguese wine.

charnel /ˈtʃɑːn(ə)l/ *n.*[1] & *a.* LME. [OFr. f. med.L *carnale* use as n. of neut. of *carnalis* CARNAL.] A *n.* Orig., a cemetery. Now (more fully *charnel-house*) a house or vault in which dead bodies or bones are piled. LME. B *adj.* Sepulchral, deathlike, ghastly. E19.

charnel /ˈtʃɑːn(ə)l/ *n.*[2] *obs.* exc. *Hist.* L15. [OFr., prob. f. L *cardinale* neut. of *cardinalis*, f. *cardo*, *-in-* hinge: see -AL[1].] A hinge, *esp.* that of a helmet.

charnockite /ˈtʃɑːnəkʌɪt/ *n.* L19. [f. Job *Charnock* (d. 1693), founder of Calcutta, whose tombstone is of this rock, + -ITE[1].] *Geol.* A granite containing hypersthene.

charnockitic /tʃɑːnəˈkɪtɪk/ *a.* M20.

Charolais /ˈʃarəʊleɪ, *foreign* ʃarɔlɛ/ *n.* Also **-ll-**. L19. [f. Monts du *Charollais* in eastern France.] (An animal of) a breed of large white beef-cattle.

Charon /ˈkɛːrən/ *n.* L15. [L f. Gk *Kharōn.*] 1 *Gk Mythol.* The ferryman conveying souls across the Styx to Hades. L15. 2 A ferryman. *joc.* M19.

charophyte /ˈkarəfʌɪt/ *n.* E20. [mod.L *Charophyta* former name of the Characeae, f. CHARA *n.*[1]: see -O-, -PHYTE.] A member of the Characeae, a group of macroscopic mainly freshwater algae marked by whorls of short branches arising from a main axis, often partly encrusted with calcium carbonate; a stonewort.

charophytic /-ˈfɪtɪk/ *a.* E20.

charoset(h) *n.* var. of HAROSETH.

charpie /ˈʃɑːpi/ *n.* L18. [Fr.: see CARPET *n.*] Old linen unravelled into short ends of thread for surgical dressings.

charpoy /ˈtʃɑːpɔɪ/ *n.* M17. [Urdu *chārpāī* f. Pers.] In the Indian subcontinent: a light bedstead.

charqui /ˈtʃɑːki/ *n.* See also JERKY *n.*[1] E17. [(Amer. Sp. *charqui, charque* f.) Quechua *cc'arki*: cf. JERK *v.*[2]] Meat, esp. beef, cut into thin slices and dried in the wind and sun.

charr *n.* var. of CHAR *n.*[2]

charro /ˈtʃɑːrəʊ/ *n.* Pl. **-os**. E20. [Mex. Sp. f. Sp. = rustic.] A Mexican cowboy, *esp.* one elaborately dressed.

charry /ˈtʃɑːri/ *a.* L18. [f. CHAR *v.*[2] or CHARCOAL: see -Y[1].] Of the nature of charcoal or a similar charred substance.

charshaf /ˈtʃarʃaf, ˈtʃɑːʃaf/ *n.* Also ***-chaf*** /-tʃaf/. E20. [Turk. *çarşaf* f. Pers. *čādor-šab* bedspread.] A headscarf worn by Turkish and Balkan women (a remnant of the veil formerly worn).

chart /tʃɑːt/ *n.* & *v.* L16. [(O)Fr. *charte* f. L *charta*: see CARD *n.*[2]] A *n.* I 1 A map. Now *spec.* (*a*) a navigator's sea map, showing coast outlines, rocks, shoals, depths of water, etc.; (*b*) an air navigator's map; (*c*) an outline map showing special features. L16. 2 A sheet of tabulated or diagrammatic information; a set of curves on a graph etc. showing fluctuations in temperature, price, etc. M19. b *spec.* A list of the currently most popular discs, tapes, etc. Usu. in *pl.* M20. II 3 A charter; a deed, document. *obs.* exc. *Sc.* E17. †4 A card; *esp.* (*a*) a playing-card; (*b*) a compass card. L17–L18.

1 *plane chart*: see PLANE *a.* 2 *test chart*: see TEST *n.*[1]

B *v.t.* Make a chart of; record in a chart; map. M19.

Comb.: **chart-buster** *colloq.* a very popular disc, tape, etc.; **chart-topping** *a.* occupying the first place in a chart of discs, tapes, etc.

charta /ˈkɑːtə/ *n.* Pl. **-tae** /-tiː/. *rare* exc. in var. of MAGNA CARTA. M17. [med.L = legal writing, charter, f. L: see CARD *n.*[2]] A charter.

chartaceous /kɑːˈteɪʃəs/ *a.* M17. [f. late L *chartaceus*, f. L *charta*: see CARD *n.*[2], -ACEOUS.] Of the nature of paper; papery.

chartae *n.* pl. of CHARTA.

†**chartel** *n.* see CARTEL.

charter /ˈtʃɑːtə/ *n.* ME. [(O)Fr. *chartre* f. L *chartula* dim. of *charta*: see CARD *n.*[2]] 1 A written document delivered by the monarch or legislature, esp. granting privileges or recognizing rights, or creating a borough, company, university, etc.; a written constitution. ME. 2 A written contract between individuals; *esp.* (*a*) *Hist.* a deed conveying land; (*b*) = CHARTER-PARTY. ME. 3 A publicly conceded right, a privilege; effective public permission; (a) licence. M16. 4 A chartered aircraft, boat, vehicle, etc. M20.

3 WORDSWORTH And mighty forms seizing a youthful fancy Had given charter to irregular hopes. *Listener* 'It's the Scroungers' Charter,' said the man in the Liverpool jeweller's shop.

Phrases: *Atlantic Charter*: see ATLANTIC *a.* 2. *blank charter*: see BLANK *a.* **Great Charter** = MAGNA CARTA. **People's Charter** the document embodying the principles and demands of the Chartists.

Comb.: **charter flight**: by chartered aircraft; **charter-land** land held by charter, freehold land; **charter-member** an original member of a society, corporation, etc.; **Charter School** *Hist.* a school established by the Charter Society; **Charter Society** *Hist.*: founded to provide Protestant education for the Catholic poor in Ireland.

charterless *a.* LME.

charter /ˈtʃɑːtə/ *v.t.* LME. [f. the n.] 1 Grant a charter to; establish by charter. LME. 2 Privilege, license. M16. 3 Hire (a ship, vehicle, aircraft, etc.) as a conveyance. L18.

chartered /ˈtʃɑːtəd/ *ppl a.* LME. [f. prec. + -ED[1].] 1 That has been chartered. LME. 2 Having membership of a professional body with a royal charter. M19.

1 **chartered libertine** a person allowed to do as he pleases. 2 *chartered accountant, engineer, librarian, surveyor*, etc.

charterer /ˈtʃɑːt(ə)rə/ *n.* ME. [f. CHARTER *n.*, *v.* + -ER[1].] 1 A freeholder; a freeman of a chartered borough. Now chiefly *Hist.* ME. 2 A person who or organization which charters a ship, vehicle, aircraft, etc. M19.

Charterhouse /ˈtʃɑːtəhaʊs/ *n.* & *a.* LME. [AN *Chartrous*, (O)Fr. *Chartreuse* alt. of earlier AN *Chartous*, OFr. *Charteuse*, f. med.L *Cart(h)usius*, f. *Cart(h)usia*: see CARTHUSIAN. Assim. to HOUSE *n.*[1] Cf. CHARTREUX.] A *n.* 1 A Carthusian monastery. Now *arch.* or *Hist.* LME. 2 In full *Charterhouse School* (or †*Hospital*). A charitable institution, later a public school, founded on the site of the Carthusian monastery in London (later moved to Godalming, Surrey). M17. B *adj.* Carthusian. LME.

charter-party /ˈtʃɑːtəpɑːti/ *n.* LME. [Fr. *charte partie* f. med.L *charta partita* divided charter, indenture.] A written contract made between a shipowner and a merchant for the hire of a ship and the delivery of the cargo.

Chartism /ˈtʃɑːtɪz(ə)m/ *n.* M19. [f. med.L CHARTA + -ISM, after the *People's Charter* (see CHARTER *n.*).] *Hist.* The principles of a British democratic reform movement of 1837–48.

Chartist /ˈtʃɑːtɪst/ *n.* & *a.* M19. [f. as prec. + -IST.] *Hist.* A *n.* An adherent of Chartism. M19. B *adj.* Of or pertaining to Chartism or Chartists. M19.

chartographer, -graphy *ns.* etc., see CARTOGRAPHER etc.

chartreuse /ʃɑːˈtrəːz; *foreign* ʃartrøːz (*pl. same*)/ *n.* E19. [Fr., fem. of *Chartreux*: see next.] 1 *Cookery.* A dish turned out from a mould, of meat, vegetables, or (now more usually) of fruit enclosed in jelly etc. E19. 2 A green or yellow liqueur of brandy and aromatic herbs etc., orig. made by the monks of La Grande Chartreuse, near Grenoble, France. M19. 3 An apple-green colour. L19.

Chartreux /ˈʃɑːtrəː, *foreign* ʃartrø/ *n.* & *a.* Now *rare* or *obs.* Pl. of n. **-eux** /-əːz, -ø/. LME. [Fr., f. (O)Fr. *Chartreuse*: see CHARTERHOUSE.] (A) Carthusian.

chartulary /ˈkɑːtjʊləri/ *n.*[1] L17. [med.L *c(h)artularius*, f. *c(h)artula*: see CARTULARY.] An archivist.

chartulary *n.*[2] var. of CARTULARY.

chary /ˈtʃɛːri/ *a.* & *adv.* [OE *ċeariġ* = OS *carag*, OHG *charag*, f. WGmc, f. base of CARE *n.*: see -Y[1].] A *adj.* †1 Sorrowful, anxious; grievous. OE–ME. †2 Dear; cherished. LME–E19. 3 Cautious, wary; shy, fastidious; frugal, sparing, ungenerous. (Foll. by *about, in, of*, (*doing*).) M16.

3 SHAKES. *Haml.* The chariest maid is prodigal enough If she unmask her beauty to the moon. SIR W. SCOTT They were more chary of their royal presence. V. GLENDINNING One would be more chary about characterizing the Anglo-Irish were it not for the fact that they themselves have not been in the least chary about it.

B *adv.* Charily. Now *rare.* L16.

charily *adv.* L16. **chariness** *n.* L16.

Charybdis /kəˈrɪbdɪs/ *n.* LME. [L f. Gk *kharubdis* a dangerous whirlpool in Gk mythol.] A danger which threatens to engulf one; *esp.* (opp. SCYLLA) either of two dangers such that to avoid one increases the risk from the other.

chase /tʃeɪs/ *n.*[1] Also (*arch.*) **chace**. ME. [OFr. *chace* (mod. *chasse*) f. Proto-Romance, f. vb whence CHASE *v.*[1]] 1 The action or an act of chasing; pursuit; hunting. ME. b A steeplechase. L19. 2 *The* or *one's* object of pursuit, as an animal, a ship, etc. ME. 3 A tract of unenclosed land reserved for hunting, *spec.* one owned by the Crown. Now chiefly *Hist.* exc. in proper names. ME. 4 The right of hunting over or of keeping animals for hunting on a tract of land. LME. 5 *Real Tennis.* The second impact of an unreturned ball, for which the player scores unless the opponent betters it by a similar and subsequent unreturned impact which lands nearer the end wall where the chase was made. LME. 6 *Hist.* The chase-guns of a ship; the part of a ship where the chase-ports are. E17.

1 *paper-chase, steeplechase*, etc. **give chase (to)** go in pursuit (of). *lead a person a chase*: see LEAD *v.*[1] **the chase** the sport of hunting. *wild-goose chase*: see WILD GOOSE.

Comb.: **chase chorus** *Jazz*: in which musicians improvise for a few bars in turn; **chase-gun, -port** *Hist.* a gun, port, in the bow or stern of a vessel for use while chasing or being chased.

chase /tʃeɪs/ *n.*[2] L16. [Fr. *châsse*: see CASE *n.*[2]] *Printing.* A metal frame for holding composed type and blocks for printing a page or sheet.

rack chase: see RACK *n.*[2]

chase /tʃeɪs/ *n.*[3] E17. [Fr. *chas* enclosed space f. Prov. *ca(u)s* f. med.L *capsum* thorax, nave of a church.] 1 The cavity of a gun barrel; the part of a gun enclosing the bore. E17. 2 A groove or furrow cut in the face of a wall etc. to receive a pipe; a trench for drain tiles etc. M19.

chase /tʃeɪs/ *n.*[4] *dial.* M17. [Cf. Fr. dial. (Norman) *chasse.*] A green lane, *esp.* one leading up to a farmhouse or field.

chase /tʃeɪs/ *v.*[1] Also (*arch.*) **chace**. ME. [OFr. *chacier* (mod. *chasser*) f. Proto-Romance var. of L *captare* frequent. of *capere* take: cf. CATCH *v.*] **1** *v.t.* Follow with intent to kill, capture, overtake, attract, etc.; pursue, run after; appear to follow thus; try to attain or achieve. ME. †**b** Persecute, harass. ME–E17. **c** Follow (a drink etc.) with (or *with*) a chaser. *colloq.* M20. **2** *v.i.* †**a** Go hunting. ME–E16. **b** Go in pursuit. Freq. foll. by *after.* LME. **c** Hurry; move with speed. Usu. w. adv. or prep. phr. LME. **3** *v.t.* Drive *away, out, from, out of*, etc. ME. **b** Put to flight, rout; dispel. *arch.* ME. **c** Drive (cattle etc.). Long *obs.* exc. *dial.* LME.

1 SWIFT We were chased by two pirates, who soon overtook us. TENNYSON Chasing each other merrily. YEATS I chased with hounds the flying deer. P. G. WODEHOUSE He drank like a fish and was always chasing girls. J. SNOW The Australians chased the 242 runs they needed to win. *chase one's tail*: see TAIL *n.*[1] *chase the dragon*: see DRAGON *n.* **chase up** *colloq.* pursue with a specific purpose. **(go and) chase oneself** *colloq.* (usu. in *imper.*) leave, go away. **2b** SIR W. SCOTT 'Horse! horse!' the Douglas cried, 'and chase!' E. O'NEILL He doesn't give wild parties, doesn't chase after musical-comedy cuties. **c** R. MACAULAY Aunt Cynthia chased off after another exciting subject. D. H. LAWRENCE The wind chases by us and over the corn. **3** J. CONRAD The ship had been chased away. G. B. SHAW A flush of interest and delight suddenly chases the growing perplexity and boredom from her face.

chaseable *a.* fit to be chased or hunted LME. **chasing** *vbl n.*[1] (*a*) the action of the vb (*contour-chasing*: see CONTOUR *n.*); (*b*) steeplechasing: LME.

chase /tʃeɪs/ *v.*[2]*t.* LME. [App. f. ENCHASE *v.*[2]] Ornament (metal) with embossed work, engrave in relief.

chasing *vbl n.*[2] (*a*) the action of the vb; (*b*) a chased design or figure: M19.

chase /tʃeɪs/ *v.*[3]*t.* E19. [f. CHASE *n.*[3]] Groove, indent.

chaser /ˈtʃeɪsə/ *n.*[1] ME. [OFr. *chacë(o)ur* (mod. *chasseur*, f. as CHASE *v.*[1]: see -ER[2]. Later senses f. CHASE *v.*[1] + -ER[1].] **1** A person who or thing which pursues, hunts, or drives away. (Foll. by *off.*) ME. **b** *spec.* An amorous pursuer of women. *colloq.* (chiefly *US*). L19. †**2a** A horse for hunting. ME–M17. **b** A horse for steeplechasing. L19. **3** *Hist.* A chase-gun. E19. **4** A drink following a drink of another kind, as water or beer after spirits, etc. *colloq.* L19.

1 *submarine chaser*: see SUBMARINE *n.*

chaser /ˈtʃeɪsə/ *n.*[2] E18. [f. CHASE *v.*[2] + -ER[1].] A person who chases metal.

chaser /ˈtʃeɪsə/ *n.*[3] L19. [f. CHASE *v.*[3] + -ER[1].] A tool for cutting grooves.

Chasid *n.* var. of HASID.

chasm /ˈkaz(ə)m/ *n.* Earlier †**chasma**, pl. **-mae, -mas.** L16. [L *chasma* f. Gk *khasma* gaping hollow.] †**1 a** An opening up of the sea, or of the earth in an earthquake. L16–M17. **b** A (supposed) rending of the firmament or vault of heaven. E17–M18. **2** A deep fissure, a wide crack. E17. **3** *fig.* A wide difference of feeling, interests, etc., a gulf; *arch.* a hiatus, a void. M17.

chasmal *a.* belonging to or of the nature of a chasm M19. **chasmed** *a.* having chasms, cleft into chasms L18. **chasmic** *a.* = CHASMAL E20. **chasmy** *a.* full of chasms; of the nature of a chasm: L18.

chasmogamy /kazˈmɒɡəmi/ *n.* E20. [f. prec. + -O- + -GAMY.] *Bot.* The opening of the perianth at the time of flowering. Opp. CLEISTOGAMY.

chasmoˈgamic, chasmogamous *adjs.* E20.

chasse /ʃas, ʃɑːs/ *n.*[1] LME. [Fr. *châsse*: see CASE *n.*[2]] A case for the relics of a saint.

chasse /ʃas, ʃɑːs/ *n.*[2] Pl. ***chasses*** /ʃas, ˈʃɑːsɪz/. M18. [Fr., abbrev. of CHASSE-CAFÉ.] A liqueur taken after coffee, tobacco, etc.; a chaser.

chassé /ʃase (*pl. same*), ˈʃaseɪ/ *n.* E19. [Fr., lit. 'chasing, chase'.] A sliding step in which one foot displaces the other in dancing.

chassé croisé /krwaze/ [lit. 'crossed'] a double *chassé* in which partners change position; *fig.* an elaborate reversal of position.

chassé /ˈʃaseɪ/ *v.* Pa. t. & pple **-éd, -é'd.** M18. [Fr. *chasser* (imper. *chassez!*) lit. 'to chase, hunt'.] **1** *v.t.* Dismiss. *arch. slang.* M18. **2** *v.i.* Execute a *chassé*. E19.

chasse-café /ʃaskafe/ *n.* Now *rare.* Pl. pronounced same. E19. [Fr., lit. 'chase-coffee'.] A liqueur taken after coffee.

chasselas /ʃaslɑ/ *n.* M17. [A village near Mâcon in France.] A variety of white grape.

chasse-marée /ʃasmare/ *n.* Pl. pronounced same. E19. [Fr., lit. 'chase-tide.'] *Hist.* A coasting lugger used by the French for smuggling and privateering.

chassepot /ʃaspo/ *n.* Pl. pronounced same. M19. [Antoine A. *Chassepot* (1833–1905), its Fr. designer.] A type of bolt-action breech-loading rifle, used by the French army between 1866 and 1874.

chasseur /ʃaˈsəː; *foreign* ʃasœːr (*pl. same*)/ *n.* M18. [Fr., f. *chasser* (see CHASE *v.*[1]) + *-eur* -OR.] **1** *Hist.* A soldier (esp. French) equipped and trained for rapid movement. M18. **2a** An attendant dressed in military style. Now *rare* or *obs.* M18. **b** A hotel messenger, esp. in France. L19. **3** A huntsman. L18.

Comb.: **chasseur sauce** a rich sauce with wine and mushrooms for poultry or game; **chicken** etc. **chasseur**: cooked in chasseur sauce.

Chassid *n.* var. of HASID.

chassis /ˈʃasi, -iː/ *n.* Pl. same /ˈʃasɪz, -iːz/. M17. [Fr. *châssis* f. Proto-Romance, f. L *capsa* CASE *n.*[2]] †**1** A window frame, a sash. M17–E18. **2** The sliding base-frame of a mounted gun. M19. **3** The base-frame of a motor vehicle etc. E20. **4** A frame carrying radio etc. equipment. M20. **5** The human or animal frame, the body. *slang.* M20.

chassisless *a.* M20.

chaste /tʃeɪst/ *a.* ME. [(O)Fr. f. L *castus.*] **1** Abstaining from unlawful or immoral or all sexual intercourse; pure, virginal. ME. †**b** Unmarried, single. ME–L16. †**2** Free from guilt, innocent. ME–M16. **3** *fig.* Undefiled, stainless. E17. **4** Decent, seemly, esp. in speech. E17. **5** Pure in taste or style, unadorned, simple; restrained, severe. M18.

3 SHAKES. *Oth.* Let me not name it to you, you chaste stars. 4 L. STERNE The Hero's horse was a horse of chaste deportment. 5 J. WARTON So chaste and correct a writer. C. HAMPTON A large, chaste desk, its only ornament a large granite crucifix.

Comb.: **chaste-tree** [cf. AGNUS CASTUS] a violet-flowered aromatic shrub of the verbena family, *Vitex agnus-castus*, native to southern Europe which is reputed to reduce sexual desire.

chastely *adv.* ME. **chasteness** *n.* LME.

†**chaste** *v.t.* Also **chasty**. ME. [OFr. *chastier* (mod. *châtier*) f. L *castigare* CASTIGATE.] **1** = CHASTEN. ME–E17. **2** Reprove, rebuke. Only in ME.

chastelain *n.* var. of CHATELAIN.

†**chastelet** *n.* see CHATELET.

chasten /ˈtʃeɪs(ə)n/ *v.t.* E16. [f. CHASTE *v.* + -EN[5].] **1** Esp. of God: discipline, punish by inflicting suffering, chastise. E16. **2** Render pure in character or style. E18. **3** *fig.* Moderate; restrain, subdue. M19.

1 TENNYSON The love Wherewith we love the Heaven that chastens us. 3 A. P. HERBERT Ernest hobbled on board, chastened by his fall, but cursing terribly.

chastener *n.* a person who or thing which chastens M16.

chastise /tʃaˈstʌɪz/ *v.t.* Also **-ize**. ME. [App. irreg. f. CHASTE *v.*] †**1** Correct the faults of; reform. ME–L17. **2** Reprove, rebuke. Long *obs.* exc. *dial.* ME. **3** Punish with a view to amendment; inflict (esp. corporal) punishment on; thrash. ME. **b** Inflict punishment for (an offence). *rare.* L16. **4** = CHASTEN 3. Now *rare* or *obs.* LME. **5** = CHASTEN 2. Now *rare* or *obs.* E17.

¶Orig., & usu. in Shakes., stressed on 1st syll.: cf. next.

chastisable *a.* that may be, or deserves to be, chastised E17. **chastiser** *n.* LME.

chastisement /ˈtʃastɪzm(ə)nt, tʃaˈstʌɪz-/ *n.* ME. [f. prec. + -MENT.] †**1** Correction of faults; (a) discipline. ME–E17. **2** Punishment, esp. corrective or disciplinary; thrashing. ME.

chastity /ˈtʃastɪti/ *n.* ME. [(O)Fr. *chasteté* f. L *castitas*, f. *castus* CHASTE *a.*: see -ITY.] **1** The quality or state of being chaste; virginity, celibacy. ME. **2** Moderation, restraint; simplicity of style or taste. M18.

1 *girdle of chastity*: see GIRDLE *n.*[1]

Comb.: **chastity belt** a garment designed to prevent the woman wearing it from having sexual intercourse.

chastize *v.* var. of CHASTISE.

†**chasty** *v.* var. of CHASTE *v.*

chasuble /ˈtʃazjʊb(ə)l/ *n.* ME. [OFr. *chesible*, later (O)Fr. *chasuble*, f. late L *casubla* obscure alt. of L *casula* little cottage, hooded cloak, dim. of *casa* house.] A sleeveless vestment worn by the celebrant at the Mass or Eucharist.

chat /tʃat/ *n.*[1] *obs.* exc. *dial.* LME. [Fr. *chats* lit. 'cats'.] **1** A catkin. LME. †**2** The winged fruit of the sycamore etc. M16–L17. **3** A small branch or twig, for kindling etc. M16.

chat /tʃat/ *n.*[2] M16. [f. CHAT *v.*] **1** Idle or frivolous talk, small talk, gossip; (now usu.) easy familiar talk. M16. **2** A light or (usu.) easy familiar conversation. M17.

1 SHAKES. *Tam. Shr.* O, how I long to have some chat with her! SWIFT Scarce list'ning to their idle chat. I. MURDOCH 'I am writing my memoirs.' 'Theatre chat?' 2 E. M. FORSTER Dear, one moment—we may not have this chance for a chat again.

Comb.: **chatline** a telephone service for conversation among a number of people on separate lines; **chat show** an entertainment of interviews, on television etc.

chat /tʃat/ *n.*[3] L17. [Prob. imit.] **1** Any of numerous small Old World thrushes with harsh calls and freq. boldly coloured plumage; *esp.* a stonechat, a whinchat. L17. **2** Any of various other small birds with harsh calls, esp. New World warblers of the genera *Granatellus* and *Icteria* (family Parulidae), and Australian birds of the family Ephthianuridae. L18.

1 *robin-chat*: see ROBIN *n.*[1] 2 *woodchat*: see WOOD *n.*[1] *yellow-breasted chat*: see YELLOW *a.*

chat /tʃat/ *v.* Infl. **-tt-**. LME. [Abbrev. of CHATTER *v.*] **1** *v.i.* Talk idly or frivolously or (now usu.) easily and familiarly. LME. †**2** *v.t.* Talk idly or familiarly of; say idly or familiarly. L15–M18. **3** *v.t.* Talk to (a person), esp. flirtatiously or with an ulterior motive. Freq. foll. by *up. slang.* L19.

1 T. F. POWYS The remainder . . chatted with one another. M. LASKI They were chatted to in the streets. P. H. JOHNSON We sat . . chatting of nothing in particular. 3 V. S. PRITCHETT The girl in red, the one you were chatting up.

château /ˈʃatəʊ, *foreign* ʃɑːto/ *n.* Pl. **-eaux** /-əʊz, *foreign* -o/. M18. [Fr.: see CASTLE *n.*[1]] A large country house in France (formerly also elsewhere); *esp.* one giving its name to wine made in its neighbourhood.

château in air, in Spain, *en Espagne* /ɒn ɛspaɲ/ = *castle in the air, in Spain* s.v. CASTLE *n.*[1] I.

Comb. **château-bottled** *a.* (of wine) bottled at the vineyard.

Chateaubriand /ʃatobrijɑ̃/ *n.* Pl. pronounced same. L19. [François René, Vicomte de *Chateaubriand* (1768–1848), Fr. writer and statesman.] A thick fillet beefsteak, grilled and garnished with herbs etc. Also *Chateaubriand grill, steak*, etc.

chatelain /ˈʃatəleɪn/ *n.* Also (earlier) **chast-** /ˈʃast-/. LME. [OFr. *chastelain* (mod. *châtelain*): see CASTELLAN.] *Hist.* = CASTELLAN I.

chatelaine /ˈʃatəleɪn/ *n.* M19. [Fr. *châtelaine* fem. of *châtelain*: see prec.] **1** A female castellan (*Hist.*); the mistress of a castle or country house. M19. **2** *Hist.* A set of short chains attached to a woman's belt for carrying keys, a watch, a pencil, etc. M19.

chatelet /ˈʃatəlɪt/ *n.* Also (earlier) †**chast-**. LME. [OFr. *chastelet* (mod. *châtelet*) dim. of *castel* CASTLE *n.*[1]: see -ET[1]. Cf. CASTELET.] *Hist.* A small castle; *spec.* a particular ancient prison in Paris.

chatellany /ˈʃatələni/ *n.* M17. [Fr. *châtellenie*, assim. to CASTELLANY.] *Hist.* = CASTELLANY.

chaton /ʃatɔ̃/ *n.* Pl. pronounced same. L16. [Fr. f. G *Kasten* (OHG, MHG *kasto*).] The part of a finger-ring in which a stone is set or on which a device is engraved.

chatoyant /ʃə'tɔɪənt, *foreign* ʃatwajɑ̃/ *n.* & *a.* Now *rare.* L18. [Fr., pres. pple of *chatoyer*: see -ANT[1].] (Of) iridescent undulating lustre.

chatta /'tʃatə, 'tʃɑːtə/ *n.* L18. [Hind. *chātā*.] In the Indian subcontinent: an umbrella.

chattel /'tʃat(ə)l/ *n.* ME. [OFr. *chatel* = Prov. *captal* f. med.L *capitale* use as n. of neut. of L *capitalis*: see CAPITAL *a.* & *n.*[2] Cf. CATTLE.] †**1 a** Property. Only in ME. **b** Livestock. *rare.* Only in 17. **2** A movable possession (in *Law* including immaterial but transferable possessions, as leases etc.); (chiefly *rhet.*) a slave, a bondman. Usu. in *pl.* ME.

2 chattels personal *Law* all movable goods. **chattels real** *Law*: such as concern the realty, as leases etc. **goods and chattels** all kinds of personal property.

Comb.: **chattel interest** (now *rare*) an interest in leasehold property; **chattel mortgage** *N. Amer.* the conveyance of chattels by mortgage as security for a debt; **chattel slave** a human being held as a chattel; **chattel slavery** = CHATTELISM.

chattelism *n.* the system of holding human beings as chattels M19.

chatter /'tʃatə/ *v.* & *n.* ME. [Imit., of frequent. formation: see -ER[5]. Cf. CHITTER.] **A** *v.* **I** *v.i.* **1** Of a bird: utter quick series of short notes (now esp. notes approaching those of the human voice). ME. **2** Of a person: talk quickly, incessantly, foolishly, or inopportunely. ME. **b** Make sounds suggestive of human chattering. E17. **3** Of the teeth: rattle together. LME. **b** Of a person: shiver, have chattering teeth. *rare.* E17. **c** Rattle with vibration. L19.

1 WORDSWORTH The jay makes answer as the magpie chatters. 2 E. FERBER They chattered on and on about little inconsequential things. **chattering classes** *colloq.* (*derog.*) the articulate professional people given to free expression of (esp. liberal) opinions on society and culture. b SHAKES. *Temp.* Like apes, that mow and chatter at me. QUILLER-COUCH A hollow in the road, across which a tiny beck . . was chattering bravely. 3 J. CARY She dressed quickly, her teeth chattering, her fingers white and weak with cold. b I. MURDOCH I was chattering with cold. c N. GORDIMER A child bore over to me a cup of milky tea chattering against its saucer.

II *v.t.* **4** Utter or say chatteringly; chatter of. ME. **5** Make (teeth) rattle. E17.

4 TENNYSON They chatter'd trifles at the door. 5 G. A. SALA Gibbering and chattering their teeth.

B *n.* **1** The chattering of birds etc.; a sound of chattering; rattling, noisy vibration. ME. **2** Incessant, trivial talk. M19.

Comb.: **chatterbox** a talkative person, esp. a child; **chattermag** *colloq.* & *dial.* a chatterbox; chatter.

chatte'ration *n.* prolonged chattering, noisy chatter M19. **chatterer** *n.* (*a*) a person who chatters; (*b*) orig. = WAXWING (*waxen chatterer*: see WAXEN *a.*); now more often, any of various other garrulous birds, *esp.* a babbler: LME. **chatteringly** *adv.* in a chattering manner M19. †**chattery** *n.* chat, chatter L18–L19. **chattery** *a.* characterized by chattering, given to chattering M19.

Chattertonian /tʃatə'təʊnɪən/ *a.* & *n.* M19. [f. *Chatterton* (see below) + -IAN.] (An admirer or student) of the English poet Thomas Chatterton (1752–70) or his pseudo-archaic literary style.

chatty /'tʃati/ *n.* L18. [Hind. *catī* f. Tamil *caṭṭi*.] In the Indian subcontinent: an earthenware pot for water.

chatty /'tʃati/ *a.* M18. [f. CHAT *n.*[2] + -Y[1].] Given to chat, fond of chatting; resembling chat.

chattily *adv.* E19. **chattiness** *n.* L19.

Chaucerian /tʃɔː'sɪərɪən/ *a.* & *n.* M17. [f. *Chaucer* (see below) + -IAN.] (An admirer, imitator, or student) of the English poet Geoffrey Chaucer (*c* 1343–1400) or his writing.

Scottish Chaucerian: see SCOTTISH *a.*

Chaucerism /'tʃɔːsərɪz(ə)m/ *n.* an expression used by or imitated from Chaucer L16.

chaud-froid /ʃəʊ'frwɑː; *foreign* ʃofrwa (*pl. same*)/ *n.* L19. [Fr., lit. 'hot-cold.'] A dish of cold cooked meat or fish in a jelly or sauce.

chaud-mellé /ʃɔːd'mɛli/ *n.* LME. [f. OFr. *chaud(e)* heated + *mellée* affray, MELLAY.] *Sc. Law* (now *Hist.*). A sudden affray arising from heated emotions; a homicide committed in hot blood and without premeditation.

chauffer /'tʃɔːfə/ *n.* LME. [Var. of CHAFER *n.*[2]; later perh. infl. by Fr. *chauffoir*, f. *chauffer*: see CHAFE *v.*] †**1** = CHAFER *n.*[2] 1. LME–E17. **2** A small portable furnace, a brazier. M19.

chauffeur /'ʃəʊfə, ʃəʊ'fəː/ *n.* & *v.* L19. [Fr. = stoker, fireman, f. *chauffer* (see CHAFE *v.*) + *-eur* -OR.] **A** *n.* †**1** A motorist. L19–E20. **2** A person employed to drive a private or hired motor car. E20. **B** *v.t.* Drive (a car) as a chauffeur; convey (a person) by car. E20.

chauffeuse /'ʃəʊfəːz, ʃəʊ'fəːz/ *n.* a female chauffeur E20.

chauki *n.* see CHOKY *n.*

chaukidar *n.* var. of CHOKIDAR.

chaulmoogra /tʃɔːl'muːgrə/ *n.* E19. [Bengali *cāul-mugrā*.] Any of several tropical Asian trees of the family Flacourtiaceae, esp. *Hydnocarpus kurzii*, whose seeds yield an oil (*chaulmoogra oil*) formerly used to treat skin diseases.

chaulmoogric *a.* (*Chem.*): *chaulmoogric acid*, a soft yellowish cyclopentene derivative, $C_{17}H_{31}COOH$, which is a major constituent of chaulmoogra oil E20.

chaung /tʃaʊŋ/ *n.* M20. [Burm.] In Myanmar (Burma), a watercourse.

chaunt *n.*, *v.* see CHANT *n.*, *v.*

chaunter *n.* see CHANTER.

chaussée /ʃose/ *n.* Pl. pronounced same. E19. [Fr.: see CAUSEY.] In France, Belgium, etc.: a causeway; a high road.

chausses /ʃoːs/ *n.pl.* L15. [Fr. = clothing for the legs.] *Hist.* Pantaloons or tight coverings for the legs and feet, esp. of mail.

¶Formerly naturalized.

chaussure /ʃosyːr/ *n.* LME. [AN *chaucer* = OFr. *chaucier* (mod. *chaussure*), Prov. *causier* shoe. Cf. med.L *calceatura*.] Footwear.

¶Formerly naturalized.

chautauqua /tʃɔː'tɔːkwə, ʃ-/ *n.* Orig. & chiefly *N. Amer.* (now *Hist.*). L19. [*Chautauqua*, a county and lake in New York State.] A summer school or similar educational course.

chauvinism /'ʃəʊv(ɪ)nɪz(ə)m/ *n.* Also **C-**. L19. [Fr. *chauvinisme*, f. as next: see -ISM.] The state or quality of being a chauvinist; chauvinistic feeling or behaviour.

B. COTTLE American hurricanes were always given women's names, a blatant piece of chauvinism. *male chauvinism*: see MALE *a.* & *n. social chauvinism*: see SOCIAL *a.*

chauvinist /'ʃəʊv(ɪ)nɪst/ *n.* & *a.* In sense A.1 also **C-**. L19. [f. Nicolas *Chauvin*, a Napoleonic veteran popularized as a character in *La cocarde tricolore* by the brothers Cogniard + -IST.] **A** *n.* **1** A bellicose patriot; a fervent supporter of a cause. L19. **2** A person who is prejudiced against or inconsiderate of those of a different sex, class, nationality, culture, etc.; *esp.* = *male chauvinist* s.v. MALE *a.* & *n.* M20. **B** *adj.* Of or pertaining to chauvinism or chauvinists; chauvinistic. L19.

chauvi'nistic *a.* bellicosely patriotic; prejudiced against or inconsiderate of those of a different sex, nationality, etc. (*male-chauvinistic*: see MALE *a.* & *n.*); showing such patriotism or prejudice: L19. **chauvi'nistically** *adv.* L20.

†**chave** *v.t.* & *i.* Also **cave**. LME–L19. [f. CHAFF *n.*[1]] Separate chaff (from).

†**chavel** *n.* see JOWL *n.*[1]

chavel /'tʃav(ə)l/ *v.* Long *obs.* exc. *dial.* Infl. **-ll-**. ME. [f. ME form of JOWL *n.*[1]] †**1** *v.i.* Talk idly, chatter. Only in ME. **2** *v.t.* Mumble (food); chew. E17.

2 *fig.*: D. H. LAWRENCE The bracken . . , broken and chavelled by the restless wild winds of the long winter.

chavender /'tʃav(ə)ndə/ *n.* Now *dial.* L15. [Obscurely f. (as) CHEVIN.] The chub.

chaw /tʃɔː/ *n.*[1] Long *obs.* exc. *Sc.* M16. [Var. of JAW *n.*[1]] †**1** A jaw. Usu. in *pl.* M16–L17. **2** Loquacity; lecturing; cheek. *Sc.* E20.

chaw /tʃɔː/ *n.*[2] *colloq.* & *dial.* E18. [Var. of CHEW *n.*: cf. CHOW *n.*[1]] An act of chewing, esp. something not for swallowing; something so chewed, *esp.* a quid of tobacco.

chaw /tʃɔː/ *v.* Now *colloq.* & *dial.* LME. [Var. of CHEW *v.*: cf. CHOW *v.*] **1** *v.t.* & *i.* Chew, now esp. without intending to swallow and in a vulgar manner. LME. †**b** *v.t.* Bite (a bullet) to make it jagged. Chiefly as *chawed* ppl a. M17–M19. **2** *v.t. fig.* Brood over, ruminate on. M16.

With advs. in specialized senses: **chaw up** *US slang* destroy, put an end to.

Comb.: **chaw-bacon** *derog.* a bumpkin, a yokel; **chaw-stick** a W. Indian climbing plant, *Gouania domingensis*, of the buckthorn family; the bark or a twig of this, chewed as a stimulant or stomachic.

chawer *n.* (*rare*) E17.

†**chawbuck** *v.t.* & *n.* As n. also **chabuk**. E17–E19. [Urdu *chābuk* f. Pers. *čābuk* horsewhip.] In India, Persia, etc.: (flog with) a whip.

chawdron /'ʃɔːdrən/ *n.* Long *obs.* exc. *dial.* Also **chald-** /'ʃɔːld-/. LME. [OFr. *chaudun* offal, pig's trotters, f. med.L *calduna*, app. f. L *calidus* hot: assim. to CHALDRON *n.*[1]] †**1** A kind of sauce made with chopped entrails, spices, etc. LME–E17. **2** *sing.* & in *pl.* Entrails, esp. as food. L16.

chawl /tʃɔːl/ *n.* L19. [Marathi *cāl* long narrow building.] In the Indian subcontinent: a type of lodging-house.

†**chawn** *n.* E17–L18. [Rel. to CHINE *n.*[1]] = CHINE *n.*[1]

chay /tʃeɪ/ *n.*[1] Also **chaya** /'tʃeɪə/. L16. [Tamil *caya*.] The root of an Indian plant, *Oldenlandia umbellata*, of the madder family, which yields a red dye.

chay *n.*[2] var. of SHAY *n.*[1]

chayote /'tʃeɪəʊti/ *n.* L19. [Sp. f. Nahuatl *chayotli*.] A vine, *Sechium edule*, native to tropical America and cultivated elsewhere for its fruit; the succulent fruit (resembling a cucumber) of this vine. Also called *chocho*.

chazan *n.* var. of HAZZAN.

Chazar *n.* & *a.* var. of KHAZAR.

cheap /tʃiːp/ *n.* Long *arch. rare.* [OE *ċēap* = OFris. *kāp*, OS *kōp* (Du. *koop*), OHG *kouf* (G *Kauf*), ON *kaup*, f. Gmc, f. L *caupo* small tradesman, innkeeper. Cf. CHAPMAN.] **1** A (good) bargain; bargaining, trade; state of the market; abundance; price, value. After ME chiefly in *good cheap*, good value, cheapness, advantageous terms, ease, plenty (passing into adj. use). OE. **2** A place of buying and selling; a market. Long *obs.* exc. as a component of proper names, as *Cheapside*, *Chepstow*, etc. OE. †**3** Merchandise, chattels; *esp.* live cattle. Only in OE.

cheap /tʃiːp/ *a.* & *adv.* L15. [Ellipt. for *good cheap*: see prec.] **A** *adj.* **1** Low in price or charge made, absolutely or in relation to value; not costly, inexpensive. L15. **b** Having or charging low prices. L16. **c** Of a fare, rate, etc.: lower than the ordinary fare etc. E18. **d** Of money: available on loan at a low rate of interest. M19. **2** Low in value, worthless, paltry. L16. **3** Lightly esteemed; *esp.* brought into contempt through overfamiliarity. L16. **4** *fig.* Easily got or made; involving little labour, effort, etc. E17. **5** In poor health, out of sorts. *slang.* L19.

1 LD MACAULAY The services of a Secretary of State . . well qualified for his post would have been cheap at five thousand. b OED He is not a cheap tailor. 2 S. JOHNSON The cheap reward of empty praise. T. STOPPARD A cynical pursuit of cheap sensationalism. 3 S. PEPYS Making the king cheap and ridiculous. 4 SHAKES. *Meas. for M.* 'Twere the cheaper way: Better it were a brother died at once Than that a sister, by redeeming him, Should die for ever. J. RUNCIMAN My kisses ain't cheap.

B *adv.* At a low price, cheaply; easily. M16.

Phrases, special collocations, & comb.: **cheap and cheerful** inexpensive but not unattractive. **cheap and nasty** of low cost and poor quality. **cheapjack** *n.* & *a.* (*a*) *n.* a hawker at a fair; (*b*) *adj.* inferior, shoddy; *cheapskate*: see SKATE *n.*[3] *dirt cheap*: see DIRT *n.* **feel cheap** *slang* feel ashamed or ill. **hold cheap** despise. **on the cheap** cheaply.

cheapie *a.* & *n.* (*dial.* & *slang*) = CHEAPO L19. **cheaply** *adv.* M16. **cheapness** *n.* M16. **cheapo** *a.* & *n.* (pl. **-os**) *slang* (something) inexpensive (cf. EL CHEAPO) M20.

†**cheap** *v.* [OE *ċēapian*, (f. different base) *ċēapian* = OS *kopian*, *kopon*, OHG *koufen*, *koufōn*, ON *kaupa*, Goth *kaupōn*, f. Gmc, f. L *caupo*: see CHEAP *n.*] **1** *v.i.* Barter; trade. OE–ME. **2** *v.t.* **a** Buy. OE–LME. **b** Bargain for; ask the price of.

ME–M19. 3 *v.t.* Offer for sale; offer *to sell.* ME–L16.

†**cheaping** *n.* (*a*) buying and selling, bargaining, trading; (*b*) a market, a market-place, (surviving in place-names as *Chipping Campden, Chipping Sodbury,* etc.): OE–L16.

cheapen /'tʃiːp(ə)n/ *v.* L16. [f. CHEAP *a., v.* + -EN[5].] 1 *v.t.* Ask the price of, bid for. *arch.* L16. 2 *v.t.* Lower the price of, make cheap; *fig.* depreciate, degrade. M17. 3 *v.i.* Become cheap (*lit.* & *fig.*). E19.

cheapener *n.* a person who cheapens something M17.

cheat /tʃiːt/ *n.*[1] LME. [Aphet. f. ESCHEAT *n.*; sense 3 of unkn. origin; later senses f. the vb.] †1 An escheat. LME–M17. †2 An item of booty or spoil. M16–E17. 3 A thing, an article, (usu. of a specified description); *spec. the* gallows. *slang* (long *arch.*). M16. †4a Cheating, fraudulence. M–L17. b A fraud, a deception, a trick. M17. 5 A person who cheats (habitually); a swindler, a deceiver; an impostor; an unfair player. M17. 6 Darnel, chess, or other grass growing as a weed among cereal crops. *N. Amer.* & *dial.* L18. 7 A card-game the point of which is to lie successfully and detect lying in others. L19.

†**cheat** *n.*[2] LME–M17. [Origin unkn.] Wheaten bread of the second quality, inferior to manchet.

¶Perh. the 2nd elem. of MANCHET.

cheat /tʃiːt/ *v.* LME. [Aphet. f. ESCHEAT *v.*] †1 *v.t.* Escheat. Only in LME. 2 *v.i.* Act fraudulently, practise deception; play unfairly. M16. b *spec.* Be sexually unfaithful. (Foll. by *on* the deceived person.) *N. Amer.* M20. 3 *v.t.* Deprive *of* by deceit; defraud; deceive, trick (*into, out of*). L16. 4 *v.t.* Beguile (time, weariness, etc.). E18. †5 *v.t.* Obtain by cheating. E–M18. 6 *v.t.* & *i. Cinemat.* Suppress or adapt (part of a film) during editing so as to create a desired illusion. E20.

2 E. F. BENSON After dinner . . she permitted herself a game of patience, and since she never cheated, it was often ten o'clock before her game was over. 3 SHAKES. *Rich. III* Cheated of feature by dissembling nature. W. CATHER I don't admire people who cheat Indians. TOLKIEN We are no phantoms, . . nor do your eyes cheat you. 4 STEELE No Lay unsung to cheat the tedious Way.

cheatable *a.* able to be cheated M17. **chea'tee** *n.* (*colloq.*) a person who is cheated E17. **cheater** *n.* †(*a*) an escheator; (*b*) a person who cheats; see also *windcheater* s.v. WIND *n.*[1]; (*c*) in *pl.* (*US slang*), spectacles: ME. **cheatery** *n.* trickery, swindling M16.

†**chebec** *n.* var. of XEBEC.

chebule /kə'buːl/ *n.* Now *rare* or *obs.* LME. [Fr. *chébule* f. It. *chebuli*, f. Pers. & Urdu *Kābulī* of Kabul.] The astringent fruit of the Indian tree *Terminalia chebula*. Also *chebule myrobalan*.

chebulic *a.* E18.

Chechen /'tʃɛtʃ(ə)n/ *n.* Pl. **-s**, same. E19. [Russ. †*chechen* (mod. *chechenets*).] A member of a N. Caucasian people forming the main part of the population of Checheno-Ingushetia, in SW Asia; the language of this people.

chechia /'ʃeɪʃɪə/ *n.* M19. [Fr. *chéchia* f. Maghribi pronunc. of Arab. *šāšiyya*, f. Arab. *Šāš* Tashkent in Uzbekistan.] A red felt cap worn in NW Africa.

check /tʃɛk/ *n.*[1] Also (long *arch.*) **cheque.** See also CHEQUE *n.*[1] ME. [f. CHECK *int.*] I 1 In *Chess*, the state or condition of a king (formerly also a queen or other powerful piece) exposed to direct attack; a move directly attacking a king etc. Formerly also *fig.*, an attack, a harmful act. ME. 2 *Falconry.* A false stoop when a hawk abandons its proper quarry and pursues crows, doves, or other prey; lesser game. LME. †3 A taunt; a rebuke. E16–M18. 4 A sudden stopping or slowing of motion; a rebuff, a repulse. E16. b A stoppage, a pause. M16. c *Hunting.* The loss of a scent. L18. d A crack or flaw in timber. L19. †5 A stoppage of wages or a fine imposed on servants in the royal household; the amount stopped. E16–E18. 6 Restraint on action; a restraining control. M16. b A person who or thing which acts as a stop or restraint. M17. 7 Control by which accuracy is secured; the means or act of testing quality. E17. 8 A token, counterfoil, ticket, or other receipt for the identification of left luggage, the reserver of a seat, etc. Chiefly *N. Amer.* E19. b A restaurant bill. Chiefly *US.* M19. 9 A counter used as a stake in a game of chance. *US.* L19. 10 A mark made against an item in an account or list indicating that it has been verified or noted; a tick. L19. II See CHEQUE *n.*[1]

Phrases: cash in one's checks: see CASH *v.*[2] 3a. **checks and balances** (chiefly *US*) constitutional means of limiting or counteracting the wrongful use of governmental power; *gen.* guarantees and counterbalancing influences. **clerk of the cheque** (*a*) an officer of the royal household keeping the roll of royal staff and having control of the yeomen of the guard; †(*b*) an officer in control of a royal port, dockyard, etc. **hand** (or **pass** etc.) **in one's checks** *fig.* (*colloq.*) die. *hatcheck boy, girl,* etc.: see HAT *n.* **in check** (*a*) *Chess* under direct attack; (*b*) under control. *overdraw check*: see OVERDRAW *n.* 2. *parity check*: see PARITY *n.*[1] *perpetual check*: see PERPETUAL *a. rain check*: see RAIN *n.*[1]

checkless *a.* (*rare*) unchecked E17.

check /tʃɛk/ *n.*[2] & *a.* LME. [Prob. abbrev. of *checker* CHEQUER *n.*[1]] A *n.* 1 A pattern of cross lines forming small squares. LME. 2 A fabric marked or woven with such a pattern. E17.

2 *tattersal check*: see TATTERSALL *n.*

B *adj.* Marked or woven with such a pattern; made of such a fabric. E16.

check *n.*[3] var. of CHICK *n.*[2]

check *n.*[4] var. of CHEQUE *n.*[1]

check /tʃɛk/ *v.*[1] LME. [Aphet. f. OFr. *eschequier* play chess, give check to, f. *eschec* CHECK *n.*[1]] 1 *v.t.* Directly threaten (an opponent's king, *transf.* one's opponent) at chess; put in check. LME. 2 *v.t.* Suddenly stop or slow the motion of; physically obstruct (an opposing player) in ice hockey etc. LME. 3 *v.i. Falconry.* Of a falcon etc.: recoil *at* or shy from the fist; abandon the quarry and fly at other prey. E16. †4 *v.t.* Stop (a person) from receiving part of his or her wages. E16–E19. 5 *v.t.* Rebuke, reprove, reprimand. Now *colloq.* E16. †6 *v.i.* & *t.* Clash or collide *with* or with. M16–M17. 7 *v.t.* Stay the onward course of, repress, restrain, (actions, growth, feelings, etc.); hold (an agent) in check or under restraint, curb; curb *oneself* in an action etc. L16. 8 *v.i.* Stop (short); restrain oneself. Formerly also *fig.*, take offence (*at*). E17. b *Hunting.* Of a dog: stop on losing a scent, or to make sure of one. M18. 9 *v.t.* Test (a statement, account, figures, work, a person working, etc.) by comparison or other investigation; examine the accuracy or condition of; inspect or investigate to ensure the satisfactoriness or suitability of. Now freq. foll. by *out, up.* L17. b *v.i.* Make a comparison or investigation, conduct a check. Freq. foll. by *on, up* (*on*). E20. 10 *v.i.* Draw a cheque (*upon, for*). *US.* E19. 11 *v.t.* Deposit (luggage etc.) for storage or dispatch (in return for a check (see CHECK *n.*[1] 8)). Chiefly *N. Amer.* M19. 12 *v.t.* Note with or indicate by a tick or other mark of verification. Also foll. by *off.* M19. 13 *v.i.* Agree when compared. Also foll. by *out.* E20.

1 *fig.*: SHAKES. *John* Thy bastard shall be king, That thou mayst be a queen and check the world. 2 S. BRETT As his finger moved towards the button, he checked it. 7 J. CARY She began to laugh and then checked herself. C. MACKENZIE You will exercise your influence . . to check such criticism. E. BOWEN She checked or attempted to hide a shiver by wrapping her arms closely across her breast. ISAIAH BERLIN This does tend to check our arrogance, to induce humility. 8 R. KIPLING The lama turned to this and that, and finally checked . . before a large alto-relief. F. TUOHY The small movements of his body checked and became total stillness. 9 BURKE I have checked this account . . and find it to be correct. A. LURIE My first reaction is to check my stockings for runs. b D. HAMMETT The District Attorney will have questioned him and checked up on him. J. DICKEY As we cleared each turn . . I kept looking for white water, and when I'd checked for that I looked along both banks. *parity checking*: see PARITY *n.*[1] 10 **checking account** *US* a current account at a bank etc. 13 M. M. ATWATER If there's finger-prints on it, and yours don't check, that'll let you out.

With advs. & preps. in specialized senses: **check in** arrive, and be recorded as arriving, at a hotel, factory, airport, etc.; record the arrival of (a person) at a hotel etc. **check into** arrive, and be recorded as arriving, at (a hotel etc.). **check out** depart, and be recorded as departing, from a hotel, factory, airport, etc.; *fig.* (*colloq.*) die; record the departure of (a person) at a hotel etc.; (see also senses 9, 13 above). **check out of** depart, and be recorded as departing, from (a hotel etc.). **check over, check through** examine or verify successive items or parts of.

checkable *a.* L19.

check /tʃɛk/ *v.*[2]*t.* LME. [f. CHECK *n.*[2] or abbrev. of *checker* CHEQUER *v.*] Mark with a pattern of crossing lines or squares.

check /tʃɛk/ *int.* ME. [Aphet. f. OFr. *eschec* (mod. *échec*) = Prov. *escac*, It. *scacco* f. Proto-Romance (med.L) *scaccus* f. Arab. f. Pers. *šāh* king, SHAH. Cf. CHESS *n.*[1], EXCHEQUER.] 1 In chess, notifying the exposure of an opponent's king to direct attack. ME. 2 Expr. assent or agreement. (Cf. CHECK *n.*[1] 10, its probable source.) *N. Amer. colloq.* E20.

2 N. MAILER 'No audience . . is going to trust a man whose wife takes a leap.' 'Check.'

check- /tʃɛk/ *comb. form.* LME. [f. CHECK *n.*[1] or *v.*[1]] In combs. in various relations w. the senses 'that serves to check or control', 'an act of checking or being checked'.

check-action a mechanism restraining a piano hammer from striking a string twice. **check-in** the act of checking in. **check-list** a (complete) list for reference and verification. **check-nut** = *lock-nut* (a) s.v. LOCK *n.*[2] **checkout** (*a*) the act of checking out; a final check; (*b*) the pay desk in a supermarket etc. (also *checkout counter, desk,* etc.). **checkpoint** a point at which documents, vehicles, etc., are checked or inspected; a time or stage at which progress etc. is assessed. **check-rail** *Railways* an extra rail laid to resist sideways pressure on a sharp curve. **check-rein** a rein attaching one horse's rein to another's bit, or preventing a horse from lowering its head. †**check-roll** a list of the names and other details of people in the service of the royal or other large household; a muster-roll. **checkroom, -stand** *N. Amer.* a room, a stand, in which 'checked' articles are placed. **check-string** *Hist.* a string used by a passenger in a carriage to signal the driver to stop. **checksum** *Computing* a modular sum of the digits in a data item, transmitted with the item to provide a check of any errors that may arise in it. **check-taker** *US* a person who takes or collects the checks or tickets for admission to a theatre etc. **check-up** a careful examination, esp. of a person's general medical condition. **check-valve** a valve preventing backward flow of liquid in a pipe etc. **checkweighman** a person who checks the weight of mined coal on behalf of miners.

checked /tʃɛkt/ *a.*[1] Also †**chequed.** LME. [f. CHECK *n.*[2], *v.*[2]: see -ED[2], -ED[1].] Marked with checks, having checks, chequered.

Time Young kids . . in checked shirts and baseball caps.

checked /tʃɛkt/ *a.*[2] Also †**chequed.** M18. [f. CHECK *n.*[1], CHEQUE *n.*[1], or CHECK *v.*[1]: see -ED[2], -ED[1].] †1 Of paper: having a counterfoil; for use as a cheque. Only in M18. 2 *gen.* That has been checked. Also *checked-in, -out, -up,* etc. L18. 3 *Phonet.* Of a syllable: ending in a consonant, closed. Of a vowel: occurring in such a syllable. L19.

checker /'tʃɛkə/ *n.*[1] M16. [f. CHECK *v.*[1] + -ER[1].] A person who or device which checks; *spec.* (*a*) a person who works at the checkout of a supermarket etc.; (*b*) a player who checks an opponent in ice hockey etc.

SPELLING *checker.*

checker *n.*[2], *n.*[3], *v.* vars. of CHEQUER *n.*[1], *n.*[2], *v.*

checkerberry /'tʃɛkəbɛri/ *n.* L18. [f. *checker* var. of CHEQUER *n.*[2] + BERRY *n.*[1]] A low creeping evergreen N. American shrub of the heath family, *Gaultheria procumbens*, with spicy-scented leaves and waxy white flowers (also called *partidge-berry, wintergreen*); the edible red fruit of this shrub.

checkered *a.* var. of CHEQUERED.

†**checklaton** *n. rare* (Spenser). Only in L16. [Alt.] = CICLATOUN.

checkmate /'tʃɛkmeɪt/ *int., n., a.,* & *v.* ME. [Aphet. f. OFr. *eschec mat* = Prov. *escac mat*, f. Arab. *šāh māt(a)* repr. Pers. *šāh māt* the king is defeated, the king is perplexed: see CHECK *int.*, MATE *a.*] A *int.* In *Chess*, notifying the putting of an opponent's king into inextricable check, by which the game is won; *transf.* notifying an adversary's defeat. ME. B *n.* (The notifying to an opponent of) the inextricable check of a king in chess; *transf.* & *fig.* final defeat or deadlock. LME. C *pred. a.* In inextricable check; *fig.* defeated. LME. D *v.t.* Give checkmate to; *fig.* defeat, frustrate. LME.

check-stone /ˈtʃɛkstəʊn/ *n.* Now *dial. rare.* L16. [Origin unkn.] A smooth round pebble; *sing.* & in *pl.* a game played with such pebbles.

checky /ˈtʃɛki/ *a.* In *Her.* also **che(c)quy**. LME. [Aphet. f. OFr. *eschequié, escheqùé*, later assim. to adjs. in -Y¹.] Chiefly *Her.* Checked, chequered; (of a field or charge) divided into three or more rows of small squares of alternate tinctures.

chedarim *n.pl.* see HEDER.

Cheddar /ˈtʃɛdə/ *n.* M17. [A village in Somerset, England.] 1 In full *Cheddar cheese.* A hard smooth-textured cheese made (orig. at Cheddar) by piling the curds and forming a smooth mass. M17. 2 *Cheddar pink*, a pink, *Dianthus gratianopolitanus*, with dull greyish leaves, in Britain found only at Cheddar Gorge. M19.

cheddaring *n.* a process or stage in the manufacture of cheese, involving the piling of the curds to form a smooth mass E20.

cheder *n.* var. of HEDER.

cheechako /tʃiːˈtʃɑːkəʊ/ *n. N. Amer. colloq.* Pl. **-os.** L19. [Chinook Jargon = newcomer.] A newly arrived immigrant to the mining districts of N. America; a greenhorn, a tenderfoot.

chee-chee *a.* var. of CHI-CHI.

cheek /tʃiːk/ *n.* [OE *ċēoce* = OFris. *ziāke*, varying w. OE *ċēace, ċēce* = (M)LG *kāke, kēke*, MDu. *kāke* (Du. *kaak*), f. WGmc.] I Of a person or animal. †1 The jaw, the jawbone; *sing.* & (usu.) in *pl.*, the chops, the fauces. OE–M16. 2 The side-wall of the mouth; the side of the face below the eye; *fig.* something suggestive of the cheek in shape, colour, etc. OE. 3 A buttock. Usu. in *pl.* L16. 4 Impertinent speech; cool confidence, effrontery; insolence. M19.

2 BYRON Ocean's cheek Reflects the tints of many a peak. 4 GEORGE MOORE If he gives me any of his cheek I'll knock him down. J. FOWLES Some even had the cheek to push their cameras through the front gate.

II *transf.* & *techn.* (All usu. in *pl.*) 5 The side post of a door, gate, etc. LME. 6 *gen.* A side. M16. 7 Either of the side-pieces of a horse's bit; the strap of a bridle passing down each side of a horse's head, to connect the headpiece with the bit. E17. 8 *Naut.* On a square-rigged ship, each of the projections on either side of a mast on which the trestle-trees rest; the outside wooden part of a block etc. E17. 9 Each of a pair of laterally arranged side-pieces forming part of a machine; *esp.* each of the jaws of a vice. M17.

Phrases etc.: **cheek by jowl** (or **†by cheek**) side by side, close together, intimate(ly). **cheek to cheek** (in dancing) with the cheeks of partners (nearly) touching. *of all the cheek* etc.: see OF *prep. tongue-in-cheek*: see TONGUE *n.* **to one's own cheek** without sharing or not shared with others. **turn the other cheek** [alluding to *Matt.* 5:39, *Luke* 6:29] permit or invite another blow, attack, etc.; refuse to retaliate. *with (one's) tongue in (one's) cheek*: see TONGUE *n.*

Comb.: **cheek-bone** (*a*) the bone above the cheek, forming the lower boundary of the orbits of the eyes; †(*b*) the jawbone; **cheek-pouch** a pouchlike enlargement of the cheek, esp. in certain monkeys; **cheek-tooth** a molar.

cheeked *a.* having a cheek or cheeks (of a specified kind) M16.

cheek /tʃiːk/ *v.t.* M16. [f. the n.] 1 Form a cheek or side to. M16. 2 Address cheekily or saucily. *colloq.* M19.

cheeky /ˈtʃiːki/ *a.* E19. [f. CHEEK *n.* + -Y¹.] Characterized by or showing cheek; insolent, impudent.

cheekily *adv.* E20. **cheekiness** *n.* M19.

cheep /tʃiːp/ *v.* & *n.* Orig. *Sc.* E16. [Imit.: cf. PEEP *v.*¹ & *n.*²] A *v.* 1 *v.i.* Utter shrill feeble sounds (like those) of a young bird. E16. 2 *v.t.* Utter with a cheeping voice. M19.

B *n.* A shrill feeble sound (as) of a young bird. L18.

not a cheep *colloq.* not the slightest sound, not a word.

cheeper *n.* E17. **cheepy** *a.* given to cheeping M19.

cheer /tʃɪə/ *n.*¹ See also CHEERS *int.* ME. [AN *chere*, OFr. *chiere* face, f. late L *cara* f. Gk *kara* head.] †1 The face; the expression of the face; countenance. ME–M19. 2 Disposition, frame of mind, mood. Now usu. w. specifying wd, esp. *good.* ME. 3 Kindly welcome or reception, hospitable entertainment (passing into sense 5). *obs.* exc. *dial.* ME. 4 Cheerfulness, gladness, mirth, joy, gaiety. LME. 5 Provisions, viands, food (for entertainment). LME. 6 A thing which gives joy or gladness; comfort; encouragement. M16. 7 A shout of encouragement, welcome, approbation, or congratulation. L17.

2 T. H. WHITE I rode away with heavy cheer. **of good cheer** stout-hearted, hopeful. **what cheer?** how do you feel? (cf. WOTCHER *int.*). 3 SHAKES. *Lucr.* She securely gives good cheer And reverend welcome to her princely guest. 4 B. RUBENS He engaged a smile . . in preparation for the cheer he would put into his voice. 5 **make good cheer** feast, revel. 6 *Times* The market took cheer . . and marked the shares up 3p. 7 J. HERRIOT The farm men didn't exactly break into a cheer but they were enormously pleased. **three cheers** successive united hurrahs (*for* a person or thing honoured). **two cheers** *iron.* mild enthusiasm.

Comb.: **cheer-leader** a person who leads collective yells, organized cheers of applause, supportive chanting, etc., esp. at a sporting event.

cheer /tʃɪə/ *n.*² Also **chir.** E19. [Nepali: imit.] In full *cheer pheasant.* A pheasant, *Catreus wallichii*, native to the Himalayan region.

cheer /tʃɪə/ *v.* LME. [f. CHEER *n.*¹] †1 *v.refl.* & *i.* With adv.: assume a particular disposition or state of mind. LME–E18. 2 *v.t.* Make of good cheer; comfort, console; make joyous, gladden, enliven. Freq. foll. by *up.* LME. †3a *v.t.* Entertain with feasting. LME–L17. b *v.t.* & *i.* Solace or comfort as food does. M16. 4 *v.t.* Encourage, inspirit, animate, incite, by word or deed (now esp. with cheers, passing into sense 7). Freq. foll. by *on.* LME. 5 *v.i.* Be or grow cheerful, enjoy oneself. Now only foll. by *up*: become cheerful, take heart. L16. 6 *v.t.* Brighten up (one's face etc.). E17. 7 *v.t.* & *i.* Salute with cheers, applause, or other indications of approbation or support. L18.

1 SHAKES. *Merch. V.* How cheer'st thou, Jessica? 2 V. S. PRITCHETT It cheers me that I live on the frontier of Camden Town and Regent's Park. G. M. FRASER Grattan didn't cheer me up by remarking that the Cumanche are cannibals. 3a DRYDEN I myself the Guests with friendly Bowls will chear. b W. H. RUSSELL A cup . . which to my mind neither cheers nor inebriates. 4 C. THIRLWALL Cheering his troops by his presence and his words. K. GRAHAME His comrades cheered him on, Mole coaxed and encouraged him . . ; but nothing could overcome his stage-fright. 5 W. FAULKNER When I gave him another sup . . , he cheered up some. 7 B. JOWETT Many of the audience cheered and applauded this. H. CARPENTER The boys were even forbidden to cheer at their own football matches.

cheerer *n.* a person who or thing which cheers L16. **cheeringly** *adv.* in a cheering manner, so as to cheer one E19.

cheerful /ˈtʃɪəfʊl, -f(ə)l/ *a.* LME. [f. CHEER *n.*¹ + -FUL.] 1 Contented, in good spirits, hopeful; willing, not reluctant. LME. 2 Inspiring contentment etc.; bright, pleasant. LME.

cheerfully *adv.* M16. **cheerfulness** *n.* LME.

cheerie-bye /tʃɪərɪˈbʌɪ/ *int. colloq.* M20. [f. next + GOODBYE.] Goodbye.

cheerio /tʃɪərɪˈəʊ/ *int. colloq.* Also **cheero** /tʃɪəˈrəʊ/. E20. [f. CHEERY + O *int.*] Expr. good wishes on parting or before drinking; goodbye; good health.

cheerless /ˈtʃɪəlɪs/ *a.* L16. [f. CHEER *n.*¹ + -LESS.] Devoid of comfort; dispiriting; gloomy.

cheerlessly *adv.* L19. **cheerlessness** *n.* M19.

cheerly /ˈtʃɪəli/ *a. arch.* L15. [f. CHEER *n.*¹ + -LY¹.] Cheerful, lively.

cheerly /ˈtʃɪəli/ *adv.* L15. [f. CHEER *n.*¹ + -LY².] Cheerily; cheeringly; *Naut.* heartily, with a will.

cheero *int.* var. of CHEERIO.

cheers /tʃɪəz/ *int. colloq.* E20. [pl. of CHEER *n.*¹] 1 Expr. good wishes, esp. before drinking; cheerio, good health. Also, goodbye. E20. 2 Expr. thanks. L20.

cheery /ˈtʃɪəri/ *a.* LME. [f. CHEER *n.*¹ + -Y¹.] Cheerful, in good spirits; genial, cheering.

cheerily *adv.* E17. **cheeriness** *n.* M19.

cheese /tʃiːz/ *n.*¹ [OE *ċēse, ċȳse* = OS *kāsi, k(i)ēsi* (Du. *kaas*), OHG *chāsi, kāsi* (G *Käse*), f. WGmc f. L *caseus.*] 1 The curds of milk (coagulated by rennet) separated from the whey and pressed into a solid mass, eaten as food; a distinct kind of this. OE. b A mass or cake of this within a rind. LME. 2 The fruit of the common mallow, *Malva silvestris*, which has a round flattened shape like a cheese. E16. 3 A conserve of fruit etc. having the consistency or form of (cream) cheese. M16. b A mass of crushed apples pressed together in the form of a cheese. E18. 4 Any object shaped like a cheese (usu. taken as being cylindrical or an oblate spheroid). M19. 5 The action of turning round rapidly and sinking down so that skirts and petticoats take the form of a cheese; a deep curtsy. (Cf. Fr. *faire des fromages.*) *arch.* M19. 6 The word 'cheese' notionally or actually pronounced to form the lips into a smile, when one is being photographed. M20.

1 *blue cheese, Cheddar cheese, cottage cheese, cream cheese, Dutch cheese, Lancashire cheese, Limburger cheese, Parmesan cheese, processed cheese, Swiss cheese*, etc. *as different as chalk and* (or *from*) *cheese*: see CHALK *n. green cheese*: see GREEN *a. hard cheese*: see HARD *a. mousetrap cheese*: see MOUSETRAP 2. 3 *damson cheese, lemon cheese*, etc.

Comb.: **cheeseboard** a board from which cheese is served; a selection of cheeses served with a meal; **cheeseburger** a hamburger with cheese in or on it; **cheesecake** (*a*) a tart(let) with a filling of sweetened curds on a pastry or biscuit-crumb base; (*b*) *slang* (orig. *US*) the display of shapely female form in advertisements, photographs, etc.; **cheesecloth** = *butter muslin* s.v. BUTTER *n.*¹; **cheese-cutter** (*a*) a knife with a curved blade used for cutting cheese; (*b*) a device for cutting cheese by pulling a wire through it; **cheese fly** a small black fly, *Piophila casei*, whose larvae feed on cheese; **cheese-head** a squat cylindrical head of a screw etc.; **cheese-knife** (*a*) = *cheese-cutter* (a) above; (*b*) a spatula used to break down curd in cheese-making; **cheese mite** a mite of the genus *Tyroglyphus*, feeding on old cheese; **cheesemonger** a dealer in cheese, butter, etc.; **cheese-pare** *v.i.* be stingy, make miserly economies; **cheese-paring** *a.* & *n.* (*a*) *adj.* stingy; (*b*) *n.* stinginess; **†cheese-rennet, †-running** lady's bedstraw, *Galium verum*, formerly used to curdle milk; **cheese skipper** the larva of the cheese fly; **cheese straw** a thin cheese-flavoured strip of pastry; **cheesewood** (the hard yellow wood of) an Australian tree of the genus *Pittosporum.*

cheese /tʃiːz/ *n.*² *slang.* E19. [Prob. f. Urdu f. Pers. *čīz* thing.] 1 *The* right or correct thing; something first-rate. E19. 2 An important or self-important person; *the* boss. Freq. as *big cheese.* Orig. *US.* E20.

cheese /tʃiːz/ *v.t. slang.* E19. [Origin unkn.] 1 Stop *it*, leave off. Esp. in *imper.* E19. 2 Bore, exasperate. Chiefly as *cheesed off*, browned off, fed up. M20.

cheeselip /ˈtʃiːzlɪp/ *n.*¹ *obs.* exc. *dial.* [OE *ċēselyb(b)*, f. CHEESE *n.*¹ + a word = ON *lyf* herb, mod.G dial. *Lüpp* rennet.] Rennet for cheese-making; the dried (calf's) stomach from which it is prepared.

cheeselip /ˈtʃiːzlɪp/ *n.*² *obs.* exc. *dial.* M16. [Origin unkn.] A woodlouse or similar crustacean.

cheesy /ˈtʃiːzi/ *a.* In sense 3 also **cheesey.** LME. [f. CHEESE *n.*¹ + -Y¹.] 1 Of, belonging to, consisting of, or of the nature of cheese; containing cheese. LME. 2 Resembling cheese in appearance etc. M18. 3 Inferior, second-rate, cheap and nasty. *slang.* L19.

cheesiness *n.* M19.

cheetah /ˈtʃiːtə/ *n.* L18. [Hind. *cītā*, f. Skt *citraka* leopard.] A swift-running spotted feline, *Acinonyx jubatus*, native to the plains of Africa and SW Asia.

cheetal *n.* var. of CHITAL.

cheewink *n.* var. of CHEWINK.

chef /ʃɛf/ *n.* E19. [Fr. = head.] A person (usu. a man) who is (usu. the chief) cook in a hotel, restaurant, etc.

chef d'école /ʃɛf dekɔl/ *n. phr.* Pl. ***chefs d'école*** (pronounced same). M19. [Fr. = head of school.] The initiator or leader of a school or style of music, painting, literature, etc.

chef-d'œuvre /ʃɛdœːvr/ *n.* Pl. ***chefs-*** (pronounced same). E17. [Fr. = chief (piece) of work.] The greatest work of an artist etc.; a masterpiece.

chef d'orchestre /ʃɛf dɔrkɛstr/ *n. phr.* Pl. ***chefs d'orchestre*** (pronounced same). M19. [Fr. = head of orchestra.] The leader or conductor of an orchestra.

chefs d'école, -d'œuvre, d'orchestre *ns.* pls. of CHEF D'ÉCOLE etc.

cheilo- /ˈkʌɪləʊ/ *comb. form.* Also **chilo-**, (bef. a vowel) **ch(e)il-**. Repr. Gk *kheilos* lip: see -O-.
cheiˈlitis *n.* (*Med.*) inflammation of the lips M19. **cheiloplastic** *a.* of or pertaining to cheiloplasty M19. **cheiloplasty** *n.* (an instance of) surgical repair of injury or deformity of the lip M19.

cheir- *comb. form* see CHIRO-.

cheiranthus /kʌɪˈranθəs/ *n.* M19. [mod.L (see below), f. Gk *kheir* hand + *anthos* flower.] A cruciferous plant of the genus *Cheiranthus* (now freq. included in the genus *Erysimum*), to which the wallflower belongs.

cheiro- *comb. form* var. of CHIRO-.

cheirology *n.* var. of CHIROLOGY.

†**cheiropteran** *n.* & *a.* var. of CHIROPTERAN.

Cheka /ˈtʃɛkə/ *n.* Also **Tch-**. E20. [Russ., f. *Che*, *ka*, pronunc. of initials of *Chrezvychaĭnaya Komissiya* Extraordinary Commission (for combating Counter-revolution, Sabotage, and Speculation).] *Hist.* An organization set up in 1917 in the USSR to investigate counter-revolutionary activities, superseded in 1922 by Ogpu.

Chekhovian /tʃɛˈkəʊvɪən/ *a.* Also **Tch-**. E20. [f. *Chekhov* (see below) + -IAN.] Of, pertaining to, or characteristic of the work of the Russian author Anton Pavlovich Chekhov (1860–1904), esp. in attaching dramatic and symbolic significance to detail.

chela /ˈkiːlə/ *n.*[1] Pl. **-lae** /-liː/. M17. [mod.L f. L *chele*, Gk *khēlē* claw.] *Zool.* A pincer-like claw of a crab, lobster, scorpion, etc.
cheˈliferous *a.* bearing chelae or claws M18. **cheliform** *a.* having the form of a chela L18.

chela /ˈtʃeɪlə/ *n.*[2] M19. [Hind. *celā*.] A disciple, a pupil, *spec.* in Hinduism.

chelate /ˈkiːleɪt/ *a.* & *n.* E19. [f. CHELA *n.*[1] + -ATE[2].] A *adj.* 1 *Zool.* Having two opposing claws or pincer-like structures. E19. 2 *Chem.* That is or involves a ligand which forms bonds to the same central atom at two or more points. E20. B *n. Chem.* A chelate compound. M20.

chelate /ˈkiːleɪt, kɪˈleɪt/ *v.t.* E20. [f. the adj.] *Chem.* Combine with in the manner of a chelate ligand.
cheˈlation *n.* the state or process of being chelated M20. **cheˈlator** *n.* a chelate ligand M20.

chelicera /kəˈlɪs(ə)rə/ *n.* Pl. **-rae** /-riː/. Also Anglicized as **chelicer** /ˈkɛlɪsə/. M19. [mod.L, f. as CHELA *n.*[1] + Gk *keras* horn.] *Zool.* Each of the anterior pair of appendages of arachnids and some other arthropods, modified as pincer-like jaws.
cheliceral *a.* L19. **chelicerate** *a.* & *n.* (an arthropod) having chelicerae E20.

cheliped /ˈkiːlɪpɛd/ *n.* M19. [f. as CHELA *n.*[1] + -I- + L *ped-*, *pes* foot.] *Zool.* Either of a pair of limbs bearing claws or pincers, found in decapod crustaceans.

Chellean /ˈʃɛlɪən/ *a.* L19. [Fr. *Chelléen*, f. *Chelles* near Paris: see -AN.] = ABBEVILLIAN *a.*

†**cheloid** *n.* & *a.* var. of KELOID.

chelonian /kɪˈləʊnɪən/ *a.* & *n.* E19. [f. mod.L *Chelonia*, f. Gk *khelōnē* tortoise: see -IA[2], -AN.] *Zool.* A *adj.* Of, pertaining to, or characteristic of the reptilian order Testudines (formerly Chelonia), which includes the tortoises, turtles, and terrapins. E19. B *n.* A reptile of this order. E19.

chelp /tʃɛlp/ *v.* & *n. dial.* E19. [Origin uncertain: perh. imit.] A *v.t.* & *i.* Chirp, squeak; chatter; cheep. E19. B *n.* Chatter; backchat. L19.

Chelsea /ˈtʃɛlsi/ *n.* E18. [A district in London on the north bank of the Thames.] 1 *Chelsea bun*, a kind of rolled currant-bun, originally made in Chelsea. E18. 2 More fully *Chelsea ware, porcelain*, etc. A kind of porcelain made at Chelsea in the 18th cent. M18. 3 *Chelsea pensioner*, an inmate of the Chelsea Royal Hospital for old or disabled soldiers. E19. 4 *Chelsea boot*, an elastic-sided boot. M20.

Cheltonian /tʃɛlˈtəʊnɪən/ *n.* & *a.* L19. [f. *Cheltenham* (see below) after ABERDONIAN etc.] (A native or inhabitant) of the town of Cheltenham in Gloucestershire; (a member or former member) of Cheltenham College or Cheltenham Ladies' College.

chemi- /ˈkɛmi/ *comb. form* of CHEMICAL *a.*: see -I-. Cf. CHEMICO-, CHEMO-.
chemilumiˈnescence *n.* the emission of (cold) light accompanying a chemical reaction L19. **chemilumiˈnescent** *a.* exhibiting chemiluminescence E20. **chemiosˈmotic** *a.* (*Biochem.*) pertaining to or involving the transfer of electrons, protons, or other species through membranes, as a mechanism of metabolic reactions M20. **chemisorb** *v.t.* [back-form.] collect by chemisorption M20. **chemiˈsorption** *n.* adsorption involving the formation of chemical bonds M20.

chemiatric /kɛmɪˈatrɪk/ *a.* & *n.* M19. [f. mod.L *chemiatria* iatrochemistry (Paracelsus), f. as prec. + Gk *iatreia* medical treatment: see -IC.] A *adj.* = IATROCHEMICAL. M19. B *n.* = IATROCHEMIST. M19.

chemic /ˈkɛmɪk/ *a.*, *n.*, & *v.* Orig. †**chymic**. L16. [Fr. *chimique*, or mod.L *chimicus*, *chym-*, for med.L *alchimicus*, f. *alchimia* ALCHEMY: see -IC.] A *adj.* 1 Alchemical. *arch.* L16. †2 = IATROCHEMICAL. E17–M18. 3 Of or belonging to chemistry. *poet.* M17. B *n.* †1 An alchemist. L16–L17. †2 = IATROCHEMIST. E–M17. †3 A chemist. M–L17. 4 Calcium or sodium hypochlorite used as bleach. *arch.* M19. C *v.t.* Infl. **-ck-**. †1 Transmute (as) by alchemy. E17–E18. 2 Bleach with a solution of calcium or sodium hypochlorite. *arch.* M19.

chemical /ˈkɛmɪk(ə)l/ *a.* & *n.* Orig. †**chym-**. L16. [f. as prec. + -AL[1].] A *adj.* †1 Alchemical. L16–M18. 2 Of, made by, or relating to, chemistry; employing chemicals. L16. b *spec.* Designating a lavatory or closet in which waste is decomposed by chemicals. M20. †3 = IATROCHEMICAL. L16–L18. 4 Of a person: engaged in the practice of chemistry; versed in chemistry. E17.
Special collocations: *chemical attraction*: see ATTRACTION 3. **chemical bond** = BOND *n.*[2] 11. **chemical engineer** an expert in chemical engineering. **chemical engineering** the science of the utilization of chemical processes in manufacturing. **chemical potential** a thermodynamic function pertaining to any one component present in a system, equal to the derivative of the free energy with respect to the quantity of that component. *chemical shift*: see SHIFT *n.* **chemical warfare**: employing chemical weapons. **chemical weapon** a weapon that depends for its effect on the release of a toxic or noxious substance.
B *n.* A distinct substance obtained by or used in a chemical process. M18.
fine chemicals: used in small amounts and in a purified state. **heavy chemicals** bulk chemicals used in industry and agriculture.
chemicalize *v.t.* treat with chemicals; use chemicals in (an activity): E20. **chemically** *adv.* E17.

chemico- /ˈkɛmɪkəʊ/ *comb. form* of CHEMICAL *a.*: see -O-. Cf. CHEMI-, CHEMO-.
chemico-ˈphysical *a.* of or pertaining to chemistry and physics M19.

chemin de fer /ʃ(ə)mɛ̃ də fɛːr, ʃəˈmã də fɛː/ *n.* L19. [Fr. = railway, lit. 'road of iron'.] A form of baccarat.

chemise /ʃəˈmiːz/ *n.* ME. [(O)Fr., f. late L *camisia* shirt, nightgown.] 1 A garment for the upper body; *esp.* a woman's loose-fitting undergarment or dress hanging straight from the shoulders. ME. 2 *Hist.* A wall with which a bastion etc. is lined as a fortification. E18. 3 *Hist.* A loose covering for a book. L19.

chemisette /ʃɛmiːˈzɛt/ *n.* E19. [Fr., dim. of prec.: see -ETTE.] 1 A bodice, resembling the upper part of a chemise. E19. 2 A piece of muslin, lace, etc., used to fill in the open front of a woman's dress. E19.

chemism /ˈkɛmɪz(ə)m/ *n. rare.* E19. [Fr. *chimisme*, parallel to *chimiste* CHEMIST: see -ISM.] Chemical action, activity, or force.

chemist /ˈkɛmɪst/ *n.* Also (*arch.*) **chym-**. LME. [Fr. *chimiste*, †*chym-* f. mod.L *chimysta*, *-ista* for *alchimista* ALCHEMIST.] †1 An alchemist. LME–M18. †2 = IATROCHEMIST. Only in E17. 3 A person skilled in chemistry; one who makes chemical investigations. E17. 4 A dealer in medicinal drugs, usu. also selling other medical goods and toiletries. M18.

chemistry /ˈkɛmɪstri/ *n.* Also (*arch.*) **chym-**. L16. [f. prec. + -RY.] 1 (The branch of science that deals with) the investigation of the substances of which matter is composed, and of the phenomena of combination and change which they display (cf. ALCHEMY); chemical reactions or properties. Also *fig.*, mysterious processes or change; imponderable interaction. L16. †2 = IATROCHEMISTRY. L17–E18.
1 *inorganic, organic, physical, surface chemistry*, etc. R. W. EMERSON The world has a sure chemistry, by which it extracts what is excellent in its children. C. SAGAN Our chemistry is delicately attuned to the temperature of the planet on which we have evolved. R. JAFFE Annabel . . hadn't been to bed with her husband for two years, except to sleep. There just wasn't any chemistry between them anymore.

chemmy /ˈʃɛmi/ *n. colloq.* E20. [Abbrev.] = CHEMIN DE FER.

chemo- /ˈkɛməʊ/ *comb. form* of CHEMICAL *a.*: see -O-. Cf. CHEMI-, CHEMICO-.
chemoprophyˈlactic *a.* of, pertaining to, or involving chemoprophylaxis M20. **chemoprophyˈlaxis** *n.* the prophylactic use of chemicals M20. **chemoreception** *n.* the response of an organism to a chemical change in its environment E20. **chemoreceptor** *n.* a sensory organ responsive to chemical stimuli E20. **chemoˈsynthesis** *n.* the formation by living organisms of carbohydrates from inorganic compounds without the agency of light E20. **chemosynˈthetic** *a.* of, pertaining to, or involving chemosynthesis M20.

chemo-autotrophic /ˌkɛməʊɔːtəˈtrəʊfɪk, -ˈtrɒf-/ *a.* M20. [f. prec. + AUTOTROPHIC.] Of micro-organisms or their metabolism: deriving energy from the oxidation of inorganic compounds.
chemo-ˈautotroph *n.* a chemo-autotrophic organism M20. **chemo-autotrophism** /-ˈtrəʊf-/ *n.* M20.

chemokinesis /kɛmə(ʊ)kɪˈniːsɪs, -kʌɪ-/ *n.* E20. [f. CHEMO- + KINESIS.] *Biol.* A kinesis in response to a particular substance.
chemokinetic /-ˈnɛtɪk/ *a.* of, pertaining to, or displaying chemokinesis E20.

chemosis /kɪˈməʊsɪs/ *n.* E18. [Gk *khēmōsis*, f. *khēmē* cockle-shell: see -OSIS.] *Med.* Oedema of the conjunctiva.

chemotaxis /kɛmə(ʊ)ˈtaksɪs/ *n.* L19. [f. CHEMO- + -TAXIS.] *Biol.* Motion of a motile cell, organism, or part towards or away from an increasing concentration of a particular substance.
chemotactic *a.* of, pertaining to, or displaying chemotaxis L19. **chemotactically** *adv.* E20.

chemotherapy /kɛmə(ʊ)ˈθɛrəpi, kiːm-/ *n.* E20. [f. CHEMO- + THERAPY.] The treatment of disease, esp. infections or cancer, by means of chemicals.
chemotheraˈpeutic(al) *adjs.* of, pertaining to, or involving chemotherapy E20. **chemotheraˈpeutically** *adv.* M20. **chemotherapist** *n.* M20.

chemotropism /kɛmə(ʊ)ˈtrəʊpɪz(ə)m/ *n.* L19. [f. CHEMO- + Gk *tropos* turning + -ISM.] *Biol.* A tropism, esp. of a plant, in response to a particular substance.
chemotropic /-ˈtrəʊpɪk, -ˈtrɒpɪk/ *a.* of, pertaining to, or displaying chemotropism L19. **chemotropically** *adv.* L19.

chempaka *n.* see CHAMPAC.

chemurgy /ˈkɛməːdʒi/ *n.* *US.* M20. [f. CHEMO- after *metallurgy*.] The chemical and industrial use of agricultural products.
cheˈmurgic(al) *adjs.* M20.

chena /ˈtʃeɪnə/ *n.* M19. [Sinhalese *sēna*, *hēna*.] In Sri Lanka (Ceylon): a clearing made for temporary cultivation; shrubby vegetation associated with shifting cultivation.

chenar /tʃɪˈnɑː/ *n.* Also **chinar**. M17. [Pers. *čenar*, *činār*.] The oriental plane tree, *Platanus orientalis* (also *chenar-tree*); the wood of this tree.

chenille /ʃəˈniːl/ *n.* M18. [Fr., lit. 'hairy caterpillar', f. L *canicula* dim. of *canis* dog.] Velvety cord with pile all round, used in trimming and bordering dresses and furniture.

chenopodium /kɛnəˈpəʊdɪəm/ *n.* L16. [mod.L, f. Gk *khēn* goose + *pod-*, *pous* foot, referring to the shape of the leaf.] A plant of the large genus *Chenopodium* (family Chenopodiaceae); a goosefoot.

ˌ**chenopodiˈaceous** *a.* of or pertaining to the family Chenopodiaceae M19.

cheongsam /tʃɪɒŋˈsam, tʃɒŋ-/ *n.* M20. [Chin. (Cantonese) = Mandarin *chángshān*.] A Chinese woman's garment with a high neck and slit skirt.

cheque /tʃɛk/ *n.*[1] Also ***check**. See also CHECK *n.*[1] E18. [Var. of CHECK *n.*[1]] **I** †**1** The counterfoil of a bank bill, draft, etc. Only in 18. †**2** A draft form having a counterfoil. E18–M19. **3** A written order to a bank etc. to pay a named sum from the drawer's account to the bearer or to (the order of) a named person; a printed form on which such an order is to be written. L18.

3 *blank cheque*: see BLANK *a.* CERTIFIED *cheque*. MARKED *cheque*. *open cheque*: see OPEN *a.* *rubber cheque*: see RUBBER *n.*[1] *traveller's* or *travellers(')* *cheque*: see TRAVELLER.

II See CHECK *n.*[1] I.

Comb.: **cheque-book** a book of printed cheques, issued to the customers of banks etc.; *attrib.* (of journalism etc., *derog.*) spending money lavishly to procure stories; **cheque card** a card issued by a bank to guarantee the honouring of cheques up to a stated value.

cheque *n.*[2] see CHECK *n.*[1]

†**chequed** *a.*[1], *a.*[2] vars. of CHECKED *a.*[1], *a.*[2]

chequeen *n.* see SEQUIN.

chequer /ˈtʃɛkə/ *n.*[1] Also **checker**. ME. [Aphet. f. EXCHEQUER *n.*] **I** †**1** A chessboard; chess. ME–E19. **2** In *pl.* (usu. treated as *sing.*). The game of draughts. *dial.* & *N. Amer.* E18. **b** In full *checkerman*. A piece in the game of draughts. *N. Amer.* M19. **II** †**3** *The* Court of Exchequer. ME–L17. †**4** *The* royal or national treasury. LME–L17. **5** A room, place, or table for accounts. *obs.* exc. *Hist.* LME. **III 6** A pattern made in squares, or with alternating colours. LME. **7** In *pl.* Squares or spots like or suggesting those which make up the design of a chessboard; *rare* the squares of an actual chessboard. E16.

Comb.: *checkerman*: see sense 2b above; **chequer-board** (the pattern of) a board for draughts or chess; **chequer-wise** *adv.* in the pattern of a chessboard; **chequer-work** work of a chequered pattern.

chequer /ˈtʃɛkə/ *n.*[2] *dial.* Also **checker**. M17. [App. = prec., from their appearance.] In *pl.* The berries of the wild service tree. Cf. CHECKERBERRY.

chequer /ˈtʃɛkə/ *v.t.* Also **checker**. See also next. LME. [f. CHEQUER *n.*[1]] **1** Diversify with a different colour or shade; variegate, mottle; break the uniformity of (*lit.* & *fig.*). LME. **2** Divide into or mark with squares, esp. of alternate colours. E17. †**3** Deposit (money) in an exchequer. E17–M18. **4** Arrange or distribute chequer-wise. L17.

1 H. ALLEN Bright golden patches shimmered and chequered the road ahead. *fig.*: DICKENS His sleep was checkered with starts and moans. 2 C. LUCAS The other . . is chequered brown and black, in half-lozenges. J. MASEFIELD Chequered by tossing boughs the moon appeared.

chequered /ˈtʃɛkəd/ *a.* Also **checkered**. LME. [f. CHEQUER *n.*[1], *v.*: see -ED[2], -ED[1].] **1** Marked like a chessboard; having a pattern of various crossing colours. LME. **2** Diversified in colour; marked with alternate light and shade; *fig.* undergoing varied fortunes, having discreditable episodes. L16.

1 **chequered flag** *Motor Racing* a flag with a black and white chequered pattern, displayed to drivers or riders at the moment of finishing a race. 2 SOUTHEY Beneath the o'er-arching forests' chequer'd shade. J. BUCHAN Ancient families with chequered pasts. *Listener* My career with 20th Century Fox was somewhat chequered. *chequered skipper*: see SKIPPER *n.*[1] 2.

†**chequin** *n.* see SEQUIN.

chequy *a.* see CHECKY.

chère amie /ʃɛːr ami/ *n. phr.* Pl. ***chères amies*** /ʃɛːrz ami/. L18. [Fr., lit. 'dear (woman) friend'.] A female lover; a mistress.

cherem /ˈxerem, h-/ *n.* Also **h-**. E19. [Heb. *ḥērem*, f. *ḥāram* devote, put under a curse.] Excommunication from the Synagogue and the Jewish community.

Cheremiss /ˈtʃɛrəmɪs/ *n.* Also **-is**, **Tch-**. Pl. **-isses**, same. M17. [Russ. †*cheremis*.] A member of a Finnic people living in Russia in the region of the middle Volga; the Finno-Ugric language of this people. Also called *Mari*.

Cherenkov radiation *n. phr.* var. of CERENKOV RADIATION.

chères amies *n. phr.* pl. of CHÈRE AMIE.

cherimoya /tʃɛrɪˈmɔɪə/ *n.* Also **chiri-** /tʃɪrɪ-/. M18. [Sp. f. Quechua, f. *chiri* cold, refreshing + *muya* circle.] (The pulpy edible fruit of) a small tree, *Annona cherimola*, native to the Andes of Peru and Ecuador.

cherish /ˈtʃɛrɪʃ/ *v.t.* ME. [(O)Fr. *chériss-* lengthened stem of *chérir*, f. *cher* dear f. L *carus*: see -ISH[2].] **1** Treat or regard (a person) affectionately; make much of; fondle. *arch.* ME. **2** Protect or tend (a child, plant, etc.) lovingly; treat with fostering care. ME. †**3** Entertain (a guest) kindly; cheer. LME–M18. †**4** Keep warm; give ease or comfort to. LME–M18. **5** Value, hold dear, cling to, (esp. hopes, feelings, ideas, etc.). LME.

5 HENRY MILLER The loss of something I had loved and cherished. P. SCOTT Both to cherish expectations and condition himself to sustain disappointments. M. LEITCH It was a good moment, one to be cherished, for he didn't know when the next one might present itself.

cherishable *a.* M17. **cherisher** *n.* LME. **cherishingly** *adv.* in a cherishing manner, tenderly E17. **cherishment** *n.* (*a*) the process or fact of cherishing; †(*b*) an indulgence; nourishment: E16.

cher maître /ʃɛːr mɛːtr/ *n. phr.* Pl. ***-s -s*** (pronounced same). E20. [Fr., lit. 'dear master'.] (A flattering form of address to) a famous writer.

chernites /kəːˈnʌɪtiːz/ *n.* E17. [Gk *khernitēs*.] *Hist.* An ivory-like marble used by the ancients.

chernozem /ˈtʃəːnəzɛm/ *n.* Also **-sem**, †**tch-**. M19. [Russ., f. *chërnyĭ* black + Slav. base *zem-* (cf. Russ. *zemlya*) earth.] A dark, humus-rich, fertile soil characteristic of temperate or cool grassland.

chernoˈzemic *a.* M20.

Cherokee /tʃɛrəˈkiː/ *a.* & *n.* L17. [Cherokee †*tsaraki* (now *tsaliki*).] **A** *adj.* Designating or pertaining to an Iroquoian Indian people inhabiting Oklahoma and N. Carolina (and formerly a large part of the southern US). L17.

Cherokee rose a fragrant white-flowered climbing rose, *Rosa laevigata*, native to China and naturalized in the US.

B *n.* Pl. same, **-s**. **1** A Cherokee Indian. E18. **2** The Iroquoian language of the Cherokee. M18.

cheroot /ʃəˈruːt/ *n.* L17. [Fr. *cheroute* f. Tamil *curuṭṭu* roll of tobacco.] A kind of cigar, orig. made in southern India, with both ends open.

Manila cheroot: see MANILA *a.* 1.

cherry /ˈtʃɛri/ *n.* & *a.* ME. [ONFr. *cherise* (treated as pl.), mod. CERISE, f. med.L *ceresia*, perh. f. orig. neut. pl. of adj. *ceraseus*, f. L *cerasus* f. Gk *kerasos*.] **A** *n.* **1** The small edible stone-fruit, dark red or yellow and red-flushed when ripe, borne by several trees of the genus *Prunus*, esp. the cultivated forms of *P. avium* (*sweet cherry*), *P. cerasus* (*sour* or *morello cherry*), or their hybrids. Also *fig.*, as a type of something red. ME. **2** Any of the trees bearing this fruit, related to the plum but with flowers in umbels or racemes. Also (chiefly w. specifying wd), any of various related trees, some of which are grown for ornament; any of several other unrelated trees resembling the cherry in some respect. LME. **b** More fully *cherry wood*. The timber of any of these trees. L18. **3** Virginity; a virgin. *slang.* E20.

1 *fig.*: P. SIDNEY Opening the cherrie of her lips. **black cherry** (*a*) a very dark ripe cherry; (*b*) *N. Amer.* (the dark fruit of) the rum-cherry, *Prunus serotina*. *sour cherry*: see SOUR *a.* **two bites, a second bite, at the cherry** more than one attempt or opportunity to do something. 2 *bird cherry*, *choke-cherry*, *flowering cherry*, *Hottentot cherry*, *Japanese cherry*, *Saint Lucie cherry*, *Suriname cherry*, etc.

Comb.: **cherry-bob** two cherries with joined stems; **cherry-bounce** *arch.* cherry-brandy; **cherry-brandy** a dark-red liqueur of brandy in which cherries have been steeped; *cherry-laurel*: see LAUREL *n.* 3; **cherry-picker** (*a*) a person who picks cherries; (*b*) in *pl.* (*Hist. slang*), the 11th Hussars (so-called from their crimson trousers); (*c*) a crane for raising and lowering persons; **cherry-pie** (*a*) a pie made with cherries; (*b*) a garden heliotrope; **cherry plum** (the fruit of) the small tree *Prunus cerasifera*; **cherry-red** (of) a bright deep red; **cherry tomato** (a plant bearing) a small deep-red variety of tomato; *cherry tree*: see sense 2 above; *cherry wood*: see sense 2b above.

B *attrib.* or as *adj.* **1** Bright deep red, of the typical colour of ripe cherries. LME. **2** Virgin. *slang.* M20.

cherry-like *a.* resembling (that of) a cherry; bright deep red: M19.

†**cherry** *v.t.* *rare* (Spenser). Only in L16. [Fr. *chérir* cherish.] Cheer, delight.

chers maîtres *n. phr.* pl. of CHER MAÎTRE.

chersonese /kəːsəˈniːs, -z/ *n. poet.* or *rhet.* E17. [L *chersonesus* f. Gk *khersonēsos*, f. *khersos* dry + *nēsos* island.] A peninsula, *spec.* that of Thrace west of the Hellespont.

chert /tʃəːt/ *n.* L17. [Origin unkn.: orig. dial.] *Geol.* Hard dense rock formed of amorphous silica, occurring as several varieties.

radiolarian chert: see RADIOLARIAN *a.*

cherty *a.* of the nature of or containing chert L18.

cherub /ˈtʃɛrəb/ *n.* Also (now *rare*) **-bin** /-bɪn/, †**-bim**. Pl. **-rubs**, (in sense 2, also) **-rubim** /-rəbɪm/. OE. [Ult. f. Heb. *kĕrūḇ*, pl. *kĕrūḇīm* (through L & Gk).] **1** In the Bible, a winged creature attending on God (and whose wings helped form the throne of God). In Christian theology, a member of the second order of the ninefold celestial hierarchy, ranking directly below the seraphim and above the thrones, and gifted with knowledge (usu. in *pl.*). Also, a conventional representation of such a being, esp. in the form of a winged (head of a) child. ME. **2** *transf.* A person, esp. a child, distinguished for cherubic qualities of beauty, innocence, etc. M16.

¶ The representation of the cherub as a child is due to a rabbinic folk-etymology explaining Heb. *kĕrūḇ* as repr. Aramaic *kĕ-rabyā* like a child.

cheˈrubic *a.* of, pertaining to, or resembling (a representation of) a cherub or cherubs; angelic; sweet and innocent: M17. †**cherubical** *a.* = CHERUBIC: only in E17. **cheˈrubically** *adv.* M19. **cheruˈbimical** *a.* = CHERUBIC L17. **cheruˈbinical** *a.* (*rare*) = CHERUBIC E17.

chervil /ˈtʃəːvɪl/ *n.* OE. [L *chaerephylla*, *-phyllum* f. Gk *khairephullon*.] An umbelliferous herb, *Anthriscus cerefolium*, with aromatic leaves; the leaves of this plant as used to flavour soups, salads, etc. Also (w. specifying wd), any of various related umbelliferous plants; *esp.* (in full *rough chervil*) *Chaerophyllum temulum*, a hedgerow plant with hairy red-spotted stems.

turnip-rooted chervil *Chaerophyllum bulbosum*, which has an edible root like a parsnip.

Cheshire /ˈtʃɛʃə/ *n.* & *a.* L16. [A county in England.] **1** In full *Cheshire cheese*. A mild crumbly cheese of a type orig. made in Cheshire. L16. **2** *grin like a Cheshire cat*, grin fixedly and broadly. L18. **3** *Cheshire acre*, a unit of area formerly current in Cheshire, equal to 10,240 sq. yards (approx. 0.857 hectare). E19.

chesil /ˈtʃɛz(ə)l/ *n.* Also (the usual form in sense 2) **chisel** /ˈtʃɪz(ə)l/. [OE *ċiosol*, *ċisel*, *ċysel* = MDu. *kezel*, LG *kesel*, OHG *kisil* (G *Kiesel*), f. WGmc base, whence MHG *kis*, G *Kies* gravel.] **1** Gravel, shingle. Long *obs.* exc. in the name (*Chesil Bank*, or *Beach*) of a long shingle ridge on the Dorset coast, enclosing a lagoon. OE. 2 Bran; coarse flour. *obs.* exc. *dial.* L15.

†**chesnut** *n.* var. of CHESTNUT.

chess /tʃɛs/ *n.*[1] ME. [Aphet. f. OFr. *esches* (mod. *échecs*), pl. of *eschec* CHECK *n.*[1]] 1 A game for two players using a chequered board of sixty-four squares with eight pieces, viz. a king, queen, two rooks, knights, and bishops, and eight pawns each, with the object of placing the opponent's king in checkmate. ME. †2 The pieces and pawns or the board used in playing. ME–E17. 3 *loosely.* Any of the various classical board games. LME.

1 : *lightning chess*: see LIGHTNING *n.* & *a.* *living chess*: see LIVING *a.*

Comb.: **chessboard** *n.* & *a.* (resembling) the board on which chess is played; **chess-clock**: displaying the accumulated time each chess-player has expended on his or her moves; **chessman** any of the pieces or pawns with which chess is played (usu. in *pl.*).

chess /tʃɛs/ *n.*[2] *obs.* exc. *dial.* LME. [Origin unkn.] 1 A tier, layer, storey; a row. LME. 2 Each of the sections into which an apple etc. may be divided. *Sc.* L18. 3 In *pl.* The parallel planks of a pontoon-bridge. E19.

chess /tʃɛs/ *n.*[3] Chiefly *N. Amer.* M18. [Origin unkn.] A grass of the genus *Bromus*, commonly found as a weed among wheat.

chess-apple /ˈtʃɛsap(ə)l/ *n.* M17. [Origin uncertain: perh. f. its spotty surface (cf. CHEQUER *n.*[2]).] The fruit of the whitebeam, *Sorbus aria*.

chessel /ˈtʃɛs(ə)l/ *n.* L17. [App. f. CHEESE *n.*[1] + WELL *n.*[1]] A cheese-making mould.

chess-tree /ˈtʃɛstriː/ *n.* ME. [f. unkn. 1st elem. + TREE *n.* (in sense 'wood').] *Naut.* A piece of wood bolted perpendicularly on a ship's side, used to confine the clew of the mainsail.

chessylite /ˈtʃɛsɪlʌɪt/ *n.* M19. [f. *Chessy*, near Lyons, France + -LITE.] *Min.* = AZURITE.

chest /tʃɛst/ *n.* [OE *čest*, *čyst*, corresp. to OFris., MDu. *kiste* (Du. *kist*), OHG *kista* (G *Kiste*), ON *kista*, f. Gmc f. L *cista* f. Gk *kistē* box.] 1 A box, a coffer; a large box of strong construction for the custody of articles of value, *esp.* one for a sailor's belongings, for tools, for medicines, etc. OE. 2 A coffin. Now *dial.* OE. 3 That part of the human or of an animal's body that is enclosed by the ribs; the thorax; the front surface of a body from neck to waist. LME. 4 The treasury or coffer of an institution; *transf.* the money in one, the funds. LME. 5 A large case into which commodities (esp. tea) are packed for transport. E18.

Phrases: **chest of drawers** a piece of furniture with a set of drawers in a frame. **chest of viols** a set of viols kept in a chest. **get a thing off one's chest** *colloq.* relieve one's feelings by disclosing something. **hold** (or **keep, play,** etc.) **one's cards close to one's chest** be reluctant to reveal one's intentions or resources. *military chest*: see MILITARY *a.*

Comb.: **chest-expander** a piece of equipment for exercising and developing the muscles of the chest and arms; **chest freezer** a low freezer with an opening top; **chest-protector** a covering or wrap of flannel etc. worn to protect the chest from cold; **chest-voice**: of the lowest speaking or singing register.

chested *a.* having a chest (of a specified kind) LME. **chestful** *n.* the quantity contained in a chest E18.

chest /tʃɛst/ *v.t.* OE. [f. the n.] 1 Put into a coffin. Now *dial.* OE. 2 Enclose in a chest; store away. OE. 3 Strike with the chest; guide or propel (a ball) with the chest. M19.

†**chesten** *n.* OE–L17. [OFr. *chastaine* (mod. *châtaigne*) f. L *castanea* f. Gk *kastanea*, *-neion*, short for *kastaneion karuon* nut of Castanaea (Pontus) or Castana (Thessaly): cf. CHESTNUT.] A chestnut; a chestnut tree.

chester /ˈtʃɛstə/ *n. obs.* exc. *Hist.* [OE *ċeaster* ult. f. L *castra*: a common elem. in place-names (also in forms *-caster*, *-cester*).] A walled town; *spec.* one that was formerly a Roman station.

chesterfield /ˈtʃɛstəfiːld/ *n.* M19. [f. an Earl of *Chesterfield*.] 1 A plain overcoat usu. with a velvet collar. M19. 2 A sofa with a padded seat, back, and ends. E20.

Chesterfieldian /tʃɛstəˈfiːldɪən/ *a.* L18. [f. *Chesterfield* (see below) + -IAN.] Relating to or characteristic of Philip Stanhope, 4th Earl of Chesterfield (1694–1773), or his writings on manners and etiquette.

Chestertonian /tʃɛstəˈtəʊnɪən/ *a.* E20. [f. *Chesterton* (see below) + -IAN.] Of, pertaining to, resembling, or characteristic of the English author Gilbert Keith Chesterton (1874–1936), or his writings.

chestnut /ˈtʃɛsnʌt/ *n.* & *a.* Also †**chesnut**. E16. [f. CHESTEN + NUT *n.*] A *n.* 1 a The edible nut of a tree of the genus *Castanea*, of the beech family; *esp.* that of *C. sativa* (also *Spanish* or *sweet chestnut*). Also (w. specifying wd), any of various fruits etc. resembling this nut. E16. b (More fully *chestnut tree*) the tree itself; (with specifying wd) any of various similar trees. Also, the wood of these trees. L16. c *ellipt.* A horse chestnut. L18. 2 A chestnut colour; a chestnut horse. (See sense B. below.) L16. 3 The small hard callosity in the skin of the horse at the inner side of the forelegs. M19. 4 A stale joke or anecdote; anything too often repeated. L19.

Phrases: *Cape chestnut*: see CAPE *n.*[1] *Chinese water chestnut*: see WATER *n.* HORSE CHESTNUT. MORETON BAY *chestnut.* **pull the chestnuts out of the fire** succeed in a hazardous undertaking on behalf of or through the agency of another (w. ref. to the fable of a monkey using a cat's paw to get roasting chestnuts from a fire). TAHITI *chestnut. water chestnut*: see WATER *n. wild chestnut*: see WILD *a.*

Comb.: **chestnut oak** any of various, chiefly N. American, oaks having leaves resembling those of the chestnut; *chestnut tree*: see sense 1b above.

B *adj.* 1 Of the colour of a chestnut; deep reddish-brown. M16. 2 Of a horse: having reddish- or yellowish-brown coloration. L17.

chestnutting *n.* the gathering of chestnuts L18. **chestnutty** *a.* (*a*) resembling the colour or flavour of a chestnut; (*b*) old and well known, frequently repeated: L19.

chesty /ˈtʃɛsti/ *a. colloq.* E20. [f. CHEST *n.* + -Y[1].] 1 Conceited, arrogant. *US.* E20. 2 Inclined to, marked by, or symptomatic of ailments of the chest. M20. 3 Having a large chest or prominent breasts. M20.

chestily *adv.* E20. **chestiness** *n.* E20.

Chesvan *n.* var. of HESVAN.

chétif /ʃetif/ *a.* E20. [Fr.] Puny, sickly, thin; miserable, wretched.

chetnik /ˈtʃɛtnɪk/ *n.* E20. [Serbo-Croat *četnik*, f. *četa* band, troop.] A guerrilla fighter in the Balkans; *spec.* (*Hist.*) one of a royalist force led by General Draža Mihajlović in occupied Yugoslavia, 1941–5.

chetty /ˈtʃɛti/ *n.* L16. [Tamil *ceṭṭi*.] (A member of) any of a group of trading castes in southern India.

chevachee /tʃɛvəˈtʃiː/ *n.* Long *obs.* exc. *Hist.* LME. [OFr. *chevauchiee*, pa. ppl formation on *chevauchier* (mod. *chevaucher*) f. late L *caballicare* ride, f. *caballus* horse.] An expedition on horseback, a raid.

chevage /ˈtʃiːvɪdʒ/ *n. obs.* exc. *Hist.* LME. [OFr. = capitation, f. *chef* head: see CHIEF *n.*, -AGE.] Capitation or poll-money paid to a lord.

cheval /ʃəval, ʃəˈval/ *n.* Pl. ***-vaux*** /-vo, -ˈvəʊ/. L15. [Fr.] The Fr. for 'horse', also 'frame', occurring in various phrases used in Eng.

cheval de bataille /də batɑːj/ [lit. 'battle-horse'] an obsession, a pet subject E19. ***chevaux de frise*** /də friːz/ [lit. 'horses of Friesland': named iron. with ref. to their use by the Frisians, who had no cavalry] a number of metal spikes set in timber to repel cavalry, or set along the top of a fence, wall, etc., to repel intruders L17. See also À CHEVAL, *pas de cheval* s.v. PAS 2, *petits chevaux* s.v. PETIT *a.*[2]

chevaleresque *a.* see CHIVALRESQUE.

chevalet /ʃəvale/ *n.* Pl. pronounced same. E19. [Fr., dim. of CHEVAL.] †1 A trestle for a bridge. Only in E19. 2 The bridge of a bowed musical instrument. L19.

cheval-glass /ʃəˈvalglɑːs/ *n.* M19. [f. Fr. CHEVAL + GLASS *n.*] A tall mirror swung on an upright frame.

chevalier /ʃɛvəˈlɪə, *foreign* ʃəvalje (*pl. same*)/ *n.* LME. [AN *chevaler*, (O)Fr. *chevalier*, f. med.L *caballarius*, f. L *caballus* horse: see -IER, -EER. Cf. CAVALIER *n.*] 1 *Hist.* A horseman, *esp.* a mounted knight. LME. 2 A chivalrous man, a gallant. M17. 3 A member of certain orders of knighthood, or of the French Legion of Honour, etc. E18.

Phrases: ***chevalier d'industrie*** /dɛ̃dystri/ [Fr., lit. 'knight of industry'] an adventurer, a swindler. PREUX *chevalier.* **the Chevalier (de St George)** James Stuart, the Old Pretender. **the Young Chevalier** Charles Edward Stuart, the Young Pretender.

chevaline /ˈʃɛvəlɪn/ *a. rare.* M16. [Fr., fem. of *chevalin*, f. CHEVAL: see -INE[1].] Of or pertaining to horses.

chevaux *n.pl.* see CHEVAL.

chevelure /ʃəvlyːr/ *n.* Pl. pronounced same. LME. [OFr. *chevelëure* (mod. *-elure*), f. L *capillatura*, f. *capillatus* haired, f. *capillus* hair: see -URE.] 1 The hair of the head, a head of hair; (formerly) a wig. LME. 2 A halo around a star etc.; a comet's coma. L17.

cheverel /ˈʃɛv(ə)r(ə)l/ *n.* & *a.* LME. [OFr. *chevrele* dim. of *chèvre* goat.] †A *n.* Kid-leather, noted for its elasticity. LME–E17. B *adj.* Of or pertaining to kid-leather; *fig.* elastic, flexible, yielding. E16.

chevesaile /ˈtʃiːvəseɪl/ *n. obs.* exc. *Hist.* LME. [OFr. *cheveçaille*, f. *chevece* collar, f. L *capitia* pl. of *capitium* opening for the head in a tunic etc.] The collar of a coat, gown, etc., often richly ornamented.

chevet /ʃəˈveɪ; *foreign* ʃəvɛ (*pl. same*)/ *n.* E19. [Fr. = pillow.] The apsidal termination of the east end of a church.

cheville /ʃəviːj/ *n.* Pl. pronounced same. L19. [Fr. = peg, pin, plug.] 1 A meaningless or redundant word or phrase inserted to round off a sentence or complete a verse. L19. 2 A peg in a stringed musical instrument. L19.

chevin /ˈtʃɛvɪn/ *n.* LME. [OFr. *chevenne*, *chevesne* (mod. *chevanne*), f. Proto-Romance f. L *capiton-*, *capito* (orig.) big-head, f. *caput*, *-it-*, head.] The chub.

Cheviot /ˈtʃɛvɪət/ *n.* In sense 2 also **c-**. L18. [f. *Cheviot* Hills on the England–Scotland border.] 1 In full *Cheviot sheep.* (An animal of) a breed of sheep from the Cheviot Hills. L18. 2 (Cloth made from) the wool of Cheviot sheep. M19.

chevisance /ˈʃɛvɪs(ə)ns/ *n.* Long *arch.* ME. [OFr., f. *cheviss-* lengthened stem of *chevir* achieve, f. *chef* head, chief: see CHIEF *n.*, -ANCE.] †1 A bringing to an end; furtherance; assistance. Only in ME. †2 Resource, remedy; an expedient. ME–M17. †3 Provision, supply; provisions; booty. ME–M17. 4 Raising money; borrowing; a loan; lending, usury; profiteering, gain. Freq. *derog.* LME. 5 (Confused by Spenser and others with *chivalry* and related wds.) Enterprise, chivalry, prowess; an exploit. L16.

chevra *n.* var. of HEBRA.

chèvre /ʃɛːvr/ *n.* M20. [Fr. = goat, esp. she-goat.] French goat's-milk cheese.

¶ See also POIL *de chèvre.*

chevrette /ʃəˈvrɛt/ *n.* M18. [Fr., dim. of prec.: see -ETTE.] †1 A machine for raising guns or mortars. M–L18. 2 A thin goatskin leather used for gloves. L19.

chevron /ˈʃɛvrən/ *n.*[1] LME. [(O)Fr. f. Proto-Romance, f. L *caper* goat: cf. L *capreoli* pair of rafters.] 1 *Her.* A charge consisting of a bent bar of an inverted V shape. LME. b This shape used in decorative art etc. E17. 2 A beam or rafter; *esp.* in *pl.*, the rafters of a roof which meet at an angle at the ridge. L16. 3 A badge in a V shape (whether inverted or not) on the sleeve of a uniform, indicating rank or length of service; a V-shaped stripe. E19.

chevronel *n.* (*Her.*) a bent bar on the escutcheon, half the breadth of the chevron L16.

†**chevron** *n.*[2] M16–E19. [App. erron. for CHEVEREL.] A glove.

chevron /ˈʃɛvrən/ *v.t.* M16. [f. CHEVRON *n.*[1] or Fr. *chevronner.*] Provide with chevrons or things arranged in a chevron pattern; make with a chevron pattern.

chevronny /ˈʃɛvrəni/ *a.* In sense 2 also **-ony.** E18. [Fr. *chevronné* pa. pple of *chevronner*, f. as CHEVRON *n.*[1]] 1 *Her.* Charged with or formed by an even number of chevrons. E18. 2 *gen.* Zigzag. L19.

chevrotain /ˈʃɛvrəteɪn/ *n.* Also **-tin** /-tɪn/. L18. [Fr., dim. of OFr. *chevrot* dim. of *chèvre* goat.] A small deerlike ruminant of the mainly southern Asian family Tragulidae. Also called *mouse deer*.

chevy *n.* & *v.* var. of CHIVVY *n.* & *v.*[1]

Chevy Chase /ˌtʃɛvi ˈtʃeɪs/ *n. phr. rhyming slang.* Now *rare.* M19. [See CHIVVY *n.* & *v.*[1]] The face.

chew /tʃuː/ *n.* See also CHAW *n.*[2], CHOW *n.*[1] ME. [f. the vb.] 1 An act of chewing. ME. 2 Something that is chewed; *spec.* a quid of tobacco. E18. 3 A chewy sweet. M20.

chew /tʃuː/ *v.* See also CHAW *v.*, CHOW *v.* [OE *ċēowan* = MLG *keuwen* (Du. *kauwen*), OHG *kiuwan* (G *kauen*), f. WGmc.] 1 *v.t.* Crush, bruise, and grind by the action of the molar teeth; grind to a pulp or indent by repeated biting; masticate (food). OE. b Injure, break, or destroy with an action resembling that of the jaws. Freq. foll. by *off, up.* M19. 2 *v.t. fig.* a Examine or plan deliberately; meditate on; turn *over* in the mind; talk *over.* ME. b Mumble; mutter inarticulately. E17. c Foll. by *out*: reprimand. *N. Amer. colloq.* M20. 3 *v.i.* Work food etc. with the teeth; champ, masticate. (Foll. by (*up*)*on* something.) LME. 4 *v.i.* Meditate, ruminate, exercise the mind, (*up*)*on, at.* L16.

1b C. RYAN The port wing . . was chewed off by the propeller of a Stirling bomber. 2a M. PRIOR He chews Revenge.

Phrases: *bite off more than one can chew*: see BITE *v.* **chewing-gum** a preparation of sweetened and flavoured gums and resins, used for prolonged chewing. *chew the cud*: see CUD *n.* **chew the rag, the fat** *slang* discuss a matter; persist in grumbling.

Comb.: **chew-stick** (*a*) = *chaw-stick* s.v. CHAW *v.*; (*b*) the root or stem of various W. African plants, used to clean the teeth.

chewable *a.* able to be chewed M19. **chewer** *n.* a person who or thing which chews E17. **chewy** *a.* suitable for chewing; needing to be chewed: E20.

†**chewet** *n.* M–L16. [Fr. *chouette.*] A jackdaw, a chough; a chatterer.

Chewings fescue /ˈtʃuːɪŋz ˈfɛskjuː/ *n. phr.* E20. [Charles *Chewings* (1859–1937), Austral. scientist who first marketed the grass (in NZ).] A variety of red fescue (*Festuca rubra*) used as a pasture and lawn grass.

chewink /tʃiːˈwɪŋk/ *n. N. Amer.* Also **chee-**. L18. [Imit.] The towhee *Pipilo erythrophthalmus.*

Cheyenne /ʃʌɪˈan/ *n.* & *a.* L18. [Canad. Fr. f. Dakota *šahíyena.*] A *n.* Pl. same, **-s**. A member of an Algonquian Indian people living in Montana and Oklahoma (orig. living between the Missouri and Arkansas rivers); the language of this people. L18. B *attrib.* or as *adj.* Of or pertaining to the Cheyenne or their language. E19.

Cheyne-Stokes /ˈtʃeɪnstəʊks/ *a.* L19. [John *Cheyne* (1777–1836), Sc. physician, and William *Stokes* (1804–78), Ir. physician.] *Med.* Designating respiration characterized by a cyclical variation of rate involving gradual decrease, cessation, and gradual increase.

ARNOLD BENNETT Symptoms of 'Cheyne-Stokes breathing', the final and worst symptom of his disease.

†**cheyney** *n.* L16–M18. [Alt. of CHINA.] A sort of worsted or woollen cloth.

chez /ʃe, *bef. a vowel* ʃez/ *prep.* M18. [Fr. f. OFr. *chiese* f. L *casa* cottage.] At the house or home of.

chi /kʌɪ/ *n.* LME. [Gk *khi.*] The twenty-second letter (*X*, *χ*) of the Greek alphabet.

chi-rho [RHO] a monogram of chi and rho representing the first two letters of Gk *Khristos* Christ. See also CHI-SQUARE.

chiack *n.* & *v.* var. of CHI-HIKE.

Chian /ˈkʌɪən, ˈkiːən/ *a.* & *n.* L16. [f. L *Chius* f. Gk *Khios* adj., f. *Khios* Chios (see below): see -AN.] A *adj.* Pertaining to or originating from the island of Chios in the Aegean. L16.

Chian turpentine: see TURPENTINE *n.* I. **Chian wine** *Hist.* wine from Chios, highly regarded in classical times.

B *n.* = *Chian wine* above. M17.

Chianti /kɪˈanti/ *n.* M19. [f. the *Chianti* Mountains, Tuscany.] A dry usu. red Italian wine, properly one made in the Chianti district of Tuscany.

chiaroscuro /kɪˌɑːrəˈskʊərəʊ/ *n.* & *a.* M17. [It., f. *chiaro* clear, bright + *oscuro* dark, OBSCURE *a.*] A *n.* Pl. **-os**. 1 A style of painting in which only light and shade are represented; black and white. M17. 2 The treatment or disposition of the light and shade, or brighter and darker masses, in a picture; or brighter and darker masses, in a picture; an effect or contrast of light and shade in a picture or in nature. L17. 3 *fig.* The use of contrast in literature etc. E19.

2 B. MOORE The sky was a shifting chiaroscuro of grays and blacks.

B *attrib.* or as *adj.* In chiaroscuro, in black and white; *fig.* marked by stylistic etc. contrasts; half-revealed. M19.

J. GROSS Strip away the rant, and what remains is a daring chiaroscuro prose.

chiaroscurist *n.* an artist distinguished for or painting in chiaroscuro L18.

chiasma /kʌɪˈazmə/ *n.* Pl. **-mas**, **-mata** /-mətə/. M19. [mod.L f. Gk *khiasma* crosspiece, decussation, f. *khiazein*: see next.] 1 *Anat.* An intercrossing or decussation; *esp.* (in full *optic chiasma*) the commissure formed between the two optic nerves. M19. 2 *Cytol.* A structure formed by chromosomes during meiosis, at which crossing over occurs. E20.

chiasmus /kʌɪˈazməs, kɪ-/ *n.* Pl. **-mi** /-mʌɪ/. M17. [mod.L f. Gk *khiasmos*, f. *khiazein* mark with a chi, f. *khi* CHI.] 1 *gen.* A diagonal or crosswise arrangement. *rare.* M17. 2 *Rhet.* The inversion in a second phrase or clause of the order of words in the first. L19.

chiastic /kʌɪˈastɪk, kɪ-/ *a.* M19. [f. Gk *khiastos* arranged crosswise, f. *khiazein*: see prec., -IC.] Characterized by chiasmus; of the form of chiasmus, with reversal of order.

B. COTTLE 'Rhymney Beer—the Best Round Here' . . with the added trick of chiastic alliteration on R, B, B, R.

chiastolite /kʌɪˈastəlʌɪt, kɪ-/ *n.* E19. [f. as prec. + -LITE.] *Min.* A form of andalusite containing carbonaceous inclusions which cause some sections of the mineral to show the figure of a cross.

chiaus /tʃaʊs, -ʃ/ *n.* Also **tchaush** /tʃaʊʃ/. L16. [Turk. *çavuş.* See also CHOUSE *n.*] A Turkish messenger, herald, or sergeant.

Chibcha /ˈtʃɪbtʃə/ *n.* & *a.* Pl. of n. same, **-s**. E19. [Amer. Sp. f. Chibcha *zipa* chief, hereditary leader.] A *n.* A member of an Indian people of Colombia having an ancient civilization; their language (now extinct), a member of the Chibchan family. E19. B *attrib.* or as *adj.* Of or pertaining to the Chibcha or their language. E19.

Chibchan /ˈtʃɪbtʃ(ə)n/ *n.* & *a.* E20. [f. prec. + -AN.] (Of) a language family of Colombia and Central America.

chibol /ˈtʃɪb(ə)l/ *n.* LME. [North. var. of OFr. *cibole* (mod. CIBOULE) f. late L *caepulla* onion-bed, f. L *caepa, cepa* onion.] †1 = CIBOULE. LME–E18. 2 A spring onion. *dial.* M19.

chibouk /tʃɪˈbuːk/ *n.* Also **-bouque**. E19. [(Fr. *chibouque* f.) Turk. *çubuk*, (earlier) *çıbık* tube, pipe.] A long Turkish tobacco-pipe.

chic /ʃiːk/ *n.* & *a.* M19. [Fr., prob. f. G *Schick* skill.] A *n.* Stylishness; elegance in dress; skill, effectiveness. M19.

punk chic: see PUNK *n.*[2] & *a.* *radical chic*: see RADICAL *a.* 2C.

B *adj.* Compar. **chic-er**; superl. **chic-est**. Stylish, elegant. M19.

chicly *adv.* E20.

chica /ˈtʃiːkə/ *n.* M19. [Amer. Sp., prob. of Amer. Indian origin.] A S. American climbing shrub, *Arrabidaea chica*, of the bignonia family; a red pigment obtained from this, and used as skin paint by peoples in the R. Orinoco region.

Chicagoan /ʃɪˈkɑːgəʊən/ *n.* Also †**-ian**. M19. [f. *Chicago* (see below) + -AN, -IAN.] A native or inhabitant of the city of Chicago in Illinois, USA.

chicana *n.* see CHICANO.

chicane /ʃɪˈkeɪn/ *n.* L17. [Fr., f. as next.] 1 = CHICANERY I. L17. †2 An instance of chicanery; a subterfuge, a quibble. L17–M18. 3 *Cards.* A hand without trumps or without cards of one suit as dealt. L19. 4 An artificial barrier or obstacle, esp. a sharp double bend, on a motor-racing track. M20.

chicane /ʃɪˈkeɪn/ *v.* L17. [Fr. *chicaner* pursue at law, quibble, of unkn. origin.] 1 *v.i.* Employ chicanery; quibble, cavil. L17. 2 *v.t.* Quibble over; argue *away* by chicanery. *rare.* L18. 3 *v.t.* Deceive by chicanery, cheat, (*into, out of,* etc.). M19.

chicaner *n.* a person who practises chicanery; a quibbler, a shifty person: L17.

chicanery /ʃɪˈkeɪnəri/ *n.* L16. [Fr. *chicanerie*, f. as prec.: see -ERY.] 1 Trickery in legal matters; the use of subterfuge and trickery in debate or action; deception; quibbling, sophistry. L16. 2 A dishonest artifice of law; a trick. L17.

chicano /tʃɪˈkɑːnəʊ, ʃɪ-, -ˈkeɪn-/ *n.* & *a.* Also **C-**. M20. [Alt. of Sp. *mejicano* Mexican, f. *Méjico* Mexico.] A *n.* Pl. **-os**. Fem. **-na** /-nə/. A N. American of Mexican origin. M20. B *adj.* Of or pertaining to chicanos; Mexican American. M20.

chich /tʃɪtʃ/ *n. obs.* exc. *dial.* Also †**cich**. LME. [Fr. *chiche* f. OFr. *cice* f. L *cicer.*] = CHICK-PEA. Also †*chich-pease.*

chicha /ˈtʃɪtʃə/ *n.* E17. [Amer. Sp. f. Cuna.] A fermented liquor made from maize in S. and Central America.

chicharron /tʃiːtʃəˈrəʊn, *foreign* tʃitʃaˈrron/ *n.* Pl. **-ones** /-əʊnɪz, *foreign* -ones/. M19. [Amer. Sp. *chicharrón.*] A piece of crackling, served as a delicacy in Mexico, parts of the southern US, etc.

chichi /ˈʃiːʃiː/ *n.* & *a.* E20. [Fr.] A *n.* Showiness, fussiness; affectation; a frilly or showy thing. E20. B *adj.* Showy, frilly, fussy; affected. M20.

chi-chi /ˈtʃiːtʃiː/ *a. Anglo-Ind.* (somewhat *derog.*). Also **chee-chee**. L18. [Perh. f. Hind. *chī-chī* fie!, supposed to be used by Eurasians.] (Esp. of a girl or woman) half-caste, Eurasian; (of speech) characteristic of the English formerly spoken by some Eurasians in India.

†**chichling** *n.* see CHICKLING.

chick /tʃɪk/ *n.*[1] Pl. **-s**, (*dial.*) **-en** (see CHICKEN *n.*[1] II). ME. [Abbrev. of CHICKEN *n.*[1]] 1 A child. *arch.* ME. 2 A chicken; a young bird, esp. before or just after hatching. LME. 3 A young woman. *slang.* E20.

1 W. MORRIS No chick or child to bless his house. 2 G. MAXWELL A moorhen chick of a few days old. 3 M. AMIS This other girl of mine, this chick, this broad called Ursula.

¶ See also DIGBY *chick.*

chick /tʃɪk/ *n.*[2] Also **check** /tʃɛk/. L17. [Urdu *chik* f. Pers. *čigh.*] In the Indian subcontinent: a screen for a doorway etc., made from split bamboo and twine.

chick /tʃɪk/ *n.*[3] L18. [Imit.] 1 A tick (of a clock etc.). *Sc.* L18. 2 The chirping call of a bird. M19.

chick /tʃɪk/ *v.i.* Long *obs.* exc. *dial.* LME. [Imit.: cf. CHIP *v.*[1]] Sprout; crack as a seed does in sprouting.

chickabiddy /ˈtʃɪkəbɪdi/ *n.* L18. [f. CHICK *n.*[1] + euphonic *-a-* + BIDDY *n.*[1]] 1 A chicken, a chick. *nursery.* L18. 2 A little one, a dear child. E19.

chickadee /ˈtʃɪkədiː/ *n. N. Amer.* M19. [Imit.] 1 Any of various titmice native to N. America. M19. 2 Used as a term of endearment to a woman. M20.

chickaree /tʃɪkəˈriː/ *n.* E19. [Imit.] A N. American red squirrel of the genus *Tamiasciurus.*

Chickasaw /ˈtʃɪkəsɔː/ *n.* & *a.* L17. [Chickasaw *čikaša.*] A *n.* Pl. **-s**, same. 1 A member of a Muskogean Indian people formerly resident in Mississippi and Alabama, but subsequently in Oklahoma. L17. 2 The language of this people. L19.

B *attrib.* or as *adj.* Of or pertaining to the Chickasaws or their language. E18.

Chickasaw Indian = sense A.1 above. **Chickasaw**

plum a wild plum, *Prunus angustifolia*, of the south-eastern US.

chicken /ˈtʃɪkɪn/ *n.*[1] & *a.* [OE *ċīcen*, *ċȳcen*, prob. ult. rel. to COCK *n.*[1] Cf. (M)Du. *kieken*, (M)LG *küken*, MHG *küchelīn* (G *Küchlein*), ON *kjúklingr*.] **A** *n.* **I** *sing.*, w. pl. **-s. 1** A young bird, esp. of the domestic fowl; (the flesh of) the domestic fowl as food. OE. **2a** A child. *arch.* LME. **b** A young and inexperienced person. E18. **c** A young woman. *slang.* M19. **3** A timorous or cowardly person. E17. **b** (The name of) a game testing courage in the face of danger. M20.

II *pl.* (*collect.*) **4** Poultry, fowl. *obs.* exc. *dial.* E17.

Phrases: **chicken à la King** cooked breast of chicken in a cream sauce with mushrooms and peppers. *chicken* CHASSEUR. **chicken Kiev** chicken breast filled with garlic butter. *chicken* (*à la*) MARENGO. *chicken* (*à la*) *Maryland*: see MARYLAND 2. **count one's chickens (before they are hatched)** be overoptimistic, be precipitate. DIGBY *chicken. like a hen with one chicken*: see HEN *n.* 1. *Maryland chicken*: see MARYLAND 2. **Mother Carey's chicken** the storm petrel. **no (spring) chicken** neither young nor inexperienced. *Surrey chicken*: see SURREY *n.*[2]

Comb.: **chicken-and-egg** *a.* designating a problem of which of two things, issues, etc., comes first, where each is viewed as the cause of the other; **chicken-breast** (*a*) a malformed projection of the breastbone; (*b*) the breast-meat of a chicken; **chicken-breasted** *a.* having a malformed projection of the breastbone; **chicken brick** an earthenware container in two halves, in which to cook a chicken etc.; **chickenburger** a cake of minced etc. chicken, usu. fried or grilled; *chicken cholera*: see CHOLERA 3; **chicken-feed** food for poultry; *colloq.* something trivial, esp. a small amount of money; **chicken-hawk** (chiefly *N. Amer.*) any of various bird-eating raptors; **chicken-heart** *fig.* a timorous or cowardly person; **chicken-hearted** *a.* timorous, cowardly; **chicken-liver** *fig.* a coward; **chicken-livered** *a.* cowardly; **chicken mite** = *red mite* (a) s.v. RED *a.*; **chickenpox** [perh. f. the mildness of the infection] a mild eruptive disease due to viral infection, chiefly affecting children; also called *varicella*; **chicken-shit** *n.* & *a.* (*slang*, chiefly *N. Amer.*) (*a*) *n.* a coward; nonsense, lies; (*b*) *adj.* cowardly; dishonest; **chicken-weed** = CHICKWEED; **chicken-wire** a light wire netting with a hexagonal mesh.

B *adj.* Cowardly; scared. *slang.* M20.

chicken *n.*[2] var. of CHIKAN.

chicken /ˈtʃɪkɪn/ *v.i. slang.* M20. [f. CHICKEN *n.*[1] & *a.*] Fail to act, back down, from motives of cowardice. Freq. foll. by *out*.

chickling /ˈtʃɪklɪŋ/ *n.* Orig. **†c(h)ichling.** M16. [f. CHICH + -LING[1].] = *grass pea* s.v. GRASS *n.* Now usu. *chickling pea*, *vetch*.

chick-pea /ˈtʃɪkpiː/ *n.* Also **†-pease.** E18. [Alt. of CHICH-*pease*: see PEA *n.*[1], PEASE.] (The seed of) a dwarf pea, *Cicer arietinum*, grown for food esp. in Asia.

chickweed /ˈtʃɪkwiːd/ *n.* LME. [f. CHICK *n.*[1] + WEED *n.*[1]] Any of numerous small white-flowered plants of the family Caryophyllaceae, and esp. of the genera *Cerastium* and *Stellaria*; spec. *S. media*, a common weed. Orig. more widely, any of various similar weedy plants.

jagged chickweed: see JAGGED *a.*[1] *mouse-ear chickweed*: see MOUSE *n. water chickweed*: see WATER *n.*

Comb.: **chickweed wintergreen** a plant of the genus *Trientalis*, of the primrose family, bearing a starry white (occas. pink) flower above a whorl of obovate leaves, esp. *T. europaea* of Eurasian upland woods and moors (cf. *star-flower* s.v. STAR *n.*[1]).

chicle /ˈtʃɪk(ə)l, -kli/ *n.* L19. [Amer. Sp. f. Nahuatl *tzictli*.] The coagulated latex of the sapodilla, *Manilkara zapota*, and several related trees, which forms the basis of chewing-gum.

chicory /ˈtʃɪk(ə)ri/ *n.* LME. [f. Fr. **†***cicorée* (mod. *chicorée*) endive, f. med.L *cic(h)orea*, ult. f. Gk *kikhorion*: cf. SUCCORY.] **1** A Eurasian blue-flowered plant of the composite family, *Cichorium intybus*, found wild by roadsides and in pastures and cultivated for its roots and crowns of leaves which are eaten blanched in salads. Also (*N. Amer.*), (the leaves of) the endive, *C. endivia.* LME. **2** The root of *C. intybus* ground and roasted as a substitute for or an additive to coffee. E19.

chid, chidden *v.* see CHIDE *v.*

chide /tʃʌɪd/ *n.* Now *rare.* ME. [f. the vb.] Wrangling; an angry rebuke.

chide /tʃʌɪd/ *v.* Now *arch.* or *literary.* Pa. t. **chided, chid** /tʃɪd/; pa. pple **chided, chidden** /ˈtʃɪd(ə)n/, **chid.** [OE *ċīdan*, of unkn. origin.] **1** *v.i.* **†a** Contend loudly, brawl, wrangle; quarrel or dispute angrily *with.* OE–M19. **b** Give loud and angry expression to dissatisfaction; scold; rail (**†***at*). ME. **2** *v.t.* Rail at, scold; rebuke; find fault with. ME. **3** *v.t.* Drive, impel, or compel by chiding, *away*, *into* or *out of* a state, position, etc. L16.

1b SWIFT You came chiding into the world. *fig.*: KEATS The silver snarling trumpets 'gan to chide. **2** S. JOHNSON Having chidden her for undutifulness. GIBBON The emperor . . chided the tardiness of the senate. **3** R. W. EMERSON Be neither chided nor flattered out of your position.

chider *n.* LME. **chiding** *n.* (*a*) the action of the vb; (*b*) a reproof, a rebuke: OE. **chidingly** *adv.* in a chiding manner L16.

chidlings *n.pl.* var. of CHITLINGS.

chief /tʃiːf/ *n.* ME. [(O)Fr. *chef*, **†***chief*, f. Proto-Romance var. of L *caput* head.] **1** A leader, a ruler, a commander; a head of a tribe, clan, organization, etc.; the head of a department, the highest official. ME. **b** *Naut. The* Chief Engineer of a (war)ship. *colloq.* L19. **†2** The chief position; first place; pre-eminence. ME–E17. **†3** The head, the top, the upper end, (*of*). LME–L16. **4** *Her.* The top part of a shield, at most one third, often one fifth of the shield. LME. **†5** *The* best part *of*; *the* height *of*, *the* prime *of*. Cf. CHIEF *a.* II. E16–E17. **6** In full *chief-rent*. Orig., a rent paid under a tenure in chief (see below). Later, a quitrent. E16.

1 THACKERAY The chief of the kitchen. G. J. WHYTE-MELVILLE Our old chief . . has been appointed to a command in India. C. G. SELIGMAN The king was paramount lord over a confederation of provincial chiefs.

Phrases etc.: **big chief, big** or **great white chief** *joc.* [after Amer. Indian speech] a person in authority, an important person. **Chief of Staff** the senior staff officer of a service or of a commander. **in chief** (*a*) (holding tenure) directly from the lord paramount, the king (*Hist.*); (holding tenure) by perpetual ground rent or feu duty; (*b*) *arch.* most of all, especially. **-in-chief** (*a*) supreme, principal, head (freq. in titles, as *Colonel-*, *Commander-*, *Commodore-*, *Editor-in-Chief*); EXAMINATION-*in-chief*; (*b*) *Hist.* holding directly from the king (as *tenant-in-chief*). *paramount chief*: see PARAMOUNT *a.* 1.

chiefdom *n.* the estate, position, or dominion of a chief L16. **chief(e)ry** *n.* (*Ir. Hist.*) the office and territory of a chief; the dues belonging to the chief or to the lord superior: L16. **chiefess** *n.* a female chief L18. **chiefless** *a.* M18. **chiefly** *a.* of or pertaining to a chief L19. **chiefship** *n.* the office and function of a chief L17.

chief /tʃiːf/ *a.* & *adv.* ME. [f. the n.] **A** *adj.* **I** (Usu. *attrib.*) **1** Formally leading or most important. (Now only of people.) ME. **2** Most important; principal, foremost, greatest. LME. **3** Prominent, leading; belonging to the highest group or the first rank. (With superl. & **†**compar.) LME. **†4** Pre-eminent in excellence; best, finest, choice. E16–M17. **5** Intimate (as friends). *Sc.* M16.

1 R. GRAFTON Vienna, which is the chiefe Citie of the Countrie. M. LOWRY The chief cook regarded the . . second cook as a creature of completely inferior station. *Chief Justice, Chief Rabbi*, etc. *Chief Constable*: see CONSTABLE 4. *little chief hare*: see LITTLE *a.* *Lord Chief Justice*: see JUSTICE *n.* **2** N. HAWTHORNE A very dear friend . . who . . had been his chief intimate. J. BUCHAN His chief regret is that he is a miserable public speaker. W. S. CHURCHILL Madras . . was the chief trading centre. **chief good** = SUMMUM BONUM. **3** W. DAMPIER The Chinese are the chiefest merchants. LD MACAULAY A chief object of the expedition.

II *absol.* (with superl. & **†**compar.) Cf. CHIEF *n.* 5. **6** *pl.* The chief people. Long *arch.* M16. **7** The most or (*obs.*) more important. E17. **8** The main part, the bulk. L17.

7 J. CHAMBERLAYNE There are six penny-post offices: the chiefest is in Threadneedle Street. **8** W. DAMPIER About which they spend the chiefest of their time. F. MARRYAT At night, when the chief of the inhabitants were in bed.

B *adv.* Chiefly, principally. *arch.* LME.

chiefly *adv.* pre-eminently; especially; above all; principally, mainly but not exclusively: LME.

chieftain /ˈtʃiːft(ə)n, -tɪn/ *n.* ME. [OFr. *chevetaine* f. late L *capitaneus* (see CAPTAIN), assim. to CHIEF *n.*] **1** The head of a body of men, an organization, state, town, etc.; the ruler, the chief. *obs.* in *gen.* sense. ME. **2** A military leader; a captain. Now *arch.* & *poet.* ME. **3** The chief of a clan or tribe. L16. **4** The captain of a band of robbers. M17.

chieftaincy *n.* the rank or position of a chieftain E17. **chieftainess** *n.* a female chieftain LME. **chieftainry** *n.* the rank, rule, or territory, of a chieftain; chieftains collectively: M18. **chieftainship** *n.* = CHIEFTAINCY L18.

chield /tʃiːld/ *n. Sc.* Also **chiel** /tʃiːl/. LME. [Var. of CHILD *n.*] A man, a lad, a fellow.

chiffchaff /ˈtʃɪftʃaf/ *n.* L18. [Imit.] A common warbler, *Phylloscopus collybita*, with a highly characteristic repetitive song.

chiffon /ˈʃɪfɒn/ *n.* & *a.* M18. [Fr., f. *chiffe* rag.] **A** *n.* **1** In *pl.* Trimmings or other adornments of women's dress. *arch.* M18. **2** A light diaphanous plain-woven fabric of silk, nylon, etc. L19. **B** *attrib.* or as *adj.* Made of chiffon; light in weight. E20.

chiffon pie: with a light-textured filling flavoured with fruit etc.

chiffony *a.* E20.

chiffonier /ʃɪfəˈnɪə/ *n.* Also **†-n(n)ière.** M18. [Fr. *chiffonnier*, *-ière*, transf. use of CHIFFONNIER.] A movable low cupboard with a sideboard top.

chiffonnade /ʃɪfəˈnɑːd; *foreign* ʃifɔnad (*pl. same*)/ *n.* L19. [Fr.] A selection of shredded or finely cut vegetables, used esp. as a garnish for soup.

chiffonnier /ʃifɔnje/ *n.* Pl. pronounced same. M19. [Fr.] A collector of scraps, a rag-picker.

†chiffonnière *n.* var. of CHIFFONIER.

chifforobe /ˈʃɪfərəʊb/ *n. US.* E20. [f. CHIFFO(NIER + WARD)ROBE.] A piece of furniture with drawers in the lower part and hanging space in the upper part.

chigger *n.* var. of JIGGER *n.*[2]

chignon /ˈʃiːnjɒ̃/ *n.* L18. [Fr., orig. = nape of the neck, f. Proto-Romance var. of L *catena* CHAIN *n.*: see -OON.] A coil or mass of hair worn by women at the back of the head.

chigoe /ˈtʃɪgəʊ/ *n.* Also (earlier) **†chique.** M17. [(Fr. *chique*) f. a W. Afr. lang.] = JIGGER *n.*[2] 1.

chi-hike /ˈtʃʌɪ(h)ʌɪk/ *n.* & *v.* Also **chi-ike;** (*Austral.* & *NZ*) **chiack** /ˈtʃʌɪak/. M19. [Origin unkn.] **A** *n.* A salutation; a noisy disturbance; jeering, banter. M19. **B** *v.* **1** *v.t.* Salute; jeer at, make fun of. L19. **2** *v.i.* Make a noisy demonstration; jeer, tease. L19.

chihuahua /tʃɪˈwɑːwə/ *n.* Also **C-.** E19. [*Chihuaha*, a city and state in Mexico.] (An animal of) a breed of very small smooth-haired dog which originated in Mexico. Also *chihuahua dog*.

chi-ike *n.* & *v.* var. of CHI-HIKE.

chikan /ˈtʃɪk(ə)n/ *n.* Also **chicken.** L19. [Urdu *chikan* f. Pers. *čikin*.] A type of hand-embroidery in the Indian subcontinent.

chikara /tʃɪˈkɑːrə/ *n.* Also **chinkara** /tʃɪŋˈkɑːrə/. M19. [Hind. *cikārā* f. Skt *chikkāra*.] In the Indian subcontinent: the mountain gazelle, *Gazella gazella*.

chikhor *n.* var. of CHUKAR.

chikungunya /tʃɪk(ə)nˈgʌnjə/ *n.* M20. [Bantu (prob. Makonde).] *Med.* A mosquito-borne viral disease resembling dengue, endemic in E. Africa and parts of Asia.

chil- *comb. form* see CHEILO-.

chilblain /ˈtʃɪlbleɪn/ *n.* M16. [f. CHILL *n.* + BLAIN.] An itching swelling, esp. on the feet or hands, due to exposure to cold and poor blood circulation.

chilblained *a.* E17.

Chilcat *n.* & *a.* var. of CHILKAT.

child /tʃʌɪld/ *n.* Also (*arch.*, esp. in sense 3) **childe, chylde.** Pl. **children** /ˈtʃɪldr(ə)n/. See also CHIELD. [OE *ċild* rel. to Goth. *kilþei* womb, *inkilþo* pregnant, as it were 'fruit of the womb'. The ME pl. *childre*, *childer* became *childeren*, *children.*] **I 1** A foetus; an infant; *spec.* (*dial.*) a female infant. OE. **2** A boy or girl. OE. **b** In biblical translations: a youth approaching or entering on manhood. LME. **3** *sing.* A youth of gentle birth. Chiefly as a title. *arch.* OE. **4** *transf.* A person who has (or is considered to have) the character, manners, or attainments of a child, esp. a person of immature experience or judgement; a childish person. ME. **5** A pupil at school. ME. **b** *spec.* A chorister. E16. †**6** A lad in service; a page, an attendant, etc. LME–E17. **7** A man, a lad, a fellow. Cf. CHIELD. Long *arch. rare.* M16.

1 SHAKES. *Wint. T.* A very pretty barne. A boy or a child, I wonder? 3 BYRON Childe Harold. 4 J. CONRAD You are not fit for diplomatic work, you know, *ma chère*. You are a mere child at it. 7 L. G. GIBBON Chris waved to the old, kind childe as he bicycled down Blawearie brae.

II As correlative to parent. **8** A son or daughter (at any age) *of* (or w. *my* etc.); an offspring of human parents. (Used chiefly, & longer, of a daughter.) OE. **b** A young animal. *rare.* L16. **9** In *pl.* Descendants; members of the tribe or clan. ME. **10** A disciple *of* a teacher; a follower or adherent *of*. Usu. in *pl.* ME. **11** *fig.* A product, derivative, extract, dependant, attachment, etc., *of*. ME.

11 SHAKES. *Rom. & Jul.* Dreams Which are the children of an idle brain. J. R. GREEN Elizabeth . . was a child of the Italian Renascence.

Phrases: **children of Israel** = ISRAEL 1. **from a child** since childhood. *poor child*: see POOR *a.* *quick with child*: see QUICK *a.* 4a. *red children*: see RED *a.* SUNDAY(*'s*) *child*. **the child unborn**: a type of innocence, ignorance, etc. **this child** *slang* (orig. *US Blacks*) I, me. **with child** *arch.* (*a*) pregnant; †(*b*) *fig.* full *of*; eager, longing, *to do*.

Comb.: **child abuse** severe maltreatment of a child, esp. by beating or neglect or sexual assault; **child allowance** a sum of money paid out or allowed against tax for a dependent child; **child-bearing** giving birth to children; **child benefit** in the UK, a State monetary allowance for each child in a family (replacing family allowance); **childbirth** giving birth to a child (*natural childbirth*: see NATURAL *a.*); **child bride** a bride who is still a child, a very young bride; **childcare** the care or oversight of a child or children, esp. by a crèche or childminder in the temporary absence of a parent or guardian, or by a local authority when a normal home life is considered to be lacking; **child guidance** the supervision of the (esp. psychological) welfare of children and adolescents, the therapeutic treatment of maladjusted children and adolescents; **child labour** the (esp. inhumane or illegal) use of children in industry or business; **childminder** a person who takes care of a child or children, esp. in the temporary absence of a parent or guardian; *spec.* a person registered with the local authority to offer paid daytime care in his or her own home for children under the age of eight; **childminding** the oversight of a child or children in the temporary absence of a parent or guardian; *spec.* the work of a registered childminder; **child-molestation** sexual abuse of a child by an adult; **child-molester** a person guilty of child-molestation; *child* PORNOGRAPHY; **childproof** *a.* that cannot be operated, opened, damaged, etc., by a child; **child psychologist** a specialist in child psychology; **child psychology** the systematic study of the psychology of children; **children's hour** (chiefly *Hist.*) an hour of recreation spent together by parents and their children in the evening; **child-resistant** *a.* = *childproof* above; **child's play** (*a*) play befitting a child; (*b*) an easy task; **child-wife** a wife who is still a child, a very young wife; **child-woman** a person between childhood and womanhood; a woman who is still like a child.

childed *a.* provided with a child or children E17. **childless** *a.* ME. **childlessness** *n.* M19. **childlike** *a.* (*a*) belonging to or becoming a child; filial; (*b*) resembling (that of) a child; possessing the qualities of a child (usu. in a good sense, as opp. *childish*): L16. **childlikeness** *n.* childlike quality E19. **childly** *a.* (*a*) childish; †(*b*) filial: OE. **childness** *n.* (*rare*) †(*a*) childish humour, childishness; (*b*) being a child: E17. **childship** *n.* (now *rare*) the relationship of child to parent; filiation, adoption: M16.

†**child** *v.* ME. [f. the n.] **1** *v.t.* Give birth to (a child); bring forth. ME–E17. **2** *v.i.* Bear a child; be delivered of a child. ME–E19.

childbed /ˈtʃʌɪl(d)bɛd/ *n.* ME. [f. CHILD *n.* + BED *n.*] **1** The state of a woman in labour; giving birth to a child. ME. **2** The bed in which a child is born. L16.

childe *n.* see CHILD *n.*

Childermas /ˈtʃɪldəmas/ *n.* *arch.* [OE *ċildramæsse*, f. *ċildra* genit. pl. of *ċild* CHILD *n.* + *mæsse* MASS *n.*[1]] **1** The festival of the Holy Innocents, 28 December, commemorating Herod's slaughter of the children (*Matt.* 2:16). OE. **2** The day of the week throughout the year corresponding to the day on which the festival last occurred. Now *dial.* E17.

childhood /ˈtʃʌɪldhʊd/ *n.* [OE *ċildhād*: see CHILD *n.*, -HOOD.] **1** The state or stage of life of a child; the time during which one is a child; the time from birth to puberty. OE. †**2** Childishness; a childish action. Only in ME. †**3** The relationship of child to parent. Only in E17.

1 *fig.* SHAKES. *Rom. & Jul.* Now I have stain'd the childhood of our joy. **second childhood** the state of childishness incident to old age; dotage.

childish /ˈtʃʌɪldɪʃ/ *a.* [OE *ċildisċ*: see CHILD *n.*, -ISH[1].] **1** Of, belonging, or proper to a child or childhood; childlike. OE. **2** Not befitting mature age; puerile, silly. LME.

childishly *adv.* LME. **childishness** *n.* E16.

children *n.* pl. of CHILD *n.*

Chile /ˈtʃɪli/ *n.*[1] Also (*arch.*) **Chili**. E19. [A S. American republic.] Used *attrib.* to designate things found in or associated with Chile.

Chile hazel: see HAZEL *n.*[1] **Chile nitre** natural sodium nitrate. **Chile pine** the monkey-puzzle tree, *Araucaria araucana*. **Chile saltpetre** = *Chile nitre* above.

chile *n.*[2] var. of CHILLI.

Chilean /ˈtʃɪlɪən/ *a.* & *n.* Also (*arch.*) **Chilian**. E18. [f. CHILE *n.*[1] + -AN.] **A** *adj.* Of or pertaining to Chile or its inhabitants. E18.

Chilean JASMINE.

B *n.* A native or inhabitant of Chile. E19.

chili *n.*[1] var. of CHILLI.

Chili *n.*[2] see CHILE *n.*[1]

chiliad /ˈkɪlɪad/ *n.* LME. [Late L *chilias*, *-ad-* f. Gk *khilias*, *-ad-*, f. *khilioi* one thousand: see -AD[1].] **1** A period of one thousand years. LME. **b** *spec.* The millennium. *rare.* E18. **2** A group of one thousand (things); a thousand. L16.

chiliagon /ˈkɪlɪag(ə)n/ *n.* L17. [f. Gk *khiliagōnos*, f. *khilioi* one thousand + *gōnia* angle.] A plane figure with a thousand straight sides and a thousand angles.

chiliahedron /kɪlɪəˈhiːdr(ə)n, -ˈhɛd-/ *n.* *rare.* Pl. **-dra** /-drə/, **-drons**. L17. [f. Gk *khilioi* one thousand + -HEDRON.] A solid figure or object with a thousand plane faces.

Chilian *a.* & *n.* see CHILEAN.

chiliarch /ˈkɪlɪɑːk/ *n.* L16. [Late L *chiliarches*, *-us* f. Gk *khiliarkhēs*, *-os*, f. *khilioi* one thousand: see -ARCH.] A commander of a thousand men.

chiliarchy *n.* †(*a*) a body of a thousand men; (*b*) the post of chiliarch: M17.

chiliasm /ˈkɪlɪaz(ə)m/ *n.* E17. [Gk *khiliasmos*, f. *khilias* CHILIAD.] The doctrine of the millennium; the belief that Christ will reign in bodily presence on earth for a thousand years.

chiliast /ˈkɪlɪast/ *n.* L16. [Late L *chiliastes* f. Gk *khiliastēs*, f. *khilias* CHILIAD.] An adherent of chiliasm; a millenarian.

chili'astic *a.* of, pertaining to, or holding the doctrine of the millennium L17.

Chilkat /ˈtʃɪlkat/ *n.* & *a.* Also **Chilcat**. M19. [Tlingit *jilḵáat*.] **A** *n.* Pl. **-s**, same. A member of a subdivision of the Tlingit Indians in Alaska. M19. **B** *adj.* Of or pertaining to this people. M19.

chill /tʃɪl/ *n.* [OE *ċele*, *ċiele*, of Gmc origin. Rel. to COLD *a.*. In branch II also f. the vb or adj.] †**I 1** *gen.* Absence of heat, cold, coldness. OE–LME.

II 2 A lowered bodily temperature, marked by shivering; feverish shivering; a sudden sensation of physical cold, which is often a first stage or symptom of illness; a feverish cold. ME. **3** A coldness of the air, water, etc., which may induce shivering; cold which has a depressing, benumbing, or penetrating effect on the body. L18. **4** *fig.* **a** A depressing influence. E19. **b** Absence of warmth of feeling or sympathy; coldness of manner. M19. **5** A metal mould, or piece of metal in a sand mould, used to cool quickly, and often to harden, the surface of molten metal brought into contact with it. L19. **6** A cloud or bloom on a surface, esp. caused by condensation. L19.

2 E. ROOSEVELT He began to complain that he felt a chill. P. F. BOLLER He contracted a chill that quickly became pneumonia. 3 G. MAXWELL She had recoiled at first from the biting chill of the water. **take the chill off** warm slightly. 4a J. MORLEY The . . prosaic results . . have thrown a chill over our political imaginations. b H. MARTINEAU To dissipate the chill by showing that we were ready to . . be sociable. 6 P. V. WHITE Basil returned with a green bottle. It was wearing a chill.

Comb.: **chill factor** *Meteorol.* the apparent lowering of the air temperature by wind.

chill /tʃɪl/ *a.* Now *literary*. LME. [Prob. f. the n.] **1** Cold to touch or feel; now usu. unpleasantly or injuriously cold; that chills or causes shivering. LME. **2** *fig.* That tends to repress warmth of feeling or enthusiasm; repressed in feeling, unemotional, austere. LME. **3** Depressingly affected by cold; having a pervading sensation of cold; sensitive or liable to cold. L16.

1 ARNOLD BENNETT The atmosphere outside the stove was chill. W. BOYD He adored the chill green drink, clear and clinking with ice-cubes. 2 T. GRAY Chill Penury repress'd their noble rage. T. HARDY A chill self-reproach. 3 M. SHELLEY They had a fire to warm them when chill.

chillness *n.* L16.

chill /tʃɪl/ *v.* LME. [Prob. f. the n.] **I 1** *v.i.* Become cold. LME. **b** Be seized with a sudden chill. M19. **c** Foll. by *out*: calm down, relax. *slang* (chiefly *US*). L20. †**2** *v.i.* Shiver with cold. LME–L16. **3** *v.t.* Make cold; affect injuriously with cold. LME. **b** Deaden or destroy with cold. E18. **4** *v.t. fig.* Affect as with cold; depress; deject, dispirit. LME. **5** *v.t.* Cool and harden (molten metal) by contact with cold metal, or by casting in a metal mould. M19. **6** *v.t.* Give a cloud or bloom to (a surface) by cold, condensation, etc. M19. **7** *v.t.* Subject (food, esp. meat, etc.) to a low but not freezing temperature, esp. to preserve it. L19.

1 DEFOE My very blood chills at the mention of the name of Newgate. 3 DRYDEN Ev'ry Lady's Blood with Fear was chill'd. 4 H. KELLER Even now the thought of those dreadful days chills my heart. *spine-chilling*. 7 B. SPOCK You boil your milk . . cool it, then chill it in the refrigerator.

II 8 *v.t.* & *i.* Warm slightly; raise or rise to temperate heat. *dial.* E19.

8 DICKENS A pint pot, the contents of which were 'chilling' on the hob.

chiller *n.* a person who or thing which chills (*spine-chiller*: see SPINE *n.*) L18. **chillingly** *adv.* in a chilling manner L16.

chilli /ˈtʃɪli/ *n.* Also **chile**, ***chili**. Pl. **chil(l)ies**, **chiles**. E17. [Sp. *chile* f. Nahuatl *chilli*.] The (dried) red pod of the pepper *Capsicum annuum* var. *longum*, used in sauces, relishes, etc., and made into a hot cayenne; cayenne made from these dried pods. Also *chilli pepper*.

chilli con carne /kɒn ˈkɑːni/ [Sp. = with meat] a Mexican dish of minced beef, beans, and chilli. **chilli relleno** /rɛˈljeɪnəʊ/ [Sp. = stuffed] a stuffed green pepper.

Comb.: *chilli pepper*: see above; **chilli powder** hot cayenne made from chillies.

chillsome /ˈtʃɪls(ə)m/ *a.* E20. [f. CHILL *n.* or *v.* + -SOME[1].] Chilling, chilly.

chillum /ˈtʃɪləm/ *n.* L18. [Hind. *chilam*.] The part of a hookah containing the tobacco etc.; *loosely* a hookah, the act of smoking, the charge of tobacco.

chillumchee /ˈtʃɪləmtʃiː/ *n.* E18. [Urdu *chilamchī*.] In the Indian subcontinent: a wash-basin of brass or tinned copper.

chilly /ˈtʃɪli/ *a.* L16. [f. CHILL *n.* + -Y[1].] **1** That chills; disagreeably cold to touch or feel. L16. **2** Affected by a chill; (feeling) rather cold; sensitive to cold. E17. **3** *fig.* Not genial; cold-mannered. M19.

chillily *adv.* M19. **chilliness** *n.* E18.

chilo- *comb. form* var. of CHEILO-.

chilopod /ˈkʌɪləpɒd/ *n.* & *a.* M19. [f. mod.L *Chilopoda* pl. (see below): see CHEILO-, -POD.] *Zool.* **A** *n.* A myriapod of the class Chilopoda, a centipede. M19. **B** *adj.* Of, pertaining to, or characteristic of Chilopoda. L19.

Chiltern Hundreds /ˌtʃɪlt(ə)n ˈhʌndrədz/ *n. phr. pl.* ME. [f. *Chiltern* Hills in S. England + HUNDRED + -S[1].] A crown manor, the administration of which is a nominal office under the Crown and so requires an MP to vacate his or her seat.

apply for the Chiltern Hundreds resign from the House of Commons.

chilver /ˈtʃɪlvə/ *n.* Now *dial.* [OE *ċilfer-*, *ċilforlomb*, corresp. to OHG *kilbur(ra)*, *-irra*: rel. to CALF *n.*[1]] In full *chilver-lamb*. A ewe-lamb.

chimaera *n.* var. of CHIMERA.

chimaeroid /kʌɪˈmɪərɔɪd, kɪ-/ *n.* & *a.* M19. [f. prec. + -OID.] (Relating to or characteristic of) a deep-sea fish of the subclass Holocephali (CHIMERA 4).

chimb *n.* var. of CHIME *n.*[2]

chime /tʃʌɪm/ *n.*[1] ME. [Prob. f. OE *ċimbal* CYMBAL, by analysis as *chime bell*.] †**1** A cymbal. Only in ME. **2** An apparatus for striking a set of bells so as to make them chime; *spec.* (usu. in *pl.*) such an apparatus used as a doorbell. LME. **3** A set of bells, or of metal bars or tubes, so attuned as to chime when struck or slightly swung. LME. **4** The series of musical sounds or tune played on such sets of bells; a chiming sound. M16. **5** The rhythm or ring of verse; *derog.* jingle. M17. **6** *fig.* A system of which all the parts are in harmony. M17. **7** *fig.* Harmony, accord, agreement. M19.

3 *musical chime*: see MUSICAL *a.* 4 J. BETJEMAN The girl of my choice, with the tilt of her nose and the chime of her voice. 6 MILTON Disproportion'd sin Jarr'd against natures chime, and with harsh din Broke the fair Musick. 7 H. MAUDSLEY Others have found no such happy chime of fact and theory.

Comb.: **chime bars** a type of glockenspiel used esp. in schools.

chime /tʃʌɪm/ *n.*[2] Also **chimb**. See also CHINE *n.*[3] LME. [Prob. identical with the n. occurring in OE *ċimstān* base, pedestal, *ċimīren* clamp-iron, *ċimbing* joint, corresp. to MDu. *kimme* (Du. *kim*) edge of a cask, MLG *kimme*, *kimm* (G *Kimme*).] The rim at the ends of a cask, formed by the ends of the staves.

chime /tʃʌɪm/ *v.*[1] ME. [Origin uncertain: the relation to CHIME *n.*[1] is obscure.] **1** *v.i.* Resound when struck; ring out; tinkle; (of a set of bells) make a series of musical sounds. ME. **2** *v.i.* Produce a musical sound from a bell by striking it; make a series of musical sounds with a set of bells. LME. **3** *v.i.* & *t.* Recite or repeat in cadence or mechanically. LME. **4** *v.t.* **a** Of a set of bells etc.: indicate (the hour) by chiming. M16. **b** Give out (a musical sound) when struck. *arch.* E17. **5** *v.t.* Bring or put (into or out of a state or place) by chiming. L16. **6** *v.t.* Make a series of musical sounds on (a set of bells); strike (a bell etc.) so that a musical sound is given out. L16. **7** *v.i.* & *t.* Jingle; rhyme (words). M17. **8** *v.i. fig.* Harmonize, agree, (*together*, *with*). L17.

1 E. WAUGH The bells of St. Bride's chimed unheard. L. DEIGHTON A clock chimed loudly. I. MCEWAN Ice chimed in glasses. 3 BYRON Let simple Wordsworth chime his childish verse. 4a G. SWIFT The mantelpiece clock chimed one in the morning. 5 SOUTHEY His enemies had the indecency to chime him out of the church. 8 W. S. CHURCHILL Her endeavours chimed with the Imperial spirit of the age.

With advs. in specialized senses: **chime in** (*a*) *v.phr.i.* join in harmoniously or in unison; (*b*) *v.phr.i.* & *t.* interject (as) a remark in agreement; (*c*) *v.phr.i.* be in complete (but usu. subordinate) accord *with*.

chime /tʃʌɪm/ *v.*[2]*t.* M19. [f. CHIME *n.*[2]] Groove or chamfer staves for the chime of (a cask).

chimer /ˈtʃʌɪmə/ *n.*[1] E17. [f. CHIME *v.*[1] + -ER[1].] A person who chimes bells etc.

chimer *n.*[2] var. of CHIMERE.

chimera /kʌɪˈmɪərə, kɪ-/ *n.* Also **chimaera**. LME. [L *chimaera* f. Gk *khimaira* she-goat, monster, f. *khimaros* he-goat.] **1** *Gk Mythol.* A fire-breathing monster, with a lion's head, a goat's body, and a serpent's tail. LME. **2** A grotesque monster represented in painting etc. LME. **3a** A bogey, a horrible phantasm. E16. **b** A wild or fanciful conception. L16. **c** A thing of hybrid character. M19. **4** (Usu. **chimaera**.) Any cartilaginous fish of the family Chimaeridae (order Holocephali), typically having erect pointed fins and a long tail. Also called *rabbit-fish*, *rat-fish*. E19. **5** *Biol.* An organism whose cells are not all derived from the same zygote. E20.

chimeric, **-ical** /-ˈmɛr-/ *adjs.* of the nature of a chimera; imaginary, fanciful, visionary; prone to entertain chimeras: M17. **chimerism** *n.* (*Biol.*) the state of being a chimera (sense 5); the occurrence of chimeras: M20.

chimere /tʃɪˈmɪə/ *n.* Also **chimer** /ˈtʃɪmə/. LME. [Obscurely rel. to Sp. *zamarra* sheepskin cloak, It. *zimarra*, *cimarra* long robe (whence Fr. *simarre*, †*chimarre* loose gown): cf. SIMAR.] A loose outer robe, *esp.* that worn by a bishop and having lawn sleeves attached.

chiminage /ˈtʃɪmɪnɪdʒ/ *n.* L16. [OFr. *cheminage* f. *chemin* road: see -AGE. In AL *cheminagium*, *chim-*.] *Feudal Law.* A toll for liberty of passage through a forest.

chimney /ˈtʃɪmni/ *n.* & *v.* ME. [(O)Fr. *cheminée* chimney, fireplace, f. late L *caminata*, perh. orig. for *camera caminata* room with a fireplace, f. L *caminus* forge, furnace, f. Gk *kaminos* oven, furnace.] **A** *n.* **1** A fireplace, a hearth. *obs.* exc. *dial.* ME. †**2** A furnace. ME–E17. †**3** A (portable) stove. LME–E17. **4** A channel or flue by which smoke from a fire, furnace, engine, etc. ascends; the part of this above a roof etc. LME. **5** *transf.* A natural opening in the earth's surface, *esp.* that of a volcano. LME. **6** More fully *lamp-chimney*. A glass tube over the wick of a lamp protecting and providing a draught for the flame. M19. **7** *Mining.* An ore-shoot. M19. **8** *Mountaineering.* A steep and narrow cleft by which a cliff or mountain face may be climbed. L19.

4 ARNOLD BENNETT To the east rose pitheads, chimneys, and kilns. P. V. WHITE The slow fire, upon which a dusty yellow light descended through the shaft that served them as a chimney. **smoke like a chimney** smoke cigarettes etc. very heavily.

Comb.: **chimney-bar** an iron bar supporting the masonry above a fireplace; **chimney-board** a board used to close up a fireplace in summer; *chimney-breast*: see BREAST *n.* 8; **chimney-corner** a warm seat within an old-fashioned fireplace; **chimney-money** *Hist.* a tax on fire-hearths, *spec.* that in England and Wales in the 17th cent.; **chimney-nook** = *chimney-corner* above; **chimney-piece** †(*a*) a picture, piece of sculpture, etc., over a fireplace; (*b*) a mantelpiece; **chimney-pot** (*a*) an earthenware or metal pipe, added to a chimney-top; (*b*) *arch.* (more fully *chimney-pot hat*) a tall silk hat; **chimney-stack** a number of chimneys standing together; a tall factory chimney; **chimney swallow** the common swallow, *Hirundo rustica*; (*N. Amer.*) = *chimney swift* below; **chimney-sweep**, **-sweeper** a person whose business is to remove soot from chimneys; **chimney swift** *N. Amer.* a swift, *Chaetura pelagica*, often nesting in chimneys; **chimney-top** the part of a chimney which rises above the roof, *esp.* the flat upper surface of this.

B *v.* **1** *v.t.* Provide with a chimney. E19. **2** *v.i. Mountaineering.* Climb *up* a chimney. M20.

chimneyless *a.* having no chimney(s) M17.

chimonanthus /kʌɪməˈnanθəs/ *n.* E19. [mod.L, f. Gk *kheimōn* winter + *anthos* flower.] A shrub of the genus *Chimonanthus*, native to China; *esp.* winter-sweet, *C. praecox*.

chimp /tʃɪmp/ *n. colloq.* L19. [Abbrev.] A chimpanzee.

chimpanzee /tʃɪmpanˈziː/ *n.* M18. [Fr. *chimpanzé* f. Kikongo.] A Central and W. African anthropoid ape of the genus *Pan*, of which there are two species, *P. troglodytes*, which resembles man more closely than does any other ape, and the pygmy chimpanzee, *P. paniscus*.

pygmy chimpanzee: see PYGMY *a.*

chin /tʃɪn/ *n.*[1] [OE *ċin(n)* = OFris. *kin*, OS *kinni* (Du. *kin*), ON *kinn* chin, lower jaw, Goth. *kinnus* cheek, f. Gmc: cogn. w. L *gena* cheek, Gk *genus* jaw.] **1** The front of the lower jaw. OE. **2** A talk, a conversation. Also redupl. *chin-chin*. *slang* (chiefly *US*). L19.

1 *double chin*: see DOUBLE *a.* & *adv.* **keep one's chin up** remain cheerful. *lead with one's chin*: see LEAD *v.*[1] *stick one's chin out*: see STICK *v.*[1] **take it on the chin** *fig.* (*a*) suffer a severe blow; (*b*) meet misfortune courageously. **up to the chin** reaching to the chin; deeply immersed *in*.

Comb.: **chin music** (chiefly *US*) talk, chatter; **chin-strap** a strap for fastening a hat etc. under the chin; *chins wag*: see WAG *v.* **chin-wag** *n.* & *v.* (*colloq.*) (*a*) *n.* chat, talk; a conversation; (*b*) *v.i.* talk, chat.

chinless *a.* (*a*) without a chin; (*b*) *fig.* lacking firmness of character (esp. in *chinless wonder*): E19. **chinned** *a.* having a chin, esp. of a specified kind L16. **chinny** *a.* marked by a conspicuous chin L19.

Chin /tʃɪn/ *n.*[2] Pl. **-s**, same. L19. [Burm. = hill-man.] A member of a people inhabiting the Chin hills and adjacent districts in Myanmar (Burma); the language of this people.

chin *n.*[3] var. of TCHIN.

Chin *n.*[4] & *a.* var. of QIN.

chin /tʃɪn/ *v.* Infl. **-nn-**. L16. [f. CHIN *n.*[1]] **I** †**1** *v.i.* Press chin to chin. Only in L16. **2** *v.t.* Bring (a fiddle etc.) up or *up* to the chin. M19. **3** *v.t.* Draw one's body up so as to bring the chin up to or above (a horizontal bar etc.) with one's feet off the ground; *refl.* raise oneself thus. E20.

3 H. ALLEN You take exercise by chinning yourself on the window bars. A. S. NEILL To ask a boy .. to chin a bar four times.

II 4 *v.i.* & *t.* Talk, chat, (to). *US slang.* L19.

China /ˈtʃʌɪnə/ *n.*[1] L16. [A country in Asia: origin of the name unkn. (not native Chinese).] **I 1** Used *attrib.* to designate things found in, obtained from, or associated with China. L16.

1 *China aster*: see ASTER *n.* 2b. **China-berry** *N. Amer.* (the fruit of) a China tree. *China crêpe*: see CRÊPE *n.* & *a.* **China-grass** ramie, *Boehmeria nivea*. **China ink** Indian ink. **China orange** the common orange, orig. from China. **China-root** (the fleshy root of) a Far Eastern shrub, *Smilax china*; also, any of certain other plants or their roots. **China rose** (*a*) the monthly rose, *Rosa chinensis*, native to China; (*b*) an ornamental shrubby hibiscus, *H. rosa-sinensis*. **China silk** a light plain-woven silk fabric. **China syndrome** the imagined movement of a nuclear reactor deep into the earth after a melt-down. **China tea** a smoke-cured tea from a small-leaved tea plant grown in China. **Chinatown** a section of a town, esp. a seaport, where Chinese live as a colony. **China tree** *N. Amer.* the azedarac; also, a wild soapberry, *Sapindus marginatus*, of the southern US. **Chinawoman** (now *arch.* or *derog.*) a female Chinese.

II 2 *ellipt.* **a** = *China-root* above. L16. **b** = *China rose* (a) above M19. **c** = *China tea* above. E20. †**3** A Chinese. E–M17.

III See next.

china /ˈtʃʌɪnə/ *a.* & *n.*[2] Also **C-**. L16. [Pers. *čīnī* f. as prec. (from attrib. uses of which early uses of the adj. are indistinguishable).] **1** (Of) a fine semi-transparent or white ceramic material; porcelain. L16. **2** Items made of this. M17. **3** In full *china plate*. A mate, a friend. *rhyming slang.* L19.

1 R. BRAUTIGAN We treat them all as if they were china. *Meissen china*, *Pinxton china*, *Plymouth china*, *Sèvres china*, etc. 3 B. BEHAN Two chinas from the same district or town.

Comb. & *special collocations*: **china-blue** (of) a greyish blue; **china clay** kaolin; **china-closet** a cabinet for keeping or displaying china; **china-mark (moth)** any of various delicately-patterned pyralid moths whose larvae feed on water plants; †**china-metal** porcelain (so called when its composition was unknown); *china plate*: see sense 3 above; **china shop**: selling china (*bull in a china shop*: see BULL *n.*[1]); **chinaware** = sense 2 above.

chinagraph *n.* a type of pencil for writing on glass, china, etc. (also *chinagraph pencil*) M20.

Chinaman /ˈtʃʌɪnəmən/ *n.* Pl. **-men**. M18. [f. CHINA *n.*[2] (branch I) or CHINA *n.*[1] (branch II) + MAN *n.*] **I 1** A dealer in porcelain. Now *rare* or *obs.* M18. **II 2** A Chinese man. Now *arch.* or *derog.* M19. **3** *Cricket.* A left-handed bowler's off-break or googly to a right-handed batsman. M20.

Phrases: **Chinaman's chance** *US colloq.* a very slight chance (usu. in neg. contexts).

chinar *n.* var. of CHENAR.

chincapin /ˈtʃɪŋkəpɪn/ *n.* Also **chinquapin** & other vars. E17. [f. Virginia Algonquian.] Any of various small N. American trees or their edible nuts; *esp.* the dwarf chestnut, *Castanea pumila.*

water chincapin the American lotus, *Nelumbo lutea.*

chinch /tʃɪn(t)ʃ/ *n.*[1] Also **chintz** /-ts/ & other vars. E17. [Sp. *chinche* f. L *cimex*, *cimic-*.] More fully *chinch-bug*. **1** A bed-bug. Now only *N. Amer.* E17. **2** A N. American bug, *Blissus leucopterus*, very destructive to cereals and other grasses. M18.

†chinch *a.* & *n.*[2] ME. [(O)Fr. *chi(n)che*.] **A** *adj.* Niggardly, miserly. Only in ME. **B** *n.* A niggard, a miser; a wretch. ME–L16.

¶Survives in CHINCHY.

chinch *v.* see CHINK *v.*[2]

chincherinchee /tʃɪntʃərɪn'tʃiː/ *n.* Also **chink-** /tʃɪŋk-/; **†tintirinties** (earlier). E20. [Imit. of the squeaky sound made by rubbing stalks together.] A white-flowered bulbous plant, *Ornithogalum thyrsoides*, native to southern Africa.

chinchilla /tʃɪn'tʃɪlə/ *n.* E17. [Sp., prob. f. Aymara or Quechua.] **I 1** A S. American rodent of the genus *Chinchilla*, with very soft grey fur. E17. **2** A cat of a silver-grey breed. L19. **3** A rabbit of a variety bred for its grey fur. Also *chinchilla rabbit*. E20. **II 4** The fur of the S. American chinchilla or of the chinchilla rabbit. E19.

chin-chin *n.* see CHIN *n.*[1] 2.

chin-chin /tʃɪn'tʃɪn/ *int.* & *v.* Now *colloq.* L18. [Chin. *qing qing* (Wade-Giles *ch'ing ch'ing*).] **A** *int.* Used as a greeting, as a farewell, and as a toast. L18. **B** *v.* Infl. **-nn-**. **1** *v.t.* Greet. L18. **2** *v.i.* Say 'chin-chin'. M19.

chinchona *n.* var. of CINCHONA.

chinchy /'tʃɪntʃi/ *a.* Now chiefly *US colloq.* LME. [f. CHINCH *n.*[2] + -Y[1].] Niggardly, miserly.

¶Not recorded between M17 and E20.

chincough *n.* see KINKCOUGH.

Chindit /'tʃɪndɪt/ *n.* M20. [Burm. *chinthé*, a mythological creature.] An Allied fighter behind the Japanese lines in Burma (Myanmar) (1943–5).

chine /tʃʌɪn/ *n.*[1] [OE *ċinu* = MDu. *kēne* (Du. *keen*) f. Gmc base of CHINE *v.*[1] Cf. CHAWN, CHINK *n.*[2]] **†1** *gen.* A fissure, a crack. OE–L16. **2** A fissure in the earth. Now only *spec.* a deep ravine in the Isle of Wight and in Dorset (chiefly in proper names). OE.

chine /tʃʌɪn/ *n.*[2] ME. [Aphet. f. OFr. *eschine* (mod. *échine*) f. Proto-Romance blend of Gmc source of SHIN *n.* and L *spina* SPINE *n.*] **1** The spine, the backbone. ME. **†2** The back. ME–L18. **3** A joint of meat containing (part of) an animal's backbone. ME. **4** *transf.* A ridge, an arête. M19.

Phrases: mourning of the chine: see MOURNING *n.*[2]

chine /tʃʌɪn/ *n.*[3] LME. [Alt. of CHIME *n.*[2]] **1** = CHIME *n.*[2] LME. **2** *Shipbuilding.* **a** That part of the waterways projecting above the deck-plank. M19. **b** The angle where the bottom lines of a ship's planking or plating meet the sides. E20.

chine /tʃʌɪn/ *v.*[1] Long *obs.* exc. *dial.* [OE *ċīnan* = OS, OHG *kīnan*, Goth. *keinan* sprout, f. Gmc: cf. CHINE *n.*[1]] **1** *v.i.* Split open, crack; sprout. OE. **†2** *v.t.* Burst, split. LME–E16.

chine /tʃʌɪn/ *v.*[2]*t.* LME. [f. CHINE *n.*[2]: cf. Fr. *échiner* break the back of.] **1** Cut along or through the backbone of (a carcass). LME. **2** Break the back of. Now *rare* or *obs.* L16.

chiné /ʃiː'neɪ/ *n.* & *a.* M19. [Fr., pa. pple of *chiner*, f. *Chine* China.] (A fabric) given a mottled pattern of (supposedly) Chinese style by colouring the warp or weft threads, or both, before weaving.

Chinee /tʃʌɪ'niː/ *n. slang* (now *arch.* or *derog.*). L19. [f. CHINESE *n.* taken as a pl.] A Chinese.

Chinese /tʃʌɪ'niːz/ *a.* & *n.* L16. [f. *China* (see CHINA *n.*[1]) + -ESE.] **A** *adj.* Of or pertaining to China. L16.

Chinese anise: see ANISE 2. *Chinese artichoke*: see ARTICHOKE 3. **Chinese block** an oblong slatted wooden block used esp. by jazz drummers. **Chinese box** each of a nest of boxes. **Chinese cabbage** an oriental brassica; spec. *B. chinensis*, with smooth-edged tapering leaves, or *B. pekinensis*, which resembles lettuce. *Chinese* CHIPPENDALE. **Chinese compliment** a pretended deference to the opinions of others, when one's mind is already made up. **Chinese copy** a slavish imitation. **Chinese gooseberry** = KIWI 4. *Chinese jute*: see JUTE *n.*[2] **Chinese lantern** (*a*) a collapsible lantern of thin coloured paper; (*b*) = ALKEKENGI. **Chinese laundry** a laundry operated by Chinese. **Chinese layering** = *air-layering* s.v. AIR *n.*[1] **Chinese leaf** = PE-TSAI; in *pl.*, the leaves of this vegetable, used in salads. *Chinese olive*: see OLIVE *n.*[1] 1b. **Chinese puzzle** an intricate puzzle or problem. **Chinese restaurant**: operated by Chinese, serving Chinese food. *Chinese tallow-tree*: see TALLOW *n.* **Chinese wall** *fig.* an insurmountable barrier. *Chinese water chestnut*: see WATER *n.* **Chinese whispers** a game in which a message is distorted by being passed around in a whisper (also called *Russian scandal*). **Chinese white** zinc oxide as a white pigment.

B *n.* Pl. same, **†-eses**. **1** A native of China; a person of Chinese descent. E17. **2** The Chinese language, a member of the Sino-Tibetan group, a tonal language with no inflections, declensions, or conjugations and having many dialects. E18.

1 *overseas Chinese*: see OVERSEAS *a.*

¶See also *Red Chinese* s.v. RED *a.*, TIBETO-CHINESE.

chinesery *n.* = CHINOISERIE L19.

Ching *n.* & *a.* var. of QING.

chink /tʃɪŋk/ *n.*[1] M16. [Obscurely rel. to CHINE *n.*[1] Cf. CHINK *v.*[1]] **1** *gen.* A fissure, a crack. M16. **2** A long narrow opening, a slit, a peep-hole; a place not fully closed and admitting the light etc. M16.

chinky *a.* characterized by or full of chinks M17.

chink /tʃɪŋk/ *n.*[2] L16. [Imit.: cf. CHINK *v.*[1]] **1** A short sharp ringing sound as of glasses or coins striking together. L16. **2a** Ready cash. *arch. colloq.* L16. **†b** In *pl.* Coins. L16–E17.

Chink /tʃɪŋk/ *n.*[3] *slang. derog.* L19. [Irreg. f. *China* (see CHINA *n.*[1]): cf. CHINKY.] A Chinese.

iron Chink: see IRON *n.* & *a.*

chink *n.*[4] see KINK *n.*[1]

chink /tʃɪŋk/ *v.*[1] LME. [Imit.: cf. CHINK *n.*[2] and Du. *kinken*.] **1** *v.i.* Emit a short, sharp ringing sound, as of coins, glasses, etc. striking together. LME. **2** *v.t.* Cause to make this sound. E17.

1 A. CARTER Spoon chinked upon soup-plate. 2 POPE He chinks his purse.

chinkle *v.i.* & *t.* chink continuously or lightly M18.

chink /tʃɪŋk/ *v.*[2]*i.* & *t.* Also (*dial.*) **chinch** /tʃɪntʃ/; (esp. *Naut.*) **chinse** /tʃɪns/. E16. [Obscurely rel. to CHINE *v.*[1]: cf. CHINK *n.*[1]] **1a** *Naut.* (Chiefly *chinse*.) Caulk (a ship, its seams), now *spec.* as a temporary measure. Also foll. by *up*. E16. **b** Fill up (cracks, esp. between bricks, tiles, the logs of a log cabin, etc.); fill up the cracks of (a building). Also foll. by *up*. Chiefly *N. Amer.* M18. **†2** (*chink* only.) Open in cracks; crack, chap. M16–L17.

chink /tʃɪŋk/ *v.*[3]*t. dial.* E19. [Origin unkn.: cf. KINK *n.*[2], *v.*[2]] Give a twist to; sprain.

chink *v.*[4] see KINK *v.*[1]

chinkara *n.* var. of CHIKARA.

chinkerinchee *n.* var. of CHINCHERINCHEE.

Chinky /'tʃɪŋki/ *n. slang.* Also **-key**, **-kie**. L19. [f. as CHINK *n.*[3] + -Y[6], -IE.] A Chinese (*derog.*); a Chinese restaurant.

chino /'tʃiːnəʊ/ *n.* & *a. US.* M20. [Amer. Sp. = toasted.] **A** *n.* Pl. **-os**. A cotton twill cloth, usu. khaki-coloured; in *pl.*, trousers made of this. M20. **B** *adj.* Of this cloth. M20.

Chino- /'tʃʌɪnəʊ/ *comb. form.* [f. *China* (see CHINA *n.*[1]) + -O-.] Chinese and, SINO-, as *Chino-Japanese* etc.

chinoiserie /ʃɪn'wɑːzəri/; *foreign* ʃinwazri (*pl. same*)/ *n.* L19. [Fr., f. *chinois* Chinese + *-erie* -ERY.] A Chinese or imitation Chinese artistic object, piece of furniture, etc.; the imitation of Chinese motifs in furniture etc.

†chinoline *n.* var. of QUINOLINE.

Chinook /tʃɪ'nʊk/ *n. N. Amer.* Also (exc. sense 1) **c-**. Pl. **-s**, same. E19. [Salish *tsinúk*.] **1** *Hist.* A member of a N. American Indian people formerly living along the Columbia river; the language of this people. E19. **2** In full *Chinook Jargon*. A pidgin composed of elements from Chinook, Nootka, English, French, and elsewhere, used in the Pacific north-west of N. America. M19. **3** In full *Chinook salmon*. A salmon, *Oncorhynchus tshawytscha*, of the N. American Pacific coast. M19. **4** In full *Chinook wind*. A warm dry wind which blows east of the Rocky Mountains. Also, a warm wet southerly wind west of them. M19.

chinovnik /tʃɪ'nɒvnɪk/ *n.* Also **tch-**. L19. [Russ.] In Russia: a government official, *esp.* a minor functionary; a (mere) bureaucrat.

chinquapin *n.* var. of CHINCAPIN.

chinse *v.* see CHINK *v.*[2]

chintz /tʃɪnts/ *n.*[1] & *a.* E17. [Hind. *chĩṭ* a spattering, stain. Mod. form a fanciful spelling of original pl.] **A** *n.* Pl. **chintzes**. Orig. **†chint**, pl. **chints**. Orig., a painted or stained calico from India. Now, a cotton cloth with a particoloured pattern, usu. fast-printed and glazed. E17. **B** *adj.* Of chintz; covered with chintz. E18.

chintzy *a.* (*a*) decorated or covered with chintz; (*b*) *fig.* unfashionable; genteel, suburban, petit bourgeois: M19.

chintz *n.*[2] var. of CHINCH *n.*[1]

chionodoxa /kʌɪənə'dɒksə/ *n.* L19. [mod.L, f. Gk *khiōn* snow + *doxa* glory.] A blue-flowered early-blooming plant of the genus *Chionodoxa* of the lily family. Also called *glory-of-the-snow*.

chip /tʃɪp/ *n.* [OE *ċipp*, *ċyp* = OS *kip* post, *kipa* stave (Du. *kip* beam of a plough), OHG *kipfa* (G dial. *Kipf(e)*) axle, stave, ON *keppr* stick, staff. Branch II perh. a different wd, rel. to CHIP *v.*[1]] **I 1** The beam of a plough. *dial.* OE.

II 2 A thin piece cut from wood; a fragment broken from stone etc. ME. **3** A thin slice or piece of bread-crust (*obs.*), fruit, potato, etc.; *spec.* a (usu. oblong) piece of potato fried or for frying, (chiefly *N. Amer.*) a potato crisp; (orig. *US*) a cold thin crisp piece of food made from seasoned flour or meal (usu. w. specifying wd). LME. **†4** A key of a spinet or harpsichord. *rare* (Shakes.). Only in L16. **5a** Wood or woody fibre split into thin strips for making hats, bonnets, baskets, etc. L18. **b** In full *chip basket*. A basket made of strips of thin wood interwoven or joined. E20. **6** A piece of dried buffalo- or cow-dung, used as fuel. Usu. in *pl. N. Amer.* M19. **7** A counter used for betting in a game of chance; a coin; in *pl.*, money. M19. **8** A blemish caused by chipping; a place on china etc. from which a chip has been knocked off. L19. **9** More fully *chip shot*. In golf, a short lofted approach-shot on to the putting-green. In soccer etc., a short lofted kick. E20. **10** A tiny wafer of semiconducting material used to make an integrated circuit, *esp.* such a wafer of silicon (also *silicon chip*). M20.

3 *corn chip*, *potato chip*, *tortilla chip*, etc. CHOCOLATE *chip*.

Phrases: (**as**) **dry as a chip** thoroughly dried up. *bargaining chip*: see BARGAIN *v.* 1. *blue chip*: see BLUE *a.* **burn** etc. **to a chip** make inedible or useless by burning, burn up. *cash in one's chips*: see CASH *v.*[2] 3a. *chip off* (or *of*) *the old block*: see BLOCK *n.* 1. *fish and chips*: see FISH *n.*[1] **hand, pass,** or **throw in one's chips** *fig.* (*US colloq.*) die. **have a chip on one's shoulder** be touchy or embittered (from a former US practice of so placing a chip as a challenge to others to knock it off). **have had one's chips** *slang* be beaten, be finished; be unable to have what one wants. **in the chips** *slang* moneyed, affluent. **not care a chip** not care at all. *pass in one's chips*: see *hand in one's chips* above. *spit chips*: see SPIT *v.*[1] *throw in one's chips*: see *hand in one's chips* above. **when the chips are down** *colloq.* when it comes to the point.

Comb.: **chip basket** (*a*) a wire basket used in deep-frying potato chips; (*b*) see sense 5b above; **chipboard** a thin pasteboard made of compressed wood chips and resin; **chip-shop** a shop selling fish and chips; *chip shot*: see sense 9 above.

chip /tʃɪp/ *v.*[1] Infl. **-pp-**. LME. [Rel. to OE *forċippian* cut off, (M)LG, (M)Du. *kippen* hatch out by chipping the shell.] **†1** *v.t.* Remove the crust of (bread); remove (the crust of bread). LME–E18. **2** *v.t.* Chap, crack. Long *obs.* exc. *dial.* LME. **3** *v.i.* Of a seed or bud: break open, germinate. Long *obs.* exc. *dial.* L15. **4** *v.t.* Of a hatching chicken etc.: crack and break open (the eggshell). E17. **5** *v.t.* Hew or cut with an axe, adze, or other implement. E17. **6a** *v.i.* Break at the edge; lose a piece from the edge or surface; be apt to do so. M19. **b** *v.t.* Cut or break at the surface or edge; shape by so cutting; carve (an inscription etc.); cut or break (a piece) *off, from,* a surface or edge. M19. **c** *v.i.* Make strokes *at* (as if) to cut or break pieces off; work *away at* so as to diminish or destroy. M19. **7** *v.t.* Harrow, hoe, (ground). *Austral* & *NZ.* E19. **8** *v.t.* Cut (esp. a potato) into chips; *US* slice (smoked dried beef) thinly. Chiefly as *chipped* ppl a. E19. **9a** *v.i.* Aim a blow *at* (*lit.* & *fig.*); poke fun *at.* E19. **b** *v.t.* Tease, chaff. *colloq.* L19. **10** *v.i.* & *t.* Foll. by *in:* **a** Put down (as) a stake, contribute (money etc.). M19. **b** Contribute to a conversation, interpose. L19. **11** *v.i.* & *t.* Kick or hit (a ball etc.) with a chip shot; bypass (an opposing player) with a chip shot. E20.

5 G. SWIFT Dick . . chips ice from the lock-gates with fingers that do not seem to feel the cold. **6a** *Ladies Home Journal* (*US*) If nail color chips between manicures. **c** H. E. BATES Workmen were chipping at snow and ice with pickaxes. *Globe & Mail* (*Toronto*) Members will chip away at the coverage extended to the consumer, if there is no regulation. **9b** J. HILTON Being chipped about that Chinese girl didn't appeal to my sense of humour. **10a** P. ACKROYD He insisted on paying the bill, he would not dream of having them chip in. R. CARVER All of us chipped in thirty-eight bucks for a funeral spray. **b** *Scottish Daily Express* Andrew quickly chipped in that there wasn't a 'bottomless pit of money'. *Stage & Television Today* Jack Lemmon and Walter Matthau—ready to chip in comments. **11** G. GREEN Chipping home the free kick for goal number five. *Guardian* Bodak broke clear . . to chip Corrigan delightfully. *Los Angeles Times* A chance to chip and putt the ball.

Comb.: **chip-axe** a small axe used in chipping timber etc. into shape; **chip-in** *Golf* a chip shot by which the ball is holed.

chipping *n.* (*a*) a small piece of wood, stone, (*obs.*) bread, etc., chipped or pared off, esp. in dressing or shaping (usu. in *pl.*); (*b*) the action of the vb: LME.

chip /tʃɪp/ *v.*[2]*i.* Chiefly *US.* Infl. **-pp-**. L18. [Imit.] Cheep, chirp.

chipping sparrow, †**bird** a N. American sparrow, *Spizella passerina.* **chip(ping) squirrel** [by erron. identification of *chip* in CHIPMUNK] a chipmunk.

Chipewyan /tʃɪpəˈwʌɪən/ *a.* & *n.* Also **-pp-**. L18. [Cree *ci:pwaya:n*, lit. '(wearing) pointed-skin (garments)'.] **A** *adj.* Designating or pertaining to an Athapaskan N. American Indian people or their language. L18. **B** *n.* Pl. **-s**, same. A member of this people; their language. E19.

chipmunk /ˈtʃɪpmʌŋk/ *n.* Also †**-muck**. M19. [f. Ojibwa *ačitamo·nʔ*.] A N. American ground-squirrel of the genus *Tamias.*

least chipmunk: see LEAST *a., n., & adv.*

chipolata /tʃɪpəˈlɑːtə/ *n.* L19. [Fr. f. It. *cipollata* dish of onions, f. *cipolla* onion.] In full *chipolata sausage.* A small (often spicy) sausage.

Chippendale /ˈtʃɪp(ə)ndeɪl/ *a.* & *n.* L19. [See below.] **A** *adj.* Designating or pertaining to an elegant style of ornamental furniture popularized in the pattern-books of the English cabinet-maker Thomas Chippendale (1718–79); designed by or in the style of Thomas Chippendale. L19. **B** *n.* A piece of Chippendale furniture. L19.

Chinese Chippendale: combining square and angular outlines with Chinese motifs.

chipper /ˈtʃɪpə/ *n.* E16. [f. CHIP *v.*[1] + -ER[1].] A person who or thing which chips; *esp.* a machine for chipping timber.

chipper /ˈtʃɪpə/ *a. colloq.* (orig. *N. Amer.*). M19. [Prob. var. of KIPPER *a.*[2], infl. by next.] Cheerful, lively.

chipper /ˈtʃɪpə/ *v. dial.* & *US.* E18. [Imit.: partly a metathesis of CHIRRUP *v.*] **1** *v.i.* Twitter; chatter. E18. **2** *v.t.* Cheer *up.* L19.

Chippewa /ˈtʃɪpəwɔː, -wɑː/ *n.* & *a.* Also **-way** /-weɪ/. Pl. of n. same, **-s**. M18. [Alt. of OJIBWA.] = OJIBWA.

¶*Chippewa(y)* is the more usual name in the US, and *Ojibwa* in Canada.

Chippewyan *a.* & *n.* var. of CHIPEWYAN.

chippie *n.*[1], *n.*[2] vars. of CHIPPY *n.*[1], *n.*[2]

chippy /ˈtʃɪpi/ *n.*[1] Orig. *US.* Also **-ie**. M19. [f. CHIP *v.*[2] + -Y[6], -IE.] **1** A small bird; *spec.* = *chipping sparrow* s.v. CHIP *v.*[2] M19. **2** A promiscuous or delinquent young woman; a prostitute; *derog.* a young woman, a girl. *slang.* L19.

chippy /ˈtʃɪpi/ *n.*[2] Also **-ie**. E20. [f. CHIP *n.* + -Y[6], -IE.] **1** A carpenter. (Cf. CHIPS.) *slang.* E20. **2** A shop selling fish and chips. *colloq.* M20.

chippy /ˈtʃɪpi/ *a. dial.* & *slang.* E17. [f. CHIP *n.* or *v.*[1] + -Y[1].] **1** That chips or breaks into small pieces easily. E17. **2** As dry as a chip, thoroughly dried up. M19. **3** Unwell, esp. with a hangover. L19. **4** Irritable. L19.

chippiness *n.* L19.

Chips /tʃɪps/ *n. slang.* L18. [Pl. of CHIP *n.*: see -S[1].] (A nickname for) a carpenter, esp. on a ship.

†**chique** *n.* see CHIGOE.

chir /tʃɪə/ *n.*[1] L19. [Hind. *cīr.*] A pine, *Pinus roxburghii*, native to the Himalayas. Also *chir pine.*

chir *n.*[2] var. of CHEER *n.*[2]

chiragh /tʃɪˈrɑːg/ *n.* L19. [Urdu f. Pers. *čirāġ* lamp, light.] A simple oil lamp used in India and adjacent countries.

chiral /ˈkʌɪər(ə)l/ *a.* L19. [f. Gk *kheir* hand + -AL[1].] Of a crystal, molecule, etc.: not superposable on its mirror image.

chiˈrality *n.* L19.

chirayta /tʃɪˈrʌɪtə/ *n.* Also **-retta** /-ˈrɛtə/. M19. [Hind. *cirāytā, ciraitā.*] (A bitter infusion made from) an Indian plant of the gentian family, *Swertia chirata.*

†**chire** *n.* see CHIVE *n.*[1]

chiretta *n.* var. of CHIRAYTA.

chirimoya *n.* var. of CHERIMOYA.

chirk /tʃəːk/ *a. US colloq.* L18. [Prob. f. next.] Lively, in good spirits.

chirk /tʃəːk/ *v.* LME. [Imit.: cf. CHARK *v.*[1]] **1** *v.i.* Grate, grind; creak; croak. Long *obs.* exc. *Sc. dial.* LME. **2** *v.i.* Chirp; squeak. LME. **3** *v.i.* & *t.* Cheer *up. US colloq.* M19.

2 O. NASH The rural squirrel in his rage Chirks like a squirrel in a cage.

chirl /tʃəːl/ *n.* & *v.* Chiefly *Sc.* E17. [Imit.] **A** *n.* A warble. E17. **B** *v.t.* & *i.* Warble. E19.

chirm /tʃəːm/ *n.* Also (now the usual form in sense 2) **charm** /tʃɑːm/. [OE *ċearm, ċierm* = OS *karm*: cf. next.] **1** Noise, din; *esp.* (*a*) the blended singing of many birds; (*b*) the noise of many children etc. chattering. Now *dial.* OE. **2** A flock (*of* finches etc.). LME.

chirm /tʃəːm/ *v.i.* Now *dial.* Also **charm** /tʃɑːm/, **sharm** /ʃɑːm/. [OE *ċirman* = MDu. *kermen, carmen* mourn, lament (Du. *kermen*), MHG *karmen.*] Cry out; *spec.* (of a bird, or a person likened to a bird) warble, chirp.

W. OWEN The birds fifed on before, . . Right down to town; and there they ceased to charm.

chiro- /ˈkʌɪrəʊ/ *comb. form.* Also **cheiro-**; (bef. a vowel) **chir-, cheir-**. [Gk *kheiro-*, f. *kheir* hand: see -O-.] Of the hand.

chiˈrognomist *n.* one practising chirognomy L19. **chiˈrognomy** *n.* the supposed estimation of character by inspection of the hand M19. **chiroˈnomic** *a.* of or pertaining to chironomy M18. **chiˈronomy** *n.* the art or science of gesticulation, or of moving the hands according to rule in oratory etc. L17.

chirograph /ˈkʌɪrəgrɑːf/ *n.* ME. [Fr. *chirographe* f. L *chirographum* f. Gk *kheirographon*, f. as CHIRO- + -GRAPH.] Chiefly *Hist.* A formal handwritten document, *esp.* an indenture of a fine.

chirographer /kʌɪˈrɒgrəfə/ *n.* LME. [AN *cirographer*, med.L *chirographarius*, f. *chirographum*: see prec., -ER[2]. In sense 2 f. CHIRO- + -GRAPHER.] **1** *Hist.* A legal officer appointed to engross fines in the Court of Common Pleas. LME. **2** A copying clerk; a person who employs handwriting. M18.

chirography /kʌɪˈrɒgrəfi/ *n.* M17. [f. CHIRO- + -GRAPHY.] (The style or character of) handwriting.

chirology /kʌɪˈrɒlədʒi/ *n.* Also **cheir-**. M17. [(Fr. *chirologie*,) f. as CHIRO- + -LOGY.] †**1** The use of manual sign language. M–L17. **2** The branch of knowledge that deals with the hand. L19.

chiroˈlogical *a.* of or pertaining to chirology (sense 2) M19. **chirologist** *n.* a person who makes the hand a subject of study M19.

chiromancy /ˈkʌɪrəmansi/ *n.* LME. [Fr. *chiromancie* f. L *chiromantia* f. Gk *kheiromanteia*, f. as CHIRO- + -MANCY.] Divination by (inspection of) the hand; palmistry.

chiromancer *n.* a practitioner of chiromancy M16. **chiroˈmantic** *a.* & *n.* [f. Gk *kheiromantis* chiromancer + -IC] (*a*) *adj.* of or pertaining to chiromancy; †(*b*) *n.* a chiromancer: E17. **chiroˈmantical** *a.* (now *rare*) = CHIROMANTIC *a.* M17. **chiromantist** *n.* (*rare*) a chiromancer M17.

chironomid /kʌɪˈrɒnəmɪd/ *a.* & *n.* L19. [mod.L *Chironomidae* (see below), f. *Chironomus* genus name f. Gk *kheironomos* pantomime dancer: see -ID[3].] **A** *adj.* Of, pertaining to, or designating the dipteran family Chironomidae, which includes many midges. L19. **B** *n.* An insect of this family. L19.

chiropodist /kɪˈrɒpədɪst, ʃɪ-/ *n.* L18. [f. CHIRO- + Gk *pod-, pous* foot + -IST.] A person who treats ailments of the feet, esp. corns, bunions, etc., (and orig. those of the hands also).

chiropody *n.* the treatment of ailments of the feet L19.

chiropractic /kʌɪrəˈpraktɪk/ *a.* & *n.* L19. [f. CHIRO- + Gk *praktikos*: see PRACTIC *n., a.*] (Concerned with or pertaining to) the diagnosis and manipulative treatment of mechanical disorders of the joints, esp. of the spine.

chiropractor *n.* a person who practises chiropractic E20.

chiropteran /kʌɪˈrɒpt(ə)rən/ *n.* & *a.* Also †**cheir-**. M19. [f. mod.L *Chiroptera* bats, f. as CHIRO- + Gk *pteron* wing: see -AN.] **A** *n.* A mammal of the order Chiroptera; a bat. M19. **B** *adj.* Of this order; pertaining to bats. M19.

Also **chiropterous** *a.* L19.

chirp /tʃəːp/ *v.* & *n.* LME. [Imit.] **A** *v.* **1** *v.i.* Of a small bird, a grasshopper, etc.: make a characteristic short sharp thin sound. Of a person: make a sound imitative of or similar to this, esp. as a greeting or as encouragement; talk merrily; *colloq.* speak *up.* LME. **2** *v.t.* Utter or express by chirping. E17. **3** *v.t.* Greet or encourage by chirping. M19. **4** *v.t.* & *i.* Cheer *up. US.* L19. **B** *n.* A short sharp thin sound (as) of a small bird, a grasshopper, etc. E19.

chirper *n.* a person who or thing which chirps; a small bird: L16. **chirping** *ppl a.* (*a*) that chirps; (*b*) merry, lively; (*c*) *arch.* producing merriment, cheering: M16.

chirpy /ˈtʃəːpi/ *a. colloq.* M19. [f. prec. + -Y[1].] Given to chirping; lively; cheerful.

chirpily *adv.* E20. **chirpiness** *n.* M19.

chirr /tʃəː/ *n.* & *v.* E17. [Imit.: cf. CHURR.] **A** *n.* A prolonged trilling sound (as) of a grasshopper etc. E17. **B** *v.i.* Make such a sound. E17.

chirrup /ˈtʃɪrəp/ *v.* & *n.* L16. [Alt. of CHIRP *v.* by trilling the *r.*] **A** *v.* **1** *v.i.* Of a bird, grasshopper, etc.: make a series of chirps, twitter. Of a person: make a sound imitative of or similar to this, esp. as a greeting or as encouragement; sing or talk merrily. L16. **2** *v.t.* Utter by chirruping. M17. **3** *v.t.* Greet or encourage by chirruping. L18. **B** *n.* A series of chirps; a twitter. M19.

chirrupy *a.* (*colloq.*) given to chirruping; lively, cheerful; chirpy: E19.

chirt /tʃəːt/ *v.* & *n. obs.* exc. *Sc.* LME. [Imit.] **A** *v.* †**1** *v.i.* Chirp. Only in LME. **2** *v.i.* Spurt out. E16. **3** *v.t.* Squeeze, press *out.* M17. **B** *n.* †**1** A chirp. Only in E17. **2** A squeeze (ejecting liquid). M19.

chiru /ˈtʃɪruː/ *n.* L19. [Prob. f. Tib.] A gazelle, *Pantholops hodgsoni*, of high plateaux in Tibet, northern India, and parts of China, the male of which has very long straight horns.

chirurgeon /kʌɪˈrəːdʒ(ə)n, tʃɪ-/ *n. arch.* ME. [OFr. *cirurgien* (mod. *chir-*): see SURGEON.] A surgeon.

chirurgery /kʌɪˈrəːdʒ(ə)ri, tʃɪ-/ *n. arch.* LME. [OFr. *cirurgerie*: see SURGERY.] Surgery.

chirurgic(al) *adjs.* surgical LME.

chisel /ˈtʃɪz(ə)l/ *n.*[1] LME. [ONFr. (mod. *ciseau*, in pl. scissors) f. Proto-Romance, f. L *cis-* (as in late L *cisorium*) var. of *caes-* stem of *caedere* to cut: see -EL[2]. Cf. SCISSORS.] 1 A cutting tool having a square bevelled end for shaping wood, stone, or metal. LME. 2 A similar surgical instrument for cutting bones. L17.

1 **cold, hot, chisel**: suitable for cutting cold, hot, metal. **full chisel** *US colloq.* at full speed. *skew chisel*: see SKEW *a.*

Comb.: **chisel-toe** a squared toe of a shoe.

chisel-like *a.* resembling (that of) a chisel M19.

chisel *n.*[2] var. of CHESIL *n.*

chisel /ˈtʃɪz(ə)l/ *v.t.* Infl. **-ll-**, ***-l-**. E16. [f. CHISEL *n.*[1]] 1 Cut, shape, etc., with a chisel; *transf.* shape, give form to. E16. 2 Cheat, defraud; treat unfairly. *slang.* E19.

1 A. MILLER You can chisel the wood out around those bolts. *fig.*: R. MACAULAY Time chiselled delicate lines in her fine clear skin.

chiselled *ppl a.* cut or shaped with a chisel; *fig.* (of features etc.) finely or clearly cut: L16.

chiseller /ˈtʃɪz(ə)lə/ *n.*[1] Also ***-eler**. E19. [f. prec. + -ER[1].] A person who cuts or shapes with a chisel; *slang* a cheat, a swindler, a confidence trickster.

chiseller /ˈtʃɪz(ə)lə/ *n.*[2] *Anglo-Ir.* Also **-elur, chisler** /ˈtʃɪzlə/. E20. [Origin unkn.] A youngster, a child, a youth.

chi-square /kʌɪˈskwɛː/ *n.* E20. [f. CHI + SQUARE *n.*: *X* is used conventionally to represent the square root of the sum of the squares of differences between observed and theoretical data.] In full *chi-square test*. A significance test used in the statistical comparison of observed and theoretical values.

chi-squared *a.* designating such a test M20.

chit /tʃɪt/ *n.*[1] LME. [Origin uncertain: perh. same as next.] †1 An animal's young; a whelp, a cub, a kitten. LME–E18. 2 A young child, a brat; a young, small, or slender woman. Usu. *derog.* E17.

2 G. SANTAYANA Some chit of a silly nurse-maid. SLOAN WILSON She was a proper woman. Not some little chit.

chit /tʃɪt/ *n.*[2] *obs.* exc. *dial.* E17. [Perh. repr. obscurely OE *ċīþ* shoot, sprout, seed, mote (in the eye), OS *kīþ* sprout, shoot, MDu. *kijt*, OHG *-kīdi* sprout, f. Gmc base also of CHINE *n.*[1]] A shoot, a sprout.

chit /tʃɪt/ *n.*[3] L18. [Abbrev. of CHITTY *n.*] A written paper, a note; a note of an order, a sum owed, etc.

chit /tʃɪt/ *v.i.* Infl. **-tt-**. E17. [f. CHIT *n.*[2]] Esp. of potatoes: sprout, germinate.

chital /ˈtʃiːt(ə)l/ *n.* Also **chee-**. L19. [Hind. *cītal*, *cittal* f. Skt *citrala* spotted.] A white-spotted deer, *Axis axis*, of southern Asia. Also called *axis (deer)*, *spotted deer*.

chitarrone /kɪtəˈrəʊni/ *n.* Pl. **-ni** /-ni/. M18. [It., augm. of *chitarra* guitar.] A double-necked lute of great length, a theorbo.

chit-chat /ˈtʃɪttʃat/ *n.* & *v.* L17. [Redupl. of CHAT *n.*[2]] A *n.* 1 Light familiar conversation. L17. 2 Subject-matter of gossip or small talk. E18. B *v.i.* Infl. **-tt-**. Gossip, chat. E19.

chit-chatty *a.* of the nature of chit-chat; gossipy: L19.

†chithe *n.* see CHIVE *n.*[1]

chitin /ˈkʌɪtɪn/ *n.* Also **†-ine**. M19. [Fr. *chitine*, irreg. f. Gk *khitōn*: see CHITON, -IN[1].] An insoluble nitrogenous polysaccharide which is the main constituent of the exoskeleton of arthropods and also occurs in fungi.

chitiniˈzation *n.* conversion into chitin L19. **chitinize** *v.t.* convert into chitin (usu. in *pass.*) L19. **chitinoid** *a.* resembling chitin L19. **chitinous** *a.* of the nature of or consisting of chitin M19.

chitlings /ˈtʃɪtlɪŋz/ *n.pl. dial.* & *US.* Also **chid-** /ˈtʃɪd-/. M19. [Contr. of pl. of CHITTERLING.] 1 Chitterlings. M19. 2 Rags, tatters. *US.* M19.

chiton /ˈkʌɪtɒn, -t(ə)n/ *n.* E19. [Gk *khitōn*; in sense 1 through mod.L *Chiton* genus name.] 1 A mollusc of the class Polyplacophora, characterized by a broad oval foot and a symmetrical dorsal shell composed of a series of eight overlapping plates. E19. 2 A long woollen tunic worn in ancient Greece. M19.

chittack /ˈtʃɪtak/ *n.* L19. [Bengali *chaṭāk*.] In the Indian subcontinent: a unit of weight equal to about 900 grains (approx. 58.3 grams).

chitter /ˈtʃɪtə/ *v.* & *n.* ME. [Imit., of frequent. formation: see -ER[5]. Cf. CHATTER.] A *v.* 1 *v.i.* (Of a bird) utter quick series of short notes, twitter; (of a squirrel etc.) chatter; *gen.* make a twittering or chattering sound. ME. 2 *v.t.* Utter by chittering. *rare.* LME. 3 *v.i.* Shiver with cold. E16. 4 *v.i.* Of the teeth: chatter. M16. B *n.* Twittering. M19.

chitter-chatter /ˈtʃɪtətʃatə/ *n.* E18. [Redupl. of CHATTER *n.*: cf. CHIT-CHAT.] Lively chattering, light gossip.

chitterling /ˈtʃɪtəlɪŋ/ *n.* ME. [Origin uncertain: perh. rel. to MHG *kutel* (G *Kutteln*) in same sense. In sense 3 treated as dim. of CHIT *n.*[1]] 1 *sing.* & (usu.) in *pl.* The smaller intestines of pigs etc., esp. when cooked as food. ME. 2 A frill, esp. down the front of a dress-shirt (prob. f. the resemblance of this to the mesentery). *obs.* exc. *dial.* L16. 3 A little child, a little brat. *derog.* L17.

chitty /ˈtʃɪti/ *n.* E17. [Hind. *ciṭṭhī* f. Skt *citra* spot, mark.] = CHIT *n.*[3]

chitty /ˈtʃɪti/ *a.* Long *obs.* exc. *dial.* E17. [f. next.] Of a face: pinched; (later) baby-like.

Comb.: **chitty-faced** *a.* having a pinched face; baby-faced.

chitty-face /ˈtʃɪtɪfeɪs/ *n.* Long *obs.* exc. *dial.* E17. [Perh. f. Fr. *chicheface* thin face: assoc. w. CHIT *n.*[1]] A person with a pinched face; (later) a baby-faced person.

chiule /tʃɪˈuːl/ *n.* M19. [AL *chiula*, *cyula* f. OE *ċīol*, *ċēol*: see KEEL *n.*[2]] *Hist.* A warship of the early Germanic or Norse invaders of Britain.

chiv /tʃɪv/ *v.* & *n. slang.* Also **sh-** /ʃ-/. E19. [Var. of CHIVE *n.*[3] & *v.*] A *v.t.* Infl. **-vv-**. Knife, stab, slash. E19. B *n.* A knife, a blade, a razor. M19.

chivalresque /ʃɪv(ə)lˈrɛsk/ *a.* Also **chevaleresque** /ʃɛvələˈrɛsk/. E19. [(f. CHIVALRY + -ESQUE after) Fr. *chevaleresque*, f. *chevalier*: see CHEVALIER.] Characteristic or suggestive of the Age of Chivalry.

chivalric /ˈʃɪv(ə)lrɪk; *poet.* ʃɪˈvalrɪk/ *a.* L18. [f. CHIVALRY + -IC.] Of or pertaining to chivalry; chivalrous.

chivalrous /ˈʃɪv(ə)lrəs/ *a.* LME. [OFr. *chevalerous*, f. *chevalier*: see CHEVALIER, -OUS.] †1 Characteristic of a medieval knight or man-at-arms; valorous. LME–E17. 2 Of or pertaining to (a knight of) the Age of Chivalry. L18. 3 Pertaining to or characteristic of the ideal knight; gallant, honourable, courteous, disinterested; *derog.* quixotic. E19.

chivalrously *adv.* LME. **chivalrousness** *n.* M19.

chivalry /ˈʃɪv(ə)lri/ *n.* ME. [(O)Fr. *chevalerie*, †*chiv-*, f. med.L *caballerius* for *caballarius*: see CHEVALIER, -ERY, -Y[3].] 1 *collect.* Knights or horsemen equipped for battle; medieval men-at-arms; gallant gentlemen. *arch.* ME. †b The cavalry of ancient Greece and Rome. E16–L18. 2 The qualities and abilities of a knight; knightly skill. *arch.* ME. †3 A feat of knightly valour; a gallant exploit. ME–E19. 4 Knighthood as a rank or order. *arch.* LME. 5 *Law.* Tenure by knight-service. *obs.* exc. *Hist.* L16. 6 The medieval knightly system with its religious, moral, and social code. M18. 7 The characteristics of an ideal knight; courage, honour, and courtesy; inclination to defend or help a weaker party. L18.

1 GIBBON A valorous knight, who charged at the head of the Spanish chivalry . . against the Moors. 2 SIR W. SCOTT The last of all the Bards was he, who sung of Border Chivalry. 7 W. HOLTBY She had evoked some masculine sentiment of protective chivalry.

Phrases: **the Age of Chivalry** the period during which the knightly social and ethical system prevailed; the period during which men behave with courage, honour, and courtesy.

†chive *n.*[1] Earlier **chire, chithe**. [OE *ċīþ* f. Gmc base also of CHINE *n.*[1], *v.*[1] Intermediate *chire* unexpl.; *chive* perh. infl. by next.] 1 A tiny shoot, a sprout; a slender blade *of* grass etc. OE–M19. 2 A filamentous organ in a flower, a stamen or pistil; the filament of a stamen. OE–E19.

chive /tʃʌɪv/ *n.*[2] Also (now *rare*) **cive** /sʌɪv/. LME. [OFr. dial. var. (whence Picard *chivot* green onion) of (O)Fr. *cive* f. L *cepa* onion. See also SITHE *n.*[2]] 1 *sing.* & (usu.) in *pl.* A small plant, *Allium schoenoprasum*, resembling the onion; the slender hollow leaves of this plant as used to flavour salads, soups, etc. LME. †2 A small bulb or bulbil, *esp.* a clove of garlic. M16–M18.

chive /tʃʌɪv, tʃɪv/ *n.*[3] & *v. slang.* Also **sh-** /ʃ-/. See also CHIV. L17. [Origin unkn.] = CHIV.

chivvy /ˈtʃɪvi/ *n.* & *v.*[1] Also **chivy, chevy** /ˈtʃɛvi/. L18. [Prob. f. *Chevy Chase*, scene of a skirmish celebrated in a Border ballad.] A *n.* 1 A hunting cry. L18. 2 A chase, a pursuit, a hunt. E19. 3 [Abbrev. of CHEVY CHASE.] The face. *slang.* L19. B *v.* 1 *v.t.* Chase; harry; worry, trouble, harass. M19. 2 *v.i.* Race, scamper. M19.

chivvy /ˈtʃɪvi/ *v.*[2] *slang.* M20. [f. CHIV *v.*] = CHIV *v.*

chivy *n.* & *v.* var. of CHIVVY *n.* & *v.*[1]

chizz /tʃɪz/ *v.* & *n. School slang.* M20. [Abbrev. of CHISEL *v.*] A *v.i.* Cheat. M20. B *n.* A swindle. M20.

chizzer *n.* a cheater M20.

chlamydia /kləˈmɪdɪə/ *n.* Pl. **-ias, -iae** /-iːː/. M20. [mod.L, f. as next: see -IA[1].] *Bacteriol.* A virus-like parasitic bacterium of the genus *Chlamydia*, some species of which cause diseases such as trachoma and psittacosis.

chlamydial *a.* M20.

chlamydomonas /ˌklamɪdəˈməʊnəs/ *n.* L19. [mod.L, f. as next + Gk *monas* MONAD.] A unicellular green freshwater alga of the genus *Chlamydomonas*.

chlamydospore /ˈklamɪdəspɔː/ *n.* L19. [f. Gk *khlamyd-* CHLAMYS + -O- + SPORE *n.*] *Bot.* & *Zool.* A spore with a thick protective coat.

chlamys /ˈklamɪs/ *n.* L17. [Gk *khlamus* mantle.] A short cloak worn by men in ancient Greece.

chloanthite /kləʊˈanθʌɪt/ *n.* M19. [f. Gk *khloanthēs* becoming green + -ITE[1].] *Min.* A nickel-rich variety of skutterudite. Also called *white nickel (ore)*.

chloasma /kləʊˈazmə/ *n.* Pl. **-mas, -mata** /-mətə/. M19. [f. Gk *khloazein* become green.] *Med.* An area of skin, usu. on the face, which is temporarily abnormally pigmented, often owing to hormonal changes.

chlor- /klɔː/ *comb. form*[1] of CHLORINE *n.* Cf. CHLORO-[2].

chloˈracne *n.* (*Med.*) a skin disease characterized by persistent lesions resembling acne, caused by regular exposure to chlorinated chemicals E20. **chloramine** *n.* an organic compound containing a chlorine atom bonded to nitrogen; *spec.* any of a group of sulphonamide derivatives used as antiseptics and disinfectants: L19. **chloˈrapatite** *n.* (*Min.*) a variety of apatite containing chlorine M19. **chlordiazeˈpoxide** *n.* a minor tranquillizer of the benzodiazepine group; (a proprietary name for the drug is LIBRIUM): M20. **chlortetraˈcycline** *n.* an antibiotic of the tetracycline group, obtained from the bacterium *Streptomyces aureofaciens* or prepared synthetically; (a proprietary name for the drug is AUREOMYCIN): M20.

chlor- *comb. form*[2] see CHLORO-[1].

chloral /ˈklɔːral/ *n.* M19. [f. CHLOR-[1] + -AL[2].] *Chem.* Trichloroacetaldehyde, CCl_3CHO, a pungent volatile liquid which is obtained by the action of chlorine on alcohol and is used esp. as a hypnotic (usu. in the form of its crystalline hydrate).

chloramphenicol /klɔːramˈfɛnɪkɒl/ *n.* M20. [f. as prec. + AMIDE + PHEN- + NITRO- + GLYCOL.] An antibiotic obtained from the bacterium *Streptomyces venezuelae* or prepared synthetically.

¶A proprietary name for this drug is CHLOROMYCETIN.

chlorate /ˈklɔːreɪt/ *n.* E19. [f. CHLORIC + -ATE[1].] *Chem.* A salt of chloric acid.

chlordane /ˈklɔːdeɪn/ *n.* M20. [f. CHLOR-[1] + INDENE + -ANE.] A viscous chlorinated derivative of indene, $C_{10}H_6Cl_8$, used as an insecticide.

chlorella /klə'rɛlə/ *n.* E20. [mod.L, dim. of Gk *khlōros* green.] A unicellular green alga of the genus *Chlorella*.

chloric /'klɔːrɪk/ *a.* E19. [f. CHLORINE *n.* + -IC: cf. CHLOROUS.] *Chem.* Of chlorine; *chloric acid*, a strongly oxidizing acid, $HClO_3$, known only as an aqueous solution.

chloride /'klɔːrʌɪd/ *n.* E19. [f. CHLORINE *n.* + -IDE.] **1** *Chem.* A compound of chlorine with a less electrovalent element or radical; a salt or ester of hydrochloric acid. E19. **2** *loosely.* A bleach or disinfectant containing a hypochlorite. E19.
chloridi'zation *n.* the process of chloridizing L19. **chloridize** *v.t.* convert (esp. metal ores) into chloride L19.

chlorinate /'klɔːrɪneɪt, 'klɒ-/ *v.t.* M19. [f. next + -ATE[3].] Treat or impregnate with chlorine (esp. as a means of disinfecting water); *Chem.* introduce one or more chlorine atoms into (a compound or molecule), usu. in place of hydrogen. Freq. as *chlorinated* ppl a.
chlori'nation *n.* M19. **chlorinator** *n.* an apparatus for chlorinating water etc. M20.

chlorine /'klɔːriːn/ *n.* E19. [f. Gk *khlōros* green + -INE[5].] A toxic yellowish-green gaseous chemical element, atomic no. 17, of the halogen group, with a strong pungent smell. (Symbol Cl.)
chlo'rinity *n.* chloride concentration (of seawater etc.) M20.

chlorine /'klɔːrʌɪn/ *a. rare.* M19. [f. as prec. + -INE[1].] Light-green.

chlorite /'klɔːrʌɪt/ *n.*[1] L18. [f. L *chloritis* f. Gk *khlōritis* a green precious stone: see CHLORO-[1], -ITE[1].] *Min.* A monoclinic basic aluminosilicate of magnesium, iron, and often other elements, which is a constituent of many rocks and forms greenish platy crystals.
chlo'ritic *a.* consisting of or containing chlorite E19. **chloriti'zation** *n.* conversion into (a form containing) chlorite L19. **chloritize** *v.t.* bring about chloritization of (usu. in *pass.*) E20. **chloritous** *a.* = CHLORITIC M19.

chlorite /'klɔːrʌɪt/ *n.*[2] M19. [f. CHLORINE *n.* + -ITE[1].] *Chem.* A salt of chlorous acid.

chloritoid /'klɔːrɪtɔɪd/ *n.* M19. [f. CHLORITE *n.*[1] + -OID.] *Min.* A basic aluminosilicate of iron and usu. also magnesium, similar to mica and varying in colour from greenish black to grey.

chloro- /'klɔːrəʊ, 'klɒrəʊ/ *comb. form*[1] of Gk *khlōros* green: see -O-. Bef. a vowel also **chlor-**.
chloro'cruorin *n.* a green respiratory pigment related to haemoglobin, present in the blood of some marine worms L19. **chlo'roma** *n.*, pl. **-mas**, **-mata** /-mətə/, *Med.* (the occurrence of) a greenish tumour of bone associated with myeloid leukaemia L19. **chloro'melanite** *n.* [Gk *khlōromelan* dark green] *Min.* a greenish-black iron-containing variety of jadeite L19. **chlo'ropal** *n.* (*Min.*) = NONTRONITE E19. **chlorophyte** *n. Bot.* †(*a*) *rare* a green plant; (*b*) a green alga: L19.

chloro- /'klɔːrəʊ, 'klɒrəʊ/ *comb. form*[2] of CHLORINE *n.*: see -O-. Cf. CHLOR-[1]. Often denoting compounds formed by replacement of one or more hydrogen atoms by chlorine, as *chlorobenzene*.
chloro'picrin *n.* [*picric acid*, from which orig. prepared] trichloronitromethane, CCl_3NO_2, a volatile, toxic, reactive liquid used as a disinfectant, pesticide, etc. M19. **chloro'platinate** *n.* a salt of chloroplatinic acid M19. **chloropla'tinic** *a.*: *chloroplatinic acid*, an acid, H_2PtCl_6, formed when platinum dissolves in aqua regia L19. **chloroprene** *n.* [ISOPRENE] 2-chloro-1,3-butadiene, C_4H_5Cl, a colourless liquid made from acetylene and hydrochloric acid, easily polymerized to neoprene M20. **chloroquine** /-kwiːn/ *n.* [QUIN(OLINE] *Pharm.* a quinoline derivative used esp. as an antimalarial M20. **chloro'thiazide** *n.* (*Pharm.*) a chlorinated thiazide used as a diuretic M20.

chlorodyne /'klɔːrədʌɪn, 'klɒr-/ *n.* M19. [f. next + ANODYNE.] A preparation containing chloroform and morphine, (esp. formerly) used as an anodyne.

chlorofluorocarbon /ˌklɔːrəʊflʊərəʊ'kɑːb(ə)n/ *n.* M20. [f. CHLORO-[2] + FLUORO- + CARBON *n.*] Any of a group of exceptionally stable compounds containing carbon, fluorine, and chlorine (analogous to the hydrocarbons), which have been used esp. as refrigerants and aerosol propellants. Abbrev. *CFC*.

chloroform /'klɒrəfɔːm, 'klɒr-/ *n.* & *v.* M19. [f. CHLORO-[2] + FORMIC.] **A** *n.* A thin colourless liquid, trichloromethane, $CHCl_3$, used as a solvent and as a general anaesthetic, its sweetish vapour producing narcosis when inhaled. M19. **B** *v.t.* Treat with chloroform; render unconscious with chloroform. Freq. *fig.* M19.
chloro'formic *a.* of, pertaining to, or like chloroform L19.

Chloromycetin /klɔːrə(ʊ)'mʌɪsɪtɪn, klɒrə(ʊ)-, ˌklɔːrəʊmʌɪ'siːtɪn/ *n.* M20. [f. CHLORO-[2] + MYCETO- + -IN[1].] (Proprietary name for) the drug chloramphenicol.

chlorophyll /'klɔːrəfɪl, 'klɒr-/ *n.* E19. [Fr. *chlorophylle* f. as CHLORO-[1] + Gk *phullon* leaf.] Any of a group of magnesium-containing green pigments which occur in plants (giving the characteristic colour to foliage etc.) and act as absorbers of light for photosynthesis.
chloro'phyllous *a.* of the nature of, containing, or characteristic of chlorophyll M19.

chloroplast /'klɔːrəplast, -plɑːst, 'klɒr-/ *n.* L19. [f. CHLORO-[1] + -PLAST.] *Bot.* A plastid containing chlorophyll.
†**chloroplastid** *n.* = CHLOROPLAST L19–E20.

chlorosis /klɒ'rəʊsɪs/ *n.* Pl. **-roses** /-'rəʊsiːz/. L17. [f. CHLORO-[1] + -OSIS.] **1** *Med.* Severe anaemia due to iron deficiency, causing a characteristic greenish pallor. Also called *greensickness*. L17. **2** *Bot.* The blanching of normally green parts of plants. Also, the abnormal turning green of other parts. E19.
chlorotic /-'rɒtɪk/ *a.* pertaining to or affected with chlorosis (in either sense) M18.

chlorous /'klɔːrəs/ *a.* M19. [f. CHLORINE *n.* + -OUS: cf. CHLORIC.] *Chem.* Of chlorine; *chlorous acid*, a weak acid, $HClO_2$, known only in aqueous solutions.

chlorpromazine /klɔː'prəʊməzɪn, -ziːn/ *n.* M20. [f. CHLOR-[1] + PROMETHAZINE.] *Pharm.* A phenothiazine derivative used as a tranquillizer, sedative, and anti-emetic.
¶Proprietary names for this drug are LARGACTIL, THORAZINE.

†**choak** *n.* var. of CHOCK *n.*[1]

†**choak** *v.* var. of CHOKE *v.*

†**choaker** *n.* var. of CHOKER.

choak-full *a.* var. of CHOCK-FULL

†**choaky** *a.* var. of CHOKY *a.*

choana /'kəʊənə/ *n.* Pl. **-nae** /-niː/. L19. [mod.L f. Gk *khoanē* funnel.] *Anat.* A funnel-shaped opening, *esp.* either of those connecting the nasal cavities to the pharynx.

choano- /'kəʊənəʊ/ *comb. form* of Gk *khoanē* funnel: see -O-.
choanocyte *n.* (*Zool.*) a flagellate cell with a collar of protoplasm at the base of the flagellum, e.g. in sponges L19.

choanoid /'kəʊənɔɪd/ *a.* M19. [f. as prec. + -OID.] *Anat.* & *Biol.* Funnel-shaped.

choate /'kəʊeɪt/ *a.* L19. [Back-form. f. INCHOATE *a.*, as if *in-* were IN-[3].] Finished, complete; fully developed.

chobdar /'tʃəʊbdɑː/ *n.* E18. [Urdu f. Pers. *čūbdār* mace-bearer.] In the Indian subcontinent: an usher bearing a staff, attending on a dignitary.

choc /tʃɒk/ *n. colloq.* L19. [Abbrev.] = CHOCOLATE *n.*
Comb.: **choc-bar**, **-ice**, a small bar of ice-cream enclosed in a thin layer of chocolate.

chocaholic *n.* & *a.* var. of CHOCOHOLIC.

chocho /'tʃəʊtʃəʊ/ *n.* Also (chiefly *Austral.* & *NZ*) **choko** /'tʃəʊkəʊ/. Pl. **-os**. M18. [Sp., of Amer. Indian origin.] = CHAYOTE.

chock /tʃɒk/ *n.*[1] Also †**choak**. See also CHUCK *n.*[4] ME. [Prob. f. ONFr. (mod. Picard *choke* big log, Norman *chouque*) var. of OFr. *ço(u)che* (mod. *souche*) log, block of wood: ult. origin unkn.] **1** A block of wood, *esp.* a wedge for stopping the motion of a cask or wheel; a block (of wood or other material) placed in front of an aeroplane wheel as a brake. ME. **2** A log, esp. for burning. *dial.* L17. **3** = CHUCK *n.*[4] 3 (now the usual form). E18.
Comb.: **chockstone** *Mountaineering* a stone wedged in a vertical cleft, used as a belay point, stance, or hold.

chock /tʃɒk/ *n.*[2] E20. [Imit.] A hollow sound such as is made by an impact on wood.

chock /tʃɒk/ *v.* E17. [f. CHOCK *n.*[1]] †**1** *v.t.* Drive in firmly. Only in E17. †**2** *v.i.* Fit *in* tightly and exactly. M17–L18. **3** *v.t.* Fit or make fast with a chock or chocks; wedge *up* tightly. M19.

chock /tʃɒk/ *adv.* Also **choke** /tʃəʊk/. L18. [Prob. f. CHOCK-FULL *a.*] Closely, tightly; close up.
chock-a-block (*a*) *Naut.* (of two blocks) run close together in a tackle; (*b*) *transf.* & *fig.* jammed together, crammed *with*.

chocker /'tʃɒkə/ *a. slang.* Also **-cka**. M20. [Abbrev. of *chock-a-block*: see prec.] Fed up; very disgruntled.

chock-full /tʃɒk'fʊl/ *a.* Also **choak-**, **choke-** /tʃəʊk-/; **chuck-** /tʃʌk-/. LME. [Origin uncertain: later assoc. with CHOCK *n.*[1], *v.*] Crammed full (*of*); packed *with*; stuffed.

choco /'tʃɒkəʊ/ *n. Austral. slang.* Also **-cko**. Pl. **-os**. M20. [Abbrev. of CHOCOLATE *soldier*.] A militiaman, a conscripted soldier.

chocoholic /tʃɒkə'hɒlɪk/ *n.* & *a.* Also **choca-**. L20. [f. next: see -AHOLIC.] **A** *n.* A person addicted to or very fond of chocolate. L20. **B** *adj.* Of or pertaining to chocoholics; addicted to or very fond of chocolate. L20.

chocolate /'tʃɒk(ə)lət/ *n.* & *a.* E17. [Fr. *chocolat* or Sp. *chocolate*, f. Nahuatl *chocolatl* article of food made from cacao seeds; infl. by unrelated *cacaua-atl* drink made from cacao.] **A** *n.* **1** A drink made of prepared chocolate (sense 2) dissolved in hot milk or water. E17. **2** An edible paste or solid made from cacao seeds by roasting, grinding, etc.; a small sweet or confection made of or covered with chocolate. M17. **3** = CACAO *n.* 3 (cf. *chocolate-tree* below). Now *rare* or *obs.* M18. **4** A dark brown colour. L18.
2 *milk chocolate*: see MILK *n.* *plain chocolate*: see PLAIN *a.*[1] & *adv.*
B *attrib.* or as *adj.* Of or resembling the colour or flavour of chocolate; dark brown. L18.
Comb. & *special collocations*: **chocolate biscuit** a chocolate-coated biscuit; **chocolate-box** a decorated box filled with chocolates; *fig.* (usu. *attrib.*) a stereotyped romantic style of prettiness; **chocolate-boxy** *a.* in chocolate-box style; **chocolate-brown** a dark rich brown; **chocolate chip** a small piece of chocolate used in making sweet biscuits and other confections; **chocolate drop** a small round sweet made of chocolate; **chocolate-house** *Hist.* a house providing chocolate as a beverage; *chocolate mousse*: see MOUSSE *n.* 2; **chocolate soldier** a chocolate figurine of a soldier; *fig.* a soldier unwilling to fight; **chocolate-tree** = CACAO *n.* 3.

chocolatey /'tʃɒk(ə)ləti/ *a.* Also **-ty**. M20. [f. prec. + -Y[1].] Made of, containing, or resembling chocolate.

chocolatier /tʃɒkə'latɪə, *foreign* ʃɔkɔlatje (*pl. same*)/ *n.* L19. [Fr., f. as CHOCOLATE: see -IER.] A maker or seller of chocolate.

chocolaty *a.* var. of CHOCOLATEY.

Choctaw /'tʃɒktɔː/ *n.* & *a.* E18. [Choctaw *čahta*.] **A** *n.* Pl. **-s**, same. **1** A member of a Muskogean Indian people originally inhabiting Mississippi and Alabama; the language of this people. E18. **b** Used as a type of an unknown or difficult language. *colloq.* M19. **2** *Skating.* A step from either edge of the skate to the other edge on the other foot in an opposite direction. Cf. MOHAWK *n.* 2. L19. **B** *attrib.* or as *adj.* Of or pertaining to the Choctaws or their language. M18.

choenix /'kiːnɪks/ *n.* E17. [Late L f. Gk *khoinix*.] *Gk Hist.* A dry measure equal to 1 quart or 1½ pints imperial measure.

choga /'tʃəʊgə/ *n.* M19. [Urdu *chogha*, *-ā* f. Pers. *čūḳā*.] A loose Afghan garment with long sleeves.

choice /tʃɔɪs/ *n.* ME. [OFr. *chois* (mod. *choix*) f. *choisir* choose, f. Proto-Gallo-Romance f. Gmc base of CHOOSE.] **1** Choosing, deciding between possibilities; a necessity to choose, a selection. ME. 2 The power, right, or faculty of choosing; option. ME. 3 A person or thing (to be) specially chosen or selected; *the* élite; *the* best *of* a group etc.; *the* pick. LME. 4 Variety and abundance to choose from; a scope or field of possibilities. L16. b An abundant and well-chosen supply. L16. †5 Care in choosing, judgement, discrimination. L16–M18. †6 Special value, estimation. *rare* (Shakes.). Only in E17. 7 An alternative. L18.

1 J. R. GREEN With this body too . . lay the choice of all future Protectors. R. L. STEVENSON At breakfast we had a choice between tea and coffee. J. BUCHAN I had before me a choice of routes, and I chose a ridge. A. LURIE You have already made your choices, taken the significant moral actions of your life. 2 E. W. LANE I have given thee thy choice of the Manner in which thou wilt die. 3 MILTON The flower and choice of many Provinces. DRYDEN For me, the Wilds and Deserts are my Choice. 4 E. HEATH Shops stocked with an immense choice of goods. 5 BACON They were collected with Iudgement, and Choice. 6 SHAKES. *All's Well* This ring he holds In most rich choice. 7 W. PALEY Death or conversion was the only choice offered to idolaters. J. D. SALINGER I didn't have any goddam choice except to leave.

Phrases: **by choice, for choice** preferably. **from choice** willingly, voluntarily. **have no choice** have no alternative. HOBSON'S CHOICE. **make** or **take one's choice** decide between possibilities. *spoilt for choice*: see SPOIL *v.*

choice /tʃɔɪs/ *a.* ME. [f. the n.] 1 Worthy of being chosen; of picked quality, select; exquisite; especially fine. ME. 2 Carefully chosen; (esp. of words) apt, appropriate. L16. 3 Careful in choosing; discriminative; making much *of*. *obs.* exc. *dial.* E17.

1 POPE In a sea of folly toss'd, My choicest Hours of Life are lost. 3 JER. TAYLOR He that is choice of his time, will also be choice of his company and choice of his actions.

choicely *adv.* LME. **choiceness** *n.* M17.

choil /tʃɔɪl/ *n.* L19. [Origin unkn.] The indentation in a knife where the edge of the blade adjoins the tang; the point at which the cutting edge ends.

choir /ˈkwaɪə/ *n.* & *v.* Also (*arch.*, earlier) **quire**. ME. [OFr. *quer* (mod. *choeur*) f. L *chorus*; sp. w. assim. to Fr. & L introduced 17.] A *n.* 1 An organized body of singers performing or leading in the musical parts of a church service. ME. 2 That part of a church appropriated to singers; *esp.* the chancel of a cathedral, minster, or large church. ME. 3 Any company of singers, esp. an organized body performing at concerts etc., a choral society; a company of singing birds, angels, etc.; *gen.* a band or collection of similar persons or things. LME. b A band of dancers or dancers and singers in non-Christian religious festivals etc. Cf. CHORUS *n.* 1b. M17. 4 (The players of) a group of musical instruments of the same class in an orchestra. E20.

Phrases: ritual choir: see RITUAL *a. ruler of the choir*: see RULER *n.*

Comb.: **choirboy** a boy who sings in a choir, esp. an ecclesiastical choir; **choirman** a man who sings in a choir; **choirmaster** the conductor of a choir; **choir nun** a nun professed to perform choir offices; **choir office** a divine service said or sung by a choir; **choir organ** [alt. of *chair organ* s.v. CHAIR *n.*[1]] the softest of three parts making up a large compound organ, with the lowest of three keyboards; **choir practice** the regular rehearsal of set pieces of music by a choir; **choir school** a school for choirboys (and other pupils) maintained by a cathedral etc.; **choir sister** = *choir nun* above; **choir-stall** a fixed seat in the choir of a church etc.

B *v.i.* & *t.* Sing as a choir. *poet. rare.* L16.

choired *a.* (*rare*) assembled in a choir; sung in chorus: L18.

choise /tʃɔɪs, -z/ *v.t.* & *i.* Long *obs.* exc. *Sc.* E16. [Alt. of CHOOSE, prob. through assim. to Fr. forms.] = CHOOSE.

choisya /ˈʃwɑːzɪə/ *n.* M19. [mod.L, f. M. J. D. *Choisy* (1799–1859), Swiss botanist: see -A[1].] A white-flowered evergreen shrub of the genus *Choisya*, of the rue family, native to Mexico and Arizona; *esp.* Mexican orange, *C. ternata.*

choke /tʃəʊk/ *n.*[1] *obs.* exc. *dial.* Also (*Sc.*) **chowk** /tʃaʊk/. ME. [Prob. var. of CHEEK *n.*; perh. also infl. by ON *kjálki* jawbone.] The fleshy part around and under the jaw; in *pl.*, the chops.

choke /tʃəʊk/ *n.*[2] E16. [f. the vb.] 1 A thing which chokes. In *pl.* formerly also, quinsy. E16. †2 A block to progress, an obstruction. L17–E18. 3 [Perh. infl. by ending of ARTICHOKE.] The central part of an artichoke. L17. 4 A constriction; *esp.* a narrowed part of a gun bore etc. M18. 5 (The sound produced by) the action of choking. M19. 6 *Electr.* A high-inductance coil which serves to smooth variations or change the phase of an alternating voltage applied to it. E20. 7 A valve in the air intake of a carburettor serving esp. to provide a richer mixture for engine starting. E20.

choke /tʃəʊk/ *v.* Also †**choak**. ME. [Aphet. f. late OE *āċēocian*, f. as A-[1] + CHEEK *n.*] I *v.t.* 1 Stop the breath of; suffocate, temporarily or finally, by squeezing the throat, blocking it up, or (of water, smoke, etc.) being unbreathable; (of emotion etc.) render speechless. ME. 2 Smother, kill (a plant, fire, etc.) by deprivation of light, air, etc.; stop the vibration of (a cymbal); *fig.* suppress (feelings, aspirations, etc.). LME †b Silence (an opponent) by an argument. M16–M17. 3 Block up (or *up*) wholly or partly; constrict (a tube) by narrowing part of it; obstruct (a channel) with sand, debris, etc. E17. 4 Fill chock-full (*lit.* & *fig.*). E18. 5 Stop (a machine or its action) by clogging or jamming; chock. E18. 6 Fit tightly *in*, ram *in*. M18. 7 Close the choke of (an internal-combustion engine, a vehicle). M20. II *v.i.* 8 Suffer a temporary or permanent stoppage of breath; become speechless through emotion etc. LME. 9 Undergo smothering, suppression, blockage, or obstruction. L16.

With advs. in specialized senses: **choke back** conceal (emotion etc.) with difficulty. **choke down** swallow (food) with difficulty; restrain oneself with an effort from uttering (words etc.). **choke off** *colloq.* stop (a person, an attempt, etc.), esp. forcibly; dissuade, discourage, rebuke.

Comb.: **choke-berry** (the red, black, or purple astringent fruit of) a N. American shrub of the genus *Aronia*, of the rose family; **choke-cherry** (the astringent cherry of) a N. American tree, *Prunus virginiana*; **choke-coil** = CHOKE *n.*[2] 6; **choke-cymbal**: equipped or able to be rapidly damped; **choke-damp** asphyxiating gas, largely carbon dioxide, accumulated in a mine, well, etc.; **choke-pear** (now *rare* or *obs.*) a hard or unpalatable pear; *fig.* something hard to accept, a difficulty; **choke-weed** a weed which chokes other plants, esp. (formerly) broomrape; **choking coil** = CHOKE *n.*[2] 6.

chokingly *adv.* in a choking manner, so as to choke E17.

choke *adv.* var. of CHOCK *adv.*

choke-full *a.* var. of CHOCK-FULL.

choker /ˈtʃəʊkə/ *n.* Also †**choaker**. M16. [f. CHOKE *v.* + -ER[1].] 1 A person who or thing which chokes. M16. 2 A clerical or other high collar. *colloq.* M19. 3 A close-fitting necklace. E20. 4 A noose of wire rope etc. tied round a log for hauling it. E20.

chokey *n.*, *a.* vars. of CHOKY *n.*, *a.*

chokidar /ˈtʃəʊkɪdɑː/ *n.* Also **chauk-**, **chowk-**, /ˈtʃaʊk-/. E17. [Urdu *chaukīdār*, f. Hind. *caukī* CHOKY *n.* + Urdu & Pers. *-dār* keeper.] In the Indian subcontinent: a watchman.

choko *n.* var. of CHOCHO.

chokra /ˈtʃəʊkrə/ *n.* L19. [Hind. *chokrā.*] In the Indian subcontinent: a boy, *esp.* one employed as a household or regimental servant.

choky /ˈtʃəʊki/ *n.* Also **chokey**; (in sense 1) **chauki** /ˈtʃaʊki/. E17. [Hindi *caukī*: in sense 2 infl. by CHOKE *v.* etc.] 1 In the Indian subcontinent: a custom or toll station; a station for horses etc.; a police station, a lock-up. E17. 2 Prison, imprisonment. *slang.* L19.

choky /ˈtʃəʊki/ *a.* Also †**choaky**; **chokey**. L16. [f. CHOKE *v.* + -Y[1].] 1 Apt to cause choking. L16. 2 Liable to or afflicted with choking. M19.

chokiness *n.* M19.

chol- *comb. form* see CHOLE-.

chola *n.* see CHOLO.

cholate /ˈkəʊleɪt, ˈkɒl-/ *n.* M19. [f. CHOLIC + -ATE[1].] *Biochem.* A salt or ester of cholic acid.

chole- /ˈkɒli/ *comb. form* of Gk *kholē* bile, gall. Bef. a vowel **chol-**.

cholagogue *n.* [Gk *kholagōgos* adj., f. *agōgos* leading, eliciting] a medicine supposed to promote the flow of bile from the gall bladder L17. **cholangi'ography** *n.* radiological examination of the bile ducts M20. **cholan'gitis** *n.* inflammation of the bile ducts L19. ˌ**cholecal'ciferol** *n.* (*Biochem.*) vitamin D_3, a compound related to calciferol, formed in the skin by ultraviolet light and present in egg yolk, liver, and fish-liver oils M20. †**choledoch** *a.* [Gk *dokhos* containing, receiving] conveying or containing bile L17–M19. **choledo'chotomy** *n.* (an instance of) surgical opening of the bile duct draining into the duodenum L19. **choleli'thiasis** *n.*, pl. **-ases** /-əsiːz/, the formation of gallstones L19.

cholecyst- /ˈkɒlɪsɪst/ *comb. form* of mod.L *cholecystis* gall bladder: see prec., CYST.

cholecy'stectomy *n.* (an instance of) surgical removal of the gall bladder L19. **cholecy'stitis** *n.* inflammation of the gall bladder M19. **cholecy'stography** *n.* radiological examination of the gall bladder E20. **cholecy'stotomy** *n.* (an instance of) surgical incision into the gall bladder L19.

cholent /ˈtʃɒl(ə)nt, ˈʃɒ-/ *n.* M20. [Yiddish *tscholnt*. Cf. SCHALET.] A Jewish Sabbath dish of slowly baked meat and vegetables, prepared on a Friday and cooked overnight.

choler /ˈkɒlə/ *n.* LME. [(O)Fr. *colère* f. L CHOLERA.] †1 = CHOLERA 2a. LME–M18. 2 *Hist.* Bile, orig. as that one of the four bodily humours believed to cause irascibility. LME. †b Bilious disorder, biliousness. LME–L17. 3 Anger; irascibility, temper. M16.

2 **choler adust** a thick black fluid formerly supposed to be secreted by the suprarenal glands and to cause melancholy; black bile (cf. ATRABILIOUS).

cholera /ˈkɒlərə/ *n.* LME. [L f. Gk *kholera*; in late L taking over the meanings of Gk *kholē* bile, anger.] †1 = CHOLER 2. LME–M16. 2a *gen.* Any of various ailments involving severe vomiting and diarrhoea. Freq. w. distinguishing wd (see below). *obs.* exc. *Hist.* E17. b *spec.* A dangerous infectious disease, endemic in Asia, which is caused by intestinal infection with the bacterium *Vibrio cholerae* and is characterized by severe vomiting and diarrhoea leading to dehydration. E19. 3 *chicken cholera, fowl cholera*, infectious pasteurellosis of fowls (orig. thought to coincide with cholera epidemics). L19.

2 W. distinguishing wds (now largely *obs.* exc. *Hist.*): **Asiatic cholera** = sense 2b. **cholera infantum** /ɪnˈfantəm/ [L = of infants] gastro-enteritis or a similar condition when occurring in a child; also called *summer cholera, summer diarrhoea*, etc. **cholera morbus** /ˈmɔːbəs/ [L = the disease cholera] = sense 2a, b. **epidemic cholera** = sense 2b. **summer cholera** = *cholera infantum* above.

Comb.: **cholera belt** *arch.* a flannel or silk waistband worn to prevent intestinal ailments.

choleraic /kɒləˈreɪɪk/ *a.* pertaining to or of the nature of cholera M19.

choleric /ˈkɒlərɪk/ *a.* ME. [(O)Fr. *cholérique* f. L *cholericus* bilious f. Gk *kholerikos*, f. *kholera* CHOLERA.] 1 *Hist.* Having choler as the predominant humour; bilious. ME. †2 Subject to, involving or causing biliousness. M16–E18. 3 Irascible; hot-tempered. L16. †4 Angry, wrathful. L16–E18. 5 = CHOLERAIC. M19.

cholesterol /kəˈlɛstərɒl/ *n.* L19. [f. CHOLE- + Gk *stereos* stiff + -OL.] *Chem.* A steroid alcohol, $C_{27}H_{45}OH$, which occurs widely in body cells and fluids, has several metabolic functions, and is a major component of atheromas and gallstones.

Also **cholesterin** *n.* (now *rare* or *obs.*) E19.

choli /ˈtʃəʊli/ *n.* E20. [Hind. *colī.*] A woman's short-sleeved bodice of a type worn in the Indian subcontinent.

choliamb /ˈkəʊlɪam(b)/ *n.* M19. [Late L *choliambus* f. Gk *khōliambos*, f. *khōlos* lame: see IAMBUS.] *Pros.* = SCAZON.

choli'ambic *n.* & *a.* (*a*) *n.* (in *pl.*) (poetry written in) this metre; (*b*) *adj.* of or pertaining to the choliamb; written in choliambs: L17.

cholic /ˈkəʊlɪk, ˈkɒl-/ *a.* M19. [Gk *kholikos*: see CHOLE-, -IC.] Biochem. *cholic acid*, a steroid acid, $C_{24}H_{40}O_5$, which is an oxidation product of cholesterol and is present (as salts) in bile.

choline /ˈkəʊliːn, -ɪn/ *n.* Also **-in** /-ɪn/. M19. [f. CHOLE- + -INE[5].] *Biochem.* A strong base, $HO{\cdot}N(CH_3)_3{\cdot}CH_2CH_2OH$, which occurs widely in living organisms as a metabolic intermediate.

choliˈnergic *a.* (*Physiol.*) releasing or involving acetylcholine as a neurotransmitter (cf. ADRENERGIC) M20. **choliˈnesterase** *n.* an enzyme which hydrolyses esters of choline; *esp.* acetylcholinesterase: M20.

cholla /ˈtʃɔɪə/ *n.* *US.* Also **choya**. M19. [Mex. Sp. use of Sp. = skull, head, of unkn. origin.] Any of various opuntias of Mexico and the south-western US.

†cholle *n.*[1], *n.*[2] vars. of JOWL *n.*[2], *n.*[3]

cholo /ˈtʃəʊləʊ/ *n.* Pl. **-os**. Fem. **chola** /ˈtʃəʊlə/. Also **C-**. M19. [Amer. Sp., f. *Chololán*, now *Cholula*, a district of Mexico.] An Indian of Latin America; a mestizo; *US* (freq. *derog.*) a lower-class Mexican.

chomer *n.* var. of HOMER *n.*[1]

chometz *n.* var. of HAMETZ.

chomp /tʃɒmp/ *v.i.* & *t.* M17. [Imit.] = CHAMP *v.* 1, 2.

Chomskyan /ˈtʃɒmskɪən/ *a.* Also **-skian**. M20. [f. *Chomsky* (see below) + -AN.] Of, pertaining to, or characteristic of Noam Avram Chomsky (1928–), US linguistic scholar, or his writings.

chon *n.* see JUN.

chondr- *comb. form* see CHONDRO-

chondrify /ˈkɒndrɪfʌɪ/ *v.t.* L19. [f. Gk *khondros* cartilage + -FY.] Convert into cartilage. Usu. in *pass.*

chondrifiˈcation *n.* L19.

chondrin /ˈkɒndrɪn/ *n.* M19. [f. as prec. + -IN[1].] A substance like gelatin, extracted from cartilage by boiling in water.

chondrite /ˈkɒndrʌɪt/ *n.* M19. [f. Gk *khondros* granule + -ITE[1].] A stony meteorite containing chondrules.

chondritic /kɒnˈdrɪtɪk/ *a.* M19.

chondro- /ˈkɒndrəʊ/ *comb. form* of Gk *khondros* cartilage, granule: see -O-. Bef. a vowel **chondr-**.

chondroˈcranium *n.* the cartilaginous skull of an embryo L19. **chondrocyte** *n.* a cartilage cell E20. **chondroˈgenesis** *n.* cartilage formation L19. **chonˈdroma** *n.*, pl. **-mas**, **-mata** /-mətə/, *Med.* a benign tumour of cartilage M19. **chondrosarˈcoma** *n.*, pl. **-mas**, **-mata** /-mətə/, *Med.* a malignant tumour arising from cartilage cells in bone L19.

chondrodite /ˈkɒndrədʌɪt/ *n.* E19. [f. Gk *khondrōdēs* granular + -ITE[1].] *Min.* A monoclinic basic silicate and fluoride of magnesium and iron, usu. occurring as yellow to dark red prisms or granules.

chondroid /ˈkɒndrɔɪd/ *a.* M19. [f. Gk *khondros* cartilage + -OID.] Resembling cartilage.

chondroitin /kɒnˈdrəʊɪtɪn/ *n.* L19. [f. CHONDRO- + -ITE[1] + -IN[1].] *Biochem.* A polysaccharide which in the form of sulphate esters is a major component of cartilage and other connective tissue.

chondrophore /ˈkɒndrəfɔː/ *n.* L19. [f. CHONDRO- + -PHORE, in sense 2 via mod.L *Chondrophora* (see below).] *Zool.* 1 A pit or projection that supports the internal hinge cartilage of a bivalve mollusc. L19. 2 Any of various pelagic hydroids of the suborder Chondrophora, consisting of polymorphic colonies or single large polyps with a chitinous float and a sail. L20.

chondrostean /kɒnˈdrɒstɪən/ *n.* & *a.* L19. [f. mod.L *Chondrostei* (see below), f. as CHONDRO- + Gk *osteon* bone: see -AN.] **A** *n.* A bony fish of the superorder Chondrostei, which includes the sturgeons and many fossil forms. L19. **B** *adj.* Of or pertaining to the Chondrostei. L19.

chondrule /ˈkɒndruːl/ *n.* L19. [f. CHONDRITE + -ULE.] A spheroidal mineral grain embedded in a meteorite.

choo-choo /ˈtʃuːtʃuː/ *n.* *colloq.* or *nursery.* E20. [Imit.] A railway (steam) train or locomotive.

chook /tʃʊk/ *n.* *Austral.* & *NZ colloq.* M20. [cf. CHUCK *n.*[2], CHUCKY.] A domestic fowl, a chicken.

chookie, -y *ns.* see CHUCKY.

choola /ˈtʃuːlə/ *n.* Also **chula**. E19. [Hind. *cūlhā* f. Skt *culli*.] In the Indian subcontinent: a fireplace, a cooking-place.

choom /tʃʊm/ *n.* *Austral.* & *NZ slang.* E20. [Alt. of CHUM *n.*[1]] An English soldier; an Englishman.

choose /tʃuːz/ *v.* Also (*arch.*) **chuse**. Pa. t. **chose** /tʃəʊz/; pa. pple **chosen** /ˈtʃəʊz(ə)n/, (*arch.* & *non-standard*) **chose**. [OE *ċēosan* = OFris. *kiāsa*, *ziāsa*, OS *kiosan* (Du. *kiezen*), OHG *kiosan*, ON *kjósa*, Goth. *kiusan*, f. Gmc, cogn. w. L *gustare* to taste.] **I** *v.t.* **1** Take by preference out of all that are available; select, pick (*out*); (w. compl.) select as. OE. **2** Decide *to do* something (rather than something else); think fit *to do*; be determined *to do*. ME. **3** Wish to have, want. *obs.* exc. *dial.* M18.

1 S. FOOTE Have unanimously chosen you Mayor. A. L. ROWSE Sir Thomas Arundell, who chose out .. this spot. D. LODGE The Poles did not choose .. the political system under which they live. 2 AV *Heb.* 9:25 Chusing rather to suffer affliction with the people of God, then to enioy the pleasures of sinne for a season. D. BOGARDE She .. didn't hear him. Or chose not to. 3 G. COLMAN Do you chuse any refreshment, Sir?

II *v.i.* **4** Make a selection; exercise choice (*between*, *from*). ME. **5** Do as one likes, take one's own way. *obs.* or *dial.* LME.

4 E. F. BENSON She knew that she must act in one way or in another way, and she had to choose.

Phrases: **cannot choose** *arch.* has or have no alternative (*but*). *choose ends*: see END *n.* **nothing to choose between** no difference between. *pick and choose*: see PICK *v.*[1]

¶ Formerly also with weak inflections.

chooser *n.* (*a*) *gen.* a person who chooses; †(*b*) *spec.* an elector: LME. **choosingly** *adv.* (*rare*) by choice M17.

choosy /ˈtʃuːzi/ *a.* *colloq.* Also **-sey**. M19. [f. prec. + -Y[1].] Particular in one's choice, fastidious.

choosiness *n.* M20.

chop /tʃɒp/ *n.*[1] LME. [f. CHOP *v.*[1]] **1** An act of chopping; a cutting stroke made with an axe or similar implement. LME. **b** A short sharp downward blow or stroke in boxing, cricket, tennis, etc. L19. **c** *sing.* & (usu.) in *pl.* A wood-chopping contest. *Austral.* & *NZ.* E20. **2** A piece chopped off; *spec.* a thick slice of meat (esp. pork or lamb) usu. including a rib. LME. **†3** A fissure, cleft, crack; a chap in the skin. L16–M19. **4** A broken motion of waves, usu. due to the action of the wind against the tide; choppiness. M19.

1 **the chop** *slang* being killed or dismissed; sudden cancellation (of a project etc.). **b** KARATE-*chop*. 2 *chump chop*, *loin chop*, etc. *Maintenon chop*: see MAINTENON 1.

Comb.: **chop-house** a (cheap) restaurant.

chop /tʃɒp/ *n.*[2] LME. [Var. of CHAP *n.*[2]] Usu. in *pl.* **1** = CHAP *n.*[2] 1, 2. LME. **†2** (A name for) a fat-faced person. L16–E17. **3** The entrance or opening of a channel, valley, etc. M17.

1 *lick one's chops*: see LICK *v.* 2 SHAKES. *1 Hen. IV*: I'll hang you for going. . . You will, chops? 3 **Chops of the Channel** the entrance from the Atlantic Ocean to the English Channel.

Comb.: **chop-fallen** *a.* = *chap-fallen* s.v. CHAP *n.*[2]

chop /tʃɒp/ *n.*[3] E17. [Hind. *chāp* stamp, brand.] **1** In the Indian subcontinent, China, etc.: a seal, an official stamp. E17. **2** A licence, permit, etc., validated by an official stamp; an official permit. E17. **3** A trade mark, a brand of goods (orig. in China). E19.

Phrases: **first chop**, **second chop** (*colloq.*) first class, second class. **no chop**, **not much chop** *Austral.* & *NZ colloq.* no good, not up to much.

chop /tʃɒp/ *n.*[4] M17. [f. CHOP *v.*[3]] A snap with the jaws or mouth.

chop /tʃɒp/ *n.*[5] Now *rare* or *dial.* exc. in *chop and change* below. L17. [f. CHOP *v.*[2]] An exchange, a barter.

chop and change a change, an alteration (usu. in *pl.*) (cf. CHOP *v.*[2] 2).

chop /tʃɒp/ *n.*[6] *W. Afr. colloq.* E19. [Origin unkn.: cf. CHOP *v.*[4]] (Prepared and cooked) food. Freq. in *comb.*

chop /tʃɒp/ *v.*[1] Infl. **-pp-**. Pa. t. & pple **-pped**, (*arch.*) **-pt**. LME. [Var. of CHAP *v.*[2]] **1** *v.t.* Cut by one or more quick heavy blows, usu. with an axe or the like. Freq. w. adv. or advb. phr. LME. **b** Strike (a ball, a person, etc.) with a short heavy (esp. edgewise) blow. L19. **2** *v.t.* Cut (*up*) into pieces, mince. LME. **3** *v.i.* Strike a short heavy (esp. edgewise) blow *at* (occas. *on*), orig. in order to cut; cut *through* with such a blow. LME. **b** In cricket, tennis, etc.: hit the ball with a short heavy (esp. edgewise) stroke. L19. **4** *v.t.* & *i.* Thrust, go, or come, (*in*, *into*) with sudden impetus or violence; drop, fall, etc., suddenly. Long *obs.* exc. *dial.* LME. **5** *v.t.* & *i.* Strike, knock. Chiefly *Sc.* Now *rare* or *obs.* LME. **†6** *v.i.* Break open in clefts or fissures; crack; chap. L16–M18. **7** *v.i.* Of the sea, waves, etc.: have a short jerky motion; break in short abrupt waves. Chiefly as *chopping* ppl a. M17.

1 AV *Micah* 3:3 They breake their bones, and chop them in pieces. E. CRISPIN I'll chop off your feet with these shears. **chopping-block** a block for chopping wood etc. on; *fig.* something sustaining continual blows. **chopping-board**: for preparing vegetables etc. on. **b** J. CLAVELL Mura had chopped his [another's] elbow with the side of his hand. 2 E. M. FORSTER Euphemia .. will not .. chop the suet sufficiently small. 3 J. T. STORY Felix .. started chopping at the chain with an axe. 4 SHAKES. *Rich. III* Chop him in the malmsey-butt in the next room. SIR W. SCOTT Lest some passing stranger should chop in between me and the prize. 7 R. H. DANA A stiff breeze .. directly against the course of the current, made an ugly, chopping sea.

chop /tʃɒp/ *v.*[2] Infl. **-pp-**. Pa. t. & pple **-pped**, (*arch.*) **-pt**. LME. [Origin uncertain: perh. var. of CHAP *v.*[1] First evidenced in *chop-church* (see below).] **1** *v.i.* & *t.* Barter, traffic (*with*); exchange by way of commerce. Long *obs.* exc. *dial.* LME. **2** *chop and change*: a *v.phr.i.* Barter, traffic, (*with*). Now chiefly *fig.*, change one's tactics, vacillate, be inconstant. L15. **b** *v.phr.t.* Barter, exchange; *fig.* make different, alter. Now *rare.* M16. **3** *v.t.* *chop logic*, engage in pedantically logical arguments. E16. **†4** *v.i.* Exchange words; answer back. L16–E17. **5** *v.i.* Change, shift; esp. *Naut.* (of the wind) veer *round*, *about*, suddenly. M17.

Comb.: **†chop-church** a trafficker in ecclesiastical benefices; **chop-logic** (*a*) disputatious argument; (*b*) a person who argues pedantically or sophistically.

chop /tʃɒp/ *v.*[3] Infl. **-pp-**. L16. [App. f. CHOP *n.*[2]] **†1** *v.t.* Take into the jaws and eat; snap *up*. L16–E18. **†2** *v.i.* Snap, bite *at*. L16–L17. **3** *v.t.* Of hounds etc.: seize (prey) before it is fairly away from cover. E17.

chop /tʃɒp/ *v.*[4] *t.* & *i.* *W. Afr. colloq.* Infl. **-pp-**. M19. [Origin unkn.: cf. CHOP *n.*[6]] Eat; kill to eat.

chop-chop /tʃɒpˈtʃɒp/ *adv.* & *int.* *Pidgin Eng.* & *colloq.* M19. [An obscure formation rendering Chin. dial. *kuai-kuai*.] Quick, quickly; hurry up!

chopin /ˈtʃɒpɪn/ *n.*[1] Chiefly *Sc.* *obs.* exc. *Hist.* ME. [(O)Fr. *chopine* f. LG *schopen* an old measure = half a pint.] A liquid measure of about one English quart.

chopin *n.*[2] var. of next.

chopine /ˈtʃɒpiːn/ *n.* *arch.* Also **chopin** /-pɪn/. L16. [App. orig. f. Sp. *chapin* = Port. *chapim*, OFr. *chapin*.] A kind of shoe raised above the ground by a cork sole or the like.

Chopinesque /ʃəʊpɪˈnɛsk/ *a.* E20. [f. *Chopin* (see below) + -ESQUE.] *Mus.* Pertaining to or resembling the compositions or pianistic style of the Polish composer Frédéric Chopin (1809–49).

chopper /ˈtʃɒpə/ *n.*[1] L15. [f. CHOP *v.*[2] + -ER[1].] A person who barters or exchanges, *esp.* (formerly) = *chop-church* s.v. CHOP *v.*[2]; a person who chops logic.

chopper /ˈtʃɒpə/ *n.*[2] M16. [f. CHOP *v.*[1] + -ER[1].] **1** A person who chops or cuts into pieces. M16. **b** A person who fells trees; a lumberman. *US colloq.* E19. **2** An implement for chopping, *esp.* a large-bladed short axe; a butcher's cleaver. E19. **3** A device for regularly interrupting a light-beam etc. E20. **4** A machine-gun or -gunner. *US slang.* E20. **5** A helicopter. *colloq.* M20. **6** A motorcycle built or adapted for speed and stripped of inessential parts. *slang* (orig. *US*). M20.

chopper /ˈtʃɒpə/ *n.*[3] L18. [Hind. *chappar.*] In the Indian subcontinent: a thatched roof.
Comb.: **chopper-cot** a camp-bed with curtains.
choppered *a.* thatched E19.

chopping /ˈtʃɒpɪŋ/ *a.* Now *rare* or *obs.* M16. [f. CHOP *v.*[1] + -ING[2].] Big and vigorous; strapping; (of a baby) bouncing.

choppy /ˈtʃɒpi/ *a.*[1] E17. [f. CHOP *n.*[1] + -Y[1].] 1 = CHAPPY *a. rare.* E17. 2 Of the sea etc.: breaking in short abrupt waves; giving a short jerky motion to things floating. M19.
choppiness *n.* L19.

choppy /ˈtʃɒpi/ *a.*[2] M19. [f. CHOP *v.*[1] + -Y[1].] Liable to change (like the wind); *fig.* unstable, vacillating.

chopstick /ˈtʃɒpstɪk/ *n.* L17. [f. Pidgin Eng. *chop* quick (cf. CHOP-CHOP) + STICK *n.*[1], rendering Chin. dial. *kuaìzi* lit. 'nimble ones'.] 1 Either of a pair of sticks of wood, ivory, etc., held in one hand, used by the Chinese etc. to lift food to the mouth. L17. 2 In *pl.* A simple tune for the piano, played with the forefinger of each hand. L19.

chopsuey /tʃɒpˈsuːi/ *n.* L19. [Chin. (Cantonese) *tsaâp suì* mixed bits.] A Chinese dish of pieces of meat or chicken fried with rice, onions, etc., often made with leftover food.

chopt *v.*[1], *v.*[2] pa. t. & pple: see CHOP *v.*[1], *v.*[2]

choragium /kɒˈreɪdʒɪəm/ *n. rare.* Pl. **-ia** /-ɪə/. L17. [L f. Gk *khorēg(e)ion* place where a chorus was trained, f. as next.] A dancing-ground.

choragus /kɒˈreɪgəs/ *n.* Also **-regus**. Pl. **-gi** /-gʌɪ, -giː/. E17. [L f. Gk *khoragos*, *-ēgos*, f. *khoros* CHORUS *n.* + *agein* to lead.] 1 A functionary at Oxford University orig. appointed to supervise the practice of music. E17. 2 Chiefly *Gk Hist.* The leader of a chorus, or of any group; *spec.* at Athens, a person who defrayed the cost of bringing out a chorus. E17.
choragic /-ˈradʒɪk, -ˈreɪdʒɪk/ *a.* of or pertaining to a choragus M18.

choral *n.* var. of CHORALE.

choral /ˈkɔːr(ə)l/ *a.* L16. [med.L *choralis*, f. L CHORUS *n.*: see -AL[1].] 1 Of or belonging to a choir; sung by a choir. L16. 2 Of, belonging to, or of the nature of a chorus; sung in chorus; containing a chorus or choruses. M17. b Of poetry, drama, etc.: said or read by a group of voices. M20. 3 *Gk Hist.* Pertaining to or forming a chorus as in ancient Greek religious festivals. M17.
Special collocations: *Choral Ode*: see ODE I. **choral service** a religious service with canticles, anthems, etc., sung in chorus (also occas. with the versicles and responses being chanted). **choral society** a society of people interested in performing choral music. *vicar choral*: see VICAR *n.* 4.
choralism *n.* choral composition; choral rendering and technique: E20. **choralist** *n.* a person who sings in a chorus M19. **chorally** *adv.* L18.

chorale /kɒˈrɑːl/ *n.* Also **-ral**. M19. [G *Choral(gesang)* tr. med.L *cantus choralis.*] 1 (A metrical hymn to) a simple tune usu. sung or played in unison, orig. in the Lutheran Church; the harmonized form of this. M19. 2 A group of singers. M20.
Comb.: **chorale prelude** an organ piece based on a chorale.

Chorasmian /kɒˈrazmɪən/ *a. poet.* E19. [f. Gk *Khorasmioi* (pl.) name of a tribe of Sogdiana + -AN.] Of, pertaining to, or designating a desert land south of the Aral Sea and about the lower course of the Oxus.

chord /kɔːd/ *n.*[1] Also †**cord**. ME. [Aphet. f. ACCORD *n.*, later infl. by next.] †1 Agreement, reconciliation; an agreement, a peace treaty. Only in ME. †2 = ACCORD *n.* 4. LME–M17. †3 *Mus.* A concord; in *pl.*, the notes added to a bass to make up a chord (sense 4). L16–M18. 4 *Mus.* A group of notes sounded usu. together, combined according to some system. M18.
4 **common chord** any note with its major or minor third and perfect fifth. *supplemental chord*: see SUPPLEMENTAL *a.*

chord /kɔːd/ *n.*[2] M16. [Refash. of CORD *n.*[1] after L *chorda.*] 1 *Anat.* = CORD *n.*[1] 3, esp. in *spinal chord*, *vocal chord*. M16. 2 A straight line joining the extremities of an arc. Cf. earlier CORD *n.*[1] 5. L16. b *Aeronaut.* The width of an aerofoil from leading to trailing edge. E20. †3 = CORD *n.*[1] I. M17–E19. 4 The string of a harp or other instrument. Chiefly *poet.* or *fig.* M17. 5 *Engin.* Either of the two principal members of the truss of a bridge. L19.
4 **strike a chord** evoke some reaction in a person. **touch the right chord** appeal skilfully to emotion; evoke sympathy.

chord /kɔːd/ *v.i. rare.* M19. [Prob. f. CHORD *n.*[1], but perh. var. of CORD *v.*[2]] Form a chord (*with*); harmonize.
chording *n.* the playing, singing, or arrangement of chords M19.

chorda /ˈkɔːdə/ *n.* Pl. **-dae** /-diː/. E19. [L.] *Anat.* = CORD *n.*[1] 3.
chorda tendinea /tɛnˈdɪnɪə/, pl. **-neae** /-nɪiː/, [mod.L = tendinous cord] any of the fine cords attaching the borders of the mitral and tricuspid valves of the heart to the papillary muscles.

chordal /ˈkɔːd(ə)l/ *a.* E17. [f. CHORD *n.*[1] or *n.*[2]: see -AL[1].] Relating to, consisting of or the nature of, a chord or chords.

chordate /ˈkɔːdeɪt/ *a.* & *n.* L19. [f. mod.L *Chordata*, f. L CHORDA: see -ATE[1].] *Zool.* A *adj.* Of, pertaining to, or characteristic of the phylum Chordata of animals which possess a notochord (for at least some part of their lives). L19. B *n.* A member of this phylum, including all vertebrates, cephalochordates (lancelets), and (usu.) urochordates. E20.

chorded /ˈkɔːdɪd/ *a.* L17. [f. CHORD *n.*[1], *n.*[2], *v.* see -ED[2], -ED[1].] Having chords; combined in chords, in harmony.

chordee /ˈkɔːdiː/ *n.* E18. [Fr. (*chaudepisse*) *cordée* corded (urethral discharge).] *Med.* Abnormal downward curvature of the erect penis.

chordophone /ˈkɔːdəfəʊn/ *n.* M20. [f. as next + -PHONE.] Any musical instrument with strings.

chordotonal /kɔːdəʊˈtəʊn(ə)l/ *a.* L19. [f. CHORD *n.*[2] + -O- + TONAL *a.*] *Zool.* Of sense-organs in insects: responsive to mechanical vibrations such as sound and bodily movements.

chore /kɔː/ *n.*[1] Long *obs.* exc. *dial.* OE. [L CHORUS *n.*. Cf. CORE *n.*[2]] †1 = CHOIR *n.* 2. OE–M17. 2 A band, a company; a group. OE. †3 A company of dancers or singers; a dance, a chorus. LME–L17.

chore /tʃɔː/ *n.*[2] & *v.* Orig. *dial.* & *US.* M18. [Unexpl. var. of CHAR *n.*[1]] A *n.* A small piece of domestic work (freq. in *pl.*); an odd job; a recurrent, routine, or tedious task. M18. B *v.i.* Do household work etc.; perform routine tasks. L18.
Comb.: **chore-boy** *N. Amer.*: employed to do odd jobs.

-chore /kɔː/ *suff.* [f. Gk *khōrein* to spread.] *Bot.* Forming ns. denoting plants whose seeds are dispersed in a particular way, as *anemochore*, *hydrochore*.

chorea /kɒˈrɪə/ *n.* L17. [L f. Gk *khoreia* dance.] *Med.* Jerky involuntary movements; a disease with symptoms of this kind.
HUNTINGTON'*s chorea*. SYDENHAM'S CHOREA.
choreal *a.* = CHOREIC *a.*[1] M19. **choreic** /kɒˈrɪɪk/ *a.*[1] pertaining to or affected with chorea L19. **choreiform** /kɒˈrɪɪfɔːm/ *a.* resembling the symptoms of chorea L19.

choree /kɒˈriː, ˈkɔːriː/ *n. rare.* L16. [Fr. *chorée* f. L *choreus* f. Gk *khoreios* pertaining to a dance.] = TROCHEE.
choˈreic *a.*[2] characterized by trochees L19.

choregraph, **choregrapher** *ns.*, etc., see CHOREOGRAPH *n.* etc.

choregus *n.* var. of CHORAGUS.

choregy /kɒˈriːdʒi, ˈkɒrɪdʒi/ *n.* M19. [Gk *khorēgia*, f. *khorēgos* CHORAGUS: see -Y[3].] *Gk Hist.* The function or position of a choragus in ancient Athens.

choreograph /ˈkɒrɪəgrɑːf/ *n. rare.* Also **choregraph** /ˈkɒrɪgrɑːf/. L19. [f. as CHOREOGRAPHY + Gk *graphos* writer.] = CHOREOGRAPHER.

choreograph /ˈkɒrɪəgrɑːf/ *v.* M20. [Back-form. f. next.] 1 *v.t.* Compose the choreography of (a ballet etc.); *fig.* arrange or combine harmoniously or for maximum effect. M20. 2 *v.i.* Compose choreography. M20.

choreographer /kɒrɪˈɒgrəfə/ *n.* Also **choregrapher** /kɒˈrɛgrəfə/. L19. [f. as next: see -GRAPHER.] The creator or arranger of a ballet, stage dance, etc.; a person skilled in choreography.

choreographic /kɒrɪəˈgrafɪk/ *a.* Also **choregraphic** /kɒrɪˈgrafɪk/. E19. [f. as next + -GRAPHIC.] 1 Of or pertaining to dancing. E19. 2 Of or pertaining to choreography or the devising of ballet or stage dances. E20.
choreographical *a.* L19. **choreographically** *adv.* E20.

choreography /kɒrɪˈɒgrəfi/ *n.* Also **choregraphy** /kɒˈrɛgrəfi/. L18. [f. Gk *khoreia* choral dancing to music + -OGRAPHY.] 1 The written notation of dancing, choreology. L18. 2 The art of dancing. M19. 3 The creation or arrangement of a ballet or stage dance; the devising of steps and figures for a ballet or stage dance; the steps and figures of a particular ballet etc. E20.
choreographist *n.* = CHOREOGRAPHER L19.

choreology /kɒrɪˈɒlədʒi/ *n.* M20. [f. as prec. + -OLOGY.] The written notation of dancing; the study and description of the movements of dancing.

chorepiscopus /kɔːrɪˈpɪskəpəs/ *n.* Pl. **-pi** /-pʌɪ, -piː/. L16. [Late L f. Gk *khōrepiskopos*, f. *khōra*, *khōros* country + *episkopos* BISHOP *n.*] *Eccl. Hist.* A country or suffragan bishop of the early Church.
chorepiscopal *a.* of or pertaining to a chorepiscopus M19.

chori- /ˈkɔːri, ˈkɒri/ *comb. form* of Gk *khōri*, *khōris* asunder, apart, used in *Bot.*
choriˈpetalous *a.* having separate petals L19.

choriamb /ˈkɒrɪam(b)/ *n.* Also in L form **choriambus** /kɒrɪˈambəs/, pl. **-bi** /-bʌɪ/. L18. [Late L *choriambus*, f. as CHOREE + IAMB.] *Pros.* A metrical foot consisting of two short syllables between two long ones.
choriˈambic *n.* & *a.* [late L *choriambicus*] (*a*) *n.* a choriambic verse, a choriamb; (*b*) *adj.* consisting of a choriamb, containing choriambs: E17.

choric /ˈkɒrɪk, ˈkɔːrɪk/ *n.* & *a.* E19. [Late L *choricus* f. Gk *khorikos*, f. *khoros* CHORUS *n.*: see -IC. As n. perh. after *heroics* etc.] A *n.* In *pl.* The verses of a (Greek) chorus. *rare.* E19. B *adj.* 1 Of, pertaining to, or resembling the chorus in a classical Greek play. M19. 2 Pertaining to a choir or chorus; choral. *rare.* L19.
chorically *adv.* M20.

chorine /ˈkɔːriːn/ *n.* Orig. & chiefly *US.* E20. [f. CHORUS *n.* + -INE[3].] A chorus girl.

chorio- /ˈkɔːrɪəʊ, ˈkɒrɪəʊ/ *comb. form* of CHORION, and also occas. of CHOROID: see -O-.
chorio-allanˈtoic *a.* of or pertaining to the chorio-allantois E20. **chorio-aˈllantois** *n.* the chorion and allantois fused together M20. **choriocarciˈnoma** *n.*, pl. **-mas**, **-mata** /-mətə/, = *chorionepithelioma* s.v. CHORION *n.* E20. **chorioretiˈnitis** *n.* = CHOROIDORETINITIS L19.

chorion /ˈkɔːrɪən/ *n.* M16. [Gk *khorion.*] 1 *Anat.* The outermost membrane enveloping the foetus in mammals, birds, and reptiles. M16. 2 *Entomol.* The outer covering or shell of an insect's egg. M19.
Comb.: **chorionepithelioma**, pl. **-mas**, **-mata** /-mətə/, *Med.* a carcinoma of maternal tissue, originating in the chorion.
choriˈonic *a.* of or pertaining to the chorion; *chorionic villus sampling*, a procedure for obtaining information about a foetus in which a sample of tissue is taken from the villi of the chorion (abbrev. *CVS*): L19.

chorist /ˈkɒrɪst, ˈkɔːrɪst/ *n.* L15. [(O)Fr. *choriste* f. med.L *chorista*, f. as CHORUS *n.* + -IST.] †1 A member of a choir. L15–M18. 2 *Gk Hist.* A member of the chorus in Greek drama. M18. 3 A person who sings in a chorus. M19.

chorister /ˈkɒrɪstə/ *n.* LME. [AN var. of OFr. *cueriste*, f. *quer* CHOIR; refash. in 16 after prec.] A member of a choir, *esp.* a choirboy; *fig.* each of a group of angels, songbirds, etc. Also (*US*), the leader of a choir.

choristership *n.* the office of chorister M16.

chorizo /tʃəˈriːzəʊ/ *n.* Pl. **-os**. M19. [Sp.] A Spanish sausage of which the chief ingredient is pork.

chorizont /kɔːrɪˈzɒnt/ *n.* Also **C-**. Pl. **-tes** /-tiːz/. M19. [Gk *khōrizontes* pl. of pres. pple of *khōrizein* to separate.] *Hist.* A grammarian who ascribed the *Iliad* and the *Odyssey* to different authors; *gen.* anyone ascribing a literary corpus to more than one author.

chorography /kɔːˈrɒgrəfi/ *n.*[1] Now *rare* or *obs.* M16. [Fr. *chorographie* or L *chorographia* f. Gk *khōrographia*, f. *khōra*, *khōros* country, district: see -GRAPHY.] The description and mapping of particular regions or districts; a description or delineation, or the natural configuration and features, of such a region.

¶Taken as intermediate in its scale between *geography* and *topography*.

chorographer *n.* E17. **choroˈgraphic** *a.* L17. **choroˈgraphical** *a.* L16. **choroˈgraphically** *adv.* L16.

chorography /kɔːˈrɒgrəfi/ *n.*[2] Now *rare* or *obs.* E18. [f. Gk *khoros* dance + -GRAPHY.] Dance notation; choreography.

choroid /ˈkɔːrɔɪd, ˈkɒr-/ *n.* & *a.* M17. [Gk *khoroeidēs* adj., for *khorioeidēs*, f. as CHORION + -OID.] *Anat.* A *n.* The pigmented vascular layer of the eyeball, situated between the retina and the sclera. M17.

B *adj.* Resembling the chorion; choroidal. M18.

choroid coat, membrane = CHOROID *n.* **choroid plexus** a network of blood-vessels in each ventricle of the brain.

choˈroidal *a.* of or pertaining to the choroid of the eye or the choroid plexus of the brain L17. **choroiˈditis** *n.* inflammation of the choroid M19.

choroido- /kəˈrɔɪdəʊ/ *comb. form* of prec.: see -O-.

choroidoretiˈnitis *n.* inflammation of the choroid and the retina M19.

chorology /kɔːˈrɒlədʒi/ *n.* L19. [f. Gk *khōra* region + -OLOGY.] (The knowledge of) the geographical distribution of an animal, plant, etc.

choroˈlogical *a.* M19.

choropleth /ˈkɒrəplɛθ/ *n.* M20. [f. as prec. + Gk *plēthos* multitude, quantity.] *Geogr.* A symbol on a choropleth map (see below). Chiefly in *choropleth map*.

Comb.: **choropleth map** a map showing the geographical distribution of a property or quantity other than by isopleths, e.g. where an average value over an area is indicated by the way the area is shaded or coloured or by a symbol within the area.

chorten /ˈtʃɔːt(ə)n/ *n.* L19. [Tib.] = CHAITYA.

chortle /ˈtʃɔːt(ə)l/ *v.* & *n.* L19. [Invented by Lewis Carroll: app. blend of CHUCKLE *v.* and SNORT *v.*[2]] A *v.i.* & *t.* Utter (with) a loud gleeful chuckle; express pleasure or satisfaction in this way. L19. B *n.* A chuckle of pleasure or satisfaction; an act of chortling. E20.

chorus /ˈkɔːrəs/ *n.* M16. [L f. Gk *khoros.*] **1a** A character in a play whose function is to speak the prologue and epilogue and comment upon events. M16. **b** *Gk Hist.* A band of organized singers and dancers in religious festivals and dramatic performances; *esp.* in Attic tragedy, such a group providing a moral and religious commentary upon events; an utterance of such a group. L16. **2** The refrain of a song in which the audience joins the performer in singing; the (repeated) main part of a popular song; a jazz improvisation on this. L16. **3** A band of singers, a choir; *spec.* in opera, oratorio, etc., the body of vocalists (as opp. to the soloists) who sing the choral parts. M17. **b** A group of organized dancers and usu. singers who provide support for the main roles in musical comedy, variety shows, etc. M19. **4** Anything sung by many at once; the simultaneous utterance of sounds by many persons, animals, etc. L17. **5** *Mus.* A composition in several (freq. four) parts each sung by several voices. L17. **6** (The sound produced by) a group of organ-pipes or stops designed to be played together; a compound stop. L18.

1a SHAKES. *Hen. V* Admit me Chorus to this history. **b** *Greek chorus*: see GREEK *a.* **2** G. DAWSON The chorus . . must be nonsense, or how could you expect the company to join in. **3** E. LINKLATER Her mother had been one of a chorus of villagers in Cavalleria Rusticana. **4** ARNOLD BENNETT He disappeared amid a wailing chorus of 'Oh, dad!' G. ORWELL Utter silence except for the chorus of the frogs. *dawn chorus*: see DAWN *n.* **in chorus** in unison, all giving utterance together. **5** *Hallelujah Chorus*: see HALLELUJAH *n.*

Comb.: **chorus girl** a young woman who sings and dances in the chorus of a musical comedy or the like; **chorus-master** the conductor of a chorus or choir.

chorus /ˈkɔːrəs/ *v.* E18. [f. the n.] **1** *v.t.* Provide with a chorus. E18. **2** *v.t.* & *i.* Sing, utter, or speak in chorus. M18.

chose /ʃəʊz/ *n.* LME. [(O)Fr. f. L *causa* matter, affair, thing.] **†1** A thing (as a vague general term). LME–M17. **2** *Law.* A thing, a chattel, a piece of property. L17.

2 chose in action a right enforceable by legal action. **chose in possession** a tangible good capable of being possessed and enjoyed, as a book, item of clothing, etc.

chose *v.* pa. t. & pple: see CHOOSE.

chose jugée /ʃoːz ʒyʒe/ *n. phr.* Pl. **-s -s** (pronounced same). L19. [Fr.] A settled or decided matter; something it is idle to discuss.

chosen /ˈtʃəʊz(ə)n/ *ppl a.* & *n.* ME. [pa. pple of CHOOSE.] Taken by preference, selected, picked out; *spec.* (*Theol.*) elect of God. *the, one's, chosen*, a person or (usu.) people chosen, esp. by God.

chosen people, chosen race the Jews; *loosely* those specially favoured by God.

choses jugées *n. phr.* pl. of CHOSE JUGÉE.

chota /ˈtʃəʊtə/ *a. Anglo-Ind.* E19. [Hind. *choṭā.*] Small, little; younger, junior.

chota hazri /ˈhɑːzri/ [Urdu *hāẓirī* breakfast] a light early breakfast. **chota peg** a small drink of whisky.

chott *n.* var. of SHOTT.

chou /ʃuː, *foreign* ʃu/ *n.* Also **choux** (pronounced same). Pl. **choux**. E18. [Fr. = cabbage f. L *caulis.*] **1** A small round cake of pastry filled with cream etc. E18. **2** A rosette or ornamental knot of ribbon, chiffon, etc., on a woman's hat or dress. L19.

Comb.: **choux pastry** a very light pastry enriched with eggs.

Chou *n.*[2] & *a.* var. of ZHOU.

Chouan /ʃwɑ̃/ *n.* Pl. pronounced same. L18. [Fr., f. 'Jean *Chouan*', an early Chouan leader, who used the cry of the *chouan* (dial.), a kind of owl.] *Fr. Hist.* A member of the irregular forces who maintained a partisan resistance in the west of France against the Republican and Bonapartist governments; a Bourbon partisan.

choucroute /ʃukrut/ *n.* M19. [Fr. f. G dial. *Surkrut* SAUERKRAUT, assim. to Fr. CHOU.] A kind of pickled cabbage.

chouette /ʃuːˈɛt/ *n.* L19. [Fr., lit. 'barn owl'.] A player in a two-handed game (e.g. backgammon, piquet) who plays against a number of others successively or in combination, esp. as a means of enabling three players to compete with one another.

chough /tʃʌf/ *n.* ME. [Prob. imit.] **1** A jackdaw or related bird. Now *rare* exc. as below. ME. **2** A small crow of the genus *Pyrrhocorax*; *spec.* (*a*) the red-legged, red-billed *P. pyrrhocorax* (orig. called *Cornish chough*), which in Britain frequents western cliffs; (*b*) *alpine chough*, a yellow-billed chough, *P. graculus*, inhabiting mountains of Continental Europe and Asia. Also (in full *white-winged chough*), an E. Australian magpie-lark, *Corcorax melanorhamphos*. LME.

choultry /ˈtʃaʊltri/ *n.* E17. [f. Malayalam *cāvaṭi*, Telugu *cāvaḍi.*] In the Indian subcontinent: an open shed used as a travellers' rest-house; the colonnade of a temple; a meeting-house, a court-house.

chou moellier /tʃaʊ ˈmɒlɪə/ *n. phr. Austral.* & *NZ.* E20. [Fr. = marrow-filled cabbage.] = *marrow-stem (kale)* s.v. MARROW *n.*[1]

chouse /tʃaʊs/ *n.* & *v.*[1] *slang* (*obs.* or *arch.*). Also **†chiaus**; **chowse**. E17. [App. var. of CHIAUS *n.*, after a Turk who received hospitality in England after claiming to be a messenger or ambassador of the Sultan.] A *n.* **I†1** A cheat, a swindler. E–M17. **†2** A person easily cheated, a dupe. M17–M18. **3** A trick, a swindle, a sham. E18. **†II 4** = CHIAUS. Only in M17. **B** *v.t.* Dupe, trick, swindle; defraud *of*; cheat *out of*. M17.

chouser *n.* a swindler, a cheat L19.

chouse /tʃaʊs/ *v.*[2]*t. US colloq.* Also **chowse**. E20. [Origin unkn.] Disturb, harry (esp. cattle).

chout /tʃaʊt/ *n.* L17. [Marathi *cauth* a fourth part.] *Hist.* In India, the blackmail of a quarter of the revenue exacted from provinces by the Mahrattas.

choux *n.* see CHOU.

chow /tʃaʊ/ *n.*[1] *Sc.* E19. [Var. of CHEW *n.*: cf. CHAW *n.*[2]] An act of chewing; something for chewing, *esp.* a quid of tobacco.

chow /tʃaʊ/ *n.*[2] L19. [Abbrev. of CHOW-CHOW.] **1** A Chinese. *slang* (chiefly *Austral.*). *derog.* L19. **2** Food. *slang* (orig. *Pidgin English*). L19. **3** A black-tongued dog of a Chinese breed, resembling a Pomeranian and usu. black or brown. L19.

chow /tʃaʊ/ *v.t.* & *i. dial.* (chiefly *Sc.*). LME. [Var. of CHEW *v.*: cf. CHAW *v.*] Chew.

chowchilla /tʃaʊˈtʃɪlə/ *n. Austral.* M20. [Imit. of the birds' calls.] Either of two logrunners of the genus *Orthonyx*, which have stiffened tail feathers and are found in eastern Australia and New Guinea.

chow-chow /ˈtʃaʊtʃaʊ/ *n.* & *a.* L18. [Pidgin Eng., ult. origin unkn.] A *n.* **1** A mixture or medley of food, as mixed pickles; *esp.* a Chinese preserve of orange peel, ginger, etc.; *gen.* (*colloq.*) food. L18. **2** = CHOW *n.*[2] **1**. *Austral. slang. derog.* M19. **3** = CHOW *n.*[2] **3**. L19. **B** *adj.* Miscellaneous, mixed, assorted; (of water) broken, choppy. M19.

chowder /ˈtʃaʊdə/ *n.* & *v.* Orig. & chiefly *N. Amer.* M18. [Origin uncertain: perh. f. Fr. *faire la chaudière* supply a pot etc. for cooking a stew of fish etc. (*chaudière* pot, cauldron).] A *n.* **1** A stew or thick soup of fish, clams, etc. M18. **2** More fully *chowder-party*. A (large) social gathering, freq. held in the open, at which chowder is cooked and served. E19. **B** *v.t.* & *i.* Prepare a chowder (of). M18.

chowderhead /ˈtʃaʊdəhɛd/ *n. colloq.* (chiefly *US*). M19. [Prob. var. of JOLTER-HEAD.] A blockhead, a muddle-headed person.

chowderheaded *a.* stupid, blockheaded E19.

chowk /tʃaʊk/ *n.*[1] M19. [Hind. *cauk.*] In the Indian subcontinent: a city market-place; a main street.

chowk *n.*[2] see CHOKE *n.*[1]

chowkidar *n.* var. of CHOKIDAR.

chow mein /tʃaʊ ˈmeɪn/ *n. phr.* L19. [Chin. *chǎo miàn* fried noodles.] A Chinese dish of fried noodles usu. in a sauce with shredded meat and vegetables.

chowry /ˈtʃaʊri/ *n.* Also **chowrie**. L18. [Hindi *caũrī* f. Skt *camara* (tail of) yak.] A fly-whisk made of hair, feathers, or (orig.) the tail of the Tibetan yak.

chowse *n.* & *v.*[1], *v.*[2] vars. of CHOUSE *n.* & *v.*[1], *v.*[2]

choya *n.* var. of CHOLLA.

chrematistic /kriːməˈtɪstɪk/ *a.* & *n.* M18. [Gk *khrēmatistikos*, f. *khrēmatizein* make money, f. *khrēma*, *-mat-* money: see -IC.] A *adj.* Of, pertaining to, or engaged in the accumulation of wealth. M18. **B** *n.* In *pl.* (treated as *sing.*). The branch of knowledge that deals with wealth; economics. M19.

chrestomathy /krɛˈstɒməθi/ *n.* M19. [Fr. *chrestomathie* or its source Gk *khrēstomatheia*, f. *khrēstos* useful + *-matheia* learning.] A collection of selected passages from an author or authors, *esp.* one compiled to assist in learning a language.

chrestomathic /krɛstə(ʊ)ˈmaθɪk/ *a.* devoted to learning useful things E19.

Chrisake *n.* & *int.* var. of CHRISSAKE.

chrism /ˈkrɪz(ə)m/ *n.* OE. [med.L *crisma*, eccl.L *chrisma*, f. Gk *khrisma*, f. *khriein* anoint.] **1** Oil mingled with balm, consecrated for use as an unguent in the administration of certain sacraments of the Christian Churches; an unguent. OE. **2** = CHRISOM **1**, **2**. OE. **3** A sacramental anointing; unction; *spec.* the ceremony of confirmation, esp. in the Orthodox Church. ME.

chrismal *a.* & *n.* (*a*) *adj.* of or pertaining to chrism; (*b*) *n.* a chrisom or similar cloth; a vessel for holding the chrism: M17. **chrismation** /krɪz'meɪʃ(ə)n/ *n.* (*obs.* exc. *Hist.*) [med.L *chrismatio(n-)*] application of the chrism, sacramental unction M16.

†chrism *v.t.* LME–L18. [med.L *chrismare*, f. as prec.] Anoint with chrism.

chrismatory /'krɪzmət(ə)ri/ *n.* LME. [med.L *chrismatorium*, f. *chrisma*, *-mat-* CHRISM *n.*: see -ORY[1].] *Chr. Ch.* The vessel containing the chrism.

chrismon /'krɪzmən/ *n.* L19. [med.L, f. *Christus* CHRIST + *monogramma* MONOGRAM.] = CHI-*rho*.

chrisom /'krɪz(ə)m/ *n.* ME. [Alt. of CHRISM *n.* through its pop. pronunc. with two syll.] **1** In full *chrisom-cloth*, *-robe*, etc. A child's white robe at Christian baptism, used as a shroud if he or she died within a month. Now *Hist.* ME. **2** In full *chrisom-child*, *-babe*, etc. A child that is less than one month old; a child that died at less than a month, or before baptism; *gen.* an infant, an innocent. ME. **†3** = CHRISM *n.* 1, 3. LME–E18.

Chrissake /'krʌɪseɪk/ *n.* & *int. informal.* Also **Chrisake**. M20. [Repr. a pronunc.] Christ's sake; for Christ's sake! (See next.)

Christ /krʌɪst/ *n.* & *int.* [OE *Crīst* = OS, OHG *Crīst*, *Krīst* f. L *Christus* f. Gk *Khristos*, use as n. of adj. meaning 'anointed', f. *khriein* anoint, tr. Heb. *māšīaḥ* MESSIAH.] **A** *n.* **1** The Messiah or Lord's Anointed of Jewish tradition. OE. **2** (The title, now usu. treated as a name, given to) Jesus of Nazareth, regarded by Christians as the fulfilment of Jewish prophecy. OE. **b** An image or picture representing Jesus. M17. **†3** In the Old Testament [rendering L *christus*]: a divinely appointed ruler or high priest. OE–E17.

Phrases & comb.: *babe in Christ*: see BABE 2. *body of Christ*: see BODY *n.* **Christ's thorn** any of various thorny shrubs popularly supposed to have formed Jesus' crown of thorns; esp. *Ziziphus spina-christi* and *Paliurus spina-christi*, two shrubs of the buckthorn family. **(for) Christ's sake!** *colloq.* expr. exasperation, surprise, impatience, etc. *soldier of Christ*: see SOLDIER *n.* **the Christ-child** Jesus as a child.

B *int.* Expr. surprise, dismay, disbelief, etc. *slang* (freq. considered *offensive*). M18.

¶See also JESUS.

Christed *a.* made one with Christ; made a partaker of Christ's nature: M17. **Christhood** *n.* the state or condition of being Christ, Messiahship LME. **Christless** *a.* without Christ or his spirit M17. **Christlike** *a.* resembling Christ; exhibiting the personal or spiritual qualities of Jesus: L17. **Christlikeness** *n.* L19. **Christly** *a.* (*a*) Christlike; (*b*) *rare* of or pertaining to Christ: OE.

Christadelphian /krɪstə'delfɪən/ *a.* & *n.* M19. [f. late Gk *Khristadelphos* in brotherhood with Christ, f. *Khristos* CHRIST + *adelphos* brother: see -IAN.] Designating or pertaining to, a member of, a religious sect founded in the US, rejecting the Christian doctrine of the Trinity and expecting the second coming of Christ.

Christ-cross /'krɪskrɒs, -krɔːs/ *n.* See also CRISS-CROSS *n.* LME. [f. *Christ's cross*.] **1** The figure of a cross (✠) in front of the alphabet in a hornbook. *obs.* exc. *Hist.* LME. **2** In full *Christ-cross-row*. The alphabet. Now *arch.* & *dial.* M16. **3** The mark of a cross in general; *esp.* one used as a signature by an illiterate. Now *dial.* or *Hist.* E17.

christen /'krɪst(ə)n/ *a.* & *n.* Long *obs.* exc. *dial.* [OE *crīsten* = OS, OHG *kristīn* f. L *christianus* CHRISTIAN *a.*] (A) Christian.

christen /'krɪs(ə)n/ *v.t.* [OE *crīstnian*, f. as prec.] **1** Convert to Christianity; make Christian. Now *obs.* or *arch.* OE. **2** Admit to the Christian Church by baptism; administer baptism to. ME. **3** Give a name to at baptism; name and dedicate (a bell, a ship, etc.) by a ceremony analogous to baptism; *gen.* give a name to. Freq. w. compl.: give as a name at baptism; call by the name of. LME. **†b** Stand as sponsor to at baptism. L15–M17. **4** Use for the first time; soil etc. through use for the first time. *colloq.* E20.

3 P. NORMAN Both of Nanny Belmayne's sons were christened with very long names. Q. CRISP It has now been christened the New End Theatre. A. BLEASDALE He was christened here in this very Church as Patrick.

christener *n.* a person who performs a christening or christenings OE. **christening** *vbl n.* (*a*) the action of the vb; (*b*) an instance of this; a ceremony of baptism: ME.

christendie /'krɪs(ə)ndi/ *n. Sc.* L18. [App. f. CHRISTIANITY, infl. by next.] Christendom.

Christendom /'krɪs(ə)ndəm/ *n.* OE. [f. CHRISTEN *a.* & *n.* + -DOM.] **†1** The state or condition of being a Christian. OE–L17. **†2** The Christian faith or religious system; Christianity. OE–M17. **3** Christians collectively; the Christian Church. OE. **b** The nations professing Christianity collectively; the Christian domain. LME. **†4** Baptism, christening; the giving of a name. ME–L17.

Christer /'krʌɪstə/ *n. N. Amer. slang.* E20. [f. CHRIST + -ER[1].] An excessively zealous, pious, or sanctimonious person.

Christian /'krɪstʃ(ə)n, -tɪən, *in sense 1b also* 'krʌɪstʃ(ə)n/ *n.* E16. [f. the adj.] **1** A member of the religion of Christ; an adherent of Christianity. E16. **b** A member of a particular sect using this name. E19. **2** A person who follows the precepts and example of Christ; a person of genuine piety. E16. **3** A (civilized) human being; a decent, respectable person. Now *colloq.* L16. **4** A variety of pear or plum. Now *rare* or *obs.* M17.

1 *Bible Christian*: see BIBLE. *Liberal Christian*: see LIBERAL *a.* MUSCULAR *Christian.*

Christianlike *a.* & *adv.* (in a manner) proper to or befitting a Christian L16.

Christian /'krɪstʃ(ə)n, -tɪən/ *a.* LME. [L *Christianus*, f. *Christus* CHRIST: see -IAN.] **1** Of a person, community, etc.: believing in, professing, or belonging to the religion of Christ. LME. **2** Of a thing: pertaining to Christ or his religion; of or belonging to Christianity. M16. **3** Showing a character consistent with Christ's teaching; of genuine piety; Christlike. L16. **4** Of or belonging to a Christian or Christians. L16. **5** Civilized, decent. Now *colloq.* L16.

Special collocations & comb.: *Christian antiquity*: see ANTIQUITY 1. (*the*) *Christian Brethren*: see BROTHER *n.* **Christian burial** burial according to the ceremonies of the Christian Church. **Christian Democrat** a member of any of various moderate European political parties having a Roman Catholic base. **Christian Democratic** *a.* designating, of or pertaining to, a party of Christian Democrats. **Christian era**: reckoned from the birth of Jesus. **Christian name** a name given (as) at baptism, a forename, a personal name. **Christian Science** the beliefs and practices of 'The Church of Christ, Scientist', a Christian body founded in the mid 19th cent. by Mary Baker Eddy in New Hampshire, USA, which holds that God and his perfect spiritual creation are the only ultimate reality, and that his law is always available to bring regeneration and healing to humanity. **Christian Scientist** an adherent of Christian Science. **Christian Socialism** a form of socialism, embracing Christianity, arising from an attempt to apply Christian precepts in everyday life. **Christian Socialist** an adherent of Christian Socialism. *Christian year*: see YEAR *n.*[1] 3b. **Court Christian** (*obs.* exc. *Hist.*) an ecclesiastical court.

Christianable *a.* (*colloq.*) [irreg.] fit to be or befitting a Christian L19. **Christianlike** *a.* & *adv.* = CHRISTIANLY L16. **Christianly** *a.* & *adv.* (*a*) *adj.* characteristic of or befitting a Christian; (*b*) *adv.* in a Christianly manner: LME.

Christiania /krɪstɪ'ɑːnɪə/ *n.* Also **c-**. E20. [Former name of Oslo, capital of Norway.] A turn in skiing in which the skis are kept in parallel, used for stopping short.

Christianise *v.* var. of CHRISTIANIZE.

Christianism /'krɪstʃ(ə)nɪz(ə)m, -tɪən-/ *n.* L16. [Fr. *christianisme* or eccl.L *christianismus* f. Gk *khristianismos* Christianity: see -ISM.] **1** Christian belief, Christianity (chiefly when compared with other 'isms'). L16. **2** Christianity of a sort. L17.

Christianity /krɪstɪ'anɪti/ *n.* ME. [OFr. *crestienté* (mod. *chrétienté*), f. *crestien* CHRISTIAN *a.*, assim. to late L *christianitas*: see -ITY.] **†1** = CHRISTENDOM 3. ME–M17. **2** The Christian faith; the doctrines of Christ and his disciples. ME. **3** The state or fact of being Christian; Christian quality or character. ME. **4** *Hist.* Ecclesiastical jurisdiction. L16.

3 MUSCULAR *Christianity*.

Christianize /'krɪstʃənʌɪz, -tɪən-/ *v.* Also **-ise**. M16. [f. CHRISTIAN *a.* + -IZE.] **1** *v.t.* Make Christian; give a Christian character to. M16. **2** *v.i.* Become Christian; act according to Christianity. M16.

Christiani'zation *n.* L18.

Christiano- /krɪstɪ'ɑːnəʊ/ *comb. form* of L *Christianus* CHRISTIAN *a.*: see -O-.

Christie /'krɪsti/ *n.* Also **-ty**. E20. [Abbrev.] = CHRISTIANIA.

Christingle /'krɪstɪŋg(ə)l/ *n.* M20. [Prob. alt. of G *Christkindl* Christmas present, (colloq.) Christ-child, after KRISS KRINGLE.] *Chr. Ch.* A lighted candle set in an orange, symbolizing Christ as the light of the world, given to each child at a children's service (the *Christingle service*) usu. held in Advent.

¶The custom is adopted from the Moravian Church.

Christmas /'krɪsməs/ *n.* & *int.* [OE *Crīstes mæsse* the mass of Christ.] **A** *n.* The festival of Christ's birth celebrated by most Christian Churches on 25 December, devoted esp. to family reunion and jollification; the season around this date. OE.

Father Christmas Santa Claus; a jolly old man dressed in red, personifying Christmas festivities. *merry Christmas*: see MERRY *a.* *white Christmas*: see WHITE *a.*

Comb.: **Christmas-box** a small present or gratuity given at Christmas esp. to employees of firms providing regular services; **Christmas bush** (chiefly *Austral.*) any of various shrubs; esp. *Ceratopetalum gummiferum*, of the family Cunoniaceae, which bears decorative fruit at Christmas-time; **Christmas card** a greetings card sent at or just before Christmas; *Christmas carol*: see CAROL *n.* 4; **Christmas Day** 25 December; **Christmas Eve** (the evening of) 24 December; **Christmas flower** any of various plants flowering at Christmas-time; *esp.* = *Christmas rose* below; **Christmas present** a gift given at Christmas; **Christmas pudding** a plum pudding eaten at Christmas; **Christmas rose** a hellebore, *Helleborus niger*, bearing white flowers in winter; **Christmas shopping**: for Christmas presents and seasonal fare; **Christmas stocking**: hung up by children on Christmas Eve for Father Christmas to fill with presents; **Christmas-tide**, **-time** the period of some days around 25 December; **Christmas tree** (*a*) an evergreen tree (usu. a Norway spruce) or artificial tree set up indoors or in the open at Christmas-time and hung with lights, presents, baubles, etc.; (*b*) *Austral.* & *NZ*, any of various trees or shrubs blooming at Christmas-time; *esp.* = POHUTUKAWA; (*c*) a device or structure suggesting a Christmas tree in appearance; *spec.* a valve manifold situated on the casing of an oil or gas well (= TREE *n.* 7(d)).

B *int.* [Alt. of *Christ*.] Expr. surprise, dismay, exasperation, etc. Freq. as *Jiminy Christmas*. L19.

¶Cf. XMAS.

Christmassy *a.* (*colloq.*) characteristic of or suitable for Christmas (festivities) L19.

Christmas /'krɪsməs/ *v. colloq.* Infl. **-s-**, **-ss-**. L16. [f. the n.] **†1** *v.t.* Provide with Christmas cheer. *rare*. Only in L16. **2** *v.i.* Celebrate Christmas. E19.

Christmas disease /'krɪsməs dɪ,ziːz/ *n. phr.* M20. [f. Stephen *Christmas*, 20th-cent. Eng. sufferer from the disease.] *Med.* = HAEMOPHILIA B.

Christo- /'krɪstəʊ/ *comb. form* of L *Christus* or Gk *Khristos* CHRIST: see -O-.

Christo'centric *a.* having Christ as its centre L19. **Christocen'tricity**, **-'centrism** *ns.* the state or condition of being Christocentric E20. **Christophany** /krɪ'stɒfəni/ *n.* a manifestation of Christ, esp. after the Resurrection M19.

Christology /krɪ'stɒlədʒi/ *n.* L17. [f. prec. + -LOGY.] That part of Christian theology dealing specifically with Christ; a doctrine or theory concerning Christ.

Christo'logical *a.* M19. **Christologist** *n.* E19.

Christy *n.* var. of CHRISTIE.

chrom- /krəʊm/ *comb. form* of CHROMIUM, used esp. in names of minerals (cf. CHROMO-).

chroma /ˈkrəʊmə/ *n.* L19. [Gk *khrōma* colour.] Purity or intensity as a colour quality, esp. in colour television etc.

chromaffin /krə(ʊ)ˈmafɪn/ *a.* E20. [f. CHROMO- + L *affinis* akin.] *Histol.* Stained brown by chromates; *spec.* designating hormone-secreting granules in the adrenal medulla.

-chromasia /krəˈmeɪzɪə/ *suff.* [f. CHROMO- + *-asia* mod.L ending on Gk model (cf. *-plasia*, *-stasia*, etc.) for ns. with a stem *-at-*: see -IA[1].] *Med.* & *Biol.* Forming ns. denoting a condition or property to do with colour, as *hyperchromasia*.

-chromasy /ˈkrəʊməsi/ *suff.* [Anglicization.] = prec.

chromat- *comb. form* see CHROMATO-.

chromate /ˈkrəʊmeɪt/ *n.* E19. [f. CHROMIC *a.* + -ATE[1].] *Chem.* A salt of chromic acid.

chromatic /krə(ʊ)ˈmatɪk/ *n.* & *a.* LME. [Fr. *chromatique* or L *chromaticus* f. Gk *khrōmatikos*, f. *khrōma*, *-mat-* colour: see -IC.] A *n.* †1 A person who preserves his 'colour'; a person who is dyed-in-the-wool. Only in LME. †2 The art of colouring in painting. L17–M18. 3 *Mus.* In *pl.* Chromatic notes, harmonies, etc. E18. 4 In *pl.* (treated as *sing.*). The science of colour. L18.

B *adj.* 1 *Mus.* Orig. (*Hist.*), designating one of three kinds of tetrachord in ancient Greek music, based on the intervals semitone, semitone, minor third. In modern music, designating, pertaining to, or including notes not belonging to the diatonic scale; (of an instrument) capable of producing (nearly) all the tones of the chromatic scale; (habitually) employing chromaticism. E17. 2 Of or produced by colour. M19. 3 Brightly coloured, colourful. M19.

1 **chromatic alteration**: raising or lowering the pitch of a note. **chromatic scale**: proceeding by semitones. **chromatic semitone** the interval between a note and its sharp or flat. 2 *chromatic aberration*: see ABERRATION *n.* 2.

chromatically *adv.* L18. **chromaticism** /-sɪz(ə)m/ *n.* (an instance of) the use of chromatic expressions, modulations, or harmonies in music L19. **chromaticity** /krəʊməˈtɪsɪti/ *n.* quality of colour determined independently of brightness E20.

chromatid /ˈkrəʊmətɪd/ *n.* E20. [f. Gk *khrōma*, *-mat-* colour + -ID[2].] *Biol.* Either of the two strands into which a chromosome divides longitudinally during cell-division.

chromatin /ˈkrəʊmətɪn/ *n.* L19. [f. as prec. + -IN [1].] *Biol.* The readily-stained material of the cell nucleus, consisting of DNA and protein.

chromatism /ˈkrəʊmətɪz(ə)m/ *n.* E18. [Gk *khrōmatismos*, f. as CHROMATID + -ISM.] 1 Natural colouring. Now *rare* or *obs.* E18. 2 Chromatic aberration. M19. 3 Hallucinatory perception of colour. E20.

chromato- /ˈkrəʊmətəʊ/ *comb. form* of Gk *khrōma*, *-mat-* colour: see -O-. Bef. a vowel **chromat-**. Cf. CHROMO-.

chromatolysis /-ˈtɒlɪsɪs/ *n.* (*Biol.*) the solution and disintegration of the chromatin of cell nuclei L19. **chromatophore** *n.* (*Biol.*) a cell or plastid containing pigment M19. **chromatoˈphoric** *a.* (*Biol.*) of or pertaining to a chromatophore L19. **chromaˈtopsia** *n.* (*Med.*) abnormally coloured vision M19.

chromatogram /krəˈmatəgram/ *n.* M20. [f. prec. + -GRAM.] A visible record of the result of a chromatographic separation.

paper chromatogram: see PAPER *n.* & *a.*

chromatograph /krəˈmatəgrɑːf/ *v.* & *n.* M19. [f. CHROMATO- + -GRAPH.] A *v.t.* †1 Represent in colours. *rare.* Only in M19. 2 Separate or analyse by chromatography. M20. B *n.* An apparatus for chromatographic separation. M20.

chromatographer /krəʊməˈtɒgrəfə/ *n.* a person who performs chromatography M20.

chromatography /krəʊməˈtɒgrəfi/ *n.* M18. [f. CHROMATO- + -GRAPHY: sense 2 f. G *Chromatographie*.] 1 The description of colours. Now *rare* or *obs.* M18. 2 Any of various methods of chemical separation or analysis which depend on the different rates of passage of the components of a mixture through a sorbent medium (the sample being dissolved in a solvent or carried in a gas). M20.

2 *paper chromatography*: see PAPER *n.* & *a.*

¶So named because in the earliest chromatographic separations the result was displayed as a number of coloured bands or spots.

chromatographic /krəʊmətəˈgrafɪk/ *a.* of, pertaining to, or involving chromatography E20. **chromatoˈgraphical** *a.* = CHROMATOGRAPHIC M20. **chromatoˈgraphically** *adv.* M20.

chromatoid /ˈkrəʊmətɔɪd/ *a.* E20. [f. CHROMATIN + -OID.] *Biol.* Resembling chromatin in staining readily.

chromatology /krəʊməˈtɒlədʒi/ *n. rare.* E19. [f. CHROMATO- + -LOGY.] The science of colours.

chrome /krəʊm/ *n.* & *v.* E19. [Fr. f. Gk *khrōma* colour: so named from the brilliant colours of its compounds.] A *n.* 1 Chromium; *esp.* chromium plate. E19. 2 A chromate or other chromium compound used in tanning or dyeing, or as a pigment. Also *ellipt.*, chrome leather. L19.

2 *Oxford chrome*: see OXFORD *a.*

Comb.: *chrome alum*: see ALUM *n.* 2; **chrome green** (*a*) chromium(III) oxide, Cr_2O_3, as a pigment; (*b*) a mixture of Prussian blue and chrome yellow (or sometimes cadmium yellow), used as a pigment (also called *zinnober green*); **chrome leather** leather tanned with chromium compounds; **chrome steel** a hard, fine-grained steel containing chromium; **chrome tanning** tanning of hides by immersion in acid solutions of chromates; **chrome yellow** lead chromate, $PbCrO_4$, used as a bright yellow pigment.

B *v.t.* (Chiefly as *chromed* ppl a. or *chroming* vbl n.) 1 Treat (textiles, hides) with a chromium compound. L19. 2 Electroplate with chromium. M20.

chromic /ˈkrəʊmɪk/ *a.* E19. [f. prec. + -IC.] *Chem.* Of or containing chromium, esp. in a higher valency (cf. CHROMOUS).

chromic acid a strongly oxidizing acid, H_2CrO_4, present in aqueous solutions of chromium(VI) oxide; this oxide itself. **chromic anhydride** chromium(VI) oxide, CrO_3, a dark red crystalline solid with powerful oxidizing properties. **chromic oxide** chromium(III) oxide, Cr_2O_3, a green amphoteric solid.

chrominance /ˈkrəʊmɪn(ə)ns/ *n.* M20. [f. CHROMO- after *luminance*.] In colour television, the colorimetric difference between a given colour and a standard colour of equal luminance.

chromite /ˈkrəʊmʌɪt/ *n.* M19. [f. CHROME or CHROMIUM + -ITE[1].] 1 *Chem.* A compound formed by reaction of chromium(III) oxide with a base. M19. 2 *Min.* The major ore of chromium, a black oxide of chromium and ferrous iron that crystallizes in the cubic system but usu. occurs in massive form. M19.

chromium /ˈkrəʊmɪəm/ *n.* E19. [f. CHROME + -IUM.] A hard white lustrous metal which is a chemical element of the transition series, atomic no. 24, and is much used in alloys and corrosion-resistant coatings. (Symbol Cr.)

Comb.: **chromium-plate** *n.* & *v.* (*a*) *n.* an electrolytically deposited protective or decorative coating of chromium; (*b*) *v.t.* electroplate with chromium; *fig.* embellish pretentiously or tastelessly.

chromo /ˈkrəʊməʊ/ *n.*[1] *colloq.* (now chiefly *Hist.*). Pl. **-os**. M19. [Abbrev.] = CHROMOLITHOGRAPH *n.*

chromo /ˈkrəʊməʊ/ *n.*[2] *Austral. slang.* Pl. **-os**. M20. [Origin unkn.] A prostitute.

chromo- /ˈkrəʊməʊ/ *comb. form* of Gk *khrōma* colour, or, less commonly, of CHROMIUM: see -O-.

chromodyˈnamics *n.* (*Particle Physics*) (more fully *quantum chromodynamics*) a quantum field theory in which the strong interaction is described in terms of an interaction between quarks mediated by gluons, both quarks and gluons being assigned a quantum number called 'colour' L20. **chromogen** *n.* (*Chem.*) a substance which can be converted to a dyestuff by the introduction of a polar group M19. **chromoˈgenic** *a.* colour-forming L19. **chromophil(e)** *a.* & *n.* (*Histol.*) (a cell) that is readily stained L19. **chromoˈphilic** *a.* (*Histol.*) readily stained L19. **chromophobe** *a.* & *n.* (*Histol.*) (a cell) that is not readily stained E20. **chromoˈphobic** *a.* (*Histol.*) not readily stained L19. **chromophore** *n.* (*Chem.*) that part of the molecule which is responsible for a compound's colour L19. **chromoˈphoric** *a.* (*Chem.*) responsible for a compound's colour L19. **chromoˈprotein** *n.* (*Biochem.*) a compound consisting of a protein bound to a metal-containing pigment or a carotenoid E20.

chromolithograph /krəʊməʊˈlɪθəgrɑːf/ *n.* & *v.* M19. [f. prec. + LITHOGRAPH *n.*, *v.*] Chiefly *Hist.* A *n.* An image printed in colours by lithography and produced by hand separation of the colours. M19. B *v.t.* Print in colours in this way. M19.

chromoliˈthographer *n.* M19. **chromolithoˈgraphic** *a.* M19. **chromoliˈthography** *n.* M19.

chromone /ˈkrəʊməʊn/ *n.* E20. [f. CHROMO- + -ONE.] *Chem.* A bicyclic ketone, $C_9H_6O_2$, e.g. coumarin; any derivative of this.

chromosome /ˈkrəʊməsəʊm/ *n.* L19. [G *Chromosom*: see CHROMO-, -SOME[3].] *Biol.* A threadlike structure of nucleic acids and protein which carries a set of linked genes and occurs singly in prokaryotes and in characteristic numbers, usu. paired, in the cell nuclei of higher organisms.

PHILADELPHIA *chromosome.*

chromoˈsomal *a.* of, pertaining to, or involving chromosomes E20. **chromoˈsomally** *adv.* as regards chromosomes, by means of chromosomes E20.

chromosphere /ˈkrəʊməsfɪə/ *n.* M19. [f. CHROMO- + -SPHERE.] *Astron.* The reddish transparent gaseous envelope surrounding the photosphere of the sun or another star.

chromoˈspheric *a.* M19.

chromous /ˈkrəʊməs/ *a.* M19. [f. CHROMIUM + -OUS.] *Chem.* Of divalent chromium. Cf. CHROMIC.

chromyl /ˈkrəʊmʌɪl, -mɪl/ *n.* M19. [f. CHROM- + -YL.] *Chem.* The divalent radical :CrO_2. Usu. in *comb.*

chronal /ˈkrəʊn(ə)l/ *a.* L19. [f. Gk *khronos* time + -AL[1].] Of or pertaining to time.

chronic /ˈkrɒnɪk/ *a.* & *n.* LME. [Fr. *chronique* f. L *chronicus* f. Gk *khronikos* of or pertaining to time, f. *khronos* time: see -IC.] A *adj.* 1 Of a disease etc.: lingering, lasting; of slow progression and often gradual onset. Cf. *acute*. LME. b Of an invalid: suffering from a chronic illness. M19. 2 *gen.* Continuous, constant, inveterate. M19. 3 Bad, intense, severe. *colloq.* E20.

2 J. S. MILL A state of chronic revolution and civil war. J. BUCHAN There was a chronic inaccuracy in him which vexed his father's soul. 3 **something chronic** *adv. phr.* severely, badly.

B *ellipt.* as *n.* A chronic invalid, sufferer, etc. M19.

chronicity /krəˈnɪsɪti/ *n.* chronic quality or condition M19.

chronical /ˈkrɒnɪk(ə)l/ *a.* M16. [f. as prec. + -AL[1].] †1 Of or relating to verbal tense. Only in M16. 2 = CHRONIC *a.* 1, 2. E17. 3 Of, pertaining to, or regulated by time. M17.

chronically *adv.* †(*a*) with regard to time; (*b*) in a chronic manner, inveterately, for a long period: M16.

chronicle /ˈkrɒnɪk(ə)l/ *n.* & *v.* ME. [AN *cronicle* var. of OFr. *cronique* (mod. *chronique*) f. L *chronica* f. Gk *khronika* annals.] A *n.* 1 A detailed and continuous record of events in order of time; a historical record in which facts are related usu. without interpretation etc. In *pl.* (treated as *sing.*) (C-), either of two historical books of the Old Testament and Hebrew Scriptures. ME. 2 A record, a register; a narrative, an account. Freq. in titles of newspapers. LME.

2 E. WAUGH Do realize that a letter need not be a bald chronicle of events.

Comb.: **chronicle drama** drama, a play, based on historical accounts; **chronicle history** *arch.* a chronicle drama.

B *v.t.* Enter in a chronicle; put on record, register. LME.

chronicler *n.* a person who writes or compiles chronicles; a recorder of events: LME.

chronique /ˈkrɒniːk; *foreign* krɔnik (*pl. same*)/ *n.* LME. [OFr. *cronique*: see prec.] A chronicle.

chronique scandaleuse /krɔnik skɑ̃dalø:z/ *n. phr.* Pl. ***-s -s*** (pronounced same). M19. [Fr.] A compilation or body of gossip, scandal, etc.

chrono- /ˈkrɒnəʊ/ *comb. form* of Gk *khronos* time: see -O-.

chronobioˈlogic *a.* = CHRONOBIOLOGICAL M20. **chronobioˈlogical** *a.* of or pertaining to chronobiology L20. **chronobiˈology** *n.* the biology of cyclical physiological phenomena M20. **chronostrati'graphic, -ical** *adjs.* of or pertaining to chronostratigraphy M20. **chronostra'tigraphy** *n.* (*Geol.*) the branch of stratigraphy that deals with the absolute ages of strata M20. **chronotropic** /-'trəʊpɪk, -'trɒpɪk/ *a.* (*Physiol.*) affecting the rate at which the heart beats M20.

chronogram /'krɒnəgram/ *n.* E17. [f. prec. + -GRAM.] A phrase etc. of which the roman-numeral letters express a date when added together (e.g. LorD haVe MerCIe Vpon Vs = 50 + 500 + 5 + 1000 + 100 + 1 + 5 + 5 = 1666).
chronogra'mmatic *a.* of or pertaining to chronograms; of the nature of a chronogram: M18. **chronogra'mmatical** *a.* (now *rare* or *obs.*) = CHRONOGRAMMATIC M17.

chronograph /'krɒnəgrɑːf/ *n.* M17. [f. CHRONO- + -GRAPH.] 1 = prec. Now *rare* or *obs.* M17. 2 An instrument for recording time with considerable accuracy; a stopwatch. M19.

chronographic /krɒnə'grafɪk/ *a.* M19. [f. as prec. + -IC.] Of or pertaining to a chronograph or chronography.
chronographical *a.* = CHRONOGRAPHIC L16. **chronographically** *adv.* M19.

chronography /krə'nɒgrəfi/ *n.* M16. [Late L *chronographia* f. Gk *khronographia*, f. as CHRONO- + -GRAPHY.] A chronological description or arrangement of past events. Also, chronology.
chronographer *n.* a chronicler, a chronologist M16.

chronological /krɒnə'lɒdʒɪk(ə)l/ *a.* E17. [f. next + -ICAL.] Of, pertaining to, relating to, or dealing with chronology; in accordance with chronology; arranged in order of time.
chronologic *a.* = CHRONOLOGICAL E17. **chronologically** *adv.* L17.

chronology /krə'nɒlədʒi/ *n.* L16. [mod.L *chronologia*, f. as CHRONO- + -LOGY.] 1 The science of computing dates; the arrangement of events according to dates or times of occurrence. L16. 2 A chronological table, list, or treatise. E17.
1 R. CUDWORTH If Chronology had not contradicted it, it would have been concluded, that he had been an Auditour of Pythagoras himself. C. S. LEWIS The chronology of this disaster is a little vague, but I know . . that it had not begun when I went there and that the process was complete very shortly after I left.
chronologer *n.* = CHRONOLOGIST L16. **chronologist** *n.* a person versed in chronology, a person who investigates the dates of events E17. **chronologize** *v.t.* †(*a*) chronicle, record; (*b*) apply chronology to, arrange chronologically: E17.

chronometer /krə'nɒmɪtə/ *n.* E18. [f. CHRONO- + -METER.] †1 *Mus.* = METRONOME. E18–M19. 2 An instrument for measuring time; *esp.* one designed to keep accurate time at all temperatures etc. and to be used at sea in determining longitude etc. by astronomical observation. E18.

chronometry /krə'nɒmɪtri/ *n.* M19. [f. as prec. + -METRY.] (The science of) the accurate measurement of time.
chrono'metric, -ical *adjs.* of or pertaining to chronometry; relating to the measurement of time: M19. **chrono'metrically** *adv.* M19.

chronoscope /'krɒnəskəʊp/ *n.* E18. [f. as prec. + -SCOPE.] A device for measuring (short) time intervals, esp. in determining (*a*) the velocity of projectiles, or (*b*) a person's reaction time.

†chrony *n.* & *v.* var. of CRONY.

chrys- *comb. form* see CHRYSO-.

chrysalid /'krɪs(ə)lɪd/ *n.* & *a.* L18. [f. as next.] A *n.* A chrysalis. L18. B *adj.* Of or pertaining to a chrysalis. E19.

chrysalides *n.pl.* see CHRYSALIS.

chrysalis /'krɪs(ə)lɪs/ *n.* Pl. **-ises** /-ɪsɪz/, (now *rare*) **-ides** /-ɪdiːz/. E17. [L *chrysal(l)is*, *-id-* f. Gk *khrūsallis*, f. *khrūsos* gold.] A pupa, esp. of a butterfly or moth; the hard sheath of this. Also *fig.*, a quiescent transitional form.
chrysaline *a.* of, pertaining to, or of the nature of a chrysalis L18. **chrysalize** *v.i.* & *refl.* (*rare*) become a chrysalis; pupate: E19. **chrysaloid** *a.* resembling a chrysalis E19.

chrysanth /krɪ'sanθ, -z-/ *n. colloq.* E20. [Abbrev.] = next.

chrysanthemum /krɪ'sanθɪməm, -z-/ *n.* M16. [L *chrysanthemum* f. Gk *khrūsanthemon*, f. as CHRYSO- + *anthemon* flower.] Any plant of the large genus *Chrysanthemum*, of the composite family. Orig. *spec.* the corn marigold, *C. segetum*; now usu., any of numerous cultivated chiefly late-blooming species or varieties placed in the genus *Dendranthema*. Also, a flower or flowering stem of such a plant.
KOREAN *chrysanthemum*.

chryselephantine /ˌkrɪsɛlɪ'fantʌɪn/ *a.* E19. [Gk *khruselephantinos*, f. *khrusos* gold + *elephant-*, *-as* elephant, ivory: see -INE[1].] Overlaid with gold and ivory, as by ancient Greek sculptors.

chrysene /'krʌɪsiːn/ *n.* M19. [Fr. *chrysène*, f. as CHRYSO- + -ENE: the first, impure, specimens were yellow.] *Chem.* A polycyclic aromatic hydrocarbon, $C_{18}H_{12}$, present in coal tar and isolated as colourless crystals.

chrysid /'krʌɪsɪd/ *n.* & *a.* L19. [f. mod.L *Chrysididae* (see below), f. *Chrysis* genus name: see CHRYSO-, -ID[3].] A *n.* A parasitic hymenopterous insect of the family Chrysididae, which includes the cuckoo wasps. L19. B *adj.* Of, pertaining to, or designating this family. E20.

chryso- /'krɪsəʊ/ *comb. form* of Gk *khrūsos* gold: see -O-. Bef. a vowel **chrys-**.
chrysarobin /krɪsə'rəʊbɪn/ *n.* [mod.L *araroba* f. Port. f. Tupi *arárowa*] a mixture of chrysophanic acid and related compounds obtained from a S. American leguminous tree, *Andira araroba*, used to treat skin ailments L19. **chrysophanic** /-'fanɪk/ *a.* [Gk *phainein* to show] (*Chem.*): *chrysophanic acid*, a yellow crystalline phenol, $C_{15}H_{10}O_4$, which is a derivative of anthraquinone and occurs in many plants and lichens M19. **chrysopo'etic** *a.* & *n.* (*rare*) (in *pl.*) [Gk *poiētikos* making] gold-making E18. **chrysotype** *n.* a photographic process employing gold chloride M19.

chrysoberyl /krɪsə'bɛrɪl/ *n.* M17. [L *chrysoberyllus*, f. as prec. + BERYL.] *Min.* Orig., a yellow-tinged variety of beryl. Now, a yellowish-green orthorhombic oxide of beryllium and aluminium which occurs as tabular crystals often of gem quality.

chrysocolla /krɪsə'kɒlə/ *n.* In sense 1 also **chrysocoll** /'krɪsəkɒl/. L16. [L *chrysocolla* f. Gk *khrūsokolla* 'gold-solder'.] 1 *Hist.* A mineral used by the ancients for soldering gold, usu. identified with borax or malachite. L16. 2 *Min.* A hydrated silicate of copper usu. occurring as green opaline crusts and masses. L18.

chrysoidine /krɪ'səʊɪdiːn/ *n.* L19. [f. Gk *khrūsoeidēs* like gold + -INE[5].] A golden-yellow dye made by diazo coupling of aniline and *m*-phenylenediamine.

chrysolite /'krɪsəlʌɪt/ *n.* LME. [OFr. *crisolite* f. med.L *crisolitus*, ult. f. Gk *khrūsolithos*, f. as CHRYSO- + -LITE.] Orig., any of various green gemstones. Now (*Min.*), a yellow variety of olivine.

chrysomelid /krɪsə(ʊ)'mɛlɪd, -'miːlɪd/ *a.* & *n.* L19. [f. mod.L *Chrysomelidae* (see below), f. *Chrysomela* genus name, f. Gk *khrusomēlon* quince (lit. 'golden apple') but infl. by Gk *khrusomēlolonthion* little golden chafer: see CHRYSO-, -ID[3].] *Zool.* A *adj.* Of, pertaining to, or designating the insect family Chrysomelidae, which comprises the leaf-beetles. L19. B *n.* A chrysomelid beetle, a leaf-beetle. L19.

chrysoprase /'krɪsəpreɪz/ *n.* ME. [OFr. *crisopace* f. L *chrysopassus*, *-prasus* f. Gk *khrūsoprasos*, f. as CHRYSO- + *prason* leek.] Orig., a golden-green precious stone, perh. a variety of beryl. Now (*Min.*), an apple-green variety of chalcedony.

chrysotile /'krɪsətʌɪl/ *n.* M19. [f. CHRYSO- + Gk *tilos* fibre.] *Min.* An asbestiform variety of serpentine.

†chrystal *n.* & *a.*, *v.* vars. of CRYSTAL *n.* & *a.*, *v.*

†chrystalline *a.* & *n.* var. of CRYSTALLINE.

chthonian /'kθəʊnɪən/ *a.* M19. [f. Gk *khthonios* (f. *khthōn* earth) + -AN.] = next.

chthonic /'kθɒnɪk/ *a.* L19. [f. Gk *khthōn* earth + -IC.] Dwelling in or beneath the earth or in the underworld; of or pertaining to the underworld.

chub /tʃʌb/ *n.* Pl. same. LME. [Origin unkn.] 1 A thick-bodied coarse-fleshed river fish, *Leuciscus cephalus*, of the carp family. Also (*N. Amer.*), any of various freshwater fishes of the carp family; any of various similar marine fishes of the family Kyphosidae (also *sea chub*). LME. †2 A lazy person; a yokel, a dolt; a lad. M16–E19.
1 RED-TAIL *chub*.
chubbed *a.* (now *rare*) short and thick, chubby L17.

Chubb /tʃʌb/ *n.* M19. [Charles *Chubb* (1773–1845), London locksmith.] In full *Chubb lock*. (Proprietary name for) a patent lock with tumblers and a device for fixing the bolt immovably should an attempt be made to pick it.

chubby /'tʃʌbi/ *a.* E17. [f. CHUB + -Y[1].] †1 Short and thick like a chub. E17–L19. 2 Round-faced; plump. E18.
chubbily *adv.* E20. **chubbiness** *n.* M19.

chuck /tʃʌk/ *n.*[1] LME. [Imit.: cf. CHUCK *v.*[1]] A soft clucking sound.

chuck /tʃʌk/ *n.*[2] L16. [Alt. of CHICK *n.*[1] after prec. Cf. CHOOK.] 1 A term of endearment, esp. as *voc.*: dear one, darling. Now *dial.* L16. 2 A chicken, a domestic fowl. *north.* L17.
1 E. BRONTË Will you come Chuck?

chuck /tʃʌk/ *n.*[3] E17. [f. CHUCK *v.*[2]] 1 A playful touch under the chin. E17. 2 = *chuck-farthing* s.v. CHUCK *v.*[2] Now *dial.* E18. 3 = CHUCKIE *n.*[1] *Sc.* E19. 4 An abrupt movement, a jerk, a toss. M19. 5 A throw from the hand; *spec.* in *Cricket*, a delivery considered to be a throw and so illegal. *colloq.* M19. 6 *the chuck*, dismissal, rejection. *slang.* L19.

chuck /tʃʌk/ *n.*[4] L17. [Var. of CHOCK *n.*[1]: cf. CHUNK *n.*[1]] 1 A chock; a chunk. Chiefly *dial.* L17. 2 A cut of beef from the neck to the ribs. E18. 3 A contrivance in a lathe etc. for holding a workpiece. E19.

chuck /tʃʌk/ *n.*[5] Now *N. Amer. colloq.* M19. [Perh. same wd as prec.] 1 Food, provisions. M19. 2 A meal; meal-time. M19.
Comb.: **chuck-wagon** a provision-cart on a ranch etc.

chuck /tʃʌk/ *n.*[6] L19. [Chinook Jargon = water.] In Canada, a large body of water.
SKOOKUM *chuck*.

chuck /tʃʌk/ *v.*[1]*i.* LME. [Imit.: cf. CHUCK *n.*[1]] 1 Make a soft clucking noise. LME. †2 Chuckle. Only in L16.

chuck /tʃʌk/ *v.*[2] E16. [Perh. f. OFr. *chuquer*, earlier form of *choquer* knock, bump, of unkn. origin.] 1 *v.t.* Give a playful touch under the chin to. E16. 2 *v.t.* Throw, toss, fling, now esp. with contempt, carelessness, or ease; throw *away*, *out*, etc. (see also specialized senses below); throw or give up; throw out; reject, abandon. (Earliest in *chuck-farthing* below.) *colloq.* L17. b *Cricket*. Deliver (a ball) with an action considered to be a throw and so illegal. *colloq.* M19. 3 *v.i.* Play chuck-farthing. *rare.* M18. 4 *v.i.* Throw a ball etc.; *spec.* in *Cricket*, deliver the ball with an action considered to be a throw and so illegal. *colloq.* E20.
2 TENNYSON England now Is but a ball chuck'd between France and Spain. W. GERHARDIE To chuck the army and enter a commercial life. P. H. GIBBS A girl who had chucked them for someone else. P. LIVELY He chucks me free concert tickets he can't use. *chuck in the towel*: see TOWEL *n.* 1. **chuck it** *slang* stop, desist.
With advs. in specialized senses: **chuck in** abandon (an activity), stop doing. **chuck off** *Austral.* & *NZ slang* sneer (*at*), chaff. **chuck out** eject, get rid of, (a troublesome or unwanted person) from a meeting, public house, etc. **chuck up** abandon, dismiss; throw over, jilt.
Comb.: **chuck-farthing** (orig.) a game in which coins were pitched at a mark and then tossed at a hole; (later) any similar game; **chuck-hole** *US* a hole or rut in a road or track.

chuck /tʃʌk/ *v.*[3]*t.* M19. [f. CHUCK *n.*[4]] Fix on a lathe by means of a chuck.

chuck /tʃʌk/ *adv.* M18. [Imit.] With direct impact.

chuck-a-luck /'tʃʌkəlʌk/ *n. N. Amer.* M19. [App. f. CHUCK *v.*[2] + connective *-a-* + LUCK *n.*] A gambling game played with dice.

chuckawalla *n.* see CHUCKWALLA.

chucker /ˈtʃʌkə/ *n.*[1] *colloq.* M18. [f. CHUCK *v.*[2] + -ER[1].] **1** A small pebble. M18. **2** A person who throws; *spec.* in *Cricket*, a bowler whose delivery of the ball is considered to be a throw and so illegal. L19. **3** *chucker-out*, a person who ejects troublesome or unwanted persons, a bouncer. L19.

chucker *n.*[2] var. of CHUKKA.

chuck-full *a.* var. of CHOCK-FULL.

chuckie /ˈtʃʌki/ *n.*[1] *Sc.* M18. [f. CHUCK *v.*[2] or *n.*[3] + -IE.] More fully *chuckie-stane, -stone*. A small pebble, a smooth stone, esp. as used in games, for skimming on water, etc.; in *pl.*, a game with pebbles or marbles.

chuckie *n.*[2] var. of CHUCKY.

chuckle /ˈtʃʌk(ə)l/ *n.* M18. [f. CHUCKLE *v.*] **1** An act of chuckling; a suppressed (formerly, a loud or convulsive) laugh; a soft cackle or clucking sound. M18. **2** Private amusement, chuckling. M19.

chuckle /ˈtʃʌk(ə)l/ *a.* E18. [Prob. rel. to CHUCK *n.*[4]: see -LE[1].] Esp. of the head: large, clumsy, blockish. Usu. in *comb.* as below.

Comb.: **chucklehead** a stupid person, a blockhead; **chuckleheaded** *a.* stupid, blockheaded; **chuckleheadedness** stupidity.

chuckle /ˈtʃʌk(ə)l/ *v.* L16. [f. CHUCK *v.*[1] + -LE[3].] **1** *v.t.* †**a** Laugh vehemently or convulsively. L16–E19. **b** Laugh to oneself; make suppressed sounds of glee etc. E19. **2** *v.t.* Call (fowl etc.) together with a chucking sound. *rare.* L17. **3** *v.i.* Of a bird: cackle or cluck softly. E19.

1b I. D'ISRAELI A tale which some antiquaries still chuckle over. **3** KEATS The chuckling linnet.

chuckler /ˈtʃʌklə/ *n.* M18. [Tamil *cakkili*.] A person of a very low caste in southern India, whose members are tanners or cobblers; a southern Indian shoemaker.

chuckwalla /ˈtʃʌkwɒlə/ *n.* Also **chuckawalla** /-kə-/. L19. [Mex. Sp. *chacahuala* f. Amer. Indian.] An iguanid lizard, *Sauromalus obesus*, of Mexico and the south-western US.

chuck-will's-widow /tʃʌkwɪlzˈwɪdəʊ/ *n.* L18. [Imit.] A large nightjar of eastern N. America, *Caprimulgus carolinensis*.

chucky /ˈtʃʌki/ *n.* Also **chuckie**; *Austral.* & *NZ* (sense 2) **chookie, -y** /ˈtʃʊki/. E18. [f. CHUCK *n.*[2] + -Y[6], -IE.] **1** A term of endearment: little one, dearie. Now *dial.* E18. **2** A chicken, a domestic fowl. *colloq.* L18.

chuddar *n.* var. of CHADAR.

chuddy *n.* var. of CHUTTY.

chufa /ˈtʃuːfə/ *n.* M19. [Sp.] (The edible nutty tuber of) the nut-grass, *Cyperus esculentus*. Also called *earth almond*.

chuff /tʃʌf/ *n.*[1] & *a.*[1] Now *dial.* LME. [Origin unkn.] **A** *n.* A rustic, a boor; a churlish person; a miser; *gen.* a person of the specified unpleasant kind. LME. **B** *adj.* Surly, gruff, morose. L18.

chuffy *a.*[1] = CHUFF *a.*[1] E18.

chuff /tʃʌf/ *n.*[2] & *a.*[2] Now *dial.* M16. [Origin unkn.] †**A** *n.* **1** A chubby cheek. Only in M16. **2** An animal's muzzle. Only in E17. **B** *adj.* **1** Chubby, fat. M16. **2** Pleased, happy. M19.

chuffy *a.*[2] plump-cheeked, chubby E17.

chuff /tʃʌf/ *n.*[3], *int.*, & *v.* Also redupl. **chuff-chuff**. E20. [Imit.] **A** *n.* & *int.* (Repr.) a sharp puffing sound, as of a steam engine. E20. **B** *v.i.* Of a steam engine etc.: work with or make a regular sharp puffing sound. E20.

chuff /tʃʌf/ *n.*[4] *slang.* M20. [Origin unkn.] The buttocks; the anus.

chuffed /tʃʌft/ *a.* *slang.* M20. [Cf. CHUFF *a.*[1], *a.*[2]] **1** Pleased. M20. **2** Displeased. M20.

chug /tʃʌg/ *n.*, *int.*, & *v.* Also redupl. **chug-chug**. M19. [Imit.] **A** *n.* & *int.* (Repr.) a muffled explosive sound as of a slowly-running internal-combustion engine or its exhaust. M19. **B** *v.i.* Infl. **-gg-**. Move with or make this sound. L19.

chukar /ˈtʃʊkɑː/ *n.* Also **chikhor** /ˈtʃɪkɔː/ & other vars. E19. [Skt *cakor(a)*.] A red-legged partridge, *Alectoris chukar*, native to Asia and SE Europe. Also *chukar partridge*.

Chukchi /ˈtʃʊktʃi, -iː/ *n.* & *a.* Also **Chukchee, Tchuktchi**, & other vars. E18. [Russ. *Chukchi* pl. (sing. *-cha*).] **A** *n.* Pl. **-s**, same. A member of a Palaeoasiatic people of extreme NE Siberia; the language of this people. E18. **B** *adj.* Designating, of, or pertaining to this people or language. E19.

chukka /ˈtʃʌkə/ *n.* Also **chucker, chukker**. L19. [Hind. *cak(k)ar* f. Skt *cakra* circle, wheel.] Each of the periods into which a game of polo is divided.

Comb.: **chukka boot** an ankle-high leather boot, as worn by polo players.

chula *n.* var. of CHOOLA.

chulo /ˈtʃulo, ˈtʃuːləʊ/ *n.* Pl. **-os** /-ɒs, -əʊz/. L18. [Sp.] A bullfighter's assistant.

chum /tʃʌm/ *n.*[1] *colloq.* L17. [Prob. short for *chamber-fellow*: orig. Oxford Univ. slang equiv. to Cambridge *crony*.] A person who shares apartments with another or others; (now usu.) an intimate friend, esp. among schoolchildren.

new chum *Austral.* & *NZ* a recent immigrant, a greenhorn.

chumship *n.* the state or condition of being chums; (the period of) intimate friendship: M19.

chum /tʃʌm/ *n.*[2] *US.* M19. [Origin unkn.] **1** Refuse from fish, *esp.* that remaining after expressing oil. M19. **2** Chopped fish thrown overboard as bait, as in trolling. L19.

chum /tʃʌm/ *n.*[3] L19. [Perh. alt. of CHUMP *n.*] *Ceramics.* A receptacle used for turning a form.

chum /tʃʌm/ *n.*[4] E20. [Chinook Jargon *tzum* (*samun*) lit. 'spotted (salmon)'.] A salmon, *Oncorhynchus keta*, of the N. American Pacific coast. Also *chum salmon*.

chum /tʃʌm/ *v.*[1] *colloq.* Infl. **-mm-**. M18. [f. CHUM *n.*[1]] **1** *v.i.* Share rooms (*with*); be very friendly (*with*). M18. **b** *chum up*, form a close friendship (*with*). L19. **2** *v.t.* Quarter (a person) *on* another to share rooms. M19.

chum /tʃʌm/ *v.*[2]*t.* & *i.* *US.* Infl. **-mm-**. L19. [f. CHUM *n.*[2]] Bait (a fishing-place) with chum; attract (fish) with chum.

chumar *n.* var. of CHAMAR.

chumble /ˈtʃʌmb(ə)l/ *v.t.* & *i.* *dial.* & *colloq.* E19. [Prob. imit.] Gnaw, nibble, peck, mumble, (*at*).

chummage /ˈtʃʌmɪdʒ/ *n.* L18. [f. CHUM *n.*[1] or *v.*[1] + -AGE.] **1** *Hist.* A fee demanded by prisoners from a new inmate; a fee paid by a person to another chummed on him, as an inducement to find alternative accommodation. L18. **2** The system of chumming one person on another. M19.

chummery /ˈtʃʌməri/ *n.* L19. [f. CHUM *n.*[1] + -ERY.] **1** Intimate friendship. L19. **2** In India: a house or apartment shared by individuals; shared quarters. L19.

chummy /ˈtʃʌmi/ *n.*[1] *arch. colloq.* M19. [Alt. of CHIMNEY *n.*] A chimney-sweeper's boy; a chimney-sweeper.

chummy /ˈtʃʌmi/ *n.*[2] *colloq.* M19. [f. CHUM *n.*[1] + -Y[6].] **1** = CHUM *n.*[1] M19. **2** A person accused or detained; a prisoner. *Police slang.* M20.

chummy /ˈtʃʌmi/ *a.* *colloq.* L19. [f. CHUM *n.*[1] + -Y[1].] Intimate, friendly, sociable.

chummily *adv.* M20.

chump /tʃʌmp/ *n.* E18. [Perh. blend of CHUNK *n.*[1] and LUMP *n.*[1] or STUMP *n.*[1]] **1** A short thick lump of wood; an end-piece. E18. **2** The thick end, esp. of a loin of lamb or mutton. M19. **3** The head. *colloq.* M19. **4** A foolish person, a blockhead. *colloq.* L19.

3 off one's chump crazy, wild with excitement, etc.

Comb.: **chump chop** a chop from the chump end; **chump end** the thick end of a loin of lamb or mutton.

Chün /tʃuːn/ *a.* & *n.* L19. [f. *Chün Chou* (see below).] (Designating) a type of thickly glazed coloured stoneware orig. made at Chün Chou in Honan province, China, during the Song dynasty.

chunam /tʃʊˈnam/ *n.* & *v.t.* L17. [Tamil *cunnāmbu* lime.] (Cover with) a cement of shell-lime and sea-sand, used chiefly in the Indian subcontinent.

chunder /ˈtʃʌndə/ *v.i.* & *n.* *Austral.* & *NZ slang.* Also **-da**. M20. [Origin unkn.] Vomit.

chunk /tʃʌŋk/ *n.*[1] & *v.*[1] L17. [App. alt. of CHUCK *n.*[4]] **A** *n.* **1** A thick lump (of wood, bread, cheese, etc.) cut or broken off. L17. **b** A block of wood. Chiefly *US.* L18. **2** A sturdy person or horse; a sturdy specimen *of*. *US.* E19. **3** A substantial amount or portion (*of*). L19. **B** *v.t.* **1** Hit with a missile; throw a missile at. *US colloq.* M19. **2** Replenish (a fire) with fuel; build (a fire) *up*. *US colloq.* M19.

chunky *a.* comprising chunks; short and thick; small and sturdy; bulky: M18.

chunk /tʃʌŋk/ *v.*[2], *n.*[2], & *int.* Also redupl. **chunk-chunk**. L19. [Imit.] **A** *v.i.* Move with or make a muffled metallic sound. L19. **B** *n.* & *int.* (Repr.) such a sound. L19.

Chunnel /ˈtʃʌn(ə)l/ *n.* *colloq.* E20. [Contr.] = *Channel Tunnel* s.v. CHANNEL *n.*[1]

chunner /ˈtʃʌnə/ *v.t.* & *i.* Chiefly *Sc.* & *US.* L16. [Prob. imit.: cf. CHANNER, CHUNTER.] Mutter, grumble, murmur querulously.

chuño /ˈtʃuɲo, ˈtʃuːnjəʊ/ *n.* E17. [Amer. Sp. f. Quechua *ch'uñu*.] (Flour prepared from) dried potatoes, as eaten by Andean Indians.

chunter /ˈtʃʌntə/ *v.i.* L17. [Prob. imit.: cf. CHANNER, CHUNNER.] Mutter, grumble, murmur querulously.

chupatti *n.* var. of CHAPATTI.

chuppah /ˈxʊpə/ *n.* Also **-a**. L19. [Heb. *ḥuppāh* cover, canopy.] A canopy beneath which Jewish marriage ceremonies are performed.

chuprassy *n.* var. of CHAPRASSI.

church /tʃəːtʃ/ *n.* [OE *ċir(i)ċe, ċyr(i)ċe* = OFris. *szereke, szurka, tzierka*, OS *kirika, kerika* (Du. *kerk*), OHG *chirihha, kiricha* (G *Kirche*), f. WGmc f. med.Gk *kurikon* for *kuriakon* use as n. (sc. *dōma* house) of neut. of *kuriakos* pertaining to the Lord, f. *kurios* master, lord. Cf. KIRK *n.*] **I** (Usu. **c-**.) A building and extended uses. **1** A building for public Christian worship, esp. of the denomination recognized by the State (cf. *chapel, oratory*); public Christian worship. OE. †**2** A temple; a mosque. OE–M17.

1 STEELE As soon as church was done, she immediately stepp'd out. **go to church** *spec.* (*colloq.*) get married. CATHEDRAL *church*. COLLEGIAL *church*. *collegiate church* s.v. COLLEGIATE *a.* *minster church*: see MINSTER 2. PARISH *church*. *Patriarchal church*: see PATRIARCHAL I.

II (Usu. **C-**.) A community or organization. **3** The body of all Christians. OE. **4** A particular organized Christian society, distinguished by special features of doctrine, worship, etc., or confined to territorial or historical limits. OE. **5** A congregation of Christians locally organized into a society for religious worship etc. OE. **6** The ecclesiastical and clerical organization of Christian society or a particular Christian society; the clergy and officers collectively or as a corporation, formerly esp. as an estate of the realm (opp. State). OE. **7** (In biblical translations) the congregation of Israelites; the faithful Israelites of the Old Testament, regarded as analogous to the Christian Church. OE. **8** A non-Christian society or movement regarded as a religion or as having the social, ethical, or spiritual qualities of a religion. LME.

3 *Doctors of the Church*: see DOCTOR *n.* *Fathers of the Church*: see FATHER *n.* **the Church Catholic**: emphasizing its universality. **the Church invisible** the whole body of Christians, past and present. **the Church militant** Christians on earth warring against evil. **the Church triumphant** Christians at peace in heaven. **the Church visible** the whole body of Christians on earth. **4** *Ancient Church, Anglican Church, Baptist Church, Catholic Church, Congregational Church, Eastern Church, Greek Church, Latin Church, Lutheran Church, Methodist Church, Nestorian Church, Orthodox Church, Presbyterian Church, Roman Catholic Church, Russian Church, Western Church*, etc. *Broad Church*: see BROAD *a.* **Church of England** the English branch of the Western or Latin Church which has rejected the Pope's supremacy since the Reformation but retained episcopacy. **Church-of-Englandism** adherence to the Church of England. **Church of Scotland** Scotland's national Presbyterian Church. *High Church*: see HIGH *a.* *Low Church*: see LOW *a.* **6** **enter, go into the Church** take holy orders, become a minister or priest. *Church and State*: see STATE *n.* *parochial church council*: see PAROCHIAL I. *Prince of the*

(*Holy Roman*) *Church*: see PRINCE *n.* 8 *Church of Scientology* etc.

Other phrases: **Holy Church** (*a*) the Church regarded as divinely instituted and guided; †(*b*) the clergy similarly regarded. **Mother Church** the Church, esp. the Roman Catholic Church, as having maternal authority or solicitude.

Attrib. & *comb.*: In the senses 'of the Church, ecclesiastical, (in England often *spec.*) of the Church of England, of a church', as *church assembly, bazaar, dignitary, door,* (US) *fair, fête, hall, -history, land, -member, -membership, officer, organ, organist, spire, steeple, tower, vestments, window*, etc. Special combs., as **church-ale** *Hist.* a periodic festive gathering held in connection with a church; **Church Army** a Church of England organization for evangelism and welfare work; **church-bell**: rung to call people to worship etc.; **church-book** a book belonging to or used in connection with a church, as a service-book, a parish register, etc.; *Church Catechism*: see CATECHISM 2; **Church Commissioners** the body managing the finances of the Church of England; **Church Congress** *Hist.* the annual meetings of the Church of England for discussion; *Church Covenant*: see COVENANT *n.*; *Church Establishment*: see ESTABLISHMENT 3; *Church Fathers*: see FATHER *n.*; **churchgoer** a person who attends the services of a church, esp. regularly; **churchgoing** (esp. regular) attendance at the services of a church; **church-government** the government or organization of a Church, esp. with regard to the exercise of authority and discipline; *church-grith*: see GRITH 2; **church-house** (*a*) a house belonging to a church or to the Church; (*b*) *US* a church, a meeting-house; *church*-LITTEN; **church-living** a benefice in the Established Church; **church mode** each of the eight modes used for plainsong and liturgical chant, each beginning on a different note and having a different pattern of tones and semitones; **church mouse**: inhabiting a church and proverbially poverty-stricken; **church-owl** the barn-owl; **church parade** attendance at church as a military etc. duty; attendance at church in a body by members of a society etc.; **church-rate** a rate levied on parishioners for the maintenance of the church and its services (formerly compulsory, now voluntary but seldom requested); **church school** a school founded by or associated with a Church, esp. the Church of England; **church-scot, -shot** *Hist.* a contribution in kind or money made or demanded for the support of the clergy; **church service** a meeting for public worship, esp. following a stated form; the order of such worship, *spec.* the order of Common Prayer of the Church of England; *Church Slavonic*: see SLAVONIC *n.*; **church-text** (now *rare*) black letter, Old English, or textura lettering and type; **churchwoman** a woman member of the Established Church; **church work** (*a*) work at building a church (proverbially slow); (*b*) work for or in connection with the Church; **churchyard** an enclosed ground in which a church stands, esp. as used for burials; *churchyard cough* a cough seeming to herald death; *Church year*: see YEAR *n.*[1]

churchdom *n.* (*rare*) status as a Church; organization as a Church: M17. **churchi'anity** *n.* (*derog.*) devotion to the Church rather than to Christianity itself M19. **churchless** *a.* not having a church or an organized Church; not belonging to a Church: M17. **churchlet** *n.* (*rare*) a small church M17. **churchlike** *a.* (*a*) befitting the Church; (*b*) like a church: L16. **churchly** *a.* pertaining to or befitting a church or the Church, ecclesiastical: OE. **churchward** *adv.* & *a.*, **churchwards** *adv.* [orig. *to churchward*] towards the church LME. **churchwise** *a.* & *adv.* after the manner of a church E17.

church /tʃəːtʃ/ *v.t.* LME. [f. the n.] **1** Bring or take (esp. a woman after childbirth) to church to receive particular rites or ministrations (usu. in *pass.*); conduct a church service of thanksgiving for (esp. a woman after childbirth). LME. **2** Call to account in church. *US local.* E19.

Churchillian /tʃəː'tʃɪlɪən/ *a.* L19. [f. family name Spencer-*Churchill* + -IAN.] Of, pertaining to, or characteristic of any of the Churchills, esp. the British statesmen Lord Randolph Churchill (1849–95) and his son Sir Winston Churchill (1874–1965). Cf. WINSTONIAN.

Churchilli'ana *n.pl.* [-ANA] sayings by Sir Winston Churchill; publications or other items concerning or associated with Churchill: M20.

churchman /'tʃəːtʃmən/ *n.* Pl. **-men**. ME. [f. CHURCH *n.* + MAN *n.*] **1** A clergyman. ME. †**2** A churchwarden. Only in 16. **3** A supporter or member of a Church; *esp.* a member of the Established Church. L17.

churchmanlike *a.* resembling or befitting a churchman M19. **churchmanly** *a.* of or befitting a churchman M19. **churchmanship** *n.* the status or quality of a churchman; churchmanly behaviour: L17.

churchwarden /'tʃəːtʃwɔːd(ə)n/ *n.* & *a.* LME. [f. CHURCH *n.* + WARDEN *n.*[1]] **A** *n.* **1** Either of two elected lay people in an Anglican parish who are the foremost representatives of the laity, with responsibility for maintaining order in the church and for looking after its movable property; *US* a church administrator. LME. **2** A long clay pipe. M19. **B** *attrib.* or as *adj.* Designating a sham Gothic style affected in church building and restoration in the early 19th cent.; in this style. M19.

churchwardenism *n.* the practice of building or restoring churches in churchwarden style M19. **churchwardenize** *v.t.* restore (a church) in churchwarden style M19. **churchwardenly** *a.* of or befitting a churchwarden L19. **churchwardenship** *n.* the position or office of churchwarden E17.

churchy /'tʃəːtʃi/ *a. colloq.* M19. [f. CHURCH *n.* + -Y[1].] **1** Obtrusively or intolerantly devoted to the Church or opposed to religious dissent. M19. **2** Like a church. L19.

churchiness *n.* L19.

churel /tʃʊ'reɪl/ *n.* E20. [Hind. *cuṛail*.] In the Indian subcontinent: the malevolent ghost of a woman who has died in childbirth, believed to spread disease.

churinga *n.* var. of TJURUNGA.

churl /tʃəːl/ *n.* In sense 2 also **ceorl** /kjəːl, tʃ-/. [OE *ċeorl* = OFris. *tzerl, tzirl*, MLG *kerle* (whence G *Kerl* fellow), (M)Du. *kerel*, f. WGmc: rel. to CARL *n.*] †**1** A man, esp. as correlative to 'wife'. OE–LME. **2** *Hist.* In the OE constitution: a man, a member of the lowest rank of freemen; an ordinary freeman ranking directly below a thane (THANE 3). After the Norman Conquest: a serf, a bondman. OE. **b** *loosely.* A person of low birth. Passing into other senses. LME. **3** A peasant, a rustic; a boor. *arch.* ME. **4** A base fellow, a rude ill-bred fellow. ME. **5** A surly or niggardly person. *arch.* M16.

churlish /'tʃəːlɪʃ/ *a.* OE. [f. prec. + -ISH[1].] **1** Of or pertaining to a churl or churls; of the rank of a churl. Long *arch.* OE. **2** Boorish, ill-bred, surly; niggardly, grudging. LME. **3** Of an animal, natural agent, etc.: violent, rough. *obs.* exc. as passing into fig. uses of sense 2. L15. **4** Of soil etc.: difficult to work, intractable. *obs.* exc. as passing into fig. uses of sense 2. L16.

churlishly *adv.* LME. **churlishness** *n.* E16.

churn /tʃəːn/ *n.* & *v.* [OE *ċyrin* = MLG *kerne, kirne*, MDu. *kerne*, ON *kirna*, f. Gmc. Sense A.2 f. the vb.] **A** *n.* **1** A butter-making machine in which milk or cream is agitated; a large milk-can (orig. one shaped like a butter-churn). OE. **2** A churning action or sensation. L19.

B *v.* **1** *v.t.* & *i.* Agitate (milk or cream) in a churn; produce (butter) thus. LME. **2** *v.t.* Stir (liquid etc.) about, cause to froth; agitate violently; turn or throw *up* violently. L17. **3** *v.i.* Move churning up water, earth, etc.; turn like a churn; (of liquid etc.) wash to and fro, foam, seethe. M18. **4** *v.t.* Foll. by *out*: produce in quantity rather than quality. E20.

2 W. HOLTBY The wagon wheels had churned the yard to treacly clay. J. BETJEMAN Bills to pay later churned up my insides. 3 S. O'FAOLÁIN Rain-water churning down the rocky valleys. R. CHANDLER The ventilator churned dully. C. S. FORESTER Churning along over Salisbury Plain on a bicycle with worn sprocket wheels. W. STYRON I felt my stomach churn and heave.

Comb.: **churn-milk** (now *dial.*) buttermilk; **churn-owl** (now *dial.*) the nightjar; **churn-staff** a staff for agitating milk or cream in a standing churn.

churna'bility *n.* the readiness (of fats in milk or cream) to form butter in churning L19. **churnable** *a.* (of fats in milk or cream) ready to form butter in churning E20. **churner** *n.* a person who or machine which churns L19. **churning** *vbl n.* (*a*) the action or process of the vb; (*b*) *colloq.* the buying and selling of a client's investments for the sole purpose of earning more commission: LME.

churr /tʃəː/ *v.* & *n.* M16. [Imit.: cf. CHIRR.] **A** *v.i.* Esp. of some birds, as the nightjar: make a deep prolonged trilling sound. M16. **B** *n.* **1** Any of various birds that make such a sound, as the partridge, the nightjar. *dial.* E17. **2** Such a sound. M19.

Churrigueresque /tʃʌrɪgə'rɛsk/ *a.* M19. [f. *Churriguera* (see below) + -ESQUE.] *Archit.* Lavishly ornamented in the late Spanish baroque style of José Churriguera (1665–1725).

churrus *n.* var. of CHARAS.

chuse *v.* arch. var. of CHOOSE.

chut /tʃʊt, ʃ-/ *int.* E19. [Imit.: cf. Fr. *chut.*] Expr. impatience.

chute /ʃuːt/ *n.*[1] & *v.* Orig. *N. Amer.* E19. [Fr. = fall (of water etc.) f. OFr. *cheoite* use as n. of fem. pa. pple of *cheoir* to fall f. L *cadere*; extended to senses of SHOOT *n.*[1] Cf. SHUTE *n.*[2]] **A** *n.* **1** A cataract or cascade of water; a steep descent in a river-bed producing a swift current. *N. Amer.* E19. **2** A sloping channel or slide, with or without water, for conveying things to a lower level; a slope for shooting rubbish down. E19. **3** A narrow passage or enclosure for cattle or sheep. L19. **4** A steep slide or roller-coaster, esp. with water at the foot, at a fairground etc. E20. **B** *v.t.* **1** Send down through a chute; drive into or pen in a chute. L19. **2** *chute the chute(s)*, ride on a chute at a fairground etc. E20.

Comb.: **chute-the-chutes** = sense A.4 above.

chute /ʃuːt/ *n.*[2] *colloq.* Also **'chute**. E20. [Abbrev.] A parachute.

chutist *n.* a parachutist E20.

chutney /'tʃʌtni/ *n.* E19. [Hindi *caṭnī*.] A pungent, orig. Indian, condiment of fruits, vinegar, spices, etc.

chutter /'tʃʌtə/ *v.i.* M20. [Imit.] Make a muffled clattering or spluttering noise.

chutty /'tʃʌti/ *n. Austral.* & *NZ slang.* Also **chuddy** /'tʃʌdi/. M20. [Origin unkn.] Chewing-gum.

chutzpah /'xʊtspə, 'hʊ-/ *n. slang.* L19. [Yiddish f. Aram. *ḥuṣpā*.] Shameless audacity, gall.

chylde *n.* see CHILD *n.*

chyle /kʌɪl/ *n.* Also in L form †**chylus**. LME. [Late L *chylus* f. Gk *khūlos* animal or plant juice.] A milky fluid containing fat droplets which drains from the lacteals of the small intestine into the lymphatic system during digestion.

receptacle of chyle: see RECEPTACLE 3a.

chyli'factive, chyli'factory *adjs.* (*rare*) producing chyle M17. **chy'liferous** *a.* bearing or containing chyle M17. **chy'lific** *a.* (now *rare* or *obs.*) producing chyle M19. **chylifi'cation** *n.* conversion into chyle E17. **chylify** *v.t.* convert into chyle M17. **chylous** *a.* pertaining to, full of, or of the nature of chyle M17. **chy'luria** *n.* (*Med.*) the presence of chyle in the urine M19.

chylo- /'kʌɪləʊ/ *comb. form* of CHYLE: see -O-.

chylo'micron *n.* a droplet of fat present in the blood or lymph after absorption from the small intestine E20. †**chylopoietic** *a.* producing chyle M18–M19.

chyme /kʌɪm/ *n.* Also in L form †**chymus**. LME. [Late L *chymus* f. Gk *khūmos* animal or plant juice.] †**1** A humour of the body; the humours collectively. Only in LME. **2** The pulpy acidic fluid which passes from the stomach to the small intestine, and consists of gastric juices and partly-digested food. E17.

chymous *a.* pertaining to or of the nature of chyme L17.

†**chymic** *a., n., & v.* see CHEMIC.

†**chymical** *a.* & *n.* see CHEMICAL.

chymist, chymistry *ns.* see CHEMIST, CHEMISTRY.

chymo- /'kʌɪməʊ/ *comb. form* of CHYME: see -O-.

chymo'trypsin *n.* a proteolytic enzyme active in the small intestine M20. ˌ**chymotryp'sinogen** *n.* an inactive precursor of chymotrypsin secreted by the pancreas and activated by trypsin M20.

†**chymus** *n.* var. of CHYME.

chypre /ʃipr/ *n.* L19. [Fr. = Cyprus, where perh. orig. made.] A heavy perfume made from sandalwood.

ciabatta /tʃə'bɑːtə, *foreign* tʃa'batta/ *n.* Pl. **-ttas, -tte** /-tte/. L20. [It. dial., lit. 'slipper' (from the shape of the loaf).] A type of moist aerated Italian bread made with olive oil; a loaf of this.

ciao /tʃaʊ/ *int. colloq.* E20. [It. dial. alt. of *schiavo* (I am your) slave f. med.L *sclavus* slave.] Hello; goodbye.

cibarian /sɪˈbɛːrɪən/ *a.* E17. [f. L *cibarius*, f. *cibus* food, + -AN.] 1 Of or pertaining to food. *rare.* E17. 2 *Entomol.* Of or pertaining to the mouthparts of an insect. M19.
cibarial *a.* (*Entomol.*) = CIBARIAN 2; *spec.* of or pertaining to the cibarium: L19. **cibarious** *a.* (*rare*) (*a*) = CIBARIAN 1; (*b*) edible: M17. **cibarium** *n.* (*Entomol.*) the preoral cavity of an insect, often specialized for the temporary storage of food or as a salivary pump M20.

†cibation *n.* L15. [Late L *cibatio(n-)*, f L *cibat-* pa. ppl stem of *cibare* to feed f. *cibus* food see -ATION.] 1 *Alch.* The seventh process, 'feeding the matter'. L15–M17. 2 *gen.* Taking food, feeding. M17–M19.

cibol *n.* see CIBOULE.

ciborium /sɪˈbɔːrɪəm/ *n.* Pl. **-ia** /-ɪə/. M16. [med.L f. Gk *kibōrion* cup-shaped seed-vessel of the Egyptian water lily, a drinking-cup made from this. Sense 1 prob. infl. by L *cibus* food.] 1 *Chr. Ch.* A receptacle for the reservation of the Eucharist, shaped like a shrine, or a cup with an arched cover. M16. 2 *Archit.* A canopy; a canopied shrine. M18.

ciboule /ˈsɪb(ə)l/ *n.* Also **cibol**. M17. [Fr.: see CHIBOL. Cf. earlier SYBOW.] The Welsh onion, *Allium fistulosum*, which resembles a spring onion.

cicada /sɪˈkɑːdə/ *n.* LME. [L *cicada*, *cicala*.] Any of the family Cicadidae of large-winged homopteran insects, the males of which make shrill chirping sounds.
periodical cicada: see PERIODICAL *a.* 2. SEVENTEEN-*year cicada*.
¶The usual name 17–18 was CIGALA.
cicad /ˈsɪkad/ *n.* a cicada M19. **cicala** *n.* a cicada L18.

cicatrice /ˈsɪkətrɪs/ *n.* Also (esp. *Med.* & *Bot.*) **cicatrix** /ˈsɪkətrɪks/. Pl. **cicatrices** /ˈsɪkətrɪsɪz; *esp. Med.* & *Bot.* sɪkəˈtrʌɪsiːz/. LME. [(O)Fr., or L *cicatrix*, *-tric-*.] 1 The scar of a healed wound, burn, etc.; a scar on the bark of a tree. LME. b *Bot.* = SCAR *n.*[2] 2. E19. 2 A mark or impression resembling a scar. L16.
cicatricial /sɪkəˈtrɪʃ(ə)l/ *a.* pertaining to or of the nature of a scar; forming a scar: L19.

cicatricula /sɪkəˈtrɪkjʊlə/ *n.* Pl. **-lae** /-liː/. Also Anglicized as **cicatricle** /sɪˈkatrɪk(ə)l/. M17. [L, dim. of *cicatrix*: see prec., -CULE.] A small mark or scar; *esp.* the germinal region of an egg.

cicatrise *v.* var. of CICATRIZE.

cicatrix *n.* see CICATRICE.

cicatrize /ˈsɪkətrʌɪz/ *v.* Also **-ise**. LME. [(O)Fr. *cicatriser*, †*-icer*, f. as CICATRICE; assim. to vbs in -IZE.] 1 *v.t.* Heal (a wound etc.) by scarring; skin over. LME. 2 *v.i.* Of a wound etc.: become healed by forming a scar. LME. 3 *v.t.* Mark with scars; scar. E18.
cicaˈtrizant *a.* & *n.* (a medicine) that cicatrizes wounds etc. M17. **cicatriˈzation** *n.* the formation of a scar in the healing of a wound etc. M16. **cicatrizer** *n.* a person who or thing which cicatrizes wounds etc. L16.

cicely /ˈsɪsɪli/ *n.* L16. [App. f. L *seselis* SESELI f. Gk, w. assim. to female forename *Cicely*.] Any of various umbelliferous plants; *esp.* (*a*) (more fully *sweet cicely*) a European plant, *Myrrhis odorata*, resembling cow parsley, with aromatic foliage and white flowers; (*b*) *N. Amer.* a member of the genus *Osmorhiza* .

cicer /ˈsɪsə/ *n.* LME. [L.] A chick-pea. Now only as mod.L genus name.

cicerone /tʃɪtʃəˈrəʊni, sɪsə-/ *n.* Pl. **-ni** /-ni/, **-nes**. E18. [It. f. L *Ciceron-*: see CICERONIAN.] A guide who understands and explains antiquities etc.

cicerone /tʃɪtʃəˈrəʊn, sɪs-/ *v.t.* L18. [f. the n.] Act as a cicerone to.

Ciceronian /sɪsəˈrəʊnɪən/ *a.* & *n.* L16. [L *Ciceronianus*, f. *Cicero*, *-on-* cognomen of Marcus Tullius *Cicero* (106–43 BC), Roman politician and orator: see -IAN.] A *adj.* Pertaining to or in the style of Cicero; eloquent, classical, rhythmical. L16. B *n.* An admirer, student, or imitator of Cicero or his works. L16.
Ciceronianism *n.* (an expression) imitating Cicero as a model of Latin style L16.

†cich *n.* var. of CHICH.

cichlid /ˈsɪklɪd/ *n.* & *a.* L19. [mod.L *Cichlidae* (see below), f. Gk *kikhlē* a kind of fish: see -ID[3].] A *n.* A tropical freshwater fish of the family Cichlidae, of which many kinds are kept in aquaria. L19. B *adj.* Of, pertaining to, or designating this family. L19.

†cichling *n.* see CHICKLING.

cicisbeo /tʃɪtʃɪzˈbeɪəʊ/ *n.* Pl. **-bei** /-ˈbeiː/, **-os**. E18. [It., of unkn. origin.] A married (orig. Italian) woman's male companion or lover.
cicisbeism /-ˈbiːɪz(ə)m/ *n.* the practice of attending a married woman as a cicisbeo M18.

ciclatoun /ˈsɪklətən/ *n.* Long *obs.* exc. *Hist.* ME. [OFr. *ciclaton*, perh. f. Arab. *siqilāṭūn*.] Cloth of gold or a similar rich material.

ciconiiform /sɪˈkəʊnɪɪfɔːm/ *a.* L19. [mod.L *ciconiiformis*, f. *ciconia* stork: see -FORM.] *Ornith.* Belonging or pertaining to the order Ciconiiformes, which includes the herons, storks, ibises, flamingos, and related birds.

†cicurate *v.t.* E17–E18. [L *cicurat-* pa. ppl stem of *cicurare* to tame f. *cicur* tame: see -ATE[3].] Tame, domesticate.

cicuta /sɪˈkjuːtə/ *n.* LME. [L *cicuta*.] Hemlock, esp. as a poison.
cicuˈtoxin *n.* a polyunsaturated alcohol that is the major toxin of water hemlock, *Cicuta virosa* L19.

cidaris /ˈsɪdərɪs/ *n.* E17. [L f. Gk *kidaris*, *kitaris*, = Heb. *keṯer* (Persian) crown, diadem.] The royal tiara or cap of state of the ancient Persians.

-cide /sʌɪd/ *suff.* [Sense 1 f. Fr. *-cide* f. L *-cida*, sense 2 f. Fr. *-cide* f. L *-cidium* cutting, killing, both f. *caedere*, *-cidere* cut, kill.] 1 Forming (usu. w. intermediate -I-) ns. w. the sense 'a person or substance that kills', as *fratricide*, *insecticide*, etc. 2 Forming (usu. w. intermediate -I-) ns. of action w. the sense 'the killing of (the first element)', as *suicide* etc.

cider /ˈsʌɪdə/ *n.* Also **cy-**. ME. [OFr. *sidre*, earlier *cisdre* (mod. *cidre*), f. eccl.L *sicera* (med.L *cisera*) f. eccl.Gk *sikera* f. Heb. *šēḵār* strong drink.] A drink made from the juice of apples (and formerly other fruit) expressed and fermented; *N. Amer.* unfermented apple juice.
Comb.: **cider apple**: from which cider is made. **cider-press**: for squeezing juice from apples.
ciderist *n.* (now *rare*) a maker or connoisseur of cider M17. **ciderkin** *n.* a weak cider made from second pressings L17. **cidery** *a.* of the nature of or resembling cider L19.

ci-devant /sidvɑ̃/ *a.* & *adv.* E18. [Fr.] Former(ly); that has been (with the person's earlier name or status).

ciel *v.* & *n.* var. of CEIL.

cieling *n.* var. of CEILING.

cierge /sɪədʒ; *foreign* sjɛrʒ (*pl. same*)/ *n.* ME. [OFr. *cerge*, (also mod.) *cierge*, f. L *cereas* wax taper, f *cera* wax.] A wax candle, *esp.* one used in religious ceremonies.

cig /sɪg/ *n. colloq.* L19. [Abbrev.] A cigarette; *occas.* a cigar, a cigarillo.

cigala /sɪˈgɑːlə/ *n.* Also **-ale** /-ɑːl/. E17. [OProv. *cigala*, Fr. *cigale*, f. as CICADA.] = CICADA.

cigar /sɪˈgɑː/ *n.* Also **segar**, (now *US colloq.* & *dial.*) **seegar** /ˈsiːgɑː/. E18. [Fr. *cigare* or its source Sp. *cigarro*, prob. f. Mayan *sik'ar* smoking.] A compact roll of tobacco-leaf for smoking.
Manila cigar: see MANILA *a.* 1. *panatela cigar*: see PANATELA 1.
Comb.: **cigar flower** a Mexican primulaceous plant, *Cuphea ignea*, with a scarlet tubular corolla tipped with black and white; **cigar-holder** a device for holding a cigar for smoking; **cigar-lighter** a device (esp. in a motor car) for lighting a cigar, cigarette, etc.; **cigar plant** = *cigar flower* above; **cigar-shaped** *a.* cylindrical with a pointed end or pointed ends.
cigaˈresque *a.* (*joc.*) having a cigar or cigars as a prominent feature M19. **cigary** *a.* of or pertaining to a heavy cigar-smoker E20.

cigarette /sɪgəˈrɛt/ *n.* Also ***-ret**. M19. [Fr., f. *cigare*: see prec., -ETTE.] A small cylinder of finely-cut tobacco or of a narcotic or medicated substance rolled in paper for smoking.
RUSSIAN *cigarette*.
Comb.: **cigarette card**, **-coupon** a picture card, a voucher, inserted by the manufacturer into a packet or box of cigarettes; **cigarette-case**: for holding cigarettes before use; **cigarette-end** the unsmoked remainder of a cigarette; **cigarette-holder** a device for holding a cigarette for smoking; **cigarette-lighter** a mechanical device for lighting cigarettes; **cigarette machine**: that dispenses (boxes or packets of) cigarettes; **cigarette-paper**: for rolling tobacco in to make a cigarette.

cigarillo /sɪgəˈrɪləʊ, -ljəʊ/ *n.* Pl. **-os**. M19. [Sp. *cigarrillo*, dim. of *cigarro* CIGAR.] A small cigar.

cigarito /sɪgəˈriːtəʊ/ *n.* Pl. **-os**. Also **-ta** /-tə/. M19. [Amer. Sp. *cigarrito*, dim. of *cigarro* CIGAR.] A cigarette.

ciggy /ˈsɪgi/ *n. colloq.* M20. [Abbrev.: see -Y[6].] A cigarette.

ciguatera /sɪgwəˈtɛːrə/ *n.* M19. [Amer. Sp., f. *cigua* sea-snail.] Poisoning due to ingestion of neurotoxins sometimes present in the flesh of tropical marine fish.

cilery /ˈsɪləri/ *n.* Now *rare* or *obs.* Also **-ll-**. M16. [Origin uncertain: perh. rel. to CEIL.] *Archit.* Drapery or foliage carved on the heads of pillars; such a carving.

cilia *n.* pl. of CILIUM.

ciliary /ˈsɪlɪəri/ *a.* L17. [f. as CILIUM + -ARY[1].] 1 Of or pertaining to the eyelashes or eyelids. L17. 2 Of, pertaining to, caused by, or involving cilia (sense 3). M19.
1 **ciliary body** the part of the eye connecting the choroid to the iris. **ciliary muscle** an annular muscle within the ciliary body controlling the shape of the lens of the eye.
Also †**ciliar** *a.* E17–E19.

ciliate /ˈsɪlɪeɪt/ *a.* & *n.* M18. [f. as prec. + -ATE[2].] A *adj.* Furnished or fringed with cilia. M18. B *n.* A protozoan of the phylum Ciliophora (formerly class Ciliophora), characterized by the presence of motile cilia. L19.
ciliated *a.* = CILIATE *a.* M18. **ciliˈation** *n.* the presence or arrangement of cilia M19.

cilice /ˈsɪlɪs/ *n.* L16. [Fr. f. L *cilicium* f. Gk *kilikion*, f. *Kilikia* Cilicia (see next).] (A garment of) haircloth.

Cilician /sɪˈlɪʃ(ə)n/ *a.* & *n.* L16. [f. *Cilicia* (see below) + -AN.] A *adj.* of or pertaining to Cilicia, an ancient district of S. Anatolia, now in S. Turkey. L16. B *n.* A native or inhabitant of Cilicia. M18.

Cilicism /ˈsɪlɪsɪz(ə)m/ *n.* M19. [f. as prec. + -ISM.] A word or expression characteristic of Cilicia.

ciliiform /ˈsɪlɪɪfɔːm/ *a.* M19. [f. CILIUM + -I- + -FORM.] Having the form of cilia.

cilio- /ˈsɪlɪəʊ/ *comb. form* of CILIUM: see -O-.
cilioˈretinal *a.* of or pertaining to the retina and ciliary body of the eye L19.

cilium /ˈsɪlɪəm/ *n.* Pl. **-ia** /-ɪə/. E18. [L.] 1 An eyelash; (the edge of) an eyelid. E18. 2 A delicate hair like an eyelash, e.g. on the margin of a leaf, or the wing of an insect. L18. 3 A hairlike appendage, usu. motile, which is found in numbers on the surfaces of some cells, and in many organisms is used in locomotion. M19.

cill *n.* & *v.* see SILL *n.*[1] & *v.*

cillery *n.* var. of CILERY.

cimarron /ˈsɪmər(ə)n, sɪməˈrəʊn/ *n. N. Amer.* Also **cimmaron**. M19. [Amer. Sp. *cimarrón* = wild, untamed, (n.) runaway slave, *cima* peak.] The Rocky Mountain sheep, *Ovis canadensis*.

cimbalom /ˈsɪmb(ə)l(ə)m/ *n.* Also **z-** /z-/. L19. [Hungarian f. It. *cembalo*, *cimbalo* CYMBALO.] A dulcimer.

cimbia /ˈsɪmbɪə/ *n.* M17. [It.] *Archit.* A fillet or ring round the shaft of a column; an apophyge.

Cimbrian /ˈsɪmbrɪən/ *n.* & *a.* M16. [f. L *Cimbri* + -AN.] A *n.* A member of an ancient people of central Europe of unknown affinities. M16. B *adj.* of or pertaining to the Cimbrians. L16.

Cimbric /ˈsɪmbrɪk/ *n.* & *a.* E17. [f. as prec. + -IC.] A *n.* †1 A Cimbrian. *rare.* Only in E17. 2 The language of the Cimbrians. M18. B *adj.* = CIMBRIAN *a.* L18.

†cime *n.* see CYME.

cimelia /sɪˈmiːlɪə/ *n.pl. rare.* M17. [Late L, pl. of *cimelium* (church) treasure f. Gk *keimēlion* anything stored up as valuable.] Treasures laid up in store.

cimeliarch *n.* (*a*) a storehouse (for treasures); (*b*) a treasurer: M17.

cimetidine /sʌɪˈmɛtɪdiːn/ *n.* L20. [f. *ci-* alt. of CY(ANO- + MET(HYL + -IDINE.] *Pharm.* An antihistamine drug which is a sulphur-containing derivative of imidazole used to treat peptic ulcers.

¶A proprietary name for this drug is TAGAMET.

cimex /ˈsʌɪmɛks/ *n.* L16. [L.] A bedbug. Now only as mod.L genus name.

cimmaron *n.* var. of CIMARRON.

Cimmerian /sɪˈmɪərɪən/ *n.* & *a.* L16. [f. L *Cimmerius* (f. Gk *Kimmerios*) + -AN.] **A** *n.* **1** A member of a people fabled to live in perpetual darkness. L16. **2** A member of a nomadic people of antiquity, the earliest known inhabitants of the Crimea, who overran Asia Minor in the 7th cent. BC. L18. **B** *adj.* **1** Of or pertaining to the legendary Cimmerians; (of darkness, night, etc.) thick, gloomy. L16. **2** Of or pertaining to the nomadic Cimmerians. M19.

cinch /sɪn(t)ʃ/ *n.* & *v.* M19. [Sp. *cincha* girth.] **A** *n.* **1** A saddle-girth used in Mexico and the western US, usu. made of twisted horsehair or cord. M19. **2** *fig.* A firm hold; *slang* a sure, safe, or easy thing, a certainty. L19. **3** A variant of the card-game all fours. L19.

2 *lead-pipe cinch*: see LEAD *n.*[1] & *a.*

B *v.* **1** *v.t.* Fix (a saddle etc.) securely by means of a girth, fix (a girth); *transf.* girdle, pull *in*, (clothing). M19. **b** *v.i.* Fix a saddle-girth. L19. **2** *v.t. fig.* Get (a person) into a tight place; secure a hold upon. L19. **b** Make certain of (something); render conclusive. *slang.* E20. **3** *v.t.* In the card-game cinch: protect (a trick) by playing a higher trump than the five. L19.

cinchocaine /ˈsɪŋkəʊkeɪn/ *n.* M20. [f. next + -CAINE.] *Pharm.* A quinoline derivative used as a very powerful local anaesthetic for surface or spinal applications.

¶A proprietary name for this drug is NUPERCAINE.

cinchona /sɪŋˈkəʊnə/ *n.* Also **chinchona** /tʃɪnˈtʃəʊnə/. M18. [mod.L, f. Countess of *Chinchón* (d. 1641), vicereine of Peru, who introduced the drug to Spain.] **1** An evergreen tree or shrub of the S. American genus *Cinchona*, of the madder family, with fragrant flowers. M18. **2** = *cinchona bark* below. Also, a drug made from cinchona bark. L18.

Comb.: **cinchona bark** the dried bark of a cinchona (as a source of quinine and other medicinal alkaloids).

cinchonicine, cinchonidine *ns.* cinchona alkaloids isomeric with cinchonine M19. **cinchonine** *n.* an alkaloid, $C_{19}H_{22}ON_2$, with febrifuge properties, found with quinine in cinchona bark E19. **cinchonism** *n.* poisoning due to excessive ingestion of cinchona alkaloids M19.

cincinnus /sɪnˈsɪnəs/ *n.* M19. [L = curl, ringlet.] *Bot.* A scorpioid cyme.

cinct /sɪŋkt/ *pred. a.* Chiefly *poet.* LME. [L *cinctus* pa. pple of *cingere* gird.] Girt, encircled, (*with*).

cincture /ˈsɪŋktʃə/ *n.* & *v.* L16. [L *cinctura*, f. as prec. + *-ura* -URE.] **A** *n.* **1** A girding, encompassing, or encircling; enclosure. L16. **2** A thing which girdles or encompasses; *spec.* a girdle or belt for the waist. M17. **b** *Archit.* The ring at the top or bottom of a column which divides the shaft from the capital or base; a ring or band encircling a column or interrupting an architrave. L17. **B** *v.t.* Gird; encompass, surround. L18.

cinder /ˈsɪndə/ *n.* & *v.* [OE *sinder* = MLG *sinder*, OHG *sintar* (G *Sinter*), ON *sindr*; w. assim. since 16 to unrelated Fr. *cendre* (L *cinis, ciner-* ashes).] **A** *n.* **1** Slag, scoria. OE. **2** In *pl.* The residue of combustion; ashes. LME. **3** *spec.* A residual piece of coal, wood, etc., whether cold or not, that has ceased to flame but has still combustible matter in it. M16.

3 burn to a cinder make inedible or useless by burning.

Comb.: **cinder-cone** a cone formed round the mouth of a volcano by debris cast up during eruption; **cinder path, track** a footpath or running-track laid with fine cinders.

B *v.t.* Reduce to cinders. LME.

cindery *a.* of the nature of a cinder; full of cinders: M16.

Cinderella /sɪndəˈrɛlə/ *n.* M19. [The heroine of a fairy tale, f. CINDER *n.* + -ELLA, after Fr. *Cendrillon*, f. *cendre* cinders, ashes + dim. ending *-illon.*] **1** A drudge; a neglected or despised partner, member of a group, etc.; a person or thing of unrecognized or disregarded merit or beauty. M19. **2** In full *Cinderella dance.* A dance stopping at midnight. L19.

cinderous /ˈsɪnd(ə)rəs/ *a.* Also **cindrous** /ˈsɪndrəs/. E17. [f. CINDER *n.* + -OUS.] Cindery.

cine /ˈsɪni/ *a.* Also (now *rare*) **k-** /k-/. See also CINE-. L19. [Abbrev.] Cinematographic.

cine camera, film, projector, etc.

cine- /ˈsɪni/ *comb. form.* [Abbrev. of CINEMATOGRAPHIC, CINEMA. Cf. prec.] **1** Cinematographic. **2** With the sense 'cinema', as *cine-goer.*

cinefluoroˈgraphic *a.* of or pertaining to cinefluorography M20. **cinefluoˈrography** *n.* the recording of a fluoroscopic image by cinephotography M20. **cinemicroˈgraphic** *a.* of or pertaining to cinemicrography M20. **cinemiˈcrography** *n.* the making of a cine film of an object, process, etc., seen with the aid of a microscope M20. **cinephoˈtography** *n.* the making of a cine film E20. **cineˈradiograph** *n.* a series of cineradiographic photographs M20. **cineradioˈgraphic** *a.* of or pertaining to cineradiography M20. **cineradiˈography** *n.* the taking of a series of X-ray photographs which can be viewed in the manner of a cine film M20.

cinéaste /ˈsɪneɪast; *foreign* sineast (*pl. same*)/ *n.* Also **cineast(e)** /ˈsɪnɪast/. E20. [Fr., f. *ciné* CINE + *-aste* as in *enthousiaste* enthusiast.] An enthusiast for or devotee of the cinema.

cinema /ˈsɪnɪmə/ *n.* Also (now *rare*) **k-** /k-/. E20. [Fr. *cinéma* abbrev. of *cinématographe* CINEMATOGRAPH *n.* Initial *k-* after Gk.] **1** = CINEMATOGRAPH *n.* E20. **2** A theatre in which cinematographic films are shown. E20. **3** Cinematography; the production of cinematographic films, esp. as an art or an industry. E20.

Comb.: **cinema-goer** a person who frequents the cinema; **cinema organ**: with extra stops and effects.

cinematheque /sɪnɪməˈtɛk/ *n.* Also *cinémathèque* /sinematɛk (*pl. same*)/. M20. [Fr. *cinémathèque*, f. as prec., after *bibliothèque* library.] A library of cinema films; a (national) repository of old films. Also, a small cinema showing artistic films.

cinematic /sɪnɪˈmatɪk/ *a.* E20. [f. CINEMA after CINEMATOGRAPH: see -IC.] Of or pertaining to the cinematograph; suitable for cinematography; suggestive of the technique, dialogue, etc., of the cinema.

cinematically *adv.* M20.

cinematize /ˈsɪnɪmətʌɪz/ *v.t.* Also **-ise.** E20. [f. as prec. + -IZE.] Adapt (a play, story, etc.) to the cinema; make a film of.

cinematograph /sɪnɪˈmatəgrɑːf/ *n.* & *v.* Also (now *rare*) **k-** /k-/. L19. [Fr. *cinématographe*, f. Gk *kinēma, kinēmat-* movement: see -GRAPH. Initial *k-* after Gk.] **A** *n.* An apparatus for producing an image in which persons and things appear to move, by rapidly projecting on to a screen a succession of photographs on a long film, often also with the reproduction of sound recorded on it; a film projector. L19. **B** *v.t.* Make a cinematographic record of. L19.

cinematographic /ˌsɪnɪmatəˈgrafɪk/ *a.* Also (now *rare*) **k-** /k-/. L19. [f. prec. + -IC. Initial *k-* after Gk.] Of or pertaining to cinematography or the cinematograph.

cinematographical *a.* E20. **cinematographically** *adv.* L19.

cinematography /ˌsɪnɪməˈtɒgrəfi/ *n.* Also (now *rare*) **k-** /k-/. L19. [f. as prec.: see -GRAPHY. Initial *k-* after Gk.] The art of taking and reproducing cinematographic films; the use of the cinematograph.

cinematographer *n.* a person who takes cinematographic films L19. **cinematographist** *n.* (now *rare*) = CINEMATOGRAPHER L19.

cinéma-vérité /sinemaverite, ˌsɪnɪməˈvɛrɪteɪ/ *n.* M20. [Fr.] (The making of) films which avoid artificiality and have the appearance of real life.

cineole /ˈsɪnɪəʊl/ *n.* Also **-ol** /-ɒl/. L19. [f. reversal of mod.L *oleum cinae* wormseed oil, f. L *oleum* oil + *cynas* an Arabian tree: see -OLE[2].] Either of two isomeric essential oils, 1,4- and 1,8-cineole; *esp.* the latter, = EUCALYPTOL.

cineraria /sɪnəˈrɛːrɪə/ *n.*[1] L16. [mod.L (former genus name), fem. of L *cinerarius* CINERARY.] Orig., the silver ragwort, *Senecio cineraria*, grown for its hoary leaves. Now, any of various garden hybrids of the allied *Pericallis cruenta*, of the Canary Islands, with corymbs of daisy-like blue, purple, etc., flower-heads, grown as pot plants.

cineraria *n.*[2] pl. of next.

cinerarium /sɪnəˈrɛːrɪəm/ *n.* Pl. **-ria** /-rɪə/. L19. [Late L *cinerarium* use as n. of neut. sing. of L *cinerarius*: see next, -ARIUM.] A place for depositing the ashes of the dead after cremation.

cinerary /ˈsɪnərəri/ *a.* M18. [L *cinerarius*, f. *ciner-, cinis* ashes: see -ARY[1].] Of or pertaining to ashes.

cinerary urn: holding the ashes of the dead after cremation.

cinereous /sɪˈnɪərɪəs/ *a.* LME. [f. L *cinereus*, f. *cinis, ciner-* ashes, + -OUS.] Of the nature of ashes; (esp. of a bird or plumage) ash-coloured.

cineritious /sɪnəˈrɪʃəs/ *a.* L17. [f. L *cinericius* f. *cinis, ciner-* ashes, + -OUS: see -ITIOUS[1].] **1** Ash-grey; also formerly used of the grey matter of the brain and spinal cord. L17. **2** Of the nature of ashes or cinders. M18.

ciné-vérité /sineverite, sɪnɪˈvɛrɪteɪ/ *n.* M20. [Fr.] = CINÉMA-VÉRITÉ.

Cingalese /sɪŋgəˈliːz/ *n.* & *a. arch.* Pl. of n. same. L16. [f. as SINHALESE, partly through Fr. *Cing(h)alais.*] = SINHALESE.

cingle /ˈsɪŋg(ə)l/ *n.* ME. [OFr. *cengle* (mod. *sangle*) f. L *cingulum, -la* girdle, f. *cingere* gird.] A girdle; a girth; a belt.

cingulum /ˈsɪŋgjʊləm/ *n.* Pl. **-la** /-lə/. M19. [L: see prec.] Chiefly *Anat.* & *Zool.* A girdle, belt, or analogous structure; *esp.* (*a*) a ridge surrounding the base of the crown of a tooth; (*b*) a gyrus of each cerebral hemisphere, partly encircling the corpus callosum.

cingular *a.* of or pertaining to a cingulum E20. **cingulate** *a.* having a cingulum; of the nature of a cingulum: E19.

cinnabar /ˈsɪnəbɑː/ *n.* & *a.* ME. [L *cinnabaris* f. Gk *kinnabari*, of oriental origin.] **A** *n.* **1** Native mercury(II) sulphide, a bright red hexagonal mineral which usu. occurs in massive form and is the only important ore of mercury; this mineral used as a pigment, vermilion. ME. **2** A moth, *Tyria jacobaeae*, with bright red wing markings. Also *cinnabar-moth.* E19. **B** *adj.* Of the colour of cinnabar; vermilion. E19.

cinnabarine *a.* consisting of or containing cinnabar; of the colour of cinnabar: L17.

cinnamic /sɪˈnamɪk/ *a.* M19. [f. L *cinnamum* CINNAMON + -IC.] *Chem.* Of cinnamon; *cinnamic acid*, the compound, 3-phenylpropenoic acid, $C_6H_5{\cdot}CHCHCOOH$, a crystalline unsaturated acid present in many resins and balsams.

cinnaˈmaldehyde *n.* the corresponding aldehyde, $C_6H_5CHCHCHO$, which is the major constituent of cinnamon and cassia oils L19. **ˈcinnamate** *n.* a salt or ester of cinnamic acid M19. **ˈcinnamyl** *n.* the radical $C_6H_5CHCHCH_2{\cdot}$; usu. in *comb.*: M19.

cinnamon /ˈsɪnəmən/ *n.* & *a.* LME. [(O)Fr. *cinnamome* f. L *cinnamomum* f. Gk *kinnamōmon*, later refash. after L *cinnamon, -mum* f. Gk *kinnamon*, f. Semitic, perh. ult. f. Malay.] **A** *n.* **1** The powdered aromatic inner bark of a southern Indian tree, *Cinnamomum zeylanicum*, used as a spice. Also, the bark of certain other trees, resembling this. LME. **2** A tree yielding cinnamon. LME. **3** The colour of cinnamon; a yellowish brown. L19.

Phrases: **wild cinnamon** an evergreen tree, *Canella winterana*, native to Florida and the W. Indies, whose bark is used as a spice; the bark of this tree.

B *adj.* Of the colour of cinnamon; yellowish brown. L17.

Comb.: **cinnamon bear** a cinnamon-coloured phase of the N. American black bear; **cinnamon fern** *N. Amer.* a large fern, *Osmunda cinnamomea*, often with cinnamon fronds; **cinnamon oil** an aromatic oil distilled from cinnamon bark; **cinnamon rose** a fragrant Eurasian rose, *Rosa majalis*; **cinnamon stone** a yellow-brown variety of garnet; **cinnamon toast** buttered toast spread with ground cinnamon and sugar.

cinq *n.* var. of CINQUE.

cinqfoil *n.* & *a.* var. of CINQUEFOIL.

cinq trous /sɛ̃:k tru/ *n. phr.* L19. [Fr. = five holes.] A form of mesh in certain types of lace in which openings are set alternately in quincunx form.

cinque /sɪŋk/ *n.* Also **cinq**. LME. [OFr. *cinc*, *cink* (mod. *cinq*) f. L *quinque* five.] **1** The five on dice; a throw of five. LME. **2** *Campanol.* In *pl.* Changes on eleven bells in which five couples of bells change places in the order of ringing. L19.

¶ Cf. earlier CINQUE PORTS, also CINQ TROUS.

cinquecento /tʃɪŋkwɪ'tʃɛntəʊ/ *n.* M18. [It. = five hundred.] The sixteenth century in Italy; the Italian style of art of this period, with reversion to classical forms.

cinquecentist *n.* a sixteenth-century Italian artist or writer L19.

cinquedea /tʃɪŋkwɪ'deɪə/ *n.* L19. [It. (Venetian), f. *cinque* five + *dea* = *dita* fingers, pl. of *dito* f. L *digitus* DIGIT.] An Italian broad-bladed dagger or short sword.

cinquefoil /'sɪŋkfɔɪl/ *n.* & *a.* Also **cinqfoil**. ME. [f. L *quinquefolium*: see CINQUE, FOIL *n.*[1]] **A** *n.* **1** Any of various plants of the genus *Potentilla*, of the rose family, with compound leaves of five leaflets. ME. **2** An ornamental design resembling the leaf of a cinquefoil, esp. inscribed in an arch or circle. LME. **B** *adj.* Shaped like the leaf of cinquefoil; decorated with cinquefoils. LME.

cinquefoiled *a.* = CINQUEFOIL *a.* E19.

†cinquepace *n.* L16–M17. [Fr. *cinq pas* five paces.] A lively dance, identified with the galliard.

Cinque Ports /sɪŋk 'pɔ:ts/ *n. phr. pl.* ME. [OFr. *cink porz* repr. L *quinque portus* five ports.] **1** Certain ports on the south-east coast of England (orig. five—Hastings, Sandwich, Dover, Romney, Hythe—later also Rye and Winchelsea) which formerly furnished the chief part of the navy and in return had many important privileges and franchises. ME. **†2** Barons of the Cinque Ports. Only in E17.

Cinzano /tʃɪn'zɑ:nəʊ/ *n.* Pl. **-os**. E20. [Name of the manufacturers.] (Proprietary name for) an Italian vermouth; a drink of this.

cion *n.* see SCION.

cipher /'sʌɪfə/ *n.* Also **cypher**. LME. [OFr. *cif(f)re* (mod. *chiffre*) f. med.L *cif(e)ra* partly through It. *cifra*, †*cifera* f. Arab. *ṣifr*: cf. ZERO *n.* & *a.* Branch II perh. a different wd: cf. CIPHER *v.*] **I 1** An arithmetical symbol, 0, of no value by itself, but used to occupy a vacant place in decimal etc. numeration. LME. **b** *fig.* A person who or thing which fills a place but is of no importance; a nonentity. L16. **2** A numeral; *esp.* an arabic numeral. LME. **†b** A symbolic character; a hieroglyph; an astrological sign. M16–M19. **3** A secret or disguised system of writing, a code used in writing; a message etc. so written; a key to such a system. E16. **†b** In *pl.* Shorthand. M16–M17. **4** An interlacing of letters, esp. the initials of a name; a monogram. M16.

1b P. G. WODEHOUSE He was.. a cipher in the home. **3** L. STRACHEY She despatched a fulminating telegram to Mr. Gladstone, not in the usual cypher, but open. PLAYFAIR *cipher*.

II 5 A continuous sounding of an organ-pipe owing to a mechanical defect. L18.

cipherdom *n.* the state of being a nonentity E20.

cipher /'sʌɪfə/ *v.* Also **cypher**. E16. [Perh. two different wds. Branch II f. the n.] **I 1** *v.i.* Of an organ: sound a note continuously owing to a mechanical defect. E16. **II 2** *v.i.* Use arabic numerals; do arithmetic. *arch.* M16. **3** *v.t.* & *i.* Write in cipher; express in a secret or disguised way; encipher. M16. **†4** *v.t. gen.* Express; delineate. (Foll. by *forth*, *out*.) L16–M17. **†5** *v.t.* Decipher. *rare* (Shakes.). Only in L16. **6** *v.t.* Bevel *away*, *off*. Now *rare* or *obs.* L17. **7** *v.t.* Calculate; work *out* arithmetically; think *out*. M19. **8** *v.t. Cricket.* Assign a zero to in the score; put out for no runs. L19.

cipherable *a.* L19. **cipherer** *n.* M17.

cipolin /'sɪpəlɪn/ *n.* Also **cipollino** /tʃɪpə'li:nəʊ/, pl. **-os**. L18. [(Fr. *cipolin* f.) It. *cipollino*, f. *cipolla* onion (L *cepa*); so called from the resemblance of its foliated structure to the coats of an onion.] An Italian marble interfoliated with veins of talc, mica, quartz, etc., showing alternations of (esp. white and green) colourings.

cippus /'sɪpəs/ *n.* Pl. **cippi** /'sɪpʌɪ/. E17. [L = post, stake.] **1** The stocks. Now *rare* or *obs.* E17. **2** *Archit.* A low column, usu. bearing an inscription, used by the ancients as a landmark, funerary monument, etc. E18.

circa /'sə:kə/ *prep.* M19. [L.] About, approximately in or at (with dates etc.).

circadian /sə:'keɪdɪən/ *a.* M20. [f. L CIRCA + *dies* day + -AN.] Of physiological activity etc.: occurring or recurring about once a day.

circar *n.* see SIRKAR.

Circassian /sə:'kasɪən/ *n.* & *a.* M16. [f. *Circassia* Latinized form of Russ. *Cherkes*: see -IA[1], -AN.] **A** *n.* **1** A native or inhabitant of Circassia, a region in the N. Caucasus; the Caucasian language of the people of this region. M16. **2** A thin worsted fabric. E19.

B *adj.* Of or pertaining to Circassia or the Circassians. M17.

the Circassian circle: a dance popular in the late 19th and early 20th cents.

Circe /'sə:si/ *n.* LME. [L *Circe*, Gk *Kirkē*, an enchantress in Gk mythol.] A dangerously attractive enchantress, a witch.

Circean /sə:'si:ən/ *a.* bewitching, dangerously attractive E17.

circensian /sə:'sɛnsɪən/ *a.* L16. [f. L *circensis* + -AN: see -IAN.] Of, pertaining to, or celebrated in the Circus in ancient Rome.

circinate /'sə:sɪnət, -eɪt/ *a.* E19. [L *circinatus* pa. pple of *circinare* make round, f. as next: see -ATE[2].] **1** *Bot.* & *Zool.* Rolled up with its apex in the centre. E19. **2** *Med.* Circular in appearance; forming circular lesions. L19.

circinately *adv.* M19. **circi'nation** *n.* (now *rare*) †(*a*) a circling or turning round; (*b*) *Bot.* circinate vernation or foliation: L16.

Circinus /'sə:sɪnəs/ *n.* E19. [L *circinus* pair of compasses.] (The name of) a small constellation of the southern hemisphere, in the Milky Way next to Centaurus; the Compasses.

circiter /'sə:sɪtə/ *prep.* L19. [L.] About, *circa*, (with dates).

circlage *n.* var. of CERCLAGE.

circle /'sə:k(ə)l/ *n.* OE. [(O)Fr. *cercle* f. L *circulus* dim. of CIRCUS: see -ULE. Respelt in 16 after L.] **I** A figure or appearance. **1** (The line enclosing) a perfectly round plane figure whose circumference is everywhere equidistant from its centre; *spec.* an imaginary circle on the celestial sphere or terrestrial globe, esp. connecting points of equal latitude, longitude, declination, etc. Also *loosely*, an imperfectly round plane figure, a ring, a closed loop. OE. **2** A luminous ring in the sky; a halo. OE. **b** The round outline or surface of a celestial object. Chiefly *poet.* M17. **3** Formerly, the sphere in which a celestial object was supposed to revolve. Now, the orbit of a planet etc. ME. **4** A ringlike marking, e.g. a fairy-ring. In various team games, a marked-off circular or semicircular area on the playing field, court, rink, etc., to which specific rules apply. LME. **b** A dark circular mark around or below the eyes, esp. due to sickness or insufficient sleep. Usu. in *pl.* M19. **†5** In urinalysis, the upper of the three layers of urine. LME–E17.

4 (In games) *centre circle*, *striking-circle*, etc.

II A material object. **6** A circular object, *esp.* a band; a ring; a crown, coronet, etc. ME. **7** The ring of a circus; *the* circus. *arch.* E17. **8** *Archaeol.* A field monument of circular shape, as a ring of standing stones, a circular ditch, a ring of pits, etc. L18. **9** A curved tier of seats in a theatre, concert hall, or cinema. M19.

6 *transit-circle*: see TRANSIT *n.* **9** *dress circle*, *family circle*, *upper circle*, etc.

III *transf.* & *fig.* **10** The area, extent, or compass *of*. Now chiefly of non-material things: the area of influence or action *of*. LME. **11** A circular course, a complete revolution; a cyclic period. LME. **12** More fully *vicious circle*. The fallacy of proving a proposition from another that rests on it for proof; an unbroken sequence of reciprocal cause and effect; an action and reaction that intensify each other. LME. **13** A completed series of parts forming a sequence. M16. **14** A set (*of* people), a coterie; a class or division of society. M17. **b** A number of people grouped round a centre of interest. E18. **c** A spiritualist seance. M19. **15** *Hist.* A territorial division, esp. in Germany under the Holy Roman Empire. L17. **16** A railway, road, etc., forming a closed loop, allowing traffic to circulate continuously; *spec.* (**C-**) a London Underground line so constructed. E19.

11 A. H. SAYCE The circle of the year. J. B. PRIESTLEY It went round us once in a wide circle. **14** P. G. WODEHOUSE The rest of his circle of acquaintance. M. GIROUARD More at home in donnish than country-house circles. **b** O. MANNING She started to rise, but the circle of women sat firm about her.

Phrases: *Antarctic Circle*: see ANTARCTIC *a.* 1. *Arctic Circle*: see ARCTIC *a.* 1. **circle of (least) confusion** the (smallest possible) circular area illuminated by the rays from a point object after refraction or reflection in a particular optical system (e.g. a camera). *circle of position*: see POSITION *n.* **circle of Willis** [Thomas *Willis* (1621–75), Eng. physician] *Anat.* a circular structure on the underside of the brain formed by several linked arteries. **come full circle** return to starting-point. **diurnal circle**: described by a celestial object in its apparent daily motion. **go round in circles** make no progress despite effort. **great circle** a circle on a sphere whose plane passes through the centre of the sphere. *inner circle*: see INNER *a.* *magic circle*: see MAGIC *a.* **†major circle** = *great circle* above. *meridian circle*: see MERIDIAN *n.*, *a.* 3. PARHELIC *circle*. *polar circle*: see POLAR *a.* PRAGUE (*linguistic*) *circle*. *primitive circle*: see PRIMITIVE *a.* & *n.* *quality circle*: see QUALITY *n.* & *a.* REPEATING *circle*. ROWLAND('s) *circle*. **run** or **rush round in circles** *colloq.* be fussily busy with little result. *sacred circle*: see SACRED *a.* *segment of a circle*: see SEGMENT *n.* 1a. **small circle** any circle on a sphere other than a great circle. *square the circle*: see SQUARE *v.* *swing around the circle*: see SWING *v.* *vertical circle*: see VERTICAL *a.* *vicious circle*: see sense 12 above. *Vienna Circle*: see VIENNA 1. *virtuous circle*: see VIRTUOUS *a.* 2.

Comb.: **circle dance** = *ring dance* s.v. RING *n.*[1]

circlewise *adv.* in the manner or form of a circle M16.

circle /'sə:k(ə)l/ *v.* LME. [f. the n.] **I** *v.t.* **1** Form a circle round; enclose in a circle. LME. **2** Move in a circle round. L16.

1 B. PLAIN White lilacs circled the brim of her straw hat. **2** P. F. BOLLER He circled the globe, visiting one country after another.

II *v.i.* **3** Move in a circle (*round*, *about*, etc.). LME. **b** *spec.* Of cavalry: sweep round on a moving flank as pivot (opp. *wheel* on a fixed flank). E18. **4** *v.i.* Stand or extend in a circle. *rare.* E17.

3 POPE While the bowl circles, and the banquet warms. C. A. LINDBERGH I was circling preparatory to landing in a clover field. **circle back** move in a wide loop towards the starting-point. **4** SIR W. SCOTT That proud ring Of peers who circled round the King.

circled *ppl a.* (*a*) that has been circled; (*b*) rounded, circular; (*c*) marked with a circle or circles: LME. **circler** *n.* E17. **circling** *n.* (*a*) the action of the vb; (*b*) a circular formation: LME.

circlet /'sə:klɪt/ *n.* LME. [f. CIRCLE *n.* + -ET[1]; perh. through Fr. †*cerclet*.] **1** A ring, band, or hoop (*spec.* one of precious metal or jewels), worn as an ornament, esp. on the head. LME. **2** A small circle. E16. **†3** A round piece of wood etc. put under a dish at table. E17–M19.

circlip /'sə:klɪp/ *n.* E20. [Blend of CIRCULAR, CIRCLE *n.*, etc. and CLIP *n.*[1]] A metal ring sprung into a slot or groove in a bar etc. to hold something in place.

circs /sə:ks/ *n.pl.* *colloq.* M19. [Abbrev.] Circumstances. Chiefly in *under the circs*.

circuit /ˈsəːkɪt/ *n.* & *v.* LME. [(O)Fr. f. L *circuitus*, f. *circuit-* pa. ppl stem of *circuire* var. of *circumire*, f. *circum* around + *ire* go.] A *n.* 1 A line that encloses an area; the distance round; the circumference. LME. †b A circlet, a crown. *rare* (Shakes.). Only in L16. 2 A space enclosed by a line; an area; an extent. LME. b *fig.* A sphere of action etc. L16. 3 The time during which a disease runs its course. *rare.* LME. 4 The action of going or moving around or about; a circular journey; a course through intermediate points back to the starting-place; a roundabout journey or course. LME. b *fig.* A revolution of time etc., a cyclic period. E17. 5 The journey of a judge etc. in a particular district to hold courts; the lawyers making the circuit. L15. b A route followed by an itinerant entertainer or competitor in sporting events; a number of places of entertainment at which productions are presented successively; a sequence of sporting events; a chain of theatres, cinemas, etc., under a single management. M19. 6 A roundabout process or mode (of reasoning, legal action, †expression, etc.). M16. 7 The district through which a judge etc. moves to hold courts. L16. 8 A group of local Methodist churches forming a minor administrative unit. M18. 9 The route followed by a confined electric current; an arrangement of interconnected devices such as transistors, resistors, etc., for achieving a particular electric effect. M18. 10 A road forming a closed loop built or used mainly for motor racing. E20. 11 A sequence of athletic exercises performed consecutively. M20.

4 R. L. STEVENSON The figure reappeared, and, making a wide circuit, began to head me off. C. P. SNOW Henry could perform a dignified circuit, Rome, Florence, Venice, . . being entertained by American acquaintances. 5b *rubber-chicken circuit*: see RUBBER *n.*[1] 9 CLOSED-*circuit*. *equivalent circuit*: see EQUIVALENT *a.* *integrated circuit*: see INTEGRATE *v.* *metallic circuit*: see METALLIC *a.* *open circuit*: see OPEN *a.* PRINTED *circuit*. SEQUENTIAL *circuit*. *short circuit*: see SHORT *a.* *solid circuit*: see SOLID *a.* & *adv.*

Comb.: **circuit board** a thin rigid board containing an electric circuit; *esp.* = PRINTED *circuit*; **circuit-breaker** an apparatus for interrupting an electric circuit, usu. as a safety measure (*oil circuit-breaker*: see OIL *n.*); **circuit court** (*a*) a court held by a circuit judge of the High Court of Justiciary in Scotland outside Edinburgh; (*b*) *US* a Federal court of authority intermediate between a district court and the Supreme Court; **circuit judge** orig., a judge who makes a circuit to hold courts; now, a judge who primarily sits in the county courts and the Crown Court or who sits on a circuit court; **circuit-training** consecutive performance of different athletic exercises.

B *v.* 1 *v.t.* Go or travel round. LME. 2 *v.i.* Go or move in a circuit. E17.

circui'teer *n.* & *v.* (*a*) *n.* a judge etc. on circuit; †(*b*) *v.i.* go on a circuit: M18. **circuiter** *n.* = CIRCUITEER *n.* M17. **circuitor** *n.* a person who goes on rounds, a travelling inspector etc. E19. **circuitry** *n.* electric circuits collectively; equipment forming a circuit or circuits: M20.

circuition /səːkjʊˈɪʃ(ə)n/ *n. arch.* M16. [L *circuitio(n-)*, f. *circuit-*: see prec., -ION.] A going round or about; *fig.* circumlocution.

circuitous /səːˈkjuːɪtəs/ *a.* M17. [med.L *circuitosus*, f *circuit-*: see CIRCUIT, -OUS.] Going a long way round, indirect, roundabout.

circuitously *adv.* L18. **circuitousness** *n.* E19.

circuity /səːˈkjuɪti/ *n.* Now *rare.* M16. [OFr. *circuité*, f. L *circuit-*: see CIRCUIT, -Y[5].] †1 Enclosure, compass, area. M–L16. 2 Circuitous quality. L16.

circulable /ˈsəːkjʊləb(ə)l/ *a.* L18. [f. CIRCULATE *v.* + -ABLE.] Able to be circulated.

circular /ˈsəːkjʊlə/ *a.* & *n.* LME. [AN *circuler*, OFr. *circulier* (mod. *-aire*), learned alt. of *cerclier* f. late L *circularis*, f. L *circulus* CIRCLE *n.*: see -AR[1].] A *adj.* 1 Having the form of a circle. LME. 2 Moving in or passing over a circle; taking place along a circle; describing a circle. LME. 3 (Of an argument) involving a vicious circle of reasoning; having the characteristics of a vicious circle. LME. 4 Of or pertaining to the circle as a mathematical figure. L16. †5 Perfect, full, complete. E–M17. 6 Circuitous, indirect. E17. 7 Moving or occurring in a cycle of repetition. M17. 8 Addressed to a circle of people, customers, etc. M17.

1 **circular saw** a toothed disc rotated by machinery for sawing. 2 **circular tour**: bringing the traveller back to the starting-place. 8 *circular letter, note*, etc.

B *n.* †1 A circular figure or space. *rare.* M16–E19. 2 A letter, notice, advertisement, etc., of which many copies are made for distribution. L18.

circularly *adv.* in a circular manner; *circularly polarized*, (of light) having a uniformly rotating plane of polarization: LME. **circularness** *n.* (*rare*) L16. †**circulary** *a.* = CIRCULAR *a.* L16–M18.

circularise *v.* var. of CIRCULARIZE.

circularity /səːkjʊˈlarɪti/ *n.* L16. [med.L *circularitas*, f. *circularis*: see CIRCULAR *a.* & *n.*, -ITY.] Circular quality, form, or movement.

S. JOHNSON A hut is constructed with loose stones, ranged . . with some tendency to circularity. J. LYONS There is no circularity involved in the statement of the problem or its proposed solution.

circularize /ˈsəːkjʊlərʌɪz/ *v.t.* Also **-ise**. L18. [f. CIRCULAR + -IZE.] 1 Make circular. L18. 2 = CIRCULATE 3. L18. 3 Send circulars to. M19.

circulari'zation *n.* L19.

circulate /ˈsəːkjʊleɪt/ *v.* L15. [L *circulat-* pa. ppl stem of *circulare*, *-ari*, f. *circulus* CIRCLE *n.*: see -ATE[3].] I *v.t.* †1 *Alch.* Subject to continuous distillation in a closed vessel, fashioned so as to return the condensed vapour to the original liquid. L15–L17. †2 = CIRCLE *v.* I. L16–L17. 3 Cause to go round, pass or hand round; put about, give currency to (a book, report, scandal, etc.); send out as a circular. L18. 4 = CIRCULARIZE 3. M20.

3 E. BOWEN Portia had to circulate the cakes. M. L. KING An enthusiastic group had mimeographed leaflets . . and by evening these had been widely circulated. 4 *Daily Telegraph* By using the . . mailing list it has circulated some 97,000 of the fund's members.

II *v.i.* †5 Gather in a circle. *rare.* Only in E16. 6 Move round in a circle or circuit; travel a course which ends at the starting-point; *spec.* (of blood, sap, or other vital fluid) flow continuously round the body. M17. 7 Pass from place to place freely and continuously; (of a newspaper etc.) pass into the hands of readers, be extensively read. M17. 8 *Math.* Of a decimal fraction, esp. of more than one figure: recur. Now *rare* or *obs.* M18. 9 Of a person: go about in a social circle; move around at a social function, talking to different people. M19. 10 Travel or walk about. Chiefly *US.* M19.

6 J. F. W. HERSCHEL The moon circulates about the earth. G. ORWELL A large jug was circulating, and the mugs were being refilled with beer. 7 EVELYN The Air . . circulates through . . to the Grate of the Stove. 9 M. O. W. OLIPHANT He came . . by no means prepared to circulate among his flock. J. WAIN Shall we circulate a bit? . . Otherwise we shan't have spoken to a soul.

Phrases: *circulating* LIBRARY. **circulating medium** the notes, gold, etc., used in exchange.

circulative *a.* having the quality of circulating or producing circulation M17.

circulation /səːkjʊˈleɪʃ(ə)n/ *n.* LME. [(O)Fr., or L *circulatio(n-)*, f. as prec.: see -ATION.] †1 *Alch.* The continuous distillation of a liquid: see CIRCULATE I. LME–M17. 2 Movement in a circle, circular motion or course. *obs.* exc. *Hist.* M16. 3 The continuous motion by which the blood travels through all parts of the body under the action of the heart; *transf.* the movement of sap in plants. M17. 4 The movement of anything such that it returns to its previous position or state after a circuit of intermediate points. M17. †5 A continuous repetition of a series of actions, events, etc. L17–M18. 6 Movement to and fro or from hand to hand etc.; the movement or exchange of currency, coin, etc., transmission or distribution of news, books, etc.; the number of copies, esp. of a newspaper, that are sold. L17. 7 A circulating medium; a currency. L18.

3 E. HEMINGWAY I slapped my arms to keep the circulation going. *collateral circulation*: see COLLATERAL *a.* 4 LANGMUIR *circulation.* 6 R. LARDNER A growing paper, with a big New York circulation. D. LODGE A wildly distorted . . version of an anecdote . . which I . . put into circulation. *bank of circulation*: see BANK *n.*[3] 3. **in circulation, out of circulation** *fig.* participating, not participating, in activities etc. 7 *medium of circulation*: see MEDIUM *n.*

circulator /ˈsəːkjʊleɪtə/ *n.* E17. [L *circulator* pedlar, quack (whence Fr. †*circulateur*), f. as CIRCULATE: see -OR.] †1 A quack, a charlatan. E17–M19. †2 A person who travels round the world; a commercial traveller. M17–M18. 3 A person who circulates information etc.; a scandalmonger. L18.

†**circulatory** *n.* M16–M18. [med.L *circulatorium*, f. as CIRCULATE: see -ORY[1].] *Alch.* An alembic having its neck bent back so as to re-enter its lower part.

circulatory /ˈsəːkjʊlət(ə)ri, səːkjʊˈleɪt(ə)ri/ *a.* E17. [f. CIRCULATE + -ORY[2]: cf. Fr. *circulatoire*. In branch II f. L *circulatorius*, f. as CIRCULATOR.] I 1 Of or pertaining to the circulation of the blood, sap, etc. E17. †2 *Alch.* For the purpose of continuous distillation. L17–E18. †II 3 Of or pertaining to a quack or charlatan. M17–L18.

circulus vitiosus /ˌsəːkjʊləs vɪʃɪˈəʊsəs, vɪtɪ-/ *n. phr.* Pl. ***-li -osi*** /-lʌɪ -ˈəʊsʌɪ/. E20. [L.] A vicious circle.

circum- /ˈsəːkəm/ *pref.* [L, f. *circum* prep. = around, about.] Used in wds adopted f. L and in Eng. wds modelled on these w. the sense 'around, about' adverbially, as *circumfuse*, *circumscribe*, and prepositionally, as *circumlittoral* etc.

circuma'djacent *a.* lying immediately around E17. †**circumagitation** *n.* motion or impulsion round or about M17–L18. **circum'ambages** *n.pl.* (*rare*) roundabout methods or modes of speech M17. **circum'gyrate** *v.t.* & *i.* (now *rare*) (cause to) turn, wheel, or roll round M17. **circumgy'ration** *n.* the act of turning, wheeling, or rolling round E17. **circumgy'ratory** *a.* marked by circumgyration M19. **circum'jovial** *a.* & †*n.* (*Astron.*) (a satellite) revolving round Jupiter L17. **circum'jovian** *a.* = CIRCUMJOVIAL *a.* M19. **circum'littoral** *a.* bordering the shore L19. **circum'lunar** *a.* moving or situated round the moon E20. **circum-me'ridian** *a.* (of a body when) at or near the meridian M19. **circum'mure** *v.t.* wall round E17. **circumnu'tate** *v.i.* (*Bot.*) perform circumnutation L19. **circumnu'tation** *n.* (*Bot.*) helical movement of the growing part of a plant L19. **circum'oral** *a.* (*Anat.* & *Zool.*) situated around the mouth M19. **circumpo'sition** *n.* (*Hort.*) the propagation of plants in a particular surrounding environment or medium; *spec.* = *air-layering* s.v. AIR *n.*[1]: M17. **circumro'tation** *n.* †(*a*) a changing about in rotation; (*b*) a revolution as of a wheel or on an axis; a complete rotation: E17. **circum'scissile** *a.* (*Bot.*) dehiscing or opening by a circular fissure M19. **circum'solar** *a.* moving or situated round the sun M19. **circum'tabular** *a.* sitting round a table E20. **circumter'restrial** *a.* moving or situated round the earth M19.

circumambient /səːkəmˈambɪənt/ *a.* & *n.* M17. [f. CIRCUM- + AMBIENT. Cf. late L *circumambire*.] A *adj.* Esp. of the air or other fluid: surrounding, encompassing. M17. B *absol.* as *n.* *The* surrounding air or atmosphere. L17.

circumambience *n.* the act or fact of surrounding E18. **circumambiency** *n.* surrounding quality or condition; an environment: M17.

circumambulate /səːkəmˈambjʊleɪt/ *v.t.* & *i.* M17. [f. CIRCUM- + AMBULATE. Cf. late L *circumambulare*.] Walk round or about.

circumambu'lation *n.* E17. **circumambulator** *n.* a person who circumambulates L18. **circumambulatory** *a.* M17.

circumbendibus /səːkəmˈbɛndɪbəs/ *n.* L17. [f. CIRCUM- + BEND *n.*[3] + L *-ibus* abl. pl. ending.] A roundabout method; a twist, a turn; a circumlocution.

Circumcellion /səːkəmˈsɛlɪən/ *n.* LME. [eccl.L *circumcelliones* pl., f. as CIRCUM- + *cella* CELL *n.*[1]] 1 *Eccl. Hist.* A Donatist fanatic in 4th-cent. Africa. Usu. in *pl.* LME. †2 A vagrant. LME–M17.

circumcircle /ˈsəːkəmsəːk(ə)l/ *n.* L19. [f. CIRCUM- + CIRCLE *n.*] A circle passing through each vertex of a polygon.

circumcise /ˈsəːkəmsʌɪz/ *v.t.* ME. [OFr. *circonciser* or *circoncis-* pa. ppl stem of *circoncire*, f. L *circumcidere* (tr. Gk *peritemnein*), f. as CIRCUM- + *caedere* to cut.] I 1 Cut off the foreskin of (a male), as a religious rite (esp. Jewish or Muslim) or for medical reasons; cut off the clitoris or the labia minora of (a female). ME. 2 *fig.* In biblical translations and allusions: purify (the heart etc.). ME. †II 3 Cut round, trim. LME–L18. †4 *fig.* Cut short, curtail, limit. M16–L17.

circumciser *n.* M16.

circumcision /sɜːkəmˈsɪʒ(ə)n/ *n.* ME. [(O)Fr. *circoncision*, f. late L *circumcisio(n-)* (tr. Gk *peritomē*), f. *circumcis-* pa. ppl stem of *circumcidere*: see prec., -ION.] I 1 The act or rite of circumcising a person, for religious or medical reasons. ME. 2 *fig.* In biblical translations and allusions: spiritual purification. LME. 3 In biblical translations and allusions: *the* Jews. LME. 4 *Eccl.* The feast of the Circumcision of Jesus, 1 January. LME. †II 5 Cutting round; a cut round. L16–M18.

circumduce /sɜːkəmˈdjuːs/ *v.t.* M16. [L *circumducere*, f. as CIRCUM- + *ducere* to lead.] †1 = next. M16–M17. 2 *Sc. Law* (now *Hist.*). Reject as legally invalid; *spec.* declare (the term) elapsed for producing proof or evidence in court proceedings. M16.

circumduct /sɜːkəmˈdʌkt/ *v.t.* L16. [L *circumduct-* pa. ppl stem of *circumducere*: see prec.] Lead or move around or about. Now *spec.* in *Anat.*, cause (an eye, a limb, etc.) to make a circular movement.

circumduction /sɜːkəmˈdʌkʃ(ə)n/ *n.* M16. [L *circumductio(n-)*, f. as prec.: see -ION.] 1 *Sc. Law* (now *Hist.*). The action of circumducing. M16. 2 The action of circumducting. M16.

circumference /səˈkʌmf(ə)r(ə)ns/ *n.* LME. [(O)Fr. *circonférence*, f. L *circumferentia*, f. *circumferre*, f. as CIRCUM- + *ferre* to carry, bear: see -ENCE.] 1 An enclosing boundary, esp. of a circle or other figure enclosed by a curve; the distance round this. LME. †2 An arc; a circle; the surface of a sphere, cylinder, or other body of circular section. LME–L18. 3 Environment. *rare.* LME. †4 A circuit; a roundabout course. M16–E18. 5 Boundary, compass, enclosure. L16.

circumfeˈrential *a.* of or pertaining to a circumference E17. **circumfeˈrentially** *adv.* M19.

circumferentor /səˈkʌmfərɛntə/ *n.* E17. [f. L *circumferent-* pres. ppl stem of *circumferre*: see prec., -OR.] A surveyor's instrument consisting of a flat bar with vertical sights at each end and a compass in the middle.

circumflex /ˈsɜːkəmflɛks/ *a.* & *n.* L16. [L *circumflexus* pa. pple of *circumflectere*, f. as CIRCUM- + *flectere* to bend, tr. Gk *perispōmenos* drawn around.] A *adj.* 1 *Gram.* Designating an angular or curved accent-mark (ˆ, ˆ, or ˜) placed over a vowel in some languages (orig. Greek) to indicate rising and falling tone, contraction, length, or special quality (of the vowel or of an adjacent consonant). L16. 2 Bent, bending round. Now *rare* in *gen.* sense. E18. 3 *Anat.* Curved; bent round another part; *spec.* designating a nerve and artery of the upper arm. M19. B *n.* 1 A circumflex accent-mark. E17. †2 Bending round, winding. E17–L18. 3 A curved line, (or {, bracketing two or more lines of writing etc. *rare.* E19.

circumflex /ˈsɜːkəmflɛks/ *v.t.* M16. [Sense 1 f. prec.; sense 2 f. L *circumflex-*, f. as prec.] 1 Write with a circumflex accent; pronounce as indicated by a circumflex accent. M16. 2 Bend or wind round. M17.

circumfluent /səˈkʌmflʊənt/ *a.* L16. [L *circumfluent-* pres. ppl stem of *circumfluere*, f. as CIRCUM- + *fluere* to flow: see -ENT.] Flowing round; surrounding.

circumfluence *n.* L19.

circumfluous /səˈkʌmflʊəs/ *a. literary.* E17. [f. L *circumfluus*, f. *circumfluere*: see prec., -OUS.] 1 Flowed round, surrounded by water. E17. 2 = CIRCUMFLUENT. M17.

circumforaneous /sɜːkəmfəˈreɪnɪəs/ *a.* Now *rare.* E17. [f. L *circumforaneus* (f. as CIRCUM- + FORUM) + -OUS.] Strolling from market to market; vagrant, vagabond; quack.

circumfuse /sɜːkəmˈfjuːz/ *v.t.* L16. [L *circumfus-* pa. ppl stem of *circumfundere*, f. as CIRCUM- + *fundere* pour.] Pour about, diffuse, (*around, about*); surround *with* or *in* a fluid medium etc.

circumfusion *n.* E17.

circumgestation /sɜːkəmdʒɛˈsteɪʃ(ə)n/ *n.* Long *rare.* M16. [f. CIRCUM- + GESTATION.] Carrying about (ceremonially or in procession).

circumincession /sɜːkəmɪnˈsɛʃ(ə)n/ *n.* Also **-session**. M17. [med.L *circumincessio(n-)* (tr. Gk *perikhōrēsis* going round), f. as CIRCUM- + *incessiō(n-)*, f. *incēdere* move, proceed: see -ION. Sp. w. *-s-* through misinterpretation as 'reciprocal indwelling'.] *Chr. Theol.* The reciprocal existence of the persons of the Trinity in one another.

circumjacent /sɜːkəmˈdʒeɪs(ə)nt/ *a.* L15. [L *circumjacent-* pres. ppl stem of *circumjacere*, f. as CIRCUM- + *jacere* lie down: see -ENT.] Situated around, adjacent on all sides. (Foll. by *to*.)

circumjacence *n.* the fact or quality of being circumjacent L19. **circumjacency** *n.* (*a*) in *pl.*, circumjacent parts; (*b*) = CIRCUMJACENCE: M18.

circumlocution /sɜːkəmləˈkjuːʃ(ə)n/ *n.* LME. [Fr., or L *circumlocutio(n-)*, f. as CIRCUM- + *locutio(n-)* LOCUTION, tr. Gk PERIPHRASIS.] Expression of meaning indirectly or in more words than necessary; evasive talk; an instance of this, a roundabout expression.

circumlocutional, -ary *adjs.* pertaining to or given to circumlocution M19. **circumlocutionist** *n.* a person who uses circumlocution M19. **circumlocutory** /sɜːkəmˈlɒkjʊt(ə)ri, sɜːkəmləˈkjuːt(ə)ri/ *a.* marked by circumlocution M17.

circumnavigate /sɜːkəmˈnavɪgeɪt/ *v.t.* M17. [f. CIRCUM- + NAVIGATE. Cf. L *circumnavigare*.] Sail round (esp. the world).

circumnavigable *a.* able to be circumnavigated L17. **circumnaviˈgation** *n.* E18. **circumnavigator** L18.

circumpolar /sɜːkəmˈpəʊlə/ *a.* L17. [f. CIRCUM- + POLAR.] 1 *Astron.* Situated or occurring above the horizon at all times of the day in a given latitude. L17. 2 Around either pole of the earth; inhabiting such a region. L17.

circumscribe /ˈsɜːkəmskrʌɪb/ *v.t.* LME. [L *circumscribere*, f. as CIRCUM- + *scribere* draw lines, write.] 1 Lay down the limits of, confine; restrict; mark off, define logically. LME. 2 Draw a line round; form the boundary of; encircle, encompass. L16. 3 *Geom.* Draw (a figure) round another, meeting it at points but not cutting it. L16. †4 Inscribe around. Only in 17.

1 SHAKES. *Haml.* Therefore must his choice be circumscrib'd. E. F. BENSON To play lawn-tennis . . in the exceedingly circumscribed court. 2 W. HOGARTH The straight line and the circular line . . bound and circumscribe all visible objects. DEFOE I was alone, circumscribed by the . . ocean.

circumscriber *n.* (*arch.*) a person who or thing which circumscribes; *spec.* a person who signs a round robin: E17. **circumscript** *a.* (now *rare*) circumscribed M16.

circumscription /sɜːkəmˈskrɪpʃ(ə)n/ *n.* LME. [L *circumscriptio(n-)*, f. *circumscript-* pa. ppl stem of *circumscribere*: see prec., -ION.] 1 An inscription around a coin etc. LME. †2 The fact or quality of being confined to definite limits of space, as a property of matter. L15–M19. 3 The action or an act of laying down limits; the fact of being limited; confinement; (a) restraint, (a) restriction; (a) definition, (a) description. M16. 4 A boundary, an outline, a periphery; a border, an edging. L16. 5 *Geom.* The action of circumscribing one figure around another. L16. 6 A circumscribed space; a district or region of definite limits. M19.

3 MILTON No injurious Alteration or Circumscription of Mens Lands. E. POUND Criticism is not a circumscription or a set of prohibitions. 4 M. BRADBURY The main horizon . . of their lives, the limit and circumscription of their world.

†**circumscriptive** *a.* pertaining to or having the attribute of circumscription (esp. of matter) L15–M18. †**circumscriptively** *adv.* L15–M18.

circumspect /ˈsɜːkəmspɛkt/ *a.* LME. [L *circumspectus* pa. pple of *circumspicere*, f. as CIRCUM- + *specere* to look.] Showing caution; cautious, wary; taking everything into account.

J. STEINBECK The brothels were quiet, orderly and circumspect. S. BELLOW He was a circumspect driver.

circumˈspection *n.* cautious observation of circumstances; circumspect action or conduct: LME. **circumˈspectious** *a.* circumspect M17. **circumˈspective** *a.* looking around; given to circumspection: M17. **circumˈspectively** *adv.* E17. **circumspectly** *adv.* LME. **circumspectness** *n.* M16.

circumsphere /ˈsɜːkəmsfɪə/ *n.* M20. [f. CIRCUM- + SPHERE *n.*, after *circumcircle*.] *Math.* A sphere that touches all the vertices of a given polyhedron. Cf. IN-SPHERE.

circumstance /ˈsɜːkəmst(ə)ns/ *n.* & *v.* ME. [(O)Fr. *circonstance* or L *circumstantia*, f. *circumstant-* pres. ppl stem of *circumstare*, f. as CIRCUM- + *stare* to stand: see -ANCE.] A *n.* I Something surrounding (*lit.* & *fig.*). †1 That which stands around or surrounds; surroundings. ME–L19. 2 In *pl.*, or *sing.* (as a non-count n.). The material, logical, or other environmental conditions of an act or event; the time, place, manner, cause, occasion, etc., of an act or event; the external conditions affecting or that might affect action, *spec.* as indicating criminality. ME. b In *sing.* (as a count n.). Any of such conditions. M16. c *spec.* In *pl.* State of financial or material welfare. E18. 3 Formality, ceremony, or fuss surrounding an act or event. Now chiefly in *pomp and circumstance*. LME. †b Importance. L16–L17. 4 Detail about the external conditions of an act or event; *arch.* circumlocution, indirectness. E16.

2 J. WEBSTER We have nought but circumstances To charge her with, about her husband's death. J. A. FROUDE Who found himself in circumstances to which he was unequal. L. P. HARTLEY A soldier has to change his mind when circumstances demand it. J. HELLER That men should die was a matter of necessity; *which* men should die, though, was a matter of circumstance. J. BARTH When I next saw her, it was under entirely different circumstances. J. FOWLES Ernestina . . was . . a victim of circumstances. b J. GALSWORTHY A solid and prolonged happiness such as perhaps no other circumstance in life had afforded him. c N. MITFORD Summer came and went without any change in Polly's circumstances.

II Something accessory. 5 An accessory matter; a particular, a detail. Usu. in *pl.* ME. †b *spec.* A material adjunct; a physical feature. L16–L18. †6 Subordinate matters or details. LME–E18. 7 The part(s) not of the essence or substance of something. *arch.* L16. 8 An incident, an occurrence; a fact. L16.

5 SWIFT The sentence of death with all the circumstances of hanging, beheading, quartering, embowelling and the like. 8 T. CAPOTE A circumstance which explained the presence of perhaps a third of the immense congregation.

Phrases: **a mere** (or **poor, remote**) **circumstance** *US colloq.* a person or thing of little or no importance. *creature of circumstance*: see CREATURE. **in no circumstances** not whatever happens; never. **in the circumstances**: owing to or making allowance for them. *narrow circumstances*: see NARROW *a.* **not a circumstance to** *US colloq.* nothing in comparison with. **under no, the, circumstances** = *in no, the, circumstances* above.

B *v.t.* †1 Subject to conditions or circumstances. LME–M18. 2 Place with regard to circumstances or relations. Chiefly as *circumstanced* ppl a. E17. †3 = CIRCUMSTANTIATE 4. M17–L18.

circumstantial /sɜːkəmˈstanʃ(ə)l/ *a.* & *n.* L16. [f. L *circumstantia* CIRCUMSTANCE *n.* + -AL[1].] A *adj.* 1 Of, pertaining to, or dependent on circumstances; adventitious, incidental. L16. 2 Detailed; particular. E17. 3 Full of ceremony or pomp. E18.

1 COLERIDGE Our political strength and circumstantial prosperity. J. R. LOWELL A principle of life is the first requirement of art; all else is circumstantial and secondary. O. SACKS The names of my patients, . . and certain other circumstantial details. **circumstantial evidence**: tending to establish a conclusion by inference from known facts which are otherwise hard to explain. 2 ADDISON We cannot be too minute and circumstantial in accounts of this nature. J. WAIN When telling a lie, make it circumstantial, load it with detail.

B *n.* In *pl.* Circumstantial matters; particulars, details; incidental or adventitious features. M17.

circumstantiˈality *n.* circumstantial quality, particularity M18. **circumstantially** *adv.* M17. †**circumstantialness** *n.* M18–E19.

circumstantiate /səːkəmˈstanʃɪeɪt/ *v.t.* Now *rare.* LME. [med.L *circumstantiat-* pa. ppl stem of *circumstantiare* to condition, f. L *circumstantia*: see CIRCUMSTANCE, -ATE[3].] †**1** Accompany as a circumstance. Only in LME. †**2** = CIRCUMSTANCE *v.* 2. Chiefly as *circumstantiated* ppl a. E17–L19. †**3** = CIRCUMSTANCE *v.* 1. M17–E18. **4** Set forth or support with circumstances or details. M17.

circumstantiaˈtion *n.* M19.

circumvallate /səːkəmˈvaleɪt, -ət/ *a.* M17. [L *circumvallatus* pa. pple, f. as next: see -ATE[2].] Surrounded (as) with a rampart; *spec.* designating certain papillae near the back of the tongue, surrounded by taste receptors.

circumvallate /səːkəmˈvaleɪt/ *v.t.* E19. [L *circumvallat-* pa. ppl stem of *circumvallare*, f. as CIRCUM- + *vallare*, f. *vallum* rampart: see -ATE[3].] Surround (as) with a rampart or entrenchment.

circumvallation /səːkəmvaˈleɪʃ(ə)n/ *n.* M17. [Late L *circumvallatio(n-)*, f. as prec.: see -ATION.] **1** The making of a rampart or entrenchment. M17. **2** A rampart, an entrenchment; *fig.* a surrounding defence. M17.

circumvent /səːkəmˈvɛnt/ *v.* LME. [L *circumvent-* pa. ppl stem of *circumvenire*, f. as CIRCUM- + *venire* come.] **1** *v.t.* Deceive, outwit, overreach; find a way round, evade (a difficulty). LME. **b** *v.i.* Employ deception or evasion. L16. **2** *v.t.* Entrap by surrounding; beset (*with*). M16. **3** *v.t.* Go round; enclose; make the circuit of. E19.

Also †**circumvene** *v.t.* (chiefly *Sc.*) L15–L18.

circumvention /səːkəmˈvɛnʃ(ə)n/ *n.* LME. [Late L *circumventio(n-)*, f. as prec.: see -ION.] The action or an act of circumventing someone; *Sc. Law* deceitful or fraudulent conduct perpetrated against a facile person.

circumvolute /səːˈkʌmvəluːt/ *v.t.* Now *rare.* L16. [L (*circumvolutare* frequent. of) *circumvolut-* pa. ppl stem of *circumvolvere* CIRCUMVOLVE.] Roll or curl round; enwrap by twisting or winding something round.

circumvolution /səːkəmvəˈluːʃ(ə)n/ *n.* LME. [f. L *circumvolut-* (see prec.) + -ION.] **1** Turning round an axis or centre; an instance of this; (a) revolution, (a) rotation. LME. **2** The winding or folding of one thing round another; a fold or turn of something so wound. L16. **3** A sinuous movement; a winding course; a twist, a coil. L16.

circumvolve /səːkəmˈvɒlv/ *v.t.* & *i.* Now *rare.* LME. [L *circumvolvere*, f. as CIRCUM- + *volvere* to turn.] **1** Rotate, revolve. LME. †**2** Wind, fold, or twist round; enwrap (*lit.* & *fig.*). L16–E19.

circus /ˈsəːkəs/ *n.* LME. [L = circle, circus, corresp. to Gk *kirkos*, *krikos* ring, circle.] **I 1** *Rom. Antiq.* A rounded or oval arena lined with tiers of seats, for equestrian and other exhibitions. LME. †**2** A circle, a ring; a road forming a closed loop. E–M18. **3** An open, more or less circular, area in a town where streets converge; a circular range of houses. M18. **4** A natural amphitheatre of hills etc. M19.

1 the Circus: the largest at Rome. **3** *Oxford Circus*, *Piccadilly Circus*, (in London), etc.

II 5 A travelling show of horses, riders, acrobats, clowns, performing animals, etc., usu. performing in a circular arena; the type of entertainment provided by such shows. L18. **6** A disturbance; a scene of lively action. *colloq.* M19. **7** An exhibition etc. at a Roman circus; *spec.* in *bread and circuses* [tr. L PANEM ET CIRCENSES], public provision of food and entertainment, esp. to assuage the populace. E20. **8** More fully *flying circus.* A squadron of aeroplanes; a group of aircraft or pilots engaged in spectacular flying. *slang.* E20. **9** A group of people performing in sports etc. together or in succession, usu. in a series of different places. *colloq.* (freq. *derog.*). M20. **10** (C-.) *The* British secret service. *slang.* M20.

5 THREE-*ring circus.*

circussy *a.* resembling or characteristic of a circus L19.

ciré /ˈsiːreɪ/ *a.* & *n.* E20. [Fr. = waxed.] (Fabric) with a smooth polished surface, obtained esp. by heating and waxing.

cire perdue /siːr pɛrdy/ *n. phr.* L19. [Fr. = lost wax.] A method of casting bronze by pouring metal over a core within a mould, into the space created by melting and running out the original wax surface of the model.

cirl bunting /səːl ˈbʌntɪŋ/ *n. phr.* L18. [f. It. *cirlo*, prob. f. *zirlare* whistle as a thrush, + BUNTING *n.*[1]] A bunting, *Emberiza cirlus*, which is resident in SW England and is distinguished by the yellow, black, and green head of the male.

†**ciron** *n.* LME–L18. [Fr.] The itch mite, *Sarcoptes scabiei.* Also = JIGGER *n.*[2] 1.

cirque /səːk/ *n.* E17. [Fr. f. L CIRCUS.] **1** = CIRCUS 1. E17. **2** A circle, a ring, a circlet. *literary.* L17. **3** *Physical Geogr.* A large bowl-shaped hollow of glacial origin at the head of a valley or on a mountainside. M19.

cirrhosis /sɪˈrəʊsɪs/ *n.* Pl. **-rrhoses** /-ˈrəʊsiːz/. Formerly also in Fr. form †**cirrhose.** E19. [mod.L f. Gk *kirrhos* orange-tawny (on account of the colour of the affected liver in many cases): see -OSIS.] *Med.* A chronic disease in which much of the liver is replaced by fibrous tissue and the organ takes on a nodular appearance. Also occas., degeneration of another organ.

cirrhotic *a.* & *n.* (*a*) *adj.* of the nature of or affected by cirrhosis; (*b*) *n.* a sufferer from cirrhosis: L19.

†**cirrhus** *n.* var. of CIRRUS.

cirri *n.* pl. of CIRRUS.

cirriferous /sɪˈrɪf(ə)rəs/ *a.* M18. [f. L *cirri-* CIRRUS + -FEROUS.] Bearing cirri.

cirriform /ˈsɪrɪfɔːm/ *a.* E19. [f. as prec. + -FORM.] **1** *Meteorol.* Having the form or appearance of cirrus. E19. **2** *Zool.* Like cirri. M19.

cirrigerous /sɪˈrɪdʒərəs/ *a.* M18. [f. as prec. + -GEROUS.] Bearing cirri.

cirripede /ˈsɪrɪpiːd/ *n.* & *a.* Also (earlier) **-ped** /-pɛd/. M19. [mod.L *Cirripeda*, *-dia* pl., f. L CIRRUS + *ped-*, *pes* foot: so called from the appearance of the legs when protruded from the valved shell.] *Zool.* (A marine crustacean) of the subclass Cirripedia, members of which (the barnacles) are generally sessile as adults and have limbs modified for filter-feeding.

cirro- /ˈsɪrəʊ/ *comb. form* of CIRRUS: see -O-.

cirroˈcumulus *n.* (*Meteorol.*) a cloud or cloud-type occurring at high altitude (usu. 5 to 13 km, 16,500 to 45,000 ft) and having the appearance of a rippled, granulated, or otherwise broken layer E19. **cirroˈstratus** *n.* (*Meteorol.*) a cloud or cloud-type occurring at high altitude (usu. 5 to 13 km, 3 to 8 miles) and forming a thin, more or less uniform layer E19.

cirrous /ˈsɪrəs/ *a.* M17. [f. CIRRUS + -OUS.] **1** *Bot.* & *Zool.* Bearing cirri; of the nature of a cirrus. M17. **2** *Meteorol.* Of or pertaining to cirrus cloud. E19.

Also **cirrose** *a.* E19.

cirrus /ˈsɪrəs/ *n.* Also †**cirrhus.** Pl. **cirri** /ˈsɪraɪ/. E18. [L = curl, fringe.] **1** A curl or tuft of hair. *rare.* E18. **2** *Bot.* A tendril. E18. **3** *Zool.* A slender, filamentary appendage, e.g. the limb of a cirripede, a barbel of certain fishes. M18. **4** *Meteorol.* A cloud-type occurring at high altitude (usu. 5 to 13 km, 16,500 to 45,000 ft) and having the appearance of wispy filamentous tufts. E19.

†**cirsocele** *n.* E18–L19. [Gk *kirsokēlē*, f. *kirsos* enlargement of a vein: see -CELE.] = VARICOCELE.

cirsoid /ˈsəːsɔɪd/ *a.* M19. [Gk *kirsoeidēs*, f. *kirsos*: see prec., -OID.] *Med.* Having the appearance of a varicose vein.

cis- /sɪs/ *pref.* In sense 2 also as attrib. adj. **cis.** [L, f. *cis* prep.] **1** Used in wds adopted f. L and in Eng. wds modelled on these w. the sense 'on this side of' (opp. TRANS-, ULTRA-), occas. retaining orientation from Rome (as *cisalpine* etc.), but usu. from the user's or the majority's position (as *cisatlantic* etc.); also occas. of time (as *cis-Elizabethan*). **2** *Chem.* (Usu. italicized.) Designating compounds in which two atoms or groups are situated on the same side of a given plane in the molecule (opp. TRANS-). L19.

cisatˈlantic *a.* on one's own side of the Atlantic L18. **cisˈlunar** *a.* on this side of the moon, between the earth and the moon L19. **cisoid** *a.* (*Chem.*) designating a compound, group, or structure in which two like atoms or groups lie on the same side of a single bond or line of bonds M20. **cispadane** *a.* on the south (Roman) side of the River Po L18. **cisˈpontine** *a.* on this side of the bridge or bridges; *spec.* on the north (orig. the better-known) side of the Thames bridges in London: M19. **cis-trans** *a.* (*Chem.*) designating isomerism characterized by *cis* and *trans* isomers M20.

cisalpine /sɪsˈalpʌɪn/ *a.* & *n.* M16. [L *cisalpinus*, f. as CIS-, ALPINE *a.* & *n.*[2]] **A** *adj.* **1** On this (the Roman) side of the Alps; south of the Alps. M16. **2** *Chr. Ch.* Of or pertaining to the Gallican Church movement. L18. **B** *n.* A member of the Roman Catholic Church who accepts the principles of the Gallican Synod of 1682. L18.

cisco /ˈsɪskəʊ/ *n.* Pl. **-oes**, same. M19. [Origin unkn.] Any of several freshwater salmonid fishes of the genus *Coregonus.*

Arctic cisco = OMUL.

Ciskeian /sɪˈskʌɪən/ *n.* & *a.* M20. [f. *Ciskei* (see below), f. CIS- + *Kei*, a river in eastern South Africa, + -AN.] (A native or inhabitant) of Ciskei, a Black African homeland and later National State within the Republic of South Africa.

cismontane /sɪsˈmɒnteɪn/ *a.* E19. [L *cismontanus*, f. as CIS-, MONTANE.] On this side of the mountains; *esp.* = CISALPINE *a.* 1.

cissoid /ˈsɪsɔɪd/ *n.* M17. [Gk *kissoeidēs*, f. *kissos* ivy: see -OID.] *Math.* A cubic curve of infinite length and having one cusp, that is the locus of certain points on the secants of a circle from a fixed point on its circumference (represented by the equation $r = a\sin^2\theta/\cos\theta$).

cissy *n.* & *a.* var. of SISSY.

cist /sɪst, kɪst/ *n.*[1] E19. [Welsh = chest.] *Archaeol.* A prehistoric burial-chamber made with stone slabs. Also, a hollowed tree-coffin.

long cist: see LONG *a.*[1] *oak cist*: see OAK *n.* & *a.*

cist /sɪst/ *n.*[2] M19. [L *cista*: see CHEST *n.*] *Gk Antiq.* A box used for sacred utensils.

Cistercian /sɪˈstəːʃ(ə)n/ *a.* & *n.* LME. [Fr. *cistercien*, f. L *Cistercium* Cîteaux, near Dijon, France (cf. med.L *Cisterciensis*): see -IAN.] **A** *adj.* Of or belonging to a monastic order founded at Cîteaux in 1098 by Robert, abbot of Molesme, as a stricter offshoot of the Benedictines. LME. **B** *n.* A monk or nun of the Cistercian order. LME.

cistern /ˈsɪstən/ *n.* ME. [OFr. *cisterne* (mod. *citerne*) f. L *cisterna*, f. as CIST *n.*[2]] **1** An artificial reservoir for storing water, *esp.* one in the roof-space of a house etc. supplying the taps, or above a water-closet. ME. **2** A large vessel for water or other liquid, *esp.* one used †(*a*) for personal washing, †(*b*) at the dinner-table. L16. **3** A natural reservoir or depression containing water, e.g. a pond. E17. **4** A fluid-filled cavity in an organism or cell; *esp.* a reservoir of cerebrospinal fluid in the subarachnoid space. E17.

cisterna /sɪˈstəːnə/ *n.* Pl. **-nae** /-niː/. L19. [mod.L f. L: see prec.] *Anat.* & *Biol.* = CISTERN 4.

cistophorus /sɪˈstɒfərəs/ *n.* Pl. **-ri** /-rʌɪ/. M19. [L f. Gk *kistophoros*, f. *kistē* CHEST *n.* + *-phoros* bearing.] A Greek coin bearing an impression of a sacred chest.

cistron /ˈsɪstrɒn/ *n.* M20. [f. CIS- + TRANS- (referring to the possibility of two genes being on the same or different chromosomes) + -ON.] *Biol.* A section of a nucleic acid molecule that codes for a specific product of transcription.

cistus /ˈsɪstəs/ *n.* M16. [mod.L f. Gk *kistos*, *-thos.*] An evergreen shrub of the genus *Cistus*, of the Mediterranean region, with large white or red flowers. Also called *rock rose.*

cistvaen *n.* var. of KISTVAEN.

cit /sɪt/ *n. arch.* M17. [Abbrev. of CITIZEN.] **1** A townsman; a shopkeeper, a trader. Occas. = CITESS 1. Usu. *contempt.* M17. **2** In *pl.* Civilian clothes, 'civvies'. *US slang.* E19.

citadel /ˈsɪtəd(ə)l, -dɛl/ *n.* M16. [Fr. *citadelle* or its source It. *cittadella* dim. of †*cittade* (var. of *città*) f. L *civitas* CITY.] **1** A fortress, *esp.* one guarding or dominating a city; *transf.* & *fig.* a stronghold. M16. 2 A meeting-hall of the Salvation Army. L19.

1 C. THIRLWALL To collect all the remaining strength . . in a mountain citadel. W. S. CHURCHILL The French had had to evacuate their troops from the citadel in Aleppo. L. TRILLING The university figured as the citadel of conservatism.

citation /sʌɪˈteɪʃ(ə)n/ *n.* ME. [(O)Fr. f. L *citatio(n-)*, f. *citat-* pa. ppl stem of *citare* CITE: see -ATION.] 1 *Law.* A summons; a document containing a summons. ME. 2 The action of citing or quoting any words or a written passage. M16. 3 A passage cited, a quotation. M16. 4 A mention in an official dispatch; a descriptive announcement of an award. E20.

4 T. ROETHKE I was graduated . . with the highest possible degree citation.

citatory /ˈsʌɪtət(ə)ri/ *a. arch.* M16. [med.L *citatorius*, f. L *citat-*: see prec., -ORY².] Having the faculty of citing or summoning; concerned with citation. Esp. in *letters citatory*.

cite /sʌɪt/ *v.t.* LME. [(O)Fr. *citer* f. L *citare* frequent. of *ciere*, *cire* set in motion, call.] 1 Summon officially before a court of (usu. ecclesiastical) law. LME. 2 *gen.* Summon; arouse, excite. Now *arch.* or *poet.* M16. 3 Quote (a book, passage, author, etc.), esp. as an authority in support of a position; adduce or mention as an example, precedent, or proof; call to mind; refer to (*as*). M16. b *spec.* Mention in an official dispatch. E20.

3 POPE I cite the whole three verses. R. GRAVES He cited Ovid as having said this, and Meleager that, in praise of a fine head of hair. J. F. KENNEDY After announcing this new industrial plan the White Paper cited the need for skilled labour. I. HAMILTON The poem's last lines—sometimes cited as a memorable evocation of urban violence.

citable *a.* able to be cited E18. †**cital** *n.* (*rare*) [-AL¹] (*a*) an impeachment; (*b*) citation, summons: L16–M18. **citer** *n.* L16.

citess /ˈsɪtɛs, sɪˈtɛs/ *n. arch.* L17. [f. (as) CIT + -ESS¹.] 1 A townswoman; a female shopkeeper or trader. *contempt. rare.* L17. †2 A female citizen. *US.* L18–E19.

cithara /ˈsɪθ(ə)rə, k-/ *n.* Also **k-** /k-/. L18. [L f. Gk *kithara*.] An ancient Greek and Roman stringed musical instrument akin to the lyre, having two arms rising vertically from the soundbox.

citharist /ˈsɪθ(ə)rɪst/ *n.* LME. [L *citharista* f. Gk *kitharistēs*, f. *kithara*: see prec., -IST.] A player on the cithara or (formerly) the cittern.

cither /ˈsɪθə/ *n.* Now *rare.* E17. [f. as CITHARA.] A cithara; a cittern.

cithern, **-ren** *ns.* vars. of CITTERN.

citied /ˈsɪtɪd/ *a.* E17. [f. CITY + -ED².] Made into or like a city; occupied by a city or cities.

citify /ˈsɪtɪfʌɪ/ *v.t.* Also **cityfy**. E19. [f. CITY + -FY.] Make urban in appearance or behaviour; impart features characteristic of a city to. Chiefly as *citified* ppl a.

citifiˈcation *n.* E20.

citizen /ˈsɪtɪz(ə)n/ *n.* & *a.* ME. [AN *citesein*, *-zein* alt. (prob. after *deinzein* DENIZEN *n.* & *a.*) of OFr. *citeain* (mod. *citoyen*) f. Proto-Romance, f. L *civitas* CITY.] A *n.* 1 An inhabitant of a city or town; *esp.* one possessing civic rights, as a freeman etc.; a town-dweller. ME. 2 A member, native or naturalized, of a (usu. specified) State or Commonwealth. LME. b *spec.* As a title or form of address during the French Revolution: supporter of the republican order. *obs.* exc. *Hist.* L18. 3 An inhabitant, an occupant, (*of*). LME. 4 A civilian. *rare.* E17.

Phrases: **citizen of the world** a person who is at home anywhere, a cosmopolitan. **Citizens' Advice Bureau** a local office giving free advice to enquirers concerning their rights or about available aid. **citizen's arrest**: by a private citizen without a warrant, allowable in certain cases, as the witnessing of an arrestable offence. **citizens' band** (designating or pertaining to) a range of radio frequencies allocated for local communication by individuals. JOHN *Citizen. second class citizen*: see SECOND CLASS *a. senior citizen*: see SENIOR *a.*

†B *adj.* Like a city- or town-dweller, city-bred. *rare* (Shakes.). Only in E17.

citizeness *n.* a female citizen L18. **citizenhood** *n.* (*a*) the state of being a citizen; (*b*) the body of citizens: L19. **citizenish** *a.* of the nature of or relating to citizens E19. **citizenly** *a.* pertaining to or characteristic of a citizen M19. **citizenry** *n.* a body of citizens, citizens collectively E19. **citizenship** *n.* the position or status of being a citizen E17.

citole /sɪˈtəʊl/ *n.* LME. [OFr. (= Prov. *citola*), obscurely f. L CITHARA: see -OLE¹.] A medieval plucked musical instrument akin to the lute, a precursor of the cittern.

citral /ˈsɪtral/ *n.* L19. [f. CITRUS + -AL².] *Chem.* A terpenoid aldehyde, $C_{10}H_{16}O$ (of which there are several isomers), which occurs widely in plants (esp. lemon-grass and citrus fruit) and has an odour of lemons.

citrate /ˈsɪtreɪt/ *n.* & *v.* L18. [f. CITRIC + -ATE¹.] A *n. Chem.* A salt or ester of citric acid. L18. B *v.t.* Treat (blood) with a solution of a citrate, esp. to prevent coagulation. Chiefly as *citrated* ppl a. E20.

citric /ˈsɪtrɪk/ *a.* L18. [f. L CITRUS + -IC.] Chem. *citric acid*, a sharp-tasting crystalline tribasic acid, $C_6H_8O_7$, present in the juice of citrus fruit and made commercially by the fermentation of sugar.

citril /ˈsɪtrɪl/ *n.* L17. [App. f. It. *citrinella* dim. of *citrina* citrine-coloured (bird).] More fully *citril finch*. A yellow-green finch, *Serinus citrinella*, resident in southern Europe.

citrin /ˈsɪtrɪn/ *n.* M20. [f. CITRUS + -IN¹.] *Biochem.* A substance consisting of one or more of a group of flavonoids which occur mainly in citrus fruit and blackcurrants and were formerly thought to be essential in the diet. Also called *vitamin P* (chiefly *US*).

citrine /ˈsɪtrɪn/ *a.* & *n.* LME. [(O)Fr. *citrin(e)* lemon-coloured f. med.L *citrinus*, f. L CITRUS: see -INE¹.] A *adj.* Of a light greenish yellow; lemon-coloured. LME. B *n.* 1 A glassy yellow variety of quartz; false topaz. L16. 2 Citrine colour. L19.

citron /ˈsɪtr(ə)n/ *n.* & *a.* E16. [(O)Fr. f. L CITRUS, after *limon* lemon.] A *n.* 1 A fruit resembling the lemon but larger, less acid, and with thicker rind. (Orig. also the lemon, and perh. the lime.) E16. 2 The tree, *Citrus medica*, which bears this fruit. Also *citron tree*. M16. 3 A light greenish-yellow colour; citrine. E17. †4 The fragrant wood of an African tree, prob. a cypress, *Tetraclinis articulata*, prized in Roman times for making furniture. M17–M18. †5 Brandy flavoured with citron or lemon peel. E–M18. B *adj.* Of a light greenish-yellow colour, citrine. E20.

citronella /sɪtrəˈnɛlə/ *n.* M19. [mod.L, dim. of prec.] A fragrant southern Asian grass, *Cymbopogon nardus*; an oil distilled from this (also *citronella oil*), often used to keep insects away.

citronellal *n.* [-AL²] a terpenoid aldehyde, $C_{10}H_{18}O$, found esp. in citronella, rose, and geranium oils L19. **citronellol** *n.* the corresponding alcohol, $C_{10}H_{20}O$, obtained from similar sources; also called *rhodinol*: L19.

citrous /ˈsɪtrəs/ *a.* E20. [f. CITRUS + -OUS.] Of the genus *Citrus*; from a tree of the genus *Citrus*.

†**citrul** *n.* LME–M18. [OFr. *citrule* (mod. *citrouille*), ult. f. L CITRUS w. dim. suff.] The watermelon. Also, the pumpkin.

citrulline /ˈsɪtrʌliːn/ *n.* Also **-in** /-ɪn/. M20. [f. med.L *citrullus* watermelon, f. as prec., + -INE⁵.] *Biochem.* An amino acid, $NH_2CONH(CH_2)_3$-$CHNH_2COOH$, which occurs in watermelons and is an intermediate in urea synthesis in animals.

citrus /ˈsɪtrəs/ *n.* E19. [L = citron tree, thuja.] A tree of the genus *Citrus*, which includes the lemon, citron, lime, orange, grapefruit, etc.; (more fully *citrus fruit*) a fruit of such a tree.

cittern /ˈsɪt(ə)n/ *n.* Also **cithern** /ˈsɪθ(ə)n/, **cithren** /ˈsɪθr(ə)n/. M16. [f. as CITHARA after GITTERN.] A wire-stringed musical instrument akin to the lute and usu. played with a plectrum, much used in the 16th and 17th cents.

Comb.: †**cittern-head** a term of abuse alluding to the grotesque carved head often found on a cittern.

city /ˈsɪti/ *n.* ME. [(O)Fr. *cité* f. L *civitas*, f. *civis* citizen: see -TY¹.] 1 A town or other inhabited place. Long *obs.* exc. *dial.* ME. 2 A large town; *spec.* a town created a 'city' by charter, esp. as containing a cathedral. Also (chiefly *US*), a municipal corporation occupying a definite area. ME. 3 The people or entire community of a city. ME. 4 *the City*, that part of London situated within the ancient boundaries and governed by the Lord Mayor and Corporation, *esp.* its business part or community, in the neighbourhood of the Exchange and the Bank of England; *loosely* financial and commercial circles. M16. 5 *Hist.* A self-governing city or city-state. M16. 6 With preceding adj. or as 2nd elem. of comb.: used to emphasize the adj. or n. of quality. *N. Amer. slang.* M20.

1 AV *Luke* 7:11 He went into a city called Nain. 2 BROWNING Hamelin town's in Brunswick By famous Hanover city. E. A. FREEMAN Birmingham and Dundee, hitherto merely boroughs, were raised to the rank of cities. *Cities of the Plain*: see PLAIN *n.*¹ 1. **city of refuge** *Hist.* an Israelite town set apart for those who had committed manslaughter. *free city*: see FREE *a. holy city*: see HOLY *a. inner city*: see INNER *a. Leonine City*: see LEONINE *a.*² 1. *Monumental City*: see MONUMENTAL. MORMON *City. mushroom city*: see MUSHROOM *n.* & *a. open city*: see OPEN *a.* **the City of God** Paradise, an ideal community in Heaven. **the City of the Seven Hills, the Eternal City** Rome. *the Granite City*: see GRANITE *a.* **the Heavenly City** Paradise. *the Windy City*: see WINDY *a.*¹ *twin city*: see TWIN *a.* & *n.* VATICAN *City*. 3 AV *Matt.* 21:10 All the city was moved, saying, Who is this? 6 *Rolling Stone* I get talking and *whoa*! Trouble city!

Comb.: **City Company** a corporation representing an ancient trade-guild; **city desk** *N. Amer.* the newspaper department for local news; **city editor**, **City editor**: (*a*) (c-) *N. Amer.* dealing with local news for a newspaper; (*b*) (C-) dealing with financial news for a newspaper or journal; **city farm** (*a*) *US* a penal institution which also functions as a farm; (*b*) a farm established within an urban area for educational purposes, as a museum, etc.; **city fathers** the persons responsible for the administration of a city; **city gent** *colloq.* a typical businessman working in the City; **city hall** *N. Amer.* municipal offices or officers; **city marshal** (*a*) see MARSHAL *n.*¹ 5b; (*b*) *US* a law officer in some cities, whose duties include the serving of summonses; *city mission*: see MISSION *n.* 4b; *city missionary*: see MISSIONARY *n.* 1; **city page** the page in a newspaper or journal dealing with financial and business news; **cityscape** a view of a city, city scenery; **city slicker** (*a*) a plausible rogue as usu. found in cities; (*b*) a smart and sophisticated city-dweller; **city-state** *Hist.* a city that is also an independent sovereign State.

cityful *n.* as many as a city will contain E19. **cityless** *a.* without a city or cities LME. **cityward** *a.*, **cityward(s)** *adv.* [orig. *to the cityward*] in the direction of a city LME.

cityfy *v.* var. of CITIFY.

cive *n.* see CHIVE *n.*²

civet /ˈsɪvɪt/ *n.*¹ M16. [Fr. *civette* f. It. *zibetto* f. med.L *zibethum* f. Arab. *zabād* (= sense 2).] 1 Any of several carnivorous mammals of the Asian and African family Viverridae, which also includes the genets and mongooses; esp. *Viverra civetta*, of subSaharan Africa. Also *civet-cat*. M16. 2 A strong musky perfume obtained from the anal glands of these animals. M16.

†**civet** *n.*² M16–E18. [Fr. *civette*, dim. of (O)Fr. *cive*: see CHIVE *n.*², -ET¹.] = CHIVE *n.*²

civet /sivɛ/ *n.*³ Pl. pronounced same. E18. [Fr., earlier *civé*, f. *cive* CHIVE *n.*²] A highly seasoned stew of hare, venison, game, etc.

civet de lièvre /də ljɛːvr/ *civet* of hare.

civet /ˈsɪvɪt/ *v.t.* E17. [f. CIVET *n.*¹] Perfume with civet.

civic /ˈsɪvɪk/ *a.* M16. [Fr. *civique* or L *civicus*, f. *civis* citizen. In sense 1 tr. L (*corona*) *civica*.] 1 *Hist.* Designating a garland of oak-leaves and acorns given in ancient Rome to one who saved a fellow citizen's life in war. M16. 2 Of or pertaining to a city; municipal; urban. M17. 3 Of or pertaining to citizenship; civil (opp. military, ecclesiastical, etc.). L18. 4 Of or proper to a citizen or citizens. L18.

1 MARVELL Our civil warrs have lost the civick crowne. 2 BYRON Butcher'd in a civic alley. R. H. TAWNEY The whole range of civic administration,

from the regulations to be made for markets . . to the control of prices, . . and rents. **civic centre** an area where municipal offices and other public buildings are situated, often in a united architectural scheme. 3 H. ARENDT A municipal law giving full civic, though not political, rights to the Jews. 4 J. S. BLACKIE He displayed a civic virtue on other occasions.

Comb.: **civic-minded** *a.* concerned with civic affairs, public-spirited.

†**civical** *a.* E–M17. **civically** *adv.* M17.

civics /ˈsɪvɪks/ *n.pl.* (usu. treated as *sing.*) Orig. *US.* L19. [f. prec. + -S¹: see -ICS.] The rights and duties of citizenship, as a subject of study.

civil /ˈsɪv(ə)l, -ɪl/ *a.*, *n.*, & *adv.* LME. [(O)Fr. f. L *civilis*, f. *civis* citizen: see -IL, -ILE.] **A** *adj.* **I** *gen.* **1** Of or pertaining to citizens as a community; relating to the internal organization of a society, State, etc. Also, of, pertaining to, or proper to citizens as individuals. LME. †**2** Civic, municipal; urban. *rare.* E16–E18. **3** Orderly; well-governed. Long *obs.* exc. *N. Ir.* & *Canad. dial.* M16. **4** In a condition of advanced social development; civilized; educated, well-bred; refined. *arch.* M16. †**5** Seemly, decent, grave. L16–L17. †**6** Humane, considerate, kind. Only in 17. **7** Polite, obliging; uneffusively courteous; not rude. E17.

1 R. HOOKER To exercise civil dominion of their own. HOR. WALPOLE The instruction of heathen children in . . civil knowledge. LD MACAULAY Compelled by civil troubles to go into banishment. 3 MILTON That Army, lately so renown'd for the civilest and best order'd in the world. 4 E. BREREWOOD Their own languages, which they held to be more civil than the Roman. SOUTHEY As in civil, so in barbarous states. 5 T. DEKKER In lookes, graue; in attire, ciuill. 7 G. SWIFT Quinn was actually civil to me, even amiable.

II *spec.* **8** Not military or naval etc.; not ecclesiastical, secular. LME. **9** Of law, a legal process, etc.: not criminal, political, or (formerly) ecclesiastical; relating to private relations between members of a community. LME. **b** Of or pertaining to Roman law or the legal systems (as of France or Germany) historically influenced by it. L16. **10** Legal as distinguished from natural; legally recognized; *spec.* (of time measurement) fixed by custom or enactment, not natural or astronomical. E17. †**11** *Theol.* Good or moral, but unregenerate. Only in 17.

8 MILTON Both in religious and civill Wisdome. B. RUSSELL The civil government had not discovered ways of preventing military insurrection.

Special collocations: **civil aviation**: not military, *esp.* commercial. **civil court** a court dealing with non-criminal cases. *civil day*: see DAY *n.* *civil* DEATH. **civil defence** the organization of civilians to preserve lives and property during and after enemy action, esp. air raids. **civil disobedience** the refusal to obey laws, pay taxes, etc., as part of a political campaign. *civil engineer*: see ENGINEER *n.* 3. *civil engineering*: see ENGINEERING *n.* 1. **civil law** *spec.* (also *the civil law*) Roman law (opp. canon or common law) or the systems of private law (as of France or Germany) historically influenced by it (the sense meant when *Civil Law* is used as a subject label in this dictionary); see also sense 9 above; **civil liberty** the state of being subject only to laws established for the good of the community; in *pl.*, one's rights to be only so subject. **civil list** (*a*) *Hist.* a list of certain items of State expenditure on civil administration; the recipients of moneys voted on this list; (*b*) an annual allowance by Parliament for the British monarch's household expenses. **civil marriage**: solemnized as a civil contract without a religious ceremony. *civil parish*: see PARISH 2. **civil rights** the rights of each citizen (*US* esp. of Blacks) to liberty, equality, etc. **civil servant** a member of the Civil Service. **Civil Service** (*a*) *Hist.* that part of the service of the East India Company carried out by covenanted servants not belonging to the army or navy; (*b*) all the non-military branches of State administration. **civil state** marital status; being single, married, divorced, etc. **civil war**: between citizens of the same country, esp. (freq. w. cap. initials) in England (1642–9), US (1861–5), or Spain (1936–9). **civil wrong** an infringement of a person's rights, as a tort of breach of contract. *civil year*: see YEAR *n.*¹

B *n.* †**1** = CIVILIAN *n.* 1. Only in LME. †**2** In *pl.* Civil matters, concerns, or affairs. M17–E18. **3** *do the civil*, act politely (*to* a person), behave in a properly polite manner. *arch. colloq.* M19.

†**C** *adv.* = CIVILLY. M17–L18.

†**civilist** *n.* (*a*) a civilian; (*b*) a politician: M16–M18. **civilly** *adv.* (*a*) in accordance with civil law; (*b*) with reference to civil matters; (*c*) in a civil manner: LME. **civilness** *n.* (*rare*) civility M16.

civilian /sɪˈvɪlj(ə)n/ *n.* & *a.* LME. [OFr. *civilien* in *droit civilien* civil law, f. as prec.: see -IAN. Later directly f. CIVIL.] **A** *n.* **1** A student of, practitioner of, or expert in civil law. Now *rare.* LME. †**2** *Theol.* A person who is good or moral, but unregenerate. E–M17. **3** *Hist.* A non-military employee of the East India Company; (later) a member of the Indian Civil Service. M18. **4** A person whose regular profession is non-military; one who is not in or of the army, navy, air force, or police. E19. **B** *attrib.* or as *adj.* Being a civilian; of or pertaining to civilians; not in or of the army, navy, air force, or police. M17.

civiliani'zation *n.* the action or result of civilianizing M20. **civilianize** *v.t.* make civilian; *spec.* convert (an armed-service post) into a civilian post: L19.

civilisation *n.* var. of CIVILIZATION.

civilise *v.* var. of CIVILIZE.

civility /sɪˈvɪlɪti/ *n.* LME. [(O)Fr. *civilité* f. L *civilitas*, f. *civilis*: see CIVIL, -ITY.] **I** Conn. w. citizenship. †**1** = CITIZENHOOD. LME–L16. †**2** Civil power. LME–M16. †**3** Polity, civil organization; *spec.* good polity, civil order. M16–L17. **4** Good citizenship; orderly behaviour. Long *obs.* exc. *N. Ir.* M16. †**5** *Theol.* Civil or moral righteousness. E–M17.

II Conn. w. civilization. **6** The state of being civilized, civilization; culture, refinement; polite or liberal education. *arch.* M16. **7** Politeness; consideration; an act or expression of politeness (usu. in *pl.*). M16. †**8** Decency, seemliness. Only in 17.

6 W. RALEIGH From them the Greekes, then barbarous, received Civilitie. DE QUINCEY Our universities, all so many recurring centres of civility. 7 LD MACAULAY He would not use the common forms of civility. J. I. M. STEWART A formally courteous person . . who felt obliged to stay put until adequate civilities had been exchanged.

Comb.: †**civility-money** a gratuity, a tip.

civilization /ˌsɪvɪlʌɪˈzeɪʃ(ə)n/ *n.* Also **-isation**. E18. [f. next + -ATION. Cf. Fr. *civilisation*.] †**1** *Law.* The process of turning a criminal action or process into a civil one; the assimilation of common law to civil law. E18–E19. **2** The state or condition of being civilized; civilized society; a highly developed state of society; a particular form, stage, or type of social development. M18. **3** The action or process of civilizing or being civilized. L18.

2 A. KOESTLER The breakdown of civilization during the Dark Ages. K. CLARK Of this ancient, rustic civilisation we have no record beyond the farmhouses themselves.

civilizational *a.* of or pertaining to civilization M19.

civilize /ˈsɪvɪlʌɪz/ *v.* Also **-ise**. E17. [Fr. *civiliser* (earlier *-zer*), f. as CIVIL: see -IZE.] **1** *v.t.* Bring out of barbarism; bring to conformity with the standards of behaviour and the tastes of a highly developed society; enlighten; refine and educate. E17. †**2** *v.t.* Subject to civil authority. E17–E18. **3** *v.i.* †**a** Behave in a civilized fashion. Only in E17. **b** Become civilized. M19.

civilizable *a.* able to be civilized M19. **civilized** *ppl a.* that has been civilized; pertaining to or characteristic of (members of) a highly-developed society; refined, educated: E17. **civili'zee** *n.* (now *rare*) a civilized person M19. **civilizer** *n.* L17.

civism /ˈsɪvɪz(ə)m/ *n.* L18. [Fr. *civisme*, f. L *civis* citizen: see -ISM.] The principles of good citizenship, esp. (& orig.) in relation to the republican order established by the French Revolution.

civvy /ˈsɪvi/ *n.* & *a. slang.* L19. [Abbrev. of CIVILIAN.] **A** *n.* **1** In *pl.* Civilian clothes. L19. **2** A civilian. E20.

B *adj.* Civilian. E20.

Civvy Street civilian (as opp. to Service) life.

clabber /ˈklabə/ *n.*¹ *Sc.* & *Ir.* Also **clauber** /ˈklɔːbə/. E19. [Gael. *clàbar*, Ir. *clábar*.] Mud, soft dirt, wet clay.

clabbery *a.* L19.

clabber /ˈklabə/ *n.*² & *v.* Chiefly *US.* E19. [Abbrev.] **A** *n.* = BONNY-CLABBER. E19. **B** *v.i.* & *t.* Curdle, turn sour. L19.

clachan /ˈklax(ə)n/ *n. Sc.* & *N. Ir.* LME. [Gael. & Ir. *clachán*.] A small village, a hamlet.

clack /klak/ *n.* & *int.* LME. [Imit.: cf. ON *klak* chirping of birds, Du. *klak*, MHG *klac*, CLAIK *n.*] **I** *n.* & *int.* Also redupl. **clack-clack(-clack)**. **1** (Repr.) the noise of continual loud talking, loud chatter. LME. **2** (Repr.) a sharp sound as of boards struck together, a metal object striking stone or wood, etc. L16. **II** *n.* **3** The clapper of a mill. *obs.* exc. *dial.* LME. **4** The human tongue. Usu. *contempt.* L16. **5** A flap-valve in a pump etc. Also *clack-valve*. M17. **6** An instrument that clacks to frighten birds away. L17. **7** A (loud) chat, a conversation. *colloq.* L18.

clack /klak/ *v.* ME. [Imit.: cf. ON *klaka* twitter, (of birds) chatter, Du. *klakken* crack, Fr. *claquer*, CLAIK *v.*] **1** *v.i.* Chatter loudly, talk continually. ME. **2** *v.i.* & *t.* (Cause to) make a clack; clatter. M16. **3** *v.i.* Of a hen etc.: cluck, cackle. E18.

1 LD MACAULAY He will sit clacking with an old woman for hours. 2 S. DELANEY The old clogs clacking along the cobbles. M. RICHLER Max clacked his tongue reproachfully.

Comb.: **clack-dish** *Hist.* = *clap-dish* s.v. CLAP *v.*¹

clacker *n.* M17.

clacket /ˈklakɪt/ *n.* L16. [Fr. *claquet*, f. *claquer* to clack: see -ET¹.] †**1** = CLACK *n.* 3, 6. L16–E17. **2** A light or repeated clacking sound; incessant chatter. E19.

clackety *a.* making a light or repeated clacking sound M19.

clacket /ˈklakɪt/ *v.i.* M16. [Fr. *claqueter*, f. as prec.] Clack lightly or repeatedly.

clad /klad/ *v.*¹*t.* Infl. **-dd-**. M16. [App. f. next.] **1** Clothe. *arch.* M16. **2** Provide with cladding. M20.

clad *v.*² pa. t. & pple: see CLOTHE.

cladding /ˈkladɪŋ/ *n.* L19. [f. CLAD *v.*¹ + -ING¹.] **1** In *pl.* Clothes. *rare.* L19. **2** A special coating or covering on a structure, material, etc.; the application of such a covering. M20.

clade /kleɪd/ *n.* M20. [Gk *klados* branch.] *Biol.* A group of organisms believed to have evolved from a common ancestor.

cladism *n.* belief in cladistics M20. **cladist** *n.* [perh. back-form. f. next] an exponent of cladistics M20.

cladistic /kləˈdɪstɪk/ *a.* M20. [f. prec. + -ISTIC.] *Biol.* Of or pertaining to clades or cladistics.

cladistically *adv.* in terms of cladistics; as regards cladistics or a cladistic relationship: M20.

cladistics /kləˈdɪstɪks/ *n.* M20. [f. prec.: see -ICS.] *Biol.* The systematic classification of groups of organisms on the basis of the order of their assumed divergence from ancestral species; systematics based on this.

clado- /ˈkleɪdəʊ, ˈkladəʊ/ *comb. form* of Gk *klados* branch, shoot, or of CLADE: see -O-.

clado'genesis *n.* (*Biol.*) the formation of a new species by evolutionary divergence of an ancestral species and species derived from it (cf. ANAGENESIS) M20. **cladoge'netic** *a.* (*Biol.*) of, pertaining to, or arising through cladogenesis M20. **cla'dogenous** *a.* (*Bot.*) growing from or borne on branches L19. **cladogram** *n.* (*Biol.*) a tree diagram of the cladistic relationship between a number of species M20.

cladoceran /kləˈdɒs(ə)r(ə)n/ *n.* & *a.* E20. [f. mod.L *Cladocera* (see below), f. as CLADO- + Gk *keras* horn (on account of the branched antennae): see -AN.] (A branchiopod crustacean) of the group Cladocera, which includes the water-fleas.

cladode /ˈkleɪdəʊd/ *n.* L19. [f. late Gk *kladōdēs* with many shoots, f. *klados* shoot.] *Bot.* A flattened leaflike stem.

cladosporium /kladəʊˈspɔːrɪəm/ *n.* L19. [mod.L (see below), f. as CLADO- + *spora* seed + -IUM.] (Infestation with) a fungus of the genus *Cladosporium*, esp. causing leaf-mould of tomatoes.

claes *n.pl.* see CLOTHES.

clag /klag/ *v.* & *n.* Chiefly *Sc.* & *north.* LME. [Perh. of Scand. origin: cf. Da. *klag*, *klagge* sticky mud, clay, *klæg*, *klæget* viscous, rel. to CLAY *n.*] **A** *v.* Infl. **-gg-**. **1** *v.t.* Bedaub or clot *with*; clog. LME. 2 *v.i.* Stick, adhere, (*to*). M16. B *n.* 1 A flaw of character; a fault. *Sc.* L16. 2 A legal encumbrance on a property etc. *Sc.* Long *rare.* L16. 3 A mass of clotted dirt in a sheep's fleece etc. M17.

claggum *n.* treacle toffee M19. **claggy** *a.* tending to form clots; sticky: L16.

claik /kleɪk/ *n.*, *int.*, & *v. Sc.* LME. [Imit.: cf. CLACK *n.* & *int.*, *v.*] A *n.* 1 More fully *claik goose.* The barnacle goose. LME. 2 Also *int.* (Repr.) the harsh call of a goose, the cluck or cackle of a hen etc. L15. 3 Chatter, gossip; a gossipy person. L18. B *v.i.* 1 Of a goose: call harshly. Of a hen etc.: cluck, cackle. E16. 2 Chatter, talk tediously. M19.

claim /kleɪm/ *n.* ME. [OFr. *claime*, f. *clamer*: see next.] I 1 A demand for something as due; a statement of one's right *to* something; a contention, an assertion; *spec.* (*a*) a formal assertion of a right to a piece of land for mining etc.; (*b*) a demand for payment in accordance with law, an insurance policy, etc.; (*c*) (in full *pay-claim*) a demand for an increase in pay; (*d*) a formal statement of the novel features in a patent. ME. 2 A right or title (*to* something); a right to make a demand ((*up*)*on* a person etc.). ME. 3 A piece of land allotted or taken for the purpose of mining etc. L18.

1 C. DAY The telephone company sent us circulars in which they made large claims. C. HILL By arbitrary arrest and imprisonment he enforced his claim to tax without Parliamentary consent. A. BRINK The Department of Justice instituted a claim for libel against the newspaper. *Court of Claims*: see COURT *n.*[1] **lay claim to** assert one's right to, claim. *no-claim(s) bonus*: see NO *a. quit claim to*: see QUIT *v. small-claims court*: see SMALL *a.* 2 J. B. PRIESTLEY Miss Trant had waived any claim to her part of the fee. R. S. THOMAS The claim Of wife and young ones. W. S. CHURCHILL His care for the Royal Navy is his chief claim upon the gratitude of his countrymen. 3 *prospecting claim*: see PROSPECT *v.* 4. **stake (out) a claim** make a claim to a piece of land for mining etc. by marking it with stakes; *fig.* make a statement of one's rights (*to*).

†II 4 A call, a shout. *rare* (Spenser). Only in L16.

Comb.: **claim-jumper** one who appropriates a mining claim already taken by another.

claimless *a.* E19.

claim /kleɪm/ *v.* ME. [OFr. *claim-* tonic stem of *clamer* to cry, call, appeal, f. L *clamare.* Cf. CLAMOUR *n.*] I *v.t.* 1 Demand as one's due or property, require as a right, (*arch.* foll. by *that, to be* + pa. ppl a.); *fig.* have as a property, achievement, or consequence, *esp.* take by death. ME. 2 Assert or demand recognition of (the fact *that*); represent oneself as having, oneself *to be, to have done*; represent oneself so as to seem *to do*; assert, contend, *that.* ME. †3 Name (as), proclaim (to be); represent (oneself) as. ME–L16. 4 Of a thing: have a right to, deserve, call for. E17.

1 C. MERIVALE He claimed that his word should be law. J. R. GREEN Every townsman could claim to be tried by his fellow-townsman. B. PYM The television screen was beginning to claim their full attention. M. M. KAYE The cholera had claimed four more lives. *Which?* You should claim a refund of the repair cost from the shop. 2 DEFOE Both sides claimed the victory. E. WAUGH Basil claimed to have eaten a girl once in Africa. G. GREENE She never claimed to like a thing that she disliked. M. HOLROYD He claimed to be a descendant of Owen Glendower. E. CRISPIN The Major could sense a journalist, or .. claimed he could. 4 J. TYNDALL One other point .. which claims our attention.

II *v.i.* 5 Put forward a claim; assert a right; represent oneself to be. Now only *spec.* make a claim for indemnity on an insurance company. ME.

5 POPE Say from what scepter'd ancestry ye claim.

claimable *a.* E17. **claimant** *n.* a person who makes a claim, esp. formally; a person who has a claim (*up*)*on*: L17. **claimer** *n.* LME.

clairaudience /klɛːrˈɔːdɪəns/ *n.* M19. [f. Fr. *clair* clear + AUDIENCE, after CLAIRVOYANCE.] The supposed faculty of perceiving, as if by hearing, what is inaudible.

clairaudient *a.* & *n.* (*a*) *adj.* having the faculty of clairaudience; of the nature of or pertaining to clairaudience; (*b*) *n.* a clairaudient person: M19.

clair-de-lune /klɛːrdəlyn, klɛːdəˈluːn/ *n.* L19. [Fr., lit. 'moonlight'.] A soft white or pale blue-grey colour; a Chinese porcelain glaze of this colour.

clair-obscure /klɛːrəbˈskjʊə/ *n.* E18. [Fr. *clair-obscur* tr. It. CHIAROSCURO.] = CHIAROSCURO.

clairschach /ˈklɑːʃəx/ *n.* Also **clar-**. L15. [Ir. *cláirseach*, Gael. *clàrsach.*] The traditional Celtic harp strung with wire.

clairschacher *n.* a person who plays the clairschach E16.

clairvoyance /klɛːˈvɔɪəns/ *n.* M19. [Fr., f. as next: see -ANCE.] 1 The supposed faculty of perceiving, as if by seeing, what is happening or exists out of sight. M19. 2 Keenness of mental perception: exceptional insight. M19.

clairvoyant /klɛːˈvɔɪənt/ *a.* & *n.* Occas. fem. **-ante**. L17. [Fr., f. *clair* clear + *voyant* pres. ppl a. of *voir* see: see -ANT[1].] A *adj.* 1 Clear-sighted, perceptive. *rare.* L17. 2 Having or exercising the faculty of clairvoyance; pertaining to clairvoyance. M19. B *n.* 1 A clear-sighted person. *rare.* L18. 2 A person having the faculty of clairvoyance. M19.

clairvoyantly *adv.* L19.

clam /ˈklam/ *n.*[1] [OE *clam* = OHG *klamma* (G dial. *Klamm*), MHG, G *klemme*, Du. *klemme, klem*, f. Gmc (rel. to CLAMP *n.*[1]).] †1 Anything that holds tight; in *pl.* bonds, bondage. Only in OE. 2 An instrument for clasping rigidly or holding fast; a clamp, vice, pair of pincers, etc.; also, a lining for the jaws of a vice. LME. 3 In *pl.* clutches, claws. Long *obs.* exc. *dial.* M16.

clam /klam/ *n.*[2] E16. [App. f. prec.] 1 A bivalve mollusc; *esp.* (*a*) *Sc.* a scallop; (*b*) an extremely large tropical bivalve, *Tridacna gigas* (usu. *giant clam*); (*c*) either of two common bivalves valued as food on the east coast of N. America, the quahog *Venus mercenaria* (also *hard* or *round clam*) and *Mya arenaria*, which has a very long siphon (also *long, longneck, soft*, or *steamer clam*). (Earliest in *clam-shell* below.) E16. 2 The mouth. *US slang.* E19. 3 A person who is close-minded, close-mouthed, etc.; a taciturn person. *US slang.* M19.

1 (*as*) *happy as a clam*: see HAPPY *a. Venus clam*: see VENUS 9. *Washington clam*: see WASHINGTON 1.

Comb.: **clambake** *US* a social gathering for eating (esp. clams and fish) outdoors; a loud and lively gathering, a jam-session; **clam-shell** (*a*) the shell of a clam; (*b*) *US slang* = sense 2 above.

clam /klam/ *n.*[3] M16. [Perh. back-form. f. CLAMMY.] †1 A soft mass. Only in M16. 2 Clamminess. L17.

clam /klam/ *n.*[4] E18. [Prob. imit.: cf. CLAM *v.*[3]] *Campanol.* The crash of two or more bells of a peal rung together.

clam /klam/ *a. obs.* exc. *dial.* ME. [Prob. rel. to next, CLOAM *n.*] Sticky; cold and damp; clammy.

clam /klam/ *v.*[1] *obs.* exc. *dial.* Infl. **-mm-**. LME. [Var. of CLEAM, perh. infl. by prec.] 1 *v.t.* Smear or spread (sticky or slimy matter) *on*; daub (*with*). LME. 2 *v.t.* Clog or choke up. E16. 3 *v.i.* Be moist and sticky; stick, adhere. M16. 4 *v.t.* Clog or entangle *with* or *in* anything sticky. L16.

clam /klam/ *v.*[2]*i.* Infl. **-mm-**. M17. [f. CLAM *n.*[2]] 1 Dig for clams, collect clams. *US.* M17. 2 Foll. by *up*: become silent, stop talking or otherwise communicating. *slang* (chiefly *N. Amer.*). E20.

clam /klam/ *v.*[3] Infl. **-mm-**. L17. [Prob. imit.: cf. CLAM *n.*[4], CLAMOUR *v.*[2]] *Campanol.* 1 *v.i.* Of bells: sound or crash together. L17. 2 *v.t.* Sound or crash (bells) together. E18.

clam *v.*[4] var. of CLEM.

clamant /ˈkleɪm(ə)nt, ˈklam-/ *a.* M17. [f. L *clamant-* pres. ppl stem of *clamare* cry out: see -ANT[1]. Cf. CLAIM *v.*] 1 Clamorous, noisy. M17. 2 *fig.* Insistent, urgent. E18.

2 *New Scientist* By 1920 the need for training and transfer of US technology was clamant.

clamantly *adv.* M19.

†**clamb** *v.* pa. t. of CLIMB *v.*

clamber /ˈklambə/ *v.* & *n.* ME. [Of frequent. form, prob. f. prec.: see -ER[5].] A *v.* 1 *v.i.* & *t.* Climb using hands and feet; climb with difficulty and effort. ME. 2 *v.i. transf.* & *fig.* a Climb or struggle (*up*) into a position of eminence; attain with effort *to.* Now *rare.* L16. b Rise upwards heavily, irregularly, or steeply. E17. c Of a plant: climb by means of tendrils. E17.

1 S. JOHNSON They can .. clamber the mountain. F. HERBERT The craft creaked as the others clambered aboard. 2b N. HAWTHORNE A tall palace of gray, time-worn stone clambered skyward. TENNYSON The narrow street that clamber'd toward the mill. c C. RAINE Ivy clambers over the sides of a rusty cot.

B *n.* An act of clambering; a climb using hands and feet. E19.

clamberer *n.* a person who or thing which clambers; formerly *esp.* a climbing plant: L16.

clame *v.* var. of CLEAM.

clamjamphrie /klamˈdʒamfri/ *n. Sc.* & *north.* Also **clan-** /klan-/, **-fry**, & other vars. E19. [Origin unkn.] Worthless or vulgar people; a mob, a rabble.

clammer *v.* see CLAMOUR *v.*[2]

clammy /ˈklami/ *a.* LME. [f. CLAM *v.*[1] or *a.* + -Y[1].] Moist, usu. cold, and sticky or slimy; damp and cold.

SOUTHEY The cold sweat stands Upon his clammy limbs. D. H. LAWRENCE The wind drifted a clammy fog across the hills. J. MASTERS The clammy sari was clinging to my body.

clammily *adv.* M19. **clamminess** *n.* E16.

clamor *n.*, *v.*[1], *v.*[2] see CLAMOUR *n.*, *v.*[1], *v.*[2]

clamorous /ˈklam(ə)rəs/ *a.* LME. [f. late L *clamorosus*, f. L *clamor*: see CLAMOUR *n.*, -OUS. Cf. OFr. *clamoreus.*] Of the nature of clamour; uttered with or accompanied by shouting; noisy; loudly and persistently complaining, appealing, or demanding; urgently claiming attention.

SHAKES. *A.Y.L.* I will be .. more clamorous than a parrot against rain. D. H. LAWRENCE Her voice was loud and clamorous. W. STYRON The night was clamorous with frogs and katydids.

clamorously *adv.* M16. **clamorousness** *n.* E17.

clamour /ˈklamə/ *n.* Also ***-or**. LME. [AN *clamur*, OFr. *clamour* f. L *clamor* rel. to *clamare*: see -OUR. Cf. CLAIM *v.*] 1 Loud shouting (by one or, freq., many), esp. in complaint, appeal, or opposition; vehement expression of feeling, esp. of discontent or disapprobation; popular outcry. LME. 2 A loud shout, an outburst of noisy utterance; a popular outcry. LME. 3 Any loud or confused noise. L16.

1 R. WHATELY Attempts .. to silence a speaker by clamour. E. LONGFORD An important section of the Army .. fell a victim to the country's clamour for economy. 2 C. THIRLWALL Interrupted in a speech by clamours of disapprobation. 3 W. IRVING The clamour of a troop of dogs. A. C. SWINBURNE The clamour of his storms. A. MACLEAN The sudden strident clamour of an alarm bell.

clamour /ˈklamə/ *v.*[1] Also ***-or**. LME. [f. the n.] 1 *v.i.* Make a clamour; raise an outcry; make a loud appeal, complaint, or demand, (*for, against, to do*). LME. 2 *v.t.* †a Disturb with clamour. Only in 17. b Move or drive *out of, into*, etc., by clamouring; put *down* by clamour. M17. 3 *v.t.* Utter or assert clamorously. M19.

1 SHAKES. *Macb.* The obscure bird Clamour'd the livelong night. A. BRIGGS The urban working classes came into the open to clamour for reform. R. SUTCLIFF If you tell me to do a thing, I will do it, without clamouring to know why.

clamourer *n.* M17.

clamour /ˈklamə/ *v.*[2]*t.* Now *rare.* Also **-or**, **clammer**. E17. [Origin uncertain: perh. rel. to CLAM *v.*[3] or a use of prec.] Silence, stop the noise of, (*spec.* bells).

¶ First recorded in Shakes.

clamp /klamp/ *n.*[1] & *v.*[1] ME. [Prob. of LG origin: cf. Du., LG *klamp*, †*klampe* (whence G *Klampe*), f. Gmc (rel. to CLAM *n.*[1]).] A *n.* 1 A brace, clasp, or band, usu. of rigid material, used for strengthening or fastening things together. ME. 2 *Naut.* Each of the thick planks in a ship's side below the shelf-piece, which support the ends of the deck-beams. L15. 3 An appliance or tool with parts which may be brought together by a screw etc. for holding or compressing. L17. 4 *Electr.* A circuit which serves to maintain at prescribed levels the voltage limits of a signal. Also *clamp circuit.* M20.

B *v.* 1 *v.t.* Patch (*up*). *Sc.* L15. 2 *v.t.* Make fast or strengthen (as) with a clamp or clamps; place or hold firmly. L17. **b** Immobilize with a wheel clamp. L20. **3** *v.i.* a *clamp down* (*on*), press down hard (on), become stricter (regarding), call a halt (to). E20. **b** *clamp down*, (of cloud, fog, etc.) descend very low, so as to prevent flying etc. M20. **4** *v.t. Electr.* Maintain the voltage limits of (a signal) at prescribed values. Freq. as *clamping* vbl n. M20.

2 R. P. WARREN To . . clamp a cigar in his left jaw. W. GOLDING A heavy hand . . clamped me down. L. DEIGHTON The . . cables were roughly clamped across the charred ends as if with artery forceps. 3a *Economist* The government clamped down firmly on all political agitation. L. LEE Suddenly the iron-frost of destitution would clamp down on the house.

Comb.: **clamp-down** an act of clamping down.

clamp /klamp/ *n.*[2] & *v.*[2] L16. [Prob. f. (M)Du *klamp* heap, rel. to CLUMP *n.*] **A** *n.* **1** A stack or pile of bricks for burning. L16. **2** A heap or pile of straw and earth covering potatoes etc. during winter; a heap or pile of turf, peat, garden rubbish, etc. E18. **B** *v.t.* Pile *up* in a clamp; store (potatoes etc.) in a clamp. M19.

clamp /klamp/ *n.*[3] & *v.*[3] Chiefly *Sc.* & *north.* L18. [Imit.: cf. CLOMP, CLUMP *n.*, *v.*] **A** *n.* A heavy step or tread; a stamp with the feet. L18. **B** *v.i.* Tread heavily, clump. E19.

clamper /ˈklampə/ *v.*[1] & *n.* Now chiefly *Sc.* M16. [f. CLAMP *v.*[1] + -ER[5].] **A** *v.t.* Put together hastily or clumsily, patch *up*, (*lit.* & *fig.*). M16. **B** *n.* **1** A metal patch or plate. *Sc.* E17. **2** A botched-up argument or charge. M17.

clamper /ˈklampə/ *v.*[2] *i.* Chiefly *Sc.* & *dial.* E19. [f. CLAMP *v.*[3] + -ER[5].] Walk or step heavily or noisily.

clan /klan/ *n.* & *v.* LME. [Gael. *clann* offspring, family, stock, f. OIr. *cland* (mod.Ir. *clann*) f. L *planta* sprout, scion, PLANT *n.*] **A** *n.* **1** A group of (esp. Highland) Scots claiming descent from a common ancestor, acknowledging a patriarchal chief, and usu. all having the same surname. LME. **2** *gen.* Any similar tribal division or group; a (large) close-knit family. E16. **3** A group of people having shared attributes; a party, a coterie, a set. Usu. *derog.* M16. **4** A group of objects, animals, plants, etc., sharing common origins or attributes. M17. **b** *Ecol.* A small local group of a dominant plant species. E20. **c** *Geol.* A group of igneous rocks of similar chemical composition. E20.

Comb.: **clansfolk** (fellow) members of a clan. **clansman** a male (fellow) member of a clan. **clanswoman** a female (fellow) member of a clan.

B *v.i.* Infl. **-nn-**. Combine (*together*) as members of a clan. L17.

clanism *n.* clan system or feeling M19. **clanny** *a.* = CLANNISH L19. **clanship** *n.* a clan system; clannish behaviour; clan membership or feeling: M18.

†**clancular** *a.* E17–M18. [L *clancularius*, f. *clanculum* adv., dim. of *clam* in secret: see -AR[2].] Secret; clandestine.

†**clancularly** *adv.* E17–M19. †**clanculary** *a.* = CLANCULAR M16–M17.

clandestine /klanˈdɛstɪn, ˈklandɛstɪn/ *a.* M16. [Fr. *clandestin* or L *clandestinus*, f. *clam* in secret: see -INE[1].] Surreptitious, secret.

clandestinely *adv.* M17. **clandeˈstinity** *n.* (surreptitious) secrecy L17.

clang /klaŋ/ *n.* & *v.* L16. [Imit., but infl. by L *clangor*, *clangere* (see next); sense A.3 f. G *Klang*. Cf. CLANK, CLINK *n.*[1], *v.*[1]] **A** *n.* **1** A loud resonant metallic sound, as of a trumpet, armour, a large bell, etc. L16. **2** The loud harsh scream of certain birds, as geese. M17. **3** Chiefly *Psychol.* (The acoustic sensation of) a sound consisting of a fundamental tone and overtones. Now *rare.* M19.

Comb.: **clang association** *Psychol.* an association of words by sound rather than meaning.

B *v.* **1** *v.i.* Move with or make a loud resonant metallic sound. L16. **2** *v.t.* Cause to make a clang; strike together with a clang. E18. **3** *v.i.* Of certain birds: utter their loud harsh cry. M19.

1 J. STEINBECK Every day the red bus clangs back and forth. A. CARTER A voice that clanged like dustbin lids.

clanger *n.* (*slang*) a blunder (esp. in *drop a clanger*, make a blunder) M20.

clangour /ˈklaŋgə/ *n.* & *v.* Also ***-or**. L16. [L *clangor*, f. *clangere* resound: see -OUR, -OR.] **A** *n.* Clanging noise; a succession or prevalence of clanging noises. L16. **B** *v.i.* Make a clangour. M19.

clangorous *a.* full of clangour E18. **clangorously** *adv.* M19.

clanjamfry, **-phrie** *ns.* vars. of CLAMJAMPHRIE.

clank /klaŋk/ *n.* & *v.* LME. [Imit., = MLG, (M)Du. *klank*, OHG *klanc*, *klank-*. Cf. CLANG, CLINK *n.*[1], *v.*[1], CLONK, CLUNK *v.* & *n.*[2]] **A** *n.* An abrupt heavy metallic sound, as of heavy pieces of metal meeting, a chain rattling, etc. LME.

B *v.* **1** *v.t.* Deposit with a clank; put *down* heavily. E17. **2** *v.i.* Make an abrupt heavy metallic sound; move with a clank or clanks. M17. **3** *v.t.* Cause to make a clank or clanks; proclaim by a clank or clanks. M18.

2 E. DARWIN Dungeons dank Where . . fetters clank. J. GALSWORTHY The iron gates clanked open. C. P. SNOW Some undergraduates came clanking through in football boots. 3 J. CLARE The beating snow-clad bell, with sounding dead, Hath clanked four. C. H. SISSON Gaolers . . Clanking their keys.

¶In isolated use bef. 17.

clankety-clank /ˌklaŋkɪtɪˈklaŋk/ *n.* a repeated clanking sound L19. **clankless** *a.* (*rare*) that does not or do not clank E19.

clannish /ˈklanɪʃ/ *a.* M18. [f. CLAN *n.* + -ISH[1].] Pertaining to or characteristic of a clan; (too much) attached to one's own clan, family, etc.

clannishly *adv.* L19. **clannishness** *n.* E19.

clap /klap/ *n.*[1] ME. [f. CLAP *v.*[1]] **I** A noise or action. **1** Noisy talk, chatter. Long *obs.* exc. *dial.* ME. **2** A sounding blow; a slap, a pat. ME. **3** A sudden stroke (*lit.* & *fig.*). *obs.* exc. *Sc.* & in *afterclap* s.v. AFTER-. ME. **4** An abrupt explosive noise, as of two hard surfaces striking one another; the report of a gun. LME. **b** *spec.* A peal of thunder. LME. **c** *spec.* The noise of the palms of the hands being struck together; (a round of) applause. L16.

2 S. JOHNSON All the forms of . . salutation, from the clap on the shoulder to the humble bow.

II A physical object. **5** = CLAPPER *n.*[1] 1; *esp.* the clapper of a mill. ME. †**6** The human tongue. ME–L16. **7** The lower mandible of a hawk. L15.

For combs. see CLAP *v.*[1]

clap /klap/ *n.*[2] *coarse slang.* L16. [f. OFr. *clapoir* venereal bubo.] Venereal disease, *esp.* gonorrhoea, (also *the clap*); an infection with this.

clap /klap/ *v.*[1] Infl. **-pp-**. Pa. t. & pple **clapped**, (*arch.*) **clapt**. [OE *clappan* = OFris. *klappia*, MLG *klappen*, OHG *klapfōn*, ON *klappa*, beside OE *clæppan* = OFris. *kleppa*, MLG *kleppen*, OHG *klepfen*: of imit. origin.] †**1** *v.i.* Throb, beat, pulsate. OE–LME. **2** *v.t.* Strike with sounding blows. *arch.* OE. **3** *v.i.* Make an abrupt explosive noise; make a loud rattling noise; *spec.* (*a*) (of a door, window, etc.) close with a bang, slam; †(*b*) rap, knock at a door etc.; (see also sense 6b). Now *arch.* & *dial.* LME. **4** *v.i.* Chatter loudly, talk continually, (= CLACK *v.* 1). Now *rare.* LME. **5** *v.t.* Cause to make an abrupt explosive noise, strike together; cause to make a loud rattling noise; *spec.* (*a*) close (a door, window, etc., *to*) with a bang, slam; †(*b*) strike (hands) reciprocally, in token of a bargain; (see also senses 6, 7). Now *arch.* & *dial.* LME. **6** *v.t.* Strike (the hands) together loudly, esp. to show approval, for warmth, as a signal, etc.; show approval of (a person, an event, etc.) by doing this. LME. **b** *v.i.* Clap the hands together; applaud by clapping hands. E16. **7** *v.t.* Of a bird: flap (the wings) audibly. LME. **8** *v.t.* Slap with the palm of the hand, as a sign of approval, in encouragement, etc.; *Sc.* & *north.* pat fondly. LME. **b** Smooth or flatten (*out*) with the palms or with a flat-surfaced object. Chiefly *north.* M16. **9** *v.t.* Put or place quickly, energetically, or unceremoniously; impose (as) with authority (*up*)*on*. LME. **10** *v.i.* †**a** Come or go suddenly or decisively; enter *into* (an activity) with alacrity. M16–M18. **b** Foll. by *on*: apply oneself energetically, set to. *colloq.* M19. **11** *v.i.* Press or lie close (*to*, *in*, etc.). Now chiefly *Sc.* L16. **12** *v.t.* **a** Foll. by *up*: make or construct hastily or without much care; chiefly (& now only) *fig.*, arrange or settle (an agreement etc.) hastily or without much care. *arch.* L16. †**b** Put or stick *together*. M17–E18.

6 S. PEPYS It was very finely sung, so as to make the whole house clap her. D. PARKER The Swedish girl raised her hands . . and clapped them twice together to summon the waiter. 9 SHAKES. *Merry W.* Clap on more sails; pursue. BYRON I have . . clapt sentinels at the doors. R. W. EMERSON He has clapped copyright on the world. E. BOWEN The ices . . were clapped between wafers. J. CHEEVER I . . clapped my hat on my head, and marched out. A. FRASER The government speedily clapped the leaders in prison. **clap eyes on** *colloq.* catch sight of, see (usu. in neg. contexts).

Comb. (partly f. CLAP *n.*[1]): **clap-bread** thin oatmeal cake; **clap-dish** *Hist.* a wooden alms-dish with a lid, carried by beggars, lepers, etc., and rattled to attract notice; **clap-net** a fowler's or entomologist's net shut by pulling a string.

clapped out *a. phr.* (*slang*) worn out, exhausted, no longer functioning M20.

clap /klap/ *v.*[2]*t. coarse slang.* Infl. **-pp-**. M17. [f. CLAP *n.*[2]] Infect with venereal disease, esp. gonorrhoea.

clapboard /ˈklapbɔːd, ˈklabəd/ *n.* & *v.* E16. [Partial tr. of CLAPHOLT.] **A** *n.* **1a** A piece of split oak used for barrel-staves and wainscoting. *obs.* exc. *Hist.* E16. **b** A weatherboard. *N. Amer.* M17. †**2** The material of such boards; such boards collectively. M16–L19. **B** *v.t.* Cover or line with clapboards. *US.* M17.

clapboarding *vbl n.* (*US*) (*a*) the action of the vb; (*b*) a covering of clapboards on a building etc.: M17.

Clapham /ˈklap(ə)m/ *n.* M19. [A district of SW London.] **1** *the Clapham Sect*, an early-19th-cent. group noted for evangelical opinions and philanthropic activity (some of whose chief members lived at Clapham). Somewhat *derog.* *obs.* exc. *Hist.* M19. **2** *the man on the Clapham omnibus*, the average man. E20.

†**clapholt** *n.* LME–E18. [LG *klappholt* = Du. *klaphout*, f. *klappen* crack + *holt* wood.] = CLAPBOARD *n.* 2.

clapmatch /ˈklapmatʃ/ *n.* Also **k-**. M18. [Du. *klapmuts*(*rob*) hooded seal, f. *klapmuts* cap with flaps.] Orig., a hooded or eared seal. Now, a female seal.

clapper /ˈklapə/ *n.*[1] & *v.* ME. [f. CLAP *v.*[1] + -ER[1].] **A** *n.* **1** A device that makes short repeated strokes or that makes a clapping or loud rattling noise; *spec.* (*a*) a contrivance in a mill for striking or shaking the hopper so as to make the grain move down to the millstones; (*b*) *Hist.* the lid of a clap-dish, or a rattle, used by beggars, lepers, etc., to attract attention; (*c*) the tongue or striker of a bell; (*d*) an instrument for frightening birds away; (*e*) *Cinemat.* (in full *clapperboard*) a device making a sharp noise for the synchronization of picture and sound. ME. **b** The human tongue. Usu. *contempt.* M17. **2** A person who claps; a claqueur. E19.

1 like the clappers *slang* very fast, very hard.

Comb.: *clapperboard*: see sense 1 above; **clapperclaw** *v.t.* (*arch.*) claw with the open hand and nails; *fig.* revile; **clapperdudgeon** *arch. slang* [app. DUDGEON *n.*[1]] a person born a beggar, a low wretch; **clapper rail** a large greyish N. American rail, *Rallus longirostris*, of coastal marshes.

B *v.* **1** *v.t.* **a** Fit a clapper to (a bell). *rare.* E16. **b** Sound (a bell) by pulling the clapper. L19. **2** *v.i.* Make a noise like a clapper. M19.

clapper /ˈklapə/ *n.*[2] ME. [AN *claper* = OFr. *clapier* f. Prov. = heap of stones, rabbit warren, of Gaulish origin.] **1** More fully *clapper bridge*. A rough bridge or raised path of stones. *dial.* ME. †**2** A rabbit burrow; a place for keeping rabbits. LME–E18.

clapt *v.* pa. t. & pple: see CLAP *v.*[1]

claptrap /ˈklaptrap/ *n.* M18. [f. CLAP *n.*[1] + TRAP *n.*[1]] **1** A device, expression, etc., to elicit applause. *arch.* M18. **2** Language used or sentiments expressed only to elicit applause; pretentious but empty assertions; nonsense. E19.

claptrappy *a.* M19.

claque /klak, klɑːk; *foreign* klak (*pl. same*)/ *n.* M19. [Fr., f. *claquer* to clap.] A hired body of applauders; *transf.* a body of sycophantic followers.

claqueur /klɑːˈkəː; *foreign* klakœːr (*pl. same*)/ *n.* M19. [Fr., f. *claquer* (see prec.) + *-eur* -OR.] A member of a claque.

clarabella /klarəˈbɛlə/ *n.* M19. [f. L *clarus*, (fem.) *-ra* clear + *bellus*, (fem.) *-lla* beautiful.] An organ-stop having a flutelike quality.

clarain /ˈklareɪn/ *n.* E20. [f. L *clarus* CLEAR *a.*, after FUSAIN.] *Geol.* One of the lithotypes of coal: a finely laminated material with a silky lustre.

Clare /klɛː/ *n.* E17. [f. St *Clare* (see below).] A nun of the Franciscan order founded by St Clare at Assisi *c* 1212. Freq. *poor Clare.*

clarence /ˈklar(ə)ns/ *n.* M19. [f. the Duke of *Clarence*, later William IV.] Chiefly *Hist.* A four-wheeled closed carriage with seats for four inside and two on the box.

Clarenceux /ˈklar(ə)nsuː/ *n.* Also †**-cieux.** LME. [AN, f. *Clarence*, an English dukedom named from Clare in Suffolk.] The second English King of Arms, having jurisdiction south of the Trent.

Clarendon /ˈklar(ə)ndən/ *n.* M19. [Prob. f. the *Clarendon* Press, Oxford.] *Typogr.* A bold condensed type with bracketed serifs, used esp. for emphasis.

claret /ˈklarət/ *a.* & *n.* LME. [OFr. (*vin*) *claret* (mod. *clairet*) orig. of light-red wines, f. *claré*: see CLARY *n.*[1]] A *adj.* †1 *claret wine* = sense B.1 below. LME–E18. 2 Of the colour of claret. M16.

B *n.* 1 Orig., wine of a yellowish or light-red colour, as distinguished from white or red wine; later, red wine generally. Now, (*a*) red wine from Bordeaux in France; *transf.* (*a*) wine of the same character from some other country. Also, a drink of such wine. E16. 2 Blood. *slang.* E17. 3 The colour of claret, (now) a reddish violet. M17.

Phrases: *riddle of claret*: see RIDDLE *n.*[2] 1. **tap a person's claret** *slang* make a person's nose bleed by a blow with the fist.

Comb. **claret-colour(ed)** (having) a reddish-violet colour.

clareˈteer *n.* (now *rare* or *obs.*) a drinker of claret L17. **clarety** *a.* E18.

clarichord /ˈklarɪkɔːd/ *n. obs.* exc. *Hist.* LME. [Alt. of CLAVICHORD by assoc. w. L *clarus* clear.] = CLAVICHORD.

clarification /ˌklarɪfɪˈkeɪʃ(ə)n/ *n.* E16. [In branch I partly f. next, partly f. Fr. *clarification*, f. as next: see -FICATION. In branch II f. eccl.L *clarificatio(n-)*, f. *clarificat-* pa. ppl stem of *clarificare*: see next, -ATION.] I 1 The action of making clear or plain to the understanding; removal of complexity, ambiguity, or obscurity. E16. 2 The action of freeing from impurities or making transparent; the process of becoming free from impurities or transparent. E17. †II 3 Glorification, transfiguration. M–L17.

clarificatory *a.* tending to, having the purpose of, or relating to, clarification M20.

clarify /ˈklarɪfʌɪ/ *v.* ME. [(O)Fr. *clarifier* f. late L *clarificare*, f. L *clarus* clear + *-ficare* -FY.] I †1 *v.t.* Declare, set forth clearly. Only in ME. 2 *v.t.* Make pure and clean, physically or (*arch.*) morally; free from impurities; *spec.* make (a liquid, butter, the air, etc.) transparent. ME. †3 *v.t.* Free from darkness or gloom; brighten, illumine. LME–L17. 4 *v.t.* Enlighten; make clear or plain to the understanding; remove complexity, ambiguity, or obscurity from (a subject, statement, etc.); remove ignorance, misconception, or error from (the mind etc.). LME. 5 *v.t.* Make unobstructed, clear, (the sight, eyes, mental vision; *arch.* the throat, the voice). LME. 6 *v.i.* Become transparent; be made clear or pure (*lit.* & *fig.*). L16. †II 7 *v.t.* Make illustrious or glorious; exalt. LME–M17.

clarifier *n.* a person who or thing which provides clarification; a vessel used in clarification: M16.

clarine /ˈklariːn/ *n.* LME. [OFr. *clarin* (mod. *clarine* in sense 2 only) by-form of *claron* CLARION.] †1 = CLARION. LME–M18. 2 A cow-bell. *rare.* E20.

clarinet /klarɪˈnɛt/ *n.* M18. [Fr. *clarinette* dim. of *clarine*: see prec., -ETTE.] 1 A woodwind instrument having a single-reed mouthpiece, holes, and keys; a player on this in an orchestra etc. M18. 2 An organ-stop of similar sound-quality. L19.

clarinettist, *-**etist** *n.* a player on the clarinet M19.

clarion /ˈklarɪən/ *n.* & *a.* ME. [med.L *clario(n-)*, f. L *clarus* clear: cf. OFr. *claron* (mod. *clairon*).] A *n.* 1 *Hist.* A shrill narrow-tubed war trumpet. ME. 2 The sound of a trumpet; any rousing sound. *poet.* M17. 3 An organ-stop of sound-quality similar to a clarion. L17.

2 MILTON The crested Cock whose clarion sounds The silent hours. K. TYNAN Her voice is a rallying-call . . a downright clarion.

B *attrib.* or as *adj.* Of a clarion; sounding like a clarion; loud and clear. LME.

clarionet /klarɪəˈnɛt/ *n.* L18. [f. prec. + -ET[1], partly f. CLARINET.] = CLARINET.

Clarisse /klaˈriːs/ *n.* L17. [Fr., f. as CLARE.] = CLARE.

clarity /ˈklarɪti/ *n.* ME. [L *claritas*, f. *clarus* clear: see -ITY.] †1 Glory, divine lustre. ME–L17. †2 Brightness, brilliancy, splendour. LME–L17. 3 Clearness (of sight, judgement, colour, sky, atmosphere, etc.); unambiguousness (of literary style, ideas, etc.). E17.

Clark /klɑːk/ *n.* E19. [William *Clark* (1770–1838), US explorer.] *Clark's crow*, *Clark('s) nutcracker*, a black, grey, and white crow, *Nucifraga columbiana*, of western N. America.

clarkia /ˈklɑːkɪə/ *n.* E19. [mod.L (see below), f. William *Clark* (1770–1838), US explorer: see -IA[1].] A plant of the American genus *Clarkia*, which includes several annuals cultivated for their white, pink, or purple flowers.

claro /ˈklɑːrəʊ/ *n.* Pl. **-os.** L19. [Sp. = light, clear.] A light-coloured cigar.

†**claro-obscuro** *n.* Only in 18. [Latinization of It. CHIAROSCURO.] = CHIAROSCURO.

clarschach *n.* var. of CLAIRSCHACH.

clart /klɑːt/ *v.* & *n. Sc.* & *north.* L17. [Origin unkn.] A *v.t.* †1 Smear or plaster (*up*)*on*. Only in L17. 2 Smear or daub with dirt. E19. B *n.* 1 Sticky dirt, mud, filth; a daub of this. E19. 2 A dirty person; a nasty thing; hypocritical talk. E19.

¶ Much older than the written record: *beclart* vb is evidenced in ME.

clarty *a.* covered in or of the nature of sticky dirt; nasty: L16.

clary /ˈklɛːri/ *n.*[1] ME. [OFr. *claré*, f. med.L (*vinum*) *claratum* clarified (wine), f. *clarare*, f. *clarus* clear: see -Y[5].] Chiefly *Hist.* A sweet drink made of wine, clarified honey, pepper, ginger, and other spices.

clary /ˈklɛːri/ *n.*[2] LME. [Fr. †*clarie* f. med.L *sclarea*: loss of initial *s* is unexpl.] An aromatic herb of the genus *Salvia*, of the mint family; esp. *S. sclarea*, native to southern Europe.

clash /klaʃ/ *n.* E16. [Imit.: cf. next.] 1 A loud discordant resonant sound as of a collision, the striking of weapons, bells rung together, cymbals, etc.; *Sc.* a blow yielding such a sound. E16. 2 A collision, a conflict, esp. of hostile opinions; a disagreement; being at variance or incompatible (*with*); a jarring or unpleasant contrast (of colour etc.). M17. 3 Chatter, idle talk; an item of (malicious) gossip. *Sc.* & *north.* M17. 4 The sound of heavy rainfall; *Sc.* & *north.* a sudden and heavy fall of rain etc. E19.

clash /klaʃ/ *v.* E16. [Imit.: cf. prec.] I *v.i.* 1 Make a loud discordant resonant sound, produce a clash; strike violently, esp. so as to produce a clash (*against*, *together*). E16. 2 Come into conflict; disagree, be at variance, be incompatible; (of colours etc.) contrast jarringly. (Foll. by *with.*) E17. 3 Talk recklessly or maliciously. *Sc.* L17.

1 MILTON Arms on Armour clashing. SIR W. SCOTT The swords clashed smartly together. O. MANNING Outside, a thunderstorm was roaring and clashing. 2 D. CARNEGIE These two clashed on every debatable subject. W. S. CHURCHILL When pleasure clashed with royal duty it was usually pleasure that won. H. KISSINGER Soviet and Chinese troops clashed in the frozen Siberian tundra.

II *v.t.* 4 Strike (together) so as to produce a clash; slam (a door etc.); *Sc.* throw violently so as to produce a clash. E16. 5 Produce or express with a clash. M17.

4 TENNYSON Sir Gareth's brand clashed his. TOLKIEN The armed men that stood near clashed their weapons. J. DICKEY I got in and clashed the car door. 5 R. ELLIS Let a gong clash glad emotion.

clasher *n.* E17.

†**clashee**, **-y** *ns.* vars. KHALASSI.

clasp /klɑːsp/ *n.* & *v.* ME. [Origin unkn.: for the terminal sounds cf. *grasp*, *hasp*, MDu. *gaspe*, *gespe* (Du. *gesp* clasp, buckle).] A *n.* 1 A contrivance of interlocking parts for fastening; a buckle, a brooch; a metal fastening of a book-cover. ME. †2 = CLASPER 2. L16–E18. 3 An embrace; an encircling grip of the hand or arm; a handshake; grasp, reach. M17. 4 A bar of silver on a medal-ribbon with the name of a battle etc. (fought during the campaign commemorated by the medal) at which the wearer was present. E19.

Comb.: **clasp-knife** a folding knife, usu. with a catch to fix the blade when open.

B *v.* I *v.t.* 1 Fasten, secure, or close with or as a clasp; fasten (a clasp). LME. 2 Provide or fit (a book etc.) with a clasp. LME. 3 *gen.* Encircle and hold closely; *loosely* & *poet.* surround, enfold. LME. 4 *spec.* Hold with close pressure of the curved hand; press (one's hands) closely together with fingers interlaced; hold closely in one's arms with hands joined; throw both arms round, embrace. LME. 5 Bend or fold tightly *around* or *over*. L18.

1 W. SHENSTONE One modest em'rald clasp'd the robe she wore. 3 T. HOOD She stood . . Clasp'd by the golden light of morn. R. MACAULAY She clasped Helen's hand in both hers. 4 GEO. ELIOT She should clasp her son again. A. G. GARDINER Two other children . . walk with the soldier, each clasping a hand. V. WOOLF She sank down . ., clasping her knees together. I. ASIMOV His hands, which had been clasped, drew apart. **clasp hands** shake hands with fervour or affection.

II *v.i.* 6 Be fastened as a clasp; hold tight; embrace; (of hands) press tightly together, esp. with interlaced fingers. M16.

6 SHAKES. *Per.* Clasping to the mast. R. WARNER I saw his hands clasp and unclasp.

clasper /ˈklɑːspə/ *n.* M16. [f. CLASP *v.* + -ER[1].] 1 A person who or thing which clasps; a means of holding fast. M16. 2 *Bot.* A tendril. L16. 3 *Zool.* Either of a pair of appendages of the male used to hold the female in copulation, esp. in certain fishes and insects. Usu. in *pl.* M19.

class /klɑːs/ *n.* & *a.* M16. [L *classis* assembly, division of the Roman people. Cf. (O)Fr. *classe.*] A *n.* 1 *Rom. Hist.* Each of the divisions or orders of the Roman people in the constitution ascribed to Servius Tullius. M16. 2 A set of students or scholars taught together; a course of instruction for a group of students; a meeting of students for instruction. M16. b All college or school students of the same standing. *N. Amer.* L17. 3 *gen.* A division according to grade or quality. E17. 4 *gen.* A group of people or things having some attribute in common; a set, a category. M17. 5a A presbytery in the Church of Scotland. Cf. CLASSIS 2. *obs.* exc. *Hist.* E18. b A subdivision of a Methodist congregation, meeting together. M18. 6 A rank or order of a society; *sing.* & in *pl.*, the members of a specified social rank; in *pl.* also (*arch.*) *the* rich or educated. M18. b The system or fact of the division of society into ranks or orders; social rank, *esp.* high rank. M19. 7 *Biol.* The principal taxonomic grouping ranking above order and below phylum or division. M18. 8 A division of candidates or competitors according to merit in an examination. E19. 9 Distinction, high quality. *colloq.* L19.

2 LYTTON I was in the head class when I left Eton. S. HEANEY My lesson note reads: Teacher will play Beethoven's Concerto Number Five And class will express themselves freely In writing. JO GRIMOND A class in first aid, which he attended. **in class** (*a*) teaching or being taught in a class; (*b*) as a member of a class. *senior class*: see SENIOR *a.* **b class of** (a specified year): all those graduating from a school or college in a particular year. 3 *high class, low class, first class, second class*, etc. **in a class of** (or **on**) **its, one's, own** unequalled. 4 COLERIDGE The class of readers, to which he means to address his communications. D. R.

HOFSTADTER The class of numbers known to be producible. *open class*: see OPEN *a.* SPECTRAL *class.* SPECTRAL-*luminosity class.* 6 *labouring, lower, master-, middle, professional (middle), socio-economic, upper (middle), working*, etc., *class* or *classes.* 8 **take a class** obtain an honours degree. 9 T. DREISER This is a special coat... It has class. **no class** *colloq.* quite inferior.

Comb.: **class action** *US* a (single) legal action brought on behalf of all the members of a group with a common interest or grievance; **class-conscious** *a.* conscious of class, *esp.* realizing and usu. participating in the conflict between one's own and other classes; **class-consciousness** the state of being class-conscious; **class-fellow** = *classmate* below; *class-leader*: see LEADER 7; **class-list** *spec.* a list of the classes obtained by candidates in an examination; **classmate** a present or past member of the same school, college, etc., class as oneself; **class-noun** *Gram.* a count noun, a common noun referring to each member of a class; **classroom** a place where a class is taught (*open classroom*: see OPEN *a.*); **class-war(fare)** conflict between social classes.

B *adj.* Having class, in the top class, classy. *colloq.* L19.

H. DE SÉLINCOURT If he'd had coaching, he'd be a class bowler. DAY LEWIS Real class your sister is.

¶ See note s.v. CLASSIS.

classless *a.* making or having no distinction of class L19. **classlessness** *n.* M20.

class /klɑːs/ *v.* E18. [f. the n.] †**1** *v.t.* Divide into classes. E18–E19. **2** *v.t.* Place in a class; assign to its proper class or group. M18. **3** *v.i.* Rank; be classed. M18.

3 **classed growth** [tr. Fr. *cru classé*] a Bordeaux wine belonging to one of the top official groupings.

classable *a.* able to be classed M19. **classer** *n.* a person who classes E19.

classes *n.* pl. of CLASS *n.*, CLASSIS.

classic /ˈklasɪk/ *a.* & *n.* E17. [Fr. *classique* or L *classicus*, f. as CLASS *n.*: see -IC.] **A** *adj.* **I 1** Of the first class, of acknowledged excellence; remarkably typical; outstandingly important. E17. **2** Of or pertaining to the standard ancient Greek and Latin authors or their works, or the culture, art, architecture, etc. of Greek and Roman antiquity generally. Cf. CLASSICAL 2. E17. **3** Known from ancient Greek or Latin authors; having literary or historic associations. E18. **4** Characteristic of the art, architecture, or literature of Greek and Roman antiquity; well-proportioned, with clarity of outline or formal design; (of style) restrained, harmonious and in accordance with established forms (cf. *romantic*). M18. **b** Of clothes: made in a simple style not much affected by changes in fashion. M20. **5** (Usu. **C-**.) Of or pertaining to a high phase of ancient Meso-American civilization *c*300–*c*900. M20.

1 C. S. LEWIS The taste for what he called 'the good, solid, old books', the classic English novelists. C. HAMPTON They tell me I'm a classic case, because my uncle raped me when I was twelve. **classic races** the five annual chief flat races for horses in England (the One Thousand Guineas, Two Thousand Guineas, Derby, Oaks, and St Leger). 2 C. KINGSLEY He had never felt the influence of classic civilization. 3 R. BURNS A few pilgrimages over some of the classic ground of Caledonia. 4 J. MORLEY That permanence, which is only secured by classic form. J. AGATE Wolfit has everything a great actor should have except classic features. **b** *classic tutu*: see TUTU *n.*[2]

†**II 6** = CLASSICAL 8. Only in M17.

B *n.* **1** A writer, artist, composer, work, or example of the first rank, acknowledged excellence, or value; orig. & *esp.* an ancient Greek or Latin writer or work of literature. In *pl.* also, *the* body of Greek and Latin literature; *the* body of literature, art, music, etc. that is considered excellent, significant, or standard. E18. **b** In *pl.* The branch of knowledge that deals with ancient Greek and Latin literature, or Greek and Roman antiquity generally. L19. **2** A scholar of Greek and Latin literature. *arch.* E19. **3** A follower of classic models. L19. **4** Each of the five classic races (see sense A.1 above). E20. **5** A garment in a classic style. M20.

1 I. D'ISRAELI Dante was the classic of his country. G. B. SHAW The glees, madrigals, and motets .. are the five English classics. D. H. LAWRENCE We like to think of the old fashioned American classics as children's books. S. BRETT 'All they ever bloody want is the Barbershop Sketch.' 'Well, it is a classic'. 2 E. M. FORSTER He was not a good classic, but good enough to take the Lower Fifth. *senior classic*: see SENIOR *a.*

classical /ˈklasɪk(ə)l/ *a.* L16. [f. L *classicus* CLASSIC + -AL[1].] **I 1** = CLASSIC *a.* 1. L16. **2** Designating, of, or pertaining to the standard ancient Greek and Latin authors or their works, or the culture, art, architecture, etc., of Greek and Roman antiquity generally; specializing in or based on the study of the Greek and Latin classics, or Greek and Roman antiquity generally. Cf. CLASSIC *a.* 2. E17. **3** Designating the form or period of a language used by ancient standard authors. M19. **4** = CLASSIC *a.* 4. M19. **5** *spec.* Designating, of, or pertaining to music characterized by clarity, regularity, and use of established forms, *esp.* that of the late 18th and early 19th cents. marked esp. by sonata form (cf. *romantic*); *loosely* designating so-called conventional or serious music as opp. to folk, jazz, pop, rock, etc. M19. **6** Designating, of, or pertaining to the form or period of an art etc. regarded as representing the height of achievement; in a long-established style of acknowledged excellence. E20. **7** Designating, of, or pertaining to the first significant period of a department of study; *spec.* (*Physics* etc.) relating to or based upon concepts and theories which predate (and hence are not subject to the postulates of) relativity and quantum mechanics, based on the theories and concepts of Newton, Maxwell, etc. E20.

1 C. HILL He is a classical example of a man who ruined himself by unsuccessful investment in the court. 2 J. BRIGHT One of the faults of a high classical education. R. V. JONES Cambridge could not find .. a classical scholar who knew any engineering. G. EWART The multitudinous / classical allusions just fill them with boredom. *classical antiquity*: see ANTIQUITY 1. 3 *classical Arabic, classical Greek, classical Hebrew, classical Latin*, etc. 4 J. RUSKIN The classical landscape .. is .. the representative of perfectly trained and civilised human life. T. E. HULME I prophesy that a period of dry, hard classical verse is coming. 5 *classical guitar*: see GUITAR *n.* 6 *classical ballet* etc. 7 *classical mechanics*: see MECHANICS 1b.

II 8 *Hist.* Of or pertaining to a classis in a Presbyterian Church. L16.

classicalism *n.* adherence to classical ideals, styles, etc.; interest in the classics: M19. **classi'cality** *n.* classical quality or character; classical scholarship; an instance of classical learning; a classical feature in art etc.: E19. **classically** *adv.* †(*a*) in classes, in order; (*b*) in (a) classical manner; in a classical style; (*c*) as regards the classics: M17.

classicise *v.* var. of CLASSICIZE.

classicism /ˈklasɪsɪz(ə)m/ *n.* M19. [f. CLASSIC + -ISM.] **1** The principles of classic literature, art, etc.; adherence to classical ideals, styles, etc. M19. **2** A classical idiom or form. L19. **3** Classical scholarship; advocacy of classical education. L19.

classicist *n.* an upholder or imitator of classical style; a student or scholar of classics; an advocate of classical education: E19. **classi'cistic** *a.* characterized by classicism M19.

classicize /ˈklasɪsʌɪz/ *v.* Also **-ise**. M19. [f. as prec. + -IZE.] **1** *v.t.* Make classic. M19. **2** *v.i.* Affect or imitate classical style etc. L19.

classification /ˌklasɪfɪˈkeɪʃ(ə)n/ *n.* L18. [Fr., f. *classe* CLASS *n.*: see -FICATION.] **1** The action of classifying. L18. **2** The result of classifying; a systematic distribution or arrangement in a class or classes. L18.

Phrases: *decimal classification*: see DECIMAL *a. periodic classification*: see PERIODIC *a.*[1] 2.

classificatory *a.* tending to, having the purpose of, or relating to classification M19.

classify /ˈklasɪfʌɪ/ *v.t.* L18. [Back-form. f. prec.] **1** Arrange in classes; assign to a class. L18. **2** Designate as officially secret or not for general disclosure. Chiefly as *classified* ppl a. M20.

classifiable *a.* able to be classified M19. **classifier** *n.* (*a*) a person or thing which classifies; (*b*) *Gram.* an element attached to or associated with nouns in certain languages, esp. indicating the class of objects to which the referent belongs: E19.

classis /ˈklasɪs/ *n.* Pl. **classes** /ˈklasiːz/. L16. [L: see CLASS *n.*] †**1** A division according to rank; a class. L16–E18. **2** In certain Protestant Churches: an inferior judicial body consisting of the elders or pastors of the parishes or churches of a district; such a district. L16. †**3** A bookcase at right angles to a wall in a library; a bay or alcove between two of these. E17–E18. †**4** A school or college class. *US.* M17–M19.

¶ Exc. in speech the pl. is usu. indistinguishable from that of CLASS *n.* Ambiguous early exs. in all but sense 1 have been regarded as belonging here.

classism /ˈklɑːsɪz(ə)m/ *n.* M19. [f. CLASS *n.* + -ISM.] Distinction or discrimination on the grounds of social class; prejudice in favour of or against others on the basis of their social class.

classist *n.* & *a.* (*a*) *n.* an adherent or practitioner of classism; (*b*) *adj.* of or pertaining to classism or classists: L20.

classy /ˈklɑːsi/ *a. colloq.* L19. [f. CLASS *n.* + -Y[1].] Of a high or superior class; stylish, smart.

classiness *n.* E20.

clastic /ˈklastɪk/ *a.* & *n.* L19. [Fr. *clastique* f. Gk *klastos* broken in pieces: see -IC.] *Geol.* (Designating) a rock consisting of fragments of pre-existing rocks.

clast *n.* [back-form.] a constituent fragment of a clastic rock M20.

clatch *n.* var. of CLETCH.

clathrate /ˈklaθreɪt/ *a.* & *n.* M19. [L *clathratus* pa. pple of *clathrare*, f. *clathri* (pl.) lattice f. Gk *klēthra* bars: see -ATE[2].] **A** *adj.* **1** Resembling lattice-work; cancellate. *rare.* M19. **2** *Chem.* Of a compound: containing molecules of one substance physically enclosed within the structure of another. M20. **B** *n.* *Chem.* A clathrate compound. M20.

cla'thration *n.* formation of a clathrate compound M20.

clatter /ˈklatə/ *n.* LME. [Prob. f. the vb: cf. MDu. *klatere*, Du. *klater* a rattle.] **1** Noisy rapid talk, loud chatter, gabble. LME. **b** *sing.* & in *pl.* Gossip; tittle-tattle. Chiefly *Sc.* L16. **2** A rattling noise as of the rapidly repeated collision of sonorous bodies that do not ring. L16.

1 T. H. WHITE Shut yer trap, .. and leave this daft clatter about Sir Lancelot. 2 S. JOHNSON The clatter of empty pots.

clattery *adv.* & *a.* (*a*) *adv.* (now *non-standard, rare*) in a clattery manner, clatteringly; (*b*) *adj.* tending to clatter, clattering: E19.

clatter /ˈklatə/ *v.* [OE (as vbl n.). Cf. (M)Du. *klateren* rattle, chatter.] **1** *v.i.* Make a clatter; move with a clatter (*along, down*, etc.). OE. **2** *v.i.* Talk noisily and rapidly, chatter loudly; *Sc.* gossip. ME. †**3** *v.t.* Say noisily and rapidly; talk noisily or indiscreetly about. ME–M18. **4** *v.t.* Cause to make a clatter. M16.

1 E. HEMINGWAY He fired two pans, the guns clattering. A. MASON The guards clattered to a halt.

clatterer *n.* LME.

clauber *n.* var. of CLABBER *n.*[1]

claucht *v.* see CLEEK *v.*

Claude Lorraine glass /klɔːd lɒˈreɪn glɑːs/ *n. phr.* Also **Claude glass**. L18. [*Claude* Gelée (1600–82), known as *Lorraine*, Fr. landscape painter.] A convex dark or coloured glass that reflects an image of diminished size and subdued colour.

Claudian /ˈklɔːdɪən/ *a.* & *n.* E18. [L *Claudianus*, f. *Claudius*: see -AN.] *Rom. Hist.* **A** *adj.* Of or pertaining to any of several distinguished Romans of the name of Claudius or the gens to which they belonged (among whose members were the emperors Tiberius, Caligula, Claudius, and Nero). E18. **B** *n.* A member of the Claudian gens. E20.

claudicant /ˈklɔːdɪk(ə)nt/ *a.* Now *rare* or *obs.* E17. [L *claudicant-* pres. ppl stem of *claudicare*: see next, -ANT[1].] Lame, limping.

claudication /klɔːdɪˈkeɪʃ(ə)n/ *n.* LME. [L *claudicatio(n-)*, f. *claudicat-* pa. ppl stem of *claudicare* to limp, f. *claudus* lame: see -ATION.] The action of limping; *intermittent claudication*, a condition of the legs, due to arterial obstruction, in which pain is induced by walking and relieved by rest.

claught *v.* see CLEEK *v.*

clause /klɔːz/ *n.* & *v.* ME. [(O)Fr. = Prov. *clauza*, for L *clausula* close of a rhetorical period, (later) conclusion of a legal formula, section of law, fem. dim. of *claus-* pa. ppl stem of *claudere* CLOSE *v.*] **A** *n.* **1** A simple sentence; a distinct part of a sentence including a subject and predicate, or one resembling this; a single passage of discourse or writing. ME. **2** A particular and separate article, stipulation, or proviso, in any formal or legal document. LME. †**3** Conclusion, *esp.* the close of a sentence. L16–E18.

1 *final clause*: see FINAL *a. subordinate clause*: see SUBORDINATE *a.* 2. **2** PRAEMUNIENTES *clause*. REOPENER *clause*. *resolutive clause*: see RESOLUTIVE 2. *saving clause*: see SAVING *ppl a. testimonium clause*: see TESTIMONIUM 2. VALENT *clause*.

B *v.i.* Construct clauses. L19.

clausal *a.* E20.

†**clauster** *n.* Also **-tre**. OE–E18. [L *claustrum* CLOISTER *n.*] A cloister, cell, or monastery.

claustral /ˈklɔːstr(ə)l/ *a.* LME. [Late L *claustralis*, f. as prec.: see -AL[1].] **1** Pertaining to a cloister or religious house; adjoining a cloister. LME. **2** Resembling (that of) a cloister; *fig.* narrow-minded. M19.

claustration /klɔːˈstreɪʃ(ə)n/ *n.* M19. [f. L *claustrum*: see CLOISTER *n.*, -ATION.] Enclosure or confinement (as) in a cloister.

†**claustre** *n.* var. of CLAUSTER.

claustrophilia /klɔːstrəˈfɪlɪə/ *n.* E20. [mod.L, f. L *claustrum* (see CLOISTER *n.*) + -O- + -PHILIA.] Irrational desire to be enclosed within a confined space.

claustrophobe /ˈklɔːstrəfəʊb/ *a.* & *n.* M20. [Back-form. f. next.] **A** *adj.* = CLAUSTROPHOBIC *a.* 2. *rare.* M20. **B** *n.* = CLAUSTROPHOBIC *n.* M20.

claustrophobia /klɔːstrəˈfəʊbɪə/ *n.* L19. [mod.L, f. L *claustrum* (see CLOISTER *n.*) + -O- + -PHOBIA.] Irrational fear of confined places.

claustrophobic /klɔːstrəˈfəʊbɪk/ *a.* & *n.* L19. [f. prec. + -IC.] **A** *adj.* **1** Prone to or suffering from claustrophobia. L19. **2** Of a place etc.: confined, restricting; inducing claustrophobia. M20. **B** *n.* A person who is prone to or suffers from claustrophobia. M20.

claustrophobically *adv.* in a claustrophobic manner; so as to induce claustrophobia: M20.

claustrum /ˈklɔːstrəm/ *n.* Pl. **-stra** /-strə/. M19. [L: see CLOISTER *n.*] *Anat.* A thin layer of grey matter in each cerebral hemisphere between the lentiform nucleus and the insula.

clausula /ˈklɔːzjʊlə/ *n.* Pl. **-lae** /-liː/. M17. [L (in med.L sense): see CLAUSE.] **1** *Mus.* The conclusion of a movement or phrase. M17. **2** *Gram.* The close or end of a period, esp. one in ancient or medieval Latin having a definable cadence. E20.

¶ See also *clausula* REBUS SIC STANTIBUS.

†**clausure** *n.* LME–E19. [Late L *clausura*: see CLOSURE.] The action of closing or enclosing; closed condition; that which encloses.

clavate /ˈkleɪveɪt/ *a.* M17. [mod.L *clavatus*, f. *clava* club: see -ATE[2].] †**1** Knobbed. Only in M17. **2** Chiefly *Bot.* Club-shaped. E19.

Also **clavated** *a.* E18.

clave /kleɪv, klɑːv/ *n.* E20. [Amer. Sp. f. Sp. *clave* keystone f. L *clavis* key.] *Mus.* Either of a pair of hardwood sticks used to make a hollow sound. Usu. in *pl.*

clave *v.*[1], *v.*[2] see CLEAVE *v.*[1], *v.*[2]

clavecin /ˈklavɪsɪn/ *n.* E19. [Fr. f. as CLAVICYMBAL.] A harpsichord, esp. in or from France.

clavecinist *n.* a (French) harpsichordist M19.

clavel /ˈklav(ə)l/ *n.* Now *dial.* L17. [OFr. (mod. *claveau*) f. med.L *clavellus* dim. of L *clavis* key: see -EL[2].] The lintel over a fireplace.

Comb.: **clavel-piece** a mantelpiece.

claver /ˈkleɪvə/ *n. Sc.* & *north.* E18. [f. CLAVER *v.*[2]] Idle garrulous talk; a piece of idle gossip.

claver /ˈklavə/ *v.*[1]*i.* Long *obs.* exc. *dial.* ME. [Origin uncertain: cf. Da. *klavre*, & mod.Du. *klaveren* clamber.] Climb, clamber.

claver /ˈkleɪvə/ *v.*[2]*i. Sc.* & *north.* L16. [Origin unkn.] Talk idly, gossip.

clavicembalo /klavɪˈtʃɛmbələʊ/ *n.* Pl. **-os**. M18. [It. f. as CLAVICYMBAL.] A harpsichord, esp. in or from Italy.

clavichord /ˈklavɪkɔːd/ *n.* LME. [med.L *clavichordium*, f. L *clavis* key + *chorda* string (see CORD *n.*[1]).] A keyboard instrument with strings activated by brass blades fixed upright in the key levers.

clavicle /ˈklavɪk(ə)l/ *n.* E17. [L *clavicula* dim. of *clavis* key: see -CULE.] *Anat.* A collar-bone.

claˈvicular *a.* E19.

clavicymbal /klavɪˈsɪmb(ə)l/ *n.* Now *arch.* or *Hist.* L15. [med.L *clavicymbalum*, f. *clavis* key + *cymbalum* CYMBAL.] A harpsichord, esp. of early date.

clavicytherium /ˌklavɪsɪˈθɪərɪəm/ *n.* Pl. **-ia** /-ɪə/. L18. [mod.L, f. L *clavis* key + CITHARA.] *Hist.* A keyboard instrument resembling an upright spinet.

clavier /ˈklavɪə; *in sense 2 also* kləˈvɪə/ *n.* E18. [(G *Klavier* f.) Fr. *clavier* f. med.L *claviarius* key-bearer, f. *clavis* key: see -ER[2].] *Mus.* **1** A keyboard. E18. **2** A keyboard instrument, esp. in or from Germany. M19.

claviform /ˈklavɪfɔːm/ *a.* E19. [f. L *clava* club + -I- + -FORM.] Club-shaped.

claviger /ˈklavɪdʒə/ *n. obs.* exc. *Hist.* M16. [L *claviger* adj., carrying a key or a club, f. *clavis* key or *clava* club + *-ger*: see -GEROUS.] A carrier or keeper of a key or keys.

Clavioline /ˈklavɪəliːn/ *n.* M20. [After CLAVICHORD etc.] (Proprietary name for) a small electronic keyboard instrument attachable to a piano.

clavis /ˈkleɪvɪs/ *n. rare.* M17. [L *clavis*.] A key.

clavus /ˈkleɪvəs/ *n.* Pl. **-vi** /-vʌɪ/. E19. [L = nail, wart.] **1** = ERGOT *n.* 1. Now *rare* or *obs.* E19. **2** *Med.* A corn, a callosity. E19. **3** = LATICLAVE. M19. **4** *Zool.* A projection resembling a fingernail; *esp.* part of the hardened forewing of a heteropteran insect. M19.

claw /klɔː/ *n.*[1] [OE *clawu* (f. the obl. cases, the orig. nom. being repr. by *clēa* CLEE) = OFris. *klē*, *klāwe*, OS *clāuua* (Du. *klauw*), OHG *klāwa* (G *Klaue*), f. WGmc.] **1** A sharp horny nail (often slender and curved) on the toes of birds and some animals; a similar structure in some arthropods; a foot with such a nail or nails. OE. †**b** A hoof; one of the parts of a (cloven) hoof. OE–M17. **2** A contrivance resembling a claw, for grappling, holding, etc.; part of the mechanism of a lock. OE. **3** A hand (*contempt.*); a bent disfigured hand. L16. **4** *Bot.* In some flowers, the narrow tapering lower part of a petal, by which it is attached. L18.

3 N. HAWTHORNE A yellow claw—the very same that had clawed together so much wealth—poked itself out of the coach-window.

Comb.: **claw-and-ball** *a.* (of furniture) having feet which represent a claw clasping a ball; **claw-hammer** a hammer with a curved split end for extracting nails.

clawed *a.* (*a*) having a claw or claws; *clawed toad*, a southern African toad, *Xenopus laevis*, freq. bred for scientific research; (*b*) (of a hand) bent and disfigured like a claw: ME. **clawless** *a.* E19. **clawlike** *a.* resembling (that of) a claw E19.

†**claw** *n.*[2] var. of CLOVE *n.*[3]

claw /klɔː/ *v.* [OE *clawian*, f. CLAW *n.*[1]] **1** *v.t.* Scratch or tear with or as with claws. OE. **2** *v.t.* & *i.* Scratch gently, so as to relieve itching or soothe. Now *Sc.* ME. **3** *v.t.* Flatter, cajole, wheedle, fawn upon. Now *dial.* LME. **4** *v.i.* Grasp, clutch, (*at* etc.); scratch *at*. LME. **5** *v.t.* Seize, grip, clutch, or pull (as) with claws. M16. **6** *v.t.* Strike as with claws; beat. Now *dial.* L16. **7** *v.i. Naut.* Beat to windward (*off*, *from*, a lee-shore etc.). E17.

2 claw the back of (now *dial.*) flatter, toady to. **3** T. ADAMS Claw me, and I will claw thee: Winke at mine, and I will not see thy faults.

With advs. in specialized senses: **claw back** regain gradually or with great effort; take back (an allowance by additional taxation etc.) **claw off** (*a*) get rid of (as an itch); †(*b*) rate soundly, scold.

Comb.: **claw-back** (*a*) [BACK *n.*[1]] a toady; (*b*) [BACK *adv.*] retrieval, recovery (of an allowance by additional taxation etc.).

clawer *n.* (*rare*) ME.

clay /kleɪ/ *n.* [OE *clǣg* = OFris. *klāy*, (M)LG, (M)Du. *klei*, f. WGmc f. Gmc base repr. also by CLEAM, CLEAVE *v.*[2], CLIMB *v.*] **1** A stiff tenacious fine-grained earth consisting mainly of hydrated aluminosilicates, which becomes more plastic when water is added, and can be moulded and dried to make bricks, pottery, etc. OE. †**b** Any substance of a tough sticky nature, as bitumen, pitch, etc. LME–L16. **2** (Moist) earth, mire, mud. ME. **3** (The material of) the human body. ME. **4** In full *clay pipe*. A tobacco-pipe made of clay. M19. **5** In full *clay pigeon*. A saucer-shaped piece of baked clay or other material, serving as a target in trap-shooting. Orig. *US.* L19.

1 YEATS Quiet as the clay-cold dead. *china clay*, *fire-clay*, *grafting-clay*, *pipeclay*, etc. *London clay*, *Oxford clay*, etc. *feet of clay*: see FOOT *n. virgin clay*: see VIRGIN *a. white clay*: see WHITE *a.* **3** *lump of clay*: see LUMP *n.*[1] **moisten** or **wet one's clay** *arch. joc.* drink. **4** *long clay*: see LONG *a.*[1]

Comb.: **clay court** a tennis-court with a clay surface; **clay ironstone** clayey iron ore, esp. argillaceous siderite; **clay mineral** any of a number of aluminosilicate minerals which occur as colloidal crystals in clay; **clay-pan** *Austral.* a natural hollow formed of clayey soil and retaining water after rain; *clay pigeon*: see sense 5 above; *clay pipe*: see sense 4 above; **clay slate** an argillaceous sedimentary rock with a slaty cleavage; **claystone** any of various rocks consisting of or resembling clay, *esp.* fine-grained mudstone.

clayen *a.* (*arch.*) of clay LME. **clayish** *a.* more or less clayey LME. **claylike** *a.* resembling clay E17.

clay /kleɪ/ *v.t.* LME. [f. the n.] Treat, cover, or dress with clay.

clayey /ˈkleɪi/ *a.* OE. [f. CLAY *n.*: see -Y[1].] **1** Full of clay; of the nature of clay; argillaceous. OE. **b** Of mortal clay. L16. **2** Smeared or soiled with clay. LME. **3** Resembling clay. L17.

clayeyness *n.* L19.

claymore /ˈkleɪmɔː/ *n.* E18. [f. Gael. *claidheamh* sword + *mór* great.] **1** *Hist.* A broadsword used by Scottish Highlanders, either two-edged, or basket-hilted and single-edged (a form introduced in the 16th cent.). E18. **b** A man armed with a claymore. M19. **2** In full *claymore mine*. A type of anti-personnel mine. M20.

claytonia /kleɪˈtəʊnɪə/ *n.* L18. [mod.L, f. John *Clayton* 18th-cent. Virginian botanist: see -IA[1].] A small succulent plant of the chiefly N. American genus *Claytonia*, of the purslane family, with white or pink flowers. Also called *spring beauty*.

-cle /k(ə)l, *after s* (ə)l/ *suff.* (not productive). Repr. Fr. *-cle* f. L *-culus*, *-a*, *-um* -CULE, as in *article*, *corpuscle*, *follicle*, *ventricle*, etc.

cleach /kliːtʃ/ *v.* Long *obs.* exc. *dial.* ME. [Prob. already in OE: cf. corresp. north. CLEEK *v.*] **1** *v.t.* & †*i.* Clutch. ME. **2** *v.t.* & *i.* Draw or get (water) in a shallow vessel. LME.

clead /kliːd/ *v.t. Sc.* & *north.* Also **cleed**. Pa. t. & pple **cled** /klɛd/. ME. [ON *klæða*, pa. t. *klædda* rel. to CLOTH, CLOTHE.] Clothe.

cleading *n.* (*a*) clothing; (*b*) a protective covering or casing, lagging: ME.

cleam /kliːm/ *v.t.* Long *obs.* exc. *dial.* Also **clame** /kleɪm/. [OE *clǣman* = MDu. *klēmen*, OHG *kleimen*, ON *kleima* daub, plaster, f. Gmc, ult. f. base repr. also by CLAY *n.*, CLEAVE *v.*[2], CLIMB *v.*, CLOAM. See also CLAM *v.*[1]] **1** Smear, bedaub, plaster. OE. **2** Cause to stick. ME.

clean /kliːn/ *n.* M19. [f. the vb.] **1** An act of cleaning. M19. **2** *Weightlifting.* The action of raising a weight from the floor to shoulder-level in a single movement. Freq. in *clean and jerk*, *clean and press*. E20.

¶ See also CLEAN-OUT, CLEAN-UP.

clean /kliːn/ *a.* [OE *clǣne* = OFris. *klēne*, *kleine*, OS *klēni* (Du. *kleen*, *klein* small), OHG *kleini* clear, delicate, neat, small (G *klein* small), f. WGmc.] **1** Free from anything that dims lustre or transparency. *obs.* exc. as passing into sense 2. OE. **2** Free from any polluting ingredient or foreign matter; unadulterated, pure, (*lit.* & *fig.*). OE. **b** In good condition, unspoiled, essentially unchanged. *colloq.* M20. **3** Free from or *of* dirt or contaminating matter; unsoiled. OE. **b** Of a ship: having a bottom free of barnacles etc. Of a whaling or fishing vessel: with nothing in the hold, empty. M17. c Of paper: blank. Of a printer's proof, a copy of writing, etc.: free from corrections or alterations. Of a document, report, etc.: bearing no adverse point or remark; listing no offence. L17. d Of a deer, a deer's horns: having shed the velvet. M19. e Of an animal, child, etc.: not fouling itself or its environment; habitually depositing or able to deposit excreta, esp. faeces, in the proper place. L19. f Free from concealed weapons, illegal substances, etc. *slang*. E20. g Of a nuclear weapon: causing relatively little fallout. M20. 4 Free from spiritual or moral pollution; chaste, innocent. (Foll. by †*of*, *from*.) OE. b Guiltless of a charge or accusation. Now *slang*, free from involvement in criminal or otherwise undesirable activity, giving no cause for suspicion. (*obs.* f. E17; recorded again E20.) ME. c Free from impropriety; not obscene. *colloq.* M19. d Free from or cured of addiction to drugs. *slang*. M20. 5 Free from ceremonial defilement or from disease. OE. b Of animals: not prohibited as food; suitable for use as food. OE. c Of an animal: avoiding food regarded as unwholesome. *arch.* M16. 6 Free from obstructions, encumbrances, unevennesses, irregularities, or non-essentials; having a simple well-defined form or line. ME. b Of timber: free from knots. E17. c Of a ship, aircraft, etc.: with tapering lines, smooth, streamlined. E18. d Of a pigeon: without feathers on the legs or feet. Of a draught horse: without long hair on the fetlocks. M19. e Giving a distinct impression to the senses; sharp and fresh. E20. 7 Complete, entire; decisive, thoroughgoing. ME. 8a Of style or language: free from faults, correct, pure. *arch.* LME. b Observing the rules or conventions of a sport or game; fair, sporting. M20. 9 Well-formed; slender and shapely; neatly made or done; skilful, adroit; smart, clever. In early use also as a vague term of approbation. LME.

1 SPENSER All of Diamond perfect pure and cleene. 2 *Times* Clean air, that is to say an atmosphere . . relatively free from pollution and contamination. 3 R. W. EMERSON A Frenchman may possibly be clean; an Englishman is conscientiously clean. A. POWELL Why aren't you wearing a clean shirt? e G. GORER When should a young child start being trained to be clean? f M. PUZO They'll frisk me . . so I'll have to be clean. 4 TENNYSON I trust That I am whole, and clean, and meet for Heaven. b A. PRICE He's . . absolutely clean No contacts. No hint of anything. c *good clean fun*. 6 E. K. KANE The clean abrupt edge of the fractures. J. STALLWORTHY Years overlap, have no clean start or end. D. BAGLEY Brooks's desk was clean, a vast expanse of solid teak unmarred by a single paper. e J. RHYS The strong taste of punch, the cleaner taste of champagne. 9 E. WALLER Thy waist is straight and clean As Cupid's shaft. D. JUSTICE Ladies . . clean of limb. J. A. MICHENER To pick off the . . animals with a clean shot.

Special collocations & phrases: (*as*) *clean as a whistle*: see WHISTLE *n.* *clean bill of health*: see BILL *n.*[3] **clean break** a quick and final break. **clean fingers** *fig.* absence of corruption or bribery. **clean hands** *fig.* absence of guilt. **clean sheet, clean slate** *fig.* a state free from commitments or imputations. *clean sweep*: see SWEEP *n.* *clean ticket*: see TICKET *n.* **come clean** *colloq.* confess, own up. *keep one's nose clean*: see NOSE *n.* *keep the party clean*: see PARTY *n.* *make a clean breast of*: see BREAST *n.* **make a clean job of** *colloq.* do thoroughly. *make a clean sweep* (*of*): see SWEEP *n.* **show a clean pair of heels** escape by speed. *the clean potato*: see POTATO *n.* **the clean thing** *US* the honest straightforward thing. *wipe the slate clean*: see SLATE *n.*[1] 3b.

cleanish *a.* fairly clean M18. **cleanness** /-n-n-/ *n.* OE.

clean /kliːn/ *v.* LME. [f. the adj.] 1 *v.t.* Make clean (*of* dirt etc.); remove the internal organs of (fish or fowl) preparatory to serving as food; eat all the food on (one's plate). LME. b Deprive (a person) of all his or her money. Cf. sense 4 below. *slang*. E20. 2 *v.i.* Become clean; make oneself clean. E18. 3 *v.t.* Foll. by *down*: clean from top to bottom; clean by brushing or wiping. M19. 4 *v.t.* Foll. by *out*: a Remove undesirable contents from; empty, strip; *slang* deprive of all available money or assets. M19. b Deal effectively with; eject; eject the occupants from. *US*. M19. 5 *v.t.* & *i.* Foll. by *up*: a *v.t.* & *i.* Make (a place, oneself, etc.) clean or tidy; clear away a mess (from). M19. b *v.t.* Acquire as gain or profit. *slang* (orig. *US*). M19. c *v.t.* Defeat; take all the money from. *slang*. L19. d *v.i.* Make a large profit. *N. Amer. slang*. E20. e *v.t.* Remove disorder, immorality, crime, etc., from; remove remaining pockets of enemy resistance from (an area). E20. 6 *Weightlifting*. Raise (a weight) from the floor to shoulder-level in a single movement. Freq. in *clean and jerk*, *clean and press*. M20.

1 *dry-clean*: see DRY *a.*

cleanable *a.* able to be cleaned L19.

clean /kliːn/ *adv.* [OE *clǣne*, *clēne*, f. the adj.] 1 In a clean manner (= CLEANLY *adv.* 1). OE. 2 Completely, outright, quite, simply. OE.

2 C. BRONTË Your proposal has almost driven me 'clean daft'. H. JAMES He had clean forgotten. R. MACAULAY The young man got clean away.

clean- /kliːn/ *comb. form*. E16. [Repr. CLEAN *a.*, *adv.*] Clean(ly).

clean-bowl *v.t.* (*Cricket*) bowl out (a batsman) or bowl down (a wicket) with a ball that hits the wicket without having touched the bat or the body of the batsman. **clean-cut** *a.* sharply outlined. **clean-living** *a.* of upright character. **clean-limbed** *a.* (of joints, a figure, etc.) well-formed, shapely. **clean-run** *a.* (of a salmon) well-fed and bright-looking, newly returned to fresh water from the sea; *fig.* (of a person) with the bloom of youth, healthy and lively. **clean-shaven** *a.* without a beard or moustache or whiskers. **cleanskin** *Austral.* an unbranded animal (cf. *clearskin* s.v. CLEAR *a.*); *slang* a person without a police record.

cleaner /ˈkliːnə/ *n.* LME. [f. CLEAN *v.* + -ER[1].] 1 A person who cleans, esp. rooms or clothes. LME. b *sing.* & (freq.) in *pl.* A shop or firm that cleans clothes or household fabrics (= *dry-cleaner* s.v. DRY *a.*). L19. 2 An instrument or machine for cleaning. L19. 3 A small marine animal which cleans larger ones of parasites, bacteria, or dead tissue. Also *cleaner fish*. M20.

1b **send** or **take to the cleaners** *fig.* (*slang*) (*a*) rob or defraud of all available money or assets; (*b*) criticize strongly or adversely.

cleanly /ˈklɛnli/ *a.* OE. [f. CLEAN *a.* + -LY[1].] †1 Morally or spiritually clean. OE–L17. †2 Free of dirt, unsoiled. ME–L16. 3 Habitually clean. E16. 4 Of an action: adroit, deft. *obs.* exc. *dial.* M16. 5 Conducing to or promoting cleanness. E17.

cleanlily *adv.* L17. **cleanliness** *n.* LME.

cleanly /ˈkliːnli/ *adv.* OE. [f. CLEAN *a.* + -LY[2].] 1 In a clean manner (= CLEAN *adv.* 1). OE. †2 = CLEAN *adv.* 2. OE–M17.

clean-out /ˈkliːnaʊt/ *n.* L19. [f. CLEAN *v.* + OUT *adv.*: see CLEAN *v.* 4.] An act of cleaning out; an emptying or removal of undesirable contents etc.

cleanse /klɛnz/ *v.* [OE *clǣnsian*, f. CLEAN *a.*] I *v.t.* 1 Make morally or spiritually clean (*of*, *from*, sin, guilt, etc.); expiate (sin or crime). OE. 2 Make free of dirt etc. Now usu. *formal* or *arch.* OE. 3 *v.t.* Chiefly in biblical translations: make ceremonially or sanitarily clean; cure (a leper etc.). *arch.* OE. 4 *v.t.* Purge, clear by evacuation. OE. 5 *v.t.* Clear, rid (*of*, *from*). ME. II *v.i.* 6 Remove sin, guilt, dirt, (*arch.*) infection, etc. ME. 7 Of cattle: pass the afterbirth. *north.* E17.

Phrases: **cleansing cream**: for removing unwanted matter from the face, hands, etc. **cleansing department** a local service of refuse collection etc. **cleansing tissue**: for removing unwanted matter from the face, hands, etc.

cleansable *a.* L15. **cleanser** *n.* a person who or thing which cleanses; *spec.* (*a*) *arch.* a purgative; (*b*) a cosmetic for cleaning the skin: OE.

clean-up /ˈkliːnʌp/ *n.* M19. [f. CLEAN *v.* + UP *adv.*[1]: see CLEAN *v.* 5.] 1 *Mining*. An act of collecting the valuable material produced during a given period of operation; the value of such material. *US*. M19. 2 A profit; a financial success or gain. *slang* (orig. *US*). L19. 3 An act of making clean or tidy; a clearing away of a mess. L19. 4 An act of removing or putting an end to disorder, immorality, crime, etc., or remaining pockets of enemy resistance. E20.

clear /klɪə/ *n.* ME. [Branch I f. the adj., branch II f. the vb.] I †1 A beautiful woman. ME–M17. †2 Brightness, clearness; translucence. L15–E18. 3 *in the clear*: a In interior extent. L17. b In profit. *N. Amer.* E20. c Free of suspicion or difficulty. M20. 4 *in clear*, not in cipher or code. M20. II 5 A clearing of the sky, weather, fog, etc. L16.

clear /klɪə/ *a.* ME. [OFr. *cler* (mod. *clair*) f. L *clarus* clear, bright, etc.] 1 Of light, a source of light: (orig.) brightly shining, brilliant; (now) pure, unclouded. Of fire: with little flame or smoke. Of a colour: pure, unmixed. ME. 2 Of the day, daylight, etc.: fully light (*arch.*). Of the weather, a period of time in respect of weather, etc.: (orig.) full of sunshine, bright; (now) free from cloud, mist, and haze. Of the sky: cloudless. ME. b *fig.* Cheerful, serene. *arch.* LME. 3 Transparent; translucent; not turbid; free from sediment etc. ME. 4 Lustrous, having a shiny surface. ME. b Of the complexion; fresh and unblemished. Formerly also of a person: having such a complexion. ME. †c Of a woman: beautiful, fair. LME–L16. †d Illustrious. LME–E17. 5 Easily seen (*lit.* & *fig.*); distinctly visible; intelligible, perspicuous, unambiguous; manifest, evident. ME. b Not in cipher or code. E20. 6 Seeing distinctly (*lit.* & *fig.*); discerning, penetrating. ME. b Confident, decided, certain. Foll. by *for*, *as to*, *on*, *about* (a fact, course of action, etc.), *that*, †*of* (a fact). E17. 7 Of a sound, a voice, etc.: ringing, pure and well-defined; distinctly audible. ME. b *Phonet.* Not velarized or retracted; *spec.* designating the palatalized, as opp. to the 'dark' or velarized, lateral consonant (/l/). L19. 8 Guileless, ingenuous; innocent, free from fault or guilt. ME. 9 Free from obstructions, obstacles, encumbrances, burden, contents, or occupants; open for passage or operations; free from the presence *of*. ME. b Free from unevennesses or irregularities. M17. 10 Free from contact; disengaged; apart, out of reach. (Foll. by *of*, *from*.) LME. 11 Of income, gain, etc.: without deduction, net. LME. 12 Free from legal, pecuniary, or other complications. L15. 13 Free from limitation or qualification; absolute, complete, entire; sheer. E16. 14 Unadulterated, pure; of the highest quality. *techn.* & *slang*. M18.

1 AV *S. of S.* 6:10 Cleare as the sunne. J. B. PRIESTLEY The clearest azure. 2 D. H. LAWRENCE It was a clear morning. C. RYAN Unlike Holland, where the weather was clear, Britain was covered by fog. 3 SWIFT A dozen or two of good clear wine. COLERIDGE The harbour-bay was clear as glass. SCOTT FITZGERALD The air so clear you could see the leaves on Sunset Mountain. 5 G. ORWELL The great enemy of clear language is insincerity. J. B. PRIESTLEY Make it clear [that] I'm not trying to sell any pictures. I. MURDOCH All the elements of his case were clear to him. P. ROTH Either I'm not making myself clear or you don't even want to begin to understand me. A. THWAITE A clear vision of Christ in majesty. 6 J. MORLEY His sight was exquisitely keen and clear. b BOSWELL We were, by a great majority, clear for the experiment. E. A. FREEMAN I am not quite clear about the date. G. GREENE He would like to be clear in his own mind as to what had happened. J. BERRYMAN I'm fairly clear . . there's no such place. 7 SHAKES. *Tr. & Cr.* Crack my clear voice with sobs. J. STEINBECK In Kino's head there was a song now, clear and soft. 8 SHAKES. *Macb.* Duncan Hath borne his faculties so meek, hath been so clear in his great office. MILTON Fame is the spur that the clear spirit doth raise. 9 POPE A clear stage is left for Jupiter to display his omnipotence. H. NELSON One of our Transports will be clear tonight. A. P. STANLEY The way was now clear to the Jordan. B. WEBB To leave the field clear for the younger men and remain a silent member. B. CHATWIN Providing the lanes were clear of ice. *the coast is clear*: see COAST *n.* 2. b W. COBBETT Several oaks . . with a clear stem of more than forty feet. 10 DEFOE We were clear of the isles. BURKE My motives are clear from private interest. H. E. BATES Ice that had been swept clear. 13 R. L'ESTRANGE You will find in all Respects the clear contrary. H. CECIL Leading by a clear eighteen lengths.

Phrases: **(as) clear as a bell** heard very distinctly. **(as) clear as day** very clear, esp. to the understanding. **(as) clear as mud** not clear at all, completely unintelligible. (*as*) *clear as a whistle*: see WHISTLE *n.* *clear* CONSCIENCE. *clear grit*: see GRIT *n.*[1] **clear soup**: containing little solid matter. **out of a clear sky** *fig.* as a complete surprise. *the clear grit*: see GRIT *n.*[1]

Comb.: **clear-air** *a.* designating atmospheric turbulence without visible signs; **clear-eyed** *a.* (*fig.*) discerning, penetrating; **clear-headed** *a.* having a clear head; able to think clearly; **clear-headedness** the quality or state of being clear-headed; **clear-obscure** = CHIAROSCURO; **clear-sighted** *a.* having clear sight, discerning; **clear-sightedness** the quality or state of being clear-sighted; **clearskin** *Austral.* an unbranded animal (cf. *cleanskin* s.v. CLEAN-); **clear-starch** *v.i.* & *t.* stiffen (linen) with colourless starch; **clearway** a road on which vehicles must not stop; **clearweed** *N. Amer.* a plant of the nettle family, *Pilea pumila*, with a semi-transparent stem; **clearwing** a day-flying moth of the family Sesiidae, members of which have largely transparent wings and mimic other insects, e.g. hornets.

clearish *a.* somewhat clear E19. **clearness** *n.* ME.

clear /klɪə/ *v.* ME. [f. the adj.] **I 1** *v.t.* Make morally or spiritually pure; expiate. *obs.* exc. as *fig.* use of senses 9, 12. ME. **2** *v.t.* Show or declare to be innocent; free from blame or suspicion. (Foll. by *of, from.*) LME. **3** *v.t.* Approve or obtain approval of (a plan etc., a person to be entrusted with secret information etc.). (Foll. by *with* an authorizing person or body.) M20.

1 SHAKES. *Lucr.* The blackest sin is clear'd with absolution. 2 ADDISON How! would'st thou clear rebellion! M. EDGEWORTH He must commit Mr. F. to gaol, unless he can clear himself. 3 A. H. COMPTON If they cleared me it would be necessary for them to clear my wife as well. M. EDWARDES The appointment had been cleared with the Prime Minister.

II 4 *v.t.* Explain, elucidate; enlighten, inform (the mind or understanding). *arch.* ME. †**b** Prove, demonstrate. ME–L18. **5** *v.t.* †**a** Fill with light; brighten (*lit.* & *fig.*). Also foll. by *up.* LME–L17. **b** Make transparent or translucent; remove cloudiness or turbidity from; clarify (a liquid). LME. **6** *v.i.* Become clear or bright. Esp. of weather also foll. by *up.* LME. **7** *v.t.* **a** Make (the voice) clear and distinct in sound. LME. **b** Make (the eyes or eyesight) clear in vision. L16. **8** *v.t.* Remove obstructions, obstacles, encumbrances, burden, contents, or occupants from; open for passage or operations; empty. (Foll. by *of,* †*from.*) Also foll. by *out.* See also *clear up* below. M16. **b** *v.i.* Become empty or unobstructed. L19. **9** *v.t.* Settle, discharge, (a debt, a bill, etc.). Also foll. by *off.* L16. †**b** *v.i.* Settle accounts *with.* L16–L18. **c** *v.t.* & *i.* Set (a person, an estate) free from debt. E17. **10** *v.t.* Free from contact, disengage; get clear *of, from.* L16. **b** *v.t.* & *i. Football, Hockey,* etc. Of a defending player: kick or hit (the ball) away from a dangerous attacking position. L19. **11** *v.t.* Remove (an obstruction, unwanted object, contents, etc.), disperse. Also foll. by *away, off, out.* See also *clear up* below. E17. **b** *v.i.* Go away; disperse; disappear. Also foll. by *away, off, out.* E19. **12** *v.t.* Pass clear of (an obstruction etc.); get clear through, away from, or over (a distance). E17. **b** Pass over or by without touching, esp. by jumping. L18. **13** *v.t.* Make (a sum) as a net gain or to balance expenses. E18. **14** *v.t.* & *i.* Pass through the formalities of (a customs office etc.). Also foll. by *out.* E18. **15** *v.t.* Pass (a cheque, bill) through a clearing-house. M19. **16** *v.i.* Remove the remains of a meal from a table etc. Also (earlier) foll. by *away.* M19.

4 GOLDSMITH Willing to clear the thing to his satisfaction. 6 THACKERAY The day did not clear up sufficiently. LD MACAULAY For a time the prospect seemed to clear. A. SILLITOE His head clearing with the sudden onset of fresh air. 8 H. MAYHEW The strathes and glens of Sutherland have been cleared of their inhabitants. J. AGATE It entirely cleared my mind of any possible doubts. D. ABSE She cleared the tea-table. R. MACAULAY Sites would be cleared for rebuilding. D. JACOBSON The soldiers began to clear a way through the throng. F. ORMSBY Other chores—a path to clear, [etc.]. *fig.*: P. ACKROYD Clearing the ground . . before he began seriously to concentrate on the work to come. **clear one's throat** rid the throat of phlegm, huskiness, etc., by slight coughing. **clear the air**: of sultriness; *fig.* of suspicion, tension, etc. *clear the coast*: see COAST *n.* 2. **clear the decks (for action)** make ready to fight (*lit.* & *fig.*). *clear the way*: see WAY *n.* 11 SOUTHEY A gentle sea-breeze began to clear the mist. M. PUZO How did he get the cops to clear everybody out and where did they go? J. FRAME Clearing the weeds and preparing the garden. E. FIGES Breakfast had been cleared away. b A. RANSOME The smoke was clearing outside. J. T. STORY Felix suddenly cleared out and drove off. T. SHARPE The Dean sat in his car and waited for the traffic to clear. 12 T. COLLINS Another mile, and I cleared the pine-ridge. b W. S. CHURCHILL Not only did he . . arrive at the fence, he cleared it in magnificent style.

With advs. in specialized senses: **clear up** (*a*) *v.phr.t.* & *i.* put (an area) into order by removing obstructions, rubbish, etc.; remove (obstructions, rubbish, etc.) to leave an area tidy; (*b*) *v.phr.t.* elucidate, solve (a mystery); cure (an infection etc.); (*c*) *v.phr.i.* (of an infection etc.) become cured, disappear; (see also senses 5, 6, 9 above).

Comb.: **clear-out** an act or period of clearing out, a removal and disposal of unwanted items or material; **clear-up** an act or period of clearing up, a removal and tidying away of obstructions, rubbish, etc.

clearage *n.* (*a*) = CLEARANCE 2; (*b*) the action of clearing: M18. **clearer** *n.* L16.

clear /klɪə/ *adv.* ME. [Partly the adj. after vbs; partly after other flat advs., esp. CLEAN *adv.*] **1** = CLEARLY 1. Now chiefly of sound, esp. in *loud and clear* s.v. LOUD *adv.* 1. ME. **2** Completely; = CLEAN *adv.* 2. Now only modifying advs. & advb. phrs. ME. **3** Brightly; with a clear light. LME. **4** So as to be clear (*of*). L16.

1 MILTON Now clear I understand. G. STEIN To make Jeff Campbell see much clearer. 2 R. L'ESTRANGE He is Now got into Clear Another story. A. LOOS The boat does not come clear up to London. 4 H. SECOMBE He leapt clear just before it plummeted down. *steer clear of*: see STEER *v.*[1]

Comb.: **clear-cut** *a.* well-defined; **clear-cut** *v.t.*, **clear-fell** *v.t.* cut down and remove every tree from (an area).

clearance /ˈklɪər(ə)ns/ *n.* M16. [f. CLEAR *v.* + -ANCE.] **1** An act of clearing or making clear; *esp.* (*a*) a removal of obstructions, encumbrances, contents, etc. (see CLEAR *v.* 8, 11); a removal of old buildings, persons, or objects, so as to clear land; (*b*) the clearing of a ship at customs; (*c*) the clearing of a cheque; (*d*) permission, authorization, esp. for an aircraft to land or take off or for a person to be entrusted with secret information etc. M16. **2** A certificate that a ship has been cleared at customs. E18. **3** A clear space allowed for the passage of two objects or parts; the distance allowed. L18. **4** A cleared space, a clearing. Now *rare* or *obs.* E19. **5** *Football, Hockey*, etc. A defensive kick or hit away from a dangerous attacking position. E20.

1 **the (Highland) clearances** *Hist.* the enforced depopulation of the Scottish Highlands.

Comb.: **clearance order**: for the demolition of buildings; **clearance sale**: to effect clearance of superfluous stock.

clear-cole /ˈklɪəkəʊl/ *n.* & *v.t.* E19. [Fr. *claire colle* clear glue or size.] (Paint with) size and whiting or white lead as a first coat in house-painting.

clearing /ˈklɪərɪŋ/ *n.* LME. [f. CLEAR *v.* + -ING[1].] **1** The action of CLEAR *v.* LME. **b** The washing of calico to remove excess dye. M19. **2** A piece of land in a forest cleared for cultivation; an open space in a forest. L17. †**3** In *pl.* The balance of a military officer's pay after deductions. L17–E19.

Comb.: **clearing-bank** a bank that is a member of a clearing-house, *spec.* of the London Clearing House; **clearing-house** a bankers' institution where cheques and bills are exchanged, so that only the balances need be paid in cash; *transf.* an agency for collecting and distributing information etc.

clearly /ˈklɪəli/ *adv.* ME. [f. CLEAR *a.* + -LY[2].] **1** Distinctly; plainly; manifestly, obviously. ME. **2** Brightly; with a clear light. Now *rare.* LME. †**3** Honestly, frankly. LME–L17. †**4** Completely; = CLEAR *adv.* 2. LME–E19. †**5** Without deduction, net. LME–M17.

1 J. TYNDALL The top of the mountain rose clearly above us. H. JAMES The moment of his mother's arrival was never clearly ascertained. G. VIDAL I remember that very clearly. I. MCEWAN It was clearly visiting time in the wards. 2 I. MURDOCH The moon shone clearly on to my bed.

clearstory *n.* see CLERESTORY.

cleat /kliːt/ *n.* & *v.* ME. [Corresp. to Du. *kloot* ball, sphere, OHG *klōz* clod, lump, wedge (G *Kloss* clod, dumpling), f. WGmc: prob. already in OE. Rel. to CLOT *n.*, CLOUT *n.*[1]] **A** *n.* **1** A wedge. ME. **2a** A projecting piece bolted on to a spar, gangway, boot, etc. to provide footing or to prevent a rope from slipping. LME. **b** A piece of wood or iron bolted on for securing ropes to or for strengthening woodwork etc. M18. **3** A wedge-shaped or other piece fastened on, or left projecting, for any purpose: as a handle etc. E17. **B** *v.t.* Fasten to, or with, a cleat; provide with cleats. E17.

cleavage /ˈkliːvɪdʒ/ *n.* E19. [f. CLEAVE *v.*[1] + -AGE.] **1** The action of splitting a crystal or rock along a line of natural fissure; *gen.* the action of splitting or dividing. Also, the state of being split, a division; the manner or direction in which a mineral or rock or *gen.* a party, opinion, etc., tends to split. E19. **b** *Biol.* Cell division; esp. of a fertilized egg cell. L19. **2** The hollow between a woman's breasts, esp. as exposed by a low-cut garment. *colloq.* M20.

1 W. LIPPMANN There is some kind of radical cleavage between the Marxian theory and the historic Soviet state. W. S. CHURCHILL Anxious to avoid a total religious cleavage with the European Powers. J. BRONOWSKI Sometimes the stone had a natural grain, sometimes the tool-maker created the lines of cleavage. b *spiral cleavage*: see SPIRAL *a.*[1]

cleave /kliːv/ *n. Anglo-Ir.* M16. [Ir. *cliabh.*] A basket.

cleave /kliːv/ *v.*[1] Now chiefly *literary*. Pa. t. **cleaved, cleft** /klɛft/, **clove** /kləʊv/, (*arch.*) **clave** /kleɪv/. Pa. pple **cleaved, cleft, clove, cloven** /ˈkləʊv(ə)n/. See also CLOVEN *ppl a.* [OE *clēofan* = OS *klioban* (Du. *klieven*), OHG *kliuban* (G *klieben*), ON *kljúfa*, f. Gmc.] **1** *v.t.* Split, esp. along the grain or line of cleavage; intersect, fissure. OE. **b** *v.t.* Separate or sever *from* by dividing or splitting. ME. **2** *v.i.* Come apart, esp. along the grain or line of cleavage. ME. **3** *v.t.* & *i.* Pierce and penetrate (air, water, etc.), make one's way through (air, water, etc.). M16. **b** *v.t.* Make (one's way, a channel, etc.) by piercing and penetrating. M19.

1 AV *Gen.* 23:3 Abraham . . claue the wood. R. MACAULAY Cleaving the forests, deep valleys ran down to the sea. 3 WORDSWORTH Through the inferior throng I clove Of the plain Burghers. E. MUIR Two towering birds cleaving the air. b E. BOWEN A steamer . . cleft a long bright furrow in the shadowy water.

cleavable *a.* able to be cloven or split M19.

cleave /kliːv/ *v.*[2] Now *literary*. Pa. t. **clave** /kleɪv/, **cleaved**; pa. pple **cleaved**. [OE *cleofian*, *clifian* (weak), *clīfan* (strong) = (i) OS *klibon* (Du. *kleven*), OHG *klebēn* (G *kleben*), (ii) OS *biklīban* (Du. *beklijven*), OHG *klīban*, ON *klífa*, f. WGmc base also of CLAY *n.*, CLIMB *v.*, CLOAM.] **1** *v.i.* Stick fast, adhere, or cling *to* (*lit.* & *fig.*). OE. †**b** Remain steadfast, continue. ME–L16. **2** *v.t.* Attach *to* (esp. *fig.*). M20.

1 BACON Water in small quantity cleaveth to any thing that is solid. L. STRACHEY More closely than ever did she cleave to the side of her mistress. B. BETTELHEIM The English translations cleave to an early stage of Freud's thought. 2 A. FRASER The real theme of the coronation—to cleave the Scottish people to their young King.

cleavelandite /ˈkliːvləndʌɪt/ *n.* E19. [f. Parker *Cleaveland* (1780–1858), US mineralogist + -ITE[1].] *Min.* A variety of albite forming thin platy crystals.

cleaver /ˈkliːvə/ *n.* LME. [f. CLEAVE *v.*[1] + -ER[1].] **1** A person who cleaves wood etc. LME. **2** An instrument for cleaving; *spec.* a butcher's chopping-tool for carcasses. L16.

cleavers /ˈkliːvəz/ *n.* (treated as *sing.* or *pl.*). Also **clivers** /ˈklɪv-/. [OE *clīfe* = OS *klība*, OHG *klība*, f. base of CLEAVE *v.*[2]] A climbing weed, *Galium aparine*, which adheres by minute hooked prickles to clothes, fur, etc. Also called *goose-grass*.

cleck /klɛk/ *v.t.* Chiefly *Sc.* LME. [ON *klekja.*] Hatch (*lit.* & *fig.*).

clecking *n.* (*a*) hatching; (*b*) a brood: M16.

cled *v.* pa. t. & pple of CLEAD *v.*

cledge /klɛdʒ/ *n. dial.* E18. [Prob. rel. to CLAG.] Clay, clayey soil; a kind of fuller's earth.

cledgy *a.* L16.

clee /kliː/ *n. obs.* exc. *dial.* [OE *clēa* (*clēo*): see CLAW *n.*[1]] = CLAW *n.*[1] 1.

cleed *v.* var. of CLEAD.

cleek /kliːk/ *n.* Chiefly *Sc.* LME. [f. the vb: cf. CLICK *n.*[3]] 1 A large hook or crook (for catching hold of something). LME. b A hold, a clutch. LME. 2 *Golf.* An iron-headed club with a straight narrow face and a long shaft, as a number one iron. *arch.* E19.

cleek /kliːk/ *v.t. Sc.* & *north.* Also **cleik**. Pa. t. & pple **claucht**, **-ght**, /klɔː(x)t/. LME. [f. as CLEACH *v.* Cf. CLICK *v.*[2]] 1 Clutch; grasp suddenly, firmly, or eagerly. LME. 2 Snatch (*out, up, off*). LME. 3 Lay hold of with a cleek. E19.

cleeve *n.* var. of CLEVE.

clef /klɛf/ *n.* L16. [Fr. f. L *clavis* key.] *Mus.* Any of several symbols placed on a particular line of a stave to indicate the name and pitch of the notes standing on that line, and hence of the other notes.

alto clef: see ALTO *a.* *bass clef*: see BASS *a.* *C clef*: see C, C. *F clef*: see F, F. *G clef*: see G, G. *soprano clef*: see SOPRANO *a.* *tenor clef*: see TENOR *a.* *treble clef*: see TREBLE *a.*

cleft /klɛft/ *n.* Also (earlier) **clift** /klɪft/. ME. [Corresp. to OHG, ON *kluft*, cogn. w. CLEAVE *v.*[1]: prob. already in OE. Assim. to next.] 1 A space or division made by cleaving; a split, a fissure, a crack, a crevice. ME. 2 *spec.* a The fork of the legs. *obs.* exc. *dial.* ME. b A split made in a tree, esp. to receive a graft. LME. c A crack of the skin, a chap; a crack in a horse's foot. L16. 3 (A piece of) split wood, esp. for fuel. Now *dial.* L15.

1 *natal cleft*: see NATAL *a.*[2] VISCERAL *cleft*.

clefted *a.* having a cleft or clefts, split M16.

cleft /klɛft/ *ppl a.* LME. [pa. pple of CLEAVE *v.*[1]: cf. CLOVEN *ppl a.*] Split apart; partly split; bifurcate.

cleft palate a congenital malformation in which there is a longitudinal fissure in the roof of the mouth. **cleft sentence** *Gram.* a sentence in which an element is emphasized by being put in a separate clause and the use of an empty introductory word, usu. *it, that,* or *what*, e.g. *it's money we want, what we want is money; it was today that I saw him; that was the King you were talking to.* **in a cleft stick** in a position allowing neither retreat nor advance; in a fix.

cleft *v.* pa. t. & pple of CLEAVE *v.*[1]

cleg /klɛg/ *n.* LME. [ON *kleggi* (Norw. *klegg*, Da. *klæg*).] A gadfly, a horsefly; *esp.* one of the common genus *Haematopota*.

cleidoic /klʌɪˈdəʊɪk/ *a.* M20. [f. Gk *kleidoō* lock up + -IC.] *Biol.* Of the egg of an oviparous land animal: completely enclosed in a membrane or shell.

cleik *v.* var. of CLEEK *v.*

cleistogamy /klʌɪˈstɒgəmi/ *n.* L19. [f. Gk *kleistos* closed + -GAMY.] *Bot.* The occurrence of permanently closed flowers in which self-fertilization occurs. Opp. CHASMOGAMY.

cleistoˈgamic, **cleistogamous** *adjs.* L19.

cleithral /ˈklʌɪθr(ə)l/ *a.* M19. [f. Gk *kleithron* bar for closing a door + -AL[1].] *Gk Archit.* Of a temple: covered in. Opp. HYPAETHRAL.

clem /klɛm/ *v. dial.* Also **clam** /klam/. Infl. **-mm-**. M16. [Repr. OE *beclemman* confine, shut in, OS *klemmian* pinch, constrain, f. WGmc, f. Gmc base also of CLAM *n.*[1]] 1 *v.t.* Pinch or waste with hunger or thirst. M16. 2 *v.i.* Suffer the pangs of hunger or thirst; starve. L16.

clematis /ˈklɛmətɪs, kləˈmeɪtɪs/ *n.* M16. [L (also, periwinkle) f. Gk *klēmatis*, f. *klēma* vine-branch.] A plant of the large genus *Clematis* of the buttercup family, with a showy calyx and no corolla, and seed-vessels often with a feathery style, most species being woody climbing shrubs, as traveller's joy, *C. vitalba*; *esp.* any of the numerous cultivated varieties.

clemency /ˈklɛm(ə)nsi/ *n.* LME. [L *clementia*, f. as next: see -ENCY.] 1 Mildness or gentleness of temper in the exercise of authority or power; mercy, leniency. LME. 2 Mildness of weather or climate. M17.

Also †**clemence** *n.* LME–L16.

clement /ˈklɛm(ə)nt/ *a.* LME. [L *clement-*, *-ens*: see -ENT.] 1 Mild and humane in the exercise of power or authority; merciful, lenient, kindly. LME. 2 Of weather or climate: mild. M19.

clemently *adv.* M16.

Clementine /ˈklɛm(ə)ntʌɪn/ *n.*[1] & *a.* LME. [med.L *Clementinus*, f. *Clemens* the adj. (see prec.) used as a pers. name: see -INE[1].] A *n.* In *pl.* The constitutions collected by Pope Clement V (1264–1314), forming the seventh book of the decretals. Also, certain apocryphal writings once attributed to Clement of Rome, a bishop of the early Church (fl. *c*AD 96). LME. B *adj.* Of or pertaining to one of the name of Clement, esp. (*a*) Clement of Rome, (*b*) Pope Clement V. E18.

clementine /ˈklɛm(ə)ntʌɪn, -tiːn/ *n.*[2] E20. [Fr. *clémentine*.] A variety of tangerine grown esp. in N. America.

clench /klɛn(t)ʃ/ *n.* See also CLINCH *n.* LME. [f. the vb.] 1 = CLINCH *n.* 1, 2, 3. LME. 2 A pun, a quibble; = CLINCH *n.* 4. *arch.* M17. 3 The action of clenching the fingers, fist, teeth, etc.; the state of being clenched together. M19.

clench /klɛn(t)ʃ/ *v.t.* See also CLINCH *v.*, CLINK *v.*[2] [OE *-clenćan* = OHG *klenken*, f. Gmc, f. base parallel to that of CLING *v.*] 1 = CLINCH *v.* 1a. OE. 2 Set firmly together, close (the fingers, fist, teeth, etc.) tightly. LME.

1 M. LEITCH Her hair was clenched in curlers. 2 J. STEINBECK He struck her in the face with his clenched fist. F. KING She clenched her jaws until they ached. *clenched fist salute*: see SALUTE *n.*[1] 3b.

clencher *n.* = CLINCHER LME.

cleome /klɪˈəʊmi/ *n.* E19. [mod.L f. Gk (Theophrastus), name of a different plant.] Any of various chiefly tropical American plants constituting the genus *Cleome*, of the caper family, notable for their very long stamens; *esp.* = *spider flower* s.v. SPIDER *n.*

clepe /kliːp/ *v. arch.* (long *rare* exc. as YCLEPT). Pa. t. & pple also †**clept**. [OE *cleopian*, *clipian* f. Gmc, rel. to OFris. *klippa*, *kleppa* ring, LG *klippen* sound, resound.] †1 *v.i.* Cry, call, (*on, to, for, after*). OE–M16. †2 *v.t.* Call (a person); summon; speak to, address. OE–M16. 3 *v.t.* Call by the name of, name. OE.

clepsydra /ˈklɛpsɪdrə/ *n.* Pl. **-dras**, **-drae** /-driː/. LME. [L f. Gk *klepsudra*, f. *kleps-* comb. form of *kleptein* steal + *hudōr* water.] An instrument used in antiquity to measure time by the flow of water; a water-clock.

†**clept** *v.* pa. t. & pple of CLEPE *v.*

cleptoparasite *n.* var. of KLEPTOPARASITE.

clerestory /ˈklɪəstɔːri/ *n.* Also ***clearstory**. LME. [f. CLEAR *a.* + STOREY: cf. AL *historia clara*.] 1 The upper part of the nave, choir, and transepts of any large church, containing a series of windows, clear of the roofs of the aisles, admitting light to the central parts of the building. LME. b A similar feature in other buildings. E16. 2 A raised section of a railway-carriage roof, containing small windows or ventilators. Chiefly *US.* L19.

Comb.: **clerestory window**: with no crosspiece dividing the light.

clergess /ˈkləːdʒɛs/ *n.* Long *arch. rare.* ME. [OFr. *clergesse* fem. of *clerc*: see CLERK *n.*, -ESS[1].] †1 A learned woman. Only in ME. 2 A female member of a religious order. LME.

clergy /ˈkləːdʒi/ *n.* ME. [Partly f. (O)Fr. *clergé* f. eccl.L *clericatus*, f. *clericus* (see CLERK, -ATE[1]); partly f. (O)Fr. *clergie*, f. *clerc* CLERK *n.* + *-ie* -Y[3], infl. by *clergé*.] 1 Learning, scholarship. Long *obs.* exc. in proverb *an ounce of mother-wit is worth a pound of clergy*. ME. †2 The state of being ordained to the Christian ministry; membership of a clerical order. ME–M16. 3 *sing.* or (usu.) *collect. pl.* The body of all persons ordained to the Christian ministry. Opp. *laity*. ME. †b Any priestly body. LME–E18. 4 In biblical translations and allusions [tr. Gk *klēros*, *klērōn* (*1 Pet.* 5:3)]: the body of all Christians. *arch.* LME.

Phrases: **benefit of clergy** *Hist.* exemption from ordinary courts of law because of membership of the clergy or (later) literacy or scholarship; also (later), exemption from the sentence for certain first offences because of literacy. *regular clergy*: see REGULAR *a.* *secular clergy*: see SECULAR *a.* 1. **without benefit of clergy** *joc.* without formal marriage etc.

Comb.: **clergyman** a man ordained to the Christian ministry, a priest; *esp.* an ordained minister of the Church of England; *clergyman's* (*sore*) *throat*, a chronic sore throat afflicting those who speak much in public; **clergywoman** †(*a*) a nun; a priestess; (*b*) (chiefly *joc.*) the wife of a clergyman; (*c*) a female minister of religion.

clergiable *a.* (*Hist.*) (of an offence etc.) admitting benefit of clergy M18.

cleric /ˈklɛrɪk/ *a.* & *n.* E17. [eccl.L *clericus* f. eccl.Gk *klērikos* belonging to the Christian ministerial order, f. *klēros* lot, heritage (as in *Acts* 1:17).] A *adj.* Of or pertaining to the clergy, clerical. Now *rare.* E17. B *n.* A person ordained to the Christian ministry. E17.

clerical /ˈklɛrɪk(ə)l/ *a.* & *n.* L15. [eccl.L *clericalis*, f. as prec.: see -AL[1].] A *adj.* 1 Orig., learned. Later *gen.*, of, pertaining to, or characteristic of (a member of) the clergy. L15. 2 Of or pertaining to a clerk or clerks; involving copying out. L18.

1 **clerical collar** an upright white collar, fastening at the back, worn by members of the clergy. 2 **clerical error** an error made in copying or writing out.

B *n.* 1 A cleric. E17. 2 In *pl.* Clerical clothes. M19.

clericalism *n.* clerical principles, rule, or influence M19. **clericalist** *n.* an adherent of clericalism M19. **cleriˈcality** *n.* (*a*) *rare* a clerical trait; (*b*) clerical quality or condition: M17. **clericaliˈzation** *n.* the action of clericalizing E20. **clericalize** *v.t.* make clerical, subject to clerical rule or influence L19. **clerically** *adv.* L18.

clerico- /ˈklɛrɪkəʊ/ *comb. form.* E19. [f. as CLERIC: see -O-.] Clerically, clerical and, as *clerico-liberal*, *-political* adjs.

clerid /ˈklɛrɪd/ *n.* & *a.* L19. [mod.L *Cleridae* (see below), f. *Clerus* genus name f. Gk *klēros*: see -ID[3].] (A beetle) of the family Cleridae.

clerihew /ˈklɛrɪhjuː/ *n.* E20. [Edmund *Clerihew* Bentley (1875–1956), Eng. writer who devised the form.] A short witty, comic, or nonsensical verse, usu. in two rhyming couplets with lines of unequal length.

clerisy /ˈklɛrɪsi/ *n.* E19. [App. after G *Klerisei*, f. as CLERIC.] A distinct class of learned or literary persons.

clerk /klɑːk/ *n.* & *v.* OE. [f. as CLERIC, reinforced by (O)Fr. *clerc* f. same source.] A *n.* 1 A man ordained to the Christian ministry, formerly esp. in minor orders, now (*arch.* or *Law*) in holy orders. OE. b A lay officer of a cathedral, parish church, university college chapel, etc. M16. 2 A literate person, a scholar. Now *arch.* or *Hist.* OE. 3 An officer in charge of records etc.; the secretary or agent of a town council, corporation, court, etc.; *spec.* a senior official in Parliament. E16. 4 A person employed in a bank, office, shop, etc., to make entries, copy letters, keep accounts and files, etc. Also, a person being trained in law. E16. 5 An assistant in a shop or hotel. *N. Amer.* L18.

Phrases: *articled clerk*: see ARTICLE *v.* 4. *Clerk of the Closet*: see CLOSET *n.* 2. **clerk of the course** the judges' secretary etc. in horse-racing or motor racing. *Clerk of the Irons*: see IRON *n.* *Clerk of the Pells*: see PELL *n.*[1] **Clerk of the Scales** the official who weighs jockeys etc. **clerk of (the) works** an overseer of building works etc. *criminous clerk*: see CRIMINOUS 3. *Deputy Clerk Register*: see REGISTER *n.*[1] *lay clerk*: see LAY *a.* *Lord Clerk Register*: see REGISTER *n.*[1] *Lord Justice Clerk*: see LORD *n.* *parish clerk*: see PARISH *n.* *reading clerk*: see READING *ppl a.*[1] *St Nicholas'(s) clerk*: see SAINT *n.* & *a.* *tally clerk*: see TALLY *n.*[1] *town clerk*: see TOWN *n.* *treason of the clerks*: see TREASON *n.*

B *v.i.* Act or work as a clerk. M16.

clerkage *n.* (*rare*) the work of a clerk; clerks collectively: M16. **clerkdom** *n.* the status or function of a clerk; clerks as a class: M19. **clerkess** *n.* (*Sc.*) a female clerk E20. **clerkhood** *n.* the status or position of a clerk ME. **clerkish** *a.* resembling or characteristic of a clerk M19. †**clerklike** *adv.* & *a.* (*rare*) (*a*) *adv.* in the manner of a clerk; (*b*) *adj.* resembling (that of) a clerk: E17–E18.

clerkly /ˈklɑːkli/ *a.* LME. [f. CLERK *n.* + -LY[1], after next.] 1 Scholarly, learned. *arch.* LME. 2 Of or pertaining to the clergy, clerical. L15. 3 Of or pertaining to fine handwriting; skilled in copying. E19. 4 Of or pertaining to an office clerk. M19.

clerkliness *n.* M16.

clerkly /ˈklɑːkli/ *adv.* LME. [f. CLERK *n.* + -LY[2], after late L *clericaliter.*] 1 In a scholarly way, learnedly. *arch.* LME. †b Cleverly, artfully. L16–E17. 2 In fine handwriting, in the manner of a good copyist. E19.

clerkship /ˈklɑːkʃɪp/ *n.* ME. [f. CLERK *n.* + -SHIP.] †1 The clergy. *rare.* Only in ME. 2 The status or position of a clerk. L15. 3 Writing by hand; style of handwriting, skilled copying. M16. 4 Scholarship, learning. *arch.* M17.

clerodendrum /klɪərəˈdɛndrəm/ *n.* Also **-dron** /-dr(ə)n/. E19. [mod.L, f. Gk *klēros* chance, lot + *dendron* tree: prob. so called because of the variable medicinal properties of the genus.] A shrub or small tree of the African and Asian genus *Clerodendrum*, of the verbena family, with fragrant showy flowers.

cleromancy /ˈklɪərəmansi/ *n.* Now *rare.* E17. [f. Gk *klēros* chance, lot + -MANCY.] Divination by lots.

cleruch /ˈklɪərʊk/ *n.* Also **k-**. M19. [Gk *klērouk̄hos* allottee, f. *klēros* chance, lot + *ekhein* have, hold.] *Gk Hist.* An Athenian granted land in a foreign State but retaining rights as a citizen at home.

cleruchy *n.* the allotment of land among cleruchs, a body of cleruchs M19.

cletch /klɛtʃ/ *n. dial.* Also **clatch** /klatʃ/. L17. [f. CLECK *v.*: cf. *bake, batch*, etc. Cf. CLUTCH *n.*[2]] A clutch of eggs, chicks, etc.; *transf.* (usu. *contempt.*) a family.

clethra /ˈkliːθrə, ˈklɛθrə/ *n.* L18. [mod.L f. Gk *klēthra* alder, which it resembles in foliage.] A tree or shrub of the genus *Clethra*, native to America and eastern Asia, with racemes of white or pink flowers. Cf. *pepperbush* s.v. PEPPER *n.*

cleuch /kl(j)uːx/ *n. Sc.* Also **-gh**. ME. [Var. of CLOUGH *n.*[1]] 1 A steep-sided ravine (= CLOUGH *n.*[1]). Freq. in place-names as *Buccleuch* etc. ME. 2 The precipitous side of a ravine; a steep descent. E16.

cleuk *n.* see CLUTCH *n.*[1]

cleve /kliːv/ *n.* Long *obs.* exc. *dial.* Also **cleeve**. ME. [Var. of CLIFF *n.* after OE pls. *cleofu, cleofum.*] 1 A cliff. ME. 2 A steep slope, a steep hillside. ME.

cleveite /ˈkliːvʌɪt/ *n.* L19. [f. Per T. *Cleve* (1840–1905), Swed. chemist + -ITE[1].] *Min.* A variety of uraninite containing rare-earth elements.

Cleveland bay /ˈkliːvlənd ˈbeɪ/ *n. phr.* L18. [f. *Cleveland*, a county of England + BAY *n.*[6]] A bay horse with black legs of a strong breed originating in the north of England.

clever /ˈklɛvə/ *a.* & *adv.* Also (*dial.*) **cliver** /ˈklɪvə/. ME. [Perh. rel. to CLEAVE *v.*[2] Cf. also LG *klöver, klever*, MDu. *klever* sprightly, brisk, smart.] A *adj.* †1 Quick or ready to catch hold. *rare.* Only in ME. 2 Manually dexterous; deft; possessing physical skill. L16. 3 Nimble, agile, active; in good health. Now *dial.* L17. 4 Lithe, clean-limbed; handsome. Now *dial.* L17. 5 Possessing mental skill or agility; talented; quick-witted. E18. 6 Of a thing or action: showing physical or mental skill or agility; ingenious. E18. 7 Handy; neat and convenient; well-made. *obs.* exc. *Canad. dial.* E18. 8 Pleasing, nice. Now *dial.* & *US colloq.* M18.

5 *too clever by half*: see HALF *n.*

Comb.: **clever-clever** *a.* ostentatiously clever, eagerly seeking to appear clever; **clever-clogs, clever Dick, clever-sticks** *colloq.* a (would-be) smart and knowing person, a know-all.

B *adv.* Cleverly. Chiefly *colloq.* & *dial.* M17.

box clever: see BOX *v.*[2]

cleve'rality *n.* (*Sc.* & *north.*) cleverness M18. **cleverish** *a.* fairly clever E19. **cleverly** *adv.* (*a*) in a clever manner; (*b*) (now *dial.* & *US*) fully, completely: L17. **cleverness** *n.* the state or quality of being clever M18.

clevis /ˈklɛvɪs/ *n.* L16. [Perh. rel. to CLEAVE *v.*[1]] A U-shaped piece of metal at the end of a beam for attaching tackle etc.; a connection in which a bolt holds one part that fits between the forked ends of another.

clew /kluː/ *n.* See also CLUE *n.* [OE *cliwen, cleowen* = MLG, Du. *kluwen*, f. base also of OHG *kliuwa, kliuwi* ball, sphere, prob. ult. rel. to CLAW *n.*[1]] †1 A globular body; a rounded mass. OE–L18. †b A round bunch or cluster. E17–E18. 2 A ball of thread or yarn. *arch.* OE. 3 *spec.* a A ball of yarn etc. used to trace a path through a maze (as in the Gk myth of Theseus in the Labyrinth); a thing which guides through perplexity, a difficult investigation, an intricate structure, etc. LME. b = CLUE *n.* 4a. E18. 4 The mythological thread of life spun by the Fates. E17. 5 *Naut.* The lower or after corner of a sail. (Earlier as CLUE *n.* 2.) E17. 6 *Naut.* The series of cords by which a hammock is suspended. M18.

Comb.: **clew-garnet** *Naut.* a tackle to clew up the courses or lower square-sails in furling; **clew-line** *Naut.* a tackle connecting the clew of a sail to the upper yard or mast; occas. = *clew-garnet* above.

clew /kluː/ *v.* See also CLUE *v.* LME. [f. the n.] 1 *v.t.* Coil *up* into a ball. LME. 2 *v.t.* Point *out* or trace (as) by a clew or clue. *rare.* E17. 3 *v.t.* & *i.* *Naut.* Draw the lower ends of (a sail) *up* to the upper yard or mast ready for furling; let *down* (a sail) by clews in unfurling. M18.

clianthus /klʌɪˈanθəs/ *n.* M19. [mod.L, app. f. Gk *klei-, kleos* glory + *anthos* flower.] An Australasian leguminous plant of the genus *Clianthus*, which includes the kaka-beak, *C. puniceus*, and Sturt's desert pea, *C. formosus*. Also called *glory pea*.

cliché /ˈkliːʃeɪ/ *n.* M19. [Fr., use as n. of pa. pple of *clicher* to stereotype, perh. of imit. origin.] 1 *Hist.* A metal stereotype or electrotype block. M19. 2 *fig.* A stereotyped expression, a hackneyed phrase or opinion; a stereotyped character, style, etc. L19.

cliché(')d *a.* hackneyed, full of clichés E20.

click /klɪk/ *n.*[1] E17. [Imit.: cf. OFr. *clique* tick of clock, Du. *klik* tick.] 1 A slight sharp sound of concussion as made by the latch of a door dropping, the impact of two billiard-balls, etc. Also (*dial.*), a quick light blow, a tap. E17. b *spec.* (Such a sound made by) a touching of a horse's fore and hind shoes, through overreaching. L19. c *Radio.* In *pl.* Atmospherics of short duration. E20. 2 A mechanism making this noise, e.g. the catch of a ratchet-wheel etc. M18. 3 A sharp non-vocal suction, used as a speech sound in certain (chiefly African) languages. E19.

Comb.: **click-beetle** a beetle of the large family Elateridae, members of which are able to spring up with a clicking sound when lying on their backs; **click-clack** *n.* & *v.i.* (make) a repeated sound like a click; **click language**: in which clicks are used.

clicky *a.* containing many clicks L19.

click /klɪk/ *n.*[2] E19. [Anglicized f. Fr. CLIQUE.] = CLIQUE.

click /klɪk/ *n.*[3] E19. [Var. of CLEEK *n.*] 1 In full *click-hook*. A large hook or crook. E19. 2 A jerk with a hook or crook. L19. 3 A manoeuvre in wrestling, whereby the opponent's foot is knocked sharply off the ground. Now *rare.* L19.

click /klɪk/ *v.*[1] L16. [Imit.: cf. CLICK *n.*[1]] 1 *v.t.* & *i.* (Cause to) make a slight sharp concussive sound; move with such a click; operate (a camera etc.) with a click. L16. b *v.i.* Of a horse: overreach and make a click by the touching of fore and hind shoes. E18. 2 *v.i. fig.* a Be successful; secure one's object; be understood; become instantly friendly, strike up a rapport. (Foll. by *with.*) *slang.* E20. b Be chosen *for*, come in *for*. *Mil. slang.* E20. c Become pregnant. *colloq.* M20. d Fall into context; begin to revive a memory. *colloq.* M20.

1 D. H. LAWRENCE She heard a latch click. E. BOWEN She . . clicked open her bag. G. ORWELL The cage door had clicked shut. J. KOSINSKI The soldiers clicked their heels. B. HINES Clicking his tongue on the roof of his mouth. 2a C. LAMBERT Attractive girls with whom he ultimately and triumphantly 'clicks'. D. CUSACK We don't seem to click. d A. BURGESS Then the name clicked, because somebody in the town had talked about Everett.

click /klɪk/ *v.*[2]*t.* Chiefly *dial.* L17. [Var. of CLEEK *v.*] Clutch; grasp suddenly, firmly, or eagerly; snatch (*up* etc.).

clicker /ˈklɪkə/ *n.* L17. [f. CLICK *v.*[1] or *v.*[2] + -ER[1].] 1 A shopkeeper's (orig. a shoemaker's) tout. L17. 2 A foreman shoemaker who cuts out the leather. L17. 3 A compositor in charge of a companionship who distributes the copy etc. E19.

clicket /ˈklɪkɪt/ *n. obs.* exc. *dial.* LME. [(O)Fr. *cliquet*, f. OFr. *clique* door-latch: see -ET[1].] 1 The latch of a door or gate. LME. †2 A latchkey. LME–L16. †3 A device for making a clicking sound, a clapper, a rattle. LME–M18.

clicket /ˈklɪkɪt/ *v.* LME. [f. the n.: cf. Fr. *cliqueter*. Branch II may be a different wd.] I 1 *v.t.* Fasten with a latch, lock. *obs.* exc. *dial.* LME. 2 *v.i.* Chatter. L16. 3 *v.i.* Make a light or repeated clicking sound. E20. II 4 *v.i.* Of a fox: be in heat; copulate. L16.

cliency /ˈklʌɪənsi/ *n. rare.* M17. [Late L *clientia*, f. as next.] = CLIENTSHIP.

client /ˈklʌɪənt/ *n.* LME. [L *client-, -ens*, earlier *cluens* use as n. of pres. pple of *cluere, cluere* hear, listen, obey: see -ENT.] I 1 A person who is under the protection and patronage of another; a dependant, a hanger-on. *arch.* LME. 2 *Rom. Hist.* A plebeian under the protection of a patrician. Cf. PATRON *n.* 4c. M16. II 3 A person who employs the services of a legal adviser; a person whose cause an advocate pleads. LME. 4 *gen.* A person using the services of any professional; a customer. E17. b A person assisted by a social worker etc. L19.

Comb.: **client state, nation**, etc.: dependent upon a larger one for trade, military aid, etc.

clientage *n.* (*a*) a body of clients; (*b*) the relation of client to patron: M17. **cliental** *a.* (*rare*) of or pertaining to a client or clients M17. **clientry** *n.* = CLIENTAGE L16. **clientship** *n.* the state or relation of a client M17.

clientele /kliːɒnˈtɛl, *foreign* kliɑ̃tɛl/ *n.* Also **-èle**. M16. [Orig. f. L *clientela*, f. as prec. Later f. Fr. *clientèle* f. L.] †1 Clientship; patronage. M16–L19. 2 A body of clients, a following; the customers (of a shop); the patrons (of a theatre etc.); persons seeking the professional advice of a lawyer, architect, etc. L16.

Clifden nonpareil /ˌklɪfd(ə)n nɒnpəˈreɪl/ *n. phr.* M18. [f. †*Clifden* (now *Cliveden*), a village in Buckinghamshire, central England + NONPAREIL.] A large Eurasian noctuid moth, *Catocala fraxini*, with blue and black hindwings.

cliff /klɪf/ *n.* [OE *clif* = OS (Du.) *klif*, OHG *klep*, ON *klif*, f. Gmc. Cf. CLEVE.] 1 A steep rock face, now *esp.* one facing the sea. OE. †2 A shore, a coast. OE–E17. 3 A steep slope, a steep hillside. Now *dial.* ME. 4 The strata of rock lying above or between coal seams. L17.

Comb.: **cliff-hanger** a serial film in which each episode ends in a desperate situation; a story etc. with the outcome excitingly uncertain; **cliff-hanging** *a.* full of suspense; **cliff swallow** a square-tailed swallow of N. and S. America, *Hirundo pyrrhonota*, which builds a jar-shaped nest of mud and straw; also called *mud swallow*.

clifflike *a.* resembling (that of) a cliff, steep and rocky M19. **cliffy** *a.* having cliffs, craggy M16.

clift /klɪft/ *n.*[1] Now *dial.* LME. [Var. of prec., by assoc. w. *clift* CLEFT *n.*] A cliff.

clifty *a.* cliffy L16.

clift *n.*[2] var. of CLEFT *n.*

climacteric /klʌɪˈmakt(ə)rɪk, klʌɪmakˈtɛrɪk/ *a.* & *n.* M16. [Fr. *climactérique* or L *climactericus*, f. Gk *klimaktērikos*, f. *klimaktēr* critical period, f. *klimax, -mak-*: see CLIMAX, -IC.] A *adj.* 1 Pertaining to or constituting a critical period in human life; critical, fatal. M16. b *Med.* Occurring at or characteristic of a period of life when (male) fertility and sexual activity are in decline; (in women) menopausal. E19. 2 = CLIMACTIC. L18. B *n.* A supposedly critical stage in human life, esp. occurring at ages that are multiples of seven years; a critical period, point, or epoch. M17.

Phrases: **grand climacteric** (designating) the 63rd year of life, supposed to be specially critical.

†**climacter** *n.* = CLIMACTERIC *n.* E–M17. **climac'terical** *a.* & †*n.* = CLIMACTERIC L16.

climactic /klʌɪˈmaktɪk/ *a.* L19. [Irreg. f. CLIMAX, prob. infl. by prec.] Of or pertaining to a climax or ascending series; of the nature of a climax.

climactically *adv.* L19.

climate /ˈklʌɪmət/ *n.* & *v.* LME. [(O)Fr. *climat* or late L *clima*, *-mat-* f. Gk *klima*, *-mat-* slope of ground, zone, region, f. *klinein* to lean, slope.] A *n.* †1 A belt of the earth's surface contained between two parallels of latitude. LME–L18. b Any region of the earth. L15–L18. 2 A region considered with reference to its atmospheric conditions or its weather. E17. 3 The prevailing atmospheric phenomena and conditions of temperature, humidity, wind, etc., (of a country or region). E17. b *fig.* The mental, moral, etc., environment prevailing in a body of people in respect of opinion, some aspect of life, etc. M17.

3 *continental climate*: see CONTINENTAL *a.* MEDITERRANEAN *climate*.

B *v.* †1 *v.i.* Sojourn in a particular climate. *rare* (Shakes.). Only in E17. 2 *v.t.* = ACCLIMATIZE. *US.* M19.

climatal *a.* = CLIMATIC M19. **climatize** *v.t.* = ACCLIMATIZE E19. †**climature** *n.* (*a*) *rare* a region; (*b*) meteorological condition resulting from latitude: E17–E19.

climatic /klʌɪˈmatɪk/ *a.* E19. [f. prec. + -IC.] Of or pertaining to climate.

climatical *a.* (*rare*) M17. **climatically** *adv.* in relation to climate L19.

climatology /klʌɪməˈtɒlədʒi/ *n.* M19. [f. CLIMATE + -OLOGY.] The branch of physical science that deals with climate.

climatoˈlogical *a.* M19. **climatoˈlogically** *adv.* L19. **climatologist** *n.* L19.

climax /ˈklʌɪmaks/ *n.* & *v.* M16. [Late L *climax* f. Gk *klimax* ladder, climax.] A *n.* 1 *Rhet.* (A figure characterized by) the arrangement of propositions or ideas in order of increasing importance, force, or effectiveness of expression. M16. †2 An ascending series or scale. M–L18. 3 The highest point reached; a peak of intensity or interest; a culmination. L18. b *spec.* The last or highest term of a rhetorical climax. M19. c *Ecol.* The final stage in a succession, at which a plant community reaches a state of equilibrium; a community that has attained this state. Freq. *attrib.* E20. d A sexual orgasm. E20. B *v.i.* & *t.* Come or bring to a climax. M19.

climb /klʌɪm/ *n.* L16. [f. the vb.] An act of climbing; a place (to be) climbed; an ascent by climbing.

at the climb *Criminals' slang* engaged as a cat burglar.

climb /klʌɪm/ *v.* Pa. t. & pple **climbed**, (*arch.*) **clomb** /kləʊm/. Pa. t. also †**clamb**. [OE *climban* = (M)LG, (M)Du. *klimmen*, OHG *klimban* (G *klimmen*), f. WGmc nasalized var. of base of CLEAVE *v.*[2] (orig. = hold fast).] I *v.i.* 1 Raise oneself by grasping or clinging, or by the aid of hands and feet; ascend a steep place. Freq. foll. by *up* (adv. & prep.). OE. b Rise with gradual or continuous motion; (of the sun, an aeroplane, etc.) go upwards, move towards the zenith; *fig.* increase steadily. OE. c *fig.* Rise in dignity, rank, or state by continued effort; ascend in the intellectual, moral, or social scale. ME. d Of a plant: creep up by the aid of tendrils or by twining. L18. 2 Slope upwards. ME. 3 Foll. by *down*: (*a*) (adv. & prep.) lower oneself (along) by grasping or clinging, or by the aid of hands and feet; (*b*) *fig.* (adv.) withdraw, esp. with ignominy, from a position taken up, abandon a declared position. ME.

1 A. RANSOME John climbed to the topmost branches of the old ash tree. J. FOWLES I climbed up the goat-paths. **climbing-frame** a structure, usu. of pipes joined together, for children to climb on. **climbing-iron** a set of spikes attachable to a boot for climbing trees or ice-slopes. *climbing perch*: see PERCH *n.*[1] *climb on the bandwagon*: see *bandwagon* s.v. BAND *n.*[3] b SHAKES. *Cymb.* Let our crooked smokes climb to their nostrils. TENNYSON The slow moon climbs. C. P. SNOW The cost of living was climbing. c H. L. MENCKEN The Japanese . . have climbed into the first rank of World Powers. *social climb*: see SOCIAL *a.* d *climbing bitter-sweet*: see BITTER-SWEET *n.* 4. 2 E. J. HOWARD The road . . climbed with a steepness only made possible by its tortuous method. 3 G. B. SHAW Climbing down the pipe. R. MACAULAY Makeshift opportunists, backing out and climbing down.

II *v.t.* 4 Ascend or mount by climbing. ME. 5 Attain or achieve by climbing. L16.

4 BYRON We . . clomb the high hill. R. MACAULAY The rich fruit orchards that climbed the wooded hills. K. VONNEGUT To climb a few rungs of the ladder of culture. *climb the ladder*: see LADDER *n.* 1b. 5 A. WELBY I've climbed the summit of some breezy hill.

Comb.: **climb-down** a withdrawal, esp. with ignominy, from a position taken up; abandonment of a declared position.

climbable *a.* M16. **climber** *n.* a person who or thing which climbs; *spec.* (*a*) a climbing plant; (*b*) *Criminals' slang* a cat-burglar; (*c*) *fig.* a person who continually seeks (esp. social) advancement (*social climber*: see SOCIAL *a.*): LME.

clime /klʌɪm/ *n.* Now chiefly *literary*. LME. [Late L *clima*: see CLIMATE.] 1 A region, esp. considered with reference to its climatic conditions. Cf. CLIMATE *n.* 1b, 2. LME. †2 = CLIMATE *n.* 1. L15–L17. 3 = CLIMATE *n.* 3; *fig.* atmosphere. L16.

clinamen /klʌɪˈneɪmɛn/ *n. literary.* Pl. **-mina** /-mɪnə/. L17. [L.] An inclination, a bias.

clinch /klɪn(t)ʃ/ *n.* L16. [Var. of CLENCH *n.*: cf. next.] 1 A thing which clutches, grips, or fixes fast; a grip, a hold. L16. 2 *Naut.* A method of fastening large ropes by a half-hitch with the end seized back on its own part; that part of a rope which is clinched. E17. 3 A fastening in which the end of a nail or bolt is beaten back or flattened after passing through something; the point of a clinched nail; a clinched nail or bolt, a nail for clinching something (also *clinch-nail*). M17. 4 A pun, a quibble; (= CLENCH *n.* 2). M17. 5 An act of clinching or riveting together; the clinching of an argument etc.; the state of being clinched. M19. 6 A struggle or scuffle at close quarters; *Boxing* a position of being too close for a full-arm blow, an act of holding after an exchange of blows. M19. b An embrace. *colloq.* (orig. *US*). E20.

clinch /klɪn(t)ʃ/ *v.* L16. [Var. of CLENCH *v.*, prob. by assim. to CLINK *v.*[2]] 1 *v.t.* a Fix securely (as) with a nail, bolt, rivet, etc.; secure (a nail, rivet, etc.) by driving the point sideways when through. L16. b *fig.* Make firm and sure (an argument, bargain, etc.); drive home; make conclusive, establish. E18. †2 *v.t.* = CLENCH *v.* 2. E17–E19. 3 *v.t. Naut.* Fasten (a rope) with a clinch. M18. 4 *v.i.* Grapple at close quarters; (of boxers) come too close for a full-arm blow. E19. b Embrace. *colloq.* (orig. *US*). L19.

1b ANTHONY SMITH His earlier, considered, authenticated and definite wish clinched the matter.

clincher *n.* a person who or thing which clinches; *esp.* a conclusive statement, argument, etc.; *clincher-built* = *clinker-built* s.v. CLINKER *n.*[1]: ME.

cline /klʌɪn/ *n.* M20. [f. Gk *klinein* to lean, slope.] 1 *Biol.* A gradation in one or more characters within a species or other taxon. M20. 2 *gen.* A continuum with an infinite number of gradations. M20.

clinal *a.* M20.

cling /klɪŋ/ *n.* M17. [f. the vb.] 1 The act of clinging; adhesion, adherence. M17. 2 A clasp; an embrace. *rare.* M17. 3 = *clingstone* (*peach*) s.v. CLING *v.* Also *cling peach.* M19.

cling /klɪŋ/ *v.* Pa. t. & pple **clung** /klʌŋ/. [OE *clingan*, corresp. to MDu. *klingen* stick, adhere. MHG *klingen* climb, f. Gmc, f. base parallel to that of CLENCH *v.*] 1 *v.i.* Adhere together in a stiff mass. Long *obs.* exc. as passing into senses 3 & 5 in *cling together.* OE. 2 *v.i.* Of an animal or vegetable body: shrink up, shrivel, wither. Now *dial.* OE. b *v.t.* Cause (an animal or vegetable body) to shrink up, shrivel, or wither. Now *dial.* M16. 3 *v.i.* Adhere or be attached (*to*) by stickiness, suction, grasping, embracing, etc.; be or remain close *to*, as if attached. ME. b *fig.* Adhere or cleave *to* in affection, fellowship, sympathy, practice, or idea; remain (stubbornly) faithful *to*. L16. †4 *v.t.* Cause to cling, make fast. L16–L18. 5 *v.t.* Cause to adhere or stick *together*. Now *dial.* E17.

2b SHAKES. *Macb.* Upon the next tree shalt thou hang alive, Till famine cling thee. 3 DICKENS The fog clings so. D. H. LAWRENCE He caught her hand and clung to it. D. WELCH The wet shorts clung to our thighs. *fig.*: JOHN BROOKE Some of the abuse heaped upon her still clings to her name. b H. L. MENCKEN The lawyers and judges cling to the idea of equality before the law.

Comb.: **cling film** thin plastic film that adheres to surfaces, used esp. for wrapping and covering foods; **clingfish** (orig. *N. Amer.*) a small marine fish of the family Gobiesocidae, having a ventral sucker enabling it to adhere to rocks etc.; also called *sea-sucker*; **clingstone** (**nectarine, peach**) a kind of nectarine or peach in which the flesh is firmly attached to the stone when ripe.

clinger *n.* E16. **clinginess** *n.* the state or quality of being clingy L18. **clinging** *a.* that clings, clingy L16. **clingingly** *adv.* M19. **clingy** *a.* tending to cling; sticky, adhesive, tenacious: E18.

clinic /ˈklɪnɪk/ *n.*[1] & *a.* Now *rare* or *obs.* E17. [L *clinicus* f. Gk *klinikos*, f. *klinē* bed: see -IC.] A *n.* 1 A person who is confined to bed by sickness etc. E17. 2 *Eccl. Hist.* A person who defers baptism until the deathbed. M17. B *adj.* Of or pertaining to the sickbed; *spec.* designating deathbed baptism, conversion, etc. (cf. CLINICAL *a.* 2). E17.

clinic /ˈklɪnɪk/ *n.*[2] M19. [Fr. *clinique* f. Gk *klinikē* the clinical art.] 1 The teaching of medicine or surgery at the bedside of a sick person, esp. in a hospital. M19. 2 A private or specialized hospital; a place or an occasion for giving medical treatment or advice, esp. in a hospital and devoted to one topic. L19. 3 A conference, class, short course, etc., on a particular subject or activity. Chiefly *N. Amer.* E20.

2 *family-planning clinic, fracture clinic, immunization clinic, post-natal clinic*, etc.

clinician /klɪˈnɪʃ(ə)n/ *n.* orig., a clinical investigator; now, a doctor having direct contact with and responsibility for patients: L19.

clinical /ˈklɪnɪk(ə)l/ *a.* L18. [f. as CLINIC *n.*[1] & *a.* + -AL[1].] 1 *Med.* Designating or pertaining to teaching given at the bedside of a sick person, esp. in a hospital, and (branches of) medicine involving the study or care of actual patients. L18. 2 *Eccl.* Administered at the sickbed to one likely to die. Cf. CLINIC *a.* M19. 3 Coldly detached and impersonal; objective, dispassionate. E20. b Bare and functional, like a hospital. M20.

1 **clinical death**: judged by direct observation of the individual's condition. **clinical medicine**: based on the observed symptoms. *clinical* THERMOMETER.

clinically *adv.* in a clinical manner; as regards clinical medicine, from the point of view of clinical medicine: M19.

clink /klɪŋk/ *n.*[1] LME. [f. CLINK *v.*[1]] 1 A sharp abrupt ringing sound, as of small metallic bodies or glasses struck together. LME. 2 Assonance, jingle. *derog.* E18. 3 A smart sharp blow. *dial.* E18. 4 Money; hard cash. *Sc. colloq.* E18.

clink /klɪŋk/ *n.*[2] *slang.* E16. [Origin unkn.: orig. applied to a prison in Southwark, London.] A prison. Esp. in *in* (*the*) *clink*.

clink /klɪŋk/ *n.*[3] L19. [Origin unkn.: cf. CLINK *v.*[3]] An internal crack in a block of metal caused by uneven heating or cooling.

clink /klɪŋk/ *v.*[1] ME. [Prob. f. (M)Du. *klinken* sound, ring, tinkle, rel. to MLG, (M)Du. *klank* sound. Cf. CLANG, CLANK.] 1 *v.t.* Cause to make a sharp abrupt ringing sound; strike together with such a clink. ME. 2 *v.i.* Move with or make a clink or clinks. LME. 3 *v.i.* Of words: jingle together; rhyme. E18. 4 *v.t.* & *i.* Put or sit *down*, go *off*, put *on*, abruptly or smartly. *Sc.* E18.

clinking *ppl a.* & *adv.* (*a*) *ppl a.* that clinks; *slang* (exceedingly) good; (*b*) *adv.* (*slang*) exceedingly: M17.

clink /klɪŋk/ *v.*[2]*t.* *Sc.* & *north.* LME. [Var. of CLENCH *v.*] Rivet; fix or fasten with nails; secure (a nail, rivet, etc.).

clink /klɪŋk/ *v.*[3]*t.* E20. [Origin unkn.: cf. CLINK *n.*[3]] Cause (metal) to fracture internally.

†**clinkard**, **-art** *ns.* vars. of CLINKER *n.*[2]

clink-clank /ˈklɪŋk-klaŋk/ *n.* & *v.* L18. [f. CLINK *n.*[1], *v.*[1] + CLANK.] A *n.* A repeated clinking sound. L18. B *v.i.* Move with or make such a sound. E20.

clinker /ˈklɪŋkə/ *n.*[1] ME. [f. CLINK *v.*[2] + -ER[1].] 1 A person who or thing which rivets or puts in nails; *fig.* a clinching argument etc. ME. 2 A clinched nail, a nail for clinching something. L19.

Comb.: **clinker-built** *a.* (of a boat) made with external planks which overlap downwards and are fastened with clinched nails.

clinker /ˈklɪŋkə/ *n.*[2] Also †**-ard**, †**-art**. M17. [Early mod.Du. *klinckaerd* (now *klinker*), f. *klinken* to ring: see CLINK *v.*[1]] 1 A very hard kind of brick employed as paving in the Netherlands. M17. 2 A brick the surface of which has vitrified, or a mass of bricks that has fused, by exposure to intense heat. M17. 3 (A piece of) stony residue from burnt coal, a furnace, etc.; slag. M18. 4 (A piece of) rough scoriaceous lava resembling furnace slag. M19.

clinkery *a.* L19.

clinker /ˈklɪŋkə/ *n.*[3] L17. [f. CLINK *v.*[1] + -ER[1].] 1 A person who or thing which clinks. L17. 2 A thing, animal, or person of the first quality; an excellent specimen. Cf. CLINKING *ppl a. slang.* M19. 3 A wrong musical note, a discord; an error in performance, a blunder. *N. Amer. slang.* M20.

clinkstone /ˈklɪŋkstəʊn/ *n.* E19. [G *Klingstein*, f. as CLINK *v.*[1] + STONE *n.*] A compact greyish-blue feldspathic rock having a metallic resonance when struck.

clino- /ˈklʌɪnəʊ/ *comb. form* of Gk *klinein* to lean, slope; in *Min.* & *Cryst.* usu. w. the sense 'monoclinic': see -O-. Cf. KLINO-.

clinochlore *n.* a hexagonal variety of chlorite rich in magnesium and aluminium and usu. poor in iron M19. **clinoˈgraphic** *a.* (*a*) (of a projection) oblique, such that no surface (esp. of a crystal) is projected as a line; (*b*) (of a curve) representing gradient as a function of altitude: L19. **clinoˈpinacoid** *n.* the plane perpendicular to the axis of symmetry in the monoclinic system L19. **clinopyˈroxene** *n.* any monoclinic pyroxene E20.

clinoid /ˈklʌɪnɔɪd/ *a.* M18. [f. Gk *klinē* bed + -OID.] *Anat.* Resembling a bed; *spec.* designating four processes of the sphenoid bone surrounding the base of the pituitary gland.

clinometer /klʌɪˈnɒmɪtə, klɪ-/ *n.* E19. [f. CLINO- + -METER.] Any of various instruments for measuring inclination or elevation, esp. of sloping ground, strata, etc.

clinquant /ˈklɪŋk(ə)nt/ *a.* & *n.* L16. [Fr., pres. pple of †*clinquer* ring, glitter, f. LG *klinken* CLINK *v.*[1]: see -ANT[1].] A *adj.* Glittering with gold and silver; tinselled. L16. B *n.* Imitation gold leaf; *fig.* literary or artistic tinsel; false glitter. L17.

clint /klɪnt/ *n.* ME. [Da. & Sw. *klint*, f. OSw. *klinter* rock.] A hard or flinty rock; *spec.* (*Geol.*) any of the masses of rock left standing between fissures (grikes) in a limestone pavement; also occas., a grike.

clinty *a.* consisting of or characterized by clints E16.

cliometrics /klʌɪəˈmɛtrɪks/ *n.* M20. [f. *Clio*, the Muse of history + METRIC *n.*[1]: see -ICS.] A method of historical research making much use of statistical information and methods.

cliometric *a.* M20. **cliometrician** /klʌɪəmɛˈtrɪʃ(ə)n/ *n.* a practitioner of cliometrics M20.

clioquinol /klʌɪə(ʊ)ˈkwɪnɒl/ *n.* M20. [f. *Cl*, chemical symbol for chlorine + IO(DINE + QUINOL(INE.] *Pharm.* A quinoline derivative that has been used as an antiseptic to treat intestinal amoebiasis, diarrhoea, and ear and skin infections; 5-chloro-8-hydroxy-7-iodoquinoline, C_9H_5NOClI.

clip /klɪp/ *n.*[1] LME. [f. CLIP *v.*[2]] 1 In *pl.* Shears, esp. for wool. LME. 2 A thing which is clipped or cut; a clipping; the whole quantity of wool shorn in any place or season. E19. b An extract from a motion picture, a television programme, etc. M20. 3 An act of clipping or shearing; a haircut. E19. 4 A smart blow or stroke. M19. 5 A rate of (esp. rapid) motion. M19.

2b *Sunday Times* The illustrative clip shown on the night featured a large Chinese family. 4 J. FOWLES I felt like giving her a good clip over the earhole. 5 H. ALLEN He splashed at a sharp clip through the ford.

clip /klɪp/ *n.*[2] L15. [f. CLIP *v.*[1]] 1 A thing which clips or clasps; an instrument or device (usu. worked by a spring) that holds an object or objects fast or together, or that attaches to an object as a marker. L15. b A linked set of cartridges for a firearm. E20. c A piece of jewellery fastened by a clip. M20. †2 Embracing; an embrace. M16–L17.

1 *bicycle-clip*, *crocodile-clip*, *hair-clip*, *paper-clip*, etc.

Comb.: **clipboard** a small board with a sprung clip for holding papers etc.

clip /klɪp/ *v.*[1] Infl. **-pp-**. Pa. t. & pple **clipped**, (*arch.*) **clipt**. [OE *clyppan* = OFris. *kleppa*, f. WGmc.] 1 *v.t.* & *i.* Clasp with the arms, embrace, hug. *arch.* & *dial.* OE. 2 *v.t.* Surround closely, encircle, encompass. *arch.* OE. 3 *v.t.* & *i.* Grip tightly; fasten with a clip; fasten (a clip). OE.

2 W. COWPER Yon fair sea, That clips thy shores. 3 E. HEMINGWAY Their carbines were clipped to the frame of the bicycles. A. MACLEAN They clipped their parachute snap catches on to the overhead wire. *Which Computer?* The ribbon . . has guides that clip onto the print head.

Comb.: **clip-on** *a.* that attaches by a clip.

clip /klɪp/ *v.*[2] Infl. **-pp-**. Pa. t. & pple **clipped**, (*arch.*) **clipt**. ME. [ON *klippa*, prob. imit.: cf. LG, Fris. *klippen*.] 1 *v.t.* Cut or trim with scissors or shears; take away (part of the hair, wool, etc.) with scissors or shears (foll. by *off*). ME. b Form or mark by so cutting or trimming. L17. 2 *spec.* a *v.t.* & *i.* Shear (sheep); cut off (a sheep's fleece etc.); cut off (a person's hair), poll. ME. b *v.t.* & *i.* Pare the edges of (coinage). LME. c *v.t.* Cut out (an article, coupon, etc.) from a newspaper etc. Chiefly *N. Amer.* L19. d *v.t.* Remove a small piece of (a railway, bus, etc., ticket) to show that it has been used. L19. e *v.t. Computing.* Process (an image) so as to remove the parts outside a certain area. M20. 3 *v.t.* & (now *dial.*) *i.* Cut short, diminish; *spec.* pronounce hurriedly and imperfectly or in a staccato fashion, omit (letters or syllables) from words. E16. 4 *v.i.* a Move the wings rapidly, fly rapidly. *arch.* E17. b Move or run quickly. *US colloq.* M19. 5 *v.t.* Hit smartly; strike against in passing. *colloq.* M19. 6 *v.t.* Swindle; rob, steal. *slang* (orig. *US*). E20.

1 W. GASS She'd be clipping the hedge. W. BOYD A neatly clipped pencil moustache. *fig.*: P. G. WODEHOUSE How your grandfather clipped six seconds off Roger Bannister's mile. **clip the wings of** trim the feathers of (a bird) so as to disable from flight; *fig.* check the aspirations of, prevent (a person) from acting. b P. PEARCE Each alcove and archway clipped in the yew-trees. 3 CARLYLE Pfalz must be reinstated, though with territories much clipped. D. CUSACK A habit of clipping her sentences till they resemble explosive bullets rather than conversation. I. MURDOCH He had given her clipped answers, minimizing everything. 5 *New Statesman* He had 'clipped him round the earhole'. *Daily Express* Tony definitely had to snatch up the filly to avoid clipping the winner's heels.

Comb.: **clip-joint** *slang* a nightclub etc. charging exorbitant prices.

clip-clop /ˈklɪpklɒp/ *n.* & *v.* L19. [Imit.] A *n.* An abrupt alternating sound as of the beating of a horse's hoofs on a hard surface. L19. B *v.i.* Infl. **-pp-**. Move with or make such a sound. E20.

Also **clippety-clop** *n.* E20.

clipe *v.* & *n.* var. of CLYPE.

clipper /ˈklɪpə/ *n.* ME. [f. CLIP *v.*[2] + -ER[1].] 1 A person who clips fleeces, hair, coinage, etc. ME. 2 An instrument for clipping; in *pl.*, shears, scissors. L16. 3a A fast sailing ship, *esp.* one with raking bows and masts. E19. b A fast horse. M19. c A first-rate person or thing, an excellent specimen. *slang.* M19.

Comb.: **clipper-built** *a.* (of a sailing ship) built for speed, with raking bows and masts; **clipper ship** = sense 3a above.

clippie /ˈklɪpi/ *n. colloq.* Also **clippy**. M20. [f. CLIP *v.*[2] + -IE, -Y[6].] A bus-conductress.

clipping /ˈklɪpɪŋ/ *n.* ME. [f. CLIP *v.*[2] + -ING[1].] 1 The action of CLIP *v.*[2] ME. 2 A piece clipped off; a paring; a shred of cloth etc.; (chiefly *N. Amer.*) = CUTTING *n.* 2c. ME.

clipping /ˈklɪpɪŋ/ *a.* L16. [f. CLIP *v.*[2] + -ING[2].] 1 That clips. L16. 2 First-rate, excellent. *slang.* M19.

clippingly *adv.* M19.

clippy *n.* var. of CLIPPIE.

clipt *v.*[1], *v.*[2] pa. t. & pple: see CLIP *v.*[1], *v.*[2]

clique /kliːk/ *n.* See also CLICK *n.*[2] E18. [(O)Fr., f. *cliquer* make a noise, f. MDu. *klikken* CLICK *v.*[1]] A small exclusive group; a coterie.

cliquish *a.* resembling or suggestive of a clique or cliques; pettily exclusive: M19. **cliquishness** *n.* M19. **cliquism** *n.* the practice of forming cliques; petty exclusiveness: M19.

cliquey /ˈkliːki/ *a.* Also **cliquy**. M19. [f. prec. + -Y[1].] Characterized by cliques; cliquish.

clish-clash /ˈklɪʃklaʃ/ *n.* & *int.* L16. [Redupl. of CLASH *n.*] 1 *n.* & *int.* (Repr.) the reciprocal or alternate clash of weapons. L16. 2 *n.* Idle gossip. *Sc.* L17.

clish-ma-claver /klɪʃməˈkleɪvə/ *n. Sc.* E18. [f. *clish-* in prec. + euphonic *-ma-* + CLAVER *n.*] Idle gossip.

clit /klɪt/ *n. slang.* M20. [Abbrev.] = CLITORIS.

clitch /klɪtʃ/ *v. obs.* exc. *dial.* See also CLUTCH *v.* [OE *clyċċan* f. Gmc.] †1a *v.t.* Crook, bend; close (the hand); clench (the fist). OE–L16. b *v.i.* Crook, bend at a joint, crouch. Only in ME. 2 *v.t.* Grasp tightly, clutch. LME. 3 *v.t.* Make fast; stick together. LME.

clitellum /klʌɪˈtɛləm/ *n.* Pl. **-lla** /-lə/. M19. [mod.L f. L *clitellae* pl., pack-saddle.] *Zool.* A raised band encircling the body of oligochaete worms and some leeches, made up of reproductive segments.

clitellar *a.* L19.

clitic /ˈklɪtɪk/ *n.* & *a.* M20. [f. EN)CLITIC, PRO)CLITIC.] *Gram.* = ENCLITIC, PROCLITIC.

clitoris /ˈklɪt(ə)rɪs/ *n.* E17. [mod.L f. Gk *kleitoris*.] A small erectile part of the female genitals in mammals and some other vertebrates.

clitoral, **cliˈtorial** *adjs.* M20. **clitoriˈdectomy** *n.* (an instance of) surgical removal of the clitoris M19.

clitter /ˈklɪtə/ *v.* & *n.* E16. [Imit.: cf. CLATTER *n.*, *v.*] A *v.* †1 *v.i.* Chatter. *rare.* E16–M19. 2 *v.t.* & *i.* (Cause to) make a thin vibratory rattling sound. M16. B *n.* A thin vibratory rattling sound. L19.

clitter-clatter /ˈklɪtəklatə/ *n.* M16. [Redupl. of CLATTER *n.*] A light or repeated clatter; garrulous talk, idle gossip.

clivers *n.* var. of CLEAVERS.

clivia /ˈklʌɪvɪə/ *n.* Also **-vea**. E19. [mod.L, f. *Clive*, maiden name of Charlotte, Duchess of Northumberland (1787–1866): see -IA[1].] A southern African amaryllid of the genus *Clivia*, with orange, red, or yellow flowers. Also called *Kaffir lily*. Cf. NATAL *lily*.

clo /kləʊ/ *n.* Orig. *US.* Pl. same. M20. [f. CLO(THING. Cf. TOG *n.* 3.] A unit expressing the heat-retaining power of clothing material.

clo' /kləʊ/ *n.pl. arch. colloq.* M19. [Abbrev.] Clothes. Esp. in *old clo'*.

cloaca /kləʊˈeɪkə/ *n.* Pl. **-cae** /-siː, -kiː/, **-cas**. L16. [L *cloaca*, *cluaca* rel. to *cluere* cleanse.] 1 An underground conduit for drainage, a sewer. Also, a water-closet. L16. 2 *Zool.* A common cavity for the release of digestive and urogenital products in birds, reptiles, amphibians, most fish, and monotremes. M19.

1 *fig.*: CARLYLE That tremendous Cloaca of Pauperism.

cloacal *a.* M17.

cloak /kləʊk/ *n.* & *v.* Also (*arch.*) **cloke**. ME. [OFr. *cloke*, *cloque*, dial. var. of *cloche* (i) bell, (ii) cloak, f. med.L *clocca*: cf. CLOCK *n.*[1]] A *n.* 1 A loose usu. sleeveless outdoor garment. ME. b *fig.* A thing which covers over and conceals; a pretext; a pretence; a covering. E16. †2 An academic or clerical gown, *esp.* a Geneva gown. M17–E18. 3 In *pl.* = *cloakroom* (b) below. M20.

1 *Inverness cloak*: see INVERNESS 2. b R. W. EMERSON Tucking up . . the ground under a cloak of snow. E. WAUGH She pretends to be a painter, but you have only to look at her work to realise it is a cloak for other activities. *Plymouth cloak*: see PLYMOUTH 1.

Comb.: **cloak-and-dagger** *a.* [tr. Fr. *de cape et d'épée*] involving or characteristic of plot and intrigue, esp. espionage; **cloak-and-sword** *a.* [tr. Sp. (*comedia*) *de capa y espada*] involving or characteristic of fighting and romance; †**cloak-bag** a bag for a cloak or other clothes; a valise; **cloakroom** (*a*) a room in which to leave cloaks, coats, hats, etc., or luggage; (*b*) *euphem.* a water-closet, a lavatory; a room containing a number of lavatories.

B *v.* 1 *v.t.* Cover with or wrap in a cloak; cover over, conceal, disguise. LME. 2 *v.i.* Put on a cloak; *fig.* dissemble. L16.

cloaking *n.* (*a*) wrapping in a cloak; concealment; (*b*) material for making cloaks: E16. **cloakless** *a.* L16.

cloam /kləʊm/ *n.* & *a. obs.* exc. *SW dial.* [OE *clām* = MDu. *cleem* potter's clay, f. WGmc deriv. of Gmc base repr. also by CLAY *n.*, CLEAM, CLEAVE *v.*², CLIMB *v.*] A *n.* Orig. *gen.*, mud, clay. Later *spec.*, earthenware, potter's clay. OE. B *adj.* Earthenware. OE.

†cloath *v.* var. of CLOTHE.

†cloaths *n.pl.* var. of CLOTHES.

clobber /ˈklɒbə/ *n.*¹ & *v.*¹ M19. [Origin unkn.] A *n.* A black paste used by cobblers to fill up and conceal cracks in leather. M19. B *v.t.* 1 Patch *up*; cobble. M19. 2 Add enamelled decoration to (porcelain, esp. blue-and-white). L19.

clobber /ˈklɒbə/ *n.*² & *v.*² *slang.* L19. [Origin unkn.] A *n.* Clothing; gear, equipment. L19. B *v.t.* Dress (oneself). Freq. foll. by *up*. Chiefly as *clobbered* ppl a. L19.

clobber /ˈklɒbə/ *v.*³*t. slang.* M20. [Origin unkn.] Hit, thrash; defeat; criticize severely.

clobiosh *n.* var. of KLABERJASS.

clochard /klɔʃaːr/ *n.* Pl. pronounced same. M20. [Fr., f. *clocher* to limp.] In France: a beggar, a vagrant.

cloche /klɒʃ, kləʊʃ/ *n.* L19. [Fr. = bell: see CLOAK.] 1 A bell-glass; a small translucent (esp. glass) cover for forcing or protecting outdoor plants. L19. 2 In full *cloche hat*. A woman's close-fitting bell-shaped hat. E20.

clocher /ˈkləʊʃə/ *n.* LME. [AN *clocher*, OFr. *clochier*, (also mod.) *clocher*, f. *cloche* bell (see CLOAK) + *-er* -ER².] A bell tower; a belfry.

clock /klɒk/ *n.*¹ LME. [MLG, MDu. *klocke* (LG, Du. *klok*), corresp. to OE *clucge*, OFris. *klokke*, OHG *glocka* (G *Glocke* bell), ON *klokka*, *klucca*, f. Gmc f. med.L *clocca*: cf. CLOAK.] †1 Orig., a bell. Later, the gong of a striking watch. LME–E18. 2 An instrument for indicating or measuring time, usu. utilizing the motion of wheels controlled by periodically wound-up springs or weights or by electricity etc., or (now) utilizing vibrating atoms, piezoelectric crystals, etc., to record and show hours, minutes, etc., by hands on a dial or by displayed figures. LME. b (Usu. **C-**.) *The* constellation Horologium. M19. 3 A watch; *esp.* a stopwatch. Now *colloq.* M16. †4 The hour as struck by the clock. E17–M18. 5 The downy seed-head of a dandelion etc. M19. 6 The human face. *slang.* E20. b A punch (in the face). *slang.* M20. 7 A dial indicating pressure, consumption, etc.; *esp.* a taximeter, a speedometer, an odometer. *colloq.* M20. 8 *Computing.* An electronic device, usu. a stable oscillator, used to initiate actions within, and to synchronize, sequential logic circuits. M20.

Phrases: *Act of Parliament clock*: see PARLIAMENT *n.* *against the clock*: see AGAINST *prep.* I. *astronomical clock*: see ASTRONOMICAL I. ATOMIC *clock*. **beat the clock** complete a task before a stated time. BIOLOGICAL *clock*. *by Shrewsbury clock*: see SHREWSBURY I. *digital clock*: see DIGITAL *a.* I. *French clock*: see FRENCH *a.* *German clock*: see GERMAN *a.*¹ **hold the clock on** ascertain the time taken by. *Jack of the clock*: see JACK *n.*¹ 2. *journeyman clock*: see JOURNEYMAN 3. *master clock*: see MASTER *n.*¹ & *a.* *musical clock*: see MUSICAL *a.* *night clock*: see NIGHT *n.* O'CLOCK. *of the clock*: see OF *prep.* *punch the clock*: see PUNCH *v.* **put the clock back** reset a clock to an earlier time; *fig.* go back to a past age or earlier state of affairs; take a retrograde step. *regulator clock*: see REGULATOR 4. **round the clock** for 24 or 12 hours without intermission; all day and night; ceaselessly. **set the clock back** = *put the clock back* above. *settler's clock*: see SETTLER 2. *speaking clock*: see SPEAKING *ppl a.* *talking clock*: see TALKING *ppl a.* **turn the clock back** = *put the clock back* above. **watch the clock** eagerly wait for a particular time, esp. the end of working hours. *water-clock*: see WATER *n.*

Comb.: **clock-face** the dial-plate of a clock; **clock golf** a lawn game in which the players putt to a hole in the centre of a circle from successive points on its circumference; **clock radio** a combined clock and radio, which can be set so that the radio will come on at a desired time; **clock tower**: built for a large clock; **clock-watch** *v.i.* eagerly wait for a particular time, esp. the end of working hours; **clock-watcher** a person who clock-watches, a person who takes care not to exceed minimum working hours.

clockwise *a.* & *adv.* in the direction of movement of the hands of a clock, moving in a curve from left to right as seen from a central position L19.

clock /klɒk/ *n.*² M16. [Origin unkn.] An ornamental pattern worked on (the side of) a sock or stocking.

clock /klɒk/ *n.*³ *dial.* M16. [Origin unkn.] A beetle; *esp.* a dor beetle or cockroach (also *black clock*).

clock /klɒk/ *v.*¹ Now *Sc.* & *north.* [OE *cloccian*, cf. MDu. *clocken* (Du. *klocken*), Sw. dial. *klokka*: cf. CLUCK *v.*] 1 *v.i.* Cluck. OE. †b *v.t.* Call (chickens etc.) by clucking. LME–E18. 2 *v.i.* Of the stomach, water, etc.: gurgle. OE. 3 *v.i.* & *t.* Of a bird etc.: sit on eggs; incubate; hatch. *Sc.* & *north.* L17.

clocker *n.*¹ (*Sc.* & *north.*) a sitting hen E19.

clock /klɒk/ *v.*²*t.* M16. [f. CLOCK *n.*²] Embroider with clocks (formerly also occas. with a similar pattern). Chiefly as *clocked* ppl a.

clocker *n.*² a person who embroiders clocks E20.

clock /klɒk/ *v.*³ L19. [f. CLOCK *n.*¹] I 1 *v.t.* Time by a clock or stopwatch. L19. 2 *v.t.* Attain or register (a stated time, distance, or speed in a race etc.). Also foll. by *up*. *colloq.* L19. 3 *v.i. clock in, on, clock out, off*, register arrival, departure, by means of an automatic recording clock; *transf.* start, stop, working; arrive, leave. E20. 4 *v.t.* Look at, watch, observe, notice. *slang.* M20. II 5 *v.t.* = CLAPPER *v.* 1b. L19. 6 *v.t.* Punch in the face; hit. *slang.* M20.

clockwork /ˈklɒkwəːk/ *n.* & *a.* E17. [f. CLOCK *n.*¹ + WORK *n.*] A *n.* A mechanism utilizing the motion of wheels controlled by periodically wound up springs (as in a clock). E17.

fig.: G. BERKELEY The clockwork of nature. M. R. MITFORD This jewel of a valet, this matchless piece of clock-work. **(as) regular as clockwork, like clockwork** smooth(ly), regular(ly), automatic(ally).

B *attrib.* or as *adj.* Operated by clockwork; of or like clockwork. M18.

S. E. FERRIER A very . . quiet, old-fashioned family, quite clock-work in our ways and hours. V. NABOKOV Mere springs and coils produced the movement of our clockwork man.

clod /klɒd/ *n.* LME. [Var. of CLOT *n.*] †1 A coagulated mass; a clot of blood etc. LME–M18. 2 A mass *of* solid matter; a lump of earth, clay, loam, etc., *esp.* one formed by ploughing. LME. b A sod, a turf. *obs.* exc. *dial.* L16. 3 A coarse cut of meat from the lower neck of an ox. L15. 4 Earth, clay, lumpy soil. L16. b *Mining.* Soft shale, esp. over a coal-seam. M19. 5 *fig.* A human body, a human being, as non-spiritual or mortal. L16. 6 *fig.* A blockhead; a clumsy awkward person; a dull unresponsive person; a dolt. Cf. CLOT *n.* 3. Now *colloq.* L16. 7 A small loaf of (esp. coarse) bread. *Sc.* L18. 8 A copper coin. *slang.* E20.

2 MILTON Two massie clods of Iron and Bras. W. SEWEL Clods and stones were thrown at him. 4 **the clod** *spec.* the earth as a place for burial. 5 SPENSER Us wretched earthly clods. 6 R. D. BLACKMORE The Doones were of very high birth, as all we clods of Exmoor knew. J. RABAN His portrait of desert life is so loving . . that one would be a clod not to be moved by it.

Comb.: **clodhopper** *colloq.* (*a*) a ploughman, an agricultural labourer; a country bumpkin; a clumsy awkward person; (*b*) a large clumsy shoe (usu. in *pl.*); **clodhopping** *a.* (*colloq.*) large and clumsy, awkward, loutish; **clodpate** *arch.* a blockhead; **clodpated** *a.* (*arch.*) blockheaded; **clodpole, -poll** a blockhead; a bumpkin, a lout.

cloddish *a.* somewhat like a clod, boorishly stolid, clumsy and awkward M19. **cloddy** *a.* †(*a*) characterized by clots, clotted, coagulated; (*b*) characterized by or full of clods; (*c*) like a clod, cloddish: LME.

clod /klɒd/ *v.* Infl. **-dd-**. LME. [f. the n.: cf. CLOT *v.*] 1 *v.t.* Clear (land) of clods etc. *obs.* exc. *Sc. dial.* LME. †2 *v.t.* Cover with clods; enclose (as) in clods. LME–E17. 3 *v.i.* & *t.* †a Clot, coagulate. LME–M18. b Stick together in clods, form into clods. Chiefly as *clodded* ppl a. M16. 4 *v.t.* Pelt with clods, throw clods, stones, etc., at; drive *away*, *out* with clods, stones, etc. Chiefly *Sc.* & *dial.* E16. 5 *v.t.* Heave, throw heavily. *Sc.* & *north.* L18.

clodder /ˈklɒdə/ *n.* Long *dial.* *rare.* LME. [f. next.] A clotted or curdled mass; a clot.

clodder *v.* var. of CLOTTER.

cloff /klɒf/ *n.* E16. [Origin unkn.] *Hist.* A proportion of the weight of certain wholesale commodities given to cover inaccuracies in retailing in smaller quantities.

clog /klɒg/ *n.* ME. [Origin unkn.] 1 A block of wood, etc., to prevent or hinder movement, loss, or escape; *fig.* an impediment, an encumbrance. ME. 2 A thick piece of wood, a log. *obs.* exc. *Sc.* LME. 3 A heavy shoe or overshoe with a wooden sole; a heavy wooden shoe with an upturned pointed toe of a type traditionally worn in the Netherlands. LME. †4 A fir cone, a pine cone. L16–E18. 5 *Hist.* A calendar cut on the sides of a square (usu. wooden) block. L17.

1 C. LAMB I never tied tin-kettle, clog, Or salt-box to the tail of dog. C. V. WEDGWOOD That clog on their action—the powerless, reduced but obstructive House of Lords.

Phrases: **clogs to clogs in three generations** the return of a family to poverty after one generation of prosperity. *pop one's clogs*: see POP *v.* 2.

Comb.: **clog-almanac** *Hist.* = sense 5 above; **clog-dance** a dance performed in clogs with rhythmic beating of the feet; *transf.* a dance imitating this; **clog-dancer** a person who performs a clog-dance.

clogger *n.* (*a*) a maker of clogs; (*b*) *slang* a player in soccer who habitually fouls in tackling: M18. **clogginess** *n.* the state or quality of being cloggy L18. **cloggy** *a.* lumpy, knotty; sticky; full of clogging matter: L16.

clog /klɒg/ *v.* Infl. **-gg-**. LME. [f. the n.] 1 *v.t.* Fasten a clog to, impede (an animal etc.) with a clog; fasten by a clog; encumber, hamper, hinder. LME. 2 *v.t.* Obstruct or encumber by stickiness. E16. 3a *v.t.* Fill up or *up* so as to hinder free passage, action, or function. L16. b *v.i.* Become filled (*up*) so as to hinder free passage, action, or function. M17. 4 *v.t.* Satiate, surfeit, cloy. *obs.* exc. *dial.* L16. 5 *v.t.* Put wooden soles on (shoes etc.). M17. 6 *v.i.* Perform a clog-dance. E20.

1 SHELLEY Superstition . . has . . clogged man to earth. A. W. KINGLAKE The whole flotilla would be clogged by the slowness of the sailing vessels. A. POWELL Extraneous detail that can clog a narrative. 2 A. T. ELLIS Her boots were clogged with mud. 3a W. DUFTON When the Eustachian tube is clogged up with mucus. H. KISSINGER The White House switchboard was clogged with congratulatory phone calls. b F. L. WRIGHT Broken stone does not clog up.

cloison /ˈklɔɪz(ə)n; *foreign* klwazɔ̃ (*pl. same*)/ *n.* L17. [Fr.] A partition, a division.

cloisonné /klwazɔne/ *a.* & *n.* M19. [Fr., pa. pple of *cloisonner* to partition, f. as prec.] More fully *cloisonné enamel*. (Designating) enamel-work or -ware in which the colours in the pattern are separated by thin strips of metal etc.

cloister /ˈklɔɪstə/ *n.* & *v.* ME. [OFr. *clo(i)stre* (mod. *cloître*) f. L *claustrum*, *clostrum* lock, bar, enclosed space, f. *claus-* pa. ppl stem of *claudere* CLOSE *v.* + *-trum* instr. suff.] A *n.* 1 A place of religious seclusion; a convent, a monastic house. ME. 2 *sing.* & (freq.) in *pl.* A covered place for walking, often round a quadrangle with a wall on the outer and a colonnade or windows on the inner side, esp. of convent, college, or cathedral buildings. ME. 3 An enclosed space, an enclosure. *obs.* exc. as passing into fig. uses of senses 1, 2. LME.

1 **the cloister** monastic life, seclusion.

Comb.: **cloister-garth** the open court enclosed by a cloister.

B *v.t.* 1 Surround (as) with a cloister; convert into a cloister. LME. 2 Enclose or shut *up* in a cloister or religious house. L16. 3 Shut up in a secluded place. L16. 4 *fig.* Confine, restrain within narrow limits. E17.

cloistered *a.* shut up (as) in a cloister; secluded, sheltered, (*lit.* & *fig.*): L16. **cloisterer** *n.* (now *rare*) a person who lives in a cloister, a monk or nun ME. **cloisterless** *a.* LME. **cloisterly** *a.* of, pertaining to, or characteristic of a cloister L16. †**cloistress** *n.* (*rare*, Shakes.) a nun: only in E17.

cloistral /ˈklɔɪstr(ə)l/ *a.* E17. [f. CLOISTER *n.* + -AL[1]; cf. med.L *claustralis*, (O)Fr. *claustral*.] Of or pertaining to a cloister; monastic; belonging to a monastic order.

cloke *n.*[1] see CLUTCH *n.*[1]

cloke *n.*[2] & *v.* see CLOAK.

cloky *n.* see CLOQUÉ.

clomb *v.* see CLIMB *v.*

clomp /klɒmp/ *v.* & *n.* Also (*Sc.*) **clomph** /klɒmf/. E19. [Imit.: cf. CLAMP *n.*[3] & *v.*[3], CLUMP *n.*, *v.*] A *v.i.* = CLUMP *v.* 1. E19. B *n.* = CLUMP *n.* 4. M19.

clone /kləʊn/ *n.* & *v.* E20. [Gk *klōn* twig, slip.] A *n.* 1 A group of organisms (orig. plants) produced by asexual means from a single ancestor to which they are genetically identical. E20. 2 An individual organism so produced; an animal or person that develops from one somatic cell of its parent and is genetically identical to that parent. L20. b Each of two or more identical people, an imitator, a double; a copy, *esp.* a microcomputer designed to simulate another (more expensive) model. L20. B *v.t.* Propagate or produce as a clone; create genetically identical copies of. M20.

clonal *a.* E20. **clonally** *adv.* M20.

clonic /ˈklɒnɪk/ *a.* M19. [f. CLONUS + -IC.] *Med.* Of, pertaining to, or of the nature of clonus. Opp. TONIC *a.* 1.

tonic-clonic: see TONIC *a.* 1.

clonk /klɒŋk/ *n.*, *int.*, & *v.* M19. [Imit.: cf. CLANK, CLINK *n.*[1], *v.*[1], CLUNK *v.* & *n.*[2]] A *n.* & *int.* (Repr.) an abrupt heavy metallic sound of impact. M19. B *v.* 1 *v.i.* Move with or make a clonk or clonks. M19. 2 *v.t.* Hit forcibly. *colloq.* M20.

clonus /ˈkləʊnəs/ *n.* E19. [L f. Gk *klonos* turmoil.] *Med.* Muscular spasm involving repeated, often rhythmic, contractions.

†**clooch** *n.* see CLUTCH *n.*[1]

cloop /kluːp/ *n.* & *v.i.* M19. [Imit.] (Make) a muted popping sound, as of a cork being drawn from a bottle.

cloose *n.* see CLOW.

cloot /kluːt/ *n.* *Sc.* & *north.* E18. [Prob. f. ON *kló* CLAW *n.*[1]] 1 (A division of) a cloven hoof. E18. 2 In *pl.* C-. The Devil. *colloq.* L18.

Clootie *n.* (*colloq.*) the Devil L18.

clop /klɒp/ *n.* & *v.* Freq. redupl. **clop-clop**. Also (now *rare*) **k-**. See also CLIP-CLOP. M19. [Imit.] A *n.* An abrupt sound as of heavy shoes or a horse's hoofs on a hard surface. M19. B *v.i.* Infl. **-pp-**. Move with or make such a sound. M19.

cloqué /ˈkləʊkeɪ/ *n.* Also Anglicized as **cloky** /ˈkləʊki/. E20. [Fr., lit. 'blistered'.] A fabric with an irregularly raised or embossed surface.

closable /ˈkləʊzəb(ə)l/ *a.* Also **close-**. E20. [f. CLOSE *v.* + -ABLE.] Able to be closed.

¶ Earlier in UNCLOSABLE.

close /kləʊs/ *n.*[1] ME. [(O)Fr. *clos* f. L *clausum* closed place, enclosure, use as n. of neut. pa. pple of *claudere* CLOSE *v.*] I 1 *gen.* An enclosed place, an enclosure. ME. 2 a An enclosure about or beside a building. Long *obs.* in *gen.* sense. ME. b *spec.* The precinct of a cathedral. Formerly also, the precinct of any sacred place, a cloister. LME. c A farmyard. Now *dial.* LME. 3 a A field, an enclosed piece of land. Now *dial.* & *Law.* LME. b A playing field at certain English public schools. L19. 4 An entry, a passage, an alleyway. Chiefly *Sc.*, an entry from a street to a common stairway or a court at the back of a building; also, a common stairway or court with such an entry. LME. 5 A (usu. short) street closed at one end, a cul-de-sac. Freq. in proper names. E18.

1 TENNYSON I lay Pent in a roofless close of ragged stones. **break a close, a person's close** *Law* trespass on another's land. 3b H. NEWBOLT There's a breathless hush in the Close to-night, Ten to make and the match to win!

†II 6 An enclosing line, a circuit, a boundary. ME–M17.

close /kləʊz/ *n.*[2] LME. [f. CLOSE *v.*] 1 An act of coming to an end; an end, a conclusion. LME. †2 The closing passage of a speech, argument, etc. L16–M18. 3 *Mus.* The conclusion of a phrase, a cadence. L16. 4 A closing or uniting together; union, junction. Chiefly *poet.* L16. 5 A closing in fight, a grapple, a struggle. *arch.* L16.

3 PLAGAL *close*.

close /kləʊs/ *a.* & *adv.* LME. [(O)Fr. *clos* f. L *clausus* pa. pple of *claudere* CLOSE *v.*] A *adj.* I Of a closed condition or its results. 1 Closed, shut; having no part left open. LME. b *Her.* Of wings: folded to the body. E17. c *Phonet.* Of a vowel: articulated with the tongue in a relatively high position. E17. 2 Shut up in prison etc., under strict restraint. Of confinement: strict. LME. 3 Concealed from observation; hidden, secret, secluded; *arch.* private, snug. LME. 4 Secretive, reticent, reserved. LME. †5 Rigorous, severe. LME–L18. 6 Enclosed, esp. with walls or barriers; shut *in* or away *from*; confined, contracted; narrow. L15. 7 Of air, atmosphere, etc.: stuffy, airless, stifling. L16. 8 Stingy, niggardly; grudging any expense. M17. 9 Restricted or limited to a privileged few. E19. 10 Under prohibition; during which something is prohibited. E19.

1 A. TROLLOPE I've brought a close carriage for him. 2 WELLINGTON Captain—is in close arrest. 3 S. JOHNSON A close room, an easy chair. I. MURDOCH She kept this interlude a close secret and never spoke of it to anyone. 4 DICKENS He was too close to name his circumstances to me. 5 J. WESLEY She had close trials from her poor, apostate husband. 6 W. OWEN Down the close, darkening lanes they sang their way. 7 A. PATON It was close and sultry, and soon there would be thunder. S. BELLOW The house was close and faintly sour with furniture polish. 8 A. S. BYATT He would break a close northern habit of meanness to provide champagne. 9 BOSW. SMITH These . . filled up the vacancies . . from among themselves, like the members of a close college.

II Of proximity of space or time. 11 Dense or compact in texture or arrangement; with no or only slight intervals. Cf. earlier B.4 below. L15. b Detailed, concentrated, searching, thorough; leaving no gaps or weaknesses. M17. 12 Of an item of clothing etc.: fitting exactly or tightly. L15. 13 Very near in relation or connection; intimate, confidential. Cf. earlier B.5 below. L16. b Of a translation etc.: following or resembling the original to a large extent. E18. 14 Very near in position; in or nearly in contact; narrowly escaped. Cf. earlier B.5 below. E17. 15 Of a contest, its outcome, etc.: nearly equal, narrowly decided. M19.

11 DRYDEN In close plantations. T. HARDY Their vans . . were drawn up . . in close file. b COLERIDGE A close reasoner. E. A. BOND Under a close cross-questioning. F. R. LEAVIS *Close analytical* study of a few poems. 13 W. PALEY In close conformity with the Scripture account. P. SCOTT No close friend by whom to be comforted. C. CONNOLLY With the sea . . his relations were always close and harmonious. P. V. WHITE We were a very close family. 14 J. HELLER The tables in the delicatessen were small and close.

B *adv.* (Some pred. uses of the adj. pass into this.) 1 In or into a closed position. LME. 2 In concealment, hiding, or strict confinement. LME. †3 Secretly, covertly. LME–M17. 4 Tightly; fast; densely, compactly; so as to leave no interstices or openings; searchingly, thoroughly. LME. 5 Very near in position, relation, or connection; in or into immediate proximity or intimacy. LME. 6 *gen.* In a close manner; closely. M17.

2 A. S. BYATT We must keep our secrets close. 4 C. THIRLWALL The closer they are examined, the more suspicious do they appear. 5 JOSEPH HALL Let us pile up all close together. J. C. POWYS The courage . . to move up close to him. I. MCEWAN They kissed and sat close.

Special collocations, comb., & phrases: *as close as it* or *one can stick*: see STICK *v.*[1] *at close range*: see RANGE *n.*[1] *close as wax*: see WAX *n.*[1] *close borough*: see BOROUGH *n.* 3. **close by** very near (to). **close call** *colloq.* = *close shave* below. **close-carpet** *v.t.* cover the whole floor of (a room) with carpet. *close communion*: see COMMUNION 5. **close-cropped** *a.* (of hair) cut very short. †**close-fights** *pl.* = *close quarters* (a) below. **close-fisted** *a.* that keeps the hand tightly shut; chiefly *fig.*, niggardly, grudging. **close-fitting** *a.* (of a garment) fitting closely to the body. **close-grained** *a.* without gaps between fibres etc. **close-handed** *a.* (*arch.*) = *close-fisted* above. **close harmony** the singing of parts within an octave or twelfth. **close-hauled** *a.* (of a ship) with sails hauled aft to sail close to the wind. **close-knit** *a.* intimately united by common interests, marriage, etc. **close-lipped** *a.* with tightly set lips; *fig.* reticent, discreet. **close mourning** *arch.* deep mourning. **close-mouthed** *a.* = *close-lipped* above. **close on** very near to, nearly. *close port*: see PORT *n.*[1] **close quarters** *pl.* (*a*) *Hist.* barriers across a ship's decks providing a place of retreat for the crew and with holes for firing at a hostile boarding party; (*b*) direct contact, esp. with an enemy; uncomfortable nearness; (*at close quarters*, very near, from a very short distance). **close-reef** *v.t.* (*Naut.*) reef closely, take in all the reefs of (a sail or ship). **close season** a period when something is forbidden by law, as the killing of game, or does not take place, as the playing of cricket or another organized sport. **close shave** a narrow escape, a near thing. **close-stool** a chamber-pot enclosed in a stool with a cover. **close thing** = *close shave* above. *close to home*: see HOME *n.* & *a.* *close to the bone*: see BONE *n.* **close to the wind** *Naut.* against the wind as nearly as is compatible with its filling the sails. **close upon** = *close on* above. *hold* etc. *one's cards close to one's chest*: see CHEST *n.* MAISON *close*. *pound close*: see POUND *n.*[2] 1a.

closen *v.t.* & *i.* make or become close(r), close up M19. **closish** *a.* fairly close M19.

close /kləʊz/ *v.* ME. [(O)Fr. *clos-* pa. ppl stem of *clore* f. L *claudere* shut, close.] 1 *v.t.* Enclose, confine, encompass; *fig.* include, contain. (Foll. by *in*, *within*.) *arch.* ME. 2 *v.t.* Cover or block (an opening); move (a lid, door, etc.) so as to cover or block an opening; cover or block up the opening(s) of (a box, room, etc.); officially prohibit access to (a public building etc.), declare to be no longer open. ME. 3 *v.i.* Become enclosed, covered or blocked up, or (esp. officially) inaccessible; become or be declared to be no longer open; move so as to cover or block an opening (foll. by *over*, (*up*)*on* a person who or a thing which has entered). LME. 4 *v.t.* Bring to an end; conclude, complete, settle (a bargain etc.). LME. 5 *v.i.* Come to an end; conclude, finish speaking or writing (*with* a particular remark etc.). LME. b *v.i.* Of stocks or shares: be *at* a particular price at the close of a day's trading. M19. 6 *v.t.* Bring closer or into contact; draw together so as to eliminate gaps or openings. LME. b Join together the uppers of (a boot or shoe). E19. c Make (an electric circuit etc.) continuous. L19. 7 *v.i.* Come closer or into contact; coalesce, meet in a common centre; draw near, approach close. LME. b Come within striking distance, come to close quarters, grapple (*with*). L16. 8 *v.i.* Come to terms, come to an agreement, (*with*); agree *with*, (*up*)*on* an offer, terms, etc. E17. 9 *v.t.* Chiefly *Naut.* Come close to or alongside of. L17.

1 W. PRYNNE They . . closed him in a monastery. TENNYSON I clung to all the present for the promise that it closed. 2 T. GRAY Now my weary lips I close. LD MACAULAY An attempt . . to close the coffee houses. P. KAVANAGH The potato-stalks closed the alleys. T. KENEALLY They closed the . . pasture gates behind them. T. BERGER He sprinkled a bit of salt into the pot before closing it with the lid. *close a gap*: see GAP *n.* *close one's eyes, heart, mind*, (*to, against*): see EYE *n.*, HEART *n.*, MIND *n.*[1] *close the books*: see BOOK *n.* *close the door on, to*: see DOOR *n.* 3 DICKENS On June 24th the eyes of the brilliant comedian closed upon the world. JAN MORRIS The Cowley works close for their annual holidays. 4 G. SAINTSBURY Dryden . . at once closed the period of his own contemporaries and opened a new one. 5 D. J. ENRIGHT I want to close by reading three poems. C. IVES The day of leaders, as such, is gradually closing. 6 E. HEMINGWAY My hands were so sore I could hardly close them over the oars. **close ranks** *fig.* maintain solidarity. 7 SHAKES. *Hen. V* As many lines close in the dial's centre. R. SUTCLIFF Closing round them as a wolf-pack closes round its prey. b C. ISHERWOOD They closed . . and staggered grappling about the room. 8 H. BELLOC Mr. Foley was glad that he came to a sensible business decision . . and closed with him. W. GOLDING I closed . . with this very advantageous offer. 9 F. MARRYAT We . . closed the admiral's ship, and the captain went on board.

With advs. in specialized senses: **close down** (*a*) *v.phr.t.* close by forcing or fastening down; (*b*) *v.phr.t.* & *i.* stop the functioning of, stop functioning, esp. permanently; (of a broadcasting station) end transmission until the next day. **close in** (*a*) *v.phr.t.* confine by covering or blocking the means of egress, hem in, enclose; (*b*) *v.phr.t.* shut with inward motion; †(*c*) *v.phr.i.* come to agreement *with*; (*d*) *v.phr.i.* come into contact or to close quarters *with*; (*e*) *v.phr.i.* come nearer so as to surround or envelop; (of days etc.) get successively shorter; (foll. by (*up*)*on*). **close off** *v.phr.t.* prevent access to by covering or blocking the means of entrance. **close out** *v.phr.t.* (*N. Amer.*) clear out (stock etc.), bring (a business etc.) to a close, dispose of, discontinue. **close up** (*a*) *v.phr.t.* confine or prevent access to by covering or blocking the opening(s); cover or block up completely; shut, esp. temporarily; bring the parts of closer together or into contact; (*b*) *v.phr.t.* (*arch.*) bring to an end; (*c*) *v.phr.i.* move closer (*to*); coalesce; become more dense or compact.

closeable *a.* var. of CLOSABLE.

closed /kləʊzd/ *ppl a.* ME. [f. CLOSE *v.* + -ED[1].] 1 *gen.* That has been closed; not open. ME. 2 Limited in number or by certain conditions; self-contained, not communicating with others. L19. b *Math.* Limited in some specified way; *esp.* (of a set) having the property that the result of a specified operation on any element of the set is itself a member of the set; also, (of a set) containing all its limit points. E20.

Special collocations & comb.: *closed book*: see BOOK *n.* **closed-circuit** *a.* (of television) for a restricted number of receivers by use of wires not waves for transmission. **closed door** *fig.* an obstacle, an impasse, a restriction; *behind closed doors*, in secret, in private. **closed-door** *a.* restricted, obstructive, secret. **closed-end** *a.* having a predetermined extent. *closed loop*: see LOOP *n.*[2] 13. **closed season** *N. Amer.* = *close season* s.v. CLOSE *a.* & *adv.* **closed shop** (the system obtaining in) a workshop or other establishment where only members of a trade union may be employed. **closed society**: characterized by a rigid system of beliefs, resisting all contact with other systems, and hostile to any structural change. **closed syllable**: ending in a consonant.

closely /ˈkləʊsli/ *adv.* LME. [f. CLOSE *a.* + -LY[2].] In a close manner; so as to be or make close.

SHAKES. *Haml.* We have closely sent for Hamlet hither. OED Henry was closely confined in the Tower. D. H. LAWRENCE He followed her closely. J. BUCHAN A sheet of yellowish parchment, covered closely with Greek characters. J. CARY He listened closely to the details of fashionable life. G. GREENE He leant closely to the canvas. J. MITCHELL The men were in closely tailored slacks or jeans.

closeness /ˈkləʊsnɪs/ *n.* LME. [f. CLOSE *a.* + -NESS.] The state or quality of being close.

SWIFT Almost stifled by the closeness of the room. H. A. L. FISHER The old Norse literature . . stands out . . for . . its closeness to the facts of life. C. FREEMAN She felt a strange closeness to the actors on the stage.

closer /ˈkləʊzə/ *n.* LME. [f. CLOSE *v.* + -ER[1].] 1 *gen.* A person who or thing which closes something; a person who or thing which forms a close. LME. 2 A worker who joins together the uppers of boots or shoes. E18. 3 A stone or brick smaller than the rest, used to end a course of brickwork etc. E18.

closet /ˈklɒzɪt/ *n.* & *a.* LME. [OFr., dim. of *clos*: see CLOSE *n.*[1], -ET[1].] A *n.* 1 A private or small room, *esp.* one used for private interviews, devotions, or study. LME. 2 The private apartment of a monarch. Now *Hist.* LME. 3 A room etc. for urination and defecation; a lavatory. L15. 4a A private repository of valuables, curiosities, etc.; a cabinet. Now chiefly in *china-closet* (passing into sense b). E17. b A cupboard, a recess for storage. Now *dial.* & *N. Amer.* E17.

2 **Clerk of the Closet** the British monarch's principal chaplain. 3 *water-closet*: see WATER *n.* 4b **come out of the closet** *fig.* stop hiding something about oneself, esp. one's homosexuality; come to public notice or view. *skeleton in the closet*: see SKELETON *n.*

Comb.: **closet play** a play to be read rather than acted.

B *attrib.* or as *adj.* Concealed, secret, private. E17.

Sunday Telegraph He was not a closet Papist intoxicated by bells and fancy vestments. **closet queen** *slang* a man who conceals his homosexuality.

closet /ˈklɒzɪt/ *v.t.* L16. [f. the n.] Shut up (or †*up*) in a closet; detain for a private consultation etc. Freq. in *pass.*, be in private consultation (*with*).

LD MACAULAY Some of the Churchmen whom he had closeted had offered to make large concessions. C. S. FORESTER He was closeted alone with Hudson for a long time.

close-up /ˈkləʊsʌp/ *n.* E20. [f. CLOSE *a.* & *adv.* + UP *adv.*[1]] A photograph or film taken at short range and showing the subject on a large scale; *fig.* an intimate and detailed description.

medium close-up: see MEDIUM *a.*

closh /klɒʃ/ *n.* E19. [Origin unkn.] A spiked upright block on the deck of a whaling vessel, on which blubber is cut up.

closing /ˈkləʊzɪŋ/ *n.* LME. [f. CLOSE *v.* + -ING[1].] The action of CLOSE *v.*, an act or instance of this; *esp.* the prohibition of access to a public building, the declaration that a shop etc. is no longer open.

early closing, *Sunday closing*, etc.

Comb.: **closing-time** the set time at which a public building or place, *spec.* a public-house, is closed.

clostridium /klɒˈstrɪdɪəm/ *n.* Pl. **-dia** /-dɪə/. L19. [mod.L f. Gk *klōstēr* spindle: see -IDIUM.] A rod-shaped anaerobic bacterium of the large genus *Clostridium*, which includes many pathogenic species, e.g. those causing tetanus, gas gangrene, botulism, and other forms of food poisoning.

clostridial *a.* of, pertaining to, or caused by such bacteria M20.

closure /ˈkləʊʒə/ *n.* & *v.* LME. [OFr. f. late L *clausura*, f. *claus-* pa. ppl stem of *claudere* CLOSE *v.*: see -URE.] A *n.* †I 1 A thing which encloses, shuts in, or confines. LME–L19. b Bound, limit, circuit. L16–M17. 2 An enclosed place; *spec.* a fortification, an entrenchment. LME–E17. 3 Enclosing. LME–E18.

II 4 An act of closing or shutting. LME. 5†a A fontanelle of the skull. LME–M16. b A thing by which another thing is closed or fastened, a fastener. E17. 6 The state or condition of being closed. M19. b *Math.* The condition or property of being closed (sense 2b); a function, operation, etc., which produces this condition; the smallest closed set that contains a given set; the closed set obtained from a given set by adding all the limit points of the latter. E20.

III 7 A bringing to an end; a conclusion; a close. LME. 8 In a legislative assembly, a decision, by vote or under rules, to put a question without further debate. L19.

8 *kangaroo closure*: see KANGAROO *n.* 3.

†IV 9 An agreement, a union, (*with*). Only in M17.

B *v.t.* Apply closure to (a motion, speakers, etc.) in a legislative assembly. L19.

clot /klɒt/ *n.* See also CLOD *n.* [OE *clot*(*t*) = MHG *kloz* (G *Klotz*), f. Gmc: cf. CLEAT, CLOUT *n.*[1]] 1 A mass of material stuck or matted together; a semi-solid lump of coagulated liquid, esp. one formed from blood exposed to air. OE. 2 = CLOD *n.* 2. Long *dial.* ME. 3 = CLOD *n.* 4. Now *rare.* LME. 4 *fig.* A clumsy awkward person; (now more commonly) a stupid person, a dolt. Cf. CLOD *n.* 6. Now *colloq.* M17.

1 R. ADAMS A flat, wet clot of dead leaves. 4 T. RATTIGAN Johnny, you clot! What about that beer?

Comb.: †**clot-bird** the wheatear; **clotpole, -poll** *arch.* = *clodpole, -poll* s.v. CLOD *n.*

clottish *a.* (*colloq.*) stupid, somewhat blockheaded M20. **clotty** *a.* (now *rare*) full of clots or lumps, inclined to clot LME.

clot /klɒt/ *v.* Infl. **-tt-**. LME. [f. the n.: cf. CLOD *v.*] 1a *v.i.* Break up clods. Long *dial.* LME. b *v.t.* Clear (land) of clods. Long *dial.* M16. 2a *v.i.* Form into clots; congeal, coagulate. LME. b *v.t.* Cause to form into clots; mat with sticky matter; cover with clots of dirt etc. L17.

2a A. KOESTLER The people were clotting into groups, chattering excitedly. D. MORRIS Blood spilled . . will clot more quickly. b D. WELCH The autumn leaves were clotted into great coloured lumps. E. BOWEN Dead leaves clotted and marred the lake.

clot-bur /ˈklɒtbəː/ *n.* Now *dial.* M16. [f. next + BUR *n.*[1]] Burdock.

clote /kləʊt/ *n.* Now *dial.* [OE *clāte* f. Gmc base meaning 'to stick': rel. to CLAY *n.*] Burdock, or another plant resembling it; the yellow water lily (also *water clote*).

cloth /klɒθ/ *n.* & *a.* [OE *clāþ* = OFris. *klāth*, *klēth*, MDu. *kleet* (Du. *kleed*), MHG *kleit* (G *Kleid*), of unkn. origin.] A *n.* Pl. **cloths**, CLOTHES. I (A piece of) fabric. 1 A piece of woven or felted material, suited for any of various purposes (identified contextually or specified), as wrapping, spreading, wiping, covering, etc. OE. b A tablecloth. ME. †c A canvas for painting on, a painted canvas. L17–E19. d *Theatr.* A large piece of painted scenery. See also BACKCLOTH 1. L19. 2 *Naut.* †a A sail. Only in LME. b The sails of a ship collectively. M17. c Each of the breadths of canvas of which a sail is composed. L17. 3 A particular length or quantity of woven fabric; a 'piece'. *obs.* exc. *dial.* LME. 4 Fabric woven or felted from animal, vegetable, mineral, or synthetic fibres; *esp.* woollen woven fabric used for clothes. LME.

1 *altar-cloth*, *dust-cloth*, *loincloth*, *neckcloth*, *tablecloth*, *tea cloth*, etc. **cloth of estate**, **state** a cloth erected over a throne or chair as a sign of rank, a canopy. †**painted cloth** a painted or embroidered wall-hanging, a tapestry. 4 *broadcloth*, *Lancaster cloth*, *long cloth*, *oilcloth*, *sackcloth*, etc. **cloth of gold, of silver**, tissue of gold, silver, threads interwoven with silk or wool. *cloth of* TARS. **cut one's coat according to one's cloth** adapt expenditure to resources, limit one's ambition to what is feasible.

II As clothing. †5a A garment. OE–LME. b Clothing, dress. ME–E19. †6 The distinctive clothing worn by employees of the same person or members of the same profession; livery. LME–E19. 7 *transf.* One's profession as shown by clothes, esp. clerical. M17.

7 *man of the cloth*: see MAN *n.* **the cloth** the clergy.

B *attrib.* or as *adj.* Made of cloth. L16.

Comb. & *special collocations*: **cloth-binding** the cover of a book in cloth over boards; **cloth-bound** *a.* having a cloth-binding; **cloth-cap** *a.* pertaining to or characteristic of the working class; **cloth-eared** *a.* (*colloq.*) having poor hearing, insensitive to sound; **cloth ears** *colloq.* (a person with) poor hearing; **cloth-head** *colloq.* a stupid person, a dolt; **cloth-headed** *a.* (*colloq.*) stupid, foolish; **cloth-worker** a maker or manufacturer of cloth; **cloth-yard shaft** *Hist.* an arrow a yard long.

clothe /kləʊð/ *v.* Also †**cloath**. Pa. t. & pple **clothed**, (*arch.*, *techn.*, & *formal*) **clad** /klad/. See also YCLAD. [OE (*ġe*)*claþod*, -*ed* ppl a., f. prec. Infl. by ON *klæða*, *klæddr* pa. t. & pple.] I *lit.* 1 *v.t.* Provide with clothes; put clothes upon; dress. (Foll. by *in*, *with*.) OE. b *spec.* Invest in a religious habit. E17. †2 *v.t.* Put on as clothing, don. Only in ME. 3 *v.t.* Cover with a cloth or cloths. LME. b *Naut.* Rig (a ship, mast, etc.). E18. 4 *v.i.* Put clothes on, dress oneself; be clothed. Now *rare.* LME.

1 SPENSER In mighty armes he was yclad anon, And silver shield. MILTON He clad Thir nakedness with Skins of Beasts. TENNYSON The hand that . . often toil'd to clothe your little ones. B. TRAPIDO Jane would . . clothe herself . . in a dowdy two-piece.

II *fig.* 5 *v.t.* Cover as with clothes or a cloth. (Foll. by *in*, *with*.) ME. 6 *v.t.* Conceal the true nature or form of, disguise. (Foll. by *in*, *with*.) LME. 7 *v.t.* Invest or endue *with* a character, attributes, etc.; endow *with* power, a liability, etc. E17. 8 *v.t.* Express (thoughts, ideas, etc.) *in*, *with*. L17.

5 SIR W. SCOTT Will spring return . . And blossoms clothe the hawthorn spray? CARLYLE Thus he [Man] is also said to be clothed with a body. H. BELLOC A wood . . clothing a rocky peak. 6 E. J. HOWARD Men had more practice at dressing up their lusts, or . . no need to clothe them. 7 BUNYAN With such gravity cloath every page. T. JEFFERSON The clauses . . clothing consuls with privileges of the law of nations.

clotheless /ˈkləʊðlɪs/ *a.* Also †**clothless**. LME. [f. CLOTH *n.* + -LESS.] Without clothes, destitute of clothing.

clothes /kləʊðz, kləʊz/ *n.pl.* Also †**cloaths**, (*Sc.* & *north.*) **claes** /kleɪz/. [OE *clāþas* pl. of CLOTH *n.*] 1 Things worn to cover the body and limbs. Freq. in comb. w. wd specifying purpose. OE. b Clothing etc. for washing; laundry. LME. †2 Swaddling-clothes. ME–M18. 3 Bedclothes. ME.

1 *bedclothes, swaddling-clothes, underclothes*, etc. *change of clothes*: see CHANGE *n.* 2. *old clothes man*: see OLD *a.*

Comb.: **clothes-bag**, **-basket**: for holding or conveying clothes to be washed; **clothes-brush** a stiff brush for removing dust, dirt, etc., from clothes; **clothes-conscious** *a.* aware of or concerned with clothes; **clothes-drier** a device for drying washed or wet clothes; *rotary clothes-drier*: see ROTARY *a.*; **clothes-hanger** a shaped piece of wood, wire, etc., from which clothes can be hung in the normal shape, a coat-hanger; **clothes-horse** a frame for airing washed clothes; *fig.*, an affectedly fashionable person; **clothes-line** a rope, wire, etc., for hanging washed clothes etc. to dry (*rotary clothes-line*: see ROTARY *a.*); *clothes-moth*: see MOTH *n.*[1] 1a; **clothes-peg**, (chiefly *N. Amer.*) **-pin** a clip or forked device of wood, plastic, etc., to hold washing on a clothes-line; **clothes-post**, **-prop** a support for a clothes-line.

clothesless *a.* = CLOTHELESS M19. **clotheslessness** *n.* L19.

clothier /ˈkləʊðɪə/ *n.* ME. [f. CLOTH *n.*: see -ER[1], -IER.] A person engaged in the cloth trade; *esp.* a seller of men's clothes.

clothing /ˈkləʊðɪŋ/ *n.* ME. [f. CLOTHE *v.* + -ING[1].] 1 The action of CLOTHE *v.* ME. 2 Clothes collectively, dress. ME. †b Bedclothes. ME–L18. †c Livery; a livery company. LME–E17. 3 Cloth-making; the cloth trade. Now *rare*. M16. 4 A covering or casing of cloth etc.; *esp.* lagging, cladding. L18. 5 *Naut.* Sails, rigging. L18.

2 *protective clothing*: see PROTECTIVE *a.* *wolf in sheep's clothing*: see WOLF *n.*

Comb.: **clothing-book** a ration book containing clothing coupons; **clothing-club** a club for the purchase or exchange of clothing by small part-payments; **clothing coupon** a ration coupon entitling the holder to a specified quantity of clothes or clothing materials.

†**clothless** *a.* var. of CLOTHELESS.

clotted /ˈklɒtɪd/ *ppl a.* E17. [f. CLOT *v.* + -ED[1]. In sense 1b prob. alt. of CLOUTED.] 1 Formed into clots or lumps; coagulated, congealed; matted in or with clots; covered with clots of blood etc. E17. b Of cream: made by scalding milk. L19. 2 *fig.* Concentrated, dense, impenetrable. L17.

2 W. EMPSON I tried to defend my clotted kind of poetry.

clotter /ˈklɒtə/ *v.i.* & *t.* Now *arch.* & *dial.* Also **clodder** /ˈklɒdə/. See also CLUTTER *v.* LME. [f. CLOT *v.* + -ER[5].] = CLOT *v.* 2.

cloture /ˈkləʊtjʊə/ *n.* & *v.* Now chiefly *US.* L19. [Fr. *clôture* f. OFr. CLOSURE.] A *n.* = CLOSURE *n.* 8. L19. B *v.t.* = CLOSURE *v.* L19.

clou /klu/ *n.* L19. [Fr., lit. 'nail, stud'.] The chief attraction, the point of greatest interest, the central idea.

cloud /klaʊd/ *n.* [OE *clūd*, prob. rel. to CLOT *n.*] 1 A mass of rock, earth, etc.; a hill. Long *obs.* exc. *local* in place-names. OE. 2 (A mass of) visible condensed water vapour suspended in the atmosphere high over the general level of the ground; in *pl.* also, the sky, the heavens. ME. 3 A thing that darkens or overshadows with gloom, trouble, suspicion, etc.; obscurity; a state of gloom, trouble, etc.; a frowning or depressed look. ME. 4 An airborne suspension of smoke, dust, etc.; a hazy aggregation of gas, particles, etc. LME. b *Astron.* A hazy area in the night sky produced by the light of distant stars; a nebula; a region of dust, gas, etc., in deep space appearing lighter or darker owing to the reflection, absorption, etc., of light. M16. 5 A great number *of* birds, insects, persons, etc., moving together. LME. 6 A thing that obscures or conceals. E16. b A region of dimness or obscurity in an otherwise clear or transparent body or liquid; a fuzzy patch or spot, *spec.* of another colour on the face of a horse. M16. c A light loosely knitted woollen scarf or shawl. Now *arch.* & *Canad. dial.* L19.

2 SHAKES. *Rom. & Jul.* She is advanc'd Above the clouds, as high as heaven itself. L. DEIGHTON Big rain clouds raced across the moon. K. A. PORTER La Condesa rose lightly as a cloud. ANTHONY HUXLEY Cloud may reduce light intensity to as little as five per cent of that of the full sun. **a cloud on the horizon** an indication of future trouble. **in the clouds** mystical, unreal, imaginary; (of a person) abstracted, inattentive. *Land of the Long White Cloud*: see LAND *n.*[1] LENTICULAR *cloud.* **on cloud seven** or **nine** *colloq.* extremely happy. **with one's head in the clouds** unrealistic(ally); living in a world of fantasy. 3 J. HEATH-STUBBS A dark cloud of suspicion broods over all. **under a cloud** out of favour, discredited. 4 H. E. BATES The tractor seemed to draw behind it a brown and smoky cloud. *blow a cloud*: see BLOW *v.*[1] *mushroom cloud*: see MUSHROOM *n.* & *a.* b MAGELLANIC *Cloud.* 5 *Oort('s)* (*comet*) *cloud*: see OORT 2. 6 C. V. WEDGWOOD The cloud of conjecture which obscures Cromwell's actions and motives.

Comb.: **cloudburst** a sudden violent rainstorm; **cloud-castle** a daydream; **cloud chamber** *Physics* a container of air or gas supersaturated with water vapour, used to detect charged particles by the condensation trails which they produce; **cloud cover** cloud that covers (much of) the sky; the extent to which the sky is covered by cloud; **cloud-cuckoo-land** [tr. Gk *Nephelokokkugia* (*nephelē* cloud, *kokkux* cuckoo) in Aristophanes' *Birds*] a fanciful or ideal realm; **cloud-hopping** (of aircraft) flying from cloud to cloud esp. for concealment; **cloud-land** utopia, fairyland; **cloudscape** a picture or picturesque grouping of clouds; **cloud seeder** a person who or thing which seeds clouds with crystals to cause rain; **cloud seeding** the seeding of clouds with crystals; **cloud street** a line of cumulus clouds formed parallel to the wind direction.

cloudless *a.* LME. **cloudlessness** *n.* M19. **cloudlet** *n.* a little cloud L18. **cloudlike** *a.* & *adv.* (*a*) *adj.* resembling (that of) a cloud; (*b*) *adv.* in the manner of a cloud: M17.

cloud /klaʊd/ *v.* LME. [f. the n.] I *v.t.* 1 Overspread or darken with clouds, gloom, trouble, etc.; throw into the shade, surpass; make dim or obscure; mar, detract from; *arch.* defame. LME. †2 Hide, conceal. L17–E18. 3 Variegate with vague patches of colour. L17.

3 **clouded leopard** a large, spotted, mainly arboreal feline, *Neofelis nebulosa*, of SE Asia. **clouded yellow** an orange or yellow and black pierid butterfly of the genus *Colias*, esp. *C. croceus*, known in Britain as a migrant from southern Europe.

II *v.i.* 4 Become overcast or gloomy. (Foll. by *over, up.*) M16.

cloudberry /ˈklaʊdbɛri, -b(ə)ri/ *n.* L16. [App. f. CLOUD *n.* + BERRY *n.*[1]] (The edible orange fruit of) a dwarf thornless bramble, *Rubus chamaemorus*, of mountain moorlands in north temperate regions.

cloudy /ˈklaʊdi/ *a.* OE. [f. CLOUD *n.* + -Y[1].] †1 Rocky, hilly. OE–LME. 2 Of or like cloud; of or pertaining to the clouds; characterized by clouds, having many clouds; obscured by cloud(s). ME. 3 Not transparent or clear. LME. b Variegated with vague patches of colour. Now *rare*. L17. 4 Darkened by ignorance etc.; (of ideas etc.) unclear, indistinct, vague. LME. 5 Darkened by misfortune, grief, anger, etc.; gloomy, sullen, frowning. LME.

cloudily *adv.* L16. **cloudiness** *n.* L16.

clough /klʌf/ *n.*[1] [OE *clōh* (in place-names) f. Gmc, rel. to OHG *klinga* (G dial. *Klinge*) ravine.] 1 A ravine, a steep valley usu. with a torrent bed. OE. 2 A cliff, a crag, a rock. Long *obs.* exc. *Sc.* LME.

clough *n.*[2] var. of CLOW.

clour /klʊə/ *n.* & *v.* *Sc.* & *north.* LME. [Origin unkn.] A *n.* †1 A knoll, a mound. LME–M17. 2 A swelling or lump (on the head) caused by a heavy blow. E16. 3 A heavy blow. L18. 4 A dent caused by a heavy blow. E19. B *v.t.* Dent; strike heavily; raise a swelling or lump on (the head) by a heavy blow. L16.

clout /klaʊt/ *n.*[1] [OE *clūt*, corresp. to (M)LG, MDu. *klūt(e)* (Du. *kluit* lump, clod), ON *klútr* kerchief: rel. to CLEAT, CLOT *n.*] I 1 A piece of cloth, leather, etc., for mending; a patch. OE. 2 A metal plate, *esp.* one fixed to an axle-tree to prevent wear. *obs.* exc. *dial.* OE. †3 A shred, esp. of cloth. ME–E17. 4 A piece of cloth (*gen.*); a cloth, *esp.* one put to squalid uses; a rag; an article of clothing. Now *arch.* & *dial.* ME. b A handkerchief. Now *dial.* & *slang.* LME. 5 In *pl.* Swaddling-clothes. Now *dial.* ME. 6 *Archery.* Orig. (*Hist.*), (a piece of canvas on a frame and laid on the ground as) the mark shot at in archery; a shot that hits the mark. Now *spec.* a target twelve times the usual size, used flat on the ground with a flag marking its centre. L16. 7 = CLOUT-NAIL. E19.

4 †**babe of clouts** a doll. **cast a clout** remove a garment.

II 8 A heavy blow. LME. 9 Personal or private influence; power of effective action, esp. in politics. *colloq.* M20.

clout /klaʊt/ *n.*[2] Long *obs.* exc. *dial.* ME. [Perh. var. of CLOT *n.* or f. as prec.] 1 A clot or clod of earth. ME. †2 In *pl.* Cream curds, clotted cream. LME–M17. 3 A stupid person. E19.

clout /klaʊt/ *v.t.* OE. [f. CLOUT *n.*[1]] I 1 Mend with a patch, patch. OE. †b Put *in, on, to*, as a patch. ME–L16. 2 Arm or protect with a metal plate; shoe with clout-nails as protection against wear. LME. †3 Put together clumsily; botch (*up*). LME–M17. 4 Cover with a cloth. *arch.* L16.

2 **clouted shoe**: studded with clout-nails as a protection against wear.

II 5 Hit hard. ME.

clouter *n.* a person who mends or patches; a botcher: ME. †**clouterly** *a.* clumsy, awkward, clownish M17–E19.

clouted /ˈklaʊtɪd/ *a.* Now *dial.* M16. [Perh. f. CLOUT *n.*[2] + -ED[2].] Of cream: clotted.

clout-nail /ˈklaʊtneɪl/ *n.* ME. [f. CLOUT *n.*[1] or *v.* + NAIL *n.*] A nail with a large flat head.

clove /kləʊv/ *n.*[1] [OE *clufu*, corresp. to the first elem. of OS *cluflōc* 'clove-leek', garlic, OHG *klovolouh* (G *Knoblauch*), f. Gmc base rel. to that of CLEAVE *v.*[1]] 1 Each of the small bulbs which make up the compound bulb of garlic, shallot, etc. OE. 2 A natural segment of a fruit. Now *rare*. M17.

clove /kləʊv/ *n.*[2] ME. [OFr. *clou de girofle* lit. 'nail of gillyflower': cf. GILLYFLOWER.] I Orig. (long *rare* in sense 1) *clove-gillyflower* & vars. 1 The dried flower-bud of a tropical myrtle, *Syzygium aromaticum*, used as a pungent aromatic spice. Usu. in *pl.* ME. 2 A clove-scented pink, *Dianthus caryophyllus*, now known only as carnations and other cultivated forms. M16.

1 **oil of cloves** a medicinal oil extracted from cloves.

II 3 In full *clove tree*. The tropical myrtle, *Syzygium aromaticum*, native to the Moluccas. L16. 4 In *pl.* A cordial flavoured with cloves. M19.

Comb.: **clove-brown** (of) the colour of cloves; medium brown; **clove carnation** = sense 2 above; *clove-gillyflower*: see branch I above; **clove pink** = sense 2 above.

clove /kləʊv/ *n.*[3] Also †**claw**. L15. [AL *clavus*, AN *clou, clove*.] *Hist.* A weight of cheese or wool, equal to 7 or 8 lbs (approx. 3.2 to 3.6 kg).

clove /kləʊv/ *n.*[4] *US.* L18. [Du. *klove*, also *kloof*, in MDu. *clove*, MLG *klove* split, cleft, rel. to CLEAVE *v.*[1]] A rocky cleft or fissure; a gap, a ravine. Chiefly in place-names.

clove *v.* see CLEAVE *v.*[1]

clove hitch /ˈkləʊv hɪtʃ/ *n. phr.* M18. [f. *clove* pa. pple of CLEAVE *v.*[1] (as showing parallel separate lines) + HITCH *n.*] A hitch by which a rope etc. is secured by passing it twice round a spar or rope etc. that it crosses at right angles.

cloven /ˈkləʊv(ə)n/ *ppl a.* ME. [pa. pple of CLEAVE *v.*[1]] Divided lengthwise; split (into pieces or to a certain depth); bifurcate.

cloven foot, hoof: of ruminant quadrupeds, of the god Pan, of the Devil (*show the cloven foot* (or *hoof*): see SHOW *v.*).

cloven *v.* see CLEAVE *v.*[1]

clover /ˈkləʊvə/ *n.* & *v.* [OE *clāfre* = (M)LG, Du. *klāver*, f. Gmc. First syll. corresp. to OS *klē*, OHG *klēo* (G *Klee*).] A *n.* Any of various leguminous plants constituting the genus *Trifolium*, with white, pink, etc., flowers in crowded heads and with trifoliate leaves; *esp.* any of several such plants grown as fodder, *T. repens* (more fully *Dutch* or *white clover*), *T. pratense* (more fully *red clover*), and *T. hybridum* (more fully ALSIKE *clover*). Cf. TREFOIL. OE.

Darling clover: see DARLING *n.*[2] **four-leaf, four-leaved, clover** (a representation of) a cloyer leaf with four leaflets, thought to bring good luck. **in clover** in ease and luxury. **Japan clover** = LESPEDEZA. *rabbit-foot clover*: see RABBIT *n.* *subterranean clover*: see SUBTERRANEAN *a.* *sweet clover*: see SWEET *a.* & *adv.*

Comb.: **clover-grass** clover; **clover leaf** (chiefly *N. Amer.*) a road intersection whose layout resembles a four-leaf clover; **clover weevil** any of various small weevils which feed on leguminous crops.

B *v.t.* Sow or cover with clover. Chiefly as *clovered* ppl a. M17.

clovery *a.* having much clover; of the nature of clover: M17.

Clovis /ˈkləʊvɪs/ *a.* M20. [See below.] Designating a prehistoric culture first found near Clovis in eastern New Mexico, USA, or its remains, esp. the typical stone projectile points with fluting at the base, which are earlier than the Folsom points (see FOLSOM).

clow /klaʊ/ *n.* Now *dial.* Also **clough**, (*Sc.* & *north.*) **cloose** /kluːs/. [OE *clūse* f. late L *clusa* var. of *clausa* closed place or way, later taken as pl.] †**1** A narrow pass. Only in OE. **2** A dam for water, a sluice. ME.

clown /klaʊn/ *n.* & *v.* M16. [Perh. of LG origin: cf. NFris. *klönne*, *klünne*, clumsy fellow, *klünj* clod, lump, etc.] **A** *n.* **1** A countryman, a rustic, a peasant, esp. when regarded as ignorant, crass, or rude. M16. **2** A person without refinement or culture; an ignoramus, a boor, an uncouth or ill-bred person. L16. **3** A fool or jester, esp. in a pantomime or circus. E17.

Comb.: **clown fish** an anemone fish, *Amphiprion percula*, which is orange-brown with black-bordered white stripes and occurs in the Indian and Pacific Oceans.

B *v.* **1** *v.*†*t.* w. *it* & *i.* Play the clown; perform as a clown. L16. **2** *v.t.* Play the clown in; portray like a clown. L19.

clownery *n.* the behaviour or acts of a clown, clownish behaviour L16. **clownish** *a.* pertaining to or characteristic of a clown; ignorant, crass, rude; jesting, boisterously comic: L16. **clownishly** *adv.* L16. **clownishness** *n.* L16. **clownship** *n.* (*a*) the estate or condition of a clown or clowns; (*b*) (with possess. adj., as *your* etc. *clownship*) a mock title of respect given to a clown: E17.

cloy /klɔɪ/ *v.* LME. [Aphet. f. ACCLOY.] †**1** *v.t.* Pierce (as) with a nail; *esp.* = ACCLOY I. LME–E18. **2** *v.t.* †**a** Stop *up*, block (a passage etc.); choke, fill *up*; clog, encumber. LME–M17. **b** Spike (a gun). Now *rare*. E17. **3** *v.t.* & *i.* Satiate, weary, or nauseate by richness, sweetness, sameness, or excess, of food, pleasure, attention, etc. (Foll. by *with*.) M16.

cloyingly *adv.* in a cloying manner or degree E20. **cloyless** *a.* that does not cloy E17. †**cloyment** *n.* (*rare*, Shakes.) satiety: only in E17. **cloysome** *a.* (*rare*) tending to cloy E17.

clozapine /ˈkləʊzəpiːn/ *n.* M20. [f. C(H)LO(RO-[2] + elems. of *benzodiazepine*.] *Pharm.* A sedative of the benzodiazepine group used to treat schizophrenia.

cloze /kləʊz/ *a.* M20. [Repr. abbrev. of CLOSURE *n.*] Designating a comprehension test or testing procedure in which the subject is asked to supply words deleted from a text.

club /klʌb/ *n.* ME. [ON *clubba* assim. form of *klumba* (cf. *klumbu-*, *klubbufótr* club-footed), rel. to CLUMP *n.*] **I 1** A heavy stick which increases in thickness and weight towards one end, used as a weapon etc. ME. **2** A stick or bat used in various ball games, esp. golf. LME. **3** Any organ, structure, etc., shaped like a club or with a knob at the end. LME. **b** The butt-end of a gun. E18. **c** Chiefly *Hist.* (A wig with) a club-shaped pigtail. L18. **4** *Cards.* [tr. Sp. *basto*, It. *bastone* (cf. BASTO, BATON *n.*) the club or cudgel figured on Sp. or It. cards.] In *pl.* (occas. treated as *sing.*), one of the four suits into which a pack of playing-cards is divided, distinguished in British cards by a trefoil leaf in black; *sing.* a card of this suit. Also occas. a card or (in *pl.*) the suit distinguished in Spanish and Italian cards by cudgels or batons. M16.

1 *Indian clubs*: see INDIAN *a.*

II †**5** Combination into one mass; *esp.* combination of contributions to make up a total sum; one share of such joint expense. M17–L18. †**6** A social meeting the expenses of which are jointly defrayed. M17–E19. †**7** A secret society, esp. with a political object. L17–M18. **8** An association of people united by some common interest; *esp.* (*a*) an association meeting periodically for a shared activity or for social purposes; (*b*) an association in which members make regular payments to a central fund or regular purchases from a central source to acquire some benefit. (Freq. w. specification of purpose, nature, or membership.) L17. **b** *spec.* An association of people formed mainly for social purposes and having premises providing meals, temporary residence, etc., for the use of members. L18. **c** A group of people, nations, etc., having something in common. M20. **9** A building, rooms, or other premises occupied or owned by a club; an establishment providing entertainment etc. to members and guests; also = *nightclub* s.v. NIGHT *n.* (Freq. w. specification as in sense 8 above.) M19.

8 *athletic club*, *benefit-club*, *book club*, *Christmas club*, *fan club*, *football club*, *social club*, *working-man's* (or *-men's*) *club*, etc. **b** A. TROLLOPE The club went on its way like other clubs, and men dined and smoked and played billiards and pretended to read. **c** *nuclear club*: see NUCLEAR *a.* **9** R. HOGGART Going with her husband to his pub or club.

Phrases: **in the (pudding) club** *slang* pregnant. **on the club** *colloq.* through a benefit-club etc. **the best club in London** *joc.* the House of Commons.

Comb.: **club (arm)chair** a thickly upholstered armchair of the type often found in clubs; **club class** an intermediate class of fare and accommodation on a passenger aircraft; **club-foot** a congenitally distorted foot, = TALIPES; also, a foot of stunted lumpy appearance; **club-footed** *a.* having a club-foot; **club-haul** *v.t.* & *i.* (*Naut.*) tack (a ship) by letting the lee-anchor down as soon as the wind is out of the sails, so bringing the head to wind, then cutting the cable and trimming the sails to the other tack when the ship pays off (a last resort); **clubhouse** the premises occupied by a club; *esp.* those attached to a golf course; **clubland** *colloq.* the vicinity of St James's in London; any area where there are many clubs; **club-law** the use of physical force as contrasted with argument; the law of the physically stronger; **club-man** (*a*) a man armed with a club; (*b*) a member of one or more clubs; **club-money** money for a club, the subscription to a benefit-club etc.; **clubmoss** any of various pteridophytes constituting the genus *Lycopodium* (family Lycopodiaceae) or formerly included in it, which are small creeping plants (unrelated to mosses) with needle-like or scalelike leaves; *lesser clubmoss*, an allied smaller mosslike plant, *Selaginella selaginoides*; **club-root** a fungal disease of turnips and other root crops, in which root galls are produced; **club-rush** a marsh or aquatic plant of the genus *Scirpus* or certain related genera of the sedge family; **club sandwich** (orig. *US*) a sandwich with two layers of filling between three slices of toast or bread, *esp.* one containing bacon, chicken, and tomato; **Club Soda** (proprietary name for) a variety of soda-water.

clubbish *a.* (*a*) resembling a club; clumsy; (now *dial.*) clownish, boorish; (*b*) fond of clubs, given to frequenting clubs: E16. **clubbism** *n.* the club system, the practice of forming clubs (orig. political clubs of the French Revolution) M19. **clubbist** *n.* (*a*) a member or supporter of the political clubs of the French Revolution, or of their principles; (*b*) a member of a club: L18. **clubby** *a.* (*US*) (*a*) identified with a club, characteristic of a club; (*b*) friendly, sociable: M19. **clublike** *a.* resembling a club; having a swelling at one end: M19. **clubster** *n.* (*a*) = *club-man* above; (*b*) *dial.* a stoat: E18.

club /klʌb/ *v.* Infl. **-bb-**. L16. [f. the n.] **1** *v.t.* Beat with or as with a club. L16. **b** Use (esp. a musket) as a club. E18. **2** *v.t.* Gather into a clublike mass, gather together, (foll. by *together*); (chiefly *Hist.*) dress (hair) in a club-shaped pigtail. E17. **3** *v.t.* Combine into a common stock or to a common end (foll. by *together*); contribute (money etc.) as one's share of a common stock; make *up* or put *together* (a sum of money etc.) by joint contributions. M17. **4** *v.i.* Combine, form into a club or mass; *esp.* combine for joint action, to make up a sum of money for a particular purpose, or (formerly) as members of a secret society. (Foll. by *together*, *with*.) M17. **5** *v.t.* *Mil.* Throw into a confused mass. E19.

1 C. G. SELIGMAN Kinnyole was clubbed to death by his own people. **2** J. PAYN London which is equal to half a dozen great towns clubbed together. **3** P. A. MOTTEUX Let every Man club his Penny towards it. G. GREENE We clubbed our butter rations. **4** S. PEPYS How he did endeavour to find out a ninepence to club with me for the coach. E. HUXLEY A group of Pakistanis . . have clubbed together to buy a joint house.

clubbable /ˈklʌbəb(ə)l/ *a.* Also **clubable**. L18. [f. CLUB *n.* + -ABLE.] Fit to be a member of a club, sociable.

clubba'bility *n.* L19. **clubbableness** *n.* M20.

clubbed /klʌbd/ *a.* LME. [f. CLUB *n.*, *v.*: see -ED[2], -ED[1].] **1** Shaped like a club; thickset. LME. **2** That has been clubbed; formed into a club; used as a club. E17.

clubber /ˈklʌbə/ *n.* M17. [f. CLUB *v.* or *n.* + -ER[1].] **1** A person who clubs or combines with others for any object; a person who belongs to a club. M17. **2** A person who wields a club. L19.

cluck /klʌk/ *n.* & *int.* E18. [f. the vb, or imit.] **A** *n.* **1** The abrupt hollow guttural sound made by a hen desiring to sit or calling its chicks. Also, any similar sound, *esp.* the click of African etc. languages (see CLICK *n.*[1] 3). E18. **2** A stupid person. Esp. in *dumb cluck*. *slang*. M20. **B** *int.* Repr. the cluck of a hen (see above). E19.

cluck /klʌk/ *v.* L15. [Imit., corresp. to MHG *klukken*, Da. *klukke*, Sw. *klucka*: cf. CLOCK *v.*[1]] **1** *v.t.* (Of a hen) summon (chicks) with clucks; summon or encourage as a hen her chicks. L15. **2** *v.i.* Utter a cluck; *fig.* express fussy concern, disapproval, etc. L16.

2 J. DOS PASSOS Fainy clacked the reins . . and clucked with his tongue. S. MILES The . . nurse . . is clucking distressedly.

clucky *a.* (of a hen) sitting or ready to sit on eggs E20.

clue /kluː/ *n.* LME. [Var. of CLEW *n.*] **1** = CLEW *n.* 3a. LME. **2** = CLEW *n.* 5. L16. **3** = CLEW *n.* 2. *arch.* E17. **4a** A fact or principle that serves as a guide, or suggests a line of inquiry, in a problem or investigation, an intricate structure, etc. E17. **b** A word, phrase, etc., indicating a word or words to be inserted in a crossword puzzle. E20. **5** The thread of a story; a train of thought. M17. †**6** = CLEW *n.* 1b. L17–E18. **7** = CLEW *n.* 5. L17. **8** = CLEW *n.* 6. M18.

4a **not have a clue** *colloq.* be ignorant or incompetent, be at a complete loss.

clueless *a.* without a clue; *colloq.* ignorant, stupid: M19. **cluelessness** *n.* M20.

clue /kluː/ *v.* M17. [Var. of CLEW *v.*] †**1** *v.t.* Follow, track. Only in M17. **2** *v.t.* & *i.* = CLEW *v.* 3. M18. **3** *v.t.* = CLEW *v.* I. M19. **4** *v.t.* Provide a clue to (a line in a crossword puzzle etc.). M20. **5** *v.t.* Inform, tell (a person). Freq. foll. by *in*, *up*. *slang*. M20.

Clumber /ˈklʌmbə/ *n.* M19. [f. *Clumber* Park in Nottinghamshire.] More fully *Clumber spaniel*. A spaniel of a slow heavily-built breed.

clump /klʌmp/ *n.* ME. [Partly f. MLG *klumpe* (LG *klump*) rel. to MDu. *klompe* (Du. *klomp*) lump, mass, & CLUMPER, CLAMP *n.*[2], CLUB *n.*; partly imit.] **1** A compact shapeless mass, a heap, a lump. ME. **b** *spec.* An agglutinated mass of blood cells, bacteria, etc. L19. **2** A cluster or compact group of or *of* trees, shrubs, or other growing things, or (*transf.*) buildings, people, etc. L16. **3** More fully *clump-sole*. A thick extra sole on a shoe. M19. **4** A heavy blow. *colloq.* L19. **5** A noise of a heavy step or tread, a non-resonant sound as of a heavy blow. Cf. CLAMP *n.*[3], CLOMP *n.* L19. **6** In *pl.* A game in which two teams try to guess an agreed word. L19.

1 E. GARRETT A baker gave me a clump o' bread. **2** V. WOOLF The fine clump of St John's wort that grew beside it. A. CARTER Discontented tradespeople stood in fretful clumps in the street. **5** W. BOYD Acutely aware of the clump of his boots on the wood.

clumpish *a.* heavy and clumsy L17. **clumpy** *a.* forming clumps; having many clumps; clumpish: E19.

clump /klʌmp/ *v.* M17. [Partly f. the n., partly imit.] **1** *v.i.* Move with or make a heavy non-resonant sound; tread heavily. Cf. CLAMP *v.*[3], CLOMP *v.* M17. **2a** *v.t.* Arrange or plant in a clump or mass. L18. **b** *v.t.* Provide with clumps of trees or other growing things. Chiefly as *clumped* ppl a. E19. **c** *v.i.* Form a clump or clumps. L19. **3** *v.t.* Hit, strike. *colloq.* M19.

1 BUNYAN Every clown with his clumping dirty shoes. F. TUOHY They clumped around in tweeds and brogues. **2a** C. BEATON Three carnations clumped together. **b** E. BOWEN A sort of outdoor drawing-room

clumped with mauve rhododendrons. c ANTHONY SMITH Further aggregation, or clumping, of the blood platelets.

clumper /ˈklʌmpə/ *n.* & *v.* Long *obs.* exc. *dial.* [OE *clympre* rel. to CLUMP *n.*] A *n.* = CLUMP *n.* I. OE. †B *v.t.* Form into lumps or masses, clot. M16–M17.

clumps /klʌmps/ *a.* Long *obs.* exc. *dial.* Also †**clumse**. E17. [Rel. to next: cf. Icel. *klumsa* lockjawed, Sw. dial. *klumsen* benumbed, dazed.] Numb with cold; awkward, stupid, lazy; gruff, surly.

clumse /klʌmz/ *v.* Long *obs.* exc. *dial.* Also **clumps** /klʌmps/. ME. [Prob. of Scand. origin: cf. Norw. dial. *klumsen* strike dumb, clog, hamper, *klumst* clumsy.] 1 *v.t.* Numb (*lit.* & *fig.*); daze, stupefy, dumbfound. Orig. & chiefly as *clumsed*, *clumst* ppl a. ME. †2 *v.i.* Be or become numb with cold. Only in LME.

clumsy /ˈklʌmzi/ *a.* L16. [f. prec. + -Y[1]: cf. Sw. *klumsig* numb, clumsy.] 1 Heavy and awkward in motion or action; awkward in shape; ungainly; lacking in grace or skill; rudely constructed; without tact. L16. †2 Numb or stiffened with cold. Only in E17.

1 I. D'ISRAELI A clumsy forgery. G. ORWELL He wrote in large clumsy capitals. A. WILSON Tom was . . clumsy; he . . knocked over full ashtrays.

clumsily *adv.* L17. **clumsiness** *n.* M17.

clunch /klʌn(t)ʃ/ *n.* LME. [Perh. f. next, or rel. to CLUMP *n.* as *bump:bunch*, *hump:hunch*.] 1 A lump. Long *obs.* exc. *dial.* LME. 2 A lumpish fellow, a lout. *obs.* exc. *dial.* E17. 3a Any of various stiff clays. Also *clunch clay*. *local.* L17. b A soft limestone used esp. for internal carved building-work. E19.

clunch /klʌn(t)ʃ/ *a.* *obs.* exc. *dial.* L18. [Prob. f. LG *Klunt*, Du. *klont* lump, clod.] Lumpy; heavy and stiff in consistency; thickset.

clung /klʌŋ/ *ppl a.* *arch.* & *dial.* ME. [pa. pple of CLING *v.*] Drawn together, shrunken; pinched with hunger. Of soil: stiff, tenacious.

clung *v.* pa. t. & pple of CLING *v.*

Cluniac /ˈkluːnɪak/ *n.* & *a.* L16. [med.L *Cluniacus*, f. *Clun(i)aeum* Cluny (or Clugny), France: see -AC.] A *n.* A monk of the monastery of Cluny, near Mâcon in France, or of the reformed Benedictine order which developed from it. L16. B *adj.* Of or pertaining to this monastery or order. L19.

clunk *n.*[1] var. of KLUNK *n.*

clunk /klʌŋk/ *v.* & *n.*[2] Orig. *Sc.* L18. [Imit.: cf. CLANK, CLINK *n.*[1], *v.*[1], CLONK.] A *v.i.* Make a hollow gurgling sound, as liquid poured from a bottle; make a dull clanking sound. L18. B *n.* Such a sound. E19.

Cluny /ˈkluːni/ *n.* L19. [See CLUNIAC.] In full *Cluny lace*. A kind of bobbin-lace for clothing etc.

clupeoid /ˈkluːpɪɔɪd/ *n.* & *a.* M19. [f. mod.L *Clupea* genus name f. L *clupea*, name of a river-fish + -OID.] (A fish) of the family Clupeidae, which includes the herring, sprat, anchovy, etc.

Also **clupeid** *n.* & *a.* L19.

cluster /ˈklʌstə/ *n.* [OE *clyster*, rarely *cluster*, also *ġeclystre*, prob. f. Gmc base also of CLOT *n.*] 1 A collection of fruit (orig. grapes), flowers, etc., growing closely together; a bunch. OE. 2 A compact group of other similar things, as persons, animals, gems, etc. LME. b *Astron.* A group of stars or galaxies forming a relatively close association. E18. c *Ling.* A group of successive consonants. E20.

2 A. P. HERBERT There was a lock every quarter of a mile, and sometimes a cluster of two or three. B. MOORE The other monks bunched in a cluster. LAYGEAR *cluster*. b GLOBULAR *cluster*. *local cluster*: see LOCAL *a.* *open cluster*: see OPEN *a.*

Comb.: **cluster bomb** an anti-personnel bomb spraying metal pellets on impact; **cluster compound** *Chem.* a compound whose structure involves a number of atoms of a metallic element bonded together as the nucleus of an ion; **cluster pine** the maritime pine, *Pinus pinaster*.

cluster /ˈklʌstə/ *v.* LME. [f. the n.] I *v.t.* Orig. & chiefly as *clustered* pa. pple & ppl a. 1 Arrange in a cluster, group closely. LME. 2 Provide or cover with clusters. (Foll. by *with*.) LME. †3 Coagulate, clot. Only in M16.

1 **clustered columns, pillars, shafts**: several close together, or disposed round and half detached from the pier. 2 SOUTHEY Mountains clustered with the fruitful pines.

II *v.i.* 4 Congregate in a cluster or clusters; grow or be situated in a cluster or clusters; gather (*a*)*round*. LME. †5 Coagulate, clot. L15–M16.

4 M. F. MAURY The . . icebergs which cluster off the Falkland Islands. K. MANSFIELD Round the ice-cream cart . . the children cluster. R. ELLISON We were a small tight group, clustered together.

clutch /klʌtʃ/ *n.*[1] Branch I also (all earlier) (*Sc.* & *north.*) **cleuk** /kluːk, klyk/, (now *dial.*) **cloke** /kləʊk/, †**clooch**, & other vars. ME. [Origin unkn.: mod. form f. CLUTCH *v.* The relationship of the various early forms is obscure.] I 1 A claw; *contempt.* a hand. Usu. in *pl.* Now chiefly *Sc.* in *gen.* sense. ME. 2 *spec.* A hand as an instrument of rapacity or cruelty, a grasping hand. Usu. in *pl.*, & in *in*, *into*, *out of*, etc., *a person's clutches* (passing into sense 3). E16. 3a Tight hold or grip; relentless control. L18. b An act of grasping *at*. M19.

2 SHAKES. *Haml.* But age . . hath caught me in his clutch. STEELE [He] escapes the Clutches of the Hangman. 3a F. MARRYAT I can't hold on ten seconds more. . . my clutch is going now.

II *clutch* only. 4 *Mech.* An arrangement for connecting or disconnecting working parts. E19. b In a motor vehicle: a device for connecting the engine to the transmission; the pedal operating this. L19.

4b *ride the clutch*: see RIDE *v.* *slip (in) the clutch*: see SLIP *v.*[1]

clutch /klʌtʃ/ *n.*[2] E18. [Prob. southern var. of CLETCH.] A set of eggs for hatching, or of birds hatched, at a single time; *transf.* (usu. *contempt.*) a closely associated group *of*.

A. L. ROWSE A clutch of leering women. D. ATTENBOROUGH The female can only lay a relatively small number of eggs in a clutch.

clutch /klʌtʃ/ *v.* ME. [Var. of CLITCH *v.*] †1a *v.i.* Bend or crook at the joint. Only in ME. b *v.t.* Incurve (the fingers), clench (the hand). L16–E18. 2 *v.t.* Seize eagerly or convulsively with the claws or fingers. LME. 3 *v.t.* Hold firmly in one's grasp, grip. E17. 4 *v.i.* Grasp or snatch *at*. M19.

2 SIR W. SCOTT With all the fingers spread out as if to clutch it. 3 D. H. LAWRENCE Alvina counted it [money] and kept it clutched in her hand. J. BERGER She dances like a bear, clutching her partner close to her. 4 H. JAMES She . . could only clutch at the hope of some inspiration. L. DURRELL The sleeper awoke and clutched at my hand.

Phrases: *clutch (at) a straw* or *straws*: see STRAW *n.*

Comb.: **clutch bag** a handbag with no handle or strap.

clutter /ˈklʌtə/ *n.* L16. [Var. of CLODDER *n.* or f. the vb: assoc. w. *cluster*, *clatter*.] †1 A clotted mass. L16–E17. 2 A confused collection; crowded disorder, untidy state, litter. M17. 3 Bustle, commotion; hubbub, disturbance; mingled rattle. Now *arch.* & *dial.* M17.

2 G. HEYER An open book lay on the ground beside it, with a clutter of newspapers and magazines. H. ACTON She was surrounded by neatness and order: there was a complete absence of clutter. 3 MILTON The clutter of their Horse, and of their Wheels. SWIFT Those ladies, who are apt to make the greatest clutter on such occasions.

clutter /ˈklʌtə/ *v.* LME. [Var. of CLOTTER *v.*, assoc. w. *cluster*, *clatter*.] 1 *v.t.* & *i.* Clot, coagulate. *obs.* exc. *dial.* LME. 2a *v.i.* Run (*together*) in confused groups, crowd (*together*). Now *rare* or *obs.* M16. b *v.t.* Heap together in confusion. *obs.* exc. *dial.* M17. 3 *v.i.* Run in bustling disorder or with a confused noise. Now chiefly *dial.* E17. 4 *v.t.* & *i.* Utter or speak confusedly, esp. habitually. M17. 5 *v.t.* Crowd untidily (*with*), litter *with*. Freq. foll. by *up*. L17.

3 DEFOE The coaches, horsemen and crowd, cluttered away, to be out of harm's way. 5 C. MCCULLERS The four walls were cluttered with calendars and crudely painted advertisements. J. FRAME Who wanted an ugly old broken-down alcoholic cluttering up precious hospital cubic feet?

†**cly** *v.* & *n.* *slang.* M16. [Perh. of LG origin: cf. LG *kleien* to scratch, claw.] A *v.t.* Take; *esp.* steal, pocket. M16–M19. B *n.* A pocket; money. L17–L19.

Comb.: **cly-faker** a pickpocket; **cly-faking** picking pockets.

Clydesdale /ˈklʌɪdzdeɪl/ *n.* L18. [The area of the River Clyde in Scotland.] 1 More fully *Clydesdale horse*. A horse of a heavy draught breed originating around Clydesdale. L18. 2 More fully *Clydesdale terrier*. A terrier of a small smooth-haired breed originating around Clydesdale. L19.

clype /klʌɪp/ *v.* & *n.* *Sc.* Also **clipe**. E18. [Obscurely f. CLEPE.] A *v.i.* Tell tales, tattle (*on*). E18. B *n.* A telltale. E19.

clypeate /ˈklɪpɪeɪt/ *a.* M19. [f. as next + -ATE[2].] *Bot.* & *Zool.* Resembling a round shield.

Also **clypeated** *a.* (*rare*) E18.

clypeus /ˈklɪpɪəs/ *n.* Pl. **-ei** /-ɪʌɪ/. M19. [L *clipeus*, *clupeus* round shield.] The broad shield-shaped frontal part of an insect's head, above the labrum.

clypeal *a.* L19.

clyster /ˈklɪstə/ *n.* & *v.* *arch.* LME. [(O)Fr. *clystère* or L *clyster* f. Gk *klustēr* syringe, f. *kluzein* rinse out.] A *n.* A medicine injected into the rectum, an enema; occas., a suppository. LME. B *v.t.* Treat with a clyster. L15.

cnemial /ˈkniːmɪəl/ *a.* L19. [f. Gk *knēmē* tibia + -AL[1].] *Ornith.* Of or pertaining to the tibia.

cnidarian /nɪˈdɛːrɪən/ *n.* & *a.* M20. [f. mod.L *Cnidaria* (see below), f. as CNIDO- + *-aria* pl. of L *-arium* -ARY[1] (cf. -ARIAN): see -AN.] *Zool.* A *n.* An animal of the invertebrate phylum Cnidaria (cf. COELENTERATE *n.*). M20. B *adj.* Of or pertaining to this phylum. M20.

cnido- /ˈknʌɪdəʊ/ *comb. form.* [f. Gk *knidē* nettle: see -O-.] *Zool.* Used in terms relating to stinging cells of coelenterates etc.

cnidoblast *n.* a cell in which a nematocyst develops L19. **cnidocil** *n.* [L CILIUM] the external irritable process of a nematocyst L19.

co- /kəʊ/ *pref.* [L, var. of COM- esp. bef. vowels, *h*, and *gn*: cf. COL-, CON-, COR-.] 1 Used in wds adopted f. L and in Eng. wds modelled on these, and as a productive pref., forming: (*a*) vbs f. vbs w. the sense 'with others', as *co-edit*, *cooperate*; (*b*) adjs. f. adjs. and advs. f. advs. w. the senses 'jointly', 'mutually', as *co-belligerent*, *coequal(ly)*; (*c*) ns. f. ns. w. the senses 'joint', as *co-author*, *co-precipitation*, and 'mutual', as *coequality*. b *Biol.* Forming names of substances which combine with others to produce an effect, or enhance the action of others, but are individually inactive, as *co-carcinogen*, *coenzyme*. 2 *Math.* Short for *complement*, in the sense 'of the complement' (as *cosine*) or 'complement of' (as *co-latitude*).

coadapˈtation *n.* mutual adaptation E19. **coaˈdapted** *a.* mutually adapted M19. **coaˈdjust** *v.t.* adjust to each other M19. **coˈadjutant** *a.* & *n.* (a person) helping another or others or with another or others E18. **co-aˈdore** *v.t.* adore conjointly (*with*) E17. **coadˈventurer** *n.* a fellow adventurer M17. **coˈagency** *n.* joint or combined agency E17. **coˈagent** *n.* a joint agent L16. **co-aˈration** *n.* cooperative ploughing or tillage, esp. as anciently practised in Wales L19. **coˈarbiter** *n.* a joint arbiter L16. **coaˈssessor** *n.* a joint assessor M17. **coaˈssume** *v.t.* assume together or conjointly (*with*) E17. **coaˈttest** *v.t.* attest together or conjointly (*with*) M17. **codeˈfendant** *n.* a joint defendant M17. **codeˈpendency** *n.* emotional dependency on supporting or caring for another person or other people L20. **codeˈterminant** *n.* each of a set of determining factors L19. **co-determiˈnation** *n.* joint determination; *spec.* of company policies by unions and workers as well as management E20. **codeˈtermine** *v.t.* jointly determine E20. **codiˈrector** *n.* a joint director M19. **co-ˈdriver** *n.* a person who takes turns in driving a vehicle, esp. in a race, rally, etc. M20. **co-ˈeditor** *n.* a joint editor L19. **coeˈffect** *n.* a joint or concomitant effect M18. **coˈenzyme** *n.* (*Biochem.*) an organic compound which combines with an enzyme to activate it E20. **co-eˈstate** *n.* an estate or state possessing equal authority or rank with another M18. **co-ˈfavourite** *n.* an equal or joint favourite, esp. in a sporting contest E20. **co-feoˈffee** *n.* (*Hist.*) a joint feoffee LME. **co-ˈfounder** *n.* a joint founder E17. **co-ˈfoundress** *n.* a joint foundress, a female joint founder M17. **co-'guardian** *n.* a joint guardian M17. **co-'guardianship** *n.* joint guardianship L19. **co-'head** *n.* a joint leader or principal L19. **co'heir** *n.* a joint heir LME. **co'heiress** *n.* a joint heiress, a female coheir M17. **co'heirship** *n.* joint heirship E17. **co'helper** *n.* a joint helper M16. **co-'heritor** *n.* a joint inheritor M16. **coindi'cation** *n.* (a) conjoint or concurrent indication E17. **co-'infinite** *a.* equally or conjointly infinite M17. **co-in'habitant** *n.* a joint inhabitant M16. **co-in'here** *v.i.* inhere together M19. **co-in'herence** *n.* joint inherence E19. **co-in'herent** *a.* jointly inherent E19. **co-in'heritance** *n.* (a) joint inheritance L16. **co-in'heritor** *n.* a joint inheritor E16. **co-instan'taneous** *a.* occurring or existing at the same moment M18. **co-instan'taneously** *adv.* simultaneously E19. **co'juror** *n.* (chiefly *Hist.*) a fellow oath-taker, one who confirms under oath the oath of another M18. **co-'labourer** *n.* a fellow labourer M19. **co-'obligant** *n.* a person under joint obligation E19. **co-'obligor** *n.* (*Law*) a person who accepts an obligation or makes a commitment along with others L18. **co-o'ccur** *v.i.* occur together or simultaneously (*with*) M20. **co-o'ccurrence** *n.* simultaneous or joint occurrence M20. **co-o'ccurrent** *a.* & *n.* (each of two or more things) occurring together or simultaneously M20. **co-om'nipotent** *a.* conjointly omnipotent M16. **co-'ossify** *v.i.* & *t.* ossify together L19. **co-'owner** *n.* a joint owner M19. **co-'ownership** *n.* joint ownership L19. **co'pastor** *n.* a joint pastor E19. **co-pro'duction** *n.* (a) joint production; *esp.* a cinematographic film produced by teams from more than one country: M20. **co-pro'moter** *n.* a joint promoter E19. **co-pro'prietor** *n.* a joint proprietor L18. **co-'regency** *n.* a joint regency M17. **co-'regent** *a.* & *n.* (a person) ruling jointly with another L18. **co-'regnant** *n.* & *a.* (a person) reigning jointly with another M17. **co-'residence** *n.* residence together, joint residence M17. **co-'ruler** *n.* a joint ruler L17. **co'seismal** *a.* & *n.* (*a*) *adj.* relating to points affected simultaneously by an earthquake; (*b*) *n.* a line or curve connecting such points: M19. **co-'sovereign** *n.* a joint sovereign, a fellow sovereign L18. **co-'sovereignty** *n.* joint sovereignty E18. **co-spe'cific** *a.* = CONSPECIFIC *a.* L19. **co'tectic** *a.* [after EUTECTIC] *Petrogr.* representing conditions under which two or more minerals etc. crystallize simultaneously from a liquid E20. **co-'tenancy** *n.* joint tenancy L19. **co-'tenant** *n.* a joint tenant M19. **cotext** *n.* the text surrounding a particular word etc. M20. **co-u'nite** *v.t.* & *i.* (*arch.*) unite together, conjoin M16. **co-'work** *v.i.* work together, cooperate E17. **co-'worker** *n.* a person who works in collaboration with another; a fellow worker: M17.

coacervate /kəʊ'asəveɪt/ *n.* E20. [Back-form. f. COACERVATION: see -ATE[1].] *Chem.* A colloid-rich viscous liquid phase which may separate from a colloidal solution on addition of a third component.

coacervate /kəʊ'asəveɪt/ *v.t.* E17. [L *coacervat-* pa. ppl stem of *coacervare*, f. as CO- + *acervare*, f. *acervus* heap: see -ATE[3].] 1 Heap together, gather into a heap. Now *rare.* E17. 2 *Chem.* Cause coacervation of. M20.

coacervation /kəʊ,asə'veɪʃ(ə)n/ *n.* LME. [L *coacervatio(n-)*, f. as prec.: see -ATION.] 1 The action of heaping together; accumulation; an accumulated mass. Now *rare.* LME. 2 *Chem.* The separation of a coacervate from a colloidal solution. E20.

coach /kəʊtʃ/ *n.* M16. [Fr. *coche* f. Hungarian *kocsi* (*szekér*) (cart) from *Kocs*, a town in Hungary.] 1 A large horse-drawn carriage; *esp.* (*a*) a State carriage; (*b*) (chiefly *Hist.*) a privately owned carriage for personal use; (*c*) *Hist.* a large closed carriage for public conveyance of passengers. M16. b A railway passenger or mail carriage; *esp.* (*US*) one not provided with beds or berths. M19. c A chartered or long-distance usu. single-decker bus. Also called *motor coach.* E20. d Economy-class seating in an aircraft. *US.* M20. 2 A cabin at the stern of a man-of-war, usu. occupied by the captain. M17. 3 A private tutor. M19. b An instructor of an athletics team, rowing crew, etc. L19. c A tame bullock, horse, etc., used as a decoy in catching wild livestock. *Austral.* L19.

1 *hackney coach, stagecoach*, etc. **drive a coach and horses, a coach and six**, etc. **through** *fig.* render (legislation etc.) useless. *sociable coach*: see SOCIABLE *a.*

Comb.: **coach-box** a coachman's seat; **coach-building** the building of motor-vehicle bodies; **coach-built** *a.* (of a motor-vehicle body) built by craftsmen, orig. using wood; **coach-dog** a Dalmatian; **coach-horse**: used for drawing a coach; *devil's coach-horse*: see DEVIL *n.*; **coach-house** an outhouse for carriages; **coachload** a large number of people travelling by coach, a coachful; **coachman** a driver of a horse-drawn carriage; **coachmanship** skill in driving a coach; *coach station*: see STATION *n.*; **coach whip** [from its whiplike stems] the ocotillo, *Fouquiera splendens*; **coachwood** *Austral.* (a tree, esp. *Ceratopetalum apetalum*, yielding) close-grained timber suitable for cabinet-making; **coachwork** the bodywork of a road or rail vehicle.

coachee *n.* (*a*) *arch. colloq.* a coachman; (*b*) *US* (chiefly *Hist.*) a long lightweight horse-drawn carriage: L18. **coachful** *n.* a coach's full complement of passengers M17. **coachy** *n.* (*arch. colloq.*) a coachman E19.

coach /kəʊtʃ/ *v.* E17. [f. the n.] 1 *v.t.* Convey in, seat in, or provide with a coach. Now *rare.* E17. 2 *v.i.* Ride or drive in a coach. M17. 3 *v.t.* Tutor, train, esp. individually or intensively (*for* an examination, competition, etc.); give hints to; prime with facts. E18. b Decoy (wild cattle, horses, etc.) with tame animals. *Austral.* L19.

2 J. HATTON The . . inn of the old coaching days. 3 C. CHAPLIN Sydney had so zealously coached me that I was almost word-perfect. H. MACMILLAN Expert scientists who . . tried to coach me in the profound mysteries of atomic theory.

coacher /'kəʊtʃə/ *n.* L16. [f. COACH *n.* or *v.* + -ER[1].] †1 A coachman. L16–E17. 2 A coach-horse. E18. 3 A person who coaches a pupil, a team, etc. L19. b = COACH *n.* 3c. *Austral.* & *NZ.* E20.

coachwhip /'kəʊtʃwɪp/ *n.* M18. [f. COACH *n.* + WHIP *n.*] 1 A whip used by a coachman. M18. 2 More fully *coachwhip snake.* A fast-moving black or brown N. American snake, *Masticophis flagellum.* M18. 3 More fully *coachwhip bird.* The Australian whipbird. L18.

coact /kəʊ'akt/ *v.* LME. [Branch I f. L *coact-* pa. ppl stem of *cogere* compel (see COGENT); branch II f. CO- + ACT *v.*] I †1 *v.t.* Compel, constrain. LME–M17. 2 *v.t.* Control. *rare.* M19. II †3 *v.t.* Enact together. *rare.* Only in L16. 4 *v.i.* Act together, cooperate. E17.

coaction *n.* (*a*) (now *rare*) compulsion, restraint, coercion; (*b*) concerted action, acting together: LME.

coactive /kəʊ'aktɪv/ *n.* & *a.* E16. [Late L *coactivus* compulsory, f. *coact-* (see prec., -IVE), or (O)Fr. *coactif, -ive.* Sense B.2 f. CO- + ACTIVE *a.*, infl. by AL *coactivus* acting jointly.] †A *n.* A compelling cause. *rare.* Only in E16. B *adj.* †1a Enforced, compulsory. L16–M17. b Compelling, coercive. Now *rare.* E17. 2 Acting in concert, taking place together. *rare.* E17.

coadjutor /kəʊ'adʒʊtə/ *n.* LME. [(O)Fr. *coadjuteur*, †*-tor*, f. late L *coadjutor*, f. as CO- + ADJUTOR.] An assistant, *esp.* one appointed to assist a bishop.

coadjutorship *n.* (*a*) the office of coadjutor; (*b*) helping cooperation: M17. **coadjutress** *n.* a female coadjutor E17. †**coadjutrice** *n.* = COADJUTRESS M16–M18. **coadjutrix** *n.* = COADJUTRESS M17.

coadunate /kəʊ'adjʊneɪt/ *v.t.* E17. [L *coadunat-* pa. ppl stem of *coadunare*, f. as CO- + *adunare*, f. as AD- + *unare*, f. *unus* one: see -ATE[3].] Unite, combine. Chiefly as *coadunated* ppl a.

coadunation /kəʊ,adjʊ'neɪʃ(ə)n/ *n.* M16. [Late L *coadunatio(n-)*, f. as prec.: see -ATION.] Union, combination.

coagment /kəʊag'mɛnt/ *v.t.* Now *rare* or *obs.* E17. [L *coagmentare*, f. *coagmentum* joining: see -MENT.] Stick together; cement. Only as *coagmented* ppl a.

coagulable /kəʊ'agjʊləb(ə)l/ *a.* M17. [Fr., or med.L *coagulabilis*, f. *coagulare* COAGULATE *v.*: see -ABLE.] Able to be coagulated.

coagula'bility *n.* L18.

coagulant /kəʊ'agjʊl(ə)nt/ *n.* & *a.* L18. [L *coagulant-* pres. ppl stem of *coagulare* COAGULATE *v.*: see -ANT[1].] (An agent, as rennet) that brings about coagulation.

coagulase /kəʊ'agjʊleɪz, -s/ *n.* E20. [f. next + -ASE.] *Biochem.* A bacterial enzyme which brings about coagulation of the blood.

†**coagulate** *a.* LME–M19. [L *coagulatus*, f. as next: see -ATE[2].] Coagulated.

coagulate /kəʊ'agjʊleɪt/ *v.* LME. [L *coagulat-* pa. ppl stem of *coagulare*, f. as COAGULUM: see -ATE[3].] 1 *v.t.* & *i.* Change from a fluid to a more or less solid state, esp. by a chemical reaction; set, solidify. LME. †b *v.i.* Solidify by evaporation; crystallize. M17–E18. 2 *v.t.* & *i.* Form as a mass; unite into a mass. E17.

1 R. KNOX Albumen . . is coagulated by heat, alcohol and the stronger acids. E. HEMINGWAY I stopped the bleeding by lying still and letting it coagulate. 2 J. HOWELL Venus . . was . . coagulated of that foam. *fig.*: J. STEINBECK Gradually their wills coagulated.

coagulative *a.* having the property of coagulating; involving or producing coagulation: E17. **coagulator** *n.* = COAGULANT *n.* E17.

coagulation /kəʊagjʊ'leɪʃ(ə)n/ *n.* LME. [(O)Fr., or L *coagulatio(n-)*, f. as prec.: see -ATION.] 1 The action or process of coagulating. LME. †b Solidification by evaporation; precipitation from a solution; crystallization. L15–E18. 2 A coagulated mass. M17.

coagulin /kəʊ'agjʊlɪn/ *n.* E20. [f. COAGULATE *v.* + -IN[1].] *Biol.* Any substance produced in the body which accelerates the coagulation of foreign proteins or of blood.

coagulometer /kəʊ,agjʊ'lɒmɪtə/ *n.* E20. [f. COAGULATE *v.* + -OMETER.] An instrument for measuring the ease or rate of coagulation of blood.

coagulum /kəʊ'agjʊləm/ *n.* Pl. **-la** /-lə/. M16. [L.] 1 A coagulant; rennet; that part of the blood that coagulates, the clotting element. Now *rare* or *obs.* M16. 2 A coagulated mass. M17.

coaita /kəʊ'ʌɪtə/ *n.* L18. [Sp. f. Tupi-Guarani *coatá* monkey.] A spider-monkey.

coak /kəʊk/ *n.* & *v.* L15. [Perh. repr. ONFr. var. of OFr. *coche*, It. *cocca* notch: cf. COCK *v.*[4]] A *n.* A tabular projection on the face of a piece of scarfed timber, to fit into a recess in the face of another which is to be joined to it, to make a firmer joint; a metal lining to such a recess. L15. B *v.t.* Join by means of coaks. L18.

coal /kəʊl/ *n.* & *v.* [OE *col* = OFris., MLG *kole* (LG *kale*), MDu. *cole* (Du. *kool*), OHG *kol(o)* (G *Kohle*), ON *kol*, f. Gmc.] A *n.* 1 A red-hot piece of carbon, charred wood, etc.; a glowing ember. Also more fully *coal of fire* (arch.), *live coal*, etc. OE. †2 A charred remnant, a cinder; cinders, ashes. Also more fully *dead coal* etc. OE–M17. †3 *sing.* & in *pl.* Charcoal. ME–M19. 4 *sing.* & (now *rare*) in *pl.* A hard opaque black or blackish mineral, mainly carbonized plant matter, found in seams or strata at or below the earth's surface and used as fuel and in the manufacture of gas, tar, etc. (With *pl.*) a piece of this ready for burning in a fire. ME.

4 *bituminous coal, black coal, blind coal, brown coal, cannel coal, coking coal, mineral coal, rough coal, round coal, sea coal, soft coal, splint-coal, steam coal, stone-coal*, etc. P. H. JOHNSON She . . went over to the fire, throwing more coals upon it. N. CALDER Fossil fuels like coal and oil. W. BRONK The coal, . . I put it on the fire.

Phrases: **call over the coals** = *haul over the coals* below. **(carry) coals to Newcastle** (bring) a thing of which there is already a plentiful supply; (do) something absurdly superfluous. **haul over the coals** [from the treatment of heretics] call to account and convict, reprimand. **heap coals (of fire) on a person's head** cause remorse by returning good for evil. *small coal*: see SMALL *a.* *white coal*: see WHITE *a.*

Comb.: **coal-bed** a stratum of coal; **coal-black** *a.* completely black; **coal-box** a receptacle for coal to supply the fire of a room; **coal-bunker** a place for storing coal in a ship etc.; **coal-cellar** a basement storage place for coal; **coal-dust** powdered coal; **coalface** an exposed surface of coal in a mine; **coalfield** a district with a series of coal strata; **coal fire** a fire made (primarily) of coal; **coal-fired** *a.* heated or driven by coal; **coalfish** = SAITHE; **coal gas** a mixture of gases (chiefly hydrogen and methane) obtained by destructive distillation of coal and used for fuel; **coal-heaver** a person employed in moving coal; **coal-heugh** *Sc.* a coalmine; **coal-hole** a small coal-cellar; **coal-house** a building etc. for the storage of coal; **coalman** a man who carries, sells, or delivers coal; **coal-master** *Hist.* the owner or lessee of a coalmine; **coal measures** the series of rocks comprising coal seams and the intervening strata; **coal-merchant** a retail seller of coal; **coal-meter** (now *arch.* or *Hist.*) a person who measures or weighs coal (formerly *spec.*, an official of the corporation of London); **coalmine** a mine in which coal is dug; **coalminer** a person who digs for coal; **coalmining** digging for coal; **coal oil** *N. Amer.* (*a*) petroleum; (*b*) paraffin; **coal-owner** *Hist.* = *coal-master* above; **coal-pit** (*a*) (now *US*) a place where charcoal is made; (*b*) a coalmine; **coal-sack** (*a*) a sack for carrying coal; (*b*) a dark patch in the Milky Way, *spec.* (also **C-**) one near the Southern Cross; **coal-scuttle** a coal-box; a bucket, usu. with a sloping lip for pouring, for carrying and holding coal for the fire of a room; **coal-seam** a stratum of coal; **coal tar** a thick black viscid liquid produced by the destructive distillation of bituminous coal, containing benzene, naphthalene, phenols, aniline, and many other organic chemicals; **coal-whipper** *Hist.* a person or apparatus raising coal from a ship's hold by means of a pulley; **coal-worker** a coalminer; a worker at a colliery; **coal-works** a colliery.

B *v.* 1 a *v.i.* Get coal; take in a supply of coal. LME. b *v.t.* Supply with coal; put coal into (a ship etc.). M19. 2 *v.t.* Convert into charcoal. *arch.* L16.

1a E. WAUGH A.. sloop which was coaling for a cruise in the Persian Gulf.

¶The vowel was short in OE and remained so in many derivatives.

coaler *n.* a ship or railway transporting coal; a tender supplying coal to a steamship: L19. **coalifi'cation** *n.* the process by which plant remains become coal E20.

coalesce /kəʊə'lɛs/ *v.* M16. [L *coalescere*, f. as CO- + *alescere* grow up, f. *alere* nourish: see -ESCE.] †1 *v.t.* Cause to grow together, unite. M16–L18. 2 *v.i.* Grow or come together to form one whole; unite; combine in a coalition. M17.

2 LD MACAULAY Who had bound himself.. never to coalesce with Pitt. C. DARWIN The granules coalesce into larger masses. M. GIROUARD The elements that were to coalesce as 'Queen Anne'.

coalescence *n.* the action or process of coalescing; union; combination in a coalition: M16. **coalescent** *a.* that coalesces M17.

coalise *v.* var. of COALIZE.

Coalite /'kəʊlʌɪt/ *n.* E20. [f. COAL *n.* + -ITE[1].] (Proprietary name for) a kind of smokeless fuel made by refining coal.

coalition /kəʊə'lɪʃ(ə)n/ *n.* E17. [med.L *coalitio(n-)*, f. *coalit-* pa. ppl stem of *coalescere* COALESCE: see -ION.] 1 Coalescence; union, fusion, combination. E17. 2 *Polit.* A temporary combination of parties etc. that retain distinctive principles. E18.

1 J. TRAPP Water and oil violently shaken together may seem to mingle, but.. there is no coalition. B. COTTLE The coalition of an emphatic name and a clear symbol has often made for fine visual advertising. 2 T. BENN All major political parties are coming to be seen for what they are—broad coalitions.

coalitioner *n.* a person who forms or joins a coalition E19. **coalitionism** *n.* the principles or advocacy of government by coalition of parties E20. **coalitionist** *n.* an adherent of a coalition or of coalitionism L18.

coalize /'kəʊəlʌɪz/ *v.i.* Now *rare*. Also **-ise**. L18. [Fr. *coaliser*, f. *coalition* f. as prec.: see -IZE.] Form a coalition.

coalizer *n.* L18.

coalmouse /'kəʊlmaʊs/ *n.* Also **cole-**. Pl. **-mice** /-mʌɪs/. [OE *colmāse*: see COAL, TITMOUSE.] = next.

coal-tit /'kəʊltɪt/ *n.* Also **cole-**. M19. [f. COAL *n.* (on account of its dark colouring) + TIT *n.*[4]] A small greyish tit, *Parus ater*. Also called *coalmouse*.

Also **coal-titmouse** *n.* (*arch.*) L18.

coaly /'kəʊli/ *a.* See also COLLY *a.* & *n.*[2] L16. [f. COAL *n.* + -Y[1].] Having much coal; covered with coal; of the nature or colour of coal.

¶Place-name evidence and the short-vowel var. *colly* suggest that the wd was already in OE.

coaming /'kəʊmɪŋ/ *n.* E17. [Origin unkn.] A raised border round the hatches etc. of a ship to keep out water. Usu. in *pl.*

coapt /kəʊ'apt/ *v.t.* Now *rare*. L16. [Late L *coaptare*, f. as CO- + *aptare*, f. *aptus* APT.] Fit or join together.

coaptation /kəʊap'teɪʃ(ə)n/ *n.* M16. [Late L *coaptatio(n-)*, f. as prec.: see -ATION.] The adaptation or adjustment of things, parts, etc., to each other; *spec.* in *Med.*, the drawing together of separated tissue, e.g. in a wound or fracture.

coarb /'kəʊɑːb/ *n.* M17. [Ir. *comharba*.] *Hist.* A successor in an ecclesiastical office of the Celtic Church.

†**coarct** *v.t.* LME. [L *coar(c)tare*, f. as CO- + *artare*, f. *artus* confined.] 1 Press or draw together. LME–E17. 2 Restrict the action of (a person). LME–E19. 3 Confine within narrow limits. LME–M17.

coarctate /kəʊ'ɑːkteɪt/ *a.* LME. [L *coar(c)tatus* pa. pple of *coar(c)tare*: see prec., -ATE[2].] 1 Pressed close together, contracted, confined. LME. 2 *Entomol.* (Of a pupa) formed within and remaining concealed by the larval cuticle; (of metamorphosis) resulting in such a pupa. E19.

coarctation /kəʊɑːk'teɪʃ(ə)n/ *n.* LME. [L *coar(c)tatio(n-)*, f. *coar(c)tat-* pa. ppl stem of *coar(c)tare*: see COARCT, -ATION.] 1 The action of compressing tightly; the state of being tightly compressed; *spec.* (*Med.*) congenital narrowing of a short section of the aorta. LME. 2 Confinement or restriction as to limits. Now *rare*. E17.

coarse /kɔːs/ *a.* LME. [Origin unkn.] I 1 Ordinary, common, inferior. Largely *obs.* exc. as passing into other senses. LME.

1 SHAKES. *Hen. VIII* Now I feel Of what coarse metal ye are moulded—envy.

II (Often inherent in earlier uses of sense I.) 2 Rough, loose, or large in texture, grain, or features; in a natural or raw state; rough or harsh to the senses. L16. b Of weather: rough, stormy. Now *dial.* L18. 3 Not delicate in perception, manner, or taste; unrefined; rude, uncivil, vulgar; (esp. of language) obscene. L17.

2 R. W. EMERSON They are full of coarse strength, rude exercise.. and sound sleep. TENNYSON Thou, My Lord, eat also, tho' the fare is coarse. J. STEINBECK His mustache was thin and coarse. A. LURIE The fine sheet.. weighed on me like a coarse blanket. C. CONRAN Spread a layer of coarse salt over the bottom of a heavy frying-pan. 3 L. STEPHEN That style of coarse personal satire of which Swift was a master. L. G. GIBBON That coarse young Guthrie brute would never thrive.

Special collocations & *comb.*: **coarse-fibred** *a.* = *coarse-grained* below. **coarse fish** any freshwater fish other than salmon or trout. **coarse fishing**: for coarse fish. **coarse-grained** *a.* (*fig.*, of a person) having a coarse nature, unrefined.

coarsely *adv.* M16. **coarsen** *v.t.* & *i.* make or become (more) coarse E19. **coarseness** *n.* M16. **coarsish** *a.* somewhat coarse M18.

coarticulate /kəʊɑː'tɪkjʊleɪt/ *v.* L16. [f. CO- + ARTICULATE *v.*] 1 *v.i.* *Anat.* Unite to form a joint. *rare*. L16. 2 *v.t.* *Phonet.* Articulate together. M20.

coarticulation /ˌkəʊɑːtɪkjʊ'leɪʃ(ə)n/ *n.* L16. [f. CO- + ARTICULATION. Sense I tr. Gk *sunarthrōsis*.] †1 Jointing together of two bones. L16–M17. 2 *Phonet.* (An) articulation of two sounds together. M20.

coast /kəʊst/ *n.* OE. [OFr. *coste* (mod. *côte*) or (in earliest use) its source L *costa* rib, flank, side. In branch II repr. mod.Fr. *côte* w. the sense 'slope, hillside', infl. by the vb.] I †1 A rib; the side of any body (human or animal); the side of anything. OE–E19. 2 Orig. more fully *coast of the sea*, *sea-coast*. The border of land near the sea; the seashore. ME. †3 A region of the earth or the heavens; a tract, a district; a part of the world. ME–M17. †4 An area or direction in relation to a person or thing; a point of the compass; a quarter. ME–E18. †5 The border of a country etc., frontier territory. Usu. in *pl.* LME–E17.

2 **clear the coast** remove an enemy or other obstacle to (dis)embarkation etc. **(from) coast to coast** across a whole island or continent. *Slave Coast*: see SLAVE *n.* & *a.* **the Coast** *esp.* (*US*) the Pacific coast of N. America. **the coast is clear** the enemy is not about to obstruct (dis)embarkation etc.; there is no chance of being hindered or observed.

II 6 A slide for tobogganing; a slide downhill on a toboggan. *N. Amer.* L18. 7 A (usu. downhill) run on a bicycle etc. without pedalling or in a motor vehicle without using the engine. L19.

Comb.: **coast disease** *Austral.* a mineral deficiency disease of sheep and cattle; **coastguard** (one of) a body of people employed to keep watch on the coasts and thus save life, prevent smuggling, etc.; **coast sickness** *Austral.* = *coast disease* above.

coastal *a.* of or pertaining to a coast M19. **coastward** *a.*, **coastward(s)** *adv.* toward or in the direction of a coast M19. **coastways** *adv.* (*arch.*) = COASTWISE *adv.* E18. **coastwise** *adv.* & *a.* (*a*) *adv.* by way of or along a coast; (*b*) *adj.* following or carried along a coast: L17.

coast /kəʊst/ *v.* LME. [OFr. *costeier* (mod. *côtoyer*), f. as prec.] I †1 *v.t.* & *i.* Keep by the side of (a person etc. moving). LME–L17. †2 a *v.t.* Go or move by the side of (a place etc.); skirt. LME–M18. b *v.i.* Lie or lead alongside; go, pass, *along*, *by*, *round*, etc. LME–M19. c *v.i.* Move in a roundabout course. *rare* (Shakes.). Only in E17. 3 *v.t.* & *i.* Proceed or travel by the edge of (the sea, a lake, a river, etc.). Now *arch.* & *dial.* LME. 4 a *v.t.* Sail by the sea-coast of, skirt the shore of. LME. b *v.i.* Sail *along*, *by*, etc., a coast; sail along a coast from port to port. M16. †5 *v.t.* & *i.* Travel around, move about, explore, scour. LME–L17. †6 a *v.t.* Border, adjoin; approach, esp. with hostility. LME–M17. b *v.i.* Border (*up*)*on*; come or be near *to*; make one's way *to*, *towards*; approach. *lit.* & *fig.* LME–E18. 7 *v.i.* Of a hawk, hound, etc.: not fly or run straight at the prey. M16.

4b **coasting vessel** = COASTER 3.

II 8 *v.i.* Slide downhill on a toboggan. *N. Amer.* L18. 9 *v.i.* Ride (usu. downhill) on a bicycle, in a motor vehicle, etc., without the use of power. L19. 10 *v.i.* *fig.* Make progress without any exertion. M20.

coastel /kəʊs'tɛl/ *n.* L20. [Blend of COAST *n.* and HOTEL.] An accommodation barge for off-shore workers, troops, etc.; a floating barracks or hotel.

coaster /'kəʊstə/ *n.* L16. [f. COAST *v.* + -ER[1].] 1 A person who sails along a coast. L16. 2 A person who lives by a sea-coast. E17. 3 A vessel employed in sailing along a coast, trading from port to port, esp. of the same country. L17. 4 a A toboggan for coasting. *N. Amer.* M19. b A roller-coaster. *N. Amer.* E20. 5 A silver tray for a decanter; a small mat for a drinking-glass etc. L19.

coat /kəʊt/ *n.* & *v.* ME. [OFr. *cote* (mod. *cotte* petticoat), f. Proto-Romance f. Frank., of unkn. origin.] A *n.* 1 An outer garment, usu. made of cloth and having long sleeves, and orig. worn by men and boys. Without specification now *esp.* a sleeved outdoor garment worn over indoor clothes for warmth; also (esp. in *coat and skirt*) a woman's tailored jacket worn with a skirt; formerly also, a close-fitting tunic coming no lower than the waist. ME. b *transf.* With qualifying colour adj. A person wearing a coat of the specified colour, esp. as a uniform. E16. †c = *coat-card* below. L16–M17. †d = *coat-money* below. E17–E18. 2 A petticoat. Usu. in *pl. obs.* exc. *dial.* LME. 3 In translations of ancient languages: any of various styles of tunic or other outer garment for the body. LME. 4 More fully *coat of arms*. A person's or corporation's distinctive heraldic bearings or shield. LME. 5 A natural covering or integument: a An animal's covering of hair, fur, feathers, etc. Also (*rare*), an animal's hide. LME. b *Anat.* A membrane etc. enclosing or lining an organ. LME. c A skin, a rind, a husk; a layer of a bulb etc. M16. †6 Clothing as indicating a profession, class, etc. L16–L18. 7 *Naut.* A piece of tarred canvas or (now usu.) of rubber fixed around a mast, bowsprits, etc., where they enter the deck, to keep water out. E17. 8 A layer of any substance, esp. paint, covering a surface; a covering laid on at one time. E17. 9 *fig.* Anything that covers or conceals. E17.

1 *car coat*, *dress coat*, *frock-coat*, *greatcoat*, *housecoat*, *Mackintosh coat*, *mandarin coat*, *Melton coat*, *overcoat*, *raincoat*, *russet coat*, *surcoat*, *tailcoat*, *trench coat*, *tuxedo coat*, *waistcoat*, etc. **coat of arms** a coat or vest embroidered with heraldic arms, a herald's tabard; (see also sense 4 above). **coat of mail** a linen or leather jacket quilted with interlaced rings or overlapping plates of steel, as defensive armour. *cut*

one's coat according to one's cloth: see CLOTH *n.* 4. *pull a person's coat*: see PULL *v.* **trail one's coat** = *trail one's coat-tails* below. **turn one's coat** desert, change sides. **b** *blue-coat*, *redcoat*, etc. **8** FIRST *coat*. *rough coat*: see ROUGH *a.*

Comb.: **coat armour** †(*a*) a coat of arms (both senses); (*b*) blazonry, heraldic arms; †**coat-card** a court-card; **coat dress** a woman's tailored dress resembling a coat; **coat-hanger** a clothes-hanger; **coat-money** *Hist.* money for providing a coat for each man in military service, *esp.* a non-parliamentary tax exacted by Charles I; **coat-tail** a tail of a coat; *on a person's coat-tails*, undeservedly benefiting from someone's progress; *trail one's coat-tails* (for someone to tread on), seek to pick a quarrel.

B *v.t.* **1** Provide with or clothe in a coat; dress. LME. **2** Cover with a surface layer or successive layers of a substance as paint, tin, etc.; (of a substance) cover (a surface) in a coat. M18.

coated *a.* wearing a coat; having a coat (of a specified kind) (*wavy-coated*: see WAVY *a.* 1d); covered *with*, *in*, a coat or coating of some substance: L16. **coa'tee** *n.* (*a*) *arch.* a close-fitting short-tailed chiefly military coat; (*b*) a woman's or infant's short coat: L18. **coatless** *a.* L16.

coath *n.* var. of COTHE *n.*

coati /kəʊ'ɑːti/ *n.* Pl. **-s**, same. E17. [Sp. & Port. f. Tupi *kua'ti.*] A Central and S. American carnivore of the genera *Nasua* or *Nasuella*, resembling a racoon and with a long flexible snout.

Also **coatimundi** /kəʊ,ɑːtɪ'mʌndi/ *n.* [Port. *cuatimundi* f. Tupi *kuatimuʔne*, f. *kuaʔti* + *muʔne* snare, trick] L17.

coating /'kəʊtɪŋ/ *n.* L16. [f. COAT + -ING[1].] **1** Material for coats. L16. **2** (An article of) clothing of the nature of a coat. L18. **3** A layer of any substance, as paint, tin, etc., spread over or covering a surface. L18.

co-author /kəʊ'ɔːθə/ *n.* & *v.* L19. [f. CO- + AUTHOR.] **A** *n.* A joint author. L19. **B** *v.t.* Be a co-author of. M20.

co-authorship *n.* L19.

coax /'kəʊaks/ *n. colloq.* M20. [Abbrev.] Coaxial cable.

coax /kəʊks/ *v.* Orig. †**cokes.** L16. [f. COKES *n.*] **1** *v.t.* Pet, fondle, caress; treat endearingly. *obs.* exc. *dial.* L16. **2** *v.t.* Persuade gradually by flattery, caresses, etc., or by continued patient trial (*to do*, *into doing*, (*in*)*to* or *out of* an action or state); get (a thing) *out of*, *from* a person by such gradual persuasion. M17. **b** *v.i.* Employ persuasive flattery, caresses, etc., or continued patient trial. M17. †**3** *v.t.* Make a fool of. L17–E19.

2 L. M. MONTGOMERY I had ever such a time coaxing her to let me come down and say good-bye. P. KAVANAGH How to coax a cheer or a laugh from a lazy crowd. DAY LEWIS A recalcitrance I could always be coaxed out of by my father's pretending I was a bear. I. COLEGATE To rake out the embers of his stove and coax it back into flame.

¶Described by Samuel Johnson as 'a low word' and prob. in use long bef. it is recorded in literature. Sense 3 is prob. the original.

coaxer *n.* E18. **coaxingly** *adv.* in a coaxing manner E18.

coaxial /kəʊ'aksɪəl/ *a.* L19. [f. CO- + AXIAL.] Sharing a common axis; situated on or rotating about the same axis. Also, using or involving coaxial cable.

coaxial cable a coaxial line; a cable consisting of several coaxial lines. **coaxial line** an electrical transmission line with two concentric conductors separated by an insulator.

coaxially *adv.* L19.

cob /kɒb/ *n.*[1] LME. [Origin unkn.] **I** With the notion 'big', 'stout'. **1** A great man, a leading man. Now *dial.* LME. †**b** A wealthy man, a miser. M16–L17. **2** A male swan. Also *cob-swan.* LME. **3** A sturdy short-legged riding-horse. E19.

II With the notion 'rounded'. **4a** In full *cob-nut*. A large kind of hazelnut; (as *cob-nut*(*s*)), any of various children's games using nuts. M16. **b** In full *cob-loaf*. A round-headed loaf. E17. **c** In full (now *dial.*) *cob-coal*. A large roundish piece of coal. E19. **d** A testicle. Usu. in *pl. dial.* E19. **e** A (baked apple) dumpling. *dial.* L19. **5a** A small stack of hay or corn. *dial.* E17. **b** A bunch or knot of hair; a chignon. M19. **6** *gen.* A lump or heap *of*. *dial.* L19.

III With the notion 'head', 'top'. †**7a** The head of a (red) herring. L16–M17. **b** In *pl.* Young herring. *Sc.* L19. **8** = CORN-COB 1. L17. **9** The seeding head of wheat, clover, etc. *dial.* M19.

8 corn on the cob maize cooked and eaten attached to the cob.

Comb.: *cob coal*: see sense 4c above; **cob-iron** (*a*) in *pl.* (*Hist.*), the irons supporting a spit; (*b*) an andiron; *cob-loaf*: see sense 4b above; **cob-meal** *US* corn-cobs ground down. *cob-nut*(*s*): see sense 4a above; **cob pipe** = CORN-COB 2.

cob /kɒb/ *n.*[2] Also **cobb.** M16. [Perh. of LG origin: cf. Du. *kobbe*, *kobmeeuw*, EFris. *sē-kobbe.*] More fully *sea-cob*. A gull, *esp.* a greater black-backed gull.

cob /kɒb/ *n.*[3] E17. [Origin unkn.] A composition of clay, gravel, and straw, used for building walls etc.

cob /kɒb/ *n.*[4] Also **cobb.** E17. [Perh. abbrev. of COBBLE *n.*] A mole or pier (as constructed of cobble-stones).

cob /kɒb/ *n.*[5] Chiefly *Anglo-Ir. obs.* exc. *Hist.* L17. [Perh. f. COB *n.*[1] I (as the largest silver coin).] A Spanish dollar or piece of eight.

cob /kɒb/ *n.*[6] *dial.* Also **cobb.** L17. [Origin unkn.] A wicker basket carried on the arm.

cob /kɒb/ *n.*[7] *US* & *dial.* Also **cobb.** E19. [f. COB *v.*[1]] A blow, a knock.

cob /kɒb/ *n.*[8] *slang.* M20. [Origin unkn.] *have, get, a cob on*, be annoyed; become angry.

cob *n.*[9] var. of KOB *n.*[1]

cob /kɒb/ *v.*[1] Infl. **-bb-.** LME. [Origin uncertain: perh. imit.] †**1** *v.i.* Fight; give blows. Only in LME. **2a** *v.t. Naut.* Strike on the buttocks with a flat instrument, as a punishment. Now *Hist.* M18. **b** *gen.* Strike. *dial.* E19. **3** *v.t.* Crush or bruise (ore). L18. **4a** *v.i.* Of seed: undergo threshing (*well* etc.). L18. **b** *v.t.* Thresh or beat out (seed). E19.

cob /kɒb/ *v.*[2]*i.* & *t. dial.* Infl. **-bb-.** L19. [Origin unkn.] Take a liking to (each other), get on well *together*.

cobalamin /kə'bɒləmɪn/ *n.* M20. [f. next + VIT)AMIN.] *Biochem.* Any of a group of cobalt-containing substances including vitamin B_{12}.

cobalt /'kəʊbɒlt, -ɔːlt/ *n.* & *a.* L17. [G *Kobalt*, KOBOLD, lit. 'fairy, demon': so called from the belief that cobalt ore was deleterious to the silver ores with which it occurred: cf. NICKEL *n.* & *a.*, WOLFRAM.] **A** *n.* **1** A hard, weakly magnetic metal which is a chemical element of the transition series, atomic no. 27, used widely in alloys. (Symbol Co.) L17. **2** In full *cobalt blue*. A deep blue pigment containing cobalt(II) oxide and alumina; the colour of such a pigment. M19.

1 *red cobalt* (*ore*): see RED *a.* *speiss-cobalt*: see SPEISS 2.

Comb.: **cobalt bloom** = ERYTHRITE; *cobalt blue*: see sense 2 above; **cobalt bomb** (*a*) a container of a cobalt radioisotope for therapeutic use; (*b*) a hydrogen bomb designed to disperse radioactive cobalt; **cobalt glance** = COBALTITE.

B *adj.* Of cobalt blue. M19.

co'baltic *a.* of or pertaining to cobalt; *spec.* of trivalent cobalt: L18. **cobal'tiferous** *a.* containing or yielding cobalt M19. **co'baltous** *a.* of divalent cobalt M19.

cobalti- /kə'bɒlti, -'bɔːlti/ *comb. form* of COBALT: see -I-. Esp. of trivalent cobalt (cf. COBALTO-).

cobalti'cyanide *n.* a salt of the complex anion $Co(CN)_6{}^{3-}$ L19.

cobaltite /'kəʊb(ə)ltʌɪt/ *n.* M19. [f. COBALT *n.* + -ITE[1].] *Min.* A cubic sulpharsenide of cobalt which usu. occurs as silvery-white metallic cubic or polyhedral crystals.

Earlier †**cobaltine** *n.* L18–L19.

cobalto- /kə'bɒltəʊ, -'bɔːlt-/ *comb. form* of COBALT: see -O-. Esp. of divalent cobalt (cf. COBALTI-). Freq. forming names of minerals.

cobb *n.* var. of COB *n.*[2], *n.*[4], *n.*[6], *n.*[7]

cobber /'kɒbə/ *n.*[1] L18. [f. COB *v.*[1] or *n.*[1] + -ER[1].] A person who breaks ore into small pieces.

cobber /'kɒbə/ *n.*[2] & *v. Austral.* & *NZ colloq.* L19. [Perh. f. COB *v.*[2]] **A** *n.* A companion; a mate; a friend. L19. **B** *v.i.* Foll. by *up*: make friends (*with*). M20.

cobble /'kɒb(ə)l/ *n.* LME. [f. COB *n.*[1] II + -LE[1].] **1** In full *cobble-stone*. A water-worn rounded stone, esp. of the size used for paving. LME. **2** In *pl.* Coal in lumps of this size. E19.

cobbly *a.* paved with cobbles L19.

cobble /'kɒb(ə)l/ *v.*[1] L15. [Back-form. f. COBBLER.] **1** *v.t.* & *i.* Mend (esp. shoes); mend roughly or clumsily; patch (*up*). L15. **2** *v.t.* Put *together* roughly or clumsily. L16. **3** *v.t.* Make by putting things together roughly or clumsily. Also foll. by *together*. M18.

cobble /'kɒb(ə)l/ *v.*[2]*t.* L17. [f. COBBLE *n.*] **1** Pelt with stones etc. *dial.* L17. **2** Pave with cobbles. M19.

cobbler /'kɒblə/ *n.* ME. [Origin unkn.] **1** A person who mends shoes. ME. **b** The last sheep to be sheared, an awkward sheep to shear, (in punning allusion to a cobbler's last). *Austral.* & *NZ colloq.* L19. **c** In *pl.* [abbrev. of *cobbler's awls* below]. Testicles; nonsense, rubbish. *slang.* M20. **2** A clumsy worker, a botcher. L16. **3** An iced drink of wine, sugar, and lemon, in a tall glass. E19. **4** A dish of fruit, or occas. other ingredients, baked with a cake topping. Orig. *US.* M19. **5** A horse chestnut used in the children's game of conkers. *dial.* L19.

Comb.: **cobbler's awls** *rhyming slang* balls, testicles; **cobbler's peg**(**s**) *Austral.* a weed of the composite family with sharp-pointed seeds, spec. *Bidens pilosa*; **cobbler's wax** a resinous substance used for waxing thread.

cobbra /'kɒbrə/ *n. Austral.* Also **cobra.** M19. [Aborig. *gabara.*] The head; the skull.

cobby /'kɒbi/ *a.* L17. [f. COB *n.*[1] I + -Y[1].] **1** Stout, hearty. *dial.* L17. **2** Headstrong; arrogant. *dial.* L18. **3** Of the nature of or like a cob (horse); shortish and thickset; stocky. L19.

Cobdenism /'kɒbd(ə)nɪz(ə)m/ *n.* M19. [f. Richard *Cobden* (1804–65), Eng. statesman and economist, its leading advocate + -ISM.] *Hist.* A policy advocating free trade, peace, and international collaboration.

Cobdenite *n.* a supporter of Cobdenism L19.

co-belligerent /kəʊbɪ'lɪdʒ(ə)r(ə)nt/ *a.* & *n.* E19. [f. CO- + BELLIGERENT.] (A nation etc.) jointly waging war.

co-belligerence, **co-belligerency** *ns.* the quality or state of being (a) co-belligerent M20.

cobia /'kəʊbɪə/ *n.* M19. [Origin unkn.] A large slender predatory game-fish, *Rachycentron canadum*, of the tropical Atlantic, Indian, and western Pacific Oceans. Also called *runner*, *sergeant-fish*.

coble /'kəʊb(ə)l/ *n.* OE. [Perh. f. Celt.: cf. Welsh *ceubal* ferry-boat, skiff, wherry, OBreton *caubal.*] A flat-bottomed boat used esp. for fishing in Scotland and NE England: in Scotland usu. a rowing boat used on rivers and lakes, in NE England a seagoing boat with oars and a lug sail.

Cobol /'kəʊbɒl/ *n.* M20. [Acronym, f. *c*ommon *b*usiness-*o*riented *l*anguage.] (The name of) a programming language designed for use in business operations.

cobra /'kəʊbrə, 'kɒbrə/ *n.*[1] M17. [Port. *cobra de capello* lit. 'snake with hood', ult. f. L *colubra* snake.] Orig. more fully *cobra de capello* /də ka'pɛləʊ/. Any of a number of venomous Asian and African snakes esp. of the genus *Naja*, which can dilate their necks to form a hood when excited.

king cobra, *spectacled cobra*, etc.

cobra *n.*[2] var. of COBBRA.

co-brother /kəʊ'brʌðə/ *n.* Pl. **-brothers, -brethren** /-'brɛðr(ə)n/. L16. [f. CO- + BROTHER *n.*] Brother in the same craft or occupation; confrère.

Coburg /'kəʊbəːg/ *n.* E19. [f. Prince Albert of Saxe-*Coburg* (1819–61), consort of Queen Victoria.] Chiefly *Hist.* **1** A two-wheeled covered carriage or cart, used esp. in the country. E19. **2** In full *Coburg loaf*. A kind of loaf. M19. **3** A thin fabric used for dresses and coat linings. M19.

cobweb /'kɒbwɛb/ *n.* Orig. †**cop**(**pe**)**-.** ME. [f. COP *n.*[2] + WEB *n.*] **1** The fine network spun by a spider to catch its prey; the material of this; *spec.* (*a*) an old web covered with dirt and dust (usu.

in *pl.*); (*b*) *Zool.* the type of web built by a cobweb spider. ME. **b** A single thread spun by a spider. M19. †**2** Threads similar to the spider's, produced by insects etc. LME–E17. **3** *fig.* Anything of flimsy, frail, or unsubstantial texture. L16. **b** *sing.* & (usu.) in *pl.* Musty rubbish. L16. **c** A subtly woven snare; an entangling mesh. M17. **4** In full *cobweb bird*. The spotted flycatcher, which uses spiders' webs in constructing its nest. E18.

3b blow, clear, away the cobwebs remove fustiness or lethargy.

Comb.: *cobweb bird*: see sense 4 above; **cobweb law** *arch.* a law which can be broken by the rich or powerful; **cobweb micrometer**: with spider's threads instead of wires; **cobweb spider** any of various spiders of the family Theridiidae, which build tangled three-dimensional webs.

cobwebbed *a.* covered or hung (as) with cobwebs E17. **cobwebbery** *n.* a structure of cobweb, *fig.* (a) subtle entangling argument: M19. **cobwebby** *a.* cobwebbed; resembling cobwebs: M18. **cobweblike** *a.* resembling (that of) a cobweb or cobwebs, cobwebby M17.

coca /ˈkəʊkə/ *n.* L16. [Sp. f. Aymara *kuka* or Quechua *koka*.] A S. American shrub, *Erythroxylum coca*; the dried leaves of this, chewed as a stimulant.

Coca-Cola /kəʊkəˈkəʊlə/ *n.* L19. [f. prec. + COLA *n.*[1]] (Proprietary name for) an American aerated soft drink.

coca-colonization /ˌkəʊkəkɒlənʌɪˈzeɪʃ(ə)n/ *n.* the spread of American culture as represented by Coca-Cola M20.

cocaine /kəˈkeɪn/ *n.* M19. [f. COCA + -INE[5].] An alkaloid, $C_{17}H_{21}NO_4$, which is present in the leaves and other parts of the coca shrub and is used as a local anaesthetic and as a stimulant.

cocainism *n.* (the condition due to) excessive use of or addiction to cocaine L19. **cocainiˈzation** *n.* treatment with cocaine L19. **cocainize** *v.t.* treat with cocaine L19.

cocarcinogen /kəʊkɑːˈsɪnədʒ(ə)n/ *n.* M20. [f. CO- + CARCINOGEN.] A substance that increases the carcinogenic effect of another.

cocarcinoˈgenic *a.* M20.

cocasse /kɔkas/ *a.* M19. [Fr.] Droll; ridiculous.

coccagee /kɒkəˈdʒiː/ *n.* E18. [Ir. *cac an ghéidh* goose-dung (from its greenish-yellow colour).] A cider apple formerly in repute; cider made from it.

Cocceian /kɒkˈsiːən/ *n.* & *a.* L17. [f. *Cocceius* (see below) Latinized form of the German surname *Koch* + -AN.] *Eccl. Hist.* An adherent of, of or pertaining to, the beliefs of the German-born dogmatic theologian Johannes Cocceius (1603–69), who held that Old Testament history was a foreshadowing of the history of Christ and his Church.

coccid /ˈkɒksɪd/ *n.* & *a.* L19. [f. COCCUS + -ID[3].] **A** *n.* A homopteran insect of the family Coccidae; a scale insect. L19. **B** *adj.* Of, pertaining to, or designating this family. E20.

coccidia *n.* pl. of COCCIDIUM.

coccidioidomycosis /kɒksɪdɪˌɔɪdəʊmʌɪˈkəʊsɪs/ *n.* Pl. **-coses** /-ˈkəʊsiːz/. M20. [f. mod.L *Coccidioides* (see below) + -O- + MYCOSIS.] *Med.* Infection with the fungus *Coccidioides immitis*, which usu. affects the lungs and is endemic in the warmer, arid regions of America. Also called *San Joaquin Valley fever*, *valley fever*.

coccidiosis /kɒkˌsɪdɪˈəʊsɪs/ *n.* Pl. **-oses** /-ˈəʊsiːz/. L19. [f. COCCIDIUM + -OSIS.] A disease of birds or mammals caused by the presence of coccidia.

coccidiostat /kɒkˈsɪdɪə(ʊ)stat/ *n.* M20. [f. as next + -O- + -STAT.] A substance administered usu. to poultry to retard the growth and reproduction of pathogenic coccidia.

coccidium /kɒkˈsɪdɪəm/ *n.* Pl. **-ia** /-ɪə/. M19. [mod.L, f. Gk *kokkid-*, *-is* dim. of *kokkos*: see COCCUS, -IUM.] †**1** *Bot.* A spherical or hemispherical conceptacle in some algae. M–L19. **2** A sporozoan of the subclass Coccidia (or suborder Eimeriorina), which includes toxoplasmas and other intracellular parasites including those of malaria (plasmodia). L19.

coccidian *n.* & *a.* (*a*) *n.* = COCCIDIUM 2; (*b*) *adj.* designating or pertaining to (parasitic) coccidia: E20.

coccinellid /kɒksɪˈnelɪd/ *n.* & *a.* L19. [mod.L *Coccinellidae* (see below), f. *Coccinella* genus name, f. L *coccineus* scarlet: see -ID[3].] **A** *n.* A beetle of the family Coccinellidae; a ladybird. L19. **B** *adj.* Of, pertaining to, or designating this family. E20.

coccolith /ˈkɒkəlɪθ/ *n.* M19. [f. Gk *kokkos* (see COCCUS) + -LITH.] A minute rounded calcareous platelet, numbers of which form the spherical shells of unicellular marine flagellates of the order Coccolithophorida.

coccoˈlithophore *n.* an organism of this order M20. **coccolithoˈphorid** *n.* & *a.* M20.

coccosphere /ˈkɒkəsfɪə/ *n.* M19. [f. as prec. + SPHERE *n.*] The shell of a coccolithophore.

cocculus indicus /ˌkɒkjʊləs ˈɪndɪkəs/ *n. phr.* Also †**cocculus india**. L16. [mod.L *cocculus* irreg. dim. of L *coccum* kermes, berry + *indicus* Indian.] The toxic dried berries of a SE Asian climbing shrub, *Anamirta cocculus* (family Menispermaceae).

coccus /ˈkɒkəs/ *n.* In sense 2 orig. †**-um**. Pl. **cocci** /ˈkɒk(s)ʌɪ, ˈkɒk(s)iː/. M18. [mod.L f. Gk *kokkos* grain, berry, seed.] **1** A scale insect, *esp.* any of those yielding cochineal, kermes, or lac. Now *rare* or *obs.* M18. **2** *Bot.* One of the separable carpels of a dry fruit. E19. **3** Any more or less spherical bacterium. L19.

coccal *a.* of or pertaining to a (bacterial) coccus; of the nature of or resembling a coccus: E20. **coccoid** *a.* of the nature of or resembling a coccus (usu. a bacterial coccus) E20.

coccy- /ˈkɒksi/ *comb. form* of COCCYX. Bef. a vowel also **coccyg-** /ˈkɒksɪdʒ, -ɪg/, **coccygo-** /ˈkɒksɪgəʊ/ (see -O-).

coccyˈdynia *n.* pain in the coccygeal region L19.

coccygeal /kɒkˈsɪdʒɪəl/ *a.* L18. [f. as next + -AL[1].] *Anat.* Of or pertaining to the coccyx.

coccyx /ˈkɒksɪks/ *n.* Pl. **-yxes, -yges** /-ɪdʒiːz/. L16. [L f. Gk *kokkux*, *-ug-* (orig.) cuckoo: from its resemblance (in humans) to a cuckoo's beak.] *Anat.* The small triangular bone forming the lower end of the spinal column in humans and some apes; the analogous part in birds or other vertebrates.

Cochin /ˈkɒtʃɪn/ *n.* M19. [*Cochin*-China, formerly a part of Fr. Indo-China, now of Vietnam.] More fully *Cochin-China* (*fowl*). A breed of poultry from Cochin-China, with feathery legs.

cochineal /ˈkɒtʃɪniːl/ *n.* L16. [Fr. *cochenille*, perh. f. L *coccinus* scarlet f. Gk *kokkos* COCCUS, or f. Sp. *cochinilla* woodlouse.] **1** (A scarlet dye made from) the dried bodies of females of a scale insect, *Dactylopius coccus*, which lives on certain cacti in Mexico and (when cultivated) elsewhere. L16. **2** The insect itself. L16.

Comb.: **cochineal insect** = sense 2 above; **cochineal plant** a shrubby cactus, *Nopalea cochenillifera*, which is the principal species on which the insect feeds.

cochlea /ˈkɒklɪə/ *n.* Pl. **-eae** /-ɪiː/. M16. [L *coc(h)lea* snail-shell, screw f. Gk *kokhlias*, prob. rel. to *kogkhē* CONCH.] †**1** A spiral staircase; an Archimedean screw. M16–L17. **2** *Anat.* The spiral cavity of the inner ear, in which the sensory reception of sound occurs. L17. **3** A snail-shell. *rare.* L17.

cochlear *a.* of or pertaining to the cochlea of the ear; *spec.* designating or pertaining to a branch of the vestibulocochlear nerve concerned with hearing (TECTORIAL *membrane of the cochlear duct*): M19. **cochleate** *a.* (chiefly *Bot.*) twisted, spiral M19. **cochleated** *a.* E18.

cochleariform /kɒklɪˈɛːrɪfɔːm/ *a.* M19. [f. L *coc(h)leare* spoon + -I- + -FORM.] Spoon-shaped.

cochlite /ˈkɒklʌɪt/ *n.* L17. [f. Gk *kokhlos* spiral sea shell + -ITE[1].] *Palaeont.* A fossil spiral shell.

cock /kɒk/ *n.*[1] [OE *cocc*, *kok* = ON *kokkr*, prob. f. med.L *coccus* (Salic Laws), of imit. origin; reinforced in ME by (O)Fr. *coq*.] **I 1** A male bird, *esp.* a male domestic fowl. As 2nd elem. of comb. also in specific names of birds (usu. distinctively of the male). OE. **b** A weathercock. LME. **c** A woodcock. M16. **2** The crowing of a domestic cock. LME. **3** The leader, the chief, the best. Usu. foll. by *of*. M16. **4** Orig., a person who fights pluckily. Now, a familiar form of address to a man, esp. in *old cock*. M17. **5** A male lobster, crab, or salmon. L17.

1 *blackcock, gorcock, heath-cock, moorcock, peacock, woodcock*, etc. **cock-of-the-north** the brambling. **cock-of-the-plains** *N. Amer.* the sage grouse, *Centrocercus urophasianus*. **cock-of-the-rock** a S. American cotinga of the genus *Rupicola*, the male of which is bright red or orange with a prominent crest. **cock-of-the-wood** (*a*) the capercaillie; (*b*) *N. Amer.* the red-crested woodpecker. **cock's egg** *dial.* a small misshapen egg. **fighting cock** a gamecock (*live like fighting cocks*, get the best of fare). *gamecock*: see GAME *n.* *sage cock*: see SAGE *n.*[1] **talk of a cock and a bull, (tell) a story** etc. **of a cock and a bull** (tell) a rambling inconsequential tale, (tell) an incredible tale, (hence *cock-and-bull story* below). See also WEATHERCOCK. **2** SHAKES. *Lear* This is the foul fiend Flibbertigibbet; he begins at curfew, and walks till the first cock. **3 cock-of-the-walk** a dominant person, a person whose supremacy in a particular circle or sphere is undisputed. **4** DICKENS Do you always smoke arter you goes to bed, old cock?

II 6 A tapped spout; a tap, a valve for controlling flow. L15. **7** A lever in a gun raised ready to be released by the trigger. M16. **8a** The pointer of a balance. E17. **b** The gnomon of a sundial. E17. **c** An overhanging bracket in a clock or watch supporting the outer end of the pivot of a wheel or pendulum. L17. **9** The penis. Cf. earlier PILLICOCK. *coarse slang*. E17. **10** *Curling*. The circle at the end of the rink at which stones are aimed. L18. **11** A cock-and-bull story; nonsense. Cf. POPPYCOCK. *slang*. M19.

6 full cock with the cock fully open. STOPCOCK. THREE-*way cock*. **turn the cock**: open it.

III [Partly f. COCK *v.*[1]] **12** The state of being cocked; a pronounced upward turn or bend; *spec.* an upward turn to the brim of a hat; a turned-up part of the brim of a hat. E17.

12 at full cock (of a firearm) with the cock lifted to the position at which the trigger will act. **at half cock** (of a firearm) with the cock lifted but not to the position at which the trigger will act; *fig.* when only half ready. KEVENHULLER *cock*.

Other phrases: †**set (the) cock on (the) hoop, set cock a hoop** [perh. repr. sense 6 but difficult to explain] (app.) turn on the tap and let the liquor run; drink without stint; abandon oneself to reckless enjoyment. *slur-cock*: see SLUR *n.*[2] 3.

Comb.: **cock-and-bull story** [f. *a story of a cock and a bull* above] an incredible tale, a false story; **cock-and-hen** *a.* including both men and women, for both sexes; **cock-bead** *Cabinet-making* a quirked or projecting bead; **cock-beaded** *a.* decorated with cock-beads; **cock-brained** *a.* foolish and light-headed, silly; **cock crow** dawn; **cock-fight**: *esp.* between cocks set to fight, as a sport; **cock-fighting** setting cocks to fight, as a sport; **cock-laird** *Sc.* a small landowner; **cock-light** *dial.* (*a*) dawn; (*b*) evening twilight; **cockmaster** *Hist.* a person who rears gamecocks; †**cock-match** a cock-fighting match; **cock-paddle** *Sc.* & *north.* the lumpfish; **cock-penny** *Hist.* a customary payment at Shrovetide, formerly made to the schoolmaster in certain schools in the north of England, orig. to defray cock-fighting or cock-throwing expenses; **cock robin** (a familiar name for) a male robin; **cocksfoot (grass)** a pasture grass, *Dactylis glomerata*, with a large branched panicle; **cockshead** *dial.* any of various meadow plants with reddish flowers, *esp.* sainfoin and red clover; **cockshoot** (now *dial.*) a broad woodland glade with nets stretched across the opening to catch woodcock; **cock-shut (time)** (now *dial.*) twilight; **cock-shy** (a throw at) an object (orig. a cock) set up to be thrown at with sticks, stones, etc.; *fig.* an object of ridicule or criticism; **cock sparrow** a male sparrow; a small lively pugnacious person; **cock-stand** *coarse slang* an erection of the penis; **cock-sucker** *coarse slang* a fellator; freq. as a generalized term of abuse; **cock-teaser** = *prick-teaser* s.v. PRICK *n.*; **cock-throppled, -throttled** *a.* (of a horse) having a long excessively curved neck; **cock-throwing** *Hist.* throwing sticks etc. at a cock tied to a post to knock it down or kill it, as a sport esp. at Shrovetide.

cock-a-doodle-doo /ˌkɒkəduːd(ə)lˈduː/ *n.* & *int.* (repr.) a cock's crow; (*nursery* or *joc.*) a cock: L16. **cockish** *a.* (*a*) strutting, self-assertive, cocky; (*b*) (now *dial.*) lecherous; (*c*) *joc.* resembling a cock: M16.

cock /kɒk/ *n.*[2] *obs.* exc. in COCKBOAT, COXSWAIN. ME. [OFr. *coque* dial. var. of *coche* = Prov. *coca*,

OIt. *cocca*, f. med.L *caudica*, f. L *caudex*, *codex* block of wood: cf. COG *n.*[1]] = COCKBOAT.

cock /kɒk/ *n.*[3] LME. [Perh. Scand. (cf. Norw. *kok* heap, lump, Da. dial. *kok* haycock, Sw. *koka* clod), but an OE wd = 'hill' has been assumed for the place-names *Cockhampstead*, *Cookham*, etc.] A small conical heap of hay etc. in a field.

cock /kɒk/ *n.*[4] Now *arch.* & *dial.* LME. [Alt.] God: used esp. in oaths and exclamations.

JONSON Cock's bodikins! we must not lose John Clay. SIR W. SCOTT Is he? . . ay, by cock and pie is he.

cock /kɒk/ *v.*[1] ME. [f. COCK *n.*[1]] †**I 1** *v.i.* & *t.* (w. *it*). Fight, quarrel. ME–E17.

II 2 *v.i.* Train or use gamecocks. Chiefly as *cocking* vbl n. M16. **3** *v.i.* Strut, swagger; brag, crow *over*. *obs.* exc. *dial.* L16. **4** *v.i.* Shoot woodcocks. Chiefly as *cocking* vbl n. L17.

III 5 †**a** *v.t.* Place (a match) in the cock of a matchlock gun. L16–M17. **b** *v.t.* Put (a firearm) in readiness for firing by raising the cock etc.; raise (the cock), draw back (the hammer), set (the trigger), in readiness for firing. M17. **6** *v.t.* Erect, stick or stand up (or *up*), jauntily or defiantly; turn or tip to one side alertly, jauntily, or defiantly; bend (a limb, a joint, etc.) at an angle. E17. **b** Turn up the brim of (a hat). M17. **7** *v.i.* Stick or stand up (or *up*) conspicuously. E17. **8** *v.t.* Foll. by *up*: bungle, make a mess of. *slang.* M20.

6 SIR W. SCOTT The wisest Captain that ever cocked the sweet gale in his bonnet. E. FIGES A small bird . . stopped to listen, its head cocked to one side. **cock an eyebrow** look quizzically (*at*). *cock a snook*: see SNOOK *n.*[2] **cock one's** (or **the**) **ears** raise or turn the ears in attention, begin to listen. **cock one's eye** glance knowingly, wink, (*at*). **cock one's eyebrows** = *cock an eyebrow* above. **cock one's hat** set one's hat jauntily on one side of the head; tip or raise one's hat jauntily, as a salutation; (see also sense 6b above). **cock one's** (or **the**) **nose** turn up one's nose in contempt or indifference. **b cocked hat** (*a*) formerly, a (three-cornered) hat with the brim permanently turned up; now, a brimless triangular hat pointed at front and back and rising to a point at the crown; *knock into a cocked hat*, defeat utterly, damage irreparably; (*b*) a note, napkin, etc., folded into the shape of a cocked hat.

cocking *n.* (*a*) the action of the vb; (*b*) *arch.* a cock-fight: ME.

cock /kɒk/ *v.*[2]*t.* & *i.* LME. [f. COCK *n.*[3]] Pile (hay etc.) into cocks.

cock /kɒk/ *v.*[3]*t.* *colloq.* & *dial.* L16. [Perh. abbrev. of COCKER *v.*[1]] Pamper, indulge; reward disproportionately. Freq. foll. by *up*.

cock /kɒk/ *v.*[4]*t.* Also **cau(l)k** /kɔːk/. M17. [Perh. f. COAK *n.*: cf. COG *v.*[3]] Secure by a dovetail, mortise and tenon, etc.

cockabully /ˈkɒkəbʊli/ *n.* *NZ.* L19. [f. Maori *kokopu*: cf. BULLY *n.*[4]] Any of various small blunt-nosed freshwater fishes, esp. of the genus *Gobiomorphus*.

cockade /kɒˈkeɪd/ *n.* Also †**-ard**. M17. [Fr. *cocarde* orig. in *bonnet à la coquarde* f. fem. of †*coquard* proud, saucy, f. *coq* COCK *n.*[1]: see -ARD. Assim. to -ADE.] A rosette, knot of ribbons, etc., worn in the hat as a badge of office or party, or as part of a livery.

cockaded *a.* having or wearing a cockade M18.

cock-a-hoop /kɒkəˈhuːp/ *a.* & *adv.* M17. [f. †*set cock a hoop* s.v. COCK *n.*[1], infl. by sense 1 of COCK *n.*[1]] **A** *adj.* Elated, boastfully triumphant. M17. **B** *adv.* †**1** *set cock-a-hoop*, elate, make boastfully triumphant. L17–E18. **2** Elatedly, with boastful triumph. E19.

Cockaigne /kɒˈkeɪn/ *n.* Also **-ayne**. ME. [OFr. *cocaigne*, as in *pais de cocaigne* fool's paradise (mod. *cocagne*), corresp. to Sp. *cucaña*, Port. *cucanha*, It. *cuccagna*, f. MLG *kokenje* small very sweet cake, dim. of *koke* CAKE *n.*] **1** An imaginary land of idleness and luxury. ME. **2** London (punningly w. reference to COCKNEY). *joc.* E19.

cockal *n.* var. of COCKALL.

cock-a-leekie /kɒkəˈliːki/ *n.* Also **cocky-** /kɒkɪ-/, **-leeky**. M18. [f. COCK *n.*[1] + LEEK: see -IE, -Y[6].] A Scottish soup made with chicken and leeks.

cockall /ˈkɒkɔːl/ *n.* *obs.* exc. *dial.* Also **-al** /-(ə)l/. M16. [Origin unkn.] †**1** A knuckle-bone, esp. (in *pl.*) as used in various games. M16–L17. **2** *sing.* & *in pl.* Any of various games using knuckle-bones. L16.

cockalorum /kɒkəˈlɔːrəm/ *n.* *colloq.* E18. [Arbitrary, f. COCK *n.*[1]] A self-important little man.

hey cockalorum, hi cockalorum, high cockalorum: (the cry in) a game like leap-frog.

cockamamie /ˈkɒkəmeɪmi/ *n.* & *a.* *slang* (orig. *US*). Also **-my**. M20. [Prob. alt. of DECALCOMANIA.] **A** *n.* A picture or design left on the skin as a transfer. M20. **B** *adj.* Muddled; implausible, incredible. M20.

cockamaroo /kɒkəməˈruː/ *n.* M19. [Origin unkn.] A variety of bagatelle played on a board or table with pins, holes, arches, and bells. Also called *Russian bagatelle*.

†**cockard** *n.* var. of COCKADE.

cockatiel /kɒkəˈtiːl/ *n.* Also **-teel**. L19. [Du. *kakatielje*, prob. dim. f. as next.] A small, delicately crested Australian parrot, *Nymphicus hollandicus*. Cf. QUARRION.

cockatoo /kɒkəˈtuː/ *n.* M17. [Du. *kaketoe* f. Malay *kakatua*: infl. by COCK *n.*[1]] **1** Any of various Australasian parrots of the family Cacatuidae, with an erectile crest. M17. **2** A lookout usu. acting on behalf of those engaged in some illegal activity. *Austral. slang.* E19. **3** A small farmer. Also *cockatoo farmer*. Cf. COCKY *n.*[2] *Austral.* & *NZ colloq.* M19.

1 *Leadbeater's cockatoo*, *rose(-breasted) cockatoo*, *sulphur-crested cockatoo*, etc.

Comb.: *cockatoo farmer*: see sense 3 above; **cockatoo fence** *Austral.* a rough fence of logs and saplings.

cockatrice /ˈkɒkətrʌɪs, -trɪs/ *n.* LME. [OFr. *cocatris* f. med.L *calcatrix*, *cauc-* fem. agent-n. f. L *calcare* to tread, track, f. *calx* heel, rendering Gk *ikhneumōn* tracker (see ICHNEUMON).] **1** A fabulous reptile, whose gaze or breath is fatal, hatched by a serpent from a cock's egg; a basilisk. LME. **b** Chiefly *Her.* A monster represented as a two-legged dragon (or wyvern) with a cock's head and a barbed tongue. E16. **2** *fig.* **a** A malicious or destructive person. Cf. BASILISK 2. E16. †**b** A prostitute, a whore. L16–M18.

cock-bill /ˈkɒkbɪl/ *n.* & *v.* Also †**-bell**. L16. [Origin unkn.] *Naut.* **A** *n.* The position of an anchor hanging from the cathead ready for dropping, or of the yards of a vessel when placed at an angle with the deck, as a sign of mourning. Only in *a-cock-bill* adv. [A *prep.*[1]], in this position. L16. **B** *v.t.* Place a-cock-bill. M19.

cockboat /ˈkɒkbəʊt/ *n.* LME. [f. COCK *n.*[2] + BOAT *n.*] A ship's small boat, *esp.* one towed behind a vessel going up or down river.

cockchafer /ˈkɒktʃeɪfə/ *n.* E18. [f. COCK *n.*[1] + CHAFER *n.*[1]] A large pale brown chafer, *Melolontha melolontha*, which often flies at night with a whirring sound. Also called *may-bug*.

cocker /ˈkɒkə/ *n.*[1] Now *dial.* [OE *cocor* = OFris. *koker*, OS *cocar(i* (Du. *koker*), OHG *kohhar(i* (G *Köcher*).] †**1** A quiver for arrows. OE–ME. **2** A high laced boot; a kind of legging. LME.

cocker /ˈkɒkə/ *n.*[2] ME. [f. COCK *v.*[1] + -ER[1].] †**1** A fighter; a quarrelsome person. Only in ME. **2** A patron of cock-fighting; a breeder or trainer of gamecocks. L17. **3** More fully *cocker spaniel*. A small spaniel of a type bred to rouse woodcock etc. E19.

cocker /ˈkɒkə/ *n.*[3] Now *dial.* Also **coker**. ME. [f. COCK *v.*[2] + -ER[1].] A person who piles hay into cocks; *gen.* a harvest-labourer.

Cocker /ˈkɒkə/ *n.*[4] E19. [Edward *Cocker* (1631–75), Eng. arithmetician, reputed author of a widely-used text.] *according to Cocker*, exact(ly), correct(ly).

cocker /ˈkɒkə/ *n.*[5] *slang* & *dial.* L19. [Cf. COCK *n.*[1] 4.] Used as a form of address.

cocker /ˈkɒkə/ *v.*[1]*t.* LME. [Origin unkn.: cf. COCK *v.*[3]] Pamper, indulge, coddle. Also foll. by *up*.

AV *Ecclus* 30:9 Cocker thy childe, and hee shall make thee afraid. S. RICHARDSON [He] cockers up that dangerous Propensity, which he ought . . to subdue. SIR W. SCOTT I have not been cockered in wantonness or indulgence.

cocker /ˈkɒkə/ *v.*[2]*i.* *obs.* exc. *Sc.* M16. [Rel. to COCKLE *v.*[2]: see -ER[5].] Rock unsteadily, totter.

cockerel /ˈkɒk(ə)r(ə)l/ *n.* ME. [Dim. of COCK *n.*[1]: see -REL.] **1** A young cock. ME. **2** A young man. *arch.* L16.

cockernony /kɒkəˈnəʊni/ *n.* *Sc.* *arch.* E18. [Origin unkn.] The gathering up of a young woman's hair in a snood.

cocket /ˈkɒkɪt/ *n.* ME. [Perh. f. L *quo quietus est* by which he is quit, the last wds of the custom-house officer's receipt. Cf. AN *cokete*, AL *coketa*, *-tum*.] **1** *Hist.* A seal of the King's Custom-House. ME. **2** Customs duty. *arch.* ME. **3** *Hist.* A sealed document certifying the payment of duty. LME.

cocket /ˈkɒkɪt/ *a.* Now *dial.* M16. [Perh. Fr. *coquet*, *-ette* gallant; in Eng. infl. by COCK *n.*[1], but cf. Fr. *coqueter* strut.] Orig., proud; pert. Now, merry, perky.

cock-eye /ˈkɒkʌɪ/ *n.* & *a.* *colloq.* E19. [App. f. COCK *v.*[1] + EYE *n.*] **A** *n.* A squinting eye. E19. **B** *adj.* = COCK-EYED *a.* L19.

cockeye pilot = BEAU GREGORY.

cock-eyed /ˈkɒkʌɪd/ *a.* *colloq.* E19. [f. prec. + -ED[2].] **1** Having a squint. E19. **2** Crooked, set aslant, not level; absurd. L19. **3** Drunk. Orig. *US.* E20.

cock-horse /ˈkɒkhɔːs, kɒkˈhɔːs/ *n.* & *adv.* M16. [f. COCK *n.*[1] or *v.*[1] + HORSE *n.*] **A** *n.* **1** A child's hobby-horse; anything a child rides astride, as a person's knee. Now chiefly in A-COCK-HORSE. M16. †**2** An exalted position, a place of triumph. Chiefly in A-COCK-HORSE. L16–E19. **3** A high-spirited horse, a stallion. L16. **4** Chiefly *Hist.* An additional horse for helping a coach uphill. L19. **B** *adv.* = A-COCK-HORSE I. M16.

cockle /ˈkɒk(ə)l/ *n.*[1] [OE *coccul*, *-el* perh. f. med.L dim. of L *coccum* berry: see -LE[2].] **1** Now usu. more fully *corn-cockle*. A purple-flowered plant, *Agrostemma githago*, of the pink family, formerly a common weed of cornfields. OE. **2** [Orig. as mistr. Gk *zizania*, L *lolium* darnel (*Matt.* 13:25).] An injurious weed of corn; a disease of corn which turns the grains black. OE.

2 *fig.*: SHAKES. *Coriol.* The cockle of rebellion, insolence, sedition.

Comb.: **cocklebur(r)** a weed of the genus *Xanthium*, of the composite family, producing fruit covered with hooked bristles.

cockle /ˈkɒk(ə)l/ *n.*[2] ME. [(O)Fr. *coquille* shell f. med.L f. med.Gk *kokhulia* pl. of *kokhulion*, for Gk *kogkhulion*, f. *kogkhē* CONCH.] **1** An edible bivalve mollusc of the genus *Cardium*, common on sandy coasts. Formerly also, any of various other bivalves. ME. **2** The shell, or a valve of the shell, of a cockle. LME. **3** A small shallow boat. M19.

Phrases: **the cockles of one's heart** one's deepest feelings (esp. in *rejoice*, *warm*, *the cockles of one's heart*).

Comb.: **cockle-hat** *Hist.* a hat with a cockle- or scallop-shell in it, worn by pilgrims; **cockle-shell** = senses 2, 3 above.

cockler *n.* a person who gathers cockles M18.

cockle /ˈkɒk(ə)l/ *n.*[3] LME. [Rel. to COCKLE *v.*[1]] A bulge or wrinkle in paper, glass, etc.; a pucker.

cockly *a.* wrinkled, puckered E16.

cockle /ˈkɒk(ə)l/ *n.*[4] L17. [Perh. f. Du. *kākel*, *kaekel*, *kāchel*, esp. in *kacheloven*, f. G *Kachel* stove-tile, *Kachelofen* stove made of these.] **1** The fire-chamber of a hop or malt kiln. Also *cockle-oast*. L17. **2** A kind of large heating stove, *spec.* one with radiating plates or chambers around which air is passed before entering for heating. Also *cockle-stove*. L18.

†**cockle** *a.* E18–E19. [Perh. f. COCKLE *n.*[2]] Whimsical.

cockle /ˈkɒk(ə)l/ *v.*[1]*i.* & *t.* M16. [Fr. *coquiller* blister (bread) in cooking (cf. *recoquiller* turn or curl up), f. *coquille* shell etc.: see COCKLE *n.*[2]] (Cause to) bulge, curl up, pucker.

cockle /ˈkɒk(ə)l/ *v.*[2]*i.* *dial.* L18. [Rel. to COCKER *v.*[2]: see -LE[3]. Cf. also COGGLE *v.*] Rock unsteadily; totter.

†cockloche *n.* Also **cockoloach**. E17–M19. [Origin unkn.] A silly coxcomb.

cock-loft /ˈkɒklɒft/ *n.* L16. [Perh. f. COCK *n.*[1] + LOFT *n.*] A small upper loft.

cockney /ˈkɒkni/ *n.* & *a.* LME. [Prob. f. COCK *n.*[1] + *-n-* of genit. pl. + EY *n.*, = cocks' egg: cf. G *Hahnenei*. Sense 2 assoc. w. COCKER *v.*[1]] **A** *n.* †**1** An egg; a small misshapen egg (= *cock's egg* s.v. COCK *n.*[1] I). LME. **2** A pampered child; a milksop. Long *obs.* exc. *dial.* LME. †**b** A wanton or squeamish woman. Only in E17. †**3** A person who lives in a town, regarded as effeminate, affected, or weakly. L16–E19. **4** A native of London, esp. of the East End or speaking its dialect; the dialect of the East End of London. Formerly somewhat *derog.* E17. **5** *Austral.* A young snapper (fish). E20.

B *adj.* **1** Pampered, effeminate, squeamish; *derog.* characteristic of a town-dweller. Now *arch.* & *dial.* L16. **2** Pertaining to or characteristic of the London cockney. M17.

2 **Cockney School** (somewhat *derog.*) a group of 19th-cent. writers belonging to London, of whom Leigh Hunt was taken as the representative.

cockneydom the domain of cockneys; cockneys collectively: M19. **cockney'ess** *n.* (now *rare*) a female cockney M19. **cockneyfi'cation** *n.* making or becoming cockney in character L19. **cockneyfy** *v.t.* & *i.* make or become cockney in character E19. **cockneyish** *a.* somewhat cockney in character E19. **cockneyism** *n.* (*a*) cockney quality; (*b*) a cockney characteristic (in idiom, pronunciation, etc.): E19. **cockneyize** *v.* (*a*) *v.t.* make cockney; (*b*) *v.i.* use cockneyisms: E19.

†cockoloach *n.* var. of COCKLOCHE.

cockpit /ˈkɒkpɪt/ *n.* L16. [f. COCK *n.*[1] + PIT *n.*[1]] **1** A pit or other place made for cock-fights. L16. **2** An arena for any struggle. L16. †**3** A theatre; the pit of a theatre. L16–M17. **4** *Naut.* The after part of the orlop deck of a man-of-war, to which the wounded were carried for treatment; the well of a sailing yacht where the steering wheel or tiller is located. E18. **5** *Aeronaut.* The space for a pilot etc. in the fuselage of an aircraft or in a spacecraft. E20. **6** The driver's seat in a racing car. M20.

cockroach /ˈkɒkrəʊtʃ/ *n.* Orig. †**cacaroch** & other vars. E17. [Sp. *cucaracha*, assim. (by 19) to COCK *n.*[1], ROACH *n.*[4]] An insect of the suborder Blattaria (order Dictyoptera), typically a stout-bodied scavenger resembling a beetle, with hardened forewings; *esp.* the large dark brown *Blatta orientalis* and *Periplaneta americana*, which infest kitchens, warehouses, etc.

German cockroach: see GERMAN *a.*[1]

cockscomb /ˈkɒkskəʊm/ *n.* Also **cock's comb**, †**coxcomb**. See also COXCOMB. LME. [f. COCK *n.*[1] + -'S[1] + COMB *n.*[1]] **I 1** The comb of a cock. LME. **II 2** Any of various plants having some resemblance to a cock's comb, *esp.* (*a*) the yellow rattle; (*b*) *Celosia cristata*, of the amaranth family, cultivated for its feathery flowers. LME. **3** A jester's cap, resembling a cock's comb. E16. †**4** The head. *joc.* L16–M19. **III** See COXCOMB I.

cockspur /ˈkɒkspəː/ *n.* In sense 1 also **cock's spur**. L16. [f. COCK *n.*[1] + -'S[1] + SPUR *n.*[1]] **1** The spur of a cock. L16. **2** *Angling.* A kind of worm. M17. **3** = FINGRIGO. M18.

Comb.: **cockspur grass** a millet, *Echinochloa crusgalli*, which is a common weed in warmer parts of the world; also called *barnyard grass*; **cockspur thorn** a N. American hawthorn, *Crataegus crus-galli*.

cocksure /kɒkˈʃʊə/ *a.* & *adv.* E16. [f. COCK *n.*[4] + SURE *a.*: assoc. w. COCK *n.*[1] is later.] **A** *adj.* **I** Of objective sureness. †**1** Absolutely safe (from danger, interference, etc.). E16–L17. †**2** Absolutely to be depended on; absolutely certain *of*, *to do*. (Of a person passing into sense 3.) E16–M19.

II Of subjective sureness. **3** Quite convinced (*of*, *about*) in one's own mind. L17. **4** Self-confident, dogmatic, presumptuous. M18.

3 F. MARRYAT 'I do believe that—I'm drunk.' 'And I'm cock sure of it.' **4** *Spectator* It was Lord Melbourne . . who said, 'I wish I was as cock-sure of anything as Tom Macaulay is cock-sure of everything.' G. GREENE He was happy, he was conceited, he was cocksure. M. RENAULT I didn't say so. I've had training enough not to make that sort of cocksure prognosis.

B *adv.* With perfect security or certainty. *arch.* L16.

cocksureness *n.* L19.

cockswain *n.* var. of COXSWAIN.

cocksy *a.* var. of COXY.

cocktail /ˈkɒkteɪl/ *a.*, *n.*, & *v.* E17. [f. COCK *n.*[1], *v.*[1] + TAIL *n.*[1]] **A** *adj.* **1** That cocks the tail or hinder part. E17. **2** (Of a horse) not thoroughbred; *fig.* (*arch.*) characteristic of an upstart, lacking in true gentility. M19.

1 **cocktail beetle** = sense B.3 below.

B *n.* **1** A cock-tailed horse; a racehorse that is not thoroughbred; *fig.* (*arch.*) a person pretending to gentility but lacking in breeding, an upstart. E19. **2** A drink of spirits with bitters, sugar, etc.; a usu. iced mixed drink with spirits. Orig. *US*. E19. **3** = *devil's coach-horse* s.v. DEVIL *n.* L19. **4** An item of food or drink, usu. a made dish such as finely-chopped fruit salad, shellfish in a sauce, etc., served as an appetizer at the beginning of a meal or as a light refreshment. E20. **5** *fig.* Any (esp. unpleasant or dangerous) mixture of substances or factors. M20.

2 *Manhattan cocktail*, *old-fashioned cocktail*, *rattlesnake cocktail*, *Sazarac cocktail*, etc. **4** *fruit cocktail*, *prawn cocktail*, *shrimp cocktail*, etc. **5** *Daily Telegraph* A 'cocktail' of drugs which included cannabis. *Molotov cocktail*: see MOLOTOV I.

Comb.: **cocktail cabinet**: for storing alcoholic drinks; **cocktail dress**: semi-formal, suitable for wearing at a cocktail party; **cocktail-mixer** a container in which a cocktail is mixed by vigorous shaking; **cocktail onion** a small pickled onion; **cocktail party**: at which cocktails or other alcoholic drinks are the principal refreshments provided; **cocktail sausage** a small sausage suitable for serving on a cocktail stick; **cocktail-shaker** = *cocktail-mixer* above; **cocktail stick** a small pointed stick on which articles of food, as onions, small sausages, etc., are served.

C *v.* **1** *v.t.* Affect with cocktails; provide with cocktails. M19. **2** *v.i.* Drink cocktails; attend cocktail parties. M20.

cock-tailed /ˈkɒkteɪld/ *a.* M18. [f. as prec. + -ED[2].] **1** Of a horse: having a docked tail. M18. **2** Having the tail or hinder part cocked up. L18.

cock-up /ˈkɒkʌp/ *n.* L17. [f. *cock up*: see COCK *v.*[1]] **1** A hat or cap cocked up in front. Now *rare*. L17. **2** A bungle, a mistake, a muddle. *slang*. M20.

cocky /ˈkɒki/ *n.*[1] *arch.* L17. [f. COCK *n.*[1] + -Y[6].] A little cock: used as a term of endearment.

cocky /ˈkɒki/ *n.*[2] *Austral.* & *NZ colloq.* L19. [f. COCK(ATOO + -Y[6].] A small farmer (= COCKATOO 3). Also *cocky farmer*.

cocky's joy *slang* (*a*) golden syrup; (*b*) treacle, molasses.

cocky /ˈkɒki/ *a.* M16. [f. COCK *n.*[1] + -Y[1].] †**1** Lecherous. Only in M16. **2** Arrogant, conceited; saucy, impertinent. M18.

cocky-leekie, **-leeky** *ns.* vars. of COCK-A-LEEKIE.

cockyolly /kɒkɪˈɒli/ *n.* *nursery* & *colloq.* M19. [Fanciful f. COCK *n.*[1]] More fully *cockyolly bird*. A small bird, a dear little bird.

coco /ˈkəʊkəʊ/ *n.* Pl. **-os**. Also **cocoa**. M16. [Port. & Sp. *coco* (orig.) grinning face, alluding to the appearance of the base of the shell. The form *cocoa* arises (app. by accident) from Johnson's Dictionary.] **I** †**1** = COCONUT I. M16–M18. **2** = COCONUT 2. M16. **3** = COCONUT 3. *slang*. E19. **II 4** The root of the taro. *W. Indies*. M18.

Comb.: **coco fibre** the fibre of the coconut husk; **coco-grass** *N. Amer.* a nut-grass, *Cyperus rotundus*; **coco matting** = COCONUT *matting*; **coco palm**, **tree** = sense 2 above.

coco *v.* var. of COCOA *v.*

cocoa /ˈkəʊkəʊ/ *n.*[1] E18. [Alt. of CACAO.] **1** = CACAO I. Now only more fully *cocoa bean*. E18. **2** The powder produced by crushing and grinding cacao beans (often with other ingredients); a drink made from this. L18. **b** A shade of brown resembling the colour of this powder. E20. **3** = CACAO 3. *rare*. L19.

Comb.: *cocoa bean*: see sense 1 above; **cocoa butter** = CACAO *butter*; **cocoa moth** = TOBACCO *moth*; *cocoa nibs*: see NIB *n.*[1] 6; **cocoa tree** = CACAO *tree*.

cocoa *n.*[2] var. of COCO *n.*

cocoa /ˈkəʊkəʊ/ *v.i.* *slang*. Also **coco**. M20. [Rhyming slang.] Say so. Only in *I should cocoa*.

cocoanut *n.* var. of COCONUT.

cocobay /ˈkəʊkəʊbeɪ/ *n.* *W. Indies*. L18. [Twi *kokobé*.] Leprosy or other skin disease.

cocobolo /kəʊkəʊˈbəʊləʊ/ *n.* Pl. **-os**. Also **-la** /-lə/. M19. [Sp. f. Arawak *kakabali*.] (The hard red wood of) a tropical American tree of the genus *Dalbergia*.

coco-de-mer /ˌkəʊkəʊdəˈmɛː/ *n.* E19. [Fr. = coco from the sea (as having been first known from the nuts found floating in the sea).] A tall palm tree *Lodoicea maldivica*, native to the Seychelles; its immense woody nut.

co-conscious /kəʊˈkɒnʃəs/ *a.* & *n.* E20. [f. CO- + CONSCIOUS.] *Psychol.* **A** *adj.* Pertaining to the conjunction of experiences within a single consciousness (applied to the supposed knowledge an omniscient god would have of the conscious acts and states of all beings). Also, of or pertaining to the experiences that are split from one another in a multiple personality. E20. **B** *n.* A hypothetical part of the subconscious. E20.

co-consciously *adv.* E20. **co-consciousness** *n.* E20.

coconut /ˈkəʊkənʌt/ *n.* Also **cocoanut**. E17. [f. COCO *n.* + NUT *n.*] **I 1** The large ovate brown hard-shelled seed of the tropical palm tree *Cocos nucifera*, which has an edible white lining enclosing a white liquid; the flesh of this. E17. **2** The tree itself. M19. **3** The human head. *slang*. M19. **II 4** *double coconut*, = COCO-DE-MER. E19.

1 SEA *coconut*.

Comb. & *phrases*: **coconut butter** the solid oil obtained from the flesh of the coconut, used in soap, candles, ointment, etc.; **coconut crab** a large terrestrial pagurid crab *Birgus latro*, which climbs palm trees to get coconuts; also called *palm-crab*, *robber crab*; **coconut ice** a sweet of sugar and desiccated coconut; **coconut matting**: made from the fibre of the nut's outer husk; **coconut milk** the liquid found inside the coconut; **coconut palm** = sense 2 above; **coconut shy** a sideshow in a fairground where balls are thrown to try to dislodge coconuts; **coconut tree** = sense 2 above; *the milk in the coconut*: see MILK *n.*

cocoon /kəˈkuːn/ *n.* & *v.* L17. [Fr. *cocon*, †*coucon* f. med. Prov. *coucoun* eggshell, cocoon, dim. of *coca* shell.] **A** *n.* **1** A silky case spun by an insect larva to protect it as a pupa, *esp.* and orig. that of the silkworm. L17. **2** *transf.* & *fig.* A similar structure made by other animals; something which encloses like a cocoon; a protective covering, esp. to prevent the corrosion of metal equipment. M19.

2 K. TYNAN Each lives in a cocoon of fantasy which the outside world can hardly penetrate. C. FRANCIS As the darkness envelops you, it is easy to believe your boat is a cocoon of safety.

B *v.* **1** *v.t.* Wrap (as) in a cocoon; spray with a protective covering. M19. **2** *v.i.* Form a cocoon. L19.

1 *Listener* Cocooned in their bungalows, isolated in their club.

cocoonery *n.* (*US*) a building or room for rearing silkworms M19.

cocopan /ˈkəʊkəʊpan/ *n.* *S. Afr.* E20. [Zulu *i-ngqukumbana*, *-bane* stumpy wagon.] A small steel truck which runs on rails, used esp. in gold-mines.

coco-plum /ˈkəʊkəʊplʌm/ *n.* L17. [f. ICACO + PLUM *n.*] = ICACO.

cocorite /ˈkəʊkərʌɪt/ *n.* L18. [f. a Brazilian or Guyanese lang.] A small S. American palm, *Maximiliana maripa*. Also *cocorite palm*.

cocotte /kɒˈkɒt/ *n.* M19. [Fr.: sense 1 f. a child's name for a hen; sense 2 f. Fr. *cocasse* f. L *cucuma* cooking vessel.] **1** A fashionable prostitute. *arch.* M19. **2** A small fireproof dish for cooking and serving one portion of food. E20.

cocoyam /ˈkəʊkəʊjam/ *n.* E20. [Prob. f. COCO *n.* 4 + YAM *n.*[1]] The edible root of taro, *Colocasia esculenta*, or of a related plant, *Xanthosoma sagittifolium*.

coctile /ˈkɒktʌɪl/ *a.* L17. [L *coctilis* baked, burnt, f. *coct-* pa. ppl stem of *coquere* to cook: see -ILE.] Of baked brick; baked.

coction /ˈkɒkʃ(ə)n/ *n.* Now *rare* or *obs.* LME. [L *coctio(n-)* digestion, (in late L) cooking, f. *coct-*: see prec., -ION.] 1 Cooking; boiling. LME. †2 Suppuration as a process regarded as necessary for the healing of wounds or diseases. L16–M19. †3 Digestion of food. E17–L19. †4 The action of heat in preparing any substance. L17–M18. †5 Preparation by a natural process leading to perfection. L17–E18.

cocus /ˈkəʊkəs/ *n.* M17. [Origin unkn.] The hard, dark, heavy wood of a W. Indian leguminous tree, *Brya ebenus*, used in turnery. Also *cocus-wood*.

cod /kɒd/ *n.*[1] [OE *cod(d)* = ON *koddi*, ODa. *kodde* (cf. COD *n.*[3]), Sw. *kudde* cushion, pillow, pad, Norw. *kodd* testicle, scrotum, f. Gmc.] 1 A bag, a wallet. Long *obs.* exc. *dial.* OE. 2 A husk, a pod. Cf. PEASECOD. *obs.* exc. *dial.* OE. 3 The scrotum; in *pl.*, the testicles. *arch.* LME. 4 The narrow-necked bag at the end of a trawl-net etc. Now usu. more fully *cod end.* M16. †b The innermost recess of a bay or inlet. L17–M18. †5 A cocoon. E17–E19.

codded *a.* (now *dial.*) (*a*) bearing pods; (*b*) in the pod or (of corn) the ear: LME.

cod /kɒd/ *n.*[2] Pl. same. ME. [Origin unkn.] More fully *codfish*. A large marine fish, *Gadus morrhua*, which inhabits the N. Atlantic and adjacent seas, and has considerable economic importance as a food fish. Also (usu. w. specifying wd), any of various other fishes related to this (in the family Gadidae) or of corresponding value in other regions.

Murray cod: see MURRAY *n.*[2] *red rock-cod*: see RED *a.*

Comb.: **cod-bank** a submarine bank frequented by cod; *codfish*: see above; **cod-line** a line used in fishing for cod; **cod-liver oil** oil expressed from the liver of the cod or a related fish, used as a rich source of vitamins A and D; **cod's-head** *fig.* a stupid person; **cod war** *colloq.* any of a number of disputes between Britain and Iceland in the period 1958–76, concerning fishing rights in Icelandic waters.

cod /kɒd/ *n.*[3] *Sc.* & *north.* LME. [ODa. *kodde*, ON *koddi* cushion, pillow (cf. COD *n.*[1]).] 1 A pillow. LME. 2 The bearing of an axle. LME.

cod /kɒd/ *n.*[4] & *a. slang.* L17. [Origin unkn.: CODGER appears much later.] A *n.* 1 A person; *esp.* an old fool, an idiot. L17. 2 A joke, a hoax; a parody. E20. B *adj.* Parodying, mock. M20.

cod /kɒd/ *n.*[5] *slang.* Also **cod(')s** /kɒdz/. M20. [Abbrev.] = CODSWALLOP.

cod /kɒd/ *v.*[1] *obs.* exc. *dial.* Infl. **-dd-**. M16. [f. COD *n.*[1]] 1 *v.i.* Produce pods. M16. 2 *v.t.* Gather the pods of. L16.

cod /kɒd/ *v.*[2]*t.* & *i. dial.* & *slang.* Infl. **-dd-**. L19. [Perh. f. COD *n.*[4]] Hoax; parody; play a joke (on).

coda /ˈkəʊdə/ *n.* M18. [It. f. L *cauda* tail.] 1 *Mus.* An independent and often elaborate passage introduced after the end of the main part of a movement. M18. b *transf.* & *fig.* A concluding event, remark, literary passage, etc. L19. 2 *Ballet.* The final section of a classical *pas de deux*; the concluding dance of a whole ballet. E20.

cod-bait *n.* see CAD-BAIT.

codder /ˈkɒdə/ *n.*[1] Now *dial.* E16. [f. COD *n.*[3] + -ER[1].] A worker in leather; a saddler.

codder /ˈkɒdə/ *n.*[2] *dial.* L17. [f. COD *n.*[1] or *v.*[1] + -ER[1].] A person who gathers pea-pods.

codder /ˈkɒdə/ *n.*[3] *US.* M19. [f. COD *n.*[2] + -ER[1].] A person or vessel engaged in fishing for cod.

†**codding** *a. rare* (Shakes.). Only in L16. [Perh. f. COD *n.*[1] 3.] Lustful.

coddle /ˈkɒd(ə)l/ *v.*[1]*t.* & *i.* L16. [Origin unkn.: cf. next.] Boil gently, parboil, stew.

coddle /ˈkɒd(ə)l/ *v.*[2] & *n.* E19. [Prob. dial. var. of CAUDLE *v.*, but perh. fig. use of prec. Cf. MOLLYCODDLE.] A *v.t.* Treat as an invalid, keep from cold and exertion, feed *up.* E19. B *n.* A person who coddles himself or herself or is coddled by others. *colloq.* M19.

coddler *n.* (*a*) *rare* = CODDLE *n.* (*b*) *egg-coddler*: see EGG *n.*: M19.

code /kəʊd/ *n.* ME. [(O)Fr. f. L *codex*: see CODEX.] 1a *Rom. Law.* Any of the systematic collections of statutes made by or for the later emperors, *esp.* that of Justinian. ME. b A systematic collection or digest of laws; a body of laws so arranged as to avoid inconsistency and overlapping. M18. †2 A collection of (chiefly religious) writings forming a book. Only in 18. 3 A set of rules on any subject; *esp.* the prevalent morality of a society or class; an individual's standard of moral behaviour. E19. 4 A system of military etc. signals esp. used to ensure secrecy; a cipher; a systematic modification of a language, information, etc., into letter, figure, or word groups or symbols for the purposes of brevity, secrecy, or the machine-processing of information; *transf.* a system by which genetic etc. information is stored. E19.

1b *criminal code*: see CRIMINAL *a.* 2. *Salic code*: see SALIC *a.*[1] 2. 3 G. ORWELL In all questions of morals they were allowed to follow their ancestral code. G. STEINER Fascism is the ultimate code of the hoodlum. *code of honour*: see HONOUR *n.* 4 U. LE GUIN He took pleasure only in writing to his friends . . in a code they had worked out at the Institute. N. CHOMSKY The phrase 'contain the expansion of China' must be understood as code for . . 'repress movements for national independence and social reconstruction in SE Asia'. *dialling code, genetic code, machine code, Morse code, Playfair code, postcode, shift code, zip code*, etc.

Comb.: **code-book** a list of symbols etc. used in a code; **code-breaker** a person who solves or breaks a code or codes; a device for breaking codes; **code-name, -number** a word, symbol, or number used for secrecy or convenience instead of an ordinary name.

code /kəʊd/ *v.* E19. [f. the n.] 1 *v.t.* Put (a message etc.) into code; represent by means of a code. E19. 2 *v.i. Biol.* Foll. by *for*: be the genetic code for (an amino acid etc.), be the genetic determiner of (a character etc.). M20.

coda'bility *n.* ability to be coded M20. **coder** *n.* a person who or thing which codes messages etc. E20.

codeine /ˈkəʊdiːn, -dɪiːn/ *n.* M19. [f. Gk *kōdeia* head, poppy-head + -INE[5].] *Chem.* A crystalline alkaloid, $C_{18}H_{21}NO_3$, obtained from opium and used as a hypnotic and analgesic.

codetta /kəʊˈdɛtə/ *n.* M19. [It., dim. of CODA.] *Mus.* A short coda; a short passage connecting sections of a movement or fugue.

codex /ˈkəʊdɛks/ *n.* Pl. **codices** /ˈkəʊdɪsiːz, ˈkɒd-/. L16. [L *codex, codic-* block of wood, block split into leaves or tablets, book.] †1 = CODE *n.* 1, 3. L16–M18. 2 A manuscript volume, esp. of ancient texts. L18. 3 A collection of pharmaceutical descriptions of drugs, preparations, etc. M19.

codger /ˈkɒdʒə/ *n.* M18. [Perh. var. of CADGER *n.*[1]] 1 A fellow, a person, esp. a strange one; an elderly man (freq. in *old codger*). *colloq.* M18. 2 A mean, stingy, or miserly (old) person; a tramp; a beggar. *dial.* L18.

codiaeum /kəʊdɪˈiːəm/ *n.* M19. [mod.L f. Indonesian *kodiho*.] *Bot.* = CROTON *n.*[1] 2.

codices *n.* pl. of CODEX.

codicil /ˈkɒdɪsɪl, ˈkəʊ-/ *n.* LME. [L *codicillus* (chiefly in pl.) dim. of *codex*: see CODEX.] 1 A supplement to a will, added by the testator for the purpose of explanation, alteration, etc., of the original contents. LME. b *transf.* & *fig.* A supplementary addition, an appendix. L18. †2 (A letter on) a writing-tablet; a letter granting a patent. M17–L18.

codi'cillary *a.* of the nature of or belonging to a codicil E18.

codicology /kəʊdɪˈkɒlədʒi/ *n.* M20. [Fr. *codicologie*, f. L *codic-*, CODEX: see -OLOGY.] The branch of knowledge that deals with manuscripts and their interrelationships.

codico'logical *a.* M20. **codico'logically** *adv.* M20.

codify /ˈkəʊdɪfʌɪ/ *v.t.* M19. [f. CODE *n.*: see -FY. Cf. Fr. *codifier*.] 1 Reduce (laws) to a code. M19. 2 Reduce to a general system; systematize. M19.

codifi'cation *n.* E19. **codifier** *n.* M19.

codilla /kəʊˈdɪlə/ *n.* L18. [App. dim. of It. CODA.] The coarse tow of flax or hemp.

codille /ˈkəʊdɪl/ *n.* L17. [Fr. f. Sp. *codillo* lit. 'elbow-joint', dim. of *codo* elbow.] In ombre, the losing of the game by the person who undertakes to win it.

codlin *n.* var. of CODLING *n.*[2]

codling /ˈkɒdlɪŋ/ *n.*[1] Pl. same. ME. [f. COD *n.*[2] + -LING[1].] A young or small cod.

codling /ˈkɒdlɪŋ/ *n.*[2] Also **-lin** /-lɪn/. LME. [AN *Quer de lion* (Fr. *Cœur de lion*) lion-heart.] 1 A cooking apple of a long tapering shape; the tree bearing this type of apple. Formerly also, any hard or unripe apple. LME. †2 A raw youth. E–M17.

Comb.: **codling-moth** a small moth, *Cydia pomonella*, whose larvae feed on apples; **codlings-and-cream** great hairy willowherb, *Epilobium hirsutum*.

codology /kɒˈdɒlədʒi/ *n. Anglo.-Ir. colloq.* E20. [f. COD *n.*[4] + -OLOGY.] Hoaxing, leg-pulling.

codominant /kəʊˈdɒmɪn(ə)nt/ *a.* & *n.* E20. [f. CO- + DOMINANT.] A *adj.* 1 Chiefly *Ecol.* Sharing dominance; of equal dominance. E20. 2 *Genetics.* Of characters, alleles: expressed independently in heterozygous offspring, without displaying dominance or recessiveness. M20. B *n.* A species etc. that is codominant. M20.

co-domini /kəʊˈdɒmɪnʌɪ/ *n.pl.* M20. [f. CO- + L *domini* pl. of *dominus* lord, ruler.] Condominium powers, *spec.* the UK and Egypt in relation to Sudan between 1899 and 1966.

codon /ˈkəʊdɒn/ *n.* M20. [f. CODE *n.* + -ON.] *Genetics.* A group of three consecutive nucleotides which together form a unit of the genetic code and determine which amino acid is added at a particular point in protein synthesis.

codpiece /ˈkɒdpiːs/ *n. obs.* exc. *Hist.* LME. [f. COD *n.*[1] 3 + PIECE *n.*] A bagged appendage to the front of a man's breeches or close-fitting hose.

codswallop /ˈkɒdzwɒləp/ *n. slang.* M20. [Origin unkn.] Nonsense, drivel.

†**cod-worm** *n.* see CAD-WORM.

coecilian *n.* var. of CAECILIAN.

coed /ˈkəʊɛd, kəʊˈɛd/ *n.* & *a. colloq.* (orig. *US*). L19. [f. COEDUCATION(AL).] A *n.* 1 A coeducational institution or system; coeducation. L19. 2 A female student at a coeducational institution. L19. B *adj.* Coeducational; of or pertaining to a coed (sense 2). L19.

coeducate /kəʊˈɛdjʊkeɪt/ *v.t.* Orig. *US.* M19. [Back-form. f. COEDUCATION.] Educate (persons of both sexes) together; educate in a coeducational institution.

coeducator *n.* a proponent or practitioner of coeducation E20.

coeducation /ˌkəʊɛdjʊˈkeɪʃ(ə)n/ *n.* M19. [f. CO- + EDUCATION.] The education of both sexes together.

coeducational *a.* of or pertaining to coeducation, practising coeducation L19.

coefficient /kəʊɪˈfɪʃ(ə)nt/ *a.* & *n.* M17. [mod.L *coefficient-*: see CO-, EFFICIENT.] A *adj.* Cooperating to produce a result. Now *rare* or *obs.* M17.

B *n.* 1 A joint or cooperating agent or factor in producing a cause. E18. 2a *Math.* A known or constant quantity placed before and multiplying another. E18. b Chiefly *Physics.* A multiplier or factor which expresses the magnitude of some property of a particular substance etc. E19.

2a **differential coefficient** = DERIVATIVE *n.* 3. b *absorption coefficient, coefficient of expansion, coefficient of friction, coefficient of permeability, pluviometric coefficient, Racah coefficient, virial coefficient*, etc.

coehorn /ˈkəʊhɔːn/ *n.* Also **cohorn**. E18. [f. Menno, Baron van *Coehoorn* (1641–1704), Du. soldier and military engineer.] *Mil. Hist.* A small bronze mortar for throwing grenades, introduced by van Coehoorn.

coelacanth /ˈsiːləkanθ/ *n.* M19. [mod.L *Coelacanthus* genus name, f. Gk *koilos* hollow + *akantha* spine, on account of its hollow-spined fins.] A crossopterygian fish of the order Actinistia, which was believed to include only fossil forms until the discovery of *Latimeria chalumnae* in the Indian Ocean in 1938.

coela'canthid *n.* & *a.* L19. **coela'canthine** *a.* L19.

-coele *suff.* var. of -CELE.

coelenterate /siːˈlɛnt(ə)rət/ *n.* & *a.* L19. [f. mod.L *Coelenterata* (see below), f. Gk *koilos* hollow + *enteron* intestine: see -ATE[2].] *Zool.* A *n.* Orig., an animal of the invertebrate phylum Coelenterata, which comprised the present-day phyla Cnidaria, Ctenophora, and sometimes Porifera (sponges). Now usu., an animal of the phylum Cnidaria (also called Coelenterata), which includes jellyfishes, hydras, sea anemones, and corals. Cf. CNIDARIAN. L19. B *adj.* Of or pertaining to this group of animals. L19.

coelenteron *n.* the central gastric cavity of a coelenterate L19.

coeliac /ˈsiːlɪak/ *a.* Also ***celiac**. M17. [L *coeliacus* f. Gk *koiliakos* f. *koilia* belly: see -AC.] *Med.* Of or pertaining to the abdominal cavity.

coeliac disease sensitivity of the lining of the small intestine to gluten, causing chronic failure to digest food properly unless gluten is strictly excluded from the diet.

†**coeliacal** *a.* E17–E18.

coelio- /ˈsiːlɪəʊ/ *comb. form* of Gk *koilia* belly: see -O-. Also ***celio-**.

coeliˈotomy *n.* (*Med.*) = LAPAROTOMY L19.

coelom /ˈsiːləm/ *n.* Also **-ome** /-əʊm/, ***cel-**, & in mod.L form **coeloma** /siːˈləʊmə/, pl. **-mata** /-mətə/. L19. [Gk *koilōma*, *-mat-* hollow, cavity.] *Zool.* The secondary body cavity of an animal, between the body wall and the gut, *spec.* one surrounded by mesoderm.

coeˈlomic *a.* pertaining to or of the nature of a coelom L19.

coelomate /ˈsiːləmeɪt/ *a.* & *n.* Also ***celomate**. L19. [f. prec. + -ATE[2].] *Zool.* A *adj.* Having a coelom. L19. B *n.* An animal having a coelom, of the group Coelomata, which includes the annelids, molluscs, arthropods, echinoderms, and chordates. L19.

coelostat /ˈsiːlə(ʊ)stat/ *n.* L19. [Irreg. f. L *caelum* sky + -O- + -STAT.] *Astron.* An instrument which by means of a rotating mirror enables celestial objects to be photographed without their diurnal motion.

coelurosaur /sɪˈljʊərəsɔː/ *n.* M20. [f. Gk *koilos* hollow + URO-[2] + -SAUR.] Any of a group of small slender theropod dinosaurs with long forelimbs.

coemption /kəʊˈɛm(p)ʃ(ə)n/ *n.* LME. [L *coemptio(n-)*, f. *coempt-* pa. ppl stem of *coemere* buy up: see -ION.] 1 The buying up of the whole supply of any commodity in the market. LME. 2 *Rom. Law.* The fictitious sale of a woman by herself or her father, usu. to her husband. L17.

coen- *comb. form* see COENO-.

coenaesthesis /siːnɛsˈθiːsɪs/ *n.* Also ***-nesth-**. Pl. **-theses** /-ˈθiːsiːz/. M19. [f. Gk *kainos* common + *aisthēsis* sensation, perception.] *Psychol.* The perception of one's whole bodily state arising from the sum of somatic sensations. Also **coenaesthesia** *n.* L19.

coeno- /ˈsiːnəʊ/ *comb. form* of Gk *koinos* common: see -O-. Bef. a vowel **coen-**.

coenˈenchyme *n.* [Gk *egkhuma* infusion] *Zool.* (*a*) a usu. calcified substance secreted by the coenosarc of some anthozoans; (*b*) = COENOSARC: L19. **coenocyte** *n.* a body of algal or fungal cytoplasm containing several nuclei, enclosed in a single membrane E20. **coenoˈcytic** *a.* of, pertaining to, or having the structure of a coenocyte E20. **coenosarc** *n.* [Gk *sarx*, *sark-* flesh] *Zool.* the soft tissue connecting the polyps of colonial coelenterates M19.

coenobite /ˈsiːnəbʌɪt/ *n.* Also ***cen-** /ˈsiːn-, ˈsɛn-/. LME. [(O)Fr. *cénobite* or eccl.L *coenobita*, f. *coenobium* f. Gk *koinobion* community life, convent, f. *koinos* common + *bios* life: see -ITE[1].] A member of a monastic community.

coenobitic, **-ical** /siːnəˈbɪtɪk, -ɪk(ə)l/ *adjs.* of or pertaining to a coenobite or coenobites, or a monastic community M17.

coenobium /sɪˈnəʊbɪəm/ *n.* Also ***cen-**. Pl. **-bia** /-bɪə/. E19. [eccl.L: see prec.] 1 = COENOBY. E19. 2 *Biol.* A cluster of unicellular organisms, e.g. green algae, that behaves as a colony. L19.

coenoby /ˈsiːnəbi/ *n.* Also ***cen-** /ˈsiːn-, ˈsɛn-/. L15. [f. as prec.] A monastic house.

coenurus /sɪˈnjʊərəs/ *n.* Pl. **-ri** /-rʌɪ/. Orig. Anglicized as †**coenure**. M19. [mod.L f. Gk *koinos* common + *oura* tail.] The hydatid of a canine tapeworm, *Multiceps multiceps*, which occurs in various intermediate hosts, esp. sheep, in which it causes staggers.

coequal /kəʊˈiːkw(ə)l/ *a.* & *n.* Now *arch.* or *literary.* LME. [L *coaequalis* of the same age: see CO-, EQUAL *a.*, *adv.*, & *n.*] A *adj.* †1 Of the same age, coeval. LME–E17. 2 Equal in rank, power, importance, etc. (*with*). LME. 3 Equivalent, coextensive (*with*). M19. B *n.* A person who is the equal of another. L16.

coeˈquality *n.* L16. **coequally** *adv.* M17.

†**coequate** *a.* E17–M18. [L *coaequatus* pa. pple of *coaequare*, f. as CO- + *aequare*: see EQUATE.] Made equal with something else.

coequate anomaly the true anomaly of a planet. Also †**coequated** *a.* L16–E18.

coerce /kəʊˈəːs/ *v.* LME. [L *coercere*, f. as CO- + *arcere* restrain.] 1 *v.t.* Forcibly constrain or impel (*into* obedience, compliance, etc.); force or compel *to do*. LME. b Enforce. Chiefly *US.* M19. 2 *v.i.* Enforce obedience; use coercive measures. L17.

coercer *n.* E19. **coercible** *a.* M17.

coercion /kəʊˈəːʃ(ə)n/ *n.* LME. [OFr. *cohercion*, *-tion* f. L *coer(c)tio(n-)* (med.L *coercio(n-)*) var. of *coercitio(n-)*, f. *coercit-* pa. ppl stem of *coercere*: see prec., -ION.] 1 Constraint, restraint, compulsion; the controlling of a voluntary agent or action by force. LME. †2 The faculty or power of coercing or punishing; the power to compel assent. E16–E18. 3 Government by force; the employment of force to suppress political disaffection and disorder. L18. 4 Physical pressure; compression. Now *rare.* M19.

coercionist *n.* a person who advocates or supports government by coercion M19.

coercive /kəʊˈəːsɪv/ *a.* & *n.* L16. [f. COERCE + -IVE.] A *adj.* 1 Of the nature of coercion; having the attribute of coercing. L16. 2 Compelling assent or belief, convincing. M17. 3 Having the power of physical pressure or compression. M17.

3 **coercive force** *Physics* = COERCIVITY.

B *n.* A coercive means or measure. M17.

coercitive *a.* (now *rare*) = COERCIVE *a.* M17. **coercively** *adv.* M17. **coerciveness** *n.* M18. **coerˈcivity** *n.* (*Physics*) the resistance of a magnetic material to changes in magnetization; *spec.* the magnetic field intensity necessary to demagnetize a given fully magnetized substance: L19.

coessential /kəʊɪˈsɛnʃ(ə)l/ *a.* L15. [eccl.L *coessentialis* (tr. Gk *homoousios* of the same substance), predicated attribute of the persons of the Trinity: see CO-, ESSENTIAL.] 1 United or inseparable in essence or being. L15. 2 Having the same substance or essence; consubstantial. L16.

coessentiˈality *n.* L17. **coessentially** *adv.* E19.

coetaneous /kəʊɪˈteɪnɪəs/ *a.* E17. [f. L *coaetaneus* contemporaneous, f. as CO- + *aetaneus*, f. *aetas* age: see -OUS.] = COEVAL *a.*

coetaneously *adv.* E19. **coetaneousness** *n.* M18.

coeternal /kəʊɪˈtəːn(ə)l/ *a.* LME. [f. eccl.L *coaeternus* (also *coaeternalis*) + -AL[1]: see CO-, ETERNAL.] Equally eternal; existing *with* another eternally.

coeternally *adv.* L16.

coeternity /kəʊɪˈtəːnɪti/ *n.* L16. [Late L *coaeternitas*: see CO-, ETERNITY.] Coeternal existence or quality; eternal existence with another.

coeval /kəʊˈiːv(ə)l/ *n.* & *a.* E17. [f. late L *coaevus*, f. as CO- + *aevum* age: see -AL[1].] A *n.* 1 A person (or thing) belonging to the same period. E17. 2 A person who is of the same age as another. M17. B *adj.* Foll. by *with*, †*to*. 1 Of equal antiquity, of contemporaneous origin. M17. 2 Of the same age, equally old. L17. 3 Existing at the same epoch; contemporary. E18. 4 Of the same duration. M18.

coeˈvality *n.* coeval quality; equality of age: M17. **coevally** *adv.* E18.

co-executor /kəʊɪgˈzɛkjʊtə/ *n.* LME. [med.L *coexecutor*: see CO-, EXECUTOR.] A joint executor.

co-executrix *n.* a joint executrix LME.

coexist /kəʊɪgˈzɪst/ *v.i.* M17. [Late L *coexistere*: see CO-, EXIST. Cf. (O)Fr. *coexister*.] Exist at the same time, in the same place, etc. (*with* another or others). Esp. of States with different ideologies: exist peacefully side by side.

coexistence /kəʊɪgˈzɪst(ə)ns/ *n.* LME. [med.L *coexistentia*: see CO-, EXISTENCE. Cf. Fr. *coexistence*.] 1 Existence together or in conjunction. LME. 2 *spec.* Existence side by side in mutual toleration of States, groups, etc., professing different ideologies. Also more fully *peaceful coexistence*. M20.

coexistent /kəʊɪgˈzɪst(ə)nt/ *a.* & *n.* M17. [f. as COEXIST: see -ENT. Cf. Fr. *coexistant*.] A *adj.* Existing together or in conjunction. M17. B *n.* A thing which coexists with something else; a concomitant. M19.

coextend /kəʊɪkˈstɛnd/ *v.t.* & *i.* E17. [f. CO- + EXTEND: cf. med.L *coextendere*.] Make or be coextensive.

coextension *n.* coincidence in extension L17.

coextensive /kəʊɪkˈstɛnsɪv/ *a.* L18. [f. CO- + EXTENSIVE.] Extending over the same space or time; coinciding in limits; of equal extension.

coextensively *adv.* M19. **coextensiveness** *n.* L17.

cofactor /ˈkəʊfaktə/ *n.* L19. [f. CO- + FACTOR *n.*] 1 *Math.* A coefficient; *spec.* the quantity obtained from a determinant or square matrix by removal of the row and column containing a given element. L19. 2 *Biochem.* Any substance (other than the substrate) whose presence is essential for the activity of an enzyme. M20.

coff /kɒf/ *v.t. Sc. arch.* Pa. t. & pple **coft** /kɒft/. LME. [Orig. only as pa. t. & pple, prob. f. MDu. *coft(e)* pa. pple of *cōpen* COPE *v.*[3]] Buy, purchase.

coffee /ˈkɒfi/ *n.* & *a.* L16. [Turk. *kahve* ult. f. Arab. *kahwa*, prob. through Du. *koffie*.] A *n.* 1 A drink made by infusion from the seeds of a shrub (see sense 3) roasted and ground or (in the East) pounded. L16. b A cupful of, or light refreshments including, this drink. L18. 2 Seeds of this shrub, either raw or roasted (and ground). E17. 3 The shrub or tree from which the seeds are obtained: any of certain members of the palaeotropical genus *Coffea* (esp. *C. arabica*), of the madder family, which bear white flowers succeeded by red berries each containing two seeds. E17. 4 The light brown colour of white coffee. E19.

Phrases: **black coffee**: served without milk or cream. **Gaelic coffee**: served with cream and (now usu. Scotch) whisky. **Irish coffee**: served with cream and Irish whiskey. KENYA *coffee*. ROBUSTA *coffee*. *Scotch coffee*: see SCOTCH *a. sergeant-major's coffee*: see SERGEANT-MAJOR *n.* 4. *Turkish coffee*: see TURKISH *a. Viennese coffee*: see VIENNESE *a.* **white coffee**: served with milk or cream.

Comb.: **coffee-and** *US slang* coffee and doughnuts; **coffee bar** a café serving coffee and light refreshments; **coffee bean** the seed of the coffee tree; **coffee-berry** (*a*) the fruit or (loosely) the seed of the coffee tree; (*b*) *US* the Kentucky coffee tree; **coffee-break** an interval, usu. between periods of work, esp. mid-morning, when coffee is drunk; **coffee cake** (*a*) *N. Amer.* a cake or sweet bread flavoured with cinnamon or topped or filled with cinnamon sugar, usu. eaten with coffee; (*b*) a coffee-flavoured cake; **coffee-coloured** *a.* (*a*) of the colour of white coffee; (*b*) (of a person) having a light brown skin colour; **coffee-cup** a cup of a special shape or size for holding coffee; **coffee-essence** concentrated extract of coffee; **coffee grounds** the granular sediment remaining in coffee after infusion; **coffee-house** *n.* & *v.* (*a*) *n.* a place where coffee and other refreshments are provided, *esp.* one used in the 17th and 18th cents. as a centre for political and literary conversation, circulation of news, etc.; (*b*) *v.i.* (*slang*) stand about gossiping, orig. while waiting for the hounds at a meet; **coffee-maker** *spec.* a device for brewing coffee; **coffee-mill** a hand-mill for grinding roasted coffee beans; **coffee-morning** a morning gathering, often in aid of charity, at which coffee is served; *coffee nibs*: see NIB *n.*[1] 6; **coffee-pot** a tall covered pot with a spout, in which coffee is made or served; **coffee-room** a public room where coffee etc. is served; formerly, the dining-room in a hotel; **coffee-shop** (*a*) a shop selling coffee beans or ground coffee; (*b*) a small restaurant, usu. attached to a hotel; **coffee-spoon** a small spoon for stirring coffee in a cup; **coffee stall** a movable structure at which coffee and other refreshments are sold; **coffee-table** a small low table for serving coffee

For other words beginning with *co-* see the entry for **co-**

(*coffee-table book* (usu. *derog.*), a large expensive lavishly illustrated book); **coffee tree** (*a*) a tree or shrub from which coffee is obtained (= sense 3 above); (*b*) *N. Amer.* a leguminous tree, *Gymnocladus dioica*, whose seeds can be used as a substitute for coffee (also more fully *Kentucky coffee tree*).

B *adj.* Of the light brown colour of white coffee. E20.

coffer /ˈkɒfə/ *n.* ME. [(O)Fr. *coffre* f. L *cophinus*: see COFFIN *n.*] **1** A box, a chest; *esp.* a strongbox in which money or valuables are kept. In *pl.* also, treasury, funds. ME. †**2** A coffin. ME–M16. †**3** An ark. ME–E18. **4** *Archit.* An ornamental sunk panel in a ceiling or soffit. M17.

1 S. SMILES Efforts to fill the coffers of Rome by the sale of indulgences.

Comb.: **coffer-dam** a watertight enclosure, usu. made of piles with clay packed between them and then pumped dry, used in the construction of bridges, in harbour works, etc.; also, a double bulkhead in a large merchant vessel, esp. a tanker, built as a safety measure between holds or oil tanks.

coffer /ˈkɒfə/ *v.t.* LME. [f. the n.] **1** Enclose (as) in a coffer; treasure *up*. *arch.* LME. **2** *Archit.* Adorn with coffers (see COFFER *n.* 4). M19.

coffering *n.* (*a*) the action of the vb; (*b*) (chiefly *Archit.*) an arrangement or structure of coffers: L18.

cofferer /ˈkɒfərə/ *n.* ME. [AN *cofrere* treasurer (= AL *cofferarius*) corresp. to OFr. *cofrier* box-maker (med.L *cofferarius*), f. as COFFER *n.*, -ER[2].] **1** *Hist.* A treasurer; *spec.* one of the treasurers of the royal household. ME. †**2** A person who makes coffers. ME–E16.

cofferet *n.* var. of COFFRET.

coffin /ˈkɒfɪn/ *n.* ME. [OFr. *cof(f)in* little basket, case f. L *cophinus* f. Gk *kophinos* basket: cf. COFFER *n.*] †**1 a** *gen.* A chest, a case, a casket, a box. ME–L17. **b** *spec.* A box in which a corpse is buried or cremated. E16. **c** *fig.* An old and unseaworthy vessel; an aircraft etc. thought likely to crash. Chiefly as *floating*, *flying*, etc., *coffin*. *colloq.* E19. †**2** A basket. LME–M16. †**3** A pastry mould for a pie, a pie-crust; a pie-dish. LME–M18. **4** A paper case or receptacle, esp. of conical shape. Now *rare* or *obs.* L16. **5** The whole of a horse's hoof below the coronet. E17. **6** The wooden frame enclosing the stone on which type was placed in a wooden printing-press. Also, the bed of a printing-machine. M17. †**7** A case in which articles are fired in a furnace. L17–L18.

1b a nail in the coffin of *fig.* something which tends to hasten or ensure the death or end of. *oak coffin*: see OAK *n.* & *a.*

Comb.: **coffin-bone** the distal phalangeal bone of a horse, enclosed within the hoof; **coffin corner** *Amer. Football* the angle between goal-line and sideline; **coffin-joint** the joint at the top of a horse's hoof; **coffin-nail** *fig.* (*slang*) a cigarette; **coffin-plate** a metal plate set in a coffin-lid, bearing the name etc. of the deceased; **coffin-ship** *colloq.* an old and unseaworthy ship (cf. sense 1c above); **coffin-stool** a stand or support for a coffin.

coffinless *a.* without a coffin, not enclosed in a coffin E19.

coffin /ˈkɒfɪn/ *v.t.* M16. [f. the n.] Enclose (as) in a coffin.

JONSON Coffin them alive In some kind clasping prison. A. P. STANLEY The coffined body lay in state at Westminster.

coffle /ˈkɒf(ə)l/ *n.* M18. [Arab. *kāfila* CAFILA.] A line of or *of* slaves or animals driven along together.

coffret /ˈkɒfrɪt/ *n.* Also **cofferet** /ˈkɒfərɪt/. L15. [OFr., dim. of *coffre*: see COFFER *n.*, -ET[1].] A small coffer.

coft *v.* pa. t. & pple of COFF.

cog /kɒg/ *n.*[1] ME. [MLG, MDu. *kogge* (Du. *kog*), whence also OFr. *cogue, koge*.] **1** *Hist.* A medieval broadly-built ship with rounded prow and stern. ME. **b** A kind of craft formerly used for local commerce on the Rivers Humber and Ouse in NE England. *obs.* exc. *dial.* M16. **2** More fully *cogboat*. = COCKBOAT. LME.

cog /kɒg/ *n.*[2] ME. [Prob. of Scand. origin: cf. synon. Sw. *kugge, kughjul* cog-wheel, Norw. *kug*.] **1** Each of a series of projections on the edge of a wheel or the side of a bar transferring motion by engaging with another such series; *fig.* an unimportant member of a large organization etc. Also, a wheel with such projections. ME. **2** Each of the short handles of the pole of a scythe. Long *dial.* L17. **3** A wedge or support fixed under anything. Chiefly *north.* L19.

1 J. ARGENTI The larger the company the greater is the feeling amongst the junior employees that they are merely small cogs in a giant wheel.

Comb.: **cog rail(way)** a rail(way) with cogs or teeth, for very steep gradients; **cog-wheel**: with cogs or teeth.

cog /kɒg/ *n.*[3] M16. [Rel. to COG *v.*[2]] †**1** An act or way of cogging at dice. M16–M17. **2** A small coin. Formerly also *gen.* (*slang*) anything used by a trickster to entice a victim. Long *obs.* exc. (*rare*) *Jamaican dial.* M16. †**3** A deception, a trick, a fraud, an imposture. E–M17.

cog /kɒg/ *n.*[4] M19. [f. COG *v.*[3]] A tenon on the end of a beam.

cog *n.*[5] var. of COGUE.

cog /kɒg/ *v.*[1] Infl. **-gg-**. L15. [f. COG *n.*[2]] **1** *v.t.* Equip (a wheel etc.) with cogs. L15. **2** *v.t.* Chock (a wheel etc.); steady with a wedge or wedges. Chiefly *north.* M17. **3** *v.t.* Roll or bloom (ingots). Also foll. by *down*. L19. **4** *v.i.* Engage with corresponding cogs or projections; *fig.* fit in, agree, work (*together*) in harmony. L19.

cog /kɒg/ *v.*[2] *arch.* Infl. **-gg-**. M16. [Origin unkn.] **1 a** *v.i.* Cheat in throwing dice. M16. **b** *v.t.* Throw (a die, dice) fraudulently to direct or control their fall; (also, by misunderstanding) load (a die, dice). M16. †**2** *v.i.* Employ fraud or deceit, cheat; employ flattery, wheedle; jest, quibble, (*with*). M16–L19. †**3** *v.t.* Cheat, flatter, (*into, out of*); get *from* a person by fraud or flattery; produce cunningly or fraudulently; foist *in* (adv.); palm off (*up*)*on*. L16–L19.

cogger *n.* M16.

cog /kɒg/ *v.*[3]*t.* & *i.* Infl. **-gg-**. E19. [App. var. of COCK *v.*[3]] Join (a beam), connect timbers etc., by means of a cog or tenon. Chiefly as *cogging* vbl n.

cogency /ˈkəʊdʒ(ə)nsi/ *n.* M17. [f. COGENT: see -ENCY.] **1** The quality of being cogent; the power of compelling conviction or assent. M17. **2** A convincing argument. *rare.* M19.

Also **cogence** *n.* (*rare*) L18.

cogeneration /ˌkəʊdʒɛnəˈreɪʃ(ə)n/ *n.* L20. [f. CO- + GENERATION.] The generation of electricity and useful heat jointly; the utilization of the steam left over from electricity generation for heating.

co'generated *a.* produced by cogeneration L20. **co'generator** *n.* a system or plant for cogeneration L20.

cogent /ˈkəʊdʒ(ə)nt/ *a.* M17. [L *cogent-* pres. ppl stem of *cogere* drive together, compel, f. as CO- + *agere* drive: see -ENT.] **1** Able to compel assent or belief; *esp.* (of an argument, explanation, etc.) persuasive, expounded clearly and logically, convincing. M17. **2** *gen.* Constraining, impelling; forcible. L17.

cogently *adv.* M17.

coggie *n.* var. of COGIE.

coggle /ˈkɒg(ə)l/ *n. obs.* exc. *dial.* LME. [Perh. var. of COBBLE *n.*] A rounded water-worn stone; a cobble.

coggle /ˈkɒg(ə)l/ *v.i.* & *t.* *Sc.* & *north.* M18. [Perh. f. prec., but cf. COCKLE *v.*[2]] Shake from side to side; totter; wobble.

coggly /ˈkɒgli/ *a.* *Sc.* & *north.* E19. [f. COGGLE *n.* or *v.* + -Y[1].] Shaky, unstable; liable to overturn.

cogida /koˈxiða, kəˈhiːdə/ *n.* E20. [Sp., lit. 'a gathering of the harvest', use as n. of fem. pa. pple of *coger* seize f. L *colligare*: see COLLIGATE *v.*] A tossing of a bullfighter by a bull.

cogie /ˈkəʊgi/ *n.* *Sc.* Also **coggie** /ˈkɒgi/. M18. [f. COGUE + -IE.] (The contents of) a small wooden bowl.

cogitable /ˈkɒdʒɪtəb(ə)l/ *a.* & *n.* LME. [L *cogitabilis*, f. *cogitare*: see COGITATE *v.*, -ABLE.] **A** *adj.* Able to be grasped by the mind; conceivable. LME. **B** *n.* A conceivable thing. Now *rare.* E17.

cogitabund /ˈkɒdʒɪtəbʌnd/ *a.* Now *rare.* M17. [L *cogitabundus*, f. *cogitare* COGITATE *v.*] Meditative, deep in thought.

cogitate /ˈkɒdʒɪteɪt/ *v.* L16. [L *cogitat-* pa. ppl stem of *cogitare* think, f. as CO- + *agitare*: see AGITATE *v.*, -ATE[3].] **1** *v.i.* & *t.* Think, ponder, meditate; devise, plan. L16. **2** *v.t.* *Philos.* Form a conception of (an object). Now *rare.* M19.

1 DICKENS Still cogitating and looking for an explanation in the fire. OED The man is cogitating mischief against us.

cogitator *n.* M19.

cogitation /kɒdʒɪˈteɪʃ(ə)n/ *n.* ME. [OFr. *cogitacion* f. L *cogitatio(n-)*, f. as prec.: see -ATION.] **1** The action of thinking; attentive consideration, reflection, meditation. ME. **b** The faculty of thinking; thought. M16. **2** A thought, a reflection. ME. **b** A plan, a design. M16.

cogitative /ˈkɒdʒɪtətɪv/ *a.* LME. [Fr. †*cogitatif, -ive*, or late L *cogitativus*, f. as COGITATE: see -IVE.] **1** Having the power or faculty of thought; thinking (as a characteristic attribute). LME. **2** Given to cogitation; thoughtful; meditative. E17.

cogitatively *adv.* M18. **cogitativeness** *n.* E19.

cogito /ˈkɒdʒɪtəʊ/ *n.* M19. [L = I think, lst pers. pres. of *cogitare* COGITATE, f. the formula *cogito, ergo sum* 'I think (or I am thinking), therefore I am' of the French philosopher René Descartes (1596–1650).] *Philos.* The principle establishing the existence of the thinker from the fact of his or her thinking or awareness.

cognac /ˈkɒnjak; *foreign* kɔɲak (*pl. same*)/ *n.* Also **C-**. L16. [*Cognac* in western France.] **1** In full *Cognac wine*. A white wine produced at Cognac. L16. **2** Orig. *cognac brandy*. French brandy, properly that distilled from the wine of Cognac; a drink of this. L17.

cognate /ˈkɒgneɪt/ *a.* & *n.* E17. [L *cognatus*, f. as CO- + *gnatus* born.] **A** *adj.* **1** Of or pertaining to kinship; descended from a common ancestor. E17. **b** *spec.* *Ling.* Of the same linguistic family; representing the same original word or root; of parallel development in different allied languages (as English *father*, G *Vater*, L *pater*). E19. **2** Akin in origin, nature, or quality. M17.

1b B. COTTLE Broom is cognate with Bramble, so the word must have something to do with spikiness. 2 J. GOAD Comets and Fiery Meteors are cognate. B. JOWETT Geometry and the cognate sciences.

Special collocations: **cognate accusative**, **object** *Gram.* a direct object whose meaning is not distinct from that of its verb (*live a good life* = live virtuously).

B *n.* **1** Chiefly *Law.* A person related by blood to another; *esp.* a relative on the mother's side; in *pl.*, descendants of a common ancestor. M18. **2** A cognate word. M19.

cognately *adv.* M20. **cognateness** *n.* E19. **cognatic** /kɒgˈnatɪk/ *a.* of, pertaining to, or reckoned through cognates (COGNATE *n.* 1) M18.

cognation /kɒgˈneɪʃ(ə)n/ *n.* Now *rare.* LME. [L *cognatio(n-)*, f. as prec.: see -ATION.] **1** The relationship of cognate persons. LME. †**2** *collect.* Kindred, relations. LME–M16. **3** Affinity, connection, relation, likeness. M16. **4** The relationship of cognate words etc. M19.

cognisable *a.*, **cognisance** *n.*, etc., vars. of COGNIZABLE etc.

cognita *n.* pl. of COGNITUM.

cognition /kɒgˈnɪʃ(ə)n/ *n.* LME. [L *cognitio(n-)*, f. *cognit-* pa. ppl stem of *cognoscere* get to know, investigate, f. as CO- + (*g*)*noscere* know: see -ION.] **1** The action or faculty of knowing, now *spec.* including perceiving, conceiving, etc., as opp. to emotion and volition; the acquisition and possession of empirical factual knowledge. LME. **b** A perception, a sensation, a notion, an intuition. L18. **2** = COGNIZANCE 4. Chiefly *Sc.* L15.

cognitional *a.* E19.

cognitive /ˈkɒgnɪtɪv/ *a.* L16. [med.L *cognitivus*, f. *cognit-*: see prec., -IVE.] Of or pertaining to cognition; based on or pertaining to empirical factual knowledge.

cognitive science the science or study of cognition or intelligence. **cognitive scientist** an expert in or student of cognitive science.

For other words beginning with *co-* see the entry for **co-**

cognitively *adv.* in a cognitive manner; with regard to or from the point of view of cognition: L19.

cognitum /ˈkɒgnɪtəm/ *n. rare.* Pl. ***-ta*** /-tə/. L19. [L, neut. pa. pple of *cognoscere*: see COGNITION.] *Philos.* An object of cognition.

cognizable /ˈkɒ(g)nɪzəb(ə)l/ *a.* Also **-isable**, **†conusable**. L17. [f. (as) COGNIZE *v.* + -ABLE.] 1 Able to be known; perceptible; recognizable. L17. 2 Able or liable to be judicially examined or tried; within the jurisdiction of a court etc. L17.

cogniza'bility *n.* M19. **cognizableness** *n.* L19. **cognizably** *adv.* E19.

cognizance /ˈkɒ(g)nɪz(ə)ns/ *n.* Also **-isance**, **†conusance**. ME. [OFr. *conis(s)aunce*, *conus-* vars. of *conoi(s)sance* (mod. *connaissance*), f. Proto-Romance, f. L *cognoscent-* pres. ppl stem of *cognoscere*: see COGNITION, -ANCE.] 1 A distinctive device or mark, as a crest, heraldic bearing, etc.; *spec.* (*Her.*) an emblem borne by all the retainers of a noble house, a badge. ME. †2 Recognition. *rare.* ME–L16. 3 Knowledge, understanding, acquaintance, awareness, now *spec.* as attained by observation or information; notice; a sphere of observation or concern. LME. 4 (The right of) dealing with a matter legally or judicially; taking judicial or authoritative notice. LME. 5 *Law.* Acknowledgement, esp. of a fine; admission of an alleged fact. Also, a plea in replevin that a defendant holds goods in the right of another as his bailee. L16.

1 T. H. WHITE The cognizance was of a silver woman on a sable field. 3 HOBBES The tree of cognizance of Good and Evill. S. JOHNSON The business from which we withdraw our cognizance is . . below our notice. R. SCRUTON A promise is made, another given, knowingly and in full cognizance of consequences. **have cognizance of** know, esp. in a legitimate or official way. **take cognizance of** attend to, not allow to go unobserved. 4 BURKE To introduce courts of justice for the cognizance of crimes.

cognizant /ˈkɒ(g)nɪz(ə)nt/ *a.* Also **-isant**. E19. [f. prec.: see -ANT[1]. Cf. earlier CONUSANT.] 1 Having knowledge, being aware (*of*). E19. b Having cognition. M19. 2 *Law.* Having cognizance or jurisdiction. M19.

cognize /kɒgˈnaɪz/ *v.* Also **-ise**. M17. [f. COGNIZANCE after *recognize* etc.] †1 *v.i.* Take judicial notice. Only in M17. 2 *v.t.* Take or have cognizance of; notice, observe; know, perceive. E19.

cognizee /kɒ(g)nɪˈziː/ *n.* Also **-isee**, **†conusee**. M16. [After COGNIZOR or its source: see -EE[1].] *Law* (now *Hist.*). The party in whose favour a fine of land was levied.

cognizor /ˈkɒ(g)nɪzɔː/ *n.* Also **-isor**, **†conusor**. M16. [AN *coniso(u)r* = OFr. *conoisseur* (later CONNOISSEUR).] *Law* (now *Hist.*). The party who levied a fine of land.

cognomen /kɒgˈnəʊmən/ *n.* Pl. **-mens**, (earlier) **†-mina**. E17. [L *cognomen*, *-min-*, f. as CO- + (*g*)*nomen* name.] 1 A surname; a nickname; *loosely* an appellation, a name. E17. 2 *Rom. Hist.* The third personal name of a Roman citizen (as Marcus Tullius *Cicero*); a fourth name or personal epithet (as Publius Cornelius Scipio *Africanus*). L19.

¶In isolated use bef. 19.

cognominal /kɒgˈnɒmɪn(ə)l/ *a.* M17. [f. L *cognominis* having the same name or f. *cognomin-*, *-men* COGNOMEN: see -AL[1].] 1 Having the same name or cognomen. M17. 2 Of or pertaining to a cognomen or surname. M17.

cognominate /kɒgˈnɒmɪneɪt/ *v.t.* E17. [L *cognominat-* pa. ppl stem of *cognominare*, f. as COGNOMEN: see -ATE[3].] Give a cognomen to; nickname; *loosely* call, style.

cognomi'nation *n.* (*a*) cognominating; (*b*) a cognomen: E17.

cognosce /kɒgˈnɒs/ *v.* Chiefly *Sc. Law.* M16. [L *cognoscere*: see COGNITION.] 1 *v.i.* Make an inquiry; take judicial cognizance of a cause etc. Now *rare* or *obs.* M16. 2 *v.t.* Judicially examine and pronounce (a person) to be of a specified status. Without compl.: declare insane. M16. 3 *v.t.* Take judicial cognizance of (a matter); investigate, examine. E17.

cognoscence /kɒgˈnɒs(ə)ns/ *n.* Now *rare.* LME. [(OFr. *cognoissance* f.) late L *cognoscentia*, f. *cognoscere*: see COGNITION, -ENCE.] 1 A heraldic cognizance or badge. LME. 2 Cognition; cognizance. L15.

cognoscent *a.* (*rare*) cognitive; cognizant: M17.

cognoscente /koɲoˈʃɛnte, kɒnjəˈʃɛnti/ *n.* Pl. ***-ti*** /-ti/. M18. [It. (now CONOSCENTE) lit. 'a person who knows', Latinized form of *conoscente* f. L *cognoscent-* pres. ppl stem of *cognoscere*: see COGNITION, -ENT.] A connoisseur; a discerning expert.

cognoscible /kɒgˈnɒsɪb(ə)l/ *a.* M17. [Late L *cognoscibilis*, f. *cognoscere*: see COGNITION, -IBLE.] 1 Knowable; recognizable. M17. †2 = COGNIZABLE 2. M17–M18.

cognosci'bility *n.* M17.

cognoscitive /kɒgˈnɒsɪtɪv/ *a.* Now *rare.* M17. [f. COGNITIVE after L *cognoscere* (see COGNITION).] = COGNITIVE.

cognovit /kɒgˈnəʊvɪt/ *n.* E18. [L *cognovit* (*actionem*) he has acknowledged (the action).] *Law* (now *Hist.*). In full *cognovit actionem* /aktɪˈəʊnɛm/. A defendant's acknowledgement that the plaintiff's cause is just; an acknowledgement of a debt.

cogue /kəʊg, kɒg/ *n.* & *v.* Chiefly *Sc.* Also **cog**. E16. [Origin unkn.] A *n.* 1 A wooden pail used for milking etc. E16. 2 A small wooden cup; a small measure of spirits etc. L17. 3 A dry measure equivalent to a quarter of a peck. M18. B *v.* †1 *v.i.* Drink spirits. M–L18. 2 *v.t.* Put into a cogue. M18.

cog(ue)ful *n.* as much as a cogue will hold L17.

cog-wood /ˈkɒgwʊd/ *n.* E18. [f. COG *n.*[2] + WOOD *n.*[1]] (The hard timber of) a W. Indian tree, *Ziziphus chloroxylon*, of the buckthorn family.

cohabit /kəʊˈhabɪt/ *v.i.* M16. [Late L *cohabitare*, f. as CO- + *habitare* HABIT *v.*] 1 *gen.* Live together (*with*). *arch.* M16. 2 *spec.* Live together as husband and wife, esp. when not legally married. M16.

cohabitant *n.* a person who lives together with another or others L16. **cohabi'tee** *n.* a person who lives with another as husband or wife without legal marriage L20. **cohabiter** *n.* a cohabitant or cohabitee E17. **cohabitor** *n.* a cohabitee L20.

cohabitation /kəʊhabɪˈteɪʃ(ə)n/ *n.* LME. [Late L *cohabitatio(n-)*, f. as CO- + *habitatio(n-)* HABITATION. Cf. (O)Fr. *cohabitation.*] 1 *gen.* Living together; community of life. *arch.* LME. 2 *spec.* Living together as husband and wife, esp. without legal marriage. M16. 3 Coexistence of or cooperation between office-holders of different political persuasions, orig. in France. L20.

cohabitational *a.* M20.

cohere /kə(ʊ)ˈhɪə/ *v.* M16. [L *cohaerere*, f. as CO- + *haerere* to stick.] 1 *v.i.* Of parts or individuals, or of a whole: stick together (*lit.* & *fig.*); become or remain united. M16. 2 *v.i.* Be consistent; be congruous in substance, tenor, or general effect. L16. †b Coincide, come together in agreement. E–M17. 3 *v.t.* Unite, cause to form a whole. *rare.* E17.

1 C. COTTON By cohering with other persons of condition. A. W. KINGLAKE The hard mass became fluid. It still cohered. W. E. H. LECKY A . . dissolution of the moral principles by which society coheres. 2 T. SHADWELL That trimming . . does not cohere with your complexion at all.

coherer *n.* an early form of radio detector, usu. consisting of a glass tube loosely filled with metal filings whose bulk electrical resistance decreased in the presence of radio waves L19. **cohering** *a.* that cohere(s); *Bot.* united externally: M17.

coherence /kə(ʊ)ˈhɪər(ə)ns/ *n.* M16. [L *cohaerentia*, f. as next: see -ENCE.] 1 The action or fact of sticking together (*lit.* & *fig.*); cohesion, union. M16. 2 Logical or clear interconnection or relation; consistency; congruity of substance, tenor, or general effect. L16. †b Coincidence, agreement. L16–L17. †3 Context; immediately surrounding discourse. L16–M18. 4 *Physics.* The property (of waveforms) of being coherent. E20.

Comb.: **coherence theory** *Philos.* either of two theories of truth positing (*a*) that coherence is the definition or criterion of truth, or (*b*) that the truth of a proposition consists in the coherence of that proposition with the set of all other true propositions.

coherency *n.* the quality of being coherent E17.

coherent /kə(ʊ)ˈhɪər(ə)nt/ *a.* M16. [f. L *cohaerent-* pres. ppl stem of *cohaerere*: see COHERE, -ENT.] †1 Logically related *to*; accordant *with*. M16–E17. 2 Of an argument, discourse, reasoning, etc.: consistent, non-contradictory, logical, in the relation of its parts; easily followed, complete and intelligible. L16. b Of a person: logical or clear in argument or expression, intelligible. E18. 3 Sticking together (*lit.* & *fig.*); united, exhibiting cohesion. L16. 4 *Physics.* (Of waves and radiation) having a constant phase relationship between different parts and so able to interfere with other waves having this property; producing such radiation. E19.

2 H. READ Too inarticulate to give a coherent account of his ambitions. P. G. WODEHOUSE A great coherent, purposeful plan. C. P. SNOW 'Are you part of a dream?' . . They were his first coherent words. b DICKENS Be plain and coherent, if you please. 3 T. H. HUXLEY These rocks are sufficiently coherent to form durable building stones. R. P. JHABVALA Their differences melted away and they became a coherent smiling group.

coherently *adv.* E17.

cohesion /kə(ʊ)ˈhiːʒ(ə)n/ *n.* M17. [f. L *cohaes-* pa. ppl stem of *cohaerere*: see COHERE, -ION.] The action or condition of sticking together or cohering; a tendency to remain united; *spec.* (*Physics*) the sticking together of particles or molecules of the same substance (cf. ADHESION).

A. GEIKIE Water . . loosens the cohesion of a steep bank. A. S. EDDINGTON The forces of cohesion between its particles. J. GROSS Social cohesion can never be as absolute as artistic unity. M. BRADBURY They had acquired a cohesion, a closeness.

cohesive /kə(ʊ)ˈhiːsɪv/ *a.* E18. [f. as prec. + -IVE.] Having the property of cohering; characterized by cohesion.

cohesively *adv.* E19. **cohesiveness** *n.* M18.

cohibit /kəʊˈhɪbɪt/ *v.t.* Now *rare.* M16. [L *cohibit-* pa. ppl stem of *cohibere* restrain, f. as CO- + *habere* have.] Restrain; restrict.

cohi'bition *n.* M16.

†Cohi Noor *n.* see KOH-I-NOOR.

coho /ˈkəʊhəʊ/ *n.* Pl. same, **-os**. Also **-oe**. M19. [Origin unkn.] A salmon, *Oncorhynchus kisutch*, of N. American coasts and rivers; also *coho salmon*. Also called *silver salmon*. .

cohobate /ˈkəʊhəʊbeɪt/ *v.t.* Long *arch.* L16. [f. mod.L *cohobare* = Fr. *cohober*: see -ATE[3].] *Chem.* Subject to repeated distillation by returning the distillate to the liquid being distilled; reflux.

†cohobation *n.* E17–L18.

cohog *n.* & *v.* see QUAHOG.

cohorn *n.* var. of COEHORN.

cohort /ˈkəʊhɔːt/ *n.* LME. [OFr. *cohorte* or L *cohors*, *-hort-* enclosure, company, crowd, f. as CO- + *hort-* as in *hortus* garden.] 1 *Rom. Hist.* A body of infantry of the Roman army, ten of which made up a legion; a body of auxiliary troops or (later) of cavalry of similar strength. LME. 2 A similar division of any other army; a band of warriors. E16. 3 A company, a band, esp. of people united in some common purpose. E18. b A group of people having a common statistical characteristic, esp. that of being born in the same year. M20. 4 A taxonomic grouping ranking above superorder and below subclass. Formerly, a grouping above order but of no fixed rank. M19. 5 An assistant, a colleague, an accomplice. Chiefly *N. Amer.* M20.

cohortation /kəʊhɔːˈteɪʃ(ə)n/ *n.* Now *rare* or *obs.* LME. [L *cohortatio(n-)*, f. as CO-, HORTATION.] (An) exhortation.

cohosh /kəˈhɒʃ/ *n.* *N. Amer.* L18. [Eastern Abnaki *kkʷàhas.*] Any of various plants having medicinal uses.

black cohosh a bugbane, *Cimicifuga racemosa.* **blue cohosh** *Caulophyllum thalictroides*, of the barberry family. **white cohosh** white baneberry, *Actaea pachypoda.*

cohue /kɔy/ *n.* Pl. pronounced same. M19. [Fr.] A mob, an unruly crowd.

cohune /kə'huːn/ *n.* Also **cahoun**. M18. [Miskito.] A Central American palm, *Orbignya cohune*. Also *cohune palm*.

coif /kɔɪf/ *n.* ME. [OFr. *coife* (mod. *coiffe*) head-dress f. late L *cofia* helmet.] 1 A close-fitting cap covering the top, back, and sides of the head. Now *Hist.* except as worn by nuns. ME. 2 A close-fitting skullcap worn under a helmet. *obs.* exc. *Hist.* ME. 3 A white cap worn by lawyers as a distinctive mark of their profession, *esp.* & later only that worn by a serjeant-at-law. *obs.* exc. *Hist.* LME.
3 **the coif** *Hist.* the position of serjeant-at-law (SERGEANT *of the coif*).

coif /kɔɪf/ *v.t.* LME. [Partly f. OFr. *coifer* (mod. *coiffer*), f. as prec.; partly f. the n.] Provide or cover with a coif; (*obs.* exc. *Hist.*) invest with a serjeant-at-law's coif.

coiff /kwɑːf, kwɒf/ *v.t.* M19. [Fr. *coiffer*: see prec.] Dress or arrange (the hair). Chiefly as *coiffed* ppl a.
Also **coiffé** /-feɪ/ *v.t.* M19.

coiffeur /kwɑː'fəː, kwɒ-; *foreign* kwafœːr (*pl. same*)/ *n.* M19. [Fr., f. as prec. + *-eur* -OR.] A hairdresser.
coiffeuse /-əːz; *foreign* -øːz (*pl. same*)/ *n.* a female hairdresser L18.

coiffure /kwɑː'fjʊə, kwɒ-; *n. also foreign* kwafyːr (*pl. same*)/ *n.* & *v.* M17. [Fr., f. as COIFF: see -URE.] A *n.* The way the hair is arranged or (formerly) the head decorated or covered; a hairstyle, a head-dress. M17. B *v.t.* = COIFF. Chiefly as *coiffured* ppl a. E20.

coign /kɔɪn/ *n.* Also **coigne**. LME. [Var. of COIN *n.*: cf. QUOIN *n.*] I = QUOIN *n.* 1 A projecting corner; a cornerstone; an angle. LME. 2 A wedge. M18.
1 R. LEHMANN They sat in a coign of the cliff. **coign of vantage** [f. Shakes. *Macb.*] a place affording a good view of something.
†II 3 = COIN *n.* II. LME–E16.

coign *v.* see QUOIN *v.*

coigning *n.* see QUOINING.

coignye *n.* var. of COYNYE.

coil /kɔɪl/ *n.*[1] Now *arch.* & *dial.* M16. [Origin unkn.] A noisy disturbance, a turmoil, a confused noise, a fuss.
keep a coil make a fuss, disturbance, etc. **this mortal coil** [f. Shakes. *Haml.*] the turmoil of life.

coil /kɔɪl/ *n.*[2] L16. [f. COIL *v.*] 1 A length of rope, cable, etc., gathered up into a number of concentric rings, the quantity of cable etc. usually wound up. L16. 2 An arrangement of a thing in a spiral or a series of concentric circles or rings; a thing so arranged. M17. 3 A single turn of a coiled thing, esp. of a snake. E19. 4 *spec.* a A piece of wire, piping, etc., wound spirally or helically. E19. b A helix of wire for the passage of electric current, esp. for the ignition in an internal-combustion engine, or around a magnetic metal core as in an electromagnet or transformer. M19. c A lock of hair twisted and made into a spiral. L19. d A roll of postage stamps, esp. for use in a stamp-machine. E20. e A flexible loop of material used as an intrauterine contraceptive device. M20. f In full *mosquito coil*. A slowly-burning spiral made with a dried paste of pyrethrum powder, which produces a smoke that inhibits mosquitoes from biting. M20.
1 *Flemish coil*: see FLEMISH *a.* & *n.* 4b *exploring coil*, *induction coil*, *repeating coil*, *Tesla coil*, *tickler coil*, etc.

coil /kɔɪl/ *v.* E16. [OFr. *coillir* (mod. *cueillir* gather) = Prov. *colhir*, Sp. *coger*, Port. *colher* (also) furl, coil rope, f. L *colligere*: see COLLECT *v.*] 1 *v.t.* Arrange (a rope etc.) in concentric rings, either on top of each other or as a flat spiral. Also foll. by *up*. E16. 2 *v.t.* Wrap or encircle in a coil or coils. *obs.* exc. *dial.* E17. 3 *v.t.* & *i.* Twist in or into a circular, spiral, or winding shape. Also foll. by *up*. M17. 4 *v.i.* Move in a spiral course or in a sinuous fashion. E19.
3 TENNYSON The long convolvuluses That coil'd around the stately stems. I. MURDOCH She coiled the .. hair into an artful bun. R. L. FOX Long tame snakes .. would .. coil themselves around the wands and garlands. 4 S. NAIPAUL The smoke coiling up from the incinerator pit.
coiled *ppl a.* that has been coiled, disposed in a coil; (of basketry, a basket) made by coiling the fibre; (of pottery, a pot) made by building up coils of clay: E17.

coin /kɔɪn/ *n.* See also COIGN *n.*, QUOIN *n.* ME. [(O)Fr. *coin*, †*coing* wedge, corner, †stamping-die, f. L *cuneus* wedge.] I 1 See QUOIN *n.* ME. †II 2 A die for stamping money; a stamped device, an impress. LME–L17. 3 A piece of metal, usu. a disc, made into money by an official stamp. LME. 4 Metal money; *slang* money, cash. LME.
3 *fig.*: F. W. ROBERTSON Words are .. the coins of intellectual exchange. *obsidional coin*: see OBSIDIONAL. **the other side of the coin** *fig.* the opposite view of a matter. 4 A. MARS-JONES In coin, two hundred pounds. **bad coin** debased currency. **false coin** imitation coin in base metal; *fig.* something spurious. **pay a person in his** or **her own coin** retaliate by similar behaviour.
Comb.: **coin-box** (a receptacle for coins in) a coin-operated telephone; **coin-op** *a.* & *n.* (*a*) *adj.* coin-operated; (*b*) *n.* a launderette etc. with automatic coin-operated machines; **coin-operated** *a.* (of a machine, lock, etc.) operated by a coin or coins.

coin /kɔɪn/ *v.*[1]*t.* ME. [OFr. *coignier* mint, f. as prec.] I 1 Make (money) by stamping metal. ME. 2 Make (metal) into money by stamping pieces of definite weight and value with authorized marks or characters. LME. 3 *fig.* a Devise, produce; fabricate, invent (esp. a new word etc.). M16. b *fig.* Make money out of or by means of. L16. c Fashion or convert (*in*)*to*. E17. †4 Stamp on a coin; figure in or on a coin. E–M17.
1 **coin money** *fig.* get money fast. 3a DISRAELI He would coin a smile for the instant. R. D. LAING The word 'psychiatry' was coined to refer to the institution of a discipline within medicine. **to coin a phrase** *iron.*: accompanying a banal remark. b W. IRVING He coined the brains of his authors. c BYRON I have not .. coin'd my cheek to smiles.
II See QUOIN *v.*
coinable *a.* M19. **coiner** *n.* (*a*) a person who coins money etc.; *esp.* a maker of counterfeit coins; (*b*) an inventor, a fabricator: ME.

coin *v.*[2] see QUOIN *v.*

coinage /'kɔɪnɪdʒ/ *n.* LME. [OFr. *coigniage*, f. as prec.: see -AGE.] 1 The action or process of coining money; the right to coin money. LME. 2 Coins collectively; a system of coins in use. LME. 3 *Hist.* The official stamping of blocks of tin; the right of doing this. LME. 4 *fig.* An invention; a coined word; the action or process of inventing or of coining words etc. E17.
2 *decimal coinage*: see DECIMAL *a.*

coincide /kəʊɪn'sʌɪd/ *v.i.* E18. [med.L *coincidere* (in Astrol.), f. as CO- + *incidere* fall upon or into. Cf. (O)Fr. *coïncider*.] 1 Occupy the same portion of space. E18. 2 Correspond in substance, nature, or character; agree exactly together or *with*. E18. b Concur *in* opinion etc. M18. 3 Occur at or during the same time. (Foll. by *with*.) E19.
2 GIBBON The true interest of an absolute monarch generally coincides with that of his people. R. D. LAING The person you take me to be, and the identity that I reckon myself to have, will coincide, by and large. 3 W. TREVOR The marriage had been arranged to coincide with the end of the Easter term.

coincidence /kəʊ'ɪnsɪd(ə)ns/ *n.* E17. [med.L *coincidentia*, f. as prec.: see -ENCE.] 1 Occupation of the same portion of space. E17. 2 Correspondence in substance, nature, character, value, etc.; exact agreement. E17. b Concurrence in opinion etc. L18. 3 Simultaneous occurrence or existence. M17. b *Physics.* The presence of ionizing particles etc. in two or more detectors simultaneously, or of two or more signals simultaneously in a circuit. M20. 4 An instance of correspondence, exact agreement, etc. M17. 5 A notable concurrence of events or circumstances without apparent causal connection. L17.
†**coincidency** *n.* (an instance of) correspondence or exact agreement E17–L18.

coincident /kəʊ'ɪnsɪd(ə)nt/ *a.* & *n.* M16. [med.L *coincident-* pres. ppl stem of *coincidere*: see COINCIDE, -ENT.] A *adj.* 1 Having the same substance, nature, character, value, etc.; in exact agreement *with*. M16. 2 Simultaneous, exactly contemporaneous. L16. 3 Occupying the same portion of space. M17. †B *n.* A coinciding thing. Usu. in *pl.* E17–M18.
coincidently *adv.* in a coincident manner, correspondingly, concurrently E17.

coincidental /kəʊɪnsɪ'dɛnt(ə)l/ *a.* E19. [f. prec. + -AL[1].] Of the nature of (a) coincidence; coinciding, esp. without apparent causal connection.
coincidentally *adv.* (*a*) = COINCIDENTLY; (*b*) by coincidence, without apparent causal connection: M19.

coining *n.* see QUOINING.

Cointreau /'kwɑːntrəʊ, *foreign* kwɛ̃tro/ *n.* E20. [Fr.] (Proprietary name for) a colourless orange-flavoured liqueur; a drink of this.

coir /'kɔɪə/ *n.* L16. [Malayalam *kayaru* cord, coir.] The fibre from the outer husk of the coconut, used for ropes, matting, etc., and as a substitute for peat in horticulture; light rope made from this.

coistrel *n.* var. of CUSTREL.

†**coit** *n.* LME–M18. [f. as COITUS.] = COITUS.

coition /kəʊ'ɪʃ(ə)n/ *n.* M16. [L *coitio(n-)*, f. *coit-* pa. ppl stem of *coire*, f. as CO- + *ire* go: see -ION.] †1 Going or coming together; mutual attraction; conjunction of planets. M16–M18. 2 = COPULATION 2. E17.

coitus /'kəʊɪtəs/ *n.* M19. [L, f. *coit-*: see prec.] = COPULATION 2.
coitus interruptus /ɪntə'rʌptəs/ withdrawal of the penis from the vagina before ejaculation. **coitus reservatus** /rɛzə'vɑːtəs/ postponement or avoidance of orgasm, to prolong sexual intercourse.
coital *a.* L19.

cojones /ko'xones, kə'həʊneɪz/ *n.pl. colloq.* M20. [Sp., pl. of *cojón* testicle.] Testicles; *fig.* courage, guts.

coke /kəʊk/ *n.*[1] & *v.*[1] LME. [Perh. same wd as COLK.] A *n.* †1 Charcoal. Only in LME. 2 *sing.* & †in *pl.* Coal deprived by dry distillation of its volatile constituents; the solid substance left after heating petrol etc. LME.
2 **go and eat coke** *slang* go away!
Comb.: **cokeman** a workman who handles coke; **coke-oven**: producing coke from coal.
B *v.t.* & *i.* Convert into coke. L18.
coking coal coal suitable for making into coke.

coke /kəʊk/ *n.*[2] & *v.*[2] *slang.* E20. [Abbrev.] A *n.* Cocaine, as a drug. E20. B *v.t.* Drug (esp. oneself) with cocaine. Also foll. by *up*. E20.
cokey *n.* a cocaine-addict E20.

Coke /kəʊk/ *n.*[3] Also **c-**. E20. [Abbrev.] Proprietary name, = COCA-COLA.

coker /'kəʊkə/ *n.*[1] L18. [f. COKE *n.*[1] & *v.*[1] + -ER[1].] A person who supervises the coking of coal; a cokeman.

coker *n.*[2] var. of COCKER *n.*[2]

†**cokes** *n.* M16–L17. [Origin unkn.] A silly fellow, a ninny, a simpleton.

†**cokes** *v.* see COAX *v.*

col /kɒl/ *n.* M19. [Fr. f. L *collum* neck.] 1 A depression in the summit-line of a mountain chain; a saddle between two peaks. M19. 2 *Meteorol.* An area of lower pressure between two anticyclones. L19.

col. /kɒl/ *n.* Pl. **cols.** (point). E20. [Abbrev.] = COLUMN 2.

col- /kɒl, *unstressed* kəl/ *pref.* Var. of L COM- bef. *l*. Cf. CO-, CON-, COR-.

cola /'kəʊlə/ *n.*[1] Also **k-**. E17. [Temne *k'ola* cola-nut.] 1 A tree of the genus *Cola*, native to W. Africa, esp. *C. acuminata*; the bitter seed of such a tree (also *cola-nut*, *-seed*). E17. 2 A carbonated drink flavoured with cola-seeds. Earliest in COCA-COLA, PEPSI-COLA. L19.
¶In sense 2 recorded as an independent wd in E20.

cola *n.*[2]*pl.* see COLON *n.*[2]

colander /'kʌləndə/ *n.* & *v.* Also **cullender**. ME. [Perh. f. OProv. *colador* (mod.Prov. *couladou*) = Sp. *colador*, f. Proto-Romance, f. L *colat-* pa. ppl stem of *colare* strain: see -OR. Cf. med.L *colatorium*, Fr. *couloir*. For the intrusive *n* cf. *messenger*, *passenger*, etc.] A *n.* A perforated vessel used as a strainer in cookery; *transf.* a similar vessel used in other processes. ME. **B** *v.t.* **1** Perforate with holes. E18. **2** Pass through a colander, strain. L19.

colation /kəˈleɪʃ(ə)n/ *n.* Long *rare.* E17. [med.L *colatio(n-)*, f. L *colat-*: see prec., -ATION.] The action of straining or passing through a strainer.

co-latitude /kəʊˈlatɪtjuːd/ *n.* L18. [f. CO- + LATITUDE.] *Astron.* The complement of latitude, i.e. the difference between latitude and 90 degrees.

†**colature** *n.* LME. [(O)Fr., or late L *colatura*, f. *colat-*: see COLANDER, -URE.] **1** The product of straining. LME–E17. **2** A strainer; *Anat.* a sphenoidal sinus. L16–L17. **3** = COLATION. M17–L18.

†**colatory** *n.* = COLATURE 2 LME–E18.

†**colbertine** *n.* Also **-een**. L17–M19. [f. *Colbert* French surname + -INE[4].] Open lace with a square ground.

colcannon /kɒlˈkanən/ *n.* L18. [Perh. f. COLE *n.*[1]] An Irish and Scottish dish of cabbage and potatoes boiled and pounded.

Colchian /ˈkɒlkɪən/ *a.* E17. [f. L *Colchis* (see below) f. Gk *Kolkhis* + -AN.] Of Colchis, the ancient name of a region east of the Black Sea, associated in Greek mythology with the quest of the Golden Fleece.

Also **Colchic** *a.* L16.

colchicine /ˈkɒltʃɪsiːn/ *n.* M19. [f. next + -INE[5].] *Chem.* A toxic yellow alkaloid, $C_{22}H_{25}NO_6$, present esp. in colchicum corms, which is used to treat gout and in plant-breeding to induce mutations.

Also †**colchicia** *n.* M–L19.

colchicum /ˈkɒltʃɪkəm, ˈkɒlk-/ *n.* L16. [L f. Gk *kolkhikon* use as n. of neut. of *Kolkhikos*, f. *Kolkhis* (with ref. to the poisonous arts of Medea): see COLCHIAN.] **1** A plant of the genus *Colchicum* of the lily family, *esp.* meadow saffron, *C. autumnale*. L16. **2** The dried corm or seed of such a plant used medicinally. L18.

†**colcothar** *n.* E17–M19. [Arab. *ḳulḳuṭār*.] Ferric oxide, rouge, formed as a residue in the distillation of sulphuric acid from ferrous sulphate.

cold /kəʊld/ *n.* Also (*Sc.* & *north.*) **cauld** /kɔːld/. [OE *cald*, *ċeald* neut., f. the adj.] **1** The opposite or the absence of heat; the prevalence of low temperature, esp. in the atmosphere; cold weather; a condition of low temperature, a cold spell. OE. **2** The sensation produced by loss of heat from the body or by exposure to a lower temperature; a cold condition of the body. OE. **b** *fig.* Lack of zeal, enthusiasm, or heartiness. ME. **3** An indisposition supposed to be caused by exposure to cold; *spec.* (also *common cold*, *cold in the head*) a viral infection causing inflammation of the mucous membranes of the nose and throat, usu. with hoarseness, running at the nose, coughing, etc. ME. **4** Cold water. Chiefly in *hot and cold*. E20.

Phrases: *catch (a) cold*: see CATCH *v.* *catch one's* DEATH *of cold*, *cold in the head*, *common cold*: see sense 3 above. **degrees of cold** degrees below freezing point. **left out in the cold** *fig.* ignored, not looked after. *streaming cold*: see STREAMING *ppl a.*

Comb.: **cold sore** an inflamed blister, esp. in or near the mouth, due to herpes simplex infection; **cold wave** *n.*[1] a spell of cold weather; a fall of temperature travelling over a large area.

cold /kəʊld/ *a.* & *adv.* Also (*Sc.* & *north.*) **cauld** /kɔːld/. [OE *cald*, (WS) *ċeald* = OFris., OS *cald* (Du. *koud*), OHG *kalt* (G *kalt*), ON *kaldr*, Goth. *kalds*, f. Gmc, rel. to L *gelu* frost.] **A** *adj.* **1** Of or at a temperature perceptibly lower than that of the living human body; of or at a relatively low temperature; characteristically or naturally so. OE. **b** Dead; *slang* unconscious. ME. **2** Not heated; having been allowed to cool after heating; (of a hearth etc.) with no fire burning; (of a tobacco-pipe etc.) not lit. OE. **3** *fig.* Void of warmth or intensity of feeling; indifferent, apathetic; cool; not cordial or friendly; (more positively) feelingless, callous. OE. **b** Sexually frigid, without sensual passion. L16. **4** *Hist.* Designating a quality associated with coldness and regarded in medieval and later times as one of four qualities inherent in all things; having a preponderance of this quality. Cf. *hot*, *dry*, *moist*. OE. **5** Gloomy, dispiriting, depressing; chilling. ME. **6** Of a person or animal, or a part of the body: feeling cold. Chiefly *pred.* LME. **7** Of soil: slow to absorb heat. LME. **8** Without power to influence; having lost the power of exciting the emotions; stale. L16. **9a** *Hunting.* Of a scent: weakened by the passage of time, faint. L16. **b** Of a participant in a children's seeking or guessing game: far from finding or guessing what is sought. M19. **10** Of a colour or colouring: suggestive of cold or a sunless day; not suggestive of light and warmth; *esp.* of a pale blue or grey tint. E18. **11** Without preparation, preliminary performance, etc.; unrehearsed. Orig. & chiefly *N. Amer.* L19. **12** At one's mercy. *colloq.* E20.

1 GOLDSMITH In the cold regions of the north. E. O'BRIEN The linoleum was cold on the soles of my feet. N. MOSLEY A spell of cold weather in which the pavements froze. **2** SCOTT FITZGERALD A plate of cold fried chicken between them. **3** STEELE Cold to what his friends think of him. T. HARDY An unprotected childhood in a cold world has beaten gentleness out of me. R. LEHMANN Cold natures are always secretive. A. C. BOULT A wonderful collection of stories which he told with such relish . . that one hesitates to retell them in cold print. **5** W. COWPER She feels . . A cold misgiving. LD MACAULAY Preston brought cold news. **6** D. H. LAWRENCE I was very cold, so I went downstairs. G. SWIFT His hands . . were still cold from walking home in the rain. **8** D. L. SAYERS The news was already 'cold'.

Phrases: **as cold as ice** very cold (*lit.* & *fig.*). *blow hot and cold*: see BLOW *v.*[1] *cauld kale het again*: see KALE *n.* *cold as charity*: see CHARITY. *go hot and cold*: see HOT *a.* **knock, lay (out), cold** *slang* knock unconscious, stun, shock severely. **leave a person cold** fail to interest or excite a person. *stone-cold sober*: see STONE *adv.*

Special collocations & comb.: **cold bath**: in cold water. *cold blood*: see BLOOD *n.* **cold-blooded** *a.* (*a*) = ECTOTHERMIC; (*b*) *fig.* without excitement or sensibility; callous, deliberately cruel. **cold call** *v.i.* & *t.* make an unsolicited call to or on (a person) to sell goods or services. **cold cathode**: that emits electrons without being heated. *cold chisel*: see CHISEL *n.*[1] I. **cold comfort** poor consolation. *cold compress*: see COMPRESS *n.* I. **cold cream** a cooling cosmetic cream, used also for softening and cleansing the skin. **cold-cream** *v.t.* apply cold cream to; take *off* by means of cold cream. **cold cuts** an assortment of cooked meats, sliced and served cold. *cold dark matter*: see *dark matter* s.v. DARK *a.* **cold deck** *US slang* a pack of cards in which the cards have been arranged beforehand. **cold-deck** *v.t.* (*US slang*) cheat (a person) by using a cold deck. **cold feet** *colloq.*: a sign of fear or cowardice; esp. in *get, have, cold feet*, refuse to proceed through fear or cowardice. **cold-finch** (*obs.* exc. *dial.*) the pied flycatcher, *Ficedula hypoleuca*. **cold frame** *Hort.*: in which small plants are grown without artificial heat. *cold front*: see FRONT *n.* 11b. **cold fusion** nuclear fusion brought about at a much lower temperature than is usually required, esp. a temperature near room temperature. *cold harbour*: see HARBOUR *n.*[1] **cold-hearted** *a.* lacking in sensibility or natural affection; unkind. *cold lead*: see LEAD *n.*[1] **cold light** light accompanied by little or no heat, e.g. luminescence. **cold meat** (*a*) meat cooled after cooking; (*b*) *slang* a corpse, corpses. *cold* OBSTRUCTION. **cold shoulder** *fig.* intentionally unfriendly treatment; esp. in *give a person the cold shoulder*. **cold-shoulder** *v.t.* treat with intentional coldness or contemptuous neglect. **cold shower**: in cold water. *cold-slaw*: see COLESLAW. *cold snap*: see SNAP *n.* 10. **cold start(ing)**: of an internal-combustion engine at ambient temperature. *cold steel*: see STEEL *n.*[1] **cold storage** storage in a refrigerator; *fig.* a state of abeyance. *cold sweat*: see SWEAT *n.* **cold table** (a table bearing) dishes of cold food. **cold tap**: dispensing cold water. **cold turkey** *slang* (*a*) *US* blunt statements; (*b*) abrupt withdrawal of drugs from an addict; the symptoms of this. **cold war** hostilities short of armed conflict, consisting in threats, violent propaganda, subversive political activities, etc.; *spec.* those formerly between the USSR and the western powers after the 1939–45 war. **cold warrior** a participant in a cold war. **cold water** *fig.* discouragement, disparagement; esp. in *pour, throw, cold water (up)on*, discourage, disparage, (a scheme etc.). **cold-water** *a.* (*a*) using or containing unheated water; (*b*) living in or characteristic of the seas of cool or polar regions; (*c*) *US* (of a house etc.) without central heating. **cold wave** *n.*[2] a kind of permanent hair-wave produced by a cold process. **cold work** the working of metal while it is cold. **cold-work** *v.t.* shape (metal) while it is cold. *ice-cold*: see ICE *n.* *stone-cold*: see STONE *n.*

B *adv.* Without any mitigation; absolutely, entirely. *US slang.* L19.

coldly *adv.* ME. **coldness** *n.* LME.

cold /kəʊld/ *v.* [OE *(a)caldian*, *ċealdian*, f. the adj.] **1** *v.i.* Become or be cold. Long *rare.* OE. †**2** *v.t.* Make cold; chill. LME–L16. **3** *v.t.* Afflict with a cold or chill. Chiefly as *colded* ppl a. *dial.* E19.

cold-short /ˈkəʊldʃɔːt/ *a.* E17. [Sw. *kallskör* (= Norw., Da. *koldskjør*), neut. *kallskört* (sc. *jern* iron), f. *kallr* cold + *skör* brittle, later assoc. with SHORT *a.* 'brittle'.] Of metal: brittle in its cold state.

coldslaw *n.* var. of COLESLAW.

cole /kəʊl/ *n.*[1] Now *rare* exc. in comb. Also †**caul**. [OE *cāwel*, *caul* = MDu. *cōle* (Du. *kool*), OHG *chōl(i)*, *chōlo*, *-a* (G *Kohl*), f. L *caulis* (later *caulus*, *-a*) stem, stalk, cabbage; reinforced by forms f. cogn. ON *kál* (cf. KALE).] **1** Cabbage, brassica. OE. **2** Soup; broth; stew. Long *obs.* exc. *dial.* LME.

Comb.: **colewort** cabbage, brassica, *esp.* a kind that does not heart. Cf. also COLESEED, COLESLAW.

cole /kəʊl/ *n.*[2] *slang.* L17. [Perh. f. COAL *n.*] Money.

-cole /kəʊl/ *suff.* [f. as -COLOUS.] Forming (*a*) ns. w. the sense 'an organism that lives or grows in or on a specified kind of habitat or material', as *limnicole*, and (*b*) adjs. w. the sense of -COLOUS, as *muscicole*.

colectomy /kəʊˈlɛktəmi/ *n.* L19. [f. COLON *n.*[1] + -ECTOMY.] Surgical removal of all or part of the colon; an instance of this.

colemanite /ˈkəʊlmənʌɪt/ *n.* L19. [f. William T. *Coleman* (1824–93), US mine-owner + -ITE[1].] *Min.* A monoclinic hydrated borate of calcium usu. occurring as white glassy prisms.

colemouse *n.* var. of COALMOUSE.

Coleoptera /kɒlɪˈɒpt(ə)rə/ *n.pl.* Rarely in sing. **-ron** /-rən/. M18. [mod.L, f. Gk *koleopteros* sheath-winged, f. *koleos* sheath + *pteron* wing: see -A[3].] (Members of) a large order of insects having the front wings modified as hard wing-cases, and comprising the beetles (including weevils).

coleopteran *n.* & *a.* (a member) of the order Coleoptera M19. **coleopterist** *n.* a person who studies beetles M19. **coleopteroid** *a.* resembling or akin to a member of the order Coleoptera L19. **coleopterous** *a.* belonging or pertaining to the order Coleoptera L18.

coleoptile /kɒlɪˈɒptʌɪl/ *n.* M19. [f. Gk *koleos* sheath + *ptilon* feather.] *Bot.* A hollow organ enclosing the first leaf of a germinating cereal grain.

coleorhiza /ˌkɒlɪə(ʊ)ˈrʌɪzə/ *n.* M19. [f. as prec. + Gk *rhiza* root.] *Bot.* The root-sheath of a germinating cereal grain.

colerake /ˈkəʊlreɪk/ *n.* Now *rare* or *obs.* Also **colrake**. LME. [Perh. f. COAL *n.* (in sense 'cinder') + RAKE *n.*[1]] An instrument for raking ashes out of an oven or furnace; a similar instrument for other purposes.

Coleridgian /kəʊlˈrɪdʒɪən/ *a.* & *n.* Also **-ean**. E19. [f. *Coleridge* (see below) + -IAN.] **A** *adj.* Of, pertaining to, or characteristic of the English poet and philosopher Samuel Taylor Coleridge (1772–1834) or his writings, opinions, etc. E19. **B** *n.* An admirer or student of Coleridge or his writing. E19.

coleseed /ˈkəʊlsiːd/ *n.* OE. [f. COLE *n.*[1] + SEED *n.* In sense 2 prob. partly f. Du. *koolzaad*: see COLZA.] †**1** Cabbage-seed. Only in OE. **2** Rape-seed; rape; = COLZA. LME.

coleslaw /ˈkəʊlslɔː/ *n.* Orig. *US* Also **cold-** /kəʊld-/. L18. [Du. *koolsla*, f. *kool* COLE *n.*[1] + *sla* SLAW.] A salad of sliced raw cabbage, now usu. with mayonnaise etc.

†**colet** *n.* LME–M18. [Abbrev.] = ACOLYTE.

coleta /kəˈleɪtə/ *n.* E20. [Sp., dim. of *cola* tail, f. L *coda*, *cauda* tail.] A pigtail, worn by a bullfighter as a mark of his profession.

cole-tit *n.* var. of COAL-TIT.

For other words beginning with *co-* see the entry for **co-**

coleus /ˈkəʊlɪəs/ *n.* M19. [mod.L f. Gk *koleos* sheath: from the form of its united filaments.] A plant of the genus *Solenostemon*, of the mint family, usu. with variegated coloured leaves.

coley /ˈkəʊli/ *n.* M20. [Prob. f. *coalfish* s.v. COAL *n.* + -Y[1].] = SAITHE.

coli /ˈkəʊlʌɪ/ *n.* Pl. same. L19. [mod.L (*Bacillus* or *Escherichia*) *coli* (species name), f. L genit. of COLON *n.*[1]] A bacterium, *Escherichia coli*, which inhabits the large intestine of humans and animals. Freq. in *comb.*

coliform *a.* belonging to a group of rod-shaped bacteria typified by *Escherichia coli* E20. **coliphage** *n.* a bacteriophage that attacks *E. coli* M20.

colibri /ˈkɒlɪbri/ *n.* L17. [Fr., Sp. f. Carib.] A large violet-eared hummingbird of the genus *Colibri*.

colic /ˈkɒlɪk/ *n.* & *a.* LME. [(O)Fr. *colique* f. late L *colicus* adj. f. COLON *n.*[1]: see -IC.] **A** *n.* An acute episodic abdominal pain, now *esp.* one arising from the twisting, obstruction, or spasm of a hollow organ. LME.

painter's colic: see PAINTER *n.*[1] RENAL *colic*.

Comb.: **colic-root** *N. Amer.* any of certain medicinal plants, *esp.* star-grass, *Aletris farinosa*.

B *adj.* **1** (Now taken to be the n. used *attrib.*) Affecting the colon; of the nature of colic. LME. **2** Pertaining to the colon. E17.

†**colical** *a.* = COLIC *a.* E17–M18. **colicky** *a.* pertaining to or of the nature of colic; subject to or producing colic: M18.

colicin /ˈkɒlɪsɪn/ *n.* Also **-ine** /-iːn/. M20. [Fr. *colicine*, f. COLI + *-c-*: see -IN[1], -INE[5].] *Bacteriol.* A bacteriocin produced by a coliform bacterium.

colin /ˈkɒlɪn/ *n.* L17. [Erron. form of Nahuatl *çolin*.] = BOBWHITE.

coliseum /kɒlɪˈsiːəm/ *n.* Also (now usual in sense 1) **colosseum**; (earlier) †**-ee**, †**-eo**. E16. [med.L *coliseum* use as n. of L *colosseus* colossal, f. as COLOSSUS. Earliest forms f. Fr. *colisée*, It. *coliseo*, f. med.L.] **1** *the Colosseum*, the amphitheatre of Vespasian at Rome. E16. †**2** Any ancient Roman amphitheatre. *rare.* L16–L18. **3** (A name given to) a large theatre or *esp.* (*N. Amer.*) a large stadium etc. L19.

¶Form *-eum* recorded M17.

colitis /kəˈlʌɪtɪs/ *n.* M19. [f. COLON *n.*[1] + -ITIS.] *Med.* Inflammation of the colon.

colk /kɒlk/ *n. obs.* exc. *dial.* LME. [Origin unkn.: cf. COKE *n.*[1]] The core of an apple, of a horn, a heart of wood, etc.

coll /kɒl/ *v.*[1]*t.* Long *obs.* exc. *dial.* Also **cull** /kʌl/. ME. [Fr. *coler* = *accoler* ACCOLL or aphet. f. ACCOLL.] Embrace, hug.

coll /kɒl/ *v.*[2]*t. obs.* exc. *Sc.* L15. [Perh. of Scand. origin: cf. ON *kollr* head, poll, shaven crown, *kolla* beast without horns, Norw. *kylla* poll, prune, cut. Cf. COW *v.*[1]] Cut off the hair of, clip, cut close.

collaborate /kəˈlabəreɪt/ *v.i.* L19. [Late L *collaborat-* pa. ppl stem of *collaborare*, f. as COL- + *laborare* LABOUR *v.*: see -ATE[3].] **1** Work jointly (*with*), esp. on a literary or scientific project. L19. **2** *spec.* Cooperate traitorously with (or *with*) an enemy. M20.

collaborateur /kɔlabɔratœːr (*pl. same*)/ *n.* = COLLABORATOR E19. **collaboˈration** *n.* M19. **collaboˈrationist** *n.* & *a.* (a person) advocating or practising collaboration E20. **collaborative** *a.* E20. **collaboratively** *adv.* L20. **collaborator** *n.* a person who collaborates E19.

collage /kɒˈlɑːʒ/ *n.* E20. [Fr. = gluing.] An abstract form of art in which photographs, pieces of paper, string, matchsticks, etc., are placed in juxtaposition and glued to a surface; a work in this form; *fig.* a jumbled collection of impressions, events, styles, etc.

collagist *n.* a person who makes collages M20.

collagen /ˈkɒlədʒ(ə)n/ *n.* M19. [Fr. *collagène* f. Gk *kolla* glue: see -GEN.] A fibrous protein that is the chief constituent of connective tissue and yields gelatin on boiling.

coˈllagenous *a.* of the nature of or containing collagen M19.

collapsar /kəˈlapsɑː/ *n.* L20. [f. COLLAPSE *v.* after *pulsar*, *quasar*.] *Astron.* A black hole formed by gravitational collapse of a star.

collapse /kəˈlaps/ *n.* E19. [f. medical L *collapsus* use as n. of pa. pple: see COLLAPSED.] (An action or instance of) collapsing; a collapsed condition.

A. J. CRONIN The operation might induce an immediate collapse. A. MARS-JONES The marshal . . waits in collapse on a chair. P. ACKROYD The entire collapse of his career. *collapse of a stout party*: see STOUT *a.*

collapse /kəˈlaps/ *v.* M18. [Back-form. f. next.] **1** *v.i.* Undergo or experience a falling in (as with the puncture of an inflated hollow body); shrink suddenly together; break down, give way, cave in. M18. **2** *v.i. transf.* & *fig.* Come to nothing, fail; experience prostration through loss of muscular or nervous power; experience a breakdown of mental energy. E19. **3** *v.t.* Cause to collapse. L19.

1 E. WAUGH The camp bed . . collapsed repeatedly. I. F. ELIS The side collapsed and half filled the pit with earth. 2 B. CHATWIN When she could work no more, she would collapse into the rocking chair. A. MOOREHEAD The little township . . has collapsed through want of trade. A. MASON The landowner collapsed where he stood, and . . was found to be dead.

collapsiˈbility *n.* the quality of being collapsible L19. **collapsible** *a.* able to be collapsed M19. †**collapsion** *n.* = COLLAPSE *n.* E17–E19.

collapsed /kəˈlapst/ *a.* E17. [f. L *collapsus* pa. pple of *collabi*, f. as COL- + *labi* fall (see LAPSE *n.*) + -ED[1].] **1** Fallen in, shrunk together, broken down. E17. **2** Ruined, fallen into decay; failed. E17. †**3** Lapsed in religion etc.; in a state of sin, fallen. E–M17. **4** Prostrated; completely broken down in mental energy. M17.

collar /ˈkɒlə/ *n.* ME. [AN *coler*, OFr. *colier* (mod. *collier*) f. L *collare*, f. *collum* neck: see -AR[1].] **1** The upright or turned-over neckband of a coat, dress, shirt, etc.; a band of linen, lace, etc., completing the upper part of a costume. Also, an ornamental chain or band worn around the neck as a badge of office etc., now *spec.* one forming part of the insignia of an order of knighthood. ME. †**2** A piece of armour for protecting the neck. ME–L16. **3** A roll around a draught animal's neck forming part of the harness through which the power of drawing is directly exerted. See also *breast collar* s.v. BREAST *n.* ME. **4** A band put around the neck of an animal (esp. a dog) to control, identify, or ornament it. LME. **5** A metal band fixed round the neck of prisoners, slaves, servants, etc. *obs.* exc. *Hist.* LME. **6** *Naut.* (Orig.) the lower end of the principal stays of a mast; (later) the rope, with a deadeye in its end, to which the stay is secured. Also, the eye in the upper end of a stay or the bight of the shrouds, which is threaded over the masthead before being set taut to hold the mast secure. LME. **7a** Orig., a boar's or pig's neck cut as a piece of meat. Now, the part of a flitch of bacon nearest the neck. L15. **b** A piece of meat (esp. from a pig's neck) or a fish rolled up and usu. tied. M17. **8** An encompassing or restraining strap or band; a ring, circle, flange, etc. in a machine. E16. **9** A wrestling move in which the opponent is tackled by the neck. L16. **10** A marking or structure resembling a collar; *esp.* a coloured stripe around an animal's or bird's neck. M17. **11** An arrest, legal apprehension. *slang.* M19.

1 *Eton collar*, *mandarin collar*, *Medici collar*, *Prussian collar*, *Shakespeare collar*, *toby collar*, etc. 3 *horse-collar*: see HORSE *n.* 4 *dog-collar*: see DOG *n.*

Phrases: *clerical collar*: see CLERICAL *a.* 1. **collar of SS, of esses** a chain consisting of a series of S's: the former badge of the House of Lancaster, still used in the costumes of some officials. **feel a person's collar** *slang* arrest or legally apprehend a person; freq. in pass. *have one's collar felt*. *hot under the collar*: see HOT *a.* **put the collar on** *slang* arrest, legally apprehend.

Comb.: **collar-beam** a horizontal beam connecting two rafters and forming with them an A-shaped roof-truss; **collar-bone** the curved bone joining the shoulder-blade to the breast-bone; the clavicle; **collar day** *Hist.*: on which knights wore the collar of their order, when taking part in any court ceremony; **collar-stud**: to fasten a detachable collar to a shirt; **collar-work** work in which a draught animal has to strain hard against the collar; *fig.* severe and close work.

collarless *a.* E17.

collar /ˈkɒlə/ *v.* M16. [f. the n.] **1** *v.t.* Put a collar on; fasten or surround as with a collar. M16. **b** *spec.* Put a collar on (a horse), esp. for the first time; break (a horse) in. L17. **2** *v.i.* Lay hold of the opponent's neck or collar in wrestling. Now *rare* or *obs.* M16. **3** *v.t.* Seize or take hold of by the collar; capture, arrest; stop and detain; *Rugby Football* lay hold of and stop (an opponent holding the ball); *slang* grab, take, appropriate, esp. illicitly. E17. **4** *v.t.* Roll up (a cut of meat, a fish, etc.) and tie with string. L17.

3 F. MARRYAT He was collared by two French soldiers, and dragged back into the battery. V. WOOLF He would collar Miss Whatshername and ask for a synopsis. JO GRIMOND The Stewart Earls and their grasping followers . . collared much of the land.

collard /ˈkɒləd/ *n. N. Amer.* & *dial.* M18. [Reduced form of *colewort* s.v. COLE *n.*[1]] A variety of cabbage which does not heart, used for greens (also *collard greens*).

collared /ˈkɒləd/ *a.* LME. [f. COLLAR *n.*, *v.*: see -ED[2], -ED[1].] **1** Wearing a collar. LME. **2** That has been collared. M17. **3** Of an animal or bird: having a bandlike marking, esp. round the neck. E19.

3 **collared dove** a grey-brown dove, *Streptopelia decaocto*, that began to colonize Britain from Europe in the 1950s and is now common. *collared lemming*: see LEMMING 1. *collared* PECCARY.

collarette /kɒləˈrɛt/ *n.* L17. [Fr. *collerette* dim. of *collier* COLLAR *n.*: see -ETTE.] **1** A woman's ornamental collar of lace, fur, etc. L17. **2** A dahlia with shortened petals immediately surrounding the centre, and flat outer petals. E20.

collate /kɒˈleɪt/ *v.* M16. [L *collat-* pa. ppl stem of *conferre*: see CONFER *v.*, -ATE[3].] **1** *Eccl.* †**a** *v.t.* Confer (a benefice) *on* a person. M16–L17. **b** *v.t.* Esp. of an Ordinary: appoint (a cleric) *to* a benefice. E17. **c** *v.i.* Make an appointment to a benefice; make appointments to benefices. E17. †**2** *v.t. gen.* Confer or bestow (*up*)*on*; grant *to*. L16–E18. **3** *v.t.* Bring together for comparison; compare carefully and exactly (esp. copies of a text or document, one such copy *with* another); put together (esp. information, or sheets to form two or more copies of a document). E17. **4** *v.t.* Examine and check the order etc. of (the sheets of a printed book, a book) by signatures; check the printed appearance and order of. L18.

collatable *a.* M19.

collateral /kɒˈlat(ə)r(ə)l/ *a.* & *n.* LME. [med.L *collateralis*: see COL-, LATERAL.] **A** *adj.* **1** Situated or placed side by side; parallel. LME. **2** *fig.* Accompanying, attendant, concomitant. LME. †**b** Of equal rank. LME–M17. **c** Parallel in time, order, development, etc.; corresponding. E16. **3** Lying aside from the main subject, issue, purpose, etc.; subordinate. LME. **4** Descended from the same ancestors but by a different line (opp. *lineal*). LME.

Special collocations: **collateral bundle** *Bot.* a vascular bundle in which the xylem and phloem lie side by side. **collateral circulation** *Anat.* an alternative route for blood when primary vessels are blocked; the channel. **collateral contract** a subsidiary contract which induces a person to enter into a main contract. **collateral damage** destruction or injury beyond that intended or expected, esp. in the vicinity of a military target. **collateral issue** *Law* a question not directly at issue. **collateral security** property etc. pledged as a guarantee for the repayment of money.

B *n.* †**1** An associate in some office, function, etc. L16–E18. †**2** An equal (in rank). E–M17. **3** A collateral kinsman or kinswoman. L17. **4** Something given as collateral security. M19. **5** *Anat.* A branch of a nerve fibre at right angles to the main part. L19.

collateˈrality *n.* E17. **collaterally** *adv.* LME.

collation /kɒˈleɪʃ(ə)n/ *n.* ME. [OFr. *collacion*, *-tion* f. L *collatio(n-)* collection, comparison, (in med.L) conference, repast, f. as COLLATE *v.*: see -ATION.] **I** Conference. **1a** In *pl.* John Cassian's *Collationes Patrum in Scetica Eremo Commorantium*, Conferences of (and with) the Egyptian Hermits (AD 415–20); *sing.* a section of this work. ME. **b** A reading in a Benedictine monastery from this work, later also from any other edifying text, before the light meal taken at

For other words beginning with *co-* see the entry for **co-**

the end of the day; this meal; *transf.* (in mod. Roman Catholic usage) a light meal in the evening of a fast-day. ME. †2 A (private or informal) conference; a discourse, a homily, a treatise. LME–M17. 3 A light meal, esp. at an unusual time. Now chiefly in *cold collation.* E16. II Bringing together. 4a A collection, esp. of money; a contribution. *obs.* exc. *Sc.* ME. b *Rom. & Sc. Law.* A bringing together of the whole estate and funds on which the children of a deceased parent have a claim in succession, including any funds etc. advanced previously to any of the children, for its subsequent equal division among them. E19. 5 The act of collating; comparison; *esp.* the textual or critical comparison of various documents, editions, etc. LME. b The recorded result of such textual etc. comparison; a set of corrections compiled after such comparison. L17. 6 The action of collating the sheets etc. of a document or printed book. M18. III 7 Conferring or bestowal (esp. of a dignity, honour, etc.). Now only *Eccl.*, the bestowal *of* a benefice on a member of the clergy; the appointment (by the Ordinary) of a member of the clergy *to* a benefice. LME. b The right of institution to a benefice. Now *rare.* L15.

co'llational *a.* of or pertaining to collation M20.

†collation *v.* M16. [f. the n.] 1 *v.t.* = COLLATE 3, 4. M16–E18. 2 *v.t.* & *i.* Entertain with or have lunch. E17–M18.

†collationer *n.* a collator; a person who lunches or has a collation: L17–L18.

collative /kɒˈleɪtɪv/ *a.* E17. [In sense 1 f. L *collativus*, f. as COLLATE + -IVE; in senses 2, 3 f. COLLATE + -IVE, perh. through Fr. *collatif.*] †1 Of a conferred or bestowed kind. Only in E17. †2 Of the nature of or formed by contribution. M17–E19. 3 That confers or can confer. (Foll. by *of.*) M17. 4 *Eccl.* Where the Ordinary collates. E18.

collator /kɒˈleɪtə/ *n.* LME. [L *collator*, f. as COLLATE: see -OR. In senses 2, 3 = med.L *collator*, Fr. *collateur.*] †1 A collector. *rare.* Only in LME. 2 A person who collates a text, edition, etc.; a person who collates the sheets of a printed book etc. E17. 3 *Eccl.* A person who collates to a benefice. E17. 4 A person who bestows. M17. 5 A machine for combining sets of punched cards, or sheets to form copies of a document. M20.

collaudation /kɒlɔːˈdeɪʃ(ə)n/ *n. arch.* E17. [L *collaudatio(n-)*, f. *collaudare*, f. as COL- + *laudare* to praise: see -ATION.] Warm praise, high commendation.

colleague /ˈkɒliːg/ *n.* E16. [Fr. *collègue* f. L *collega* partner in office, f. as COL- + *leg-* stem of *lex* law, *legare* depute.] A fellow official or worker, esp. in a profession or business.

colleagueship *n.* the position or relation of a colleague M17.

colleague /kəˈliːg/ *v. obs.* exc. *Sc.* M16. [OFr. *colliguer*, later *colléguer* f. L *colligare* bind together, f. as COL- + *ligare* bind.] †1 *v.t.* Join in alliance, associate. M16–M18. 2 *v.i.* Unite, cooperate; conspire. (Foll. by *with, together.*) M16.

collect /ˈkɒlɛkt, -lɪkt/ *n.* ME. [(O)Fr. *collecte* f. L *collecta* gathering, collection, (in late L) assembly, meeting, use as n. of fem. pa. pple of *colligere*: see COLLECT *v.*] 1 A short prayer said by the minister in Anglican and Roman Catholic liturgies, *esp.* one before the first reading in the Eucharist and varying according to the day or season. ME. †2 The action or an act of collecting (esp. money). LME–M16. †3 A meeting, esp. for worship. LME–E18. †4 A group of things collected or occurring together. LME–L19.

collect /kəˈlɛkt/ *pa. pple* & *ppl a.* Long *arch.* LME. [L *collectus* pa. pple of *colligere*: see next.] Collected.

collect /kəˈlɛkt/ *v.* LME. [(O)Fr. *collecter* or med.L *collectare*, f. L *collect-* pa. ppl stem of *colligere*, f. as COL- + *legere* collect, assemble, choose, read.] I 1 *v.t.* Assemble into one place or group. LME. b *v.t.* Obtain or seek out (specimens, stamps, books, etc.) to add to others, esp. as a hobby. M18. c *v.i.* Maintain and add to a collection of similar things, esp. as a hobby. L19. 2a *v.t.* Get or receive (money, contributions, etc.) from a number of people. M17. b *v.i.* Receive donations or (*colloq.*) a payment. M19. 3 *v.t.* Get from a place of deposit; call for. *colloq.* L19. 4 *v.t.* Attract (a group of people) to oneself, serve as a focus for. M20.

1 J. RUSKIN Collecting materials for my work on Venetian architecture. **collect eyes** intentionally attract several people's attention. 2b J. JOHNSTON Those collecting for some charity.

II 5 *v.t.* Deduce, infer, gather. Foll. by simple obj. subord. cl., obj. and inf. LME. 6 *v.t.* Regain control over (one's thoughts or feelings, oneself); summon up (courage). E17. 7 *v.i.* Come together, gather, assemble; accumulate. L18. 8 *v.t.* Cause (a horse) to bring its legs compactly under itself and be better able to respond to the rider. M19.

5 G. HEYER I collect, from something Stavely said to me, that already she doesn't like it. 7 LD MACAULAY A force was collecting at Bridport.

collect /kəˈlɛkt/ *adv.* & *a.* Orig. *US.* E20. [Imper. of COLLECT *v.*] A *adv.* On the condition that the recipient (of a parcel, telephone call, etc.) pays, in some cases at the time of delivery. E20.

M. DE LA ROCHE She arranged for coal to be sent collect.

B *adj.* Sent in this way. E20.

collectable /kəˈlɛktəb(ə)l/ *a.* & *n.* Also **-ible**. M17. [f. COLLECT *v.* + -ABLE, -IBLE.] A *adj.* 1 Able to be collected. M17. 2 Worth collecting; of interest to a collector. L19. B *n.* A book etc. worth collecting. Usu. in *pl.* M20.

collectanea /kɒlɛkˈtɑːnɪə, -ˈteɪn-/ *n.* M17. [L *collectanea* neut. pl., f. *collect-* (see COLLECT *v.*), as used as adj. in *Dicta collectanea* of Caesar, and as n. in *Collectanea* of Solinus.] As *pl.*, passages, remarks, etc., collected from various sources. As *sing.*, a miscellany.

collectar /ˈkɒlɛktɑː/ *n.* Also **-are**. ME. [med.L *collectarium*, f. *collecta* COLLECT *n.*: see -ARIUM.] *Chr. Ch.* A book of collects.

Also **collectarium** /kɒlɛkˈtɑːrɪəm, -ˈtɛːr-/ *n.*, pl. **-ia** /-ɪə/, **-iums** M19.

collected /kəˈlɛktɪd/ *ppl a.* E17. [f. COLLECT *v.* + -ED[1].] 1 In command of one's thoughts or feelings; self-possessed. E17. 2 Gathered together; *spec.* (of a horse) with its legs brought compactly under itself. L17.

collectedly *adv.* L17. **collectedness** *n.* M17.

collectible *a.* & *n.* see COLLECTABLE.

collection /kəˈlɛkʃ(ə)n/ *n.* LME. [(O)Fr. f. L *collectio(n-)*, f. *collect-*: see COLLECT *v.*, -ION.] 1 The action or an act of collecting or gathering together. LME. b The action or an act of collecting taxes, or money for a definite purpose (e.g. in church or at a meeting); money so collected. L15. †2 A summary, an abstract. LME–E18. 3 A group of things collected or gathered together, e.g. literary items, specimens, works of art, or fashionable clothes. LME. b An accumulation of material. L17. 4 The district under the jurisdiction of a collector of taxes or customs. L15. †5 The action of inferring; an inference. E16–E18. 6 In *pl.* A college examination held at the beginning or end of each term at Oxford (hence occas. elsewhere). L18.

1 L. MACNEICE A red letter-box fastened to a telegraph pole—four collections a week. A. THWAITE Parcelling up the garbage for Collection. b D. H. LAWRENCE The collection arrived with the last hymn. 3 R. G. COLLINGWOOD A new collection of all the Roman inscriptions . . in Britain. P. ROTH We have an excellent classical record collection.

collective /kəˈlɛktɪv/ *a.* & *n.* LME. [(O)Fr. *collectif, -ive* or L *collectivus*, f. *collect-*: see COLLECT *v.*, -IVE.] A *adj.* 1 Denoting or representing a number of individuals or items. LME. 2 Formed by collection; constituting a collection; taken as a whole, aggregate. L16. †3 That deduces or infers. *rare.* Only in M17. 4 Pertaining to or derived from a number of individuals taken or acting together. M17.

1 J. LOCKE The great collective idea of all bodies whatsoever, signified by the name *world.* **collective noun**: denoting, in the singular, more than one individual, e.g. *committee, flock.* 2 W. TAYLOR A collective edition of his works. **collective fruit** *Bot.* a fruit formed by the aggregation of carpels from several flowers, as in the mulberry. 4 W. LIPPMANN The socialist contention that the collective ownership of the means of production will produce . . men who are purged of acquisitiveness and aggression. **collective bargaining** negotiation of wages etc. by an organized body of employees. **collective farm**: consisting of the holdings of several farmers run as a joint enterprise, esp. in the former USSR. **collective ownership** State ownership (of land, the means of production) for the benefit of all. **collective security** *Polit.* the policy or principle of the alliance of several countries to strengthen the security of each. **collective unconscious** in Jungian psychology, the part of the unconscious that derives from ancient ancestral experience and is common to all.

B *n.* 1 A collective noun. E17. 2 A collective body, whole, or organization; *esp.* a collective farm. M17.

collectively *adv.* in a collective manner; in a body, jointly: L16. **collectiveness** *n.* M17.

collectivise *v.* var. of COLLECTIVIZE.

collectivism /kəˈlɛktɪvɪz(ə)m/ *n.* M19. [f. prec. + -ISM, after Fr. *collectivisme.*] Collective ownership of land and the means of production, as a political principle; the practice or principle of giving the group priority over the individual.

collectivist *n.* & *a.* (*a*) *n.* an advocate of collectivism; (*b*) *adj.* of or pertaining to collectivism or collectivists: L19. **collecti'vistic** *a.* L19.

collectivity /kɒlɛkˈtɪvɪti/ *n.* M19. [f. COLLECTIVE + -ITY: in senses 2 and 3 after Fr. *collectivité.*] 1 Collective quality. M19. 2 Collectivism. L19. 3 A group or community of people bound together by common beliefs or interests. L19. 4 An aggregate, a whole. L19.

3 S. NEILL He uses the term . . in the plural . . for the churches as a collectivity in which a common faith and a common order prevail. 4 J. Z. YOUNG The relation of the individual to the collectivity of men.

collectivize /kəˈlɛktɪvʌɪz/ *v.t.* Also **-ise**. L19. [f. COLLECTIVE + -IZE.] Establish or organize in accordance with principles of collectivism.

co,llectivi'zation *n.* the process or policy of collectivizing L19.

collector /kəˈlɛktə/ *n.* LME. [AN *collectour* f. med.L *collector*, f. *collect-*: see COLLECT *v.*, -OR.] 1 A person who collects money; an official who receives money due, as taxes or rent. LME. b *Hist.* In India, the chief administrative official of a district, whose special duty was the collection of revenue. L18. 2 A person who or thing which collects or gathers together; *spec.* a person who collects and keeps specimens, works of art, etc.; formerly also, a compiler. M16. b A part of various electrical machines that receives or attracts current. L18. c The part of a transistor into which charge-carriers flow from the base. M20.

2 **collector's item, piece** a thing of sufficient beauty, rarity, or interest to be placed in a collection. *ticket-collector*: see TICKET *n.*

collectorate *n.* the district in which a collector (sense 1) has jurisdiction L18. **collectorship** *n.* (*a*) the position or office of a collector; (*b*) an Indian collectorate: E16.

colleen /kɒˈliːn, ˈkɒliːn/ *n. Anglo-Ir.* E19. [Ir. *cailín* dim. of *caile* countrywoman, girl: see -EEN[2].] A girl.

college /ˈkɒlɪdʒ/ *n.* LME. [(O)Fr. *collège* or its source L *collegium* association, partnership, guild, corporation, f. *collega* COLLEAGUE *n.*] 1 An organized body of people performing certain common functions and sharing special privileges. LME. †2 An assemblage or company *of* individuals. LME–M18. b [Repr. G *Collegium.*] A reunion, a meeting of companions. E18. 3 A community of clergy living together on a foundation for religious service etc. Now chiefly *Hist.* LME. 4a An independent self-governing corporation of teachers and scholars, *esp.* one within or associated with a university; an American or (formerly) Scottish university, *esp.* a small US university that offers a limited curriculum or teaches only to the first degree.

LME. **b** An institution for professional or vocational training or study, e.g. in music, agriculture, or theology; a higher educational institution for those who have left school, other than a university (sometimes also other than a polytechnic), usu. having a bias towards technical or vocational subjects; a school for pupils over the school-leaving age. Also, the name of some modern public schools and smaller private ones. M19. **5a** The building or set of buildings occupied by a college (sense 4). LME. **b** Without article: some college, known or unknown; attendance at a college or university. M18. **6** *Hist.* A hospital, almshouse, or similar charitable foundation. L17. **7** A prison, a reformatory. *slang.* L17. **8** A course of lectures at a foreign university. E18.

1 **College of Arms**, (*colloq.*) **College of Heralds** a corporation recording armorial bearings and lineages. **College of Justice** all those who participate in the administration of justice in the Court of Session in Scotland (*Senator of the College of Justice*: see SENATOR 3). ELECTORAL *college*. **Heralds' College** = *College of Arms* above. **Sacred College** the Pope's council of cardinals, which elects a new pope, usu. from amongst their number (*Dean of the Sacred College*: see DEAN *n.*[1] 6). *College of Preceptors, College of Surgeons*, etc. 2 DRYDEN Thick as the college of the bees in May. 3 *College of the Propaganda*: see PROPAGANDA *n.* 1. 4a *Eton College, Harvard College, New College*, etc. **college of education** an institution for training schoolteachers. *junior college*: see JUNIOR *a.* *senior college*: see SENIOR *a.* **b** *Cheltenham Ladies' College, Lancing College, sixth-form college, tertiary college*, etc. *military college, technical college*, etc. **5b** DISRAELI College had ruined me. *New Society* A young social worker, fresh out of college and with all the right letters after his name. **be at college** attend a college or university. **go to college** attend or begin attending a college or university.

Comb.: **college living** a benefice in the gift of a college; **college pudding** a small plum pudding for one person.

colleger *n.* (*a*) a member of a college or (formerly) of the same college; *spec.* each of the 70 foundation scholars at Eton College; (*b*) *slang* a mortarboard: M16.

collegial /kəˈliːdʒɪəl, -dʒ(ə)l/ *a.* LME. [(O)Fr. *collégial* or late L *collegialis*, f. *collegium*: see COLLEGE, -IAL.] **1** = COLLEGIATE *a.* 1. LME. **2** Of or pertaining to a (university etc.) college. E17. **3** Pertaining to or involving a body of people associated as colleagues. E17.

1 **collegial church** a collegiate church.

collegiˈality *n.* the relationship of, or appropriate to, colleagues; *spec.* joint responsibility, esp. of Roman Catholic bishops in church government: L19. **collegially** *adv.* M17.

collegian /kəˈliːdʒɪən, -dʒ(ə)n/ *n.* & *a.* LME. [med.L *collegianus*, f. *collegium*: see COLLEGE, -IAN.] **A** *n.* **1** A past or present member of a college; a foundation scholar, a colleger. LME. **2** A prisoner. *slang.* E19. **B** *adj.* = COLLEGIAL. *rare.* M17.

collegianer *n.* (*a*) (*obs.* exc. *Sc.*) = COLLEGIAN *n.* 1; †(*b*) a colleague: M16.

collegiate /kəˈliːdʒ(ɪ)ət/ *a.* & *n.* LME. [Late L *collegiatus* member of a college (in med.L as adj.), f. *collegium* COLLEGE: see -ATE[1], -ATE[2].] **A** *adj.* **1** Of the nature of, constituted as, a college. LME. **2** Of or pertaining to colleagues; corporate, combined. LME. **3** Of, pertaining to, or characteristic of a college or college students. M16. **b** *spec.* Designed for use by college students or others of similar educational standard. *US.* L19. **4** Composed of colleges. M19.

3 DEFOE A collegiate life did not suit me. J. KEROUAC He liked to dress sharp, slightly on the collegiate side.

Special collocations: **collegiate church** (*a*) a church that is endowed for a chapter of canons or prebends but is not a cathedral; (*b*) *Sc.* & *US* a church in the joint charge of two ministers. **collegiate Gothic** *US* (in) a style of Gothic architecture associated with old colleges.

B *n.* **1** A member of a college. *obs.* exc. *US.* E17. †**b** An inmate of a prison or asylum. *slang.* L17–M18. †**2** A colleague. Only in 17. **3** A collegiate dictionary. *US.* L19.

collegiately *adv.* E17.

collegiate /kəˈliːdʒɪeɪt/ *v.t.* M16. [f. prec.: see -ATE[3].] Constitute as a college or a collegiate church.

collegium /kəˈliːdʒɪəm/ *n.* Pl. **-ia** /-ɪə/. L19. [L: see COLLEGE.] **1** In full *collegium musicum* /ˈmjuːzɪkəm/, pl. *collegia musica* /ˈmjuːzɪkə/. A society of amateurs for performing music, now *esp.* one attached to a German or US university. L19. **2** *Hist.* [Repr. Russ. *kollegiya*.] An advisory or administrative board in Russia. E20.

collembolan /kəˈlɛmbələn/ *n.* & *a.* L19. [f. mod.L *Collembola* (see below), f. Gk *kolla* glue + *embolon* peg, stopper (with ref. to the insect's ventral tube, which can secrete an adhesive substance): see -AN.] **A** *n.* A minute wingless insect of the order Collembola; a springtail. L19. **B** *adj.* Of or pertaining to the order Collembola or collembolans. L19.

collenchyma /kəˈlɛŋkɪmə/ *n.* M19. [f. Gk *kolla* glue + *egkhuma* infusion.] *Bot.* Tissue strengthened by the thickening of cell walls, as in young shoots.

collenˈchymatous *a.* L19.

Colleries /ˈkɒlərɪz/ *n.pl.* M18. [Tamil *kaḷḷar* thieves.] A Dravidian people of SE India.

Colles fracture /ˈkɒlɪs ˈfraktʃə/ *n. phr.* Also **Colles's** /ˈkɒlɪsɪz/. L19. [Abraham *Colles* (1773–1843), Ir. surgeon.] *Med.* Fracture of the lower end of the radius accompanied by backward displacement of the hand.

collet /ˈkɒlɪt/ *n.*[1] & *v.* LME. [(O)Fr., dim. of *col* f. L *collum* neck: see -ET[1].] **A** *n.* †**1 a** A piece of armour for the neck. *Sc.* LME–E17. **b** The neckband of a garment; a necklet. M16–M17. **2** A circular metal ring on a spindle or lining in a hole; *Engin.* a slit sleeve with an external taper which tightens when pushed into an internally tapered socket in a lathe mandrel etc. E16. **3** A metal flange or setting for a precious stone. E16. †**4** *Glass-making.* The portion of glass left on the end of a blowing-iron after the removal of the finished article. See also CULLET. M17–L18. **B** *v.t.* Set in or provide with a collet. E17.

collet *n.*[2] see CULET *n.*[2]

colleterial /kɒlɪˈtɪərɪəl/ *a.* L19. [f. Gk *kollan* to glue + *-ētēr* agent-suff. + -IAL.] *Entomol.* Of a gland: secreting the materials which form the ootheca.

†**colley** *n.* var. of COLLIE.

colliculus /kəˈlɪkjʊləs/ *n.* Pl. **-li** /-lʌɪ, -liː/. M19. [L, dim. of *collis* hill: see -CULE.] *Anat.* A small protuberance; *spec.* any of those of the roof of the midbrain, of which there are two pairs involved respectively in vision and hearing.

collicular *a.* L19.

collide /kəˈlʌɪd/ *v.* E17. [L *collidere* clash together, f. as COL- + *laedere* hurt by striking.] **1** *v.t.* Bring into violent contact, strike together. Now *rare* or *obs.* exc. *techn.* E17. **2** *v.i.* Come into collision (*with*); strike or dash together. E18. **b** *fig.* Be in conflict, clash, conflict. M19.

collider *n.* (*Physics*) a particle accelerator in which two beams are made to collide L20.

collidine /ˈkɒlɪdiːn/ *n.* M19. [f. Gk *kolla* glue + -IDINE.] *Chem.* Any of a number of isomeric trimethyl and methylethyl derivatives of pyridine, found in coal tar.

collie /ˈkɒli/ *n.* Also **-y**, †**-ey**. M17. [Perh. f. COAL (f. its colour) + -IE, -Y[6]: cf. COLLY *a.* & *n.*[2]] A sheepdog of an orig. Scottish breed with a long pointed nose and usu. long hair. Also *collie-dog*.

bearded collie: see BEARDED 1. *border collie*: see BORDER *n.* *rough collie*: see ROUGH *a.*

collier /ˈkɒlɪə/ *n.* ME. [f. COAL + -IER.] **1** A maker of wood charcoal. *obs.* exc. *US.* ME. †**2** A person who carries coal or charcoal for sale. L15–E19. **3** A person who works in a coalmine; a coalminer. M16. **4** A ship carrying coal; a member of the crew of such a ship. E17. **5** In full *collier-aphid, fly*, etc. A black aphid, *Aphis fabae*. *obs.* exc. *US.* M18. **6** The swift. *dial.* L18.

colliery /ˈkɒlɪəri/ *n.* M17. [f. prec. + -Y[3].] **1** A place where coal is worked; a coalmine and its buildings. M17. †**2** Ships employed in the coal trade; one such vessel. E–M18.

collieshangie /kɒlɪˈʃaŋi/ *n.* *Sc.* M18. [Origin unkn.] A noisy quarrel; a confused fight.

colligable /ˈkɒlɪgəb(ə)l/ *a.* M20. [f. COLLIGATE *v.* + -ABLE.] *Ling.* Capable of forming part of a colligation.

colligaˈbility *n.* M20.

†**colligance** *n.* LME–E18. [OFr., or med.L *colligantia* f. L *colligare*: see COLLEAGUE *v.*, -ANCE.] Attachment together; connection.

colligate /ˈkɒlɪgət/ *a.* Long *rare.* L15. [L *colligatus* pa. pple, f. as next: see -ATE[2].] Bound together, attached.

colligate /ˈkɒlɪgeɪt/ *v.* M16. [L *colligat-* pa. ppl stem of *colligare*, f. as COL- + *ligare* bind: see -ATE[3].] †**1** *v.t.* Bind or fasten together. M16–L18. **2** *v.t.* Join or unite *with*. E17. **3** *v.t.* Unite in a class or order; *spec.* in *Logic*, connect together (isolated facts) by a general notion or hypothesis. L17. **4** *v.i.* *Ling.* Of a word-class or other functional category: be in colligation *with*. M20.

coˈlligative *a.* of or pertaining to the binding together of molecules E20.

colligation /kɒlɪˈgeɪʃ(ə)n/ *n.* LME. [OFr., or L *colligatio(n-)*, f. as prec.: see -ATION.] †**1** Physical binding together; connection. LME–M17. **2** Conjunction, alliance; union. M17. **3** *Logic.* The connection of a number of isolated facts by a general notion or hypothesis; a group of facts so connected. M19. **4** *Ling.* Juxtaposition or grouping in syntactic relation of particular word-classes or other functional categories; a sequence of word-classes etc. in syntactic relation. M20.

colligible /ˈkɒlɪdʒɪb(ə)l/ *a.* Now *rare.* M17. [f. stem of L *colligere* COLLECT *v.* + -IBLE.] That may be collected.

collimate /ˈkɒlɪmeɪt/ *v.* E17. [f. L *collimare* erron. reading in some eds. of Cicero for *collineare* aim: see -ATE[3].] †**1** *v.i.* Level or aim at a mark. Only in Dicts. E17–L18. **2** *v.t.* Orig. *Astron.* Correct the direction of (telescopes or other devices, rays of light, etc.); make accurately parallel. M19.

collimator *n.* a device for collimating; *esp.* (*a*) a small telescope for collimating another; (*b*) a device for producing a beam of parallel rays: M19.

collimation /kɒlɪˈmeɪʃ(ə)n/ *n.* L17. [f. as prec.: see -ATION.] The action of collimating (sense 2) a telescope, light-beam, etc. Also, correct or parallel alignment, absence of divergence.

collinear /kɒˈlɪnɪə/ *a.* M18. [f. COL- + LINEAR.] †**1** Lying in the same plane. *rare.* Only in M18. **2** In the same straight line. M19.

collineˈarity *n.* M19. **collinearly** *adv.* M19.

Collins /ˈkɒlɪnz/ *n.*[1] M19. [A surname.] (In full *John* or *Tom Collins*) a cocktail consisting of gin mixed with soda, lemon or lime juice, and sugar; (usu. w. specifying wd, as *brandy Collins*) this cocktail made with a different spirit.

Collins /ˈkɒlɪnz/ *n.*[2] *colloq.* E20. [William *Collins*, a character in Jane Austen's *Pride & Prejudice*.] A letter of thanks for hospitality or entertainment, sent by a departed guest.

†**colliquation** *n.* E17. [med.L *colliquatio(n-)*, f. as next: see -ATION. Cf. Fr. †*colliquation*.] **1** Melting, fusion, liquefaction. E17–M18. **2** *Med.* Wasting away of the body; disintegration of tissue into pus etc.; excessive fluidification of the bodily humours, esp. the blood. E17–M18.

colliquative /kɒˈlɪkwətɪv/ *n.* & *a.* Now *rare.* LME. [f. med.L *colliquat-* pa. ppl stem of *colliquare*, f. as COL- + *liquare* liquefy, melt, + -IVE. Cf. Fr. †*colliquatif*.] †**A** *n.* A medicine to dissolve or reduce bodily solids. *rare.* Only in LME. **B** *adj.* Having the power or effect of liquefying; *Med.* causing the body to waste away, characterized by wasting away of the body. M17.

collision /kəˈlɪʒ(ə)n/ *n.* LME. [Late L *collisio(n-)*, f. *collis-* pa. ppl stem of *collidere* COLLIDE *v.*: see -ION.] **1** The action of striking against something with force; the action or an act of colliding; (a) violent encounter of a moving body, esp. a ship or vehicle, with another or with a fixed object. LME. **b** *Computing.* An instance of two or more records being assigned the same location in memory.

Also, an instance of different sources or nodes attempting to send a signal simultaneously along a shared line. M20. †2a Synaeresis of two vowels. M16–L17. b Dissonant conjunction of speech sounds. M17. 3 *fig.* The encounter of opposed ideas, interests, factions, etc.; a clash, a conflict. M17. b The action of coming into contact (with no notion of violence or hostility); coincidence, conjunction. Now *rare* or *obs.* M17.

1 E. RUTHERFORD The number of collisions of the particle with the atom. J. WAIN His head came into painful collision with a wooden crate. M. SHADBOLT His brakes squealed, to avoid a collision with a truck. 3b S. JOHNSON By the fortuitous collision of happy incidents.

Comb.: **collision bulkhead** a strong watertight bulkhead built in the bows of a ship to prevent flooding after a collision; **collision course** a course or action bound to end in a collision (*lit.* & *fig.*); **collision-mat** *Naut.* a mat with oakum on one face for putting over a hole made by a collision; **collision quarters, stations** pre-assigned positions to be taken up by the crew and passengers of a ship etc. in the event of a collision.

collisional *a.* pertaining to or resulting from collision, esp. of microscopic particles L19. **collisionally** *adv.* M20. **collisionless** *a.* M20.

colloblast /ˈkɒləʊblast/ *n.* E20. [f. Gk *kolla* glue + -O- + -BLAST.] *Zool.* = *lasso-cell* s.v. LASSO *n.*

collocable /ˈkɒləkəb(ə)l/ *a.* M20. [f. next + -ABLE.] *Ling.* Capable of forming part of a collocation.

collocaˈbility *n.* M20.

collocate /ˈkɒləkeɪt/ *v.* E16. [L *collocat-* pa. ppl stem of *collocare*, f. as COL- + *locare* to place, LOCATE: see -ATE[3].] 1 *v.t.* Place side by side or in some relation; set in a place or position; *spec.* in *Ling.*, juxtapose (a word) with another so as to form a collocation. E16. 2 *v.i.* *Ling.* Be habitually juxtaposed *with*, form a collocation. M20.

collocative *a.* of the nature of or pertaining to collocation E19.

collocation /kɒləˈkeɪʃ(ə)n/ *n.* LME. [L *collocatio(n-)*, f. as prec.: see -ATION.] The action of collocating; the state of being collocated; a disposition, an arrangement; *spec.* in *Ling.*, (esp. habitual) juxtaposition or association of a particular word with other particular words, a group of words so associated.

colloˈcational *a.* of or pertaining to collocation L19.

collocutor /ˈkɒləkjuːtə, kəˈlɒkjʊtə/ *n.* M16. [Late L *collocutor*, f. *collocut-* pa. ppl stem of *colloqui*, f. as COL- + *loqui* talk: see -OR.] A participant in a conversation or dialogue.

one's collocutor the person with whom one is talking.

colˈlocutory *a.* of the nature of conversation or dialogue L18.

collodion /kəˈləʊdɪən/ *n.* Also (*rare*) **-ium** /-ɪəm/. M19. [f. Gk *kollōdēs* gluelike, f. *kolla* glue: cf. -ODE[1].] A solution of pyroxylin in ether, used to apply a thin gummy film in photography and surgery.

collodionize *v.t.* treat with collodion M19.

collogue /kɒˈləʊg/ *v.* E17. [Prob. alt., by assoc. w. L *colloqui*, of COLLEAGUE *v.*] †1 *v.i.* a Speak flatteringly; deal flatteringly *with*. E17–E18. b Feign agreement or belief. E–M17. 2 *v.i.* a Intrigue, collude, conspire, (*with*). Now *dial.* M17. b Talk confidentially (*with*). E19. 3 *v.t.* Influence by flattery, coax. *obs.* exc. *dial.* L17.

colloid /ˈkɒlɔɪd/ *a.* & *n.* M19. [f. Gk *kolla* glue + -OID.] A *adj.* Of the nature or appearance of glue; *Med.* characterized by the formation of colloid; *Chem.* = COLLOIDAL. *rare* in *gen.* sense. M19.

B *n.* 1 *Med.* & *Anat.* A jelly-like substance; *esp.* (*a*) one characteristic of certain cancers; (*b*) one normally present in the follicles of the thyroid gland. M19. 2 *Chem.* A non-crystalline substance consisting of ultramicroscopic particles (often large single molecules); such a substance dispersed in another phase, esp. to form a viscous solution having special properties. M19.

2 *protective colloid*: see PROTECTIVE *a.* 3a.

colloidal /kəˈlɔɪd(ə)l/ *a.* M19. [f. prec. + -AL[1].] *Chem.* Of, pertaining to, or of the nature of a colloid.

colloiˈdality *n.* M19. **colloidally** *adv.* as a colloid; in the manner of a colloid: E20.

collop /ˈkɒləp/ *n.*[1] LME. [f. Scand. wd repr. by OSw. *kolhuppadher* roasted on coals (f. *kol* COAL *n.* + *huppa* leap, cf. SAUTÉ), Sw. *kalops*, dial. *kollops* dish of stewed meat.] 1 In *pl.* Orig., fried bacon and eggs. Later (in *collops and eggs*), fried bacon. Now *dial.* LME. 2 A slice of meat (orig. fried or grilled); an escalope. LME. b In *pl.* (A dish of) minced or chopped meat. *dial.* M17. †3 A piece of flesh; *fig.* an offspring. E16–M17. 4 A thick fold of flesh on the body. Now *Sc.* & *dial.* M16. 5 *fig.* A slice; a piece cut off. L16.

2b *Scotch collops*: see SCOTCH *a.*

Comb.: **Collop Monday** (now *dial.*) the Monday before Shrove Tuesday, on which bacon and eggs would be served.

collop /ˈkɒləp/ *n.*[2] *Anglo-Ir.* L17. [Ir. *colp(th)ach* heifer, bullock.] A full-grown cow or horse; *transf.* the quantity of grass or area of pasture needed for a cow for one year.

collophane /ˈkɒləfeɪn/ *n.* E20. [G *Kollophan*, f. as COLLOID + Gk *-phanēs* showing, f. *phainein* to show.] *Min.* A cryptocrystalline calciferous form of apatite which occurs in fossilized bone and other organic deposits.

Also **coˈllophanite** *n.* M19.

colloque /kəˈləʊk/ *n.* Now *rare.* L15. [Fr. f. L COLLOQUIUM.] †1 A place for conversation. *rare.* Only in L15. †2 A conversation, a conference. L16–L17. 3 = COLLOQUY 2. M19.

colloquial /kəˈləʊkwɪəl/ *a.* & *n.* M18. [f. L COLLOQUIUM + -AL[1].] A *adj.* 1 Conversational; in or of talk, oral. M18. 2 Belonging to familiar speech and writing; not used in formal or elevated language. M18. B *n.* Colloquial speech or language. E20.

colloquialism *n.* colloquial style, esp. of language; a colloquial expression: L18. **colloquialist** *n.* (*a*) a person who uses colloquialisms; (*b*) a good talker: E19. **colloquiˈality** *n.* (now *rare*) = COLLOQUIALISM E19. **colloquially** *adv.* L18.

colloquise *v.* var. of COLLOQUIZE.

colloquist /ˈkɒləkwɪst/ *n.* L18. [f. as prec. + -IST.] An interlocutor.

colloquium /kəˈləʊkwɪəm/ *n.* Pl. **-ia** /-ɪə/, **-iums.** L16. [L, f. as COL- + *loqui* speak.] †1 A conversation, a dialogue. L16–M18. 2 A conference; *spec.* an academic conference or seminar. M19.

colloquize /ˈkɒləkwʌɪz/ *v.i.* Also **-ise.** E19. [f. as prec. + -IZE.] Engage in colloquy.

colloquy /ˈkɒləkwi/ *n.* LME. [L COLLOQUIUM: see -Y[4].] 1 A discourse, a dialogue, (spoken or written); an act of conversing; a conversation. LME. b Conversation, dialogue. E19. 2 *Eccl.* A judicial and legislative court in a Reformed or Presbyterian Church. L17.

collotype /ˈkɒlətʌɪp/ *n.* L19. [f. Gk *kolla* glue + -O- + -TYPE.] A thin sheet of gelatin which may be exposed to light, treated with reagents, and used to make a print by lithography; a print so made.

collow /ˈkɒləʊ/ *v.* & *n.* *obs.* exc. *dial.* ME. [Origin uncertain: perh. repr. OE vb f. COALY (see note s.v.). Cf. COLLY *a.* & *n.*[2], *v.*[2]] A *v.t.* Make black with coal-dust; blacken, begrime. ME. B *n.* Soot; smut; grime. L17.

colluctation /kɒlʌkˈteɪʃ(ə)n/ *n.* *arch.* E17. [L *colluctatio(n-)*, f. *colluctat-* pa. ppl stem of *colluctari*, f. as COL- + *luctari* wrestle, strive.] A wrestling or struggling together; a conflict, opposition.

collude /kəˈl(j)uːd/ *v.* E16. [f. L *colludere* have a secret agreement, f. as COL- + *ludere* play.] 1 *v.i.* Conspire, plot, connive; act in secret concert. (Foll. by *with* a person, *in* an act etc.) E16. †2 *v.t.* Stir up or bring about by collusion. L18–M19.

colluder *n.* M17.

collusion /kəˈl(j)uːʒ(ə)n/ *n.* LME. [(O)Fr., or L *collusio(n-)*, f. *collus-* pa. ppl stem of *colludere*: see prec., -ION.] 1 Secret agreement or understanding for nefarious purposes; conspiracy; fraud, trickery. LME. b An instance of this. Now *rare.* L16. 2 *Law.* An agreement between two or more people, esp. ostensible opponents in a suit, to act to the prejudice of a third party or for an improper purpose. LME.

collusive /kəˈl(j)uːsɪv/ *a.* L17. [f. L *collus-* (see prec.) + -IVE.] Characterized by or given to collusion.

collusively *adv.* M18.

collusory /kɒˈluːz(ə)ri/ *a.* Now *rare.* E18. [Late L *collusorius*, f. as prec.: see -ORY[2].] = COLLUSIVE.

colluvial /kəˈl(j)uːvɪəl/ *a.* E19. [f. next + -AL[1].] 1 Of or pertaining to a colluvies. *rare.* E19. 2 *Physical Geogr.* Of, pertaining to, or of the nature of colluvium. L19.

colluvies /kəˈl(j)uːviːz/ *n.* Now *rare* or *obs.* Pl. same. M17. [L *colluvies*, f. *colluere* rinse, f. as COL- + *luere* wash.] 1 A collection of foul matter, *esp.* a discharge from an ulcer. M17. 2 A confluence (of waters etc.). M17. 3 *fig.* A rabble, a hotchpotch. M17.

colluvium /kəˈl(j)uːvɪəm/ *n.* M20. [L, f. as prec.: see -IUM.] *Physical Geogr.* Material which accumulates at the foot of a steep slope.

colly *n.*[1] var. of COLLIE.

colly /ˈkɒli/ *a.* & *n.*[2] Long *dial.* E17. [Var. of COALY.] A *adj.* Sooty, grimy; coal-black. E17. B *n.* 1 Soot, smut. E18. 2 The blackbird. E19.

†**colly** *v.*[1]*i.* LME–L18. [OFr. *coleier*, *coloier* turn the neck, f. *col* neck.] Move the neck; (of a bird) turn the head from side to side.

colly /ˈkɒli/ *v.*[2]*t.* Now *arch.* & *dial.* L16. [Var. of COLLOW *v.*] Blacken with coal-dust or soot; begrime.

Collyridian /kɒlɪˈrɪdɪən/ *n.* & *a.* M16. [Late L *collyridianus*, f. *collyrida* f. Gk *kolluris*, *-id-* cake, dim. of *kollura* roll of coarse bread: see -AN.] *Eccl. Hist.* A *n.* A member of a sect idolatrously offering cakes to the Blessed Virgin, which consisted mainly of women and originated in Thrace in the 4th cent. AD. M16. B *adj.* Of or pertaining to this sect. E19.

collyrium /kəˈlɪrɪəm/ *n.* Pl. **-ia** /-ɪə/. LME. [L *collyrium* f. Gk *kollurion* poultice, eye ointment, f. *kollura* (see prec.).] 1 A medicinal application for the eyes, an eye-lotion. LME. 2 A cosmetic application for the eyes, as kohl. *rare.* E17. 3 A suppository. M18.

Colly-west /ˈkɒlɪwɛst/ *adv.*, *n.*, & *a.* *dial.* Also **Collywest.** E19. [f. *Collyweston*, a village in Northamptonshire.] A *adv.* Awry, askew. E19. B *n.* Nonsense. M19. C *adj.* Contrary, contradictory. L19.

collywobbles /ˈkɒlɪwɒb(ə)lz/ *n.pl.* *colloq.* E19. [Fanciful formation f. COLIC + WOBBLE *n.*] Rumbling in the intestines; stomach-ache; a feeling of apprehension (with intestinal symptoms).

Colmar /ˈkɒlmə/ *n.* E18. [Perh. f. the town in Alsace.] A fan fashionable in Queen Anne's reign.

colobine /ˈkɒləbʌɪn/ *a.* & *n.* M20. [f. mod.L *Colobinae* (see below), f. as COLOBUS: see -INE[1].] *Zool.* A *adj.* Of, pertaining to, or characteristic of the subfamily Colobinae (family Cercopithecidae) of mainly leaf-eating Old World monkeys, which have sacculated stomachs and lack cheek pouches. M20. B *n.* A monkey of this subfamily, a leaf-monkey. M20.

colobium /kəˈləʊbɪəm/ *n.* Pl. **-ia** /-ɪə/. E17. [Late L f. Gk *kolobion*, f. *kolobos* curtailed.] A half-sleeved or sleeveless tunic worn by the early clergy, by monks, and by monarchs at their coronation.

coloboma /kɒləʊˈbəʊmə/ *n.* Pl. **-mas, -mata** /-mətə/. M19. [mod.L f. Gk *kolobōma* the part removed in mutilation, f. *kolobos* curtailed: see -OMA.] *Med.* A congenital malformation of the eye causing e.g. a notch in the iris or in an eyelid.

colobus /ˈkɒləbəs/ *n.* M19. [mod.L f. Gk *kolobos* curtailed (on account of the shortened thumbs).] An African leaf-eating monkey of the genus *Colobus*. Also *colobus monkey*.

colocynth /ˈkɒləsɪnθ/ *n.* Orig. also in L form †**colocynthis.** M16. [L *colocynthis* f. Gk *kolokunthis*, *-id-*: cf. COLOQUINTIDA.] The bitter-apple, *Citrullus colocynthis*, a plant of the gourd family, whose pulpy fruit furnishes a bitter purgative drug. Also, the fruit or the drug.

Cologne /kəˈləʊn/ *n.* In sense 2 now usu. **c-**. M17. [Fr. = G *Köln*, f. L *Colonia (Agrippina)*, a German city on the Rhine.] 1 *Cologne earth*, †*Cologne's earth*, a brown pigment prepared from lignite, orig. from near Cologne. M17. 2 Eau-de-Cologne or other lightly-scented toilet water. Also *Cologne water*. E19.

colombophile /kəˈlʌmbəfʌɪl/ *n.* & *a.* L19. [Fr., f. *colombe* pigeon f. as COLUMBA: see -PHIL.] **A** *n.* A pigeon-fancier. L19. **B** *adj.* Pigeon-fancying. L19.

colometry /kəʊˈlɒmɪtri/ *n.* L19. [Gk *kōlometria*, f. *kōlon* limb, clause: see -METRY.] *Palaeogr.* The division of texts by cola.

coloˈmetric *a.* L19. **coloˈmetrical** *a.* E20. **coloˈmetrically** *adv.* E20.

colon /ˈkəʊlən, -lɒn/ *n.*[1] LME. [L f. Gk *kolon*, (also) food, meat.] *Anat.* The greater part of the large intestine extending from the caecum to the rectum. Formerly (*pop.*), the belly, the guts.

sigmoid colon: see SIGMOID *a.* 2. *transverse colon*: see TRANSVERSE *a.*

coˈlonic *a.* of or pertaining to the colon; affecting the colon: E20.

colon /ˈkəʊlən/ *n.*[2] Pl. in sense 1 **cola** /ˈkəʊlə/, in sense 2 **-s**. M16. [L f. Gk *kōlon* limb, clause.] 1 In *Class. Pros.* & *Rhet.*, (a pause of intermediate length before) a distinct section of a complex sentence or rhythmical period. In *Palaeogr.*, a clause or group of clauses written as a line or taken as a standard of measure in ancient manuscripts or texts. M16. 2 A punctuation mark consisting of two dots placed one above the other (:), indicating a discontinuity of grammatical construction, though one less than that indicated by a period or full stop, and now esp. marking antithesis, illustration, quotation, or listing (sometimes with a dash :—), or between numbers in a proportion, reference, etc. See also SEMICOLON. E17.

colon /kɒˈlɒn/ *n.*[3] E17. [Fr. f. L *colonus*: see COLONY.] 1 A husbandman. *rare*. E17. 2 *Hist.* A colonial settler or farmer, esp. in a French colony. M20.

colón /kəʊˈləʊn/ *n.* Pl. **colones** /kəʊˈləʊnɪz/, **colons**. L19. [f. Sp. Cristóbal *Colón* Christopher Columbus (see COLUMBUS).] The basic monetary unit of Costa Rica and of El Salvador, equal to 100 céntimos in Costa Rica and 100 centavos in El Salvador.

colonel /ˈkəːn(ə)l/ *n.* Also †**coro-**, (esp. in titles) **C-**. M16. [Fr. †*coronel*, later *colonnel* (now *colonel*), f. It. *colonnello*, f. *colonna* COLUMN.] 1 The highest-ranking officer of a regiment; an officer ranking next above a lieutenant colonel and next below a brigadier in military rank. Also (esp. in the southern US) used as a courtesy title to minor government officials and to former military men. M16. 2 *Hist.* A holder of any of various military ranks in ancient armies. M16.

1 *Colonel Blimp*: see BLIMP 3. **colonel-general** an officer in charge of all the regiments of an (esp. foreign) army: freq. an honorary rank. **Colonel-in-Chief**: an honorary rank. LIEUTENANT *colonel*.

¶The form †*coronel* prevailed in writing until M17 and is also the source of the mod. pronunc. The 1773 edition of Johnson's *Dictionary* records only /ˈkɒl-/.

colonelcy *n.* the post, rank, or commission of a colonel L18. **colonelling** *n.* playing the colonel; trying to raise a regiment: M17. **colonelship** *n.* = COLONELCY L16.

colonial /kəˈləʊnɪəl/ *a.* & *n.* L18. [f. COLONY + -AL[1], perh. after Fr. *colonial*.] **A** *adj.* 1 Of or pertaining to a colony or colonies, esp. a British Crown Colony. Now freq. *derog.* L18. **b** Pertaining to or characteristic of the period of the British colonies in America before they became the US; built or designed in a style of this period. *N. Amer.* L18. **c** Dealing in produce from a colony or colonies. L19. 2 Of animals or plants: living in colonies. L19.

1 R. CONQUEST A state ruled by a foreign marshal condemns colonial oppression. **colonial goose** *Austral.* & *NZ* stuffed boned roast leg of mutton. **Colonial Office** *Hist.* the Government department in charge of colonies. 2 N. TINBERGEN Like many colonial birds, gulls are very vociferous.

B *n.* 1 A native or inhabitant of a colony. M19. 2 A house etc. built in colonial style. *N. Amer.* M20.

colonially *adv.* M19.

colonialism /kəˈləʊnɪəlɪz(ə)m/ *n.* L18. [f. prec. + -ISM.] 1 The practice or policy of maintaining colonies; now freq. *derog.*, the alleged policy of exploitation of backward or weak peoples. L18. 2 Colonial manners or practices. Now *rare*. M19. 3 A colonial expression or idiom. L19.

colonialist *n.* & *a.* (*a*) *n.* an adherent of colonialism; (*b*) *adj.* of or pertaining to colonialists or colonialism: E19.

colonisation *n.*, **-ise** *v.* vars. of COLONIZATION, -IZE.

colonist /ˈkɒlənɪst/ *n.* E18. [f. COLONIZE: see -IST.] 1 A settler in a new country; an inhabitant of a colony. E18. **b** An established but non-indigenous plant or animal. L19. 2 *US Polit.* A party supporter planted in a district to increase the party's vote in an election. M19.

colonization /kɒlənʌɪˈzeɪʃ(ə)n/ *n.* Also **-isation**. L18. [f. prec. + -ATION.] 1 The establishment of a colony or colonies. (Foll. by *of* a place.) L18. **b** The occupation by a plant or animal species of an area from which it was formerly absent. E20. 2 *US Polit.* The planting of party supporters in a district to increase the party's vote at an election. M19.

colonizationism *n.* (*US Hist.*) the principles of colonizationists M19. **colonizationist** *n.* (*US Hist.*) an advocate of the colonization of Africa by Blacks from America M19.

colonize /ˈkɒlənʌɪz/ *v.* Also **-ise**. E17. [f. COLONY: see -IZE.] 1 *v.t.* Establish a colony in. E17. **b** Of plants or animals: establish themselves in (an area). Cf. COLONIZATION 1b. M19. 2 *v.t.* Establish in a colony. M17. 3 *v.i.* Establish a colony or colonies; join a colony. E19. 4 *v.i.* & *t.* *US Polit.* Plant (party supporters) in a district, plant party supporters in (a district), to increase the party's vote at an election. M19.

1 G. STEINER The uprooted peoples began colonizing Asia Minor. 2 *Encycl. Brit.* Permission . . to colonize 300 families.

colonizable *a.* M19. **colonizer** *n.* L18.

colonnade /kɒləˈneɪd/ *n.* E18. [Fr. (earlier †*-ate*), f. *colonne* COLUMN, after It. *colonnato*, †*-ata*: see -ADE.] 1 *Archit.* A series of columns placed at regular intervals and supporting an entablature. E18. 2 *transf.* A row of trees etc. M18.

colonnaded *a.* having a colonnade E19.

colonnette /kɒləˈnɛt/ *n.* L19. [Fr., dim. of *colonne* COLUMN: see -ETTE.] *Archit.* A small column.

colony /ˈkɒləni/ *n.* LME. [L *colonia* farm, settlement, f. *colonus* tiller, settler, f. *colere* cultivate: see -Y[3].] **I** 1 *Rom. Hist.* A garrison settlement, usu. of veteran soldiers, in a conquered territory. LME. †2 A farm; a rural settlement. M16–M17. 3 *Gk Hist.* An independent city founded by emigrants L16.

II 4 A settlement in a new country; a body of settlers forming a community fully or partly subject to the mother State; the territory of such settlers. M16. 5 A community of animals or plants of one kind forming a physically connected structure or otherwise living in close proximity; the place of habitation of such a group. L17. 6 A body of people of a particular nationality or occupation in a city or country, esp. if living more or less in isolation or in a special quarter; a segregated group; the district, quarter, etc., inhabited by such a group. E18.

4 HOBBES Colonies sent from England, to plant Virginia. S. JOHNSON A ship stored for a voyage to the colonies. 5 R. DAWKINS Blackheaded gulls nest in large colonies. D. ATTENBOROUGH Coral polyps . . working together in colonies. 6 *Time* The Nudist colony on an island in the Seine.

colopexy /ˈkəʊləpɛksi, kəʊləˈpɛksi/ *n.* L19. [mod.L *colopexia*, f. as COLON *n.*[1] + -O- + Gk *pēxis* fixing: see -Y[3].] The surgical attachment of part of the colon to the abdominal wall; an instance of this.

colophon /ˈkɒləf(ə)n/ *n.* E17. [Late L *colophon* f. Gk *kolophōn* summit, finishing touch.] 1 A crowning or finishing touch. *rare*. E17. 2 A statement, sometimes with a device, at the end of a manuscript or printed book, giving information about its authorship, production, etc. (as the printer's name and date and place of printing). L18. **b** A publisher's or printer's imprint; *loosely* a publisher's device, esp. on a title-page. M20.

1 C. CONNOLLY One of the colophons of literature, one of those great writers who put full stop to a form of art, was Marcel Proust.

colophony /kəˈlɒfəni, ˈkɒləfəʊni/ *n.* ME. [L *colophonia* for *Colophonia resina* resin of Colophon (a town in Lydia).] Rosin.

coloquintida /kɒləˈkwɪntɪdə/ *n.* Now *rare* or *obs.* LME. [med.L, f. as COLOCYNTH.] = COLOCYNTH. Also *fig.*, a bitter medicine.

color *n.*, *v.*, **colorable** *a.* see COLOUR *n.*, *v.*, COLOURABLE.

Coloradan /kɒləˈrɑːd(ə)n/ *n.* & *a.* L19. [f. as next + -AN.] A native or inhabitant of, of or pertaining to, the State of Colorado, USA.

Also **Coloradian**, **Coloradoan** *n.* & *a.* M19.

Colorado beetle /kɒləˌrɑːdəʊ ˈbiːt(ə)l/ *n. phr.* M19. [*Colorado*, a State of the US.] A yellow black-striped beetle, *Leptinotarsa decemlineata*, which is native to N. America and is a serious pest of potato crops. Also *Colorado potato beetle*.

colorant *n.* see COLOURANT.

coloration /kʌləˈreɪʃ(ə)n/ *n.* Also **colour-**. E17. [Fr., or late L *coloratio(n-)*, f. *colorat-* pa. ppl stem of *colorare* COLOUR *v.*: see -ATION.] Colouring, the method of putting on or arranging colour; the natural, esp. variegated, colouring of plants and animals.

protective coloration: see PROTECTIVE *a.* *warning coloration*: see WARNING *ppl a.*

coloratura /kɒlərəˈtjʊərə, -ˈtʊ-/ *n.* M18. [It. f. late L *coloratura*, f. *colorat-*: see prec., -URE.] 1 Florid passages in vocal music, with runs, trills, etc.; the singing of these. M18. 2 A singer of coloratura, esp. a soprano. M20.

Also **colorature** *n.* (*rare*) [G *Coloratur*] E19.

colorectal /kəʊləʊˈrɛkt(ə)l/ *a.* M20. [f. COLON *n.*[1] + RECTAL: see -O-.] *Med.* Pertaining to or affecting the colon and the rectum.

colored *a.* & *n.* see COLOURED.

colorific /kʌləˈrɪfɪk, kɒl-/ *a.* L17. [Fr. *colorifique* or mod.L *colorificus*, f. L *color* COLOUR *n.*: see -FIC.] Producing colour(s); highly coloured (*lit.* & *fig.*).

colorimeter /kʌləˈrɪmɪtə, kɒl-/ *n.* M19. [f. L *color* COLOUR *n.* + -IMETER. Cf. Fr. *colorimètre*.] An instrument for measuring intensity of colour.

coloriˈmetric(al) *adjs.* of or pertaining to a colorimeter or colorimetry L19. **coloriˈmetrically** *adv.* by means of a colorimeter E20. **colorimetry** *n.* the measurement of intensity of colour L19.

coloring, **-ist** *ns.*, **-ize** *v.* see COLOURING etc.

coloss /kəˈlɒs/ *n. arch.* Also **-osse**. M16. [Fr. *colosse* f. L COLOSSUS.] = COLOSSUS.

colossal /kəˈlɒs(ə)l/ *a.* E18. [Fr., f. as prec.: see -AL[1].] 1 Of or like a colossus; gigantic, huge, (in scope, extent, or amount). E18. 2 Tremendous; remarkable, splendid, delightful. *colloq.* L19. 3 *Archit.* Of an order: more than one storey high. M20.

colossally *adv.* M19.

colosse *n.* var. of COLOSS.

colossean /kəˈlɒsɪən/ *a. arch.* Also †**-ian**. E17. [f. L *colosseus*, f. as COLOSSUS: see -EAN, -IAN.] = COLOSSAL 1.

colosseum *n.* see COLISEUM.

Colossian /kəˈlɒsɪən/ *n.* & *a.*[1] E16. [f. *Colossae* (see below) + -IAN.] **A** *n.* A native or inhabitant of Colossae, an ancient city in Phrygia, Asia Minor. In *pl.* (treated as *sing.*), St Paul's Epistle to the Colossians, a book of the New Testament. E16. **B** *adj.* Of or pertaining to Colossae or the Colossians. L19.

†**colossian** *a.*[2] see COLOSSEAN.

colossus /kəˈlɒsəs/ *n.* Pl. **-ssi** /-sʌɪ/, **-ssuses**. LME. [L f. Gk *kolossos* applied by Herodotus to the statues of Egyptian temples.] 1 A statue of much more than life size, as that said to have stood astride the entrance to the harbour of Rhodes in ancient Greece. LME. 2 A gigantic or overawing person or thing; an empire etc. personified as standing astride over dominions. E17.

colostomy /kəˈlɒstəmi/ *n.* L19. [f. COLON *n.*[1] + Gk *stoma* mouth + -Y[3].] (The making of) a surgical incision in the colon to provide an artificial anus through the abdominal wall in cases of stricture etc.

colostrum /kəˈlɒstrəm/ *n.* Also (earlier) †**-tra**. L16. [L.] The first milk of a mammal after parturition.

colotomy /kəˈlɒtəmi/ *n.* M19. [f. COLON *n.*[1] + -TOMY.] Surgical incision into the colon; an instance of this.

colour /ˈkʌlə/ *n.* Also ***color**. ME. [OFr. *colur*, *colour* (mod. *couleur*) f. L *color*: see -OUR.] **I 1** A particular tint; one, or any mixture, of the constituents into which light can be separated as in the spectrum, including (loosely) black and white. ME. **b** A conventional colour used in heraldry, as gules, vert, etc.; a tincture, *esp.* one other than a metal or a fur. LME. **c** *Bot.* A colour other than green. M19. **2** Facial complexion; hue of the skin as reflecting a physical or mental state. ME. **b** *spec.* Ruddiness of face. Also, a flush, a blush. ME. **c** Hue of skin pigmentation; (dark) skin pigmentation, esp. as giving rise to prejudice, discrimination, etc. LME. **3** The sensation produced on the eye by spectral resolution or (selective) surface reflection etc. of rays of light; the property of so producing different sensations on the eye. Cf. *black*, *white*. LME. **4a** *Art.* The general effect produced by all the colours of a picture. M17. **b** The representation of colour by contrasts of light and dark in an engraving or monochrome. Also, the (relative) blackness of printed type. L18. **c** (The use of) two or more colours, not just black and white, in photography or cinematography; (the use of) nearly natural colours in a reproductive medium. L19.

1 DAY LEWIS Her hair . . was a rich auburn colour. E. LONGFORD The colours the Duke preferred were gay and warm; no greens, blues, black or white. *liver colour*, *mouse-colour*, *stone-colour*, *strawberry colour*, etc. **2b** S. O'FAOLÁIN A sturdy woman with fresh colour in her cheeks. A. JACKSON A word of praise would bring A colour to her cheek. **c** L. VAN DER POST A spirit . . at work among us all no matter what our race or colour. **3** E. BOWEN The façade, dun stucco, . . never altered in colour except at sunset.

II 5 A colouring matter; pigment; paint. ME. **6** *sing.* & (usu.) in *pl.* A coloured device, badge, article or set of clothing, etc., worn as a symbol of a party, membership of a club, a jockey's employer, etc. LME. **b** In *pl.* The distinctive colours of a school, college, club, etc., team, crew, or the like, as conferred to denote selection as a representative member; selection to represent a school etc. L19. **c** A person who has gained colours. M20. **7** A naval or nautical flag; either of the pair of silk flags (*the King's* or *Queen's colour* and *the regimental colour*) carried by a regiment. In *pl.* also, a regiment, the armed forces, (now chiefly in *with the colours*). L16. **b** In *pl.* More fully *pair of colours*. An ensign's commission. *arch.* E18. **c** In *pl.* A national flag. Also, two or more symbolic flags usually displayed or carried together. L19. **d** In *pl.* A nautical ceremony at which a flag is saluted as it is raised or lowered. E20. **8** *Mining.* (A particle of) gold. M19. **9** *Snooker.* Any of the balls other than the white cue-ball and the reds. E20.

5 *Ladies Home Journal* (US) If nail color chips between manicures, simply brush on a fresh coat of color. **6** SIR W. SCOTT The servants . . wore the colours of the Prince's household. *National Review* (US) Its green, yellow, and white colors are splashed over public buildings. **7** SHAKES. *3 Hen. VI* Sound trumpets; let our bloody colours wave. **c** J. DOS PASSOS The Commanding General never permits a flag to be carried past him without uncovering and remaining so until the colors have passed.

III 10 (An) outward appearance, (a) show, (a) semblance *of*. ME. **11** General complexion or tone; character, kind, mood; import, shade of meaning. ME. **12** A specious or plausible reason; a pretext; an excuse. LME. **b** *Law.* An apparent or *prima facie* right, as *colour of title*; a plausible but really false plea intended to make the point to be decided appear to be one of law and not of fact. M16. **13** In *pl.* Rhetorical modes or figures; ornaments of style or diction. LME. **14** Timbre, sound-quality; variety of musical expression, modulation (of the voice etc.). L16. **15** Evocative description, detailed characterization; picturesqueness in literature. Earliest in *local colour*: see LOCAL *a.* L19. **16** *Particle Physics.* A quantized property of quarks which differentiates them into three varieties (called blue, green, and red) and is thought to be the source of the strong interaction. L20.

11 O. CROMWELL Nor can it be urged that my words have the least colour that way. THACKERAY Pendennis . . took his colour very readily from his neighbour. T. KENEALLY The colour of his opinion . . was generally anti-monarchist and Papist. **12** JAS. MILL An enterprise . . which . . afforded a colour for detaining the troops. **14** S. HAZZARD His voice . . had a mature colour, resonant, almost beautiful. *Los Angeles Times* The reading had vitality and color, balances that brought the all-important flute part . . to the fore.

Phrases etc.: **change colour** *spec.* of a person: (*a*) turn pale; (*b*) blush, flush. **come off, through, with flying colours** come successfully through a test etc., win credit. **complementary colour** a colour that combined with a given colour makes white or black. *dead colour*: see DEAD *a.* & *adv.* *false colours*: see FALSE *a.* *FOUR-colour problem*. *full-colour*: see FULL *a.* **gain** or **get one's colours, give a person his** or **her colours** be included, include a person, in a sports team, esp. as a regular member. **give colour to** = *lend colour to* below. **haul down one's colours** admit defeat. *high colour*: see HIGH *a.* *horse of another colour*: see HORSE *n.* **lend colour to** (*a*) afford a pretext to; (*b*) give plausibility to. *liturgical colours*: see LITURGICAL *a.* *local colour*: see LOCAL *a.* **nail one's colours to the mast** (*a*) persist, refuse to give in; (*b*) commit oneself to some party or plan of action. *off colour*: see OFF *prep.* & *a.* **paint in bright colours** *fig.* describe optimistically. **person of colour** a non-White person. *primary colour*: see PRIMARY *a.* *primitive colour*: see PRIMITIVE *a.* & *n.* RACING *colours*. *r-colour*: see R, R I. *scheme of colour*: see SCHEME *n.*[1] 7b. *secondary colour*: see SECONDARY *a.* **see the colour of a person's money** receive some evidence of forthcoming payment from a person. **show one's (true) colours** reveal one's (true) party or character. *solid colour*: see SOLID *a.* & *adv.* *stand of colours*: see STAND *n.*[1] 15b. *strike one's colours*: see STRIKE *v.* *the King's*, *Queen's*, or *regimental colour*: see sense 7 above. *turn colour*: see TURN *v.* **under colour of** under pretext or pretence of; under the alleged authority of. *vowel colour*: see VOWEL *n.* **with the colours** serving in the armed forces.

Attrib. & *comb.*: Esp. with ref. to photographic etc. reproduction in colour, as *colour camera*, *photograph*, *photography*, *print*, *slide*, *transparency*, etc. Special combs., as **colour atlas** a chart giving examples of a series of shades of colour; **colour bar** legal or social discrimination between White and non-White persons; **colour-blind** *a.* unable to distinguish certain colours; (esp. of animals) unable to distinguish colours at all; **colour-blindness** the condition of being colour-blind; **colour-box** a paintbox; **colour-change** *spec.* a change in the colour of an animal's coat, skin, etc., for camouflage or protection; **colour code** a guide or code using certain colours as a standard method of identification; **colour-code** *v.t.* identify by means of a standard colour; **colour constancy** the effect whereby the intrinsic colour of an object is perceived as almost constant despite changes in the colour of the illumination; **colour-fast** *a.* dyed in colours that will not easily fade or wash out; **colour-fastness** the quality of being colour-fast; **colour film** (*a*) a cinema film produced in nearly natural colours; (*b*) a film suitable for producing colour photographs; **colour-filter** a photographic filter that absorbs light of certain colours; **colour guard** an honour guard carrying colours; **colour hearing** = *coloured hearing* s.v. COLOURED *a.* 1; **colour-index** a measure of colour; *spec.* (*a*) *Astron.* the difference between the photographic and visual magnitudes of a star, or between the apparent magnitudes at two standard wavelengths; (*b*) *Geol.* a number representing the relative proportions of dark-coloured (ferromagnesian) and pale-coloured minerals in an igneous rock; **colour-light** *a.* designating (esp. railway) signals using coloured electric lights; **colour line** a social or occupational demarcation between White and non-White persons; **colour-man** (*a*) a dealer in paints; (*b*) a dye-worker; **colour-phase** a genetic or seasonal variation in the colour of the skin, pelt, or feathers of an animal or bird; **colour-plate** each of a set of plates used in printing in colour; a print made from such plates; **colour prejudice**: against persons of particular skin colour; **colour scheme** a (deliberate) conjunction of colours, esp. in interior decoration or garden-planting; **colour-sergeant** the senior sergeant of an infantry company; a sergeant in an honour guard who carries one of the colours; **colour supplement** a supplement containing coloured illustrations, published with a newspaper etc. otherwise printed without colour; **colour television**: reproducing nearly natural colours, not just black and white; **colour temperature** *Astron.* & *Photogr.* the temperature at which a black body would emit radiation of the same colour as the body in question; **colourtype (process)** = THREE-*colour process*; **colour-wash** *n.* & *v.t.* (paint with) coloured distemper; **colourway** a coordinated combination of colours.

colourful *a.* full of colour; *fig.* full of interest, excitement, force, etc., flamboyant: L19. **colourfully** *adv.* E20. **colourfulness** *n.* E20. **colourless** *a.* (*a*) *gen.* without colour; (*b*) without distinctive character, vividness, or picturesqueness; neutral: LME. **colourlessly** *adv.* L19. **colourlessness** *n.* L17. **coloury** *a.* (*a*) *colloq.* characterized by or rich in colour; (*b*) (of hops, coffee beans, etc.) having a colour indicative of good quality: M19.

colour /ˈkʌlə/ *v.* Also ***color**. ME. [OFr. *colourer* (mod. *colorer*) f. L *colorare*, f. *color* COLOUR *n.*] **1** *v.t.* Give colour to; paint, stain, dye. Also *fig.*, embellish, adorn, make vivid or picturesque. ME. **2** *v.t.* Disguise; render specious or plausible; misrepresent. LME. †**3** *v.t.* Lend one's name to; represent or deal with as one's own. LME–E18. **4** *v.i.* Turn red in the face, blush. Also foll. by *up*. E17. **5** *v.i.* *gen.* Take on colour; change colour; become coloured. M17. **6** *v.t.* Imbue with its own tone or character; condition, influence. M19.

1 *Church Times* Finish the picture by joining the dots. . . Colour it with crayons or felt-tips. *Globe & Mail* (*Toronto*) Her dances are romantically coloring the world after nature. **2** DICKENS The evidence has been suppressed and coloured. **4** D. LESSING Anna, conscious that she was colouring, met his eyes with an effort. **6** G. M. TREVELYAN The aristocratic influence which coloured many aspects of life.

With advs. in specialized senses: **colour in** fill in by colouring. **colour over** cover by colouring.

colourer *n.* E17.

colourable /ˈkʌlərəb(ə)l/ *a.* Also ***color-**. LME. [OFr. *colorable* having bright colours; in sense 2 f. COLOUR *n.*: see COLOUR *n.*, -ABLE.] **1** Having an appearance of truth or right; specious, plausible. LME. **b** Pretended; feigned; counterfeit. LME. †**2** Possessed of colour; having much colour. E17–E18.

coloura'bility *n.* L19. **colourably** *adv.* LME.

colourant /ˈkʌlər(ə)nt/ *n.* Also ***color-**. L19. [f. COLOUR *v.* + -ANT[1].] A colouring agent.

colouration *n.* var. of COLORATION.

coloured /ˈkʌləd/ *a.* & *n.* Also ***color-**. LME. [f. COLOUR *v.*, *n.*: see -ED[1], -ED[2].] **A** *adj.* **1** Having colour (strictly, exclusive of black or white); having been coloured. Also *fig.*, (of literary style etc.) embellished, adorned, made picturesque; imbued with a particular tone or character, conditioned, influenced. LME. †**2** Made to look well; specious; feigned. LME–E17. **3** Having a specified colour or type of complexion. LME. **4** Having a skin of a colour other than white; wholly or partly of non-White descent; of or belonging to a Black people; for the separate use of Blacks. (Cf. BLACK *a.* 2b.) Now freq. considered *racially offensive*. E17. **b** *spec.* (**C-**.) Designating South Africans of mixed descent; of, belonging to, or for the separate use of the South African population group of mixed descent. E19.

1 W. GASS They have some colored sheets—one lavender, one rose, one wine. C. HAYES Coloured pencils have the same graphic qualities as pastels. **coloured hearing** accompaniment of the hearing of sounds with the perception of certain colours. **3** *cream-coloured*, *flesh-coloured*, *fresh-coloured*, *mulberry-coloured*, *pink-coloured*, *sky-coloured*, *tabby-coloured*, etc. **4** S. LONGSTREET Poor white and colored high yaller. *New Yorker* The 'colored balcony', with its separate entrance, once a regular feature of Southern theatres. **b** *Cape Coloured*: see CAPE *n.*[1]

B *n.* Also (*S. Afr.*) C-. A coloured person. Freq. in *pl.* M20.

colouring /ˈkʌlərɪŋ/ *n.* Also ***color-**. LME. [f. COLOUR *v.* + -ING[1].] **1** The action of COLOUR *v.* LME. **2** Matter which imparts colour. LME. **3** The effect of the application of colour; the style in which anything is coloured, or in which an artist employs colour. Also, a coloured drawing, a painting. E18. **b** Pervading character, tone, or aspect. M18. **c** Facial complexion; usual hue of the skin. M20.

3c *protective colouring*: see PROTECTIVE *a.*

Comb.: **colouring book** a book of outline drawings designed to be coloured in (usu. by children).

colourise *v.* var. of COLOURIZE.

colourist /ˈkʌlərɪst/ *n.* Also ***color-**. L17. [f. COLOUR *n.* + -IST, after It. *colorista* (whence Fr. *coloriste*).] A painter skilful in colouring; an adept user of colour (*lit.* & *fig.*).

colouˈristic *a.* of or pertaining to a colourist or artistic colouring L19.

colourize /ˈkʌlərʌɪz/ *v.t.* Also ***color-**; **-ise**. E17. [f. COLOUR *n.* + -IZE.] = COLOUR *v.* 1; *spec.* colour (a black and white film) by means of a computer.

Video World We urge you to shun any 'colorized' tapes and stick with the original black and white.

colouriˈzation *n.* coloration, colouring; (as *Colorization*, US proprietary name for) the process or technique of colourizing: M18. **colourizer** *n.* a colouring agent or process; (as *Colorizer*, US proprietary name for) a colourizing process: L19.

-colous /ˈkələs/ *suff.* [f. L *-colus* inhabiting, f. *colere* inhabit: see -OUS.] Forming adjs. w. the senses 'living or growing in or on', 'frequenting', as *calcicolous*, *nidicolous*.

colpo- /ˈkɒlpəʊ/ *comb. form*. Bef. a vowel **colp-**. [f. Gk *kolpos* womb: see -O-.] Forming ns. (and their derivs.) w. the sense 'of the vagina'.

colposcope *n.* an instrument which can be inserted into the vagina for examination of the cervix of the womb M20. **colˈposcopy** *n.* internal examination by means of a colposcope M20. **colˈpotomy** *n.* (an instance of) surgical incision into the wall of the vagina E20.

colportage /ˈkɒlpɔːtɪdʒ/ *n.* M19. [Fr., f. *colporter*: see next, -AGE.] The work of a colporteur; the peddling of books, newspapers, bibles, etc.

colporteur /ˈkɒlpɔːtə, kɒlpɔːˈtəː/ *n.* L18. [Fr., f. *colporter* prob. alt. of *comporter* f. L *comportare* transport, f. as COM- + *portare* carry (cf. PORTER *n.*[2]).] A pedlar of books, newspapers, etc., *esp.* one employed by a religious society to distribute bibles and other religious tracts.

colrake *n.* var. of COLERAKE.

colsa *n.* var. of COLZA.

colt /kəʊlt/ *n.*[1] OE. [Origin uncertain: cf. Sw. *kult*, *kulter*, *kulting*, applied to half-grown animals and boys.] **1** Orig., a young horse or animal of the horse kind; in early biblical translations, a young camel. Now, a young male horse that has been taken from the dam but is not fully grown, *spec.* (esp. of a racehorse) that is under the age of 4 or 5. Cf. FILLY, FOAL *n.* OE. **2** A person likened to a colt; *spec.* †(*a*) a lascivious person; (*b*) a young or inexperienced person, esp. in sports; a member of a junior team; *esp.* a cricketer during his first season; (*c*) a frisky or frolicsome person. ME. **3** The barrister who attended on a serjeant-at-law at his induction. *slang. obs.* exc. *Hist.* M18. **4** A short piece of weighted rope used as a weapon, *spec.* (*Naut.*) a similar instrument used for corporal punishment. *slang.* M18.

Comb.: **colt foal** a male foal; **colt-pixie** a mischievous sprite in the form of a ragged colt; **coltsfoot** [tr. med.L *pes pulli*] a plant of the composite family, *Tussilago farfara*, with yellow flowers and heart-shaped leaves; also occas., any of certain other plants resembling this (*sweet coltsfoot*: see SWEET *a.* & *adv.*); **colt's tail** a cloud with a ragged edge, regarded as portending rain; **colt's tooth** (*a*) one of the first set of teeth of a horse; (*b*) youthful desires; inclination to friskiness, frolicking, or lasciviousness.

colthood *n.* M19. **coltish** *a.* (*a*) of, pertaining to, or like a colt or colts; wild, frisky, untamed; †(*b*) lascivious, salacious: LME. **coltishly** *adv.* M16. **coltishness** *n.* M17.

Colt /kəʊlt/ *n.*[2] M19. [Samuel *Colt* (1814–62), US inventor.] (Proprietary name for) a type of firearm, *esp.* a type of repeating pistol.

colt /kəʊlt/ *v.* L16. [f. COLT *n.*[1]] **1** *v.i.* Frisk or run wild as a colt (usu. implying wantonness). *obs.* exc. *dial.* L16. †**2** *v.t.* Make a fool of; cheat. L16–E17. †**3** *v.t.* Copulate with. *rare* (Shakes.). Only in E17. **4** *v.i.* Fall in, cave in; collapse. *dial.* L17. **5** *v.t.* Beat with a colt (see COLT *n.*[1] 4). *slang.* M18.

colting *n.* (*a*) the action of the vb; (*b*) *slang* a beating with a colt: M19.

colter *n.* see COULTER.

coluber /ˈkɒljʊbə/ *n.* LME. [L *coluber*, *-bris*.] A snake; *spec.* a colubrid. Now only as mod.L genus name.

colubrid /ˈkɒljʊbrɪd/ *n.* & *a.* L19. [mod.L *Colubridae* (see below), f. as prec.: see -ID[3].] *Zool.* **A** *n.* A snake of the large family Colubridae, to which most typical non-venomous snakes belong. L19. **B** *adj.* Of, pertaining to, or designating this family. L19.

colubrine /ˈkɒljʊbrʌɪn/ *a.* E16. [L *colubrinus*, f. as COLUBER: see -INE[1].] **1** Of or belonging to a snake; snakelike. E16. **2** *Zool.* Colubrid; *spec.* of or pertaining to the subfamily Colubrinae of colubrid snakes with solid teeth. M19.

colugo /kəˈluːgəʊ/ *n.* Pl. **-os**. L18. [Origin unkn.] A flying lemur.

colulus /ˈkɒljʊləs/ *n.* Pl. **-li** /-lʌɪ, -liː/. E20. [mod.L, dim. of *colus* distaff.] *Zool.* A sclerite at the base of and between the front spinnerets in many spiders.

Columba /kəˈlʌmbə/ *n.* L18. [L *columba* dove, pigeon.] (The name of) a constellation of the southern hemisphere near Canis Major; the Dove.

columbaceous /kɒl(ə)mˈbeɪʃəs/ *a.* L17. [f. as prec. + -ACEOUS.] Of the nature of a dove or pigeon; dovelike.

Columban /kəˈlʌmb(ə)n/ *a.* & *n.* L19. [f. *Columba* (see below) + -AN.] **A** *adj.* Of, pertaining to, or characteristic of the Irish missionary St Columba of Iona (*c* 521–97), or his followers. L19. **B** *n.* A disciple of St Columba. L19.

columbarium /kɒl(ə)mˈbɛːrɪəm/ *n.* Pl. **-ia** /-ɪə/, **-iums**. M18. [L *columbarium*, f. as COLUMBA: see -ARIUM.] **1** A vault or building with niches for the reception of cinerary urns; a niche in such a vault etc. M18. **2** A pigeon-hole; a columbary. E19.

columbary /ˈkɒl(ə)mb(ə)ri/ *n.* M16. [f. as prec.: see -ARY[1].] A pigeon-house, a dovecote.

columbiad /kəˈlʌmbɪad/ *n.* L18. [f. as next + -AD[1].] **1** An epic of America. Chiefly as a poem title. L18. **2** A kind of heavy cast-iron cannon formerly used in the US army. E19.

Columbian /kəˈlʌmbɪən/ *a.* & *n.* M18. [f. mod.L *Columbia* poet. name for America, f. as COLUMBUS: see -AN.] **A** *adj.* Of or pertaining to America, esp. at the time of its discovery by Christopher Columbus; *spec.* of or pertaining to the United States. M18. **B** *n.* An American; a native or inhabitant of the United States. *obs.* exc. *Hist.* L18.

columbic /kəˈlʌmbɪk/ *a.* Now *rare* or *obs.* E19. [f. COLUMBIUM + -IC.] *Chem.* Of or pertaining to columbium (niobium).

columbic acid = NIOBIC *acid*.

columbate *n.* = NIOBATE E19.

columbine /ˈkɒl(ə)mbʌɪn/ *n.*[1] ME. [OFr. *colombine* f. med.L *columbina* (*herba*) dovelike (plant), f. *columba* pigeon, the flower being likened to five clustered pigeons: see -INE[1].] Aquilegia, esp. *Aquilegia vulgaris*.

Columbine /ˈkɒl(ə)mbʌɪn/ *n.*[2] E18. [Fr. f. It. *Colombina* use as n. of fem. of *colombino* dovelike in gentleness.] Orig., a servant-girl in *commedia dell'arte*. Now, the sweetheart of Harlequin in pantomime.

columbine /ˈkɒl(ə)mbʌɪn/ *a.* & *n.*[3] Now *rare*. LME. [(O)Fr. *columbin(e)* f. L *columbinus* f. *columba* dove: see -INE[1].] **A** *adj.* **1** Of, pertaining to, or of the nature of a dove; dovelike. LME. **2** Dove-coloured. LME. **B** *n.* Dove-colour. E17.

columbite /kəˈlʌmbʌɪt/ *n.* E19. [f. next + -ITE[1].] *Min.* The chief ore of niobium, an orthorhombic oxide of iron, manganese, and niobium (usu. with some tantalum), occurring usu. as red prismatic crystals.

columbium /kəˈlʌmbɪəm/ *n.* Chiefly *US*. Now *rare* or *obs.* E19. [f. mod.L *Columbia* poet. name for America, f. *Columbus* (see next), + -IUM.] *Chem.* = NIOBIUM (symbol Cb).

Columbus /kəˈlʌmbəs/ *n.* L16. [Christopher *Columbus* (1451–1506), Genoese explorer, discoverer of America.] An explorer, a discoverer.

¶ See also *Knight of Columbus* s.v. KNIGHT *n.*

columel /ˈkɒljʊmɛl/ *n. rare.* E17. [L *columella*, dim. of *columna*: see COLUMN, -EL[2].] A small column.

columella /kɒljʊˈmɛlə/ *n.* Pl. **-llae** /-liː/. L16. [L: see prec.] A structure or organ resembling a small column; *esp.* †(*a*) the uvula; (*b*) the axis of the cochlea; (*c*) the axis of a spiral shell; (*d*) *Bot.* the axis of a fruit composed of several carpels; the axis of the spore-producing body of certain plants; (*e*) *Zool.* one of the ossicles of the middle ear of birds, reptiles, and amphibians.

columellar *a.* E19.

column /ˈkɒləm/ *n.* LME. [Partly f. OFr. *columpne* (mod. *colonne*, after It. *colonna*), partly f. its source L *columna* pillar.] **1** *Archit.* A long vertical, often slightly tapering, cylinder usu. surmounted by an entablature and forming part of an arcade or colonnade, or standing alone as a monument. LME. **b** *fig.* A support, a prop. E17. **2** A vertical division of text on a page; a vertical array of figures or other information in a table. LME. **b** A part of a newspaper, sometimes more or less than a column of print, devoted (esp. regularly) to a special subject or writer. M19. **3** A structure or object likened to a column (sense 1), as part of an animal body, part of a machine, etc. LME. **b** *Bot.* The structure formed by the union of the style and stamens, or of staminal filaments, esp. in the orchids. E19. **4** *Mil.* A narrow-fronted deep formation of troops or armoured vehicles etc. in successive lines. LME. **b** *Naut.* A body or division of ships. E19. **5** A vertical cylindrical mass of liquid or vapour. L17. **6** A party, a faction. Chiefly *US*. E20.

1 W. S. MAUGHAM Long halls, the roof supported by sculptured columns. A. WILSON The towering column of the Duke of York. COUPLED *columns*. OSIRIDE *column*. 2 G. K. CHESTERTON Adding up a column in a ledger. b R. CAMPBELL Then through my weekly columns I may pour The sentiments that dowagers adore. *advertisement column*, *agony column*, *gossip column*, etc. *funny column*: see FUNNY *a.* *personal column*: see PERSONAL *a.* *social column*: see SOCIAL *a.* **the columns of** (a newspaper): its contents; (*our columns*, used by the newspaper itself). 3 TENNYSON The knotted column of his throat. *pulsed column*: see PULSED *ppl a.* *rectifying column*: see RECTIFY *v.* 2. *spinal column*: see SPINAL *a.* *vertebral column*: see VERTEBRAL *a.* 2. 4 *transf.*: R. LOWELL A mother skunk with her column of kittens. *column of* ROUTE. **dodge the column** *colloq.* shirk a duty; avoid work. *fifth column*: see FIFTH *a.* 5 L. VAN DER POST I spotted two more columns of smoke.

Comb.: **column-inch** the quantity of print occupying one inch length of column.

columniform /kəˈlʌmnɪfɔːm/ *a.* shaped like a column E19.

columna /kəˈlʌmnə/ *n. rare.* Pl. **-nae** /-niː/. L17. [L: see COLUMN *n.*] **1** *Bot.* = COLUMN 3b. L17. **2** *Anat.* A column-shaped part of the body. M18.

columnal /kəˈlʌmn(ə)l/ *a.* & *n.* M18. [f. COLUMN + -AL[1].] **A** *adj.* Columnar. Now *rare*. M18. **B** *n.* *Zool.* A segment or joint of the stem of a crinoid. L19.

columnar /kəˈlʌmnə/ *a.* E18. [Late L *columnaris*, f. *columna* COLUMN: see -AR[1].] **1** Of the nature or form of a column or columns. E18. **2** Written or printed in columns. M19. **3** Characterized by or raised on columns. M19.

Also †**columnary** *a.* L16–E18.

columnated /ˈkɒl(ə)mneɪtɪd/ *a.* Also **-iated** /-ɪeɪtɪd/. E18. [f. L *columnatus*, f. *columna* COLUMN, + -ED[1]. Form w. *-i-* after COLUMNIATION.] = COLUMNED 1.

columned /ˈkɒl(ə)md/ *a.* L18. [f. COLUMN *n.* + -ED[2].] 1 Furnished with columns; supported on columns. L18. 2 Divided into columns. E19. 3 Like a column, columnar. M19.

columniated *a.* see COLUMNATED.

columniation /kəlʌmnɪˈeɪʃ(ə)n/ *n.* M17. [f. L *columnatio(n-)*, f. *columna* COLUMN, after INTERCOLUMNIATION.] *Archit.* The employment of columns; the arrangement of columns.

columnist /ˈkɒl(ə)m(n)ɪst/ *n.* E20. [f. COLUMN + -IST.] A journalist who regularly contributes to a newspaper a column, esp. of miscellaneous comment on people and events.

¶ See also *fifth columnist* s.v. FIFTH *a.*

colure /kəˈljʊə/ *n.* LME. [Late L *coluri* pl. f. Gk *kolourai* (sc. *grammai* lines) pl. of *kolouros* truncated, f. *kolos* docked + *oura* tail (so called because their lower part is permanently cut off from view).] *Astron.* Either of the two great circles passing through the celestial poles and intersecting the ecliptic at either the equinoxes or the solstices.

coly /ˈkəʊli/ *n.* M19. [f. mod.L *Colius* f. Gk *kolios* a kind of woodpecker.] = *mousebird* s.v. MOUSE *n.*

colza /ˈkɒlzə/ *n.* Also **colsa**. E18. [Fr. (Walloon) *kolza*, earlier *colzat* f. LG *kōlsāt*, Du. *koolzaad*, f. *kool* COLE *n.*[1] + *zaad* SEED *n.*] Rape, rape-seed; = COLESEED 2.

com- /kɒm, *unstressed* kəm/ *pref.* Repr. L *com-* (= *cum* prep. 'with') in senses 'with', 'together', 'jointly'; also 'completely', and hence *intensive*. Used bef. *b*, *p*, *m*, and a few words beginning with vowels or *f*; assim. to COL- bef. *l*, COR- bef. *r*; reduced to CO- bef. vowels generally, *h*, and *gn*; as CON- bef. other consonants. As a living prefix chiefly in form CO-.

coma /ˈkəʊmə/ *n.*[1] Pl. **-mae** /-miː/. E17. [L f. Gk *komē* hair of the head.] 1 *Bot.* The top of a plant; *esp.* a terminal tuft of bracts or leaves; a leafy crown of branches; a tuft of silky hairs at the end of some seeds. E17. 2 *Astron.* The diffuse hazy region surrounding the nucleus of a comet. M18. 3 An optical aberration causing the image of an off-axis point to be flared, like a comet with a diverging tail; the flared image itself. M19.

coˈmatic *a.* E20.

coma /ˈkəʊmə/ *n.*[2] M17. [mod.L f. Gk *kōma*, *-mat-*, rel. to *koitē* bed, *keisthai* lie down.] *Med.* A prolonged state of unconsciousness from which the patient cannot be roused. Formerly also, an unnatural heavy sleep.

Comb.: **coma vigil** †(*a*) a prolonged state of drowsiness in which the patient nevertheless cannot sleep; (*b*) a state in typhus fever etc. in which the patient lies unconscious but with eyes wide open.

Coma Berenices /ˈkəʊmə bɛrɪˈnʌɪsiːz/ *n. phr.* L17. [L, f. as COMA *n.*[1] + *Berenice* (*c*273–221 BC), wife of Ptolemy III of Egypt, whose hair was said to have been stolen from the temple of Venus and afterwards placed in the heavens.] (The name of) an inconspicuous constellation of the northern hemisphere, between Boötes and Virgo; = BERENICE'S HAIR.

comae *n.* pl. of COMA *n.*[2]

Comanche /kəˈmantʃi/ *n.* & *a.* E19. [Sp. f. Shoshonean.] A *n.* Pl. **-s**, same. 1 A member of a N. American Indian people of Texas and Oklahoma. E19. 2 The Shoshonean language of this people. M19. B *attrib.* or as *adj.* Of or pertaining to the Comanches or their language. E19.

co-mate /ˈkəʊmeɪt, kəʊˈmeɪt/ *n.* L16. [f. CO- + MATE *n.*[2]] A companion, a mate.

comatose /ˈkəʊmətəʊs/ *a.* L17. [f. Gk *kōmat-* (see COMA *n.*[1]) + -OSE[1].] 1 In a coma; of the nature of coma. L17. 2 *transf.* Drowsy, lethargic. E19.

Also †**comatous** *a.* M17–L18.

comb /kəʊm/ *n.*[1] See also KAME. [OE *camb*, *comb* = OS *camb* (Du. *kam*), OHG *kamb* (G *Kamm*), ON *kambr*, f. Gmc.] I 1 A toothed strip of bone, horn, metal, plastic, etc., for untangling, arranging, or keeping in place the hair. See also CURRY-COMB *n.*, *horse-comb* s.v. HORSE *n.* OE. 2 Something resembling this in function, structure, etc., as (*a*) a toothed instrument for separating and dressing textile fibres; (*b*) a toothed structure for graining painted work; (*c*) the pair of abdominal appendages in a scorpion; an analogous structure in other animals; (*d*) a row of brass points for collecting the electricity in an electrostatic generator; (*e*) *Austral.* & *NZ* the lower, fixed cutting-piece of a sheep-shearing machine. ME. 3 The action or an act of combing. E20.

1 *fine-tooth comb*: see FINE *a.* *redding-comb*: see REDD *v.*[2] *Spanish comb*: see SPANISH *a.* *tooth-comb*: see TOOTH *n.*

II 4 The red fleshy crest on the head of the domestic fowl, esp. the male; so called from its serrated form (cf. COCKSCOMB 1); an analogous growth in other birds. OE. 5 Something resembling a cock's comb in position or appearance, as (*a*) the crest of a helmet; the upright blade on a morion; (*b*) (now *dial.*) the crest or top of a bank, hill, etc.; the ridge formed between ruts; (*c*) the upper corner of a gun-stock, against which the cheek is placed in firing; (*d*) the crest of a wave. OE.

4 **cut the comb of** humiliate, make less conceited. *white comb*: see WHITE *a.*

III (Not found in the cognates.) 6 = HONEYCOMB *n.* 1 (earlier). ME.

6 *virgin comb*: see VIRGIN *a.*

Comb.: **comb-back** a high-backed Windsor chair with a straight top rail; **comb-brush** (*a*) a brush to clean combs; †(*b*) a lady's maid; **comb-jelly** *Zool.* a ctenophore; *comb-tailed paradise fish*: see PARADISE *n.*

combed *a.* (esp. of a cock) having a comb M16. **combless** *a.* without a comb or crest L16. **comblike** *a.* resembling (that of) a comb E17. **comby** *a.* (*a*) full of holes like a honeycomb; (*b*) *Geol.* having layers with parallel crystals like the teeth of a comb: L18.

comb /kəʊm/ *n.*[2] Now chiefly *dial.* Also **come** /kəʊm, kuːm/, **coomb** /kuːm/. LME. [Prob. f. Gmc base repr. also by G *Keim*.] The radicle of the grain, which develops during malting and is then dried up by roasting and separated.

comb *n.*[3], *n.*[4] vars. of COOMB *n.*[1], *n.*[2]

comb /kəʊm/ *v.* LME. [f. COMB *n.*[1], repl. KEMB *v.*] 1 *v.t.* **a** Draw a comb through (the hair); curry (a horse). LME. **b** Dress (wool, flax, etc.) with a comb, so as to separate and arrange the fibres. L16. **c** Scrape or rake with an action like that of a comb. M17. 2 *v.i.* Of a wave: roll over and break with a foamy crest. Orig. *US*. E19. 3 *v.t.* Search minutely and systematically. (Earlier in BEACHCOMBING.) *colloq.* E20. 4 *v.t.* Of a ship: turn into line with (the track of a torpedo) to avoid being hit. M20.

1 **comb a person's head with a three-legged stool** & vars. (now *dial.*), give a person a thrashing. **comb out** comb through (the hair) after setting and drying it, or to remove knots; *fig.* search or bombard systematically; single out for removal (orig. persons fit for military service). c R. HUGHES The wind had combed up some quite hearty waves. 2 K. KESEY The swells at the mouth of the jetty were combing higher than the boat. 3 H. INNES I combed the 'Situations Vacant' columns of the papers. B. MALAMUD He combed the crowded streets, searching for Susskind.

Comb.: **comb-out** an act of combing something out (*lit.* & *fig.*).

combat /ˈkɒmbat, ˈkʌm-, -ət/ *n.* M16. [Fr., f. *combattre* f. late L *combattere*, f. as COM- + var. of *batuere* fight.] 1 A fight or armed encounter between two persons, parties, animals, etc.; a duel. More explicitly *single combat*. M16. 2 *gen.* A fight, fighting, between opposing forces (usu. on a smaller scale than (a) battle); a conflict, strife. L16.

1 *judicial combat*: see JUDICIAL *a.* *judiciary combat*: see JUDICIARY *a.* 3. **trial by combat** *Hist.* legal decision of a dispute by single combat. 2 B. JOWETT Is courage only a combat against fear and pain? H. WOUK Her life passed in combat with an incompetent world. *attrib.*: F. FITZGERALD These officers were professional soldiers. Most of them had combat experience. UNARMED *combat*.

Comb.: **combat boots, jacket**: (of a type) worn by soldiers in actual combat; **combat fatigue** mental illness due to stress in wartime combat (= *battle fatigue*); *combat jacket*: see *combat boots* above.

combat /ˈkɒmbat, ˈkʌ-, -ət/ *v.* M16. [Fr. *combattre*: see prec.] 1 *v.i.* Fight or do battle (*with*, *against*), esp. in single combat. M16. 2 *v.t.* Fight with, oppose in armed conflict. Now chiefly *fig.* L16.

2 A. HAILEY Details of the types of offences involved and methods being used to combat them.

combater *n.* (*rare*) L16.

combatant /ˈkɒmbət(ə)nt, ˈkʌm-/ *a.* & *n.* In sense A.1 freq. **-tt-**. LME. [OFr., pres. pple of *combattre*: see COMBAT *n.*, -ANT[1].] A *adj.* 1 *Her.* Poised for combat; *esp.* rampant with the forepaws raised as if in fight (usu. said of two lions facing each other). LME. 2 *gen.* Fighting, ready to fight; *esp.* taking part in active fighting during a war (opp. *non-combatant*). M17. B *n.* A participant in an armed contest, in early use esp. in single combat; a participant in active fighting during a war (opp. *non-combatant*); *gen.* a contender, an opponent. L15.

combative /ˈkɒmbətɪv, ˈkʌm-/ *a.* M19. [f. COMBAT *v.* + -IVE.] Having a propensity for combat, pugnacious.

combatively *adv.* M19. **combativeness** *n.* (orig. *Phrenol.*) E19. **combativity** /-ˈtɪvɪti/ *n.* E20.

combattant *a.* see COMBATANT.

combe *n.* var. of COOMB *n.*[2]

comber /ˈkəʊmə/ *n.*[1] ME. [f. COMB *v.* + -ER[1].] 1 A person who, or a machine which, combs wool, cotton, etc. ME. 2 A long curling wave, a breaker. Cf. BEACHCOMBER 2. M19. 3 A person who searches minutely and systematically. Earliest & chiefly in BEACHCOMBER 1. M19.

comber /ˈkɒmbə/ *n.*[2] M18. [Origin unkn.] A fish of the sea-perch family, *Serranus cabrilla*. Cf. GAPER 3.

combie /ˈkɒmbi/ *n. colloq.* L19. [Abbrev.: cf. COMBS.] *sing.* & (usu.) in *pl.* A combination garment, combinations.

combinable /kəmˈbʌɪnəb(ə)l/ *a.* M18. [f. COMBINE *v.*[1] + -ABLE.] Able to be combined.

combinaˈbility *n.* E20.

combinate /ˈkɒmbɪnət/ *a. rare.* L16. [Late L *combinatus* pa. pple of *combinare* COMBINE *v.*[1]: see -ATE[2].] 1 Combined. L16. †2 Betrothed, bound by oath. Cf. COMBINE *v.*[1] 2. *rare* (Shakes.). Only in E17.

combination /kɒmbɪˈneɪʃ(ə)n/ *n.* LME. [OFr. (mod. *combinaison*) or L *combinatio(n-)*, f. *combinat-* pa. ppl stem of *combinare*: see COMBINE *v.*[1], -ATION.] 1 The action of combining two or more things; combined state. LME. **b** A combined set or series of things; a compound thing, *esp.* a compound word or taxonomic name. M16. 2 The association of people for a common (formerly usu. illegal) purpose; an association of people so formed. LME. †**b** Agreement, compact. *rare* (Shakes.). Only in E17. **c** A small instrumental band. Cf. COMBO. E20. 3 **a** *Math.* A selection of a given number of elements from a larger number of elements, without regard to the order of the elements chosen. Cf. PERMUTATION. L17. **b** A particular sequence of letters or numbers chosen in setting a combination lock (see below); the lock itself. M19. **c** *Chess.* A sequence of forcing moves with a specific goal. L19. 4 *Chem.* The union of substances to form a compound (whose properties differ from those of the original substances); the state of being united in a compound; a compound so formed. M18. 5 In *pl.* A single undergarment for the body and legs (= *combination garment* below). L19. 6 A motorcycle with side-car attached. E20.

1 E. O'NEILL Consider these two inventions of mine in combination. C. FRANCIS Bad visibility and a sudden squall are a dangerous combination.

Comb.: **combination garment** = sense 5 above; **combination laws** laws (repealed in 1824) directed against workpeople combining to obtain an increase in wages, etc.; **combination lock** a lock (as of a safe or strongroom) controlled by a dial or dials, in which letters or numbers have to be arranged in a particular sequence to release the lock; **combination room** at Cambridge University, a common-room, *esp.* a senior common-room (*senior combination room*: see SENIOR *a.*); **combination tone** a note produced by the combined sounding of two other notes, a resultant tone.

combinational *a.* L17.

combinative /ˈkɒmbɪnətɪv/ *a.* M19. [f. prec. + -IVE: see -ATIVE.] 1 Able or tending to combine; relating to combination. M19. 2 *Philol.* Of a sound-change: occurring under the influence of adjoining sounds. Opp. ISOLATIVE 2. L19. 3 *Chess.* Using combinations. E20.

combinatorial /ˌkɒmbɪnəˈtɔːrɪəl/ *a.* E19. [f. as next + -AL¹.] Of or pertaining to mathematical combinations. Esp. in *combinatorial analysis*.
ˌ**combinatoriˈality** *n.* M20. **combinatorially** *adv.* M20.

combinatory /ˈkɒmbɪnət(ə)ri, kɒmbɪˈneɪt(ə)ri/ *a.* M17. [f. COMBINATION + -ORY¹.] 1 = COMBINATIVE 1. M17. 2 *Logic.* Designating or pertaining to a branch of symbolic logic concerned esp. with substitution and elimination of variables. E20.
combinatorics /-ˈtɒrɪks/ *n.* the study of possible combinations or configurations M20.

combine /ˈkɒmbʌɪn/ *n.* E17. [f. next.] †1 A conspiracy, a plot. Only in E17. 2 An alliance of people or organizations to further their commercial, political, etc., ends, freq. by underhand means. L19. 3 In full *combine harvester.* A combined reaping and threshing machine. E20.

combine /kəmˈbʌɪn/ *v.*¹ LME. [OFr. *combiner* or late L *combinare* join two by two, f. as COM- + *bini* two at a time.] 1 *v.t.* Unite, join together; associate (persons etc.) in a joint action, feeling, etc. LME. b Cause to coalesce or form one body; *Chem.* cause to enter into combination. L18. c Possess or show (esp. disparate qualities or features) at the same time. E19. †2 *v.t.* Bind by oath. Cf. COMBINATE 2. *rare* (Shakes.). Only in E17. 3 *v.i.* Unite together for a common purpose; form an association, esp. for some economic, social, or political objective. E17. 4 *v.i.* Come together in one body, coalesce; *Chem.* unite to form a compound, enter into combination. E18.
1 JAS. MILL A sense of common danger might.. combine them in operations of defence. c W. S. MAUGHAM She combined great good nature with a proper degree of toughness. 2 SHAKES. *Meas. for M.* For my poor self, I am combined by a sacred vow, and shall be absent. 3 G. B. SHAW When wolves combine to kill a horse. 4 **combining weight** *Chem.* the equivalent of an element.
†**combinement** *n.* = COMBINATION *n.* E17–E19. **combiner** *n.* †(*a*) a conspirator; (*b*) a person who or thing which combines: E16.

combine /ˈkɒmbʌɪn/ *v.*²*t.* E20. [f. COMBINE *n.* 3.] Harvest with a combine harvester.

combined /kəmˈbʌɪnd/ *a.* LME. [f. COMBINE *v.*¹ + -ED¹.] 1 United or coupled; resulting from a combination. LME. 2 Performed by agents acting in concert. E17.
1 A. KNOX When a collective and combined effect is to be produced. B. SPOCK Inoculations against these three diseases can be given together in a combined form. R. K. NARAYAN The hall was a passage, .. drawing-room, study, everything combined. **combined pill** an oral contraceptive containing both an oestrogen and a progestogen. 2 LD MACAULAY One vigorous and combined struggle for emancipation. **combined operation**: in which several branches of the armed forces (or some other organization) cooperate.
combinedly /-nɪd-/ *adv.* M17. **combinedness** *n.* M19.

combing /ˈkəʊmɪŋ/ *n.* M16. [f. COMB *v.* + -ING¹.] 1 The action of COMB *v.* M16. 2 In *pl.* Hairs combed off. M17.
1 BEACHCOMBING.
Comb.: **combing wool** long-stapled wool suitable for combing and spinning into worsted.

combining /kəmˈbʌɪnɪŋ/ *n.* M16. [f. COMBINE *v.*¹ + -ING¹.] The action of COMBINE *v.*¹ Also (*rare*), an instance of combining.
Comb.: **combining form** a form of a word used (only) in compounds, as *Indo-* repr. *Indian* in *Indo-European*.

comble /kɔ̃ːbl/ *n.* Pl. pronounced same. M19. [Fr. f. L *cumulus* heap.] A culminating point, a crowning touch.

combo /ˈkɒmbəʊ/ *n. slang.* Pl. **-os.** L19. [f. COMB(INATION + -O.] 1 A White man who lives with an Aboriginal woman. *Austral.* L19. 2 Combination, partnership (in various senses). Chiefly *N. Amer.* E20. 3 A small instrumental band, esp. of jazz musicians. Cf. COMBINATION 2C. E20.

comboloio /kɒmbəˈləʊjəʊ, kɒmvəˈlɔɪjəʊ/ *n.* Pl. **-os.** E19. [mod.Gk *kompoloi.*] A Muslim rosary of ninety-nine beads.

combretaceous /kɒmbrɪˈteɪʃəs/ *a.* M19. [f. mod.L *Combretaceae*, f. genus name *Combretum*: see next, -ACEOUS.] Of or pertaining to the Combretaceae, a family of tropical trees and shrubs allied to the myrtles.

combretum /kɒmˈbriːtəm/ *n.* E19. [mod.L f. L *combretum* (Pliny), an unidentified plant.] A tree or (often climbing or trailing) shrub of the genus *Combretum*, of the family Combretaceae (see prec.).

combs /kɒmz/ *n.pl. colloq.* Also **coms.** M20. [Abbrev.: cf. COMBIE.] A combination garment, combinations.

comburent /kəmˈbjʊər(ə)nt/ *a.* & *n. rare.* Also **-ant.** L16. [L *comburent-* pres. ppl stem of *comburere* burn up: see -ENT.] A *adj.* Burning; causing combustion. L16. B *n.* A substance that causes combustion. M19.

comburgess /kɒmˈbəːdʒɪs/ *n.* LME. [f. COM- + BURGESS *n.*, after med.L *comburgensis.*] *Hist.* 1 A fellow citizen or freeman of a borough; a fellow burgess. LME. 2 In certain English boroughs, up to 1835: any of the municipal magistrates chosen by and from among their fellow burgesses, and associated with the alderman. M17.

combust /kəmˈbʌst/ *a.* LME. [L *combustus* pa. pple of *comburere* burn up: cf. OFr. *combust.*] †1 Burnt; *spec.* acted on by fire, calcined. LME–E19. 2 *Astrol.* Of planets in or near conjunction: so near the sun (*spec.* within 8°30′) as to have their influence destroyed by it. LME.

combust /kəmˈbʌst/ *v.* L15. [f. (as) prec.] 1 *v.t.* Now chiefly *Sci.* Subject to combustion; *spec.* (*arch.*) calcine. L15. 2 *v.i.* Chiefly *Sci.* Undergo combustion. M20.

combustible /kəmˈbʌstɪb(ə)l/ *a.* & *n.* E16. [(O)Fr., or med.L *combustibilis*, f. *combust-*: see next, -IBLE. Cf. earlier INCOMBUSTIBLE.] A *adj.* 1 Able to be consumed by fire, suitable for burning. E16. 2 *fig.* Easily kindled to violence or passion. M17. B *n.* A combustible substance. L17.
combustiˈbility *n.* L15. **combustibleness** *n.* (*rare*) M17. **combustibly** *adv.* (*rare*) L16.

combustion /kəmˈbʌstʃ(ə)n/ *n.* LME. [(O)Fr., or late L *combustio(n-)*, f. *combust-*, pa. ppl stem of *comburere* burn up.] 1 Consumption or destruction by fire. LME. 2 *Chem.* Chemical change, *spec.* oxidation, marked by the production of heat and light. Also, a process of slow oxidation not accompanied by light, as in the animal body, in the decomposition of organic matter, etc. LME. †3 *Med.* A burn; inflammation. LME–M17. †4 *Astrol.* Obscuration by proximity to the sun (see COMBUST *a.* 2). LME–M18. 5 *fig.* Violent excitement or commotion. Now *rare.* L16.
2 *internal-combustion engine*: see INTERNAL *a.* *spontaneous combustion*: see SPONTANEOUS *a.* 3. 5 MALCOLM X This is the situation which permitted Negro combustion to slowly build up to the revolution-point.
Comb.: **combustion chamber** a space in which combustion takes place, as of gases in a boiler-furnace or fuel in an internal-combustion engine; **combustion-tube** a heat-resistant tube in which organic compounds are burnt (used in quantitative analysis).
†**combustious** *a.* combustible; marked by combustion; *fig.* raging, turbulent: L16–E19.

combustive /kəmˈbʌstɪv/ *a.* L16. [f. L *combust-* (see prec.) + -IVE.] †1 *Med.* Pertaining to a boil (cf. COMBUSTION *n.* 3). Only in L16. 2 †a Having the quality of causing combustion. M17–E19. b Pertaining to or marked by combustion. M19.

come /kʌm/ *n.*¹ [OE *cyme* f. Gmc, f. base of next; assim. to the vb in ME. Later f. the vb.] †1 Approach, arrival, coming. OE–LME. 2 *come-and-go*, passage to and fro. L18. 3 A flow or flood *of* water. M19. 4 Semen; sexual fluid. *slang.* M20.

come *n.*² var. of COMB *n.*²

come /kʌm/ *v.* Pa. t. **came** /keɪm/; pa. pple **come.** [OE *cuman* = OFris. *kuma*, OS *cuman* (Du. *komen*), OHG *queman*, *coman* (G *kommen*), ON *koma*, Goth. *qiman*, f. Gmc.] *gen.* An elementary intrans. vb of motion expressing movement towards the speaker or a point where he or she mentally places himself or herself, towards the person spoken to, or towards the person spoken of. Opp. *go.* I *v.i.* Of (actual or attributed) spatial motion. 1 Move towards one; *esp.* reach one thus; arrive. (Foll. by *to do*, *and do*, vbl n. in A *prep.*¹ 8, pple in -ING².) OE. 2 Of an inanimate thing or involuntary agent: move or be brought hither, or *to* a specified place. (Following constructions as sense 1.) ME. 3 Be reached, pass *into* view, as a result of a person's actual or notional advance; take a specified position in relation to something else. ME. 4 Reach or extend without actual motion (as far as or *to* a specified point or level). LME.
1 MILTON He at their invoking came. DICKENS When will you come to see me? TENNYSON I never came a-begging for myself. OED Come and see us. J. FOWLES If someone came looking for them. 2 J. CONRAD The scented air of the garden came to us. 3 W. STUBBS Beneath these comes the free class of labourers. 4 R. H. MOTTRAM The bed came so far down the little room.
II *v.i.* With the idea of movement subordinated. 5 Of an event, a fate, etc.: happen *to* a person or thing. OE. 6 Pass into the possession of a person etc. (Foll. by *to.*) ME. b Of a thing: be normally available or on sale (*in* a size, colour, etc., or *with* certain features etc.). M20. 7 Be perceived or thought. (Foll. by *into*, *to.*) ME. b Take shape in one's imagination or mind; issue as speech. M18. 8 Be derived, emanate, (*from*); be the result or descendant *of.* ME. 9 Pass or be brought *into* or *to* a situation or state. E16. 10 Of butter: form. Of a liquid: solidify, coagulate. M17.
6 *easy come, easy go.* 7 TENNYSON There came a sound. b G. GREENE Trying to write a book that simply would not come. 8 V. WOOLF That's what comes of putting things off. 9 C. HILL Laud had come into favour at court. *come into contact, fashion, play, prominence*, etc.
III *v.i.* With an idea of time or succession involved. 11 a Foll. by *to*, *to do*: reach in the course of orderly treatment. ME. b Foll. by *to*: reach, as an end or result. L15. 12 Arrive or occur in due course. ME. b With following future date (*colloq.*) or period of time (*dial.*): when that date comes, when that period has elapsed. ME. 13 Happen, come about. ME. 14 Foll. by *to*, *to do*: attain or be brought to (a specified state) by events or development. ME. 15 With compl.: become, get to be (in a specified condition); turn out by experience to be. ME. 16 Reach orgasm. Also foll. by *off.* *slang.* E17.
11a DEFOE When I come to consider that part. b V. WOOLF How difficult to come to any conclusion! 12 SWIFT The day came for my departure. G. GREENE After the steak-and-kidney pie came a treacle tart. b T. COLLINS He was married, three years ago come Boxing Day. 13 COVERDALE *1 Sam.* 1:4 Whan it came vpon a daye that Elcana offred. 14 E. HEMINGWAY Later he had come to like it. I. MURDOCH It came to rest. 15 DICKENS The brown-paper parcel had 'come untied'.
IV *v.t.* 17 Traverse (a route, a distance). E17. 18 Approach (a specified age) as the next birthday. Chiefly as *coming* pres. pple. L17. 19 Play (a dodge, a trick); behave as. (Foll. by *over* the person taken in.) L18. 20 Achieve; succeed in doing. Chiefly as *come it. US* & *dial.* E19.
19 J. CARY She apologised for coming the don.
V *spec.* uses of parts of the vb. 21 In *imper.* a An invitation or encouragement to do something, usu. with the speaker. OE. b An exclam. expressing mild protest, remonstrance, or impatience at someone. ME. 22 *coming* pres. pple: a response to a call, 'I am coming.' E18.
Phrases: (A selection of cross-refs. only is included.) **as (tough etc.) as they come** *colloq.*: supremely so. *come a cropper*: see CROPPER *n.*² *come a gutser*: see GUTSER *n.* *come a long way*: see WAY *n.* **come and go** (*a*) come to a place and depart again; (*b*) be first

present and then absent; (of time) arrive and pass. *come a purler*: see PURLER I. *come a stumer*: see STUMER 1b. *come clean*: see CLEAN *a. come easy to*: see EASY *adv.* I. *come home (to)*: see HOME *adv. come home to roost*: see ROOST *n.*[1] *come home with the milk*: see MILK *n. come in one's way*: see WAY *n.* **come into one's head** occur to one. *come into question*: see QUESTION *n. come into the world*: see WORLD *n.* **come it over** *colloq.* seek to impose on or to impress deceptively. **come it strong** *slang* go to excessive lengths, use exaggeration. *come naturally to*: see NATURALLY I. *come of age*: see AGE *n.* 2. **come off it** *colloq.* stop talking or acting like that; stop trying to fool the hearer; (usu. in *imper.*). **come one's way** become available or accessible to one; happen to one. *come one's ways*: see WAY *n. come on strong, come out strong*: see STRONG *adv. come out in the wash*: see WASH *n. come rain or shine*: see RAIN *n.*[1] *come short*: see SHORT *adv.* †*come short home*: see HOME *adv. come tardy off*: see TARDY *adv.* **come the old soldier over** *slang* seek to impose on (someone), esp. on grounds of greater experience or age. *come the raw prawn (on, over, with)*: see PRAWN *n. come the* ROTHSCHILD. **come to a bad end** meet with ruin or disgrace. **come to an end** terminate, end. **come to a point** taper. **come to think of it** *colloq.* when one considers; on reflection. *come true*: see TRUE *a., n., & adv. come unstuck*: see UNSTICK *v.* **come what may** whatever may happen. *everything coming one's way*: see WAY *n. have another think coming*: see THINK *n.* **have it coming to one** *colloq.* have one's just deserts coming. *how come?*: see HOW *adv. kingdom come*: see KINGDOM *n.* 4. *let 'em all come*: see LET *v.*[1] *not come to much*: see MUCH. *see a person coming*: see SEE *v. see it coming*: see SEE *v. shape of things to come*: see SHAPE *n.*[1] *take things as they come*: see TAKE *v. the world to come*: see WORLD *n.* **to come** (*a*) *pred.* in the future; (*b*) *postpositive* future; (*c*) *absol.* the future. *when a person's ship comes home* (or *in*): see SHIP *n.* I.

With advs. in specialized senses: (See also phrases above.) **come about** (*a*) happen, come to pass; (*b*) = *come round* (a) below; (*c*) (now *rare* or *obs.*) (of the wind) = *come round* (d) below; (of a boat) change direction. **come abroad** *arch.* come out from seclusion, appear. *come across*: see ACROSS *adv.* 2. **come again** (*a*) return; (*b*) recover from faintness etc.; (*c*) (as *interrog. imper.*) what did you say?; (*d*) (of a racehorse) regain speed. **come along** (*a*) move onward (toward or with the speaker); freq. in *imper.* (*colloq.*), make haste or an effort; (*b*) make progress; (*c*) arrive, turn up. **come amiss** happen out of order; be unacceptable; (usu. in neg.). **come apart** fall into pieces (*come apart at the seams*: see SEAM *n.*[1]). **come away** (*a*) (of a plant) grow rapidly; (*b*) become detached; (*c*) be left *with* an impression, feeling, etc. **come back** (*a*) return, esp. to memory, or to a former state of popularity; (*b*) regain consciousness; (*c*) *N. Amer.* retort, retaliate; (*d*) (of an athlete) regain form, or the initiative in an event. **come by** pass by. **come down** (*a*) come to a place regarded as lower; *spec.* fall, (of an aircraft) land; *come down to earth* (colloq.), return to reality; (*b*) lose social status; (*c*) become lower in cost or value; (*d*) *come down on* or *upon*: attack suddenly or severely; make a heavy call on; punish, reprimand; (*e*) survive from an earlier time, be handed down; (*f*) *colloq.* pay out, give money, (foll. by *with* money etc.); (*g*) *Austral., NZ, & S. Afr.* (of a river) flow in flood; (*h*) *come down to*: be basically a matter of; amount to, mean in essence; *come down to it*, get to basic principles; (*i*) become ill (*with*); (*j*) decide (*in favour of* etc.); (*k*) end a period of residence in a university. **come forward** approach the front; offer oneself for a task, post, etc.; make advances (*lit.* & *fig.*). **come in** (*a*) enter a house or a room; (*b*) come into use; become fashionable or seasonable; (*c*) invade, occupy; become a partner in a company; *come in on*, join (an enterprise); †(*d*) *come in unto*, have sexual intercourse with; †(*e*) submit (*to* an adversary); (*f*) (of a time or a season) begin; †(*g*) *come in with*, meet, fall in with; (*h*) be brought or given in; be received as income; (*i*) enter into a narrative, list, etc.; find a place, esp. with reference to manner or position; *where a person comes in*, what his or her role is, how his or her interests are advanced, (usu. in *interrog.*); *where a person came in* (colloq.), back where he or she started or at a stage reached previously; *come in nowhere*: see NOWHERE *adv.* 3; †(*j*) *Fencing* get within the opponent's guard; (*k*) arrive, reach a destination; take a specified place in a race; (*l*) *come in for*: receive, esp. incidentally; attract (criticism etc.); *come in for it* (colloq.), incur punishment or a rebuke; (*m*) come to power, be elected; (*n*) *dial.* & *US* (of a cow) calve; (*o*) *Cricket* begin an innings; (*p*) (of the tide) advance; (*q*) be (useful etc.) as something to have available; (*r*) *come in on* or *upon*, enter one's thoughts; (*s*) begin radio transmission; start speaking, in a discussion. *come near*: see NEAR *adv.*[2] **come off** (*a*) come away from, leave (esp. a port or mooring); (*b*) emerge from a contest etc. in a specified manner or state; (*come off second-best*: see SECOND-BEST *a.* & *adv.*, *come off with flying colours*: see COLOUR *n.*); †(*c*) (of a thing) turn out, come to a result; (*d*) take place; †(*e*) pay; †(*f*) get off, escape; (*g*) become detached; be detachable; (*h*) *colloq.* be successful or effective; (*i*) *US slang* = *come off it* in Phrases above; (*j*) fall from a horse, a bicycle, etc.; (*k*) *Cricket* cease bowling; (*l*) (of a show) reach the end of its run; (*m*) cease to be assigned to (a task etc.); cease to use (*come off the pill*: see PILL *n.*[3] 1c); (see also sense 15 above). **come on** (*a*) continue coming; advance, esp. to attack; arrive having come *from* a previous place of arrival; (*b*) supervene; begin *to* rain or blow; (*c*) make progress, improve; thrive; (*d*) arise to be discussed or dealt with; (*e*) appear on stage or a scene of action; begin to be heard on the radio or telephone, or be seen on a cinema or television screen; (*f*) *Cricket* begin to bowl; (*g*) in *imper.*: hurry up; follow me; please do what I ask; I defy you. **come out** (*a*) come out of a place, *spec.* to fight; begin a strike; leave a place where it was fixed or held; (*b*) become public, become known; (of a card) be played; (of a game of patience) go to the finish, with all cards played and their desired arrangement achieved; (*c*) be published; (*d*) (of a plant, disease, etc.) come into visible development; *Photogr.* give rise to a satisfactory image; become covered *in* a rash etc.; (*e*) show or declare oneself publicly (*for* or *against* something); *spec.* cease to conceal one's homosexuality; (*f*) (of a girl) make her formal entry into upper-class society; make a début on stage; (*g*) (of the sun etc.) emerge from cloud; become visible; (*h*) show itself prominently; become explicit; (*i*) finish up (in a certain way or at a certain value), esp. after a contest or a calculation; (*j*) extend, project; (*k*) (of a stain or mark) be removed; (*l*) *come right out* (*with it*) (N. Amer. colloq.), speak frankly or tactlessly; (*m*) *come out of*: emerge from (a place); be brought from; pass out of (a state); proceed or result from; (*n*) *come out with*, utter; blurt. **come over** (*a*) come, in the process crossing an obstacle or travelling a distance; (*b*) change sides, to one's own; (*c*) pass over during distillation; (*d*) *colloq.* (with following adj.) have a specified feeling come over one; adopt a specified manner; (*come over all unnecessary*: see UNNECESSARY *a.* 1); (*e*) convey one's meaning or an impression; (*come over big*: see BIG *adv.*). **come round** (*a*) come with the passage of time, recur; (*b*) come in the course of a circuit or a circuitous route; (*c*) make an informal or casual visit; (*d*) (of the wind) change to a more favourable quarter; hence, change for the better, esp. after faintness, bad temper, etc.; be converted to another person's opinion. *come short*: see SHORT *adv.* **come through** (*a*) survive an experience; attain an end; (*come through with flying colours*: see COLOUR *n.*); (*b*) arrive after passing through a system, process, etc.; (*c*) act as desired or expected; provide what is required; (*d*) succeed in giving a favourable impression. **come to** (*a*) *Naut.* cease moving, heave to; (*b*) (*obs.* exc. *dial.*) recover one's calmness or good humour; (*c*) regain consciousness; revive. **come up** (*a*) come to a place regarded as higher, *spec.* to London; come into residence at a university; (of food) be vomited; (*b*) approach close *to*; *be coming up*, be approached in the course of travel; *come up smiling*, emerge cheerfully and undaunted from an unpleasant experience; (*c*) originate; come into use or fashion; (*d*) appear above the soil; rise through water or above its surface; (*e*) attain or be equal *to* a certain standard; *come up to scratch*: see SCRATCH *n.*[1]; (*f*) *Naut.* come to a specified direction; change course towards the wind; (*g*) come forward from the rear; get abreast (*with*); *be come up with* (US), be outwitted; (*h*) be presented in court, or *for* a decision, sale, etc.; (*i*) arise, occur; be mentioned in talk; (*j*) (of theatre lights) become brighter; (of something cleaned or renovated) look cleaner or brighter; (*k*) *coming up* (colloq.): said when food is about to be served; (*l*) *marry come up!* see MARRY *int.*; (*m*) *come up with* (colloq.), produce in response to a challenge.

With preps. in specialized senses: (See also Phrases above.) **come across** meet or find by chance. **come at** (*a*) (now *dial.*) approach, come to; (*b*) reach, get access to, esp. with effort; (*c*) come suddenly and aggressively towards; (*d*) *Austral.* & *NZ colloq.* agree to do or accept. **come before** (*a*) be presented for consideration by (a judge, court, etc.); (*b*) be given priority over. *come between*: see BETWEEN *prep.* 5. **come by** get hold of, obtain; receive. **come for** = *come at* (c) above. **come into** †(*a*) accede to, fall in with; (*b*) come into possession of, esp. as an heir; (see also sense 9 above). **come of** become of, happen to; (see also sense 8 above). **come on** = *come upon* below. **come over** †(*a*) surpass; (*b*) take possession of (*fig.*), affect persuasively; (*c*) happen to, befall (a person); influence for the worse; (*d*) *colloq.* get the better of by craft. **come to** (*a*) *come to oneself, one's senses*: regain consciousness; recover from excitement, passion, etc.; (*b*) add up to, cost, amount to (*lit.* & *fig.*), be equivalent to; *if it comes to that, come to that* (colloq.), in fact; (*c*) result in; tend towards (a condition disapproved of). **come under** (*a*) be classed as, be included under; (*b*) become subject to (an influence etc.). **come upon** (*a*) attack, esp. suddenly; (*b*) affect in an overwhelming or supernatural way; (*c*) make a demand or claim upon; (*d*) = *come across* above; (*e*) become a burden or charge on.

Comb.: **come-at-able** *a.* (*colloq.*) accessible; obtainable; **come-between** a person who or thing which intervenes; **come-by-chance** *colloq.* an illegitimate child; **comedown** a downfall; a drop in status or official position; **come-hither** *n.* & *a.* (*colloq.*) (*a*) *n.* enticement, allure; (*b*) *adj.* enticing, flirtatious; **come-off** (*a*) a conclusion, finish; (*b*) an excuse for non-performance; **come-outer** *US* a person who dissociates himself or herself from an organization; **come-o'-will** *Sc.* a thing that comes of its own accord; an illegitimate child.

comeback /'kʌmbak/ *n.* L19. [f. *come back* s.v. COME *v.*] **1** An act of retaliation; a retort, a critical reaction; an opportunity to seek redress. *slang.* L19. **2** A sheep three-quarters merino and one quarter crossbred; the skin or fleece of such a sheep. *Austral.* & *NZ.* L19. **3** A return to a former favourable position; a reinstatement. E20. **4** A person who has come back; *spec.* a ghost. E20.

Comecon /'kɒmɪkɒn/ *n.* M20. [Abbrev. of *Council for Mutual Economic Assistance* (or *Aid*), tr. Russ. *Sovet Ėkonomicheskoĭ Vzaimopomoshchi.*] An economic association of Communist countries, chiefly in eastern Europe.

†**co-meddle** *v.t. rare.* Also **commeddle**. Only in E17. [f. CO-, COM- + MEDDLE *v.*] Mix or mingle together.

comedian /kə'miːdɪən/ *n.* L16. [Fr. *comédien*, f. *comédie* COMEDY: see -IAN.] **1** A writer of comedies. L16. **2** A comic actor; occas., any actor. E17. **3** An entertainer whose act is designed to make the audience laugh; an amusing person (freq. *iron.*). L19.

2 *low comedian*: see LOW *a.* & *n.*[4] **3** *alternative comedian*: see ALTERNATIVE *a.* 3b.

comedic /kə'miːdɪk, -'mɛ-/ *a.* M17. [L *comoedicus* f. Gk *kōmōdikos*, f. *kōmōdia* COMEDY: see -IC.] Of or pertaining to comedy; comic.

comédie /kɔmedi/ *n.* Pl. pronounced same. E19. [Fr.: see COMEDY.] **1** *comédie larmoyante* /larmwajɑ̃t/, pl. *-antes* /-ɑ̃t/ [Fr. *larmoyant* weeping], a sentimental, moralizing comedy. E19. **2** *comédie humaine* /ymɛn/, pl. *-aines* /-ɛn/ [Fr. *humain* HUMAN *a.*, humane], the sum of human activities; a literary portrait of this. L19. **3** *comédie noire* /nwaːr/, pl. *-res* /-r/ [Fr. *noir* black], a macabre or farcical rendering of a violent or tragic theme. Cf. BLACK *a.* 8b. M20.

comedienne /kəmiːdɪ'ɛn, -mɛ-/ *n.* Also **-éd-** /-eɪd-/. M19. [Fr., fem. of *comédien* COMEDIAN.] A female comedian.

alternative comedienne: see ALTERNATIVE *a.* 3b.

comedietta /kəmiːdɪ'ɛtə/ *n.* M19. [It., f. *comedia* (now *-mm-*) f. L *comoedia* COMEDY + *-etta* -ET[1].] A short or slight comedy.

comedist /'kɒmədɪst/ *n.* E19. [f. COMEDY + -IST.] A writer of comedies.

comedo /'kɒmɪdəʊ, kə'miːdəʊ/ *n.* Pl. **comedos**, **comedones** /kɒmɪ'dəʊniːz/. M19. [L = glutton, f. *comedere* eat up (see COMESTIBLE).] *Med.* A blackhead.

comedy /'kɒmɪdi/ *n.* LME. [(O)Fr. *comédie* f. L *comoedia* f. Gk *kōmōidia*, f. *kōmōidos* comic actor, comic poet, f. *kōmos* revel + *aoidos* singer (f. *aeidein* sing).] **1 a** A narrative poem with a happy ending. *obs.* exc. in *The Divine Comedy* [tr. *La Divina Commedia*] of Dante. LME. **b** A drama (on stage, film, or radio) with a happy ending, chiefly representing everyday life and of a light, amusing, and often satirical character; any literary composition with similar characteristics. E16. **2 a** A genre of drama etc. characterized by its depiction of amusing characters or incidents and an informal style. LME. **b** Humour; humorous behaviour. L19. **3** A humorous or farcical incident in life; such incidents collectively. L16.

1b SHAKES. *L.L.L.* A consent, Knowing aforehand, of our merriment, To dash it like a Christmas comedy. T. RANDOLPH A pleasant Comedie entituled Hey for Honesty.. translated out of Aristophanes his Plutus. BYRON All comedies are ended by a marriage. 2b F. HURST Come on,.. cut the comedy.

Phrases: *alternative comedy*: see ALTERNATIVE *a.* 3b. **comedy of manners**: in which modes and manners of society are satirically or amusingly portrayed. *low comedy*: see LOW *a.* & *n.*[4] *musical comedy*: see MUSICAL *a.* SITUATION *comedy*.

¶Cf. TRAGEDY.

comeling /ˈkʌmlɪŋ/ *n.* Now *arch.* & *dial.* ME. [f. COME *v.* + -LING[1].] A newcomer, an immigrant; a stranger.

comely /ˈkʌmli/ *a.* ME. [Prob. aphet. f. BECOMELY. Cf. MHG *komlich* suitable (beside *bekōme* suitably; G dial. *komm-*, *kömmlich*), Du. †*komlick* fitting.] 1 Pleasing to the eye; *esp.* (of a person) attractive without being beautiful. ME. 2 Pleasing to the moral sense or aesthetic taste; becoming, proper, decorous. ME. 3 *gen.* Pleasing, agreeable. *arch.* ME.

2 R. HOGGART A good and comely life.

comelily *adv.* (now *rare* or *obs.*) ME. **comeliness** *n.* LME.

come-on /ˈkʌmɒn/ *n.* & *a. slang.* L19. [f. *come on* s.v. COME *v.*] A *n.* 1 A dupe. L19. 2 A swindler. E20. 3 An enticement, an invitation to approach. E20. B *adj.* Enticing. E20.

comer /ˈkʌmə/ *n.* LME. [f. COME *v.* + -ER[1].] 1 A person who comes; a visitor. Usu. qualified by prec. adj. or pref. LME. 2 A person who shows promise. *colloq.* L19.

1 *first comer, home-comer, incomer, newcomer*, etc. **all comers** anyone who chooses to come or take part; a sporting event open to anyone. *late comer*: see LATE *a.*

comes /ˈkəʊmiːz/ *n.* Pl. **comites** /-ɪtiːz/. M18. [L = companion, f. as COM- + *ire*, *it-* go.] *Mus.* An answering or imitating voice in a canon or fugue; the answer itself. Opp. DUX I.

comestible /kəˈmɛstɪb(ə)l/ *a.* & *n.* L15. [(O)Fr. f. med.L *comestibilis*, f. L *comest-* pa. ppl stem of *comedere* eat up, f. as COM- + *edere* eat: see -IBLE.] †A *adj.* Edible. L15–L17. B *n.* An article of food. Usu. in *pl.* Usu. *formal* or *joc.* M19.

comet /ˈkɒmɪt/ *n.* & *a.* Also †**-eta**. LOE. [((O)Fr. *comète* f.) L *cometa* f. Gk *komētēs* long-haired (star), f. *komaein* wear the hair long, f. *komē* hair.] A *n.* 1 *Astron.* A celestial object that orbits the sun in a highly elliptical path and, when in the vicinity of the sun, usu. has a bright hazy head and a long more diffuse tail. LOE. b *fig.* A portent; a herald. L16. 2 A card-game ancestral to Newmarket. L17.

1 *Oort('s) comet cloud*: see OORT 2.

Comb.: **comet-finder, -seeker** a telescope of low power and large field of view, used in searching for comets; **comet-year**: in which a notable comet has appeared.

B *adj.* Designating wine made in a comet-year, supposed to have superior qualities. M19.

cometary *a.* of or pertaining to a comet or comets; like a comet: M17. **coˈmetic, -ical** *adjs.* cometary; *fig.* blazing; portentous; erratic: M17.

come-uppance /kʌmˈʌp(ə)ns/ *n. colloq.* M19. [f. COME *v.* + UP *adv.*[1] + -ANCE.] One's deserts (for misbehaviour etc.).

comfit /ˈkʌmfɪt/ *n.* & *v.* ME. [OFr. *confit(e)* f. L *confectum*, *-ta* use as n. of neut. and fem. of *confectus* pa. pple of *conficere* prepare: see CONFECT *v.*] A *n.* A sweet containing a nut, seed, etc., preserved with sugar. ME. †B *v.t.* Preserve, pickle; make (a nut, fruit, etc.) into a comfit. LME–M18.

†**comfiture** *n.* var. of CONFITURE.

comfort /ˈkʌmfət/ *n.* ME. [OFr. *confort* f. Proto-Romance, f. late L *confortare*: see next.] 1 Strengthening, encouragement; aid, support; a support, a source of strength; refreshment. Now only in *aid and comfort* (arch., in Law). ME. †2 Pleasure, enjoyment; gladness. ME–M16. 3 Relief or support in distress or affliction; consolation, solace; the state of being consoled. ME. 4 A person who or thing which affords consolation; a cause of satisfaction or relief. LME. 5 A thing that produces or ministers to a state of physical and mental ease; a thing that makes life easy. Usu. in *pl.* M17. 6 A state of physical and material well-being; the condition of being comfortable. E19. 7 A warm quilt. *US.* M19.

3 H. FIELDING Others applying for comfort to strong liquors. GEO. ELIOT She had.. a sense of solemn comfort. 4 D. M. MULOCK Growing up to be a help and comfort to my father. E. M. FORSTER His comfort was that the pater's eyes were opened at last. 5 S. JOHNSON Before they quit the comforts of a warm home. J. HELLER Some new comfort Orr had installed .. running water, wood-burning fireplace, cement floor. 6 JAN MORRIS The heads of colleges live in almost unrivalled comfort, in lovely old houses with attentive servants. R. COBB Edward driving, which he did much too fast for my comfort.

Phrases: *cold comfort*: see COLD *a.* **creature comforts** good food, clothes, etc. *curate's comfort*: see CURATE *n.* *letter of comfort*: see LETTER *n.*[1] *Southern Comfort*: see SOUTHERN *a.*

Comb.: **comfort station** *US* a public lavatory.

comfortful *a.* full of comfort, comforting M16. **comfortless** *a.* without comfort; dreary, cheerless: LME. **comfortlessly** *adv.* M16.

comfort /ˈkʌmfət/ *v.* ME. [OFr. *conforter* f. late L *confortare* strengthen, f. as COM- + *fortis* strong.] †1 *v.t.* Strengthen (morally or physically); encourage, hearten; invigorate, refresh. ME–E18. †2 *v.t.* Give delight or pleasure to; gladden; entertain. ME–E17. †3 *v.t.* Lend support to; give relief to; assist, aid. ME–L18. 4 *v.t.* Soothe in grief and trouble; console; solace. ME. †b *v.i.* Take comfort. *rare* (Shakes.). Only in E17. 5 *v.t.* Allay physical discomfort; make comfortable. L19.

1 COVERDALE *2 Sam.* 2:7 Let youre hande now therfore be comforted, and be ye stronge. R. COPLAND The water.. that conforteth and clereth the syght. 2 SHAKES. *Jul. Caes.* To keep with you at meals, comfort your bed, and talk to you sometimes. 3 J. AYLIFFE Guilty of comforting and assisting the Rebels. WORDSWORTH She quite forgot to send the Doctor To comfort poor old Susan Gale. 4 S. RICHARDSON She comforted herself, that Sir Charles would to able to soften their resentments. E. HEMINGWAY I comforted her and she stopped crying. 5 M. E. BRADDON Refreshed by the coffee and comforted by the warmth of the stove.

comfortable /ˈkʌmf(ə)təb(ə)l/ *a.* & *n.* ME. [AN *confortable*, f. as prec.: see -ABLE.] A *adj.* I Active. †1 Giving mental or spiritual delight; pleasant; pleasing to the senses. ME–M18. †b Satisfactory; *colloq.* tolerable, fairly good. M17–E18. 2 Strengthening (morally, spiritually, or †physically); sustaining; encouraging, reassuring. *arch.* LME. †b Helpful, serviceable. L16–E18. 3 Affording or conveying consolation; comforting; consolatory. *arch.* LME. 4 Such as to obviate hardship, save trouble, and promote content; ministering to comfort; freeing from anxiety or concern. M18. b (Of a margin) large enough to avoid any challenge or doubt; (of a victory) achieved with ease. M20.

2 G. BERKELEY The comfortable expectation of Immortality. **the Comfortable Words** four scriptural passages following and confirming the absolution in some Eucharistic rites. b DEFOE Their.. canoes which had been so comfortable to them. 3 SHAKES. *All's Well* Be comfortable to my mother.., and make much of her. 4 N. SHUTE On the table at a comfortable height for Elspeth. P. REDGROVE A very comfortable income.

II Passive & neutral. †5 Consoled; cheerful. L16–M18. 6 At ease, free from hardship, pain, and trouble; enjoying comfort; having ample money for one's needs; having an easy conscience. L18. b Undisturbed; complacent; placidly self-satisfied. *colloq.* M19.

6 OED I am not.. quite comfortable about the matter. E. M. FORSTER Would she not be more comfortable.. at the hotel? W. FAULKNER She was of comfortable people—not the best in Jefferson, but good people enough. b B. PYM The comfortable assumption of so much that could be left to the women.

B *n.* †1 A source of comfort; a creature comfort. M17–L18. 2 A warm article of clothing, a comforter; *US* a warm quilt. M19.

comfortableness *n.* L16. **comfortably** *adv.* in a comfortable manner; so as to be comfortable; (*comfortably off*, having ample money for one's needs): LME.

†**comfortative** *a.* & *n.* LME. [OFr. *confortatif*, *-ive* f. late L *confortativus*, f. *confortare*: see COMFORT *v.*, -ATIVE.] A *adj.* Strengthening, reviving; cheering. LME–L17. B *n.* A thing which strengthens or revives, *esp.* a restorative medicine or cordial. LME–L19.

comforter /ˈkʌmfətə/ *n.* LME. [Partly f. AN *confortour* = OFr. *confortëor*, f. as COMFORT *v.*, -OUR, -ER[2]; partly (as a title of the Holy Spirit) tr. eccl.L *consolator* rendering Gk *paraklētos* PARACLETE.] 1 A person who or thing which gives comfort. LME. †2 A small kind of spaniel. L16–E19. 3a A warm garment; *spec.* a long woollen scarf. E19. b A warm quilt. *N. Amer.* M19. 4 A baby's dummy teat of rubber etc. L19.

1 *Job's comforter*: see JOB *n.*[3] **The Comforter** *Chr. Theol.* the Holy Spirit.

†**comfortive** *a.* & *n.* LME–E19. [f. COMFORT *v.* + -IVE.] = COMFORTATIVE.

comfortress /ˈkʌmfətrɪs/ *n.* Now *rare.* LME. [OFr. *conforteresse* fem. of *confortère* comforter: see -ESS[1].] A female comforter.

comfrey /ˈkʌmfri/ *n.* ME. [AN *cumfirie*, OFr. *confi(e)re* (mod. dial. *confier* etc.), also *confierge*, f. med.L *cumfiria* for L *conferva*, f. *confervere* heal, (lit.) boil together, f. as CON- + *fervere* boil.] A plant of the genus *Symphytum*, of the borage family; esp. *S. officinale*, which has rough leaves and bears drooping clusters of white or purple flowers, and was formerly much used to treat wounds.

comfy /ˈkʌmfi/ *a. colloq.* E19. [Abbrev.: see -Y[1].] Comfortable.

comfily *adv.* E20.

comic /ˈkɒmɪk/ *a.* & *n.* L16. [L *comicus* f. Gk *kōmikos* f. *kōmos* revel: see -IC.] A *adj.* 1 Pertaining to or in the style of comedy. L16. 2 Causing or meant to cause laughter; facetious; burlesque; funny. M18.

2 W. S. MAUGHAM Our use of the same word.. had a comic effect, so that we were obliged to laugh. J. IRVING I promise.. to perform comic stunts and make you laugh all night.

Special collocations: **comic book** a book of strip cartoons. **comic opera**: with much spoken dialogue, and usu. humorous treatment. **comic paper** = sense B.3 below. **comic relief** comic episodes in a play etc. intended to offset more serious portions; the relaxation of tension etc. provided by such episodes. **comic strip** a strip cartoon telling a comic story.

B *n.* †1 A comic writer; = COMEDIAN I. E17–M18. †2a A comic actor; = COMEDIAN 2. E17–E18. b An entertainer whose act is designed to make the audience laugh; an amusing person. Cf. COMEDIAN 3. E20. 3 A light or amusing paper; a periodical with narrative mainly in pictures (orig. and chiefly for children); in *pl.* also, comic strips in a newspaper etc. L19. b A comic film, television programme, etc. E20.

3 HORROR *comic*.

¶Cf. TRAGIC.

comical /ˈkɒmɪk(ə)l/ *a.* LME. [f. as prec. + -AL[1].] †1 = COMIC *a.* I. LME–E18. †2 Of style, subject, etc.: befitting comedy, trivial, low. L16–L17. †3 Like the ending of a comedy, happy, fortunate. L16–L17. 4 Causing laughter; humorous, jocose, funny; ludicrous, risible. L17. 5 Strange, odd; difficult to deal with; out of sorts, unwell. *colloq.* & *dial.* L18.

comiˈcality *n.* comic quality; a comical thing: L18. **comically** *adv.* E17. **comicalness** L17.

Comice /ˈkɒmɪs/ *n.* L20. [Fr. = association, co-operative, spec. the *Comice Horticole* of Angers, France, where the variety was developed.] A kind of pear, = *Doyenne du Comice* s.v. DOYENNE *n.*[1]

comico- /ˈkɒmɪkəʊ/ *comb. form.* [f. L *comicus*, Gk *kōmikos*: see COMIC, -O-.] Forming chiefly adjs. w. the sense 'comic and', as *comico-tragic(al)* etc.

†**comilitant** *n.* & *a.* var. of COMMILITANT.

Cominform /ˈkɒmɪnfɔːm/ *n.* M20. [f. *Com(munist Inform(ation (Bureau).)* *Hist.* A former Soviet-led agency of international Communism in Europe.

Cominformist *a.* & *n.* supporting, a supporter of, the Cominform or Soviet rather than national (esp. Yugoslavian) Communist policy M20.

coming /ˈkʌmɪŋ/ *n.* ME. [f. COME *v.* + -ING[1].] 1 The action of COME *v.*; a movement towards or arrival at a specified or understood point, time, or result. Also foll. by adv. or prep. ME. †2 A means of access, an approach; *coming in*, a means of entrance, an entry. LME–E18. 3 *comings in*, revenues, receipts. L16.

1 MILTON At his coming to the Crown. T. S. ELIOT A cold coming we had of it. R. GITTINGS His financial position at coming-of-age. A. POWELL A . . dance on the 'coming out' of a daughter. *second coming*: see SECOND *a.*

coming /ˈkʌmɪŋ/ *a.* LME. [f. COME *v.* + -ING[2].] 1 That comes. Also foll. by adv. LME. 2 Inclined to make or meet advances; ready, eager, complaisant, forward. *arch.* L16. 3 Likely to be important in the future, rising into prominence. M19.

1 *have (got) another guess coming*: see GUESS *n.* 3 H. ROBBINS People will pay to see the pictures. . . It's the coming thing.

comingle *v.* var. of COMMINGLE.

Comintern /ˈkɒmɪntəːn/ *n.* E20. [Russ. *Komintern*, f. *kom(munisticheskiĭ* communist + *intern(atsional'nyĭ* international.] The Third International (see INTERNATIONAL *n.* 2).

comitadji /kɒmɪˈtadʒi/ *n.* Also **komitadji, komitaji.** E20. [Turk. *komitacı* lit. 'member of a (revolutionary) committee'.] A member of a band of irregular soldiers in the Balkans; *spec.* (*Hist.*) a Balkan rebel against the Ottoman Empire before the war of 1914–18.

comital /ˈkɒmɪt(ə)l/ *a.* M19. [med.L *comitalis*, f. *comit-*, *comes* in sense 'a count': see -AL[1].] Of or pertaining to a count or earl; of the rank of a count or earl.

comitant /ˈkɒmɪt(ə)nt/ *a.* & *n. rare.* E17. [L *comitant-* pres. ppl stem of *comitari* accompany, f. *comit- comes* companion: see -ANT[1].] (Something) accompanying; (a) concomitant.

comitative /ˈkɒmɪtətɪv/ *a.* M19. [f. L *comitat-* pa. ppl stem of *comitari* (see prec.), + -IVE.] *Gram.* Expressing accompaniment or association.

comitatus /kɒmɪˈteɪtəs/ *n.* Pl. same. L19. [L *comitatus*, f. *comit-*, *comes* companion: see -ATE[1].] *Hist.* A body of warriors, nobles, etc., attached to the person of a king or chieftain; the status of such a body.

See also POSSE COMITATUS.

comites *n.* pl. of COMES.

comitia /kəˈmɪʃə, -ʃɪə/ *n.pl.* (also treated as *sing.*). E17. [L, pl. of *comitium* assembly, f. as COM- + *-itium*, f. *it-*, *ire* go.] 1 *gen.* An assembly. *rare.* E17. 2 An assembly of the Fellows of the Royal College of Physicians, London. L17. 3 *Rom. Hist.* An assembly of the Roman people to elect magistrates and pass legislation. M18.

comitial /kəˈmɪʃ(ə)l, -ʃɪəl/ *a.* M16. [L *comitialis*, f. as prec.: see -AL[1].] 1 *Rom. Hist.* Of or pertaining to the comitia. M16. †2 Designating or pertaining to any of various Presbyterian or political assemblies. L16–L18.

comity /ˈkɒmɪti/ *n.* M16. [L *comitas*, f. *comis* courteous: see -ITY.] 1 Courtesy, civility; kindly and considerate behaviour towards others. M16. 2a *comity of nations*, *international comity*, the friendly recognition as far as is practicable by nations of each other's laws and usages. M19. b An association of or *of* nations etc. for mutual benefit; the community of civilized nations. M19.

2b C. R. ATTLEE Germany was back in the comity of nations. P. USTINOV Voices which spoke for Russia in the comity of civilised people.

comma /ˈkɒmə/ *n.* L16. [L f. Gk *komma* piece cut off, short clause.] 1 In *Class. Pros.* & *Rhet.*, a phrase or group of words shorter than a colon (COLON *n.*[2] 1); *loosely* (now *rare* or *obs.*) a short clause or phrase within a sentence. L16. †b A clause or short passage of a treatise or argument. L16–L17. 2 A punctuation mark (now ,) indicating the least discontinuity of grammatical construction, also used to separate (groups of) figures etc. L16. b A short pause such as may be indicated by a comma. L16. c *fig.* A break of continuity, an interval, a pause. E17. 3 *Mus.* A definite minute interval or difference of pitch. L16. 4 In full *inverted comma*. A comma (sense 2) placed upside down (single or paired) above the line before a quotation; in *pl.* also, quotation marks (including the erect comma(s) or apostrophe(s) above the line closing a quotation). E18. 5 In full *comma butterfly*. A nymphalid butterfly, *Polygonia c-album*, having a white comma-shaped mark on the underside of the wing. M18. 6 In full *comma bacillus*. A cholera bacillus (of curved shape). L19.

command /kəˈmɑːnd/ *n.* LME. [f. the vb.] 1 The act of commanding; an authoritative statement that a person must do something; an order, bidding; a commandment. LME. b A symbolic expression which defines an operation in a computer; a signal initiating the performance of such an operation. M20. 2 The faculty of commanding; rule, control; the exercise or tenure of authority, esp. naval or military. Also, a commander's position. LME. b Those in command. Esp. in *the high(er) command*, the army commander-in-chief and his staff. E20. 3 Power of control, sway, mastery, possession. M16. b Domination from an elevated or superior strategic position; range of vision, outlook, prospect. E17. c Despotism, coercion. *rare.* L17. 4 A body of troops, a district, etc., under a commander (esp. naval or military) or one particular authority; a unit of an army, air force, etc., organized for a particular duty or operating in a particular area. L16.

1 **at** or **by a person's command** in pursuance of a person's bidding. **word of command** the customary order for movement in drill; spoken signal to begin. 2 DRYDEN He assumed an absolute command over his readers. LD MACAULAY The places and commands which he held under the Crown. C. S. FORESTER The command of a regular brigade of cavalry. **in command (of)** commanding, in control (of). *second in command*: see SECOND *a.* **under (the) command of** commanded by. 3 B. JOWETT Having gifts of courage . . and command of money and friends. I. COMPTON-BURNETT Duncan . . had lost his command of himself. **at command** ready to be used at will. **command of language** skill in speech, articulacy. b K. DIGBY I . . gott my fleete out of command of the fortes. DRYDEN The steepy stand, which overlooks the vale with wide command. 4 G. CATLIN Colonel Dodge ordered the command to halt. B. HORROCKS Before the war Western Command had always been regarded as a backwater. *Bomber Command, Coastal Command, Fighter Command, Strike Command, Support Command, Transport Command*, etc.

Comb.: **command language** *Computing* a source language composed chiefly of a set of commands or operators, used esp. for communicating with the operating system of a computer; *spec.* a job control language; **command module** the control compartment of a spacecraft; **Command Paper** a paper laid by command of the Crown before Parliament etc.; **command performance** a theatrical etc. performance given by royal command; **command post** the headquarters of a military unit.

command /kəˈmɑːnd/ *v.* ME. [AN *comaunder*, OFr. *comander* (mod. *commander*) f. late L *commandare*, f. as COM- + *mandare* commit, enjoin: cf. COMMEND *v.*] I 1 *v.t.* Lay down as a command; give a command or commands to; order, bid, enjoin, with authority and influence. (With a command, a person etc. given a command (historically an indirect obj.), or both as object(s); a person etc. *to do*, (arch.) *do*, †*to* a thing; *that* something (*should*) *be* done; a person or thing *to be* + pa. pple.) ME. b *v.i.* Issue commands. LME. 2 *v.t. ellipt.* a Order to come or go *to*, *from*, *away*, etc. *arch.* LME. †b Order to be sent or given; demand. L16–L18. 3 *v.t.* Have authority over; be in command of (forces, a ship, etc.); be in control of; master, restrain, (oneself, one's passions, etc.). LME. b *v.i.* Have authority or control; be in command, be supreme. L16. 4 *v.t.* Have (a person etc.) at one's call; have (money, skill, etc.) at one's disposal or within easy reach. M16. 5 *v.t.* Deserve and get; exact, compel. L16. 6 *v.t.* Dominate from an elevated or superior strategic position; look down on or over. E17. b *v.i.* Dominate by looking down *over*; have a commanding position. E17.

1 AV *Acts* 25:6 He . . commanded Paul to be brought. W. BLACKSTONE The rule of life which religion commands. J. B. PRIESTLEY 'Go to Liverpool at once,' he commanded. E. O'NEILL His Imperial Majesty commands that you stop talking. T. CAPOTE When the next boy commanded him to halt, he at once obeyed. 2a MILTON Commanded home for doing too much. b SHAKES. *Cymb.* You have commanded of me these most poisonous compounds. 3 C. MARLOWE The haughty Dane commands the narrow seas. M. EDGEWORTH: F. commanded his temper. b DEFOE Colonel Forbes . . commanded at the siege. 4 A. C. BOULT Eugène Ysaÿe commanded a breadth of tone as a violinist which remains unmatched. H. WILSON Whether A or B can in fact command a majority in the House of Commons. **yours to command** *arch.*: a formula used for closing a letter. 5 K. TYNAN He could not command my sympathy nor even . . my interest. F. HERBERT He . . commanded their attention with a knuckle rap against the table. 6 J. RUSKIN My bedroom window commanded . . a very lovely view. E. BOWEN Combe Farm commanded the valley.

†II 7 *v.t.* Commend, recommend, confide, LME–M16.

commandable *a.* LME.

commandant /kɒmənˈdant, ˈkɒməndant; -ɑːnt/ *n.* L17. [Fr. *commandant*, It., Sp. *commandante*; in sense 2 Afk. *kommandant*: see COMMAND *v.*, -ANT[1].] 1 A commanding officer, esp. of a particular force, a military academy, etc. L17. 2 In *S. Afr. Hist.*, the leader of a Boer commando. Now, an officer in the South African armed forces ranking between a major and a colonel. L18.

2 **commandant-general** a commander-in-chief.

commandantship *n.* the office or position of commandant M19.

Commandaria /kɒmənˈdɛːrɪə/ *n.* Also **-eria** /-ɪərɪə/. E20. [med.L *commandaria* (from being made on the former commanderies): see COMMANDERY 1.] A sweet red or dark brown wine from Cyprus.

commandeer /kɒmənˈdɪə/ *v.t.* E19. [Afk. *kommandeer* f. Du. *commanderen* f. Fr. *commander* COMMAND *v.*] Seize (men or goods) for military service; take arbitrary possession of.

commander /kəˈmɑːndə/ *n.* ME. [OFr. *comandere*, *-ëor*, AN *comandour*, (mod. *commandeur*), f. Proto-Romance, f. late L *commandare*: see COMMAND *v.*, -ER[2].] 1 A person who commands; a person who has the control or disposal *of*; a ruler, a leader. ME. 2 *spec.* a An officer in command of a ship, a military force, etc.; a naval officer ranking next below a captain; an officer in charge of a London police district. LME. b *Hist.* The administrator of a commandery of a knightly order. E17. c More fully *knight commander*. A member of a higher class in some orders of knighthood. E19. 3 A large wooden mallet. L16. †4a A surgical instrument for reducing dislocations. L17–L18. b A mechanical device for straightening, reshaping, etc. L19.

1 **Commander of the Faithful**: a title of the Caliphs. 2a *master and commander*: see MASTER *n.*[1] *wing commander*: see WING *n.*

Comb.: **commander-in-chief** a supreme commander.

commandership *n.* the office or position of commander E17.

Commanderia *n.* var. of COMMANDARIA.

commandery /kəˈmɑːndəri/ *n.* Also **-dry** /-dri/. LME. [Fr. *commanderie*, f. as COMMANDER: see -ERY. Partly f. med.L *commendaria*, f. *commenda* benefice.] 1 *Hist.* An estate, manor, etc., belonging to a religious and military order of knights, as the Knights Hospitallers. LME. b A conventual priory of a non-military religious order. M16. †2 An ecclesiastical or other benefice held *in commendam*. M16–E19. †3 The tenure of command. L16–M17. 4 The rank of commander in an order of knighthood; a benefice or pension attached to such a commandership. E17. †5 A district under a commander. M17–E19.

commanding /kəˈmɑːndɪŋ/ *a.* L15. [f. COMMAND *v.* + -ING[2].] 1 Possessing or exercising command; ruling; controlling. L15. 2 Indicating or expressing command; (of a person,

For other words beginning with *co-* see the entry for **co-**

looks, ability, etc.) dignified, exalted, impressive. L16. 3 Dominating by an elevated or superior strategic position; (of a hill, position, etc.) affording command, giving a wide view. M17.

commandingly *adv.* LME. **commandingness** *n.* (*rare*) commanding quality L19.

commandite /kɒmən'diːt; *foreign* kəmɑ̃dit/ *n.* M19. [Fr., f. *commander* in sense 'entrust'.] A form of partnership in which a person may advance capital with no functions and strictly limited liability.

commandment /kə'mɑːn(d)m(ə)nt/ *n.* ME. [OFr. *comandement* (mod. *comm-*), f. *comander* COMMAND *v.*: see -MENT.] 1 *gen.* An authoritative order or injunction. *arch.* ME. 2 *spec.* A divine command. ME. †3 The action or fact of commanding; bidding. LME–L17. †4 Authority, sway, rule; military command. LME–M17. 5 *Law.* The offence of inducing another to break the law. *obs.* exc. *Hist.* E17.

2 *eleventh commandment*: see ELEVENTH *a.* **the Ten Commandments** those given by God to Moses on Mount Sinai (*Exod.* 20:1–7); *arch. colloq.* the ten fingernails (esp. of a woman).

commando /kə'mɑːndəʊ/ *n.* Pl. **-os.** L18. [Port. (now *comando*), f. *commandar* COMMAND *v.*] 1 A party, orig. of Boers or burghers in South Africa, called out for military purposes, a militia; *S. Afr. Hist.* a unit of the Boer army made up of the militia of an electoral district; a raiding-party, a raid, orig. against Black tribesmen; participation in such a raid. L18. 2 (A member of) a unit of British amphibious shock troops; (a member of) a similar unit elsewhere. M20.

1 **(up)on commando** engaged in a commando; on militia service in the Boer army.

†**commandore** *n.* see COMMODORE.

commandress /kə'mɑːndrɪs/ *n.* Now *rare.* L16. [f. COMMANDER + -ESS[1].] A female commander.

commandry *n.* var. of COMMANDERY.

commeasurable /kɒ'mɛʒ(ə)rəb(ə)l/ *a.* L17. [f. COM- + MEASURABLE.] = COMMENSURABLE.

commeasure /kə'mɛʒə/ *v.t.* E17. [f. COM- + MEASURE *v.*] Measure as an exact equivalent; be equal to in measure, be coextensive with.

comme ci, comme ça /kɔm si kɔm sa/ *adv.* & *a. phr.* M20. [Fr., lit. 'like this like that'.] So-so, middling(ly).

†**commeddle** *v.* var. of CO-MEDDLE.

commedia dell'arte /kɒm'meːdia dɛll'arte, kɒ'mɛdɪə dɛl'ɑːteɪ/ *n. phr.* L19. [It. = comedy of art.] The improvised popular comedy in Italian theatres between the 16th and 18th cents. with stock characters.

comme il faut /kɔm il fo, kɒm iːl fəʊ/ *adv.* & *pred. a. phr.* M18. [Fr., lit. 'as it is necessary'.] Proper(ly), correct(ly), as it should be (esp. of behaviour).

commemorate /kə'mɛməreɪt/ *v.t.* L16. [L *commemorat-* pa. ppl stem of *commemorare*, f. as COM- + *memorare* relate, f. *memor* (see MEMORY): see -ATE[3].] 1 Mention. Now *spec.* mention as worthy of remembrance; celebrate in speech or writing. L16. 2 Preserve in memory by some solemnity or celebration. M17. 3 Of a thing: be a memorial of. M18.

commemorative *a.* that commemorates a person, event, etc. L16. **commemoratively** *adv.* M17. **commemorator** *n.* a person who commemorates a person, event, etc. M19.

commemoration /kəmɛmə'reɪʃ(ə)n/ *n.* LME. [(O)Fr., or L *commemoratio(n-)*, f. as prec.: see -ATION.] 1 An act of commemorating by some solemnity or celebration. LME. b *Chr. Ch.* A service or part of a service in memory of a saint or some sacred event. LME. c A public memorial. M17. d An annual celebration at Oxford University in memory of the founders and benefactors of a college or the university. Cf. ENCAENIA. M18. 2 Recital, mention. Now *spec.* eulogistic or honourable mention. L16.

Comb.: **commemoration ball** an Oxford college dance held at a time close to commemoration.

commence /kə'mɛns/ *v.* ME. [OFr. *com(m)encier* (mod. *commencer*) f. Proto-Romance, f. L COM- + *initiare* INITIATE *v.* In sense 3 tr. med.L *incipere.*] 1 *v.t.* Begin (an action, *doing*, *to do*), enter upon. ME. 2 *v.i.* Make a start or a beginning; come into operation. LME. 3 *v.i.* & *t.* Take an academic degree, esp. a higher degree, (*in* a particular faculty etc.); take the academic degree of (MA etc.); graduate from university etc. LME. 4 As *copular v.* Begin to be or with being; begin to act or work as. *arch.* M17.

4 J. WESLEY The wandering thoughts.. then commence sinful. A. DOBSON Who had already commenced poet as an Eton boy.

commenceable *a.* M17. **commencer** *n.* (*a*) *gen.* a person who commences; †(*b*) *spec.* a person taking an academic degree, esp. a higher degree; *US* a college student about to graduate: LME.

commencement /kə'mɛnsm(ə)nt/ *n.* ME. [(O)Fr., f. as prec.: see -MENT.] 1 The action, process, or time of beginning. ME. 2 The taking of an academic degree, esp. a higher degree; (at certain universities, esp. in the US) the ceremony of degree conferment. LME.

†**commend** *n.* L15. [Partly f. Fr. *commende*, partly f. the vb.] 1 (A) commendation. L15–M17. 2 A greeting, a compliment. L15–M17. 3 = COMMENDAM. *Sc.* L15–E16.

1 SHAKES. *Per.* He had need mean better than his outward show Can any way speak in his just commend.

commend /kə'mɛnd/ *v.* ME. [L *commendare*, f. as COM- + *mandare* commit, entrust: cf. COMMAND *v.*] 1 *v.t.* Mention or present as worthy of acceptance or approval; praise, extol; recommend. ME. b *v.t.* Esp. in greetings: recommend (oneself, another) to kindly remembrance, convey kind greetings from (a person) *to* another. *arch.* LME. c *v.i.* Give praise. M18. 2 *v.t.* Entrust, commit, (*to*, now only *to* a person's care or keeping). LME. †3 *v.t.* Adorn, grace. M16–M17. 4 *v.t. Eccl. Hist.* Bestow *in commendam.* E17. 5 *v.t. Hist.* Place under the personal protection of a feudal lord. M19.

1 J. LONDON He had been commended for his brilliant description of the Socialist meeting. F. M. NICHOLS It commends itself to all the theologians who are either learned, or honest and candid. E. BOWEN Mr. Lee-Mittison.. commended him to their good graces with a general wave of the hand. **highly commended** (of a competitor) just missing the prize-list. b **commend me to** give my kind greetings to; *colloq.* give me by choice, (*iron.*) I prefer. 2 T. BECON Commend to memory the fifteenth chapter of Corinthians. J. BUCHAN I commended my soul to my Maker.

commender *n.* (now *rare*) L16.

commenda *n.* see COMMENDAM.

commendable /kə'mɛndəb(ə)l/ *a.* LME. [(O)Fr. f. L *commendabilis*, f. as COMMEND *v.*: see -ABLE.] Deserving of commendation or approval; laudable.

commendableness *n.* M17. **commendably** *adv.* LME.

commendador /kəmɛndə'dɔː/ *n.* L16. [Sp. *comendador* COMMANDER.] Chiefly *Hist.* A Spanish or Venetian commander.

commendam /kə'mɛndam/ *n.* Also (now *rare*) **-da** /-də/, †**-dum.** M16. [eccl.L, accus. sing. of *commenda* in *dare* etc. IN COMMENDAM.] *Eccl. Hist.* The custody of a benefice in the absence of a regular incumbent; the benefice or office so held.

commendatary /kə'mɛndət(ə)ri/ *n.* & *a.* Now *rare.* M16. [med.L *commendatarius*, f. *commendat-*: see next, -ARY[1].] A *n.* In *Eccl. Hist.*, = COMMENDATOR 1; *gen.* a commissioner. M16. B *adj.* = COMMENDATORY *a.* 2. E17.

commendation /kɒmɛn'deɪʃ(ə)n/ *n.* ME. [(O)Fr. f. L *commendatio(n-)*, f. *commendat-* pa. ppl stem of *commendare* COMMEND *v.*: see -ATION.] 1 *Chr. Ch.* Usu. in *pl.* A liturgical office, orig. ending with the prayer *Tibi, Domine, commendamus* (to You, Lord, we commend), commending the souls of the dead to God, said before burial or cremation and at any subsequent memorial service. ME. 2 The action of commending; approval, praise; recommendation. LME. 3 An expression of approval; a recommendation; in *pl.* also (*arch.*), respects, compliments, greetings. L15. 4 *Hist.* The delivery by a freeman of himself and his possessions to the protection of a feudal lord. E19.

commendator /'kɒməndeɪtə/ *n.* E16. [L *commendator* f. as prec.: see -OR.] 1 *Eccl. Hist.* A person holding a benefice *in commendam.* E16. 2 A Spanish commander. Now *rare* or *obs.* L16.

commendatore /kɒmɛndə'tɔːri/ *n.* L19. [It., f. as prec.] A knight of an Italian order of chivalry.

commendatory /kɒ'mɛndət(ə)ri/ *a.* & *n.* M16. [Late L *commendatorius*, f. as COMMENDATOR: see -ORY[2].] A *adj.* 1 Commending, recommending. M16. 2 *Eccl. Hist.* Holding a benefice *in commendam.* L17. †B *n.* 1 = COMMANDER 2b. M16–M18. 2 = COMMANDERY 1. L16–M18. 3 = COMMENDATOR 1. L16–E18. †4 A commendatory fact or word. M17–E18. 5 = COMMENDAM. M18–M19.

commensal /kə'mɛns(ə)l/ *a.* & *n.* LME. [Fr., or its source med.L *commensalis*, f. as COM- + *mensa* table: see -AL[1].] A *adj.* 1 Eating at or pertaining to the same table. LME. 2 *Biol.* Of, pertaining to, or exhibiting commensalism. L19. B *n.* 1 Any of a company eating at the same table. Formerly also *spec.*, an oppidan at Eton College. LME. 2 *Biol.* A commensal organism. L19.

commensalism *n.* (*Biol.*) an association between two species in which one benefits and the other is neither harmed nor benefited (cf. SYMBIOSIS) L19. **commen'sality** *n.* the habit of eating at the same table E17.

commensurable /kə'mɛnʃ(ə)rəb(ə)l, -sjə-/ *a.* M16. [Late L *commensurabilis*, f. as COM- + *mensurabilis* MENSURABLE: see -ABLE.] 1 Measurable by the same standard (*to*, *with*); (of numbers, magnitudes, etc.) having a ratio that may be expressed as a ratio of two integers. M16. 2 Proportionate (*to*). Now *rare.* M17.

commensura'bility *n.* L16. **commensurableness** *n.* M16. **commensurably** *adv.* M17.

commensurate /kə'mɛnʃ(ə)rət, -sjə-/ *a.* M17. [Late L *commensuratus*, f. as COM- + *mensuratus* pa. pple of *mensurare*: see MEASURE *v.*, -ATE[2].] 1 Of equal extent, coextensive, (*with*, *to*). M17. 2 Proportionate (*to*, *with*). M17. 3 Corresponding in nature (*with*, *to*); belonging to the same category. Now *rare.* M17.

commensurately *adv.* L17. **commensurateness** *n.* M17.

†**commensurate** *v.t.* M17. [f. (as) prec.: see -ATE[3].] 1 Make commensurate *to.* M17–E18. 2 Reduce to a measure or standard, measure. Only in M17.

commensuration /kəmɛnʃə'reɪʃ(ə)n, -sjə-/ *n.* Now *rare.* E16. [Senses 1, 2 f. COM- + MENSURATION; sense 3 f. late L *commensuratio(n-)*, f. as prec.: see -ATION.] 1 The measuring of things against or in comparison with each other. E16. †2 An act of measuring; a measurement. M16–L17. 3 Relationship of measurements etc., proportion. E17.

comment /'kɒmɛnt/ *n.* LME. [L *commentum* invention, contrivance, interpretation, comment, f. *comment-* pa. ppl stem of *comminisci* devise, contrive.] †1 An expository treatise; a commentary. LME–L19. 2 An explanatory note; a remark; a criticism; an opinion, now esp. as conveyed by the media; *fig.* (of an event etc.) an illustration, an elucidating example. LME. 3 Critical matter added to illustrate the text of a book etc. L16. 4 Animadversion, criticism, remark. M19. 5 *Ling.* The part of a sentence giving new information about the topic or theme of an utterance or discourse. Cf. RHEME 2. M20.

2 G. CRABBE Bibles with cuts and comments. V. GLENDINNING No one can go and post a letter without a comment being made. 4 E. ROOSEVELT It would cause great comment if I cancelled them [engagements] at the last moment.

Phrases: **no comment** *colloq.* (*a*) I decline to answer the question; (*b*) there is no need for me to express an opinion. *social comment*: see SOCIAL *a.*

comment /'kɒmɛnt/ *v.* LME. [f. prec. or Fr. *commenter*; in sense 1, f. med.L *commentare*, L *-ari* frequent. of L *comminisci* (see prec.).] †1 *v.t.* Devise, contrive, invent. LME–L16. 2 *v.i.* Write explanatory notes (*up*)*on*; make (esp.

unfavourable) remarks (*on, upon, that*). LME. 3 *v.t.* Provide with comments, make comments on; annotate. *arch.* L16. †4 *v.i.* Remark mentally; meditate. L16–E17.

2 DAY LEWIS He would act the biblical stories on which he was commenting. C. RYAN Eisenhower never commented on him except in private.

commenter, **-or** *n.* a person who comments; a commentator: LME.

commentary /ˈkɒmənt(ə)ri/ *n.* & *v.* LME. [L *commentarius*, *-ium* use as n. (sc. *liber* book, *volumen* volume) of adj. f. *commentari*: see prec., -ARY[1].] A *n.* 1 An expository treatise; a series of comments or annotations on a text. LME. b Chiefly *Hist.* A memoir, an informal historical record. Usu. in *pl.* L15. c A spoken description of an event, performance, etc., accompanying a radio or television broadcast, a cinema film, etc. L19. 2 *transf.* & *fig.* A comment, a remark, an illustration. M16. 3 Exposition, annotation, systematic commenting, acting as commentator. M17.

1c *running commentary*: see RUNNING *ppl a.* 2 T. GUNN There will be no speech from / the scaffold, the scene must / be its own commentary.

B *v.* †1 *v.i.* Comment (*up*)*on*. Only in E17. 2 *v.t.* Annotate. *rare.* M17.

commentate /ˈkɒmənteɪt/ *v.* LME. [In isolated early use f. L *commentat-*: see next, -ATE[3]. In mod. use back-form. f. COMMENTATOR.] 1 *v.t.* = COMMENT *v.* 3. *rare.* LME. 2 *v.i.* Act as a commentator. M19.

commentation /kɒmənˈteɪʃ(ə)n/ *n.* LME. [L *commentatio(n-)*, f. *commentat-* pa. ppl stem of *commentari*: see COMMENT *v.*, -ATION.] †1 A comment; a commentary. LME–E18. †2 (Comment which is) mere invention or concoction. M17–M18. 3 Commenting. M19.

commentator /ˈkɒmənteɪtə/ *n.* LME. [L *commentator*, f. *commentat-*: see prec., -OR.] A writer or speaker of a commentary; a person who comments on current events, esp. on radio or television.

commentaˈtorial *a.* of, pertaining to, or characteristic of a commentator or commentators E19. **commentatorship** *n.* M18.

commentitious /kɒmenˈtɪʃəs/ *a.* Now *rare* or *obs.* E17. [f. L *commenticius*, *-tius*, f. *comment-*: see COMMENT *n.*, -ITIOUS[1].] Fictitious, lying.

commerce /ˈkɒməːs/ *n.* M16. [Fr. *commerce* or L *commercium* trade, trafficking, f. as COM- + *merx*, *merc-* merchandise.] 1 Dealings, social intercourse; converse with God, with spirits, passions, thoughts, etc. M16. 2 Buying and selling; the exchange of merchandise or services, esp. on a large scale. L16. b A gambling card-game in which players exchange cards with a spare hand. Also, a derivative of this in which cards are obtained by purchase from the dealer or by exchange with one's neighbour. E18. †3 A mercantile transaction; an affair, a concern. L16–E18. 4 Sexual intercourse. *arch.* E17. †5 Interchange (of ideas, letters, etc.). E17–M18. †6 Means of communication. M17–M18.

2 *Chamber of Commerce*: see CHAMBER *n.* 2. *standard of commerce*: see STANDARD *n.* 7b.

commerce /kəˈməːs/ *v.i. arch.* L16. [Partly f. the n., partly f. Fr. *commercer*.] †1 Carry on trade. L16–M17. 2 Communicate or associate *with*. L16.

commercial /kəˈməːʃ(ə)l/ *a.* & *n.* L16. [f. COMMERCE *n.* + -IAL.] A *adj.* 1 Engaged in commerce; of, pertaining to, or bearing on commerce. L16. 2 Of a chemical etc.: unpurified. M18. 3 Interested in financial return rather than artistry; likely to make a profit; regarded as a mere matter of business. L19. 4 Of radio or television broadcasting: funded by the revenue from broadcast advertising. M20.

Special collocations: **commercial art**: used in advertising etc. **commercial college**, **school**, etc.: giving instruction in commercial subjects. *commercial docks*: see DOCK *n.*[3] *commercial school*: see *commercial college* above. *commercial traveller*: see TRAVELLER 2c. **commercial vehicle**: used or suitable for transporting fare-paying passengers or merchandise.

B *n.* 1 A commercial traveller; a person engaged in commerce. *arch.* M19. 2 A broadcast advertisement; a broadcast programme containing an advertisement. M20.

2 *spot commercial*: see SPOT *n.* & *a.*

commerciaˈlese *n.* (an instance of) the language or diction of the commercial world E20. **commercialism** *n.* (*a*) the principles and practice of commerce; excessive adherence to financial return as a measure of worth; (*b*) a commercial custom or expression: M19. **commercialist** *n.* a person engaged in commerce; an adherent of commercialism: E19. **commerciˈality** *n.* M19. **commercialize** *v.t.* render (merely) commercial, derive commercial profit from M19. **commercially** *adv.* L18.

commère /kɒmɛː, ˈkɒmɛː/ *n.* Pl. pronounced /-ɛː, -ɛːz/. E20. [Fr. (see CUMMER), fem. of COMPÈRE.] A female compère.

commie /ˈkɒmi/ *n.* & *a. slang.* Also **C-**. M20. [Abbrev.: see -IE.] (A) Communist.

†**commigration** *n.* E17–M18. [L *commigratio(n-)*, f. *commigrat-* pa. ppl stem of *commigrare*: see COM-, MIGRATE, -ATION.] Migration, esp. on a large scale.

†**commilitant** *n.* & *a.* Also **comil-**. L16. [L *commilitant-* pres. ppl stem of *commilitare* soldier with: see COM-, MILITATE, -ANT[1].] A *n.* A fellow soldier. L16–E18. B *adj.* Fighting in alliance. *rare.* Only in M19.

commilito /kəˈmɪlɪtəʊ/ *n.* Pl. ***commilitones*** /kəmɪlɪˈtəʊniːz/. Also Anglicized as †***-ton***. LME. [L, f. as COM- + *milit-*, *miles* soldier.] A fellow soldier, a comrade in arms.

comminate /ˈkɒmɪneɪt/ *v.t.* & *i.* E17. [f. L *comminat-*: see next, -ATE[3].] Anathematize.

comminator *n.* L17.

commination /kɒmɪˈneɪʃ(ə)n/ *n.* LME. [L *comminatio(n-)*, f. *comminat-* pa. ppl stem of *comminari*, f. as COM- + *minari* threaten: see -ATION.] 1 Threatening of divine vengeance; denunciation. LME. 2 A recital of divine threats against sinners in the Anglican liturgy for Ash Wednesday; the service that includes this. M16.

comminatory /ˈkɒmɪnət(ə)ri/ *a.* E16. [med.L *comminatorius*, f. *comminat-*: see prec., -ORY[2].] Threatening; denunciatory.

commingle /kɒˈmɪŋg(ə)l/ *v.i.* & *t. literary.* Also **comingle** /kəʊˈmɪŋg(ə)l/. E17. [f. COM-, CO- + MINGLE *v.*] Mingle together.

comminute /ˈkɒmɪnjuːt/ *v.t.* E17. [L *comminut-* pa. ppl stem of *comminuere*, f. as COM- + *minuere* lessen.] 1 Reduce to small fragments; break down or grind into small particles. E17. 2 Divide (property etc.) into small portions. M19.

1 **comminuted fracture**: producing multiple fragments of bone.

commiˈnution *n.* L16. **comminutor** *n.* a machine that breaks up solids, esp. of sewage M19.

commis /ˈkɒmi/ *n.* Pl. same (pronounced same, /-iːz/). L16. [Fr., use as n. of pa. pple of *commettre* entrust f. as COMMIT.] †1 A deputy, a clerk. L16–E19. 2 A junior waiter or chef. M20.

commiserable /kəˈmɪz(ə)rəb(ə)l/ *a.* E17. [f. next + -ABLE.] Deserving commiseration.

commiserate /kəˈmɪzəreɪt/ *v.* L16. [L *commiserat-* pa. ppl stem of *commiserari*, *-are*, f. as COM- + *miserari* lament, pity, f. *miser* wretched: see -ATE[3].] 1 *v.i.* Feel compassion (*arch.*); condole (*with*). L16. 2 *v.t.* Feel or express compassion for; condole with. *arch.* E17.

1 V. SACKVILLE-WEST They would commiserate now with her in being left alone. W. GOLDING Philip commiserated; . . pointed out the agony of my choice.

commiseratingly *adv.* with commiseration M19. **commiserative** *a.* given to or showing commiseration, compassionate E17. **commiseratively** *adv.* E17.

commiseration /kəmɪzəˈreɪʃ(ə)n/ *n.* M16. [L *commiseratio(n-)*, f. as prec.: see -ATION.] 1 The action of commiserating; (the expression of) compassion; pity. M16. 2 A feeling or expression of compassion; a condolence. Usu. in *pl.* E17.

1 A. TOFFLER Moving one's household . . is a cause for commiseration rather than congratulation. 2 W. GOLDING I asked that my commiserations for his sickness . . should be conveyed.

commish /kəˈmɪʃ/ *n. colloq.* E20. [Abbrev.] (A) commission.

commissaire /kɒmɪˈsɛː/ *n.* M18. [Fr.: see next.] = COMMISSARY.

commissar /kɒmɪˈsɑː/ *n.* LME. [Fr. *commissaire* f. med.L *commissarius* COMMISSARY. In sense 2 f. Russ. *komissar* f. Fr.] †1 A deputy, a delegate, a commissary. Chiefly *Sc.* LME–M18. 2 *Hist.* The head of a government department in the USSR. E20.

commissarial /kɒmɪˈsɛːrɪəl/ *a.* E18. [f. med.L *commissarius* COMMISSARY + -AL[1].] Of or pertaining to a commissary.

commissariat /kɒmɪˈsɛːrɪət/ *n.* In sense 1 usu. **-ot**. L16. [Partly f. med.L *commissariatus*, f. as next; partly f. Fr. *commissariat*: see -ATE[1].] 1 *Sc. Law* (now *Hist.*). The office, jurisdiction, or district of a commissary. L16. 2 A department, esp. military, for the supply of food etc.; food supplied. L18. 3 *Hist.* A government department in the USSR. E20.

commissary /ˈkɒmɪs(ə)ri/ *n.* LME. [med.L *commissarius* officer in charge, f. *commiss-*: see next, -ARY[1].] 1 A deputy, a delegate, a commissioned representative. LME. 2 *Eccl.* The representative of the bishop in part of his diocese, or of an absent bishop. LME. 3a The Vice-Chancellor of Oxford University. *obs.* exc. *Hist.* LME. b An assessor in the Vice-Chancellor's court at Cambridge University. L18. 4a *Mil.* An officer charged with the supply of food etc. to soldiers. L15. b A store for provisions etc.; *spec.* a restaurant in a film studio etc. *US.* L19. 5 A senior police officer in France. L18. 6 *Sc. Law* (now *Hist.*). A judge in a commissary court. E19. 7 = COMMISSAR 2. E20.

Comb. & phrases: **commissary court** *Sc. Law* (now *Hist.*) a court which exercised jurisdiction in marriage, testamentary affairs, etc.; **commissary general** a chief or head commissary.

commissaryship *n.* L16.

commission /kəˈmɪʃ(ə)n/ *n.* ME. [(O)Fr. f. L *commissio(n-)*, f. *commiss-* pa. ppl stem of *committere* COMMIT: see -ION.] I 1 Authority; *esp.* delegated authority to act in a specific capacity or manner. ME. b *spec.* Authority to act as agent for another in trade; (a) payment to an agent proportional to the amount involved in a transaction, a percentage on the amount involved. E17. 2 A command, an instruction. LME. 3 A warrant conferring authority, *esp.* that of officers in the army, navy, and air force, above a certain rank; an office or rank conferred by such a warrant. LME. 4 A body of people with delegated authority to act in a specific capacity or manner; the office or department of such a body or of a commissioner. L15. 5 A charge or matter entrusted to a person to perform; an order for the execution of a particular work. L16. 6 The entrusting of or *of* authority, a charge, etc. (*to*); the admitting of a warship etc. to active service. L19.

1 LD MACAULAY Dundee . . had summoned all the clans which acknowledged his commission. b V. S. NAIPAUL Some of them wanted a fifteen-cent commission on every copy. W. C. KETCHUM Galleries . . have been known to take merchandise at no commission. 2 E. A. FREEMAN They gave him no direct commission to bind them to any consent. 3 H. COX Commissions of inquiry are issued by the Crown. B. CHATWIN The colonel had recently resigned his commission. 5 M. HOLROYD His first commission in portraiture was to paint an old lady living in Eaton Square. J. RATHBONE I have a commission to find you.

II 7 The committing of or *of* a crime, sin, etc. LME. 8 An offence, crime, etc., committed. *rare.* M17.

Phrases: *Commission of Array*: see ARRAY *n.* 3. *commission of lunacy*: see LUNACY 1. *commission of oy and terminer*: see OY *int.*[2] *commission of sewers*: see SEWER *n.*[1] **commission of the peace** (the authority given to) Justices of the Peace. *High Commission*: see HIGH *a.* **in commission** (*a*) in the exercise of (delegated authority); (*b*) (of an office) placed by warrant in the charge of a body of people, instead of the ordinary constitutional administrator; (*c*) (of a warship, aircraft, etc.) manned, armed, and ready for active service. **on commission** with payment proportional to the amount involved in a transaction, (paid) on a pro rata basis. **out of commission** not in service; not in working order, unable to function. *override one's commission*: see OVERRIDE *v.* *overriding commission*: see OVERRIDE *v.* **Royal Commission** a commission of inquiry or a committee appointed by the Crown at the instance of the Government. **sin of commission** the doing of a thing which ought not to have been done (opp. *sin of omission*).

Comb.: **commission-agent** a person who transacts business for another on commission; *spec.* a bookmaker; †**commission-officer** a commissioned officer.

commission /kə'mɪʃ(ə)n/ *v.* M17. [f. the n.] **1** *v.t.* Empower by a commission, give authority; entrust with an office or duty. Foll. by *to do.* M17. **b** Send on a mission *to, to do.* L17. **c** Give (an artist etc.) a commission *to do.* E19. **2** *v.t.* Give (a person) a commission for a rank in the army, navy, or air force. Cf. earlier COMMISSIONED 1. E18. **3** *v.t.* Give (an officer) command of a ship. L18. **4** *v.t.* Admit (a warship, aircraft, etc.) to active service; prepare (a warship, aircraft, etc.) for active service; bring (a machine, equipment, etc.) into operation. L18. **b** *v.i.* Of a warship, aircraft, etc.: commence active service. E20. **5** *v.t.* Give a commission for, order, (a particular piece of work, the execution of a work, †an article of merchandise). L18.

1 G. VIDAL Giles was commissioned to find a boat. c G. GREENE I've been commissioned to do a Life of General Gordon. 2 F. CHICHESTER I was commissioned as a Flying Officer. 5 R. BURNS The books I commissioned in my last. K. CLARK The princely patrons . . commissioned quantities of manuscripts.

commissional *a.* of or pertaining to a commission M16. †**commissionate** *v.t.* & *i.* = COMMISSION *v.* L16–E19.

commissionaire /kəmɪʃə'nɛː/ *n.* M17. [Fr. *commissionnaire* f. as COMMISSIONER.] **1** A person entrusted with small commissions; a messenger. Now *rare.* M17. **2** A member of an association of pensioned soldiers organized for employment as messengers, porters, etc. (now *Hist.*). Hence, a uniformed door-attendant at a theatre, cinema, large shop, office, etc. M19.

commissioned /kə'mɪʃ(ə)nd/ *a.* L17. [f. COMMISSION *n.*, *v.*: see -ED[2], -ED[1].] **1** Of an officer in the army, navy, or air force: holding a rank conferred by a commission. Opp. *non-commissioned.* L17. **2** *gen.* That has been commissioned. M18.

commissioner /kə'mɪʃ(ə)nə/ *n.* LME. [med.L *commissionarius* n., f. *commissio(n-)*: see COMMISSION *n.*, -ER[2].] **1** A person appointed by commission, as the head of the Metropolitan Police in London, a delegate to the General Assembly of the Church of Scotland, etc.; a member of a commission or of any of certain government boards. LME. **b** A representative of supreme authority in a district, department, etc. L15. **2** A bookmaker. *slang.* Now *rare.* M19.

1 *Charity Commissioner, Civil Service Commissioner, commissioner of sewers, Parliamentary Commissioner for Administration*, etc. **Commissioner for Oaths** a solicitor authorized to administer an oath to a person making an affidavit. *High Commissioner*: see HIGH *a.* **Lord (High) Commissioner** the representative of the Crown at the General Assembly of the Church of Scotland.

commissionership *n.* E19.

commissive /kə'mɪsɪv/ *a.* E19. [f. COMMISSION *n.* + -IVE, after *omissive.*] Of an act etc.: actually done or committed, involving active agency.

commissure /'kɒmɪsjʊə/ *n.* LME. [L *commissura*, f. *commiss-*: see COMMISSION *n.*, -URE.] **1** *gen.* A juncture, a seam. LME. **2** A joint between two bones; *esp.* a suture. Now *rare* or *obs.* M16. **3** The line or point where lips or eyelids meet. M18. **4** Any of several bundles of nerve tissue which connect the two sides of the central nervous system in the brain or spinal cord. E19. **5** *Bot.* The line of junction of the cohering faces of two carpels (in umbellifers). M19.

commis-voyageur /kɔmi vwajaʒœːr/ *n.* Pl. pronounced same. M19. [Fr.] A commercial traveller.

commit /kə'mɪt/ *v.* Infl. **-tt-**. LME. [L *committere* join, practise, entrust, (in med.L) consign to custody, f. as COM- + *mittere* put, send (see MISSION *n.*, *v.*).] **I** *v.t.* **1** Entrust or consign for treatment or safe keeping (*to* a person, a person's care, etc., *to* the earth, the flames, etc.). LME. **2** Consign officially to custody as a (suspected) criminal or as insane; send to prison etc., esp. until trial. (Foll. by *to.*) LME. †**3** Charge with a duty or office. LME–M16. **4** Be the doer of (a crime, a sin, a blunder, etc.): LME. †**5** Connect, fasten. M16–L17. **6** Refer (a parliamentary bill etc.) to a committee. L16. **7** Engage (parties) as opponents; embroil. *arch.* E17. **8** Expose to risk; involve (character, honour, etc.). L18. **b** Pledge (oneself) by implication; bind (a person, oneself, *to* a course of action); dedicate (oneself) morally (*to* a doctrine or cause). L18.

1 **commit to memory** learn so as to be able to recall. *commit to paper*: see PAPER *n.* & *a.* **commit to writing** record in writing. 2 H. MARTINEAU The magistrates committed the prisoners to the House of Correction for one month each. E. ALBEE I'm rather worried about you. About your mind. . . I think I'll have you committed. R. TRAVERS He was charged with wilful murder and formally committed for trial. 4 *commit adultery, mayhem, murder, suicide*, etc. 8 T. JEFFERSON The importance of restraining individuals from committing the peace and honor of the two nations. b H. JAMES Your offer has been before me only these few minutes, and it's too soon for me to commit myself to anything. SLOAN WILSON He had written, 'Maybe—don't commit us.'

II *v.i.* †**9** Commit an offence; commit adultery. M16–M17. **10** Commit a (suspected) criminal to prison etc. E19.

committable *a.* M17. **committed** *ppl a.* that has been committed; *spec.* obliged to adhere (*to* a course of action), morally dedicated (*to* a doctrine or cause), having a political, artistic, etc., commitment: LME. **committer** *n.* E16. **committible** *a.* M17.

commitment /kə'mɪtm(ə)nt/ *n.* L16. [f. prec. + -MENT.] **1** The action of officially consigning a person to custody; imprisonment, esp. until trial. L16. **b** A warrant or order consigning a person to prison etc. M18. †**2** The action of committing an offence etc. E17–M18. **3** The action of referring a parliamentary bill etc. to a committee. E17. **4** *gen.* The action of entrusting or consigning for treatment or safe keeping. L17. **5** The action of committing oneself or another to a course of action etc. L18. **b** [tr. Fr. *engagement.*] (Moral, political, artistic, etc.) involvement restricting freedom of action. M20. **6** An engagement, an obligation; an act of committing oneself. M19.

committal /kə'mɪt(ə)l/ *n.* E17. [f. as prec. + -AL[1].] The action of committing; commitment, esp. (*a*) of an offence, (*b*) of a person to custody or confinement, (*c*) of a body or ashes to the grave or the sea at burial or to the fire at cremation.

Comb.: **committal proceedings**: in a magistrates' court to determine whether a case should go for trial to a Crown Court.

committee /*in branch I* kɒmɪ'tiː; *in branch II* kə'mɪti/ *n.* L15. [f. COMMIT + -EE[1].] **I** An individual. **1** A person to whom some charge, trust, or function is committed. *obs.* in *gen.* sense. L15. **b** *Hist.* A director of the East India Company. L17. **c** *Hist.* A member of the highest management board of Guy's Hospital, London. E18. **2** *Law.* A person entrusted with the charge of another or of his or her property; *US* a person who has been judicially committed to the charge of another because of insanity or retardation. M18.

II An aggregate of people. **3** A body of two or more people appointed for some special function by, and usu. out of, a (usu. larger) body; *esp.* such a body appointed by Parliament etc. to consider details of proposed legislation. L16. †**4** A meeting or session of such a body. M17–M18.

3 **Committee of the whole House** the whole House of Commons when sitting as a committee. *joint committee*: see JOINT *a. National Hunt Committee*: see NATIONAL *a. Rules Committee*: see RULE *n. select committee*: see SELECT *a. standing committee*: see STANDING *a. steering committee*: see STEER *v.*[1]

Comb.: **committee-man, -woman**: a member of a committee or committees.

commix /kɒ'mɪks/ *v.t.* & *i.* Now *arch.* or *poet.* Pa. pple **-mixed, -mixt**. LME. [Orig. pa. pple, f. L *commixtus*, f. as COM- + *mixtus* (see MIX *v.*).] Mix, blend.

commixtion /kɒ'mɪkstʃ(ə)n/ *n.* Also †**-mixion**. LME. [Late L *commixtio(n-)*, f. L *commixt-* pa. ppl stem of *commiscere*, f. as COM- + *miscere* (see MIX *v.*).] **1** = COMMIXTURE 1. *obs.* exc. *Sc. Law*, the mixing together of materials belonging to different owners. LME. †**2** Sexual intercourse. LME–L17. †**3** = COMMIXTURE 2. LME–M17.

commixture /kɒ'mɪkstʃə/ *n.* L16. [Late L *commixtura*, f. *commixt-*: see prec., -URE.] **1** The action or an act of mixing together. L16. **2** The state of being mixed together; a mixture, a compound. L16. †**3** = COMPLEXION *n.* 1. *rare* (Shakes.). Only in L16.

Commo /'kɒməʊ/ *n. derog. slang* (chiefly *Austral.* & *NZ*). Also **c-**. Pl. **-os**. M20. [Abbrev.: see -O-.] A Communist.

commodatum /kɒmə'deɪtəm/ *n.* Pl. **-ta** /-tə/. L17. [L, use as n. of neut. of *commodatus* pa. pple of *commodare* accommodate, lend.] *Rom.* & *Sc. Law.* A free loan, for use, of anything not perishable or consumable.

Also **commodate** /'kɒmədət/ *n.* (now *rare* or *obs.*) E18.

commode /kə'məʊd/ *n.* L17. [Fr., use as n. of *commode* adj.: see next.] **1** A tall head-dress formerly worn by women, consisting of a wire framework covered with silk or lace. L17. **2** A chest of drawers or chiffonier of the decorative kind found esp. in 18th-cent. drawing-rooms. M18. **3** A lavatory, a privy. *arch. rare.* E19. **4** A chamber-pot enclosed in a chair or box with a cover. M19.

†**commode** *a.* M17. [Fr. f. L *commodus*: see COMMODIOUS.] **1** Convenient, suitable. M17–M18. **2** Accommodating: usu. in a bad sense. E–M18.

commodification /kəˌmɒdɪfɪ'keɪʃ(ə)n/ *n.* L20. [f. COMMODITY: see -FICATION.] The action of turning something into or treating something as a (mere) commodity.

commodious /kə'məʊdɪəs/ *a.* LME. [Fr. *commodieux* or med.L *commodiosus*, f. L *commodus* convenient, f. as COM- + *modus* measure: see -OUS.] †**1** Beneficial, profitable, useful. LME–M18. **2a** Convenient, serviceable; *spec.* convenient as accommodation or shelter. Foll. by *for, to. arch.* M16. **b** Conveniently roomy, spacious. M16. †**3** Of life, living: endowed with conveniences. M16–M17. †**4** Opportune. E17–M18. †**5** Of a person: accommodating. *rare* (Shakes.). Only in E17.

2a DEFOE The Isle of Caldey . . safe and commodious for Men of War. b H. JAMES The smoking-room . . was . . high, light, commodious.

commodiously *adv.* LME. **commodiousness** *n.* M16.

commodity /kə'mɒdɪti/ *n.* LME. [(O)Fr. *commodité* or L *commoditas*, f. *commodus*: see prec., -ITY.] †**I1** Suitability; fitting utility; convenience, as a property of something. LME–L17. **2a** A person's convenience. LME–M19. **b** (An) advantage, (a) benefit; (selfish) interest. E16–M19. **c** Expediency. L16–L18. **d** Profit, gain. L16–M17. **3** Opportunity, occasion. M16–M17.

II4 A thing of use or value; *spec.* a thing that is an object of trade, *esp.* a raw material or agricultural crop. LME. **b** *fig.* A thing one deals in or makes use of. L16. †**5** A quantity *of* wares; *spec.* one lent on credit by a usurer for resale, usu. to the usurer himself. L16–M17.

4 R. K. NARAYAN Bullock carts . . loaded with coconut, rice and other commodities for the market. b A. G. GARDINER Prettiness is the women's commodity. 5 SHAKES. *Meas. for M.* Here's young Master Rash; he's in for a commodity of brown paper and old ginger, . . of which he made five marks ready money.

commodore /'kɒmədɔː/ *n.* Orig. also †**commandore**. L17. [Prob. f. Du. *komandeur* f. Fr. *commandeur* COMMANDER.] **1a** A naval officer ranking above a captain and below a rear admiral. L17. **b** A commodore's ship; the principal or the second ship of a group. Now *rare* or *obs.* L17. **2** The senior captain of a company of ships or of a shipping line. M19. 3 The senior officer of a yacht-club. M19. 4 *air commodore*, a commissioned rank in the Royal Air Force, above a group captain and below an air vice-marshal. E20.

common /ˈkɒmən/ *n.* See also COMMONS. ME. [Partly repr. Fr. *commune* (see COMMUNE *n.*[1]); partly L *commune* use as n. of neut. of *communis*; partly f. the adj.] †1 The community, the general body of people; occas., the State. ME–M17. †2 The common people, often as an estate of the realm. ME–M18. 3 An area of land held jointly by all the members of a community; in mod. use, a piece of open waste land or of common land. ME. 4 *Chr. Ch.* The parts of a service used for each of a certain class of occasions, e.g. saint's days, where no individual psalm, lesson, etc., is appointed. Cf. PROPER *n.* 2. ME. 5 *Law.* A right to make a particular kind of use of land or water owned by another. Also *right of common*. LME. 6 *ellipt.* Common sense. *slang.* E20.

5 *common of pasture, common of piscary, common of turbary*, etc.

Phrases: **in common** †(*a*) generally; ordinarily; (*b*) in joint use or possession; (*c*) *Law* (held or owned) by two or more people each having undivided possession but with distinct, separately transferable interests (TENANCY *in common*); (cf. *in severalty* (a) s.v. SEVERALTY); (*d*) that is common to both or all; jointly *with*. **the common** what is usual or ordinary; now chiefly in *out of the common*, unusual.

common /ˈkɒmən/ *a.* & *adv.* ME. [OFr. *comun* f. L *communis*.] A *adj.* I Of a public or non-private nature. 1 Shared alike by all the persons or things in question, or by all humankind (foll. by *to*, (rare) *between*); having the same relationship to all the persons or things in question. ME. 2 Belonging to more than one as a result of joint action or agreement. ME. 3 Of or belonging to the community or a civic authority. ME. 4 Free to be used by everyone; public. ME. 5 Generally known; *spec.* (of an offender or offence) public, notorious, habitual. ME. 6 Of general application. LME. †7 [L *communis*.] Generally accessible, affable. LME–E17.

1 ADDISON Faults common to both Parties. H. E. BATES Weeping to each other in common grief. *Common Celtic, Germanic*, etc. 2 CHAUCER This was the commune voys of every man. W. TREVOR They walked towards a common goal. 3 TENNYSON He sow'd a slander in the common ear. *common council, hall, hangman, seal*, etc. 4 *common alehouse, lodging-house*, etc. 5 J. WESLEY Baptized liars and common swearers. *common nuisance* etc.

II Of ordinary occurrence or quality. 8 Of frequent or ordinary occurrence; prevalent; usual. ME. 9a Of a person: undistinguished by rank or position; belonging to the general body of people. ME. b Unrefined, vulgar. M19. 10 Undistinguished by any special or superior quality; ordinary. LME. 11 Of the most familiar type. LME.

8 T. HARDY The Coggans . . were as common among the families of this district as the Avons and Derwents among our rivers. D. DU MAURIER That endless yattering, so common in women. 9a ADDISON Songs and Fables . . in Vogue among the common People. R. WEST Even common soldiers had considerable opportunity for advancement. b JILLY COOPER Nanny Ellis said it was . . common to play with children whose friends were in trade. 10 JOSEPH HALL Dayes, whether common or sacred. G. MACDONALD Here . . was no common mind. 11 B. FRANKLIN Common fire . . as well as electrical fire. G. WHITE Flocks of the common linnet.

III 12 In New Testament and derived use [= Hellenistic Gk *koinos*]: not ceremonially clean. ME.

IV Technical uses. 13 *Math.* Of a quantity: belonging equally to two or more quantities. LME. 14 *Gram.* a Of a noun: applicable to any of an indefinite class of entities, not just one, or denoting a general property or quality. Opp. *proper*. LME. b Designating a gender to which both masculine and feminine words belong; (of a word) belonging to this gender. M16. 15 *Pros.* Of a syllable: optionally either short or long. L17.

13 *common factor, common multiple*, etc.

Phrases & special collocations: *by common consent*: see CONSENT *n.* 2. *common astrologer*: see ASTROLOGER 2. **common carrier** a person who undertakes as a business to transport any goods or any person in a specified category. *common centaury*: see CENTAURY 2. *common chord*: see CHORD *n.*[1] 4. *common cold*: see COLD *n.* 3. **Common Council** a town or city council, now only in London or US. **Common Councilman** a member of a Common Council. **common crier** a town crier. *common denominator*: see DENOMINATOR 1. **Common Era** the Christian era. **common field** *Hist.* a field belonging to the members of a local community as a whole. **common form** what is usually done and of no special significance. **common ground** something on which two parties agree or in which both are interested in negotiation, conversation, etc. **common ground dove** = TOBACCO *dove*. **common gull** a migratory gull, *Larus canus*, widespread on coasts and lowlands in northern and eastern Eurasia and north-west N. America. *common hunt*: see HUNT *n.*[1] **common informer** *Hist.* a person who sued for the penalty payable by an offender in cases where part or all of the penalty was given to anyone who would sue for it, not only the aggrieved party. *common jackal*: see JACKAL *n.* 1. **common jury** *Hist.*: for which no qualification of rank or property was required. **common knowledge** something known to most people. **common land** (*a*) land subject to rights of common; (*b*) open waste land. *common laurel*: see LAUREL *n.* 3. **common lizard** = *viviparous lizard* s.v. VIVIPAROUS 1. *common* LOGARITHM. *common* MALLOW. *common maple*: see MAPLE *n.* 1. **Common Market** the European Economic Community, an economic association of certain European countries with internal free trade and free movement of labour, and common external tariffs and internal policies on agriculture etc. *common* MERGANSER. **common metre** an iambic metre for hymns in which the verse has four lines with 8, 6, 8, and 6 syllables. *common* MICA. *common opal*: see OPAL *n.* 1. **common or garden** *colloq.* ordinary. *common* PEAFOWL. *common pleas*: see PLEA *n.* *common* POMPANO. **common prayer** prayer in which worshippers publicly unite; *esp.* (*C- P-*) the public worship of the Church of England as prescribed in the *Book of Common Prayer*, orig. in 1549. *common privet*: see PRIVET 1. **common property** *fig.* = *common knowledge* above. *common* REDSTART. *common recovery*: see RECOVERY 4. *common roller*: see ROLLER *n.*[2] *common* ROOIBEKKIE. **common-room** a room in a college, school, etc., to which all members in a certain category have common access for social or business purposes; the members using it; (*junior common-room*: see JUNIOR *a.*, *middle common-room*: see MIDDLE *a.*, *senior common-room*: see SENIOR *a.*). *common* RORQUAL. *common ryegrass*: see RYEGRASS 2. *common salt*: see SALT *n.*[1] 1. **common sandpiper** a migratory Old World sandpiper, *Actitis hypoleucos*, with olive-brown and white plumage. *common scold*: see SCOLD *n.* 1. *common scrub-fowl*: see SCRUB *n.*[1] *common scurvy-grass*: see SCURVY *n.* *common seal*: see SEAL *n.*[1] 1. *common* SENSORIUM. *common sensory*: see SENSORY *n.* 2. **Common Serjeant** a circuit judge who has duties in the City of London and sits in the Central Criminal Court. *common shore*: see SHORE *n.*[3] *common shoveler*: see SHOVELER 2. *common shrimp*: see SHRIMP *n.* 1. *common silverbill*: see SILVER *n.* & *a.* *common situs*: see SITUS 2b. *common snapping turtle*: see SNAPPING *ppl a.* 3. *common snipe*: see SNIPE *n.* 1. *common soldier*: see SOLDIER *n.* 1. *common sole*: see SOLE *n.*[3] *common St John's wort*: see SAINT *n.* & *a.* **common stock** *N. Amer.* the ordinary shares of a company. *common stork's-bill*: see STORK *n.* *common suit*: see SUIT *n.* 1b. *common* TEGU. **common tern** the widespread migratory tern *Sterna hirundo*. **common time** *Mus.*: in which there are two or four beats, esp. four crotchets, in a bar. *common toadfish*: see TOADFISH 1. *common twayblade*: see TWAYBLADE 1. *common valerian*: see VALERIAN 1. *common violet*: see VIOLET *n.* 1. *common vole*: see VOLE *n.*[2] *common* WALLAROO. *common* WOMBAT. **common year** a year of 365 days beginning on 1 January. *least, lowest common multiple*: see MULTIPLE *n.* *make common cause with*: see CAUSE *n.* *the common rustic*: see RUSTIC *n.* 3.

B *adv.* Commonly. *obs.* exc. *US colloq.* ME.

commonish *a.* rather common L18.

†**common** *v.* ME. [Orig. a form of COMMUNE *v.*, with stress shifted to 1st syll. In branch III f. COMMON *n.*, *a.*, COMMONS.] I 1 *v.i.* Associate *with*, have (esp. sexual) intercourse *with*. ME–M16. 2 *v.t.* Share (*with*), communicate (*to*). LME–M16. 3 *v.t.* Tell, declare, publish. LME–M16. 4 *v.i.* Participate, share *in*, *with*. LME–E17. II = COMMUNE *v.* II. 5 *v.t.* & *i.* = COMMUNE *v.* 6. LME–E16. 6a *v.i.* = COMMUNE *v.* 5a. LME–M18. b *v.t.* = COMMUNE *v.* 5c. LME–E17. III 7 *v.i.* Exercise a right of common. E16–E19. 8 *v.i.* Eat at a common table. L16–M18.

commonable /ˈkɒmənəb(ə)l/ *a.* E17. [f. prec. + -ABLE.] 1 Of an animal: able to be pastured on common land. E17. 2 Of land: able to be held in common; suitable for the exercise of rights of common. M17.

commonage /ˈkɒmənɪdʒ/ *n.* E17. [f. COMMON *n.*, *v.* + -AGE.] 1a = COMMON *n.* 5, *esp.* common of pasture. E17. b Common land; a common. L18. c The condition of being subject to rights of common. E19. 2 The common people. M17.

commonality /kɒməˈnalɪti/ *n.* LME. [By-form of next.] †1a = COMMONALTY 1a. LME–L17. b = COMMONALTY 1b. Only in L17. c = COMMONALTY 3. Only in L17. 2a Possession in common; the sharing of features or attributes; the state of having something in common (*with*). (*rare* bef. M20.) M16. b A shared feature or attribute. L20. 3 = COMMONALTY 2. L16.

commonalty /ˈkɒmən(ə)lti/ *n.* See also prec. ME. [OFr. *comunalté* f. med.L *communalitas*, f. L *communis*: see COMMON *a.*, -ALITY.] †1 a The people of a nation, city, etc.; a community, a body politic. ME–M17. b A republic, a democracy. E–M17. 2 The common people. ME. 3 A corporate body. LME. 4 The general body *of* humankind etc. M16.

commoner /ˈkɒmənə/ *n.* ME. [med.L *communarius*, f. *communa* COMMUNE *n.*[1]: see -ER[2].] †1 A citizen, a burgess. ME–M17. 2 Any of the common people; now, anyone below the rank of peer. LME. †3 A person who shares in anything. LME–M17. 4 A member of the House of Commons. Now *rare*. LME. 5 A person who has a right of common. LME. †6 A prostitute. Only in 17. 7 At some English educational institutions: a student without financial support from his college, paying for his own commons; a student without a college scholarship etc. Cf. PENSIONER 5. E17.

commonership *n.* the situation of being a commoner E20.

commonise *v.* var. of COMMONIZE.

†**commonitory** *a.* & *n.* M16. [Late L *commonitorius*, f. L *commonit-* pa. ppl stem of *commonere* remind forcibly, f. as COM- + *monere* advise: see -ORY[2].] A *adj.* Serving to advise or admonish. M16–M18. B *n.* A warning. E18–M19.

†**commonition** *n.* (*rare*) (giving of) a formal admonition M18–M19.

commonize /ˈkɒmənʌɪz/ *v.* Also **-ise**. M19. [f. COMMON *a.* + -IZE.] 1 *v.i.* Pool food and share a meal (*with*). *colloq.* M19. 2 *v.t.* Make common; *spec.* give (a proper noun) a meaning other than as a proper noun. M19.

commoniˈzation *n.* M20.

common law /ˈkɒmən lɔː/ *n. phr.* ME. [tr. med.L *jus commune*.] 1 The part of English law that is applied by national courts but is not fully prescribed by statute, purporting instead to be derived from ancient usage and judicial decisions. Opp. *equity*, *civil law*, *statute law*. ME. b The body of English law as adopted and adapted by the different States of the US. E19. †2 The general law of a community or of the Church, as opp. to local or personal rules and customs. LME–M16.

Comb.: **common-law husband**: in a common-law marriage; **common-law lawyer** = COMMON LAWYER; **common-law marriage** a marriage recognized in some jurisdictions as valid under common law though not brought about by a civil or ecclesiastical ceremony; *pop.* a relationship in which a man and woman cohabit for a period long enough to suggest stability; **common-law wife**: in a common-law marriage.

common lawyer *n. phr.* a lawyer versed in, or practising, common law L16.

commonly /ˈkɒmənli/ *adv.* ME. [f. COMMON *a.* + -LY[2].] †1 Generally, universally. ME–M17. †2 Together. ME–M16. 3 As a general thing; usually, ordinarily. ME. †4 Closely, familiarly. ME–L16. †5 Publicly. LME–L16.

3 GIBBON More than commonly deficient in those qualities. B. JOWETT Writings commonly attributed to

Plato. 5 AV *Matt.* 28:15 This saying is commonly reported among the Iewes vntill this day.

commonness /ˈkɒmənnɪs/ *n.* M16. [f. COMMON *a.* + -NESS.] 1 The state or quality of being common. M16. 2 *spec.* Lack of excellence or distinction. E19.

commonplace /ˈkɒmənpleɪs/ *n.*, *a.*, & *v.* M16. [Orig. two wds, tr. L *locus communis* tr. Gk *koinos topos* general theme.] A *n.* †1 *Rhet.* A passage of general application; a leading text. M–L16. 2a A notable passage or quotation entered in a book for future use. M16. †b A commonplace-book. M16–M18. 3 An ordinary topic; an opinion or statement generally accepted; a platitude. M16. †4 A thesis or discourse on a set theme. M17–E18. 5 Anything usual or trite; ordinary or trite matter. M18. 6 Ordinariness; lack of distinction. M19. 7 *the commonplace*, that which is ordinary and without novelty. M19.

3 D. H. LAWRENCE He was nervous . . , chattering the conventional commonplaces. JOHN BROOKE A commonplace of school history books. 5 S. RICHARDSON Common subjects afford only commonplace. 6 G. M. TREVELYAN Local traditions were yielding to nationwide commonplace.

Comb.: **commonplace-book** a book of commonplaces (sense 2a).

B *adj.* Of the nature of a commonplace; lacking originality, trite. E17.

C *v.* 1 *v.i.* Utter commonplaces. E17. †2 *v.i.* Speak in support of a thesis. M17–M18. 3 *v.t.* Extract noteworthy items from (a text); arrange under general headings; enter in a commonplace-book. M17.

commonplaceness *n.* E19. **commonplacer** *n.* †(*a*) a commonplace-book; (*b*) a person who keeps a commonplace-book: M17.

commons /ˈkɒmənz/ *n.pl.* ME. [Pl. of COMMON *n.*] I Common people. 1 *Hist.* The common people, as distinguished from those of noble, knightly, or gentle rank. ME. †2 The burgesses of a town. ME–E18. 3a The third estate in the English or other similar constitution (in early use excluding the clergy), as represented by the Lower House of Parliament. ME. b (C-.) The representatives in Parliament of this estate; the Lower House. ME.

3b **House of Commons** the Lower House of Parliament, its buildings.

II Provisions in common. 4a Provisions shared in common, esp. in a college or a religious community; the share due to each person; formerly also, the cost of this. ME. b Treated as *sing.* A common table; a dining-hall; formerly, at Oxford University, a definite portion of food supplied by one's college at a set price. M17. 5 Rations; daily fare. M16.

4b T. C. WOLFE Food was . . very cheap: at the college commons, twelve dollars a month. 5 **short commons** insufficient food.

common sense /kɒmən ˈsɛns/ *n. phr.* & *a.* Also **common-sense**, **commonsense**. M16. [Repr. Gk *koinē aisthēsis*, L *sensus communis*.] A *n. phr.* 1 An internal sense formerly regarded as uniting the impressions of the five senses in a common consciousness. *obs.* exc. *Hist.* M16. 2a Ordinary or normal understanding, as possessed by all except the insane and the mentally handicapped. M16. b Good sound practical sense in everyday matters; general sagacity. E18. c A thing in accordance with common sense. E19. 3 The collective sense or judgement of humankind or of a community. L16. 4 *Philos.* The faculty by which certain beliefs are generally accepted without philosophical enquiry or influence from religious teaching etc. M18.

B *adj.* (With hyphen or as one wd.) Based on common sense; that is in accord with common sense. M19.

R. G. COLLINGWOOD The world they represent is not the common-sense world, it is the world of delirium.

common'sensible *a.* = COMMONSENSICAL M19. **common'sensibly** *adv.* L19. **common'sensical** *a.* possessing or marked by common sense M19. **ˌcommonsensi'cality** *n.* E20. **common'sensically** *adv.* L19.

commonty /ˈkɒmənti/ *n.* Now only *Sc.* LME. [OFr. *comuneté*: see COMMUNITY.] †1 = COMMONALTY 2. LME–M17. †2 A community, a body politic. LME–E16. 3 Common possession. LME. 4 = COMMON *n.* 5. *Sc.* LME. 5 = COMMON *n.* 3. *Sc.* LME.

commonweal /ˈkɒmənwiːl/ *n. arch.* ME. [Orig. two wds, f. COMMON *a.* + WEAL *n.*[1]] 1 = COMMONWEALTH 2. ME. 2 (Usu. two wds.) Common well-being; the general good. LME.

commonwealth /ˈkɒmənwɛlθ/ *n.* LME. [Orig. two wds, f. COMMON *a.* + WEALTH.] 1 = COMMONWEAL 2. *arch.* LME. 2 The body politic; a nation, viewed as a community in which everyone has an interest. E16. 3 *fig.* Any aggregate of persons or things united by some common factor. M16. b A company of actors who share the takings instead of receiving a salary. E19. 4 A republic; a democracy. E17. b A state of the US, esp. as a formal title of some of them. L18. 5 *the Commonwealth*: a *Hist.* The republican government in England between 1649 and 1660. M17. b The federated states of Australia. L19. c [f. sense 3.] A free association of the UK with certain independent States (orig. subject to Britain) and dependencies which all acknowledge the British monarch as its Head. Also *British Commonwealth (of Nations)*. E20.

3 BURKE Writers on publick law have often called this aggregate of nations a commonwealth. **commonwealth of learning** learned people collectively. *commonwealth of letters*: see LETTER *n.*[1] **commonwealth of nations** the nations viewed as a community of states. 5a *Lord Protector of the Commonwealth*: see PROTECTOR 2b. c **the New Commonwealth** countries of the British Commonwealth that have become independent since 1945. **the Old Commonwealth** Canada, Australia, and New Zealand.

Comb.: **Commonwealth Day** a day each year commemorating the British Commonwealth (formerly called Empire Day); **Commonwealth preference** the practice of charging lower tariffs on imports from Commonwealth countries; **commonwealth's-man** †(*a*) a person devoted to the public good; (*b*) *Hist.* an adherent of the Commonwealth in the 17th cent.; †(*c*) a republican.

commorant /ˈkɒmər(ə)nt/ *a.* Now *rare* or *obs.* M16. [L *commorant-* pres. ppl stem of *commorari* tarry, abide, f. as COM- + *morari* delay: see -ANT[1].] Resident.

commorancy *n.* (a) residence, (an) abode L16. †**commoration** *n.* residing, abiding E17–M19.

commorient /kəˈmɔːrɪənt/ *a.* & *n.* M17. [L *commorient-* pres. ppl stem of *commori*, f. as COM- + *mori* die: see -ENT.] †A *adj.* Of or pertaining to simultaneous death. Only in M17. B *n.* Pl. **commorientes** /kəmɔːrɪˈɛntiːz/, **commorients**. A person who dies at the same time as another; *Law* each of two or more people dying on the same occasion (as in the same accident or other disaster) and connected by way of disposing of assets one to the other on death (usu. in *pl.*). M18.

commot /ˈkɒmət/ *n.* Also **-ote** /-əʊt/. L15. [Welsh *cymwd*, *kymwt* (now *cwmwd*) neighbourhood, locality.] *Welsh Hist.* A territorial division subordinate to a cantred.

commotion /kəˈməʊʃ(ə)n/ *n.* LME. [(O)Fr., or L *commotio(n-)*, f. as COM- + *motio(n-)* MOTION *n.*] †1 Mental or emotional disturbance. LME–M18. 2 Public disorder; (an) insurrection. LME. 3a (A) physical disturbance, more or less violent. LME. b (A) bustle; (a) noisy confusion. E17. †4 Continuous or recurring motion. E16–M17.

3a SOUTHEY The billows' commotion. b P. PEARCE There was a commotion of voices and footsteps.

commove /kəˈmuːv/ *v.t. arch.* LME. [Orig. f. OFr. *commovoir* (see COM-, MOVE *v.*); later f. MOVE *v.* after L *commovere*.] Move violently; agitate, arouse, (*lit.* & *fig.*); excite. Chiefly as *commoved* ppl a.

R. L. STEVENSON He who has seen the sea commoved with a great hurricane.

communal /ˈkɒmjʊn(ə)l, kəˈmjuː-/ *a.* L15. [OFr. *communel* (mod. *-al*) f. late L *communalis*, f. *communis* COMMON *a.*: see -AL[1].] †1 Unanimous. *rare.* Only in L15. 2 Of, pertaining to, or belonging to a commune, esp. (C-) the Paris Commune. E19. 3 Of or for the community or a community, for common use; shared by all, general. M19.

3 R. FRY The greatest art has always been communal. C. MCCULLOUGH The bathroom and kitchen were communal, shared by all the tenants. F. WELDON The communal guilt which the male sex appears to bear in relation to women. *communal* MARRIAGE.

commu'nality *n.* community of feeling, solidarity E20. **communali'zation** *n.* the action of communalizing L19. **communalize** *v.t.* make (esp. land) communal L19. **communally** *adv.* L19.

communalism /ˈkɒmjʊn(ə)lɪz(ə)m/ *n.* L19. [f. prec. + -ISM.] The principle of the communal organization of society.

communalist *n.* an adherent of communalism L19. **communa'listic** *a.* L19.

communard /ˈkɒmjʊnɑːd/ *n.* L19. [Fr., f. as next + -ARD.] A member of a commune; *esp.* (C-) an adherent of the Paris Commune; a communalist.

commune /ˈkɒmjuːn/ *n.*[1] L17. [Fr. f. med.L *communia* neut. pl. of L *communis* COMMON *a.* taken as fem. sing. in sense 'group of people having a common life'.] I 1 A French territorial division, the smallest for administrative purposes; a similar division elsewhere. L17. 2 Hist. *the Commune (of Paris)*, *the Paris Commune*: (*a*) a body which usurped the municipal government of Paris during the French Revolution; (*b*) the communalistic government temporarily established in Paris in 1871. L18. 3 A communal settlement, orig. in a Communist country; a group of people not all of one family sharing living accommodation and goods. E20. II 4 *Hist.* The commonalty; a corporate body. E19.

commune /ˈkɒmjuːn/ *n.*[2] E19. [f. next.] The action of communing; converse, communion.

commune /kəˈmjuːn, ˈkɒmjuːn/ *v.* ME. [OFr. *comuner* share, f. *comun* COMMON *a.*: cf. COMMON *v.*] I = COMMON *v.* I. †1 *v.i.* = COMMON *v.* 1. ME–E19. †2 *v.t.* = COMMON *v.* 2. ME–M16. †3 *v.t.* = COMMON *v.* 3. LME–M16. †4 = COMMON *v.* 4. Only in LME. II †5a *v.i.* Confer, consult, converse, (*with* a person, *of*, (*up*)*on* a matter). ME–M18. b *v.i.* Have an intimate (esp. mental or spiritual) exchange or discussion (*with* a friend, one's heart, etc., *together*); feel in close touch *with* (nature etc.). LME. †c *v.t.* Confer about, discuss, debate. L16–M17. †6a *v.t.* Administer Holy Communion to; = COMMUNICATE *v.* 3b. ME–E16. b *v.i.* Receive Holy Communion; = COMMUNICATE *v.* 3a. Now chiefly *US*. M16.

communer *n.* (long *rare*) LME.

communicable /kəˈmjuːnɪkəb(ə)l/ *a.* LME. [(O)Fr., or late L *communicabilis*, f. *communicare*: see COMMUNICATE *v.*, -ABLE.] †1 Communicating, having intercommunication. LME–L17. 2 Able to be communicated to others. M16. 3 Communicative, affable. *arch.* M16.

2 E. A. PARKES An animal poison . . communicable from person to person. H. READ A vision . . too mystical to be wholly communicable.

communica'bility *n.* M17. **communicableness** *n.* E17. **communicably** *adv.* E17.

communicant /kəˈmjuːnɪk(ə)nt/ *a.* & *n.* L15. [L *communicant-* pres. ppl stem of *communicare*: see COMMUNICATE *v.*, -ANT[1].] A *adj.* †1 Of existence: shared *with*. *rare.* Only in L15. 2 Sharing, participating; having a part in common. *rare.* M16. 3 Providing communication, communicating. *rare.* L17. 4 Receiving Holy Communion, esp. regularly. *rare.* M19. B *n.* 1 A person who receives Holy Communion, esp. regularly. M16. 2 A person who or thing which makes a communication; a person who imparts information. L16.

†**communicate** *a.* LME–E18. [L *communicatus* pa. pple, f. as next: see -ATE[2].] Extrinsic; communicated.

communicate /kəˈmjuːnɪkeɪt/ *v.* E16. [L *communicat-* pa. ppl stem of *communicare* impart, share, etc., f. *communis* COMMON *a.* + *-ic-* formative of factitive vbs: see -ATE[3].] 1 *v.t.* Impart, transmit, (something intangible or abstract, as heat, motion, feeling, disease, etc., *to*, *spec.* information, news, etc., *to*, †*with*). E16. †**b** Give, bestow, (something material). L16–M18. **2** *v.t.* Share in, partake of; use or enjoy in common (*with*); share *with. arch.* E16. †**b** *v.i.* Have a share, participate. (Foll. by *in*, *with*.) L16–E18. **3a** *v.i.* Receive Holy Communion. M16. **b** *v.t.* Administer Holy Communion to. M16. †**c** *v.t.* Celebrate, give, or receive (the Eucharist). M17–E18. †**4** *v.refl.* Make oneself familiar; have intercourse or converse. (Foll. by *to*, *with*.) M16–L18. **5** *v.i.* Make or maintain social contact; convey or exchange information etc.; succeed in evoking understanding. (Foll. by *with*.) L16. **6** *v.i.* Of rooms, vessels, etc.: have a common connecting door, aperture, channel, etc., (*with*); open into one another. M18.

1 E. F. BENSON She read her other letter . . and communicated the contents. V. BRITTAIN I tried to communicate my enthusiasm for Oxford to the family circle. A. POWELL The stagnant character of those streets seemed to communicate itself to one's limbs. 2 JONSON Thousands, that communicate our loss. W. WALLACE Nor was he the only acquaintance with whom Schopenhauer communicated some of his . . means. 5 E. B. TYLOR No means of communicating with others but by signs. *Listener* They buy only pictures that will communicate readily. B. EMECHETA She and Francis communicated only in monosyllables. *Acorn User* There are many variable parameters to be agreed before two computers can communicate. 6 H. JAMES The library, which communicated with the office. OED Their apartments are separate, but they communicate by a door.

communication /kəmjuːnɪˈkeɪʃ(ə)n/ *n.* LME. [f. as prec.: see -ATION.] **1** The action of communicating heat, feeling, motion, etc.; *spec.* the transmission or exchange of information, news, etc. LME. **b** In *pl.* The science and practice of transmitting information. M20. †**2** Conference; a conversation. LME–E17. **3** Social contact, personal intercourse. LME. **b** Sexual intercourse. Long *arch.* L18. †**4** Shared possession, common participation; a similarity; a sharing. LME–L18. **5** Something communicated; (a piece of) information; a written paper of information, observations, comments, etc. L15. **6** Access or means of access between persons or places; a means of communicating; a connecting door, passage, road, telephone line, etc.; in *pl.* spec. *Mil.*, the means of transport between a base and a front. L17. **7** A meeting of a Masonic lodge. L19.

1 J. B. PRIESTLEY The telegram was . . the common method of communication. 3 DEFOE They had little knowledge or communication one with another. 5 OED I have read your communication to the *Academy*. M. PEAKE Very little communication passed between . . these outer quarters and those who lived *within* the walls. 6 J. LUBBOCK To protect our communications with India and Australia.

Phrases: **in communication (with)** †(*a*) in conference with; (*b*) actively communicating (with), able to communicate actively (with). PRIVILEGED *communication*.

Comb.: **communication cord** a cord or chain for pulling by a passenger to stop a train in an emergency; **communication(s) satellite** an artificial satellite for broadcast communications; **communication(s) theory** the branch of knowledge that deals with language and other means of conveying or exchanging information.

communicational *a.* M20. **communicationally** *adv.* L20.

communicative /kəˈmjuːnɪkətɪv/ *a.* LME. [Late L *communicativus*, f. as prec.: see -IVE. Cf. (O)Fr. *communicatif*, *-ive*.] **1** Having the quality or habit of communicating. Now *spec.* ready to impart information etc.; open, talkative. LME. †**2** Able to be communicated. E17–M18. **3** Of or pertaining to communication. L17.

1 JER. TAYLOR An evil so communicative that it doth . . work like poison. W. COWPER Communicative of the good he owns. A. LURIE When drinks are served people become more lively and communicative.

communicatively *adv.* M17. **communicativeness** *n.* M17.

communicator /kəˈmjuːnɪkeɪtə/ *n.* M17. [f. COMMUNICATE *v.* + -OR.] A person who or thing which communicates.

attrib.: D. ADAMS The . . Captain pressed a communicator button.

communicatory *a.* (now *rare*) tending or pertaining to communication M17.

communion /kəˈmjuːnjən/ *n.* LME. [(O)Fr., or L *communio(n-)*, f. *communis* COMMON *a.*: see -ION. The religious uses depend on eccl.L.] **I1** Sharing, holding or being held in common, community; fellowship; (an) association in action, relation, or function. LME. **2** Communication, social contact. E17. **3** Intimate mental or spiritual communing. *literary*. E19.

1 AV *2 Cor.* 6:14 What fellowship hath righteousness with unrighteousness? and what communion hath light with darkness? A. WILSON Three elderly English scholars with no real communion of feeling except their nationality. 2 W. RALEIGH The Israelites never had any communion or affairs with the Ethiopians. 3 R. FORD That health of body and soul which ever rewards a close communion with Nature.

II4 The fellowship or mutual recognition between members of one Church, esp. between branches of the Catholic Church. Also, an organized body of people united by common religious faith and rites; *esp.* a body professing one branch of the Christian faith. LME. **5** Also **C-**. (Participation in) the Eucharist. Also more fully *Holy Communion*. LME.

4 *communion of saints*: see SAINT *n.* & *a.* *lay communion*: see LAY *a.* 5 **close Communion**: restricted to selected Church members; esp. among Baptists, to those baptized by immersion. **Communion in both kinds**: in which both the consecrated elements of bread and wine are administered. **Communion in one kind**: in which only one consecrated element is administered. **free Communion** = *open Communion* below. *lay communion*: see LAY *a.* **open Communion**: administered to any Christian believer. **strict Communion** = *close Communion* above.

Comb.: **Communion-cloth** = *altar-cloth* s.v. ALTAR *n.*; **Communion-cup, -plate**, etc.: used for the consecrated elements at Holy Communion; **Communion-rail** a rail in front of an altar or Communion table behind which people can receive Communion; **Communion table** the table or altar at which Holy Communion is celebrated.

communionist *n.* (*a*) *rare* = COMMUNICANT *n.* 1; (*b*) an adherent of a specified (*strict* etc.) type of Communion: M17.

communiqué /kəˈmjuːnɪkeɪ/ *n.* M19. [Fr., use as n. of pa. pple of *communiquer* communicate.] An official communication; *esp.* an official statement reporting on a meeting, conference; etc.

communise *v.* var. of COMMUNIZE.

communism /ˈkɒmjʊnɪz(ə)m/ *n.* M19. [Fr. *communisme*, f. *commun* COMMON *a.*: see -ISM.] (A theory advocating) a system of society with property vested in the community and each member working for the common benefit according to his or her capacity and receiving according to his or her needs; *spec.* (usu. **C-**) the movement or political party advocating such a system, esp. as derived from Marxism and seeking the overthrow of capitalism by a proletarian revolution; the communistic form of society established in the 20th cent. in the former USSR and elsewhere.

communist /ˈkɒmjʊnɪst/ *n.* & *a.* Also **C-**. M19. [Fr. *communiste*, f. as prec.: see -IST.] **A** *n.* An adherent of communism. M19. **B** *adj.* Of or pertaining to communists or communism; adhering to communism. M19.

commuˈnistic *a.* of, pertaining to, or characteristic of communism M19. **commuˈnistically** *adv.* L19.

communitarian /kəmjuːnɪˈtɛːrɪən/ *n.* & *a.* M19. [f. COMMUNITY + -ARIAN, after *unitarian* etc.] **A** *n.* A member of a community practising cooperation and some communism. M19. **B** *adj.* Of, pertaining to, or characteristic of communitarians or their type of community. E20.

communitorium *n.* a communitarian residence or settlement M19.

community /kəˈmjuːnɪti/ *n.* LME. [OFr. *communeté* (mod. *communité*), assim. to its source L *communitas*, f. *communis* COMMON *a.*: see -ITY. Cf. COMMONTY.] **I** A body of individuals. †**1** The commons as opp. to peers etc.; the common people. LME–E18. **2** An organized political, municipal, or social body; a body of people living in the same locality; a body of people having religion, profession, etc., in common; a body of nations unified by common interests (freq., w. cap. initial, in the title of an international organization). LME. **b** *The* members of such a body collectively. L18. **3** A monastic, socialistic, etc., body of people living together and holding goods in common. E18. **4** A group of animals etc. living or acting together; *Ecol.* a group of interdependent plants or animals growing or living together in natural conditions or inhabiting a specified locality. M18.

2 C. G. SELIGMAN They live in small communities or hunting bands. J. BRAINE The Thespians gave me . . the sense of belonging, of being part of a community. DAY LEWIS We were an ordered little unit . . , a Protestant enclave in a Catholic community. *European Defence Community*, *European Economic Community*, etc. *satellite community*: see SATELLITE *n.* 3b. 4 *open community*: see OPEN *a.*

II A quality or state. **5** The state of being shared or held in common; joint ownership or liability. M16. **6** (A) common character; (an) agreement; (an) identity. L16. **7** Social intercourse; communion; fellowship, sense of common identity. L16. †**8** Commonness, ordinary occurrence. L16–M17. **9** Life in association with others; society; the social state. M17.

5 H. G. WELLS Our community of blood with all mankind. H. J. LASKI Wallace traces these evils to private property and . . sees no remedy save community of possessions. 6 WORDSWORTH The points of community in their nature. A. STORR Men who form a close association based upon a community of ideas cannot avoid passionate controversy. 7 M. SHELLEY There can be no community between you and me; we are enemies. P. GOODMAN During depression . . there is more community. 9 STEELE [Marriage] is the foundation of community, and the chief band of society. S. NAIPAUL The decaying cities where the sense of community, of human belongingness, had been destroyed.

Comb.: **community architect**: working in consultation with the local community in designing housing and other amenities; **community architecture**: as practised by community architects; **community centre** (a part of) a building providing social, recreational, and educational facilities for a neighbourhood; **community charge** a community tax; *spec.* (*Hist.*) in Britain, a short-lived tax levied by local authorities on every adult; **community chest** *US* a fund for charity and welfare work in a community; **community college** *N. Amer.*: esp. for members of the local community providing further and higher education; **community home** an institution for young offenders and other juveniles in need of custodial care; **community hospital** *US* a local general hospital esp. for short-term patients; **community leader** a prominent and active member or office-holder within a particular community; **community medicine** the branch of medicine that deals with matters of health and disease as they affect communities as a whole; **community policeman, police officer**, etc.: involved in community policing; **community policing**: by officers intended to have personal knowledge of and involvement in the community which they police; **community service order**: for a convicted offender to perform a stipulated period of unpaid work helping the community or a member of it; **community singing**: in chorus by a large gathering of people; **community spirit** a feeling of membership of a community; **community tax** (a) local tax on members of a community; **community worker** a person who works in a community to promote its welfare.

communize /ˈkɒmjʊnʌɪz/ *v.t.* Also **-ise**. L19. [f. L *communis* COMMON *a.* + -IZE.] Make (land etc.) common property; make communistic.

communiˈzation *n.* M19.

commutable /kəˈmjuːtəb(ə)l/ *a.* M17. [L *commutabilis*, f. as COMMUTE *v.*; in sense 2 f. COMMUTE *v.*: see -ABLE. Cf. earlier INCOMMUTABLE.] **1** Exchangeable; convertible into money; that can be compounded for. M17. **2** Of a place: able to be commuted from or to; within commuting distance. (Foll. by *from* (a place), *to*.) L20.

commutaˈbility *n.* L18.

commutate /ˈkɒmjuːteɪt/ *v.* M17. [L *commutat-* pa. ppl stem of *commutare*: see COMMUTE *v.*, -ATE³.] †1 *v.i.* Change. *rare*. Only in M17. 2 *v.t.* Regulate the direction of (an electric current), esp. to make it a direct current. L19.

commutation /kɒmjʊˈteɪʃ(ə)n/ *n.* LME. [(O)Fr., or L *commutatio(n-)*, f. as prec.: see -ATION.] †1 Exchange, barter. LME–M18. †2 Change, alteration. E16–M19. 3 *Rhet.* A figure of speech involving a reversal of word order. *rare*. M16. 4 Interchange, replacement, substitution; *spec.* (*a*) substitution of one kind of payment or penalty for another; *Law* a reduction in severity in the penalty imposed; (*b*) *Math.* interchange of the order of two quantities added, operated on, multiplied, etc.; (*c*) *Ling.* substitution of one sound for another to produce a different word, as a test of separate phonemes. L16. 5 Regulation of the direction of an electric current; the action of a commutator. L19.

Comb.: **commutation ticket** *US* a season ticket.

commutative /kəˈmjuːtətɪv, ˈkɒmjʊtətɪv/ *a.* M16. [(O)Fr. *commutatif, -ive* or L *commutativus*, f. as COMMUTATE: see -IVE.] 1 Of or pertaining to exchange or transactions between people. Chiefly & now only in *commutative justice*. M16. 2 Pertaining to or involving substitution; *Math.* governed by or stating the condition that the result of a binary operation is unchanged by interchange of the order of quantities, e.g. that $a \times b = b \times a$. M19. 3 Pertaining to or involving commutation of a penalty etc. M19.

2 B. RUSSELL The associative, commutative and distributive laws.

commutatively *adv.* L17. **commutativeness** *n.* = COMMUTATIVITY L19. **commutaˈtivity** *n.* the ability of two or more quantities to commute E20.

commutator /ˈkɒmjʊteɪtə/ *n.* M19. [f. (as) COMMUTATE + -OR.] A thing which commutes; *spec.* a device for commutating an electric current.

commute /kəˈmjuːt/ *v.* & *n.* LME. [L *commutare* change wholly, exchange, f. as COM- + *mutare* change.] A *v.* 1 *v.t.* Change (*into*); exchange, substitute, (*for*); interchange (two things). LME. 2 *v.t. spec.* Change (an obligation etc.) *for, into* another by making a payment etc.; change (one kind of payment or penalty) *for, into* another; change (a punishment) *to* another less severe; convert into money. M17. 3 *v.i.* Compensate *for*; serve as a substitute *for*. Now *rare*. M17. 4 *v.t.* Commutate (an electric current). L19. 5 *v.i.* Buy and use a commutation ticket (*US*); travel by public or private conveyance between one's home and one's place of work; travel *between* regularly or frequently. (Earlier in COMMUTER.) L19. 6 *v.i. Math.* Have a commutative relation (*with*). E20.

1 T. KEN He and the Beasts seem Natures to commute, They act like Reason, and he like the Brute. 2 J. S. MILL The legislature . . might commute the average receipts of Irish landowners into a fixed rent charge. E. BOWEN I commuted my pension. A. KOESTLER He waited a year for his execution, then the sentence was commuted to lifelong imprisonment. 5 J. ARCHER The 8.17 train so favoured by those who commute from Oxford to London every day.

B *n.* A journey on a commutation ticket (*US*); a journey by public or private conveyance between one's home and one's place of work. M20.

commuter /kəˈmjuːtə/ *n.* Orig. *US*. M19. [f. COMMUTE *v.* + -ER¹.] A person who commutes to work.

commutual /kəˈmjuːtʃʊəl, -tjʊəl/ *a.* Chiefly *poet.* Also †**comutual**. E17. [f. COM-, CO- + MUTUAL *a.*] Mutual, reciprocal.

comose /ˈkəʊməʊs/ *a.* L18. [L *comosus*, f. as COMA *n.*²: see -OSE¹.] Of seeds etc.: hairy, downy. Also **comous** *a.* M17.

comozant *n.* see CORPOSANT.

comp /kɒmp/ *n. colloq.* L17. [Abbrev.] 1 = COMPANY *n.* 3d. L17. 2 = COMPOSITOR 3. L19. 3 = COMPETITION 2. E20. 4 = ACCOMPANIMENT I. M20.

comp /kɒmp/ *v.i.* & *t. colloq.* L19. [Abbrev.] 1 Work as a compositor (on), compose. L19. 2 Play an accompaniment (to); accompany. M20.

compact /ˈkɒmpakt/ *n.*¹ L16. [L *compactum* use as n. of neut. pa. pple of *compacisci* make an agreement: see COM-, PACT *n.* Cf. OFr. *compact*.] 1 An agreement or contract made between two or more parties. L16. †2 Confederacy, plot, conspiracy. L16–M17.

1 *social compact*: see SOCIAL *a.*

compact /ˈkɒmpakt/ *n.*² L16. [f. next.] 1 An object or body of compacted material; a combination; a compact state. Now *rare*. L16. 2 A small flat case for face-powder etc., usu. with a mirror in the lid. Also *powder compact*. E20. 3 A medium-sized motor car. *N. Amer.* M20.

compact /kəmˈpakt, *in sense 1 also* ˈkɒmpakt/ *a.* LME. [L *compactus* pa. pple, f. as COMPACT *v.*¹ Cf. (O)Fr. *compact* adj.] 1 Closely or neatly packed together; dense; economical of space; not straggling or gangling; not diffuse; (of style etc.) condensed, terse. LME. 2 Made up *of*, composed *of*. M16.

1 K. AMIS A compact city with no suburbs to speak of. P. DAVIES A star that has imploded . . and become so compact that even its atoms are crushed. **compact car** *N. Amer.* a medium-sized car. **compact disc**: on which sound, information, etc., is recorded digitally as a spiral pattern of pits and bumps for reproduction or retrieval using a laser beam. 2 V. SACKVILLE-WEST Of such small . . and mutual courtesies was their relationship compact.

compactly *adv.* E17. **compactness** *n.* M17.

compact /kəmˈpakt/ *v.*¹*t.* Pa. pple (earlier) **compact** (*arch.*), **-ed**. LME. [L *compact-* pa. ppl stem of *compingere*, f. as COM- + *pangere* fasten. Cf. prec.] 1 Join or press firmly together; combine closely; compress, condense. LME. 2 Devise; make up (or †*up*), compose (*of*). M16. †3 Confirm, give consistency to. *rare* (Shakes.) Only in E17.

compactedly *adv.* (*rare*) compactly M17. **compactedness** *n.* compactness M17. **compactor** *n.* a person who or thing which compacts. L16.

†**compact** *v.*² Pa. pple **compact, -ed**. M16. [L *compact-* pa. ppl stem of *compacisci*: see COMPACT *n.*¹] 1 *v.i.* Make a compact or agreement (*with*). M16–L17. 2 *v.t.* Join in a compact; plan by a compact. L16–M17.

compaction /kəmˈpakʃ(ə)n/ *n.* LME. [L *compactio(n-)*, f. as COMPACT *v.*¹: see -ION. Cf. OFr. *compaction*.] The action, process, or result of making or becoming compact; *spec.* the action or process of inducing the particles of a substance (as soil, concrete, etc.) to combine more tightly.

compactum /kəmˈpaktəm/ *n.* E20. [L, use as n. of neut. of *compactus*: see COMPACT *a.*] A structure or device intended to hold a number of articles; a container; *spec.* a wardrobe.

†**compacture** *n.* L15–M17. [L *compactura*, f. as COMPACT *v.*¹: see -URE.] Manner of putting closely together; compact structure.

compadre /kɒmˈpɑːdri/ *n.* Chiefly *US*. M19. [Sp. = godfather, hence benefactor, friend. Cf. GOSSIP *n.*] Companion, friend, (freq. as a form of address).

compages /kəmˈpeɪdʒiːz/ *n.* Pl. same. Also (earlier) †**-age**. M16. [L *compages*, f. as COM- + *pag-* base of *pangere* fasten, fix. Earliest form assoc. w. ns. in -AGE.] 1 The joining of parts into a whole; solid structure; consistency. Now *rare*. M16. 2 A whole formed by the joining of parts; a framework, a complex structure, (*lit.* & *fig.*). M17.

compaginate /kəmˈpadʒɪneɪt/ *v.t.* Now *rare*. E17. [Late L *compaginat-* pa. ppl stem of *compaginare*, f. *compago, -agin-* compages: see -ATE³.] Join or fit firmly together; connect, unite, (*lit.* & *fig.*).

compagiˈnation *n.* M17.

compagnon de voyage /kɔ̃paɲɔ̃ də vwajaːʒ/ *n. phr.* Also ***du*** /dy/. Pl. ***compagnons de voyage*** (pronounced same). M18. [Fr.] A travelling companion, a fellow traveller.

compander /kəmˈpandə/ *n.* Also **-or**. M20. [Blend of COMPRESSOR and EXPANDER.] *Telecommunications.* A device that improves the signal-to-noise ratio of reproduced or transmitted sound by compressing the range of amplitudes of the signal before transmission, and then expanding it on reproduction or reception.

compand *v.t.* [back-form.] subject to the action of a compander L20.

†**companiable** *a.* Also **-anable**. ME–E19. [OFr. *compaignable*, f. as COMPANY *v.*: see -ABLE.] Sociable, companionable.

†**compan(i)ableness** *n.* L16–L18.

companion /kəmˈpanjən/ *n.*¹ & *v.* ME. [OFr. *compaignon* f. Proto-Romance, f. L COM- + *panis* bread.] A *n.* I 1 A person who associates with or accompanies another; an associate *in*, a sharer *of*. ME. †b A (worthless) person, a fellow. L16–M18. †2 Each of two or more people associated in a specific or legal relation. M16–M18. 3 (Also C-.) A member of an order of knighthood. Now *spec.* a member of the lowest grade of some orders of distinction. M16. 4 A person, usu. a woman, who is paid to live with and accompany another. M18. 5 A journeyman. *obs.* exc. *Hist.* L18.

3 *Companion of the Bath* etc.

II 6 A necessary guide or aid to a particular pursuit; *esp.* (*a*) a handbook or reference book to a specific subject, locality, etc. (freq. as part of the title); (*b*) (a piece of) equipment combining several requisites. E18. 7 A thing that matches or closely resembles another. L18. 8 A star etc. that accompanies another; *esp.* the fainter component of a double star system. E19.

Phrases: *boon companion*: see BOON *a.* **companion in arms** a fellow-soldier. **Companion of Honour** a member of a British order for those who have rendered conspicuous service to the nation. **Companion of Literature** (a recipient of) an honour conferred by the Royal Society of Literature. *free companion*: see FREE *a.* *lady's companion*: see LADY *n.* & *a.* *native companion*: see NATIVE *a.*

Attrib. & *comb.*: In the sense 'that is a companion, that matches', as *companion piece, volume*, etc. Special combs., as **companion-cell** *Bot.* a specialized elongated parenchymatous cell connected to a sieve-tube in the phloem of some flowering plants; **companion-set** a set of fireside implements on a stand; **companion star** = sense 8 above.

B *v.* 1 *v.*†*refl.* & *i.* Keep company, consort, *with*. *literary.* E17. 2 *v.t.* Go or be with as a companion; accompany (*lit.* & *fig.*). E17.

companionage *n.* (a list of) the body of companions of various orders L19. **companionhood** *n.* = COMPANIONSHIP M19. **companionless** *a.* E19. †**companionry** *n.* (chiefly *Sc.*) = COMPANIONSHIP L16–E18.

companion /kəmˈpanjən/ *n.*² M18. [Alt., by assoc. w. prec., of Du. †*kompanje* (now *kampanje*) quarterdeck f. OFr. *compagne* f. It. (*camera della*) *compagna* storeroom for provisions.] *Naut.* 1 A raised window-frame on a quarterdeck for lighting cabins etc. below. Also, a wooden covering over the entrance to the master's cabin in some small ships. M18. 2 In full *companion ladder*. A ladder giving access from deck to deck; the ladder to the quarterdeck used by officers. M19. 3 In full *companion-way*. The staircase to a cabin. M19.

Comb.: **companion-hatch** a wooden covering over the companion-way; **companion hatchway** an opening in a deck leading to a cabin; *companion ladder*: see sense 2 above; *companion-way*: see sense 3 above.

companionable /kəmˈpanjənəb(ə)l/ *a.* E17. [Alt. of COMPAN(I)ABLE after COMPANION *n.*¹] 1 Fitted for companionship; sociable, friendly; agreeable as company. E17. 2 Fitted to go *with* or match. *rare*. E19.

companionaˈbility *n.* E19. **companionableness** *n.* L17. **companionably** *adv.* L17.

companionate /kəmˈpanjənət/ *a.* M17. [f. COMPANION *n.*¹ + -ATE².] †1 Companioned. Only in M17. 2 Designating a proposed form of marriage providing for divorce by mutual consent without any further legal obligations. E20.

companioned /kəmˈpanjənd/ *a.* E19. [f. COMPANION *n.*¹, *v.*: see -ED², -ED¹.] Having, or accompanied by, a companion or companions.

¶Earlier in UNCOMPANIONED (in different sense).

companionship /kəm'panjənʃɪp/ *n.* M16. [f. COMPANION *n.*^{1} + -SHIP.] 1 The state of being or having a companion or companions; association or presence as a companion or companions; fellowship. M16. b An association, a fellowship. M19. 2 *Hist.* The state of being a journeyman. L18. 3 An organized group of people; *spec.* (*Printing Hist.*) a company of compositors working together under a clicker. E19. 4 Usu. **C-**. The dignity of a Companion in an order of knighthood etc. L19.

company /'kʌmp(ə)ni/ *n.* ME. [AN *compainie*, OFr. *compa(i)gnie*, f. Proto-Romance source of COMPANION *n.*^{1}: see -Y^3. Infl. in commercial sense by It. *compagnia*, in mil. sense by Fr. *compagnie*.] 1 Companionship, fellowship, society. ME. †b Sexual intercourse. ME–E17. 2 A number of individuals assembled or associated together; a body of people combined for some common object. ME. 3 *esp.* a A body of soldiers; *spec.* a subdivision of an infantry battalion usu. commanded by a major or a captain. ME. b (A corporation historically representing) a medieval trade guild. LME. c A party of actors, entertainers, (formerly) musicians, etc. E16. d A legal association formed to carry on some commercial or industrial undertaking. M16. e In full *ship's company*. The entire crew of a ship. E17. f A social party or assembly. M17. g A unit of Guides. E20. 4 Persons assembled or associated together; the social world (*arch.*); persons or a person whose presence prevents solitude or privacy; *esp.* guests. LME. b The partner(s) whose names do not appear in the style or title of a firm. Chiefly in *and Company*. M16. c The person or persons with whom one voluntarily or habitually associates. E17.

1 H. JAMES He found his own company quite absorbing. N. MOSLEY My child was quiet in the company of the others. 2 V. WOOLF Gulls rode gently swaying in little companies of two or three. 4 OED I hoped we should be private here, but I find we have company. R. LARDNER I do love to have company once in a while, just a few congenial friends. c BURKE Unfortunate in the choice of his political company.

Phrases: **bad, good,** etc., **company** (*a*) a dull, lively, etc., companion; (*b*) unsuitable, suitable, etc., companions. *bear company*: see BEAR *v.*^{1} **err** etc. **in good company** do no more than better people have done. *free company*: see FREE *a. good company*: see *bad company* above. **in company with** together with. JOHN *Company*. *join company*: see JOIN *v.* 2. *joint-stock company*: see JOINT *a.* **keep company (with)** associate habitually (with); *arch. colloq.* court. **keep a person company** accompany or stay with a person. **know a person by his** or **her company, by the company he** or **she keeps** deduce a person's character from his or her habitual companions, resorts, etc. LIMITED *company*. LIMITED-*liability company*. MIXED *company*. *parent company*: see PARENT *n.* 3b. *part company*: see PART *v. present company excepted*: see PRESENT *a. private company*: see PRIVATE *a. proprietary company*: see PROPRIETARY *a.* 2. *public company*: see PUBLIC *a.* & *n. repertory company*: see REPERTORY 3c. *ship's company*: see sense 3e above. STATUTORY *company*. *subsidiary company*: see SUBSIDIARY *a.* 1. **the Company** *US slang* the Central Intelligence Agency. *transfer company*: see TRANSFER *n.*

Comb.: **company car**: owned (or leased) and maintained by a commercial company for the use of an employee; **company law**: concerned with legally established companies; **company officer** a captain or lower commissioned officer; *company promoter*: see PROMOTER 1b; *company sergeant-major*: see SERGEANT-MAJOR *n.* 2.

company /kʌmp(ə)ni/ *v.* Now *dial., arch.,* & *literary*. ME. [OFr. *compaignier*, f. *compaing* nom. of (the accus. form) *compaignon* COMPANION *n.*^{1}] 1 *v.t.* Accompany. ME. †2 *v.t.* Associate in companionship (*with*). LME–L16. 3 *v.i.* Keep company (*with, together*). LME. †b Cohabit *with*. LME–L17.

comparable /'kɒmp(ə)rəb(ə)l/ *a.* LME. [(O)Fr. f. L *comparabilis*, f. *comparare*: see COMPARE *v.*^{1}, -ABLE.] 1 Able to be compared (*with*). LME. 2 Worthy of comparison; fit to be compared (*to*). LME.

compara'bility *n.* M19. **comparableness** *n.* M18. **comparably** *adv.* LME.

comparatist /kəm'parətɪst/ *n.* M20. [f. next + -IST. Cf. Fr. *comparatiste*.] A user of comparative methods, esp. in the study of language and literature.

comparative /kəm'parətɪv/ *a.* & *n.* LME. [L *comparativus*, f. *comparat-* pa. ppl stem of *comparare*: see COMPARE *v.*^{1}, -ATIVE.] A *adj.* 1 *Gram.* Designating the degree of comparison expressing more (or less) of a quality or attribute; designating a form etc. of an adjective or adverb expressing this degree of comparison (e.g. with inflection, as English -ER^3; with modifier, as English *more*; with a word from a different root, as English *better* corresponding to *good*). Cf. *superlative*. LME. 2 Considered, estimated, or perceptible by comparison; relative. L16. †3 Fertile in (insulting) comparisons. *rare* (Shakes.). Only in L16. 4 Of or involving comparison; *esp.* involving comparison across different branches of a science or subject of study. E17. †5 Serving as a basis for comparison. *rare* (Shakes.). Only in E17. †6 Comparable, worthy to be compared, (*to*). M17–E19.

2 B. JOWETT The comparative claims of pleasure and wisdom. C. S. FORESTER From the peril of the top to the comparative safety of the mainyard. 4 *comparative anatomy, grammar, law, linguistics, philology, religion*, etc.

B *n.* †1 A thing or person to be compared, a rival, an equal. L15–E17. 2 *Gram.* A comparative form etc. of an adjective or adverb; the comparative degree. M16.

comparatively *adv.* by way of comparison, somewhat, rather: L16. **comparativist** *n.* a comparatist; a student of comparative linguistics or literature: L19.

comparator /kəm'parətə/ *n.* L19. [f. L *comparat-* (see prec.) + -OR.] A device for making comparative measurements, esp. against a standard.

optical comparator: see OPTICAL *a.*

compare /kəm'pɛː/ *n.*^{1} Now *literary*. E16. [Var. of COMPEER *n.*, assim. to COMPARE *v.*^{1} Cf. next.] An equal, a rival. Chiefly in *have no compare*, *without compare* (in which merges into next).

compare /kəm'pɛː/ *n.*^{2} Chiefly *literary*. E16. [f. COMPARE *v.*^{1}, perh. also infl. by *without compare* (see prec.).] Comparison. Chiefly in *beyond, past*, etc., *compare*.

compare /kəm'pɛː/ *v.*^{1} LME. [(O)Fr. *comparer* f. L *comparare* pair, match, f. *compar* like, equal, f. as COM- + *par* equal.] 1 *v.t.* Liken, pronounce similar, (*to*). LME. 2 *v.i.* Be compared; bear comparison; be on terms of equality *with*. LME. 3 *v.t.* Consider or estimate the similarity or dissimilarity of (one thing or person *to* another esp. in quality, *with* another esp. in quantity or detailed nature, two things or persons); observe the similarity or relation between (passages in a book etc.). L15. 4 *v.i.* Draw a comparison; make comparisons. L16. 5 *v.t. Gram.* Form the comparative and superlative degrees of (an adjective or adverb). E17.

1 R. GRAVES It is hardly complimentary to Parrot, an undeniably handsome bird, to compare my grandson to him. **not to be compared to** greatly inferior or superior to. 2 SPENSER Art, stryving to compare with Nature. OED This compares favourably with the inertness of England. 3 R. G. COLLINGWOOD To compare the two accounts . . given by Thucydides and Aristotle. G. VIDAL How dull he is, thought Caroline, comparing him unfavourably with Jim. **compare notes** compare each other's observations etc., exchange ideas and opinions. 4 C. S. LEWIS The pernicious tendency to compare and to prefer. 5 W. WARD Words of one syllable are usually compared by *er*, and *est*.

comparer *n.* M17.

†**compare** *v.*^{2}*t. rare.* M–L16. [L *comparare*, f. as COM- + *parare* get ready, provide, etc. Cf. OFr. *comparer*.] Get, obtain, acquire.

SPENSER To fill his bags, and richesse to compare.

comparison /kəm'parɪs(ə)n/ *n.* ME. [OFr. *comparesoun* (mod. *-aison*) f. L *comparatio(n-)*, f. *comparat-* pa. ppl stem of *comparare*: see COMPARE *v.*^{1}, -ISON.] 1 The action or an act of likening, or representing as similar. ME. 2 Capacity of being likened or compared; comparable condition or character. (Always with negative expressed or implied.) ME. 3 The action or an instance of observing and estimating similarities, differences, etc. LME. 4 *Gram.* The action of comparing an adjective or adverb; the relationship expressed in the (potential) comparing of qualities or attributes. Now chiefly in *degree* or *grade of comparison* below. LME. 5 A simile; an illustrative instance, a parallel, an analogy. LME.

1 B. JOWETT The comparison of philosophy to a yelping she-dog. 2 SHAKES. *Tr. & Cr.* Troilus is the better man of the two. . O Jupiter! There's no comparison. 3 **bear, stand, comparison (with)** admit of being compared favourably (with). **beyond (all) comparison** totally different in quality. **in comparison with** compared to. PAIRED *comparison*. 4 **degree** or **grade of comparison** each of the degrees of relationship expressed in the (potential) comparing of qualities or attributes: the positive or absolute, when no comparison is made; the comparative, when two are compared; the superlative, when more than two are compared. 5 A. P. HERBERT It was like an unconvincing third act of a promising play—though this comparison did not occur to Jane.

compart /kəm'pɑːt/ *v.t.* L16. [OFr. *compartir* or late L *compartiri* share with another, f. as COM- + *partiri* divide, share.] †1 Divide and share. L16–E17. 2 Lay out in accordance with a plan. E17. 3 Subdivide; partition; divide into compartments. L18.

compartition /kɒmpɑː'tɪʃ(ə)n/ *n.* E17. [med.L *compartitio(n-)*, f. *compartit-* pa. ppl stem of *compartiri*: see prec., -ION.] 1 The distribution and disposition of the parts of a plan. E17. †2 Division and sharing with another. Only in M17.

compartment /kəm'pɑːtm(ə)nt/ *n.* & *v.* As n. also †**copart(i)ment**. M16. [Fr. *compartiment* f. It. *compartimento*, f. *compartire* f. late L *compartiri*: see COMPART *v.*, -MENT.] A *n.* 1 A division or separate part, orig. of a design; a division separated by partitions; *spec.* (*a*) *Her.* a panel, grassy mount, etc., below a shield; †(*b*) a discrete section or feature of a formal garden; (*c*) a partitioned-off division of a railway carriage; (*d*) a watertight division of a ship; (*e*) a section of a parliamentary bill with an allotted time for consideration. M16. †2 = COMPARTITION 1. E–M18.

1 J. F. W. HERSCHEL They divide the spectrum into compartments. S. T. WARNER The most peculiar stockings, like gloves, with a compartment for each toe. R. P. GRAVES Housman began to keep his friendships in separate compartments. *watertight compartment*: see WATERTIGHT *a.*

B *v.t.* Divide or put into compartments (*lit.* & *fig.*). M19.

compartmen'tation *n.* division into compartments M20.

compartmental /kɒmpɑːt'mɛnt(ə)l/ *a.* M19. [f. prec. + -AL^1.] Consisting of or pertaining to a compartment or compartments; characterized by division into compartments.

,compartmentali'zation *n.* division or separation into compartments (*lit.* & *fig.*) E20. **compartmentalize** *v.t.* divide into compartments, place in separate compartments, (*lit.* & *fig.*) E20. **compartmentally** *adv.* M20.

†**compartner** *n.* L16–E18. [f. COM- + PARTNER *n.*] A co-partner.

compass /'kʌmpəs/ *n., adv.,* & *a.* ME. [(O)Fr. *compas*, f. *compasser*: see next.] A *n.* †1 (Skilful or crafty) contriving; ingenuity, cunning; a crafty contrivance. ME–L16. 2 *sing.* & (usu.) in *pl.* An instrument for drawing circles and arcs or measuring distances between points, most commonly consisting of two legs connected at one end by a movable joint. Also *pair of compasses*. ME. b In *pl.* (Usu. **C-**.) *The* constellation Circinus. E19. †3a A circle; a circular thing. ME–L17. b An arc (*obs.* in *gen.* use); *spec.* the curved path of an arrow, or the angle of elevation determining this. LME. c A circular course, a round; a roundabout journey, a detour. *arch.* LME. 4 The line or boundary enclosing an area, the perimeter; measurement round, circumference. ME. 5 A circumscribed area or space; area, extent. ME. 6 An instrument for navigation or orientation showing the magnetic or true north, and bearings from it (in its simplest form a magnetized needle turning on a pivot). LME. 7 *fig.* Limits, range, scope. M16. b *Mus.* The range of tones of a voice or musical instrument. L16. c Moderation, due limits. *obs.* exc. *dial.* L16.

2 *beam-compass(es)*, *bow-compass(es)*, *calliper compasses*, etc. *universal compass*: see UNIVERSAL *a.* 3c **fetch a compass** *arch.* make a circuit or detour, *fig.* act or speak in a roundabout way. 4 T. HERBERT The Caspian Sea is in compasse neere three thousand miles. 5 C. THIRLWALL The . . towering hopes of Athens demanded that the new wall should inclose a larger compass. 6 *box the compass*: see BOX *v.*[3] GYROCOMPASS. *liquid compass*: see LIQUID *a.* & *n.* *magnetic compass*: see MAGNETIC *a.* *MARINER's compass.* *point of the compass*: see POINT *n.*[1] 16. PRISMATIC *compass*. *variation of the compass*: see VARIATION 8. 7 H. JAMES A peculiar girl, but the full compass of whose peculiarities had not been exhibited before. A. G. GARDINER Things to which we can give no name . . because they are outside the compass of our speech.

†B *adv.* 1 In circumference. ME–L16. 2 In an arc, curvedly. LME–M17.

C *adj.* Round, circular, curved. Now only in technical collocations (see below). E16.

Comb. & *special collocations*: *compass card*: see CARD *n.*[2] 2b; **compass course**: indicated by a compass, but not actually followed because of deviation caused by wind, currents, etc.; **compass plane** a convex plane for smoothing curved surfaces; **compass-plant** *N. Amer.* any of various plants in which the leaves or branches are aligned north and south so as to avoid the midday sun, *esp.* the plant *Silphium laciniatum*, of the composite family; **compass rose** a graduated circle on a chart, from which bearings can be taken; **compass-saw** a handsaw with a narrow blade for cutting curves; **compass timber** *Shipbuilding* timber steamed and curved to take the desired shape; **compass window** a bay-window with a semicircular curve.

compassless *a.* without a (mariner's) compass. M19.

compass /ˈkʌmpəs/ *v.* Now chiefly *literary.* ME. [(O)Fr. *compasser* (now only) measure as with compasses, repr. Proto-Romance vb f. L COM- + *passus* step, PACE *n.*[1] Branch II f. prec.] I 1 *v.t.* Contrive or devise, esp. by underhand means. ME. 2 *v.t.* a Surround or hem in on all sides, enclose. Freq. extended by *round, about.* ME. b Encircle or surround *with* something, †*in* the arms. LME. 3 *v.t.* & †*i.* Go round, make a circuit of; traverse from end to end. LME. †4 *v.t.* & *i.* Consider, ponder. LME–M16. 5 *v.t.* Seize, grasp. Now only *fig.*, grasp with the mind, comprehend. E16. 6 *v.t.* Accomplish, achieve (an objective); succeed in obtaining (something desired). M16.

1 J. L. MOTLEY England, whose desolation is thus sought and compassed. 2a AV *Ps.* 118:12 They compassed mee about like Bees. POPE Like the sea they compass all the land. 3 C. KINGSLEY A generation which will compass land and sea to make one proselyte. 5 SHELLEY Why this should be, my mind can compass not. 6 T. KYD We, for all our wrongs, can compasse no redresse. LD MACAULAY Men who would unscrupulously employ corruption . . to compass their ends. G. MAXWELL They painted . . as much of the walls as their diminutive statures and a broken ladder could compass.

II 7 *v.t.* & *i.* Bend round or into a circle, curve. Now chiefly of timber. M16.

compassable *a.* attainable L16. **compasser** *n.* (now *rare*) L15.

compassion /kəmˈpaʃ(ə)n/ *n.* ME. [(O)Fr. f. eccl.L *compassio(n-)*, f. *compass-* pa. ppl stem of *compati* suffer with: see COM-, PASSION *n.*] †1 Participation in another's suffering; fellow-feeling, sympathy. ME–E17. 2 Pity inclining one to show mercy or give aid. Freq. in *have compassion on.* ME. †3 Sorrowful emotion, grief. ME–L16.

Comb.: **compassion fatigue** indifference to charitable appeals resulting from the frequency of such appeals.

compassion /kəmˈpaʃ(ə)n/ *v.t. rare.* L16. [f. prec., or Fr. †*compassionner*, f. as prec.] Have compassion on, pity.

compassionable *a.* †(*a*) compassionate; (*b*) deserving compassion, pitiable: M16.

compassionate /kəmˈpaʃ(ə)nət/ *a.* L16. [f. Fr. *compassionné* pa. pple of †*compassionner* (see prec.) + -ATE[2].] 1 Feeling or showing compassion or sympathy for others. L16. b Granted out of compassion rather than from legal obligation. M19. †2 Displaying sorrowful emotion. *rare* (Shakes.). Only in L16. †3 Exciting compassion, pitiable. M17–M18.

1b **compassionate allowance**: granted when an ordinary pension or allowance is not permissible under official rules. **compassionate leave**: granted on grounds of bereavement, family illness, etc.

compassionately *adv.* E17. **compassionateness** *n.* E17.

compassionate /kəmˈpaʃəneɪt/ *v.t. arch.* L16. [f. prec., or Fr. †*compassionner*: see COMPASSION *v.*, -ATE[3].] Regard or treat with compassion, feel pity for.

compassive /kəmˈpasɪv/ *a. arch.* LME. [AN, OFr. *compassif, -ive* or late L *compassivus*, f. *compass-*: see COMPASSION *n.*, -IVE.] Compassionate, sympathetic.

compaternity /kɒmpəˈtəːnɪti/ *n.* LME. [med.L *compaternitas*, f. *compater* godfather, f. as COM- + *pater* father: see -ITY.] The (spiritual) relationship between a child's godfathers (or godparents), or between them and the actual parents.

compatible /kəmˈpatɪb(ə)l/ *a.* LME. [Fr. f. med.L *compatibilis*, f. late L *compati* suffer with: see COMPASSION *n.*, -IBLE.] I 1 Able to be admitted or employed together or to coexist in the same subject; consistent, congruous. Of people: able to live or work in harmony together, mutually congenial, well-suited. (Foll. by *with*, †*to*.) LME. 2 *spec.* a Of substances, esp. drugs: able to be used together without altering or adversely affecting the individual properties of each. L19. b Of blood, organs, etc.: able to be introduced into the body by transfusion, transplantation, etc., without immune response. E20. c Of two flowers (on the same or different plants): able to fertilize each other. See also SELF-COMPATIBLE *a.* E20. d Of television pictures transmitted in colour: able to be received in black and white by a monochrome set. M20. e Of computer hardware or software: able to be used on more than one system without special modification. L20.

1 W. BROOME Our poets have joined together such qualities as are by nature the most compatible. V. SACKVILLE-WEST To keep your estimate as low as is compatible with your own reasonable profit. S. HILL How many tastes we share, how compatible we are, Mrs Clemency! e *upward-compatible*: see UPWARD *adv.*

†II 3 Participating in another's sufferings; sympathetic. L15–E17.

compatiˈbility *n.* the quality or state of being compatible (*with*) (UPWARD *compatibility*) E17. **compatibleness** *n.* (now *rare*) E17. **compatibly** *adv.* M18.

compatriot /kəmˈpatrɪət, -ˈpeɪt-/ *n.* & *a.* L16. [(O)Fr. *compatriote* f. late L *compatriota* (tr. Gk *sumpatriōtēs*): see COM-, PATRIOT *n.*] A *n.* A fellow countryman or countrywoman. L16. B *adj.* Belonging to the same country. M18.

compatriˈotic *a.* of or pertaining to compatriots; belonging to the same country: E19. **compatriotism** *n.* the position of being compatriots; compatriotic feeling: L18.

compear /kəmˈpɪə/ *v.i. Sc. obs.* exc. *Law.* LME. [OFr. *comper-* tonic stem of *compareir* f. L *comparere*, f. as COM- + *parere* come into view: cf. APPEAR *v.*] Appear, present oneself; *esp.* (*Law*) appear in court, either in person or by counsel.

compearance *n.* appearance, esp. in court LME.

compeer /kəmˈpɪə/ *n.* & *v.* LME. [OFr. *comper*: see COM-, PEER *n.*[1]] A *n.* 1 A person of equal rank or standing. See also COMPARE *n.*[1] LME. 2 A companion, an associate. LME. †B *v.t.* Be the equal of, rival. E17–M19.

compel /kəmˈpɛl/ *v.t.* Infl. **-ll-**. LME. [L *compellere*, f. as COM- + *pellere* drive.] 1 Constrain, force, oblige, (a person). (Foll. by *to do*, (*in*)*to* an action etc.). LME. 2 Force to come or go (in some direction); drive or force together. Now *literary.* LME. †3 Take by force, extort, requisition. LME–E19. 4 Bring about or evoke by force. L17.

1 J. S. C. ABBOTT Russia should unite her arms with ours, and compel that power to peace. R. SCRUTON A law-making body is powerless unless it can compel the judges to apply its laws. 2 DRYDEN Attended by the chiefs who sought the field, (Now friendly mix'd, and in one troop compell'd). SCOTT FITZGERALD Wedging his . . arm imperatively under mine, Tom Buchanan compelled me from the room. 4 P. LARKIN His passionate sincerity compelled complete attention.

compellaˈbility *n.* the quality or state of being (esp. legally) compellable L19. **compellable** *a.* that may be compelled or constrained (*to do, to*); *spec.* (*Law*) that may be made to attend court or give evidence: LME. **compeller** *n.* L16. **compelling** *ppl a.* that compels; *spec.* that compels strong interest or feeling or admiration: E17. **compellingly** *adv.* M17.

compellation /kɒmpəˈleɪʃ(ə)n/ *n. arch.* E17. [L *compellatio(n-)*, f. *compellat-* pa. ppl stem of *compellare* accost, address, f. stem of *compellere*: see prec., -ATION, and cf. APPELLATION.] 1 Addressing or calling upon anyone; a salutation, an address. E17. 2 Addressing by a particular name or title; style of address; a name or title used in speaking of a person or thing, an appellation. M17.

compend /ˈkɒmpɛnd/ *n.* Now *rare* or *obs.* L16. [L COMPENDIUM: cf. STIPEND.] A compendium, an epitome.

compendia *n.pl.* see COMPENDIUM.

†**compendiary** *n.* & *a.* L16. [L *compendiarius* short, and *-arium* neut. sing. used as n.; f. as COMPENDIUM, -ARY[1].] A *n.* A compendium, an epitome. L16–E17. B *adj.* Compendious, brief; expeditious. E17–E19.

compendiate /kɒmˈpɛndɪeɪt/ *v.t.* Long *rare.* E17. [L *compendiat-* pa. ppl stem of *compendiare* shorten, abridge, f. as COMPENDIUM: see -ATE[3].] Sum up concisely.

V. NABOKOV Seldom does a casual snapshot compendiate a life so precisely.

compendious /kəmˈpɛndɪəs/ *a.* LME. [(O)Fr. *compendieux* f. L *compendiosus*, f. as next: see -OUS.] †1 Of a route, method, etc.: saving time or space, expeditious. LME–L18. 2 Containing the essential facts in a small compass; comprehensive but fairly brief. LME.

compendiously *adv.* LME. **compendiousness** *n.* LME.

compendium /kəmˈpɛndɪəm/ *n.* Pl. **-iums**, **-ia** /-ɪə/. L16. [L, orig. 'profit, saving', f. as COM- + *pendere* weigh.] I 1 A work presenting in brief the essential points of a subject; a digest, an epitome. L16. 2 *fig.* An embodiment in miniature. E17. †3 Saving of labour, space, etc. M17–E19. II 4 An assortment, a varied collection. L19. 5 a In full *compendium of games.* A box containing assorted table-games. L19. b A package of stationery for letter-writing. E20.

compenetrate /kəmˈpɛnɪtreɪt/ *v.t.* L17. [f. COM- + PENETRATE.] Penetrate in every part, pervade; penetrate mutually.

compeneˈtration *n.* E19.

compensable /kəmˈpɛnsəb(ə)l/ *a.* M17. [Fr., f. *compenser* f. L *compensare*: see next, -ABLE.] Chiefly *Law.* Able to be compensated for, justifying compensation.

compensate /ˈkɒmpɛnseɪt/ *v.* M17. [L *compensat-* pa. ppl stem of *compensare* weigh (one) against another, f. as COM- + *pensare*, frequent. of *pendere* weigh: see -ATE[3].] 1 *v.t.* Counterbalance, make amends for. (Foll. by *with, by.*) M17. 2 *v.i.* Serve as a recompense or adequate substitute (*for*); make up *for.* M17. 3 *v.t.* Make amends to, recompense. (Foll. by *for.*) E19. 4 *v.t.* Provide (a pendulum etc.) with an arrangement to neutralize the effects of variations in temperature. E19. 5 *v.i.* (foll. by *for*) & *t. Electr.* Neutralize (a magnetomotive or electromotive force); correct (an undesired characteristic or effect) in a device or circuit. M19. 6 *v.i. Psychol.* Offset a supposed deficiency or a frustration by developing another characteristic. E20.

1 W. DAMPIER The benefit of it would not compensate the danger. 2 I. COMPTON-BURNETT The hard moments were more than compensated for by the good ones. 3 R. WARNER Nothing could compensate him for what he was about to lose.

¶Formerly pronounced w. stress on 2nd syll.

compensatingly *adv.* so as to compensate E19. **compensative** /kəmˈpɛnsətɪv, kɒmpɛnˈseɪtɪv/ *a.* = COMPENSATORY M17. **compensator** *n.* a person who or thing which compensates M19. **compensatory**

/kəmˈpɛnsət(ə)ri, kɒmpɛnˈseɪt(ə)ri/ *a.* providing, effecting, or aiming at compensation. E17.

compensation /kɒmpɛnˈseɪʃ(ə)n/ *n.* LME. [(O)Fr. f. L *compensatio(n-)*, f. as prec.: see -ATION.] **1** The action of compensating; the condition of being compensated. LME. **b** *Physiol.* The counterbalancing of a deficiency by an increase in functional power elsewhere. M19. **c** *Electr.* Neutralization of a magnetomotive or electromotive force; correction of an undesired characteristic or effect in a device or circuit. M19. **d** *Psychol.* (The result of) offsetting a supposed deficiency or a frustration by development of another characteristic. E20. **2** A thing that compensates or is given to compensate (*for*); a counterbalancing feature or factor; amends, recompense; *spec.* money given to compensate loss or injury, or for requisitioned property. L16. **b** Salary, wages, remuneration. *N. Amer.* L18.

1 W. J. BATE When we cannot attain wealth, and therefore, by compensation, dismiss it as unimportant. 2 D. CUSACK This place [a girls' school] has all the disadvantages of a nunnery with none of the compensations. G. BROWN The Germans made available a million pounds for compensation to British subjects for their sufferings under Nazi persecution.

Comb.: **compensation-balance**, **-pendulum**: designed so as to neutralize the effects of temperature variation; **compensation water**: supplied from a reservoir to a stream in time of drought.

compensational *a.* E19.

compère /ˈkɒmpɛː/ *n.* & *v.* Also **compere**. M18. [Fr., orig. 'godfather in relation to the actual parents', f. med.L *compater*: see COMPATERNITY.] **A** *n.* **†1** An elderly man who lavishes gifts on a younger woman. Only in M18. **2** A person in a cabaret act, radio or television show, etc., who introduces the performers, comments on the turns, etc. E20. **B** *v.t.* & *i.* Act as compère (to). M20.

compesce /kəmˈpɛs/ *v.t. arch.* Long only *Sc.* LME. [L *compescere.*] Restrain, repress.

compete /kəmˈpiːt/ *v.i.* E17. [L *competere* in its late sense of 'strive for (something) together with another', f. as COM- + *petere* aim at.] Be a rival, bear comparison (*with* another, *in* a quality); strive, contend, take part in a competition, (*with* or *against* another, *for* a thing, *in doing*); strive for superiority *in*; be commercially competitive.

R. HEBER There was none who could compete with him in renown of learning. W. S. JEVONS The stores . . compete with shopkeepers, and induce them to lower their prices. A. STORR If an animal is competing with another for food, it needs to be aggressive. A. C. BOULT To compete at Henley is a wholly delightful experience. *Washington Post* If the Mexican industry is able to compete in its own market, that will guarantee that it will be able to compete in foreign markets.

competence /ˈkɒmpɪt(ə)ns/ *n.* L16. [f. COMPETENT *a.*: see -ENCE.] **†1** = COMPETENCY I. L16–M18. **2** An income adequate to support life; the condition of having this, easy circumstances. M17. **3** Power, ability, capacity, (*to do*, *for* a task etc.); *spec.* legal authority, qualification, or admissibility, right to take cognizance. E18. **b** The ability of a stream or current to carry fragments of a certain size. L19.

2 S. JOHNSON They . . growled away their latter years in discontented competence. R. H. TAWNEY To be content with a modest competence and to shun the allurements of riches. 3 H. HALLAM The court of session . . . possessed no competence in criminal proceedings. N. CHOMSKY What the speaker of a language knows implicitly (what we may call his *competence*). R. V. JONES The construction of radio receivers was just within the competence of the average man.

competency /ˈkɒmpɪt(ə)nsi/ *n.* L15. [f. as prec.: see -ENCY. Branch II f. L *competent-* in the earlier sense of *competere* (see COMPETENT *a.*).] **I†1** An adequate supply (*of*). L15–M18. **2** = COMPETENCE 2. L16. **3** = COMPETENCE 3. L16. **†II 4** Rivalry, competition. L16–M17.

competent /ˈkɒmpɪt(ə)nt/ *n.* M17. [eccl.L *competent-*, *-ens* use as n. of pres. pple of *competere* in its later sense: see COMPETE, -ENT.] *Eccl. Hist.* A candidate for baptism.

competent /ˈkɒmpɪt(ə)nt/ *a.* LME. [(O)Fr. *compétent* or its source L *competent-* pres. ppl stem of *competere* in its earlier sense 'coincide, be fitting' (cf. COMPETE): see -ENT.] **†1 a** *gen.* Suitable, appropriate. LME–L18. **b** *spec.* Appropriate to a person's rank or status. *arch.* LME. **2** Sufficient or adequate in amount, extent, or degree. LME. **†b** Moderate, no more than adequate. E16–L18. **3** *Law.* Legally authorized or qualified, able to take cognizance, (of a witness, evidence) eligible, admissible. LME. **4** *gen.* Belonging *to* as a rightful possession; permissible, legitimate. E17. **5** *gen.* Having adequate skill, properly qualified, effective. (Foll. by *to do*, *at*, *for*, *in.*) M17. **b** Of a stream, current: able to carry fragments of a certain size. L19. **c** *Med.* Esp. of a valve or sphincter: functioning normally. L19.

1b K. E. DIGBY If she [a widow] depart from the castle, then a competent house shall be provided for her. 2 JAS. MILL Mr. Pitt's bill . . being now supported by a competent majority. 4 W. BLACKSTONE It is not competent to the defendant to allege fraud in the plaintiff. 5 G. B. SHAW I should not be competent to deal with it, as I am not a technical expert in medicine. D. H. LAWRENCE Extremely competent at motor-cars and farming. R. WARNER He was never brilliant but he used to be competent enough.

competently *adv.* LME.

competition /kɒmpɪˈtɪʃ(ə)n/ *n.* E17. [Late L *competitio(n-)*, f. *competit-* pa. ppl stem of *competere*: see COMPETE *v.*, -ITION.] **1** The action of competing or contending with others (*for* supremacy, a position, a prize, etc.). E17. **b** *spec.* Striving for custom between rival traders in the same commodity. L18. **c** *Biol.* The interaction between two or more organisms, populations, or species that share a limited environmental resource. M19. **2** An event in which persons or teams compete; a match, a contest, a trial of ability. E17. **3** The person or persons competing with one; the opposition in a contest. E20.

1 J. S. MILL Opening all objects of ambition . . to general competition. J. RABAN Ice-cream vans . . playing different tunes in furious competition. b *imperfect competition*: see IMPERFECT *a.* 2 JO GRIMOND They played together . . in the foursomes competition known as the Calcutta Cup.

Comb.: **competition-wallah** *Anglo-Ind. colloq.* an Indian Civil Servant appointed by competitive examination.

competitioner *n.* a competitor; a person who enters a service etc. by competition: M17.

competitive /kəmˈpɛtɪtɪv/ *a.* E19. [f. L *competit-* (see prec.) + -IVE.] **1** Of, pertaining to, involving, characterized by, or decided by competition. Of a person: with a strong urge to compete. E19. **2** Of a price etc.: comparing favourably with that of other traders. E20.

1 **competitive examination**: for a position, office, bursary, etc.

competitively *adv.* M19. **competitiveness** *n.* L19. **competiˈtivity** *n.* M20.

competitor /kəmˈpɛtɪtə/ *n.* E16. [Fr. *compétiteur* or L *competitor*, f. as COMPETE: see -OR.] **1** A person who competes, a contestant; a rival, esp. in trade. E16. **†2** An associate, a partner. L16–L17.

competitorship *n.* E17. **competitory** *a.* marked by or subject to competition; competitive: E18. **competitress** *n.* (now *rare*) a female competitor M17.

compilation /kɒmpɪˈleɪʃ(ə)n/ *n.* LME. [(O)Fr. f. L *compilatio(n-)*, f. *compilat-* pa. ppl stem of *compilare*: see next, -ATION.] **1** The act of compiling; the state of being compiled. LME. **2** A thing compiled; a collection from various sources. LME.

Comb.: **compilation film** a film, esp. a documentary, compiled from various pieces (chiefly) shot for a different purpose.

ˈcompilator *n.* a compiler LME. **compilatory** /kəmˈpʌɪlət(ə)ri/ *a.* of a compiler or a compilation E19.

compile /kəmˈpʌɪl/ *v.t.* ME. [(O)Fr. *compiler* put together, collect, or its presumed source L *compilare* plunder, plagiarize.] **1** Collect (materials) into a list, volume, etc. ME. **2** Make up (a volume etc.) of materials from various sources. LME. **†3** Compose (a poem, story, etc.). LME–L16. **†4** Make up, build. L15–L17. **†5** Heap or gather together. L16–E19. **6** In *Cricket* etc., accumulate (a specified high score). L19. **7** *Computing.* Cause (a program etc.) to be changed from a high-level language into machine language or a low-level language designed for execution. M20.

1 L. STEPHEN Compiling notes to the Iliad from Eustathius. 2 V. CRONIN The Princess began compiling a Russian dictionary.

†compilement *n.* (*a*) a structure; an accumulation; (*b*) = COMPILATION: E17–M19. **compiler** *n.* (*a*) a person who compiles materials, a volume, etc.; †(*b*) an author, a composer; (*c*) *Computing* a program for putting other programs into a form suitable for a particular computer: ME.

compital /ˈkɒmpɪt(ə)l/ *a.* M17. [L *compitalis*, f. *compitum* place where roads cross: see -AL[1].] *Rom. Antiq.* Of or pertaining to crossroads; *spec.* designating shrines of domestic gods placed at street corners.

complacence /kəmˈpleɪs(ə)ns/ *n.* LME. [med.L *complacentia*, f. as COMPLACENT: see -ENCE.] **†1** Pleasure; (a) satisfaction. LME–M18. **b** An object or source of pleasure and satisfaction. *rare* (Milton). Only in M17. **2** = COMPLACENCY I. L15. **†3** Complaisance. E17–M18.

complacency /kəmˈpleɪs(ə)nsi/ *n.* M17. [f. as prec.: see -ENCY.] **1** Tranquil pleasure, self-satisfaction, esp. when uncritical or unwarranted. M17. **†2** = COMPLACENCE I. M17–L19. **†3** (A) contented acquiescence or consent. M17–E18. **4** Complaisance. *arch.* M17.

complacent /kəmˈpleɪs(ə)nt/ *a.* M17. [L *complacent-* pres. ppl stem of *complacere*, f. as COM- + *placere* please: see -ENT.] **†1** Pleasant. M17–L18. **2** Tranquilly pleased, self-satisfied, esp. uncritically or unwarrantedly. M18. **3** Complaisant. *arch.* L18.

†complacential *a.* characterized by complacency; complaisant: M17–M19. **complacently** *adv.* E19.

complain /kəmˈpleɪn/ *v.* & *n.* LME. [(O)Fr. *complaign-* pres. stem of *complaindre*, f. Proto-Romance (med.L) *complangere*, f. L COM- + *plangere* lament: cf. PLAIN *v.*] **A** *v.* **†1** *v.t.* Bewail, lament. LME–E18. **†2** *v.i.* & *refl.* Give expression to sorrow. LME–M17. **3** *v.i.* & *†refl.* Express dissatisfaction. (Foll. by *about*, (arch.) *against*, *at*, *of*, *that*, †(*up*)*on.*) LME. **b** Make a formal statement of a grievance; lodge a complaint, bring a charge. LME. **†4** *v.t.* Express dissatisfaction with. Only in 16. **5** *v.i.* & *†refl.* Suffer physically, be unwell. *obs.* exc. *dial.* E17. **6** *v.i. transf.* & *fig.* Emit a mournful sound; (of a mast, rudder, etc.) groan, creak. L17.

With preps. in specialized senses: **complain of** announce that one is suffering from (a headache, an illness, etc.); (see also sense 3 above).

B *n.* Complaint. Now *poet.* L15.

complainable *a.* (*rare*) lamentable, to be complained of LME. **complainer** *n.* (*a*) *Law* (esp. *Sc.*) = COMPLAINANT *n.* 1; (*b*) a person who complains: LME. **complainingly** *adv.* in a complaining manner, querulously LME.

complainant /kəmˈpleɪnənt/ *a.* & *n.* LME. [Fr. *complaignant* pres. pple of *complaindre*: see prec., -ANT[1].] **A** *adj.* (Formally) complaining. Now *rare.* LME. **B** *n.* **1** *Law.* A plaintiff in certain lawsuits; a person who alleges that a crime has been committed. LME. **2** *gen.* A person who complains. E16.

complaint /kəmˈpleɪnt/ *n.* LME. [(O)Fr. *complainte* use as n. of fem. pa. pple of *complaindre*: see COMPLAIN.] **1** The expressing or an expression of grief; (a) lamentation; *spec.* a plaintive poem, a plaint. *arch.* LME. **2** The expressing or an expression of grievance or injustice suffered; *spec.* a formal accusation or charge, an allegation of a crime; the plaintiff's initial pleading in a civil action. LME. **3** A bodily ailment. E18. **4** A subject or ground of dissatisfaction or grievance; a grievance that one wishes to express. M18.

2 O. MANNING Veering between complaint and a tolerant acceptance of suffering. A. POWELL One of Uncle Giles's chief complaints that he had been 'put' into the army. 4 D. JACOBSON Everything is fine. He has no complaints.

complaintive *a.* (*rare*) given to complaint M17.

complaisance /kəm'pleɪz(ə)ns/ *n.* M17. [(O)Fr., f. as next: see -ANCE.] 1 Politeness; deference; willingness to please others; acquiescence. M17. 2 An act showing complaisance. M18.

complaisant /kəm'pleɪz(ə)nt/ *a.* M17. [Fr. = obliging, pres. pple of *complaire* acquiesce in order to please, repr. L *complacere*: see COMPLACENT, -ANT[1].] Disposed to please; obliging, courteous; accommodating.

E. M. FORSTER So she did want to talk about her broken engagement. Always complaisant, he put the letter away. **complaisant husband** = MARI COMPLAISANT.

complanate /'kɒmpləneɪt/ *v.* & *a.* M17. [L *complanat-* pa. ppl stem of *complanare* make level, f. as COM- + *planare*, f. *planus* flat, level: see -ATE[3], -ATE[2].] †A *v.t.* Make plane, flatten. M17–E18. B *adj.* Made plane, flattened. M19.

compla'nation *n.* L17.

compleat *a.* & *adv.* see COMPLETE *a.* & *adv.*

complect /kəm'plɛkt/ *v.t.* E16. [L *complecti*, *-ere* embrace, encircle, f. as COM- + *plectere* plait, twine.] †1 Embrace (*lit.* & *fig.*). E16–M17. 2 Connect together; interweave (*lit.* & *fig.*). L16.

complected /kəm'plɛktɪd/ *a.* *US dial.* & *colloq.* E19. [App. f. COMPLEXION.] Having a (specified) complexion.

complement /'kɒmplɪm(ə)nt/ *n.* LME. [L *complementum*, f. *complere*: see COMPLETE *a.* & *adv.*, -MENT. Cf. COMPLIMENT *n.*] †1a Completing, fulfilling. LME–E18. b Completeness, fullness. Chiefly & now only *Her.* of the moon. E17. 2 A thing which puts the finishing touches to a thing; the perfection, the consummation, the culmination. (Foll. by *of.*) LME. 3 The quantity or amount that completes or fills, the totality. (Foll. by *of.*) L16. b The full number required (to man a ship, fill a conveyance, etc.). E17. 4 A thing which, when added, completes or makes up a whole; either of two mutually completing parts. L16. b *Math.* & *Astron.* The angle which when added to a given angle makes 90°. Cf. SUPPLEMENT *n.* 1c. L16. c That colour which, mixed with another, produces white. M19. d *Gram.* A word, phrase, or clause added to the verb of a sentence to complete the predicate, esp. to a verb of incomplete predication. Also, a restrictive relative clause identifying or defining the noun (in Eng. often introduced by *that*, as in *the fact that*). L19. e *Physiol.* A group of proteins present in blood plasma and tissue fluid, which by combining with an antigen-antibody complex can bring about the lysis of foreign cells. E20. f *Computing.* The number related to a given number in such a way that their sum is a number consisting entirely of 9s (in the decimal system), 1s (in the binary system), etc. Also, such a number increased by one. M20. †5 A completing accessory. L16–L17. †6 A personal accomplishment or quality. L16–M17. †7a A ceremony, a formal observance. L16–M17. b Civility, politeness. Cf. COMPLIMENT *n.* 3. L16–L17. c = COMPLIMENT *n.* 1, 2. L16–E18.

2 STEELE Men rather seek for Money as the Complement of all their Desires. 3 ADAM SMITH That full complement of riches which is consistent with the nature of its laws. b G. GREENE A full complement of passengers would have numbered only fourteen. 4 T. ROETHKE Such a course could provide a real complement to existing courses. d *objective complement*: see OBJECTIVE *a.* & *n.*

Comb.: **complement-fixation**, **-fixing** *Med.* the reaction of complement (sense 4e) with an antigen-antibody complex, freq. as the basis of a diagnostic test.

complementizer *n.* (*Gram.*) a word, suffix, etc., that introduces a complement clause M20.

complement /'kɒmplɪmɛnt/ *v.* E17. [f. the n.] †1 *v.i.* & *t.* (w. *it*). Employ ceremony or formal courtesy. Cf. COMPLIMENT *v.* 1. Only in 17. †2 *v.t.* = COMPLIMENT *v.* 2. M17–M18. 3 *v.t.* Complete, form the complement to. M17.

complementer *n.* E17.

complemental /kɒmplɪ'mɛnt(ə)l/ *a.* L16. [f. COMPLEMENT *n.* + -AL[1]. Cf. COMPLEMENTAL.] I†1 Formal, ceremonious. L16–L17. 2 Of the nature of a complement; complementary (*to*). E17. †3 Accessory. Only in M17. †4 Personally accomplished. Only in M17.

2 **complemental male** *Zool.* a small, often degenerate, male which may accompany hermaphrodite or female specimens of some cirripedes.

†II 5 Complimentary. E17–E18.

complementally *adv.* L16.

complementary /kɒmplɪ'mɛnt(ə)ri/ *a.* E17. [f. as prec. + -ARY[1].] †1 Formal, ceremonious. E–M17. 2 Forming a complement (*to*), completing; (of two or more things) complementing each other. E19. 3 Designating or pertaining to medicine that involves methods or means not recognized by the majority of medical practitioners, not given full official recognition, or not based on modern scientific knowledge. L20.

2 **complementary angles**: whose sum is 90°. *complementary colour*: see COLOUR *n.* **complementary distribution** *Ling.*: of sounds, forms, etc., in mutually exclusive contexts. **complementary function** *Math.* that part of the general solution of a linear differential equation which is the general solution of the associated homogeneous equation obtained by substituting zero for the terms not containing the dependent variable.

complementarily *adv.* E20. **complemen'tarity** *n.* complementary relationship; *spec.* (*Physics*) the capacity of two contrasted theories (e.g. the wave and particle theories of light) together to explain a body of phenomena, although each separately accounts for only some aspects: E20.

complementation /ˌkɒmplɪmɛn'teɪʃ(ə)n/ *n.* M20. [f. COMPLEMENT *v.*, *n.* + -ATION.] 1 *Gram.* Complementary distribution. Also, addition of a word, phrase, or clause as a complement. M20. 2 *Genetics.* The phenomenon by which the effects of two different non-allelic mutations in a gene are partly or entirely cancelled out when they occur together. M20. 3 *Math.* & *Computing.* The action of finding the complement of a numerical quantity. M20. 4 The action of doing something that is complementary to something else. L20.

completable /kəm'pliːtəb(ə)l/ *a.* M19. [f. COMPLETE *v.* + -ABLE.] Able to be completed.

complete /kəm'pliːt/ *a.* & *adv.* Also (now only in sense A.4, *arch.*) **compleat**. LME. [(O)Fr. *complet* or L *completus* pa. pple of *complere* fill up, finish, fulfil, f. as COM- + base of *plenus* full.] A *adj.* 1 Having all its parts or elements; entire, full, total. LME. b Of a formal logical or mathematical system: such that no new axiom can be added that is independent of the existing axioms and consistent with them. M20. 2 Finished, concluded, having run its full course. LME. 3 Without defect, perfect. LME. 4 Fully accomplished, consummate. E16. 5 Having the maximum extent or degree, thorough. M17.

1 G. CHAPMAN A coach . . Stately and complete. A. SILLITOE The drawn curtains . . made the blackout complete. 2 POPE Behold Villario's ten years toil compleat. 3 S. JOHNSON The praise had been compleat had his friend's virtue been equal to his wit. 4 I. WALTON The Compleat Angler. 5 DEFOE The greatest and best principles are often illustrated . . by their completest contraries. A. N. WILSON The Bodger's action made Monty look a complete fool.

Phrases: **complete with** having as an important accompaniment.

B *adv.* Completely. Now *dial.* LME.

¶In L16, E17 freq. stressed on 1st syll.

completely *adv.* LME. **completeness** *n.* E17.

complete /kəm'pliːt/ *v.* LME. [f. the adj. Cf. Fr. *compléter*.] 1 *v.t.* Bring to an end, finish, conclude. LME. b *v.i.* Conclude the legal transfer or sale of real estate. E19. 2 *v.t.* Make whole or perfect; fill up the amount or number of; add what is required to (a questionnaire etc.). LME. †b Give a full title or degree to; invest fully with a rank or office. M17–E18. 3 *v.t.* Accomplish, fulfil (a vow, hope, etc.). *rare.* LME.

1 M. MEYER He never completed the work. P. ACKROYD He decided to complete his course for a bachelor's degree in three years. 2 WORDSWORTH All that love can do . . to complete the man, Perfect him, made imperfect in himself. 3 POPE To town he comes, completes the nation's hope.

†**completement** *n.* completion M17–E19. **completer** *n.* E18. **completive** *a.* having the attribute of completing, serving for completion (*of*) M17.

completion /kəm'pliːʃ(ə)n/ *n.* L15. [L *completio(n-)*, f. *complet-* pa. ppl stem of *complere*: see COMPLETE *a.* & *adv.*, -ION.] 1 Accomplishment, fulfilment. L15. 2 *gen.* The action of completing; the condition of being completed. L15. b *ellipt.* Completion of the purchase of property. E20.

completory /kəm'pliːt(ə)ri/ *n.* & *a.* L15. [Late and med. (eccl.) L *completorius*, (n.) *-ium*, f. as prec.: see -ORY[1], -ORY[2].] A *n.* 1 = COMPLINE. L15. 2 A thing which affords completion. M17. B *adj.* Affording completion (*of*). M17.

complex /'kɒmplɛks/ *n.* M17. [L *complexus* n., f. pa. ppl stem of *complectere* (see next); later interpreted as use as n. of next.] 1 A complex whole; a group of related elements; an assemblage of related buildings, units, etc. M17. 2 *Chem.* A substance or species formed by the combination of simpler ones; *spec.* a species (charged or neutral) in which a central usu. metal atom is bonded to a set of outer or ligand atoms, ions, or molecules (cf. COORDINATION *compound*). L19. 3 In *Psychoanalysis*, a related group of usu. repressed ideas, attitudes, and desires causing mental or behavioural abnormality; *colloq.* an obsession. E20.

1 A. TUCKER Names being . . necessary for gathering our ideas, and holding them together in a complex. *Downside Review* Russia is a culture-complex in itself. K. CLARK That complex of memories and instincts which are awakened . . by the word 'beauty'. D. LODGE The Inner Ring, an exhilarating complex of tunnels and flyovers. *leisure complex*: see LEISURE *n.* & *a.* 2 SYNAPTONEMAL *complex*. 3 *inferiority complex*, *Oedipus complex*, etc.

com'plexant *n.* (*Chem.*) a constituent of a complex; a species which forms a complex: M20.

complex /'kɒmplɛks/ *a.* M17. [Fr. *complexe* or its source L *complexus* pa. pple of *complectere*, *complecti* encompass, embrace, comprehend, comprise, assoc. w. *complexus* plaited.] 1 Consisting of parts, formed by combination, composite. M17. b *Chem.* Of a substance or species: formed by combination of compounds, of the nature of a complex (COMPLEX *n.* 2). L20. 2 Intricate, not easily analysed or disentangled, complicated. E18. 3 *Math.* Containing real and imaginary parts. M19.

1 **complex sentence** *Gram.*: with a subordinate clause or subordinate clauses. 2 SOUTHEY As they weave The complex crossings of the mazy dance. C. FRANCIS He was a complex personality, with glaring faults as well as superhuman virtues. 3 **complex conjugate** each of two complex numbers having their real parts identical and their imaginary parts of equal magnitude but opposite sign. **complex number**: of the form $a + ib$ where a and b are real numbers and i is the square root of -1.

com,plexifi'cation *n.* the action of complexifying E20. **com'plexify** *v.t.* & *i.* make or become (more) complex M19. **complexly** *adv.* †(*a*) collectively; (*b*) in a complex manner: M17. **complexness** *n.* E18.

complex /kəm'plɛks, 'kɒmplɛks/ *v.* L15. [L *complex-* stem of *complexus*: see prec. Later senses prob. f. the adj. or n.] †1 *v.t.* Join, attach. Only in L15. 2 *v.t.* Combine into a complex whole; complicate. *rare.* M17. 3 *Chem.* a *v.t.* (Cause to) form a complex with. M20. b *v.i.* Form a complex (*with*). M20.

complexion /kəm'plɛkʃ(ə)n/ *n.* & *v.* ME. [(O)Fr. f. L *complexio(n-)* combination, association, (in late L) physical constitution, f. as prec.: see -ION.] A *n.* †1 Physical constitution or nature (orig. as constituted by the bodily humours). ME–M18. 2 *Hist.* The combination of supposed qualities (*cold* or *hot*, *moist* or *dry*), or of the four bodily humours, in a certain proportion, regarded in medieval and later times as determining the nature of a body, plant, etc.; the type of constitution attributed to this combination. LME. †b A bodily humour; a collection of humours. LME–L17. 3 A habit of mind, a disposition. *obs.* exc. as *fig.* use of sense 4. LME. 4 The natural colour, texture, and appearance, of the skin, esp. of the face. L16. b *transf.* Colour, visible aspect, appearance. L16. 5

fig. Character, aspect. L16. †6 Complication; (a) combination. E17–M19.

5 G. B. SHAW What you say puts a very different complexion on the matter. L. WOOLF People of varying political complexion.

B *v.t.* †1 Constitute by combination of various elements. LME–M17. 2 Give a colour or tinge to. E17.

complexional *a.* †(*a*) of or pertaining to physical or mental constitution; (*b*) of or pertaining to skin colour and texture: LME. **complexionally** *adv.* M17. †**complexionary** *a.* M17–E18. **complexioned** *a.* †(*a*) having a (specified) physical or mental constitution; (*b*) having a (specified) colour and texture of skin; having a (specified) character or aspect: LME. **complexionless** *a.* (of a person) pale, colourless M19.

complexity /kəmˈplɛksɪti/ *n.* L17. [f. COMPLEX *a.* + -ITY. Cf. Fr. *complexité*.] 1 Complex nature or structure. L17. 2 A complex condition; a complication. L18.

†**complexive** *a.* M17–M19. [L *complexivus*, f. *complex-* stem of *complexus*: see COMPLEX *a.*, -IVE.] Comprehensive.

complexus /kəmˈplɛksəs/ *n.* L19. [f. as COM- + PLEXUS.] A complicated system; a complex.

compliable /kəmˈplʌɪəb(ə)l/ *a. arch.* M17. [f. COMPLY + -ABLE.] 1 Compliant. M17. †2 Reconcilable, accordant. M17–M18.

compliance /kəmˈplʌɪəns/ *n.* M17. [f. COMPLY + -ANCE.] †1 Complaisance. M17–M18. †2 Agreement; accord. M17–M19. 3 The action of complying with a request, command, etc.; an instance of so complying. (Foll. by *with*, (arch.) *to*.) M17. †b *spec.* (Expedient) conformism in religion or politics. L17–M19. c (An instance of) unworthy submission to a request, command, etc. E18. 4 *Physics.* The property of a body or material of undergoing elastic deformation, or (of gases) change in volume, when a force is applied; the extent of this under specified conditions. M20.

Also **compliancy** *n.* M17.

compliant /kəmˈplʌɪənt/ *a.* & *n.* M17. [f. COMPLY + -ANT[1].] A *adj.* 1 Disposed to comply, yielding. M17. †2 Pliant, yielding to physical pressure. M17–L18. †B *n.* A person who complies. Only in M17.

compliantly *adv.* E19.

complicacy /ˈkɒmplɪkəsi/ *n.* E19. [f. COMPLICATE *v.*: see -ACY.] 1 Complexity. E19. 2 A complicated structure or condition. M19.

complicate /ˈkɒmplɪkət/ *a. arch.* LME. [L *complicatus* pa. pple, f. as next: see -ATE[2].] Compound, complex; intricate; involved. Also, interwoven.

†**complicateness** *n.* M17–E19.

complicate /ˈkɒmplɪkeɪt/ *v.t.* E17. [L *complicat-* pa. ppl stem of *complicare*, f. as COM- + *plicare* fold: see -ATE[3].] †1 Combine intimately, intertwine; fold together; entangle. E17–E18. †2 Compose or compound *of*. E17–E18. 3 Make (more) complex or intricate. M17. 4 Combine or mix up *with* in a complex or involved way. L17.

complicated *a.* that has been complicated; *esp.* intricate, involved, confused, complex: M17. **complicatedly** *adv.* L19. **complicatedness** *n.* M18. **complicative** *n.* & *a.* †(*a*) *n.* (*rare*) a complicating force, principle, etc.; (*b*) *adj.* complicating, causing complication: M17.

complication /kɒmplɪˈkeɪʃ(ə)n/ *n.* LME. [(O)Fr., or late L *complicatio(n-)*, f. as prec.: see -ATION.] 1 An involved condition or structure; an entangled state of affairs; a complicating circumstance; a secondary disease or condition aggravating a previous one. LME. †2a The action of combining intimately, folding together, or compounding; the condition of being so combined etc. Only in 17. b The action of making (more) complicated; the condition of being complicated, complexity. L18.

1 W. PALEY That complication of probabilities by which the Christian history is attested. T. ROETHKE I've had pharyngitis with complications. 2b R. L. STEVENSON A woodyard of unusual extent and complication.

complice /ˈkʌmplɪs/ *n. arch.* LME. [(O)Fr. f. late L *complex*, *complic-* (adj.) confederate, f. as COM- + *plic-* as in *plicare* to fold.] †1 *gen.* An associate. LME–L19. 2 *spec.* An accomplice. LME.

complicit /kəmˈplɪsɪt/ *a.* L20. [Back-form. f. COMPLICITY.] Having or showing complicity, that is a party to or involved *in* wrongdoing.

Independent The absurd notion . . that all these people are complicit in some criminal conspiracy.

complicity /kəmˈplɪsɪti/ *n.* M17. [Sense 1 f. prec., sense 2 f. COMPLICATE *v.*: see -ITY.] 1 Partnership or involvement in wrongdoing. M17. 2 Complexity. Now *rare.* M19.

complier /kəmˈplʌɪə/ *n.* E17. [f. COMPLY + -ER[1].] †1 An accomplice. E–M17. 2 A person who complies *with* a request, command, etc., (formerly) a fashion etc. M17. †b *spec.* A conformist in religion or politics, esp. for expediency. M17–M18.

compliment /ˈkɒmplɪm(ə)nt/ *n.* M17. [Fr. f. It. *complimento* repr. Proto-Romance var. of L *complementum* COMPLEMENT *n.*] 1 A polite expression of praise or approval; a neatly-turned remark or an act implying praise or approval. M17. 2 Polite praise, complimentary language. M17. 3 A formal greeting, esp. as the accompaniment to a message, note, present, etc. Usu. in *pl.* (Formerly foll. by *of*.) M17. 4 A gift, a present. Now *arch.* & *dial.* E18.

1 *pay* (arch. *make, pass*) *a compliment.* 3 *make, pay, present, send*, etc., *one's compliments.*

Phrases: *Chinese compliment*: see CHINESE *a.* **compliments of the season** greetings appropriate to the (Christmas) season. **return the compliment** give one compliment in return for another; *fig.* retaliate or give a benefit in a similar way.

Comb.: **compliment slip** a small piece of paper conveying formal greetings.

compliment /ˈkɒmplɪmɛnt/ *v.* L17. [Fr. *complimenter*, f. as prec. Cf. earlier COMPLEMENT *v.*] 1 *v.i.* Employ ceremony or formal courtesy; pay compliments. L17. 2 *v.t.* Address with formal courtesy; pay a compliment to (a person, *on* a thing), congratulate (*up*)*on*; present (a person *with* a thing) as a mark of courtesy. E18.

complimenter *n.* M18.

complimental /kɒmplɪˈmɛnt(ə)l/ *a.* L17. [f. COMPLIMENT *n.* + -AL[1]. Cf. COMPLEMENTAL.] †1 Formal, ceremonious. L17–E18. 2 Complimentary. *arch.* & *dial.* E18.

complimentally *adv.* L17.

complimentary /kɒmplɪˈmɛnt(ə)ri/ *a.* E18. [f. as prec. + -ARY[1].] Expressive of or implying praise or approval; (of a person) given to paying compliments, paying a compliment; of the nature of a compliment, given free of charge by way of a compliment.

complimentarily *adv.* E19.

compline /ˈkɒmplɪn, -ʌɪn/ *n.* Also **-in** /-ɪn/. ME. [Alt., prob. after *matines*, *matins*, of (O)Fr. *complie* (now *complies*), use as n. of fem. pa. pple of †*complir* complete, f. Proto-Romance var. of L *complere* (see COMPLETE *a.* & *adv.*).] *Eccl.* The seventh and last of the daytime canonical hours of prayer; the office, orig. directed to be said immediately before retiring for the night, appointed for this hour.

complish /ˈkʌmplɪʃ/ *v.t.* Long *arch. rare.* LME. [OFr. *compliss-* lengthened stem of *complir* complete: see prec., -ISH[2]. Later perh. aphet. f. ACCOMPLISH.] Fulfil, accomplish.

complot /ˈkɒmplɒt/ *n.* Now *rare.* M16. [(O)Fr. = †dense crowd, secret project, of unkn. origin: assoc. w. PLOT *n.*] A conspiracy, a plot; an intrigue.

complot /kəmˈplɒt/ *v.t.* & *i.* Now *rare.* Infl. **-tt-**. L16. [Fr. *comploter*, f. as prec.] Combine in plotting (some act, usu. criminal).

†**complotment** *n.* conspiracy, plot L16–E18. **complotter** *n.* L16.

Complutensian /kɒmpluːˈtɛnsɪən/ *a.* M17. [f. L *Complutensis*, f. *Complutum* (see below), + -IAN.] Of or pertaining to the Spanish town of Complutum (later Alcalá de Henares); *spec.* designating the earliest polyglot bible, published there in the early 16th cent.

compluvium /kəmˈpluːvɪəm/ *n.* Pl. **-ia** /-ɪə/. M19. [L, f. *compluere* flow together.] *Rom. Antiq.* A square opening in the roof of the atrium, through which fell the rainwater collected from the roof.

comply /kəmˈplʌɪ/ *v.* L16. [f. It. *complire* f. Catal. *complir*, Sp. *cumplir*, f. L *complere*: see COMPLETE *a.* & *adv.*] †1 *v.t.* Fulfil, accomplish. *rare.* L16–M17. †2 *v.i.* Observe the formalities of courtesy and politeness. (Foll. by *with* a person). E–M17. †3 *v.i.* Agree *with*, *together*; (foll. by *with*) suit. Only in 17. 4 *v.i.* Foll. by *with*: accommodate oneself to (a person, circumstances, customs, etc.). *obs.* exc. as passing into sense 5. M17. †b Conform in religion or politics. Only in M17. 5 *v.i.* Act in accordance with or *with* a request, command, etc. M17. †b Consent or agree *to*, *to do*. L17–E18. †6 *v.i.* Ally oneself *with*. Only in M17. †7 *v.t.* Make conform *to*. M–L17. 8 *v.i.* Of a thing: fit *with*, adapt itself *to*. Long *obs.* exc. *dial.* L17.

5 H. JAMES She . . prepared to comply with their aunt's demands. H. WILSON The Ministry did not agree with it and did not propose to comply. ANTHONY SMITH Friends do not always comply with expectation.

compo /ˈkɒmpəʊ/ *n.*[1] Pl. **-os**. E19. [Abbrev. of COMPOSITION.] Stucco, plaster.

compo /ˈkɒmpəʊ/ *n.*[2] *Austral.* & *NZ slang.* M20. [Abbrev. of COMPENSATION.] Compensation, *esp.* that paid for an industrial injury.

compo /ˈkɒmpəʊ/ *a.* L19. [Abbrev.] = COMPOSITE *a.*

compo rations: made up of various tinned foods, designed to last several days, and carried in a large pack.

†**compone** *v.* see COMPOUND *v.*

componé *a.* var. of COMPONY.

component /kəmˈpəʊnənt/ *n.* & *a.* M16. [L *component-* pres. ppl stem of *componere*: see COMPOUND *v.*, -ENT.] A *n.* †1 A compounder. Only in M16. 2 A constituent part; *spec.*: (*a*) any of the separate parts of a motor vehicle, machine, etc.; (*b*) *Math.* & *Physics* each of a set of vectors (e.g. forces) which when combined are equivalent to a given vector; (*c*) *Chem.* each of the constituents of a phase system which together constitute the minimum number necessary in specifying the composition of the system. M17. B *adj.* Composing, constituting, making up, constituent. M17.

componential /kɒmpəˈnɛnʃ(ə)l/ *a.* of or pertaining to components; *spec.* (*Ling.*) designating the analysis of distinctive sound units or grammatical elements into phonetic or semantic components: M20. **componentry** *n.* components collectively M20.

compony /kɒmˈpəʊni/ *a.* Also **-né**. L16. [(O)Fr. *componé*: see -Y[5].] *Her.* Composed of a single row of squares of two alternate tinctures, gobony.

comport /ˈkɒmpɔːt/ *n.* L19. [App. abbrev. of Fr. *comportier* var. of COMPOTIER.] = COMPOTE 3, COMPOTIER.

comport /kəmˈpɔːt/ *v.* Now *literary.* LME. [L *comportare*, f. as COM- + *portare* carry, bear. Cf. (O)Fr. *comporter*.] †1 *v.t.* & *i.* Foll. by *with*. Endure, tolerate. LME–M19. 2 *v.i.* Foll. by *with*: agree with, suit, befit. L16. 3 *v.refl.* & †*i.* Behave. E17.

†**comportance** *n.* carriage, bearing, behaviour; agreement, compliance: L16–M17.

comportment /kəmˈpɔːtm(ə)nt/ *n.* L16. [Fr., f. *comporter* f. as prec.: see -MENT.] Personal bearing, demeanour; behaviour.

compos /ˈkɒmpɒs/ *a.* E19. [Abbrev.] = COMPOS MENTIS.

See also NON COMPOS.

composant *n.* see CORPOSANT.

compose /kəmˈpəʊz/ *v.* LME. [(O)Fr. *composer*, based on L *componere* (see COMPOUND *v.*) but re-formed after L pa. pple *compositus* and (O)Fr. *poser*: see POSE *v.*[1]] I Put together. 1 *v.t.* Make by assembling parts; make up, construct. *obs.* exc. as below. LME. †b Fashion, frame. L15–L17. 2 *spec.* a *v.t.* Construct in words, write as author, produce in literary form. LME. b *v.t.* Construct in notes of music, produce in musical form; set (words) to music. L16. c *v.i.* Construct a work or works in words or music; engage in literary or musical creation. E17. 3 *v.t.* In *pass.* (orig. of sense 1, but now assoc. w. sense 6). Be made up, be formed; be constituted *of*, consist *of*. M16. 4 *v.t. Printing* & *Typogr.* Arrange (characters) by hand or machine, or electronically, in the order to be reproduced in print; set (an article, book, etc.) in type or otherwise prepare for printing. M17. 5 *v.t.* Put together to form a whole; *spec.* arrange artistically. M17. 6 *v.t.* Constitute, make up, be the constituents or material of. (See also sense 3 above.) M17.

2a DAY LEWIS A few poems in her own handwriting, composed after her marriage. P. ROTH To compose in my head . . the first lines of an introductory lecture. b J. GLASSCO She busied herself composing a sonata for violin. 3 SHAKES. *Much Ado* He is compos'd and fram'd of treachery. JO GRIMOND The British Army was composed of Generals and 3-ton lorries. 4 **composing-stick** an instrument, usu. of adjustable width, in which metal type is assembled with spaces to form lines before being put on a galley. 6 B. RUSSELL A good society is a means to a good life for those who compose it.

II Arrange, adjust. 7 *v.t.* Settle (a dispute), pacify (contending persons, a region); arrange (any matter) properly or successfully. LME. b *v.i.* Come to a settlement. *rare* (Shakes.). E17. 8 *v.t.* Arrange in a particular manner or for a particular purpose (specified or understood, esp. in proper order or in a position of rest); arrange (one's face, features, etc.) so as to conceal one's feelings. M16. b Lay out (a corpse). L17. 9 *v.t.* Dispose (esp. the mind, oneself) calmly and collectedly (*to* or *for* an action or state, *to do* something); calm, pacify, tranquillize. E17. 10 *v.t.* Quiet (a noise etc.). *arch.* E17.

7 TENNYSON It then remains . . to compose the event. L. VAN DER POST You must compose your differences with one another. 8 L. A. G. STRONG She had been able to compose herself in a suitable attitude of meditation. N. ALGREN She composed her features and her hair. 9 SOUTHEY I would fain compose my thoughts for action. W. MARCH She sat down to compose herself. J. BARZUN Intellect . . should calm and compose the soul.

composable *a.* †(*a*) *rare* adapted for composition; (*b*) able to be composed; suitable for setting to music: E17. **composal** *n.* (now *rare*) the act or action of composing M17. **composed** *a.* that has been composed; *spec.* †(*a*) compound, composite; (*b*) calm and self-possessed; expressive of calm and self-possession: L15. **composedly** *adv.* M17. **composedness** *n.* E17.

composer /kəm'pəʊzə/ *n.* M16. [f. prec. + -ER[1].] 1 *gen.* A person who or thing which composes. (Foll. by *of*.) M16. 2 *esp.* †a A compositor. L16–E18. b A person who composes music. L16. c An author, a writer, (*of*). E17.

composite /'kɒmpəzɪt; *in sense B.5* -zʌɪt/ *a.* & *n.* In *Archit.* orig. †**-ita**. LME. [Fr., or L *compositus* pa. pple of *componere*: see COMPOUND *v.*, -ITE[2].] A *adj.* 1 *Math.* †a Of a number: composed of more than one digit. Only in LME. b Of a number: being the product of two or more factors greater than unity; not prime. M18. 2 *Archit.* Designating the fifth classical order, a compound of Ionic and Corinthian. M16. 3 *gen.* Made up of various parts or elements, compound; made of constituents that remain recognizable. L17. 4 *Biol.* Made up of a number of separate simple parts or individual organisms; *spec.* (*Bot.*) belonging to or designating the large plant family Compositae, in which the so-called flower is a head of many florets sessile on a common receptacle and surrounded by a common involucre of bracts, as in the daisy, dandelion, etc. M18. 5 Of a railway carriage: with compartments of different classes. M19. B *n.* †1 *Math.* A number composed of more than one digit. Only in LME. 2 *Archit.* The composite order. M16. 3 *gen.* A composite thing, a composite material, a compound. M17. 4 A composite plant. M19. 5 A resolution compiled from several independent resolutions, put before a Party Conference, Trades Union Congress, etc. Cf. earlier COMPOSITE *v.* L20.

compositely *adv.* M19. **compositeness** *n.* L19.

composite /kɒmpə'zʌɪt/ *v.t.* & *i.* M20. [f. the n.] Combine (independent resolutions) into one resolution for putting before a Party Conference, Trades Union Congress, etc.

composition /kɒmpə'zɪʃ(ə)n/ *n.* LME. [(O)Fr. f. L *compositio(n-)*, f. *composit-* pa. ppl stem of *componere*: see COMPOUND *v.*, -ION.] I The action. 1 The action of combining; the fact of being combined; combination. LME. 2 The forming of or *of* a thing by the combination of parts etc.; formation, construction. LME. 3 The combination of mathematical quantities, forces, etc. L15. 4 The settling of a debt etc. by some arrangement. L15. 5a The combination (according to various rules and principles) of lexical items into a compound word. M16. b The arrangement of words into sentences, and sentences into poetry or prose. M16. †6 The putting (of things) into proper order. L16–M19. 7 *Philos.* †a Synthetic reasoning; reasoning from the universal to the particular. L16–M18. b The combination of two terms or propositions to form a compound term or proposition; (chiefly as *fallacy of composition*) the invalid move from a proposition about individual members or subsets of a set or class taken separately to a proposition about the set or class itself. E18. 8 The composing of anything to be recited or read; the practice or art of literary production. L16. 9 The action or art of composing music. L16. 10 The arranging of the elements of a drawing, painting, sculpture, photograph, etc., so as to form an aesthetically pleasing whole. L16. 11 *Printing* & *Typogr.* The setting of type by hand or machine. See also PHOTOCOMPOSITION. M19.

8 ARNOLD BENNETT He sat down to the composition of his letter. 9 M. TIPPETT What Mozart wrote in a letter about composition. 10 E. H. GOMBRICH This . . gave the artist of the Middle Ages a new freedom to experiment with more complex forms of composition.

II The mode, with the resulting condition or state. 12 The manner in which a thing is composed or made up; the state or condition resulting from or constituted by combination; the combination of physical and mental qualities that make up a person. LME. 13 The state or quality of being composite. M16. 14 The artistic manner or style in which words, visual elements, or musical notes, are put together. M16. †15 Consistency. *rare* (Shakes.). Only in E17.

12 H. JAMES Her stature, like most other points in her composition, was not unusual. J. REED Trotsky announced its composition: 100 members, of which 70 Bolsheviki. B. SPOCK The water and sugar are put in to make the mixture more like mother's milk in composition. *organic composition* (*of capital*): see ORGANIC *a.*

III The product. 16 A substance or preparation formed by the combination or mixture of various ingredients; *esp.* a compound artificial substance serving the purpose of a natural one. LME. 17a An agreement, a contract; a treaty, a truce. *arch.* LME. b A compromise. L16. 18 A condition consisting in the combination (material, practical, or ideal) *of* several things; a combination, an aggregate, a mixture. M16. 19a A piece of writing, a literary production; in schools etc., a piece of writing as an exercise in expressing oneself in prose. L16. b A piece of music. M17. c A painting, drawing, sculpture, photograph, etc., consisting of several elements aesthetically combined; *transf.* a harmonious natural scene. M18. 20 An agreement for the payment of a sum of money in lieu of a larger sum or some other obligation; payment of this by agreement; the sum of money so paid. L16.

16 *attrib.*: R. CHANDLER The gates folded back on a black composition driveway. 18 R. W. EMERSON He seemed . . to be a composition of several persons. 19a J. D. SALINGER I didn't have to do any work in English at all hardly, except write compositions once in a while. b Y. MENUHIN The Solo Sonata is . . the most important composition for violin alone since Bach. c K. CLARK The carefully constructed compositions of the later Giotto.

compositional *a.* E19. **compositionally** *adv.* M20. †**compositure** *n.* = COMPOSITION 12 E17–E18.

compositive /kəm'pɒzɪtɪv/ *a.* L16. [f. COMPOSITE *a.* & *n.* or prec.: see -IVE.] Involving or using composition; synthetic.

compositor /kəm'pɒzɪtə/ *n.* LME. [AN *compositour* = (O)Fr. *-eur*, f. L *compositor*, f. *composit-*: see COMPOSITION, -OR.] †1 An umpire, an arbiter, a peace-maker. *Sc.* LME–E18. 2 The composer or compiler of a literary work. *rare*. M16. 3 *Printing*. A person who sets type by hand, corrects composed matter, makes up pages, and assembles them for printing; *loosely* a person who sets type by machine. M16.

composi'torial *a.* of or pertaining to composers or compositors E19.

compositum /kəm'pɒzɪtəm/ *n.* Pl. **-ta** /-tə/, **-tums**. M17. [L, neut. pa. pple of *componere*: see COMPOUND *v.*] = COMPOSITION 16, 18.

compos mentis /ˌkɒmpɒs 'mɛntɪs/ *pred. a. phr.* E17. [L.] In one's right mind, having control of one's mind, not mad.

See also NON COMPOS MENTIS.

compossible /kəm'pɒsɪb(ə)l/ *a.* M17. [OFr. f. med.L *compossibilis*: see COM-, POSSIBLE. Cf. earlier INCOMPOSSIBLE.] Possible in conjunction, compatible, (*with*).

compossi'bility *n.* M17.

compost /'kɒmpɒst/ *n.* LME. [OFr. *composte* (mod. COMPOTE) f. L *compos(i)ta, -tum* use as n. of fem. and neut. pa. pple of *componere* COMPOUND *v.*] 1 A composition, a combination, a compound. LME. †2 A preparation of preserved fruit etc.; = COMPOTE 1. LME–E18. 3 A mixed manure of organic origin; loam soil or some other medium with added organic matter to grow plants in; *fig.* a mixture of ingredients. LME.

Comb.: **compost heap, pile**: of garden refuse, soil, etc., used for the quick production of compost.

compost /'kɒmpɒst/ *v.t.* L15. [OFr. *composter*, f. as COMPOST *n.*] Treat with or make into compost.

compostable *a.* L20.

composture /kəm'pɒstʃə/ *n.* Long *obs.* exc. *dial.* E17. [OFr., f. as prec.: see -URE.] 1 Composition. E17. †2 Compost, manure. *rare* (Shakes.). Only in E17.

composure /kəm'pəʊʒə/ *n.* L16. [f. COMPOSE *v.* + -URE.] †1 The action of composing or compounding; = COMPOSITION I. L16–M18. †2a *gen.* The mode or form of composition, the state of being composed; = COMPOSITION II. E17–M19. b *spec.* Calmness and self-possession, tranquil demeanour. M17. †3 A product of composing; = COMPOSITION III. E17–L18.

compotation /kɒmpə(ʊ)'teɪʃ(ə)n/ *n.* L16. [L *compotatio(n-)* (in Cicero tr. Gk *sumposion* SYMPOSIUM): see COM-, POTATION.] A drinking-session, a carouse.

'**compotator** *n.* a fellow drinker M18. **com'potatory** *a.* E19.

compote /'kɒmpəʊt, -ɒt/ *n.* Also **-ôte**. L17. [Fr.: see COMPOST *n.*] 1 (A dish of) fruit preserved or cooked in a syrup; a fruit salad, stewed fruit, esp. with or in a syrup. L17. 2 A dish of stewed pigeon. M18. 3 A bowl-shaped dessert dish with a stem; a dish for stewed fruit etc. Cf. COMPORT *n.*, next. L19.

compotier /kɔ̃pɔtje/ *n.* Pl. pronounced same. M18. [Fr., f. as prec.: see -IER.] = COMPOTE 3.

compotus *n.* var. of COMPUTUS.

compound /'kɒmpaʊnd/ *n.*[1] M16. [f. COMPOUND *a.*] 1 A compound thing, a compound substance; *spec.* (*a*) a compound word; (*b*) *Chem.* a substance consisting of two or more elements chemically combined in fixed proportions by weight; (*c*) a compound (steam) locomotive. M16. 2 A union, combination, or mixture *of* ingredients, parts, etc. E17. 3 Compounding, composition. L17.

1 R. FRY This attempt to isolate the elusive element of the pure aesthetic reaction from the compounds in which it occurs. N. G. CLARK A group of compounds known as paraffin hydrocarbons. BINARY *compound*. *open compound*: see OPEN *a.* 2 S. BRETT The smell of the house—a compound of used cooking oil, beer and wet cardboard.

compound /'kɒmpaʊnd/ *n.*[2] L17. [Port. *campon* or Du. *kampoeng*, f. Malay *kampung*, *-ong* enclosure, small village.] 1 In SE Asia, the Indian subcontinent, etc.: an enclosure in which a house or factory stands. L17. 2 In S. Africa: an enclosure in which miners live. L19. **3** A large fenced-in space in a prison, concentration camp, etc.; a pound. E20.

compound /ˈkɒmpaʊnd/ *a.* LME. [Orig. pa. pple of †*compo(u)ne*: see next, -ED[1].] **1** Made up of several ingredients; consisting of several parts or elements; *spec.* (*a*) *Biol.* consisting of a number of distinct units, organisms, etc.; (*b*) *Gram.* (of a word) made up of more than one word or root; (of a tense) formed using an auxiliary verb; (*c*) *Optics* (of a lens) consisting of two or more different lenses mounted as a single unit. LME. **2** Combined, collective. E18.

Special collocations: **compound engine** (*a*) a steam engine in which the same steam is made to expand successively in different sets of cylinders; (*b*) an aero-engine utilizing the kinetic energy of the exhaust (as a turbofan or turboprop). **compound eye** *Zool.* an eye (e.g. of an insect) composed of many simple units (ommatidia) each forming a facet of the whole organ. **compound fracture**: with the skin pierced by a bone end and involving a risk of infection. *compound interest*: see INTEREST *n.* **compound interval** *Mus.*: exceeding one octave. **compound leaf**: divided into a number of leaflets (which may themselves be further divided). **compound locomotive**: working on the principle of the compound (steam) engine. *compound machine*: see MACHINE *n.* 4b. **compound order** *Archit.* the composite order. *compound pendulum*: see PENDULUM *n.* *compound* PISTIL. *compound* RACEME. **compound sentence** *Gram.*: formed by coordination of two or more simple sentences. **compound time** *Mus.*: having beats with the value of a dotted note. *compound umbel*: see UMBEL I.

compoundness *n.* M18.

compound /kəmˈpaʊnd/ *v.* Also (earlier) **†-o(u)ne**. LME. [(O)Fr. *compo(u)n-* pres. stem of *compondre* f. L *componere*, f. as COM- + *ponere* to place. Mod. form (E16) after EXPOUND.] **I†1** *v.t.* Put together, join. LME–M17. **2** *v.t.* Combine, mix, (material or immaterial elements). (Foll. by *with*.) LME. **b** *Gram.* Combine (words or roots) to form a larger word. M16. **c** Combine (mathematical quantities etc.) so as to obtain a resultant or composite quantity. Also, reckon as compound interest, increase (as) by compound interest. L16. **d** Add to, increase, complicate, (esp. difficulties etc.). M20. **3** *v.t.* Make up by the combination of various ingredients or elements. (Foll. by *of*, *from*.) LME. **4** *v.t.* Construct, form, compose. *obs.* exc. as passing into sense 3. LME. **†5** *v.t.* Go to make up, constitute. E17–E18.

2 SHAKES. *2 Hen. IV* Only compound me with forgotten dust. I. MURDOCH A vague . . pain in which portions of jealousy and wounded pride were compounded with a profound sense of homelessness. **d** A. HAILEY If the first was a mistake, then at least we need not compound it. **3** A. J. CRONIN Andrew . . began . . to compound an anti-pyretic mixture. Jo GRIMOND The feeling was compounded of several fears. **4** B. JOWETT Meletus . . has been compounding a riddle.

II 6 *v.i.* Agree, come to terms, settle a matter, now *spec.* by mutual concession or compromise or as in sense 7. (Foll. by *with* a person, *for* a thing.) LME. **7** *v.i. spec.* **a** Come to a settlement by paying money, agree on a payment, (*with* a person, *for* a thing); substitute a money payment or some other lighter performance for or *for* a liability or obligation; settle a debt by partial repayment; discharge a recurrent payment in a lump sum. L15. **b** Accept terms of settlement in lieu of prosecution; accept payment in lieu of one's full claims. (Foll. by *for*.) L16. **8** *v.t.* Settle, compose, (a matter, esp. a dispute etc.), now *spec.* by mutual concession or compromise or as in sense 9. E16. **9** *v.t. spec.* **a** Settle (a debt) by partial repayment; settle (any matter) by payment of money. M17. **b** Accept money for; condone (an offence etc.) for money; settle privately; forbear prosecution of (a felony) from private motives. L17.

compoundable *a.* E17. **compounded** *a.* (*a*) that has been compounded; formed by combination of various ingredients or elements; †(*b*) compound, composite, complex: L16.

compounder /kəmˈpaʊndə/ *n.* M16. [f. prec. + -ER[1].] **1** A person who settles quarrels; *derog.*, a compromiser. *obs.* exc. *Hist.*, a supporter of the conditional restoration of James II. M16. **2** A person who compounds for a liability, debt, or charge; one who compounds a felony or offence. M16. **3** A person who makes a compound of ingredients. E17.

†compoune *v.* see COMPOUND *v.*

comprador /kɒmprəˈdɔː/ *n.* Also **-ore**. E17. [Port. = buyer, f. late L *comparator*, f. *comparare* purchase, f. as COM- + *parare* furnish.] **†1** A house steward in the European households of SE Asia, the Indian subcontinent, etc. E17–E19. **2** The Chinese chief agent of a foreign business-house in China; *fig.* an agent of a foreign power. M19.

comprecation /kɒmprɪˈkeɪʃ(ə)n/ *n.* E17. [L *comprecatio(n-)*, f. *comprecat-* pa. ppl stem of *comprecari*, f. as COM- + *precari* pray: see -ATION.] Communal prayer; joint supplication.

comprehend /kɒmprɪˈhɛnd/ *v.t.* ME. [OFr. *comprehender* or L *comprehendere*, f. as COM- + *prehendere* seize.] **I 1** Grasp mentally, understand. ME. **2** Apprehend with the senses, esp. the sight. *arch.* LME. **†3** Accomplish, overtake, attain (*lit.* & *fig.*). LME–E17. **†4** *lit.* Lay hold of, seize. *rare.* L16–M17.

1 J. S. MILL The majority . . cannot comprehend why those ways should not be good enough for everybody. S. KAUFFMANN To know him better than anyone, to comprehend him. B. MALAMUD Speak more slowly so that we can comprehend everything you say.

II †5 Summarize; sum up. LME–E17. **6** Include, contain, comprise, take in; encompass. LME.

6 COVERDALE *2 Chron.* 2:6 The heauens of all heauens maye not comprehende him. M. DRAYTON Some swelling source (Whose plentie none can comprehend in bounds). R. HAKLUYT The second Volume comprehendeth the principall Navigations . . to the South. J. AUSTEN Far from comprehending him or his sister in their father's misconduct. M. H. ABRAMS In many later mimetic theories everything is comprehended in two categories.

comprehendingly *adv.* in a comprehending manner, intelligently M19.

comprehensible /kɒmprɪˈhɛnsɪb(ə)l/ *a.* L15. [Fr. *compréhensible* or L *comprehensibilis*, f. *comprehens-* pa. ppl stem of *comprehendere*: see prec., -IBLE. Cf. earlier INCOMPREHENSIBLE.] **1** That may be understood; conceivable, intelligible. (Foll. by *to*.) L15. **2** That may be included, contained, or comprised. E16.

comprehensiˈbility *n.* M18. **comprehensibly** *adv.* M18.

comprehension /kɒmprɪˈhɛnʃ(ə)n/ *n.* LME. [Fr. *compréhension* or L *comprehensio(n-)*, f. *comprehens-*: see prec., -ION.] **I 1** The act, fact, or faculty of understanding, esp. of writing or speech; mental grasp. LME. **b** *spec.* The setting or answering of questions on a set passage to test or improve linguistic understanding, esp. as a school exercise. M20. **2** An understanding, an adequate notion, (*of*). L16. **†3** An act of grasping physically. *rare.* M17–M18. **II 4** The action of including, containing, or comprising; the fact or condition of being so included etc. LME. **b** *Eccl. Hist.* The inclusion of Nonconformists in the Church of England. M17. **5** The faculty or quality of including; inclusiveness. E17. **6** *Logic.* The sum of the attributes included in a concept; intension. E18.

comprehensive /kɒmprɪˈhɛnsɪv/ *a.* & *n.* E17. [Fr. *compréhensif, -ive* or late L *comprehensivus*, f. *comprehens-*: see COMPREHENSIBLE, -IVE.] **A** *adj.* **1** Comprising or including much or all; of large content or scope. E17. **b** Inclusive *of*. M17. **c** *spec.* Designating a secondary school or a system of education which provides for children of all intellectual or other abilities. M20. **2** Characterized by mental comprehension; embracing many mental sympathies etc. E17. **3** *Logic.* Understood in intension as opp. to extension. Now *rare* or *obs.* E18.

1 M. FRAYN A comprehensive lexicon of all the multi-purpose monosyllables used by headline-writers. D. HALBERSTAM He wanted more coverage than any other paper; he was determined . . to be comprehensive.

B *n.* A comprehensive school. M20.

comprehensively *adv.* LME. **comprehensiveness** *n.* M17. **comprehensiviˈzation** *n.* the action of comprehensivizing M20. **comprehensivize** *v.t.* make (a school, an education system) comprehensive M20.

†comprehensor *n.* M17–E18. [f. L *comprehens-* (see COMPREHENSIBLE) + -OR.] A person who has attained to full (religious) comprehension.

†compresbyter *n.* L16–E18. [eccl.L, f. as COM-, PRESBYTER.] A fellow presbyter.

compresence /kɒmˈprɛz(ə)ns/ *n.* M17. [f. COM- + PRESENCE.] Presence together; co-presence.

compresent *a.* present together; co-present: E20.

compress /ˈkɒmprɛs/ *n.* L16. [Fr. *compresse*, f. as next.] **1** A soft linen pad for compressing an artery, applying a medicine, etc.; a piece of cloth, usu. wet and covered with a waterproof bandage, applied to reduce inflammation, etc. (also *cold compress*, *water compress*). L16. **2** A machine for pressing cotton-bales etc. in a compact form for transport etc. M19.

compress /kəmˈprɛs/ *v.t.* LME. [OFr. *compresser* or late L *compressare* frequent. of L *comprimere*, or f. *compress-* pa. ppl stem of *comprimere*: see COM-, PRESS *v.*[1]] **1** Press together, squeeze, (separate things, a hollow thing reducing its capacity, a substance making it more dense); flatten (as) by pressure; reduce to smaller volume; *fig.* condense, concentrate. LME. **b** Increase the density of (a fluid) mechanically by increasing the mass contained in a fixed volume or reducing the volume of a fixed mass. L17. **†2** Repress, keep under restraint. E16–M19. **†3** Embrace sexually. E17–E18.

1 R. C. HUTCHINSON Bickerings at Westminster could be compressed . . into a few columns of the big daily newspapers. M. FRAYN As if he had compressed a whole week's emotional energy into that one burst of anger.

compressed *a.* (*a*) that has been compressed; *compressed air*, air that is at greater than atmospheric pressure; (*b*) *Zool.* & *Bot.* flattened laterally: L16.

compressible /kəmˈprɛsɪb(ə)l/ *a.* L17. [f. prec. + -IBLE.] **1** Able to be compressed. L17. **2** *Med.* Of the pulse: so faint that it appears to vanish under the pressure of the finger; thready. Now *rare.* M19.

compressiˈbility *n.* the quality of being compressible; *Physics* (a measure of) the ability of a fluid to be compressed: L17.

compression /kəmˈprɛʃ(ə)n/ *n.* LME. [(O)Fr. f. L *compressio(n-)*, f. *compress-*: see COMPRESS *v.*, -ION.] **1** The action or act of compressing; the state or condition of being compressed. LME. **2a** In a steam engine, the reduction in volume of the steam left in the cylinder after the exhaust is closed at the end of the exhaust stroke. M19. **b** The (amount of) reduction in volume of the air-fuel mixture in an internal-combustion engine before ignition. L19.

Comb.: **compression ratio** the ratio of the maximum to minimum volume in the cylinder of an internal-combustion engine measured before and after compression; **compression stroke** the stroke of the piston compressing the air-fuel mixture in the cylinder of an internal-combustion engine.

compressional *a.* L19.

compressive /kəmˈprɛsɪv/ *a.* LME. [(O)Fr. *compressif, -ive*, or med.L *compressivus*, f. *compress-*: see COMPRESS *v.*, -IVE.] **1** Having the attribute or function of compressing; tending to compress. LME. **†2** Consisting in or caused by compression. LME–M17.

compressor /kəmˈprɛsə/ *n.* M19. [f. COMPRESS *v.* + -OR.] An instrument or device for compressing; *spec.* a machine, or part of a machine, for compressing air or other gases, esp. for motive power.

compressure /kəmˈprɛʃə/ *n.* M17. [med.L *compressura*, f. *compress-*: see COMPRESS *v.*, -URE.] Compression; pressing together.

comprise /kəmˈprʌɪz/ *v.t.* Also **-ize**. LME. [Fr. *compris(e)* pa. pple of *comprendre* COMPREHEND. Cf. APPRISE *v.*[1]] **†1 a** Lay hold of, seize; *Sc.* seize legally. LME–L17. **†b** Grasp mentally, perceive, comprehend. LME–L17. **2** Include, contain; extend to, encompass; consist of, be made up of.

LME. †b Enclose, hold. L15–M17. c Summarize, sum up. E16. †3 Write as author, compile, compose. L15–E17. 4 Make up, constitute, compose; in *pass.*, be composed *of*, consist *of*. L18.

2 C. BRONTË In her own single person she could have comprised the duties of a first minister and a superintendent of police. MAX-MÜLLER The registers .. comprised a period of 200,000 years. M. MEYER The ground floor comprised the shop, a tiny waiting room and the kitchen. c W. PALEY Comprising what he delivered within a small compass. 4 L. DURRELL A few such sketches comprise the whole portrait of the author.

comprisable *a.* E17.

compromise /ˈkɒmprəmʌɪz/ *n.* & *a.* LME. [(O)Fr. *compromis* f. L *compromissum* use as n. of neut. pa. pple of *compromittere* consent to arbitration, f. as COM- + *promittere* PROMISE *v.*] A *n.* I †1 A joint agreement made by contending parties to abide by the decision of an arbitrator. LME–L16. b = COMPROMISSION 2. E18–L19. 2 Settlement by an arbitrator; arbitration. Now *rare* or *obs.* LME. 3 Settlement of a dispute by mutual concession; a concession offered to settle a dispute. E16. 4 The finding of an intermediate way between (or *between*) conflicting requirements, courses of action, etc., by modification of each; a thing that results from or embodies such an arrangement. E18.

3 SHAKES. *Rich. II* Warr'd he hath not, But basely yielded upon compromise That which his noble ancestors achiev'd with blows. 4 LD MACAULAY Logic admits of no compromise The essence of politics is compromise. SCOTT FITZGERALD A compromise between the serious and the trivial.

II 5 A putting in peril; an exposure to risk. E17.

B *adj.* That is, or serves as, a compromise (sense A.4 above). M19.

compromise /ˈkɒmprəmʌɪz/ *v.* LME. [f. the n.] I †1 *v.t.* Refer (something) *to* another for decision. LME–M17. †2 *v.t.* In *pass.* Be agreed by mutual concession. LME–L18. 3 *v.i.* Come to terms by mutual concession; make a compromise. LME. 4 *v.t.* †a Settle (a matter in dispute between others). L16–L18. b Of a contending party: settle (a difference with or *with* another) by mutual concession; come to terms about. L17.

3 S. RICHARDSON To induce him to compromise on those terms. M. MEYER Politicians .. invariably compromised with their ideals.

II 5 *v.t.* Bring under suspicion or into danger, esp. by indiscreet action; imperil (a reputation etc.). L17.

5 R. CHURCH The spot of ink on his trousers .. did not compromise his dignity. T. SHARPE The shopgirls they had compromised.

compromiser *n.* †(*a*) an arbitrator in a dispute; (*b*) a person who compromises or advocates compromise: L15.

compromission /kɒmprəˈmɪʃ(ə)n/ *n.* LME. [(O)Fr., or med.L *compromissio(n-)*, f. L *compromiss-* pa. ppl stem of *compromittere*: see COMPROMISE *n.* & *a.*, -ION.] 1 Submission of a dispute to arbitration. LME. 2 Delegation of the responsibility of electing to chosen representatives. LME.

†**compromit** *v.* LME. [L *compromittere*: see COMPROMISE *n.* & *a.*] 1 *v.refl.* & in *pass.* Bind themselves etc., be bound, jointly to accept an arbitrator's decision. LME–M16. 2 *v.t.* Refer to arbitration; settle by arbitration or compromise. LME–L17. 3 *v.i.* & *t.* Delegate (an election or one's right to vote). Only in 16. 4 *v.t.* = COMPROMISE *v.* 5. *US.* L18–L19.

†**comprotector** *n.* M17–M18. [f. COM- + PROTECTOR.] A joint protector.

comprovincial /kɒmprəˈvɪnʃ(ə)l/ *n.* & *a.* LME. [Late L *comprovincialis* f. L COM- + *provincialis* PROVINCIAL.] A *n.* A bishop of the same province. LME. B *adj.* Belonging to the same province. M16.

†**compt** *n.* var. of COUNT *n.*[1]

†**compt** *a.* LME–L18. [L *comptus* pa. pple of *comere* dress (hair), adorn.] Having the hair dressed. Of a person, a style of discourse: elegant, polished.

†**compt** *v.* var. of COUNT *v.*

†**comptable** *a.* & *n.* var. of COUNTABLE *a.* & *n.*

compter *n.* see COUNTER *n.*[1]

compte rendu /kɔ̃t rɑ̃dy/ *n. phr.* Pl. **-s -s** (pronounced same). E19. [Fr. = account rendered.] A report, a review, a statement.

comptes rendus *n. phr.* pl. of COMPTE RENDU.

†**compting** *vbl n.* var. of COUNTING.

comptoir /kɔ̃twɑː/ *n.* Pl. pronounced same. E18. [Fr.: see COUNTER *n.*[1]] A commercial agency or factory in a foreign country.

Comptometer /kɒm(p)ˈtɒmɪtə/ *n.* L19. [App. f. Fr. *compte* COUNT *n.*[1] + -OMETER.] (Proprietary name for) a type of calculating-machine.

Compton effect /ˈkɒm(p)tən ɪˌfɛkt/ *n. phr.* E20. [f. A. H. *Compton* (1892–1962), US physicist.] *Physics.* The increase in wavelength that occurs when X-rays and gamma rays are scattered.

†**comptrol** *v.* var. of CONTROL *v.*

comptroller /kənˈtrəʊlə/ *n.* L15. [Var. of CONTROLLER by erron. assoc. w. COUNT *n.*[1] (late L COMPUTUS).] A controller: now only in the titles of some financial and legal officers in government and the royal household.

Comptroller and Auditor General.

†**comptrolment** *n.* var. of CONTROLMENT.

compulsative /kəmˈpʌlsətɪv/ *a. rare* (Shakes.). E17. [f. L *compulsat-* pa. ppl stem of *compulsare* frequent. of *compellere* COMPEL + -IVE.] Of the nature of compulsion.

compulsatively *adv.* M19.

†**compulsator** *n.* see COMPULSITOR.

†**compulsatory** *a.* E16–E19. [f. as COMPULSATIVE: see -ORY[2].] Of the nature of compulsion; compulsory.

†**compulsatorily** *adv.* M–L18.

compulse /kəmˈpʌls/ *v.t. rare.* LME. [OFr. *compulser* f. L *compulsare*: see COMPULSATIVE.] Compel, oblige.

compulsion /kəmˈpʌlʃ(ə)n/ *n.* LME. [(O)Fr. f. late L *compulsio(n-)*, f. L *compuls-* pa. ppl stem of *compellere* COMPEL: see -ION.] 1 The action, or an act, of compelling; the condition of being compelled; coercion, obligation. LME. 2 *Psychol.* An irresistible impulse to behave in a certain way, esp. despite one's conscious intent or wish. E20.

1 T. LEWIN The tribute .. would not be forthcoming except on compulsion. **under compulsion** because one is compelled. 2 A. J. CRONIN An inner compulsion so powerful as to be irresistible.

compulsitor /kəmˈpʌlsɪtə/ *n.* Orig. †**-ator.** E16. [med.L *compulsatorius* adj., f. L *compulsat-*: see COMPULSATIVE, -OR.] *Sc. Law.* An act, instrument, or proceeding that orders or compels.

compulsive /kəmˈpʌlsɪv/ *a.* & *n.* L16. [med.L *compulsivus*, f. L *compuls-*: see COMPULSION, -IVE.] A *adj.* 1 = COMPULSORY *a.* 2. L16. †2 = COMPULSORY *a.* 1. E17–M19. 3 *Psychol.* Of the nature of or resulting from a compulsion; characterized by a compulsion. E20. 4 Of an entertainment etc.: that compels one's continued attention. M20.

3 R. D. LAING His compulsive tendency to act in a feminine way. R. HAYMAN He was compulsive about personal cleanliness. 4 *Listener* John Cole, Gerald Kaufman and Took's Endpiece are all compulsive reading.

B *n.* 1 A compelling force. *rare.* M17. 2 A person subject to a psychological compulsion. M20.

compulsively *adv.* E17. **compulsiveness** *n.* E18.

compulsory /kəmˈpʌls(ə)ri/ *n.* & *a.* E16. [med.L *compulsorius*, f. L *compuls-*: see COMPULSION, -ORY[2].] A *n.* Something that compels or is obligatory; *esp.* a legal mandate compelling obedience. E16.

B *adj.* 1 Produced by compulsion; enforced; compelled. L16. 2 Compelling, coercive. M17.

1 *compulsory purchase*: see PURCHASE *n.* 6a.

compulsorily *adv.* M17. **compulsoriness** *n.* M19.

compunction /kəmˈpʌŋkʃ(ə)n/ *n.* ME. [(O)Fr. *componction* f. eccl.L *compunctio(n-)*, f. L *compunct-* pa. ppl stem of *compungere* prick sharply, sting, f. as COM- + *pungere* prick: see -ION.] 1 Pricking or stinging of the conscience or the heart; uneasiness of mind after wrongdoing; remorse. ME. b In weakened sense: a slight or passing regret for a minor misdeed, a scruple (sometimes including pity for the person wronged). E18. †2 Pity. LME–L18. †3 The action of pricking or puncturing. LME–M17.

compunctious /kəmˈpʌŋkʃəs/ *a.* E17. [f. prec. + -OUS.] 1 Of the nature of, expressive of, compunction. E17. 2 Having compunction. E19.

compunctiously *adv.* M19.

compurgation /kɒmpəːˈgeɪʃ(ə)n/ *n.* M17. [med.L *compurgatio(n-)*, f. L *compurgat-* pa. ppl stem of *compurgare* purge completely: see COM-, PURGATION.] 1 The action of clearing a person from a charge by the oaths of a number of others; *gen.* vindication; vindicating evidence. M17. 2 *Hist.* The ancient mode of trial and purgation by means of a number of compurgators. M19.

1 SIR W. SCOTT My evidence is necessary to the compurgation of ane honest gentleman.

compurgator /ˈkɒmpəːgeɪtə/ *n.* M16. [med.L, f. L COM- + *purgator*, f. *purgat-*: see PURGATION, -OR. Cf. OFr. *compurgateur*.] 1 *Hist.* A person who swore in favour of the character or credibility of an accused person when the latter swore an oath declaring his innocence. M16. 2 *gen.* A person who vouches for another; a character witness. E17.

comˈpurgatory *a.* E17.

computable /kəmˈpjuːtəb(ə)l/ *a.* E17. [L *computabilis*, f. *computare*: see COMPUTE *v.*, -ABLE.] Able to be computed.

computaˈbility *n.* L19.

computation /kɒmpjʊˈteɪʃ(ə)n/ *n.* LME. [L *computatio(n-)*, f. *computat-* pa. ppl stem of *computare*: see COMPUTE *v.*, -ATION.] 1 The action or process of reckoning; calculation; the use of a computer. LME. 2 A result got by calculation. E18.

computational *a.* L19. **computationally** *adv.* M20.

†**computator** *n.* L16–M18. [L, f. *computat-*: see prec., -OR.] A person who calculates.

compute /kəmˈpjuːt/ *n.* Now *rare.* LME. [In sense 1 f. Fr. *comput*; in sense 2, f. next.] †1 = COMPUTUS 1. LME–M16. 2 Calculation. Now chiefly in *beyond compute.* L16.

compute /kəmˈpjuːt/ *v.* E17. [Fr. *computer* or L *computare*, f. as COM- + *putare* settle (an account), reckon.] 1 *v.t.* Determine by calculation or computation; estimate, reckon. E17. 2 *v.i.* Make reckoning; use a computer. M17. †3 *v.i.* Of numbers: make up, count. *rare* (Milton). Only in M17.

1 S. PEPYS He hath computed that the rents .. comes to 600,000*l.* per annum. SWIFT The souls in this kingdom are computed to be 1,500,000. F. CHICHESTER I uncased the slide rule, and computed the sun's true bearing. **computed (axial) tomography** = *computerized (axial) tomography* s.v. COMPUTERIZE; abbrevs. *CAT, CT.*

computer /kəmˈpjuːtə/ *n.* Also **-or.** M17. [f. prec. + -ER[1].] 1 A person who makes calculations; *spec.* a person employed for this in an observatory etc. M17. 2 An apparatus for making calculations; *spec.* an automatic electronic machine for making rapid calculations or controlling operations that are expressible in numerical or logical terms. L19.

2 *computer program, programmer, terminal,* etc. *personal computer*: see PERSONAL *a.*

Comb.: **computer-aided, -assisted** *adjs.* performed with the aid of a computer, esp. when previously performed without; **computer dating** the use of facilities provided by a computer to find potential partners for people; **computer-friendly** *a.* suitable for use with computers, compatible with computers; (of a person) well-disposed towards computers, computerate; **computer game** (a software package for) a game played on a computer; *computer graphics*: see GRAPHIC *n.* 1b, 4; **computer language** any of numerous systems of rules, words, and symbols for writing computer programs or representing instructions etc.; **computer literacy** = COMPUTERACY; **computer-literate** *a.* = COMPUTERATE; **computer-readable** *a.* = *machine-readable* adj. s.v. MACHINE *n.*; **computer science** the branch of knowledge that deals with the construction, operation, programming, and applications of computers; **computer scientist** a specialist in computer science; **computer virus** = VIRUS 4.

computeracy *n.* [after LITERACY] the quality of being computerate L20. **computerate** *a.* [after LITERATE *a.*] able to use computers, familiar with the operation of computers L20. **compute'rese** *n.* (*a*) the symbols and rules of a programming language; (*b*) the jargon associated with computers: M20. **computerist** *n.* a (frequent) user of computers L20. **computeri'zation** *n.* the action or result of computerizing something M20. **computerize** *v.t.* equip with a computer; perform or produce by computer; *computerized* (*axial*) *tomography*, tomography in which the X-ray scanner makes many sweeps of the body and the results are processed by computer to give a cross-sectional image (abbrevs. *CAT*, *CT*): M20.

computist /ˈkɒmpjʊtɪst/ *n.* LME. [med.L *computista*, f. late L COMPUTUS: see -IST.] 1 A person skilled in calendrical or astronomical reckoning. LME. †2 A keeper of accounts. L16–L17.

compu'tistic(al) *adjs.* M20.

computor *n.* var. of COMPUTER.

computus /ˈkɒmpjʊtəs/ *n.* Also **-pot-** /-pət-/. M19. [Late L = computation, f. L *computare* COMPUTE *v.*] *Hist.* 1 A medieval set of tables for astronomical and calendrical calculations. M19. 2 A reckoning; an account. M19.

comrade /ˈkɒmreɪd/ *n.* Orig. also †**camerade**. M16. [Fr. *camerade*, *camarade* f. Sp. *camarada* barrack-room, chamber-fellow, f. *camara* chamber f. L CAMERA: see -ADE.] 1 Orig., a person who shared the same room or tent, *esp.* (also *comrade-in-arms*) a fellow soldier; hence, an associate (usu. male) in friendship, occupation, or fortune; an equal with whom one is on familiar terms. M16. 2 *spec.* A fellow socialist or communist. Freq. used before a name and as a form of address or reference. L19. 3 A (young) Black radical political activist in South Africa. L20.

comradeliness *n.* comradely nature or behaviour M20. **comradely** *a.* characteristic of or befitting a comrade L19. **comradery** *n.* = COMRADESHIP L19. **comradeship** *n.* the relationship of comrades; camaraderie: E19.

comrogue /ˈkɒmrəʊg/ *n. arch.* E17. [f. COM- + ROGUE *n.*] A fellow rogue.

coms *n.pl.* var. of COMBS.

comsat /ˈkɒmsat/ *n.* M20. [Abbrev. of *communication satellite*.] A satellite used for telecommunication.

Comstockery /ˈkɒmstɒk(ə)ri/ *n.* Also **c-**. E20. [f. Anthony *Comstock* (1844–1915), member of the New York Society for the Suppression of Vice + -ERY.] Excessive opposition to supposed immorality in the arts; prudery.

Comstocker *n.* a person who advocates or practises Comstockery E20.

comte /kɔ̃ːt (*pl. same*); kɔːnt, kɒmt/ *n.* E17. [Fr.: see COUNT *n.*[2]] A French nobleman corresponding in rank to an English earl.

¶Rare bef. L19.

Comtean *a.* var. of COMTIAN.

comtesse /kɔ̃tes (*pl. same*); kɔːnˈtɛs, kɒm-/ *n.* E20. [Fr., f. as prec. + -ESS[1].] A French noblewoman corresponding in rank to an English countess.

Comtian /ˈkɔ̃ːntɪən, ˈkɒmt-/ *a.* Also **-ean**, **c-**. M19. [f. *Comte* (see below) + -IAN, -EAN.] Of or deriving from Auguste Comte (1798–1857), French philosopher and founder of positivism.

Comtism *n.* Comtian philosophy, positivism M19. **Comtist** *n.* & *a.* (*a*) *n.* an advocate or follower of Comtism; (*b*) *adj.* = COMTIAN: M19.

Comus /ˈkəʊməs/ *n.* L16. [L f. Gk *kōmos* revel.] Revelry personified; a revel.

†**comutual** *a.* var. of COMMUTUAL.

con /kɒn/ *n.*[1] L16. [f. CON *adv.*] A reason, argument, or arguer against. Chiefly in *pros and cons* s.v. PRO *prep.* etc.

con /kɒn/ *n.*[2] *obs.* exc. *dial.* E17. [Perh. f. Fr. *cogner* strike, thump.] A rap with the knuckles, a knock.

con /kɒn/ *n.*[3] Also **conn**. E19. [f. CON *v.*[2]] The action or post of conning a ship.

con /kɒn/ *n.*[4] *colloq.* (orig. *US*). L19. [Abbrev.] In *comb.* = CONFIDENCE, as *con artist*, *con man*, *con trick*, etc.; *ellipt.* a confidence trick, a confidence trickster.

short con: see SHORT *a.*

con /kɒn/ *n.*[5] *slang.* L19. [Abbrev.] A convict; a criminal conviction.

con /kɒn/ *n.*[6] *slang.* E20. [Abbrev.] = CONSTRUE *n.*

con /kɒn/ *n.*[7] *colloq.* M20. [Abbrev.] A convenience: only in MOD CON.

con /kɒn/ *v.*[1] Also (long *obs.* exc. *dial.*) **cun** /kʌn/. OE. [Partly form of CAN *v.*[1], w. vowel extended f. OE 1st & 3rd person sing. pres.; partly OE *cunnian*, *-ode* (wk) f. WGmc deriv. of base of CAN *v.*[1]] †I Senses repl. by CAN *v.*[1] Infl. as CAN *v.*[1] 1 *v.t.* & *i.* Know. OE–L17. 2 *v.i.* (usu. w. inf.) Know how to; have the capacity or be able to. ME–L15.

1 N. FAIRFAX That [this] should be . . I no more conne, than that. 2 CAXTON I sholde not conne telle the harme . . that he hath doon.

II Senses not repl. by CAN *v.*[1] Infl. **-nn-**. 3 *v.t.* Express, make known (gratitude, displeasure, etc.). *obs.* exc. in *con thanks* below. OE. 4 *v.t.* Study, learn by heart; peruse; scan. Freq. foll. by *over*. LME.

3 ELIZ. I We con you many laudes for having so neerely approched the villainous Rebel. **con thanks** (now *arch.* & *dial.*) acknowledge one's gratitude; thank. 4 S. BUTLER To con the Authors Names by rote. R. S. SURTEES The Baronet conned the . . matter over in his mind. J. GALSWORTHY He opened *The Times* . . and . . set himself steadily to con the news.

con /kɒn/ *v.*[2]*t.* & *i.* Also †**cann**, ***conn**, †**cun**. Infl. **-nn-**. E17. [App. weakened form of COND.] Direct the steering of (a ship).

con /kɒn/ *v.*[3]*t. slang.* Infl. **-nn-**. L19. [f. CON *n.*[4]] Persuade; dupe, swindle.

con /kɒn/ *adv.* L16. [Abbrev. of CONTRA.] Against a proposition etc. Chiefly in *pro and con* (occas. *con and pro*) s.v. PRO *prep.*, *adv.*, etc.

con- /kɒn, *unstressed* kən/ *pref.* Var. of L COM- bef. *c*, *d*, *f*, *g*, *j*, *n*, *q*, *s*, *t*, *v*, and occas. bef. vowels (*conurbation*). Cf. CO-, COL-, COR-.

conacre /ˈkɒneɪkə/ *n.* & *v.* E19. [f. CORN *n.*[1] + ACRE *n.*] *Ir. Hist.* A *n.* The letting by a tenant of small portions of land prepared for crop or grazing. E19. B *v.t.* Sublet (land) in this manner. M19.

conalbumin /kənˈalbjʊmɪn/ *n.* E20. [f. CON- + ALBUMIN.] *Biochem.* An iron-binding albumin present in egg-white, resembling transferrin.

con amore /kɒn əˈmɔːreɪ, *foreign* kon aˈmoːrɛ/ *adv. phr.* M18. [It. = with love.] With devotion or zeal; *Mus.* (as a direction) with tenderness.

conarium /kəˈnɛːrɪəm/ *n. obs.* exc. *Hist.* Also †**-ion**. M17. [mod.L f. Gk *kōnarion* dim. of *kōnos* pine cone.] *Anat.* The pineal gland.

conation /kəˈneɪʃ(ə)n/ *n.* E17. [L *conatio(n-)*, f. *conat-* pa. ppl stem of *conari* endeavour: see -ATION.] †1 An attempt, an endeavour. Only in E17. 2 *Philos.* The desire to perform an action; volition; voluntary or purposive action. M19.

conative /ˈkɒnətɪv, ˈkəʊ-/ *n.* & *a.* †(*a*) *n.* (*rare*) an endeavour, striving; (*b*) *adj.* of, pertaining to, or characteristic of conation: L17. **'conatively** *adv.* M20.

conatus /kəˈneɪtəs/ *n.* Pl. same /-tuːs/, **-tuses**. M17. [L, f. *conari*: see prec.] A purposive or seemingly purposive force or impulse; an effort, striving.

con brio /kɒn ˈbriːəʊ, *foreign* kon ˈbrio/ *adv. phr.* E19. [It.] *Mus.* A direction: with vigour.

concamerate /kɒnˈkaməreɪt/ *v.t.* E17. [L *concamerat-* pa. ppl stem of *concamerare* vault: see CON-, CAMERA, -ATE[3].] 1 Vault, arch over. Now *rare* or *obs.* E17. 2 Divide into chambers or cells. Chiefly as *concamerated* ppl a. M18.

concame'ration *n.* (*a*) vaulting, a vaulted roof etc. (*lit.* & *fig.*); (*b*) (each of the chambers or the chambered formation resulting from) division into a number of separate cells: M17.

concatenate /kənˈkatɪneɪt/ *a.* L15. [Late L *concatenatus* pa. pple, f. as next: see -ATE[2].] Linked together, concatenated.

concatenate /kənˈkatɪneɪt/ *v.t.* L16. [Late L *concatenat-* pa. ppl stem of *concatenare*, f. as CON- + *catena* CHAIN *n.*: see -ATE[3].] Link together (chiefly *fig.*); connect as by a chain.

concatenation /kənkatɪˈneɪʃ(ə)n/ *n.* E17. [Fr. *concaténation* or late L *concatenatio(n-)*, f. as prec.: see -ATION.] 1 Union by linking together, esp. in a series or chain; concatenated condition. E17. 2 A concatenated series or system; an interdependent or unbroken sequence. M17.

1 G. H. LEWES The necessary concatenation of ideas which should reproduce the concatenation of objects. 2 J. RUSKIN This vile concatenation of straight lines. U. LE GUIN Obscure concatenations of effect/cause/effect.

concaulescence /kɒnkɔːˈlɛs(ə)ns/ *n.* L19. [f. CON- + CAULESCENT + -ENCE.] *Bot.* Coalescence of two axes, e.g. of a leaf-stalk and main stem.

concause /ˈkɒnkɔːz/ *n.* E17. [med.L *concausa*, f. as CON- + CAUSE *n.*] A cooperating cause.

con'causal *a.* M17.

concave /ˈkɒnkeɪv, kɒnˈkeɪv/ *n.* M16. [OFr. f. the adj. (see next: cf. L *concava* hollows), or ellipt. use of next.] †1 A hollow; a (cylindrical or spherical) cavity, the bore of a gun etc. M16–E19. 2 The concave inner surface of a vault, arch, hemisphere, etc.; freq. the vault of the sky, the vault of heaven. Chiefly *poet.* M16. 3 A concave lens, mirror, etc. E17. 4 A concave piece of a machine, as the part of a thresher in which the cylinder works etc. Chiefly *US*. L19.

concave /ˈkɒnkeɪv, *pred. also* kɒnˈkeɪv/ *a.* LME. [L *concavus*, f. as CON- + *cavus* hollow (perh. through (O)Fr. *concave*).] †1 Having an internal cavity; hollow. LME–M17. 2 Having an outline or surface curved like the interior of a circle or sphere; the reverse of convex. LME.

2 *concave lens*, *mirror*, etc.

concavely *adv.* L19. **concaveness** *n.* M18.

concave /ˈkɒnkeɪv/ *v.t.* LME. [OFr. *concaver* or L *concavare*, f. as prec.] Make concave; hollow out; *rare* vault, arch over. Orig. & chiefly as *concaved* ppl a.

concavity /kɒnˈkavɪti/ *n.* LME. [(O)Fr. *concavité* or late L *concavitas*, f. as CONCAVE *a.*: see -ITY.] 1 A hollow, a cavity. LME. 2 The concave surface or side of an arch, hemisphere, etc.; a hollow vault. L15. 3 The quality or condition of being concave. L16.

concavo- /kɒnˈkeɪvəʊ/ *comb. form.* [f. CONCAVE *a.* + -O-.] Concavely, concave and —.

concavo-'concave *a.* concave on both sides L19. **concavo-'convex** *a.* concave on one side and convex on the other (and thinnest in the centre: cf. CONVEXO-CONCAVE) L17.

conceal /kənˈsiːl/ *v.t.* ME. [OFr. *conceler* f. L *concelare*, f. as CON- + *celare* hide.] 1 Keep secret (*from*); refrain from disclosing or divulging. ME. 2 Put, remove, or keep out of sight or notice; hide. LME.

1 SIR W. SCOTT Concealing from him all knowledge of who or what he was. R. GRAVES Augustus had always great difficulty in concealing his dislike for Tiberius as a son-in-law. **concealed land** (*obs.* exc. *Hist.*) land withheld from the monarch without a proper title (used esp. of land that had been in monastic possession before the Reformation). 2 SMOLLETT There was a blind that concealed us from the view. I. FLEMING He had a vast belly that he concealed behind roomy trousers and well-cut . . suits. M. GIROUARD Their apparent artlessness concealed a great deal of sophistication. *transf.*: W. TREVOR He pressed his face into the pillow to conceal the sound of . . sobbing. **concealed lighting** artificial lighting in which the fitments are hidden from view.

concealable *a.* (*rare*) able to be concealed M17.

concealer /kənˈsiːlə/ *n.* L15. [AN *concelour*, f. as prec.: see -OUR, -ER[2].] 1 A person who conceals. L15. 2 *Law* (now *Hist.*). A person who sought to disturb possessors of concealed lands (see prec.) by surreptitiously procuring spurious grants of Crown rights. L16.

concealment /kənˈsiːlm(ə)nt/ *n.* ME. [OFr. *concelement*, f. as CONCEAL: see -MENT.] 1 The concealing or keeping secret (of information); *Law* the non-disclosure of a known fact by a party to a contract. ME. b The holding of land against the monarch's rights, without a proper title. *obs.* exc. *Hist.* E17. 2 *gen.* The action of concealing or keeping secret; the action of hiding or obscuring anything from view. L16. †3 Secret knowledge; a secret, a mystery. L16–E17. 4 The condition of being concealed; the capacity for concealing; in *pl.*, conditions or surroundings that conceal. E17.

1 A. S. TAYLOR The concealment of pregnancy is no offence in the English Law, but the concealment of.. the *birth* of a child is a misdemeanour. 2 J. GALSWORTHY The concealment of his satisfaction had been merely instinctive. 3 SHAKES. *1 Hen. IV* A worthy gentleman, Exceedingly well read, and profited In strange concealments. 4 OED He has absconded, and is still in concealment. C. MORGAN He is like a man secretly in love;.. speak her name, and his agony shines through all his concealments. R. WARNER I stepped forward a little from my place of concealment.

concede /kənˈsiːd/ *v.* L15. [Fr. *concéder* or L *concedere* withdraw, yield, f. as CON- + *cedere* CEDE.] 1 *v.t.* Admit to be true, allow, grant (a proposition); acknowledge the justice, propriety, etc., of (a statement, claim, etc.); (occas.) allow formally for the sake of argument. L15. b *v.t.* & *i.* Acknowledge (defeat) esp. in an election; admit defeat in (an election, a constituency, etc.). Orig. *US.* E19. 2 *v.t.* Grant, yield, or surrender (anything asked for or claimed, as a right, privilege, etc.); fail to prevent an opponent in a contest from scoring (a goal, points, runs, etc.), lose (a game, match, etc.). M17. 3 *v.i.* Make a concession. *rare.* L18.

1 J. GILBERT The law itself was not conceded to have been unjust. DICKENS Conceding, for a moment, that there is any analogy between a bee and a man. H. JAMES Her claim to figure was questioned, but she was conceded presence. HARPER LEE If you'll concede the necessity of going to school. T. BENN Government and industry will have to concede that workers have a part to play in the management of the economy. 2 H. T. BUCKLE Free trade was conceded to the West Indian Islands. H. READ Perhaps he conceded too much to the romantic idealism of his public. 3 BURKE When.. I wished you to concede to America, at a time when she prayed concession at our feet.

conceder *n.* M19.

conceit /kənˈsiːt/ *n.* LME. [f. CONCEIVE *v.* after *deceit* etc.] I 1 That which is conceived in the mind, a conception, a notion, an idea. *obs.* exc. *Sc.* LME. †2 The faculty of mental conception; apprehension, understanding. LME–E19. 3 Personal opinion, judgement, estimation. Usu. w. qualifying adj., as *good, bad*, etc., *conceit (of oneself)*. *arch.* & *dial.* LME. 4 Favourable opinion, esteem. Now *dial.* exc. in *out of conceit* below. LME. 5 Overestimation of oneself or one's personal qualities; personal vanity. E17.

1 T. FULLER Fluent in language to express their conceits. C. LAMB A glimmering conceit of some such thing. 2 WORDSWORTH His own conceit the figure planned. 3 B. FRANKLIN A remonstrance.. containing a submissive conceit, that one hundred thousand pounds.. would answer. F. KING She always had a good conceit of herself, that one. **in one's own conceit** in one's own judgement. 4 ADAM SMITH The landlord's conceit of his own superior knowledge. **out of conceit** no longer pleased *with.* 5 K. GRAHAME He got so puffed up with conceit that he made up a song .. in praise of himself.

II 6 A fancy article; anything quaintly decorative; a pretty trifle. *obs.* exc. *Sc.* LME. 7 A fanciful, ingenious, or witty expression; *esp.* a far-fetched comparison or elaborate and intricate figure of speech, image, etc. Also, the use of such expressions etc. E16. 8 A fanciful notion; a fancy; a whim; the faculty of imagination. M16.

7 POPE Some to conceit alone their taste confine. J. R. GREEN Religious enthusiasm had degenerated into the pretty conceits of Mariolatry. 8 R. GREENE In conceit build castles in the sky. D. WELCH It was an old conceit of my aunt's to carry the predominant colour of her party decorations into the food itself.

†III 9 Conception of offspring. LME–L16. 10 An illness or affliction of the mind or the body. M16–E17.

10 H. PEACHAM Hee tooke a conceipt and dyed.

conceitless *a.* (*rare*) without conceit LME. **conceity** *a.* (chiefly *Sc.*) full of conceits, conceited L16.

conceit /kənˈsiːt/ *v. arch.* & *dial.* M16. [f. the n.] I *v.t.* †1 Form a conception of; apprehend. M16–E17. 2 Fill or inspire with a conceit or fancy. L16. 3 Take a fancy to, like. L16. 4 Imagine, fancy, think. E17. †5 Conceive as a purpose or design, plan. E–M17.

1 SHAKES. *Jul. Caes.* Him and his worth and our great need of him You have right well conceited. 2 F. HALL To conceit ourselves that our progeny will be satisfied with our English. 3 M. R. MITFORD I shall never conceit the sight of a perch again. 4 J. PRIESTLEY Arts of sorcery which they conceit that he learned in Egypt. J. R. SEELEY Conceiting himself to be made of better clay than other men.

†II 6 *v.i.* Form a conception; think, imagine, consider. L16–E19.

conceited /kənˈsiːtɪd/ *a.* M16. [f. CONCEIT *n.*, *v.*: see -ED[2], -ED[1].] I Chiefly f. the n. †1a Having intelligence, wit, a mind, of a particular kind; clever, witty, amusing. M16–L17. b Of a person, a person's work: ingenious, clever; *spec.* (of a writer, literary style, etc.) characterized by a use of literary conceits (see CONCEIT *n.* 7). Only in L16. 2 Fanciful or fantastical in manner, habit, etc.; whimsical; fastidious. L16. 3 Having an opinion (of a particular kind; †*absol.* good); -minded, -disposed. Long *dial.* L16. 4 Having too high an opinion of or (*rare*) *of* one's own beauty, ability, etc.; vain, self-satisfied. (See also SELF-CONCEITED.) E17.

1a ROBERT BURTON The Egyptians.. are commended to be.. a conceited merry Nation. W. LILLY Humane, rationall, and pleasantly conceited. b SHAKES. *Lucr.* A piece Of skilful painting.. Which the conceited painter drew so proud. 3 J. SELDEN The people well-conceited of the King's aims. 4 J. H. NEWMAN The less a man knows, the more conceited he is of his proficiency. G. GREENE 'You ought to be grateful,' he told her in his light cocksure conceited manner.

II f. the vb. 5 Conceived, devised; fancied; imaginary. Now *rare* or *obs.* L16. †6 Ingenious; fancy. L16–L17.

conceitedly *adv.* L16. **conceitedness** *n.* †(*a*) cleverness, imagination; (*b*) self-conceit, vanity: E17.

conceivable /kənˈsiːvəb(ə)l/ *a.* & *n.* LME. [f. next + -ABLE. Cf. Fr. *concevable.*] A *adj.* Able to be (mentally) conceived; imaginable; supposable; (just) possible. LME.

E. A. FREEMAN It is just conceivable that Duncan refused homage to Cnut. L. DURRELL They are coming in from everywhere now, at every conceivable angle and speed.

B *n.* A conceivable thing. M17.

conceiva'bility *n.* E19. **conceivableness** *n.* LME. **conceivably** *adv.* E17.

conceive /kənˈsiːv/ *v.* ME. [(O)Fr. *conceiv-* tonic stem of *concevoir* repr. L *concipere*, f. as CON- + *capere* take.] I In a physical sense. 1 *v.t.* & *i.* Become pregnant (with); in *pass.*, be created in the womb, be engendered. ME. †2 *v.t.* In *pass.* Be made or become pregnant. LME–M17. †3 *v.t. transf.* Take on (any state or condition); catch (fire etc.). LME–M18.

1 AV *Gen.* 30:19 And Leah conceived againe, and bare Iacob the sixth sonne. W. F. HOOK He preached the Lord Jesus Christ, who.. was conceived by the Holy Ghost. F. RAPHAEL In those two years Rachel conceived two children. 2 C. MARLOWE A princess-priest, Conceiv'd by Mars, Shall yield to dignity a double birth. 3 C. LUCAS The lightest waters most readily conceive igneous motion.

II Of mental processes. 4 *v.t.* Take or admit into the mind; become affected or possessed with. ME. 5 *v.t.* & *i.* Form a mental representation (of or *of*); devise (a purpose, idea, plan, etc.); think, imagine. ME. 6 *v.t.* Grasp mentally; take in, comprehend; understand. *arch.* LME. 7 *v.t.* & †*i.* Take into one's head; be of the opinion; fancy. LME.

4 M. EDGEWORTH He had conceived a dislike.. for this lady. 5 BUNYAN I can better conceive of them with my Mind, then speak of them with my Tongue. W. COWPER He first conceives, then perfects his design. R. J. SULLIVAN His system.. ill conceived and worse arranged. G. GREENE He was incapable of conceiving the pain he might cause others. I. MURDOCH He could not conceive of anybody enjoying Danby's company. 6 SHAKES. *Merry W.* Nay, conceive me, conceive me, sweet coz. B. MARTIN All this I conceive perfectly well. 7 J. SELDEN I am the rather induced to conceive charitably of those times. J. S. MILL He ought, I conceive, to be warned of the danger. R. H. MOTTRAM Words.. in what he conceived to be French.

III Other senses after L. †8 *v.t.* Encompass, comprise, comprehend. LME–L16. †9 *v.t.* Institute (an action at law). LME–L16. 10 *v.t.* Formulate, express in words etc.; couch. Usu. in *pass.* LME.

10 GIBBON His answer was conceived in the tone of insult and defiance.

conceivement *n.* (*rare*) conception E17. **conceiver** *n.* L16.

concelebrate /kɒnˈsɛlɪbreɪt/ *v.* L16. [L *concelebrat-* pa. ppl stem of *concelebrare*, f. as CON-, CELEBRATE: see -ATE[3].] †1 *v.t.* Celebrate together or in great numbers; extol loudly. L16–E17. 2 *v.i.* (Of priests) celebrate mass, the Eucharist, etc., together; *esp.* (of a newly ordained priest) celebrate mass etc. *with* the ordaining bishop. L19.

concele'bration *n.* M19.

concent /kənˈsɛnt/ *n.* & *v.* Now *rare* or *obs.* L16. [L *concentus*, f. *concinere* sing together, harmonize, f. as CON- + *canere* sing. Cf. CONCINNATE *v.*] A *n.* Harmony (of sounds, or *fig.*), concord, accord; a harmonious combination of voices etc. L16. †B *v.t.* & *i.* Harmonize. L16–M17.

concenter *v.* see CONCENTRE.

concentrate /ˈkɒns(ə)ntreɪt/ *a.* & *n.* M17. [f. as next + -ATE[2], or directly f. the vb.] A *adj.* Concentrated. *arch.* M17. B *n.* A concentrated substance; a concentrated form of something, esp. animal foodstuff. L19.

concentrate /ˈkɒns(ə)ntreɪt/ *v.* M17. [Latinized form of CONCENTRE, or analogical formation on Fr. *concentrer*: see -ATE[3].] I *v.t.* 1 Bring towards or collect at a centre; cause to converge or be focused (*on* a point, objective, etc.). M17. 2 *Chem.* Increase the strength of (a solution, mixture, etc.), e.g. by evaporation of solvent. L17. b Bring (ore etc.) to a state of greater purity by mechanical means. L19. 3 Bring into closer union the parts of; reduce in compass (with concomitant increase in intensity etc.). M18.

1 D. BREWSTER The different rays concentrated by the lens. BOSW. SMITH Here Hannibal.. concentrated the forces which had been gathered from such distant countries. G. CLARE To concentrate over-powering affection exclusively on one other human being. R. DAHL Fury and hate can concentrate a man's mind to an astonishing degree. 2 C. DARWIN The sap is concentrated by boiling, and is then called treacle. 3 C. BRONTË The obstinacy of my whole sex.. was concentrated in me.

II *v.i.* 4 Collect or come together at a centre; become intensified. M17. 5 Employ all one's power or attention *on*; focus one's mental efforts (*on*). E20.

4 ISAAC TAYLOR Church Power.. concentrating around the See of Rome. 5 I. COMPTON-BURNETT He .. put the matter aside to concentrate on other things. J. H. BURN Morphine may produce drowsiness and inability to concentrate.

concentrated *a.* (*a*) brought together, wholly directed towards one point or thing, intensified; (*b*) *Chem.* (of solutions etc.) relatively strong (opp. *dilute*), *fig.* intense: L17. **concentratedly** *adv.* L19. **concentratedness** *n.* (*rare*) L19. **concentrator** *n.* a person who or thing which concentrates; *esp.* an apparatus which concentrates liquids etc.: M19.

concentration /kɒns(ə)nˈtreɪʃ(ə)n/ *n.* M17. [f. prec. + -ATION.] 1 The action of concentrating; the state of being concentrated; a concentrated collection or mass. M17. †2a The chemical separation of gold etc. from an alloy. L17–L18. b *Chem.* The strengthening of a solution by removal (e.g. by evaporation) of solvent; the condition so produced; the amount of solute per unit volume of a solution. L18. c The mechanical removal of unwanted portions from an ore etc. L19. 3 The bringing of parts or elements closer together; the act of condensing. M19. 4 The continued focusing of mental powers and faculties on a particular object. M19.

1 WELLINGTON The concentration of your force in one position. J. R. GREEN This concentration of all power in the hands of a single man. E. MOONMAN The main concentration of West Indians is to be found in Brixton, London. 2b P. PARISH Injections ensure that the drug reaches a high concentration in the blood. 3 M. ARNOLD Epochs of concentration cannot well endure for ever; epochs of expansion.. follow them. J.

RUSKIN My affected concentration of language. 4 DAY LEWIS Aged voters who.. through failing sight or powers of concentration confused C. S. with C. D. Lewis.

Comb.: **concentration camp**: for the detention of non-combatants, political prisoners, internees, etc., esp. in Nazi Germany (w. connotations of inhuman privations endured by the inhabitants).

concentrative /ˈkɒns(ə)ntreɪtɪv/ *a.* E19. [f. CONCENTRATE *a.* & *n.* + -IVE.] That concentrates; characterized by concentration.

concentrativeness *n.* E19.

concentre /kɒnˈsɛntə/ *v.* Also ***-ter**. L16. [Fr. *concentrer*, f. as CON- + CENTRE *v.*: cf. CONCENTRATE *v.*] **I** *v.t.* **1** Bring into closer union, draw into a smaller space or area; intensify or strengthen in this way. L16. **2** Bring to or draw towards a common centre; collect (thoughts, faculties, etc.) and give them a common direction or purpose; form a centre or meeting-point for. M17. †**3** *Chem.* = CONCENTRATE *v.* 2. M17–E19. **II** *v.i.* †**4** Agree, coincide. L16–M18. **5** Converge; collect at, move towards a common centre. M17.

concentric /kənˈsɛntrɪk/ *a.* LME. [(O)Fr. *concentrique* or med.L *concentricus*, f. as CON- + CENTRE *n.*: see -IC.] Having a common centre (*with, to*); situated or occurring around the same centre; consisting of more or less circular parts surrounding a common centre.

R. BENTLEY The concentric Revolutions of the Planets about the Sun. P. WARNER A concentric castle broke away from the old pattern of linear defence.. and instead had a system of enclosed squares. **concentric bundle** *Bot.* a vascular bundle in which one kind of vascular tissue completely surrounds the other. **concentric cable** = COAXIAL *cable*.

concentrical *a.* = CONCENTRIC M16. **concentrically** *adv.* E18. †**concentricate** *v.t.* = CONCENTRATE *v.* 1, 3 M17–L18. **concentricity** /-ˈtrɪsɪti/ *n.* the state or quality of being concentric E19.

concentus /kɒnˈsɛntəs/ *n. rare.* E17. [L: see CONCENT.] Singing together in harmony; a harmonious combination of voices etc.

concept /ˈkɒnsɛpt/ *n.* M16. [Late L *conceptus*, f. pa. ppl stem of *concipere*: see CONCEIVE.] †**1** = CONCEIT *n.* M–L16. **2** A product of the faculty of conception; an idea of a class of objects, a general notion; a theme, a design. M17.

2 B. RUSSELL Awareness of universals is called *conceiving*, and a universal of which we are aware is called a *concept*. R. M. PIRSIG The motorcycle.. a system of concepts worked out in steel. D. LESSING The concept of ownership of land was unknown to them: land belonged to itself. *attrib.*: S. BRETT Great Expectations.. was a concept restaurant, themed wittily around the works of Dickens.

conceptacle /kənˈsɛptək(ə)l/ *n.* E17. [Fr., or L *conceptaculum*: see CON-, RECEPTACLE.] †**1** A receptacle. E17–M19. **2** †**a** *Anat.* A vessel or cavity of the body. E–M17. **b** *Biol.* A structure resembling a cavity that contains the reproductive cells in some plants and animals of simple organization. M18.

conception /kənˈsɛpʃ(ə)n/ *n.* ME. [(O)Fr. f. L *conceptio(n-)*, f. *concept-* pa. ppl stem of *concipere*: see CONCEIVE, -ION.] **1** The action of conceiving, or the fact of being conceived, in the womb. ME. **2** That which is conceived: (*a*) an embryo, a foetus; †(*b*) a child. LME. **3** The action or faculty of conceiving in the mind; apprehension, imagination; the formation of a concept. LME. **4** That which is conceived in the mind; an idea, a notion; a concept. E17. †**b** A mere fancy. *rare* (Shakes.). Only in E17. **5** Something originated in the mind; a design, plan; an original idea; a mental product of invention. E17. **b** Origination in the mind; planning. E19. †**6** The generation or production of plants and minerals. Only in M17.

1 R. DAWKINS Our genes are doled out to us at conception. *Immaculate Conception*: see IMMACULATE. 2 *false conception*: see FALSE *a.* 3 A. EINSTEIN We are drifting toward a catastrophe beyond conception. **in my conception** to my mind, in my view. 4 J. BUTLER As impossible.. as for a blind man to have a conception of colours. *Washington Post* Ronald Reagan has.. altered the conception of the President's role. **have no conception of** be unable to imagine. 5 W. H. PRESCOTT It was a bold conception, that of constructing a fleet to be transported across forest and mountain before it was launched.

conceptional *a.* pertaining to, or of the nature of, a conception or idea M19. **conceptionist** *n.* (*a*) a person who deals with conceptions; (*b*) (**C-**) a member of a Catholic order named in honour of the Immaculate Conception: L18. †**conceptious** *a.* (*rare*, Shakes.) apt to conceive, prolific: only in E17.

conceptive /kənˈsɛptɪv/ *a.* M17. [L *conceptivus*, f. *concept-*: see prec., -IVE.] That conceives; apt to conceive; of or pertaining to conception. (Rarely in a physical sense.)

conceptively *adv.* in a (mentally) conceptive manner M19. **conceptiveness** *n.* E19.

conceptual /kənˈsɛptjʊəl/ *a.* M17. [med.L *conceptualis*, f. as CONCEPT *n.*: see -AL[1].] Of or pertaining to mental conception or concepts.

¶ Rare bef. M19.

conceptualism *n.* (*a*) the scholastic doctrine that universals exist as mental concepts (only); (*b*) the doctrine that the mind is capable of forming a mental image corresponding to a general term: M19. **conceptualist** *n.* & *a.* an adherent of, pertaining to or marked by, conceptualism M19. **conceptuaˈlistic** *a.* L19. **conceptuaˈlistically** *adv.* M20. **conceptually** *adv.* as a concept L19.

conceptualize /kənˈsɛptjʊəlʌɪz/ *v.t.* & *i.* Also **-ise**. L19. [f. prec. + -IZE.] Form a concept or idea (of).

conceptuaˈlizable *a.* M20. **conceptualiˈzation** *n.* E20. **conceptualizer** *n.* L20.

conceptus /kənˈsɛptəs/ *n.* M18. [L = conception, embryo, f. *concept-* pa. ppl stem of *concipere*: see CONCEIVE.] The product of conception in the womb, esp. in the early stages of pregnancy.

concern /kənˈsəːn/ *n.* L16. [f. the vb. Cf. *regard, respect.*] **I 1** Reference, respect, relation. Now *spec.* important relation, importance, interest, (chiefly in *of concern* (*to*)). L16. **2** A practical or business relation. Usu. in *pl.* L17. **3** Solicitous regard, anxiety. L17. **b** In the Society of Friends, a conviction of the divine will. E18. **4** Active interest, a share *in*. E18.

1 A. W. HADDAN A truth of deep concern to men's souls. 2 H. FIELDING I know Mr. Nightingale.. and have formerly had concerns with him. DAY LEWIS His proper concern is with the object to be created. **have no concern with** have nothing to do with. 3 DRYDEN Without concern he hears.. Of.. distant war. M. AMIS She looks at me with such gentle concern, such protective concern. 4 **have a concern in** have an interest or share in.

II 5 A matter that relates to some person or thing; in *pl.* affairs. L17. **6** A matter that affects or touches one; a subject that excites one's interest, attention, or care. L17. **7** A business organization; a firm. L17. **8** An affair, an intrigue; an incident. Now *dial.* L17. **9** A material contrivance; a (complicated or cumbrous) thing. *colloq.* E19.

5 R. L. CHALONER The Battery subalterns.. Chat about minor military concerns. 6 A. MACLEAN The Treasury's basic concern is money. A. MCCOWEN It was no concern of mine if his mother had married his uncle. 7 J. CHEEVER Mr. Nudd had inherited.. a wool concern. *going concern*: see GOING *ppl a.* 9 J. CARLYLE A steel-pen, which is a very unpliable concern.

concern /kənˈsəːn/ *v.* Also (*dial.*, esp. in sense 5) **consarn** /kənˈsɑːn/. LME. [(O)Fr. *concerner* or late L *concernere* sift, distinguish, (in med.L) have respect or reference to, f. as CON- + *cernere* sift.] **I 1** *v.t.* Have relation or reference to. LME. **2** *v.t.* Affect; have a bearing on; involve. LME. **3** *v.t.* & †*i.* Be of importance (to); be the concern of. L15. **4** *v.t.* Engage the attention of; implicate; cause anxiety to. Usu. in *pass.* L16. **b** *refl.* Interest oneself *with, in, about, to do.* M17. **5** *v.t.* in *imper.* (expr. impatience). Confound, bother. *US* & *dial.* E19.

1 TINDALE *Acts* 28:31 Teachynge those thinges which concerned the lorde Jesus. **as concerns** with regard to. 2 B. JOWETT Music is concerned with harmony and rhythm. R. G. COLLINGWOOD What the different people concerned were trying to do. W. CATHER It's a confidential matter, and concerns another person. 3 SHAKES. *Oth.* The importancy of Cyprus to the Turk.. it more concerns the Turk than Rhodes. 4 M. EDGEWORTH Accused of being concerned in a riot. E. BOWEN At the minute, breakfast was what concerned her. LYNDON B. JOHNSON Eisenhower was deeply concerned about the disintegration in Laos. **to whom it may concern**: used to introduce a statement or testimonial. b R. GRAVES I never concern myself with high politics.

†**II 6** *v.t.* Distinguish, discern. LME–L16.

†**concernancy** *n. rare* (Shakes.). Only in E17. [f. prec. + -ANCY.] = CONCERNMENT.

concerned /kənˈsəːnd/ *ppl a.* Also (*dial.*, esp. in sense 2) **consarned** /kənˈsɑːnd/. M17. [f. CONCERN *v.* + -ED[1].] **1** Interested, involved; troubled, anxious; showing concern. (Foll. by *about, for, in, with*, etc., (now usu. in neg. & interrog. contexts) *to do.*) M17. **b** *spec.* Having a social conscience, involved in social or moral issues. M20. **2** Confounded, deuced. *US* & *dial.* M19.

1 E. M. FORSTER I am really concerned at the way those girls go on. E. BOWEN Braithwaite was clearing tea away with a concerned face. **as, so, far as one is concerned** as regards one's interests.

concernedly /-nɪdli/ *adv.* M17. **concernedness** /-nɪdnɪs/ *n.* L17.

†**concerning** *n.* L16–M17. [f. CONCERN *v.* + -ING[1].] The taking of concern; concernment; a concern.

concerning /kənˈsəːnɪŋ/ *ppl a. arch.* M17. [f. CONCERN *v.* + -ING[2]. Cf. earlier UNCONCERNING.] That is of concern; distressing; important.

concerning /kənˈsəːnɪŋ/ *prep.* LME. [f. prec., prob. modelled on a similar use of Fr. *concernant.*] Regarding, touching, in reference or relation to; about.

concernment /kənˈsəːnm(ə)nt/ *n.* E17. [f. CONCERN *v.* + -MENT.] **1** A matter concerning a person or thing; an interest. *arch.* E17. **2** An affair; a business; a concern. E17. **3** The fact of concerning or having reference; relation. M17. **4** Importance, weight, moment. M17. **5** Participation *in*, involvement *with*; interference. M17. **6** A feeling of interest, solicitude, anxiety, etc. M17.

2 DRYDEN I do not think it my Concernment to defend it. 3 R. BURTHOGGE Mind.. free from all.. concernment with matter. 4 R. W. EMERSON Secrets of highest concernment. 6 R. LOWELL He showed concernment for his soul.

concert /ˈkɒnsət/ *n.* E17. [Fr. f. It. *concerto*, f. *concertare*: see next. See also earlier CONSORT *n.*[2]] **1** Accordance of sounds; a (harmonious) combination of voices, instruments, etc. (Now only as a *transf.* or *fig.* use of another sense.) E17. **2** Agreement in a plan or design; union formed by such agreement; accordance, harmony. M17. **3** A musical performance in which several performers take part; *loosely* a solo recital. L17. **b** A dancing performance consisting of single items, folk-dances, etc. (in contrast to a full-scale ballet). E20. †**4** A company or set of musicians; a choir. E–M18.

1 W. S. CHURCHILL The foundations were laid for a closer concert between the two peoples in facing the problems of the world. 2 W. C. BRYANT The linden.. Hums with a louder concert.

Phrases: **Concert of Europe** *Hist.* the chief European powers acting together. **in concert** (*a*) acting jointly and in harmony (*with*); (*b*) performing music before a live audience, not in a recording studio etc. *sacred concert*: see SACRED *a.*

Comb.: **concert-goer** a person who regularly attends concerts; **concert grand** a grand piano of the largest size, suitable for concerts; **concert hall** a hall for the public performance of concerts; **concert-master** the leader of an (esp. American or Continental) orchestra; **concert overture** *Mus.* a piece like an operatic overture but intended for independent performance; **concert party** (*a*) a group of performers who give variety concerts; (*b*) *Stock Exch.* a number of parties who separately invest in a company with the concealed intention of using their holdings as a single block; **concert performance** (of an opera etc.): without scenery, costume, or action; **concert pitch** the (international standard) pitch to which musical instruments are tuned for concerts; *fig.* a state of unusual efficiency or readiness.

concertize *v.* (*a*) *v.i.* give a concert or concerts; (*b*) *v.t.* arrange for performance in concert: L19.

concert /kənˈsəːt/ *v.* L16. [Fr. *concerter* f. It. *concertare* bring into agreement or harmony, of unkn. origin.] †**1** *v.t.* Bring to agreement or unity. L16–L17. 2 *v.t.* Arrange to carry out, agree (plans, action, etc.) with or *with* another person etc. or others; contrive by mutual agreement; plan or effect (coordinated action). L17. 3 *v.i.* Arrange a matter by agreement *with* someone; act in harmony *with*. E18. 4 *v.i.* Sing or play in concert. *rare*. E19.

2 C. THIRLWALL The insurrection seems not to have been judiciously concerted. D. ACHESON I hoped that the North Atlantic Treaty countries would concert their policies. J. G. FARRELL The inability of the sepoys to concert an attack with all their disparate forces. 3 A. F. DOUGLAS-HOME The Homes were the peacemakers, . . charged to concert with their English opposite number to keep order.

concerted *ppl a.* (*a*) arranged by mutual agreement, done in concert, coordinated; (*b*) *Mus.* arranged in parts for several voices or instruments; (*c*) united in action or intention; earlier in UNCONCERTED: E18.

concertante /kɒntʃəˈtanti/ *a.* & *n.* Pl. of n. **-ti** /-ti/. E18. [It., ppl a. of *concertare*: see prec.] *Mus.* Formerly, (designating) those instrumental parts present throughout a piece of music. Now, (a piece of music) containing one or more solo parts (usu. of less prominence or weight than in a concerto) playing with an orchestra; also, designating such a part.

sinfonia concertante: see SINFONIA I.

concerti *n.pl.* see CONCERTO.

concerti grossi *n. phr. pl.* see CONCERTO GROSSO.

concertina /kɒnsəˈtiːnə/ *n.*, *a.*, & *v.* M19. [f. CONCERT *n.* + -INA[1].] A *n.* 1 A portable free-reed musical instrument consisting of a pair of bellows usu. polygonal in form, with a set of finger-studs at each end controlling valves which admit wind to the reeds. M19. 2 In full *concertina wire*. Wire used for entanglements. E20. B *attrib.* or as *adj.* (Able to be) compressed or closed like a concertina; involving such action. E20. C *v.t.* & *i.* Shut up like a concertina; compress; collapse; wrinkle. E20.

concertinist *n.* a person who plays the concertina L19.

concertino /kɒntʃəˈtiːnəʊ/ *n.* Pl. **-os**. L18. [It., dim. of next.] *Mus.* 1 A small or short concert. *rare*. L18. 2 The solo instrument(s) in a concerto. E19. 3 A simple or short concerto. L19.

concerto /kənˈtʃəːtəʊ, -tʃɛːtəʊ/ *n.* Pl. **-tos**, **-ti** /-ti/. E18. [It., f. *concertare*: see CONCERT *v.*] *Mus.* Orig., a composition for various combinations of instruments. Now, a composition (in the classical form usu. in three movements) for one, or sometimes more, solo instruments accompanied by orchestra.

fig.: J. T. STORY A mad concerto of wildly excited bees and birds. **double**, **triple**, **concerto**: for two, three, solo instruments.

concerto grosso /kənˌtʃəːtəʊ ˈgrɒsəʊ/ *n. phr.* Pl. **-ti -ssi** /-tiː -siː/. E18. [It. = big concerto.] *Mus.* A baroque concerto characterized by the use of a small group of solo instruments alternately with the full orchestra; a modern imitation of this.

concessible /kənˈsɛsɪb(ə)l/ *a.* M18. [f. L *concess-* (see next) + -IBLE.] That can be conceded.

concession /kənˈsɛʃ(ə)n/ *n.* LME. [(O)Fr., or L *concessio(n-)*, f. *concess-* pa. ppl stem of *concedere*: see CONCEDE, -ION.] 1 The action or an act of conceding something asked or required. LME. 2 A grant of land or other property made by a government or ruling power. LME. b A piece of land or territory so allotted. M18. c A grant or lease of a small area or of a portion of premises for some specified purpose; the business premises etc. established there. *N. Amer.* E20. 3 A right or privilege granted by a government or ruling power. M16. b A right or privilege granted by a commercial organization to an individual or company; a reduction in price for a certain category of person. M20. 4 Admission of a point claimed in argument. E17.

1 HOBBES The Right whereby the Kings did rule, was founded in the very concession of the People. E. LANGLEY Jim's concession to the evening was to wash his sweater. 4 SIR T. BROWNE He [Satan] endeavours to propagate the unbelief of witches, whose concession infers his coexistency.

concessional *a.* M20. **concessionary** *a.* & *n.* (*a*) *adj.* pertaining to or of the nature of concession; (*b*) *n.* = CONCESSIONAIRE: M18. **concessioner** *n.* (*US*) = CONCESSIONAIRE L19. **concessionist** *n.* a person who advocates concession E19.

concessionaire /kənsɛʃəˈnɛː/ *n.* Also **-nn-**. M19. [Fr. *concessionnaire*, f. as prec. + *-aire* -ARY[1].] The holder of a concession or grant, esp. of the use of land or trading rights.

concessive /kənˈsɛsɪv/ *a.* & *n.* E18. [Late L *concessivus*, f. *concess-*: see CONCESSION, -IVE.] A *adj.* 1 *Gram.* (Of a preposition or conjunction) introducing a phrase or clause which might be expected to preclude the action of the main clause but does not; designating such a phrase or clause. E18. 2 *gen.* Of the nature of or tending to concession. L19. B *n. Gram.* A concessive particle, clause, etc. M18.

concessively *adv.* M17. **concessiveness** *n.* L19.

concessor /kənˈsɛsə/ *n. rare*. M17. [Late L, f. *concess-*: see CONCESSION, -OR.] A person who concedes.

concetto /kənˈtʃɛtəʊ/ *n.* Pl. **-tti** /-ti/. M18. [It., f. as CONCEPT.] = CONCEIT *n.* 7.

concettism *n.* use of or fondness for conceits in literature M19. **concettist** *n.* a writer who makes use of conceits L19.

conch /kɒŋk, kɒn(t)ʃ/ *n.* Pl. **conchs** /kɒŋks/, **conches** /ˈkɒn(t)ʃɪz/. Also ***conk** /kɒŋk/, pl. **-s**. LME. [L CONCHA f. Gk *kogkhē* mussel, cockle, shell-like cavity.] 1 Orig., a bivalve mollusc such as the oyster or mussel. Now, any of various prosobranchiate marine snails chiefly of the family Strombidae and Melongenidae, esp. of the genus *Strombus*, in which the outer whorl of the shell has a triangular outline and a wide lip, and often juts towards the apex; the shell of this or any other large gastropod. LME. b Such a shell used as a wind instrument, e.g. in Hindu temples; *esp.* (*Rom. Mythol.*) the shell blown by the Tritons in place of a trumpet. M18. 2 An ancient Roman shallow bowl or vessel. LME. 3 *Archit.* (The domed roof of) a semicircular apse. M19. 4 *Anat.* The concha of the ear. Now *rare* or *obs.* M19. 5 A White person of low social status inhabiting the Florida Keys or N. Carolina, *esp.* one of Bahamian origin. *US colloq.* M19.

1 **crown conch** either of two Caribbean gastropods of the genus *Melongena* (family Melongenidae), which have heavy spiny shells. **fighting conch** either of two heavy Caribbean conches of the genus *Strombus*. *queen conch*: see QUEEN *n.* **spider conch** = SCORPION *shell*.

conched *a.* having a conch or conchs M19.

concha /ˈkɒŋkə/ *n.* Pl. **-chae** /-kiː/. L16. [L: see prec.] 1 *Anat.* & *Zool.* A part or structure resembling a shell, *esp.* (*a*) the central concavity of the auricle leading to the auditory meatus; (*b*) (more fully *nasal concha*) the turbinate bone. L16. 2 *Archit.* = CONCH 3. E17.

conˈchiferous *a.* producing or bearing shells, characterized by the presence of shells E19.

conche /kɒntʃ/ *n.* & *v.* E20. [Fr. = CONCH.] A *n.* A shell-shaped part of a machine used to work chocolate during its manufacture. E20. B *v.t.* Mix or knead (chocolate) in such a machine. E20.

conchie /ˈkɒnʃi/ *n. slang.* Also **conchy**. E20. [Abbrev.] A conscientious objector.

conchiolin /ˈkɒntʃɪəʊlɪn/ *n.* L19. [f. L CONCHA + *-iola* dim. suff. + -IN[1].] *Biochem.* A scleroprotein forming the basis of the shells of molluscs.

†conchite *n.* L17–M18. [Gk *kogkhitēs* (*lithos*) shelly (stone): see -ITE[1].] *Palaeont.* A fossil shell; a petrified shell.

conchitic /kɒŋˈkɪtɪk/ *a.* E19. [f. as prec. + -IC.] *Geol.* Having many (fossil) shells.

conchoid /ˈkɒŋkɔɪd/ *n.* E18. [f. CONCH + -OID.] *Math.* Any of a family of quartic curves resembling a conch shell in outline, represented by the equation $(x-a)^2(x^2+y^2)=b^2x^2$.

conchoidal /kɒŋˈkɔɪd(ə)l/ *a.* M17. [f. as prec. + -AL[1].] 1 *Math.* Pertaining to or resembling a conchoid. M17. 2 *Geol.* Designating or displaying a fracture (of a rock or mineral) characterized by smooth shell-like convexities and concavities. E19.

conchoidally *adv.* in a conchoidal form L19.

conchology /kɒŋˈkɒlədʒi/ *n.* L18. [f. Gk *kogkho-*, *kogkhē* shell + -LOGY.] The branch of zoology that deals with shells and shellfish.

conchoˈlogical *a.* E19. **conchoˈlogically** *adv.* M19. **conchologist** *n.* L18.

conchy *n.* var. of CONCHIE.

†conchyliology *n.* L18–L19. [f. L *conchylium* shellfish f. Gk *kogkhulion* dim. of *kogkhulē* = *kogkhē* CONCH: see -OLOGY.] = CONCHOLOGY.

concierge /ˈkɒnsɪɛːʒ; *foreign* kɔ̃sjɛrʒ (*pl. same*)/ *n.* M16. [Fr. f. OFr. *cumcerges* etc. = med.L *consergius*, prob. ult. f. L *conservus* fellow slave.] 1 The warden of a house, castle, or prison; (the title of) a high official in France and other European states, having custody of a royal palace etc. *obs.* exc. *Hist.* M16. 2 In France etc.: a doorkeeper, porter, etc., for a building, esp. a block of flats. L17.

†concile *v.t.* LME–M18. [L *conciliare*: see CONCILIATE.] Reconcile; conciliate.

†conciliable *n.* see CONCILIABULE.

conciliable /kənˈsɪlɪəb(ə)l/ *a. rare*. M17. [f. as CONCILE + -ABLE.] Able to be conciliated; reconcilable.

conciliabule /kənˈsɪlɪəbjuːl/ *n.* Also (earlier) **†-able**. E16. [L *conciliabulum* place of assembly, f. *concilium* assembly.] A small or secret assembly; a conventicle.

conciliar /kənˈsɪlɪə/ *a.* L17. [med.L *conciliarius* counsellor: see -AR[2].] Of or pertaining to (esp. ecclesiastical) councils.

conciliarism *n.* a theory of ecclesiastical government embodying the principle that Church councils constitute the highest authority M20. **conciliarist** *n.* a supporter of conciliarism M20. **conciliarly** *adv.* by a council M17.

conciliate /kənˈsɪlɪeɪt/ *v.* M16. [L *conciliat-* pa. ppl stem of *conciliare* combine, unite physically, procure, win, f. *concilium* COUNCIL: see -ATE[3].] †1 *v.t.* Procure, get as an addition. M16–L18. 2 *v.t.* Gain (goodwill, esteem, etc.) by soothing or pacifying acts. M16. 3 *v.t.* Reconcile, make accordant or compatible. L16. b *v.i.* Effect a reconciliation, arbitrate, mediate, (*between*). L20. 4 *v.i.* Make friends (*with*). *rare*. M18. 5 *v.t.* Overcome the distrust or hostility of; placate, pacify. L18.

2 LD MACAULAY The arts which conciliate popularity. 3 GIBBON Conciliating the qualities of a soldier with those of a philosopher. 5 A. FRASER The acute financial demands of his foreign policy left him no choice but to conciliate Parliament.

conciliative *a.* = CONCILIATORY E19. **conciliator** *n.* a person who or thing which conciliates L16.

conciliation /kənsɪlɪˈeɪʃ(ə)n/ *n.* M16. [L *conciliatio(n-)*, f. as prec.; see -ION.] 1 The action of conciliating; reconcilement; the use of conciliating measures. M16. 2 *spec.* The process of seeking agreement between the parties in an industrial dispute, without recourse to arbitration. L19.

conciliatory /kənˈsɪlɪət(ə)ri/ *a.* L16. [f. as CONCILIATE + -ORY[2].] Tending or calculated to conciliate; showing a spirit of conciliation.

conciliatorily *adv.* E20. **conciliatoriness** *n.* M19.

concinnate /kənˈsɪnət/ *a. rare*. M16. [L *concinnatus* pa. pple, f. as next: see -ATE[2].] Concinnated.

concinnate /kənˈsɪneɪt/ *v.t.* Now *rare*. E17. [L *concinnat-* pa. ppl stem of *concinnare* f. as next: see -ATE[3].] Put together fitly; arrange skilfully or neatly; set right.

concinnity /kənˈsɪnɪti/ *n.* M16. [L *concinnitas*, f. *concinnus* skilfully put together: see -ITY.] 1 Skilful fitting together; harmonious arrangement. M16. 2 Studied elegance of style. L16.

concinnous *a.* †(*a*) *Mus.* harmonious; (*b*) of elegant style: M17.

†concional *a.* M17–E18. [L *contionalis*, *conc-*, f. *contio(n-)* (later *conc-*) contr. of *conventio(n-)* CONVENTION: see -AL[1].] Of or pertaining to a public assembly or public speaking.

†**concionary** *a.* = CONCIONAL M17–E18. †**concionator** *n.* [L *contionator*] a person who makes speeches, a preacher E17–M19.

concipient /kən'sɪpɪənt/ *a. rare.* E19. [L *concipient-* pres. ppl stem of *concipere* CONCEIVE.] That conceives, conceiving.

concise /kən'sʌɪs/ *a.* L16. [Fr. *concis(e)* or L *concisus* divided, broken up, brief, pa. pple of *concidere*, f. as CON- + *caedere* to cut.] Of speech, writing, a person, style, etc.: brief but comprehensive in expression.

concisely *adv.* L17. **conciseness** *n.* M17.

concision /kən'sɪʒ(ə)n/ *n.* LME. [L *concisio(n-)*, f. *concisus*: see prec., -ION.] 1 A cutting to pieces, a cutting up; *spec.* (in biblical translations and allusions) circumcision. LME. †b A schism. M16–E18. 2 The quality or state of being concise; conciseness. L18.

concitation /kɒnsɪ'teɪʃ(ə)n/ *n.* Long *rare.* M16. [L *concitatio(n-)*, f. *concitat-* pa. ppl stem of *concitare* stir up, excite, f. as CON- + CITE: see -ATION.] Stirring up, agitation.

conclamation /kɒŋklə'meɪʃ(ə)n/ *n.* E17. [L *conclamatio(n-)*, f. *conclamat-* pa. ppl stem of *conclamare*, f. as CON- + *clamare* shout: see -ATION.] A loud calling out of many together, esp. in lamentation for the dead.

conclave /'kɒŋkleɪv/ *n.* LME. [Fr. f. L *conclave*, f. as CON- + *clavis* key.] †1 a *gen.* A private room, an inner chamber. LME–M18. b *spec.* The meeting-place of the cardinals of the Roman Catholic Church for the election of a pope. LME. 2 A private meeting or close assembly. M16. b *spec.* An assembly of cardinals for the election of a pope; *loosely* the body of cardinals. E17.

2 **in conclave** (of cardinals or *gen.*) meeting privately or behind closed doors.

conclavist *n.* †(*a*) any of the cardinals in conclave; (*b*) a person attendant upon a cardinal in conclave: E17.

conclude /kən'kluːd/ *v.* ME. [L *concludere*, f. as CON- + *claudere* close, shut.] I†1 *v.t.* Overcome in argument, convince. ME–E18. 2 *v.t.* Shut up, enclose; include, comprise. *arch.* LME. †b Restrict, confine. M16–L17. 3 *v.t.* †a Debar, restrain (*from*). LME–E18. b Bind, oblige. *obs.* exc. *Law.* LME.

2 TENNYSON I dreamt Of some vast charm concluded in that star. 3b J. LOCKE The consent of the majority shall .. conclude every individual.

II 4 *v.t.* Bring to a close or end; wind up; finish; say or write in conclusion. LME. 5 *v.i.* Of a thing: come to a close or end; terminate. LME. 6 *v.i.* Make an end of an action; finish, close. Freq. foll. by *by*, *with*. E16.

4 SHAKES. *Rom. & Jul.* His fault concludes .. The life of Tybalt. DAY LEWIS Invariably concluding my discourse with 'In the name of the Father [etc.]'. J. CONRAD 'Aren't you astonished?' concluded the gaunt student. 5 SHAKES. *Ven. & Ad.* Her heavy anthem still concludes in woe. 6 T. HOOD My paper being filled .. I must conclude with kind regards to Emily.

III 7 *v.t.* Arrive at as a judgement or opinion by reasoning; infer, deduce. Foll. by simple obj., the obj. *to be* something, *that*. LME. †8 *v.t.* Of a person, argument, etc.: demonstrate, prove. With constructions as sense 7. LME–L18. †9 *v.i.* Be conclusive. E16–E18. 10 *v.i.* Form a conclusion (*from*, *to*, (*up*)*on*). E16.

7 H. POWER We cannot but conclude such Prognostics to be within the circle of possibilities. BURKE The greatest part of the governments .. must be concluded tyrannies. E. M. FORSTER Am I to conclude .. that he is a Socialist? 10 M. NOVAK So one must conclude from the eagerness with which Americans purchase 'how to' books.

IV 11 *v.t.* Bring (a matter) to a decision; settle, arrange finally. LME. 12 *v.t.* & †*i.* Come to a decision, determine, resolve. Foll. by *that*, *to do*, †*of*, †(*up*)*on*. LME. †b *v.i.* Agree, make terms (*with*). LME–L17.

11 H. MACMILLAN He wished to conclude a German peace treaty. 12 SHAKES. *Lucr.* They did conclude to bear dead Lucrece thence. S. PEPYS We judged a third man is necessary, and concluded on .. Warren. C. M. YONGE She .. concluded that she would wait.

concludent *a.* (now *rare* or *obs.*) [L *concludent-*: see -ENT] conclusive, decisive L16. **concluder** *n.* E17.

conclusible /kən'kluːzɪb(ə)l/ *a. rare.* M17. [f. L *conclus-* (see next) + -IBLE.] Able to be concluded.

conclusion /kən'kluːʒ(ə)n/ *n.* LME. [(O)Fr., or L *conclusio(n-)*, f. *conclus-* pa. ppl stem of *concludere*: see prec., -ION.] 1 The end, finish, or termination of a speech, writing, etc.; *esp.* a final section summarizing the main points. LME. 2 The issue, the final result, the outcome. LME. 3 The result of a discussion or examination of an issue; final resolution, decision, agreement. LME. 4 A judgement or statement arrived at by reasoning; an inference, a deduction. LME. b *Logic.* A proposition derived from two previous propositions (the premisses) in a syllogism; a deduction from premisses. L15. †c The action of concluding or inferring. *rare.* M16–M17. †5 A proposition, a dictum, a dogma; a problem, a riddle; an experiment. LME–L17. 6 The settling or final arranging (of a treaty etc.). M16. 7 *Law.* a An act by which a person debars himself or herself; an estoppel. M16. b *Sc. Law.* The clause of a summons which states the remedy sought. E19.

2 I. MURDOCH One who has brought a difficult piece of navigation to a successful conclusion. 3 W. RALEIGH Their standing out, hindred not the rest from proceeding to conclusion. 4 J. TYNDALL The sober conclusions of science. G. BROWN People soon came to the conclusion that the letter must have been written by me. 6 E. HEATH The conclusion of the Test Ban Treaty was a diplomatic triumph.

Phrases: *foregone conclusion*: see FOREGONE *ppl a.*[1] **in conclusion** in the end, finally, to conclude. *jump to conclusions*: see JUMP *v.* **try conclusions with** engage in a trial of skill etc. with.

conclusive /kən'kluːsɪv/ *a.* L16. [Late L *conclusivus*, f. as prec.: see -IVE.] †1 Summing up. Only in L16. 2 Concluding; occurring at or forming the end; final. Now *rare.* E17. 3 Ending all argument; decisive, convincing. M17.

3 R. GRAVES They should have provided more conclusive evidence of poisoning. P. H. JOHNSON The brisk and conclusive tone of a dentist who has completed a patient's fillings.

conclusively *adv.* M16. **conclusiveness** *n.* L17. **conclusory** *a.* relating or tending to a conclusion M19.

concoct /kən'kɒkt/ *v.* Pa. pple **concocted**, †**concoct**. M16. [L *concoct-* pa. ppl stem of *concoquere* lit. 'cook together', f. as CON- + *coquere* cook.] †1 *v.t.* Digest (food): see CONCOCTION *n.* M16–E19. †2a *v.t.* Refine, purify (metals, minerals, etc.) by the action of heat. M16–M19. b *v.t.* & *i.* Cook, bake, boil; undergo cooking. L16–M19. †3 *v.t.* & *i.* Ripen, bring or come to maturity. L16–E19. b *v.t.* Produce naturally, secrete. E17–M18. 4 *v.t.* Prepare (esp. a soup, a drink) from a variety of ingredients. L17. 5 *v.t.* Devise or make up (a story, scheme, etc.) by elaborate or concerted planning; fabricate. L18.

4 M. MITCHELL Eating .. the dessert concocted by Mammy from corn meal and dried huckleberries. J. B. MORTON An Indian .. concocted the foulest smell on earth to drive the snake out. 5 C. THIRLWALL The whole project, concocted with such elaborate preparations. T. DREISER He would have to concoct some excuse.

concocter, **-tor** *n.* M17. **concoctive** *a.* †(*a*) digestive; (*b*) pertaining to the concoction of a mixture, a story, etc.: L16.

concoction /kən'kɒkʃ(ə)n/ *n.* M16. [L *concoctio(n-)*, f. as prec.: see -ION.] †1 Digestion (of food). M16–E19. †2 Ripening, maturation. M16–M19. 3 The elaborate composition of a story, scheme, etc. to suit a purpose; a fabricated story etc. E19. 4 The preparation of a dish, potion, etc., from a variety of ingredients; a thing so concocted. M19.

1 **first, second, third concoction**: the three stages of digestion formerly recognized (*a fault* or *error in the first concoction* (*fig.*), a fault etc. in the initial stage).

concolorous /kən'kʌlərəs/ *a.* M19. [f. L *concolor*, f. as CON- + *color* COLOUR *n.*: see -OUS.] *Bot. & Zool.* Of a uniform colour; of an identical colour *with*.

concomitance /kən'kɒmɪt(ə)ns/ *n.* M16. [med.L *concomitantia*: see next, -ANCE.] 1 The fact of being concomitant; subsistence together; an instance of this. M16. 2 *Theol.* (The doctrine of) the coexistence of the body and blood of Christ in each Eucharistic element singly (esp. the bread). M16.

Also **concomitancy** *n.* M17.

concomitant /kən'kɒmɪt(ə)nt/ *a.* & *n.* E17. [Late L *concomitant-* pres. ppl stem of *concomitari* accompany: see -ANT[1].] A *adj.* Of a quality, circumstance, etc.: occurring along with something else, accompanying. (Foll. by *with*, (now *rare*) *of*, †*to*.) E17.

M. L. KING A numerical growth in church membership does not necessarily reflect a concomitant increase in ethical commitment.

B *n.* 1 An attendant quality, state, circumstance, etc.; an accompaniment. (Foll. by *of*.) E17. †2 A person who accompanies another; a companion. M17–L18.

1 E. FROMM Joy is the concomitant of productive activity.

concomitantly *adv.* M17.

concord /'kɒŋkɔːd/ *n.*[1] ME. [(O)Fr. *concorde* f. L *concordia*, f. *concors*, *concord-* of one mind, f. as CON- + *cor*, *cord-* heart.] 1 Agreement or harmonious relations between persons, nations, etc. ME. b A treaty establishing harmony between nations. LME. 2 Agreement or harmony between things, esp. musical notes sounded together. ME. b *Mus.* A chord which is in itself satisfying to the ear and does not require resolution. Cf. DISCORD *n.* 3. L16. 3 *Law.* An agreement made in court respecting the conveyance of a fine of lands by which a deforciant acknowledged that the lands in question were the property of the complainant. *obs.* exc. *Hist.* L15. 4 *Gram.* Agreement between words in gender, number, case, person, etc. M16.

1 MILTON Love-quarrels oft in pleasing concord end. b W. H. PRESCOTT Abiding by the concord of Salamanca. 2 SHAKES. *Merch. V.* The man that .. is not mov'd with concord of sweet sounds. 4 *false concord*: see FALSE *a.*

Concord /'kɒŋkɔːd/ *n.*[2] M19. [US place-name.] 1 In full *Concord coach*, *wagon*. A type of stagecoach orig. made at Concord, New Hampshire. M19. 2 In full *Concord grape*. A variety of table grape developed at Concord, Massachusetts. M19.

concord /kən'kɔːd/ *v.* LME. [(O)Fr. *concorder* f. L *concordare*, f. *concord-*: see CONCORD *n.*[1] Sense 3 is back-form. f. next.] 1 *v.i.* Be in or come into agreement or harmony. LME. 2 *v.t.* Bring into harmony, reconcile. Now *rare.* LME. †b Agree upon, decide by agreement. LME–M17. 3 *v.t.* Make a concordance to (a text); arrange in a concordance. M20.

concordable *a.* (now *rare* or *obs.*) in full accord LME.

concordance /kən'kɔːd(ə)ns/ *n.* & *v.* LME. [(O)Fr. f. med.L *concordantia*, f. *concordant-*: see CONCORDANT, -ANCE.] A *n.* 1 Agreement, concord; an instance of this. LME. †b Harmony of sounds. L15–L17. †2a A parallel passage in a book, esp. the Bible; a citation of such passages. LME–E18. b An alphabetical arrangement of the principal words in a book (orig. the Bible) or author, with a list (and usu. citations) of the passages in which each occurs. Orig. in *pl.* LME. B *v.t.* Make a concordance to (a book etc.). L19.

concordancer *n.* a compiler of a concordance L19.

concordancy /kən'kɔːd(ə)nsi/ *n.* Now *rare.* L16. [f. as prec.: see -ANCY.] Agreement, concord.

concordant /kən'kɔːd(ə)nt/ *a.* L15. [(O)Fr. f. L *concordant-* pres. ppl stem of *concordare*, f. *concord-*: see CONCORD *n.*[1], -ANT[1].] 1 Agreeing; harmonious; unanimous; consistent. L15. 2 *Geol.* Corresponding in direction with the planes of adjacent or underlying strata. E20.

1 SHELLEY Then dulcet music swelled Concordant with the life-strings of the soul. J. TYNDALL These different methods have given concordant results. W. STUBBS The common concordant and unanimous consent of all and singular.

concordantly *adv.* LME.

concordantial /kɒŋkɔːˈdanʃ(ə)l/ *a.* M17. [f. med.L *concordantia*: see CONCORDANCE, -AL[1].] Pertaining to a literary concordance.

concordat /kənˈkɔːdat/ *n.* E17. [Fr., or L *concordatum* use as n. of neut. pa. pple of *concordare* agree on: see next, -AT[1].] An agreement, a compact; now *esp.* one between the Vatican and a secular government relating to matters of mutual interest.

concordatory /-dət-/ *a.* L19.

concordatum /kɒŋkɔːˈdɑːtəm/ *n.* E17. [L = 'a thing agreed upon': see prec.] *Hist.* An Order in Council relating to the disposal of a special fund (the *concordatum-fund*) for extraordinary expenses in Ireland voted annually by the British Parliament; a payment made under such an order.

concorporate /kənˈkɔːp(ə)rət/ *a.* LME. [L *concorporatus* pa. pple of *concorporare* incorporate, f. as CON- + *corpus, corpor-* body: see -ATE[2].] United in one body.

concorporate /kənˈkɔːpəreɪt/ *v. arch.* M16. [L *concorporat-* pa. ppl stem of *concorporare*: see prec., -ATE[3].] 1 *v.t.* Form into one body. M16. †2 *v.i.* Coalesce into one body. E17–E18.

concorpoˈration *n.* E17.

concours d'élégance /kɔ̃kur delegɑ̃ːs/ *n. phr.* Pl. same. M20. [Fr. = contest of elegance.] A parade of motor vehicles in which prizes are awarded for the most elegant-looking.

concourse /ˈkɒŋkɔːs/ *n.* LME. [(O)Fr. *concours* f. L *concursus*, f. *concurs-* pa. ppl stem of *concurrere* CONCUR.] 1 A flocking or meeting together; a running or flowing together; confluence. LME. †b A concurrence of times or circumstances; process (of time, events). Also, a conjunction of planets etc. LME–L18. 2 An assemblage of persons or things; a crowd, throng. LME. †3 The (place of) meeting of lines, surfaces, etc. LME–E19. †4 Concurrence in action or causation, cooperation. LME–M19. 5 An open central area in a large public building, railway station, etc. Orig. *US.* M19.

1 M. HALE The product of chance, or fortuitous concourse of particles of matter. DRYDEN Hears.. The noise and busy concourse of the mart. 2 MILTON Under some concourse of shades. M. HOLROYD A great concourse of people gathered at the grave. 5 M. BRADBURY He crosses the main concourse of the university.. where paths cross, crowds gather.

concreate /kɒŋkriːˈeɪt/ *v.t.* Now *rare* or *obs.* E17. [eccl.L *concreat-* pa. ppl stem of *concreare*: see CON-, CREATE *v.*] Create together. Chiefly as *concreated* ppl a.

concreative *a.* created or creating together M17.

†**concredit** *v.t.* L16–E19. [L *concredit-* pa. ppl stem of *concredere*: see CON-, CREDIT *n.*] Commit, entrust.

concremation /kɒŋkrɪˈmeɪʃ(ə)n/ *n. rare.* M18. [f. CON- + CREMATION.] 1 Cremation together. M18. 2 Burning to ashes. M19.

concrement /ˈkɒŋkrɪm(ə)nt/ *n. rare.* M17. [f. CON- + *-crement*, after *increment* etc.] A growing together; a concretion.

concrescence /kənˈkrɛs(ə)ns/ *n.* E17. [f. CON- + *-crescence*, after *excrescence* etc.] †1 Growth by assimilation. Only in E17. 2 A concretion. Now *rare* or *obs.* E17. 3 *Biol.* The coalescence or growing together of parts originally separate; *spec.* that of the lips of the blastopore to form the body of an embryo. L19.

concrescent *a.* growing together E20.

concrete /ˈkɒŋkriːt/ *a.* & *n.* LME. [Fr. *concret* or L *concretus* pa. pple of *concrescere* grow together, f. as CON- + *crescere* grow.] A *adj.* 1 Formed by cohesion of parts into a mass, solidified, solid; grown together. Also, compounded of various ingredients, composite. Now *rare* or *obs.* LME. 2 *Gram.* & *Logic.* Of a term or noun: denoting a substance or thing as distinct from a quality, state, or action (opp. *abstract*). Formerly also, designating a quality regarded as adherent to a substance, or a term expressing such a quality, i.e. the adjective, e.g. *white* (paper etc.), as distinct from the quality abstracted from the substance and expressed by an abstract noun, e.g. *whiteness.* LME. 3 Embodied in material form or existing as an actual example; real, tangible: opp. *abstract.* Of an idea, proposal, etc.: relating to realities or actual instances; specific, definite. M17. 4 [the n. used attrib.] Made or consisting of concrete. L19.

3 R. FRY Metaphysical ideas so vague as to be inapplicable to concrete cases. Y. WINTERS The concept is rendered concrete by the image of Cupid. H. MACMILLAN I was to announce the Bond as a concrete proposal. R. MACDONALD My witnesses aren't entirely dependable. We need concrete evidence. **concrete music** = MUSIQUE CONCRÈTE. *concrete operations*: see OPERATION 6b. **concrete poetry, verse**: in which the meaning is conveyed visually, by means of patterns of words or letters and other typographical devices. **concrete universal** (*Philos.* etc.) (something expressing) a universal in which the general and the particular or individual are combined; an organized unity. *concrete verse*: see *concrete poetry* above. 4 D. MORRIS The city is not a concrete jungle, it is a human zoo.

B *n.* I 1 A concrete noun or term. *rare.* LME. 2 A concreted mass; a concretion. Now *rare* or *obs.* exc. as below. M17. 3 A heavy-duty building material made from a mixture of broken stone or gravel, sand, cement, and water, which forms a stonelike mass on hardening; paving etc. made of this. M19.

3 E. FERBER Tramping of restless feet on the concrete. *reinforced concrete*: see REINFORCE *v.*

II 4 *absol.* That which is concrete. Esp. in *in the concrete*, in the sphere of concrete reality, concretely. M16.

Comb.: **concrete-mixer** = *cement-mixer* s.v. CEMENT *n.*

concretely *adv.* in a concrete form, manner, or sense M17. **concreteness** *n.* M18. **concretize** *v.t.* render concrete, esp. opp. abstract L19. **concretiˈzation** *n.* the action of concretizing; the state of being concretized: M20.

concrete /kənˈkriːt; *in sense 3* ˈkɒŋkriːt/ *v.* L16. [f. prec.] 1 *v.t.* (freq. in *pass.*) & *i.* Unite into a mass by cohesion or coalescence of particles; make or become solid. L16. †b *v.t.* Unite, combine (sensations, ideas, etc.). E18–E19. 2 *v.t.* Give concrete expression to (an abstract thing). M17. 3 *v.t.* Cover or pave with concrete; embed or set in concrete. L19.

1 C. LYELL Ochreous sand, concreted.. into a kind of stone. 2 J. CONRAD Precious dreams that concrete the most cherished.. of his illusions.

ˈ**concreter** *n.* a builder or worker with concrete L19.

concretion /kənˈkriːʃ(ə)n/ *n.* M16. [Fr. *concrétion* or L *concretio(n-)*, f. *concret-* pa. ppl stem of *concrescere*: see CONCRETE *a.* & *n.*] 1 The action or process of growing together or uniting in one mass; coalescence. M16. b Congelation or coagulation of a liquid. E17. †2 Union with a material thing. E17–M18. 3 A concreted mass (*of*); a lump, a nodule. E17. b *spec. Med.* A calculus or hardened deposit in the body. M17. c *Geol.* A nodule of distinct mineral composition occurring (usu. around a nucleus) in sedimentary rock. M19. 4 The action of expressing (an idea etc.) in concrete form; an embodiment in concrete form. M17.

concretionary *a.* (esp. *Geol.*) formed by concretion; marked by or consisting of concretions: M19.

†**concrew** *v.i. rare* (Spenser). Only in L16. [f. ACCRUE by substitution of CON-, perh. after OFr. *concrëu.*] Grow into a mass.

concubinage /kɒnˈkjuːbɪnɪdʒ/ *n.* LME. [Fr., f. as CONCUBINE: see -AGE.] The cohabiting of a man and a woman who are not legally married; the practice of keeping, or the state of being, a concubine.

concubinary /kɒnˈkjuːbɪnəri/ *a.* & *n.* E16. [med.L *concubinarius*, f. L *concubina*: see next, -ARY[1].] A *adj.* Relating to concubinage. Of a person: living or born in concubinage. E16. B *n.* A person who lives in concubinage. L16.

concubine /ˈkɒŋkjʊbʌɪn/ *n.* & *v.* ME. [(O)Fr. f. L *concubina, concubinus*, f. as CON- + *cubare* to lie.] A *n.* 1 A woman who cohabits with a man without being his wife, a kept mistress; (in polygamous societies) a secondary wife. ME. †2 A woman's lover. LME–M16. B *v.t.* †1 Take as a concubine. Only in L16. 2 Provide with a concubine or concubines. *rare.* E19.

conˈcubinal *a.* (*rare*) M17.

†**conculcate** *v.t.* M16–E18. [L *conculcat-* pa. ppl stem of *conculcare*, f. as CON- + *calcare* tread: see INCULCATE.] Trample under foot.

†**conculcation** *n.* LME–E19.

concupiscence /kənˈkjuːpɪs(ə)ns/ *n.* ME. [(O)Fr. f. late L. *concupiscentia*, f. *concupiscent-* pres. ppl stem of *concupiscere* inceptive of *concupere*, f. as CON- + *cupere* desire.] Eager or inordinate desire; immoderate sexual desire, lust; *Theol.* desire for worldly things.

C. CHAPLIN There's a dame that arouses my concupiscence But she looks very expensive.

concupiscent *a.* eagerly desirous, lustful M18. **concupiscently** *adv.* LME.

concupiscible /kənˈkjuːpɪsɪb(ə)l/ *a.* LME. [Late L *concupiscibilis*, f. *concupiscere*: see prec., -IBLE.] 1 Of the nature of concupiscence; vehemently desirous, lustful. LME. †2 Greatly to be desired or lusted after. L15–M18.

1 **concupiscible principle** etc.: (in Platonic philosophy) one of the two parts of irrational human nature (the other being the *irascible*). 2 L. STERNE Never did thy eyes behold.. anything.. more concupiscible.

†**concupy** *n. rare* (Shakes.). Only in E17. [Perh. abbrev. of CONCUPISCENCE.] Lust, concupiscence.

¶By some interpreted as a perversion of CONCUBINE *n.*

concur /kənˈkəː/ *v.i.* Infl. **-rr-**. LME. [L *concurrere*, f. as CON- + *currere* run.] †1 a Run together violently, collide; rush together in battle. LME–L17. †b Run or flow together to a meeting-point. Of lines etc.: converge. M16–E19. 2 Act in concert, cooperate. Of causes etc.: combine (to produce a result). LME. 3 Agree or express agreement. (Usu. foll. by *with.*) LME. †b Of things: agree in character etc., accord (*with*). M16–L18. 4 Happen or occur together, coincide. Of characteristics: be combined in the same person or thing. L16.

2 R. JAMESON One of the plane angles which concur to the formation of the solid angle. GEO. ELIOT I concurred with our incumbent in getting up a petition against the Reform Bill. 3 H. FIELDING Mr. Alworthy by no means concurred with the opinion of those parents. G. VIDAL Let me know.. if you concur in my plan. G. SWIFT We concur It's Sunday, without a doubt. b HOR. WALPOLE It was now twilight, concurring with the disorder of his mind. 4 A. BAIN When two pleasures concur, the result is a greater pleasure.

concurrence /kənˈkʌr(ə)ns/ *n.* LME. [f. next or med.L *concurrentia*: see -ENCE.] †1 Concentration (of mind). Only in LME. 2 a Joint action, cooperation. E16. b Agreement, assent. M17. 3 A running together in time or space: a Coincidence of events or circumstances. E17. b The (point of) meeting of lines. M17. 4 Rivalry, competition. (In later use a Gallicism.) *arch.* E17.

2b BURKE I had the fortune to find myself in perfect concurrence with a large majority in the house. T. HARDY With a mutual glance of concurrence the two men went into the night together. 3a J. FOSTER The most opportune concurrence of circumstances.

Also **concurrency** *n.* L16.

concurrent /kənˈkʌr(ə)nt/ *a.* & *n.* LME. [L *concurrent-* pres. ppl stem of *concurrere*: see CONCUR, -ENT.] A *adj.* 1 Occurring or operating simultaneously or side by side. LME. b Of lines etc.: meeting in or tending towards the same point. E18. 2 Acting in conjunction; cooperating. M16. 3 Expressing agreement. Of things: accordant, consistent. M16.

1 J. WILLIAMS The concurrent existence of two distinct systems of jurisprudence. 2 H. E. MANNING He.. gives them the concurrent assistance of his own power. 3 J. BROWN By Shouts of Sympathy or concurrent Approbation.

B *n.* 1 A rival claimant, a competitor. (In later use a Gallicism.) *arch.* L16. 2 A concurrent circumstance, a contributory cause. M17.

concurrently *adv.* LME.

concursion /kənˈkəːʃ(ə)n/ *n.* Now *rare* or *obs.* M16. [L *concursio(n-)*, f. *concurs-* pa. ppl stem of *concurrere*: see CONCUR, -ION.] A running or rushing together.

concuss /kən'kʌs/ *v.t.* L16. [L *concuss-* pa. ppl stem of *concutere*, f. as CON- + *quatere* shake.] 1 Shake violently, disturb. Chiefly *fig.* L16. **b** *Med.* Affect with concussion. L17. 2 Force by threats (*into*, *to do*); intimidate. *arch.* (chiefly *Sc.*). E19.

concussive *a.* of the nature of, producing, or pertaining to concussion L16.

concussion /kən'kʌʃ(ə)n/ *n.* LME. [L *concussio(n-)*, f. as prec.; see -ION.] 1 *Med.* Temporary unconsciousness or incapacity due to a blow on the head. LME. 2 *gen.* The action of shaking violently; the shock of impact. L15. 3 Extortion by threats or violence, esp. by a ruling power. Now *rare* or *obs.* L16.

2 R. BRADBURY The ocean rose and fell with prolonged concussions. C. RYAN The ground shook constantly from the concussion of heavy explosives.

†**cond** *v.t.* Also **cund**. Orig. **condie**, **-due**. ME. [(O)Fr. *conduire* f. L *conducere* CONDUCT *v.*] 1 Conduct, guide. Only in ME. 2 = CON *v.*[2] E17–E19. 3 Direct (fishing boats etc.) towards a shoal of herring etc. E17–M19.

conde /'kɒnde/ *n.* Also **C-**. M17. [Sp. f. L *comes*, *comitis*: see COUNT *n.*[2]] A Spanish count.

condemn /kən'dɛm/ *v.t.* ME. [OFr. *condem(p)ner* (mod. *condamner*) f. L *condem(p)nare*, f. as CON- + DAMN *v.*] 1 Give judgement against, convict; sentence *to* punishment, *to be* punished; *esp.* sentence to death. ME. 2 Pronounce an adverse judgement on; express strong disapproval of; censure, blame; reject. Of words, looks, actions, etc.: incur or bring about condemnation of. LME. 3a Consign to perdition; damn. LME. **b** Force into or limit to an unwelcome or unpleasant action or state; *esp.* in *pass.*, be doomed *to* some condition or *to do* something. M17. 4 Pronounce guilty *of* (a crime, fault, etc.). *arch.* M16. 5 Close permanently, block up (a door, window). M16. 6 Pronounce (smuggled goods, prizes of war, etc.) legally forfeited. E18. 7 Pronounce officially to be unfit for use, consumption, or habitation. E18. **b** Pronounce judicially (land etc.) as converted or convertible to public use. *US.* M19. 8 Pronounce incurable. M19.

1 POPE The thief condemn'd, in law already dead. 2 OED Their looks condemn them. W. S. CHURCHILL Opinion . . has on the whole condemned Rupert's resolve to fight. C. HAUGHEY I condemn the Provisional I.R.A. and all its activities. 3b J. MORSE A tract of sea . . condemned to perpetual calms. A. S. NEILL A society that condemns poor women to slave for sixteen hours a day. 4 T. HEYWOOD She was condemned of incest and buried alive. 7 E. COXHEAD Though it had been condemned twenty years before, a house is a house. I. MURDOCH These trees had . . been condemned as unsafe.

condemnable /-mn-/ *a.* M16. **condemningly** *adv.* with condemnation M19.

condemnation /kɒndɛm'neɪʃ(ə)n/ *n.* LME. [Late L *condemnatio(n-)*, f. *condemnat-* pa. ppl stem of *condemnare*: see prec., -ATION.] 1 The action of condemning; judicial conviction; censure; the fact of being condemned. LME. 2 The state or condition of being condemned. M16. 3 A ground or reason for condemning. M16. 4 A sentence of forfeiture; *spec.* (*US*) the judicial assignment of property to public purposes, or in payment of a debt. M19.

1 J. R. ACKERLEY Irregular relationships were regarded with far greater condemnation in Victorian times. R. A. KNOX The condemnation to hell of all infants that had died without baptism. 2 MILTON To whom belongs But condemnation, ignominy and shame. 3 SHAKES. *Cymb.* Speak, or thy silence on the instant is Thy condemnation and thy death.

condemnator /kən'dɛmnətə/ *a.* & *n.* Chiefly *Sc.* E16. [Fr. †*condemnatoire* f. as next.] *Law.* A *adj.* Condemnatory; *esp.* (of a decree) in favour of the plaintiff. E16. †**B** *n.* A condemnatory sentence or decree. M16–M17.

condemnatory /kən'dɛmnət(ə)ri/ *a.* L16. [med.L *condemnatorius*, f. *condemnat-*: see CONDEMNATION, -ORY[2]. Cf. prec.] Having the character of condemning; expressing condemnation.

condemned /kən'dɛmd/ *a.* LME. [f. CONDEMN + -ED[1].] 1 Pronounced to be at fault or guilty; under sentence of condemnation. LME. **b** Confounded, damned. *arch. colloq.* (chiefly *US*). M19. 2 Set aside for or pertaining to persons sentenced to death. Chiefly in *condemned cell*: see CELL *n.*[1] L17. 3 Officially pronounced unfit for use, consumption, or habitation. L18.

condensate /'kɒnd(ə)nseɪt/ *n.* L19. [f. CONDENSE *v.* + -ATE[2].] A product of chemical or physical condensation.

condensate /kən'dɛnsət, -seɪt/ *a.* Now *rare* or *obs.* L15. [L *condensat-* pa. ppl stem of *condensare*: see CONDENSE *v.*, -ATE[2].] Condensed, thickened, increased in density.

condensate /kən'dɛnseɪt/ *v.t.* & *i.* Now *rare* or *obs.* M16. [f. as prec.: see -ATE[3].] Condense.

condensator *n.* (*rare*) a condenser E19.

condensation /kɒndɛn'seɪʃ(ə)n/ *n.* E17. [Late L *condensatio(n-)*, f. as prec.: see -ATION. Cf. (O)Fr. *condensation*.] 1 The act or process of condensing; *spec.* the conversion of a substance from a state of gas or vapour to a liquid (occas., a solid) condition. E17. 2 Condensed condition; a condensed mass; condensed material, esp. of water on the inside of cold windows etc. E17. 3 The compression of thought or meaning into a few words; *esp.* the abridgement of a book etc.; the result of this. L18. 4 *Chem.* In full *condensation reaction*. A reaction in which two molecules combine to form a larger molecule, strictly with the elimination of a small molecule such as H_2O. L19. 5 *Psychoanalysis.* The fusion of two or more images or ideas into a single composite or new image, esp. in a dream; the carrying of more than one symbolic meaning by an image. E20.

Phrases: KNOEVENAGEL *condensation*. *surface condensation*: see SURFACE *a.*

Comb.: *condensation reaction*: see sense 4 above; **condensation trail** = *vapour trail* s.v. VAPOUR *n.*

†**condense** *a.* LME–L18. [L *condensus*: see next.] Dense, condensed.

condense /kən'dɛns/ *v.t.* & *i.* LME. [(O)Fr. *condenser* or L *condensare*, f. *condensus* very dense: see CON-, DENSE *a.*] 1 Make or become (more) dense; increase in density; thicken; concentrate. LME. 2 Reduce or be reduced from gas or vapour to a liquid (occas. a solid) condition. M17. 3 Bring or come together closely; *esp.* express (writing, speech, etc.) in few(er) words, make concise. E19.

1 B. LOVELL The contemporary view that the stars condensed from the interstellar gas clouds. **condensed milk**: thickened by evaporation and sweetened. 2 E. STILLINGFLEET The air was condensed into clouds. D. LODGE Their breath condenses on the chill, damp air. 3 CONAN DOYLE Is this too condensed, or can you follow it clearly? J. HELLER Gold condensed the piece further by four hundred words.

condensa'bility *n.* the quality of being condensable E19. **condensable** *a.* that may be condensed M17. **condensedly** *adv.* with condensation (esp. of expression) L19. **condensery** *n.* a factory for making condensed milk E20. **condensible** *a.* = CONDENSABLE L18.

condenser /kən'dɛnsə/ *n.* L17. [f. prec. + -ER[1]. Cf. Fr. *condenseur*.] 1 *gen.* A person who or thing which condenses. L17. 2 A vessel, apparatus, etc., in which vapour is reduced to liquid (occas. solid) form; *esp.* a chamber in a steam engine in which steam is condensed on leaving the cylinder; *Chem.* a device for condensing vapour during distillation etc. M18. 3 *Electr.* = CAPACITOR. L18. 4 A lens or system of lenses for concentrating light. L18.

2 *Liebig('s) condenser*: see LIEBIG 2. 3 *padder condenser*: see PADDER *n.*[2] 3.

condensity /kən'dɛnsɪti/ *n.* E17. [Fr. †*condensité* or late L *condensitas*, f. *condensus*: see CONDENSE *v.*, -ITY.] †1 Density. E17–E19. 2 Condensed quality, pithiness. L19.

†**conder** *n.* E17. [f. COND *v.* + -ER[1].] 1 A person who, stationed on high ground, signals the direction taken by shoals of herring etc. to fishing boats. E17–M19. 2 A person who cons a ship. L17–E19.

condescend /kɒndɪ'sɛnd/ *v.* ME. [(O)Fr. *condescendre* f. eccl.L *condescendere* stoop (fig.), (in med.L) accede, agree to, f. as CON- + DESCEND.] I Make concession (to). †1 *v.i.* & (*rare*) *refl.* Yield, defer, accommodate oneself (*to*); accede, consent (*to*); come to agreement, concur. ME–L18. †2 *v.t.* Concede, vouchsafe; agree upon, consent to. LME–L18.

1 G. DOUGLAS Thay [singers] condiscend sa weill in ane accord. W. DRUMMOND The three estates . . together condescended to the raising of an army. W. GODWIN He was resolved to condescend no further to the whims of a person. 2 J. SPALDING It was condescended among his friends, that twenty-four gentlemen . . should weekly attend. T. JEFFERSON No answers having yet been condescended.

II Come down voluntarily. †3 *v.i.* Come or go down, descend. LME–L17. 4 *v.i.* Be gracious enough *to do* something, stoop voluntarily *to* an action, though showing one's feelings of dignity or superiority. Now freq. *iron.* LME. 5 *v.i.* Disregard one's superiority *to* a person; show kindness to an inferior; behave patronizingly (*to*). E17.

4 S. SMILES [They] condescended to the meanest employments, for the purpose of disarming suspicion. E. F. BENSON Dismiss Johnson . . and get somebody who will condescend to garden. 5 P. S. WORSLEY The god, condescending to his child. P. SCOTT The . . subalterns . . gave themselves airs. . . They even condescended to the Area Commander.

III Come to a point. †6 *v.i.* Come *to* a particular point (in narration etc.) LME–E16. 7 *v.i.* Come to particulars; particularize, elaborate (*up*)*on*. *obs.* exc. *Sc.* LME.

condescendence *n.* (*a*) condescension; compliance; (*b*) *Sc.* a specification of particulars: E17. **condescendency** *n.* (now *rare* or *obs.*) condescension M17. **condescender** *n.* (*rare*) M17.

condescending /kɒndɪ'sɛndɪŋ/ *a.* M17. [f. prec. + -ING[2].] †1 Consenting. Only in M17. 2 That condescends, characterized by condescension; patronizing. E18. 3 Going into details, particularizing. *Sc.* L18.

condescendingly *adv.* M17.

condescension /kɒndɪ'sɛnʃ(ə)n/ *n.* M17. [Obs. Fr. (now *condescendance*), f. (orig.) eccl.L *condescensio(n-)*, f. L *condescens-* pa. ppl stem of *condescendere*: see CONDESCEND, -ION.] †1 The fact or action of acceding or consenting; concession. M17–E18. †2 The action of stooping to something unworthy. M17–L18. 3 Voluntary disregarding of a superior position; affability to inferiors; a consciously gracious or patronizing act or manner. M17. 4 Gracious, considerate, or submissive deference shown to another; complaisance. Now *rare* or *obs.* M17.

3 R. L. STEVENSON I had come . . to prove in a thousand condescensions that I was no sharer in the prejudice of race. I. MURDOCH I had never been spontaneously approached by a publisher before and such condescension rather turned my head. 4 H. FIELDING Their extreme servility and condescension to their superiors.

†**condescensive** *a.* characterized by or given to condescension M17–E19.

condictio /kən'dɪkʃɪəʊ/ *n.* Pl. **-dictiones** /-dɪkʃɪ'əʊniːz/. Also Anglicized as †**-diction**. L18. [L *condictio(n-)*, f. *condict-* pa. ppl stem of *condicere*, f. as CON- + *dicere* say: see -ION.] *Rom. Law.* A formal claim of debt or restitution.

†**condie** *v.* see COND.

condign /kən'dʌɪn/ *a.* LME. [(O)Fr. *condigne* f. L *condignus* wholly worthy, f. as CON- + *dignus* worthy.] †1 Equal in worth or dignity (*to*). LME–M19. 2 Of a person or thing: worthy, deserving. Now *rare* or *obs.* LME. 3 Worthily deserved, merited, appropriate; adequate. *obs.* in *gen.* sense. LME. **b** *spec.* Of punishment, retribution, etc.: appropriate to the crime, well-deserved and severe. E16.

1 S. DOBELL Rank after mingling rank . . but each condign. 2 H. BRADSHAW As most condigne to beare the principalitie. 3 SHAKES. *L.L.L.* Speak you this in my praise? . . In thy condign praise. **b** BOSW. SMITH To wreak condign vengeance on the common oppressor. *Times* Punishment for perjury had to be condign and commensurate with the gravity of the offence.

condignly *adv.* LME. **condignness** /-n-n-/ *n.* L16.

condignity /kən'dɪgnɪti/ *n.* M16. [med.L *condignitas*, f. *condignus*: see prec., -ITY.] 1 *Scholastic Theol.* Merit acquired by man through actions performed in reliance on the Holy Spirit; grace earned by works, as opp. to that freely given. M16. †2 *gen.* Worthiness, merit; what one deserves. L16–M17.

condiment /ˈkɒndɪm(ə)nt/ *n.* & *v.* LME. [L *condimentum*, f. *condire* preserve, pickle, embalm, by-form of *condere* preserve: see -MENT.] **A** *n.* A substance used to give relish to food; seasoning. LME. **B** *v.t.* Season or flavour with a condiment; spice. *rare.* LME.

condimental /kɒndɪˈmɛnt(ə)l/ *a.* of or belonging to a condiment; spicy: E17.

condisciple /kɒndɪˈsʌɪp(ə)l/ *n. arch.* LME. [L *condiscipulus* fellow-scholar: see CON-, DISCIPLE *n.*] A fellow disciple; a fellow scholar or student.

†**condite** *v.t.* LME. [L *condit-* pa. ppl stem of *condire*: see CONDIMENT.] **1** Preserve with salt, spices, etc.; pickle. LME–E18. **2** Embalm. Only in M17. **3** Season, flavour. M–L17.

condition /kənˈdɪʃ(ə)n/ *n.* ME. [OFr. *condicion* (mod. *condition*) f. L *condicio(n-)* agreement, situation, etc., rel. to *condicere* agree upon, promise, f. as CON- + *dicere* declare, say: see -ION.] **I** A convention, proviso, etc. **1** A thing demanded or required as a prerequisite to the granting or performance of something else; a stipulation. ME. †**b** *ellipt.* As conj. = *on condition that* below. Only in E17. **2** A thing on whose existence or fulfilment that of another depends; a prerequisite. In *pl.*, circumstances, *esp.* those necessary for a thing's existence. ME. †**3** A restriction, a qualification, a limitation. LME–M19. †**4** An agreement; a covenant, a treaty. L15–E18. **5** A provision in a will, contract, etc., on which the legal force or effect of the document depends. L16. **6** *Gram.* A conditional clause. M19. **7** A subject, course, etc., in which a student must pass an examination within a stated time to maintain provisionally granted status. *US.* M19.

1 MILTON Wilt thou enjoy the good, Then cavil the conditions? G. F. KENNAN A list of twenty-one conditions on which .. Communist groups .. would be admitted to the Third International. **on condition that** with the condition that, provided that. POTESTATIVE *condition. resolutive condition*: see RESOLUTIVE 2. b SHAKES. *Tr. & Cr.* Condition I had gone barefoot to India. 2 G. J. ROMANES Environment .. or the sum total of the external conditions of life. G. MURRAY It is .. a necessary condition of social living, that we are individuals as well as members of a social whole. 3 J. BRAMHALL We are absolutely without condition glad of our own liberty. 4 SHAKES. *Merch. V.* If you repay me not .. such sum or sums as are Express'd in the condition. 5 **conditions of sale** the provisions under which a sale by auction takes place.

II State, mode of being. **8** A particular mode of being of a person or thing; a state; circumstances of wealth; social position. ME. **b** *spec.* A state resulting from a physical or mental illness; sickness, a malady. E20. †**9** Mental disposition; moral nature; temper. In *pl.*, personal qualities; ways, morals; behaviour. LME–M19. †**10** Nature, character, quality; a characteristic, an attribute. LME–E18.

8 W. H. PRESCOTT In the middle classes; and even in those of humbler condition. M. ESSLIN The act of waiting as an essential and characteristic aspect of the human condition. **change one's condition** (now *arch.* & *dial.*) get married. **in a certain** (or **a delicate, an interesting**) **condition** *euphem.* pregnant. **in, out of, condition** in good, bad, condition; physically fit, unfit. *in mint condition*: see MINT *n.*[1] **in no condition** certainly not fit enough *to do*. *race condition*: see RACE *n.*[1] 3c. *spheroidal condition*: see SPHEROIDAL 2. b T. S. ELIOT The condition is curable. 9 AV 2 *Macc.* 15:12 A good man, .. gentle in condition, well spoken also. SIR W. SCOTT Miss Bell Fergusson, a woman of the most excellent conditions. 10 A. DAY A man shaped as you see, and as bold in condition as he appeareth in shew. SHAKES. *Two Gent.* Here is the cate-log .. of her condition .. She can fetch and carry. .. She can milk.

Comb.: **condition-powder** a medicinal powder to keep an animal in condition.

condition /kənˈdɪʃ(ə)n/ *v.* L15. [OFr. *condicionner* (mod. *-tionner*) or med.L *condicionare* (*-tion-*), f. *condicio(n-)*: see prec.] **I** *v.i.* **1** Negotiate about conditions; make conditions; bargain *with*, *for*. *arch.* L15.

II *v.t.* **2** Stipulate for; make (something) a condition; agree by stipulation *to do* something. *arch.* M16. **3** Make conditional. Usu. foll. by *on*, *upon*. M16. **4** Govern, determine; impose conditions on; be essential to. E17. **5** Charge (a bond) with clauses or conditions. L17. **6** *Philos.* Subject to the qualifying conditions of finite existence or cognition. Now *rare.* E19. **7** Admit (a student) to a class on the condition of passing an examination within a stated time. (Cf. CONDITION *n.* 7.) *US.* M19. **8** Test the condition, state, or quality of (a textile etc.). M19. **9** Bring into a desired state or condition (*for*); make fit (esp. dogs, horses, etc.). M19. **b** Teach, accustom (a person, animal, etc.) to adopt certain habits, attitudes, etc.; establish a conditioned reflex or response in. (Foll. by *to do*, *to* a thing etc.) E20.

4 M. GIROUARD Their ideas of beauty were conditioned by what they disliked about their parents. 9 *air-conditioning*: see AIR *n.*[1] b ALDOUS HUXLEY His conditioning has laid down rails along which he's got to run. He can't help himself. A. STORR Repeated positive reinforcement has conditioned him to favourable self-appraisal. *verbal conditioning*: see VERBAL *a.* 2.

conditional /kənˈdɪʃ(ə)n(ə)l/ *a.* & *n.* LME. [OFr. *condicionel* (mod. *-tionnel*) or late L *condicionalis*, f. *condicio(n-)*: see CONDITION *n.*, -AL[1].] **A** *adj.* **1** Subject to one or more conditions; depending (*on*, *upon*); not absolute; made or granted on certain conditions or terms. LME. **2** *Gram.* & *Logic.* Expressing or including a condition or supposition. M16.

1 W. LIPPMANN The fulfillment of this promise is .. conditional upon the ability .. to define equality. P. BLANCHARD Such conditional endearments as, 'My love to the little Sarah Margaret. I love her if she is a good girl and learns to read.' A. LURIE His parents' affection .. was always conditional on good behaviour. **conditional agreement** *Law* an agreement dependent on the happening of an uncertain event. **conditional discharge** *Law* an order made by a criminal court whereby an offender may be sentenced for the original offence if a further offence is committed within a fixed period. **conditional offer** *spec.* of a place at a university, college, etc., subject to the attainment of specified grades in forthcoming examinations. **conditional sale agreement** *Law* a contract for the sale of goods under which ownership does not pass to the buyer until the instalments have been paid, although the buyer has possession. 2 A. BAIN The conditional clause is introduced by 'if'. **conditional mood** *Gram.*: used in the consequent clause of a conditional sentence.

B *n.* Chiefly *Gram.* & *Logic.* A word, clause, proposition, etc., expressing or including a condition; the conditional mood. M16.

conditionalism *n.* (*Theol.*) the doctrine of conditional survival after death L19. **conditionalist** *a.* & *n.* of or pertaining to, a believer in, conditionalism L19. **conditioˈnality** *n.* the state or quality of being conditional M17. **conditionally** *adv.* (*a*) in a conditional manner, subject to conditions; †(*b*) on condition (*that*): LME.

conditionate /kənˈdɪʃ(ə)nət/ *a.* & *n.* LME. [med.L *condicionatus* (*-tion-*) pa. pple, f. as next: see -ATE[2].] **A** *adj.* Conditioned; subject to or limited by conditions. Now *rare* or *obs.* LME. **B** *n.* A conditional thing, a contingency. L17.

conditionate /kənˈdɪʃ(ə)neɪt/ *v.* M16. [med.L *condicionat-* pa. ppl stem of *condicionare*: see CONDITION *v.*, -ATE[3].] †**1** *v.t.* & *i.* Agree on (conditions); stipulate. M16–M17. **2** *v.t.* Limit as a condition; be, or act as, a condition of. L16.

conditioned /kənˈdɪʃ(ə)nd/ *a.* LME. [f. CONDITION *n.*, *v.*: see -ED[2], -ED[1].] **I** f. the n. **1** Having a (specified) disposition or temperament; in a particular condition or state. LME. **2** Placed in certain conditions; circumstanced, situated. M19.

1 SHAKES. *Merch. V.* The kindest man, the best condition'd and unwearied spirit In doing courtesies. *ill-conditioned*, *well-conditioned*, etc. 2 COLERIDGE In countries well governed and happily conditioned.

II f. the vb. **3** Subject to conditions or limitations; dependent on a condition; not absolute or infinite. M17. **4** Brought into a desired state; with the balance of certain qualities adjusted. E20. **5** Taught to accept certain habits, attitudes, standards, etc.; accustomed *to*. M20.

3 *absol.*: W. HAMILTON The Conditioned is that which is alone conceivable or cogitable. 4 H. G. WELLS They had no properly mixed and conditioned air. **conditioned reflex** a reflex response to a non-natural stimulus established by training in a person, animal, etc. *air-conditioned*: see AIR *n.*[1] 5 R. CHURCH My father, long conditioned to bullying, refused to be intimidated.

conditioner /kənˈdɪʃ(ə)nə/ *n.* L16. [f. CONDITION *v.* + -ER[1].] †**1** A person who makes conditions. Only in L16. **2** A substance, appliance, etc., the use of which improves the condition of something. L19.

2 *air-conditioner*, *hair conditioner*, etc.

condo /ˈkɒndəʊ/ *n. colloq.* (orig. *US*). Pl. **-os.** M20. [Abbrev.] = CONDOMINIUM 2.

condolatory /kənˈdəʊlət(ə)ri/ *a.* M18. [f. next after *consolatory*.] Expressive of or intending condolence.

condole /kənˈdəʊl/ *v.* L16. [Chr.L *condolere*, f. as CON- + *dolere* suffer pain, grieve.] **I** *v.i.* †**1** Sorrow greatly, grieve, lament. L16–M17. **2** Grieve *with*; express sympathy *with* a person *on* a loss etc.; express condolence. L16.

1 R. TOFTE For my Sinnes fore Heauen I do condole. 2 H. MARTINEAU Three quarters of her acquaintance came to condole. S. T. WARNER Condole with her, and listen to her sorrows.

II *v.t.* †**3** Grieve over, bewail, lament (a loss, misfortune, etc.); *refl.* grieve, lament. L16–L18. †**4** Grieve with (a person); express commiseration of or sympathy with. L16–L18. **5** Express formal regret at (a bereavement etc.). Now *rare.* L16.

3 S. RICHARDSON A person .. whose sufferings I condole. 4 ADDISON They are comforted and condoled .. by their fellow-citizens. 5 H. ELLIS Elizabeth had sent to condole the death of Frederick the Second.

condolement *n.* †(*a*) lamentation; (*b*) (an expression of) condolence: L16. **condoler** *n.* E18. **condolingly** *adv.* in a condoling manner, with condolence E18.

condolence /kənˈdəʊl(ə)ns/ *n.* E17. [f. prec. + -ENCE. In sense 2 also infl. by Fr. *condoléance*.] †**1** Sympathetic grief; sorrowing with and for others. E17–E18. **2** Outward expression of sympathy for another's grief; *esp.* a formal declaration of regret for a person's bereavement, misfortune, etc. Freq. in *pl.* E17.

2 J. GALSWORTHY Kindness .. would frequently result in visits of condolence being made. H. CECIL The usual congratulations between the plaintiff and his legal advisers and .. condolences between Martin and his legal advisers.

†**condolency** *n.* (*a*) = CONDOLENCE; (*b*) compassion, commiseration: E17–E19.

condolent /kənˈdəʊl(ə)nt/ *a.* LME. [L *condolent-* pres. ppl stem of *condolere*: see CONDOLE, -ENT.] †**1** Sorrowing greatly. LME–L15. **2** Compassionate; expressing sympathetic grief. L15.

condom /ˈkɒndəm/ *n.* E18. [Origin unkn.] A contraceptive or prophylactic sheath that can be worn on the penis during sexual intercourse. See also *female condom* s.v. FEMALE *a.*

condominium /kɒndəˈmɪnɪəm/ *n.* E18. [mod.L, f. as CON- + DOMINIUM.] **1** Joint control of a State's affairs vested in two or more other States. E18. **2** A set of flats, group of cottages, etc., rented or bought by a group of people; a unit of property so held. *N. Amer.* M20.

condonation /kɒndəʊˈneɪʃ(ə)n/ *n.* E17. [L *condonatio(n-)*, f. as next: see CON-, DONATION.] The forgiveness or overlooking, esp. by implication, of an offence.

condone /kənˈdəʊn/ *v.t.* M19. [L *condonare* deliver up, surrender, favour by not punishing, f. as CON- + *donare* give.] **1** Forgive or overlook (an offence; freq. a spouse's adultery); *esp.* forgive tacitly by not allowing the offence to affect one's relations with the offender. M19. **2** Of an action, fact, etc.: atone for (an offence); make (a wrong) appear forgivable. E19. **3** Approve, sanction, esp. reluctantly; acquiesce in. M20.

1 G. B. SHAW Is it your intention not only to condone my son's frauds, but to take advantage of them? 2 I. MURDOCH The vague illumination of lofty notions which may seem to condone all kinds of extravagance. 3 K. KESEY Like the whole thing had been planned by him, or at least condoned and authorized.

condonable *a.* L19. **condoner** *n.* M19.

condor /ˈkɒndɔː/ *n.* E17. [Sp. *cóndor* f. Quechua *kuntur*.] Either of two very large vultures, *Vultur gryphus*, native to the Andes of S. America (more fully *Andean condor*), and *Gymnogyps californianus*, of the mountains of California (more fully *Californian condor*).

condottiere /kɒndɒtˈtjere/ *n.* Pl. ***-ri*** /-ri/. Also †***-iero***. L18. [It., f. *condotta* a contract, f. fem. pa. pple of *condurre* conduct, f. as next.] *Hist.* A leader or member of a troop of mercenaries (orig. and esp. in Italy).

conduce /kənˈdjuːs/ *v.* LME. [L *conducere* bring together, hire, contribute, f. as CON- + *ducere* to lead.] I *v.t.* †1 Lead, conduct, bring (*lit.* & *fig.*). Foll. by *to*. LME–M17. †2 Engage for money, hire. *Sc.* L15–L17. †3 Bring about, bring to effect. Only in E16.

II *v.i.* 4 Foll. by *to*: lead or tend towards, contribute to; promote, encourage. L15. †5 Gather together, start. *rare* (Shakes.). Only in E16.

4 W. S. CHURCHILL This has not conduced to the national interest. R. WILBUR All bitter things conduce to sweet. Y. MENUHIN These circumstances not conducing to slumber, I spent the rest hour holding forth. 5 SHAKES. *Tr. & Cr.* Within my soul there doth conduce a fight Of this strange nature.

conducement *n.* (long *rare*) (*a*) the action or quality of conducing (*to*); (*b*) a thing that conduces, tendency: M16. **conducible** *a.* (*obs.* exc. *Sc.*) that conduces; expedient, serviceable M16.

conducive /kənˈdjuːsɪv/ *a.* & *n.* M17. [f. prec. after *conductive* etc.: see -IVE.] A *adj.* Foll. by *to*: conducing or tending to (a specified end); tending to promote or encourage. M17. B *n.* That which conduces (*to*). *rare*. L18.

conduciveness *n.* L17.

conduct /ˈkɒndʌkt/ *n.*[1] Orig. †**conduit**. See also CONDUIT *n.* ME. [(OFr. *conduit* f.) L *conductus*, f. *conduct-* pa. ppl stem of *conducere*: see CONDUCE.] I 1 Provision for guidance or conveyance; an escort, a convoy; a pass. *obs.* exc. in SAFE-CONDUCT. ME. 2 The action of conducting; guidance, leading (*lit.* & *fig.*). LME. †3 A guide, a leader (*lit.* & *fig.*). LME–L18. 4 More fully *conduct-money*. Money paid for travelling expenses, esp. (*Hist.*) to provide conveyance for men furnished for military service; an impost levied under this head by Charles I. E16. 5 Conveyance, esp. of liquid by a channel. *rare*. M16.

1 SHAKES. *Cymb.* I desire of you a conduct overland to Milford Haven. 2 S. JOHNSON Travelling together under the conduct of chance. W. GILPIN Under his conduct we climbed the steep.

II 6 Leadership, command, management. LME. 7 The action or manner of carrying on a proceeding, business, etc.; management, handling; the execution of a work of art or literature, etc. LME. 8 Aptitude for leadership; skill in managing affairs; practical address, discretion. *arch.* M16. 9 Manner of conducting oneself; behaviour, esp. in its moral aspect. M16. b A proceeding, a course of conduct. Now *rare* or *obs.* E18.

6 W. ROBERTSON The conduct of these troops was committed to Andrew de Foix. 7 J. REYNOLDS He perfectly understood.. the conduct of the background. T. ARNOLD Those engaged in the conduct of the school. R. V. JONES Those responsible for the conduct of the war. 8 DRYDEN Thus conduct won the prize when courage fail'd. 9 A. POWELL Conduct obnoxious.. in one person may be.. tolerated in another. *disorderly conduct*: see DISORDERLY *a.* 1. b JAS. MILL A conduct which demanded the most serious consideration.

†III See CONDUIT *n.*

Comb.: **conduct book** etc.: for recording a person's offences and punishments; *conduct-money*: see sense 4 above.

conduct /ˈkɒndʌkt/ *n.*[2] LME. [L *conductus* pa. pple of *conducere* hire.] 1 In full *conduct priest*. A hired or salaried chaplain. *obs.* exc. *Hist.* LME. b An Eton College chaplain. E18. †2 A hired workman. L15–M17.

conduct /kənˈdʌkt/ *v.* Pa. t. & pple **conducted**, †**conduct**. Orig. †**conduit**. See also CONDUIT *v.* LME. [(O)Fr. *conduite* pa. pple of *conduire* f. L *conducere* CONDUCE, assim. to L *conductus*: see CONDUCT *n.*[1]] I 1 *v.t.* Lead, guide (*lit.* & *fig.*); escort. LME. b *v.i.* Lead *to*, conduce *to*. M19. 2a *v.t.* Direct, be the commander of (an army, siege, etc.). *arch.* LME. b *v.t.* Manage, carry on (a business, transaction, process, etc.); preside over (a meeting etc.). M17. c *v.t.* & *i.* Act as conductor of (an orchestra, choir, musical performance, etc.). L18. 3a *v.t.* Convey, serve as a channel for (fluids etc.). LME. b *v.t.* & *i.* Transmit (heat, electricity, etc.) by conduction; be a conductor of heat or electricity. M18. †4 *v.t.* = CONDUCE *v.* 2. L15–M16. 5 *v.refl.* Behave oneself in a specified way. E18.

1 P. MORTIMER He conducted me round the factory. **conducted tour**: led by a guide on a fixed itinerary. b R. FIRBANK An elm-lined lane that conducted to the farmyard gates. 2b E. BOWEN She saw him conducting a funeral.. leaning.. over the yawn of the grave to scatter his handful of earth. P. G. WODEHOUSE You can't conduct a delicate negotiation like this over the telephone. D. ADAMS The greatest experiment ever conducted—to find.. the Ultimate Answer of Life, the Universe, and Everything. 3a H. MARTINEAU Air would be conducted into the recesses of the groves.

†II See CONDUIT *v.*

conducting *vbl n.* the action of the vb; *esp.* the directing of an orchestra by a conductor: L15. **conducting** *ppl a.* that conducts; *esp.* = CONDUCTIVE *a.* 2: M17.

conductance /kənˈdʌkt(ə)ns/ *n.* L19. [f. prec. + -ANCE.] The conducting power of an electrical conductor or component, equal (for direct currents) to the reciprocal of resistance.

mutual conductance: see MUTUAL *a.* *specific conductance*: see SPECIFIC *a.*

conductible /kənˈdʌktɪb(ə)l/ *a.* *rare*. M19. [f. CONDUCT *v.* + -IBLE.] Capable of conducting heat etc.; able to be conducted.

conductiˈbility *n.* M19.

conductimetric /kəndʌktɪˈmɛtrɪk/ *a.* M20. [f. CONDUCTIVITY + -METRIC.] *Chem.* = CONDUCTOMETRIC.

conduction /kənˈdʌkʃ(ə)n/ *n.* M16. [(O)Fr., or L *conductio(n-)*, f. *conduct-*: see CONDUCT *n.*[1], -ION.] †1 = CONDUCT *n.*[1] 1. M16–M17. †2 = CONDUCT *n.*[1] 6, 7, 8. M16–M19. 3 Hiring. *obs.* exc. *Rom. Law*. M16. 4 The conveyance *of* fluid through a pipe etc. (usu. w. ref. to natural processes). E17. 5 Transmission (of heat, electricity, etc.) by contact between the particles of matter; the transmission of impulses along nerves. E19.

Comb.: **conduction band** *Physics* an energy band partly filled by electrons, which can move freely and so conduct electricity.

conductitious /kɒndʌkˈtɪʃəs/ *a.* Now *rare* or *obs.* E17. [L *conducticius*, *-tius*, f. *conduct-* pa. ppl stem of *conducere* hire: see -ITIOUS[1]. Cf. CONDUCT *n.*[2]] Hired, for hire.

conductive /kənˈdʌktɪv/ *a.* E16. [f. CONDUCT *v.* + -IVE.] †1 a *gen.* Having the property of conducting or leading (*lit.* & *fig.*). E16–M17. b *spec.* Having the power of conducting heat, electricity, etc.; of, pertaining to, or involving the conduction of heat, electricity, etc. M19. †2 Conducive (*to*). E17–E18.

conductively *adv.* by means of conduction L19.

conductivity /kɒndʌkˈtɪvɪti/ *n.* M19. [f. prec. + -ITY.] *Physics* etc. (A measure of) the property or power of a substance of conducting heat or electricity; conductance per unit volume; the property of tissue of conveying nerve impulses.

ELECTRICAL *conductivity*. *specific conductivity*: see SPECIFIC *a.* *thermal conductivity*: see THERMAL *a.*

Comb.: **conductivity water** water of high purity (and hence extremely low electrical conductivity) used in laboratory measurements of conductivity of solutions.

conductometer /kɒndʌkˈtɒmɪtə/ *n.* L19. [f. CONDUCTIVITY + -OMETER.] An instrument for measuring electrical conductivity.

conductoˈmetric *a.* (*Chem.*) of, pertaining to, or involving the measurement of electrical conductivity, esp. as the means of determining the end-point in titration E20. **conductometry** *n.* E20.

conductor /kənˈdʌktə/ *n.* LME. [OFr. *conduitor*, (also mod.) *conducteur*, f. L *conductor*, f. *conduct-*: see CONDUCT *n.*[1], -OR.] 1 A (military) commander. Long *obs.* exc. *Hist.* LME. 2 A leader, a guide. L15. 3 A person who directs or manages. L16. b The director of an orchestra, choir, etc., who indicates rhythm etc. by gestures made with the hands or a baton. L18. 4 A person who hires; a tenant. *obs.* exc. *Rom. Law*. M17. 5 A thing which conducts or forms a channel for the passage of something; *esp.* a substance or device which conducts heat or electricity (freq. w. specifying wd). M18. 6 An official responsible for collecting fares and general supervision on a bus, tram, etc.; *US* a guard on a train. E19.

5 *bus-conductor*, *tram-conductor*. 6 *bad conductor*, *good conductor*, *non-conductor*, etc. *lightning conductor*: see LIGHTNING *n.* & *a.* SEMICONDUCTOR.

Comb.: **conductor-rail**: transmitting the current to an electric train etc.

conducˈtorial *a.* of, pertaining to, or characteristic of a conductor (esp. of music) M19. **conductorship** *n.* the office or function of (musical) conductor E19.

conductress /kənˈdʌktrɪs/ *n.* E17. [f. prec.: see -ESS[1].] A female conductor (esp. in a bus etc.).

conductus /kənˈdʌktəs/ *n.* Pl. **-ti** /-tʌɪ/. E19. [med.L: see CONDUCT *n.*[1]] *Medieval Mus.* A type of composition of the 12th and 13th cents. with metrical Latin text.

conduit /ˈkɒndɪt, -jʊɪt/ *n.* Also †**conduct**. See also CONDUCT *n.*[1] ME. [Orig. form of CONDUCT *n.*[1]] I 1 A (natural or artificial) channel or pipe for conveying liquids etc. ME. b A tube or trough for protecting insulated wires; a length of this. L19. 2 A fountain. *arch.* ME. 3 *Archit.* A passage, esp. underground. *rare*. E17.

1 W. D. THORNBURY The volcanic plug formed when lava in the conduit of a volcano solidifies. P. MATTHIESSEN Water.. dripping sonorously onto slate conduits that conduct it to a.. caldron. *fig.*: L. TRILLING The family is the conduit of cultural influences. 2 D. G. ROSSETTI The conduits round the garden sing.

†II See CONDUCT *n.*[1]

Comb.: **conduit-pipe** a tubular conduit.

†**conduit** *v.* LME. [Orig. form of CONDUCT *v.* Sense 2 f. prec.] 1 See CONDUCT *v.* LME. 2 *v.t.* Convey (as) through a conduit. LME–E17.

conduplicate /kənˈdjuːplɪkət/ *a.* L18. [L *conduplicatus* pa. pple of *conduplicare*, f. as CON- + DUPLICATE *v.*: see -ATE[2].] *Bot.* Of a leaf: folded lengthwise along the middle.

conduplication /kəndjuːplɪˈkeɪʃ(ə)n/ *n.* Now *rare*. E17. [L *conduplicatio(n-)*, f. as prec.: see -ATION.] A doubling, a repetition.

condurango *n.* var. of CUNDURANGO.

condylarth /ˈkɒndɪlɑːθ/ *n.* L19. [f. *Condylarthra* (see below), f. Gk *kondulus* knuckle, CONDYLE + *arthron* joint.] A member of the order Condylarthra of extinct mammals of the Palaeocene and Eocene periods, the ancestors of some recent ungulates.

condylarthrosis /ˌkɒndɪlɑːˈθrəʊsɪs/ *n.* Pl. **-throses** /-ˈθrəʊsiːz/. M19. [f. next + ARTHROSIS.] *Anat.* (A) condyloid articulation.

condyle /ˈkɒndɪl, -dʌɪl/ *n.* M17. [Fr. f. L *condylus* f. Gk *kondulos* knuckle.] *Anat.* A rounded usu. cartilage-covered process at the end of a bone, articulating with another bone.

OCCIPITAL *condyle*.

condylar *a.* of or pertaining to a condyle L19. **condyloid** *a.* resembling, pertaining to, or (of articulation) involving a condyle M18.

condyloma /kɒndɪˈləʊmə/ *n.* Pl. **-mas, -mata** /-mətə/. LME. [L f. Gk *kondulōma* callous knob or lump, f. *kondulos*: see prec., -OMA.] *Med.* A large papilloma or warty growth of the skin, usu. in the genital region, of viral or syphilitic origin.

condylomatous *a.* of the nature of a condyloma M19.

Condy's fluid /ˈkɒndɪz ˈfluːɪd/ *n. phr.* M19. [Henry Bollmann *Condy*, 19th-cent. Eng. chemical manufacturer.] A strong solution of sodium manganate or permanganate, used as a disinfectant.

cone /kəʊn/ *n.* LME. [Fr. *cône* f. L *conus* f. Gk *kōnos* pine cone, geometrical cone, apex, etc.] **I 1** †**a** An apex, a vertex, an angle. LME–E18. **b** The pointed tip of a helmet etc. E17. **2** A more or less conical reproductive structure found in the conifers and related plants, consisting of overlapping scales; a strobilus. M16. **3** *Math.* A surface or solid figure generated by the straight lines drawn from a fixed point (the vertex) to a circle or other closed curve in a plane not containing the vertex. M16. **4** A cocoon. Now *rare* or *obs.* L18.

3 **oblique** (**circular**) **cone**: in which the vertex does not lie perpendicularly above the centre of the circle. **right** (**circular**) **cone**: in which the vertex lies perpendicularly above the centre of the circle. *scalene cone*: see SCALENE *a.* 1.

II *transf.* f. sense 3. **5** Any object or structure having a shape resembling that of a geometrical cone; a conical mass *of* any substance. L16. **6** In full *cone-shell*. (The conical shell of) a marine gastropod of the family Conidae and esp. of the genus *Conus*. L18. **7** A cone-shaped mountain or peak; *esp.* one of volcanic origin. M19. **8** *Anat.* Any of the cone-shaped red-, green-, or blue-sensitive cells in the retina of the eye which function best in bright light and are essential for acute vision. Cf. ROD *n.* 9b. M19. **9** A black conical object hoisted by coastguards as a gale-warning, the position of the cone conveying information about wind direction etc. M19. **10** = CORNET *n.*[1] 3b. E20. **11** A conical marker used to direct traffic. M20.

5 *null cone*: see NULL *a.* PYROMETRIC *cone*. SEGER *cone*. *Southern Cone*: see SOUTHERN *a.* *Staffordshire cone*: see STAFFORDSHIRE I. 6 *textile cone*: see TEXTILE *a.* I.

Comb.: **coneflower** any of several N. American plants belonging to the genus *Rudbeckia* and related genera of the composite family, having flowers with conelike centres; **cone-in-cone** *Geol.* a structure of concentric cones displayed by some concretions in sedimentary rocks, due to crystallization around an axis; **cone-sheet** *Geol.* a discordant igneous intrusion or dyke (usu. one of a concentric series), having the form of an inverted hollow cone; *cone-shell*: see sense 6 above; **cone wheat** = RIVET *n.*[2]

conelike *a.* resembling (that of) a cone, cone-shaped, conical M17.

cone /kəʊn/ *v.* L15. [f. the n.] **1** *v.t.* Shape like a cone; provide with a cone. Chiefly as *coned* ppl a. L15. **2** *v.i.* Of a tree: bear or produce cones. L19. **3** *v.t.* Concentrate a number of searchlight beams (or streams of tracer shells) upon (an aircraft). M20. **4** *v.t.* Mark or close *off* (an area, esp. of road) with conical markers. L20.

coning *vbl n.* (*a*) the action of the vb; the condition of being coned, esp. (of a wheel) in having a tapering tread; (*b*) the slanting upwards of helicopter rotor blades when in motion: M19.

conessine /kəˈnɛsiːn/ *n.* M19. [f. *Conessi* (see below) + -INE[5].] A bitter alkaloid, $C_{24}H_{40}N_2$, obtained chiefly from the seeds and bark of an Asian tree, *Holarrhena* (formerly *Conessi*) *antidysenterica*, and used to treat amoebic dysentery.

Conestoga /kɒnɪˈstəʊgə/ *n.* & *a.* Pl. **-s**, (in sense 1, also) same. L17. [Prob. f. Iroquoian; in senses 2 & 3 f. *Conestoga*, a town in Pennsylvania.] **1** A member of, of or pertaining to, an Iroquoian Indian people formerly inhabiting parts of Pennsylvania and Maryland. Also called *Susquehannock*. L17. **2** In full *Conestoga wagon*. A large travelling-wagon. *obs.* exc. *Hist.* E18. **3** A heavy breed of horse. Also *Conestoga horse* etc. E19.

coney *n.* see CONY.

confab /ˈkɒnfab/ *n.* & *v.* *colloq.* E18. [Abbrev.] **A** *n.* = CONFABULATION 1. E18. **B** *v.i.* Infl. **-bb-**. = CONFABULATE 1. M18.

confabulate /kənˈfabjʊleɪt/ *v.i.* E17. [L *confabulat-* pa. ppl stem of *confabulari* to converse, f. as CON-, FABLE *v.*: see -ATE[3].] **1** Converse together, chat (*with*). E17. **2** *Psychiatry.* Fabricate imaginary experiences as a compensation for loss of memory. E20.

confabulator *n.* a person who confabulates M17.

confabulatory *a.* of confabulation; chatty, colloquial: M17.

confabulation /kənfabjʊˈleɪʃ(ə)n/ *n.* LME. [L *confabulatio(n-)*, f. as prec.: see -ATION.] **1** Talking together, conversation, chat; a familiar conversation. LME. **2** *Psychiatry.* The invention of imaginary experiences to fill gaps in memory; an account so fabricated. E20.

1 M. KEANE Delicious confabulations with her sisters on the endless subject of clothes. P. L. FERMOR After some whispered confabulation, they decided to have pity on me.

confarreation /kənfarɪˈeɪʃ(ə)n/ *n.* L16. [L *confarreatio(n-)*, f. *confarreat-* pa. ppl stem of *confarreare* unite in marriage by offering bread, f. as CON- + *farreum* spelt-cake: see -ATION.] *Rom. Hist.* The highest and most solemn form of marriage among the patricians of ancient Rome, made by offering a cake made of spelt in the presence of the Pontifex Maximus or Flamen Dialis and ten witnesses. Cf. DIFFARREATION.

confect /ˈkɒnfɛkt/ *n.* E16. [med.L *confectum*, *-ta* use as n. of pa. pple of *conficere*: see next. Cf. COMFIT.] A confection, a comfit.

confect /kənˈfɛkt/ *v.t.* Now chiefly *literary.* LME. [L *confect-* pa. ppl stem of *conficere* put together, f. as CON- + *facere* make.] **1** Put together from various ingredients, make up. LME. **2** Make into a confection; prepare (food). Now *rare* or *obs.* LME.

1 BACON The Confecting of the Ointment. D. ATTENBOROUGH Faked monsters . . confected in the Far East from bits and pieces of dissimilar creatures and . . sold to gullible travellers.

confection /kənˈfɛkʃ(ə)n/ *n.* ME. [(O)Fr. f. L *confectio(n-)* preparation, f. as prec.: see -ION.] **1** A preparation made by mixing; *esp.* a medicinal preparation of various drugs (often with a sweetening and preserving agent). Now *rare* or *obs.* exc. as below. ME. **b** A prepared dish or delicacy; *esp.* a sweet preparation of fruit, spices, sugar, chocolate, etc. Also *fig.*, a light and pleasing piece of music, literature, etc. LME. †**c** A deadly potion. L15–M17. **2** Making or preparation by mixture of ingredients; mixing, compounding; the making of preserves or confectionery. LME. †**3** State of preparation; composition, constitution. LME–L17. **4** A fashionable article of women's dress. (Orig. a Gallicism.) L19.

1b *fig.*: J. CAREY He knew he could manufacture the high-souled confection that his readers wanted. 2 THACKERAY Pots of jam of her confection. 4 G. HEYER A dazzling confection with a high crown, a huge, upstanding poke-front, pomona green ribbons, and . . ostrich plumes.

confection /kənˈfɛkʃ(ə)n/ *v.t.* M16. [f. the n.: cf. Fr. *confectionner*.] **1** Make into a confection; make up as a seasoned delicacy etc. M16. **2** Put together (a fashionable article of clothing). (Orig. a Gallicism.) M19.

confectionary /kənˈfɛkʃ(ə)n(ə)ri/ *n.* & *a.* L16. [f. CONFECTION *n.* + -ARY[1]. Cf. med.L *confectionarius* a maker of confectionery, apothecary.] **A** *n.* **1** A confection, a sweet delicacy, a comfit. L16. †**2** A maker of confections. E–M17. **3** A place where confections are kept or prepared. E17. **4** The art or business of a confectioner, = CONFECTIONERY 2. M18. **B** *adj.* Of the nature of a confection; of or pertaining to confections or confectionery. M17.

confectioner /kənˈfɛkʃ(ə)nə/ *n.* L16. [f. CONFECTION *v.* + -ER[1].] A maker of confections, cakes, chocolates, pastries, etc., now esp. for public sale.

confectionery /kənˈfɛkʃ(ə)n(ə)ri/ *n.* M18. [f. prec. + -Y[3]: see -ERY.] **1** A thing, *collect.* things, made or sold by a confectioner. M18. **2** The art or business of a confectioner (cf. CONFECTIONARY *n.* 4); a confectioner's shop. E19.

†**confeder** *v.t.* & *i.* LME–E17. [(O)Fr. *confédérer* f. L *confoederare*: see CONFEDERATION.] = CONFEDERATE *v.*

confederacy /kənˈfɛd(ə)rəsi/ *n.* LME. [AN, OFr. *confederacie*, f. stem of *confederer*, *confederacion*: see CONFEDERATION, -ACY.] **1** A union between persons, groups, States, etc., for mutual support or joint action; a league, an alliance. LME. **b** A league etc. for an unlawful purpose; a conspiracy. LME. **2** The condition or fact of being confederate; union for joint action; conspiracy. LME. **3** A collective body of people, groups, etc., united by league; *esp.* a union of States, a confederation. L17.

1 W. ROBERTSON A general confederacy against the Ottoman power. 2 V. SACKVILLE-WEST They looked at each other with a glance of confederacy. 3 W. IRVING The literary world is made up of little confederacies.

confederal /kənˈfɛd(ə)r(ə)l/ *a.* L18. [f. CONFEDERATION after *federal*.] Pertaining to a confederation, *spec.* (*US Hist.*) to the early organization of the US under the Articles of Confederation of 1781.

confederate /kənˈfɛd(ə)rət/ *a.* & *n.* LME. [Late (eccl.) L *confoederatus*, f. as CON- + FEDERATE *a.*] **A** *adj.* **1** Allied; united in a confederacy. LME. **2** *Hist.* (**C-**.) Designating, of, or pertaining to the eleven Southern States of the US that seceded from the Union 1861–65. M19. **B** *n.* **1** A person confederated with another or others; an ally; a conspirator, an accomplice. L15. **2** *Hist.* (**C-**.) A person belonging to or supporting the Confederate States of America. M19.

confederate /kənˈfɛdəreɪt/ *v.t.* & *i.* M16. [Prob. f. prec.: see -ATE[3].] Bring, form, or come into a league, alliance, confederacy, or conspiracy (*with*).

confederator *n.* (now *rare* or *obs.*) [AN *confederatour*] a confederate, a conspirator LME.

confederation /kənfɛdəˈreɪʃ(ə)n/ *n.* LME. [OFr. *confederacion* (mod. *-tion*) or late L *confederatio(n-)*, f. L *confederat-* pa. ppl stem of *confoederare*, f. as CON- + *foederare* league together, f. *foedus*, *foeder-* league, treaty.] **1** The action of confederating; the condition of being confederated: union (esp. of States) for mutual support or joint action; a league, an alliance. LME. **2** A number of parties united in an alliance or league; *esp.* a body of States joined in more or less permanent union. E17.

Phrases: **articles of confederation** provisions by which parties confederate; *spec.* (*US Hist.*) those adopted by the thirteen original colonies at the Continental Congress of 1777.

confederative /kənˈfɛd(ə)rətɪv/ *a.* E19. [Fr. *confédératif*, *-ive*, f. *confédération*: see prec., -IVE.] Of or relating to confederates or confederating.

confer /kənˈfəː/ *v.* Infl. **-rr-**. LME. [L *conferre*, f. as CON- + *ferre* bring.] †**1** *v.t.* Bring together, gather, collect. LME–E17. **2** *v.i.* Converse, hold conference, take counsel, (*with*). LME. †**b** *v.t.* Discuss. M16–L17. †**3** *v.i.* Contribute (*unto*, *to*). E16–E18. †**4** *v.t.* Bring into comparison (*with*). E16–M18. **5** *v.t.* Give, grant, or bestow (a title, degree, favour, etc.). (Foll. by *on*, *upon*, †*to*, †*unto*.) M16.

4 SHAKES. *Temp.* Confer fair Milan With all the honours on my brother. H. JAMES The character conferred on the scene by a cold spring rain. R. SCRUTON The Rent Acts confer powers to interfere in contractual bargaining.

conferˈee *n.* a participant in a conference; the recipient of a grant, honour, etc.: L18. **conferment** *n.* the action of granting or bestowing M17. **conferrable** *a.* that may be conferred M17. **conferrer** *n.* M16.

conference /ˈkɒnf(ə)r(ə)ns/ *n.* & *v.* E16. [Fr. *conférence*, or med.L *conferentia*, f. as prec. + -ENCE.] **A** *n.* **1** Orig., conversation, talk. Now, the action of conversing or taking counsel on serious or important matters. E16. **b** (The facility for) telephonic conversation among more than two people on separate lines. Usu. *attrib.* M20. †**2** Bringing together, collection; collation, comparison. M16–M17. **3** A formal (esp. annual) meeting held by any organization, association, etc., for consultation and discussion. L16. **4** (**C-**.) (The annual assembly of) the central governing body of the Methodist Church or of some other religious groups. M18. **5** = CONFERRENCE. M19. **6** An association in commerce (esp. of shipping companies) etc.; an association of sports teams or athletic clubs which usually play each other. L19. **7** (Usu. **C-**.) A late variety of pear with a flecked dark green skin. L19.

1 SHAKES. *Jul. Caes.* Nor with such free and friendly conference As . . of old. S. LEWIS There was a conference of four union officials as to whether the . . coal-miners . . should strike. **in conference** engaged in consultation, at a meeting. **news conference, press conference** an interview given to journalists by a person or persons in order to make an announcement or answer questions. 3 *Lambeth Conference*: see LAMBETH 1.

Comb.: **conference centre** a building or complex for the holding of conferences; a place where a conference is held.

B *v.i.* Confer; hold or attend a conference. Freq. as *conferencing* vbl n. M19.

conférencier /kɔ̃ferɑ̃sje/ *n.* Pl. pronounced same. L19. [Fr.] A lecturer, a public speaker; a (leading) member of a conference; a compère.

conferential /kɒnfəˈrɛnʃ(ə)l/ *a.* M19. [f. med.L *conferentia*: see CONFERENCE, -AL[1].] Of or relating to (a) conference.

conferral /kənˈfəːr(ə)l/ *n.* Chiefly *US.* L19. [f. as next + -AL[1].] Conferment, conferrence.

conferrence /kənˈfəːr(ə)ns/ *n.* L19. [f. CONFER + -ENCE.] Conferment, bestowal, (esp. of degrees). Cf. CONFERENCE 5.

conferva /kənˈfəːvə/ *n. obs.* exc. *Hist.* Pl. **-vae** /-viː/. M18. [L, perh. = comfrey.] *Bot.* Any of a large group of filamentous cryptogams, esp. simple freshwater green algae, formerly constituting a heterogeneous and variously-defined genus *Conferva*.

confess /kənˈfɛs/ *v.* LME. [OFr. *confesser* f. Proto-Romance, f. L *confessus* pa. pple of *confiteri* acknowledge, f. as CON- + *fateri* declare, avow.] 1 *v.t.* Acknowledge; declare, disclose, (a secret, one's sins, esp. to a priest); admit (a crime, fault, weakness, etc.); concede, grant. Foll. by simple obj., *that*, a person or thing *to be*, †*to have done*, oneself to be. LME. 2 *v.t.* Acknowledge one's belief in, *that*; acknowledge the character or claims of; admit as legally valid. LME. 3 *v.refl.* & *i.* Make a formal confession of one's sins, esp. to a priest. LME. 4 *v.t.* Of a priest etc.: hear the confession of, act as confessor to. LME. 5 *v.t.* Make known by circumstances; be evidence of; attest. Now *poet.* L16. 6 *v.i.* Admit the truth of a (criminal) charge. L16. 7 *v.i.* Foll. by *to*: admit, acknowledge, (a charge, fault, weakness, etc.). L18.

1 SHAKES. *Per.* I here confess myself the King of Tyre. E. PEACOCK A distorted knowledge, it must be confessed, of religious duty. J. STEINBECK It would be interesting to know what sins she confessed. G. F. KENNAN Instead . . of confessing their real plight, they made efforts to conceal it. N. MAILER I must confess that this conversation bores me. M. BRADBURY They confessed things to each other. 2 WYCLIF My soule magnefieþ þe Lord, for I confesse þat he is greet. *Alternative Service Book* Grant that we . . who confess thy name may be united in thy truth. 3 *Book of Common Prayer* Bewail your own sinful lives, confess yourselves to Almighty God with full purpose of amendment of life. SHAKES. *Rom. & Jul.* Come you to make confession to this Father? . . To answer that, I should confess to you. 5 SIR W. SCOTT Even . . Magnus himself had confessed the influence of the sleepy god. 7 SOUTHEY I confess to having made free with his tail and his hoofs and his horns. G. B. SHAW A young fellow who is manly enough to confess to an obvious disadvantage.

confessant *n.* a person who confesses or makes a confession, esp. as a religious duty E17. **confessedly** /-sɪdli/ *adv.* admittedly; avowedly: M17. **confe'ssee** *n.* a person who is confessed by a priest; the priest to whom a person confesses: E17.

confessio /kənˈfɛsɪəʊ/ *n.* Pl. **-os.** M19. [med.L *confessio(n-)* CONFESSION.] = CONFESSION 8.

confession /kənˈfɛʃ(ə)n/ *n.* LME. [(O)Fr. f. L *confessio(n-)*, f. *confess-* pa. ppl stem of *confiteri* CONFESS *v.*: see -ION.] 1 The making known or acknowledging of one's own fault, offence, etc.; acknowledgement before proper authority of the truth of a criminal charge. LME. 2 The acknowledging of sin or sinfulness with repentance and desire of absolution, either as a formal public religious act or privately to a priest as a religious duty. LME. 3 Concession of the truth of a statement, agreement. Now *rare* or *obs.* LME. 4 The declaration of a belief; avowal, profession (of faith etc.). LME. 5 That which is confessed; the matter confessed; *esp.* a statement of one's guilt in a crime etc. LME. 6 That part of the public litany of most Christian Churches in which a general acknowledgement of sinfulness is made. LME. 7 In full *confession of faith.* A statement setting out essential religious doctrine, a creed; a statement of one's principles in any matter. M16. b The body of people sharing a confession of faith. M17. 8 A tomb in which a martyr etc. is buried, the whole structure erected over such a tomb; a part of, or the crypt or shrine under, the altar in which relics are placed. L17.

confessionary *n.* †(*a*) = CONFESSIONAL *n.* 2; (*b*) = CONFESSION 8: M17. **confessionary** *a.* of or pertaining to confession E17. **confessionist** *n.* an adherent of a particular religious confession or sect M16. **confessionless** *a.* without a confession; faithless: L19.

confessional /kənˈfɛʃ(ə)n(ə)l/ *n.* L16. [Fr. f. It. *confessionale* f. med.L *confessionale* neut. sing. of adj. *confessionalis*, f. *confessio(n-)*: see prec., -AL[1].] †1 A payment for hearing or giving permission to hear confession. Only in L16. 2 A stall, desk, etc., where a priest (usu. of the Roman Catholic Church) hears confessions. E18. b The act or practice of confessing to a priest. E19.

confessional /kənˈfɛʃ(ə)n(ə)l/ *a.* LME. [f. CONFESSION + -AL[1].] 1 Of the nature of or pertaining to confession. LME. 2 Of or pertaining to confessions of faith or doctrinal systems; denominational; holding or according with certain doctrines or beliefs. L19.

confessor /kənˈfɛsə, *in sense 3 also* ˈkɒnfɛsə/ *n.* OE. [AN *confessur*, OFr. *confessour* (mod. *-eur*) f. eccl.L *confessor*, f. *confess-*: see CONFESSION, -OR.] 1 A person avowing his religion in the face of danger, and adhering to it despite persecution, but not suffering martyrdom. OE. 2 A person who makes confession or public acknowledgement of religious belief etc., or (later) of a crime, sin, etc. ME. 3 A priest who hears confessions. ME.

1 **(Edward) the Confessor** Edward, King of England 1042–66, canonized in 1161.

confe'ssorial *a.* of or pertaining to a confessor M19. **confessorship** *n.* the function or office of confessor M17.

confetti /kənˈfɛti/ *n.* (orig. *pl.* but now usu. treated as *sing.*). E19. [It., pl. of *confetto* COMFIT.] Coloured paper shapes showered on the bride and bridegroom by the guests at a wedding. In Italy (the earlier sense), real or imitation bonbons thrown during carnival etc.

confidant /kɒnfɪˈdant, ˈkɒnfɪdant/ *n.* Fem. & in sense 2 **-ante**. M17. [Alt. of CONFIDENT *n.*, prob. to repr. pronunc. of Fr. *confidente*: see CONFIDENT, -ANT[1].] 1 A person entrusted with knowledge of one's private affairs (orig. esp. one's love affairs) or thoughts. M17. 2 A type of settee usu. with seats at each end separated from the main seat by upholstered divisions. Also, a sociable. L18.

confide /kənˈfʌɪd/ *v.* LME. [L *confidere*, f. as CON- + *fidere* trust.] 1 *v.i.* Trust or have faith; place trust or confidence *in*. LME. 2 *v.i.* & *t.* Trust, believe, have confidence, (*that*). *arch.* L15. 3 *v.t.* Impart as a secret or in confidence *to* (now also *in*) a person; entrust (an object of care, a task, etc.) *to*. M18. 4 *v.i.* Foll. by *in*: take (a person) into one's confidence, talk confidentially to. L19.

1 HOBBES Some other whom they confide in for protection. 2 T. JEFFERSON They confide that the next election gives a decided majority in the two Houses. 3 E. M. FORSTER He was confiding secrets to people whom he had scarcely seen. J. REED One confided to me . . that the counter-revolution would begin at midnight. J. W. KRUTCH He must . . confide his destiny to the whims of developing technology. A. HALEY To confide in his mother something he had kept carefully guarded from anyone. 4 S. BELLOW We no longer confide in each other; in fact, there are many things I could not mention to her.

confider *n.* M17. **confiding** *a.* †(*a*) trusty, trustworthy; (*b*) trustful; imparting or inclined to impart confidences: M17. **confidingly** *adv.* L19. **confidingness** *n.* L17.

confidence /ˈkɒnfɪd(ə)ns/ *n.* & *v.* LME. [L *confidentia*, f. *confident-* pres. ppl stem of *confidere* CONFIDE: see -ENCE. Cf. (O)Fr. *confidence.*] **A** *n.* 1 Firm trust, reliance, faith (*in*). LME. 2 Assurance arising from reliance on oneself, circumstances, etc.; self-reliance, boldness. LME. b Excessive assurance; presumption, impudence. *arch.* L16. 3 A source of trust. *arch.* LME. 4 Assured expectation; the state of feeling certain (*of*). M16. 5 The confiding of private matters with mutual trust; confidential intimacy. L16. †6 Trustworthiness. M17–E19. 7 A confidential communication. M18.

1 SHAKES. *Rich. II* The King reposeth all his confidence in thee. H. JAMES She had but a limited confidence in her brother's judgement. *level of confidence*: see LEVEL *n.* 4d. *vote of confidence, vote of no confidence*: see VOTE *n.* 2 S. JOHNSON He . . was able to address those whom he never saw before with ease and confidence. M. DRABBLE The dress gave me a certain superficial confidence. D. ADAMS Feeling that he was the most important person in the Universe gave him the confidence to believe that something would turn up. b S. PEPYS Willetts confidence in sitting cheek by jowl by us. 3 AV *Prov.* 3:26 For the Lord shalbe thy confidence. 4 W. TEMPLE The very Confidence of Victory . . makes Armies victorious. 5 **in confidence** confidentially, as a secret. **in the confidence of** allowed to know the private thoughts or affairs of. **take into one's confidence** confide in. 6 **person of confidence** a confidential agent. 7 B. CASTLE Elizabeth tends to make a lot of confidences at these times.

Comb.: **confidence coefficient** *Statistics* the particular probability used in defining a confidence interval, representing the likelihood that the interval will contain the parameter; **confidence game** *US* = *confidence trick* below; **confidence interval** *Statistics* a range of values so defined that there is a specified probability that the value of a parameter of a population lies within it; **confidence level** = *confidence coefficient* above; **confidence limit** *Statistics* either of the extreme values of a confidence interval; **confidence man**: who practises a confidence trick; **confidence trick** a swindle in which the victim is persuaded to entrust money or valuables to the swindler; **confidence trickster** a person who practises a confidence trick.

B *v.t.* Swindle by means of a confidence trick. *US slang.* L19.

Also **confidency** *n.* (*rare*) E17.

confident /ˈkɒnfɪd(ə)nt/ *a.* & *n.* L16. [In sense 1 f. L *confident-* (see prec.); in later senses and as n. f. Fr. *confident(e)* f. It. *confidente* f. L.] **A** *adj.* †1 Trustful, confiding. L16–M17. 2 Having firm trust or expectation; fully assured, certain. (Foll. by *of, in, that*). L16. 3 Self-reliant, bold; sure of oneself, one's course, etc.; having no fear of failure. L16. b Overbold; presumptuous, impudent. *arch.* L16. c Assertive; dogmatic. E17. †4 Trustworthy, dependable. E17–E18. 5 Confidential, entrusted with secrets. Now *rare* or *obs.* E17.

2 SHAKES. *Cymb.* Confident I am Last night 'twas on mine arm. G. VIDAL My father died, confident that death did not exist. 3 S. JOHNSON His accusers were confident and loud. N. ALGREN He left with a confident, executive stride, a man who'd be rich in six weeks if not in five. b H. FIELDING A confident slut. c G. BERKELEY Your confident and positive way of talking.

B *n.* A person in whom another confides; a confidant. E17.

confidently *adv.* L16.

confidential /kɒnfɪˈdɛnʃ(ə)l/ *a.* M17. [f. prec. + -IAL, infl. by CONFIDENCE.] †1 Confident, bold. *rare.* M–L17. 2 Indicating private intimacy; inclined to impart confidences, confiding. M18. 3 Spoken or written in confidence; not intended for public knowledge. L18. 4 Enjoying another's confidence; entrusted with secrets; charged with a secret task. E19.

confidenti'ality *n.* M19. **confidentially** *adv.* in a confidential manner; as a confidence: L17. **confidentialness** *n.* L19.

configurate /kənˈfɪgjʊreɪt/ *v.t.* Now *rare.* M16. [L *configurat-* pa. ppl stem of *configurare*: see CONFIGURE, -ATE[3].] Frame; give a configuration to.

configurative /-rətɪv/ *a.* of or pertaining to configuration L18.

configuration /kənfɪɡəˈreɪʃ(ə)n, -ɡjʊ-/ *n.* M16. [L *configuratio(n-)*, f. as prec.: see -ATION. Cf. (O)Fr. *configuration.*] 1 *Astron.* & *Astrol.* Relative position, apparent or actual, of celestial objects; *esp.* = ASPECT *n.* 4. M16. 2 *gen.* The (result of) arrangement of the parts or elements of something; internal structure, conformation, outline. M17. 3 *Chem.* The fixed three-dimensional relationship of the atoms in a molecule. L19. 4 *Physics.* The distribution of electrons among the energy levels of an atom, or of nucleons among the energy levels of a nucleus, as specified by quantum numbers. E20. 5 *Psychol.* = GESTALT. E20. 6 *Computing.* The configuring of (the constituent parts of) a computer system; the way the constituent parts of a computer system are configured, the units or devices required for this. M20.

configurational *a.* E20. **configurationally** *adv.* E20. **configurationism** *n.* a theory that stresses configurations, *esp.* gestalt psychology E20.

configure /kənˈfɪɡə/ *v.t.* LME. [L *configurare* fashion after a pattern, f. as CON- + *figurare* FIGURE *v.*] 1 Fashion according *to* a model (esp. w. allus. to *Phil.* 3:10). Now *rare.* LME. 2 Put together in a certain configuration; shape, fashion. M17. 3 *spec. Computing.* Interconnect or interrelate (a computer system or elements of it) so as to fit it for a designated task. M20.

confine /ˈkɒnfʌɪn, *poet. also* kɒnˈfʌɪn/ *n.* LME. [Fr. *confins*, †*confines*, f. L *confinia* pl. of *confine* and *confinium*, f. *confinis* bordering, f. as CON- + *finis* end, limit (pl. *fines* territory). Branch II f. L *confinis* n. f. adj.] I 1 A boundary, a frontier, a limit, a borderland, (*lit.* & *fig.*). Usu. in *pl.* LME. †2 A region, a territory. Usu. in *pl.* LME–L17. 3 Confinement, limitation. *poet.* L16. b A place of confinement. Now *rare.* E17.

1 R. L. STEVENSON That .. sort of tragedy which lies on the confines of farce. P. S. BUCK His heart swelled and stopped as though it met sudden confines. B. LOVELL Star systems .. outside the confines of the Milky Way. 3 R. BURNS Think on the dungeon's grim confine.

†II 4 In *pl.* Neighbours. M–L16.

confineless *a.* (*rare*) unlimited E17.

confine /kənˈfʌɪn/ *v.* E16. [Fr. *confiner*, f. as prec., prob. after It. *confinare.*] 1 a *v.i.* Have a common boundary *with*; border *on*, be adjacent *to*. Now *rare.* E16. †b *v.t.* Border on. Only in 17. †2 *v.t.* Banish. L16–M17. 3 *v.t.* Keep *in* a place, *within* or *to* limits or a defined area; restrict, secure. (*lit.* & *fig.*) L16. b Shut up, imprison (*in*, †*into*). E17. 4 *v.t.* Oblige (a person) to remain indoors, in bed, etc., through illness, bad weather, etc. (Foll. by *to.*) Usu. in *pass.* M17. b In *pass.* Be in childbirth. L18.

3 B. T. WASHINGTON He .. had to confine himself to the deck of the ship. W. S. CHURCHILL In the Middle Ages education had largely been confined to training the clergy. J. UPDIKE Border patrols have been instituted to confine the nomads. b SHAKES. *Temp.* She did confine thee .. Into a cloven pine. C. S. FORESTER It is here that the slaves were confined during the middle passage. 4 G. BERKELEY I have been confined three weeks by gout. P. BARKER Gradually .. her health got worse, until she was confined to the house and almost bedridden.

confinable *a.* able to be confined (earlier in UNCONFINABLE) E17. **confined** *a.* that has been confined; (of a space) cramped, restricted: L16. **confinedly** /-nɪdli/ *adv.* (earlier in UNCONFINEDLY) L17. **confinedness** /-nɪdnɪs/ *n.* M17.

confinement /kənˈfʌɪnm(ə)nt/ *n.* M17. [f. prec. + -MENT.] 1 The action of confining; the state or condition of being confined; imprisonment; restriction, limitation. M17. 2 The condition of being in childbirth; delivery, *accouchement.* L18.

1 *solitary confinement*: see SOLITARY *a.*

confiner /kənˈfʌɪnə/ *n.* L16. [f. CONFINE *n.* or *v.* + -ER[1].] †1 A borderer, a neighbour. L16–L17. †2 An inhabitant. L16–E17. 3 A person who or thing which confines. *rare.* M17.

confinity /kənˈfɪnɪti/ *n.* Now *rare.* M16. [(O)Fr. *confinité* or med.L *confinitas*, f. *confinis*: see CONFINE *n.*, -ITY.] The position of bordering, contiguity.

confirm /kənˈfəːm/ *v.t.* ME. [OFr. *confermer* (later *confirmer*) f. L *confirmare*, f. as CON- + *firmare* strengthen, f. *firmus* FIRM *a.*] 1 Make firm or firmer; establish (power, possession, etc.) more firmly, settle. ME. 2 Make valid by formal assent; ratify, sanction; ratify the appointment etc. of (a person) *to* or *in* a position etc.; ratify the bestowal etc. of (a dignity, estate, etc.) *to* a person. ME. 3 Administer the religious rite of confirmation to. ME. 4 Strengthen, establish, encourage (a person) *in* a habit, opinion, disposition, etc. Also *absol.* (now *rare*), strengthen morally or (formerly) physically. ME. 5 Corroborate, verify, put beyond doubt. LME. †6 Affirm, maintain *that.* LME–M17. †7 Assure, convince. E17–L18.

1 SHAKES. *1 Hen. VI* His alliance will confirm our peace. 2 R. HOLINSHED He was confirmed bishop of Couentrie. SHAKES. *3 Hen. VI* Confirm the crown to me and to mine heirs. GIBBON This modest sentence was confirmed by the emperor. 4 BYRON To laugh him out of his supposed dismay .. Perhaps .. to confirm him in it. b J. RUSKIN Men .. whose hearts [were] confirmed, in the calm of these holy places. 5 E. M. FORSTER Inside, the clock struck ten. .. Other clocks confirmed it. A. KOESTLER This suspicion is confirmed by the inquiry. B. BAINBRIDGE Before Adolf could confirm or deny that he had any such problem. 7 J. FLETCHER We are all confirm'd 'twas a sought quarrel.

confirmaˈbility *n.* (*Philos.*) the quality or condition of being confirmable M20. **confirmable** *a.* able to be confirmed M17. **confirˈmand** *n.* a candidate for (religious) confirmation M18. **confirmatory** *a.* tending to confirm; confirmative: M17. **confirmed** *a.* that has been confirmed; firmly established, permanent, unlikely to change, inveterate: LME. **confirˈmee** *n.* (*a*) *Law* a person to whom a confirmation is made; (*b*) *Eccl.* a person who is confirmed: E17. **confirmer** *n.* a person who or thing which confirms L16. **confirmor** *n.* (*Law*) a party who confirms a voidable estate etc. E17.

confirmation /kɒnfəˈmeɪʃ(ə)n/ *n.* ME. [(O)Fr. f. L *confirmatio(n-)*, f. *confirmat-* pa. ppl stem of *confirmare*: see prec., -ATION.] 1 A rite administered to baptized persons, esp. at the age of discretion to admit to full membership in various Christian Churches. In Judaism, the ceremony of *bar mitzvah* or *bat mitzvah*. ME. 2 The formal act of ratifying an appointment, election, decision, etc. ME. 3 The action of making (more) firm; establishing, settling. LME. 4 The action of corroborating or verifying; proof; a confirmatory statement or circumstance. LME. 5 *Law.* An act by a person ratifying a voidable estate. L15. b *Sc. Law.* A ratification of the testamentary appointment of an executor, or the first appointment for a case of intestacy, by court order. L15.

Comb.: **confirmation theory** inductive logic.

confirmative /kənˈfəːmətɪv/ *n.* & *a.* L16. [L *confirmativus* adj., f. *confirmat-*: see prec., -IVE.] †A *n.* A thing that expresses confirmation. Only in L16. B *adj.* Having the property of confirming. M17.

confirmatively *adv.* M19.

confiscate /ˈkɒnfɪskeɪt/ *v.t.* Pa. pple & ppl a. **-ated**, (*arch.*) **-ate** /-ət/. M16. [L *confiscat-* pa. ppl stem of *confiscare*, f. as CON- + *fiscus* chest, treasury: see -ATE[3].] 1 Appropriate to the public treasury (as a penalty); adjudge to be forfeited to the State. M16. 2 Deprive of property as forfeited to the State. *arch.* E17. 3 Seize as by authority or summarily. E19.

3 A. MCCOWEN When he discovered me reading Dostoievsky .. he turned white and confiscated the book.

conˈfiscable *a.* liable to confiscation M18. **confiˈscatable** *a.* M19. **confiscator** *n.* a person who confiscates M18. **confiscatory** /kɒnˈfɪskət(ə)ri/ *a.* of the nature of or tending to confiscation L18.

confiscation /kɒnfɪˈskeɪʃ(ə)n/ *n.* L15. [L *confiscatio(n-)*, f. as prec.: see -ATION.] 1 The action of CONFISCATE *v.*; seizure (of property) as legally forfeited, summary appropriation. L15. b Unjust seizure; robbery under legal sanction. M19. 2 Confiscated property. *rare.* L18.

†**confisk** *v.t.* LME–E17. [OFr. *confisquer* f. L *confiscare*: see CONFISCATE.] = CONFISCATE.

confitent /ˈkɒnfɪt(ə)nt/ *n.* E17. [L *confitent-* pres. ppl stem of *confiteri*: see CONFESS, -ENT.] A person who confesses; a penitent.

Confiteor /kɒnˈfɪtɪɔː/ *n.* ME. [L = I confess, first wd of the formula *Confiteor Deo Omnipotenti* I confess to Almighty God, etc.] *RC Ch.* A form of prayer confessing sins, used in the Mass and some other sacraments.

confiture /ˈkɒnfɪtjʊə; *foreign* kɔ̃fityːr (*pl. same*)/ *n.* Also †**comf-**. LME. [(O)Fr., f. *confit*: see COMFIT, -URE. Readopted in 19 from mod.Fr.] †1 A preparation of drugs. *rare.* Only in LME. 2 A preparation of preserved fruit etc.; a confection. M16.

confix /kənˈfɪks/ *v.t.* E17. [f. CON- + FIX *v.*] Fix firmly, fasten.

conflab /ˈkɒnflab/ *n. colloq.* (chiefly *US*). L19. [Alt.] = CONFAB *n.*

conflagrate /ˈkɒnfləɡreɪt/ *v.* M17. [L *conflagrat-* pa. ppl stem of *conflagrare* burn up, f. as CON- + *flagrare* blaze: see -ATE[3].] 1 *v.i.* Catch fire. M17. 2 *v.t.* Set ablaze; burn up. L18.

conflagrant /kənˈfleɪɡr(ə)nt/ *a.* on fire, blazing M17. **conflagrator** *n.* an incendiary (person) M17.

conflagration /kɒnfləˈɡreɪʃ(ə)n/ *n.* L15. [L *conflagratio(n-)*, f. as prec.: see -ATION.] 1 The burning up *of* anything; consumption by fire. L15. 2 A great and destructive fire. M17. †3 *transf.* Severe inflammation; (a) high fever. L17–E19.

1 HOBBES The day of Judgment, and Conflagration of the present world. 2 P. ACKROYD Warehouse after warehouse going up in the general conflagration.

ˈ**conflagrative** *a.* productive of conflagration E19.

conflate /ˈkɒnfleɪt/ *a.* L16. [L *conflatus* pa. pple, f. as next: see -ATE[2].] Put together from various elements. Now *spec.* formed by fusion of two textual readings.

conflate /kənˈfleɪt/ *v.t.* LME. [L *conflat-* pa. ppl stem of *conflare* kindle, achieve, fuse, f. as CON- + *flare* blow.] †1 Fuse, melt down (metal). LME–M17. 2 Put together; compose; bring about. E17. 3 Combine, blend (two things, esp. two variant texts etc.) into one. L19.

2 D. PIPER Attempts .. to conflate an ideal poet, with Pope's image dominant. 3 A. H. MCNEILE The custom of the former [Matthew] was to conflate the language of his sources when they overlapped.

conflation /kənˈfleɪʃ(ə)n/ *n.* LME. [Late L *conflatio(n-)* fanning (of fire), fusion, f. as prec.: see -ATION.] The action or process of CONFLATE *v.*; the result of conflating, *esp.* a composite textual reading.

conflict /ˈkɒnflɪkt/ *n.* LME. [L *conflictus*, f. *conflict-* pa. ppl stem of *confligere* strike together, clash, contend, fight, f. as CON- + *fligere* strike.] 1 A fight, a battle, a (prolonged) struggle between opposing forces (*lit.* & *fig.*); fighting, strife; the clashing or variance of opposed principles, beliefs, etc.; *Psychol.* (the emotional distress due to) the opposition of incompatible wishes etc. in a person. LME. 2 Collision (of physical bodies), dashing together. Now *rare.* M16.

1 W. S. CHURCHILL At every point .. the opposing causes came into conflict. JOHN BROOKE The conflict between successive generations is part of the law of life. F. FITZGERALD Many Americans persisted in thinking of the Vietnamese conflict as a civil war. D. HALBERSTAM He felt a powerful conflict of loyalties and interests.

conflictful *a.* M20. **conflictual** /kənˈflɪktʃʊəl/ *a.* pertaining to, characterized by, or involving conflict M20.

conflict /kənˈflɪkt/ *v.* LME. [L *conflict-*: see prec.] 1 *v.i.* Fight, struggle (*with*). *lit.* & *fig.* LME. †2 *v.t.* Engage in battle, assault; *fig.* buffet with adversity. L16–M17. 3 *v.i.* Of principles, interests, etc.: clash; be incompatible. M17.

1 W. COWPER These Two with Hector and his host Conflicted. 3 T. H. GREEN The perplexities of conscience .. in which duties appear to conflict with each other. H. MOORE Many other artists have had the same two conflicting sides in their natures.

confliction *n.* the action or condition of conflicting L17. **conflictive** *a.* (*rare*) of a conflicting nature or tendency M19.

conflow /kɒnˈfləʊ/ *v.i.* E17. [f. CON- + FLOW *v.*] Flow together (*with*).

confluence /ˈkɒnflʊəns/ *n.* LME. [Late L *confluentia*, f. as next: see -ENCE.] 1 a A flowing together or union of rivers etc. LME. b The place where two or more rivers etc. unite. M16. c A combined flow or flood. E17. 2a A gathering together or flocking of people etc. LME. b A numerous concourse or assemblage of people etc.; a multitude. LME.

confluent /ˈkɒnflʊənt/ *a.* & *n.* L15. [L *confluent-* pres. ppl stem of *confluere*, f. as CON- + *fluere* flow: see -ENT.] A *adj.* 1 Coalescing with one another so as to form one continuous mass or surface. L15. 2 Of streams, roads, etc.: flowing or running together so as to form one, uniting. E17. 3 Flowing together in a body. E18.

1 C. DARWIN The surrounding dark zones become confluent. 2 A. GEIKIE Numerous confluent valleys, whose united waters . . enter the sea. 3 M. PRIOR The whole ocean's confluent waters swell.

B *n.* †1 The place where rivers etc. unite. Only in E17. 2 A stream etc. joining another, *spec.* one of nearly equal size. M17.

confluently *adv.* L19.

conflux /ˈkɒnflʌks/ *n.* E17. [Late L *confluxus*, f. as CON- + *fluxus* FLUX *n.*] = CONFLUENCE.

confocal /kɒnˈfəʊk(ə)l/ *a.* & *n.* M19. [f. CON- + FOCAL.] A *adj.* Having a common focus or common foci. M19. B *n.* A figure having the same focus as another. E20.

conform /kənˈfɔːm/ *a.* & *adv.* LME. [Fr. *conforme* f. late L *conformis*, f. L CON- + *forma* shape, FORM *n.*] A *adj.* 1 = CONFORMABLE *a.* 1, 2. Now *rare* or *obs.* LME. †2 Conforming religiously, conformist. M17–E18. B *adv.* In conformity *with*, *to*. *Sc.* E16.

†**conformly** *adv.* LME–M18.

conform /kənˈfɔːm/ *v.* ME. [(O)Fr. *conformer* f. L *conformare*, f. as CON- + *formare* FORM *v.*[1]] 1 *v.t.* Foll. by *to*: form (something) according to (some model); make like. ME. 2 *v.t.* (freq. *refl.*) Bring into harmony or conformity; adapt. ME. 3 *v.i.* Act conformably or in conformity *to*; comply with rules or general custom; yield or show compliance. LME. b *spec.* Chiefly *Hist.* Comply with the usages of the Church of England. E17. 4 *v.i.* Foll. by *to*, *with* (of things): follow in form or nature. L15. †5 *v.t.* Bring into accord or mutual agreement. M17–E18.

1 R. HOOKER It truly conformeth us unto the image of Jesus Christ. 2 J. R. LOWELL The life of a nation . . should be conformed to certain principles. 3 M. MCCARTHY He had tried to conform to an ideal of the English butler. E. FROMM Most people are not even aware of their need to conform. 4 R. DODSLEY The path . . conforms to the water . . accompanying this semicircular lake into another winding valley. H. NEMEROV Bent To conform with the curve of the rim.

conformance *n.* the action of conforming, conformity E17. **conformer** *n.* a person who conforms, a conformist E17.

conformability /kənfɔːməˈbɪlɪti/ *n.* M19. [f. next + -ITY.] The quality or condition of being conformable; *spec.* (*Geol.*) the relation of strata, one of which rests on, and lies parallel to, the other.

conformable /kənˈfɔːməb(ə)l/ *a.* & *adv.* L15. [med.L *conformabilis*, f. *conformare*: see CONFORM *v.*, -ABLE.] A *adj.* 1 Disposed or accustomed to conform; tractable; compliant *to*. L15. b *spec.* Chiefly *Hist.* Conforming to the usages of the Church of England. L16. 2 According in form or character *to*; similar *to*. E16. 3 Corresponding so as to fit; consistent; harmonious; fitting. (Foll. by *to*, *with*.) M16. 4 *Geol.* Of strata in contact: lying in the same direction. Of a formation etc.: displaying conformability. E19.

1 SHAKES. *Tam. Shr.* And bring you from a wild Kate to a Kate Conformable as other household Kates. 2 G. BERKELEY The supposed circulation of the sap . . is in no sort conformable or analagous to the circulation of the blood. 3 J. BUCHAN He felt it necessary to erect his own sanctuary, conformable to his modest but peculiar tastes.

B *adv.* in conformity with; conformably *to*. L16.

conformableness *n.* M16. **conformably** *adv.* in a conformable manner, in conformity *with*, according *to*, compliantly; *Geol.* with conformability: E16.

conformal /kənˈfɔːm(ə)l/ *a.* M17. [In sense 1 f. L *conformalis*, f. as CON- + *formalis* formal. In sense 2 f. G *conform* + -AL[1].] 1 = CONFORMABLE. *rare.* M17. 2 *Math.* Conserving the size of all angles in the representation of one surface on another; *spec.* (in map-making) orthomorphic. L19.

conformally *adv.* L19.

conformation /kɒnfɔːˈmeɪʃ(ə)n/ *n.* E16. [L *conformatio(n-)*, f. *conformat-* pa. ppl stem of *conformare* CONFORM *v.*: see -ATION.] 1 The action of coming or bringing into conformity (*to*); adjustment, adaptation (*to*). E16. 2 The forming or fashioning of a thing in all its parts. E17. 3 The manner in which a thing is formed; structure, organization. M17. b *Chem.* Each of the three-dimensional structures that may be adopted by a particular molecule and can interconvert freely esp. by rotations around single bonds. M20.

Phrases: *vice of conformation*: see VICE *n.*[1] 2b.

conformational *a.* M20. **conformationally** *adv.* M20.

conformism /kənˈfɔːmɪz(ə)m/ *n.* E20. [Fr. *conformisme* or f. (as) next + -ISM. Cf. earlier NONCONFORMISM.] The action, practice, or principle of conforming; belief in conforming.

conformist /kənˈfɔːmɪst/ *n.* & *a.* M17. [f. CONFORM *v.* + -IST.] A *n.* A person who conforms *to* any usage or practice; *spec.* (chiefly *Hist.*) a person who conforms to the usages of the Church of England. (Cf. NONCONFORMIST.) M17.

occasional conformist: see OCCASIONAL *a.* 1.

B *adj.* That conforms; of or pertaining to conformists. M17.

conformity /kənˈfɔːmɪti/ *n.* LME. [(O)Fr. *conformité* or late L *conformitas*, f. *conformare*: see CONFORM *v.*, -ITY.] 1 Correspondence in form or manner (*to*, *with*); agreement in character; likeness; congruity. LME. 2 Action in accordance with some standard; compliance (*with*, *to*); acquiescence. L15. b *spec.* Chiefly *Hist.* Compliance with the usages of the Church of England. E17.

2b *occasional conformity*: see OCCASIONAL *a.* 1.

confound /kənˈfaʊnd/ *v.t.* ME. [AN *confundre*, *-foundre*, (O)Fr. *confondre* f. L *confundere* pour together, mix up, f. as CON- + *fundere* pour.] 1 Overthrow, defeat, ruin, (now usu. a scheme, hope, etc.). ME. †b Waste; spend. L16–E18. 2 As a (mild) imprecation: curse, damn. ME. 3 Discomfit; abash; put to shame. Usu. in *pass.* (Chiefly w. allus. to biblical use.) ME. 4 Throw into confusion or disorder; perplex. LME. 5 Mix up so that the elements become difficult to distinguish; confuse. LME. 6 Mix up in idea; fail to distinguish. L16.

1 F. WELDON A further confounding of Hilda's ill-wishes. A. S. BYATT The local prodigy returning . . to astonish and confound prophecy. b SHAKES. *1 Hen. IV* He did confound the best part of an hour In changing hardiment with great Glendower. 2 O. CROMWELL One of them was heard to say . . 'God damn me, God confound me; I burn, I burn.' J. BUCHAN Confound the day I ever left the herdin'! 3 MILTON Silent, and in face Confounded long they sate. 4 C. DARWIN This difficulty for a long time quite confounded me. 5 S. JOHNSON I came by it [the money] in a very uncommon manner, and would not confound it with the rest. 6 K. DOUGLAS I see men as trees suffering / or confound the detail and the horizon.

confoundable *a.* (*rare*) E19. **confounded** *a.* & *adv.* (*a*) *adj.* that has been confounded; accursed, damnable; (*b*) *adv.* confoundedly: LME. **confoundedly** *adv.* †(*a*) in a perplexed or confused manner; (*b*) cursedly, damnably: L17. **confoundedness** *n.* M17. **confounder** *n.* a person who confounds LME.

†**confrairy** *n.* LME–M18. [OFr. *confra(i)rie*, f. as CONFRÈRE: see -Y[3].] = CONFRATERNITY 1.

confrater /kənˈfreɪtə/ *n.* L16. [med.L *confrater*: see CONFRÈRE.] A member of a brotherhood, esp. of monks.

confraternity /kɒnfrəˈtəːnɪti/ *n.* LME. [(O)Fr. *confraternité* f. med.L *confraternitas*, f. *confrater*: see next, FRATERNITY.] 1 A brotherhood; an association of men united for some (esp. religious) purpose, or in some profession. LME. 2 Brotherly union or communion. L17.

confrère /ˈkɒnfrɛː/ *n.* LME. [(O)Fr. f. med.L *confrater*: see CON-, FRIAR.] †1 A fellow member of a fraternity. LME–L17. 2 A fellow member of a profession, scientific body, etc. M18.

confrérie /kɔ̃freri/ *n.* Pl. pronounced same. E19. [Fr., f. as prec.] A religious brotherhood; an association or group of people having similar interests, jobs, etc.

†**confrication** *n.* LME–L18. [Late L *confricatio(n-)*, f. *confricat-* pa. ppl stem of *confricare*, f. as CON- + *fricare* rub: see -ATION.] Rubbing together, friction.

confront /kənˈfrʌnt/ *v.t.* M16. [Fr. *confronter* f. med.L *confrontare*, f. L CON- + *frons*, *front-* forehead, face, FRONT *n.*] 1 Stand or meet facing, esp. in hostility or defiance; stand against, oppose. M16. 2 Bring together face to face; bring face to face *with*. M16. b Set (a thing) face to face or side by side *with* another for purposes of comparison; compare. E17. 3 Place (a thing) facing *to*; set in contrast *to*. *rare.* M17.

1 LD MACAULAY John Hampden . . had the courage . . to confront the whole power of the government. QUILLER-COUCH I am only coarse when confronted by respectability. 2 BURKE When and where the parties might be examined and confronted. G. GREENE A criminal should be confronted with his crime, for he may . . betray himself. b B. JOWETT The old order of things makes so poor a figure when confronted with the new.

confronter *n.* a person who or thing which confronts L16. **confrontment** *n.* (now *rare*) E17.

confrontation /kɒnfrənˈteɪʃ(ə)n/ *n.* E17. [f. prec. + -ATION. Cf. med.L *confrontatio(n-)* boundary, Fr. *confrontation.*] 1 The bringing of people face to face, esp. of an accused and the accuser(s), etc., for the purpose of establishing the truth. E17. 2 The action of bringing things together for comparison. M17. 3 Hostile opposition of countries, parties, etc., with or without actual conflict. M20.

confrontational *a.* characterized by or leading to (hostile) confrontation; aggressive, uncompromising: L20.

Confucian /kənˈfjuːʃ(ə)n/ *n.* & *a.* M19. [f. *Confucius* (see below, Latinization of *Kongfuze* Kong the master) + -AN.] A *n.* A follower of the Chinese philosopher Confucius (551–479 BC). M19. B *adj.* Of or pertaining to Confucius, his teaching, or his followers. M19.

Confucianism *n.* the doctrines or system of Confucius and his followers M19. **Confucianist** *n.* & *a.* an adherent of, of or pertaining to, Confucianism M19.

confusable /kənˈfjuːzəb(ə)l/ *a.* & *n.* M19. [f. CONFUSE *v.* + -ABLE. Cf. CONFUSIBLE.] A *adj.* Able to be, or liable to be, confused. M19. B *n.* A thing, esp. a word, that is liable to be confused with another. Usu. in *pl.* L20.

confusaˈbility *n.* M19.

†**confuse** *a.* ME–M18. [(O)Fr. *confus(e)* f. L *confusus* pa. pple of *confundere* CONFOUND.] Confused.

†**confusely** *adv.* LME–M18.

confuse /kənˈfjuːz/ *v.t.* ME. [Orig. *confused* pa. pple, f. as prec. + -ED[1]; active voice is back-form., only in isolated use bef. 19.] †1 Rout, bring to ruin. Only in ME. 2 Discomfit in mind or feelings; abash, bewilder, perplex. LME. 3 Throw into disorder or confusion. LME. 4 Mix up or mingle physically. Only in *pass.* M16. 5 Mix up in the mind; fail to distinguish. E17.

2 R. HUGHES Question her . . , perhaps frighten her, at any rate confuse her and make her contradict herself. F. WELDON The signposts were turned the wrong way round to confuse German spies. 3 DICKENS I fear I might confuse your arrangements by interfering. ALDOUS HUXLEY His thoughts were confused, but the muddle was bright and violent . . not foggily languid. 4 T. MEDWIN Their arms, legs, and bodies were confused together. 5 J. RUSKIN We in reality confuse wealth with money. DAY LEWIS I have been confused with the . . aviator, Cecil Lewis.

confused *a.* that has been confused; bewildered, perplexed; disorderly, chaotic, lacking clear distinction of elements: LME. **confusedly** /-zɪdli/ *adv.* E16. **confusedness** /-zɪdnɪs/ *n.* L16. **confusible** *a.* (*a*) = CONFUSABLE; †(*b*) confusing, involving confusion: LME. **confusing** *ppl a.* perplexing, bewildering M19. **confusingly** *adv.* M19. †**confusive** *a.* that tends to confuse E17–L18.

confusible /kənˈfjuːzɪb(ə)l/ *a.* & *n.* LME. [f. CONFUSE *v.* + -IBLE.] A *adj.* †1 Confusing; involving confusion. *rare.* LME–E16. 2 =

CONFUSABLE *a.* M19. **B** *n.* = CONFUSABLE *n.* Usu. in *pl.* L20.

confusion /kən'fju:ʒ(ə)n/ *n.* ME. [(O)Fr., or L *confusio(n-)*: see CON-, FUSION.] **1** Discomfiture, ruin. *arch.* ME. **2** Mental discomfiture, putting to shame; embarrassment, perplexity. ME. **3** Mixture in which the distinction of the elements is lost. Now *rare* or *obs.* ME. **4** The action of throwing into disorder. LME. **5** A disordered condition; disorder. LME. **b** Tumult; civil commotion. M16. **6** Failure to distinguish. LME. **7** The quality of being confused, indistinct or obscure. E18.

1 MILTON With ruin upon ruin, rout on rout, Confusion worse confounded. P. O'BRIAN 'Confusion to Boney,' they said, and drank their glasses dry. 2 COVERDALE *Ps.* 30:1 In the, O Lorde, is my trust: let me neuer be put to confucion. G. GREENE The woman . . rose in confusion at the sight of the strangers coming in. 3 *Book of Common Prayer* One altogether, not by confusion of substaunce: but by vnitie of person. 4 BACON The first great judgement of God upon the ambition of man was the confusion of tongues. 5 S. BECKETT In this immense confusion one thing alone is clear. 6 E. CLODD That confusion between names and things which marks all primitive thinking. 7 A. BUTLER Confusion . . in writing is indeed without excuse. *circle of (least) confusion*: see CIRCLE *n.* 1.

confusional *a.* characterized by (mental) confusion L19.

confusticate /kən'fʌstɪkeɪt/ *v.t. colloq.* L19. [Fanciful alt. of CONFOUND or CONFUSE *v.*] Confuse, confound, perplex.

confutation /kɒnfjʊ'teɪʃ(ə)n/ *n.* LME. [Fr., or L *confutatio(n-)*, f. *confutat-* pa. ppl stem of *confutare*: see next, -ATION.] The action or an instance of confuting; disproof; the complete argument in which a thing is confuted.

confute /kən'fju:t/ *v.t.* E16. [L *confutare* check, restrain, answer conclusively, f. as CON- + base of *refutare* refute.] **1** Prove (an argument or opinion) to be false, invalid or defective; refute. E16. **2** Prove (a person) to be wrong; convict of error by argument or proof. M16. **3** Render futile, bring to naught. L16.

1 H. ALLEN There are certain expressions at times upon the faces of some women that utterly confute the doctrine of original sin but confirm predestination. 2 MILTON Satan stood A while as mute confounded what to say . . confuted and convinced.

confutable *a.* able to be confuted M17. **confutative** *a.* tending to confutation M17. **confuter** *n.* a person who confutes L16.

conga /'kɒŋgə/ *n.* & *v.* M20. [Amer. Sp. f. Sp. fem. of *congo* of or pertaining to Congo.] **A** *n.* **1** A Latin American dance usu. performed by people in single file who take three steps forward and then kick. M20. **2** In full *conga drum*. A tall, narrow, low-toned drum that is beaten with the hands. M20. **B** *v.i.* Pa. t. & pple **conga'd**, **congaed**. Perform the conga. L20.

congé /kɔ̃ʒe (*pl. same*); 'kɔ̃:ʒeɪ, 'kɒnʒeɪ/ *n.* Also (now *rare*) ***congee*** /'kɒndʒi:/. LME. [OFr. *congié* (mod. *congé*) f. L *commeatus* passage, leave to pass, furlough, f. *commeare* go and come, f. as CON- + *meare* go, pass.] **1** Permission (for any act). Now *rare* or *obs.* LME. **2** Ceremonious leave-taking. LME. **†3** Formal permission to depart. L15–L18. **4** A bow. *arch.* L16. **5** [f. mod.Fr.] Unceremonious dismissal. Chiefly *joc.* M19.

2 QUILLER-COUCH You don't stop to touch your hat when you makes your congees.

Phrases: ***congé d'élire*** /,kɒnʒeɪ deɪ'lɪə/ [Fr., 'to elect'] royal permission to a cathedral chapter or a monastic body to fill a vacant see or abbacy by election.

¶Formerly naturalized, but now usu. treated as mod.Fr. in the current senses.

congé *v.* var. of CONGEE *v.*[2]

congeal /kən'dʒi:l/ *v.* LME. [(O)Fr. *congeler* f. L *congelare*, f. as CON- + *gelare* freeze, f. *gelu* frost.] **I** *v.t.* **1** Convert by cooling from a soft or fluid state to a solid one; freeze. LME. **†2** Make crystalline or solid by any means. LME–E18. **3** Make (a liquid, esp. the blood) viscid or jelly-like. LME.

1 *fig.*: S. JOHNSON Curiosity . . may be dissipated in trifles or congealed by indolence. 3 *fig.*: SHAKES. *Tam. Shr.* Too much sadness hath congeal'd your blood.

II *v.i.* **4** Become solid by cooling; freeze. LME. **5** Become solid by any process. LME. **6** Of a liquid: stiffen into a viscid or jelly-like consistency; coagulate. LME.

congealable *a.* E17. **congealment** *n.* (*a*) the act or process of congealing; (*b*) a congealed mass: LME.

congee /'kɒndʒi:/ *n.*[1] & *v.*[1] Also **conjee**. L17. [Tamil *kañci*.] **A** *n.* Water in which rice has been boiled. L17.

Comb.: **congee-house** *arch. slang* a military detention room or cell (where inmates are fed on congee).

B *v.t.* Pa. t. & pple **congeed**. Starch with rice-water. L17.

congee *n.*[2] see CONGÉ *n.*

congee /'kɒndʒi:/ *v.*[2] Also **congé**. Pa. t. & pple **congeed**. ME. [OFr. *congeer*, *congier*, f. as CONGÉ *n.*] **†1** *v.t.* Dismiss. ME–M16. **†2** *v.t.* Give official permission to. LME–M16. **3** *v.i.* Pay one's respects on leaving; say goodbye. *obs.* exc. *dial.* E17. **4** *v.i.* Bow in courtesy or obeisance. *arch.* E17.

congelation /kɒndʒɪ'leɪʃ(ə)n/ *n.* LME. [(O)Fr., or L *congelatio(n-)*, f. *congelat-* pa. ppl stem of *congelare* CONGEAL: see -ATION.] **1a** The action or process of freezing. LME. **b** A frozen condition; a frozen mass. L17. **2a** Solidification; *spec.* crystallization. LME. **b** A concretion. E17. **3** Coagulation, clotting. LME.

†congelative *a.* producing cold; tending to congeal or to crystallize: LME–E18.

congener /'kɒndʒɪnə, kɒn'dʒi:nə/ *n.* & *a.* M18. [L, f. as CON- + *gener-*, *genus* race, stock.] **A** *n.* **1** A thing or person of the same kind or class as another. M18. **2** A by-product in the making of spirits or wines which gives the drink a distinctive character. *US.* M20. **B** *adj.* Congeneric; akin. M19.

con'generate *a.* (*rare*) congeneric M17.

congeneric /kɒndʒɪ'nɛrɪk/ *a.* M19. [f. as prec. + -IC.] Of the same genus, kind, or race; allied in nature or origin.

Also **con'generous** *a.* M17.

congenial /kən'dʒi:nɪəl/ *a.* E17. [f. CON- + GENIAL *a.*[1]] **1** Of a person: sharing the same disposition or temperament. Of a thing or attribute: kindred; of similar character. (Foll. by *with*, *to*.) E17. **b** Suited to the nature of anything. (Foll. by *to*.) M18. **c** Agreeable; matching one's taste or inclination. (Foll. by *to*.) L18. **†2a** Innate; congenital. M17–L18. **b** Connected with one's birth. L17–L18. **†3** = CONGENERIC. M17–E19.

congeni'ality *n.* E17. **congenially** *adv.* M18.

congenital /kən'dʒɛnɪt(ə)l/ *a.* L18. [f. L *congenitus*, f. as CON- + *genitus* pa. pple of *gignere* beget: see -AL[1].] Existing from birth; that is such from birth.

M. LOWRY I was not a congenital idiot. G. BOURNE The delivery of a child suffering from congenital syphilis.

congenitally *adv.* M19. **†congenite** *a.* connate; congenital; innate: E17–E19.

conger /'kɒŋgə/ *n.*[1] ME. [(O)Fr. *congre* f. L *congrus*, *conger* f. Gk *goggros*.] More fully *conger eel*. Any eel of the family Congridae, comprising scaleless sea-eels usu. found in coastal waters; spec. *Conger conger*, a European conger reaching up to 3 metres in length and caught for food.

conger /'kɒŋgə/ *n.*[2] L17. [Origin unkn.] *Hist.* An association of booksellers who sold or printed books for their common advantage.

congeries /kɒn'dʒɪəri:z, -ɪz, -ɪi:z/ *n.* Pl. same. M16. [L *congeries* heap, pile, f. *congerere*: see CONGEST *v.*] A collection of disparate or unsorted items; a rag-bag.

Also **'congery** *n.* M19.

congest /kən'dʒɛst/ *v.* LME. [L *congest-* pa. ppl stem of *congerere* collect, heap up, f. as CON- + *gerere* bear, carry.] **†1** *v.t.* Bring or gather together; heap up, accumulate. LME–M19. **2** *v.t.* Affect with congestion. Chiefly as *congested* ppl a. M19. **3** *v.i.* Gather together; congregate. L19.

2 *Daily Telegraph* Congested town centres.

congestive *a.* involving or produced by congestion M19.

congestion /kən'dʒɛstʃ(ə)n/ *n.* LME. [(O)Fr. f. L *congestio(n-)*, f. as prec.: see -ION.] **1** Excessive accumulation of fluid in a part of the body: now only of blood in blood-vessels or of mucus in the respiratory tract. LME. **2a** The action of heaping together in a mass; accumulation. L16. **b** A heap, a pile. M17. **3** Obstructive or disruptive overcrowding. M19.

2a C. IVES Congestion of personal property tends to limit the progress of the soul. 3 J. CHEEVER The noise and congestion of the city.

congiary /'kɒndʒɪəri/ *n.* E17. [L *congiarium*, f. as next: see -ARY[1].] *Rom. Hist.* A quantity of oil, wine, etc., or money given for distribution as a gift among the people or the soldiers.

congius /'kɒndʒɪəs/ *n.* Pl. **-ii** /-ɪʌɪ/. LME. [L.] *Rom. Hist.* A liquid measure of one eighth of an amphora, equal to about 6 imperial pints.

†conglaciate *v.* M17. [L *conglaciat-* pa. ppl stem of *conglaciare* freeze up, f. as CON- + *glaciare* turn to ice, f. *glacies* ice: see -ATE[3].] **1** *v.t.* Make into or like ice. M17–E19. **2** *v.i.* Become ice, freeze. M17–E19.

†conglaciation *n.* M17–M18.

conglobate /'kɒŋgləbeɪt, -ət/ *a.* M17. [L *conglobatus* pa. pple, f. as next: see -ATE[2].] Formed or gathered into a ball; rounded, globular.

conglobate /'kɒŋgləbeɪt/ *v.t.* & *i.* M17. [L *conglobat-* pa. ppl stem of *conglobare*, f. as CON- + *globare* make into a ball, f. *globus* ball, GLOBE: see -ATE[3].] = CONGLOBE.

conglo'bation *n.* the action of conglobating; a rounded formation: L16.

conglobe /kɒn'gləʊb/ *v.t.* & *i.* M16. [Fr. *conglober* or L *conglobare*: see prec.] Gather or form into a rounded compact mass.

conglobulate /kɒn'glɒbjʊleɪt/ *v.i. rare.* M18. [f. L *globulus* GLOBULE after CONGLOBATE *v.*] Collect into a rounded or compact mass.

conglobu'lation *n.* E20.

conglomerate /kən'glɒm(ə)rət/ *a.* & *n.* LME. [L *conglomeratus* pa. pple of *conglomerare*, f. as CON- + *glomer-*, *glomus* ball: see -ATE[2].] **A** *adj.* **1** Consisting of distinct parts gathered together into a more or less rounded mass; clustered. LME. **2** *Geol.* Of the nature of or forming a conglomerate. E19. **B** *n.* **1** *Geol.* A coarse-grained sedimentary rock composed of rounded fragments embedded in a matrix of a cementing material such as silica. E19. **2** A mixture of heterogeneous elements. M19. **3** A commercial or industrial corporation formed by the merger or takeover of a number of diverse enterprises; a company with subsidiaries operating in different, unrelated markets. M20.

conglome'ratic *a.* (*Geol.*) of the nature or character of conglomerate M19. **conglomerator** *n.* an industrialist who manages a conglomerate or forms conglomerates L20. **conglome'ritic** *a.* = CONGLOMERATIC M19.

conglomerate /kən'glɒməreɪt/ *v.* L16. [L *conglomerat-* pa. ppl stem of *conglomerare*: see prec., -ATE[3].] **1** *v.t.* Form into a more or less rounded mass; heap together. Now *rare* or *obs.* L16. **2** *v.t.* & *i.* Collect into a coherent or compact body (*lit.* & *fig.*). L16.

2 V. WOOLF Infinite numbers of dull people conglomerated round her.

conglomeration /kənglɒmə'reɪʃ(ə)n/ *n.* E17. [Late L *conglomeratio(n-)*, f. as prec.: see -ATION.] **1** The action of conglomerating. E17. **2** A cluster; a heterogeneous mixture. M19.

conglutinate /kɒn'glu:tɪneɪt/ *v.* Now *rare.* LME. [L *conglutinat-* pa. ppl stem of *conglutinare*, f. as CON- + *glutinare* to glue, f. *glutin-*, *gluten* glue: see -ATE[3].] **1** *v.i.* Stick together, cohere (*lit.* & *fig.*). Orig. (now *obs.*) of a fracture or wound: knit together, close and heal. LME. **2** *v.t.* Unite (a wounded part, broken bone, etc.); heal. LME. **3** *v.t.* Cause to cohere; fasten firmly together. LME.

congluti'nation *n.* LME.

Congo /'kɒŋgəʊ/ *n.*[1] Pl. **-oes**. E19. [Place-name: see branch I.] **I 1** Used *attrib.* to designate things associated (actually or mentally) with the Congo, a region in west central Africa on either side of the Zaire (Congo) River, or with any of the countries in it called Congo (now represented by Zaire and the People's Republic of the Congo), or with American Blacks from it. E19. 2 In full *Congo dance*. A kind of dance formerly performed by American Blacks and subsequently Whites of the southern US. E19. 3 In full *Congo eel, snake*. Any of various large salamanders found in shallow water in the south-eastern and central US and having tiny, inconspicuous legs: *Amphius means*, with four legs, or *Siren lacertina* or *S. intermedia*, each with two forelegs only. M19. 4 *Hist.* A Black from the Congo. M19.

1 **Congo pea** (an edible seed of) a cajan, *Cajanus cajan*. *Congo* PEAFOWL.

II 5 Used *attrib.* to designate various azo dyes mostly derived from benzidine or tolidine. L19.

Congo'ese *a.* & *n.* (now *rare*) = CONGOLESE L18.

†congo *n.*[2] & *v.* see CANGUE.

congo *n.*[3] var. of CONGOU.

Congolese /kɒŋgəˈliːz/ *a.* & *n.* E20. [Fr. *Congolais*, f. as CONGO *n.*[1]: see -ESE.] A *adj.* Of or pertaining to (the) Congo (see CONGO *n.*[1] I) or its people. E20. B *n.* Pl. same. A native or inhabitant of (the) Congo; the language of the Congolese. E20.

congou /ˈkɒŋguː, -gəʊ/ *n.* Also **C-, congo, k-**. E18. [Abbrev. f. (Cantonese) Chin. *kungfüch'a*, (Mandarin) *gōngfu chá* tea made for refined tastes, f. *gōngfu* effort + *chá* TEA *n.*] A kind of black China tea. Also *congou tea*.

congrats /kənˈgrats/ *n.pl. colloq.* L19. [Abbrev.] Congratulations. Usu. as *int.*

Also **congratters** *n.pl.* [-ER[6]] E20.

congratulate /kənˈgratjʊleɪt/ *v.* M16. [L *congratulat-* pa. ppl stem of *congratulari*, f. as CON- + *gratulari* manifest one's joy, f. *gratus* pleasing: see -ATE[3].] †1 *v.t.* Express joy or satisfaction at (an event or circumstance, *to* or *with* a person); celebrate *with* some act. M16–E19. 2a *v.t.* Express sympathetic joy to (a person, *on, upon, †for* an event or circumstance). M16. b *v.i.* Offer congratulations. M17. c *v.refl.* Think oneself fortunate; feel satisfaction at an achievement. (Foll. by *on, upon, that.*) M17. †3 *v.i.* Rejoice along *with* another. (Foll. by *on, upon, for.*) L16–E19. †4 *v.t.* Give a salutation to. L16–E17. †5 *v.t.* Rejoice at, welcome (an event). E17–M18.

congratulant *a.* & *n.* (*a*) *adj.* that congratulates; (*b*) *n.* a congratulator: M17. **congratulative** *a.* (*rare*) congratulatory M19. **congratulator** *n.* a person who congratulates M17. **congratulatory** *a.* conveying congratulations E16.

congratulation /kəngratjʊˈleɪʃ(ə)n/ *n.* LME. [L *congratulatio(n-)*, f. as prec.: see -ATION.] 1 The action of congratulating. LME. 2 In *pl.* Congratulatory expressions. Freq. as *int.*, well done! M17.

†congree *v.i. rare.* L16–M19. [f. CON- + GREE *v.*] Accord.

†congreet *v.i. rare* (Shakes.). Only in L16. [f. CON- + GREET *v.*[1]] Greet mutually.

congregant /ˈkɒŋgrɪg(ə)nt/ *n.* L19. [L *congregant-* pres. ppl stem of *congregare*: see CONGREGATE *v.*, -ANT[1].] A member of a (Jewish) congregation.

congregate /ˈkɒŋgrɪgət/ *a.* Now *rare*. LME. [L *congregatus* pa. pple, f. as next: see -ATE[2].] Congregated. Also, collective.

congregate /ˈkɒŋgrɪgeɪt/ *v.t.* & *i.* LME. [L *congregat-* pa. ppl stem of *congregare* collect together, f. as CON- + *greg-*, *grex*, flock: see -ATE[3].] Collect or gather together into a crowd or mass; meet or assemble in a body, flock.

SHELLEY The north wind congregates in crowds The floating mountains of the silver clouds. R. L. STEVENSON That city of gold to which adventurers congregated. R. P. WARREN People, almost a crowd, were beginning to congregate.

congregated *ppl a.* (*a*) assembled or collected together; †(*b*) organized congregationally: E17. **congregative** *a.* tending to congregate L16. **congregator** *n.* a person who congregates M17.

congregation /kɒŋgrɪˈgeɪʃ(ə)n/ *n.* LME. [(O)Fr. *congrégation* or L *congregatio(n-)*, f. as prec. see -ATION.] 1 The action of congregating or collecting into a crowd or mass. LME. 2 *gen.* A gathering, an assemblage, a company. LME. 3 (Freq. **C-**.) A general assembly of (certain, esp. senior resident) members of a university. LME. 4 In the Bible, the collective body, or an actual assembly, of the Israelites in the wilderness. LME. 5 *RC Ch.* A body of people obeying a common religious rule. LME. b An administrative subdivision of the papal curia, *spec.* a permanent committee of cardinals. L17. 6 A body of people assembled for religious worship or to hear a preacher; the body of people regularly attending a particular church etc. E16. 7 *Sc. Hist.* The party of Protestant Reformers during the reign of Mary Stuart. M16.

2 SHAKES. *Haml.* A foul and pestilent congregation of vapours. O. HENRY The.. outlaws seemed to be nothing more than a congregation of country bumpkins. J. S. HUXLEY A congregation of black snakes.. convoluted in their mating ceremonies. 5 *Congregation of the Propaganda*: see PROPAGANDA *n.* 1. 6 I. COMPTON-BURNETT We shall see you all in church this evening, I hope? We want very much to have a full congregation. *lead the prayers of a congregation*: see LEAD *v.*[1]

congregationer *n.* †(*a*) = CONGREGATIONALIST; (*b*) *Sc. Hist.* a member of the party of Protestant Reformers (see CONGREGATION *n.* 7): M17. **congregationist** *n.* †(*a*) = CONGREGATIONALIST; (*b*) a member of a Roman Catholic congregation (see CONGREGATION 5): M17.

congregational /kɒŋgrɪˈgeɪʃ(ə)n(ə)l/ *a.* & *n.* M17. [f. prec. + -AL[1].] A *adj.* 1 Of or pertaining to a congregation; performed by a congregation. M17. 2 (**C-**.) Of, pertaining or adhering to, Congregationalism. M17. B *n.* (**C-**.) A Congregationalist. *rare*. M17.

Congregationalist *n.* a member or adherent of a Congregational church L17. **congregationalize** *v.t.* make congregational M19. **congregationally** *adv.* L19.

Congregationalism /kɒŋgrɪˈgeɪʃ(ə)n(ə)lɪz(ə)m/ *n.* E18. [f. prec. + -ISM.] A system of ecclesiastical organization that leaves the legislative, disciplinary, and judicial functions to the individual churches and congregations; adherence to a Congregational church (in England and Wales such churches were largely merged in the United Reformed Church from 1972).

congress /ˈkɒŋgrɛs/ *n.* & *v.* LME. [L *congressus*, f. *congress-* pa. ppl stem of *congredi* go together, meet, f. as CON- + *gradi* proceed, step.] A *n.* †1 An encounter in combat. LME–E18. 2 A coming together (of persons, †of things); a meeting. E16. 3 = COPULATION 2. Now *arch.* or *literary*. L16. 4 Social intercourse. *arch.* E17. 5 A formal meeting or assembly of delegates etc. for discussion, esp. of people belonging to a particular body or engaged in special studies. L17. 6 (**C-**.) The national legislative body of the US during any two-year term, comprising the House of Representatives and the Senate. Also, the corresponding body in some other countries. L18.

2 J. WOODWARD A fortuitous Congress of Atoms. DISRAELI Never was a congress of friendship wherein more was said and felt. 3 J. R. ACKERLEY It did not enter my head.. that my father might still be having congress with my mother. 5 *Church Congress*: see CHURCH *n.* 6 *Continental Congress*: see CONTINENTAL *a.* *Member of Congress*: see MEMBER *n.* 2.

Comb.: **congress boot** a high boot with elastic sides; **Congressman**: belonging to the US Congress; **Congress Party** a broadly-based political party in India, arising directly from the Indian independence movement (which met as the *Indian National Congress* from 1885); **Congresspeople, -person, -woman**: belonging to the US Congress.

B *v.i.* Meet in congress, come together, assemble. *rare*. M19.

con'gression *n.* (*rare*) [L *congressio(n-)*] †(*a*) hostile encounter; †(*b*) = CONGRESS *n.* 3; (*c*) = CONGRESS *n.* 2: LME. **congressist** *n.* (*rare*) a member or supporter of a congress L19.

congressional /kənˈgrɛʃ(ə)n(ə)l/ *a.* L17. [f. CONGRESS after L *congressio(n-)*; see -ION, -AL[1].] Of or pertaining to a congress, esp. (**C-**) the legislative Congress of the US.

congressionalist *n.* a supporter of a congress L19.

Congreve /ˈkɒŋgriːv/ *n.* E19. [Sir William *Congreve* (1772–1828), Eng. inventor.] *Hist.* 1 In full *Congreve rocket*. A military rocket of a kind invented by Congreve. E19. 2 In full *Congreve match*. A friction match of a kind invented by Congreve. M19.

†congrue *v.i. rare.* (Shakes.). Only in E17 [OFr. *congruer* or L *congruere*: see CONGRUENT.] Agree, accord.

congruence /ˈkɒŋgrʊəns/ *n.* LME. [L *congruentia*, f. *congruent-*: see next, -ENCE.] 1 = CONGRUITY 2. LME. †2 *Theol.* = CONGRUITY 4. LME–M17. 3 Accordance, correspondence, consistency. M16. 4 Grammatical agreement or correctness E18. 5 *Math.* The relationship between two congruent numbers; an equation expressing this. L19.

congruency *n.* (*a*) congruence; (*b*) *Math.* a system of lines depending on two parameters: L15.

congruent /ˈkɒŋgrʊənt/ *a.* LME. [L *congruent-* pres. ppl stem of *congruere* meet together, agree, correspond, f. as CON- + *ruere* fall, rush: see -ENT.] 1 Agreeing or corresponding (*with*) in character, accordant. LME. †b Fitting, proper. LME–E18. 2 *Math.* a Of geometrical figures: coinciding exactly when superimposed. E18. b Of numbers: giving the same remainder when divided by a given number, called the modulus. Cf. RESIDUE *n.* 4. L19.

congruently *adv.* LME.

Congruism /ˈkɒŋgrʊɪz(ə)m/ *n.* L19. [Fr. *congruisme*, f. *congru* f. L *congruus*: see CONGRUOUS, -ISM.] *Theol.* The doctrine which derives the efficacy of grace from its adaptation to the character and circumstances of the person called.

Congruist *n.* a person who holds the doctrine of Congruism E18.

congruity /kənˈgruːɪti/ *n.* LME. [Fr. *congruité* or late L *congruitas*, f. as next: see -ITY.] 1 The quality of being congruous; agreement in character or qualities; accordance, harmony. LME. b An instance or point of correspondence, agreement, etc. Usu. in *pl.* E17. 2 Accordance with what is right or appropriate; fitness, propriety. LME. †3 Grammatical agreement or correctness; propriety of speech. LME–E18. 4a *Scholastic Theol.* The appropriateness of God's conferment of grace as a reward for the performance of good works. (Cf. *condignity*.) M16. b = CONGRUISM. M17. †5 *Math.* Coincidence, congruence. M17–M18. 6 Harmony of the parts of a whole, coherence. E19.

congruous /ˈkɒŋgrʊəs/ *a.* L16. [f. L *congruus* agreeing, suitable + -OUS.] 1 Accordant, conformable, *with*. L16. 2 Fitting, appropriate. L16. †3 Grammatically correct. Only in M17. 4 *Math.* Coincident, congruent. Now *rare* or *obs.* M17. 5 Coherent. M18.

congruously *adv.* L16. **congruousness** *n.* M18.

conhydrine /kənˈhʌɪdriːn/ *n.* M19. [f. CONIINE + HYDRATE *n.* + -INE[5].] *Chem.* A piperidine derivative, $C_8H_{17}NO$, found together with coniine in hemlock.

coni *n.* pl. of CONUS.

conic /ˈkɒnɪk/ *a.* & *n.* L16. [mod.L *conicus* f. Gk *kōnikos*, f. *kōnos*: see CONE *n.*, -IC.] A *adj.* 1 Of or pertaining to a cone. L16. 2 = CONICAL *a.* 1. E17.

1 **conic section** any of a group of curves (circle, ellipse, parabola, hyperbola) formed by the intersection of a right circular cone and a plane.

B *n.* 1 In *pl.* (treated as *sing.*). The branch of mathematics that deals with the cone and the figures that may be generated from it. Now *rare*. L16. 2 A conic section. L19.

conicity /kəˈnɪsɪti/ *n.* conicalness L19. **conicoid** *n.* any of the bodies or surfaces that can be generated by the rotation of conic sections M19.

conic- *comb. form* see CONICO-.

conical /ˈkɒnɪk(ə)l/ *a.* L16. [f. as CONIC + -AL[1].] 1 Shaped like a cone; tapering regularly to a point from a more or less circular base. L16. 2 = CONIC *a.* 1. L16.

1 *conical pendulum*: see PENDULUM *n.* 2 **conical projection** a map projection in which a spherical surface is projected on to a cone (usu. with its vertex above one of the poles).

conically *adv.* M17. **conicalness** *n.* M18.

conico- /'kɒnɪkəʊ/ *comb. form.* Bef. a vowel also **conic-**. E19. [Repr. Gk *kōniko-*, *-kos* CONIC: see -O-.] Used adverbially to form adjs. w. the sense 'nearly —, but with a tendency to be conical', as *conico-cylindrical*, *-hemispherical*, etc.

conicopoly /kɒnɪ'kɒpəli/ *n. obs.* exc. *Hist.* L17. [Tamil *kanakka-piḷḷai* account-man.] A non-European clerk or accountant in the Indian subcontinent.

conidium /kəʊ'nɪdɪəm/ *n.* Pl. **-ia** /-ɪə/. L19. [mod.L, f. Gk *konis* dust: see -IDIUM.] An asexual spore in certain fungi (where it forms at the tip of a specialized hypha) and in some bacteria resembling fungi.

conidial *a.* of, pertaining to, or of the nature of a conidium or conidia L19. **conidiophore** *n.* a hypha bearing a conidium L19. **conidi'ophorous** *a.* bearing conidia L19.

conifer /'kɒnɪfə, 'kəʊn-/ *n.* M19. [L *conifer* adj., cone-bearing, f. *conus* CONE *n.*: see -FER.] A gymnospermous tree or shrub of the order Coniferales, members of which typically bear cones and evergreen needle-like leaves and include the pines, firs, cedars, larches, spruces, yews, etc.

coniferi'zation *n.* conversion of woodland to coniferous forest; planting with coniferous trees: M20.

coniferous /kə'nɪf(ə)rəs/ *a.* M17. [f. as prec.: see -FEROUS.] Cone-bearing, that is a conifer; pertaining to or consisting (predominantly) of conifers.

coniform /'kəʊnɪfɔːm/ *a.* L18. [f. L *conus*, *coni-* CONE *n.* + -FORM.] Cone-shaped, conical.

coniine /'kəʊniːn/ *n.* M19. [f. L CONIUM + -INE[5].] *Chem.* A volatile oily liquid alkaloid, 2-propylpiperidine, $C_8H_{17}N$, which is the active principle of hemlock, *Conium maculatum*.

conium /'kəʊnɪəm/ *n.* M19. [L f. Gk *kōneion* hemlock.] An umbelliferous plant of the genus *Conium*; *esp.* hemlock, *C. maculatum*; an extract of any plant of this genus used medicinally.

†**conject** *v.t.* & *i.* LME. [L *conjectare* frequent. of *conjicere* throw together, put together in speech or thought, conclude, f. as CON- + *jacere* throw.] 1 = CONJECTURE *v.* 3, 4. LME–M18. 2 Plot, plan. LME–M16. 3 = CONJECTURE *v.* 1. LME–E17.

†**conjector** *n.* [AN *conjectour*, OFr. *-eur*] a person who conjectures; a soothsayer, a guesser: LME–M18.

conjectural /kən'dʒɛktʃ(ə)r(ə)l/ *a.* M16. [Fr. f. L *conjecturalis*, f. *conjectura*: see next, -AL[1].] 1 Of the nature of, involving, or depending on conjecture. M16. 2 Given to making conjectures. M17.

conjectu'rality *n.* (*rare*) M17. **conjecturally** *adv.* LME.

conjecture /kən'dʒɛktʃə/ *n.* LME. [(O)Fr., or L *conjectura* conclusion, inference, f. *conject-* pa. ppl stem of *conjicere*: see CONJECT, -URE.] †1 The interpretation of signs or omens; divination; (a) prognostication. LME–L17. †2 Supposition. *rare*. LME–L16. 3 (The formation or offering of) an opinion or conclusion based on insufficient evidence or on what is thought probable; guesswork, a guess, (a) surmise; *spec.* in textual criticism, (the proposal of) a reading not actually found in the text. E16. †4 A ground or reason for conclusion (short of proof). E16–M17.

1 MILTON To cast Ominous conjecture on the whole success. 2 SHAKES. *Hen. V* Now entertain conjecture of a time When creeping murmur . . Fills . . the universe. 3 G. MURRAY You cannot study the future. You can only make conjectures about it. C. V. WEDGWOOD Contemporary hearsay and conjecture (of which there was much).

conjecture /kən'dʒɛktʃə/ *v.* LME. [(O)Fr. *conjecturer* f. late L *conjecturare*, f. L *conjectura* (see prec.). Cf. CONJECT.] †1 *v.t.* & *i.* Infer from signs or omens; divine, prognosticate. LME–M17. †2 *v.t.* Conclude, infer, or judge from appearances or probabilities. LME–E17. 3 *v.t.* Form or offer as an opinion or conclusion on admittedly insufficient grounds; guess, surmise; propose as a conjectural reading. M16. 4 *v.i.* Form a conjecture; indulge in guesswork. (Foll. by *about*, (arch.) *of*, †*at*.) L16.

3 M. W. MONTAGU I conjecture them to be the remains of that city. T. HARDY I . . conjectured that these hours of absence were spent in furtherance of his plan. V. CRONIN Catherine's feelings . . can only be conjectured. 4 BARONESS ORCZY Perhaps he was going to Greenwich, or . . . but Marguerite ceased to conjecture.

conjecturable *a.* that may be conjectured L16. **conjecturer** *n.* †(*a*) a fortune-teller, an augur; (*b*) a maker of conjectures: E17.

conjee *n.* & *v.* var. of CONGEE *n.*[1] & *v.*[1]

conjobble /kən'dʒɒb(ə)l/ *v.t.* & *i. colloq.* Now *rare* or *obs.* L17. [f. CON- and perh. JOB *n.*[1], *v.*[2] or JABBER, + -LE[3].] Arrange (matters); discuss.

conjoin /kən'dʒɔɪn/ *v.* LME. [(O)Fr. *conjoign-* pres. stem of *conjoindre* f. L *conjungere*, f. as CON- + *jungere* JOIN *v.*] I *gen.* 1 *v.t.* & *i.* Join or become joined together; unite, combine. LME.

1 J. SPEED Many fresh springs . . meet and conjoine in the vallies. A. J. AYER It is common to find belief in a transcendent god conjoined with belief in an after-life.

II *spec.* 2 *v.t.* & *i.* Of planets: be or come into conjunction (with). LME. 3 *v.t.* & †*i.* Join or combine in action or purpose; ally. LME. †4 *v.t.* Join in marriage. LME–M17. †5 *v.i.* = COPULATE 2. L16–E17.

conjoined *ppl a.* joined together, combined, allied; *Her.* (of charges) connected together, placed so as to touch: L16. **conjoiner** *n.* M17.

conjoint /kən'dʒɔɪnt/ *a.* (orig. *pa. pple*). LME. [(O)Fr., pa. pple of *conjoindre*: see prec.] Conjoined; united, combined; conjunct.

conjointly *adv.* ME.

conjugacy /'kɒndʒəgəsi/ *n.* M17. [f. CONJUGATE *a.* + -ACY.] †1 Married state. *rare*. Only in M17. 2 Chiefly *Math.* Conjugate condition. L19.

conjugal /'kɒndʒʊg(ə)l/ *a.* E16. [L *conjugalis*, f. *conjug-*, *-ju(n)x* consort, spouse, f. as CON- + stem of *jugum* yoke: see -AL[1]. Cf. (O)Fr. *conjugal*.] Of or relating to marriage, matrimonial; of or pertaining to a husband or wife in their relationship to each other.

I. WALTON The hearing of such conjugal faithfulness will be Musick to all chaste ears. **conjugal rights** those rights (esp. to sexual relations) supposedly exercisable in law by each partner in a marriage on the other. **conjugal rites** the wedding ceremony; *arch.* sexual intercourse.

conju'gality *n.* M17. **conjugally** *adv.* E17.

conjugate /'kɒndʒʊgət/ *a.* & *n.* L15. [L *conjugatus* pa. pple of *conjugare*: see next, -ATE[2].] A *adj.* 1 *gen.* Joined together, *esp.* coupled; connected, related. L15. 2 *Math.* & *Physics.* Joined or paired in some reciprocal relation (*to*); *spec.* (of two complex numbers) such that each is the complex conjugate of the other. L17. 3 *Bot.* Of leaves etc.: growing in or as a pair. L18. 4 *Gram.* Of words: derived from the same root (as one another). M19. 5 *Biol.* Of gametes: fused. M19. 6 *Bibliogr.* Of a pair of leaves: united with each other in being part of a single sheet of paper. L19.

Special collocations: **conjugate acid, base** (*Chem.*): related to each other by the gain or loss of a proton (e.g. acetate ion is the conjugate base of acetic acid, the latter the conjugate acid of the former). **conjugate angle, arc** *Math.*: either of a pair whose sum is 360°. **conjugate axis** *Math.* the axis of a conic that bisects the principal or transverse axis. *conjugate base* (Chem.): see *conjugate acid* above. **conjugate deviation** *Ophthalm.* a forced, persistent turning of the eyes to one side, their direction in relation to each other remaining unaltered. **conjugate diameter** (*a*) *Anat.* the distance between the front and rear of the pelvis, *spec.* determined from the sacral promontory to the back of the pubic symphysis; (*b*) *Math.* = *conjugate axis* above. **conjugate focus** either of two points so situated in relation to a lens that light from an object placed at one of them forms an image at the other. **conjugate solution** *Chem.* either of a pair of solutions which may be formed by two partially miscible liquids and exist together in equilibrium at a given temperature, the solute in one solution being the solvent in the other.

B *n.* 1 *Gram.* Either of a group of words sharing the same root. L16. 2 Any conjugated thing. E17.

2 *complex conjugate*: see COMPLEX *a.* 3.

conjugate /'kɒndʒʊgeɪt/ *v.* M16. [L *conjugat-* pa. ppl stem of *conjugare*, f. as CON- + *jugare* join, yoke, marry, f. *jugum* yoke: see -ATE[3].] 1 *v.t. Gram.* Inflect (a verb) in its various forms of voice, mood, tense, number, and person. M16. 2 *v.t.* Yoke together, join, unite. *rare*. L16. 3 *v.i.* Unite sexually. Now chiefly *Biol.*, unite in conjugation (sense 4). L18. 4 *v.t. Biochem.* Bring into conjugation (sense 5) *with*. Usu. in *pass.* M20.

conjugated /'kɒndʒʊgeɪtɪd/ *a.* L16. [f. prec. + -ED[1].] 1 That has been conjugated; conjugate. L16. 2 *Chem.* Of, pertaining to, designating, or containing a (chain or ring) system of two or more double bonds linked by alternate single bonds. L19.

conjugation /kɒndʒʊ'geɪʃ(ə)n/ *n.* LME. [L *conjugatio(n-)*, f. *conjugat-*: see CONJUGATE *v.*, -ATION.] 1 *Gram.* The scheme of all the inflectional forms belonging to a verb; a division of verbs according to general inflectional differences. LME. b The setting forth (in speech or writing) of a verb's conjugation. M16. c In Semitic languages, any of several sets of inflectional forms that give a passive, reflexive, causative, etc., meaning to the simple verb. L16. †2 *Anat.* A group of conjoined parts; *esp.* each of the several pairs of cerebral nerves. L16–E18. 3 The action of joining together or uniting; the condition of being conjugated or joined together; conjunction, union. E17. †b An assemblage, a combination. E17–E18. 4 *Biol.* The fusion of gametes in sexual reproduction; the union of simple organisms for the exchange of genetic material. M19. 5 *Biochem.* The (reversible) combination of a substance such as a protein with one of a different kind. M20.

1 RICHARD MORRIS The verbs of the strong conjugation . . form the past tense by a change of the root-vowel. V. S. NAIPAUL Her grammar . . included a highly personal conjugation of the verb to be.

conjugational *a.* M19. **conjugationally** *adv.* L19.

conjunct /'kɒndʒʌŋkt/ *n.* L16. [f. next.] †1 A conjoined whole. *rare*. Only in L16. 2 A person or thing conjoined or associated with another. M17. 3 = CONJUNCTURE. M19.

conjunct /kən'dʒʌŋkt/ *a.* (orig. *pa. pple*). LME. [L *conjunctus* pa. pple of *conjungere*, f. as CON- + *jungere* join. Cf. CONJOINT.] 1 Joined together; conjoined, combined; associated, esp. in a subordinate capacity. Also (*Sc. Law*), immediately associated. LME. 2 *Law* (chiefly *Sc.*). Pertaining to or involving several persons jointly. L15. 3 Constituted by the conjunction of several elements; united, joint. E16. 4 *Mus.* Designating motion by steps from one degree of a scale to the next (i.e. by intervals of a second); proceeding by or involving such steps. Opp. DISJUNCT *a.* 3. L17.

1 **conjunct person** *Sc. Law* an associate in an offence; *esp.* a person so closely involved with another as to be liable to the presumption of collusion or connivance. **conjunct probation, proof** *Sc. Law* (leading of) evidence restricted to the rebuttal of the averments of the opposing party in an action, but not introducing new points.

conjunctly *adv.* jointly LME.

conjunction /kən'dʒʌŋkʃ(ə)n/ *n.* LME. [(O)Fr. *conjonction* f. L *conjunctio(n-)*, f. *conjunct-* pa. ppl stem of *conjungere*: see prec., -ION.] 1 The action or an act of conjoining; the fact or condition of being conjoined; (a) union, (a) connection. LME. b *Alch.* A mixing or union of substances. LME. †c Union in marriage; sexual union. M16–E19. 2 *Astron.* & *Astrol.* An alignment of three celestial objects; *spec.* the apparent coincidence or proximity of two celestial objects as viewed from the earth. LME. 3 *Gram.* An uninflected word, other than a relative pronoun, used to connect clauses or sentences, or to coordinate words in the same clause. (One of the parts of speech.) LME. †4 A junction; a joint. LME–L17. 5 A number of things, persons, etc., conjoined or associated together; a combination, an association. M16. 6 An occurrence of events or circumstances in combination. L17. 7 *Logic.* A proposition of the form (*p* and *q*), which is true only when both *p* and *q* (and any further conjoined statements) are true. E20.

1 A. BRIGGS A conjunction of some of his own supporters with his enemies. **in conjunction** together, jointly, (*with*). 2 **inferior, superior, conjunction**: of an inferior planet with the sun, when the planet and the earth are on the same side, opposite sides, of the sun. 3 *subordinating conjunction*: see SUBORDINATE *v.* 5 A. W. KINGLAKE A strong man and a good cause make a formidable conjunction. 6 H. T. BUCKLE [This] required a peculiar conjunction of events.

conjunctional *a.* of the nature of or pertaining to a conjunction M17. **conjunctionally** *adv.* M19.

conjunctiva /kɒndʒʌŋkˈtʌɪvə, kənˈdʒʌŋktɪvə/ *n.* LME. [med.L (*tunica*) *conjunctiva* conjunctive (membrane): see next.] The delicate mucous membrane that covers the front of the eye (except over the cornea) and lines the inside of the eyelids.

conjunctival *a.* of or pertaining to the conjunctiva M19.

conjunctive /kənˈdʒʌŋktɪv/ *a.* & *n.* LME. [Late L *conjunctivus*, f. *conjunct-*: see CONJUNCTION, -IVE.] A *adj.* 1 *Gram.* Of the nature of a conjunction; having the function of connecting, *spec.* uniting the sense as well as the construction. LME. b Of the mood of a verb: used only in conjunction with another verb, subjunctive. M18. 2 *gen.* Having the property or effect of uniting or joining; connective. L15. 3 Conjunct, conjoined, united. E17. 4 *Logic.* Of, pertaining to, or characterized by the conjunction of statements etc. L17. B *n.* 1 *Gram.* A conjunction; *spec.* one uniting the sense as well as the construction. L16. b (A verb in) the conjunctive mood. E19. †2 = CONJUNCTIVA. M17–M18. 3 *Logic.* A conjunctive proposition or syllogism. M19.

conjunctively *adv.* E17. **conjunctiveness** *n.* M18.

conjunctivitis /kəndʒʌŋktɪˈvʌɪtɪs/ *n.* M19. [f. CONJUNCTIVA + -ITIS.] Inflammation of the conjunctiva.

conjuncture /kənˈdʒʌŋktʃə/ *n.* E17. [f. CONJUNCTION by suffix-substitution, partly after Fr. (mod. *conjoncture*) f. It. *congiuntura*, f. as CONJUNCT *n.* + -URE.] 1 A meeting *of* circumstances or events; a state of affairs, a juncture. E17. †2 = CONJUNCTION 2. E17–E19. †3 The action of joining together; the fact or state of being joined; a joining, a combination. M17–L18.

conjuration /kʌndʒʊˈreɪʃ(ə)n, (*esp. in sense 1*) kɒndʒʊ(ə)-/ *n.* LME. [OFr. *conjuracion*, (also mod.) *-ation*, f. L *conjuratio(n-)*, f. *conjurat-* pa. ppl stem of *conjurare* CONJURE *v.*: see -ATION.] 1 An act of swearing together; a making of a common oath; a banding together, a conspiracy. *arch.* LME. 2 A solemn appeal to something sacred or binding; a solemn entreaty. *arch.* LME. 3 The effecting of something supernatural by the invocation of a name of power or by an incantation. LME. 4 An incantation, a spell, a charm; a form of words used in conjuring. LME. 5 The performance of magic tricks, conjuring; a conjuring trick. M18.

conjurator /ˈkɒndʒʊ(ə)reɪtə/ *n.* LME. [AN *conjuratour* or med.L *conjurator*, f. *conjurat-*: see prec., -ATOR.] A person joined with others by an oath; a fellow-conspirator.

conjure /ˈkʌndʒə/ *n.* LME. [In isolated early use f. OFr.; later (L19) f. the vb.] †1 = CONJURATION 3. Only in LME. †2 = CONJURATION 1. Only in M16. 3 *W. Indies* & *US Blacks.* Magic. L19.

Comb.: **conjure doctor, man** a witch-doctor; **conjure woman** a witch.

conjure /ˈkʌndʒə; *in senses 1, 2* kɒnˈdʒʊə/ *v.* ME. [(O)Fr. *conjurer* plot, exorcise, adjure f. L *conjurare* band together by an oath, conspire, (in med.L) invoke, f. as CON- + *jurare* swear.] I 1 *v.t.* Constrain (a person to some action) by appeal to an oath or something sacred; call upon in the name of some supernatural being. ME. 2 *v.t.* Appeal solemnly to (a person) *to do* something; beseech, implore. ME. 3 *v.t.* Call upon (a demon, spirit, etc.) to appear or act, by invocation or incantation. ME. 4 *v.i.* Orig., invoke a demon etc., use incantation or spells. Now, produce magical effects by trickery. ME. †5 *v.t.* Affect by incantation; charm, bewitch. LME–M19. 6 *v.t.* Effect, produce, bring (*out*), convey (*away*), by magic or a conjuror's trick; evoke. Freq. *fig.* M16.

2 CARLYLE A Letter from the Queen, conjuring him to return without delay. 4 **a name to conjure with**: of great importance. **conjuring trick** a magical effect achieved by sleight of hand or other natural means. 6 R. B. SHERIDAN What has conjured you to Bath? W. COWPER To conjure clean away the gold they touch. A. RANSOME As if she had somehow herself conjured the whole of High Topps into existence. S. HAZZARD Having perpetually conjured the sight of him in fancy. **conjure up** bring into existence as if by magic, cause to appear to the mind or eye, evoke.

†II 7 *v.i.* Swear together; band together by oath; conspire. LME–M17. 8 *v.t.* Link by oath in an association or conspiracy. Usu. in *pass.* M16–E18.

8 MILTON The third part of Heav'ns Sons Conjur'd against the highest.

conjuror /ˈkʌndʒərə; *in sense 3* kɒnˈdʒʊərə/ *n.* Also **-er**. ME. [Partly f. prec., partly f. AN *conjurour*, OFr. *conjurere*, *-eor* f. med.L *conjurator* CONJURATOR: see -OR, -ER[1], -ER[2].] 1 A person who practises conjuration; a magician, a wizard, a sorcerer. ME. 2 A person who performs conjuring tricks. E18. 3 A person who is bound with others by an oath. Only in Dicts. M19.

1 **no conjuror** a person of limited intelligence or ability.

conjuress *n.* a female conjuror; a sorceress: L16. **conjurorship** *n.* L17.

conjury /ˈkʌndʒəri/ *n.* M19. [f. CONJURE *v.* after *augury*, *injury*, etc.] Conjurors' tricks, magic.

conk /kɒŋk/ *n.*[1] *slang.* E19. [Perh. alt. of CONCH.] 1 The nose; the head. E19. 2 A punch on the nose or head; a blow. L19.

conk /kɒŋk/ *n.*[2] Orig. *US.* M19. [App. var. of CONCH.] The fruiting body of a bracket fungus, esp. the fungus *Trametes pini*; infestation of timber by such a fungus.

conky *a.* affected with conk E20.

conk *n.*[3] var. of CONCH.

conk /kɒŋk/ *v.*[1]*t. slang.* E19. [f. CONK *n.*[1]] Punch, esp. on the nose or head; hit, strike; kill.

conk /kɒŋk/ *v.*[2]*i. slang.* E20. [Origin unkn.] Of a machine etc.: break down, fail or show signs of failing. Of a person: collapse, die. Usu. foll. by *out*.

conker /ˈkɒŋkə/ *n.* Also occas. **conquer**. M19. [Perh. f. CONCH, assoc. w. CONQUER *v.*] Orig., a snail-shell; now, a horse chestnut. In *pl.*, a game played orig. with snail-shells, now with horse chestnuts on strings, in which each player tries to break with his or her own that held by the opponent. Cf. earlier CONQUEROR 2.

conkering *vbl n.* see CONQUERING.

con moto /kɒn ˈməʊtəʊ, *foreign* kɔn ˈmoto/ *adv. phr.* E19. [It. = with movement.] *Mus.* A direction: with spirited movement.

conn *n.* var. of CON *n.*[3]

conn *v.* see CON *v.*[2]

connate /ˈkɒneɪt/ *a.* M17. [Late L *connatus* pa. pple of *connasci*, f. as CON- + *nasci* be born: see -ATE[2].] 1 Existing in a person from birth; innate, congenital. M17. 2 Of the same or similar nature; allied; congenial. M17. 3 *Bot.* & *Zool.* Of parts or organs: congenitally united, so as to form one part or organ. L18. 4 Formed at the same time, coeval. E19. 5 *Geol.* Of water: trapped in a sedimentary rock during its deposition. E20.

connately *adv.* L19. **connateness** *n.* M17.

connation /kəˈneɪʃ(ə)n/ *n.* M19. [f. as prec.: see -ATION.] *Biol.* Connate condition (see CONNATE 3).

connatural /kəˈnatʃ(ə)r(ə)l/ *a.* L16. [Late L *connaturalis*, f. as CON- + NATURAL *a.*] 1 Innate; belonging inherently or naturally (*to*). L16. 2 Of the same or similar nature, cognate. E17.

connatuˈrality *n.* E17. **connaturalize** *v.t.* make connatural M17. **connaturally** *adv.* M17. **connaturalness** *n.* E17.

connect /kəˈnɛkt/ *v.* LME. [L *connectere*, f. as CON- + *nectere* bind, fasten.] I *v.i.* Usu. foll. by *with*. 1 Be united physically, make contact, join on; be related or associated; form a logical sequence. (*rare* bef. 18.) LME. b Of a train, aeroplane, etc.: have its arrival timed to allow passengers in it to transfer to another (specified) train etc. M19. c Hit the target (*with* a blow, kick, etc.). *colloq.* E20. d Make a mental or practical connection; realize interconnections. E20. e Make contact with a person, esp. for the purpose of buying drugs: cf. CONNECTION 9. *slang* (orig. *US*). E20. f Succeed in communicating with the audience or reader; be meaningful. M20.

1 A. TUCKER One all-comprehensive plan; wherein . . all the parts connect with one another. F. TUOHY For her the word connected still with guilt. b F. L. OLMSTED The train was advertised to connect here with a steamboat for Norfolk. d E. M. FORSTER Live in fragments no longer. Only connect, and the beast and the monk, robbed of the isolation that is life to either, will die. f *Listener* A magazine programme . . has probably done its job if one of its items connects.

II *v.t.* 2 Join, link, fasten together, (two things, one thing *to* or *with* another); link in sequence or coherence. M16. 3 Associate in occurrence or action. Usu. in *pass.*, be to do *with*. E18. b Associate mentally. M18. 4 Unite (a person) with another or others by relationship or marriage, by common interests, etc. Usu. in *pass.* or *refl.* M18. 5 Establish telephone communication for (a person) (*with*). E20.

2 S. JOHNSON The authour connects his reasons well. JAS. MILL The Conjunctions are distinguished from the Prepositions by connecting Predications. DAY LEWIS The ponds . . were connected one to another by a tiny . . stream. L. DEIGHTON The super highway that connects Reggio to Naples. 3 J. BENTHAM A very busy amateur in everything that is in any way connected with mechanics. W. F. HARVEY For some time there was nothing to connect me with the crime. b D. H. LAWRENCE It did not occur to her to connect the train's moving on with the sound of the trumpet.

connectable *a.* = CONNECTIBLE L19. **connectiˈbility** *n.* the quality of being connectible E20. **connectible** *a.* able to be connected M18. **connecting** *ppl a.* serving to connect or join (*connecting-rod*: transmitting motion from the piston to the crankpin etc. in an engine) L17.

connected /kəˈnɛktɪd/ *a.* E18. [f. prec. + -ED[1].] 1 Joined together, conjoined; *esp.* joined in sequence, coherent. E18. 2 Related; having relationships or associations (of a specified nature). L18.

1 SIMPLY *connected*. *T-connected*: see T, T 2. 2 **well connected** related to or associated with persons of good social position or influence.

connectedly *adv.* L18. **connectedness** *n.* L17.

connecter *n.* see CONNECTOR.

Connecticutter /kəˈnɛtɪkʌtə/ *n.* L19. [f. *Connecticut* (see below) + -ER[1].] A native or inhabitant of the State of Connecticut, USA.

connection /kəˈnɛkʃ(ə)n/ *n.* Also (earlier, now usual only in sense 6b) **-nex-**. LME. [L *connexio(n-)*, f. *connex-* pa. ppl stem of *connectere*: see CONNECT, -ION. Mod. sp. after *connect*.] 1 *gen.* The action or an act of connecting or joining; the state of being connected. LME. b The connecting of parts of an electric circuit; the making of electrical contact. M19. c A linking by telephone communication. L19. 2 A connecting part; *spec.* a link between electrical components, a means of making electrical contact. LME. 3 (A) causal or logical relationship or association; (an) interdependence. E17. 4 (A) contextual relation. Esp. in *in this* (*the same, another*, etc.) *connection*. E18. 5 Personal dealing; a personal relationship or association. (Foll. by *with*.) M18. b A sexual relationship, sexual intercourse. *arch.* L18. 6 A body of people united by political, commercial, or other ties; a body of customers or clients. M18. b *spec.* (**-nex-**.) In the Methodist Church or its offshoots: a denomination, an interrelated system of congregations. M18. 7 (A) family relationship, as by marriage or distant consanguinity. Freq. in *pl.* L18. b A person connected with another or others by marriage or distant consanguinity; an acquaintance, *esp.* one who has prestige or influence. L18. 8 The scheduled meeting of one train, aeroplane, etc., with another on another route, for the transfer of passengers; the facilities or arrangements for this. M19. 9 A purchase of illegal drugs; a person who peddles or supplies these; an organization dealing in illegal drugs. *slang* (orig. *US*). M20.

1 C. DARWIN This connection of the former and present buds by ramifying branches. J. BRYCE The connection of Church and State. b SCOTT CONNECTION. 3 E. W. ROBERTSON There was a close connexion during the early feudal period between rank and wealth. J. CONRAD The voice returned, stammering words without connection. 4 R. PORSON Martin took the sentence out of its connection. 5 F. RAPHAEL She cared little for her parents' world and had no connexion with it. 6 LD MACAULAY At the head of a strong parliamentary connection. 7 LD MACAULAY He was, by hereditary connection, a Cavalier. J. FENTON He was always Boasting of his connections. b S. H. ADAMS [John Quincy Adams] may well have been a connection of our line. 8 L. MACNEICE I missed my connection in Glasgow and had to spend the day there.

connectional /kəˈnɛkʃ(ə)n(ə)l/ *a.* Also (in sense 2 always) **-nex-**. M19. [f. prec. + -AL[1].] 1 Of, pertaining to, or of the nature of a connection. M19. 2 *spec.* Of or pertaining to a Methodist connection. M19.

connectionalism *n.* the organization of a Church by a system of connections L19.

connective /kəˈnɛktɪv/ *a.* & *n.* M17. [f. CONNECT *v.* + -IVE, repl. earlier CONNEXIVE.] A *adj.* Serving or tending to connect. M17.

connective tissue *Anat.* fibrous tissue connecting and binding the more specialized tissues and organs of the body.

B *n.* 1 *Gram.* & *Logic.* A connecting word or particle. M18. 2 *Bot.* The part of the filament which connects the lobes of the anther. M19.

connectival /kɒnɛkˈtʌɪv(ə)l/ *a.* (*Bot.*) of the connective M19. **connectively** *adv.* L16. **connecˈtivity** *n.* (chiefly *Math.* & *Logic*) the state, property, or degree of being (inter)connected L19.

connector /kəˈnɛktə/ *n.* Also (esp. of a person) **-er**. L18. [f. as prec. + -OR, -ER[1].] A person who or thing which connects; *esp.* a device for keeping two parts of an electrical conductor in contact.

Connemara /kɒnɪˈmɑːrə/ *n.* M19. [A region in the west of Co. Galway, Republic of Ireland.] Used *attrib.* to designate things found in or associated with Connemara.

Connemara marble a banded serpentinous marble. **Connemara pony** a small hardy breed of horse.

conner /ˈkɒnə, *in sense 1 also* ˈkʌn-/ *n.*[1] OE. [f. CON *v.*[1] + -ER[1].] 1 A person who tests or examines; an inspector. Cf. *aleconner* s.v. ALE *n.* *arch.* OE. 2 A person who cons or studies diligently. E19.

conner *n.*[2] var. of CUNNER.

connex /ˈkɒnɛks/ *n.* LME. [OFr. *connexe* annexe, dependence, f. med.L, f. pa. pple of L *connectere*: see CONNECT *v.*] †1 A connected circumstance or property. LME–L17. 2 *Sc. Law* (now *Hist.*). An item of property connected with another. Always in conjunction w. *annex*. M16.

†**connex** *v.t.* M16. [OFr. *connexer*, app. f. *connexe* adj., f. L *connexus* pa. pple of *connectere*: see CONNECT.] 1 Join or fasten together. M16–E18. 2 Connect logically or practically; associate. M16–M19.

connexion *n.* see CONNECTION.

connexional *a.* see CONNECTIONAL.

connexity /kəˈnɛksɪti/ *n.* E17. [(O)Fr. *connexité*, f. *connexe*: see CONNEX *v.*, -ITY.] Connected quality, connectedness.

†**connexive** *a.* L16. [L *connexivus*, f. *connex-* pa. ppl stem of *connectere*: see CONNECT, -IVE.] 1 *Logic.* Conditional; (of a proposition) whose clauses are connected together as antecedent and consequent. L16–E18. 2 *Gram.* Conjunctive. M17–L18. 3 Connective. L18–M19.

conning-tower /ˈkɒnɪŋtaʊə/ *n.* L19. [f. CON *v.*[2] + -ING[1] + TOWER *n.*[1]] The (armoured) pilot-house of a warship; the superstructure of a submarine from which the vessel may be directed when on or near the surface.

conniption /kəˈnɪpʃ(ə)n/ *n.* *N. Amer. colloq.* M19. [Prob. invented.] A fit of rage or hysteria; in *pl.*, hysterics. Also *conniption-fit*.

connivance /kəˈnʌɪv(ə)ns/ *n.* Also (earlier, now only in sense 3) **-vence**. L16. [Fr. *connivence* or L *conniventia*, f. *connivere*: see next, -ENCE.] †1 *lit.* Winking. L16–E17. 2 The action of conniving (*at* or *in* a person's misconduct); assistance in wrongdoing by conscious failure to prevent or condemn; tacit permission. L16. 3 *Bot.* & *Zool.* (Usu. **-vence**.) Tendency to converge. M19.

connivancy *n.* (*arch.*) connivance E17.

connive /kəˈnʌɪv/ *v.* E17. [Fr. *conniver* f. L *connivere*, f. as CON- + a stem rel. to *nictare* (see NICTITATE).] I *v.i.* 1 Foll. by *at*: shut one's eyes to (a thing one dislikes but is resigned to), pretend ignorance of, overlook. *arch.* E17. †2 Foll. by *at*: regard (an offender) sympathetically. E17–M18. 3 Foll. by *at*: turn a blind eye to (an action one ought to oppose, but which one secretly sympathizes with); be secretly accessory to. M17. †4 Remain inactive or dormant. *rare* (Milton). M–L17. 5 Be in secret complicity, conspire, (*with*). L18. 6 *Bot.* & *Zool.* Converge (gradually). *rare.* M19.

1 LD MACAULAY The government thought it expedient occasionally to connive at the violation of this rule. 2 CHESTERFIELD You must renounce courts, if you will not connive at knaves and tolerate fools. 3 S. SMILES The maritime population .. actively connived at their escape. 5 SIR W. SCOTT Dost thou connive with the wolves in robbing thine own fold?

II *v.t.* †7 Connive at (a fault, offence, etc.). E17–M19.

conniver *n.* M17.

connivence *n.* see CONNIVANCE.

connivent /kəˈnʌɪv(ə)nt/ *a.* E17. [L *connivent-* pres. ppl stem of *connivere* CONNIVE: see -ENT.] †1 Disposed to connive at or overlook offences. E–M17. 2 *Anat.* Designating the circular folds (now usu. called *plicae circulares*) in the mucous membrane of the small intestine. Long *rare* or *obs.* L17. 3 *Bot.* & *Zool.* Of parts: gradually convergent, approaching at the extremity. M18.

connoisseur /kɒnəˈsəː/ *n.* & *v.* E18. [(O)Fr. (now *connaisseur*), f. OFr. *conoiss-* pres. ppl stem of *conoistre* (mod. *connaître*) know + *-eur* -OR.] A *n.* A person with a thorough knowledge and critical judgement of a subject, esp. one of the fine arts; an expert in any matter of taste, e.g. wines, foods. (Foll. by *of*, *in*.) E18.

R. CHURCH I loved pencils... I collected them as a connoisseur. K. CLARK Lord Burlington was a connoisseur, collector and arbiter of taste.

B *v.i.* & *t.* Be a connoisseur (of). *rare.* E19.

connoisseurship *n.* the role or activity of a connoisseur; proficiency as a connoisseur: M18.

connotation /kɒnəˈteɪʃ(ə)n/ *n.* LME. [med.L *connotatio(n-)*, f. *connotat-* pa. ppl stem of *connotare*: see CONNOTE, -ATION.] †1 Something implied as a condition or accompaniment; a concomitant symptom. Only in LME. 2 An association or idea suggested by a word in addition to its primary meaning; implication. M16. 3 *Logic.* Orig., the subject of which an attribute is predicated. Later, the attribute connoted by a term. M17. 4 The sum of what a word implies; meaning, signification. M19.

2 V. PACKARD The words instant coffee seemed loaded with unfortunate connotations.

connotational *a.* pertaining to or involving connotation M20.

connotative /ˈkɒnəteɪtɪv, kəˈnəʊtətɪv/ *a.* E17. [med.L *connotativus*, f. *connotat-*: see prec., -IVE.] Having the quality of connoting; *esp.* implying or implied in addition to the primary meaning.

connotative term *Logic* a term which, while denoting a subject, also connotes its attributes.

connotatively *adv.* M19.

connote /kəˈnəʊt/ *v.t.* M17. [med.L *connotare*, f. as CON- + *notare* NOTE *v.*[1]] 1 Of a word etc.: signify or imply in addition to the primary meaning. M17. 2 Of a fact etc.: imply as a consequence or condition; suggest. M17. 3 *Logic.* Orig., imply (the subject) in which an attribute inheres, while primarily signifying the attribute itself. Now, with inverted use: imply (the attributes involved), while denoting the subject. E19. 4 Include in its signification; mean, signify. M19.

1 M. PATTISON Deism .. connotes along with natural religion a negation of the .. Christian revelation. 2 IDWAL JONES A gate that connoted landed respectability.

connubial /kəˈnjuːbɪəl/ *a.* M17. [L *connubialis*, f. *connubium* wedlock, f. as CON- + *nubere* marry: see -AL[1].] 1 Of or pertaining to marriage or the married state; matrimonial. M17. 2 Married, wedded; of or pertaining to a spouse. E19.

connubiˈality *n.* the married state, wedlock; in *pl.*, customs characteristic of wedlock: M19. **connubially** *adv.* M19.

connumerate /kəˈnjuːməreɪt/ *v.t.* *rare.* Pa. pple & ppl a. **-ated**, †**-ate**. LME. [Late L *connumerat-* pa. ppl stem of *connumerare*, f. as CON- + NUMERATE *v.*] Reckon or count together.

connumeˈration *n.* M17.

conodont /ˈkəʊnədɒnt/ *n.* M19. [f. Gk *kōnos* cone + -ODONT.] Any of various Palaeozoic toothlike fossils of uncertain affinity.

conoid /ˈkəʊnɔɪd/ *a.* & *n.* L16. [Gk *kōnoeidēs* cone-shaped; f. *kōnos* CONE *n.*: see -OID.] A *adj.* Resembling a cone in shape; more or less conical. L16. B *n.* 1 A solid generated by the revolution of a conic section about its axis; *esp.* a paraboloid or hyperboloid. L16. 2 A body of similar shape to a cone. L18.

coˈnoidal *a.* pertaining to, of the shape of, or resembling a conoid L16. **coˈnoidic** *a.* (*rare*) = CONOIDAL E19. **coˈnoidical** *a.* (*rare*) = CONOIDAL L17.

conoscente /konoʃˈʃɛnte/ *n.* Pl. ***-ti*** /-ti/. M18. [It.] = COGNOSCENTE.

†**conquassate** *v.t.* M17–M18. [L *conquassat-*: see next, -ATE[3].] Shake hard, agitate.

†**conquassation** *n.* LME–L18. [L *conquassatio(n-)*, f. *conquassat-* pa. ppl stem of *conquassare*, f. as CON- + *quassare* frequent. of *quatere* shake: see -ATION.] Severe shaking; agitation.

conquer *n.* var. of CONKER *n.*

conquer /ˈkɒŋkə/ *v.* ME. [OFr. *conquerre* f. Proto-Romance f. L *conquirere* seek for, procure, gain, win, f. as CON- + *quaerere* seek.] I *v.t.* †1 Acquire, get possession of; attain to. ME–M16. 2 Acquire by force of arms, win in war; subjugate (a country etc.) by force. ME. 3 Overcome (an opponent) by force; vanquish. ME. 4 *transf.* & *fig.* Overcome or subdue (habit, passion, etc.) by an effort of will; get the better of; master; gain by a struggle; win the affections or sexual favours of. LME. b Climb successfully and reach the top of (a mountain). L19.

1 CAXTON Brenne had .. conquerd a grete lordship thurgh maryage. 2 A. ALISON At all hazards we must conquer a maritime peace. H. A. L. FISHER They had conquered Syria and Egypt. 3 R. W. EMERSON The Germans, whom the Romans found hard to conquer in two hundred .. years. 4 C. HILL The idea of conquering poverty through conquering idleness. A. LURIE I conquered the impulse to hide in my room.

II *v.i.* 5 Be the conqueror; make conquests; be victorious. ME.

5 SHAKES. *Rich. III* Arm, fight, and conquer, for fair England's sake! W. H. PRESCOTT Cortez .. did not conquer from the mere ambition of conquest.

conquerable *a.* able to be conquered L15. **conqueress** *n.* (now *rare*) a female conqueror LME. **conqueringly** *adv.* (*rare*) in a conquering manner, victoriously E17. **conquerless** *a.* (*poet. rare*) invincible L16.

conquering /ˈkɒŋk(ə)rɪŋ/ *vbl n.* In sense 2 usu. **conk-**. ME. [f. prec. + -ING[1]. See also CONQUEROR 2, CONKER.] 1 The action of CONQUER *v.* ME. 2 Playing at conkers. *colloq.* E19.

conqueror /ˈkɒŋk(ə)rə/ *n.* ME. [AN *conquerour*, OFr. *-eor* (obl.), f. as CONQUER *v.*: see -OR.] 1 A person who conquers; a person who subjugates a nation; a victor. ME. 2 = CONKER. E19.

1 **(William) the Conqueror** King William I of England.

conquest /ˈkɒŋkwɛst/ *n.* ME. [OFr. *conquest(e)* (mod. *conquête*), repr. use as n. of neut. and fem. of Proto-Romance pa. pple of CONQUER *v.*] 1 The action or an act of gaining by force of arms;

military subjugation (of a country etc.). ME. **2** The action or an act of overcoming by force or by an effort of will; mastery; (a) winning of a person's affections or sexual favours; (a) successful climbing to the top of a mountain. ME. **3** Something acquired by force of arms; *esp.* conquered territory; *fig.* a person whose affections or sexual favours have been won. ME. **4** *Sc. Law.* (The acquisition of) property gained otherwise than by inheritance. *obs.* exc. *Hist.* LME.

1 HOBBES Conquest . . is the Acquiring of the Right of Soveraignty by Victory. **the (Norman) Conquest** the acquisition of the English crown by William of Normandy in 1066. 2 SHAKES. *3 Hen. VI* I must yield . . by my fall, the conquest to my foe. W. S. MAUGHAM When he made the customary advances he discovered to his relief, for he was not a man who considered that resistance added a flavour to conquest, that she was no prude. ALDOUS HUXLEY The so-called 'conquest of space'. 3 SHAKES. *Jul. Caes.* What conquest brings he home? What tributaries follow him to Rome. G. SANTAYANA Young boys . . look for some easy conquest among . . country wenches.

conquest /ˈkɒŋkwest/ *v.t.* Chiefly *Sc.* & *north.* Pa. t. & pple **-quested**, †**-quest**. ME. [f. the n.] **1** Acquire, get possession of. Long only *Sc. Law* (now *Hist.*), acquire (property) otherwise than by inheritance. ME. †**2** Conquer; vanquish. LME–M17.

conquistador /kɒŋˈkwɪstədɔː/ *n.* Pl. **-dors**, **-dores** /-dɔːrɪz/. M19. [Sp.] A conqueror; *spec.* any of the Spanish conquerors of Mexico and Peru in the 16th cent.

Conradian /kɒnˈradɪən/ *a.* E20. [f. Joseph *Conrad* (original name Teodor Józef Konrad Korzeniowski: see below) + -IAN.] Of, pertaining to, or characteristic of Joseph Conrad (1857–1924), Polish-born writer of novels in English, or his work.

con-rod /ˈkɒnrɒd/ *n. colloq.* M20. [Abbrev.] A connecting-rod.

consanguine /kɒnˈsaŋgwɪn/ *a.* E17. [Fr. *consanguin(e)* f. L *consanguineus*: see next.] Consanguineous.

consanguineous /kɒnsaŋˈgwɪnɪəs/ *a.* E17. [f. L *consanguineus* of the same blood, f. as CON- + *sanguis, -inis* blood: see -OUS.] **1** Related by descent from a common ancestor; of or pertaining to blood relationship. E17. **2** *Rom. Law.* Related as children of the same father (opp. *uterine*); pertaining to those so related. M19.

2 *brother consanguineous, consanguineous brother*: see BROTHER *n.*

consanguineal *a.* = CONSANGUINEOUS 1 L18. **consanguinean** *a.* = CONSANGUINEOUS E18. **consanguineously** *adv.* L19.

consanguinity /kɒnsaŋˈgwɪnɪti/ *n.* LME. [L *consanguinitas*, f. *consanguineus*: see prec., -ITY.] **1** Relationship by descent from a common ancestor; blood relationship. LME. †**2** *collect.* Blood relations, kin. *rare.* LME–E18.

1 *fig.*: S. JOHNSON Such is the consanguinity of our intellects.

consarcination /kɒnˌsɑːsɪˈneɪʃ(ə)n/ *n.* Now *rare* or *obs.* M17. [f. L *consarcinat-* pa. ppl stem of *consarcinare* patch together, f. as CON- + *sarcinare* to patch: see -ATION.] Patching together; a heterogeneous combination.

consarn *v.*, **consarned** *ppl a.* see CONCERN *v.*, CONCERNED.

conscience /ˈkɒnʃ(ə)ns/ *n.* ME. [(O)Fr. f. L *conscientia* privity of knowledge, consciousness, f. *conscire* be privy to, f. as CON- + *scire* know: see -ENCE.] †**I1** One's inmost thought, one's mind or heart. ME–E17. **2** (An) inward knowledge or consciousness; (an) internal conviction; mental recognition or acknowledgement (*of*). LME–M19. **3** Reasonableness, understanding. *rare* (Shakes.). Only in E17.

1 SHAKES. *Hen. V* I will speak my conscience of the King: I think he would not wish himself anywhere but where he is. 2 HOBBES Mankind, from conscience of its own weaknesse.

II4 A moral sense of right or wrong; a sense of responsibility felt for private or public actions, motives, etc.; the faculty or principle that leads to the approval of right thought or action and condemnation of wrong. ME. †**5** Conscientious observance *of*, regard *to*. LME–L17. **6** Practice of or conformity to what is considered right; conscientiousness. *arch.* LME. †**7** Sense of guilt with regard to a thought or action; scruple, compunction, remorse. LME–E17.

4 E. PEACOCK With several twinges of conscience. R. MACAULAY David can do as he likes . . , it is between him and his conscience. E. ROOSEVELT Working conditions which no one with any social conscience would tolerate today. 6 A. C. SWINBURNE The care and conscience with which their scenes were wrought out.

Phrases: **bad** or **guilty conscience** a conscience troubled by feelings of remorse, guilt, or sin; a consciousness that one's thoughts or actions are or have been wrong. **case of conscience** [tr. L *casus conscientiae*] a matter in which a conflict of principles has to be resolved by one's conscience. **clear** or **good conscience** a conscience untroubled by feelings of remorse, guilt, or sin; a consciousness that one's thoughts or actions are or have been right. **for conscience** (or **conscience') sake** in order to satisfy one's conscience. **freedom** or **liberty of conscience** freedom of all citizens of a State to practise the religion of their choice. *good conscience*: see *clear conscience* above. *guilty conscience*: see *bad conscience* above. **have on one's conscience** feel guilty about. **in all conscience** *colloq.* by any reasonable standard. **keep a person's conscience** ensure that he or she forms sound moral judgements. *liberty of conscience*: see *freedom of conscience* above. †**make (a) conscience of** have scruples about. *prick of conscience*: see PRICK *n.* **prisoner of conscience** a person detained or imprisoned because of his or her religious or political beliefs. *social conscience*: see SOCIAL *a.* *soul and conscience*: see SOUL *n.*

Comb.: **conscience clause**: (in a law etc.) ensuring respect for the consciences of those affected; **conscience money**: sent to relieve the conscience, esp. in payment of evaded income tax; **conscience-smitten, -stricken, -struck** *adjs.* made uneasy by a bad conscience.

conscienced *a.* having a conscience (of a specified nature) M16. **conscienceless** *a.* LME.

conscient /ˈkɒnʃɪənt/ *a.* Now *literary.* E17. [L *conscient-* pres. ppl stem of *conscire*: see prec., -ENT.] Conscious.

conscientious /kɒnʃɪˈɛnʃəs/ *a.* E17. [Fr. *consciencieux* f. med.L *conscientiosus*, f. L *conscientia*: see CONSCIENCE, -OUS.] Obedient to conscience, (habitually) governed by a sense of duty; done according to conscience; scrupulous, painstaking; of or pertaining to conscience.

C. KINGSLEY She became a Baptist from conscientious scruples. T. COLLINS Ida was an untiring and conscientious worker. **conscientious objector** a person who makes use of a conscience clause to refuse to conform to a regulation etc.; *esp.* a person who for reasons of conscience objects to military service.

conscientiously *adv.* M17. **conscientiousness** *n.* M17.

conscionable /ˈkɒnʃ(ə)nəb(ə)l/ *a.* Now *rare* or *obs.* M16. [f. CONSCIENCE (w. /-s/ erron. taken as pl. suff. -S[1]) + -ABLE.] Having a conscience; showing a regard for conscience; conscientious, scrupulous.

¶See UNCONSCIONABLE.

conscionableness *n.* E17. **conscionably** *adv.* M16.

conscious /ˈkɒnʃəs/ *a.* & *n.* L16. [f. L *conscius* knowing something with others, knowing in oneself, f. *conscire*: see CONSCIENCE, -OUS.] **A** *adj.* †**1** Having guilty knowledge (*of*). L16–E19. **2** Orig. more fully †*conscious to oneself*. Knowing or perceiving within oneself, aware. Foll. by *of* a fact, one's sensations, thoughts, etc., external circumstances, an external object, *that*. Also *absol.* (*poet.*), well aware. E17. **b** As 2nd elem. of comb.: aware of, concerned about. E20. **3** Of an inanimate thing: privy to, sharing in, or witnessing human thoughts and actions, external events, etc. Chiefly *poet.* E17. †**4** Foll. by *to*: sharing in the knowledge of, aware of, privy to. M17–E19. **5** Of an emotion, quality, etc.: of which one is aware; felt, sensible. M17. **6** Having or manifesting the faculty of consciousness (CONSCIOUSNESS 3). L17. **7** Self-conscious, affected. E18. **8** Aware of what one is doing or intends to do. Of an action etc.: realized by the doer, planned, deliberate. M19. **9** Having the mental faculties in an active and waking state. M19.

1 HENRY MORE She being conscious, did . . make confession of her wickedness. 2 LD MACAULAY He must have been conscious that, though he thought adultery sinful, he was an adulterer. T. HARDY Conscious that . . his accents and manner wore a roughness not observable in the street. I. MCEWAN He walked towards them slowly, . . conscious of their attention. S. HAZZARD She found them insufficiently conscious of their disadvantage. SELF-CONSCIOUS. b *class-conscious, clothes-conscious, health-conscious*, etc. 3 SOUTHEY If the conscious air had caught the sound. 5 GOLDSMITH His face became pale with conscious guilt. B. RUSSELL Fear—deep, scarcely conscious fear. 6 J. B. MOZLEY Man . . as a conscious being. *conscious subject*: see SUBJECT *n.* 5c. 7 POPE The conscious simper, and the jealous leer. L. P. HARTLEY This florid woman, with her air of conscious Edwardian gentility. 8 B. F. WESTCOTT A . . sequence . . which few will attribute to . . a conscious design. L. STEPHEN Pope was . . a conscious and deliberate artist. 9 T. HOLMES The sister reported that he had become conscious, having recognized her.

B *n. The* conscious mind. E20.

¶Cf. SUBCONSCIOUS, UNCONSCIOUS.

consciously *adv.* L17.

consciousness /ˈkɒnʃəsnɪs/ *n.* M17. [f. prec. + -NESS.] **1** Internal knowledge or conviction, esp. of one's own guilt, innocence, deficiencies, etc. M17. **2** The state or fact of being mentally aware *of* anything; the perception *that*. L17. **3** The state or faculty, or a particular state, of being aware of one's thoughts, feelings, actions, etc. L17. **4** The totality of the thoughts, feelings, impressions, etc., of a person or group; such a body of thoughts etc. relating to a particular sphere; a collective awareness or sense. L17. **5** The state of having the mental faculties awake and active; the waking state. E19.

1 B. JOWETT Happy in the consciousness of a well-spent life. 2 ADAM SMITH A consciousness that . . this species of cultivation . . is more profitable. H. JAMES He enjoyed the consciousness of their having a secret together. 3 J. LOCKE Consciousness is the perception of what passes in a Man's own mind. WORDSWORTH Consciousnesses not to be subdued. 4 M. HOWITT The commencement of a moral consciousness. *stream of consciousness*: see STREAM *n.* 5 D. L. SAYERS He became gradually weaker and lost consciousness.

Comb.: **consciousness-raising** increasing (esp. social, political, or moral) sensitivity or awareness.

¶Cf. SUBCONSCIOUSNESS, UNCONSCIOUSNESS.

conscribe /kənˈskraɪb/ *v.t.* L15. [L *conscribere*: see CONSCRIPT *a.*] †**1** Write, compose. *rare.* Only in L15. †**2a** *gen.* Enrol, levy (an army); enlist (a soldier). M16–M17. **b** *spec.* = CONSCRIPT *v.* E19. †**3** Circumscribe, limit. L16–E18.

conscript /ˈkɒnskrɪpt/ *n.* L18. [Fr. *conscrit* f. L *conscriptus*: see next.] A person enlisted by conscription for military etc. service.

conscript /ˈkɒnskrɪpt/ *a.* LME. [L *conscriptus* pa. pple of *conscribere* write down, list, enrol, f. as CON- + *scribere* write.] **1** Enrolled or elected as a Roman senator or *transf.* as a member of any legislative or administrative body. Chiefly in *conscript fathers* [L *patres conscripti*, orig. *patres et conscripti*], Roman senators, legislators, etc., collectively. LME. **2** Of a soldier, an army, etc.: enlisted or raised by conscription. E19.

conscript /kənˈskrɪpt/ *v.t.* Orig. *US.* E19. [Back-form. f. next.] Enlist by conscription; recruit compulsorily.

C. RYAN Conscripted into the *Wehrmacht*. *fig.*: L. LEE Winter and summer . . conscripted our thoughts.

conscription /kənˈskrɪpʃ(ə)n/ *n.* LME. [Late L *conscriptio(n-)* levying of troops, f. as CONSCRIPT *a.*: see -ION. In sense 3 after Fr.] †**1** Writing down together, putting in writing. Also (*rare*), conjoint signature. LME–E17. †**2** *gen.* Enrolment or enlistment of soldiers. E16–M17. **3** Compulsory enlistment for State service, esp. military service. E19.

conscriptionist *n.* an advocate of (military) conscription E20. **conscriptive** *a.* involving or having (military) conscription E20.

consecrate /ˈkɒnsɪkrət/ *a. arch. rare.* LME. [L *consecratus* pa. pple, f. as next: see -ATE[2].] Consecrated, hallowed.

consecrate /ˈkɒnsɪkreɪt/ *v.t.* LME. [L *consecrat-* pa. ppl stem of *consecrare*, f. as CON- + *sacrare* dedicate, f. *sacer* SACRED: see -ATE[3].] 1 Set apart as sacred (*to*); dedicate solemnly to a sacred or religious purpose; make fit for religious use. LME. b *spec.* Give sacramental character to (the Eucharistic elements of bread and wine) by performing the appropriate rite. E16. 2 Ordain (a bishop, monarch, etc.) to office. LME. 3 Dedicate or devote *to* a particular purpose or pursuit. M16. †4 Devote or doom *to* destruction etc. L16–M17. †5 Apotheosize, deify. E17–M18. 6 Make an object of veneration or regard; sanctify; sanction by usage. L17.

1 R. HOOKER The custom of the primitive church in consecrating holy virgins . . unto the service of God. *Book of Common Prayer* If the consecrated bread or wine be all spent . . the Priest is to consecrate more. 3 W. H. PRESCOTT His whole life was consecrated to letters. 6 J. LINGARD Writers, whose reputation consecrates their opinions.

consecrated *ppl a.* that has been consecrated; *esp.* (of a church, churchyard, ground, etc.) set apart by episcopal dedication for public worship or the burial of the dead, and having the ecclesiastical and legal status thus conferred: M16. **consecrator** *n.* M16. **consecratory** *a.* that consecrates E17.

consecration /kɒnsɪˈkreɪʃ(ə)n/ *n.* LME. [(O)Fr. *consécration* or L *consecratio(n-)*, f. as prec.: see -ATION.] 1 The action of consecrating to a sacred or religious purpose; setting apart as sacred, devoting to religious use; *esp.* (*a*) the formal dedication of a church, churchyard, ground, etc., by a bishop for public worship or the burial of the dead; (*b*) the giving of the sacramental character to the Eucharistic elements of bread and wine. LME. b An act of so consecrating; in *pl.* also, consecrated things. Long *arch.* M16. 2 (The ceremony of) ordination to a holy office. LME. 3 *Rom. Hist.* Apotheosis, deification. L15. 4 Dedication or devotion to a particular purpose or pursuit. L18. 5 Sanction by law, custom, or usage. M19.

consectary /kənˈsɛktəri/ *n.* L16. [f. L *consectarius* adj., logically following (also *consectaria* n.pl.), f. *consectari* frequent. of *consequi*: see next, -ARY[1].] A consequence; a deduction, a conclusion, a corollary.

consecution /kɒnsɪˈkjuːʃ(ə)n/ *n.* LME. [L *consecutio(n-)*, f. *consecut-* pa. ppl stem of *consequi* follow closely, overtake, f. as CON- + *sequi* pursue: see -ION.] †1 Attainment. *rare.* LME–E17. 2 (A) logical sequence; (an) inference; a train of reasoning. M16. 3 (A) succession, (a) sequence of events, phenomena, etc. M16. b *Mus.* (A) succession of similar intervals. M17.

consecutive /kənˈsɛkjʊtɪv/ *a.* E17. [Fr. *consécutif*, *-ive*, f. med.L *consecutivus*, f. *consecut-*: see prec., -IVE.] 1 Following continuously; following one's or its predecessor in uninterrupted sequence. E17. †2 Consequent (*to*). M17–M19. 3 Proceeding in logical sequence. M18. 4 *Mus.* Of intervals of the same kind, esp. fifths or octaves: occurring adjacently between the same two parts. E19. 5 *Gram.* Expressing consequence or result. L19.

1 T. COLLINS Mrs. B. has . . three consecutive husbands in heaven. 3 CONAN DOYLE The first consecutive account of the affair. 5 C. T. ONIONS Relative Clauses with Final or Consecutive meaning sometimes take *shall* (*should*).

Special collocations & phrases: **consecutive points, poles** = *consequent points* s.v. CONSEQUENT *a.* *waw consecutive*: see WAW *n.*[3]

consecutively *adv.* M17. **consecutiveness** *n.* E19.

consenescence /kɒnsɪˈnɛs(ə)ns/ *n.* *rare.* L17. [f. CON- (intensifier) + SENESCENCE.] Simultaneous or parallel senescence; general decay.

consension /kənˈsɛnʃ(ə)n/ *n.* *rare.* L16. [L *consensio(n-)*, f. as CONSENSUS: see -ION.] Agreement.

consensual /kənˈsɛnsjʊəl, -ʃʊəl/ *a.* M18. [f. as next + -AL[1].] 1 Relating to or involving consent or consensus. M18. 2 *Physiol.* Involving reflex response of the nervous system to stimulation of a sense-organ; *spec.* designating the reaction of both eyes to a stimulus applied only to one. E19.

1 **consensual contract** *Rom. Law*: requiring only the consent of the parties.

consensually *adv.* L19.

consensus /kənˈsɛnsəs/ *n.* M17. [L = agreement, f. *consens-* pa. ppl stem of *consentire*: see CONSENT *v.*] 1 Agreement or unity of or *of* opinion, testimony, etc.; the majority view, a collective opinion; (an agreement by different parties to) a shared body of views. M17. 2 Sympathetic or concordant action (of bodily organs etc.). Now *rare* or *obs.* M19.

1 M. HUNTER No single group has the right to ignore a consensus of thoughtful opinion. C. P. SNOW The general consensus appears to be that the murder story is unproven. *attrib.*: T. BENN Consensus politics draws its inspiration from many sources in all political parties.

¶Rare bef. M19.

consent /kənˈsɛnt/ *n.* ME. [OFr. *consente*, f. as next.] 1 Voluntary agreement to or acquiescence in a proposition etc.; compliance, permission. ME. 2 Agreement by a number of people as to a course of action etc. Now only in *by common consent*, (arch.) *with one consent*, unanimously. LME. 3 Agreement in feeling, sympathy; harmony, accord. *arch.* LME. 4 Unity of opinion, a consensus. *arch.* E16. †5 Feeling, opinion. Only in L16. †6 *Physiol.* A sympathetic relation between one organ and another. E17–L18.

1 HOBBES The Consent of a Subject to Soveraign Power. N. MITFORD I must have your consent as I'm not of age until May. *Proverb*: Silence gives consent. **age of consent** the age above which consent, esp. of a girl to sexual intercourse, is valid in law. 2 W. COWPER But sing and shine by sweet consent. 3 POPE The World's great harmony, that springs From Order, Union, full Consent of things. 4 W. PALEY We are far from a perfect consent in our opinions or feelings. 5 SHAKES. *1 Hen. VI* By my consent, we'll even let them alone.

consent /kənˈsɛnt/ *v.* ME. [(O)Fr. *consentir* f. L *consentire*, f. as CON- + *sentire* feel.] I *v.i.* 1 Be of the same opinion, agree (*with* a person, *that*, †*to* a doctrine etc.). *arch.* ME. 2 Express willingness, give permission, agree (*to* a proposal etc., *to do*, *that*). ME. †3 Come to agreement. LME–M17. †4 Be in accord or harmony. LME–L18. †5 Act or react in sympathy. Only in M18.

1 SHAKES. *A.Y.L.* All your writers do consent that ipse is he. 2 BYRON And whispering 'I will ne'er consent'—consented. E. M. FORSTER Mr. Beebe consented to run—a memorable sight. **consenting adult**: who willingly takes part in a particular action, esp. a homosexual act. 4 BACON Thinges like and consenting in qualitie.

II *v.t.* †6 Allow, agree to, consent to. LME–L17.

consenter *n.* ME. **consentingly** *adv.* (*a*) with consent or willing acquiescence; †(*b*) by common consent: LME. **consentive** *a.* (*rare*) = CONSENTIENT L15.

consentaneous /kɒns(ə)nˈteɪnɪəs/ *a.* L16. [f. L *consentaneus*, f. *consentire*: see prec., -ANEOUS.] 1 Unanimous, done by common consent; concurrent. L16. 2 Accordant, suited (*to*, *with*). E17.

consentaˈneity *n.* consentaneous quality L18. **consentaneously** *adv.* L16. **consentaneousness** *n.* M17.

consentant /kənˈsɛntənt/ *a.* *rare.* LME. [(O)Fr., pres. pple of *consentir* CONSENT *v.*: see -ANT[1].] Consenting.

consentient /kənˈsɛnʃ(ə)nt/ *a.* E17. [L *consentient-* pres. ppl stem of *consentire*: see CONSENT *v.*, -ENT.] 1 Agreeing, unanimous. E17. b Acting together, concurrent. M18. c Exhibiting or involving the body's ability to act as a unified whole in reflex response to sensory stimuli. L19. 2 Consenting, accordant, (*to*). M17.

consentience *n.* L19.

consequence /ˈkɒnsɪkw(ə)ns/ *n.* LME. [(O)Fr. *conséquence* f. L *consequentia*, f *consequent-* pres. ppl stem of *consequi* follow closely: see CONSECUTION, -ENCE.] 1 A thing or circumstance which follows as an effect or result from something preceding. LME. 2 A logical result or inference. LME. 3 Importance, moment, weight. M16. b *spec.* Importance in rank and position; social distinction. E17. c *spec.* Assumed sense of importance. L18. 4 The action or condition of following as a result upon something antecedent; the relation of an effect to its cause; the following of a logical conclusion from premisses. L16. †b Sequence; succession; course. L16–E18. 5 *Astrol.* Motion from an earlier to a later sign of the zodiac or from west to east. Now *rare* or *obs.* L17. 6 In *pl.* (usu. treated as *sing.*). A pencil-and-paper game in which a narrative is devised, usu. describing the meeting of a man and woman, and its consequences, each player contributing a part in ignorance of what has gone before. L18.

1 J. LE CARRÉ A minor heart attack as a consequence of stress and overwork. 3 H. JAMES This defect was of no great consequence. 4 MILTON Such fatal consequence unites us three. b HOBBES They thought the Names . . sufficiently connected when . . placed in their natural consequence.

Phrases: **in consequence**, *arch.* **by consequence** as a result (*of*). **of consequence** (*a*) important, significant; (*b*) *arch.* as a result. †**of good, bad**, etc., **consequence** with good, bad, etc., results. **of no consequence** unimportant. **take the consequences** accept whatever results from one's choice or act, *esp.* accept punishment.

†**consequency** *n.* = CONSEQUENCE 1, 2, 4 M16–E18.

consequent /ˈkɒnsɪkw(ə)nt/ *n.* LME. [(O)Fr. *conséquent*, f. as next (use as n. of pres. pple).] †1 = CONSEQUENCE 1. LME–M18. †2a = CONSEQUENCE 2. LME–M19. b *spec.* The second part of a conditional proposition, dependent on the antecedent. E17. †3 A follower; a pursuer. M16–M17. 4 A thing which follows something else in time or order (without necessary causal connection); *Math.* (now *rare*) the second of two quantities linked by some relationship or operation (e.g. a ratio). L16.

consequent /ˈkɒnsɪkw(ə)nt/ *a.* LME. [(O)Fr. *conséquent* f. L *consequent-*: see CONSEQUENCE, -ENT.] 1 Following as an effect or result (*on*, *upon*, *to*), resulting. LME. 2 Following as an inference or logical conclusion. LME. †3 Following in time or order; subsequent. L16–M18. 4 Observing or characterized by logical sequence; logically consistent. M19. 5 *Physical Geogr.* Of a stream, valley, etc.: having a course or character corresponding to the original slope of the land surface before it began to be eroded. Cf. OBSEQUENT *a.* 1, SUBSEQUENT *a.* 2b. L19.

1 J. LONDON Reaction and exhaustion consequent upon the hard day. P. ROSE Innocence of the female nude and consequent shock when confronted with one.

Special collocations: **consequent points** magnetic poles in excess of the usual pair in any magnetized body.

consequential /kɒnsɪˈkwɛnʃ(ə)l/ *a.* E17. [f. L *consequentia* CONSEQUENCE + -AL[1].] 1 Following, esp. as an (immediate or eventual) effect, or as a logical inference; of the nature of a consequence. E17. 2 Characterized by logical sequence or consistency. Now *rare.* M17. 3 Of consequence; important, significant. Now only of a person: having social consequence. E18. 4 Self-important. M18.

1 S. TURNER Wars and their consequential burthens. **consequential damages, losses**: that follow or result from an act, but not directly and immediately. 2 COLERIDGE A consistent and strictly consequential Materialism.

consequentialism *n.* the belief that the morality of an action is to be judged solely from its consequences M20. **consequentialist** *n.* & *a.* (*a*) *n.* an advocate of consequentialism; (*b*) *adj.* pertaining to or advocating consequentialism: M20. **consequentiˈality** *n.* E19. **consequentially** *adv.* E17. **consequentialness** *n.* (*rare*) L17.

consequently /ˈkɒnsɪkw(ə)ntli/ *adv.* & *conj.* LME. [f. prec. + -LY[2].] †1 *adv.* In following time or order; subsequently. LME–E17. †2 *adv.* With proper sequence or connection of thought etc.; consistently. LME–L18. 3 *adv.* & *conj.* As a consequence or result, therefore, accordingly. LME.

3 B. T. WASHINGTON There was no provision made in the house . . , and consequently a fire had to be built in the yard. SCOTT FITZGERALD Rosemary still

thought her money was miraculously lent to her and she must consequently be very careful of it.

†conservacy *n.* M16–M18. [AN *conservacie* f. AL *conservatia* by-form of L *conservatio(n-)* CONSERVATION: see -ACY.] = next.

conservancy /kən'sə:v(ə)nsi/ *n.* M18. [Alt. of prec.: see -ANCY.] 1 A commission, (formerly) court, etc., controlling a port, river, etc.; a similar body concerned with other environmental resources. M18. 2 Official preservation of a resource, e.g. forests. M19.

conservate /'kɒnsəveɪt/ *v.t. rare.* M19. [L *conservat-* pa. ppl stem of *conservare*: see CONSERVE *v.*, -ATE³.] Conserve; preserve.

conservation /kɒnsə'veɪʃ(ə)n/ *n.* LME. [(O)Fr., or L *conservatio(n-)*, f. *conservat-* pa. ppl stem of *conservare*: see CONSERVE *v.*, -ATION.] 1 The action of keeping from harm, decay, loss, or waste; careful preservation. LME. b The preservation *of* existing conditions, institutions, rights, etc. LME. c The preservation of the environment, esp. of natural resources. E20. 2 Official charge and care of rivers, sewers, forests, etc.; conservancy. L15. 3 *Physics.* (A principle stating) the invariance of the total quantity *of* energy (or any of certain other physical properties) possessed by a system of bodies not subject to external action. M19. 4 The preserving of fruit etc. L19.

3 *conservation of energy, mass, momentum*, etc.

Comb.: **conservation area** an area containing noteworthy buildings etc. which is specially protected by law from undesirable changes; **conservation law**: stating the conservation (sense 3) of a particular physical property (under some or all circumstances or in certain interactions).

conservational *a.* M19. **conservationist** *n.* a proponent or advocate of (esp. environmental) conservation L19.

conservatism /kən'sə:vətɪz(ə)m/ *n.* M19. [f. next + -ISM.] 1 (Usu. **C-**.) The doctrine and practice of Conservatives; Toryism. M19. 2 Reluctance to make changes; conservative principles in politics, theology, etc. M19.

conservatist *n.* & *a.* (*rare*) (*a*) *n.* a person preferring the preservation of institutions etc. unchanged; (*b*) *adj.* conservative: M19. **conservatize** *v.t.* & *i.* (*rare*) make or become conservative M19.

conservative /kən'sə:vətɪv/ *a.* & *n.* LME. [Late L *conservativus*, f. L *conservat-*: see CONSERVATION, -ATIVE.] A *adj.* 1 Characterized by a tendency to preserve or keep intact and unchanged; preservative (*of*). LME. b *Physics.* Characterized by conservation (sense 3). L19. 2 (Usu. **C-**.) Of, supporting, or characteristic of the Conservative Party (see below) of Great Britain, or an analogous political party in another country. M19. 3 Characterized by caution, moderation, or reluctance to make changes; (of views, taste, etc.) avoiding extremes. M19. b Of an estimate etc.: purposely low. E20.

1 J. RUSKIN Jealously conservative of old things, but conservative of them as pillars, not as pinnacles. 3 N. MITFORD Being conservative by nature I was glad to see that the decoration of the room had not been changed. L. GOULD The white shirt, tie and conservative navy-blue suit. b *Daily Telegraph* The distances quoted are conservative.

Special collocations: *Conservative and Unionist Party*: see *Conservative Party* below. **Conservative Jew** an adherent of Conservative Judaism. **Conservative Judaism** a movement favouring certain non-essential adaptations or relaxations of Jewish law and tradition. **Conservative Party**, (since 1912 more fully) **Conservative and Unionist Party** a British political party which developed from the old Tory Party in the 1830s, and is generally disposed to maintain traditional institutions and promote individual enterprise. **conservative surgery**: that seeks to preserve tissues as far as possible.

B *n.* 1 A preserving agent or principle; a preservative. LME. 2 (Usu. **C-**.) A member or supporter of the British Conservative Party, or of an analogous party elsewhere; a Tory. In early use, a supporter of Sir Robert Peel. M19. 3 A conservative person. M19.

conservatively *adv.* M19. **conservativeness** *n.* M19. **conservativism** *n.* = CONSERVATISM M19.

conservatoire /kən'sə:vətwɑ:, *foreign* kɔ̃sɛrvatwa:r (*pl. same*)/ *n.* L18. [Fr. f. It. CONSERVATORIO.] An academy of music or other performing arts, esp. in France or elsewhere in Continental Europe. Cf. CONSERVATORIO, CONSERVATORIUM, CONSERVATORY *n.* 5.

conservator /*esp. in sense 1* 'kɒnsəveɪtə, *esp. in sense 2* kən'sə:vətə/ *n.* LME. [AN *conservatour*, (O)Fr. *conservateur* f. L *conservator* keeper, preserver, f. *conservat-*: see CONSERVATION, -OR.] 1 A preserver, a keeper. LME. 2 An official custodian of a museum etc.; a member of a conservancy. LME.

conservatorship *n.* M17. **con'servatrix** /-trɪks/ *n.*, pl. **-trices** /-trɪsi:z/, [L *conservatrix*] a female conservator LME.

conservatoria *n.pl.* see CONSERVATORIUM.

conservatorio /kənsə:və'tɔ:rɪəʊ/ *n.* Pl. **-os.** L18. [It., f. as CONSERVATORY *n.*] An (Italian or Spanish) academy of music or other performing arts. Cf. CONSERVATOIRE, CONSERVATORIUM, CONSERVATORY *n.* 5.

¶ Orig. an Italian hospital or school for orphans and foundlings where a musical education was given.

conservatorium /kənsə:və'tɔ:rɪəm/ *n.* Pl. **-iums, -ia** /-ɪə/. M19. [G & mod.L, f. as CONSERVATORY *n.*: see -ORIUM.] An academy of music or other performing arts, esp. in Germany, Austria, or Australia. Cf. CONSERVATOIRE, CONSERVATORIO, CONSERVATORY *n.* 5.

conservatory /kən'sə:vət(ə)ri/ *n.* M16. [Late L *conservatorium* use as n. of neut. of *conservatorius* adj., f. *conservat-*: see CONSERVATION, -ORY¹. In branch II after It. CONSERVATORIO, Fr. CONSERVATOIRE.] I †1 A thing which preserves; a preservative. M16–M17. †2 A place where things are preserved, stored, or kept securely; a repository; a reservoir of water. E17–L18. 3 A greenhouse for tender plants; a room, esp. attached to a house, designed for the growing or displaying of plants. M17. II †4 A hospital or school for orphans and foundlings. Only in 17. 5 An academy of music or other performing arts. Cf. CONSERVATOIRE, CONSERVATORIO, CONSERVATORIUM. Chiefly *N. Amer.* E19.

conservatory /kən'sə:vət(ə)ri/ *a.* L16. [Late L *conservatorius*: see prec., -ORY².] 1 Adapted to conserve; preservative. L16. 2 = CONSERVATIVE *a.* 3. Now *rare.* E19.

conserve /kən'sə:v, 'kɒnsə:v/ *n.* LME. [(O)Fr. (= It., Sp., med.L *conserva*) f. as next.] †1 A preservative. LME–L16. †2 A preserve; a store; a hoard. LME–M17. 3 A confectionary or (formerly) medicinal preparation of fruit etc. preserved in sugar; jam, esp. made from fresh fruit. LME.

conserve /kən'sə:v/ *v.t.* LME. [(O)Fr. *conserver* f. L *conservare*, f. as CON- + *servare* keep.] 1 Keep from harm, decay, loss, or waste, esp. with a view to later use; preserve with care. LME. †b Keep alive or flourishing. LME–L17. c *Physics.* Maintain (energy etc.) unchanged in total quantity according to a conservation law. Usu. in *pass.* L19. †2 Keep (a commandment etc.); observe (a custom or rite). LME–M17. 3 Preserve (fruit etc.) in sugar or by similar means; make into a conserve. L15.

1 EVELYN Draw them out of the ground before the frost, and conserve them in a warm place. R. DAWKINS Emperor penguins conserve heat by huddling together.

conservable *a.* [Late L *conservabilis*] E17. **conserver** *n.* LME.

consider /kən'sɪdə/ *v.* LME. [(O)Fr. *considérer* f. L *considerare* examine, perh. f. as CON- + *sider-*, *sidus* constellation, star.] 1 *v.t.* Look at attentively; survey; scrutinize. *arch.* LME. 2 *v.i.* Look attentively. Long *arch.* LME. 3 *v.t.* Give mental attention to; think over, meditate or reflect on; pay heed to, take note of; weigh the merits of. LME. b Give mental attention to the fact *that*; reflect or take note of *how, whether, who, why*, etc. LME. 4 *v.i.* Think carefully, reflect. (Foll. by *of* (arch.), †*on*.) LME. †5 *v.t.* Estimate; reckon. LME–M16. 6 *v.t.* Take into account; show regard for; make allowance for. LME. b In *pa. pple* in an *absol.* clause: being taken into account. Now chiefly in *all things considered*. LME. 7 *v.t.* Regard in a certain light or aspect; look upon *as*; think or take *to be* (or absol.). M16. b Be of the opinion *that*; suppose *to do, to have done*. M19. †8 *v.t.* Recognize in a practical way; remunerate; recompense. L16–L17. 9 *v.t.* Think highly of; esteem; respect. *arch.* L17.

1 MILTON And with inspection deep Consider'd every Creature. 2 AV *Lev.* 13:13 The Priest shall consider: and behold, if the leprosie haue couered al his flesh, he shal pronounce him cleane. 3 SHAKES. *Lear* Is man no more than this? Consider him well. J. SIMMS Just before I went to Germany I had considered returning to Japan. b T. HARDY He paused . . to consider how they might have got there. 4 G. K. CHESTERTON But consider a moment; do not condemn me hastily. 7 A. LANG Consider yourself under arrest! N. MITFORD A determination to show people what she considered to be their proper place and keep them in it. b OED I consider him to have acted disgracefully. J. CONRAD She considered herself to be of French descent. D. H. LAWRENCE I consider this is really the heart of England. 8 SHAKES. *Meas. for M.* You that have worn your eyes almost out in the service, you will be considered. 9 S. JOHNSON A pamphlet . . which was . . enough considered to be both seriously and ludicrously answered.

considered *ppl a.* (*a*) maturely reflected on, done etc. after careful thought; (*b*) *arch.* highly thought of, respected: E17. **considerer** *n.* LME. **consideringly** *adv.* thoughtfully; in a considering manner, tone, or attitude: M17.

considerable /kən'sɪd(ə)rəb(ə)l/ *a.*, *n.*, & *adv.* LME. [med.L *considerabilis* worthy to be considered, f. L *considerare*: see prec., -ABLE.] A *adj.* †1 That may be considered or viewed. *rare.* LME–M17. †2 That should be considered or taken into account; notable. L16–E18. 3 Worthy of consideration or regard; of consequence. (Passing into sense 4.) E17. 4 Worthy of consideration by reason of magnitude; somewhat large in amount, extent, duration, etc.; a good deal of (an immaterial or (chiefly *US*) material thing). M17.

3 W. FIELD The daughter of a considerable potter in that neighbourhood. 4 CONAN DOYLE A great wandering house, standing in a considerable park. D. L. SAYERS She evidently gave considerable thought to the subject. W. BOYD The flow of traffic was considerable.

B *n.* †1 A thing to be considered; a point etc. worth considering. M–L17. 2 A fair amount or quantity (*of*), a good deal, much. *US.* L17.

2 W. FAULKNER Maybe a considerable of almost anything else. I. SHAW I've heard considerable about you.

C *adv.* = CONSIDERABLY. Now *US* & *dial.* L17.

considera'bility *n.* (*rare*) M17. **considerableness** *n.* (now *rare*) M17. **considerably** *adv.* †(*a*) in a way or to a degree that ought to be noticed; (*b*) to a large extent, much, a good deal: M17.

†considerance *n.* LME–L16. [OFr. f. L *considerantia*, f. stem of *considerare*: see CONSIDER, -ANCE.] The action or an act of considering; reflection.

SHAKES. *2 Hen. IV* After this cold considerance, sentence me.

considerate /kən'sɪd(ə)rət/ *a.* L16. [L *consideratus* pa. pple of *considerare*: see CONSIDER, -ATE². Cf. earlier INCONSIDERATE.] 1 Marked by or showing careful thought; deliberate; prudent, thoughtful. *arch.* L16. 2 Showing consideration for the circumstances, feelings, well-being, etc., of others; thoughtful for others. E18.

1 J. LOCKE None of the Definitions . . are so perfect . . as to satisfy a considerate inquisitive Person. SIR W. SCOTT Foster . . paced the room twice with the same steady and considerate pace. 2 J. G. FARRELL The Major's considerate inquiries about . . the state of her health. M. KEANE She shut the drawer carefully—she was gently considerate to all furniture.

considerately *adv.* M16. **considerateness** *n.* M17.

consideration /kənsɪdə'reɪʃ(ə)n/ *n.* LME. [(O)Fr. *considération* f. L *consideratio(n-)*, f. *considerat-* pa. ppl stem of *considerare*: see CONSIDER, -ATION.] †1 The action of viewing with the eyes or mind; beholding. LME–M17. 2 The keeping of a subject before the mind; attentive thought; reflection; meditation. LME. b In *pl.* Thoughts, reflections. L15. 3 The action of taking into account; the fact of being taken into account. LME. 4 The taking into account of anything as a reason or motive; a fact or circumstance taken, or to be taken, into account. LME. 5 Regard for the circumstances, feelings, comfort, etc., of another; considerateness. LME. 6a *Law*. Something given, done, or forborne in return for the promise or act of another party. M16. b Something given in payment; a reward; a remuneration; a compensation. E17. 7 Estimation; esteem; importance; consequence. *arch.* L16.

2 M. AMIS Deciding, after mature consideration, against the hamburger. 3 M. W. MONTAGU I.. speak .. without any consideration, but that of your figure and reputation. 4 E. WAUGH Those with whom price is not a primary consideration. S. BELLOW Returning once more to practical considerations, he must be very careful. 5 S. DELANEY She's not got a bit of consideration in her. 7 LD MACAULAY A man of the first consideration.

Phrases: **in consideration of** in return for; on account of. **take into, leave out of, consideration** make, fail to make, allowance for. **under consideration** being considered. *valuable consideration*: see VALUABLE *a.* 1.

†considerative *a.* LME–E19. [OFr. *consideratif, -ive* f. med.L *considerativus* reflective, thoughtful; later f. CONSIDERATE + -IVE.] = CONSIDERATE.

considering /kən'sɪd(ə)rɪŋ/ *prep., conj., & adv.* LME. [Absol. use of pres. pple or vbl n. of CONSIDER: see -ING[2], -ING[1].] A *prep. & conj.* When one considers (*that*); taking into account (the fact *that*). LME.

F. SMITH The Evening was pleasant, and also warm, considering we were amongst Ice. H. JAMES Considering its great fury the storm took long to expend itself.

B *adv.* Considering the circumstances; taking everything into account. *colloq.* M18.

M. R. MITFORD We went on very prosperously, *considering*; as people say of a young lady's drawing, or a Frenchman's English, or a woman's tragedy.

consign /kən'sʌɪn/ *v.* LME. [Fr. *consigner* f. L *consignare* attest with a seal, f. as CON- + *signare* SIGN *v.*] †1 *v.t.* Mark with the sign of the cross; *spec.* confirm; dedicate *to, unto* thus. LME–E18. †2 *v.t.* Attest, confirm, ratify. LME–M19. 3 *v.t.* Entrust or commit to another's charge or care. E16. b Deposit (money). M16. †4 *v.i.* Foll. by *to*: agree to, subscribe to; submit to the same terms as. *rare* (Shakes.). L16–E17. 5 *v.t.* Make over as a possession, deliver formally or commit *to* a state, fate, etc. M17. 6 *v.t.* Deliver or transmit (goods) for sale etc. or custody; send (goods) by carrier, rail, etc., (*to*). M17.

5 C. RAYNER I would have consigned them both to perdition. P. ACKROYD To escape from the academic career to which his family seemed to have consigned him.

†**consignatary** *n.* a consignee L17–M18. **consi'gnee** *n.* a person to whom goods are consigned L18. **consigner** *n.* a person who consigns M17. **consignor** *n.* a person who dispatches goods to another L18.

consignation /kɒnsɪg'neɪʃ(ə)n/ *n.* Now *rare.* M16. [L *consignatio(n-)* (in med.L senses), f. *consignat-* pa. ppl stem of *consignare*: see prec., -ATION.] †1 The action of marking with the sign of the cross. M16–M19. 2 The action of paying over or depositing money; a sum deposited. M16. †3 Sealing; confirmation; attestation. E17–M19. †4 (Formal) delivery; consigning *to* a state or condition. Only in 17. 5 = CONSIGNMENT 3. E18.

consigne /kɔ̃siɲ/ *n.* Pl. pronounced same. M19. [Fr., f. *consigner* give instructions to a sentinel.] 1 An order given to a sentinel; a password. *rare.* M19. 2 A left-luggage office in France. L19.

consignificant /kɒnsɪg'nɪfɪk(ə)nt/ *a. rare.* E17. [f. as CONSIGNIFY: see -ANT[1].] Conjointly significant; having a meaning in combination.

Also **consignificative** *a.* (*rare*) M17.

consignification /ˌkɒnsɪgnɪfɪ'keɪʃ(ə)n/ *n. rare.* E18. [med.L *consignificatio(n-)*, f. *consignificat-* pa. ppl stem of *consignificare*: see next, -ATION.] Joint or conjoint signification; connotation.

consignify /kɒn'sɪgnɪfʌɪ/ *v.t. & i. rare.* E17. [med.L *consignificare*, f. L CON- + *significare* SIGNIFY.] Signify in conjunction (*with*).

consignment /kən'sʌɪnm(ə)nt/ *n.* M16. [f. CONSIGN + -MENT.] 1 The action of sealing or dedicating with a sign. *rare.* M16. 2 The action or an act of handing over; committal, delivery. M17. 3 The action of consigning goods for sale etc. or custody. E18. 4 A quantity of goods consigned for sale etc. or custody. E18.

consilient /kɒn'sɪlɪənt/ *a.* M19. [f. CON- + L *-silient-, -ens* jumping (as in *resilient-, -ens* RESILIENT), after *concurrent.*] Of inductions from different phenomena, etc.: concurrent, agreeing.

consilience *n.* the fact or condition of being consilient M19.

consimilar /kɒn'sɪmɪlə/ *a.* Now *rare.* M16. [f. L *consimilis*, f. as CON- + *similis*: see SIMILAR.] †1 Homogeneous. M16–M17. 2 Entirely similar, like. M17.

consimi'larity *n.* (*rare*) mutual likeness M17.

consist /kən'sɪst/ *v.i.* LME. [L *consistere* stand still, remain firm, exist, f. as CON- + *sistere* place, stand firm or still. Cf. Fr. *consister.*] I 1 Foll. by *in*: †a Exist or reside in; be located or inherent in. LME–E19. b Be constituted or composed of (actions, qualities, etc.; *arch.* material things); have its essential features in. L16. †2 Exist together as compatible facts; be compatible (*with*). M16–M19. 3 Have a settled existence; subsist, hold together, exist. *arch.* M16. †b Stand firm, remain, stay; have its place. M16–M17. 4 Be made up or composed *of*. M16. †5 Be based or rest (*up*)*on*. M16–M17. 6 Be consistent, be congruous, harmonize, (*with*). M17.

1b S. BUTLER Moral government consists .. in rewarding the righteous, and punishing the wicked. I. MURDOCH Part of my unease about my cousin consisted in a fear that he would succeed in life and I would fail. 2 J. WESLEY Costiveness cannot long consist with Health. 3 AV *Col.* 1:17 He is before all things, and by him all things consist. 4 C. A. LINDBERGH His education consisted largely of home study. J. SIMMS The group consisted of five string players and two singers. 6 G. GROTE Appetites are to be indulged only so far as consists with some .. approved end.

†II 7 Insist (*up*)*on. rare.* E16–E17.

†**consisting** *ppl a.* (*a*) cohering, united; (*b*) = CONSISTENT 4: E17–E18.

consistence /kən'sɪst(ə)ns/ *n.* L16. [Fr. *consistance*, †*-ence* or late L *consistentia*, f. *consistent-* pres. ppl stem of *consistere*: see prec., -ENCE.] †1 Standing or remaining still; a state of rest; a settled condition, *spec.* in the life of an organism when it is fully grown. L16–M18. 2†a Matter dense enough to cohere. L16–L18. b Material coherence and permanence of form; solidity sufficient to retain form. E17. 3 = CONSISTENCY 2. E17. †4 (A) union, (a) combination. M17–E18. 5 = CONSISTENCY 3, 3b. L17.

1 EVELYN I hope I have brought my affaires almost to a Consistence. 2b T. THOMSON Cubic crystals without consistence, .. resembling a jelly. 3 P. V. WHITE Soup .. of a milky .. consistence.

consistency /kən'sɪst(ə)nsi/ *n.* L16. [f. (as) prec.: see -ENCY.] 1 = CONSISTENCE 2b. L16. 2 The degree of firmness with which the particles of a substance cohere; degree of density, esp. of thick liquids. M17. 3 The quality, state, or fact of being consistent; agreement (*with* something, *of* things etc.); uniformity, regularity. M17. b The agreement of parts or elements with each other, esp. as a personal attribute in life or conduct; constancy of principle etc. E18. †4 A settled condition. L17–E18.

3 W. PALEY To question the consistency of the two records. P. V. PRICE Branded wines make consistency of quality possible. b R. W. EMERSON A foolish consistency is the hobgoblin of little minds.

consistent /kən'sɪst(ə)nt/ *a. & adv.* L16. [L *consistent-* pres. ppl stem of *consistere*: see CONSIST, -ENT.] A *adj.* †1 Consisting *in, of*, composed *of*. L16–L17. †2 Remaining still; settled, durable. Only in 17. †3 Coexisting (*with*). *rare.* M17–M18. †4 Holding together as a coherent material body; firm, solid. M17–M19. 5 Agreeing in substance or form; congruous, compatible (*with*, †*to*), not contradictory; marked by uniformity or regularity. M17. b *Logic.* Of an axiom system: leading to no theorems that contradict each other. E20. c *Statistics.* Of an estimate etc.: approaching the true value of the quantity estimated more closely as the sample size is increased. E20. 6 Of a person, conduct: constantly adhering to the same principles of thought or action. M18.

5 SIR T. BROWNE An habite .. not consistent with the words of our Saviour. H. T. BUCKLE The most consistent of all combinations .. great ignorance with great arrogance. H. CECIL Since a regular backer of horses .. is usually a loser, repeated and consistent wins excite suspicion. 6 B. JOWETT Let us be consistent then, and either believe both or neither. W. S. CHURCHILL Two generations of consistent House of Commons parsimony.

B *adv.* Consistently. Now *rare* or *obs.* M18.

consistently *adv.* in accordance *with*; with consistency; uniformly: E18.

consistometer /kɒnsɪ'stɒmɪtə/ *n.* E20. [f. CONSISTENCY + -OMETER.] An instrument for measuring the consistency of a viscous or plastic material.

consistorial /kɒnsɪ'stɔːrɪəl/ *a.* LME. [(O)Fr., or med.L *consistorialis*, f. late L *consistorium*: see CONSISTORY, -AL[1].] 1 Of or pertaining to a consistory. LME. 2 Of or pertaining to Church government by consistories; Presbyterian. M16.

consistorially *adv.* (*rare*) E17. †**consistorical** *a.* = CONSISTORIAL E17–M18.

consistorian /kɒnsɪ'stɔːrɪən/ *a. & n.* L16. [L *consistorianus*, f. *consistorium*: see next, -AN.] †A *adj.* = CONSISTORIAL. L16–M17. B *n.* †1 A settled inhabitant. *rare.* Only in L16. 2 A Presbyterian. *obs.* exc. *Hist.* E17.

consistory /kən'sɪst(ə)ri/ *n.* ME. [AN *consistorie* = (O)Fr. *consistoire* f. late L *consistorium*, f. as CONSIST: see -ORY[1].] †I 1 A place where councillors meet, a council-chamber. ME–M18. †2 A court, a company surrounding a throne. Also, a court of judgement. ME–L17. 3 A meeting of councillors, a council. *obs.* exc. *Hist.* or *poet.* LME. II Eccl. senses. 4 (Usu. C-.) A bishop's court for ecclesiastical causes and offences; a diocesan court, held by the chancellor or commissary of a diocese. (Now only in the Anglican Church.) Also *Consistory Court.* ME. 5 (A meeting of) the council of the Pope and cardinals. LME. 6 In the Reformed Protestant Churches, a court of presbyters. L16. 7 In the Lutheran Church, a supervisory board of clerical officers. L17.

consociate /kɒn'səʊʃɪət, -sɪət/ *a. & n.* LME. [L *consociatus* pa. pple, f. as next: see -ATE[2], -ATE[1].] A *adj.* Associated; united in fellowship. LME. B *n.* A partner, an associate. L16.

consociate /kɒn'səʊʃɪeɪt, -səʊsɪ-/ *v.* L16. [L *consociat-* pa. ppl stem of *consociare*, f. as CON- + *sociare* to associate, f. *socius* fellow: see -ATE[3].] 1 *v.t.* Bring into association or partnership; join in action. L16. 2 *v.i.* Enter into association or union; keep company *with*. M17.

consociation /kɒnsəʊʃɪ'eɪʃ(ə)n, -səʊsɪ-/ *n.* L16. [L *consociatio(n-)*, f. as prec.: see -ATION.] 1 The action or fact of associating together; combination. L16. 2 Fellowship, companionship (*with*). E17. 3 An alliance or confederation, esp. of Congregational or Presbyterian churches in an area. Now *Hist.* exc. *US.* E17. b A council of Congregational churchmen. *US.* L18. 4 *Ecol.* A small climax community or division of a plant association characterized by a single dominant species. E20. 5 A political system in which power is shared by representatives of different or antagonistic social groups. M20.

consociational *a.* L19. **consociationalism** *n.* the principle or practice of political consociation M20.

consol *n.* see CONSOLS.

consolable /kən'səʊləb(ə)l/ *a.* M17. [f. CONSOLE *v.* + -ABLE. Cf. earlier INCONSOLABLE, UNCONSOLABLE.] Able to be consoled.

consolamentum /kənsəʊlə'mentəm/ *n.* Pl. **-ta** /-tə/. L19. [mod.L, f. L *consolari*: see CONSOLE *v.*] *Eccl. Hist.* The spiritual baptism of the Cathars.

†consolate *v.t.* Pa. pple **-ated,** (earlier) **-ate.** L15–E19. [L *consolat-*: see CONSOLATION, -ATE[3].] = CONSOLE *v.*

consolatio /kɒnsə'leɪʃɪəʊ, -'lɑːtɪəʊ/ *n.* Pl. ***-iones*** /-ɪ'əʊniːz/. M20. [L: see next.] A thing written to expound philosophical or religious themes as comfort for the misfortunes of life.

consolation /kɒnsə'leɪʃ(ə)n/ *n.* LME. [(O)Fr. f. L *consolatio(n-)*, f. *consolat-* pa. ppl stem of *consolari*: see CONSOLE *v.*, -ATION.] 1 The action of consoling; alleviation of sorrow or mental distress; the state of being consoled. LME. 2 A fact, event, etc., that serves to console. LME.

Comb.: **consolation prize**: given to a competitor who has just missed a main prize.

consolationes *n.* pl. of CONSOLATIO.

†consolator *n.* M16–M18. [L *consolator*, f. *consolat-*: see CONSOLATION, -OR.] A consoler.

consolatory /kən'sɒlət(ə)ri, -'səʊl-/ *a.* & *n.* LME. [L *consolatorius*, f. as prec.: see -ORY[2].] A *adj.* Tending or intended to console. LME. †B *n.* A consolatory speech or composition. M–L17.

consolatrix /kɒnsə'leɪtrɪks/ *n. rare.* Pl. **-trices** /-trɪsiːz/. M17. [Late L, fem. of L CONSOLATOR: see -TRIX.] A female consoler.

console /'kɒnsəʊl/ *n.* M17. [Fr., perh. f. *consolider* consolidate.] 1 *Archit.* An ornamental flat-sided bracket or corbel, usu. incorporating a volute at each end. M17. 2 In full *console table*. A table supported by consoles, and either fixed to a wall or free-standing. E19. 3 A cabinet containing the keyboards, stops, and pedals of an organ. L19. 4 A cabinet for audio equipment, a television set, etc. E20. 5 A cabinet or panel where switches, meters, and controls are grouped together. M20.

5 M. BRADBURY The booking clerk prints the tickets on a large console. *New Yorker* An enormous computer console.

console /kən'səʊl/ *v.t.* M17. [Fr. *consoler* f. L *consolari*, f. as CON- + *solari* soothe.] Comfort in disappointment or distress.

J. CHEEVER He . . consoled himself with whiskey. C. FREEMAN No one wiped away the tears or consoled him.

consolement *n.* L18. **consoler** *n.* M18.

consolidate /kən'sɒlɪdeɪt/ *v.* Pa. pple **-ated,** (*arch.*) **-ate** /-ət/. E16. [L *consolidat-* pa. ppl stem of *consolidare*, f. as CON- + *solidare* make firm or solid, f. *solidus* SOLID *a.*: see -ATE[3].] I *v.t.* 1 Combine (estates, laws, debts, companies, etc.) into a single whole. E16. †b Unite and so heal (a wound, fracture, or rupture). M16–L18. 2 Strengthen, give firmness to (esp. political power or an established system). M16. 3 Make (more) solid. M17.

1 **consolidated annuities** the Government annuities of the UK (representing part of the National Debt) which in 1751 were consolidated into a single stock, now called CONSOLS. **Consolidated Fund** a British government fund, formed by amalgamation in 1786, which receives the product of various taxes etc. and pays the interest on the National Debt and other agreed regular charges. 2 R. NIEBUHR Religion may consolidate benevolent sentiments and lodge their force in the will. A. J. TOYNBEE The Incas came, saw, conquered, and consolidated their conquests.

II *v.i.* 4 Unite solidly or compactly; become solid or firm; make one's position more secure. E17.

consolidator *n.* E18.

consolidation /kənsɒlɪ'deɪʃ(ə)n/ *n.* LME. [Late L *consolidatio(n-)*, f. as prec.: see -ATION.] 1 The action or an act of uniting or amalgamating; combination into a single whole. LME. 2 The action or an act of making (more) solid or compact. E17. 3 (A) strengthening, esp. of power, position, or organization. E17.

consolidationist *n.* an advocate of federal rule in the US M19.

consols /'kɒns(ə)lz/ *n.pl.* L18. [f. abbrev. of *consolidated annuities* + pl. -s[1].] An undated British government stock representing the consolidated annuities (see CONSOLIDATE) and now bearing interest at 2½ per cent. Also, Consolidated Loan stock, an undated British government stock first issued in 1926 and bearing interest at 4 per cent.

¶ Sing. *consol* is used *attrib.* & *Comb.*

consommé /kən'sɒmeɪ/ *n.* E19. [Fr., use as n. of pa. pple of *consommer* f. L *consummare*: see CONSUMMATE *v.*] A clear, orig. meat, soup.

consonance /'kɒns(ə)nəns/ *n.* LME. [(O)Fr., or L *consonantia*, f. *consonant-*: see next, -ANCE.] 1 Agreement, harmony, concord. LME. 2 Resemblance or correspondence of sounds, now esp. consonants, in different words or syllables. L16. 3 (A) pleasing combination of sounds. L16. 4 *Mus.* A consonant interval. E17. b The sounding of two or more notes in harmony. L17.

1 W. S. CHURCHILL His conversion to Christianity . . was also in consonance with his secular aims.

consonancy *n.* (*arch.*) = CONSONANCE 1, 2, 3 LME.

consonant /'kɒns(ə)nənt/ *n.* ME. [OFr. f. L *consonant-*, *consonans* (sc. *littera* letter) pres. pple of *consonare* sound together, f. as CON-, SONANT.] 1a A letter of the alphabet that represents a consonantal sound. ME. b An elementary speech sound other than a vowel, in which the air-stream is at least partly obstructed, and which in forming a syllable is usu. combined with a vowel. E17. †2 = CONSONANCE 4. LME–E18.

1b *stop consonant*: see STOP *n.*[2] 18b.

Comb.: **consonant shift** a systematic change in consonantal sounds during the evolution of a language.

conso'nantal *a.* of the nature of a consonant; pertaining to or involving a consonant or consonants: L18. **consonanted** *a.* having consonants (of a specified kind) L19. **conso'nantic** *a.* (*rare*) M19. **consonantism** *n.* the use of consonants; the system or character of the consonants in a language or a word: M19.

consonant /'kɒns(ə)nənt/ *a.* LME. [OFr., pres. pple of *consoner* (mod. *-nn-*), f. L *consonare*: see prec., -ANT[1].] 1 In agreement or accordance (*with*); compatible; agreeable, accordant (*to*). LME. †b Consistent, unvarying. M16–M18. 2 Harmonious; *Mus.* constituting a concord. L15. 3 Of words etc.: corresponding in sound; exhibiting consonance. M17.

1 HENRY MORE Divine Truth will be found every-where consonant to itself. L. A. G. STRONG After as short an interval as was consonant with decency . . he married Miss Jones.

consonantly *adv.* M16.

consonous /'kɒns(ə)nəs/ *a. rare.* M17. [f. L *consonus*, f. as CON- + *sonus* sounding: see -OUS.] Harmonious.

†consopition *n.* M17–E18. [L *consopitio(n-)*, f. *consopit-* pa. ppl stem of *consopire* lull to sleep, f. as CON- + *sopire* (same sense): see -ITION.] A lulling to sleep; a dulling of the senses.

con sordino /kɒn sɔː'diːnəʊ/ *adv.* & *a. phr.* E19. [It.: see SORDINO.] *Mus.* (Played) with a mute or (*con sordini* /-iː/) mutes.

consort /'kɒnsɔːt/ *n.*[1] LME. [Fr. f. L *consort-*, *consors* sharing in common, partner, f. as CON- + *sors* portion, lot.] 1 A partner, a companion; a colleague. Now *rare* or *obs.* exc. as below. LME. 2a A partner in marriage or sexual relations; a husband or wife, esp. of a monarch. L16. b An animal's mate. L18. 3 A ship sailing in company with another. E17.

2a W. BLACKSTONE The queen of England is either queen regent, queen consort, or queen dowager. J. CLAVELL A man could have as many consorts as he wished, but only one wife at one time. *fig.*: ISAAC TAYLOR That love which is to be the consort of knowledge. *Prince Consort*: see PRINCE *n.*

con'sortion *n.* (*arch.*) [L *consortio(n-)*] keeping company; alliance: L17. **consortism** *n.* (*rare*) symbiosis L19. **consortship** *n.* (now *rare*) the situation of being a consort; partnership, fellowship: L16.

consort /'kɒnsɔːt/ *n.*[2] L16. [Partly f. next, suggested by L CONSORTIUM; partly (branch II) early form of CONCERT *n.*] I Conn. w. next. †1 A number consorting together; a fellowship, a partnership; a company. L16–L18. 2 Accord; agreement. L16.

1 J. GLANVILL Instances must be . . examined singly and in consort. 2 J. HILTON Conway, in whom a mystical strain ran in curious consort with scepticism.

II †3 Musical harmony or accord; a harmonious combination of voices or instruments. L16–E18. 4 A company of musicians who regularly perform together. L16. †5 = CONCERT *n.* 3. L17–L18.

consort /kən'sɔːt/ *v.* L16. [In sense 1 f. CONSORT *n.*[1]; in other senses prob. a reinforcement of SORT *v.*, infl. by prec.] †1 *v.t.* Accompany; escort, attend. L16–E17. 2 *v.t.* Associate in a common lot; class or bring together (*with*). L16. 3 *v.i.* & †*refl.* Habitually associate (*with*), esp. as a companion or a lover. L16. 4 *v.i.* Accord, harmonize. (Foll. by *to*, *with*.) L16. 5 *v.t.* & *i.* Musically play, sing, or sound together. *arch.* L16.

1 SHAKES. *L.L.L.* Sweet health and fair desires consort your Grace! 2 E. BLUNDEN The men with whom I was now consorted. 3 R. W. EMERSON Men consort in camps and towns. D. CARNEGIE Fearing that he might be consorting with another woman. P. L. FERMOR I would travel on foot . . and only consort with peasants and tramps.

consortium /kən'sɔːtɪəm/ *n.* Pl. **-ia** /-ɪə/, **-iums.** E19. [L, f. *consors* CONSORT *n.*[1]] 1 Partnership, association. *rare.* E19. 2 *Law.* The companionship, affection, and assistance which each spouse in a marriage is entitled to receive from the other. M19. 3 An association of organizations or States formed for commercial or financial purposes. L19. 4 A group; an assortment. M20.

4 E. HUXLEY A consortium of odours in which dried and pickled fish predominate. JO GRIMOND The consortium of Majors present, of whom I was one.

†consound *n.* OE–E19. [(O)Fr. *consoude* f. late L *consolida* comfrey, f. L *consolidare* CONSOLIDATE *v.*] Any of certain herbs to which healing properties were attributed; *esp.* comfrey.

conspecific /kɒnspə'sɪfɪk/ *a.* & *n.* M19. [f. CON- + SPECIFIC.] (An organism or individual) of the same species.

†conspectuity *n. rare* (Shakes.). Only in E17. [App. joc. f. L CONSPECTUS + -ITY.] Faculty of sight, vision.

conspectus /kən'spɛktəs/ *n.* M19. [L, f. *conspect-* pa. ppl stem of *conspicere* (see next).] 1 A comprehensive mental survey. M19. 2 A summary, a synopsis. M19.

conspicuous /kən'spɪkjʊəs/ *a.* M16. [f. L *conspicuus*, f. *conspicere* look at attentively, f. as CON- + *specere* look (at): see -OUS.] 1 Clearly visible, striking to the eye. M16. 2 Obvious, plainly evident; attracting notice; remarkable, noteworthy. E17. 3 Of expenditure etc.: lavish, with a view to enhancing one's prestige. L19.

2 J. RUSSELL One provision was conspicuous . . by its absence.

conspi'cuity *n.* the state or quality of being conspicuous; ease of visibility: E17. **conspicuously** *adv.* E17. **conspicuousness** *n.* M17.

conspiracy /kən'spɪrəsi/ *n.* LME. [AN *conspiracie* alt. of (O)Fr. *conspiration* f. L *conspiratio(n-)*, f. *conspirat-* pa. ppl stem of *conspirare*: see CONSPIRE, -ATION, -ACY.] 1 The action or an act of conspiring; (a) combination of people for an unlawful or a reprehensible purpose; an agreement so to combine, a plot. LME. 2 In a neutral or good sense: combination for one purpose. *arch.* M16.

1 **conspiracy of silence** an agreement not to mention something.

conspirator /kən'spɪrətə/ *n.* LME. [AN *conspiratour*, (O)Fr. *-eur*, f. L *conspirator*, f. *conspirat-*: see prec., -OR.] A person who conspires or is engaged in a conspiracy.

conspirative *a.* conspiratorial L19. **conspira'torial** *a.* pertaining to or characteristic of a conspirator or conspiracy; suggestive of a conspirator: M19. **conspira'torially** *adv.* E20. **conspiratory** *a.* conspiratorial E19. **conspiratress** *n.* a female conspirator L18.

conspire /kən'spʌɪə/ *v.* LME. [(O)Fr. *conspirer* f. L *conspirare* agree, combine, f. as CON- + *spirare* breathe.] 1 *v.i.* a Combine secretly (*with*) for an unlawful or reprehensible purpose, esp. treason, murder, or sedition; agree secretly. (Foll. by *against*, *to do*.) LME. b Combine in action or aim (*with*); cooperate by or as by intention (*to do*). M16. **2** *v.t.* Plot (something unlawful, evil, or hostile). *arch.* LME. †**3** *v.i.* Concur, agree in spirit, sentiment, etc. M16–M18.

1 I. MURDOCH We all conspired not to tell him.

conspirant *n.* & *a.* (*rare*) [Fr.] (*a*) *n.* a conspirator; (*b*) *adj.* conspiring: E17. **conspi'ration** *n.* (now *rare* or *obs.*) [Fr.] = CONSPIRACY ME. **conspirer** *n.* LME.

constable /'kʌnstəb(ə)l, 'kɒn-/ *n.* ME. [OFr. *cunestable*, *cone-* (mod. *connétable*) repr. late L *comes stabuli* lit. 'count (head officer) of the stable'.] **1** *Hist.* The principal officer of the household, administration, or army of a monarch or nobleman; *spec.* one of the chief officers of the French, English, or Scottish royal household. ME. **2** The governor or warden of a royal fortress or castle. ME. **3** A military officer. Long *rare.* ME. **4** An officer of the peace. ME. **b** A police officer of the lowest rank. Also more fully *police constable.* M19.

4 **Chief Constable** the head of the police force of a county etc. **High Constable** *Hist.* the principal officer of the peace in a hundred or similar administrative area. **outrun** or **overrun the constable** go too far, overstep the bounds of moderation; overspend, get into debt. **parish** or **petty constable** *Hist.* an officer of a parish or township whose duties included being a conservator of the peace. **special constable** a person sworn in to assist the police on special occasions.

†**constablery** *n.* = CONSTABLEWICK ME–M18. **constableship** *n.* the office of constable LME. **constablewick** *n.* (*arch.*) (*a*) the district under a constable; (*b*) constableship: LME.

constabulary /kən'stabjʊləri/ *n.* L15. [med.L *con(e)stabularia* use as n. (sc. *dignitas* rank) of fem. of *con(e)stabularius*: see next.] **1** The district under the charge of a constable. L15. †**2** = CONSTABLESHIP. E16–M18. **3** The organized body of constables or police in an area. M19.

constabulary /kən'stabjʊləri/ *a.* E19. [med.L *con(e)stabularius*, f. *con(e)stabulus* CONSTABLE: see -ARY[1].] **1** Of or pertaining to police officers, the police force, or (formerly) petty constables. E19. **2** Of the nature or function of constables. M19.

Also **constabular** *a.* M19.

constancy /'kɒnst(ə)nsi/ *n.* L15. [L *constantia*, f. *constant-*: see next, -ANCY.] **1** The state or quality of being constant in mind; steadfastness, firmness, fortitude. L15. **2** Steadfastness of attachment to a person or a cause; fidelity. M16. †**3** Certainty. M–L16. **4** The property of being invariable; unchangingness. L16. †**b** Perseverance. *rare* (Shakes.). Only in E17. **5** Something permanent; a permanent arrangement. E18.

4 *Encycl. Brit.* Size, shape, brightness, and colour. Perceptual constancy tends to prevail for these. **5 for a constancy** as a permanent arrangement.

†**constance** *n.* [Fr.] = CONSTANCY 1, 2, 4b ME–M17.

constant /'kɒnst(ə)nt/ *a.* & *n.* LME. [(O)Fr. f. L *constant-* pres. ppl stem of *constare* stand firm, f. as CON- + *stare* stand: see -ANT[1].] **A** *adj.* **1** Staying firm in mind or purpose; steadfast, resolute. LME. **2** Steadfast in attachment (*to* a person or cause), faithful, true. LME. **3** Unchanging in condition, form, or magnitude; unvarying. M16. †**4a** Permanent; always maintained. M16–E19. **b** Continuing without intermission, incessant; unremitting; frequently occurring; (of a person) continually engaged in a particular activity. M17. †**5** Confident; certain. M16–M17. †**6** Not on the move, settled, steady. L16–M18.

1 MILTON The best-resolved of men, The constantest. 2 POPE Tho' fortune change, his constant spouse remains. E. BOWEN She had been constant to the good resolutions made on her honeymoon. 4b MILTON A constant reader of Saint Paul's Epistles. W. LIPPMANN In the industrial revolution there is constant technical change. *constant* ATTENDANCE *allowance.*

B *n.* **1** *Math.* A numerical quantity which does not vary, or is assumed not to vary; *Sci.* a number expressing a relation, property, etc., and remaining the same in all circumstances or for the same substance in the same conditions. M19. **b** *Logic.* The name of, or a symbol representing, a particular individual, class, proposition, etc. M20. **c** *Computing.* = LITERAL *n.* 3. L20. **2** *fig.* A constant element or factor. M19.

1 *Avogadro('s) constant*, *Boltzmann('s) constant*, *cosmical constant*, *cosmological constant*, *dielectric constant*, *gas constant*, *Planck('s) constant*, *solar constant*, *tidal constant*, etc. 2 L. DURRELL The more I knew her the less predictable she seemed; the only constant was the frantic struggle to break through the barriers.

constantan /'kɒnst(ə)ntan/ *n.* E20. [f. prec. + arbitrary *-an*.] A copper-nickel alloy used in electrical work for its high resistance, which varies little with temperature.

Constantia /kən'stanʃə/ *n.* L18. [An estate near Cape Town.] Any of the wines produced on the Constantia farms near Cape Town, South Africa, famous for their sweet dessert wines. Also *Constantia wine.*

Constantinian /kɒnst(ə)n'tɪnɪən/ *a.* M17. [f. *Constantine* (see below) + -IAN.] Of or pertaining to the Roman Emperor Constantine the Great or his period (306–37).

Constantinopolitan /kɒn,stantɪnə'pɒlɪt(ə)n/ *a.* LME. [Late L *Constantinopolitanus*, f. *Constantinopolis* = Gk *Kōnstantinou polis* city of Constantine: see -AN.] Of or pertaining to Constantinople (formerly Byzantium and now Istanbul in Turkey), or the Eastern Empire or Church.

constantly /'kɒnst(ə)ntli/ *adv.* LME. [f. CONSTANT *a.* + -LY[2].] **1** Steadfastly, faithfully. *arch.* LME. †**2** Confidently. M16–M17. †**3** Continuously, permanently. M16–E17. **4** Uniformly, regularly. M17. **5** Continually, incessantly. L17.

constatation /kɒnstə'teɪʃ(ə)n/ *n.* E20. [Fr., f. as next: see -ATION.] **1** The process of ascertaining or verifying; something verified. E20. **2** A statement, an assertion. M20.

constate /kən'steɪt/ *v.t. rare.* L18. [Fr. *constater*, f. L *constat* 3rd person sing. pres. indic. of *constare*: see CONSTANT.] Establish, ascertain, state.

constative /'kɒnstətɪv, kən'steɪtɪv/ *a.* & *n.* E20. [f. L *constat-* pa. ppl stem of *constare*, after G *konstatierend*: see CONSTANT, -IVE.] **A** *adj.* **1** *Gram.* Of a use of the aorist tense: indicating that the action has taken place, rather than emphasizing its initiation or completion. E20. **2** Able to be true or false. M20. **B** *n.* A statement able to be true or false. M20.

constellate /'kɒnstələt, kɒn'stɛlət/ *a.* M17. [Late L *constellatus*, f. as CON- + *stellatus* STELLATE *a.*] **1** Formed into a constellation; clustered together. M17. **2** Studded with stars. M19.

constellate /'kɒnstəleɪt/ *v.* L16. [f. as prec. (see -ATE[3]), infl. by CONSTELLATION.] †**1** *v.t. Astrol.* **a** Predict by means of the stars; cast a horoscope for; affect with or fashion under stellar influence. L16–M19. **b** In *pass.* Be predestined (*to*) by one's stars. M17–E19. **2** *v.t.* Form into a constellation or group. M17. **3** *v.i.* Cluster together like stars in a constellation. M17. **4** *v.t.* Adorn thickly, as with stars. L17.

2 S. JOHNSON He . . must . . constellate in himself the scattered graces which shine single in other men. H. T. LANE Every immediate purpose we have is constellated with the great purpose—perfection. 4 P. L. FERMOR Miniatures and silhouettes constellate the spaces between the portraits.

constellation /kɒnstə'leɪʃ(ə)n/ *n.* ME. [(O)Fr. f. late L *constellatio(n-)*, f. as CON- + *stella* star: see -ATION.] †**1** *Astrol.* The relative positions of the stars (i.e. planets), as supposed to influence events; *esp.* their positions at the time of someone's birth; character, as so influenced. ME–M19. **2** A group of fixed stars with a traditional imaginary outline as seen in the sky. LME. **3** A group or cluster, esp. of brilliant things; *Psychol.* a group of associated ideas or personality components. E17.

3 R. BOYLE A Constellation of fair Ladies.

constellatory /kɒn'stɛlət(ə)ri/ *a. rare.* M17. [f. prec. + -ORY[2].] †**1** *Astrol.* Pertaining to constellations (sense 1) or the casting of horoscopes from them. M17–E19. **2** Pertaining to or of the nature of a constellation; like that of a constellation. E19.

consternate /'kɒnstəneɪt/ *v.t.* M17. [L *consternat-* pa. ppl stem of *consternare* lay prostrate, terrify, f. as CON- + *sternare* lay low: see -ATE[3].] Fill with consternation; dismay. Usu. in *pass.*

consternation /kɒnstə'neɪʃ(ə)n/ *n.* E17. [Fr., or L *consternatio(n-)*, f. as prec.: see -ATION.] Amazement or dismay such as to cause mental confusion.

†**constipate** *a.* LME–M18. [L *constipatus* pa. pple, f. as next: see -ATE[2].] Constipated.

constipate /'kɒnstɪpeɪt/ *v.t.* M16. [L *constipat-* pa. ppl stem of *constipare*, f. as CON- + *stipare* press, cram: see -ATE[3].] **1** Affect (a person, the bowels) with constipation; render costive. Chiefly in *pass.* M16. †**b** Make (body tissue) more compact; constrict (a pore or duct). E17–M18. **c** *fig.* Hinder or obstruct abnormally. L19. †**2** Crowd, pack, or press closely together; condense, thicken (a fluid). M16–M18.

constipated *a.* affected with constipation, costive; characteristic of or associated with constipation: M16.

constipation /kɒnstɪ'peɪʃ(ə)n/ *n.* LME. [(O)Fr., or late L *constipatio(n-)* crowding together, (in med.L) costiveness, f. as prec.: see -ATION.] †**1a** Contraction or constriction of passages or tissues of the body. LME–M17. **b** Irregularity and difficulty in defecation. M16. **c** *fig.* Abnormal lack of efficacy or ease. E19. †**2** Compression or condensation of matter. E17–E18.

constituency /kən'stɪtjʊənsi/ *n.* M19. [f. next: see -ENCY.] **1** All the people entitled to vote for a particular seat or member in a public, esp. a legislative, body; the area or population represented by an elected member. M19. **2** A body of customers, supporters, etc. L19.

constituent /kən'stɪtjʊənt/ *n.* & *a.* L15. [(Partly through Fr. *constituant*) f. L *constituent-* pres. ppl stem of *constituere* CONSTITUTE *v.*: see -ENT.] **A** *n.* **1** A person who appoints another as agent or representative. L15. **2** A voting member or an inhabitant of a constituency. E18. **3** A constituent part (*of*); an element of a complex whole. M18.

3 F. NORRIS As the spot grew larger, it resolved itself into constituents. *immediate constituent*: see IMMEDIATE *a.*

B *adj.* †**1** That makes a thing what it is; characteristic. M17–M19. **2** That goes to make up; *esp.* that jointly constitute a whole. (Foll. by *of.*) M17. **3** That appoints or elects a representative. M18. **4** Able to frame or alter a (political) constitution. L18.

1 W. WHEWELL To each degree of pressure . . there is a constituent temperature corresponding. 2 W. PALEY The constituent parts of water. L. MACNEICE Tone of voice or syntax or rhythm . . found . . to be not only formal but constituent of meaning. 4 *New York Times* Voters will elect a 60-member Constituent Assembly to write a new constitution and name an interim president.

constituently *adv.* M19.

constitute /'kɒnstɪtjuːt/ *v.* Pa. pple **-tuted**, †**-tute**. LME. [L *constitut-* pa. ppl stem of *constituere* establish, appoint, f. as CON- + *statuere* set up.] **1** *v.t.* **a** Make up, go to form; be the constituent parts or material of. LME. **b** Frame or make by combination of elements. Usu. in *pass.*, of bodily or mental constitution. L16. **c** Make (a thing) what it is; determine. M19. **2** *v.t.* (w. compl.). **a** Appoint (a person) to the office or post of. LME. **b** Set (a person, oneself, a thing) up as. M16. †**3** *v.t.* Set, place, (*in* a specified situation etc.). L15–L19. **4**†**a** *v.i.* Make laws. L15–M17. **b** *v.t.* Make, establish, (a law etc.). (Formerly foll. by subord. cl.) Now *rare* or *obs.* M16. **c** *v.t.* Establish (an institution etc.); give legal form to. M16.

1a L. DEIGHTON The lectures and diagrams that would constitute the afternoon briefing. A. FRASER His marriageability constituted about his only ace. **b** E. F. BENSON She was so constituted that she had to object. **2a** DEFOE We constituted him captain. **b** J. A. FROUDE The will of a single man . . cannot be allowed to constitute itself an irremoveable obstacle to a great national good.

constituter *n.* (now *rare*) L17. **constitutor** *n.* M16.

constitution /kɒnstɪˈtjuːʃ(ə)n/ *n.* ME. [(O)Fr., or L *constitutio(n-)*, f. as prec.: see -ION.] **I 1** *Hist.* A decree, an ordinance, a law, a regulation. ME. †**2** A body of rules, customs, or laws. Cf. sense 4b. Only in ME. **3** The way in which a thing is constituted or made up; composition, make-up. M16. **b** The character of the body as regards health, strength, vitality, etc. M16. **c** Condition of mind; (a) disposition, (a) temperament. L16. **4a** The manner in which a State is organized, esp. as regards the location of ultimate power. E17. **b** The set of fundamental principles according to which a State is constituted and governed; a body of rules prescribing the major elements of the structure and activities of any organization. M18.

3 SHAKES. *Twel. N.* The excellent constitution of thy leg. H. MARTINEAU That..is the fault of the constitution of society. b R. LEHMANN Thanks to his excellent constitution he rallied steadily. 4a H. HALLAM The original constitution of England was highly aristocratical. b M. PATTISON Any further change in the constitution of the University. *unwritten constitution, written constitution.*

II 5 The action of constituting. LME. †**6** The action of decreeing or ordaining. LME–M17.

constitutioned *a.* having a constitution (of a specified kind) E18.

constitutional /kɒnstɪˈtjuːʃ(ə)n(ə)l/ *a.* & *n.* L17. [f. prec. + -AL[1].] **A** *adj.* **1** Of, belonging to, or inherent in a person's constitution. L17. **2** Affecting a person's constitution, *spec.* beneficially. M18. **3** Forming an essential part. M18. **4** In harmony with or authorized by the constitution of a State etc. Cf. *unconstitutional.* M18. **5** Of, pertaining to, or dealing with the constitution of a State or States, etc. L18.

1 L. STEPHEN Pope's constitutional irritability. 4 W. LIPPMANN While in free societies opposition is a constitutional function, in authoritarian societies it is treason. **constitutional government, monarchy, sovereign**: limited by a constitution or its forms.

B *n.* **1** = CONSTITUTIONALIST *n.* 2. L18. **2** A walk taken (esp. regularly) for the sake of one's health or well-being. E19.

constitutioˈnality *n.* L18. **constitutionalize** *v.* (*a*) *v.t.* make constitutional; (*b*) *v.i.* (*colloq.*) take a constitutional: M19.

constitutionalist /kɒnstɪˈtjuːʃ(ə)n(ə)lɪst/ *n.* & *a.* M18. [f. prec. + -IST.] **A** *n.* **1** A person who studies or writes on the constitution of a State. M18. **2** A supporter of constitutional principles, or of a particular constitution. L18. **B** *adj.* Of, pertaining to, or being a constitutionalist or constitutionalists. M19.

constitutionalism *n.* constitutional government; adherence to constitutional principles: M19.

constitutionally /kɒnstɪˈtjuːʃ(ə)n(ə)li/ *adv.* M18. [f. as prec. + -LY[2].] **1** By virtue of one's constitution; by nature. M18. **2** In accordance with the constitution of a State etc. Cf. *unconstitutionally.* M18. **3** As regards the constitution (of a thing or a person). M18.

constitutive /ˈkɒnstɪtjuːtɪv/ *a.* L16. [Late L *constitutivus* confirmatory, defining, f. as CONSTITUTE *v.*: see -IVE.] **1** Having the power of constituting; giving formal or definite existence or expression to something. L16. **2** = CONSTITUTIONAL *a.* 3. E17. **3** Forming a part; constituent. M17. **4** With *of*: that constitutes. M17. **5** *Biochem.* Designating or pertaining to an enzyme which is continuously produced in an organism rather than depending on the presence of an inducer. M20.

1 B. BROWN The great constitutive ideas which have moulded powerfully the institutions of society. W. NOLL Constitutive equations defining the particular ideal material we wish to study.

constitutively *adv.* M17. **constitutiveness** *n.* (*rare*) L17. **ˌconstituˈtivity** *n.* (*Biochem.*) the property of being constitutive (sense 5) M20.

constrain /kənˈstreɪn/ *v.* ME. [OFr. *constraindre* (mod. *contraindre*), pres. stem *constraign-*, f. L *constringere* bind tightly together, f. as CON- + *stringere* (see STRAIN *v.*[1]).] **1a** *v.t.* & *i.* Compel or oblige (a person; *to* or *into* a course of action, state, etc.; *to do*); urge irresistibly or by necessity. ME. **b** *v.t.* Bring about by compulsion. E17. **c** *v.t. Mech.* Restrict the motion of (a body or particle) to a certain path. M19. †**2** *v.t.* Force out; produce by effort or straining. LME–E18. †**3** *v.t.* Afflict, distress. LME–M19. **4** *v.t.* Confine forcibly; imprison. LME. **b** *fig.* Limit, keep within bounds. E17. †**5** *v.t.* Constrict, contract. LME–L17. †**6** *v.t.* Take by force; ravish. L16–L17.

1a POPE Some rule, that guides, but not constrains. J. FULLER The season constrained them to carry on the harvest. b I. WATTS Sufficient testimony to constrain our assent.

constrainable *a.* LME. **constrained** *a.* that has been constrained; not natural; embarrassed; (earlier in UNCONSTRAINED): E16. **constrainedly** /-nɪdli/ *adv.* M16. **constrainer** *n.* (*rare*) LME.

constraint /kənˈstreɪnt/ *n.* LME. [OFr. *constreinte* use as n. of fem. of pa. pple of *constraindre* (see prec.).] **1** Coercion, compulsion. LME. †**2** Oppression, affliction. LME–L16. **3** Restriction of liberty; something that restricts freedom of action or (*Mech.*) of motion. L16. **4** Restricted expression of natural feelings and impulses; a constrained manner. E18.

1 E. A. FREEMAN How far the electors acted under constraint. 3 M. MCCARTHY Social constraints. 4 V. WOOLF There was always some constraint between them.

constrict /kənˈstrɪkt/ *v.t.* M18. [L *constrict-* pa. ppl stem of *constringere*: see CONSTRAIN.] **1** Draw together as by an encircling pressure; make more narrowly confined (*lit.* & *fig.*); compress. M18. **2** Cause (living tissue) to contract. M18.

constricted *a.* drawn together or narrowed by constriction; narrow as if compressed: M18. **constrictive** *a.* [L *constrictivus*] †(*a*) checking discharge from or distention of a part of the body; (*b*) pertaining to, characterized by, or causing constriction: LME.

constriction /kənˈstrɪkʃ(ə)n/ *n.* LME. [Late L *constrictio(n-)*, f. as prec.: see -ION.] **1** The action of making narrower or smaller as by an encircling pressure; the state of being so contracted. LME. **2** A thing which constricts or limits. M17. **3** A feeling of tightness in a part of the body. L18. **4** A constricted part. E19.

4 *primary constriction*: see PRIMARY *a.* *secondary constriction*: see SECONDARY *a.*

constrictor /kənˈstrɪktə/ *n.* & *a.* E18. [mod.L, f. as prec. + -OR.] **A** *n.* **1** A snake that kills by compressing, *esp.* = BOA *constrictor.* E18. **2** A constrictor muscle. M18. **B** *adj. Anat.* That draws together or narrows a part. M19.

constringe /kənˈstrɪndʒ/ *v.* *literary.* L16. [L *constringere*: see CONSTRAIN.] **1** *v.t.* & *i.* Constrict (tissue): see CONSTRICT 2. L16. **2** *v.t.* = CONSTRICT 1. Now *rare* or *obs.* E17. **3** *v.t.* Cause to contract, as by cold etc. M17.

constringent /kənˈstrɪndʒ(ə)nt/ *a.* E17. [L *constringent-* pres. ppl stem of *constringere*: see CONSTRAIN, -ENT.] Causing constriction.

constringency *n.* L17.

construable /kənˈstruːəb(ə)l/ *a.* M17. [f. CONSTRUE *v.* + -ABLE.] Able to be construed.

construaˈbility *n.* M19.

construal /kənˈstruːəl/ *n.* M20. [f. CONSTRUE *v.* + -AL[1].] An act or the action of construing; (an) interpretation.

construct /ˈkɒnstrʌkt/ *n.* L19. [f. the vb.] **1** *Semitic Gram.* The construct state. L19. **2** *Ling.* A group of words forming a phrase. L19. **3a** *Psychol.* An object of perception or thought constructed by combining sense-impressions. L19. **b** *gen.* Anything constructed, esp. by the mind; a concept. E20.

construct /ˈkɒnstrʌkt/ *a.* E19. [f. pa. pple of next.] *Semitic Gram.* Designating the state or form of a noun when it precedes another noun that has an attributive or possessive relationship to it (usu. expressible in English by *of* or *in*).

construct /kənˈstrʌkt/ *v.t.* Pa. pple **constructed,** (*arch.*) **construct.** LME. [L *construct-* pa. ppl stem of *construere*, f. as CON- + *struere* lay, pile, build.] **I 1** Make by fitting parts together; build, erect. LME. **b** Form in the mind, devise. M18. **2** Find a geometrical construction for (a problem); draw precisely (a geometrical figure). E18. **3** *Gram.* Combine (words) according to grammatical rules. M19. †**II 4** Interpret, understand (in a certain way). *Sc.* E17–M18.

constructible *a.* M19. **constructor,** †**-er** *n.* †(*a*) a person who construes or interprets; (*b*) a person who constructs: E17.

constructio ad sensum /kɒnˌstrʌktɪəʊ ad ˈsɛnsəm/ *n. phr.* L19. [mod.L, lit. 'construction according to the sense'.] *Gram.* The overriding of grammatical requirements by those of word-meaning, so that, for example, a plural verb is used with a singular collective noun.

construction /kənˈstrʌkʃ(ə)n/ *n.* LME. [(O)Fr. f. L *constructio(n-)*, f. as CONSTRUCT *v.*: see -ION.] **I** Construing. **1** *Gram.* The syntactical relationship between words in a sentence etc.; the action of arranging words in accordance with established usage so as to convey the desired sense; an instance or type of this. LME. **2** An explanation or interpretation of a text, statement, statute, etc.; an interpretation put upon conduct, facts, etc.; the (good, bad, etc.) way in which these are taken by others. L15.

1 M. MCCARTHY The ablative absolute as a construction in English. *pregnant construction*: see PREGNANT *a.*[1] 2 R. D. LAING The construction we put on this behaviour. *strict construction*: see STRICT *a.*

II Constructing. **3** The action of constructing something (material or mental); the art or science of doing this. LME. **b** The action or method of drawing precisely a geometrical figure or a diagram. L16. **4** The manner in which something is arranged; structure, disposition. L16. **5** A constructed thing; a material or mental structure. L18.

3b *mechanical construction*: see MECHANICAL *a.* 5 *ideal construction*: see IDEAL *a.*

Comb.: **construction camp, railway,** etc.: used or engaged in the construction of a railway or similar undertaking.

constructional *a.* of, pertaining to, or engaged in construction; structural, belonging to the original structure: M18. **constructionally** *adv.* L19. **constructionism** *n.* = CONSTRUCTIVISM 1 E20. **constructionist** *n.* (*a*) (with *strict* or *loose*) a person who puts a strict or a loose construction upon something, *spec.* the US Constitution; (*b*) a constructivist: M19.

constructive /kənˈstrʌktɪv/ *a.* M17. [Late L *constructivus*, f. as CONSTRUCT *v.*: see -IVE.] **1** Resulting from a certain interpretation; inferred, not directly expressed; such in law though not in fact. M17. **2** Of or pertaining to construction; structural. E19. **3** Tending to construct or build up something non-material; contributing helpfully, not destructive. M19. **4** Of or pertaining to constructivism. E20. **5** *Math.* Of a proof: showing how an entity may in principle be constructed or arrived at in a finite number of steps. Also, accepting as valid only proofs of this kind. M20.

1 *constructive blasphemy, contempt, dismissal,* etc. **constructive delivery** *Law* delivery of goods to the buyer under a hire-purchase agreement. 3 *constructive criticism.*

constructively *adv.* L17. **constructiveness** *n.* E19.

constructivism /kənˈstrʌktɪvɪz(ə)m/ *n.* E20. [f. prec. + -ISM, after Russ. *konstruktivizm.*] **1** An orig. Russian artistic movement or style which makes use of three-dimensional, usu. non-representational, arrangements of different materials. E20. **2** *Math.* A view which admits as valid only constructive proofs and entities demonstrable by them. M20.

constructivist *a.* & *n.* (*a*) *n.* an exponent or advocate of constructivism; (*b*) *adj.* of or pertaining to constructivism or constructivists: E20.

†**constructure** *n.* E17–M19. [OFr., or late L *constructura*, f. as CONSTRUCT *v.*: see -URE.] = CONSTRUCTION II.

construe /kənˈstruː, ˈkɒnstruː/ *n.* Now *rare.* M19. [f. the vb.] An act of grammatical construing; a verbal translation.

construe /kənˈstruː/ *v.* LME. [L *construere* CONSTRUCT *v.*, (in late L) construe (sense 4).] **1** *v.t.* Give the sense of (a word, passage, legal document, etc.); expound; interpret. (Foll. by *as, into, to be.*) LME. **2** *v.t.* Interpret, understand (an action, thing, or person) in a specified way; put a construction on. (Foll. by *as*, †*for*, *into*, *to be*, and w. double obj.) LME. 3 *v.t.* Deduce, infer. LME. 4 *v.t.* & *i.* Analyse the grammatical construction of (a sentence); translate word for word; translate orally. LME. 5 *v.t.* Combine (a word) grammatically with or *with* others. LME.

2 D. L. SAYERS Whether the offer.. could reasonably be construed into a motive for murder. 3 I. HAMILTON How *little* of his life.. can be construed from the poems.

†**constuprate** *v.t.* M16–L17. [L *constuprat-* pa. ppl stem of *constuprare*, f. as CON- + *stuprare* ravish, f. *stuprum* defilement: see -ATE³.] Ravish, violate.

†**constupration** *n.* E17–M18.

consubstantial /kɒnsəbˈstanʃ(ə)l/ *a.* LME. [eccl.L *consubstantialis* (tr. Gk *homoousios*), f. as CON- + SUBSTANTIAL.] Of the same substance or essence (esp. in *Chr. Theol.* of the three persons of the Trinity).

consubstantialist *n.* (*Chr. Theol.*) a believer the consubstantiality of the persons of the Trinity, or in the doctrine of consubstantiation M17. **ˌconsubstantiˈality** *n.* [eccl.L *consubstantialitas*] identity of substance or essence M16. **consubstantially** *adv.* L16.

consubstantiate /kɒnsəbˈstanʃɪət/ *a.* M17. [Late L *consubstantiatus*, f. as next: see -ATE².] United in substance or essence.

consubstantiate /kɒnsəbˈstanʃɪeɪt/ *v.* L16. [f. late L *consubstantiat-* ppl a. (cf. med.L *consubstantiare*), f. as CON-, SUBSTANTIATE.] 1 *v.t.* Unite in one common substance. L16. †2 *v.i. Chr. Theol.* Believe in consubstantiation. L17–E18.

consubstantiation /ˌkɒnsəbstanʃɪˈeɪʃ(ə)n, -sɪ-/ *n.* L16. [mod.L *consubstantiatio(n-)*, f. as CON- after *trans(s)ubstantiatio(n-)* TRANSUBSTANTIATION.] 1 *Chr. Theol.* (The doctrine of) the real substantial presence of Christ's body and blood together with the bread and wine in the Eucharist. L16. †2 The action or an act of making consubstantial. M17–L18.

1 MILTON The Lutheran holds Consubstantiation.

consubstantiationist *n.* (*Chr. Theol.*) a believer in consubstantiation E19.

consuetude /ˈkɒnswɪtjuːd/ *n.* LME. [OFr., or L *consuetudo*, f. *consuetus* pa. pple of *consuescere* accustom, use, f. as CON- + *suescere* become accustomed: see -TUDE.] 1 Custom, esp. as having legal force. Chiefly *Sc.* LME. 2 Familiarity; acquaintance. E19.

consueˈtudinal *a.* customary, consuetudinary; *spec.* in *Celtic Gram.*, designating or in a mood expressing customary action: M17.

consuetudinary /kɒnswɪˈtjuːdɪnəri/ *a.* & *n.* LME. [Late L *consuetudinarius*, f. as prec.: see -ARY¹.] A *adj.* Customary. LME. B *n.* A written collection of the customs of a particular locality or body, esp. of a religious house or order. LME.

consul /ˈkɒns(ə)l/ *n.* LME. [L, rel. to *consulere* take counsel.] 1 *Hist.* a Either of two annually elected magistrates who jointly exercised supreme authority in the Roman Republic; a holder of a corresponding title (without the function) in the Roman Empire. LME. b Each of the three chief magistrates of the French Republic, from 1799 to 1804, the first of whom was head of State. E19. 2 *Hist.* A medieval earl or count. L15. †3 A member of a council. E16–M18. †4 A foreign official or magistrate; *spec.* a representative head of the merchants of a particular nation resident in a foreign town. E16–L18. 5 An agent appointed by a State to reside in a foreign town to protect the interests of the State's subjects and assist its commerce. M16.

1b **First Consul** Napoleon Bonaparte. 5 **consul general** [GENERAL *a.*]: of the highest status, usu. having jurisdiction over other consuls.

consulage *n.* consular charge or dues L16. **conṡulˈless** *n.* (*arch.*) the wife of a consul E19. **consulship** *n.* the post of consul; the term of office of a consul: M16.

consular /ˈkɒnsjʊlə/ *a.* & *n.* LME. [L *consularis*, f. as CONSUL: see -AR¹.] A *adj.* Of, pertaining to, or of the nature of a consul. LME. B *n.* Chiefly *Hist.* A person of consular rank. LME.

consulary *a.* (now *rare* or *obs.*) = CONSULAR *a.* L16.

consulate /ˈkɒnsjʊlət/ *n.* LME. [L *consulatus*, f. as CONSUL: see -ATE¹.] 1 *Hist.* A consular government; the period of this in France (1799–1804); the post or position of governing consuls. LME. †2 A body of councillors called consuls. L15–E17. 3 The post or establishment of a (modern) consul. L17.

consult /kənˈsʌlt, ˈkɒnsʌlt/ *n.* M16. [In sense 1 f. L *consultum*, f. *consultus* pa. pple of *consulere* CONSULT *v.*; in other senses f. Fr. *consulte* f. med.L *consulta* use as n. of fem. of L *consultus*.] 1 *Hist.* A decree of the Roman senate. M16. 2 The action or an act of consulting; (a) consultation. Now *rare*. M16. 3 *Hist.* A meeting for consultation; *spec.* a secret meeting for seditious purposes. M17.

consult /kənˈsʌlt/ *v.* E16. [(O)Fr. *consulter* f. L *consultare* frequent. of *consult-* pa. ppl stem of *consulere* take counsel.] 1 *v.i.* Deliberate, take counsel, confer, (*with* someone; *about*, *upon* a matter). E16. †2 *v.t.* Confer about, deliberate upon, consider. M16–E18. b Meditate, plan, contrive. M16–M17. 3 *v.t.* & *i.* foll. by *for*, †*with*). Take into consideration, have consideration for, (the interest, feelings, good, etc., of a person or persons). M17. 4 *v.t.* Ask advice of, seek counsel or a professional opinion from; refer to (a source of information); seek permission or approval from for a proposed action. M17.

1 W. COWPER The gods all sat consulting. 2 CLARENDON Many things were there consulted for the future. b R. EDEN They consulted to burne the shyppe. 3 ADDISON Those whose Safety I would principally consult. SOUTHEY For the general weal Consulting first. 4 A. A. MILNE You must *never* go down to the end of the town without consulting me. G. VIDAL Maximus consulted forbidden oracles. I. WALLACE He consulted his wristwatch. **consulting room**: *spec.* in which a doctor examines patients.

consultable *a.* M17. **consulˈtee** *n.* a person consulted M19. **consulter** *n.* (*a*) = CONSULTOR (b); †(*b*) = CONSULTOR (a): L16. †**consultive** *a.* = CONSULTATIVE E17–E19. **consultor** *n.* (*a*) a person who gives advice, esp. officially; (*b*) a person who consults: E17.

consulta /kɒnˈsʌltə/ *n.* Also (earlier) †**-to**. L17. [It., Sp., & Port., f. as CONSULT *n.*] A meeting of council (in Italy, Spain, or Portugal); a record of such a meeting.

consultant /kənˈsʌlt(ə)nt/ *n.* L17. [Prob. f. Fr., f. L *consultant-* pres. ppl stem of *consultare* CONSULT *v.*: see -ANT¹.] 1 A person who consults. L17. 2 A consulting physician; *spec.* a clinician in the highest grade of the British hospital service, having independent charge of patients. L19. 3 A person who gives professional advice or services in a specialist field. L19.

consultancy *n.* the work or position of a consultant; a department of consultants: M20.

†**consultary** *a.* var. of CONSULTORY.

consultation /kɒnsəlˈteɪʃ(ə)n/ *n.* LME. [(O)Fr., or L *consultatio(n-)*, f. L *consultat-* pa. ppl stem of *consultare* CONSULT *v.*: see -ATION.] 1 A meeting in which parties consult together, or one person consults another, *spec.* on a medical or legal matter. LME. 2 *Law* (now *Hist.*). A writ by which a cause removed from an ecclesiastical court to a civil court was returned to ecclesiastical jurisdiction. E16. 3 The action of consulting; deliberation. M16.

1 E. F. BENSON The two held consultation.

consultative /kənˈsʌltətɪv/ *a.* L16. [f. CONSULT *v.* + -ATIVE.] Of or pertaining to consultation; having the right to advise but not to decide on an issue.

consultatory /kənˈsʌltət(ə)ri/ *a.* E17. [Late L *consultatorius*, f. *consultat-*: see CONSULTATION, -ORY².] Pertaining to or serving for consultation; consultative.

consulting /kənˈsʌltɪŋ/ *ppl a.* M17. [f. CONSULT *v.* + -ING²; in sense 2 tr. Fr. (*médicin*) *consultant* f. obs. sense of *consulter* give professional counsel.] 1 That consults, that asks advice. M17. 2 Designating a person who makes a business of giving professional advice, esp. in specialized areas to those in the same profession. E19.

2 *consulting architect*, *engineer*, etc. **consulting physician** a physician who is consulted by colleagues or patients in special cases; a consultant.

†**consulto** *n.* see CONSULTA.

consultory /kənˈsʌltəri/ *a.* Now *rare* or *obs.* Also †**-ary**. E17. [f. CONSULTATION + -ORY².] = CONSULTATORY.

consumable /kənˈsjuːməb(ə)l/ *a.* & *n.* M17. [f. CONSUME + -ABLE.] A *adj.* Able to be consumed, as by fire; suitable for consumption as food. M17. B *n.* An article intended for consumption, not for repeated use. Usu. in *pl.* E19.

consume /kənˈsjuːm/ *v.* LME. [(Partly through Fr. *consumer*) f. L *consumere*, f. as CON- + *sumere* take.] I *v.t.* 1a Destroy by or like fire or (formerly) disease; cause to vanish (*away*), as by evaporation. LME. b *fig.* Engage the full attention or interest of (a person); engross. Chiefly as *consumed* ppl a. (foll. by *with*, *by*), *consuming* ppl a. LME. c In optative form in angry imprecations: damn. Long *dial.* M18. 2 Occupy or waste (time, or a period of time). LME. 3 Spend (money or goods), esp. wastefully. LME. 4 Use so as to destroy; take up and exhaust; use up. E16. 5 Eat up, drink down; devour. L16.

1b SCOTT FITZGERALD He was consumed with wonder at her presence. E. CALDWELL His career.. would be his consuming interest for many years. D. CAUTE I was consumed by a passion that I've recently been able to diagnose as ambition. 2 M. L. KING Most of my early evenings were consumed in this fashion. 4 A. MACLEAN The *Morning Rose* consumed a great deal of fuel. 5 J. HERRIOT I had consumed several whiskies.

II *v.i.* †6 Waste away with disease or grief. LME–L17. 7 Decay, rot. E16. 8 Burn away (*lit.* & *fig.*). L16.

consumingly *adv.* so as to consume or be consumed; exceedingly: M16.

consumed /kənˈsjuːmd/ *ppl a.* & *adv.* LME. [f. prec. + -ED¹.] 1 *adj.* That has been consumed (esp. *fig.*) LME. †2 *adj.* & *adv.* Confounded(ly), damn(ably). E18–L19.

consumedly /-mɪdli/ *adv.* †(*a*) confoundedly, damnably; (*b*) *arch.* excessively, extremely: E18.

consumer /kənˈsjuːmə/ *n.* LME. [f. as prec. + -ER¹.] 1 A person who or thing which squanders, destroys, or uses up. LME. 2 A user of an article or commodity, a buyer of goods or services. Opp. *producer*. L17.

Comb.: **consumer durable** an article for domestic use which does not need to be rapidly replaced; **consumer goods**: used in their own right, esp. domestically, not for manufacturing etc.; **consumer research** investigation of the wants and opinions of those who might buy a product; **consumer resistance** sales resistance from consumers.

consumerism *n.* (*a*) protection of the interests of consumers; (*b*) preoccupation with consumer goods and their acquisition: M20. **consumerist** *a.* & *n.* (a person) advocating or involved in the protection of consumers' interests L20. **consumeˈristic** *a.* L20.

consummate /ˈkɒnsʌmət/ *a.* (orig. *pa. pple*). LME. [L *consummatus* pa. pple, f. as next: see -ATE².] †1a Completed; fully accomplished. LME–M19. b Of a marriage: consummated. M16–M18. †2 Having in it finality. Only in LME. 3 Of a thing: complete, perfect. *arch.* E16. 4 Of the highest degree; supreme, utmost. M16. 5 Of a person: fully accomplished; supremely skilled. M17.

4 P. G. WODEHOUSE A sweeping and consummate vengeance. C. HILL His consummate skill. 5 R. FRY The prince of craftsmen, the consummate technician.

consummately *adv.* E17. **consummateness** *n.* (*rare*) E20.

consummate /ˈkɒnsəmeɪt, -sjʊ-/ *v.* M16. [L *consummat-* pa. ppl stem of *consummare*, f. as CON- + *summa* SUM *n.*, *summus* highest, supreme: see -ATE³.] 1 *v.t.* Bring to completion; accomplish, fulfil, finish. M16. 2 *v.t.* & (now *rare*) *i.* Complete (marriage) by sexual intercourse. M16. 3 *v.i.* Fulfil or perfect itself. M19.

consummator *n.* L16. **consummatory** /kənˈsʌmət(ə)ri/ *a.* = CONSUMMATIVE *a.*; *spec.* designating an (animal or human) action that is an end in itself: M17.

consummation /kɒnsəˈmeɪʃ(ə)n, -sjʊ-/ *n.* LME. [(O)Fr. *consommation* or L *consummatio(n-)*, f. as prec.: see -ATION.] **1** The action of consummating (esp. a marriage). LME. **2** A conclusion, an end (in time), *spec.* that of the world. LME. **3** The action of perfecting; the condition of full development; acme; a desired end or goal. LME.

3 *Time* The meal in preparation and its consummation at the table. F. WARNER A perfect end The consummation of a life of prayer.

consummative /ˈkɒnsəmeɪtɪv, kənˈsʌmətɪv/ *a.* L17. [f. as CONSUMMATE *v.* + -IVE.] That consummates or tends to consummate.

consummatively *adv.* E17. **consummativeness** *n.* (*rare*) E18.

consumpt /kənˈsʌm(p)t/ *n.* Chiefly *Sc.* E18. [L *consumpt-*: see next.] = CONSUMPTION 4.

consumption /kənˈsʌm(p)ʃ(ə)n/ *n.* LME. [(O)Fr. *consomption* f. L *consumptio(n-)*, f. *consumpt-* pa. ppl stem of *consumere* CONSUME: see -ION.] **1** The action or fact of consuming by use, waste, eating, etc. (see CONSUME *v.*). LME. **2** Wasting of the body by disease; (formerly) a wasting disease; now *spec.*, severe pulmonary tuberculosis. LME. **3** Decay, wasting away, wearing out. E16. **4** The purchase and use of or *of* goods, material, or energy; the amount or rate of this. M17.

1 *fig.*: W. OWEN To borrow a book for Dorothy's immediate consumption. 2 M. GIROUARD Galloping consumption forced him to spend more . . time on the south coast. 4 *specific* (*fuel*) *consumption*: see SPECIFIC *a.*

†**consumptioner** *n.* a consumer M17–M18.

consumptive /kənˈsʌm(p)tɪv/ *a.* & *n.* M17. [med.L *consumptivus*, f. L *consumpt-*: see prec., -IVE.] **A** *adj.* **1** Tending to consume; wasteful, destructive. M17. **2** Affected by or pertaining to a wasting disease; *spec.* of or pertaining to, having or tending to, pulmonary tuberculosis. M17. **3** Of or for economic consumption. M19.

2 U. BENTLEY She lay . . on the sofa, . . looking romantically consumptive.

B *n.* **1** A person with consumption. M17. †**2** A destructive or corrosive agent. L17–L18.

consumptively *adv.* L17. **consumptiveness** *n.* M18.

contabescence /kɒntəˈbɛs(ə)ns/ *n.* Now *rare* or *obs.* M17. [f. L *contabescent-* pres. ppl stem of *contabescere* waste away: see -ENCE.] Wasting away, atrophy; *Bot.* suppression of pollen formation in the anthers of flowers.

contabescent *a.* M19.

contact /ˈkɒntakt/ *n.* E17. [L *contactus*, f. *contact-* pa. ppl stem of *contingere* touch closely, border on, f. as CON- + *tangere* touch. Cf. Fr. *contact*.] **1** The state or condition of touching; an instance of touching. E17. **b** The touching of electrical conductors to permit the flow of current; a device for effecting this; each of the conductors involved. M19. **2** *Math.* The touching of a straight line and a curve, of two curves, or of two surfaces. M17. **3** Meeting, communication. E19. **4a** A person who has been exposed to infection by proximity to someone suffering from an infectious disease. E20. **b** A person who can be called upon for assistance, information, etc.; a business etc. acquaintance who may be useful. M20. **5** = *contact lens* below. Usu. in *pl. colloq.* M20.

1b *break contact, make, contact.* 3 R. K. NARAYAN His lifelong contact with tough men had hardened him. V. GRISSOM I was in radio contact with . . the helicopters which were on their way to pick me up. 5b J. DIDION He was a good contact He knew a lot of things.

Phrases: **come in(to) contact with** touch, meet, come across, be brought into communication with. SLIDING *contact*.

Comb.: **contact breaker** a contrivance for breaking an electric circuit automatically; **contact flight, flying** navigation of an aircraft by the observation of landmarks; **contact healing** *Spiritualism* the healing of illness by physical contact with a medium; **contact herbicide**: that affects a plant only when it comes into contact with it, not when it is taken up through the roots; **contact lens** a small glass or plastic lens placed on the surface of the eyeball to correct faulty vision; **contact man** a go-between; a man who carries or supplies information; **contact metamorphism** *Geol.*: due to contact with or proximity to an igneous intrusion; **contact print, -printing** *Photogr.* a print made by, the making of prints by, passing light through a negative on to sensitized paper, glass, or film held in direct contact with the negative; **contact process** *Chem.*: for making sulphuric acid by means of the oxidation of sulphur dioxide in the presence of a solid catalyst; **contact screen** a halftone screen made on a film base; **contact sport** a sport in which the participants necessarily come into bodily contact with one another.

contact /ˈkɒntakt, kənˈtakt/ *v.* M19. [f. the n.] **1** *v.t.* Bring into or place in contact. *rare.* M19. **2** *v.i.* Come into or be in contact (*with*). L19. **3** *v.t.* Come into contact with; get in touch with. E20.

contactable *a.* M20. **contactor** *n.* a device for making and breaking an electric circuit E20.

contadina /kontaˈdiːna, kɒntəˈdiːnə/ *n.* Pl. ***-ne*** /-ne, -ni/, ***-nas***. E19. [It., fem. of next.] An Italian peasant girl or peasant woman.

contadino /kontaˈdiːno, kɒntəˈdiːnəʊ/ *n.* Pl. ***-ni*** /-ni/, ***-nos***. M17. [It., f. *contado* county, (peasant population of) agricultural area round a city: cf. -INE[1].] An Italian peasant or countryman.

contagion /kənˈteɪdʒ(ə)n/ *n.* LME. [L *contagio(n-)*, f. as CON- + base of *tangere* to touch: see -ION. Cf. Fr. *contagion*.] **1** A contagious disease; a plague, a pestilence. *fig.* a contagious moral disease, corruption. LME. **2** Harmful contagious influence or quality (chiefly *fig.*). LME. **3** The communication of disease from body to body by direct or indirect contact. E17. **4** *Med. Hist.* A substance or agent by which a contagious disease is transmitted. E17. †**b** A poison that infects the blood. *rare* (Shakes.). Only in E17. **5** In a good or neutral sense: the infectious quality or influence of an emotion, action, etc. M17.

1 M. L. KING Hate is a contagion; . . it grows and spreads as a disease. 2 E. P. THOMPSON The tendency of the Methodists . . to keep their members apart from the contagion of the unconverted. 5 J. A. FROUDE The contagion of example.

contagionist *n.* (*obs.* exc. *Hist.*) a believer in the contagiousness of a particular disease or particular diseases E19.

contagious /kənˈteɪdʒəs/ *a.* LME. [Late L *contagiosus*, f. as prec.: see -OUS.] **1** Communicating disease or corruption by contact. LME. †**2** Apt to breed disease, pestilential; *gen.* harmful, noxious. LME–L18. **3** Of a disease: infectious by direct or indirect contact; communicable. LME. **4** Charged with the agents (as bacteria etc.) of a communicable disease. L16. **5** *fig.* Of an emotion etc.: infectious, quickly affecting others. E17.

1 *fig.*: SOUTHEY Ere the contagious vices of the court Polluted her. 2 R. HAKLUYT The Winter comming . . with much contagious weather. 3 **contagious abortion** brucellosis in cattle, as producing abortion. 4 DEFOE Their breath, their sweat, their very clothes were contagious. 5 CONAN DOYLE The faculty of deduction is certainly contagious, Watson. . . It has enabled you to probe my secret.

contagiously *adv.* LME. **contagiousness** *n.* L15.

contagium /kənˈteɪdʒɪəm/ *n.* Pl. **-ia** /-ɪə/. M17. [L, var. of *contagio(n-)* CONTAGION.] †**1** *gen.* Contagion. Only in M17. **2** *spec.* = CONTAGION 4. L19.

contain /kənˈteɪn/ *v.* ME. [Repr. tonic stem of (O)Fr. *contenir* f. L *continere*, f. as CON- + *tenere* hold.] **I** Have in it. **1** *v.t.* Include as a part or the whole of its substance or content; comprise. ME. **b** Of a measure: be equal to (so much or many of another). LME. **c** *Math.* Of a number: be divisible by, esp. without a remainder. Usu. in *pass.* L16. †**2** *v.t.* Extend over, take up. LME–M18. **3** *v.t.* Have inside itself, (be able to) hold within itself. LME. **4** *v.t.* Have (an area, a space, etc.) within its boundaries, enclose (*between, within*); *Math.* form the boundary of (a geometric figure). Usu. in *pass.* LME.

1 J. TYNDALL The rock . . contains a good deal of iron. T. HARDY The next letter . . contained . . a statement of his position. 2 SWIFT A complete history . . would contain twelve large volumes in folio. 3 A. URE Waggons . . containing each 53 cwts. J. BUCHAN The side pocket . . contained an old . . cigar case. 4 OED The space contained between the orbits of Mars and Jupiter.

II Restrain, control. **5** *v.t.* Restrain, keep in check, repress, (oneself, one's emotions etc., †another). (Foll. by †*from* an action etc.) ME. **b** *v.i.* Control oneself or one's emotions. Now *rare.* E17. †**6** *v.refl.* & *i.* Behave. ME–L15. **7** *v.t.* Restrict, limit, confine. Now *esp.* keep (a hostile force, ideology, etc.) within certain boundaries; prevent from moving or extending. LME. †**8** *v.t.* Retain in a desired state or order. (Foll. by *in*, *within*.) M16–M19. †**b** Keep in one's possession or control. L16–M17.

5 SPENSER To contayne the unruly people from a thousand evill occasions. E. BOWEN She could hardly contain herself for apprehension and pleasure. D. LESSING She made efforts to contain her feelings. b AV *1 Cor.* 7:9 But if they cannot conteine, let them marry. 7 A. DAVIS The collective anger was so great that the people could not be contained. Defiant throngs pressed forward through the doors of the building. C. RYAN The assault was aimed at containing the fifteenth Army. 8 GIBBON That he could . . contain in obedience . . his wide-extended dominions.

containable *a.* (earlier in UNCONTAINABLE) L17. **contained** *ppl a.* (*a*) included, enclosed, held; (*b*) restrained, showing self-restraint, reserved (see also SELF-CONTAINED): LME. **containing** *n.* (*a*) the action of the vb; †(*b*) that which is contained; contents: LME. **containment** *n.* the action or fact of containing or holding; restraint; *esp.* the action of preventing a hostile force etc. from expanding into other areas: M17.

container /kənˈteɪnə/ *n.* LME. [f. prec. + -ER[1].] A person who or thing which contains something; a receptacle designed to contain some particular thing(s); *spec.* a large boxlike receptacle of standard design, used for the transportation of goods.

Comb.: **container-lorry**: transporting goods loaded in a container; **container-ship, -train**: designed to carry goods stored in containers.

containerize *v.t.* pack into or transport by means of containers M20.

contaminate /kənˈtamɪneɪt/ *v.t.* Pa. pple & ppl a. **-ated**, (*arch.*) **-ate** /-ət/. LME. [L *contaminat-* pa. ppl stem of *contaminare*, f. *contamen, -min-*, contact, pollution, f. base of *tangere* touch: see -ATE[3]. Cf. CONTAGION.] **1** Make impure by contact or mixture; pollute, corrupt, infect. LME. **2** *spec.* **a** Subject to contamination by radioactivity. E20. **b** Subject to textual contamination. E20.

contaminant *n.* something which contaminates, a contaminating substance M20. **contaminative** *a.* that contaminates E19. **contaminator** *n.* E19.

contamination /kəntamɪˈneɪʃ(ə)n/ *n.* LME. [L *contaminatio(n-)*, f. as prec.: see -ATION.] **1** The action of making impure or polluting; defilement, infection. LME. **b** *spec.* The introduction or presence of radioactivity where it is harmful or undesirable. E20. **2** Something which contaminates; an impurity. E19. **3a** The blending of two or more stories, plots, etc., into one. L19. **b** *Ling.* The blending of forms of similar meaning or use in order to produce a form of a new type. L19. **c** *Textual Criticism.* A blending of manuscripts resulting in readings from different traditions occurring in the same (group of) manuscript(s). E20.

contango /kənˈtaŋɡəʊ/ *n.* & *v.* M19. [Prob. arbitrary, on the analogy of L 1 pres. sing. in *-o*, perh. w. notion '(I) make contingent'.] *Comm.* **A** *n.* Pl. **-os**. A premium paid by a buyer of stock to postpone transfer to a future settling day. Cf. BACKWARDATION. M19.

Comb.: **contango day** the eighth day before a settling day.

B *v.t.* Pay contango on (stocks or shares). E20.

conte /kɔ̃ːt/ *n.* Pl. pronounced same. L19. [Fr.] A short story, as a form of literary composition; *spec.* a medieval narrative tale.

conteur /kɔ̃tœːr (*pl. same*)/ *n.* a composer of *contes*; a narrator: M19.

Conté /ˈkɒnteɪ/ *a.* Also **c-**. M19. [Nicolas Jacques *Conté* (1755–1805), Fr. inventor.] Designating a kind of pencil, crayon, or chalk which Conté developed.

contemn /kənˈtɛm/ *v.t.* Now chiefly *literary.* LME. [OFr. *contemner* or L *contemnere*, f. as

CON- + *temnere* despise.] Treat as of small value, view with contempt; disregard; despise, scorn.

contemner, -or *n.* E16. **contemningly** *adv.* (now *rare*) in a contemning or scornful manner L15.

contemper /kən'tɛmpə/ *v.t.* Now *rare* or *obs.* L16. [Fr. †*contempérer* or L *contemperare* temper by mixing, f. as. CON- + TEMPER *v.*¹] 1 Mingle together. L16. 2 Temper, moderate, qualify. E17. 3 Adjust (*to*) by tempering. E17.

†**contemperate** *v.t.* Pa. pple **-ated,** (earlier) **-ate.** L15–M18. [L *contemperat-* pa. ppl stem of *contemperare*: see prec., -ATE³.] = CONTEMPER.

contemperature /kən'tɛmp(ə)rətʃə/ *n.* Now *rare* or *obs.* M16. [f. as prec. after TEMPERATURE.] The action or product of blending together; a harmonious mixture.

contemplable /kən'tɛmpləb(ə)l/ *a. rare.* E17. [L *contemplabilis*, f. *contemplari*: see CONTEMPLATE, -ABLE.] That may be contemplated.

contemplamen /kɒntəm'pleɪmɛn/ *n. rare.* L17. [mod.L, f. *contemplari*: see CONTEMPLATE.] An object of contemplation.

contemplant /kən'tɛmpl(ə)nt/ *n.* & *a. rare.* E17. [L *contemplant-* pres. ppl stem of *contemplari*: see next, -ANT¹.] †A *n.* A person who contemplates. Only in E17. B *adj.* That contemplates. L18.

contemplate /'kɒntɛmpleɪt, -təm-/ *v.* L16. [L *contemplat-* pa. ppl stem of *contemplari*, f. as CON- + *templum* open space for observation, temple: see -ATE³.] 1 *v.i.* Meditate (†*on*), muse; be occupied in contemplation. L16. 2 *v.t.* Meditate on, ponder; view mentally; consider in a particular aspect, regard. L16. 3 *v.t.* & †*i.* foll. by *on*. Look at with continued attention; gaze on, observe thoughtfully. E17. 4 *v.t.* Regard as possible, expect, take into account as a contingency. L18. b Have in view as a purpose; intend. E19.

1 SOUTHEY Julian was silent then, and sate contemplating. I. D'ISRAELI Too deeply occupied with their own projects to contemplate on those of others. 2 S. TURNER [It] must not be contemplated as a barbarism of the country. J. LONDON He would have . . to do a thousand and one things that were awful to contemplate. *contemplate one's navel*: see NAVEL 1. 3 J. CONRAD She continued to contemplate . . the bare and untidy garden. 4 E. F. BENSON Failure, however, she did not contemplate. b A. CHRISTIE We are not contemplating arresting anyone at present. B. WEBB I am . . contemplating a course of reading on music and musicians.

†**contemplatist** *n.* a person given to contemplation M17–M19.

contemplation /kɒntɛm'pleɪʃ(ə)n, -təm-/ *n.* ME. [(O)Fr. f. L *contemplatio(n-)*, f. as prec.: see -ATION.] 1 Religious musing; devout meditation. ME. 2 *gen.* The action of thinking about or of pondering over a thing continuously; musing, meditation. ME. b A state or period of meditation or study. Also, a meditation expressed in writing (usu. in *pl.*). E16. 3 The action of viewing as a possibility or as a purpose; taking into account; prospect, intention. LME. †b Request, petition. LME–M16. 4 The action of gazing on or looking at attentively or thoughtfully. L15. 5 (A) matter for contemplation. Now *rare.* E18.

2 M. DE LA ROCHE Each absorbed in contemplation of his own thoughts. J. GLASSCO I sat down . . and gave myself up to contemplation. 3 **in contemplation** in mind; under serious consideration. 5 S. JOHNSON Everything must supply you with contemplation.

contemplative /kən'tɛmplətɪv/; *in senses A.2, 3 also* 'kɒntɛmpleɪtɪv, -təm-/ *a.* & *n.* ME. [(O)Fr. *contemplatif, -ive* or L *contemplativus*, f. as CONTEMPLATE: see -ATIVE.] A *adj.* 1 Devoted or given up to religious contemplation and prayer. ME. 2 *gen.* Given to contemplation; meditative, thoughtful. ME. 3 Characterized by, of the nature of, or tending to contemplation. LME.

1 Esp. in *contemplative life* [L *vita contemplativa*]. 3 W. BLACK Smoking a contemplative cigar under the . . starlight.

B *n.* A person devoted to meditation or religious contemplation; a person who leads the contemplative life. ME.

contemplatively *adv.* LME. **contemplativeness** *n.* M18.

contemplator /'kɒntɛmpleɪtə, -təm-/ *n.* LME. [L *contemplator*, f. as CONTEMPLATE: see -OR. Partly f. CONTEMPLATE + -OR.] A person who contemplates something; a person given to or engaged in contemplation.

†**contemporane** *a.* & *n.* Also **-an.** LME. [f. as CONTEMPORANEOUS.] A *adj.* Contemporaneous (*with*). LME–L16. B *n.* A contemporary. M16–M18.

contemporaneity /kəntɛmp(ə)rə'niːəti, -'neɪɪti/ *n.* L18. [f. next + -ITY. Cf. Fr. *contemporanéité*. See also COTEMPORANEITY.] Contemporaneous condition or state.

contemporaneous /kəntɛmpə'reɪnɪəs, kɒn-/ *a.* M17. [f. L *contemporaneus*, f. as CON- + *tempus, tempor-* time: see -OUS. See also COTEMPORANEOUS.] 1 Existing or occurring at the same time (*with*). M17. 2 Of the same historical or geological period (*with*); of the same age. M19.

contemporaneously *adv.* E19. **contemporaneousness** *n.* E19.

contemporary /kən'tɛmp(ə)r(ər)i/ *n.* & *a.* M17. [med.L *contemporarius*, f. as CON- + *tempus, tempor-* time, after L *contemporaneus* (see prec.) and late L *contemporalis* (see CON-, TEMPORAL *a.*¹): see -ARY¹. See also COTEMPORARY.] A *adj.* 1 Belonging to the same time; existing or occurring together in time. (Foll. by *with*, †(*un*)*to*.) M17. 2 Equal in age, coeval. M17. 3 Occurring at the same moment or during the same period; contemporaneous, simultaneous. M17. 4 Modern or ultra-modern in style or design. M19.

1 M. PATTISON Writers contemporary with the events they write of. G. M. TREVELYAN The . . changes in Scottish mind and manners . . did not come to any serious collision with the . . church, such as marked contemporary movements of opinion in France. 2 J. SULLIVAN The water is as ancient as the earth, and contemporary with it. 4 A. TATE It was often said of T. S. Eliot that his poems were *very* contemporary but that his ideas . . were all frozen in the past.

B *n.* A person who lives at the same time as or is the same age as another or others; *transf.* a journal etc. published at the same time as another. M17.

contemporarily *adv.* (*a*) contemporaneously; (*b*) in a contemporary manner: M18. **contemporariness** *n.* M17.

contemporize /kən'tɛmpəraɪz/ *v.t.* & *i.* Also **-ise.** M17. [f. late L *contemporare* + -IZE.] (Cause to) synchronize.

contempt /kən'tɛm(p)t/ *n.* LME. [L *contemptus*, f. *contempt-* pa. ppl stem of *contemnere* CONTEMN.] 1 The action of scorning or despising; the mental attitude in which something or someone is considered as worthless or of little account. LME. 2 The condition of being held worthless or of being despised; dishonour, disgrace. LME. 3 *Law.* Disobedience or open disrespect to the monarch's lawful commands or to the authority of Parliament or another legislative body; (in full *contempt of court*) disobedience or open disrespect to, or interference with the proper administration of justice by, a court of law. LME. 4 A scornful or disrespectful act; *esp.* an act in contempt of a court of law. L16. †5 An object of contempt. E17–M19.

1 P. G. WODEHOUSE A true woman's contempt for consistency. C. P. SNOW She said it dismissively and with contempt. *beneath contempt*: see BENEATH *prep.* 3. 2 **bring, fall, into contempt** make, become, despised. **have** or **hold in contempt** despise. 3 **in contempt (of court)** in the position of having committed contempt and not having purged this offence. 4 J. WESLEY Our sins are so many contempts of this highest expression of his love.

†**contempt** *v.t.* Pa. pple **-ed,** (earlier) **contempt.** LME–E19. [L *contempt-* (see prec.).] = CONTEMN.

contemptible /kən'tɛm(p)tɪb(ə)l/ *a.* & *n.* LME. [(O)Fr., or late L *contemptibilis*, f. as prec.: see -IBLE.] A *adj.* 1 Worthy only of contempt; despicable. LME. 2 Expressing contempt, full of contempt. *obs.* exc. *dial.* L16.

B *n.* A contemptible person or thing. *rare* exc. as below. M17.

Old Contemptibles *Hist.* the British army in France in 1914 (w. ref. to the German Emperor's alleged mention of a 'contemptible little army').

contempti'bility *n.* E17. **contemptibleness** *n.* L16. **contemptibly** *adv.* LME.

contemptuous /kən'tɛm(p)tjʊəs/ *a.* M16. [med.L *contemptuosus*, f. as CONTEMPT *n.*: see -UOUS.] †1 Defying or despising law and public order. M16–L17. 2 Exciting or worthy of contempt; despicable. Now *rare.* M16. 3 Showing or full of contempt; disdainful, scornful, insolent. L16.

2 SHAKS. *2 Hen. VI* Contemptuous base-born callet as she is. 3 P. WARNER Henry . . had at first been contemptuous of Strongbow. L. O'FLAHERTY Proud, contemptuous, closed lips and an arrogant expression.

contemptuously *adv.* E16. **contemptuousness** *n.* M17.

contend /kən'tɛnd/ *v.* LME. [OFr. *contendre* or L *contendere*, f. as CON- + *tendere* stretch, strive.] 1 *v.i.* Be in rivalry, compete, vie, (*with* a person, *for* a thing). LME. 2 *v.i.* Engage in conflict, fight (*with* a person, *for* a thing); strive *with* or *against* feelings, natural forces, difficulties, etc. L15. †3 *v.i.* Make great efforts; endeavour. L15–E19. b Proceed with effort. L16–E17. 4 *v.i.* Argue (*with*, *against*, etc.) M16. 5 *v.t.* Maintain, assert, (*that*). M16. †6 *v.t.* Dispute (an object). *rare.* L17–L18.

1 H. FIELDING Nature and fortune . . seem to have contended which should enrich him most. W. LIPPMANN The pulling and pushing of interested groups contending for the assistance of the sovereign power. 2 SHAKS. *Coriol.* In ambitious strength I did Contend against thy valour. POPE Strength of Shade contends with strength of Light. D. H. LAWRENCE The only thing he had to contend with was the colliers setting snares for rabbits. 3 SWIFT Contending to excel themselves and their fellows. 5 H. J. LASKI The Nonjurors might with justice contend that they had right on their side. 6 SOUTHEY From his grasp Wrench the contended weapon.

†**contendent** *n.* & *a.* (*a*) *n.* a person who contends; (*b*) *adj.* contending: M16–E19. **contender** *n.* a person who contends or is given to contention M16.

contenement /kən'tɛnɪm(ə)nt/ *n. obs.* exc. *Hist.* E16. [OFr., or med.L *contenementum*, f. as CON- + TENEMENT.] Land held by a feudal tenant; property necessary for the maintenance of status.

¶Used to render *contenementum* in Magna Carta, a word of which the precise meaning is uncertain.

content /'kɒntɛnt/ *n.*¹ LME. [med.L *contentum*, pl. *contenta* things contained, use as n. of *contentus* pa. pple of *continere* CONTAIN.] I 1 In *pl.* & †*sing.* What is contained (in a vessel, object, book, document, etc.). (Foll. by *of* or possess.) LME. b In full *table of contents* (or †*content*). A summary of the subject-matter of a book (usu. a list of the titles of chapters etc.). L15. †2 *sing.* & in *pl.* (treated as *sing.* or *pl.*). Tenor, purport, (of a document etc.). LME–M17. 3 The sum of the constituent elements of something (usu. immaterial); the substance as opp. to the form; the amount (of a specified element or material component) contained or yielded. M19. b *Psychol.* [tr. G *Inhalt.*] The totality of the constituents of a person's experience at any particular moment. L19.

1 W. COWPER A letter ought not to be estimated by the length of it, but by the contents. J. CHEEVER She dumped the contents of her handbag onto the counter. 2 MILTON Terms of weight, Of hard contents. 3 W. D. WHITNEY The inner content or meaning of words. M. SCHORER Works [of literature] with the most satisfying content. M. AMIS Her life was disastrously free of neurotic content. F. HOYLE The moisture content of the air. *local content*: see LOCAL *a.*

II 4 Containing capacity; volume; (now *rare*) area, extent. LME. †b A portion of material or of space of a certain extent. L16–L17.

Comb.: **content word** a word having an independent lexical meaning (as a noun, adjective, verb, etc.) as opp. to one expressing primarily a grammatical relationship (as a preposition, conjunction, auxiliary, etc.).

con'tentual *a.* (*Philos.* & *Psychol.*) pertaining to or dealing with content (as opp. to form) E20.

content /kən'tɛnt/ *n.*² LME. [Perh. f. next. Cf. Sp., Port., It. *contento.*] †1 Payment, compensation for something done. *rare*. LME–M17. 2 Satisfaction, pleasure; contented state. L15. †3 A source of satisfaction; in *pl.*, pleasures, delights. L16–E18. †4 Acquiescence; unquestioning acceptance. M17–M18. 5 A sweet beverage, served hot or cold. *obs.* exc. *Sc.* L17.

2 DRYDEN In Concord and Content The Commons live, by no Divisions rent. K. MANSFIELD A look of deep content shone in her eyes. **to one's heart's content** to the full extent of one's desires. 4 POPE The sense they humbly take upon content.

contentful *a.* (now *rare*) full of content M16. **contentless** *a.* (now *rare*) discontented E17.

content /kən'tɛnt/ *pred. a.* & *n.*[3] LME. [(O)Fr. f. L *contentus* that is satisfied, pa. pple of *continere* (fig.) repress, restrain: cf. CONTAIN *v.*] A *adj.* 1 Desiring nothing more; satisfied (*with* what one has, *with* things as they are); contented, not unwilling *to do*, †*that*. LME. 2 Pleased, gratified: *arch.* exc. in *well content*. LME. 3 As *int.* Agreed! All right! *obs.* exc. in the House of Lords expr. formal assent or (*not content*) dissent (corresp. to *ay* and *no* in the House of Commons). L16.

1 L. URIS Abdul Kadar was content to play a waiting game. DAY LEWIS As a small child, I was content enough with the life around me. R. HARRIES I am content But I'm not happy. 2 TENNYSON So the three . . Dwelt with eternal summer, ill-content. 3 SHAKES. *1 Hen. VI* Content: I'll to the surgeon's.

B *n.* In the House of Lords: an affirmative or (*not content*) dissenting voter. E17.

content /kən'tɛnt/ *v.* LME. [(O)Fr. *contenter* f. Proto-Romance (med.L) *contentare*, f. *contentus*: see prec.] 1 *v.t.* Satisfy; be enough for. LME. b *refl.* Foll. by *with*, (arch.) *to do*: be satisfied or not unhappy with; accept or do no more than. LME. †c *v.i.* Be content, acquiesce. LME–L16. †2 *v.t.* Pay in full, reimburse, make good. LME–E19. †3 *v.t.* Please, gratify, delight. M16–L17.

1 SHAKES. *A.Y.L.* I will content you if what pleases you contents you. E. M. FORSTER No ordinary view will content the Miss Alans. b S. JOHNSON Most men, when they should labour, content themselves to complain. P. G. WODEHOUSE George Pennicut contented himself with saying 'Goo!' He was a man of few words. C. MCCULLOUGH Ashamed to sit with a great plate of meat . . when the people of the country contented themselves with bread. 2 J. USSHER To content the workeman for his paynes. SIR W. SCOTT A certain sum of sterling money to be presently contented and paid to him.

contentable *a.* able to be contented L16.

contentation /kɒntɛn'teɪʃ(ə)n/ *n. arch.* LME. [med.L *contentatio(n-)*, f. *contentat-* pa. ppl stem of *contentare*: see prec., -ATION. Cf. OFr. *contentacion*.] †1 Compensation; payment in satisfaction. Also, expiation of sin. LME–M17. †2 Satisfying of the conscience, allaying of doubt. L15–M17. †3 The action of contenting; the fact of being contented. L15–E18. 4 Contented condition. M16. †5 A source of satisfaction or pleasure. M16–L17.

contented /kən'tɛntɪd/ *a.* E16. [f. CONTENT *v.* + -ED[1].] Satisfied, not displeased; not disposed to complain; willing to be content *with*; willing *to do*.

contentedly *adv.* M16. **contentedness** *n.* M17.

contention /kən'tɛnʃ(ə)n/ *n.* LME. [(O)Fr., or L *contentio(n-)*, f. *content-* pa. ppl stem of *contendere*: see CONTEND, -ION.] 1 Strife, dispute, verbal controversy; a dispute or quarrel. LME. 2 Earnest exertion, endeavour. *arch.* M16. 3 Competition; (an act of) rivalry. L16. 4 A point contended for in argument. M17.

1 *fig.*: SHAKES. *Oth.* The great contention of the sea and skies Parted our fellowship. *bone of contention*: see BONE *n. draw the saw of contention*: see SAW *n.*[1] 3 **in contention** competing; in a position to win. 4 B. MAGEE My central contention . . is that Wagner's music expresses . . repressed and highly charged contents of the psyche.

contentional *a.* of the nature of contention E19.

contentious /kən'tɛnʃəs/ *a.* LME. [(O)Fr. *contentieux* f. L *contentiosus*, f. *content-*: see prec. -IOUS.] 1 Characterized by, involving, or subject to contention; disputed. LME. 2 Of or pertaining to differences between contending parties. L15. 3 Given to contention; quarrelsome. L15.

1 GLADSTONE Forbearing to raise contentious issues. 2 **contentious jurisdiction** *Law* right of jurisdiction in disputes between contending parties. 3 AV *Prov.* 21:19 Better to dwell in the wildernesse, then with a contentious and an angry woman.

contentiously *adv.* M16. **contentiousness** *n.* L16.

contentive /kən'tɛntɪv/ *a.* Now *rare.* L17. [Fr. *contentif, -ive*, f. as CONTAIN + -IVE.] That contains, having containing power.

contentment /kən'tɛntm(ə)nt/ *n.* LME. [Fr. *contentement*, f. as CONTENT *v.*: see -MENT.] †1 Payment of a claim. LME–E17. 2 The action of satisfying; satisfaction. *arch.* L15. †3 Pleasure, delight, gratification. L16–L18. †4 A source of satisfaction or pleasure; a delight. L16–L17. 5 The fact, condition, or quality of being contented; tranquil happiness, contentedness. (Foll. by *with*, †*in*.) L16.

conterminal /kɒn'tɜːmɪn(ə)l/ *a.* M17. [Alt. of CONTERMINOUS with substitution of suff. -AL[1]. Cf. COTERMINAL.] = COTERMINOUS 1.

conterminate /kɒn'tɜːmɪnət/ *a.* Now *rare.* L16. [Late L *conterminatus* pa. pple, f. as next: see -ATE[2].] = COTERMINOUS.

†**conterminate** *v.i.* M17–E19. [Late L *conterminat-* pa. ppl stem of *conterminare*, f. as next: see -ATE[3].] Be conterminous in space or time; have a common limit.

conterminous /kɒn'tɜːmɪnəs/ *a.* M17. [f. L *conterminus*, f. as CON- + TERMINUS: see -OUS. See also COTERMINOUS.] 1 Having a common boundary (*with*), adjacent (*to*). M17. 2 Meeting at their ends. M18. 3 Coextensive in space, time, or meaning. E19.

conterminously *adv.* M19. **conterminousness** *n.* E20.

†**conterraneous** *a.* M17–E18. [f. L *conterraneus*, f. as CON- + *terra* land: see -OUS.] Of or belonging to the same country.

contessa /kɒn'tɛsə/ *n.* Also (esp. in titles) **C-**. E19. [It. f. med.L *comitissa*: see COUNTESS.] An Italian countess.

contest /'kɒntɛst/ *n.* M17. [f. the vb, or Fr. *conteste*, f. *contester* CONTEST *v.*] 1 A controversy; debate, argument. *arch.* M17. 2 A struggle for victory, for an objective, etc.; conflict, strife. M17. 3 A competition; amicable contention for a prize etc. M17.

1 EDWARD WARD He was, without Contest, As grand a Rebel as the best. 3 G. VIDAL They were in serious contest to determine who could spit the farthest. JAN MORRIS The Boat Race is a straight contest, start to finish. *beauty-contest* etc.

contest /kən'tɛst/ *v.* L16. [L *contestari* call to witness, introduce (a suit) by calling witnesses, initiate (an action), f. as CON- + *testari* bear witness.] †1 *v.t.* Swear to (a fact or statement). L16–E17. †2 *v.t.* Attest. *rare.* L16–M17. †3 *v.t.* Call to witness, adjure. Only in E17. 4 *v.i.* Strive in argument (*with, against*), wrangle. E17. 5 *v.i. gen.* Strive, contend. E17. 6 *v.i.* Contend in rivalry, compete. E17. 7 *v.t.* Dispute by fighting; struggle or fight for. E17. 8 *v.t.* Debate, argue (a point etc.); call in question. M17. b *spec.* Challenge the legality of (the result of an election). Chiefly *N. Amer.* L18. 9 *v.t.* Set in contention. *rare.* L17. 10 *v.t.* Contend or compete in (an election etc.) or for (a seat in Parliament etc.). E18.

5 POPE For Forms of Government let Fools contest. 7 R. S. THOMAS Before Wars were contested. JOHN BROOKE Great Britain and France contested the supremacy of Western Europe. 8 DRYDEN A fifth Rule (which one may hope will not be contested). J. CHEEVER I'm going to declare that contract null and void, and if Murchison contests it, we'll drag him into court. 9 M. AYRTON Contesting the inertness of the mud against the spring in the rib.

contestee /kɒntɛs'tiː/ *n.* (*US*) a candidate whose election is contested L19. **contester, -or** *n.* a person who contests L19.

contestable /kən'tɛstəb(ə)l/ *a.* E18. [f. prec. + -ABLE. Cf. earlier INCONTESTABLE.] Able to be contested; open to question or argument, disputable.

contestant /kən'tɛst(ə)nt/ *n.* M17. [Fr., pres. pple of *contester* CONTEST *v.*: see -ANT[1].] A person who contests. Now usu. a person who takes part in a competition.

contestation /kɒntɛ'steɪʃ(ə)n/ *n.* M16. [L *contestatio(n-)*, f. *contestat-* pa. ppl stem of *contestari*: see CONTEST *v.*, -ATION; partly through Fr.] †1a Adjuration; solemn appeal or protest. M16–E18. b *Eccl. Hist.* In the Gallican liturgy, the prayer immediately preceding the Canon of the Mass. E18. †2 Confirmation by sworn testimony; solemn asseveration. L16–M17. 3 A disputation; controversy, argument. E17. b An assertion contended for, a contention. L19. 4 The action of struggling against each other; conflict. E17. 5 Competition; rivalry. Latterly *Sc.*. Now *rare.* E17.

†**contex** *v.t.* Also **context**. Pa. pple **context(ed)**. M16–L18. [L *contexere, context-*: see next.] Weave together (*lit.* & *fig.*)

context /'kɒntɛkst/ *n.* LME. [L *contextus*, f. *context-* pa. ppl stem of *contexere* weave together, f. as CON- + *texere* weave.] †1 = CONTEXTURE 3. LME–M17. †2 = CONTEXTURE 4. M16–M17. 3 The part or parts immediately preceding or following a passage or word as determining or helping to reveal its meaning; the surrounding structure as determining the behaviour of a grammatical item, speech sound, etc. M16. b *fig.* Ambient conditions; a set of circumstances; relation to circumstances. M19.

3 CONAN DOYLE That phrase 'Lion's Mane' haunted my mind. I knew that I had seen it somewhere in an unexpected context. **out of context** without relation to context and with consequently misleading implication. b L. P. HARTLEY Applied to another context, the thought struck him unpleasantly. N. PODHORETZ Much less Marxist . . though equally given to the seeing of things in historical and social context. **in this context** in this connection.

contextless *a.* M20.

†**context** *v.* see CONTEX.

contextual /kən'tɛkstjʊəl/ *a.* E19. [f. CONTEXT *n.* after *textual*.] Of or belonging to the context; depending on the context.

contextual definition: see DEFINITION 2.

contextualism *n.* (*a*) any philosophical doctrine emphasizing the importance of the context of inquiry in a particular question; (*b*) in literary criticism, the setting of a work in its cultural context: E20. **contextualist** *n.* an exponent or adherent of contextualism M20. **contextually** *adv.* E19.

contextualize /kən'tɛkstjʊəlʌɪz/ *v.t.* Also **-ise**. M20. [f. prec. + -IZE.] Place in or treat as part of a context; study in context.

contextuali'zation *n.* M20.

contexture /kən'tɛkstʃə/ *n.* Now *literary.* E17. [Fr., prob. f. med.L, f. L CON- + *textura* TEXTURE *n.*] 1 The action of weaving or linking together to form a connected whole (*lit.* & *fig.*); the fact or manner of being woven or linked together; structure, constitution. E17. 2 A mass of things interwoven together; a fabric (*lit.* & *fig.*). E17. 3 The putting together of words and sentences in connected composition; the construction of a text. E17. 4 A connected literary structure, a continuous text. E17. 5 = CONTEXT *n.* 3. E17.

contignation /kɒntɪg'neɪʃ(ə)n/ *n. arch.* L16. [L *contignatio(n-)*, f. *contignat-* pa. ppl stem of *contignare* join together with beams, f. as CON- + *tignum* building material, piece of timber: see -ATION.] 1 A structure formed by joining timbers together, a framework; *spec.* a floor, storey, or stage so formed. L16. 2 The joining together of beams or boards; jointing. M17.

contiguity /kɒntɪ'gjuːɪti/ *n.* E16. [Late L *contiguitas*, f. L *contiguus*: see next, -ITY.] 1 Contact (*lit.* & *fig.*); close proximity. E16. b *Psychol.* The proximity of ideas or impressions in place or time, as a principle of association. M18. †2 A contiguous thing. Only in M17. 3 A continuous mass. Now *rare.* L18.

contiguous /kən'tɪgjʊəs/ *a.* E16. [f. L *contiguus* touching together, f. *contingere*: see CONTINGENT, -OUS.] 1 Neighbouring, in close proximity. E16. 2 Touching, in contact; adjoining. Foll. by *to*. E17. 3 Next in order, successive. E17. †4 Continuous. Only in E18.

1 L. P. HARTLEY They occupied contiguous deck-chairs. 2 S. JOHNSON An heiress whose land lies contiguous to mine. 3 D. HARTLEY Two contiguous Moments of Time. 4 DEFOE The notion of the Hills being contiguous, like a wall that had no gates.

†**contigual** *a.* = CONTIGUOUS LME–M17. **contiguously** *adv.* M17. **contiguousness** *n.* M17.

continence /ˈkɒntɪnəns/ *n.* ME. [(O)Fr., or L *continentia*, f. *continent-* pres. ppl stem of *continere* restrain: see CONTAIN, -ENCE.] **I 1** Self-restraint. ME. **2** *spec.* Sexual self-restraint; *esp.* complete sexual abstinence. LME. **3** The possession of normal voluntary control over excretory functions. Opp. earlier *incontinence.* E20. †**II 4** Continuity. Only in E18.

continency *n.* (now *rare*) = CONTINENCE 1, 2 E16.

continent /ˈkɒntɪnənt/ *n.* L15. [In branches I & II f. use as n. of L *continent-* (see prec.); branch I also infl. by the adj. In branch III corresp. to Fr. *continent*, It. *continente*, repr. ellipt. use of L *terra continens* continuous land.] †**I 1** A person who is continent in appetites; a person under a vow of continence. L15–E18.

II 2 That which contains or holds something; *fig.* that which comprises or sums up something. Now *rare.* M16. †**3** Containing area; capacity. Only in 17.

2 G. MACDONALD Stealing from the significance of the content by the meretricious grandeur of the continent.

III 4 A continuous tract of land. *obs.* exc. as in sense 6 below. M16. †**b** Land as opp. to water; the earth. Only in L16. †**c** The globe of the sun or moon. E–M17. **5** The main land, as distinguished from islands, peninsulas, etc.; mainland. Now chiefly in *the Continent* (*of Europe*), the mainland of Europe as distinct from the British Isles. L16. **6** Any of the main continuous bodies of land (in *Geol.*, continental crust) on the earth's surface (of which six are now recognized—Europe, Asia, Africa, N. and S. America, Australia, Antarctica). E17. **7** *US Hist.* The colonies or states of America collectively, esp. at the time of the War of Independence. M18.

4 P. ERONDELLE That part of New France which is one Continent with Virginia. 5 DEFOE It is not known whether that country be an island or the continent. 6 *fig.*: CARLYLE Continents of parchment. See also SUBCONTINENT. *the Dark Continent*: see DARK *a.*

continent /ˈkɒntɪnənt/ *a.* LME. [L *continent-*: see CONTINENCE, -ENT.] **I 1** Characterized by self-restraint; temperate. LME. **2** *spec.* Sexually self-restrained; chaste. LME. †**3** Restraining, restrictive. *rare* (Shakes.). L16–E17. **4** Capable of containing; capacious. *rare.* M19. **5** Having normal voluntary control over one's excretory functions. Opp. earlier *incontinent.* M20.

3 SHAKES. *Macb.* My desire all continent impediments would o'erbear That did oppose my will.

†**II 6** Continuous in space; connected *to, with.* LME–L17. **7** Continuous in duration; *Med.* (of a fever etc.) not intermittent. E17–L18.

6 R. GRAFTON The mayne and continent land of the whole worlde.

continently *adv.* (*a*) in moderation, chastely, temperately; †(*b*) *rare* continuously: LME.

continental /kɒntɪˈnɛnt(ə)l/ *a.* & *n.* M18. [f. CONTINENT *n.* + -AL[1].] **A** *adj.* **1** Of or pertaining to a continent. M18. **2** (Usu. **C-**.) Belonging to or characteristic of the continent of Europe. M18. **3** *US Hist.* Of or belonging to the colonies or States of America collectively, esp. at the time of the War of Independence. L18.

Special collocations: **Continental breakfast** a light uncooked breakfast of coffee, rolls, etc. **continental climate**: having wide seasonal variations of temperature (characteristic of continental interiors far from the moderating influence of the sea). **Continental Congress** *US Hist.* each of the three congresses held by the American colonies in revolt against British rule in 1774, 1775, and 1776 respectively. **continental crust** *Geol.* the sialic crust which forms the earth's large land masses and the continental shelf (cf. SIAL). **Continental day** a school day extending from early morning to early afternoon, as is customary in many countries of mainland Europe. **continental drift** the continuing slow movement of the continents (due to the movement of the lithospheric plates on the upper layer of the earth's mantle) which has brought them to their present positions. *continental quilt*: see QUILT *n.* 1. **Continental roast** (designating) dark-roasted coffee beans with a taste associated with mainland Europe. **continental shelf** the bed of the shallow sea area bordering a continent. **continental slope**: between the outer edge of the continental shelf and the ocean bed. **Continental Sunday** Sunday as a day of recreation rather than of rest and worship. **Continental System** *Hist.*: Napoleon's plan to blockade England in 1806.

B *n.* **1** *US Hist.* **a** A soldier of the continental army in the War of Independence. L18. **b** A currency note of an early US issue that rapidly depreciated; *colloq.* the least possible amount. L18. **2** A native or inhabitant of a continent, *spec.* (usu. **C-**) of the continent of Europe. E19.

1b M. TWAIN He didn't give a continental for anybody.

continentalist *n.* (*a*) *US Hist.* an advocate of the federation of the States after the War of Independence; (*b*) = CONTINENTAL *n.* 2: L18. **continenˈtality** *n.* (*a*) the condition of being continental; (*b*) *spec.* the properties characteristic of a continental climate: L19. **continentalize** *v.* (*a*) *v.i.* (*rare*) make a continental tour; (*b*) *v.t.* make continental, impart a continental character to: M19. **continentally** *adv.* L18.

contingence /kənˈtɪndʒ(ə)ns/ *n.* LME. [f. as next: see -ENCE.] **1** = CONTINGENCY 1, 5. Now *rare.* LME. **2** Touching, contact. M16. †**3** Connection, affinity. M16–E17.

contingency /kənˈtɪndʒ(ə)nsi/ *n.* M16. [Late L *contingentia* in its med.L sense of circumstance, contingency: see next, -ENCY.] **I 1 a** *Philos.* The condition of being free from necessity with regard to existence, action, etc.; openness to the effect of chance or free will. M16. **b** *gen.* The quality or condition of being contingent; uncertainty of occurrence; chance. E17. **2** A thing dependent on an uncertain event. L16. **3** A thing that may happen at a later time; a condition that may or may not be present in the future. E17. **4** A thing incident to another; an incidental expense etc. E17. **5** A chance occurrence; a concurrence of events, a juncture. E17.

1b L. STERNE 'Twas a matter of contingency, which might happen or not. T. PYNCHON The War, the absolute rule of chance, their own pitiable contingency here, in its midst. 2 D. ACHESON Its thoroughness in preparation left no contingencies uncovered. 3 W. COBBETT All the . . ever-varying contingencies of marriage, number of children, etc. 4 C. V. WEDGWOOD He was compelled . . to modify his plan to meet unexpected and sometimes unwelcome contingencies. O. NASH Ready with a quip for any conversational contingency. 5 A. TROLLOPE Some settled contingencies to be forthcoming on their father's demise.

II 6 Close relationship or connection (*spec.* in *Sc. Law*, between processes); affinity. E17. †**7** Touching, contact. M–L17.

Comb.: **contingency fund**: set aside to deal with possible future or incidental expenses. **contingency plan**: to take account of a possible future event or circumstance.

contingent /kənˈtɪndʒ(ə)nt/ *a.* & *n.* LME. [L *contingent-* pres. ppl stem of *contingere* be contiguous, be in connection or in contact, befall, f. as CON- + *tangere* to touch.] **A** *adj.* **I 1** Of uncertain occurrence; liable to happen or not. LME. **b** Incidental (*to*). M18. **2** *Philos.* Of a proposition etc.: that may or may not be true or false. L16. **b** Dependent for its existence on something else; non-essential. E17. **3** Happening by chance; fortuitous. E17. **4** Conditional; dependent *on, upon.* E17. †**5** Not predetermined by necessity; free. E17–L18. †**6** Subject to accident etc.; at the mercy of; chance. E18–M19. **7** *Law.* Dependent on a foreseen probability; provisionally liable to exist or take effect. E18.

1 GEO. ELIOT The results of confession were not contingent, they were certain. 2b H. T. BUCKLE The senses only supply what is finite and contingent. I. MURDOCH There are some parts of London which are necessary and others which are contingent. 3 M. BRADBURY An accident is a happening, . . a chance or a contingent event. 4 W. S. MAUGHAM The best opening . . was contingent on his putting in a considerable amount of capital. 5 RICHARD WATSON If human actions are not Contingent, what . . of the morality of actions? 7 F. MARRYAT We are not looked upon as actual, but only contingent, inheritors of the title.

II 8 In contact, touching; tangential. Now *rare.* L16.

B *n.* **1** A chance occurrence; an accident. M16. **2** A thing that may or may not happen; a possibility. E17. **3** The proportion falling to a person on a division; a quota. E18. **4** Troops contributed to form part of an army etc.; *gen.* a group contributed to a larger one or having a similar origin. (The usual sense.) E18.

4 I. MURDOCH The Finch contingent had tactfully not stayed to lunch. JO GRIMOND The Viking contingents going to or from the Crusade.

continˈgential *n.* & *a.* (*rare*) (*a*) *n.* a non-essential; (*b*) *adj.* of a contingent nature, non-essential: M17. **contingently** *adv.* LME.

continua *n.* pl. of CONTINUUM.

continual /kənˈtɪnjʊəl/ *a.* ME. [(O)Fr. *continuel*, f. as CONTINUE: see -AL[1].] **1** Always happening; very frequent and without cessation; *arch.* regularly recurring. ME. **b** *Law.* Of a claim: formally reiterated within statutory intervals in order that it might not be deemed to be abandoned. *obs.* exc. *Hist.* E16. †**2** Perpetually existing or acting; unchanging in position. LME–M19. †**3** Forming a connected whole or continuous series; unbroken in expanse etc. LME–M18. †**4** Of a disease: chronic, not intermittent. E16–M18.

1 J. GALSWORTHY 'Why did she marry me?' was his continual thought. C. BROOKS Her devotion is continual whereas that of the poet is sporadic. 2 N. HAWTHORNE Beating it down with the pressure of his continual feet. 3 H. SAVILE A deepe masse of continuall sea.

continuˈality *n.* (*rare*) E19. **continually** *adv.* ME. **continualness** *n.* (*rare*) E17.

continuance /kənˈtɪnjʊəns/ *n.* LME. [OFr., f. as CONTINUE: see -ANCE.] **1** The action of making something continue or allowing something to continue; the maintaining or prolonging of an action, process, etc. LME. **2** *Law.* The adjournment of a suit or trial until a future date or for a period. Now only *US.* LME. **3** The action of continuing in something; perseverance, persistence. *arch.* LME. **4** The lasting or enduring of an action, state, etc.; duration. LME. **5** The action or fact of remaining in or *in* a place, state, etc. LME. **6** Course or length of time; a continuing period. *arch.* LME. †**7** Continuity. LME–M18. †**8** The quality of lasting or having lasted; permanence, durability; antiquity. E16–L17. **9** = CONTINUATION *n.* 5. Now *rare* or *obs.* M16.

1 ADDISON His own preservation, or the continuance of his species. C. SAGAN This is a tradition worthy of continuance. 4 T. HALE Any Voyage not exceeding five or six years continuance. 5 SHAKES. *1 Hen. VI* Cloy'd With long continuance in a settled place. 6 R. L. STEVENSON I have . . seen him re-peruse it for a continuance of minutes.

†**continuando** *n.* Pl. **-os**. L17–M18. [L = by continuing.] *Law.* A continuation or repetition of alleged acts, or an alleged act, of trespass; *gen.* a continuation.

continuant /kənˈtɪnjʊənt/ *a.* & *n.* E17. [Partly f. Fr., pres. pple of *continuer*; partly f. L *continuant-* pres. ppl stem of *continuare*: see CONTINUE, -ANT[1].] **A** *adj.* **1** Continuing, persisting in time; remaining in force. E17. **2** *Phonet.* Of a consonant: of which the sound can be prolonged as desired, articulated without complete obstruction of the air-stream, (as *f, n, r, s*). L19. **B** *n.* **1** *Phonet.* A continuant consonant. M19. **2** *Philos.* A thing that retains its identity although its states and relations may be changed. E20.

†**continuantly** *adv.* LME–L16.

†**continuate** *a.* (orig. *pa. pple*). L15. [L *continuatus* pa. pple, f. as next: see -ATE[2].] **1** Continued; long-continued, lasting. L15–M17. **2** Continuous; uninterrupted. M16–M17.

†**continuate** *v.t.* L16–M19. [L *continuat-*: see next, -ATE[3].] Make continuous in space or time.

continuation /kəntɪnjʊˈeɪʃ(ə)n/ *n.* LME. [(O)Fr. f. L *continuatio(n-)*, f. *continuat-* pa. ppl stem of *continuare*: see CONTINUE, -ATION.] †**1** The action of continuing in something; = CONTINUANCE 3. LME–L15. †**2** Continuity in space or of substance. LME–E18. 3 The action or fact of remaining in a state; continuous or prolonged existence or operation. LME. †b The action or fact of remaining in a place. M–L17. 4 *Sc. Law.* Adjournment, prorogation. Long *rare.* LME. 5 Something which continues another thing; an additional part or parts. LME. 6 The carrying on or resumption of an action, course, story, etc. L16. 7 *Stock Exch.* The carrying over an account to the next settling day. E19. 8 In *pl.* Gaiters (as a continuation of knee-breeches worn by bishops etc.); trousers (as a continuation of the waistcoat). *arch. slang.* E19.

3 G. B. SHAW To impose a continuation of marriage on people who have ceased to desire to be married. 5 J. GARDNER The page four continuation of a front-page story. **with continuation of days** *Sc. Law* with allowance for the possible adjournment of the matter to a date later than that cited.

Comb.: **continuation day** = *contango day* s.v. CONTANGO *n.*; **continuation school** *Hist.* a school for the additional teaching in spare time of those who had left full-time education.

continuative /kənˈtɪnjʊətɪv/ *n.* & *a.* M16. [Late L *continuativus*, f. *continuat-*: see prec., -ATIVE.] A *n.* A thing that serves to produce continuity (esp. of expression etc.) or to express continuance. M16. B *adj.* 1 Tending or serving to continue something. L17. 2 Expressing continuance. L19.

continuator /kənˈtɪnjʊeɪtə/ *n.* M17. [f. L *continuat-* (see CONTINUATION) + -OR. In sense 2 repr. Fr. *continuateur.*] 1 A person who continues or maintains continuity. M17. 2 A person who continues work begun by another; *esp.* a person who writes a continuation of another's work. M17.

continue /kənˈtɪnjuː/ *v.* ME. [(O)Fr. *continuer* f. L *continuare* make or be continuous, f. *continuus* CONTINUOUS. In branch III infl. by CONTAIN.] I *v.t.* 1 Carry on, maintain, persist in, not stop, (an action, usage, etc.). ME. 2 Cause to last or endure; prolong (something external to the agent); keep on in a place, a condition, etc. LME. 3 Take up, resume, (a narrative, journey, etc.); form a prolongation of, extend; be a sequel to. LME. b With direct speech as obj.: proceed or resume by saying. E18. 4 *Law.* Adjourn, prorogue. Chiefly *Sc.* LME. †5 Connect, attach *to.* LME–M17.

1 G. BANCROFT To continue the struggle. E. HEMINGWAY Come to the Soviet Union and continue your studies there. 2 S. JOHNSON Almighty God who hast continued my life to this day. W. IRVING He was continued in his office. 3 SHAKES. *2 Hen. IV* Our humble author will continue the story, with Sir John in it. D. BREWSTER If we continue backwards the rays . . they will meet at *m.* M. ARNOLD The man of intelligence was continued by successors like . . Euler. b J. CONRAD 'It's an official statement,' he continued.

II *v.i.* 6 Persist in action or (of a person, now *rare*) in or *in* a course of action; persevere, keep on. ME. 7 Remain in existence or in its present condition; last, endure. LME. 8 Remain in or *in* a place or state. With compl., not stop being, not become other than. LME. 9 Go on *doing*; not cease *to do.* LME. 10 Proceed in one's discourse, resume. E18.

6 SHAKES. *Macb.* I have known her continue in this a quarter of an hour. J. H. BLUNT The persecution continued with unabated rigour. 7 BROWNING Let what now exists continue. D. CARNEGIE Our friendship continued to his death. 8 W. WHISTON The Deity would continue their friend. S. JOHNSON Your English style still continues in its purity and vigour. J. AUSTEN Frederica is made wretched by his continuing here. G. M. FRASER The weather continues fine. 9 LD MACAULAY He continued to offer his advice daily. W. GASS They would certainly continue growing.

†III 11 *v.t.* Contain. LME–L16.

continuable *a.* L18. **continuer** *n.* a person who or thing which continues M16.

continued /kənˈtɪnjuːd/ *ppl a.* LME. [f. prec. + -ED[1].] 1 Carried on without cessation; constant. LME. 2 Extended unbroken or uninterrupted in space or time; carried on in a series or sequence. LME.

Special collocations: **continued fraction** *Math.* a fraction of infinite length whose denominator is a quantity plus a fraction, which latter fraction has a similar denominator, and so on. **continued proportionals** *Math.* quantities belonging to a series such that the ratio between every two adjacent terms is the same. **continued story** *US* a serial story.

continuity /kɒntɪˈnjuːɪti/ *n.* LME. [(O)Fr. *continuité* f. L *continuitas*, f. *continuare*: see CONTINUE, -ITY.] 1 The state or quality of being continuous; connectedness; unbroken succession; logical sequence. LME. 2 A continuous or connected whole; an unbroken course or series. E17. 3 Uninterrupted duration. *rare.* M17. 4 A detailed scenario of a film; the maintenance of consistency or of a continuous flow of action in a cinema or television sequence; (commentary etc. providing) linkage between items in a broadcast. E20.

1 WELLINGTON The continuity of the frontier. J. BERGER Neither by way of his children . . nor by way of society can he find any sense of succession or continuity. **law of continuity**: that all changes in nature are continuous, not abrupt. **solution of continuity** the fact or condition of being or becoming discontinuous; fracture; rupture; (orig. *Med.* w. ref. to injury to the body). 2 COLERIDGE A chain that ascends in a continuity of links. 3 D. BREWSTER The severity and continuity of his studies.

Comb.: **continuity girl, man,** etc., *Cinemat.*: responsible for ensuring the necessary agreement of detail between different filmings.

continuo /kənˈtɪnjʊəʊ/ *n.* Pl. **-os.** E18. [It. = continuous.] A figured bass, a thorough bass, (= *basso continuo* s.v. BASSO); an accompaniment, usu. for keyboard, improvised from this. Also, the instrument(s) playing this part.

continuous /kənˈtɪnjʊəs/ *a.* M17. [f. L *continuus* uninterrupted, f. *continere* hang together, f. as CON- + *tenere* hold: see -OUS.] 1 Characterized by continuity; extending in space without a break; uninterrupted in time or sequence; acting without interruption; connected. M17. 2 *Gram.* Designating an aspect or tense of the verb expressing continuing action or action in progress, or a particular form expressing this aspect or tense. L19.

1 C. DARWIN In most cases the area inhabited by a species is continuous. B. JOWETT The power of . . continuous thought is very rare. W. STYRON A dog howls on and on . . , a continuous harsh lonely cry.

Special collocations: **continuous assessment** the evaluation of a student's progress based on work done throughout a course as well as or instead of by examination. **continuous creation** creation of the universe or of matter in it regarded as occurring continuously rather than in a particular event. **continuous function** *Math.* a function whose graph is a continuous (unbroken) curve; a function such that as the value of x approaches a given value a, the value of $f(x)$ approaches that of $f(a)$ as a limit. **continuous stationery**: with sheets joined together and folded alternately. **continuous wave** *Physics* an electromagnetic wave of constant amplitude.

continuously *adv.* L17. **continuousness** *n.* E19.

continuum /kənˈtɪnjʊəm/ *n.* Pl. **-nua** /-njʊə/. M17. [Use as n. of neut. sing. of L *continuus*: see prec.] A continuous thing, quantity, or substance; a continuous series of elements passing into each other; *Math.* the set of real numbers.

A. E. SMAILES No longer . . a . . dichotomy of town and country; rather it is an urban-rural continuum. E. FIGES This endless continuum of days. *space–time continuum*: see SPACE *n.*

Comb.: **continuum hypothesis** *Math.*: that there is no transfinite cardinal between the cardinal of the set of positive integers and that of the set of real numbers.

contline /ˈkɒntlʌɪn/ *n.* M19. [Perh. alt. of *cant-line* s.v. CANT *n.*[1]] *Naut.* = *cant-line* s.v. CANT *n.*[1]

conto /ˈkɒntəʊ/ *n.* Pl. **-os.** E17. [Port. f. L *computus* COUNT *n.*[1]] In Portugal, Brazil, etc.: a million reis; a thousand escudos or cruzeiros.

contoid /ˈkɒntɔɪd/ *a.* & *n.* M20. [f. *cont* contr. of CONSONANT *n.* + -OID.] *Phonet.* (Designating or pertaining to) a speech sound of the consonantal type. Cf. VOCOID.

contorni *n.* pl. of CONTORNO.

contorniate /kɒnˈtɔːnɪət/ *a.* & *n.* L17. [Fr., or It. *contorniato*, f. *contorniare* to surround, border, edge.] A *adj.* Of a medal, coin, etc.: having a deep furrow round the disc, within the edge. L17. B *n.* A contorniate coin or medal; *esp.* any of certain brass pieces of Nero and other Roman emperors. E19.

contorno /kɒnˈtorno/ *n. literary.* Pl. **-ni** /-ni/. M18. [It. = circuit, contour.] A contour, an outline of a figure.

†**contorsion** *n.* var. of CONTORTION.

contort /kənˈtɔːt/ *v.t.* LME. [L *contort-* pa. ppl stem of *contorquere*, f. as CON- + *torquere* twist.] Twist, esp. out of normal shape; distort by twisting.

R. P. JHABVALA He . . contorts himself so as to dig himself in the base of his spine. A. CARTER A face contorted by pain.

contorted *ppl a.* (*a*) twisted, esp. out of shape, distorted; (*b*) (of petals etc.) overlapping at one margin and overlapped at the other: E17.

contortion /kənˈtɔːʃ(ə)n/ *n.* Also †**-sion.** LME. [L *contortio(n-)*, f. as prec.: see -ION. Cf. Fr. *contorsion.*] 1 (An act of) twisting, esp. of the face or body; distortion by twisting or writhing. LME. 2 A contorted condition, state, or form. M17.

1 R. W. EMERSON The contortions of ten crucified martyrs. 2 W. BLACK The curious contortions of the rocks.

contortionist *n.* a person who practises contortion; *esp.* an acrobat who adopts unusual postures; *fig.* a person who contorts meanings etc. M19.

contortuplicate /kɒntɔːˈtjuːplɪkət/ *a.* E19. [L *contortuplicatus*, f. *contortus* twisted together + *-plicatus* folded: see -ATE[2].] *Bot.* Twisted back upon itself.

contour /ˈkɒntʊə/ *n.* & *v.* M17. [Fr. f. It. *contorno*, f. *contornare* draw in outline, f. as CON- + *tornare* to turn.] A *n.* 1 The outline of a figure, object, topographical feature, etc.; *spec.* a line separating differently-coloured parts of a design etc. Freq. in *pl.* M17. b Artistic quality of outline. L18. 2 In full *contour line.* A line, passing through points of equal elevation (or depth) on a map, as one of a series drawn at regular height intervals; a similar but imaginary line on the ground. M19. 3 *Phonet.* A particular level or a sequence of varying levels of pitch, tone, or stress. M20.

1 R. L. STEVENSON The sides . . bulging outward with the contour of the ship. J. ANTHONY Her firm tawny body whose contours reminded me of the low-lying Tunisian hills. 2 F. J. MONKHOUSE The contours are numbered on the upper side of each line, which indicates . . uphill and downhill directions, placing the figures in a row above one another.

Comb.: **contour-chasing** *slang* flying close to the ground following the contours of the landscape; **contour feather**: any of those that form the outline of a bird; *contour line*: see sense 2 above; **contour map**: showing contour lines; **contour ploughing**: along lines of a constant altitude to minimize soil erosion.

B *v.t.* 1 Mark with contour lines. M19. 2 Cause (a road etc.) to follow the contours of the terrain etc.; shape so as to match a particular form. L19. 3 Follow the contour of. E20.

contourné /kɒnˈtʊəneɪ/ *a.* E18. [Fr.] *Her.* Turned about, towards the sinister side.

contra /ˈkɒntrə/ *adv., prep.,* & *n.* LME. [L = against (adv. & prep.), abl. fem. of a compar. f. *com, cum* with.] A *adv.* On or to the contrary; contrariwise. Chiefly in *pro and contra* s.v. PRO *prep.* etc. LME.

B *prep.* Against. LME.

C *n.* 1 The contrary or opposite (side); an opposing factor or argument. Chiefly in *pros and contras* s.v. PRO *prep.* etc. LME. 2 Also **C-.** [Sp.] A counter-revolutionary in Nicaragua, *esp.* one opposing the government. Cf. SANDINISTA. L20.

1 PER CONTRA.

contra- /ˈkɒntrə/ *pref.* [L *contra-*, f. as prec. Freq. through It., Sp.] Used in wds adopted (ult.) f. L and in Eng. wds modelled on these, w. the sense 'against, opposing, contrary', forming chiefly vbs and vbl derivatives, as *contradict,* (*-diction, -dictory*), *contradistinguish, contra-indicate, contravene*; in *Mus.* forming the names of instruments and organ-stops having a pitch of an octave below that of the instrument etc. named, as *contrabass, contrabassoon.* Not a very productive pref. in mod. Eng., the usual form being COUNTER-.

contraband /ˈkɒntrəband/ *n.* & *a.* L16. [Sp. *contrabanda* f. It. *contrabando* (now *-bb-*), f. *contra-* CONTRA- + *bando*: see BAN *n.*[1]] A *n.* 1 Illegal or prohibited trade; smuggling. L16. 2 Something whose import or export is prohibited; smuggled goods. L16. 3 In full *contraband of war*. Something forbidden to be supplied by neutrals to belligerents. M18. 4 During the American Civil War: a Black slave, *esp.* a fugitive or captured slave. (From a decision of General Butler in 1861 that such slaves were contraband of war.) *US* (*obs.* exc. *Hist.*). M19. B *adj.* Forbidden to be imported or exported; concerned with smuggled goods etc.; *fig.* forbidden, illegitimate, unauthorized. M17.

¶Earlier Anglicized as COUNTERBAND.

contrabandist *n.* a smuggler E19. **contraban'dista** *n.* [Sp.] a smuggler M19.

contraband /ˈkɒntrəband/ *v.t.* Long *rare.* E17. [f. prec. Cf. COUNTERBAND *v.*] Import (prohibited goods); smuggle. Chiefly as *contrabanded* ppl a.

contrabass /ˈkɒntrəbeɪs/ *n.* & *a.* E19. [It. *contrabasso* (now *-bb-*), Fr. *contrebasse*, f. as CONTRA- + BASS *n.*[2]] *Mus.* A *n.* 1 (A part within) the octave below the normal (bass) range. E19. 2 A double-bass. L19. B *attrib.* or as *adj.* Designating an instrument with range an octave lower than the usual type, as *contrabass tuba*. L19.

¶Earlier Anglicized as COUNTERBASS.

contra'bassist *n.* a double-bass player L19.

contrabasso /kɒntrəˈbasəʊ/ *n.* Pl. **-bassos**, **-bassi** /-ˈbasi/. E19. [It.: see prec.] 1 = CONTRABASS *n.* 2. E19. 2 = CONTRABASS *n.* 1. M19.

contra-bassoon /kɒntrəbəˈsuːn/ *n.* L19. [f. CONTRA- + BASSOON.] = *double* BASSOON.

contraception /kɒntrəˈsɛpʃ(ə)n/ *n.* L19. [f. CONTRA- + CONCEPTION.] The prevention of pregnancy from being a consequence of sexual intercourse; the use of contraceptive methods.

contraceptive /kɒntrəˈsɛptɪv/ *n.* & *a.* L19. [f. CONTRA- + CONCEPTIVE.] A *n.* A device, drug, etc., which serves to prevent uterine conception (or implantation of the ovum) while allowing sexual intercourse. L19. B *adj.* Serving to prevent pregnancy from being a consequence of sexual intercourse. E20.

contraceptively *adv.* E20.

contraconscientiously /ˌkɒntrəkɒnʃɪˈɛnʃəsli/ *adv. rare.* M17. [f. CONTRA- + CONSCIENTIOUSLY.] Against conscience.

contract /ˈkɒntrakt/ *n.*[1] ME. [OFr. (mod. *contrat*) f. L *contractus*, f. *contract-* pa. ppl stem of *contrahere*, f. as CON- + *trahere* draw.] 1 A binding agreement between two or more parties, *spec.* one enforceable by law; as (*a*) (the earliest use) a formal agreement to marry, betrothal; (*b*) a business agreement for the supply of goods or the performance of work at a specified price or rate; (*c*) the conveyance of property. ME. b An arrangement for someone to be killed, usu. by a hired assassin. *slang.* M20. 2 A document in which an agreement is set out for signature by the parties concerned. E17. †3 Mutual attraction. E–M17. 4 The branch of law relating to contracts. M19. 5 The commitment to make a stated number of tricks in a hand of bridge. Also *ellipt.*, contract bridge. E20.

1 *quasi-contract*, *subcontract*, etc. *collateral contract*: see COLLATERAL *a. consensual contract*: see CONSENSUAL *a.* 1. *nude contract*: see NUDE *a.* 2. *privity of contract*: see PRIVITY 5. *social contract*: see SOCIAL *a.* **under contract** party to a legal contract. *yellow dog contract*: see YELLOW *a.*

Comb.: *contract bridge*: see BRIDGE *n.*[2]; **contract killer** a hired assassin; **contract work**: done according to the terms of an agreement to supply a service, commodity, etc. (formerly often w. derog. connotation).

contract /kənˈtrakt/ *ppl a.* & *n.*[2] LME. [OFr., var. of *contrait* f. L *contractus* pa. pple of *contrahere*: see prec.] A *ppl a.* = CONTRACTED. Now *rare* or *obs.* LME. B *n.* †1 A paralytic. Only in L15. †2 An abridgement, an epitome. Only in M17. 3 A contracted form or word; an abbreviation. *rare.* M17.

contract /kənˈtrakt/, *in sense 5 also* ˈkɒntrakt/ *v.* Pa. t. & pple **-ed**, (earlier) †**contract**. LME. [Orig. pa. pple: see prec. Cf. (O)Fr. *contracter.*] I Agree on, make a contract. 1 *v.t.* Formally enter into (marriage). LME. b Engage formally, affiance. M16. 2 *v.t. gen.* Agree on, establish by agreement, undertake mutually, enter on. Now *rare.* M16. 3 *v.i.* Enter into an agreement (*to do*, *for* an action, a thing to be done, etc.), esp. a business or legal engagement. M16. 4 *v.t.* Arrange (work) to be done by contract; let *out* by contract. L19. b Place under contract (*for*). M20. 5 *v.i.* & *refl.* a Foll. by *out* (*of*): arrange for one's exemption or exclusion from (the provisions of a law etc.); decline or refuse to take part in (a scheme etc.). L19. b Foll. by *in*(*to*): arrange for one's subjection to (the provisions of a law etc.); agree to take part in (a scheme etc.). E20.

1 I. MURDOCH She wondered if having failed in one marriage she should hastily contract another. b SHAKES. *Wint. T.* But come on, Contract us fore these witnesses. 2 R. HAKLUYT We have contracted an inviolable amitie, peace and league with the aforesaid queene. 3 EVELYN This Dutchman had contracted with the Genoese for all their marble. S. UNWIN Harrison . . had contracted with my uncle to write a book.

II 6 *v.t.* Enter into, form (a friendship, a habit, etc.); bring on oneself; incur (a liability, debt, etc.); become infected with, catch (a disease, illness). LME.

6 S. PEPYS And he contract the displeasure of the world. CHESTERFIELD Contract a habit of correctness and elegance. G. GISSING He died of a cold contracted on one of his walks.

III Draw together, narrow, shrink. †7 *v.t.* Bring together, collect, concentrate. LME–L18. 8 *v.t.* Cause to shrink, bring the parts of (a muscle etc.) together; knit (the brow); stiffen by contraction. E16. 9 *v.t.* Reduce in extent, amount, or scope; make smaller, narrow; limit, confine. L16. b *Ling.* Shorten (a word, syllable, etc.) by combination or elision of elements. E17. †c Abridge, summarize; *refl.* write or speak briefly. E17–M18. 10 *v.i.* Become smaller in extent or volume; shorten, shrink. M17.

7 B. HARRIS The king contracted formidable forces near Sedan. 8 SHAKES. *Timon* Aches contract and starve your supple joints! J. STEINBECK The house cracked loudly as the cooler night air contracted the wood. 9 S. JOHNSON Selfishness has contracted their understandings. W. LIPPMANN The economic area must be contracted to exclude competitors. 10 J. TYNDALL In passing from the solid to the liquid state, ice . . contracts. B. RUBENS His stomach contracted . . in agonizing cramps.

contractable *a.* liable to be contracted L19. **contractant** *n.* (*rare*) a contracting party M16. **contracti'bility** *n.* the quality of being contractible M18. **contractible** *a.* capable of contracting, contractile M17. **contractive** *a.* having the property of contracting; of the nature of contraction; tending to produce contraction: E17.

†**contractation** *n.* Also **contrat-**. M16–E18. [Sp. *contratación* trade, business transaction, w. assim. to CONTRACT *v.*, -ATION.] Mutual dealing, exchange.

Comb.: **contractation-house** an exchange or treasury in Seville where contracts were made in connection with the West Indian trade.

contracted /kənˈtraktɪd/ *ppl a.* M16. [f. CONTRACT *v.* + -ED[1].] †1 Engaged to be married, betrothed. M16–E17. 2 Arranged by contract, established by agreement. Now *rare* exc. in *contracted-in*, *-out*, that has contracted into, out of, a scheme etc. (see CONTRACT *v.* 5). L16. 3 Made smaller by contraction; shrunken, narrowed; condensed, concise; restricted, narrow. L16. †4 Collected, combined. Only in E17. 5 Incurred, acquired. M17.

contractedly *adv.* E17. **contractedness** *n.* M17.

contractee /kɒntrakˈtiː/ *n.* L19. [f. CONTRACT *n.*[1] or *v.* + -EE[1].] A person with whom a contract is made.

contractile /kənˈtraktʌɪl/ *a.* E18. [f. CONTRACT *v.* + -ILE.] Capable of or producing contraction.

W. B. CARPENTER The contractile tissues, by which the movements of plants are produced. **contractile vacuole** a vacuole in some protozoans which expels excess liquid on contraction.

contrac'tility *n.* L18.

contraction /kənˈtrakʃ(ə)n/ *n.* LME. [(O)Fr. f. L *contractio(n-)*, f. *contract-*: see CONTRACT *n.*[1], -ION.] I 1 The action of contracting; the state of being contracted; decrease in extent, shortening, shrinking, narrowing; limitation; *esp.* (a) shortening of a muscle or muscles in response to a nerve impulse, generating tension in the muscle(s) and frequently producing movement. LME. 2a Abbreviation of a writing etc.; (an) abridgement; condensation, conciseness. Now *rare* or *obs.* L16. b *Ling.* The shortening of a word, syllable, etc. by combination or elision; a contracted form of a word etc. E18. 3 The action of drawing together or back. *rare.* E17.

1 L. P. HARTLEY Not expansion but contraction of personality was what he sought. 2a A. C. SWINBURNE A poem of . . exquisite contraction and completeness. 3 D. H. LAWRENCE The cattle . . ducked their heads . . in sudden contraction from her.

II 4 The action of agreeing on or establishing by contract; *spec.* the action of contracting marriage. Now *rare.* L16. 5 The action of incurring or acquiring a debt, disease, habit, etc. L17.

Comb.: **contraction joint** a joint in a structure (esp. of concrete) to allow for contraction of the material.

contractional *a.* relating to or produced by contraction L19.

contractor /kənˈtraktə/ *n.* E16. [Late L, f. *contract-* (see CONTRACT *n.*[1]) or directly f. CONTRACT *v.*: see -OR.] 1 A person who enters into a contract or agreement. Now chiefly *spec.* a person or firm that undertakes work by contract, esp. for building to specified plans. E16. 2 A thing that contracts or causes contraction; *spec.* (more fully *contractor muscle*) a contracting muscle. E17.

contractual /kənˈtraktʃʊəl/ *a.* M19. [f. L *contractus* CONTRACT *n.*[1] + -AL[1]. Cf. Fr. *contractuel.*] Pertaining to or of the nature of a contract.

contractually *adv.* E20.

contractural /kənˈtraktʃ(ə)r(ə)l/ *a.* E20. [f. prec. w. erron. *r.*] = prec.

contracture /kənˈtraktʃə/ *n.* M17. [Fr., or L *contractura*, f. (as) *contract-*: see CONTRACT *n.*[1], -URE.] *Med.* A condition of shortening and hardening of tissue, esp. muscles and tendons, often leading to deformity and rigidity of joints.

contractured *a.* affected by contracture L19.

contradance *n.* var. of CONTREDANSE.

contradict /kɒntrəˈdɪkt/ *v.* L16. [L *contradict-* pa. ppl stem of *contradicere*, orig. *contra dicere* speak against.] †1 *v.t.* Speak against; oppose in speech; forbid. L16–M18. 2 *v.t.* & *i.* Deny a statement made by (a person); affirm the contrary of (a statement etc.). L16. 3 Of a statement, action, etc.: be contrary to, go counter to. L16.

contradictable *a.* M19. **contradictor** *n.* L16.

contradiction /kɒntrəˈdɪkʃ(ə)n/ *n.* LME. [(O)Fr. f. L *contradictio(n-)*, f. as prec.: see -ION.] 1 The action of speaking against or opposing; gainsaying, opposition. LME. 2 The action of declaring to be untrue or erroneous; affirming the contrary; denial. LME. 3 A statement containing propositions or terms which are at variance with one another; a contradictory proposition. LME. b More fully *contradiction in terms*. A statement, phrase, etc., which appears to be self-contradictory. E18. 4 A state of opposition in things compared; variance; logical inconsistency. L16. 5 A contradictory act, fact, or condition; an inconsistency. E17. 6 A statement contradicting another. E18. 7 A person or thing made up of contradictory qualities. M18.

1 STEELE There are those who pursue their own Way out of a Sourness and Spirit of Contradiction. 2 SHAKES. *Ant. & Cl.* Without contradiction I have heard that. 3 HOBBES Both parts of a contradiction cannot possibly be true. b B. JOWETT A virtuous tyrant is a contradiction in terms. 4 GEO. ELIOT The contradiction between men's lives and their professed beliefs had pressed upon him. 5 S. JOHNSON An attempt to make contradictions consistent. 6 OED An official contradiction of the recent rumours. 7 POPE Woman's at best a contradiction still.

contradictious /kɒntrəˈdɪkʃəs/ *a.* E17. [f. CONTRADICT *v.* + -IOUS.] †**1** Characterized by contradiction; contrary. E17–M18. **2** Self-contradictory; involving a contradiction in terms. *arch.* M17. **3** Inclined to contradict; disputatious. L17.

contradictiously *adv.* E17. **contradictiousness** *n.* M17.

contradictive /kɒntrəˈdɪktɪv/ *a.* M17. [f. CONTRADICT + -IVE.] **1** Of contradictory quality or tendency. M17. †**2** = CONTRADICTIOUS 3. M–L17.

contradictively *adv.* M19. **contradictiveness** *n.* E19.

contradictory /kɒntrəˈdɪkt(ə)ri/ *n.* & *a.* LME. [Late L *contradictorius*, f. as CONTRADICT + -ORY².] **A** *n.* **1** *Logic.* A proposition, assertion, or principle that contradicts another. LME. **2** The opposite, the contrary. M19.

1 A. J. AYER It is impossible that a proposition and its contradictory should neither of them be true. 2 T. ARNOLD A place the very contradictory . . of the hill Difficulty.

B *adj.* **1a** Mutually opposed or inconsistent; inconsistent in itself; (of two propositions) so related that one and only one must be true. M16. **b** Having the quality of contradicting; making denial. E17. **2** Of opposite character or tendency; diametrically opposed, contrary. M18. **3** Inclined to contradict. L19.

1a STEELE If we sit down satisfy'd with such contradictory accounts. **contradictory terms** *Logic:* of the form A and not-A, which admit of no intermediate. b A. TROLLOPE Two answers which were altogether distinct, and contradictory one of the other. **contradictory opposition** *Logic:* between contradictory propositions. 2 J. BUTLER There is nothing in the human mind contradictory . . to virtue.

contradictorily *adv.* (*a*) in a way that contradicts; (*b*) *Logic* with contradictory opposition: L16. **contradictoriness** *n.* M18.

contradistinct /kɒntrədɪˈstɪŋkt/ *a.* E17. [f. CONTRA- + DISTINCT *a.* Cf. COUNTERDISTINCT.] Contradistinguished; distinct and in contrast (*to*, *from*).

contradistinction /kɒntrədɪˈstɪŋkʃ(ə)n/ *n.* M17. [f. CONTRA- + DISTINCTION. Cf. earlier COUNTERDISTINCTION.] The action of contradistinguishing; distinction by contrast or opposition.

H. A. L. FISHER A country which . . must, in contradistinction to the prevailing misery of the continent, have presented a spectacle of rare . . prosperity.

contradistinctive /kɒntrədɪˈstɪŋktɪv/ *a.* M17. [f. CONTRA- + DISTINCTIVE.] Serving to contradistinguish. Also (*rare*), expressing contradistinction.

contradistinctively *adv.* E19.

contradistinguish /kɒntrədɪˈstɪŋgwɪʃ/ *v.t.* E17. [f. CONTRA- + DISTINGUISH *v.* Cf. COUNTERDISTINGUISH.] Distinguish (*from* or †*to* another) by contrast or opposition.

T. JEFFERSON When the common law and statute law began to be contra-distinguished. COLERIDGE Doctrines . . which contra-distinguish the religion as Christian. M. ARNOLD The development which contradistinguishes the Hellene from the barbarian.

contrafacta *n.* pl. of CONTRAFACTUM.

contrafactual /kɒntrəˈfaktʃʊəl/ *a.* M20. [f. CONTRA- + FACTUAL *a.*] *Philos.* = COUNTERFACTUAL *a.*

contrafactum /kɒntrəˈfaktəm/ *n.* Pl. **-ta** /-tə/. M20. [mod.L, use as n. of neut. pa. pple of med.L *contrafacere* to counterfeit: see COUNTERFEIT *a.* & *n.*] *Early Mus.* A rearrangement of a vocal composition whereby the music is retained and the words altered.

contrafagotto /kɒntrəfəˈgɒtəʊ/ *n.* Pl. **-tti** /-ti/. L19. [It. (now *-trof-*).] = *double* BASSOON.

contrafissure /kɒntrəˈfɪʃə/ *n.* Now *rare* or *obs.* L17. [f. CONTRA- + FISSURE *n.*] *Med.* A fracture (of the skull) in a part opposite to the site of the blow.

contraflexure /kɒntrəˈflɛkʃə/ *n.* L19. [f. CONTRA- + FLEXURE.] The condition of being bent or curved in opposite directions; the point or piece at which this occurs.

contraflow /ˈkɒntrəfləʊ/ *n.* M20. [f. CONTRA- + FLOW *n.*¹] Flow in the opposite direction or in opposite directions; *esp.* (a system allowing) movement of road traffic alongside and in a direction contrary to the established or usual flow. Freq. *attrib.*

contragredient /kɒntrəˈgriːdɪənt/ *a.* M19. [f. CONTRA- + L *-gredient-* pres. ppl stem (in comb.) of *gradi* proceed, step: see -ENT.] *Math.* Characterized by change in an opposite sense (*to*), or in opposite senses, under equivalent substitution.

contrahent /ˈkɒntrəhənt/ *postpositive a.* & *n.* Now *rare* or *obs.* E16. [L *contrahent-* pres. ppl stem of *contrahere*: see CONTRACT *v.*, -ENT.] (A person etc.) entering into a contract.

contrail /ˈkɒntreɪl/ *n.* M20. [Contr.] A condensation trail.

contra-indicant /kɒntrəˈɪndɪk(ə)nt/ *n.* E17. [f. CONTRA- + INDICANT.] A contra-indication.

contra-indicate /kɒntrəˈɪndɪkeɪt/ *v.t.* M17. [f. CONTRA- + INDICATE. Cf. COUNTER-INDICATE.] Chiefly *Med.* Give indications contrary to; *esp.* act as an indication against the use of (a particular treatment etc.). Usu. in *pass.*

I. HAMILTON In the course of drug treatment alcohol would have been 'contraindicated'.

contra-indication /ˌkɒntrəɪndɪˈkeɪʃ(ə)n/ *n.* E17. [f. CONTRA- + INDICATION. Cf. COUNTER-INDICATION.] A contrary indication; *esp.* a symptom, circumstance, etc., which tends to make a particular course of (remedial) action inadvisable.

contrair /ˈkɒntrɛː/ *a.*, *n.*, *adv.*, *prep.* Chiefly & now only *Sc.* LME. [(O)Fr. *contraire*: see CONTRARY *a.*] **A** *adj.* & *n.* (The) contrary. LME. **B** *adv.* Contrariwise. LME. **C** *prep.* Against, in opposition to. LME.

contralateral /kɒntrəˈlat(ə)r(ə)l/ *a.* L19. [f. CONTRA- + LATERAL *a.*] *Med.* Belonging to or occurring on the opposite side of the body. Opp. *ipsilateral.*

contralto /kənˈtraltəʊ/ *n.* & *a.* M18. [It., f. as CONTRA- + ALTO: cf. COUNTER-TENOR.] *Mus.* **A** *n.* Pl. **-os**. The lowest female voice or (formerly) highest adult male voice; a singer having such a voice; a part written for such a voice. M18. **B** *adj.* Possessing, belonging to, or written for a contralto voice. M18.

contra mundum /ˌkɒntrə ˈmʌndəm/ *adv. phr.* M18. [L *contra mundum*.] Against the world; defying or opposing everyone.

contranatant /kɒntrəˈneɪt(ə)nt/ *a.* E20. [f. CONTRA- + NATANT *a.*] Of the migration of fish: against the current. Opp. DENATANT.

contranaˈtation *n.* the act of migrating against the current E20.

contranatural /kɒntr(ə)ˈnatʃər(ə)l/ *a.* M17. [f. CONTRA- + NATURAL *a.*] Opposed to what is natural; contrary to nature.

contrapose /kɒntrəˈpəʊz/ *v.t.* E17. [f. CONTRA- + POSE *v.*¹ after L *contraponere*. Cf. earlier COUNTERPOSE.] **1** Set in opposition or against each other. E17. **b** Foll. by *to*: contrast directly with. E20. **2** *Logic.* Convert (a proposition) by contraposition. M19.

contraposit /kɒntrəˈpɒzɪt/ *v.t.* L19. [Back-form. f. next.] = CONTRAPOSE 2.

contraposition /kɒntrəpəˈzɪʃ(ə)n/ *n.* M16. [Late L *contrapositio(n-)*, f. *contraposit-* pa. ppl stem of *contraponere*, f. as CONTRA- + *ponere* to place: see -ITION. Cf. COUNTERPOSITION.] **1** *Logic.* The conversion of a proposition from *all A is B* to *all not-B is not-A*. M16. **2** *gen.* Opposition, antithesis, contrast. L16.

contrapositive /kɒntrəˈpɒzɪtɪv/ *n.* & *a.* M19. [f. L *contraposit-*: see prec., -IVE.] **A** *n.* A thing characterized by contraposition; *Logic* a contrapositive proposition. M19. **B** *adj.* Of, belonging to, or produced by contraposition. L19.

contrapositively *adv.* M19.

contrapposto /kontrapˈposto/ *n.* Pl. **-ti** /-ti/. E20. [It., pa. pple of *contrapporre* f. L *contraponere* CONTRAPOSE *v.*] In the visual arts, an arrangement of a figure in which the action of the arms and shoulders contrasts as strongly as possible with that of the hips and legs; a twisting of a figure on its own axis.

contra proferentem /ˌkɒntrə prɒfəˈrɛntɛm/ *adv. phr.* E20. [L.] *Law.* Against the party which proposes or adduces a contract or a condition in a contract.

contraption /kənˈtrapʃ(ə)n/ *n. colloq.* E19. [Perh. f. CONTRIVE *v.*¹ (cf. *conceive*, *conception*), assoc. w. TRAP *n.*¹] A strange machine; a device, a contrivance.

contrapuntal /kɒntrəˈpʌnt(ə)l/ *a.* M19. [f. It. *contrapunto* (now *-pp-*) f. med.L as COUNTERPOINT *n.*¹ + -AL¹.] *Mus.* Of, pertaining to, or of the nature of counterpoint; according to the rules of counterpoint.

contrapuntally *adv.* L19. **contrapuntist** *n.* a person skilled in counterpoint L18.

contra-remonstrant /kɒntrərɪˈmɒnstr(ə)nt/ *n.* E17. [f. CONTRA- + REMONSTRANT *n.*] A person who remonstrates in answer or opposition to a remonstrance.

contra-remonstrance *n.* a remonstrance drawn up in answer to a previous one L17. **contra-remonstrancer** *n.* (*rare*) = CONTRA-REMONSTRANT E17.

contrariant /kənˈtrɛːrɪənt/ *prep.*, *a.*, & *n.* LME [(O)Fr., pres. pple of *contrarier*: see CONTRARY *v.*, -ANT¹.] †**A** *prep.* Acting contrary to, in opposition to. Only in LME. **B** *adj.* **1** Opposed, repugnant, contrary *to*. M16. **2** Mutually opposed or antagonistic. M16. †**3** Unfavourable, prejudicial; adverse. M16–M17. **C** *n.* A person who or thing which is opposed to another in purpose or nature. M17.

contrariantly *adv.* L18.

contrariety /kɒntrəˈrʌɪəti/ *n.* LME. [(O)Fr. *contrariété* f. late L *contrarietas*, f. *contrarius*: see CONTRARY *a.* etc., -ITY.] **1** Opposition in nature, quality, or action; contrariness; disagreement, inconsistency. LME. **b** An antagonistic action or fact; a discrepancy. LME. **2** Opposition to one's purpose or advantage; an adversity, a mishap. LME. **3** *Logic.* Contrary opposition. LME.

1 MILTON In the words of our Saviour there can be no contrariety. GEO. ELIOT With an odd contrariety to her former niceties she liked his rough attire. b W. DE LA MARE O riddle of life that is An endless war 'twixt contrarieties. 2 SIR T. BROWNE The tempests and contrarieties of winds.

contrarious /kɒnˈtrɛːrɪəs/ *a. arch.* ME. [OFr. f. med.L *contrariosus*, f. L *contrarius*: see CONTRARY *a.* etc., -OUS.] †**1** Of opposed character or tendency, repugnant (*to*). ME–M17. **2** Mutually opposed, antagonistic; inconsistent. Now *rare* or *obs.* ME. †**3** Opposed in purpose, hostile. ME–M16. **4** Characterized by self-willed or refractory opposition; perverse; = CONTRARY *a.* 3b. ME. **5** Of a thing: opposed to one's interests; adverse. ME.

contrariously *adv.* LME. **contrariousness** *n.* LME.

contrariwise /kənˈtrɛːrɪwʌɪz, ˈkɒntrərɪwʌɪz/ *adv.* LME. [f. CONTRARY *a.* + -WISE.] **1** On the other hand, on the contrary. LME. **2** In the opposite way or order; vice versa; in opposite directions; in the opposite direction; on opposite sides. LME. **3** In opposition (*to*); *esp.* with self-willed opposition, perversely. L16.

contra-rotating /kɒntrərəʊˈteɪtɪŋ/ *a.* M20. [f. CONTRA- + *rotating* pres. ppl a. of ROTATE *v.* Cf. COUNTERROTATE.] Rotating in the opposite direction or in opposite directions, esp. about the same shaft.

contra-rotation /kɒntrərəʊˈteɪʃ(ə)n/ *n.* E18. [f. CONTRA- + ROTATION.] Rotation in an opposite direction.

contrary /ˈkɒntrəri, *in sense A.3b* kənˈtrɛːri/ *a.*, *n.*, *adv.*, & *prep.* ME. [AN *contrarie*, (O)Fr. *contraire* f. L *contrarius*, f. *contra* CONTRA: see -ARY¹. Cf. CONTRAIR.] **A** *adj.* **1** Opposed in nature or tendency; mutually opposed. (Foll. by *to*, †*than*, †*from*.) ME. †**b** Different, other. L16–L17. **2** The opposite, the other (of two things). ME. †**b** Opposite to the proper or right thing; wrong. *rare* (Shakes.). Only in L16. **3** Of a person, an action, etc.: †**a** Actively opposed, hostile. ME–M17. **b** Characterized by self-willed or refractory opposition, perverse; (= earlier CONTRARIOUS 4). *colloq.* M18. **4a** Of wind: impeding, unfavourable. LME. †**b** *gen.* Of a thing: opposed to one's well-being or interests, unfavourable. L15–M18. **5** Opposite in position or direction. LME.

1 C. BEATON Artificial perfumes were contrary to her tastes. B. BETTELHEIM A passionate struggle raging between two contrary impulses. *contrary to nature*: see NATURE *n.* 2 SPENSER All ignorant of her contrary sex. 3a J. BARGRAVE In despite of the Spaniards, to whom he was much contrary. b J. MASEFIELD I was my folk's contrary son; I bit my father's hand right through. 4b W. WHISTON The remedies . . proved contrary to his case. 5 GOLDSMITH A quite contrary way from that in which they then marched.

Special collocations & comb.: **contrary-minded** *a.* of the contrary opinion. **contrary opposition** *Logic* the opposition of contrary propositions and terms. **contrary proposition** *Logic* either of two propositions each of which denies every case of the other. **contrary terms** *Logic* terms which are at opposite ends of a single scale, as *black* and *white*. **contrary-to-fact** *a.* counterfactual, untrue.

B *n.* **1** *The* exact opposite or reverse of what has previously been mentioned. ME. **2** An object, fact, quality, etc., that is the exact opposite of something else; in *pl.*, things of the same class showing the most difference. LME. **b** *Paper-making.* A foreign body or any substance which resists pulping. Usu. in *pl.* E20. †**3** The opposite position or side. LME–E17. †**4** (An act of) opposition or hostility. LME–M16. †**5** An adversary. LME–E17. †**6** A denial, an opposing statement. M16–M19. **7** *Logic.* A contrary term or proposition. M16.

1 A. STORR An individual who, in early life, believed himself to be inadequate, is driven to . . prove the contrary. **on the contrary** on the other hand, in contradistinction; far from it. **to the contrary** to the opposite effect. 2 N. PEVSNER The need for considering national character in contraries or polarities. **by contraries** by direct contrast; in direct opposition to logic or expectation. b *pernicious contrary*: see PERNICIOUS *a.*[1]

C *adv.* **1** In opposition (*to*). LME. **2** On the other hand, on the contrary. *arch.* LME. **3** Adversely, unfavourably. L15. **4** In an opposite or very different way. L16. †**5** In the opposite direction. E–M17.

1 W. S. CHURCHILL The Royalist commanders . . , contrary to all previous conventions, were . . shot. 2 N. CULPEPER The seed thereof contrary doth bind the belly. 3 SHAKES. *Rom. & Jul.* What storm is this that blows so contrary?

†**D** *prep.* Against, contrary to. LME–M16.

contrary /ˈkɒntrəri, kənˈtrɛːri/ *v.* ME. [(O)Fr. *contrarier* oppose, f. late L *contrariare*, f. L *contrarius*: see CONTRARY *a.* etc.] **1** *v.t.* Oppose, thwart; contradict; do what is contrary to. *obs.* exc. *dial.* ME. †**2** *v.i.* Act, speak, or write in opposition. LME–L16.

contra-seasonal /kɒntrəˈsiːz(ə)n(ə)l/ *a.* M20. [f. CONTRA- + SEASONAL.] Unusual for the time of year; contrary to the seasonal norm.

contra-seasonally *adv.* M20.

contrast /ˈkɒntrɑːst/ *n.* L16. [Fr. *contraste* f. It. *contrasto* strife, opposition, f. *contrastare* withstand, strive, f. med.L *contrastare*: see next.] †**I1** Contention, strife. L16–M18.

II2 In the visual arts, the juxtaposition of different forms, colours, etc., to heighten the total effect. E18. **3** A thing or person having noticeably different qualities (*to*). E18. **4** Comparison of things showing striking differences; (an instance of) display of opposing qualities; manifest difference. M18. **5** *Psychol.* The modification or intensification of a sensation by the juxtaposition of another (freq. opposite) sensation; *spec.* (the interaction producing) a change of the perceived appearance of an object caused by adjacent objects etc. L19. **6** The degree of difference between tones in a photograph, television picture, etc. E20.

2 M. GIROUARD Colour contrasts between brown stock bricks, red brick dressings, and white woodwork. SIMULTANEOUS *contrast.* 3 I. D'ISRAELI Buckingham offered a provoking contrast to his master. 4 J. TYNDALL The contrast between the two waters was very great. ARNOLD BENNETT She was . . especially pale by contrast with the black of her . . dress. G. MAXWELL A labouring dog-paddle in amazing contrast to his smooth darting grace below water. M. DRABBLE The area attracted her strongly, in its violent seedy contrasts, its juxtaposition of the rich and the poor.

Comb.: **contrast medium** a substance introduced into a subject in order to improve the visibility of organs etc. during radiography.

contrasty *a.* (esp. of a photograph, television picture, etc.) showing a high contrast L19.

contrast /kənˈtrɑːst/ *v.* L15. [In branch I f. OFr. *contrester* f. med.L *contrastare*, f. L *contra-* CONTRA- + *stare* to stand; in branch II f. Fr. *contraster* f. It. *contrastare*, ult. f. L (as I).] †**I1** *v.t.* & *i.* Withstand, fight (against); resist. L15–L17.

II2 *v.t.* **a** In the visual arts, juxtapose so as to bring out differences of form, colour, etc., and thus heighten the total effect. L17. **b** *gen.* Set (two things, one *with* or *to* another) in opposition so as to show their differences. E18. **3** *v.t.* Set off (each other) by opposition or contrast; offer or form a contrast to (usu. in *pass.*, foll. by *by*, *to*). *arch.* L17. **4** *v.i.* Form a contrast; show a striking difference on comparison (*with*). E18.

2a DRYDEN Contrasted by contrary motions, the most noble parts foremost in sight. b THOMAS HUGHES He contrasted our hero with the few men with whom he generally lived. E. M. FORSTER Our business is not to contrast the two, but to reconcile them. 3 J. F. COOPER The dark foliage of the evergreens was brilliantly contrasted by the glittering whiteness of the plain. C. P. SNOW My mother's thin beak of a nose contrasted itself to Aunt Milly's bulbous one. 4 A. WILSON The deep voice . . contrasted oddly with the tiny body. J. FRAME Her sudden energy contrasted with Henry's sudden exhaustion.

contrastive /kənˈtrɑːstɪv/ *a.* M19. [f. prec. + -IVE.] Forming a contrast; standing in contrast (*to*); concerned with contrasts.

contrastively *adv.* E19. **contrastiveness** *n.* M20.

contra-suggestible /kɒntrəsəˈdʒɛstɪb(ə)l/ *a.* E20. [f. CONTRA- + SUGGESTIBLE.] *Psychol.* Tending to respond to a suggestion by believing or doing the contrary.

contra-suggestiˈbility, **-suggestion** *ns.* the tendency to believe or do the contrary of what is suggested E20.

†**contratation** *n.* var. of CONTRACTATION.

contrate /ˈkɒntreɪt/ *a.* L15. [med.L, Proto-Romance *contrata* adj.: see COUNTRY.] †**1** Opposed, contrary, adverse. *rare.* Only in L15. **2** *contrate wheel*, a crown wheel, esp. in a watch mechanism. L17.

contratenor /ˈkɒntrətɛnə/ *n.* M16. [It. *contratenore*, f. *contra-* CONTRA- + TENOR *n.*[1]] *Mus.* = COUNTER-TENOR. Now only *Hist.*, a part written against the tenor in the same range.

contravallation /kɒntrəvəˈleɪʃ(ə)n/ *n.* L17. [Fr. *contrevallation* or It. *contravallazione*, f. L *contra-* CONTRA- + *vallatio(n-)*, f. late L *vallare* entrench, f. *vallum* rampart: see WALL *n.*[1], -ATION.] *Hist.* A chain of redoubts and breastworks constructed by besiegers for protection against sorties of the garrison.

contravariant /kɒntrəˈvɛːrɪənt/ *n.* & *a.* M19. [f. CONTRA- + VARIANT, after *covariant.*] *Math.* **A** *n.* A contravariant quantity. M19. **B** *adj.* Of a tensor etc.: such that the order of items has to be inverted for certain transformations and equations to hold (as in $F(f*g) = F(g)*F(f)$). M20.

contravene /kɒntrəˈviːn/ *v.* M16. [Late L *contravenire*, f. as CONTRA- + *venire* come. Cf. Fr. *contrevenir.*] **I** *v.t.* **1** Go counter to; infringe (a law, rule, etc.); (of a thing) conflict with. M16. **2** Oppose in argument; contradict, dispute, deny. E18.

1 BURKE Either to conform to the tenour of the article, or to contravene it. D. ADAMS The band's public address system contravenes local strategic arms limitations treaties. 2 T. H. HUXLEY Are those conclusions so firmly based that we may not contravene them?

II *v.i.* †**3** Foll. by *to*: infringe; contradict. *Sc.* L16–M17.

contravener *n.* M16.

contravention /kɒntrəˈvɛnʃ(ə)n/ *n.* M16. [(O)Fr. f. med.L *contraventio(n-)*, f. as CONTRA-, CONVENTION.] The action of contravening; infringement.

P. G. WODEHOUSE The dealers . . in direct contravention of their professed object in life, had refused to deal.

contrayerva /kɒntrəˈjəːvə/ *n.* M17. [Sp., lit. 'counter-herb', i.e. one used as an antidote, f. *contra-* CONTRA- + *yerva* (now *hierba*) herb.] (The root of) any of several tropical American plants of the genus *Dorstenia*, of the mulberry family, used medicinally (formerly against snake-bites).

†**contre-approach** *n.* see COUNTER-APPROACH.

contrecoup /ˈkɔ̃ːtrəkuː/ *n.* M18. [Fr., f. *contre* against + *coup* blow.] **1** A repercussion, an adverse consequence. *rare.* M18. **2** *Med.* An injury of a part (esp. one side of the brain) resulting from a blow on the opposite side. M19.

contrectation /kɒntrɛkˈteɪʃ(ə)n/ *n.* Long *rare.* E17. [L *contrectatio(n-)*, f. *contrectat-* pa. ppl stem of *contrectare*, f. as CON- + *tractare* to touch: see -ATION.] Handling, touching, fingering.

contredanse /ˈkɒntrədɑːns, *foreign* kɔ̃trədɑ̃ːs (*pl. same*)/ *n.* Also **contradance**. E19. [Fr., alt. of COUNTRY *dance* by assoc. w. *contre* against, opposite.] A country dance, *esp.* a social dance of which quadrille is a variant; a piece of music for such a dance.

contre-jour /ˈkɔ̃ːtrəʒʊə/ *n.* E20. [Fr., f. *contre* against + *jour* daylight.] *Photogr.* Back-lighting. Usu. *attrib.*

contretemps /ˈkɔ̃ːtrətɔ̃ː, ˈkɒn-/ *n.* Pl. same /-z/. L17. [Fr., orig. 'motion out of time', f. *contre* against + *temps* time.] **1** *Fencing.* Orig., a thrust made at an inopportune moment or at the same time as one's opponent makes one. Now, a feint made with the intention of inducing a counter-thrust. L17. **2** An unexpected or untoward occurrence, esp. of an embarrassing kind; a hitch, a mishap. E18. **b** A disagreement, an argument, a dispute. *colloq.* M20. **3** *Dancing.* A (ballet) step danced on the offbeat. Also, an academic ballet step involving a partial crossing of the feet and a small jump from a knees-bent position. E18.

2 E. M. FORSTER The son . . took every little contretemps as if it were a tragedy. b M. EDWARDES The Zambian President had had a particularly unpleasant contretemps with the Rhodesians.

contribuent /kənˈtrɪbjʊənt/ *n.* M19. [L *contribuent-* ppl stem of *contribuere*: see CONTRIBUTE, -ENT.] A contributing factor or person.

contributable /kənˈtrɪbjʊtəb(ə)l/ *a.* E17. [f. CONTRIBUTE + -ABLE.] **1** Liable to contribute, subject to contribution. E17. **2** To be contributed, payable as a contribution. E19.

†**contributary** *a.* LME. [f. next + -ARY[1]: cf. late L *contributarius* jointly taxed, CONTRIBUTORY.] **A** *adj.* **1** Paying or liable to pay tribute etc. Of property: subject to a tax. LME–M17. **2** Contributing to a common stock, purpose, or result. Of a stream: tributary. LME–E19. **B** *n.* A person who contributes. L16–E17.

contribute /kənˈtrɪbjuːt, ˈkɒntrɪbjuːt/ *v.* M16. [L *contribut-* pa. ppl stem of *contribuere*, f. as CON- + *tribuere* grant.] **1a** *v.t.* Supply or pay along with others to a common fund or stock (*lit.* & *fig.*). M16. **b** *v.i.* Make a contribution. E17. **2a** *v.i.* Play a part in the achievement of a result. Foll. by *to*, *to do*. E17. **b** *v.t.* Provide (agency or assistance) *to* a common result or purpose. M17. **3** *v.t.* & *i.* Supply (literary work) for publication in a magazine etc. M19.

1a S. JOHNSON Every hand is open to contribute something. b L. STEFFENS The local corporations contributed heavily to the Tammany campaign fund. S. BRETT Walter Proud didn't contribute to the conversation. 2a J. TYNDALL If I thought his presence would in any degree contribute to my comfort. b L. DURRELL The high magnification . . and the heat haze . . contributed a feathery vibration to the image.

contribution /kɒntrɪˈbjuːʃ(ə)n/ *n.* LME. [(O)Fr., or late L *contributio(n-)*, f. as prec.: see

-ION.] 1 A payment imposed on a body of people, a levy, an impost; *esp.* (*Hist.*) one imposed on a district by an army of occupation. Also, the action of paying such a levy. LME. 2 Something paid or given (voluntarily) to a common fund or stock; an action etc. which helps to bring about a result; the action of contributing. L16. b A writing forming part of a joint literary work; *esp.* an article contributed to a magazine or newspaper. E18. 3 *Law.* The payment by each of the parties concerned of his or her share in a common loss or liability. M17.

1 LD MACAULAY An infantry regiment.. had levied contributions on the people of that town. **lay under contribution** (esp. of an army) exact an imposition from. 2 AV *Rom.* 15:26 To make a certaine contribution for the poore sainctes.. in Hierusalem. B. JOWETT He makes a distinction.. which is a real contribution to the science of logic. *superannuation contribution*: see SUPERANNUATION 2.

contributive /kən'trɪbjʊtɪv/ *a.* L16. [f. CONTRIBUTE + -IVE.] That contributes; tending to contribute (*to*).

contributor /kən'trɪbjʊtə/ *n.* LME. [AN *contributour* (mod.Fr. *-eur*), f. as prec.: see -OUR, -OR.] †1 A person who pays a tax or tribute. LME–M17. 2 A person or body that contributes to a common fund or stock; a person who or thing which contributes to a result. M16. b A writer who contributes to a joint literary work; *spec.* one who writes articles for a newspaper or magazine. M18.

contributory /kən'trɪbjʊt(ə)ri/ *a.* & *n.* LME. [med.L *contributorius*, f. as CONTRIBUTE: see -ORY[2]. Cf. CONTRIBUTARY.] A *adj.* 1 Contributing to a common fund or undertaking. LME. b Of things: subject to a contribution or tax. L15. †c Paying tribute to the same lord. M16–E17. 2 Contributing to a result; partly responsible. M17. 3 Relating to or of the nature of contribution; *spec.* (of a pension or insurance scheme) in which the premiums are paid partly by the employee and partly by the employer. M19.

2 CLARENDON Contributory to our own destruction. **contributory negligence** *Law* negligence on the part of a person injured to take proper precautions against the injury.

B *n.* 1 A person who or thing which contributes. LME. 2 *Law.* A person who is bound, on the winding up of a company, to contribute towards the payment of its debts. M19.

†contrist *v.t.* LME–E19. [(O)Fr. *contrister* f. L *contristare*, f. as CON- + *tristis* sad.] Make sad, distress.

contrite /'kɒntraɪt/ *a.* ME. [(O)Fr. *contrit, -ite* f. L *contritus* pa. pple of *conterere*, f. as CON- + *terere* rub, grind (see TRITE *a.*).] 1 Crushed or broken in spirit by a sense of wrongdoing; sincerely penitent; (of an action, speech, etc.) showing contrition. ME. †2 Physically bruised or crushed; abraded. M17–M18.

1 L. WOOLF She was miserably contrite, saying that she had no excuse. W. STYRON His manner.. became apologetic, civilized, almost contrite.

contritely *adv.* LME. **contriteness** *n.* (*rare*) L17.

†contrite *v.t.* LME. [f. L *contrit-*: see next.] Chiefly as *contrited* ppl a. 1 Bruise, crush, abrade. LME–M18. 2 Make contrite. L15–E19.

contrition /kən'trɪʃ(ə)n/ *n.* ME. [(O)Fr. f. late L *contritio(n-)*, f. *contrit-* pa. ppl stem of *conterere*: see CONTRITE *a.*, -ION.] †1 The action of bruising or pounding, esp. so as to pulverize. ME–L17. 2 The condition of being distressed in mind for some fault or injury done; *spec.* complete penitence for sin (cf. ATTRITION 1). ME.

2 G. GREENE How easily we believe we can slide out of our guilt by a motion of contrition. R. A. KNOX Contrition must be accompanied by the desire to put things right.

contrivance /kən'traɪv(ə)ns/ *n.* E17. [f. next + -ANCE.] 1 A thing contrived as a means to an end; an expedient, a stratagem; a trick. E17. b A device, an arrangement, an invention. Freq. *derog.* M17. 2a The action of contriving or ingeniously bringing about; machination (in a bad sense), trickery. M17. b Arrangement of parts according to a plan; design. L17. 3 Inventive capacity. M17. †4 The way in which an object etc. is contrived. M17–M19.

1 J. BUCHAN A clumsy contrivance to persuade me that I was unsuspected. b P. G. WODEHOUSE One of those silk contrivances.. which you tie round your waist instead of a waistcoat. 2a M. ELPHINSTONE He escaped.. by the contrivance of his mother. b T. REID The marks of good contrivance which appear in the works of God.

contrive /kən'traɪv/ *v.*[1] ME. [OFr. *controver* (with suff. stress), *contreuve* (with stem stress), mod.Fr. *controuver* invent, f. med.L *contropare* compare, prob. f. as CON- + *tropus* TROPE.] I *v.t.* 1 Plan or design with ingenuity or skill; devise, invent; (in a bad sense) plot. ME. 2 Discover (the answer to a problem etc.); find out; imagine, guess. *obs.* exc. *dial.* LME. 3 Find a means of effecting; find a way *to do*, manage (freq. *iron.*, unintentionally or fortuitously). LME. 4 Bring by ingenuity *into* a position or form. Now *rare.* L16.

1 K. GRAHAME Scheming and planning and contriving how to get your property back. A. J. CRONIN Using sticks and a blanket, Stephen contrived a primitive shade over the cart. M. AMIS The tirade hadn't been contrived wholly for Rachel's benefit. 3 SHELLEY Prophecies.. Contrive their own fulfilment. H. JAMES How a place in the deepest depths of Essex.. could contrive to look so suburban. J. GALSWORTHY Somehow he must contrive to see her! 4 O. HENRY To contrive the rope into an ingenious noose-bridle.

II *v.i.* 5 Form schemes, conspire (*with, against*). LME–M17. 6 Manage household affairs etc. resourcefully; get by (well etc.). *arch.* M18.

5 SHAKES. *Jul. Caes.* The Fates with Traitors do contrive.

contrivable *a.* able to be contrived M17. **contrived** *a.* that has been contrived (in a particular way); obviously planned, artificial, not spontaneous: LME. **contrivement** *n.* (*arch.*) = CONTRIVANCE 1, 2, 4 L16. **contriver** *n.* a person who contrives; a skilful deviser; a (good, bad, etc.) manager: LME.

†contrive *v.*[2]*t.* LME. [App. irreg. f. L *contrivi* etc. perf. of *conterere*: see CONTRITE *a.*] 1 Wear down, defeat (an enemy). Only in LME. 2 Pass, spend (time). M–L16.

2 SHAKES. *Tam. Shr.* Please ye we may contrive this afternoon, And quaff carouses to our mistress' health.

control /kən'trəʊl/ *n.* Also **†-oul.** L16. [f. next, or Fr. *contrôle*, f. *contrôler*: see next.] 1 The act or power of directing or regulating; command, regulating influence. L16. 2 The action of holding in check; restraint; self-restraint; prevention of the spread of something unwanted; regulation of the numbers of an animal species etc. L16. 3 A means of restraining or regulating; a check; *spec.* a measure adopted to regulate prices, consumption of goods, etc. L16. 4 A person or body that acts as a guide or check; a controller. L18. b *Spiritualism.* An agency held to direct the actions of or to convey messages through a medium. L19. c A member of an intelligence organization who personally directs the activities of a spy; a spymaster. M20. 5 A standard of comparison for checking inferences deduced from an experiment; *spec.* a patient, specimen, etc., similar to the one(s) being investigated but not subjected to the same treatment. Freq. *attrib.* L19. 6 A device or mechanism for controlling the operation of a machine, esp. the direction, speed, etc., of an aircraft or vehicle. Usu. in *pl.* E20. 7 A military or other checkpoint; a point on a motor rallying etc. course where contestants must halt to have particulars recorded, or a section where speed is controlled. E20. 8 *Cards.* Esp. in bridge, (possession of) a card which will enable its holder to win a trick in a given suit at a desired moment. E20. 9 *Computing.* A key on a keyboard that produces an effect rather than a graphic character (such as movement of a cursor), and is usu. used in conjunction with a character key. Also more fully *control key.* M20.

1 G. B. SHAW Any Act transferring the theatres to the control of a licensing authority. DAY LEWIS The cart.. swayed behind the ass, which Keyes.. lost all control of. M. TIPPETT This process of imagination is outside our control. 2 J. BEATTIE Lust that defies controul. D. CUSACK My God! What control! If she'd only cried. N. TINBERGEN Attempts at gull control by taking the eggs. 3 D. HUME The particular checks and controuls provided by the constitution. 4 H. H. MILMAN He could not be a resident.. control upon the Doge. c B. FORBES He sat with his KGB control.., listening.. as the details of his new assignment were explained. 6 A. BLOND He took over the controls and landed the plane.

Phrases: *arms control*: see ARM *n.*[2] BIOLOGICAL *control. birth control*: see BIRTH *n.*[1] *board of control*: see BOARD *n. dual control*: see DUAL *a. locus of control*: see LOCUS *n.*[1] **out of control** not or no longer subject to proper direction or restraint. *quality control*: see QUALITY *n.* & *a. remote control*: see REMOTE *a. social control*: see SOCIAL *a. span of control*: see SPAN *n.*[1] *throttle control*: see THROTTLE *n.* 2b. **under control** subject to proper direction; *fig.* in proper order.

Comb.: **control board** (*a*) = *control panel* below; (*b*) a board of control; **control experiment**: used to verify another experiment, using conditions identical except in one respect; *control key*: see sense 9 above; **control panel** a surface on which are mounted switches, dials, etc., for the remote control of electrical or other apparatus; **control rod**: of neutron-absorbing material used to control the rate of reaction in the core of a nuclear reactor; **control room** a room in or from which an operation is controlled; **control surface** a movable surface or aerofoil used to control the aerodynamic behaviour of an aircraft etc.; *control tower*: see TOWER *n.*[1] 3f; **control unit** a self-contained controlling device; *esp.* the element in a central processing unit which accepts and decodes instructions from the main memory and sends executive signals to other units.

control /kən'trəʊl/ *v.t.* Also **†-oul, †comptrol.** Infl. **-ll-**. LME. [AN *contreroller*, Fr. †*conteroller* (now *contrôler*), f. med.L *contrarotulare*, f. *contrarotulus* copy of a roll, f. *contra* against + *rotulus* ROLL *n.*[1]] 1a Check or verify and hence regulate (accounts etc.), orig. by comparison with a duplicate register. LME. b *gen.* Check the accuracy of (a statement etc.). *arch.* M16. 2a Exercise power or influence over; dominate, regulate. L15. b Restrain from action, hold in check (emotions etc.). Freq. *refl.* M16. c Curb the growth or spread of. M19. †3 Take to task, reprove (a person); censure, object to (a thing). E16–M18. 4†a Overpower, subdue. L16–M18. b *Law* (now *Hist.*). Overrule (a judgement etc.). E18. 5 Subject to verification by a control experiment. Chiefly as *controlled* ppl a. M19.

1b SIR T. MORE He shalbe sure seldome to meete any manne.. by whom hys tale might be controlled. 2a W. S. CHURCHILL The militia must be controlled by the Lord-Lieutenants of the counties. E. L. DOCTOROW By controlling the speed of the moving belts he could control the workers' rate of production. **controlled drug, substance**: restricted by law in respect of use and possession. **controlling interest** the ability of a person or group to determine the policy of a company, esp. through owning a majority of the stock. b B. C. BRODIE Difficulty in controlling his temper. N. COWARD You're far too temperamental. Try to control yourself. c C. S. FORESTER Fire would be.. difficult to control in the sails and the rigging.

controlla'bility *n.* the quality or condition of being (easily) controllable E20. **controllable** *a.* able to be controlled or restrained L16.

controller /kən'trəʊlə/ *n.* See also COMPTROLLER. LME. [AN *contrerollour*, f. *contreroller*: see CONTROL *v.*, -ER[2].] 1 A person who keeps a duplicate register so as to exercise a check on a treasurer or person in charge of accounts; an official appointed to supervise expenditure; a steward. (Freq. COMPTROLLER.) LME. †2 A (censorious) critic. M16–E17. 3 A person who or thing which controls or regulates. M16. b A device or mechanism by means of which the operation of a machine can be regulated. L19.

3 *quality controller*: see QUALITY *n.* & *a.*

Comb.: **controller-general** an official exercising overall responsibility.

controllership *n.* the office of controller L15.

controlment /kən'trəʊlm(ə)nt/ *n.* *arch.* Also **†compt-**. LME. [f. CONTROL *v.* + -MENT.] †1 The checking or verifying and regulating of accounts. LME–E18. 2 Control; direction, regulation; restraint, check. L15. †3 Censure, reproof. M16–M17.

†controul *n.*, *v.* vars. of CONTROL *n.*, *v.*

†controverse *n.* E16–M17. [(O)Fr. f. L *controversia* CONTROVERSY *n.*] A dispute, a controversy.

†controverse *v.t.* L16–M18. [Orig. as pa. ppl a., f. Fr. *controversé*, earlier *controvers* f. L *controversus*: see CONTROVERSY.] Make the subject of controversy, dispute.

controversial /kɒntrəˈvəːʃ(ə)l/ *a.* L16. [Late L *controversialis*, f. *controversia* CONTROVERSY *n.*: see -AL[1].] 1 Subject to controversy; forming an object of debate, disputed; *loosely* about the merits of which opinions are divided. L16. 2 Of or pertaining to controversy; polemical. M17. 3 Given to controversy; disputatious. M17.

1 J. WILSON As controversial a point as the authorship of Junius. C. HAMPTON If I didn't disgust at least a substantial minority, I wouldn't be controversial. 2 W. STUBBS The .. object of his writing was didactic rather than controversial.

controversialism *n.* controversial spirit or practice M19. **controversialist** *n.* a person who engages in or is skilful in controversy M18. **controversiˈality** *n.* controversial nature L20. **controversially** *adv.* L17.

controversion /kɒntrəˈvəːʃ(ə)n/ *n.* L17. [OFr. f. late L *controversio(n-)*, f. L *controversus*: see next, -ION.] 1 A turning in the opposite direction (*lit.* & *fig.*). L17. †2 A controversy, a dispute. L17–M18. 3 The action of controverting. M18.

controversy /ˈkɒntrəvəːsi, kənˈtrɒvəsi/ *n.* & *v.* LME. [L *controversia*, f. *controversus* disputed, f. *contro-* var. of *contra-* CONTRA- + *versus* pa. pple of *vertere* turn: see -Y[3].] A *n.* 1 Disputation on a matter of opinion or (formerly) rival claims. LME. 2 A (prolonged) argument or debate, *esp.* one conducted in public. LME.

1 H. E. MANNING This text has been the subject of endless controversy. **beyond** or **without controversy** unquestionably. *draw the saw of controversy*: see SAW *n.*[1] 2 A. TOFFLER A fierce controversy is .. raging today among biologists over the .. ethical issues arising out of eugenics.

†B *v.i.* Engage in controversy. *rare.* L16–M19.

controvert /ˈkɒntrəvəːt, kɒntrəˈvəːt/ *v.* M16. [f. L *contro-* in *controversus* + *vertere*: see prec.] 1 *v.t.* a Make a subject of verbal contention; argue about, debate. M16. †b Dispute (a right, possession, etc.); contest (an election). L16–M19. 2 *v.i.* Engage in controversy (*with*). M16. 3 *v.t.* Attempt to disprove; argue against, deny (an idea). E17.

1a H. FIELDING A point which was controverted between Mr. Thwackum and Mr. Square. 3 A. G. GARDINER The idea .. was too foolish to be controverted.

controverter *n.* L16. **controˈvertible** *a.* debatable E17. **controvertist** *n.* a controversialist M17.

contubernal /kənˈtjuːbən(ə)l/ *n.* & *a.* E17. [L *contubernalis* tent-companion, f. as CON- + *taberna* hut, booth: see -AL[1]. Cf. L *contubernium* occupation of a tent in common.] A *n.* An intimate companion, a comrade. E17. B *adj.* Of or relating to cohabitation (as the only form of marital relationship recognized among slaves in ancient Rome). L19.

contumacious /kɒntjʊˈmeɪʃəs/ *a.* L16. [f. as next: see -ACIOUS.] 1 Obstinately disobedient to authority; stubbornly perverse; *spec.* (chiefly *Hist.*) wilfully disobedient to the summons or order of a court. L16. †2 Of a disease: resistant to treatment. Only in 17.

contumaciously *adv.* E17. **contumaciousness** *n.* M17.

contumacy /ˈkɒntjʊməsi/ *n.* ME. [L *contumacia*, f. *contumax*, *-ac-*, perh. f. as CON- + *tumere* swell: see -Y[3].] 1 Obstinate disobedience to authority; stubborn perverseness; *spec.* (chiefly *Hist.*) wilful disobedience to the summons or order of a court. ME. b An act of disobedience. E18. †2 Resistance of a disease to treatment. M16–M17.

Also **contuˈmacity** *n.* (*rare*) LME.

contumelious /kɒntjʊˈmiːlɪəs/ *a.* LME. [OFr. *contumelieus* (mod. *-eux*) f. L *contumeliosus*, f. *contumelia*: see next, -OUS.] 1 Of a word, action, etc., (formerly) a person: scornfully insulting, insolent, reproachful. LME. †2 Shameful, ignominious. M16–M17.

1 SHAKES. *1 Hen. VI* With scoffs, and scorns, and contumelious taunts. TENNYSON Curving a contumelious lip.

contumeliously *adv.* M16. **contumeliousness** *n.* M17.

contumely /ˈkɒntjuːmɪli, -tjuːmli/ *n.* LME. [OFr. *contumelie* f. L *contumelia*, perh. f. as CON- + *tumere* swell.] 1 (An instance of) contemptuously insulting language or treatment, scornful and humiliating rudeness. LME. 2 Disgrace, ignominy. L15.

1 R. GRAVES The Rhodians, seeing him deprived of .. his magisterial powers .. began to treat him .. with contumely.

contund /kənˈtʌnd/ *v.t.* LME. [L *contundere*, f. as CON- + *tundere* beat, thump.] 1 Pound, beat small. Now *rare* or *obs.* LME. 2 Bruise; beat, thrash. Now only *joc.* M17.

†conturbation *n.* LME–E19. [L *conturbatio(n-)*, f. *conturbat-* pa. ppl stem of *conturbare*, f. as CON- + *turbare* disturb: see -ATION.] Disturbance (physical or mental).

contuse /kənˈtjuːz/ *v.t.* LME. [L *contus-* pa. ppl stem of *contundere*: see CONTUND.] 1 Injure (a part of the body) without breaking the skin; bruise. LME. †2 Pound, beat small. M16–E17.

contusive /-ˈtjuːsɪv/ *a.* producing contusion; of or pertaining to contusions: L18.

contusion /kənˈtjuːʒ(ə)n/ *n.* LME. [Fr. f. L *contusio(n-)*, f. as prec.: see -ION.] 1 Injury to the body without breaking of the skin, bruising; a bruise. LME. †2 The action of pounding or beating small. E17–M18.

conundrum /kəˈnʌndrəm/ *n.* L16. [Origin unkn.] †1 Used as a term of abuse for a person (perh. a crank or a pedant). *rare.* Only in L16. †2 A whim, a fancy. E17–E18. †3 A play on words, a pun. M17–L18. 4 A riddle with a punning answer; a puzzle; a hard question. L17. 5 A thing one is puzzled to think of a name for. *Sc. rare.* E19.

conurbation /kɒnəːˈbeɪʃ(ə)n/ *n.* E20. [f. CON- + L *urbs*, *urbis* city + -ATION.] An aggregation of contiguous towns or urban areas forming a single community in some respects.

conure /ˈkɒnjʊə/ *n.* M19. [mod.L *Conurus* former genus name, f. Gk *kōnos* CONE *n.* + *oura* tail.] Any of numerous Central and S. American parrots belonging to the genera *Aratinga*, *Pyrrhura*, and related genera.

conus /ˈkəʊnəs/ *n.* Pl. **-ni** /-naɪ/. L19. [L: see CONE *n.*] 1 *Anat.* A structure or organ resembling a cone. L19. 2 *Med.* A pale crescent-shaped or annular patch next to the optic disc resulting from atrophy of the choroid and exposure of the sclera. L19.

1 **conus arteriosus** /ɑːˌtɪərɪˈəʊsəs/ [L = arterial] the upper and anterior part of the right ventricle of the heart. **conus medullaris** /mɛdəˈlɑːrɪs/ [L = medullary] the conical lower extremity of the spinal cord.

†conusable *a.*, **-ance** *n.* vars. of COGNIZABLE, -ANCE.

†conusant *a.* M17–E19. [OFr. (also *-is(s)ant*, *-ois(s)ant*) pres. pple of *conuistre*, *-oistre* (mod. *connaître*) f. L *cognoscere*: see COGNITION, -ANT[1].] = COGNIZANT.

†conusee, **-or** *ns.* vars. of COGNIZEE, -OR.

convalesce /kɒnvəˈlɛs/ *v.i.* L15. [L *convalescere*, f. as CON- + *valescere* grow strong, f. *valere* be strong or well.] Regain health after an illness, injury, etc., esp. through a period of rest or reduced activity.

Q. BELL They .. were sent off to Bath to convalesce.

convalescence /kɒnvəˈlɛs(ə)ns/ *n.* L15. [Fr. f. L *convalescentia*, f. as next: see -ENCE.] (A period of) gradual recovery after illness, injury, etc.

Also **convalescency** *n.* (*rare*) M17.

convalescent /kɒnvəˈlɛs(ə)nt/ *a.* & *n.* M17. [L *convalescent-* pres. ppl stem of *convalescere*: see CONVALESCE, -ENT.] A *adj.* 1 (Gradually) recovering from illness, injury, etc. M17. 2 *attrib.* Of or for persons in convalescence. E19.

2 *convalescent home*, *hospital*, etc.

B *n.* A convalescent person. M18.

convalidate /kənˈvalɪdeɪt/ *v.t. rare.* M17. [med.L *convalidat-* pa. ppl stem of *convalidare*, f. as CON- + VALIDATE.] Strengthen, confirm; ratify, give legal effect to.

convaliˈdation *n.* E16.

convect /kənˈvɛkt/ *v.* L19. [Back-form. f. next.] 1 *v.t.* Transport by convection. L19. 2 *v.i.* Be convected; undergo convection. L20.

convection /kənˈvɛkʃ(ə)n/ *n.* E17. [Late L *convectio(n-)*, f. *convect-* pa. ppl stem of *convehere*, f. as CON- + *vehere* carry: see -ION.] †1 The action of carrying. *rare.* Only in E17. 2 (The transport of heat by) the relative movement of parts of a fluid differing in density (and usu. temperature); *spec.* in *Meteorol.*, upward motion of warmer (less dense) air or downward motion of cooler (denser) air. M19.

Comb.: **convection cell** a self-contained convective zone in which upward motion of warmer fluid in the centre is balanced by downward motion of cooler fluid at the periphery.

convectional *a.* of, pertaining to, or induced by convection; *spec.* (of rain) resulting from the condensation of water vapour carried into the upper atmosphere by convection: L19.

convective /kənˈvɛktɪv/ *a.* M19. [f. L *convect-*: see prec., -IVE.] 1 Having the property of conveying. M19. 2 Of, relating to, or resulting from convection. M19.

convectively *adv.* M19.

convector /kənˈvɛktə/ *n.* E20. [f. CONVECTION: see -OR.] More fully *convector heater*. A type of heater employing convection to warm a room.

†convell *v.t.* M16. [L *convellere*, f. as CON- + *vellere* tear, pull, pluck.] 1 Refute completely, overthrow. M16–E18. 2 Tear, wrench. *rare.* M–L17.

convenable /ˈkɒnvɪnəb(ə)l/ *a.*[1] Long *rare.* Also (earlier) †**cov-**. ME. [AN, OFr. *covenable*, later *conv-*, f. *co(n)venir* agree f. L *convenire*: see CONVENE, -ABLE. Form in *conv-* f. LME.] 1 Appropriate, suitable; becoming, congruous. ME. †2 Convenient. ME–M17.

convenable /kənˈviːnəb(ə)l/ *a.*[2] M17. [f. CONVENE + -ABLE.] Able to be convened.

convenance /kɔ̃vnɑ̃ːs/ *n.* Pl. pronounced same. L15. [Fr., f. *convenir* f. L *convenire*: see next, -ANCE.] †1 Agreement, concurrence. *rare.* L15–L17. 2 Conventional propriety or usage; in *pl.*, the proprieties. M19.

¶Formerly naturalized.

convene /kənˈviːn/ *v.* LME. [L *convenire* assemble, agree, suit, f. as CON- + *venire* come.] I 1 *v.i.* & *refl.* Come together, meet, assemble, esp. for a common purpose; (of things) occur together. LME. 2 *v.t.* Summon (a person) before a tribunal; *esp.* (at Cambridge University) bring (a student) before a college court of discipline. LME. 3 *v.t.* Cause (individuals, a collective body, an assembly) to come together; convoke. M16.

1 D. G. ROSSETTI The murmuring courts Where the shapes of sleep convene! D. ACHESON The UN Atomic Energy Commission was convening for discussions. 3 V. SACKVILLE-WEST More intimate parties, where only twenty guests .. were convened. A. E. STEVENSON President Eisenhower convened a White House Conference on Education.

II 4 *v.i.* Agree, accord, harmonize. Long *rare.* LME.

4 THACKERAY Articles which the marriage-monger cannot make to convene at all, tempers .. tastes, etc.

convener /kənˈviːnə/ *n.* Also **-or.** M16. [f. prec. + -ER[1], -OR.] †1 A person who assembles with others. M16–M17. 2 A person who convenes a meeting; *esp.* an official who arranges (and presides at) meetings of a committee or other body. L17.

convenership *n.* L19. **convenery** *n.* (*Sc.*) an assembly, a convention M19.

convenience /kənˈviːnɪəns/ *n.* & *a.* LME. [L *convenientia*, f. as CONVENIENT: see -ENCE. Cf. CONVENIENCY.] A *n.* †1 Agreement; congruity; an agreement. (CONVENIENCY 1 recorded later.) LME–M17. †2 Suitability by nature; fitness. LME–M18. b Moral fitness, propriety. (Earlier CONVENIENCY 2b.) Only in L17. 3a The quality of being convenient generally; suitability. LME. b The quality of being personally convenient; material advantage; personal comfort; trouble-saving. (Earlier CONVENIENCY 3b.) E18. 4a A convenient state; an advantage. E17. b An opportune occasion. (Earlier CONVENIENCY 4b.) L17. 5 A material arrangement or appliance conducive to personal comfort, ease of action, or saving of trouble; a utensil. Usu. in *pl.* (Earlier CONVENIENCY 5.) L17. b *spec.* A conveyance. Now *rare* or *obs.* L17. c *spec.* A privy, a lavatory. Now esp. in *public convenience.* M18.

2 SHAKES. *All's Well* The Duke will lay upon him all the honour That good convenience claims. 3a J. Q. ADAMS The convenience . . of decimal arithmetic for 'calculation'. b J. K. GALBRAITH We associate truth with convenience—with what most closely accords with self-interest. JO GRIMOND A . . causeway of cobbles laid for the convenience of walkers. 4 B. PLAIN A fine convenience it was, to have water running in the kitchen. 5a J. E. T. ROGERS Necessary conveniences for the homestead.

Phrases: **at one's convenience** in a way or at a time convenient to one. **at one's earliest convenience** as soon as one can. *flag of convenience*: see FLAG *n.*[4] LEATHERN *convenience.* **make a convenience of** use (a person) without consideration of his or her feelings. **marriage of convenience** a marriage that is not primarily a love-match and serves another purpose. MODERN *convenience.*

B *attrib.* or as *adj.* Designed for convenience, that is convenient. Orig. *US.* M20.

convenience food pre-prepared food needing a minimum of further treatment and suitable for use whenever desired. **convenience store**: stocking a wide range of goods and remaining open outside usual shopping hours.

convenience /kən'viːnɪəns/ *v.t.* M17. [f. the n.] Afford convenience to, suit; accommodate.

conveniency /kən'viːnɪənsi/ *n.* Now *rare.* L15. [f. as CONVENIENCE *n.*: see -ENCY.] †1 = CONVENIENCE *n.* I. L15–E18. †2 = CONVENIENCE *n.* 2. E16–M17. b = CONVENIENCE *n.* 2b. L16–M17. 3a = CONVENIENCE *n.* 3a. E17. b = CONVENIENCE *n.* 3b. E17. †4a = CONVENIENCE *n.* 4a. M17–L18. b = CONVENIENCE *n.* 4b. M17. 5 = CONVENIENCE *n.* 5. M17.

convenient /kən'viːnɪənt/ *a.* LME. [L *convenient-* pres. ppl stem of *convenire*: see CONVENE, -ENT.] †1 Foll. by *to, for*: in accordance with the nature of; in keeping with; befitting, becoming. LME–L17. †2 Morally suitable, proper. LME–E18. †3 Suitable (*to* or *for* a purpose, the circumstances, etc.); appropriate, due. LME–L18. 4 Personally suitable, well-adapted to one's purpose or situation; available or occurring at a suitable moment; favourable, comfortable; trouble-free. L15. 5 Within easy reach; readily accessible; near (*to*) in space or time. *colloq.* E19.

2 AV *Eph.* 5:4 Neither filthinesse, nor foolish talking, nor iesting, which are not conuenient. 3 SHAKES. *Mids. N. D.* Here's a marvellous convenient place for our rehearsal. J. WESLEY Many were destitute of convenient clothing. 4 E. A. FREEMAN It had once been convenient to forget, it was now equally convenient to remember. G. GISSING I thought five o'clock . . would be a convenient time. BETTY SMITH His red trousers had a convenient hole . . so that his tail could stick out. 5 THACKERAY Heretics used to be brought thither convenient for burning hard by.

conveniently *adv.* LME.

convenor *n.* see CONVENER.

convent /'kɒnv(ə)nt, -vɛnt/ *n.* Also **cov-** /'kɒv-/ (long *obs.* exc. in names, as *Covent Garden*, London). ME. [AN *covent*, OFr. *convent* (mod. *couvent*), f. L *conventus* assembly, company, f. *convent-* pa. ppl stem of *convenire* CONVENE. Cf. COVIN.] †1 A gathering, an assembly. ME–M17. †2 A company; *spec.* (*a*) the twelve apostles; (*b*) a company of twelve (or thirteen including a superior) religious persons. ME–M16. 3 A religious community (usu. Christian) living together under discipline; a religious institution founded for communal living; now *esp.* such a community of or institution for women (cf. *monastery*). ME. 4 The buildings or estate occupied by such a community. LME.

Comb.: **convent school**: conducted by members of a convent.

con'ventical *a.* (*rare*) of or pertaining to a convent M18.

convent /kɒn'vɛnt/ *v. obs.* exc. *Hist.* M16. [L *convent-* pa. ppl stem of *convenire* CONVENE.] 1 *v.t.* & *i.* = CONVENE *v.* I. M16. †2 *v.i.* Be convenient, suit. *rare* (Shakes.). Only in E17.

conventicle /kən'vɛntɪk(ə)l/ *n.* & *v.* LME. [L *conventiculum* (place of) assembly, formally dim. of *conventus* meeting: see CONVENT *n.*] **A** *n.* †1 A (regular) assembly or meeting. LME–M17. 2 A meeting or assembly of a private, clandestine, irregular, or illegal nature. *obs.* exc. as below. LME. b *spec.* A clandestine or unlawful religious meeting, esp. (*Hist.*) of Nonconformists or Dissenters in England, or of Covenanters in Scotland. E16. 3 A place of (irregular etc.) meeting; esp. (*Hist.*, formerly *derog.*) a Nonconformist or Dissenting meeting-house. LME. †4 A small convent. M16–E17.

Comb.: **Conventicle Acts** *Hist.*: of the reign of Charles II, suppressing religious meetings not conforming to the Church of England.

†**B** *v.t.* & *i.* Form into a conventicle; hold or frequent conventicles. L16–E18.

†**conventicleer** *n.* = CONVENTICLER M17–E18. **conventicler** *n.* an attender of conventicles LME.

convention /kən'vɛnʃ(ə)n/ *n.* LME. [(O)Fr. f. L *conventio(n-)* meeting, covenant, f. *convent-*: see CONVENT *v.*, -ION.] **I1** An assembly or gathering of people; esp. a formal meeting for deliberation, legislation, etc. LME. b *spec. Hist.* A meeting of Parliament, or of the Scottish Estates, without the formal summons usually required. M16. c In the US, an assembly of delegates of a political party for the purpose of nominating a candidate for the presidency, etc. E19. †2 The action of coming together, meeting, or assembling; an assemblage, a union. L15–L18. †3 The action of summoning before a person in authority. L16–E19. 4 The action of convening a meeting etc. M17.

1 T. DREISER There was a convention of dentists in the city. c *national convention*: see NATIONAL *a.* 2 J. HOWELL Venice is . . a Convention of little Ilands.

II5 An agreement or covenant between parties; an agreement creating legal relations. LME. b *spec.* A diplomatic agreement between States, now *esp.* one less formal than a treaty. E17. c *spec.* An agreement between belligerents as to the suspension of hostilities, exchange or treatment of prisoners, etc. L18. 6 General agreement or consent, deliberate or implicit, as to any custom, usage, behaviour, etc. L18. b Accepted social behaviour, esp. if merely formal or repressively artificial. M19. 7 A generally accepted rule or practice based on custom, usage, etc. L18. b *Cards.* A prearranged method of play or bidding, esp. in bridge, used to convey information. M19.

5 *Geneva Convention(s)*: see GENEVA *n.*[1] 6 G. B. SHAW A man . . is by convention the master and lawgiver of the hearthstone. 7 G. GREENE I may have been christened—it's a social convention isn't it? L. P. HARTLEY Bound by the moral conventions of the eighteenth century.

conventio'neer *n.* (orig. *US*) = CONVENTIONER M20. **conventioner** *n.* a member of a convention, a person who attends conventions L17. **conventionist** *n.* †(*a*) a party to a convention or agreement; (*b*) = CONVENTIONER: M18.

conventional /kən'vɛnʃ(ə)n(ə)l/ *a.* & *n.* L15. [Fr. *conventionnel* or late L *conventionalis*, f. as prec.: see -AL[1].] **A** *adj.* 1 Relating to, based on, or of the nature of a formal agreement or convention, e.g. between States. L15. b *Cards.* Of, pertaining to, or characterized by a convention (sense 7b) or conventions. M19. 2 Relating to or depending on agreed social usage, custom, etc.; arbitrarily or artificially determined. M18. b Accepting social conventions; in accordance with accepted (artificial) standards or models, orthodox; lacking originality, spontaneity, or realism. M19. c Of weapons, warfare, power stations, etc.: non-nuclear. M20. 3 Of, pertaining to, or of the nature of a convention or assembly. E19.

2 H. BLAIR The connexion between words and ideas may . . be considered as arbitrary and conventional. b L. W. MEYNELL Tall poplars silhouetted . . resembling the conventional trees of a child's Noah's Ark. T. S. ELIOT I'm not a person of liberal views. I'm very conventional. A. TOFFLER It is conventional wisdom to assert that the age of the entrepreneur is dead.

B *n.* 1 *absol.* That which is conventional. E19. 2 = CONVENTIONALIST I. *rare.* L19.

conventionally *adv.* M19.

conventionalise *v.* var. of CONVENTIONALIZE.

conventionalism /kən'vɛnʃ(ə)n(ə)lɪz(ə)m/ *n.* M19. [f. CONVENTIONAL + -ISM.] 1 Adherence to or regard for what is conventional. M19. 2 An instance of mere convention, a conventional usage etc. M19. 3 *Philos.* A doctrine holding that a priori truths are true by virtue of linguistic convention. Also, a doctrine holding that at least some apparently empirical scientific laws are in fact postulates. M20.

conventionalist /kən'vɛnʃ(ə)n(ə)lɪst/ *n.* E19. [f. as prec. + -IST.] 1 *Hist.* A supporter of the French National Convention of 1792. E19. 2 A person who follows conventional usage etc. M19. 3 *Philos.* An adherent of conventionalism. M20.

conventionality /kənvɛnʃə'nalɪti/ *n.* M19. [f. CONVENTIONAL + -ITY.] 1 The quality or state of being conventional. M19. 2 A conventional thing or practice; in *pl.*, *the* forms and usages established as fit and proper by society. M19.

conventionalize /kən'vɛnʃ(ə)n(ə)lʌɪz/ *v.t.* Also **-ise**. M19. [f. CONVENTIONAL + -IZE.] Render conventional, treat conventionally.

conventionali'zation *n.* L19.

conventionary /kən'vɛnʃ(ə)n(ə)ri/ *a.* E17. [med.L *conventionarius*, f. L *conventio(n-)*: see CONVENTION, -ARY[1].] Designating or holding tenure on terms fixed by agreement rather than custom.

conventual /kən'vɛntjʊəl/ *a.* & *n.* LME. [med.L *conventualis*, f. L *conventus* CONVENT *n.*: see -AL[1].] **A** *adj.* 1 Of or belonging to a convent; characteristic of a convent. LME. 2 (**C-**.) Designating or pertaining to the Franciscan Conventuals (see sense B.1 below). E18.

1 M. BEERBOHM A conventual hush in her voice.

B *n.* 1 (**C-**.) A member of a branch of the Franciscans in which the friars live in large convents and follow a less strict rule. Cf. *Observant.* M16. 2 A member or inmate of a convent. E17.

conventually *adv.* LME.

converge /kən'vəːdʒ/ *v.* L17. [Late L *convergere* incline together, f. as CON- + L *vergere* bend, turn, incline.] 1 *v.i.* Tend to meet in a point; approach nearer together as if to meet or join (*on* a point). L17. 2 *v.i. Math.* Of an infinite series: have the property that as more terms are taken, in order from the first, their sum gets closer and closer to a definite limit. E18. 3 *v.t.* Cause to approach each other or come together. L18.

1 P. PEARCE Footsteps were coming to the house, converging on it from different directions. *fig.*: B. WEBB Our points of view are slowly converging. 3 **converging lens**: causing light rays to converge.

converger *n.* a person whose thought is convergent M20.

convergence /kən'vəːdʒ(ə)ns/ *n.* E18. [f. CONVERGENT: see -ENCE.] 1 The action, fact, or property of converging; tendency to come together at a point. E18. 2 *Biol.* The tendency of distinct animals and plants to evolve similar structural or physiological characteristics under similar environmental conditions. M19. 3 *Meteorol.* & *Oceanogr.* A place where airflows or ocean currents meet, characteristically marked by upwelling (of air) or downwelling (of water). M20.

3 *Antarctic convergence*: see ANTARCTIC *a.*

convergency *n.* convergent quality, convergence E18.

convergent /kən'vəːdʒ(ə)nt/ *a.* E18. [Late L *convergent-* pres. ppl stem of *convergere*: see CONVERGE, -ENT.] 1 Converging; of or pertaining to convergence; *Math.* (of an infinite series) that converges (CONVERGE 2). E19. 2 *Biol.* Characterized by or displaying evolutionary convergence (CONVERGENCE 2). L19. 3 *Psychol.* Of thought: tending to reach only the most rational result. Cf. DIVERGENT 2. M20.

2 *pointwise convergent*: see POINTWISE *adv.* 2.

conversable /kən'vəːsəb(ə)l/ *a.* L16. [Obs. Fr. = affable etc. f. med.L *conversabilis*, f. L *conversari*: see CONVERSE *v.*, -ABLE. See also CONVERSIBLE *a.*[2]] 1 That may be conversed with. Now *esp.* pleasant in conversation, disposed to converse. L16. 2 Of or pertaining to social converse. M17.

conversableness *n.* L17. **conversably** *adv.* M17.

conversance /kən'vəːs(ə)ns/ *n.* E17. [f. next: see -ANCE.] The state or quality of being conversant (*with*).

Also **conversancy** *n.* L18.

conversant /kən'vəːs(ə)nt/ *a.* & *n.* ME. [(O)Fr., pres. pple of *converser*: see CONVERSE *v.*, -ANT[1].] **A** *adj.* †1 Living or passing time habitually or frequently *in* or in a specified place. ME–E19. 2 Associating regularly *with* (also †*in*, †*among*); on familiar terms *with*. ME. 3 Occupied or engaged *with* (also †*in*, †*among*, †*about*); having to do *with*. LME. 4 Well versed or experienced *in*, familiar *with*, (a subject). LME. †5 Of a thing: well known, familiar. LME–M17.

1 T. PENNANT On marshy . . grounds, where they are conversant. 2 STEELE I am afraid you have been very little conversant with Women. 3 W. LILLY A meer Fisherman, or man conversant in water. C. G. B. DAUBENY Chemistry . . had . . been conversant merely with the qualities of matter. 4 B. EMECHETA Men who were conversant with the goings-on in world politics. M. MOORCOCK My mother . . was conversant in all forms of literature and learning.

†**B** *n.* A familiar acquaintance. L16–L17.

conversation /kɒnvə'seɪʃ(ə)n/ *n.* ME. [(O)Fr. f. L *conversatio(n-)*, f. *conversari* CONVERSE *v.*: see -ATION.] †1 The action of living or having one's being *in*, *among*. ME–E18. †2 The action of consorting (*with*); intimacy. ME–L18. 3 Behaviour, mode of life. *arch.* ME. 4 Sexual intercourse or relations. *obs.* exc. in *criminal conversation* (see CRIMINAL *a.* 1). LME. 5 The informal interchange of information, ideas, etc., by spoken words; ability or proficiency in this. L16. **b** An informal spoken interchange, a talk. L17. †6 Occupation or acquaintance *with* (an object of study etc.). L16–E18. †7 A circle of acquaintance; company. E17–E18. †8 A social gathering, an at-home. Cf. CONVERSAZIONE. L17–L18.

1 G. STANHOPE Proneness to Idolatry, which a long Conversation in Egypt had disposed them to. 2 MILTON The good and peace of wedded conversation. 3 AV *Ps.* 50:23 Him that ordereth his conversation aright. 5 S. JOHNSON We had *talk* enough, but no *conversation*; there was nothing *discussed*. A. POWELL Neither of the girls had much conversation. **make conversation** converse, esp. only as a social duty. **b** J. T. STORY They . . held a long . . conversation in Italian. 7 CLARENDON His Domestick Conversation . . were all known Papists.

Comb.: **conversation card** *Hist.* a card containing a sentence for use in a question-and-answer game; **conversation chair** a type of upright chair on which the occupant sits astride, facing the back; **conversation lozenge** a lozenge with an inscribed motto; **conversation piece** (*a*) a type of genre painting involving a portrait group posed in a landscape or domestic setting; (*b*) a subject serving as a topic of conversation on account of its unusualness etc.; **conversation-stopper** *colloq.* a remark etc. that admits of no reply; something outrageous or startling.

conversationist *n.* = CONVERSATIONALIST L17.

conversational /kɒnvə'seɪʃ(ə)n(ə)l/ *a.* L18. [f. prec. + -AL[1].] 1 Of or pertaining to conversation; characteristic of or appropriate to conversation. L18. 2 Fond of or good at conversation. L18.

conversationalist *n.* a participant in conversation; a person who is good at conversation: E19. **conversationally** *adv.* E19.

conversative /kən'vəːsətɪv/ *a. rare.* M17. [f. CONVERSE *v.* + -ATIVE.] †1 Of or fitted for social intercourse, sociable. Only in M17. 2 = CONVERSATIONAL 2. E18.

conversazione /ˌkɒnvəsatsɪ'əʊni/ *n.* Pl. **-nes**, **-ni** /-ni/. M18. [It. = conversation.] 1 In Italy, an evening gathering for conversation and recreation. M18. †2 An at-home. L18–E19. 3 A social gathering for discussion of the arts, literature, etc.; an educational soirée. L18.

converse /'kɒnvəːs/ *n.*[1] LME. [f. as CONVERSE *a.*[2]] 1 A form of words derived from another by the transposition of some terms; a thing or action which is the exact opposite of another; *the* opposite or contrary. LME. 2 *Math.* A proposition whose premiss and conclusion are the conclusion and premiss of another. L16. 3 *Logic.* A converted proposition (CONVERT *v.* 4). M17.

converse /'kɒnvəːs/ *n.*[2] Now *literary* or *arch.* L15. [f. the vb.] 1 Social communication, intercourse. *obs.* exc. as passing into senses 2, 3. L15. 2 Informal spoken interchange of ideas etc., conversation. L16. †**b** A conversation. M17–L18. 3 Spiritual or mental intercourse, communion. M17. †4 = CONVERSATION 6. M17–E18. †5 = CONVERSATION 3. M17–E18.

2 I. MURDOCH Ann was sitting . . in close converse with Douglas Swann. 3 W. SHENSTONE With Nature here high converse hold.

¶ Orig. with pronunc. as the vb.

converse /'kɒnvəːs/ *a.*[1] & *n.*[3] ME. [(O)Fr. *convers* f. L *conversus* (use as n. of) pa. pple of *convertere* CONVERT *v.*] †**A** *adj.* Converted in mind or feeling. Only in ME. **B** *n.* †1 A religious convert. LME–L15. 2 *Hist.* = CONVERSUS. LME.

converse /'kɒnvəːs/ *a.*[2] L16. [L *conversus* turned about, transformed: see prec.] That is the opposite of something expressed or implied; reversed; contrary.

conversely /'kɒnvəːsli, kən'vəːsli/ *adv.* E19.

converse /kən'vəːs/ *v.* LME. [(O)Fr. *converser* f. L *conversari*, middle voice of *conversare* turn round, f. as CON- + *versare* frequent. of *vertere* turn.] **I** *v.i.* †1 Live, dwell, (*in*, *among*). LME–E18. †2 Consort, be familiar; have sexual relations; deal, trade. Foll. by *with*. LME–E19. 3 Be engaged *in*; have to do, be conversant, *with*. *obs.* exc. as *fig.* use of sense 5. L16. 4 Communicate, interchange ideas, (*with*). *obs.* in *gen.* sense. L16. 5 Commune *with*. L16. 6 Engage in conversation, talk, (*with* a person, *on* or *about* a subject). E17. **II** *v.t.* †7 Associate with; talk with. M17–E18.

converser *n.* L16.

conversi *n.* pl. of CONVERSUS.

conversible /kən'vəːsɪb(ə)l/ *a.*[1] *rare.* M16. [Late L *conversibilis*, f. *convers-*: see CONVERSION, -IBLE.] Able to be converted or transposed.

conversible /kən'vəːsɪb(ə)l/ *a.*[2] E18. [Alt. of CONVERSABLE after -IBLE.] = CONVERSABLE.

conversion /kən'vəːʃ(ə)n/ *n.* ME. [(O)Fr. f. L *conversio(n-)*, f. *convers-* pa. ppl stem of *convertere*: see CONVERT *v.*, -ION.] **I** Change in character, nature, etc. 1 *Theol.* The turning of sinners to God; a change from sinfulness to righteousness. ME. 2 The action of bringing a person over, or the fact of being brought over, to a particular belief or opinion, *spec.* to a religious faith. LME. 3 The action or an act of changing or being changed (*to* or *into* something else); (esp. structural) alteration for a different function. LME. **b** *spec.* The structural adaptation of (part of) a building for new purposes; (a part of) a building so modified. E20. **c** *Gram.* Change of the function or class of a word; zero derivation. E20. **d** *Rugby* & *N. Amer. Football.* The action or an act of scoring immediately following a try, by kicking the ball over the crossbar from a place-kick. E20. **e** The transformation of fertile into fissile material in a nuclear reactor. M20. †4 *Mil.* The converting of files into ranks; a change of front to a flank. L16–M19.

2 S. LEWIS To be picked out as a missionary within half an hour of his conversion! OED Conversion to Free Trade principles. 3 BACON Artificiall Conuersion of Water into Ice. P. NORMAN Conversion of the High Street shop into a café.

II Turning. †5 The action or an act of turning (*to* a particular direction) or of directing *to* some object; turning round, revolution, rotation; turning back, returning, *spec.* the solstice. LME–E18. 6 Transposition, inversion; *spec.* in *Logic*, (an instance of) the transposition of the subject and predicate of a proposition to form a new proposition. M16. †7 *Rhet.* = ANTISTROPHE 1. Also = APOSTROPHE *n.*[1] M16–M18. 8 *Law.* The action of wrongfully dealing with goods in a manner inconsistent with the owner's rights. E17.

8 N. BACON Fraudulent conversion of Treasure-trove.

III Change by substitution. 9 The change of moneys, stocks, units in which a quantity is expressed, etc., into others of a different kind. M16. †**b** (A) translation into another language. L16–M17. 10 *Law.* (An instance of) the changing of real property into personalty, or of joint into separate property, or vice versa. L18. 11 *Psychiatry.* The manifestation of a mental disturbance as a physical disorder or disease. L19.

Comb.: **conversion factor** (*a*) an arithmetical multiplier for converting a quantity expressed in one set of units into an equivalent expressed in another; (*b*) *Econ.* the manufacturing cost of a product relative to the cost of raw materials; **conversion hysteria**, **symptom**, etc. *Psychiatry*: manifesting conversion (sense 11 above).

conversionism *n.* preoccupation with bringing about the religious conversion of others L19. **conversionist** *n.* a person advocating or preoccupied with the religious conversion of others L19.

conversive /kən'vəːsɪv/ *a.* E17. [Obs. Fr. *conversif*, *-ive* = med.L *conversivus*, f. *convers-*: see prec., -IVE.] †1 = CONVERSE *a.*[2] E–M17. 2 Having the power or function of conversion. M17.

2 *waw conversive*: see WAW *n.*[3]

conversus /kən'vəːsəs/ *n.* Pl. **-versi** /-'vəːsʌɪ/. L18. [L: see CONVERSE *a.*[1] & *n.*[3]] *Hist.* A lay member of a monastery or convent, *esp.* one entering monastic life as a mature person.

convert /'kɒnvəːt/ *n.* & *a.* M16. [f. the vb, superseding and perh. infl. by synon. CONVERSE *n.*[3] Cf. VERT *n.*[2]] **A** *n.* A person (newly) converted to a religious faith, an opinion, a belief, etc. M16. †**B** *adj.* 1 Converted to a religious faith. E17–E19. 2 *convert brother*, *sister*, = CONVERSUS. M–L17.

convertism *n.* the system or practice of making converts E18. †**convertist** *n.* (*a*) = CONVERT *n.*; (*b*) = CONVERTER 2: E17–M18.

convert /kən'vəːt/ *v.* ME. [(O)Fr. *convertir* f. Proto-Romance var. of L *convertere* turn about, transform, f. as CON- + *vertere* turn.] **I** Turn. †1 *v.t.* Give a different direction to, turn about; direct. ME–L18. †2 *v.t.* Cause to return; restore. LME–M17. 3 *v.t.* Turn or apply *to* (another or a specific use), divert; *spec.* in *Law*, appropriate illegally *to one's own use*. LME. 4 *v.t.* Reverse in position, sense, or direction; invert, transpose. *obs.* exc. *Logic*, transpose the terms of (a proposition). LME.

1 SHAKES. *Sonn.* The eyes . . now converted are . . and look another way. GOLDSMITH The two kings . . agreed to convert their whole attention to the rescuing Jerusalem.

II Change in nature etc. 5 *v.t.* & †*i. Theol.* (Cause to) turn from a sinful to a righteous life. ME. 6 *v.t.* & *i.* (Cause to) turn to and adopt a particular faith, belief, opinion, course of action, etc.; *spec.* (cause to) adopt Christianity. (Foll. by *to*.) ME. †7 *v.t.* & *i.* (Cause to) change in mental state, disposition, etc. LME–L16. 8 *v.t.* Turn or change (*in*)*to* something different; change in character or function, transform. LME. †**b** Assimilate, digest. LME–M17. **c** *spec.* Make structural alterations in (a building). E19. 9 *v.i.* Undergo change or transformation (*to*, *into*). Now *esp.* be able or designed to be changed. M16. 10 *v.t.* & *i. Football.* Complete (a try, touchdown, etc.) by scoring a goal; score from (a penalty kick, place-kick, etc.). L19.

6 C. POTOK Many . . went away converted to his way of thinking. C. FREEMAN He marries a *goyisheh maidel* who converts and becomes more Jewish than any of them. D. CUPITT There were hopes of converting the Emperor . . and so eventually . . the whole country. 8 MILTON That . . lessens The sorrow, and converts it nigh to joy. R. HOGGART They convert an electric-kettle into a lethal weapon. A. HAILEY Night college classes . . converted young Paulsen to a graduate engineer. 9 S. WEINBERG The neutrons began to convert to protons. *Sunday Telegraph* The sofa . . converts into a double bed.

III Change by substitution. †11 *v.t.* Translate (*into* another language) M16–M17. 12 *v.t.* Change by substitution of something equivalent; change (moneys, stocks, etc.) into others of a different kind; express in terms of different units. M16. b *Law.* Change from real property to personalty, or from joint to separate property, or vice versa. L18.

12 LYNDON B. JOHNSON To convert their dollars into gold at the official rate of $35 an ounce. D. STOREY Struggling to convert a fraction of a yard into feet and inches.

converted *ppl a.* & *n.* (*a*) *adj.* that has been converted; (*b*) *n.pl.* the people who have been converted, as a class (*preaching to the converted*: see PREACH *v.*): L16. **convertive** *a.* (*rare*) (*a*) characterized by turning; (*b*) having the property of converting: E17.

convertend /ˈkɒnvətɛnd/ *n.* M19. [L *convertendus*, *-um* to be converted, gerundive of *convertere* CONVERT *v.*: see -END.] *Logic.* The proposition as it stands before conversion (CONVERSION 6).

converter /kənˈvəːtə/ *n.* M16. [f. CONVERT *v.* + -ER[1].] 1 A person who converts one thing into another, or who converts a thing to his or her own use. M16. 2 A person who makes converts. L16. 3 An apparatus for converting or transforming one thing into another; *spec.* (*a*) a refractory-lined retort in which air or oxygen can be passed through a charge of metal or ore in certain metallurgical (esp. steel-making) processes; (*b*) a device for altering the nature of an electrical current, esp. for the interconversion of alternating current and direct current or of analogue and digital data signals; (*c*) (in full *converter reactor*) a nuclear reactor that transforms fertile material into fissile material. M19.

3 BESSEMER *converter*. CATALYTIC *converter*. *rotary converter*: see ROTARY *a.*

convertible /kənˈvəːtɪb(ə)l/ *a.* & *n.* LME. [(O)Fr. f. L *convertibilis*, f. *convertere* CONVERT *v.*: see -IBLE.] A *adj.* 1 Interchangeable; (of terms) synonymous. LME. b *Logic.* That may be legitimately transposed by conversion (CONVERSION 6). L16. †2 Able to be turned or directed. L15–M17. 3 Able to be changed (*into* or *to* something else). M16. b Of a motor car etc.: having a roof that can be folded down or removed. E20. 4 Able to be converted to a religion, belief, opinion, etc. E19. 5 Able to be turned to a particular use or purpose. E19. 6 Able to be converted by exchange; *esp.* (*a*) (of paper money) able to be converted into coin; (*b*) (of currency etc.) that may be converted into gold or US dollars; (*c*) (of a bond, stock, etc.) that may be converted into other shares, esp. ordinary shares. M19. B *n.* 1 In *pl.* Interchangeable or synonymous things or terms. E17. 2 A motor car etc. with a folding or removable roof. E20. 3 A convertible bond etc. M20.

converti'bility *n.* M18. **convertibly** *adv.* E18.

convertiplane /kənˈvəːtɪpleɪn/ *n.* M20. [f. prec. + AEROPLANE *n.*] A type of aircraft combining certain features of the helicopter with those of a conventional aeroplane.

convertite /ˈkɒnvətʌɪt/ *n.* *arch.* M16. [f. CONVERT *n.* or *v.* + -ITE[1], after Fr. *converti* use as n. of pa. pple of *convertir* to convert.] 1 A person converted to righteousness or approved conduct; *spec.* a reformed prostitute. M16. 2 A convert to a religion, belief, etc. L16.

convex /ˈkɒnvɛks, *pred. also* kɒnˈvɛks/ *a.* & *n.* L16. [L *convexus* vaulted, arched. Cf. (O)Fr. *convexe*.] A *adj.* Having an outline or surface curved like the exterior of a circle or sphere; the reverse of concave. L16.

convex lens, mirror, etc.

B *n.* †1 A convex surface or body; a vault etc. as viewed from above or (*poet.*) below. E17–L18. 2 The convex part of something. E18. 3 A convex lens, mirror, etc. E18.

1 MILTON This huge convex of Fire . . immures us round Ninefold.

convexly *adv.* M18. **convexness** *n.* M18.

convex /ˈkɒnvɛks/ *v.t.* & *i.* L16. [f. the adj.] Make or become convex; bow or bend outwards. Orig. & chiefly as *convexed* ppl a.

convexity /kɒnˈvɛksɪti/ *n.* L16. [L *convexitas*, f. *convexus*: see CONVEX *a.* & *n.*, -ITY. Cf. Fr. *convexité*.] 1 The quality or condition of being convex. L16. 2 A convex curve, surface, side, or part. E17.

convexo- /kənˈvɛksəʊ/ *comb. form.* [f. CONVEX *a.* & *n.* + -O-.] Convexly, convex and —.

convexo-'concave *a.* convex on one side and concave on the other (and thickest in the centre: cf. CONCAVO-CONVEX) L17. **convexo-'convex** *a.* convex on both sides L19.

convey /kənˈveɪ/ *v.* & *n.* ME. [OFr. *conveier* (mod. *convoyer* CONVOY *v.*), f. med.L *conviare*, f. as CON- + *via* way.] A *v.t.* †1 Escort; convoy. ME–E18. 2 Lead, guide. Long *rare* (*Sc.*). ME. 3 Take from one place to another; transport, carry. LME. 4 Remove, take *away* (esp. secretly or clandestinely); make away with; *esp.* steal. *arch.* LME. 5 Transmit, transfer (esp. something immaterial); communicate, impart (a benefit, influence, sentiment, etc.); express, carry as a meaning. LME. †b Transfer secretly or furtively. E17–E18. †6 Bring down by succession, derive; transmit to posterity, hand down. LME–M18. †7 Carry on (an affair, business, etc.); manage. LME–M17. 8 *Law.* Transfer by deed or legal process. L15. 9 Act as a channel, path, or medium for the movement of; conduct. M16.

3 E. WAUGH They conveyed her to a nursing-home in Wimpole Street. I. MURDOCH She plucked a leaf, and conveyed it to her mouth. 4 SMOLLETT Teresa . . was . . detected in the very act of conveying a piece of plate. 5 HOBBES Any influence . . but such as is conveighed . . from the Soveraign Authority. V. WOOLF Her manner conveyed an extraordinary degree of sympathy. P. G. WODEHOUSE He could convey to Ruth that he thought her a . . neglected wife. G. GREENE He seemed to be looking for words . . with which to convey his meaning. 7 SHAKES. *Lear* I will . . convey the business as I shall find means. 9 DRYDEN Thro' reeden Pipes convey the Golden Flood. S. P. WOODWARD The auditory nerves convey impressions of sound.

†B *n.* 1 = CONVOY *n.* 2. LME–L17. 2 Conveyance. L16–E17.

conveyable *a.* †(*a*) having the quality of conveying; (*b*) that may be conveyed: M16.

conveyance /kənˈveɪəns/ *n.* LME. [f. prec. + -ANCE.] 1 The action of carrying or transporting; transport. LME. †2 Conduct (*of* an affair etc.), execution; skilful or cunning management; sleight of hand. LME–E18. b A secret or cunning device, an artifice, a trick. M16–M17. 3a Nimble carrying off; stealing. *arch.* L15. †b *gen.* Removal, riddance. M16–M17. 4 Transference, handing from one to another; *esp.* communication or imparting (*of* a thing, *to* a person). L15. †5 The conveying of meaning by words; expression; manner of expression, style. L15–L18. 6 Escorting; conduct. Long *arch. rare.* E16. 7 *Law.* (A document effecting) the transfer of the legal title to property. E16. 8 A conducting or communicating channel or medium; a passage. Now only *spec.* a conducting pipe in an organ. M16. 9 The conducting or transmission of fluid, heat, electricity, etc. L16. 10 A means of transport, a vehicle. L16.

7 *innocent conveyance*: see INNOCENT *a.*

conveyancer /kənˈveɪənsə/ *n.* E17. [f. prec. + -ER[1].] 1 = CONVEYER 1. E17. 2 A lawyer who prepares documents for the conveyance of property. M17.

conveyancing /kənˈveɪənsɪŋ/ *n.* L17. [f. CONVEYANCE + -ING[1].] †1 Deceitful contrivance. Only in L17. 2 (The branch of the law that deals with) the preparation of documents for the conveyance of property. E18.

conveyer /kənˈveɪə/ *n.* Also (the usual form in sense 4) **-or**. E16. [f. CONVEY *v.* + -ER[1], -OR.] 1 *gen.* A person who or thing which conveys something. E16. †2 A deft thief. M–L16. 3 A person who transfers property. M17. 4 A mechanical contrivance for conveying articles or materials during manufacture or processing; *esp.* (in full *conveyor belt*) an endless moving belt of rubber, canvas, etc., for this purpose. E19.

4 *fig.*: G. CLARE For Grandmother this conveyor-belt production of sons must have been traumatic.

conveyorize *v.t.* equip with a conveyor, carry out by means of a conveyor M20.

convict /ˈkɒnvɪkt/ *n.* L15. [f. original pa. pple & ppl a. of next, w. subsequent shift of stress.] 1 *gen.* A person judicially convicted of a criminal offence. *arch.* L15. 2 *spec.* A criminal serving a sentence of imprisonment or (*Hist.*) penal servitude, transportation, etc. L18.

convictism *n.* (*Hist.*) the system of penal settlements for convicts; the body of convicts so treated: M19.

convict /kənˈvɪkt/ *v.* Pa. pple & ppl a. **convicted**, (earlier, now *arch.*) **convict**. ME. [L *convict-* pa. ppl stem of *convincere* CONVINCE.] I *v.t.* 1 Prove to be guilty by judicial procedure; declare guilty by the verdict of the jury or by the decision of the judge. (Foll. by *of*, †*for*, †*to have done*.) ME. b Prove or declare guilty of an error or reprehensible conduct. LME. †2 = CONVINCE 3. ME–M17. †3 Demonstrate, prove. LME–M18. †4 Overcome; vanquish; conquer. LME–E17. 5 Cause (a person) to admit or realize his or her sinfulness or error. E16. 6 Disprove; refute. *arch.* M16.

1 COVERDALE A convicte transgressour of the lawe. J. CONRAD A city clerk . . gets himself convicted of a common embezzlement. b J. MORLEY Convicted . . of want of sensibility. 4 SHAKES. *John* A whole armado of convicted sail Is scattered and disjoin'd from fellowship. 5 B. JOWETT He is supposed to have a mission to convict men of self-conceit. 6 G. GROTE No man shall be able to convict you in dialogue.

II *v.i.* 7 Bring in a verdict of guilty, make a conviction. M19.

7 J. THURBER The testimony . . was, under the law, not enough to convict.

convictable *a.* L18.

conviction /kənˈvɪkʃ(ə)n/ *n.* LME. [L *convictio(n-)*, f. as prec.: see -ION.] 1 Proof of guilt by judicial procedure; (a) declaration of guilt by the verdict of the jury or by the decision of the judge; the fact or condition of being convicted of an offence. LME. †2 Proof or detection of error; confutation; exposure. L16–E18. 3 The act of convincing someone of something. Now *rare.* M17. 4 Awakened consciousness of sin; a feeling of one's own sinfulness. M17. 5 The condition of being convinced; strong belief on the ground of satisfactory reasons or evidence; convincing quality of expression; a settled belief or opinion. L17.

1 A. URE The perjury of the witnesses placed an effectual barrier against conviction. L. DURRELL Impossible to secure convictions against people unless caught *in flagrante delicto*. **summary conviction**: by judge or magistrates without a jury. 3 J. SULLIVAN To require something more for the conviction of the experimentalist. 5 S. JOHNSON A painful conviction of his defects. O. WISTER Every good man in this world has convictions about right and wrong. F. WELDON Her lack of conviction showed through: the words on the page rang false. *carry conviction*: see CARRY *v.* *courage of one's convictions*: see COURAGE *n.* 4.

convictive /kənˈvɪktɪv/ *a.* E17. [f. CONVICT *v.* + -IVE.] Having the power of producing conviction, convincing.

convictively *adv.* M17. **convictiveness** *n.* M17.

convictor /kənˈvɪktə/ *n.* M17. [L = a person who lives with another, f. *convict-* pa. ppl stem of *convivere*, f. as CON- + *vivere* live: see -OR.] A person who eats at a communal table; a boarder, esp. in a Roman Catholic seminary etc.

convince /kənˈvɪns/ *v.t.* M16. [L *convincere* convict of error, refute, f. as CON- + *vincere* overcome.] I †1 Overcome; vanquish. M16–M17. †2 Overcome in argument; confute. M16–E18. 3 Persuade to believe firmly the truth (*of*, *that*); satisfy by argument or evidence; in *pass.*, be firmly persuaded. E17. b Prevail upon, persuade *to do*. Chiefly *N. Amer.* M20. 4 Bring (a person) to an awareness *of* his or her sinfulness or error. M17.

1 SHAKES. *Macb.* His two chamberlains Will I with wine and wassail so convince That memory . . shall be a fume. 2 MILTON Satan stood . . confuted and convinced Of his weak arguing and fallacious drift. 3 SCOTT FITZGERALD I suspected that he was pulling my

leg, but a glance.. convinced me otherwise. M. DRABBLE I couldn't convince him that I didn't care. M. AMIS Herbert.. seems pretty well convinced it will be him.

†II 5 = CONVICT v. I. M16–L18. 6 Demonstrate, prove; expose in its true character; prove (a quality etc.) *of* its possessor. M16–M18. 7 Disprove; refute. M16–E17.

convinced *ppl a.* firmly persuaded L17. **convincement** *n.* conviction E17. **convincer** *n.* M17. **convincing** *a.* that convinces; able to convince: E17. **convincingly** *adv.* M17. **convincingness** *n.* M17.

convincible /kən'vɪnsɪb(ə)l/ *a.* M17. [Late L *convincibilis*, f. *convincere*: see prec., -IBLE.] Orig., able to be convicted. Now, able to be convinced.

†convival *n.* & *a.* E17. [L *convivalis*: see CONVIVIAL, -AL¹.] A *n.* A guest. Only in E17. B *adj.* = CONVIVIAL. M17–M18.

convive /kɔ̃viːv (*pl. same*), 'kɒnvʌɪv/ *n.* M17. [(Fr. f.) L *conviva*, f. *convivere* live together with, f. as CON- + *vivere* live.] A member of a company who eat together, a fellow feaster.

†convive *v.i. rare* (Shakes.). Only in E17. [L *convivere*: see prec.] Feast together.

convivial /kən'vɪvɪəl/ *a.* M17. [L *convivialis*, *convivalis* (cf. CONVIVAL), f. *convivium* feast, f. as CON- + *vivere* live: see -IAL.] 1 Of or befitting a feast or banquet; festive. M17. 2 Fond of feasting and good company; jovial. E18.

1 J. CONRAD He sang his praises.. over a convivial glass. 2 W. COWPER The plump convivial parson.

convivialist *n.* a person of convivial habits E19. **convivi'ality** *n.* the quality of being convivial; (the enjoyment of) festivity; convivial spirit: L18. **convivially** *adv.* E19.

convocate /'kɒnvəkeɪt/ *v.t. arch.* Pa. pple & ppl a. **-ate** /-ət/ (earlier), **-ated**. M16. [L *convocat-* pa. ppl stem of *convocare*: see CONVOKE, -ATE³.] Call or summon together.

convocation /kɒnvə'keɪʃ(ə)n/ *n.* LME. [L *convocatio(n-)*, f. as prec.: see -ATION.] 1 The action of calling together or assembling by summons; the state or fact of being called together. LME. 2 *gen.* An assembly of people called together or summoned. LME. 3 A provincial assembly of the clergy. Now *spec.* a synod of the Anglican clergy of the province of Canterbury or York. LME. 4 A legislative or deliberative assembly of certain universities. E16. †5 The parliament of tinners in Cornwall. Cf. STANNATOR. Only in 18.

convocational *a.* M17.

convoke /kən'vəʊk/ *v.t.* L16. [L *convocare* call together, f. as CON- + *vocare* call.] Call together; summon to assemble.

R. L. STEVENSON Where soft joys prevail, where people are convoked to pleasure. D. ACHESON That the President convoke a world-disarmament committee.

convolute /'kɒnvəluːt/ *a.* & *n.* L18. [L *convolutus* pa. pple, f. as next.] A *adj.* 1 *Bot.* & *Zool.* Rolled longitudinally upon itself, as a leaf in the bud. L18. 2 *gen.* Convoluted. M19. B *n.* Something of a convoluted form; a convolution. M19.

convolute /'kɒnvəluːt/ *v. rare.* L17. [L *convolut-*: see CONVOLUTION.] †1 *v.t.* Twist or coil round (something); embrace. L17–E18. 2 *v.t.* & *i.* Twist or wind about; coil up. (Earlier as CONVOLUTED.) E19.

convoluted /'kɒnvəl(j)uːtɪd/ *a.* L18. [f. prec. + -ED¹.] Coiled, twisted; complex, involved.

M. LASKI Elaborately convoluted fire-irons. B. CASTLE A convoluted statement of wonderful circularity.

convolution /kɒnvə'luːʃ(ə)n/ *n.* M16. [med.L *convolutio(n-)*, f. L *convolut-* pa. ppl stem of *convolvere*: see next.] 1 A fold, turn, or twist (of something coiled); a complexity. M16. b *spec.* Any of the folds of the surface of the brain. E17. 2 The action of coiling, twisting, or winding together; the condition of being convoluted. L16. 3 *Math.* An integral function of two or more given functions f_1, f_2, f_3, ... of the type $\int\int f_1(x)f_2(y-x)f_3(z-y)\,dxdydz$; an analogous summation. M20.

convolutional *a.* = CONVOLUTIONARY L19.

convolutionary *a.* of or pertaining to a convolution or convolutions, esp. of the brain E20.

convolve /kən'vɒlv/ *v.* L16. [L *convolvere*, f. as CON- + *volvere* to roll.] †1 *v.t.* Enclose in folds. L16–L18. 2 *v.t.* Roll together; coil; twist. Freq. as *convolved* ppl a., convoluted. M17. †3 *v.t.* In *pass.* Be contorted. M17–L18. 4 *v.i.* Revolve together. E19.

convolvulaceous /kənvɒlvjʊ'leɪʃəs/ *a.* M19. [f. mod.L *Convolvulaceae* (see below), f. as next: see -ACEOUS.] *Bot.* Of or pertaining to the family Convolvulaceae, to which belong convolvulus and numerous other twining plants.

convolvulus /kən'vɒlvjʊləs/ *n.* Pl. **-luses**, **-li** /-lʌɪ, -liː/. M16. [L = bindweed, f. as CONVOLVE.] Any member of the large genus *Convolvulus* of twining plants (e.g. some bindweeds) with slender stems and trumpet-shaped flowers; *loosely* = BINDWEED I.

convoy /'kɒnvɔɪ/ *n.* Orig. *Sc.* E16. [(O)Fr. *convoi*, f. as next.] †1 Conduct (of oneself or of affairs). *Sc.* Only in 16. 2 An escort for courtesy's sake or for guidance or protection; *esp.* (*a*) a funeral train or cortège; (*b*) a group of warships escorting unarmed vessels. E16. 3 The act of escorting as a courtesy or for guidance or protection; protection afforded by an escort. M16. 4 An individual, company, supply of provisions, etc., under (protective) escort; a group of merchant ships, vehicles, etc., travelling under escort or together. L16. †5a A conducting medium, channel, way, or path. L16–M17. b A brake for conducting a vehicle down an incline. Now *rare* or *obs.* M18. †6 A guide; a conductor. E17–E18.

2 P. HOLLAND Heavie funerals and convoies of the dead. DRYDEN And with a convoy send him safe away. 3 MILTON Through this adventurous glade.. to give him safe convoy. 4 A. HARDY Great merchant fleets, sailing in armed convoys. B. PLAIN A rumbling convoy of army vehicles.

Phrases: **in convoy** (travelling) under escort with others, as a group, together.

convoy /'kɒnvɔɪ/ *v.t.* Orig. &, exc. in the usual mod. sense (4), chiefly *Sc.* LME. [(O)Fr. *convoyer* var. & mod. form of *conveier* CONVEY.] 1 Convey, carry. Now *rare.* LME. †2 Conduct or carry through (an affair); manage. LME–L18. 3 Escort, conduct; accompany (as a guide). *arch.* LME. 4 Escort with, or as, an armed force for protection; *esp.* (of a warship) escort merchant vessels in a convoy. L15. †5 Conduct or lead (a band of men); conduct or drive (a vehicle). E16–M17.

convoyance *n.* (now *rare* or *obs.*) M16. **convoyer** *n.* L15.

convulsant /kən'vʌls(ə)nt/ *a.* & *n.* L19. [Fr., pres. pple of *convulser* CONVULSE.] (A drug) that produces convulsions. Cf. ANTICONVULSANT.

convulse /kən'vʌls/ *v.* & *n.* M17. [L *convuls-* pa. ppl stem of *convellere* pull violently, wrench, f. as CON- + *vellere* pluck, pull.] A *v.* 1 *v.t.* Shake violently; agitate or disturb severely. M17. 2 *v.t.* Affect with violent involuntary contraction of the muscles, producing contortion of the body or limbs; throw into convulsions. Usu. in *pass.* M17. 3 *v.i.* Become convulsed; go into convulsions. L17. 4 *v.t.* Throw into a violent fit of laughter. M18.

1 I. D'ISRAELI A revolution.. was to convulse England for many years. H. ROTH Suddenly a blind, shattering fury convulsed him. 3 S. HILL The limbs perked and convulsed before going still again. 4 M. HOLROYD If one caught sight of the other.. she would be convulsed with giggles.

B *n.* = CONVULSION. *rare.* E19.

convulsion /kən'vʌlʃ(ə)n/ *n.* M16. [Fr., or L *convulsio(n-)*, f. as prec.: see -ION.] 1 *Med.* Orig., cramp; spasms. Now, a violent involuntary contraction of the muscles producing contortion of the body or limbs. Freq. in *pl.* M16. †2 The action of wrenching; the condition of being wrenched. L16–E19. 3 Violent agitation or upheaval; social or political disturbance; violent natural disturbance, esp. produced by an earthquake etc. Usu. in *pl.* M17. 4 In *pl.* A violent fit of laughter. M18.

1 J. C. POWYS A person.. shaken by the convulsions of some terrible fit. 2 MILTON Those two massy pillars With horrible convulsion to and fro He tugged, he shook. 3 DISRAELI Her voice was choked with the convulsions of her passion. W. S. CHURCHILL The awful convulsions which would.. shiver into fragments the structures of the nineteenth century. E. F. BENSON The most terrific convulsion of Nature.

convulsional *a.* (*rare*) of, pertaining to, or of the nature of convulsion(s) M19. **convulsionist** *n.* (*Hist.*) (*a*) = CONVULSIONARY *n.*; (*b*) = CATASTROPHIST *n.*: E19.

convulsionary /kən'vʌlʃ(ə)n(ə)ri/ *n.* & *a.* M18. [f. prec. + -ARY¹, after Fr. *convulsionnaire.*] A *n. Hist.* A member of a sect of Jansenist fanatics in France in the 18th cent., who repeatedly threw themselves into convulsions. M18. B *adj.* 1 Pertaining to, affected with, or marked by convulsion(s). L18. 2 *Hist.* Of or pertaining to the convulsionaries. E19.

convulsive /kən'vʌlsɪv/ *a.* E17. [f. CONVULSE *v.* + -IVE. Cf. Fr. *convulsif.*] 1 Of the nature of or characterized by convulsion(s). E17. 2 Affected with convulsion(s). L17. 3 Producing convulsion(s). L17.

1 T. COLLINS The convulsive sobs which the girl vainly tried to repress. 3 DRYDEN Convulsive rage possess'd Her trembling limbs, and heav'd her lab'ring breast.

convulsively *adv.* L18. **convulsiveness** *n.* L19.

cony /'kəʊni/ *n.* Also (the usual form in *Her.*) **coney**; (*obs.* exc. as in sense 4b, where now the only form) **cunny** /'kʌni/. ME. [AN *coning*, OFr. *conin*, f. L *cuniculus*. In senses 4a & (esp.) 4b infl. by CUNT.] 1 A rabbit. Now *arch.* & *dial.* exc. *Her.* ME. 2 The skin or fur of a rabbit. ME. 3a A rock hyrax. (In biblical translations and allusions tr. Heb. *šāpān.*) LME. b A pika. *N. Amer.* L19. 4†a Used as a term of endearment or (later) abuse for a woman. Cf. CUNT 2. E16–L17. b The female genitals, the vulva, (= CUNT I). *coarse slang.* E17. †5 A dupe. Latterly only in *cony-catcher* below. L16–E19. 6 A sea bass, *Cephalopholis fulva*, of the tropical Atlantic. Also called *nigger fish*. (See also *cony-fish* below.) L19.

Comb.: **†cony-catch** *v.t.* dupe, gull; **†cony-catcher** (*a*) a person who catches rabbits; (*b*) a person who catches dupes, a swindler; **cony-fish** *dial.* a burbot; **cony-garth** (now *dial.*) a rabbit warren; **cony-wool** the fur of the rabbit.

¶The historical pronunc. is /'kʌni/, but during the 19th cent. this was superseded by /'kəʊni/ except in, and perh. partly because of, sense 4b.

conynger /'kʌnɪndʒə/ *n.* Long *obs.* exc. *dial.* Also **conyger** /'kʌnɪdʒə/, **conygree** /'kʌnɪgriː/, & other vars. ME. [OFr. *con(n)iniere* var. of *con(n)il(l)iere* f. med.L *cunicularium*, pl. *-aria*, f. L *cuniculus* rabbit: see -ARY¹.] A rabbit warren.

conyza /kə'nʌɪzə/ *n.* LME. [L f. Gk *konuza.*] Orig., fleabane (genus *Inula*) or a similar plant. Now, a plant of the genus *Conyza* (which formerly included *Inula* species), of the composite family.

coo /kuː/ *v.* & *n.* M17. [Imit.] A *v.* 1 *v.i.* Of a pigeon: make its natural soft murmuring sound. Of a person, esp. an infant: make a sound similar to this. M17. 2 *v.i.* Converse caressingly or amorously. Chiefly in *bill and coo* s.v BILL *v.*¹ 2b. L17. 3 *v.t.* Utter or express by cooing. L18. B *n.* A sound (as) of a pigeon. E18.

cooer *n.* M19. **cooingly** *adv.* in a cooing manner E19.

coo /kuː/ *int. slang.* Also **coo-er** /kuː'ɜː/. E20. [Imit.] Expr. surprise or incredulity.

cooba(h) *n.* var. of COUBA.

cooee /'kuːi, -iː/ *n.*, *int.*, & *v.* Chiefly *Austral.* & *NZ.* Also **cooey**. L18. [Imit. of a signal used by Aborigines and copied by settlers.] A *n.* & *int.* (A call or cry) used as a signal to draw attention to the caller. L18.

within (a) cooee (of) *colloq.* within hailing distance (of), within easy reach (of), near (to).

B *v.i.* Utter this call. E19.

coo-er *int.* see COO *int.*

cooey *n.*, *int.*, & *v.* var. of COOEE.

coof /kuːf/ *n. Sc.* E18. [Origin unkn.] A dull spiritless person.

cook /kʊk/ *n.* OE. [pop.L *cocus* for L *coquus*.] 1 A person (orig. *spec.* a male) who cooks, esp. as an occupation; a person responsible for the preparation of food for the table. OE. b *fig.* A person who falsifies or concocts something. *rare.* E17. 2 *Chess.* An unforeseen second solution that spoils a problem, position, etc. L19.

1 *Proverb*: Too many cooks spoil the broth. *plain cook*: see PLAIN *a.*[1] & *adv.*

Comb.: **cook-general**, pl. **cooks-general**, a domestic servant who does both housework and cookery; **cook-maid** a maid who cooks or assists a cook; **cook's knife** a general-purpose kitchen knife. (See also combs. of COOK *v.*)

cookess *n.* (*rare*) a female cook LME. **cookless** *a.* without a cook M19.

cook /kʊk/ *v.* LME. [f. the n.] 1 *v.i.* Act as cook; prepare food for eating with the application of heat. LME. 2a *v.t.* Prepare for eating with the application of heat. L15. b *v.i.* Of food: undergo the process of being cooked. M19. c *v.t.* & *i.* Prepare (opium) for use by heating. L19. 3 *v.t.* Concoct, make *up*, invent. E17. 4 *v.t.* Falsify; alter surreptitiously to produce a desired result. *colloq.* M17. 5 *v.t.* Ruin, spoil, defeat; *spec.* in *Chess*, spoil (a problem, position, etc.) by discovering an alternative solution. M19. 6 *v.t.* & *i.* Make or become radioactive. *colloq.* M20. 7 *v.i.* Play music with excitement or inspiration; perform or proceed well. *slang.* M20.

3 W. GOLDING I don't think there's a scientific explanation though . . you may cook one up. 4 *Times* The evidence about the bribes was the evidence of . . gentlemen who cooked the books. 5 H. ROBBINS You can't afford to sit still . . If you do, you're cooked.

Phrases: **cook a person's goose** *slang* spoil a person's plans, cause a person's downfall. **cook on the front burner, cook with gas** *N. Amer. slang* be on the right lines, be on the way to rapid success. *pressure cook*: see PRESSURE *n.* **what's cooking?** *colloq.* what is happening? what is being planned?

Comb.: **cookbook** a cookery book; *gen.* an instruction manual, a detailed account or list; **cook-camp** *N. Amer.* the part of a camp where the cooking is done; a building used as kitchen and eating-room; **cook-chill** *v.* & *n.* (*a*) *v.t.* cook and then immediately refrigerate (food) for later reheating; (*b*) *n.* the process or practice of cook-chilling food; **cookhouse, cook-room** an outdoor or camp kitchen; a ship's galley; **cook-shack** *N. Amer.* a shack used for cooking; **cookshop** an eating-house; *NZ* a sheep station's kitchen; **cook-stove** *US* a cooking-stove; **cooktop** a cooking unit, usu. with hot plates or burners, built into or fixed on the top of a cabinet etc.; **cookware** utensils used in cooking.

cookable *a.* & *n.* (something) that may be cooked M19.

cookee *n.* see COOKIE *n.*[2]

cooker /ˈkʊkə/ *n.* M19. [f. COOK *v.* + -ER[1].] 1 A person who concocts or manipulates something. M19. 2 A stove or other apparatus used for cooking; a vessel in which something is cooked. L19. 3 A fruit, esp. an apple, or other eatable, which cooks well, and is better eaten cooked than raw. L19.

2 *electric cooker, gas cooker, pressure cooker, slow cooker*, etc.

Comb.: **cooker hood** a canopy or hood above a cooker for extracting smells, smoke, etc.

cookery /ˈkʊk(ə)ri/ *n.* LME. [f. COOK *n.* or *v.* + -ERY.] 1 The art or practice of cooking; the preparation of food using heat. LME. 2 A place for cooking, a kitchen. Now *US.* L16. 3 The action of concocting a work, falsifying figures, etc. E18. 4 (An item of) cooked food. *rare.* M18.

Comb.: **cookery book** a book of recipes and instructions for cooking.

cookie /ˈkʊki/ *n.*[1] Orig. chiefly *Sc.* & *N. Amer.* Also **cooky**. E18. [Du. *koekje* dim. of *koek* cake.] 1 Any of various small cakes; (orig. *N. Amer.*) a small flat sweet cake, a biscuit. In Scotland also, a plain bun. E18. 2 A woman, *esp.* an attractive girl; a person of a specified kind. *slang.* E20. 3 A bomb. *Air Force slang.* M20.

1 **the way the cookie crumbles** *colloq.* (chiefly *N. Amer.*) how things turn out, the unalterable state of things. 2 W. R. BURNETT He's a real tough cookie and you know it.

Comb.: **cookie-cutter** (chiefly *N. Amer.*) a device with sharp edges for cutting dough for biscuits etc. into particular shapes; **cookie jar** a jar for biscuits etc.; *transf.* & *fig.* a place where good things are kept, a source of good things; **cookie-pusher** *US colloq.* a diplomat who devotes time to protocol and social engagements rather than to work, a person only superficially effective in his or her work; **cookie sheet** (chiefly *N. Amer.*) a flat metal tray on which biscuits etc. may be cooked.

cookie /ˈkʊki/ *n.*[2] Also (chiefly *N. Amer.*) **cookee, cooky.** L18. [f. COOK *n.* + -Y[6], -IE.] (A name for) a cook; *esp.* (*N. Amer.*) an assistant cook in a camp.

cooking /ˈkʊkɪŋ/ *vbl n.* M17. [f. COOK *v.* + -ING[1].] The action of COOK *v.*; style of this.

home cooking, plain cooking, etc.

Attrib. & *comb.*: In the sense 'suitable for or used in cooking', as *cooking apple, sherry*, etc. Special combs., as *cooking range*: see RANGE *n.*[1]; **cooking-stove** a stove used for cooking; **cooking top** = *cooktop* s.v. COOK *v.*

cookout /ˈkʊkaʊt/ *n.* Also **cook-out**. M20. [f. COOK *n.*, *v.* + OUT *adv.*] A gathering at which food is cooked in the open air; a barbecue.

Cook's tour /kʊks ˈtʊə, ˈtɔː/ *n. phr.* E20. [Thomas *Cook* (1808–92), Eng. travel agent.] A tour or journey in which many places are visited, often briefly.

cooky *ns.* vars. of COOKIE *n.*[1], *n.*[2]

cool /kuːl/ *n.* LME. [f. the adj.] 1 That which is cool or moderately cold; the cool part, place, time, etc. LME. 2 = COOLNESS I. Now *rare.* LME. 3 Composure, relaxedness. Esp. in *keep, lose, one's cool. slang.* M20.

1 M. SINCLAIR Papa walked in the garden in the cool of the evening. 3 S. BELLOW My interviewer's detachment or professional cool. *blow one's cool*: see BLOW *v.*[1]

cool /kuːl/ *a.* [OE *cōl* = MLG, MDu. *kōl* (Du. *koel*) f. Gmc, f. base also of COLD *a.*] 1 Moderately cold; agreeable and refreshing, in contrast with heat or cold; producing or maintaining a feeling of coolness; suggestive of coolness. OE. 2 Not affected by passion or emotion; undisturbed, calm. OE. b Assured and unabashed where diffidence might be expected; calmly audacious in making a proposal or demand. E19. 3 Lacking enthusiasm or warmth of interest; lacking in cordiality. L16. 4 Of a sum of money: actual, no less than. (Chiefly used as an intensive.) *colloq.* E18. 5 (Of jazz music, a jazz musician) restrained or relaxed in style (opp. *hot*); characteristic of those who favour relaxed music; *gen.* good, excellent, admirably up to date, stylish. *colloq.* M20.

2 D. LESSING Very cool, clear and efficient, she found . . a new flat and settled into it. b A. CHRISTIE Cool customer. Not giving anything away, is he? *Survey* A cool lack of morality is not . . a guarantee of foreign policy successes. A. EDEN A deed of cool and outstanding bravery. 3 E. GASKELL He had been friendly, though the Cranford ladies had been cool. 4 A. SILLITOE Mam collected a cool five hundred in insurance and benefits. 5 *Observer* They got long, sloppy haircuts . . and no-press suits with fat lapels. Very cool.

Phrases: *cool as a cucumber*: see CUCUMBER 2. **leave a person cool** not particularly excite or interest a person. *play it cool*: see PLAY *v.*

Special collocations & comb.: **cool box** an insulated box for keeping food cool. **cool chamber**: where perishable goods may be kept cool. **cool-headed** *a.* not easily excited; calm. **cool-house** a greenhouse kept at a cool temperature. **cool-store**: where perishable goods may be kept cool. **cool tankard** *arch.* a cooling drink, usu. made of wine, water, lemon-juice, spices, and borage.

coolish *a.* somewhat cool E18. **coolly** /-(l)li/ *adv.* L16.

cool /kuːl/ *v.* [OE *cōlian* = OS *cōlon*, f. Gmc, f. base of prec.: cf. KEEL *v.*[1]] 1 *v.i.* Become less hot; *fig.* become less zealous or ardent, lose the heat of excitement or passion. Freq. foll. by *down, off*, (*US colloq.*) *out.* OE. †b Of a thing: lose its opportuneness. *rare* (Shakes.). L16–E17. †c Of the senses: become cold with fear. *rare* (Shakes.). Only in E17. 2 *v.t.* Make less hot; cause to lose heat; *fig.* make less zealous or ardent, diminish the intensity of (strong feeling, resolve). Also foll. by *down*, (*US colloq.*) *out.* ME. b Deprive (a thing) of its opportuneness. *rare.* E18. 3 *v.t.* Kill. *US slang.* M20.

1 SCOTT FITZGERALD The rain cooled . . to a damp mist. T. MORRISON You want to calm down. . . Cool out. M. MEYER Strindberg cooled on the idea, the project lapsed. 2 B. SPOCK Bring to a boil, . . then cool it down to body temperature. B. PLAIN The hard slick metal cooled her burning shoulders and back.

Phrases: **cool it** *slang* calm down, relax, go more slowly. **cool one's heels** rest; be kept standing or waiting. *keep* or *save one's* BREATH *to cool one's porridge.*

coolabah /ˈkuːləbɑː/ *n. Austral.* Also **-lib-** /-lɪb-/, & other vars. L19. [Kamilaroi *gulubaa.*] More fully *coolabah tree.* Any of various eucalypts, esp. *Eucalyptus microtheca*, which is usu. found by watercourses.

coolamon /ˈkuːləmən/ *n. Austral.* Also **-liman** /-lɪmən/. M19. [Kamilaroi *gulaman.*] A vessel made of wood or bark for carrying water etc.

coolant /ˈkuːl(ə)nt/ *n.* M20. [f. COOL *v.* + -ANT[1], after LUBRICANT.] A cooling agent; *esp.* (*a*) a liquid used to cool and lubricate a cutting tool; (*b*) a fluid for removing heat from an engine or a nuclear reactor.

cooler /ˈkuːlə/ *n.* L16. [f. COOL *v.* + -ER[1].] 1 Something that cools or makes cool (*lit.* & *fig.*); *N. Amer.* a refrigerator, an insulated picnic-box, jug, etc. L16. b A cooling medicine (*arch.*); a cooling drink; a long drink, now *esp.* one containing some alcohol or for mixing with alcohol; a mixture of wine and soda-water, a spritzer. E17. 2 A vessel in which something is cooled; *spec.* one used for cooling the wort in brewing, or for crystallizing the syrup in sugar-refining. L16. b Something which cools water; a place where or machine from which cool drinking-water is available. *N. Amer.* M19. 3 A prison, a prison cell. *slang.* L19.

Cooley's anaemia /ˈkuːlɪz əˈniːmɪə/ *n. phr.* Also ***anemia.** M20. [Thomas B. *Cooley* (1871–1945), US paediatrician.] *Med.* = THALASSAEMIA *major.*

Coolgardie safe /kuːlˈgɑːdi seɪf/ *n. phr. Austral.* M20. [A town in Western Australia + SAFE *n.*] A food safe made of netting and cooled by strips of fabric suspended round it with their ends in water.

coolibah *n.* var. of COOLABAH.

coolie /ˈkuːli/ *n.* & *a.* Also **-ly**. L16. [Sense A.1 f. as KOLI. Sense A.2 f. Hind. & Telugu *kūlī* day-labourer, prob. f. Tamil Telugu *kūli* hire; assoc. w. Urdu *ḳulī* slave f. Turk.] A *n.* 1 = KOLI *n.* Now *rare* or *obs.* L16. 2 A (non-European) hired labourer or burden-carrier in India, China, and elsewhere. M17. b A person from the Indian subcontinent, a person of Indian descent. *derog.* & usu. considered *racially offensive. S. Afr.* L19.

B *attrib.* or as *adj.* That is a coolie; of or pertaining to coolies. E19.

coolie hat a broad conical hat, usu. made of straw, similar to those worn in Asia by coolies.

cooliman *n.* var. of COOLAMON.

cooling /ˈkuːlɪŋ/ *vbl n.* ME. [f. COOL *v.* + -ING[1].] The action of COOL *v.* (Foll. by *down, off.*)

Comb.: **cooling-off period**: to allow time for reflection before committing oneself; *cooling-pond*: see POND *n.* 2a; **cooling tower** a tall tower for cooling hot water from an industrial process before reuse.

coolness /ˈkuːlnɪs/ *n.* OE. [f. COOL *a.* + -NESS.] 1 The condition of being or feeling moderately cold. OE. 2 *fig.* Freedom from excitement. M17. 3 Lack of enthusiasm or friendly warmth. L17. 4 Calm and unabashed assurance. M18. 5 *Jazz.* A relaxed or cool quality or style. M20.

coolth /kuːlθ/ *n.* M16. [f. COOL *a.* + -TH[1]: cf. WARMTH.] = COOLNESS I.

¶Rare bef. 20.

cooly *n.* & *a.* var. of COOLIE.

coom /kuːm/ *n.* L16. [In senses 1, 2 app. a var. of CULM *n.*[1] In sense 3 prob. a different wd.] 1 Soot. *obs.* exc. *Sc.* & *north.* L16. 2 Coal dust or refuse. *obs.* exc. *Sc.* & *north.* E17. 3 A black grease or dust from axles or bearings. E18.

coomy *a.* dirty with coom E19.

coomb /kuːm/ *n.*[1] Also **comb.** [OE *cumb* prob. identical w. older LG *kumb*, HG *kump(f)*, mod.LG, HG *kumm*, mod.G *Kumme.*] †1 A vessel, a cup. Only in OE. †2 A brewing tub or vat. LME–M19. 3 A dry unit of capacity equal to four bushels. LME.

coomb /kuːm/ *n.*[2] Also **comb(e)**, **coombe**. [OE *cum(b)* f. Brit.: cf. CWM.] A deep hollow or valley, esp. on the side of a hill; a valley running up from the sea.

¶Not found in OE or ME literature, but occurring from early times in charters in place-names belonging to the south of England, many of which survive, e.g. *Batscombe*, *Southcombe*. Its present general use goes back to L16.

coomb *n.*[3] var. of COMB *n.*[2]

coon /kuːn/ *n.* & *v.* Chiefly *N. Amer.* M18. [Abbrev. of RACOON.] A *n.* I 1 = RACOON. M18. II Applied to persons. 2 *Hist.* One of the US Whigs (1834–56), who had the racoon as an emblem. M19. 3 A sly knowing person. *colloq.* M19. 4 A Black. *slang. derog.* & usu. considered *racially offensive* M19. 5 A member of any of the colourfully costumed competing dance troupes which parade through the streets of Cape Town during an annual New Year carnival. *S. Afr.* E20.

Comb. & phrases: **a coon's age** *US slang* a long time; *a gone coon*: see GONE *a.* 1; **coon-dog**, **-hound** *US* a dog trained to hunt racoons; **coonskin** *n.* & *a.* (*a*) *n.* (a cap etc. made from) the skin of a racoon; (*b*) *adj.* made from coonskin; **coon song** *arch.* (now usu. considered *racially offensive*) (a popular song resembling) a song sung by Blacks.

B *v.t.* & *i.* Creep along (a branch etc.) clinging close like a racoon. M19.

coon-can /ˈkuːnkan/ *n.* L19. [Perh. f. Sp. *¿con quién?* with whom?] A card-game of Mexican origin, for two players and ancestral to (gin) rummy. Formerly also, a form of this played with two packs each with two jokers.

coonjine /ˈkuːndʒʌɪn/ *v.* & *n.* *US slang.* L19. [Origin unkn.] A *v.i.* & *t.* Walk or carry in a waddling shuffling manner (orig. associated with Black riverboat loaders); sing songs while doing this. L19. B *n.* A waddling shuffling walk. M20.

coontie /ˈkuːnti/ *n.* *US.* Also **-tah** /-tə/. L18. [Seminole *kunti.*] Any of several low-growing palmlike cycads of the genus *Zamia*, native to tropical and subtropical America; the arrowroot yielded by these plants.

coop /kuːp/ *n.*[1] ME. [= MLG, MDu. *kūpe* (Du. *kuip* tub, vat) = OS *kōpa*, OHG *kuofa* (G *Kufe*) cask, f. L *cupa*, med.L *copa* tun, barrel.] †1 *gen.* A basket. Only in ME. 2 A wickerwork basket used in catching fish. ME. 3 A cage or pen for confining poultry etc. ME. 4 A narrow place of confinement; *slang* a prison. L18.

Phrases: **fly the coop** *N. Amer. slang* leave abruptly.

coop /kuːp/ *n.*[2] E19. [Origin unkn.] A small heap of soft material, esp. manure.

coop *n.*[3] var. of COUP *n.*[2]

coop /kuːp/ *v.t.* L16. [f. COOP *n.*[1]] 1 Put or confine (poultry etc.) in a coop. (Foll. by *up.*) L16. 2 Confine (a person) in an irksomely small space. Formerly also, confine (a thing or substance) within a vessel or narrow limits. Usu. foll. by *up.* L16. 3 Surround with a protective grating or fence. Now *rare* or *obs.* M17.

2 P. G. WODEHOUSE He had had a boring afternoon, cooped up in his room. R. SUTCLIFF Cooped within doors all winter long.

co-op /ˈkəʊɒp/ *n.* & *a.* *colloq.* M19. [Abbrev.] = COOPERATIVE; *spec.* a cooperative society, store, or (*N. Amer.*) dwelling.

Spare Rib This press is a co-op . . so please don't ask to see the boss . . or the manager. *New Yorker* We bought a co-op overlooking the Hudson on Riverside Drive.

cooper /ˈkuːpə/ *n.* & *v.* ME. [MDu., MLG *kūper*, f. as COOP *n.*[1]: see -ER[1].] A *n.* 1 A skilled worker who makes and repairs wooden vessels formed of staves and hoops, as casks, tubs, etc. ME. b A crew member on a ship who repairs casks etc. E17. 2 A person engaged in the trade of sampling, bottling, or retailing wine. E16. 3 A bottle-basket used in wine cellars. E19. 4 A drink composed of a mixture of stout and porter, orig. drunk by the coopers in breweries. L19.

Comb.: **cooper-shop** *arch.* a shop selling wine.

B *v.t.* 1 Make or repair the staves or hoops of (casks etc.); equip or secure with hoops. E18. 2 Put or stow in casks. M18. 3 Foll. by *up*: get into a presentable form. *colloq.* E19. 4 Ruin, spoil. *slang.* M19.

cooperage /ˈkuːp(ə)rɪdʒ/ *n.* L15. [f. COOPER *n.* + -AGE.] 1 Cooper's work; a cooper's products. L15. 2 Money payable for a cooper's work. M17. 3 A cooper's workshop. E18.

cooperant /kəʊˈɒpər(ə)nt/ *a.* & *n.* Also **co-operant**. LME. [eccl.L *cooperant-* pres. ppl stem of *cooperari*: see COOPERATE *v.*, -ANT[1].] A *adj.* Working together or for the same purpose. LME. B *n.* A cooperating agent or factor. *rare.* M16.

cooperancy *n.* (*a*) the state of being cooperant; †(*b*) cooperation: M17.

cooperate /kəʊˈɒpərət/ *a.* Also **co-operate**. M19. [f. COOPERATION after *corporation*, *corporate*, etc.] Caused to cooperate; brought into cooperation; cooperative.

cooperate /kəʊˈɒpəreɪt/ *v.i.* Also **co-operate**. L16. [eccl.L *cooperat-* pa. ppl stem of *cooperari*, f. as CO- + *operari* OPERATE: see -ATE[3].] 1 Of things: concur in producing an effect. L16. 2 Of people: work together for the same purpose or in the same task. Of an individual: act jointly with or *with* another (*in* a task, (*arch.*) *to* an end); participate in a joint or mutual enterprise. E17. 3 Practise economic or industrial cooperation. E19.

2 C. ODETS We want to make your boy famous, a millionaire, but he won't let us—won't co-operate D. MAY The French Vichy government . . co-operated erratically with the Germans.

cooperation /kəʊˌɒpəˈreɪʃ(ə)n/ *n.* Also **co-operation**. LME. [L *cooperatio(n-)*, f. as prec.: see -ATION. Later partly, through Fr. *coopération.*] 1 The action of working together for the same purpose or in the same task. LME. 2 The combination of a number of individuals in an economic activity so that all may share the benefits. E19.

1 C. BROOKE-ROSE Structures of power . . depend on the assistance and cooperation of innumerable individuals. 2 H. FAWCETT The essential characteristic of cooperation is a union of capital and labour.

cooperationist *n.* a person who practises or advocates cooperation M19.

cooperative /kəʊˈɒp(ə)rətɪv/ *a.* & *n.* Also **co-operative**. E17. [Late L *cooperativus*, f. as COOPERATE *v.*: see -IVE. Later partly, through Fr. *coopératif.*] A *adj.* 1 Working together, acting jointly; willing to cooperate; of or pertaining to cooperation. E17. 2 Pertaining to economic or industrial cooperation; based on the principle of cooperation; *N. Amer.* (of a dwelling) jointly owned or leased by the occupiers. E19.

1 H. H. MILMAN Four great principles . . mutually cooperative. G. BROWN The Boilermakers, often accused of being troublemakers . . , proved splendidly cooperative. 2 **cooperative farm**: in which the profits are shared by all those involved in it. **cooperative society** a union of people for the production or distribution of goods, in which the profits are shared by the members. **cooperative store** a store or shop belonging to a cooperative society, the profits being shared among the members and customers.

B *n.* 1 A cooperationist; a member of a cooperative society. *rare.* E19. 2 A cooperative society or store; an organization or business owned by its workers or those who use its services. L19. 3 A dwelling jointly owned or leased by the occupiers. *N. Amer.* M20.

cooperatively *adv.* M19. **cooperativeness** *n.* M17. **coopera'tivity** *n.* L20. **cooperativi'zation** *n.* the action of organizing or restructuring as a cooperative or as cooperatives M20.

cooperator /kəʊˈɒpəreɪtə/ *n.* Also **co-operator**. LME. [eccl.L = fellow-worker, f. as COOPERATE *v.*: see -OR.] 1 A person who cooperates. LME. 2 A cooperationist; a member of a cooperative society. E19.

Cooper pair /ˈkuːpə pɛː/ *n. phr.* M20. [L. N. *Cooper* (b. 1930), US physicist.] A loosely bound pair of electrons with opposite spins and moving with the same speed in opposite directions, held to be responsible for the phenomenon of superconductivity; a similar bound pair of atoms in a superfluid.

For other words beginning with *co-* see the entry for **co-**

Cooper's hawk /ˈkuːpəz hɔːk/ *n. phr.* E19. [William *Cooper* (1798–1864), US naturalist.] A N. American bird of prey, *Accipiter cooperii*, resembling but smaller than the goshawk.

coopery /ˈkuːp(ə)ri/ *n.* LME. [f. COOPER *n.* + -Y[3]: see -ERY.] = COOPERAGE 1.

co-opt /kəʊˈɒpt/ *v.* Also ***coöpt**. M17. [L *cooptare*, f. as CO- + *optare* choose.] 1 *v.t.* & *i.* Elect (a person) to a body by the votes of its existing members. M17. 2 *v.t.* Absorb into a larger (esp. political) group; take over, adopt, (an idea etc.). *N. Amer.* M20.

co-optable *a.* L20. **co-optee** *n.* a person who is co-opted M20. **co-option** *n.* the action of co-opting L19. **co-optive** *a.* pertaining to co-option; (composed of members) chosen by co-option: L19.

co-optate /kəʊˈɒpteɪt/ *v.t.* Now *rare.* Also ***coöp-**. E17. [L *cooptat-* pa. ppl stem of *cooptare*: see prec., -ATE[3].] = CO-OPT. Formerly more widely, elect, choose, admit to a body.

co-optative *a.* = CO-OPTIVE L19.

co-optation /kəʊɒpˈteɪʃ(ə)n/ *n.* Also ***coöp-**. M16. [L *cooptatio(n-)*, f. as prec.: see -ATION.] Election into a body by the votes of its existing members. Formerly more widely, election, adoption.

coordinate /kəʊˈɔːdɪnət/ *a.* & *n.* Also **co-ordinate**, ***coör-**. M17. [f. CO- + L *ordinatus* (see ORDINATE *a.*) after earlier SUBORDINATE *a.*] A *adj.* 1 Of the same order; equal in rank (*with*); *Gram.* designating each clause of a compound sentence. Opp. SUBORDINATE *a.* M17. 2 Involving coordination, coordinated. M18. 3 *Chem.* Designating a type of covalent bond in which one atom, ion, or molecule provides both the shared electrons. E20. 4 Designating a university having separate classes or colleges for men and women students or a college, esp. for women, of such a university. *US.* E20.

B *n.* 1 *Math.* Each of a set of two or more quantities used to define the position of a point, line, or plane, by reference to a fixed system of lines, points, etc. E19. 2 A person or thing of the same rank as another; an equal; an equivalent; *US* a coordinate college. M19. 3 In *pl.* Clothes matching in colour, fabric, or other features. M20.

1 *Cartesian coordinates*, *homogeneous coordinates*, *polar coordinates*, *rectangular coordinates*, *trilinear coordinates*, etc. 2 *Publishers Weekly* Kirkland College in Clinton, N.Y., the women's co-ordinate of prestigious Hamilton College for men.

coordinately *adv.* L17.

coordinate /kəʊˈɔːdɪneɪt/ *v.* Also **co-or-**, ***coör-**. M17. [f. CO- + L *ordinare* (see ORDINATE *v.*), after SUBORDINATE *v.*] 1 *v.t.* Make coordinate or equal; place or class in the same rank or division. M17. 2 *v.t.* Cause (things or persons) to function together or occupy their proper place as parts of an interrelated whole. M19. 3 *v.i.* Act in the proper order for the production of a particular result. M19. 4 *v.t.* & *i.* *Chem.* Be or become linked *with* or *to* (an atom or atoms) by a coordinate bond; form a coordinate bond or coordination compound (with). E20.

1 **coordinating conjunction** *Gram.*: placed between words, phrases, clauses, or sentences of equal rank, e.g. *and*, *but*. 2 D. LESSING Nothing would work if someone didn't co-ordinate things.

coordinative *a.* †(*a*) involving coordination; (*b*) placing in proper order, coordinating: M17. **coordinator** *n.* (*a*) a person who or thing which coordinates; (*b*) *Gram.* a coordinating conjunction: M19.

coordination /kəʊˌɔːdɪˈneɪʃ(ə)n/ *n.* Also **co-ordination**, ***coör-**. E17. [(O)Fr., or late L *coordinatio(n-)*, f. L CO- + *ordinatio(n-)* ORDINATION.] †1 Orderly combination. E–M17. 2 The action or result of placing in the same degree or rank. M17. 3 The action or result of placing things in due order or relation to each other; the harmonious functioning together of different interrelated parts. M19. 4 *Chem.* The formation or existence of a coordinate bond; linking by means of a coordinate bond. E20.

3 E. H. ERIKSON Man's . . highly specialized brain-eye-hand coordination.

Comb.: **coordination compound** *Chem.*: containing coordinate bonds, esp. between a central atom (usu. of a metal) and a definite number of other atoms or groups; **coordination number** *Chem.* (*a*) the number of atoms linked to the central atom or group in a coordination compound; (*b*) the number of ions surrounding a molecule or ion in a crystal.

coot /kuːt/ *n.*[1] ME. [Prob. of LG origin: cf. Du. *koet.*] 1 An aquatic bird, *Fulica atra*, belonging to the rail family, with black and dark grey plumage and the upper mandible extended backwards to form a white plate on the forehead; any other bird of the genus *Fulica*, esp. *F. americana* of N. America. ME. 2 Any of various other swimming or diving birds, *esp.* (*a*) the guillemot; (*b*) the water rail; (*c*) the moorhen. *dial.* ME. 3 A silly person; a man, a chap. *colloq.* M18.

1 *as bald as a coot, bald coot, baldicoot*: see BALD *a.* 3 X. HERBERT He's a good sort of coot. R. CHANDLER The widow of an old coot with whiskers.

coot /kuːt/ *n.*[2] *Sc.* Also †**cute.** E16. [Of LG origin.] 1 The ankle joint. E16. 2 The fetlock of a horse. Now *rare.* L17.

Cootamundra /kuːtəˈmʌndrə/ *n.* E20. [A town in New South Wales, Australia.] More fully *Cootamundra wattle.* A small Australian tree, *Acacia baileyana*, with feathery foliage and fluffy golden flowers.

cooter /ˈkuːtə/ *n.*[1] E19. [Origin unkn.] Any of several freshwater turtles of the southern US, esp. of the genus *Pseudemys*. Cf. SLIDER 4.

cooter *n.*[2] var. of COUTER.

cootie /ˈkuːti/ *n. slang.* Also **k-.** E20. [Perh. f. Malay *kutu* a biting insect.] A body louse.

cootie /kuːti/ *a. Sc.* Also **cooty.** L18. [f. COOT *n.*[2] + -Y[1].] Of a bird: having feathered legs.

cop /kɒp/ *n.*[1] OE. [Origin unkn. Several different wds may be represented.] 1 The top of something, esp. a hill. OE. †**b** A crest on a bird's head. L15–L18. 2 A conical heap of unbound barley, hay, etc. *dial.* E16. 3 A conical ball of thread wound on a spindle in a spinning-machine. L18. 4 A hedge bank; an embankment. *dial.* E19.

cop /kɒp/ *n.*[2] Long *obs.* exc. *dial.* LME. [Abbrev. of ATTERCOP.] A spider.

cop /kɒp/ *n.*[3] *obs.* exc. *dial.* L17. [Origin unkn.] A movable frame used to extend the surface of a farm cart for bulky loads.

cop /kɒp/ *n.*[4] *slang.* M19. [f. COP *v.*[2], COPPER *n.*[2]] 1 A police officer. M19. 2 A capture, an arrest. Chiefly in *a fair cop* s.v. FAIR *a.* L19. 3 An acquisition; a welcome chance or opportunity. Chiefly *Austral.* & *NZ.* L19. 4 Value or use, esp. in something acquired. Chiefly w. neg. E20.

1 **cops and robbers** a children's game of hiding and chasing. *motor cop*: see MOTOR *n.* & *a.* *silent cop*: see SILENT *a.*

Comb.: **cop-shop** a police station.

cop /kɒp/ *v.*[1]*t.* Now *dial.* Infl. **-pp-.** M16. [f. COP *n.*[1]] Heap up; stack.

cop /kɒp/ *v.*[2] *slang* (orig. *dial.*). Infl. **-pp-.** E18. [Prob. var. of CAP *v.*[2]] 1 *v.t.* Capture, catch; get, obtain; steal. E18. 2 *v.t.* w. *it* (the usual form), *one*, & *i.* w. *out.* Get into trouble, be punished; die. L19. 3 *v.t.* Strike (a person). (Foll. by *one.*) L19. 4 *v.i.* Foll. by *out*: escape; drop out of something; evade a responsibility or decision; go back on a promise. M20.

Phrases: *cop a packet*: see PACKET *n.* 3. *cop a plea*: see PLEA *n.* 2c.

copacetic /kəʊpəˈsɛtɪk, -ˈsiːt-/ *a. N. Amer. slang.* Also **-set-.** E20. [Origin unkn.] Excellent; in good order.

copaiba /kəʊˈpʌɪbə/ *n.* Also **-va** /-və/. E17. [Port. *copaíba* (whence Sp. *copaiba*) f. Tupi *copaíba*, Guarani *cupaíba.*] A balsam of aromatic odour and acrid taste obtained from S. American leguminous trees of the genus *Copaifera* and used in medicine and the arts. Formerly also, a tree yielding this.

copal /ˈkəʊp(ə)l/ *n.* L16. [Sp. f. Nahuatl *copalli* incense.] A hard translucent odoriferous resin obtained from various tropical trees and used to make a fine transparent varnish. Also *gum copal.*

copalm /ˈkəʊpɑːm/ *n.* L18. [Louisiana Fr. *copalme* f. *palme de copal* (cf. prec.).] The N. American liquidambar or sweet gum tree, or its timber; a balsam (liquid storax) got from it.

coparcenary /kəʊˈpɑːs(ə)n(ə)ri/ *n.* & *a.* E16. [f. CO- + PARCENARY. The adj. by assoc. w. -ARY[1].] *Law.* **A** *n.* 1 Joint heirship; the status of a coparcener. E16. 2 Copartnership; joint ownership. L16. **B** *adj.* Of or pertaining to coparceners. M19.

coparceny *n.* = COPARCENARY *n.* M16.

coparcener /kəʊˈpɑːs(ə)nə/ *n.* LME. [f. CO- + PARCENER.] *Law.* A person who shares equally with others in the inheritance of an undivided estate or in the rights to it (in the UK now as equitable interests).

†**copart(i)ment** *ns.* vars. of COMPARTMENT *n.*

copartner /kəʊˈpɑːtnə/ *n.* LME. [f. CO- + PARTNER.] A person who shares or takes part with another (*in* any activity, undertaking, etc.). Formerly = COPARCENER.

copartnership *n.* the relationship of copartners; a company or association of copartners: L16. **copartnery** *n.* (a) copartnership L17.

copasetic *a.* var. of COPACETIC.

†**copataine** *n. rare* (Shakes.). Only in L16. [Origin unkn.] A sugar-loaf hat.

cope /kəʊp/ *n.*[1] ME. [med.L *capa* var. of late L *cappa* CAP *n.*[1]] †1 A long cloak or cape worn outdoors. ME–M18. 2 *Eccl.* A semicircular cloak of rich material worn in processions and on other, chiefly non-Eucharistic, occasions. ME. 3 *fig.* Anything likened to a cloak or canopy; *esp.* the vault of heaven, the firmament. LME. 4 *Founding.* The upper or outer part of a flask. M19.

3 ADDISON The dark cope of night. W. DE LA MARE Heaven's midnight cope. **under the cope of heaven** *arch.* in all the world.

Comb.: **copestone** the top or head stone of a building; chiefly *fig.*, a finishing touch.

†**cope** *n.*[2] E16–L18. [f. COPE *v.*[1] or f. OFr. *co(l)p*: see COPE *v.*[1]] An encounter in combat.

cope /kəʊp/ *n.*[3] E16. [f. COPE *v.*[3]] †1 *God's cope*, a very large sum. E–M16. 2 A bargain. Now *dial.* M16. 3 A duty payable by Derbyshire miners for permission to raise lead ore. M17.

Comb.: **copeman**, †**copes-** *arch.* a merchant.

cope /kəʊp/ *v.*[1] ME. [OFr. *co(l)per* (mod. *couper*) strike, cut, f. *co(l)p* blow f. med.L *colpus*: see COUP *n.*[1] Cf. COUP *v.*[2]] **I** *v.i.* 1 Strike, hit; come to blows *with*; engage or meet (*together*) in battle. *arch.* & *dial.* ME. 2 Contend successfully *with* (an opponent, difficulty, situation, etc.); *colloq.* deal competently with one's life or situation. L16. 3 Have to do *with*; come into contact or relation *with. arch.* L16.

2 E. A. FREEMAN An army able to cope with the insurgents. B. PYM It wasn't as if Marcia was an invalid or unable to cope.

II *v.t.* †4 Meet. L16–E17. †5 Match (something) *with* an equivalent. *rare* (Shakes.). Only in L16.

cope /kəʊp/ *v.*[2] LME. [f. COPE *n.*[1]] 1 *v.t.* Supply with or dress in a cope. Chiefly as *coped* ppl a. LME. 2 *v.t.* Cover with or as with a coping. E16. 3 *v.i.* & *t.* (Cause to) slope down or hang *over* like a coping. E17. 4 *v.t.* Cover as with a vault or canopy. E18.

cope /kəʊp/ *v.*[3] LME. [MDu., (M)LG *kōpen* rel. to OHG *koufen*, *koufōn*: see CHEAP *v.*] †1 *v.t.* Buy. LME–L16. 2 *v.t.* Exchange, barter (*away*). Now *dial.* L16. †3 *v.i.* Make an exchange or bargain. L16–E17.

cope /kəʊp/ *v.*[4]*t.* L16. [App. f. OFr. *coper* cut: see COPE *v.*[1]] Cut or pare (the beak or talons of a hawk).

cope /kəʊp/ *v.*[5]*t.* Long *obs.* exc. *dial.* E17. [Origin unkn.] Tie or sew up or *up* the mouth of (a ferret); stop (a person) from talking.

copek *n.* var. of KOPEK.

†**copemate** *n.* Also **copes-.** M16. [f. COPE *v.*[1] + MATE *n.*[2], w. assim. to *cope(s)man.*] 1 An adversary. M16–M17. 2 A partner, a colleague; a companion; *spec.* a lover, a spouse. L16–L17. 3 A man. *colloq.* or *contempt.* L16–M18.

copen /ˈkəʊp(ə)n/ *n. N. Amer.* E20. [Abbrev. of *Copenhagen*, Eng. form of Da. *København*, the capital of Denmark.] In full *copen blue.* A strong light blue colour.

copepod /ˈkəʊpɪpɒd/ *n.* & *a.* L19. [mod.L *Copepoda* pl., f. Gk *kōpē* handle, oar + -POD.] **A** *n.* A crustacean of the class Copepoda, which comprises small aquatic, mostly marine, organisms without a carapace and with paddle-like feet used for swimming. L19. **B** *adj.* Of or pertaining to a copepod or copepods. L19.

coˈpepodan *a.* pertaining to or characteristic of copepods L19. **coˈpepodid** *a.* & *n.* (*a*) *adj.* designating or characteristic of certain free-swimming stages in the development of some copepods, following naupliar stages; (*b*) *n.* a copepodid individual: E20. **coˈpepodous** *a.* = COPEPODAN L19.

coper /ˈkəʊpə/ *n.* M16. [f. COPE *v.*[3] + -ER[1].] A dealer, a merchant; *spec.* a horse-dealer.

Copernican /kəˈpəːnɪk(ə)n/ *a.* & *n.* M17. [f. *Copernicus* (see below) Latinized form of *Koppernigk* + -AN.] **A** *adj.* Of or pertaining to the Polish astronomer Copernicus (1473–1543) or his theory that the planets, including the earth, revolve around the sun. M17. **B** *n.* A person who holds the Copernican theory. M17.

Copernicanism *n.* (belief in) the Copernican theory E19.

coperta /kəˈpəːtə/ *n.* L19. [It. = covering, f. *coprire* to cover f. L *coperire*, *cooperire* COVER *v.*[2]] A transparent lead glaze given as a final glaze to some majolica.

†**copesmate** *n.* var. of COPEMATE.

cophosis /kəˈfəʊsɪs/ *n.* Now *rare* or *obs.* M17. [Gk *kōphōsis*, f. *kōphos* deaf: cf. -OSIS.] *Med.* Complete deafness.

copia /ˈkəʊpɪə/ *n.* M16. [L *copia*: see COPY *n.*[1]] An abundance, a plentiful supply.

copia verborum /vəːˈbɔːrəm/ an abundance of words, a copious vocabulary.

copiability *n.*, **copiable** *a.* vars. of COPYABILITY, COPYABLE.

copiapite /ˈkəʊpɪəpʌɪt/ *n.* M19. [f. *Copiapó* a city in Chile + -ITE[1].] *Min.* A yellow, triclinic, hydrated basic sulphate of ferric and ferrous iron and often other metals, usu. occurring as loose masses of tiny tabular crystals.

copier /ˈkɒpɪə/ *n.* L16. [f. COPY *v.*[1] + -ER[1].] 1 A person who makes copies of documents, works of art, etc. L16. 2 An imitator. L17. 3 A machine that produces facsimile copies of documents; a photocopier. E20.

copilot /ˈkəʊpʌɪlət/ *n.* E20. [f. CO- + PILOT *n.*] A second pilot in an aircraft.

coping /ˈkəʊpɪŋ/ *n.* M16. [f. COPE *v.*[2] + -ING[1].] A course of masonry or tiling on the top of a wall, usu. sloping so as to deflect rain.

Comb.: **coping saw** a very narrow saw held taut in a U-frame, similar to but longer than a fretsaw and used for cutting curves in wood; **coping-stone** a stone forming part of a coping; *fig.* a pinnacle, a finishing touch.

copious /ˈkəʊpɪəs/ *a.* & *adv.* LME. [(O)Fr. *copieux* or L *copiosus*, f. *copia*: see COPY *n.*[1], -IOUS.] **A** *adj.* 1 Existing or produced in abundance; plentiful. LME. 2 Yielding an abundance *of.* Formerly also, having an abundant supply of or *of* something, rich *in.* LME. 3 Profuse in speech; diffuse or exuberant in style. Of a language: having a large vocabulary. LME. †4 Numerous, multitudinous. LME–M18. 5 Having much information. L15.

2 J. DALRYMPLE A.. toune copious in citizenis. J. GAY Newgate's copious market. W. COWPER Copious of flow'rs. W. H. PRESCOTT More copious sources of knowledge. 5 H. JAMES A copious diary.

B *adv.* Copiously. *arch.* L18.

copiously *adv.* LME. **copiousness** *n.* LME.

†**copist** *n.* M16–L18. [Fr. *copiste* or its source med.L *copista*, f. *copiare* COPY *v.*[1]: see -IST.] = COPYIST.

copita /kəʊˈpiːtə/ *n.* M19. [Sp., dim. of *copa* f. pop.L *cuppa* CUP *n.*] A tulip-shaped sherry glass of a type traditionally used in Spain; a glass of sherry.

coplanar /kəʊˈpleɪnə/ *a.* L19. [f. CO- +

PLANAR.] *Math.* Situated or acting in the same plane.

copla'narity *n.* M19.

copolymer /kəʊ'pɒlɪmə/ *n.* M20. [f. CO- + POLYMER.] *Chem.* A composite polymer formed by copolymerization and composed of units of more than one kind.

copolymerization /ˌkəʊpɒlɪmərʌɪ'zeɪʃ(ə)n, kəʊˌpɒl-/ *n.* Also **-isation**. M20. [f. CO- + POLYMERIZATION.] *Chem.* The polymerization together of two or more different compounds to form a polymer that contains part of each.

co'polymerize *v.i.* & *t.* M20.

†coportion *n. rare* (Spenser). Only in L16. [f. CO- + PORTION *n.*] A joint portion.

cop-out /'kɒpaʊt/ *n. slang.* M20. [f. COP *v.*[2] + OUT *adv.*: see COP *v.*[2] 4.] 1 An escape, esp. from reality; a pretext, an excuse; an evasion of responsibility. M20. 2 An escapist, a drop-out. M20.

copped /'kɒpɪd, kɒpt/ *a.* OE. [f. COP *n.*[1] + -ED[2].] I *lit.* †1 Polled. Only in OE. 2 Crested. Now *dial.* ME. 3 Having a peak. LME. II *fig.* 4 Saucy; peevish. Now *Sc.* LME. 5 Conceited. *dial.* M17.

†coppel *n.* & *v.* var. of CUPEL.

copper /'kɒpə/ *n.*[1] & *a.* [OE *copor, coper* corresp. to MDu. *coper* (Du. *koper*), ON *koparr*, f. Gmc (whence also MLG *kopper*, OHG *kupfar* (G *Kupfer*)), f. late L *cuprum* f. L *cyprium* (*aes*) lit. '(metal) of Cyprus', so called from its most noted ancient source.] A *n.* 1 A malleable and ductile reddish metal which is a chemical element of the transition series, atomic no. 29, used esp. for electrical conductors and as the base of alloys. (Symbol Cu.) OE. 2 A copper or iron vessel for boiling water, esp. for cooking or laundry; a copper mug. E17. 3 = COPPERPLATE *n.* 2. M17. 4 A bronze or copper coin; money composed of such coins. E18. 5 Any of various reddish-orange butterflies of the genus *Lycaena* (family Lycaenidae), of which only the small copper, *L. phlaeas*, is now common in Britain. L18. 6 In *pl.* The throat. *slang.* M19. 7 In *pl.* Shares in a copper-mining company. L19. 8 A ceremonial copper sheet used by N. American Indians. L19.

1 PITCHY *copper ore. purple copper (ore)*: see PURPLE *a. red copper ore*: see RED *a. rose copper*: see ROSE *a. ruby copper*: see RUBY *a. set copper*: see SET *a. velvet copper ore*: see VELVET *n.* & *a.* 6 **hot coppers** a throat and mouth parched through excessive drinking.

B *adj.* 1 Made of copper; *fig.* worthless. L16. 2 Of the colour of copper. L17.

Comb. & *special collocations*: **Copper Age** a prehistoric period when copper was used in a particular culture but not bronze; **copper beech** a kind of beech with copper-coloured leaves; **copper-belly** (*a*) = COPPERHEAD 1a; (*b*) a harmless N. American water snake, *Natrix erythrogaster*, having a red belly; **copper belt** an area of central Africa where much copper is mined; **copper-bit** a soldering-iron bit made of copper; **copper-bottomed** *a.* (esp. of a ship) having a bottom covered with copper; *fig.* thoroughly sound or reliable; **copper-captain** a sham (ship's) captain; **copper-cut** a copperplate engraving; **copper-fasten** *v.t.* (*fig.*) make more secure, establish firmly; **copper-fastened** *a.* (of a ship) fastened with copper bolts; **copper glance** *Min.* = CHALCOCITE; **copper-headed** *a.* having a copper-coloured head; relating to a copperhead (sense 2 or 3); *copper-knob*: see *copper-nob* below; **copper loss** loss of energy as a result of electrical resistance in the copper conductors of machinery etc.; **copper-nickel** [G *Kupfernickel*, f. its resemblance to copper] *Min.* = NICCOLITE; **copper-nob, -knob** *colloq.* a red-haired person; **copper-nose** a red nose caused by disease, intemperance, etc.; *copper pyrites*: see PYRITES 2; **copperskin** *US slang* an American Indian; *copper* VITRIOL.

copperish *a.* (*rare*) somewhat coppery M17. **coppery** *a.* resembling copper, esp. in colour; containing copper: E18.

copper /'kɒpə/ *n.*[2] *slang.* M19. [f. COP *v.*[2] + -ER[1].] A police officer.

come or **turn copper** inform on someone. *copper's nark*: see NARK *n.* 1a.

copper /'kɒpə/ *v.*[1] M16. [f. COPPER *n.*[1]] 1 *v.t.* Cover or sheathe with copper. M16. 2 *v.t.* & *i.* Place a copper coin on (a card) in faro to indicate a bet against it; bet against anything; place (such a bet). M19. 3 *v.t.* Give a false colour to by means of salts of copper. L19.

copperer *n.* a person who works in copper ME.

copper /'kɒpə/ *v.*[2] *slang.* L19. [f. COPPER *n.*[2]] 1 *v.t.* Arrest. L19. 2 *v.t.* & *i.* Inform the police (about). L19.

copperas /'kɒp(ə)rəs/ *n.* LME. [(O)Fr. *couperose* f. med.L *cup(e)rosa* lit. 'flower of copper', ult. f. late L *cupri-* comb. form of L *cuprum* copper + *rosa* ROSE *n.*, after Gk *khalkanthon*.] Ferrous sulphate heptahydrate, $FeSO_4 \cdot 7H_2O$, a green crystalline compound used in inks and pigments and in medicine. Formerly also, the sulphate of copper or zinc.

†blue copperas copper sulphate. **green copperas** ferrous sulphate heptahydrate. **†white copperas** zinc sulphate.

Comb.: **†copperas-stone** marcasite.

copperhead /'kɒpəhed/ *n.* L18. [f. COPPER *n.*[1] & *a.* + HEAD *n.*] 1 More fully *copperhead snake*: a A venomous but rarely fatal N. American pit viper, *Agkistrodon contortrix*. L18. b A venomous but unaggressive Australian snake, *Denisonia superba*, of the cobra family, Elapidae. L19. 2 *Hist.* In the American Civil War, a Northerner who sympathized with the South. M19. 3 An American Indian. *US.* Now *rare* or *obs.* M19.

copper Maori *n. phr.* var. of KOPA MAORI.

copperplate /'kɒpəpleɪt/ *n.* & *v.* M17. [f. COPPER *n.*[1] + PLATE *n.*] A *n.* 1 A plate, or plates, made of copper. M17. 2 *spec.* A polished printing plate of copper on which a design is engraved or etched. M17. 3 A print made with a copperplate. M17. 4 An English style of handwriting (a kind of round hand) for which the copybooks were printed from copperplates; round neat handwriting. M18. 5 Engraving or printing done from copperplate. E19. B *v.t.* Engrave on and print from a copperplate. E19.

coppersmith /'kɒpəsmɪθ/ *n.* ME. [f. COPPER *n.*[1] + SMITH *n.*] 1 A person who works in copper. ME. 2 The crimson-breasted barbet, *Megalaima haemacephala*, of SE Asia (so called from its metallic note). M19.

coppice /'kɒpɪs/ *n.* & *v.* Also **†cop(p)y**. LME. [OFr. *copeïz*, ult. f. Proto-Romance vb (whence COPE *v.*[1]) f. med.L *colpus*: see COUP *n.*[1] Cf. COPSE *n.*[1] & *v.*] A *n.* A small wood of undergrowth and small trees, grown for periodic cutting. LME.

Comb.: **coppice-wood** = *copsewood* s.v. COPSE *n.*[1]

B *v.* 1 *v.t.* Grow or treat as a coppice; cut down periodically. LME. 2 *v.i.* Of a tree: produce new shoots from a stump. L19.

copping /'kɒpɪŋ/ *vbl n.* L18. [f. COP *n.*[1] + -ING[1].] The formation of cops of thread.

copple /'kɒp(ə)l/ *n.* Long *obs.* exc. *dial.* in *copple-crown*. LME. [Dim. of COP *n.*[1]: see -LE[1].] 1 More fully *copple-crown*. A crest on a bird's head, = COP *n.*[1] 1b. LME. †2 A small summit or piece of rising ground. *rare.* Only in E17.

†coppled *a.* (*a*) crested; (*b*) rising conically to a point: E17–E18. **†coppling** *a.* swelling upwards towards a summit L17–M18.

†coppy *n.* & *v.* var. of COPPICE.

copra /'kɒprə/ *n.* L16. [Port. & Sp. f. Malayalam *koppara*.] Dried coconut kernels, from which oil is obtained.

co-precipitation /ˌkəʊprɪsɪpɪ'teɪʃ(ə)n/ *n.* M20. [f. CO- + PRECIPITATION.] *Chem.* The simultaneous precipitation of two or more compounds from a solution; the removal of a compound from solution by causing it to bind to a precipitate.

co-pre'cipitate *v.t.* deposit by co-precipitation M20.

co-presence /kəʊ'prez(ə)ns/ *n.* E19. [f. CO- + PRESENCE.] Presence together.

co-present *a.* E19.

copro- /'kɒprəʊ/ *comb. form* of Gk *kopros* dung: see -O-.

copro'lalia *n.* the use of obscene language, esp. as a symptom of mental illness or organic brain disease L19. **coprolite** *n.* [-LITE] (a piece of) fossilized dung E19. **copro'litic** *a.* pertaining to or containing coprolite; of the nature of coprolite: E19. **coprolith** *n.* [-LITH] a mass of hardened faeces in the appendix or bowel; also, a coprolite: L19. **co'prology** *n.* (the treatment of) filthy subjects in literature or art M19. **copro'mania** *n.* an obsession with faeces L19. **copro'maniac** *n.* a person with copromania E20. **copro'phagia** *n.* = COPROPHAGY E20. **copro'phagic** *a.* involving or engaging in the eating of dung E20. **co'prophagous** *a.* [-PHAGOUS] (esp. of a beetle) that eats dung E19. **co'prophagy** *n.* the eating of dung L19. **coprophil(e)** *n.* [-PHIL] a person with coprophilia M20. **copro'philia** *n.* an undue interest in faeces and defecation M20. **copro'philic** *a.* & *n.* (*a*) *adj.* of, pertaining to, or exhibiting coprophilia; (*b*) *n.* a coprophilic person: E20. **co'prophilous** *a.* exhibiting coprophilia; (esp. of a fungus) that grows on dung: L19. **co'prophily** *n.* = COPROPHILIA E20. **copro'porphyrin** *n.* any of several porphyrins present in urine and faeces, esp. in certain diseases E20. **copro'zoic** *a.* [Gk *zōē* life] (of an animal) living in or feeding on dung M20.

coprosma /kə'prɒzmə/ *n.* L19. [mod.L *Coprosma*, f. as COPRO- + Gk *osmē* smell.] A plant of the genus *Coprosma* (family Rubiaceae), which comprises small evergreen trees and shrubs found in Australasia.

co-prosperity /kəʊprɒ'sperɪti/ *n.* M20. [f. CO- + PROSPERITY.] Joint prosperity; *spec.* (*Hist.*) in *co-prosperity sphere*, the parts of eastern and south-eastern Asia which Japan aimed to control in the war of 1939–45 and which were mostly occupied by her.

cops *n.* var. of COPSE *n.*[2]

copse /kɒps/ *n.*[1] & *v.* L16. [Syncopated f. COPPICE.] A *n.* 1 = COPPICE *n.* L16. 2 Undergrowth, *esp.* the low trees and undergrowth of a copse. M18.

Comb.: **copsewood** †(*a*) a copse; (*b*) the low trees and undergrowth of a copse.

B *v.t.* 1 = COPPICE *v.* 1. L16. 2 Cover with a copse. M18.

copsy *a.* planted with copses M18.

copse /kɒps/ *n.*[2] Long *obs.* exc. *dial.* Also **cops**. [OE *cops, cosp* = OS *cosp* fetter.] †1 A shackle, a fetter, a manacle. OE–ME. 2 A hasp for fastening a door or gate. L15. 3 A clevis. Cf. earlier COPSOLE. L18.

copsole /'kɒps(ə)l/ *n.* Long *obs.* exc. *dial.* Also **-sil**. M16. [App. f. prec. + obscure 2nd elem.] A clevis; = COPSE *n.*[2] 3.

Copt /kɒpt/ *n.* & *a.* E17. [Fr. *Copte* or mod.L *Cop(h)tus* f. Arab. *al-ḳibṭ, al-ḳubṭ* Copts f. Coptic *Gyptios*, f. Gk *Aiguptios* Egyptian: see AL-[2].] A *n.* An Egyptian not of Arab descent; a member of the Coptic Church. E17. B *adj.* = COPTIC *a.* M17.

copter /'kɒptə/ *n. colloq.* (chiefly *N. Amer.*). Also **'c-**. M20. [Abbrev.] = HELICOPTER *n.*

Coptic /'kɒptɪk/ *n.* & *a.* M17. [f. COPT + -IC.] A *n.* The medieval language of Egypt, now used only in the liturgy of the Coptic Church. M17. B *adj.* Of or pertaining to the Copts; designating or pertaining to the Monophysite Christian Church in Egypt. L17.

copula /'kɒpjʊlə/ *n.* E17. [L = connection, linking of words, f. as CO- + *apere* fasten: see -ULE.] 1 *Logic* & *Gram.* That part of a proposition which connects the subject and the predicate; the verb *be* as a mere sign of predication; a verb with a similar function. E17. 2 A connection, a link. M17. 3 *Anat.* A part (e.g. a bone or ligament) connecting other parts. Now *rare* or *obs.* L17.

copular *a.* M19.

copulate /'kɒpjʊleɪt/ *v.* LME. [L *copulat-* pa. ppl stem of *copulare* fasten together, f. as prec.: see -ATE[3].] †1 *v.t.* Join, link together. LME–E19. 2 *v.i.* Of a male and female: have copulation, unite sexually (*with*). E17.

copulatory *a.* pertaining to or used for copulation M19.

copulation /kɒpjʊ'leɪʃ(ə)n/ *n.* LME. [(O)Fr. f. L *copulatio(n-)*, f. as prec.: see -ATION.] 1 *gen.* The action of linking together two things or ideas; the state of being linked. Now *rare* or *obs.* LME. 2 The physical union of male and female (esp. animals) by means of their genitals, as in the act of procreation; sexual intercourse. L15. 3 Grammatical or logical connection. L16.

copulative /'kɒpjʊlətɪv/ *a.* & *n.* LME. [(O)Fr. *copulatif, -ive* or late L *copulativus*, f. as

COPULATE: see -IVE.] A *adj.* 1 Serving to connect, esp. (*Gram.*) words or clauses that are joined in sense (opp. *disjunctive*), or subject and predicate (or complement); involving such connection. LME. 2 *Zool.* & *Anat.* = COPULATORY. M19. B *n.* 1 *Gram.* A copulative conjunction or particle. M16. †2 In *pl.* Persons about to be joined in marriage. *joc. rare* (Shakes.). Only in L16.

copulatively *adv.* E17.

copy /ˈkɒpi/ *n.*[1] & *a.* ME. [(O)Fr. *copie* f. L *copia* abundance, plenty; the med.L & Proto-Romance sense 'transcript' arose f. such phrs. as *copiam describendi facere* give the power (permission) of transcription.] A *n.* I 1 A piece of written or printed matter that reproduces the contents of another; a transcript, *spec.* (*Law*, now *Hist.*) of a manorial court roll; a specimen of penmanship made in imitation of a model. ME. b Anything (regarded as) made to reproduce the appearance of something else (a picture, personality, etc.). L16. 2 An original from which a copy is to be made; *spec.* a specimen of penmanship. L15. †b *fig.* A pattern, an example. L16–L18. 3a Matter or text prepared for printing, *spec.* the wording of an advertisement. Formerly also, a passage or manuscript of such matter. L15. b Something which lends itself to interesting narration in a newspaper etc. M19. 4 Each of the written or printed specimens of a work or publication. M16. †5 A copyright work; copyright. L16–L18. †6 = COPYHOLD *n.* Cf. earlier B. below. E–M17. 7 A particular size of paper, now disused. E18.

1b D. HUME Of this impression there is a copy taken by the mind. R. CAMPBELL Lilian Bayliss.. photographed the house, and sent me a copy of it. 3a Q. BELL Repeated failures to float magazines, to produce copy on time. b G. B. SHAW Socialist speeches which make what the newspapers call 'good copy'. 4 E. J. HOWARD He picked up a copy of *Country Life*.

†II 8 Abundance, plenty, copiousness. LME–M17.

Phrases: **copy of verses** a short verse composition, esp. in Greek or Latin as an exercise. †**copy of one's countenance** a mere outward show of what one would do or be; a pretence. *Chinese copy*: see CHINESE *a. fair copy*: see FAIR *a. rough copy*: see ROUGH *a. set a copy to*: see SET *v.*[1] *soft copy*: see SOFT *a. top copy*: see TOP *a. working copy*: see WORKING *n.*

Comb.: **copyboard** a part of a camera that holds a document ready for photographing; **copydesk** *US*: where copy is edited for printing; **copy-edit** *v.t.* read and edit for printing; **copy editor** a person who reads and edits copy for printing; †**copy-money**: paid to an author for his or her manuscript or copyright; **copyreader** = *copy editor* above; **copy-taster** a person who selects what is to be published; **copy-typist** a person who makes typewritten transcripts of documents or recorded dictation; **copywriter** a person who writes or prepares copy, esp. advertising copy, for publication.

†B *adj.* = COPYHOLD *a.* E16–M17.

†**copy** *n.*[2] var. of COPPICE *n.*

copy /ˈkɒpi/ *v.*[1] LME. [(O)Fr. *copier* f. med.L *copiare* f. L *copia* (see COPY *n.*[1]).] 1 *v.t.* Make a copy of (a text, work of art, etc., also foll. by *out*); transcribe (*from* an original); design or produce by making a copy of something else (foll. by *from* the original). LME. b *Computing.* Read (data stored in one location), read the data in (a disc etc.), and reproduce in another. (Foll. by *from* one, *into*, *to* another.) M20. c Send a copy of (a document) *to* a person etc. L20. 2 *v.t.* Imitate, follow the example of; follow in behaviour, mode, etc. M17. 3 *v.i.* Imitate or follow the example of another or others; make a copy or copies rather than create something original. (Foll. by *after*, *from*.) L17.

1 R. W. EMERSON The potters copied his ugly face on their stone jugs. B. HINES He copied age, address and other details from the record card. 2 T. HARDY This scheme of extinction by death was but tamely copying her rival's method. 3 J. RUSKIN No painter who is worth a straw ever will copy.

Comb.: **copycat** *n.*, *a.*, & *v.* (*colloq.*) (*a*) *n.* an unimaginative or slavish imitator; (*b*) *attrib. adj.* characterized by or consisting in imitation; (*c*) *v.t.* imitate unimaginatively. **copying-pencil**: used for indelible writing and for duplicating by a direct-transfer process.

†**copy** *v.*[2] var. of COPPICE *v.*

copyable /ˈkɒpɪəb(ə)l/ *a.* Also **copiable**. M18. [f. COPY *v.*[1] + -ABLE.] Able to be copied.

copyaˈbility *n.* M20.

copybook /ˈkɒpɪbʊk/ *n.* & *a.* M16. [f. COPY *n.*[1] + BOOK *n.*] A *n.* 1 A book containing copies of accounts etc. Now *US.* M16. 2 A book containing specimens of handwriting for learners to copy. L16.

2 *blot one's copybook*: see BLOT *v.* 1.

B *adj.* 1 Of a conventional or trite nature. M19. 2 Accurate, exemplary. E20.

copyhold /ˈkɒpɪhəʊld/ *n.* & *a.* LME. [f. COPY *n.*[1] + HOLD *n.*[1]] *Hist.* A *n.* 1 Tenure of land according to the custom of the manor to which it belonged, as recorded in transcripts of the manorial court rolls. LME. 2 An estate, land, held by copyhold. LME. B *adj.* Held by copyhold; relating to or of the nature of copyhold. E16.

copyholder /ˈkɒpɪhəʊldə/ *n.* LME. [f COPY *n.*[1] + HOLDER[1].] 1 *Hist.* A person who held an estate or land in copyhold. LME. 2 A clasp for holding copy while it is set or keyboarded. L19. 3 An assistant who reads copy aloud to a proofreader. L19.

copyist /ˈkɒpɪɪst/ *n.* M17. [f. COPY *v.*[1] + -IST. Cf. COPIST.] A person who copies (esp. documents) or imitates.

copyism *n.* the practice of copying, esp. slavishly, (slavish) imitation E19.

copyright /ˈkɒpɪrʌɪt/ *n.* & *a.* E18. [f. COPY *n.*[1] + RIGHT *n.*[1]] A *n.* The exclusive right, given to the originator or his or her assignee for a fixed number of years, to reproduce or perform a literary, musical, cinematic, etc., work and to authorize others to do the same. E18.

Comb.: **copyright library**: entitled to a free copy of every book published in Britain.

B *adj.* Protected by copyright. L19.

copyright /ˈkɒpɪrʌɪt/ *v.t.* E19. [f. the n.] Secure copyright for.

copyrightable *a.* L19.

coq *n.* var. of COQUE *n.*[2]

coq au vin /kɒk əʊ vɛ̃/ *n. phr.* M20. [Fr., lit. 'cock in wine'.] Chicken cooked in wine.

coque /kɒk/ *n.*[1] E19. [Fr. = shell.] †1 *Bot.* = COCCUS 2. *rare.* Only in E19. 2 A loop, a looped bow. Now *spec.* a small loop of ribbon in the trimming of a woman's hat. E19.

coque /kəʊk/ *n.*[2] Also **coq** /kɒk/. E20. [Fr. *coq* = COCK *n.*[1]] In full *coque feather*. A cock's feather used in the trimming of a hat etc.

coquelicot /ˈkəʊklɪkəʊ/ *n.* & *a.* L18. [Fr. = red poppy, var. of *coquerico* cock-a-doodle-doo.] (Of) the colour of the red poppy, a brilliant orange-red.

†**coqueluche** *n.* E17–L19. [Fr., of unkn. origin.] Orig., an epidemic catarrh; later, whooping cough.

coquet /kɒˈkɛt/ *n.* & *a.* L17. [Fr., dim. of *coq* COCK *n.*[1]; as adj. = forward, wanton, gallant. The n. was formerly both masc. & fem.; later the fem. became *coquette.*] A *n.* 1 A man given to flirting or coquetry. L17. †2 = COQUETTE *n.* L17–E19. B *adj.* Coquettish. L17.

coquet /kɒˈkɛt/ *v.* Also **-ette**. L17. [Fr. *coqueter*, f. as prec.] 1 *v.i.* & †*t.* w. *it.* Of a woman, or (formerly) a man: flirt (*with*). L17. †2 *v.t.* Flirt with. Only in 18. 3 *v.i.* Dally, trifle, or toy (*with* a matter etc.). L18.

3 W. E. H. LECKY Lady Townshend.. coquetted with Methodism as with Popery.

coquetry /ˈkɒkɪtri, ˈkəʊ-/ *n.* M17. [Fr. *coquetterie*, f. *coqueter* COQUET *v.*: see -RY.] 1a Behaviour intended to excite admiration or love in the opposite sex merely for the sake of vanity or mischief; flirtation. Formerly, attractive pertness in a woman. M17. b A coquettish act. M18. 2 Trifling or dalliance with a cause etc. without serious interest in it. L18.

coquette /kɒˈkɛt/ *n.* & *a.* M17. [Fr., fem. of *coquet*: see COQUET *n.* & *a.*, -ETTE.] A *n.* 1 A woman who trifles with men's affections; a woman given to flirting or coquetry. M17. b *male coquette*, = COQUET *n.* 1. Now *rare* or *obs.* L18. 2 A crested hummingbird of the genus *Lophornis*. M19. B *adj.* = COQUET *a.* M18.

coquettish *a.* like (that of) a coquette; characterized by coquetry: E18. **coquettishly** *adv.* L18. **coquettishness** *n.* L19.

coquette *v.* var. of COQUET *v.*

coquilla nut /kəʊˈkɪl(j)ə nʌt/ *n. phr.* M19. [App. Sp. or Port. dim. of *coca* shell f. OSp.: see COQUINA.] The nut of the Brazilian palm tree *Attalea funifera*, the hard shell of which is used by turners.

coquimbite /kəʊˈkɪmbʌɪt/ *n.* M19. [f. *Coquimbo*, province of Chile + -ITE[1].] A hexagonal hydrated ferric sulphate, $Fe_2(SO_4)_3 \cdot 9H_2O$, occurring as coloured crystals that dehydrate in air to a white powder.

coquina /kəʊˈkiːnə/ *n.* M19. [Sp. = shellfish, cockle, f. OSp. *coca* f. med.L by-form of L CONCHA.] A soft white limestone composed of broken marine shells cemented together and used for building in the W. Indies and Florida. Also *coquina rock, stone*.

coquito /kəʊˈkiːtəʊ/ *n.* Pl. **-os**. M19. [Sp., dim. of *coco* coconut.] The Chilean wine palm, *Jubaea chilensis*, which yields palm honey and fibre. Also *coquito palm*.

cor /kɔː/ *n.* LME. [Heb. *kōr*.] *Hist.* A Hebrew measure of capacity of about 400 litres (100 gallons), = HOMER *n.*[1]

cor /kɔː/ *int. slang.* M20. [Alt. of *God*.] Expr. surprise, alarm, etc.

cor blimey = GORBLIMEY *int.*

cor- /kɒ, *unstressed* kə/ *pref.* Var. of L COM- bef. *r*. Cf. CO-, COL-, CON-.

†**coracine** *n.* E17–M18. [L *coracinus*, f. Gk *korax* raven: so called from its black colour: see -INE[1].] A fish resembling a perch, found in the River Nile.

coracle /ˈkɒrək(ə)l/ *n.* M16. [Welsh *corwg(l)*, *cwrwgl* coracle (= Gael., (O)Ir. *curach* (small) boat: cf. CURRACH).] A small boat made of wickerwork covered with watertight material, used on lakes and rivers in Wales and Ireland.

coraco- /ˈkɒrəkəʊ/ *comb. form.* [f. next: see -O-.] *Anat.* Pertaining to or connecting the coracoid and, as *coracohumeral*.

coracoid /ˈkɒrəkɔɪd/ *a.* & *n.* M18. [mod.L *coracoides* f. Gk *korakoeidēs* raven-like, f. *korax* raven, crow: see -OID.] *Anat.* A *adj.* Designating or pertaining to a short projection of the human shoulder-blade that extends towards the breastbone and resembles a crow's beak. Also, designating or pertaining to a bone in birds and reptiles homologous with this, forming the distal or ventral element of the scapular arch. M18. B *n.* The coracoid process or bone. E19.

coraˈcoidal *a.* L19.

coradgee *n.* see KORADJI.

coraggio /koˈraddʒo, kɒˈrɑːdʒəʊ/ *int.* E17. [It.] Courage! (see COURAGE *n.* 4b).

corah /ˈkɔːrə/ *n.* & *a.* E19. [Hindi *korā* new, unbleached.] A *n.* An Indian-pattern silk handkerchief. E19. B *adj.* Of silk: undyed. L19.

coral /ˈkɒr(ə)l/ *n.* & *a.* ME. [OFr. (mod. *corail*) f. L *corallum*, *-alium* f. Gk *korallion*, *kouralion*.] A *n.* I 1 A usu. hard calcareous substance secreted by many marine polyps as an external skeleton for support and habitation, and occurring in both single specimens and extensive accumulations; a similar substance produced by other lime-secreting marine organisms. Orig. *spec.* the red variety of this. ME. 2 A particular kind of coral or coral-producing polyp. L16. 3 A piece of red coral used as an ornament etc. E17. 4 A toy of polished coral or other hard material given to teething babies. E17.

1 *pink coral*, *red coral*, *white coral*, etc. *precious coral*: see PRECIOUS *a. stony coral*: see STONY *a.* 2 D. ATTENBOROUGH The profusion of shapes and colours of the corals.

II *transf.* & *fig.* 5 Anything bright red or (formerly) precious. ME. 6 The unimpregnated roe of the lobster (which turns red when boiled). M18. 7 In full *coral-snake*. Any of various snakes with some red colour; *esp.* any venomous elapid snake with red, black, and yellow bands. M18.

B *adj.* **1** Made or formed of coral. LME. **2** Of the colour of red coral. E16.

Comb. & *special collocations*: **coral-berry** a N. American shrub (*Symphoricarpos orbiculatus*) of the honeysuckle family, with deep-red berries; **coral fern** *Austral.* any fern of the genus *Gleichenia*, the members of which form dense mats; **coral insect** = *coral polyp* below; **coral island**: formed by the accumulation of coral on a coral reef or an undersea mountain top; **coral-limestone** coralline limestone; **coral pea** any leguminous plant of the genus *Kennedia*, which comprises trailing and climbing shrubs native to Australia and bearing showy, usu. red, flowers; **coral-pink** *a.* & *n.* (of) the colour of red coral; **coral-plant** †(*a*) any plant resembling coral; (*b*) a tropical American tree or large shrub, *Jatropha multifida*, of the spurge family, bearing scarlet flowers; (*c*) a Central American shrub of the genus *Russelia*, of the figwort family, *esp.* the red-flowered *R. equisetiformis*; **coral polyp** a polyp that produces coral; **coral rag** rubbly limestone composed chiefly of petrified coral; **coral-red** *n.* & *a.* (of) the colour of red coral; **coral reef**: composed chiefly of coral or similar calcareous material of plant or animal origin; **coral-root** (*a*) a cruciferous woodland plant, *Cardamine* (or *Dentaria*) *bulbifera*, with scaly rhizomes and purple flowers; (*b*) (more fully *coral-root orchid*) any member of the genus *Corallorhiza* of brown saprophytic orchids with much-branched coral-like roots, esp. *C. trifida*; *coral-snake*: see sense 7 above; **coral spot** (a disease of shrubs caused by) the fungus *Nectria cinnabarina*; **coral tree** †(*a*) branched coral; (*b*) any of numerous tropical or subtropical thorny leguminous shrubs and trees constituting the genus *Erythrina*, with showy red or orange flowers; **coral vine** = CORALLITA; **coral-wood** (*a*) a hard red cabinet wood from Central and S. America; (*b*) the SE Asian tree *Adenanthera pavonina*, which yields a red wood used in furniture; **coralwort** = *coral-root* (a) above.

coralled *a.* covered with coral E18. **co'ralliform** *a.* shaped like coral E19. **cora'lligenous** *a.* producing coral E19. **coral-like** *a.* resembling coral; having a crustose or branching form: M19. **coral-like** *a.* resembling coral M19.

coral /'kɒr(ə)l/ *v.t. rare.* Infl. **-ll-**, ***-l-**. M17. [f. prec.] Make red like coral.

coraleta, -ita *ns.* vars. of CORALLITA.

coralline /'kɒrəlʌɪn/ *n.*[1] M16. [It. *corallina* dim. of *corallo* CORAL *n.*] **1** A seaweed of the genus *Corallina* (family Corallinaceae), having a calcareous jointed stem; any plant of the family Corallinaceae, which comprises lime-secreting red algae. M16. **2** A marine animal, esp. a bryozoan, which lives in colonies resembling coral. E18.

coralline /'kɒrəlʌɪn/ *a.* & *n.*[2] M17. [Fr. *corallin*, *-ine* or late L *corallinus*, f. L *corallum* CORAL *n.*: see -INE[1].] **A** *adj.* **1** Of the colour of red coral. M17. **2** Of the nature of coral; formed of or from coral. M17. **3** Resembling coral; *spec.* (of an alga) belonging to the family Corallinaceae (see CORALLINE *n.*[1] 1). M19.

2 JOHN PHILLIPS Coralline oolite and calcareous grits.

B *n.* Coral. L18.

corallita /kɒrə'liːtə/ *n.* Also **coraleta, -ita**. L19. [Amer. Sp. *coralito* dim. of Sp. *coral* CORAL *n.*] A climbing vine, *Antigonon leptopus*, of the knotgrass family that grows in the W. Indies and as an ornamental elsewhere and has pink flowers.

corallite /'kɒrəlʌɪt/ *n.* E19. [f. as CORALLUM + -ITE[1].] *Palaeont.* **1** A fossil coral. E19. **2** The cuplike skeleton of a single coral polyp. M19.

coralloid /'kɒrəlɔɪd/ *a.* & *n.* E17. [f. as next + -OID.] (An organism) resembling coral.

cora'lloidal *a.* M17.

corallum /kə'raləm/ *n.* M19. [L = CORAL *n.*] The calcareous skeleton of a colony of coral polyps.

coram /'kɔːrəm/ *prep.* M16. [L.] The L for 'before, in the presence of', occurring in various phrases used in Eng.

coram judice /'juːdɪsi/ [L *judex, judic-* judge] before a judge, i.e. a properly constituted or an appropriate court. ***coram nobis*** /'nəʊbɪs/ [L *nos* we] before us (the monarch), i.e. in the King's or Queen's Bench. ***coram populo*** /'pɒpjʊləʊ/ [L *populus* people] in public.

Coramine /'kɔːrəmiːn, 'kɒr-/ *n.* E20. [f. *cor-* (origin unkn.) + AMINE.] *Pharm.* (Proprietary name for) nikethamide.

cor anglais /kɔːr 'ɑːŋgleɪ, 'ɒŋgleɪ/ *n. phr.* L19. [Fr., lit. 'English horn'.] A musical instrument like an oboe but lower in pitch; a player of this. Also, an organ reed-stop of similar quality.

coranto /kɒ'rantəʊ/ *n.*[1] *obs.* exc. *Hist.* Pl. **-os**. M16. [Alt., by addition of It. ending, of Fr. COURANTE.] = COURANTE.

coranto /kɒ'rantəʊ/ *n.*[2] *obs.* exc. *Hist.* Pl. **-os**. E17. [Alt. of Fr. *courant* or Eng. COURANT *n.*[1] in same way as prec.] = COURANT *n.*[1]

corban /'kɔːban/ *n.* ME. [pop.L f. New Testament Gk *korban* f. Heb. *qorbān* offering, f. *qāraḇ* approach.] †**1** The treasury of the Temple at Jerusalem; *transf.* a church treasury. ME–M17. **2** An offering or sacrifice made to God by the ancient Hebrews. LME.

†**corbe** *n. rare* (Spenser). Only in L16. [Abbrev.] = CORBEL *n.* 2.

corbeau /'kɔːbəʊ/ *n.* & *a.* E19. [Fr. = crow, raven: see CORBEL.] In the drapery trade, (of) a dark green colour verging on black.

corbeil /'kɔːbeɪl/ *n.* E18. [(O)Fr. *corbeille* basket f. late L *corbicula* dim. of *corbis* basket.] †**1** A basket filled with earth and placed on a parapet to protect defending soldiers. *rare.* Only in E18. **2** *Archit.* A representation in stone of a basket of flowers. M18.

corbeille /kɔː'beɪj/ *n.* E19. [Fr.: see prec.] An elegant basket of flowers or fruit.

corbel /'kɔːb(ə)l/ *n.* & *v.* LME. [OFr. *corbel* (mod. *corbeau*) crow, raven, corbel, dim. of *corp* f. L *corvus* raven: see -EL[2].] **A** *n.* †**1** A raven. Only in LME. **2** A projection of stone, timber, etc., jutting out from a wall to support weight. LME. **3** A short timber laid longitudinally under part of a beam to give a better bearing on the supporting wall or pier. E18.

Comb.: **corbel-stone** = sense 2 above; **corbel-table** a projecting course resting on a series of corbels.

B *v.i.* & *t.* Infl. **-ll-**, ***-l-**. (Cause to) stick *out* like or on a corbel. M19.

corbelled *a.* provided with corbels; fashioned as a corbel: M19. **corbelling** *n.* corbels collectively; work consisting of corbels: M16.

corbicula /kɔː'bɪkjʊlə/ *n.* E19. [Late L: see CORBEIL.] = *pollen basket* s.v. POLLEN *n.*

corbie /'kɔːbi/ *n. Sc.* LME. [f. OFr. *corb* var. of *corp* (see CORBEL) + -IE.] A raven; a carrion crow. Also *corbie-crow*.

Comb.: **corbie-gable**: having corbie-steps; **corbie messenger** [after *Gen.* 8:7]: who returns too late or not at all; **corbie-steps** projections in the form of steps on the sloping sides of a gable.

corbin /'kɔːbɪn/ *n.* Long *obs.* exc. in comb. ME. [OFr. f. as prec.: cf. L *corvinus* of or pertaining to a raven.] A raven.

Comb.: **corbin-bone** the lower end of a deer's breastbone (customarily thrown to the birds).

corcass /'kɔːkəs/ *n.* L18. [Ir. *corcach* marsh.] A salt-marsh bordering certain Irish rivers.

corchorus /'kɔːk(ə)rəs/ *n.* Now *rare* or *obs.* exc. as a genus name. M18. [Gk *korkhoros* blue pimpernel, jute.] = KERRIA.

¶Formerly placed in the genus *Corchorus*.

corcule /'kɔːkjuːl/ *n.* Now *rare* or *obs.* Also **corcle** /-k(ə)l/, **corculum** /-kjʊləm/. L18. [L *corculum* dim. of *cor* heart: see -ULE.] The embryo in a plant seed.

cord /kɔːd/ *n.*[1] & *a.* ME. [(O)Fr. *corde* f. L *chorda* f. Gk *khordē* gut, string of musical instrument. Cf. CHORD *n.*[2]] **A** *n.* **I** *lit.* **1** (A piece of) string or rope composed of several strands twisted or woven together; now *esp.* a thick string or light rope. ME. **b** (A piece of) electric flex. Chiefly *N. Amer.* L19. †**2** A string of a musical instrument. Cf. CHORD *n.*[2] 4. ME–M19. **3** Any structure in the body that is long, flexible, and rounded like a cord; *spec.* = UMBILICAL *cord*. LME. **4** *sing.* & (usu.) in *pl.* Stringhalt of horses. Now *rare* or *obs.* E16. †**5** = CHORD *n.*[2] 2. M–L16. **6** A measure of cut wood, esp. firewood (usu. 128 cu. ft, approx. 3.62 cu. metres). E17. **7** A raised cordlike rib on cloth; ribbed cloth, *esp.* corduroy; in *pl.* (*colloq.*), corduroy trousers. L18.

1 T. PYNCHON Binds his hands and feet with scarlet silk cords. **the cord** *spec.* the hangman's rope. *bungee cord, light cord, rip cord, whipcord*, etc. **3** S. KING Clamped so tightly . . that the cords in his wrist stood out. *spermatic cord, spinal cord, vocal cords*, etc.

II *fig.* **8** A moral or emotional tie. LME.

8 R. L. STEVENSON The cords of discipline. *silver cord*: see SILVER *n.* & *a.*

Comb.: **cord-drill**: worked by a cord twisted round it and pulled to and fro; **cord-grass** any of several spartina grasses, valuable in binding coastal mud-flats; **cord-ornamented** *a.* (*Archaeol.*) (of pottery) decorated by pressing cord into the soft clay; **cordwood** wood stacked in cords; firewood cut in standard (usu. 4-ft) lengths.

B *attrib.* or as *adj.* **1** Made of ribbed cloth, esp. corduroy. M19. **2** *Archaeol.* Of pottery: cord-ornamented. E20.

1 MOLLIE HARRIS He always wore thick brown cord trousers.

cordless *a.* (of an electrical appliance) working without connection to the mains, battery-powered: E20. **cordlike** *a.* resembling (that of) (a) cord E17. **cordy** *a.* (*rare*) of or like cord E17.

†**cord** *n.*[2] var. of CHORD *n.*[1]

cord /kɔːd/ *v.*[1] LME. [f. CORD *n.*[1]] **1** *v.t.* Provide with a cord or cords. LME. **2** *v.t.* Fasten or tie with cord. L15. **3** *v.t.* Stack (wood) in cords. M17. **4** *v.i.* Of a muscle or vein: form a visible ridge on the skin; become visibly hard or taut. Cf. earlier CORDED 2b. M20.

2 DICKENS Miss Charity called to him to come and cord her box. **4** M. RENAULT The vein . . corded and stood out.

corder *n.* a person who or thing which fastens with a cord or forms a cord LME.

cord /kɔːd/ *v.*[2]*t.* & *i.* Long *Sc. rare.* ME. [Aphet. Cf. CHORD *v.*] = ACCORD *v.*

cordage /'kɔːdɪdʒ/ *n.* L15. [(O)Fr., f. as CORD *n.*[1]: see -AGE.] Cords or cordlike ridges collectively; *esp.* a ship's rigging.

†**cordal** *n.* LME–E19. [OFr. *corda(i)l*, f. as CORD *n.*[1]: see -AL[1].] A cord, esp. of a heraldic robe.

†**cordant** *a.* ME–M19. [Aphet.] = ACCORDANT.

cordate /'kɔːdeɪt/ *a.* M17. [L *cordatus* wise, in mod.L heart-shaped f. *cor(d-)* heart: see -ATE[2].] †**1** Wise, prudent. M17–M18. **2** *Bot.* & *Zool.* Heart-shaped; pointed at one end and rounded and indented at the other. M18.

†**cordated** *a.* = CORDATE 2: only in 18.

cordax *n.* var. of KORDAX.

corded /'kɔːdɪd/ *a.* LME. [f. CORD *n.*[1] + -ED[2].] **1** Having cords; in the form of cords. LME. **2** Having a ribbed appearance or texture. M18. **b** Of part of the body: with muscles or veins forming a visible ridge on the skin. Of a muscle or vein: forming such a ridge, visibly hard or taut. L19.

2 **corded ware** cord-ornamented ware, esp. of a neolithic people of Thuringia (also called *Schnurkeramik*).

Cordelier /kɔːdɪ'lɪə/ *n.* LME. [(O)Fr., f. as CORDELLE: see -IER.] **1** A Franciscan Observant (so called from the knotted cord worn round the waist). LME. **2** A member of a political club of the French Revolution which met in a former convent of the Cordeliers. M19.

cordelière /kɔːdɛlɪ'ɛː/ *n.* M16. [Fr., f. as prec.] †**1** A kind of coarse knotted work in embroidery. M–L16. **2** *Her.* A loosely knotted silver cord around armorial bearings of women (in Britain only occasionally, and denoting a widow). E18.

cordelle /kɔː'dɛl/ *n.* & *v.* E16. [(O)Fr., dim. of *corde* CORD *n.*[1]: see -EL[2].] **A** *n.* †**1** A rope, esp. on a ship. *Sc.* E16–E17. **2** A ship's towing-line. *N. Amer.* E19. **B** *v.t.* & *i.* Give a tow (to) with a cordelle. *N. Amer.* E19.

cordia /'kɔːdɪə/ *n.* E19. [mod.L (see below), f. E. *Cordus* (1486–1535) and his son V. *Cordus* (1515–44), Ger. botanists: see -IA[1].] Any of various (sub)tropical shrubs and trees of the genus *Cordia*, of the borage family, grown as ornamentals or for timber.

cordial /'kɔːdɪəl/ *a.* & *n.* ME. [med.L *cordialis*, f. *cor(d-)* heart: see -IAL.] **A** *adj.* †**1** Of or belonging to the heart. ME–M17. **2** Heartfelt, earnest, warm; warm and friendly without showing intimacy. ME. 3 Stimulating, invigorating; reviving. LME.

2 R. W. DALE A cordial abhorrence of what is sensual. J. HILTON Sanders was very cordial and said he hoped to meet us again.

B *n.* A medicine, food, or drink to stimulate the circulation and invigorate; a flavoured and sweetened drink. ME.

cordially *adv.* LME.

cordialise *v.* var. of CORDIALIZE.

cordiality /kɔːdɪˈalɪti/ *n.* E17. [f. CORDIAL *a.* + -ITY.] Cordial quality; heartfelt warmth; warm friendliness without intimacy.

cordialize /ˈkɔːdɪəlʌɪz/ *v.* Also **-ise**. L18. [f. as prec. + -IZE.] 1 *v.t.* Make into a cordial. L18. 2 *v.t.* Make cordial or friendly. *rare.* E19. 3 *v.i.* Be or become cordial (*with*), be on friendly terms. Chiefly *Sc.* M19.

cordierite /ˈkɔːdɪərʌɪt/ *n.* E19. [f. P. L. A. *Cordier* (1777–1861), Fr. geologist + -ITE[1].] *Min.* An aluminium and magnesium silicate occurring in an altered state in metamorphic rocks and otherwise as blue, transparent or translucent, orthorhombic crystals which are pleochroic and have been used as gems.

cordiform /ˈkɔːdɪfɔːm/ *a.* E19. [f. L *cor(d-)* heart + -I- + -FORM.] Heart-shaped; = CORDATE 2.

cordillera /kɔːdɪˈljɛːrə/ *n.* E18. [Sp., f. *cordilla* dim. of *cuerda* f. L *chorda* CORD *n.*[1]] Each of a series of parallel mountain ridges or chains, esp. in the Andes; an extensive belt of mountains, valleys, etc., esp. as a major continental feature.

cordilleran *a.* L19.

cordiner *n.* see CORDWAINER.

cording /ˈkɔːdɪŋ/ *n.* L16. [f. CORD *n.*[1], *v.*[1] + -ING[1].] 1 Cords collectively. L16. 2 The action of fastening with or hanging by a cord; the arrangement of cords in a loom. E17.

cordite /ˈkɔːdʌɪt/ *n.* L19. [f. CORD *n.*[1] (from its stringlike appearance) + -ITE[1].] A smokeless explosive used in guns, made from gun-cotton, nitroglycerine, and petroleum jelly.

cordoba /ˈkɔːdəbə, -və/ *n.* E20. [F. Fernández de *Córdoba* (fl. 1524), Sp. governor of Nicaragua.] The basic monetary unit of Nicaragua, equal to 100 centavos.

cordon /ˈkɔːd(ə)n; *in sense 4 also foreign* kɔrdɔ̃ (*pl. same*)/ *n.* LME. [It. *cordone* augm. of *corda* CORD *n.*[1] & (O)Fr. *cordon* dim. of *corde* CORD *n.*[1]: cf. -OON.] 1 An ornamental cord or braid worn on the person. LME. 2 *Fortif.* A course of stones where a parapet meets a rampart, or forming a coping on the inner wall of a ditch. L16. 3 *Archit.* A projecting band of stone on the face of a wall. E18. 4 A ribbon forming part of the insignia of an order of knighthood. E18. 5 A line or circle of troops etc. positioned to prevent passage to or from a guarded area; a system of police roadblocks. M18. **b** A guarded line between districts affected with a disease and those unaffected, to prevent its spread. E19. 6 A fruit tree trained to grow as a single stem, usu. against a wall. L19.

cordoned *a.* decorated with the cordon of an order M16.

cordon /ˈkɔːd(ə)n/ *v.t.* M16. [Fr. *cordonner*, f. *cordon*: see prec.] †1 Ornament with a cordon. *rare.* Only in M16. †2 Twist into a cord. *rare.* Only in E17. 3 Cut *off* or surround (as) with a cordon of police etc. L19.

cordon bleu /ˌkɔːdɔ̃ ˈbləː/ *n.* & *a. phr.* M18. [Fr., f. as CORDON *n.* + *bleu* BLUE *a.*] **A** *n.* Pl. **-s -s** (pronounced same). 1 (A person having) a supreme distinction; *spec.* a first-class cook. M18. 2 *Hist.* A blue ribbon signifying the highest order of chivalry under the Bourbon kings. L18. **B** *adj.* Of cooking: first-class. M20.

cordon sanitaire /ˌkɔːdɔ̃ sanɪˈtɛː/ *n. phr.* Pl. **-s -s** (pronounced same). M19. [Fr., f. as CORDON *n.* + *sanitaire* sanitary.] = CORDON *n.* 5b.

fig.: B. WARD The Allies succeeded in creating a *cordon sanitaire* of buffer-states to cut Communism off from Europe.

cordovan /ˈkɔːdəv(ə)n/ *a.* & *n.* L16. [Sp. *cordován* (now *-bán*) n., *-ano* adj., f. *Córdova* (now *-oba*) f. L *Corduba* Córdoba (see below).] **A** *adj.* Of or pertaining to the city of and province of Córdoba in Spain; made of cordovan. L16. **B** *n.* 1 A kind of pliable fine-grained leather used esp. for shoes, made orig. at Córdoba from goatskin and now from horsehide. L16. †2 A skin of this leather. M17–E19.

Cordtex /ˈkɔːdtɛks/ *n.* M20. [f. CORD *n.*[1] + TEXTILE.] (Proprietary name for) fuse cable consisting of a core of explosive material in a plastic and textile sheath.

corduroy /ˈkɔːdərɔɪ/ *n.* & *a.* L18. [Prob. f. CORD *n.*[1] + DUROY.] **A** *n.* 1 A coarse cotton velvet with thick ribbing. L18. 2 In *pl.* Corduroy trousers. *colloq.* L18. 3 A road made of logs laid together transversely; ground made up into such a road. M19. **B** *adj.* 1 Made of corduroy. L18. 2 Having ridges and furrows like corduroy; *spec.* (of a road etc.) made of logs laid together transversely. L18.

corduroyed *a.* wearing corduroy M19.

corduroy /ˈkɔːdərɔɪ/ *v.t.* M19. [f. the n.] Make as a corduroy road; cross (a swamp etc.) with such a road.

cordwain /ˈkɔːdweɪn/ *n. arch.* LME. [OFr. *cordewan, cordoan*, f. *Cordoue* f. Sp. *Córdova*: see CORDOVAN.] = CORDOVAN *n.* 1.

SIR W. SCOTT Shoes of Spanish cordwain fastened with silver buckles.

cordwainer /ˈkɔːdweɪnə/ *n. arch.* Also (now *Sc.*) **cordiner** /ˈkɔːd(ə)nə/. ME. [AN *cordewaner* = OFr. *cordoanier* (mod. *cordonnier*), f. as prec.] A worker in cordwain, a shoemaker.

¶Now only in names of guilds etc.

cordwainery *n.* shoemaker's work M19. **cordwaining** *n.* = CORDWAINERY M18.

core /kɔː/ *n.*[1] ME. [Origin unkn.] **I** 1 The hard central part of an apple, pear, quince, etc., containing the seeds. ME. †**b** *fig.* Something that sticks in one's throat, something one cannot get over. LME–M17. 2 An unburnt part in the middle of a piece of coal, limestone, etc. LME. 3 The hard centre of a boil. M16.

3 *fig.*: R. NORTH The Canker, or Coar, of the late Rebellion was torn out by this loyal Acknowledgment.

II 4 The innermost part or heart of anything (*lit.* & *fig.*), *spec.* of timber or of one's person. LME.

4 SHAKES. *Haml.* In my heart's core, ay, in my heart of heart. WELLINGTON Our system is rotten to the core. S. BARING-GOULD A solid core of fact. P. PORTER The fire storm bit out the core of Dresden.

III A central portion that is separated from the rest. 5 A piece cut out and removed from the middle of something, esp. the ground or the seabed. M17. 6 A central portion that is left; *spec.* (*Archaeol.*) a piece of stone left as a waste product after the removal of flakes to make implements. E19.

IV 7 *gen.* A central part of different character. Chiefly *techn.* M17. 8 An internal mould filling the space to be left hollow in a casting. E18. 9 A length of soft iron forming the centre of an electromagnet or an induction coil. M19. **b** Each of an array of small magnetic units in a computer whose magnetization is reversed by passing a current through a nearby wire. M20. 10 The central strand of a rope or an electric cable. M19. 11 The central part of the earth; *spec.* that within the mantle, with a radius of 3500 km (2200 miles). L19. 12 *Physics.* The part of an atom other than the valency electrons. E20. 13 The part of a nuclear reactor that contains the fissile material. M20.

Phrases etc.: *hard core*: see HARD *a.* *soft-core*: see SOFT *a.* *red core*: see RED *a.*

Attrib. & *comb.*: In sense 'central, basic, fundamental', as *core vocabulary* etc. Special combs., as **core area** a central geographical area in which characteristic elements are concentrated; **core curriculum** a group of basic subjects whose study is compulsory and to which optional ones may be added; **core implement, tool** *Archaeol.* a stone tool shaped by the removal of waste and trimming flakes from a block or nodule; **core loss** energy loss in electrical machinery by hysteresis and eddy currents in cores; **core sampler** a device for extracting a core from the seabed etc.; **core-sampling** drilling of the seabed etc. so as to extract cores as samples; *core tool*: see *core implement* above.

coreless *a.* E19.

core /kɔː/ *n.*[2] E17. [Partly var. of CHORE *n.*[1], partly Anglicized spelling of CORPS.] 1 A body or company of people; *spec.* the players in a curling match, a rink. Chiefly *Sc.* E17. 2 A gang of miners working together in one shift. L18. 3 A shift in a Cornish mine. L18.

core /kɔː/ *v.t.* LME. [f. CORE *n.*[1]] 1 Take out the core of. LME. 2 In *pass.* Be enshrined. E19. 3 Hollow *out* by using a core (in founding) or extracting one. L19.

corer *n.* (*a*) a device for extracting cores from fruit; (*b*) = *core sampler* s.v. CORE *n.*[1]: L18.

coreal *n.* var. of CORIAL.

†**Corean** *n.* & *a.* see KOREAN.

†**Coreis** *n.* see KOREISH.

†**Coreis(h)** *n.pl.* & *a.* see KOREISH.

corelation /kəʊrɪˈleɪʃ(ə)n/ *n.* Also **co-relation**. M19. [f. CO- + RELATION.] Mutual relation; correlation.

corelative /kəʊˈrɛlətɪv/ *a.* & *n.* Also **co-relative**. M18. [f. CO- + RELATIVE.] (A) correlative.

corelatively *adv.* L19.

co-religionist /kəʊrɪˈlɪdʒ(ə)nɪst/ *n.* Also ***corel-**. E19. [f. CO- + RELIGION + -IST.] An adherent of the same religion.

corella /kəˈrɛlə/ *n.* L19. [App. Latinized form of Aborig. *ca-rall.*] The long-billed cockatoo, *Cacatua tenuirostris*, a white Australian bird that can be taught to talk.

coreopsis /kɒrɪˈɒpsɪs/ *n.* M18. [mod.L, f. Gk *koris* bug + *opsis* appearance, in ref. to the shape of the seeds.] A plant of the mostly American genus *Coreopsis*, of the composite family, comprising annuals and perennials with rayed usu. yellow flowers, some of which are grown as garden flowers.

co-respondent /kəʊrɪˈspɒnd(ə)nt/ *n.* Also ***corespondent**. M19. [f. CO- + RESPONDENT.] *Law.* A person with whom a married person, esp. a married woman, is alleged to have committed adultery.

co-respondent's shoes *joc.* men's two-toned shoes.

corf /kɔːf/ *n.* Pl. **corves** /kɔːvz/. LME. [(M)LG, (M)Du. *korf* = OHG *chorp, korb* (G *Korb*), f. L *corbis* basket.] †1 A basket. LME–E17. 2 A large basket formerly used for conveying, hoisting, or delivering mined coal or ore; the tub which has superseded it. M17. 3 A container through which water can flow for keeping fish etc. in it alive. L17.

Corfiote /ˈkɔːfɪəʊt/ *n.* & *a.* Also **-ot** /-ət/. M19. [f. *Corfu* (see below) after CYPRIOT.] (A native or inhabitant) of the Greek island of Corfu.

corgi /ˈkɔːgi/ *n.* E20. [Welsh, f. *cor* dwarf + *ci* dog.] A dog of a small short-legged breed of Welsh origin, with a head resembling that of a fox. Also *Welsh corgi*.

coriaceous /kɒrɪˈeɪʃəs/ *a.* L17. [f. late L *coriaceus*, f. as CORIUM: see -ACEOUS.] 1 Resembling leather in texture or appearance; leathery. L17. 2 Made of leather. *rare* (*affected*). E19.

corial /kɔːrɪˈɑːl/ *n.* Also **-eal**. L18. [Amer. Sp. f. Arawak *kuljara*: cf. CURIARA.] In Guyana, a dugout canoe with pointed ends.

coriander /kɒrɪˈandə/ *n.* ME. [(O)Fr. *coriandre* f. L *coriandrum* f. Gk *koriannon.*] 1 An annual umbelliferous plant, *Coriandrum sativum*, native to southern Europe and Asia Minor and with aromatic fruit used for flavouring. ME. 2 = *coriander seed* below. Also, the leaves of coriander, as a culinary item. M16.

Comb.: **coriander seed** (*a*) the globose fruit of coriander, *esp.* the dried ripe fruit; (*b*) *slang* (now *rare* or *obs.*) money.

†**Corinth** *n.* ME. [(O)Fr. *Corinthe* (AN *Corauntz*) f. L *Corinthos* f. Gk *Korinthos*: see next.] **I** 1 *raisins of Corinth*, (orig.) *of Corauntz* [see CURRANT], currants. ME–E17. 2 (**c-**.) See CURRANT. ME. **II** 3 In *pl.* Natives or inhabitants of Corinth. LME–M17. 4 A brothel. E17–L18.

Corinthian /kəˈrɪnθɪən/ *n.* & *a.* E16. [f. L *Corinthius* f. Gk *Korinthios*, f. *Korinthos* Corinth (see below): see -AN.] **A** *n.* 1 A native or inhabitant of Corinth, a city of ancient and modern Greece. In *pl.* (treated as *sing.*), either of St Paul's two Epistles to the Corinthians, books of the New Testament. E16. †2 A wealthy man; a profligate idler; a licentious man; a brazen-faced man. L16–L19. 3 A man about town. E19. 4 A wealthy amateur of sport. L19.

B *adj.* 1 Of or pertaining to Corinth. L16. 2 *Archit.* Designating the lightest and most ornate of the three classical orders, characterized by bell-shaped capitals with rows of acanthus leaves giving graceful volutes and helices. E17. 3 Profligate, licentious; given to luxurious dissipation. *arch.* M17. 4 After the elegant style of the art of Corinth; too brilliant. M19. 5 Amateur (in sport). (Earlier in CORINTHIANISM.) L19.

1 **Corinthian brass, bronze** an alloy produced at Corinth, much prized for ornaments, said to be of gold, silver, and copper; *fig.* effrontery, shamelessness. 5 *transf.*: *Sunday Times* Against the hardened professionals of the treasury, Hattersley's is a decidedly corinthian team.

Corinthia'nesque *a.* approximating to the Corinthian architectural style M19. **Corinthianism** *n.* amateurism in sport E19. **Corinthianize** *v.i.* (*a*) *arch.* live licentiously; (*b*) imitate the Corinthian order of architecture: E19.

Coriolis /kɒrɪ'əʊlɪs/ *a.* (*attrib.*). E20. [G. G. *Coriolis* (1792–1843), Fr. engineer.] Pertaining to or designating the effect whereby a body moving relative to a rotating frame of reference is accelerated in that frame in a direction perpendicular to its motion and to the axis of rotation.

Coriolis acceleration, Coriolis force, etc.

corium /'kɔːrɪəm/ *n.* E19. [L = skin, hide, leather.] 1 *Entomol.* A hardened part at the base of the forewings of heteropteran insects, next to the clavus. E19. 2 = DERMIS. M19. 3 *Hist.* A suit of leather armour composed of overlapping flaps. M19.

co-rival /kəʊ'rʌɪv(ə)l/ *n.* & *a.* L17. [Partly f. CO- + RIVAL *n.* & *a.*, partly var. of CORRIVAL.] (A person) who is one of two or more joint rivals.

co-rivalry *n.* M19.

cork /kɔːk/ *n.*[1] & *a.* ME. [Du., LG *kork* f. Sp. *alcorque* cork soled sandal, f. Arab. AL-[2] + (prob.) Sp. Arab. *kurk, kork* ult. f. L *quercus* oak, (in some parts of Iberia) cork-oak.] A *n.* 1 A buoyant light-brown material that is obtained from the cork-oak, being the cork (sense 1b) of that tree. ME. b *Bot.* The material forming the outer layer of the periderm in parts of some higher plants, providing protection by its impermeability to air and water. Also called *phellem.* L19. 2 A sandal, sole, or heel made of cork. Now *Hist.* LME. 3 A piece of cork used as a float for a fishing-line or a person swimming. L15. 4 A cylindrical or tapering stopper for a bottle, made of cork or other material. M16. 5 An evergreen oak, *Quercus suber*, which is native to the Mediterranean and has the distinctive property of producing more cork after some is removed. M16.

1 BURNT *cork.*

B *attrib.* or as *adj.* Made of or with cork. E18.

Comb. & *special collocations*: **cork cambium** the tissue of a plant's periderm that gives rise to cork on its outer surface and phelloderm on its inner; **cork-jacket**: made with cork, to support a person in the water; **cork lino(leum)**: made of canvas backed with a mixture of linseed oil and ground cork; **cork-oak** = sense 5 above; **cork-tipped** *a.* (of a cigarette) having a filter of corklike material; **cork tree** (*a*) = sense 5 above; (*b*) any of several deciduous trees of eastern Asia belonging to the genus *Phellodendron* of the rue family and having corklike bark; **corkwing** a small European wrasse (*Crenilabrus melops*); **corkwood** (a tree yielding) any very light and porous wood, esp. *Leitneria floridana*, a rare deciduous shrub or tree of the south-eastern US, and the whau, *Entelea arborescens*, of New Zealand.

corklike *a.* resembling (that of) cork M19.

cork /kɔːk/ *n.*[2] ME. [Gael. & (O)Ir. *corcur* (orig.) purple f. L *purpur.*] A purple or red dye obtained from certain lichens.

cork *n.*[3] see CALK *n.*

cork /kɔːk/ *v.*[1]*t.* E16. [f. CORK *n.*[1]] †1 Provide with a cork as a sole, float, etc. E16–M19. 2 Stop (a bottle etc.) with a cork. M17. 3 Shut *up* or confine with or as with a cork; bottle *up* (feelings). Also foll. by *down.* M17. 4 Blacken with burnt cork. E19.

corked *ppl a.* that has been corked; (of wine) tasting of the cork, impaired by a defective cork: E16.

cork *v.*[2] see CALK *v.*[1]

corkage /'kɔːkɪdʒ/ *n.* M19. [f. CORK *n.*[1] or *v.*[1] + -AGE.] A charge made by a hotel or restaurant for serving a bottle of liquor, esp. one not supplied by it.

corker /'kɔːkə/ *n.* & *a.* E18. [f. CORK *v.*[1] + -ER[1].] A *n.* 1 A person who puts corks into bottles. Formerly perh. also a person who cut cork into stoppers. E18. 2 *fig.* Something that puts an end to a matter; an astonishing or surpassingly good thing or person. *colloq.* M19. B *adj.* Astonishing, surpassingly good, stunning. *NZ colloq.* M20.

corking /'kɔːkɪŋ/ *n.* M17. [f. CORK *n.*[1], *v.*[1] + -ING[1].] 1 The action of CORK *v.*[1] M17. 2 The development or presence of a corky taste in wine. E20.

corking /'kɔːkɪŋ/ *a. slang.* L19. [f. CORKER + -ING[2].] Exceptionally fine, excellent, or large.

corkingly *adv.* E20.

†corking-pin *n.* E18–M19. [App. f. alt. of CALKIN + PIN *n.*] A pin of the largest size.

corkir /'kɔːkə/ *n. Sc.* Also **k-**. E18. [Gael. *corcur*: see CORK *n.*[2]] A lichen, *Lecanora tartarea*, which yields a red dye.

corks /kɔːks/ *int. slang.* E20. [Alt. of COCK *n.*[4] or blend of this and LAWK.] Expr. astonishment or dismay.

corkscrew /'kɔːkskruː/ *n.*, *v.*, & *a.* E18. [f. CORK *n.*[1] + SCREW *n.*[1]] A *n.* 1 An instrument for drawing a cork from a bottle, comprising a steel helix with a (usu. transverse) handle. E18. 2 Something, esp. a curl, with a spiral twist. M19.

Comb.: **corkscrew rule**: that the direction of the magnetic field produced by an electric current following a spiral path is that which a corkscrew would have if it were turned in the same way as the current.

B *v.* 1 *v.t.* & *i.* Move or twist in a spiral course. L18. 2 *v.t.* Get *out of* someone by devious means or with effort. M19. C *adj.* Spirally twisted. E19.

THACKERAY Little corkscrew ringlets. TENNYSON Up the cork-screw stair.

corkscrewy *a.* L19.

corky /'kɔːki/ *a.* E17. [f. CORK *n.*[1] + -Y[1].] 1 Light, frivolous; buoyant, lively; restive. *colloq.* E17. †2 Dry and stiff; withered. Only in E17. 3 *gen.* Resembling cork. M18. 4 Having a taste of cork; corked. L19.

corkiness *n.* M19.

Corliss /'kɔːlɪs/ *a.* M19. [G. H. *Corliss* (1817–88), US engineer.] *Mech.* Designating (a steam engine employing) a kind of valve-gear with an oscillatory rotary motion.

corm /kɔːm/ *n.* M19. [mod.L *cormus* f. Gk *kormos* trunk of a tree with the boughs lopped off.] An underground rounded, swollen portion of the stem of some perennial plants which develops buds, leaves, and roots and each year dries up after giving rise to new corms.

cormorant /'kɔːm(ə)r(ə)nt/ *n.* & *a.* ME. [OFr. *cormaran* (mod. *cormoran*) f. med.L *corvus marinus* sea-raven. For final *t* cf. *peasant, tyrant.*] A *n.* 1 A large lustrous-black fish-eating water-bird, *Phalacrocorax carbo*, having a long neck and bill and found near many coasts; any bird of the same family (Phalacrocoracidae) of dark fish-eating water-birds. ME. 2 *fig.* An insatiably greedy person or thing. E16. B *attrib.* or as *adj.* Greedy; rapacious. M16.

corn /kɔːn/ *n.*[1] [OE *corn* = OFris., OS, OHG, ON *korn*, Goth. *kaurn* f. Gmc; rel. to L *granum* GRAIN *n.*[1]] 1 A small hard particle, as of sand or salt. Long *dial.* OE. 2 *spec.* The small hard seed or fruit of a plant; *esp.* a cereal seed. OE. 3 The seed, collectively, of a cereal plant; grain; *esp.* that of the chief cereal of a district, as in England wheat, in Scotland oats. OE. b More fully *Indian corn.* Maize. Without qualifying adj. chiefly *N. Amer.* E17. c More fully *corn-whiskey.* Whiskey distilled from maize. *US.* E19. 4 Cereal plants as a standing or a harvested crop. OE. 5 In *pl.* Cereal crops. Now *dial.* OE. †6 A single stalk or plant of a cereal. *rare.* LME–L16. 7 Something corny (CORNY *a.*[1] 5), *esp.* old-fashioned or sentimental music. *colloq.* M20.

2 BARLEY-CORN. PEPPERCORN. 3 TENNYSON A sack of corn. b POPCORN. 4 SHAKES. *Hen. VIII* Her foes shake like a field of beaten corn.

Phrases: **acknowledge the corn** admit defeat, a charge, etc. **corn in Egypt** a plentiful supply (in allusion to *Gen.* 42:2). *corn on the cob*: see COB *n.*[1] 8. *Indian corn*: see sense 3b above. *lye corn*: see LYE *v. soft corn*: see SOFT *a. sweet corn*: see SWEET *a.* & *adv.*

Comb.: **corn baby** [alt. of KIRN *n.*[2]] = *corn dolly* below; **corn beef** corned beef; **corn borer** any of several moths (or their larvae) whose larvae bore into corn, *esp.* (more fully *European corn borer*) a pyralid moth, *Ostrinia* (*Pyrausta*) *nubilalis*, of Europe and N. America, and (more fully *south-western corn borer*) a grass moth, *Diatraea* (*Zeadiatraea*) *grandiosella* of the southern US; **corn brandy** whiskey; **corn-bread** *N. Amer.* bread made of the meal of maize; **corn bunting** a brown bunting, *Miliaria calandra*, of the open countryside; **corn cake** *US* corn-bread made in the form of flat cakes; one of these cakes; **corn chandler** a dealer in corn; **corn circle** = *crop circle* s.v. CROP *n.* *corn-cockle*: see COCKLE *n.*[1] 1; *corn crib*: see CRIB *n.* 8; **corn dance** *US* any dance connected with the sowing or harvesting of maize among N. American Indians or Blacks; **corn dodger** *US* a type of cake of corn-bread; **corn dolly** [alt. of KIRN *n.*[2]] a symbolic or decorative figure made of plaited straw; **corn ear worm** a moth, *Heliothis armigera* or *H. zea*, whose larvae are a major pest of cultivated plants, esp. of maize in N. America; a larva of this moth; **corn exchange** a building where corn is or used to be bought and sold; **corn-factor** a dealer in corn; **corn-fed** *a.* fed on grain, esp. maize; *fig.* (*colloq.*) plump, well-fed; *Jazz slang* old-fashioned, trite; **cornfield**: in which corn is grown; **corn-flag** any plant of the genus *Gladiolus* (see GLADIOLUS); **cornflake** (*a*) in *pl.*, a kind of breakfast cereal made from toasted and flavoured flakes of maize meal; (*b*) a flake of this cereal; **cornflour** (*a*) fine flour got from maize, used in making puddings, corn syrup and corn sugar, adhesives, etc.; (*b*) flour got from rice or other grain; **corn-ground**: on which corn is grown; **corn-house** †(*a*) a granary; (*b*) *US*= *corn crib* s.v. CRIB *n.* 8; **corn-husk** *N. Amer.* the husk of coarse leaves enclosing an ear of maize; **corn-husker** *N. Amer.* a machine which or person who strips the husks from the ears of maize; **corn-husking** *N. Amer.* the separation of maize husks; a convivial gathering that begins with this task; **Corn Laws** laws regulating the corn trade; *esp.* those in England restricting the import of corn, repealed in 1846; **corn lily** = IXIA 2; **corn marigold** a tall annual plant of the composite family, *Chrysanthemum segetum*, with yellow flowers like daisies and occurring as a weed on cultivated land; **cornmeal** meal made from corn, *spec.* in Scotland oatmeal, in N. America, meal of maize; **†cornmonger** a dealer in corn; **corn-oil**: made from the germ of maize for use as a salad and cooking oil; **corn parsley** a glaucous parsley, *Petroselinum segetum*, of chalky banks and fields; **corn-pipe** a rustic musical instrument made of a stalk of corn; *corn pone*: see PONE *n.*[2]; **corn-popper** *N. Amer.* a device for making popcorn; *corn poppy*: see POPPY *n.* 1; **corn-rent**: paid in corn, or determined annually by the price of corn; **corn-roast** *N. Amer.* a party at which green maize is roasted and eaten; **corn rose** (*a*) = *corn poppy* above; (*b*) the cockle (COCKLE *n.*[1] 1, 2); **corn-salad** a plant of the genus *Valerianella* in the valerian family, esp. *V. locusta* or *V. eriocarpa*, annuals grown as salad plants in Europe; **corn-shuck(ing)** *N. Amer.* = *corn-husk(ing)* above; *corn silk*: see SILK *n.*; **corn smut** a smut fungus, *Ustilago zeae*, that attacks maize; the disease it causes; **corn snake** a long non-venomous snake, *Elaphe guttata*, common in the US; **corn snow** *US* coarse wet snow resulting from alternate thawing and freezing; *corn spurrey*: see SPURREY 1; **corn-stalk** (*a*) a stalk of corn; (*b*) *slang* an Australian, esp. one from New South Wales, Australia; **cornstarch** (chiefly *N. Amer.*) = *cornflour* (a) above; **corn sugar** *US* glucose sugar, esp. when made from cornflour; **corn syrup** *N. Amer.* glucose syrup, esp. when made from cornflour; *corn whiskey*: see sense 3c above; **corn-worm** a moth larva or other insect destructive to grain.

corn /kɔːn/ *n.*[2] LME. [AN = (O)Fr. *cor* f. L *cornu* horn.] A small, horny, usu. tender area of thickened skin, esp. on the foot, caused by undue pressure.

tread on a person's corns: see TREAD *v.*

corn /kɔːn/ *v.* LME. [f. CORN *n.*[1]] I *v.t.* †1a Provision with corn. *rare.* Only in LME. b Give (a horse) a feed of oats. *Sc.* M18. 2 Form (esp. gunpowder) into grains, as by sieving. M16. 3 Sprinkle or preserve with salt. M16. 4 Plant with corn; grow corn on. M17. II *v.i.* †5 Become granular. M16–L17. 6 Of a cereal or legume: form seeds in the ear or pod. M17.

cornada /kɔrˈnaða, kɔːˈnɑːdə/ *n.* Pl. **-as** /-as, -əz/. M20. [Sp., f. *cuerno* f. L *cornu* horn.] The goring of a bullfighter by a bull; a wound so caused.

cornage /ˈkɔːnɪdʒ/ *n.* L16. [OFr., f. *corn(e)* f. L *cornu* horn: see -AGE. In med.L *cornagium*.] *Hist.* A feudal service, being a form of rent fixed by the number of horned cattle.

¶The term was formerly widely misunderstood, and explained as a duty to blow a horn to warn of a border incursion etc.

corn-ball /ˈkɔːnbɔːl/ *n.* & *a.* M19. [f. CORN *n.*[1] + BALL *n.*[1]] A *n.* 1 A sweet consisting of a ball of popcorn and syrup. *US.* M19. 2 A corn-ball person. *slang.* M20. B *adj.* = CORNY *a.*[1] 5. *slang.* M20.

cornbrash /ˈkɔːnbraʃ/ *n.* E19. [f. CORN *n.*[1] + BRASH *n.*[2]] *Geol.* An earthy fossiliferous limestone occurring widely in England in a thin formation of Jurassic age.

corn-cob /ˈkɔːnkɒb/ *n.* L18. [f. CORN *n.*[1] + COB *n.*[1]] 1 The cylindrical woody part to which the grains are attached in an ear of maize. L18. 2 More fully *corn-cob pipe.* A tobacco-pipe made from a corn-cob. M19.

corncrake /ˈkɔːnkreɪk/ *n.* LME. [f. CORN *n.*[1] + CRAKE *n.*[1]] A slender brown bird, *Crex crex*, of the rail family which has a harsh grating cry and lives in grassland. Also called *landrail*, *meadow crake*.

cornea /ˈkɔːnɪə/ *n.* LME. [Short for med.L *cornea tela* horny web, f. L *corneus* CORNEOUS.] The transparent circular outer covering at the front of the eye, over the iris and pupil.

luna cornea: see LUNA 2C.

corneal *a.* E19.

†corned *a.*[1] E16–M19. [f. Fr. *corné* f. L *corneus* CORNEOUS: see -ED[2].] Horned; pointed.

corned /kɔːnd/ *a.*[2] L16. [f. CORN *n.*[1], *v.*: see -ED[2], -ED[1].] 1 Granulated. L16. 2 Preserved or cured with salt. E17. 3 Drunk, intoxicated. Cf. CORNY *a.*[1] 4. *slang.* L18. 4 Bearing seeds or grains; having the seeds developed. E19.

2 **corned beef** beef preserved with salt and often tinned.

cornel /ˈkɔːn(ə)l/ *n.*[1] Long *obs.* exc. *dial.* LME. [OFr. *cornal* var. of *cornée*, *cornier* CORNER *n.*] A corner; an angle (of a building etc.).

cornel /ˈkɔːn(ə)l/ *n.*[2] & *a.* LME. [OFr. *corn(e)ille*, *cornolle* (mod. *cornouille*) f. L *cornus.*] A *n.* 1 Long only more fully *cornel wood.* The wood of the cornelian cherry, formerly used for weapons because of its hardness. LME. 2 Either of two plants, (orig. & more fully *cornel tree*) the cornelian cherry (*Cornus mas*), and the dogwood (*Cornus sanguinea*); any of various other plants of the genus *Cornus*, which comprises mostly deciduous shrubs and trees. M16. 3 More fully *cornel berry*, *fruit.* The fruit of the cornelian cherry, of the size and shape of an olive. L16. 4 [tr. L *cornus.*] A javelin made of cornel wood. *literary.* E17. B *adj.* Made of cornel wood. L17.

cornelian /kɔːˈniːlɪən/ *n.*[1] Also **carnel-** /kɑːˈniːl-/. LME. [OFr. *corneline* (mod. *cornaline*); cf. med.L *corneolus*, later *cornelius.* Var. *carn-* after L *carnis*, *caro* flesh, etc.] A dull red or reddish-white kind of chalcedony.

cornelian /kɔːˈniːlɪən/ *n.*[2] E17. [f. CORNEL *n.*[2] + -IAN.] Now only more fully *cornelian cherry.* A European flowering shrub or small tree, *Cornus mas*, of the dogwood family which bears edible fruit and is grown as an ornamental; the fruit itself (= CORNEL *n.*[2] 3).

cornemuse /ˈkɔːnəmjuːz; *foreign* kɔrnəmyːz (*pl. same*)/ *n.* LME. [(O)Fr., prob. f. *cornemuser* play the cornemuse, f. *corner* sound a horn (f. *corne* horn f. L *cornu*) + *muser* play the musette.] An early form of bagpipe; a kind of mouth-blown bagpipe of the present-day in France and Belgium.

corneo- /ˈkɔːnɪəʊ/ *comb. form.* [f. CORNEA: see -O-.] *Med.* Of or pertaining to the cornea and, as *corneo-iritis.*

corneous /ˈkɔːnɪəs/ *a.* Now *techn.* M17. [f. L *corneus*, f. *cornu* horn: see -EOUS.] Horny.

corner /ˈkɔːnə/ *n.* ME. [AN *corner*, OFr. *cornier* f. Proto-Romance f. L *cornu* horn, tip, corner: see -ER[2].] 1 A place where the converging sides or edges of something meet, forming an angular projection. ME. 2 A projecting angle or extremity, esp. where two streets meet, or a road etc. changes direction. ME. b A triangular piece cut from the hind end of a side of bacon. L19. 3 The small space included between meeting sides or edges, esp. of a room. ME. b Each of the diagonally opposite angles of a boxing or wrestling ring, where a contestant rests between rounds and is attended by a second or seconds; *transf.* a boxer's or wrestler's second(s). M19. 4 A secluded or remote region; somewhere that readily escapes notice. ME. b A part of anywhere, even the smallest or most secluded. E16. 5 A distant part; a quarter *of* the earth. Formerly also, a direction. LME. 6 A landmark or surveyor's mark at the angle of a plot of land. *US.* L17. 7 A point in whist and certain other card-games. M18. 8 *Comm.* The speculative purchase by a syndicate of all the available supply of a stock or commodity, so as to make speculative sellers unable to meet their obligations except by coming to the syndicate on its own terms; any combination to raise prices by securing a monopoly. M19. 9 A share in something, esp. the proceeds of a robbery. *dial.* & *slang.* L19. 10 In some field games, a free kick or hit after an opponent has sent the ball over his or her own goal-line, taken from the nearest corner (as in soccer) or from a point on the goal-line or sideline at or towards the corner (as in hockey). Also *corner-kick*, *-hit.* L19.

1 GOLDSMITH The corners of the mouth. J. TYNDALL The corner of a window. T. COLLINS I regarded him out of the corner of my eye. *fig.*: J. K. JEROME There are one or two corners about you that are not perfect. *Oxford corners*: see OXFORD *a.* 2 *Daily Mirror* Youngsters . . hanging around on street corners. *cut a corner, cut corners*: see CUT *v.* **just (a)round the corner** *colloq.* close at hand; imminent. **turn the corner** pass round a corner into another street; *fig.* pass from worsening to improving, esp. in an illness. 3 DAY LEWIS Dark corners or passages of the houses we occupied. *cosy corner*: see COSY *a.* 2. *tight corner*: see TIGHT *a.* **drive someone, paint oneself, into a corner** *fig.* force someone, bring oneself, into a difficult situation from which there is no escape. *every nook and corner*: see NOOK *n.* 3b. *puss in the corner*: see PUSS *n.*[1] **within the four corners** within the scope or extent *of.* b *neutral corner*: see NEUTRAL *n.* & *a.* 4 JOSEPH HALL Whatever private contract may be transacted in corners betwixt the parties. B. JOWETT A dark corner of the human mind. L. P. HARTLEY This small corner of Wales. *hole-and-corner*: see HOLE *n.*[1] **keep a corner** reserve a small place. b H. CONWAY My friend must have seen every nook and corner in the house. J. BUCHAN No corner of the globe left unexplored. 5 SHAKES. *Much Ado* Sits the wind in that corner? MAX-MÜLLER Carried to all the corners of the earth. 8 R. H. TAWNEY Speculators who had made a corner in wheat. *fig.*: S. BELLOW I don't have a corner on troubles. You've got your own. 9 **stand one's corner** contribute or pay for one's share. 10 *Norwich Mercury* His goal-bound effort was deflected for a corner. *long corner*: see LONG *a.*[1] *short corner*: see SHORT *a.*

Comb.: **cornerback** in certain field sports, as American football, hurling, (a player in) a defensive position on the wing; **corner-boy** a street rough, a loafer esp. in Ireland (cf. *corner-man* below); **†corner-cap** a cap with four (or three) corners, worn by divines and members of a university; **†corner-creeper** *fig.* an underhand and stealthy person; **corner cupboard**: fitted into the corner of a room; **corner flag**: marking a corner of the playing area in football, hockey, and lacrosse; **corner-forward** in hurling, (a player in) an attacking position on the wing; *corner-hit*, *-kick*: see sense 10 above. **corner-man** (*a*) a street rough, a loafer (cf. *corner-boy* above); (*b*) a performer at either end of a row of blackface minstrels, playing bones or tambourine and contributing comic effects; (*c*) = CORNERER; **corner shop** a shop at a street corner; any small local shop, as distinct from a supermarket etc.; **cornerstone** [after late L (Vulgate) *lapis angularis*] a stone forming the projecting angle of a wall; *fig.* an indispensable or essential part, a basis on which something depends; **corner throw** (*a*) in certain ball-games, a free throw of the ball from a corner of the playing area; (*b*) *Judo* = SUMI-GAESHI.

cornerless *a.* L16. **cornerwise** *adv.* so as to form a corner; diagonally: L15. **cornery** *a.* having many corners L16.

corner /ˈkɔːnə/ *v.* ME. [f. the n.] 1 *v.t.* Provide with corners. Usu. in *pass.* ME. 2 *v.t.* Place in a corner. LME. 3 *v.t.* Drive into a corner or a place from where escape is impossible; *fig.* put into a difficult or embarrassing position. E19. 4 *v.i.* Abut *on* at a corner; meet at an angle. *US.* E19. 5 *v.t. Comm.* Operate in (a stock etc.) or against (a dealer) by means of a corner; control (a market) in this way. M19. 6 *v.t.* Go round (a corner) in a road, racetrack, etc. M19. 7 *v.i.* Go round a corner, take corners, esp. in a specified manner. E20.

1 MILTON The Imperial City . . corner'd with four white Towers. 3 M. TWAIN The little Lady Jane turned to Tom and cornered him with this question. J. COLVILLE Our 51st Division is cornered at St. Valéry and has been ordered to surrender. 4 N. HAWTHORNE A pew cornering on one of the side-aisles. 5 E. WILSON His employers . . had succeeded in cornering the market and wanted to keep up the price. 7 *Times* Letting plenty of fresh air into the car, . . driving smoothly with no fast cornering or sudden braking.

cornerer *n.* a person who makes a corner in a stock or commodity M19.

cornered /ˈkɔːnəd/ *a.* ME. [f. CORNER *n.*, *v.*: see -ED[2], -ED[1].] Having a corner or corners. Freq. as 2nd elem. of comb., as *three-cornered*, *sharp-cornered*, etc.

cornet /ˈkɔːnɪt/ *n.*[1] In sense 1 now usu. **-tt.** LME. [(O)Fr. dim. of Proto-Romance var. of L *cornu* horn: see -ET[1].] I *Mus.* 1a *Early Mus.* Orig., a wind instrument made of a horn or resembling a horn. Later = CORNETTO. Also, a player of such an instrument. LME. b Orig. †*cornet-à-piston(s).* A valved brass instrument used chiefly in bands, similar to a trumpet but shorter and with a wider mouth; a player of this instrument. M19. 2 Any of various organ-stops suggestive of a cornet(t), esp. a powerful mixture stop. M17. II 3a A piece of paper rolled into a conical form and twisted at the tip, for carrying sugar, salt, etc. M16. b A conical wafer, esp. one filled with ice-cream. E20. †4 A farrier's instrument formerly used for blood-letting. Also *cornet-horn.* L16–M18. 5 In gold assaying, a small flat coil into which the sample is rolled after cupellation, prior to the removal of silver by nitric acid. E19.

corˈnet(t)ist *n.* a player of the cornet(t) L18.

cornet /ˈkɔːnɪt/ *n.*[2] M16. [(O)Fr. *cornette* dim. of *corne* horn, orig. collect., f. Proto-Romance alt. of L *cornua* pl. of *cornu* horn: see -ET[1].] 1 *Hist.* A kind of ladies' head-dress; the large white, winged head-dress formerly worn by the Sisters of Charity. M16. †2 The standard of a troop of cavalry. L16–M19. 3 A company of cavalry. *obs.* exc. *Hist.* L16. 4 Chiefly *Hist.* The fifth commissioned officer in a troop of cavalry, who carried the colours. L16. 5 Formerly, the mounted bearer of a standard or colour. Now only *Sc.*, the chief rider and standard-bearer of a burgh at the riding of the marches. E18.

4 C. V. WEDGWOOD The King was seized by a party of soldiers under Cornet Joyce.

cornetcy *n.* the rank of a cornet M18.

cornett *n.* see CORNET *n.*[1]

cornetto /kɔːˈnɛtəʊ/ *n.* Pl. **-tti** /-ti/, **-ttos.** L19. [It., dim. of CORNO.] *Early Mus.* A straight or curved wooden wind instrument with finger-holes and a cup-shaped mouthpiece; a player of this instrument. Cf. CORNET *n.*[1] 1a.

cornflower /ˈkɔːnflaʊə/ *n.* E16. [f. CORN *n.*[1] + FLOWER *n.*] 1 Any of several flowers that grow in corn, esp. *Centaurea cyanus*, a tall, usu. blue, annual formerly common as a weed; a flower or flowering stem of such a plant. E16. 2 A soft purplish-blue colour. Also *cornflower blue.* E20.

cornice /ˈkɔːnɪs/ *n.* & *v.* Also (now *dial.*) **-ish** /-ɪʃ/. M16. [Fr. *corniche*, †*-ice*, †*-isse* f. It. *cornice*, perh. f. L *cornix*, *cornic-* crow (cf. etym. of CORBEL) but w. blending of a deriv. of Gk *korōnis* coping-stone.] A *n.* 1 *Archit.* A horizontal, usu. moulded projection crowning the outside of a building or structure; *spec.* the uppermost part of an entablature, above the frieze. M16. 2 An ornamental moulding running round the wall of a room near the ceiling; a picture-rail. L17. 3 An overhanging ledge of ice or snow at the edge of a steep ridge or cliff. L19. **B** *v.t.* Provide with a cornice; finish as with a cornice. Chiefly as *corniced* ppl a. M18.

cornicing *n.* work consisting of a cornice or cornices L17.

corniche /ˈkɔːnɪʃ, kɔːˈniːʃ/ *n.* M19. [Fr.: see prec.] A road along the edge of a cliff; any coastal road with panoramic views. Also *corniche road.*

cornicle /ˈkɔːnɪk(ə)l/ *n.* M16. [L *corniculum* dim. of *cornu* horn: see -CULE.] A small projecting part of an animal; *spec.* each of a pair of erect dorsal tubules on an aphid which secrete a waxy liquid as a defence against predators.

corniculate /kɔːˈnɪkjʊlət/ *a.* M17. [L *corniculatus*, f. as prec.: see -ATE[2].] Having horns or hornlike projections; shaped like a horn.

corniculate cartilage either of a pair of small conical lumps of elastic cartilage in the larynx articulating with the arytenoid cartilages.

cornify /ˈkɔːnɪfʌɪ/ *v.t.* E17. [f. L *cornu* horn + -I- + -FY.] †1 Cuckold. Only in E17. 2 Turn (tissue) into horny material; keratinize. Chiefly as *cornified* ppl a. M19.

cornifiˈcation *n.* M19.

cornigerous /kɔːˈnɪdʒ(ə)rəs/ *a.* M17. [f. L *corniger*, f. as prec.: see -GEROUS.] Having horns; producing horny material.

cornish *n.*[1] & *v.* see CORNICE.

Cornish /ˈkɔːnɪʃ/ *a.* & *n.*[2] LME. [f. *Corn-* in *Cornwall* (see below) + -ISH[1].] **A** *adj.* Of or belonging to Cornwall, a county in SW England. LME.

Cornish boiler a cylindrical horizontal boiler with a single flue through its middle. *Cornish chough*: see CHOUGH 2. **Cornish cream** clotted cream. **Cornish engine** a kind of single-acting beam engine first used in Cornwall for pumping up water. **Cornishman** a man who is a native of Cornwall. *Cornish moneywort*: see *moneywort* s.v. MONEY *n.* **Cornish pasty** a pasty containing seasoned meat and cooked vegetables.

B *n.* The Brittonic language formerly spoken in Cornwall. M16.

cornist /ˈkɔːnɪst/ *n.* Now *rare* or *obs.* E19. [Fr. *corniste*, f. *corne* horn f. L *cornu*: see -IST.] A horn player.

corno /ˈkɔːnəʊ/ *n.* Pl. **corni** /-iː/. E19. [It. f. L *cornu* horn.] *Mus.* A horn, *esp.* a French horn.

corno da caccia /da ˈkatʃə/ [lit. 'hunting horn'] a natural horn. **corno di bassetto** /diː baˈsɛtəʊ/ (*a*) = BASSET-HORN; (*b*) a kind of organ reed-stop of 8-ft pitch. **corno inglese** /ɪŋˈɡleɪzeɪ/ [lit. 'English horn'] = COR ANGLAIS.

cornopean /kɔːˈnəʊpɪən/ *n.* M19. [Obscurely f. CORNET *n.*[1]] *Mus.* 1 = CORNET *n.*[1] 1b. Now *rare* or *obs.* M19. 2 A kind of organ reed-stop of 8-ft pitch, similar to a trumpet stop. M19.

corn-row /ˈkɔːnrəʊ/ *n.* & *v.* M18. [f. CORN *n.*[1] + ROW *n.*[1]] **A** *n.* 1 A row of (Indian) corn. *N. Amer.* M18. 2 Each of a line of small braids made close to the head, as in the hairstyle of some Blacks (usu. in *pl.*); a hairstyle in which the head is covered in this way. L20. **B** *v.t.* Arrange (hair) in corn-rows. L20.

cornstone /ˈkɔːnstəʊn/ *n.* E19. [f. CORN *n.*[1] + STONE *n.*] *Geol.* A concretionary earthy limestone characteristic of the Old and the New Red Sandstone.

cornu /ˈkɔːnjuː/ *n.* Pl. **-ua** /-juːə/. L17. [L = horn.] *Anat.* Any formation with a shape likened to a horn, as (*a*) either of the two lateral cavities of the womb, into which the Fallopian tubes pass; (*b*) each of three elongated parts of each of the lateral ventricles of the brain; (*c*) a horn-shaped process on the thyroid cartilage or certain bones (as the hyoid and the coccyx).

cornual *a.* L19.

Cornu- /ˈkɔːnjuː/ *comb. form.* M18. [f. next.] Cornish and, as *Cornu-Breton, -British* adjs.

cornua *n.* pl. of CORNU.

Cornubian /kɔːˈnjuːbɪən/ *a.* L18. [f. med.L *Cornubia* Cornwall + -AN.] Cornish.

cornucopia /kɔːnjʊˈkəʊpɪə/ *n.* E16. [Late L *cornucopia* f. L *cornu copiae* horn of plenty (a mythical horn able to provide whatever is desired).] 1 A goat's horn depicted as a horn of plenty, overflowing with flowers, fruit, and corn; an ornamental vessel or other representation of this. E16. 2 *fig.* An overflowing stock; an abundant source. E17.

2 JO GRIMOND Archie . . was a cornucopia of agricultural and other information.

cornucopian *a.* pertaining to or characteristic of a cornucopia; overflowingly abundant: E17.

cornus /ˈkɔːnəs/ *n.* M19. [L = dogwood.] A plant of the genus *Cornus* of the dogwood family. Cf. CORNEL *n.*[2] 2.

cornute /kɔːˈnjuːt/ *v.*, *n.*, & *a.* L16. [L *cornutus* horned, f. *cornu* horn.] **A** *v.t.* Cuckold. *arch.* L16. †**B** *n.* 1 A retort for distillation. E17–M18. 2 A cuckold. E17–E18. **C** *adj.* = CORNUTED. *rare.* E18.

†**cornutor** *n.* a man who makes cuckolds L17–M18.

cornuted /kɔːˈnjuːtɪd/ *a.* E17. [f. as prec. + -ED[1].] 1a Having horns or hornlike projections. E17. b Shaped like a horn. M19. 2 Cuckolded. *arch.* E17.

cornuto /kɔːˈn(j)uːtəʊ/ *n.* Now *rare* or *obs.* Pl. **-os.** LME. [It., f. as CORNUTE.] A cuckold.

corny /ˈkɔːni/ *a.*[1] LME. [f. CORN *n.*[1] + -Y[1].] 1 Of beer: tasting strongly of malt. Long *obs.* exc. *dial.* LME. 2 Of or pertaining to corn. L16. 3 Producing corn; having much corn, as a crop or as grains. L16. 4 Drunk, intoxicated. Cf. CORNED *a.*[2] 3. *dial.* E19. 5 Rustic, unsophisticated; ridiculously or tiresomely old-fashioned or sentimental; trite. *colloq.* M20.

corniness *n.* (*colloq.*) the quality of being corny (sense 5) M20.

corny /ˈkɔːni/ *a.*[2] E18. [f. CORN *n.*[2] + -Y[1].] Having corns on the feet; pertaining to corns on the feet.

corocoro /kɔːrəʊˈkɔːrəʊ/ *n.* Pl. ***-os.*** E17. [Malay *kurakura.*] A style of boat with outriggers used in the Malay archipelago.

corody *n.* var. of CORRODY.

corolla /kəˈrɒlə/ *n.* L17. [L, dim. of *corona* CROWN *n.*] 1 A little crown. *rare.* L17. 2 The whorl of modified leaves (petals), separate or combined, that form the inner, coloured, envelope of a flower and are its most conspicuous part. M18.

Comb.: *corolla-tube*: see TUBE *n.* 10.

†**corol** *n.* = COROLLA 2 M18–M19. **coroˈllaceous** *a.* having or being a corolla L18. **corolline** *a.* pertaining to the corolla M19.

corollary /kəˈrɒləri/ *n.* & *a.* LME. [L *corollarium* money paid for a garland, present, gratuity, deduction, f. prec.: see -ARY[1].] **A** *n.* 1a A proposition, esp. in geometry, appended to one that has already been demonstrated as following immediately from it; an immediate inference. LME. b A practical consequence, a result. L17. †2 An addition to a speech or composition; an appendix; a concluding or crowning part. E17–E18. 3 Something additional or surplus. E17. †4 A proposition, a thesis. M17–E19.

1a LYTTON That is scarcely a fair corollary from my remark. b W. LIPPMANN When advanced nations adopt collectivism, and its inevitable corollary, the self-contained economy.

B *adj.* Of the nature of a corollary; appended as an inference; accompanying, supplementary; resulting. LME.

Coromandel /kɒrə(ʊ)ˈmand(ə)l/ *n.* & *a.* M19. [The *Coromandel* coast, SE India.] **A** *n.* Calamander. Also *Coromandel ebony, wood.* M19. **B** *adj.* Designating oriental lacquerware, esp. folding screens, having incised decorations and orig. transhipped on the Coromandel coast. L19.

corona /kəˈrəʊnə/ *n.*[1] Pl. **-nas, -nae** /-niː/. OE. [L = CROWN *n.*] †1 = CROWN *n.* 1. Only in OE. 2 *Archit.* A part of a cornice having a broad vertical face, usu. of considerable projection, and lying below the cyma. M16. 3a A small circle of light sometimes seen round the sun, moon, or other luminary; *esp.* one due to diffraction by water droplets, often prismatically coloured with red on the outside. Cf. HALO *n.* M17. b The irregularly shaped area of light seen around the moon's disc in a solar eclipse; the hot, highly rarefied, outermost gaseous envelope of the sun responsible for this; a similar envelope around other celestial objects. M19. 4 Any of various parts of the human body (as of a tooth or the penis), or of an animal's, that are likened to a crown. E18. 5 *Bot.* a An appendage on the top of certain seeds, as those of a dandelion. M18. b The cup-shaped or trumpet-shaped outgrowth of perianth tissue in the centre of the flower of a daffodil or other narcissus. Also, the ring of filaments in the flower of the passion-flower. M19. 6 A circular chandelier in a church. E19. 7 A glow around a conductor when the electric field is strong enough to ionize the air but not strong enough to cause a spark. E20.

Phrases: **Corona Australis** /ɒˈstreɪlɪs/ [L *australis* AUSTRAL *a.*] (the name of) a small constellation of the southern hemisphere, on the edge of the Milky Way next to Sagittarius. **Corona Borealis** /bɔːrɪˈeɪlɪs/ [L *borealis* BOREAL] (the name of) a small constellation of the northern hemisphere, between Boötes and Hercules.

Corona /kəˈrəʊnə/ *n.*[2] Also **c-.** L19. [f. (formerly proprietary) name *La Corona* (Sp., lit. 'the crown').] A brand of Havana cigar; a long straight-sided cigar.

coronach /ˈkɒrənək, -x/ *n.* E16. [Gael. *corranach*, f. *comh-* together + *rànach* outcry.] †1 An outcry of a crowd. *Sc.* E16–L17. 2 A funeral lamentation in the Scottish Highlands or Ireland. M16.

coronagraph /kəˈrəʊnəɡrɑːf/ *n.* Also **corono-.** L19. [f. CORONA *n.*[1] + -GRAPH.] An instrument for observing or photographing the sun's corona, esp. other than during an eclipse.

coronaˈgraphic *a.* L19.

coronal /ˈkɒrən(ə)l/ *n.* ME. [App. f. AN f. *cor(o)une* CROWN *n.* In sense 3 prob. f. med.L *coronalis.* Cf. CROWNAL *n.*] **I** 1 A circlet, esp. of gold or gems, for the head; a coronet. ME. 2 A wreath for the head; a garland. L16. **II** *Anat.* †3 The coronal bone (see next, sense 1). LME–M18.

coronalled *a.* bearing a coronal LME.

coronal /kəˈrəʊn(ə)l, ˈkɒr(ə)n(ə)l/ *a.* LME. [Fr., or L (& med.L) *coronalis*, f. *corona* CROWN *n.*: see -AL[1]. Cf. CROWNAL *a.*] 1 Of or pertaining to the crown of the head. LME. †2 Pertaining to a crown or crowning. M16–M17. 3 Of or pertaining to a corona, esp. that of the sun. M18. 4 *Phonet.* Designating or pertaining to speech sounds produced with the tip or blade of the tongue raised towards the hard palate. L19.

1 **coronal bone** (now *rare*) the frontal bone. **coronal plane**: dividing the body vertically into front and back halves.

coronary /ˈkɒr(ə)n(ə)ri/ *a.* & *n.* E17. [L *coronarius*, f. as prec.: see -ARY[1].] **A** *adj.* †1 Suitable for use in making garlands. Only in 17. 2 Of the nature of or resembling a crown; pertaining to or forming a crown. *obs.* exc. in *coronary gold* below. M17. 3 *Anat.* Pertaining to or designating blood-vessels, nerves, and ligaments which encircle a part. L17. 4 Pertaining to or designating the second phalangeal bone of a horse's foot. M19.

2 **coronary gold** [tr. L *coronarium aurum*] *Hist.* money awarded in lieu of a crown to a victorious Roman general. 3 D. WATERSON The coronary ligament consists of the folds of peritoneum which are reflected from the liver to the diaphragm. **coronary artery** either of two arteries that supply the tissues of the heart with blood. **coronary thrombosis**: occurring in a coronary artery.

B *n.* †1 A plant or flower suitable for use in making garlands. Only in L17. 2 The coronary bone of a horse. M19. 3 A coronary blood-vessel; a coronary thrombosis. L19.

coronate /ˈkɒr(ə)neɪt/ *v.t.* Pa. pple **-ate** (*arch.*), **-ated.** LME. [L *coronat-* pa. ppl stem of *coronare* CROWN *v.*[1]: see -ATE[3].] Crown.

coronated /ˈkɒr(ə)neɪtɪd/ *ppl a.* L17. [f. as prec. + -ED[1].] *Bot.* & *Zool.* Having something resembling a crown.

coronation /kɒrəˈneɪʃ(ə)n/ *n.* LME. [(O)Fr. f. med.L *coronatio(n-)*, f. as CORONATE *v.*: see

-ATION. Cf. CROWNATION.] 1 The action or an act of crowning; *spec.* the ceremony of investing a monarch or monarch's consort with a crown as an emblem of royal status. LME. 2 *fig.* The crowning or completion *of* a work. L16. †3 = CARNATION *n.*³ Only in L16.

Attrib. & *comb.*: Designating articles produced to commemorate a particular coronation, as *coronation mug*. Special combs., as **coronation oath**: taken by a monarch at his or her coronation. **Coronation Street** [a fictitious street in, and the title of, a television series] (characteristic of) a working-class street in the middle of an industrial city in the north of England.

†coronel *n.* see COLONEL *n.*

coroner /ˈkɒr(ə)nə/ *n.* ME. [AN *cor(o)uner*, f. *cor(o)une* CROWN *n.* (see -ER²), f. the L title *custos placitorum coronae* guardian of the pleas of the crown; in med.L *coronarius*, later *coronator*. Cf. CROWNER *n.*²] 1 Orig., an officer of the royal household responsible for safeguarding the private property of the Crown. Now, a legal officer with local or national jurisdiction who holds inquests on deaths of those who may have died by violence or accident, and also on treasure trove. ME. 2 The chief officer of a sheading in the Isle of Man. L16.

1 **coroner's jury**: composed of 7–11 persons, appointed to decide an issue of fact at a coroner's inquest.

coronership *n.* the office of coroner LME.

coronet /ˈkɒr(ə)nɪt/ *n.* & *v.* LME. [OFr. *coronet(t)e* dim. of *corone* CROWN *n.*: see -ET¹. Cf. CRONET, CROWNET.] A *n.* 1 A small or inferior crown, *esp.* one denoting noble or royal but not sovereign rank; a heraldic representation of this. LME. 2 A band of beautiful or precious materials worn as an ornament on the head, now esp. as part of a woman's formal dress. L16. 3 A garland of flowers for the head. L16. 4 The lowest part of the pastern of a horse, forming a ridge round the top of the hoof. Cf. earlier CRONET 3, CROWNET 2. L17. 5 A moth, *Craniophora ligustri*, with greenish or brownish forewings. Also *coronet moth*. E19. 6 = BUR *n.*¹ 4. L19.

3 OBSIDIONAL *coronet*.

B *v.t.* Infl. -t-, *-tt-. Adorn with a coronet; confer a coronet or noble title upon. Chiefly as *coronet(t)ed* ppl a. M18.

coronilla /kɒrəˈnɪlə/ *n.* L18. [mod.L, dim. of L *corona* CROWN *n.*] Any leguminous plant of the genus *Coronilla*, comprising evergreen and deciduous shrubs and herbaceous plants bearing usu. yellow flowers in umbels.

coronis /kəˈrəʊnɪs/ *n.* M17. [L f. Gk *korōnis* flourish at end of book or chapter.] †1 An end, a conclusion. *rare*. Only in M17. 2 *Gk Gram.* A sign, ', placed over a Greek vowel as a mark of contraction or crasis. M19.

coronium /kəˈrəʊnɪəm/ *n.* L19. [f. CORONA *n.*¹ + -IUM.] An element formerly thought to exist in the sun's corona, producing spectral lines now attributed to highly ionized atoms of other elements.

coronograph *n.* var. of CORONAGRAPH.

coronoid /ˈkɒr(ə)nɔɪd/ *a.* & *n.* M18. [f. Gk *korōnē* crow, anything hooked, coronoid process + -OID.] A *adj. Anat.* Pertaining to or designating projections of bone likened to a crow's beak. M18.

coronoid fossa a hollow immediately above the trochlea on the anterior surface of the condyle of the humerus, into which the coronoid process of the ulna fits when the arm is bent. **coronoid process** (*a*) a flattened triangular projection directed upwards and forwards on the ramus of the mandible; (*b*) a projection from the front of the upper end of the ulna, immediately below the olecranon.

B *n. Zool.* A membrane bone in the lower jaw of certain lower vertebrates, projecting upwards behind the teeth. L19.

coroplast /ˈkɔːrəplast, -plɑːst/ *n.* L19. [Gk *koroplastēs*, f. *korē* girl, doll: see -PLAST.] *Antiq.* A maker of terracotta figures.

corozo /kəˈrəʊzəʊ/ *n.* Pl. -os. M18. [Sp., var. of dial. *carozo* stone or core of fruit.] Any of several S. American palm trees, *esp.* the ivory-nut palm, *Phytelephas macrocarpa*, and the American oil-palm, *Corozo* (*Elaeis*) *oleifera*.

Comb.: **corozo nut** the seed of *Phytelephas macrocarpa*, from which vegetable ivory is obtained.

corp. /kɔːp/ *n. colloq.* Also **corp** (no point). E20. [Abbrev.] = CORPORAL *n.*² 1.

corpocracy /kɔːˈpɒkrəsi/ *n.* L20. [Blend of CORPORATE *a.* and BUREAUCRACY.] Bureaucratic organization as manifested in large companies, esp. where a rigid hierarchical structure leads to inefficiency; a company characterized by such organization; such companies collectively.

ˈ**corpocrat** *n.* an executive within a corpocracy L20. **corpoˈcratic** *a.* pertaining to or characteristic of corpocracy or corpocracies L20.

corpora *n.pl.* see CORPUS.

corporal /ˈkɔːp(ə)r(ə)l/ *n.*¹ OE. [(O)Fr., or med.L *corporale* use as n. (sc. *pallium* PALL *n.*¹) of neut. of *corporalis* CORPORAL *a.*] *Chr. Ch.* †1 A certain ancient Eucharistic vestment. OE–M17. 2 A (now square) cloth on which the chalice and paten are placed during the Eucharist, before the consecration; a smaller cloth placed over the chalice, a pall. LME.

corporal /ˈkɔːp(ə)r(ə)l/ *n.*² M16. [Fr., obs. var. of *caporal* f. It. *caporale* (of which there appears to have been a Venetian form †*corporale*), prob. f. *corpo* f. L CORPUS, *corpor-* body (of troops) w. assim. to It. *capo* head: cf. CORPORAL *a.*] 1 A non-commissioned officer in the army, air force, or marines who ranks next below a sergeant. M16. 2 *Hist.* Orig., a petty officer on board a warship responsible for teaching the use of small arms; later (also *ship's corporal*), a superior petty officer who attended solely to police matters under the master-at-arms. E17. 3 A freshwater fish, *Semotilus corporalis*, of the carp family. *US*. L19.

1 *orderly corporal*: see ORDERLY *a.* **the little Corporal** Napoleon.

corporalship *n.* †(*a*) a body of soldiers under the command of a corporal; (*b*) the position or rank of a corporal: L16.

corporal /ˈkɔːp(ə)r(ə)l/ *a.* LME. [OFr. (mod. *-el*) f. L *corporalis*, f. CORPUS, *corpor-* body: see -AL¹.] 1 Of or belonging to the human body; bodily; personal. LME. †b Having a body, embodied. L15–M17. †2 Of the nature of matter; physical, material. LME–E18.

1 MILTON Corporal pleasure. S. RICHARDSON Taking his corporal leave of her. THACKERAY A quite unheroic state of corporal prostration.

Special collocations: **corporal oath** *arch.*: ratified by touching a sacred object. **corporal punishment**: inflicted on the body, now esp. by flogging.

corporally *adv.* L15.

corporality /kɔːpəˈralɪti/ *n.* LME. [Late L *corporalitas*, f. L *corporalis*: see prec., -ITY.] 1 Material or corporeal existence; body. LME. 2 Embodied existence or condition. Now *rare*. M17.

corporas /ˈkɔːp(ə)rəs/ *n.* ME. [OFr. *corporaus* (earlier *-als*) nom. sing. of *corporal* CORPORAL *n.*¹] = CORPORAL *n.*¹ 2.

corporate /ˈkɔːp(ə)rət/ *a.* L15. [L *corporatus* pa. pple, f. as next: see -ATE².] 1 Forming or being a corporation; having a legal existence distinct from that of the individuals who compose it. L15. b Of or belonging to a corporation, esp. (now) an industrial corporation, or a group of people; collective, joint. E17. †2 Pertaining to or affecting the body. L15–E17. †3 Corpulent. E16–L18. †4 Having a body; material. L16–M19.

1 *body corporate*: see BODY *n.* **corporate town**: having municipal rights. *county corporate*: see COUNTY *n.*¹ b H. CARPENTER Auden was not sociable at school and kept out of corporate activities. S. BELLOW Lawyers and corporate executives. *corporate image*: see IMAGE *n.* **corporate name**: under which a corporation engages in legal acts. **corporate raider** a person who or organization which attempts to take over companies against their wishes or interests. **corporate State**: governed by representatives not of geographical areas but of vocational corporations of the employers and employees in each industry etc.

corporately *adv.* L15.

corporate /ˈkɔːpəreɪt/ *v. arch.* Pa. pple **-ate(d)**. LME. [L *corporat-* pa. ppl stem of *corporare*, f. CORPUS, *corpor-* body: see -ATE³.] 1 *v.t.* & (*rare*) *i.* Unite or combine in one body; embody. LME. †2 *v.t.* Form into a corporation, incorporate. LME–M17.

corporation /kɔːpəˈreɪʃ(ə)n/ *n.* LME. [Late L *corporatio(n-)*, f. as prec.: see -ATION.] †1 The action or result of incorporating. LME–M16. 2 A body of people that has been given a legal existence distinct from the individuals who compose it; a single person with a separate legal existence; a fictitious person created by statute, royal charter, etc.; *spec.* (*a*) (more fully *municipal corporation*) the civic authorities of a borough, town, or city; (*b*) a large industrial company. LME. b An incorporated company of traders who orig. controlled their particular trade in a place. M16. c A body of people. M16. 3 A protruding or prominent abdomen. Formerly, the body. *colloq.* M18.

2 BROWNING A thousand guilders! The Mayor looked blue; so did the Corporation too. *Encycl. Brit.* The company was liquidated and replaced by a public corporation, the British Broadcasting Corporation. **corporation aggregate**: comprising more than one individual. **corporation sole**: comprising only one individual at any one time, as a king or bishop.

Comb.: **corporation tax**: levied on companies' profits.

corporational *a.* M19.

corporatism /ˈkɔːp(ə)rətɪz(ə)m/ *n.* L19. [f. CORPORATE *a.* + -ISM.] The principles or practice of corporate action or organization, esp. in a corporate State.

corporatist *a.* L19.

corporative /ˈkɔːp(ə)rətɪv/ *a.* M19. [f. as prec. + -IVE.] = CORPORATE *a.* 1b.

corporativism *n.* = CORPORATISM M20.

corporatize /ˈkɔːp(ə)rətʌɪz/ *v.t.* Also **-ise**. L20. [f. CORPORATE *a.* + -IZE.] Convert (a State body) into an independent commercial company.

corporator /ˈkɔːp(ə)reɪtə/ *n.* L18. [Irreg. f. CORPORATION + -OR.] A member of a corporation, esp. a municipal corporation.

corporeal /kɔːˈpɔːrɪəl/ *a.* & *n.* LME. [Late L *corporealis*, f. L *corporeus*, f. CORPUS, *corpor-* body: see -AL¹.] A *adj.* 1 Of the nature of matter, material. LME. 2a Of the nature of the body rather than the spirit; bodily; mortal. E17. †b Pertaining to or affecting the body, corporal. E18–M19. 3 *Law.* Tangible; consisting of material objects. L17.

2a J. STRYPE Any manner of corporeal presence in the Sacrament. D. PIPER The full corporeal presence of that massive torso. b W. HAMILTON The infliction of corporeal punishment. 3 W. BLACKSTONE Corporeal hereditaments consist wholly of substantial and permanent objects.

B *n.* In *pl.* Corporeal things; *Law* corporeal possessions. M17.

corporealism *n.* materialism L17. †**corporealist** *n.* a materialist M17–M19. **corporeˈality** *n.* corporeal quality or state; bodily nature: M17. **corporealiˈzation** *n.* the action of corporealizing M19. **corporealize** *v.t.* render or represent as corporeal L18. **corporeally** *adv.* in a corporeal manner; bodily: M17. †**corporeous** *a.* = CORPOREAL E17–M19.

corporeity /kɔːpəˈriːɪti, -ˈreɪɪti/ *n.* E17. [Fr. *corporéité* or med.L *corporeitas*, f. L *corporeus*: see prec., -ITY.] 1 The quality of being or having a material body. E17. 2 (A) bodily substance. M17. 3 Material or physical nature. Formerly also, relative density. M17.

2 E. H. PLUMPTRE A subtle attenuated corporeity . . investing the soul.

†corporify *v.t.* M17. [f. L CORPUS, *corpor-* body + -FY, perh. through Fr. *corporifier*.] 1 Make material, *esp.* convert into liquid or solid. M17–E18. 2 Incorporate (itself) into a material substance. M17–E18.

†**corporification** *n.* the action or result of making material; embodiment: M17–M19.

corporosity /kɔːpəˈrɒsɪti/ *n.* *US humorous colloq.* M19. [f. as prec. + -OSITY.] A person's body or bodily bulkiness.

your corporosity you (as a greeting).

corposant /ˈkɔːpəzant/ *n.* Also **composant** /ˈkɒmp-/, **comozant** /ˈkɒməz-/. M16. [OSp., Port., & It. *corpo santo* holy body.] A luminous corona sometimes seen in the air adjacent to a ship or aircraft during a storm, esp. near pointed objects such as mastheads.

corps /kɔː; *foreign* kɔːr/ *n.* Pl. same /kɔːz, *foreign* kɔːr/. L16. [Fr. f. L CORPUS body. Cf. CORE *n.*[2]] **1** A tactical division of an army; an organized body of troops assigned to a special duty or a particular kind of work (medical, ordnance, intelligence, etc.). (Earliest in *corps de garde* below.) L16. **2** A body of people engaged (collectively or as individuals) in a particular activity. M18. **3** A students' society in a German university. L19.

2 J. B. MORTON Tips . . given away by a corps of bookies. *Sunday Times* A 200-strong international Press corps.

Phrases: ***corps à corps*** /a kɔːr/ in close, esp. bodily, contact. ***corps de ballet*** /də balɛ, də 'baleɪ/, pl. same, the company of supporting dancers in a ballet; the ballet-dancers at a theatre. ***corps de garde*** /də gard, də 'gɑːd/, pl. same, a small body of soldiers stationed on guard or as sentinels; the post they occupy, a guard-room, a guard-house. ***corps d'élite*** /delit, deɪ'liːt/, pl. same, a select group, a body of specially picked people. ***corps de logis*** /də lɔʒi/, pl. same, [lit. 'body of dwelling'] the main (part of a) building. ***corps diplomatique*** /diplɔmatik, dɪpləma'tiːk/, pl. **-*iques*** (pronounced same) = *diplomatic corps* s.v. DIPLOMATIC *a.* 2. ESPRIT *de corps*.

Comb.: **corpsman** *US* an enlisted medical auxiliary in the army or navy.

corpse /kɔːps/ *n.* & *v.* Orig. †**corps** (pl. **corps(es)**). ME. [Alt. of CORSE *n.* after L *corpus*, Fr. *corps* body. The inserted *p* was at first mute, as in Fr., but began to be pronounced before 1500. The final *e* was rare bef. 19, but then became standard, providing differentiation from CORPS. Cf. also CORPUS.] **A** *n.* †**1** The living body of a person or animal. ME–E18. **2** A dead (usu. human) body. LME. †**3** The main portion or body *of*; a body or corpus *of* (law etc.). LME–M17. **4** *Hist.* The endowment of an ecclesiastical or (formerly) civil office, esp. a prebend. M16.

2 *walking corpse*: see WALKING *ppl a.*

Comb.: **corpse-candle** (*a*) a lambent flame seen in a churchyard and superstitiously believed to portend a coming death or funeral route; (*b*) a lighted candle, esp. of unbleached wax, placed beside a corpse before burial; **corpse-light** = *corpse-candle* (a) above; *corpse-reviver*: see REVIVER *n.*[1] 1c.

B *v.* **1** *v.t.* Kill. *slang.* M19. **2** *v.t.* Confuse (an actor) in the performance of his or her part; spoil (a piece of acting) by some blunder. *slang.* M19. **3** *v.i.* Spoil a piece of acting by some blunder, as forgetting one's lines or laughing; burst out laughing at an inappropriate moment. *slang.* L19.

corpsy *a.* resembling or characteristic of a corpse; cadaverous: L19.

corpulence /'kɔːpjʊl(ə)ns/ *n.* LME. [(O)Fr., f. as next: see -ENCE.] †**1** Size or habit of body. LME–L15. **2** Bulk of body; excessive bulk, obesity. M16.

corpulency /'kɔːpjʊl(ə)nsi/ *n.* M16. [L *corpulentia*, f. as CORPULENT: see -ENCY.] †**1** = CORPULENCE 1. M16–E17. **2** = CORPULENCE 2. L16.

corpulent /'kɔːpjʊl(ə)nt/ *a.* LME. [L *corpulentus*, f. CORPUS body: see -ULENT.] †**1** Of the nature of a physical body; solid, dense, gross. LME–M17. **2** Bulky of body; fleshy, fat. LME. †**3** Corporeal, material. LME–M17.

cor pulmonale /kɔː pʌlmə'nɑːli, -eɪli/ *n. phr.* M19. [f. L *cor* heart + mod.L *pulmonalis*, *-e* (f. L *pulmo(n-)* lung).] *Med.* †**1** The right auricle and ventricle of the heart. Only in M19. **2** Disease, esp. enlargement, of the right side of the heart as a result of disease of the lungs or their blood-vessels. M20.

corpus /'kɔːpəs/ *n.* Pl. **corpora** /'kɔːp(ə)rə/, **corpuses**. LME. [L = body.] **1** The body of a person or animal. Now *joc.* LME. **2** *Anat.* Any of various masses of tissue in the body that have a distinct structure or function. Chiefly in phrs. below. L17. **3** A body or collection of writing, knowledge, etc.; the whole body *of* a particular category of literature etc. E18. **b** *spec.* A body of spoken or written material on which a linguistic analysis is based. M20. **4** Principal or capital, as opp. to interest or income. *arch.* M19. **5** *Bot.* The inner layers of cells in an apical meristem, which divide mainly periclinally and contribute to volume growth. Cf. TUNICA *n.*[1] 2. M20.

3 GLADSTONE Assaults on the corpus of Scripture. A. BEVAN The accumulated corpus of knowledge in his own particular field.

Phrases: **corpus callosum** /kə'ləʊsəm/, pl. **-sa** /-sə/, [L, neut. of *callosus* tough] a broad band of nerve fibres joining the two hemispheres of the brain. **corpus cavernosum** /kavə'nəʊsəm/, pl. **-sa**, /-sə/ [L, neut. of *cavernosus* containing hollows] either of two masses of erectile tissue forming the bulk of the penis and the clitoris. **Corpus Christi** /'krɪsti/, pl. **Corpus Christis** /-ɪz/, [L, genit. of *Christus* Christ] a holy day in parts of the Western Church in commemoration of the Holy Eucharist, observed on the first Thursday after Trinity Sunday. **corpus delicti** /dɪ'lɪktiː/ [L, genit. of *delictum* offence] *Law* all the facts that go to make a breach of the law; *pop.* concrete evidence of a crime, *esp.* a corpse. **corpus juris, iuris** /'dʒʊərɪs, 'jʊə-/ [L, genit. of *jus* law] a body of law. **corpus juris canonici** /kə'nɒnɪsiː/ [L, genit. of *canonicus* CANONIC] the chief collection of law in the Western Church until 1917. **corpus juris civilis** /sɪ'vɪlɪs/ [L: see CIVIL] the body of Roman civil law based on Justinian's compilation. **corpus luteum** /'luːtɪəm, 'ljuː-/, pl. **-tea** /-tɪə/, [L, neut. of *luteus* yellow] a hormone-secreting body that develops in the ovary after the ovum is discharged, degenerating after a few days unless pregnancy has begun. **corpus spongiosum** /spʌndʒɪ'əʊsəm/, pl. **-sa** /-sə/, [L, neut. of *spongiosus* porous] a mass of erectile tissue alongside the corpora cavernosa of the penis and terminating in the glans. **corpus striatum** /strʌɪ'eɪtəm/, pl. **-ta** /-tə/, [L, neut. of *striatus* grooved] part of the basal ganglia of the brain, comprising the caudate and lentiform nuclei. **corpus vile** /'vʌɪli/, pl. **-lia** /-lɪə/, [L, neut. of *vilis* cheap] something that can be made the object of experimentation because of no intrinsic worth.

corpuscle /'kɔːpʌs(ə)l/ *n.* M17. [L *corpusculum* dim. of CORPUS: see -CULE. Cf. CORPUSCULE.] **1** A minute particle of matter; an atom; a molecule. *arch.* M17. **b** *Hist. Sci.* An electron. L19. **2** A minute structure forming a distinct part of the body; *esp.* a blood cell; an encapsulated sensory nerve ending. M18.

2 *Malpighian corpuscle*, *Meissner's corpuscle*, *Pacinian corpuscle*, *red* (*blood*) *corpuscle*, *white* (*blood*) *corpuscle*, etc.

corpuscular /kɔː'pʌskjʊlə/ *a.* M17. [f. as prec. + -AR[1].] **1** Involving the idea or hypothesis of corpuscles. M17. **2** Of or pertaining to corpuscles; consisting of or being corpuscles. L17.

1 **corpuscular theory** *Hist. Sci.*: that light consists of a stream of particles; also called *emission theory*.

corpuscu'larian *a.* & *n.* (*a*) *adj.* = CORPUSCULAR 1; (*b*) *n.* (*Hist. Sci.*) a person who believed that matter, or light, is composed of corpuscles: M17.

corpuscule /kɔː'pʌskjuːl/ *n. arch.* Also (earlier) in L form **-culum** /-kjʊləm/, pl. **-la** /-lə/. M17. [f. as CORPUSCLE.] = CORPUSCLE.

corpusculated *a.* = CORPUSCULAR 2 M19. **corpusculous** *a.* = CORPUSCULAR 2 L19.

†**corrack** *n.* var. of CURRACH.

corrade /kə'reɪd/ *v.t.* E17. [L *corradere*, f. as COR- + *radere* scrape.] †**1** Scrape together (*lit.* & *fig.*). E–M17. **2** Wear down by scraping. Now only *Geol.*, subject to corrasion. M17.

corral /kə'rɑːl/ *n.* & *v.* L16. [Sp. & OPort. *corral*, Port. *curral*: cf. CRAWL *n.*[1], KRAAL *n.*] **A** *n.* **1** An enclosure for horses, cattle, etc. Chiefly *N. Amer.* L16. **2** An enclosure in which to trap and capture wild animals. M19. **3** A defensive enclosure formed of wagons in an encampment. M19. **B** *v.* Infl. **-ll-**. **1** *v.t.* & *i.* Form (wagons) into a corral. M19. **2** *v.t.* Shut up (as) in a corral, confine. M19. **3** *v.t.* Obtain, get hold of. *N. Amer. colloq.* M19.

corrasion /kə'reɪʒ(ə)n/ *n.* E17. [f. L *corras-* pa. ppl stem of *corradere*: see CORRADE, -ION.] †**1** The action of scraping together (*fig.*). *rare.* Only in E17. **2** *Geol.* The local wearing away of part of the earth's surface by moving air, water, ice, etc., and matter transported by them. L19.

correct /kə'rɛkt/ *a.* L16. [Fr. f. L *correctus* pa. pple, f. as next. Cf. earlier INCORRECT.] **1** Free from error; accurate; in accordance with fact, truth, or reason. L16. **2** Conforming to acknowledged standards of style, manners, or behaviour; proper. L17.

1 LD MACAULAY Mr. Hunt is . . quite correct in saying that [etc.] G. GORDON Trying to open a safe without knowing the correct combination. 2 S. JOHNSON The best and correctest authours. R. FORD The correct thing is to have the owner's name worked in on the edge. D. ABSE Rabbi Shatz in his correct black homburg.

correctly *adv.* L17. **correctness** *n.* L17.

correct /kə'rɛkt/ *v.* Pa. pple **corrected**, †**correct**. ME. [L *correct-* pa. ppl stem of *corrigere*, f. as COR- + *regere* lead straight, direct.] **I** *v.t.* **1** Put right (an error or fault). ME. **2** Cure (a person) *of* a fault; admonish, or point out the faults of, with a view to amendment. ME. **3** Punish for faults of character or conduct (with a view to amendment). *arch.* LME. **4** Put (a thing) right; substitute what is right for the errors in; mark errors in (a proof etc.). LME. **5** Remove or prevent the harmful effect of, counteract. M16. †**6** Reduce to order, reclaim from wildness. L16–E18. **7** Bring (the body) into a healthy state. E17. **8** Adjust (a numerical result or reading) to allow for departure from standard conditions. L18.

1 W. S. CHURCHILL Having made a mistake . . he went back and corrected it. 2 C. BURNEY Pleasure . . in seeing one of my own children corrected of all natural defects. E. BLUNDEN He corrected me for carrying an untrimmed . . stick. T. F. POWYS He always corrected himself. 4 E. WAUGH I sit with a blue pencil correcting history essays. 5 D. BREWSTER Take a prism of each with such angles that they correct each other's dispersion as much as possible. J. A. FROUDE The heart . . corrects the folly of the head.

II *v.i.* **9** Make a correction or corrections. L15.

correctable *a.* able to be corrected LME. **correctible** *a.* = CORRECTABLE L19.

correction /kə'rɛkʃ(ə)n/ *n.* ME. [(O)Fr. f. L *correctio(n-)*, f. as prec.: see -ION.] **1 a** The action of putting right or indicating errors. ME. **b** An act or instance of emendation; that which is substituted for what is wrong, esp. in a text. E16. †**2** Reproof of a person for a fault of character or conduct. (Foll. by *of* the fault.) ME–E19. **3** Chastisement, disciplinary punishment; *esp.* corporal punishment. *arch.* LME. **4** The neutralization of anything harmful or unpleasant. LME. **5** Adjustment of a numerical result; the quantity added or subtracted in this. M18.

1 **under correction** subject to correction, esp. by a higher authority. 3 **house of correction** *Hist.* an institution where vagrants and minor offenders were confined and set to work.

Comb.: **correction fluid** a (usu. white) liquid that can be painted over a typed or written error leaving a blank surface on which to type or write afresh; **correction(s) officer, official** *N. Amer.* a prison officer.

correctional *a.* of or pertaining to correction L18. †**correctioner** *n.* (*rare*, Shakes.) a person who administers correction: only in L16.

correctitude /kə'rɛktɪtjuːd/ *n.* L19. [f. CORRECT *a.* + RECTITUDE.] Correctness; *esp.* conscious correctness of behaviour.

corrective /kə'rɛktɪv/ *a.* & *n.* M16. [(O)Fr. *correctif*, *-ive*, or late L *correctivus*, f. as CORRECT *v.*: see -IVE.] **A** *adj.* Having the property or function of correcting or of counteracting what is harmful. M16.

corrective justice, *corrective training*.

B *n.* **1** Something that restores to a healthy condition. E17. †**2** A correction, an emendation. L17–M18. **3** Something that tends to counteract an evil, put right an error, etc. (Foll. by *of*, *to*.) M18.

3 H. T. BUCKLE Patriotism is a corrective of superstition. R. W. EMERSON The criticism of memory as a corrective to first impressions.

correctively *adv.* E17.

corrector /kə'rɛktə/ *n.* LME. [AN *cor(r)ectour*, (O)Fr. *correcteur* f. L *corrector*, f. as CORRECT *v.*: see -OR.] **1** A person who points out errors and indicates what is right; a critic; *spec.* (also *corrector of the press*, *press corrector*) a proofreader. LME. **2** A person who exercises discipline or inflicts punishment. LME. **3** As an official title: a controller; a director; a religious superior. LME.

4 Something that provides a means of correction or prevents error. E17. †5 = CORRECTIVE *n.* I. E17–L18.

correctory *a.* (now *rare* or *obs.*) of the nature of a corrector or correction E17. **correctress** *n.* (now *rare*) a female corrector E17. **†correctrice** *n.* = CORRECTRESS M16–E18.

Correggiesque /kɒˌrɛdʒɪˈɛsk/ *a.* M18. [f. *Correggio* (see below) + -ESQUE.] Characteristic of, or in the style of, the Italian painter Antonio Allegri Correggio (*c* 1489–1534); consciously elegant and charming or with soft outlines, in the manner of Correggio.

Correggiescity *n.* (*rare*) Correggiesque style M18.

corregidor /kəˈrɛgɪdɔː/ *n.* Pl. **corregidores** /kərɛgɪˈdɔːriːz/, **-ors.** L16. [Sp. agent-n. f. *corregir* f. L *corrigere* CORRECT *v.*] The chief magistrate of a Spanish town or a town in former Spanish territory.

correlate /ˈkɒrəleɪt, -rɪl-/ *n.* M17. [Prob. f. as next: see -ATE[1].] 1 Either of two or more related things, esp. that imply or are complementary to one another. M17. 2 Something corresponding or analogous. E19.

correlate /ˈkɒrəleɪt, -rɪl-/ *v.* M18. [Back-form. f. next.] 1 *v.i.* Have a mutual relation; be correlative or correlated (*with, to*). M18. 2 *v.t.* Bring into mutual relation; establish the likely relation between. (Foll. by *with.*) M19. 3 *v.t.* In *pass.* Be regularly connected or related; exhibit a correlation. M19.

1 G. GROTE Ethical obligation correlates . . with ethical right. *Scientific American* The number of nights when the aurora is seen correlates well with the number of spots on the sun. 2 N. BOHR It has been possible to correlate each term with the occurrence of electron orbits of a given type. 3 G. GORER Class is not directly correlated with income.

correˈlatable *a.* L19.

correlation /kɒrəˈleɪʃ(ə)n, -rɪ-/ *n.* M16. [med.L *correlatio(n-)*, f. as COR- + *relatio(n-)* RELATION. Cf. CORELATION.] 1 Mutual close or necessary relation of two or more things; *spec.* an interdependence of variable quantities; the degree of such interdependence. M16. 2 The action of correlating. L19.

1 K. PEARSON A sensible correlation (*circa* 0.18) between fertility and height in the mothers of daughters. W. LIPPMANN A real correlation of cause and effect.

Comb.: **correlation coefficient** a number between +1 and −1 calculated so as to represent the linear interdependence of two variables or sets of data.

correlational *a.* of, pertaining to, or employing correlation M20.

correlative /kəˈrɛlətɪv/ *a.* & *n.* M16. [med.L *correlativus*, f. as COR- + late L *relativus* RELATIVE. Cf. Fr. *corrélatif, -ive*; CORELATIVE.] A *adj.* 1 Related each to the other; occurring together; analogous; *Gram.* (of two words) corresponding to each other and regularly used together, (of a construction) formed with such words. (Foll. by *with, to.*) M16. 2 Having or involving a relation such that each implies the other; mutually interdependent. (Foll. by *with, to.*) L17. 3 *Math.* Of geometric figures, propositions, etc.: such that points in one correspond to lines (in two dimensions) or to planes (in three) in the other, and vice versa. L19.

1 ISAAC TAYLOR Such utterances of desire, or hope, or love, as seem to suppose the existence of correlative feelings. P. G. PERRIN *Either* . . . *or* Correlative conjunctions. 2 J. LOCKE Husband and wife, and such other correlative terms. G. GROTE Correlative rights and duties.

B *n.* A correlative thing or word. M16.

objective correlative: see OBJECTIVE *a.* & *n.*

correlatively *adv.* M17. **correlativeness** *n.* M18. **correlaˈtivity** *n.* L19.

correption /kəˈrɛpʃ(ə)n/ *n.* LME. [L *correptio(n-)*, f. *corrept-* pa. ppl stem of *corripere*, f. as COR- + *rapere* snatch: see -ION.] †1 (A) reproof. LME–M18. 2 *Gram.* Shortening in pronunciation; an instance of this. *rare.* L19.

correspond /kɒrɪˈspɒnd/ *v.* LME. [(O)Fr. *correspondre* f. med.L *correspondere*, f. as COR- + L *respondere* RESPOND *v.*] I *v.i.* 1 Be congruous or in harmony (*with*), be agreeable or conformable (*to*). LME. 2 Have a similar or analogous character, form, or function; agree in position, amount, etc. (Foll. by *to, with.*) E16. 3 Communicate (*with*) by the interchange of letters or (formerly) any other (esp. secret) means. E17. †4 Respond in like manner. (Foll. by *to, with.*) M17–E19.

1 R. FRY To consider . . how far the pictured past corresponds to any reality. J. BARZUN Difficulty obtaining employment corresponding to their . . talents. 2 H. J. STEPHEN Their general assembly, corresponding with our House of Commons. G. MAXWELL To transpose them until each ball and socket corresponded. *Times* Radiation of 21.1 cm wavelength, corresponding with a frequency of about 1430 megahertz. 3 DEFOE To correspond with him, by the passages of the mountains. D. BREWSTER Locke and Newton had corresponded on the prophecies of Daniel.

II *v.t.* †5 Answer to, agree with, suit. M16–L17.

corresponder *n.* (now *rare*) a person who corresponds, a correspondent L18.

correspondence /kɒrɪˈspɒnd(ə)ns/ *n.* LME. [(O)Fr. f. med.L *correspondentia*, f. *correspondent-*: see next, -ENCE.] 1 Congruity, harmony, agreement; (a) similarity of character, form, or function; (an) analogy. LME. b *Math.* A relation between two sets such that each element of one is associated with a specified number of elements in the second set, and each element of the second is associated with a specified number of elements in the first. M19. †2 A concordant or sympathetic response. M16–L17. †3 Relations, a relationship, between persons or communities, usu. of a specified nature. L16–M19. †4 Dealings between individuals, esp. of a secret or illicit nature; communication for purposes of trade; an instance of this. L16–L18. 5 Vital or active communication; an instance of this. E17. 6 Communication by letters to and fro; letters exchanged, sent, or received; an exchange of letters. M17.

1 J. BUTLER The correspondence of actions to the nature of the agent renders them natural. E. B. PUSEY The correspondence of the punishment with the sin. F. SMYTH The gunsmith . . pointed out the points of correspondence between the bullets. b **one-to-one correspondence**: in which each element of one set is associated with just one element of the second, and vice versa. 3 MARVELL Our ill correspondence with the French Protestants. 5 C. LAMB Sun-dials . . holding correspondence with the fountain of light. 6 F. NORRIS A correspondence had been maintained between the two. E. WELTY He had dispatched all his correspondence promptly.

Comb.: **correspondence college**: that instructs by means of correspondence; **correspondence course** a course of instruction conducted by correspondence; **correspondence principle** *Physics*: that in the limit the laws of quantum theory pass into those of classical physics; **correspondence school**: that instructs by means of correspondence; **correspondence theory** *Philos.*: that the definition or criterion of truth is that true propositions correspond to the facts.

correspondency *n.* (now *rare*) = CORRESPONDENCE (now only sense 1) L16.

correspondent /kɒrɪˈspɒnd(ə)nt/ *a.* & *n.* LME. [(O)Fr. *correspondant* or med.L *correspondent-* pres. ppl stem of *correspondere* CORRESPOND: see -ENT.] A *adj.* 1 = CORRESPONDING 1. (Foll. by *to, with.*) *arch.* LME. †2 Responsive; compliant, submissive. E17–M18.

1 WELLINGTON The . . price has been . . increased without any correspondent improvement in the quality of the goods. J. RUSKIN Sculptural sketching, exactly correspondent to a painter's light execution of a background.

B *n.* 1 A thing that corresponds to something else. M17. †2 A person who has (esp. secret) communication with another; an accomplice. M17–L18. 3a A writer of letters. M17. b A person employed to contribute matter for publication in a newspaper or magazine or for broadcasting, esp. from a particular place or on a particular subject. Formerly, a contributor of letters to a periodical. E18. 4 A person with whom one has business dealings, esp. at a distance. L17.

3a P. H. JOHNSON She was a poor correspondent, her letters brief and schoolgirlish. b *Brussels correspondent, chess correspondent, political correspondent, special correspondent, war correspondent*, etc.

correspondential /ˌkɒrɪspɒnˈdɛnʃ(ə)l/ *a.* pertaining to correspondence or a correspondent E19. **correspondently** *adv.* correspondingly L15. **correspondentship** *n.* the post of correspondent for a newspaper etc. M19.

corresponding /kɒrɪˈspɒndɪŋ/ *ppl a.* L16. [f. CORRESPOND + -ING[2].] 1 That corresponds to something else; analogous, equivalent, proportional. L16. 2 That corresponds by letter. M18.

2 **corresponding member** an honorary member of a learned society who lives at a distance and has no voice in its discussions.

correspondingly *adv.* M19.

corresponsive /kɒrɪˈspɒnsɪv/ *a.* Now *rare.* E17. [f. COR- + RESPONSIVE.] = CORRESPONDING 1.

corrida /kɔːˈriːdə, *foreign* kɔˈrriða/ *n.* L19. [Sp., lit. 'course (of bulls)'.] In full *corrida de toros* /də ˈtɔːrəʊz, *foreign* ðe ˈtoros/. A bullfight; bullfighting.

corridor /ˈkɒrɪdɔː/ *n.* L16. [Fr. f. It. *corridore* alt., by assim. to *corridore* runner, of *corridoio* running place, f. *correre* run f. L *currere.*] †1 *Fortif.* = *covered way* (a) s.v. COVERED *a.* L16–E18. 2 A passage or covered way between two places. E17. 3 An outdoor covered way round the inside of a quadrangle or the court of a building. M17. 4 A long passage in a building, *esp.* one with many doors to side rooms; a similar passage in a railway carriage, with doors to the compartments. E19. 5 A strip of territory that runs through that of another State and secures access to the sea or some desired part. E20. 6 A belt of land or a route where traffic is concentrated or to which it is confined; *spec.* = *air corridor* s.v. AIR *n.*[1] E20.

4 **corridors of power** places or society where covert influence is exerted in government. 6 C. RYAN They were charged with holding open the corridor . . over which British armour would drive. *Economist* The area is something of a corridor for commuter traffic.

Comb.: **corridor carriage, coach** a railway carriage with a corridor; **corridor train**: made up of carriages with corridors.

corrie /ˈkɒri/ *n.* Chiefly *Sc.* M16. [Gael., (O)Ir. *coire* cauldron, hollow.] A circular hollow on a mountainside; a cirque.

Corriedale /ˈkɒrɪdeɪl/ *n.* & *a.* *NZ.* E20. [An estate in N. Otago, NZ.] (Designating) a sheep of a New Zealand breed yielding both wool and meat; the breed itself.

corrigendum /kɒrɪˈdʒɛndəm/ *n.* Pl. **-da** /-də/. E19. [L, neut. gerundive of *corrigere* CORRECT *v.*] Something requiring correction, *spec.* in a book. In *pl. esp.* errors listed with the corrections alongside.

corrigible /ˈkɒrɪdʒɪb(ə)l/ *a.* LME. [Fr. f. med.L *corrigibilis*, f. L *corrigere* CORRECT *v.*: see -IBLE. Cf. earlier INCORRIGIBLE.] †I1 Deserving punishment; punishable by law. LME–M17. 2 Able to be corrected; rectifiable; (of a fault or weakness) capable of improvement or reformation. L15. 3 Of a person: receptive to admonishment or punishment. L16. †II4 Corrective. Only in E17.

corrigiˈbility *n.* M18.

corrival /kəˈraɪv(ə)l/ *n.* & *a.* *arch.* L16. [Fr., or L *corrivalis*: see COR-, RIVAL *n.* & *a.* Cf. CO-RIVAL.] A *n.* 1 A person who is one of two or more joint rivals, a person with rival claims; *esp.* a rival suitor. L16. †2 A person having equal rights; a partner. Only in L16. B *adj.* Rival. M17.

†corrivality *n.* L16–M17. **†corrivalry** *n.* [cf. CO-RIVALRY] E–M17. **†corrivalship** *n.* the situation of a corrival E17–M18.

corroborant /kəˈrɒb(ə)r(ə)nt/ *a.* & *n.* E17. [Fr., or L *corroborant-* pres. ppl stem of *corroborare*: see next, -ANT[1].] A *adj.* Strengthening, invigorating. E17. B *n.* 1 A corroborant agent; a tonic. M18. 2 A fact which corroborates a statement etc. E19.

corroborate /kəˈrɒbəreɪt/ *v.t.* Pa. pple **-ated,** (long *arch.*) **-ate** /-ət/. M16. [L *corroborat-* pa. ppl stem of *corroborare*, f. as COR- + *roborare* strengthen, f. *robur, robor-* strength: see -ATE[3].] †1 Make stronger materially. M16–E19. †2 Strengthen (the body or spirit), act on (a part) as a restorative; invigorate. M16–E19. 3 Strengthen (a faculty, power, etc.) or (a person) *in* a quality. *arch.* M16. 4 Confirm formally (a law etc.). *arch.* M16. 5 Support (a statement, argument, etc.) with agreeing statements; provide or be additional evidence for, confirm. E18.

4 W. CRUISE For the purpose of corroborating the conveyance. 5 J. TYNDALL This observation corroborates those of Professor Forbes. A. BRINK Under oath his wife corroborated his evidence.

corroborator *n.* L17. **corroboratory** *a.* = CORROBORATIVE *a.* M17.

corroboration /kərɒbəˈreɪʃ(ə)n/ *n.* LME. [Fr., or late L *corroboratio(n-)*, f. as prec.: see -ATION.] †1 Strengthening. LME–E19. 2a Legal confirmation. *arch.* M16. b Confirmation of a statement etc. by additional evidence. M18. 3 Something which corroborates. M16.

corroborative /kəˈrɒb(ə)rətɪv/ *a.* & *n.* L16. [Fr. *corroboratif, -ive*, f. as CORROBORATE: see -IVE.] A *adj.* Having the quality of corroborating; *esp.* confirmatory. L16. †B *n.* = CORROBORANT *n.* 1. E17–E19.

corroboratively *adv.* M19.

corroboree /kəˈrɒbəri/ *n.* & *v.* L18. [Aborig.] A *n.* 1 A night-time dance of Australian Aborigines, which may be either festive or warlike; a song or chant for this. L18. 2 A noisy gathering; a disturbance. L19. B *v.i.* Take part in a corroboree; dance. M19.

corrode /kəˈrəʊd/ *v.* LME. [L *corrodere*, f. as COR- + *rodere* gnaw.] 1 *v.t.* Gradually destroy or wear away, esp. through chemical action or disease. Formerly also, of water, erode by physical action. LME. †2 *v.t.* Of an animal: eat into, gnaw away. M16–M19. 3 *v.i.* Cause corrosion. E17. 4 *v.i.* Undergo corrosion, be corroded. E19.

1 A. HIGGINS A paraffin lamp much corroded by rust. *fig.*: M. L. KING Dignity is . . corroded by poverty. 3 *fig.*: GOLDSMITH Suffering this jealousy to corrode in her breast.

corrodaˈbility *n.* = CORRODIBILITY L20. **corrodable** *a.* = CORRODIBLE L20. **corrodent** *a.* & *n.* (now *rare* or *obs.*) (*a*) *adj.* corrosive; (*b*) *n.* a corrosive agent: L16. **corroder** *n.* a person who or thing which causes corrosion L17.

corrodiary /kəˈrəʊdɪəri/ *n.* M17. [AN *corrōdiārius* f. AL *corrodium* CORRODY: see -ARY[1].] *Hist.* A recipient of a corrody.

corrodible /kəˈrəʊdɪb(ə)l/ *a.* M17. [f. CORRODE + -IBLE. Cf. CORROSIBLE.] Able to be corroded; susceptible to corrosion.

corrodiˈbility *n.* M18.

corrody /ˈkɒrədi/ *n.* Also **coro-**. LME. [AN *corodie*, AL *corrodium* var. of *corredium*, f. OFr. *conrei, conroi* (mod. *corroi*), f. *correier* CURRY *v.*[1]] *Hist.* Provision for maintenance, esp. as given regularly by a religious house; a pension.

corrosible /kəˈrəʊzɪb(ə)l/ *a.* E18. [f. L *corros-*: see next, -IBLE.] = CORRODIBLE.

corrosiˈbility *n.* L17.

corrosion /kəˈrəʊʒ(ə)n/ *n.* LME. [OFr., or late L *corrosio(n-)*, f. L *corros-* pa. ppl stem of *corrodere* CORRODE: see -ION.] The action or process of corroding; the state, esp. of a metal, of having been partly altered or destroyed by slow chemical action.

fig.: S. JOHNSON Peevishness . . wears out happiness by slow corrosion.

corrosive /kəˈrəʊsɪv/ *a.* & *n.* LME. [OFr. *corosif, -ive* (mod. *corr-*) f. med.L *corrosivus*, f. L *corros-*: see prec., -IVE.] A *adj.* 1 Having the property of corroding, tending to corrode. LME. 2 *fig.* Destructive, consuming; fretting, wearing. LME.

1 J. HELLER The corrosive blot of some crawling disease. *corrosive sublimate*: see SUBLIMATE *n.* 1. 2 R. HOOKER A pensive and corrosive desire.

B *n.* 1 A drug, remedy, etc., that destroys tissue. LME. 2 A chemical that causes corrosion. L15.

corrosively *adv.* L17. **corrosiveness** *n.* L16.

corrugate /ˈkɒrʊgeɪt/ *v.* Pa. pple **-ated**, (now chiefly *Bot.* & *Zool.*) **-ate** /-ət/. LME. [L *corrugat-* pa. ppl stem of *corrugare*, f. as COR- + *rugare*, f. *ruga* wrinkle: see -ATE[3].] 1 *v.t.* Wrinkle (skin); mark with or bend into (usu. parallel) ridges and furrows. LME. 2 *v.i.* Become corrugated. M18.

1 J. BUCHAN Trees . . whose roots corrugated the path. S. HILL A corrugated tin roof. **corrugated iron** iron or steel sheeting bent into a uniform series of parallel ridges and hollows to give added rigidity and strength. **corrugated paper**: with parallel flutings (for added rigidity and strength) and a flat backing sheet attached on one or both sides.

corrugation /kɒrəˈgeɪʃ(ə)n/ *n.* E16. [(O)Fr., or med.L *corrugatio(n-)*, f. as prec.: see -ATION.] 1 The action of corrugating; the state of being corrugated. E16. 2 A wrinkle, furrow, etc., of a corrugated surface. E19.

2 J. PACKER Poor car on the corrugations!

corrugator /ˈkɒrəgeɪtə/ *n.* L18. [f. (as) CORRUGATE + -OR.] 1 *gen.* A thing which or person who causes corrugation. L18. 2 *spec.* Either of two muscles which contract the eyebrows in frowning. M19.

corrupt /kəˈrʌpt/ *a.* ME. [OFr., or L *corruptus* pa. pple of *corrumpere* destroy, mar, bribe, f. as COR- + *rumpere* break.] 1 Depraved; infected with evil; perverted. ME. 2 Turned from a sound into an unsound condition; infected with decay; mouldy, rotten; rotting. *arch.* LME. 3 Influenced by bribery; perverted from fidelity. LME. 4 Of a language, text, etc.: unconsciously or accidentally altered from the original or correct form; containing errors or alterations; debased. LME.

1 H. REED Charles II came back . . with tastes as corrupt as his morals. 3 BURKE A corrupt representative of a virtuous people. **corrupt practice** *spec.* any of various illegal practices (as bribery, personation) in connection with elections (usu. in *pl.*). 4 T. PYNCHON The 'Whitechapel' edition . . abounds in such corrupt and probably spurious lines.

corruptly *adv.* LME. **corruptness** *n.* M16.

corrupt /kəˈrʌpt/ *v.* LME. [f. the adj.] I *v.t.* 1 Render morally unsound; destroy the moral purity or chastity of; defile. LME. 2 Make mouldy or rotten; turn from a sound into an unsound condition; contaminate, infect. *arch.* LME. 3 Induce to act dishonestly or unfaithfully; bribe. LME. †4 Pervert the text or sense of (a law etc.) for evil ends. LME–E18. 5 Mar, spoil in quality. Now *rare* or *obs.* E16. 6 Destroy the purity of (a language) or the correctness of (a text); unconsciously or accidentally alter (a word of a language). M17.

1 C. MACKENZIE Letting a rascal . . corrupt the minds of children. B. PLAIN The hidden envy that can corrupt old age. 2 W. LITHGOW The infectious air, that corrupted the blood of strangers. 3 MILTON The greatest part Of Mankind they corrupted to forsake God their Creator.

II *v.i.* 7 Putrefy, rot; decompose. *arch.* LME. 8 Undergo moral decay; degenerate. L16. 9 Cause corruption; destroy moral purity. L19.

9 LD ACTON Power tends to corrupt and absolute power corrupts absolutely.

corruptedly *adv.* in a corrupted manner E17. **corruptedness** *n.* the state of being corrupted M17. **corrupter, -or** *n.* a person who or thing which corrupts LME. **corruptful** *a.* (*rare*) fraught with corruption L16. **corruptless** *a.* (*arch.*) not subject to corruption E17. **corruptress** *n.* (now *rare*) a female corrupter E17.

corruptible /kəˈrʌptɪb(ə)l/ *a.* ME. [eccl.L *corruptibilis*, f. L *corrupt-*: see next, -IBLE.] 1 Perishable, mortal; subject to decay. ME. 2 Capable of moral corruption; open to bribery. LME.

1 SOUTHEY The soul Inhabits still its corruptible clay.

corruptiˈbility *n.* LME. **corruptibleness** *n.* LME. **corruptibly** *adv.* L16.

corruption /kəˈrʌpʃ(ə)n/ *n.* ME. [(O)Fr. f. L *corruptio(n-)*, f. *corrupt-* pa. ppl stem of *corrumpere*: see CORRUPT *a.*, -ION.] 1 Putrefaction; decay, esp. of a dead body. Formerly also more widely, decomposition of any kind, of organic or inorganic substances. ME. 2 Moral deterioration; depravity; an instance or manifestation of this. ME. 3 A corrupting influence; a cause of deterioration or depravity. ME. 4 Perversion of a person's integrity in the performance of (esp. official or public) duty or work by bribery etc. LME. 5 Evil nature; anger, temper. Now *dial.* LME. 6 Decomposed or putrid matter; pus. *obs.* exc. *dial.* LME. 7 The unconscious or accidental alteration of a word, text, etc., in transmission; a word or passage so altered. L15. 8 (A) change for the worse of an institution, custom, etc.; a departure from a state of original purity. M17.

2 V. KNOX Seminaries of young ladies . . are in danger of great corruption. 3 B. JOWETT The love of money is the corruption of states. 4 HOBBES The frequent corruption and partiality of Judges. 5 A. BRONTË I am no angel, and my corruption rises against it. 7 G. K. CHESTERTON Whether Notting Hill . . is a corruption of Nothing-ill.

Phrases: **corruption of blood** *Hist.* the effect of attainder by which the person attainted could neither inherit, retain, nor transmit land.

corruptionist *n.* a person who supports or practises corruption, esp. in public affairs E19.

corruptive /kəˈrʌptɪv/ *a.* LME. [(O)Fr. *corruptif, -ive* or eccl.L *corruptivus*, f. L *corrupt-*: see prec., -IVE.] 1 Tending to corrupt. LME. †2 Subject or liable to corruption. L16–L17.

corruptively *adv.* M17.

†**cors** *n.* see CORSE *n.*

corsac /ˈkɔːsak/ *n.* M19. [Russ. *korsak* f. Turki *karsak*.] A fox, *Vulpes corsac*, of the steppes of central Asia.

corsage /kɔːˈsɑːʒ, ˈkɔːsɑːʒ/ *n.* LME. [(O)Fr., f. *cors* (mod. CORPS): see -AGE.] †1 The body, the trunk; size and shape of body. LME–M17. 2 The bodice of a woman's dress. E19. 3 A posy for the front of a woman's dress. E20.

corsair /ˈkɔːsɛː/ *n.* M16. [Fr. *corsaire* f. med.L *cursarius*, f. *cursa*, *cursus* hostile inroad, plunder, a spec. use of L *cursus* COURSE *n.*[1]] 1 *Hist.* a A privateersman of the Mediterranean, esp. the Barbary coast; a pirate. M16. b A privateering ship; a pirate ship. Also *corsair ship*. M17. 2 Either of two nocturnal reduviid bugs of the western and southern US, of the genus *Rasahus*, which can give a painful bite. E20.

corse /kɔːs/ *n.* Also (the only form in sense 4) †**cors**. ME. [OFr. *cors* (mod. CORPS). Cf. CORPSE *n.*] †1 = CORPSE *n.* 1. ME–L16. 2 = CORPSE *n.* 2. Now *poet.* & *arch.* ME. †3 A ribbon or band serving as ground for an ornamented girdle, garter, etc. ME–M16. †4 *Archit.* A slender pillar surmounted by a pinnacle or figure and close to but not supporting a wall. L15–M19.

Comb.: †**corse-present** a customary gift due to the clergy from the effects of a deceased householder.

corse /kɔːs/ *v.t.* Long *obs.* exc. *dial.* Also **course**. ME. [Origin unkn. Cf. COSS *v.*, SCORSE *v.*[1]] Barter, exchange, buy and sell, (esp. horses).

corser *n.* a dealer, a jobber; *esp.* (more fully *horse-corser*) a horse-dealer: LME.

corselet *n.* var. of CORSLET.

corselette /kɔːs(ə)ˈlɛt, ˈkɔːs(ə)lɛt/ *n.* E20. [f. prec.: see -ETTE.] A foundation garment combining girdle and brassière.

corset /ˈkɔːsɪt/ *n.* & *v.* ME. [(O)Fr., dim. of *cors* (mod. CORPS): see -ET[1].] A *n.* 1 *Hist.* A close-fitting laced or stiffened outer bodice or gown worn by women; a similar garment worn by men. ME. 2 *sing.* & in *pl.* A woman's close-fitting undergarment for giving shape and support to the figure, formerly with lacing and stiffening. L18. 3 A close-fitting support worn because of injury, weakness, or deformity, esp. of the thorax or spine. M19.

2 *fig.*: *Listener* It imprisons the state in a bureaucratic corset designed to restrict development.

B *v.t.* 1 Fit or provide with a corset. Chiefly as *corseted* ppl a., *corseting* vbl n. M19. 2 *fig.* Place restraints or controls on; force *into*. M20.

corsetless *a.* L19. **corsetry** *n.* (*a*) the making or fitting of corsets; (*b*) corsets collectively: E20.

corsetière /ˈkɔːsɪtjɛː/ *n.* M19. [Fr., fem. of *corsetier*, f. as prec.: see -IER.] A woman who makes or fits corsets.

Corsican /ˈkɔːsɪk(ə)n/ *n.* & *a.* M18. [f. *Corsica* (see below) + -AN.] A *n.* A native or inhabitant of Corsica, an island in the Mediterranean; the dialect of Italian spoken there. M18. B *adj.* Of or pertaining to Corsica. M18.

Phrases: **Corsican pine** a tall slender pine (a subspecies of the Austrian pine *Pinus nigra*) which is native to southern Europe and has been introduced into Britain. **the Corsican (ogre, robber,** etc.) Napoleon, who was born in Corsica.

†corsie *n.* & *a.* Also **corsive**. LME. [Syncopated f. CORROSIVE.] A *n.* **1** = CORROSIVE *n.* LME–M17. **2** A cause of trouble and grief, a grievance. M16–L19. B *adj.* = CORROSIVE *a.* L16–E17.

corslet /ˈkɔːslɪt/ *n.* Also **corselet**. L15. [(O)Fr., dim. of *cors* (mod. CORPS): see -LET.] **I 1 a** *Hist.* A piece of armour covering the body, orig. from the head to the thighs, later just the upper trunk. L15. **†b** A soldier wearing a corslet. L16–E18. **2** A usu. tight-fitting garment covering the trunk. E16. **3** = CORSELETTE. M20. **II 4** The thorax or prothorax of an insect, esp. a beetle. M18.

corsned /ˈkɔːsnɛd/ *n.* [OE *cor-snǣd*, f. *cor* choice, trial + *snǣd* bit, piece, f. *snīdan* to cut.] *Hist.* A piece of bread consecrated by exorcism which in pre-Conquest times an accused person was required to swallow without harm to demonstrate his or her innocence.

Corso /ˈkɔːsəʊ/ *n.* Also **c-**. Pl. **-os**. L17. [It. = course, main street f. L *cursus* COURSE *n.*[1]] In Italy and some other Mediterranean countries: a procession of carriages; a social promenade; a street given over to this, or where races etc. were formerly held.

Cortaillod /kɔːˈtʌɪjəʊ/ *n.* & *a.* L19. [Place in the canton of Neuchâtel, Switzerland.] A *n.* A red table wine made in the canton of Neuchâtel, Switzerland, from Pinot grapes. L19. B *adj.* *Archaeol.* Designating or pertaining to an early neolithic culture of Switzerland, represented esp. by lakeside sites. M20.

cortège /kɔːˈteɪʒ/ *n.* M17. [Fr. f. It. *corteggio*, f. *corteggiare* attend court, f. *corte* COURT *n.*[1]] A train of attendants; a procession of people, esp. mourners.

Cortes /ˈkɔːtɛs, -z/ *a.* Pl. same. M17. [Sp. & Port., pl. of *corte* COURT *n.*[1]] The legislative assembly of Spain or (*Hist.*) Portugal or any of various medieval Spanish kingdoms.

cortex /ˈkɔːtɛks/ *n.* Pl. **-tices** /-tɪsiːz/. LME. [L = bark.] **1** An outer layer of a part in an animal or plant, as of the kidney or a hair; *spec.* (*Anat.*) the outer layer of the cerebrum, composed of folded grey matter and playing an important role in consciousness; a similar layer of the cerebellum; *Bot.* a layer of plant tissue between the epidermis and the central vascular tissue. LME. **†2** *fig.* An outer shell or husk. M17–M18. **3** The bark of a tree, or the peel or rind of a plant, as used medicinally; *spec.* cinchona bark. L17.

1 *adrenal cortex*: see ADRENAL *a.* *motor cortex*: see MOTOR *n.* & *a.* *visual cortex*: see VISUAL *a.*

Corti /ˈkɔːti/ *n.* L19. [A. *Corti* (1822–88), It. histologist.] Anat. *organ of Corti*, a sense-organ on the basilar membrane of the cochlea, containing sensory hair cells.

cortical /ˈkɔːtɪk(ə)l/ *a.* M17. [med.L *corticalis*, f. L *cortic-*, CORTEX: see -AL[1].] **1** Belonging to or forming a cortex. M17. **†2** *fig.* Superficial, external. M17–M19.

corticated /ˈkɔːtɪkeɪtɪd/ *a.* M17. [f. L *corticatus* derived from bark, f. *cortic-*, CORTEX: see -ATE[2], -ED[1].] *Bot.* & *Zool.* Having a cortex; having a bark, rind, or other outer layer.

Also **corticate** /-eɪt, -ət/ *a.* M19.

corticene /ˈkɔːtɪsiːn/ *n.* Also **-ine**. L19. [f. L *cortic-*, CORTEX + -ENE, -INE[4].] A floor-covering material made from ground cork.

cortices *n.* pl. of CORTEX.

cortici- /ˈkɔːtɪsi/ *comb. form* of CORTEX: see -I-. Cf. CORTICO-.

corti'cifugal *a.* = CORTICOFUGAL L19. **corti'cipetal** *a.* = CORTICOPETAL L19.

corticine *n.* var. of CORTICENE.

cortico- /ˈkɔːtɪkəʊ/ *comb. form* of CORTEX: see -O-. Used esp. w. ref. to the adrenal and cerebral cortices. Cf. CORTICI-.

cortico'fugal *a.* [L *fugere* flee] (of a nerve fibre) originating in and running from the cerebral cortex L19. **corticoid** *n.* = CORTICOSTEROID M20. **cortico'petal** *a.* [L *petere* seek] (of a nerve fibre) originating outside and running into the cerebral cortex L19. **cortico'steroid** *n.* any of the steroid hormones produced in the adrenal cortex, which are concerned with one or other of electrolyte balance, carbohydrate metabolism, anti-inflammatory activity, and sexuality; any analogous synthetic steroid: M20. **cortico'sterone** *n.* [-STERONE] a corticosteroid, $C_{21}H_{30}O_4$, which is converted in the body to aldosterone M20. **cortico'trop(h)ic** *a.* = ADRENOCORTICOTROP(H)IC M20. **cortico'trop(h)in** *n.* the adrenocorticotropic hormone M20.

corticolous /kɔːˈtɪkələs/ *a.* M19. [f. L *cortic-*, CORTEX + -COLOUS.] *Bot.* Of a plant, esp. a lichen: growing on bark. Cf. SAXICOLOUS.

Also **'corticole** *a.* L19.

cortile /korˈtiːle, kɔːˈtiːli/ *n.* E18. [It., deriv. of *corte* COURT *n.*[1]] An enclosed usu. roofless and arcaded area within or attached to an Italian building.

cortina /kɔːˈtʌɪnə, -ˈtiːnə/ *n.* M19. [Late L = CURTAIN *n.*] A thin weblike structure left hanging from the cap of mushrooms etc. after the lower edge of the partial veil separates from the stalk; the partial veil itself.

cortisol /ˈkɔːtɪsɒl/ *n.* M20. [f. next + -OL.] = HYDROCORTISONE.

cortisone /ˈkɔːtɪzəʊn/ *n.* M20. [f. 17-hydroxy-11-dehydroxy*cortico*ster*one*, chemical name: see CORTICOSTERONE.] A steroid hormone, $C_{21}H_{28}O_5$, produced in the adrenal cortex and made synthetically, that is used as an anti-inflammatory and anti-allergy agent.

corundum /kəˈrʌndəm/ *n.* E18. [Tamil *kuruntam*, Telugu *kuruvindam*.] Aluminium oxide, Al_2O_3, a very hard mineral occurring in many rocks as hexagonal crystals of various colours (some of gem quality, as sapphires, rubies, etc.), and made synthetically for use in abrasives, refractories, and bearings.

coruscant /kɒˈrʌsk(ə)nt/ *a.* L15. [L *coruscant-* pres. ppl stem of *coruscare*: see next, -ANT[1].] Glittering, sparkling, (*lit.* & *fig.*).

coruscate /ˈkɒrəskeɪt/ *v.i.* E18. [L *coruscat-* pa. ppl stem of *coruscare* vibrate, glitter: see -ATE[3].] Flash; sparkle, glitter, (*lit.* & *fig.*).

D. CECIL A flight of comic fantasy, coruscating with grotesque images and . . plays on words.

coruscation /kɒrəˈskeɪʃ(ə)n/ *n.* L15. [L *coruscatio(n-)*, f. as prec.: see -ATION.] A quivering flash or glow of light; a display of such flashes.

L. M. MONTGOMERY Reflecting the sunlight back from its window in several little coruscations of glory.

corvée /ˈkɔːveɪ/ *n.* ME. [(O)Fr. = Prov. *corroada* f. Proto-Romance use as n. (sc. *opera* work) of L *corrogata* neut. pl. pa. pple of *corrogare* summon, f. as COR- + *rogare* ask.] A day's unpaid work required of a vassal by a feudal lord; forced labour exacted as a tax, *spec.* that on public roads in France before 1776; *fig.* an unpleasant duty, an onerous task.

corver /ˈkɔːvə/ *n.* E18. [f. CORF + -ER[1].] A maker of corves.

corves *n.* pl. of CORF.

corvette /kɔːˈvɛt/ *n.* M17. [Fr., ult. dim. of (M)Du. *korf* basket, kind of ship: see CORF, -ETTE.] *Hist.* **1** Orig., a kind of small French vessel using both oars and sail. Later, a warship with a flush deck and one tier of guns. Now *Hist.* M17. **2** An escort vessel smaller than a frigate used esp. for protecting convoys against submarines in the war of 1939–45. M20.

corvid /ˈkɔːvɪd/ *n.* & *a.* M20. [mod.L *Corvidae* (see below), f. L *corvus* raven: see -ID[3].] (A bird) of the passerine family Corvidae, which includes crows, jays, magpies, choughs, and ravens.

corvina /kɔːˈviːnə/ *n.* L18. [Sp. & Port., f. as next.] Any of several marine fishes of the family Sciaenidae, *esp.* an American food fish of the genus *Cynoscion*.

corvine /ˈkɔːvʌɪn/ *a.* M17. [L *corvinus*, f. *corvus* raven: see -INE[1].] Of or pertaining to a raven or crow; of the crow kind.

†corviser *n.* OE–E18. [AN *corvoiser*, OFr. *co(u)rvoisier*, f. *courveis* leather f. L *Cordubensis* of Córdoba, f. *Corduba*: see CORDOVAN, -ER[1].] A shoemaker; = CORDWAINER.

Corvus /ˈkɔːvəs/ *n.* L17. [L *corvus* raven.] (The name of) an inconspicuous constellation of the southern hemisphere south of Virgo; the Crow, the Raven.

Corybant /ˈkɒrɪbant/ *n.* Pl. **Corybants, Corybantes** /kɒrɪˈbantiːz/. LME. [L *Corybas, -bant-* f. Gk *Korubas*.] *Gk Hist.* A priest of the fertility and nature goddess Cybele, whose worship involved wild dances and ecstatic states.

cory'bantic, C- *a.* resembling (that of) the Corybants; wild, frenzied: M17.

Corycian /kəˈrɪʃɪən, -ʃ(ə)n, -sɪən/ *a.* M16. [f. L *Corycius* of or belonging to Corycus or the Corycian cave f. Gk *Kōrukios*, f. *Kōrukos* Corycus: see -IAN.] **1** *Gk Mythol.* Designating a large cave on Mount Parnassus in Greece and the nymphs, daughters of Pleistos, supposed to live there. M16. **2** Of or pertaining to Corycus in Cilicia (now Curco in Turkey). E20.

corydalis /kəˈrɪdəlɪs/ *n.* E19. [mod.L f. Gk *korudallis* crested lark (w. allus. to the flower, likened to the bird's spur), f. *korus* helmet: cf. LARKSPUR.] A plant of the genus *Corydalis*, of the poppy family, comprising mostly rhizomatous or tuberous herbaceous perennials with racemose flowers. Also (w. specifying wd), a plant of any of several related genera.

corymb /ˈkɒrɪmb/ *n.* E18. [Fr. *corymbe* or L *corymbus* f. Gk *korumbos* summit, cluster of fruit or flowers.] **1** *Bot.* An inflorescence whose lower flower stalks are proportionally longer so that the flowers form a flat or slightly convex head. Formerly also, a discoidal head of a composite flower. E18. **2** A cluster of ivy berries or grapes. E18.

co'rymbiform *a.* having the form of a corymb L19. **corymbose** *a.* growing in or as a corymb; of the nature of a corymb: L18. **corymbosely** *adv.* M19.

corymbiferous /kɒrɪmˈbɪf(ə)rəs/ *a.* M17. [f. L *corymbifer* bearing clusters of berries, f. *corymbus*: see prec., -FEROUS.] **1** Bearing berries. *rare* (Dicts.). M17. **2** *Bot.* Bearing corymbs; belonging to an obsolete division of the family Compositae called Corymbiferae. Now *rare* or *obs.* L17.

corynebacterium /ˌkɒrɪnɪbakˈtɪərɪəm, kəˌrɪn-/ *n.* Pl. **-ia** /-ɪə/. E20. [mod.L, f. Gk *korunē* club + BACTERIUM.] A bacterium of the genus *Corynebacterium* of Gram-positive club-shaped rods, of which some species cause disease in plants, animals, or man (e.g. diphtheria).

coryneform /kəˈrɪnɪfɔːm/ *a.* M20. [f. Gk *korunē* club + -FORM.] Resembling or being a corynebacterium.

coryphaeus /kɒrɪˈfiːəs/ *n.* Pl. **-phaei** /-ˈfiːʌɪ/. E17. [L f. Gk *koruphaios* chief, chorus-leader, f. *koruphē* head, top.] **1** The leader of a chorus. E17. **2** The leader of a party, sect, school of thought, etc. E17. **3** A post of assistant to the Choragus that formerly existed in Oxford University. M19.

coryphée /ˈkɒrɪfeɪ/ *n.* E19. [Fr. f. as prec.] A leading dancer of a *corps de ballet*.

coryphodon /kəˈrɪfədɒn/ *n.* M19. [mod.L, f. Gk *koruphē* head, top + -ODON.] A large extinct herbivorous quadruped of the fossil genus *Coryphodon* (order Pantodonta), which lived in late Palaeocene and early Eocene times.

Also **co'ryphodont** *n.* L19.

coryza /kəˈrʌɪzə/ *n.* E16. [L f. Gk *koruza* nasal mucus, catarrh.] Acute catarrhal inflammation of the nose; *esp.* the common cold.

coryzal *a.* E20.

cos /kɒs/ *n.*[1] Also **C-**. L17. [*Cos*, one of the Dodecanese islands.] In full *cos lettuce*. A variety of lettuce with long smooth leaves (orig. introduced from Cos).

cos /kɒz, -s/ *n.*[2] M18. [Abbrev.] *Math.* Cosine (of).

cos /kɒz, kəz/ *adv.* & *conj. dial.* & *colloq.* Also **'cos**. E19. [Alt. of 'CAUSE.] = BECAUSE.

Cosa Nostra /ˈkəʊzə ˈnɒstrə/ *n. phr.* M20. [It. = our thing.] The American branch of the Mafia.

cosaque /kɒˈzɑːk/ *n.* M19. [App. f. Fr. *Cosaque* COSSACK.] = CRACKER 3b.

coscinomancy /ˈkɒsɪnəmansi/ *n.* E17. [med.L *coscinomantia* f. Gk *koskinomantis*, f. *koskinon* sieve: see -MANCY.] Divination by the turning of a sieve (held on a pair of shears etc.).

coscoroba /kɒskəˈrəʊbə/ *n.* E19. [mod.L of unkn. origin.] In full *coscoroba swan*. A small S. American swan, *Coscoroba coscoroba*, with white plumage and bright pink legs and feet.

cose /kəʊz/ *v.*[1]*i. colloq.* M19. [Back-form. f. COSY *a.*] Make oneself cosy.

cose *v.*[2] var. of COSS *v.*

cosec /ˈkəʊsɛk/ *n.* M18. [Abbrev.] *Math.* Cosecant (of).

cosecant /kəʊˈsiːk(ə)nt, -ˈsɛk-/ *n.* E18. [mod.L *cosecant-*: see CO-, SECANT.] *Math.* The secant of the complement of a given angle; in a right-angled triangle containing the angle, the ratio of the hypotenuse to the side opposite the angle. Abbrev. COSEC.

coset /ˈkəʊsɛt/ *n.* E20. [f. CO- + SET *n.*[2]] *Math.* A subset of a group composed of all the products obtained by multiplying each element of a subgroup in turn by one particular element of the group.

cosh /kɒʃ/ *n.*[1] & *v. colloq.* Also **k-**. M19. [Origin unkn.] A *n.* A heavy stick or bludgeon; a truncheon. M19.

Comb.: **cosh boy** a youth or man who uses or carries a cosh.

B *v.t.* Strike with a cosh. L19.

fig.: J. BARNES Some writers . . sneak in at the back door and cosh the reader with a highly personal style.

cosher *n.* a person who uses a cosh; *slang* a police officer: L19.

cosh /kɒʃ, kɒˈseɪtʃ/ *n.*[2] L19. [f. COS *n.*[2] + *h* (for *hyperbolic*).] *Math.* Hyperbolic cosine (of).

cosher /ˈkɒʃə/ *v.*[1]*i.* L16. [f. Ir. *cóisir* feast.] *Ir. Hist.* Quarter oneself as the guest of another, esp. a dependant or kinsman; live at another's expense.

cosherer *n.* a person who coshers or lives by coshering M17. **coshery** *n.* entertainment for themselves and their followers exacted by Irish chiefs from their dependants L16.

cosher /ˈkɒʃə/ *v.*[2]*t.* M19. [Origin unkn.] Pamper; coddle. (Foll. by *up*.)

co-signatory /kəʊˈsɪgnət(ə)ri/ *n.* & *a.* Also **cosig-**. M19. [f. CO- + SIGNATORY.] (A person or State) who signs a treaty, cheques, etc., jointly with another.

cosine /ˈkəʊsʌɪn/ *n.* E17. [f. CO- + SINE *n.*] *Math.* The sine of the complement of a given angle; in a right-angled triangle containing the angle, the ratio of the adjacent side to the hypotenuse. Abbrev. COS *n.*[2]

hyperbolic cosine a hyperbolic function defined by $y = \frac{1}{2}(e^x+e^{-x})$. LOGARITHMIC *cosine*.

†cosins *n.* Only in E18. [f. the name of the maker.] A kind of corset or bodice.

Coslettize /ˈkɒzlɪtʌɪz/ *v.t.* Also **c-**, **-ise**. E20. [f. T. W. *Coslett* (fl. 1906), Eng. chemist + -IZE.] Give (iron or steel) a rustproof coating of phosphate by boiling in dilute phosphoric acid.

cosmea /ˈkɒzmɪə/ *n.* E19. [mod.L, f. COSMOS *n.*[2]: see -A[1].] = COSMOS *n.*[2]

cosmetic /kɒzˈmɛtɪk/ *n.*, *a.*, & *v.* E17. [Fr. *cosmétique* f. Gk *kosmētikos*, f. *kosmein* arrange, adorn, f. *kosmos* COSMOS *n.*[1]: see -IC.] A *n.* 1 *sing.* & in *pl.* The art of adorning or beautifying the body. E17. 2 A preparation for use in beautifying the face, skin, or hair. M17.

B *adj.* 1 Able or used to beautify a person's appearance, esp. the complexion; of or pertaining to cosmetics. M17. 2 Of surgery: aimed at improving or modifying the appearance. Of a prosthetic device: re-creating the normal appearance. E20. 3 *fig.* Intended merely to improve appearances; superficial. M20.

2 *Observer* His metal alloy legs . . are finished with cosmetic shoes. 3 J. BAYLEY The alterations . . are not much more than cosmetic. *Daily Telegraph* The ferry was able to sail . . despite 'cosmetic' damage to the bows.

C *v.t.* Infl. **-ck-**. Treat with cosmetics; apply a cosmetic to. L19.

cosmetical *a.* M16. **cosmetically** *adv.* L19. **cosmetician** /kɒzməˈtɪʃ(ə)n/ *n.* (chiefly *N. Amer.*) an expert in cosmetics, a beautician E20. **cosmeticize** /-sʌɪz/ *v.t.* treat with cosmetics; *fig.* make superficially presentable: E19.

cosmetology /kɒzmɪˈtɒlədʒi/ *n.* M19. [Fr. *cosmétologie*, f. as prec.: see -OLOGY.] †1 A book on dress and personal hygiene. *rare.* Only in M19. 2 The art and practice of beautifying the face, hair, and skin; the branch of science that deals with this as a technical skill. M20.

cosmetologist *n.* E20.

cosmic /ˈkɒzmɪk/ *a.* M17. [f. COSMOS *n.*[1] + -IC, after Fr. *cosmique* (f. Gk *kosmikos*, f. *kosmos* COSMOS *n.*[1]).] †1 Of this world. Only in M17. 2 Of or pertaining to the universe as an ordered system or totality; universal; immense, infinite. M19. 3 Belonging to the universe as distinguished from the earth; extraterrestrial. L19. 4 Characteristic of the vast scale of the universe. L19. 5 [after Russ. *kosmicheskiĭ*.] Of or pertaining to travel through space. M20.

2 W. D. WHITNEY The great cosmic law of gravitation. H. NICOLSON The Civil War . . as a cosmic clash between strong men and massive principles. C. SAGAN A deep and common wish . . to have human affairs matter in the cosmic context. 4 J. TYNDALL Cosmic ranges of time. 5 *Daily Telegraph*: Cosmic flights.

Special collocations: **cosmic dust** minute particles of matter in or from space. *cosmic string*: see STRING *n.* 18b. **cosmic radiation, rays** radiation of great energy (chiefly atomic nuclei) which originates in space and reaches the earth from all directions (also more fully *primary cosmic radiation*); radiation that this gives rise to in the atmosphere (also more fully *secondary cosmic radiation*).

cosmical /ˈkɒzmɪk(ə)l/ *a.* M16. [f. as prec.: see -ICAL.] †1 Pertaining to the earth; geographical. *rare.* M16–E19. 2 *Astron.* Of the rising or setting of a star: occurring at sunrise. M16. 3 = COSMIC 2, 3, 4. L17.

3 **cosmical constant** = COSMOLOGICAL *constant*.

cosmically /ˈkɒzmɪk(ə)li/ *adv.* M16. [f. COSMIC or prec.: see -ICALLY.] 1 *Astron.* Coincidently with the rising of the sun. M16. 2 In a cosmic manner; in relation to the cosmos. M19.

cosmism /ˈkɒzmɪz(ə)m/ *n.* M19. [f. COSMOS *n.*[1] + -ISM.] The view that the universe is a self-existent, self-acting whole explicable purely in scientific terms.

cosmist *n.* a believer in cosmism M19.

cosmo- /ˈkɒzməʊ/ *comb. form.* [Gk *kosmo-* f. *kosmos* COSMOS *n.*[1]: see -O-.] Used in wds adapted f. Gk and in Eng. wds modelled on these, w. the sense 'world, universe'.

cosmoˈcentric *a.* centred in the cosmos M19. **cosmoˈchemical** *a.* of or pertaining to cosmochemistry M20. **cosmoˈchemically** *adv.* from a cosmochemical point of view M20. **cosmoˈchemistry** *n.* the branch of science that deals with the chemical properties of stars etc. and the cosmic distribution of elements and compounds M20. **cosmodrome** *n.* [after AERODROME] in the countries of the former USSR a launching site for spacecraft M20. **cosmogeˈnetic** *a.* = COSMOGENIC (a) L19. **cosmoˈgenic** *a.* (*a*) of or pertaining to cosmogeny; (*b*) of cosmic origin: E20. **cosˈmogeny** *n.* the origin or evolution of the universe M19. **cosmoˈrama** *n.* a peep-show containing views of all parts of the world E19. **cosmoˈramic** *a.* belonging to or of the nature of a cosmorama E19. **cosmoˈthetic** *a.* that posits or assumes an external world M19.

cosmogony /kɒzˈmɒgəni/ *n.* L17. [Gk *kosmogonia* creation of the world, f. as COSMOS *n.*[1]: see -GONY.] 1 A theory or account of the origin of the universe; the branch of science that deals with the origin of the universe. L17. 2 The creation of the universe. M18.

1 C. SAGAN The Babylonian cosmogony enshrined in Genesis.

cosmoˈgonic(al) *adjs.* E19. **cosmogonist** *n.* †(*a*) a person who holds that the world had a beginning in time; (*b*) a person who studies cosmogony or propounds a cosmogony: L17.

cosmographer /kɒzˈmɒgrəfə/ *n.* E16. [f. late L *cosmographus* f. Gk *kosmographos*, f. as COSMO- + -GRAPH: see -ER[1]. Cf. (O)Fr. *cosmographe*.] A person skilled in cosmography. Formerly also, a geographer.

cosmography /kɒzˈmɒgrəfi/ *n.* LME. [Fr. *cosmographie* or late L *cosmographia*, f. Gk *kosmographia*, f. as COSMO-: see -GRAPHY.] 1 An overall description or representation of the universe or the earth. LME. 2 The science which deals with the general features and disposition of the universe, including the earth. Formerly also, geography. E16.

cosmoˈgraphic *a.* E19. **cosmoˈgraphical** *a.* M16. **cosmoˈgraphically** *adv.* M16. **cosmographist** *n.* (*rare*) = COSMOGRAPHER M17.

Cosmoline /ˈkɒzmə(ʊ)liːn/ *n.* Also **c-**. L19. [f. COSM(ETIC + -OL + -INE[5].] (Proprietary name for) petroleum jelly.

cosmological /kɒzməˈlɒdʒɪk(ə)l/ *a.* L18. [f. next: see -ICAL.] Of or pertaining to cosmology.

cosmological argument: for the absolute existence of God from the contingent existence of things. **cosmological constant** an arbitrary constant in the field equations of general relativity.

cosmologically *adv.* M19.

cosmology /kɒzˈmɒlədʒi/ *n.* M17. [Fr. *cosmologie* or mod.L *cosmologia*, f. as COSMO- + -LOGY.] 1 The science of the evolution and structure of the universe; a theory or postulated account of this. M17. 2 The branch of philosophy or metaphysics which deals with the universe as a whole. M18.

1 S. WEINBERG The big bang cosmology. P. DAVIES The expanding universe is now a cornerstone of cosmology.

cosmologist *n.* a person who studies cosmology or propounds a cosmology L18.

cosmonaut /ˈkɒzmənɔːt/ *n.* M20. [f. COSMO- after *aeronaut* and Russ. *kosmonavt*.] An astronaut, *esp.* a Soviet astronaut.

cosmoˈnautic(al) *adjs.* M20. **cosmoˈnautics** *n.pl.* (usu. treated as *sing.*) = ASTRONAUTICS M20.

cosmopolis /kɒzˈmɒp(ə)lɪs/ *n.* M19. [f. COSMO- + -POLIS.] A cosmopolitan city; a capital city, a world capital.

cosmopolitan /kɒzməˈpɒlɪt(ə)n/ *n.* & *a.* M17. [f. next + -AN: cf. METROPOLITAN.] A *n.* 1 A person who treats the whole world as his or her country; a person with no national attachments or prejudices. M17. 2 A plant or animal found all over the world. M20.

B *adj.* 1 Belonging to all or many parts of the world; not restricted to any one country or region. M19. 2 Free from national limitations or attachments; having characteristics suited to or arising from an experience of many countries. M19. 3 Containing people from many different countries. E20.

2 LD MACAULAY That cosmopolitan indifference to constitutions and religions. A. KOESTLER Cosmopolitan by nature and education, wherever she was she was at home.

cosmopolitanism *n.* (*a*) cosmopolitan character; (*b*) *Hist.* (in Soviet usage) disparagement of Russian traditions and culture: E19. **cosmopolitanize** *v.t.* make cosmopolitan L19. **cosmopolitanly** *adv.* L19.

cosmopolite /kɒzˈmɒp(ə)lʌɪt/ *n.* & *a.* E17. [Fr. f. Gk *kosmopolitēs*, f. as COSMO- + *politēs* citizen.] A *n.* 1 = COSMOPOLITAN *n.* 1. E17. 2 = COSMOPOLITAN *n.* 2. M19. B *adj.* = COSMOPOLITAN *a.* E19.

ˌcosmopoˈlitical *a.* [after *political*] relating to all States and polities L16. **cosmopolitism** *n.* = COSMOPOLITANISM (a) L18.

cosmos /ˈkɒzmɒs/ *n.*[1] ME. [Gk *kosmos* order, ornament, world.] 1 The universe as an ordered whole. ME. 2 Harmony, order. M19. 3 An ordered system of ideas etc. L19.

cosmos /ˈkɒzmɒs/ *n.*[2] E19. [mod.L f. as prec.] A tropical American plant of the genus *Cosmos*, of the composite family, having flowers of various bright colours; esp. *C. bipinnatus*, an annual with single blossoms on long stems that is cultivated as a garden plant.

†cosmos *n.*[3] var. of KUMIS.

coss *n.* var. of KOS.

coss /kɒs/ *v.t.* & *i.* Chiefly *Sc.* Also **cose** /kəʊz/. LME. [Origin unkn. Cf. CORSE *v.*, SCORSE *v.*[1]] Barter, exchange.

Cossack /ˈkɒsak/ *n.* & *a.* L16. [Russ. *kazak* (whence Fr. *Cosaque*) f. Turkic = vagabond, nomad, adventurer; later infl. by Fr. Cf. KAZAKH.] A *n.* 1 A member of a people living in southern and SW Russia, noted as horsemen from early times and formerly serving as border guards for Poland and pre-Communist Russia. L16. 2 A high boot. E19. 3 In *pl.* Baggy trousers pleated into a waistband. E19. 4 A police officer, *esp.* a member of a strikebreaking force. *slang.* M19.

B *adj.* Of, pertaining to, or being a Cossack or Cossacks. E19.

Cossack boot = sense A.2 above. **Cossack hat** a brimless hat widening towards the top. **Cossack post** *Hist.* an outpost of a few mounted men under a non-commissioned officer or senior soldier. **Cossack trousers** = sense A.3 above.

cosset /'kɒsɪt/ *n.* & *v.* M16. [Perh. f. AN *coscet, cozet* cottager f. as COTSET.] A *n.* 1 A lamb brought up by hand. M16. 2 A petted child; a spoiled person. L16. B *v.* 1 *v.t.* Pamper; pet, fondle. M17. 2 *v.i.* Indulge in pampering; nestle *up.* L19.

†**cossic** *a.* M16–M19. [It. *cossico*, f. *cosa* thing, tr. Arab. *šay'* lit. 'something, thing', unknown quantity in an equation: see -IC.] Algebraic.

Also †**cossical** *a.* L16–E19.

cossid /'kɒsɪd/ *n.* L17. [Pers. f. Arab. *ḳāṣid* foot-messenger, courier.] *Hist.* In the Indian subcontinent: a running messenger.

cossie /'kɒzi, -s-/ *n. slang* (chiefly *Austral.*). Also **cozzie** /-z-/. E20. [f. COS(TUME + -IE.] A swimsuit, a pair of swimming-trunks.

†**cost** *n.*[1] OE–L16. [L *costum*, COSTUS f. Gk *kostos* f. Arab. *ḳusṭ* f. Skt *kuṣṭha*.] = COSTMARY.

¶Survives in *alecost* s.v. ALE; COSTMARY.

cost /kɒst/ *n.*[2] ME. [AN *cost*, OFr. *coust* (mod. *coût*), f. *couster*: see COST *v.*] 1 What must be given in order to acquire, produce, or effect something; the price (to be) paid for a thing. ME. b What a thing originally cost. L19. 2 In *pl.* Charges, expenses; *obs.* exc. *Law*, the expenses of litigation, prosecution, or other legal transaction, *esp.* those allowed in favour of the winning party or against the losing party. ME. 3 Expenditure of time or labour; what is borne, lost, or suffered in accomplishing or gaining something. (Now chiefly in phrs. or with *of.*) ME. †4 Outlay, expenditure. LME–L18. †5 What money etc. is expended on; a costly thing. *rare.* LME–L16.

4 ADDISON No Art or Cost is omitted to make the Stay . . agreeable.

Phrases: **at all costs, at any cost** whatever the cost may be. **at cost** at the initial cost; at cost price. **at the cost of** at the expense of losing (something). *bill of costs*: see BILL *n.*[3] **cost of living** the financial outlay required for the basic necessities of life. **count the cost** consider the risks, disadvantages, or repercussions of an action. **know to one's cost** have learned by bitter experience. *prime cost*: see PRIME *a.* *social cost*: see SOCIAL *a.* **to a person's cost** with loss or disadvantage to him or her. *unit cost*: see UNIT *n.*[1] & *a.* *with costs*: see WITH *prep.*

Comb.: **cost accountant**: engaged in cost accounting; **cost accounting** the recording and review of all the costs incurred in a business, as an aid to management (*current cost accounting*: see CURRENT *a.*); **cost-benefit analysis, study**, etc.: assessing the relation of the cost of an operation to the value of the resulting benefits; **cost clerk**: who records all the costs incurred in a business, as an aid to management; **cost-effective** *a.* providing a satisfactory return for the outlay; **cost-of-living index**: measuring the change with time in the level of retail prices; **cost-plus** *a.* designating or pertaining to a pricing system in which a fixed profit factor is added to the cost incurred; **cost price**: at which a merchant etc. buys; **cost-push** *n.* & *a.* (caused by) increasing costs, esp. pay, rather than increasing demand as agents of inflation.

costless *a.* without cost, free E16. **costlessness** *n.* an absence of any expense M19.

cost /kɒst/ *n.*[3] Now *rare.* L16. [OFr. *coste* (mod. *côte*) rib f. L *costa.*] *Her.* A cottise, esp. when borne singly.

cost /kɒst/ *v.* Pa. t. & pple **cost**, (in branch II) **costed**. LME. [OFr. *coster, couster* (mod. *coûter*) f. Proto-Romance var. of L *constare* stand firm, be fixed, stand at a price, f. L CON- + *stare* stand.] I *v.t.* w. advb. obj. & *i.* 1 *v.t.* Be acquired or acquirable at, be bought or maintained for, necessitate the expenditure of, (so much). Also w. the person buying, spending, etc. as indirect obj. LME. 2 *v.t.* Necessitate or involve the expenditure of (time, trouble, etc.), loss or sacrifice of (some valued possession), suffering of (some penalty etc.). Also w. the person losing, suffering, etc., as indirect obj. LME. 3 *v.i.* Be expensive; prove costly. Also w. pers. indirect obj. *colloq.* E20.

1 SHAKES. *Oth.* His breeches cost him but a crown. 2 G. HERBERT Good words are worth much and cost little. T. H. HUXLEY His eagerness to witness the spectacle cost him his life. R. KIPLING The horses were stampeded . . and . . it cost a day and a half to get them together again. *cost an arm and a leg*: see ARM *n.*[1] **cost a person dear(ly)** involve a heavy penalty on a person. 3 SCOTT FITZGERALD I like them but my God they cost. M. KENYON 'That call was from Chicago.' 'It must have cost him.'

II *v.t.* w. simple obj. 4 *v.t.* Determine the cost of producing (an article) or undertaking (a piece of work). L19.

¶In senses 1, 2 the vb has no pass. either with the price or the pers. indirect obj. as subj. and the price can be expressed by an adv., as *dearly*. The simple obj. in Eng. and Fr. goes back to a L abl. or genit.

costing *vbl n.* the determination of the cost of producing or undertaking something; *sing.* & in *pl.*, the cost so arrived at: L19. **costing** *ppl a.* costly; spiritually exhausting or expensive: E20. **costingly** *adv.* in a costly or costing way E20. **costingness** *n.* the quality of being costing E20.

cost- *comb. form* see COSTO-.

costa /'kɒstə/ *n.*[1] Pl. **costae** /'kɒstiː/. M19. [L.] Chiefly *Bot.* & *Zool.* A rib or riblike structure; *esp.* the main vein running along the anterior edge of an insect's wing.

Costa /'kɒstə/ *n.*[2] *joc.* M20. [Sp. (= COAST *n.*, f. as prec.), in *Costa Brava, Costa del Sol*, etc.] A coast: in pseudo-Sp. names of resort areas with a specified characteristic or location.

Costa Geriatrica /dʒerɪ'atrɪkə/: largely frequented or inhabited by elderly people.

costae *n.* pl. of COSTA *n.*[1]

costal /'kɒst(ə)l/ *a.* & *n.* M17. [Fr. f. mod.L *costalis*, f. as COSTA *n.*[1]: see -AL[1].] A *adj.* 1 *Anat.* Of or pertaining to the ribs. M17. 2 Chiefly *Bot.* & *Zool.* Pertaining to or of the nature of a costa. M19.

1 *costal pleura*: see PLEURA *n.*[1] 1.

B *n.* †1 The side. Only in M17. 2 *Anat.* & *Zool.* A costal vein, muscle, plate, etc. E19.

co-star /'kəʊstɑː/ *n.* Orig. *US.* E20. [f. CO- + STAR *n.*[1]] A cinema or stage star appearing with one or more other stars of equal importance; an actor or actress receiving star billing with another.

co-star /'kəʊstɑː/ *v.* Orig. *US.* Infl. **-rr-**. E20. [f. CO- + STAR *v.*] 1 *v.i.* Perform as a co-star. E20. 2 *v.t.* Include as a co-star or co-stars. E20.

costard /'kɒstəd, 'kʌst-/ *n.* ME. [AN, f. *coste* rib f. L COSTA *n.*[1]: see -ARD. Cf. CUSTARD *n.*[2]] 1 A large ribbed kind of apple. ME. 2 The head. *joc. arch.* M16.

Costa Rican /'kɒstə 'riːk(ə)n/ *a.* & *n.* M19. [f. *Costa Rica* (see below) + -AN.] A *adj.* Of, pertaining to, or characteristic of the Central American country of Costa Rica. M19. B *n.* A native or inhabitant of Costa Rica. M19.

costate /'kɒsteɪt/ *a.* E19. [L *costatus* ribbed, f. as COSTA *n.*[1]: see -ATE[2].] *Bot.* & *Zool.* Having a rib or ribs.

Also **costated** *a.* M19.

co-State /'kəʊsteɪt/ *n.* Also **-state**. L18. [f. CO- + STATE *n.*] A State allied with another. (Foll. by *of.*)

costean /kɒ'stiːn/ *v.* & *n.* Orig. *Corn.* Also **-een**. L18. [f. Corn. *cotha* to drop + *stean* tin.] *Mining.* A *v.i.* Sink pits through the surface soil to the underlying rock in order to establish the direction of a lode. L18. B *n.* A pit sunk in costeaning; a trench cut to expose the width of a seam. Also *costean pit.* L18.

coster /'kɒstə/ *n.*[1] Long *obs.* exc. *Hist.* ME. [AN = OFr. *costier* side, something by the side, hanging, f. *coste* f. L COSTA *n.*[1]: see -ER[2].] A hanging for a bed, the walls of a room, an altar, etc.

coster /'kɒstə/ *n.*[2] *colloq.* M19. [Abbrev.] = COSTERMONGER.

costerdom *n.* = COSTERMONGERDOM L19. **costering** *n.* = COSTERMONGERY M19.

costermonger /'kɒstəmʌŋgə/ *n.* & *a.* E16. [f. COSTARD + MONGER.] A *n.* Orig., an apple-seller. Now, a person who sells fruit, vegetables, etc., from a street-barrow. E16. B *adj.* Base, scoundrelly. Now *rare* or *obs.* L16.

costermongerdom *n.* costermongers collectively; the realm of costermongers: L19. **costermongering** *n.* = COSTERMONGERY M19. **costermongery** *n.* the occupation of a costermonger M19.

costive /'kɒstɪv/ *a.* LME. [AN, OFr. *costivé* f. L *constipatus*: see CONSTIPATE *v.*] 1 Constipated. LME. †2 Tending to prevent evacuation of the bowels. M16–M17. 3 Slow or reluctant in action; niggardly; reticent. L16.

3 L. A. G. STRONG The parrot was still very costive in the matter of speech.

costively *adv.* M19. **costiveness** *n.* LME.

costly /'kɒs(t)li/ *a.* & *adv.* LME. [f. COST *n.*[2] + -LY[1].] A *adj.* 1 That costs much; expensive; sumptuous. LME. 2 Lavish in expenditure; extravagant. *arch.* M17.

1 **costly colours** an obsolete card-game. 2 DRYDEN To curse the Costly sex.

†B *adv.* In a costly manner; sumptuously. LME–E17.

costliness *n.* M16.

costmary /'kɒstmɛːri/ *n.* LME. [f. COST *n.*[1] + (St) MARY.] An aromatic perennial plant of the composite family, *Balsamita major*, formerly used for flavouring ale; alecost.

costo- /'kɒstəʊ/ *comb. form.* Bef. a vowel **cost-**. [f. L COSTA *n.*[1]: see -O-.] Of or pertaining to the ribs and —.

costocla'vicular *a.* of or pertaining to the ribs and clavicle M19.

costrel /'kɒstr(ə)l/ *n.* Long *obs.* exc. *dial.* LME. [OFr. *costerel* flagon, prob. dim. of *costier*: see COSTER *n.*[1], -EL[2].] A bottle for wine etc. with an ear or ears by which it may be hung from the waist; a wooden keg similarly used.

costume /'kɒstjuːm/ *n.* & *v.* E18. [Fr. f. It. = custom, fashion, habit, f. L *consuetudo, -din-*: see CUSTOM *n., a., & adv.*] A *n.* 1 In historical and literary art: the custom and fashion proper to the time and locality in which a scene is set. E18. 2 The style or fashion of clothing, hair, etc., of a particular country, class, or period. E19. 3 Fashion of clothing appropriate to a particular occasion or season; a garment for a particular activity. E19. b The dress or attire worn by an actor in a play etc. L19. c *spec.* A swimsuit. L19. 4 A complete set of outer garments; a woman's matching jacket and skirt or dress. M19.

1 J. REYNOLDS Hardly reconcileable to strict propriety, and the costume, of which Raffaele was in general a good observer. 2 H. JAMES She sought to . . make up for her diffidence of speech by a fine frankness of costume. J. MARQUAND The Chinese in their silk robes the only persons clinging to a national costume. 3 DISRAELI A Court costume. A. GRAY The costumes they would wear at the fancy-dress ball. *bathing-costume, swimming-costume*, etc.

Comb.: **costume jewellery** artificial jewellery worn to decorate clothes; **costume piece, play**: in which the actors wear historical costume.

B *v.t.* Provide with or dress in a costume. Chiefly as *costumed* ppl a. E19.

costumer *n.* = COSTUMIER M19. **co'stumery** *n.* arrangement of costumes; costumes collectively: M19.

costumier /kɒ'stjuːmɪə/ *n.* M19. [Fr., f. *costumer* COSTUME *v.*] A person who makes or deals in costumes; *esp.* a person who sells or hires out theatrical costumes and properties.

costus /'kɒstəs/ *n.* L16. [L: see COST *n.*[1]] More fully *costus root.* The aromatic root of the Kashmiri plant *Saussurea costus*, of the composite family, which yields an oil used in perfumery.

cosy /'kəʊzi/ *a., n., & v.* Orig. *Sc.* Also ***cozy**. E18. [Origin unkn.] A *adj.* 1 Of a person: comfortably sheltered, snug. E18. 2 Of a place: sheltered; warm and comfortable, inviting. L18. 3 Of a person or thing: warmly intimate or friendly; *derog.* complacent, smug, unadventurous, parochial. E20.

1 N. COWARD I feel completely lost, completely bewildered. . . I don't feel any too cosy. 2 R. BURNS In some cozie place, They close the day. **cosy corner** an upholstered seat for fitting into the corner of a room; a

corner so furnished. 3 C. P. SNOW It was mildly ironic . . to find her set on seeing him a cosy, bourgeois success. *Daily Mail* A cosy chat.

B *n.* 1 More fully *tea cosy*, *egg cosy*. A covering for keeping a teapot or a boiled egg warm. M19. 2 [Perh. suggested by Fr. *causeuse*.] A cosy seat; *spec.* a canopied seat for two. L19.

C *v.* †1 *v.i.* Be cosy. *dial.* Only in L19. 2 *v.t.* Reassure; deceive to prevent suspicion or alarm. Also foll. by *along*. *colloq.* M20. 3 *v.i.* Foll. by *up to*: snuggle up to; become friendly with; ingratiate oneself with. *colloq.* (chiefly *N. Amer.*). M20.

2 M. SHARP Her impulse . . was to cosy Mr Clark on every point.

cosily *adv.* E18. **cosiness** *n.* M19.

cot /kɒt/ *n.*^{1} [OE *cot* = MLG, MDu., ON *kot*, f. Gmc base (cf. ON *kytja* hovel) rel. to that of COTE *n.*^{1}] 1 A (small) cottage; a humble dwelling. Now chiefly *poet.* & *literary*. OE. 2 A small erection for shelter or protection; = COTE *n.*^{1} 2. Usu. in *comb.*, as *bell-cot*, *dovecot*. ME. 3 A protective covering; *spec.* a finger-stall. *obs.* exc. *dial.* E17.

1 F. QUARLES Poor cots are ev'n as safe as princes halls.

Comb.: **cot-house** *Sc.* & *dial.* (*a*) a small cottage; *spec.* in Scotland, the house of a cottar; (*b*) an outhouse, a shed; **cotland** *Hist.* a piece of land (about 5 acres, 2 hectares) attached to a peasant's cot; **cotman** *Hist.* a tenant of a cot or cottage; *Sc.* a cottar; **cot-town** *Sc.* a hamlet of cot-houses.

cot /kɒt/ *n.*^{2} *dial.* ME. [AN, perh. identical with med.L *cot(t)um* bed-quilt, stuffed mattress.] 1 Wool matted together in the fleece. ME. 2 A tangled mass (of hair, weeds, etc.). M19.

cot /kɒt/ *n.*^{3} *Anglo-Ir.* M16. [(O)Ir. *coite*, Gael. *coit*.] A small roughly-made boat; a dugout.

cot /kɒt/ *n.*^{4} M17. [Hind. *khāṭ* bedstead, couch, hammock.] 1 a A light bedstead. *Anglo-Ind.* M17. b A portable or folding bed; a camp-bed. *US.* M19. c A type of bed or wheeled stretcher used in hospitals. *US.* L19. 2 *Hist.* A canvas bed in a wooden frame suspended from deck-beams, in which naval officers etc. used to sleep. M18. 3 A small bed for a child: orig., one suspended so as to swing between uprights; now, a bed with high sides to stop the child from falling out; a bed in a children's hospital. Cf. CRIB *n.* 5. E19.

1b R. JARRELL She just slept on the cot in her office. c P. GALLICO Sitting on the edge of his cot in the Brothers of Man Mission House.

Comb.: **cot-case** a person too ill to leave bed; **cot-death** a sudden unexplained death of a baby in its sleep.

cot /kɒt/ *n.*^{5} M18. [Abbrev.] *Math.* Cotangent (of).

cot /kɒt/ *v.*^{1}*t.* Infl. **-tt-**. E19. [f. COT *n.*^{1}] Put (a sheep) in a cote.

cot /kɒt/ *v.*^{2}*t.* & *i.* *dial.* Infl. **-tt-**. L19. [f. COT *n.*^{2} Cf. earlier COTTED *a.*^{1}] Tangle or mat together.

cotangent /kəʊˈtandʒ(ə)nt/ *n.* E17. [f. CO- + TANGENT *n.*] *Math.* The tangent of the complement of a given angle. Abbrev. COT *n.*^{5}

cote /kəʊt/ *n.*^{1} [OE *cote* corresp. to LG *kote*, f. Gmc base rel. to that of COT *n.*^{1}] 1 A cottage, a cot. Now *dial.* OE. 2 A light building or enclosure for sheltering or confining animals or for storing something; *spec.* a sheepfold. Now usu. in *comb.*, as *dovecote*, *sheep-cote*. LME.

Comb.: **cote-house** *Sc.* & *dial.* = *cot-house* s.v. COT *n.*^{1}

cote /kəʊt/ *n.*^{2} Now *rare* or *obs.* L16. [f. COTE *v.*^{1}] The action (of a dog) of making a hare alter course by 'coting' another dog.

cote /kəʊt/ *v.*^{1}*t.* Now *rare* or *obs.* M16. [Perh. f. OFr. *coster* proceed by the side of, follow closely, f. *coste* side f. L COSTA *n.*^{1}] 1 Of either of two dogs in coursing: pass (the other dog) at an angle so as to cause the hare etc. to alter course. M16. 2 *transf.* & *fig.* Pass by; exceed, surpass. M16.

cote /kəʊt/ *v.*^{2}*t.* M17. [f. COTE *n.*^{1}] Put (an animal) in a cote.

†**cote** *v.*^{3} & *n.*^{3} see QUOTE *v.* & *n.*^{2}

coteau /kɒˈtəʊ, *foreign* kɔto/ *n.* *N. Amer.* Pl. **-eaus**; **-eaux** /-o/. M19. [Fr. = slope, hillside f. OFr. *costel*, f. *coste*: see COST *n.*^{3}, -EL^2.] Any of various kinds of elevated geographical features, as a plateau, a divide between valleys, etc.

cote-hardie /ˈkəʊthɑːdi/ *n.* ME. [OFr., f. *cote* COAT *n.* + *hardie* bold (see HARDY *a.*).] *Hist.* A medieval close-fitting sleeved tunic, worn by both sexes.

cotemporaneity /kəʊˌtɛmp(ə)rəˈniːɪti, -ˈneɪɪti/ *n.* Now *rare.* E19. [Alt. of CONTEMPORANEITY: see CO-.] = CONTEMPORANEITY.

cotemporaneous /kəʊˌtɛmpəˈreɪnɪəs/ *a.* Now *rare.* M19. [Alt. of CONTEMPORANEOUS: see CO-.] = CONTEMPORANEOUS.

cotemporary /kəʊˈtɛmp(ə)rəri/ *a.* & *n.* Now *rare.* M17. [Alt. of CONTEMPORARY: see CO-.] = CONTEMPORARY.

¶Although condemned by some, during 18 *cotemporary* almost ousted *contemporary*, only to become less frequent again.

coterell /ˈkɒt(ə)r(ə)l/ *n.* LME. [OFr. *coterel*, med.L *coterellus*, dim. of OFr. *cotier* COTTIER.] *Feudal Hist.* = COTTAR 1.

¶Recorded from late OE in surnames. Cf. COTSET, COTSETLA.

coterie /ˈkəʊt(ə)ri/ *n.* E18. [Fr. (in OFr. = tenants holding land together), ult. f. MLG *kote* COTE *n.*^{1}: see -ERY.] 1 A small exclusive group with common interests; *esp.* a select social group. E18. 2 A meeting of such a group. E19.

1 M. DRABBLE She found herself elected to an honorary membership of the fastest, smartest . . coterie.

coterminal /kəʊˈtəːmɪn(ə)l/ *a.* Now *rare.* M19. [f. CO- + TERMINAL *a.* Cf. CONTERMINAL.] = COTERMINOUS 2.

coterminous /kəʊˈtəːmɪnəs/ *a.* L18. [Alt. of CONTERMINOUS: see CO-.] 1 Having a common boundary (*with*). L18. 2 Coextensive (*with*) in space, time, or meaning. M19.

coth /kɒθ/ *n.* L19. [f. COT *n.*^{5} + *h* (for hyperbolic).] *Math.* Hyperbolic cotangent (of).

cothe /kəʊð/ *n.* Also **coath**. [OE *coþu*, *cope*.] †1 Sickness; an attack of something. OE–LME. 2 A disease of the liver in animals, esp. sheep. *dial.* L18.

cothe /kəʊð/ *v.t.* *obs.* exc. *dial.* LME. [f. the n.] Give (a sheep) cothe or rot. Formerly, give any disease to.

cothurn /ˈkəʊθəːn, kəʊˈθəːn/ *n.* Now *rare.* E17. [Fr. *cothurne* f. L COTHURNUS.] = next.

cothurned *a.* wearing cothurns L19.

cothurnus /kəʊˈθəːnəs/ *n.* Pl. **-ni** /-nʌɪ/. E18. [L f. Gk *kothornos*.] = BUSKIN 2.

fig.: F. W. FARRAR St. Paul cannot always wear the majestic cothurnus, yet his lightest words are full of meaning.

cothurnal *a.* of or pertaining to the cothurnus; tragic: E17. **cothurnate** *a.* wearing cothurni; tragic in style: E17.

co-tidal /kəʊˈtʌɪd(ə)l/ *a.* M19. [f. CO- + TIDAL.] Of a line: connecting places where high tide occurs at the same time. Of a chart etc.: showing such lines.

cotillion /kəˈtɪljən/ *n.* & *v.* In senses A.1, B. also **cotillon** /kəˈtɪljən; *foreign* kɔtijɔ̃ (*pl. same*)/. E18. [Fr. *cotillon* petticoat, dance, dim. of *cotte* COAT *n.*] A *n.* 1 Any of several dances with elaborate steps and figures; *spec.* (*a*) an 18th-cent. French social dance based on the contredanse; (*b*) *US* a quadrille; (*c*) (in full *German cotillion*) a complex dance in which one couple leads the other couples through a variety of figures and there is a continual change of partners. E18. 2 A formal ball, *esp.* one at which débutantes are presented. *US.* L19. B *v.i.* Dance a cotillion. M19.

cotinga /kəˈtɪŋɡə/ *n.* L18. [Fr. f. Tupi *cutinga*.] A passerine bird of the tropical American family Cotingidae or its type genus *Cotinga*, including many noted for their brilliant plumage.

cotise *n.* & *v.* var. of COTTISE.

cotoneaster /kətəʊnɪˈastə/ *n.* M18. [mod.L, f. L *cotoneum* QUINCE + -ASTER.] A shrub or small tree of the European and northern Asian (esp. Himalayan and Chinese) genus *Cotoneaster*, of the rose family, with small pink or white flowers and red or black berries.

cotonnade *n.* & *a.* var. of COTTONADE.

†**cotquean** *n.* M16. [f. COT *n.*^{1} + QUEAN.] 1 The wife of a cotman. M16–E17. 2 A coarse scolding woman. L16–M17. 3 A man who occupies himself with housework and women's concerns. L16–E19.

co-trimoxazole /kəʊtrʌɪˈmɒksəzəʊl/ *n.* L20. [f. CO- + TRIM(ETHOPRIM + SULPHAMETH)OXAZOLE.] A synergistic mixture of sulphamethoxazole and trimethoprim used to treat many bacterial infections.

†**cots** *n.* E16–E18. [Alt. Cf. CUTS.] God's: used in oaths and exclamations.

cotset /ˈkɒtsɛt/ *n.* [OE *cotsǣta*, f. COT *n.*^{1} + *sǣta*, f. var. of Gmc base of SIT *v.* See also COSSET.] *Feudal Hist.* = COTTAR 1.

¶Not recorded from ME until use as a historical term in 19. In early use chiefly Latinized. Cf. next, COTERELL.

cotsetla /kɒtˈsɛtlə/ *n.* Also **-setle** /-sɛt(ə)l/. OE. [f. COT *n.*^{1} + OE *-sǣtla* settler.] *Feudal Hist.* = COTTAR 1.

¶Not recorded from ME until use as a historical term in 19. Cf. prec., COTERELL.

Cotswold /ˈkɒtswəʊld/ *n.* M16. [*Cotswold* Hills (see below).] 1 Used *attrib.* to designate things originally produced or found in the Cotswold Hills, a range mainly in Gloucestershire noted for their sheep pasture. M16. 2 *ellipt.* A Cotswold sheep; Cotswold cheese. M19.

1 **Cotswold cheese** double Gloucester cheese with chives (and onions). **Cotswold lion** *joc.* a Cotswold sheep. **Cotswold sheep** a sheep of a long-woolled breed.

cotta /ˈkɒtə/ *n.* M19. [It. f. Proto-Romance, whence also COAT *n.*] *Chr. Ch.* A short surplice.

cottabus /ˈkɒtəbəs/ *n.* Also **-os**. E19. [L f. Gk *kottabos*.] *Hist.* An amusement at drinking parties in ancient Greece, in which the dregs in one's cup had to be flicked into a metal basin so as to strike it noisily.

cottage /ˈkɒtɪdʒ/ *n.* LME. [AN *cotage*, AL *cotagium*, f. COT *n.*^{1}, COTE *n.*^{1}: see -AGE.] 1 A small modest dwelling of the kind for long occupied by poorer country people. LME. †2 A small temporary shelter. M16–L18. 3 Without implication of poverty: any moderate detached country or suburban residence. M18. 4 A private summer holiday residence. *N. Amer.* L19. 5 A one-storey house, a bungalow. *Austral.* L19. 6 One of a group of small detached dwelling units forming part of a larger complex, as in a hotel or institution. *N. Amer.* M20.

1 *love in a cottage*: see LOVE *n.* 3 **cottage orné(e)** /ˈɔːneɪ/ a villa in the form of a cottage with an ornate design.

Comb.: **cottage-bonnet** a woman's close-fitting straw bonnet fashionable in the early 19th cent.; **cottage cheese** a soft white cheese made from unpressed curds; **cottage hospital** a small hospital without resident medical staff; **cottage industry**: carried on partly or wholly in people's homes; **cottage loaf**: of two round masses, a smaller on top of a larger; †**cottage lecture** an address given by a clergyman in a layman's home; **cottage piano** a small upright piano; **cottage pie** a pie of minced meat and potatoes under mashed potatoes; (*loosely*) = *shepherd's pie* s.v. SHEPHERD *n.*

cottaged *a.* †(*a*) *rare* lodged in a cottage or humble dwelling; (*b*) set with cottages: M17. **cottag(e)y** *a.* resembling or suggestive of a cottage M19.

cottager /ˈkɒtɪdʒə/ *n.* M16. [f. prec. + -ER^1.] 1 *gen.* A person, esp. a rural labourer, living in a cottage. M16. 2 *spec.* = COTTAR 2. L18. 3 A person with a private summer holiday residence. *N. Amer.* L19.

cottar /ˈkɒtə/ *n.* Also **-er**. LOE. [f. COT *n.*^{1} + -ER^1 (Sc. *-ar*): cf. med.L *cotarius* COTTIER. In earliest uses perh. repr. OFr. *cot(i)er* COTTIER.] 1 *Feudal Hist.* A villein who held a cot with an attached plot of land in return for working for his lord part of the time. (In early use chiefly in surnames. Not recorded from ME until use as a historical term in 19. Cf. COTSET, COTSETLA.) LOE. 2 In Scotland: a tenant occupying a farm cottage, sometimes with a small plot of land, orig. in return for labouring on the farm as required, now usu. as part of a contract of employment with the farmer. LME. 3 *Ir. Hist.* = COTTIER *n.* 2. L18.

For other words beginning with *co-* see the entry for **co-**

cottary *n.* var. of COTTERY.

cotted /ˈkɒtɪd/ *a.*[1] L18. [f. COT *n.*[2] + -ED[2].] Matted, tangled.

cotted /ˈkɒtɪd/ *a.*[2] E19. [f. COT *n.*[1] + -ED[2].] Dotted or lined with cottages; cottaged.

cotter /ˈkɒtə/ *n.*[1] ME. [Origin unkn.: see COTTEREL.] In machinery etc.: a pin, wedge, or bolt which passes into a hole and holds two parts together.

Comb.: **cotter-pin** (*a*) a cotter of circular cross-section; (*b*) a split pin for keeping a cotter in place.

cotter *n.*[2] var. of COTTAR *n.*

cotter /ˈkɒtə/ *v.*[1] Chiefly *dial.* L16. [Origin unkn.: cf. COTTED *a.*[1]] 1 *v.t.* Cause to thicken or coagulate; *esp.* scramble (an egg). L16. 2 *v.t.* & *i.* Form into a tangled mass; entangle, mat. L18. 3 *v.i.* Shrivel or shrink *up.* E19.

cotter /ˈkɒtə/ *v.*[2]*t.* M17. [f. COTTER *n.*[1]] Fasten (esp. a window-shutter) with a cotter.

cotterel /ˈkɒt(ə)r(ə)l/ *n. dial.* LME. [Closely rel. to COTTER *n.*[1], which may be a shortened form, or the primitive of which this is a dim.] 1 A hook, crane, or bar from which a pot is hung over a fire. *south.* & *Canad.* LME. 2 = COTTER *n.*[1] *north.* L16.

cottery /ˈkɒtəri/ *n. Sc. obs.* exc. *Hist.* Also **-ary**. L15. [f. *cotter* COTTAR: see -ERY. Cf. COTERIE.] A cottar's holding.

cottice *n.* & *v.* var. of COTTISE.

cottid /ˈkɒtɪd/ *n.* L19. [mod.L *Cottidae* (see below), f. *Cottus* genus name: see -ID[3].] Any acanthopterygian fish of the family Cottidae, including the sculpins and other small mostly marine fishes of the northern hemisphere.

cottier /ˈkɒtɪə/ *n.* ME. [OFr. *cotier* (in med.L *cotarius*), ult. f. Gmc base of COT *n.*[1]: see -IER.] 1 Orig. = COTTAR 1. Now, a rural labourer living in a cot or cottage. ME. 2 *Ir. Hist.* A peasant who rented a smallholding under a system of tenure (*cottier tenure*) by which land was let annually in small portions direct to the labourers, the rent being fixed by public competition. M19.

cottise /ˈkɒtɪs/ *n.* & *v.* Also **cottice, cotise**. L16. [Fr. *cotice* (earlier †*cotisse*), leather thong.] *Her.* A *n.* A charge like the bend etc. that it runs alongside but one quarter of its width, usu. occurring in a pair, one on each side of the bend etc. (originating as a stylized leather band). L16. B *v.t.* Border (a bend etc.) with a pair of cottises. Chiefly as *cottised* ppl a. L16.

cotton /ˈkɒt(ə)n/ *n.*[1] & *a.* LME. [(O)Fr. *coton* f. Arab. *kuṭn*, *kuṭun*, in Sp. Arab. *kuṭūn*: cf. ACTON.] A *n.* 1 The soft white fibrous substance which surrounds the seeds of various plants of the tropical and subtropical genus *Gossypium*, used for making thread and cloth. LME. b A similar substance found in other plants. M16. 2 (In full *cotton-plant*) a plant of the genus *Gossypium*, of the mallow family, that yields cotton or is cultivated for cotton; such plants collectively, as a crop. LME. 3a Cloth or fabric made from cotton; a cotton fabric or garment (usu. in *pl.*). LME. b Thread spun from cotton yarn. M19. †4 The pile of fustian. Only in L15.

Phrases etc.: *absorbent cotton*: see ABSORBENT *a.* **French cotton** the floss surrounding the seeds of the mudar, *Calotropis procera*. *gun-cotton*: see GUN *n.* *lavender cotton*: see LAVENDER *n.*[2] NANKEEN *cotton*. *silk cotton*: see SILK *n.* & *a.* **spit cotton** *US colloq.* spit white saliva; have a mouth parched by thirst; *fig.* be very angry. *Upland cotton*: see UPLAND *a.*

Comb.: **cotton batting** *N. Amer.* cotton wool; **cotton belt** the cotton-producing region of the southern US; **cotton-boll weevil** = *boll-weevil* s.v. BOLL *n.*[1]; **cotton-bush** (*a*) a cotton-plant; (*b*) *Austral.* any of several low downy drought-resistant shrubs, esp. *Bassia aphylla*; **cotton cake** a mass of compressed cotton-seed used as cattle feed; **cotton candy** *N. Amer.* candyfloss; **cotton famine** *Hist.* the failure of the supply of cotton to the English cotton-mills during the American Civil War; **cotton-fish** *Austral.* = *cotton-spinner* (b) below; **cotton flannel** a strong cotton fabric with a raised nap; **cotton gin** a machine for separating cotton fibre from the seed; **cotton-grass** a sedge of the genus *Eriophorum*, the fruiting heads of which bear long white cottony hairs; *esp.* (more fully *common cotton-grass*) *E. angustifolium*, characteristic of wet bogs, and (more fully *hare's-tail cotton-grass*) *E. vaginatum*, common in damp moorland; **cotton-leaf worm** the larva of a moth, *Alabama argillacea*, which feeds on the leaves of the cotton-plant in America; **cotton lord** a wealthy manufacturer of cotton yarn or goods; **cotton-mouth (moccasin)** = *water moccasin* s.v. MOCCASIN 2; **cotton-picking** *n.* & *a.* (*a*) *n.* the harvesting of cotton; *US* a social gathering to mark this occasion; (*b*) *adj.* (*N. Amer. slang*) unpleasant, damned, confounded; *cotton-plant*: see sense 2 above; **cotton plush** = *cotton flannel* above; **cotton-powder** an explosive made from gun-cotton; **cotton-rat** a rodent, *Sigmodon hispidus*, common in the southern US; **cotton-sedge** = *cotton-grass* above; **cotton-seed** the seed of the cotton-plant, from which an edible oil is obtained; **cotton-spinner** (*a*) a worker who spins cotton; a cotton-manufacturer; (*b*) *Austral.* a sea-cucumber of the genus *Holothuria*, which shoots out long white threads (Cuvierian organs) when disturbed; **cotton-stainer** an insect of the heteropteran genus *Dysdercus*, esp. *D. suturellus*, which feeds on cotton bolls and stains the fibre reddish; **cotton state** any of the States of the southern US of which cotton is or was a major product; *spec.* (w. cap. initials) Alabama; **cottontail** a rabbit of the N. American genus *Sylvilagus*, most species of which have a white fluffy underside to the tail; **cotton-thistle** a tall white-felted thistle, *Onopordum acanthium*, often grown in gardens; Scotch thistle; **cotton-top** (in full *cotton-top tamarin*) a brown and cream tamarin, *Saguinus oedipus*, of northern Colombia, with a crest of white hair; **cotton tree** (*a*) any of various tropical trees (of the genera *Bombax* and *Ceiba*) producing a cottony floss; (*b*) *dial.* the wayfaring-tree, *Viburnum lantana*; (*c*) the N. American plane, *Platanus occidentalis*; (*d*) = *cottonwood* (a) below; (*e*) either of two Australian trees, *Hibiscus tiliaceus* and *Cochlospermum heteronemum*; **cotton waste** waste cotton yarn, used to clean machinery etc.; **cottonweed** any of several related plants of the composite family with hoary pubescent stems and leaves, esp. *Otanthus maritimus* of maritime sands in southern and western Europe; **cottonwood** (*a*) any of various N. American poplars with cottony hairs surrounding the seeds; (*b*) a downy-leaved Australian shrub of the composite family, *Bedfordia salicina*; (*c*) *NZ* = TAUHINU; **cotton-worm** = *cotton-leaf worm* above. See also COTTON WOOL.

B *attrib.* or as *adj.* Made of cotton. M16.

cottonize *v.t.* reduce (flax, hemp, etc.) to a short staple resembling cotton M19. **cottony** *a.* resembling cotton; consisting of or covered with soft hairs like cotton (*cottony-cushion scale*, an Australian scale insect, *Icerya purchasi*, which infests citrus trees): L16.

†**cotton** *n.*[2] E16–M19. [Perh. f. prec. in sense 'down, nap'.] A coarse woollen fabric formerly made in NW England (*Manchester cotton* and *Kendal cotton*), and in Wales (*Welsh cotton*).

cotton /ˈkɒt(ə)n/ *v.* ME. [f. (as) COTTON *n.*[1] Cf. Fr. *cotonner.*] I *lit.* 1 Pad, wrap, or block with cotton (wool). ME. †2a *v.t.* Give a nap or finish to (cloth). L15–L16. b *v.i.* Of cloth etc.: take on a nap. E17–E19.

II *fig.* 3 *v.i.* Prosper, succeed. *obs.* exc. *dial.* M16. 4 *v.i.* Of a person or thing: get on well, be in harmony, (*with*, *together*). M16. 5 *v.i.* Behave in a friendly or warm way. (Foll. by *together*, *with*.) M17. 6 *v.i.* Be drawn *to*, take a liking *to*. E19.

4 C. BURY The vaulted roof of a cathedral . . did not 'cotton' with lively ideas. 5 W. CONGREVE I love to see 'em hug and cotton together, like Down upon a Thistle. 6 E. BIRNEY I was workin in a store. . . Dint cotton much to the job, though.

With advs. in specialized senses: **cotton on** *slang* (*a*) take a liking *to*; (*b*) get wise (*to*), understand. **cotton up** *arch.* make friendly overtures (*to*).

cottoner *n.* a person who puts a nap on cloth ME.

cottonade /kɒtəˈneɪd/ *n.* & *a.* Also **cotonnade**. E19. [Fr. *cotonnade*, f. as COTTON *n.*[1]: see -ADE.] (Made of) any of various coarse cotton fabrics.

Cottonian /kɒˈtəʊnɪən/ *a.* E18. [f. *Cotton* (see below) + -IAN.] Of or pertaining to the English antiquary and book-collector Sir Robert Cotton (1570–1631); *spec.* designating the library he formed, now in the British Library, London.

cottonocracy /kɒtəˈnɒkrəsi/ *n.* M19. [f. COTTON *n.*[1]: see -CRACY.] Cotton lords as a class.

Cottonopolis /kɒtəˈnɒp(ə)lɪs/ *n.* M19. [f. COTTON *n.*[1] + -O- + -POLIS.] The city of Manchester, in NW England, once a centre of the British cotton trade.

cotton wool /kɒt(ə)n ˈwʊl/ *n.* & *a. phr.* LME. [f. COTTON *n.*[1] + WOOL *n.*] A *n.* 1 Raw cotton as gathered from the bolls of the cotton-plant. Now *US.* LME. 2 Raw cotton prepared for use as packing or wadding; this substance with its natural wax removed, used as a soft absorbent material. M19. b *fig.* Excessive comfort or protection. M19. B *attrib.* or as *adj.* Made of or resembling cotton wool; protected as if with cotton wool. M17.

cotton-ˈwoolly *a.* resembling cotton wool E20.

cotwal *n.* var. of KOTWAL.

cotyledon /kɒtɪˈliːd(ə)n/ *n.* M16. [L = navelwort f. Gk *kotulēdōn* cup-shaped cavity, f. *kotulē* cup, socket.] 1 *Anat.* Each of the distinct patches of villi on the foetal chorion of ruminants; each of the analogous lobes or their constituent lobules in the disc of the human placenta, each lobule containing a branching chorionic blood-vessel. M16. 2 A succulent of the largely southern African genus *Cotyledon* or one of the European species formerly included in it, *esp.* navelwort. E17. 3 *Bot.* A seed-leaf, a primary leaf in the embryo of a higher plant (in angiosperms borne either singly (in monocotyledons) or in pairs (in dicotyledons), in gymnosperms borne in numbers varying from 2 to 15 or more). L18.

cotyledonary, **cotyledonous** *adjs.* marked by the presence of cotyledons; pertaining to or of the nature of a cotyledon: M19.

cotyloid /ˈkɒtɪlɔɪd/ *a.* M18. [f. Gk *kotuloeidēs*, f. *kotulē*: see prec., -OID.] *Anat.* Cup-shaped; *spec.* designating the acetabulum (*cotyloid cavity*) and parts connected with it.

couac /kuˈak/ *n.* L19. [Fr.: imit.] *Mus.* A quacking sound made by bad blowing on the clarinet, oboe, or bassoon.

couba /ˈkuːbə/ *n. Austral.* Also **coo-**, **-bah**. L19. [Aborig.] An acacia, *Acacia salicina*, with a drooping habit of growth.

coucal /ˈkuːk(ə)l, ˈkʊkɑːl/ *n.* E19. [Fr., said to be f. *couc*(*ou* cuckoo + *al*(*ouette* lark.] Any of numerous non-parasitic birds of the cuckoo family that belong to the genera *Centropus* and *Coua*, found in Africa, southern Asia, Australia, and Madagascar.

couch /kaʊtʃ/ *n.*[1] ME. [(O)Fr. *couche*, f. as COUCH *v.*] 1 A frame, with what is spread over it, on which to lie down; anything on which one sleeps. Now *arch.* or *literary.* ME. 2 The den or lair of an animal, esp. an otter. LME. 3 A piece of furniture for reclining or sitting on, *esp.* one with a low back and an arm at one end. LME. b *spec.* The couch on which a doctor's or psychiatrist's patient reclines for examination or treatment. M20. 4 *Malting.* A layer of grain laid on the floor to germinate after steeping; the floor itself. E17. 5 A layer, a stratum, a bed; *esp.* a layer of paint. M17.

1 LD MACAULAY Hospitality could offer little more than a couch of straw. 3 L. JONES Both of you sit on this couch where I'm sitting. *casting couch*: see CASTING *n.*

Comb.: **couch potato** *slang* a person whose spare time is spent lounging about, esp. watching television.

couch /kaʊtʃ, kuːtʃ/ *n.*[2] L16. [Var. of QUITCH.] Any of various esp. rhizomatous grasses occurring as weeds, esp. *Elymus repens*. Also (w. specifying wd), any of several other grasses of the genus *Elytrigia*. Also *couch grass*.

onion couch: see ONION *n.*

couchy *a.* full of couch grass; resembling couch grass: L18.

couch /kaʊtʃ/ *v.* ME. [(O)Fr. *coucher* f. L *collocare*: see COLLOCATE.] I Lay down flat, and related senses. †1 *v.t.* Lay (things); place, set down, esp. horizontally or in layers. ME–L18. 2 *v.t.* & *i.* Embroider with gold thread etc. laid flat on the surface. LME. 3 *v.t.* Cause to lie down, lay down (a person, one's head, etc.); put to bed; *refl.* lie down. Now only of an animal and as *couched* ppl a., laid or lying (as) on a couch. LME. †4 *v.t.* Cause to crouch. Chiefly as *couched* ppl a., prostrated, cowering. LME–E18. 5 *v.t. Malting.* Spread (grain) on a floor to germinate. M16. 6 *v.t. Paper-making.* Lay (a sheet of pulp) on a felt etc. to be pressed. M18.

For other words beginning with *co-* see the entry for **co-**

1 R. SURFLET An vnderstorie .. to couch your wines and cidres in. 3 KEATS Two fair creatures, couched side by side in deepest grass. E. MUIR The tractors lie .. like dank sea-monsters couched and waiting. 4 SHAKES. *Lucr.* Like a falcon tow'ring in the skies, Coucheth the fowl below with his wings' shade.

II Place, arrange. †7 *v.t.* Place in a lodging. LME–L17. †8 *v.t.* Collect *together*; include *in* a list etc. or *under* a heading. LME–E18. 9 *v.t.* Put together, arrange, (words etc.); put into writing or speech; express. Now always foll. by *in* certain *terms, words*, etc. E16. 10 *v.t.* Hide (a meaning, idea, etc.) *under, in*. M16. 11 *v.t.* Hide, conceal; place in concealment. Now *rare* or *obs.* L16.

9 K. M. E. MURRAY The flowery language in which he couched his eloquent speeches. 10 J. CAIRD Materialistic metaphors under which our spiritual conceptions are couched.

III Lower, bring down. 12 *v.t.* a Lower (a spear etc.) to the position of attack; level (a gun etc.). L15. b Lay down, bring down, or lower, (a part of the body etc.). E17. 13 *v.t.* & *i. Surg.* Treat (a cataract, a patient, etc.) by displacing the opaque lens of the eye downwards into the vitreous by means of a needle. L16.

12a T. GRAY To arms! cried Mortimer, and couch'd his quiv'ring lance. 13 *fig.*: DE QUINCEY She it was .. that first couched his eye to the sense of beauty.

IV Lie. 14 *v.i.* Lie, esp. at rest or in sleep. Now chiefly of a wild animal: lie in its lair. LME. 15 *v.i.* Crouch, cower, in fear, obedience, submission, etc. Formerly also, stoop under a burden. LME. 16 *v.i.* Lie in ambush, lurk. L16. 17 *v.i.* Of leaves etc.: lie in a heap for decomposition. L18.

14 W. OWEN I have couched in exactly twelve different rooms. *fig.*: R. BROOKE Raindrops couching in cool flowers. 15 J. BAILLIE Like spaniel couching to his lord. 16 TENNYSON Sir Launcelot passing by Spied where he couch'd.

couching *n.* (*a*) the action of the vb; (*b*) *Embroidery* couched work (*surface couching*: see SURFACE *a.*): LME.

couchancy /ˈkaʊtʃ(ə)nsi/ *n.* L17. [f. COUCHANT: see -ANCY.] *Law* (now *Hist.*). The fact of being couchant. Only in LEVANCY *and couchancy*.

couchant /ˈkaʊtʃ(ə)nt/ *a.* LME. [(O)Fr., pres. pple of *coucher* COUCH *v.*: see -ANT[1].] 1 Esp. of an animal: lying down; couching. LME. 2 *Her.* Of an animal: lying on its belly with its head up, lodged. Usu. *postpositive*. E16. †3 Lying hidden, lurking. M17–E18.

1 *levant and couchant*: see LEVANT *a.*

couché /ˈkuːʃeɪ/ *a.* M18. [Fr., pa. pple of *coucher* COUCH *v.*] *Her.* Of a shield: shown tilted, with the sinister corner uppermost.

couchee /ˈkuːʃeɪ; *foreign* kuʃe (*pl. same*)/ *n.* L17. [Fr. *couché* var. of *coucher* lying down, going to bed, use as n. of *coucher* COUCH *v.* Cf. LEVEE *n.*[1]] An evening reception.

coucher /ˈkaʊtʃə/ *n.*[1] LME. [App. AN, f. base of (O)Fr. *couche*: see COUCH *n.*[1], -ER[2]. Cf. Fr. *coucheur.*] 1 A person lying down (*rare*); *Sc.* a laggard, a coward. LME. †2a A large book; *esp.* a large breviary permanently on a desk in a church etc. LME–M16. b More fully *coucher-book*. A large cartulary or register. E17–L19.

coucher /ˈkaʊtʃə/ *n.*[2] M18. [f. COUCH *v.* + -ER[1]: cf. Fr. *coucheur, couchart.*] *Paper-making.* A person who or thing which couches pulp to be pressed.

couchette /kuːˈʃɛt; *foreign* kuʃɛt (*pl. same*)/ *n.* E20. [Fr., lit. 'little bed', f. as COUCH *n.*[1]: see -ETTE.] A (Continental) railway carriage in which the seats convert into sleeping-berths; such a berth.

coudé /kuːˈdeɪ/ *a.* & *n.* L19. [Fr., pa. pple of *couder* bend at right angles, f. *coude* elbow f. L *cubitum* CUBIT.] (Of, pertaining to, or designating) a telescope in which the rays are bent to focus at a fixed point off the axis.

Couéism /ˈkuːeɪɪz(ə)m/ *n.* E20. [Emile *Coué* (1857–1926), Fr. psychologist + -ISM.] A system of psychotherapy by systematic auto-suggestion, usu. of an optimistic nature.

Coué *n.* & *v.* (*a*) *n.* Couéism; (*b*) *v.t.* bring (oneself) *into* or *out of* a certain state by Couéism; produce by Couéism: E20. **Couéist** *n.* a person who practises or advocates Couéism E20. **Coué'istic** *a.* of or pertaining to Couéism, resembling Couéism M20.

Couette /kuːˈɛt/ *n.* M20. [M. F. A. *Couette*, 19th-cent. Fr. physicist.] *Physics.* Used *attrib.* with ref. to the work of Couette in hydrodynamics.

Couette flow flow of a Newtonian fluid between two parallel surfaces one of which is moving relative to the other. **Couette viscometer** a viscometer consisting of two concentric cylinders with liquid in between them, the torque on one cylinder being measured when the other is rotated.

cougar /ˈkuːgə/ *n.* Chiefly *N. Amer.* Also (now *rare*) **-guar** /-gjʊə, -gwə/. L18. [Fr. *couguar*, †*-gar* abbrev. f. mod.L *cuguarcarana* f. Guarani *cuguaçurana.*] = PUMA.

cough /kɒf/ *n.* ME. [f. the vb.] 1 A tendency to cough; a disorder of the respiratory tract manifesting itself in bouts of coughing. Formerly *the cough*. ME. 2 A single act of coughing; a sudden expulsion of air from the lungs with a noise produced by abrupt opening of the glottis. M18. b The sound of a shell being fired or bursting. *colloq.* E20.

1 SHAKES. *2 Hen. IV* What disease hast thou? .. A whoreson cold, sir, a cough, sir. *smoker's cough*: see SMOKER. *whooping-cough*: see WHOOPING *ppl a.* 2 JOYCE He announced his presence by that gentle .. cough which so many have tried .. to imitate.

Comb.: **cough candy** *N. Amer.* = *cough-sweet* below; **cough drop** (*a*) a medicated lozenge taken to relieve a cough; (*b*) *slang* an awkward or disagreeable person or thing; **cough medicine, mixture** a medicinal concoction for the relief of a cough; **cough-sweet**: medicated to relieve a cough.

cough /kɒf/ *v.* ME. [f. imit. base repr. by OE *cohhetan* shout, (M)LG, (M)Du. *kuchen* cough, MHG *kūchen* breathe, exhale (G *keuchen* pant).] 1 *v.i.* Expel air from the lungs with a sudden effort and a noise produced by the abrupt opening of the glottis, usu. in order to remove something obstructing or irritating the air passages. ME. b Of an engine etc.: make a noise like coughing, esp. when starting; misfire. Of a gun: fire shells. L19. c Confess, give information. *slang.* E20. 2 *v.t.* Express by coughing. LME. 3 *v.t.* With advs.: bring into a specified position or condition by coughing (see also below). LME.

1 YEATS It was but the cart-horse coughing. G. B. SHAW Pothinus coughs admonitorily. J. H. BURN The reluctance of the patient to cough and to clear his airways. b J. HARVEY Machines coughed and started. c M. PROCTER Slade would never 'cough' while there was no evidence.

With advs. in specialized senses: **cough away** bring (one's life etc.) to an end with coughing. **cough down** put down or silence (a speaker) by coughing. **cough out** = *cough up* (a) below. **cough up** (*a*) *v.phr.t.* eject by coughing, say with a cough; *slang* disclose, confess, give information; (*b*) *v.phr.t.* & *i.* (*slang*) bring out or produce (esp. money) reluctantly.

cougher *n.* a person who coughs E17. **coughing** *n.* the action of the vb; the sound of a person, engine, etc., coughing: LME.

couguar *n.* see COUGAR.

coul *n.* var. of COWL *n.*[2]

could *v.* etc.: see CAN *v.*[1]

coulée /kuːˈleɪ, ˈkuːli/ *n.* Also **-lee**, (sense 1) ***-lie** /ˈkuːli/. E19. [Fr. = (lava) flow, f. L *colare* filter, strain, (in Proto-Romance) flow, f. *cōlum* strainer.] 1 (The bed of) an intermittent stream; a dry valley; a gulch or valley with steep sides. *N. Amer. dial.* E19. 2 *Geol.* A stream of molten or solidified lava. M19.

couleur /kuːˈləː/ *n.* M19. [Fr. = COLOUR *n.*] In the game rouge-et-noir, the section of the table in which are placed bets, that the colour of the first card dealt will be the same as that of the winning row.

couleur de rose /kulœːr də roːz/ *n.* & *a. phr.* LME. [Fr. = rose colour.] A *n. phr.* Rose-colour, pink; *fig.* optimism, cheerfulness. LME. B *adj. phr.* Rose-coloured, pink; *fig.* optimistic, cheerful. L18.

coulibiac /kuːlɪˈbjak/ *n.* Also **k-**. L19. [Russ. *kulebyaka.*] A Russian pie of fish or meat, cabbage, etc.

coulie *n.* see COULÉE.

coulisse /kuːˈliːs/ *n.* E19. [Fr., use as n. of fem. of *coulis* sliding: see CULLIS *n.*[1] Cf. PORTCULLIS.] 1 *Theatr.* Each of the side scenes of a stage; *sing.* & (usu.) in *pl.*, the space between them, the wings. E19. 2 A groove in which a sluice-gate or other movable partition slides up and down. M19. 3 The body of outside dealers on the Paris Bourse; similar dealers in other stock exchanges; the place where they deal. L19. 4 A corridor; *fig.* a place of informal discussion or negotiation. E20.

couloir /ˈkuːlwɑː; *foreign* kulwaːr (*pl. same*)/ *n.* E19. [Fr. = channel, f. *couler* pour (f. L *colare* filter) + *-oir* -ORY[1].] A steep gully on a mountainside.

Coulomb /ˈkuːlɒm/ *n.* In sense 2 **c-**. M19. [C. A. de *Coulomb* (1736–1806), Fr. physicist.] *Physics.* 1 Used *attrib.* and in *possess.* with ref. to Coulomb's work in electrostatics. M19. 2 The SI unit of electric charge; the quantity of electricity conveyed in one second by a current of one ampere. (Symbol C.) L19.

1 **Coulomb force** the electrostatic force of attraction or repulsion exerted by one charged particle on another. **Coulomb interaction** the electrostatic interaction between charged particles. **Coulomb('s) law**: that like charges repel and opposite charges attract, with a force proportional to the product of the charges and inversely proportional to the square of the distance between them.

cou'lombian, C- *a.* = COULOMBIC E20. **cou'lombic, C-** *a.* of or pertaining to Coulomb or the force, laws, etc., named after him M20.

coulometer /kuːˈlɒmɪtə/ *n.* E20. [f. prec. + -METER.] An electrolytic cell for finding the amount of electricity that has flowed in electrolysis by measuring the products of the process.

coulo'metric *a.* pertaining to or employing coulometry M20. **coulometry** *n.* the use of a coulometer; chemical analysis in which quantities are determined from the amount of electricity needed for their electrolysis: M20.

coulter /ˈkəʊltə/ *n.* Also ***colter**. OE. [L *culter* knife, ploughshare.] The vertical cutting blade fixed in front of the share in a plough.

Comb.: **coulterneb** *dial.* the puffin (from the shape of its bill).

coumarin /ˈkuːmərɪn/ *n.* M19. [Fr. *coumarine*, f. *coumarou* f. Port. & Sp. *cumarú* f. Tupi, substance from tonka beans: see -IN[1].] An aromatic chromone, $C_9H_6O_2$, with the smell of new-mown hay, occurring in various plants and used in perfumery etc.

coumarone /ˈkuːmərəʊn/ *n.* Also **cum-**. L19. [f. prec. + -ONE.] *Chem.* A colourless liquid (C_8H_6O) present in coal tar, which is related to coumarin and is used in making synthetic resins; any derivative of this.

Comb.: **coumarone resin** any of various thermoplastic resins produced by polymerizing coumarone with indene and used esp. in the rubber and varnish industries.

council /ˈkaʊns(ə)l, -sɪl/ *n.* OE. [AN *cuncile*, *concilie* f. L *concilium* assembly, meeting, f. as CON- + *calare* call, summon.] I An assembly. 1 An assembly of ecclesiastics (with or without laymen) convened to regulate doctrine or discipline in the Church or to settle disputes between the ecclesiastical and civil powers. OE. †2 *gen.* An assembly called together for any purpose. Only in ME. 3 An assembly or meeting for consultation or advice. ME. 4 In New Testament translations: (a meeting of) the Sanhedrin. LME.

1 *diocesan council, ecumenical council, general council*, etc. 3 *Cabinet Council, family council*, etc.

II A body of counsellors or councillors. 5 A body of people chosen as advisers on matters of state. ME. 6 The local administrative body of a village, parish, town, or larger area. LME. 7 A deliberative committee sharing the administration of a society or institution. M17.

6 *city council, county council, district council, parish council, regional council, town council*, etc.

Phrases: *Aulic Council*: see AULIC. *Common Council*: see COMMON *a.* **council of war** (*a*) an assembly of officers of the armed services called together usu. in a special emergency; *fig.* a meeting held to discuss a plan of action; (*b*) *Hist.* in some foreign countries, a permanent advisory committee on military affairs. **Great Council** *Hist.* (occas.) = WITENAGEMOT; (more often) an assembly under the Norman kings of tenants-in-chief and great ecclesiastics, out of which the House of Lords developed. **in council** in consultation or deliberation in a council. **King** or **Queen in Council** the Privy Council as issuing Orders in Council or receiving petitions etc. *Nicene Council*: see NICENE *a.* 1. *Order in Council*: see ORDER *n. privy council*: see PRIVY *a. Queen in Council*: see *King in Council* above. *Second* VATICAN *Council*. VATICAN *Council. wages council*: see WAGE *n.*

Comb.: **council-board** a table at which councillors sit; councillors in session; **council-book** a book in which the acts of a council are registered; the register of Privy Counsellors; **council-chamber** a room used for council meetings; **council estate** an estate of council houses; **council-fire** a fire kindled by N. American Indians when in council; **council flat**: owned and let by a local council; **council-general** a general or common council; **council-house** (*a*) a house in which a council meets; in Scotland, a town hall; (*b*) a house used by N. American Indians when in council; (*c*) a house owned and let by a local council; **council school**: supported by a town or county council; **council-table** (*a*) a council-board; †(*b*) the Privy Council; **council tax** a tax levied by local authorities (from 1993, replacing the community charge) based on the band in which the estimated capital value of a property falls.

¶ Conf. w. COUNSEL *n.* until 16.

councillor /ˈkaʊns(ə)lə/ *n.* Also ***-ilor**. LME. [Alt. of COUNSELLOR by assim. to prec.] An official member of a council.

county councillor, parish councillor, etc. *privy councillor*: see PRIVY *a.*

councillorship *n.* the office or position of councillor L16.

councilman /ˈkaʊns(ə)lmən, -sɪl-/ *n.* Pl. **-men**. M17. [f. COUNCIL *n.* + MAN *n.*] A member of a council, esp. a local council, in the City of London or the US.

Common Councilman: see COMMON *a.*

councilmanic /-ˈmanɪk/ *a.* M19.

councilor *n.* see COUNCILLOR.

counsel /ˈkaʊns(ə)l/ *n.* ME. [OFr. *c(o)unseil* (mod. *conseil*) f. L *consilium* consultation, plan, deliberating body, rel. to *consulere*: see CONSULT *v.*] **I** 1 (A piece of) advice, (a) direction, esp. when the result of deliberation. ME. **b** *Theol.* Any of the advisory declarations of Christ and the Apostles, given as a means of attaining greater moral perfection. LME. 2 Interchange of opinions; deliberation, consultation. ME. †3 The ability to counsel or give advice; judgement, prudence, sagacity. ME–M17. 4 The result of deliberation; a resolution, a purpose; a plan. ME. 5 A secret purpose or opinion; a secret. Long *obs.* exc. w. *keep* (see below). ME.

1 S. JOHNSON The counsels of philosophy and the injunctions of religion. SAKI Francesca . . not only sought his counsel but frequently followed it.

II Cf. COUNCIL. †6 *gen.* A body of advisers. ME–M16. **b** A counsellor. LME–M17. 7 Usu. *collect. pl.* A body of legal advisers engaged in the direction or conduct of a court case. LME. **b** (Pl. usu. same.) A legal adviser; a barrister, an advocate (in Scotland etc.). L17.

7 LD DENNING They went off to their solicitors. They saw counsel. **b** *New Statesman* Counsel is holding the photograph the wrong way up. Jo GRIMOND I was briefed as junior counsel to defend a man charged with murder.

Phrases: **counsel of despair** an action to be taken when all else fails. **counsel of perfection** advice designed to guide one towards moral perfection (see *Matt.* 19:21); ideal but impracticable advice. †**in counsel** in private, in confidence. **keep counsel** *arch.* observe secrecy. **keep one's (own) counsel** keep one's secret; be reticent. †**keep someone's counsel** keep a secret which someone has committed to one. **King's** or **Queen's Counsel** a senior barrister appointed on the recommendation of the Lord Chancellor. *leading counsel*: see LEADING *ppl a. Parliamentary Counsel*: see PARLIAMENTARY *a. purge of partial counsel*: see PURGE *v.* 4b. *Queen's Counsel*: see *King's Counsel* above. **take counsel** consult (*with*).

counselless /-l-l-/ *a.* without counsel ME.

counsel /ˈkaʊns(ə)l/ *v.* Infl. **-ll-**, ***-l-**. ME. [OFr. *cons(e)illier* (mod. *conseiller*) f. L *consiliari*, f. *consilium*: see prec.] 1 *v.t.* Give or offer counsel or counselling to (a person); advise (*to do*). ME. **b** *v.i.* Give or offer counsel (†*to* a course or purpose). Now *rare* or *obs.* LME. 2 *v.t.* Recommend (a plan, suggestion, etc.; *that*). ME. †3 *v.t.* Ask counsel of, consult. ME–M16. 4 *v.i.* Take counsel with others, deliberate. ME.

1 LYTTON Since we have thus met, I will pause to counsel you. J. MCPHEE The passenger . . counselled the pilot to stay with the principal stream in sight. 2 E. M. FORSTER His mother . . would be pleased; she had counselled the step. M. EDWARDES Armstrong counselled that we should moderate the letter.

counsellable *a.* (*a*) willing to be counselled; (*b*) (of a thing) advisable: M16. **counseˈllee** *n.* a person who receives counselling M20.

counselling /ˈkaʊns(ə)lɪŋ/ *vbl n.* Also ***-eling**. ME. [f. prec. + -ING[1].] The action of COUNSEL *v.*; *spec.* a therapeutic procedure in which a usu. trained person adopts a supportive non-judgemental role in enabling a client to deal more effectively with psychological or emotional problems or gives advice on practical problems.

Listener Some students need counselling or even psychological treatment in these testing years.

counsellor /ˈkaʊns(ə)lə/ *n.* Also ***-elor**. ME. [(O)Fr. *conseiller* f. L *consiliarius* (see -ARY[1]), and OFr. *conseillour*, (O)Fr. *-eur* f. L *consiliator*: see -OR.] 1 A person who gives or offers counsel; an adviser; *spec.* a person who provides counselling as a therapy. ME. 2 More fully *counsellor-at-law*. A person whose profession is to give legal advice to clients and conduct their cases in court; a barrister, an advocate. Now chiefly *Ir.* & *US*. LME. 3 A senior officer in the British diplomatic service, esp. in one of the larger embassies; a senior officer in the Foreign and Commonwealth Office. E20.

Phrases: **Counsellor of State** any of a group of people appointed to act for the British monarch during a temporary absence abroad. *privy counsellor*: see PRIVY *a.*

count /kaʊnt/ *n.*[1] Also †**compt**. ME. [OFr. *co(u)nte* (mod. *compte* reckoning, *conte* tale) f. late L *computus* calculation, f. *computare* COMPUTE *v.*] 1 The action of counting; a calculation. ME. **b** The counting aloud of up to ten seconds by the referee when a boxer or wrestler is knocked down or otherwise unable to rise (ten seconds marking a knockout). E20. 2 A reckoning as to money or property; a statement of moneys received and expended, an account. LME. 3 *fig.* = ACCOUNT *n.* 3. *arch.* L15. 4 The result of a numerical calculation; a sum total. L15. **b** A number expressing the fineness of yarn, e.g. the length per unit mass of yarn. Also *yarn count*. M19. **c** *Physics.* The detection of an ionizing event by a Geiger counter etc.; an event so detected. E20. 5 Estimation, consideration; the way of estimating; regard, notice. L15. 6 In *Law*, a charge in an indictment; *fig.* any of several points under discussion. L16.

1 P. G. WODEHOUSE In actual count of time, he was no longer in his first youth. M. MOORCOCK About fifty titles, at the present count. **keep, lose, count** be aware, fail to know, how many there have been. **b out for the count** defeated, *spec.* in *Boxing* or *Wrestling* by being unable to rise within ten seconds; **take the count** be defeated. 3 SHAKES. *Oth.* When we shall meet at compt This look of thine will hurl my soul from heaven. 4 J. A. MICHENER The count was at its maximum, around forty million. *blood count, pollen count*, etc. **c** *Nature* An intensity of 20 counts s^{-1}. 5 E. B. BROWNING Of miserable men, he took no count. 6 A. T. ELLIS You are entirely wrong on both counts.

Comb.: **count noun** *Gram.* a noun denoting something of which there is more than one, a countable noun, in English usu. a noun which has a plural and is used with an indefinite article (opp. *mass noun*).

count /kaʊnt/ *n.*[2] Also (esp. in titles) **C-**. LME. [OFr. *conte* (mod. *comte*), f. L *comes, comit-* companion, overseer, attendant, etc., (in late L) occupant of a State office, f. as COM- + *it-* pa. ppl stem of *ire* go.] A foreign nobleman corresponding to a British earl.

Count Palatine: see PALATINE *a.*[1]

Comb.: **count-bishop, -cardinal**: who holds both the temporal and the spiritual dignities designated.

countship *n.* the position, domain, or jurisdiction of a count E18.

count /kaʊnt/ *v.* Also †**compt**. LME. [OFr. *c(o)unter* reckon, relate (mod. *compter* reckon, *conter* relate), f. L *computare* COMPUTE *v.*] **I** *v.t.* 1 Find the number of, esp. by assigning successive numerals to the members of; repeat numerals in order up to (a selected number). LME. **b** Foll. by *out*: (*a*) complete a count of ten seconds over (a boxer or wrestler unable to rise), adjudge to be knocked out after a count; (*b*) count while taking from a stock; (*c*) procure an adjournment of (the House of Commons) when fewer than forty members are present; (*d*) in children's games, select (a player) for a special role or dismissal by counting with the words of a rhyme etc. E19. **c** Foll. by *up*: find the sum of. L19. **d** Foll. by *down*: mark (time remaining before an event) by counting backwards to zero; mark the time remaining to (an event) by so counting. M20. 2 (With double obj., or obj. and compl.) consider to be; regard *as*, (*arch.*) take *for*. LME. 3 Reckon, estimate, (at such a price, in such terms, etc.). Formerly also, esteem, value. LME. †4 Tell, relate, recount. LME–L18. 5 Include in a reckoning or plan; take into consideration. E16. **b** Foll. by *in, out*: include, exclude, (a person) as a participant or supporter. *colloq.* M19. †6 Impute, put down to the account of. Foll. by *to*. M16–E18.

1 ALDOUS HUXLEY 'One, two, three . . . '; the seekers . . began to count their hundred, aloud. E. BIRNEY He counted the flies on the ceiling. **be counting the days, hours**, etc., be waiting impatiently for an event a few days, hours, etc., ahead. *count heads*: see HEAD *n. count noses*: see NOSE *n. count one's beads*: see BEAD *n.* 2. *count one's blessings*: see BLESSING *n. count one's chickens*: see CHICKEN *n.*[1] *count sheep*: see SHEEP *n. count (up to) ten*: see TEN *n.* 2. 2 E. M. FORSTER I count myself a lucky person. J. BUCHAN America. . . Among her citizens I count many of my closest friends. I. MURDOCH Mor still counted Tim as one of his best friends. 3 H. L. MENCKEN Nearly all of them count success in terms of money. 5 R. GRAFTON He is not counted in the number of kinges. E. ALBEE Martha hasn't been sick a day in her life, unless you count the time she spends in the rest home. *count the cost*: see COST *n.*[2]

II *v.i.* †7 Take account *of*; think (much, lightly, etc.) *of*; care *for*. LME–M19. 8 Reckon, make a reckoning. Now only in *count without*, not take into account. LME. 9 Repeat or list numerals in order (foll. by *from* one numeral, (*up*) *to* or *down to* another); foll. by *down*: repeat numerals in descending order to zero, esp. when launching a rocket etc. Also, do arithmetic, conduct reckoning. L16. 10 Foll. by (*up*)*on*: make the basis of one's plans; expect confidently; depend or rely on (a future contingency). M17. †11 *Law.* Plead in a court of law; state a plaintiff's case. Foll. by *upon*: make the basis of a plea. M17–E19. 12 With compl.: amount to, be in number. *arch.* E19. 13 Be regarded or considered *as*. M19. 14 Be included in the reckoning (*against, in someone's* or *something's favour*); be important, be significant; (foll. by *for*) be worth *much, little, nothing*, etc. M19.

7 SHAKES. *Two Gent.* So painted, to make her fair, that no man counts of her beauty. 9 M. ARNOLD To count by tens is the simplest way of counting. 10 ADDISON We . . may possibly never possess what we have so foolishly counted upon. 13 B. PYM He didn't count as an ordinary man who went out to work. 14 THOMAS HUGHES Oxford ought to be the place . . where money should count for nothing. J. RHYS It is the small things that count.

'count /kaʊnt/ *n.* *dial.* M19. [Aphet.] = ACCOUNT *n.* 4. Cf. COUNT *n.*[1] 5, *no-'count* s.v. NO *a.*

countable /ˈkaʊntəb(ə)l/ *a.* & *n.* As adj. also †**compt-**. LME. [OFr. *contable* (mod. *comptable*), f. as COUNT *v.*: see -ABLE.] **A** *adj.* †1 Answerable (*to*), accountable (*for*). LME–E19. 2 Able or fit to be counted; *spec.* in *Math.*, = DENUMERABLE. LME. †3 Sensitive *to*. Only in E17. 4 *Gram.* Of a noun: denoting something of which there is more than one, able to form a plural or be used with an indefinite article. Cf. *count noun* s.v. COUNT *n.*[1] M20. **B** *n.* *Gram.* A countable thing, a countable noun. E20.

counta'bility *n.* the property of being countable L20. **countably** *adv.* (*Math.*) in a denumerable way E20.

countdown /ˈkaʊntdaʊn/ *n.* M20. [f. COUNT *n.*[1] or *v.* + DOWN *adv.*: see COUNT *v.* 1d.] The action or an act of counting numerals in reverse order to zero, esp. in the procedure for launching a rocket etc.; (the procedures carried out in) the period of time so marked.

fig.: *Times* The count-down begins for the first Test match.

countenance /ˈkaʊnt(ə)nəns, -tɪn-/ *n.* ME. [AN *c(o)untenaunce*, (O)Fr. *contenance* bearing, behaviour, mien, contents, f. *contenir*: see CONTAIN, -ANCE.] **I** †**1** Bearing, demeanour; conduct. ME–E18. †**2** Appearance, aspect; mere show, pretence. ME–M19. **3** The expression on a person's face. ME. **b** The face. LME. **4** Calmness of appearance, composure. ME. †**5** A sign, a gesture. LME–M16.

3 J. LONDON The man flung past Martin with an angry countenance. b P. GALLICO She.. peered up into his countenance long and searchingly.

II †**6** Manner towards others as expressing good or ill will. LME–M17. **7** Appearance of favour to one side; moral support. L16.

7 H. JAMES He had given countenance to the reprehensible practice of gaming.

†**III 8** One's position in the world, standing; credit, repute. LME–L18.

Phrases: **change countenance** change expression as a result of emotion. †**for (a) countenance** for appearance's sake. **keep a person in countenance** keep a person from being disconcerted, esp. by a show of support. **keep one's countenance** maintain composure, *esp.* refrain from laughing. **lose countenance** become embarrassed. **(put) out of countenance** (make) disconcerted.

countenanced *a.* having a countenance (of a specified kind) L16.

countenance /ˈkaʊnt(ə)nəns, -tɪn-/ *v.* LME. [f. the n.] **I** *v.i.* †**1** Gesture. Only in LME. †**2** Assume a particular demeanour; behave (*as if*), pretend. L15–E16.

II *v.t.* †**3** Face *out*, persist in maintaining; (of a thing) bear *out*, confirm. E16–E17. **4** Give approval to; sanction, permit; favour, encourage. M16. †**5** Make a show of, feign. *rare* (Spenser). Only in L16. †**6** Keep in countenance (by acting in accordance with); be in keeping with. *rare* (Shakes.). Only in E17.

4 SHAKES. *2 Hen. IV* I beseech you, sir, to countenance William Visor.. against Clement Perkes. C. POTOK He disagreed with Reb Saunders.. but he would countenance no slander against his name. 6 SHAKES. *Macb.* As from your graves rise up.. To countenance this horror!

countenancer *n.* a person who gives approval, support, or encouragement E17.

counter /ˈkaʊntə/ *n.*[1] Also (now only in sense 6) **compter**. ME. [AN *count(e)our*, OFr. *conteo(i)r* (mod. *comptoir*), f. med.L *computatorium*, f. L *computare* COMPUTE *v.*: see -ER[2]. Not formally distinguished in AN f. source of next. Cf. also COMPTOIR.] **I 1** Something used in counting or keeping count; *esp.* a small disc of metal, plastic, etc., used for keeping account or as a piece marking position etc. in a game. ME. **2** An imitation coin; a token representing a coin. Also, debased coin; *contempt.* money generally; anything worthless. LME.

II †**3** A table or desk for counting money. ME–L16. †**4** A counting-house. LME–E19. **5** A banker's or money-changer's table; the table etc. in a shop on which money is counted out and across which goods are delivered; a similar structure where service is provided in a library, cafeteria, etc. L17.

5 M. INNES A counter ineptly piled with *démodé* goods. *nail to the counter*: see NAIL *v.* **over the counter** (*a*) by ordinary purchase in a shop, *spec.* without prescription; (*b*) by direct transaction outside the stock exchange system. **under the counter** surreptitiously, *esp.* illegally.

III Also **C-**. **6** The prison attached to a city court; *esp.* (the name of) any of certain prisons for debtors in London, Southwark, and elsewhere. *obs.* exc. *Hist.* LME. †**7** The office, court, or hall of justice of a mayor. L15–M18.

Comb.: **counter-caster** *arch.* & *poet.* a person who reckons with counters, *derog.* an arithmetician; **counter-jumper** *colloq.* (*derog.*) a shop assistant; **counter lunch**: served at the counter of a public house etc.; **counterman** a man who serves at a counter.

counter /ˈkaʊntə/ *n.*[2] LME. [Partly f. AN *count(e)our*, OFr. *conteor* f. L *computator*, f. *computare* COMPUTE *v.*: see -OR. Partly f. COUNT *v.* + -ER[1]. Cf prec., COUNTOUR.] †**1** = COUNTOUR. LME–L15. **2** A person who counts or calculates. LME. **3** An apparatus for counting; *spec.* (*Physics*) = RADIATION *counter*. E19.

3 *Geiger counter, rev counter, scintillation counter*, etc. *kern counter*: see KERN *n.*[2] *proportional counter*: see PROPORTIONAL *a.* 2.

counter /ˈkaʊntə/ *n.*[3] LME. [f. COUNTER-.] **1** *Hunting.* The opposite direction to that taken by the game. LME. **2** The contrary, the opposite. LME. **3** *Mus.* A voice or part contrasting with (and usu. lower than) the principal melody or part. Also, a counter-tenor voice or part. LME. **4** The enclosed part of a printed or written character. L19. **5** *Skating.* A figure in which the body is revolved in a direction opposite to that in which it was revolved in the previous turns. L19.

counter /ˈkaʊntə/ *n.*[4] L15. [Fr. *contre* corresp. to It. *contro*, use as n. of prep., f. as CONTRA.] **1** *Fencing.* A circular parry. L15. **2** *Boxing.* A blow returned in response to the opponent's. M19.

counter /ˈkaʊntə/ *n.*[5] E16. [Origin uncertain: perh. rel. to COUNTER *n.*[3]] **1** The part of a horse's breast between the shoulders and under the neck. Now *rare.* E16. **2** The curved part of the stern of a ship. E17.

counter /ˈkaʊntə/ *n.*[6] M19. [Abbrev. of COUNTERFORT.] The back part of a boot or shoe, round the heel.

counter /ˈkaʊntə/ *a.* L16. [Independent use of COUNTER-.] Acting in opposition; lying or tending in the opposite direction; opposed, opposite; duplicate, serving as a check.

K. CLARK The loose swinging movement, the twist and counter twist. U. LE GUIN This idea was so counter to Shevek's habits of thinking that.. he suppressed it at once.

counter /ˈkaʊntə/ *v.* ME. [In branch I aphet. f. ENCOUNTER *v.*; in branch II infl. by COUNTER-, COUNTER *n.*[4]] †**I 1** *v.t.* & *i.* Meet. ME–E19. **2** *v.t.* & *i.* (w. *with*). Meet in opposition; engage in combat. ME–E19.

II 3 *v.t.* Act or speak against; contradict, oppose; answer with a countermove; counterbalance. LME. **b** *Boxing* & *Wrestling.* Meet (a blow, move, etc.) with or *with* a counterblow, countermove, etc. E19. †**4** *v.i.* Engage in argument; retort *against*, dispute *with*. LME–L16. **5** *v.i.* Make a move or reply in response; respond (*with*); *Boxing* & *Wrestling* give a counterblow, make a countermove. M19.

3 J. C. POWYS The revolutionary ideas of the man were countered by the inflexible Toryism of the woman. b J. B. MORTON She countered my double-lock with a half-Nelson. 5 J. AGATE Coming up to me and saying: 'Sir, a bone to pick with you,' and me countering with.. 'Madam, a whole skeleton!'.

counter /ˈkaʊntə/ *adv.* LME. [(O)Fr. *contre* f. as CONTRA. Due mainly to analysis of vbs etc. in COUNTER-.] **1** In the opposite direction; back again. LME. †**2** In opposite directions to each other. Only in 17. **3** In opposition; contrary. M17.

1 **go, hunt,** or **run counter**: in a direction opposite to that taken by the quarry. 3 CARLYLE Sigismund voted clearly so, and Jobst said nothing counter. **run counter to** be or act contrary to.

counter- /ˈkaʊntə/ *pref.* [AN *countre-*, (O)Fr. *contre-*, f. as CONTRA-.] A freely productive pref. forming vbs, ns., and adjs. **1** Forming vbs f. vbs, w. the senses 'against, in the opposite direction', as *counteract*, *counterbrace*, etc.; 'with the opposite effect, so as to rival or frustrate', as *countercharm*, *counterwork*, etc.; 'in response, reciprocally', as *counterargue*, *counter-claim*, etc. **2** Forming ns. f. ns., w. the senses 'contrary, opposed (in direction or effect), reciprocal', as *counter-attack*, *countercurrent*, *countermarch*, *counter-reformation*, etc.; also 'corresponding, matching', as *counterbalance*, *counterfoil*, etc.; 'substitute, secondary', as *counterdrain*, *counterearth*, etc.; 'false', as *counterprophet* etc. **3** Forming adjs. f. adjs. and ns., w. the senses 'contrary to, in opposition to', as *counternatural* etc.; 'turned in the opposite direction, placed on opposite sides', as *counterpassant* etc.; 'reversed, interchanged', as *counter-coloured* etc.

counter-agency *n.* agency in opposition (*to* something) M19. **counter-agent** *n.* = COUNTERACTIVE *n.* E19. **counter-arch** *n.* & *v.* (*a*) *n.* an inverted arch opposite to another arch; an arch connecting counterforts at the top; (*b*) *v.t.* provide or support with a counter-arch: E18. **counter-'argue** *v.t.* & *i.* argue against or in return M17. **counter-argument** *n.* an argument on the opposite side or against anything M19. **counter-attack** *n.* & *v.* (*a*) *n.* an attack (*lit.* & *fig.*) in reply to an attack by an enemy or opponent; (*b*) *v.t.* & *i.* make a counter-attack (on): L19. **counter-attraction** *n.* an attraction of a contrary tendency; a rival attraction, tending to draw attention away from another M18. **counter-battery** *n.* †(*a*) a counter-attack made with artillery; (*b*) a battery raised against another: L16. **counterbid** *n.* a bid made in return, *esp.* a takeover bid made in response to another bid for the same company M20. **counter-bill** *n.* the counterpart or duplicate of a bill L16. **counterblast** *n.* an energetic declaration or action in opposition (*to*) M16. **counterblow** *n.* a blow given in return; a blow resulting from a rebound: M17. **counterbond** *n.* a bond to indemnify a person who has entered into a bond for another L16. **counter-book** *n.* a duplicate account-book to serve as a check E17. **counterbuff** *n.* & *v.* †(*a*) *n.* a counterblow; a rebuff; an exchange of blows; (*b*) *v.t.* (*arch.*) strike in return; meet (a blow) with another blow; rebuff: L16. †**counter-cast** *n.* (*rare*, Spenser) an antagonistic artifice: only in L16. **countercharge** *n.* a charge brought in opposition to another or against an accuser E18. **countercharge** *v.t.* (*a*) charge with an opposing or contrary charge; †(*b*) oppose with a contrary charge: E17. **counter-charm** *n.* a counteracting charm E17. **counter'charm** *v.t.* (now *rare*) neutralize the effect of (a charm), affect with an opposing charm L16. **counter-claim** *n.* & *v.* (*a*) *n.* a claim made in response to another or by a defendant; (*b*) *v.t.* & *i.* make a counter-claim (against); L18. **counter-claimant** *n.* a person who makes a counter-claim L19. **counter'clockwise** *a.* & *adv.* = ANTICLOCKWISE L19. **counter-'coloured** *a.* (*Her.*) having the tinctures interchanged in opposite or corresponding parts; counterchanged: L16. †**counter-componed** *a.* = COUNTER-COMPONY L16–E18. **counter-com'pony** *a.* (*Her.*) composed of two conjoined rows of squares of alternate tinctures E17. **countercross** *v.i.* (*rare*) cross in contrary directions E17. **counter'cultural** *a.* of, pertaining to, or characteristic of a counterculture L20. **counterculture** *n.* a mode of life deliberately deviating from established social practices; a group that has adopted such a lifestyle: L20. **counter'culturist** *n.* a person who belongs to or shows sympathy with a counterculture L20. †**countercuff** *n.* a blow given in return or to parry another L16–E18. **countercurrent** *n.* & *a.* (*a*) *n.* an opposite flow or trend; (*b*) *adj.* running in the opposite direction; involving countercurrents: L16. **counter'currently** *adv.* against another current M20. **countercycle** *n.* an economic change or trend stimulated by a government to mitigate or compensate for the effects of fluctuation in business or in the national economy M20. **counter'cyclical** *a.* of or pertaining to a countercycle, having the nature or effect of a countercycle M20. **counter-disen'gage** *n.* & *v.* (*Fencing*) (*a*) *n.* the action of disengaging; a riposte made by this means; (*b*) *v.i.* disengage and make a thrust as the opponent changes the engagement: L18. **counter-disen'gagement** *n.* = COUNTER-DISENGAGE *n.* L19. †**counterdistinct** *a.* = CONTRADISTINCT M–L17. †**counterdistinction** *n.* = CONTRADISTINCTION: only in 17. †**counterdistinguish** *v.t.* = CONTRADISTINGUISH E17–M18. **counter-earth** *n.* (*Hist. Sci.*) = ANTICHTHON 2 M19. **counter-élite** *n.* an élite that replaces another élite after the latter is overthrown M20. **counter-em'battled** *a.* (*Her.*) (of an ordinary) embattled on both sides with the battlements on one side opposite the indentures on the other (cf. BRETESSY) M19. **counter-e'namel** *v.t.* enamel on the back as well as the front L19. **counter-'espionage** *n.* action directed against espionage by an enemy L19. **counter-'etch** *v.* & *n.* (*a*) *v.t.* treat (a lithographic plate) with dilute acid to make it clean and receptive to grease; (*b*) *n.* the process of counter-etching; the acid solution used for it: E20. **counter-evidence** *n.* evidence tending to rebut other evidence M17. **counter-ex'tend** *v.t.* (*Med.*) exercise counter-extension on (a limb etc.) M17. **counter-extension** *n.* (*Med.*) the action of pulling on or holding the upper part of a limb so as to oppose extension applied to the lower part M19. **counter-faller** *n.* (*Spinning*) in a mule, a wire which passes between the yarns, when pressed down by the faller wire, so as to keep the tension uniform M19. **counter-fire** *n.* & *v.* (*a*) *n.* a fire lit deliberately in order to combat a heath or forest fire; (*b*) *v.i.* use a counter-fire: L19. **counter'fleury, -'flory** *a.* (*Her.*) (of an ordinary) having flowers on each side set opposite each other in pairs L16. **counter-'flowered** *a.* = COUNTERFLEURY L18. **counterfoil** *n.* the complementary part of a cheque, official receipt, etc., with a note of the particulars, retained by the person issuing such a document E18. **counterforce** *n.* & *a.* (*a*) *n.* a force acting or maintained in opposition to another; (*b*) *adj.* based on or involving nuclear retaliation against military forces or bases: E17. **counter-go'bony** *a.* (*Her.*) = COUNTER-COMPONY M19. **counter-'indicate** *v.t.* = CONTRA-INDICATE L19. **counter-indication** *n.* = CONTRA-INDICATION M18. **counter-influence** *n.* an opposing influence M19. †**counter-influence** *v.t.* influence in the opposite direction: only in M17. **counter-intelligence** *n.* activity intended to stop information from reaching the enemy, counter-espionage; an agency or service engaged in this: M20. **counter-interro'gation** *n.* cross-examination E19. **counter-in'tuitive** *a.* contrary to intuition M20. **counter-ion** *n.* an ion of opposite charge associated with a substance or particle M20. **counter'irritant** *n.* (*Med.*) something used to produce irritation of the skin in order to counteract a more deep-seated symptom or disease; *fig.* an irritant that acts as a distraction from another: M19. **counterirri'tation** *n.* (the use of) a counterirritant M19. **counterlath** *n.* & *v.* (*a*) *n.* a lath or rafter laid between two more substantial or more accurately placed ones; (*b*) *v.t.* provide with counterlaths or counterlathing: M17. **counterlathing** *n.* laths for plastering nailed to fillets on beams or timber M19. †**counter-letter** *n.* a letter countermanding another letter E17–E19. **counter-marque** *n.* (*obs.* exc. *Hist.*) reprisals against letters of marque E16. **counter-mart** *n.* (*obs.* exc. *Hist.*) [alt.] = COUNTER-MARQUE E18. **counter'match** *v.t.* †(*a*) *rare* match (one thing) against another; (*b*) be a match for, counterbalance: L16. **countermeasure** *n.* an action taken to counteract a danger, threat, etc. E20. **countermelody** *n.* a subordinate melody accompanying a principal one M20. **countermissile** *n.* a missile designed to intercept and destroy another missile, an anti-missile missile M20. **counter-motion** *n.* (*a*) motion in the opposite direction; (*b*) a motion contrary to one already proposed: E17. **countermove** *n.* & *v.* (*a*) *n.* a move or action in opposition to another; (*b*) *v.i.* move in an opposite direction or opposite directions: M19. **countermovement** *n.* a movement in opposition, a contrary movement E19. **counter-offensive** *n.* (esp. *Mil.*) an offensive action designed to allow escape from a defensive situation M20. **counter-offer** *n.* an offer made in return, esp. by a company to one making a takeover bid for it L18. **counter-opening** *n.* an opening opposite another, *esp.* a surgical one LME. †**counterpace** *n.* (*a*) *rare* a movement in a contrary direction; (*b*) a step taken against something: L16–M18. **counter-passant** *a.* (*Her.*) walking in opposite directions, repassant E17. **counter-passion** *n.* (*a*) a passion opposed to or the opposite of another; †(*b*) an outburst of passion against something: L16. **counter-penalty** *n.* [tr. Gk *antitimēsis*] *Gk Hist.* the penalty which an accused person who had been pronounced guilty suggested in opposition to that called for by the accuser M19. **counter-plea** *n.* (*Law*) an answer to a plea or request, giving arguments why it should not be admitted E16. **counterplot** *n.* a plot contrived to defeat another plot E17. **counterplot** *v.* (*a*) *v.i.* make a counterplot *against*; (*b*) *v.t.* plot against, frustrate by a counterplot: L16. **counter-pole** *n.* the opposite pole M19. **counter-'potent** *a.* (*Her.*) (of a fur) having potents of the same tincture arranged base to base as in countervair E17. **counter-pressure** *n.* opposite or contrary pressure M17. †**counter-price** *n.* [tr. Gk *anti-lutron* in *I Tim.* 2:6] a ransom L17–E18. **counter-pro'ductive** *a.* having the opposite of the desired effect; tending to act against the attainment of an objective: M20. **counterproof** *n.* †(*a*) proof to the contrary; (*b*) *Printing* an impression taken from a freshly printed image, appearing the same way round as the image on the original printing surface: E17. **counter'prove** *v.t.* †(*a*) disprove; (*b*) take a counterproof of: L17. **counter-question** *n.* a question put in response to another person's question M19. **counter-'questioning** *n.* the asking of counter-questions M19. **counter-revo'lution** *n.* a revolution opposed to an earlier one or reversing its results L18. **counter-revo'lutionary** *n.* & *a.* (*a*) *n.* a person who takes part in, supports, or works for a counter-revolution; (*b*) *adj.* pertaining to or of the nature of a counter-revolution: L18. **counter-rhythm** *n.* a subordinate rhythm acting as counterbalance to a main rhythm E20. **counter-'salient** *a.* (*Her.*) (of two animals borne as charges) salient in opposite directions E17. **counter-scale** *n.* the opposite scale (of the balance) (chiefly *fig.*) M17. **counter-se'cure** *v.t.* (*a*) secure (a person) against the risk he or she incurs by becoming security for another; (*b*) give an additional security to: M17. **countersense** *n.* [Fr. *contresens*] a meaning opposed to the true sense M17. **countershading** *n.* coloration (esp. of a bird or animal) in which parts normally in shadow are light and those exposed to the sky are dark L19. **countershaft** *n.* an intermediate shaft transmitting drive from one shaft to another or to an individual machine M19. **counterslope** *n.* (*a*) the opposite slope of a hill etc.; a slope in the opposite direction; (*b*) an overhanging slope: M19. **counter-spell** *n.* a spell against something; a spell to dissolve another spell: E18. **counterspy** *n.* a spy engaged in counter-espionage M20. **counterstain** *n.* & *v.* (*a*) *n.* an additional dye used in a microscopy specimen to produce a contrasting background to the parts of interest or to make clearer the distinction between different kinds of tissue etc.; (*b*) *v.t.* & *i.* treat with or use a counterstain: L19. **counter-step** *n.* a step in opposition or in the opposite direction E18. **counter-stroke** *n.* (*a*) a stroke given in return; (*b*) = CONTRECOUP *n.* 2: L16. **countersubject** *n.* (*Mus.*) a second or subsidiary subject, esp. accompanying the subject or its answer in a fugue M19. †**countersway** *v.t.* forcibly move or incline to the opposite side M17–E18. **counter-tide** *n.* a tide running against the main or usual current L16. **counter-title** *n.* (*Law*) a title to property in opposition to another title E19. **counter-trade** *n.* (*a*) = ANTITRADE *n.*; (*b*) international trade in which goods are exchanged instead of cash paid: E20. **countertype** *n.* †(*a*) = ANTITYPE; (*b*) a parallel, a counterpart; (*c*) an opposite type: E17. **counter'vair** *n.* (*Her.*) a variety of vair in which the bells or shield-shaped forms of the same tincture are placed base to base M18. **counterva'llation** *n.* (*rare*) = CONTRAVALLATION L17. **counter'value** *n.* & *a.* (*a*) *n.* equivalent value; (*b*) *adj.* based on or involving nuclear retaliation against civilian targets: M17. **counterview** *n.* †(*a*) a view from opposite sides or in opposite directions; a contrasting or confronting position; (*b*) *rare* the opposite opinion: L16. **counter-walk** *n.* (now *rare* or *obs.*) a smaller parallel path as an accessory to a main path M17.

counteract /kaʊntər'akt/ *v.t.* L17. [f. COUNTER- 1 + ACT *v.*] 1 Hinder or defeat by contrary action; neutralize the action or effect of. L17. †2 Act in opposition to; oppose. E18–M19.

1 T. H. HUXLEY The weight upon the upper surface is counteracted by the upward pressure of the air on the under surface. A. STORR The therapist may be able to counteract the depressive's negative view of his own accomplishments. 2 J. WILLOCK I had counteracted his intentions often before, especially in going to sea . . against his inclinations.

counteractant *n.* = COUNTERACTIVE *n.* L19. **counteraction** *n.* (*a*) the action of counteracting; opposition; (*b*) a counteracting influence or force: M18. **counteractive** *a.* & *n.* (*a*) *adj.* tending to counteract; (*b*) *n.* a counteracting agent or force: E19.

counter-approach /'kaʊnt(ə)rəprəʊtʃ/ *n.* Also (earlier) †**contre-**. L17. [Fr. *contre-approche*, f. *contre-* COUNTER- + *approche* APPROACH *n.*] *Mil.* A work constructed outside permanent fortifications by a besieged force, to check and command the works of the besiegers. Usu. in *pl.*

counterbalance /'kaʊntəbal(ə)ns/ *n.* L16. [f. COUNTER- 2 + BALANCE *n.*] †1 The opposite side of a balance. *rare*. Only in L16. 2 A weight used to balance another weight; *spec.* one used to balance the weight of a rotating or an ascending and descending part, so as to facilitate movement. E17. 3 *fig.* A power, influence, emotion, etc., which balances the effect of a contrary one. M17.

counterbalance /kaʊntə'bal(ə)ns/ *v.t.* L16. [f. COUNTER- 1 + BALANCE *v.*] †1 Of a person: weigh or balance (one thing) against another. (Foll. by *to*, *with*.) L16–E17. 2 Of a thing: act as a counterbalance to. E17. 3 *fig.* Balance or cancel the effect of. M17.

†**counterband** *n.*, *a.*, & *v.* E16. [Alt. of Sp. *contrabanda* CONTRABAND *n.*: see COUNTER-.] A *n.* & *adj.* = CONTRABAND *n.* & *a.* E16–E19. B *v.t.* = CONTRABAND *v.* M17–E18.

counterbass /'kaʊntəbeɪs/ *n.* Long *rare* or *obs.* Also **-base**. L16. [f. COUNTER- 2 + BASS *n.*[2] after It. CONTRABASSO.] *Mus.* = CONTRABASS *n.* 1.

counterbore /'kaʊntəbɔː/ *n.* L19. [f. COUNTER- 2 + BORE *n.*[1]] 1 A drilled hole that has a flat-bottomed enlargement at its mouth. L19. 2 A drill whose bit has a uniform smaller diameter near the tip, for drilling counterbores in one operation. L19.

counterbore /'kaʊntəbɔː; *in sense 1* kaʊntə'bɔː/ *v.* E17. [Sense 1 f. COUNTER- 1 + BORE *v.*[1]; sense 2 f. the n.] 1 *v.i.* Bore in the opposite direction. Now *rare* or *obs.* E17. 2 *v.i.* & *t.* Drill a counterbore (in). L19.

counterchange /'kaʊntətʃeɪndʒ/ *n.* L16. [Fr. *contrechange* (= It. *contraccambio*), f. as COUNTER-, CHANGE *n.*] 1 Exchange of one thing for another. Long *rare*. L16. †b Equal or equivalent return; requital. L16–M17. †2 Transposition. L16–E17. 3 Patterning in which a dark motif on a light ground alternates with the same motif light on a dark ground. L19.

counterchange /'kaʊntətʃeɪndʒ/ *v.* LME. [Fr. *contrechanger*, f. as COUNTER-, CHANGE *v.*] 1 *v.t. Her.* Interchange the tincture of (a charge) with that of the field when the latter is of two tinctures; interchange (tinctures) in this way. Chiefly as *counterchanged* ppl a. LME. b Chequer; mark *with* contrasting shades etc. E17. †2 *v.t.* Exchange for or *for* another. L16–M17. 3 *v.t.* Change to the opposite (position, state, quality); transpose. Long *rare*. E17. 4 *v.i.* Change places or parts. M19.

countercheck /'kaʊntətʃɛk/ *n.* M16. [f. COUNTER- 2 + CHECK *n.*[1]] 1 A rebuke or reproof in reply to or in return for one given; a retort. Long *rare*. M16. 2 A restraint that opposes something; a check. L16. 3 A restraint that operates against another restraint. M19.

countercheck /'kaʊntətʃɛk/ *v.t.* L16. [f. COUNTER- 1 + CHECK *v.*[1]] †1 Rebuke or reprove in return or as an expression of opposition. Only in L16. 2 Check or arrest by contrary action. L16.

counterfactual /kaʊntə'faktʃʊəl/ *a.* & *n.* M20. [f. COUNTER- 3 + FACTUAL *a.* Cf. CONTRAFACTUAL.] *Philos.* A *adj.* Pertaining to or expressing what has not happened or is not the case. M20. B *n.* A counterfactual conditional statement. M20.

counterfactually *adv.* contrary to fact M20.

†**counterfeisance** *n.* L16–M17. [OFr. *contrefaisance*, f. *contrefaire*: see next, -ANCE.] The action of counterfeiting; deceit, fraud, imposture.

counterfeit /'kaʊntəfɪt, -fiːt/ *a.* & *n.* LME. [AN *co(u)ntrefet*, (O)Fr. *contrefait* pa. pple of *contrefaire* f. Proto-Romance (med.L) *contrafacere*, f. as CONTRA- + L *facere* make.] A *adj.* (orig. *pa. pple*). 1 Made in imitation, not genuine; made of inferior materials; forged. LME. 2 Pretended, feigned, sham; falsely represented or representing oneself to be (what is denoted by the noun). LME. †b Misrepresenting oneself, deceitful. M16–M18. †3 Made to a pattern, fashioned. LME–M16. †4 Disguised, transformed in appearance. LME–E18. †5 Misshapen, deformed. LME–L16. †6 Represented in a picture, writing, etc.; portrayed. L16–M19.

1 W. S. JEVONS It is difficult to make any counterfeit gold or silver. M. HOLROYD A counterfeit Van Dyck to hang in his dining-room. 2 T. CHALMERS The counterfeit and the worthless Poor do a world of mischief to the cause of beneficence. J. H. NEWMAN I also warn you against a counterfeit earnestness. *counterfeit crank*: see CRANK *n.*[3] 6 SHAKES. *Haml.* Look here upon this picture and on this, the counterfeit presentment of two brothers.

B *n.* 1 A false or spurious imitation; something not genuine; something made of inferior materials; a forgery. LME. †2 a A representation in painting, sculpture, etc.; an image; a portrait. LME–M19. b *fig.* A copy, a likeness. *arch.* L16. †3 A pretender, an impostor. L15–M18. †4 A deformed person. M–L16.

1 J. ARBUTHNOT He has the original deed .. the others are counterfeits. LD MACAULAY One who does not value real glory, will not value its counterfeit. 2a SHAKES. *Merch. V.* What find I here? Fair Portia's counterfeit! b J. D. LONG Entranced at such A counterfeit of his own filial love.

counterfeitly *adv.* M16. **counterfeitness** *n.* M16.

counterfeit /ˈkaʊntəfɪt, -fiːt/ *v.* ME. [AN *countrefeter*, f. *countrefet* pa. pple: see prec.] I *v.t.* 1 Imitate (an action, thing, etc.) with intent to deceive; make a fraudulent imitation of (money etc.). ME. †2 Assume the character of (a person); pass oneself off as, impersonate. ME–E17. †3 Imitate, without intending to deceive; follow the example of (a person); copy (a fashion etc.). ME–E17. 4 Feign (a feeling, state, etc.). Formerly also, pretend *to be, that*. LME. 5 Have the appearance of; resemble, be like. LME. 6 Make in fraudulent imitation of something else; devise (something spurious) and pass it off as genuine. LME. †7 Make in imitation, without intending to deceive. LME–L16. †8 Represent by a picture, in writing, etc.; delineate, portray. LME–M17. †9 Put a false or deceptive appearance on; disguise, falsify; adulterate. LME–E18.

1 G. BERKELEY That it be felony to counterfeit the notes of this bank. K. AMIS He .. moved off counterfeiting a heavy limp. 2 BACON To counterfeite and personate the second sone of Edward the Fourth, supposed to be murdered. 3 JAMES I Counterfeiting the maners of others. M. WROTH Her complexion .. never was .. equald, or could be counterfeited. 4 SHAKES. *A.Y.L.* Take a good heart and counterfeit to be a man. S. JOHNSON To counterfeit happiness which they do not feel. 5 S. LEACOCK The scales of the fish counterfeit the glistening water of the brook. 6 T. HERBERT He lost a Ring of Gold .. he conceals the loss, and counterfeits another like it of silver. 9 DEFOE I counterfeited my voice.

II *v.i.* 10 Make pretence, practise deceit. Long *rare*. LME.

10 SHAKES. *Twel. N.* Are you not mad indeed, or do you but counterfeit?

counterfeiter *n.* (*a*) a maker of fraudulent imitations, *spec.* a maker of counterfeit coins; (*b*) a pretender, a dissembler; (*c*) an imitator (with no intent to deceive): LME.

counterfort /ˈkaʊntəfɔːt/ *n.* L16. [Fr. *contrefort*, f. OFr. *contreforcier* prop, buttress.] A buttress or projecting piece of masonry to support and strengthen a wall or terrace, esp. as part of a fortification.

counterglow /ˈkaʊntəgləʊ/ *n.* M19. [f. COUNTER- 2 + GLOW *n.*, as tr. G *Gegenschein.*] = GEGENSCHEIN.

counterguard /ˈkaʊntəgɑːd/ *n.* E16. [Fr. *contregarde*, f. as COUNTER-, GUARD *n.*] †1 An extra guard to act as a check on another, or as a reserve defence. E16–M17. 2 *Fortif.* A narrow detached rampart immediately in front of an important work to prevent it from being breached. L16.

countermand /kaʊntəˈmɑːnd/ *n.* L15. [OFr. *contremand*, f. as next.] 1 A command or order that revokes or annuls a previous one. L15. †2 A prohibition. L16–L17. 3 *Law.* An action that has the effect of making void something previously executed. E17.

countermand /kaʊntəˈmɑːnd/ *v.t.* LME. [OFr. *contremander* f. med.L *contramandare*, f. as CONTRA- + L *mandare* command.] I Implying the cancellation of an earlier command. 1 Command the opposite of; revoke (a command) by a contrary one. LME. †2 Order (a person *to do* something, or *that* something be done) in reversal of a command already issued. LME–M16. 3 Recall (a person, forces, etc.) by a contrary order. LME. 4 Stop or prohibit (what has been commanded, ordered, or allowed); cancel an order for (goods etc.). M16.

1 Q. BELL She proposed .. a second visit to the shop to countermand the order. W. GOLDING I can find no one who has the authority to countermand this singularly foolish order. 3 GOLDSMITH Our regiment is countermanded.

II Without the implication of branch I. †5 Go counter to or oppose the command of (a person in authority) L16–M17. †6 Give a command against, prohibit. L16–M17. †7 Control, keep under command. L16–M17. †8 Counteract; counterbalance. M17–E18.

7 C. MARLOWE And all the sea my galleys countermand.

countermandable *a.* E17. **countermander** *n.* (now *rare*) M17.

countermarch /ˈkaʊntəmɑːtʃ/ *n.* L16. [f. COUNTER- 2 + MARCH *n.*[3]] 1 A march (*lit.* & *fig.*) in the opposite direction. L16. 2 *Mil. Hist.* An evolution by which a column turns to face in the opposite direction while retaining the same order, so that those at the front are finally at the rear. M17. 3 A march held as a demonstration opposing another march. M20.

countermarch /ˈkaʊntəmɑːtʃ/ *v.i.* & *t.* E17. [f. COUNTER- 1 + MARCH *v.*[2]] 1 *Mil. Hist.* (Cause to) execute a countermarch. E17. 2 (Cause to) march in a contrary direction; march back. M17.

countermark /ˈkaʊntəmɑːk/ *n.* E16. [Fr. *contremarque*, f. as COUNTER-, MARQUE *n.*[2]] An additional mark placed on something already marked, e.g. for increased security; a second watermark.

countermine /ˈkaʊntəmʌɪn/ *n.* & *v.* LME. [f. COUNTER- 2 + MINE *n.*] A *n.* 1 *Mil.* A subterranean excavation made by defenders to intercept one made by besiegers. LME. 2 *fig.* A counterplot. L16. B *v.* 1 *v.t.* & *i.* Make a countermine (against). L16. 2 *v.t.* Defeat by a counterplot. L16. 3 *v.i.* Lay mines intended to explode an enemy's mines. L19.

counterminer *n.* L17.

countermure /ˈkaʊntəmjʊə/ *n.* E16. [(O)Fr. *contremur*, f. as COUNTER- + *mur* wall.] 1 A defensive wall raised inside another wall, in case of a breach in the latter. E16. 2 An outer wall round a city. M16. 3 A wall or mound raised outside a fortress to help besiegers. M16. 4 *fig.* A strong defence. L16.

countermure /ˈkaʊntəmjʊə/ *v.t.* LME. [Fr. *contremurer*, f. as prec.] Defend with a countermure.

counter-order /ˈkaʊntərɔːdə/ *n.* L18. [f. COUNTER- 2 + ORDER *n.*] An order contrary to or reversing a previous order.

counter-order /kaʊntərˈɔːdə/ *v.t.* M17. [f. COUNTER- 1 + ORDER *v.*] Give an order against, countermand.

†**counterpane** *n.*[1] L15. [AN *countrepan*, f. as COUNTER- + OFr. *pan* piece, part.] 1 = COUNTERPART *n.* 2, 3, 4. L15–L17. 2 *Law.* The counterpart of an indenture. E16–L17.

counterpane /ˈkaʊntəpeɪn/ *n.*[2] E17. [Alt. of COUNTERPOINT *n.*[2] by assim. to PANE *n.*[1]] A bedspread, usu. woven in raised figures, quilted, etc.; a quilt.

counterpart /ˈkaʊntəpɑːt/ *n.* LME. [f. COUNTER- 2 + PART *n.* after (O)Fr. *contrepartie.*] 1 *Law.* The opposite part of an indenture; each of two or more similar copies of a deed or lease, *esp.* one not regarded as the principal one. LME. 2 Either of two parts which fit and complete each other; a person or thing forming a natural complement to another. M17. †3 A duplicate, an exact copy. L17–E18. 4 A person or thing so like another as to appear a duplicate; an equivalent; a person or thing with an exactly comparable function etc., esp. at a different time or in a different context. L17. 5 *Mus.* A part written to accompany another. E18.

2 HAZLITT Popular fury finds its counterpart in courtly servility. 4 W. IRVING A full-length portrait .. the very counterpart of his visitor of the preceding night. H. CARPENTER The middle-class Englishman of 1851, like his counterpart a century later.

Comb.: **counterpart fund** a sum of money in local currency equivalent to goods or services received from abroad.

counterpoint /ˈkaʊntəpɔɪnt/ *n.*[1] & *v.* LME. [In branch I f. (O)Fr. *contrepoint* f. med.L *contrapunctum, cantus contrapunctus* song pricked or marked opposite (i.e. to the original melody), f. as CONTRA- + med.L *punctus* musical note, use as n. of L pa. pple of *pungere* prick. In branch II directly f. COUNTER- 2 + POINT *n.*[1]] A *n.* I 1 The art or practice of combining two or more musical parts in accordance with definite rules so that they are heard simultaneously as independent lines; the style of composition in which this is done; *fig.* a pleasing or effective combination of contrasting things. LME. b A melody or part added to another in counterpoint. M16. 2 The combination of two types of rhythm in a line of verse. L19.

1 S. BRETT The depressing nature of his surroundings seemed, by counterpoint, to enhance his sunny mood. *quadruple counterpoint*: see QUADRUPLE *a.* **strict counterpoint**: according to rules as an academic exercise, not as an actual composition.

II †3 A contrary point (in an argument). M16–E17. 4 The opposite point. Formerly, the antithesis. L16.

B *v.* 1 *v.i.* Compose or play musical counterpoint. *rare.* L19. 2 *v.t.* Write or add a counterpoint to. L19. 3 *v.t.* Set in contrast (*against*); emphasize by juxtaposition the contrast between. M20.

†**counterpoint** *n.*[2] LME–L17. [OFr. *contrepointe*, f. alt. of med.L *culcit(r)a puncta* quilted mattress, f. *culcit(r)a* cushion, mattress + *puncta* fem. of *punctus* (see prec.).] A quilted bed-cover; a counterpane.

counterpoise /ˈkaʊntəpɔɪz/ *n.* LME. [OFr. *countrepeis, -pois* (mod. *contrepoids*), f. as COUNTER- + POISE *n.*[1]] 1 A weight which balances another weight or establishes equilibrium against a force. LME. 2 Something of equivalent force, effect, etc., on the opposite side. LME. †b A compensation; an equivalent. L16–E17. 3 The state of being balanced; equilibrium. L16. 4 A horizontal network of conductors connected to a transmitting aerial just above the ground to reduce losses to earth. E20. 5 A conductor or network of conductors buried in the ground and connected to an electricity pylon in order to reduce the risk of flash-overs caused by lightning. M20.

2 T. COLLINS Deeming my birth and education a sufficient counterpoise to her wealth. b SHAKES. *All's Well* To whom I promise A counterpoise, if not to thy estate A balance more replete. 3 MILTON The pendulous round earth with ballanc't Aire In counterpoise.

counterpoise /ˈkaʊntəpɔɪz/ *v.* LME. [f. tonic stem of OFr. *contrepeser*, f. as COUNTER-, PEISE *v.* Later assim. to the n.] 1 *v.t.* a Balance in power, quality, or effect; compensate for. LME. b Balance by a weight on the opposite side or acting in opposition; counterbalance. M16. †2 *v.i.* Act as a counterbalance (*to, with, against*). LME–M16. 3 *v.t.* Bring into or keep in equilibrium. LME. †4 *v.t.* & *i.* Consider or ponder carefully. LME–L17. 5 *v.t.* Compare (a thing) *with* another to ascertain their relative values. L17.

1a H. FIELDING A weakness which may counterpoise this merit. b W. HARRISON One shilling of siluer in those daies did counterpeise our common ounce. 2 T. NORTON Such a bitternesse of sorrow .. as may in balaunce counterpaise with the trust of pardon. 5 SOUTHEY Who in the deceitful scales Of worldly wisdom, dare to counterpoise The right with the expedient.

counterpoison /ˈkaʊntəpɔɪz(ə)n/ *n.* M16. [Fr. *contrepoison*, f. as COUNTER-, POISON *n.*] 1 A medicine that counteracts the effect of a poison; an antidote (*lit.* & *fig.*). M16. 2 An opposite poison. L18.

counterpose /kaʊntəˈpəʊz/ *v.t.* L16. [f. COUNTER- 1 + POSE *v.*[1], w. influence of COUNTERPOISE *v.* on sense. Cf. CONTRAPOSE.] Set against or in opposition; counterbalance.

counterposition /ˈkaʊntəpəzɪʃ(ə)n/ *n.* L16. [f. COUNTER- 2 + POSITION *n.*, in sense 1 after CONTRAPOSITION.] 1 = CONTRAPOSITION 2. L16. 2 An opposite position. M19.

counterpunch /ˈkaʊntəpʌn(t)ʃ/ *n.* & *v.* L17. [f. COUNTER- 2 + PUNCH *n.*[1]] A *n.* 1 A punch used to make a depression in the face of a typefounder's punch corresponding to an enclosed non-printing part of a letter. L17. 2 A boxer's counter; a punch or an attack given in return. M20. B *v.* 1 *v.t.* Form by means of a counterpunch. L17. 2 *v.i.* Of a boxer etc.: make a counterpunch or counterpunches. Chiefly as *counterpunching* vbl n. M20.

counterpuncher *n.* a defensive boxer; a person who retaliates readily or well: M20.

counter-reformation /ˈkaʊntərɛfə,meɪʃ(ə)n/ *n.* Also **Counter-Reformation**. M19. [f. COUNTER- 2 + REFORMATION *n.*[1]] The activity in the Roman Catholic Church in the 16th and early 17th cents. directed towards countering the effects of the Protestant Reformation.

counter-roll /ˈkaʊntərəʊl/ *n. obs.* exc. *Hist.* E17. [Fr. †*contrerolle* (now *contrôle*), f. med.L *contrarotulus*: see CONTROL *v.*] A copy of a roll or document, kept for purposes of checking.

†**counterrollment** *n.* the making of an entry in a counter-roll: only in L16.

counterrotate /kaʊntərəʊˈteɪt/ *v.i.* M20. [f. COUNTER- 1 + ROTATE *v.*] Rotate in opposite directions, esp. about the same axis; (of a propeller) have blades that do this. Chiefly as *counterrotating* ppl a. (cf. CONTRA-ROTATING).

counterscarp /ˈkaʊntəskɑːp/ *n.* L16. [Fr. *contrescarpe* f. It. *controscarpa*, f. as CONTRA-, SCARP *n.*[2]] **1** The outer wall or slope of a ditch surrounding a fortification; this slope together with the glacis beyond it. L16. **2** *fig.* A means of defence; a protective barrier. E17.

counter-seal /ˈkaʊntəsiːl/ *n.* & *v.* Now *Hist.* E17. [OFr. *contre-seel*, f. as COUNTER-, SEAL *n.*[2]] **A** *n.* A smaller seal impressed on the reverse of a main seal for further security or sanction. Also, the reverse side of a seal. E17. †**B** *v.t.* Seal with a counter-seal. *rare* (Shakes.). Only in E17.

countersign /ˈkaʊntəsʌɪn/ *n.* L16. [Fr. *contresigne* f. It. *contrasegno* (now *contrassegno*), f. as CONTRA- + *segno* f. L *signum* SIGN *n.*] **1** A sign or signal made in response to another sign; *spec.* a password given on request. L16. **2** A special sign or mark put on something for the purpose of authentication, identification, or reference. L16.

countersign /ˈkaʊntəsʌɪn/ *v.t.* M17. [Fr. *contresigner*, f. as COUNTER-, SIGN *v.*] †**1** Mark with a countersign. Only in M17. **2** Sign (a document) near or in addition to another signature; add one's signature to (a document already signed by another). L17. **3** *fig.* Confirm, sanction, ratify. M19.

2 C. PEBODY The Secretary of State . . had countersigned the warrant for his arrest.

counterˈsignature *n.* an additional signature M19.

countersink /ˈkaʊntəsɪŋk/ *v.* & *n.* L18. [f. COUNTER- 1 + SINK *v.*] **A** *v.t.* Pa. t. & pple **-sunk** /-sʌŋk/. **1** Sink the head of (a screw, bolt, etc.) in a countersink so that it does not protrude. L18. **2** Enlarge the outer part of (a drilled hole) by bevelling the edge. Cf. earlier COUNTERSUNK. M19. **B** *n.* **1** A tool for countersinking. L18. **2** A conical enlargement of the outer part of a drilled hole for receiving the head of a screw etc. M19.

countersunk /ˈkaʊntəsʌŋk/ *n.* L18. [f. pa. pple of COUNTERSINK *v.*] = COUNTERSINK *n.* 2.

counter-tenor /kaʊntəˈtɛnə/ *n.* LME. [OFr. *contreteneur* f. It. †*contratenore*, f. as CONTRA- + *tenore* f. L TENOR *n.*[1] Cf. CONTRATENOR.] **1** A part higher than a tenor for a man's voice; a male alto. Formerly, a man's part written against the tenor in the same range. LME. **2** A singer with a counter-tenor voice. E16. **3** A counter-tenor voice. L18.

counter-turn /ˈkaʊntətəːn/ *n.* L16. [f. COUNTER- 2 + TURN *n.* In branch I tr. Gk *antistrophē*.] †**I 1** *Pros.* The continued repetition of the same word at the end of successive clauses. *rare.* Only in L16. †**2** = ANTISTROPHE *n. rare.* Only in M17. **II 3** An unexpected development in the plot of a play etc. at its climax. M17. **4** A turn in the opposite direction. M18.

countervail /kaʊntəˈveɪl/ *v.* & *n.* LME. [AN *countrevaloir* repr. L *contra valere* be of worth against: see CONTRA, VAIL *v.*[1]] **A** *v.* †**1** *v.t.* Be equivalent to in value. LME–M17. **2** *v.t.* Make up for (damage, trouble, etc.), be compensation for. Formerly also, give compensation for. LME. **3** *v.i.* **a** Be of equal force or weight on the contrary side; avail *against*. (Also foll. by †*with*, †*for*.) LME. †**b** Be equivalent or equal; vie *with*. M–L16. **4** *v.t.* Equal, match; be equivalent to. *arch.* M16. †**b** Make an equivalent return for, reciprocate. L16–M17. **5** *v.t.* Avail or be effective against; offset the effect of, counterbalance. M16. †**6** *v.t.* Act against or resist with equal physical force. L16–M17.

2 ADDISON It . . more than countervails all the calamities and afflictions which can possibly befal us. 3a H. A. L. FISHER Such is human nature that great calamities provoke . . countervailing efforts. 5 *Sunday Times* Philby's accession to secret work did something to countervail the rather strong MI5 bias. **countervailing duty**: put on imports to offset a subsidy in the exporting country or a tax on similar goods not from abroad.

B *n.* Something which countervails; an equivalent. Now *rare* or *obs.* L15.

counterweigh /kaʊntəˈweɪ/ *v.* LME. [f. COUNTER- 1 + WEIGH *v.*: cf. COUNTERPOISE *v.*] **1** *v.t.* Mentally weigh (things) against each other. Now *rare* or *obs.* LME. **2** *v.i.* Act as a counterbalance (*lit.* & *fig.*); weigh evenly (*with*, *against*). E16. **3** *v.t.* = COUNTERBALANCE *v.* 2, 3. E19.

counterweight /ˈkaʊntəweɪt/ *n.* L17. [f. COUNTER- 2 + WEIGHT *n.*] A counterbalancing weight.

counterwork /ˈkaʊntəwəːk/ *n.* L16. [f. COUNTER- 2 + WORK *n.*] **1** Work to counteract other work; an opposing act. L16. **2** *Mil.* A work raised in opposition to those of the enemy. M17.

counterwork /ˈkaʊntəwəːk/ *v.* Pa. t. & pple **-worked**, (*arch.*) **-wrought** /-rɔːt/. E17. [f. COUNTER- 1 + WORK *v.*] **1** *v.i.* Work in opposition or with contrary intent. E17. **2** *v.t.* Work against, counteract, frustrate. E17.

counterworker *n.* a person who opposes or works in opposition M19.

countess /ˈkaʊntɪs/ *n.* Also (esp. in titles) **C-**. ME. [OFr. *cuntesse*, *contesse* (mod. *comtesse*) f. med.L *comitissa* fem. of *comes*, *comit-*: see COUNT *n.*[2], -ESS[1].] **1** The wife or widow of an earl or a count; a woman holding the rank of earl or count in her own right. ME. **2** A roofing-slate of a middle size. Cf. DUCHESS 4, LADY *n.* II. E19.

countess-ship *n.* (*rare*) the quality, position, or personality of a countess E17.

counting /ˈkaʊntɪŋ/ *vbl n.* †**compt-**. LME. [f. COUNT *v.* + -ING[1].] The action of COUNT *v.*

counting of the omer: see OMER 2.

Comb.: **counting-frame** an abacus; **counting-house** an office, *esp.* one where accounts are kept; **counting number** *Math.* = *natural number* s.v. NATURAL *a.*; **counting-room** (chiefly *US*) a counting-house.

countless /ˈkaʊntlɪs/ *a.* L17. [f. COUNT *n.*[1] + -LESS.] That cannot be counted or valued; *esp.* too many to be counted.

SHAKES. *Ven. & Ad.* And one sweet kiss shall pay this countless debt. TOLKIEN They saw the torches, countless points of fiery light.

countour /ˈkaʊntə/ *n.* Also **-tor**, **C-**. ME. [AN *count(e)our* lawyer: see COUNTER *n.*[2]] †**1** An accountant; an official who assisted in collecting or auditing the county dues. Only in ME. **2** *Law.* A legal pleader; a serjeant-at-law. *obs.* exc. *Hist.* ME.

countrify /ˈkʌntrɪfʌɪ/ *v.t.* *rare* exc. as COUNTRIFIED. Also **countryfy**. M17. [f. next + -FY.] Give characteristics of the country to; make rural or rustic. Usu. in *pass.*

countrified *ppl a.* (*a*) having country manners and character; rustic, unsophisticated; (*b*) (of scenery) rural, of the kind seen in the country: M18.

country /ˈkʌntri/ *n.* & *a.* ME. [OFr. *cuntrée* (mod. *contrée*) f. med.L, Proto-Romance *contrata* use as n. (sc. *terra* land) of fem. of adj. f. L CONTRA: see -Y[5].] **A** *n.* **1** An expanse of land; a region. ME. **b** Land, territory; *esp.* land with distinct characteristics or associated with (the work of) a particular person. L19. **2** An area of land defined in terms of human occupation, e.g. owned by the same lord or inhabited by speakers of the same language. Formerly, a county, a barony. ME. **b** The fox-hunting area of any one hunt. M19. **3** The territory of a nation; a region constituting an independent State, or a province etc. which was formerly independent and is still distinct in institutions, language, etc. ME. **4** With *possess.* or *absol.* The land of one's birth, citizenship, residence, etc.; one's native land, one's homeland. ME. **5** *The* areas away from cities and conurbations; *the* part of a State outside the capital. ME. **b** More fully *country and western* (*music*), *country music*. Popular music of a style originating in folk music of the rural southern US in which the fiddle, guitar, and banjo were dominant instruments. M20. **6** The people of a district or State; the national population, esp. as electors. Usu. *the country*. ME. **7** *Law.* A jury. *arch.* ME. **8** In full *country rock*. Rock enclosing a mineral deposit or an igneous intrusion. Formerly, rock pierced by lodes other than the principal one. L17. **9** *Naut.* A region of the sea. Now *rare* or *obs.* M18. **10** *Cricket. The* outfield. *slang.* L19.

1 N. SHUTE A country of gracious farms on undulating hilly slopes. b T. KENEALLY Back again in country where the horse was futile. P. MORTIMER Constable country, of course. You care for Constable? *fig.*: A. HAILEY The trio walked deeper into computer country, past rows of . . metal and glass cabinets. 2 SIR W. SCOTT The fort . . constructed for the express purpose of bridling the country of the MacGregors. 3 M. L. KING There were only three independent countries in . . Africa. 4 S. DECATUR Our country! In her intercourse with foreign nations, may she always be in the right, but our country, right or wrong. TENNYSON If love of country move thee there at all. YEATS My country is Kiltartan Cross, My countrymen Kiltartan's poor. G. B. SHAW We call it justice . . or our duty to king and country. 5 V. WOOLF He would give up London . . and live in the country. 6 AV *Gen.* 41:57 All countreys came into Egypt . . for to buy corne. T. STOPPARD The country . . looks to its elected representatives to set a moral standard. 7 H. COX When the prisoner has . . put himself 'upon the country'.

Phrases etc.: **across country** across fields etc., not keeping to (main) roads (cf. CROSS-COUNTRY). **appeal to the country** test the opinion of the electorate by (calling) a general election. *Black Country*: see BLACK *a. country and western* (*music*): see sense 5b above. CROSS-COUNTRY. DOWN-COUNTRY. *free country*: see FREE *a. God's* (*own*) *country*: see GOD *n.* **go to the country** = *appeal to the country* above. *high country*: see HIGH *a. inside country*: see INSIDE *a.* **line of country** a subject etc. with which a person is familiar. *live off the country*: see LIVE *v. Low Countries*: see LOW-COUNTRY. *Lucky Country*: see LUCKY *a. Never Never Country*: see NEVER. *north country*: see NORTH *adv.*, *a.*, *n.*, & *v. old country*: see OLD *a. Queen and country*: see QUEEN *n. red country*: see RED *a. satellite country*: see SATELLITE *n.* 3a. *serve one's country*: see SERVE *v.*[1] SOUTH *country*. *the old country*: see OLD *a. third country*: see THIRD *a.* & *n. town and country planning*: see TOWN *n.* **unknown country** an unfamiliar place or topic. UP-COUNTRY. *West Country*: see WEST *a.*

B *attrib.* or as *adj.* (rarely *pred.*). **1** Of or pertaining to rural as distinct from urban districts; situated or living in the country; belonging to or characteristic of the country, esp. as contrasted with the town. ME. †**2** Of the country, district, or part of the world implied; national. Usu. with possess. or demonstr. adj. LME–E18. **3** Of or belonging to India (or other foreign country) as distinguished from European. *obs.* exc. *Hist.* L16.

1 C. H. WARREN He is country to the core—and Cotswold country at that. G. GORER In a society as urban as that of modern England, country ways represent a survival of earlier patterns. 2 DRYDEN Talk not of our country ladies: I declare myself for the Spanish beauties. 3 T. S. RAFFLES Since the conquest . . a very extensive trade has been carried on in country ships.

Comb. & *special collocations*: **country club** a sporting and social club in a rural district; **country cousin** a countrified relation or other person who is out of place in a city or among city-dwellers; **country dance** an English rural, native, or traditional dance, *esp.* one with couples face to face in long lines (cf. CONTREDANSE); **country dancing** the performing of country dances; **country-folk** (*a*) = *country-people* (a) below; (*b*) (*obs.* exc. *dial.*) = *country-people* (b) below; **country gentleman**: having landed property in a rural area; **country house** a substantial rural residence, *esp.* one of a country gentleman; *country jake*: see JAKE *n.*[1]; *country mouse*: see MOUSE *n.*; *country music*: see sense A.5b above; **country party** a political party supporting agricultural against manufacturing, or national against sectional, interests; **country-people** (*a*) people who live in the country; †(*b*) (with *possess.*) compatriots; *country put*: see PUT *n.*[2]; **country road** †(*a*) a public road made and maintained by a country or province; (*b*) a road leading through a rural area; **country rock** (*a*) see sense A.8 above; (*b*) a blend of country and western and rock music; *country seat*: see SEAT *n.* 11b; **countryside** (*a*) the land and scenery of the country; (*b*) (the inhabitants of) a region or regions in the country; **country-wide** *a.* extending throughout the whole of a nation.

¶ The original stress was on the final syllable, as still in ballads.

countryship *n.* relationship based on (a common) country E17.

countryfy *v.* var. of COUNTRIFY.

countryman /ˈkʌntrɪmən/ *n.* Pl. **-men**. ME. [f. COUNTRY + MAN *n.*] **1** A man (in *pl.* also, people) of a (specified or indicated) country or district. ME. **2** A man (in *pl.* also, people) of one's own country; a compatriot. Usu. w. *possess.* LME. **3** A man (in *pl.* also, people) living in the country, *esp.* one following country ways. L16.

1 *North countryman.* WHAT *countryman?* 2 B. JOWETT Simonides is a countryman of yours. 3 A. F. DOUGLAS-HOME My father was a countryman, and a naturalist, and on the right interpretation of wind or weather depended the action of the day. **countryman's treacle** (now *dial.*) (*a*) garlic, *Allium sativum*; †(*b*) rue, *Ruta graveolens*.

countrywoman /ˈkʌntrɪwʊmən/ *n.* Pl. **-women** /-wɪmɪn/. LME. [f. as prec. + WOMAN *n.*] **1** A female compatriot. Usu. with *possess.* LME. **2** A woman of a (specified or indicated) country or district. L16. **3** A woman who lives in the country, *esp.* one following country ways. L17.

2 NORTH *countrywoman*.

county /ˈkaʊnti/ *n.*[1] & *a.* ME. [AN *counté*, OFr. *cunté*, *conté* (mod. *comté*), f. L *comitatus*, f. *comes*, *comit-*: see COUNT *n.*[2], -Y[5].] **A** *n.* **1** *Hist.* The meeting or court held periodically under the sheriff for the transaction of shire business; a particular session of this court. ME. **2** The domain or territory of a count. *obs.* exc. in *county palatine* s.v. PALATINE *a.*[1] LME. **3** Each of the territorial divisions of Great Britain and Ireland, long forming the chief unit for administrative, judicial, and political purposes and orig. equivalent to the English shire; *Hist.* an English city or town given the status and powers of a county. LME. **b** An administrative division in a British colony or Commonwealth country; in the US, an administrative division next in rank below a state. L17. **4** The people or ratepayers of a county collectively; *esp.* (members of) county families. M17.

3 *Home Counties*: see HOME *a.* *the Six Counties*: see SIX *a.* *the Twenty-six Counties*: see TWENTY *a.*

Comb.: **county borough** *Hist.* a large borough ranking as a county for administrative purposes; **county commissioner** (*a*) a justice of the peace on the commission of a county; (*b*) *US* an elected administrative officer of a county; **county corporate** *Hist.* a city or borough ranking as an administrative county; **county council** the representative governing body of an administrative county; **county court** a court with local civil (and in some countries criminal) jurisdiction; *Hist.* = sense 1 above; **county-court** *v.t.* (*colloq.*) sue in the county court, esp. for debt; **county cricket**: between teams representing counties; **county family**: belonging to the nobility or gentry, with an ancestral seat in a particular county; **county hall** a building where county administration is carried on or (*Hist.*) the county quarter sessions, assizes, etc., were held; **county library** a public library run by a county authority; **county school**: supported by a county council; **county seat** *US* the place which is the administrative centre of a county; **county town** the chief town or administrative capital of a county.

B *adj.* Having the social status or characteristics of county families. E20.

C. ISHERWOOD Mummy's bringing her up to be very county.

†**county** *n.*[2] M16–M19. [App. f. AN *counte* or OFr. and It. *conte* (see COUNT *n.*[2]), with unusual retention of the final vowel, and infl. in form by prec.] = COUNT *n.*[2]

coup /kuː; *foreign* ku (*pl. same*)/ *n.*[1] LME. [(O)Fr. f. med.L *colpus* f. L *colaphus* f. Gk *kolaphos* blow with the fist. Reintroduced f. Fr. in 18 in branch II.] †**I 1** A blow given or received in combat. LME–M16.

II 2 A stroke or move that one makes; *esp.* a notable or strikingly successful move. L18. **b** = COUP D'ÉTAT. M19. **c** *Hist.* Among N. American Indians: the act of touching an enemy, as a deed of bravery; the act of first touching an item of the enemy's in order to claim it. M19. **3** *Billiards.* The direct pocketing of the cue-ball, which is a foul stroke. L18.

2 W. GERHARDIE I made a bold *coup* to regain my tottering prestige. *grand coup*: see GRAND *a.*[2] *Vienna coup*: see VIENNA 1.

Phrases: ***coup d'essai*** /dɛsɛ/ *rare* [lit. 'stroke of trial'] a first attempt. ***coup de force*** /də fɔrs/ [lit. 'stroke of force'] a sudden violent action. ***coup de foudre*** /də fudr/ [lit. 'stroke of lightning'] a sudden unforeseen event; love at first sight. ***coup de glotte*** /də glɔt/ a glottal stop. ***coup de grâce*** /də grɑːs/ [lit. 'stroke of grace'] a blow by which a person condemned or mortally hurt is put out of his or her misery; a decisive finishing stroke. ***coup de main*** /də mɛ̃/ [lit. 'stroke of hand'] (chiefly *Mil.*) a surprise attack. ***coup de maître*** /də mɛːtr/ a master-stroke. ***coup de poing*** /dəpwɛ̃/ [lit. 'stroke of fist'] *Archaeol.* (now *rare*) a hand-axe. ***coup de soleil*** /də sɔlɛːj/ an attack of sunstroke. ***coup de théâtre*** /də teɑːtr/ a theatrical hit; a sensational or dramatically sudden action or turn of events, *spec.* in a play. ***coup de vent*** /də vɑ̃/ [lit. 'stroke of wind'] a whirlwind; a gale. ***coup d'œil*** /dœj/ [lit. 'stroke of eye'] a comprehensive glance; a general view; *Mil.* the action or faculty of rapidly sizing up a position and estimating its advantages etc.

Comb.: **coup stick** among N. American Indians, a stick used to touch the enemy in a coup.

coup /kuːp, kaʊp/ *n.*[2] Now *dial.* Also **cowp**; **coop** /kuːp/. LME. [Perh. same wd as COOP *n.*[1]] A cart or wagon with closed sides and ends for moving dung, lime, etc.

coup /kaʊp/ *n.*[3] *Sc.* M16. [f. COUP *v.*[2]] **1** A fall; an upset. M16. **2** A place for emptying rubbish, a dump. L19.

coup /kuːp/ *v.*[1]*t.* ME. [Fr. *couper*, OFr. *co(l)per*: see COPE *v.*[1]] †**1** Cut; slash. Only as *couped* ppl a. Only in ME. **2** Chiefly *Her.* Cut clean off; depict as having an extremity cut off in a straight line. Chiefly as *couped* ppl a. E16.

2 *Times* The bust appearing on coins will be 'couped', or cut off above the shoulders.

coup /kaʊp/ *v.*[2] *Sc.* LME. [Prob. same wd as COPE *v.*[1]] †**1** *v.i.* Strike; come to blows. Only in LME. **2** *v.t.* Overturn, upset; empty out, as from a cart or wheelbarrow by tilting. L16. **3** *v.i.* Be overturned or upset; fall or tumble over; capsize. L18.

2 *coup the crans*: see CRAN *n.*[1] 3. *coup the creels*: see CREEL *n.*[1]

coup-cart /ˈkaʊpkɑːt/ *n.* Now *dial.* ME. [Origin uncertain: assoc. w. COUP *n.*[2], *n.*[3], or *v.*[2]] **1** = COUP *n.*[2] ME. **2** A cart with a body that tips up to release the load. M18.

coup d'état /kuː deɪˈtɑː, *foreign* ku deta/ *n. phr.* Pl. **coups d'état** /kuːz deɪˈtɑː, *foreign* ku deta/, **coup d'états** /kuː deɪˈtɑːz/. M17. [Fr. lit. 'blow of State'.] A violent or illegal change in government. Formerly also, any sudden and decisive stroke of State policy.

coupe /kuːp/ *n.*[1] L19. [Fr. = goblet f. med.L *cuppa*: see CUP *n.*] **1** A shallow dish; a short-stemmed glass. L19. **2** A dessert of ice-cream, fruit, etc., served in a glass coupe. E20.

coupe /kuːp/ *n.*[2] E20. [Fr. = felling, f. as COUP *v.*[1]] A periodic felling of trees; an area so cleared.

coupé /ˈkuːpeɪ/ *n.* In sense 3b also ***coupe** /kuːp/. E18. [Fr., f. as next. In branch II abbrev. of *carrosse coupé* lit. 'cut carriage'. Cf. earlier COUPEE.] **I 1** Formerly = COUPEE *n.* Now, a step in ballet in which one foot displaces another and weight is transferred to it. E18. **2** *Fencing.* A movement of the sword similar to a disengage, but effected by drawing the sword along and over the point of the opponent's. L19. **II 3a** Chiefly *Hist.* A four-wheeled carriage with a seat for two inside and an outside seat for the driver. M19. **b** An enclosed two-door motor car with two or four seats and (now) usu. a sloping rear. E20. **4** *Hist.* **a** The front or after compartment of a Continental stagecoach. M19. **b** An end compartment in old railway carriages, with seats on one side only. M19.

3b **coupé de ville** /də viːl/ [lit. 'of town'] a car in which the passenger seats are roofed and the driver's seat open or adapted to open.

coupé /ˈkuːpeɪ/ *a. rare.* L16. [Fr., pa. pple of *couper* cut: see COUP *v.*[1]] *Her.* Couped, cut off. Cf. COUP *v.*[1] 2.

coupee /kʊˈpiː, ˈkuːpi/ *n.* & *v. obs.* exc. *Hist.* L17. [f. as COUPÉ *n.*] **A** *n.* A dance step in which the dancer rests on one foot and passes the other forward or backward in a kind of salutation; a bow made while advancing. L17. **B** *v.i.* Perform a coupee; make a bow or salutation in dancing. L17.

coupla *a.* see COUPLE *n.* 5.

couple /ˈkʌp(ə)l/ *n.* ME. [OFr. *cople*, *cuple* (mod. *couple*) f. L COPULA.] **I** A union of two; a pair. **1** A married or engaged man and woman; a set of two people who are habitual companions, live together, etc.; a set of two people associated as partners in a dance etc. ME. **b** (Pl. after numeral often same.) A pair of animals consisting of a male and a female. LME. **2** Either of a pair of inclined rafters that form the main support of a roof. Usu. in *pl.* ME. †**3** = COUPLET 1. *rare.* ME–L16. **4a** (Pl. after numeral often same.) A brace of hunting dogs; a brace of rabbits. LME. **b** A ewe and her lamb. E18. **5** *gen.* Two individuals (persons, animals, or things) of the same sort considered together. Also (w. following quantifier) passing into *adj.* LME. **b** *ellipt.* A couple of alcoholic drinks. *colloq.* M20. **6** *Mech.* A pair of equal but opposite forces acting along parallel lines, tending to cause rotation. M19. **7** A set of two plates of different conducting materials in electrical contact, between which a voltage arises. M19.

1 STEELE A very loving Couple. *happy couple*: see HAPPY *a.* 2 *main couple*: see MAIN *a.* 4a MALORY A noyse as hit hadde ben a thyrtty couple of houndes. 5 J. MCPHEE A couple of tributaries came into the river, the first from the east, the second from the west. **a couple more** (*a.* & *adv.*) (about) two more. **a couple of —**, **a coupla —** [repr. colloq. pronunc.: see A *prep.*[2]] (*US colloq.*) **a couple —** a pair of, (approximately) two. **b** R. KEVERNE Stopped at the 'Swan' for a couple.

II That which unites two. †**8** Union in marriage; the marriage bond; sexual union. ME–E17. **9** *sing.* & (usu.) in *pl.* A brace, a leash, or joined collars for holding two hunting dogs together. LME. †**10** *Gram.* A connecting word or particle, a copula. L16–E18.

8 T. CORYAT To be begotten in the honest and chast couple of marriage. 9 *go, hunt, run, in couples.*

couple /ˈkʌp(ə)l/ *v.* ME. [OFr. *copler*, *cupler* (mod. *coupler*) f. L *copulare* COPULATE.] **I** *v.t.* **1** *gen.* Fasten or link (two things) together or *together*; fasten or link (one thing) *to* another; join, connect. ME. **b** *Chem.* Cause to combine chemically with, esp. with the elimination of a simple molecule. E20. **2** Join or link (immaterial things), associate in thought or speech, (*together*, *with* or *to* something else). ME. †**3a** Join in marriage or sexual union (*together*, *to*). ME–M18. **b** Mate (animals); mate (one animal) *with* another. E18. **4** Bring (persons) together or *together* in pairs or as companions or partners; pair (one person) *with* another, attach (one person) *to* another. Formerly also, match or engage as opponents in a contest. LME. **5** Tie or fasten (hunting dogs) together in pairs or as a pair; pair (one dog) *with* or attach (one dog) *to* another by a leash etc. LME. **6** Connect (one thing) *to* another for joint or coordinated operation; *esp.* connect (one group of pipes in an organ) *to* another by means of a coupler. E19. **7** Connect (railway vehicles *together*, one railway vehicle *to* another) by a coupling. M19. **8** Bring about a coupling between (oscillating systems, subatomic particles, etc.); in *pass.*, interact *with*, be physically or causally connected *to*. Cf. COUPLING 4. L19. **9** *Physics.* Cause to pass, transfer, (*into*, *out of*). L20.

1 POPE Measuring syllables and coupling rhymes. SHELLEY My young lambs coupled two by two With willow bands. 2 W. H. DIXON A man who coupled acts with words. SAKI Their names had naturally been coupled in the match-making gossip of the day. R. V. JONES The background of the Grenadiers coupled with seven years in the O.T.C. 3 SWIFT A parson who couples all our beggars. 4 WORDSWORTH See Latimer and Ridley in the might Of Faith stand coupled for a common flight. 5 P. DRABBLE Coupling young hounds to their elders and betters. 7 C. JACKSON When her Pullman had finally been coupled between two cars of the new train. P. THEROUX The engine was being coupled to the coach. 8 *Scientific American* The predatory adaptation of the lynx meant that the populations of both caribou and arctic hares were tightly coupled to the snowshoe hare population. 9 *Physics Bulletin* The energy is coupled out of the laser using a . . beam divider.

II *v.i.* 10 = COPULATE 2. LME. 11 Come together in a pair; join with another as a companion. Formerly also, engage (*with* another) in a contest. L15. 12 Be able or intended to be coupled (*with*, *to*, etc.). M20.

12 *Nature* One arm . . couples directly into the Hersch cell.

couple-close /'kʌp(ə)lkləʊs/ *n.* L16. [App. f. Fr. *couple* COUPLE *n.* + *close* closed, shut.] 1 *Her.* Either of a pair of cottises in the form of narrow chevrons one quarter the width and often bordering an ordinary chevron. L16. 2 A pair of couples in a roof. M19.

coupled /'kʌp(ə)ld/ *ppl a.* LME. [f. COUPLE *v.* + -ED[1].] 1 Tied, joined, linked, or associated together in pairs. LME. 2 Of a horse or other quadruped: having a specified type of conformation from the forequarters to the hindquarters, as *short-coupled*, *well-coupled*, etc. M17.

1 **coupled columns** *Archit.* columns disposed in pairs close together, with wider intervals between the pairs.

†couplement *n.* M16. [OFr., f. as COUPLE *v.*: see -MENT.] 1 The act of coupling; the fact of being coupled. M16–M18. 2 A couple, a pair. L16–E19.

coupler /'kʌplə/ *n.* M16. [f. COUPLE *v.* + -ER[1].] 1 A person who couples, or couples things together. M16. 2 A thing that couples or links things together; *spec.* a device in an organ, harpsichord, etc., for connecting two manuals, a manual with a pedal, or two keys, so that both can be played with a single motion. M17. 3 *Photogr.* A compound in a developer or an emulsion which combines with the products of development to form an insoluble dye, part of the image. M20. 4 In full *acoustic coupler*. A modem which converts digital signals from a computer into audible sound signals and vice versa, so that the former can be transmitted and received over telephone lines. M20.

coupleress *n.* (*rare*) a female coupler; a procuress: M19.

couplet /'kʌplɪt/ *n.* L16. [(O)Fr., dim. of *couple* COUPLE *n.*: see -ET[1].] 1 A pair of successive lines of verse, esp. when rhyming together and of the same length. L16. 2 *gen.* A pair, a couple. E17. 3 *Archit.* A window of two lights. M19. 4 *Mus.* A duplet. L19.

1 *heroic couplet*: see HEROIC *a.*

couple'teer *n.* a writer of couplets; a versifier: E19.

coupling /'kʌplɪŋ/ *n.* ME. [f. COUPLE *v.* + -ING[1].] I An action or state. 1 Joining in couples; (a) pairing, (a) linking. ME. 2 (An act of) sexual intercourse. LME. 3 *Genetics.* More fully *gametic coupling* = LINKAGE 2. Now *rare.* E20. 4 *Physics.* A mutual dependence of oscillations or oscillatory systems; an interaction, esp. by means of an electromagnetic etc. field. E20. b A causal relationship. L20.

1 R. W. EMERSON Their realistic logic, or coupling of means to ends. 2 I. MCEWAN One of the most desolating couplings known to copulating mankind. 4 *Scientific American* The howl was caused by acoustic coupling between the transducers. B. LOVELL A magnetic coupling between the Sun and the planetary disk. *loose coupling*: see LOOSE *a.*

II A thing joining or joined. 5 *gen.* Something that couples things or is used to join things together. M16. 6 A transverse timber connecting a pair of inclined ones in a roof. L16. †7 *sing.* (usu.) in *pl.* = COUPLE *n.* 9. Only in 17. 8 A device for connecting parts of machinery, esp. in order to transmit motion; *spec.* (*a*) a device for connecting two shafts; (*b*) a link by which two railway vehicles are connected in a train. E19. 9 (The conformation of) the part of the body of a horse or other quadruped between the forequarters and the hindquarters. L19. 10 The recording on the other side or the remainder of a gramophone record; a pair of recordings on the same record. M20.

8 *universal coupling*: see UNIVERSAL *a.* 10 *Gramophone* The only modern rival in this coupling.

Comb.: **coupling coefficient**: representing the degree of coupling between electric circuits etc.; **coupling constant** *Physics*: representing the strength of the interaction between a particle and a field; **coupling-pin**: that secures the connection between a train's carriages, a lorry's cab and trailer, etc.; **coupling-reins**: that couple a pair of horses together; **coupling-rod**: that connects two cranks so that they turn as one, e.g. in a steam engine.

coupon /'kuːpɒn/ *n.* & *v.* E19. [Fr. = piece cut off, slice, f. *couper* to cut: see COPE *v.*[1], -OON.] A *n.* 1 A detachable portion of a stock certificate which is given up in return for a payment of interest; any detachable ticket entitling the holder to something, esp. the purchase of rationed goods. E19. b The nominal rate of interest on a fixed-interest stock. M20. 2 A voucher issued with a product for the purchaser to exchange for cash or goods; part of a printed wrapper etc. used similarly. E20. 3 Part of an advertisement which a reader can fill in and send to the advertiser for more information or as an order for goods. E20. 4 An entry-form for a competition, esp. for a football pool. E20. 5 *Hist.* A recommendation given by a party leader to a parliamentary candidate. E20.

2 *cigarette coupon* etc. 4 *football coupon*, *pools coupon*, etc.

Comb.: **coupon bond**: on which interest is paid by coupons; **coupon-clipper** *colloq.* (*a*) *US* a person with a large number of coupon bonds; a wealthy person; (*b*) a person who cuts out and uses coupons (for discounts on goods, etc.) from newspapers and magazines; **coupon-free** *a.* obtainable without coupons.

B *v.t.* 1 *Hist.* Give party approval to (a parliamentary candidate). E20. 2 Ration by means of coupons. M20.

coupon(n)ed *a.* (*a*) having or bearing a coupon; (*b*) that has been couponed: L19.

coupure /kuː'pjʊə/ *n.* E18. [Fr., f. *couper* cut: see COPE *v.*[1], -URE.] *Mil.* A ditch or trench, *esp.* one dug for defence; in *Fortif.*, a passage cut through the glacis to facilitate sallies by the besieged.

courage /'kʌrɪdʒ/ *n.* & *v.* ME. [OFr. *corage*, *curage* (mod. *courage*) f. Proto-Romance, f. L *cor* heart: see -AGE.] A *n.* †1 The heart as the seat of feeling etc.; disposition, nature. ME–M17. †2 What is in one's mind; purpose; desire, inclination. ME–E17. †3a Anger; pride, haughtiness; boldness. LME–E17. b Spirit, vigour. L15–E17. c Sexual vigour; lust. E16–E17. 4 The quality of character which shows itself in facing danger undaunted or in acting despite fear or lack of confidence. LME. b As *int.* Take courage! Cheer up! L16.

4 R. H. HUTTON Illusions from which . . men have had the courage to break free. E. LONGFORD Ney faced the firing squad with the courage to be expected of 'the bravest of the brave'. **courage of one's convictions** the courage to act in accordance with one's beliefs. **Dutch courage** *colloq.* temporary boldness induced by drinking alcohol. *moral courage*: see MORAL *a.* **take one's courage in both hands** nerve oneself to a venture.

†B *v.t.* Encourage. LME–E17.

couraged *a.* having courage (now only in comb., as *high-couraged*) L15. **courageless** *a.* (now *rare*) without courage L16.

courageous /kə'reɪdʒəs/ *a.* ME. [AN *corageous*, OFr. *corageus* (mod. *courageux*), f. as COURAGE: see -OUS.] 1 Having or showing courage; brave, valiant. ME. †2 Eager (*to do* something). Only in ME. †3 Virile, vigorous, lusty. LME–L16.

courageously *adv.* LME. **courageousness** *n.* LME.

courant /kʊ'rant/ *n.*[1] & *a.* E17. [Fr., pres. pple of *courir* run f. L *currere*: see -ANT[1]. Cf. CORANTO *n.*[2]] A *n.* †1 A running string. Only in E17. †2 An express messenger or message. E17–E18. 3 A newspaper. *obs.* exc. in titles of newspapers. E17. B *adj. Her.* Of an animal: running. E18.

†**couranteer** *n.* a journalist E–M18.

courant *n.*[2] see next.

courante /kʊ'rɒ̃(n)t, -rɑːnt/ *n.* Also **-rant** /-'rant/. L16. [Fr., use as n. of fem. pres. pple of *courir*: see COURANT *n.*[1] & *a.* Cf. CORANTO *n.*[1]] 1 A court dance of the 16th and 17th cents. characterized by glides and light hops. L16. 2 *Mus.* A piece of music for this dance; a piece of music in triple time, *esp.* one which forms a movement of a suite. L16.

†courb *v.i.* & *t.* Also **curb**. LME–E19. [(O)Fr. *courber* f. L *curvare* CURVE *v.*] Bend, bow.

courbash *n.* & *v.* var. of KOURBASH.

courbette /kʊə'bɛt/ *n.* M17. [Fr. f. It. *corvetta*: see CURVET.] A leap in *haute école* in which a trained horse rears up and jumps forward on the hind legs without the forelegs' touching the ground.

coureur /kurœːr/ *n.* Pl. pronounced same. E18. [Fr. = (wood-)runner.] *Hist.* In full *coureur de bois* /də bwa/. A woodsman, trader, etc., of French origin in Canada and the northern US.

courge /kʊəʒ/ *n.* M19. [Fr. = GOURD f. OFr. *cohourde* f. L *cucurbita*.] A basket for holding live bait, towed behind a fishing boat.

courgette /kʊə'ʒɛt/ *n.* M20. [Fr., f. as prec.: see -ETTE.] A small variety of vegetable marrow. Also called *zucchini*.

courida /kuːrɪ'dɑː/ *n.* E19. [Prob. f. Carib.] In Guyana, the black mangrove.

courier /'kʊrɪə/ *n.* & *v.* LME. [Fr. †*courier* (now *courrier*) f. It. *corriere* (med.L *currerius*), f. *correre* to run f. L *currere*: see -IER. In sense 1 f. OFr. *coreor* (mod. *coureur*) f. Proto-Romance, f. L *currere*.] A *n.* 1 A running messenger, a messenger sent in haste; a special messenger. Also in titles of newspapers. LME. b A messenger for an underground or espionage organization. E20. †2 *Mil.* A light horseman acting as skirmisher or scout. E16–E17. 3 A person employed on a journey to make the necessary travel arrangements, now esp. to assist and guide a party of tourists. L16.

1 H. KISSINGER I sent a courier to Bonn . . with personal letters to Bahr and Rush.

B *v.t.* & *i.* Attend or travel as a courier. E19.

course /kɔːs/ *n.*[1] & *adv.* As adv. also **'course**. ME. [(O)Fr. *cours* f. L *cursus*, f. *curs-* pa. ppl stem of *currere* run; reinforced by (O)Fr. *course* f. Proto-Romance use as n. of fem. pa. pple.] A *n.* I Action, direction, or place of running. †1 A run; a gallop. ME–L17. 2 Onward movement in a particular path, as of a celestial object, a ship, etc. ME. †3 Impetus; force. ME–E16. 4 The charge of combatants in a battle or tournament; a bout, an encounter. *obs.* exc. *Hist.* ME. †5a Running (of liquids); flow, flux. ME–M17. b The faculty or opportunity of moving, flowing, etc. LME. †c Circulation (of money etc.); currency. LME–E16. 6 The ground on which a race is run; the route to be taken, with any obstacles to be negotiated, in a race (passing into sense 26). ME. b More fully *golf course*. An area of land on which golf is played. L19. 7 The path taken by a moving body, a stream, etc., *esp.* the intended route of a ship or aircraft; the line of a mountain chain etc. ME. b A channel in which water flows; a watercourse. LME. c The direction in which a ship or aircraft is travelling. M16. d In *pl.* The points of the compass. E17. 8 A race. *arch.* LME. 9 The pursuit of game (esp. hares) with greyhounds by sight rather than scent. LME. †10 A fashionable riding or driving place. M17–M18.

2 S. JOHNSON They slackened their course. 5b AV *2 Thess.* Pray for us, that the word of the Lord may have free course. 6 A. E. T. WATSON A familiar phrase on the turf is 'horses for courses'. . . The Brighton Course is very like Epsom, and horses that win at one meeting often win at the other. *racecourse*, *racing-course*, etc. 7 F. L. WRIGHT The course of the sun as it goes from

east to west. c L. MACNEICE In sight of Stornoway harbour the captain altered his course.

II *fig.* Of time, events, or action. **11** The continuous process (of time), succession (of events); progress through successive stages. ME. †**b** Length (in time), duration. M17–E18. **12** Habitual or regular manner of procedure; custom, practice. ME. **13** Life viewed as a race that is run; a person's career. LME. †**14** The purport or general drift of a narrative. M16–E18. †**15** Appointed order of succession. M16–E17. **16** A line of conduct, a person's method of proceeding. L16.

11 L. STRACHEY In the ordinary course, the Queen never saw a Tory. R. P. WARREN At some time or other during the course of almost every meeting of the board. A. C. BOULT Richter's influence on the whole course of British music was immense. **13** M. HANMER Where he made an end of his course. **16** DISRAELI Our wisest course will be to join the cry. E. PEACOCK He had made up his mind to a certain course of action.

III (Each member of) a consecutive series. **17** Each of the successive divisions of a meal, as soup, meat, pudding, etc. ME. **18a** A row, a layer. *obs.* exc. in *Building*. LME. **b** A single horizontal row of bricks etc. in a wall. LME. **c** *Mus.* A group of strings tuned to the same note and placed side by side so that they can be plucked together. L19. **d** A row of knitted stitches. M20. †**19** Any of several successive attacks, as of a disease or of the dogs in bear-baiting. LME–E19. †**20a** The time for anything which comes to each person in turn; (a person's) turn. LME–M17. **b** Each of two or more groups of people who take turns. L15–M17. **21** In *pl.* A woman's periods. M16. **22** A set of things, esp. (*Hist.*) candles, made or used at the same time. M16. **23** A planned or prescribed series of actions, esp. lessons etc. or therapeutic measures; the content of or a text for such a series of lessons. M16. **b** *Eccl.* The prescribed series of prayers for the seven canonical hours. L16. **24** *Campanol.* The successive shifting of the order in which a particular bell is struck; a series of changes which brings the bells back to their original order. L17. **25** A particular mode of rotating crops; a cycle of crop rotation. M18. **26** A series of fences, obstacles, etc., to be negotiated in a race, competition, or exercise; these and the ground on which they are situated (passing into sense 6). L19.

20a G. HAVERS Trouble and peace . . comfort and discontent, come all of them by courses. **23** GIBBON A regular course of study and exercise was judiciously instituted. P. H. NEWBY They gave him a course of drugs. *fig.*: T. DUNCAN It's a wonderful short course in human nature, being a doctor's son in a town of eight hundred. *correspondence course, crash course, orientation course, refresher course, (thick) sandwich course*, etc. **26** M. C. SELF The course is set up with a variety of jumps placed around the hall or ring. *assault course, obstacle course*, etc.

IV **27** A sail bent to the lowest yard on the mast of a square-rigged ship, esp. on the foremast, mainmast, or mizen-mast. LME.

Phrases: **a matter of course** the natural or expected thing. †**by course** (*a*) in due course; duly; (*b*) by turns, alternately. *clerk of the course*: see CLERK *n.* **course of nature** the ordinary recurring processes of nature. *damp(-proof) course*: see DAMP *n. horses for courses*: see HORSE *n.* **in course** (*a*) (now *Eccl.*) in order, in turn; †(*b*) = *in due course* below; (*c*) (now *non-standard*) naturally, of course. **in course of** in the process of (construction, being constructed, etc.). **in due course** in the usual or natural order; at about the expected time. **in the course of** while *doing*; during the progress or length of (*in the course of things*, in the ordinary sequence of events). *main course*: see MAIN *a. middle course*: see MIDDLE *a.* **of course** (*a*) (now *rare* exc. in *a matter of course* above) customary, natural, to be expected; (*b*) in the ordinary course of things, as a natural result; (*c*) naturally, obviously; admittedly. **off course** not on course. **on course** †(*a*) in the ordinary course of things; (*b*) following the right path or direction or (*fig.*) the course that will have the desired or specified result. *par for the course*: see PAR *n.*[1] 4. *reciprocal course*: see RECIPROCAL *a.* **run its course** complete its natural development. *shape one's course*: see SHAPE *v. stay the course*: see STAY *v.*[1] **take its course** = *run its course* above. *warn off the course*: see WARN *v.*[1] 7c.

Comb.: **course-book**: for use on a course of study; *course unit*: see UNIT *n.*[1] 2d; **courseware** material for a training course, esp. in computing.

B *adv.* = *of course* (c) above. *colloq.* L19.

†**course** *n.*[2] var. of KOS.

course /kɔːs/ *v.*[1] LME. [f. the n.] †**1** *v.t.* Persecute, harass. LME–E17. **2** *v.i.* Gallop about, run, career; flow swiftly. L15. †**b** *fig.* Run *over* or *through* a set of particulars, writings, etc. L16–M18. **3** *v.t.* Exercise, run, (a horse). L15. **4** *v.t.* & *i.* Hunt (game) with hounds; *spec.* hunt (hares etc.) with greyhounds by sight rather than scent; use (greyhounds) to hunt hares in this way. E16. **5** *v.i.* Direct one's course; take a course. M16. **6** *v.t. gen.* Chase, pursue; follow quickly. L16. †**7** *v.t.* Chase with blows; thrash. L16–E17. †**8** *v.i.* Run a course (in a fight or tournament). *rare* (Spenser). Only in L16. **9** *v.t.* Move swiftly over (a place) or along (a path). E18.

2 P. LARKIN The rain courses in cart-ruts down the deep mud lane. **b** MILTON It were tedious to course through all his writings.

coursing *n.* the action of the vb; *spec.* the sport of hunting hares etc. with greyhounds by sight rather than scent: E16.

course *v.*[2] var. of CORSE *v.*

course libre /kurs libr/ *n. phr.* Pl. **-s -s** (pronounced same). M20. [Fr. = free course.] A bullfight, as in France, in which the bull is baited but not killed.

courser /ˈkɔːsə/ *n.*[1] ME. [Orig. repr. OFr. *courseur* f. L *cursor* CURSOR; later prob. f. COURSE *v.*[1] or *n.*[1] + -ER[1]. In sense 4 after mod.L *Cursorius* genus name, lit. 'adapted to running'.] †**1** A runner in a race. ME–M17. †**2** A chaser, a pursuer. L16–L17. **3** A dog used for coursing; a person who goes coursing. E17. **4** Any of several long-legged birds of the Old World genus *Cursorius* and allied genera, related to the pratincoles, which are found in open usu. arid parts of Africa and Asia. M18.

courser /ˈkɔːsə/ *n.*[2] ME. [OFr. *corsier* (mod. *coursier*) f. Proto-Romance f. L *cursus* COURSE *n.*[1]: see -ER[2].] **1** A swift horse. Formerly, a large powerful horse ridden in battle. Now *poet.* ME. **2** A stallion. *obs.* exc. *Sc.* LME.

courses libres *n. phr.* pl. of COURSE LIBRE.

court /kɔːt/ *n.*[1] ME. [AN *curt* f. OFr. *cort* (mod. *cour*) f. Proto-Romance f. L *cohors*, *cohort-*: see COHORT.] **I** An enclosed area. **1** A clear space enclosed by walls or buildings; at Cambridge University, a college quadrangle. ME. **b** A subdivision of a building open to the general roof. M19. **2** A large building or set of buildings standing in a courtyard; a large house, *Hist.* a manor house. Now only in proper names. ME. **3** A walled or marked-off quadrangular area for playing one of certain games involving the striking of a ball, as tennis, squash, etc.; a marked-off division of such an area. E16. **4** A confined yard opening off a street; a yard surrounded by houses and communicating with the street by an entry. L17.

3 *badminton court, croquet court, fives court, squash court, tennis-court*, etc. *clay court, grass court, hard court*, etc. **4** V. WOOLF Jacob's rooms . . were in Neville's Court.

II A princely residence or household. **5** The place where a monarch etc. lives and holds state. ME. **b** In full *court shoe*. A woman's light shoe with a low-cut upper and often a high heel. L19. **6** The establishment and surroundings of a monarch with his or her retinue. With or without determiner (article, possess. or demonstr. adj., etc.). ME. **7** The monarch with his or her ministers and councillors as the ruling power. Treated as *sing.* ME. **8** A monarch's retinue; the body of courtiers collectively. Treated as *pl.* ME. **9** Formal assembly of the monarch and his or her retinue. Chiefly in *hold, keep court*. ME. **10** Homage; flattering attention, courtship. Chiefly in *pay* (or *make*) *court* (*to*). L16.

5 SHAKES. *A.Y.L.* Dispatch you with your safest haste, And get you from our court. LD MACAULAY The quarters of William now began to present the appearance of a court. **6** N. MITFORD No tiara, no necklace, what will the poor child wear at Court? **8** THACKERAY The king and the whole court. *fig.*: H. ACTON A life of generous affluence surrounded by a court of writers and artists. **9** DRYDEN That sweet isle where Venus keeps her court.

III A place of law or administration. **11** (A session of) an assembly of judges or other persons acting as a tribunal legally appointed to hear and determine causes. Also more fully *court of law, justice, judicature*. ME. **12** A place or hall in which justice is administered. With or without determiner (article, possess. or demonstr. adj., etc.). ME. **13** (A meeting of) the members or the managers of a company collectively. E16. **b** A local branch of certain friendly societies. M19.

Phrases: *civil court*: see CIVIL *a. contempt of court*: see CONTEMPT *n.* 3. *Court of Appeal(s)*: see APPEAL *n.* 1. *Court of Arches*: see ARCH *n.*[1] 1. *Court of Audience*: see AUDIENCE 2. *Court of Augmentations*: see AUGMENTATION 1. *Court of Cassation*: see CASSATION *n.*[1] *court of chancery*, etc.: see CHANCERY 2. **Court of Claims**: in which claims, *spec.* (*US*) against the government, are adjudicated. *court of first instance*: see INSTANCE *n.* **court of inquiry** a tribunal appointed in the armed forces to investigate a matter and decide whether a court martial is called for. *court of judicature, justice, law*: see sense 11 above. *court of peculiars*: see PECULIAR *n. Court of Piepowders*: see PIEPOWDER. *court of record*: see RECORD *n. Court of Request(s)*: see REQUEST *n. court of review*: see REVIEW *n.* **Court of Rome** the papal Curia. **Court of St James's** the British monarch's court. *Court of Session*: see SESSION *n.* 4b. *Court of Star Chamber*: see STAR *n.*[1] & *a. criminal court*: see CRIMINAL *a.* 2. *customary court*: see CUSTOMARY *a.* 1. *Divisional Court*: see DIVISIONAL 2. **General Court** a legislative assembly, *spec.* that of Massachusetts or New Hampshire. **go to court** take legal action. *High Court*: see HIGH *a. High Court of Justiciary*: see JUSTICIARY *n.*[2] **High Court of Parliament** Parliament. *higher court*: see HIGHER *a.* **hold court** *fig.* preside over one's admirers etc. *Inn of Court*: see INN *n. in open court*: see OPEN *a. juvenile court*: see JUVENILE *a. last-court*: see LAST *n.*[3] *laugh out of court*: see LAUGH *v. lower court*: see LOWER *a. magistrates' court*: see MAGISTRATE 3. *motor court*: see MOTOR *n.* & *a. Orphan's Court*: see ORPHAN *n.* 1. **out of court** (*a*) (of a plaintiff) having forfeited his or her claim to be heard; (*b*) (of a settlement) reached before the hearing or judgement; (*c*) *fig.* not worthy of consideration, having no claim to be considered. *prevotal court*: see PREVOTAL *a. rule of court*: see RULE *n. service court*: see SERVICE *n.*[1] *small-claims court*: see SMALL *a. spiritual court*: see SPIRITUAL *a.* 2. *standing rule of court*: see RULE *n. suit of court*: see SUIT *n.* 1a. *superior court*: see SUPERIOR *a. Supreme Court*: see SUPREME *a.* 2. *Supreme Court of Judicature*: see JUDICATURE. **the ball is in your court** *fig.* you must be next to act. *the Verge of the Court*: see VERGE *n.* 9. *ward of court*: see WARD *n.* 15a.

Comb.: **court-card** [orig. *coat-card*: see COAT *n.*] a playing-card other than a joker or a tarot, bearing the representation of a human figure (king, queen, jack, etc.), typically ranking above the sequence of numerals; *Court Christian*: see CHRISTIAN *a.*; **court circular** a daily report of the doings of the court issued to the press; **court-craft** (*a*) the art practised or required at court; (*b*) skill in the movements and positioning of a tennis player; **court cupboard** a 16th- or 17th-cent. sideboard for displaying plate etc., *esp.* one consisting of three open shelves and sometimes a small cupboard in the upper half; **court-day**: on which a (legal etc.) court is held or a prince holds court; **court dress** formal dress as worn at court; **court fool** = *court jester* below; **court-hand** a style of handwriting used in English courts of law until prohibited there by an act of 1731; †**court holy water** insincere flattery; **court-house** (*a*) a building in which courts of law are held; (*b*) *US* the seat of government of a county; (*c*) *US* a building containing the main administrative offices of a county; **court jester**: kept to entertain a court; *court leet*: see LEET *n.*[1] 1; **court-man** a (male) courtier; **court-metre** = DRÓTTKVÆTT; **court order**: given by a court of law and requiring a party to do or refrain from doing a specified act; **court party** a political party advocating the interests of the court; **court-plaster** [from its former use for beauty spots by ladies at court] sticking-plaster made of silk coated with isinglass; **court roll** *Hist.* a record of a manorial court giving the holdings, rents, successions, etc., of the tenants; **courtroom**: in which a court of law is held; *court shoe*: see sense 5b above; **court tennis** *N. Amer.* real tennis; **court week** *US*: during which the county court meets; **courtyard** a court (sense 1 above), *esp.* one adjacent to a house.

courtlet *n.* a small or petty court M19. **courtlike** *a.* after the manner of the Court; courtly, elegant, polite:

M16. **courtling** *n.* (*a*) a young or minor courtier; †(*b*) any courtier: L16.

†court *n.*[2] ME–E18. [Origin unkn.] A kind of cart.

court /kɔːt/ *v.* E16. [After OIt. *corteare* (mod. *corteggiare*), OFr. *courtoyer* (mod. *courtiser*), f. *cort* COURT *n.*[1]] †**1** *v.i.* Be or reside at court. E–M16. †**2** *v.t.* w. *it.* Act the courtier. M16–M17. **3** *v.t.* Seek the favourable attention of, pay courteous attention to. L16. **4** *v.t.* Try to win the affection of, esp. with a view to marriage; woo. L16. **5** *v.i.* Behave amorously; conduct a courtship. L16. **6** *v.t.* Set out to gain or win (popularity etc.). L16. **7** *v.t.* Allure, entice (*from*, *to do*, etc.). E17. **8** *v.t.* Unwisely invite, incur the risk of, (inquiry, disaster, etc.). M20.

3 GOLDSMITH To flatter kings, or court the great. 4 M. PUZO He had been courting his second wife in Spain, trying to get her to marry him. *fig.*: W. MOTHERWELL Their broad sheets court the breeze. 5 R. BURNS When feather'd pairs are courting. 6 E. J. HOWARD 'Are you glad I'm back?' she asked the children—hearing herself courting their approbation. 7 S. JOHNSON An interval of calm sunshine courted us out to see a cave on the shore. 8 G. B. SHAW A prophet who . . courted and suffered a cruel execution. K. TYNAN A dramatist could inject a shot of colloquialism into a tragic aria without courting bathos.

courter *n.* a person who courts E17.

court-baron /kɔːtˈbar(ə)n/ *n.* LME. [AN, earlier *court de baroun* (AL *curia baronis*) court of the baron.] *Hist.* A usu. annual court for dealing with small civil disputes, consisting of the freehold tenants of a manor under the presidency of the steward.

court bouillon /kur bujɔ̃/ *n. phr.* M17. [Fr., f. *court* short (f. as CURT) + BOUILLON.] A stock made from wine, vegetables, etc., in which fish is boiled.

courteous /ˈkɔːtjəs/ *a.* ME. [OFr. *corteis*, *curteis* (mod. *courtois*) f. Proto-Romance (as COURT *n.*[1]) + *-ensis* -ESE (*-eous* replacing *-eis* in 16.)] **1** Having manners such as befit the court of a prince; polite, kind, considerate, in manner or approach. ME. †**2** Of a superior: gracious. ME–E19. **3** Of a deed, quality, etc.: appropriate to a courteous person, showing courtesy. ME.

courteously *adv.* ME. **courteousness** *n.* LME.

†courtepy *n.* ME–M19. [MDu. *korte pïe*, f. *kort* (f. as CURT) + *pïe* (mod. *pij*) coat, habit.] A short coat of coarse material worn in medieval times.

courtesan /kɔːtɪˈzan/ *n.* Also **-zan**. M16. [Fr. *courtisane* f. It. †*cortigiana* fem. of *cortigiano* courtier, f. *corte* COURT *n.*[1]] A prostitute, *esp.* one whose clients are wealthy or upper-class.

courtesanship *n.* the practice and position of a courtesan, high-class prostitution M19.

courtesy /ˈkɔːtɪsi/ *n.* & *a.* In sense A.4 also **curtesy**. See also CURTSY *n.* ME. [OFr. *curtesie*, *co(u)r-* (mod. *courtoisie*), f. as COURTEOUS: see -Y[3].] **A** *n.* **1** Courteous behaviour; graceful politeness or consideration towards others. ME. **2** Courteous disposition, courteousness. Formerly also, nobleness, benevolence. ME. **3** A courteous act or expression. ME. **4** *Law* (now *Hist.*). A tenure by which a husband, after his wife's death, held certain kinds of property which she had inherited. Also *courtesy of England*, *of Scotland*. ME. †**5a** Customary expressing of respect by action or gesture, esp. to a superior. Chiefly in *make*, *do courtesy*. E16–M17. **b** A curtsy. *arch.* L16. †**6** A moderate quantity. (Earlier as CURTSY *n.* 1.) M16–E17.

1 I. COMPTON-BURNETT She was your guest, and entitled to courtesy at your hands. 2 A. WILSON Sir Edgar's old-world courtesy never deserts him.

Phrases: **by courtesy** by favour, not by right. **(by) courtesy of** with the kind permission of, through the good offices of, with thanks to. †*remember one's courtesy*: see REMEMBER 1.

Comb.: **courtesy call** a social call made for no more special reason than that of general courtesy; **courtesy cop** *slang* a police officer whose duty it is to persuade motorists etc. by polite firmness to drive well; **courtesy light** a light in a motor vehicle which comes on automatically when a door is opened; **courtesy title** a title of no legal validity given by social custom, *esp.* that of a peer's son or daughter.

B *attrib.* or as *adj.* (Supplied) free of charge, as a courtesy. Chiefly *N. Amer.* M20.

D. LODGE He tries to read a courtesy copy of *Time*.

courtesy /ˈkɔːtɪsi/ *v.* L16. [f. the n.: cf. CURTSY *v.*] †**1** *v.t.* Treat with courtesy. Only in L16. **2** *v.i.* & (*rare*) *t.* Curtsy (to). M17.

courtezan *n.* var. of COURTESAN.

courtier /ˈkɔːtɪə/ *n.* ME. [AN *courte(i)our*, f. OFr. *courtoyer*: see COURT *v.* Ending assim. to -IER through *-e(y)er*.] **1** A person who attends or frequents a royal court. ME. †**2** A wooer. E17–M18.

courtierism *n.* the practice or quality of a courtier M19. **courtierly** *a.* having the characteristics of a courtier L19. **courtiership** *n.* the practice or position of a courtier M16.

courtly /ˈkɔːtli/ *a.* ME. [f. COURT *n.*[1] + -LY[1].] **1** Such as befits a royal court; polished, refined, markedly courteous. ME. †**2** Of or pertaining to a royal court. L15–L19. **3** Given to flattery; obsequious. E17.

1 F. BURNEY I could but accede, though I fear with no very courtly grace. **courtly love** a highly conventionalized medieval tradition of chivalric love and etiquette first developed by the troubadours of southern France (cf. AMOUR COURTOIS).

courtliness *n.* L15.

courtly /ˈkɔːtli/ *adv.* L15. [f. as prec. + -LY[2].] In courtly fashion.

court martial /kɔːt ˈmɑːʃ(ə)l/ *n. phr.* Pl. **courts martial, court-martials**. Also †**court marshal**. LME. [f. COURT *n.*[1] + MARTIAL *a.*, in early use freq. identified w. MARSHAL *n.*[1]] †**1** A court presided over by the Constable and Marshal of England. LME–M17. **2** A judicial court held in one of the armed forces under its disciplinary code. M16.

court-martial /kɔːtˈmɑːʃ(ə)l/ *v.t.* Infl. **-ll-**, ***-l-**. M19. [f. prec.] Try by court martial.

court of guard /kɔːt əv ˈgɑːd/ *n. phr.* L16. [Alt.] *Hist.* = CORPS *de garde*.

courtship /ˈkɔːtʃɪp/ *n.* L16. [f. COURT *n.*[1] + -SHIP.] †**1** Courtliness of manners; courteous behaviour. L16–E18. †**2** The state befitting a court or courtier; position at court, courtiership. L16–M17. †**3** Court-craft; diplomacy, flattery, etc. L16–M18. †**4** The activity of paying courteous attentions. L16–E18. **5** The activity or period of courting a woman with a view to marriage. L16. **b** Animal behaviour that precedes and leads up to copulation. L18. **6** The action of enticing or seeking to win over. E18.

5 F. ASTAIRE They were married after a brief courtship. 6 BYRON In vain from side to side he throws His form, in courtship of repose.

couscous /ˈkuːskuːs/ *n.*[1] Also **kouskous, couscoussou** /ˈkuːskuːsuː/. E17. [Fr. f. Arab. *kuskus*, *kuskusū*, prob. of Berber origin. Cf. CUSCUS *n.*[1]] A spicy N. African dish of crushed wheat or coarse flour steamed over broth, freq. with meat or fruit added; the granules of flour from which this dish is made.

couscous *n.*[2] var. of CUSCUS *n.*[2]

couscoussou *n.* var. of COUSCOUS *n.*[1]

cousin /ˈkʌz(ə)n/ *n.* & *a.* ME. [OFr. *cosin*, *cusin* (mod. *cousin*) f. L *consobrinus* mother's sister's child, f. as CON- + *sobrinus* second cousin, f. *soror* sister.] **A** *n.* **1** The child of one's uncle or aunt. Also *first cousin*. ME. **2** Any collateral relative. Formerly *esp.* a nephew or niece; now always, a relative at least as distant as a first cousin. ME. †**3** *Law.* One's next of kin; a person one was next of kin to. LME–M17. **4** (Also **C-**.) **a** A title used by a monarch in formally addressing another monarch or a nobleman of the same realm. LME. **b** As *voc.* Friend. Freq. w. following pers. name. Now chiefly *dial.* LME. **5** *fig.* A person or thing having affinity of nature to another. LME. †**6** A prostitute (cf. AUNT 3). Also, a dolt. Also *Cousin Betty*. *slang*. L16–M19. **7** A person of a kindred race or nation. M19.

2 SHAKES. *Much Ado* How now, brother! Where is my cousin, your son? W. FAULKNER Some remote maiden cousins of his mother. 5 B. JOWETT The Sophist is the cousin of the parasite and flatterer. 7 J. C. JEAFFRESON Our American cousins.

Phrases & comb.: *call cousin(s)*: see CALL *v.* *Cousin Betty*: see sense 6 above. **cousin-in-law**, pl. **cousins-in-law**, a cousin's wife or husband; a cousin of one's wife or husband. **Cousin Jack** *slang* a Cornishman. **cousin once, twice**, etc., **removed** (*a*) the child, grandchild, etc., of a cousin; (*b*) the cousin of a parent, grandparent, etc. *first cousin*: see sense 1 above. *kissing cousin*: see KISSING *ppl a.* *parallel cousin*: see PARALLEL *a.* *Scotch cousin*: see SCOTCH *a.* **second, third**, etc., **cousin** a child of a parent's first, second, etc., cousin.

B *adj.* Kindred, related. LME.

CHAUCER The wordes moote be cosyn to the dede.

cousinage *n.* = COUSINHOOD ME. **cousiˈness** *n.* (now *rare*) a female cousin LME. **cousinhood** *n.* (*a*) the relation of being a cousin or cousins, kinship; (*b*) (a body of) cousins or kinsfolk: LME. **cousinliness** *n.* cousinly behaviour or character E20. **cousinly** *a.* characteristic of or befitting a cousin; behaving like a cousin: E19. **cousinry** *n.* a body of cousins or kinsfolk M19. **cousinship** *n.* (*a*) kinship, cousinhood; *fig.* relationship; (*b*) action proper to a cousin: L16.

cousin /ˈkʌz(ə)n/ *v.t.* M17. [f. the n.] Call cousin, claim kinship with.

cousin-german /kʌz(ə)nˈdʒəːmən/ *n.* Pl. **cousins-german**, †**cousin-germans**. ME. [Fr. *cousin germain*: see COUSIN *n.*, GERMAN *a.*[2]] **1** = COUSIN *n.* 1. ME. **2** = COUSIN *n.* 5. M16.

couteau /kuto, ˈkuːtəʊ/ *n.* Pl. ***couteaux*** /kuto/, ***couteaus*** /ˈkuːtəʊz/. L17. [Fr. f. as next.] Chiefly *Hist.* A large knife used as a weapon.

couteau de chasse /kuto də ʃas, ˈkuːtəʊ də ʃas/ a hunting-knife.

coutel /kuːˈtɛl/ *n.* LME. [OFr. f. L *cultellus* knife.] *Hist.* A dagger, a knife used as a weapon.

couter /ˈkuːtə/ *n. slang. obs.* exc. *Hist.* Also **coo-**. M19. [Perh. f. Danubian Romany *cuta* gold coin.] A sovereign (the coin).

couth /kuːθ/ *a.* (orig. *pa. pple*) & *n.* [OE *cūþ* pa. pple of *cunnan* CAN *v.*[1] In sense A.7 back-form. f. UNCOUTH.] **A** *adj.* †**1** *pa. pple* & *adj.* Known. OE–E17. †**2** Of a person: well known, familiar. OE–M16. †**3** Famous, renowned. OE–M16. †**4** Acquainted (*with*, *of*). OE–LME. **5** Kind, agreeable. *Sc.* LME. **6** Comfortable, snug, cosy. *Sc.* M18. **7** Cultured, well-mannered, refined. L19. **B** *n.* Good manners, refinement. M20.

couthie, couthy *a.* & *adv.* (*Sc.*) (*a*) *adj.* kindly, agreeable; comfortable, cosy; (*b*) *adv.* genially, kindly: E18. **couthly** *adv.* (*a*) (now *Sc.*) familiarly, kindly; †(*b*) certainly, dearly: OE.

coutil /kʊˈtɪl/ *n.* M19. [Fr. f. OFr. *keutil*, f. *keute*, *coute* mattress f. L *culcita*: cf. QUILT *n.*] A strong cotton-based fabric used esp. in foundation garments.

couture /kuːˈtjʊə/ *n.* E20. [Fr. f. OFr. *cousture* sewing f. late L *consutura*, f. L *consutus* pa. pple of *consuere* sew together, f. as CON- + *suere* sew.] Dressmaking; (the design and making of) fashionable garments, esp. French ones.

HAUTE COUTURE. MAISON *de couture*.

couturier /kuːˈtjʊərɪeɪ, -rɪə/ *n.* a fashion designer, *esp.* a leading French one L19. **couturière** /kuːˈtjʊərɪɛː/ *n.* a female dressmaker or couturier E19.

couvade /kuːˈvɑːd/ *n.* M19. [Fr., f. *couver* hatch f. L *cubare* lie: see -ADE 1.] A custom in some cultures by which a man takes to his bed and goes through certain rituals when his wife bears a child.

¶Adopted in Fr. in this sense in M19 owing to a misunderstanding of *faire la couvade*, 'sit doing nothing' in earlier writers.

couvert /kuvɛːr/ *n.* Pl. pronounced same. M18. [Fr.: see COVERT *n.*] = COVER *n.*[1] 5.

couverture /ˈkuːvətjʊə/ *n.* M20. [Fr. = covering: see COVERTURE.] (A layer of) chocolate for coating sweets and cakes.

couvre-pied /kuvrəpje (*pl. same*)/ *n.* Also ***-pieds*** /-pje/. E19. [Fr., lit. 'cover foot', f. *couvrir* COVER *v.*[1]] A rug to cover the feet.

covalent /kəʊˈveɪl(ə)nt/ *a.* E20. [f. CO- + -VALENT.] *Chem.* Of, pertaining to, or characterized by covalency.

covalent bond: formed by the sharing of electrons, usu. in pairs by two atoms in a molecule.

covalence, covalency *ns.* (the linking of atoms by) a covalent bond; the number of covalent bonds that an atom can form: E20. **covalently** *adv.* by a covalent bond M20.

covariance /kəʊ'vɛːrɪəns/ *n.* L19. [In sense 1 f. COVARIANT; in sense 2 f. CO- + VARIANCE.] **1** *Math.* The property of being covariant; the property of a function of retaining its form when the variables are linearly transformed. L19. **2** *Statistics.* The mean value of the product of the deviations of two variates from their respective means. M20.

covariancy *n.* covariance; covariation: L19.

covariant /kəʊ'vɛːrɪənt/ *n.* & *a.* M19. [f. CO- + VARIANT.] **A** *n.* *Math.* A function of the coefficients and variables of a given function which is invariant under a linear transformation except for a factor equal to a power of the determinant of the transformation; a covariant quantity. M19. **B** *adj.* Changing in such a way that mathematical interrelations with another simultaneously changing quantity or set of quantities remain unchanged; correlated; *esp.* (*Math.*) having the properties of a covariant; of or pertaining to a covariant. E20.

covariation /ˌkəʊvɛːrɪ'eɪʃ(ə)n/ *n.* E20. [f. CO- + VARIATION.] Correlated variation.

co-'vary *v.i.* change simultaneously with something else, while preserving interrelations between the two unchanged M20.

cove /kəʊv/ *n.*[1] & *v.* [OE *cofa* chamber = MLG *cove*, MHG *kobe* (G *Koben*) stable, pigsty, ON *kofi* hut, shed, f. Gmc. Cf. CUB *n.*[2]] **A** *n.* **1** A small chamber, cell, etc. Only in OE exc. in *cove and key* (now *Hist.*) closet or chamber and key (used in reference to the functions and rights of the mistress of a house). OE. **2a** A hollow or recess in a rock; a cave. *Sc.* & *north.* OE. **b** A steep-sided recess in a mountainside. E19. **3** A sheltered recess among hills, woods, etc.; a narrow valley. LME. **4** *Archit.* A concave arch; the curved junction of a wall with the ceiling or floor. E16. **5** A sheltered recess in a coast; a small bay, creek, or inlet where boats may shelter. L16.

3 M. HOWITT Small farm-houses . . in the little coves of the valleys.

B *v.* †**1** *v.i.* & *t.* (w. *it*). Shelter in a cove. *rare.* M17–E18. **2** *v.t.* Give an arched or vaulted form to; provide (a ceiling) with a cove. Chiefly as *coved* ppl a. M18.

2 H. SWINBURNE The mosques . . are rounded into domes and coved roofs.

covelet *n.* a small cove L19. **coving** *n.* (*a*) an arched or vaulted piece of building; coved work; (*b*) in *pl.*, the inclined sides of a fireplace: E18.

cove /kəʊv/ *n.*[2] *slang* (esp. *Austral.*). M16. [Perh. f. Romany *kova* thing, person, or rel. to COFF *v.*] A fellow; a chap.

covellite /kəʊ'vɛlʌɪt/ *n.* M19. [f. N. *Covelli* (1790–1829), It. chemist + -ITE[1].] *Min.* A blue hexagonal copper sulphide usu. occurring as massive coatings and disseminations with other copper minerals.

coven /'kʌv(ə)n/ *n.* LME. [Var. of COVIN.] †**1** = COVIN I. LME–E17. **2** A company of witches who regularly meet together; *fig.* a secret or inward-looking group of associates. M17.

†**covenable** *a.* see CONVENABLE *a.*[1]

covenant /'kʌv(ə)nənt/ *n.* ME. [OFr. *covenant* use as n. of pres. pple (later and mod. *convenant*) of *co(n)venir* agree f. L *convenire* CONVENE: see -ANT[1].] **1** A mutual agreement between two or more people to do or refrain from doing certain acts; the undertaking of either party in such an agreement. ME. †**b** A term of an agreement. LME–E17. **2** *Law.* A formal agreement or promise of legal validity; *esp.* in *Eng. Law*, a promise or contract under seal. ME. **b** A clause of agreement contained in a deed. E17. †**3** The matter agreed between two parties, or undertaken or promised by either; agreed wages, rent, etc. ME–M18. **4** In biblical translations and allusions, an engagement entered into by God with a person, nation, etc. ME. **b** = DISPENSATION 5. E19. **5** *Chr. Ch.* The engagement with God which is entered into by believers at their baptism, or admission into the Visible Church. M16. **6** *Sc. Hist.* (**C-**.) An agreement signed by Presbyterians for the maintenance of their form of Church government in Scotland (*National Covenant*, 1638) and in England and Scotland (*Solemn League and Covenant*, 1643). M17.

4 MILTON And makes a Covenant never to destroy The Earth again by flood.

Phrases: *ark of the Covenant*: see ARK 2. **Church Covenant** the formal agreement made by the members of a Congregational church in order to constitute themselves a distinct religious society. **Covenant of Works, of Grace** *Theol.*: the two relations which are represented as subsisting between God and Man, before the Fall of Man and since the Atonement. **Day of the Covenant** *S. Afr.* a national holiday observed annually on 16 December, on which a vow made by the Voortrekkers before the battle at Blood River on that day in 1838 is honoured. **deed of covenant** a deed in which one party covenants to pay stated sums to another over a stated period of time. **land of the Covenant** the promised land, Canaan. *National Covenant*: see sense 6 above. **New Covenant** the New Testament. **Old Covenant** the Old Testament. *restrictive covenant*: see RESTRICTIVE *a.* 3. *Solemn League and Covenant*: see sense 6 above.

cove'nantal *a.* of or pertaining to a covenant E19.

covenant /'kʌv(ə)nənt/ *v.* ME. [f. the n.] **1** *v.i.* Enter into a covenant (*for*, *to do*). ME. **2** *v.t.* Agree formally to give or do (something); make a deed of covenant for (a sum). LME. **3** *v.t.* Stipulate (*that*). LME.

1 T. ARNOLD Did you not covenant to write to me first? 2 C. H. PEARSON She refused to pay the witch . . the sum covenanted.

covenan'tee *n.* the person to whom a promise by covenant is made M17. **covenantor** *n.* the party who is to perform the obligation expressed in a covenant M17.

covenanted /'kʌv(ə)nəntɪd/ *ppl a.* M17. [f. prec. + -ED[1].] **1** Of a thing: agreed on, established, or secured by covenant. M17. **2** Of a person: having entered into a covenant, bound by a covenant; *spec.* in *Hist.* (*a*) *Sc.* (also **C-**) having subscribed to the National Covenant or the Solemn League and Covenant; (*b*) having entered into a covenant with the East India Company or (later) the Secretary of State for India to become a regular member of the Indian Civil Service. M17.

covenanter /'kʌv(ə)nəntə, *in sense 2 also* kʌvə'nantə/ *n.* In sense 2 also **C-**. L16. [f. as prec. + -ER[1].] **1** *gen.* A person who enters into a covenant. L16. **2** *Sc. Hist.* A subscriber to or adherent of the National Covenant or the Solemn League and Covenant. M17.

covent *n.* see CONVENT *n.*

Coventry /'kɒv(ə)ntri, 'kʌv-/ *n.* L16. [A city in the English Midlands.] †**1** In full *Coventry blue*. A kind of blue embroidery thread formerly manufactured at Coventry. L16–E17. †**2** *Coventry bells*, = *Canterbury bell(s)* s.v. CANTERBURY *n.*[1] 1. L16–L18. **3** *send to Coventry*, refuse to associate with or speak to; ostracize. M18.

cover /'kʌvə/ *n.*[1] ME. [f. COVER *v.*[2] or partly a var. of COVERT *n.*] **I** A thing which covers. **1** *gen.* A thing which is put on or which lies over something. ME. †**2a** A piece of armour; an article of clothing. ME–L18. **b** More fully *bed-cover*. A cloth for putting on a bed, *spec.* a quilt; in *pl.*, bedclothes. E19. **3** A lid. LME. **4** The binding, wrapper, or case of a book; either of the boards forming the front and back of a book; an outer page of a magazine. L16. **5** An envelope or other wrapper for a letter; *spec.* a stamped envelope of philatelic interest. M18. **6** *Cricket.* = *cover-point* (a) s.v. COVER *v.*[2]; *the covers*, cover-point and extra cover-point. M19. **7** *Textiles.* A design that is printed over another design in resist work. Also *cover pattern*. L19. **8** *Comm.* Funds adequate to cover or meet a liability or to secure against contingent loss. L19. **b** Adequate insurance against loss, damage, etc.; the state of being protected by this. E20. **9** In full *cover version*. A recording of a previously recorded song etc., *esp.* one made to take advantage of the latter's publicity or success. M20.

1 W. BUCKLAND The alluvial cover which rests upon the rocks of this district. 2b D. RUNYON He just pulls the covers up over his head and lies there.

II A thing which conceals. **10** A thing which serves for shelter or concealment; a shelter; a hiding place. LME. **b** A disguise, a screen; *spec.* a spy's assumed identity or activity as concealment. L16. **c** The partner who screens the operations of a pickpocket. E19. **11** Woodland, undergrowth, etc., that serves to shelter or conceal wild animals or game. E18. **b** The vegetation covering the surface of the ground. E20. **12** Protection from attack, *esp.* that provided by a supporting force etc.; a force providing such protection. E19.

10 J. BUCHAN There was not cover in the whole place to hide a rat. C. MILNE When a storm broke we took cover. D. BOGARDE Leaving . . under cover of night. b B. JOWETT Under the cover of rhetoric much higher themes are introduced. A. PRICE The precipitate withdrawal to Holland when it looked as though his cover had been blown. 11b *Discovery* This denudation of forest cover is due to human interference.

III [Fr. COUVERT.] **13** The utensils laid for each person's use at table; a plate, napkin, knife, fork, spoon, etc., a place-setting. E17.

13 H. ALLEN The man . . began to lay covers for two.

Phrases: *break cover*: see BREAK *v.* *extra cover*: see EXTRA *a.* **first-day cover** an envelope postmarked with the date on which its stamp was first issued. **from cover to cover** from beginning to end (of a book). *loose cover*: see LOOSE *a.* *open cover*: see OPEN *a.* *paper cover*: see PAPER *n.* & *a.* **take cover** use natural or prepared shelter (against attack). **under cover to** in an envelope or other postal packet addressed to. **under separate cover** in another envelope or postal packet.

Comb.: **cover charge** a charge for service added to that for food and drink in a restaurant; **cover crop** a usu. leguminous crop sown to protect the soil or to enrich it by being ploughed under; **cover-drive** *Cricket* a drive past cover-point; **cover-girl** a young woman whose picture appears on the front cover of a magazine; **cover-glass** a slip of glass used to cover a specimen for the microscope; **cover note**: certifying the existence of a current insurance policy; **cover-slip** = *cover-glass* above; **cover story** (*a*) a fictitious life history etc. concocted as a false identity for a person; (*b*) a news story illustrated or mentioned on the front cover of a magazine; *cover version*: see sense 9 above.

cover /'kəʊvə/ *n.*[2] Chiefly *dial.* E20. [f. COVE *n.*[1] + -ER[1].] A person who lives in a cove.

cover /'kʌvə/ *v.*[1] Long *obs.* exc. *dial.* Orig. †**acover**. [OE *ācofrian* corresp. to OHG *ir-koboron* f. L *recuperare* RECUPERATE. Aphet. ME to *cover* (infl. by OFr. *co(u)vrer* get, acquire: cf. Fr. *recouvrer* RECOVER *v.*[1]), which became thereafter the only form.] **1** *v.t.* Get, gain, obtain, attain. OE. †**b** *v.i.* Get *to*, *out of*, *up*, etc. OE–L15. †**2** *v.t.* Recover, regain. OE–LME. †**3** *v.t.* Restore, relieve (a person etc.); heal (a wound). OE–E17. **4** *v.i.* Recover (from sickness etc.); regain health; be restored. OE.

cover /'kʌvə/ *v.*[2] ME. [OFr. *cuvrir*, *covrir* (mod. *couvrir*) f. L *cooperire*, f. as CO- + *operire* to cover.] **I 1** *v.t.* Put or lay something over or in front of (an object) so as to conceal, protect, or enclose it; put a covering or cover on (*spec.* a book). (Foll. by *with*.) ME. †**b** Put a roof on or over. LME–M18. **c** Put a cloth on (a table). M16. **2** *v.t.* Clothe (a body); wrap or enclose (a limb etc.); enclose (a chair etc.) *in* fabric. ME. **3** *v.t.* & *i.* Put a hat etc. on (one's head); in *pass.*, put on or wear a hat etc. ME. **4** *v.t.* Serve as a covering to; lie or be over (an object) so as to conceal, protect, or enclose it. ME. **5** *v.t.* Occur here and there over the whole surface of; cause the surface of (something) to be overlain or marked (foll. by *with*, *in*). ME. **6** *v.t.* Of a stallion, bull, etc.: copulate with. M16. **b** Of a bird: sit on (eggs). E17. **7** *v.t.* **a** In wagering, match (a coin etc.) with another of equal value. E19. **b** Play a higher-ranking card on top of (a card already played). L19. **c** Make a cover version of (a song etc.). M20.

1 A. B. SOYER Cover the saucepan for an instant. R. C. HUTCHINSON The winter sun had . . been covered by fresh clouds. J. THURBER He wore a cap to cover his baldness. P. MORTIMER I covered my face with my hands. **cover one's feet** (in biblical translations) urinate; defecate. 2 V. WOOLF Six yards of silk will cover one body. W. PLOMER An Empire sofa . . had been newly covered in striped lavender satin. *fig.*: H. FIELDING He stood . . covered with confusion. **cover oneself with glory** be remarkably successful. 3 SHAKES. *A.Y.L.* Good ev'n. . . Nay, prithee be cover'd. J. HELLER Her head was covered in a knitted cap. 4 J. TYNDALL Pines . . covered with the freshly-fallen snow. I. MURDOCH A wet scarf covered her hair. G. GREENE

For other words beginning with *co-* see the entry for **co-**

One wall was almost covered by a large roller map. 5 W. COWPER Gardens, fields and plains Were cover'd with the pest. J. R. GREEN Art and literature covered England with great buildings and busy schools. R. BROOKE The breeze moves in the trees . . And covers you with white petals. *Observer* He . . was covered in ink.

II 8 *v.t. gen.* Shield; protect; shelter; be a means of defence or protection for. ME. **9** *v.t. gen.* Hide or screen from view; conceal, prevent the perception or discovery of. ME. **10** *v.t.* Aim a gun at; have within firing-range; command (territory etc.) from a superior position. L17. **b** In *Tennis* etc., have (an area) within the scope of one's play; in various team games, be responsible for defence in (an area). L19. **11** *v.t.* Include within its application or scope; deal with, provide for. L18. **b** Report on or photograph for the press; attend or investigate as a journalist. L19. **12** *v.t.* a *Mil.* Stand directly behind or in line with. L18. **b** In *Cricket*, stand behind (another fielder) so as to be able to stop the balls he or she misses; in various team games, mark (an opponent). M19. **13a** *v.t.* Of a pickpocket's partner: screen the operations of (the pickpocket). E19. **b** *v.t.* & *i.* Of a medical practitioner: act for or cooperate improperly with (an unqualified practitioner). L19. **c** *v.t.* & *i.* w. *for*. Stand in for (an absent colleague); take (a class) for an absent teacher. M20. **14** *v.t.* a Pass over (ground); traverse (a given distance). E19. **b** Extend over, be co-extensive with; occupy (a period or area). M19. **15** *v.t.* Be sufficient to defray (expenses), pay (a dividend etc.), or meet (a liability); compensate for (a loss or risk); protect by insurance. E19. **b** *v.i.* Insure oneself; provide cover. L19.

8 H. NELSON She was an American Vessel, although covered by British Papers. J. SEACOME Cannon . . to cover the Ships in the Harbour. *Granta* We moved back slowly . . , covering the battalion's retreat. 9 SOUTHEY Thou shalt wish The earth might cover thee. D. LODGE He forced a laugh to cover his embarrassment. *cover a person's tracks*: see TRACK *n.* 11 BURKE Mr. Fox's general principle fully covered all this. K. AMIS I cover the medieval angle for the History Department here. b P. LIVELY The paper is sending her to cover a party conference. 14a J. BUCHAN The hill-top . . from which the eye may cover half the southern midlands. K. M. E. MURRAY In three days they covered at least fifty miles. b A. CARNEGIE During the period which these events cover I had made repeated journeys to Europe. D. MURPHY Letters . . covering more than twenty foolscap pages. *cover much ground, cover the ground*: see GROUND *n.* 15 *Times* With the dividend covered three times there is unlikely to be any danger to shareholders.

With advs. in specialized senses: **cover in** complete the covering of (something) by adding the upper layer or part; provide with a roof. **cover over** cover the whole surface of; overlay; cover with something that overhangs. **cover up** (*a*) *v.phr.t.* conceal under a cover; cover over; (*b*) *v.phr.t.* & *i.* conceal (a misdeed), assist in a deception.

Comb.: **covering letter, note**: sent with an enclosure and indicating its contents. **cover-point** (*a*) *Cricket* (the position of) a fielder a little in front of the batsman on the off side, further from the pitch than point; (*b*) *Lacrosse* a player who is positioned just in front of point; **cover-shame** (*a*) something used to conceal shame; (*b*) the shrub savin (as an abortifacient); **cover-slut** an apron, a pinafore; **cover-up** (*a*) something designed to conceal a crime or restrict knowledge of misconduct; (*b*) a high-necked garment; a coverall.

coverable *a.* able to be covered L20. **coverer** *n.* a person who or thing which covers ME.

coverage /ˈkʌv(ə)rɪdʒ/ *n.* Orig. *US.* E20. [f. COVER *v.*[1] + -AGE.] **1** The area, range, etc., that is covered; *spec.* the area or number of people reached by a particular broadcasting station or advertising medium. E20. **2** The action of covering something for the press; the fact or extent of being included in news reports, broadcasts, etc.; reporting. M20.

1 G. MILLERSON The longer the focal length of the lens . . , the narrower its coverage. 2 *Economist* Soviet radio gave greater radio coverage to this peace congress.

coverall /ˈkʌvərɔːl/ *n.* & *a.* M19. [f. COVER *v.*[1] + ALL.] **A** *n.sing.* & in *pl.* Something that covers entirely, *esp.* a full-length protective outer garment. M19. **B** *adj.* That covers entirely. L19.

coverchief /ˈkʌvətʃɪf/ *n.* Long *obs.* exc. *Hist.* ME. [OFr. *cuevre-chief*, (also mod.) *couvre-chef*: see KERCHIEF *n.*] = KERCHIEF *n.*

covercle /ˈkʌvək(ə)l/ *n.* LME. [OFr. *covercle* (mod. *couvercle*) f. L *cooperculum*, f. *cooperire* COVER *v.*[1]] †**1** A cover; a lid. LME–L19. **2** *Bot.* & *Zool.* Any natural structure acting as a lid; an operculum. *rare.* L17.

covered /ˈkʌvəd/ *a.* LME. [f. COVER *n.*[1], *v.*[2]: see -ED[2], -ED[1].] **1** Having a cover, covering, or lid. LME. †**2** Hidden; secret; ambiguous. LME–L16. **3** Sheltered, protected, screened. Now *rare* or *obs.* exc. in *covered way* below. L15. **4** Overgrown with vegetation. Now only as 2nd elem. of comb., as *moss-covered, weed-covered*, etc. M17. **5** Roofed or closed in overhead. M17. **6** Wearing one's hat. M17.

5 *covered bridge, covered market, covered wagon.*

Special collocations: **covered way** (*a*) *Fortif.* a strip of land beyond the outer edge of a ditch and protected by a parapet; (*b*) a path that is roofed in.

covering /ˈkʌv(ə)rɪŋ/ *n.* ME. [f. COVER *v.*[2] + -ING[1].] **1** The action of COVER *v.*[2] ME. **2** Something which covers or is adapted to cover; a cover. ME. †**b** *spec.* A lid. L15–M17.

1 *short covering*: see SHORT *a.*

coverlet /ˈkʌvəlɪt/ *n.* Also **-lid** /-lɪd/. ME. [AN *covrelet, -lit*, f. *covre-* pres. stem of OFr. *covrir* COVER *v.*[2] + *lit* bed.] **1** A bedspread; a counterpane. ME. **2** A covering of any kind; a cover. LME.

co-versed /kəʊˈvəːst/ *a.* Now *rare.* E18. [f. CO- + VERSED *a.*] Math. *co-versed sine*, the versed sine of the complement of an angle.

covert /ˈkʌvə, ˈkʌvət/ *n.* ME. [OFr. (mod. *couvert*) use as n. of masc. pa. pple of *cuvrir, covrir* COVER *v.*[2]] **1** *gen.* A covering. ME. **2** = COVER *n.*[1] 10. ME. **3** A flock or company of coots. Long *rare.* LME. **4** A place which gives shelter to wild animals or game; *esp.* a thicket. L15. †**5** = COVERTURE 8. Chiefly in *under covert.* M16–E18. **6** *Ornith.* More fully *covert feather*. A feather covering the base of wing or tail feathers. Also called *tectrix*. Usu. in *pl.* L16.

Comb.: **covert cloth** a medium-weight fabric with a twill weave; **covert coat** a short light overcoat worn for shooting, riding, etc.; **covert coating** = *covert cloth* above; *covert feather*: see sense 6 above.

covert /ˈkʌvət, ˈkəʊvəːt/ *a.* ME. [OFr. (mod. *couvert*) pa. pple of *cuvrir, covrir* COVER *v.*[2]] **1** Covered; hidden; sheltered. Now *rare.* ME. **2** Secret, concealed; disguised. ME. **3** Of a person: secretive, sly. ME. **4** Of a word: of hidden or obscure meaning. Now *rare.* LME. **5** *Law.* Of a woman: married (formerly as under the authority or protection of her husband). L15.

1 WORDSWORTH This covert nook reports not of his hand. 2 N. CHOMSKY Unless intervention is discreet and covert, there will be protest, disaffection. 3 SHAKES. *Rich. III* He was the covert'st shelt'red traitor That ever liv'd.

Special collocations: **covert way** = *covered way* (*a*) s.v. COVERED. FEME *covert. pound covert*: see POUND *n.*[2] 1a.

covertly *adv.* LME. **covertness** *n.* LME.

covert-baron /ˈkʌvətbar(ə)n/ *a.* & *n. obs.* exc. *Hist.* E16. [AN *couverte baroun*, orig. *coverte de barun* covered by a husband: see prec., BARON.] **A** *adj.* = COVERT *a.* 5. E16. **B** *n.* The condition of being a married woman. Chiefly in *under covert-baron*. Cf. COVERT *n.* 5, COVERTURE 8. L16.

coverture /ˈkʌvətjʊə/ *n.* ME. [OFr. (mod. *couverture*), f. *covrir* COVER *v.*[2] or late L *coopertura* (f. ppl stem of L *cooperire* COVER *v.*[2]): see -URE.] †**1** A bed-cover; a coverlet. ME–L17. †**2** Clothing; a garment; a horse's trappings. ME–E17. **3** *gen.* (A) covering. Formerly also, a cover (of a dish, book, letter, etc.). LME. **4** An overhead covering; a canopy. Now *rare.* LME. **5** Protective covering; (a) shelter, (a) refuge. LME. **6** Concealing covering; (a) disguise. LME. **b** *fig.* Concealment; dissimulation, deceit. Now *rare.* LME. †**7** A pretext, a pretence. LME–M16. **8** The legal status of a married woman (formerly as under the authority and protection of her husband); a woman's married state. Esp. in *during the coverture, under coverture.* M16.

5 SPENSER Agaynst his cruell scortching heate, Where hast thou couerture? 6 I. BARROW Shrowded under the coverture of other Persons and Names.

covess /kəʊˈvɛs/ *n. slang.* L18. [f. COVE *n.*[2] + -ESS[1].] A woman, a girl.

covet /ˈkʌvɪt/ *v.* ME. [OFr. *coveitier, cu-* (mod. *convoiter*) f. Proto-Romance, f. L *cupiditas* CUPIDITY.] **1** *v.t.* Desire; *esp.* desire eagerly, long for. ME. **2** *v.t.* Long for (what belongs to another); desire culpably. ME. †**3** *v.t.* Desire with concupiscence; desire sexually. ME–L16. †**4** *v.i.* Have inordinate or culpable, esp. sexual, desire. Foll. by *for, after, against.* LME–E16.

1 J. ARBUTHNOT They covet subacid Liquors, and abhor fat and oily things. F. BURNEY Her mind . . coveted to regain its serenity. D. HALBERSTAM He did not covet small-bore social acceptance. 2 C. JACKSON She coveted the necklace and made up her mind to own it.

covetable *a.* highly desirable ME. **coveter** *n.* a person who covets or is given to coveting LME. **covetingly** *adv.* with great longing LME.

covetise /ˈkʌvətiːs/ *n.* Long *arch.* ME. [OFr. *coveitise* (mod. *convoitise*) alt. w. suffix-change of *coveitié, covoitié* f. L *cupiditas* CUPIDITY: see -ISE[1], -ICE[1].] Inordinate or ardent desire; lust; *spec.* excessive desire for wealth etc.; covetousness.

covetous /ˈkʌvɪtəs/ *a.* ME. [OFr. *coveitous* (mod. *convoiteux*) f. Proto-Gallo-Romance, f. L *cupiditas* CUPIDITY: see -OUS.] **1** Having an ardent or excessive desire. Foll. by *of*, †*for*; *to do, have, be.* ME. **2** Culpably or inordinately desirous of gaining wealth or possessions; greedy, grasping; avaricious. ME. **3** Of an action: proceeding from cupidity. LME.

covetously *adv.* LME. **covetousness** *n.* †(*a*) inordinate desire (*of*); (*b*) culpable desire: L15.

covey /ˈkʌvi/ *n.*[1] ME. [OFr. *covée* (mod. *couvée*), use as n. of fem. pa. pple of *cover* f. L *cubare* lie.] **1** A brood or flock of partridges (or occas. of grouse etc.); a family of partridges etc. keeping together during the first season. ME. **2** A party, group, etc., *of* persons or things. ME.

2 V. WOOLF Coveys of nursemaids pushed perambulators.

covey /ˈkəʊvi/ *n.*[2] *slang.* E19. [f. COVE *n.*[2] + -Y[6].] A little chap or fellow.

†**covid** *n.* L17–E19. [Port. *côvado* f. L *cubitum* CUBIT.] An Indian unit of length varying from 36 to 14 inches.

covin /ˈkʌvɪn/ *n.* Also **-ine**. See also COVEN. ME. [OFr. *covin(e)* f. med.L *convenium*, f. L *convenire* CONVENE. Cf. CONVENT *n.*] **I** †**1** A number of people allied together; a company, a band. ME–E16. **2** A collusion between two or more to the prejudice of another; a secret plan or agreement. Now *rare* or *obs.* LME. **3** Fraud; deceit; treachery. *arch.* LME. †**4** Secret contrivance or intent. Only in LME. †**5** State, character. LME–L15. **II 6** = COVEN 2. *Sc.* M19.

Comb.: **covin-tree** *Sc.* a large tree in front of a Scottish mansion where the laird met or took leave of his visitors etc.

covinous *a.* (now *rare*) collusive; fraudulent: L16. **covinously** *adv.* (now *rare*) M16.

cow /kaʊ/ *n.*[1] & *a.* Pl. **cows**, (*arch.*) **kine** /kʌɪn/, (*Sc.* & *north.*) **kye** /kʌɪ/. [OE *cū* = OFris. *kū*, OS *kō* (Du. *koe*), OHG *kuo, chuo* (G *Kuh*), ON *kýr*, f. Gmc, f. IE base also of L *bos*, Gk *bous*.] **A** *n.* **I 1** A domesticated female ox, *esp.* one that has calved (kept for milk etc.); any mature female bovine animal. OE. **b** A domestic bovine animal (regardless of sex or age). Orig. *US.* M19. **2** The female of various other large animals, as the elephant, rhinoceros, whale, seal, etc. E18. **II** †**3a** A faint-hearted person. L16–E17. **b** A woman, *esp.* a coarse or unpleasant one. *slang. derog.* L17. **c** An objectionable person, thing, or situation. *Austral.* & *NZ slang.* L19.

3b C. MACKENZIE Silly cow! She ought to know better. c F. D. DAVISON Looking for work's a cow of a game!

Phrases: *bull-and-cow*: see BULL *n.*[1] & *a.* *Lucanian cow*: see LUCANIAN *a.* *muley cow*: see MULEY *n.* & *a.*[1] *sacred cow*: see SACRED *a.* *Sussex cow*: see SUSSEX 1. *the tune the (old) cow died of*: see TUNE *n.* **till the cows come home** *colloq.* for an indefinitely long period.

Comb.: **cow-baby** (*obs.* exc. *dial.*) a childish timorous person; **cowbail** *Austral.* & *NZ* [BAIL *n.*[2]] a cowshed; **cowbane** any of several marsh umbellifers poisonous to cattle, esp. *Cicuta virosa* of Europe and *C. maculata* and *Oxypolis rigidior* of the US; **cow-banger** *dial., Austral.* & *NZ slang* a small dairy farmer; a worker on a dairy farm; **cowbell** (*a*) a bell hung round a cow's neck to indicate its whereabouts; (*b*) a bell without a clapper used as a percussion instrument; **cowberry** (the red acid fruit of) an evergreen bilberry, *Vaccinium vitis-idaea*, of upland moors; red whortleberry; **cowbind** the twining plant white bryony, *Bryonia dioica*; **cowbird** *US* any of several related N. American orioles, esp. *Molothrus ater*, which associate with cattle for the insects stirred up in grazing; **cow-camp** *US* an encampment of cowboys; **cow-catcher** (chiefly *N. Amer.*) an apparatus fixed in front of a locomotive to push aside cattle and other obstructions; **cow chip** *N. Amer.* a dried cow-pat; **cow-cocky** *Austral.* & *NZ slang* a small dairy farmer; **cow-creamer** an antique cream-jug in the form of a cow; **cow-fish** (*a*) the manatee; (*b*) any of several trunkfishes with hornlike spines over the eyes, esp. *Lactophrys quadricornis*; **cow-flap, -flop** (*a*) *dial.* the foxglove; (*b*) *dial.* & *US* = *cow-pat* below; **cow-gait, -gate** *Hist.* a pasture where a cow may be grazed; right of grazing cattle, as on common land; †**cow-gun** *Naut. slang* a heavy naval gun; **cow-hand** a person employed to tend or ranch cattle; **cow-heel** (a dish made from) the heel of a cow or ox stewed to a jelly; **cowherd** [HERD *n.*[2]] a person who tends grazing cattle; **cowhide** *n.* & *v.* (*a*) *n.* (leather made from) the hide of a cow; *US* a whip made of cowhide; (*b*) *v.t.* flog with a cowhide whip; **cow-hitch** *Naut.* an improperly tied knot which slips under strain; **cow-hocked** *a.* (of a horse or dog) having hocks that turn inwards like a cow's; **cow-horse** *US* a horse used in herding or driving cattle; **cow-house** a cowshed; **cow-hunt** *US*: for strayed cattle; **cow-keeper** a dairyman; a dairy farmer; **cow-lady** *dial.* a ladybird; **cow-lick** a projecting lock of hair, esp. on the forehead; **cowman** (*a*) a cowherd; (*b*) = COWBOY *n.* 3; **cow-pad** = *cow-pat* below; **cow parsley** a tall hedgerow umbellifer, *Anthriscus sylvestris*, with white flowers and finely-cut leaves; **cow parsnip** a tall hedgerow umbellifer, *Heracleum sphondylium*, with whitish flowers and segmented leaves; hogweed; **cow-pat** a roundish patch of cow-dung; **cowpea** a leguminous plant, *Vigna unguiculata*, grown as fodder in southern Europe and the southern US; its seed, eaten as pulse; **cow pen** an enclosure for cows; **cow-pen** *v.t.* pen cows on (land); **cowpoke** *N. Amer. colloq.* = COWBOY *n.* 3; **cow pony** *US*: trained for use in cattle-ranching; **cowpox** a viral disease of cows which produces vesicles on teats and udders and the virus of which is used in vaccination against smallpox; **cowpuncher** *N. Amer. colloq.* = COWBOY *n.* 3; **cow-run** a common on which cows pasture; **cow shark** a shark of the family Hexanchidae, with six or seven gill openings on either side of the head instead of the usual five; **cowshed** a shed for cows not at pasture; a milking-shed; **cow-shot** *Cricket slang* a clumsy attacking shot made by hitting across the ball, usu. in the direction of midwicket; **cow-skin** *n.* & *v.t.* = *cowhide* above; **cow-spanker** *Austral.* & *NZ slang* = *cow-banger* above; **cow-tail** †(*a*) the bushy tail of the Tibetan yak used as a fly-whisk; (*b*) the coarsest grade of wool, sheared from the sheep's hind legs; **cow town** *N. Amer.* (*a*) a town that is a local centre in a cattle-raising area; (*b*) a small isolated or unsophisticated town; **cow-tree** a Venezuelan tree, *Brosimum utile*, of the mulberry family, with a juice looking and tasting like cow's milk; any of several other tropical American trees with a milky juice; **cow-wheat** (orig.) *Melampyrum arvense*, a Eurasian cornfield weed of the figwort family with pinkish bracts; (now) any plant of the same genus, *esp.* (more fully *common cow-wheat*) *M. pratense* of woods and heaths.

B *attrib.* or as *adj.* Of a domesticated ox or other large animal (orig. of a calf): female. OE.

¶Cf. BULL *n.*[1] & *a.*

cow /kaʊ, kuː/ *n.*[2] *Sc.* L15. [f. OFr. *coe, coue* (mod. *queue*) tail, or f. COW *v.*[1]] A twig; a tufted stem of heather; a bunch of these, *esp.* a besom or a birch.

cow /kaʊ/ *n.*[3] *Sc.* E16. [Origin unkn.] A hobgoblin; an object of terror. Cf. WORRICOW *n.*

cow /kaʊ/ *n.*[4] *dial.* M18. [Var. of COWL *n.*[1]] = COWL *n.*[1] 4.

cow /kaʊ, kəʊ/ *v.*[1]*t.* *Sc.* E16. [Var. of COLL *v.*[2]: cf. *knowe, pow* for *knoll, poll.*] 1 Crop the hair of; clip, cut short. E16. 2 Surpass, outdo. M19.

cow /kaʊ/ *v.*[2]*t.* L16. [Prob. f. ON *kúga* oppress, tyrannize over (Norw. *kue*, MSw. *kufwa*, Sw. *kuva*).] Frighten or browbeat into humility or submission; overawe, intimidate. Freq. foll. by *into*.

C. ACHEBE He seemed the quiet type and . . a little cowed by his beautiful, bumptious wife. M. ESSLIN The individual cowed into conformism by society.

cowabunga /kaʊəˈbʌŋɡə, kɑːwə-/ *int. slang* (esp. *children's*). M20. [Prob. fanciful.] Expr. exhilaration, delight, or satisfaction, or as an excited call to action.

cowage /ˈkaʊɪdʒ/ *n.* Also **cowhage**. See also COWITCH. M17. [Hind. *kawãc, -āc.*] The stinging hairs on the pods of a leguminous vine, *Mucuna pruriens*, formerly used as an antidote for intestinal worms; the plant itself; its pods.

cowan /ˈkaʊən/ *n.* L16. [Origin unkn.] 1 A dry-stone-waller; *derog.* a person who does a mason's work without having been apprenticed to the trade. *Sc.* L16. 2 A person who is not a Freemason. E18.

coward /ˈkaʊəd/ *n., a., & v.* ME. [OFr. *cuard* (later *couard*) f. Proto-Romance var. of L *cauda* tail (cf. sense B.2 below): see -ARD.] **A** *n.* A person who shows unworthy fear in the face of danger, pain, or difficulty; a person with little or no courage. ME.

B *attrib.* or as *adj.* 1 Cowardly. ME. 2 *Her.* Of a lion or other animal: having the tail drawn in between the hind legs. E16.

1 POPE The Coward-Counsels of a tim'rous Throng.

†**C** *v.t.* 1 Weaken the courage of, make afraid. ME–L17. 2 Call, or show to be, a coward. M–L17.

cowardize *v.t.* make cowardly, daunt E17. **cowardness** *n.* (*obs.* exc. *Sc.*) cowardice LME. †**cowardship** *n.* cowardice ME–E17.

cowardice /ˈkaʊədɪs/ *n.* ME. [OFr. *couardise*, f. *couard*: see prec., -ISE[1], -ICE[1].] Cowardly quality; lack of courage.

moral cowardice: see MORAL *a.*

cowardly /ˈkaʊədli/ *a.* M16. [f. COWARD + -LY[1].] 1 Acting like a coward; having little or no courage. M16. 2 Characteristic of a coward; proceeding from a spirit of cowardice. L16.

1 SHAKES. *Hen. V* The cowardly rascals that ran from the battle. 2 LD MACAULAY The affront was not only brutal, but cowardly.

cowardliness *n.* L15.

cowardly /ˈkaʊədli/ *adv.* LME. [f. COWARD *a.* + -LY[2].] In the manner of a coward; with base avoidance of danger.

cowardy /ˈkaʊədi/ *a. colloq.* M19. [f. COWARD *n.* + -Y[1].] Cowardly. Esp. in the children's taunt *cowardy (cowardy) custard* (CUSTARD *n.*[2]).

cowboy /ˈkaʊbɔɪ/ *n.* & *a.* Esp. in sense A.1 also **cow boy, cow-boy.** E17. [f. COW *n.*[1] + BOY *n.*] **A** *n.* 1 A boy who tends cows. E17. 2 *US Hist.* In the War of Independence, a member of a band of pro-British marauders operating near New York. L18. 3 *N. Amer.* A mounted cattle-herder or rancher; *spec.* one employed to drive large herds of cattle to new pastures, shipping-points, etc., in the days of open ranges, *c*1865–90 (later a stock character in the genre of westerns). M19. 4 A boisterous, unruly, or aggressive young man. *slang.* E20. 5 A reckless or irresponsible motorist. *colloq.* M20. 6 A person who undercuts established traders or operators with an inferior service or product; an unqualified or unauthorized trader or operator; a trader or operator who employs sharp practices. *colloq.* L20.

3 **cowboys and Indians** a children's game in which conflicts between cowboys and American Indians are imitated. 4 *drugstore cowboy*: see DRUG *n.*[1]

Comb.: **cowboy boots** high-heeled, freq. richly ornamented, boots of a style worn by cowboys.

B *attrib.* or as *adj.* Irresponsible, dubiously legal; providing an inferior service or product; employing sharp practices. *colloq.* M20.

Times A 'cowboy' carpet fitter has left a trail of complaints in South Yorkshire.

cower /ˈkaʊə/ *v.* ME. [MLG *kūren* lie in wait (whence G *kauern*), of unkn. origin.] 1 *v.i.* Stand or squat in a bent position; crouch, esp. for shelter or in fear. ME. 2 *v.t.* Lower, bend down. *rare* exc. *Sc.* L18.

1 F. BOWEN The dog cowers at the sight of the whip. J. STEINBECK He crouched cowering against the wall.

coweringly *adv.* in the manner of a person who cowers E19.

cowey *a.* var. of COWY.

cowhage *n.* var. of COWAGE.

cow-heart /ˈkaʊhɑːt/ *n.* Now *dial.* M18. [Alt., after COW *n.*[1], HEART *n.*] A coward.

cow-'hearted *a.* faint-hearted, timorous, cowardly M17.

cowish /ˈkaʊɪʃ/ *n.* E19. [Prob. N. American Indian.] An umbelliferous plant of the Oregon region, *Lomatium cous*; its edible root.

cowish /ˈkaʊɪʃ/ *a.* L16. [f. COW *n.*[1] + -ISH[1].] 1 Like a cow. L16. †2 Cowardly. L16–E17.

cowitch /ˈkaʊɪtʃ/ *n.* M17. [Alt. of COWAGE by assoc. with *itch*.] = COWAGE.

cowl /kaʊl/ *n.*[1] & *v.* [OE *cug(e)le, cūle*, corresp. to MLG, MDu. *cōghel*, OHG *cucula, cugula, chugela* (G *Kugel, Kogel*), f. eccl.L *cuculla* f. L *cucullus* hood of a cloak. In ME reinforced by *kuuele* f. OE *kufle* and prob. by (O)Fr. *coule.*] **A** *n.* 1 A hooded sleeveless garment worn by monks. Also, a full cloak with wide sleeves worn by members of Benedictine orders. OE. 2 The hood of such a garment. L16. 3 Monkhood, monasticism; a monk. M17. 4 A vented covering fitted on top of a chimney or ventilation shaft to improve the draught. (Earlier as COW *n.*[4]) E19.

3 POPE What differ more (you cry) than crown and cowl?

Comb.: **cowl neck** a neck on a woman's garment that hangs in draped folds.

B *v.t.* 1 Clothe (as) with a monk's cowl; make a monk of. M16. 2 Draw over like a cowl. E19.

1 R. D. BLACKMORE Mountains, cowled with fog. 2 H. E. BATES A sort of black cloak . . half like the garment, cowled over the head, that nuns or nurses wear.

cowled *a.* wearing or provided with (something resembling) a cowl LME.

cowl /kaʊl/ *n.*[2] Now *arch.* & *dial.* Also **coul.** [OE *cȳfel* app. f. OFr. *cuvele* f. late L *cupella* dim. of *cupa* tub, vat.] A tub or large vessel for water etc.; *esp.* one with two ears, for carrying by two people on a cowl-staff (see below).

Comb.: **cowl-staff** a stout stick for carrying a burden, supported on the shoulders of two bearers.

cowle /kaʊl/ *n.* *Anglo-Ind.* L17. [Arab. *ḳawl* utterance, declaration.] A written agreement; *esp.* (a) safe-conduct or amnesty.

cowling /ˈkaʊlɪŋ/ *n.* E20. [f. COWL *n.*[1] + -ING[1].] The removable covering over the engine etc. of an aeroplane or motor vehicle.

cowp *n.* var. of COUP *n.*[2]

Cowper's gland /ˈkaʊpəz gland/ *n. phr.* M18. [William *Cowper* (1666–1709), Eng. anatomist.] = BULBO-URETHRAL *gland.*

Cowperian /kaʊˈpɪərɪən/ *a.* L19. **Cowpe'ritis** *n.* inflammation of a bulbo-urethral gland L19.

cowrie /ˈkaʊ(ə)ri/ *n.* Also **cowry.** M17. [Hind. *kauṛī.*] 1 A small gastropod, *Cypraea moneta*, of the Indian Ocean; its polished shell, formerly used as money in parts of Africa and southern Asia. Also *money-cowrie.* M17. 2 (The usu. smooth glossy shell of) any gastropod of this genus or the family Cypraeidae, marked by an oval shape and narrow elongated opening. M19.

cowslip /ˈkaʊslɪp/ *n.* [OE *cūslyppe, cūsloppe*, f. as COW *n.*[1] + SLIP *n.*[1]: cf. OXLIP, SLOP *n.*[2]] 1 A spring-flowering primula, *Primula veris*, of dry grassy banks and pastures, bearing drooping umbels of fragrant yellow flowers; (with specifying wd) any of various other plants resembling this. Also, a flowering stem of such a plant. OE. 2 The marsh marigold, *Caltha palustris*. *US.* M19.

1 **American cowslip** any of various N. American plants bearing umbellate mostly purple or white flowers with reflexed petals that constitute the genus *Dodecatheon*, of the primrose family; esp. *D. meadia.* **Cape cowslip** = LACHENALIA. *Virginia cowslip*: see VIRGINIA I. *Virginian cowslip*: see VIRGINIAN *a.*

cowslipped *a.* covered with cowslips L18. **cowslipping** *n.* the gathering of cowslips L19.

cowson /ˈkaʊs(ə)n/ *n. slang. derog.* M20. [f. COW *n.*[1] + SON *n.*[1], after *whoreson.*] A detestable person or (occas.) thing.

J. R. ACKERLEY A cowson of a place.

cowy /ˈkaʊɪ/ *a.* Also **-ey.** L19. [f. COW *n.*[1] + -Y[1].] Of, pertaining to, or characteristic of a cow.

cox /kɒks/ *n.*[1] & *v.* M19. [Abbrev. of COXSWAIN.] A *n.* A coxswain, esp. of a racing boat. M19. B *v.t.* & *i.* Act as the cox of (a boat); be a cox. L19.
coxless *a.* L19.

Cox /kɒks/ *n.*[2] Also **Cox's** /ˈkɒksɪz/. M19. [R. *Cox*, amateur Eng. fruit-grower, who first raised it (1825).] In full *Cox's orange pippin*. A leading variety of eating apple with a red-tinged green skin.

coxa /ˈkɒksə/ *n.* Pl. **coxae** /ˈkɒksiː/. LME. [L = hip.] †1 *Anat.* The thigh; the thigh-bone. Only in LME. 2 *Anat.* The hip; the hip-bone. *rare.* L17. 3 *Zool.* The segment nearest the body in the leg of an insect or other arthropod. E19.
coxal *a.* E19. **coˈxalgia** *n.* [Gk *algos* pain] pain in the hip-joint M19. **coˈxalgic** *a.* pertaining to or affected with coxalgia L19.

coxcomb /ˈkɒkskəʊm/ *n.* Also †**cockscomb,** †**cock's comb.** See also COCKSCOMB. M16. [Var. of COCKSCOMB.] 1 Orig., a fool, a simpleton. Now, a conceited showy empty-headed person; a fop. M16. 2 See COCKSCOMB II.
1 GOLDSMITH Fond to be seen she kept a bevy Of powdered coxcombs at her levy.
†**coxcombly** *a.* = COXCOMBICAL L16–E19. **coxcombry** /-kəmri/ *n.* †(*a*) foolishness; (*b*) coxcombical quality; a coxcombical trait or act: E17.

coxcombical /kɒksˈkəʊmɪk(ə)l, -ˈkɒm-/ *a.* E18. [f. prec. + -ICAL.] Resembling, pertaining to, or characteristic of a coxcomb; foolishly conceited.
coxcombic *a.* = COXCOMBICAL L18. **coxcombiˈcality** *n.* coxcombical quality; a coxcombical act: M18. **coxˈcombically** *adv.* M18.

†**coxen** *n.* Also **-on.** E17–M18. [Repr. pronunc.] = COXSWAIN.

coxopodite /kɒkˈsɒpədʌɪt/ *n.* L19. [f. COXA + -O- + Gk *pous, pod-* foot + -ITE[1].] *Zool.* The segment nearest the body in the leg of an arthropod, esp. a crustacean.
coxopoˈditic *a.* L19.

Cox's *n.* see COX *n.*[2]

Coxsackie virus /kɒkˈsaki ˌvʌɪrəs, kʊk-/ *n. phr.* Also **c-** & as one wd. M20. [*Coxsackie* in New York State, where the first cases were found.] Any of a group of enteroviruses which cause various respiratory, neurological, and muscular diseases in man.

coxswain /ˈkɒks(ə)n, -sweɪn/ *n.* & *v.* Also **cockswain.** ME. [f. COCK *n.*[2] + SWAIN *n.*] A *n.* The steersman of a ship's boat, lifeboat, racing boat, etc.; the senior petty officer on board a small ship, submarine, etc. ME. B *v.t.* & *i.* Act as the coxswain of (a boat); be a coxswain. E20.
coxswainless *a.* L19. **coxswainship** *n.* L19.

coxy /ˈkɒksi/ *a. dial.* & *slang.* Also **cocksy.** E18. [f. COCK *n.*[1] + -SY.] Impudent, bumptious, cocky.
coxiness *n.* M19.

coy /kɔɪ/ *n.* Now *dial.* E17. [Du. *kooi*, †*koye*, a parallel development to MDu. *kouwe* (Du. dial. *kouw* cage), = MLG *kaue* f. L *cavea* CAGE *n.* Cf. DECOY *n.*] 1 A place for entrapping wildfowl; = DECOY *n.* I. E17. 2 In full *coy-duck*. A decoy-duck. E17.

coy /kɔɪ/ *a.* ME. [(O)Fr. *coi*, earlier *quei*, f. Proto-Romance var. of L *quietus* QUIET *a.*] †1 Quiet, still. Chiefly in *bear, hold, keep* (*oneself*) *coy*. ME–M17. 2 Displaying modest backwardness, shy; *spec.* (of a (young) woman) unresponsive to amorous advances, esp. in an affected or coquettish way. Of behaviour, a look, etc.: suggesting or marked by this quality. LME. b Affecting reluctance to make a statement or give information; archly reticent. M20. †3 Distant in manner, disdainful. L15–M17. 4 Chary or shy *of*; reluctant *to*. L16. 5 Of a place or thing: withdrawn from view or access; secluded. M17.
2 SHAKES. *Ven. & Ad.* 'Tis but a kiss I beg; why art thou coy?
coyish *a.* (now *rare*) M16. **coyly** *adv.* LME. **coyness** *n.* L16.

coy /kɔɪ/ *v.* LME. [f. COY *a.*, or perh. orig. aphet. f. ACCOY.] †1 *v.t.* Calm, make quiet. LME–M16. †2 *v.t.* Stroke or touch soothingly; caress. LME–L17. †3 *v.t.* Coax; win over by caresses. L15–L18. 4 *v.i.* & (usu.) *t.* w. *it*. Behave coyly; affect modesty or reserve. *arch.* L16. †5 *v.i.* Disdain *to do*. *rare* (Shakes.). Only in E17. 6 *v.t.* Disguise (affection etc.) in a coy manner. *rare.* L19.

coydog /ˈkɔɪdɒg/ *n. N. Amer.* M20. [f. COYOTE + DOG *n.*] A hybrid between a coyote and a wild dog.

†**coyn** *n.* see QUINCE.

coynye /ˈkɔɪn(j)i/ *n.* Also **coignye, coyne** /kɔɪn/. LME. [Ir. *coinneamh*.] *Ir. Hist.* Food and entertainment exacted by chiefs for the billeting of their attendants; a tax imposed in place of this.

coyote /ˈkɔɪəʊt, kɔɪˈəʊti/ *n.* & *v.* Pl. same, **-s.** M18. [Mex. Sp. f. Nahuatl *coyotl*.] A *n.* A small nocturnal wolflike animal, *Canis latrans*, of western N. America, noted for its mournful howling. Also called *prairie-wolf*. M18.
Comb.: **coyote diggings** small lateral shafts sunk by miners in California, resembling the holes of the coyote.
B *v.i. Mining.* Make a small lateral tunnel from a shaft etc. *US slang.* M19.

coypu /ˈkɔɪpuː/ *n.* Also **-pou.** Pl. same, **-s.** L18. [Araucanian.] A S. American semi-aquatic rodent, *Myocastor coypus*, resembling a beaver, bred for its fur (nutria) and now naturalized in parts of Europe and the US.

coz /kʌz/ *n. arch.* M16. [Abbrev.] Cousin. (Usu. as a form of address.)

coze /kəʊz/ *n.* & *v.* E19. [App. f. Fr. *causer* chat, perh. assoc. w. *cozy*, COSY.] A *n.* A long intimate talk. E19. B *v.i.* Converse in a friendly way; have a long chat. E19.

cozen /ˈkʌz(ə)n/ *v.t.* L16. [Perh. f. It. †*cozzonare* act as a horse-breaker, cheat, f. *cozzone* middleman, broker f. L *cocio(n-)*, *coctio(n-)* dealer. Cf. also OFr. *coçoner* act as a middleman with, ult. f. same L source.] 1 Cheat, trick, (*of, out of*); trick, beguile, *into*. L16. 2 Deceive, mislead. L16.
cozenage *n.* the practice or an act of cozening; (a) deception, (a) fraud: L16. **cozener** *n.* a cheat, an impostor M16.

cozy *a., n.,* & *v.* see COSY.

cozzie *n.* var. of COSSIE.

crab /krab/ *n.*[1] [OE *krabba* = (M)LG, (M)Du. *krabbe*, ON *krabbi* rel. to MLG *krabben* CRAB *v.*[1], ON *krafla* scratch.] 1 Any of numerous decapod crustaceans of the section Brachyura, which have the first pair of legs modified into pincers and can move in any direction, including sideways and backwards; *esp.* any of the edible kinds found near sea-coasts; the flesh of any of these used as food. Also (w. qualification), any of various similar crustaceans and arachnids. OE. 2a (Usu. **C-**.) *The* constellation and zodiacal sign Cancer. OE. b *the Crab* (*nebula*), a nebula in the constellation Taurus, the remnant of a supernova outburst observed in 1054. M19. 3 In full *crab-louse* (otherwise usu. in *pl.*). A parasitic insect, *Phthirus pubis*, infesting the pubic and other hair in humans. M16. 4 Any of various contrivances (orig. one with claws) for hoisting or hauling heavy weights; *esp.* (*a*) a kind of capstan without a drumhead; (*b*) a portable winch; (*c*) the lifting-gear of a travelling crane. E17. 5 In *pl.* The lowest throw in the game of hazard, two ones. Formerly also, hazard. Cf. *crab's eyes* (c) below, CRAPS. M18. 6 [After G *Krebs*.] A book returned unsold to the publisher. *colloq.* L19.
1 *fiddler-crab, hermit-crab, horseshoe crab, land-crab, peeler crab, red crab, robber-crab, shore crab, soldier-crab, soft crab, spider crab, velvet crab, velvet fiddler crab, velvet swimming crab, violet crab*, etc. **catch a crab** (in rowing) get one's oar jammed under water, as if it were being held down by a crab; also, miss the water with the stroke.
Comb.: **crab-catcher** *W. Indies* a heron which feeds on crabs, *esp.* the green heron *Butorides striatus*; †**crab-fish** = sense 1 above; **crab-grass** †(*a*) glasswort; (*b*) (orig. *US*) a creeping grass; esp. *Digitaria sanguinalis*, widespread as a weed in warmer parts of the world; **crab-harrow** a harrow with bent teeth for breaking up deeply ploughed land; **crab-hole** *Austral.* a depression in the ground attributed to the action of a land-crab; *crab-louse*: see sense 3 above; *Crab nebula*: see sense 2b above; **crab plover** a gregarious large-billed white and black crab-eating wading bird, *Dromas ardeola*, of coasts around the Indian Ocean; **crab-pot** a wickerwork trap for catching crabs; **crab's-eye** (*a*) a calcareous concretion from the stomach of a crayfish etc., formerly used in powdered form as an absorbent and antacid (usu. in *pl.*); (*b*) in *pl.*, (the scarlet, black-tipped seeds of) the jequirity; (*c*) in *pl.*, (*slang*) = sense 5 above; **crab-spider** a spider of the family Thomisidae which runs sideways like a crab.
crabber *n.*[1] a person who fishes for crabs; a boat used in crabbing: LME. **crablike** *a.* & *adv.* (*a*) *adj.* resembling (that of) a crab; (*b*) *adv.* = CRABWISE *adv.*: L16. **crabwise** *adv.* & *a.* (*a*) *adv.* moving sideways or backwards like a crab; (*b*) *adj.* = CRABLIKE *a.*: E20.

crab /krab/ *n.*[2] LME. [Perh. alt. of SCRAB *n.* by assoc. with prec. or CRABBED. Sense 3 in later use back-form. f. CRABBED.] 1 The wild apple, a native fruit of northern Europe, smaller than the cultivated apple and noted for its sour, astringent flavour. Also, the fruit of an ornamental crab (see sense 2 below). LME. 2 In full *crab tree*. The European tree, *Malus sylvestris*, which bears the wild apple. Also, any of various small-fruited trees of the genus *Malus* grown for ornament, e.g. the Siberian crab, *M. baccata*. LME. 3 A sour or cross-grained person. L16.
Comb.: **crab-apple** = senses 1, 2 above; **crab-stick** a stick made from the wood of the crab tree; *fig.* a bad-tempered person; **crab-stock** a young crab tree used as a stock for grafting on; *crab tree*: see sense 2 above.

crab /krab/ *n.*[3] Also **carap(a)** /kəˈrap(ə)/. M18. [f. *carap*, Antillean name f. Carib = oil.] A S. American tree, *Carapa guianensis*, of the mahogany family.
Comb.: **crab-nut** the seed of the crab; **crab-oil** the oil obtained from crab-nuts, used in lamps and as an anthelmintic; **crabwood** the timber of the crab.

crab /krab/ *n.*[4] *colloq.* L19. [f. CRAB *v.*[1]] The action or an instance of finding fault or complaining; a reason for fault-finding or complaint, a grouse.

crab /krab/ *v.*[1] Infl. **-bb-.** L16. [(M)LG *krabben* rel. to CRAB *n.*[1]] 1 *v.t.* & *i. Falconry.* Of hawks: scratch and fight (each other). L16. 2 *v.t.* Obstruct the progress or success of (a scheme etc.); spoil the plans of (a person). *colloq.* E19. 3 *v.t.* Criticize, find fault with. *colloq.* M19. 4 *v.i.* Grumble, complain (*at, about*). *colloq.* L19.
2 C. SANDBURG You're trying to crab my act. 3 R. MACAULAY It is a pity to crab all governments and everything they do. 4 B. TRAPIDO If you don't come he'll crab on at us about the expense.
crabber *n.*[2] a person who criticizes or complains E20.

crab /krab/ *v.*[2] Infl. **-bb-.** M17. [f. CRAB *n.*[1]] 1 *v.i.* Fish for or take crabs. Chiefly as *crabbing* vbl n. M17. 2 *v.i. Naut.* Drift sideways to leeward. M19. 3 *v.t.* & *i. Aeronaut.* Turn (an aircraft) into the wind to offset drift. E20. 4 *v.t.* & *i. gen.* Move (something), move oneself, sideways or obliquely like a crab. M20.

crab /krab/ *v.*[3]*t.* Infl. **-bb-.** L19. [Origin unkn.] In worsted finishing: wind (cloth) on a roller under tension and subject it to hot water or steam, to prevent subsequent cockling or wrinkling. Chiefly as *crabbing* vbl n.

crabbed /ˈkrabɪd, krabd/ *a.* ME. [Orig. f. CRAB *n.*[1] (cf. DOGGED *a.*), with ref. to the gait and habits of the crab, which suggest a cross-grained disposition: cf. LG *krabbe* cantankerous man, *krabbig* contentious, cross-grained. Later assoc. with CRAB *n.*[2]] 1 Of a person: orig., objectionably perverse or wayward; later, irritable, cantankerous (passing into sense 5). ME. b In a bad mood; cross, irritated. Orig. & chiefly *Sc.* LME. †c Of words, facial expression, etc.: indicating irritability or anger. LME–M17. †2 Unpleasant to the taste, unpalatable. LME–E17. †3a Of a tree, stick, etc.: crooked, gnarled. E16–L17. b Of weather, terrain: rough, rugged. *obs.* exc. *dial.* L16. 4a Of writings, an author, etc.: hard to understand or interpret; involved, intricate. M16. b Of handwriting: hard to decipher. E17. 5 Like a crab-apple; *fig.* sour-tempered, morose. M16.
crabbedly *adv.* LME. **crabbedness** *n.* LME.

crabby /ˈkrabi/ *a.* M16. [f. CRAB *n.*[1] (in sense 3, partly f. CRAB *n.*[2]) + -Y[1].] †1 Crooked; perplexing. M–L16. 2 Resembling the crab (CRAB *n.*[1]). Formerly *spec.*, moving obliquely. L16. 3 Bad-tempered; morose. L18.

crack /krak/ *n.* In sense 3 also †**crake**. ME. [Corresp. to MDu. *crak*, OHG, G *Krach*: cf. CRACK *v.*] I Of sound, & derived senses. 1 A sudden sharp loud noise (as) of something breaking or exploding, of a whip, a rifle, thunder, etc. ME. 2a Formerly, a cannon-shot. Now (*colloq.*), a rifle-shot. LME. b An attempt, a try. Chiefly in *have a crack at*. *colloq.* (orig. *US*). E19. c A sharp blow. *colloq.* M19. 3a Boastful talk; an instance of this. Also, a flagrant lie. Now *dial.* LME. b A gossip, an intimate talk; in *pl.*, items of gossip. *Sc.* & *north.* E18. c A witty or sarcastic remark; a wisecrack. *colloq.* (orig. *US*). L19. d Amusement provided by conversation; congenial conversation. Chiefly in *for the crack*. *Anglo-Ir. colloq.* M20. 4 A short space of time, a moment. Esp. in *in a crack*. *colloq.* E18.

1 **a (fair) crack of the whip** *colloq.* a (fair) chance to act, participate, or prove oneself. **crack of doom** *arch.* the thunder-peal of the Day of Judgement. 2b B. SCHULBERG Maybe I'll give another agency first crack at it instead. 3c J. THURBER Insinuations, reflections, or . . cracks about old boy friends . . should be avoided. 4 **crack of dawn** the moment when dawn breaks.

II Breaking or the result of it. 5 A slight opening formed by the breaking of a hard substance; a fissure. L15. b *spec.* A gap between floorboards. *US.* E19. c The chink left when a door etc. is not quite closed. L19. 6 A deficiency or flaw (in an immaterial thing). M16. b A mental flaw; a mania, a craze. E17. 7 An incomplete break or fracture, in which the parts still cohere. L16. 8 Cracked or broken tone (as of a boy's voice at puberty). E17. 9 A burglary. *arch. Criminals' slang.* E19.

5 F. A. KEMBLE Centipedes . . come out of the cracks . . of the walls. **paper over the cracks** *fig.* use temporary expedients to disguise confusion or disagreement. 6b STEELE The Upholsterer, whose Crack towards Politicks I have . . mentioned. 8 SHAKES. *Cymb.* Though now our voices Have got the mannish crack.

III Transferred or doubtfully derived senses. †10 A pert lively boy. L16–L17. 11 A sportsman, horse, etc., of outstanding excellence. M17. †12 A woman of bad reputation; a prostitute. L17–L18. 13 Cocaine heated with baking-powder until hard and broken into small pieces for smoking or inhaling. Orig. *US slang.* L20.

Comb.: **crackhead** *slang* a person who habitually takes crack; **crack house** *slang* a place where crack is bought and sold.

crackless *a.* free from cracks or flaws E17.

crack /krak/ *a. colloq.* L18. [f. CRACK *n.* II.] Pre-eminent in a particular sphere, first-class.

J. K. JEROME Crack shots, winners of Queen's prizes. P. USTINOV Soldiers of several crack regiments.

crack /krak/ *v.* Also †**crake**. [OE *cracian* = (M)Du. *krāken*, OHG *krahhōn* (G *krachen*).] I With chief ref. to sound. 1 *v.i.* Of a thing breaking, of thunder, a gun, a whip, etc.: make a sudden sharp or explosive noise. OE. b *v.t.* Strike with a resounding blow. Now *dial.* or *colloq.* LME. c *v.t.* Cause (a whip etc.) to make a sharp noise. M17. 2 *v.t.* Utter or tell, esp. suddenly or with éclat. Now only in *crack a joke* or with the spoken words of a joke or wisecrack as obj. ME. 3 *v.i.* Talk big, boast. Now *dial.* LME. †b *v.t.* Claim boastfully *that*, a person or thing *to be*. M16–L17. 4 *v.i.* Discuss the news, gossip, chat. *Sc.* & *north.* LME.

1 POPE Silks russle, and tough Whalebones crack. J. STEINBECK The flame cracked up among the twigs. b X. HERBERT Don't be cheeky or I'll crack you. 2 T. HOCCLEVE Not a worde dar he crake. B. SCHULBERG 'Yeah,' Sammy cracked, 'you should have been there'. 3 CARLYLE My sleep was nothing to crack of.

II With chief ref. to breaking. 5 *v.t.* Break (esp. something hard and hollow) with a sudden sharp noise. ME. 6a *v.i.* & *t.* (Cause to) snap or break in two. *arch.* ME. b *v.i. fig.* Break down, give way, yield (to torture etc.), succumb to pressure. Cf. *crack up* (b) below. M17. 7a *v.i.* & *t.* (Cause to) break without complete separation of parts. LME. b *v.t.* Open up fissures in. M17. c *v.t.* Break or crush (esp. corn) into small particles. *US.* M19. 8 *transf.* & *fig.* a *v.t.* Damage (something immaterial) so that it is no longer sound. Formerly esp. in †*crack credit*. M16. b *v.t.* Impair the reasoning power of. E17. c *v.t.* & *i.* With ref. to the voice, esp. in puberty or old age: make or become hoarse or dissonant, like a cracked bell. E17. 9 *v.t.* Open and drink (a bottle of liquor). *colloq.* L16. 10 *v.t.* Find the solution to (a problem, code, etc.). E17. 11 *v.t.* Break into (a house, safe, etc.). *Criminals' slang.* E18. 12 *v.t.* Decompose (heavy oils) by heat or pressure so as to produce lighter hydrocarbons, such as petrol. M19.

5 N. MOSLEY His head was like an egg that you crack and it runs over the egg cup. 6a *fig.*: SHAKES. *Cymb.* He could not But think her bond of chastity quite crack'd. b N. MAILER They both cracked . . They couldn't stop laughing. 7 W. SALMON Some Colours . . will crack when they are dry. D. W. JERROLD There's four glasses broke and nine cracked. 8a A. WOOD [This] . . hath much crak'd his Reputation. b STEELE Lest this hard . . student should . . crack his brain with studying. c G. VIDAL Gallus's voice cracked with anger.

III Of sudden action. 13 *v.t.* Move with a jerk or sudden movement; snatch *out*, clap *on*. M16. 14 *v.i.* Travel with speed; rush *along*, press *on*. Chiefly *Naut.* exc. in *get cracking* below. M19.

Phrases: **crack a crib** *Criminals' slang* burgle a house. **crack hardy** or **hearty** *Austral.* & *NZ slang* put on a show of courage in the face of misfortune or difficulty. **crack on sail** *Naut.* hoist additional sails to increase speed. **crack the whip** *fig.* enforce one's authority. **get cracking** *colloq.* set to work briskly. *take* or *use a sledgehammer to crack a nut*: see SLEDGEHAMMER *n.*

With advs. in specialized senses: **crack down (on, upon)** *colloq.* take severe repressive measures (against). **crack up** *colloq.* (*a*) extol, praise; in *pass.* (usu. in neg. contexts), be asserted in glowing terms *to be*; (*b*) collapse under strain etc.; suffer a nervous breakdown; collapse with laughter.

crack /krak/ *int.* & *adv.* L17. [f. CRACK *n.*, *v.*] A *int.* Repr. a cracking sound. L17. B *adv.* With a crack. M18.

crack- /krak/ *comb. form.* L15. [Partly repr. the stem of CRACK *v.*, usu. with a following obj.; partly for CRACKED.] 1a That cracks (the 2nd elem. of the comb.). b That cracks. 2 Cracked.

crack-brain a crazy person, a crank. **crack-brained** *adj.* crazy, cranky. †**crack-halter** = *crack-rope* n. below. **crack-headed** *a.* crazy, cranky. **crack-hemp** = *crack-rope* n. below. **crack-jaw** *n.* & *a.* (a word that is) difficult to pronounce. **crackpot** *n.* & *a.* (*a*) *n.* a crazy person; an eccentric or unpractical person; (*b*) *adj.* crazy, cranky, eccentric, unpractical. †**crack-rope** *n.* & *a.* (*a*) *n.* a person fit to be hanged, a gallows-bird; a rogue; (*b*) *adj.* fit to be hanged; roguish. **crack-voiced** *a.* having a broken voice. **crack-willow** a willow, *Salix fragilis*, with branches that break off readily.

crackajack *n.* & *a.* var. of CRACKERJACK.

crackdown /ˈkrakdaʊn/ *n. colloq.* M20. [f. *crack down* s.v. CRACK *v.*] An instance of cracking down, a taking of severe repressive measures.

cracked /krakt/ *ppl a.* Also †**crackt**. E16. [f. CRACK *v.* + -ED[1].] 1 That has cracked or been cracked; broken. E16. b *spec.* Broken or crushed into coarse particles. Orig. *US.* M19. 2 *fig.* Flawed, unsound; blemished in reputation etc. *arch.* E16. 3 Deranged, slightly mad, crazy; infatuated. Now *colloq.* E17.

1 SHAKES. *1 Hen. IV* We must have bloody noses and crack'd crowns. DICKENS The lips were parched and cracked in many places. R. WEST She forced her voice, and only achieved a cracked whisper. b *cracked corn, rice, wheat*, etc. 2 T. DEKKER A most false and crackt Latin oration. SWIFT A cracked chambermaid. 3 D. JACOBSON He was a little cracked—it could be seen in his remote, pale eyes.

Comb.: **cracked-pot** *n.* & *a.* (*fig.*) = *crackpot* s.v. CRACK-.

crackedness *n.* unsoundness of mind E20.

cracker /ˈkrakə/ *n.* LME. [f. CRACK *v.* + -ER[1].] 1 A noisy boastful person. Also, an extravagant liar. LME. b A flagrant lie. *colloq.* E17. 2 An instrument for cracking or crushing something, esp. (*sing.* & (usu.) in *pl.*) for cracking nuts. Also, an installation for cracking hydrocarbons. M16. 3 A kind of firework that explodes with a sharp report or series of reports. L16. b A cylindrical paper structure made so as to break with a bang when its ends are pulled, used on festive occasions, and often containing a paper hat, a motto or joke, a small toy or novelty, etc. M19. 4 The pintail duck (so called from its alarm call). *local.* M17. 5 A thin dry biscuit. M18. b A light crisp made of rice or tapioca flour. Usu. w. specifying wd. M20. 6 Orig., a frontier outlaw. Later, a 'poor white' in certain of the southern States of the US, esp. Florida and Georgia. *derog. US.* M18. 7 A horsehair attachment to the end of a whiplash, to enhance its cracking. *US, Austral.*, & *NZ.* M19. 8 An outstandingly good person or thing. *colloq.* E20.

2 *cat cracker, nutcracker*, etc. 3b *Christmas cracker*. 5 *cream cracker* etc. b *prawn cracker, shrimp cracker*, etc.

Comb.: **cracker-barrel** *n.* & *a.* (*N. Amer.*) (*a*) *n.* a barrel in which crackers (biscuits) are packed; (*b*) *adj.* (of philosophy, a philosopher, etc.) homespun; **cracker-bush** an Australian tree of the spurge family, *Petalostigma glabrescens*, with a fruit that splits open with a loud report.

crackerjack /ˈkrakədʒak/ *n.* & *a. colloq.* (orig. *US*). Also **crackajack**. L19. [Fanciful formation f. CRACK *v.* or CRACKER.] A *n.* 1 Something exceptionally good of its kind. Also, a very skilful person. L19. 2 A sweet made of popcorn and syrup. (Orig. a proprietary name.) E20. B *adj.* Of outstanding excellence, first-rate. E20.

crackers /ˈkrakəz/ *pred. a. slang.* E20. [f. CRACKER *n.*: see -ER[6]. Cf. CRACKED 3.] Crazy, mad; infatuated.

cracket *n.* see CRICKET *n.*[3]

cracking /ˈkrakɪŋ/ *a.* & *adv.* LME. [f. CRACK *v.* + -ING[2].] A *adj.* 1 That cracks or breaks. LME. †2 Bragging; boastful. E16–L17. 3 (Of pace) very fast; very good, outstanding. *slang.* M19. B *adv.* Outstandingly, very. *slang.* E20.

crackle /ˈkrak(ə)l/ *n.* L16. [f. the vb.] †1 A child's rattle. Only in L16. 2 A crackling sound. M19. 3 A network of fine cracks induced in the glaze of china, pottery, glass, etc., for decorative effect. Also = *crackle-ware* below. M19.

2 E. GLASGOW The crackle of the leaves underfoot. F. WELDON The transistor radio produced only crackle. *snap, crackle, (and) pop*: see SNAP *n.*

Comb.: **crackle-ware** a kind of china marked by a crackle in the glaze.

crackle /ˈkrak(ə)l/ *v.* LME. [f. CRACK *v.*: see -LE[3].] 1 *v.i.* Emit a succession of slight cracking sounds. Formerly also (*contempt.*), trill or quaver in singing. LME. b *fig.* Sparkle with vigour or animation. M20. 2 *v.t.* Cause to emit a crackling sound; break with a crackling sound. E17.

1 C. HARDWICK Huge logs blazed and crackled. D. H. LAWRENCE The wind made the canvas crackle. 2 J. STEINBECK His fingers crackled the paper in his pocket.

crackled *ppl a.* (*a*) (of roast pork) having the skin crisp and hard (see CRACKLING *n.* 3); (*b*) (esp. of ceramics etc.) marked by many small cracks. E17. **crackly** *a.* having a tendency to crackle M19.

crackling /ˈkraklɪŋ/ *n.* L16. [f. prec. + -ING[1]. Cf. SCRATCHING *n.*[1]] 1 The action of CRACKLE *v.* L16. 2 In *pl.* a The residue of tallow-melting, used to feed dogs. L16. b The residue of hogs' fat after the lard has been fried out. *dial.* & *US.* M19. 3 The crisp skin of roast pork. E18. b Sexually attractive women collectively. Esp. in *a (nice) bit of crackling*. *slang.* Freq. considered *offensive.* M20. 4 Crackle-ware. L19.

cracknel /ˈkrakn(ə)l/ *n.* LME. [Alt. of (O)Fr. *craquelin* f. MDu. *krākeline*, f. *krāken* CRACK *v.*] A light crisp kind of biscuit.

cracksman /ˈkraksmən/ *n. Criminals' slang.* Pl. **-men**. L18. [f. CRACK *n.* 9 + -'S[1] + MAN *n.*] A burglar. Also, a person who breaks open safes.

†**crackt** *ppl a.* var. of CRACKED.

crack-up /ˈkrakʌp/ *n. colloq.* E20. [f. *crack up* s.v. CRACK *v.*] An instance of cracking up, a collapse under strain etc.; a nervous breakdown.

cracky /ˈkraki/ *a.* L15. [f. CRACK *n.* or *v.* + -Y[1].] 1 Full of cracks or fissures; inclined to crack. L15. 2 Full of conversation; talkative, affable. *Sc.* & *north.* E19. 3 Cracked in the head, crazy. *colloq.* M19.

crackiness *n.* (*colloq.*) craziness M19.

cracovienne /krəkəʊvɪ'ɛn/ *n.* M19. [Fr., fem. adj. f. *Cracovie* Kraków (Cracow), a city in southern Poland.] A lively Polish dance; a ballet dance in a Polish style. Also called *krakowiak*.

-cracy /krəsi/ *suff.* [Repr. Fr. *-cratie*, med.L *-cratia*, Gk *-kratia* power, rule (*kratos* strength, authority).] In or forming ns. referring to types of government or ruling class, as *democracy*, *aristocracy*, etc. From the *o* which regularly precedes the suffix in words of Gk origin a form *-ocracy* has been inferred which has been added to certain English words (mainly in nonce-formations), as *meritocracy*.

cradle /'kreɪd(ə)l/ *n.* [OE *cradol*, perh. f. the same base as OHG *kratto*, MHG, G *Kratte* basket.] **I 1** A little bed or cot for an infant, *esp.* one mounted on rockers or swinging. OE. **2** Any bed or place of repose. *poet.* ME. **3** *fig.* The place in which a thing begins or is nurtured in its earlier stage; the beginning. (Foll. by *of*.) L16. **4** *Naut.* A bedstead for a wounded seaman. Now *rare.* E19.

1 **(from the) cradle to (the) grave** throughout one's whole life. **from the** or **one's cradle** from infancy (to any stage in life). See also *cat's cradle* s.v. CAT *n.*[1] 3 A. BEVAN The district which was the cradle of heavy industry in Britain.

II *techn.* **5** A framework of bars, cords, rods, etc., used as a support or protection; a grating, a structure resembling a hurdle. LME. **6** A framework on which a ship or boat rests during construction or repairs or down which it is slid when launched. E16. **7** A wooden frame attached to a scythe, with a row of long curved teeth parallel to the blade, which enable the cut corn to be laid more evenly. L16. **8** *Med.* A framework to protect an injured limb etc. from the weight of bedclothes. E18. **b** A frame placed round the neck of an animal to prevent it from biting an injury or sore. M19. **9** *Engraving.* A chisel-like tool with a serrated edge, which is rocked to and fro over a metal plate to produce a mezzotint ground. Also called *(mezzotint) rocker.* L18. **10** A trough on rockers in which auriferous earth or sand is shaken in water in order to separate the gold. E19. **11** A framework on or in which a person is supported to work on the vertical face of a building, ship, etc. L19. **12** A rest or support for a telephone receiver not in use. E20. **13** *Cricket.* A device used to deflect a ball thrown on it in practising short-range fielding. M20.

Comb.: **cradle-board** among N. American Indians, a board to which an infant is strapped; **cradle-cap** *(a)* a cap worn by a baby; *(b)* an area of yellowish or brownish scales that sometimes forms on the top of a baby's head; the condition of having this, seborrhoeic eczema of the scalp in a baby; **cradle Catholic** a person who has been a Roman Catholic from birth; **cradle-rocker** *(a)* any of the curved bars fitted under a child's cradle to enable it to rock; *(b)* a person who rocks a child's cradle; **cradle-roof** a roof of semi-cylindrical shape, divided into panels by wooden ribs; **cradle-scythe** a scythe fitted with a cradle (sense 7). **cradle-snatch** *v.t.* & *i.* (*slang*) have a love affair with or marry (a much younger person); **cradle-snatcher** *slang* a person who has a love affair with or marries a much younger person; **cradle-song** a lullaby.

cradle /'kreɪd(ə)l/ *v.* LME. [f. the n.] **I** *v.t.* **1** Lay in, or as in, a cradle; rock to sleep; hold or shelter as in a cradle. LME. **2** Nurture, shelter, or rear in infancy (*lit.* & *fig.*). E17. **3** Mow (corn etc.) with a cradle-scythe. M18. **4** *techn.* Support in or on a cradle; raise (a vessel) to a higher level by a cradle. L18. **5** Wash (auriferous earth etc.) in a miner's cradle. M19. **6** Support the back of (a picture etc.) by ribs and transverse narrow strips. L19. **7** Replace (a telephone receiver) on its cradle. M20.

1 W. STYRON Her head was cradled against the inside of her arm.

II *v.i.* **8** Lie as in a cradle. *rare* (Shakes.). Only in E17.

cradler *n.* a person who or thing which cradles; formerly *esp.* a person who mows with a cradle-scythe: M18.

cradling /'kreɪdlɪŋ/ *n.* E19. [f. prec. + -ING[1].] **1** The action of CRADLE *v.* E19. **2** *Archit.* A wooden or iron framework, esp. in a ceiling. E19.

craft /krɑːft/ *n.* [OE *cræft* = OFris. *kraft*, OS *kraft* (Du. *kracht*), OHG, G *Kraft*, ON *kraptr* (in sense I only). The transference to 'skill, art, occupation' is Eng. only.] **†I 1** Strength, power, force. OE–E16. **2** Skill, art; ability in planning or constructing; ingenuity, dexterity. Now chiefly as 2nd elem. of comb. OE. **†b** *spec.* Occult art, magic. ME–L15. **†c** Human skill; art as opp. to nature. LME–L16. **†3** An artifice, a device, a skilful contrivance; *spec.* a magical device. OE–M16. **4** In a bad sense: **†a** A deceitful action; a trick, a fraud. OE–L17. **b** Skill or art applied to deceive or overreach; guile, cunning. ME. **5** An art, trade, or profession requiring special skill or knowledge, esp. manual dexterity. OE. **b** The members of a trade or handicraft collectively; a trade union, guild, or company of craftsmen. LME. **†6** Scholarship; a branch of learning, a science. ME–M16.

2 *handicraft, priestcraft, stagecraft, statecraft, witchcraft, woodcraft,* etc. 4b J. CONRAD With her it was very difficult to distinguish between craft and innocence. 5 C. PRIEST I determined to learn country crafts: weaving, woodwork, pottery. S. SPENDER Painting is largely a craft . . whereas writing is largely cerebral. *handicraft* etc. *arts and crafts*: see ART *n.*[1] *the gentle craft*: see GENTLE *a.* **b the Craft** the brotherhood of Freemasons.

II Vehicles, equipment, etc. **7** (Pl. same (*collect.*, the earliest use), **†-s**.) A boat, esp. of small size; a vessel; a machine for flying in or for travelling in space. LME. **8** *collect.* (usu. treated as *pl.*). Implements used in catching and killing fish. Now *rare.* L17.

7 L. T. C. ROLT The water was packed with crowded, flag-bedecked craft. *aircraft, spacecraft,* etc. *small craft*: see SMALL *a.*

Comb.: **craft-brother** one of the same craft or trade; **craft-conscious** *a.* aware of the value of craftsmanship; **craft-guild** a guild of people of the same craft or trade; **craftsmaster** *arch.* *(a)* a person skilled in a particular craft or trade; †*(b)* a master of deceitful craft or cunning; **craftspeople** artisans; **craftsperson** an artisan; **craftswoman** a female artisan; **craft-union** a trade union of people of the same skilled craft; **craftwork** work in a handicraft, (the production of) items of handicraft.

¶ Cf. ART *n.*[1]

craftless *a.* OE.

craft /krɑːft/ *v.* ME. [f. the n.] **†1** *v.t.* Attain, win. *rare.* Only in ME. **2** *v.t.* Make or construct skilfully. (In isolated use bef. M20.) LME. **†3** *v.i.* Act craftily; use one's craft or skill. E16–E17.

2 T. KENEALLY One of the prisoners, a jeweller . . had been crafting a present.

craftsman /'krɑːftsmən/ *n.* Also **†craftman.** Pl. **-men.** LME. [f. CRAFT *n.* + -'S[1] + MAN *n.*] **1** A person who practises a handicraft; an artisan. LME. **2** A person who cultivates one of the fine arts, = ARTIST 3. L19. **3** A private soldier in the Royal Electrical and Mechanical Engineers. M20.

craftsmanship *n.* M17.

crafty /'krɑːfti/ *a.* [OE *cræftig* = OS *kraftag, -ig*, OHG *kreftig* (G *kräftig*), ON *krǫptugr*: see CRAFT *n.*, -Y[1].] **†1** Strong, powerful. OE–ME. **2** Skilful, dexterous, clever, ingenious. Now *arch.* & *dial.* OE. **3** Cunning, artful, wily. ME.

2 W. MORRIS His crafty hands are busy yet. 3 B. HARRIS The most crafty Cheats are held the best Politicians. LD MACAULAY Had not his crafty schemes been disconcerted.

Comb.: **†crafty-sick** *a.* feigning sickness.

craftily *adv.* OE. **craftiness** *n.* LME.

crag /krag/ *n.*[1] Also (*Sc.* & *north.*) **craig** /kreɪg/ ME. [Of Celt. origin. Sense 3 prob. a different wd.] **1** A steep rugged rock; a rough rock detached or projecting. ME. **†2** As a material: rock. LME–E19. **3** *Geol.* Deposits of shelly sand found in East Anglia; the Pliocene and Miocene strata to which these belong. M18.

1 A. MASON That barren . . land of crags and precipices. **crag and tail** *Geol.* a rock formation which is steeply rugged on one side and gently sloping on the other.

Comb.: **crag-bound, crag-fast** *adjs.* (of a person or animal) trapped on a crag and unable to go either up or down; **cragsman** a person accustomed to or skilled in climbing crags.

crag /krag/ *n.*[2] Chiefly *Sc.* & *north.* Also **craig** /kreɪg/. LME. [Prob. f. LDu.: cf. MLG *krage*, MDu. *crāghe*, Du. *kraag*. Cf. SCRAG *n.*[1]] **1** The neck. LME. **b** The throat. L18. **†2** A neck of mutton or veal. LME–M18.

cragged /'kragɪd/ *a.* LME. [f. CRAG *n.*[1] + -ED[2].] **1** Rugged, rough. LME. **2** Formed into or having many crags. M16.

craggedness *n.* L16.

craggy /'kragi/ *a.* LME. [f. CRAG *n.*[1] + -Y[1].] **1** Having many crags; of the nature of a crag, steep and rugged. LME. **2** Of a person, a face, etc.: rough or rugged in form. M16. **3** *fig.* Hard to deal with; rough, difficult. Now *rare.* L16.

cragginess *n.* E17.

craig *n.*[1], *n.*[2] see CRAG *n.*[1], *n.*[2]

craigie /'kreɪgi/ *n. Sc.* & *north.* E18. [f. *craig*, CRAG *n.*[2] + -IE.] = CRAG *n.*[2]

crake /kreɪk/ *n.*[1] Also (*Sc.*) **craik.** ME. [ON *kráka, krákr*, of imit. origin: cf. CROAK.] **1** A crow, a raven. *north.* ME. **2** A bird of the family Rallidae, *esp.* any of the shorter-billed kinds such as the corncrake and the members of the genus *Porzana* (cf. RAIL *n.*[3]). LME. **3** The harsh cry of the corncrake. M19.

2 CORNCRAKE. SORA *crake*. **spotted crake** *Porzana porzana*, a brown skulking marsh bird with a high, sharp call.

†crake *n.*[2] see CRACK *n.*

crake /kreɪk/ *v.*[1]*i.* LME. [Prob. imit.] **1** Utter a harsh grating cry. LME. **2** Of a door etc.: grate harshly, creak. Now *Sc.* & *dial.* M17.

†crake *v.*[2] var. of CRACK *v.*

crakow /'krakaʊ/ *n. obs.* exc. *Hist.* LME. [*Cracow, Kraków*, or Fr. *Cracovie*, in Poland: see CRACOVIENNE.] A boot or shoe with a very long pointed toe, worn in the 14th cent.

cram /kram/ *v.* & *n.* [OE (*ġe*)*crammian* corresp. to MLG *kremmen*, ON *kremja* squeeze, pinch, f. Gmc. Rel. to Du. *krammen* cramp, clamp, MHG *krammen* claw.] **A** *v.* Infl. **-mm-**. **1** *v.t.* Fill (a space, receptacle, etc.) completely, esp. by force or compression; overfill. (Foll. by *with*.) OE. **2** *v.t.* Feed to excess (*spec.* poultry etc. to fatten them up, *with* food). ME. **b** *v.i.* Eat greedily or to excess, stuff oneself. M16. **3** *v.t.* Force or stuff (something) *into* a receptacle, space, etc., which it overfills, *down* someone's throat, etc. LME. **4** *v.t.* Convince (a person) of a false or exaggerated statement. *slang.* L18. **5** *v.t.* & *i.* Prepare for an examination etc. by intensive coaching or study; study (a subject) intensively for an examination etc. *colloq.* E19. **6** *v.t.* Urge on forcibly (a horse). *arch. slang.* E19.

1 A. J. CRONIN A large chilly basement, crammed to the ceiling with second-hand goods. J. G. FARRELL An enormous letter, crammed with confidences. 3 E. REVELEY Most working parents . . have to cram everything into two tightly organized days. 5 THOMAS HUGHES He had been well crammed in his science. A. S. NEILL I crammed Botany and Zoo for my degree and I know nothing about either. J. GALSWORTHY They were cramming for an important examination.

B *n.* **1** In *pl.* Food used to fatten poultry or other livestock. *dial.* E17. **2** A dense crowd, a crush, a squeeze. *colloq.* E19. **3** The action of cramming for an examination etc.; information crammed. *colloq.* E19. **4** A lie. *slang.* M19.

Comb.: **cram-full** *a.* as full as cramming can make it; **cram-jam** *v.t.* & *adv.* (*colloq.* & *dial.*) (fill) cram-full;

crammable *a.* (of information) able to be crammed M19.

†crambe *n.* M16. [L f. Gk *krambē*: usu. w. ref. to *crambe repetita* (Juvenal). Cf. next.] **1** Cabbage (in *fig.* contexts as something distasteful repeated); distasteful repetition. Also *crambe bis cocta* [med.L = twice cooked]. M16–M18. **2** = CRAMBO 2, 3. E17–E19.

cramble /'kramb(ə)l/ *v.i.* Long *obs.* exc. *dial.* Also **crammle** /'kram(ə)l/. L16. [Imit.: cf. SCRAMBLE *v.*] **†1** Of roots, stems, etc.: creep about, twine. Only in L16. **2** Hobble, crawl. E17.

crambo /'krambəʊ/ *n.* E17. [Alt. of CRAMBE, on an It. or Sp. model.] **†1** A particular fashion in drinking. Only in E17. **2** A game in which one player gives a word or line of verse to which each of the others has to find a rhyme. M17. **3** Rhyme, rhyming. *derog.* L17. **†4** Distasteful repetition; = CRAMBE I. L17–E18.

2 **dumb crambo** a game in which one side has to guess a word chosen by the other side, after being given a word which rhymes with it, by acting in mime various words until they find it.

crammer /ˈkramə/ *n.* M17. [CRAM *v.* + -ER[1].] 1 A person who or an apparatus which crams poultry etc. M17. 2 A person who or an institution which crams pupils for an examination etc. E19. 3 A lie. *slang.* M19.

crammle *v.* var. of CRAMBLE.

cramoisy /ˈkramɔɪzi/ *a.* & *n. arch.* LME. [Early It. *cremesi* and OFr. *crameisi* (mod. *cramoisi*) ult. f. Arab. *ḳirmizī*, f. *ḳirmiz* KERMES: cf. CRIMSON.] Crimson (cloth).

cramp /kramp/ *n.*[1] LME. [OFr. *crampe* f. MLG, MDu. *krampe* = OHG *krampfo* rel. to OS *kramp*, OHG, G *Krampf*, uses as n. of an adj. meaning 'bent' (OHG *krampf*, ON *krappr* narrow, OE *crampiht*). Cf. next, CRIMP *v.*[1]] 1 Involuntary painful contraction of a muscle or muscles, often caused by cold, a slight strain, etc.; an instance of this. LME. 2 Any of various diseases of animals, *esp.* a disease affecting the wings of hawks. Now *rare.* LME.

1 E. BLISHEN A tendency to sensational cramp . . I would fall writhing to the ground, my leg muscles knotted. J. DOS PASSOS Her belly was all knotted up with a cramp. SCRIVENER'S *cramp. writer's cramp*: see WRITER.

Comb.: **cramp-bone** the kneecap of a sheep, formerly believed to be a charm against cramp; **cramp fish** the electric ray or torpedo; **cramp-ring** a ring believed to be efficacious against cramp etc., *esp.* (*Hist.*) one of those consecrated by the English monarch on Good Friday for this purpose.

crampy *a.*[1] liable to or suffering from cramp; inducing cramp; of the nature of cramp: LME.

cramp /kramp/ *n.*[2] LME. [MDu. *krampe* (whence G *Krampe*, Fr. *crampe*) = OS *krampo*, of same ult. origin as prec.] 1 = CRAMPON 2. *obs.* exc. *dial.* LME. 2 = CRAMP-IRON 2. LME. 3 A portable tool or press with a movable part which can be screwed up so as to hold things together. Cf. CLAMP *n.*[1] 3. M17. 4 *fig.* A constraining force or power; a cramping restraint. E18. 5 A footplate of iron etc. worn on ice to secure one's grip or, if polished, to skate on. Cf. CRAMPET 3, CRAMPON 2. E19.

4 H. MATTHEWS His genius was embarrassed by the cramp . . of the French literary laws.

crampy *a.*[2] restricting, confining M19.

cramp /kramp/ *a.* L17. [Origin uncertain: perh. f. CRAMP *n.*[1] or *v.*] 1 Difficult to make out; crabbed; cramped. L17. 2 Constrained, narrow; cramping. L18.

crampness *n.* M19.

cramp /kramp/ *v.* LME. [f. CRAMP *n.*[1], *n.*[2]] I Conn. w. CRAMP *n.*[1] 1 *v.t.* Affect with cramp. Usu. in *pass.* LME. †2 *v.t.* Cause (a person) to be seized with cramp. L16–L17.

II Conn. w. CRAMP *n.*[1] and (esp.) CRAMP *n.*[2] †3 *v.t.* Compress or squeeze with irons in punishment or torture. (Opp. to *rack.*) M16–E18. 4 *v.t.* Restrict or confine narrowly. Also foll. by *up.* E17. 5 *v.t.* & *i.* Deflect or turn to one side. *US.* L19.

4 ALDOUS HUXLEY He has only narrowed . . his life; and . . cramped his intellect. B. SPOCK The shoes big enough so that the toes aren't cramped. *Country Life* A car . . with a very cramped interior. **cramp a person's style** restrict a person's natural behaviour, prevent a person from acting freely. 5 J. DICKEY The river hooked and cramped.

III Conn. w. CRAMP *n.*[2] 6 *v.t.* Fasten or secure with a cramp or cramps. M17.

cramped *a.* (*a*) that has been cramped; (*b*) (of handwriting) small and difficult to read: L17.

crampet /ˈkrampɪt/ *n.* LME. [App. f. CRAMP *n.*[2]] 1 = CRAMP-IRON 2. LME. 2 The chape of the scabbard of a sword. L15. 3 = CRAMPON 2, formerly *esp.* one used by curlers, to enable the player to remain steady while delivering the stone; a footboard used for the same purpose. Orig. *Sc.* M17. 4 A wall-hook. E20.

cramp-iron /ˈkrampʌɪən/ *n.* M16. [f. CRAMP *n.*[2] + IRON *n.*] †1 = CRAMPON 2. M16–L18. 2 A small metal bar with the ends bent so as to hold together two pieces of masonry, timber, etc. L16.

crampon /ˈkrampən/ *n.* Also ***crampoon** /kramˈpuːn/ ME. [(O)Fr. f. Frank.: cf. CRAMP *n.*[2]] 1 = CRAMP-IRON 2. Also, a metal bar with the end bent in the form of a hook; a grappling-iron. ME. 2 A small plate of iron etc. set with spikes and fastened to the foot in order to give a better grip on ice or steep inclines. L18.

cramponny /kramˈpɒni/ *a.* Also **-nnée** /-neɪ/. E18. [Fr. *cramponnée*, f. as prec.] *Her.* Of a cross: having a right-angled hook at the end of each limb.

crampoon *n.* see CRAMPON.

cran /kran/ *n.*[1] *Sc.* LME. [Var. of CRANE *n.*[1]] I 1 The crane; the heron. Now *rare* or *obs.* LME. 2 The swift. M19.

II 3 An iron instrument to support a pot or kettle over a fire. M18.

3 **coup the crans** *fig.* have an upset, come to grief.

cran /kran/ *n.*[2] *Sc.* L18. [Gael. *crann*, perh. identical with *crann* 'lot', applied to the share of fish given to each man engaged.] A measure for fresh herrings, equal to 37½ gallons (170 litres, or about 750 fish).

cranage /ˈkreɪnɪdʒ/ *n.* LME. [f. CRANE *n.*[1] + -AGE.] (Dues paid for) the use of a crane to hoist goods.

cranberry /ˈkranb(ə)ri/ *n.* M17. [f. G *Kranbeere*, LG *kranebeere* lit. 'crane berry'.] 1 (The acid bright red fruit of) any of several Eurasian or American dwarf hardy shrubs of the genus *Vaccinium*, of the heath family, esp. *V. oxycoccos*, and the larger American *V. macrocarpon*. M17. 2 Any of various shrubs of similar appearance, the fruits of which may be used in cooking as a substitute for cranberries. M19.

2 **bush cranberry** a N. American bush, *Viburnum trilobum*, allied to the guelder rose. **native cranberry** *Austral.* (the fruit of) either of two shrubs of the epacris family, *Styphelia sapida* and *Astroloma humifusum*.

Comb.: **cranberry bush** = *bush cranberry* above; **cranberry jelly, sauce**: made with cranberries and eaten as a relish with turkey etc; **cranberry tree** = *bush cranberry* above.

¶ Orig. adopted by N. American colonists.

crance /krans/ *n.* M19. [Perh. f. Du. *krans* garland. Cf. CRANTS.] *Naut.* An iron cap on the outer end of the bowsprit, through which the jib-boom passes; a boom-iron.

cranch /krɑːn(t)ʃ/ *v.* & *n.* Also (exc. in sense B.1) **craunch** /krɔːn(t)ʃ/. M17. [Prob. imit.: cf. SCRANCH.] A *v.t.* & *i.* Crunch, crush or grind noisily. M17. B *n.* 1 *Mining.* A part of a stratum or vein left when excavating, to support the roof. M18. 2 A crunch. E19.

crane /kreɪn/ *n.*[1] & *a.* See also CRAN *n.*[1] [OE *cran* = MLG *krān*, *krōn*, MDu. *crāne* (Du. *kraan*), OHG *krano* (G *Kran* in sense 2), rel. to L *grus*, Gk *geranos.*] A *n.* 1 Any of various large birds of the family Gruidae, with long legs, neck, and bill; *esp.* one of the common European species *Grus grus*, ash-grey in colour. Also (*Austral.*), the brolga. OE. b A heron; an egret; a stork; a shag. *dial.* or *local* exc. as below. LME. c (Usu. **C-**.) *The* constellation Grus. L17. 2 A machine for moving heavy weights, usu. consisting of a vertical post capable of rotation on its axis, a projecting arm or jib over which passes the chain, rope, etc., from which the load is suspended, and a barrel round which the chain or rope is wound. ME. b Any of various similar mechanical contrivances, as (*a*) a machine for weighing goods, constructed on the principles of a crane for moving heavy loads; (*b*) an upright revolving axis with a horizontal arm for suspending a pot, kettle, etc., over the fire; (*c*) *Naut.* in *pl.*, projecting pieces of iron, timber, etc., on board a ship, to support a boat or spar; (*d*) a moving platform for a camera. E18. 3 A bent tube used to draw liquor out of a vessel; a siphon. M17. 4 More fully *water-crane.* An apparatus consisting of an elevated tank and tube, for supplying water, esp. to a locomotive. M17.

1 *demoiselle crane, sand-hill crane, whooping crane*, etc. *wattled crane*: see WATTLED 2. b **blue crane** (*a*) *Austral.* the white-faced heron, *Ardea novaehollandiae*; (*b*) *S. Afr.* = STANLEY *crane.* 2 *luffing crane*: see LUFF *v. travelling crane*: see TRAVELLING *ppl a.*

Comb.: **crane-colour** ashy-grey; **crane-coloured** *a.* of crane-colour; **crane-driver** a person who drives and operates a crane; **crane-fly** a long-legged two-winged fly of the family Tipulidae, a daddy-long-legs; **crane line** *Naut.* any of a set of small ropes set up to prevent the lee backstays from chafing against the yards of a square-rigged ship when running before the wind (usu. in *pl.*); **craneman** a man in charge of a crane (sense 2); **crane-neck** (chiefly *Hist.*) an iron bar uniting the back and front timbers of a carriage; **crane-necked** *a.* (*a*) (chiefly *Hist.*) having a crane-neck; (*b*) (esp. of a person) having a long neck like a crane's; **cranesbill** (*a*) any of the plants constituting the genus *Geranium* (family Geraniaceae), characterized by five-petalled purple, violet, pink, etc., flowers and long-beaked fruits; (*b*) a kind of surgical forceps with long jaws.

B *adj.* †1 Crane-coloured. Only in E16. 2 Cranelike, long and lanky. L17.

cranelike *a.* resembling (that of) a crane L19.

crane /kreɪn/ *n.*[2] Now *arch. rare.* LME. [Fr. *crâne* f. as CRANIUM.] The skull, the cranium.

crane /kreɪn/ *v.* L16. [f. CRANE *n.*[1]] 1 *v.t.* Hoist or lower (as) with a crane or similar apparatus. L16. 2 *v.t.* & *i.* Stretch (the neck, *arch.* the head) like a crane; lean or bend forward with outstretched neck. L18. b *v.i.* Of a camera mounted on a crane: alter range or direction. Usu. foll. by adv. M20. 3 *v.i.* In the hunting field, pull up at a hedge etc. and look over before jumping; *fig.* (*colloq.*) hesitate at a danger, difficulty, etc. E19.

1 SIR W. SCOTT Being safely craned up to the top of the crag. 2 J. WAIN He began craning to see over people's heads. B. CHATWIN Ganders hissed and craned their necks. 3 BYRON He clear'd hedge, ditch, and double post, and rail, And never *craned.*

crang *n.* var. of KRENG.

crani- *comb. form* see CRANIO-.

cranial /ˈkreɪnɪəl/ *a.* E19. [f. CRANIUM + -AL[1].] Of or pertaining to the cranium.

cranial index the ratio of the width of the skull to its length, usually expressed as a percentage. **cranial nerve** each of twelve pairs of nerves arising directly from the brain and passing through separate apertures in the cranium.

craniate /ˈkreɪnɪət/ *n.* & *a.* L19. [mod.L *craniatus*, f. as CRANIUM: see -ATE[2].] (An animal) having a skull or cranium.

cranio- /ˈkreɪnɪəʊ/ *comb. form* of Gk *kranion* skull: see -O-. Bef. a vowel also **crani-**.

cranio-facial *a.* of or pertaining to both the cranium and the face. L19. **cranіˈometry** *n.* the science of measuring the differences in size and shape of skulls M19. **craniˈopathy** *n.* any disease of the cranium L19. **cranioplasty** *n.* (an instance of) a surgical operation to reconstruct or alter the shape of part of the skull L19. **cranio-spinal** *a.* of or pertaining to both the cranium and the spine L19. **craniotome** *n.* a special instrument used for (esp. obstetric) craniotomy L19. **craniˈotomy** *n.* a surgical operation involving opening the skull; *esp.* in obstetric surgery, the perforation of the skull of a dead foetus during difficult labour: M19.

craniology /kreɪnɪˈɒlədʒi/ *n.* E19. [f. prec. + -LOGY.] †1 Phrenology. E–M19. 2 The branch of knowledge that deals with the size, shape, and character of skulls of different races etc. M19.

cranioˈlogical *a.* of or pertaining to craniology E19. **cranioˈlogically** *adv.* M20. **craniologist** *n.* one who practises or is versed in craniology E19.

cranium /ˈkreɪnɪəm/ *n.* Pl. **-ia** /-ɪə/, **-iums**. LME. [med.L *cranium* f. Gk *kranion* skull.] 1 The bones enclosing the brain; the bones of the whole head, the skull. LME. 2 The head. *joc.* M17.

crank /kraŋk/ *n.*[1] [OE *cranc-* in *crancstæf* weaver's implement (cf. *crencestre* female weaver), rel. to *crincan*, parallel to *cringan* fall in battle. Cf. MHG, G, Du. *krank* sick (a fig. devel. of the primary notion of something bent or crooked).] 1 A part of an axle or shaft bent at right angles, used to communicate motion or for converting reciprocal into circular motion, or vice versa. OE. 2 An elbow-shaped connection in bell-hanging. M18. 3 An elbow-shaped support or bracket. M18. 4 *Hist.* A revolving disc to which a regulated pressure could be applied, turned by prisoners as a punishment. M19.

Comb.: **crank-axle** (*a*) the driving-axle of an engine or machine; (*b*) a carriage axle with the ends bent twice at a right angle to lower the body while permitting the use of large wheels; **crankcase** the case or covering in which a crankshaft is enclosed; **crankpin** a pin by which a connecting-rod is attached to a crank; **crankshaft** a shaft driven by a crank; **crank-wheel** a wheel acting as a crank; *esp.* one having near its circumference a pin to which the end of a connecting-rod is attached as to a crankpin.

crank /kraŋk/ *n.*[2] M16. [Prob. ult. f. as prec.; in sense 6 back-form. f. CRANKY *a.*] †**1** An inaccessible hole or crevice; a cranny; a chink. M16–M19. **2** A crook, a bend; a crooked path, course, or channel; *fig.* a deceit, a wile. Long *obs.* exc. *Sc.* L16. **3** A fanciful turn of speech; a conceit. L16. **4** In *pl.* Slight ailments; aches. *dial.* E19. **5** An eccentric notion or action; a crotchet, a whim, a caprice. Cf. earlier CRANKUM 2. M19. **6** An eccentric person; *esp.* a person subject to a whimsical enthusiasm. Orig. *US.* M19.

3 MILTON Quips, and cranks, and wanton wiles. 5 T. S. ELIOT The critic . . should endeavour to discipline his personal prejudices and cranks. 6 L. T. C. ROLT Amateurs and cranks aired their theories. M. SHADBOLT The man beside him looks normal, no crank.

†**crank** *n.*[3] *slang.* M16–E17. [Du. or G *krank* sick: see CRANK *n.*[1]] In full *counterfeit crank.* A person who feigned sickness for the purpose of begging.

crank /kraŋk/ *a.*[1] LME. [Origin unkn.] †**1** Strong, vigorous; in good condition. LME–M17. **2** Lively, brisk; cheerful; aggressively or impudently high-spirited. Now *dial.* & *US.* L15.

crankly *adv.* (now *rare*) M16.

crank /kraŋk/ *a.*[2] E17. [Origin uncertain: perh. conn. w. next or w. CRANK *n.*[1]] More fully *crank-sided.* Of a ship: liable to capsize, esp. through being built too deep or narrow, or through having too little ballast to carry full sail.

fig. : T. MOORE Things, which . . Still serve to ballast, with convenient words, A few crank arguments for speeching lords.

crankness *n.* L16.

crank /kraŋk/ *a.*[3] E18. [f. CRANK *n.*[1] or back-form. f. CRANKY *a.*] **1** Crooked, distorted; angularly twisted or bent. *Sc.* E18. **2** Awkward or difficult to pronounce, understand, or do. *obs.* exc. *Sc.* E18. **3** Infirm, in poor health; weak, ailing. *dial.* E19. **4** Of machinery etc.: in a shaky condition, in poor order; working with difficulty. M19.

2 SWIFT Hard, tough, crank, gutt'ral, harsh, stiff names. 4 CARLYLE The machinery of laughter took some time to get in motion, and seemed crank and slack.

crankous *a.* (*Sc.*) irritable, fretful L18.

crank /kraŋk/ *v.*[1]*i.* L16. [f. CRANK *n.*[2]] Twist and turn about; move in a sharply winding course; zigzag. Now chiefly w. allus. to Shakes. (see below).

SHAKES. *1 Hen. IV* See how this river comes me cranking in, And cuts me from the best of all my land . . a monstrous cantle out.

crank /kraŋk/ *v.*[2] L18. [f. CRANK *n.*[1]] **1** *v.t.* Bend at right angles; bend sharply. L18. **2** *v.t.* Provide with a crank, attach a crank to. M19. **3** *v.t.* Fasten with a crank. L19. **4** *v.t.* Draw *up* by means of a crank; operate by a crank. L19. **5** *v.t.* & *i.* Turn (an engine) with a crank. E20. **b** *v.t.* & *i.* Foll. by *up*: start (an engine of a motor vehicle) by turning a crank, *slang* increase (speed etc.) by intensive effort. E20. **c** *v.i.* Inject narcotics. Also foll. by *up. slang.* L20.

5 J. B. PRIESTLEY The car refused to start again. . . She cranked away until she was breathless. E. WAUGH The taxi-driver . . got out of his seat and cranked up the engine.

crank /kraŋk/ *v.*[3]*i.* E19. [App. imit.] Make a jarring or grating sound.

crankle /ˈkraŋk(ə)l/ *n.* L16. [f. the vb or f. CRANK *n.*[1], *n.*[2] + -LE[1]. Cf. CRINKLE-CRANKLE.] A bend, a twist; an angular prominence.

crankle /ˈkraŋk(ə)l/ *v.* L16. [Frequent. of CRANK *v.*[1]: see -LE[3].] **1** *v.i.* Bend in and out; wind; follow a zigzag course. L16. †**2** *v.t.* Cause to follow a zigzag course; wrinkle (a surface). L16–E18.

crankum /ˈkrankəm/ *n.* M17. [Fanciful formation f. CRANK *n.*[2]] †**1** In *pl.* = CRINKUM. Only in M17. **2** = CRANK *n.*[2] 5. Cf. CRINKUM-CRANKUM. E19.

cranky /ˈkraŋki/ *a.* L18. [Perh. orig. f. CRANK *n.*[3]; also infl. by assoc. w. CRANK *n.*[2]: see -Y[1].] **1** Sickly; in poor health; ailing. *dial.* L18. **2** Awkward; difficult to please; ill-tempered. E19. **3** Subject to whims; odd, eccentric. M19. **4** Out of order; working badly; shaky. M19. **5** Crooked; full of crannies. M19. **6** = CRANK *a.*[2] M19.

2 M. FRENCH The baby . . was cranky and hungry. 3 R. MACAULAY It's shockingly cranky, anyway, all this Morris craze of yours. E. P. THOMPSON William Blake seems no longer the cranky untutored genius. 5 W. S. LANDOR No curling dell, no cranky nook.

crankily *adv.* M19. **crankiness** *n.* M19.

crannog /ˈkranəg/ *n.* E17. [Ir. *crannóg*, Gael. *crannag* timber structure, f. *crann* tree, beam.] An ancient fortified dwelling constructed in a lake or marsh in Scotland or Ireland.

cranny /ˈkrani/ *n.*[1] & *v.* LME. [OFr. *crané* (see -Y[5]) pa. pple of vb (implied by *craneüre* notch) f. (O)Fr. *cran*, f. pop.L *crena* incision, notch.] **A** *n.* A small narrow opening or hole; a chink, a crevice, a crack. LME.

every nook and cranny: see NOOK *n.* 3b.

B *v.i.* †**1** Open in crannies or chinks. LME–E17. **2** Penetrate into crannies. *rare.* E19.

crannied *a.* (*a*) having crannies; (*b*) *rare* formed like a cranny: LME.

cranny /ˈkrani/ *n.*[2] M17. [Origin unkn.] A rod of iron etc. used in forming the necks of glass bottles.

cranreuch /ˈkranrəx/ *n. Sc.* L17. [f. Gael. *crann* tree + *reodhadh* freezing.] Hoar-frost.

crants /krants/ *n. obs.* exc. *Hist.* Pl. same. M16. [Du. *krans*, G *Kranz* garland, wreath: cf. CRANCE.] †**1** A form of candle-holder. *Sc.* M–L16. **2** A garland, a chaplet, a wreath. L16.

†**crany** *n.* E16–M18. [Alt.] = CRANIUM.

crap /krap/ *n.*[1] LME. [Corresp. to Du. *krappe* rel. to *krappen* pluck off, cut off. Cf. OFr. *crappe* siftings, AL *crappa* chaff.] †**1** The husk of grain; chaff. LME–L15. **2** Any of various plants, *esp.* buckwheat or a weed growing among corn, as darnel, charlock, etc. *dial.* LME. **3a** *sing.* & (usu.) in *pl.* The residue formed in boiling, melting, or rendering fat; crackling. *dial.* L15. **b** The dregs of beer etc. *dial.* M19. †**4** A scrap. Only in 16. **5** Money. *slang* or *dial.* L17. **6** Faeces; an act of defecation. Also, rubbish, nonsense; something worthless, inferior, or offensive. *coarse slang.* L19.

6 T. ROETHKE I'm writing a lot of inane crap. J. T. FARRELL One who hadn't backed down or taken any crap.

Comb.: **crap-artist** *coarse slang* a liar, a boaster, an exaggerator.

†**crap** *n.*[2] E18–E19. [Du. *krap.*] Madder.

crap /krap/ *n.*[3] *arch. slang.* E19. [Du. *krap* cramp, clamp.] *The* gallows.

crap *n.*[4] see CRAPS.

crap /krap/ *v.*[1]*t. arch. slang.* Infl. **-pp-**. L18. [f. CRAP *n.*[3]] Hang (on the gallows). Usu. in *pass.*

crap /krap/ *v.*[2] *coarse slang.* Infl. **-pp-**. M19. [f. CRAP *n.*[1] In sense 4 perh. f. or infl. by CRAPS.] **1** *v.i.* Defecate. M19. **2** *v.t.* & *i.* Lie, boast, or exaggerate (to); act deceitfully (to). M20. **3** *v.i.* Mess or fool *around* (*with*). *US.* M20. **4** *v.i.* Foll. by *out*: be unsuccessful; withdraw from a game etc. *US.* M20.

crapaud /ˈkrapəʊ/ *n.* ME. [OFr. *crapau(l)t* (mod. *crapaud*), med.L *crapaldus.*] †**1** A toad. ME–M17. †**2** More fully *crapaud-stone.* A toadstone. LME–L16. **3** An edible bullfrog, *Leptodactylus pentadactylus*, of S. and Central America. M20.

¶ See also JOHNNY *Crapaud.*

crapaudine /ˈkrapədiːn, krapəˈdiːn/ *n.* LME. [(O)Fr. f. med.L *crapaudinus, -ina*, f. as prec.: see -INE[1].] **1** = TOADSTONE *n.*[1] Long *obs.* exc. *Hist.* LME. **2** An ulcer on the coronet of a horse. M18.

crape /kreɪp/ *n.* & *a.* E16. [Fr. CRÊPE *n.*] **A** *n.* **1** Transparent but dull black gauze with a crimped surface, esp. for mourning dress; a band of this, esp. worn round a hat etc. as a sign of mourning. Formerly also, a piece of crape worn as a mask. E16. **2** A kind of thin worsted used for clerical dress; *transf.* a clergyman. *obs.* exc. *Hist.* L17. **B** *attrib.* or as *adj.* Made of crape. M16.

Special collocations & *comb.*: **crape-fern** a New Zealand fern, *Leptopteris superba*, with tall dark-green plumes. **crape hair** artificial hair for an actor's false beard etc. **crape-myrtle** a Chinese ornamental shrub, *Lagerstroemia indica*, of the purple loosestrife family, with pink, white, or purplish crinkled petals.

crapy *a.* (*a*) resembling crape; (*b*) of crape, clothed in crape: M19.

crape /kreɪp/ *v.t.* E18. [f. the n. For sense 1 cf. Fr. *crêper*, CRÊPE *v.*] †**1** Crimp, make wrinkled or crinkled; curl (hair). E18–E19. **2** Cover, clothe, or drape with crape. E19.

crapper /ˈkrapə/ *n. coarse slang.* M20. [f. CRAP *v.*[2] + -ER[1].] A water-closet, a lavatory.

crappie /ˈkrapi/ *n.* Also **croppie** /ˈkrɒpi/. M19. [Origin unkn.] A N. American freshwater sunfish of the genus *Pomoxis*, *esp.* (in full *white crappie*) *P. annularis* and (in full *black crappie*) *P. nigromaculatus.*

crappit-head /ˈkrapɪthɛd/ *n. Sc.* E19. [Cf. Du. *krappen* cram.] The head of a haddock stuffed with the roe, oatmeal, suet, and spices.

crappy /ˈkrapi/ *a. coarse slang.* M19. [f. CRAP *n.*[1] + -Y[1].] Rubbishy; disgusting.

craps /kraps/ *n. N. Amer.* Also (usual in comb.) **crap**. E19. [App. alt. of *crabs*: cf CRAB *n.*[1] 5.] **1** A game of chance played with two dice. E19. **2** A losing throw of 2, 3, or 12 in craps. L19.

1 shoot craps play craps.

Comb.: **crap game** a game of craps; **crapshooter** a player at craps; **crapshooting** playing at craps.

crapulence /ˈkrapjʊl(ə)ns/ *n.* E18. [f. next: see -ENCE.] **1** Sickness or indisposition resulting from intemperance in drinking or eating. E18. **2** Intemperance, esp. in drinking. E19.

†**crapulency** *n.* (*rare*) = CRAPULENCE 2: only in M17.

crapulent /ˈkrapjʊl(ə)nt/ *a.* M17. [Late L *crapulentus* very drunk, f. L *crapula* inebriation f. Gk *kraipalē* drunken headache: see -ULENT.] **1** Of or pertaining to crapulence; suffering from the effects of intemperance. M17. **2** Given to intemperance. L19.

crapulous /ˈkrapjʊləs/ *a.* M16. [Late L *crapulosus*, f. L *crapula*: see prec., -ULOUS.] **1** Characterized by intemperance; debauched. M16. **2** Suffering from the effects of intemperance in drinking; resulting from drunkenness. M18.

crapuˈlosity *n.* inclination to drunkenness or gluttony M16. **crapulousness** *n.* M19.

craquelure /ˈkrakljʊə, *foreign* kraklyːr/ *n.* E20. [Fr.] A network of small cracks in the pigment or varnish on the surface of a painting.

crare *n.* var. of CRAYER.

crases *n.* pl. of CRASIS.

crash /kraʃ/ *n.*[1] & *a.*[1] E16. [f. the vb.] **A** *n.* †**1** A bout of revelry, fighting, etc.; a short spell, a spurt. E16–M18. **2** A sudden loud noise as of a violent collision or of shattering; the sound of thunder, loud music, etc.; violent percussion or breakage. L16. **3** *Hunting.* The outcry made by hounds when they find the game. L18. **4** *fig.* A sudden ruin, failure, or collapse, esp. of a financial undertaking or of a computer system. L18. **5** A violent impact or fall; *esp.* the collision of a vehicle or aircraft with another, with a fixed object, or with land or water; (the wreckage at) the scene of such a collision. E20.

2 POPE The whole forest in one crash descends. J. CHEEVER The crash of the sea outside. A. AYCKBOURN A distant crash of colliding vehicles. 4 J. W. KRUTCH A depression by comparison with which that following the crash of 1929 would seem like boom time. 5 *Daily Telegraph* 70 feared dead in rail crash.

Comb.: **crash barrier**: along a carriageway, racetrack, etc., to stop out-of-control vehicles; **crash cymbal**: suspended by a cord and struck with a drumstick; **crash-dive** *n.* & *v.* (*a*) *n.* a sudden dive made by a submarine in an emergency; a dive by an aircraft ending in a crash; (*b*) *v.i.* make a crash-dive; **crash-halt** a sudden stop by a vehicle; **crash-helmet**: worn, esp. by motorcyclists, to protect the head in case of a crash; **crash-helmeted** *a.* wearing a crash-helmet; **crash-land** *v.i.* make a crash-landing;

crash-landing a landing by an aircraft with a crash, usu. without lowering the undercarriage; **crash pad** *slang* a place to sleep, esp. in an emergency; **crash-stop** = *crash-halt* above; **crash-tackle** *v.* & *n.* (*Football*) (*a*) *v.t.* & *i.* tackle vigorously; (*b*) *n.* a vigorous tackle.

B *attrib.* or as *adj.* Done rapidly, intensively, or urgently. M20.

crash course, diet, programme, etc.

crashworthiness *n.* the quality in an aircraft or motor vehicle that increases its safety in the event of a crash M20. **crashworthy** *a.* relatively well able to withstand a crash M20.

crash /kraʃ/ *n.*[2] & *a.*[2] E19. [Russ. *krashenina* dyed coarse linen.] (Made of) a coarse plain fabric of linen etc.

crash /kraʃ/ *v.* & *adv.* LME. [Imit., perh. partly suggested by *craze* and *dash*.] A *v.* I *v.i.* 1 Break into pieces with a crash, shatter noisily; make a crash; move or go with a crash (usu. w. adv. or adv. phr.). LME. †2 Make a grating or gnashing noise; gnash. LME–L16. 3 Collide violently with an obstacle etc.; run violently *into*; (of an aircraft or member of an aircrew) fall violently on to land or sea. E20. 4 *fig.* Be ruined, esp. financially; fail, come to grief; (of a computer system etc.) fail or stop working, with loss of data; *colloq.* be heavily defeated. E20. 5 Go *in*, *into* without authorization, invitation, etc. *colloq.* E20. 6 Go to bed, go to sleep. Also foll. by *out*. *slang*. M20.

1 W. OWEN Your guns may crash around me. I'll not hear. I. MURDOCH The glass crashed into pieces on the floor. D. M. THOMAS She heard them crashing through the undergrowth, close behind her. 3 N. MAILER A Jap plane had crashed in the swamp. *Daily Telegraph* A car crashed into a bus stop queue. 4 T. S. ELIOT I must give up the *Criterion* before my health crashes. J. BUCHAN A highbrow financier who . . had just crashed. 5 D. RUNYON He hears rumours of the party, and just crashes in. 6 *It* You can only crash here one night.

II *v.t.* 7 Break into pieces with a crash; shatter, smash. Now *rare*. LME. †8 Gnash (the teeth); crush with the teeth. M16–M18. 9 Throw or drive with a crash; cause (a vehicle etc.) to crash. M19. 10 Enter or pass without authorization; intrude at (a party etc.) without an invitation. E20.

7 POPE Full on his Ankle dropt the pond'rous Stone, Burst the strong Nerves, and crash'd the solid Bone. 9 S. O'FAOLÁIN He could . . see the bigger of the two crash his fist into the face of the other. V. SCANNELL The one Who . . crashed his bike Doing a ton. 10 R. FULLER I hope you'll forgive me crashing your excellent party. **crash the gate** gatecrash. *gatecrash*: see GATE *n.*[1]

B *adv.* With a crash. M18.

THOMAS HUGHES Crash went the slight deal boards.

crasher *n.* (*a*) a thing which crashes or makes a crash; a loud, percussive blow; (*b*) a person who intrudes uninvited at a party etc., = *gatecrasher* s.v. GATE *n.*[1]: M19. **crashing** *ppl a.* (*a*) that crashes; (*b*) *colloq.* overwhelming (esp. in *crashing bore*): L16. **crashingly** *adv.* (*colloq.*) overwhelmingly (esp. boring) L20.

crasis /ˈkreɪsɪs/ *n.* Pl. **crases** /ˈkreɪsiːz/. M16. [Gk *krasis* mixture, combination.] †1 The blending of the constituents or humours of an animal body etc., either as a permanent characteristic or as constituting a particular state of health. M16–M19. 2 A mixture, a combination. *rare*. L17. 3 *Gk Gram.* The contraction of two adjacent vowels into one long vowel or diphthong, esp. at the end of one word and beginning of the next. M19.

crass /kras/ *a.* L15. [L *crassus* solid, thick, fat.] 1 Coarse, thick, dense, gross, (in physical constitution or texture). Now *rare*. L15. 2 Grossly stupid, dull, or insensitive. M17.

2 GEO. ELIOT Crass minds . . whose reflective scales could only weigh things in the lump. R. A. KNOX There is such a thing, you see, as crass ignorance. U. BENTLEY My action now struck me as crass and blundering.

crassly *adv.* M17. **crassness** *n.* M16.

crassitude /ˈkrasɪtjuːd/ *n.* LME. [L *crassitudo*, f. as prec.: see -TUDE.] †1 Thickness of dimension. LME–E18. †2 Thickness of consistency; coarseness of physical constitution. E17–E19. 3 Gross stupidity, dullness, or insensitivity. L17.

crassula /ˈkrasjʊlə/ *n.* Pl. **-lae** /-liː/, **-las**. LME. [med.L dim. of L *crassus* thick: see -ULE.] 1 Orig., any of certain kinds of stonecrop, *esp.* orpine, *Sedum telephium*. Now, any of numerous succulent herbaceous plants and shrubs constituting the related, chiefly southern African, genus *Crassula*, some of which are grown as house-plants. LME. 2 *Bot.* A thickening between the pits of gymnosperm tracheids, made up of primary wall and intercellular material. M20.

-crat /krat/ *suff.* [Repr. Fr. *-crate*, f. adjs. in *-cratique*, f. as -CRACY.] In or forming ns. w. the sense 'a supporter or member of a -CRACY', as *aristocrat, plutocrat*, etc.

-cratic(**al**) *suffs.* in or forming adjs.

cratch /kratʃ/ *n.*[1] ME. [OFr. *creche* (mod. CRÈCHE) f. Proto-Romance f. Gmc base also of CRIB *n.*] 1 A rack for feeding animals out of doors; (now *dial.*) a manger. ME. 2 A wooden grating; a sparred frame or rack. *dial.* LME.

cratch /kratʃ/ *v.* & *n.*[2] *obs.* exc. *dial.* ME. [Origin uncertain: its meaning associates it w. MLG, MDu. *kratsen*, OHG *krazzōn* (G *kratzen*), OSw. *kratta* to scratch.] †A *v.* 1 *v.t.* & *i.* Scratch. ME–M16. 2 *v.t.* Snatch (as) with claws; grab. LME–L16. B *n.* †1 Scratching, an itch. Only in ME. 2 In *pl.* A sore condition of the feet of horses or sheep; scratches (see SCRATCH *n.* 2a). E16.

crate /kreɪt/ *n.* & *v.* LME. [Perh. f. Du. *krat* tailboard of a wagon, †box of a coach, of unkn. origin; sense 1 appears in AL as *crata*.] A *n.* †1 A hurdle. LME–E16. 2 A large wickerwork basket or hamper for carrying crockery, glass, etc.; any openwork, wood-framed, or partitioned case or basket for carrying fragile goods. LME. 3 An (old) aeroplane or other vehicle. *slang*. E20.

B *v.t.* Pack in a crate. L19.

Comb.: **crateman** *arch.* a hawker of pottery.

crateful *n.* as many as a crate will hold L19.

crater /ˈkreɪtə/ *n.* & *v.* E17. [L f. Gk *kratēr* bowl, mixing-vessel.] A *n.* I 1 A bowl- or funnel-shaped hollow forming the mouth of a volcano. E17. 2 A bowl-shaped cavity, esp. one made by the explosion of a mine, shell, or bomb. M19. b *spec.* A cavity (usu. with a raised rim) on the moon, a planet, etc., formed by the impact of a meteorite or larger celestial body. M19. II 3 (Usu. **C-**.) (The name of) an inconspicuous constellation of the southern hemisphere, between Hydra and Virgo; the Cup. M17. 4 *Gk Antiq.* A large wide-mouthed bowl in which wine was mixed with water. M18.

Comb.: **crater-lake** a lake formed by the collection of water in the crater of an inactive volcano.

B *v.* 1 *v.i.* Yield inwards to form a crater. *rare*. L19. 2 *v.t.* Form a crater in, esp. by an explosive. E20.

crateral *a.* pertaining to or resembling a (volcanic) crater M19. **crateriform** *a.* shaped like a (volcanic) crater; *Bot.* bowl-shaped: M19. **craterlet** *n.* a small crater, esp. on the moon L19. **crater-like** *a.* resembling (that of) a crater M19. **craterous** *a.* (*a*) crater-like; (*b*) having many craters: M19.

craton /ˈkratɒn/ *n.* M20. [Alt. of KRATOGEN.] *Geol.* A large stable block of the earth's crust that has resisted deformation over a geologically long period; a shield. Also called *kratogen*.

cra'tonic *a.* M20.

craunch *v.* & *n.* see CRANCH.

†cravant *a.*, *n.*, & *v.* see CRAVEN.

cravat /krəˈvat/ *n.* & *v.* M17. [Fr. *cravate* appellative use of *Cravate* f. G *Krabat*(*e*), (dial.) *Krawat* f. Serbo-Croat *Hrvat* CROAT.] A *n.* A neckerchief, a necktie, a scarf tied round the neck; orig., a scarf of lace, linen, etc., tied in a bow with flowing ends, worn by men and women; now usu., a neckerchief or loosely fastened broad necktie, worn by men. M17. B *v.* Infl. **-tt-**. 1 *v.t.* Provide or cover with a cravat. E19. 2 *v.i.* Put on a cravat. E19.

crave /kreɪv/ *v.* & *n.* [OE *crafian* f. Gmc, rel. to ON *krǫf* a request, *krefja*.] A *v.* I *v.t.* 1 Demand, esp. as a legal right; claim as one's own or one's due. Long *dial. rare* exc. *Sc.* OE. †b Summon, prosecute. OE–ME. 2 Ask earnestly, courteously, or humbly for (a thing), *to do*, *that* something be done, (foll. by *of*, *from* the person asked); beg (a person, *for*, *to do*, †a thing). ME. b *spec.* Ask (a debtor) for payment. *Sc.* LME. c Beg to know. L16. 3 Long for, desire earnestly. LME. 4 Require, call for. *arch.* M16.

2 SHAKES. *Rom. & Jul.* Madam, your mother craves a word with you. DRYDEN I must crave leave to tell you. J. HACKET The Keeper craved to be heard. SIR W. SCOTT The crown, says he, canna be craved to prove a positive. T. H. WHITE I crave the privilege of being the very first . . to address you with it. c SMOLLETT He craved my name. 3 POPE If, when the more you drink, the more you crave, You tell the Doctor. W. C. WILLIAMS Lonesome creatures craving affection, not only craving it, but actively going out to get it. I. MURDOCH What I now abjectly craved was to see Palmer. 4 SHAKES. *Rich. II* His designs crave haste.

II *v.i.* 5 Beg (*for*); long *for*, yearn (*for*, *after*). ME.

5 H. T. BUCKLE They taught the men of their generation to crave after the unseen. ALDOUS HUXLEY Being obsessed with time and our egos, we are for ever craving and worrying. P. BROOK He confuses a sort of intellectual satisfaction with the true experience for which he craves.

B *n.* 1 *Sc. Law.* A demand or claim addressed to a court. E18. 2 A craving. M19.

craver *n.* ME. **craving** *n.* the action of the vb; an instance of this; a strong desire, an intense longing: ME. **cravingly** *adv.* in a craving manner E17.

craven /ˈkreɪv(ə)n/ *a.*, *n.*, & *v.* Also (earlier) **†cravant**. ME. [Perh. f AN abbrev. of OFr. *cravanté* overcome, vanquished, pa. pple of *cravanter* crush, overwhelm, f. Proto-Romance, f. L *crepant-* pres. ppl stem of *crepare* rattle, burst; later assim. to pa. pples in -EN[6].] A *adj.* †1 a Vanquished, defeated. Only in ME. b *cry craven*, acknowledge defeat, surrender. *arch.* M17. 2 Cowardly, abjectly pusillanimous. LME. †b *spec.* Of a cock: unwilling to fight. L16–M17.

2 SIR W. SCOTT The poor craven bridegroom said never a word. SAKI To turn back would seem rather craven.

B *n.* 1 A confessed or acknowledged coward. L16. 2 A cock that is unwilling to fight. Long *arch.* L16.

C *v.t.* Make craven. E17.

SHAKES. *Cymb.* Against self-slaughter There is a prohibition so divine That cravens my weak hand.

cravenly *adv.* E17. **cravenness** /-n-n-/ *n.* (*rare*) M19.

craw /krɔː/ *n.*[1] LME. [f. or cogn. w. MLG *krage* (whence Icel. *kragi*), MDu. *crāghe* (Du. *kraag*) neck, throat, gullet = MHG *krage* (G *Kragen*), of unkn. origin. The limitation of sense is peculiar to Eng.] 1 The crop of birds or insects. LME. 2 *transf.* The stomach (of man or animals) *joc.* or *derog.* E16.

1 **stick in one's craw** *fig.* be unacceptable.

craw *n.*[2] & *a.*, *n.*[3], *v.* see CROW *n.*[1] & *a.*, *n.*[2], *v.*

craw-craw /ˈkrɔːkrɔː/ *n.* Also **kraw-kraw**. L18. [App. f. Du. *kraauwen* to scratch.] In W. Africa: a skin disease with itching due to nematode infestation.

crawfish *n.* & *v.* see CRAYFISH.

crawk /krɔːk/ *v.i.* & *n.* M19. [Imit.] (A) squawk, (a) croak.

crawl /krɔːl/ *n.*[1] M17. [Port. *curral*: cf. CORRAL *n.*, KRAAL *n.*] 1 In the W. Indies, an enclosure or building for keeping hogs. M17. 2 An enclosure in water, or a tank or reservoir, for holding live turtles, fish, sponges, etc. L17. 3 = KRAAL *n.* 1. *arch.* L18.

crawl /krɔːl/ *n.*[2] E19. [f. the vb.] 1 The action or an act of crawling; a slow rate of movement. E19. b In full *pub-crawl*, (arch.) *gin-crawl*. A journey taking in several pubs or drinking-places, with one or more drinks at each. *colloq.* L19. 2 A high-speed swimming stroke with alternate overhand arm movements and rapid kicks of the legs. Also *crawl stroke*. E20.

1 P. LEACH A real crawl, moving along deliberately with his tummy right off the floor, is very unusual before six months. S. KING Time slowed to an inchworm's crawl.

crawl /krɔːl/ *v.* ME. [Origin unkn.: cf. Sw. *kravla*, Da. *kravle*.] I *v.i.* 1 Move slowly, dragging the body along close to the ground etc., as a child on hands and knees, a short-limbed reptile or quadruped, a snake, worm, or other limbless creature, etc. Cf. CREEP *v.* I. ME. **2** Of ground etc.: be covered or swarming *with* crawling things; be filled *with*. ME. **3** Walk or move along with a slow or laborious motion. LME. **b** Move stealthily, sneakingly, or abjectly. E17. **c** Behave abjectly or ingratiatingly (*to*). *colloq.* L19. **4** Of a plant: spread over a surface with extending stems or branches. Cf. CREEP *v.* 4. M17. **5** Feel a creepy sensation. Cf. CREEP *v.* 5. L19. **6** Swim with a crawl stroke. E20.

1 J. GAY Slow crawl'd the snail. R. C. HUTCHINSON My grandson, nearly a year old, . . had hardly tried to crawl yet. M. ESSLIN A mythical universe peopled by lonely creatures crawling through the mud on their bellies. 2 I. HAY Country districts crawling with troops. W. STEVENS The place is crawling with books. 3 SHAKES. *Mids. N. D.* I can no further crawl. N. MAILER Southbound traffic whose drivers were crawling by at five miles an hour. S. BRETT Time crawled by. **crawling peg** *Econ.* a system whereby the exchange rate can be frequently and marginally adjusted. *kerb-crawling*: see KERB *n.* **pub-crawl** engage in a pub-crawl (CRAWL *n.*[2] 1b). **b** SHAKES. *Hen. VIII* Cranmer . . Hath crawl'd into the favour of the King. **c** A. SACHS I don't actually crawl to them but I am so eager to win their approval. 4 MILTON A green mantling vine That crawls along the side of yon small hill. 5 *make a person's flesh crawl*: see FLESH *n.*

II *v.t.* **7** Crawl on or over. *rare.* M17.

crawlingly *adv.* in a crawling manner L17. **crawly** *a.* having or suggestive of the sensation of insects etc. crawling on one's skin, creepy; (see also CREEPY-*crawly*): M19.

crawler /ˈkrɔːlə/ *n.* E17. [f. prec. + -ER[1].] **1** A person or creature that crawls along the ground etc. E17. **2** An idler, a loafer. *Austral. arch.* E19. **3** A slow-moving domestic animal. *Austral. arch.* M19. **4** A cab or cab-driver moving slowly along the streets in search of a fare; (a driver of) any slow-moving vehicle. M19. **5** An abject or obsequious person, a sycophant. L19. **6** *sing.* & (usu.) in *pl.* A baby's overall for crawling in. L19. **7** In full *crawler tractor*. A tractor moving on an endless chain. E20.

1 *night crawler*: see NIGHT *n.* 4 *kerb-crawler*: see KERB *n.*

cray /kreɪ/ *n.* Chiefly *Austral.* & *NZ.* E20. [Abbrev.] = CRAYFISH *n.* 1, 2.

crayer /krɛː/ *n.* Also **crare**. ME. [OFr. *crayer* etc., in med.L *craiera*, *creiera*.] *Hist.* A small trading vessel.

crayfish /ˈkreɪfɪʃ/ *n.* & *v.* Also **craw-** /ˈkrɔː-/ (see note below); (earlier) †**crevice** & other vars. ME. [OFr. *crevice*, *-is* f. Frank. corresp. to OHG *krebiz* (G *Krebs*) CRAB *n.*[1]; 2nd syll. assim. to FISH *n.*[1]] **A** *n.* Pl. same, **-es** /-ɪz/. **1** Any of various long-bodied freshwater decapod crustaceans of the infraorder Astacidea. ME. **2** Orig., any large, esp. edible, crustacean; a lobster, (formerly) a crab. Now *spec.* a spiny lobster. LME. **3** (*craw-*.) A political renegade. *US colloq.* M19. **B** *v.i.* **1** Fish for crayfish. Chiefly as *crayfishing* vbl n. M19. **2** (*craw-*.) Retreat, back *out*. *US colloq.* M19. **3** (*cray-*.) Move like a crayfish; *fig.* act in a cowardly or scheming manner. *Austral.* E20.

¶The form *crayfish* is used in sense B.3, and in Britain is usual in sense A.1; the form *crawfish* is used in senses A.3 and B.2, and in Britain is usual in sense A.2.

crayon /ˈkreɪən/ *n.* & *v.* M17. [Fr., f. *craie* f. L *creta* chalk, clay: see -OON.] **A** *n.* **1** A small stick or pencil of charcoal or chalk, wax, etc., coloured with pigment, for drawing. M17. **b** *in crayon(s)*, drawn with a crayon or crayons. M17. **2** A drawing made with a crayon or crayons. M17. **B** *v.t.* **1** Draw with a crayon or crayons. M17. **2** *fig.* Sketch (*out*), rough *out*. M18.

craze /kreɪz/ *n.* L16. [f. the vb.] †**1** A crack, a breach, a flaw; an infirmity. L16–E19. **2** An insane fancy, a mania, a crazy condition. E19. **3** A temporary enthusiasm. L19.

3 G. SWIFT There's a craze at the moment for films with heroes who are actually admired because they are half robots. B. GUEST African sculpture . . was the latest craze of the avant-garde.

craze /kreɪz/ *v.* LME. [Perh. f. ON (cf. Sw. *krasa* crunch, *kras* in phr. *gå i kras* fly into pieces, *slå i kras* dash to pieces).] **I** *v.t.* **1** Break in pieces, shatter; bruise, damage. LME–E19. **2** Crack; *spec.* produce small cracks on (pottery glaze etc.). LME. **3** Impair in physical health, make infirm. Usu. in *pass. arch.* L15. **4** Impair in intellect, make insane. Usu. in *pass.* L15. **5** *fig.* Impair; ruin financially. Usu. in *pass.* Long *arch.* M16.

2 A. R. AMMONS Mesquite roots crazed the stone. 3 MILTON Till length of years And sedentary numbness craze my limbs. 4 SHAKES. *Lear* The grief hath craz'd my wits.

II *v.i.* †**6** Be broken, shattered, or bruised; suffer damage. LME–M19. †**7** Become infirm or diseased. *rare.* Only in M17. **8** Go mad, become crazy. E19. **9** Of pottery glaze etc.: develop small cracks. M19.

crazed *a.* that has been crazed; insane, crazy: LME.

crazia /ˈkrɑːtsɪə/ *n.* Pl. **-ie** /-ɪeɪ/. L18. [It. f. G *Kreuzer* KREUTZER.] An ancient Tuscan copper coin, the twelfth part of a lira.

crazy /ˈkreɪzi/ *a.*, *n.*, & *adv.* E16. [f. CRAZE *v.* or *n.* + -Y[1].] **A** *adj.* †**1** Infirm, ailing, sickly. E16–L19. **2** Full of cracks or flaws; (esp. of a ship or a building) shaky, unsound. L16. **b** Of paving, a quilt, etc.: made of irregular pieces fitted together. L19. **3** Of a person, action, etc.: insane, mad; absurd. E17. **b** Extremely enthusiastic (*about*). *colloq.* E19. **c** Unrestrained, exciting, excellent. *slang* (orig. *US*). E20.

1 SHAKES. *1 Hen. VI* Some better place, Fitter for sickness and for crazy age. 2 ADAM SMITH The house is crazy . . and will not stand very long. QUILLER-COUCH A crazy, rusty blunderbuss hung over the fireplace. 3 J. BRAINE As they say in the films, I'm just a crazy mixed-up kid. (*as*) *crazy as a loon*: see LOON *n.*[2] *crazy as a two-bob watch*: see WATCH *n.* **crazy like** (or **as**) **a fox** *colloq.* (orig. *US*) very cunning or shrewd. **like crazy** *colloq.* (orig. *US*) like mad. **b crazy about, for** *spec.* infatuated with, in love with.

Special collocations & comb.: **crazy ant** an ant with fast or erratic movement, *esp.* the tropical ant *Prenolepsis longicornus*. **crazy bone** *US* the funny-bone. **crazy-pave** *v.t.* cover with crazy paving.

B *n.* A mad or eccentric person. *colloq.* M19.

C *adv.* Extremely, excessively. *slang* (chiefly *US*). L19.

crazily *adv.* M17. **craziness** *n.* E17.

creagh /krɛk, -x/ *n.* Chiefly *Anglo-Ir.* & *Sc. obs.* exc. *Hist.* Also **creach**. E19. [Gael. & Ir. *creach* plunder.] **1** A foray. E19. **2** Booty; prey. E19.

creaght /kreɪt, krɛxt/ *n.* & *v.* Chiefly *Anglo-Ir. obs.* exc. *Hist.* L16. [Ir. *caeraigheacht*, f. *caera* sheep.] **A** *n.* A nomadic herd of cattle, freq. including the drovers. L16. **B** *v.i.* Take cattle from place to place to graze. E17.

creak /kriːk/ *v.* & *n.* ME. [Imit.: cf. CRAKE *v.*[1], CROAK *v.*] **A** *v.* **1** *v.i.* Of a crow, rook, goose, etc.: utter a harsh cry. Long *rare*. ME. **2** *v.i.* Speak in a strident or querulous tone. *obs.* exc. as passing into sense 3. LME. **3** *v.i.* Make a harsh squeaking or grating sound. L16. **b** Move with a creak or creaks. M19. **4** *v.t.* Cause to make a creak or creaks. E17.

3 TOLKIEN The pine-trees . . creaking and cracking in the wind. **creaking gate** *fig.* a chronic invalid (likely to outlive others more healthy). **b** J. G. WHITTIER A single hay-cart down the dusty road Creaks slowly. 4 SHAKES. *All's Well* Creaking my shoes on the plain masonry.

B *n.* A strident noise, as of an ungreased hinge etc.; a harsh squeak. E17.

J. STEINBECK He heard the creak of the leather of the saddle. S. HEANEY The treble Creak of her voice like the pump's handle.

creakily *adv.* in a creaky manner; with a creaky sound: E20. **creakingly** *adv.* = CREAKILY M19. **creaky** *a.* characterized by creaking; apt to creak: M19.

cream /kriːm/ *n.*[1] *obs.* exc. *Hist.* ME. [OFr. *cresme* (mod. *chrême*) f. eccl.L *chrisma* unction: see CHRISM *n.*] = CHRISM *n.*

cream /kriːm/ *n.*[2] & *a.* ME. [OFr. *creme*, *craime*, *cresme* (mod. *crème* fem.) repr. blending of late L *cramum*, *crama* (perh. of Gaulish origin) with eccl.L *chrisma* CHRISM *n.*] **A** *n.* **1** The part of milk with high fat content, which collects at the top of the milk and which by churning is made into butter. ME. **2** A fancy dish or pudding of which cream is an ingredient, or which has the appearance and consistency of cream. LME. **b** More fully *cream sherry*. A full-bodied sweet sherry. L19. **c** A sweet or biscuit with a creamy filling. M20. **3** *The* most excellent element or part; *the* most outstanding group of people within a larger group; *the* quintessence. L16. **4** The part of a liquid that gathers at the top; a head of scum, froth, etc. (Implied earlier in CREAM *v.* 1a.) M17. **b** The liquid rich in droplets or particles of the dispersed phase that forms a separate (esp. upper) layer in an emulsion or suspension when it is allowed to stand or is centrifuged. E20. **5** A creamlike preparation used cosmetically or medicinally. E18. **6** *ellipt.* Cream colour; a cream-coloured horse, rabbit, etc. L18.

1 *clotted cream*, (dial.) *clouted cream*, *Cornish cream*, *dairy cream*, *Devonshire cream*, *double cream*, *full cream*, *half cream*, *ice-cream*, *single cream*, *sour cream*, *whipping cream*, etc. 3 R. DAVIES The successful Parisian entertainer, drawing the cream of society to his little theatre. S. BRILL These auto and steel pensions are the cream of the crop. 5 GOLDSMITH In vain she tries her paste and creams To smooth her face or hide its seams.

Phrases: **burnt cream** = *crème brûlée* s.v. CRÈME 1. *cold cream*: see COLD *a.* **cream of chicken, tomato,** etc., **(soup)** a chicken etc. soup made with cream or milk. **cream of tartar** purified and crystallized potassium bitartrate, used in medicine etc.; *cream of tartar fruit* (Austral.), the fruit of the baobab; *cream of tartar tree* (Austral.), the baobab. *night cream*: see NIGHT *n.* *peaches and cream*: see PEACH *n.*[1] SWISS *cream*. *vanishing cream*: see VANISH *v.* *violet cream*: see VIOLET *n.*

Comb.: **cream bun, cake**: filled with cream; **cream cheese** a soft rich kind of cheese made of unskimmed milk and cream; a cheese of this kind; **cream colour** the colour of the cream of milk, a yellowish white; **cream-coloured** *a.* of cream colour, yellowish white; **cream cracker** a crisp unsweetened biscuit; **cream-cups** a Californian and Mexican plant of the poppy family, *Platystemon californicus*, with yellow or cream-coloured flowers; **cream horn** a pastry shaped like a horn and filled with cream and jam; **cream ice** (an) ice-cream; **cream nut** a Brazil nut; **cream puff** (*a*) a puff pastry filled with cream; (*b*) an unimportant person or thing; (*c*) an effeminate person; a male homosexual; **cream sauce**: made with cream or milk; *cream sherry*: see sense 2b above; **cream soda** a carbonated drink of vanilla-flavoured soda water; **cream soup**: made with cream or milk; **cream tea** an afternoon tea which includes bread or scones with jam and (clotted) cream; **creamware** earthenware of a rich cream colour.

B *adj.* Cream-coloured; yellowish-white. M19.

creamlike *a.* resembling (that of) cream M19.

cream /kriːm/ *v.* LME. [f. CREAM *n.*[2]] **1** *v.i.* **a** Of a liquid: form a scum or frothy layer on the surface; foam. LME. **b** Of milk: form cream. L16. **c** Of an emulsion or suspension: form cream, separate into cream and another layer. E20. **2** *v.t.* Separate as cream; take the best or any specified part of; gather as the cream. Usu. foll. by *off*. E17. **3** *v.t.* Skim the cream from the surface of (milk). E18. **4** *v.t.* Make or flavour with cream; prepare (fish, chicken, etc.) in a cream sauce. Chiefly as *creamed* ppl a. M18. **5** *v.t.* & *i.* Add cream to (tea, coffee, etc.). E19. **6** *v.t.* **a** Cause or allow (milk, an emulsion or suspension) to form cream. L19. **b** Work (butter and sugar, mashed potatoes and milk, etc.) into a creamy consistency. L19. **c** Defeat heavily; ruin, wreck. *colloq.* (orig. *US*). E20. **7** *v.t.* Treat (the skin) with a cosmetic cream. E20.

2 A. BEVAN The industrialists . . were not prepared to allow any substantial part of their profits to be creamed off for welfare expenditure. *Times Educ. Suppl.* Creaming is another potential problem: do the magnet schools attract the most able staff and pupils to the detriment of other schools in the area? 6b D. CANFIELD You put the silver around, while I cream the potatoes.

creamer /ˈkriːmə/ *n.* M19. [f. prec. + -ER[1].] **1** A flat dish for skimming the cream off milk; a machine for separating cream. M19. **2** A jug for cream. Orig. *US.* L19. **3** A cream or milk substitute for adding to coffee, tea, etc. L20.

creamery /ˈkriːm(ə)ri/ *n.* M19. [f. CREAM *n.*[2] + -ERY, through Fr. *crémerie*.] 1 A shop where milk, cream, butter, etc., are sold. M19. 2 A butter-factory. L19.

Comb.: **creamery butter** factory-made butter as distinguished from that made at a private dairy.

creamometer /kriːˈmɒmɪtə/ *n.* L19. [f. as prec. + -OMETER, after LACTOMETER.] An instrument for measuring the percentage of cream in a sample of milk.

creamy /ˈkriːmi/ *a.* LME. [f. CREAM *n.*[2] + -Y[1].] 1 Containing (much) cream. LME. 2 Resembling cream; soft and rich; of a soft or rich cream colour. E17.

creamily *adv.* with a creamy tint or surface; in a creamy or smooth manner: E20. **creaminess** *n.* L17.

creance /ˈkriːəns/ *n.* ME. [(O)Fr. *créance* f. med.L *credentia*, f. L *credere* believe: see -ANCE. Cf. CREDENCE.] †1 The mental action or condition of believing; faith. ME–E17. b The thing believed; one's faith; a creed. LME–M17. †2 Credit (personal and commercial); reputation; trust. ME–L15. 3 *Falconry.* A long fine cord attached to a hawk's leash to prevent escape during training; a line used to confine the game at which a hawk is flown. L15.

crease /kriːs/ *n.*[1] & *v.* L16. [Prob. a var. of CREST *n.* (formerly also w. long vowel): cf. OFr. *cresté* wrinkled, furrowed.] A *n.* 1 A line or mark produced on the surface of anything by folding or pressing; a fold; a wrinkle; a ridge. L16. 2 *Archit.* A curved or ridge tile. E18. 3 *Cricket.* A line defining the legitimate position of bowler and batsman. M18. b In ice hockey and lacrosse, the area marked out in front of the goal. L19.

1 M. E. BRADDON Never mind the creases in that blue frock. J. GALSWORTHY Very well dressed, with special creases down their evening trousers. T. KENEALLY His cheeks folded themselves . . into creases of apparent contentment. 3 BOWLING-*crease*. POPPING *crease*. *return crease*: see RETURN *n.*

B *v.* 1 *v.t.* Make a crease or creases in or on the surface of; wrinkle; fold in a crease; *fig.* (*slang*) convulse with laughter, amuse highly, (usu. foll. by *up*). L16. 2 *v.t.* Stun (a horse etc.) by a grazing shot in the ridge of the neck. E19. b Stun (a person); graze with a bullet; kill; exhaust physically. *slang* (orig. *US*). E20. 3 *v.i.* Become creased; fall into creases; *fig.* (*slang*) be convulsed with laughter, be highly amused, (usu. foll. by *up*). L19.

1 G. A. BIRMINGHAM Major Kent . . creased his trousers and dressed for dinner every night. F. HERBERT A smile creased his mouth. 3 OED A material that is apt to crease. B. CHATWIN He creased with laughter, and clung to his stomach as if he were never going to stop.

creased *a.* having a crease or creases, wrinkled, folded in a crease M16. **creaser** *n.* a person who or thing which creases L19. **creasy** *a.* full of creases M19.

crease *n.*[2] var. of KRIS.

create /kriːˈeɪt/ *a.* (orig. *pa. pple*). *arch.* LME. [L *creatus* pa. pple, f. as next: see -ATE[2].] Created.

create /kriːˈeɪt/ *v.* LME. [L *creat-* pa. ppl stem of *creare* bring forth, produce: see -ATE[3]. Earliest as pa. pple *created*, an extension (see -ED[1]) of CREATE *a.*] I *v.t.* 1 Of a divine agent: bring into being; *esp.* form out of nothing. Also w. obj. & compl. LME. 2 *v.t.* Invest (a person) with (a rank, title, etc.). LME. 3 *v.t.* Make, form, or constitute for the first time or afresh; bring into legal existence; invent. (Implied earlier in CREATION 2.) L16. 4 *v.t.* Cause, occasion, produce, give rise to, (a condition, set of circumstances, etc.) L16. 5 Of an actor: be the first to represent (a role) and so give it its character. L19. 6 Design (a costume, dress, etc.); design and execute a scheme of interior decoration for (a room etc.). E20.

1 MAX-MÜLLER And the gods consulted a second time how to create beings that should adore them. F. HALL God created man a moral creature. 2 R. GRAFTON He created two Dukes. W. S. CHURCHILL He was created Earl of Marlborough. 3 W. CRUISE The word heirs is not necessary to create a fee simple. R. LYND He . . wished to create an Irish civilization that would be as acceptable ultimately to the old Unionists as to the Nationalists. J. FOWLES These characters I create never existed outside my own mind. 4 L. NAMIER They accepted a measure which under normal conditions would have created an uproar. C. RAYNER Her gown belled and lifted, . . creating a waft of air. 5 S. BRETT You dare to offer me the job of understudy to a part I CREATED! 6 J. BUCHAN If ever I . . had a house of my own, I would create just such a room. *Daily Telegraph* A brown mixture tweed suit . . created by Schiaparelli.

II *v.i.* 7 Create things, bring something into being. L16. 8 *v.i.* Make a fuss, complain loudly, (*about*). *slang.* E20.

7 J. RUSKIN It is only for God to create without toil. 8 K. FARRELL If my old man doesn't get 'is bit of fish at one . . he'll create.

creatable *a.* L17.

creatine /ˈkriːətiːn/ *n.* M19. [Irreg. f. Gk *kreas* (stem *kreo-*) flesh + -INE[5].] *Biochem.* A guanidine derivative, $C_4H_9N_3O_2$, present in living animal tissue, esp. muscle.

creatinine /krɪˈatɪniːn/ *n.* M19. [f. prec. + -INE[5].] *Biochem.* An alicyclic compound, $C_7H_4N_3O$, which is produced by metabolism of creatine and excreted in the urine.

creation /kriːˈeɪʃ(ə)n/ *n.* LME. [(O)Fr. *création* f. L *creatio(n-)*, f. as CREATE *v.*: see -ION.] 1 The action of a divine agency in creating something, esp. the world; the fact of being created by divine agency. LME. b *The* creating of the world; *the* beginning of the world, as a point in time. L16. 2 *gen.* The action of making, forming, producing, or constituting for the first time or afresh; invention; causation, production. LME. 3 The action of investing with a title, dignity, or function. LME. 4 That which divine agency has created; the created world; creatures collectively. E17. 5 An original (esp. imaginative) production of human intelligence or power. E17. b *spec.* The first representation by an actor of a dramatic character or role; a dramatic character as portrayed by a particular actor. L19. c A costume, dress, etc., as the work of its designer. L19.

1b M. INNES For the first time since the creation every continent and every sea was under fire. 2 C. LYELL The creation of a new lake, the engulphing of a city, or the raising of a new island. E. LONGFORD The creation of the Metropolitan Police force was in every sense the child of Peel's foresight and labour. P. DAVIES The big bang represents the creation of the physical universe. CONTINUOUS *creation*. 4 K. AMIS Hell . . Is eternal banishment from God And from the whole of his creation. **beat, lick, whip, creation** *US colloq.* surpass everything. *lords of (the) creation*: see LORD *n.* 5 J. GALSWORTHY Those stripey, streaky creations of Monet's.

Comb.: **creation science** the interpretation of scientific knowledge according to belief in the literal truth of the Bible, esp. as regards the origins of matter, life, and man.

creational *a.* (*rare*) M17. **creationism** *n.* a system or theory of creation; *spec.* (*a*) the theory that God creates a soul for every human being at conception or birth (opp. *traducianism*); (*b*) the theory which attributes the origin of matter, biological species, etc., to a special creation (opp. *evolutionism*); *esp.* = CREATION *science*: M19. **creationist** *n.* an adherent of creationism M19.

creative /kriːˈeɪtɪv/ *a.* L15. [f. CREATE *v.* + -IVE: cf. OFr. *creatif*, *-ive*, med.L *creativus*.] 1 Having the quality of creating; able to create; of or pertaining to creation; *spec.* inventive, imaginative, showing imagination as well as routine skill; intended to stimulate the imagination. L15. 2 Productive *of*. E19.

1 *creative art, artist, literature, writer, writing*, etc. **creative accountancy, accounting** *colloq.* modification of accounts to achieve a desired end; falsification of accounts that is misleading though not illegal. 2 H. MARTINEAU Laws and customs cannot be creative of virtue: they may encourage and help to preserve it; but they cannot originate it.

creatively *adv.* M19. **creativeness** *n.* E19. **creaˈtivity** *n.* creative power or faculty; ability to create: L19.

creator /kriːˈeɪtə/ *n.* ME. [(O)Fr. *creatour*, *-tur* (now *créateur*) f. L *creator*, f. as CREATE *v.*: see -OR.] 1 The divine agent creating from nothing, God. ME. 2 *gen.* A person who or thing which creates or gives origin to something. L16. b A person who creates a dramatic character or role. L19. c A person who creates or designs a costume etc. E20.

1 AV *Eccles.* 12:1 Remember now thy Creatour in the dayes of thy youth. 2 MILTON Custom was the creator of prelaty.

creatorship *n.* M19. **creatress** *n.* a female creator L16. **creatrix** /-trɪks/ *n.*, pl. **-trices** /-trɪsiːz/, [L] = CREATRESS L16.

creature /ˈkriːtʃə/ *n.* See also CRITTER. ME. [(O)Fr. *créature* f. late L *creatura*, f. as CREATE *v.*: see -URE.] 1 *gen.* A created thing; a created being. ME. †b The created universe; creation. ME–E17. c A material comfort, a thing that promotes well-being. Also *good creature*. *arch.* E17. 2 An animate being; an animal (often as distinct from a human being). ME. b *spec.* A farm animal; in *pl.*, cattle. *US dial.* M17. 3 A human being, a person. Freq. w. specifying wd of admiration, contempt, patronage, etc. ME. 4 A person who owes his or her fortune to, and remains subservient to, another; a puppet. L16. 5 A result or product *of*. M17.

1 W. COWPER The first boat or canoe that was ever formed . . was a more perfect creature in its kind than a balloon at present. c **the creature** *colloq.* intoxicating liquor, *esp.* whisky. 2 D. ATTENBOROUGH Several creatures . . quite unlike any other animals that we know, living or fossil. 3 SHAKES. *Rich. III* There is no creature loves me. STEELE Decent Dresses being often affected by the Creatures of the Town. E. BLISHEN This woman was a charming creature. 4 LD MACAULAY The corporations were filled with his creatures. 5 E. G. WHITE If we are creatures of circumstance, we shall surely fail of perfecting Christian characters. W. MAXWELL We were both creatures of the period . . 16heavy-businessman-father-and-the-oversensitive-artistic-son. **creature of habit** a person whose behaviour is guided by habit.

Comb.: *creature comforts*: see COMFORT *n.* 5.

creatural *a.* pertaining to creatures; of the nature of a creature: M17. **creaturehood** *n.* the condition of a creature L19. **creatureliness** *n.* creaturely state or quality M19. **creaturely** *a.* creatural; characteristic of a creature: M17. **creatureship** *n.* the state or condition of a creature M17.

creave *v.* see CREE.

crebrity /ˈkriːbrɪti/ *n. rare.* M17. [L *crebritas*, f. *creber* frequent: see -ITY.] Frequency.

crèche /krɛʃ, kreɪʃ/ *n.* L18. [Fr.: see CRATCH *n.*[1]] 1 A model of the infant Jesus in the manger with attending figures, often displayed at Christmas. L18. 2 A day nursery for infants and young children. M19.

cred /krɛd/ *n.*[1] *slang.* L20. [Abbrev.: earliest in *street cred* s.v. STREET *n.*] = CREDIBILITY *n.*

cred /krɛd/ *n.*[2] *slang.* L20. [Abbrev.] Credit on goods, services, etc.

credal /ˈkriːd(ə)l/ *a.* Also **creedal**. M19. [f. CREED *n.* + -AL[1], sp. w. single *e* after L *credere* etc.] Of or pertaining to a creed; characterized by a creed.

credence /ˈkriːd(ə)ns/ *n.* ME. [(O)Fr. *crēdence* f. med.L *credentia*, f. L *credent-* pres. ppl stem of *credere* believe: see -ENCE.] 1 Belief, acceptance as true. ME. 2 Trustworthiness; credit, repute. *obs.* exc. in *letter of credence*, a letter of recommendation or introduction, esp. of an ambassador. ME. †b A document furnishing credentials; a message entrusted to an embassy etc. LME–L18. †3 Trust, confidence *in*, reliance *on* (a person, authority, etc.). LME–M16. †4 Safekeeping, charge, care. L15–L16. †5a = CREDENZA. M16–M19. b *Eccl.* In full *credence shelf, table*, etc. A small side-table, shelf, or niche for the Eucharistic elements before consecration. E19.

1 H. JAMES This programme seemed almost too agreeable for credence. J. CHEEVER An evangelical credence in the romance and sorcery of business success. **attach, give, credence to** believe.

credent *a.* (*rare*) (*a*) believing, trustful; †(*b*) having credit or repute; credible: L16.

credenda /krɪˈdɛndə/ *n.pl.* M17. [L, neut. pl. of gerundive of *credere* believe.] Things to be believed; matters of faith.

credential /krɪˈdɛnʃ(ə)l/ *a.* & *n.* LME. [med.L *credentialis*, f. *credentia* CREDENCE: see -AL[1], -IAL.] A *adj.* Recommending or entitling to credit or confidence. *rare.* LME.

B *n.* A letter of recommendation or introduction, esp. of an ambassador; an indication of trustworthiness or achievement. Usu. in *pl.* M17.

F. BURNEY The whole ceremony of delivering his credentials to the King in state. J. B. MOZLEY The superiority of the virtues is no credential to the motive. W. C. WILLIAMS I was approached by a young chap at my office door who showed me his credentials. J. C. RANSOM They scarcely had the credentials to judge of such matters.

credentialled, ***-ialed** *a.* furnished with credentials L19.

credenza /krɪˈdɛnzə/ *n.* L19. [It. f. med.L *credentia*: see CREDENCE.] A sideboard, a cupboard, a buffet.

credibility /krɛdɪˈbɪlɪti/ *n.* M16. [med.L *credibilitas*, f. as next: see -ITY.] The quality of being credible; good reputation.

Comb.: **credibility gap** a disparity between facts and what is said or written about them, esp. officially.

credible /ˈkrɛdɪb(ə)l/ *a.* LME. [L *credibilis*, f. *credere* believe: see -IBLE.] **1** Believable; worthy of belief or support. LME. **b** Of a threat etc.: convincing. M20. †**2** Ready, willing, or inclined to believe. LME–L17. †**3** Creditable, reputable. M17–E18.

1 W. SEWEL Which I noted down from the mouth of credible persons. J. A. FROUDE When the falsehood ceased to be credible the system which was based upon it collapsed.

credibleness *n.* = CREDIBILITY L16. **credibly** *adv.* LME.

credit /ˈkrɛdɪt/ *n.* M16. [Fr. *crédit* f. It. *credito* or L *creditum* use as n. of neut. pa. pple of *credere* believe, put trust in.] **1** Belief, faith, trust. M16. †**b** Something believed; a report. *rare* (Shakes.). Only in E17. †**2** Trustworthiness, credibility; authority (on which testimony is accepted). M16–M19. **3** Reputation. Now *spec.* good reputation, good name. M16. **4** Power derived from character or reputation, personal influence. M16. †**5** Safekeeping, charge, care. M16–M17. **6** Trust in a person's ability and intention to pay at a later time for goods, services, etc., supplied; consent or opportunity for deferring payment; the length of time for which payment may be deferred. M16. **b** Reputation for solvency and honesty. L16. **7** A source of commendation or honour *to*; something creditable. L16. **8** Acknowledgement of merit (*for*, *of* an action etc.); honour. E17. **b** In full *pass-with-credit*. A grade above 'pass' in an examination. E20. **9** A sum at a person's disposal in the books of a bank etc.; a note, bill, etc., acting as security against a loan etc. E17. **10** The acknowledgement of payment by entry in an account; (a sum entered on) the credit side (see below) of an account. Opp. DEBIT *n.* 2. M18. **11** A certificate or other acknowledgement of a student's completion of (part of) a course of study; a unit of study for completion of which such official acknowledgement is given. Chiefly *N. Amer.* E20. **12** An acknowledgement of a contributor's services to a film, broadcast programme, etc. Usu. in *pl.* E20.

1 GIBBON Charges like these may seem to deserve some degree of credit. **2** T. FULLER I dare take it on the credit of an excellent witness. D. HUME The abstract philosophy of Cicero has lost its credit. **3** W. COWPER John Gilpin was a citizen of credit and renown. **4** W. H. PRESCOTT Granvelle . . was not slow to perceive his loss of credit with the regent. **6** DEFOE He buys his wool . . at two or three months' credit. S. UNWIN The good lady in the shop, evidently feeling that as a regular customer I was entitled to credit, . . said I could pay the halfpenny the next time. **b** SHAKES. *Merch. V.* Try what my credit can in Venice do. **7** DICKENS You are a credit to the school. M. DRABBLE Her name could be a credit and not a shame. **8** N. O. BROWN The credit for recognizing the central importance of the excremental theme in Swift belongs to Aldous Huxley. G. F. KENNAN These ventures . . were serious mistakes. They reflected no credit on the governments that sent them.

Phrases: **do credit to** enhance the reputation of, reflect well on. **get credit for** be given credit for. **give a person credit for** enter (a sum) to a person's credit; *fig.* ascribe (usu. a good quality or achievement) to a person, acknowledge in a person's favour. **give credit to** (*a*) believe (a story etc.); (*b*) allow to have goods or services on credit. **letter of credit** †(*a*) = *letter of credence* s.v. CREDENCE 2; (*b*) an order authorizing a person to draw money from the writer's correspondent in another place; a letter from an importer's bank guaranteeing payment to the exporter for specified goods. *line of credit*: see LINE *n.*[2] **on credit** with payment to be made at a later time by agreement. *postwar credit*: see POSTWAR *a.* *revolving credit*: see REVOLVING *a.* *social credit*: see SOCIAL *a.* *Social Credit League*: see SOCIAL *a.* *Social Credit Party*: see SOCIAL *a.* **to a person's credit** on the credit side of a person's account; *fig.* to a person's advantage, in a person's favour. **vote of credit** the voting by Parliament of a sum on account in anticipation of the annual estimates.

Comb.: **credit account** an account to which goods and services may be charged on credit; **credit card** a card issued by a bank, business, etc., authorizing the acquisition of goods and services on credit; **credit insurance** insurance against bad debts; **credit note** a written acknowledgement of a sum credited, as for goods returned; **credit rating** an estimate of a person's ability and intention to pay his or her debts in due course; **credit sale**: of goods or services charged to a credit account; **credit side** the side or column of an account, conventionally the right-hand side, in which credits are entered; **credit squeeze** the restriction of financial credit facilities through banks etc.; **credit title** a credit (sense 12) at the beginning or end of a cinema or television film; **credit transfer** a method of payment by which a sum is transferred from one person's bank account to another's; **credit union** a non-profit-making money cooperative whose members can borrow from pooled savings at low interest rates; **creditworthiness** the extent to which a person, firm, etc., is creditworthy; **creditworthy** *a.* (*a*) (now *rare*) trustworthy; (*b*) qualified to receive commercial credit.

credit /ˈkrɛdɪt/ *v.* M16. [f. the n. or f. L *credere* (see prec.).] **1** *v.t.* & †*i.* w. *to*. Believe; put faith in. M16. †**2** *v.t.* Supply with goods etc. on credit. M16–M19. †**3** *v.t.* Entrust (a person) *with*, (a thing) *to*. L16–M18. **4** *v.t.* Bring into credit or estimation; do credit to. Now *rare*. L16. **5** *v.t.* Enter a sum on the credit side of (an account) or of the account of (a person), (foll. by *with* the sum); enter (a sum) on the credit side of an account (foll. by *to* the account, the person whose account is credited). L17. **b** *fig.* Ascribe (usu. a good quality or achievement) *to*; ascribe a good quality, achievement, etc., to (a person: foll. by *with* the quality etc.) M19.

1 L. DURRELL An absurdity so patent that I could hardly credit it. C. P. SNOW I found it impossible to credit that I had much will. **4** S. PALMER Smatterers in science . . neither instruct the company, nor credit themselves. **5b** H. L. MENCKEN Very little of the extraordinary progress of medicine . . is to be credited to the family doctor. L. TRILLING Hegel . . credits him with great wit.

creditable /ˈkrɛdɪtəb(ə)l/ *a.* E16. [f. CREDIT *n.* or *v.* + -ABLE.] †**1** Credible. E16–E19. **2** That brings credit or honour (*to*). M17. †**b** Respectable, decent. L17–M19. †**3** Qualified to receive commercial credit, creditworthy. L18–E19. **4** Able to be ascribed *to*. E20.

creditaˈbility *n.* L19. **creditableness** *n.* M17. **creditably** *adv.* L17.

Creditiste /krɛdɪˈtiːst/ *n.* & *a.* M20. [Fr.] (An adherent) of the Quebec wing of the Social Credit party in Canada.

creditor /ˈkrɛdɪtə/ *n.* LME. [AN *creditour*, (O)Fr. *créditeur* f. L *creditor*, f. *credit-* pa. ppl stem of *credere*: see CREDIT *n.*, -OR.] **I1** A person who gives credit for money or goods; a person to whom a debt is owing. LME. **2** The credit side of an account. Formerly also, a sum entered in this. M16. †**II3** A person who stands surety. LME–E16.

creditress *n.* (now *rare*) a female creditor E17. **creditrix** /-trɪks/ *n.* (now *rare*), pl. **-trices** /-trɪsiːz/, [L] = CREDITRESS E17.

credo /ˈkriːdəʊ, ˈkreɪ-/ *n.* Pl. **-os.** ME. [L *credo* I believe. Cf. CREED *n.*] **1** The Apostles' Creed, the Nicene Creed, (from their first word). Now *esp.* a musical setting of the Nicene Creed. ME. **2** *gen.* A creed, a set of opinions or principles. L16.

credulity /krɪˈdjuːlɪti/ *n.* LME. [(O)Fr. *crédulité* f. L *credulitas*, f. *credulus*: see next, -ITY.] Orig., belief, faith, readiness to believe. Now *spec.* overreadiness to believe, disposition to believe on weak or insufficient grounds.

Also **ˈcredulence** *n.* (*rare*) M17.

credulous /ˈkrɛdjʊləs/ *a.* L16. [f. L *credulus*, f. *credere* believe: see -ULOUS.] **1** Disposed to believe. Now *spec.* disposed to believe too readily. (Foll. by *of*.) L16. **2** Of behaviour etc.: characterized by or showing credulity. M17.

credulously *adv.* M17. **credulousness** *n.* L16.

Cree /kriː/ *n.* & *a.* Also (earlier) †**Cris.** M18. [Canad. Fr. *Cris* abbrev. of earlier *C(h)ristinaux* f. Algonquian (now *kinistino:*).] **A** *n.* Pl. **-s**, same. **1** A member of an Indian people of central N. America. M18. **2** The Algonquian language of this people. E19. **B** *attrib.* or as *adj.* Of or pertaining to the Cree or their language. M18.

cree /kriː/ *v.* Chiefly *dial.* Also **creave, creeve,** /kriːv/. LME. [(O)Fr. *crever* burst, split f. L *crepare* crackle, crack.] †**1** *v.i.* Burst, split. Only in LME. **2** *v.t.* Soften (grain) by boiling. E17. **3** *v.t.* Pound into a soft mass. E19. **4** *v.i.* Become soft or pulpy by soaking or boiling. M19.

creed /kriːd/ *n.* OE. [f. as CREDO.] **1** A brief formal summary of Christian doctrine, *esp.* each of those known as the (Apostles') Creed, the Athanasian Creed, and the Nicene Creed. OE. **2** A repetition of the Creed as an act of devotion, esp. as part of the Mass. LME. **3** A system of religious belief. M16. **4** A set of opinions or principles on any subject; *esp.* a political philosophy. E17. **5** Belief or confidence *in*; an article of faith. *rare*. E19.

1 *Apostles' Creed*: see APOSTLE. *Athanasian Creed*: see ATHANASIAN *a.* *Nicene Creed*: see NICENE *a.* **2. the Creed** *spec.* the Apostles' Creed. **3** JOHN BROOKE The history and doctrines of Christianity according to the creed of the Church of England. **4** R. W. EMERSON The cynical creed . . of the market. G. STEINER Communism . . is a creed penetrated . . by a sense of the values of intellect and art.

creedless *a.* without a creed M19. **creedlessness** *n.* M19.

creed /kriːd/ *v.t.* & *i.* Long *obs.* exc. *dial.* E17. [L *credere*, after prec.] Believe.

creedal *a.* var. of CREDAL.

creek /kriːk/ *n.*[1] Also **crick** /krɪk/. ME. [ON *kriki* chink, nook, or (O)Fr. *crique* f. ON. Perh. partly also f. MDu. *krēke* (Du. *kreek* creek, bay).] **I1** An inlet on a sea-coast or in the tidal estuary of a river. ME. **2** A small port or harbour; an inlet within the limits of a haven or port. L15. **3** A short arm of a river. L16. **4** A tributary of a river; a stream, a brook. *N. Amer.*, *Austral.*, & *NZ*. E17. **5** *transf.* A valley extending from a plain into a highland area. M17. **II**†**6** A cleft in the face of a rock etc. Also, the cleft between the buttocks. ME–M17. †**7** A trick, an artifice, a contrivance. LME–E17. **8** A narrow or winding passage; an out-of-the-way corner, a nook. *obs.* exc. *dial.* L16. †**9** A bend, a turning, a winding. L16–L17.

Phrases etc.: *fly-up-the-creek*: see FLY *v.* *up shit creek*: see SHIT *n.* **up the creek** *slang* (*a*) in a tight corner, in trouble; *spec.* pregnant; (*b*) crazy, eccentric.

creeklet *n.* a little creek L16. **creeky** *a.* full of creeks M16.

creek /kriːk/ *n.*[2] *obs.* exc. *Sc.* M16. [Corresp. to early mod.Du. *kriecke*, f. earlier Du. *kriecken*, *krieckelen*, mod.Du. *krieken*, break or burst through as the daylight. See also SKREEK.] Dawn; break *of* day.

Creek /kriːk/ *n.*[3] & *a.* E18. [f. CREEK *n.*[1]] **A** *n.* Pl. **-s**, same. **1** A member of a N. American Indian confederacy of the Muskogee and some other peoples; a member of the Muskogee. E18. **2** The Muskogean language of the Muskogee. L19. **B** *attrib.* or as *adj.* Of or pertaining to the Muskogee or their language, or the confederacy including the Muskogee. E18.

creel /kriːl/ *n.*[1] & *v.* Orig. *north.* & *Sc.* ME. [Origin unkn.] **A** *n.* **1** A large wicker basket, now esp. for fish. ME. **b** An angler's fishing-basket. E19. **2** A trap made of wickerwork for catching fish, lobsters, etc. LME.

Phrases: **coup the creels** *Sc.* fall head over heels; meet with a mishap. **in a creel** *Sc.* in a state of temporary mental aberration.

B *v.t.* 1 Put into a creel. E16. 2 In certain marriage customs in Scotland: make (a newly married man) go through some ceremony with a creel. L18.

creelful *n.* as much as a creel will hold E19.

creel /kriːl/ *n.*[2] L18. [Perh. same wd as prec.] 1 *gen.* A framework, a rack. L18. 2 A frame for holding bobbins in a spinning-machine. M19.

creeler *n.* a person who attends to a creel in a spinning-machine. M19.

creep /kriːp/ *n.* L15. [f. the vb.] 1 The action or an act of creeping; slow and stealthy motion. L15. 2a A gradual bulging of or a bulge in the floor in a coalmine, owing to pressure on the pillars. E19. b *Geol.* The gradual (esp. downhill) movement of soil, disintegrated rock, etc., owing to gravity, atmospheric changes, etc. Also, the gradual displacement of strata or the earth's crust by expansion, contraction, compression, etc. L19. c *Metall.* Gradual change of shape under stress. E20. 3a An enclosure with a small entrance for animals; *spec.* a feeding-enclosure with an entrance admitting only young animals. E19. b A low arch under a railway embankment, road, etc.; an opening in a hedge etc. for an animal to pass through. L19. 4 A shivering or shuddering sensation, esp. caused by dread or revulsion. Chiefly in *the creeps*. *colloq.* E19. 5 A dislikeable, tiresome, or fawning person. *slang* (orig. *US*). L19. 6 A sneak-thief. *slang.* E20.

1 **the creep** *slang* stealthy robbery. 4 M. MITCHELL The live oaks with their waving curtains of grey moss gave Scarlett the creeps.

¶Rare bef. 19.

creep /kriːp/ *v.* Pa. t. & pple **crept** /krɛpt/. [OE *crēopan* = OFris. *kriapa*, OS *criopan*, ON *krjūpa*, f. Gmc.] I *v.i.* 1 Move dragging the body close to the ground, as a person on all fours, a short-limbed reptile or quadruped, (formerly) a snake, worm, or other limbless creature, etc. Cf. CRAWL *v.* I. OE. 2 Move timidly, slowly, softly, or stealthily. ME. 3 *fig.* Advance by imperceptible degrees, develop gradually; insinuate oneself *into*; come *in*, *up*, etc., unobserved. ME. b Proceed or exist abjectly; behave timidly, diffidently, or unambitiously. L16. 4 (Of a plant) spread over or along a surface with extending stems or branches; extend like a creeping plant. LME. 5 Of a person: shiver or shudder with dread, revulsion, etc.; feel as if things were creeping over one's skin. Of the flesh or skin: feel as if things were creeping over it, through dread, revulsion, etc. LME. 6 Drag a river, the seabed, etc., with a creeper. L18. 7 Of a mine floor, soil, metal, etc.: undergo creep (see CREEP *n.* 2). M19. 8 Of a liquid: cover a surface as a thin film. L19. 9 Commit robbery with stealth. *slang.* E20.

1 T. HERBERT Land Tortoyses so great that they will creepe with two mens burthens. DAY LEWIS A hole in the hedge . . through which I must creep if I was to play with the neighbour's children. †**creep to the Cross** etc., advance towards the crucifix on one's knees or prone, in the Roman Catholic service on Good Friday. 2 SHAKES. *A.Y.L.* The whining schoolboy . . creeping like snail Unwillingly to school. J. G. WHITTIER The mists crept upwards. B. PYM She grew cold at last and crept back to bed. 3 B. JOWETT The licence of which you speak very easily creeps in. E. WELTY A sudden alert, tantalized look would creep over the little man's face. b POPE Wit that can creep, and Pride that licks the dust. 4 A. P. STANLEY Vineyards creep along the ancient terraces. *gill-creep-by-ground*: see GILL *n.*[1] 5 *make a person's flesh creep*: see FLESH *n.*

II *v.t.* †10 Advance towards (the Cross) on one's knees or prone. L15–L16. 11 Creep along or over. *rare.* M17. 12 Foll. by *in*: introduce or increase gradually or imperceptibly. M20.

Comb.: **creep-hole** a hole through which a person creeps; a hole into which an animal etc. creeps; **creep-joint** *US slang* (*a*) a gambling game that shifts location each night; (*b*) a brothel or other seedy place of resort, esp. where patrons are robbed; **creep-mouse** *n.* & *a.* (*a*) *n.* pretending to be a mouse in playing with a small child; (*b*) *adj.* furtive, timid, shy.

creepage *n.* gradual movement; *spec.* leakage of electricity: E20.

creeper /ˈkriːpə/ *n.* OE. [f. prec. + -ER[1].] 1 A person who creeps (*lit.* & *fig.*). OE. b A trainee tea-planter, esp. in Sri Lanka (Ceylon). Now *arch.* or *Hist.* L19. 2 A creature that creeps. LME. b A bird that climbs up trees, over bushes, etc. Formerly *spec.* the treecreeper. M17. 3a A grapnel, *spec.* one used for dragging a river, the seabed, etc. LME. b A small iron firedog. Now *dial.* or *Hist.* M16. 4 A plant that creeps along the ground, up a wall, etc. E17. 5 *Cricket* etc. A bowled ball that travels low along the ground, a daisy-cutter. M19. 6 In *pl.* Soft-soled shoes (also BROTHEL-*creepers*). *slang.* E20.

1 *New Yorker* Though Brian was clever enough at his books he was no swot or creeper. 2b *brown creeper*. *honey-creeper, treecreeper, wallcreeper, woodcreeper*. 4 *caustic creeper*: see CAUSTIC *a.* I. RANGOON *creeper*. *Virginia creeper*: see VIRGINIA I. *Virginian creeper*: see VIRGINIAN *a.*

creepered *a.* covered with a creeping plant, esp. Virginia creeper L19.

creepie /ˈkriːpi/ *n.* *Sc.* & *dial.* M17. [f. CREEP *v.* + -IE, -Y[6].] A low stool.

creeping /ˈkriːpɪŋ/ *ppl a.* OE. [f. CREEP *v.* + -ING[2].] That creeps.

creeping barrage a curtain of gunfire moving ahead of advancing troops. **creeping buttercup** a common buttercup, *Ranunculus repens*, with strong spreading stems which root at nodes. **creeping Jenny** a trailing loosestrife, *Lysimachia nummularia*, with yellow flowers in the axils of glossy paired roundish leaves; also called *moneywort*. **creeping Jesus** *slang* an abject or hypocritical person. *creeping palsy*: see PALSY *n.*[1] I. **creeping paralysis** locomotor ataxia. *creeping soft-grass*: see SOFT *a.* *creeping thistle*: see THISTLE *n.* I.

creepingly *adv.* M16.

creepy /ˈkriːpi/ *a.* L18. [f. CREEP *v.* or *n.* + -Y[1].] 1 Characterized by creeping, given to creeping. L18. 2 Having or producing a creeping of the flesh; eerie, uncanny. M19.

2 A. TROLLOPE It is dark and cold and what I call creepy Do you ever fancy that perhaps you will see a ghost some day? J. GALSWORTHY The creepy feeling that it gave him, of a man missing. T. PYNCHON Women avoid him . . . he's creepy.

Comb.: **creepy-crawly** *a.* & *n.* (*a*) *adj.* that creeps and crawls; sneaking, servile; (of feelings etc.) eerie, uncanny; (*b*) *n.* a creature that creeps and crawls, an insect.

creese *n.* var. of KRIS.

creesh /kriːʃ/ *n.* & *v.* *Sc.* Also **creish**. LME. [OFr. *craisse* = *graisse* f. L *crassa* thick, fat; cf. GREASE *n.*] A *n.* 1 Grease, fat. LME. 2 A smart blow. L18. B *v.t.* Grease. L15.

creeshy *a.* greasy M16.

creeve *v.* see CREE.

creish *n.* & *v.* var. of CREESH.

crémaillère /kremɑjɛːr/ *n.* Pl. pronounced same. E19. [Fr., formerly *cramaillère*, f. *cramail* pot-hanger, chimney-hook.] *Fortif.* A zig-zag or indented inside line of a parapet.

cremaster /krɪˈmastə/ *n.* L17. [Gk *kremastēr*, f. *krema-* hang.] 1 *Anat.* The muscle of the spermatic cord, by which the testicle can be partially raised. L17. 2 *Entomol.* The tip of the abdomen of the pupa of an insect, serving as an anchorage point. L19.

cremas'teric *a.* of or pertaining to the cremaster (muscle) L19.

cremate /krɪˈmeɪt/ *v.t.* L19. [L *cremat-* pa. ppl stem of *cremare* burn, or back-form. f. next: see -ATE[3].] Consume (a corpse) by fire, burn.

cremator *n.* a person who cremates corpses etc.; a crematory furnace: L19.

cremation /krɪˈmeɪʃ(ə)n/ *n.* E17. [L *crematio(n-)*, f. as prec.: see -ATION.] The action of cremating; *spec.* the burning of a corpse as a means of disposing of it instead of burial; an instance of this.

cremationist *n.* an advocate of cremation L19.

crematorium /krɛməˈtɔːrɪəm/ *n.* Pl. **-ia** /-ɪə/, **-s**. L19. [mod.L, f. as CREMATE: see -ORIUM.] A place for cremating corpses.

crematory /ˈkrɛmət(ə)ri/ *a.* & *n.* L19. [f. CREMATE *v.* + -ORY[1], -ORY[2].] A *adj.* Of or pertaining to cremation. L19. B *n.* = CREMATORIUM. Now chiefly *N. Amer.* L19.

crème /krɛm (*pl. same*); kreɪm/ *n.* Also ***crême***. E19. [Fr. = CREAM *n.*[2]] 1 Cream; a cream, a custard. Used esp. in names of desserts and liqueurs (see below). E19. 2 *crème de la crème* /də la, lɑː/, the pick of society; the élite. M19.

1 ***crème brûlée*** /bryle, ˈbruːleɪ/ [Fr. = burnt] a cream or custard dessert topped with caramelized sugar. ***crème caramel*** /karamɛl, ˈkarəmɛl/ a custard dessert made with whipped cream and eggs and topped with caramel. ***crème Chantilly*** /ʃɑ̃tiji, ʃanˈtɪli/ whipped cream sweetened and flavoured with vanilla. ***crème de cacao*** /də kakao, kəˈkɑːəʊ/ a chocolate-flavoured liqueur. ***crème de menthe*** /də mɑ̃ːt, ˈmɑːnt, ˈmɒnθ/ a peppermint-flavoured liqueur. ***crème de noyau*** /də nwajo, ˈnwʌɪəʊ/ an almond-flavoured liqueur. ***crème renversée*** /rɑ̃vɛrse, ˈrɛnvəːseɪ/ [Fr. = inverted] a custard turned out of a mould.

Cremnitz white /ˈkrɛmnɪts ˈwʌɪt/ *n. phr.* Also **K-**. L19. [f. G *Kremnitz*, (formerly also) *C-*, Kremnica, a town in Slovakia + WHITE *n.*] A white lead pigment used as a paint base.

cremnophobia /krɛmnəˈfəʊbɪə/ *n.* E20. [f. Gk *krēmnos* overhanging cliff + -O- + -PHOBIA.] Irrational fear of precipices or steep places.

cremona /krɪˈməʊnə/ *n.*[1] M17. [Alt. of KRUMMHORN.] = CROMORNE, KRUMMHORN 2.

Cremona /krɪˈməʊnə/ *a.* & *n.*[2] L17. [A town in Lombardy.] (Designating) an old Italian violin of fine quality, *spec.* one made in Cremona in the 17th and early 18th cents.

cremor /ˈkrɛmə/ *n.* Now *rare.* E17. [L: erron. assoc. w. Fr. CRÈME.] A thick juice or liquid; a broth. Also, a scum gathering on the top of a liquid.

crenate /ˈkriːneɪt/ *a.* L18. [mod.L *crenatus*, f. pop.L *crena* (in late gloss) notch, incision, of unkn. origin: see -ATE[2].] *Bot.*, *Zool.*, etc. = next.

cre'nation *n.* a crenated formation, a crenature; crenated condition: M19. **crenature** /ˈkrɛnətjʊə, ˈkriː-/ *n.* a rounded tooth or denticulation on the margin of a leaf etc. E19.

crenated /ˈkriːneɪtɪd/ *a.* L17. [f. as prec. + -ED[1].] *Bot.*, *Zool.*, etc. Having a notched edge or rounded teeth; finely scalloped.

crenel /ˈkrɛn(ə)l/ *n.* Also **crenelle** /krɪˈnɛl/. L15. [OFr. (mod. *créneau*) f. Proto-Gallo-Romance dim. of pop.L *crena* (see CRENATE). Cf. KERNEL *n.*[2]] Each of the open spaces or indentations in a battlemented parapet, orig. used for shooting through etc.; an embrasure. In *pl.*, battlements.

crenel /ˈkrɛn(ə)l/ *v.t.* Infl. **-l(l)-**. L17. [(O)Fr. *créneler*, f. as prec. Cf. KERNEL *v.*[2]] Indent the edge of; crenellate. Chiefly as *crenelled* ppl a.

crenellate /ˈkrɛn(ə)leɪt/ *v.t.* Also **-elate**. E19. [f. as prec. + -ATE[3].] Provide with battlements or embrasures.

crene'llation *n.* the action of crenellating; the condition of being crenellated; a battlement: M19.

crenelle *n.* see CRENEL *n.*

crenellé /ˈkrɛnəli/ *a.* Also **-lly**. L16. [Fr. *crénelé* pa. pple of *créneler*: see CRENEL *v.*] *Her.* Having battlements, or indentations similar to battlements.

crenulate /ˈkrɛnjʊleɪt/ *a.* L18. [mod.L *crenulatus*, f. *crenula* dim. of *crena*: see CRENATE, -ATE[2].] 1 *Bot.* & *Zool.* Of a leaf, a shell, etc.: minutely crenate; finely scalloped. L18. 2 *Physical Geogr.* Of a shoreline: having many small irregular bays due to the erosion of rock of varying hardness. E20.

crenulated *a.* = CRENULATE 1 E19. **crenu'lation** *n.* a crenulated formation M19.

creodont /ˈkriːədɒnt/ *n.* & *a.* L19. [mod.L *Creodonta* (see below), f. Gk *kreas* flesh + -ODONT.] *Palaeont.* A member of, of or pertaining to, the order Creodonta of extinct carnivorous mammals, from the Palaeocene, Eocene, and Oligocene epochs.

creole /ˈkriːəʊl/ *n.* & *a.* Also (esp. in strict use of sense A.1 & corresp. uses of the adj.) **C-**. E17. [Fr. *créole*, earlier *criole* f. Sp. *criollo* prob. f. Port. *crioulo* Black born in Brazil, home-born slave, f. *criar* nurse, breed f. L *creare* CREATE *v.*] A *n.* 1 A descendant of European settlers or (occas.) of Black slaves, in the W. Indies or Central or S. America; a descendant of French settlers in the southern US, esp. Louisiana. Also *loosely*, a person of mixed European and Black descent. E17. 2 A former pidgin language that has

developed into the sole or native language of a community. L19.
Phrases: SCOTCHMAN *hugging a Creole*.

B *adj.* **1** That is a creole; of, pertaining to, or characteristic of a creole or creoles. M18. **2** Of an animal or plant: bred or grown in the W. Indies etc. but not of indigenous origin; of local origin or production. M18.

1 V. S. NAIPAUL Old creole woman from 42 owe six dollars. E. L. ORTIZ Serve with . . any creole soup. *Scientific American* Creole languages throughout the world exhibit the same uniformity and even the same grammatical structures that are observed in Hawaii.

cre'olian *n.* & *a.* (now *rare*) = CREOLE *n.* I, *a.* I L17. **creolism** *n.* (now *rare*) creole descent L18. **creolist** *n.* an expert in or student of creole languages M20. **creo'listics** *n.* the branch of linguistics that deals with creole languages L20.

creolize /'kri:əʊlʌɪz, 'krɪ-/ *v.* Also **-ise**. E19. [f. prec. + -IZE.] **1** *v.i.* Relax in an elegant fashion in a warm climate. *rare.* E19. **2** *v.t.* Naturalize in the W. Indies, Central or S. America or Louisiana. M19. **3** *v.t.* Make (a language) into a creole. L19.

creoli'zation *n.* the action or process of creolizing someone or something; the process by which a pidgin language develops into a creole: L19.

creophagous /krɪ'ɒfəgəs/ *a.* Also **k-**. L19. [Gk *kreophagos*, f. *kreas* flesh: see -PHAGOUS.] Flesh-eating, carnivorous.

creophagy /-dʒi/ *n.* the eating of flesh L19.

creosol /'kri:əsɒl/ *n.* M19. [f. CREOS(OTE + -OL.] *Chem.* A colourless liquid phenolic ether, $C_8H_{10}O_2$, forming the chief constituent of wood-tar creosote.

creosote /'kri:əsəʊt/ *n.* & *v.* M19. [G *Kreosote*, f. Gk *kreo-* comb. form of *kreas* flesh + *sōtēr* saviour, *sōteria* safety, intended to mean 'flesh-saving', w. ref. to its antiseptic properties.] **A** *n.* **1** A colourless oily liquid distilled from wood tar, having powerful antiseptic properties. M19. **2** More fully *creosote oil.* A dark brown oil distilled from coal tar and used as a wood preservative. M19. **B** *v.t.* Treat (wood etc.) with creosote. M19.

crêpe /kreɪp/ *n.* & *a.* Also **crepe**. See also CRAPE *n.* & *a.* L18. [Fr., earlier †*crespe*, use as n. of OFr. *crespe* curled, frizzed f. L *crispus* curled. Cf. CRISP *n.*, *a.*] **A** *n.* **1** A fine cotton or gauzelike fabric with a crinkled surface. L18. **2** = *crêpe rubber* below. E20. **3** A very thin pancake. E20.

1 China crêpe, crêpe de Chine /də 'ʃi:n/ a fine crêpe of silk or a similar fabric. *romaine crêpe*: see ROMAINE 2. **3 crêpe Suzette** /su:'zɛt/ a thin dessert pancake served in a spirit or liqueur.

B *attrib.* or as *adj.* Made of crêpe; resembling crêpe. L18.

crêpe paper thin crinkled paper resembling crêpe. **crêpe rubber** a type of raw rubber rolled into thin sheets with a corrugated surface, used for shoe-soles etc. **crêpe sole** a layer of crêpe rubber forming the underside of a shoe. *pale crêpe rubber*: see PALE *a.*

crêp(e)y *a.* resembling crêpe L19.

crêpe /kreɪp/ *v.t.* E19. [Fr. *crêper.*] Crimp, frizz (hair). Cf. CRAPE *v.* I.

crêpé /-pi/ *ppl a.* (of the hair) crimped, frizzed E19. **crêping** *vbl n.* (*a*) crimping or frizzing of hair; (*b*) production of crêpe rubber or crêpe paper: L19.

crêpeline /'kreɪpəli:n/ *n.* Also **-oline**. L19. [Fr., dim. of CRÊPE *n.*] A thin light dress-material made of silk or silk and wool.

crepine /'krɛpi:n/ *n. obs.* exc. *Hist.* Also **crespin(e)** /'krɛspi:n, -ɪn/ M16. [OFr. *crespine* (mod. *crépine*), f. *crespe*: see CRÊPE *n.* & *a.*] A ladies' net or caul for the hair; a ruffled part of a hood. Also, a frill or fringe for a bed, dais, etc.

crépinette /kreɪpɪ'nɛt/ *n.* L19. [Fr., dim. of *crépine* caul: see -ETTE.] A kind of flat sausage consisting of minced meat and savoury stuffing wrapped in pieces of pork caul.

crepitate /'krɛpɪteɪt/ *v.i.* E17. [L *crepitat-* pa. ppl stem of *crepitare* crackle, f. *crepare* rattle: see -ATE[3].] †**1** Break wind. E17–M18. **2** *Entomol.* Of a (bombardier) beetle: eject a pungent fluid with a sudden sharp report. E19. **3** Make a crackling sound; *Med.* (of the lungs) make the sound of crepitation (sense 2). M19.

crepitant *a.* crackling, crepitating E19.

crepitation /krɛpɪ'teɪʃ(ə)n/ *n.* M17. [Fr. *crépitation* or late L *crepitatio(n-)*, f. as prec.: see -ATION.] **1** A crackling or sharp rattling sound. M17. **2** *Med.* A crackling sound in the lungs heard on auscultation, arising in the alveoli during inhalation, often a symptom of lung disease. Also = CREPITUS I. M19.

crepitus /'krɛpɪtəs/ *n.* E19. [L, f. *crepare* rattle etc.] *Med.* **1** A crackling sound or sensation caused by friction between bone and cartilage or between the fractured parts of a bone. Also = CREPITATION 2. E19. **2** The breaking of wind. *rare.* L19.

crepitous *a.* of the nature of or such as to produce crepitus E19.

crêpoline *n.* var. of CRÊPELINE.

crépon /'kreɪpɒn/ *n.* & *a.* L19. [Fr., f. as CRÊPE *n.* & *a.* see -OON.] (Made of) a fabric resembling crêpe; but heavier.

crept *v.* pa. t. & pple of CREEP *v.*

crepuscle *n.* see CREPUSCULUM.

crepuscular /krɪ'pʌskjʊlə, krɛ-/ *a.* M17. [f. next + -AR[1]: cf. Fr. *crépusculaire.*] **1** Resembling the twilight of morning or evening; dim, indistinct; not yet fully enlightened. M17. **2** Of or pertaining to twilight. M18. **3** *Zool.* Appearing or active by evening twilight. E19.

1 J. L. MOTLEY The state of crepuscular civilization to which they have reached.

crepusculum /krɪ'pʌskjʊləm, krɛ-/ *n.* Also Anglicized as **crepuscle** /'krɛpʌs(ə)l/, **crepuscule** /'krɛpəskju:l/. LME. [L, rel. to *creper* dusky, dark.] The period of half-dark at the beginning or end of the day; twilight, dusk.

crepusculine *a.* (*rare*) of or pertaining to twilight, dusky M16. **crepusculous** *a.* = CREPUSCULAR I M17.

†**crescence** *n.* L15–M18. [L *crescentia*: see CRESCENT *n.*, -ENCE.] Growth; increase.

crescendo /krɪ'ʃɛndəʊ/ *adv.*, *a.*, *n.*, & *v.* L18. [It., pres. pple of *crescere* to increase f. L *crescere* grow.] **A** *adv.* & *adj. Mus.* (A direction:) with a gradual increase in loudness. L18.

B *n.* Pl. **-dos**, **-di** /-di/. **1** *Mus.* A gradual increase in loudness; a passage (to be) played or sung with such an increase. L18. **2** A progressive increase in force or effect; a progress towards a climax. L18. **3** A climax. E20.

2 J. B. PRIESTLEY The shock . . coming at the end of a long crescendo of excitement, cut the last binding thread of self-control. **3** P. G. WODEHOUSE The babble at the bar had risen to a sudden crescendo.

C *v.i.* Increase gradually in loudness or intensity. E20.

crescent /'krɛs(ə)nt/ *n.* See also CROISSANT. LME. [AN *cressaunt*, OFr. *creissant* (mod. *croissant*) f. L *crescent-* pres. ppl stem of *crescere* grow: see -ENT. In 17 assim. to L.] **1** The waxing moon during the period between new moon and full. LME. **2** The convexo-concave figure of the waxing or waning moon during the first or last quarter, esp. when very new or very old. LME. **3** A representation of this phase of the moon, esp. (*a*) as an ornament; (*b*) *Her.* as a charge or a cadence mark for a second son in England; (*c*) as a badge or emblem adopted by the Turks, and hence Muslims in general, as a military and religious symbol (analogous to the Christian cross); *fig.* (**C-**) *the* Turkish power, *the* Muslim religion, esp. as a political force. LME. **4** *gen.* Anything of the shape of the new or old moon; a crescent-shaped figure. L17. **5** *spec.* A street or terrace of houses built in a crescent shape or arc. M18. **6** *spec.* A croissant. Chiefly *N. Amer.* L19.

2 SHELLEY The moon's argentine crescent hung In the dark dome of heaven. **4** T. BEWICK The breast [of a bird] is distinguished by a crescent of pure white. R. WEST Sandy hair which curved across the front of her head in a high hollow crescent.

Phrases: *Fertile Crescent*: see FERTILE *a.* I. *olive crescent*: see OLIVE *n.*[1] & *a. Red Crescent*: see RED *a. Turkish crescent*: see TURKISH *a.*

crescen'tade *n.* [after *crusade*] (*a*) a religious war waged under the Turkish flag; (*b*) a jihad or holy war for Islam: M19. **crescented** *a.* formed as a crescent or new moon E19. **crescentic** /krɪ'sɛntɪk/ *a.* crescent-shaped M19. **crescentric** /krɪ'sɛntrɪk/ *a.* (*rare*) = CRESCENTIC M19.

crescent /'krɛs(ə)nt/ *a.* L16. [L *crescent-* pres. ppl stem of *crescere* grow: see prec., -ENT.] **1** Growing, increasing, developing, esp. as or like the moon's figure. L16. **2** Shaped like the new or old moon; convexo-concave. E17.

1 SHAKES. *Ant. & Cl.* My powers are crescent, and my auguring hope Says it will come to th' full. **2** W. H. RUSSELL New Orleans is called the 'crescent city' in consequence of its being built on a curve of the river. *Scientific American* Two fine pictures of crescent Mars.

crescent roll a croissant.

crescive /'krɛsɪv/ *a.* M16. [f. L *crescere* grow + -IVE.] Growing.

cresol /'kri:sɒl/ *n.* M19. [f. *cres-* for CREOSOTE + -OL.] *Chem.* Each of three isomeric crystalline phenols (*ortho-*, *meta-*, and *para-*methylphenol), $(CH_3)C_6H_4OH$, present in coal tar creosote and used as disinfectants.

crespin(e) *n.* see CREPINE.

cress /krɛs/ *n.* [OE *cressa*, *cresse*, *cærse*, *cerse* = MLG *kerse*, MDu. *kersse*, *korsse* (Du. *kers*), OHG *kresso*, *kressa* (G *Kresse*), f. WGmc.] *sing.* & (now *rare*) in *pl.* Any of various plants belonging to Cruciferae or occas. other families, usu. with pungent edible leaves; esp. = *garden cress* s.v. GARDEN *n.*

Indian cress, Pará cress, penny cress, rock cress, swine cress, watercress, etc. *mustard and cress*: see MUSTARD *n.*

¶ Until 19 usu. in pl.

cresset /'krɛsɪt/ *n.* LME. [OFr. *cresset*, *craisset*, f. *craisse* var. of *graisse* oil, GREASE *n.*: see -ET[1].] *Hist.* A metal vessel, usu. mounted on a pole, for holding oil, coal, etc., to be burnt for light.

fig.: SIR W. SCOTT The moon . . hung her dim dull cresset in the heavens.

Comb.: †**cresset-light** a blazing cresset; the light of a cresset; a beacon-light.

cresson /krɛsɔ̃/ *n.* M17. [Fr. = CRESS.] †**1** In *pl.* Cress. *rare.* Only in M17. **2** A shade of green resembling that of watercress. L19.

crest /krɛst/ *n.* ME. [OFr. *creste* (mod. *crête*) f. L *crista* tuft, plume.] **1** An erect plume of feathers, horsehair, etc., fixed to the top of a helmet or head-dress; any ornament worn similarly as a cognizance. ME. **b** (The apex of) a helmet. ME. **2** A comb, tuft of feathers, etc., on a bird's or animal's head. LME. **3** *Her.* A figure or device, often a representation of an animal or bird, placed on a wreath, coronet, etc., and borne above the shield and on the helmet in a coat of arms or used separately as a cognizance on seals, plate, notepaper, etc. LME. **b** *Archery.* A coloured identifying pattern below the fletching of an arrow. E20. **4** The head, summit, or top of or *of* anything, esp. a hill or mountain. LME. **5** *Archit.* The finishing of stone, metal, etc., which surmounts a roof-ridge, wall, etc. LME. **6** An elevated ridge; *spec.* (*a*) the ridge of a mountain, pass, bank, etc.; (*b*) *Fortif.* the top line of a parapet or slope; (*c*) a balk or ridge in a field between two furrows; (*d*) the curling foamy top of a wave; the peak of a wave. LME. **7** The ridge of the neck of a horse, dog, lion, etc.; an animal's mane. L16. **8** A raised ridge on the surface of any object; *esp.* (*Anat.*) a ridge running along the surface of a bone. L16.

1 T. H. WHITE Many were vain enough to have these armorial crests . . but Sir Lancelot always contented himself with a bare helmet. **b** MILTON On his crest Sat horror plum'd. **2** E. T. GILLIARD The cockatoos . . differ from other parrots in having the crest erectile and usually greatly elongated. **3** SHAKES. *Tam. Shr.* What is your crest—a coxcomb? **4** *fig.*: V. SACKVILLE-WEST Her relations with Sebastian would seem to have reached the crest of their perfection. **6** I. MURDOCH The sea is agitated, very dark blue with white crests. **on the crest of the wave** *fig.* at the most favourable moment in one's progress. **8** *frontal crest, occipital crest, parietal crest, sagittal crest*, etc. *neural crest*: see NEURAL *a.* I.

Comb.: **crestfallen** *a.* (*a*) with drooping crest; *fig.* dejected, abashed; (*b*) (of a horse) having the ridge of the neck hanging to one side. **crest-line** (*a*) a series of ridges; (*b*) the skyline of a ridge.

cresting *n.* (*a*) *Archit.* an ornamental ridging to a wall or roof; (*b*) ornamental edging on a chair, settee, etc.: M19. **crestless** *a.* L16.

crest /krɛst/ *v.* LME. [f. the n.] **1** *v.t.* Provide with a crest. LME. **2** *v.t.* Mark with long streaks (w. allus. to the streaming hair of a crest). *rare.*

L16. 3 *v.t.* Serve as a crest to, top, crown. E17. 4 *v.i.* Erect one's crest; raise oneself proudly. *obs.* exc. *dial.* E18. 5 *v.t.* Reach the crest or summit of (a hill, wave, etc.). M19. 6 *v.i.* (Of a wave) form or rise into a crest; *gen.* peak. M19.

3 SOUTHEY Broad battlements Crested the bulwark. 5 J. H. NEWMAN In this inquisitive age, when the Alps are crested, and seas fathomed. 6 S. KING The boy's temperature had crested at a giddy one hundred and five degrees.

crested /ˈkrɛstɪd/ *a.* LME. [f. CREST *n.*, *v.*: see -ED², -ED¹.] 1 Wearing or having a crest; *spec.* designating plants and animals distinguished by a crest. LME. 2 *Her.* Esp. of a bird: having a crest of a different (specified) tincture from that of the body. L16. †3 Having raised lines or striae; ribbed. L16–M19. 4 Having a raised ridge. M19.

1 D. H. LAWRENCE The bird lifted its crested head. E. WAUGH A fat order for crested note-paper. *crested argus, crested dog's-tail, crested kingfisher, crested penguin*, etc. **crested newt** a large newt, *Triturus cristatus*, the male of which has a tall crest along its back and tail in the breeding season, and which is found from Britain to central Asia. **crested tit** a small tit, *Parus cristatus*, which has a short crest and is found in coniferous forests from western Europe to the Urals. **great crested grebe** a large grebe, *Podiceps cristatus*, which has a black crest and chestnut and black ear ruffs, and is found in many areas of the Old World.

Creswellian /krɛzˈwɛlɪən/ *a.* & *n.* E20. [f. *Creswell* Crags in Derbyshire (where the phase is well represented) + -IAN.] *Archaeol.* A *adj.* Designating or pertaining to a cultural period of the late palaeolithic in NW Europe, esp. Britain, roughly contemporary with the later part of Magdalenian. E20. B *ellipt.* as *n.* The Creswellian period. M20.

cresyl /ˈkriːsʌɪl, -sɪl/ *n.* M19. [f. CRES(OL + -YL.] *Chem.* Each of three isomeric radicals, $CH_3C_6H_4O·$, derived from the cresols. Usu. in *comb.*

cresylic *a.* of cresyl; *cresylic acid*, a mixture of cresols and other phenols distilled from coal tar: M19.

cretaceous /krɪˈteɪʃəs/ *a.* & *n.* In *Geol.* usu. **C-**. L17. [f. L *cretaceus*, f. *creta* chalk: see -ACEOUS.] A *adj.* 1 Of the nature of chalk; chalky. L17. 2 *Geol.* Designating or pertaining to the last period of the Mesozoic era, following the Jurassic and preceding the Tertiary, in which many chalk deposits were formed and flowering plants first appeared. M19. B *n.* *Geol.* The Cretaceous period; the system of rocks dating from this time. M19.

cretaceously *adv.* M19.

Cretan /ˈkriːt(ə)n/ *a.* & *n.* L16. [L *Cretanus*, f. *Creta* f. Gk *Krētē* Crete: see -AN.] A *adj.* Of or belonging to the island of Crete in the eastern Mediterranean (at one time supposed to contain many liars). L16.

B *n.* A native or inhabitant of Crete. L16.

T. HARDY He was perfectly truthful towards men, but to women lied like a Cretan.

cretic /ˈkriːtɪk/ *a.* & *n.* L16. [L *creticus* f. Gk *krētikos*, f. *Krētē*: see prec., -IC.] *Class. Pros.* (Designating) a metrical foot consisting of one short syllable between two long. Cf. AMPHIMACER.

cretin /ˈkrɛtɪn/ *n.* L18. [Fr. *crétin* f. Swiss Fr. *creitin*, *crestin* f. L *Christianus*: see CHRISTIAN *a.*] 1 *Med.* A person afflicted with cretinism. L18. 2 A fool; a person who behaves stupidly. L19.

cretinism *n.* the condition of a cretin; *Med.* mental handicap, deficient growth, and coarseness of the skin and facial features due to congenital lack of thyroid hormone: E19. **cretinize** *v.t.* reduce to cretinism M19. **cretinoid** *a.* resembling a cretin or cretinism L19. **cretinous** *a.* pertaining to or characteristic of a cretin; of the nature of cretinism: M19.

cretize /ˈkriːtʌɪz/ *v.i.* Now *rare* or *obs.* Also **-ise**. M17. [Gk *krētizein*, f. *Krētē* Crete.] Behave in a manner attributed to Cretans, lie.

cretonne /krɛˈtɒn, ˈkrɛtɒn/ *n.* L19. [Fr., of unkn. origin.] A strong unglazed fabric printed on one or both sides with a (usu. large floral) pattern, used for chair covers, curtains, etc.

Creutzfeldt-Jakob disease /krɔɪtsfɛltˈjakɒb dɪˌziːz/ *n. phr.* L20. [f. H. G. *Creuzfeldt* (1885–1964) + A. M. *Jakob* (1884–1931), German neurologists.] A transmissible, usu. fatal, disease of the middle-aged and elderly in which there is degeneration of nerve cells in the brain, causing mental, physical, and sensory disturbances such as dementia and seizures.

crevasse /krɪˈvas/ *n.* E19. [Fr. (OFr. *crevace*): see CREVICE *n.*¹] 1 A (usu. deep) fissure or chasm in the ice of a glacier; *transf.* a deep crack or chasm. E19. 2 A breach in the bank or levee of a river, canal, etc. *US.* E19.

crevasse /krɪˈvas/ *v.* M19. [Fr. *crevasser*, f. as prec.] 1 *v.t.* Fissure with crevasses. Chiefly as *crevassed* ppl a. M19. 2 *v.i.* Form crevasses. Chiefly as *crevassing* vbl n. M19.

crève /krɛv/ *n.* L19. [Abbrev.] = CRÈVECOEUR.

crèvecoeur /ˈkrɛvkəː/ *n.* M19. [Fr., lit. 'split heart' (from the shape of the comb).] A variety (usu. black) of the domestic fowl, of French origin.

crevice /ˈkrɛvɪs/ *n.*¹ ME. [OFr. *crevace* (mod. CREVASSE *n.*), f. *crever* to burst, split f. L *crepare* rattle, crack, break with a crash.] 1 An opening produced by a crack, esp. in rock, a building, etc.; a cleft; a fissure; a chink. ME. 2 *spec.* *Mining.* A fissure in which a deposit of ore or metal is found. M19.

1 J. BALDWIN Dirt was in every corner, angle, crevice of the monstrous stove.

creviced *a.* M16. **crevicing** *n.* (*N. Amer. Mining*) the working of a crevice or crevices M19.

†**crevice** *n.*² see CRAYFISH.

crew /kruː/ *n.*¹ LME. [OFr. *creüe* (mod. *crue*) increase, use as n. of fem. pa. pple of *croistre* (mod. *croître*) f. L *crescere* grow, increase.] I *gen.* †1 An augmentation or reinforcement of a military force; a company of soldiers. LME–L16. 2 Any organized armed band. L16. 3 A number of people associated together; a company. L16. b An assemblage of animals or things. E17. 4 A number of people classed together; a set, a gang, a mob. L16.

2 W. GILPIN Those crews of outlawed banditti, who .. plundered the country. 3 MILTON Mirth, admit me of thy crew. 4 J. GALSWORTHY He was not of 'that catch-penny crew,' new paid off.

II *spec.* 5 A squad of workers under an overseer; an organized unit of workers. L17. 6 A squad of sailors on a warship under the direction of a petty officer or with some particular duty. L17. 7 A body of people manning a ship, boat, aircraft, spacecraft, train, etc.; such people other than the officers. Also, a person single-handedly manning a yacht etc. L17. 8 A team of people concerned with the technical aspects or a specified technical aspect of making a film, recording, etc. M20.

7 N. SHUTE Besides her eleven officers she carried a crew of about seventy petty officers and enlisted men. 8 *camera crew, film crew, sound crew*, etc.

Comb.: **crew cut** a closely cropped style of haircut for men and boys (app. first adopted by boat crews at Harvard and Yale Universities); **crew-cut** *a.* (of hair) closely cropped all over; (of a person) having a crew cut; **crewman** a member of a crew; **crew neck** (orig. *US*) a round neckline, esp. of a sweater, fitting closely to the throat as on vests worn by oarsmen.

crew *n.*² var. of CRUE.

crew /kruː/ *v.*¹ M20. [f. CREW *n.*¹] 1 *v.i.* Act as (a member of) a crew (*for*). M20. 2 *v.t.* Act as (a member) of the crew of; supply crew for. M20.

1 F. CHICHESTER Martin had crewed for me in a number of races.

crew *v.*² see CROW *v.*

crewel /ˈkruːəl/ *n.* & *a.* L15. [Origin unkn.] A *n.* 1 A thin loosely twisted worsted yarn, used esp. for tapestry and embroidery. L15. 2 = *crewel-work*, sense B.2 below. L19. B *attrib.* or as *adj.* 1 *gen.* Made of or with crewel. *obs.* exc. *dial.* M16. 2 *crewel-work*, (embroidery with) a design worked in worsted on a ground of linen or cloth. M19. 3 Of or pertaining to crewel-work; for use in crewel-work; embroidered with crewel-work. L19.

crewelist *n.* a person who works crewel-work L19.

crewels /ˈkruːəlz/ *n.pl.* *Sc.* Long *arch.* L16. [Fr. *écrouelles.*] Scrofula.

criard /kriaːr/ *a.* Also (Fr. fem.) ***criarde*** /kriaːrd/. M19. [Fr.] Shrill; garish.

crib /krɪb/ *n.* [OE *crib(b)* = OFris. *cribbe*, OS *kribbia* (Du. *krib(be)*, OHG *krippa* (G *Krippe*). In branch III f. the vb.] I 1 A barred receptacle for fodder etc.; a manger, *esp.* that in which the infant Jesus was said to be laid. OE. b A model of the manger-scene at Bethlehem. L19. 2 A stall in a cowshed. Now *dial.* ME. †3 A wickerwork basket, pannier, etc.; a hop-picker's bin. LME–M19. 4 A small house, a cabin, in NZ *spec.* at the seaside, a holiday resort, etc.; a hovel; a narrow room; *fig.* a confined space. L16. b A house, an apartment; *spec.* a public house, a saloon; a brothel. *slang.* M19. 5 A small bed for a child, with barred or latticed sides; also occas., a cradle. Cf. COT *n.*⁴ 3. M17. 6 Food, provisions; a light meal or snack. Now chiefly *Austral.* & *NZ.* M17. 7 A rack used in salt-making for drying salt after boiling. Now *rare* or *obs.* L17. 8 In full *corn crib.* A bin or ventilated building for storing maize. *US.* L17. b A storage bin or receptacle for other commodities, tools, etc. M19. 9 A framework of bars or spars for strengthening, support, etc. L17. b *spec.* A small raft of boards etc. *N. Amer.* L18. c Heavy crossed timbers used in foundations in loose soil, to support a pier, to form a dam, etc., (also more fully *cribwork*); a structure of such timbers. E19. d A framework lining the shaft of a mine. M19.

2 AV *Prov.* 14:4 Where no Oxen are, the crib is cleane. 4 SHAKES. *2 Hen. IV* Why rather, sleep, liest thou in smoky cribs .. Than in the perfum'd chambers of the great. *fig.*: A. H. CLOUGH The world .. Whithersoever we turn, still is the same narrow crib. b *crack a crib*: see CRACK *v.*

II 10 In the game of cribbage, the set of cards given to the dealer by himself or herself and each other player; *colloq.* the game of cribbage. L17.

III 11 A translated version for (esp. illegitimate) use by students. *colloq.* E19. 12 A plagiarism; a translation taken from a crib. *colloq.* M19.

Comb.: **crib-biter** a horse given to crib-biting; *fig.* a grumbler; **crib-biting** a horse's habit of seizing a manger, door, or projection in the teeth and at the same time noisily drawing in breath; *cribwork*: see sense 9c above.

crib /krɪb/ *v.* Infl. **-bb-**. LME. [f. the n.] †1 *v.i.* Feed from a crib. *rare.* Only in LME. 2 *v.t.* Shut up (as) in a crib; confine in a small space; hamper. E17. b Place (maize etc.) in a crib. *US.* E18. 3 *v.t.* Provide with a crib or cribs. M17. 4 *v.t.* Pilfer, purloin, steal; appropriate furtively (a small part of something). *colloq.* M18. 5 *v.t.* & *i.* Copy (a passage, a translation, etc.) unfairly or without acknowledgement; plagiarize. *colloq.* L18. 6 *v.i.* Of a horse: engage in crib-biting. M19. b *fig.* Complain, grumble. *colloq.* E20.

2 SHAKES. *Macb.* I am cabin'd, cribb'd, confin'd, bound in. 5 A. S. NEILL There has been no real authority on education, and I do not know of any book from which I can crib. A. S. BYATT An essay .. clearly largely cribbed from C. S. Lewis.

cribbage /ˈkrɪbɪdʒ/ *n.* M17. [Origin uncertain: cf. CRIB *n.* 10.] 1 A card-game for two, three, or four players, played with a complete pack and a board with pegs and holes for scoring, in which the dealer scores also from the cards given to him or her as discards from each player's hand. M17. 2 The action of cribbing; something cribbed. *rare.* M19.

Comb.: **cribbage-board**: for scoring at cribbage; **cribbage-faced** *a.* (*arch.*) pockmarked.

cribble /ˈkrɪb(ə)l/ *n.* Now *rare* or *obs.* LME. [(O)Fr. *crible* f. pop.L var. of L *cribrum* sieve.] †1 Bran, coarse meal, etc., remaining in a sieve after the fine flour has been sifted out; *spec.* a particular quality of coarse meal. LME–E18. 2 A sieve. M16.

Comb.: †**cribble bread**: made of this particular quality of coarse meal.

cribellum /krɪˈbɛləm/ *n.* Pl. **-lla** /-lə/. L19. [Late L, dim. of *cribrum* sieve: see -ELLUM.] *Zool.* An additional spinning-organ, having numerous fine pores, situated in front of the spinnerets in certain spiders.

ˈ**cribellate** *a.* having a cribellum E20. ˈ**cribellated** *a.* = CRIBELLATE *a.* E20.

criblé /kriblе/ *n.* & *a.* L19. [Fr., f. as CRIBBLE.] (Designating) a type of engraving with small punctures or depressions on a wood or metal ground.

¶ See also MANIÈRE CRIBLÉE.

cribo /'kriːbəʊ, 'krʌɪbəʊ/ *n.* Pl. **-os.** L19. [Origin unkn.] = *indigo snake* s.v. INDIGO *n.*

cribriform /'krɪbrɪfɔːm/ *a.* M18. [f. L *cribrum* sieve + -I- + -FORM.] *Anat.* & *Bot.* Having numerous small holes; perforated like a sieve.

cribriform plate the part of the ethmoid bone which forms the roof of the nasal cavity and is traversed by the olfactory nerves.

cribrose /krʌɪ'brəʊs/ *a.* M19. [f. L *cribrum* sieve: see -OSE[1].] Chiefly *Bot.* & *Anat.* Perforated like a sieve.

Also †**cribrous** *a.* L17-E18.

Crichton /'krʌɪt(ə)n/ *n.* E19. [James *Crichton* of Clunie (1560-85?), a Scottish prodigy of intellectual and knightly accomplishments.] More fully *Admirable Crichton.* A person who excels in all kinds of studies and pursuits; a person noted for supreme competence.

crick /krɪk/ *n.*[1] LME. [Origin unkn.] A sudden painful stiffness of the muscles in the neck, back, etc.

crick *n.*[2] var. of CREEK *n.*[1]

crick /krɪk/ *v.*[1]*i.* E17. [Imit.: cf. Fr. *criquer*, *cric* int. Cf. CRICKET *n.*[1]] Make a sharp abrupt chirping sound, as a grasshopper.

crick /krɪk/ *v.*[2]*t.* M19. [f. CRICK *n.*[1]] Produce a crick in (the neck etc.).

crick-crack /'krɪkkrak/ *n.* & *int.* M16. [Redupl. of CRACK *n.* Cf. Fr. *cric crac*, Du. *krikkrakken* crackle.] (Repr.) a repeated sharp, explosive, or light cracking noise.

cricket /'krɪkɪt/ *n.*[1] ME. [(O)Fr. *criquet* †grasshopper, cricket, f. *criquer* crackle, of imit. origin: cf. (M)Du. *krekel* cricket, f. imit. base.] Any of various jumping, chirping orthopterous insects of the family Gryllidae; *esp.* (more fully *house-cricket*) *Acheta domestica*, formerly a familiar insect living indoors near fireplaces, ovens, etc., or (more fully *field-cricket*) *Gryllus campestris*, found in meadows etc. Also (w. specifying wd), any of various other insects related to or resembling the crickets.

J. G. HOLLAND Mullens had become as cheerful and lively as a cricket. BALM-CRICKET. **bush-cricket** any of various mainly arboreal grasshoppers of the family Tettigoniidae, having very long antennae; also called *long-horned grasshopper.* **mole-cricket** any large nocturnal burrowing orthopteran of the family Gryllotalpidae; esp. *Gryllotalpa gryllotalpa.* MORMON *cricket.*

Comb.: **cricket-frog** a small N. American tree frog of the genus *Acris*, noted for its clicking call; **cricket-teal** *dial.* the garganey.

cricket /'krɪkɪt/ *n.*[2] & *v.* L16. [Origin unkn.] **A** *n.* An open-air game played with ball, bats, and wickets, between two sides now usu. of eleven players each; (in full *indoor cricket*) a form of the game played indoors; the playing of this game. L16.

Phrases: **not cricket** *colloq.* infringing the codes of fair play between honourable opponents in any sphere. *French cricket*: see FRENCH *a.* *snob-cricket*: see SNOB *n.*[2]

Comb.: **cricket bag** a long bag for carrying a cricketer's bat etc.; **cricket-bat** a bat [BAT *n.*[1] 2] used in cricket; *cricket-bat willow*, a glabrescent variety of white willow, *Salix alba* var. *caerulea*, which provides the best wood for cricket-bats.

B *v.i.* Play cricket. L17.

¶ Many changes have been made in the character of the game since the 17th cent., when the bats were like hockey-sticks, the wicket of two stumps with one long bail, and the ball trundled along the ground.

cricke'tana *n.pl.* publications or other items concerning or associated with cricket M19. **cricketer** *n.* a person who plays cricket M18.

cricket /'krɪkɪt/ *n.*[3] Now *dial.* Also (*north.*) **cracket** /'krakɪt/. M17. [Origin unkn.] A low wooden stool; a footstool.

crickey *int.* var. of CRIKEY.

crickle-crackle /'krɪk(ə)l krak(ə)l/ *n. rare.* M17. [Redupl. of CRACKLE *n.*: cf. CRICK-CRACK.] A repeated crackling.

crico- /'krʌɪkəʊ/ *comb. form.* [Gk *kriko-* comb. form of *krikos* = *kirkos* ring: see -O-.] *Anat.* Of or pertaining to the cricoid cartilage.

crico-'thyroid *a.* of or pertaining to the cricoid and thyroid cartilages M19.

cricoid /'krʌɪkɔɪd/ *a.* & *n.* M18. [mod.L *cricoides* ring-shaped f. Gk *krikoeidēs*, f. *krikos* ring: see prec., -OID.] *Anat.* **A** *adj.* Designating, of or pertaining to, the cartilage which forms the lower and back part of the larynx. M18. **B** *n.* The cricoid cartilage of the larynx. M19.

†**cricoidal** *a.* = CRICOID *a.*: only in L17.

cri de cœur /kri də kœːr/ *n. phr.* Pl. ***cris de cœur*** (pronounced same). E20. [Fr. = cry of or from the heart.] An appeal in distress.

cried *v.* pa. t. & pple of CRY *v.*

crier /'krʌɪə/ *n.* LME. [AN *criour*, OFr. *criere*, nom. of *crieur*, f. *crier*: see CRY *v.*, -OUR, -ER[2].] **1** A person who cries. LME. **2** *spec.* **a** An officer who makes public announcements in a court of justice or (more fully *common crier*, *town crier*) in a town. LME. **b** A person who cries goods for sale. Now *arch.* or *Hist.* M16.

crikey /'krʌɪki/ *int. slang.* Also **crickey** /'krɪki/. M19. [Alt. of CHRIST.] Expr. astonishment.

crim /krɪm/ *n. slang* (chiefly *Austral.*). E20. [Abbrev.] A criminal.

†**crimble** *v.* & *n.* var. of CRUMBLE.

crim. con. /krɪm 'kɒn/ *n. arch. colloq.* L18. [Abbrev.] = *criminal conversation* s.v. CRIMINAL *a.*

crime /krʌɪm/ *n.* ME. [(O)Fr. *crime*, †*crimne* f. L *crimen* judgement, accusation, offence, f. reduced base of *cernere* decide, give judgement.] **1** Sinfulness, wickedness; wrongdoing, sin. *arch.* ME. **2** An act or omission constituting an offence (usu. a grave one) against an individual or the State and punishable by law. Also, a soldier's offence against regulations. LME. **b** *gen.* An evil or injurious act; a grave offence; *colloq.* a shameful act. E16. **3** Such acts collectively; violation of law. LME. †**4** Charge, accusation; matter of accusation. LME-M17.

1 MILTON One next himself in power, and next in crime. **2** B. SPOCK Stealing is a serious crime. **b** P. BAILEY It's no crime, looking one's age. **3** GOLDSMITH I was imprisoned, though a stranger to crime.

Phrases: **crime of passion** = CRIME PASSIONNEL. *perfect crime*: see PERFECT *a.* SCENE(*s*)*-of-crime.* *the* SCENE *of the crime.*

Comb.: **crime-buster** *slang* a person engaged in crime-busting; **crime-busting** *slang* the defeating of organized crime, the detection and arrest of criminals; **crime-sheet** *Mil.* a record of offences; **crime wave** a sudden brief increase in the number of crimes committed; **crime writer** an author who writes about real or fictional (usu. violent) crimes.

crimeful *a.* (now *rare*) full of crime, criminal L16. **crimeless** *a.* free from crime, innocent M16.

crime /krʌɪm/ *v.t.* LME. [f. the n.] Now chiefly *Mil.* Charge with or convict of an offence.

Crimean /krʌɪ'mɪən/ *a.* M19. [f. *Crimea* (see below) + -AN.] Of, pertaining to, or characteristic of the Crimea, a peninsula between the Sea of Azov and the Black Sea.

Crimean Gothic an East Germanic language, supposedly a dialect or descendant of Gothic, which continued to be used in the Crimea down to the 16th cent. **Crimean shirt**: of a type worn by workers in the Australian and New Zealand bush. **the Crimean War**: between Russia and Turkey (supported by her allies, including Britain and France), 1854-6, chiefly fought in the Crimea.

crime passionnel /krim pasjənɛl/ *n. phr.* Pl. ***-s -s*** (pronounced same). E20. [Fr.] A crime, esp. murder, due to sexual jealousy.

crimes /krʌɪmz/ *int. slang.* L19. [Alt. of CRIMINE.] Expr. astonishment.

crimes passionnels *n. phr.* pl. of CRIME PASSIONNEL.

criminal /'krɪmɪn(ə)l/ *a.* & *n.* LME. [Late L *criminalis* f. L *crimin-*, *crimen* CRIME *n.*: see -AL[1].] **A** *adj.* **1** Of the nature of or involving a crime punishable by law; *gen.* of the nature of a grave offence, wicked; *colloq.* deplorable. LME. **2** Relating to crime or its punishment. LME. **3** Guilty of a crime or grave offence. L15.

1 G. K. CHESTERTON That kind of thing is really criminal; it's against the public good. *Offshore* It would have been criminal to spend each moment . . waiting on the beach in a country which has so much to explore. **criminal conversation** (now *arch.* or *Hist.*) adultery. **criminal libel**: calculated to provoke a breach of the peace. **2** GIBBON They no longer possessed the administration of criminal justice. **criminal code** a system of jurisprudence to be applied in criminal cases. **criminal court**: having jurisdiction over criminal prosecutions. **criminal law**: concerned with the punishment of offenders, opp. *civil law.* **criminal lawyer**: whose practice lies in the criminal courts. *criminal record*: see RECORD *n.* 4b. **3** I. MURDOCH He felt alien, almost criminal, hoping that no one would notice him.

B *n.* **1** A person guilty or convicted of a crime. E17. †**2** A person accused of a crime. M-L17.

1 *common criminal*: see COMMON *a.* **2** DRYDEN Was ever criminal forbid to plead?

criminalism *n.* the state or practice of a criminal L19. **criminalist** *n.* an expert in criminal law M17. **criminally** *adv.* (*a*) according to criminal law; (*b*) in a criminal manner, so as to constitute crime: E16. **criminalness** *n.* (long *rare*) criminality M17. **criminaloid** *n.* a person with a tendency towards crime, a first or occasional offender, as opp. to a habitual criminal L19.

criminalistic /ˌkrɪmɪnə'lɪstɪk/ *a.* E20. [f. prec. + -ISTIC.] Of or pertaining to criminals or their habits; tending towards criminality.

criminalistics /ˌkrɪmɪnə'lɪstɪks/ *n.* E20. [f. as prec.: see -ICS. Cf. G *Kriminalistik.*] The use of the physical sciences in investigating crimes.

criminality /krɪmɪ'nalɪti/ *n.* E17. [Fr. *criminalité* f. med.L *criminalitas*, f. as CRIMINAL: see -ITY.] The quality or fact of being criminal.

criminate /'krɪmɪneɪt/ *v.t.* M17. [L *criminat-* pa. ppl stem of *criminare*, f. *crimin-*, *crimen* CRIME *n.*: see -ATE[3].] **1** Charge with crime; represent as criminal. M17. **2** Prove guilty of crime; incriminate. Now *rare.* M17. **3** Censure (a thing or action) as criminal; blame severely, condemn. M17.

crimi'nation *n.* the action or an act of criminating; (a) severe accusation or censure: L16. **criminative** *a.* tending to or involving crimination, accusatory M18. **criminator** *n.* a person who criminates, an accuser LME. **criminatory** *a.* criminative L16.

crimine /'krɪmɪni/ *int. arch. slang.* Also **-iny.** L17. [Alt. of CHRIST.] Expr. astonishment.

criminology /krɪmɪ'nɒlədʒi/ *n.* L19. [f. L *crimin-*, *crimen* CRIME *n.* + -OLOGY.] The branch of knowledge that deals with crime.

crimino'logical *a.* L19. **criminologist** *n.* M19.

criminous /'krɪmɪnəs/ *a.* LME. [AN *criminous*, OFr. *crimineux*, f. L *criminosus*, f. *crimin-*, *crimen* CRIME *n.*: see -OUS.] **1** Of the nature of a crime; marked by crime or grave offence; criminal. Long *rare.* LME. †**2** Accusing of crime; involving crimination. LME-M17. **3** Of a person: guilty of crime. Now only in *criminous clerk*, a member of the clergy guilty of a crime. *arch.* M16.

criminously *adv.* E17. **criminousness** *n.* M17.

criminy *int.* var. of CRIMINE.

crimmer *n.* var. of KRIMMER.

crimp /krɪmp/ *n.*[1] M17. [Origin unkn.] †**1** Used as a term of abuse or reproach. *rare.* Only in M17. †**2** An agent or contractor for unloading coal-ships. L17-L18. **3** *Hist.* An agent whose business was to entrap men for service in the army, navy, etc., esp. by decoying or pressing them. Also *transf.* & *fig.* (*arch.*) a deceptive or coercive agent. M18.

crimpage *n.* (*Hist.*) a payment made to a crimp for his services M18.

crimp /krɪmp/ *n.*[2] M17. [f. CRIMP *v.*[1] Sense 1 may be a different wd.] **1** *Hist.* A particular card-game, perh. a gambling game involving turning up the corner of a card on which a bet was placed. M17. †**2** *be in the crimps*, be well dressed. Only in L17. **3** A curl, a wave, esp. made in the hair with a hot iron etc. or occurring naturally in a sheep's fleece (usu. in *pl.*); a crease, a pleat, a fold. M19. **b** The wavy condition of a sheep's fleece. M19.

3 L. M. ALCOTT It's too wet. Shouldn't have a crimp left if I went out such a day as this. C. SANDBURG Respectable people With the right crimp in their napkins. **put a crimp in** *fig.* (*N. Amer. slang*) thwart, interfere with.

crimp /krɪmp/ *a. arch.* L16. [App. conn. w. CRIMP *v.*[1]: cf. MHG *krimpf* crooked, curved. See also CRUMP *a.*[2]] **1** Friable, brittle; crisp. L16. **2** Of hair, feathers, etc.: crimped, artificially curled. M18.

crimp /krɪmp/ *v.*[1] [OE *ġecrympan*: cf. (M)LG, (M)Du. *krimpen* shrink, wrinkle, shrivel = OHG *krimphan* (MHG *krimpfen*).] **1** *v.t.* Compress into pleats or folds; frill; make waves or curls in (esp. hair, with a hot iron etc.); make narrow wrinkles or flutings in; corrugate. (*rare* bef. 18.) OE. †**2** *v.i.* Be compressed, pinched, or indented. *rare.* Only in LME. **3** *v.t.* Cause (the flesh of fish) to contract and become firm by gashing or cutting it before rigor mortis has set in; *transf.* slash, gash. L17. **4** *v.t.* Bend or mould (leather) into shape for the uppers of boots, a saddle, etc. L19.

crimp /krɪmp/ *v.*[2]*t.* E19. [f. CRIMP *n.*[1]] *Hist.* Entrap for service in the army, navy, etc.

crimper /ˈkrɪmpə/ *n.*[1] E19. [f. CRIMP *v.*[1] + -ER[1].] **1** A person who crimps fish, hair, etc.; *slang* a hairdresser. E19. **2** Any of various devices, or machines for crimping cloth, hair, leather, metal, etc. L19.

crimper /ˈkrɪmpə/ *n.*[2] M19. [f. CRIMP *v.*[2] + -ER[1].] *Hist.* = CRIMP *n.*[1] 2.

crimple /ˈkrɪmp(ə)l/ *n.* Now *dial.* & *US.* LME. [Rel. to next. Cf. also CRUMPLE *n.*] A crease, a wrinkle, a narrow fold, a crinkle.

crimple /ˈkrɪmp(ə)l/ *v.* Long *dial.* LME. [Perh. a dim. & iterative of CRIMP *v.*[1]: see -LE[3].] **1** *v.i.* (Esp. of the legs) be or become incurved or drawn together; be lame, limp, hobble. LME. **2** *v.i.* & *t.* Wrinkle, crinkle, curl. LME.

Crimplene /ˈkrɪmpliːn/ *n.* Also **c-**. M20. [Prob. f. CRIMP *n.*[2] + TERY)LENE.] (Proprietary name for) a synthetic yarn and fabric with good resistance to creasing.

crimpy /ˈkrɪmpi/ *a.* L19. [f. CRIMP *n.*[2] or *v.*[1] + -Y[1].] Having a crimped appearance; frizzy, curly.

crimson /ˈkrɪmz(ə)n/ *a.*, *n.*, & *v.* LME. [OSp. *cremesín*, Fr. †*cramoisin*, & other Proto-Romance forms, all ult. f. Arab. *ḳirmizī*, f. *ḳirmiz* KERMES. Cf. CRAMOISY.] **A** *adj.* **1** Of a rich deep-red colour inclining to purple. LME. **2** *fig.* Sanguinary. *arch.* L17.

1 J. RHYS His face crimson with heat. **crimson clover** a red-flowered clover, *Trifolium incarnatum*, formerly grown for fodder. 2 J. S. BLACKIE The crimson crime, the basest in the book.

B *n.* **1** Crimson colour or pigment. LME. †**2** Crimson cloth. LME–E17.

C *v.* **1** *v.t.* Make crimson. E17. **2** *v.i.* Become crimson, blush. E19.

1 J. BUCHAN The sun crimsoned the distant olive-green forests. 2 H. JAMES I felt myself crimson and I covered my face with my hands.

crimsony *a.* somewhat crimson, resembling crimson M19.

crin /krɪn, *foreign* krɛ̃/ *n.* & *a.* E20. [Fr. (OFr. CRINE *n.*) = horsehair.] (Of) a fabric made wholly or partly from horsehair.

crinal /ˈkrʌɪn(ə)l/ *a.* M17. [L *crinalis*, f. *crinis* hair: see -AL[1].] Of or pertaining to the hair.

crine /krʌɪn/ *n.* E17. [OFr. (mod. CRIN) = hair of the head, mane, or its source L *crinis* hair.] **1** Hair; a head of hair. *rare.* E17. **2** Each of the small, hairlike feathers which grow around the cere of a hawk. Usu. in *pl.* L19.

crine /krʌɪn/ *v.i.* & *t. Sc.* E16. [App. f. Gael. *crion* wither.] Shrivel, wither; contract through dryness, heat, etc.

crined /krʌɪnd/ *a.* L16. [f. (as) CRINE *n.* + -ED[2].] *Her.* Having the hair or mane of a different (specified) tincture from the body; maned.

crinet /krɪˈnɛt/ *n.* L15. [f. as CRINE *n.* or CRIN + -ET[1].] †**1** = CRINE *n.* 2. Usu. in *pl.* L15–L18. **2** = CRINIÈRE. *obs.* exc. *Hist.* L16.

cringe /krɪn(d)ʒ/ *n.* L16. [f. the vb.] A servile or fawning obeisance; cringing.

THACKERAY Performing cringes and congees like a court-chamberlain. THOMAS HUGHES Alternative fits of swagger & cringe.

cringe /krɪn(d)ʒ/ *v.* ME. [Corresp. to OE *crinġan*, *crinċan* yield, fall in battle, OFris. *krenza*, Du. *krengen* heel over, and rel. to ON *krangr* weak, frail, *kranga* creep along, MLG, Du., MHG *krenken* weaken, injure, OFris., (M)LG, MHG, G *krank* sick, ill, slight (cf. CRANK *n.*[1]).] **I** *v.i.* **1** Contract the muscles of the body involuntarily; shrink; cower. ME. **2** Bow timorously or servilely (*to*). L16. **3** Behave obsequiously (*to*). E17.

1 L. M. MONTGOMERY Bridges that made Anne's flesh cringe with . . fear. J. STEINBECK The dogs cringed to the ground and whined piteously. D. LODGE Some of the things I'm supposed to say . . make me cringe with embarrassment. 2 T. T. LYNCH You should bow to most people, but cringe to nobody. 3 LD MACAULAY To teach the people to cringe and the prince to domineer.

II *v.t.* †**4** Draw in or contract (part of the body); distort (the neck, face, etc.). L16–M17. †**5** Cringe to (a person); usher cringingly. E17–E19.

4 SHAKES. *Ant. & Cl.* Till like a boy you see him cringe his face And whine aloud. 5 BYRON Hence, and bow and cringe him here!

cringeling *n.* (*rare*) a cringing creature L17. **cringer** *n.* a person who cringes, an obsequious or servile person L16. **cringing** *a.* that cringes; obsequious, servile: L16. **cringingly** *adv.* M19. **cringingness** *n.* L17.

cringle /ˈkrɪŋg(ə)l/ *n.* & *v.* E17. [LG *kringel* dim. of *kring* circle, ring: cf. CRANK *n.*[1], CRANKLE *n.*, *v.*, CRINKLE *n.*, *v.*] **A** *n.* **1** *Naut.* A ring or eye of rope containing a thimble for another rope to pass through. E17. **b** A rope or wire for fastening a gate etc. *dial.* L18. **2** A crinkle. *dial.* E19. **B** *v.t.* Fasten (*up*) with a cringle. *dial.* E17.

¶Perh. ME in place-names (= CRINKLE *n.*).

crinière /krɪˈnjɛː/ *n.* Also †**-ier**. L16. [Fr. = mane, f. as CRINE *n.*, CRIN.] Chiefly *Hist.* A protective covering for the neck and throat of a warhorse. Also called *crinet*.

crinigerous /krɪˈnɪdʒ(ə)rəs/ *a.* M17. [f. L *crinis* hair + -GEROUS.] Having or bearing hair.

crinite /ˈkrʌɪnʌɪt/ *a.* L16. [L *crinitus* pa. pple of *crinire* cover or provide with hair, f. *crinis* hair: see -ITE[2]. Cf. OFr. *crinite.*] Hairy; having a hairlike appendage or hairy tufts.

crinkle /ˈkrɪŋk(ə)l/ *n.* L16. [Prob. f. the vb, but app. earlier (ME) in place-names. Cf. CRINGLE.] A twist, a bend, a wrinkle, a ripple, esp. in a line or surface. Formerly also, a circle.

Comb.: **crinkle-cut** *a.* (of chipped potatoes) machine-cut with regularly ridged surfaces.

crinkliness *n.* crinkly condition E20. **crinkly** *a.* full of crinkles; characterized by crinkling sounds: E19.

crinkle /ˈkrɪŋk(ə)l/ *v.* LME. [Frequent. f. base of OE *crinċan* (see CRINGE *v.*) + -LE[3].] **1** *v.i.* Form twists or bends; contract into wrinkles or ripples. LME. **2** *v.i.* Cringe; *fig.* recede from one's purpose. *obs.* exc. *dial.* E17. **3** *v.t.* Twist, bend; wrinkle; ripple; crimp (the hair). E19. **4** *v.i.* Make sharp rustling or crackling sounds. M19.

1 T. C. WOLFE Huge crinkled lettuces. P. V. WHITE Her face would . . crinkle under the influence of impatience or anger. 3 G. GREENE An expression of glee crinkled the man's face. W. BOYD The fishponds . . were . . crinkled by a breeze.

crinkle-crankle /ˈkrɪŋk(ə)lkraŋk(ə)l/ *n.*, *a.*, & *adv.* Chiefly *dial.* L16. [Redupl. of CRANKLE *n.*, partly after CRINKLE *n.* Cf. CRINKUM-CRANKUM.] **A** *n.* A zigzag; something zigzag. L16. **B** *a.* & *adv.* (Twisting) in and out; zigzag. M19.

†**crinkum** *n. slang.* Also **grincome**. E17–L19. [Origin unkn.] *sing.* & (usu.) in *pl.* Venereal disease; syphilis.

crinkum-crankum /krɪŋkəmˈkraŋkəm/ *n.* & *a.* M17. [Fanciful redupl. of CRANK *n.*[1], *n.*[2]: cf. CRANKUM, CRINKLE-CRANKLE.] **A** *n.* An intricate or convoluted thing; an elaborate device. Also, a crooked course (*lit.* & *fig.*), deviousness. M17. **B** *adj.* Intricate, convoluted, elaborate. L18.

crinoid /ˈkrʌɪnɔɪd/ *n.* & *a.* M19. [Gk *krinoeidēs* adj., lily-like, f. *krinon* lily: see -OID.] **A** *n.* Any echinoderm of the class Crinoidea, members of which are characterized by cup-shaped bodies and usu. branched arms, and include sea-lilies, feather-stars, and many fossil forms. M19. **B** *adj.* Of or pertaining to the Crinoidea. M19.

criˈnoidal *a.* of or pertaining to crinoids M19.

crinoline /ˈkrɪn(ə)lɪn/ *n.* & *a.* M19. [Fr., irreg. f. L *crinis* hair (Fr. CRIN) + *līnum* thread (Fr. *lin* flax).] **A** *n.* **1** A stiff fabric made of horsehair and cotton or linen thread, used for linings, hats, etc., and formerly for skirts and to expand a petticoat. M19. **2** *Hist.* A stiff petticoat, orig. of this fabric, worn under a skirt to support or distend it; hence, a hooped petticoat. M19. **3** *Hist.* A netting fitted round warships as a defence against torpedoes. L19. **B** *attrib.* or as *adj.* Made of crinoline. M19.

crinolined *a.* wearing (a) crinoline M19.

crinosity /krʌɪˈnɒsɪti/ *n. rare.* M17. [f. L *crinis* hair: see -OSITY.] Hairiness.

crio- /ˈkriːəʊ/ *comb. form* of Gk *krios* ram: see -O-.

criosphinx *n.* a sphinx having a ram's head M19.

criollo /krɪˈɒləʊ/ *n.* & *a.* Also **C-**. Pl. of n. **-os**. L19. [Sp. = native to the locality: see CREOLE.] **1** (Designating or pertaining to) a native of Spanish S. or Central America, esp. one of pure Spanish descent. L19. **2** (Designating) a cacao tree of a variety producing thin-shelled beans of high quality. E20. **3** (Designating) any of various S. or Central American breeds of domestic animal, *esp.* a small horse bred from S. American and Arab stock, or cattle of Spanish ancestry. M20.

crip /krɪp/ *n. N. Amer. slang* (freq. considered *offensive*). E20. [Abbrev.] A cripple.

cripes /krʌɪps/ *int. slang.* E20. [Alt. of CHRIST.] Expr. astonishment.

cripple /ˈkrɪp(ə)l/ *n.* & *a.* [OE (Northumb.) *crypel* = OLG *krupil*, & OE *crēopel* = MLG, MDu. *krēpel*, f. Gmc: cogn. w. CREEP *v.*] **A** *n.* **I 1** A person (permanently) impaired in movement by an injury or defect, *esp.* one unable to walk normally; a lame person. OE. **2** *transf.* & *fig.* **a** A sixpence. Cf. BENDER 4. *arch. slang.* L18. **b** A maimed or lamed animal or bird, esp. a game-bird. M19. **c** A person (permanently) impaired or deficient in some other way, specified or understood. E20. **d** A vehicle, ship, etc., that is unfit to proceed or for service. E20. **3** *sing.* & in *pl.* A crippling disease of cattle. *dial.* & *Austral.* L19.

1 D. MURPHY My mother returned . . as a complete cripple, unable to walk from the sitting-room to the downstairs lavatory, or to wash or dress herself, or to brush her hair. 2c *Times* There would still be the emotional and psychological cripples among our children.

II 4 A low opening in a wall. Chiefly in proper name *Cripplegate*. ME. **5** A swamp or low-lying tract of land overgrown with trees or shrubs. *US.* L17.

B *adj.* Crippled. *obs.* exc. *dial.* ME.

SHAKES. *Hen. V* And chide the cripple tardy-gaited night Who like a foul and ugly witch doth limp So tediously away.

crippledom, -hood *ns.* the condition of being a cripple M19.

cripple /ˈkrɪp(ə)l/ *v.* ME. [f. the n.] **1** *v.t.* Make a cripple of (a person); lame. ME. **b** *transf.* & *fig.* Disable, impair; have a severe adverse effect on. L17. **2** *v.i.* Hobble; walk lamely. Now chiefly *Sc.* ME.

1 G. GREENE A local farmer who had been crippled as a boy, losing his right arm in an accident. b H. NELSON The lower masts, yards, and bowsprit all crippled. A. TOFFLER Lack of an education will cripple a child's chance in the world of tomorrow.

crippler *n.* (*a*) a person or thing which cripples; (*b*) *slang* something astonishingly good: M17. **crippling** *a.* (*a*) that cripples; (*b*) *slang* astonishingly good: L16. **cripplingly** *adv.* so as to cripple or disable; to a crippling extent: L19.

†**Cris** *n.* & *a.* see CREE.

cris de cœur *n. phr.* pl. of CRI DE CŒUR.

crise /kriːz/ *n.* Pl. pronounced same. LME. [Fr.] = CRISIS.

crise de conscience /də kɔ̃sjɑ̃ːs/ a crisis of conscience. ***crise de nerfs*** /də nɛːr/ [= of nerves] a fit of hysterics.

¶Formerly fully naturalized.

crisis /ˈkrʌɪsɪs/ *n.* Pl. **crises** /ˈkrʌɪsiːz/, (*rare*) **crisises**. LME. [Medical L f. Gk *krisis* decision, judgement, event, issue, turning-point of a disease, f. *krinein* decide.] **1** The turning-point of a disease. LME. †2 *Astrol.* A conjunction of the planets determining the issue of a disease or a critical point in the course of events. L16–M17. 3 *gen.* A turning-point, a vitally important or decisive stage; a time of trouble, danger, or suspense in politics, commerce, etc., or in personal life. E17. †4 A judgement, a decision. E17–E18. †5 A criterion; a token. E–M17.

3 J. GALSWORTHY When his son-in-law . . had that financial crisis, due to speculation in Oil Shares, James made himself ill worrying over it. E. ROOSEVELT The threat of war was just over the horizon and no one else had the prestige and the knowledge to carry on through a crisis. M. HOLROYD She coped with crises ranging from burst hot-water bottles to outbreaks of measles. J. CRITCHLEY What the alienists call 'a crisis of identity'. *mid-life crisis*: see MID-LIFE *a.*

Comb.: **crisis management** the action or practice of taking managerial action only when a crisis has developed.

crisp /krɪsp/ *n.* ME. [App. f. the adj.: cf. CRAPE *n.* & *a.*, CRÊPE *n.* & *a.*] †1 A light fabric like crêpe; a head-covering or veil made of this. ME–E17. †2 A crisp kind of pastry. Only in LME. †3 A curl (of hair); *esp.* a short or close curl. M–L17. 4 The crackling of roast pork. Now *dial.* L17. 5 A thing overdone by roasting etc. Orig. *US.* M19. 6 More fully *potato crisp.* A fried thin slice of potato, usu. eaten cold from a packet. Usu. in *pl.* Cf. CHIP *n.* 3. E20. 7 A crisp piece of pastry or chocolate. L20.

5 **burn to a crisp** make inedible or useless by burning.

crisp /krɪsp/ *a.* OE. [L *crispus* curled. Branch II may result from symbolic interpretation of the sound of the wd.] I 1 Of hair: curly; now *esp.* stiff and closely curling, frizzy. Also, having such hair. OE. †2 Of fabric: crinkly, like crêpe. Only in ME. 3 *gen.* Having a crinkled or rippled surface. *arch.* LME. 4 *Bot.* Having a crinkled or wavy edge, crispate. M18.

II 5 Hard or firm but fragile; brittle. M16. 6 *transf.* & *fig.* Stiff, not limp; neat, clearly defined; decisive in manner, brisk. E19. 7 Of the air, of a day as regards atmosphere, etc.: frosty; bracing. M19.

5 J. M. NEALE When the snow lay round about, Deep and crisp and even. F. KING As crisp as a dead leaf. **crispbread** a thin crisp biscuit of crushed rye etc. 6 WILKIE COLLINS Such a crisp touch on the piano. T. DREISER A gift . . for making crisp and cynical remarks. S. J. PERELMAN Her crisp white nurse's uniform. P. V. PRICE The crisp, almost bitterly dry white wine. A. N. WILSON The crisp creases of his trouser knees.

crispen *v.t.* & *i.* make or become (more) crisp M20. **crispish** *a.* somewhat crisp M20. **crisply** *adv.* E19. **crispness** *n.* LME.

crisp /krɪsp/ *v.* ME. [f. the adj. Cf. L *crispare.*] 1 *v.t.* Crimp, crinkle. ME. 2 *v.i.* Curl in short stiff folds or waves. E16. 3 *v.t.* Make crisp (CRISP *a.* II). E17. 4 *v.i.* Become crisp (CRISP *a.* II). E19.

crisper *n.* a person who or thing which crisps or curls; *esp.* a container or compartment in a refrigerator for keeping salads etc. crisp and fresh: M19.

crispate /ˈkrɪspeɪt/ *a.* M19. [L *crispatus* pa. pple of *crispare* curl: see -ATE².] Crisped; *spec.* in *Bot.* & *Zool.*, having a crinkled or wavy edge.

crispation /krɪˈspeɪʃ(ə)n/ *n.* Now *rare.* E17. [f. L *crispat-* pa. ppl stem of *crispare* curl: see -ATION.] 1 (A) curled condition; curliness; (an) undulation. E17. 2 A slight contraction of a muscle etc. or of the skin, as in goose-flesh. E18.

crispature /ˈkrɪspətjʊə/ *n. rare.* M18. [f. as prec.: see -URE.] (A) crisp or curled condition.

Crispin /ˈkrɪspɪn/ *n. arch.* Also **c-**. E18. [Patron saint of shoemakers.] (A name given to) a shoemaker.

crispy /ˈkrɪspi/ *a.* LME. [f. CRISP *a.* + -Y¹.] 1 Curly, wavy, crinkly. LME. 2 Crisp, brittle; brisk. E17.

1 W. MORRIS His crispy hair of gold. 2 B. W. ALDISS They ate chow mein, sweet and sour pork and crispy noodles.

crispiness *n.* M17.

criss-cross /ˈkrɪskrɒs/ *n.*, *a.*, & *adv.* Also **crisscross**. E17. [Reduced form of CHRIST-CROSS, latterly treated as redupl. of CROSS *n.*] A *n.* 1 = CHRIST-CROSS. Now *arch.* & *dial.* exc. *Hist.* E17. 2 A crossing of lines, currents, etc.; a network of crossing lines. L19. 3 The state of being at cross purposes. E20. B *adj.* In crossing lines; marked by crossings or intersections. M19. C *adv.* Crosswise; at cross purposes. L19.

criss-cross /ˈkrɪskrɒs/ *v.t.* & *i.* E19. [f. prec.] Mark or work with a criss-cross pattern; move crosswise; cross or intersect repeatedly.

B. HINES Hundreds of knife cuts had criss-crossed the surface into tiny geometrical figures. E. CRISPIN Power-lines . . criss-crossing one another at all angles. S. SONTAG The metaphoric uses of TB and cancer crisscross and overlap.

crissum /ˈkrɪs(ə)m/ *n.* L19. [mod.L, f. *crissare* move the haunches.] *Ornith.* The region of the vent of a bird, including the under-tail coverts.

crissal *a.* of or pertaining to the crissum; *crissal thrasher*, a brown N. & Central American thrasher, *Toxostoma dorsale*, with rufous under-tail coverts: L19.

crista /ˈkrɪstə/ *n.* Pl. **-stae** /-stiː/. M19. [L: see CREST *n.*] Chiefly *Anat.* & *Zool.* A ridge, a crest.

cristate /ˈkrɪsteɪt/ *a.* M17. [L *cristatus*, f. as prec.: see -ATE².] Chiefly *Anat.* & *Zool.* Crested; having the form of a crest or ridge.

Also **cristated** *a.* (now *rare*) E18.

cristobalite /krɪˈstəʊbəlʌɪt/ *n.* L19. [f. Cerro San Cristóbal, a locality in Mexico: see -ITE¹.] *Min.* A variety of silica of which there is a stable high-temperature cubic form and a metastable low-temperature tetragonal form, and which occurs as massive deposits (e.g. in opal) and as small usu. octahedral crystals.

crit /krɪt/ *n. colloq.* Also **crit.** (point). M18. [Abbrev.] †1 A critic. Only in M18. 2 (Literary, textual, etc.) criticism; a critique. E20. 3 Critical mass. M20.

2 *lit. crit*: see LIT. *a.*

criteria *n.* pl. of CRITERION.

criteriology /krʌɪˌtɪərɪˈɒlədʒi/ *n.* L19. [f. next: see -OLOGY.] The study or analysis of criteria; the branch of logic that deals with criteria.

criterioˈlogical *a.* pertaining to criteriology; dealing with criteria: M20. **criterioˈlogically** *adv.* M20.

criterion /krʌɪˈtɪərɪən/ *n.* Occas. (Latinized) **-ium** /-ɪəm/. Pl. **-ia** /-ɪə/. E17. [Gk *kritērion* means of judging, test, f. *kritēs* judge.] 1 A principle, standard, or test by which a thing is judged, assessed, or identified. E17. †2 A (supposed) organ or faculty of judging. M–L17.

1 A. BEVAN Medical treatment and care . . should be made available to rich and poor alike in accordance with medical need and by no other criterion. J. L. AUSTIN Hoping to find a criterion to distinguish statements from performatives. RAYLEIGH(*'s*) *criterion. Richardson('s) criterion*: see RICHARDSON *n.*² 1.

¶ Throughout 17 freq. in Gk characters.

criterial *a.* M20.

crithomancy /ˈkrɪθəmansi/ *n.* M17. [f. Gk *krithē* barley-corn: see -MANCY.] Divination by meal strewn over animals sacrificed.

critic /ˈkrɪtɪk/ *n.*¹ L16. [L *criticus* f. Gk *kritikos*, use as n. of adj. f. *kritēs* judge: see -IC.] 1 A person who pronounces judgement; *esp.* a censurer. L16. 2 A judge or writer on the qualities of literary or artistic works; a professional reviewer of books, musical or dramatic performances, etc.; a person skilled in textual criticism. E17.

2 *drama critic, literary critic, music critic, television critic*, etc. *New Critic*: see NEW *a.*

criticling *n.* = CRITICASTER M18.

†**critic** *n.*² see CRITIQUE *n.*

critic /ˈkrɪtɪk/ *a.* Now *rare.* LME. [Fr. *critique*, f. late L *criticus*, f. as CRITIC *n.*¹] †1 = CRITICAL 1, 2. LME–E17. †2 = CRITICAL 4. L16–M17. 3 = CRITICAL 5. E17.

†**critic** *v.* Infl. **-ck-**. E17. [Fr. *critiquer*, f. as CRITIQUE *n.*] 1 *v.i.* Play the critic. Only in 17. 2 *v.t.* Criticize; censure. L17–M18.

critical /ˈkrɪtɪk(ə)l/ *a.* M16. [f. late L *criticus* (see CRITIC *a.*) + -AL¹.] I 1 Of or pertaining to the crisis of a disease; determining the issue of a disease. M16. 2 *gen.* Of, pertaining to, or constituting a crisis; of decisive importance, crucial; involving risk or suspense. E17. 3 *Math.* & *Physics.* Constituting or relating to a point of transition from one state etc. to another. M19. b Of a nuclear reactor etc.: maintaining a self-sustaining chain reaction. M20.

2 H. MACMILLAN We made a serious error, at a critical moment when France was already nervous and uncertain. H. KISSINGER Their need for American grain was critical. A. HAILEY They were vulnerable, critical installations and could take weeks to repair or replace completely.

II 4 Given to judging, esp. unfavourably; fault-finding, censorious. L16. 5 Skilful at or engaged in criticism, esp. of literature or art; providing textual criticism. L16. b Belonging to criticism. M18. †6 Involving careful judgement or observation; nice, exact, punctual. M17–M19.

4 SHAKES. *Oth.* I am nothing if not critical. W. GOLDING She was severe and very critical of my playing. 5 J. M. MURRY These two finely critical minds—in their separate provinces the finest critical minds we have in England to-day. A. WILSON A critical edition of the text of *Lamia*.

Special collocations & phrases: **critical angle** the angle of incidence at which a ray of light must strike an interface with a less dense medium so as to be refracted parallel to the interface. *critical apparatus*: see APPARATUS 2C. **critical damping** *Physics* damping just sufficient to prevent oscillations. **critical mass** the mass of a body of fissile material of critical size (see below). **critical path** a sequence of stages determining the minimum time needed for the execution of an entire project. **critical point** a set of conditions of temperature, pressure, and density at which a liquid and its vapour become indistinguishable. **critical pressure** the pressure required to liquefy a gas at its critical temperature. **critical size** the minimum size of a body of a given fissile material which is capable of sustaining a nuclear chain reaction. **critical temperature**: above which a gas cannot be liquefied by pressure. **critical volume** the volume of unit mass of a gas or vapour at its critical temperature and pressure. **go critical** (of a nuclear reactor etc.) begin to sustain a nuclear chain reaction. *New Critical*: see NEW *a.*

critiˈcality *n.* the state or quality of being critical; *esp.* the condition of sustaining a nuclear chain reaction: M18. **critically** *adv.* M17. **criticalness** *n.* M17.

criticaster /krɪtɪˈkastə, ˈkrɪtɪkastə/ *n.* L17. [f. CRITIC *n.*¹ + -ASTER.] A petty or inferior critic.

criticise *v.* var. of CRITICIZE.

criticism /ˈkrɪtɪsɪz(ə)m/ *n.* E17. [f. (as) CRITIC *n.*¹ + -ISM.] I 1 The action of passing judgement; *esp.* fault-finding, censure. E17. 2 The investigation of the text, character, composition, and origin of literary documents. M17. 3 The art or practice of estimating the qualities and character of literary or artistic works; the work of a critic. L17. 4 The critical philosophy of Kant (based on critical examination of the faculty of knowledge). Now *rare* or *obs.* M19.

2 **textual criticism**: dealing with and seeking the correct reading of a text, esp. a manuscript text, of an author. **the higher criticism**: dealing with the origin, character, etc., of texts, esp. of biblical writings. **the lower criticism** the textual criticism of the Bible. 3 *literary criticism*: see LITERARY *a. New Criticism*: see NEW *a. practical criticism*: see PRACTICAL *a.*

II 5 An act of criticizing; a critical analysis, article, essay, or remark. E17. †6 A nicety, a subtlety; a quibble. Only in 17.

criticist *n.* an adherent of the critical philosophy of Kant L19.

criticize /ˈkrɪtɪsʌɪz/ *v.* Also **-ise**. M17. [f. as prec. + -IZE.] 1 *v.i.* Pass judgement, esp. unfavourably; find fault, be censorious. (Foll. by †(*up*)*on.*) M17. 2 *v.t.* Discuss critically. M17. 3 *v.t.* Censure; find fault with. E18.

1 MILTON His Criticizing about the sound of Prayers. 2 BOLINGBROKE The verses I sent you are very bad . . you would do them too much honour, if you criticized them. J. KOSINSKI Each of them would criticize the others and himself, giving praise where due, pointing out shortcomings. 3 SWIFT To criticise his gait, and ridicule his dress. E. LONGFORD His wife was criticizing him for not giving enough to charity.

criticizable *a.* M19. **criticizer** *n.* L17.

critico- /ˈkrɪtɪkəʊ/ *comb. form.* E19. [After Gk *kritiko-*, f. *kritikos*: see CRITIC *n.*¹, -O-.] Critically, critical and —, as *critico-historical, -theological*, etc.

critique /krɪˈtiːk/ *n.* Orig. †**critic**. M17. [Fr., ult. f. Gk *kritikē* (sc. *tekhnē*) the critical art, criticism.] 1 Criticism; *esp.* the art of criticism. M17. 2 A criticism; *esp.* a critical analysis, article, or essay. M17.

1 R. BENTLEY I do not expect from our Editors much sagacity in way of Critic. 2 G. STEINER The student and the person interested in the current of literature reads reviews and critiques of books rather than the books themselves. E. FROMM Marx's whole critique of capitalism and his vision of socialism.

critique /krɪˈtiːk/ *v.t.* M18. [f. the n.] Discuss critically; write a critique of; make a critical assessment of.

critter /ˈkrɪtə/ *n. dial.* & *joc.* Also **-ur**. E19. [Var. of CREATURE.] A creature, *esp.* an ox, cow, or horse; *derog.* a person.

crivvens /ˈkrɪv(ə)nz/ *int. slang.* E20. [Alt. of CHRIST, perh. after *heavens!*] Expr. astonishment or horror.

crizzle /ˈkrɪz(ə)l/ *v.t.* & *i.* Now *dial.* E17. [Perh. dim. of CRAZE *v.*: see -LE[3].] (Cause to) become rough on the surface, as glass etc. by scaling, or water beginning to freeze.

cro /krəʊ/ *n.*[1] LME. [OIr. *cró* wound, violent death, Gael. *cró* blood.] *Celtic Hist.* Compensation payable for the killing of a man, according to his rank.

†**cro** *n.*[2] var. of CRUE.

croak /krəʊk/ *v.* & *n.* ME. [Imit. Cf. OE *crakettan*.] A *v.* 1 *v.i.* Of a frog or raven: make its characteristic deep harsh sound. ME. 2 *v.i.* Of a person: speak in a hoarse manner; *fig.* talk dismally or despondently. Formerly also, groan, cry. LME. †3 *v.i.* Of the stomach or bowels: rumble. M16–L18. 4 *v.t.* Say or proclaim with a croak or dismally. E17. 5 *v.i.* Die. *slang.* E19. 6 *v.t.* Kill; murder. *slang.* E19.

B *n.* A deep harsh sound made by a frog or raven; a sound likened to this. M16.

A. ALVAREZ His throat was raw and tender and the words came out in a formless croak.

croaky *a.* like a croak; hoarse: M19.

croaker /ˈkrəʊkə/ *n.* E17. [f. prec. + -ER[1].] 1 A person or animal that croaks; *spec.* any fish of the family Sciaenidae (= DRUM *n.*[1] 3b). E17. 2 A person who talks dismally or despondently; a prophet of evil. E17. 3 A doctor, *esp.* a prison doctor. *slang* (chiefly *US*). M19.

Croat /ˈkrəʊat/ *n.* & *a.* M17. [mod.L *Croatae* pl. f. Serbo-Croat *Hrvat*.] A *n.* = CROATIAN *n.*; *Hist.* a soldier of a French cavalry regiment composed mainly of Croatians. M17. B *adj.* = CROATIAN *a.* E19.

¶ See also SERBO-CROAT.

Croatian /krəʊˈeɪʃɪən, -ʃ(ə)n/ *n.* & *a.* M16. [f. mod.L *Croatia*, f. *Croatae*: see prec., -IAN.] A *n.* A native or inhabitant of Croatia, one of the Balkan States; the language of Croatia, a form of Serbo-Croat language written in the Roman alphabet. M16. B *adj.* Of or pertaining to Croatia, its people, or its language. E17.

¶ See also SERBO-CROATIAN.

croc /krɒk/ *n.* L19. [Abbrev.] = CROCODILE *n.* 1, 4.

mock croc imitation crocodile skin.

crocard *n.* var. of CROCKARD.

crocean /ˈkrəʊsɪən/ *a.*[1] *rare.* E17. [f. L *croceus*, f. as CROCUS *n.*[1]: see -AN.] Of the colour of saffron.

Also **croceate** *a.* M19.

Crocean /ˈkrəʊtʃɪən, ˈkrəʊsɪən/ *a.*[2] Also **-ian**. E20. [f. *Croce* (see below) + -AN, -IAN.] Of, pertaining to, or characteristic of the Italian philosopher and statesman Benedetto Croce (1866–1952) or his idealistic 'philosophy of the spirit'.

croche /krəʊtʃ/ *n.* L16. [Fr., cogn. w. (O)Fr. *croc* hook f. ON *krókr*: cf. CROOK *n.*] One of the knobs at the top of a stag's horn.

crochet /ˈkrəʊʃeɪ, -ʃi/ *n.* & *v.* M19. [Fr., dim. of *croc* with *-ch-* f. *crochié*, *crochu* hooked: see prec., -ET[1].] A *n.* A kind of knitting done using a single hooked needle to form intertwined loops; knitted material made in this way. M19.

Comb.: **crochet hook** the needle used in crochet work.

B *v.* 1 *v.t.* Make in crochet. L19. 2 *v.i.* Do crochet work. L19.

Crocian *a.* var. of CROCEAN *a.*[2]

crocidolite /krə(ʊ)ˈsɪdəlʌɪt/ *n.* M19. [f. Gk *krokis*, *-id-* nap of woollen cloth + -O- + -LITE.] A blue or green fibrous variety of riebeckite mined as a source of asbestos which is strong but has low heat resistance.

crocin /ˈkrəʊsɪn/ *n.* M19. [f. L *crocus* (see CROCUS *n.*[1]) + -IN[1].] A yellowish carotenoid glycosidic pigment, $C_{44}H_{64}O_{24}$, which is the colouring matter in saffron and some other kinds of crocus.

crock /krɒk/ *n.*[1] [OE *croc*, *crocca* rel. to synon. ON *krukka* and prob. to OE *crōg* small vessel (= OHG *kruog*, G *Krug*), *crūce* pitcher (= OS *krūka*, Du. *kruik*, MHG *kruche*).] 1 An earthenware vessel. OE. 2 A metal pot. *dial.* L15. 3 A broken piece of earthenware, *esp.* one used for covering the hole in a flowerpot. M19.

crock /krɒk/ *n.*[2] LME. [Perh. of Flem. origin, but appropriate wds have a different vowel, as MDu. *kraecke* (Du. *krak*), Flem. *krake*; presumably rel. to CRACK *v.*] 1 An old ewe. *Sc.* LME. 2 An old broken-down horse. L19. 3 A weak or debilitated person; a hypochondriac. *colloq.* L19. 4 An old worn-out vehicle, ship, etc. *slang.* E20.

crock /krɒk/ *n.*[3] *obs.* exc. *dial.* M17. [Origin unkn.] Dirt; a smut.

crock *n.*[4] see CRUCK.

crock /krɒk/ *v.*[1]*t.* Now *dial.* L16. [f. CROCK *n.*[1]] Put away (as) in a crock.

crock /krɒk/ *v.*[2] M17. [f. CROCK *n.*[3]] 1 *v.t.* Make dirty or grimy. M17. 2 *v.i.* Of a coloured article: impart its colour to something else. Of a colour or dye: transfer to something else. M19.

crock /krɒk/ *v.*[3] *colloq.* M19. [f. CROCK *n.*[2]] 1 *v.i.* Become feeble or decrepit; break down. Also foll. by *up*. M19. 2 *v.t.* Injure, damage. Also foll. by *up*. L19.

2 *Times* I had 'crocked' my knee at hockey.

crockard /ˈkrɒkɑːd/ *n.* Also **crocard**. ME. [AN f. OFr. *crocard*.] *Hist.* One of various base coins of foreign origin current in the reign of Edward I.

crocked /krɒkt/ *a. slang.* E20. [Perh. f. CROCK *v.*[3] + -ED[1].] Intoxicated.

†**crocker** *n.* ME–E18. [f. CROCK *n.*[1] + -ER[1].] A potter.

crockery /ˈkrɒk(ə)ri/ *n.* E18. [f. CROCKER: see -ERY.] Earthenware vessels, esp. for household use; pottery. Also *crockery-ware*.

crocket /ˈkrɒkɪt/ *n.* ME. [ONFr., var. of (O)Fr. *crochet* CROTCHET *n.*[1]] †1 A curl of some kind. Only in ME. 2 In Gothic architecture, each of a series of small projecting decorative features (usu. buds or leaves) on the sides of a pinnacle, gable, etc. L17. 3 = CROCHE. L19.

crocketed *a.* having crockets E19.

Crockford /ˈkrɒkfəd/ *n. colloq.* L19. [J. *Crockford* (1823–65), who first issued it.] (A copy of) *Crockford's Clerical Directory*, a directory of living Anglican clergy published periodically since 1858.

crocodile /ˈkrɒkədʌɪl/ *n.*, *a.*, & *v.* ME. [OFr. *cocodrille* (mod. *crocodile*) f. med.L *cocodrillus* for L *crocodilus* f. Gk *krokodilos*. Refash. after L & Gk, 16–17.] A *n.* 1a Any of a group of tropical and subtropical reptiles (sometimes treated as a family, Crocodylidae) related to alligators; any crocodilian. ME. b The skin of the crocodile (or alligator). E20. 2 *fig.* A person who makes a show of sorrow hypocritically or for a malicious purpose (as the crocodile was said to do in fable). L16. 3 A sophism in which an opponent is presented with a choice in the form of a question, but either of the two contrary answers leads to his or her defeat. E18. 4 A long line of children etc. walking together; a long procession of moving objects close together. *colloq.* L19.

1 *Nile crocodile*: see NILE 1. *Nilotic crocodile*: see NILOTIC *a.* 1.

Comb.: **crocodile bird** the Egyptian black-headed plover, *Pluvianus aegyptius* (family Glareolidae), which eats insects parasitic on crocodiles; **crocodile clip** a metal spring clip with long serrated jaws, used for making temporary electrical connections.

B *attrib.* or as *adj.* Feigned; hypocritical. M16.

G. S. FABER A crocodile affectation of clemency. **crocodile tears** false or affected sorrow.

C *v.i.* Walk in a crocodile. L19.

crocodiling *n.* = ALLIGATORING M20.

crocodilian /krɒkəˈdɪlɪən/ *a.* & *n.* M17. [f. L *crocodilus* (see prec.) + -IAN.] A *adj.* †1 Treacherous; that feigns sorrow. Only in M17. 2 Pertaining to or being a crocodilian. M19. B *n.* A reptile of the group including crocodiles and alligators; *spec.* one of the order Crocodylia, which also includes the caymans, the gharials, and numerous extinct animals, all large lizard-like semi-aquatic carnivores with a long tail and snout and a covering of horny and bony plates. M19.

crocoite /ˈkrəʊkəʊʌɪt/ *n.* M19. [Orig. Fr. *crocoise* f. Gk *krokoeis* saffron-coloured, f. *krokos* (see next); alt. to *crocoisite*, then to *crocoite*: see -ITE[1].] *Min.* Lead chromate occurring as bright orange monoclinic crystals. Also called *red lead ore*.

crocus /ˈkrəʊkəs/ *n.*[1] LME. [L f. Gk *krokos* of Semitic origin: cf. Heb. *karkōm*, Arab. *kurkum*.] 1 A plant of the genus *Crocus*, of the iris family, which comprises small plants with corms and single bright (often yellow or purple) flowers that usu. appear in spring. LME. b *autumn crocus*, an autumn-flowering plant of the genus *Colchicum*, *esp.* meadow saffron, *C. autumnale*. E19. 2 Saffron. LME. 3 Ferric oxide obtained as a reddish or purplish powder by calcination of ferrous sulphate and used for polishing metal; any of various red or yellow powders obtained from metals by calcination. M17. 4 A quack doctor. *slang.* L18.

1 *saffron crocus*: see SAFFRON *n.* 1.

crocus /ˈkrəʊkəs/ *n.*[2] & *a.* Now *US* & *W. Indies dial.* L17. [Origin uncertain: perh. the same wd as prec.] (Made of) a coarse heavy cloth used esp. for making bags and (formerly) cheap clothing.

V. S. REID I see my bro' take a crocus bag with him to the beach.

Croesus /ˈkriːsəs/ *n.* M17. [L form of the name of a king of Lydia (in Gk *Kroisos*) in the 6th cent. BC who was famous for his wealth.] A very rich person.

croft /krɒft/ *n.*[1] OE. [Origin unkn.] A piece of enclosed land used for tillage or pasturage; *esp.* a plot of arable land attached to a house. Also, a smallholding worked by a tenant; *esp.* one in the Highlands and Islands of Scotland comprising a plot of arable land attached to a house and a right of pasturage in common with others.

toft and croft: see TOFT *n.*[1] 1.

crofting *n.* the system of land tenure by crofters; a crofter's holding: L16.

croft /krɒft/ *n.*[2] *rare.* L15. [MDu. *crofte* (MLG *kruft*) cave, hole f. med.L *crupta* f. L *crypta* CRYPT.] A crypt; a cavern. See also UNDERCROFT.

crofter /ˈkrɒftə/ *n.* L18. [f. CROFT *n.*[1] + -ER[1].] A person who rents and cultivates a croft, esp. in the Highlands and Islands of Scotland.

¶ Recorded ME as a surname, which may be the same wd.

Crohn's disease /ˈkrəʊnz dɪˌziːz/ *n. phr.* M20. [B. B. *Crohn* (1884–1983), US pathologist.] A chronic inflammatory disease of the gastro-intestinal tract, esp. the colon and ileum, causing ulcers and fistulae.

†**croisade, -ado** *ns.* see CRUSADE *n.*

†**croises** *n.pl.* E17–M19. [Fr. *croisés* pl. of *croisé* use as n. of pa. pple of *croiser* cross f. OFr. *cruisier*, *croisier* f. eccl.L *cruciare*, f. L *cruc-*, *crux* cross.] Crusaders.

croisette /krwɒˈzɛt/ *n.* L17. [Fr., dim. of *croix* CROSS *n.*] A small cross.

¶ Rare bef. 20.

croissant /ˈkrwasɒŋ/ *n.* L16. [Fr.: see CRESCENT *n.*] †1 Var. of CRESCENT *n.* 1–4. L16–L17. 2 A flaky pastry roll in the shape of a crescent. L19.

Croix de Guerre /krwa də gɛːr/ *n. phr.* Pl. same. E20. [Fr., lit. 'cross of war'.] A French medal instituted in 1915 for individual gallantry in war.

cro'jack *n.* var. of CROSS-JACK.

Crokerism /ˈkrəʊkərɪz(ə)m/ *n.* M19. [f. *Croker* (see below) + -ISM.] *Hist.* The political principles of J. W. Croker (1780–1857), Conservative opponent of the Reform Bill.

Cro-Magnon /krəʊˈmanjɔ̃, -ˈmagnən/ *a.* & *n.* M19. [A hill near Les Eyzies, Dordogne department, France, containing a cave in which the skeletons were found.] A *adj.* Pertaining to or designating an individual of the type represented by certain skeletons found in 1868 in upper palaeolithic deposits, belonging to tall people with long skulls and short wide faces who were of physically modern type; pertaining to or designating any example of physically modern man of the early upper palaeolithic of western Europe. M19. B *n.* A Cro-Magnon man. M20.

cromb *n.* & *v.* var. of CROME.

crombec /ˈkrɒmbɛk/ *n.* E20. [Fr., f. Du. *krom* crooked + *bek* beak.] Any African warbler of the genus *Sylvietta.*

crome /krəʊm, kruːm/ *n.* & *v.* Now *dial.* Also **cromb.** LME. [Repr. an OE wd rel. to CRUM *a.*] A *n.* A hook, a crook. Formerly also, a claw, a talon. LME. B *v.t.* Seize or draw with a crook. M16.

Cromerian /krəʊˈmɪərɪən/ *a.* & *n.* E20. [f. *Cromer* (see below) + -IAN.] A *adj.* 1 *Geol.* & *Palaeont.* Designating or pertaining to a series of estuarine and freshwater deposits rich in fossils which outcrop at Cromer, Norfolk, and the interglacial or stratigraphic stage in the Middle Pleistocene when they were formed. Also, designating or pertaining to a much longer period in the Early and Middle Pleistocene that includes this interglacial as a warm period. E20. 2 *Archaeol.* Designating or pertaining to a supposed culture formerly thought to be represented by remains that were found in Pliocene deposits near Cromer but are no longer thought to be artefacts. E20. B *n.* 1 *Archaeol.* A person of the Cromerian culture. E20. 2 *Geol.* The Cromerian interglacial or its deposits. M20.

cromlech /ˈkrɒmlɛk/ *n.* L17. [Welsh, f. *crom* fem. of *crwm* bowed, arched + *llech* (flat) stone, LECH *n.*[1]] A dolmen; any megalithic chamber-tomb.

cromoglycate /krəʊməˈglʌɪseɪt/ *n.* M20. [f. alt. of CHROMO(NE + GLYC(EROL + -ATE[1].] *Pharm.* A drug whose sodium salt is inhaled to prevent asthmatic attacks and allergic reactions.

cromorne /krəʊˈmɔːn/ *n.* E18. [Fr. f. G KRUMMHORN.] An organ reed stop, usu. of 8-ft pitch, suggestive of a krummhorn or (later) a clarinet in sound; = CREMONA *n.*[1], KRUMMHORN 2.

Cromwell /ˈkrɒmwɛl/ *n.* M19. [Oliver *Cromwell*: see next, CROMWELLIAN *a.* 1.] 1 In full *Cromwell chair.* A dining-chair with a square seat and slightly sloping back, both being stuffed and covered with leather. M19. 2 In full *Cromwell shoe.* A shoe with a large buckle or bow. L19.

Cromwellian /krɒmˈwɛlɪən/ *a.* & *n.* M17. [f. *Cromwell* (see below) + -IAN.] A *adj.* 1 Of, pertaining to, or characteristic of Oliver Cromwell (1599–1658), English soldier, statesman, and Puritan leader of the Parliamentary forces in the English Civil War and Lord Protector 1653–8. M17. 2 Designating a Cromwell chair. E20. B *n.* A supporter of Cromwell; one of the English settlers in Ireland following Cromwell's defeat of the Irish and the Act of Settlement of 1652; a descendant of such a settler. L17.

crone /krəʊn/ *n.* LME. [Prob. MDu. *croonje, caroonje* carcass, old ewe f. ONFr. *caroigne* (mod.Fr. *charogne*) CARRION, cantankerous or mischievous woman. Sense 1 perh. directly f. ONFr.] 1a A withered old woman. LME. b A worn-out old man. *rare.* M17. 2 An old ewe. Also *crone sheep.* M16.

†**cronet** *n.* E16. [Syncopated f. CORONET. Cf. CROWNET.] 1 A head of a tilting spear, usu. with three or four short spreading points. E16–M18. 2 = CORONET *n.* 1, 2. M16–E17. 3 = CORONET *n.* 4. E17–E18.

Cronian /ˈkrəʊnɪən/ *a. rare.* E17. [f. Gk *Kronios* belonging to Kronos (Saturn) + -AN.] Designating the frozen sea of the north.
MILTON Two Polar Winds blowing adverse upon the Cronian sea.

cronk /krɒŋk/ *a. Austral. colloq.* L19. [Cf. CRANK *a.*[3]] (Of a racehorse) unfit to run, run dishonestly; *gen.* unsound; fraudulent.

crony /ˈkrəʊni/ *n.* & *v.* Also †**ch-**. M17. [f. Gk *khronios* long-lasting, long-continued, f. *khronos* time. Orig. university slang, the Gk wd being perverted to the sense 'contemporary'.] A *n.* An intimate friend or associate. M17.
ARNOLD BENNETT The two were regular cronies for about a couple of months. E. HEATH The beer cellar where Hitler and his cronies had first met.
B *v.i.* Associate (*with*) as a crony. E19.
cronyism *n.* friendship, fondness for the company of cronies; *US* the appointment of friends to political posts without due regard to their qualifications: M19.

croo *n.* var. of CRUE.

crood /kruːd/ *v.i. Sc.* E16. [Imit.] = CROODLE *v.*[2]

croodle /ˈkruːd(ə)l/ *v.*[1]*i. dial.* L18. [Origin unkn.] Crouch down; draw oneself together, as for warmth; nestle; cling close *to* a person.

croodle /ˈkruːd(ə)l/ *v.*[2]*i.* E19. [f. CROOD + -LE[3].] Coo like a dove.

crook /krʊk/ *n.* & *a.* ME. [ON *krókr* hook, barb, peg, bend, corner (Sw. *krok,* Da. *krog*).] A *n.* I 1 An implement, weapon, or tool of hooked form; a hook. ME. 2 A shepherd's staff, one end of which is hooked for catching a sheep's leg. LME. 3 The pastoral staff of a bishop etc., shaped like a shepherd's crook. LME. 4 A sharply curved part or appendage of anything. LME. 5 A curve, a bend, e.g. of a river. LME. 6 A small piece of ground; an odd corner. LME. †7 *Typogr.* A bracket, a parenthesis. L16–M18. 8 A crooked or incurved piece of timber; *spec.* = CRUCK. E19. 9 A curved piece of tubing which can be fitted to a wind instrument to change its pitch. Cf. SHANK *n.* 4g. M19.
1 R. S. SURTEES Crooks, from whence used to dangle . . legs of . . mutton. 4 M. SINCLAIR With a dead child in the crook of her arm.
II †10 A trick, an artifice, a wile. ME–L16. 11 A professional criminal; a rogue, a swindler. *colloq.* L19.
III 12 An act of crooking or bending something. ME.
Phrases: by hook or by crook: see HOOK *n.* **crook in one's lot** *Sc.* something untoward or distressing; a trial, an affliction. **on the crook** *slang* dishonestly.
B *adj.* 1 Crooked (*lit.* & esp. *fig.*). Now chiefly *Austral.* & *NZ.* E16. 2 Of a thing or situation: bad; unpleasant; unsatisfactory. *Austral.* & *NZ.* L19. 3 Annoyed; angry. (Foll. by *on, at.*) *Austral.* & *NZ.* E20. 4 Out of sorts; injured. *Austral.* & *NZ.* E20.
1 B. CRONIN The crook business man is in a decided minority. 2 D. IRELAND Things were crook at Tallarook. 3 P. V. WHITE His mum went crook, and swore. 4 X. HERBERT He's got a crook heart.
Comb.: **crook-back** (*a*) a hunchback; †(*b*) a crooked back; **crook-backed** *a.* hunchbacked; **crookneck** *N. Amer.* a squash with a recurved neck.
crookdom *n.* the realm of crooks E20. **crookery** *n.* the state of being a crook; the dealings of crooks; the world of crooks: E20. **crookish** *a.* characteristic or suggestive of crooks or crooked dealings E20.

crook /krʊk/ *v.* ME. [f. the n.] 1 *v.t.* Make into a curved or angular form; bend. ME. 2 *v.i.* Be or become crooked in form. ME. 3 *v.i.* Bow as a sign of reverence or humility. Now *rare* or *obs.* ME. 4 *v.t. Polo.* Interpose one's stick in front of (an opponent's). L19.
1 **crook one's elbow** or **little finger** *slang* drink alcohol, esp. to excess.

crooked /ˈkrʊkɪd; *in sense A.5 usu.* krʊkt/ *a.* & *adv.* ME. [f. CROOK *n.* + -ED[2], prob. after ON *krókóttr* crooked, cunning.] A *adj.* 1 Bent from a straight form; twisted, awry. ME. 2 Of a person: deformed; bowed with age. ME. †b Of a horse: broken down, old and decrepit. ME–L17. 3 *fig.* Not straightforward; deviating from uprightness of character or conduct; dishonest; corrupt. ME. 4 Dishonestly come by; stolen. *colloq.* M19. 5 = CROOK *a.* 3. (Foll. by *on.*) *Austral.* & *NZ. slang.* M20.
1 O. HENRY His smile became crooked. 3 M. PUZO A crooked police official.
Comb.: **crooked-necked squash** *US* = *crookneck* s.v. CROOK *n.*
B *adv.* In or into a crooked position. M16.
K. A. PORTER A young officer with his cap knocked crooked.
crookedly *adv.* LME. **crookedness** *n.* (*a*) the quality or state of being crooked; (*b*) a crooked part; a crooked act: LME.

crooken /ˈkrʊk(ə)n/ *v.t.* Now *dial.* M16. [Irreg. f. CROOK *v.* + -EN[5].] Make crooked; bend.

Crookes /krʊks/ *n.* L19. [See below.] Used *attrib.* and in *possess.* with ref. to the inventions and observations of the English physicist Sir William Crookes (1832–1919).
Crookes('s) dark space: between the negative glow and the cathode of a low-pressure discharge tube. **Crookes('s) glass, lens**: made so as to absorb ultraviolet light. **Crookes('s) radiometer** an evacuated globe containing four vanes which have one side blackened and jointly spin when heat radiation impinges on them. **Crookes('s) space** = *Crookes('s) dark space* above. **Crookes('s) tube** a highly evacuated electron tube in which stratified electric discharges can be produced.

croon /kruːn/ *v.* & *n.* L15. [MLG, MDu. *krōnen* lament, groan (Du. *kreunen*), of imit. origin.] A *v.* 1 *v.i.* Make a low murmuring sound; *esp.* sing a popular sentimental song in a low smooth voice. L15. 2 *v.i.* Make a continued loud, deep sound; bellow; boom. *Sc.* & *north.* E16. 3 *v.t.* Sing or say in a low murmuring voice; *esp.* sing (a popular sentimental song) in a low smooth voice. L16.
3 *Fortune* Rudy Vallée crooning I'm a Dreamer. C. ISHERWOOD 'Poor little Mummy, . . little Muttchen,' he crooned.
B *n.* 1 A loud, deep sound. *Sc.* & *north.* E16. 2 A low murmuring sound. E18.
crooningly *adv.* in a crooning manner E20.

crooner /ˈkruːnə/ *n.* E18. [f. CROON *v.* + -ER[1].] 1 The grey gurnard, *Eutrigla gurnardus* (from the noise it makes when landed). *Sc.* E18. 2 A person who croons; *spec.* a person who sings in a crooning style. L19.

croove *n.* var. of CRUIVE.

crop /krɒp/ *n.* [OE *crop* corresp. to MLG, MDu. *kropp,* OHG, G *Kropf,* ON *kroppr*; further relations uncertain.] I 1a A pouchlike enlargement of the gullet of many birds in which food is stored and prepared for digestion; an analogous organ in insects and some other animals. OE. b *transf.* & *fig.* The stomach; the throat. Now *dial.* ME. 2 The head of a flower, herb, etc., esp. as picked for use; an ear of corn. Now *dial.* OE. 3 The top of a tree; a topmost branch. Now *dial.* ME. 4 The upper part of a whip or (now *Sc.*) a fishing-rod; the whole stock of a whip; *spec.* (more fully *riding-crop, hunting-crop*) a short whipstock with a loop instead of or as well as a lash. LME. 5 *Archit.* The foliate part of a finial. L15. 6 *gen.* The top of anything material. *Sc.* E16.
II 7 [From sense 2.] The annual produce of cultivated plants, esp. the cereals, whether in the field or gathered. ME. 8 The yield of any natural product in a particular season or locality; a plant etc. which is periodically harvested. LME. 9 The entire tanned hide of an animal. LME. 10 A quantity produced or appearing, esp. at one time. L16.
7 JOSEPH HALL The Husbandman looks not for a crop in the wild desart. J. H. B. PEEL Is the crop really ready? 8 POPE Fields waving high with heavy crops. G. B. SHAW Their first crop of potatoes. W. FAULKNER Cotton is a speculator's crop. 10 G. B. SHAW The world's crop of infamy. M. MCCARTHY This new crop of girls was far less idealistic . . than their mothers.
III [f. the vb.] 11 A joint of or *of* meat; a piece cut off anything. LME. 12 An earmark made by cutting off part of the ear, esp. of an animal. M17. 13 An outcrop of rock. E18. 14 A conspicuously short haircut. L18.
Phrases: Eton crop: see ETON 5. *green crop*: see GREEN *a. lop and crop*: see LOP *n.*[2] 1. *main crop*: see MAIN *a. neck and crop*: see NECK *n.*[1] *sour crop*: see SOUR *a. standing crop*: see STANDING *a.*

Comb.: **crop circle** a circular area in a field of standing crops (esp. wheat or another cereal) in which the stalks have been flattened to the ground, usu. in concentric rings; **crop-dusting** the spraying of crops with powdered insecticide etc. from the air; †**crop-ear** (an animal or person with) an ear that has been cropped; **crop-eared** *a.* (*a*) having the ears cropped; (*b*) *arch.* having the hair cut short and close to the head so that the ears are conspicuous, in a style favoured by Puritan supporters of Parliament in the English Civil War (cf. PRICK-EARED 2); **crop-full** *a.* having a full crop or stomach (*lit.* & *fig.*); *crop husbandry*: see HUSBANDRY *n.* 2; **crop-mark** a local variation in the colour or growth of a crop, esp. when seen from the air, caused by a varying depth of soil (used to detect the presence of buried archaeological features); **crop-over** the end of the sugar cane harvest on a W. Indian plantation; the accompanying celebration; **crop-sick** *a.* (now *dial.*) having an upset stomach, esp. through overindulgence.

†**crop** *a.* M17–E19. [f. the n.] Having the ears or hair cropped.

crop /krɒp/ *v.* Infl. **-pp-**. Pa. t. & pple **cropped**, (*arch.*) **cropt**. ME. [f. the n.] **1** *v.t.* Remove the top or terminal parts of (a plant); pick (a flower or fruit). ME. **2** *v.t.* & *i.* Of an animal: bite off the top of (grass etc.) in feeding. LME. **3** *v.t.* Cut off short (*lit.* & *fig.*); cut short the ears of (a person or animal) or the hair of (a person, a head); trim the pages of (a book); cut off or mask unwanted areas of (a photograph etc.). E16. **4** *v.t.* Reap, harvest; cull (animals). E17. **5** *v.i.* Bear or yield a crop. E17. **6** *v.t.* Raise a crop on; sow or plant with a crop. E17. **b** *v.i.* Grow crops; work as a farmer. *US.* M19. **7** *v.i.* *Geol.* Of a stratum etc.: appear at the surface. Usu. foll. by *out* or *up*. M17. **8** *v.i.* Foll. by *up*: occur unexpectedly or incidentally. M19. **9** *v.i.* Foll. by *out*: come out or disclose itself incidentally. M19.

2 E. GLASGOW The stony hillside where sheep were cropping. W. DE LA MARE His horse moved, cropping the dark turf. 3 CARLYLE By the hundred and the thousand, men's lives are cropt. A. J. CRONIN A beard, cropped close on cheek and chin. *Vogue* Cropped black top. 4 *Nature* The cropping of whales. 6 L. MACNEICE They won't crop their farms regularly. SHARECROP *n.* & *v.* 8 J. GALSWORTHY That nonsense of the separate room had cropped up again!

cropper /ˈkrɒpə/ *n.*[1] ME. [f. CROP *v.* or *n.* + -ER[1].] **I 1** A person or thing which crops or trims; *spec.* a shearing machine or implement for cutting metal; a person who uses one. ME. **2** A person who raises a crop. L16. **3** A plant which yields a crop of a specified kind or in a specified way. M19.

2 *sharecropper*: see SHARE *n.*[2]

II 4 A pigeon of a breed that is able greatly to puff up its crop; a pouter-pigeon. M17.

cropper /ˈkrɒpə/ *n.*[2] *colloq.* M19. [Perh. f. *neck and crop* s.v. NECK *n.*[1]] A heavy fall; *fig.* a severe misfortune, personal failure, etc.

come a cropper fall heavily; be ruined, suffer sudden misfortune.

Cropper /ˈkrɒpə/ *n.*[3] Also **c-**. L19. [H. S. *Cropper*, Eng. manufacturer.] A kind of small treadle platen printing machine.

croppie *n.* var. of CRAPPIE.

croppy /ˈkrɒpi/ *n.* L18. [f. CROP *n.* + -Y[1].] *Hist.* A person who has his or her hair cut short; *spec.* (*a*) (also *croppy-boy*) one of the Irish rebels of 1798, who showed their sympathy with the French Revolution in this way; (*b*) *Austral.* an escaped convict.

cropt *v.* pa. t. & pple: see CROP *v.*

croquet /ˈkrəʊkeɪ, -ki/ *n.* & *v.* M19. [Origin uncertain: perh. f. north. Fr. var. of Fr. CROCHET.] **A** *n.* **1** A game played on a lawn in which mallets are used to drive wooden etc. balls in a particular order through hoops fixed in the ground. M19. **2** The act of croqueting another ball. L19. **B** *v.t.* & *i.* Drive away (the ball of an opponent) or the ball of (an opponent), after hitting it with one's own, by placing the two in contact and striking one's own with the mallet. M19.

croquette /krɒˈkɛt/ *n.* E18. [Fr., f. *croquer* to crunch: see -ETTE.] A small ball or roll of vegetable, minced meat, or fish (to be) fried in breadcrumbs.

croquis /krɔki, krəʊˈkiː/ *n.* Pl. same /-i, -iːz/. E19. [Fr., f. *croquer* to sketch.] A rough draft; a sketch.

crore /krɔː/ *n.* Pl. same, **-s**. E17. [Hind. *k(a)roṛ* f. Skt *koṭi*.] In the Indian subcontinent: ten million, a hundred lakhs. (Foll. by *of.*)

Bangladesh Times Lakhs and crores of people. F. A. MEHTA Capital equipment exported . . was under a crore of rupees. *Nature* The 1976–77 budget on oil exploration at Rupees 42 crores (42 million dollars).

crosier /ˈkrəʊzɪə, -ʒə/ *n.* Also **-z-**. ME. [Partly f. OFr. *croisier* (med.L *cruciarius*) cross-bearer, f. *crois* CROSS *n.*; partly f. OFr. *crocier*, *crossier* bearer of a bishop's crook, f. *croce* (mod. *crosse*) f. Gmc base also of CRUTCH *n.*: see -IER.] **I 1** A person who bears a processional cross in front of an archbishop. Now *Hist.* ME. †**2** The bearer of a bishop's crook. LME–M16. **3** = CROOK *n.* 3. E16. **4** An archbishop's processional cross. E18. **II** †**5** The constellation of the Southern Cross; in *pl.*, its four chief stars. M16–E18. **6** The curled tip of a young fern. L19.

crosiered *a.* E18.

cross /krɒs/ *n.* See also CROSS-. LOE. [ON *kross* f. OIr. *cros* (corresp. to Gael. *crois*, Welsh *croes*) f. late L var. of L CRUX, *cruc-*, whence also OFr. *croiz*, *crois* (mod. *croix*).] **I 1** A monument consisting of or surmounted by an upright and a short transverse piece, symbolizing the Cross of Jesus (sense 3 below). LOE. **b** A market-place; a market. Now *dial.* L16. **2** A tall upright stake usu. with a transverse beam, to which a person was fastened as a mode of execution in the ancient world. ME. **3** *spec.* (Also **C-**.) The particular structure on which Jesus was crucified. ME. **4** *Chr. Ch.* A devotional and liturgical act in which a hand or digit traces the shape of a cross on the body of oneself or another, usu. on the forehead or by touching in turn the forehead, chest, each shoulder, and the chest again. Now usu. *sign of the cross.* ME. **5** A model of a cross (sense 2 above) as a religious emblem in a church, an ornament worn round the neck, etc. ME. **6** A staff surmounted by a cross and carried in religious processions, esp. as an archbishop's emblem of office. ME. **7 a** (Also **C-**.) The Christian religion. ME. **b** *Chr. Ch.* (Also **C-**.) The atonement accomplished by Christ through his Crucifixion and death. LME. **8** An affliction seen as to be borne with Christian patience; any source of personal trouble or vexation. ME. **9** A more or less elaborate representation of a cross on a surface, as a religious symbol. ME. **10** A figure of a cross stamped on one side of a coin; a coin bearing such a figure; any coin. *arch.* ME. **11** A mark or figure consisting of two short lines cutting one another, usu. at right angles; any object seen as having a similar shape. LME. **12** A stylized representation of a cross used as a heraldic device. LME. **b** An order of knighthood or a decoration for valour having a cross as its emblem; the emblem itself; a recipient of such an honour. L17. **13** *the Cross* (more fully *the Southern Cross*), (the name of) a small but conspicuous constellation of the southern hemisphere, lying in the Milky Way near Centaurus and having a cross- or kite-shaped group of four bright stars pointing approximately north–south. M16. **14** A surveyor's instrument having two sights at right angles to one another. M17.

2 *Calvary cross*, *cross Calvary*: see CALVARY 1. *holy cross*: see HOLY *a.* *St Cross*: see SAINT *n.* & *a.* 3 *Invention of the Cross*: see INVENTION *n.* *St Cross*: see SAINT *n.* & *a.* *Station of the Cross*: see STATION *n.* 10. *the Way of the Cross*: see WAY *n.* 5 A. WILSON A small opal cross on her ample bosom. *creep to the cross*: see CREEP *v.* 1. 8 ALDOUS HUXLEY We all have our cross to bear. J. CARY My father was . . a cross and burden to his family. **10 cross and** (or **or**) **pile** (*a*) *arch.* the obverse and (or) reverse of a coin; a coin; money; †(*b*) (usu. w. *cast*, *throw*, etc.) a toss-up (*lit.* & *fig.*). 11 EVELYN The body of the Church formes a Crosse. D. STOREY Examining the marks, the ticks, the crosses. *long cross*: see LONG *a.*[1] *noughts and crosses*: see NOUGHT *pron.* & *n.* 4. 12 *Celtic cross*, *Greek cross*, *Latin cross*, *Lorraine cross*, *Maltese cross*, *St Andrew's cross*, *St Anthony('s) cross*, *St George's cross*, *tau cross*, *Teutonic cross*, etc. b *Distinguished Flying Cross*, *George Cross*, *Iron Cross*, *Military Cross*, *Victoria Cross*, etc. **Grand Cross** the highest degree of any of certain orders of knighthood having a cross-shaped decoration.

II †**15 a** A crossed position. Chiefly in *on cross* (surviving as ACROSS *adv.*). LME–M17. **b** *the cross*, the diagonal across the warp of a material, the bias. Chiefly in (*cut* etc.) *on the cross*. L19. **16** A place where two lines or routes cross each other. M16. **17** An instance of being thwarted, a disappointment. L16. **18** An intermixture of animal breeds or of plant varieties or species; an animal or plant so produced, a hybrid. M18. **b** A thing or person intermediate in character or appearance *between* two different things or persons. L18. **19 a** *the cross*, dishonest or fraudulent practices; criminal activities. *slang.* E19. **b** A fraudulent deed or arrangement. *slang.* E19. **20** A transverse movement; *Theatr.* a movement from one side of the stage to the other; a blow in boxing that crosses the opponent's lead; a cross-pass. M19.

17 W. H. DIXON Anne was suffering from a cross in love. 18 FIRST *cross*. *reciprocal cross*: see RECIPROCAL *a.* b R. S. SURTEES A cross between a military dandy and a squire. G. MAXWELL The studio came to look like a cross between a monkey-house and a furniture repository. **19a on the cross** dishonest(ly), criminal(ly). 20 J. DEMPSEY The right cross, deadliest of all counterpunches. See also CROSS-.

¶ In OE only in place-names.

crossless *a.* L15.

cross /krɒs/ *a.* See also CROSS-. E16. [Partly attrib. use of the n., partly ellipt. use of CROSS *adv.*] **1** Lying across; extending from side to side; transverse; (of a cricket bat) held slanting. E16. **b** Of a wind: blowing across one's course. Of a sea: running across the direction of the wind; composed of two sets of waves crossing each other. E17. **2** Contrary, opposed, (*to*). Now usu. *attrib.* M16. **3** Adverse, unfavourable; not in accord with one's desire. M16. **4** *attrib.* Involving interchange or reciprocal action. L16. †**5** Inclined to quarrel or disagree; perverse. L16–M19. **6** Annoyed, ill-tempered (*at*, *with*, †*to*); expressing or showing annoyance or ill temper. M17. **7** Dishonest; dishonestly come by. *slang.* E19. **8** Of an animal or plant: crossbred; hybrid. L19.

1 *fig.*: DISRAELI How many cross issues baffle the parties. b DICKENS In the cross-swell of two steamers. 3 T. DEKKER Such crosse fortune! DEFOE We had but a cross voyage. 6 J. AUSTEN I have never had a cross word from him. A. J. CRONIN He was cross with her for being out of sorts.

crossly *adv.* L16. **crossness** *n.* L16.

cross /krɒs/ *v.* ME. [f. CROSS *n.*] **1** *v.t.* Make the sign of the cross on or over (esp. oneself, as an act of devotion or reverence or to invoke divine protection). ME. **2** *v.t.* Draw a line or lines across; (usu. foll. by *off*, *out*) cancel in this way. LME. **3** *v.t.* Of a line etc.: intersect; lie or pass across. LME. **b** *v.i.* Intersect, lie or pass across each other. L17. **c** *v.t.* Bestride (a horse). M18. **4** *v.t.* Place crosswise (*with*); set (things) across one another; place (one thing) *over* another. L15. **5 a** *v.i.* Pass (*over*) from one side or end to or *to* the other. L15. **b** *v.t.* Pass over (a line, boundary, etc.); go or travel across (a region etc.). L16. **c** *v.t.* Of a thing: extend across. L16. **d** *v.t.* Carry or take (something) across. E19. **e** *v.t.* & *i.* *Football* etc. Pass (the ball) across the pitch, esp. from a wing to the centre. M20. **6** *v.t.* **a** Thwart; resist the wishes of; oppose (a plan etc.). M16. †**b** Contradict; contravene. L16–M18. †**c** Debar *from*. *rare.* L16–M17. **7 a** *v.t.* Meet in one's way, esp. adversely. *arch.* L16. **b** *v.t.* & †*i.* (w. *on*, *upon*). Come across, encounter. Now *rare.* L17. **8 a** *v.t.* Meet and pass; pass in an opposite direction; (of a letter etc.) be on its way at the same time as (one to the sender from the recipient). L18. **b** *v.i.* (Of a letter etc.) be on its way at the same time as one to the sender from the recipient (foll. by *with*); (of letters etc. between two people) be on their way at the same time. L18. **9** *v.t.* Breed (an animal or plant) with or *with* one of a different breed, variety, etc.;

modify by this means. L18. **10** *v.t.* Act dishonestly towards (a person) or in (a matter). *slang.* E19.

2 THACKERAY I have . . crossed the t's and dotted the i's. E. BOWEN Hermione . . crossed off the days on her calendar. **3b** A. MASON A pair of stout sticks had been thrust into the ground slantwise so that they crossed near the top. **4** M. KEANE They crossed and uncrossed their legs clumsily. S. PLATH I sat . . and crossed my right ankle over my left knee. **5a** R. ADAMS We will cross to the further side of the river. T. STOPPARD French enters and crosses to his place. C. P. SNOW They had to cross, to the island in the middle of the road. **b** H. JAMES If he crossed that threshold. J. CONRAD I crossed the landing to my sitting-room. N. COWARD If we crossed Siberia by train. **c** O. HENRY A little river . . crossed by a hundred little bridges. **6** C. WILSON When crossed, he had an explosive temper. **8a** C. LAMB Now and then a solitary gardening man would cross me. K. M. E. MURRAY His letter crossed an apology from Wheatley. **b** DICKENS This letter will cross with your second.

Phrases, & with advs. in specialized senses: **cross a cheque** draw or print two parallel lines across a cheque, so that it has to be paid into a bank account. **cross a person's hand** or **palm (with silver)** give her or him a coin as payment for fortune-telling (orig. describing a cross with it in the palm). *cross my heart (and hope to die)*: see HEART *n.* *cross one's bridge when one comes to it*: see BRIDGE *n.*[1] 1. **cross one's face** appear briefly in one's expression. **cross one's fingers** crook one finger over another to bring good luck. **cross one's heart** make the sign of the cross over one's heart in attestation of sincerity. **cross one's mind** come suddenly into one's thoughts. **cross one's path** meet, esp. so as to obstruct or thwart; pass across one's path in front of one. **cross over** (*a*) *Biol.* (of chromosome segments) undergo crossing over (CROSSING *over*); (*b*) *euphem.* die; (see also senses 4, 5a above). **cross swords** *fig.* have a fight, controversy, or overt rivalry, (*with*). *cross the floor*: see FLOOR *n.* *cross the T*: see T, T 2. *cross the t's*: see T, T 1. **cross wires** accidentally connect telephone circuits so that one call is heard with another; *fig.* have a misunderstanding; (usu. in *pass.*). **get one's wires crossed** = *cross wires* above. **keep one's fingers crossed** keep one finger over another to bring good luck; be in suspenseful hope (*that*).

crossable *a.* M19. **crosser** *n.* M16.

cross /krɒs/ *prep.* & *adv.* See also CROSS-. M16. [Aphet. f. ACROSS.] **A** *prep.* = ACROSS *prep.* 1, 2, 3. Now *dial.* or *poet.* exc. as CROSS-. M16. **B** *adv.* †**1** = ACROSS *adv.* 2. L16–L18. †**2** In a contrary way *to.* E17–M18. **3** = ACROSS *adv.* 3. Now *rare.* E17.

cross- /krɒs/ *comb. form.* [Repr. CROSS *n., a., prep.* & *adv.*] In combs. in various relations and with various senses, as 'a cross', 'transverse(ly)', 'in opposition', 'across'. (In some a hyphen is optional, others are customarily written as two wds or as one.)

cross-accent *n.* (*Mus.*) a syncopated accent, syncopation M20. **cross-action** *n.* a legal action brought on the same subject by a defendant against a plaintiff or another defendant M19. †**cross-aisle** *n.* (an arm of) a transept LME–L18. **cross-beak** *n.* = CROSSBILL *n.* L17. **cross-beam** *n.* a transverse beam L15. **cross-bearer** *n.* a person who carries or wears a cross; *esp.* one who carries an archbishop's cross before him in procession: M16. **cross-bearings** *n.pl.* (*Naut.*) bearings of two or more objects from one point, or of one object from two or more points, which enable the single position to be found given the others E19. **cross-'bedding** *n.* (*Geol.*) layering within a stratum and at an angle to the main bedding plane L19. **cross-bench** *n.* each of the benches in the House of Lords where peers sit who have no party allegiance (usu. in *pl.*) M19. **cross-'bencher** *n.* a member of either House of Parliament who sits on the cross-benches or asserts his or her independence of party allegiance L19. **crossbones** *n.pl.* a figure of two crossed thigh bones as an emblem of death (usu. under the figure of a skull: see *skull and crossbones* s.v. SKULL *n.*[1]) L18. **cross-border** *a.* (*a*) that forms a border across a fabric etc.; (*b*) passing, occurring, or performed across a border between two countries etc.: L19. **cross bun** *n. phr.* (usu. more fully *hot cross bun*): marked with a cross, traditionally for eating on Good Friday M18. **cross-'buttock** *n.* & *v.* (*a*) *n.* a throw in which a wrestler throws an opponent head first over his or her hip; (*b*) *v.t.* throw in this way: E18. **cross-'buttocker** *n.* (a wrestler who uses) a cross-buttock E19. **cross-channel** *a.* passing or situated across a channel, esp. the English Channel L19. **cross-co'nnect** *v.t.* connect (each of a set of wires etc.) to a non-corresponding wire etc. in another set L19. **cross-co'nnection** *n.* a cross-connected arrangement L19. **cross-corner** *n.* a diagonally opposite corner of a quadrilateral; *at cross-corners with* (fig.), directly contrary to: E19. **cross-corre'lation** *n.* a correlation between two different series of measurements etc. E20. **cross-'country** *a., adv.,* & *n.* (*a*) *adj.* & *adv.* (going, leading, or taking place) across fields etc. rather than along (main) roads; (of a flight) involving landing at a point distant from the take-off point and the practice of air navigation; (*b*) *n.* a cross-country run, flight, etc.; cross-country running, skiing, etc.: M18. **cross-court** *a.* (of a stroke in tennis etc.) hit diagonally across the court E20. **cross-cousin** *n.* either of two cousins who are children of a brother and sister L19. **cross crosslet** *n. phr.* a Greek cross in which each limb is crossed L15. **cross-'cultural** *a.* pertaining to or involving different cultures or comparison between them M20. **cross-'culturally** *adv.* in cross-cultural terms M20. **cross-'date** *v.t.* (*Archaeol.*) date by correlation with the chronology of another culture, site, etc. M20. **cross-division** *n.* (an instance of) division of a group according to more than one principle, producing problems of classification E19. **cross-'dress** *v.i.* wear clothes of members of the opposite sex L20. **cross-'dresser** *n.* a transvestite L20. **cross-exami'nation** *n.* a spell of, or the action of, cross-examining E19. **cross-e'xamine** *v.t.* examine with minute and persistent questioning; (of a barrister etc.) question (a witness for the other side) in order to weaken evidence previously given or elicit evidence favourable to the barrister's own side: M17. **cross-eyed** *a.* having one or both eyes turned inwards in a squint L18. **cross-fade** *v.* & *n.* (*Broadcasting*) (*a*) *v.i.* fade out one sound while fading in another; (*b*) *n.* an act of cross-fading: M20. **cross-'fenced** *a.* (*US*) having additional fencing inside a fenced enclosure L20. **cross-fertili'zation** *n.* fertilization in which the fusing gametes come from different individuals; *fig.* the fruitful interchange of ideas, information, etc.: M19. **cross-'fertilize** *v.* (*a*) *v.t.* fertilize with gametes from another individual of the same species; cross-pollinate; *fig.* help or promote by interchange of ideas, information, etc.; (*b*) *v.i.* employ cross-fertilization (*lit.* & *fig.*): M19. **cross-fingering** *n.* on a woodwind instrument, a method or the action of changing a note by a semitone by uncovering one hole part of the way along the instrument and covering up one or more of the holes nearer the open end; an instance of this: L19. **crossfire** *n.* lines of gunfire crossing one another from different positions; *fig.* (danger due to) attacks from different quarters: M19. †**cross-fixed** *a.* crucified E17–M19. **cross fox** *n. phr.* = *patch fox* s.v. PATCH *n.*[1] M19. **cross-'garnet** *n.* a hinge composed of a short vertical piece fastened to a door frame and a longer horizontal one fastened to the face of the door M17. **cross-'gartered** *a.* (*Hist.*) having garters crossed on the legs L16. **cross-'gartering** *n.* (*Hist.*) the wearing of garters crossed on the legs E17. **cross-'grained** *a.* & *adv.* (*a*) *adj.* (of wood) having a grain that deviates from the longitudinal direction; *fig.* difficult to deal with, perverse; (*b*) *adv.* across the grain (*lit.* & *fig.*): M17. **cross-'grainedness** *n.* perversity, irritability M17. **cross-guard** *n.* a guard on a sword, dagger, etc., consisting of a short transverse bar M19. **cross-hair** *n.* = CROSS-WIRE L19. **cross-'handed** *a.* & *adv.* (*a*) *adj.* having the hands crossed; (of a boat) rowed with hands crossed; (*b*) *adv.* with the hands crossed: M19. **cross-handled** *a.* having a handle in the form of a cross E19. **cross-hatch** *v.t.* engrave with two sets of parallel lines crossing each other; shade in this way; mark with crossing lines: E19. **cross-'index** *v.t.* index under another heading as a cross-reference L19. **cross-in'fection** *n.* transfer of infection, esp. to a hospital patient with a different infection etc. M20. **cross-keys** *n.pl.* two keys depicted in the form of an X, as in the papal arms M16. **cross-kick** *v.* & *n.* (*a*) *v.i.* kick a football across the field; (*b*) *n.* a kick across a football field: E20. **cross-legged** *adv.* & *a.* (*a*) *adv.* with the legs crossed at the ankles and bent outwards; (*b*) *adj.* lying with one leg laid over the other; sitting cross-legged: M16. **cross-light** *n.* a light which crosses another and illuminates parts which the other leaves in shade M19. **cross-line** *n.* (*a*) a line drawn across another; (*b*) a fishing-line stretched across a stream with many hooks attached: LME. **cross-link** *n.* & *v.* (*Chem.*) (*a*) *n.* a bond, atom, or short chain of atoms that connects two long chains in a polymer molecule etc.; (*b*) *v.t.* & *i.* form a cross-link (with): M20. **cross-'linkage** *n.* (*Chem.*) a cross-link M20. **cross-'lots** *adv.* (*N. Amer. dial.*) by a short cut E19. **cross-member** *n.* a structural member across the width of a motor-vehicle chassis E20. **cross-multiplication** *n.* a method of multiplying together quantities given in feet and inches, etc., without reducing them to one denomination; also called *duodecimals*: E18. **cross-pass** *n.* a pass across a football etc. field E20. **crosspatch** *n.* an ill-tempered person L17. **cross-path** *n.* a path that crosses between two roads or points M16. **cross-peen, -pein** *a.* (of a hammer) having a peen that lies crossways to the length of the shaft L19. **crosspiece** *n.* a transverse component of a structure etc. E17. **cross-plough,** (*N. Amer.* & *arch.*) **-plow** *v.t.* plough (a field etc.) across the furrows of a previous ploughing M17. **cross-ply** *a.* & *n.* (designating) a tyre in which successive layers of fabric have their cords running diagonally, crossways to each other M20. **cross-point** *n.* †(*a*) some kind of dance step; (*b*) a compass point between two of the cardinal points: L16. **cross-'pollinate** *v.t.* (*Bot.*) subject to cross-pollination E20. **cross-polli'nation** *n.* the pollination of one plant with pollen from another plant L19. **cross-'posting** *n.* a move to a different department or industry M20. **cross product** *n. phr.* = *vector product* s.v. VECTOR *n.* M20. **cross 'purpose** *n. phr.* conflicting purpose: in *pl.* (treated as *sing.*), a parlour game involving mismatched questions and answers; *at cross purposes*, with a misunderstanding of each other's meaning or intention: M17. **cross-'question** *n.* & *v.* (*a*) *n.* a question put by way of cross-examination; (*b*) *v.t.* interrogate with questions that tend to check previous answers; cross-examine: L17. **cross-re'act** *v.i.* take part in a cross-reaction M20. **cross-re'action** *n.* the reaction of an antibody with an antigen other than the one which gave rise to it M20. **cross-'reading** *n.* a reading continued across adjacent columns of a newspaper etc. so as to produce a comic effect L18. **cross-re'fer** *v.i.* & *t.* refer from or *from* one place in a book or list to or *to* another; provide with a cross-reference: L19. **cross-'reference** *n.* & *v.* (*a*) *n.* a reference to another place in a book, list, etc., where the same subject or word is treated; (*b*) *v.t.* provide with a cross-reference; refer *to* another place by means of a cross-reference: M19. **cross-rhythm** *n.* simultaneous use of more than one rhythm; an instance of this: E20. †**cross-row** *n.* the alphabet; = *Christ-cross-row* s.v. CHRIST-CROSS 2: E16–L17. **cross-ruff** *n.* & *v.* (*a*) *n.* an obsolete card-game; a sequence of play in bridge etc. in which partners alternately trump each other's leads; (*b*) *v.t.* & *i.* play (in) a cross-ruff: L16. **cross-saddle** *n.* & *adv.* (*a*) *n.* a saddle on which the rider sits astride; (*b*) *adv.* astride a saddle: L19. **cross-sea** *n.*: running across the wind, or having two sets of waves crossing M19. **cross slide** *n. phr.* a sliding part on a lathe or planing machine which is supported by the saddle and carries the tool in a direction at right angles to the bed of the machine L19. **cross-springer** *n.* (*Archit.*) a rib that extends diagonally in vaulting E19. **cross-staff** *n.* (*arch.*) (*a*) an archbishop's cross; a bishop's crook; (*b*) an instrument formerly used for finding the altitude of the sun: LME. **cross-stitch** *n.* & *v.* (*a*) *n.* a stitch formed of two stitches that make a cross; needlework characterized by such stitches; (*b*) *v.t.* sew or embroider with cross-stitches: M17. **cross-street** *n.* a street crossing another or connecting two streets M17. **cross-'subsidize** *v.t.* subsidize out of the profits of another business or activity M20. **cross-'subsidy** *n.* the financing of losses arising from one business or activity out of profits from another, which may be deliberately increased for the purpose M20. **crosstalk** *n.* unwanted transfer of signals from one circuit, channel, etc., to another; *fig.* repartee; conversation: L19. **cross-tie** *n.* a transverse connecting piece, *esp.* (*N. Amer.*) a railway sleeper E19. **cross-tongue** *n.* a slip of wood with the grain running crossways, used to strengthen a joint L19. **cross-town** *a.* & *adv.* (*N. Amer.*) (that goes or leads) across a town L19. **cross-tree** *n.* (*a*) in *pl.*, a pair of horizontal struts attached to a mast, esp. athwart-ships to spread the rigging or support a top; (*jack cross-tree*: see JACK *n.*[1]); (*b*) *poet.* = CROSS *n.* 3: E17. **cross-vault(ing)** *ns.* (*Archit.*): formed by the intersection of two or more vaults M19. **cross-'voting** *n.* voting for a party not one's own or for more than one party L19. **crosswalk** *n.* (*a*) a path or walk that crosses another; (*b*) *N. Amer.* & *Austral.* a pedestrian crossing: M18. **crosswind** *n.* a wind blowing across one's course E20. **cross-wire** *n.* a fine wire at the focus of an optical instrument, crossing the field of view, to aid in positioning or measuring M19. **crossword** *n.* (more fully *crossword puzzle*) a puzzle in which words crossing one another, usu. horizontally and vertically in a chequered pattern of squares, have to be filled in from clues provided E20. **crosswort** *n.* any of various plants with leaves arranged in a cross, or whorl of four, esp. *Cruciata laevipes*, a straggling hedgerow plant of the madder family L16.

crossbar /'krɒsbɑː/ *n.* M16. [f. CROSS- + BAR *n.*[1]] **1** A bar fixed across something, esp. a bicycle frame or a goal. M16. **2** A transverse line or stripe. L16. †**3** = *bend sinister* s.v. BEND *n.*[2] 2. M17–M18.

crossbar /ˈkrɒsbɑː/ *v.t.* Infl. **-rr-**. L16. [Partly f. CROSS- + BAR *v.*, partly f. prec.] **1** Mark crosswise (*with*); draw bars or stripes across. L16. **2** Put or fix a bar or bars across. E17.

crossbill /ˈkrɒsbɪl/ *n.* L17. [f. CROSS- + BILL *n.*²] Any bird of the genus *Loxia* of the finch family, occurring widely in the northern hemisphere and having mandibles that cross one another when the bill is closed.

cross-bill /ˈkrɒsbɪl/ *n.* M17. [f. CROSS- + BILL *n.*³] *Hist.* A bill filed in the Court of Chancery by a defendant against the plaintiff or other defendants in the same suit.

†**crossbite** *v.* & *n.* M16. [f. CROSS- + BITE *v.*] A *v.t.* **1** Cheat in return; dupe, deceive. M16–M19. **2** Censure bitingly or bitterly. L16–M18. B *n.* A swindle; a deception. L16–E18.

crossbow /ˈkrɒsbəʊ/ *n.* LME. [f. CROSS- + BOW *n.*¹] **1** An orig. medieval weapon for propelling missiles with great force, comprising a bow, usu. of metal, fixed to the end of a wooden stock that has a groove to hold the missile, a trigger to release it, and often a crank for drawing the cord tight. LME. **2** A man armed with a crossbow. Usu. in *pl.* L15.

Comb.: **crossbowman** = sense 2 above.

crossbred /ˈkrɒsbrɛd/ *ppl a.* & *n.* M19. [f. CROSS- + BRED *ppl a.*] A *ppl a.* Bred from parents of different breeds or varieties; (of wool) obtained from a crossbred sheep. M19. B *n.* A crossbred animal; wool from a crossbred sheep. L19.

crossbreed /ˈkrɒsbriːd/ *n.* L18. [f. CROSS- + BREED *n.*] A breed produced by crossing; an individual of such a breed.

crossbreed /ˈkrɒsbriːd/ *v.t.* Pa. t. & pple **-bred** /-brɛd/. L17. [f. CROSS- + BREED *v.*] Produce or modify by crossing different breeds, varieties, etc.

cross-check /ˈkrɒstʃɛk/ *n.* M20. [f. CROSS- + CHECK *n.*¹] A method or act of cross-checking.

cross-check /ˈkrɒstʃɛk/ *v.t.* M20. [f. CROSS- + CHECK *v.*¹] **1** In ice hockey and lacrosse, obstruct (an opponent) with the use of the length of one's stick. M20. **2** Check by reference to additional sources, calculations, etc. M20.

cross-cut /ˈkrɒskʌt/ *n.* L18. [f. CROSS- + CUT *n.*²] **1** *Mining.* A cutting made across the course of a vein or the general direction of the workings. L18. **2** A direct route going diagonally or transversely across. E19. **3** A cross-cut saw. M19. **4** A cross-section, a representative sample. M20.

cross-cut /ˈkrɒskʌt/ *a.* M17. [Partly f. the vb; partly f. CROSS- + CUT *ppl a.*] **1** Designed for cutting across. M17. **2** Cut across; having transverse cuts. M19.

1 cross-cut saw: having a handle at each end for two people to cut across the grain of timber.

cross-cut /ˈkrɒskʌt/ *v.* Infl. **-tt-**. Pa. t. & pple **-cut**. L16. [f. CROSS- + CUT *v.*] **1** *v.t.* Cut transversely. L16. **2** *v.t.* & *i. Cinemat.* Switch back and forth between (two or more sequences) in editing a film; alternate (one sequence) with another; employ this technique. M20.

crosse /krɒs/ *n.* M19. [Fr. *crosse*, OFr. *croce* bishop's crook: see CROSIER.] The stick used in lacrosse, having a curved L-shaped or triangular frame at one end with a piece of netting in the angle.

cross-head /ˈkrɒshɛd/ *n.* & *v.* E19. [f. CROSS- + HEAD *n.*] A *n.* **1** A block at the end of a piston rod of a steam engine which slides between straight guides and communicates motion to an attached connecting-rod. E19. **2** Any transverse structure at the top of a machine etc. M19. **3** A heading printed across a column or page within the text of an article. L19. B *v.t.* Provide with a printed cross-head (sense 3 above). L19.

cross-heading *n.* = CROSS-HEAD *n.* 3 L19.

crossing /ˈkrɒsɪŋ/ *n.* LME. [f. CROSS *v.* + -ING¹.] **1** The action or an act of making or marking with the sign of the cross; the action or an act of drawing lines across; striking *off* or *out* by drawing lines across. LME. **2** The action or an act of passing, lying, or placing across; the action or an act of passing in an opposite direction. LME. **3** The action or an act of thwarting; an act of resistance or opposition. L16. **4** Dishonest practice. *rare.* L16. **5a** A place at which a river or road is crossed; *esp.* a designated part of a road where crossing is facilitated. M17. **b** The intersection of two roads, two railway lines, etc., or of one with another. L17. **c** The part of a cruciform church where the transepts cross the nave. M19. **6** The action or an instance of crossbreeding. M19.

5a *pedestrian crossing, pelican crossing, zebra crossing,* etc. b *grade crossing*: see GRADE *n. level crossing*: see LEVEL *a.* 6 C. SAGAN Such crossings are about as reasonable as the mating of a man and a petunia.

Comb.: **crossing over** *Biol.* the exchange of chromosome segments between paired homologous chromosomes, resulting in a mixture of parental characters in offspring; **crossing sweeper** *Hist.* a person who sweeps a street crossing.

cross-jack /ˈkrɒsdʒak, ˈkrɒdʒɪk/ *n.* Also **cro'jack**. E17. [f. CROSS- + JACK *n.*³] A sail bent to the lower yard of a mizen-mast of a square-rigged ship; (in full *cross-jack yard*) such a yard.

crosslet /ˈkrɒslɪt/ *n.* LME. [f. CROSS *n.* + -LET, after AN *croiselete*; cf. OFr. *croisete* (mod. *croissete*).] **1** *Her.* A small cross. LME. **2** A small object in the form of a cross. LME.

1 CROSS CROSSLET.

crossleted *a.* decorated with a crosslet or crosslets E19.

crossopterygian /ˌkrɒsɒptəˈrɪdʒɪən/ *a.* & *n.* Also **C-**. M19. [f. mod.L *Crossopterygii*, *-ia* (f. Gk *krossos* tassel, (in pl.) fringe + *pterux*, *pterug-* fin + -IA²) + -AN.] A *adj.* Of, pertaining to, or designating a group of mostly extinct bony fish with fleshy lobed fins and a cranium divided into two parts, from which amphibians and other land vertebrates are thought to have evolved. M19. B *n.* A crossopterygian fish. M19.

crossover /ˈkrɒsəʊvə/ *n.* & *a.* L18. [f. *cross over* s.v. CROSS *v.*] A *n.* **1** (A) fabric having the design running across from selvage to selvage instead of lengthways. L18. **2** A wrap worn round the shoulders and crossed in front. M19. **3** A short length of track joining two adjacent lines of a railway or tramway. L19. **4** The action or process of crossing over; an instance of this, *esp.* (*Biol.*) an individual with a genetic character produced by crossing over; a chromatid resulting from crossing over. E20. **b** The process by which a piece of recorded music gains popularity (unexpectedly or through marketing) with an audience outside that usual for its particular genre or style; a song or record gaining such popularity. L20.

B *adj.* That crosses over; characterized by crossing over; having a part that crosses over. L19.

crossover distortion *Electronics*: occurring where a signal changes from positive to negative or vice versa. **crossover network** a filter in a loudspeaker unit that divides the signal and delivers different parts to bass and treble speakers etc. **crossover vote, voter, voting** *US*: switching support from the expected political party or candidate to another.

crossroad /ˈkrɒsrəʊd/ *n.* & *a.* E18. [f. CROSS- + ROAD *n.*] A *n.* **1** A road crossing another; a road joining two main roads; a byroad. E18. **2** *sing.* & (usu.) in *pl.* treated as *sing.* A place where two roads cross; *fig.* a situation in which two courses of action or two lines of development diverge; a critical turning-point in life, a career, etc. L18.

2 *dirty work at the crossroads*: see DIRTY *a.*

B *adj.* Passing by crossroads; situated at a crossroads; *fig.* (*US*) small, cheap. L18.

cross-section /krɒsˈsɛkʃ(ə)n/ *n.* & *v.* M19. [f. CROSS- + SECTION *n.*] A *n.* **1** A cut made through an object or substance, esp. through its narrow dimension; a surface exposed in this way; the area the surface has or would have; a diagram representing what such a cut would reveal. M19. **2** *fig.* A typical or representative sample, group, etc. E20. **3** *Physics.* A numerical quantity, expressed as an area, representing the likelihood that a particle will undergo a specified interaction with another particle. E20.

2 E. GRIERSON The jury, a fair cross-section of the community.

B *v.t.* Make a cross-section of; cut into a cross-section. L19.

cross-sectional *a.* L19.

crossway /ˈkrɒsweɪ/ *n.* ME. [f. CROSS- + WAY *n.*] **1** *sing.* & in *pl.* (treated as *sing.* or *pl.*). A place where two roads or paths cross. ME. **2** = CROSSROAD I. L15.

crossway /ˈkrɒsweɪ/ *adv.* & *a.* LME. [f. CROSS- + -WAY.] A *adv.* = CROSSWISE *adv.* LME. B *adj.* Placed or running across; transverse. E19.

crossways /ˈkrɒsweɪz/ *a.* & *adv.* ME. [f. CROSS- + -WAYS.] †A *adj.* = CROSSWAY *a.* Only in ME. B *adv.* = CROSSWISE *adv.* LME.

crosswise /ˈkrɒswʌɪz/ *adv.* & *a.* LME. [f. CROSS- + -WISE.] A *adv.* **1** In the form of a cross. LME. **2** Transversely, across. L16.

1 S. JOHNSON A church built crosswise. 2 F. L. WRIGHT A tremendous spaciousness . . cut up crosswise or lengthwise.

B *adj.* = CROSSWAY *a.* E20.

Crostarie /krɒsˈtɑːri/ *n. Sc.* L17. [Gael. *crostàraidh*, *-tàra* cross of gathering.] = FIERY *cross*.

crotal /ˈkrɒt(ə)l/ *n.*¹ & *a.* Also **crottle**. M18. [Gael., Ir.] (Of the golden-brown colour of) any dye-producing lichen.

crotal /ˈkrəʊt(ə)l/ *n.*² L18. [L CROTALUM or Fr. CROTALE.] A usu. small bell or rattle that wholly encloses the pellet that sounds it.

crotala *n.* pl. of CROTALUM.

crotale /ˈkrəʊt(ə)l/ *n.* M20. [Fr. f. L CROTALUM.] A small tuned cymbal; a kind of castanet or clapper; a crotalum.

crotaline /ˈkrəʊt(ə)lʌɪn/ *a.* & *n.* M19. [mod.L *Crotalinae* (see below), f. *Crotalus*, name of the genus that includes rattlesnakes, f. as CROTALUM: see -INE¹.] A *adj.* Of, pertaining to, or designating the viperid subfamily Crotalinae, which comprises the pit vipers and rattlesnakes. Cf. VIPERINE *a.* 3b. M19. B *n.* A snake of this subfamily. Cf. VIPERINE *n.* L19.

crotalum /ˈkrɒt(ə)l(ə)m, ˈkrəʊ-/ *n.* Pl. **-la** /-lə/. M18. [L f. Gk *krotalon*.] An ancient clapper or castanet whose two halves were struck together with the finger and thumb.

crotch /krɒtʃ/ *n.* M16. [Perh. ult. rel. to OFr. *croche* crosier, CROOK *n.*, but partly var. of CRUTCH *n.*] †**1** A fork used in agriculture or the garden. M–L16. †**2** = CRUTCH *n.* I. M–L16. **3** A support in the form of a stake or rod with a forked end. L16. **4** A fork of a tree or bough. L16. **5** The place where the legs join the trunk (of the human body or a garment). L16. **6** A fork of a river or road. Chiefly *US.* L17. **7** *Naut.* = CRUTCH *n.* 4. M18.

crotched *a.* (now *US*) forked L16. **crotchless** *a.* (of a garment) having a hole cut so as to leave the genitals uncovered L20.

crotchet /ˈkrɒtʃɪt/ *n.*¹ ME. [(O)Fr. *crochet* dim. of *croc* hook: see -ET¹.] **1** A hook, as an instrument or implement, or (formerly) an ornamental fastener. ME. **b** A hooklike organ or process. L17. **2** *Archit.* = CROCKET 2. LME. **3** *Mus.* The symbol for a note lasting half as long as a minim, and twice as long as a quaver, having a solid black head and a straight stem with no hook; a note of this length. LME. **4** A whimsical fancy; a perverse belief or preference, usu. about a trivial matter. L16. **5** A fanciful literary, artistic, or mechanical device. E17. **6** *Typogr.* A square bracket. *obs.* exc. *Hist.* L17.

crotche'teer *n.* a person with a crotchet, *esp.* one who obtrudes his or her crotchets in politics etc. E19. **crotchetiness** *n.* crotchety character M19. **crotchety** *a.* peevish, given to crotchets; of the nature of a crotchet: E19.

†**crotchet** *n.*² M17–L18. [f. CROTCH + -ET¹.] = CROTCH 3.

crotchet /ˈkrɒtʃɪt/ *v.* Long *rare.* L16. [f. CROTCHET *n.*¹] †**1** *v.t.* & *i. Mus.* Break up (a longer note) into crotchets. L16–E17. †**2** *v.t.* Affect with crotchets or whimsical fancies. *rare.* Only in E17. **3** *v.t. Archit.* Ornament with crockets. L19.

crotey /ˈkrəʊti/ *v.* & *n.* Long *arch.* LME. [App. f. an AN & OFr. vb f. OFr. *crote* (mod. *crotte*) dung.] A *v.i.* & *t.* Of a hare etc.: void (excrement). LME. **B** *n.* In *pl.* = CROTTELS. LME.

croton /ˈkrəʊt(ə)n/ *n.*[1] M18. [Gk *krotōn* sheep-tick (which the seeds of the croton, sense 1, resemble).] **1** Any plant of the genus *Croton* of the spurge family, comprising strong-scented tropical and subtropical herbs, shrubs, and trees, several of which yield economically important products (as cascarilla, croton oil). M18. **2** Any plant of the genus *Codiaeum* of the spurge family, comprising evergreen shrubs and trees from Asia; esp. *Codiaeum variegatum*, cultivated as a pot plant for its brilliant glossy leaves. L19.

Comb.: **croton oil** an evil-smelling oil from the seeds of the E. Indian tree *Croton tiglium*, formerly used as a violent purgative.

Croton /ˈkrəʊt(ə)n/ *n.*[2] *US.* M19. [A river near New York.] **1** In full *Croton water*. Water, esp. (orig.) water from the Croton River, utilized from 1842 to supply New York. M19. **2** *Croton bug*, = *German cockroach* s.v. GERMAN *a.*[1] M19.

crottels /ˈkrɒt(ə)lz/ *n.pl.* L16. [App. dim. of OFr. *crot(t)e*: see CROTEY, -EL[2].] The globular lumps of dung from hares etc.

crottle *n.* & *a.* var. of CROTAL *n.*[1] & *a.*

crouch /kraʊtʃ/ *n.*[1] Long *obs.* exc. *Hist.* [OE *crūć* f. L *cruc-*, CRUX.] A cross. Latterly only in *Crouchmas*, the festival of the Invention of the Cross, formerly observed on 3 May.

crouch /kraʊtʃ/ *v.* & *n.*[2] LME. [Perh. f. OFr. *crochir* be bent, f. *croche* (see CROTCH).] **A** *v.* **1** *v.i.* Of a person: stand (or sit) low with the legs bent close to the body, as for concealment or shelter or in fear; formerly also, bend low in reverence. Of an animal: stand low with bent legs and tense body, in fear or readiness to spring. LME. **2** *v.i.* Behave submissively or fawningly. E16. **3** *v.t.* Bend (the knee, one's head, etc.), esp. in a cringing way. E18.

1 OED To *cower* concerns chiefly the head and shoulders: to *crouch* affects the body as a whole. S. BECKETT He crouched over the fire trying to get warm. **crouched burial** *Archaeol.*: with the body in a crouching posture, usu. on its side. 2 SIR W. SCOTT I crouch to no one—obey no one.

B *n.* **1** An act of crouching. L16. **2** A crouching posture used at the start of a race. E20.

Comb.: **crouchback** *n.* & *a.* (*obs.* exc. *Hist.*) (*a*) *n.* (a person who has) a hunched back; (*b*) *adj.* hunchbacked; **crouch start** = sense 2 above.

crouchant *a.* crouching L16. **croucher** *n.* L16. **crouchingly** *adv.* in a crouching manner M19.

†crouched *a.* see CRUTCHED *a.*[1]

Crouch ware /ˈkraʊtʃ wɛː/ *n. phr.* L18. [Origin unkn.] Brownish salt-glazed stoneware made in Staffordshire in the early 17th cent.

croup /kruːp/ *n.*[1] ME. [(O)Fr. *croupe* f. Proto-Romance f. Gmc base rel. to CROP *n.*] The rump, the hindquarters, esp. of a horse or other beast of burden.

croup /kruːp/ *n.*[2] M18. [f. the vb.] A harsh brassy painful cough with difficult breathing (and often stridor) in a child with severe laryngitis; any respiratory infection with this symptom.

croupal, croupous, croupy *adjs.* characteristic of or accompanied by croup; affected with croup: M19.

croup /kruːp/ *v.i.* *obs.* exc. *dial.* E16. [Imit.] Give a hoarse cry; croak.

croupade /kruˈpeɪd/ *n.* M17. [Fr. f. It. *groppata* (w. assim. to Fr. *croupe* CROUP *n.*[1]), f. It. *groppa* croup.] *Horsemanship.* A single leap with the hind legs brought up under the belly. Also, a high kick with the hind legs with forelegs on the ground.

croupier /ˈkruːpɪə, -pɪeɪ/ *n.* E18. [Fr. (orig. a person who rides behind on the croup), f. as CROUP *n.*[1]: cf. -IER.] **†1** A person who stands behind a gambler to give support and advice. Only in E18. **2** A person who rakes in and pays out the money or tokens at a gaming-table. M18. **3** An assistant chairman sitting at the lower end of the table at a public dinner. L18.

†croupon *n.* LME–L18. [(O)Fr., f. as CROUP *n.*[1]: see -OON.] A croup; a person's buttocks; the hinder part of something; a crupper.

crouse /kruːs/ *a.* & *adv.* *Sc.* & *north.* ME. [Prob. f. LG or OFris.; agrees in form with LG, MLG, MHG *krus* (G *kraus*) crisp, and in sense with Du. *kroes* (f. LG) cross, annoyed, G *kraus* sullen.] **A** *adj.* **1** Touchy, captious. Formerly also, angry. ME. **2** Bold; forward, cocky; conceited. ME. **3** In good spirits; vivacious, pert; jolly. LME. **4** Cosy, comfortable. E19. **B** *adv.* Boldly, confidently; vivaciously. LME.

crousely *adv.* (*Sc.*) L16.

croustade /kruˈstɑːd/ *n.* M19. [Fr., f. OFr. *crouste* (mod. CROÛTE) or It. *crostata* tart (f. *crosta* crust).] A crisp piece of bread or pastry hollowed to receive a savoury filling.

croûte /krut/ *n.* Pl. pronounced same. E20. [Fr.: see CRUST *n.*] A crisp piece of toasted or fried bread; a croûton. See also EN CROÛTE.

croûton /ˈkruːtɒn; krutɔ̃ (*pl. same*)/ *n.* Also **crouton**. E19. [Fr., f. CROÛTE.] A small piece of toasted or fried bread served with soup or as a garnish.

crove *n.* var. of CRUIVE.

crow /krəʊ/ *n.*[1] & *a.* Also (*Sc.* & *north.*) **craw** /krɔː, krɑː/. [OE *crāwe* corresp. to OS *krāia* (Du. *kraai*), OHG *krāwa, krāja, krā* (G *Krähe*), f. WGmc base of CROW *v.*] **A** *n.* **I 1** Any of various large, mostly glossy black passerine birds of the genus *Corvus* (family Corvidae), e.g. a rook, raven, or jackdaw; *esp.* (*a*) (more fully *carrion crow*) a uniformly black bird, *Corvus corone*, of western Europe and parts of Asia; (*b*) (more fully *hooded crow*) a subspecies of *Corvus corone* having a grey mantle and underparts, found in northern and eastern Europe and parts of Asia; (*c*) (more fully *American crow*) the common crow of N. America, *Corvus brachyrhynchos*. Also, any bird of the family Corvidae (e.g. a magpie, chough, or jay), *esp.* a large black one. OE. **b** (Usu. **C-**.) *The* constellation Corvus. M17. **2** An iron bar with a curved, usu. beaklike, end for use as a lever. Now usu. *crowbar*. LME. **3** A grappling hook. *obs.* exc. *Hist.* M16. **4** A kind of door-knocker. *obs.* exc. *Hist.* L16. **5** A person who pitches sheaves to a stacker. *NZ colloq.* L19. **6** A girl or woman, *esp.* one who is old or ugly. Also *old crow*. *slang.* E20.

1 *Clark's crow, hooded crow, pied crow, rain crow, saddleback crow*, etc. **as the crow flies** in a straight line. *eat crow*: see EAT *v.* **have a crow to pick, pluck**, or **pull** have something disagreeable to settle or a fault to find *with* someone. *starve the crows*: see STARVE *v.* 5. **stone the crows** expr. surprise or disgust. *wattled crow*: see WATTLED 2. **white crow** *fig.* a rare thing or event.

II 7 (**C-**.) Pl. **-s**, same. A member of a N. American Indian people formerly occupying a region south of the Yellowstone River, Montana, and subsequently a reservation in that State; the Siouan language of this people. E19.

Comb.: **crow-bait** an old horse; old horses; *crowbar*: see sense 2 above; **crowberry** [prob. tr. G *Krähenbeere*] (the usu. black flavourless berry of) a low heathlike evergreen shrub of the genus *Empetrum* (family Empetraceae); (the berry of) a small evergreen shrub of the genus *Corema* of the same family; **crow-bill** a forceps for extracting bullets etc. from wounds; **crow-blackbird** *US* a grackle of the genus *Quiscalus*; **crow-boy**: employed to scare crows away from farmland; **crow-eater** *Austral. slang* a South Australian; **crow-flower** any of various wild flowers, *esp.* the buttercup; **crow garlic** a common wild garlic, *Allium vineale*; **crow-hop** *v.* & *n.* (*a*) *v.i.* hop like a crow with both feet at the same time; *US* (of a horse) jump with an arched back and stiffened legs; (*b*) *n.* a crow-hopping action; **crow-quill** a quill from a crow's wing, used for fine writing; a small fine pen for map drawing etc.; **crow's nest** a lookout platform high up a ship's mast etc.; **crow step** a step of a corbie-gable; **crowstepped** *a.* having corbie-steps; **crow-toe** *arch.* & *dial.* any of various wild flowers, *esp.* (*a*) a bluebell, (*b*) a buttercup (cf. CROWFOOT 1).

B *adj.* **1** *Mining.* Of ore, rock, etc.: of poor or impure quality. *Sc.* & *north.* L18. **2** (**C-**.) Of or pertaining to the Crows or their language. E19.

crow /krəʊ/ *n.*[2] Also (*Sc.* & *north.*) **craw** /krɔː, krɑː/. ME. [f. CROW *v.*] A cry (as) of a crow; the joyful cry of a baby.

crow /krəʊ/ *n.*[3] M17. [Rel. to MHG (*ge*)*kroese*, *kroes* (G *Gekröse* mesentery, calf's pluck, goose's giblets), MDu. *croos*, Du. *kroost* entrails, giblets.] The mesentery of an animal.

crow /krəʊ/ *v.i.* Also (*Sc.* & *north.*) **craw** /krɔː, krɑː/. Pa. t. **-ed**, (esp. sense 1) **crew** /kruː/. [OE *crāwan*, corresp. to OHG *krāen* (G *krähen*), f. WGmc vb of imit. origin.] **1** Of a cock: utter its characteristic loud shrill cry. OE. **2** Express gleeful triumph; exult loudly or prominently (*over*); swagger, boast. LME. **3** Give an inarticulate joyful cry. L16.

2 A. S. NEILL A public accusation might make him crow and show off what a tough guy he was. CLIVE JAMES Nor is there any reason to crow about things going wrong. 3 R. C. HUTCHINSON He was not one who smiled often or who crowed as other babies do.

crowd /kraʊd/ *n.*[1] ME. [Welsh CRWTH.] **1** = CRWTH. *obs.* exc. *Hist.* ME. **2** A fiddle. Now *dial.* E17.

crowd /kraʊd/ *n.*[2] M16. [f. CROWD *v.*[1]] **1** A number of people gathered together so as to press upon or impede each other; any large group of people in one place, *esp.* an audience, a mass of spectators. M16. **b** A group of actors representing a crowd. L19. **2** *sing.* & in *pl.* A large number *of* people or things considered collectively. E17. **3** *The* multitude, *the* masses. L17. **4** A set of associates; a set, a lot. *colloq.* M19.

2 J. B. PRIESTLEY The first to be swept away were the crowds of middle-men. 3 T. GRAY Far from the madding crowd's ignoble strife. 4 J. P. DONLEAVY The theatrical crowd he knocked around with.

Phrases: **crowd of sail** an unusual number of sails hoisted for speed. **follow the crowd** conform with the majority. **will, would pass in a crowd** is not conspicuously below the average, esp. in appearance.

Comb.: **crowd-puller** *colloq.* an event, person, or thing which attracts a large audience or mass of spectators.

crowd /kraʊd/ *v.*[1] [OE *crūdan* corresp. to MLG, MDu. *kruden* (Du. *kruien* push in a wheelbarrow).] **†1** *v.i.* Exert pressure. OE–ME. **2** *v.i.* Press on, hurry, (orig. of a ship or its crew). Now *US colloq.* OE. **3** *v.t.* Press, push, formerly esp. in a barrow. Now *US* & *dial.* ME. **4** *v.i.* Push one's way into a confined space or through a crowd. Now *rare.* LME. **5** *v.i.* Congregate closely so as to press upon one another; come or go (*in, round, upon*, etc.) in a crowd; flock, throng. LME. **6** *v.t.* Cram (things) *in* or *into* a small space or a short time; compress; pack closely together. L16. **7** *v.t.* Press closely about; hamper by pressure of numbers; come aggressively or uncomfortably close to (a person). E17. **8** *v.t.* Fill as a crowd does, occupy densely; cram *with*, fill to excess or encumbrance *with*. E17. **9** *v.t.* Approach (a specified age) closely. *US colloq.* M20.

3 O. HENRY Then official duties crowded the matter from his mind. 5 M. SPARK The girls crowded around each other. D. MAHON Everyone Crowds to the window. 6 LD MACAULAY The experience of years is crowded into hours. 7 E. J. BANFIELD Don't crowd a fellow. Go to a rock of your own. G. BOYCOTT We crowded him with as many men as we could get near the bat. 8 A. S. NEILL The poems that crowd the average school-book. H. MACMILLAN Four days .. crowded with colour and even excitement.

Phrases, & with advs. in specialized senses: **crowd (on) sail** hoist a large number of sails for speed. **crowd out** †(*a*) force out by pressure of a crowd; (*b*) exclude by crowding. **crowd the mourners** *US colloq.* exert undue pressure, hurry in an unseemly manner.

¶Rare bef. 17.

crowdedness *n.* a crowded state E19.

†crowd *v.*[2]*i.* ME–M18. [Imit.] Crow, croak, screech.

crowd /kraʊd/ *v.*[3]*i.* *obs.* exc. *dial.* LME. [f. CROWD *n.*[1]] Play a fiddle or (formerly) a crwth.

crowder /ˈkraʊdə/ *n.*[1] Now *dial.* & *Hist.* ME. [f. CROWD *n.*[1] or *v.*[3] + -ER[1].] A player on a crwth; a fiddler.

crowder /ˈkraʊdə/ *n.*[2] L16. [f. CROWD *v.*[1] + -ER[1].] A person who crowds; a member of a crowd.

crowdie /ˈkraʊdi/ *n.*[1] *Sc.* & *north.* Also **-y.** E16. [Origin unkn.] Meal and water stirred into a thick gruel; porridge.

crowdie /ˈkraʊdi, *Sc. also* ˈkrʌdi/ *n.*[2] Also **-y.** E19. [f. CRUD *n.* + -IE.] Soft cheese made from or with buttermilk or sour milk, orig. in Scotland.

crowdy *n.*[1], *n.*[2] vars. of CROWDIE *n.*[1], *n.*[2]

crowfoot /ˈkrəʊfʊt/ *n.* Pl. **-feet** /-fiːt/, in sense 1 usu. **-foots**. LME. [f. CROW *n.*[1] + FOOT *n.*] 1 Any of various wild flowers, *esp.* a buttercup or other member of the genus *Ranunculus*. LME. 2 *Naut.* A number of short lines spreading from a single eye or block. L16. 3 = CROW'S-FOOT 1. E17. 4 *Mil.* A caltrop. L17.

1 *urchin crowfoot*: see URCHIN *n.* & *a.*

crow-ˈfooted *a.* (*a*) *Sc.* having crow steps; (*b*) having crow's-feet about the eyes: E19.

†**crowl** *v.i.* E16–E18. [Imit.] Of the stomach or bowels: rumble.

crown /kraʊn/ *n.* ME. [AN *corune*, OFr. *corone* (mod. *couronne*) f. L *corona* wreath, chaplet f. Gk *korōnē* something bent (*korōnis* crown). Cf. CORONA.] **I** 1 An ornamental object worn on the head by a monarch as a symbol of sovereignty and usu. made of or adorned with precious metals and jewels. ME. 2 A (freq. idealized or imaginary) wreath or circlet worn on the head for personal adornment or as a mark of honour or victory; *transf.* & *fig.* any honourable distinction or reward given as a mark of honour or victory, a championship. ME. 3 A chief adornment; a culminating attribute, event, etc. LME. 4 The authority symbolized by a crown; a monarch's rule or sovereignty. LME. 5 *the crown*, *the Crown*, the monarch in his or her official character; the supreme governing power under a monarchical constitution. L16.

1 J. MASEFIELD The Kings go by with jewelled crowns. AV *Matt.* 27:29 When they had platted a crowne of thornes, they put it vpon his head. 2 G. B. SHAW You shall have a laurel crown of gold. Superb fighter. *Guardian* The Venezuelan .. will defend his World Boxing Association crown. 3 H. KELLER What I consider my crown of success is the happiness and pleasure that my victory has brought dear Teacher. 4 JOHN BROOKE The Crown suffered from the conflict between King and heir apparent. 5 L. STRACHEY The Crown intended to act independently of the Prime Minister. DEMESNE *of the Crown*.

II Something having a figure of a crown. 6 An ornament, figure, or sign (esp. of an inn) having the shape of a crown or depicting a crown. ME. 7 Any of various coins, orig. bearing the figure of a crown; *esp.* an English or British coin of the value of 5 shillings or (now) 25 pence; a krona, krone, or koruna of some other European countries. LME. 8 (Usu. **C-**.) (More fully *Northern Crown*) *the* constellation Corona Borealis; (more fully *Southern Crown*) *the* constellation Corona Australis. M16. 9 A size of paper orig. watermarked with a crown (now usu. 15 × 20 inches, 381 × 508 mm). E18.

6 S. PEPYS To the Crown .. and there supped. T. PARKER To be a sergeant major and have a crown on my sleeve.

III Something with the circular form of a crown or wreath. †10 A cleric's tonsure. ME–M16. 11 = CORONA 3a. M16. 12 In full *crown glass*. Lead-free glass made from alkali-lime silicates, used as an optical glass of low dispersion and formerly for windows (orig. made in circular sheets by blowing and whirling). E18. 13 = CORONA 6. M19.

IV The top of something. 14 The top of the head; the head itself. ME. 15 The top of a hat or cap. L15. 16 The rounded summit of a mountain, hill, or mound. L16. 17 The leafy head of a tree or shrub. L16. b The cluster of leaves on the top of a pineapple. L17. 18 The highest, central part of an arch or arched surface, e.g. a road with a camber; the surface of a crown green. M17. 19 The flattened or rounded roof of a tent or building. E18. 20 The top, with the ear or canons, of a bell. M18. 21 The part of a tooth which projects from the gums; an artificial structure made to cover or replace this. E19. 22 The part of a root or tuber from which the stem arises; the underground bud of a herbaceous perennial. M19. 23 The part of an anchor where the shank meets the arms. M19. 24 The part of a cut gem above the girdle. L19.

Comb. & *phrases*: **Crown Agents** a body orig. appointed by the British Government to act as commercial and financial agents in Britain for the colonies, but now offering a similar service to foreign governments and international bodies; **crown and anchor** a gambling game played with three dice each bearing a crown, an anchor, and the four card suits, and played on a board similarly marked; **crown bowler** a player of crown bowls; **crown bowling, bowls**: played on a crown green; **crown cap** a cork-lined metal cap which is crimped on to a bottle top; **Crown colony** a British colony in which the Crown has some power of legislation or appointment; **crown cork** = *crown cap* above; **crown court** (*a*) *Hist.* the court in which the criminal business of an assize was dealt with; (*b*) (with cap. initials) a court of criminal jurisdiction in England and Wales which replaced in 1971 the assizes and quarter sessions and sits in various towns; **Crown Derby** china made at Derby after *c*1784 with a crown as an additional mark; **crown ether** *Chem.* a polyether with a large molecule that is approximately flat and circular and selectively binds metal ions; **crown fire** a forest fire that spreads from treetop to treetop; **crown gall** a bacterial disease of many plants, marked by galls on the roots and lower stem; *crown glass*: see sense 12 above; **crown graft** a graft in which scions are inserted between the inner bark and the sapwood; **crown green** a bowling-green with the middle higher than the sides; **crown imperial** *Bot.* a fritillary, *Fritillaria imperialis*, native to northern India, Pakistan, Iran, and Afghanistan, having a cluster of leaves and bell-like flowers at the top of a tall, largely bare stem; **crown jewels** jewels forming part of royal regalia or associated with a royal house; *transf.* & *fig.* the most beautiful feature or possession, the most valuable asset; *slang* a man's genitals; **crown land** land belonging to the British Crown or (in parts of the Commonwealth) the Government; **crown lens**: made of crown glass and usu. forming one component of an achromatic lens; **Crown Office** (*a*) an office of the King's or Queen's Bench (now the King's or Queen's Bench Division of the High Court) dealing with criminal and ministerial business; (*b*) part of the Central Office of the High Court (orig. an office of Chancery concerned with the sealing of certain documents); **crown of thorns (starfish)** a starfish, *Acanthaster planci*, which has spines on its upper surface and feeds on coral polyps; **crown-piece** = sense 7 above; **crown prince** [tr. G *Kronprinz*, etc.] a male heir apparent to a throne; a non-reigning head of a royal house; *fig.* a likely successor in any office; **crown princess** the wife of a crown prince; a female heir to a throne; **Crown privilege** the right of the Crown and Ministers acting on its behalf to withhold a document from court on the grounds that it is in the public interest to do so; *Crown Prosecution Service*: see PROSECUTION 5; **crown roast** a roast of pork, lamb, or veal consisting of rib-pieces arranged in a circle like a crown; **crown rot** a fungus disease of rhubarb; **crown rust** a rust affecting cereals and other grasses; **crown saw**: having teeth on the edge of a hollow cylinder; **crown vetch** a trailing plant, *Coronilla varia*, of the bean family, that has pink and white flowers, native to Europe and used for ground cover in the US; **crown-wearing** *Hist.* a ceremonial appearance of a medieval monarch with his crown and regalia; **crown wheel** a gearwheel with teeth parallel to its axis, *esp.* one in the differential of a motor vehicle; *French crown*: see FRENCH *a.*; *jewel in the crown*: see JEWEL *n.* 2; *Minister of the Crown*: see MINISTER *n.* 3a; NAVAL *crown*; *obsidional crown*: see OBSIDIONAL; *Pleas of the Crown*: see PLEA *n.*; *triple crown*: see TRIPLE *a.* & *adv.*; *veneer crown*: see VENEER *n.* 5; *wear a crown*: see WEAR *v.*[1]

crownless *a.* E19. **crownlet** *n.* a little crown E19.

crown /kraʊn/ *v.*[1] ME. [AN *coruner*, OFr. *coroner* (mod. *couronner*) f. L *coronare*, f. *corona* CROWN *n.*] **I** *v.t.* 1 Place a crown or wreath on the head of. ME. 2a Invest with a regal crown; officially give (a person) the dignity of a monarch etc. Also with the title as compl. ME. b Endow with honour, dignity, plenty, or other desirable thing. Now *poet.* M16. 3 Surmount (something) *with*; occupy the top of; form a crowning ornament to. LME. b Cover as a crown does, constitute a crown for. E17. 4 Fill to overflowing. L16. 5 Put the finishing touch to, complete worthily. L16. 6 Bring to or bless with a successful outcome; be the happy fruit of. E17. 7 Adorn the surface of (something) *with* what is beautiful, rich, or splendid. L17. 8 Hit (a person) on the head. *colloq.* M18. 9 *Draughts.* Make (a piece) a king by placing another on top of it. M19. 10 *Dentistry.* Protect the remains of (a tooth) by fixing an artificial crown on to it. L19.

2a E. PERRONET To crown Him Lord of All. *fig.*: AV *Ps.* 8:5 Thou .. hast crowned him with glory and honour. b AV *Ecclus* 19:5 He that resisteth pleasures, crowneth his life. 3 T. RICKMAN The walls are crowned by a parapet. E. WAUGH A brimless top-hat crowned his venerable head. S. PLATH Doctor Gordon's private hospital crowned a grassy rise. *Adweek* (*US*) One Florida bar is serving a shot of pepper vodka spiked with horseradish and crowned with either a clam or an oyster. 5 W. IRVING A bottle of wine to crown the repast. **crown all** end with something that confirms and surpasses everything previous, esp. bad luck. 6 E. PEACOCK Success did not immediately crown his efforts.

II *v.i.* 11 Rise to a rounded summit, arch. M18. 12 *Med.* Of a baby's head in labour: fully appear in the vaginal opening prior to emerging, without receding between contractions. M20.

crown /kraʊn/ *v.*[2]*t.* *obs.* exc. *dial.* E17. [f. CROWNER *n.*[2]] Hold a coroner's inquest on.

crownal /ˈkraʊn(ə)l/ *n. arch.* E16. [By-form of CORONAL *n.*] = CORONAL *n.* 1, 2.

crownal /ˈkraʊn(ə)l/ *a. rare.* M16. [By-form of CORONAL *a.*] = CORONAL *a.*

crownation /kraʊˈneɪʃ(ə)n, kruː-/ *n. obs.* exc. *dial.* M16. [By-form of CORONATION w. assim. to *crown*.] = CORONATION 1.

crowned /kraʊnd/ *a.* ME. [f. CROWN *n.*, *v.*[1]: see -ED[2], -ED[1].] 1 That has been crowned. ME. 2 Surmounted by a crown; headed by a monarch. LME. †3 Consummate, perfect; sovereign. LME–M17. 4 Brimming, abundant, bounteous. Long *rare.* E17. 5 Having a crown or top (of a specified description); crested. M17.

1 **crowned head** a king, a queen. 5 **crowned crane** either of two African cranes of the genus *Balearica*, with prominent crests, *B. paronina* of central Africa and *B. regulorum* of southern Africa; also called *Kavirondo crane*. **crowned pigeon** each of three large pigeons with ornate crests, of the genus *Goura*, native to New Guinea and adjacent islands; also called *goura* (*Victoria crowned pigeon*: see VICTORIA 6).

crowner /ˈkraʊnə/ *n.*[1] LME. [f. CROWN *v.*[1] + -ER[1].] 1 A person who crowns someone or something. LME. 2 A thing that crowns all. *US.* E19. 3 A fall in which the head is struck. M19.

crowner /ˈkraʊnə, ˈkruː-/ *n.*[2] Now *dial.*, *arch.*, & *joc.* LME. [By-form of CORONER w. assim. to *crown*.] 1 = CORONER 1. LME. 2 A commander of troops from a county, a colonel. *Sc. obs.* exc. *Hist.* L16.

†**crownet** *n.* LME. [By-form of CORONET *n.*, CRONET.] 1 = CORONET *n.* 1, 2. LME–M19. 2 = CORONET *n.* 4. E17–E18.

crowning /ˈkraʊnɪŋ/ *a.* E17. [f. CROWN *v.*[1] + -ING[2].] 1 That crowns, that bestows a crown. *rare.* E17. 2 Forming the crown or acme; consummating; highest, most perfect. M17.

2 **crowning glory** the most beautiful feature or possession, the greatest achievement; *spec.* a woman's hair.

crow's-foot /ˈkrəʊzfʊt/ *n.* Also **crowsfoot**. Pl. **-feet** /-fiːt/. LME. [f. CROW *n.*[1] + -'S[1] + FOOT *n.*] 1 A small wrinkle at the outer corner of the eye. Usu. in *pl.* LME. †2 *Naut.* = CROWFOOT 2. E17–E19. 3 *Mil.* A caltrop, = CROWFOOT 4. M17. 4 In *pl.* Numerous small creases or wrinkles in a fabric. M20.

crow's-footed *a.* having crow's-feet about the eyes M19.

†**croy** *n.* var. of CRUE.

croze /krəʊz/ *n.* E17. [Perh. f. Fr. *creux*, *creuse*, OFr. *crues*, *cros* hollow.] 1 A groove in the end of a stave of a cask to receive the edge of the head. E17. 2 A cooper's tool for making such grooves. M19.

croze /krəʊz/ *v.t.* M19. [f. prec. or Fr. *creuser*, OFr. *croser* hollow out, f. as prec.] Make a croze in.

crozier *n.* var. of CROSIER.

cru /kry (*pl. same*), kruː/ *n.* & *a.* Also **crû**. E19. [Fr., f. *crû* pa. pple of *croître* grow.] (The grade or quality of wine produced in) a French vineyard or wine-producing region; (designating) French wine of a specified quality.

P. V. PRICE Just below the classed growths come the *crus bourgeois* .. then the *crus artisans*. **cru classé** /klase, 'klaseɪ/, pl. ***-s -s*** (pronounced same) [= classified] = *classed growth* s.v. CLASS *v.* 3. ***grand cru*** /grɑ̃, grand/ (pl. ***grands crus*** /grɑ̃ kry/, ***grand crus*** /grand 'kru:z/) [= great] (designating) a wine of superior quality. PREMIER CRU.

crub /krʌb/ *n.* Long *obs.* exc. *dial.* M16. [Metathetic var.] = CURB *n.*

crubeen /krʊ'bi:n, 'kru:bi:n/ *n. Anglo-Ir.* M19. [Ir. *crúibín* dim. of *crúb* claw, hoof, paw.] The foot of an animal; *esp.* a (cooked) pig's trotter.

cruces *n.pl.* see CRUX.

cruche /kru:ʃ/ *n.* M19. [Fr. = pitcher.] = CRUSE.

crucial /'kru:ʃ(ə)l/ *a.* E18. [Fr., f. L *cruc-*, *crux* cross: see -IAL. In sense 2 f. *instantia crucis* (Bacon) crucial instance.] 1 Chiefly *Anat.* Of the form of a cross, cruciate. Now *rare.* E18. 2 That finally decides between hypotheses; relating or leading to decision between hypotheses; decisive; critical; *colloq.* very important. M19. b Excellent. *slang.* L20.

2 J. MARTINEAU Crucial experiments for the verification .. of his theory. DAY LEWIS The most crucial and agonising decisions I have been faced with have arisen from personal relationships. G. GORDON Did it encourage their secretaries and junior executives to feel they belonged to some crucial organization?

cruci'ality *n.* M20. **crucially** *adv.* L19. **crucialness** *n.* L20.

crucian /'kru:ʃ(ə)n/ *n.* M18. [f. alt. of LG *karus(s)e*, *karutze* (G *Karausche*) ult. f. as CORACINE: see -AN.] More fully *crucian carp.* A European cyprinid fish, *Carassius carassius*, with an olive green or reddish-brown back, paler sides, and bright reddish-bronze fins.

†**cruciat** *n.* see CRUSADE *n.*

cruciate /'kru:ʃɪət, -eɪt/ *n.* & *a.* L17. [med.L *cruciatus*, f. L *cruc-*, *crux* cross: see -ATE[2].] *Anat., Bot.,* & *Zool.* A *n.* †1 A cross-shaped incision. Only in L17. 2 A cruciate ligament. L20.

B *adj.* Cross-shaped; in the form of a cross. E19.

cruciate ligament either of two ligaments in the knee-joint which cross each other and connect the femur and tibia.

cruciate /'kru:ʃɪeɪt/ *v.t. arch.* Pa. pple †**-ate** (earlier), **-ated.** LME. [Orig. pa. pple, f. L *cruciatus* pa. pple of *cruciare* torture, f. *cruc-*, *crux* cross: see -ATE[3]. Sense 2 is f. eccl.L.] 1 Torture; torment; excruciate. LME. †2 Crucify. M16–M17.

cruciation /kru:ʃɪ'eɪʃ(ə)n/ *n.* Long *rare.* LME. [OFr., or eccl.L *cruciatio(n-)*, f. as prec.: see -ATION.] Torture; torment.

crucible /'kru:sɪb(ə)l/ *n.* & *v.* LME. [med.L *crucibulum* night-lamp, crucible, f. L *cruc-*, *crux* cross.] A *n.* 1 A melting-pot, usu. of earthenware, for metals etc. LME. b A hollow or basin for collecting molten metal etc. at the bottom of a furnace. M19. 2 *fig.* A place or occasion of severe test or trial. M17. B *v.t.* Put into or melt in a crucible. *rare.* L18.

crucifer /'kru:sɪfə/ *n.* M16. [Chr.L, f. L *cruc-*, *crux* cross: see -FER.] 1 *Eccl.* A cross-bearer in processions. M16. 2 *Bot.* A cruciferous plant. M19.

cruciferous /kru:'sɪf(ə)rəs/ *a.* M17. [f. as prec. + -OUS.] 1 Bearing, wearing, or adorned with a cross. M17. 2 *Bot.* Of, pertaining to, or characteristic of the family Cruciferae, which comprises plants having flowers with four equal petals arranged crosswise (as cabbage, mustard, cress, stock, etc.). M19.

crucified /'kru:sɪfʌɪd/ *a.* & *n.* ME. [f. CRUCIFY + -ED[1].] A *adj.* That has been crucified; nailed or otherwise fastened to a cross. ME. B *n. the Crucified*, Jesus Christ. M16.

crucifix /'kru:sɪfɪks/ *n.* ME. [(O)Fr. f. eccl.L *crucifixus* f. L *cruci fixus* fixed to a cross: cf. CRUCIFY.] †1 *the crucifix*, Jesus on the Cross. ME–M17. 2 A model, figure, or image of (Jesus on) the Cross. ME. 3 *Gymnastics.* A position in exercises on parallel rings, in which the body is held rigid with arms stretched horizontally. M20.

crucifixion /kru:sɪ'fɪkʃ(ə)n/ *n.* LME. [eccl.L *crucifixio(n-)*, f. *crucifix-* pa. ppl stem of *crucifigere* CRUCIFY: see -ION.] 1 The action or an act of crucifying or putting to death on a cross; *spec.* (C-) the crucifying of Jesus. LME. b A picture or other representation of the Crucifixion of Jesus. M19. 2 The action or an act of crucifying or mortifying passions, sins, the flesh, etc. E18.

cruciform /'kru:sɪfɔ:m/ *a.* M17. [f. L *cruc-*, *crux* cross + -I- + -FORM.] Cross-shaped; in the form of a cross.

A. W. CLAPHAM These .. churches .. show a highly developed plan which is sometimes cruciform.

crucify /'kru:sɪfʌɪ/ *v.t.* ME. [(O)Fr. *crucifier* f. Proto-Romance alt. of eccl.L *crucifigere*, f. L *cruci figere* fix to a cross: see CRUX, FIX *v.*] 1 Put to death by nailing or otherwise fastening to a cross (an ancient mode of capital punishment, considered by the Greeks and Romans to be especially ignominious). ME. 2 Mortify, destroy the power of, (passions, sins, the flesh etc.). ME. 3 Cause extreme mental or (now less commonly) physical pain to; torment; persecute. E17.

3 H. ROBBINS Somebody has to be held up before the stockholders and crucified so that they can say: 'See, it was all his fault. He was to blame!' *Listener* He would be severely beaten up, then subjected to some crucifying punishment and, if that did not teach him, very probably executed.

crucifier *n.* ME.

cruciverbalist /kru:sɪ'və:b(ə)lɪst/ *n.* L20. [f. L *crucis*, *crux* cross + *verbum* word: see VERBALIST.] An enthusiast for crossword puzzles; a compiler or solver of crossword puzzles.

cruck /krʌk/ *n.* Also (now *dial.*) **crock** /krɒk/. L16. [Prob. var. of CROOK *n.*] Either of a pair of curved timbers, forming with other pairs the framework of a house.

crud /krʌd/ *n.* Also (*US slang*) **crut** /krʌt/. LME. [Earlier form of CURD *n.*] I 1 See CURD *n.* LME. II 2 Filth, excrement; undesirable foreign matter; *fig.* nonsense, rubbish. *slang* (orig. *US*). M20. 3 Disease, *esp.* venereal or skin disease; any horrible disease. *slang* (orig. *US Army*). M20. 4 A despicable or undesirable person or thing. *slang* (orig. *US*). M20.

crud *v.* see CURD *v.*

crudded *a.* see CURDED.

cruddle *v.* see CURDLE *v.*

cruddy /'krʌdi/ *a.* LME. [Earlier form of CURDY *a.*] 1 See CURDY *a.* LME. 2 Filthy, dirty; unpleasant, unsavoury. *slang* (orig. *US*). M20.

crude /kru:d/ *a.* & *n.* LME. [L *crudus* raw, rough, cruel.] A *adj.* I 1 In the natural or raw state; not changed by any process or preparation; not manufactured, refined, tempered, etc. LME. †b *spec.* Of food: uncooked. M16–L18. c Designating the insoluble fibre left when vegetable matter is boiled alternately in dilute acids and alkalis, corresponding roughly to its indigestible part. L19. 2 Of bodily humours, secretions, etc.: not pure, unnatural, morbid. Of food in the stomach: undigested, not fully digested. *arch.* LME. †b Characterized by or affected with indigestion. Only in 17. 3 Of fruit: unripe; sour. *arch.* M16. 4 Of a disease etc.: in an early or undeveloped stage. Now *rare* or *obs.* M17.

1 G. RAWLINSON Sometimes the crude and the burnt brick were used in alternate layers. **crude oil** unrefined petroleum. *crude turpentine*: see TURPENTINE *n.* 1.

II *fig.* 5 Not completely thought out or worked up; lacking finish or maturity of treatment; roughly or inexpertly planned, executed, or made. E17. 6 Rude, blunt, rough; unrefined; lacking subtlety or sophistication; unmitigated; brutally plain; characterized by coarseness of thought, feeling, action, or character. M17. 7 *Gram.* (Of a word) uninflected; being or forming the base or stem which undergoes inflection. Now *rare* or *obs.* E19. 8 *Statistics.* Unadjusted; not corrected by reference to modifying circumstances. L19.

5 DISRAELI The crude opinions of an unpractised man. J. M. MURRY A fair example of Keats' poetry at the beginning of the four years—crude and naïve, but spontaneous in feeling. C. G. SELIGMAN Their dwellings are crude semi-circular shelters of branches. 6 R. LYND The humour was crude; but it went home to the honest Victorian heart. C. BROWN I knew I was kind of crude, right off the streets of Harlem. ANNE STEVENSON Windless gardens / walled to protect eccentric vegetation / from a crude climate.

B *n.* Crude oil. L19.

crudely *adv.* M17. **crudeness** *n.* M16.

†**crudelity** *n.* LME–E18. [OFr. *crudelitie* or L *crudelitas* CRUELTY.] = CRUELTY.

crudify /'kru:dɪfʌɪ/ *v.t.* L19. [f. CRUDE *a.* + -FY.] Make (more) crude.

crudifi'cation *n.* E20.

crudités /krydite, 'kru:dɪteɪ/ *n.pl.* M20. [Fr.: see next.] Mixed raw vegetables as an hors d'oeuvre.

crudity /'kru:dɪti/ *n.* LME. [(O)Fr. *crudité* or L *cruditas*, f. *crudus*: see CRUDE, -ITY.] I 1 Impurity, unnaturalness, or morbidity of bodily humours, secretions, etc.; in *pl.*, impure etc. bodily humours. Also, the state of being undigested or indigestible in the stomach; undigested or indigestible matter; indigestion. *arch.* LME. 2 The state or quality of being raw, unprocessed, unrefined, untempered, etc., or (*arch.*) unripe or sour; an instance of this; in *pl.* also, raw or (*arch.*) unripe products or substances. E17. 3 The early or undeveloped stage of a disease etc. Now *rare* or *obs.* E18.

II *fig.* 4 A crude idea, statement, literary work, etc.; the state or quality of being crude in planning, execution, thought, expression, action, etc. M17.

4 ADDISON This Author, in the last of his Crudities, has amassed together a Heap of Quotations. G. B. SHAW Beside themselves by the crudity of his notions of government.

crue /kru:/ *n. Sc.* & *dial.* Also **crew, croo,** †**cro(y).** ME. [Gael. *crò*, Ir. *cró* sheepfold, pen.] 1 = CRUIVE 1. ME. 2 A dam or other structure to protect a river-bank. *Sc.* E16. 3 = CRUIVE 2, 3. M16.

cruel /krʊəl/ *a., n., adv.,* & *v.* ME. [(O)Fr., f. L *crudelis* rel. to *crudus*: see CRUDE.] A *adj.* Compar. **-l(l)er**, superl. **-l(l)est.** 1 Disposed to inflict suffering; having or showing indifference to or pleasure in another's pain; merciless; pitiless; hard-hearted. ME. 2 Painful; distressing; *colloq.* difficult to bear, hard. ME. †3 Fierce; savage. ME–L17. †4 Severe; strict; rigorous. ME–L17.

1 S. JOHNSON The meanest and cruelest of human beings. H. JAMES It was cruel to bewilder her. E. O'BRIEN I could feel her cruel eyes on me. 2 SWIFT I have got a cruel cold, and staid within all this day. A. N. WILSON She had died .. with cruel and unannounced suddenness.

B *absol.* as *n.* A cruel person. Now *arch.* & *poet.* LME.

POPE Canst thou, oh cruel, unconcerned survey Thy lost Ulysses on this signal day?

C *adv.* Cruelly; distressingly; exceedingly, very. *obs.* exc. *dial.* L16.

D *v.t.* Infl. **-l(l)-.** Spoil; destroy all chance of success with. *Austral. slang.* M20.

cruellie *n.* (*colloq.*) a cruel joke, remark, comment, etc. M20. **cruelly** *adv.* in a cruel manner; to a cruel degree; excessively: ME. **cruelness** *n.* (*rare*) ME.

cruelty /'krʊəlti/ *n.* ME. [OFr. *crualté* (mod. *cruauté*) f. Proto-Romance var. of L *crudelitas*, f. *crudelis*: see prec., -ITY.] 1 The quality of being cruel, disposition to inflict suffering, delight in or indifference to another's pain, mercilessness, pitilessness, hard-heartedness, esp. as exhibited in action. Also, an instance of this. ME. †2 Severity (of pain); strictness; rigour. ME–M17.

1 *mental cruelty*: see MENTAL *a.*[1] *Theatre of Cruelty*: see THEATRE *n.*

Comb.: **cruelty man** *colloq.* an officer of the National Society for the Prevention of Cruelty to Children, the Royal Society for the Prevention of Cruelty to Animals, or a similar organization.

†**cruentous** *a. rare.* M17–L19. [f. L *cruentus* bloody + -OUS.] Bloody, mixed with blood.

cruet /ˈkruːɪt/ *n.* ME. [AN dim. of OFr. *crue* f. OS *krūka* (Du. *kruik*) = OE *crūce*, MHG *krūche* (G *Krauche*) rel. to CROCK *n.*[1]] 1 *Eccl.* A small vessel to hold wine or water for use in the celebration of the Eucharist etc. ME. 2 Formerly, any small bottle or vial for liquids. Now *spec.* a small stoppered glass bottle etc. for vinegar, oil, etc., for the table; (in extended use) a caster for holding salt, pepper, etc. (usu. in *pl.*, such casters with or without a vinegar bottle etc.); also, (in full *cruet-stand*) a stand for cruets. LME.

2 T. PYNCHON Tall cruets of pale banana syrup to pour oozing over banana waffles.

cruise /kruːz/ *n.* E18. [f. the vb.] 1 A voyage in which a ship sails to and fro over a particular region, esp. for the protection of shipping or for pleasure; a sail for pleasure making for no particular place or calling at a series of places. E18. 2 *transf.* A similar journey by land or air; a journey, or part of a journey, at cruising speed. M18. 3 *Forestry.* A survey or estimate of the amount of timber in a particular area. Chiefly *US.* E20. 4 In full *cruise missile.* A low-flying missile carrying a warhead, which is guided continuously to its target by computer. M20.

Comb.: **cruise control** (a device providing) the facility for maintaining a motor vehicle at a predetermined constant speed without use of the accelerator pedal; **cruise liner** a liner designed for holiday cruises; *cruise missile*: see sense 4 above; **cruise ship** = *cruise liner* above; **cruiseway** an inland waterway intended chiefly for pleasure cruising; **cruisewear** clothes suitable for wearing on a holiday cruise.

cruise /kruːz/ *v.* M17. [Prob. f. Du. *kruisen* to cross, f. *kruis* CROSS *n.*] 1 *v.i.* & *t.* Sail to and fro (over), esp. for the protection of shipping or for pleasure; sail for pleasure making for no particular place or calling at a series of places. M17. 2 *v.i.* & *t. transf.* Walk or travel about making for no particular place or calling at a series of places (in); *esp.* (of a vehicle or driver) drive around at random, esp. slowly when patrolling, looking for passengers, etc.; walk or drive around looking for amusement, a sexual partner, etc. L17. 3 *v.i.* & *t. Forestry.* Search (forest land) for saleable timber; search for (such timber). (Earlier in CRUISER 2.) Chiefly *US.* E20. 4 *v.i.* (Of an aircraft, motor vehicle, etc.) travel comfortably and economically at less than top speed; *transf.* & *fig.* move at a comfortable speed, progress easily. E20.

1 J. CONRAD The *Amelia* was cruising off the peninsula. *Nature* He cruised the waters of Newfoundland and Northern Labrador in a small sailboat and in a kayak .. on vacations with his family. 2 A. HAILEY She continued to cruise the district in her sports convertible. H. CARPENTER The habit of 'cruising'—picking up boys for casual sex. *Times* As the taxi drivers cruise Islamic streets, they listen to cassettes of the latest American disco hits. 4 C. A. LINDBERGH If the *Spirit of St. Louis* can cruise at 1750 r.p.m. with this load, I have *more* than enough fuel to reach Paris. *Which?* Even on motorways they will cruise happily at 70 mph. *Times* Prideaux Boy cruised up to the leaders on the home turn.

Comb.: **cruising radius, range**, the maximum distance that the fuel capacity of a ship or aircraft will allow it to travel and return at cruising speed; **cruising speed** the best economic travelling speed for a ship, aircraft, or vehicle.

cruiser /ˈkruːzə/ *n.* L17. [Du. *kruiser*, f. *kruisen*: see prec.] 1 A ship that cruises, formerly *esp.* a privateer. Now, a high-speed warship less heavily armed than a battleship. L17. b A yacht constructed or adapted for cruising; a motor vessel designed for pleasure cruises. L19. 2 *Forestry.* a A person who searches forest land for saleable timber. Chiefly *US.* L19. b A long-legged boot of a type worn by cruisers for timber. *US.* E20. 3 In some science fiction: an aircraft, a spacecraft. E20. 4 A police patrol car. *N. Amer.* E20. 5 A person who walks or drives around looking for amusement, a sexual partner, etc. E20. 6 A person sailing on a pleasure cruise. M20.

1 *battle-cruiser*: see BATTLE *n.* b *cabin cruiser*: see CABIN *n. through-deck cruiser*: see THROUGH- *comb. form.*

Comb.: **cruiserweight** (of) a boxing weight, equivalent to light heavyweight; (a boxer) of this weight.

cruisie *n.* var. of CRUSIE.

cruive /kruːv/ *n.* Orig. & chiefly *Sc.* Also **croove**; **crove** /krəʊv/. ME. [Prob. f. CRUE w. parasitic *v*, but cf. CORF.] 1 A coop of wickerwork or spars placed in tideways etc. to trap salmon or other fish. ME. 2 A hovel, a hut, a cabin. *Sc.* L15. 3 A pen for livestock; *esp.* a pigsty. *Sc.* L16.

†crull *a.* Only in ME. [MDu. *krul* rel. to MLG *krus* crisp, curly.] Curly.

¶The base of CURL(ED).

†crulled *a.* see CURLED.

cruller /ˈkrʌlə/ *n. N. Amer.* E19. [Du. *kruller*, f. *krullen* to curl.] A small cake made of dough containing eggs, butter, sugar, etc., twisted or curled and deep-fried until crisp.

crum *n.*[1] & *v.*[1] see CRUMB *n.* & *v.*[1]

crum *n.*[2] see CRUMBS.

crum /krʌm/ *a.* & *v.*[2]*t.* Long *obs.* exc. *Sc.* & *north.* Also **crumb**. [OE *crumb* = OFris., OS *krumb*, OHG *krump*, *krumb-* (G *krumm*), f. WGmc var. of base of CRAMP *n.*[1]] (Make) crooked or curved.

crumb /krʌm/ *n.* & *v.*[1] Also (earlier, now *rare*) **crum**. [OE *cruma* = MDu. *crūme* (Du. *kruim*), MLG, MDu. *crōme*, MHG, G *Krume*. The parasitic *b* appears in 16: cf. *dumb*, *thumb*.] A *n.* 1 A small particle; *esp.* a small fragment of bread, cake, etc., such as breaks off by rubbing etc. OE. b In soil, a more or less spheroidal compound particle. Cf. *crumb structure* below. E20. c In rayon manufacture, a particle of cellulose. E20. 2 The soft inner part of (a loaf, roll, or slice of) bread. LME. 3 *fig.* A very small particle or portion of something immaterial; an atom; a scrap. (Foll. by *of*.) M16. 4 A body-louse. *US slang.* M19. b A lousy or filthy person; an objectionable, worthless, or insignificant person. *slang* (orig. *US*). E20.

1 J. FOWLES He brings me food, but I have touched *not one crumb.* **gather, pick, up one's crumbs** (*obs.* exc. *dial.*) recover strength or health; improve in condition. 3 T. D'URFEY To beg Some Crumbs of Comfort. 4b H. M. RIDEOUT A couple of crumbs want to kill you.

Comb.: **crumb-bum** *slang* = sense 4b above; **crumb structure** the (porous) structure or condition of soil when its particles are largely aggregated into crumbs (sense 1b).

B *v.* 1 *v.t.* Break into crumbs or small fragments. LME. †2 *v.i.* Fall into crumbs; crumble. M16–E19. 3 *v.t.* Thicken or cover with crumbs. L16.

1 H. JAMES The way he crumbed up his bread. 3 BUNYAN A Dish of Milk well Crumbed.

crumblet *n.* (*rare*) a little crumb E17.

crumb *a.* & *v.*[2] var. of CRUM *a.* & *v.*[2]

crumble /ˈkrʌmb(ə)l/ *v.* & *n.* Also **†crim-**. LME. [Prob. repr. an OE vb, ult. f. same Gmc base as CRUMB *n.*: see -LE[3].] A *v.t.* & *i.* Break or fall into crumbs, particles, or fragments, (*lit.* & *fig.*); disintegrate; (cause to) go to pieces. LME.

EVELYN Marbles with their deepest inscriptions crumble away. D. C. PEATTIE The termites live on the Joshua tree, .. crumbling the fortress from within. G. SWIFT My father did not crumble at my mother's death. *the way the cookie crumbles*: see COOKIE *n.*[1] 1.

B *n.* 1 A crumb, a particle, a fragment. *rare.* L16. 2 Crumbly or crumbled substance. *rare* in *gen.* sense. M19. 3 Flour, fat, and sugar etc. mixed to a crumbly consistency, usu. topping cooked fruit; a dish of this. M20.

crumbling *n.* (*a*) the action of the vb; (*b*) in *pl.*, crumbled particles, debris: M17.

crumbly /ˈkrʌmbli/ *a.* & *n.* As n. also **crumblie**. E16. [Orig. f. CRUMB *n.* + -LY[1]; later f. CRUMBLE *v.* + -Y[1].] A *adj.* †1 Consisting of crumbs; crumbed. E16–E17. 2 Liable to crumble, friable. M18. B *n.* A person considered very old or senile, esp. by teenagers. Cf. WRINKLY *n. slang* (*derog.*). L20.

crumbliness *n.* E19.

crumbs /krʌmz/ *n.* & *int.* Also **crums**; (as n.) **crum**. L19. [Alt. of CHRIST.] A *n. by crumbs*, = sense B below. L19. B *int.* Expr. astonishment, consternation, or dismay. L19.

crumby /ˈkrʌmi/ *a.* Also (earlier, now freq. in sense 4) **crummy**. M16. [f. CRUMB *n.* + -Y[1].] †1 Crumbly. M16–E18. 2a Of the nature of the crumb of bread. L16. b Full of crumbs; scattered or covered with crumbs. M18. 3 Plump; comely; rich. *arch. slang.* E18. 4 Lousy, filthy, dirty, untidy; inferior, shoddy, distasteful. *slang.* M19.

crumbiness, crumminess *n.* M20.

crumen /ˈkruːmɛn/ *n.* L19. [L *crumena* purse.] *Zool.* The suborbital gland in certain deer and antelopes, which secretes a waxy substance.

crumhorn *n.* var. of KRUMMHORN.

crummie /ˈkrʌmi/ *n. Sc.* & *north.* Also **-y**. E18. [f. CRUM *a.* + -IE, -Y[6].] A cow with crooked horns; (a name for) any cow.

crummy /ˈkrʌmi/ *n.*[1] *N. Amer. slang.* E20. [f. CRUMBY *a.*] = CABOOSE 3. Also, an old or converted vehicle for transporting workmen etc.

crummy *n.*[2] var. of CRUMMIE.

crummy *a.* see CRUMBY.

†crump *n.*[1] M17. [f. CRUMP *a.*[1]] 1 A hump on the back. *rare.* Only in M17. 2 A humpbacked person. L17–M18.

crump /krʌmp/ *n.*[2] M19. [f. CRUMP *v.*[2]] 1 A hard abrupt hit. *colloq.* & *dial.* M19. 2 (The sound of) the explosion of a heavy shell or bomb; a shell or bomb that explodes heavily. *Army slang.* E20. 3 A violent burst in the floor, walls, or ceiling of a mine. E20.

crump /krʌmp/ *a.*[1] *obs.* exc. *dial.* [OE *crump* (= OHG *krumpf*) by-form, prob. intensive, of *crumb* CRUM *a.*] Esp. of the body: crooked.

crump /krʌmp/ *a.*[2] *Sc.* & *north.* L18. [By-form of CRIMP *a.*] = CRIMP *a.* 1.

crump /krʌmp/ *v.*[1]*i.* & *t. obs.* exc. *dial.* ME. [f. CRUMP *a.*[1] Cf. CRIMP *v.*[1]] Bend into a curve; crook; curl up.

crump /krʌmp/ *v.*[2] M17. [Imit.] 1 *v.t.* & *i.* Esp. of a horse or pig: eat with a muffled crunch. M17. 2 *v.i.* Of snow, snow-covered ground: crunch dully under the feet. L18. 3 *v.t.* & *i.* Chiefly *Cricket.* Strike hard and abruptly. L19. 4 *Army slang.* a *v.t.* & *i.* Bombard with or fire heavy shells or bombs. E20. b *v.i.* Explode with a crump. E20.

crumper *n.* (*colloq.* & *dial.*) a large heavy person or thing; a large specimen of its kind: M19.

crumpet /ˈkrʌmpɪt/ *n.* L17. [Origin uncertain: perh. conn. w. *crumb* CRUM *v.*[2]] †1 A thin griddle-cake. L17–M19. 2 A soft cake made with flour and yeast and cooked on a griddle or other hot surface, now usu. of a type intended for toasting and eating with butter etc. M18. 3 The head. Esp. in *barmy in* or *on the crumpet*, wrong in the head, mad. *slang.* L19. 4 *old crumpet*: used as a familiar form of address. *slang.* E20. 5 A sexually attractive woman; women collectively; sexual intercourse with a woman. *slang.* Freq. considered *offensive.* M20.

5 **bit, piece, of crumpet** a (desirable) woman.

crumple /ˈkrʌmp(ə)l/ *n.* L16. [f. the vb. Cf. CRIMPLE *n.*] A crushed fold, a wrinkle.

†crumple *a.* (*attrib.*) ME–M19. [f. the vb.] Crumpled. Usu. in *comb.*, as *crumple-horned* adj.

crumple /ˈkrʌmp(ə)l/ *v.* ME. [f. CRUMP *v.*[1] or *a.*[1] + -LE[3]. Cf. CRIMPLE *v.*] I *v.t.* 1 Make crooked, bend together, contort, now esp. by crushing. ME. 2 Crush into irregular creases; crush together or *up* into a creased state; ruffle, wrinkle, crinkle. M16. 3 *fig.* Cause to collapse or give way; deprive of strength or energy. Also foll. by *up.* M19.

2 LYTTON Don't crumple that scarf. M. SHADBOLT To crumple the page into a ball and throw it away. 3 R. KIPLING For the sickness gets in as the liquor dies out, An' it crumples the young British soldier.

II *v.i.* 4 Shrivel up or *up*; become crooked or bent together, now esp. by crushing; become creased, wrinkle, crinkle. LME. 5 *fig.* Collapse, give way; lose strength or energy. Also foll. by *up.* L19.

Comb.: **crumple zone** an area of a motor vehicle designed to crumple and absorb impact.

crumpled *a.* that has been crumpled; *spec.* (of the horns of cattle) bent spirally, curly: ME. **crumpler** *n.* (*a*) a person who or thing which causes crumpling; (*b*) a fall by a horse and rider in which both are doubled up: M19. **crumply** *a.* M19.

crums *n.* & *int.* var. of CRUMBS.

crunch /krʌn(t)ʃ/ *n.* & *a.* M19. [f. the vb.] **A** *n.* **1** An act or the action of crunching; a crunching sound. M19. **2** A crisis; a crucial moment; a decisive event; a showdown. Also, the main problem, a sticking-point. M20.

1 E. K. KANE Listening to the half-yielding crunch of the ice. S. W. BAKER The hippo . . killed him by one crunch. 2 W. S. CHURCHILL At the crunch he was sure he could count on his influence. J. I. M. STEWART Wouldn't Tony, in a crunch, do as you tell him? *Irish Times* The real crunch—a problem which can be solved only through pragmatic global politics. **when it comes to the crunch, when the crunch comes** when it comes to the point, in a showdown.

B *attrib.* or as *adj.* Critical, decisive, crucial. L20.

G. BOYCOTT The crunch period was approaching fast; at lunch there were only eleven overs to go before the new ball was due. R. D. LAING The first, decisive, crunch decision.

crunch /krʌn(t)ʃ/ *v.* E19. [Var. of CRANCH *v.* w. assim. to *munch*, *crush*.] **1** *v.t.* & *i.* Crush with the teeth, esp. noisily; chew or bite with a crushing noise. E19. **2** *v.i.* Make or move with a crunching sound; be crushed or ground under foot etc. with a crunching sound. E19. **3** *v.t.* Cause to make a crunching sound; crush or grind under foot etc. with a crunching sound. M19.

1 H. WILLIAMSON She ate her prey, holding it in her fore-paws and crunching with her head on one side. L. GOULD He reads the paper and crunches his toast. *number-crunch*: see NUMBER *n.* 2 D. WELCH The cinders crunched under our feet. W. PLOMER We crunched over the gravel path into the chapel. P. V. WHITE The car was crunching on the drive. 3 C. BRONTË A sound of heavy wheels crunching a stony road. T. KENEALLY His feet crunched the stiff frost.

cruncher *n.* (*a*) *slang* a crucial question, a sticking-point, a decisive blow; (*b*) see *number-cruncher* s.v. NUMBER *n.*: M20. **crunchiness** *n.* the quality of being crunchy L19. **crunchingly** *adv.* in a crunching manner, with a crunching action or sound M19. **crunchy** *a.* fit for crunching or being crunched, crisp E20.

crunk /krʌŋk/ *v.* & *n.* Long *obs.* exc. *dial.* M16. [Cf. Icel. *krúnka* to croak.] **A** *v.i.* Of a bird: utter a hoarse harsh cry. M16. **B** *n.* The harsh cry of a bird; a croak. M19.

crunkle /ˈkrʌŋk(ə)l/ *v.*[1]*t.* Chiefly *north.* LME. [Parallel to CRINKLE *v.*] Wrinkle, rumple, crinkle. Chiefly as *crunkled* ppl a.

crunkle /ˈkrʌŋk(ə)l/ *v.*[2]*i.* L19. [Imit.] Make a harsh dry sound as by grinding the jaws, etc.

crunode /ˈkruːnəʊd/ *n.* L19. [Irreg. f. L *crux* cross + NODE.] *Math.* A point on a curve where it intersects itself; a node with two real tangents.

cruˈnodal *a.* L19.

crunt /krʌnt/ *n.* & *v.* *Sc.* L18. [Prob. imit.: cf. CRUMP *n.*[2], *v.*[2]] **A** *n.* A blow on the head. L18. **B** *v.t.* Strike on the head. E20.

cruor /ˈkruːɔː/ *n.* Now *rare* or *obs.* M17. [L.] Coagulated blood, gore.

crupper /ˈkrʌpə/ *n.* & *v.* ME. [AN *cropere*, OFr. *cropiere* (mod. *croupière*), f. Proto-Romance, f. base of CROUP *n.*[1]: see -ER[2].] **A** *n.* **1** A strap buckled to the back of a saddle and looped under the horse's tail, to prevent the saddle from slipping forward. ME. **2** *transf.* The hindquarters of a horse. L16. **b** A person's buttocks. Chiefly *joc.* L16. **3** *Hist.* A piece of armour covering the hindquarters of a horse. M17. **4** *Naut.* More fully *crupper-chain*. A chain to secure a jib-boom down in its saddle. M19. **B** *v.t.* Equip with a crupper, put a crupper on. Chiefly as *cruppered* ppl a. L18.

crura *n.* pl. of CRUS.

crural /ˈkrʊər(ə)l/ *a.* L16. [Fr., or L *cruralis*, f. *crus*, *crur-* leg: see -AL[1].] *Anat.* Of or pertaining to the leg, *spec.* that part between the knee and ankle. Also, of or pertaining to the crura cerebri.

crus /krʌs/ *n.* Pl. **crura** /ˈkrʊərə/. E18. [L: see prec.] **1** *Anat.* The leg or hind limb; *spec.* the part from the knee to the ankle, the shank. E18. **2** Any of various elongated processes or parts of a structure occurring in pairs; *esp.* (in full *crus cerebri* /ˈsɛrɪbrʌɪ/ [= of the brain]) either of two symmetrical nerve tracts of the midbrain linking the pons and the cerebral hemispheres. E18.

crusade /kruːˈseɪd/ *n.* Also (earlier) †**crois-**, †**-ado**, (earliest, in senses 1, 2) †**cruciat**, & other vars. Also (esp. in sense 1) **C-**. LME. [In early use f. med.L *cruciata*, f. L *cruc-*, *crux* cross; later (16) partly f. Fr. *croisade* alt. of *croisée* (f. *crois* CROSS *n.*) by assim. to Sp., partly f. Sp. *cruzada* (f. *cruz* CROSS *n.*): see -ADE, -ADO.] **1** A war or expedition instigated by the Church for alleged religious ends; *spec.* (*Hist.*) any of several Christian military expeditions made in the 11th, 12th, and 13th cents. to recover Jerusalem and the Holy Land from the Muslims (freq. in *pl.*). LME. †**2** A papal bull authorizing a crusade. LME–L18. **3** *Hist.* In the Spanish kingdoms, a levy of money, originally intended to finance expeditions against the Moors, afterwards diverted to other purposes. L16. †**4** The symbol of the cross, the badge worn by crusaders. E17–E18. **5** A vigorous movement or enterprise against poverty or a similar social evil; a personal campaign undertaken for a particular cause. L18.

1 R. W. EMERSON The power of the religious sentiment . . inspired the crusades. 5 P. MORTIMER God and my grandfather headed the crusade for compulsory education in Melksham.

crusade /kruːˈseɪd/ *v.i.* M18. [f. the n.] Engage in a crusade.

crusader /kruːˈseɪdə/ *n.* Also (*Hist.*) **C-**. M18. [f. CRUSADE *n.* or *v.* + -ER[1].] A person who engages in a crusade.

crusado *n.*[1] see CRUZADO.

†**crusado** *n.*[2] see CRUSADE *n.*

cruse /kruːz/ *n.* *arch.* [OE *crūse* = MHG *krūse* (G *Krause*), ON *krús*; reinforced in ME by (M)LG *krūs*.] A small earthenware pot or jar; a drinking-vessel. Also *fig.* (w. allus. to *1 Kings* 17:16), a seemingly slight resource which is in fact not readily exhausted (more fully *widow's cruse*).

THACKERAY He had dipped ungenerously into a generous mother's purse, basely . . spilt her little cruse.

crush /krʌʃ/ *n.* ME. [f. the vb.] †**1** The noise of violent percussion; clashing; a crash. Only in ME. **2** An act of crushing; violent compression or pressure that bruises, breaks down, injures, or destroys; destruction by crushing. L16. **3** A bruise or injury caused by crushing. Now *rare* or *obs.* E17. **4** The crowding together of a number of things; a crowded mass, esp. of people. E19. **b** A crowded social gathering. *colloq.* M19. **c** A group of people; *spec.* a body or unit of troops, a regiment. *slang.* E20. **5** In full *crush-pen*. A fenced passage with one narrow end for handling cattle, sheep, etc. M19. **6** (A person who is the object of) an infatuation. *slang.* L19. **7** *Croquet.* In full *crush stroke*. A foul stroke made when a mallet touches a ball that is in contact with a peg or hoop other than in playing it away. E20. **8** A drink made from the juice of crushed fruit. E20.

2 ADDISON The wrecks of matter, and the crush of worlds. *fig.*: S. JOHNSON A heavy crush of disaster. 4 DICKENS A crush of carts and chairs and coaches. b LD MACAULAY I fell in with her at Lady Grey's great crush. 6 M. LASKI The pupil with a crush who would . . give unstinting doglike devotion. **have, get** etc., **a crush on** be, become, infatuated with.

Comb.: **crush bar** a place in a theatre, opera-house, etc., for the audience to buy drinks in the intervals; **crush barrier** a (temporary) barrier for restraining a crowd; **crush-hat** a soft hat which can be crushed flat; *spec.* a hat constructed with a spring so as to collapse, an opera-hat; *crush-pen*: see sense 5 above; **crush-room** *arch.* a room or area in a theatre, opera-house, etc., for the audience to walk about during the intervals; *crush stroke*: see sense 7 above.

crush /krʌʃ/ *v.* ME. [AN *crussir*, *corussier*, OFr. *croissir*, *cruissir* gnash (the teeth), crash, crack, f. Proto-Romance: ult. origin unkn.] **I 1** *v.t.* Compress forcibly so as to break, bruise, injure, or destroy. ME. **b** Crumple or crease (a fabric, dress, etc.) by pressure or rough handling; give (a fabric etc.) a crumpled or crinkled finish (chiefly as *crushed* ppl a.). L19. **2** *v.t.* Bruise, pound, break down into small pieces; reduce to powder, pulp, etc., by pressure. LME. **3** *v.t.* Press or squeeze forcibly (*against*, *into*, *out of*, *through*, etc.); force out or *out* by pressing or squeezing. L16. **4** *v.t.* *fig.* Break down the strength or power of; extinguish, stamp *out* (actions, feelings, etc.); subdue, overwhelm. L16. **5** *v.t.* Drink, quaff, (a glass of wine, pot of ale, etc.). *arch.* L16. **6** *v.i.* Become crushed. M18. **7** *v.i.* Advance or make one's way by pressing, squeezing, pushing, etc. M18. **8** *v.i.* *Croquet.* Touch with a mallet a ball that is in contact with a peg or hoop other than in playing it away (constituting a foul stroke). Chiefly as *crushing* vbl n. & ppl a. L19.

1 T. HERBERT Some . . cast themselves in the way and are crusht to death. L. LEE A man . . crushed a glass like a nut between his hands. b OED Her bonnet and dress were all crushed. *Belfast Telegraph* Crushed velvet for curtains. 2 M. DONOVAN The apples had . . been well crushed and pressed. 3 SHAKES. *1 Hen. IV* To crush our old limbs in ungentle steel. R. CHANDLER She bent to crush out her cigarette. R. ELLISON I was crushed against a huge woman. R. BRADBURY Wine was being crushed from under the grape-blooded feet of dancing vintners' daughters. 4 GIBBON His enemies were crushed by his valour. E. J. HOWARD While she was with him, she was able to crush these feelings of guilt. C. HAMPTON The urban guerrilla movement was said to be crushed and finished. 5 SIR W. SCOTT You shall crush a cup of wine to the health of the Fathers of the city. 6 G. MACDONALD I heard hailstones crush between my feet and the soft grass. 7 J. T. FARRELL He arose, crushed out to the aisle, walked to the exit. 8 **crushing stroke** = CRUSH *n.* 7.

†**II 9** *v.t.* & *i.* Dash together with the sound of violent percussion; clash, crash. Chiefly as *crushing* vbl n. Only in LME.

crushable *a.* able to be crushed, esp. without damage (earlier in UNCRUSHABLE) M19. **crushing** *ppl a.* that crushes; *esp.* overwhelming: L16. **crushingly** *adv.* E19.

crusher /ˈkrʌʃə/ *n.* L16. [f. prec. + -ER[1].] **1** A person who or thing which crushes or compresses forcibly. L16. **2** An overwhelming person, thing, or event; a crushing blow or retort. *colloq.* M19. **3** A police officer. *slang.* M19. **b** A ship's corporal; a regulating petty officer. *Naut. slang.* E20.

1 *Daily Telegraph* The cars were dropped into the crusher complete with tyres, engines, seats and instruments. 2 THACKERAY She *is* a crusher, ain't she now? C. DICKSON That's where he had a very bad bit of luck, a crusher, the thing that did for him.

crusie /ˈkruːzi/ *n.* *Sc.* Also **cruisie**. E16. [Perh. repr. Fr. *creuset* crucible.] A small lamp with a handle, burning oil or tallow (also *crusie lamp*). Also, a type of triangular candlestick.

crusily /ˈkruːsɪli/ *a.* Also **-lly**. L16. [OFr. *crusillé* var. of *croisillé*, f. (O)Fr. *croisille* dim. of *croix* CROSS *n.*: see -Y[5].] *Her.* Of a shield or charge: strewn with cross crosslets rather than crosses.

Crusoe /ˈkruːsəʊ/ *v.* & *n.* L19. [See ROBINSON CRUSOE.] **A** *v.i.* Live as a castaway; live a solitary open-air life. Chiefly as *Crusoeing* vbl n. L19. **B** *n.* A castaway; an independent and resourceful person isolated from others (physically or intellectually etc.); = ROBINSON CRUSOE *n.* E20.

crust /krʌst/ *n.* ME. [OFr. *crouste* (mod. CROÛTE) f. L *crusta* rind, shell, incrustation.] **1** The hard outer part of (a loaf, roll, or slice of) bread; a portion of this; a hard dry scrap of bread; a piece of bread as a meagre means of sustenance; *slang* (chiefly *Austral.* & *NZ*) a livelihood, a living. ME. **2** The pastry forming the covering of a pie. LME. **3** A hard dry formation on the skin covering a burn, ulcer, etc., or caused by a skin disease; a scab. LME. **4** A more or less hard coating or deposit on the surface of anything; an incrustation; a deposit on the sides of a bottle, thrown by some ports and other wines; a harder layer over soft snow. LME. **5** A plank cut from the outside of a tree-trunk. Long *obs.* exc. *dial.* L15. **6** Orig., the upper surface or layer of the ground. Now *Geol.*, the outer rocky portion of the earth (*spec.* those parts above the Mohorovičić discontinuity), the moon, a planet, etc. M16. **7** A crusty person. Long *arch.* L16. **8** The hard external covering of an animal (esp. a crustacean) or plant; a shell, a husk. Now *rare* or *obs.* E17. **9** *fig.* A deceptive outward appearance; a superficial hardness of demeanour etc; *slang* impudence, effrontery (cf. RIND *n.*[1] 3c). M17. **10** In leather manufacture, the state of skins when tanned but not yet dyed or coloured. Chiefly in *in the crust.* L17.

1 KEATS Love in a hut, with water and a crust, Is—Love, forgive us!—cinders, ashes, dust. E. DE MAUNY 'What do you do for a crust?' 'I work on a newspaper.' S. BRETT Anchovy paste sandwiches with the crusts cut off. 3 H. JOLLY This treatment clears the scalp . . although crusts may reappear. 4 P. CAREY A dry crust of spittle marked the corners of her mouth. J. GRIGSON The cream takes 1½ hours to form its crust. 9 F. W. ROBERTSON Break through the crust of his selfishness. P. G. WODEHOUSE The blighter had the cold, cynical crust to look me in the eyeball without a blink.

Phrases: *continental crust*: see CONTINENTAL *a.* OCEANIC *crust. upper crust*: see UPPER *a.*

crustless *a.* without a crust, having the crust removed E20.

crust /krʌst/ *v.* LME. [f. the n.] **1** *v.i.* Form or become covered with a crust. LME. **2** *v.t.* Cover (as) with a crust; form into a crust. M16. **3** *v.t.* Hunt (deer etc.) on the crust of snow. *N. Amer.* M19.

1 T. PYNCHON Blood darkened and crusting at the lesion in his neck. 2 WILKIE COLLINS The dirt of half a century, crusted on the glass. J. A. FROUDE The truth had been crusted over with fictions. C. MCCULLERS A thin coat of ice crusted the puddles.

crusta /ˈkrʌstə/ *n.* Pl. **crustae** /ˈkrʌstiː/. E19. [L: see CRUST *n.*] **1** Chiefly *Anat.* & *Med.* A hard outer layer, rind, shell, or incrustation. E19. **2** *Antiq.* A thin plate of embossed metal, etc., inlaid on a vessel, wall, or other object. M19.

1 **crusta petrosa** /pɛˈtrəʊsə/ [= hard, like rock] the cement of a tooth.

crustacean /krʌˈsteɪʃ(ə)n/ *n.* & *a.* M19. [f. mod.L *Crustacea* (see below), use as n. of neut. pl. of *crustaceus* adj.: see CRUSTACEOUS, -AN.] *Zool.* **A** *n.* Any member of the large class Crustacea of mainly aquatic, hard-shelled arthropods including the crab, lobster, shrimp, woodlouse, etc. M19. **B** *adj.* Of or pertaining to the Crustacea. M19.

crustaceology /krʌˌsteɪʃɪˈɒlədʒi/ *n.* E19. [f. as prec. + -OLOGY.] The branch of zoology that deals with the Crustacea.

crustaceoˈlogical *a.* E19. **crustaceologist** *n.* M19.

crustaceous /krʌˈsteɪʃəs/ *a.* M17. [f. mod.L *crustaceus*, f. L *crusta* CRUST *n.*: see -ACEOUS.] **1** Pertaining to or of the nature of a crust or hard integument; (of a lichen) crustose. M17. **2** Of an animal: having a hard integument. M17. **3** *Zool.* Of, pertaining to, or resembling the Crustacea; crustacean. M17.

†crustade *n.* see CUSTARD *n.*[1]

crustal /ˈkrʌst(ə)l/ *a.* M19. [f. L *crusta* CRUST *n.* + -AL[1].] Of or pertaining to a crust, esp. that of the earth, moon, etc.

†crustarde *n.* see CUSTARD *n.*[1]

crustate /ˈkrʌsteɪt/ *a.* M17. [L *crustatus*, f. *crusta* CRUST *n.*: see -ATE[2].] Crusted, crustaceous.

crustated *a.* = CRUSTATE L18. **cruˈstation** *n.* the formation of a crust; an incrustation: M17.

crusted /ˈkrʌstɪd/ *a.* LME. [f. CRUST *n.* or *v.*: see -ED[2], -ED[1].] Having a crust; (of wine, esp. port) having deposited a crust; *fig.* antiquated, venerable.

T. HARDY Fine old crusted characters who had a decided taste for living without worry.

crustose /krʌˈstəʊs/ *a.* L19. [L *crustosus*, f. *crusta* CRUST *n.*: see -OSE[1].] Of the nature of a crust; crustaceous. Of a lichen: having a thin thallus which adheres closely to the substrate like a crust.

crusty /ˈkrʌsti/ *a.* LME. [f. CRUST *n.* + -Y[1].] **1** Resembling a crust, hard; having a crisp crust. Of wine, esp. port: crusted. LME. **2** *fig.* Of a person, disposition, etc.: short-tempered, irritable; curt. L16.

M. R. MITFORD His loaves, which are crusty, and his temper, which is not.

crustily *adv.* L16. **crustiness** *n.* E17.

crut *n.* see CRUD *n.*

crutch /krʌtʃ/ *n.* [OE *cryć(ć)* = OS *krukka* (Du. *kruk*), OHG *krucka* (G *Krücke*), ON *krykkja*, f. Gmc. Rel. to CROOK *n.* See also CROTCH *n.*] **I 1** A staff to support a lame or infirm person in standing or walking, now usu. with a crosspiece at the top to fit under the armpit, or a curved rest to take the weight on the forearm. Freq. in *pair of crutches.* OE. **2** Orig., the raised part of a saddle in front and rear. Now, the forking front of a saddle-tree, which supports the pommel; also, a forked rest for the leg in a side-saddle. E17. **3** A support or prop with a forked or concave top. Cf. CROTCH *n.* 3. M17. **4** *Naut.* Any of various forked contrivances in a ship or boat, as (*a*) a support for a boom, mast, spar, etc., when not in use, (*b*) a rowlock. In *pl.* also, crooked timbers or bands of iron etc. bolted to the stern-post and the sides of a vessel. M18. **5** = CROTCH *n.* 5. M18. **6** In a mechanical clock, a fork at the end of the arm hanging down from the axis of the anchor-escapement, which supports the pendulum rod. M18. **7a** A handle of a tool etc. with a crossbar. M19. **b** An implement consisting of a shaft and crosspiece, used in dipping sheep. (Implied earlier in CRUTCH *v.* 3.) Chiefly *Austral.* & *NZ.* E20.

1 A. HAILEY Some walking with the aid of canes, a few on crutches. *walk on crutches*: see WALK *v.*[1] 3 CAPT. COOK The hunters fix their crutches in the ground, on which they rest their firelocks. 5 S. RAVEN I hope . . your bloody cousin gets hit in the crutch by a cricket ball.

II 8 *fig.* A person who or thing which provides support against faltering. L16.

crutch /krʌtʃ/ *v.* M17. [f. the n.] **1** *v.t.* Support as with a crutch or crutches; prop *up*, sustain. M17. **2** *v.i.* & *t.* with *it*, *one's way*. Go on crutches, limp. E19. **3** *v.t.* Push (a sheep) into a dip with a crutch. Chiefly *Austral.* & *NZ.* L19. **4** *v.t.* Clip the wool or hair from the hindquarters of (a sheep, dog, etc.). Chiefly *Austral.* & *NZ.* E20.

1 DRYDEN Two fools that crutch their feeble sense on verse. G. W. THORNBURY Old crippled buildings . . crutched up with posts and logs. 2 *Dirt Bike* Using a stick he found on the ground, he crutched his way over to it.

crutched /ˈkrʌtʃɪd/ *a.*[1] Also (earlier) **†crouched**; **C-.** L16. [f. CROUCH *n.*[1] + -ED[2], after L *cruciferi*, *sanctae crucis*.] Chiefly *Hist.* Designating a friar of any of various religious congregations noted for their bearing or wearing a cross.

crutched /krʌtʃt/ *a.*[2] E18. [f. CRUTCH *n.* + -ED[2].] Furnished with a crutch; resembling a crutch.

crux /krʌks/ *n.* Pl. **cruxes** /ˈkrʌksɪz/; **cruces** /ˈkruːsiːz/. M17. [L = CROSS *n.*] **1** (A representation of) a cross. Chiefly in *crux ansata* /anˈseɪtə/, pl. *cruces ansatae* /-tiː/, [= with a handle] = ANKH. M17. **2** A difficult matter, a puzzle; the decisive point at issue; the central point. E18. **3** (Usu. **C-.**) (The name of) the constellation of the Southern Cross (see CROSS *n.* 13). M19.

2 E. DOWDEN The consideration of a textual crux in itself sharpens the wits. L. MACNEICE The crux of the story is the great gulf separating the people of the sea from human beings.

cruzado /kruːˈzɑːdəʊ/ *n.* In sense 1 also (earlier) **crusado** /kruːˈseɪdəʊ/. Pl. **-os.** M16. [Port., use as n. of adj. = bearing a cross.] **1** *Hist.* Any of various Portuguese gold or silver coins bearing the figure of a cross. M16. **2** The principal monetary unit of Brazil between 1988 and 1990, equal to 1000 cruzeiros. L20.

cruzeiro /kruːˈzɛːrəʊ/ *n.* Pl. **-os.** E20. [Port., lit. 'large cross'.] A monetary unit of Brazil, formerly the basic unit superseding the milreis, later equal to one-thousandth of a cruzado, now the basic unit, equal to one hundred centavos.

crwth /kruːθ/ *n.* M19. [Welsh: cf. Gael. *cruit* harp, violin, Ir. *cruit* small harp, OIr. *crot* harp, cithara. Adopted earlier as CROWD *n.*[1]] An old Celtic musical instrument with three, or later six, strings which was held against the chest and played by bowing and plucking.

cry /krʌɪ/ *n.* ME. [(O)Fr. *cri*: Proto-Romance f. as the vb.] **1** A loud inarticulate sound made by a person to express grief, pain, or other strong emotion. Also, the making of such a sound. ME. **2** A loud excited utterance of words; a shout. Formerly also, shouting, calling out. ME. **†b** Clamour, tumultuous noise. ME–E16. **3** A loud importunate call; an appeal (*for* mercy, help, etc.). ME. **4** A summons (orig. formal). Now only *Sc.* ME. **5a** *gen.* A loud public announcement; a proclamation, an edict. Long *obs.* exc. *Hist.* ME. **b** In *pl.* The proclamation of marriage-banns: cf. CRY *v.* 4e. Long *obs.* exc. *Sc.* ME. **c** A public complaint or outcry against a wrong. *obs.* exc. in *hue and cry* (see HUE *n.*[2]). ME. **d** A proclamation of goods or business in the streets; a street vendor's special call. M17. **6a** Public report or rumour. ME. **b** The public voice as expressing approval or condemnation. Hence, an opinion generally expressed. E17. **7** The loud natural utterance of an animal, bird, etc., *esp.* the distinctive call of one. ME. **b** *spec.* The yelping of hounds giving chase. LME. **†8a** A company or troop of people, esp. soldiers. In later use *contempt.* and infl. by sense 8b. ME–M17. **b** A pack of hounds. L16. **9** A word or phrase shouted to encourage or rally people, esp. soldiers in battle; a watchword. M16. **b** *spec.* A political or electioneering slogan or rallying-cry. L18. **10** A fit of weeping. *colloq.* E19. **11** The creaking noise made by tin when bent. L19.

1 J. GOWER With such weping and with such cry Forth . . he goth. M. ARNOLD We shall not meet [our doom] . . With women's tears and weak complaining cries. TENNYSON In one blind cry of passion and of pain. D. DU MAURIER She saw the Christmas tree . . and gave a cry of pleasure. 2 POPE With the hunter's cry the grove resounds. 3 AV *Prov.* 21:13 Whoso stoppeth his eares at the cry of the poore. M. BRAGG The miners' cry for the Eight-Hour Day had grown into a practicable demand. 5a LD BERNERS Kyng yuoryn made a crye thorow all the cyte that euery man sholde be armed. 6a SHAKES. *Oth.* Faith, the cry goes that you marry her. b STEELE Then the Cry would be, Images were put up for the . . ignorant People to worship. E. LONGFORD There is a general cry throughout France against the occupation. 7 N. TINBERGEN The clear, . . resounding cries of the Herring Gulls. 8a SHAKES. *Haml.* Would not this . . get me a fellowship in a cry of players, sir? 9 W. MORRIS Ho, friends, and ye that follow, cry my cry! *battle-cry*, *rallying-cry*, *war cry*, etc. b D. BREWSTER The Tory election cry . . was 'the Church in danger'.

Phrases: **a far cry** (chiefly *fig.*) a very long distance (*from*, *to*). **a good cry** *colloq.* a prolonged or violent fit of weeping that relieves the feelings. **cry from the heart** a *cri de cœur*. **great, much, cry and little wool** (the proverbial result of shearing pigs) a lot of fuss with little effect, a lot of fuss about nothing. **in full cry** in hot pursuit. **†out of (all) cry** excessively. **within cry of** within calling distance of.

cry /krʌɪ/ *v.* Pa. t. & pple **cried** /krʌɪd/. ME. [(O)Fr. *crier* f. L *quiritare* raise a public outcry (lit. 'call on the *Quirites* or Roman citizens for help').] **1** *v.t.* Ask for earnestly or in a loud voice. *arch.* ME. **†b** Call for, demand, require. E17–L18. **2** *v.i.* Call out or *out* in a loud voice, esp. in seeking mercy, help, etc., or in expressing emotion. (Foll. by *to*, *†unto*, *†(up)on* a person addressed, *for* a person or thing desired, *to do* a thing desired, (arch.) *against* a cause of complaint.) ME. **b** *fig.* Of a thing: call *for*, suggest strongly the need *for*. ME. **3** *v.t.* Utter (esp. specified words) in a loud voice. ME. **4** *v.t.* Announce publicly in a loud voice; proclaim. ME. **b** Of a street vendor or auctioneer: announce (a sale, goods for sale). LME. **c** Give oral notice of (things lost or found). Now *arch.* or *Hist.* L16. **†d** Extol; = *cry up* below. Only in E17. **e** Proclaim the marriage banns of. Now *Sc.* & *US dial.* L18. **5** *v.i.* Utter inarticulate exclamations of distress; wail. ME. **b** *v.i.* & *t.* With little or no idea of sound: weep, shed (tears). (Foll. by *for* a person or thing desired.) M16. **c** *v.refl.* Bring oneself into a specified state by weeping. E17. **d** *v.t.* *cry one's eyes out*, weep bitterly. Also *cry one's heart out*: see HEART *n.* E18. **6** *v.i.* Of an animal, bird, etc.: utter a loud (esp. distinctive) call. Of a hound: yelp as when giving chase. ME.

1 CAXTON Whan they repente . . and crye their god mercy. DEFOE The Portuguese cry quarter. W. IRVING 'I cry your mercy,' said I, 'for mistaking your age.' *cry craven*: see CRAVEN *a.* 1b. *cry halves*: see HALF *n.* b

SOUTHEY The innocent blood cried vengeance. 2 SPENSER The damned ghosts.. with sharp shrilling shrieks do bootlesse cry. SHAKES. *Wint. T.* How he cried to me for help. D. G. ROSSETTI She is cried upon In all the prayers my heart puts up. E. O'NEILL I.. cried to be buried with her. **be crying out for** be asking urgently for, be in urgent need of. *cry (a person) mercy*: see MERCY *n.* **cry for the moon** ask for what is unattainable, ask the impossible. **for crying out loud!** *colloq.*: expr. exasperation, impatience, or surprise. b C. THIRLWALL Injuries and insults.. which cried aloud for vengeance. 3 R. RAYMOND Where so many voices cry encouragement, it is well that one should speak warning. E. M. FORSTER 'The field's cut!' Helen cried excitedly. *cry aim*: see AIM *n.* 3. *cry cupboard*: see CUPBOARD *n.* 4. *cry harrow*: see HARROW *int. cry havoc*: see HAVOC *n. cry quits*: see QUITS *a. cry roast meat*: see ROAST *a. cry shame (up)on*: see SHAME *n. cry uncle*: see UNCLE *n. cry wolf (too often)*: see WOLF *n.* 4 TENNYSON She sent a herald forth, And bade him cry, with sound of trumpet, all The hard condition. b W. H. AUDEN A pedlar still, .. I no longer cry my wares. *cry stinking fish*: see STINKING *a.* 5 SHAKES. *Much Ado* If you hear a child cry in the night, you must call to the nurse. b C. KINGSLEY He.. cried salt tears from sheer disappointment. E. WAUGH The boy took out a handkerchief and began to cry quietly. *a shoulder to cry on*: see SHOULDER *n. cry all the way to the bank*: see BANK *n.*[3] 3. *cry on a person's shoulder*: see SHOULDER *n. cry over spilt milk*: see MILK *n. give something to cry about, for*: see GIVE *v.* c *cry oneself to sleep* etc. 6 W. FULKE Frogs crying.. forewarne us of a tempest. BYRON Hark, hark! the sea-birds cry!

With advs. in specialized senses: **cry back** (in hunting) go back on one's tracks; revert to an ancestral type. **cry down** (*a*) proclaim unlawful or forbidden; publicly disclaim responsibility for; disparage, decry; †(*b*) overcome or silence by louder or more vehement crying out. **cry off** excuse oneself from a commitment, decline to keep a promise. †**cry out** be in childbirth. **cry up** proclaim the merits of, extol.

cry-baby /ˈkrʌɪbeɪbi/ *n.* & *v. colloq.* M19. [f. CRY *n.* or *v.* + BABY *n.*] A *n.* A person easily reduced to childish tears. M19. B *v.i.* Behave like a cry-baby; be easily reduced to childish tears or complaints. *US.* E20.

crying /ˈkrʌɪɪŋ/ *a.* LME. [f. CRY *v.* + -ING[2].] 1 That cries. LME. 2 *fig.* Of a problem, an evil, etc.: that calls for notice or urgent action; flagrant. E17.

2 DAY LEWIS Some crying need for self-protection. F. DHONDY It was nothing less than a crying shame for a workers' government to treat the workers so.

cryingly *adv.* E19.

cryo- /ˈkrʌɪəʊ/ *comb. form.* Also (occas.) **kryo-**. [f. Gk *kruos* frost, icy cold: see -O-.] Used in *Sci.* w. the sense 'of, involving, or producing very low temperatures'.

cryobiˈology *n.* the biology of organisms, tissues, etc., cooled to temperatures below those at which they normally function M20. **cryogen** *n.* (*Chem.*) a substance used to induce very low temperatures; a freezing mixture: L19. **cryoˈglobulin** *n.* (*Biochem.*) any of a group of proteins which occur in the blood in certain disorders and may be precipitated when cooled outside the body M20. **cryopreˈcipitate** *n.* a substance precipitated by controlled freezing; *spec.* an extract rich in a haemostatic factor obtained as a residue when frozen blood plasma is thawed: L20. **cryopreserve** *v.t.* subject to cryopreservation L20. **cryopreserˈvation** *n.* the cooling of living matter to below the freezing point of water in order to prolong its life L20. **cryoprobe** *n.* an ultra-cooled probe employed in cryosurgery M20. **cryoproˈtectant** *n.* an agent used for cryoprotection L20. **cryoproˈtection** *n.* protection against freezing M20. **cryopump** *n.* a vacuum-pump which uses a liquefied gas such as helium to freeze out the gases in a volume M20. **cryosphere** *n.* the permanently frozen part of the earth's surface M20. **cryostat** *n.* (*a*) an apparatus for maintaining a very low steady temperature; (*b*) a cold chamber in which frozen tissue is divided with a microtome; the microtome itself: E20. **cryoˈsurgery** *n.* surgery using local application of intense cold usu. in order to freeze and destroy unwanted tissue M20. **cryoˈtherapy** *n.* the use of extreme cold in the treatment of disease M20. **cryoturˈbation** *n.* physical disturbance to the soil caused by freezing (and thawing) of water in the soil M20.

cryoconite /krʌɪəˈkəʊnʌɪt/ *n.* Also (earlier) †**k-**. L20. [f. CRYO- + Gk *konis* dust + -ITE[1].] A powdery material of aeolian origin forming layered deposits in holes in glaciers, ice sheets, etc.

cryogenic /krʌɪə(ʊ)ˈdʒɛnɪk/ *a.* E20. [f. CRYO- + -GENIC.] Of or pertaining to the production of very low temperatures and their effects.

cryoˈgenics *n.* the branch of physics and technology that deals with the production of very low temperatures and their effects M20.

cryolite /ˈkrʌɪəlʌɪt/ *n.* E19. [f. CRYO- + -LITE: named from large deposits in Greenland.] *Min.* A monoclinic fluoride of sodium and aluminium which occurs usu. as white or colourless massive deposits and is used as a flux in the electrolytic smelting of aluminium.

cryonics /krʌɪˈɒnɪks/ *n.* M20. [Contr. of CRYOGENICS.] The practice or technique of deep-freezing the bodies of those who have died of an incurable disease, in the hope that some cure for it will be discovered in the future.

cryonic *a.* M20. **cryonically** *adv.* L20. **cryonicist** /-sɪst/ *n.* L20.

cryophorus /krʌɪˈɒf(ə)rəs/ *n.* E19. [mod.L, f. as CRYO- + Gk *-phoros*: see -PHORE.] An instrument for illustrating the freezing of water by evaporation.

cryoscopy /krʌɪˈɒskəpi/ *n.* E20. [f. CRYO- + -SCOPY.] The determination of the freezing point of liquids, esp. (in medical diagnosis) that of blood or urine compared with distilled water; *Chem.* the measurement of the lowering of the freezing point of a liquid by a substance dissolved in it (used in the calculation of molecular weight).

cryoˈscopic *a.* of or pertaining to cryoscopy E20. **cryoˈscopically** *adv.* E20.

crypt /krɪpt/ *n.* LME. [L *crypta* f. Gk *kruptē* vault, use as n. of fem. of *kruptos* hidden.] †1 A grotto, a cavern. Only in LME. †2 An underground passage or tunnel. Only in M17. 3 An underground chamber or vault; *spec.* one under a church, used as a burial place etc. L18. 4 *transf.* & *fig.* A recess, a secret hiding place. M19. 5 *Anat.* A small tubular gland, pit, or recess. M19.

5 *crypt of* LIEBERKÜHN.

cryptal *a.* M19.

crypt- *comb. form* see CRYPTO-.

crypta /ˈkrɪptə/ *n.* Now *rare*. Pl. **-tae** /-tiː/. M16. [L: see CRYPT.] †1 = CRYPT 1, 2, 3. M16–E18. 2 = CRYPT 5. M19.

cryptanalysis /krɪptəˈnalɪsɪs/ *n.* Orig. *US.* E20. [f. CRYPT- + ANALYSIS.] The practice or art of solving cryptograms by analysis; code-breaking.

crypˈtanalyst *n.* an expert in cryptanalysis E20. **cryptanaˈlytic(al)** *adjs.* of or pertaining to cryptanalysis M20.

cryptand /ˈkrɪptand/ *n.* L20. [f. CRYPTO- + -AND.] *Chem.* A bicyclic compound whose molecule contains a cavity able to hold metal cations. Cf. next.

cryptate /ˈkrɪpteɪt/ *n.* M20. [f. as prec. + -ATE[1].] *Chem.* An organometallic complex in which a metal cation is held inside a cryptand.

cryptic /ˈkrɪptɪk/ *n.* & *a.* E17. [Late L *crypticus* f. Gk *kruptikos*, f. *kruptē*: see CRYPT, -IC.] A *n.* †1 A secret method. Only in E17. 2 A cryptogrammic puzzle. M20.

B *adj.* 1 Secret, mystical; mysterious; obscure in meaning; enigmatic. E17. b Of a crossword (clue): indicating the answer(s) in a way that is not straightforward. M20. 2 *Zool.* Of markings, coloration, etc.: serving to camouflage an animal etc. in its natural environment. L19.

1 F. W. CROFTS 'It just shows. You never know'; with which rather cryptic remark the interview closed. C. S. LEWIS That cryptic knight who comes and goes we know not whence or whither. J. T. STORY Covered in cryptic figures and names, like a code.

cryptical *a.* = CRYPTIC *a.* 1 E17. **cryptically** *adv.* L17.

crypto /ˈkrɪptəʊ/ *n. colloq.* Pl. **-os**. M20. [Use of next as separate wd.] A person who secretly supports a political group; *spec.* a crypto-Communist.

crypto- /ˈkrɪptəʊ/ *comb. form.* Bef. a vowel or *h* also **crypt-**. [Gk *kruptos* hidden: see -O-.] Forming words, mostly scientific terms, modelled on Gk compounds, w. the sense 'concealed, secret, not visible to the naked eye', as *cryptogram, cryptobranchiate*. Hence as a freely productive elem. forming ns. and adjs. w. the sense 'unavowed(ly), not overt(ly)', as *crypto-Communist, -Fascist, -Semite.*

cryptobiosis /-bʌɪˈəʊsɪs/ *n.* (*Biol.*) a state of existence in which metabolic activity is reduced to an undetectable level without disappearing altogether M20. **cryptobiˈotic** *a.* †(*a*) designating primitive organisms presumed to have existed in earlier geological periods but to have left no trace of their existence; (*b*) = CRYPTOZOIC 1; (*c*) pertaining to or in a state of cryptobiosis: E20. **cryptoˈbranchiate** *a.* (esp. of certain divisions of crustaceans, gastropods, etc.) having the gills concealed L19. **crypto-ˈCalvinist** *n.* in 16th-cent. Germany, a Lutheran suspected of harbouring Calvinist sympathies; a Philippist: M18. **cryptoˈcrystalline** *a.* crystalline, but so finely structured that its crystals are not visible even under a microscope M19. **cryptoˈgenic** *a.* (of a disease) of obscure or uncertain origin E20. **cryptolect** *n.* a secret or coded language L20. **cryptophyte** *n.* †(*a*) a cryptogam; (*b*) a plant that bears perennating buds below the surface of the ground: M19. **crypˈtorchid** *n.* & *a.* (*Med.*) (a person) suffering from or exhibiting cryptorchidism L19. **crypˈtorchidism** *n.* (*Med.*) a condition in which one or both of the testes fail to descend into the scrotum L19. **cryptovolˈcanic** *a.* (*Geol.*) (of a structure) that is, or is presumed to be, of volcanic origin although exposed material does not afford direct evidence of volcanic activity E20. **cryptozooˈlogical** *a.* of or pertaining to cryptozoology M20. **cryptozoˈologist** *n.* an expert in or student of cryptozoology M20. **cryptozoˈology** *n.* the search for and study of creatures (e.g. the Loch Ness monster) whose supposed existence is evidenced by tradition, unsubstantiated reports, etc. M20. **cryptozoon** /-ˈzəʊɒn/ *n.*, pl. **-zoa** /-ˈzəʊə/, (*a*) *Geol.* a reef-forming Cambrian fossil, thought to derive from algae; (*b*) *Zool.* (in *pl.*) cryptozoic organisms: L19.

cryptococcosis /ˌkrɪptəʊkəˈkəʊsɪs/ *n.* Pl. **-ccoses** /-ˈkəʊsiːz/. M20. [f. mod.L *Cryptococcus* (see below) + -OSIS.] *Med.* Infestation with a yeastlike fungus, *Cryptococcus neoformans*, usu. attacking the lungs and central nervous system. Also called *torulosis*.

cryptoˈcoccal *a.* of or pertaining to *Cryptococcus* or cryptococcosis L20.

cryptogam /ˈkrɪptəʊgam/ *n.* M19. [Fr. *cryptogame* f. mod.L *cryptogamae* (sc. *plantae*) fem. pl. of *cryptogamus* adj., f. as CRYPTO- + Gk *gamos* marriage: so called because the means of reproduction was not apparent.] Any plant of the Linnaean division Cryptogamia (now disused), which embraced all non-flowering plants, as ferns, mosses, algae, fungi, etc. (opp. PHANEROGAM). Now *rare* exc. as *vascular cryptogam*, any plant of the group that includes ferns and their allies (e.g. horsetails and clubmosses), which resemble flowering plants in possessing a vascular system.

cryptoˈgamic *n.* & *a.* (*a*) *n.* a cryptogam; (*b*) *adj.* belonging to the Cryptogamia: E19. **crypˈtogamist** *n.* a botanist specializing in cryptogams M19. **crypˈtogamous** *a.* = CRYPTOGAMIC *a.* L18.

cryptogram /ˈkrɪptəgram/ *n.* L19. [f. CRYPTO- + -GRAM.] Something written in cipher; a coded message.

cryptoˈgrammic, **cryptogrammˈatic(al)** *adjs.* of, pertaining to, or of the nature of a cryptogram L19. **cryptoˈgrammatist** *n.* a person who encodes or decodes messages L19. **cryptoˈgrammist** *n.* = CRYPTOGRAMMATIST E20.

cryptograph /ˈkrɪptəgrɑːf/ *n.* M19. [f. CRYPTO- + -GRAPH.] 1 A cryptogram. M19. 2 A device for encoding or decoding messages. L19.

cryptography /krɪpˈtɒgrəfi/ *n.* M17. [mod.L *cryptographia*: see CRYPTO-, -GRAPHY.] 1 The practice or art of encoding messages. M17. 2 Cryptanalysis. M20.

crypˈtographer *n.* a person who encodes messages M17. **cryptoˈgraphic** *a.* of, pertaining to, or of the nature of cryptography E19. **crypˈtographist** *n.* a cryptographer M19.

cryptology /krɪpˈtɒlədʒi/ *n.* M17. [f. CRYPTO- + -LOGY.] 1 Secret speech or communication; mysterious or enigmatic language. M17. 2 The practice or art of encoding and decoding messages; the knowledge of codes. M20.

cryptomeria /krɪptə(ʊ)ˈmɪərɪə/ *n.* M19. [mod.L, f. as CRYPTO- + Gk *meros* part (because the seeds are concealed by scales).] (The wood of) an ornamental evergreen tree *Cryptomeria* *japonica*, allied to the cypresses, native to Japan and China. Also called *Japan(ese) cedar*.

cryptonym /ˈkrɪptənɪm/ *n.* L19. [f. CRYPTO- + -NYM.] A secret name, a code-name.

cryptonymous /krɪpˈtɒnɪməs/ *a.* whose name is secret, of the nature of a cryptonym L19.

cryptoporticus /krɪptə(ʊ)ˈpɔːtɪkəs/ *n.* L17. [L, f. as CRYPTO- + *porticus* gallery.] *Class. Archit.* An enclosed gallery having side-walls with openings instead of columns. Also, a covered or subterranean passage.

cryptozoic /krɪptə(ʊ)ˈzəʊɪk/ *a.* & *n.* L19. [f. CRYPTO- + -ZOIC.] A *adj.* 1 *Zool.* Of a small invertebrate: living hidden in the leaf litter or soil. Opp. PHANEROZOIC *a.* I. L19. 2 *Geol.* Usu. **C-**. Precambrian, esp. as marked by a dearth of fossil remains. E20. B *n. Geol.* The Cryptozoic period. M20.

crystal /ˈkrɪst(ə)l/ *n.* & *a.* Also †**chr-**. LOE. [(O)Fr. *cristal* f. L *crystallum* f. Gk *krustallos* ice.] A *n.* †1 (Clear) ice. (A literalism of translation.) LOE–M16. 2 A mineral clear and transparent like ice; *esp.* a form of quartz having these qualities (now more fully *rock-crystal*: see ROCK *n.*[1]). LOE. b Pure clear water. *poet.* L16. 3 A piece of rock-crystal or a similar mineral; *esp.* a crystal ball (see below). LME. b An eye. Usu. in *pl. poet.* L16. 4 *Chem.* & *Min.* An aggregation of atoms or molecules of a substance with an ordered internal structure and the external form of a solid enclosed by symmetrically arranged plane faces; a solid with a regular arrangement of atoms etc. E17. b Used in old names of chemical salts of crystalline form. Usu. in *pl. arch.* M17. 5 [ellipt. for *crystal-glass* below.] A highly transparent form of glass, flint glass; *loosely* fine cut glass. Hence, glass vessels etc. of this material. M17. b A vessel etc. made of this glass; *spec.* the glass over the face of a watch. M17. 6 A crystalline piece of a semiconductor used in electronic devices as a detector, rectifier, etc. E20.

2 (*as*) *clear as crystal*. MIXED *crystal*. *twin crystal*: see TWIN *n.* 5. 3 JAMES I The Seer looks into a Chrystal or Berryl, wherein he will see the answer. 4 D. PAGE Granite is composed of crystals of felspar, quartz and mica. *crystal form*: see FORM *n.* 1d. *liquid crystal*: see LIQUID *a.* & *n.* *plastic crystal*: see PLASTIC *a.* & *n.*[3] b *crystals of tartar* etc. 5 A. LURIE The stainless-steel tableware.., the utility glassware..had been replaced with silver and crystal.

B *attrib.* or as *adj.* 1 Made of crystal. LME. 2 Like crystal; clear as crystal. LME.

2 G. DURRELL Peering..through a fathom of crystal water at the sea bottom.

Comb. & *special collocations*: **crystal axis** each of the three directions chosen to define the edges of the unit cell of a crystal; **crystal ball** a globe-shaped piece of rock-crystal, used in crystal-gazing; **crystal-clear** *a.* completely clear, transparent, unclouded, (*lit.* & *fig.*); **crystal-gazer** a person who engages in crystal-gazing; a clairvoyant; **crystal-gazing** concentrating one's gaze on a crystal to see images forecasting the future or representing distant events; *fig.* unfounded speculation about the future; **crystal-glass** [G *Krystallglas*] = sense 4 above; **crystal lattice** the space lattice underlying the arrangement of atoms or molecules in a crystal; also, the arrangements of points occupied by the atoms or molecules or of the atoms or molecules themselves; **crystal set** *Hist.* a primitive form of radio receiving set using a crystal touching a metal wire as the rectifier; **crystal violet** an aniline dye used as a microscopical stain and as an antiseptic in the treatment of skin infections.

cryˈstallic *a.* (*rare*) (*a*) of, pertaining to, or like crystal; (*b*) of or pertaining to crystals or their formation: M17. **crystaˈlliferous** *a.* containing or yielding crystals L19. **cryˈstalliform** *a.* having a crystalline form L18. **crystal-like** *a.* resembling (that of) a crystal L19.

crystal /ˈkrɪst(ə)l/ *v.t.* Also †**chr-**. Infl. **-ll-**, ***-l-**. L17. [f. the n.] Convert into crystal, crystallize.

crystallin /ˈkrɪst(ə)lɪn/ *n.* M19. [f. L *crystallum* CRYSTAL *n.* + -IN[1].] *Biochem.* Any of various globulins contained in the lens of the eye.

crystalline /ˈkrɪst(ə)lʌɪn, *poet. also* krɪˈstalɪn/ *a.* & *n.* Also †**chr-**. ME. [(O)Fr. *cristallin* f. L *crystallinus* f. Gk *krustallinos*, f. *krustallos*: see CRYSTAL *n.* & *a.*, -INE[2].] A *adj.* 1 Clear and transparent like crystal; *fig.* perfectly clear to the understanding. ME. 2 Made or consisting of crystal (rock-crystal or glass). E16. 3 Having the form or structure of a crystal; composed of crystals. E17. b Of or pertaining to crystals and their formation. *rare.* M19.

1 T. GRAY She eyes the clear chrystalline well. J. BUCHAN There was a crystalline sharpness of outline in the remotest hills. **crystalline heaven**, **sphere**(s) *Hist.* a sphere (or two spheres) postulated by medieval astronomers between the primum mobile and the firmament. †**crystalline humour** the substance of the lens of the eye. *crystalline lens*: see LENS *n.* 2a.

B *n.* 1 *Hist.* The crystalline heaven (see sense A.1 above). LME. 2 The crystalline lens or (formerly) humour of the eye. LME. 3 Rock-crystal; a crystal, a crystalline rock. *rare.* M16.

crystaˈllinity *n.* crystalline quality; degree of crystallization: L19.

crystallisation *n.*, **crystallise** *v.* vars. of CRYSTALLIZATION, -IZE.

crystallite /ˈkrɪst(ə)lʌɪt/ *n.* E19. [f. CRYSTAL *n.* & *a.* + -ITE[1].] †1 Volcanic rock in a crystalline state after fusion and slow cooling. E–M19. 2 A minute body, lacking definite crystalline form, found in glassy volcanic rocks etc.; an incipient crystal. Formerly also = MICROLITE. L19. b An individual crystal or grain in a metal or other polycrystalline substance. E20. c A region within a volume of cellulose or other polymer with a degree of structural ordering as in a crystal. Also called *micelle*. E20.

crystaˈllitic *a.* (of the nature) of a crystallite; consisting of or containing crystallites: M19.

crystallization /krɪst(ə)lʌɪˈzeɪʃ(ə)n/ *n.* Also **-isation**. M17. [f. next + -ATION.] 1 The action or process of crystallizing (*lit.* & *fig.*). M17. 2 A product of crystallizing, a crystallized formation, (*lit.* & *fig.*). L17.

1 H. J. LASKI The age which saw the crystallization of the party-system. **water of crystallization** water forming an essential part in the structure of some crystals, esp. hydrated salts. 2 W. IRVING Salt springs ..forming beautiful crystallizations.

crystallize /ˈkrɪst(ə)lʌɪz/ *v.* Also **-ise**. L16. [f. CRYSTAL *n.* & *a.* + -IZE.] †1 *v.t.* Convert into crystal or ice. L16–L18. 2 *v.t.* & *i.* (Cause to) become crystalline in form or structure. M17. 3 *fig.* a *v.t.* Give a definite or permanent shape to (something vague or unformed). M17. b *v.i.* Assume a definite or permanent shape. E19. 4 *v.t.* Preserve (fruit, ginger, etc.) by impregnating and coating with crystals of sugar. Chiefly as *crystallized* ppl a. L19.

2 **crystallize out** separate in the form of crystals from a solution. *crystallized* VERDIGRIS. 3a G. MURRAY The writers who have most..revelation about them do not crystallize their revelation into formulae. b J. MCCARTHY This vague impression crystallised into a conviction. J. LONDON Just as my style is taking form, crystallizing.

crystallizable *a.* capable of crystallizing or being crystallized L18. **crystallizer** *n.* a person who or an apparatus which crystallizes E17.

crystallo- /ˈkrɪst(ə)ləʊ/ *comb. form* of Gk *krustallos* CRYSTAL *n.*: see -O-.

crystalloˈblastic *a.* (*Geol.*) (of rock texture) characteristic of or produced by recrystallization in a metamorphic process E20. **crystallo-ceramie** /-ˈsɛrəmi/ *n.* the technique of embedding decorative ceramic objects in clear glass, esp. in paperweights; objects made by this technique: E19. **crystallomancy** *n.* divination by means of a crystal E17.

crystallogenesis /krɪst(ə)ləʊˈdʒɛnɪsɪs/ *n.* L19. [f. prec. + -GENESIS.] The formation of crystals, esp. as a branch of study in science.

crystallogenic *a.* leading to the formation of crystals M19. **crystaˈllogeny** *n.* crystallogenesis M19.

crystallography /krɪstəˈlɒɡrəfi/ *n.* E19. [f. CRYSTALLO- + -GRAPHY.] The scientific study of the structure and properties of crystals and their classification.

X-RAY *crystallography*.

crystallographer *n.* E19. **crystalloˈgraphic(al)** *adjs.* pertaining to crystallography or to crystals scientifically considered E19. **crystalloˈgraphically** *adv.* with regard to or by means of crystallography M19.

crystalloid /ˈkrɪst(ə)lɔɪd/ *n.* & *a.* Now *rare.* LME. [f. CRYSTAL *n.* & *a.* + -OID.] A *n.* †1 The substance of the lens of the eye. Only in LME. 2 *Chem.* A crystalline substance, capable of dissolving in water and, when dissolved, of diffusing through a membrane. M19. 3 *Bot.* A crystal-like granule formed by the precipitation of protein, found in seeds and other storage organs. L19. B *adj.* Of crystalline form; pertaining to or of the nature of a crystalloid. M19.

crystaˈlloidal *a.* = CRYSTALLOID *a.* M19.

csardas /ˈtʃɑːdɑːʃ, ˈzɑːdəs/ *n.* Also **cz-**. Pl. same. M19. [Hungarian *csárdás*, f. *csárda* inn.] A Hungarian dance usu. having a slow start and a rapid wild finish, with many turns and leaps; a piece of music for this dance.

C sol fa *n.* var. of CESOLFA.

ctenidium /tɪˈnɪdɪəm/ *n.* Pl. **-dia** /-dɪə/. L19. [mod.L f. Gk *ktenidion* dim. of *kteis*, *kten-* comb.] *Zool.* Each of the respiratory organs or gills in a mollusc, consisting of an axis with a row of projecting filaments; a row of spines like a comb in some insects.

ctenidial *a.* L19.

ctenoid /ˈtiːnɔɪd/ *n.* & *a.* M19. [f. Gk *kteis*, *kten-* comb + -OID.] A *n.* A member of a former order of fishes comprising those with ctenoid scales. Now *rare* or *obs.* M19. B *adj.* Of the scales of certain fishes: having marginal projections like the teeth of a comb. Of a fish: having such scales. L19.

ctenophore /ˈtiːnəfɔː, ˈtɛn-/ *n.* L19. [f. mod.L *ctenophorus*, f. as prec.: see -PHORE.] *Zool.* Any animal of the phylum Ctenophora, comprising pelagic marine creatures resembling jellyfish and moving by means of stiff cilia borne on comblike plates. Also called *comb-jelly*.

cteˈnophoral *a.* of or pertaining to the Ctenophora or a ctenophore M19. **cteˈnophoran** *a.* & *n.* (*a*) *adj.* = CTENOPHORAL; (*b*) *n.* = CTENOPHORE: L19. **ctenoˈphoric** *a.* = CTENOPHORAL L19.

cuadrilla /kwadˈriʎa, kwɒdˈriːljə/ *n.* Pl. ***-as*** /-as, -əz/. M19. [Sp.: see QUADRILLE *n.*[2]] A company of people; *esp.* a matador's team.

cuartel /kwarˈtel, kwɔːˈtɛl/ *n.* M19. [Sp., f. *cuarta* quarter f. *cuarto* fourth f. L *quartus*.] A military barracks in Spain and Spanish-speaking countries.

cuatro *n.* var. of QUATRO.

cub /kʌb/ *n.*[1] & *v.*[1] M16. [Origin unkn.] A *n.* 1 A young fox. M16. 2 A young bear, wolf, lion, tiger, etc.; a young whale. L16. 3 An awkward unpolished youth. E17. b An apprentice, a beginner; *spec.* (in full *cub reporter*) a young or inexperienced newspaper reporter. M19. 4 (**C-**.) More fully *Cub Scout* (formerly *Wolf Cub*). A member of the junior branch of the Scout Association. E20.

3 THACKERAY He thinks it necessary to be civil to the young cub. b attrib.: *cub engineer*, *pilot*, etc.

B *v.* Infl. **-bb-**. 1 *v.t.* & *i.* Give birth to (a cub or cubs). M18. 2 *v.i.* Hunt fox-cubs. L19.

cubhood *n.* the state or period of being a cub M19.

cub /kʌb/ *n.*[2] & *v.*[2] Now *dial.* M16. [Prob. f. LG: cf. EFris. *kübbing*, *kübben* in same sense, LG *kübbing*, *kübje* shed or lean-to for cattle. Cf. COVE *n.*[1]] A *n.* A stall, pen, or shed for cattle; a coop, a hutch. Also, a crib for fodder. M16. B *v.t.* Infl. **-bb-**. Coop *up*. E17.

cubage /ˈkjuːbɪdʒ/ *n.* M19. [f. CUBE *n.*[1] or *v.* + -AGE.] Cubature; cubic content.

Cuba libre /ˈkjuːbə ˈliːbreɪ/ *n. phr.* Pl. **Cuba libres**. L19. [Amer. Sp. = free Cuba (a toast during the Cuban War of Independence, 1895–8).] A long drink usu. containing lime-juice and rum.

Cuban /ˈkjuːbən/ *a.* & *n.* L16. [f. *Cuba* (see below) + -AN.] (A native or inhabitant) of Cuba, an island in the W. Indies.

Cuban heel a broad straight-fronted moderately high shoe heel.

cubature /ˈkjuːbətjʊə/ *n.* L17. [f. CUBE *v.* after QUADRATURE.] The determination of the cubic content of a solid.

cubbish /ˈkʌbɪʃ/ *a.* E19. [f. CUB *n.*[1] + -ISH[1].] Resembling a cub; awkward, unpolished.

cubbishly *adv.* L19. **cubbishness** *n.* E19.

cubby /ˈkʌbi/ *n.* M17. [Rel. to CUB *n.*[2]] 1 A straw basket. *Sc.* M17. 2 In full *cubby-hole*. A small closet, a confined space, *esp.* one used for storage. E19. 3 An enclosure containing bait and a hidden trap for animals. *N. Amer.* E20.

Comb.: **cubby house** something that children playing pretend is a house; *esp.* a toy house.

cube /kjuːb/ *n.*[1] & *a.* M16. [(O)Fr., or its source L *cubus* f. Gk *kubos*.] A *n.* 1 A solid contained by six equal squares; a regular hexahedron. M16. b A block of something so or similarly shaped; a cubical object. E17. 2 *Math.* The product obtained by multiplying a number by the square of that number; the third power *of* a quantity. M16. 3 An extremely conventional or conservative person. (Cf. *square*.) *slang.* M20.

1b *ice-cube, sugar-cube*, etc. *double cube*: see DOUBLE *a.* & *adv. Necker('s) cube*: see NECKER *n.*[1] RUBIK('S) *cube*.

B *adj.* 1 = CUBIC *a.* 1, 2. Now chiefly in *cube root* below, *cube sugar*. L16. 2 Following a measurement: of the form of a cube with edges of the stated length. E18.

1 R. P. WARREN He took all the cube sugar that was in the bowl. **cube root** that number of which the given number is the cube. 2 J. D. DANA Some of these were six feet cube.

cube /ˈkuːbeɪ, ˈkjuː-/ *n.*[2] Also **cubé**. E20. [Amer. Sp. *cubé*.] Any of various S. American shrubby leguminous plants of the genus *Lonchocarpus* with roots containing the insecticide rotenone; (an extract from) the roots of such a plant.

cube /kjuːb/ *v.t.* L16. [f. the n.] 1 *Math.* Raise (a number) to the third power; find the cube of. L16. 2 Determine the cubic content of. M17. 3 Cut into small cubes; dice. M20.

cuber *n.* a machine for cutting meat etc. into cubes M20.

cubeb /ˈkjuːbɛb/ *n.* ME. [(O)Fr. *cubèbe*, †*quibibe* (med.L *cubeba*, *quibiba*) f. Sp. Arab. *kubēba* for Arab. *kubāba*.] The pungent berry of a SE Asian shrub of the pepper family, *Piper cubeba*, used in medicine (esp. crushed in medicated cigarettes) and cookery. Usu. in *pl.*

cubic /ˈkjuːbɪk/ *a.* & *n.* L15. [(O)Fr. *cubique* or its source L *cubicus* f. Gk *kubikos*, f. *kubos* CUBE *n.*[1]: see -IC.] A *adj.* 1 *Math.* Relating to or involving a third power but no higher one; of three dimensions; of the third degree. L15. 2 = CUBICAL 2. M16. b Belonging to or being a crystal system in which there are three crystallographic axes equal in length and mutually perpendicular. L19. 3 Of three dimensions; solid; *esp.* designating a volume equal to that of a cube whose edge is a specified unit of length. M17.

1 *cubic* RESIDUE. 2 **cubic nitre** sodium nitrate. 3 *cubic centimetre, cubic foot*, etc.

B *n. Math.* †1 = CUBE *n.*[1] 2. Only in L15. 2 A cubic expression, equation, or curve. L18.

cubica /ˈkjuːbɪkə/ *n.* & *a.* M19. [Sp.] (Of) a fine worsted fabric, similar to shalloon.

cubical /ˈkjuːbɪk(ə)l/ *a.* L15. [f. CUBIC + -AL[1].] 1 = CUBIC *a.* 1. Now *rare.* L15. 2 Having the shape or form of a cube. L16. 3 = CUBIC *a.* 3. L16.

cubically *adv.* L15. **cubicalness** *n.* (*rare*) E18.

cubicle /ˈkjuːbɪk(ə)l/ *n.* LME. [L *cubiculum*, f. *cubare* recline: see -CULE.] †1 A bedroom. LME–E16. 2 A small individual sleeping compartment. M19. 3 Any small partitioned space to accommodate one or two people; *spec.* = CARREL 2. E20. 4 A chamber or compartment to hold switch-gear. E20.

cuˈbicular *n.* & *a.* †(*a*) *n.* (chiefly *Sc.*) an attendant in a bedroom; a chamberlain; (*b*) *adj.* of or belonging to a bedroom: LME.

cubiculum /kjuːˈbɪkjʊləm/ *n.* Pl. **-la** /-lə/. M19. [L: see CUBICLE.] A sleeping-chamber (now *joc.*); *Archit.* a chapel or oratory attached to a church.

Also †**cubiculo** *n.* (*rare*, Shakes.): only in E17.

cubiform /ˈkjuːbɪfɔːm/ *a.* M18. [f. L *cubus* CUBE *n.*[1] + -I- + -FORM.] Having the form of a cube.

cubism /ˈkjuːbɪz(ə)m/ *n.* Also **C-**. E20. [Fr. *cubisme*, f. as CUBE *n.*[1]: see -ISM.] An artistic movement begun by Picasso and Braque in which perspective with a single viewpoint was abandoned and use was made of, initially, simple geometric shapes or interlocking semi-transparent planes and, later, solid objects stuck on the canvas.

cubist *n.* & *a.* (*a*) *n.* a practitioner or adherent of cubism; (*b*) *adj.* of or pertaining to cubists or cubism: E20. **cuˈbistic** *a.* somewhat cubist, in a style resembling that of cubism E20. **cuˈbistically** *adv.* E20.

cubit /ˈkjuːbɪt/ *n.* ME. [L *cubitum* elbow, forearm, cubit.] 1 *Hist.* A unit of length approximately equal to the length of the forearm. ME. †2 The forearm; the ulna. LME–M19. 3 The analogous part of the forelimb of a bird or quadruped. Now *rare.* E18.

cubital /ˈkjuːbɪt(ə)l/ *a.* LME. [L *cubitalis*, f. *cubitus* CUBIT: see -AL[1].] 1 *Hist.* Of the length of a cubit. LME. 2 *Anat.* Pertaining to the elbow or (formerly) the forearm or ulna. LME. 3 Of or pertaining to the cubitus or the cubit of an animal, esp. an insect. E19.

cubitus /ˈkjuːbɪtəs/ *n.* E19. [L: see CUBIT.] *Entomol.* †1 The fourth joint in the first pair of legs in an insect. Only in E19. 2 The fifth longitudinal vein from the anterior edge of an insect's wing. L19.

cubito- *comb. form* [see -O-] of the cubitus and —: L19.

cuboctahedron /ˌkjuːbɒktəˈhiːdr(ə)n, -ˈhɛd-/ *n.* Also **cubo-octa-** /ˌkjuːbəʊɒktə-/. Pl. **-dra** /-drə/, **-drons**. M19. [f. CUBE *n.*[1] + -O- + OCTAHEDRON.] A solid of fourteen faces formed by cutting off the corners of a cube so as to add eight equilateral triangular faces corresponding to those of an octahedron.

cuboctahedral *a.* E19.

cuboid /ˈkjuːbɔɪd/ *a.* & *n.* E19. [mod.L *cuboides* f. Gk *kuboeidēs*, f. *kubos* CUBE *n.*[1]: see -OID.] A *adj.* Resembling or approximating to a cube in form, cuboidal. E19.

cuboid bone, a squat bone on the outer side of the foot, next to the fourth and fifth metatarsals.

B *n.* 1 The cuboid bone. M19. 2 A solid with six faces that are rectangular but not all equal; an object with a cuboid shape. L19.

cuˈboidal *a.* resembling or approximating to a cube in form; *Anat.* of or pertaining to the cuboid bone; (of epithelium) composed of cuboidal cells: E19.

cuck /kʌk/ *v.*[1]*i.* *obs.* exc. *Hist.* in comb. LME. [Of Scand. origin: cf. Icel. *kúka* defecate, *kúkur* excrement).] Defecate.

Comb.: **cucking-stool** *Hist.*, †**cuck-stool** a chair in which disorderly women etc. were punished by ducking or exposure to public ridicule.

cuck /kʊk/ *v.*[2]*i.* L17. [Back-form. f. CUCKOO.] = CUCKOO *v.* 1.

cuckold /ˈkʌk(ə)ld/ *n.* & *v.* LOE. [ONFr. var. of OFr. *cucuault*, f. *cucu* CUCKOO + *-ald*, *-aud*, *-ault* pejorative suff.] A *n.* A man whose wife is adulterous. *derog.* LOE. B *v.t.* Make a cuckold of. L16.

†**cuckoldly** *a.* = CUCKOLDY L16–M18. **cuckoldom** *n.* (*a*) the state or position of a cuckold; †(*b*) = CUCKOLDRY (a): L16. **cuckoldry** *n.* (*a*) the action of making a cuckold of a man; †(*b*) = CUCKOLDOM (a): E16. **cuckoldy** *a.* (*arch.*) having the character or qualities of a cuckold (freq. as a general term of abuse) E17.

cuckoo /ˈkʊkuː/ *n.*, *int.*, *a.*, & *v.* ME. [OFr. *cucu* (mod. *coucou*) of imit. origin: cf. L *cuculus*, Gk *kokkux*. Superseded OE *ġēac* GOWK.] A *n.* 1 A migratory Eurasian grey or brown speckled bird, *Cuculus canorus*, which leaves its eggs in the nests of other birds and has a distinctive cry, the first hearing of which is regarded as a harbinger of spring. ME. b Any bird of the cosmopolitan family Cuculidae, including cuckoos, the roadrunner, and the anis. L18. 2 Also *int.* (Repr.) the call of the cuckoo; an imitation of this. ME. 3 A person who behaves like a cuckoo; *spec.* (*slang*) a silly person. L16.

1 SPENSER The merry Cuckow, messenger of Spring. b **chestnut-bellied cuckoo** a large brownish cuckoo of Jamaica, *Hyetornis pluvialis*; also called *hunter*, *old man*. EMERALD *cuckoo*. KLAAS'S CUCKOO. SHINING *cuckoo*. 3 O. W. HOLMES We Americans are all cuckoos,—we make our homes in the nests of other birds. J. K. JEROME Give us a hand here, can't you, you cuckoo; standing there like a stuffed mummy. **cuckoo in the nest** an unwanted intruder.

Comb.: **cuckoo-bud** *dial.* any of various plants (in Shakes. perh. a buttercup); **cuckoo clock**: in which the hours are sounded by an imitation of the cuckoo's call (often with an imitation cuckoo appearing); **cuckoo-flower** any of various spring wild flowers, esp. *Cardamine pratensis*, a cruciferous plant with small pink flowers (also called *lady's-smock*); **cuckoo-land** = *cloud-cuckoo-land* s.v. CLOUD *n.*; *cuckoo roller*: see ROLLER *n.*[2]; **cuckoo scab** *NZ* & *Austral.* a skin disease of sheep; **cuckoo shrike** any of various tropical Old World passerines of the family Campephagidae, which resemble shrikes; **cuckoo's mate** the wryneck; **cuckoo's meat** wood sorrel; **cuckoo-spit, cuckoo-spittle** a frothy secretion exuded on plants by larvae of insects of the family Cercopidae (frog-hoppers or spittle-bugs); **cuckoo wasp** any wasp of the family Chrysididae, which includes solitary wasps of a metallic blue or green colour which lay eggs in the nests of other wasps and bees; **cuckoo wrasse** a nest-building European wrasse, *Labrus mixtus*.

B *adj.* 1 Of or pertaining to the cuckoo; resembling the cuckoo and its uniformly repeated call. Usu. *attrib.* E17. 2 Crazy; foolish. *slang.* E20.

1 A. HELPS Tired of hearing this cuckoo exclamation. 2 M. GILBERT She must be cuckoo.

C *v.* 1 *v.i.* Utter the call of the cuckoo. E17. 2 *v.t.* Repeat incessantly and without variation. M17.

cuckoo-pint /ˈkʊkuːpʌɪnt, -pɪnt/ *n.* Earlier †**-pintle**. LME. [f. prec. + PINT(LE, w. ref. to the shape of the spadix.] The wild arum, *Arum maculatum*.

cuckquean /ˈkʌkwiːn/ *n.* & *v.* Long *rare.* M16. [f. CUCK(OLD + QUEAN.] A *n.* A woman whose husband is adulterous. M16. †B *v.t.* Make a cuckquean of. L16–M17.

cucujo *n.* var. of CUCUY.

cuculiform /kəˈkjuːlɪfɔːm/ *a.* L19. [mod.L *Cuculiformes*, f. L *cuculus* cuckoo + -FORM.] *Ornith.* Belonging or pertaining to the order Cuculiformes, which comprises the cuckoo family (Cuculidae) and the turaco family (Musophagidae).

cucullate /ˈkjuːkʌleɪt, kjʊˈkʌlət/ *a.* L18. [Late L *cucullatus*, f. *cucullus* hood: see -ATE[2].] *Bot.* & *Zool.* Shaped like a hood or cowl.

cucullately *adv.* M19.

cucullated /ˈkjuːkʌleɪtɪd/ *a.* M17. [f. as prec. + -ED[1].] 1 *Bot.* & *Zool.* Cucullate. M17. 2 Wearing a hood, cowled. M18.

cucumber /ˈkjuːkʌmbə/ *n.* LME. [L *cucumis*, *cucumer-*, whence OFr. *cocombre* (mod. *concombre*) to which the Eng. wd was assim.] 1 A trailing vine of the gourd family, *Cucumis sativus* native to southern Asia, whose fruit is the cucumber (sense 2). LME. 2 The long fleshy fruit of this plant, usu. eaten sliced in salads or sandwiches, or pickled when young (see GHERKIN). LME. 3 Any of various related or similar plants or their fruits. M16. 4 *sea cucumber*, a holothurian; formerly, some shellfish mentioned by Pliny. E17. 5 In full *cucumber tree*. Any of several American magnolias, esp. *Magnolia acuminata*, with small cucumber-shaped fruit. *US.* L18.

2 **cool as a cucumber** perfectly cool or self-possessed. 3 **squirting cucumber** a plant of the gourd family, *Ecballium elaterium*, whose fruit when ripe expels its seeds and pulp with force.

Comb.: **cucumber beetle** *N. Amer.* any of several beetles which attack cucumbers, corn, and other plants; **cucumber mosaic** a virus disease of cucurbits spread by cucumber beetles and aphids and causing mottling and stunting; **cucumber tree** (*a*) a tropical Asian tree of the oxalis family, *Averrhoa bilimbi*, with edible astringent cucumber-shaped fruit; (*b*) see sense 5 above.

cucumiform /kjʊˈkjuːmɪfɔːm/ *a.* M19. [f. L *cucumis* cucumber + -FORM.] Of the shape of a cucumber.

cucurbit /kjʊˈkəːbɪt/ *n.* LME. [(O)Fr. *cucurbite* f. L *cucurbita*.] 1 A plant of the gourd family, Cucurbitaceae. Formerly, a gourd. LME. 2 A vessel or retort (orig. gourd-shaped) for chemical or alchemical use. *obs.* exc. *Hist.* LME.

cucurbitaceous /kjʊˌkəːbɪˈteɪʃ(ə)s/ *a.* E19. [f. mod.L *Cucurbitaceae* (see below), f. L *cucurbita* gourd: see -ACEOUS.] *Bot.* Of or pertaining to the family Cucurbitaceae, which comprises trailing or climbing plants with fleshy fruits, as the gourd, melon, pumpkin, cucumber, etc.

cucuy /kəˈkuːi/ *n.* Also **cucujo** /kəˈkuːjəʊ/, pl. **-os**, & other vars. L16. [Sp. *cucuyo* f. Haitian creole.] A luminous W. Indian click beetle, *Pyrophorus noctilucus*.

cud /kʌd/ *n.* & *v.* [OE *cudu*, earlier *cwudu*, *cwidu* = OHG *quiti*, *kuti* glue (G *Kitt* cement, putty).] **A** *n.* **1** The partly digested food which a ruminating animal brings back into its mouth from its first stomach for further chewing. OE. **2** Any substance used by a person to keep in the mouth and chew. (Cf. QUID *n.*[3]) Now *dial.* OE.

Phrases: **chew the cud** *fig.* reflect meditatively, ruminate.

B *v.* Infl. **-dd-**. **1** *v.t.* Chew as cud; ruminate upon. *rare.* M16. **2** *v.i.* Of an animal: chew the cud. M20.

cudbear /ˈkʌdbɛː/ *n.* M18. [Alt. of *Cuthbert* by Cuthbert Gordon, 18th-cent. Sc. chemist who patented the powder: cf. CUDDY *n.*[2]] A purple or violet powder used for dyeing, prepared from various lichens, esp. *Ochrolechia tartarea*. Also, this lichen.

†**cudden** *n.*[1] L17–M19. [Origin unkn.] A fool, a dolt.

cudden *n.*[2] var. of CUDDING.

cuddie *n.* var. of CUDDY *n.*[3]

cuddikie *n.* see CUDEIGH.

cudding /ˈkʌdɪŋ/ *n.* Chiefly *Sc.* Also **-din**, **-den**. L17. [Gael. *cudainn*: cf. CUDDY *n.*[3]] **1** = CHAR *n.*[2] Now *rare* or *obs.* L17. **2** = CUDDY *n.*[3] M19.

cuddle /ˈkʌd(ə)l/ *v.* & *n.* E16. [Perh. f. COUTH + -LE[3].] **A** *v.* **1** *v.t.* Hold in an affectionate embrace, hug and fondle. E16. **2** *v.i.* Settle close and snug to another or together. (Foll. by *up.*) E18. **3** *v.i.* & *refl.* Curl oneself *up* in preparing to sleep; lie down to sleep. E19. **B** *n.* An affectionate hug, a close embrace. E19.

¶Rare bef. 18.

cuddleable *a.* (*colloq.*) = CUDDLY (b) E20. **cuddlesome** *a.* = CUDDLY (b) L19. **cuddly** *a.* (*a*) given to cuddling; (*b*) that invites cuddling M19.

cuddy /ˈkʌdi/ *n.*[1] M17. [Prob. f. early mod.Du. *kajute*, *kaiuyte* (now *kajuit* whence Fr. *cajute*) f. (O)Fr. *cahute* shanty, of unkn. origin.] **1** *Naut.* A room or cabin in a ship; *esp.* (*a*) one where the captain and passengers eat; (*b*) a shelter or locker in the bow of a small boat. M17. **2** *gen.* A small room, closet, or cupboard. L18.

cuddy /ˈkʌdi/ *n.*[2] E18. [Perh. a use of *Cuddy*, pet-form of male forename *Cuthbert*: cf. NEDDY *n.*] **I 1** A donkey. Chiefly *Sc.* E18. **2** A stupid person, an ass. Chiefly *Sc.* M19. **3** A (small) horse. Chiefly *north.* & *Austral.* M20. **II 4** A lever mounted on a tripod for lifting stones etc. M19.

Phrases: *Scotch cuddy*: see SCOTCH *a.*

cuddy /ˈkʌdi/ *n.*[3] *Sc.* Also **cuddie**. L18. [Gael. *cudaig*: cf. CUDDING.] The coalfish, *esp.* a young one.

†**cuddy** *n.*[4] var. of next.

cudeigh /ˈkʌdɪx/ *n.* Also **cuddikie** /ˈkʌdɪki/, †**cuddy**. LME. [Repr. (O)Ir. & Gael. *cuid oidhche* (*cuid* share, part, meal, *oidhche* night).] **1** *Ir.* & *Sc. Hist.* A supper and night's entertainment due to a lord from his tenant; a rent or present in lieu of this. LME. †**2** *transf.* A gift, a bribe; a premium on a loan. *Sc.* E18–E19.

cudgel /ˈkʌdʒ(ə)l/ *n.* & *v.* [OE *cyċġel*, of unkn. origin.] **A** *n.* **1** A short thick stick used as a weapon; a club. OE. **2** In *pl.* The use of cudgels; the art of combat with cudgels. M17.

1 take up the cudgels *fig.* engage in a vigorous debate (*for* etc.) **2** ADDISON They learned to Box and play at Cudgels.

Comb.: **cudgel-play**, **cudgel-playing** = sense 2 above.

B *v.* Infl. **-ll-**, ***-l-**. **1** *v.t.* Beat (as) with a cudgel. L16. **2** *v.i.* Wield a cudgel or cudgels. Chiefly as *cudgelling* vbl n. L18.

1 : *cudgel one's brains*: see BRAIN *n.*

cudgeller *n.* L16.

cudgerie /ˈkʌdʒəri/ *n.* *Austral.* L19. [Aborig. *gajari.*] Any of several Australian trees, *spec.* the southern silver ash, *Flindersia schottiana*, an evergreen rainforest timber tree (family Rutaceae).

†**cuds** *n.* L16–M17. [Alt.] God's: used in oaths and exclamations.

Also †**cudso** *n.*: only in E18.

cudweed /ˈkʌdwiːd/ *n.* M16. [f. CUD *n.* + WEED *n.*[1]] Any of various erect herbaceous plants of the composite family, esp. of the genera *Gnaphalium* and *Filago*, with hairy or downy foliage.

cudwort /ˈkʌdwɔːt/ *n.* M16. [f. CUD *n.* + WORT *n.*[1]] = prec.

†**cue** *n.*[1] LME. [Repr. pronunc. of Q.] **1** The sum of half a farthing, formerly denoted in college accounts by the letter q (for L *quadrans* quarter). LME–E17. **2** A particular small quantity of bread, beer, etc. *Univ. slang.* E17–M19.

cue /kjuː/ *n.*[2] M16. [Origin unkn.] **I 1 a** *Theatr.* A particular word or phrase in a play etc. which serves as a signal to another actor to enter or begin a speech. M16. **b** *Mus.* In an orchestral or vocal score, a short passage from another part written in small notes as a signal to a performer of an approaching entry. L19. **c** *Cinemat.* & *Broadcasting.* A prearranged signal for action to begin or end; *spec.* a mark on a film serving as a signal for a film editor or projectionist. M20. **2** An indication or hint of when or how to speak, behave, etc. M16. **3** The part assigned to one to play; the proper course to take. L16. **4** *Psychol.* A feature of a perception or of something perceived that is used as an aid in the brain's interpretation of the perception. E20. **5** A facility for playing a tape recording during a fast forward wind, so that it can be stopped when a particular recording is reached. L20.

1a M. RENAULT An actor who dries up on the crucial cue for which the scene is waiting. **2** E. F. BENSON Lucia had not been thinking of this . . but she picked up her cue instantaneously.

II 6 A mood, a disposition, a frame of mind. Now *rare.* M16.

Phrases: **cue and review** a tape-recording cue facility combined with a similar one for fast rewind. **on cue** (as if) in response to a signal; at the correct moment. **take one's cue from** follow the example or advice of.

Comb.: **cue-bid** *n.* & *v.i.* (*Bridge*) (make) an artificial bid, inviting a particular response from one's partner, for exploratory or informative purposes; **cue card**: held beside a camera for an announcer etc. to read from while looking into the camera.

cue /kjuː/ *n.*[3] M18. [Var. of QUEUE *n.*] **1** A long plait of hair worn hanging down behind, a pigtail. M18. **2** The long straight tapering rod, now usu. of wood tipped with leather, with which the white ball is struck in billiards, snooker, etc. M18.

Comb.: **cue-ball** the white ball which is to be struck with the cue in billiards, snooker, etc.

cueist *n.* a player of billiards, snooker, etc.; a person skilled in the use of a cue: L19.

cue /kjuː/ *n.*[4] *colloq.* E20. [Abbrev.: cf. CUKE.] = CUCUMBER 2.

cue /kjuː/ *v.*[1]*t.* Now *rare.* L18. [f. CUE *n.*[3] Cf. QUEUE *v.*] Form or twist (the hair) into a cue.

cue /kjuː/ *v.*[2]*t.* E20. [f. CUE *n.*[2]] Provide with a cue or signal; lead *in* by means of a cue.

A. COOKE Cued by my mention of some of the great names, he went off into a bout of marvellous total recall.

cueca /ˈkwɛkə/ *n.* E20. [Amer. Sp. f. ZAMACUECA.] A lively S. American dance. Also called *marinera*.

cue-owl /ˈkjuːaʊl/ *n.* *rare.* M19. [It. *chiù*, *ciù*, f. the sound of its cry.] The European scops owl, *Otus scops*.

cuesta /ˈkwɛstə/ *n.* E19. [Sp. = slope f. L *costa*: see COAST *n.*] Orig. (*US dial.*), a steep slope that terminates a gently sloping plain; a plain in this configuration. Now (*Geogr.*), a ridge with a gentle slope on one side and a steep one on the other, a scarp and dip.

cuff /kʌf/ *n.*[1] LME. [Origin unkn.] **1** A mitten, a glove. Long *obs.* exc. *Canad. dial.* LME. **2 a** A distinctive part at the end of a long sleeve, consisting of the sleeve itself turned back or a band of material sewn on; a separate band of linen worn round the wrist. L15. **b** A turn-up on a trouser leg. Chiefly *N. Amer.* E20. **3** A handcuff. Usu. in *pl.* M17. **4** An inflatable bag which is wound round a limb when blood pressure is measured. E20.

Phrases: *French cuff*: see FRENCH *a.* **off the cuff** *colloq.* extempore, without preparation. **on the cuff** *colloq.* (*a*) *US* on credit; (*b*) *NZ* beyond what is appropriate or conventional. *rotator cuff*: see ROTATOR 1. *shoot one's cuffs*: see SHOOT *v.*

Comb.: **cuff-link** a device which goes through two buttonholes in a cuff to hold its two sides together.

cuffless *a.* L19.

cuff /kʌf/ *n.*[2] M16. [f. CUFF *v.*[2]] A blow, *esp.* one given with the open hand.

W. C. WILLIAMS He was my boss and many a time he gave me a cuff over the ears. **go, fall, to cuffs** (now *rare*) come to blows, start fighting.

cuff /kʌf/ *n.*[3] *slang. contempt.* E17. [Origin unkn.: cf. CUFFIN.] An old man, *esp.* a miserly one.

cuff /kʌf/ *n.*[4] Chiefly *Sc.* M18. [Origin unkn.: cf. SCUFF *n.*[2], SCRUFF *n.*[2]] The nape *of* the neck.

rotator cuff: see ROTATOR 1.

Cuff /kʌf/ *n.*[5] *US colloq.* Now *rare* & considered *derog.* M18. [Abbrev.] = CUFFEE.

cuff /kʌf/ *v.*[1]*t.* E16. [f. CUFF *n.*[1]] **1** Provide with a cuff or cuffs. Chiefly as *cuffed* ppl a. E16. **2** Handcuff. *rare.* L17.

1 *Daily Telegraph* Flannel trousers, deeply cuffed.

cuffing *vbl n.* (*a*) the action of the vb; (*b*) the pathological accumulation of lymphocytes etc. in a ring within a blood-vessel: L17.

cuff /kʌf/ *v.*[2] M16. [Perh. imit.: cf. G slang *kuffen* thrash, Sw. *kuffa* thrust, push.] **1** *v.t.* Strike, esp. with the open hand; buffet. M16. **2** *v.i.* Deal or exchange blows; scuffle. E17. **3** *v.t.* Discuss, talk *over*, (a tale, a matter); tell (a tale). *dial.* M18.

1 B. CHATWIN She cuffed him when he tried to make love to her. W. GOLDING The wind . . did not clear the sky but cuffed the air this way and that.

cuffer *n.* (*a*) *arch.* a person who cuffs; a fighter; (*b*) *dial.* & *slang* a yarn, a story: M17.

Cuffee /ˈkʌfi/ *n.* *US colloq.* Now *rare* & considered *derog.* Also **Cuffy**, **c-**. E18. [A pers. name formerly common among Blacks.] **1** (A nickname for) a Black. E18. **2** A black bear. E19.

cuffin /ˈkʌfɪn/ *n.* *Criminals' slang.* M16. [Origin unkn.: cf. CHUFF *n.*[1]] = COVE *n.*[2]

Cuffy *n.* var. of CUFFEE.

Cufic *a.* var. of KUFIC.

cufuffle *n.* var. of KERFUFFLE.

cui bono /kwiː ˈbɒnəʊ, kuːiː-, ˈbəʊnəʊ/ *int.* (*interrog.*), *a.*, & *n. phr.* E17. [L = to whom (is it) a benefit?] **A** *int.* (*interrog.*) What is the purpose (of)? Who stands to gain (and so might be responsible)? E17. **B** *adj. phr.* Of or pertaining to the question *cui bono?* M18. **C** *n. phr.* The question *cui bono?* M19.

cuirass /kwɪˈras/ *n.* & *v.* Also †**curats**. LME. [OFr. *cuirace*, later *curas*, *-ace* (mod. *cuirasse*), f. alt. (after (O)Fr. *cuir* leather) of Proto-Romance use as n. of fem. of L *coriaceus* adj., f. *corium* leather: see -ACEOUS.] **A** *n.* **1** *sing.* & in *pl.* A piece of armour for the body (orig. of leather); *spec.* a piece reaching down to the waist, and consisting of a breastplate and a backplate, buckled or otherwise fastened together. In *sing.* occas., the breastplate alone. LME. **2** = BUCKLER *n.* 3. E17. **3** The armour-plating of a ship etc. M19. **4** A close-fitting sleeveless bodice, often stiffened with metal trimmings or embroidery, formerly worn by women. L19. **5** In full *cuirass respirator.* A respirator which encloses the trunk but not the limbs. M20. **B** *v.t.* Cover or protect (as) with a cuirass. M19.

cuirassed *a.* provided with cuirasses; protected (as if) by a cuirass: E19.

cuirassier /kwɪrəˈsɪə/ *n.* M16. [Fr., f. as prec.: see -IER.] A cavalry soldier wearing a cuirass.

cuir-bouilli /kwɪəˈbuːlji, *foreign* kyirbuji/ *n.* Long *obs.* exc. *Hist.* LME. [Fr. = boiled leather.] Leather boiled or soaked in hot water and, when soft, moulded into any required form, which it retains on becoming dry and hard (formerly often used for armour).

cuir-ciselé /kwɪəˈsiːzleɪ, *foreign* kyirsizle/ *a.* M20. [Fr. = engraved leather.] (Of a design on a leather binding) cut in relief with a pointed tool; having such a design.

Cuisenaire rod /kwiːzəˈnɛː rɒd/ *n. phr.* M20. [Georges *Cuisenaire* (*c*1891–1976), Belgian educationalist.] Each of a set of wooden rods, of different length and colour according to the number they represent, used in teaching children about numbers.

¶ *Cuisenaire* is a proprietary name.

cuish *n.* var. of CUISSE.

cuisine /kwɪˈziːn/ *n.* L18. [Fr. = kitchen f. L *coquina, cocina,* f. *coquere* to cook: cf. KITCHEN.] A culinary establishment; cookery as an art, esp. as characteristic of a particular country or establishment.

batterie de cuisine: see BATTERIE 2. **cuisine bourgeoise** /ˈbʊəʒwaːz/ [middle-class] plain (French) home cooking. NOUVELLE CUISINE.

cuisinier *n.* a (French) cook M19.

cuisse /kwɪs/ *n.* Also **cuish** /kwɪʃ/. ME. [Orig. in pl. f. OFr. *cuiss(i)eus* pl. of *cuissel* f. late L *coxale,* f. *coxa* hip.] In *pl.*, armour for protecting the front of the thighs; *sing.* a thigh-piece.

†cuit *a.* & *n.* Also **cute**. LME–M18. [Fr. (f. L *coctus*), pa. pple of *cuire* f. L *coquere* cook, boil.] (A wine, liquor, etc.) made thicker by boiling down, and sweetened.

cuiter /ˈkuːtə/ *v.t. Sc.* L17. [Origin unkn.] Attend to (a person) with kindly assiduity.

cuittle /ˈkuːt(ə)l/ *v.t. Sc.* M16. [Origin unkn.] 1 Curry (favour); wheedle, coax. M16. 2 Tickle. L18.

cuivré /ˈkiːvreɪ, *foreign* kyivre/ *adv.* & *n.* M20. [Fr., pa. pple of *cuivrer* play with a brassy tone, f. *cuivre* COPPER *n.*[1] f. late L *cuprum.*] *Mus.* (With) a harsh strident tone (in a brass instrument).

cuke /kjuːk/ *n. colloq.* (chiefly *N. Amer.*). E20. [Abbrev.: cf. CUE *n.*[4]] = CUCUMBER *n.* 2.

culbut /ˈkʌlbʌt/ *v.i.* & *t. rare.* L17. [Fr. *culbuter,* f. *cul* buttocks + *buter* BUTT *v.*[1]] Overturn backwards; drive back in disorder.

culch /kʌltʃ/ *n. local* & *US.* Also **cultch**. M17. [Origin unkn. Cf. SCULCH.] 1 The mass of stones, old shells, etc., of which an oyster-bed is formed. M17. 2 *gen.* Rubbish, refuse. M18.

culching *n.* the practice of strewing an oyster-bed with culch L19.

culchie /ˈkʌl(t)ʃi/ *n.* & *a. Anglo-Ir. slang* (freq. *derog.*). Also **-shie** /-ʃi/. M20. [Perh. alt. of 1st part of *Kilti*magh, a country town in County Mayo, Ireland.] A *n.* A country bumpkin; a provincial or rustic person. M20. B *attrib.* or as *adj.* Of, pertaining to, or characteristic of a culchie, provincial, rustic. L20.

Culdee /ˈkʌldiː/ *n.* & *a.* LME. [med.L *culdeus* alt. (after L *cultor Dei* worshipper of God) of *Kel(e)deus,* f. OIr. *céle Dé, céile Dé* anchorite, lit. 'client of God' (*Dé* genit. of *Día* god).] A *n.* A member of an ancient Scoto-Irish religious order, found from the 8th cent. onwards. LME. B *adj.* Of or pertaining to the Culdees. L19.

Cul'dean *a.* E19.

cul-de-lampe /kydlɑ̃p/ *n.* Pl. ***culs-*** (pronounced same). E18. [Fr., lit. 'bottom of lamp'.] 1 *Archit.* An ornamental support or pendant of inverted conical form. E18. 2 *Typogr.* An ornament, often based on an inverted conical form, placed at the end of a passage of text. Now *rare.* E19.

cul-de-sac /ˈkʌldəsak, kʊldəˈsak/ *n.* Pl. **culs-de-sac** (pronounced same), **cul-de-sacs**. M18. [Fr. = sack-bottom.] 1 *Anat.* A vessel, tube, sac, etc., open only at one end; the closed end of such a vessel. M18. 2 A street, passage, etc., closed at one end; a blind alley; *Mil.* a position in which an army is hemmed in on all sides except behind. L18.

culdoscopy /kʌlˈdɒskəpi/ *n.* M20. [f. prec. + -O- + -SCOPY.] *Med.* Visual examination of a woman's pelvic viscera by means of an endoscope passed through the vaginal wall.

'culdoscope *n.* an endoscope designed for this M20.

-cule /kjuːl/ *suff.* [Repr. Fr. *-cule* f. L *-culus, -cula, -culum,* dim. suff.: cf. -CLE, -UNCLE.] Forming (orig. dim.) ns., as *molecule, crepuscule,* etc. The L endings *-culus, -cula, -culum,* are retained in some (esp. technical) wds f. L.

culet /ˈkʌlɪt/ *n.*[1] *obs.* exc. *Hist.* M16. [OFr. *cueillete* f. med.L *collecta* sum collected.] A sum collected from all those who are obliged to pay it; an assessment, a rate.

culet /ˈkjuːlɪt/ *n.*[2] Also (earlier) **collet** /ˈkɒlɪt/. L17. [Fr., dim. of *cul* bottom: see -ET[1].] 1 The horizontal base of a diamond, formed by the blunting of a point, when the stone is cut as a brilliant. L17. 2 A piece of armour for protecting the hinder part of the body below the waist. M19.

culex /ˈkjuːlɛks/ *n.* In sense 2 also **C-**. Pl. **-lices** /-lɪsiːz/. L15. [L = gnat.] †1 A gnat. Only in L15. 2 Any mosquito of the genus *Culex,* which includes the common house mosquito. Also more fully *culex mosquito.* E19.

†culgee *n. Anglo-Ind.* M17. [Urdu f. Pers. *kalġī.*] 1 A rich figured silk used for turbans, gowns, etc. M17–M18. 2 A jewelled plume on a turban. E18–M19.

culici- /ˈkjuːlɪsi/ *comb. form* of L *culic-,* CULEX: see -I-. Also **culi-**.

culici'cidal *a.* pertaining to or being a culicicide L19. **culicicide** *n.* [-CIDE] an insecticide for destroying mosquitoes E20. **culi'cidal** *a.* = CULICICIDAL L19. **culicide** *n.* = CULICICIDE *n.* E20. **culicifuge** *n.* [-FUGE] a substance applied to the body or to clothing in order to keep mosquitoes away L19.

culicine /ˈkjuːlɪsiːn/ *n.* & *a.* E20. [mod.L *Culicini, -nae,* f. L *culic-,* CULEX: see -INE[1].] *Entomol.* (Pertaining to or designating) a mosquito of a group that contains the genus *Culex* but not *Anopheles.*

culinary /ˈkʌlɪn(ə)ri/ *a.* M17. [L *culinarius,* f. *culina* kitchen: see -ARY[1].] 1 Of or pertaining to a kitchen or cookery. M17. 2 Of a vegetable etc.: fit for cooking. M18.

culi'narian *a.* (*rare*) of or pertaining to a kitchen E17. **culinarily** *adv.* (*rare*) M19.

cull /kʌl/ *n.*[1] & *a.* E17. [f. CULL *v.*[1]] A *n.* 1 An act of culling; a selection; *spec.* the process of selecting and killing surplus or inferior animals from a flock etc. E17. 2 An animal selected in a cull; *spec.* an inferior farm animal. L18. 3 *sing.* & in *pl.* Inferior or refuse timber. Chiefly *N. Amer.* E19. 4 *gen.* In *pl.* Items picked out as surplus or inferior. Chiefly *dial.* L19.

1 *Times Lit. Suppl.* A list of the words and phrases I'd found.. showing an average daily cull from an intelligent newspaper. *Guardian* A cull of 375 seals is to be allowed.. this summer.

B *attrib.* or as *adj.* Selected in a cull; rejected as surplus or inferior. L18.

Times Some cull apples go, at a low price, into cider manufacture.

cull /kʌl/ *n.*[2] *slang* & *dial.* L17. [Perh. f. CULLY.] = CULLY.

cull /kʌl/ *v.*[1] ME. [OFr. *coillier,* (also mod.) *cueiller* f. Proto-Romance f. L *colligere* COLLECT *v.*] 1 *v.t.* Choose from a fairly large number; pick, select. (Foll. by *from,* (arch.) *out.*) ME. b *v.t.* & *i.* Select (livestock etc.) according to quality; select from a flock and kill (surplus or inferior animals etc.); *N. Amer.* remove (timber) as inferior. E19. 2 *v.t.* Gather, pick, (flowers, fruit, etc.). M17. 3 *v.t.* Subject (something containing or consisting of many items) to a process of selection. E18.

1 G. CRABBE Words aptly culled, and meanings well express. H. CARPENTER His wide general knowledge, culled from his father's library. b *transf.*: T. KENEALLY The limpers, the coughers, were culled at the beginning of each stage and executed.

culler *n.* a person who culls or selects (esp. inferior or surplus items) LME.

cull *v.*[2] var. of COLL *v.*[1]

cullender *n.* & *v.* var. of COLANDER.

cullet /ˈkʌlɪt/ *n.* E19. [Var. & extension of use of COLLET *n.*[1] 4.] Broken or scrap glass which is melted down for reuse.

†cullible *a.* Only in E19. [f. CULL *n.*[2], CULLY + -IBLE. No corresp. vb *cull* is recorded.] Easily made a fool of; gullible.

†cullibility *n.* gullibility E18–M19.

culling /ˈkʌlɪŋ/ *n.* LME. [f. CULL *v.*[1] + -ING[1].] 1 The action of selecting or picking out; *spec.* the selective killing of surplus or inferior animals. LME. 2 An item picked out; *spec.* an old or inferior animal taken out from a flock. Freq. in *pl.* E17.

cullion /ˈkʌljən/ *n.* LME. [OFr. *coillon* (mod. *couillon*) f. Proto-Romance, f. L *coleus, culleus* bag, testicle f. Gk *koleos* sheath.] 1 A testicle. Now *rare.* LME. 2 A base despicable person; a rascal. *arch.* L16. 3 In *pl.* An orchid. Now *rare.* E17.

†cullionly *a.* rascally, base E17–E19.

cullis /ˈkʌlɪs/ *n.*[1] Now *rare.* LME. [OFr. *colëiz* (mod. *coulis*) use as n. of adj. f. Proto-Romance, f. L *colare* strain, flow (whence Fr. *couler*).] A strong broth of meat, fowl, etc., boiled and strained.

cullis /ˈkʌlɪs/ *n.*[2] M19. [Fr. COULISSE.] *Archit.* A grooved timber, a gutter, a channel.

cully /ˈkʌli/ *n.* & *v. slang.* M17. [Origin unkn.] A *n.* 1 A person who is cheated or imposed upon; a dupe; a simpleton. Now *rare.* M17. 2 A man; a mate, a pal. L17. †B *v.t.* Make a fool of, cheat, take in. L17–M19.

culm /kʌlm/ *n.*[1] ME. [Prob. rel. to COAL *n.*] 1 Soot, smut. *obs.* exc. *Sc.* ME. 2 Coal-dust, slack, esp. of anthracite. E17. 3 Anthracite. M18. 4 *Geol.* (Also **C-**.) The material of a set of Carboniferous strata (*the Culm Measures*) in SW England, mostly shale and limestone with occasional thin coal seams. Also, this set of strata. M19.

†culm *n.*[2] *rare.* L16–E19. [Abbrev. of CULMEN.] The summit, the culminating point.

culm /kʌlm/ *n.*[3] M17. [L *culmus.*] *Bot.* The stem of a plant; *esp.* the jointed stem of grasses and sedges.

culmen /ˈkʌlmɛn/ *n.* M17. [L, contr. of *columen* top, summit, etc.] 1 The top, the summit; *fig.* the acme, the culminating point. M17. 2 The upper ridge of a bird's bill. M19. 3 *Anat.* An anterior part of the vermis of the cerebellum bounded by deep fissures. L19.

culmiferous /kʌlˈmɪf(ə)rəs/ *a.*[1] E18. [f. CULM *n.*[3] + -FEROUS.] *Bot.* Having a jointed hollow stalk, like grasses.

culmiferous /kʌlˈmɪf(ə)rəs/ *a.*[2] M19. [f. CULM *n.*[1] + -FEROUS.] *Geol.* Containing or producing culm.

culminant /ˈkʌlmɪnənt/ *a.* E17. [Late L *culminant-* pres. ppl stem of *culminare*: see next, -ANT[1].] 1 (Of a celestial object) at its greatest altitude, on the meridian; *gen.* at its greatest height. E17. 2 Forming the highest point; topmost. M19.

culminate /ˈkʌlmɪneɪt/ *v.* M17. [Late L *culminat-* pa. ppl stem of *culminare* exalt, extol, f. *culmen, -min-* summit: see -ATE[3].] 1 *v.i.* Of a celestial object: reach its greatest altitude, be on the meridian. M17. 2 *v.i. gen.* Reach its highest point; rise to an apex or summit. (Foll. by *in.*) M17. 3 *v.i.* Reach its climax or point of highest development. (Foll. by *in.*) M17. 4 *v.t.* Bring to a climax; form the summit or climax of, crown. (*rare* bef. L19.) M17.

2 O. SITWELL Almost every hill culminates in a tower. 3 H. J. LASKI The speculative mania which culminated in the South Sea Bubble. HENRY MILLER Did my life really lead up to this culminating moment? *Nature* The warm period in the present century has culminated. 4 *New Scientist* Feynman and.. Gell-Mann, whose work culminated a period of feverish experimental and theoretical development.

culmination /kʌlmɪˈneɪʃ(ə)n/ *n.* M17. [f. prec.: see -ATION.] I 1 The attainment by a celestial object of its highest altitude; the act of reaching the meridian. M17. 2 *Geol.* A part of a fold, esp. a nappe, where the strata were at their highest before they were eroded. E20. 3 *Geol.* A locally highest part in a fold system which rises and falls in axial as well as transverse directions; a high point between two saddles. M20. II *fig.* 4 The attainment of the highest or climactic point; that in which something culminates, the crown, the consummation, (*of*). M17.

culotte /kjuːˈlɒt, *foreign* kylɔt/ *n.* Pl. pronounced same. M19. [Fr. = knee-breeches. Cf. SANSCULOTTE.] 1 Knee-breeches. *rare.* M19. 2 *sing.* & (usu.) in *pl.* A woman's garment that hangs like a skirt but has separate legs, as in trousers; a divided skirt. E20. 3 A fringe of soft hair on the back of the forelegs of some dogs. E20.

culpa /ˈkʌlpə/ *n.* M19. [L: see next.] *Law.* Neglect resulting in damage, negligence.

culpable /ˈkʌlpəb(ə)l/ *a.* & *n.* ME. [(O)Fr. *coupable* f. L *culpabilis*, f. *culpare* to blame, f. *culpa* fault, blame: see -ABLE.] A *adj.* 1 Guilty (*of*, †*in* an offence), criminal; deserving punishment. Now *rare* or *obs.* ME. †2 Foll. by *of*: deserving, liable to, (punishment, judgement, etc.). LME–E17. 3 Deserving censure; blameworthy. L16.

1 G. P. R. JAMES The greatest crime of which a man could render himself culpable. **culpable homicide** *Sc. Law* homicide not amounting to murder. 3 HOBBES What circumstances make an action laudable, or culpable.

†B *n.* A guilty person, a culprit. ME–M18.

culpaˈbility *n.* L17. **culpableness** *n.* LME. **culpably** *adv.* in a culpable manner, to a culpable degree M17.

culpose /kʌlˈpəʊs/ *a.* M19. [f. L *culpa* fault + -OSE[1], after *dolose.*] *Rom. Law.* Characterized by (criminal) negligence.

culprit /ˈkʌlprɪt/ *n.* L17. [Perh. f. misinterpretation as a form of address of written abbrev. *cul. prist* for AN *Culpable: prest d'averrer notre bille* '(You are) guilty: (we are) ready to aver our indictment'. In sense 3 infl. by L *culpa* fault.] 1 *Law.* A person arraigned for high treason or felony. Only in the formula *Culprit, how will you be tried?*, said by the clerk to a prisoner who has pleaded not guilty. Long *obs.* exc. *Hist.* L17. 2 A person accused of a criminal offence. E18. 3 A person who is guilty of an offence; a person responsible for a fault. M18.

2 M. PRIOR An author is in the condition of a culprit: the public are his judges. 3 L. URIS We will find the culprit and he will tell us where he has planted the bomb.

culrach /ˈkʌlreɪx/ *n. obs.* exc. *Hist.* Also **-reach.** LME. [App. f. Gael. *cùl* back + *ràth(an)* surety.] *Sc. Law.* A surety given to a court when a case is removed from its jurisdiction to that of another court.

culs-de-lampe *n.* pl. of CUL-DE-LAMPE.

culs-de-sac *n.pl.* see CUL-DE-SAC.

culshie *n.* & *a.* var. of CULCHIE.

cult /kʌlt/ *n.* & *a.* E17. [Fr. *culte* or its source L *cultus* worship, f. *colere* inhabit, cultivate, protect, honour with worship.] A *n.* †1 Worship; reverential homage rendered to a divine being. Only in 17. 2 A system of religious worship, esp. as expressed in ceremonies, ritual, etc. L17. 3 Devotion or homage paid to a person or thing; *esp.* a fashionable enthusiasm; *derog.* a transient fad of an in-group. E18.

1 EVELYN God, abolishing the cult of Gentile idols. 2 K. CLARK The cult of the Virgin. G. VIDAL Like a priest of a pagan cult he began to perform the ritual of arranging plates. 3 M. GIROUARD The cult of aestheticism was brought to England . . by Swinburne and Walter Pater.

B *attrib.* or as *adj.* That is the object of a cult; involving or involved in a cult; cultic. E20.

Punch There has been a small cult-following for West. *Listener* One of the stars . . has become an unlikely cult hero.

cultch *n.* var. of CULCH.

cultic /ˈkʌltɪk/ *a.* L19. [f. CULT *n.* + -IC, perh. after G *kultisch.*] Of or pertaining to a (religious) cult.

cultically *adv.* M20.

cultigen /ˈkʌltɪdʒ(ə)n/ *n.* E20. [f. *cultivated* pa. pple of CULTIVATE + -GEN.] A plant species or variety known only in cultivation, *esp.* one with no known wild ancestor.

cultish /ˈkʌltɪʃ/ *a.* E20. [f. CULT *n.* + -ISH[1].] Of the nature of, resembling, or belonging to a cult, esp. one regarded as eccentric or unorthodox.

Daily Telegraph Her kind of clowning . . seems to exercise a cultish appeal.

cultishness *n.* M20.

cultism /ˈkʌltɪz(ə)m/ *n.*[1] L19. [Sp. *cultismo*, f. *culto* polished, ult. f. L *cultus* pa. pple of *colere*: see CULT, -ISM.] = GONGORISM.

cultist *n.*[1] = GONGORIST M19.

cultism /ˈkʌltɪz(ə)m/ *n.*[2] M20. [f. CULT *n.* + -ISM.] The principle, system, or practice of a cult or cultic activity.

cultist *n.*[2] a devotee of a cult M20. **culˈtistic** *a.* E20.

cultivable /ˈkʌltɪvəb(ə)l/ *a.* L17. [(O)Fr., f. *cultiver* CULTIVATE *v.*: see -ABLE.] Able to be cultivated.

¶Earlier in UNCULTIVABLE.

cultivaˈbility *n.* L19.

cultivar /ˈkʌltɪvɑː/ *n.* E20. [f. next + VAR(IETY.] A plant variety that has arisen in cultivation.

cultivate /ˈkʌltɪveɪt/ *v.t.* M17. [med.L *cultivat-* pa. ppl stem of *cultivare* (cf. (O)Fr. *cultiver*), f. *cultivus* in *cultiva terra* arable land (cf. OFr. *terres cultives*), f. L *cult-* pa. ppl stem of *colere*: see CULT, -IVE, -ATE[3].] I *lit.* 1 Prepare and use (soil) for crops; bring (land) into a state of cultivation. M17. b Break up (ground) with a cultivator. M19. 2 Give attention to (a plant) to promote growth, improve fertility, etc.; produce or raise by agriculture or horticulture. L17. b = CULTURE *v.* 2. L19.

2 C. PRIEST The previous owners had cultivated fruit and vegetables, but everything was now overgrown.

II *fig.* 3 Promote the growth of, devote oneself to the development of, (an art, sentiment, faculty, etc.); foster. M17. 4 *spec.* Foster (another person's friendship, good opinion, etc.) in relation to oneself. L17. b Pay attention to (a person); seek to win the favour or friendship of; court. E18. 5 Improve and develop (a person, his or her mind, manners, etc.) by education or training. Freq. as *cultivated* ppl a. L17. 6 Pay attention to, practise, cherish, (a sentiment, skill, pursuit, etc.), esp. with the object of acquiring it or improving oneself in it. M18.

3 A. S. NEILL I try hard to cultivate their sense of humour and their imagination. 4 S. RICHARDSON He was more solicitous to cultivate her mamma's good opinion, than hers. b D. L. SAYERS Bunter has been cultivating Hannah Westlock almost to breach of promise point. 6 J. BUCHAN That air of brisk competence which shy women often cultivate in self-defence.

Phrases: **cultivate one's garden** *fig.* attend to one's own affairs.

cultivataˈbility *n.* (*rare*) the quality of being cultivable L19. **cultivatable** *a.* cultivable M19.

cultivation /kʌltɪˈveɪʃ(ə)n/ *n.* L17. [Fr., f. *cultiver*: see prec., -ATION.] 1 The action of cultivating (*lit.* & *fig.*). L17. b = CULTURE *n.* 3. L19. 2 The state of being cultivated, esp. in mind or manners; refinement. M19. 3 A culture of bacteria etc. L19.

1 DEFOE I saw several Sugar Canes, but wild, and for want of Cultivation, imperfect. JAS. HARRIS The cultivation of every liberal accomplishment. C. W. DILKE The amount of land under cultivation. *shifting cultivation*: see SHIFTING *a.* 1. 2 J. GROSS Reviewers . . assumed an imposing degree of cultivation among their readers.

Comb.: **cultivation bank, ridge, terrace** *Archaeol.* a steplike feature formed naturally or artificially on a cultivated hillside.

cultivator /ˈkʌltɪveɪtə/ *n.* M17. [f. CULTIVATE + -OR, prob. after Fr. *cultivateur.*] 1 A person who cultivates something (*lit.* & *fig.*). M17. 2 An implement or machine for breaking up the ground and uprooting weeds. M18.

cultrate /ˈkʌltrət/ *a.* M19. [L *cultratus*, f. *culter* knife: see -ATE[2].] *Zool.* & *Bot.* Shaped like a knife; sharp-edged.

culˈtrated *a.* = CULTRATE L18. **cultriform** *a.* [-FORM] = CULTRATE E19.

culturable /ˈkʌltʃ(ə)rəb(ə)l/ *a.* L18. [f. CULTURE *v.* + -ABLE.] Able to be cultured or cultivated (*lit.* & *fig.*); cultivable.

Lancet Culturable acid-fast microorganisms.

cultural /ˈkʌltʃ(ə)r(ə)l/ *a.* M19. [f. L *cultura* tillage + -AL[1].] 1 Of or pertaining to cultivation, esp. of the mind, manners, etc. M19. 2 Of or pertaining to culture in a society or civilization. L19. 3 Of or pertaining to the culture of micro-organisms, tissues, etc. E20.

2 : *cultural* ANTHROPOLOGY. **cultural attaché** an embassy official whose function is to promote cultural relations between his own country and that to which he is accredited. *cultural* RELATIVISM. **Cultural Revolution** an extreme reform movement in China, 1966–76, which sought to combat revisionism by the restoration of pure Maoist doctrine.

culturally *adv.* L19.

culture /ˈkʌltʃə/ *n.* ME. [Fr., or its source L *cultura*, f. *cult-*: see CULTIVATE, -URE.] I †1 A cultivated field or piece of land. ME–M18. 2 The action or practice of cultivating the soil; tillage. LME. 3 The action or practice of cultivating a crop or raising certain animals (as fish, oysters, bees); the production of silk. E17. b The action or process of causing bacteria, tissue, etc., to grow in prepared media; a growth of cells or spores so obtained. L19.

3 F. FITZGERALD Their method of rice culture was far superior to any other in SE Asia. b F. SMYTH He worked in a cancer research centre, managed to smuggle out a cancer culture. *pure culture*: see PURE *a.*

II 4 The cultivation or development of the mind, manners, etc.; improvement by education and training. E16. 5 Refinement of mind, tastes, and manners; artistic and intellectual development; the artistic and intellectual side of civilization. E19. 6 A particular form, stage, or type of intellectual development or civilization in a society; a society or group characterized by its distinctive customs, achievements, products, outlook, etc. M19. 7 The distinctive customs, achievements, products, outlook, etc., of a society or group; the way of life of a society or group. L19.

4 R. W. DALE The Jewish system was intended for the culture of the religious life. *physical culture*: see PHYSICAL *a.* 5 M. ARNOLD The great men of culture. E. SHINWELL Of what use is culture to a labourer? 6 P. DAVIES The common interest in astronomy among such diverse cultures as the Sumerians and the N. American Indians. D. ATTENBOROUGH This . . results in a community having shared skills and knowledge, shared ways of doing things—in short, a culture. **the two cultures** literature and science, as disciplines that tend to be mutually incompatible or hostile. 7 A. S. BYATT Working-class culture. **material culture** the physical objects which give evidence of the type of culture developed by a society or group. *pop culture*: see POP *a.*

Comb.: **culture-bound** *a.* restricted in character, outlook, etc., by belonging to a particular culture; **culture pearl** a cultured pearl; **culture shock**: experienced by a person who finds himself or herself in a notably unfamiliar or uncongenial cultural environment; **culture vulture** *joc.* a person who devotes much time and effort to acquiring culture.

culturist *n.* (*a*) a person engaged in the culture of crops etc. (*physical culturist*: see PHYSICAL *a.*); (*b*) an advocate of culture: E19. **cultureless** *a.* uncultivated (*lit.* & *fig.*); lacking culture: E19.

culture /ˈkʌltʃə/ *v.t.* E16. [Fr. †*culturer* or med.L *culturare*, f. as prec.] 1 Subject to culture; cultivate (*lit.* & *fig.*). Now *rare* exc. as CULTURED. E16. 2 Maintain (bacteria etc.) in artificial conditions that promote growth. E20.

-culture /ˈkʌltʃə/ *suff.* [f. AGRICULTURE.] Forming ns. denoting the raising or breeding of a certain kind of organism, or in a certain kind of environment, as *apiculture*, *aquaculture*, *aviculture*.

cultured /ˈkʌltʃəd/ *a.* M18. [f. CULTURE *n.*, *v.*: see -ED[2], -ED[1].] 1 Of ground, a plant, etc.: subjected to or produced by cultivation. Chiefly *poet.* M18. 2 Improved by education and training; possessed of culture; refined, cultivated. L18. 3 Caused to develop by artificial means or in an artificial nutrient medium. E20.

2 C. FREEMAN For all her cultured background Sara had lived in poverty. 3 *Nature* Experiments with nuclei from cultured tadpole cells. **cultured pearl**: formed by an oyster after the insertion of a suitable foreign body.

culturology /kʌltʃəˈrɒlədʒi/ *n.* M20. [G *Kulturologie*, f. *Kultur* culture + *-ologie* -OLOGY.] The science or study of culture or cultures as a branch of anthropology.

culturoˈlogical *a.* M20. **culturologist** *n.* M20.

cultus /ˈkʌltəs/ *n.* M17. [L, f. pa. ppl stem of *colere*: see CULT.] †1 = CULT *n.* 1. *rare.* Only in M17. 2 A system of religious worship or ritual; a cult. M19.

cultus-cod /ˈkʌltəskɒd/ *n. N. Amer.* L19. [f. Chinook Jargon *cultus* good-for-nothing, f.

Lower Chinook *kəltas* in vain, + COD *n.*[3]] = *lingcod* s.v. LING *n.*[1]

-culum, -culus *suffs.* see -CULE.

culver /ˈkʌlvə/ *n.* Now *dial.* & *poet.* [OE *cul(u)fre, culfer* f. L *columbula* dim. of *columba* dove, pigeon.] A pigeon, *esp.* the woodpigeon.

culverin /ˈkʌlv(ə)rɪn/ *n.* L15. [(O)Fr. *coulevrine* (cf. med.L *colubrina*, *colo-*, It. *colubrina*), f. *couleuvre* snake f. Proto-Romance f. L *colubra, coluber* snake: see -INE[1].] *Hist.* 1 A kind of handgun. L15. 2 A large cannon long in proportion to its bore. E16.

culveri'neer *n.* a soldier armed with or in charge of a culverin E16.

culverkeys /ˈkʌlvəkiːz/. *n.* Now *dial.* In branch I also **-key** /-kiː/. E17. [f. CULVER + KEY *n.*[1]] I 1 The wild hyacinth. E17. 2 The cowslip. M18. II 3 The seed-pods of the ash. L18.

culvert /ˈkʌlvət/ *n.* & *v.* L18. [Origin unkn.] A *n.* 1 An enclosed channel or conduit for carrying a stream under an embankment, road, etc. L18. 2 A conduit for electric cables. L19. B *v.t.* Provide or lay with culverts; enclose in a culvert. L19.

culvertage /ˈkʌlvətɪdʒ/ *n.* E17. [OFr., f. *culvert* villein f. med.L *collibertus* freed serf, in cl.L fellow freedman, f. as COL- + *libertus* freedman: see -AGE.] *Hist.* The state or condition of a villein; degradation to the position of a villein.

cum /kʌm/ *prep.* LME. [L = with.] 1 Combined with: used in names of combined parishes. LME. 2 With: chiefly in L phrs. and Eng. ones imitating them. L16. 3 And also: denoting a dual or combined nature or function. L19.

1 *Chorlton-cum-Hardy, Stow-cum-Quy*, etc. 2 **cum dividend** (with ref. to share prices) with a dividend about to be paid. **cum grano (salis)** /ˌgrɑːnəʊ ˈsɑːlɪs/ [L] with a grain of salt, with reservations. **cum laude** /ˈlɔːdi, ˈlaʊdeɪ/ (chiefly *N. Amer.*) [L = praise] (a degree, diploma, etc.) with distinction, with honours. MAGNA CUM LAUDE. SUMMA CUM LAUDE. 3 R. KIPLING Motor-bike-*cum*-side-car trips. K. CROSSLEY-HOLLAND He was the poet cum priest cum doctor.

cumacean /kjʊˈmeɪʃ(ə)n/ *a.* & *n.* Also **C-**. L19. [f. mod.L *Cumacea* (see below), f. *Cuma* genus name f. Gk *kuma*: see CYMA, -ACEAN.] *Zool.* A *adj.* Of or pertaining to the Cumacea, an order of small sessile-eyed marine crustaceans resembling prawns and living in mud or sand. L19. B *n.* A cumacean animal. L19.

Cumaean /kjʊˈmiːən/ *a.* & *n.* M18. [f. *Cumae* (L *Cumae*, Gk *Kumē*) (see below) + -AN.] A *adj.* Of or pertaining to Cumae, an ancient city on the Italian coast near Naples; *spec.* designating the Sibyl of Virgil's *Aeneid*, who had her seat nearby. M18. B *n.* A native or inhabitant of Cumae. M20.

Cuman /ˈkjuːmən/ *n.* & *a.* Also **K-**. Pl. of n. **-s**, same, (earliest) †**Cumani**. L16. [med.L *Cumani* pl., perh. ult. f. the river *Kuma* in the northern Caucasus.] = KIPCHAK.

Also **Cu'manian** *n.* & *a.* M19.

cumarone *n.* var. of COUMARONE.

cumbent /ˈkʌmbənt/ *a.* M17. [L *-cumbent-* pres. ppl stem of *-cumbere* (only in compounds, as *recumbere* etc.) lie down, nasalized stem corresp. to *cubare* lie: see -ENT.] Esp. of a statue: lying down, reclining.

cumber /ˈkʌmbə/ *n.* ME. [f. the vb or aphet. f. ENCUMBER *n.*] †1 Overthrow, destruction, rout. Only in ME. 2 A thing which cumbers, an encumbrance; a hindrance, an obstruction; a burden (*lit.* & *fig.*). LME. 3 Trouble, distress; embarrassment, inconvenience. Now *arch. rare.* E16. 4 The action or quality of encumbering; the fact of being encumbered; hindrance, obstruction. M16. 5 Pressure of business; in *pl.* affairs that occupy and trouble one. Now *rare* or *obs.* M17.

2 A. UTTLEY Hay chambers . . with their cumber of past days . . parts of spinning-wheels, giant presses, cheese-stones. 4 J. RUSKIN Of other prefatory matter . . the reader shall be spared the cumber.

cumberless *a.* M16.

cumber /ˈkʌmbə/ *v.t.* ME. [Prob. aphet. f. ACCUMBER, ENCUMBER *v.*] †1 Overwhelm, overthrow, destroy. ME–L16. 2 Benumb; stiffen with cold. Chiefly as *cumbered* ppl a. *obs.* exc. *Sc.* ME. 3 Incommode, bother. Formerly also, harass, distress, trouble. ME. †4 Perplex, puzzle. LME–E17. 5 Hamper, hinder; get or be in the way of (a person, a person's movement, etc.). LME. 6 Occupy obstructively or inconveniently; burden, load. LME.

3 AV *Luke* 10:40 But Martha was cumbred about much seruing. 5 BROWNING Body shall cumber Soul-flight no more. C. S. FORESTER They were cumbered with greatcoats and swords. 6 G. A. BIRMINGHAM Out-of-date theological books . . were cumbering my over-full shelves. *fig.*: D. CECIL Cumbered with the permanent care of a mentally afflicted sister.

Comb.: **cumber-ground** *arch.* a person who or thing which uselessly occupies the ground; an unprofitable occupant of a position.

cumberer *n.* a person who or thing which cumbers LME. **cumberment** *n.* †(*a*) the state of being cumbered; (*b*) (now *rare* or *obs.*) an encumbrance: ME.

Cumberland /ˈkʌmbələnd/ *n.* M17. [A former English county, now part of Cumbria.] 1 Used *attrib.* to designate things originating in or associated with Cumberland. M17. 2 More fully *Cumberland and Westmorland.* A style of wrestling in which the wrestlers stand chest to chest and clasp hands, the first to break hold or to touch the ground other than with the feet being the loser. E19.

1 **Cumberland ham**: cured separately from the rest of the carcass. **Cumberland pig** a lop-eared white pig of a breed now extinct. **Cumberland sauce** a piquant sauce served esp. as a relish with cold meat. **Cumberland sausage** a type of coarse-grained sausage traditionally made in a continuous strip from which the amount required is cut off.

cumbersome /ˈkʌmbəs(ə)m/ *a.* LME. [f. CUMBER *v.* + -SOME[1].] †1 Of a place or way: presenting obstruction, difficult to pass through. LME–L17. 2 Causing trouble or annoyance; full of trouble; wearisome, oppressive. Now *rare* or *obs.* E16. 3 Inconvenient in size, weight, or shape; unwieldy, clumsy to handle. L16. 4 *fig.* Involving effort but serving no purpose; needlessly complicated or indirect. M17.

3 J. G. FARRELL The cat . . had become too big and cumbersome to remain on her lap. 4 HENRY MORE Cumbersome Ceremonies. D. LESSING Government had become so enormous, so cumbersome, so ridden with bureaucracy.

cumbersomely *adv.* L17. **cumbersomeness** *n.* L16.

cumble /ˈkʌmb(ə)l/ *v.t.* & (*rare*) *i.* *obs.* exc. *dial.* ME. [(O)Fr. *combler* load etc. f. L *cumulare*: see CUMULATE *v.*] Deprive or become deprived of strength or power; *esp.* stiffen with cold.

cumbly /ˈkʌmli/ *n.* Also **cumly**. L17. [Hind. *kamlī* f. Skt *kambala*.] In the Indian subcontinent: a blanket, a coarse woollen cloth.

†**cumbrance** *n.* ME. [f. CUMBER *v.* + -ANCE.] 1 The action of cumbering; the state of being cumbered. ME–M17. 2 A source of trouble or annoyance. LME–M17. 3 An encumbrance. M–L17.

Cumbrian /ˈkʌmbrɪən/ *a.* & *n.* M18. [f. med.L *Cumbria*, f. Welsh *Cymry* Welshmen or Brittonic wd meaning 'compatriots': see -AN.] A *adj.* Of, pertaining to, or native to the ancient British kingdom of Cumbria, or the modern English county of Cumbria (formerly Cumberland and Westmorland), or the area of NW England that was anciently Cumbria, esp. the former county of Cumberland or the Lake District. M18. B *n.* A Cumbrian person. L18.

Cumbric /ˈkʌmbrɪk/ *n.* & *a.* M20. [f. as prec. + -IC.] (Of) the Celtic language of the ancient British kingdom of Cumbria.

cumbrous /ˈkʌmbrəs/ *a.* LME. [f. CUMBER *n.* + -OUS.] †1 = CUMBERSOME 1. LME–M19. †2 = CUMBERSOME 2. LME–M17. 3 = CUMBERSOME 3. LME. 4 *fig.* = CUMBERSOME 4. M18.

cumbrously *adv.* LME. **cumbrousness** *n.* M16.

cumdach /ˈkuːdɑːx/ *n.* L19. [Ir. *cumhdach*.] *Ir. Hist.* An ornamented casket for keeping manuscript books.

cumene /ˈkjuːmiːn/ *n.* M19. [f. L *cuminum* CUMIN + -ENE.] Any of a group of isomeric derivatives, C_9H_{12}, of benzene; *spec.* $C_6H_5CH(CH_3)_2$, a liquid made from propylene and benzene and used in making phenol and acetone.

cumin /ˈkʌmɪn/ *n.* Also **-mm-**. [OE *cymen* f. L *cuminum* f. Gk *kuminon*, of Semitic origin: cf. Heb. *kammōn*, Arab. *kammūn*. Superseded in ME by forms f. OFr. *cumin, comin* f. L.] 1 An umbelliferous plant, *Cuminum cyminum*, similar to fennel and native to the Mediterranean; the small aromatic fruit of this, used in curry powders etc. and as a source of oil. OE. 2 With specifying wd: any of various similar plants. L16.

2 **black cumin** fennel-flower, *Nigella sativa*, a Mediterranean plant of the buttercup family whose seeds are used for seasoning. **sweet cumin** the anise, *Pimpinella anisum*.

cumly *n.* var. of CUMBLY.

cummer /ˈkʌmə/ *n.* *Sc.* Also **kimmer** /ˈkɪmə/. ME. [(O)Fr. *commère* f. eccl.L *commater, -tr-*, f. as COM- + *mater* MOTHER *n.*[1]] 1 A godmother. ME. 2 A female companion or close friend. E16. 3 A woman; *spec.* a young girl; a witch; a midwife. M18.

cummerbund /ˈkʌməbʌnd/ *n.* E17. [Urdu *kamar-band* loin- or waist-band f. Pers., f. *kamar* waist, loins + Pers. & Urdu *-bandī* a tie, a band.] A usu. wide sash worn round the waist.

cummin *n.* var. of CUMIN.

cummingtonite /ˈkʌmɪŋtənʌɪt/ *n.* E19. [f. *Cummington*, Massachusetts, US + -ITE[1].] *Min.* A magnesium iron silicate of the amphibole group occurring as brownish fibrous crystals in some metamorphic rocks.

cumquat *n.* var. of KUMQUAT.

cumshaw /ˈkʌmʃɔː/ *n.* E19. [Chin. (dial.) *gǎmsiâ*, (Mandarin) *gǎnxiè* (phr. used by beggars), f. *gǎn* be grateful + *xiè* thank.] In China: a gratuity, a tip.

cumulate /ˈkjuːmjʊlət/ *a.* & *n.* M16. [L *cumulatus* pa. pple, f. as next: see -ATE[2].] A *adj.* Heaped up, massed. M16. B *n.* An igneous rock that was formed by particles in a magma settling to the bottom. M20.

cumulately *adv.* (*rare*) M19.

cumulate /ˈkjuːmjʊleɪt/ *v.* M16. [L *cumulat-* pa. ppl stem of *cumulare*, f. *cumulus* a heap: see -ATE[3].] 1 *v.t.* & (*rare*) *i.* Gather in a heap; heap up; accumulate. M16. 2 *v.t.* Combine *with* something additional. M17. b Combine (successive lists, e.g. of books) into a single comprehensive list, esp. at regular intervals. E20. 3 *v.t.* Put the finishing touches to, crown, culminate. *arch.* M17.

2 E. EDWARDS Allowed him to cumulate the councillorship with the corregidorship. 3 MARVELL To cumulate all this happiness, they had this new Law against the Fanaticks.

cumulated *a.* that has been cumulated; (of cloud) formed into cumuli; *Chem.* involving two double bonds attached to the same carbon atom: M17.

cumulation /kjuːmjʊˈleɪʃ(ə)n/ *n.* E17. [Late L *cumulatio(n-)*, f. as prec.: see -ATION.] 1 The action of heaping up; a mass, a heap; accumulation. Chiefly *fig.* E17. †2 The taking of higher and lower university degrees together. Cf. ACCUMULATION 3. Only in M17. 3 (A list obtained by) the process of cumulating lists of book titles. E20.

cumulative /ˈkjuːmjʊlətɪv/ *a.* E17. [f. CUMULATE *v.* + -IVE. Cf. Fr. *cumulatif, -ive*.] †1 Such as is formed by accumulation (rather than organic growth). Only in E17. 2 Formed by or arising from accumulation; increasing in quantity or effect by successive additions. M17. b Of a statistical function: concerned with all the values of a variate up to and (usually) including the one specified. M20. 3 *Law* (now *Hist.*). Of jurisdiction: shared. M17. 4 Tending to accumulate. L19.

1 BACON As for knowledge which man receiveth by teaching, it is cumulative and not original. 2 H. KISSINGER The cumulative total of Americans killed in action since 1961 . . stood at over 31,000. R. HAYMAN The cumulative effect of working six hours a day for six days a week.

Special collocations: **cumulative error**: increasing, or not decreasing, as more observations are taken into account. **cumulative preference share**: entitling the holder to an annual dividend which, if it cannot be paid in any year, accrues until it can. **cumulative vote, voting**: in which each voter has as many votes as there are candidates and may give all to any one of them.

cumulatively *adv.* M17. **cumulativeness** *n.* L19.

cumulet /ˈkjuːmjʊlɪt/ *n.* L19. [f. CUMULUS + *-et* of unkn. origin.] A high-flying variety of the domestic pigeon.

cumuliform /ˈkjuːmjʊlɪfɔːm/ *a.* L19. [f. CUMULUS + -I- + -FORM.] *Meteorol.* Of cloud etc.: developed in a predominantly vertical direction.

cumulo- /ˈkjuːmjʊləʊ/ *comb. form* of CUMULUS: see -O-.

cumulo'nimbus *n.* (*Meteorol.*) a cloud or cloud-type resembling cumulus but towering and massive, often with the top spread out like an anvil L19. **cumulo'stratus** *n.* (*Meteorol.*) = STRATOCUMULUS E19.

cumulous /ˈkjuːmjʊləs/ *a.* E19. [f. next + -OUS.] Of the nature of or resembling a cumulus cloud or cumuli.

M. PEAKE Dense and cumulous smoke.

cumulus /ˈkjuːmjʊləs/ *n.* Pl. **-li** /-lʌɪ, -liː/. M17. [L.] 1 A heap, a pile; an accumulation; the conical top of a heap. M17. 2 *Meteorol.* (A cloud-type consisting of) rounded masses of cloud heaped on each other and having a horizontal base at usu. a low altitude. Also *cumulus cloud.* E19. 3 *Anat.* (The material of) a mass of follicular cells surrounding an oocyte in an ovarian follicle. Also *cumulus oophorus.* M19.

2 W. BOYD Great ranges of purple cumulus loomed in the sky.

cun *v.*[1] see CON *v.*[1]

†**cun** *v.*[2] var. of CON *v.*[2]

Cuna /ˈkuːnə/ *n.* & *a.* Also **K-**. M19. [Cuna.] A *n.* Pl. **-s**, same. 1 A member of an Indian people of the isthmus of Panama. M19. 2 The Chibchan language of this people. E20. B *attrib.* or as *adj.* Of or pertaining to the Cunas or their language. M19.

cunabulum /kjʊˈnabjʊləm/ *n. rare.* Pl. **-la** /-lə/. L18. [f. L *cunabula* neut. pl., f. *cunae* cradle: see -ULE. Cf. INCUNABULUM.] A cradle (*lit.* & *fig.*); in *pl.*, the place where something began or was nurtured.

Cunarder /kjuːˈnɑːdə/ *n.* M19. [f. *Cunard* (see below) + -ER[1].] A ship belonging to the Cunard Line, founded by Sir Samuel Cunard (1787–1865) as the first regular steamship line for transatlantic passenger traffic.

cunctation /kʌŋ(k)ˈteɪʃ(ə)n/ *n.* L16. [L *cunctatio(n-)*, f. *cunctat-* pa. ppl stem of *cunctari* delay: see -ATION.] The action of delaying; tardy action.

cunctatious *a.* (*rare*) prone to delay M19. **'cunctative** *a.* (*rare*) = CUNCTATIOUS E17.

cunctator /kʌŋ(k)ˈteɪtə/ *n.* E17. [L, f. *cunctat-*: see prec., -OR.] A person who acts tardily, a delayer.

¶Often used w. ref. to Q. Fabius Maximus Cunctator, Roman general in the war against Hannibal.

'cunctatory *a.* (*rare*) disposed to delay M19.

cunctipotent /kʌŋ(k)ˈtɪpət(ə)nt/ *a. rare.* L15. [Late L *cunctipotent-*, *-ens* f. *cunctus* all, after cl.L *omnipotens* OMNIPOTENT *a.*] Omnipotent.

†**cund** *v.* var. of COND.

cundurango /kʌndʊˈraŋgəʊ/ *n.* Also **con-** /kɒn-/. Pl. **-os**. L19. [Sp., f. Quechua *cuntur* CONDOR + *anku* nerve, tendon.] A S. American climbing plant, *Marsdenia cundurango*, an extract of the bark of which has been used therapeutically; its bark.

cuneal /ˈkjuːnɪəl/ *a.* Now *rare* or *obs.* L16. [med. or mod.L *cunealis*, f. cl.L *cuneus* wedge: see -AL[1].] Wedge-shaped.

cuneate /ˈkjuːnɪət/ *a.* E19. [f. L *cuneus* wedge + -ATE[2]: cf. *caudate.*] Wedge-shaped; (of a leaf, petal, etc., or its base) triangular with the narrow end at the point of attachment.

cuneated *a.* = CUNEATE E18. **cune'atic** *a.* = CUNEATE M19.

cuneiform /ˈkjuːnɪɪfɔːm, -nɪf-/ *a.* & *n.* Also **-nif-** /-nɪf-/. L17. [Fr. *cunéiforme* or mod.L *cuneiformis*, f. L *cuneus* wedge: see -FORM.] A *adj.* 1 Having the form of a wedge; wedge-shaped. L17. 2 Designating or pertaining to (inscriptions composed of) writing in wedge-shaped impressed strokes, usu. in clay, in ancient inscriptions of Assyria, Persia, etc. E19.

1 **cuneiform bone** each of three bones in the tarsus that articulate with a bone of the metatarsus in front and with the navicular bone behind.

B *n.* 1 *Anat.* A cuneiform bone. M19. 2 Cuneiform writing. M19.

cuneiformist *n.* a specialist or expert in cuneiform L19.

cunet *n.* var. of CUNIT.

cunette /kjʊˈnɛt/ *n.* L17. [Fr. f. It. *cunetta* ditch.] *Fortif.* A trench along the middle of a dry ditch or moat, serving as a drain or obstacle etc.

cuniculus /kjʊˈnɪkjʊləs/ *n.* Pl. **-li** /-lʌɪ, -liː/. M17. [L = rabbit, underground passage.] An underground passage or mine; *spec.* (*Archaeol.*) an underground drain of preclassical times in Italy.

cunicular *a.* †(*a*) living underground; (*b*) of or pertaining to cuniculi: M18.

cuniform *a.* & *n.* var. of CUNEIFORM.

cu-nim /kjuːˈnɪm/ *n. colloq.* Also **-nimb** /-ˈnɪmb/. M20. [Abbrev.] Cumulonimbus; a cumulonimbus cloud.

cunit /ˈkjuːnɪt/ *n.* Also **-et** /-ət/. M20. [f. C (= a hundred) + UNIT *n.*[1]] A unit of stacked wood equal to 100 cu. ft (approx. 2.83 cu. metres).

cunjee *n.* var. of CUNJIE.

cunjevoi /ˈkʌndʒɪvɔɪ/ *n.* In sense 2 also **-boi** /-bɔɪ/. L19. [Aborig.] 1 A tall Australian plant (*Alocasia macrorrhiza*) of the arum family whose corms were formerly cooked as food. L19. 2 A kind of sea squirt found on Australian reefs and rocks and used as bait. E20.

cunjie /ˈkʌndʒi/ *n. Austral. colloq.* Also **-jee**. M20. [Abbrev. of prec.] = CUNJEVOI 2.

cunner /ˈkʌnə/ *n.* Also **conner** /ˈkɒnə/. E17. [Perh. assoc. w. CONDER 1.] Either of two wrasses, *Crenilabrus melops* of the Mediterranean and eastern Atlantic and *Tautogolabrus adspersus* of the Atlantic coast of N. America.

cunnilingus /kʌnɪˈlɪŋgəs/ *n.* L19. [L = a person who licks the vulva, f. *cunnus* female external genitals + *lingere* to lick.] Stimulation of a woman's genitals with the tongue.

cunnilingue /ˈkʌnɪlɪŋ/ *n.* & *v.* (*a*) *n.* a person who performs cunnilingus; (*b*) *v.t.* & *i.* perform cunnilingus (on): L19.

cunning /ˈkʌnɪŋ/ *n.* ME. [Perh. f. ON *kunnandi* knowledge, accomplishments, f. *kunna* know (see CAN *v.*[1]), but may be vbl n. f. CUN *v.*[1]] †1 Knowledge; learning, erudition. ME–M17. †2 The capacity or faculty of knowing; wit, wisdom, intelligence. ME–M16. 3 Knowledge how to do something; skill, dexterity. *arch.* ME. †4 An art, a craft; a branch of knowledge; *esp.* occult art, magic. LME–L16. 5 Skill in deceit or evasion; selfish cleverness or insight. LME.

3 AV *Ps.* 137:5 Let my right hand forget her cunning. 5 R. GRAVES To pride themselves on their cunning in avoiding detection.

cunning /ˈkʌnɪŋ/ *a.* ME. [ON *kunnandi* knowing, pres. pple of *kunna*: see prec.] †1 Learned; knowledgeable (*in* a subject). ME–M17. 2 Possessing practical knowledge or skill; dexterous. *arch.* ME. b Ingenious, skilfully contrived or executed. LME. 3 Possessing magical knowledge or skill. Only in *cunning man*, *woman. obs.* exc. *Hist.* L16. 4 Skilled in deceit or evasion; artful, crafty; exhibiting or characterized by craftiness. L16. 5 Possessing keen intelligence or wit; clever. Now *rare.* L17. 6 Attractively quaint; charming; picturesque. *N. Amer.* M19.

2b P. BARRY A cunning little camera. 4 DICKENS His black eyes were restless, sly, and cunning.

cunningly *adv.* LME. **cunningness** *n.* LME.

cunny *n.* see CONY.

cunt /kʌnt/ *n. coarse slang.* ME. [Corresp. to ON *kunta* (Norw., Sw. dial. *kunta*, Da. dial. *kunte*), OFris., MLG, MDu. *kunte*, f. Gmc.] 1 The female genitals, the vulva. ME. 2 A very unpleasant or stupid person. E20.

cup /kʌp/ *n.* OE. [pop.L *cuppa*, prob. f. L *cupa* tub.] 1 A small open vessel, usu. hemispherical or nearly so, with or without a handle or handles, used for drinking from; now *spec.* a single-handled one with matching saucer for certain hot drinks (*coffee-cup*, *teacup*, etc.). Also, the bowl of a more ornamental drinking-vessel that has a stem or a lid. OE. b *fig.* Something to be endured or enjoyed; fate, (esp. unhappy) experience. ME. 2 *spec.* a *Chr. Ch.* = CHALICE 2. ME. b An ornamental vessel, typically of silver and comprising a bowl with a stem and base, that is offered as a prize in a competitive event. M17. 3 A cup with the drink it contains; the contents of a cup; a cupful. LME. b *Chr. Ch.* The wine administered at the Eucharist. L16. c Wine, beer, cider, or fruit juice to which other ingredients have been added for flavouring, usu. served chilled from a bowl or jug; a drink of this. L18. d *Cookery.* A standard measure of capacity equal to half a US pint (0.237 litre, 8.33 British fluid ounces). Chiefly *N. Amer.* M19. 4 In *pl.* & †*sing.* The drinking of intoxicating liquor; drunken revelry. Usu. & now only in *in one's cups*, while intoxicated, (formerly) while drinking. LME. 5 *Surg.* A vessel used for cupping. Also, a vessel to receive a measured amount of blood (usu. 4 ounces) in blood-letting. Now *Hist.* LME. 6 A natural structure in a plant or animal having the form of a cup or bowl, e.g. the calyx of a flower, the corona of a narcissus flower, the cupule of an acorn, the socket of a bone. LME. 7 (Usu. **C-**.) *The* constellation Crater. M16. 8 In *pl.* One of the four suits in packs of playing-cards in Italy, Spain, and Spanish-speaking countries, and in tarot packs. E19. 9 A rounded cavity, small hollow, or depression in the ground; *spec.* †(*a*) a small deep depression forming a hazard on a golf course; (*b*) (the liner of) each of the holes into which a golf ball is played. E19. 10 A manufactured article resembling a cup or bowl. M19. b The part of a brassière to contain or support one breast. M20.

1 **between** or **(be)twixt cup and lip** while something is on the point of being achieved. *cup of assay*: see ASSAY *n.* 5. *cup of estate*: see ESTATE *n.* 4. **cup of tea** *fig.* (*colloq.*) a person of a specified kind; *different cup of tea*, a quite different situation etc.; *one's cup of tea*, what interests or suits one. *loving-cup*: see LOVING *ppl a. mazer cup*: see MAZER 2. *paper cup*: see PAPER *n.* & *a.* TREMBLEUSE *cup.* TUMBLER *cup.* b A. SEEGER We drained deeper the deep cup of life. 2b A. E. HOUSMAN The still-defended challenge-cup. 3 C. THIRLWALL A cup of poison had been prepared for him. C. M. YONGE All ready for tea! . . Won't you . . have a cup, Amy? *kiss the cup*: see KISS *v.* c R. MACAULAY A glassful of hock cup, full of fruit and vegetables. 6 W. SHENSTONE The cowslip's golden cup. *buttercup* etc. *Indian cup*: see INDIAN *a.* NEPTUNE'*s cup. optic cup*: see OPTIC *a.* PAINTED *cup.* 10 *grease cup*: see GREASE *n.* b K. KESEY Did she wear a B cup, he wondered, or a C cup.

Comb.: **cup-and-ball** *Hist.* a toy consisting of a cup at the end of a stem to which a ball is attached by a string, the object being to toss the ball and catch it in the cup or on the spike end of the stem; the game played with this; = BILBOQUET 2; **cup-and-cone** *a.* designating a metal fracture in which one surface consists of a raised rim enclosing a flat central portion into which the other surface fits; **cup-and-ring** *a.* (*Archaeol.*) designating marks cut in megalithic monuments consisting of a circular depression surrounded by concentric rings; **cupbearer** a person who serves wine, esp. as an officer of a royal or noble household; **cup-cake**: baked in a small open container or from ingredients measured in cupfuls; **Cup Final** the final match in a competition for a (football etc.) cup; **cup-fungus** any of various ascomycetous fungi in which the spore-producing layer develops as the lining of a shallow cup; **cup grease** a lubricating grease for use in grease cups; **cup hook**: for screwing into a cupboard etc. and hanging cups and mugs on; **cup-lichen** a lichen, *Cladonia pyxidata*, with cup-shaped processes arising from the thallus; **cup-marked** *a.* (*Archaeol.*) designating megalithic monuments marked with a circular depression; **cup-moss** = *cup-lichen* above; **cup-mushroom** = *cup-fungus* above; **cup shake** = *ring shake* s.v. RING *n.*[1]; *cup-tie*: see TIE *n.*[1] 5b.

cupful *n.* as much as a cup will hold; *spec.* (*N. Amer.*) an 8-fluid-ounce measure in cookery: ME.

cuplike *a.* resembling a cup, esp. in shape; deeply concave: M19.

cup /kʌp/ *v.* Infl. **-pp-**. LME. [f. the n.] 1 *v.t. Hist.* Apply a cupping-glass to; bleed (a person) by means of a cupping-glass placed over an incision in a vein. LME. †2 *v.t.* Supply with liquor; make drunk, intoxicate. *rare.* Only in E17. 3 *v.t.* Receive, place, or hold as in a cup; place the curved hand round. M19. 4 *v.i.* Form a cup; be or become cup-shaped. M19. 5 *v.t.* Make concave or cup-shaped; form into a cup. E20.

3 R. WEST Aunt Lily had an elbow on the table and cupped her chin in one hand. 5 X. FIELDING The despatcher . . cupped his hand to my ear.

cupboard /ˈkʌbəd/ *n.* & *v.* LME. [f. CUP *n.* + BOARD *n.*] A *n.* 1 A table on which to display cups and plates etc.; a sideboard. *obs.* exc. in *court cupboard* s.v. COURT *n.*[1] LME. †2 A set of vessels for the table. E16–L17. 3 A recess or piece of furniture with a door and usu. shelves for storing crockery, provisions, or other small items. M16. 4 Food, provisions, etc. Chiefly in *cry cupboard*, crave for food. Now *rare* or *obs.* L17.

3 *skeleton in the cupboard*: see SKELETON *n.*

Comb.: **cupboard love**: simulated for the sake of what one can get by it.

B *v.t.* Place or keep (as) in a cupboard. *rare.* E17.

cupel /ˈkjuːp(ə)l/ *n.* & *v.* Also †**coppel**. E17. [Fr. *coupelle* dim. of *coupe* CUP *n.*: see -EL[2].] A *n.* A shallow vessel made of a refractory material which absorbs impurities when gold or silver is melted in it. E17.

fig.: DISRAELI Money is to be the cupel of their worth.

B *v.t.* Infl. **-ll-**, ***-l-**. Assay or refine in a cupel; subject to cupellation. M17.

cupeˈllation *n.* assaying or refining using a cupel; separation of silver from lead in this way: L17.

cupferron /ˈkʌpfɛrən, ˈkjuːp-/ *n.* E20. [G, f. L *cuprum* copper + *ferrum* iron + *-on*.] *Chem.* A compound, $C_6H_5N(NO)ONH_4$, used as a quantitative precipitant for iron, titanium, zirconium, and certain other metals and formerly as a reagent for copper.

Cupid /ˈkjuːpɪd/ *n.* LME. [L *Cupido* personification of *cupido* desire, love, f. *cupere* to desire.] The Roman god of love, son of Mercury and Venus (represented as a beautiful naked winged boy with a bow and arrows); (also **c-**) a representation of the god; a beautiful young boy.

Cupid's bow (the upper edge of) the upper lip etc. shaped like the double-curved bow carried by Cupid. **Cupid's dart** (*a*) the conquering power of love; (*b*) in *pl.*, rutilated quartz; (*c*) a herbaceous perennial of the composite family, *Catananche caerulea*, with blue or white flowers.

cupidity /kjuːˈpɪdɪti/ *n.* LME. [Fr. *cupidité* or its source L *cupiditas*, f. L *cupidus* eagerly desirous, f. *cupere* to desire: see -ID[1], -ITY.] 1 Inordinate desire to appropriate another's wealth or possessions; greed for gain. LME. 2 *gen.* Inordinate longing or lust; covetousness; an ardent desire. *arch.* M16.

1 W. GOLDING She had a variety of . . brilliant hair-ribbons; and I . . desired them with hopeless cupidity. 2 COLERIDGE The cupidity for dissipation and sensual pleasure.

Cupidon /ˈkjuːpɪdɒn; *foreign* kypidɔ̃ (*pl. same*)/ *n.* Chiefly *poet.* Also **c-**. E19. [Fr. = CUPID.] A beautiful youth; a cupid, an Adonis.

cupidone /ˈkjuːpɪdəʊn/ *n.* M19. [Fr. = prec.] = *Cupid's dart* (c) s.v. CUPID.

cupie *n.* var. of KEWPIE.

cupola /ˈkjuːpələ/ *n.* M16. [It. f. late L *cupula* little cask, small burying-vault, dim of *cupa* cask.] 1 A rounded vault or dome forming the roof of (part of) a building; *spec.* a small rounded dome forming or adorning a roof; the ceiling of a dome. M16. b Something likened to such a dome. M17. 2 A tall usu. cylindrical furnace, open at the top and tapped at the bottom, for melting metal that is to be cast. Also *cupola furnace.* E18. 3 *Anat.* The small dome-shaped end of the cochlear duct. E19. 4 A revolving dome for protecting mounted guns on a warship etc. M19. 5 *Geol.* A small dome-shaped projection on the top of a larger igneous intrusion. E20.

cupola'd, **cupolaed** *a.* provided with a cupola E16.

cuppa /ˈkʌpə/ *n. colloq.* Also **cupper**. M20. [Repr. *cup of* as spoken.] A cup of tea (or coffee).

cupped /kʌpt/ *a.* L18. [f. CUP *n.* or *v.*: see -ED[2], -ED[1].] 1 Shaped like a cup; having a rounded depression or hollow. L18. 2 Lying as if in a cup. L19.

cupper /ˈkʌpə/ *n.*[1] ME. [f. as prec.: see -ER[1].] †1 A cup-maker; a cup-bearer. ME–M17. 2 *Hist.* A person who performed the surgical operation of cupping. E19.

cupper /ˈkʌpə/ *n.*[2] *slang.* E20. [f. CUP *n.* + -ER[6].] A series of intercollegiate matches played in competition for a cup at Oxford University. Usu. in *pl.*

cupper *n.*[3] var. of CUPPA.

cupping /ˈkʌpɪŋ/ *n.* LME. [f. CUP *n.* or *v.* + -ING[1].] 1 *Hist.* A procedure for drawing blood by applying a heated cup to the scarified skin. Also *wet cupping.* LME. b A similar procedure without scarification, as a counterirritant. Also *dry cupping.* M18. 2 The drinking of intoxicating liquor; a drinking-bout. E17. 3 The formation of a concavity; the assumption of a curved or hollow shape. L19. 4 The process of forming a depression in sheet metal by forcing a plunger into it when it is placed over a die. E20. 5 Cuppiness in metal; the flaws present in cuppy wire. E20.

Comb.: **cupping-glass** a wide-mouthed glass vessel for use in cupping (sense 1); **cupping-test**: of the ductility of metal by means of cupping.

cuppy /ˈkʌpi/ *a.* L19. [f. CUP *n.* + -Y[1].] 1 Cup-shaped; concave, hollow. L19. 2 Of ground: full of shallow depressions. Of (the position of) a golf ball: in such a depression. L19. 3 Of drawn metal, esp. wire: having internal cavities liable to lead to a cup-and-cone fracture. E20.

cuppiness *n.* the state or condition (of metal) of being cuppy E20.

cupr- *comb. form* see CUPRO-.

cuprammonium /kjuːprəˈməʊnɪəm/ *n.* M19. [f. prec. + AMMONIUM.] A complex ion of copper and ammonia, $Cu(NH_3)_4^{++}$, solutions of which dissolve cellulose.

Comb.: **cuprammonium rayon**: made from cellulose dissolved in cuprammonium solution.

cuprammonia *n.* liquid containing cuprammonium ions M19.

cuprea bark /ˈkjuːprɪə bɑːk/ *n. phr.* L19. [f. late L *cuprea* fem. of *cupreus* CUPREOUS + BARK *n.*[2]] The coppery-red bark of a S. American tree of the madder family, *Remijia pedunculata* (and *R. purdieana*), a source of quinine.

cupreous /ˈkjuːprɪəs/ *a.* M17. [f. late L *cupreus*, f. as next: see -OUS.] 1 Of the nature of copper; containing or consisting of copper. M17. 2 Looking like copper; copper-coloured. E19.

cupric /ˈkjuːprɪk/ *a.* L18. [f. late L *cuprum* COPPER *n.*[1] + -IC.] *Chem.* Of copper in the divalent state.

cuprate *n.* a salt containing divalent copper M19.

cupriferous /kjuːˈprɪf(ə)rəs/ *a.* L18. [f. as prec. + -FEROUS.] Yielding or containing copper.

cuprite /ˈkjuːprʌɪt/ *n.* M19. [f. as next + -ITE[1].] Native cuprous oxide, a red cubic mineral important as an ore of copper.

cupro- /ˈkjuːprəʊ/ *comb. form* of late L *cuprum* COPPER *n.*[1]: see -O-. Bef. a vowel **cupr-**.

cupro-ˈnickel *n.* an alloy of copper and nickel, esp. in the proportions 3:1 as used in the 'silver' coinage of the UK E20.

cuprous /ˈkjuːprəs/ *a.* M17. [Partly (orig.) f. late L *cuprum* COPPER *n.*[1], partly f. CUPRIC: see -OUS.] Cupreous; *Chem.* of copper in the monovalent state.

cupule /ˈkjuːpjʊl/ *n.* Also **-ula** /-jʊlə/. LME. [Late L *cupula*: see CUPOLA. Cf. Fr. *cupule.*] 1 *Bot.* A cuplike structure associated with the reproductive parts of certain plants; *spec.* (*a*) the woody involucre partly enclosing an acorn; (*b*) the case at the base of a kernel or grain on a corn-cob. LME. 2 *Zool.* & *Anat.* A small cup-shaped organ, as the sucker of a cuttlefish etc.; *esp.* (as *cupula*) one of the gelatinous masses into which sensory hairs protrude in a semicircular canal of the ear. E19. 3 A small cup-shaped depression on a surface. L19.

cupular *a.* shaped like a cupule L19. **cupulate** *a.* cupular; having a cupule: M19.

cur /kəː/ *n.* ME. [Prob. orig. in *cur-dog*, perh. f. ON *kurr* grumbling, *kurra* murmur.] 1 Orig., a dog. Now *spec.* a worthless, low-bred, or snappish dog. Also *cur-dog.* ME. 2 A surly, ill-bred, or cowardly fellow. E16. †3 Either of two fishes, the red gurnard (*Aspitrigla cuculus*) and the bullhead (*Cottus gobio*). Also *cur fish.* L16–M18. 4 The goldeneye, *Bucephala clangula.* *dial.* E17.

1 C. CONNOLLY I feel like a cringing cur kicked about in a crowd.

curship *n.* (*rare*) (with possess. adj., as *your* etc. *curship*) a mock title of respect M17.

curable /ˈkjʊərəb(ə)l/ *a.* LME. [(O)Fr., or its source late L *curabilis*, f. *curare* CURE *v.*: see -ABLE.] 1 Able to be cured; remediable (*lit.* & *fig.*). LME. †2 Able to cure; curative. L15–E17.

curaˈbility *n.* LME. †**curableness** *n.* M17–E18.

curaçao /kjʊərəˈsəʊ/ *n.* Also **-oa**, **C-**. Pl. **-s**. E19. [*Curaçao*, a Caribbean island of the Lesser Antilles producing oranges used in the flavouring.] A sweet liqueur of spirits flavoured with the peel of bitter oranges.

curacy /ˈkjʊərəsi/ *n.* LME. [f. CURATE *n.*: see -ACY.] The office or position of curate; *Hist.* the benefice of a perpetual curate.

curandero /kuranˈdero/ *n.* Pl. **-os** /-ɒs/. Fem. ***-dera*** /-ˈdera/. M20. [Sp., f. *curar* to cure f. L *curare.*] In Spain and Latin America: a healer who uses folk remedies.

curare /kjʊˈrɑːri/ *n.* L18. [(Sp. & Port. f.) Carib wd repr. also by WOURALI.] A resinous bitter substance obtained from the bark and stems of various tropical and subtropical S. American plants of the genus *Strychnos*, esp. the vine *S. toxifera*, and from the similar *Chondrodendron tomentosum*, which paralyses the motor nerves and was formerly used as an arrow poison by S. American Indians and in surgery etc. to relax the muscles.

fig.: P. ACKROYD The lethargy of the will, the curare that annihilates the nervous elements of thought and motion.

ˈcurarine *n.* an alkaloid obtained from curare (now replaced in medicine by tubocurarine) M19. **curariˈzation** *n.* the action or process of curarizing; the state of being curarized: L19. **ˈcurarize** *v.t.* administer curare to; produce temporary paralysis in by the administration of curarine or a drug with similar action: L19.

curassow /ˈkjʊərəsəʊ/ *n.* L17. [Alt. of *Curaçao*: see CURAÇAO.] Any of various gallinaceous birds of the family Cracidae similar to turkeys, native to Central and S. America; *esp.* (also *black curassow*) *Crax alector*, with greenish-black plumage.

helmeted curassow a Venezuelan curassow, *Crax pauxi*, which has a large casque at the base of the bill; also called *pauxi*.

†**curat** *n.* M16–E17. [Back-form f. *curats* var. of CUIRASS.] *sing.* & in *pl.* = CUIRASS.

curatage /ˈkjʊərətɪdʒ/ *n.* M18. [f. next + -AGE.] †1 The post of guardian; the provision of guardians. Only in M18. 2 A residence provided for a curate. L19.

curate /ˈkjʊərət/ *n.* ME. [med.L *curatus* a person who has a cure or charge (of a parish), f. *cura*: see CURE *n.*[1], -ATE[1].] I A person holding a spiritual charge. 1 *gen.* A ecclesiastical or spiritual pastor. *arch.* ME. 2 A member of the clergy engaged as a paid assistant or deputy to an incumbent in the Church of England or in the Roman Catholic Church in Ireland. M16. 3 The priest of a Roman Catholic parish in Continental Europe. M17. II A person holding a temporal charge. †4 A curator; an overseer. LME–M17. 5 In Ireland: an assistant to a person selling spirits etc.; a bartender. E20.

Phrases & comb.: **curate-in-charge**: appointed to take charge of a Anglican parish during the incapacity or suspension of the incumbent. **curate's comfort** a cake-stand with two or more tiers. **curate's egg** something of very mixed character, partly good and partly bad. **curate's friend** = *curate's comfort* above. *perpetual curate*: see PERPETUAL *a.*

†**curateship** *n.* the post or position of curate, a curacy L16–M19. **cu'ratic(al)** *adjs.* L19.

curate /kjʊ(ə)'reɪt/ *v.*[1]*t.* E18. [Back-form. f. CURATOR.] †**1** *v.i.* Provide a record of curation. *rare.* Only in E18. **2** *v.t.* Act as the curator of (a museum, exhibits, etc.); look after and preserve. L19. **3** *v.i.* Perform the duties of a curator; store and preserve exhibits etc. Chiefly as *curating* vbl n. E20.

curate /'kjʊərət/ *v.*[2]*i.* M19. [f. the n.] Act as curate.

curation /kjʊ(ə)'reɪʃ(ə)n/ *n.* LME. [OFr. *curacion* f. L *curatio(n-)*, f. *curat-*: see CURATOR, -ATION.] †**1** Healing, cure. LME–L17. **2** Guardianship, esp. of a collection of preserved or exhibited items. M18.

curative /'kjʊərətɪv/ *a.* & *n.* LME. [Fr. *curatif, -ive* f. med.L *curativus*, f. L *curat-*: see next, -ATIVE.] **A** *adj.* **1** Of or pertaining to the curing of disease, healing of wounds, etc. LME. **2** Able or tending to cure; *fig.* remedial, corrective. M17. **B** *n.* A curative agent. M19.

curatively *adv.* M19. **curativeness** *n.* L19.

curator /kjʊ(ə)'reɪtə/; *in branch I also* 'kjʊərətə/ *n.* LME. [Partly f. (O)Fr. *curateur*, partly f. its source L *curator*, f. *curat-* pa. ppl stem of *curare*: see CURE *v.*, -OR.] **I** Senses derived through Fr. †**1** = CURATE *n.* 1. Only in LME. **2** Now chiefly *Sc. Law.* A person appointed as guardian of a minor or other person legally unfit to conduct his or her own affairs. LME. **II** Senses directly f. L. **3** A person in charge, a manager, a steward. M17. **4** The officer in charge of a museum, library, or other collection; a keeper, a custodian. M17. **5** In some universities, a board member or official with responsibility for overseeing property or for choosing professors. L17. **6** *Hist.* Any of various public officers under the Roman Empire. E18.

cura'torial *a.* M18. **cu'ratorship** *n.* the post or position of a curator L16. **'curatory** *n.* curatorship; guardianship: LME.

curatory /'kjʊərət(ə)ri/ *a.* LME. [L *curatorius*, f. *curator*: see prec., -ORY[2]. In mod. use referred to *cūrāre* CURE *v.*] Curative.

curatrix /kjʊ(ə)'reɪtrɪks/ *n.* Pl. **-trices** /-trɪsiːz/, **-trixes.** L16. [Late L, fem. of L CURATOR: see -TRIX.] A female curator or guardian.

†**curats** *n.* var. of CUIRASS.

curb /kəːb/ *n.* See also KERB *n.* L15. [Prob. f. CURB *v.*[2] Cf. CRUB.] **I 1** A chain or strap passing under the lower jaw of a horse and attached to the bit, used chiefly as a check. L15. **2** *fig.* Anything that curbs or restrains; a check, a restraint. E17.

1 W. HOLTBY The big horse pulled at the curb. 2 *Time* Italy has imposed curbs on Japanese motorcycles.

II Senses corresp. to Fr. *courbe* curve. **3** A hard swelling on a horse's leg; the disease characterized by this. E16. **4** A curve, an arc. *obs.* exc. *dial.* E17. **5** A mould or template for marking out curved work. L18.

III An enclosing (orig. curved) framework or border. **6** A frame round the top of a well or a brewer's copper; the frame of a trapdoor or skylight. E16. **7** A raised margin or edging, as a fender round a hearth. M18. **8** An edging of stone etc. to a pavement or raised path; = KERB *n.* 3. Now *N. Amer.* L18. **9** A circular ring or plate round the edge of a dome or other circular structure; the base of a well. (Earlier as KERB *n.* 2.) E19.

Comb.: **curb-bit**, **-bridle**: fitted with a curb; **curb-chain**: acting as a horse's curb; **curb-plate** the curb of a dome or a well; the horizontal timber where the upper and lower slopes of a curb roof meet; **curb roof**: of which each face has two slopes, the lower one being the steeper; **curb service** *N. Amer.* service by a shop etc. to customers in cars at the street kerb; **curbstone** = *kerbstone* s.v. KERB *n.*

curbed *a.* having a curb; *fig.* checked, restrained: L16. **curbless** *a.* (*rare*) without curb or restraint E19.

curb /kəːb/ *v.*[1]*t.* See also KERB *v.* M16. [f. the n.] **1** Put a curb on (a horse); check or restrain by means of a curb. M16. **2** *fig.* Restrain; keep in check. (Foll. by †*of*, †*from*.) L16. **3** = KERB *v.* Now *N. Amer.* M19.

2 J. BERGER If we curb the power of monarchy and rely upon parliamentary government. A. HAILEY Nim curbed a sharp reply.

curber *n.* a person who or thing which restrains E17.

†**curb** *v.*[2] var. of COURB.

curbash *n.* & *v.* var. of KOURBASH.

curby /'kəːbi/ *a.* M19. [f. CURB *n.* + -Y[1].] Of a horse's leg: liable to be affected with curb.

curbily *adv.* L19.

curch /kəːtʃ/ *n.* *Sc.* LME. [Erron. sing. repr. OFr. *cuevrechés* pl. of *couvrechef*: see COVERCHIEF. Cf. KERCH *n.*[1]] A woman's head-covering or kerchief.

curculio /kəː'kjuːlɪəʊ/ *n.* Pl. **-os.** M18. [L = corn-weevil.] Any of various beetles of the family Curculionidae, comprising the weevils.

curcuma /'kəːkjʊmə/ *n.* LME. [med.L f. Arab. *kurkum* (Pers. *karkam*) f. Skt *kuṅkuma* saffron.] Turmeric (the substance and the plant).

curd /kəːd/ *n.* Also (earlier, now *dial.*) **crud** /krʌd/. LME. [Origin unkn. Cf. CRUD *n.*] **1** The coagulated substance formed (naturally or artificially) by the action of acids or rennet on milk, and made into cheese or eaten as food; a mass of this. Often in *pl.* LME. **2** Any similar substance, as a conserve. LME. **b** The edible head of such brassicas as cauliflower and broccoli. M18. **c** The fatty substance found between the flakes of flesh in boiled salmon. E19.

1 *Nursery rhyme*: Little Miss Muffet Sat on a tuffet Eating some curds and whey. 2 *lemon curd, lime curd*, etc.

Comb.: **curd cheese** soft cheese made from unfermented curds; **curd soap** a white soap made of tallow and soda.

curdlike *a.* resembling curds M17.

curd /kəːd/ *v.* Also (earlier, now *dial.*) **crud** /krʌd/, infl. **-dd-.** LME. [f. the n.] **1** *v.t.* & *i.* Make into or become curd; coagulate; congeal. LME. †**2** *v.t.* Curdle (blood). *rare* (Shakes.). Only in E17.

curded /'kəːdɪd/ *a.* Also (earlier, now *dial.*) **crudded** /'krʌdɪd/. LME. [f. CURD *n.*, *v.*: see -ED[2], -ED[1].] **1** Formed into (something like) curd; congealed. LME. **2** Having curd or a curd. LME.

curdle /'kəːd(ə)l/ *n.* *rare.* L16. [f. the vb.] The act or product of curdling; a curd.

curdle /'kəːd(ə)l/ *v.t.* & *i.* Also (earlier, now *dial.*) **cruddle** /'krʌd(ə)l/. L16. [Frequent. of CURD *v.*: see -LE[3].] Turn into curd or a soft semi-solid substance resembling it; form curd (in); coagulate, congeal.

fig.: E. BOWEN Mist, at freezing-point, curdled under the headlights. **curdle someone's blood** horrify or terrify someone.

curdler *n.* something which causes curdling; *spec.* a story etc. that curdles the blood: M19. **curdly** *a.* apt to curdle; of a curdled nature: L17.

curdy /'kəːdi/ *a.* Also (earlier, now *dial.*) **cruddy** /'krʌdi/. LME. [f. CURD *n.* + -Y[1]. Cf. CRUDDY.] **1** Full of curdlike coagulations; curdlike in consistency or appearance. LME. **2** Full of curd or curds. E16.

2 SPENSER His cruell woundes with cruddy bloud congeald.

curdiness *n.* E19.

†**curdy** *v.t.* *rare* (Shakes.). Only in E17. [f. the adj.] Make curdlike; congeal.

cure /kjʊə/ *n.*[1] ME. [(O)Fr. f. L *cura* care.] **I**†**1** Care, heed, concern; anxiety. ME–E17. †**2** Care committed to a person, responsibility; a duty, an office. ME–M17. **3** *Eccl.* **a** More fully *cure of souls.* The spiritual charge or oversight of parishioners etc. ME. **b** A parish; the people under the charge of a priest; a sphere of spiritual ministry. L15. †**4** Medical treatment. LME–E18. **5** Successful medical treatment; the action or process of healing a sick person, an illness, etc.; a thing that does this, a remedy. LME. **6a** A particular method or course of medical treatment. M19. **b** A period of residence at a health-resort, under medical regimen, in order to restore or benefit one's health. Cf. KURSAAL. L19.

5 E. S. TURNER Physical cures happen at Lourdes and the phenomenon cannot be ignored. T. S. ELIOT Tried to impose upon me Your own diagnosis, and prescribe your own cure. *miracle cure*: see MIRACLE *n.* 6a A. FLINT In order to carry out . . the 'milk-cure', . . milk . . should be taken largely. *rest-cure*: see REST *n.*[1] b W. S. MAUGHAM The cure at Montecatini had not done him the good he expected.

II 7 The curing or preserving of fish, pork, etc.; a catch of fish so treated. M18. **8** The process of curing rubber or plastic; the degree of hardness produced. E20.

cureless *a.* incurable, irremediable M16. **curelessly** *adv.* M19.

cure /kjʊə/ *n.*[2] *slang.* M19. [Abbrev. of CURIOSITY, with play on CURE *n.*[1]: cf. CURIO.] An odd person; a funny fellow.

cure /kjʊə/ *v.* LME. [(O)Fr. *curer* take care of, clean f. L *curare* care for, cure.] †**1** *v.t.* & *i.* Take care (of); take trouble; care (for). LME–E17. †**2** *v.t.* & *i.* Take charge of the spiritual interests of (a parish etc.). LME–L16. †**3** *v.t.* Treat surgically or medically. LME–L16. **4** *v.t.* Restore to health, relieve *of* an illness, an evil. LME. **5** *v.t.* Heal (an illness, a wound); remedy, remove, (an evil). LME. **6** *v.i.* Effect a cure. Freq. in *kill or cure* s.v. KILL *v.*[2] L16. †**7** *v.i.* Be cured, get well again. *rare.* L16–L18. **8** *v.t.* Prepare for keeping by salting, drying, etc.; preserve (meat, fish, tobacco, etc.). E17. **9** *v.i.* Undergo preservation by salting etc. M17. **10** *v.t.* Vulcanize (rubber); change physical properties of, esp. harden, (plastic) chemically during manufacture; harden (concrete). M19. **11** *v.i.* Undergo vulcanization; harden, set. E20. **12** *v.i.* Stay at a health resort in order to follow a health-improving regimen. E20.

4 G. STEIN He tried to cure the boy of his bad ways and make him honest. 5 J. FREEMAN The pain that never the new years may cure. B. SPOCK Dehydration fever . . can always be cured immediately by giving fluid. 8 D. L. SAYERS A farmer who cured his own bacon. 11 G. BOYCOTT Cement which has cured too quickly.

curer *n.* (*a*) a person who or thing which cures illness etc.; (*b*) a person whose occupation is to cure fish etc.: L16.

curé /kyre/ *n.* Pl. pronounced same. M17. [Fr. f. med.L *curatus*: see CURATE *n.*] A parish priest in France and French-speaking countries.

cure-all /'kjʊərɔːl/ *n.* L18. [f. CURE *v.* + ALL.] A universal remedy, a panacea. Formerly, a plant with healing properties.

Curetonian /kjʊə'təʊnɪən/ *a.* & *n.* M19. [f. *Cureton* (see below) + -IAN.] (Designating) the Syriac version of the Gospels discovered and edited by the Revd William Cureton (1808–64).

curettage /kjʊə'retɪdʒ, kjʊərɪ'tɑːʒ/ *n.* L19. [Fr., f. as next: see -AGE.] *Surg.* The scraping or cleaning of an internal surface of an organ or body cavity with a curette; a common operation on the womb which consists of this (see *dilatation and curettage* s.v. DILATATION 1).

curette /kjʊə'ret/ *n.* & *v.* M18. [Fr., f. as CURE *v.*: see -ETTE.] *Surg.* **A** *n.* A small instrument resembling a scoop used to remove material by a scraping action, esp. from the womb. M18. **B** *v.t.* & *i.* Scrape or clean with a curette. L19.

curettement *n.* (*rare*) curettage E20. **curetting** *n.* (*a*) use of a curette; (*b*) in *pl.*, material removed with a curette: L19.

curf /kəːf/ *n.* M19. [Alt. of CARF.] A cherty limestone found in one of the strata of Portland stone.

curfew /'kəːfjuː/ *n.* ME. [AN *coeverfu*, OFr. *cuevrefeu* (mod. *couvrefeu*), f. tonic stem of *cuvrir* COVER *v.*[1] + *feu* fire.] **I 1** A regulation, widespread in medieval Europe, by which fires had to be covered or extinguished at a fixed hour each evening, indicated by the ringing of a bell; (also *curfew-bell*) the bell itself; the time of its ringing; the practice of ringing a bell at a fixed hour each evening (for any purpose). ME. †**b** The ringing of a bell at a fixed hour each morning. L16–E18. **2** A regulation forbidding people to be out of doors (at all, or occas. except under specified conditions) between certain hours, usu. of the night; the time of effectiveness of such a regulation; *transf.* (the time of effectiveness of) any restriction on movement at night. L19.

1 C. LYELL At nine o'clock, a . . curfew tolls . . after which no coloured man is permitted to be abroad. 2 K. AMIS The unbreakable midnight curfew her father had put on her evenings out till she was turned eighteen. G. GREENE The curfew had been lifted.

II 3 A cover for a fire. Now *rare.* E17.

curfuffle *n.* var. of KERFUFFLE.

curfuffle /kəˈfʌf(ə)l/ *v.t. Sc.* L16. [f. (perh.) Gael. *car* twist, bend, turn about + FUFFLE. Cf. KERFUFFLE.] Disorder; ruffle.

curia /ˈkjʊərɪə/ *n.* Pl. **-iae** /-iiː/, **-ias.** E17. [L.] 1 *Hist.* Each of the ten divisions into which each of the three tribes of ancient Rome was divided; a similar division in another ancient city; the senate of an ancient Italian town, as distinguished from that of Rome. E17. 2 A court of justice, counsel, or administration, esp. of the Roman Catholic Church or (*Hist.*) under the feudal system. E18. 3 (**C-.**) *The* Vatican tribunals, congregations, and other institutions through which the Pope directs the work of the Roman Catholic Church; *the* government departments of the Vatican. M19.

curial /ˈkjʊərɪəl/ *n.* & *a.* LME. [Fr. *curiale* n., *curial(e)* adj., f. L *curialis*, f. as prec.: see -AL[1].] A *n.* †1 A courtier. Only in LME. 2 *Hist.* A member of an ancient Roman or Italian curia. L17. B *adj.* †1 Courtly. L15–M16. 2 Of or pertaining to a curia. L17.

curialism *n.* a curial or courtly system, *esp.* Vaticanism L19. **curialist** *n.* a member or supporter of the papal Curia M19. **curiaˈlistic** *a.* of or pertaining to curialists or curialism L19.

†curiality *n.* LME–M19. [OFr. *curialité*, med.L *curialitas*, f. *curialis* CURIAL.] What pertains to a court; courtliness; courtesy, favour.

curiara /kuːrɪˈɑːrə/ *n.* E20. [Amer. Sp. f. Carib *culiala*: cf. CORIAL.] In Venezuela and Colombia: a dugout canoe.

curiate /ˈkjʊərɪət/ *a.* M16. [L *curiatus*, f. as CURIA: see -ATE[2].] *Hist.* Of or pertaining to the Roman curiae.

curie /ˈkjʊəri/ *n.* In sense 2 usu. **C-.** E20. [Pierre (1859–1906) and Marie (1867–1934) *Curie*, co-discoverers of radium.] *Physics.* 1 A unit of radioactivity equal to 3.7×10^{10} disintegrations per second; a quantity of radioactive material with this activity. Formerly, a quantity of a decay product of radium in radioactive equilibrium with 1 gram of radium. E20. 2 *Curie point, temperature*, a temperature at which the type of magnetism or electrical behaviour exhibited by a substance changes, *spec.* that at which a substance loses its ferromagnetism on being heated and becomes paramagnetic. E20.

curing /ˈkjʊərɪŋ/ *vbl n.* LME. [f. CURE *v.* + -ING[1].] 1 Healing, cure. Now *rare.* LME. 2 The process of preparing fish etc. for preservation by salting, drying, etc. L17. 3 The process of curing rubber etc. M19.

curio /ˈkjʊərɪəʊ/ *n.* Pl. **-os.** M19. [Abbrev. of CURIOSITY: cf. CURE *n.*[2]] An *objet d'art*, souvenir, etc., valued as a curiosity or a rarity; an unusual person.

curiologic /kjʊərɪəˈlɒdʒɪk/ *a.* & *n.* Also **†cyrio-.** M17. [Irreg. f. Gk *kuriologikos* speaking literally, opp. *sumbolikos* symbolic.] A *adj.* Designating or pertaining to that form of hieroglyphic writing in which objects are represented by pictures. M17. B *n.* In *pl.* (treated as *sing.*). Representation by picture-writing. E19.

curiological *a.* E19. **curiologically** *adv.* M18.

curiosa /kjʊərɪˈəʊsə/ *n.pl.* L19. [L *curiosa* neut. pl. of *curiosus*: see CURIOUS.] Curiosities, oddities; *spec.* erotic or pornographic books.

curiosa felicitas /kjʊərɪˌəʊsə fəˈlɪsɪtɑːs/ *n. phr.* M18. [L, lit. 'careful felicity'.] A studied appropriateness of expression.

curiosity /kjʊərɪˈɒsɪti/ *n.* LME. [OFr. *curiouseté* (mod. *curiosité*) f. L *curiositas*, f. *curiosus*: see CURIOUS, -ITY.] I As a personal attribute. †1 Carefulness; scrupulousness; fastidiousness. LME–M18. †2 Skill, cleverness, ingenuity. LME–M18. 3a Inquisitiveness about matters that do not concern one. Formerly also, any undue or inquisitive desire to know or learn. LME. b A desire or inclination to know or learn about something, esp. what is novel or strange. E17. †4 A fancy, a whim; a hobby. E17–E18. †5 Scientific or artistic interest; connoisseurship. M17–E19.

3a L. DURRELL I spied upon her . . from curiosity to know what she might be doing or thinking. b D. MORRIS Our curiosity, our inquisitiveness, urges us on to investigate all natural phenomena.

II As a quality of things. †6 Careful or elaborate workmanship; delicacy or elegance of construction. LME–E19. 7 The quality of being interesting on account of novelty or strangeness. L16.

III A matter or thing embodying this quality. †8 A subtle or abstruse matter of investigation; a nicety. LME–E18. †9 A matter receiving undue attention; a vanity. LME–E18. †10 A curious detail or trait. M17–M18. 11 A curious, rare, or strange object. M17.

8 DONNE Troubling the peace of the Church, with . . inextricable curiosities. 11 H. JAMES He had been to China and brought home a collection of curiosities.

curioso /kjʊərɪˈəʊzəʊ/ *n. arch.* Pl. **-si** /-si/, **-sos.** M17. [It.] Orig., a person with a keen interest in matters of science and art. Later, a connoisseur.

curious /ˈkjʊərɪəs/ *a.* & *adv.* ME. [OFr. *curios* (mod. *curieux*) f. L *curiosus* careful, assiduous, inquisitive, f. *cura* care: see CURE *n.*[1], -OUS.] A *adj.* I As a subjective quality of people. 1 Having a wish to see or to know; eager to learn, esp. about what does not concern one; inquisitive. ME. †2 Careful, attentive, solicitous. LME–L18. 3 Having high standards; fastidious, particular; cautious. *obs.* exc. *dial.* LME. †4 Skilful, clever, ingenious. LME–M19. †5 Having expertise as a connoisseur or virtuoso. L16–M19. †6 Accurate in observation or investigation; (of the eye etc.) sharp, perceptive. L16–E19.

1 F. NORRIS Annixter, curious for details, forbore, nevertheless, to question. 4 HOR. WALPOLE That neat and curious painter Vander Heyden.

II As an objective quality of things etc. †7a Of an inappropriately searching nature; abstruse, subtle; occult. ME–M18. b Of an investigation etc.: characterized by special care; meticulous. Now *rare.* E16. †c Very accurate, exact, precise. E17–E19. †8a Elaborately or carefully made or prepared. LME–M19. b Performed with or requiring skill. L17–L18. †9 Exquisite, excellent, fine. LME–E19. †10 Interesting, noteworthy. LME–E19. 11 Deserving or arousing curiosity; somewhat surprising; strange, queer. E18. 12 Of an action etc.: prompted by curiosity. M19. 13 *euphem.* Erotic; pornographic. L19.

7b DISRAELI A subject which demands the most curious investigation. c J. SELDEN Your curious learning and judgment. R. HOOKE The most curious Mathematical Instruments. 9 S. PEPYS A very calm, curious morning. 10 J. RICHARDSON Statues, Intaglias, and the like Curious Works of Art. J. REYNOLDS It is curious to observe, that [etc.]. 11 R. CAMPBELL Father had some very curious cranky habits mostly concerned with the telephone. E. ROOSEVELT She was not exactly a hunchback, but she had a curious figure. **curiouser and curiouser** more and more curious; increasingly strange. 12 DICKENS She stole a curious look at my face. 13 I. MONTAGU The bookseller's catalogue labelled 'Erotica' or 'Curious'.

Comb.: **curious-minded** *a.* having an inquisitive or a strange mind.

†B *adv.* Curiously. LME–M18.

curiously *adv.* ME. **curiousness** *n.* LME.

curium /ˈkjʊərɪəm/ *n.* M20. [f. as CURIE + -IUM.] A radioactive metallic chemical element of the actinide series, atomic no. 96, which is produced artificially. (Symbol Cm.)

curl /kəːl/ *n.* L16. [f. the vb.] 1 A lock of hair of a spiral or coiled form. L16. b The state (of hair) of being curled. M19. 2 Anything of a spiral or incurved shape; a coil. E17. 3 A ripple or wave on water. M17. b The curved top of a wave about to break. M20. 4 The action or an act of curling, esp. by a cricket ball or a bowler. L18. 5 A disease of plants in which the shoots or leaves are curled up and imperfectly developed. L18. 6 *Math.* The vector product of the operator ∇ (see DEL) and any given vector. L19.

1 SHAKES. *Haml.* Hyperion's curls, the front of Jove himself. MONTAGUE *curl.* b **in curl** (of hair) curled. **out of curl** (of hair) having become straight (*go out of curl* fig., lose one's drive or energy). 2 E. BOWEN The steamer's smoke hung in curls on the clear air. 3b P. O'BRIAN He saw the vast breaking wave with the *Waakzaamheid* broadside on in its curl. 4 **curl of the lip** a curving of the upper lip, expressive of scorn or disgust.

Comb.: **curl-paper** a piece of paper with which hair is twisted into a curl; **curl-pate** *arch.* (a person with) a curly head; **curl-pated** *a.* (*arch.*) curly-haired.

curlless /-l-l-/ *a.* M19.

curl /kəːl/ *v.* LME. [Orig. pa. pple, f. (as) CURLED. See also QUERL.] 1 *v.t.* Bend round or twist into curls or a spiral shape. LME. b Ripple, make waves on, (water). L16. 2 *v.i.* Of hair, a fleece: form curls, be susceptible to curling. M16. †3 *v.t.* Curl the hair of. Cf. CURLED 2. L16–M17. 4 *v.i.* Adopt an incurved form or posture. Freq. foll. by *up.* M17. b Foll. by *up*: collapse, lose energy. *slang.* L19. c Shrink or writhe with shame, horror, etc. Freq. foll. by *up.* E20. d *v.i.* Foll. by *up*: settle oneself cosily. M20. 5 *v.i.* Move in spiral convolutions or undulations. E18. 6 *v.i.* Play at curling. *Sc.* E18. 7 *Cricket.* a *v.i.* Of a ball: turn in after pitching; turn in its flight before pitching. M19. b *v.t.* Of a bowler: cause (the ball) to swing in the air. E20.

1b POPE Soft zephyrs curling the wide, watery main. 4 W. GASS I wanted to curl up, face to my thighs. c P. G. WODEHOUSE I'm going to . . look him in the eye . . and watch him curl up at the edges. d R. JARRELL I'll bet *you've* often curled up in a window-seat with *Little Women.* 5 J. FOWLES The breeze . . sent little waves curling . . along the shingle.

Phrases & comb.: **curl a person's hair** *fig.* (*colloq.*) horrify or shock a person. **curl one's** or **the lip** curve the upper lip slightly on one side, as an expression of scorn or disgust. **curl the mo** *v.* & *a.* (*Austral. slang*) [MO *n.*[2]] (*a*) *v.* succeed brilliantly, win; (*b*) *adj.* (w. hyphens), excellent, outstanding. **make a person's hair curl** = *curl a person's hair* above. **want to curl up and die** wish to escape from a highly embarrassing situation; feel mortified.

curlingly *adv.* in a curling manner E17.

curled /kəːld/ *a.* Orig. **†crulled.** LME. [Earliest use f. CRULL *a.*, later f. CURL *n.*, *v.*: see -ED[2], -ED[1]. Metathesized form also LME.] 1 Formed into curls; having a spiral or wavy form. LME. 2 Having the hair in curls. L16. 3 Of potatoes: affected with curl. L18. 4 Of wood, esp. maple: having a wavy or curly grain. L18.

1 *curled* KALE. *curled(-leaved)* MALLOW.

curler /ˈkəːlə/ *n.* M17. [f. CURL *v.* + -ER[1].] 1 A player at the game of curling. (Earlier than the vb.) M17. 2 A person who or thing which produces curls; *spec.* a clasp, roller, etc., used to curl the hair. M18.

curlew /ˈkəːl(j)uː/ *n.* ME. [(O)Fr. *courlieu* var. of *courlis*, orig. imit. of the bird's cry, but prob. assim. to OFr. *courliu* courier, messenger, f. *courre* run + *lieu* place.] 1 Any bird of the genus *Numenius*, comprising waders with long slender down-curved bills; *esp.* one of the common European species *N. arquata.* Cf. *stone curlew* s.v. STONE *n.*, *a.*, & *adv.* ME. †2 [tr. L *coturnix*, Gk *ortux.*] In biblical translations and allusions: a quail. ME–E16.

1 *Eskimo curlew*: see ESKIMO *a.* HUDSONIAN *curlew. Jack curlew*: see JACK *n.*[1] *slender-billed curlew*: see SLENDER *a.*

curlicue /ˈkəːlɪkjuː/ *n.* & *v.* Also **curly-.** M19. [f. CURLY + CUE *n.*[1] or *n.*[2]] A *n.* A fantastic curl or twist; *US* a caper. M19. B *v.t.* & *i.* Bend elaborately or fantastically. M19.

curlie-wurlie *n.* see CURLY-WURLY.

curling /ˈkəːlɪŋ/ *n.* LME. [f. CURL *v.* + -ING[1].] 1 The action of CURL *v.*; a curl, an undulation. LME. 2 A game played on ice in Scotland and elsewhere, in which large circular stones are slid along a defined area (the *rink*) towards a mark (the *tee*). (Earlier than the corresponding sense of the vb.) M17.

Comb.: **curling-iron, -pin**: used for curling the hair; **curling rink** (a building containing) an area of ice prepared and marked for the game of curling; **curling-stone**: used in playing curling (now a large polished circular stone with an iron handle on top); **curling-tongs** metal tongs which are heated and around which strands of hair are wound to put a curl in them.

curly /ˈkəːli/ *a.* L18. [f. CURL *n.* + -Y[1].] 1 Of hair: having curls, in curls. L18. 2 Of a curled form; wavy. L18. 3 Having curly hair. E19. 4 = CURLED 4. E20.

2 *curly* KALE. LINCOLNSHIRE *Curly-Coat(ed)*.

¶See also *get, have, by the short and curlies* s.v. SHORT *a.*

curliness *n.* E19.

curlycue *n.* & *v.* var. of CURLICUE.

curly-wurly /kəːlɪˈwəːli/ *n.* & *a. colloq.* As n. also **curlie-wurlie**. L18. [Redupl. of CURLY.] A *n.* A fantastically curling ornament. L18. B *adj.* Twisting and curling. M19.

curmudgeon /kəːˈmʌdʒ(ə)n/ *n.* L16. [Origin unkn.] A churlish or miserly person.

curmudgeonly *a.* miserly, niggardly, churlish L16.

curmurring /kəˈmʌrɪŋ/ *n. Sc.* L18. [Imit.] A low rumbling, growling, or murmuring sound.

curn /kəːn/ *n. north.* Long only *Sc.* ME. [Perh. rel. to KERN *n.*[2]] †1 In *pl.* Grain. Only in ME. 2 A grain. LME. 3 A small quantity; a few. E17.

curny *a.* granular E19.

curple /ˈkəːp(ə)l/ *n. Sc.* Now *rare.* L15. [Var. of CRUPPER *n.* w. metathesis & dissimilation of /r/ to /l/.] 1 A crupper for a horse etc. L15. 2 The buttocks. L18.

curr /kəː/ *v.* & *n.* LME. [Imit.] A *v.i.* Make a low murmuring sound; coo; purr. LME. B *n.* A curring sound. M19.

currach /ˈkʌrə(x)/ *n.* Also **-agh**, **†corrack**. LME. [Ir., Gael. *curach* small boat: cf. CORACLE.] In Ireland and Scotland: a small boat made of slats or laths covered with watertight material (formerly hide, now usu. tarred canvas).

curragh /ˈkʌrə(x)/ *n.*[1] M17. [Ir. *currach* marsh, Manx *curragh* moor, bog, fen.] In Ireland and the Isle of Man: marshy waste ground.

the Curragh a level stretch of open ground in Co. Kildare, Ireland, famous for its racecourse and military camp.

curragh *n.*[2] var. of CURRACH.

currajong *n.* var. of KURRAJONG.

currance *n.* var. of CURRENCE.

currant /ˈkʌr(ə)nt/ *n.* Also **†corinth**. E16. [Abbrev. of *raisins of Corauntz* f. AN *raisins de Corauntz* for (O)Fr. *raisins de Corinthe* lit. 'grapes of Corinth' (their original place of export): see CORINTH.] 1 A dried fruit of a dwarf seedless variety of grape grown in the eastern Mediterranean region, used in cookery. E16. 2 The small round edible berry of certain shrubs of the genus *Ribes*. L16. 3 A shrub producing this berry or (usu. edible) fruit resembling it (also *currant-bush*); any shrub of the genus *Ribes*. M17.

Phrases: BLACKCURRANT. **flowering currant** a N. American shrub, *Ribes sanguineum*, grown for its conspicuous crimson flowers; also (*US*) a yellow-flowered currant, *R. aureum*. **Indian currant** = *coral-berry* s.v. CORAL *n.* & *a.* REDCURRANT. **white currant** (the whitish berry of) a cultivar of the redcurrant, *Ribes rubrum*.

Comb.: **currant borer** *US*, **currant clearwing** a black and yellow clearwing, *Ramosia tipuliformis*; its larva, which bores into the canes of currant bushes; **currant jelly** a preserve made from the strained juice of boiled currants heated and mixed with sugar; **currant tomato** a tomato with tiny fruits, *Lycopersicon pimpinellifolium*.

currawong /ˈkʌrəwɒŋ/ *n. Austral.* E20. [Aborig. *garraway*.] Any of various large woodland songbirds of the Australian genus *Strepera*, similar to the magpie.

†currence *n.* Also **-ance**. L16. [f. as next: see -ENCE.] 1 = CURRENCY 1. Only in L16. 2 = CURRENCY 2, 5. M17–M19.

currency /ˈkʌr(ə)nsi/ *n.* & *a.* M17. [f. CURRENT *a.*: see -ENCY.] A *n.* 1 The fact or condition of flowing; a current, a stream. *rare.* M17. 2 The fact or quality of being in circulation as a medium of exchange. L17. 3 The money or other commodity which is in circulation as a medium of exchange. E18. b *spec.* A medium of exchange which differs in value from that used for official reckoning, e.g. local money formerly used in British colonies (usu. contrasted w. *sterling*); *fig.* (*Austral.*) a native-born Australian. *arch.* M18. 4 The course *of* time; the time during which something runs its course. E18. 5 The fact or quality of being generally accepted; prevalence (of an idea, report, etc.). E18.

3 G. BOYCOTT Having surrendered all our local currency . . we had no money to buy food or a drink. *hard currency*: see HARD *a.* *managed currency*: see MANAGED 2. *postal currency*: see POSTAL *a.* *reserve currency*: see RESERVE *n.* & *a.* *soft currency*: see SOFT *a.* 4 J. R. MCCULLOCH During the entire currency of the lease. 5 G. F. KENNAN The . . prejudiced views about Russian Communism that were beginning to find currency in Western officialdom. N. PODHORETZ When I was in college, the term WASP had not yet come into currency.

Comb.: **currency note** a note issued as a medium of exchange, *esp.* one of the £1 and 10s. notes first issued by the Treasury during the 1914–18 war.

B *attrib.* or as *adj.* Native-born Australian. *arch.* E19.

Landfall She spoke the King's English like a currency lass.

current /ˈkʌr(ə)nt/ *n.* LME. [OFr. *corant* (mod. *courant*) use as n. of the pres. pple: see next.] 1 Something which flows; *spec.* a portion of a body of water, air, etc., moving in a definite direction. LME. 2 The flow of a river etc. M16. 3 The slope given to a gutter, roof, etc., to enable water to run off. L16. 4 The course of time or of events. L16. 5 Course or progress in a defined direction; tendency, drift, (of events, opinions, etc.). L16. 6 (A) flow of electricity; the rate of this, measured as quantity of charge per second. M18. b *Particle Physics.* A transfer or exchange of a subatomic particle, esp. as mediating an interaction between other particles. M20.

1 N. CALDER The Gulf Stream, the warm current that runs . . across the Atlantic. *Japan current, Japanese current, Labrador current*, etc. 2 W. IRVING A river with high banks and deep rapid current. 4 T. CHALMERS The whole current of my restless and ever-changing history. 5 K. CLARK All the intellectual currents of the time. L. P. HARTLEY Did she . . think that a new experience . . could change the current of an author's work? 6 *alternating current, direct current. fig.*: M. M. KAYE He saw her exchange a brief glance with Ash, and . . it seemed . . that an invisible current leapt between them. *dark current*: see DARK *a.* TOWNSEND *current*.

Comb.: **current bedding** *Geol.*: with a direction produced by a current of water or air at the time of deposition.

currentless *a.* M19.

current /ˈkʌr(ə)nt/ *a.* ME. [OFr. *corant* (mod. *courant*) pres. pple of *courre* (mod. *courir*) f. L *currere* to run, sp. assim. to L: see -ENT, -ANT[1].] 1 Running; flowing. Now *rare.* ME. b Running easily and swiftly; flowing smoothly. Now *rare.* L15. 2a Of money: in circulation, in general use as a medium of exchange. L15. †b Genuine, authentic. L16–M18. 3 Generally reported or known; prevalent; generally accepted, established by common consent, (passing into sense 4). M16. 4 (Of time) now passing, in progress; belonging to the current period of time. E17.

3 DRYDEN A word which is not current English. W. C. WILLIAMS A story current in Paris at the time. 4 DICKENS We must call the current number for that date the Christmas number.

Special collocations & phrases: *current account, account current*: see ACCOUNT *n.* **current affairs, events** matters of public interest in progress. **current asset** *Comm.* an asset in the form of cash or expected to be converted into it, e.g. stock. **current cost accounting** a method of accounting in which assets are valued on the basis of their current replacement cost and increases in their value as a result of inflation are excluded from calculations of profit. **go (†for) current** be generally accepted as true or genuine. **pass (†for) current** = *go (for) current* above.

currently *adv.* LME. **currentness** *n.* (now *rare*) L16.

currente calamo /kəˌrenteɪ ˈkaləməʊ/ *adv. phr.* L18. [mod.L, lit. 'with the pen running on'.] Extempore; without deliberation or hesitation.

curricle /ˈkʌrɪk(ə)l/ *n.* LME. [L CURRICULUM.] †1 The running or course of one continuous thing or several consecutive things. LME–E18. 2 Chiefly *Hist.* A light open two-wheeled carriage, usually drawn by two horses abreast. M18.

curricula *n.* pl. of CURRICULUM.

curricular /kʌˈrɪkjʊlə/ *a.* L18. [f. (as) next + -AR[1].] 1 Of or pertaining to driving or carriages. *rare.* L18. 2 Of or pertaining to a curriculum. E20.

curriculum /kʌˈrɪkjʊləm/ *n.* Pl. **-la** /-lə/. E19. [L = running, course, race-chariot, f. *currere* to run.] A course of study at a school, university, etc.; the subjects making up such a course.

national curriculum: see NATIONAL *a.*

curriculum vitae /kʌˌrɪkjʊləm ˈviːtʌɪ, ˈvʌɪtiː/ *n. phr.* Pl. **curricula vitae** /kʌˈrɪkjʊlə/. E20. [f. as prec. + L *vitae* of life.] A brief account of one's life or career, esp. as required in an application for employment.

†currie *n.* var. of CURRY *n.*[2]

currier /ˈkʌrɪə/ *n.*[1] LME. [OFr. *corier* f. L *coriarius*, f. *corium* leather: see -ER[2]. In sense 2 f. CURRY *v.*[1] + -ER[1].] 1 A person who curries tanned leather. LME. 2 A person who curries horses etc. M16.

†currier *n.*[2] M16–M19. [Origin unkn.] A firearm of the same calibre and strength as the harquebus, but with a longer barrel.

currish /ˈkəːrɪʃ/ *a.* L15. [f. CUR + -ISH[1].] 1 Like a cur in nature; snappish, quarrelsome; mean-spirited, base. L15. 2 Relating to or resembling a cur(-dog). M16.

currishly *adv.* E16. **currishness** *n.* LME.

curry /ˈkʌri/ *n.*[1] L16. [Tamil *kaṟi*.] (A dish of) meat, fish, vegetables, etc., cooked with a mixture of strong spices and turmeric; (in full *curry powder*) a mixture of strong spices and turmeric used in making such a dish.

give a person curry *Austral. slang* abuse, reprove, express anger at, a person. *Madras curry, vindaloo curry*, etc.

Comb.: **curry paste, sauce**: made with curry powder; *curry powder*: see above.

†curry *n.*[2] Also **currie**. E16–M19. [Fr. *curée*, earlier OFr. *cuirée*; gen. referred to *cuir* leather: see -Y[5], QUARRY *n.*[1]] The parts of an animal killed in hunting that were given to the hounds; the cutting up and disembowelling of the game.

curry /ˈkʌri/ *v.*[1] ME. [OFr. *correier* (mod. *courroyer*) arrange, equip, curry (a horse) f. Proto-Romance, f. L CON- + Gmc base of READY *a.*] 1 *v.t.* Groom (a horse etc.) with a curry-comb. ME. b Dress (the hair); dress the hair of. L16. 2 *v.t.* Treat (tanned leather) by soaking, scraping, beating, etc., to improve its properties. LME. 3 *v.t.* Beat, thrash, (a person). LME. †4 *v.i.* & *t.* Employ flattery (with). LME–M19. 5 *v.t. curry favour* [alt. of *curry favel* below], seek to win favour or ingratiate oneself (*with* a person) by flattery etc. E16. †b Seek to win (goodwill, friends, etc.) by flattery etc. L16–E19.

1 **†curry favel** [lit. 'the fallow or chestnut horse': see FAVEL] use insincere flattery etc. to gain personal advantage. 5 G. VIDAL 'I was a close follower in the first few years,' I said, currying favor. b COLERIDGE Currying pardon for his last liberalism by charging . . himself with the guilt of falsehood.

curry /ˈkʌri/ *v.*[2]*t.* M19. [f. CURRY *n.*[1]] Flavour or prepare with curry or curry powder.

curry-comb /ˈkʌrɪkəʊm/ *n.* & *v.* L16. [f. CURRY *v.*[1] + COMB *n.*[1]] A *n.* A toothed instrument used for getting coarse dirt out of the coat of a horse etc. or for cleaning brushes for a horse etc. L16. B *v.t.* Rub down or groom with a curry-comb. E18.

curse /kəːs/ *n.* See also CUSS *n.* OE. [Origin unkn.] 1 An utterance of God, or of a person invoking God, consigning or intending to consign a person or thing to destruction, divine vengeance, misery, etc.; *spec.* a formal ecclesiastical censure, a sentence of excommunication. OE. 2 A profane oath; an imprecation. OE. 3 An evil supposedly inflicted by divine or supernatural power in response to an imprecation or as retributive punishment. ME. b A thing which blights or blasts; a bane. L16. c *the curse*, menstruation. *colloq.* M20. 4

Something that is cursed; an accursed person or thing. LME. **b** An annoying, wretched, or despicable person. L18. **5** In *pl.* as *int.* Expr. strong annoyance. L19.

2 SHAKES. *Mids. N. D.* I give him curses, yet he gives me love. 3 H. B. STOWE This is God's curse on slavery! b W. BUCHAN Many people look upon the necessity . . of earning . . bread by labour, as a curse.

Phrases: **Curse of Scotland** the nine of diamonds in a pack of cards. *not be worth* or *care a tinker's curse*: see TINKER *n.* 1. *tinker's curse*: see TINKER *n.* **under a curse** feeling or liable to the effects of a curse.

curseful *a.* (*rare*) fraught with curses LME.

curse /kəːs/ *v.* Pa. pple **cursed,** (now *rare*) **curst**. See also CUSS *v.* OE. [f. the n. Cf. ACCURSE.] **1** *v.t.* Utter against (a person or thing) words intended to consign their object to destruction, divine vengeance, misery, etc.; anathematize, excommunicate. OE. **2** *v.t.* Speak impiously against (fate, God, etc.); blaspheme. OE. **3** *v.t.* Pour maledictions upon; swear at. ME. **b** In subjunct. w. no subj. expressed: damn, confound. M18. **4** *v.i.* Utter curses; swear in anger or irritation. ME. **5** *v.t.* Afflict with or *with* an evil regarded as the result of divine wrath or malignant fate. Usu. in *pass.* LME.

3 HUGH WALPOLE He cursed Foster for a meddling, cantankerous fanatic. C. FREEMAN The rain that she had been cursing . . now seemed like a blessing. b L. STERNE Curse the fellow. . . I am undone for this bout. 4 A. MACLEAN Morris Schaffer . . cursed fluently as . . a cup of scalding coffee emptied itself over his thigh. 5 B. EMECHETA Leprosy was a disease with which the goddess . . cursed anyone who dared to flout one of the town's traditions. A. KOESTLER The serpent . . was cursed . . to walk on its belly.

curser *n.* ME.

cursed /ˈkəːsɪd, kəːst/ *a.* & *adv.* Also (usual in sense 4) **curst** /kəːst/. See also CUSSED. ME. [pa. pple of prec.: see -ED[1]. Cf. ACCURSED.] **A** *adj.* **1** Under a curse. ME. **2** Deserving or bringing a curse or misery; heinously wicked; execrable, detestable. ME. **3** Damned, confounded. LME. **4** Malignant; perversely disagreeable or cross. Long *obs.* exc. *dial.* & as CUSSED. LME. **†5** Fierce, savage, vicious. LME–L18.

3 SWIFT I have cut my thumb with this cursed knife.

B *adv.* Damnably; very. E18.

cursedly *adv.* LME. **cursedness** *n.* ME.

†cursh *n.* var. of QURSH.

cursillo /kurˈsiʎo; kʊəˈsiːjəʊ, -ˈsiːljəʊ/ *n.* Pl. **-os** /-ɒs, -əʊz/. M20. [Sp., lit. 'little course'.] A short course of study etc., *spec.* of intensive religious studies and exercises, orig. for Roman Catholics in Spain.

cursillista /kursiˈʎista, kʊəsiːˈ(l)jɪstə/ *n.* a person who has participated in a *cursillo* M20.

cursitor /ˈkəːsɪtə/ *n.* E16. [Legal AN *coursetour* f. med.L *cursitor*, f. *cursus* COURSE *n.*[1]] **1** Each of twenty-four officers of the Court of Chancery who until 1835 made out all the common or routine writs for their respective counties. *obs.* exc. *Hist.* E16. **†2** A tramp, a vagabond. M16–E18. **†3** A courier. L16–M17.

Comb.: **Cursitor Baron** a baron of the former Court of Exchequer appointed for fiscal rather than legal expertise.

cursive /ˈkəːsɪv/ *a.* & *n.* L18. [med.L *cursivus*, f. L *curs-* pa. ppl stem of *currere* to run: see -IVE.] **A** *adj.* Designating writing, esp. in ancient manuscripts, in which the pen etc. is not raised after each character; written in this style, in a running hand. L18. **B** *n.* A manuscript in cursive writing. M19.

cursively *adv.* (*rare*) †(*a*) in continuous succession; (*b*) in cursive writing: E17. **cursiveness** *n.* (*rare*) cursive quality E19.

cursor /ˈkəːsə/ *n.* ME. [L = runner, f. *curs-*: see prec., -OR.] **†1** A runner, a running messenger. ME–M17. **2** A part of a mathematical or surveying instrument which can be slid back and forwards; *spec.* the transparent slide with a fine line with which the readings on a slide-rule are taken. L16. **3** A movable visual marker forming part of a VDU display, showing where the next character to be keyed will appear. M20.

†cursorary *a. rare* (Shakes.). Only in E17. [f. as prec. + -ARY[1].] = CURSORY 1.

cursorial /kəːˈsɔːrɪəl/ *a.* M19. [f. as next + -AL[1].] *Zool.* Having limbs adapted for running.

cursory /ˈkəːs(ə)ri/ *a.* E17. [L *cursorius*, f. as CURSOR: see -ORY[2].] **1** Passing rapidly over a thing or subject; hasty, hurried; superficial. E17. **†2** Travelling. *rare.* E–M17. **3** *Hist.* Designating informal lectures at medieval universities given, esp. by bachelors, in addition to the prescribed lectures by authorized teachers. M19.

1 T. HARDY Since he could not call at her father's . . cursory encounters . . were what the acquaintance would have to feed on. E. F. BENSON The whole place, as could be seen at the most cursory glance, had been laid out with skill and care.

cursorily *adv.* hastily, superficially E17. **cursoriness** *n.* E18.

curst *a.* see CURSED.

curst *v.* pa. pple: see CURSE *v.*

cursus /ˈkəːsəs/ *n.* Pl. same, **-uses**. M18. [L = course, f. *currere* to run.] **1** *Archaeol.* A neolithic structure consisting of a long straight avenue, usu. closed at the ends, formed by two earthen banks with a ditch on the outer side of each. M18. **2** A stated order of daily prayer or worship. M19. **3** One of the cadences which mark the ends of sentences and phrases, esp. in Greek and Latin prose; the use of such cadences in accordance with definite rules. E20. **4** In full *cursus honorum* /ɒˈnɔːrəm/ [= of honours]. An established hierarchy of positions through which a person may be promoted. E20.

curt /kəːt/ *a.* LME. [L *curtus* cut short, mutilated, abridged.] **1** Short, shortened. *arch.* LME. **2** Of words, manner, etc.: concise, terse; discourteously brief. M17.

2 C. P. SNOW Pictures drawn by himself of what, from the curt descriptions, he imagined the saga heroes to have looked like. D. DU MAURIER I barely answered him, and he must have thought me curt.

curtly *adv.* M17. **curtness** *n.* M18.

curtail /kəːˈteɪl/ *v.t.* L15. [f. CURTAL, from 16 assoc. w. *tail* and perh. later w. Fr. *tailler* to cut.] **1** Shorten in length, duration, extent, or amount; abridge, reduce. L15. **2** Deprive *of*. L16. **3** Cut short the tail of. Now *rare* or *obs.* L16.

1 A. J. AYER The freedom of expression . . may have to be curtailed when it threatens the security of the state. I. MURDOCH My account is curtailed, but omits nothing of substance. 2 SHAKES. *Rich. III* I—that am curtail'd of this fair proportion.

curtailer *n.* a person who curtails E18. **curtailment** *n.* L18.

curtail-step /kəːteɪlˈstɛp/ *n.* M18. [Origin of 1st elem. unkn.] The lowest step of a stair with the outer end carried round in a semicircle or scroll.

curtain /ˈkəːt(ə)n/ *n.* ME. [OFr. *cortine* (mod. *courtine*) f. late L *cortina* (Vulgate), rendering Gk *aulaia*, f. *aulē* court (= L *cohort-*, *cort-*).] **1** A piece of cloth or other material suspended by the top so as to form a screen, and usu. able to be moved sideways or upwards. ME. **2** Something (material or immaterial) that covers, conceals, divides, or hangs like a curtain. LME. **3** More fully *curtain-wall*. The plain wall of a fortification, connecting two towers etc.; a plain enclosing wall not supporting a roof. M16. **4** A screen which is lowered to separate the stage of a theatre from the auditorium (raised at the start of the action and lowered at the end). L16. **5** *Theatr.* **a** In full *curtain-call*. An audience's summons to a performer or performers to take a bow after the curtain has fallen. L19. **b** The fall of the curtain at the end of a scene etc.; a finale; in *pl.* (*slang*), the end, *esp.* a final downfall. L19. **6** In *pl.* A wrinkled effect resembling a draped curtain on a painted surface etc. *colloq.* E20. **7** In full *curtain of fire* etc. A concentration of gunfire etc. serving to create a barrier. E20.

1 W. S. MAUGHAM Heavy lace curtains over the window shut out the light. **draw, pull, the curtain**(s) draw the curtain(s) back so as to reveal, or forward so as to cover, what is behind. 2 C. M. YONGE Her lilac-spotted bonnet . . with a huge curtain serving for a tippet. J. CHEEVER They sat . . in the shelter of the dense foliage, watching the moving curtain of rain. *bamboo curtain*: see BAMBOO *n.* 4 **behind the curtain** behind the scenes, away from public view. *iron curtain*: see IRON *n.* & *a.* *safety curtain.* 5a L. MACNEICE The music stopped, the dancers took their curtain. b P. KAVANAGH We will wait and watch the tragedy to the last curtain. B. SCHULBERG In court it looks like curtains for her. 7 T. HORSLEY We . . began our glide through the curtain of lead towards the inner harbour.

Comb.: *curtain-call*: see sense 5a above; **curtain-fire** gunfire forming a curtain; **curtain-hook**: used to fasten a curtain to a curtain-rail; **curtain lecture** a wife's private reproof to her husband (orig. behind bed-curtains); **curtain line** *Theatr.* the last line of a play, act, or scene; **curtain-rail**: from which a curtain is suspended esp. by means of sliding hooks; **curtain-raiser** a short opening piece performed before the principal play; *fig.* any preliminary event; **curtain-ring**: used to fasten a curtain to the rail or rod; **curtain-rod**: from which a curtain is suspended by means of sliding rings; **curtain-up** the beginning of a stage performance; *curtain-wall*: see sense 3 above.

curtainless *a.* L18.

curtain /ˈkəːt(ə)n/ *v.t.* ME. [f. the n.] Provide, cover, surround, screen, or shut *off* (as) with a curtain or curtains.

curtal /ˈkəːt(ə)l/ *n.* & *a.* L15. [Fr. *courtault*, *-auld* (now *courtaud*), f. *court* short (ult. f. as CURT) + pejorative suff. *-ault*.] **A** *n.* **1** A kind of short-barrelled cannon. *obs.* exc. *Hist.* L15. **2** A horse or other animal with its tail docked; anything cut short. Now *rare* or *obs.* E16. **†3** A rogue with a short cloak. *slang.* M16–E18. **4** *Mus.* An early form of bassoon. L16. **B** *adj.* **†1** Shortened, short; abridged, curtailed; brief. L16–M17. **†2** Of an animal: with a docked tail. L16–M17. **3** *curtal friar*, a friar with a short gown. *arch.* E17.

curtal-axe /ˈkəːt(ə)laks/ *n. obs.* exc. *Hist.* Also (earlier) **†curtelace**. M16. [Alt. of CUTLASS by assim. to prec. and AXE *n.*[1]] A cutlass; a heavy slashing sword.

Curtana /kəːˈtɑːnə, -ˈteɪnə/ *n.* ME. [AL *curtana* fem. (sc. *spatha* sword) f. AN *curtain*, OFr. *cortain*, name of Roland's sword, so called because it had broken at the point when thrust into a block of steel, f. *cort* CURT.] The unpointed sword borne before the British monarch at the Coronation, emblematically considered the sword of mercy.

curtate /ˈkəːteɪt/ *a.* L17. [L *curtatus* pa. pple, f. as next: see -ATE[2].] **1** *Geom.* & *Astron.* Shortened by being projected on to a plane. L17. **2** *Econ.* & *Statistics.* Calculated for the number of full years in a period, excluding any odd fraction of a year. L19.

curtation /kəːˈteɪʃ(ə)n/ *n.* L16. [f. L *curtat-* pa. ppl stem of *curtare*, f. *curtus*: see CURT, -ATION.] **†1** *Alch.* The shorter process for transmuting base metals into gold. L16–L17. **2** *Astron.* The difference between the actual and the curtate distance. Now *rare* or *obs.* E18.

†curtaxe *n. rare* (Spenser). Only in L16. [Alt.] = CURTAL-AXE.

†curtelace *n.* see CURTAL-AXE.

curtesy *n.* see COURTESY *n.*

curtilage /ˈkəːt(ɪ)lɪdʒ/ *n.* ME. [AN = OFr. *co(u)rtillage*, f. *co(u)rtil* small court, kitchen garden, f. *cort* COURT *n.*[1]: see -AGE.] A small court, yard, or piece of ground attached to a house and forming one enclosure with it.

curtsy /ˈkəːtsi/ *n.* & *v.* Also **-sey**. E16. [Syncopated f. COURTESY *n.*] **A** *n.* **†1** = COURTESY *n.* 6. Only in 16. **†2** = COURTESY *n.* 5a. M–L16. **†3** = COURTESY *n.* 1, 2, 3. L16–M17. **4** An obeisance. Now *spec.* a woman's or girl's salutation made by lowering the body and bending the knees. Freq. in *make* or *drop a curtsy*. L16. **B** *v.i.* & (*rare*) *t.* Make a curtsy (to). M16.

curucui /kʊərʊˈkuːɪ/ *n.* L17. [Repr. Tupi *surucuá*, of imit. origin.] The blue-crowned trogon, *Trogon curucui*, native to S. America.

curule /ˈkjʊəruːl/ *a.* M16. [L *curulis*, f. *currus* chariot, f. *currere* to run.] *Hist.* Designating a seat inlaid with ivory and shaped like a camp-stool with curved legs, used by the highest magistrates of ancient Rome; (of a magistrate etc.) entitled to sit on such a seat; *gen.* of high civic dignity.

curvaceous /kəːˈveɪʃəs/ *a.* M20. [f. CURVE *n.* + -ACEOUS.] Having many, or conspicuous, curves; *esp.* (of a woman or a woman's figure) shapely.

H. HOBSON Sharon; lissome and curvaceous in a revealing leopard-spotted bikini. D. PIPER The grand generalizing and curvaceous amplitude of the baroque.

curvant /'kəːv(ə)nt/ *a. rare.* L15. [L *curvant-* pres. ppl stem of *curvare* CURVE *v.*] Curving.

curvated /kəː'veɪtɪd/ *a. rare.* E18. [f. L *curvat-* (see CURVATURE) + -ED¹.] Curved; of a curved form.

curvation /kəː'veɪʃ(ə)n/ *n.* LME. [L *curvatio(n-)*, f. *curvat-*: see next, -ATION.] Curvature; a curving motion.

curvature /'kəːvətʃə/ *n.* LME. [OFr. f. L *curvatura*, f. *curvat-* pa. ppl stem of *curvare* CURVE *v.*: see -URE.] **1** The action of curving or bending; the fact or manner of being curved; curved form. LME. **b** *spec.* in *Sci.* (The degree of) the deviation of a curve from a straight line, or of a curved surface from a plane; an analogous property of a space of three or more dimensions. E18. **2** A curved portion of anything; a curve. LME.

1 J. CHEEVER A tall man with an astonishing.. curvature of the spine. **b centre, radius, of curvature**: those of the circle which passes through a curve at a given point and has the same tangent and curvature at that point.

curve /kəːv/ *a.* & *n.* LME. [L *curvus* bent, curved.] **A** *adj.* Curved. Now *rare* or *obs.* exc. as passing into attrib. use of the n. LME.

B *n.* **1** A line of which no part is straight. L17. **b** A (straight or curved) line showing how one quantity varies with another, e.g. time; a graph. M19. **2** A curved form, outline, etc.; a curved thing or part; *spec.* the curving line of a woman's figure (usu. in *pl.*). E18. **3** A template used for drawing curved lines. Also *French curve.* L19. **4** *Baseball.* In full *curve ball.* A ball which deviates from the path it would otherwise take, because of spin put on it by the pitcher. L19. **5** A parenthesis, a round bracket. *US.* E20.

1 *geodesic curve, Jordan curve, loxodromic curve*, etc. **b** *Listener* The population curve has slowed down. *characteristic curve, J-curve*, etc. **2** P. G. WODEHOUSE I can remember the days.. when every other girl you met.. had as many curves as a Scenic Railway. P. THEROUX The track was perfectly straight—not a curve in it anywhere.

Comb.: *curve ball*: see sense 4 above; **curve-fitting** the finding of (the equation of) the curve which most closely represents the points on a graph.

curveless *a.* E19. **curvesome** *a.* (of a woman or a woman's figure) shapely M20.

curve /kəːv/ *v.* LME. [L *curvare*, f. as prec.] **1** *v.t.* Bend or shape so as to form a curve. LME. **b** *Baseball.* Throw (a ball) so that it is a curve ball. L19. **2** *v.i.* Have or take a curved form or path. L16.

curvedly *adv.* (*rare*) in a curved manner L19. **curvedness** *n.* (*rare*) curvature L17. **curvingly** *adv.* in a curving manner E20.

curvet /kəː'vɛt/ *n.* & *v.* L16. [It. *corvetta* dim. of *corva*, early form of *curva* curve, f. L *curva* fem. of *curvus* bent, curved.] **A** *n.* A horse's leaping or frisking motion; *spec.* = COURBETTE. L16.

B *v.i.* Infl. **-t(t)-**. (Of a horse or rider) perform a curvet; *gen.* leap (about), frisk. L16.

P. G. WODEHOUSE He curveted past me into the sitting room.

curvi- /'kəːvi/ *comb. form.* M19. [f. L *curvus* bent, curved + -I-.] Having or consisting of (a) curved (what the second elem. denotes), as *curvidentate, curviform.*

curvilineal /kəːvɪ'lɪnɪəl/ *a.* M17. [f. prec. after RECTILINEAL.] = next.

curvilinear /kəːvɪ'lɪnɪə/ *a.* E18. [f. as prec. after RECTILINEAR.] Consisting of or contained by a curved line or lines; of the form of a curved line; *Archit.* designating a style of Decorated tracery characterized by ornate ogee curves with a continuous flow from curve to curve.

ˌ**curviline'arity** *n.* M19. **curvilinearly** *adv.* E19.

curvity /'kəːvɪti/ *n.* Now *rare* or *obs.* LME. [Fr. *curvité* or late L *curvitas*, f. L *curvus* bent, curved: see -ITY.] Curvature; a curve; *fig.* crookedness of conduct or character.

curvous /'kəːvəs/ *a. rare.* L17. [f. CURVE *n.* + -OUS.] Curved; crooked.

curvy /'kəːvi/ *a.* E20. [f. CURVE *n.* + -Y¹.] Having a curve or curves; full of curves.

curviness *n.* L20.

cuscus /'kʊskʊs/ *n.*¹ L16. [Arab. *kuskus*: see COUSCOUS *n.*¹] The grain of African millet, an article of food in Africa and Asia.

cuscus /'kʌskʌs/ *n.*² Also **couscous** /'kuːskuːs/. M17. [Fr. *couscous* f. Du. *koeskoes* f. native Moluccas name.] Any of several phalangers of the genus *Phalanger* and related genera, native to New Guinea and N. Australia.

cuscus /'kʌskʌs/ *n.*³ Also **khus-khus**. E19. [Urdu & Pers. *ḵaskas*.] (The sweet-scented root of) a grass, *Vetiveria zizanioides*, used in the Indian subcontinent to make fans and screens.

cusec /'kjuːsɛk/ *n.* E20. [Abbrev. of *cubic foot per second.*] A unit of flow of rivers etc. equal to one cubic foot per second.

cush /kʊʃ/ *n. colloq.* L19. [Abbrev. of CUSHION *n.*] A cushion, *esp.* that of a billiard-table.

cushat /'kʌʃət/ *n.* Chiefly *Sc.* & *north.* OE. [Origin unkn. Cf. QUEEST.] The woodpigeon.

cushaw /kʊ'ʃɔː, 'kuːʃɔː/ *n. US.* L16. [Origin unkn.] A winter curved-necked squash (crookneck); a variety of this.

cush-cush /'kʊʃkʊʃ/ *n.* L19. [Perh. ult. of Afr. origin.] A yam, *Dioscorea trifida*, native to S. America and cultivated for its edible tubers.

Cushing /'kʊʃɪŋ/ *n.* M20. [Harvey W. *Cushing* (1869–1939), US surgeon, who described the condition.] *Med.* **1** *Cushing's syndrome*, a syndrome of hypertension, obesity, metabolic disorders, etc., caused by overproduction of hormones by the adrenal cortex. M20. **2** *Cushing's disease*, Cushing's syndrome accompanied and caused by a tumour of the pituitary gland. M20.

Cushingoid, c- *a.* similar to (that of) Cushing's syndrome; resembling a patient with Cushing's syndrome: L20.

cushion /'kʊʃ(ə)n/ *n.* ME. [OFr. *co(i)ssin, cu(i)ssin*, (also mod.) *coussin*, f. Proto-Gallo-Romance form ult. f. L *coxa* hip, thigh.] **1** A mass of soft or yielding material, esp. stuffed into a bag of cloth, silk, etc., used to give support or comfort to the body in sitting, reclining, or kneeling. ME. **b** A similar item for supporting a book in a pulpit. E17. **c** The seat of a judge or ruler. M17. **2** An object resembling a cushion; *spec.* (*a*) a small soft pad for sticking pins in to keep them ready for use, a pincushion; (*b*) *Hist.* a bustle; (*c*) a pad worn by women under the hair; (*d*) a sweet in the shape of a cushion. L16. **3a** The fleshy part of the buttock of a horse, pig, etc. E18. **b** The frog of a horse's hoof; the coronet just above the hoof. L19. **4** A thing acting as a cushion, esp. by providing protection or support; *spec.* (*a*) (*Billiards, Snooker*, etc.) the sides of the table from which the balls rebound; (*b*) the steam left in the cylinder of a steam engine as a buffer to the piston; (*c*) the body of air supporting a hovercraft etc. L18. **5** A dense compact mass of foliage. L19.

Phrases: *lady's cushion*: see LADY *n.* & *a.* *ride (the) cushions*: see RIDE *v.* *squab cushion*: see SQUAB *n.* 2b. *thump a cushion*: see THUMP *v.* 1a.

Comb.: **cushion capital** *Archit.*: resembling a cushion pressed down by a weight; **cushion-dance** *Hist.* a ring dance formerly danced at weddings, in which women and men alternately knelt on a cushion to be kissed; **cushion star** any of various small short-armed starfish, esp. of the genera *Asterina* and *Porania*; **cushion stitch** a flat embroidery stitch used to fill in backgrounds; **cushion-thumper** *colloq.* a violent preacher; an evangelist.

cushionless *a.* M19. **cushion-like** *adv.* & *a.* (*a*) *adv.* in the manner of a cushion; (*b*) *adj.* resembling a cushion: M17. **cushiony** *a.* M19.

cushion /'kʊʃ(ə)n/ *v.t.* M18. [f. the n.] **1** Rest, seat, set, (a person or thing) on or against a cushion; prop *up* with cushions. M18. **2** Provide or protect (as) with a cushion or cushions; mitigate the effects of (as) with a cushion. E19. **3** Suppress quietly. E19. **4** Form into a cushion of steam or air. L19. **5** *Billiards, Snooker*, etc. Leave, place, or rebound (a ball) against the cushion. Now *rare.* L19.

2 *Listener* Action.. to cushion the economy against a recession. H. FAST She looked for a role instead, always cushioning her defeats with Martin Spizer's promises. **3** C. BRONTË There my courage failed: I preferred to cushion the matter.

cushioned /'kʊʃ(ə)nd/ *a.* M18. [f. CUSHION *n.*, *v.*: see -ED², -ED¹.] **1** In the form of a cushion; cushion-shaped. M18. **2** Provided with a cushion or cushions. L18. **3** Seated on or supported by a cushion; *fig.* protected from harm or adverse effects. E19.

Cushite /'kʊʃʌɪt/ *n.* & *a.* Also **K-**. M19. [f. *Cush*, an ancient country in the Nile valley + -ITE¹.] **A** *n.* **1** A member of an ancient people of E. Africa, south of Egypt. M19. **2** Cushitic. M20. **B** *adj.* Of or pertaining to this people. M19.

Cushitic /kʊ'ʃɪtɪk/ *a.* & *n.* Also **K-**. E20. [f. prec. + -IC.] (Designating, of, or pertaining to) an Afro-Asiatic language family of NE Africa.

cushla-machree /ˌkʊʃləmə'kriː/ *n. Anglo-Ir.* E19. [f. Ir. *cuisle* pulse + *mo* my + *chroidhe* heart: see ACUSHLA, MACHREE. Cf. MACUSHLA.] As a form of address: my dear, darling.

cushy /'kʊʃi/ *a. colloq.* (orig. *Anglo-Ind.*). E20. [Urdu *ḵušī* pleasure, f. Pers. *ḵuš*.] Of a post, task, etc.: easy, comfortable, esp. more so than might be expected.

cushiness *n.* M20.

cusimanse *n.* var. of KUSIMANSE.

cusk /kʌsk/ *n. US.* E17. [Origin unkn.: cf. TORSK.] **1** The burbot. *rare.* E17. **2** The torsk. L19.

Comb.: **cusk-eel** any of a group of mostly small marine eel-like fishes of the family Ophidiidae.

cusp /kʌsp/ *n.* L16. [L *cuspis, -id-* point, apex.] **1** *Astrol.* The initial point or entrance of a house. L16. **2** *gen.* An apex, a pointed end or tip, *spec.* that of a canine tooth or a leaf. M17. **3** Each of the pointed ends of the crescent moon, the partly eclipsed sun, etc. L17. **4** *Geom.* A point at which two branches of a curve come together and share a common tangent, as if a point describing the curve had its motion reversed there. M18. **5** *Archit.* A projecting point between adjacent small arcs in Gothic tracery, arches, etc. E19.

cuspate *a.* cusp-shaped L19. **cuspated** *a.* (*Archit.*) cuspidated M19. **cusped** *a.* having a cusp or cusps E19. **cusping** *n.* (*Archit.*) cusp-shaped stonework; a cusp-shaped part of a window etc.: M19.

cusparia /kʌ'spɛːrɪə/ *n.* L19. [mod.L *Cusparia* genus name f. Amer. Sp. f. Galibi *cuspare*.] More fully *cusparia bark.* = ANGOSTURA *bark.*

cuspid /'kʌspɪd/ *n.* M18. [L *cuspid-*: see CUSP, -ID².] **1** *Geom.* = CUSP 4. M18. **2** A cusped tooth. L19.

cuspidal /'kʌspɪd(ə)l/ *a.* M17. [f. as prec. + -AL¹.] †**1** Belonging to the apex (of a cone). Only in M17. **2** Of a tooth: cuspidate. M19. **3** *Geom.* Having, relating to, or being a cusp. L19.

cuspidate /'kʌspɪdət, -deɪt/ *a.* L17. [mod.L *cuspidatus*, f. *cuspidat-* pa. ppl stem of *cuspidare* provide with a point, f. *cuspid-*: see CUSP, -ATE².] Having a cusp or a sharp point; *spec.* (*a*) (of a leaf) tapering to a rigid point; (*b*) designating a canine tooth.

cuspidated /'kʌspɪdeɪtɪd/ *a.* M17. [f. as prec. + -ED¹.] Having a cusp or cusps.

cuspidation /kʌspɪ'deɪʃ(ə)n/ *n.* M19. [f. L *cuspidat-*: see prec., -ATION.] *Archit.* Ornamentation with cusps; cusps collectively.

cuspides *n.* pl. of CUSPIS.

cuspidor /'kʌspɪdɔː/ *n.* Chiefly *N. Amer.* M18. [Port. = spitter, f. *cuspir* to spit f. L *conspuere*: see -OR.] A spittoon.

cuspis /'kʌspɪs/ *n.* Now *rare.* Pl. **cuspides** /-pɪdiːz/. M17. [L: see CUSP.] = CUSP 2.

cuss /kʌs/ *n. colloq.* (orig. *US*). L18. [Var. of CURSE *n.* Sense 1 later often regarded as abbrev. of CUSTOMER.] **1** A person, a creature; *esp.* a detestable, perverse, or obstinate one. L18. **2** A curse; a profane oath. M19.

1 P. LIVELY I am going to need you, though I will never let on, being the obstinate cuss that I am. **2** *tinker's cuss*: see TINKER *n.*

Comb.: **cuss-word** a swear-word.

cuss /kʌs/ *v.t.* & *i. colloq.* (orig. *US*). E19. [Var. of CURSE *v.*] Curse, swear (at).
cuss a person out *US* silence, intimidate, or subdue a person by swearing at him or her.

cussed /ˈkʌsɪd/ *a. colloq.* (orig. *US*). M19. [Var. of CURSED.] Cursed; detestable; *esp.* perversely disagreeable or cross, obstinate, pig-headed (cf. CURSED 4).
cussedly *adv.* M19. **cussedness** *n.* M19.

custard /ˈkʌstəd/ *n.*[1] Also (earlier) †**crusta(r)de**. LME. [f. OFr. *crouste* CRUST *n.*: see -ADE. Forms without *-r-* also LME.] Orig., a kind of open pie containing meat or fruit covered with broth or milk, thickened with eggs, sweetened, and spiced. Now, a sauce made of heated sweetened milk with cornflour or egg, etc.; egg-custard.
Comb.: **custard-apple** the fruit of any of several trees of the genus *Annona* (family Annonaceae), characterized by sweet yellow pulp, esp. the bullock's heart, *A. reticulata*, and sweetsop, *A. squamata*; (also *custard-apple tree*) a tree bearing such a fruit; **custard marrow** a variety of summer squash, *Cucurbita pepo* var. *melopepo*, having round flattened fruits scalloped at the edges; also called *simlin*; **custard-pie** *n.* & *a.* (*a*) *n.* an open pie with a filling of cold thick custard; *fig.* slapstick comedy (in which such pies are commonly used as missiles); (*b*) *adj.* slapstick; **custard powder** a preparation of cornflour etc. for making custard.
custardy *a.* L19.

custard /ˈkʌstəd/ *n.*[2] *colloq. derog.* M19. [Alt. of COSTARD.] A person. Only in the children's taunt *cowardy (cowardy) custard*
J. M. BARRIE Father's a cowardy custard.

custock *n.* var. of CASTOCK.

custode /kʌˈstəʊdi, *foreign* kuˈstɔde/ *n.* Pl. **-di** /-di/. M19. [It. f. L *custos*, *-od-*.] A person who has the custody of something; a guardian; a custodian.

custodee /kʌstəˈdiː/ *n.* E19. [f. L *custod-* (see CUSTODY) or CUSTODY: see -EE[1].] A person entrusted with the custody of anything.

custodes *n.* pl. of CUSTOS.

custodi *n.* pl. of CUSTODE.

custodial /kʌˈstəʊdɪəl/ *a.* & *n.* L18. [f. L *custodia* CUSTODY + -AL[1]] A *adj.* Relating to custody or guardianship; of or pertaining to imprisonment or forcible institutionalization. L18.
H. H. GODDARD Those.. technically called *imbeciles*, also require more or less custodial care. T. BERGER While I was on my lunch.. the custodial staff watched the door for me. *Guardian* The first person to be given a custodial sentence under the Health and Safety Act.
B *n. Eccl.* A receptacle for sacred objects. M19.

custodiam /kʌˈstəʊdɪəm/ *n. obs.* exc. *Hist.* M16. [L, accus. sing. of *custodia* CUSTODY (from the wording of the grant).] *Law.* A three-year grant by the exchequer of lands etc. in possession of the Crown.

custodian /kʌˈstəʊdɪən/ *n.* L18. [f. CUSTODY + -AN, after *guardian*.] 1 A person who has custody; a guardian, a keeper, esp. of a public building. L18. 2 *Sport.* A goalkeeper or wicket-keeper. *colloq.* & *joc.* E20.
custodianship *n.* M19.

custodier /kʌˈstəʊdɪə/ *n.* Now *Sc.* L15. [f. as next + -ER[1].] A custodian.

custody /ˈkʌstədi/ *n.* LME. [L *custodia*, f. *custos*, *-od-* guardian: see -Y[3].] 1 Safe-keeping; protection; care; guardianship. LME. 2 Imprisonment. L15.
1 T. CAPOTE He was returned to the custody of his father. D. LESSING Enough to prevent him from divorcing her and gaining custody of Tommy. 2 *protective custody*: see PROTECTIVE *a.* *remand in custody*: see REMAND *v.* 1b. **take into custody** arrest.

custom /ˈkʌstəm/ *n.*, *a.*, & *adv.* ME. [AN *custome*, *-ume*, OFr. *co(u)stume* (mod. *coutume*), f. alt. of L *consuetudo*, *-din-*, f. *consuescere* become accustomed, f. as CON- + *suescere* become accustomed.] A *n.* 1 A habitual or usual practice; a common way of behaving; usage, fashion, habit. ME. b *Law.* An established usage which by long continuance has acquired the force of a law or right. ME. c The practising of something habitually; the fact of being or becoming accustomed. E16. 2 A customary service, rent, or due paid to a lord or ruler. *obs.* exc. *Hist.* ME. 3 Orig., duty levied by a lord or local authority on commodities on their way to market, *esp.* that levied in the name of the monarch on imports and exports. Now, in *pl.*, such duty levied by a government on imports, the area at a port etc. where goods are examined for this purpose. LME. 4 The practice of habitually giving business to any particular shop etc.; regular business; regular customers. L16.
1 N. MITFORD The English custom which keeps the men in the dining-room after dinner. R. HOGGART Individuals.. who are not paid but by custom are supplied with drinks. I. FLEMING It was his custom, when unpleasant things had to be said, to sweeten his breath. †**custom of women** menstruation. *old Spanish custom*: see SPANISH *a.* b W. BLACKSTONE The will of the lord was to be interpreted by the custom of the manor. c J. INGELOW Custom makes all things easy. 3 **The Customs** the department of the Civil Service that levies customs duties. 4 P. G. WODEHOUSE The head waiter came up and suggested that we should take our custom elsewhere.
Comb.: **custom-house** an office (esp. in a port) at which customs are collected or administered; **customs union** a group of States with an agreed common tariff and usu. free trade with each other.
B *adj.* Made or done to order for individual customers; (of a place or person) specializing in such work. Chiefly *N. Amer.* exc. in *custom car* below. M19.
T. STERLING He had designed the murder for one woman and no other. It was a perfect custom fit. H. HORWOOD We do a lot of custom sawing..—cutting logs that people bring to us.
Special collocations: **custom car**: built or modified to the owner's design. **custom clothes** etc. (chiefly *N. Amer.*): made to the customer's order.
C *adv.* In response to individual requirements; for an individual customer. Only in comb. w. following vb or pa. pple. Chiefly *N. Amer.* exc. in *custom-built*, *-made*. M20.
M. MCLUHAN Custom-make your own book by simply Xeroxing a chapter from this one, a chapter from that one. *Offshore Engineer* We'll custom-install a compact Total Cementing Concept system for your platform.

custom /ˈkʌstəm/ *v.* LME. [OFr. *costumer*, f. *costume*: see prec.] 1 *v.t.* Make customary or usual; practise habitually. *obs.* exc. as *customed* pa. pple. LME. 2 *v.t.* & (*rare*) *i.* Accustom, habituate, (oneself or another); in *pass.*, be accustomed (*to do* something). *arch.* LME. †3 *v.t.* Pay duty or toll on; pass through a custom-house. L15–E18. 4 *v.t.* Bestow one's custom on; frequent as a customer. Now *rare.* L16.
2 E. SMITHER The eyes of a nightbird customed to the splash of the sea.

customable /ˈkʌstəməb(ə)l/ *a.* & *adv.* ME. [AN *custumable*, OFr. *cost-*, f. as CUSTOM *n.*: see -ABLE.] A *adj.* †1 Customary, usual. ME–M17. †2 Of a person: accustomed (*to*); wont (*to do*); (w. agent-n.) habitual. ME–L16. 3 Liable to duty, dutiable. *rare.* LME.
2 R. PECOCK King Saul was a wickid customable synner.
†**B** *adv.* Customarily; habitually. ME–M17.
†**customableness** *n.* LME–M18. **customably** *adv.* (now *dial.*) customarily; habitually, usually: ME.

customal *n.* var. of CUSTUMAL.

customary /ˈkʌstəm(ə)ri/ *n.* Also **custu-** /ˈkʌstjʊ-/. LME. [med.L *custumarius* use as n. of the adj.: see next.] 1 The customs of a country etc. collectively, esp. as set down in a book or legal document. LME. 2 *Eccl.* = CONSUETUDINARY *n.* L19.

customary /ˈkʌstəm(ə)ri/ *a.* E16. [med.L *custumarius*, f. *custuma* f. AN *custume*: see CUSTOM *n.*, -ARY[1].] 1 *Law* (now *Hist.*). Subject to or held by customs (CUSTOM *n.* 2), esp. of a manor. E16. 2 *Law.* Established by custom, based on custom, (rather than common law or statute). L16. 3 According to custom; commonly done etc.; usual. E17.
1 J. WILKINSON If any customarie tenant or copiholder hold two parcels of land by herriot service. **customary court** a manorial court which exercised jurisdiction over the copyhold tenants and administered the customary law of the manor. 2 *Encycl. Brit.* The origin of international customary law is frequently found in earlier treaty clauses.. subsequently.. taken for granted. 3 G. SANTAYANA Anxious talk had kept them up for a full hour beyond their customary bed-time. R. P. GRAVES During their fourth year at St John's, it was customary for men to live in lodgings.
customarily *adv.* E17. **customariness** *n.* M17.

customer /ˈkʌstəmə/ *n.* LME. [Orig. f. AN *custumer* or med.L *custumarius*; in some senses newly f. CUSTOM *n.*: see -ER[1].] †1 A person who acquires ownership by long use or possession. Only in LME. †2 A person who collects customs, a customs officer. LME–L19. 3 A person who makes a purchase or gives business, esp. habitually to any particular seller or establishment. LME. †4 A person with whom one has dealings; an associate, a companion. LME–E17. b A common woman; a prostitute. *rare* (Shakes.). Only in E17. 5a A person of a specified character to deal with. *colloq.* L16. b A fox that affords good sport in the field. M19. †6 = CUSTUMAL *n.* E17–L18.
3 P. THEROUX Everyone in Colón looks unemployed, even the shopkeepers: not a customer in sight. 5a *awkward customer*, *cool customer*, *queer customer*, *ugly customer*, etc.

customize /ˈkʌstəmaɪz/ *v.t.* Orig. *US.* Also **-ise.** M19. [f. CUSTOM *n.* + -IZE.] Make or modify to order or according to individual requirements.
customizable *a.* L20. **customiˈzation** *n.* L20. **customizer** *n.* M20.

custos /ˈkʌstɒs/ *n.* Pl. **custodes** /kʌˈstəʊdiːz/, (orig.) †**-oses.** LME. [L.] A keeper, a guardian, a custodian. Now chiefly in titles f. mod.L.
custos rotulorum /rəʊtjʊˈlɔːrəm/ [L = keeper of the rolls] the principal Justice of the Peace of a county, who has nominal custody of the records of the commission of the peace.

custrel /ˈkʌstr(ə)l/ *n.* Also **coistrel** /ˈkɔɪstr(ə)l/. L15. [In sense 1 corresp. in meaning to OFr. *coustillier*, *-illeur* soldier armed with a *coustille* (a double-edged sword); sense 2 (not in Fr.) perh. infl. by CUSTRON.] 1 *Hist.* An attendant on a knight or man-at-arms. L15. 2 As a term of reproach: knave, fool. Now *rare* (chiefly *Sc.*). E16.

custron /ˈkʌstr(ə)n/ *n.* Now *Sc.* ME. [OFr. *coistron*, nom. *cuistre* scullion, f. pop.L *coquistro*, *-on-* shopkeeper.] A scullion; a base-born fellow; a rogue.

custumal /ˈkʌstjʊm(ə)l/ *n.* Also **-tom-** /-təm-/. L16. [med.L *custumale* customs-book, neut. of *custumalis*, f. *custuma* = OFr. *co(u)stume* CUSTOM *n.*: see -AL[1].] *Law.* A written collection of the customs of a city etc.

custumary *n.* var. of CUSTOMARY *n.*

cut /kʌt/ *n.*[1] *obs.* exc. *dial.* ME. [Perh. f. the vb (as CUT *n.*[2]).] 1 A lot that is drawn. Chiefly in *draw cuts* (orig. †*draw*, †*lay cut*), cast lots by the chance drawing of sticks, straws, etc., of unequal length. ME. †2 A person's lot, fate, etc.; fate or fortune as a ruler of events. ME–M17.

cut /kʌt/ *n.*[2] LME. [f. the vb.] **I** A result of cutting. 1 A piece (esp. of meat or cloth) cut off; *spec.* each of the joints of meat into which a butcher divides a carcass; *Sc.* & *north.* a certain quantity of yarn; *N. Amer.* a quantity of timber etc. harvested; *N. Amer.* (a light snack of) a slice of meat (*obs.* exc. in *cold cuts*: see COLD *a.*). LME. b A part of a field cut or for cutting at one time. *US.* M18. c A number of sheep or cattle taken out of a flock or herd. *US, Austral.*, & *NZ.* L19. d *fig.* A share of profits or takings; commission. *slang.* E20. 2 A long narrow opening in a surface, esp. the skin, made by something sharp; an incision; a gash. M16. 3 An incision made in the edge of a garment etc. for ornament. M16. 4a A passage cut or dug out; a new channel made for a river; a railway cutting. M16. b A natural narrow opening or passage by water; a channel, a strait; a creek, an inlet. *obs.* exc. *dial.* L16. 5 A design engraved on a block of wood (formerly also copper or steel) for printing; an electrotype; an illustration made with such a block etc. M17. 6 A gramophone record or recording; a version of a film after editing. M20.

1 M. EDGEWORTH Mary spun nine cuts a day. E. DAVID Recipes for the cheaper cuts of meat. 2 J. STEINBECK A long deep cut in his chin . . , a deep bleeding slash. J. HOOKER Stones with red marks like cuts of a rusty axe. SPEEDY *cut*. 5 WOODCUT. 6 *lateral cut*: see LATERAL *a*. *rough cut*: see ROUGH *a*.

II An act of cutting. **7** An act or utterance that wounds the feelings; a blow, a shock. M16. **8** A stroke or blow given with a sharp-edged instrument, as a knife, sword, etc.; *Fencing* a stroke given with the edge of the weapon as distinguished from the point; an act of cutting a person's hair, a haircut, (cf. sense 18 below). L16. **b** A sharp stroke with a whip, cane, etc. See also *upper-cut* s.v. UPPER *a*. E18. **9** The act of cutting a pack of cards; the card obtained by cutting. L16. **10** The excision or omission of part of a play, film, book, etc. E17. **11** A step in which a dancer cuts (CUT *v*. 29). L17. **12** A deliberate refusal to recognize or acknowledge another person. *colloq*. L18. **13** An act of absenting oneself from a class etc. Chiefly *US*. M19. **14** A stroke made by cutting in cricket, tennis, etc. M19. **15** A reduction in price, rate of pay, service offered, etc. Also, a temporary cessation of the availability of electricity, gas, water, or telephone communication. L19. **16** *Cinemat*. An immediate transition from one scene to another. M20.

7 R. BOLTON A most cruel cut to a troubled conscience. 8 T. H. WHITE Waving his blade and trying to get a cut at him. **cut and thrust** the use of both the edge and the point of one's sword while fighting; *fig*. lively interchange of argument etc. *second cut*: see SECOND *a*. b A. BRINK He tried to protest against Jonathan's sentence of six cuts . . By that time the flogging had . . been administered. **the cuts** *Austral*. & *NZ slang* the cane, as a child's punishment. 14 *late cut*: see LATE *a*. *square cut*: see SQUARE *a*. 15 *power cut* etc.

III A thing that cuts. **17** A passage, course, or way straight across, esp. as contrasted with a longer way round. Now chiefly *US* exc. in *short cut* below. L16.

17 A. FONBLANQUE The cut across the fields is shut up. E. BOWEN Crossing . . Oxford Street, they took a cut through Mayfair. **near cut** (now *Sc*.), **short cut** a shorter route to a place than the usual or expected (*lit*. & *fig*.).

IV A style of cutting. **18** The way something is cut; fashion, style, (of clothes, hair, etc.); *spec*. (freq. w. specifying wd) a hairstyle created by cutting, a haircut. L16.

18 S. BELLOW The German cut of his overcoat. *crew cut*, *urchin cut*, etc. *fig*.: J. CARLYLE These Londoners are all of the cut of this woman. **a cut above** noticeably superior to. *the cut of a person's jib*: see JIB *n*.[1]

Comb.: **cut-line** (*a*) *Rackets* the line above which a served ball must strike the wall; (*b*) a caption to an illustration.

†cut *n*.[3] L15. [f. pa. pple of CUT *v*.] **1** Used as a term of abuse. L15–E19. **2** A labouring horse; a gelding. E16–E17.

cut /kʌt/ *ppl a*. LME. [f. CUT *v*.] **1** That has been cut. LME. **b** Of a garment: having the edges etc. indented or slashed for ornament or as a fashion. LME. **2** Drunk. *slang*. L17.

1 *Farmers Weekly* Extensive pot plant and cut flower nurseries. *clean-cut*, *clear-cut*, etc. **cut and dried** *fig*. completely decided, prearranged; (of ideas etc.) ready-made, without freshness or originality. *fine-cut*: see FINE *adv*. *single cut*: see SINGLE *a*. & *adv*.

Special collocations & comb.: **cut glass** *n*. & *a*. (*a*) *n*. glass that has been ornamented by having patterns cut into it by grinding and polishing; (*b*) *adj*. made of cut glass; *fig*. characterized by (excessively) careful enunciation. **cut loaf** a sliced loaf. **cut paper**: cut into a desired shape, usually for decorative purposes. **cut-price**, **-rate** *adjs*. selling or sold at a reduced price. **cut splice** *Naut*. two ropes spliced together to form an eye. **cut-under** *US* a horse-drawn vehicle with part of the body cut away to allow the front wheels to turn underneath it.

cut /kʌt/ *v*. Infl. **-tt-**. Pa. t. & pple **cut**. See also CUT, CUTTED *ppl adjs*. ME. [Rel. to Norw. *kutte*, Icel. *kuta* cut with a little knife, *kuti* little blunt knife. Prob. already in OE.] **I** Make an incision (in, through, etc.). **1** *v.t*. Penetrate or wound with a sharp-edged thing; make an incision in. ME. **b** *fig*. Wound the feelings of (a person), hurt deeply. Chiefly in *cut to the heart*, *the quick*. ME. **2** *v.t*. Divide with a knife or other sharp-edged instrument into two or more pieces; sever (string, cord, etc.); carve (meat); slice (a loaf, a cake). ME. **3** *v.t*. & *i*. Divide (what grows) with an edged instrument in order to take the part detached; hew (timber), mow (grass), etc.; divide the stalk of and gather (a flower). ME. **b** *v.t*. Cut the crop on (land). L18. **†4** *v.t*. Break up, reduce, or dissolve the viscidity of (a liquid, phlegm, etc.). LME–M18. **5** *v.i*. Make an incision; be capable of making an incision. LME. **6a** *v.i*. Be or become cut; admit of being cut (esp. with a good, bad, etc., result). M16. **b** *v.t*. Of land etc.: yield as a crop. M18. **7** *v.t*. Make a narrow opening through (a dyke etc.), breach the bank of (a canal), esp. to permit the escape of water. L16. **8** *v.t*. & *i*. Strike sharply with a whip, cane, etc. Of a whip etc.: cause a painful blow. E17. **9** *v.t*. In full *cut open*. Separate the leaves of (a book) by cutting the folds of the sheets. L18. **10** *v.i*. *Fencing*. Attempt a cut at an opponent. M19.

1 N. MOSLEY The edge of the pipe cut his mouth, which bled. *fig*.: ADDISON Tormenting thought! it cuts into my soul. b F. BURNEY He says something so painful that it cuts us to the soul. 2 I. MURDOCH Julius . . began to cut it straight across into narrow black strips. *that one could cut with a knife*: see KNIFE *n*. 3 *fig*.: J. GATHORNE-HARDY By war and legislation, the wealth of the upper classes had been effectively cut into. 5 EVELYN Cut close to the stem. *fig*.: G. HERBERT The tongue is not steel, yet it cuts. 6 OED The cloth does not cut to advantage.

II Separate, shorten, etc., by cutting. **11** *v.t*. **a** Separate or remove by cutting; sever from the main body; remove (lines etc.) from a text; *Computing* remove (information, esp. text) for placing elsewhere (cf. PASTE *v*. 1b). (Foll. by *from* or other prep., advb. compl.) ME. **†b** Cut off, isolate, *from*. L16–L18. **12** *v.t*. Shorten or reduce by cutting off a portion; trim, prune. ME. **13** *v.t*. *fig*. Curtail, abridge; shorten (a text etc.) by omitting part; reduce (a price, wage, service, etc.); cancel, abolish, (a service etc.); stop (one's talking). LME. **14** *v.t*. Reduce the intensity of (a colour etc.); *esp*. dilute or adulterate (alcohol, a drug, etc.). Chiefly *N. Amer*. M19. **15** *v.t*. Outdo, beat, surpass. Chiefly *US*. L19. **16** *v.t*. & *i*. *Cinemat*. Edit (a film); make an immediate transition *to* another shot. E20. **17** *v.t*. & *i*. (Cause to) cease running or operating. M20.

11 P. THOMAS We were obliged . . to cut the Raft adrift. P. THOMPSON Halfpenny-worths of bread cut off the loaf. 12 J. BUCHAN The lawn was . . cut with a scythe instead of a mower. N. FREELING His hair needed cutting. 13 *Observer* We didn't cut the fares; the voters did. *Times* British Telecom . . denied suggestions that 15,000 jobs might be cut. 14 G. VIDAL He did not cut his wine with water. 16 N. KNEALE Cut—to the excavation. 17 H. ROBBINS The motors cut and died away.

III Make by cutting. **18** *v.t*. Make or form by cutting, engraving, carving, etc. ME. **b** Make a sound recording of, esp. on a gramophone record; make (a sound recording). M20. **19** *v.t*. Make by excavation or digging; make (one's way) thus (*lit*. & *fig*.). L16. **20** *v.t*. Perform, execute, (an action, gesture, or display, esp. of a striking or surprising kind). E17.

18 W. S. MAUGHAM The clever dressmaker had cut her frock to conceal youthful plumpness. J. BUCHAN I cut a walking-stick of hazel. A. CARTER The key gleamed as freshly as if it had just been cut. *transf*.: S. C. HALL His features were finely cut. 19 LD MACAULAY He cut his way gallantly through them. A. H. MARKHAM Cutting a road through the hummocks. 20 W. IRVING Two of us . . saw a fellow . . cutting queer antics.

IV Pass through as in cutting. **21** *v.t*. & *i*. Divide, separate, intersect, run into or *through*, (by virtue of position rather than motion). LME. **22** *v.i*. Cross (*over*), pass straight *through*, *across*, esp. as a shorter way. M16. **23** *v.t*. & *i*. Move sharply through or *through* (the air, water); cleave. Chiefly *literary* & *poet*. L16. **24a** *v.i*. Run away or *away*, make *off*, escape; move sharply or suddenly. Now *colloq*. L16. **b** *v.t*. Of a vehicle: move sharply in front of (another); pass recklessly or illegally. M20. **25** *v.t*. & *i*. Come across, hit upon (a path, trail, etc.). Chiefly *US*. L19.

21 J. G. WHITTIER Yon spire . . That cuts the evening sky. I. TODHUNTER If two straight lines cut one another. 22 S. BARSTOW We cut across the grass to the shelter. 24 THOMAS HUGHES We all cut upstairs after the Doctor. E. NESBIT You'll be late for your grub! . . Then cut along home.

V Contextual, ellipt., & techn. uses. **26a** *v.t*. Castrate. LME. **b** *v.t*. & *i*. Operate (on) to remove a stone. *arch*. M16. **c** *v.t*. Circumcise. *rare*. M17. **†27** *v.i*. & *t*. Speak, talk, say. *slang*. E16–E19. **28** *v.t*. & *i*. Divide (a pack of cards) by lifting the upper half (or thereabouts) and either revealing one of the cards at the join to determine at random a dealer, trump suit, seating position, etc., or placing the upper half face down for the lower half to be replaced on it, to conceal the identity of the last card dealt; select (a card) by cutting a pack. M16. **29** *v.i*. Execute a dance movement by springing from the ground and twiddling the feet one in front of the other alternately. Now *Hist*. E17. **30** *v.i*. Of a horse: strike and bruise the inside of the fetlock with the shoe or hoof of the opposite foot. M17. **31a** *v.t*. Renounce (an acquaintance); refuse to recognize or acknowledge (a person) on meeting or passing. M17. **†b** *v.i*. Break off acquaintance or connection (*with*). L18–E19. **c** *v.t*. Absent oneself from, choose not to attend. L18. **32** *v.t*. Have (a tooth) appear through the gum. L17. **33** *v.i*. *Naut*. Cut the cable in order to get quickly under way. E18. **34** *v.i*. & *t*. **a** *Cricket*. (Of a ball) turn sharply after pitching; (of a bowler) make (a ball) do this. E19. **b** *Cricket*. Hit (a ball) with the bat nearly horizontal, esp. (backward of) square on the offside. M19. **c** Slice (a golf ball). L19. **d** *Croquet*. Drive (a ball) away obliquely by a stroke from another ball. L19.

31c E. BOWEN Next day, Sunday, she cut chapel.

Phrases: *cut a caper*, *capers*: see CAPER *n*.[2] **cut a corner** take the shortest course around a corner, pass round a corner as directly as possible, esp. on the wrong side of the road; *fig*. scamp a piece of work; (*cut a corner off*: see *cut off a corner* below). *cut a dash*: see DASH *n*.[1] *cut a figure*: see FIGURE *n*. *cut a long story short*: see SHORT *a*. **cut and run** (*a*) *Naut*. cut the cable and make sail without waiting to weigh anchor; (*b*) *colloq*. hurry off, run away. **cut a person dead** completely refuse to recognize him or her. *cut a person some slack*: see SLACK *n*.[3] *cut a* (or *the*) *rug*: see RUG *n*.[2] *cut a shine*: see SHINE *n*. *cut a splash*: see SPLASH *n*.[1] 3. *cut a* (*wide*) *swath*: see SWATH *n*.[1] **cut both ways** have good and bad effect; (of an argument) support both sides. **cut corners** *fig*. scamp work, do nothing inessential. *cut each other's throats*: see THROAT *n*. **cut ice** *slang* have influence or importance, achieve something (chiefly in neg. contexts). *cut it fine*: see FINE *a*. *cut loose*: see LOOSE *a*. *cut one's coat according to one's cloth*: see CLOTH *n*. 4. **cut one's eye-teeth** acquire experience, attain worldly wisdom. **cut one's losses** abandon a losing speculation in good time. *cut one's lucky*: see LUCKY *n*.[2] *cut one's own throat*: see THROAT *n*. **cut one's stick** *slang* make off. **cut one's teeth on** *fig*. acquire experience from. *cut open*: see sense 9 above. *cut out work for a person*: see WORK *n*. *cut short*: see SHORT *adv*. *cut the cackle*: see CACKLE *n*. 2. *cut the comb of*: see COMB *n*.[1] 4. *cut the* GORDIAN *knot*. *cut the grass*, *the ground from under a person's feet*: see GRASS *n*., GROUND *n*. *cut the mustard*: see MUSTARD *n*. *cut the painter*: see PAINTER *n*.[2] *cut the throat*, *cut the throat of something*: see THROAT *n*. **cut to pieces** destroy (a military division etc.) by inflicting heavy losses. *have one's work cut out*: see WORK *n*. *rotary cutting*: see ROTARY *a*.

With advs. & preps. in specialized senses: **cut back** (*a*) *v.phr.t*. shorten, prune, (a branch etc.); (*b*) *v.phr.t*. & *i*. reduce (expenditure, production, etc.), curtail; economize; (*c*) *v.phr.i*. & *t*. (*Cinemat*.) repeat part of a previous scene, esp. for dramatic effect; return (so far) in doing this. **cut down** (*a*) *v.phr.t*. bring or throw down by cutting; (*b*) *v.phr.t*. kill by the sword or disease; (*c*) *v.phr.t*. = sense 15 above; (*d*) *v.phr.t*. & *i*. curtail, abridge; reduce consumption or expenses; *cut down to size*: see SIZE *n*.[1] 6b. **cut in** (*a*) *v.phr.i*. come in abruptly (*between*); interpose in conversation; (*b*) *v.phr.i*. join in a card-game by taking the place of a player who cuts out; (*c*) *v.phr.i*. take a dance-partner from another; (*d*) *v.phr.i*. obstruct the path of a vehicle one has just overtaken by returning to one's own side of the road too soon; (*e*) *v.phr.t*. (*slang*) give a share of profits etc. to (a person); (*f*) *v.phr.t*. & *i*. incorporate into a film sequence; switch into an electric circuit; (of a motor etc.) begin operating. **cut off** (*a*) remove or detach (as) by cutting (*cut off one's nose to spite one's face*: see NOSE *n.*); (*b*) bring to an abrupt end or (esp. early) death; (*c*) intercept (a supply, communication); stop the availability of (electricity, gas, water, or telephone communication); break the telephone connection of (a caller) during a call; (*d*) conceal from view; exclude *from* access, influence, etc.; (*e*) *cut off a corner, cut a corner off*, take a short cut that saves going round it; (*f*) *cut off with a shilling*, disinherit (bequeathing a trivial sum to demonstrate that the disinheritance was intentional). **cut out** (*a*) *v.phr.t.* take out by cutting; omit (part of a text etc.); *colloq.* stop (an action) (usu. *imper.* in *cut it out*); (*b*) *v.phr.t.* (*Naut.*) surprise and carry off (a ship) by getting between it and the shore; (*c*) *v.phr.t.* (chiefly *US*) separate (an animal) from the herd; (*d*) *v.phr.t.* = sense 15 above; (*e*) *v.phr.t.* fashion or shape (esp. a garment) by cutting; *fig.* make suitable *for* a particular purpose (usu. in *pass.*); *have one's work cut out*: see WORK *n.*; (*f*) *v.phr.i.* & †*t.* leave, or exclude from, a card-game after an unfavourable card has been cut; (*g*) *v.phr.t.* & *i.* disconnect from an electric circuit; (of a motor etc.) cease operating; (*h*) *v.phr.i.* (*Austral.* & *NZ*) finish shearing or some other activity. **cut up** (*a*) *v.phr.t.* cut in pieces; divide by cutting; *fig.* destroy utterly, mar irretrievably; criticize severely; (*b*) *v.phr.i.* (*slang*, of a deceased person) turn out (well etc.), as to the amount of fortune left; (*c*) *v.phr.t.* distress (greatly); (usu. in *pass.*); (*d*) *v.phr.t.* root up by cutting; (*e*) *v.phr.i.* & *t.* (*N. Amer. colloq.*) show off; behave (in a specified way), esp. badly; *cut up capers, shines*, etc., behave in a mischievous or frolicsome way; (*f*) *cut up rough* (colloq.), behave in a quarrelsome, aggressive, or unruly way.

Comb.: **cut-and-come-again** *n.* & *a.* (allowing) the act or faculty of helping oneself as often as one likes, abundance; **cut-and-cover** (*a*) *US* a mode of ploughing whereby the furrow-slice is turned over on an unploughed strip; (*b*) a method of building a tunnel by making a cutting which is then lined and covered in; **cut-and-fill** the process or result of removing material from a place and depositing it nearby; **cutgrass** any grass of the genus *Leersia* of Europe and N. America, with tiny hooks on the blades able to cut the skin; **cut moth** = *cutworm* (b) below; **cutworm** (*a*) a caterpillar that eats young shoots near ground level, *esp.* that of the turnip moth; (*b*) any of various noctuid moths with such caterpillars.

cutaneous /kjuːˈteɪnɪəs/ *a.* L16. [f. mod.L *cutaneus* (f. L *cutis* skin): see -ANEOUS.] Of, pertaining to, or affecting the skin.

cut-away /ˈkʌtəweɪ/ *a.* & *n.* M19. [f. CUT *ppl a.* + AWAY *adv.*] A *adj.* 1 Of a coat: having the skirt cut back from the waist. M19. 2 Of a diagram etc.: with some parts of the object omitted, to reveal the interior. M20. 3 *Cinemat.* Designating a shot filmed separately from the shot to which it is subsequently joined in editing. M20. B *n.* 1 A cut-away coat. M19. 2 *Cinemat.* A cut-away shot. M20.

cut-back /ˈkʌtbak/ *n.* L19. [f. *cut back* (inf. & pa. pple): see CUT *v.*] 1 A plant which has been pruned hard. L19. 2 *Cinemat.* A scene which is a return to a previous action. E20. 3 A reduction in expenditure, production, etc. M20.

cutch /kʌtʃ/ *n.* M18. [Malay *kachu.*] = CATECHU.

cutcha *a.* & *n.* var. of KUTCHA.

cutcherry /kʌˈtʃɛri/ *n.* Also **cutchery** /ˈkʌtʃəri/. E17. [Hind. *kacahrī, kacerī.*] In the Indian subcontinent: an office; a court-house.

†**cute** *n.*[1] var. of COOT *n.*[2]

†**cute** *n.*[2] var. of CUIT *n.*

cute /kjuːt/ *a.*[1] *colloq.* E18. [Aphet. f. ACUTE.] 1 Clever, keen-witted, shrewd; ingenious. E18. 2 Attractive, pretty; quaint, fascinating. E19.

2 P. MORTIMER She's ever so cute—blue eyes.

cutely *adv.* M18. **cuteness** *n.* M18.

†**cute** *a.*[2] var. of CUIT *a.*

cutesy /ˈkjuːtsi/ *a.* M20. [f. CUTE *a.*[1] + -SY.] Dainty or quaint to an affected degree.

cutey *n.* var. of CUTIE.

Cuthbert /ˈkʌθbət/ *n.* L17. [Male forename: in senses 1 & 2 f. St *Cuthbert* (*c*635–87), bishop of Lindisfarne.] 1 (*St*) *Cuthbert's beads*, detached and perforated joints of fossil crinoids found along the Northumbrian coast. L17. 2 *Cuthbert duck, St Cuthbert's duck*, the eider duck, which breeds in the Farne Islands. L17. 3 A man who deliberately avoids military service; *esp.* in the war of 1914–18, one who did so by securing a post in a Government office or the Civil Service; a conscientious objector. *slang. derog.* E20.

cuticle /ˈkjuːtɪk(ə)l/ *n.* L15. [L *cuticula* dim. of *cutis* skin: see -CULE.] 1 Orig., a membrane of the body. Now *spec.* the epidermis. L15. b The area of dead skin at the base of a fingernail or toenail. E20. 2 Any of various outer layers in a plant or animal, *esp.* a non-cellular protective film covering the epidermis in a plant or insect. M17. †3 A thin film formed on the surface of a liquid; a thin coating left by the evaporation of brine etc. M17–E18.

cuticula /kjuːˈtɪkjʊlə/ *n.* E17. [f. as prec.] The cuticle of an insect or (formerly) the skin.

cuticular /kjuːˈtɪkjʊlə/ *a.* L16. [f. as prec. + -AR[1].] Of or pertaining to a cuticle, resembling a cuticle.

cuticulariˈzation *n.* the process or result of cuticularizing L19. **cuticularize** *v.t.* change into a cuticle; cover with cutin: L19.

cutie /ˈkjuːti/ *n. slang.* Also **cutey**. M18. [f. CUTE *a.*[1] + -IE.] A cute person; *esp.* an attractive young woman.

cutikin /ˈkuːtɪkɪn/ *n. Sc.* E19. [f. COOT *n.*[2] + -KIN.] A gaiter, a spat.

cutin /ˈkjuːtɪn/ *n.* M19. [f. CUTIS + -IN[1].] *Bot.* A hydrophobic substance in the cuticle of plants, consisting of highly polymerized esters of fatty acids.

cutiniˈzation *n.* the process or result of cutinizing L19. **cutinize** *v.t.* change into cutin, impregnate with cutin L19.

cut-in /ˈkʌtɪn/ *n.* & *a.* L19. [f. *cut in* (inf. & pa. pple): see CUT *v.*] A *n.* 1 An act of cutting in. L19. 2 Something that is cut in, *esp.* an interposed scene in a film. E20. 3 A device for completing an electric circuit, esp. automatically. E20.

B *adj.* Designating something that is cut in. L19.

cutis /ˈkjuːtɪs/ *n.* E17. [L = skin.] *Med.* The skin; the dermis. Now chiefly w. following L adjs., forming the names of skin conditions.

cutis laxa, cutis marmorata.

cutlass /ˈkʌtləs/ *n.* L16. [Fr. *coutelas* f. Proto-Romance, f. L *cultellus* (see next) + augm. suff. *-aceum*: cf. CURTAL-AXE.] A short sword with a flat slightly curved blade, *esp.* that with which sailors were formerly armed; a machete.

Comb.: **cutlass-fish** any of various long slender marine fishes of the family Trichiuridae, with long jaws and sharp teeth; esp. *Trichiurus lepturus*, a silvery-coloured fish of the Atlantic, caught for food in the tropics.

cutler /ˈkʌtlə/ *n.* ME. [(O)Fr. *coutelier*, f. OFr. *coutel* (mod. *couteau*) knife f. L *cultellus* dim. of *culter* COULTER: see -ER[2].] A person who makes, deals in, or repairs knives, forks, and similar utensils.

cutlery /ˈkʌtləri/ *n.* ME. [(O)Fr. *coutellerie*, f. as prec.: see -ERY.] The craft or trade of a cutler; *collect.* knives and other wares made or sold by cutlers, *esp.* knives, forks, and spoons for use at table.

cutlet /ˈkʌtlɪt/ *n.* E18. [Fr. *côtelette*, formerly *costelette* dim. of *coste* (now *côte*) rib f. L *costa*: see -EL[2], -ETTE. Assim. to CUT *n.*[2], -LET.] A neck-chop of mutton or lamb; a small piece of veal etc. for frying; a similarly shaped cake of minced meat etc.

Maintenon cutlet: see MAINTENON 1. **nut cutlet** a cutlet-shaped savoury cake of chopped nuts and other ingredients.

cutling /ˈkʌtlɪŋ/ *n.*[1] Long *obs.* exc. *dial.* M17. [f. CUTLER, CUTLERY + -ING[1]. Cf. also CUTTLE *n.*[2]] The business or occupation of a cutler; the making of cutlery.

cutling /ˈkʌtlɪŋ/ *n.*[2] Long *obs.* exc. *dial.* L17. [Origin unkn.] Husked oat grains; coarse oatmeal.

cut-off /ˈkʌtɒf/ *n.* & *a.* M17. [f. *cut off* (pa. pple & inf.): see CUT *v.*] A *n.* 1 A portion or quantity cut off. M17. b An oxbow lake. L19. 2 An artificial channel cut to shorten the course of a river or to join two bodies of water. L18. 3 A shorter section of a river where it has cut across the neck of a bend; *US* a bayou. E19. 4 A land route which serves as a short cut. E19. 5 (A device for producing) an interruption or cessation of flow; an instance of being cut off or cut short. M19. b *Electr.* A sudden drop in amplification or responsiveness at a certain frequency. M20. 6 In *pl.* Shorts, *esp.* ones made by cutting short a pair of jeans. Chiefly *N. Amer.* L20.

1 *Scientific American* Cutoffs discarded during the manufacture of new cotton goods. 5 *fig.*: G. B. SHAW His death . . seems to me a complete cut-off.

B *adj.* 1 That is cut off; *spec.* isolated; remote. E19. 2 That cuts off; that stops a flow. M19. 3 That constitutes a limit. E20.

1 J. F. FIXX Cut-off jeans. 3 R. QUIRK We take this level as our cut-off point in choosing samples of English for inclusion.

cut-ˈoffness *n.* E20.

cut-out /ˈkʌtaʊt/ *a.* & *n.* L18. [f. *cut out* (pa. pple & inf.): see CUT *v.*] A *adj.* Made by cutting out; of or pertaining to a piece cut out. L18.

B *n.* 1 A space or outline where something has been cut out. M19. 2 A device for automatically breaking an electric circuit under certain circumstances. L19. 3 An act of separating animals from a herd. *US.* L19. 4 Something that is cut out or intended for cutting out; *spec.* a preprinted figure that can be cut out of paper or card; *Theatr.* a flat piece of board painted to simulate scenery etc. E20. 5 The end of shearing; the end of shearing a particular group. *Austral.* & *NZ.* E20. 6 A middleman, an intermediary, esp. in espionage. *slang.* M20.

1 *Practical Wireless* Cut-outs are provided for the only two connections which must pass beneath them. 2 *Which?* All the kettles we tested have a safety cut-out. 4 *fig.*: W. GOLDING It reveals Philip to me as a person in three D, as more than a cut-out.

Comb.: **cut-out box** *US* a fuse-box.

cut-over /ˈkʌtəʊvə/ *n.* & *a.* L19. [f. *cut over* (inf. & pa. pple): see CUT *v.*] A *n. Fencing.* An offensive disengage executed over the opponent's blade. L19. B *adj.* Of land etc.: having had the saleable timber felled and removed. L19.

cutpurse /ˈkʌtpəːs/ *n. arch.* LME. [f. CUT *v.* + PURSE *n.*] A person who stole by cutting purses from the girdles from which they were suspended; a pickpocket, a thief.

†**cuts** *n.* L17–E18. [Alt. Cf. COTS.] God's: used in oaths and exclamations.

cuttable /ˈkʌtəb(ə)l/ *a.* LME. [f. CUT *v.* + -ABLE.] Able to be cut.

cuttanee /ˈkʌtəniː/ *n.* E17. [Urdu *katānī* f. Arab. *kattān* flax, linen.] *Hist.* Cloth of silk, cotton, or both, usu. striped and sometimes decorated, imported from India or Malaya and used esp. for quilts and upholstery.

cutted /ˈkʌtɪd/ *ppl a.* Long *obs.* exc. *dial.* LME. [f. CUT *v.* + -ED[1].] 1 = CUT *ppl a.* 1. LME. †2 Wearing a short skirt or cloak. LME–E17. 3 Curt, testy. Cf. CUTTY *a.* 2. M16.

cuttee /kʌˈtiː/ *n.* E19. [f. CUT *v.* + -EE[1].] A person who is cut socially.

cutter /ˈkʌtə/ *n.* ME. [f. CUT *v.* + -ER[1]. Branch III perh. a different wd.] I A person who cuts. 1 *gen.* A person who cuts (*lit.* & *fig.*); (with specifying wd) a person who shapes etc. things by cutting. Also w. advs., as *cutter-in, -out.* ME. 2 *spec.* a A person who cuts hair. LME. b A person who castrates animals. Now *dial.* M16. c Orig., a tailor. Now, a person in a tailoring establishment who takes measurements and cuts the cloth. L16. d A person who cuts or edits film. E20. 3 A person overready to use a weapon; a bully; a cutthroat, a highway-robber. *arch.* M16.

1 J. PYCROFT A good cutter at the wicket. C. E. MULFORD The cutters-out rode after some calf.

II A thing. 4 An implement or tool that cuts; the cutting part of a machine. M17. 5 *Mining.* A crack or fissure intersecting the lines of stratification; the cleavage of slate (usu. in *pl.*). *dial.* M18. 6 A fine kind of brick which can be sawn and rubbed smooth, formerly used esp. for arches. M19. 7 A pig heavier than a porker but lighter than a baconer. E20. 8 An animal yielding an inferior grade of meat. E20. 9 *Cricket.* A ball that turns sharply after pitching. M20.

4 A. ALVAREZ The younger man mangled his cigar's sleek end with the cutter. attrib.: *cutter-bar, -head*, etc.

III 10 A ship's boat fitted for rowing and sailing, and used for carrying light stores, passengers, etc. M18. 11 Orig., a small fore-and-aft rigged boat with one mast, more than one head-sail, and a running bowsprit, formerly used esp. as a fast auxiliary. Now also, a sailing-yacht with one mainsail and two foresails; a light pilot or patrol vessel. M18. 12 A light horse-drawn sleigh. *N. Amer.* E19.

Phrases: *laver cutter*: see LAVER *n.*[3] *off cutter*: see OFF *prep.* & *a.* *rotary cutter*: see ROTARY *a.* *silage cutter*: see SILAGE *n.* *top cutter*: see TOP *a.*

cutthroat /ˈkʌtθrəʊt/ *n.* & *a.* Also **cut-throat**. M16. [f. CUT *v.* + THROAT *n.*] A *n.* 1 An assassin, a murderer; a violent criminal. M16. †2 A kind of firearm. *Sc.* M16–M17. †3 A lantern, *esp.* one whose light could be completely obscured. M17–E19. 4 Any of several games of chance; *esp.* (more fully *cutthroat bridge, poker*, etc.) a card-game for three or more players in which players score individually and not in partnership. E19. 5 The mustang grape. Also *cutthroat grape.* L19. 6 In full *cutthroat finch, weaver.* A small African bird, *Amadina fasciata*, of the waxbill family, the male of which has a red mark round the throat. L19. 7 In full *cutthroat trout.* A N. American trout, *Salmo clarki*, that has red markings under its jaw and is a game and food fish in the US. L19. 8 In full *cutthroat razor.* A razor with a long blade fixed in a handle, as opp. to a safety razor. M20. B *attrib.* or as *adj.* That is or has the character of an assassin; (of a place) such as might be frequented by violent criminals; (of competition) merciless, intense. M16.

cutting /ˈkʌtɪŋ/ *n.* ME. [f. CUT *v.* + -ING[1].] 1 The action of CUT *v.* Also w. advs., as *cutting out, up*, etc. ME. 2 A piece cut off; *esp.* a shred etc. made in preparing or trimming an object for use. Also, a quantity of timber etc. suitable for cutting. ME. b A small shoot, branch, etc., cut off a plant for use in propagation. L17. c A paragraph or short article cut from a newspaper etc. Also *newspaper cutting, press cutting.* M19. †3 An intersection of two lines; a portion of a line between two intersections. L16–E18. 4 A figure, representation, etc., produced by cutting; a carving etc. L18. 5 A large gully or trench made through higher ground so that a road etc. can pass through with little change of slope. M19. 6 In *pl.* Low-grade fragments of ore, esp. when mixed with better quality; small fragments produced by a coal-cutting machine or brought up in rock drilling. L19.

1 *rotary cutting*: see ROTARY *a.*

Comb. (perh. partly f. next): **cutting compound** an abrasive substance used to smooth and blend paintwork on a motor vehicle; **cutting edge** *n.* & *a.* (*a*) *n.* an edge that cuts; *fig.* the factor with most implications, the most significant factor; the forefront of a movement etc.; (*b*) *adj.* pioneering, innovative; **cutting horse** *US*: trained in separating cattle from a herd; **cutting-out scissors** large scissors for cutting patterns from fabric; **cutting room** a room where the cutting of material, meat, etc., is carried out, *esp.* (*Cinemat.*) where film is cut and edited.

cutting /ˈkʌtɪŋ/ *a.* LME. [f. CUT *v.* + -ING[2].] 1 That cuts. LME. 2 *fig.* Acutely wounding to the mind, sensibilities, etc.; sharp, hurtful. L16. †3 Violent, swaggering; that is a cutthroat or bully. L16–L17.

1 H. MARTINEAU You don't know . . what a cutting wind it is. **cutting grass** (*a*) any of several grasses or sedges of Australia and New Zealand with sharp-edged leaves or stems, esp. *Gahnia psittacorum*; (*b*) = *cane-rat* s.v. CANE *n.*[1] 2 C. BRONTË He can say the driest, most cutting things in the quietest of tones.

cuttingly *adv.* L16.

cuttle /ˈkʌt(ə)l/ *n.*[1] [OE *cudele*, corresp. to OLFrank. *cudele*, Norw. dial. *kaule*, f. base of COD *n.*[1], w. allus. to its ink-bag.] = CUTTLEFISH.

Comb.: **cuttle-bone** the thick light shell inside a cuttlefish, now crushed for use as a dietary supplement for cage-birds.

†**cuttle** *n.*[2] M16–L17. [App. f. OFr. *coutel* (mod. *couteau*): see CUTLER.] A knife; a cutter.

cuttle /ˈkʌt(ə)l/ *v.i. rare. obs.* exc. *dial.* LME. [Origin unkn.] Whisper; talk privately and confidentially.

cuttlefish /ˈkʌt(ə)lfɪʃ/ *n.* Pl. **-es** /-ɪz/, (usu.) same. L16. [f. CUTTLE *n.*[1] + FISH *n.*[1]] Any of various marine cephalopods of the genus *Sepia* or order Sepioidea, having an elongated body with an undulating lateral fin, ten arms, a cuttle-bone, and the habit of ejecting a black fluid when alarmed; *loosely* a squid, an octopus.

cuttoe /ˈkʌtəʊ/ *n.* Chiefly *US.* Also **-o**, pl. **-o(e)s**. M17. [Fr. COUTEAU.] = COUTEAU.

cutty /ˈkʌti/ *a.* & *n.* M17. [f. *cut* pa. pple of CUT *v.* + -Y[6].] A *adj.* 1 Cut short; exceptionally short. *Sc.* & *north.* M17. 2 Testy, short-tempered. Cf. CUTTED 3. *Sc.* & *north.* E19. 3 Capable of cutting, sharp. Chiefly *NZ* in *cutty grass* below. E20.

1 R. BURNS Her cutty sark, o' Paisley harn . . In longitude tho' sorely scanty. **cutty stool** *Sc.* a low stool; *esp.* (*Hist.*) a particular seat in a church on which offenders had to sit, to be publicly rebuked during divine service. 3 **cutty grass** *NZ* = *cutting grass* (a) s.v. CUTTING *a.*

B *n.* 1 A short pipe; *Sc.* a short spoon. M18. 2 A wren. *Sc.* & *dial.* L18. 3 A short stumpy young woman; (also *joc.*) a short-tempered or naughty woman or girl. *Sc.* E19.

cut-up /ˈkʌtʌp/ *n.* & *a.* L18. [f. *cut up* (inf. & pa. pple): see CUT *v.*] A *n.* 1 A distressing event, a deep loss. L18. 2a A practical joke; an event at which there is much fooling around. *rare.* Chiefly *N. Amer.* M19. b A person who plays the fool; a boisterous person. Chiefly *N. Amer.* L19. 3 An article of hosiery made from one of a series of pieces cut from a long length rather than being knitted fully-fashioned. M19. B *adj.* That has been or is cut up. L19.

cutwater /ˈkʌtwɔːtə/ *n.* M17. [f. CUT *v.* + WATER *n.*] 1a The forward curve of a ship's stem, the part that divides the water. M17. b A wedge-shaped end of the pier of a bridge, serving to divide the current, break up ice, etc. L18. 2 The black skimmer, *Rhynchops nigra*, of N. America. *US.* M18.

cutwithe /ˈkʌtwɪð/ *n. obs.* exc. *dial.* Also **-withy** /-wɪði/. M16. [f. CUT *ppl a.* + WITHE *n.*] A bar etc. at the front of a plough or harrow to which the gear of a draught animal may be attached.

cutwork /ˈkʌtwəːk/ *n.* LME. [f. CUT *ppl a.* + WORK *n.*] 1 Garments or embroidery with the edges cut into elaborate shapes, as a medieval fashion; embroidery or lace with parts cut out and the edges oversewn or filled with needlework designs; appliqué work in which the pattern is cut out and sewn on. LME. 2 *gen.* Work produced by cutting or carving. M17. †3 Flower-beds cut in the turf so as to form elaborate patterns. L17.

cuvée /kjuːˈveɪ, *foreign* kyve (*pl. same*)/ *n.* M19. [Fr. = vatful, f. *cuve* f. L *cupa* cask, vat.] The contents of a vat of wine; a particular blend or batch of wine.

cuvette /kjuːˈvɛt/ *n.* L17. [Fr., dim. of *cuve*: see prec., -ETTE.] 1 *Fortif.* = CUNETTE. L17. 2 A shallow vessel for holding liquid; a transparent vessel with flat sides for holding a spectrophotometric sample etc. E18. 3 A large clay basin or crucible used in making plate glass. M19. 4 *Geol.* A basin in which sedimentation is occurring or has occurred. E20.

Cuvierian /kjuːˈvɪərɪən/ *a.* M19. [f. *Cuvier* (see below) + -IAN.] Of, pertaining to, or named after the French naturalist Georges Cuvier (1769–1832); characteristic of his methods or system of classification.

cwm /kʊm/ *n.* M19. [Welsh = COOMB *n.*[2]] A bowl-shaped valley or hollow in (Welsh) mountains; *Physical Geogr.* = CIRQUE *n.* 3.

-cy /sɪ/ *suff.* [Repr. L *-cia, -tia*, Gk *-k(e)ia, -t(e)ia*: see -Y[3].] Forming ns. of state or quality (orig. and esp. in forms such as -ACY, -ANCY, -CRACY, -ENCY, -MANCY), as *bankruptcy, captaincy, chaplaincy, idiocy, normalcy*, etc.

cyan /ˈsʌɪən/ *n.* & *a.* L19. [Gk *kuan(e)os* dark blue.] (Of) a greenish-blue colour. Also more fully *cyan-blue.*

cyan- *comb. form* see CYANO-.

cyanamide /sʌɪˈanəmʌɪd/ *n.* M19. [f. prec. + AMIDE.] *Chem.* Cyanogen amide, a weakly acidic crystalline solid, CN_2H_2, or a salt of this, esp. (in full *calcium cyanamide*) that of calcium, $CaCN_2$, used as a fertilizer.

Comb.: **cyanamide process**: for making calcium cyanamide by the action of nitrogen on calcium carbide at high temperature.

cyanate /ˈsʌɪəneɪt/ *n.* M19. [f. CYANIC + -ATE[1].] *Chem.* A salt or ester of isocyanic acid, containing the ion NCO^- or one of the groups ·N=CO and ·OC≡N (= ISOCYANATE), or of the hypothetical cyanic acid HONC.

cyanelle /sʌɪəˈnɛl/ *n.* M20. [f. CYAN-: see -EL[2].] *Bot.* A blue-green alga in symbiosis within a protozoan.

cyaneous /sʌɪˈeɪnɪəs/ *a. rare.* L17. [f. L *cyaneus* f. Gk *kuaneos*: see CYAN, -OUS.] Deep blue, azure.

cyanic /sʌɪˈanɪk/ *a.* E19. [f. CYAN- + -IC.] 1 *Chem.* Of cyanogen; *cyanic acid*, a colourless, volatile, strongly acidic liquid, unstable above 0°C, HN:C:O (= ISOCYANIC *acid*; *esp.* the hypothetical isomer of this, HO·CN. E19. 2 Blue, azure. *rare.* M19.

cyanicide /sʌɪˈanɪsʌɪd/ *n.* L19. [f. next + -CIDE.] Any substance present in a metal ore which reacts detrimentally with the cyanide used in a metal extraction process.

cyanide /ˈsʌɪənʌɪd/ *n.* & *v.* E19. [f. CYAN- + -IDE.] A *n. Chem.* A salt or ester of hydrocyanic acid, containing the group ·CN or the ion CN^- (in *Org. Chem.* = NITRILE); such a salt as the type of a powerful poison; the sodium, calcium, or other salt used in the extraction of gold, silver, or other metals from their ores. E19. B *v.t.* 1 Treat (ores of gold, silver, etc.) with cyanide solution in order to form a soluble complex with the metal, as part of an extraction process. L19. 2 Case-harden (steel etc.) by immersion in a molten cyanide. E20.

cyaniˈdation *n.* (metal extraction involving) the treatment of ores with cyanides L19.

cyanin /ˈsʌɪənɪn/ *n.* M19. [f. CYAN- + -IN[1].] *Chem.* A violet anthocyanin present as a pigment in many flowers, e.g. cornflower, dahlia, violet.

cyanidin /sʌɪˈanɪdɪn/ *n.* the aglycone of cyanin (usu. isolated as the chloride $C_{15}H_{11}O_6Cl$) E20.

cyanine /ˈsʌɪəniːn/ *n.* L19. [f. as prec. + -INE[5].] 1 In full *cyanine dye.* Any of a large class of synthetic dyestuffs having a molecular structure typically containing two heteroaromatic ring systems joined by one or more carbon atoms. L19. 2 A blue pigment that is a mixture of cobalt blue and Prussian blue. L19.

Comb.: **cyanine blue** (*a*) a blue cyanine dye; (*b*) = sense 2 above; *cyanine dye*: see sense 1 above.

cyanite *n.* var. of KYANITE.

cyano- /ˈsʌɪənəʊ/ *comb. form.* Bef. a vowel or *h* **cyan-**. [Gk *kuan(e)os* dark blue: see -O-.] Dark blue; *Chem.* cyanogen, cyanide.

cyanoˈacrylate *n.* a substance of a class forming exceptionally strong adhesives M20. **cyanobacˈterium** *n.*, pl. **-ria**, a blue-green alga L20. **cyanoˈchroite** *n.* [Gk *khroia* colour] *Min.* a monoclinic hydrated sulphate of copper and potassium occurring as blue tabular crystals or crystalline crusts M19. **cyanocoˈbalamin** *n.* (*Biochem.*) a form of vitamin B_{12} containing a cyanide group bonded to the central cobalt atom of the cobalamin molecule M20. **cyanolabe** *n.* [Gk *lab-* base of *lambanein* take] *Physiol.* a blue-sensitive pigment in the cones of the retina M20. **cyanometer** /sʌɪəˈnɒmɪtə/ *n.* an instrument for measuring the blueness of the sky E19. **cyanometry** /sʌɪəˈnɒmɪtri/ *n.* the measurement of the blueness of the sky L19. **cyanophilous** /sʌɪəˈnɒfɪləs/ *a.* (*Biol.*) readily stained by blue and green dyes L19. **cyanoˈphycin** *n.* (*Biochem.*) a polypeptide that is the principal constituent of the food storage granules of most cyanobacteria L19. **cyanophyte** *n.* (*Bot.*) a blue-green alga M20. **cyanophytic** /-ˈfɪtɪk/ *a.* (*Bot.*) of or pertaining to a cyanophyte or the cyanophytes M20. **cyanotrichite** /-ˈtrɪkʌɪt/ *n.* [Gk *trikh-, thrix* hair] *Min.* an orthorhombic hydrated basic sulphate of copper and aluminium, occurring as blue fibrous crystals M19. **cyaˈnurate** *n.* (*Chem.*) a salt or ester of cyanuric acid

M19. †**cyanuret** *n.* = CYANIDE *n.* E–M19. **cya'nuric** *a.* (*Chem.*) designating polymers of cyanogen; *cyanuric acid*, a colourless crystalline tribasic heterocyclic acid, $C_3H_3O_3N_3$, obtained by dry distillation of urea: M19.

cyanogen /sʌɪ'anədʒ(ə)n/ *n.* E19. [Fr. *cyanogène*, f. as CYANO- + -GEN, as being related chemically to Prussian blue.] *Chem.* A colourless flammable highly toxic gas, $(CN)_2$, chemically one of the pseudohalogens.

cyanogenic /sʌɪənə'dʒɛnɪk/ *a.* M20. [f. CYANO- + -GENIC.] *Biochem.* Capable of producing (hydrogen) cyanide; containing a cyanogen group in the molecule.
cyanogenesis *n.* cyanogenic property M20. **cyanoge'netic** *a.* = CYANOGENIC E20.

cyanosis /sʌɪə'nəʊsɪs/ *n.* Pl. **-noses** /-'nəʊsiːz/. M19. [mod.L f. Gk *kuanōsis* blueness, f. as CYAN- + -OSIS.] *Med.* A blue discoloration of the skin due to deficient oxygenation of the blood.
'**cyanosed** *a.* affected with cyanosis M19. **cyanotic** /-'nɒtɪk/ *a.* pertaining to, of the nature of, or affected with cyanosis M19.

cyathi *n.* pl. of CYATHUS.

cyathiform /sʌɪ'aθɪfɔːm/ *a.* L18. [f. next + -I- + -FORM.] Chiefly *Bot.* Shaped like a cup widened at the rim.

cyathium /sʌɪ'aθɪəm/ *n.* Pl. **-ia** /-ɪə/. L19. [mod.L, f. Gk *kuathion* dim. of *kuathos* CYATHUS.] *Bot.* The characteristic inflorescence of the spurges (genus *Euphorbia*), consisting of a cup-shaped involucre of fused bracts enclosing several greatly reduced male flowers and a single female flower; the involucre forming part of such an inflorescence.

cyathus /'sʌɪəθəs/ *n.* Pl. **-thi** /-θʌɪ/. LME. [L f. Gk *kuathos.*] *Class. Antiq.* A cup or ladle used for drawing wine from a bowl. Also, a wineglass as a measure of volume (usu. about 50 ml.).

cybernation /sʌɪbə'neɪʃ(ə)n/ *n.* M20. [f. next + -ATION.] Control of processes, communities, etc., by machines.
'**cybernate** *v.t.* place under machine control (usu. in *pass.*) M20.

cybernetics /sʌɪbə'nɛtɪks/ *n.* M20. [f. Gk *kubernētēs* steersman, f. *kubernan* to steer: see -ICS.] The science of systems of control and communications in living organisms and machines.
cybernetic *a.* of or pertaining to cybernetics M20. **cybernetician** /-nɪ'tɪʃ(ə)n/, **cyberneticist** /-sɪst/ *ns.* an expert in cybernetics M20.

cyberpunk /'sʌɪbəpʌŋk/ *n.* L20. [Blend of prec. and PUNK *n.*[2]] Science fiction featuring punk styles and attitudes.

cyberspace /'sʌɪbəspeɪs/ *n.* L20. [f. prec. + SPACE *n.*] The notional environment within which electronic communication occurs, esp. when represented as the inside of a computer system; space perceived as such by an observer but generated by a computer system and having no real existence; the space of virtual reality.

cyborg /'sʌɪbɔːg/ *n.* M20. [Blend of CYBERNETIC *a.* and ORGANISM.] A person whose physical tolerances or capabilities are extended beyond normal human limitations by a machine etc.; an integrated man-machine system.

cybotaxis /sʌɪbə'taksɪs/ *n.* E20. [f. Gk *kubos* CUBE *n.*[1] + -TAXIS.] *Physics.* The arrangement of molecules in a liquid in transitory aggregates each having approximately crystalline structure.
cybotactic *a.* of, pertaining to, or exhibiting cybotaxis E20.

cycad /'sʌɪkad/ *n.* M19. [f. mod.L *Cycas* genus name, f. supposed Gk *kukas*, scribal error for *koikas* accus. pl. of *koix* Egyptian doum-palm: see -AD[1].] An evergreen palmlike gymnospermous plant of the order Cycadales (including many fossil forms), and esp. of the genus *Cycas*, some members of which yield sago.
cy'cadean *a.* of, pertaining to, or resembling (that of) a cycad M19. **cy'cadeoid** *a.* & *n.* (of, pertaining to, or designating) a cycadophyte of the extinct Mesozoic order Bennettitales (of Cycadeoidales) M19. **cyca'daceous** *a.* of or pertaining to a cycad or the cycads, or the family Cycadaceae M19. **cycadophyte** *n.* a plant of the group Cycadophyta, which includes cycads and related fossil forms M20.

Cycladic /sɪ'kladɪk, sʌɪ-/ *a.* E20. [f. L *Cyclades* (see below) f. Gk *Kuklades* (*nēsoi* islands), f. *kuklos* circle: see -IC.] Of or pertaining to the Cyclades, a group of Greek islands in the Aegean Sea; *spec.* designating or pertaining to the prehistoric civilization of these islands.

cyclamate /'sɪkləmeɪt, 'sʌɪk-/ *n.* M20. [Contr. of *cyclohexylsulphamate.*] *Chem.* Any salt of cyclohexylsulphamic acid, $C_6H_{11}{\cdot}NHSO_3H$; *esp.* the sodium or calcium salt used as an artificial sweetening agent.

cyclamen /'sɪkləmən/ *n.* M16. [med.L f. L *cyclaminos, -on* f. Gk *kuklaminos*, perh. f. *kuklos* circle, w. ref. to the bulbous roots of the plant.] **1** Any of various plants of the Eurasian genus *Cyclamen*, of the primrose family, usu. with reflexed twisted petals and including several kinds cultivated as pot plants. M16. **2** A pink colour characteristic of some cyclamen flowers. E20.

cyclas /'sɪkləs/ *n.* M19. [L f. Gk *kuklas* a woman's garment with a border all round it.] *Hist.* A close-fitting tunic; *spec.* a surcoat made shorter in front than behind and worn over armour.

cycle /'sʌɪk(ə)l/ *n.* LME. [Fr., or late L *cyclus* f. Gk *kuklos* circle: in sense 5 an abbrev.] **1** A recurrent period of definite duration; a period in which a certain series of events or phenomena is completed, usu. as part of a repeating succession of similar periods; *loosely* an age. LME. **2** A circle or orbit in the heavens. *arch.* M17. **3** A recurrent round or course of events or phenomena; a series of successive events through which something runs to completion. M17. **b** *spec.* (chiefly *Sci.*). A recurring series of successive operations, reactions, or states, e.g. in the working of an internal-combustion engine, in the alternation of an electric current or a wave, or in the metabolism of an organism. Also (*ellipt.*), a cycle per second (= HERTZ 2). M19. **c** *Ling.* More fully *transformational cycle* (The application of) a set of transformational rules operating successively at each level of structure. M20. **4** A complete set or series; *spec.* a series of poems, songs (more fully *song cycle*), etc., composed round a central event or idea. M17. **5** A bicycle, tricycle, or similar machine. L19.
1 TENNYSON Better fifty years of Europe than a cycle of Cathay. CONAN DOYLE If the cycle of nine days holds good then we shall have the Professor at his worst to-night. *lunar* (or *Metonic*) *cycle, Sothic cycle, Victorian cycle*, etc. 3 SHELLEY Or hadst thou waited the full cycle, when Thy spirit should have filled its crescent sphere. E. WILSON He seems to have imagined history as a series of repetitive cycles. L. D. STAMP As the cycle of erosion progresses . . the surface is reduced to a monotonous level . . plain. D. LODGE An almost unbroken cycle of grants, fellowships, leaves of absence and alcoholic cures. *vicious cycle*: see VICIOUS *a.* **b** *carbon cycle, Carnot's cycle, Krebs cycle, life cycle, menstrual cycle, open cycle, Otto cycle, Rankine cycle, Stirling cycle, thermal cycle, tricarboxylic acid cycle*, etc. 4 R. MACAULAY The Arthurian cycle, the cycle of Charlemagne, . . the cycle of Christ—these are the European folk tales which filled the Middle Ages. A. C. BOULT Our last pre-war memory is Toscanini's Beethoven Cycle. 5 *motor cycle, pedal cycle*, etc.
Comb. (chiefly sense 5): **cycle clip** = BICYCLE *clip*; **cycle track, way**: reserved for cyclists.

cycle /'sʌɪk(ə)l/ *v.i.* M19. [f. the n.] **1** Move in or pass through cycles; complete a cycle. M19. **2** Ride a cycle (*spec.* a bicycle). L19.
2 **cycling lizard** = RACEHORSE *lizard.*
cycler *n.* = CYCLIST 2 L19. **cycling** *vbl n.* the action of the vb; *spec.* the riding of bicycles as a sport or recreation L19.

cycli *n.* pl. of CYCLUS.

cyclian /'sʌɪklɪən/ *a. rare.* L17. [f. Gk *kuklios* circular, cyclic + -AN.] = CYCLIC (esp. sense 3b).

cyclic /'sʌɪklɪk/ *a.* L18. [Fr. *cyclique* or L *cyclicus* or Gk *kuklikos*: see CYCLE *n.*, -IC.] **1** Of, pertaining to, or of the nature of, a cycle; moving or recurring in cycles. L18. **2** Of or belonging to a cycle of legends, poems, etc. E19. **3** *Gk Pros.* Of a dactyl or anapaest: occupying in scansion only three time units instead of four. M19. **4** *Math.* Of or pertaining to a circle or other closed curve; (of a polygon) having all its vertices lying on a circle. M19. **b** Of a group: having the property that each element of the group can be expressed as a power of one particular element. L19. **5** *Bot.* Of a flower: having its parts arranged in whorls. L19. **6** *Chem.* Having a molecular structure containing one or more closed rings of atoms. L19.
1 U. LE GUIN The whole universe is a cyclic process, an oscillation of expansion and contraction, without any before or after. 2 SHELLEY Episodes of that cyclic poem written by Time upon the memories of men.
¶ Orig. pronunc. (now *rare*) /'sɪk-/.
cyclicity /sʌɪ'klɪsɪti/ *n.* L20.

cyclical /'sʌɪklɪk(ə)l/ *a.* E19. [f. as prec. + -AL[1].] = CYCLIC (esp. sense 1).
cyclically *adv.* L19.

cyclin /'sʌɪklɪn/ *n.* L20. [f. CYCLE *n.* + -IN[1].] *Biochem.* Any of several proteins associated with the cycle of cell division which are thought to initiate certain processes of the division.

cyclise *v.* var. of CYCLIZE.

cyclist /'sʌɪklɪst/ *n.* M19. [f. CYCLE *n.* + -IST.] **1** A person who recognizes cycles in the course of phenomena etc. *rare.* M19. **2** A person who rides a cycle (without specification usu. a bicycle), esp. habitually. L19.
2 *motor cyclist*: see MOTOR *n.* & *a. trick cyclist*: see TRICK *a.*

cyclitis /sɪ'klʌɪtɪs/ *n.* M19. [f. Gk *kuklos* circle + -ITIS.] *Med.* Inflammation of the ciliary body of the eye.

cyclize /'sʌɪklʌɪz/ *v.t.* & *i.* Also **-ise.** M20. [f. CYCLIC + -IZE.] *Chem.* (Cause to) undergo a reaction which results in the formation of a closed ring of atoms.
cycli'zation *n.* E20.

cyclo- /'sʌɪkləʊ/ *comb. form.* [f. Gk *kuklos* circle, or directly f. CYCLE *n.*, CYCLIC: see -O-.] **1** Forming ns. and adjs. w. the sense 'circular, cyclic, of circles or cycles'. **2** *Chem.* Prefixed to names of hydrocarbons to form names of cyclic hydrocarbons with rings of corresponding numbers of carbon atoms (as *cyclobutane, -pentadiene, -pentane*, etc.), or used more generally w. the sense 'involving cyclic compounds'. **3** With the sense 'of bicycles or cycling'.
cyclo-a'ddition *n.* an addition reaction in which a cyclic molecule is formed M20. **cyclo'alkane** (*Chem.*) = CYCLOPARAFFIN M20. **cyclo-cross** *n.* cross-country racing on bicycles M20. **cyclo'dextrin** *n.* (*Chem.*) a compound whose molecule is a ring of six to eight cyclic hexoses linked end to end M20. **cyclodi'alysis** *n.* (*Med.*) an operation for relieving glaucoma by surgically detaching the ciliary body of the eye from the sclera E20. **cyclogiro** *n.*, pl. **-os**, a rotor aircraft obtaining lift from aerofoils rotating about a horizontal axis M20. **cyclograph** *n.* an instrument for tracing circular arcs E19. **cyclo'hexane** *n.* a colourless liquid cycloparaffin, C_6H_{12}, obtained in petroleum or by hydrogenating benzene, and widely used as a solvent L19. **cyclomor'phosis** *n.*, pl. **-phoses** /-'fəʊsiːz/, (*Biol.*) a seasonal change in form undergone by some planktonic organisms E20. **cyclo'paraffin** *n.* any saturated cyclic hydrocarbon E20. **cyclo'plegia** *n.* (*Med.*) paralysis of the ciliary muscle of the eye E20. **cyclo'plegic** *a.* & *n.* (*a*) *adj.* pertaining to or producing cycloplegia; (*b*) *n.* a substance that produces cycloplegia: E20. **cyclo'propane** *n.* (*Chem.*) a flammable gaseous hydrocarbon, C_3H_6, used chiefly as an anaesthetic M20. **cyclo'rrhaphous** *a.* [Gk *rhaphē* seam] *Entomol.* of or pertaining to the very large suborder Cyclorrhapha of dipteran insects characterized by the emergence of the adult from the puparium through a circular split L19. **cyclo'sporin** *n.* [mod.L *polysporum* (see below) + -IN[1]] (more fully *cyclosporin A*) a cyclic oligopeptide produced by the fungus *Trichoderma polysporum* and used as an immunosuppressive drug to prevent the rejection of grafts and transplants L20. **cyclostrophic** /-'strəʊfɪk, -'strɒfɪk/ *a.* (*Meteorol.*) designating the force acting on a wind as a consequence of the curvature of its path; (of a wind) dominated by such forces: E20. **cyclothem** *n.* [Gk *thema* something laid down, THEME] *Geol.* a sedimentary deposit whose structure shows evidence of a cyclic process of deposition M20.

cycloid /'sʌɪklɔɪd/ *n.* & *a.* M17. [f. Gk *kukloeidēs* adj., circular: see CYCLE *n.*, -OID.] **A** *n.* **1** *Math.* A curve traced by a point on the circumference of a circle (or occas. in some other fixed relation to it) as the circle rolls along a straight line. M17. 2 *Psychiatry.* = CYCLOTHYMIC *n.* E20. B *adj.* 1 *Zool.* Designating fish-scales of approximately circular form with concentric striations; having such scales. M19. 2 *Psychiatry.* = CYCLOTHYMIC *a.* E20.

cy'cloidal *a.* (*Math.*) of, pertaining to, or of the form of a cycloid (CYCLOID *n.* 1) E18.

cyclometer /sʌɪ'klɒmɪtə/ *n.* M17. [f. CYCLO- + -METER.] †1 A person concerned with measuring the circle. *rare.* Only in M17. 2 An instrument for measuring arcs of circles. E19. 3 An apparatus attached to the wheel of a cycle for measuring the distance travelled. L19.

cyclometry *n.* the measurement of circles; squaring the circle: M17.

Cyclon *n.* var. of ZYKLON.

cyclone /'sʌɪkləʊn/ *n.* M19. [Prob. f. Gk *kuklōma* wheel, coil of a snake, f. *kuklos* circle: the change of *m* to *n* is unexpl.] 1 A storm or atmospheric disturbance involving circular motion of winds. *obs.* in *gen.* sense. M19. b A violent hurricane of limited diameter. M19. c *Meteorol.* A pressure system characterized by a low central barometric pressure and an anticlockwise (northern hemisphere) or clockwise (southern hemisphere) circulation; a depression. M19. 2 A centrifugal machine for separating solids. Freq. *attrib.* L19.

Comb.: **cyclone cellar** *US*: intended to give shelter during a cyclone (in the US).

cyclonic /sʌɪ'klɒnɪk/ *a.* of, pertaining to, of the nature or characteristic of a cyclone M19. **cy'clonically** *adv.* L19.

cyclonite /'sʌɪklənʌɪt/ *n.* E20. [f. CYCLO- + NITRO- (as elems. of alternative chemical name), with ending assim. to -ITE[1].] A high explosive, chemically 1,3,5-trinitrohexahydro-1,3,5-triazine, $(N(NO_2)CH_2)_3$. Also called *hexogen*, *RDX*.

Cyclop *n.* see CYCLOPS.

cyclopaedia /sʌɪklə'piːdɪə/ *n.* Also **-pedia**. E17. [Abbrev.] †1 = ENCYCLOPEDIA 1. Only in 17. 2 = ENCYCLOPEDIA 2. E18.

cyclopaedic *a.* M19.

Cyclopean /sʌɪklə'piːən, -'kləʊpɪən/ *a.* Also **Cyclopian** /*usu.* sʌɪ'kləʊpɪən/. L16. [f. L *Cyclopeus*, *-pius* f. Gk *Kuklōpios*, f. *Kuklōps* CYCLOPS: see -EAN, -IAN.] 1 Belonging to or resembling the Cyclopes; monstrous, huge. L16. 2 Of (esp. ancient) masonry: made with massive irregular or crudely-shaped blocks. E19.

cyclopedia *n.* var. of CYCLOPAEDIA.

Cyclopes *n.pl.* see CYCLOPS.

cyclopia /sʌɪ'kləʊpɪə/ *n.* M19. [f. CYCLOPS + -IA[1].] *Zool.* & *Med.* The fusion of two eyes into one central eye (whether as a normal condition or a malformation).

Cyclopian *a.* see CYCLOPEAN.

Cyclopic /sʌɪ'klɒpɪk/ *a.* *rare.* M17. [Gk *Kuklōpikos*, f. *Kuklōps* CYCLOPS: see -IC.] Cyclopean; monstrous.

†**Cyclopical** *a.* L16–M17.

cyclopoid /'sʌɪkləpɔɪd/ *a.* & *n.* M19. [f. mod.L CYCLOPS + -OID.] *Zool.* A member of, belonging to or resembling, the order Cyclopoida of copepods, typified by the cyclopes.

Cyclops /'sʌɪklɒps/ *n.* In sense 2 usu. **c-**. Pl. **Cyclopes** /sʌɪ'kləʊpiːz/, same, (sense 1) **-ses**. In sense 1 also (*rare*) **-op**, pl. **-ops**. LME. [L *Cyclops* f. Gk *Kuklōps* lit. 'round-eyed', f. *kuklos* circle + *ōps* eye.] 1 *Gk Mythol.* A member of a race of one-eyed giants who forged thunderbolts for Zeus. LME. 2 A free-swimming copepod of the genus *Cyclops*, characterized by having a single centrally-placed eye. M19.

cyclorama /sʌɪklə'rɑːmə/ *n.* M19. [f. CYCLO- after *panorama* etc.] 1 A panoramic scene arranged on the inside of a cylindrical surface, to be viewed by a central spectator. M19. 2 *Theatr.* A large (curved) backcloth or wall at the rear of a stage for displaying a background, esp. of the sky. E20.

cyclosis /sʌɪ'kləʊsɪs/ *n.* M19. [Gk *kuklōsis* encirclement.] 1 *Biol.* Circulatory motion, e.g. of cytoplasm within a cell. M19. 2 *Physics* etc. The existence of cycles; cyclic behaviour. L19.

cyclostome /'sʌɪkləstəʊm/ *n.* M19. [f. CYCLO- + Gk *stoma* mouth.] A fish of the former taxon Cyclostomata (now incorporated in Agnatha: cf. AGNATHAN), which includes primitive forms (the lampreys and hagfishes) having a round sucking mouth.

cyclo'stomatous *a.* M19.

cyclostyle /'sʌɪkləstʌɪl/ *n.* & *v.* L19. [f. CYCLO- + STYLE *n.*] A *n.* An apparatus for printing copies of writing by means of a stencil-plate, orig. one cut with a pen bearing a small toothed wheel which perforated sheets of waxed paper. L19. B *v.t.* Print or copy using a cyclostyle. L19.

cyclothymia /sʌɪklə'θʌɪmɪə/ *n.* E20. [f. CYCLO- + Gk *thumos* mind, temper + -IA[1].] *Psychiatry.* Behaviour characterized by an alternation of mood between depression and elation; manic-depressive behaviour.

cyclothyme, **cyclo'thymic** *adjs.* & *ns.* (*a*) *adj.* of, pertaining to, or exhibiting cyclothymia; manic-depressive; (*b*) *n.* a person with cyclothymia: E20.

cyclotomy /sʌɪ'klɒtəmi/ *n.* L19. [f. CYCLO- + -TOMY.] 1 *Math.* The division of a circle into a given number of equal parts. L19. 2 Surgical cutting of the ciliary muscle of the eye; an instance of this. L19.

cyclo'tomic *a.* (*Math.*) of or pertaining to cyclotomy L19.

cyclotron /'sʌɪklətrɒn/ *n.* M20. [f. CYCLO- + -TRON.] *Physics.* An apparatus for accelerating with an electric field charged atomic particles revolving in a magnetic field.

cyclus /'sʌɪkləs/ *n.* Pl. **-li** /-lʌɪ, -liː/. E19. [L.] A cycle of myths, poems, songs, etc.

cyder *n.* var. of CIDER.

cydippe /sʌɪ'dɪpi/ *n.* M19. [mod.L (see below) f. Gk *Kudippē*, a Nereid.] A ctenophore of the genus *Pleurobrachia* (formerly *Cydippe*).

cydippid *n.* & *a.* (a larval ctenophore) resembling an adult of the order Cydippida L19.

cygnet /'sɪgnɪt/ *n.* LME. [f. OFr. *ci(g)ne* (mod. *cygne*) or its ult. source L *cycnus*, *cyg-* swan f. Gk *kuknos*: see -ET[1].] A young swan.

Cygnus /'sɪgnəs/ *n.* M16. [L *cygnus* swan: see prec.] (The name of) a large constellation of the northern hemisphere, in the Milky Way between Hercules and Pegasus; the Swan.

cylices *n.pl.* see KYLIX.

cylinder /'sɪlɪndə/ *n.* L16. [L *cylindrus* f. Gk *kulindros* roller, f. *kulindein* to roll.] I 1 A solid geometrical figure generated by a straight line fixed in direction and describing with one of its points a closed curve, esp. a circle (in which case the figure is a *circular cylinder*, its ends being parallel circles). L16. 2 A (solid or hollow) body, object, or part having this shape, exemplified by a roller, straight tree-trunk, pencil, etc. L16.

1 *scalene cylinder*: see SCALENE *a.* 1. 2 VASCULAR *cylinder.*

II *spec.* 3 A chamber in which a fluid exerts pressure on a piston or analogous part, e.g. in a steam or internal-combustion engine. L17. 4 A metal roller used in printing. M18. 5 *Watchmaking.* The cylindrical recess, cut away to allow the passage of the escape wheel, on the verge of the balance in a particular kind of escapement (called *cylinder escapement*). M18. 6 A hollow barrel-shaped object of baked clay, covered with cuneiform script and buried under the foundations of a Babylonian or Assyrian temple; a small stone of similar shape used in antiquity as a seal. M19. 7 *Hist.* A cylindrical phonograph record. L19. 8 A cylindrical container for liquefied gas etc. E20.

3 **fire** (or **function** etc.) **on all cylinders** *fig.* work at full power.

Comb.: **cylinder bore** a cylinder-bored gun; **cylinder-bored** *a.* having an unrifled bore of uniform diameter; *cylinder escapement*: see sense 5 above; **cylinder head** the end cover of a cylinder in an internal-combustion engine, against which the piston compresses the cylinder contents; **cylinder lock**: having the keyhole and tumbler mechanism contained in a cylinder; **cylinder oil**: of a kind suitable for lubricating steam engine valves and pistons; **cylinder press** a printing machine in which the printing surface is carried on a flat bed and pressure is applied by a revolving cylinder; **cylinder saw** a crown saw.

cylindered *a.* having a cylinder or cylinders (of a specified number or kind) L19.

cylindraceous /sɪlɪn'dreɪʃəs/ *a.* L17. [f. prec. + -ACEOUS.] = CYLINDRICAL 1.

cylindric /sɪ'lɪndrɪk/ *a.* L17. [mod.L *cylindricus* f. Gk *kulindrikos*, f. *kulindros* CYLINDER: see -IC.] Cylindrical.

cylindricity /sɪlɪn'drɪsɪti/ *n.* M19.

cylindrical /sɪ'lɪndrɪk(ə)l/ *a.* M17. [f. as prec. + -AL[1].] 1 Shaped like a cylinder. M17. 2 Of, pertaining, or relating to a cylinder. M17.

2 **cylindrical projection** a map projection in which part of a spherical surface is projected on to a cylinder which is then unrolled into a plane.

cylindrically *adv.* M17. **cylindricalness** *n.* E18.

cylindriform /sɪ'lɪndrɪfɔːm/ *a.* L19. [f. L *cylindrus* CYLINDER + -I- + -FORM.] = CYLINDRICAL 1.

cylindrite /sɪ'lɪndrʌɪt/ *n.* L19. [f. Gk *kulindros* CYLINDER + -ITE[1].] *Min.* A blackish-grey metallic sulphide of lead, antimony, and tin, occurring usu. as cylindrical masses.

cylindro- /sɪ'lɪndrəʊ/ *comb. form* of Gk *kulindros* CYLINDER: see -O-.

cylindro-'conical *a.* of cylindrical form with one end conical M19. **cylindro-co'noidal** *a.* of cylindrical form with one end conoidal L19.

cylindroid /'sɪlɪndrɔɪd/ *n.* & *a.* M17. [f. prec. + -OID.] A *n.* A figure or body resembling a cylinder; a cylinder of elliptical section. M17. B *adj.* Resembling a cylinder in shape; somewhat cylindrical. M19.

cylin'droidal *a.* (*a*) of the form of a cylindroid; (*b*) = CYLINDROID *a.*: M19.

cylindroma /sɪlɪn'drəʊmə/ *n.* Pl. **-mas**, **-mata** /-mətə/. L19. [f. CYLINDRO- + -OMA.] *Med.* A cutaneous or dermal tumour having a cylindrical structure.

cylix *n.* var. of KYLIX.

cyma /'sʌɪmə/ *n.* M16. [mod.L f. Gk *kuma* billow, wave, wavy moulding, f. *kuein* become pregnant.] 1 *Archit.* An ogee moulding of a cornice. M16. 2 *Bot.* = CYME *n.* 2. E18.

1 **cyma recta** /'rɛktə/ [= straight]: having the concave part of the curve uppermost. **cyma reversa** /rɪ'vəːsə/ [= reversed]: having the convex part of the curve uppermost.

cymagraph *n.* an instrument for tracing the contours of mouldings M19.

†**cymaise** *n.* M17–M18. [Fr. f. as CYMATIUM.] *Archit.* = CYMA 1.

cymar *n.* var. of SIMAR.

cymatium /sɪ'matɪəm, -'meɪʃəm/ *n.* Pl. **-tia** /-tɪə, -ʃə/. M16. [L *cymatium* ogee, Ionic volute f. Gk *kumation* dim. of *kuma* CYMA.] *Archit.* = CYMA 1.

cymbal /'sɪmb(ə)l/ *n.* & *v.* OE. [L *cymbalum* f. Gk *kumbalon*, f. *kumbē* cup, hollow vessel. Readopted in ME f. (O)Fr. *cymbale* f. L.] A *n.* A musical instrument consisting of a concave plate of brass or bronze, which is struck against another or with a stick etc. to produce a ringing or clashing sound. Formerly also *loosely*, any of various other percussion instruments. OE.

ride cymbal: see RIDE *n.* 4c. *top cymbal*: see TOP *a.*

B *v.i.* & *t.* Infl. **-l(l)-**. Play on cymbals. *rare.* LME.

cymbalist *n.* a cymbal player M17.

cymbalo /'sɪmbələʊ/ *n.* Pl. **-os**. L19. [It. *cembalo*, *cim-* f. L *cymbalum* CYMBAL *n.* Cf. CIMBALOM.] A dulcimer.

cymbidium /sɪm'bɪdɪəm/ *n.* E19. [mod.L (see below), f. Gk *kumbē* cup: so called from a hollow recess in the flower-lip.] An epiphytic orchid of the large tropical Asian and Australasian genus *Cymbidium*.

cymbiform /'sɪmbɪfɔːm/ *a.* E19. [f. L *cymba* boat + -I- + -FORM.] Boat-shaped.

cyme /sʌɪm/ *n.* In sense 1 also †**cime**. E18. [Fr. *cyme*, *cime* summit, top f. pop. form of L CYMA.] †1 The unopened head of a plant. *rare.* Only in E18. 2 *Bot.* An inflorescence (freq. forming a more or less flat head) in which the primary axis bears a single flower which develops first, flowers of secondary and higher order axes developing successively later. Cf. RACEME. L18.

cymose *a.* of the nature of a cyme; bearing or arranged in cymes: E19.

cymene /ˈsʌɪmiːn/ *n.* M19. [f. Gk *kuminon* CUMIN + -ENE.] *Chem.* Each of three isomeric liquid aromatic hydrocarbons, 1-methyl-2(or 3 or 4)-isopropylbenzene, $C_{10}H_{14}$, one or more of which are present in oil of cumin and other volatile oils.

cymling *n.* see SIMLIN.

cymoid /ˈsʌɪmɔɪd/ *a.* E19. [f. CYMA + -OID.] Resembling a cyma or a cyme.

cymophane /ˈsʌɪməfeɪn/ *n.* E19. [f. Gk *kumo-kuma* CYMA + *-phanēs* showing.] Chrysoberyl, now *spec.* of a chatoyant variety used for gems.

cymotrichous /sʌɪˈmɒtrɪkəs/ *a.* E20. [f. as prec. + -TRICH + -OUS.] *Anthropol.* Having wavy hair; (of hair) wavy.

cymotrichy *n.* the state or condition of having wavy hair E20.

Cymric /ˈkɪmrɪk/ *a.* M19. [f. Welsh *Cymru* Wales, *Cymry* the Welsh + -IC.] Welsh.

†cynanche *n.* M16–M19. [Late L f. Gk *kunagkhē* canine quinsy, sore throat, f. *kun-*, *kuōn* dog + *agkhein* to throttle: cf. QUINSY.] Quinsy or a similar inflammatory complaint.

cynanthropy /sɪˈnanθrəpi/ *n. rare.* L16. [Fr. †*cynanthropie* (after *lycanthropie*, LYCANTHROPY f. Gk *kun-*, *kuōn* dog. Cf. Gk *kunanthrōpos* of a dog-man.] A form of madness in which a person believes himself or herself to be a dog and behaves accordingly.

cyne- /ˈkɪnə, *foreign* ˈkynə/ *comb. form.* Long *obs.* exc. *Hist.* OE. [Cf. KING *n.*] Royal: occurring in certain OE compounds retained by historians.

cynebót *n.* [BOOT *n.*[1]] compensation paid to the people for the murder of the king.

cynegetics /sɪnɪˈdʒɛtɪks/ *n.pl. rare.* M17. [f. Gk *kunēgetikos* adj., f. *kunēgetēs* hunter, f. *kun-*, *kuōn* dog + *hēgetēs* leader: see -ICS.] The chase, hunting.

cynegetic *a.* relating to the chase E18.

cynghanedd /kəŋˈhɑːnɛð/ *n.* M19. [Welsh.] An intricate system of alliteration and rhyme in Welsh poetry.

cynic /ˈsɪnɪk/ *n.* & *a.* M16. [L *cynicus* adj. f. Gk *kunikos* lit. 'doglike, churlish', prob. f. *Kunosarges* gymnasium where Antisthenes taught, but assoc. with *kun-*, *kuōn* dog: see -IC.] A *n.* 1 (C-.) Any of a sect of ancient-Greek philosophers founded by Antisthenes (a pupil of Socrates), who had an ostentatious contempt for ease and pleasure. M16. 2 A cynical person; one who sarcastically doubts or despises human sincerity and merit. L16.

2 G. MEREDITH Cynics are only happy in making the world as barren to others as they have made it for themselves.

B *adj.* 1 a = CYNICAL *a.* 1. L16. b (C-.) Belonging to or characteristic of the sect of Cynics. M17. 2 Of or suggesting a dog; canicular. *rare.* E17.

cynicism /-sɪz(ə)m/ *n.* (*a*) (C-) the philosophy of the Cynics; (*b*) cynical disposition or quality: L17. **cynism** *n.* (*rare*) [Fr. *cynisme*] = CYNICISM M19.

cynical /ˈsɪnɪk(ə)l/ *a.* L16. [f. as prec. + -AL[1].] 1 Resembling or characteristic of the Cynic philosophers: distrustful or incredulous of human goodness and sincerity; sneering. L16. 2 Of dogs, canine. Chiefly *joc. rare.* E17.

1 R. WEST We were experts in disillusion, we had learned to be cynical about fresh starts. S. NAIPAUL One is led to the cynical conclusion that most had been opposed to the draft rather than to the war itself; passionately dedicated to saving their own skins.

cynically *adv.* E17.

cyno- /ˈsʌɪnəʊ, ˈsɪnəʊ/ *comb. form* of Gk *kun-*, *kuōn* dog: see -O-.

cynoˈlogical *a.* of or pertaining to cynology E20. **cyˈnology** *n.* the branch of science that deals with dogs L19. **cynoˈphobia** *n.* irrational fear of dogs L19.

cynocephalus /sʌɪnəˈsɛf(ə)ləs, sɪn-/ *n.* Pl. **-li** /-lʌɪ, -liː/. ME. [L f. Gk *kunokephalos* adj. = dog-headed, f. as prec. + *kephalē* head.] 1 A member of a fabled race of men with dogs' heads. ME. 2 A baboon or other primate having a doglike head. *obs.* exc. as mod.L name of a genus of Asian flying lemurs. E17.

cynocephalous *a.* dog-headed M19.

cynodont /ˈsʌɪnədɒnt/ *n.* & *a.* L19. [f. CYNO- + -ODONT. Cf. earlier DICYNODONT.] *Palaeont.* A *n.* A Triassic mammal-like reptile with well developed specialized teeth. L19. B *adj.* Designating or pertaining to a cynodont. L19.

cynosure /ˈsɪnəzjʊə, ˈsʌɪn-, -sjʊə/ *n.* L16. [Fr., or L *Cynosura* f. Gk *kunosoura*, f. *kunos* genit. sing. of *kuōn* dog + *oura* tail.] 1 (C-.) *The* constellation Ursa Minor, or *the* polestar which it contains. Now *rare* or *obs.* L16. 2 A thing which serves for guidance or direction. *arch.* L16. 3 A thing which or person who is the centre of attraction or admiration. E17.

2 JOSEPH HALL For the guidance of our either caution or liberty . . the onely Cynosure is our Charity. 3 CARLYLE The fair young Queen . . the cynosure of all eyes. M. MEYER Rome . . . the cynosure of contemporary writers and artists.

Cynthia /ˈsɪnθɪə/ *n. poet.* L16. [L, a name of the goddess Diana, born on Mount Cynthus in Delos: see -IA[1].] The moon personified as a goddess.

cyperus /sʌɪˈpɪərəs, ˈsʌɪpərəs/ *n.* LME. [L *cyperus* f. Gk *kupeiros*, *kuperos* an aromatic marsh-plant.] A sedge of the genus *Cyperus* (family Cyperaceae); *esp.* (English) galingale.

cyperaceous /sʌɪpəˈreɪʃəs/ *a.* of or pertaining to the family Cyperaceae M19.

cyphel /ˈsʌɪf(ə)l/ *n.* LME. [App. Gk *kuphella* the hollows of the ears.] Orig., the houseleek, *Sempervivum tectorum*. Now (more fully *mossy cyphel*), a cushion-forming alpine plant, *Minuartia sedoides*, of the pink family, with sessile apetalous flowers.

cypher *n.*, *v.* vars. of CIPHER *n.*, *v.*

cyphonism /ˈsʌɪfənɪz(ə)m/ *n.* E18. [Gk *kuphōnismos*, f. *kuphōn* crooked piece of wood, f. *kuphos* bent: see -ISM.] *Gk Hist.* Punishment of offenders by means of a wooden pillory fastened to the neck.

†cyphosis *n.* see KYPHOSIS.

cypraea /sʌɪˈpriːə/ *n.* E19. [mod.L (see below), f. *Cypria*, a name of Venus.] A gastropod of the large genus *Cypraea*; a cowrie.

cy pres /siː preɪ/ *adv.* & *a. phr.* E19. [AN = Fr. *si près* as near (as).] *Law.* As near as possible (to the intentions of a testator or donor when these cannot be precisely followed).

cypress /ˈsʌɪprəs/ *n.*[1] ME. [OFr. *cipres* (mod. *cyprès*) f. late L *cypressus* f. Gk *kuparissos*, of alien origin: sp. later assim. to L.] 1 An evergreen coniferous tree of the Eurasian and N. American genus *Cupressus* having flattened shoots with scalelike leaves; *esp.* (also *Italian cypress*) *C. sempervirens*, a tall, often fastigiate, tree native to southern Europe and the Middle East, with dark foliage and hard durable wood. Also *cypress tree.* ME. b With specifying wd: any of numerous trees or shrubs related to or resembling the true cypresses. M16. c Foliage of *C. sempervirens* regarded or used as a symbol of mourning. L16. 2 The wood of any of these trees. ME.

1 G. DURRELL An admonishing finger of black cypress against the sky. b **African cypress** a conifer of the African genus *Widdringtonia.* **bald cypress** *Taxodium distichum*, a N. American conifer of water margins, often with exposed root-buttresses. **false cypress** a conifer of the N. American and Asian genus *Chamaecyparis*, closely related to *Cupressus.* LAWSON'S CYPRESS. *Monterey cypress*: see MONTEREY 2. *Nootka cypress*: see NOOTKA *a.* 1. SITKA *cypress.* **summer cypress** = BELVEDERE 2. **swamp cypress** = *bald cypress* above. c TENNYSON That remorseless iron hour Made cypress of her orange flower. *attrib.*: O. WILDE The quenched-out torch, the lonely cypress-gloom.

Comb.: **cypress-knee** an exposed root-buttress of bald cypress; **cypress pine** a small Australian conifer of the genus *Callitris*; **cypress spurge** a European spurge, *Euphorbia cyparissias* (freq. cultivated), with numerous pale green linear leaves, suggesting a miniature conifer; **cypress-vine** a tropical American climbing plant with scarlet flowers, *Ipomoea quamoclit*, of the bindweed family.

cypress /ˈsʌɪprəs/ *n.*[2] Now *rare* or *obs.* LME. [Alt. of CYPERUS, app. confused w. prec.] (English) galingale.

cypress /ˈsʌɪprəs/ *n.*[3] & *a.* Now *rare* or *obs.* LME. [AN *cipres*, *cypres* f. OFr. *Cipre*, *Cypre* (mod. *Chypre*) the island of Cyprus.] A *n.* A textile fabric originally brought from Cyprus; *spec.* (a piece of) a light transparent material of silk and hair resembling crape, formerly often worn (as crape) in mourning. LME. B *attrib.* or as *adj.* Made of or resembling this fabric. M16.

Cyprian /ˈsɪprɪən/ *a.* & *n.* L16. [f. L *Cyprius* of Cyprus (see CYPRIOT) + -AN.] A *adj.* Of or pertaining to Cyprus. Formerly often *transf.*, of prostitutes, lewd (from the ancient fame of Cyprus for the worship of Aphrodite or Venus). L16. B *n.* A Cypriot. Formerly also, a lewd person, a prostitute. L16.

Cyprianic /sɪprɪˈanɪk/ *a.* L17. [mod.L *Cyprianicus*, f. *Cyprianus* (see below): see -IC.] Of, pertaining to, or characteristic of St Cyprian (Thascius Caecilius Cyprianus), Bishop of Carthage, martyred AD 258.

cyprides *n.* pl. of CYPRIS.

cyprinodont /sɪˈprʌɪnədɒnt/ *n.* & *a.* M19. [f. as next + -ODONT.] A *n.* A member of the family Cyprinodontidae of small tropical and warm-temperate freshwater fishes. M19. B *adj.* Of, pertaining to, or designating this family. L19.

cyprinoid /ˈsɪprɪnɔɪd/ *a.* & *n.* M19. [f. L *cyprinus* carp f. Gk *kuprinos* + -OID.] A *adj.* Resembling or related to the carp; belonging to the large superfamily Cyprinoidea which includes Cyprinidae (see below) and several other families. M19. B *n.* A cyprinoid fish. M19.

cyprinid *n.* & *a.* (*a*) *n.* a fish of the family Cyprinidae, which includes the carps and minnows; (*b*) *adj.* of, pertaining to, or designating this family: L19. **cypˈriniform** *n.* & *a.* (*a*) *n.* a fish of the order Cypriniformes, which includes the carps, loaches, and suckers; (*b*) *adj.* of or pertaining to this order; carplike: L19.

Cypriot /ˈsɪprɪət/ *n.* & *a.* Also **-ote** /-əʊt/. L16. [Gk *Kupriōtēs*, f. *Kupros* Cyprus. Cf. CYPRIAN.] A *n.* 1 A native or inhabitant of Cyprus, an island in the eastern Mediterranean; a person descended from inhabitants of Cyprus. L16. 2 The (ancient or modern) Greek dialect of Cyprus. L19. B *adj.* Of or pertaining to Cyprus or Cypriots. L19.

Greek, **Turkish**, **Cypriot**: of Greek, Turkish, extraction.

cypripedium /sɪprɪˈpiːdɪəm/ *n.* L18. [mod.L (see below), f. Gk *Kupris* Aphrodite + *pedilon* slipper.] An orchid of the genus *Cypripedium*, to which the lady's slipper orchids belong.

cypris /ˈsʌɪprɪs/ *n.* Pl. **-ides** /-ɪdiːz/. M19. [mod.L (see below) f. Gk *Kupris* Aphrodite.] A freshwater ostracod of the genus *Cypris*. Also, a cirripede larva at a stage (following the *nauplius*) in which it acquires a shell like that of a *Cypris* ostracod and becomes anchored to a rock etc.

cypsela /ˈsɪpsɪlə/ *n.* Pl. **-lae** /-liː/. L19. [mod.L f. Gk *kupselē* hollow vessel, chest, etc.] *Bot.* An achene with the calyx attached, as in plants of the composite family.

Cyrenaic /sʌɪrɪˈneɪɪk/ *n.* & *a.* L16. [L *Cyrenaicus* f. Gk *Kurēnaikos*, f. *Kurēnē* Cyrene, an ancient Greek colony in N. Africa.] *Hist.* A *n.* A philosopher belonging to a hedonistic school founded by Aristippus of Cyrene during the 4th cent. BC. L16. B *adj.* Designating or belonging to this school. M17.

Cyrenaican /sʌɪrɪˈneɪɪk(ə)n/ *a.* & *n.* E17. [f. as prec. + -AN.] A *adj.* Of or pertaining to Cyrenaica, a region of N. Africa (now part of Libya), or its people. E17. B *n.* A native or inhabitant of Cyrenaica. M20.

Cyrenian /sʌɪˈriːnɪən/ *a.* & *n.* As adj. also **-ean**. E17. [f. L *Cyrene* Cyrene (see CYRENAIC) + -IAN, -EAN. In senses A.2, B f. Simon of Cyrene (*Matt.* 27:32 etc.), helper of Jesus on the road to Calvary.] A *adj.* 1 = CYRENAIC *a.* E17. 2 Designating or pertaining to an organization for helping the destitute. L20. B *n.* A member of the Cyrenian organization; a helper of the destitute. L20.

Cyrillic /sɪˈrɪlɪk/ *a.* & *n.* E19. [f. St *Cyril* (826–69), apostle of the Slavs, author of the Glagolitic alphabet (from which Cyrillic was later derived): see -IC.] (Designating, written in, or pertaining to) an alphabet or script used in writing Old Church Slavonic and some modern

Slavonic languages (e.g. Russian, Bulgarian, Serbian).

†cyriologic *a.* var. of CURIOLOGIC.

cyrto- /ˈsəːtəʊ/ *comb. form* of Gk *kurtos* curved: see -O-.

cyrtolite *n.* (*Min.*) a variety of zircon containing uranium and rare-earth elements and freq. having convex crystal faces: M19. **cyrˈtometer** *n.* an instrument for measuring or recording curves of the body L19.

†cyssors *n.pl.* var. of SCISSORS.

cyst /sɪst/ *n.* E18. [Late L CYSTIS.] **1** A thin-walled hollow organ or cavity in an animal or plant, containing a liquid secretion; a sac, a vesicle, a bladder. E18. **2** *Med.* A sac or cavity of abnormal character, containing fluid; a structure enclosing a larva of a parasitic worm etc. E18. **3** A cell or cavity enclosing reproductive bodies, an embryo, etc. M19.

2 MEIBOMIAN *cyst*. NEURENTERIC *cyst*.

cystlike *a.* resembling (that of) a cyst M19.

cyst- /sɪst/ *comb. form* of Gk *kustis* bladder, cyst, used bef. a vowel. Cf. CYSTI-, CYSTO-.

cyˈstalgia *n.* (*Med.*) pain in the urinary bladder L19. **cyˈstectomy** *n.* (an instance of) surgical removal of a cyst or (usu.) of the urinary bladder L19.

cysteine /ˈsɪstiːiːn, -tiːn, -teɪn, -tiːn/ *n.* Also **-ein**. L19. [f. CYSTINE + -EINE.] *Biochem.* A sulphur-containing amino acid, $HS{\cdot}CH_2CH(NH_2)$-COOH, which occurs in proteins, notably keratins, often in the form of cystine. Cf. CYSTINE.

¶Increasingly pronounced as a disyllable (cf. *protein*), leading to confusion with CYSTINE.

cysti- /ˈsɪsti/ *comb. form* of Gk *kustis* bladder, cyst. Cf. CYST-, CYSTO-.

cystiform *a.* of the form of a bladder or cyst M19.

cystic /ˈsɪstɪk/ *a.* M17. [Fr. *cystique* or mod.L *cysticus*: see CYSTIS, -IC.] **1** Pertaining to or connected with the gall bladder. M17. **2** *Med.* Of the nature of a cyst; characterized by the formation of cysts; containing cysts. E18. **3** Of or pertaining to the urinary bladder. E19. **4** Enclosed in a cyst. M19.

1 *cystic artery, duct*, etc. **2** *cystic* FIBROSIS.

cysticercus /sɪstɪˈsəːkəs/ *n.* Pl. **-ci** /-saɪ/. M19. [mod.L (orig. the name of a supposed genus), f. as CYSTI- + Gk *kerkos* tail.] *Zool.* A larval tapeworm, esp. of the family Taeniidae, at a stage in which the scolex is invaginated, typically found as a cyst in the muscle tissue of the host.

cysticercoid *a.* & *n.* (pertaining to, resembling, or of the nature of) a cysticercus M19.

cystid /ˈsɪstɪd/ *n.* M19. [f. CYSTIS + -ID[3].] *Palaeont.* A cystoid.

Also **cyˈstidean** *n.* M19.

cystidium /sɪˈstɪdɪəm/ *n.* Pl. **-dia** /-dɪə/. M19. [mod.L, f. Gk *kustis* CYST: see -IDIUM.] *Bot.* A sterile body projecting from the spore-bearing surface of a basidiomycete.

cystine /ˈsɪstiːn, -tɪn/ *n.* M19. [f. Gk *kustis* bladder + -INE[5]: orig. isolated from urinary calculi.] *Biochem.* A base, $C_6H_{12}N_2O_4S_2$, which is in effect an oxidized dimer of cysteine (with which it is readily interconvertible), and is the form in which cysteine often occurs in organic tissue.

cystiˈnosis *n.*, pl. **-noses** /-ˈnəʊsiːz/, *Med.* an inherited metabolic disorder resulting in the accumulation of cystine in the body M20. **cystinotic** /-ˈnɒt-/ *a.* exhibiting cystinosis, containing excessive amounts of cystine M20. **cystiˈnuria** *n.* (*Med.*) the abnormal presence of cystine in the urine, usu. as a result of an inherited disorder of amino-acid metabolism M19.

†cystis *n.* M16–M18. [Late L f. Gk *kustis* bladder.] A cyst.

cystitis /sɪˈstaɪtɪs/ *n.* L18. [f. CYST- + -ITIS.] *Med.* Inflammation of the urinary bladder.

cysto- /ˈsɪstəʊ/ *comb. form* of Gk *kustē* = *kustis* bladder, cyst: see -O-. Cf. CYST-, CYSTI-.

cystocarp *n.* (*Bot.*) the fruiting body of the gametophyte in some algae of the subclass Florideae L19. **cystocele** *n.* (*Med.*) prolapse of the base of the urinary bladder in women E19. **cystolith** *n.* (*Bot.*) a hard mineralized ingrowth of the wall of cells in the epidermis of certain plants M19. **cystometer** /sɪˈstɒmɪtə/ *n.* an instrument for measuring the internal pressure and volume of the urinary bladder E20. **cystometry** /sɪˈstɒmɪtri/ *n.* measurement of the internal pressure and volume of the urinary bladder M20. **cystoscope** *n.* an instrument for internal examination of the urinary bladder L19. **cyˈstoscopy** *n.* examination of the urinary bladder with a cystoscope E20. **cyˈstostomy** *n.* (an instance of) the surgical formation of a (semi-)permanent artificial opening in the urinary bladder E20. **cyˈstotomy** *n.* (an instance of) surgical incision into the urinary bladder L19.

cystoid /ˈsɪstɔɪd/ *a.* & *n.* L19. [f. Gk *kustis* bladder + -OID.] **1** *Med.* (Of the nature of) a cyst. *rare.* L19. **2** *Palaeont.* A member of, of or pertaining to, the order Cystoidea of fossil echinoderms. L19.

cytase /ˈsaɪteɪz/ *n.* L19. [f. CYTO- + -ASE.] *Biochem.* An enzyme, present in some plant seeds, capable of hydrolysing the hemicellulose constituents of cell walls of plants.

cytaster /ˈsaɪtastə/ *n.* L19. [f. CYTO- + ASTER.] *Biol.* A star-shaped structure formed in the cytoplasm of a cell prior to the onset of cell division. Cf. ASTER *n.* 3.

-cyte /saɪt/ *suff.* [f. Gk *kutos* receptacle.] Forming ns. denoting (usu. mature) cells, as *erythrocyte*. Cf. -BLAST.

Cytherean /sɪθəˈriːən/ *n.* & *a.* M18. [f. L *Cytherea*, a name of Venus, f. *Cythēra* Kithira, an Ionian island: see -AN.] **A** *n.* A votaress of Venus; a temple prostitute. M18. **B** *adj.* Of or pertaining to Venus (goddess or planet). M19.

cytidine /ˈsaɪtɪdiːn/ *n.* E20. [f. CYTO- + -IDINE.] *Biochem.* A nucleoside composed of cytosine linked to ribose.

cytidylic /saɪtɪˈdɪlɪk/ *a.* M20. [f. prec. + -YL + -IC.] Biochem. *cytidylic acid*, a nucleotide composed of a phosphoric acid ester of cytidine, present in most DNA and RNA.

cytisine /ˈsɪtɪsiːn/ *n.* M19. [f. next + -INE[5].] *Chem.* A poisonous alkaloid, $C_{11}H_{14}N_2O$, present in laburnum and numerous other leguminous plants.

cytisus /ˈsɪtɪsəs/ *n.* M16. [L f. Gk *kutisos*.] Orig., a shrubby plant mentioned by classical writers; *spec.* a southern European medick, *Medicago arborea*. Now, any of a large genus of leguminous shrubs, mostly native to southern Europe, including some brooms and (formerly) laburnum.

cyto- /ˈsaɪtəʊ/ *comb. form* of Gk *kutos* receptacle: see -O-. Freely used in *Biol.* etc. to form ns. and adjs. w. the sense 'of a cell or cells'.

cytoarchitecˈtonic *a.* (*Med.*) pertaining to the arrangement of cells in a tissue; *spec.* designating numbered areas of the cerebral cortex which are characterized by the arrangement of their cells and are each associated with particular functions: E20. **cytoarchitecˈtonics** *n.* (treated as *sing.* or *pl.*) *Med.* the cytoarchitectonic properties of something; the field of study that deals with these: M20. **cytoarchiˈtectural** *a.* (*Med.*) = CYTOARCHITECTONIC M20. **cytoarchiˈtecturally** *adv.* (*Med.*) from a cytoarchitectonic point of view M20. **cytoˈarchitecture** *n.* (*Med.*) = CYTOARCHITECTONICS M20. **cytoˈcentrifuge** *n.* a centrifuge used for depositing cells suspended in a liquid on a slide for microscopic examination M20. **cytochalasin** /-kəˈleɪsɪn/ *n.* [Gk *khalasis* dislocation] any of several fungal metabolites used in research for their property of interfering with cell processes M20. **cytoˈchemical** *a.* of or pertaining to cytochemistry M20. **cytoˈchemistry** *n.* the chemistry of living cells, esp. as studied microscopically E20. **cytochrome** *n.* any of various compounds consisting of haem bonded to a protein, which function as electron transfer agents in many biochemical reactions, esp. in cellular respiration E20. **cytoˈcidal** *a.* that kills living cells E20. **cyˈtogamy** *n.* †(*a*) fusion of cells; (*b*) simultaneous autogamy of two individual protozoans in contact, with no exchange of material between them: E20. **cytokine** *n.* any of various hormones secreted by certain cells of the immune system L20. **cytokinin** /-ˈkaɪnɪn/ *n.* (*Biochem.*) = KININ 2 M20. **cyˈtolysis** *n.* dissolution or disruption of cells, esp. by an external agent E20. **cytoˈlytic** *a.* pertaining to or bringing about cytolysis E20. **cytoˈmegalic** *a.* (*Med.*) characterized by enlarged cells; *spec.* designating a disease caused by a cytomegalovirus: M20. **cytoˈmegalovirus** *n.* (*Med.*) a kind of herpesvirus which usually produces very mild symptoms in an infected person but may cause severe neurological damage in people with weakened immune systems and in the newborn (abbrev. *CMV*) M20. **cytomorˈphosis** *n.* the series of morphological changes undergone by a cell during its existence E20. **cytoˈpathic**, **-pathoˈgenic** *adjs.* of, pertaining to, or producing damage to living cells M20. **cytopaˈthology** *n.* the pathology of cells; the branch of science that deals with cells as affected by disease: M20. **cytoˈphilic** *a.* having an affinity for living cells; *spec.* designating antibodies which attach themselves to cells other than at the cells' specific combining sites: E20. **cytoˈskeletal** *a.* of or pertaining to a cytoskeleton M20. **cytoskeleton** *n.* a network of protein filaments and tubules in the cytoplasm of many eukaryotic cells that contributes to their shape and coherence M20. **cytosol** *n.* the aqueous component of cytoplasm M20. **cytoˈsolic** *a.* of or pertaining to cytosol L20. **cytotaˈxonomy** *n.* taxonomy based on cytological (and esp. cytogenetic) study M20. **cytoˈtoxic** *a.* toxic to cells E20. **cytoˈtoxin** *n.* a substance toxic to cells E20. **cytotropic** /-ˈtrəʊpɪk, -ˈtrɒpɪk/ *a.* exhibiting cytotropism; having an affinity for cells: M20. **cytotropism** /-ˈtrəʊp-/ *n.* the tendency of cells to move towards or (*negative cytotropism*) away from each other E20.

cytogenetics /ˌsaɪtəʊdʒəˈnɛtɪks/ *n.* M20. [f. prec. + GENETICS.] *Biol.* The branch of science that deals with the behaviour and properties of chromosomes.

cytogenetic *a.* †(*a*) of or pertaining to cell generation; (*b*) of or pertaining to cytogenetics: L19. **cytogenetical** *a.* = CYTOGENETIC (b) M20. **cytogenetically** *adv.* M20. **cytogeneticist** /-sɪst/ *n.* M20.

cytoid /ˈsaɪtɔɪd/ *a.* L19. [f. as prec. + -OID.] Resembling a living cell.

cytology /saɪˈtɒlədʒi/ *n.* L19. [f. as prec. + -LOGY.] The science of the structure and functions of the cells of organisms.

cytoˈlogic *a.* (chiefly *US*) = CYTOLOGICAL M20. **cytoˈlogical** *a.* of or pertaining to cytology L19. **cytoˈlogically** *adv.* E20. **cytologist** *n.* L19.

cytophotometry /ˌsaɪtəʊfəˈtɒmɪtri/ *n.* M20. [f. as prec. + PHOTOMETRY.] *Biol.* The investigation of the contents of cells by measuring the light they allow through after staining.

cytophoˈtometer *n.* a photometer for use in cytophotometry M20. **cytophotoˈmetric** *a.* M20. **cytophotoˈmetrically** *adv.* by means of cytophotometry L20.

cytoplasm /ˈsaɪtəplaz(ə)m/ *n.* L19. [f. as prec. + PLASMA.] *Biol.* The material contained within a cell, other than the nucleus.

cytoˈplasmic *a.* of, pertaining to, or of the nature of cytoplasm L19.

cytosine /ˈsaɪtəsiːn/ *n.* L19. [f. as prec. + -OSE[2] + -INE[5].] *Biochem.* A derivative of pyrimidine which is one of the bases of nucleic acids, paired with guanine in double-stranded DNA; 2-oxy-4-aminopyrimidine, $C_4H_5N_3O$.

cyul /kiːl/ *n.* E17. [AL *cyula* f. OE *cēol*, *ciol* KEEL *n.*[2]] *Hist.* A N. European sailing vessel or war-galley of the period before the Norman Conquest.

czar *n.* var. of TSAR.

czardas *n.* var. of CSARDAS.

czarevich *n.* var. of TSAREVICH.

czarevna *n.* var. of TSAREVNA.

czarina *n.* var. of TSARINA.

czaritsa *n.* var. of TSARITSA.

Czech /tʃɛk/ *n.* & *a.* E19. [Pol. spelling of Czech *Čech* n. (cf. Czech *Čechy* Bohemia, *český* adj., Bohemian).] **A** *n.* **1** A native or inhabitant of Bohemia, the Czech Republic, or (*Hist.*) Czechoslovakia. E19. **2** The Slavonic language of Bohemia. L19. **B** *attrib.* or as *adj.* Of or pertaining to the Czechs or their language; Bohemian, Czechoslovakian. E19.

Czechoslovak /tʃɛkəʊˈsləʊvak/ *n.* & *a.* E20. [f. as next, after SLOVAK.] = next.

Czechoslovakian /ˌtʃɛkə(ʊ)sləˈvakɪən/ *n.* & *a.* E20. [f. *Czechoslovakia* (see below) + -AN.] **A** *n.* A native or inhabitant of Czechoslovakia, a former State in central Europe comprising most of the territories of Bohemia, Moravia, and Slovakia. Also *loosely*, the Czech or Slovak language. E20. **B** *adj.* Of or pertaining to Czechoslovakia or its peoples. E20.

D

D, d /diː/, the fourth letter of the modern Eng. alphabet and of the ancient Roman one, corresp. to Gk *delta*, Heb. *daleth*. The sound normally represented by the letter is a voiced alveolar plosive consonant. Pl. **D's, Ds**. See also DEE *n*.

I 1 The letter and its sound. **2** The shape of the letter. **b** *Billiards* etc. The semicircle marked on the table in the baulk area, with its diameter part of the baulk line, from which a player must play after retrieving the cue-ball by hand.

2 D-ring a D-shaped metal ring through which a strap etc. can pass. **D-shaped** *a.* having a shape or a cross-section like the capital letter D.

II Symbolical uses. **3** Used to denote serial order; applied e.g. to the fourth group or section, sheet of a book, etc. **4** *Mus.* (Cap. D.) The second note of the diatonic scale of C major. Also, the scale of a composition with D as its keynote. **5** The fourth hypothetical person or example. **6** *Math.* (Usu. italic *d*.) In calculus, used before variables to indicate a derivative, e.g. in *dy/dx*, the derivative of *y* with respect to *x*. **7** (Usu. cap. D.) Designating the fourth-highest class (of academic marks, population as regards affluence, etc.). **8** The roman numeral for 500. [Understood to be half of CIƆ, earlier form of M = 1,000.] **9** *Chem.* Orig. italic *d*, now only as a small capital D: applied to (a compound having) a configuration about an asymmetric carbon atom analogous to that of an arbitrarily chosen compound (now D-glyceraldehyde for organic compounds). Also, as D(+), D(−), further denoting respectively dextro- or laevorotation of polarized light by the compound. [Extended use of *d* = dextrorotatory.] **10** *D-layer*, the lowest stratum of the ionosphere.

III 11 Abbrevs.: (A small selection only is given here. Those all in caps. or small caps. also occur with a full stop after each letter; some of those all in caps. also occur (i) with initial cap. only, (ii) in small caps.) **D.** = (*US*) Democrat; Distinguished (in decorations); Doctor (in academic degrees). **D** = defence (in *D-notice*, an official request to British news editors not to publish items on specified subjects, for reasons of security); (*Chem.*) deuterium; dimension, dimensional, (esp. in *3-D*, three-dimensions, -dimensional). **d.** = (*colloq.*) damn (adj. & adv.), damned; daughter; day; (*colloq.*) decent (esp. in *jolly d.*); delete; departs; depth; deputy; died; (in former British currency) [L] *denarius, -rii* penny, pence. **d** = (as *pref.*) deci-; (*Chem.*) (as *pref.*) dextrorotatory (cf. sense 9 above); (*Physics & Chem.*) diffuse: orig. designating one of the four main series (S, P, D, F) of lines in atomic spectra, now more frequently applied to electronic orbitals, states, etc., possessing two units of angular momentum (as *d-electron, d-orbital*, etc.); (*Particle Physics*) a quark flavour associated with a charge of −⅓ (cf. DOWN *a.* 5). **DA** = deposit account; (*US*) District Attorney. **D/A** = (*Computing*) digital to analogue. **d.a.** = duck's arse (haircut: see DUCK *n.*[1]). **da** = (as *pref.*) deca-. **Dak.** = Dakota. **Dan.** = Daniel (in the Bible). **d. and c.** (*Med.*) = dilatation and curettage. **DAT** = digital audio tape. **dB** = decibel(s). **DBE** = Dame Commander (of the Order) of the British Empire. **DBS** = direct-broadcast satellite, direct broadcasting by satellite. **DC** = (*Mus.*) da capo; direct current (*AC/DC*: see A, A); District Commissioner; District of Columbia. **DCB** = Dame Commander (of the Order) of the Bath. **DCC** = digital compact cassette. **DCL** = Doctor of Civil Law. **DCM** = Distinguished Conduct Medal. **DCMG** = Dame Commander (of the Order) of St Michael and St George. **DCVO** = Dame Commander of the Royal Victorian Order. **DD** = Doctor of Divinity. **DDR** = [G] *Deutsche Demokratische Republik* German Democratic Republic. **DDT** = *d*ichloro*d*iphenyl*t*richloroethane, a chlorinated hydrocarbon ($CCl_3CH(C_6H_4Cl)_2$) widely employed as an insecticide. **DE** = Delaware. **Dec.** = December. **dec.** = deceased; (*Cricket*) declared. **deg.** = degree(s). **Del.** = Delaware. **Dem.** (*US*) = Democrat. **dep.** = departs; deputy. **Dept.** = Department. **DES** = Department of Education and Science. **Deut.** = Deuteronomy (in the Bible). **DEW** = distant early warning. **DF** = [L] *Defensor Fidei* Defender of the Faith; direction-finder, -finding. **DFC** = Distinguished Flying Cross. **DFM** = Distinguished Flying Medal. **DG** = [L] *Dei gratia* by the grace of God; *Deo gratias* thanks to God; director-general. **DHSS** (*Hist.*) = Department of Health and Social Security. **DI** = Defence Intelligence. **dia.** = diameter. **dim.** = diminuendo. **DIN** /*freq.* dɪn/ = [G] *Deutsche Industrie-Norm* German industrial standard. **Dip.** = Diploma. **Dip. Ed.** /*freq.* dɪp 'ɛd/ = Diploma in Education. **Dip. H.E.** = Diploma of Higher Education. **Dip. Tech.** /*freq.* dɪp 'tɛk/ = Diploma in Technology. **Div.** = Division. **DIY** = do-it-yourself. **DJ** = dinner jacket; disc jockey. **D.Litt.** = [L] *Doctor Litterarum* Doctor of Letters. **DL** = Deputy Lieutenant. **dl** = decilitre(s). **DM, D-mark** = Deutschmark. **dm** = decimetre(s). **D.Mus.** = Doctor of Music. **DMZ** = demilitarized zone. **DNB** = Dictionary of National Biography. **do.** = ditto. **DOA** = dead on arrival (at hospital etc.). **DOD** = (*US*) Department of Defense. **DOE** = Department of the Environment. **DOH** = Department of Health. **dol.** = dollar(s). **DORA** /'dɔːrə/ (*Hist.*) = Defence of the Realm Act, an act providing the British Government with wide powers during the war of 1914–18. **doz.** = dozen. **DP** = data processing; displaced person. **D.Phil.** = Doctor of Philosophy. **DPP** = Director of Public Prosecutions. **Dr** = Doctor. **Dr.** = Drive (in addresses). **dr.** = drachm(s); drachma(s); dram(s). **DRAM** /'diːram/ *Computing* = dynamic random access memory. **DS** = dal segno; disseminated sclerosis. **DSC** = Distinguished Service Cross. **D.Sc.** = Doctor of Science. **DSIR** (chiefly *Hist.*) = Department of Scientific and Industrial Research. **DSM** = Distinguished Service Medal. **DSO** = (Companion of the) Distinguished Service Order. **DSS** = Department of Social Security. **DT** = delirium tremens. **DTI** = Department of Trade and Industry. **DTs** /diː'tiːz/ = delirium tremens. *DUKW*: see DUCK *n.*[4] **DV** = [L] *Deo volente* God willing. **d.w.t.** = dead weight tonnage. **dwt.** [L *denarius* penny] = pennyweight. **Dy** (*Chem.*) = dysprosium. **dyn** = dyne(s).

'd *v.* see HAVE *v.*, SHALL *v.*, WILL *v.*[1]

-d, -'d *suffs.* see -ED[1], -ED[2].

da /dɑː/ *n. nursery* & *dial.* M19. [Abbrev. of DADA *n.*[1]] Father. Cf. DAD *n.*[1], DADA *n.*[1]

dab /dab/ *n.*[1] ME. [f. the vb.] **I 1** A slight or undecided blow; a tap, a peck, a jab; *fig.* a slight or casual effort. ME. **2** A gentle blow or tap with a soft substance; a brief application of a sponge, handkerchief, etc., to a surface without rubbing. M18. **3** A blob of some soft or moist substance dabbed or dropped on something; a small amount, a smear. M18. **b** In *pl.* Fingerprints. *slang.* E20.

1 SMOLLETT Giving us several dabs with its beak. DICKENS Making two dabs at him in the air with her needle. **3** WILL ROGERS I had . . half way decided to get a little dab of some kind of stock. E. WAUGH The clownish dabs of rouge high on the cheekbones. B. PYM Purple jelly with a dab of synthetic cream.

II 4 A wet or dirty cloth or garment. *obs.* exc. *dial.* E18. **5** An unfortunate or unkempt person; a small child. *obs.* exc. *dial.* M18.

dab /dab/ *n.*[2] LME. [Origin unkn.] Any of several small coastal flatfishes of the family Pleuronectidae; spec. *Limanda limanda*, common in British waters. Also, the flesh of these as food.

dab /dab/ *n.*[3] *colloq.* L17. [Origin unkn.] An expert, one who is skilful or adept (*at*, occas. *in*). Also *dab hand*.

dab /dab/ *v.* Infl. **-bb-**. ME. [Imit. Cf. DABBLE, DIB *v.*] **1** *v.t.* Strike lightly or undecidedly, hit feebly, pat, peck. ME. **2** *v.t.* Press briefly with a cloth, sponge, etc., without rubbing; apply (a substance) in this manner. Also, daub, plaster. L16. **3** *v.t.* Put down roughly or carelessly. Now *dial.* L18. **4** *v.i.* Aim a light or hesitant blow *at*; press gently *at*. Orig. *Sc.* E19.

2 J. TYNDALL I dip my brush . . . and dab it against the paper. V. WOOLF She walked about the room, dabbing her wet cheeks with a towel. L. LEE The porridge was dabbed on our plates from a . . spoon. **4** OED If you go near the nest, the hen will dab at you. F. TUOHY Mrs. Peverill drank some tea and dabbed at her mouth with a handkerchief.

dabber *n.* a person who or thing which dabs; *spec.* a rounded pad used by printers etc. to apply ink, colour, etc., to a surface: L18.

dab /dab/ *adv.* E17. [f. the vb.] With a dab, abruptly; *colloq.* exactly, squarely.

dabble /'dab(ə)l/ *v.* M16. [Du. †*dabbelen*, or f. DAB *v.* + -LE[3].] **1** *v.t.* Moisten or soil by sprinkling, splashing, or dipping into water or other liquid; move, splash (the hands, feet, etc.) in water etc. M16. **2** *v.i.* Move the feet, hands, bill, etc., in shallow water; paddle. E17. **3** *v.i.* Engage *in* or work *at* a pursuit in a desultory manner. E17. **b** Meddle, interfere. *obs.* exc. *dial.* M17.

1 T. TROLLOPE I dabbled a handkerchief in a neighbouring fountain. M. MITCHELL She . . dabbled her burning feet in the cool water. **2** WORDSWORTH Where the duck dabbles 'mid the rustling sedge. **dabbling duck** any of the tribe Anatini of mostly freshwater ducks that habitually feed in shallow water by dabbling or upending, exemplified by the mallard, teal, shoveler, etc. **3** D. L. SAYERS The idle rich gentleman who dabbles in detection.

dabbler *n.* a person who or thing which dabbles; a dilettante: E17.

dabby /'dabi/ *a.* Now *dial.* L16. [f. DAB *n.*[1] + -Y[1].] Damp, moist; (of clothes) wet and clinging.

dabchick /'dabtʃɪk/ *n.* Also (*obs.* exc. *dial.*) **dob-** /'dɒb-/, **dop-** /'dɒp-/, & other vars. M16. [f. *dab-* perh. rel. to 2nd elem. of DIVE-DAP (cogn. w. DEEP *a.*, DIP *v.*, DOP *v.*) + CHICK *n.*[1]] The little grebe, *Tachybaptus ruficollis*; *US* the pied-billed grebe, *Podilymbus podiceps*. Also (*dial.*), the moorhen.

Dabitis /'dabɪtɪs/ *n.* L16. [L = you will give, taken as a mnemonic, A indicating a universal affirmative proposition and I a particular affirmative proposition.] *Logic.* An indirect mood of the first syllogistic figure, in which the major premiss is universal and affirmative and the minor premiss and conclusion are particular and affirmative.

daboia /də'bɔɪə/ *n.* L19. [Hind. *daboyā* lit. 'lurker', f. *dabnā* lurk.] = RUSSELL'S VIPER.

dabster /'dabstə/ *n.* E18. [f. DAB *n.*[3] or *n.*[1] + -STER.] **1** A person skilled at something, an expert. Chiefly *dial.* E18. **2** An incompetent or careless worker, a person who dabbles. L19.

da capo /dɑː 'kɑːpəʊ/ *adv. phr.* E18. [It. = from the beginning.] *Mus.* A direction: repeat from the beginning.

dace /deɪs/ *n.* Also †**darse**. Pl. same. LME. [OFr. *dars* nom. of *dart* dace (= DART *n.*).] For loss of *r* cf. BASS *n.*[1] Cf. DARE *n.*[1]] A European freshwater cyprinoid fish, *Leuciscus leuciscus*; *US* any of several small cyprinoid fishes.

dacha /'datʃə/ *n.* Also **datcha**. M19. [Russ. = grant of land.] In Russia: a small country house or villa.

dachs /daks/ *n. colloq.* Pl. same. L19. [Abbrev.] = next.

dachshund /'dakshʊnd, -s(ə)nd/ *n.* L19. [G = badger-dog.] An animal of a German breed of dog with short legs and a long body, orig. used to hunt badgers.

Dacian /'deɪʃ(ə)n, -sjən/ *n.* & *a.* L16. [f. *Dacia* (see below) + -AN.] **A** *n.* A native or inhabitant of Dacia, an ancient Roman province containing the Carpathian Mountains and Transylvania; the language of this region, a Thracian dialect. L16. **B** *adj.* Of or pertaining to Dacia, its people, or their language. L18.

dacite /'deɪsʌɪt/ *n.* L18. [f. as prec. + -ITE[1].] *Geol.* A volcanic rock resembling andesite but containing free quartz.

dacitic /-'sɪtɪk/ *a.* of the nature of or containing dacite M20.

dacker /'dakə/ *v. Sc.* & *north.* Also **daiker** /'deɪkə/. L16. [Origin unkn.: perh. two wds. In branch II cf. MFlem. *daeckeren.*] **I 1** *v.t.* & *i.* Search, ransack; search for or *for.* L16. **II 2** *v.i.* Waver, totter, stagger; saunter; work irregularly, potter. M17.

dacoit /də'kɔɪt/ *n.* & *v.* L18. [Hind. *ḍakait*, f. *ḍākā* gang-robbery.] **A** *n.* A member of an Indian or Myanmar (Burmese) band of armed robbers. L18. **B** *v.t.* & *i.* Plunder as a dacoit. L19.

dacoity *n.* [Hind. *ḍakaitī*] (an act of) robbery with violence committed by dacoits E19.

Dacron /'dakrɒn, 'deɪ-/ *n.* Also **d-**. M20. [Invented name: cf. NYLON.] (Proprietary name for) polyethylene terephthalate used as a textile fabric.

¶Another proprietary name for this substance is TERYLENE.

dacryo- /'dakrɪəʊ/ *comb. form* of Gk *dakruon* tear: see -O-. Used in *Med.*

dacryoade'nalgia *n.* pain in a lacrimal gland M19. **dacryoade'nitis** *n.* inflammation of a lacrimal gland M19. **dacryocy'stitis** *n.* inflammation of a tear-sac M19.

dacryon /'dakrɪən/ *n.* L19. [Gk *dakruon* tear.] *Anat.* In the cranium, the point of juncture of the lacrimal and frontal bones with the frontal process of the maxilla.

dactyl /'daktɪl/ *n.* LME. [L *dactylus* f. Gk *daktulos* finger, date, dactyl (from its three joints).] **1** *Pros.* A metrical foot consisting of one long syllable followed by two short syllables, or, in English etc., of one stressed syllable followed by two unstressed syllables; a verse composed of or containing such feet. LME. †**2** A date (fruit). LME–M17. **3** A terminal part of a jointed claw, limb, etc.; *rare* a digit. L19.

1 J. GALSWORTHY 'This young Bōsinney' (he made the word a dactyl in opposition to general usage of a short o) 'has got nothing.'

dactylic /dak'tɪlɪk/ *a.* & *n.* L16. [L. *dactylicus* f. Gk *daktulikos*, f. *daktulos*: see prec., -IC.] *Pros.* **A** *adj.* Composed of or containing dactyls; of or pertaining to a dactyl or dactyls. L16.

dactylic hexameter: see HEXAMETER.

B *n.* A dactylic verse or line. Usu. in *pl.* L18.

dactylically *adv.* L19.

dactylio- /dak'tɪlɪəʊ/ *comb. form* of Gk *daktulios* finger-ring: see -O-.

dactyliomancy *n.* divination by means of a finger-ring E17.

dactylo- /'daktɪləʊ/ *comb. form* of Gk *daktulos* finger: see -O-.

dactylogram *n.* a fingerprint E20. **dactylographer** /-'lɒgrəfə/ *n.* (*a*) a person who takes or studies fingerprints; (*b*) *rare* a typist: E20. **dactylology** /-'lɒlədʒi/ *n.* the art of communicating by signs made with the fingers M17. **dactylopodite** /-'lɒpədʌɪt/ *n.* (*Zool.*) the terminal joint of a crustacean limb L19. **dactyloscopy** /-'lɒskəpi/ *n.* the examination of fingerprints E20. **dactylo'zooid** *n.* (*Zool.*) a mouthless cylindrical zooid in some hydrozoans L19.

dad /dad/ *n.*[1] M16. [Perh. imit. of infants' first speech: cf. DADA *n.*[1], DADDY.] **1** Father. *colloq.* M16. **2** Used as a form of address to a man other than one's father. *slang* (esp. *Jazz*). M20.

dad /dad/ *n.*[2] & *int. colloq.* (now chiefly *US*). L17. [Alt.: cf. DOD *n.*[3] & *int.*] God: used in oaths and exclamations.

dad /dad/ *v.* & *n.*[3] *Sc.* & *north.* Also **daud**. L16. [Imit.: cf. DOD *v.*[2]] **A** *v.t.* Infl. **-dd-**. Knock, beat; shake with knocking or beating. L16. **B** *n.* **1** A knock, a thump. E18. **2** A large piece, a lump. L18.

dada /'dadə/ *n.*[1] *colloq.* (*nursery*). L17. [f. as DAD *n.*[1]] = DAD *n.*[1] 1.

Dada /'dɑːdɑː/ *n.*[2] & *a.* Also **d-**. E20. [Fr., title of a review first appearing at Zürich in 1916, lit. 'hobby-horse'.] (Of, pertaining to, or designating) an international movement in art and literature about 1915–20, which repudiated conventions and reason and intended to shock.

Dadaism *n.* the theory or practice of Dada E20. **Dadaist** *n.* & *a.* (*a*) *n.* an adherent or practitioner of Dada; (*b*) *adj.* of or pertaining to Dadaism or Dadaists: E20.

†**da-da** *int. nursery* & *colloq.* L17–M18. [Origin unkn.: cf. TA-TA.] Goodbye.

dadder /'dadə/ *v.i.* Long *obs.* exc. *dial.* LME. [f. obscure 1st elem. + -ER[5]. Cf. DADE, DODDER *v.*, DIDDER *v.*, DITHER *v.*] Quake, tremble.

daddle /'dad(ə)l/ *n. dial.* L18. [Origin unkn.] The hand, the fist.

daddle /'dad(ə)l/ *v.i. dial.* Also (*Sc.* & *north.*) **daidle** /'deɪd(ə)l/. L18. [f. 1st elem. of DADDER + -LE[3]. Cf. DAWDLE *v.*, DODDLE *v.*] Walk unsteadily, like a small child; dawdle.

daddy /'dadi/ *n.* E16. [f. as DAD *n.*[1] + -Y[6]. Cf. also DADA *n.*[1]] **1** Father. *colloq.* E16. **2** A man; a man in charge; (*US*, chiefly *Jazz*) a husband, a woman's lover. Also *daddy-o*. Chiefly *voc. slang.* M19. **3** The doyen *of*; a superlative example *of. colloq.* E20.

2 B. BEHAN He was the daddy of the wing and what he claimed was his. *sugar daddy*: see SUGAR *n.* 3 M. FRANKLIN I never felt such a daddy of a thirst on me before.

Comb.: **daddy-long-legs** *colloq.* (*a*) a crane-fly; (*b*) (chiefly *US*) a long-legged spider, a harvestman.

dade /deɪd/ *v.t.* Long *obs.* exc. *dial.* L16. [1st elem. of DADDER.] Lead and support (a person who totters, esp. a child learning to walk).

dado /'deɪdəʊ/ *n.* Pl. **-os**. M17. [It. = die, cube, f. L. *datum*: see DIE *n.*[1]] *Archit.* **1** The plain portion of a pedestal between the base and the cornice. Cf. DIE *n.*[1] 3. M17. **2** The lower part of an interior wall when faced or coloured differently from the upper part. L18.

Comb.: **dado-rail** a moulding round the wall of a room to protect it from damage by furniture pushed against it.

dae *v.* see DO *v.*

daedal /'diːd(ə)l/ *n. rare.* Also **ded-**. M17. [L *Daedalus*: see DAEDALIAN.] **1** A skilful or ingenious artificer like Daedalus. M17. **2** A maze, a labyrinth. L17.

daedal /'diːd(ə)l/ *a. literary.* Also **ded-**. L16. [L *daedalus* f. Gk *daidalos* skilful, variegated.] **1** Skilful, inventive, ingenious. L16. **2** Of the earth etc.: rich in natural wonders; variously adorned. L16. **3** Complex, intricate; like a maze. M17.

Daedalian /dɪ'deɪlɪən/ *a.* Also **Ded-**, **-ean**. L16. [Sense 1 f. as prec.; sense 2 f. L *Daedaleus*, Gk *daidaleos*, f. *Daedalus* (Gk *Daidalos*), legendary builder of the Cretan labyrinth, and maker of wings for himself and Icarus: see -IAN, -EAN.] †**1** = DAEDAL *a.* 2. Only in L16. **2** In the manner of Daedalus; ingenious, intricate, labyrinthine. E17.

Daedalic /'diːdəlɪk/ *a.* Also **Ded-**. M20. [f. as prec. + -IC.] *Archaeol.* Designating or pertaining to a Greek (chiefly Dorian) sculptural style of the 7th cent. BC.

daemon *n.*, **daemonic** *a.*, **daemonism** *n.*, etc., see DEMON *n.*[1] etc.

dafadar /dʌfə'dɑː/ *n. obs.* exc. *Hist.* Also **duff-**. E19. [Pers. & Urdu *dafʿadār.*] A non-commissioned officer in the British Indian army or police.

daff /daf/ *n.*[1] Now *north.* ME. [Origin uncertain: cf. DAFT.] A person deficient in sense or spirit; a simpleton; a coward.

daff /daf/ *n.*[2] *colloq.* E20. [Abbrev.] = DAFFODIL 2.

daff /daf/ *v.*[1] M16. [f. DAFF *n.*[1]] **1** *v.i.* Play the fool. Chiefly *Sc.* M16. **2** *v.t.* Daunt. *north.* L17.

daff /dɑːf/ *v.*[2]*t. arch.* L16. [Var. of DOFF.] †**1** Put off (as clothes); divest oneself of. *rare* (Shakes.). L16–E17. **2** Put or turn aside; waive. L16. †**b** Put off (with an excuse etc.). *rare* (Shakes.) Only in E17.

2 SHAKES. *1 Hen. IV* The . . Prince of Wales, And his comrades that daff'd the world aside And bid it pass.

daffadowndilly /dafədaʊn'dɪli/ *n.* Chiefly *dial.* & *joc.* L16. [Playful extension of DAFFODIL: cf. DAFFODILLY.] = DAFFODIL 2.

daffle /'daf(ə)l/ *v.i. dial.* & *colloq.* L18. [f. DAFF *v.*[1] + -LE[3].] Become silly; act stupidly; falter.

daffodil /'dafədɪl/ *n.* M16. [Alt. of AFFODILL. The initial *d* is unexpl.] †**1** = ASPHODEL. M16–E17. **2** A narcissus, *esp.* one with yellow flowers; *spec.* a western European plant, *Narcissus pseudonarcissus*, native in woods etc. and widely cultivated, having a bright yellow corona as long as the perianth segments (cf. NARCISSUS 1); a flower or flowering stem of such a plant, esp. as the Welsh national emblem. M16. **3** The colour of the daffodil; (bright) yellow. Freq. *attrib.* M19.

daffodilly *n.* (*dial.* & *poet.*) = DAFFODIL 1, 2 M16.

Daffy /'dafi/ *n.*[1] *arch.* Also **d-**. L17. [Thomas *Daffy* (d. 1680), Eng. clergyman.] In full *Daffy's elixir*. Orig., a medicine given to infants to which gin was commonly added. Later (*slang*), gin itself.

daffy /'dafi/ *n.*[2] *colloq.* (orig. *dial.*). L18. [Abbrev. of DAFFODILLY.] = DAFFODIL 2.

daffy /'dafi/ *a. dial.* & *slang.* L19. [f. DAFF *n.*[1] or *v.*[1] + -Y[1].] = next.

daft /dɑːft/ *a.* See also DEFT. [OE *gedæfte* f. Gmc, f. stem also of Goth. *gadaban* become, be fitting.] †**1** Mild, meek, humble. OE–ME. **2** Silly; lacking in intelligence; stupid; reckless, wild. ME. **3** Of unsound mind; crazy. LME. **4** Madly frolicsome; giddy. *Sc.* L16.

2 D. LODGE This was not . . quite such a daft development as it seems on first consideration. *daft as a brush*: see BRUSH *n.*[2] 3. 3 T. ARNOLD I hope you will not think I ought to . . adjourn to the next asylum for daft people. 4 SIR W. SCOTT Ay, ay—they were daft days thae—but they were a' vanity and waur.

daftie *n.* (*colloq.*) a daft person L19. **daftly** *adv.* E18. **daftness** *n.* M16.

dag /dag/ *n.*[1] LME. [Origin unkn.: cf. TAG *n.*[1]] †**1** A pendent pointed portion of something; a pointed ornamental division made in the lower edge of a garment. LME–E17. †**2** = AGLET *n.* 1, 2. LME–E17. **3** In full *dag-lock*. A lock of wool clotted with dung about the hind legs of a sheep. Usu. in *pl.* Now chiefly *Austral.* & *NZ.* E17. **4** An extraordinary person; a character; a tough but amusing person. *Austral.* & *NZ slang.* E20.

3 **rattle one's dags** *Austral.* & *NZ slang* hurry up.

Comb.: **dag-boy** etc.: employed to remove dags from wool or sheep; *dag-lock*: see sense 3 above.

daggy *a.* (chiefly *Austral.* & *NZ*) (of a sheep or wool) clotted with dags E20.

dag /dag/ *n.*[2] LME. [(O)Fr. *dague* lit. 'long dagger', f. Prov. or It. *daga.*] **1** A metal pin, bolt, etc.; a pointed implement. LME. **2** The simple straight pointed horn of a young stag. M19.

dag /dag/ *n.*[3] Orig. *Sc. obs.* exc. *Hist.* M16. [Gael., of unkn. origin.] A kind of heavy pistol or handgun.

dag /dag/ *v.*[1] Infl. **-gg-**. LME. [Rel. to or f. DAG *n.*[1]] **1** *v.t.* Cut the edge of (a garment) into jags; slash. Long *rare.* LME. **2** *v.t.* Clog with dirt; bemire. Now *dial.* L15. **b** *v.i.* Trail in the dirt or wet. *dial.* M19. **3** *v.t.* Cut the dags from (sheep). Chiefly *Austral.* & *NZ.* E18.

†**dag** *v.*²*t.* Infl. **-gg-**. LME–E19. [Rel. to (O)Fr *dague* DAG *n.*²] Pierce or stab (as) with a pointed weapon.

dageraad /ˈdagərɑːd/ *n. S. Afr.* Also **daggerhead** /ˈdagəhɛd/. M19. [Afk. f. Du. = daybreak (from its colour).] A brilliantly coloured marine fish, *Chrysoblephus cristiceps*, of the family Sparidae.

dagesh /ˈdɑːgɛʃ/ *n.* & *v.* M16. [Heb. *dāgēš*.] *Heb. Gram.* A *n.* A point or dot placed within a Hebrew letter, denoting either that it is doubled or that it is not aspirated. M16. B *v.t.* Mark with a dagesh. M18.

Dagestan /dɑːgəˈstɑːn/ *n.* Also **-gh-**. E20. [A district of the eastern Caucasus.] In full *Dagestan rug*. A rug with a geometric design, handwoven in Dagestan.

dagga /ˈdagə/ *n.*¹ *S. Afr.* L17. [Afk. f. Nama *daχa*.] Indian hemp, *Cannabis sativa* subsp. *indica*, used as a narcotic; any indigenous plant of the genus *Leonotis* which is similarly used.

dagga /ˈdɑːgə/ *n.*² *S. Afr.* L19. [Zulu, Xhosa *udaka* mud, clay, mortar.] A kind of mortar made of mud and cow-dung, often combined with ox-blood.

dagger /ˈdagə/ *n.*¹ & *v.* LME. [Perh. f. DAG *v.*² + -ER¹, infl. by (O)Fr. *dague* (see DAG *n.*³).] A *n.* 1 A short stabbing-weapon with a pointed and edged blade. LME. b Something that wounds grievously. L16. 2 Chiefly *Naut.* A piece of wood standing upright or aslant. Also = *dog-shore* s.v. DOG *n.* M17. 3 *Typogr.* A mark resembling a dagger (†); an obelisk. E18. 4 Any of a number of noctuid moths chiefly of the genus *Apatele* with a dark marking in the shape of a dagger on the forewings. M19.

Phrases: **at daggers drawn** on the point of fighting, in bitter enmity, (*with*). **double dagger** a mark like a dagger but with a second crosspiece near the foot (‡). **look daggers** stare angrily (*at* a person). *Spanish dagger*: see SPANISH *a.* †**speak daggers** speak angrily or woundingly. *wooden dagger*: see WOODEN *a.*

Comb.: **dagger-board** *Naut.* a sliding centreboard; **dagger plant** a yucca, *Y. aloifolia*, having sharp-edged and pointed leaves;

B *v.t.* Stab with a dagger. M16.

daggered *a.* armed with a dagger LME.

dagger /ˈdagə/ *n.*² *Austral.* & *NZ.* L19. [f. DAG *n.*¹ + -ER¹.] 1 A person who removes dags from wool. L19. 2 In *pl.* Hand-shears. L19.

daggerhead *n.* var. of DAGERAAD.

daggett /ˈdagɪt/ *n.* M19. [Russ. *dëgot'* tar.] A dark oil obtained by distilling birch-bark, used in the preparation of Russia leather.

daggle /ˈdag(ə)l/ *v.* Now chiefly *dial.* M16. [Frequent. of DAG *v.*¹: see -LE³.] 1 *v.t.* Orig., clog with wet mud; wet and soil (a garment etc.) by trailing through mud etc. Later, wet by splashing etc. M16. 2 *v.t.* & *i.* Drag or trail about (through mud etc.). L17.

Comb.: **daggle-tail** *n.* = DRAGGLE-TAIL *n.*; **daggle-tailed** *a.* = DRAGGLE-TAILED.

daggly *a.* (esp. of weather) wet L18.

Daghestan *n.* var. of DAGESTAN.

dago /ˈdeɪgəʊ/ *n. slang* (*derog.* & usu. considered *racially offensive*). Orig. *US.* Pl. **-o(e)s**. M19. [Alt. of Sp. DIEGO.] 1 A Spaniard; a Portuguese; an Italian; any foreigner. M19. 2 The Spanish language; the Italian language. E20.

Comb.: **dago red** *US* cheap red wine, esp. from Italy.

dagoba /ˈdɑːgəʊbə/ *n.* E19. [Sinhalese *dāgaba* f. Pali *dhātu-gabbha* receptacle for relics.] A stupa or dome-shaped structure containing Buddhist relics.

Dagon /ˈdeɪgɒn/ *n.* LME. [L f. Gk *Dagōn* f. Heb. *dāgōn*, perh. f. *dāgān* corn, but derived by folk etym. f. *dāg* fish.] The national god of the ancient Philistines, prob. a corn-god, but later represented with the head, chest, and arms of a man, and the tail of a fish.

Daguerrean /dəˈgɛrɪən/ *a.* Also **-eian**. M19. [f. *Daguerre* (see next) + -AN.] Pertaining to Daguerre or the daguerreotype. Also (now *rare* or *obs.*), photographic.

daguerreotype /dəˈgɛrə(ʊ)tʌɪp/ *n.* & *v.* Also **-rro-**. M19. [Fr. *daguerréotype*, f. Louis-Jacques-Mandé *Daguerre* (1789–1851), the inventor: see -O-, -TYPE.] A *n.* (A photograph taken by) an early photographic process using an iodine-sensitized silver(ed) plate and mercury vapour. M19. B *v.t.* Photograph by the daguerreotype process. M19.

Dagwood /ˈdagwʊd/ *n. N. Amer.* L20. [*Dagwood* Bumstead, comic-strip character who makes and eats such sandwiches.] In full *Dagwood sandwich*. A thick sandwich filled with mixed meats and cheeses with a variety of seasonings and dressings.

dah /dɑː/ *n.*¹ Also **dao** /daʊ/. M19. [Burm.] A short heavy sword, used also as a knife, esp. in Myanmar (Burma).

dah /dɑː/ *n.*² M20. [Imit.] = DASH *n.*¹ 2c.

dahabeeyah /dɑːhəˈbiːjə/ *n.* Also **-biah**. M19. [Arab. *ḏahabīya* = golden (*sc.* boat), orig. the gilded state barge of the Muslim rulers of Egypt.] A large sailing boat, used on the Nile.

dahlia /ˈdeɪlɪə/ *n.* E19. [f. Andreas *Dahl* (1751–89), Swed. botanist + -IA¹.] 1 Any of various Central American plants of the genus *Dahlia*, of the composite family, many of which (esp. *D. pinnata*) are cultivated for their many-coloured single or double flowers. E19. 2 A shade of red. M19.

1 *blue dahlia*: see BLUE *a.*

Dahoman /dəˈhəʊmən/ *n.* & *a.* Also **-mean** /-mɪən/. L18. [f. *Dahomey* (see below) or the tribal name *Dahomeh* + -AN.] *Hist.* A *n.* A member of the people of the former W. African kingdom of Dahomey, or of the modern State of Dahomey (now called Benin), occupying much of the former territory. L18. B *adj.* Of or pertaining to Dahomey, its people, or their language. L18.

dai /dʌɪ, ˈdɑːi/ *n.* L18. [Urdu *dāī*, f. Pers. *dāyah*.] In the Indian subcontinent and Iran: a nurse; a wet-nurse; a midwife.

daidle *v.* see DADDLE *v.*

daiker *n.* var. of DAKER.

Dáil /dɔɪl/ *n.* E20. [Ir. *Dáil* (*Éireann*) assembly (of Ireland).] In full *Dáil Éireann* /ˈɛːr(ə)n/. The lower house of the Parliament of the Republic of Ireland.

daily /ˈdeɪli/ *a.* & *n.* LME. [f. DAY *n.* + -LY¹: cf. OE *-dæġlić*.] A *adj.* Of or belonging to each day; produced, occurring, or working on every day or weekday. LME.

daily bread: see BREAD *n.*¹ *daily dozen*: see DOZEN *n.* 1.

B *n.* 1 A daily newspaper. M19. 2 Daily bread; food; livelihood. *rare.* E20. 3 A domestic cleaner or charwoman who comes in daily. M20. 4 In *pl.* The first prints from cinematographic takes, made rapidly for film producers or editors; the rushes. M20.

dailiness *n.* daily quality or occurrence; humdrum routine: L16.

daily /ˈdeɪli/ *adv.* LME. [f. DAY *n.* + -LY².] Every day or weekday; day-by-day; constantly.

J. BUCHAN I was daily growing narrower in my outlook on the present.

daimio *n.* var. of DAIMYO.

daimon /ˈdʌɪməʊn/ *n.* M19. [Gk *daimōn*: see DEMON *n.*¹] An attendant or indwelling spirit, one's genius, = DEMON *n.*¹ 2.

daimonic /-ˈməʊnɪk, -ˈmɒnɪk/ *a.* E20.

daimyo /ˈdʌɪmɪəʊ, -mjəʊ/ *n.* Also **-io**. Pl. **-os**. E18. [Jap., f. *dai* great + *myō* name.] In feudal Japan, any of the chief land-owning nobles, vassals of the shogun.

†**daint** *a.* & *n.* L16–M17. [Abbrev.] = DAINTY *a.*, *n.*

†**daintly** *adv.* M–L16.

dainteth /ˈdeɪntɪθ/ *n.* Long *obs.* exc. *Sc.* Now *rare.* Also **-ith**. ME. [OFr. *deintiet* older form of *deintié* DAINTY *n.*] = DAINTY *n.*

daintify /ˈdeɪntɪfʌɪ/ *v.t.* L18. [f. DAINTY *a.* + -FY.] Make dainty.

daintihood /ˈdeɪntɪhʊd/ *n. rare.* L18. [f. DAINTY *a.* + -HOOD.] Daintiness.

daintily /ˈdeɪntɪli/ *adv.* ME. [f. DAINTY *a.* + -LY².] †1 Excellently; finely; handsomely; delightfully. ME–M17. 2 In a dainty manner; delicately; nicely; elegantly; deftly. LME. †3 Rarely; sparingly. L15–L16.

2 SHAKES. *Tit. A.* Why, there they are, both baked in this pie, Whereof their mother daintily hath fed. J. L. WATEN Our piebald mare . . trotted easily and daintily.

daintiness /ˈdeɪntɪnɪs/ *n.* M16. [f. DAINTY *a.* + -NESS.] 1 The quality of being fine, handsome, delightful etc. Now only of food: choiceness. M16. 2 Niceness; fastidiousness; delicacy. M16. 3 Elegance; neatness; deftness. L16.

daintith *n.* var. of DAINTETH.

dainty /ˈdeɪnti/ *n.* ME. [AN *dainté*, OFr. *daintié*, *deintié* f. L *dignitas* worthiness, worth, beauty, f. *dignus* worthy: see -TY¹.] I†1 Estimation, regard; affection. ME–E16. †2 Choice quality, sumptuousness. Only in ME. †3 Liking *to do* or *see* something; delight. ME–E16. †4 Fastidiousness. Only in L16. II 5 Something estimable, choice, or pleasing, *esp.* something pleasing to the palate, a delicacy. ME.

dainty /ˈdeɪnti/ *a.* & *adv.* ME. [f. prec.] A *adj.* 1 Handsome; choice; delightful. Now chiefly *dial.* ME. 2 Pleasing to the palate. LME. 3 (Now the predominant sense.) Of delicate beauty; small and graceful. LME. †4 Precious; rare; scarce. LME–L17. 5 Of a person: having delicate tastes or sensitivities; fastidious, particular; (over)nice. M16.

1 CHAUCER Full many a deynte hors hadde he in stable. 2 MILTON The daintiest dishes shall be serv'd up last. 5 SHAKES. *Macb.* And let us not be dainty of leave-taking, But shift away. R. L. STEVENSON I was surprised to find them so dainty in their notions.

B *adv.* Daintily. *rare.* E17.

daiquiri /ˈdʌɪkɪri, ˈdak-/ *n.* E20. [*Daiquiri*, a rum-producing district in Cuba.] A cocktail containing rum and lime-juice.

dairi /ˈdʌɪri/ *n. arch.* E17. [Jap. = (palace of the) emperor, f. *dai* inside + *ri* within.] The emperor of Japan.

dairy /ˈdɛːri/ *n.* & *v.* ME. [f. DEY *n.*¹ + -ERY, -RY.] A *n.* 1 A room or building for keeping milk and cream and making butter, cheese, etc.; a shop for milk etc.; a company that distributes milk etc.; *NZ* a local shop selling groceries (including milk) and other goods. ME. 2 A dairy farm; that department of a farm or farming which is concerned with the production of milk etc. ME.

Comb.: **dairy cattle, cow**, etc.: kept for milk production; **dairy cream** real cream made from milk; **dairy factory** (chiefly *NZ*): for making butter and cheese; **dairy farm, farming**: concerned largely with the keeping of cows for milk production; **dairy-free** *a.* containing no milk product; **dairymaid** a woman employed in a dairy; **dairyman** (*a*) a man employed in a dairy or in dairy farming; (*b*) a man who deals in dairy products; **dairy products** milk and its derivatives (cream, butter, cheese, etc.).

B *v.* 1 *v.i.* Keep a dairy farm; produce milk and dairy products. Chiefly as *dairying* vbl n. M17. 2 *v.t.* Keep or feed (cows) for milk. *rare.* L18.

dais /ˈdeɪɪs, deɪs/ *n.* Also (*Sc.*) **deas** /*also* diːs/. ME. [OFr. *deis* (mod. *dais*) f. med.L DISCUS table.] †1 A raised table in a hall, at which distinguished persons sat at feasts etc.; the high table. ME–L16. 2 The raised platform in a hall etc. for the high table, seats of honour, throne, etc. ME. b *gen.* A raised platform. M19. 3 A seat; a bench; a settle. *Sc.* & *north.* ME.

2 *chamber of dais*: see CHAMBER *n.* 1.

¶In sense 2 largely obs. for several centuries until revived by historical and antiquarian writers *c*1800, with the disyllabic spelling-pronunciation.

daisy /ˈdeɪzi/ *n.*, *a.*, & *v.* [OE *dæġes ēaġe* day's eye, the disc of the flower being revealed in the morning.] A *n.* 1 A small European wild and garden plant of the composite family, *Bellis perennis*, with a flower of yellow disc and white rays (also *common daisy*). Also, a flower-head or flowering stem of this plant; a flower-head resembling that of the daisy. OE. 2 (A flowering stem of) any of various similar plants. Usu. w. specifying wd. LME. 3 A first-rate person or thing. (Earlier as sense B.2.) *US slang.* M19.

1 *fresh as a daisy*: see FRESH *a.* **pushing up the daisies** *slang* dead and buried. 2 *African daisy*, *Michaelmas daisy*, *moon-daisy*, *ox-eye daisy*, *Shasta daisy*, etc.

Comb.: **daisy-bush** a shrub of the Australasian genus *Olearia*, of the composite family; **daisy-chain** *n.* & *v.* (*a*) *n.* a string of daisies with the stems threaded together; *fig.* a linked series of persons or things; (*b*) *v.i.* & *t.* form into a linked series; **daisy-cutter** (*a*) a horse that steps low in trotting; (*b*) (*Cricket* etc.) a bowled ball that travels low along the ground (cf. CREEPER 5); **daisy roots** *rhyming slang* boots; **daisy tree** = *daisy bush* above; **daisy wheel** a circular element in some electric printers, typewriters, etc., which carries the type on radiating spokes.

B *attrib.* or as *adj.* 1 Resembling a daisy. E17. 2 First-rate, excellent. *slang* (chiefly *US*). M18.

2 E. WALLACE I'll introduce you to the daisiest night club in town.

C *v.t.* Cover or adorn with daisies. Chiefly as *daisied* ppl a. E17.

daisy-like *a.* resembling (that of) a daisy L19.

dak /dɑːk, dɔːk/ *n.* Also **dawk**. E18. [Hind. *ḍāk*.] In the Indian subcontinent: orig., post or transport by relays; now, postal service, delivery of letters, mail.

Comb.: **dak-bungalow** a travellers' resting-house, orig. one on a dak route.

daker /ˈdeɪkə/ *n.* Also **daiker**. LME. [OFr. *dacre*, *dakere*, med.L *dacra* var. of *dicra*: see DICKER *n.*[1]] *Hist.* = DICKER *n.*[1] 1.

daker-hen /ˈdeɪkəhɛn/ *n. dial.* M16. [Origin unkn.] The corncrake.

dakhma /ˈdɑːkmə/ *n.* M19. [Pers.] = *tower of silence* s.v. TOWER *n.*[1]

Dakin /ˈdeɪkɪn/ *n.* E20. [H. D. *Dakin* (1880–1952), Brit. chemist.] Med. *Dakin's fluid, solution*, an antiseptic solution of sodium hypochlorite.

Dakota /dəˈkəʊtə/ *n.* & *a.* E19. [Dakota *Dakhóta*, lit. 'allies'.] A *n.* Pl. **-s**, same. 1 A member of a N. American Indian people inhabiting the upper Mississippi and Missouri river valleys. Also called *Sioux*. E19. 2 The Siouan language of this people. M19. B *attrib.* or as *adj.* Of or pertaining to the Dakota or their language. E19.

Dakotan /dəˈkəʊt(ə)n/ *n.* & *a.* L19. [f. *Dakota* (see below) f. as prec.: see -AN.] (A native or inhabitant) of the former US territory of Dakota or the States of North and South Dakota into which it is now organized.

dal *n.* var. of DHAL.

Dalai Lama /dalʌɪ ˈlɑːmə/ *n. phr.* L17. [Mongolian *dalai* ocean + LAMA *n.*] The chief lama of the dominant Tibetan Buddhist order, widely regarded as the spiritual leader of the Tibetan people.

dalasi /dɑːˈlɑːsiː/ *n.* Pl. same, **-s**. L20. [Name of a previous local coin.] The basic monetary unit of The Gambia, equal to 100 butut.

Dalcroze /dalˈkrəʊz/ *a.* & *n.* E20. [Émile Jaques-*Dalcroze* (1865–1950), Swiss music teacher and composer.] (Designating or pertaining to) eurhythmics as developed by Dalcroze.

dale /deɪl/ *n.*[1] [OE *dæl* corresp. to OFris. *del*, OS (Du.) *dal*, OHG *tal* (G *Tal*), ON *dalr*, Goth. *dal(s)*, f. Gmc.] 1 A valley, esp. in N. England. In literary Eng. chiefly *poet.* OE. †2 A hole in the ground, a hollow. OE–L15.

1 TENNYSON Till over down and over dale All night the shining vapour sail. *dale and down*: see DOWN *n.*[1] 2. *hill and dale*: see HILL *n.*

Comb.: **dales folk, dalesman**, etc.: inhabiting dales in N. England.

dale /deɪl/ *n.*[2] Now *rare* or *obs.* E17. [Prob. f. Fr. *dalle* conduit, tube, etc. f. ON *dæla* bilge-water conduit; cf. LG, Du. *daal* in same sense.] A conduit for carrying off water from a (ship's) pump.

dale *n.*[3] see DOLE *n.*[1]

Dalecarlian /dɑːlɪˈkɑːlɪən/ *n.* & *a.* M19. [f. *Dalecarlia* (see below) + -AN.] (A native or inhabitant) of Dalecarlia (now more usually called Dalarna), a province of central Sweden.

dalek /ˈdɑːlɛk/ *n.* M20. [Invented wd.] An alien machine-organism appearing in the BBC television science-fiction series *Dr Who*; *gen.* a ruthless automaton, a robot.

Daliesque /dɑːlɪˈɛsk/ *a.* M20. [f. *Dali* (see below) + -ESQUE.] Resembling or characteristic of the work of the Spanish painter Salvador Dali (1904–89), esp. in the use of partly abstract improbable juxtapositions; surrealistic.

†**Dalilah** *n.* var. of DELILAH.

dalle /dal/ *n.* Pl. pronounced same. E18. [Fr. f. LDu., rel. to DEAL *n.*[2]] A flat slab of stone, marble, or terracotta, used for flooring, esp. of an ornamental kind.

dallage /dalaːʒ/ *n.* flooring with *dalles* M19.

dalles /dalz/ *n.pl. US.* L18. [Fr., pl. of *dalle* conduit, tube, etc. Cf. DALE *n.*[2]] In the western US, rapids where a river is compressed into long narrow troughlike channels.

dalliance /ˈdalɪəns/ *n.* ME. [f. DALLY *v.* + -ANCE.] †1 Talk, chat; conversation. ME–L15. †2 Waste of time in trifling; idle delay. LME–L16. 3 Amorous toying, (an) idle flirtation. LME. 4 Idle or frivolous action; trifling (*with* a matter). M16.

2 SHAKES. *Com. Err.* My business cannot brook this dalliance. 3 POPE The lewd dalliance of the queen of love. A. FRASER Did their summer dalliance have more serious consequences than either intended? 4 W. H. PRESCOTT He continued to live in idle dalliance.

Dally /ˈdali/ *n.* & *a. NZ colloq.* M20. [Abbrev.] (A) Dalmatian.

dally /ˈdali/ *v.* ME. [OFr. *dalier* to converse, chat (frequent in AN), of unkn. origin.] †1 *v.i.* Talk or converse lightly or idly; chat. Only in ME. 2 *v.i.* Amuse oneself with a person or thing; toy; sport, flirt, trifle, *with*. LME. 3 *v.i.* Idle, linger, delay. M16. †4 *v.t.* Put off or defer by trifling. L16–E19. 5 *v.t.* Fritter *away* (time, opportunity, etc.). L17.

2 V. SACKVILLE-WEST He liked to dally with pretty and sycophantic women. C. CONNOLLY After dallying with the Church, he plunged into the world of letters. 3 V. WOOLF Hugh Whitbread ruminated, dallying there in front of the shop window.

dallier *n.* M16.

Dalmatian /dalˈmeɪʃ(ə)n/ *n.* & *a.* L16. [f. *Dalmatia* (see below) + -AN.] A *n.* 1 A native or inhabitant of Dalmatia, a region on the Adriatic coast of Croatia. L16. 2 A dog of a breed characterized by its short-haired white coat with many dark spots, formerly used as a carriage-dog. E19. 3 A Romance language formerly spoken by natives of Dalmatia. E20.

B *adj.* Of or pertaining to Dalmatia or its inhabitants. E17.

Dalmatian dog = sense A.2 above.

dalmatic /dalˈmatɪk/ *n.* & *a.* Also **D-**. LME. [(O)Fr. *dalmatique* or L *dalmatica* use as n. (sc. *vestis* robe, made of Dalmatian wool) of *Dalmaticus* of Dalmatia: see prec., -IC.] (Designating) a wide-sleeved ecclesiastical vestment with two stripes, worn by deacons and bishops on certain occasions, or a similar robe worn by monarchs and emperors esp. at coronations.

Dalradian /dalˈrɑːdɪən/ *a.* L19. [f. *Dalrad-*, altered form of *Dalriada* an ancient kingdom of Scotland and N. Ireland + -IAN.] *Geol.* Designating or pertaining to a series of metamorphosed sedimentary and volcanic rocks of early Cambrian age found in a belt extending from the west coast of Ireland to the southern highlands of Scotland.

dal segno /dal ˈseɪnjəʊ/ *adv. phr.* L19. [It. = from the sign.] *Mus.* A direction: go back to the point indicated by the sign (not the beginning). Cf. AL SEGNO.

dalt /dɔːlt/ *n. Sc.* Also **dault**. L18. [Gael. *dalta*.] A foster-child.

dalton /ˈdɔːlt(ə)n/ *n.* M20. [John *Dalton* (see next).] *Chem.* = ATOMIC *mass unit*: chiefly used in expressing the molecular weight of proteins.

Daltonian /dɔːlˈtəʊnɪən/ *a.* & *n.* E19. [f. John *Dalton* (1766–1844), Eng. chemist and sufferer from colour-blindness: -IAN.] A *adj.* Relating to Dalton or the atomic theory first enunciated by him. E19. B *n.* A person affected with daltonism (see next). M19.

daltonism /ˈdɔːlt(ə)nɪz(ə)m/ *n.* M19. [Fr. *daltonisme*, f. as prec. + -ISM.] Colour-blindness; *esp.* protanopia.

Dalton plan /ˈdɔːlt(ə)n plan/ *n. phr.* E20. [*Dalton*, Massachusetts, US, location of the first school to use the plan.] A system of education in which pupils are made responsible for the completion of assignments over fairly long periods.

Daltonize *v.t.* manage or arrange by the Dalton plan E20.

dam /dam/ *n.*[1] ME. [(M)LG, (M)Du. = OFris. (also *dom*), MHG *tam* (G *Damm* from LG), from a base repr. also by OE *for)demman*, OFris. *demmen*, Goth. *faur)dammjan* dam up, close up, of unkn. origin.] 1 A barrier constructed to hold back water and raise its level, so as to form a reservoir or prevent flooding. ME. b In full *beaver-dam*. A barrier constructed in a stream by beavers. M17. c A causeway through fens. E19. 2 A body of water confined by a barrier or embankment. Now *local.* ME. 3 An area of flat land from which water has been drained. *local.* E17. 4 A partition or enclosure for excluding or confining fluids. E18. b *spec.* In full *rubber dam*. A rubber sheet used to keep saliva from the teeth during dental operations. Chiefly *N. Amer.* L19.

1 *mill-dam*: see MILL *n.*[1] *water over the dam*: see WATER *n.* 4 *coffer-dam*: see COFFER *n.*

Comb.: **dam-head** *Sc.* a weir on a river for diverting the water into a mill-race.

dam /dam/ *n.*[2] ME. [Alt. of DAME.] †1 = DAME I. Only in ME. 2 A (human) mother. Now *derog.* ME. 3 A female parent (of animals, now usu. quadrupeds). Correl. to *sire*. (Earlier as DAME II). LME.

dam /dam/ *n.*[3] Chiefly *Sc.* L16. [Fr. DAME lady, a piece in draughts (*jeu de dames*).] Each of the pieces in the game of draughts. Now only in *pl.*, the game of draughts.

dam /dɑːm/ *n.*[4] *obs.* exc. *Hist.* L18. [Hind. *dām*.] An Indian copper coin of the value of one-fortieth of a rupee.

dam /dam/ *v.t.* Infl. **-mm-**. LME. [f. DAM *n.*[1], repl. OE compound vb *fordemman*.] Furnish or confine with a dam; block *up*, hold *back*, obstruct, (*lit.* & *fig.*).

W. C. WILLIAMS The complete damming up of all my creative capacities. R. BRAUTIGAN The boards dammed up the creek enough to form a huge bathtub there.

dam(') *a.* & *adv.* var. of DAMN *a.* & *adv.*

†**dama** *n.*[1] see TAMMAR.

Dama *n.*[2] see DAMARA.

damage /ˈdamɪdʒ/ *n.* ME. [OFr. (mod. *dommage*), f. *dam*, *damme* loss, damage, prejudice f. L *damnum* loss, hurt: see DAMN *v.*, -AGE.] 1 Loss or detriment to one's property, reputation, etc. *arch.* ME. 2 Harm done to a thing or (less usually, chiefly *joc.*) person; *esp.* physical injury impairing value or usefulness. LME. †3 A disadvantage, an inconvenience; a misfortune. LME–E18. 4 *Law.* †*sing.* & (now) in *pl.* A sum of money claimed or awarded in compensation for loss or injury. LME. 5 Cost, expense. Esp. in *what's the damage?* how much is there to pay? *slang.* M18.

1 CHAUCER As moche to oure damage as to oure profit. 2 DEFOE She was leaky, and had damage in her hold. S. WEIGHELL In our industry we have the power to cause enormous damage to the economy. *collateral damage*: see COLLATERAL *a.* VACCINE *damage.* 3 T. SHELTON The Damage is . . that I have no money here about me. 4 W. LIPPMANN An injured workman should not have to sue, but should receive damages according to a definite schedule. *consequential damages*: see CONSEQUENTIAL *a.* 1. *exemplary damages*: see EXEMPLARY *a.* 4. *with damages*: see WITH *prep. vindictive damages*: see VINDICTIVE 1. 5 BYRON I must pay the damage, and will thank you to tell me the amount of the engraving.

Comb.: **damage control** action taken to alleviate the effects of damage after an accident etc.; the taking of such action; **damage limitation** action taken to limit the effects of damage after a hostile attack, accident, error, etc.; the taking of such action.

damage /ˈdamɪdʒ/ *v.t.* ME. [OFr. *damagier*, f. as prec.] Injure (a thing) so as to diminish its value or usefulness; cause harm (now rarely physically) to (a person), *esp.* detract from the reputation of.

A. LURIE Charlie didn't kill himself, after all, .. didn't even damage much furniture. G. GREENE They would like to disrupt us, damage morale and hurt us with the Americans. M. AMIS I feel strangely protective of little Martin here: .. I would hate to damage him, or see him damaged. **damaged goods** merchandise which has deteriorated in quality. VACCINE-*damaged*.

damageable *a.* †(*a*) causing loss or injury; (*b*) liable to be damaged: L15. **damagement** *n.* (*rare*) [OFr.] the action of damaging; the fact of being damaged: E17. **damagingly** *adv.* so as to cause damage, hurtfully M19.

damage-feasant /damɪdʒˈfiːz(ə)nt/ *a.* & *n.* L16. [OFr. *damage fesant* (mod. *dommage faisant*) doing damage.] *Law.* (Causing or involving) damage done on a person's land by animals or goods of another, which would justify the landowner in distraining them until compensated.

daman /ˈdamən/ *n.* M18. [Arab. *damān ʼisrāʼīl* lit. 'lamb of Israel'.] The rock hyrax.

Damara /ˈdɑːmərə, ˈdam-/ *n.* Also **Dama** /ˈdɑːmə/. Pl. **-s**, same. E19. [Nama.] More fully *Hill, Berg*, or *Mountain Damara*. A member of a people of the mountainous parts of SW Africa, who have adopted the Nama language.

Damascene /ˈdaməsiːn, daməˈsiːn/ *n.* & *a.* See also DAMSON. LME. [L *Damascenus* f. Gk *Damaskēnos*, f. *Damaskos* Damascus, f. Semitic name (Heb. *dammeśeq*, Arab. *dimašk, dimišk*).] A *n.* 1 A native or inhabitant of the city of Damascus in Syria. LME. 2 (Usu. **d-**.) (An item of) damascened work; a pattern characteristic of damascened work. Formerly also, the fabric damask. L15. B *adj.* 1 Of or pertaining to the city of Damascus. M16. 2 (Usu. **d-**.) Of or pertaining to the damascening of metal or the fabric damask. M16.

damascene /ˈdaməsiːn, daməˈsiːn/ *v.t.* M19. [f. the adj. Cf. earlier DAMASKEEN *v.*] 1 Ornament (metal, a metal object) with inlaid designs in gold or silver; inlay (a design) thus. M19. 2 Produce or ornament (steel, a blade, etc.) with the watered pattern produced in welding. M19.

damascener *n.* a person who damascenes metal M19.

Damascus /dəˈmaskəs/ *a.* Orig. in It. form †**Damasco.** E17. [attrib. use of name of city of Damascus, f. L f. Gk *Damaskos*: see DAMASCENE *n.* & *a.*] *Hist.* Designating (objects of) damask steel.

damask /ˈdaməsk/ *n.* & *a.* LME. [L DAMASCUS, prob. through AN. Cf. Fr. *damas.*] A *n.* 1 A richly-figured woven material (orig. of silk) with a pattern visible on either side, orig. produced at Damascus. Also, a twilled table linen with woven designs shown by reflection of light. LME. 2 The colour of the damask rose (see below); velvety pink or light red, esp. as the colour of a woman's complexion. L16. 3 Damask steel (see below); the wavy pattern characteristic of this. E17.

2 KEATS She .. Blush'd a live damask.

B *adj.* 1 (Originally) made at or associated with Damascus. LME. 2 Of the colour of the damask rose; blushing. L16. 3 Made of the fabric damask. E17. 4 Made of or characteristic of damask steel. E17.

Special collocations: **damask rose** a rose of an old sweet-scented species, *Rosa damascena*, grown esp. to make attar. **damask steel** *Hist.* steel made at Damascus, or in the manner employed there, with a characteristic wavy surface-pattern resulting from the method of repeated heating and hammering together of strips of steel and iron. **damask violet** = DAME'*s violet*. **damask work** damascened work.

damask /ˈdaməsk/ *v.t.* M16. [f. the n.] Freq. as *damasked* pa. pple & ppl a. 1 Weave with richly-figured designs. M16. 2 = DAMASCENE *v.* L16. 3 Cause to have the colour of a damask rose. *poet.* L16. 4 Ornament with an intricate or variegated pattern. E17. 5 Deface or destroy by stamping or marking with lines or figures. L17. †6 Warm (wine). *slang.* L17–L18.

3 SHAKES. *Sonn.* I have seen roses damask'd .. But no such roses see I in her cheeks. 4 MILTON On the soft downie Bank damaskt with flours.

damaskeen /daməˈskiːn/ *v.t.* Also **-squine.** L16. [Fr. *damasquiner*, f. *damasquin(e)* f. It. *damaschino*, f. *Damasco* Damascus.] = DAMASCENE *v.*

dame /deɪm/ *n.* ME. [(O)Fr., earlier †*damme* f. L *domina* fem. corresp. to *dominus* lord. Cf. DAM *n.*[2], DAN *n.*[1], DOM *n.*[1], DON *n.*[1]] I 1 A female ruler or head. *obs.* in *gen.* sense. ME. †2 A form of address: my lady, madam. (Orig. the fem. corresp. to *sire*, later applied only to women of lower rank.) ME–E18. 3 (Used as a title preceding the name of) a woman of rank, formerly *spec.*, the wife or widow of a knight or baronet, now *spec.* a woman Knight Commander or holder of Grand Cross in the Order of the Bath, the Order of the British Empire, the Royal Victorian Order, or the Order of St Michael and St George. ME. b Used as a title preceding the name of an abstraction personified as a woman, as *Dame Fortune, Dame Nature*, etc. ME. 4 (Used before the surname of) the mistress of a household, an elderly matron, or a housewife. Now *arch.* & *dial.* ME. 5 (Used as a title preceding the name of) the superior of a nunnery, an abbess, prioress, etc.; *spec.* (as a formal title of) a Benedictine nun who has made her solemn profession. LME. 6 A woman, a lady. Now *arch., poet., joc.*, or *slang* (chiefly *N. Amer.*). M16. 7 *Hist.* (Used before the surname of) the mistress of a children's school. M17. 8 At Eton College: one of a class of women (at one time also men) who keep boarding-houses for oppidans but are not attached to the teaching staff. M18. 9 A comic character in modern pantomime, that of a middle-aged woman, traditionally played by a man. E20.

1 MILTON Sovran of Creatures, universal Dame. 4 SHAKES. *Wint. T.* This day she was .. Both dame and servant; welcom'd all; serv'd all. 6 W. H. AUDEN If you pass up a dame, you've yourself to blame.

†II 10 = DAM *n.*[2] 2. ME–E19. 11 = DAM *n.*[2] 3. ME–E18.

Comb.: **dame-school** *Hist.* a primary school of a kind kept by elderly women; **dame's violet** a cruciferous plant, *Hesperis matronalis*, with pale lilac flowers which have no scent until evening.

dame de compagnie /dam də kɔ̃paɲi/ *n. phr.* Pl. ***dames de compagnie*** (pronounced same). L18. [Fr., lit. 'lady of company'.] A paid female companion.

dame d'honneur /dam dɔnœːr/ *n. phr.* Pl. ***dames d'honneur*** (pronounced same). E19. [Fr., lit. 'lady of honour'.] A maid of honour, a lady-in-waiting.

dames de compagnie, d'honneur *n. phrs.* pls. of DAME DE COMPAGNIE, D'HONNEUR.

damfool /ˈdamfuːl/ *a.* & *n. colloq.* Also **damn-fool.** L19. [f. DAMN *a.* + FOOL *n.*[1]] (A person who is) thoroughly foolish or stupid.

dam'foolery *n.* E20. **dam'foolishness** *n.* L19.

dammar /ˈdamə/ *n.* Also **-er.** L17. [Malay *damar* resin.] Any of various resins used to make varnish etc. obtained from eastern Asian and Australasian conifers, esp. of the genera *Agathis* (cf. KAURI) or *Shorea* (cf. SAL *n.*[2]). Also (in full *dammar-pine, -tree*), a tree yielding this.

damme /ˈdami/ *int.* & *n. arch.* E17. [Alt.] Damn me!; this oath, or (formerly) a person using this or similar oaths.

dammer *n.* var. of DAMMAR.

dammit /ˈdamɪt/ *int.* M19. [Alt.] Damn it!

as — as dammit very — indeed.

damn /dam/ *n.* E17. [f. the vb.] 1 An utterance of the word 'damn'; an oath, an imprecation. E17. 2 A negligible amount (in *not to care* (or *give*) *a damn, not worth a damn*, etc.). *colloq.* M18.

1 R. B. SHERIDAN The best terms will grow obsolete. Damns have had their day. 2 LD MACAULAY How they settle the matter I care not .. one twopenny damn. *not be worth* or *care a tinker's damn*: see TINKER *n.* 1.

damn /dam/ *a.* & *adv. colloq.* Also **dam, dam(n)'.** L18. [Abbrev.] = DAMNED *a.* 4 & *adv.* (Formerly freq. printed *d*—; abbrev. *d.*)

E. WALLACE It's none of your dam' business. N. COWARD We .. intended to damn well get on with it. D. STUART You one of those damn' Yankee reporters? **a damn sight** a great deal (*better, more*, etc.). *damn-all*: see ALL *pron.* & *n.* 3. *damn-fool*: see DAMFOOL.

damn /dam/ *v.* ME. [OFr. *dampner*, (also mod.) *damner* f. L *dam(p)nare* (orig.) inflict loss upon, f. *damnum* loss, damage, expenditure.] †1 *v.t.* Pronounce to be guilty; condemn judicially, sentence, (*to* a penalty or fate). ME–L19. 2 *v.t.* Pronounce to be bad, a failure, etc.; censure, denounce; condemn esp. by public expression of disapproval. ME. 3 *v.t.* (Of God) condemn to eternal punishment; doom to hell; cause the damnation or condemnation of; be the ruin of. Also (*colloq.*) in imprecations, freq. in imper. or optative form (for *God* etc. *damn* —), expr. anger, hatred, contempt, irritation, etc. ME. b *v.i.* as *int.* Expr. anger, irritation, displeased surprise or realization, etc. Cf. DAMNATION *n.* 3. M20. 4 *v.i.* & *t.* Say 'damn' (at), swear (at), curse. E17.

2 W. GODWIN We should [not] totally damn a man's character for a few faults. W. S. CHURCHILL The Fabian Society .. damned all revolutionary theory and set about the propagation of a practical Socialist doctrine. **damn with faint praise** commend so feebly as to imply disapproval. 3 DICKENS I will see them d—d before I make any further alteration. T. F. POWYS He .. damned the gate to Hell because it would not open. G. GORER It may not be necessary to believe that any soul is permanently damned. E. WAUGH No one is damned except by his own deliberate act. **damn your** (or **my** etc.) **eyes!** *arch.*: expr. contempt etc. **I'll be damned**: expr. astonishment etc. **I'm** (or **I'll be**) **damned if I** —: I certainly do not —, I will not —. b N. BALCHIN I shall have to let go of the other wrench. Damn and blast. 4 G. B. SHAW I don't mind your damning and blasting .. but there is a certain word I must ask you not to use.

damner *n.* LME. **damningly** *adv.* so as to damn or condemn, to a damning degree E18.

damna *n.* pl. of DAMNUM.

damnable /ˈdamnəb(ə)l/ *a.* & *adv.* ME. [OFr. *dampnable*, (also mod.) *damnable* f. L *dam(p)nabilis*, f. *dam(p)nare*: see prec., -ABLE.] A *adj.* 1 Subject to divine condemnation; deserving damnation. ME. 2 Worthy of condemnation, reprehensible, detestable; accursed, confounded. LME.

1 SMOLLETT Those enthusiasts who look upon every schism from the established articles of faith as damnable. 2 T. HEARNE This is a damnable Shame. J. HAWKES What was admirable when it concerned only the transport of the finest materials to build the greatest buildings has become damnable when dictated by commercial expediency.

†B *adv.* Damnably, extremely. E17–E18.

damna'bility *n.* M16. **damnably** *adv.* †(*a*) so as to deserve or incur damnation; (*b*) in a damnable way, to a damnable extent; reprehensibly, detestably, confoundedly, extremely: LME.

damnation /damˈneɪʃ(ə)n/ *n.*, *a.*, & *adv.* ME. [OFr. *dampnation*, (also mod.) *damnation* f. L *dam(p)natio(n-)*, f. *dam(p)nat-* pa. ppl stem of *dam(p)nare*: see DAMN *v.*, -ATION. See also DEMNITION.] A *n.* 1 The action of condemning, the fact of being condemned; condemnation. ME. 2 *Theol.* Condemnation to eternal punishment in hell; perdition; the cause of such condemnation. ME. 3 As *int.* Expr. anger, irritation, displeased surprise or realization, etc. Cf. DAMN *v.* 3b. E17.

1 H. SIDDONS The fatal cough, well known to authors as the sure forerunner of dramatic damnation. 2 SHAKES. *Merch. V.* 'Twere damnation To think so base a thought.

B *adj.* & *adv.* = DAMNED *a.* 4 & *adv. colloq.* M18.

F. MARRYAT The damned Frenchman and his damnation horse.

damnatory /ˈdamnət(ə)ri/ *a.* L17. [L *damnatorius*, f. *damnat-*: see prec., -ORY[2].] 1 Conveying or causing censure or condemnation. L17. 2 *Theol.* Conveying a sentence of damnation in hell; incurring damnation. M18.

damned /damd, *poet. also* ˈdamnɪd/ *a.*, *n.*, & *adv.* LME. [f. DAMN *v.* + -ED[1].] A *adj.* †1 Doomed, condemned, sentenced. LME–E19. 2 *Theol.* Condemned to eternal punishment; consigned to hell. LME. 3 Deserving damnation, worthy of a curse. *obs.* exc. as passing into senses

2, 4. M16. 4 Accursed, damnable; confounded, infernal. (Formerly freq. printed *d—*, *d—d*; abbrev. *d.*) *colloq.* L16.

1 C. LAMB The reveries of the cell-damned murderer. 4 H. B. FEARON There was 'nothing in America but d—d Yankees and rogues'. THACKERAY You would be a d— fool not to take the place. CONAN DOYLE Many people .. would think that this insistence had reached the point of damned impertinence.

B *n.* 1 *absol.* as *n.pl. The* souls in hell. E16. 2 *one's damnedest*, one's utmost, *esp.* one's very best effort. M19.

C *adv.* Damnably; extremely. *colloq.* M18.

damn-fool *a.* & *n.* var. of DAMFOOL.

damnify /ˈdamnɪfʌɪ/ *v.t.* E16. [OFr. *damnefier*, *dam(p)nifier* f. L *damnificare* injure, condemn, f. L *damnificus* hurtful, f. *damnum*: see DAMN *v.*, -FY.] 1 Cause loss or inconvenience to; hurt (financially, in reputation, etc.). Now *rare* (chiefly *Law*). E16. 2 Injure or damage physically. *obs.* exc. *dial.* M16. †3 Destroy. Only in 17.

damnifiˈcation *n.* E17.

damnosa hereditas /damˌnəʊsə hɪˈrɛdɪtas/ *n. phr.* M19. [L = inheritance that causes loss.] An inheritance, tradition, etc., bringing more burden than profit.

damnum /ˈdamnəm/ *n.* Pl. **-na** /-nə/. E19. [L = hurt, harm, damage.] *Law.* A loss, a wrong.

Damocles /ˈdaməkliːz/ *n.* M18. [L f. Gk *Damoklēs*, of a flatterer whom Dionysius of Syracuse (4th cent. BC) feasted while a sword hung by a hair above him.] *sword of Damocles*, *Damocles('s) sword*, an imminent danger, a constant threat, esp. in the midst of prosperity.

Damoˈclesian *a.* L19.

damoiseau /ˈdamɪzəʊ, *foreign* damwazo/ *n.* Long *arch.* Pl. **-eaux** /-əʊz, *foreign* -o/. L15. [Fr., later form of OFr. *damoisel* masc., corresp. to fem. *damoiselle* (mod. *demoiselle*): see DAMSEL.] A young man of gentle birth, not yet a knight.

damosel, -zel *n.* see DAMSEL.

damp /damp/ *n.* ME. [(M)LG = vapour, steam, smoke (so in mod.Du.) = (O)HG *dampf* steam, f. WGmc.] I 1 A noxious exhalation; now *spec.* (usu. w. specifying wd) a harmful vapour or gas occurring in a coalmine. ME. †2 A visible vapour; fog, mist. E17–E19. 3 Moisture in the air, on a surface, or diffused through a solid; (a state or period of) slight wetness or high humidity. (The ordinary current sense.) E18.

1 *after-damp, black damp, choke-damp, fire-damp*, etc. 3 T. S. SURR We keep fires in all the rooms by turns, so that no damp has come to the tapestry. LONGFELLOW Amid the chills and damps Of the vast plain where death encamps. *rising damp*: see RISING *a.*

II †4 A dazed condition, a stupor. M16–E18. 5 A check, a discouragement. L16. 6 A state of dejection; a depression, a chill. E17.

4 ADDISON I felt a general Damp and a Faintness all over me. 5 BURKE Those accidents that cast an occasional damp upon trade. 6 W. H. PRESCOTT This news struck a damp into the hearts of the Castilians.

Comb.: **damp course** a layer of damp-proof material laid in a wall near ground level to keep moisture from rising; **damp-proof** *a.* & *v.t.* (make) impervious to damp; *damp-proof course* = *damp course* above.

dampy *a.* †(*a*) vaporous, foggy; (*b*) somewhat damp: E17.

damp /damp/ *a.* L16. [f. the n.] †1 Affected with or showing stupefaction or depression. L16–M19. †2 Of the nature of or pertaining to a noxious exhalation. M17–M18. 3 Slightly wet, moist; permeated with moisture. E18.

1 MILTON With looks Down cast and damp. 3 G. BERKELEY A cold, damp, sordid habitation, in the midst of a bleak country. N. COWARD I'm still damp from the bath. J. C. POWYS Damp odours .. of dew-soaked grasses and river mud. **damp-dry** *v.t.* dry to the state of being only damp. *damp squib*: see SQUIB *n.* 1.

damply *adv.* L19. **dampness** *n.* M17.

damp /damp/ *v.* LME. [f. the n.] 1 *v.t.* Stifle, choke, extinguish, dull. LME. †b Benumb, daze (the faculties etc.). L16–E18. c *Physics* & *Music.* Stop or reduce the vibration of (a string or other oscillating body); impose or act as a resisting influence on (an oscillation or vibration) so that it is progressively reduced in amplitude or stopped. M19. 2 *v.t.* Depress, discourage, check (zeal, hopes, etc.). M16. 3 *v.t.* Moisten. E17. 4 *v.i.* Foll. by *off*: (of a plant) die from fungal attack in damp conditions. M19.

1 BACON All shutting in of Air .. dampeth the Sound. **damp down** heap (a fire, furnace, etc.) with ashes etc. to retard combustion. c CRITICAL *damping.* 2 J. CLARE Sorrow damps my lays. P. G. WODEHOUSE It kind of damps you to come to a place where the youngest member is about eighty-seven. L. DURRELL They tempered her enthusiasm without damping it.

dampen /ˈdamp(ə)n/ *v.* M16. [f. DAMP *a.* or *v.* + -EN[5].] 1 *v.t.* Dull, depress, discourage. M16. b = DAMP *v.* 1C. L19. 2 *v.i.* Become dull, depressed, or damp. L17. 3 *v.t.* Make damp, moisten. E19.

dampener *n.* a thing that dampens; *US* a contrivance for moistening linen etc.: L19.

damper /ˈdampə/ *n.* M18. [f. DAMP *v.* + -ER[1].] 1 A person who or thing which damps or depresses the spirits. M18. 2a A contrivance in a piano for damping or stopping the vibrations of the strings. Also, the mute of a horn etc. L18. b Any device for damping mechanical or other vibrations; *spec.* (*a*) a shock absorber on a motor vehicle; (*b*) a conductor serving to reduce hunting in an electric motor or generator. M19. 3 A movable metal plate in a flue or chimney, used to control the combustion by regulating the draught. L18. 4 Something which takes the edge off appetite. L18. 5 An unleavened cake made of flour and water and baked in hot ashes. Chiefly *Austral.* & *NZ.* E19. 6 A device for dampening or moistening. E19.

1 HOR. WALPOLE Sussex is a great damper of curiosity. B. BAINBRIDGE A room so lofty and so full of draughts as to put the damper on any occasion.

Comb.: **damper pedal** = *sustaining pedal* (a) s.v. SUSTAINING.

dampish /ˈdampɪʃ/ *a.* L16. [Orig. f. DAMP *n.* + -ISH[1]; later treated as f. DAMP *a.*] †1 Vaporous, foggy, misty. L16–M17. 2 Somewhat damp or moist. M17.

dampishly *adv.* E17. **dampishness** *n.* E17.

damsel /ˈdamz(ə)l/ *n.* In sense 1 also **damosel, -ozel**, /daməˈzɛl/. ME. [OFr. *dameisele, damisele* (mod. *demoiselle*), alt. (after *dame*) of *danzele, donsele* f. Proto-Gallo-Romance dim. of L *domina* lady: see DAME. Cf. DAMOISEAU.] 1 A young unmarried woman, orig. one of noble birth. Now *literary, arch.*, or *joc.* ME. b *spec.* A maid-in-waiting. *obs.* exc. *literary* & *arch.* ME. 2 [Cf. *1 Kings* 1:1–4.] A hot iron for warming a bed. *obs.* exc. *Hist.* E18. 3 A projection on the spindle of a millstone for shaking the shoot of the hopper. L19.

1 P. G. WODEHOUSE In the Middle Ages .. practically everybody whose technical rating was that of Damsel was in distress and only too willing to waive the formalities in return for services rendered.

Comb.: **damselfish** any of numerous brightly coloured tropical marine fishes of the family Pomacentridae; **damselfly** any slender insect of the suborder Zygoptera (order Odonata), like a dragonfly but with wings or equal length folded over the body when resting.

damson /ˈdamz(ə)n/ *n.* & *a.* Orig. †**damascene**. LME. [L *damascenum* (*prunum* plum) of Damascus: cf. DAMASCENE *n.* & *a.*] A *n.* A small dark-purple plum borne by the tree *Prunus insititia*. Also, the tree itself. LME.

Comb.: **damson cheese** a solid preserve of damsons and sugar; **damson plum** (*a*) the damson or (usu.) a larger plum resembling it; (*b*) (the edible purple fruit of) a neotropical tree, *Chrysophyllum oliviforme*, of the sapodilla family.

B *adj.* Of a dark-purple or purplish-brown colour. M17.

dan /dan/ *n.*[1] Long *arch.* ME. [OFr., also *dam* (mod. *dom*) f. L *dominus* master, lord: cf. DOM *n.*[1], DON *n.*[1]] Used as an honourable title preceding a name: master, sir.

SPENSER Dan Chaucer, well of English undefyld.

dan /dan/ *n.*[2] L17. [Origin unkn.] A small buoy, used as a marker in deep-sea fishing or in minesweeping. Also *dan buoy.*

Dan /dan/ *n.*[3] M18. [A town in the territory of Dan, one of the twelve tribes of Israel, taken to represent the northern limit of Israelite settlement in biblical times, as Beersheba was taken to represent the southern limit (*Judg.* 20:1 etc.).] *from Dan to Beersheba*, over the whole extent, to the furthest extremity.

dan /dan/ *n.*[4] M20. [Jap.] Each of the (numbered) grades of the advanced level of proficiency in judo, karate, etc. (also *dan grade*); a person who has reached (a specified grade of) this level. Cf. KYU.

Danaert /ˈdanət/ *n.* Also **dannert**. M20. [Its 20th-cent. Ger. inventor.] In full *Danaert wire*. Spring steel wire, usually barbed and in a spiral form, used in defensive warfare.

danaid /ˈdaneɪɪd/ *n.* & *a.* L19. [f. as next + -ID[3].] *Entomol.* = next.

danaine /ˈdaneɪʌɪn/ *n.* & *a.* L19. [f. mod.L *Danainae* (see below), f. *Danaus* genus name: see -INE[1].] *Entomol.* A *n.* A butterfly of the family Danaidae or Danainae, exemplified by the monarch or milkweed. L19. B *adj.* Of or belonging to this family. L19.

danaite /ˈdɑːnəʌɪt, ˈdeɪn-/ *n.* M19. [f. J. Freeman *Dana* (1793–1827), US chemist + -ITE[1].] *Min.* A cobaltiferous variety of arsenopyrite.

Danakil /ˈdanəkɪl, dəˈnɑːk(ə)l/ *n.* & *a.* Also **Dankali** /daŋˈkɑːli/. L19. [Arab. *danākil* pl. of *dankalī*.] A *n.* A member of a widely-spread Hamitic people of Djibouti and NE Ethiopia; the Cushitic language of this people. Also called *Afar*. L19. B *adj.* Of or pertaining to this people, their language, or their lands. E20.

danalite /ˈdeɪnəlʌɪt, ˈdɑːn-/ *n.* M19. [f. James D. *Dana* (1813–95), US mineralogist + -LITE.] *Min.* A cubic silicate and sulphide of beryllium and iron, crystallizing in the cubic system and usu. occurring as reddish octahedrons.

danburite /ˈdanbjʊrʌɪt/ *n.* M19. [f. *Danbury*, Connecticut, US + -ITE[1].] *Min.* An orthorhombic calcium borosilicate, usu. occurring as colourless, yellow, or brownish prisms.

dance /dɑːns/ *n.* ME. [(O)Fr. *dance*, (also mod.) *danse*, f. as next.] 1 The action or an act of dancing; a single round or turn of dancing; the art or practice of dancing. ME. 2 An arrangement of steps and movements constituting a specific form of dancing, often given a particular name. LME. b A musical composition for dancing to or in a rhythm suitable for dancing to. E16. 3 A social gathering for the purpose of dancing. LME. 4 *fig.* A course of action, a proceeding; a game. Now only in set phrs. below. LME.

2 *ballroom dance, barn dance, clog-dance, country dance, Highland dance, morris dance, square dance, sword dance, tap-dance, war dance*, etc. 3 *dinner-dance, tea dance*, etc.

Phrases: **begin the dance** *fig.* take the lead in a course of action. *dance macabre*: see MACABRE *n.* **Dance of Death** an allegorical representation of Death leading people of all conditions in the dance to the grave, popular in the Middle Ages; = DANSE MACABRE. *dance of macabre*: see MACABRE *a.* **lead a person a (merry) dance** cause a person a lot of trouble esp. by leading him or her on a lengthy pointless course. **lead the dance** = *begin the dance* above. *song and dance*: see SONG *n.*[1] *St Vitus'(s) dance*: see SAINT *n.* & *a.* *waggle dance*: see WAGGLE *n.*

Comb.: **dance band** a band that plays music (suitable) for dancing to; **dance-card** a card bearing the names of (a woman's) prospective partners at a dance; **dance-drama** a drama in which all the action is expressed by dancing; **dance floor** a usu. uncarpeted area of flooring reserved for dancing; **dancehall** (orig. *US*) a place where public dances are held; **dance hostess** (*a*) a woman who holds a dance at her house etc.; (*b*) a woman dancing-partner (see *dancing-partner* (b) s.v. DANCING *vbl n.*); **dance-house** (chiefly *US*) a dancehall; **dance programme** a dance-card.

dance /dɑːns/ *v.* ME. [OFr. *dancer*, (also mod.) *danser* f. Proto-Romance, of unkn. origin.] 1 *v.i.* Move with rhythmical steps, leaps, glides, and other gestures, usually in time to a musical accompaniment, alone or with a partner or set. ME. b Of an animal: perform, after training, simple rhythmic movements. M16. 2 *v.i.* Of a person or animal: leap, spring, move up and down, from excitement or strong emotion. Of the heart, blood, etc.: move in a lively way. LME. 3 *v.t.* Perform (dance steps); perform the steps and movements of (a particular dance). LME. 4 *v.t.* Move or toss up and down with a dancing jerky motion; dandle. LME. 5 *v.i.* Of an insect, inanimate thing, etc.: bob up and down, move about, esp. in the air or on the surface of water. M16. 6 *v.t.* Lead in a dance, cause to dance; remove, put bring, etc., *off*, *away*, *to*, etc., by dancing. M17.

2 TENNYSON Yniol's heart Danced in his bosom, seeing better days. 3 R. DAVIES Makes you want to grab someone and dance ring-a-ring-o-roses. 4 R. P. JHABVALA She.. picked up the child and danced her up and down in her arms. 5 C. P. SNOW The midges were dancing over the water. A. HIGGINS She saw firelight dancing on the kitchen walls and over the ceiling. 6 R. BOLT You'd dance him to the Tower—You'd dance him to the block! A. MASON The music danced him, on and on, towards its consummation.

Phrases: *dance* ATTENDANCE (*on*). †**dance barefoot** *fig.* (of an elder daughter) remain single while a younger daughter is married. **dance to** or **after a person's tune, pipe**, etc., follow a person's lead, do as a person demands. **dance upon nothing** *arch.* be hanged.

danceable *a.* (*colloq.*) suitable for dancing; fit to dance with: M19.

dancer /ˈdɑːnsə/ *n.* LME. [f. DANCE *v.* + -ER[1].] 1 A person who dances; *spec.* a person who dances professionally in public. LME. 2 In *pl.* Stairs. *arch. slang.* L17. 3 In *pl.* More fully *merry dancers*. The aurora borealis. Chiefly *Sc.* E18. 4 *Hist.* In *pl.* A sect of enthusiasts who arose in 1374 in Flanders and were noted for their wild dancing. M18. 5 A housebreaker, *esp.* one who enters through the roof of a building. *slang.* M19.

1 *ballet dancer, clog-dancer, morris dancer, tap-dancer*, etc.

danceress *n.* (long *rare*) LME.

dancercise /ˈdɑːnsəsʌɪz/ *n.* Also **-ize**. M20. [f. DANCE *n.* + EXERCISE *n.*] Dancing performed as physical exercise.

dancette /dɑːnˈsɛt/ *n.* E19. [Inferred f. next.] *Archit.* A zigzag or chevron moulding.

dancetté /ˈdɑːnsəti/ *a.* Also **-tty**. E17. [Alt. of Fr. *danché*, *denché*, earlier †*dansié* f. late L adj., f. L *dens*, *dent-* tooth.] *Her.* Having (esp. three) large, deep indentations.

dancing /ˈdɑːnsɪŋ/ *vbl n.* ME. [f. DANCE *v.* + -ING[1].] The action of DANCE *v.*; style of this.

ballroom dancing, clog-dancing, disco dancing, morris dancing, tap-dancing, etc.

Comb.: **dancing-master, -mistress** a teacher of dancing; **dancing-partner** (*a*) a person with whom one dances; (*b*) an expert dancer engaged to act as teacher or partner as required; **dancing-school** a school for instruction in dancing.

dancing /ˈdɑːnsɪŋ/ *ppl a.* M16. [f. DANCE *v.* + -ING[2].] That dances.

dancing DERVISH. **dancing-girl** a female professional dancer, esp. a member of a group.

dancingly *adv.* M17.

dandelion /ˈdandɪlʌɪən/ *n.* LME. [Fr. *dent-de-lion*, rendering med.L *dens leonis* lion's tooth: so called from the usu. strongly-toothed leaves.] Any of numerous composite plants constituting the genus *Taraxacum*, which are characteristic of grassland and have heads of bright yellow ligulate florets, stems containing a milky juice, and leaves in a basal rosette; a flower or flowering stem of this plant. Also (*Austral.*), Cape-weed, *Cryptostemma candulaceum*.

Comb.: **dandelion-clock** = CLOCK *n.*[1] 5; **dandelion coffee** (a drink prepared from) dried dandelion roots; **dandelion greens** *N. Amer.* fresh dandelion leaves used as a green food or herb.

dander /ˈdandə/ *n.*[1] *Sc.* L18. [Origin unkn.] A calcined cinder from a forge etc.

dander /ˈdandə/ *n.*[2] L18. [Rel. to DANDRUFF.] Dandruff, scurf, esp. as found in the hair of animals.

dander /ˈdandə/ *n.*[3] *colloq.* (orig. *US*). M19. [Origin unkn.] Temper, anger, indignation.

get one's dander up become angry.

dander /ˈdandə/ *v.* & *n.*[4] *Sc.* & *north.* Also **daun(d)er** /ˈdɔːn(d)ə/. L16. [Frequent. (see -ER[5]), perh. rel. to DADDER, DADDLE *v.*, etc.] A *v.i.* 1 Stroll, saunter; walk aimlessly. L16. 2 Talk incoherently, ramble; make a trembling sound, vibrate. E18. B *n.* A stroll, a saunter. E19.

dandiacal /danˈdʌɪək(ə)l/ *a.* M19. [f. DANDY *n.*[2] after *hypochondriacal* etc.] Dandyish, dandified.

Dandie /ˈdandi/ *n.* L19. [Abbrev.] = next.

Dandie Dinmont /dandɪ ˈdɪnmənt/ *n.* E19. [A character in Sir Walter Scott's novel *Guy Mannering*.] (A dog of) a breed of terrier from the Scottish borders, with short legs, a long body, and a rough coat.

dandify /ˈdandɪfʌɪ/ *v.t. colloq.* E19. [f. DANDY *n.*[2] + -FY.] Make like a dandy; smarten up. Freq. as *dandified* ppl a.

dandifiˈcation *n.* the act of dandifying; a dandified ornament: E19.

dandilly /ˈdandɪli/ *n.* & *a. Sc.* E16. [App. a deriv. of DANDLE *v.*] A *n.* A pet, a darling. E16. B *adj.* Petted, spoiled. M18.

dandiprat /ˈdandɪprat/ *n. arch.* Also **dandy-**. E16. [Origin unkn.] †1 A small 16th-cent. coin, worth three halfpence. E16–M17. 2 A small, insignificant, or contemptible fellow; a young boy, an urchin. M16.

dandizette /dandɪˈzɛt/ *n.* Also **dandy-**. E19. [f. DANDY *n.*[2], after Fr. *grisette* etc.: see -ETTE.] A female dandy.

dandle /ˈdand(ə)l/ *v.* M16. [Origin unkn.] 1 *v.t.* Move (a child etc.) lightly up and down in the arms or on the knee; *gen.* move lightly up and down. M16. 2†a *v.t.* Trifle, play, or toy with. M16–M17. b *v.i.* Play or toy (*with*). *rare.* E19. 3 *v.t.* Make much of, pet, pamper. M16.

1 S. BECKETT Perhaps she had dandled me on her knees while I was still in swaddling clothes. G. HOUGH An apple tree Dandled its fruit.

dandler *n.* L16. **dandling** *n.* (*obs.* exc. *dial.*) a dandled child, a darling E17.

dandruff /ˈdandrʌf/ *n.* Also (now *rare*) **-iff** /-ɪf/. M16. [1st elem. obscure, 2nd perh. identical w. ROVE *n.*[2]] Dead skin in small scales entangled in the hair, esp. when excessive as in seborrhoea.

dandruffy *a.* like dandruff, having much dandruff M19.

dandy /ˈdandi/ *n.*[1] L17. [Hindi *ḍā̃ḍī*, f. *ḍā̃ḍ* staff, oar.] 1 *Hist.* A boatman on the Ganges. L17. 2 In the Indian subcontinent, a type of litter, carried by two men. L19.

dandy /ˈdandi/ *n.*[2] L18. [Perh. abbrev. of JACK-A-DANDY, the last elem. of which may be identical w. *Dandy*, pet-form of male forename *Andrew*.] I 1 A man whose style of dress is ostentatiously elegant or fashionable; a fop, a beau. L18. 2 A very good thing of its kind; *the* best. *colloq.* L18.

1 R. FRY An exquisite and refined intellectual dandy living in a society of elegant frivolity. S. GIBBONS Mr. Neck was a great dandy, who usually changed his button-hole twice a day. 2 J. RUNCIMAN The barque looked a real dandy.

II App. transf. applications to things considered neat or trim. 3 A bantam fowl. *dial.* E19. 4 *Naut.* A sloop or cutter with a jigger-mast right aft, on which a mizen-lugsail is set. M19. 5 In full *dandy roll(er)*. A wire roller used to compress the fibres of a partly-formed web of paper, which also simultaneously imparts the watermark. M19.

Comb.: **dandy-brush** a stiff brush used for cleaning horses; **dandy-cart** (now *rare*) a kind of spring-cart; **dandyfunk** *Naut.* hard tack soaked in water and baked with fat and molasses; **dandy-horse** *Hist.* an early form of bicycle, in which the rider achieved propulsion by pushing the ground with each foot alternately; **dandy-line** a weighted fishing-line with cross-pieces at short intervals, each of which has a hook on either end; *dandy roll(er)*: see sense 5 above.

dandydom *n.* the condition of a dandy; the world of dandies: M19. **dandyish** *a.* like a dandy, foppish E19. **dandyishly** *adv.* M19. **dandyism** *n.* the character, style, or manners of a dandy E19.

dandy /ˈdandi/ *n.*[3] E19. [W. Indian alt. of DENGUE.] More fully *dandy-fever*. Dengue.

dandy /ˈdandi/ *a.* & *adv.* L18. [f. DANDY *n.*[2]] A *adj.* 1 Splendid, first-rate; very good of its kind. *colloq.* (orig. *US*). L18. 2 Of, belonging to, or characteristic of a dandy or dandies; affectedly neat, trim, or smart. E19.

1 R. LARDNER She plays a dandy game of bridge, lots better than her husband. *fine and dandy*: see FINE *a.*

B *adv.* Finely, splendidly. *N. Amer. colloq.* E20.

dandyprat *n.* var. of DANDIPRAT.

dandyzette *n.* var. of DANDIZETTE.

Dane /deɪn/ *n.* [OE *Dene* (repr. in *Denmark*), superseded in ME by forms f. ON *Danir* pl. (late L *Dani*).] 1 A native or inhabitant of Denmark, a Scandinavian country between the North Sea and the Baltic; orig. & *Hist.*, any Norse invader of England between the 9th and 11th cents. OE. 2 More fully *Great Dane* (An animal of) a large, powerful, short-haired breed of dog, between the mastiff and the greyhound in type. L18.

Comb.: **Dane gun** *W. & S. Afr.* a primitive gun of a kind orig. introduced by Danish traders; **Danes' blood, daneweed** (now *rare*) danewort; **danewort** [so called because orig. supposed to spring up where Danish blood was spilt in battle] a herbaceous elder, *Sambucus ebulus*.

Danebrog *n.* var. of DANNEBROG.

Danegeld /ˈdeɪngɛld/ *n.* Also (now *rare*) **-gelt** /-gɛlt/. LOE. [f. ON genit. of *Danir* (pl.) Danes + *gjald* payment, tribute (cf. GELD *n.*); = ODa. *Danegjeld*.] 1 *Eng. Hist.* An annual tax, imposed orig. (it is believed) to provide funds for the protection of England against the Danes (but often identified with the tribute exacted by the Danes in the late 10th century), and continued as a land tax. LOE. 2 A sum of money paid or demanded in order to ensure safety against a more powerful enemy; protection money. E20.

dane-hole *n.* var. of DENE-HOLE.

Danelaw /ˈdeɪnlɔː/ *n.* [Late OE *Dena lagu* Danes' law.] *Hist.* 1 The Danish law formerly in force over that part of England which was occupied by Danes from the 9th to the 11th cents. LOE. 2 *The* part of northern and eastern England over which this law prevailed. M19.

dang /daŋ/ *v.*[1] & *n. colloq.* L18. [Euphem. alt.] A *v.t.* = DAMN *v.* 3. L18. B *n.* = DAMN *n.* E20.

dang *v.*[2] see DING *v.*[1]

danger /ˈdeɪn(d)ʒə/ *n.* ME. [AN *da(u)nger*, OFr. *dangier* (mod. *danger*) f. Proto-Romance, f. L *domnus*, *dominus* lord, master: see -ER[2].] †1 Power of a lord or master, jurisdiction; power to harm or injure. ME–M19. †b Liability (to loss, punishment, etc.). LME–L17. †2 Difficulty (made or raised); reluctance; chariness. ME–E16. †3 Mischief, harm, damage. LME–L16. 4 Liability or exposure to harm or injury; risk, peril. Also, an instance or cause of this; an unwelcome possibility *that*. LME. b The position or indication of a railway signal directing stoppage or caution. M19.

1 *fig.*: SHAKES. *Haml.* Keep you.. Out of the shot and danger of desire. **in a person's danger** at the mercy of or under obligation to a person. 4 TOLKIEN The desire to eat hobbits, had seemed the chief danger in Gollum. M. DRABBLE I sensed danger on every side. **in danger of** likely to incur, do, etc. **out of danger** unlikely to die of a present illness or injury.

Comb.: **danger angle** *Naut.* the angle enclosed by lines drawn from two known points to the point marking the limit of safe approach for a vessel to a danger to navigation; **danger line** a real or imaginary line marking the division between safety and danger; **danger list** a (notional) list of patients (in a hospital) whose lives are in danger (chiefly in *on the danger list*, dangerously ill); **danger man** someone perceived as posing a particular threat (in sport etc.); **danger money** a payment made beyond basic wages for dangerous work; **danger signal** an indicator of impending danger, *esp.*, on a railway, a red light or a semaphore signal in the 'on' position.

†**dangerful** *a.* dangerous E16–E19. **dangerless** *a.* (now *rare*) without danger LME. **dangersome** *a.* (*obs.* exc. *dial.*) dangerous M16.

danger /ˈdeɪn(d)ʒə/ *v.t.* Now *rare.* LME. [OFr. *dangerer*, f. *dangier*: see prec.] †1 Render liable. LME–M17. 2 Expose to danger; endanger, imperil, risk. L15. †3 Harm, injure. M16–E17.

dangerous /ˈdeɪn(d)ʒ(ə)rəs/ *a.* ME. [AN *da(u)ngerous*, OFr. *dangereus* (mod. *-eux*), f. as DANGER *n.*: see -OUS.] †1 Difficult to deal with or to please; arrogant; uncooperative; fastidious. ME–L16. b Cautious, reserved, chary (*of*). LME–M17. 2 Fraught with or causing danger; involving risk; perilous, hazardous; unsafe. LME. †3 Hurtful, injurious. M–L16. 4 Extremely ill; at risk (of death) from an illness or injury. Now *dial.* & *US colloq.* E17.

2 *Drive* Since December the charges of dangerous driving and causing death by dangerous driving have been abolished. A. THWAITE The dangerous possibility that she might grow up to resemble her mother. **dangerous drug** a powerful drug, *esp.* one that can cause addiction.

dangerously *adv.* in a dangerous manner; to a dangerous degree: L16. **dangerousness** *n.* M16.

dangle /ˈdaŋg(ə)l/ *a.* & *n.* E17. [f. the vb.] A *adj.* Dangling. *rare.* E17. **B** *n.* The act of dangling; something that dangles. M18.

dangle /ˈdaŋg(ə)l/ *v.* L16. [Imit.: cf. NFris. *dangeln*, Sw. *dangla*, Da. *dangle*, parallel to Icel., Sw. *dingla*, Da. *dingle*. See -LE[3].] **1** *v.i.* Hang loosely, swaying to and fro. L16. **b** *spec.* Hang from the gallows, be hanged. L17. **2** *v.t.* Make (a thing) hang loosely and sway to and fro; hold suspended loosely; keep (hopes etc.) hanging uncertainly or as a temptation. E17. **3** *v.i.* Hang *after*, hover, as an unofficial follower, aspirant lover, etc. *arch.* E17.

1 F. L. WRIGHT When sitting on the high chairs . . their short legs would dangle. M. FRAYN A cigarette dangled permanently from her lips. 2 C. SANDBURG He dangles herring before prospective customers. 3 LD MACAULAY Heirs of noble houses . . dangling after actresses.

danglement *n.* dangling M19. **dangler** *n.* (*a*) something that dangles, a dangling object or part; (*b*) *arch.* a hanger-on, a dallying follower: E18. **dangling** *ppl a.* (*a*) that dangles; (*b*) *Gram.* lacking a proper grammatical connection; *dangling participle*, a participle in an absolute clause or phrase whose subject is omitted, with possible ambiguity: L16. **dangly** *a.* loosely hanging and swaying L19.

Danic /ˈdeɪnɪk/ *a. rare.* E17. [med.L *Danicus*, f. *Dania* Denmark: see -IC.] Danish.

Daniel /ˈdanj(ə)l/ *n.* L16. [The prophet *Daniel*, introduced as a shrewd judge in the apocryphal Book of Susanna.] An upright judge; a person of infallible wisdom.

¶ First recorded in Shakes.

Daniell /ˈdanj(ə)l/ *n.* M19. [John F. *Daniell* (1790–1845), Eng. physicist.] *Physics.* **1** In full *Daniell('s) battery* or *cell*. An electrochemical cell having an amalgamated zinc cathode standing in dilute sulphuric acid and a copper anode in a solution of copper sulphate, the electrolytes being in contact usu. through a porous pot or plate. M19. **2** *Daniell's hygrometer*, a hygrometer in which the cooling is produced by the forced evaporation of ether. M19.

Danish /ˈdeɪnɪʃ/ *a.* & *n.* [OE *Denisć* = ON *Danskr*, f. Gmc, superseded by forms f. AN *danes*, OFr. *daneis* (mod. *danois*) f. med.L *Danensis* f. late L *Dani* Danes. Later assim. to adjs. in -ISH[1].] **A** *adj.* Of or pertaining to Denmark in Scandinavia, the Danes, or their language. OE.

Danish axe *Hist.* a kind of battleaxe with a very long blade. **Danish blue** (**cheese**) a soft white cheese from Denmark, with blue mould veins. **Danish dog** the Great Dane. **Danish modern** a plain, simple style of furniture made of light coloured wood. **Danish pastry** a rich pastry cake topped with icing, nuts, etc., sometimes with a filling.

B *n.* **1** The North Germanic language of Denmark. LME. **2** A Danish pastry. *colloq.* M20.

Danishry *n.* (*obs.* exc. *Hist.*) the people of Danish descent (in Britain) LME.

Danism /ˈdeɪnɪz(ə)m/ *n.* M19. [f. DANE + -ISM.] A Danish idiom or expression. Also (*rare*), favour towards Denmark.

Danite /ˈdanʌɪt/ *n.* M16. [f. *Dan* one of the twelve sons of the patriarch Jacob + -ITE[1].] *Hist.* **1** A member of the Hebrew tribe founded by Dan. M16. **2** A member of an alleged secret order of Mormons, supposed to have arisen in the early days of the sect to act as spies and suppress disaffection. M19.

dank /daŋk/ *v.*, *a.*, & *n.* ME. [Prob. of Scand. origin: cf. Sw. *dank* marshy spot, ON *døkk* pit, pool.] **A** *v.t.* (Esp. of rain, mist, etc.) wet, damp, moisten; dampen (the spirits). *obs.* exc. *dial.* ME.

B *adj.* **1** Wet, watery; oozy. (Now esp. of ground, marshes, etc.) LME. **2** Unpleasantly or unwholesomely damp and cold. L16. **b** Growing in damp places. E19.

1 R. COBB A big Victorian house . . with a dank, dripping, overgrown garden. 2 O. NASH I do not like the foggy fall . . The dank, rheumatic air. B. PLAIN The house smelled dank and musty. b SHELLEY Dock, and henbane, and hemlock dank.

†**C** *n.* Wetness, damp; a wet place, a pool, a marsh. LME–M17.

dankish *a.* M16. **dankly** *adv.* E19. **dankness** *n.* L16. **danky** *a.* somewhat dank, dampish M16.

Dankali *n.* & *a.* var. of DANAKIL.

†**danna** *n.* see DUNNY *n.*

Dannebrog /ˈdanəbrɒg/ *n.* Also ***Dane-***. E18. [Da., f. *Danne-*, *Dane-* Danish + *brog* breech, cloth.] The Danish national flag.

order of *Dannebrog*, *Dannebrog* order: a Danish order of knighthood.

dannert *n.* var. of DANAERT.

Dano- /ˈdeɪnəʊ/ *comb. form.* [f. L *Danus* DANISH + -O-.] Danish and —, Denmark or the Danes in connection with —.

Dano-Norwegian *a.* & *n.* (designating or pertaining to) the Danish language as modified and used in Norway after its separation from Denmark L19.

danse du ventre /dɑ̃ːs dy vɑ̃ːtr/ *n. phr.* Pl. ***danses du ventre*** (pronounced same). L19. [Fr.] A belly-dance.

danse macabre /dɑ̃ːs makɑːbr, -ka-/ *n. phr.* Pl. ***-s -s*** (pronounced same). L19. [Fr. Earlier Anglicized as *dance (of) macabre*: see MACABRE.] The Dance of Death; a musical piece or passage representing or suggestive of this.

danses du ventre, danses macabres *n. phrs.* pls. of DANSE DU VENTRE, MACABRE.

danseur /dɑ̃sœːr/ *n.* Pl. pronounced same. E19. [Fr., f. *danser* (see DANCE *v.*) + *-eur* -OR.] A male ballet-dancer.

danseur noble /nɔbl/ the partner of a ballerina. PREMIER DANSEUR.

danseuse /dɑ̃søːz/ *n.* Pl. pronounced same. E19. [Fr.] A female dancer; a ballerina. PREMIÈRE DANSEUSE.

†**Dansk** *a.* M16–E17. [Da., Sw. *Dansk*, Icel. *Danskur.*] = DANISH *a.*

†**Dansker** *n.* (*rare*, Shakes.) a Dane: only in E17.

dante /ˈdanti/ *n.* Also **-ta** /-tə/. E17. [Sp. *ante*, *dante* elk, buffalo, *danta* tapir; It. *dante*; ult. f. Arab. *lamṭ* North African oryx.] The American tapir.

Dantean /ˈdantɪən, danˈtiːən/ *a.* & *n.* L18. [f. *Dante* (see below) + -AN, -EAN.] **A** *adj.* Of or pertaining to the Italian poet Dante Alighieri (1265–1321) or his writing; in the style of or reminiscent of Dante's works. L18. **B** *n.* An admirer or student of Dante or his writing. M19.

Danˈtesque *a.* in the style of or reminiscent of Dante's works E19.

danthonia /danˈθəʊnɪə/ *n.* E20. [mod.L, f. Étienne *Danthoine*, 19th-cent. Fr. botanist: see -IA[1].] Any of various tufted pasture grasses of the large genus *Danthonia*, chiefly of Australia and New Zealand. Also called *wallaby-grass*.

Dantonist /ˈdantənɪst/ *n.* M19. [f. *Danton* (see below) + -IST.] A follower of Georges Jacques Danton (1759–94), one of the leaders in the French Revolution.

†**Dantzig** *a.* var. of DANZIG.

Danubian /daˈnjuːbɪən/ *a.* M19. [f. med.L *Danubius*, *Danuvius* f. Gk *Danoubios* + -IAN.] Of, pertaining to, or bordering on the River Danube, which rises in the Black Forest in SW Germany and flows into the Black Sea; of or pertaining to the prehistoric cultures of the surrounding region.

Danzig /ˈdanzɪg/ *a.* Now *arch.* or *Hist.* Also †**-tzig**. L16. [A city (now *Gdańsk*) in Poland.] Of Danzig or its region (formerly *esp.* designating timber or beer).

Dao, Daoism *ns.* vars. of TAO, TAOISM.

dap /dap/ *n.* M19. [f. the vb. Sense 3 perh. a different wd.] **1** The bounce of a ball; the skip of a stone on water. *dial.* M19. **2** In fishing: a bait made to bob lightly on the surface. E20. **3** A rubber-soled shoe; a sports shoe, a plimsoll. *slang.* E20.

dap /dap/ *v.* Infl. **-pp-**. M17. [App. parallel to DAB *v.*, the final *p* expressing a lighter touch. Cf. also DOP *v.*] **1** *v.i.* Fish by making the bait bob lightly on the water. M17. **2** *v.t.* Use as bait in this mode of fishing. M17. **3** *v.i.* Rebound, bounce; hop or skip like a stone across water. M19. **4** *v.i.* Dip lightly or suddenly into water. L19.

1 J. BUCHAN He had gone off . . to dap for trout in the park lake.

dapatical /dəˈpatɪk(ə)l/ *a. rare.* E17. [f. late L *dapaticus*, f. L *dapem* feast + -AL[1].] Sumptuous, costly.

daphne /ˈdafni/ *n.* LME. [Gk *daphnē* laurel, bay tree, *Daphnē* a nymph who escaped Apollo's advances by being changed into a laurel.] Orig., a laurel or bay tree. Now, a flowering shrub of the genus *Daphne*, of the mezereon family; *esp.* spurge laurel, *D. laureola*.

Comb.: **daphne heath** *Austral.* any of various flowering shrubs of the genus *Brachyloma*, of the epacris family.

Daphnean /ˈdafnɪən/ *a.* L16. [f. L *Daphnaeus*, f. Gk *Daphnaios*, f. as prec.: see -EAN.] †**1** Of laurel. Only in L16. **2** Pertaining to or characteristic of the nymph Daphne (see prec.); pertaining to or showing maidenly timidity or modesty. E17.

daphnia /ˈdafnɪə/ *n.* Pl. same. M19. [mod.L (see below), f. as DAPHNE: see -IA[1].] A freshwater cladoceran of the genus *Daphnia*; a water-flea.

daphnin /ˈdafnɪn/ *n.* E19. [f. mod.L *Daphne* genus name f. as DAPHNE: see -IN[1].] *Chem.* A bitter glycoside occurring in some shrubs of the genus *Daphne*.

daphnetin /ˈdafnɪtɪn/ *n.* a yellow crystalline compound, 7,8-dihydroxycoumarin, $C_9H_6O_4$, the aglycone of daphnin M19.

dapifer /ˈdapɪfə/ *n. obs.* exc. *Hist.* M17. [Late L, f. *daps*, *dap-* food, feast: see -FER.] A person who brings food to the table; the steward in a monarch's or noble's household.

dapper /ˈdapə/ *a.* LME. [MLG, MDu. = heavy, powerful, strong, stout (Du. = bold, valiant) = OHG *tapfar* heavy, weighty, firm (late MHG, G *tapfer* brave), ON *dapr* sad, dreary.] **1** Neat, trim, smart in dress or appearance. LME. **2** *spec.* Of a small person, esp. a man; smart in movements etc., active, sprightly. E17.

1 A. WOOD Mounting my dapper nagg, Pegasus. A. N. WILSON Those walks . . with her father, in those days rather dapper, with yellow kid gloves, and an Inverness cape. 2 R. W. EMERSON We are dapper little busybodies, and run this way and that superserviceably.

dapperling *n.* a little dapper fellow E17. **dapperly** *adv.* LME. **dapperness** *n.* M16.

dapple /ˈdap(ə)l/ *n.* L16. [f. DAPPLED or DAPPLE *a.*] **1** Each of many roundish patches of colour or shade on a surface. Usu. in *pl.* L16. **2** Dappled condition or effect; mottled marking. L16. **3** An animal, esp. a horse, with a dappled coat. M17.

1 J. R. LOWELL To watch the dapples of sunlight on the grass. 2 G. MAXWELL The dapple of changing cloud shadow upon the shoulders of the hills.

dapple /ˈdap(ə)l/ *a.* L15. [f. DAPPLED. Perh. earlier in DAPPLE GREY.] Dappled.

dapple /ˈdap(ə)l/ *v.* L16. [f. DAPPLED.] **1** *v.t.* Variegate with rounded spots or patches of colour or shade. L16. **2** *v.i.* Become dappled. L17.

1 SHAKES. *Much Ado* The gentle day . . Dapples the drowsy east with spots of grey. 2 BYRON Methought that mist of dawning gray Would never dapple into day.

dappled /ˈdap(ə)ld/ *a.* LME. [Origin uncertain: perh. f. ON *depill* spot (cf. Norw. *dape* puddle). Cf. next.] Marked with spots or patches of a different colour or shade; speckled, mottled.

J. RUSKIN Beeches cast their dappled shade. J. C. OATES His lovely gray-and-white dappled Shetland pony.

Comb.: **dappled-grey** *a.* & *n.* = next.

dapple grey /dap(ə)l ˈgreɪ/ *a.* & *n. phr.* LME. [Perh. f. *dappled-grey* (see prec.) or alt. of an unattested comb. *apple-grey* (cf. ON *apalgrár*, OHG *aphelgrāo* (G *apfelgrau*), Du. *appelgrauw*, = Fr. *pommelé* dapple grey).] **A** *adj.* Of a horse: grey variegated with spots or patches of a darker shade. LME. **B** *n. phr.* A horse of this colour. LME.

daps /dap/ *n.pl. obs.* exc. *dial.* L16. [Origin unkn.] **1** Ways, modes of action. L16. **2** Likeness, image in ways or appearance. M18.

dapsone /ˈdapsəʊn/ *n.* M20. [f. *di*(para-*amino-phenyl*)*sulphone* (alternative systematic name).] *Pharm.* A crystalline bacteriostatic compound, bis(4-aminophenyl)sulphone, $(H_2NC_6H_4)_2SO_2$, used esp. in the treatment of leprosy.

Darapti /dəˈrapti/ *n.* M16. [A mnemonic of scholastic philosophers, first used in med.L, A indicating a universal affirmative proposition and I a particular affirmative proposition.] *Logic.* The first valid mood of the third syllogistic figure, in which a particular affirmative conclusion is drawn from two universal affirmative premisses.

Darby /ˈdɑːbi/ *n.* L16. [A personal surname, perh. in some cases repr. the usual pronunc. of the English city *Derby*.] **I 1 a** (*Father*) *Darby's bands*, some rigid form of band for debtors. Long *obs.* exc. *Hist.* L16. **b** (Usu. **d-**.) In *pl.* Handcuffs; (formerly) fetters. *slang.* L17. †**2** Ready cash. *slang.* L17–L18. **3** A kind of plasterer's float, usu. with two handles. E19. **4** In full *Darby kelly*, also *Darby kel.* = BELLY *n.* 2, 4. *rhyming slang.* E20.

II 5 [Perh. f. characters in a poem published in 1735 in the *Gentleman's Magazine*.] *Darby and Joan*, a devoted old married couple. L18.

Comb.: **Darby and Joan club**: for elderly people.

Darbyite /ˈdɑːbɪʌɪt/ *n.* M19. [f. John *Darby* (1800–82), founder of the sect + -ITE[1].] A member of the Plymouth Brethren, *spec.* of the Exclusive Brethren.

darcy /ˈdɑːsi/ *n.* Pl. **-cies**, **-cys**. M20. [H. P. G. *Darcy* (1803–58), Fr. hydrologist and waterworks inspector.] *Physics.* A cgs unit of permeability to fluid flow, being the permeability of a medium that allows a flow of 1 cubic centimetre per second of 1 centipoise viscosity under a pressure gradient of 1 atmosphere/centimetre.

Dard /dɑːd/ *n.* & *a.* M19. [Dard.] **A** *n.* A member of any of several peoples inhabiting eastern Afghanistan, northern Pakistan, and Kashmir; (any of) a group of Indic languages spoken by these peoples. M19. **B** *attrib.* or as *adj.* Of or pertaining to these peoples or (any of) their languages. L19.

Dardic *a.* & *n.* (*a*) *adj.* = DARD *a.*; (*b*) *n.* a Dard language: E20.

Dardan /ˈdɑːd(ə)n/ *a.* & *n. rare.* E17. [L *Dardanus*.] (A) Trojan.

Also **Dardanian** /-ˈdeɪnɪən/ *a.* L16.

†**dare** *n.*[1] L15–M18. [A sing. f. †*darse* var. of DACE.] = DACE.

dare /dɛː/ *n.*[2] Now *colloq.* L16. [f. DARE *v.*[1]] **1** An act of defiance; a challenge. L16. **2** Boldness. *rare.* L16.

1 BUNYAN Sin is the dare of God's justice. LYNDON B. JOHNSON I wanted to see if I could keep up this arduous task. In a way, I made myself a dare. 2 SHAKES. *1 Hen. IV* It lends . . A larger dare to our great enterprise.

dare /dɛː/ *n.*[3] M19. [f. DARE *v.*[2]] A contrivance for catching larks by fascinating them.

dare /dɛː/ *v.*[1] 3 sing. pres. usu. **dare** bef. expressed or implied inf. without *to*; otherwise **dares**. Pa. t. in this position occas. **dare**; otherwise **dared**; (*arch.* & *dial.*) **durst** /dəːst/. Pa. pple **dared**. Informal abbrev. forms: **daren't** /dɛːnt/ = *dare not*; **durstn't** /ˈdəːs(ə)nt/ = *durst not*. [OE *durran*, pres. *dearr*, *durron*, pa. *dorste*, a preterite-pres. vb, corresp. to OFris. *dūra*, OS *gidurran*, OHG *giturran*, Goth. *gadaursan*, f. Gmc bases f. IE, whence Skt *dhṛṣ-*, Gk *tharsein* be bold.] **I** *v.i.* **1** Have sufficient courage or impudence; be so bold (as). (Foll. by (*to*) *do*.) OE. **2** *ellipt.* Dare to go, venture. *poet.* LME.

1 AV *John* 21:12 None of the disciples durst aske him, Who art thou? W. IRVING No one would dare to desert. J. BUCHAN He would have gone himself, but he dared not. G. VIDAL I don't dare mention his name to my family. **I dare say**, (*informal*) **daresay** I am prepared to believe, I do not deny, it is very likely. **I dare swear** I feel sure that. *I dare* UNDERTAKE. 2 DRYDEN Nor dare beyond the Reed.

II *v.t.* **3** Challenge, defy, (a person). (Foll. by *to* an action, *to do*.) L16. **4** Venture to meet or be exposed to, meet defiantly; have enough courage for (an action), venture on. E17.

3 F. MARRYAT You wish to dare me to it—well, I won't be dared to anything. DYLAN THOMAS Gomer Owen kissed her when she wasn't looking because he was dared. P. GOODMAN He promptly dared the others to jump off the roof. 4 SWIFT Should some sourer mongrel dare too near an approach. JAS. HOGG To . . dare In his dark home the sullen bear. G. A. WAGNER Against his will he'd dared A dreadful danger.

darer *n.* E17.

dare /dɛː/ *v.*[2] *obs.* exc. *dial.* [OE *darian* f. stem also of MDu. and LG *bedaren* appease, calm, Flem. *verdaren* amaze.] †**1** Lie hidden, lurk. OE–LME. **2** *v.i.* Lie motionless, crouch, esp. in fear; tremble with fear. ME. †**3** *v.i.* Gaze fixedly; stare in amazement or terror. ME–M16. **4** *v.t.* Daze; fascinate. M16. **5** Daunt, terrify, paralyse with fear. E17.

dare-all /ˈdɛːrɔːl/ *n.* & *a.* M19. [DARE *v.*[1] + ALL *pron.*] **A** *n.* A person who or thing which defies all adversity. Also, a weatherproof covering. *rare.* M19. **B** *adj.* Bold, reckless. E20.

daredevil /ˈdɛːdɛv(ə)l/ *n.* & *a.* L18. [f. DARE *v.*[1] + DEVIL *n.*] (A person who is) recklessly daring.

CONAN DOYLE He is about the most daredevil rider in England. D. JACOBSON A team of French dare-devils turning their cars over and over.

daredevilry *n.* reckless daring M19.

†**dareful** *a. rare.* Only in E17. [f. DARE *n.*[2] or *v.*[1] + -FUL.] Full of daring or defiance.

darg /dɑːg/ *n. Sc.*, *north.*, & *Austral.* Also †**dark**, (earliest) †**dawark**. LME. [Syncopated f. *daywork*.] **1** A day's work; a particular amount of work, a task. LME. **2** The result or product of a day's work. L15.

¶Mod. form recorded f. M16.

daric /ˈdarɪk/ *n.* M16. [Gk *Dareikos* (sc. *statēr* stater): see -IC.] *Hist.* A gold coin of ancient Persia, named from the first King Darius. Also, a silver Persian coin of similar design.

Darii /ˈdɛːrɪʌɪ/ *n.* M16. [A mnemonic of scholastic philosophers, first used in med.L, A indicating a universal affirmative proposition and I a particular affirmative proposition.] *Logic.* The third valid mood of the first syllogistic figure, in which a particular affirmative conclusion is drawn from a universal major premiss and a particular affirmative minor premiss.

daring /ˈdɛːrɪŋ/ *n.* E17. [f. DARE *v.*[1] + -ING[1].] The action of DARE *v.*[1]; adventurous courage, boldness, audacity.

daring /ˈdɛːrɪŋ/ *a.* L16. [f. DARE *v.*[1] + -ING[2].] Bold, adventurous, audacious; unconventional.

B. PYM I wonder what could possibly be regarded as too daring to publish nowadays. G. SWIFT Dad was involved in a succession of daring operations in France.

daringly *adv.* E17. **daringness** *n.* E17.

dariole /ˈdarɪəʊl/ *n.* LME. [(O)Fr.] **1** An individual sweet or savoury dish of various kinds; now *spec.* one made in a dariole mould. LME. **2** In full *dariole mould*. A small metal mould shaped like a flower-pot and used for making such a dish. M19.

Darjeeling /dɑːˈdʒiːlɪŋ/ *n.* L19. [A town and district in West Bengal.] In full *Darjeeling tea*. A high-quality tea grown in the mountainous regions of northern India.

dark /dɑːk/ *n.*[1] ME. [f. the adj.] **1** The absence of light, darkness; a dark time or place; night, nightfall. ME. **2** Obscurity; secrecy; ignorance. E17. **3** A dark colour or shade; *esp.* a part of a painting in shadow. L17.

1 DEFOE The Darks of Hell. J. RHYS I . . stayed away till dark. A. LURIE I couldn't see his face in the dark. **after dark** at night. **dark of the moon** the time when there is no moonlight. **leap** or **shot in the dark** *fig.* an action of which the outcome cannot be foreseen. **whistle in the dark** keep up one's courage, esp. by a show of confidence. **2 be, keep, in the dark** be, keep, in a state of ignorance about some matter. 3 J. ROSENBERG Rembrandt's light becomes most selective and evocative, through its peculiar interpenetration with the darks.

Comb.: **dark-adaptation** adjustment of the eye to low intensity of light; **dark-adapted** *a.* (of the eye) adjusted to low intensity of light; **darkfall** dusk, nightfall.

darksome *a.* (now chiefly *poet.*) somewhat dark (*lit.* & *fig.*); gloomy, sombre, obscure: M16.

†**dark** *n.*[2] var. of DARG.

dark /dɑːk/ *a.* [OE *deorc*, prob. f. Gmc base; perh. rel. to OHG *tarnjan* (G *tarnen*) conceal.] **I** *lit.* **1** Devoid of or deficient in light; unilluminated. OE. **2** Reflecting or transmitting little light; gloomy, sombre. OE. **3** Of colour, an object, etc.: approaching black in hue; having intensity or depth of colour. LME. **b** Of a person, or the complexion: having brown or black hair or skin, not blond. LME.

1 O. HENRY The alley was dark except for one patch of light. SCOTT FITZGERALD It was a dark night with no moon. †**keep a person dark** keep a person confined in a darkened room (as the insane were formerly kept). 2 J. CONRAD A . . vision of dark peaks. S. SPENDER Dusk drops a dark cloak. 3 SOUTHEY Her dark hair floating on the morning gale. SIR W. SCOTT The bound of dark-brown doe. **b** P. S. BUCK She had always been a dark woman, her skin ruddy and brown.

II *fig.* **4** Devoid of moral or spiritual light; evil, wicked, sinister; foul, atrocious. OE. **5** Gloomy, dismal, sullen, sad. OE. **b** Of facial expression: clouded with anger or dislike, frowning. L16. **6** Obscure in meaning; indistinct. LME. **7** Partially or totally blind. *obs.* exc. *dial.* LME. **8** Unenlightened, uninformed, ignorant. LME. **9** Hidden from view or knowledge; concealed, secret. E17. **b** Of a person: reticent, secretive. L17. **10** Of whom or of which little is known. M19. **11** In *superl.* Of part of a region (orig. of Africa): most remote, inaccessible, and uncivilized. Now chiefly *joc.* L19. **12** *Phonet.* Velarized, retracted; *spec.* designating the velarized, as opp. to the 'clear' or palatalized, lateral consonant (/l/). L19. **13** Of a theatre etc.: closed, not in use. E20.

4 C. V. WEDGWOOD Colonel Harrison . . had assured the King that nothing dark or underhand would be done to him. I. MURDOCH A man destined by dark forces to commit a murder for which he had no will. 5 J. STEINBECK They're a dark people with a gift for suffering way past their deserving. **b** A. LURIE The dark spiteful glance of . . your enemy. 6 L. STRACHEY The issue grew doubtful and more dark. 8 MILTON What in me is dark Illumine, what is low raise and support. 9 DICKENS He hid himself . . kept himself dark. **keep something dark** *colloq.* keep something secret. **b** POPE And Lyttelton a dark, designing knave. 11 H. M. STANLEY Through Darkest Africa. C. COOPER They shunted him off to darkest Somerset.

Special collocations & comb.: **Dark Age** (*a*) the period between the end of the Bronze Age and the beginning of the historical period in Greece and other Aegean countries; (*b*) = *Dark Ages* (a) below. **Dark Ages** (*a*) the Medieval period, now usu. the earlier part, between the fall of Rome and the appearance of vernacular documents; *transf.* an unenlightened or ignorant period; an age of which little is known; *joc.* an obscure or little-regarded period before the present; (*b*) = *Dark Age* (a) above. **dark arches (moth)** a noctuid moth, *Apamea monoglypha*, with highly variable brown or black wing-coloration. **dark current** the electric current flowing in a photoelectric device when no radiation is incident on it. **dark days**: of adversity. **dark glasses** spectacles with tinted lenses. **dark horse** a racehorse whose form is little known; *fig.* a person, esp. a competitor, about whom little is known. **dark lantern**: with means for concealing its light. **dark lines** (in a spectrum) absorption lines. **dark matter** *Astron.* matter whose existence is postulated to account for the dynamical behaviour of galaxies, but which has not been detected (*cold dark matter*: in the form of exotic weakly interacting particles; *hot dark matter*: in the form of high-energy randomly moving particles soon after the big bang). **dark night (of the soul)** a period of spiritual aridity suffered by a mystic etc., *transf.* a period of anguish or despair. **darkroom**: from which all actinic rays, such as daylight, have been excluded, for photographic developing etc. **dark space** any of several non-luminous areas in a vacuum tube traversed by an electric discharge. **the Dark Continent** Africa, esp. in the time before it was fully explored by Europeans.

darkful *a.* (*rare*) full of darkness OE. **darkish** *a.* LME. **darkly** *adv.* OE.

dark /dɑːk/ *v.* OE. [f. the adj.] **1** *v.t.* & *i.* Make or become dark, darken. *obs.* exc. *dial.* OE. **2** *v.i.* Lie concealed, lurk. Now only (*dial.*), listen furtively, eavesdrop. ME. **3** *v.t. fig.* Obscure, dim, sully. Now *rare* or *obs.* LME.
¶Largely superseded by DARKEN.

darken /ˈdɑːk(ə)n/ *v.* ME. [f. DARK *a.* + -EN⁵.] **1** *v.t.* & *i.* Make or become devoid of or deficient in light. ME. **2** *v.t. fig.* Cast a shadow over; cloud, tarnish; eclipse. LME. **b** *v.i.* Become gloomy or sad; cloud with anger. M18. **3** *v.t.* & *i.* Make or become blind or dim-sighted. Now chiefly *fig.* M16. **4** *v.t.* & *i.* Make or become obscure in meaning or intelligibility. M16. **5** *v.t.* & *i.* Make or become darker in hue or colour. E18.
1 MILTON When Night darkens the Streets. E. BOWEN Day darkened over the Channel, the skyline vanished. 2 SHAKES. *Coriol.* And you are dark'ned in this action, sir, Even by your own. S. C. HALL Domestic affliction . . darkened the later years of his life. **darken a person's door(s)** make a visit, esp. an unwelcome one (usu. in neg. contexts). b SIR W. SCOTT His displeasure seemed to increase, his brow darkened. 3 AV *Ps.* 69:23 Let their eyes be darkened, that they see not. 4 AV *Job* 38:2 Who is this that darkeneth counsel by words without knowledge? LYTTON The vision darkens from me.
¶Largely superseding DARK *v.*

darkey, **darkie** *ns.* vars. of DARKY.

darkle /ˈdɑːk(ə)l/ *v.* E19. [Back-form. f. next.] **1** *v.i.* Become dark or gloomy. E19. **2** *v.i.* Appear dimly or indistinctly. E19. **3** *v.t.* Make obscure, darken. L19.

darkling /ˈdɑːklɪŋ/ *adv.*, *a.*, & *n.* LME. [f. DARK *n.*¹ + -LING².] **A** *adv.* In the dark. LME.
B *adj.* **1** Being or taking place in the dark. M18. **2** Characterized by darkness or obscurity. M18.
Special collocations: **darkling beetle** = TENEBRIONID *n.*
C *n.* = DARK *n.*¹ E20.
Also **darklings** *adv.* (*rare*) M17.

darkmans /ˈdɑːkmənz/ *n. slang.* Now *rare* or *obs.* M16. [f. DARK *a.*: for 2nd elem. cf. LIGHTMANS, TOGEMANS.] The night.

darkness /ˈdɑːknɪs/ *n.* OE. [f. DARK *a.* + -NESS.] **1** Partial or total absence of light. OE. **2** *fig.* Lack of spiritual or intellectual light; wickedness, evil; ignorance. ME. **b** Death. LME. **3** The quality of being dark in hue or colour. LME. **4** Blindness, dimness of sight. Now chiefly *poet.* LME. **5** Unhappiness, distress, gloom. LME. **6** Secrecy, mystery; obscurity. LME.
2 ADDISON The Darkness and Superstition of later Ages. **Prince of Darkness** Satan, the Devil. 4 TENNYSON His eyes . . Were shrivell'd into darkness in his head. 5 SHELLEY The darkness of deepest dismay.

darky /ˈdɑːki/ *n. slang.* Also **-key**, **-kie**. L18. [f. DARK *a.* + -Y⁶.] **1** The night, darkness. L18. **2** A Black. *colloq.* (freq. considered *derog.*). L18. **3** A dark lantern. *arch.* E19.

darl /dɑːl/ *n. colloq.* (chiefly *Austral.*). M20. [Abbrev.] = DARLING *n.*¹

darling /ˈdɑːlɪŋ/ *n.*¹ & *a.* Also †**dear-**. OE. [f. DEAR *a.*¹, *n.* + -LING¹.] **A** *n.* **1** A person who is dearly loved. Freq. as a form of address. OE. **2** A favourite, a pet; an object of indulgent affection. OE. **3** A lovable person, an endearing creature. L18.
1 TENNYSON Answer, darling, answer, no. M. GEE Then he would kiss her and call her his darling. 2 H. ROBBINS Mark was the columnists' darling He was always good for an item. Q. BELL A nervous, delicate boy, his mother's darling.
B *adj.* **1** Best-loved, dearest, favourite. L16. **2** Lovable; *colloq.* (*affected*) sweetly pretty or charming. E19.
1 COLERIDGE His [the devil's] darling sin Is pride that apes humility. 2 QUEEN VICTORIA Short clothes with darling little stockings and . . pink satin shoes—really too darling!

Darling /ˈdɑːlɪŋ/ *n.*² L19. [A river in western New South Wales, Australia.] Used *attrib.* to designate things associated with the area of the River Darling, esp. in names of plants growing there.
Darling clover sweet fenugreek, *Trigonella suavissima*, a fragrant herb growing along watercourses. **Darling lily** a bulbous plant of the amaryllis family, *Crinum flaccidum*, with large white or pink flowers. **Darling pea** either of two leguminous plants of the genus *Swainsona*, *S. galegifolia* and *S. greyana*, with flowers which are poisonous to sheep; also called *poison-bush*. **Darling shower** *local* a dust-storm.

darling /ˈdɑːlɪŋ/ *v.t.* L19. [f. DARLING *n.*¹] Address as 'darling'.
T. RATTIGAN Wonderful the way you stage people darling each other.

darlint /ˈdɑːlɪnt/ *n.* & *a. dial.* & *joc.* L19. [Alt.] = DARLING *n.*¹ & *a.*

darn /dɑːn/ *n.*¹ E18. [f. DARN *v.*¹] A place in a garment repaired by darning.

darn /dɑːn/ *n.*², *a.*, & *adv. slang* (orig. *US*). Also ***dern**, ***durn**, /dəːn/. L18. [Euphem. alt.] = DAMN *n.*, *a.* & *adv.*
dar'nation *n.*, *a.*, & *adv.* = DAMNATION *n.* 3, *a.* & *adv.* L18.

darn /dɑːn/ *v.*¹ E17. [Perh. f. DERN *v.*¹: cf. MDu. *dernen* stop holes in (a dyke).] **1** *v.t.* & *i.* Mend (a garment, fabric, esp. knitted material) by filling in the damaged area with interwoven yarn. E17. **2** *v.t.* Ornament or embroider with darning-stitch. L19.
2 **darned net** net embroidered so as to resemble lace.

darn /dɑːn/ *v.*²*t. slang* (orig. *US*). Also ***dern**, ***durn**, /dəːn/. L18. [Alt. of DAMN *v.*] In imprecations, freq. in imper. or optative form: damn.
darned *ppl a.* & *adv.* = DAMNED *a.* 4 & *adv.* E19.

darn *v.*³ var. of DERN *v.*¹

darnel /ˈdɑːn(ə)l/ *n.* ME. [Origin unkn.: cf. Walloon dial. *darnelle* (= Fr. *ivraie*).] A grass of the genus *Lolium*; esp. *L. temulentum*, formerly common as a weed in cornfields in Europe and Asia.
fig.: H. BARROW [Satan] sowing his darnel of errors and tares of discord among them. *red darnel*: see RED *a.*

darner /ˈdɑːnə/ *n.* E17. [f. DARN *v.*¹ + -ER¹.] **1** A person who repairs garments, fabric, etc., by darning. E17. **2** A darning-machine. Also, a tool used in darning; a darning-needle, a darning-egg. L19.

darning /ˈdɑːnɪŋ/ *n.* E17. [f. DARN *v.*¹ + -ING¹.] **1** The action of DARN *v.*¹; mending fabric using interwoven stitches. E17. **b** (Embroidering with) darning-stitch. L19. **2** Articles darned or to be darned. L19.
Comb.: **darning-ball**, **-egg**, **-last**, etc., a curved piece of wood or other smooth hard material used to stretch and support material being darned; **darning-cotton**: of a kind suitable for darning with; *darning-egg*, *-last*: see *darning-ball* above; **darning-machine**: for repairing garments, fabric, etc., by darning; **darning-needle** a long thick needle with a large eye, suitable for darning with (*devil's darning-needle*: see DEVIL *n.*); **darning-stitch** a large running stitch as used in darning; **darning-wool**: of a kind suitable for darning with.

daroga /dəˈrəʊgə/ *n.* M17. [Pers. & Urdu *dārogā*.] In the Indian subcontinent: orig., a governor or chief officer, a head of police or excise; now, a police sub-inspector.

†**darrein** *a.* E16–M19. [AN, OFr. *derrein*, *darrein*, whence OFr. *derrenier*, (also mod.) *dernier* last.] *Law.* Last, ultimate, final; = DERNIER.

†**darse** *n.* var. of DACE.

darshan /ˈdɑːʃən/ *n.* E20. [Hindi pronunc. of Skt *darśana* sight, seeing, f. *dṛś-* to see.] In the Indian subcontinent etc.: the opportunity or occasion of seeing a holy person or the image of a deity.

dart /dɑːt/ *n.* ME. [OFr. (mod. *dard*), accus. of *darz*, *dars*, f. Frank. = spear, lance, repr. by OE *daroþ*, OHG *tart*, ON *darraðr*; in senses 2 and 4 f. the vb.] **1** A small pointed missile shot or thrown as a weapon; *poet.* an arrow. ME. **b** A small pointed missile, usu. with a feather or plastic flight, thrown at a target in a game; in *pl.*, the indoor game played with such missiles and a circular target. E20. †**2** In full *dart-snake*, *-serpent*. A snake or snakelike lizard with characteristic darting movements. L16–M19. **3** An animal organ resembling a dart in shape or function; *spec.* (*a*) (now only *poet.*) the sting of a venomous insect etc.; (*b*) a calcareous pointed organ in some gastropods forming part of the reproductive system. M17. **4** An act of darting; a sudden rapid movement. E18. **5** In full *dart-moth*. Any of a large group of noctuid moths, most having dart-shaped markings on their wings. E19. **6** *Dressmaking.* A stitched tapered tuck for shaping a garment. L19. **7** A plan, a scheme; a good idea; a fancy; a favourite. *slang* (chiefly *Austral.*). Now *rare.* L19.
1 *fig.* & *transf.*: W. M. PRAED The lightning's vivid dart. E. BLUNDEN Shrapnel shells, uncoiling their . . smoke downwards while their white-hot darts scoured the acre below. CUPID's *dart. heart and dart*: see HEART *n.* 4 A. TROLLOPE She . . prepared herself for a dart at the door.
Comb.: **dartboard** a circular target with numbered sectors used in the game of darts; **dartman** a soldier armed with darts; *dart-moth*: see sense 5 above; **dart-sac** a hollow organ in some gastropods, secreting the reproductive dart; *dart-serpent*, *-snake*: see sense 2 above.

dart /dɑːt/ *v.* LME. [f. the n. Cf. Fr. *darder*.] **1** *v.t.* Pierce with a dart or other pointed weapon. Now *rare.* LME. **2** *v.i.* (now *rare*) & *t.* Throw or shoot (a dart or similar missile). M16. **3** *v.t.* Send out suddenly and rapidly, make a rapid movement with; cast (a glance etc.) quickly and keenly. L16. **4** *v.i.* Move like a dart, swiftly and suddenly; start rapidly in some direction; make rapid changes of direction. E17.
3 F. HERBERT The old eyes darted a hard glance at Jessica. R. P. JHABVALA He darted the tip of his tongue over his lips. 4 V. WOOLF The firelight darting and making the room red. W. S. MAUGHAM His restless eyes darted here and there like a hare trying to escape a pursuer. E. MANNIN Lizards darted up and down the trunks of the palms.

†**dartars** *n.* L16–M18. [Fr. DARTRE.] A kind of scab on the chin of sheep.

darter /ˈdɑːtə/ *n.* M16. [f. DART *v.* + -ER¹.] **I 1** A person who throws or shoots darts. Now usu. *Hist.* M16. **2** A person who or thing which darts or moves swiftly. E19. **II** †**3** = DART *n.* 2. E17–E19. **4** Any of a number of long-necked fish-eating birds of the genus *Anhinga*, esp. of any of the Old World species. Cf. ANHINGA. L18. **5** Any of numerous small quick-moving N. American percid fishes belonging to the genus *Etheostoma* and related genera. M19. **6** In full *darter dragonfly*. A dragonfly that darts to and fro from a particular perch when flying; *spec.* = LIBELLULID. M20.

Dartford warbler /dɑːtfəd ˈwɔːblə/ *n. phr.* L18. [*Dartford* in Kent, England, near where the bird was first seen.] A small dark warbler, *Sylvia undata*, of Europe and N. Africa.

dartle /ˈdɑːt(ə)l/ *v.t.* & *i. rare.* M19. [Dim. & iterative of DART *v.*: see -LE³.] Dart or shoot out repeatedly.

Dartmoor /ˈdɑːtmʊə, -mɔː/ *n.* M19. [A moorland plateau in Devon, England.] **1** *Dartmoor pony*, (an animal of) a breed of small shaggy pony native to Dartmoor. M19. **2** *Dartmoor sheep*, (an animal of) a hardy variety of sheep bred on Dartmoor. M19.

dartos /ˈdɑːtɒs/ *n.* M17. [Gk = flayed.] *Anat.* The muscle of the scrotal skin.
dartoid *a.* of the nature of, resembling, or pertaining to the dartos L19.

dartre /ˈdɑːtə/ *n.* Now *rare* or *obs.* E19. [Fr. f. med.L *derbita*, of Gaulish origin.] A skin ailment or scab, *esp.* herpes. Cf. DARTARS.
dartrous *a.* M19.

Darwin /ˈdɑːwɪn/ *n.* L19. [Charles *Darwin*: see next.] **1** In full *Darwin tulip*. A tall late-flowering type of tulip with self-coloured flowers rectangular in outline in their lower part. L19. **2** *Darwin's finch*, any of a diverse group of related buntings of the Galapagos Islands adapted to a wide range of ecological niches and used by Darwin to illustrate speciation. Usu. in *pl.* M20. **3** (**d-**.) A unit of rate of change in evolution, corresponding to variation by a factor *e* (= 2.718...) in one million years. M20.

Darwinian /dɑːˈwɪnɪən/ *a.* & *n.* L18. [f. *Darwin*, a family name (sense 1 Erasmus, sense 2 his grandson Charles) + -IAN.] **A** *adj.* **1** Of or pertaining to the English physician, naturalist, and poet Erasmus Darwin (1731–1802), his speculations, or his poetical style. L18. **2** Of or pertaining to the English naturalist Charles Robert Darwin (1809–82) or his views, esp. his theory of the evolution of species. (The predominant sense.) M19.

2 **Darwinian tubercle** *Anat.* a small projection on the edge of the human ear, present in the foetus and sometimes persisting in the adult, hypothesized to be a vestige of the pointed ear of primates.

B *n.* A follower of Erasmus or (more commonly) Charles Darwin; an adherent of Charles Darwin's theory of evolution. E19.

Darwinianism *n.* = DARWINISM E19.

Darwinise *v.* var. of DARWINIZE.

Darwinism /ˈdɑːwɪnɪz(ə)m/ *n.* M19. [f. as DARWINIAN + -ISM.] **1** The doctrines or hypotheses of Erasmus Darwin. *rare*. M19. **2** The biological theories of Charles Darwin concerning the evolution of species, etc. M19.

Darwinist *n.* L19. **Darwiˈnistic** *a.* L19.

Darwinize /ˈdɑːwɪnʌɪz/ *v.* Also **-ise**. L19. [f. as prec. + -IZE.] **1** *v.i.* Speculate after the manner of Erasmus or Charles Darwin. L19. **2** *v.t.* Affect or influence by Darwinian theories of evolution. E20.

das /das, dɑːs/ *n.* L15. [Du. = G *Dachs*: cf. DASSIE.] †**1** A badger. Only in L15. **2** A rock hyrax, *Procavia capensis*, = DASSIE 1. *S. Afr.* L18.

Dasein /ˈdɑːzaɪn/ *n.* M19. [G, f. *dasein* exist, f. *da* there + *sein* be.] *Philos.* In Hegelian terms, existence, determinate being; in existentialism, human existence, the being of a person in the world.

dash /daʃ/ *n.*[1] LME. [f. DASH *v.*[1]] **1** A violent blow, stroke, impact, or collision. LME. **2** A stroke or line (usu. short and straight) made with or as with a pen etc., esp. (*a*) drawn through writing for erasure, (*b*) forming part of a character or used as a flourish, (*c*) marking a parenthetic clause, break in sense, omission, substitution, etc., or separating distinct portions of matter. M16. **b** *Mus.* A short vertical mark (ˈ) placed above or beneath a note to indicate that it is to be performed staccato, esp. more so than when marked with a dot (see DOT *n.*[1] 4b). M19. **c** The longer of the two signals (the other being the dot) which in various combinations make up the letters of the Morse alphabet. M19. **3** A hasty stroke of the pen. L16. †**4** A sudden blow; affliction; discouragement. L16–M18. **5** A splash, splashing; the sound of water striking or being struck. L16. **6** A small quantity (*of* something) mingled with something else; a slight admixture or infusion; a tinge. L16. **7** A small portion (of colour etc.) thrown on a surface; a splash of colour; something laid roughly on a surface. E18. **8** A showy appearance; showy behaviour. Chiefly in *cut a dash* below. E18. **9** (Capacity for) vigorous and spirited action. L18. **10** The dasher of a churn. L18. **11** A sudden impetuous movement; a rush; a sudden vigorous attack. E19. **12** A race run in one heat; a sprint. Chiefly *N. Amer.* M19. **13** = DASHBOARD 1. M19.

1 *fig.*: SHAKES. *1 Hen. VI* She takes upon her bravely at first dash. 2 *swung dash*. 5 W. COWPER Music not unlike The dash of Ocean on his winding shore. 6 E. BLUNDEN He went off, leaving a dash of bitterness in my mild draught of content. 7 J. T. BENT Syra is almost entirely a white town, relieved now and again by a dash of yellow wash. *pebble-dash*: see PEBBLE *n.* 9 WELLINGTON The affair . . was occasioned . . by the imprudence of the officer, and the dash and eagerness of the men. 11 G. STEIN She made a rapid dash out of the door.

Phrases: **cut a dash** make a brilliant show. **do one's dash** *Austral. colloq.* become played out. **have a dash at** *colloq.* make an attempt at. **make a dash for** try to reach by quickness, rush towards.

Comb.: **dashlight** a light on the dashboard of a motor vehicle.

dash /daʃ/ *n.*[2] Also †**dashee**. E17. [(Guinean *dashee* f.) Port. *das* ult. f. L DATA.] In W. Africa, a gift or commission; *slang* a bribe.

dash /daʃ/ *v.*[1] ME. [Prob. of imit. origin: an appropriate base is repr. by Sw. *daska*, Da. *daske* beat, but no older Scand. forms are recorded.] **I** *v.t.* **1** Strike with violence so as to shatter, smash; strike violently against. ME. **2** Knock, drive, throw, or thrust (*away*, *down*, *out*, etc.) with violence; fling, impel with destructive contact *against* or *into* something. ME. **3** Splash or splatter *with* mud etc. Also, put *out* by splashing water on (a fire). LME. **4** *fig.* Destroy, frustrate, (now esp. a person's hopes etc.). E16. **5** Depress; daunt; confound, abash. M16. **6** Qualify *with* some (freq. inferior) admixture; dilute, mix. M16. **7 a** Draw a dash through. Now *rare* or *obs.* M16. **b** Mark with a dash; underline. L18. **8** Write or sketch rapidly without premeditation. Usu. foll. by *off* or *down*. E18. **9** In mild imprecations, freq. in imper. or optative form: damn. E19.

1 SHAKES. *Temp.* A brave vessel . . Dash'd all to pieces! S. HAZZARD Refinement was a frail construction continually dashed by waves of a raw . . humanity. 2 SIR W. SCOTT Dashing from him the snake which was about to sting him. A. J. CRONIN He . . seized a vase . . and dashed it hard upon the floor. V. ACKLAND The rain drops dashed themselves against . . the windscreen. 3 DICKENS Rows of fire-buckets for dashing out a conflagration. TENNYSON Deep tulips dash'd with fiery dew. 4 V. WOOLF I . . dashed my pleasure by losing my Roman brooch. J. BUCHAN Years . . of zeal and hope not yet dashed by failure. 5 SHAKES. *Oth.* I see this hath a little dash'd your spirits. 6 C. J. LEVER Dash the lemonade with a little maraschino. 8 K. TYNAN Like watching a series of lightning water-colours, dashed off by a master. 9 DICKENS Dash it, Tony . . you really ought to be careful.

II *v.i.* **10** Move, fall, or throw itself with violence; come *against* etc. with violent collision. ME. **11** Rush with impetuosity or spirit; move about, ride, run, etc., in a great hurry. ME. **12** Make a display; cut a dash. L18.

10 E. PEACOCK The full force of the Atlantic is dashing on the cliffs. 11 J. STEINBECK Jack-rabbits . . dashed away in long jolting steps. J. RABAN I had . . lost most of my eagerness to dash headlong into new places. 12 T. S. SURR That blade dashes most confoundedly . . he is a princely fellow, to be sure.

dashed *a.* & *adv.* (*a*) *adj.* that has been dashed; *euphem.* damned; (*b*) *adv.* confoundedly: M17. **dashy** *a.* (*colloq.*) given to cutting a dash E19.

dash /daʃ/ *v.*[2]*t.* Also †**dashee**. E18. [f. DASH *n.*[2]] In W. Africa, give as a gift or commission; *slang* bribe.

dash /daʃ/ *adv.* L17. [f. DASH *v.*[1]] With a dash. See also SLAPDASH *adv.*

dashboard /ˈdaʃbɔːd/ *n.* M19. [f. DASH *v.*[1] or *n.*[1] + BOARD *n.*] **1 a** A board of wood or leather in the front of a carriage to keep out mud. M19. **b** A panel beneath the windscreen of a motor vehicle, in an aircraft, etc., containing instruments and controls. E20. **2** *Archit.* A sloping board to carry off rainwater from the face of a wall. L19.

†**dashee** *n.*, *v.* vars. of DASH *n.*[2], *v.*[2]

dasheen /daˈʃiːn/ *n.* Orig. *W. Indies*. L19. [Origin unkn.] A cultivated variety of taro.

dasher /ˈdaʃə/ *n.* L18. [f. DASH *v.*[1] + -ER[1].] **1** A person who or thing which dashes; *colloq.* a person who cuts a dash, a stylish person; *Austral.* a daring gambler. L18. **2** A contrivance for agitating cream in a churn. M19. **3** = DASHBOARD 1. *US*. M19.

Dashera *n.* var. of DUSSEHRA.

dashiki /ˈdɑːʃiki/ *n.* M20. [Prob. f. Yoruba f. Hausa: cf. Krio *da(n)shiki*.] A loose brightly coloured W. African shirt, also worn by Blacks in America etc.

dashing /ˈdaʃɪŋ/ *n.* LME. [f. DASH *v.*[1] + -ING[1].] **1** The action of DASH *v.*[1] LME. **2** = DASH *n.*[1] 7. L16.

2 *pebble-dashing*: see PEBBLE *n.*

dashing /ˈdaʃɪŋ/ *a.* LME. [f. DASH *v.*[1] + -ING[2].] **1** That dashes. LME. **2** Spirited, lively, impetuous. L18. **3** Given to cutting a dash, stylish. L18.

Special collocations: **Dashing White Sergeant** a lively country dance performed in sets of three.

dashingly *adv.* E19. **dashingness** *n.* M20.

dashpot /ˈdaʃpɒt/ *n.* M19. [f. DASH *v.*[1] + POT *n.*[1]] A hydraulic device for damping shock or vibration, a hydraulic buffer.

†**dasje** *n.* var. of DASSIE.

Dassera *n.* var. of DUSSEHRA.

dassie /ˈdasi/ *n.* *S. Afr.* Also †**dasje**. L18. [Afk. f. Du. *dasje* dim. of DAS *n.*] **1** A rock hyrax, *Procavia capensis*, = DAS *n.* 2. L18. **2** A sparid coastal fish, *Diplodus sargus*, with a black tail-spot; the blacktail. M19.

dassievanger /ˈdasɪfaŋə, -vaŋə, *foreign* ˈdasifaŋər/ *n.* *S. Afr.* M19. [Afk., f. as prec. + *vanger* catcher.] An eagle; *esp.* Verreaux's eagle, *Aquila verreauxii*.

dastard /ˈdastəd, ˈdɑː-/ *n.*, *a.*, & *v.* LME. [Prob. f. *dazed* pa. pple & ppl a. of DAZE *v.* + -ARD, infl. by DOTARD *n.*[1] & *a.*[1]] **A** *n.* †**1** A dullard; a stupid person. LME–M16. **2** A mean, base, or despicable coward, *esp.* one who does malicious acts in a skulking way. L15. **B** *adj.* = DASTARDLY. L15. †**C** *v.t.* = DASTARDIZE. L16–M17.

†**dastardice** *n.* = DASTARDY L16–M18. **dastardize** *v.t.* (now *rare*) make a dastard of, cow M17. **dastardy** *n.* (*arch.*) base or mean cowardice, dastardliness L16.

dastardly /ˈdastədli, ˈdɑː-/ *a.* M16. [f. prec. + -LY[1].] †**1** Dull, stupid. Only in M16. **2** Resembling or characteristic of a dastard; showing mean or despicable cowardice. L16.

dastardliness *n.* M16.

dastur /dəˈstʊə/ *n.*[1] Also **destour**. M17. [Pers. *dastūr*, f. OPers. *dastōbār* prime minister, Zoroastrian high priest.] A chief priest of the Parsees.

dastur /dəˈstʊə/ *n.*[2] Also **dustoor**. L17. [Urdu *dastūr* f. Pers.] In the Indian subcontinent: custom, usage. Also = DASTURI.

dasturi /dəˈstʊəri/ *n.* Also **dustoory**. E17. [Urdu *dastūrī*, f. as prec.] In the Indian subcontinent: a customary fee, a perquisite.

dasylirion /dasɪˈlɪrɪən/ *n.* M19. [mod.L, f. Gk *dasus* thick + *leirion* lily.] Any plant of the genus *Dasylirion* of the lily family, comprising plants of Mexico and the south-western US which have white bell-shaped flowers and are often cultivated as greenhouse evergreens.

dasypygal /dasɪˈpʌɪg(ə)l/ *a.* L19. [f. Gk *dasupugos*, f. *dasus* hairy + *pugē* buttocks: see -AL[1].] *Zool.* Having hairy buttocks.

dasyure /ˈdasɪjʊə/ *n.* M19. [Fr. f. mod.L *dasyurus*, f. Gk *dasus* rough, hairy + *oura* tail.] Any of a number of carnivorous arboreal catlike marsupials of the genus *Dasyurus*, native to Australia and New Guinea.

URSINE *dasyure*.

dat /dat/ *demonstr. pron.*, *adj.*, *adv.*, & *conj.* *Black English* & *dial.* L17. [Repr. a pronunc.] = THAT.

data /ˈdeɪtə/ *n.* M17. [L, pl. of DATUM.] **I** *pl.* & *collect. sing.* **1** Things given or granted; things known or assumed as facts, and made the basis of reasoning or calculation. M17. **2** Facts, esp. numerical facts, collected together for reference or information. L19. **3** The quantities, characters, or symbols on which operations are performed by computers and other automatic equipment, and which may be stored and transmitted in the form of electrical signals, records on magnetic, optical, or mechanical recording media, etc. M20.

1 E. F. BENSON She had to make the best plans on the data that were hers. 2 B. LOVELL These data confirmed . . that the surface of Venus must have a high temperature. 3 *Computer Weekly* They have done little to analyse and interpret this data.

II *sing.* **4** A piece of information, a statistic. *rare*. E19.

Comb.: **data bank** a place where data are stored in large amounts; **database** an organized store of data for computer processing; *data capture*: see CAPTURE *n.* 6; **data communications** the use of communication networks and devices to transmit digital information; **data entry** the process or operation of inputting data to a computer system; **dataglove** a device worn like a glove and containing sensors linked to a representation of a hand in a computer display, allowing the manual manipulation of images in virtual reality; **data link** a telecommunications link over which data are transmitted; *data-logger*: see LOGGER *n.*[1] 2; **data processing** the performance by automatic means of any operations on empirical data, such as classifying or analysing them; **data processor** a machine for data processing; **data protection** the legal regulation of access to data stored in computers; **data retrieval** the obtaining of data stored on a computer system; **data sheet** a leaflet containing a summary of useful information on a subject; **data stream** = STREAM *n.* 5e; **data structure** the way data are organized in a computer, in so far as it affects the use or modification of the data; **data terminal**: at which a person can enter data into a computer-based system or receive data from one; **data type** a particular kind of data item, as defined by the values it can take or the operations that can be performed on it.

¶ The sing. uses are freq. regarded as erroneous.

datacom(s) *n.* = *data communications* above L20.

datal /ˈdeɪt(ə)l/ *a.*[1] M19. [f. DATE *n.*[2] + -AL[1].] Containing or including the date (as of a charter). Also (*rare*), chronological.

datal *a.*[2] var. of DAY-TALE.

datary /ˈdeɪt(ə)ri/ *n.* E16. [med.L *datarius*, *-ria*, f. *datum* DATE *n.*[2]: see -ARY[1].] **1** An officer of the papal court, charged with the duty of registering and dating all documents issued by the Pope, and of representing the Pope in matters relating to grants, dispensations, etc. E16. **2** The function or office of dating papal documents etc. E17.

datcha *n.* var. of DACHA.

date /deɪt/ *n.*[1] ME. [(O)Fr. (mod. *datte*) f. L *dactylus* f. Gk *daktulos* finger, toe, date (see DACTYL); so called from the finger-like leaf-shape.] **1** The fruit of the date-palm (see below), an oblong one-seeded drupe with sweet pulp, growing in clusters. ME. **b** More fully *soppy date*. A foolish, comic, or sentimental person. *colloq.* E20. **2** More fully *date-palm*. A palm tree of the genus *Phoenix*; esp. *P. dactylifera*, source of most commercially-grown dates, native to northern Africa and western Asia. LME.

Comb.: *date-palm*: see sense 2 above; **date-plum** (the fruit of) any of several kinds of persimmon, esp. *Diospyros kaki* and *D. virginiana*.

date /deɪt/ *n.*[2] ME. [(O)Fr. f. med.L *data* use as n. of fem. of *datus* pa. pple of *dare* give. Derived f. the L formula used in dating letters, e.g. *Data* (sc. *epistola*) *Romae*, '(letter) given at Rome'.] **1** The day of the month; the day of the month, the month, or the year of an event; the time or period at which something happened or the time at which something is to happen. ME. **b** A statement in a document, letter, book, or inscription, of the time (and often place) of execution, writing, publication, etc. LME. **2** Term of life or existence; season; duration. ME. **3** The period to which something old belongs; the age (of a thing or person). LME. **4** The limit or end of a period of time or of the duration of something. *arch.* LME. **5a** An appointment or engagement at a particular time (esp. with a person of the opposite sex); a social activity engaged in by two people. *colloq.* L19. **b** The person with whom such an appointment is made. *colloq.* (orig. *US*). E20. **c** A theatrical, musical, etc., engagement or performance; a place where such a performance is given (esp. as part of a tour). *colloq.* E20.

1 GOLDSMITH Not far remov'd the date, When commerce proudly flourish'd through the state. E. WAUGH A date was fixed for the wedding. A. BURGESS 714 to 768, if you want his dates. 2 MILTON Ages of endless date Founded in righteousness. 3 E. A. FREEMAN Rich in antiquities of Roman date. 4 W. COWPER All has its date below; the fatal hour Was registered in Heaven ere time began. 5a E. BOWEN He won't be in for supper. He's got a date. b J. D. SALINGER There were about a million girls . . waiting for their dates to show up. c P. G. WODEHOUSE He proposed to teach it a few simple tricks and get it dates on television.

Phrases: *bear date*: see BEAR *v.*[1] *blind date*: see BLIND *a.* *double date*: see DOUBLE *a.* & *adv.* **out of date** old-fashioned; obsolete. *sell-by-date*: see SELL *v.* **to date** to the present time or moment; until now. *up to date*: see UP *adv.*[1] *up-to-date*: see UP *adv.*[1] *use-by date*: see USE *v.*

Comb.: **date-cancel** *v.t.* cancel by a written or stamped date; **date-letter** a letter stamped on gold or silver plate, pottery, etc., denoting the year of manufacture; **date-line** (*a*) an internationally recognized line from the north to the south pole, partly along meridian 180° from Greenwich, east and west of which the date differs; (*b*) a line in a newspaper at the head of a dispatch, special article, etc., giving the date (and usu. place) of writing; **date-lined** *a.* (of an article etc.) having a (specified) date-line; **date-mark** a mark showing the date; *spec.* = *date-letter* above; **date rape**: of a girl or woman by a person she is dating or with whom she is on a date; **date-stamp** *n.* & *v.* (*a*) *n.* (the impression made by) an adjustable rubber stamp etc. used to record the date of delivery, receipt, etc., of a letter, parcel, bill, etc.; (*b*) *v.t.* mark with a date-stamp.

date /deɪt/ *v.* LME. [f. prec.] **1** *v.t.* Mark with a date. LME. **2** *v.t.* Fix or ascertain the date or time of; reckon as beginning *from*; reckon chronologically. LME. **b** *v.i.* Count the time; reckon. M18. **c** *v.t.* & *i.* Mark as or bear evidence of being of a certain date; make, be, or become outdated. *colloq.* L19. **d** *v.t.* Assign *to* a specified date. E20. **3** *v.t.* Put an end or period to; assign a duration to. Long *rare.* L16. **4** *v.i.* Assign itself or be assigned to a particular time; have its origin *from*. E19. **5** *v.i.* Bear date; be written or addressed *from* (a specified place). M19. **6** *v.t.* & *i.* Make or have a date (with); *esp.* do so regularly, go out with (a person). Also foll. by *up*. *colloq.* (orig. *US*). E20.

1 J. AUSTEN The letter . . was dated from Rosings at eight o'clock in the morning. 2 N. PODHORETZ Several short passages . . that the student was expected to date within ten years or so. c H. BELLOC All the middle and early Victorians are already dating—except Macaulay. M. MCCARTHY It was wiser not to use slang because it dated you so quickly. d E. T. LEEDS This find can be dated by coins to about A.D. 290. 4 E. K. KANE The house dated back as far as the days of Matthew Stach. J. L. WATEN Father's affection for Ginger dated from this encounter. **date back** to have existed since. 5 D. G. ROSSETTI Dante's sonnet probably dates from Ravenna. 6 N. SHUTE Every girl was dated up by a negro. J. D. SALINGER She was dating this terrible guy . . that went to Choate. O. SACKS She never dated . . variously maintaining that she despised, hated, or feared the other sex.

dat(e)able *a.* M19. **dated** *a.* (*a*) marked or assigned with a date; (*b*) *colloq.* outdated, old-fashioned; (*c*) (long *rare*) having a fixed term: L16. **dater** *n.* E17.

dateless /ˈdeɪtlɪs/ *a.* L16. [f. DATE *n.*[2] + -LESS.] **1** Having no limit or fixed term; endless; not likely to become out of date. L16. **2** Not bearing a date, undated. Also, timeless. M17. **3** Crazed; insensible; foolish. Chiefly *dial.* L17. **4** Indefinitely ancient, immemorial. L18.

datelessly *adv.* M20. **datelessness** *n.* M17.

dating /ˈdeɪtɪŋ/ *vbl n.* L17. [f. DATE *v.* + -ING[1].] **1** *gen.* The action of DATE *v.* L17. **2** (A particular technique used in) the determination of the age of a rock, fossil, archaeological specimen, etc. E20. **3** The act or practice of making dates (DATE *n.*[2] 5), esp. regularly. *colloq.* M20.

2 *carbon dating*, *potassium-argon dating*, *radiocarbon dating*, *rubidium-strontium dating*, *tree-ring dating*, etc.

dation /ˈdeɪʃ(ə)n/ *n.* Long *obs.* exc. *Law.* M17. [(O)Fr., or L *datio(n-)*, f. *dat-* pa. ppl stem of *dare* give: see -ION.] The action of giving or conferring; that which is given.

Datisi /dəˈtʌɪsʌɪ/ *n.* M16. [A mnemonic of scholastic philosophers, first used in med.L, A indicating a universal affirmative proposition, and I a particular affirmative proposition.] *Logic.* A valid mood of the third syllogistic figure, in which a universal affirmative major premiss and a particular affirmative minor yield a particular affirmative conclusion.

dative /ˈdeɪtɪv/ *a.* & *n.* LME. [L *dativus* of giving, f. *dat-* pa. ppl stem of *dare* give: see -IVE. In grammar (sc. *casus*) tr. Gk (*ptōsis*) *dotikē* (see CASE *n.*[1]).] **A** *adj.* **1** *Gram.* Designating, being in, or pertaining to a case in inflected languages expressing the indirect object or recipient (equivalent to modern English *to* or *for* w. the noun etc.). LME. **2** *Law.* In a person's gift; (of an office etc.) removable, temporary; *Sc.* given by a magistrate etc., not by disposition of law. L15. †**3** Of the nature of a gift; conferred or bestowed as a gift. L16–M17.

1 **dative absolute** in some inflected languages, a construction resembling the Latin ablative absolute, in which a noun and participle in the dative case form an adverbial clause of time, cause, or coexistence. 2 **executor dative**: named by a court, not by a testator.

B *n.* *Gram.* *The* dative case; a word, form, etc., in the dative case. LME.

datival /dəˈtʌɪv(ə)l/ *a.* E19. **datively** *adv.* M19.

dato *n.* var. of DATUK.

datok *n.* var. of DATUK.

datolite /ˈdeɪtəlʌɪt/ *n.* E19. [f. Gk *dateisthai* to divide + -O- + -LITE.] *Min.* A monoclinic hydrated basic silicate of boron and calcium, occurring as glassy prisms (colourless when pure).

dattock /ˈdatək/ *n.* L19. [Cf. Krio, Wolof *dita*.] (The hard wood, resembling mahogany, of) a W. African leguminous tree, *Detarium senegalense*.

datuk /ˈdɑːtək/ *n.* Also **-ok**, **dato** /ˈdɑːtəʊ/ (pl. **-os**), **datu** /ˈdɑːtuː/. M19. [Malay *dato'*, *datok* elder (as a term of address and a title) (in Indonesian *datuk*), and Tagalog *datò* ruler.] A landowner or chief in northern Borneo, the Philippines, and some adjacent areas.

datum /ˈdeɪtəm/ *n.sing.* Pl. DATA. M18. [L, neut. pa. pple of *dare* give.] A thing given or granted; a thing known or assumed as a fact, and made the basis of reasoning or calculation; a fixed starting-point for a series of measurements etc.

datum-line, *datum-point*, etc. ORDNANCE *datum*. *sense datum*: see SENSE *n.*

datura /dəˈtjʊərə/ *n.* L16. [mod.L (see below) f. Hind. *dhatūrā*. Cf. DEWTRY.] Any of various plants of the genus *Datura* (all containing toxic or narcotic alkaloids), of the nightshade family; *esp.* the thorn-apple, *D. stramonium*.

daturine *n.* = ATROPINE M19.

daub /dɔːb/ *n.* LME. [f. the vb.] **1** Material for daubing; plaster, clay, etc., for surface-coating, esp. mixed with straw and applied to laths or wattles to make walls. LME. **2** An act or instance of daubing. M17. **3** A patch or smear of some moist substance. M18. **4** A coarsely executed painting. M18.

1 *wattle and daub*: see WATTLE *n.*[1] 1. 3 A. BURGESS Sandwiches with a raw onion and a daub of mustard. 4 W. COWPER That he discerns The difference of a Guido from a daub.

daubster *n.* a crude or inartistic painter, a dauber L19. **dauby** *a.* of the nature of (a) daub M17.

daub /dɔːb/ *v.* LME. [OFr. *dauber* f. L *dealbare* whiten, whitewash, plaster, f. *de-* DE- I + *albus* white.] **I** *v.t.* **1** Coat or cover *with* plaster, mortar, clay, etc., esp. in building walls. LME. **2** Cover or coat *with* a moist, sticky, greasy, or dirty substance; smear; soil, stain. LME. †**3** *fig.* Cover or conceal with a plausible exterior; whitewash, gloss over. M16–L18. **4** Smear or lay on (a moist or sticky substance, plaster, etc.); apply (paint) crudely. (Foll. by *on*.) L16. **5** Cover with tasteless finery. *obs.* exc. *dial.* L16. **6** Paint crudely or inartistically. M17.

2 R. SUTCLIFF Their bodies daubed with strange designs in woad and madder. *fig.*: W. COWPER I would not be a king to be . . daubed with undiscerning praise. 3 S. FIELDING The painted canvas is most innocent; but the daubed hypocrite most criminal. 4 R. MACAULAY She's quite clever at drawing, and daubs on her paint rather amusingly. 6 DRYDEN A lame, imperfect piece, rudely daubed over with . . too much haste.

II *v.i.* **7** Apply a plaster etc. coating; paint crudely or inartistically. E16. **8** *fig.* Put on a false show; dissemble, flatter. *obs.* exc. *dial.* E17. †**9** Practise bribery. M17–L18.

7 A. TROLLOPE He . . daubed away briskly at the background.

daubing *n.* (*a*) the action of the vb; (*b*) = DAUB *n.*: LME.

daube /dəʊb, *foreign* doːb (*pl. same*)/ *n.* E18. [Fr.] A braised meat (usu. beef) stew with wine, spices, etc.

À LA *daube*. EN DAUBE.

Daubenton's bat /ˈdɔːbəntənz bat, dəʊbɑ̃ˈtɔ̃z/ *n. phr.* L19. [f. Jean Marie *Daubenton* (1716–?1800), Fr. naturalist + BAT *n.*[3]] A small Eurasian bat, *Myotis daubentoni*.

dauber /ˈdɔːbə/ *n.* ME. [AN *daubour*, *-ber*, or directly f. DAUB *v.* + -ER[1].] **1** A person who builds with daub, a plasterer. *obs.* exc. *Hist.* ME.

2 A crude or inartistic painter. M17. 3 = *mud-dauber* (a) s.v. MUD *n.*[1] Chiefly *US.* M19.

daubery *n.* the practice of daubing; the work of a dauber: M16.

daubréeite /dəʊˈbreɪʌɪt/ *n.* L19. [f. Gabriel Auguste *Daubrée* (1814–96), Fr. mineralogist + -ITE[1].] *Min.* A tetragonal basic oxychloride of bismuth, colourless when pure, occurring as massive or scaly secondary deposits.

daubréelite /dəʊˈbreɪlʌɪt/ *n.* L19. [f. as prec. + -LITE.] *Min.* A cubic sulphide of chromium and iron occurring in iron meteorites.

daud *v.* & *n.* var. of DAD *v.* & *n.*[3]

daughter /ˈdɔːtə/ *n.* & *a.* [OE *dohtor* = OFris. *dochter*, OS *dohtar* (Du. *dochter*), OHG *tohter* (G *Tochter*), ON *dóttir*, Goth. *dauhtar*, f. Gmc f. IE, whence also Skt *duhitṛ*, Gk *thugatēr*.] A *n.* 1 A female human being in relation to either or both of her parents. Also, a female offspring of an animal. OE. 2 A female descendant; a female member of a family, nation, etc. Also, a woman who is the spiritual or intellectual product *of* a specified person or thing. OE. 3a Used as a term of affectionate address to a woman or girl, by an older or superior person. *arch.* OE. b A young woman. *arch.* LME. 4 A thing (usu. personified as female) as the product, reflex, or dependant of something else. ME. b *Physics.* A nuclide formed by the disintegration of another. M20.

1 SHAKES. *Lear* The dear father would with his daughter speak. 2 J. WESLEY A daughter of affliction came to see me. TENNYSON A daughter of our meadows. 3a AV *Matt.* 9:22 But Iesus . . said, Daughter, bee of good comfort, thy faith hath made thee whole. 4 WORDSWORTH Stern Daughter of the Voice of God! O Duty! OED Carthage the famous daughter of Tyre.

Phrases: *daughter of Eve*: see EVE *n.*[1] **Daughters of the American Revolution**: a patriotic American women's society. **Duke of Exeter's daughter** an instrument of torture supposedly invented by a Duke of Exeter. GUNNER*'s daughter*.

B *attrib.* or as *adj.* (Freq. w. hyphen.) That is a daughter (esp. *fig.*). E17.

Word The passive could have existed in Proto-Indo-European, rather than in its daughter languages.

Special collocations & *comb.*: **daughter atom** = sense 4b above. **daughterboard** a printed circuit board which contains subsidiary components of a microcomputer etc. and which may be connected to a motherboard. **daughter cell** *Biol.* a cell formed by division or budding etc. of another. **daughter element** = sense 4b above. **daughter-in-law**, pl. **daughters-in-law**, (*a*) the wife of one's son; †(*b*) a stepdaughter.

daughterhood *n.* (*a*) the condition of being a daughter; (*b*) daughters collectively: M19. **daughterless** *a.* LME.

daughterly /ˈdɔːtəli/ *a.* M16. [f. prec. + -LY[1].] Such as becomes a daughter; filial.

daughterliness *n.* M17.

Daulian /ˈdɔːlɪən/ *a. literary* (*affected*). L19. [f. mod.L *Daulias* nightingale f. Gk, lit. 'woman of Daulis', Procne, who in Gk mythol. was changed into a nightingale: see -AN.] *Daulian bird*, the nightingale.

dault *n.* var. of DALT.

dauncy /ˈdɔːnsi/ *a. US* & *dial.* M19. [Var. of DONSIE.] Sickly; delicate.

daun(d)er *v.* & *n.* var. of DANDER *v.* & *n.*[4]

daunomycin /dɔːnəʊˈmʌɪsɪn/ *n.* M20. [f. *Daunia*, a former region of S. Italy, + -o- + -MYCIN.] *Pharm.* = next.

daunorubicin /dɔːnəʊˈruːbɪsɪn/ *n.* M20. [f. as prec. + *-rubi-* red (cf. RUBICUND).] *Pharm.* An antibiotic used to treat various forms of cancer.

daunt /dɔːnt/ *v.* & *n.* ME. [AN *daunter*, OFr. *danter*, var. of *donter* (mod. *dompter*) f. L *domitare* frequent. of *domare* to tame.] A *v.t.* I†1 Overcome, subdue; control; quell. ME–E18. 2 Discourage, dispirit, intimidate. ME. 3 Tame, break in (an animal). Long *obs.* exc. *dial.* LME. 4 Daze, stupefy. *obs.* exc. *dial.* L16. 5 Press (salted herring) into the barrel with a daunt. Chiefly *Sc.* E18.

2 W. PLOMER I had felt a little daunted by the extreme modishness of her clothes and by her poise. R. MACAULAY Such barriers to religion, which daunt those not brought up to them.

†II 6 Dandle, fondle. Cf. DAUT. ME–L15.

B *n.* 1 The act of daunting; intimidation; a check. Now *dial.* & *Sc.* LME. 2 A wooden disc used to press down herring in barrels. Chiefly *Sc.* M19.

daunter *n.* E16. **daunton** *v.t.* (*Sc.*) daunt M16.

dauntless /ˈdɔːntlɪs/ *a.* L16. [f. prec. + -LESS.] Not to be daunted; bold, intrepid; persevering.

dauntlessly *adv.* E19. **dauntlessness** *n.* M18.

dauphin /ˈdɔːfɪn, ˈdəʊfã/ *n.* & *a.* Also D-. LME. [Fr. (OFr. *daulphin*: see DOLPHIN), family name of the lords of Viennois or Dauphiné. Cf. also DELPHIN.] A *n.* 1 *Hist.* (The title of) the eldest son of the King of France, from 1349 to 1830. LME. †2 A dolphin. *rare.* Only in L16. †B *attrib.* or as *adj.* = DELPHIN *a.* Only in E18.

dauphinate *n.* (*Hist.*) the rule or jurisdiction of a dauphin (cf. earlier DOLPHINATE) L19. **dauphiness** /ˈdɔːfɪnɛs/ *n.* (*Hist.*) the wife of a dauphin (cf. earlier DOLPHINESS) L17.

daut /dɔːt/ *v.t. Sc.* Also **dawt**. E16. [Origin unkn. Cf. DAUNT *v.* 6.] Pet, fondle, make much of.

davenport /ˈdav(ə)npɔːt/ *n.*[1] Also **devon-** /ˈdɛv(ə)n-/. M19. [Prob. f. Capt. *Davenport*, for whom early examples were made in late-18th cent.] 1 A kind of escritoire fitted with drawers and a hinged writing-slab. M19. 2 A large sofa. *US.* M20.

Davenport /ˈdav(ə)npɔːt/ *n.*[2] M19. [See below.] More fully *Davenport china, porcelain, ware*, etc. A kind of earthenware made by the Davenport family firm at Longport, Staffordshire, England, between 1793 and 1882.

Davidic /deɪˈvɪdɪk, də-/ *a.* M19. [f. *David* (see below) + -IC.] Of or pertaining to David (d. *c*970 BC), king of Judah and later of all Israel, traditionally regarded as author of the Psalms.

Also **Davidical** *a.* E19.

Davis /ˈdeɪvɪs/ *n.* M20. [Sir Robert H. *Davis* (1870–1965), Eng. inventor.] Used *attrib.* to designate a breathing apparatus designed to enable a person to escape from a submerged submarine.

davit /ˈdavɪt, ˈdeɪv-/ *n.* L15. [AN, OFr. *daviot*, later *daviet* (mod. *davier*), dim. of *Davi* David.] A (curved) crane mounted on a ship for hoisting objects inboard or outboard; orig. one mounted at the bow for use in hoisting the anchor. Now freq. either of a pair of cranes used for suspending or lowering a ship's boat.

davy /ˈdeɪvi/ *n.*[1] *slang.* M18. [Abbrev.] An affidavit.

Davy /ˈdeɪvi/ *n.*[2] E19. [Sir Humphry *Davy* (1778–1828), Eng. chemist.] In full *Davy lamp*. A miners' safety-lamp invented by Davy, in which the flame is surrounded with wire-gauze so as to prevent its transmission to explosive gases outside the lamp.

Davy Jones /deɪvi ˈdʒəʊnz/ *n. phr. Naut. slang.* E18. [Origin unkn.] The evil spirit of the sea. Chiefly in *Davy Jones's locker*, the deep, esp. as the grave of those who perish at sea.

daw /dɔː/ *n.* LME. [Rel. to OHG *tāha* (G dial. *Tach*), beside MHG *dāhele, tāle* (G *Dohle*): prob. already in OE. Cf. CADDOW *n.*[1]] 1 = JACKDAW. LME. 2 A simpleton; a lazy person; a slattern. LME.

daw /dɔː/ *a.* M19. [Origin unkn.] Of a pale primrose colour, as the eyes of certain gamefowl.

daw /dɔː/ *v. obs.* exc. *Sc.* [OE *dagian*, corresp. to MDu. *daghen*, Du., LG *dagen*, OHG *tagēn* (G *tagen*), f. WGmc base of DAY *n.*] 1 *v.i.* Dawn. OE. †2 *v.i.* & *t.* Waken, revive. ME–L17.

†dawark *n.* see DARG.

dawdle /ˈdɔːd(ə)l/ *v.* & *n.* M17. [Prob. f. dial. origin. Cf. DADDLE *v.*, DODDLE *v.*] A *v.* 1 *v.i.* Idle, waste time; loiter, dally. M17. 2 *v.t.* Waste, fritter *away* (time etc.). M18.

1 HENRY MILLER The breakfast . . was the one ceremony of the day over which she dawdled and lingered. *fig.*: D. MORRIS While our reproductive systems raced ahead, our brain-growth dawdled behind.

B *n.* A person who dawdles; an act of dawdling. M18.

dawdler *n.* E19.

dawg /dɔːg/ *n. dial.* & *joc.* L19. [Repr. a pronunc.] = DOG *n.*

dawing /ˈdɔːɪŋ/ *n. obs.* exc. *Sc.* OE. [f. DAW *v.* + -ING[1].] Dawn, daybreak.

dawk *n.* var. of DAK.

dawn /dɔːn/ *n.* L16. [f. the vb.] 1 The first appearance of light in the sky before sunrise; daybreak. L16. 2 *fig.* The beginning, rise, or first appearance *of* something; an incipient gleam *of*. M17.

1 *crack of dawn*: see CRACK *n.* 4. *false dawn*: see FALSE *a.* 2 S. JOHNSON From the dawn of manhood to its decline. C. LAMB You could see the first dawn of an idea stealing slowly over his countenance.

Comb.: **dawn chorus** the early-morning singing of birds; **dawn man** an extinct primitive man; formerly *esp.* Piltdown man; **dawn raid** (*a*) a surprise attack at dawn; (*b*) *Stock Exch. slang* a swift operation early in trading whereby a broker buys for a client a markedly increased holding in a company; *dawn redwood*: see REDWOOD *n.*[1] 2.

dawn /dɔːn/ *v.i.* L15. [Back-form. f. next, largely repl. DAW *v.*] 1 Of the morning, the day, etc.: begin to grow light. L15. 2 Begin to brighten (as) with the light of dawn. M17. 3 *fig.* Begin to appear or develop; become visible or evident. E18. b Of ideas, facts, etc.: begin to become evident to the mind, be perceived. Usu. foll. by *on*, *upon* a person. M19.

1 J. BARTH I saw him more clearly as the day dawned. 2 TENNYSON I waited underneath the dawning hills. 3 LD MACAULAY In the year 1685 . . his fame . . was only dawning. H. L. MENCKEN It was not until skepticism arose in the world that genuine intelligence dawned. b D. LODGE The awful truth dawned upon him: Radio One was like this all the time. C. WILSON It dawned on him that the alchemists were talking in symbols. H. CARPENTER The realisation had dawned that the apparent triumphs of the Industrial Revolution had produced widespread misery.

dawning /ˈdɔːnɪŋ/ *n.* ME. [Alt. of DAWING after Scand. (OSw. *daghning*, Sw., Da. *dagning*).] 1 The beginning of daylight; daybreak, dawn; *transf.* the east. Now chiefly *poet.* ME. 2 *fig.* The first gleam, the appearance, the beginning, (*of* something). E17.

1 C. KINGSLEY Oh sing, and wake the dawning. 2 W. H. PRESCOTT The dawnings of a literary culture.

dawt *v.* var. of DAUT.

day /deɪ/ *n.* [OE *dæġ* = OFris. *dei*, OS (Du.) *dag*, OHG *tac* (G *Tag*), ON *dagr*, Goth. *dags*, f. Gmc.] I (The time of) sunlight. 1 The time during which the sun is above the horizon; the interval of light between two nights. OE. 2 Daybreak, dawn. Now *rare* or *obs.* ME. 3 Daylight, the light of day. ME. 4 Any of the perpendicular divisions or lights of a mullioned window. *arch.* LME. 5 *Mining.* The surface of the ground over a mine. M17.

1 N. CARPENTER The longest day is equall to the longest night. S. KING The day was overcast and drippy. 2 H. NELSON This morning at day we fell in with a Spanish . . Ship. 3 DEFOE It was broad day.

II As a unit of time. 6 The time for one rotation of the earth on its axis; the period of twenty-four hours as a unit of time, esp. from midnight to midnight. Also (*Astron.*), a single rotation of a planet in relation to its primary. OE. b A day of notable eventfulness etc. *colloq.* E20. 7 This period of time, esp. the civil day, treated as a point or unit of time, a particular date, etc. OE.

6 D. BREWSTER We may regard the length of the day as one of the most unchangeable elements in the system of the world. R. S. THOMAS So the days will drift into months. P. CHEYNEY Life is what you make it. Rome wasn't built in a day. b E. HEMINGWAY I say. We have had a day . . I must have been blind [drunk]. 7 DAY LEWIS I was born next day—April 27th, 1904.

III A specified or appointed day. 8 A specific period of twenty-four hours, the whole or part of which is assigned to some particular purpose, observance, or action; the date of a specified festival etc. (freq. w. specifying wd(s)). OE. b The period of time in each day, established by law or usage, during which work is customarily done; a working-day. M19. 9 A date agreed on; a day for a regular event, as being at home for guests, seeing patients at a clinic, etc. ME. 10 The day of a battle or contest; (victory in) a battle. L15.

8 J. CHEEVER The day of the flower show. *Ascension Day, birthday, Boxing Day, Christmas Day, Father's Day, holiday, Labour Day, Lady Day, May Day, New Year's Day, pay-day, St Andrew's day, St Swithin's day, washday, wedding day, workday*, etc. b R. TANGYE A great agitation . . in favour of a nine hours' day. M. MCCARTHY A little light chatter about her day in the store. 9 DRYDEN Or if my debtors do not keep their day. MRS H. WARD We found she was in town, and went on her 'day'. 10 T. TUSSER The battell is fought, thou hast gotten the daye. J. MCCRAE These . . died not knowing how the day had gone.

IV A space of time, a period. 11 *sing.* & in *pl.* The time during which something exists or takes place; a period, a time, an era; *the* current period. Also (with possess. pers. n. or pron.) the period of a person's rule, activity, career, or life; one's lifetime; time of action, period of power or influence. OE. 12 Time allowed in which to be ready for something, esp. payment; delay, respite; credit. Long *rare*. LME. 13 A space of time (freq. of a defined extent). *obs.* exc. *Sc.* LME.

11 DRYDEN I at Naples pass my peaceful Days. M. L. KING The Hitlers and the Mussolinis have their day, and for a period they may wield great power. J. C. OATES A popular tune of the day. *Proverb*: Every dog has his day. *school-days* etc.

Phrases: *a good day's work*: see WORK *n.* **all (the) day (long)** throughout the day, from daybreak to nightfall. **all in the** or **a day's work** part of the normal routine, a matter of course. *(an) eight days*: see EIGHT *a.* **any day** at any time, under any conditions. *as clear as day*: see CLEAR *a.* **astronomical day** = *solar day* below. **at the end of the day** in the final reckoning. **better days** times of greater prosperity. *break of day*: see BREAK *n.* 4. **call it a day** decide that one has worked at a task long enough, cease working (for the day, for the present, or finally); be satisfied with what one has done. *carry the day*: see CARRY *v.* **civil day**: as used for time reckoning in ordinary affairs. **day after day** each day as a sequel to the preceding one, esp. in an unvarying sequence. **day and night**: throughout these or in both alike. **day by day** on each successive day, daily without ceasing. *day in, day out*: see IN *adv.* *Day of Atonement*: see ATONEMENT. **day off** a day away from work, school, etc. *Day of Judgement, Judgement Day*: see JUDGEMENT. *day of* RECKONING. **day of rest** *spec.* the Sabbath. *day of retribution*: see RETRIBUTION 2. *day of the Covenant*: see COVENANT *n.* *day of the week*: see WEEK *n.* *day of truce*: see TRUCE *n.* **day out** a day away from home etc., an excursion. *days of grace*: see GRACE *n.* **day-to-day** continuous(ly), routine(ly). *dish of the day*: see DISH *n.* 3a. *dog days*: see DOG *n.* *dominical day*: see DOMINICAL *a.* 1. *eight days*: see *an eight days* above. *Ember day*: see EMBER *a.* **end one's days** pass the last part of one's life, die. *equinoctial day*: see EQUINOCTIAL *a.* *evil day(s)*: see EVIL *a.* *eye of day*: see EYE *n.* *fifth day*: see FIFTH *a.* FIRST *day*. FOURTH *day*. **from day to day** continuously or without interruption from one day to another. **have had its day** be of no further use or effect. *high day*: see HIGH *a.* **if he's** etc. **a day** at least (a particular age etc.) **in this day and age** at the present time, as things are at the present. *last day(s)*: see LAST *a.* **late in the day** *fig.* late in the proceedings; *esp.* so late as to be of doubtful use. *light of day*: see LIGHT *n.* *Lord's day*: see *(the) Lord's day* below. *lunar day*: see LUNAR *a.* *make a day of it*: see MAKE *v.* *make a person's day*: see MAKE *v.* *mean solar day*: see MEAN *a.*[2] **natural day** (*a*) = sense 1 above; (*b*) = sense 6 above (the usual sense). **night and day** = *day and night* above. **not one's day** a day when things go badly for one. **of a day** transitory, ephemeral. **one day** on some unspecified day, past or future. *one fine day, one of these fine days*: see FINE *a.* **one of these days** before long. **one of those days** a day of misfortune. **on one's day** at the time of one's best achievement etc., when at one's best. *open day*: see OPEN *a.* *order of the day*: see ORDER *n.* *red letter day*: see RED *a.* SALAD *days*. *second day*: see SECOND *a.* SIDEREAL *day*. *solar day*: see SOLAR *a.*[1] *some day*: see SOMEDAY *adv.* **that will be the day** that will be worth waiting for, *iron.* that will never happen. **these days** *adv.* nowadays, at present. **The Day** [tr. G *der Tag*] a day expected to be marked by an important event, esp. a military conflict or victory. *(the) Lord's day*: see LORD *n.* *the other day*: see OTHER *a.* *this day* MONTH. **those were the days** (particular) past times were good or *iron.* bad (in comparison with the present). *time of day*: see TIME *n.* *to* or *until one's dying day*: see DYING *a.*[1] **to this day** at the present time as in the past, still, yet. *twelfth day*: see TWELFTH *a.* VARNISHING *day*. *wait the day*: see WAIT *v.* *win the day*: see WIN *v.*[1] *with continuation of days*: see CONTINUATION 5. WORKING *day* See also WEEKDAY.

Comb.: **day-bed** a bed for daytime sleep or rest; a sofa, a couch; **day blindness** = HEMERALOPIA; **daybook** (*a*) *arch.* a journal, a diary; formerly also, a nautical logbook; (*b*) an account-book in which esp. sale transactions are entered at once for later transfer to a ledger; **day-boy** a schoolboy who attends a boarding-school but lives at home; **daybreak** dawn, the first light of day; **day care** the supervision of young children during the day, esp. while a parent or guardian is at work; **day centre** a place providing social, recreational, or other facilities for elderly or handicapped persons during the day; **day-dawn** *poet.* daybreak; **day-flower** any of various plants of the genus *Commelina* of the spiderwort family, having short-lived flowers usually blue in colour; **day-fly** a mayfly, living only a few hours or days; **day-girl** a schoolgirl who attends a boarding-school but lives at home; **day labour** work performed as a daily task, daily labour; labour hired by the day; **day labourer**: hired by the day; **day letter** *US Hist.* a low-priority telegram sent by day; **day lily** any of various plants of the genus *Hemerocallis* of the lily family, with yellow, reddish, or purplish flowers lasting only for a day; **daylong** *a.* & *adv.* (lasting) for a whole day; **daymare** [after *nightmare*] a frightening or oppressive trance or hallucinatory condition experienced while awake; **day-nursery** (*a*) a room for children in the daytime; (*b*) a place where young children are looked after while a parent or guardian is at work; **day-owl** an owl that hunts by day, *esp.* the short-eared owl; **day-peep** *arch.* earliest dawn; **day release** a system of allowing employees days off work to follow educational courses; **day return** (a ticket) at a reduced rate for a journey made both ways in one day; **day-room** a room used by day only; *esp.* a common living-room at a boarding school, a common-room for inmates of a hospital, etc.; †**day-rule** a rule or order which permitted a prisoner to go beyond the confines of prison for one day; **day-school** a school attended daily during the week, esp. as opp. to Sunday, night-, or boarding-school; **day shift** a shift worked during the daylight hours, as opp. to the night shift; **daysman** (*a*) *arch.* an arbitrator, a mediator; (*b*) a day labourer; **day-spring** *arch.* & *poet.* dawn; **day-star** (*a*) the morning star; (*b*) (chiefly *poet.*) the sun; **daytime** the time of daylight; **daywork** (*a*) (*obs.* exc. *dial.*) a day's work; †(*b*) the amount of land able to be ploughed in a day; (*c*) work paid for according to the time worked.

dayless *a.* †(*a*) without redress, resource, or result; (*b*) *poet.* devoid of daylight, dark: LME.

†**day** *v.* ME. [Branch I var. of DAW *v.* assim. to DAY *n.*; branch II f. DAY *n.*] I *v.i.* 1 Dawn. ME–M16. II *v.t.* 2 Submit (a matter) to arbitration, decide by arbitration. LME–E17. 3 *year and day*, subject to a statutory period of a year and a day. E16–E17. 4 Measure by the day; provide with days. E17–M19.

Dayak *n.* & *a.* var. of DYAK.

dayan /da'jɑːn/ *n.* Pl. **-nim** /-nɪm/, **-s**. L19. [Heb. *dayyān*, f. *dān* to judge.] A religious judge in a Jewish community.

daydream /'deɪdriːm/ *n.* & *v.* M17. [f. DAY *n.* + DREAM *n.*[2]] A *n.* A fancy or reverie (esp. of happiness) indulged in while awake; a fantasy, a castle in the air. M17. B *v.* 1 *v.i.* Indulge in a daydream; become lost in one's imaginings. E19. 2 *v.t.* Imagine in a daydream; transport (oneself) imaginatively in a daydream. L19.

daydreamer *n.* a person who daydreams, esp. habitually M19.

Day-Glo /'deɪgləʊ/ *n.* & *a.* Also **dayglo** & other vars. M20. [f. DAY *n.* + GLOW *n.*] A *n.* (Proprietary name for) fluorescent paint or other colouring material. M20. B *adj.* Coloured (as) with Day-Glo; (of colour) vivid, luminous, fluorescent. M20.

daylight /'deɪlʌɪt/ *n.* ME. [f. DAY *n.* + LIGHT *n.*] 1 The light of day. Also *fig.*, the full light of knowledge and observation; openness, publicity. ME. 2 The time of daylight, the daytime; *spec.* dawn. ME. 3 In *pl.* The vital organs. Formerly also, the eyes. *slang.* M18. 4 A clear visible interval, as between boats in a race, the rim and contents of a wineglass, a rider and the saddle, etc. E19.

1 *burn daylight*: see BURN *v.* 8b. **let daylight into** *slang* make a hole in, stab, shoot. **see daylight** *fig.* understand what was previously puzzling. 3 **beat, scare**, etc., **the living daylights out of** beat, scare, etc. severely.

Comb.: *daylight robbery*: see ROBBERY *n.* 3; **daylight-saving** the use of modified time to give longer evening daylight esp. in summer, by making clocks show a later time.

days /deɪz/ *adv.* Now *colloq.* & *US.* OE. [f. DAY *n.* + -S[3], later identified w. -S[1]. Cf. NIGHTS *adv.*] During the day, by day.

day-tale /'deɪteɪl/ *a.* Chiefly *dial.* Also **da(y)tal** /'deɪt(ə)l/. M16. [f. DAY *n.* + TALE *n.* reckoning etc.] Designating work, wages, a worker, etc., reckoned, paid, or engaged by the day.

daze /deɪz/ *n.* L17. [f. the vb.] †1 Mica. L17–L18. 2 A dazed condition (*lit.* & *fig.*); (a state of) stupefaction or bewilderment. E19.

2 DAY LEWIS In a daze of pure satisfaction. D. BAGLEY Conscious but in a daze, hardly aware of what was happening.

daze /deɪz/ *v.* ME. [Orig. in pa. pple f. ON *dasaðr* weary or exhausted from cold or exertion. Cf. ON *dasask* (v.refl.) become exhausted, *dasi* lazy fellow, Sw. *dasa* lie idle.] I *v.t.* 1 Stupefy, bewilder (a person), as by a blow on the head, drink, etc.; stun, confuse. Freq. as *dazed* ppl a. ME. 2 Benumb, blight, or destroy with cold. *Sc.* & *north.* ME. 3 Confound or bewilder (the vision) by excessive light or brilliance; dazzle (*lit.* & *fig.*). Chiefly *poet.* E16.

1 G. MACDONALD She looked dazed, perhaps from the effects of her fall. D. MURPHY I was so dazed with joy that I could hardly speak. 3 TENNYSON The sudden light Dazed me half-blind.

II *v.i.* †4 Be or become stupefied or bewildered; be benumbed with cold; remain inactive or torpid. ME–E16. †5 Be or become dazzled; gaze stupidly. LME–M17. 6 Of meat, bread, etc.: become spoiled by being cooked at the wrong temperature. Of wood etc.: become rotten or spoiled from dampness etc. Chiefly as *dazed* ppl a. *Sc.* & *north.* L17.

dazedly /-zɪdli/ *adv.* in a dazed manner LME. **dazedness** *n.* the state or condition of being dazed LME. **dazy** *a.* (*rare*) in a dazed condition E16.

dazibao /'dɑːdzəbaʊ/ *n.* Pl. same. M20. [Chin. *dàzìbào*, f. *dà* big + *zì* character + *bào* newspaper, poster.] In the People's Republic of China, a wall-poster written in large characters expressing an (esp. political) opinion.

dazzle /'daz(ə)l/ *v.* & *n.* L15. [f. DAZE *v.* + -LE[3].] A *v.* 1 *v.i.* Of the eyes: lose the faculty of steady vision, esp. from gazing at too bright a light. *arch.* L15. 2 *v.t.* Confuse or dim (the sight, eye, etc.), bewilder (a person), with an excess of light, intricate motion, an incalculable number, etc. E16. 3 *v.t.* & *i.* Delude or surprise (the mind, a person) by a brilliant or showy display or prospect; confuse or impress *by* or *with* brilliance etc.; temporarily overcome (a person's judgement etc.) in this way. M16. 4 *v.t.* Outshine, dim, eclipse, (chiefly *fig.*). *rare.* L16.

1 J. WEBSTER Cover her face; mine eyes dazzle. 2 B. PYM She opened her eyes but was . . too dazzled by the sun to be able to see. 3 L. STEPHEN Pope seems to have been dazzled by the amazing vivacity of the man. M. ARNOLD A style to dazzle, to gain admirers everywhere. 4 N. HAWTHORNE This church was dazzled out of sight by the Cathedral.

B *n.* 1 A dazzled state or condition. *rare.* E17. 2 An act of dazzling; a brightness, glitter, etc., that dazzles the vision; a bright confusing light. M17. 3 More fully *dazzle paint*. Paint patterned on a ship to deceive an enemy about its type or course. E20.

2 A. MASON The dazzle of armour too bright to look at in the sun. *fig.*: J. RUSKIN Amidst the tumult and the dazzle of their busy life.

Comb.: *dazzle paint*: see sense 3 above; **dazzle-painted** *a.*, **-painting** camouflaged, camouflaging, by dazzle paint.

dazzlement *n.* (*a*) the act of dazzling; a cause of dazzling; (*b*) a dazzled condition: M17. **dazzler** *n.* (see also BOBBY-DAZZLER) L18. **dazzling** *ppl a.* †(*a*) that is or becomes dazzled; (*b*) that dazzles the eyes, mind, etc.; bright, brilliant, or splendid to a degree that dazzles: L16. **dazzlingly** *adv.* E17.

dbx /diːbiː'ɛks/ *n.* L20. [f. *db* = decibel + *x* = expander.] (Proprietary name for) a device designed to increase the dynamic range of reproduced sound.

D-Day /ˈdiːdeɪ/ *n.* E20. [f. D for *day* + DAY *n.*] **1** The day on which a particular (esp. military) operation is scheduled to begin; *spec.* (an anniversary of) 6 June 1944, when Allied forces invaded German-occupied northern France. E20. **2** The day of conversion of a country to decimal currency (in Britain, 15 February 1971). M20.

de- /diː, dɪ/ *pref.* [f. or after L *de-* f. *de* adv. & prep., = off, from. In privative sense 3 partly through Fr. *dé-* f. OFr. *des-* f. L *dis-*, treated as identical w. L *de-* (cf. DIS-).] **1** In vbs (w. derivs.) of L origin w. the senses 'down, down from, down to', as *depend, depress*, etc., 'off, away, aside', as *decline, deduce, desist*, etc., 'completely, thoroughly', as *declaim, denude, derelict*, etc., 'to exhaustion', as *deliquesce* etc., or in a bad sense, as *deceive, deride, detest*, etc. **2** In or after late L w. the sense 'repeatedly, over again', as *decomposite, decompound*, etc. **b** In adjs. w. the sense 'formed from (what is denoted by the root noun)', as *de-adjectival, denomial, deverbal*, etc. **3** With privative sense (denoting removal or reversal), in vbs f. L, as *decorticate* etc., f. Fr., as *debauch, defrock*, etc., and as a freely productive pref., forming vbs (w. derivs.) f. vbs, as *de-acidify, decentralize, decentralization, de-escalate, depressurize, desegregate*, etc., or f. ns., as *defuse, de-ice, delouse, detrain*, etc.

de-accession /diːəkˈsɛʃ(ə)n/ *v.* & *n.* L20. [f. DE- 3 + ACCESSION *v.*] **A** *v.t.* & *i.* Officially remove (an item) from the listed holdings of a library, museum, etc., esp. for sale or disposal. L20. **B** *n.* The action or process of de-accessioning items; a de-accessioned item. L20.

deacon /ˈdiːk(ə)n/ *n.* Also (esp. as a title) **D-**. OE. [eccl.L *diaconus* f. Gk *diakonos* servant, in eccl.Gk Christian minister.] **I** *Chr. Ch.* **1 a** In the early Church, an appointed minister of charity (see *Acts* 6:1–6). OE. **b** In the episcopal Churches, a member of the third order of the ministry, ranking below bishops and priests and having the functions of assisting the priest in divine service (esp. the celebration of the Eucharist), parish work, etc. OE. **c** In Nonconformist Churches, an officer appointed or elected to attend to secular matters affecting the congregation. M16. †**2** A set of Eucharistic garments worn by a deacon. LME–M16.

1b *cardinal deacon*: see CARDINAL *a.* 3.

II †**3** = LEVITE *n.* 1. OE–LME. **4** The president of an incorporated craft or trade in any town; a master craftsman, a thoroughly capable man. *Sc.* LME. **5** A junior officer in a Masonic lodge. L18. **6** (The hide of) a very young or aborted calf. *US colloq.* L19.

Comb.: **deacon-seat** *N. Amer.* a long seat in a log-cabin, cut from a single log.

deaconate *n.* (*a*) deaconship; (*b*) a body of deacons: L19. **deaconhood** *n.* (*rare*) = DEACONATE LME. **deaconship** *n.* the position or office of deacon LME.

deacon /ˈdiːk(ə)n/ *v.t.* M19. [f. the n.] **1** Read aloud (a hymn etc.) one or two lines at a time, before it is sung. Freq. foll. by *off*. *US colloq.* M19. **2** Pack (fruit etc.) with the finest specimens on top; *gen.* alter so as to deceive, display deceptively. *US colloq.* M19. **3** Admit to the office of deacon. L20.

deaconess /diːkəˈnɛs, ˈdiːk(ə)nɪs/ *n.* Also (esp. as a title) **D-**. LME. [f. DEACON *n.* + -ESS[1], after L *diaconissa*.] *Chr. Ch.* **1 a** In the early Church, a woman performing diaconal duties among other women. LME. **b** In some modern Churches, a woman with functions analogous to those of a deacon. E17. **2** (**D-**.) A member of any of several Protestant orders of women, with educational and charitable aims. M19. **3** A deacon's wife. *rare.* M19.

deaconry /ˈdiːk(ə)nri/ *n.* L15. [f. as prec. + -RY.] **1** The position or office of deacon; deaconship. L15. **2** A body of deacons. L17. **3** *RC Ch.* A chapel or charitable institution, in the charge of a cardinal deacon. L17.

deactivate /diːˈaktɪveɪt/ *v.t.* M20. [f. DE- 3 + ACTIVATE *v.*] Render inactive; make less (chemically) reactive.

deactiˈvation *n.* E20. **deactivator** *n.* a substance which deactivates (chemically) M20.

dead /dɛd/ *n.*[1] OE. [f. the adj.] **1** A dead person. Chiefly *collect.*, those or all who have died. OE. **2** The dead period *of* a particular time, season, etc. M16. **3** *Mining.* In *pl.* Earth or rock containing no ore. M17.

1 I. MURDOCH The dead are the victims of the living. J. C. OATES Even the dead were washed out of their graves. **dead's part** *Sc. Law* the part of an estate whose disposal is decidable by the testator or by the law of intestacy. **from the dead** from among those who are dead, from a state of death. **on the dead** *US slang* in dead earnest, honestly. *walking dead*: see WALKING *ppl a.* **2** W. S. CHURCHILL Driven in dead of winter along the mountain roads covered with snow.

dead *n.*[2] see DEATH.

dead /dɛd/ *a.* & *adv.* [OE *dēad* = OFris. *dād*, OFr. *dōd* (Du. *dood*), OHG *tōt* (G *tot*), ON *dauðr*, Goth. *dauþs*, f. Gmc, f. pa. pple of ult. base of DIE *v.*[1]] **A** *adj.* **I 1** That has ceased to live; deprived of life. OE. **2** Having lost sensation or vitality; benumbed, insensible. Also *hyperbol.*, exhausted, drained of strength, worn out. ME. **3** Foll. by *to*: completely insensible or unresponsive to; unappreciative of; hardened against. Also, as good as dead in a particular respect or capacity; *spec.* legally cut off from all civil rights. ME. **4** Devoid of living organisms; barren, infertile. ME. **5** Destitute of spiritual life or energy. LME. **6** Not endowed with life; inanimate; inert. LME. †**7** Causing death; deadly, mortal. LME–E17. **8** [Partly attrib. use of DEAD *n.*[1]] Of, pertaining or relating to a dead person, animal, etc., or a death. Also, (of a hedge or fence) made of dead plants etc. L15. **9** No longer in use or existence; obsolete; past; *esp.* (of a language etc.) no longer spoken. L16.

1 DEFOE He was shot dead. S. JOHNSON Macbean.. is dead of a suppression of urine. DAY LEWIS A semi-circle of drive.. littered with dead leaves. **2** OED She fell on the floor in a dead faint. A. HIGGINS My feet have gone dead on me. **3** N. BACON He that is in a monastery is dead to all worldly affairs. SHELLEY Sensual, and vile; Dead to all love. *Washington Post* Rome.. dismissed as culturally dead. **4** HENRY MILLER The arid surface of dead planets. **5** W. COWPER He lives, who lives to God alone, And all are dead beside. **6** ADDISON There are some living creatures which are raised but just above dead matter. **7** SHAKES. *Wint. T.* Though full of our displeasure, yet we free thee From the dead blow of it. **8** W. COMBE What the medical people call a dead case.. a consultation.. to discover the disorder of which their patient died. **9** TENNYSON My doubts are dead. J. IRVING Old East Norse is a dead language.

II 10 Without vigour or animation, lifeless. OE. **b** Of a racehorse: not intended to win, fraudulently run to prevent its winning. *slang.* M19. **11** Without motion, unmoving; still, standing; (of a mechanical part) not designed to move independently. OE. **12** Without active force or practical effect; ineffectual, inoperative. ME. **13** Without commercial, social, or intellectual activity; marked by inactivity, dull; (of capital, stock, etc.) lying unutilized, unprofitable, unsaleable. ME. **14** Deprived of or wanting a vital or characteristic quality; extinguished, extinct; spent, burnt-out; flat, dull, lustreless. ME. **b** Of an electric circuit, conductor, etc.: not carrying or transmitting a current; not connected. Of a microphone, telephone, etc.: not transmitting sounds. E20. **15** Of sound: muffled, without resonance, dull. Of a room etc.: allowing minimal acoustic reverberation. LME. **16** Characterized by absence of physical motion or sound; profoundly quiet or still. Of ground etc.: lacking resilience or springiness; *Mil. colloq.* naturally sheltered from a line of fire. Of a house (*slang*): uninhabited. M16. **17** Characterized by complete and abrupt cessation of motion, action, or speech. M17. **18** *Games.* Of the ball: not in play, (temporarily) inactive. Also (*Golf*), so close to a hole that the putt is deemed to be unmissable. M17. **19** *Archit.* Lacking its ostensible purpose; false, blind; inoperative. E19.

10 L. HUTCHINSON A bare dead description. R. W. EMERSON Active intellect and dead conservatism. **11** I. WALTON From the dead, still water, into the sharp streames and the gravel. O. G. GREGORY The dead pulley is fixed to the axis and turns with it. **12** J. H. NEWMAN So earnest for a dead ordinance. **13** R. KNOX And now caps were become a very dead commodity. J. A. FROUDE It was the dead season; but there were a few persons still in London. **14** EVELYN It will not ferment.. and then the Cider will be dead, flat, and soure. DRYDEN The dead colour of her face. H. COLERIDGE The crackling embers on the hearth are dead. **b** I. MURDOCH There was a big electric torch, but the battery was dead. **16** SHAKES. *Meas. for M.* 'Tis now dead midnight. **17** DICKENS The answer spoilt his joke, and brought him to a dead stop. **18** B. JOHNSTON A ball does *not* become dead when it strikes an umpire. **19** R. FORSYTH A.. bridge.. the dead arches of which have been fitted up as a town-hall.

III 20 Unrelieved, unbroken; profound, deep; (of the state of the tide) lowest; (of pull, strain, etc.) applied to its utmost against an unmoving body. M16. **21** Absolute, complete, entire, thorough, downright; unerring, certain, sure; exact. L16. **22** Of an expense etc.: unrelieved, complete, utter. Of an outlay: unproductive, without returns. E18.

20 D. LIVINGSTONE I crossed it at dead low-water. TENNYSON We heard In the dead hush the papers.. Rustle. J. R. LOWELL To reduce all mankind to a dead level of mediocrity. **21** R. SHARROCK Till the seed.. be come to a full and dead ripeness. SIR W. SCOTT This is a dead secret. THACKERAY He is a dead hand at piquet. **22** W. COBBETT Those colonies are a dead expense to us.

Phrases: **dead and gone** or **buried** *rhet.* in one's grave, deceased; *fig.* past, over. **dead as a doornail** quite dead. **dead as mutton** quite dead. **dead as the** or **a dodo** extinct, entirely obsolete. **dead from the neck up** *colloq.* brainless, stupid, doltish. **dead to the wide** *slang* (*a*) = *dead to the world* below; (*b*) totally exhausted. **dead to the world** unconscious, fast asleep. *lay dead*: see LAY *v.*[1] *the dead ring* (*of*): see RING *n.*[2] *top dead centre*: see TOP *a.* **wouldn't be seen dead in** (or **with**) *colloq.* shall have nothing to do with, refuse to wear etc.

Special collocations & comb.: **dead(-and)-alive** alive without animation, dull, spiritless, monotonous. **dead-ball line** *Rugby Football* a line behind the goal-line beyond which the ball is considered out of play. **dead bat** *Cricket* a bat held loosely so that the ball strikes it and immediately falls to the ground. *dead body*: see BODY *n.* **dead-born** *a.* (chiefly *dial.*) born dead. **dead centre** (*a*) the exact centre; (*b*) = *dead point* below; (*c*) in a lathe, the centre which does not revolve. *dead cert*: see CERT *n.* **dead colour** the first or preparatory layer of colour in a painting. **dead-colour** *v.t.* paint in dead colour. †**dead-doing** *a.* killing, murderous. *dead duck*: see DUCK *n.*[1] **deadeye** *Naut.* a round flat three-holed block for extending shrouds. **deadfall** (chiefly *N. Amer.*) (*a*) a trap with a falling weight to kill an animal, a snare (*lit.* & *fig.*); (*b*) a tangled mass of fallen trees etc.; (*c*) a disreputable drinking or gambling place. **dead-fire** a corposant, taken as a presage of death. *dead giveaway*: see GIVEAWAY *n.* 2. **dead hand** (*a*) [tr.] = MORTMAIN; (*b*) posthumous control, *esp.* an undesirable persisting posthumous influence. **dead-hearted** *a.* callous, insensible. **dead heat** a race in which two or more competitors finish exactly level. **dead-heat** *v.i.* run a dead heat (*with* another competitor). **dead horse** *fig.* something no longer of use, something it is pointless to attempt to revive, (*flog a dead horse*, waste energy on something unalterable). **dead house** *arch. colloq.* a mortuary. **dead letter** (*a*) a writing etc. taken literally without reference to its spirit or intention, and so useless or ineffective; (*b*) a law no longer observed, a disused practice; (*c*) an unclaimed or undelivered letter. **dead lift** (*a*) a lift made without mechanical assistance or other advantage; an exertion of the utmost strength to lift or move something (esp. beyond one's strength); (*b*) (now *arch.* & *dial.*) an extremity, a hopeless case (chiefly in *at a dead lift*). **deadlight** (*a*) *Naut.* a strong shutter fixed inside or outside a porthole etc. to keep out water in a storm; (*b*) *Sc.* = *corpse-candle* (a) s.v. CORPSE *n.*; **deadline** (*a*) a line, constituting a piece of tackle etc., that does not move or run; (*b*) a line beyond which it is not permitted or possible to go; (*c*) a time-limit, *esp.* the time by which an article etc. scheduled for publication must be completed. **dead load** a load of constant and invariable weight. **dead loss** (*a*) a complete and unrelieved (financial) loss; (*b*) *colloq.* a useless or contemptible person or thing. **dead march** a slow solemn march for a funeral etc., a funeral march. **dead-melt** *v.t.* keep (a metal) at a melting temperature until it is perfectly fluid and no more gas is evolved. **dead-nettle** any of various labiate plants of or allied to the genus *Lamium*, with leaves like those of stinging nettles but without stinging hairs; *esp.* (*a*) (more fully *red dead-nettle*) *L. purpureum*, a European weed with pinkish-purple flowers; (*b*) (more fully *white dead-nettle*) *L. album*, a Eurasian hedge plant with large white flowers; (*c*) *yellow dead-nettle* = *yellow archangel* s.v. ARCHANGEL 2. †**dead palsy**: producing complete insensibility or immobility of the affected part. **dead pay** [cf. Fr. *morte-paye*] †(*a*) (a soldier etc. receiving) pay continued after active service has ceased; (*b*) *Hist.* a soldier etc. actually dead or discharged but for whom nevertheless pay is claimed; pay drawn in this way. **dead point** the position of a crank in direct line with the connecting rod and not exerting torque. **dead reckoning** estimation of the position of a ship, aeroplane, etc., by log, compass, etc., when observations are impossible. *dead set*: see SET *n.*[1] 4, 5. **dead shot** an unerring marksman. *dead soldier*: see SOLDIER *n.* **dead-stick landing**: of an aircraft with the engine(s) stopped. **dead stock, deadstock** (*a*) (as two wds) commercially inactive or unproductive stock, capital, etc.; (*b*) (as one wd) farm machinery etc. (as opp. *livestock*). **dead time** *Physics* the period after the recording of a pulse etc. when a detector is unable to record another. **dead-tongue** (chiefly *dial.*) a poisonous umbellifer, hemlock water dropwort, *Oenanthe crocata*. **dead water** (*a*) the neap tide; (*b*) water without any current, still water; (*c*) *Naut.* the eddy water just behind the stern of a ship under way. **dead weight** (*a*) a heavy unrelieved weight or burden; an inert mass; (*b*) the weight of cargo, fuel, crew, and passengers carried by a ship etc.; (*c*) *fig.* a debt not covered by assets; (*d*) the weight of an animal after it has been slaughtered and prepared as a carcass. **dead well**: sunk to a porous stratum to carry off surface or refuse water. **dead white** (*a*) flat or lustreless white; (*b*) pure white. **dead wood** (*a*) wood no longer alive; *fig.* a person or persons, a thing or things, regarded as useless or unprofitable; (*b*) *Naut.* solid blocks of timber fastened just above the keel at each end of a ship, to strengthen her structure. **dead work** (*a*) unproductive work (in mining etc.); †(*b*) = *upper works* (a) s.v. UPPER *a.*

B *adv.* **1** To a degree suggesting death; with extreme inactivity, stillness, etc.; profoundly; to extremity. LME. **2** Utterly, entirely, absolutely, quite, exactly. Now *colloq.* L16. **3** Directly, straight. E19. **4** With an abrupt cessation of motion or action. M19.

1 J. CARLYLE Whether I fainted, or suddenly fell dead-asleep. **dead drunk** so drunk as to be insensible or immobile. 2 W. F. HOOK One horse . . which soon became dead lame. R. COBB The train came in dead on time. SLOAN WILSON You're just like the others—dead ordinary. *dead broke, dead certain, dead right, dead sure,* etc. **dead on** exactly right. *dead to rights*: see RIGHT *n.*[1] 3 J. CONRAD It loomed up dead to leeward. **dead against** directly opposed or opposite to (*lit.* & *fig.*). 4 E. POUND Don't make each line stop dead at the end.

¶The compar. *deader* and superl. *deadest* are in use where the sense permits.

deadish *a.* (now *rare*) LME. **deadness** *n.* L16.

dead /dɛd/ *v.* OE. [f. the adj. Superseded by DEADEN.] **I** *v.i.* †**1** = DEADEN 5. OE–M17. **II** *v.t.* **2** Cause to die, kill. Now *nursery*. LME. †**3** = DEADEN 3. LME–L17. †**4** = DEADEN 1. E17–M18. †**5** = DEADEN 2. Only in 17.

dead-beat /ˈdɛdbiːt, *as pred. adj.* dɛdˈbiːt/ *a.*, *n.*, & *v.* E19. [f. DEAD *adv.* + BEAT *ppl a.*] **A** *adj.* **1** Completely exhausted; at the end of one's resources. *colloq.* E19. **2** Of an escapement etc.: without recoil. L19. **B** *n.* A worthless sponging idler, a loafer (orig. *US*); a man down on his luck (orig. *Austral.*). *colloq.* M19. **C** *v. colloq. rare.* **1** *v.t.* Exhaust, wear out. M19. **2** *v.t.* & *i.* Sponge (on), cheat. L19.

dead-ˈbeaten *a.* exhausted L19.

deaden /ˈdɛd(ə)n/ *v.* M17. [f. DEAD *a.* + -EN[5]. Superseding DEAD *v.*] **I** *v.t.* **1** Deprive of some effective physical quality, as flavour, lustre, sharpness, etc.; make (sound) dull or indistinct. M17. **b** Make impervious to sound. E20. **2** Destroy or reduce the energy of (motion). M17. **3** Deprive of vitality, force, etc.; dull, benumb; make dead or insensible *to*. L17. **4** Deprive (tissue etc.) of life, kill; *spec.* (*US*) kill (trees), clear (ground) of trees, by ringbarking. L18.

1 E. BOWEN Grass which had seeded between the cobbles . . deadened her steps. 3 A. S. NEILL A bairn does like the dramatic; prosiness deadens its wee soul at once. M. SHADBOLT He was given injections to deaden pain.

II *v.i.* **5** Become dead; *esp.* lose vitality, vigour, brightness, feeling, etc. E18.

5 SOUTHEY The dash Of the out-breakers deaden'd.

deadener *n.* M19. **deadeningly** *adv.* in a deadening manner, so as to deaden M20.

dead-end /dɛdˈɛnd; *as attrib. adj.* ˈdɛdɛnd/ *n.*, *a.*, & *v.* L19. [f. DEAD *a.* + END *n.*] **A** *n.* (Also as two wds.) The closed end of a passage etc., a cul-de-sac; *fig.* a job, policy, course of action, etc., with no prospects of advancement. L19.

B *adj.* Closed at the end, leading nowhere; *fig.* having no possibilities for advancement, promotion, etc. L19.

dead-end kid a young slum-dwelling tough, a juvenile delinquent.

C *v.t.* & *i.* Bring or come to a dead-end. E20.

deadhead /ˈdɛdhɛd/ *n.* & *v.* Also **dead-head**. L16. [f. DEAD *a.* + HEAD *n.*] **A** *n.* †**1** = CAPUT MORTUUM. L16–E18. **2** A disposable or unmoving mechanical part. M19. **3** A non-paying theatre-goer, passenger, etc. *colloq.* (orig. *US*). M19. **b** An empty train, vehicle, etc. *US colloq.* M20. **4** A useless or unenterprising person; one who contributes nothing to an activity etc., a hanger-on. *colloq.* L19. **5** In full *deadhead log*. A sunken or submerged log. *N. Amer.* E20. **6** A faded flower-head, esp. when still attached to the plant. M20. **B** *v.* **1** *v.t.* & *i.* Enter or admit to a theatre etc. without payment; (allow to) travel free. *US colloq.* M19. **2** *v.i.* & *t.* Drive or travel in (a train, vehicle, etc.) with no passengers or cargo. *colloq.* (orig. *US*). E20. **3** *v.t.* Remove a dead flower or flowers from (a plant). M20.

de-adjectival /ˌdiːadʒɛkˈtʌɪv(ə)l/ *a.* M20. [f. DE- 2 + ADJECTIVAL.] *Gram.* Derived from an adjective.

deadlock /ˈdɛdlɒk/ *n.* & *v.* L18. [f. DEAD *a.* + LOCK *n.*[2]] **A** *n.* **1** A condition or situation in which no progress or activity is possible; a complete standstill; lack of progress due to irreconcilable disagreement or equal opposing forces. L18. **2** A lock which opens and shuts only with a key (as opp. to a spring-lock); occas., a padlock. M19. **B** *v.t.* & *i.* Bring or come to a state of deadlock. L19.

deadlocked *a.* (of negotiation, conflict, etc.) in which no progress is possible L19.

deadly /ˈdɛdli/ *a.* OE. [f. DEAD *a.* + -LY[1].] †**I 1** Subject to death, mortal. OE–M19. **2** In danger of death; of or belonging to death. ME–E17.

II 3 Causing fatal injury or serious damage; mortal; poisonous, venomous, pestilential. OE. **4** *Chr. Theol.* Of sin: entailing damnation, mortal (as opp. *venial*), *esp.* designating each of the seven chief or cardinal sins. ME. **5** Aiming or involving an aim to kill or destroy; implacable; internecine. ME. **6** Resembling or suggestive of death; deathlike, esp. in unconsciousness or physical prostration; (of darkness, gloom, silence, etc.) intense; *colloq.* dreary. ME. **7** Excessive, intense. *colloq.* M17. **8** Of aim etc.: accurate. E20.

3 J. BEATTIE Tho' Fortune aim her deadliest blow. TOLKIEN To wield his sword with left hand more deadly than his right had been. *deadly* NIGHTSHADE. 5 G. F. KENNAN A deadly, implacable, snakelike enmity. 6 SHAKES. *Com. Err.* I know it by their pale and deadly looks. 7 CARLYLE Why such deadly haste to make money?

deadlily *adv.* (*rare*) E17. **deadliness** *n.* ME.

deadly /ˈdɛdli/ *adv.* OE. [f. DEAD *a.* + -LY[2].] †**1** In a way that causes death; mortally, fatally; *Theol.* in a way entailing damnation. OE–E19. †**2** Implacably, to the death. ME–M17. **3** In a manner resembling or suggesting death; as if dead. ME. **4** Extremely, excessively. *colloq.* L16. **5** In a dead manner; like a dead thing. *rare.* L16.

3 J. CONRAD Being so deadly white . . like a horrible . . invalid. 4 M. KEANE A deadly dull display of barometers.

dead man /dɛd ˈman/ *n. phr.* Pl. **dead men** /ˈmɛn/. Also (now *rare*) **deadman** /ˈdɛdman/, pl. **deadmen**. OE. [f. DEAD *a.* + MAN *n.*] **I** *lit.* **1** A man who is dead. OE. **II** *transf.* & *fig.* **2** In *pl.* Empty liquor bottles. *slang.* L17. †**3** A loaf charged to a customer but never delivered. *slang.* M18–L19. †**4** A dummy at whist etc. Only in L18. **5** *Naut.* In *pl.* Reef- or gasket-ends left dangling when a sail is furled. E19. **6** Any of various objects buried in or secured to the ground for the purpose of providing anchorage or leverage. M19. **7** A scarecrow. *dial.* M19.

Phrases: **dead man's** or **men's bells** *Sc.* the foxglove. †**dead man's eye** = *deadeye* s.v. DEAD *a.* etc. **dead man's** or **men's fingers** (*a*) any of various orchids, *esp.* the early purple orchid; (*b*) a soft coral, *Alcyonium digitata*; (*c*) the divisions of the gills in a crab or lobster. **dead man's hand** (*a*) = *dead man's fingers* (a), (b) above; (*b*) the male fern, *Dryopteris filix-mas*. **dead man's handle, pedal**, etc., a control in an electric train etc. which acts as a safety device by automatically cutting off the current if released; an emergency brake in a motor lorry etc. **dead man's thumb** (*a*) the early purple orchid; (*b*) = *dead man's fingers* (b) above. *dead man men's bells, fingers*: see *dead man's bells, fingers* above. *dead men's shoes*: see SHOE *n.*

deadpan /ˈdɛdpan/ *a.*, *n.*, *adv.*, & *v.* Also (esp. as n.) **dead pan**. E20. [f. DEAD *a.* + PAN *n.*[1]] **A** *adj.* Expressionless, impassive, unemotional; detached, impersonal. E20.

I. BAIRD Matt's eyes lost their cold deadpan look. *Listener* The Baron's marvellously deadpan tall tales.

B *n.* (A person with) a deadpan expression; a deadpan demeanour or style. M20.

C *adv.* With a deadpan face; in a deadpan manner. M20.

D *v.t.* & *i.* Infl. **-nn-**. Speak, perform, behave, etc., with a deadpan face or in a deadpan manner. M20.

Dead Sea /dɛd ˈsiː/ *n. phr.* ME. [f. DEAD *a.* + SEA *n.*, tr. L *mare mortuum*, Gk *hē nekra thalassa*.] The inland sea into which the River Jordan flows, which has no outlet and is noted for its bitter, saline waters and arid surroundings; *gen.* (**d- s-**) any sea considered to be devoid of life.

Comb.: **Dead Sea apple, fruit** (*a*) a legendary fruit, of attractive appearance, which dissolved into smoke and ashes when held; (*b*) either of two plants with showy fruit, *Solanum sodomeum*, an African nightshade naturalized in the Mediterranean region, and a mudar, *Calotropis procera*; the fruit of either of these plants; (*c*) *fig.* any outwardly desirable object which on attainment turns out to be worthless; any hollow disappointing thing; **Dead Sea Scrolls** a collection of ancient Jewish scrolls and fragments discovered in caves in the area of Qumran, a region on the north-western shore of the Dead Sea, between 1947 and 1956.

de-aerate /diːˈɛːreɪt/ *v.t.* L18. [f. DE- 3 + AERATE.] Remove air from.

de-aeˈration *n.* M19.

deaf /dɛf/ *a.* & *n.* [OE *dēaf* = OFris. *dāf*, OS *dōf* (Du. *doof*), OHG *toup* (G *taub*), ON *daufr*, Goth. *daufs*, *daubs*, f. Gmc, f. IE base repr. also by Gk *tuphlos* blind.] **A** *adj.* **1** Without hearing; defective in the sense of hearing. OE. **b** Insensitive to certain kinds of sound, musical rhythm, harmony, etc. Foll. by *to* or in *comb.*, as *tone-deaf* etc. L18. **2** Lacking its essential quality or characteristic; hollow, barren; insipid. Now chiefly *dial.* OE. **3** Not giving ear *to*; unwilling to hear or pay attention *to*; unresponsive, uncompliant. ME. †**4** Of a sound: so dull as to be hardly or indistinctly heard; muffled. E17–E18.

1 SIR W. SCOTT Lady Suffolk is a little deaf. E. LONGFORD He was to be stone deaf in the left ear for life. *fig.*: SHELLEY Have its deaf waves not heard my agony? *deaf as an adder, a beetle, a post*, etc. 3 J. L. WATEN Although their voices floated out into the kitchen I was deaf to them. **fall on deaf ears** be ignored. **turn a deaf ear (to)** pretend not to hear, be unresponsive (to an appeal etc.).

B *absol.* as *n.* A deaf person. Long only *collect. pl.*, *the* class of deaf people. OE.

Special collocations & comb.: **deaf adder** (*a*) the slow-worm; (*b*) *US* a hognose snake. **deaf-aid** a hearing-aid. **deaf and dumb** neither able to hear nor to speak; *the* class of deaf and dumb people. **deaf-and-dumb alphabet, language** a system of manual signs for communication with the deaf, = *finger spelling* s.v. FINGER *n.* **deaf-dumbness** the condition of being deaf and dumb. **deaf-nettle** *dial.* a dead-nettle. **deaf nut** a nut with no kernel; *fig.* something hollow or worthless.

deafish *a.* E17. **deafly** *adv.* (*a*) without hearing (*lit.* & *fig.*); (*b*) dully, indistinctly: ME. **deafness** *n.* OE.

deaf /dɛf/ *v.t.* Now *arch.* & *dial.* LME. [f. the adj.: cf. earlier DEAVE. Superseded by DEAFEN.] 1 = DEAFEN 1. LME. 2 = DEAFEN 2. M17.

deafen /ˈdɛf(ə)n/ *v.t.* L16. [f. DEAF *a.* + -EN[5]. Superseding DEAF *v.*] 1 Make deaf; deprive of hearing by noise, temporarily or permanently. L16. 2 Make (a sound) inaudible; drown *by* a louder sound. E19. 3 *Building.* Make (a floor etc.) soundproof. Now chiefly *Sc.* E19.

1 M. W. MONTAGU Hunting horns . . that almost deafen the Company. **deafening silence** *iron.* a conspicuous or significant failure to comment on a matter or otherwise respond.

deafened *a.* & *n.* (*a*) *adj.* that has been made deaf (now esp. permanently); (*b*) *n. the* class of deafened people: E17. **deafeningly** *adv.* so as to deafen M19.

deafferent /diːˈaf(ə)r(ə)nt/ *v.t.* E20. [f. DE- 3 + AFFERENT *a.*] *Biol.* & *Med.* Interrupt or destroy the afferent connections of (nerve cells); deprive of afferent connection with the central nervous system.

deafferen'tation *n.* M20.

de-afforest /diːəˈfɒrɪst/ *v.t.* M17. [med.L *deafforestare*, f. as DE- 1, AFFOREST. Cf. DEFOREST, DISAFFOREST, DISFOREST.] *Hist.* = DISAFFOREST 1.

de-affore'station *n.* M17.

deaf mute /dɛf ˈmjuːt/ *n.* & *a. phr.* Also (esp. as adj.) **deaf-mute.** M19. [f. DEAF *a.* + MUTE *a.* & *n.*[2] after Fr. *sourd-muet.*] A *n. phr.* A deaf and dumb person. M19. B *adj.* Both deaf and dumb; of or pertaining to the deaf and dumb. M19.

deaf-'mutism *n.* the condition of being both deaf and dumb M19.

deal /diːl/ *n.*[1] [OE *dǣl* = OFris., OS *dēl* (Du. *deel*), OHG, G *Teil*, Goth. *dails*, f. Gmc base also of DOLE *n.*[1]] †1 A part or division of a whole; a portion, section. OE–M18. 2 A portion allowed to anyone; a share. Now *dial.* OE. 3 A (specified, now usu. *great* or *good*) quantity, amount, or number (*of*). Also (*colloq.*) *absol.*, a considerable quantity, a lot, much. In adv. phrs.: to a specified degree or extent. OE.

1 AV *Num.* 15:9 A meate offering of three tenth deales of flowre. EVERYDEAL, HALFENDEAL, SOMEDEAL. 3 J. RAY So vast a deal of room, that 40,000 people may shelter . . in it. K. GRAHAME In the winter time the Rat slept a great deal. J. GALSWORTHY A deal of mortals in this world, and not enough imagination to go round! J. G. COZZENS Quite a good deal younger than her husband. R. MACAULAY I have a great deal to say to you, my child.

deal /diːl/ *n.*[2] ME. [MLG, MDu. *dele* plank, floor (Du. *deel* plank), corresp. to OHG *dil*, *dilo*, *dillo*, *dilla* (G *Diele* floorboard, floor), ON *þilja* OE *þille*, f. Gmc.] 1 A piece of sawn timber (now always fir or pine wood) of standard size; a plank or board of fir or pine; timber in such planks or boards. Also more fully *deal board.* ME. 2 Fir or pine timber. E17.

2 *attrib.*: S. HEANEY The deal table where he wrote. **red deal** the wood of the Scots pine, *Pinus sylvestris.* **white deal** the wood of the Norway spruce, *Picea abies*, or of the silver fir, *Abies alba.* **yellow deal** = *red deal* above.

Comb.: *deal board*: see sense 1 above; **deal-fish** a N. Atlantic fish, *Trachipterus arcticus*, belonging to the ribbonfish family Trachipteridae, with laterally compressed body (likened to a deal).

deal /diːl/ *n.*[3] L15. [f. the vb.] †1 Dealings, intercourse. *Sc.* L15–L16. 2 The distribution of cards to players before a round of play; a player's turn for this; the round of play following this; the set of hands dealt to players. E17. 3 An act of trading or of buying or selling; a business transaction, a bargain, an arrangement; *esp.* a private or secret arrangement entered into by parties for their mutual benefit. *colloq.* M19.

3 H. F. PRINGLE Deals and counterdeals between Tammany and anti-Tammany Democrats. P. G. WODEHOUSE If you don't wish to meet my terms, the deal is off. J. DIDION It was kind of a Swiss Family Robinson deal down there. *big deal!*: see BIG *a.* **a fair deal** equitable treatment, honest dealing. **a raw** or **rough deal** harsh or unfair treatment. *a square deal*: see SQUARE *a. new deal*: see NEW *a.*

deal /diːl/ *v.* Pa. t. & pple **dealt** /dɛlt/. [OE *dǣlan* = OFris. *dēla*, OS *dēljan* (Du. *deelen*), OHG, G *teilen*, ON *deila*, Goth. *dailjan*, f. Gmc, f. base of DEAL *n.*[1]] I†1 *v.t.* Divide. OE–L16. †2 *v.t.* & (*rare*) *i.* Separate, part (*from*). OE–LME. †3 *v.t.* Divide (property etc.) in due shares, portion out; share *with* another or others. OE–M16. 4 *v.t.* Distribute, give out (gifts etc.) among a number of recipients; (*esp.* of Providence etc.) deliver as share or deserts (*to* a person). Freq. foll. by *out.* OE. 5 *v.t.* Cause to be received, administer, deliver (esp. a blow (*lit.* & *fig.*)). ME. 6 *v.t.* & *i.* Distribute (cards) to the players in a game or round; give a player (such or so many cards) in dealing. E16. b *v.t.* Include (a person) *in* those to whom cards are dealt; *fig.* include (someone) *in* an undertaking, give (a person) a share or part. *colloq.* (orig. *US*). M20.

1 CAXTON This kyngdome of Northumberland was first deled in two prouynces. 3 COVERDALE *Josh.* 8:2 Ye shal deale amonge you their spoyle & catell. 4 M. ARNOLD Has thou yet dealt him, O life, thy full measure? K. AMIS A woman in a corner sweet-shop . . who had dealt out the lollies . . to the school kids. 5 DRYDEN By fits he deals his fiery bolts about. E. BOWEN You dealt us a knock, you know. You gave us a fright. 6 C. COTTON He that deals hath the advantage of this game. *transf.*: M. AMIS I picked up the stack of mail . . and dealt myself one off the bottom. b W. GARNER If they won't deal us in we may end up having to steal it.

II†7 *v.i.* Engage *with* in conflict; contend. OE–E18. †8 *v.i.* Take part *in*, share or participate *in* or *with*, partake *of.* OE–L15. 9 *v.i.* Have to do, have dealings *with* (esp. w. neg.); *arch.* negotiate, treat *with*, esp. in an underhand or secret way; do business, trade *with* a person, *in* goods etc., (*lit.* & *fig.*). ME. 10 *v.i.* Foll. by *with*: be concerned with (a thing) in any way; busy or occupy oneself with, esp. with a view to discussion or refutation. Also, take (esp. punitive or corrective) measures regarding, cope with, handle (a difficult person, situation, etc.). ME. 11 *v.i.* Foll. by *with* or *by*: behave towards, treat (a person etc.) (in a specified way). Also *absol.*, act towards people generally (in a specified way), conduct oneself. ME. †12 *v.i.* Take action, act, proceed (*in* a matter). ME–M17. 13 *v.i.* Set to work, practise (*up*)*on. arch. rare.* L16.

7 MILTON Brutish that contest and foule, When Reason hath to deal with force. 9 JONSON Now have they dealt with my pothecary to poison me. I. WATTS True Logic is not that noisy thing that deals all in dispute and wrangling. E. A. FREEMAN One of the charges . . was that of dealing with a familiar spirit. W. H. AUDEN War is but a kind of trading: Instead of cheese, it deals in lead. 10 LD MACAULAY A power more than sufficient to deal with Protector and Parliament together. B. PYM His notes dealt almost entirely with religion. F. WELDON The way to deal with Hilda was to agree with what she said, while believing none of it. 11 EARL OF CHATHAM If we would deal fairly by ourselves. SWIFT They had better give up now, if she will not deal openly. 12 SHAKES. *Much Ado* Do not you meddle; let me deal in this. 13 SHAKES. *Rich. III* Two deep enemies . . Are they that I would have thee deal upon.

Phrases: *wheel and deal*: see WHEEL *v.*

dealable *a.* (*rare*) able to be dealt *with*; suitable for dealing: M17.

dealbate /diːˈalbət/ *a. rare.* LME. [L *dealbatus* pa. pple of *dealbare*: see next, -ATE[2].] Presenting a white appearance; whitened.

dealbation /diːalˈbeɪʃ(ə)n/ *n.* LME. [L *dealbatio(n-)*, f. *dealbat-* pa. ppl stem of *dealbare*: see DAUB *v.*, -ATION.] The action of whitening; blanching, bleaching.

de-alcoholize /diːˈalkəhɒlʌɪz/ *v.t.* Also **-ise.** M19. [f. DE- 3 + ALCOHOL *n.* + -IZE.] Remove the alcohol from (wine etc.). Chiefly as *de-alcoholized* ppl a.

dealer /ˈdiːlə/ *n.* OE. [f. DEAL *v.* + -ER[1].] 1 A person who divides, distributes, or delivers something; *spec.* the player dealing at cards. OE. 2 A person who has dealings *with* another or others, *in* an affair, etc.; an agent, a negotiator. Now chiefly as *transf.* use of sense 4. OE. 3 A person who acts (in a specified way) in relation to others. Now usu. in *comb.*, as below. M16. 4 A person or (in *pl.*) firm dealing in merchandise, a trader; *spec.* one buying and selling articles of a particular commodity. L16. 5 A jobber on a stock exchange. See also BROKER-*dealer.* E18.

2 DEFOE A sorcerer . . or dealer with the Devil. SWIFT Small dealers in wit and learning. 3 *double-dealer*: see DOUBLE *a.* & *adv. plain dealer*: see PLAIN *a.*[1] & *adv.* 4 *antique-dealer*, *horse-dealer*, *money-dealer*, etc.

dealership *n.* the position, business, etc., of a dealer; an authorized trading establishment: E20.

dealing /ˈdiːlɪŋ/ *n.* LME. [f. as prec. + -ING[1].] 1 Division, distribution, delivering (of gifts, blows, cards, etc.); sharing *out.* LME. 2 *sing.* & (now usu.) in *pl.* Friendly or business communication (*with*); personal connection or association (*with*). LME. 3 *sing.* & in *pl.* Mode of acting towards others, treatment of others; conduct, behaviour. (Foll. by *with* the person(s) towards whom the behaviour is directed.) L15. 4 *sing.* & in *pl.* Trading, trafficking; buying and selling, esp. of a particular commodity. M17.

3 *plain dealing*: see PLAIN *a.*[1] & *adv.*

dealkylation /ˌdiːalkɪˈleɪʃ(ə)n/ *n.* E20. [f. DE- 3 + ALKYLATION.] *Chem.* The removal of an alkyl group from a compound.

de'alkylate *v.t.* remove an alkyl group from M20.

dealt *v.* pa. t. & pple of DEAL *v.*

deambulation /dɪˌambjʊˈleɪʃ(ə)n/ *n.* E16. [L *deambulatio(n-)*, f. *deambulat-* pa. ppl stem of *deambulare* walk about, f. as DE- 1 + AMBULATION.] The action of walking about; a walk.

de'ambulate *v.i.* (*rare*) E17.

deambulatory /dɪˈambjʊlət(ə)ri/ *n.* & *a.* LME. [med.L *deambulatorium* n., *-orius* adj., f. *deambulat-*: see prec., -ORY[1], -ORY[2].] A *n.* A place to walk in for exercise; *esp.* a covered walk or cloister. LME. B *adj.* Walking about; peripatetic. E17.

deaminate /dɪˈamɪneɪt/ *v.t.* E20. [f. DE- 3 + AMINE + -ATE[3].] *Chem.* Remove an amino group or groups from.

deami'nation *n.* E20.

dean /diːn/ *n.*[1] Also (esp. as a title) **D-.** ME. [AN *de(e)n*, OFr. *d(e)ien* (mod. *doyen*), f. late L *decanus* chief of a group of ten, f. L *decem* ten, after *primanus* member of the first legion, perh. infl. by Gk *deka* ten.] I *Chr. Ch.* 1 The head of the chapter of a cathedral or a collegiate church. ME. 2 More fully *rural dean.* A member of the clergy exercising supervision (under the bishop or archdeacon) over a group of parochial clergy within a division of an archdeaconry. ME. b More generally, a member of the clergy invested with a specified charge and having a particular jurisdiction. M17. 3 *Hist.* [tr. eccl.L *decanus.*] The head of ten monks in a monastery. LME.

2b *Dean of peculiars*: see PECULIAR *n. Dean of the Arches*: see ARCH *n.*[1] 1.

II *gen.* †4 A head, chief, or commander of a division of ten. LME–L15. 5 *Hist.* More fully *Dean of guild.* An officer of a medieval guild who summoned members to attend meetings etc. Also (*Sc.*), the head of the guild or merchant-company of a royal burgh, latterly usu. a member of the town council. LME. 6 The leader or senior member of any body; a doyen. LME. 7 The head of a university faculty or department, or of a medical school. Also (*N. Amer.*), the registrar or secretary of a university or college faculty. E16. 8 In a college or university (esp. Oxford or Cambridge), a fellow, or each of a number of fellows (formerly and still sometimes resident) with disciplinary and advisory functions. L16.

6 **Dean of Faculty** the president of the Faculty of Advocates in Scotland. **Dean of the Sacred College** the senior member of the Sacred College, usu. the oldest of the Cardinal Bishops, who presides in the consistory in the absence of the Pope. 7 **dean's list** *N. Amer.* a list of students receiving special recognition from the dean of a college or university for academic excellence. 8 *junior dean*, *senior dean*, etc.

deaness *n.* (*a*) *Chr. Ch.* a woman who is head of a female chapter; (*b*) *joc.* the wife of a dean: M18. **deanship** *n.* the office, position, or rank of a dean; *joc.* (*his Deanship* etc.) used as the title of a dean: M16.

dean *n.*[2] var. of DENE *n.*[1]

deaner /ˈdiːnə/ *n. slang* (chiefly *Austral.* & *NZ*). *obs.* exc. *Hist.* Also **deener.** M19. [Prob. ult. f. DENARIUS, DENIER *n.*[2]] A shilling.

deanery /ˈdiːnəri/ *n.* LME. [f. DEAN *n.*[1] + -ERY, after AN *denrie*.] 1 The position or office of a dean. LME. 2 The group of parishes presided over by a rural dean. Formerly also, the jurisdiction of a dean. LME. 3 The official residence of a dean. L16.

de-Anglicize /diːˈaŋglɪsʌɪz/ *v.t.* Also **-ise**. L19. [f. DE- 3 + ANGLICIZE.] Remove English characteristics or influence from.
de-Anglici'zation *n.* E20.

dear /dɪə/ *a.*[1], *n.*, & *int.* [OE *dēore*, (WS) *dīere* = OFris. *diore*, OS *diuri* (Du. *dier* beloved, *duur* high-priced), OHG *tiuri* distinguished, worthy, costly (G *teuer*), ON *dýrr*, f. Gmc.] A *adj.* †1 Glorious, noble, honourable, worthy. OE–E17. 2 Regarded with esteem and affection; beloved; loved, cherished; precious *to*. Freq. used in speech in addressing a person (sometimes as a merely polite or iron. form), and as part of the polite introduction (or occas. subscription) of a letter, esp. in a formula denoting the degree of formality involved. OE. b Affectionate, loving, fond. Now *rare* exc. as passing into sense 2c. L16. c Lovable, endearing, sweet. *colloq.* M18. †3 Highly esteemed; high in worth or value; valuable; important. OE–E17. 4 High in price or charge made, absolutely or in relation to value; costly, expensive. OE. b Having or charging high prices. ME. c Of money: available on loan only at a high rate of interest. L19. 5 Heartfelt; earnest. L16.

1 SHAKES. *1 Hen. IV* Dear men Of estimation and command in arms. 2 T. WYATT Therewith all sweetly did me kiss And softly said, 'Dear heart how like you this?' JER. TAYLOR I am.. Dear Sir, your obliged and most affectionate friend and servant J. Taylor. D. H. LAWRENCE My dear Lady Ottoline,—I arrived home safely. E. WAUGH No, no, dear boy. You are to lunch with Jo. J. D. SALINGER The kind of information that will be very, very dear to your heart. W. VAN T. CLARK As if I were an old, dear friend she was worried about. b I. WALTON Sir Henry Wotton, a dear lover of this Art. J. KEBLE My dear love to — and —. 3 SHAKES. *Sonn.* And with old woes new wail my dear time's waste. 4 T. FULLER The dearest town in England for fuel. D. DU MAURIER Any stuff like this is dear, but it will last for years. 5 G. B. SHAW My father-in-law's dearest wish was to be a teacher and a preacher.

Phrases: **be dear of** be kind or thoughtful of (a person, *to do* something). **Dear John (letter)** *colloq.* a letter from a woman to an absent fiancé, husband, etc., notifying him of the end of their relationship and her attachment to another man. **for dear life** as though life itself were at stake. **hold dear** regard with affection, value highly.

B *n.* 1 (With or, as a form of address, also without possess.) a person dear to one; a dear one, a darling, a lovable or endearing person. Cf. DEAREST 3. ME. 2 (*the*) *dear knows* = *God knows* s.v. KNOW *v.* E19.

1 SPENSER From that day forth Duessa was his deare. M. EDGEWORTH 'Really, my dear', answered she, 'I can't say.' R. MACAULAY Aunt Stanley was a great dear; treated one always as a friend. K. AMIS The two things are completely different, dear. B. PYM I don't grudge the old dears a lunch.

C *int.* Expr. surprise, distress, sympathy, regret, etc. L17.

dear, dear! I am sorry, concerned, etc. **dear me!**, **oh dear!** I am shocked, surprised, disappointed, etc.

dear /dɪə/ *a.*[2] *arch.* OE. [Origin unkn.] †1 Brave, strenuous, hardy. Only in OE. 2 Hard, severe, grievous; fell, dire. OE. †3 Difficult. Only in ME.

2 SHAKES. *Sonn.* Made lame by Fortune's dearest spite. SHELLEY Now I forget them at my dearest need.

dear /dɪə/ *v.t.* LME. [f. DEAR *a.*[1]] †1 Make dear or expensive; raise the price of. *Sc.* Only in LME. 2 Endear. *rare.* E17. 3 Make a fuss *over* a person. *rare.* L18. 4 Address as 'dear'. E19.

4 F. MARRYAT Don't dear *me*, Sir Hurricane, I am not one of *your dears.*

dear /dɪə/ *adv.* [OE *dīore*, *dēore* = OHG *tiuro* (G *teuer*).] 1 At a high price; at great cost. OE. 2 Fondly, earnestly, dearly. *arch.* ME.

1 P. GALLICO Buy cheap and sell dear. *cost a person dear*: see COST *v.* 2. **dear-bought** bought at a high price, obtained at great cost. 2 SHAKES. *Rom. & Jul.* Rosaline, that thou didst love so dear.

dearborn /ˈdɪəbɔːn/ *n. US.* E19. [Prob. f. Gen. Henry *Dearborn* (1751–1829).] A kind of light four-wheeled wagon.

dearest /ˈdɪərɪst/ *n.* LME. [Superl. of DEAR *a.*[1] used absol.] †1 *The* most noble or worthy people. Only in LME. †2 *The* highest price offered. Only in LME. 3 With, or as a form of address, also without possess.: the person(s) most dear to one, dearest one. Cf. DEAR *n.* L16.

3 H. MARTINEAU Do not exhaust yourself at once, dearest. *nearest and dearest*: see NEAR *a.*

dearie /ˈdɪəri/ *n.*, *a.*, & *int.* Also **deary**. L17. [Dim. of. DEAR *a.*[1], *n.*, & *int.*: see -IE, -Y[6].] A *n.* Chiefly as a form of address, with or without possess.: little dear, darling. L17. B *adj.* Attractively small, tiny. *dial.* L17. C *int.* Expr. sorrow, dismay, etc. Chiefly in *dearie me!*, dear me, alas. L18.

†dearling *n.* & *a.* var. of DARLING *n.*[1] & *a.*

dearly /ˈdɪəli/ *adv.* [OE *dēorlīce* = OS *diurlīco*, OHG *tiurlīhho*, f. as DEAR *a.*[1] + -LY[2].] †1 In a precious, worthy, or excellent manner; finely, richly. OE–E17. 2 As one who is held dear; affectionately, fondly. Now usu. modifying *love*, *like*, etc. ME. 3 Earnestly, in a heartfelt manner; keenly. Now usu. in a weakened sense: very much, greatly. ME. 4 At a high price, at great cost, (freq. *fig.*). L15.

2 MILTON His dearly-loved mate. 3 SHAKES. *A.Y.L.* My father hated his father dearly. A. PRICE He would dearly have liked a pint now himself. 4 E. K. KANE All the dearly-earned documents of the expedition. B. PYM I valued my independence very dearly. *cost a person dearly*: see COST *v.* 2.

dearness /ˈdɪənɪs/ *n.* ME. [f. DEAR *a.*[1] + -NESS.] 1 The quality of being held dear. Also, intimacy, (mutual) affection, fondness. ME. †b An expression or token of affection. M17–E18. 2 The quality of being dear in price; expensiveness, costliness. M16.

1 G. BURNET The dearness that was between them, was now turned..to..enmity. I. GURNEY The dearness of common things, Beechwood, tea, plate shelves.

dearth /dəːθ/ *n.* & *v.* ME. [f. DEAR *a.*[1] + -TH[1]. Cf. OS *diur(i)þa*, OHG *tiurida*, *diurida*, ON *dýrð*.] A *n.* 1 Scarcity and dearness of food; formerly, a famine. ME. 2 A scarcity *of* anything; a practical deficiency; want or lack *of* a quality. ME. 3 Costliness, high price. *obs.* exc. *Sc.* E17.

1 GIBBON The fertility of Egypt supplied the dearth of Arabia. J. UPDIKE In this time of crisis and dearth, our human resources must be conserved. 2 W. JAMES The veriest lack and dearth of your imagination. K. TYNAN Nor is there a dearth of English actors; the land is alive with them.

B *v.t.* Make dear in price; cause a dearth of. Long *obs.* exc. *Sc.* LME.

deary *n.*, *a.*, & *int.* var. of DEARIE.

deas *n.* see DAIS.

deasil /ˈdɛs(ə)l, ˈdjɛʃ(ə)l/ *adv.* & *n.* Chiefly *Sc.* Also **deisal**, & other vars. L18. [Gael. *deiseil*.] A *adv.* In the direction of the sun's apparent course (considered as lucky), clockwise. L18. B *n.* Movement in a clockwise direction, esp. round a particular object. L18.

death /dɛθ/ *n.* Also (*obs.* exc. *Sc.*) **dead** /dɛd/, (*Sc.*) **deid** /diːd/. [OE *dēaþ* = OFris. *dāth*, OS *dōþ* (Du. *dood*), OHG *tōd* (G *Tod*), ON *dauðr*, Goth. *dauþus*, f. Gmc base ult. also of DIE *v.*[1]: see -TH[1].] 1 The act or fact of dying; the end of life; the final and irreversible cessation of the vital functions of an animal or plant. OE. b An instance of a person's dying. E18. c Cessation of life in a particular part or tissue. E19. 2 The state of being dead; the state or condition of being without life, animation, or activity. OE. 3 *transf.* & *fig.* a The lack or loss of spiritual life; the loss or deprivation of particular rights, privileges, etc. (chiefly in *civil death* below). OE. b The ceasing to be, extinction, or annihilation of something. LME. 4 A cause or occasion of death; something that kills or renders liable to death; an offence punishable by death (*for* a person *to do* something); *poet.* a deadly weapon, poison, etc. OE. 5 A general mortality caused by an epidemic disease; plague, pestilence. Now chiefly in *Black Death* (see BLACK *a.*). LME. †6 *Hunting.* A note sounded on the horn at the death of the quarry; the mort. LME–M18. 7 Bloodshed, slaughter, murder. *arch.* E17. 8 As *int.* Expr. vehement anger, surprise, etc. Cf. 'SDEATH. *arch.* E17.

1 J. R. SEELEY The Greek did not believe death to be annihilation. DAY LEWIS My mother's untimely death. C. V. WEDGWOOD The hideous death designed by the law for traitors. *personified*: MILTON Over them triumphant Death his Dart Shook; but delaid to strike. TENNYSON Into the jaws of Death.. Rode the six hundred. 2 OED His eyes were closed in death. 3a TINDALE *Rom.* 8:6 To be carnally mynded, is deeth. b SHELLEY From the lamp's death to the morning ray. 4 POPE The clam'rous lapwings feel the leaden death. GOLDSMITH A school would be his death. 5 R. HOLINSHED A great death of the pestilence reigned in London. 7 BACON Not to suffer a man of death to live. 8 SHAKES. *Oth.* Death and damnation! O!

Phrases: **a fate worse than death** *arch.* (*euphem.* or *joc.*) being raped; seduction. **as sure as death** *colloq.* quite certain(ly). **at death's door** in imminent danger of or very close to death through illness etc. **be death on** *slang* be skilful at killing (prey etc.) or dealing with. **be the death of** cause the death of (freq. *hyperbol.*). *Black Death*: see BLACK *a. brain death*: see BRAIN *n.* **catch one's death (of cold)** *colloq.* contract a fatal chill etc. (usu. *hyperbol.*). **civil death** the loss of a citizen's privileges through outlawry, banishment, etc. *clinical death*: see CLINICAL I. *Dance of Death*: see DANCE *n. die the death*: see DIE *v.*[1] **do to death** (*a*) *arch.* kill; (*b*) *fig.* overdo, repeat too frequently. **everlasting death** damnation. *flog to death*: see FLOG *v.* **in at the death** present in the hunting-field etc. when the quarry is killed; *gen.* present at the ending of any enterprise. **like death warmed up** *slang* notably ill or exhausted in appearance. **like grim death** with all one's strength. *living death*: see LIVING *a.* **put to death** kill, *esp.* execute. *sudden death*: see SUDDEN *a. the gate(s) of death*: see GATE *n.*[1] *the kiss of death*: see KISS *n.* **to death** (*a*) so as to kill or be killed esp. in a specified way, as *burn, stone to death*, etc. (see also *do to death*, *put to death* above); fatally, mortally; (*b*) *fig.* utterly, at or beyond the point of endurance, to excess, (as *scared, sick, tickled, tired to death*; see also *worked to death* below). **to the death** = *to death* above: now only *lit.*, (*fight, pursue*, etc.) until death results. *Wall of Death*: see WALL *n.*[1] *white death*: see WHITE *a.* **worked to death** *fig.* hackneyed. **worse than death** *arch.* = *a fate worse than death* above.

Comb.: **death adder** (*a*) *dial.* the deaf adder; (*b*) any of various venomous elapid snakes of the genus *Acanthophis*; *esp.* a thick-bodied Australian snake, *A. antarcticus*; **deathbed** †(*a*) the grave; (*b*) the bed etc. on which a person died or will die (*deathbed repentance* etc., a last-minute change of conduct or policy); **death-bell** a passing-bell; **death-bird** a carrion bird, a bird associated with or presaging death; **deathblow** a blow etc. that causes death (*lit.* & *fig.*); **death cap** the poisonous toadstool *Amanita phalloides*; *death cell*: see CELL *n.*[1]; **death certificate** an official document stating the time, place, cause, etc., of a person's death; **death cup** = *death cap* above; **death-day** (the anniversary of) the day of a person's death; **death-dealing** *a.* lethal; **death duties, duty** *Hist.* & *colloq.* tax levied on a dead person's estate; **death-fire** = *corpse-candle* (a) s.v. CORPSE *n.*; **death grant** a statutory payment towards funeral expenses made by the State to the appropriate relative of a dead person; **death-head** = *death's head* (a) below; **death house** (*a*) a place where someone has died; (*b*) *US* a group of death cells; **death-in-life** life that lacks any satisfaction or purpose, living death; **death-knell** the tolling of a bell to mark a person's death; *fig.* an event etc. that heralds the end of something; **death-mask** a cast taken of a dead person's face; **death-or-glory** *a.* brave to the point of foolhardiness, dashing, reckless (*Death-or-Glory Boys*, in the British army, the 17th Regiment of Lancers); **death penalty** *the* penalty of death, capital punishment; **death-place** the place where a person died or will die; **death rate** the ratio of the number of deaths to the population, usu. calculated per thousand of population per year; **death-rattle** a rattling sound in a dying person's throat; **death-ray** a ray (imaginary or actual) capable of killing; **death-roll** a list or the number of those killed in an accident, a battle, an epidemic, etc.; **death row** *US colloq.* the area of a prison where prisoners under sentence of death are confined; **†death's face** = *death's head* (a) below; **death's head** (*a*) (a figure or representation of) a skull, esp. as an emblem of mortality; (*b*) *death's head (hawk)moth*, a large dark hawkmoth, *Acherontia atropos*, having pale markings on the back of the thorax resembling a skull; **death-sick** *a.* mortally ill; **deathsman** *arch.* an executioner;

death-song [cf. G *Todesgesang, Totengesang*] a song sung immediately prior to one's death or the death of another, or to commemorate the dead; **death-stricken, -struck** *adjs.* (*arch.*) subject to a mortal illness, wound, etc.; **death tax** *US* = *death duty* above; **death throe(s)** the final violent anguish, struggle, etc., of a dying person or animal or *fig.* of a custom, practice, etc., coming to an end; **death-toll** = *death-roll* above; **death-trap** an unsuspectedly unhealthy or dangerous place, structure, etc.; **death-warrant** a warrant for the execution of a convicted person; *fig.* any action etc. which signals the abolition or end of a custom, practice, etc.; **death-watch** (*a*) any of various insects making a sound like a watch ticking, once supposed to portend death; *spec.* (in full *death-watch beetle*) a beetle, *Xestobium rufovillosum*, whose larvae bore in old wood and are notably destructive to house timbers, furniture, etc.; (*b*) a vigil kept beside a dying person; **death-wish** [tr. G *Todeswunsch*] a wish, esp. an unconscious wish, for the death of oneself or another; **death-wound** a mortal wound.

deathlike *a.* †(*a*) deadly, fatal; (*b*) resembling death: M16. **deathling** *n.* (*rare*) a person subject to death, a mortal L16.

deathful /ˈdɛθfʊl, -f(ə)l/ *a.* ME. [f. DEATH + -FUL.] 1 Fatal, destructive, deadly. ME. 2 Subject to death, mortal. *arch. rare.* E17. 3 Having the appearance of death, deathly. M17.

deathfully *adv.* E19. **deathfulness** *n.* M17.

deathless /ˈdɛθlɪs/ *a.* L16. [f. DEATH + -LESS.] Not subject to death; immortal, undying, unending.

E. A. FREEMAN The deathless name of Godwine. I. MURDOCH Zeus deplores the sight of deathless beings involved in the pointless horrors of morality. Q. CRISP My jumbled speech would be translated into deathless prose.

deathlessly *adv.* M19. **deathlessness** *n.* L17.

deathly /ˈdɛθli/ *a.* [OE *dēaþlić* (= OHG *tōdlīh*), f. as DEATH + -LY¹.] 1 Subject to death, mortal. Long *rare.* OE. 2 Causing death, fatal, deadly. *arch.* ME. 3 Of the nature of or resembling death; deathlike; gloomy, pale, etc., as death. ME. 4 Of or pertaining to death. *poet.* M19.

deathliness *n.* ME.

deathly /ˈdɛθli/ *adv.* ME. [In early use f. DEATH + -LY², later f. the adj.] †1 In a way causing or tending to death. Only in ME. 2 To a degree resembling or suggestive of death. L19.

deathward /ˈdɛθwəd/ *adv.* & *a.* LME. [f. DEATH + -WARD.] A *adv.* Orig. (arch.) *to deathward*, †*to one's deathward.* In the direction of death, towards death. LME. B *adj.* Tending or moving towards death. M19.

Also **deathwards** *adv.* E19.

deathy /ˈdɛθi/ *adv.* & *a. arch.* or *poet.* L18. [f. DEATH + -Y¹.] A *adv.* To a degree resembling or suggestive of death, deathly. L18. B *adj.* Of the nature or character of death, deathly. E19.

deathiness *n.* E19.

deaurate /dɪˈɔːrət/ *a.* Now *rare* or *obs.* LME. [Late L *deauratus* pa. pple, f. as next: see -ATE².] Gilded, golden.

deaurate /dɪˈɔːreɪt/ *v.t.* Now *rare* or *obs.* M16. [Late L *deaurat-* pa. ppl stem of *deaurare* gild, f. L *aurum* gold: see -ATE³.] Gild over, make golden. Chiefly as *deaurated* ppl a.

deauˈration *n.* M17.

deave /diːv/ *v.* Now *Sc.* & *north.* [OE *-dēafian*, f. as DEAF *a.* Cf. DEAF *v.*] †1 *v.i.* Become deaf. *rare.* OE–LME. 2 *v.t.* Deafen; stun, worry, or confuse with din or talk. ME.

deb /dɛb/ *n. colloq.* E20. [Abbrev.] = DÉBUTANTE 2.

debs' or **deb's delight** an eligible young man in fashionable society.

†debacchation *n.* M17–M18. [Late L *debacchatio(n-)*, f. L *debacchat-* pa. ppl stem of *debacchari* rave as a bacchanal, f. *de-* DE- 1 + *bacchari*, f. *Bacchus* god of wine: see -ATION.] Noisy or drunken raving; a drunken revel.

débâcle /deɪˈbɑːk(ə)l, dɪ-/ *n.* Also **debacle**. E19. [Fr., f. *débâcler* unbar, f. *dé-* DE- 3 + *bâcler* to bar.] 1 A breaking-up of ice in a river; a sudden flood or rush of water carrying along debris. E19. 2 A sudden and ignominious collapse or defeat; a confused rush, a rout. M19.

2 L. URIS The British suffered one debacle after another. Dunkirk! Crete! Greece! J. GROSS The extent to which Liberal attitudes survived the debacle of the party as such.

debag /diːˈbag/ *v.t. slang.* Infl. **-gg-**. E20. [f. DE- 3 + BAG *n.*] Remove the trousers from, as a punishment or joke.

deballast /diːˈbaləst/ *v.t.* M20. [f. DE- 3 + BALLAST *n.* & *v.*] Remove ballast from (a ship etc.).

debamboozle /diːbamˈbuːz(ə)l/ *v.t. colloq.* E20. [f. DE- 3 + BAMBOOZLE.] Undeceive, enlighten, disabuse.

debar /dɪˈbɑː/ *v.t.* Infl. **-rr-**. LME. [Fr. *débarrer*, OFr. *desbarrer*, f. *des-* DE- 3 + *barrer* to bar.] 1 Exclude, shut out *from* (†*of*) a place or condition; prevent *from doing*; deprive of. LME. 2 Prohibit, obstruct, prevent (an action etc.). L15.

1 SHAKES. *Sonn.* I . . that am debarr'd the benefit of rest. A. STORR This disability need not debar a man from being a conscientious and valuable priest. 2 T. SPENCER The dore when it is shut, debarres all entrance.

debarment *n.* the act of debarring, the fact of being debarred M17.

debarbarize /diːˈbɑːbərʌɪz/ *v.t.* Also **-ise**. E19. [f. DE- 3 + BARBARIZE.] Free from barbarous character, make not barbarous.

debark /diːˈbɑːk/ *v.*¹*t.* & *i.* M17. [Fr. *débarquer*, f. *dé-* DE- 3 + *barque* BARK *n.*³] = DISEMBARK.

debark /diːˈbɑːk/ *v.*²*t.* M18. [f. DE- 3 + BARK *n.*²] Strip (a tree etc.) of its bark.

debark /diːˈbɑːk/ *v.*³*t.* M20. [f. DE- 3 + BARK *n.*¹] Deprive (a dog) of the ability to bark.

debarkation /diːbɑːˈkeɪʃ(ə)n/ *n.* M18. [f. DEBARK *v.*¹ + -ATION.] The action of disembarking; *esp.* the unloading of troops, supplies, or equipment from a ship or aircraft.

debarrass /dɪˈbarəs/ *v.t.* Now *rare.* L18. [Fr. *débarrasser*, f. *dé-* DE- 3 + (*em*)*barrasser* EMBARRASS.] = DISEMBARRASS.

debase /dɪˈbeɪs/ *v.t.* M16. [f. DE- 1 + BASE *n.*¹, *v.* Cf. ABASE.] †1 Lower in position or rank, humiliate. M16–E19. †2 Decry, belittle, depreciate. M16–M18. 3 Lower in quality, value, or character, corrupt; adulterate; degrade. L16. b *spec.* Decrease the value of (coinage) by alloying etc. E17.

3 S. JOHNSON Words which convey ideas of dignity . . are in time debased. I. MURDOCH They simply resented their stepfather . . as a debased version of human existence.

debasedness *n.* the quality or condition of being debased E18. **debasement** *n.* (*a*) the action or process of debasing; debased condition; †(*b*) abasement: L16. **debaser** *n.* E17.

débat /deba/ *n.* Pl. pronounced same. L19. [Fr. = DEBATE *n.*] A poetic discussion between persons, personifications, or abstractions, on a question of morality, politics, or love, common in medieval European literature.

debatable /dɪˈbeɪtəb(ə)l/ *a.* Also **debateable**. LME. [OFr., f. *debatre*, or AL *debatabilis*, f. as DEBATE *v.* + -ABLE.] 1 Open to question or argument, controversial. LME. 2 Of or pertaining to land or territory on the border of two countries and claimed by each, *spec.* (*Hist.*) designating the tract between the Rivers Esk and Sark on the border between England and Scotland. LME.

debate /dɪˈbeɪt/ *n.* ME. [OFr. *debat* (mod. *débat*), f. as next.] 1 Strife, dissension, quarrelling, (formerly) fighting; a quarrel. Long *arch.* ME. 2 Contention in argument, (a) discussion; *esp.* (a) formal discussion of a matter in a legislature or public assembly. LME. b = DÉBAT. M19.

2 J. COLVILLE Big debate on Finland this evening, during which the P.M. won great personal success. J. HERRIOT It was a matter of debate whether she was a widow or separated. *full-dress debate*: see FULL *a.*

debate /dɪˈbeɪt/ *v.* LME. [OFr. *debatre* (mod. *débattre*) f. Proto-Romance, f. L *dis-* (cf. DE- 3) + *battere* to fight.] 1 *v.*†*i.* & *t.* Contend, fight (over), quarrel (about). *arch.* LME. 2 *v.t.* & *i.* Argue, discuss, esp. formally in a public assembly etc.; take part in debate (about). LME. 3 *v.t.* & *i.* Consider in one's mind, deliberate (on), ponder. LME. †4 *v.t.* Defend, fight for. *Sc.* L15–E17.

1 SPENSER Well could he tourney, and in lists debate. DRYDEN The boys and Latian youth debate The martial prizes on the dusty plain. 2 TOLKIEN They debated long on what was to be done. B. LOVELL The existence of extragalactic systems had been debated for centuries. **debating club, society**: whose members meet for debating. **debating point** a minor point open to argument, esp. one used to gain advantage in debate. 3 W. MORRIS Debating in her mind of this and that. HARPER LEE I was debating whether to stand there or run.

†**debatement** *n.* the act of debating; discussion, contention, strife: M16–M17. **debater** *n.* a person who debates, or is skilled in debate. LME.

debateable *a.* var. of DEBATABLE.

debauch /dɪˈbɔːtʃ/ *n.* Now chiefly *literary.* E17. [Fr. *débauche*, f. as next.] 1 A bout of excessive indulgence in sensual pleasures; an orgy, a spree. E17. 2 The habit or practice of sensual indulgence. L17. 3 *transf.* & *fig.* An excess. L17. 4 A debauchee. Long *obs.* exc. *dial.* L17.

1 S. PEPYS My head akeing all day from last night's debauch. 2 J. S. BLACKIE All debauch is incipient suicide. 3 G. ORWELL An enormous debauch of work.

debauch /dɪˈbɔːtʃ/ *v.* Now chiefly *literary.* Also †**debosh**. L16. [Fr. *débaucher*, OFr. *desbaucher*, f. *des-* DE- 3 + elem. of unkn. origin.] I *v.t.* †1 Turn away, entice, or seduce from allegiance or duty. (Foll. by *from* a leader etc., *to* an action etc.) L16–E19. 2 Pervert from virtue or morality, corrupt, deprave, esp. by intemperance or sensual indulgence. L16. b Seduce (a woman) from chastity. E18. †3 Damage in reputation, disparage. E–M17. 4 Deprave, vitiate, (the senses, judgement, etc.). M17.

1 JAS. MILL To betray their master and debauch his army. 2 J. TILLOTSON To debauch himself by intemperance and brutish sensuality. 4 SIR W. SCOTT They debauch the spirit of the ignorant and credulous with mystical trash.

II *v.i.* 5 Indulge riotously or to excess in sensual pleasures. Now *rare* or *obs.* E17.

debaucher *n.* E17.

debauched /dɪˈbɔːtʃt/ *a.* Now chiefly *literary.* Also (*arch.*) **deboshed** /dɪˈbɒʃt/. L16. [f. prec. + -ED¹.] That has been debauched; dissolute, licentious.

debauchedly *adv.* (now *rare*) M17. **debauchedness** *n.* (now *rare*) E17.

debauchee /dɪbɔːˈtʃiː, -ˈʃiː/ *n.* Now chiefly *literary.* M17. [Fr. *débauché* pa. pple of *débaucher*: see DEBAUCH *v.*, -EE¹.] A person addicted to sensual indulgence; an excessively sensual person.

debauchery /dɪˈbɔːtʃ(ə)ri/ *n.* Now chiefly *literary.* E17. [f. DEBAUCH *v.* + -ERY.] 1 Excessive indulgence in sensual pleasures; immorality, licentiousness. E17. †2 Seduction from duty or virtue; corruption. E18–M19.

debby /ˈdɛbi/ *n. colloq.* E20. [f. DEB *n.* + -Y⁶.] = DÉBUTANTE 2.

debby /ˈdɛbi/ *a. colloq.* M20. [f. DEB *n.* + -Y¹.] Of, pertaining to, or characteristic of a débutante or fashionable society.

debeak /diːˈbiːk/ *v.t.* M20. [f. DE- 3 + BEAK *n.*¹] Remove the upper part of the beak of (a bird) to prevent cannibalism etc.

debel /dɪˈbɛl/ *v.t.* Now *rare* or *obs.* Infl. **-ll-**. LME. [L *debellare*, f. *de-* DE- 1 + *bellare* wage war, f. *bellum* war.] Subdue in battle, conquer, vanquish.

†**debellation** *n.* conquest, subjugation LME–M19.

de bene esse /diː ˌbɛni ˈɛsi; deɪ/ *adv. phr.* E17. [L = of well-being.] *Law.* As conditionally allowed for the present.

debenture /dɪˈbɛntʃə/ *n.* LME. [L *debentur* are owing or due, 3rd person pl. pres. indic. pass. of *debere* owe, occurring as the first wd of a certificate of indebtedness: final syll. assim. to -URE.] 1 A voucher issued in the royal household or by government enabling the recipient to claim the sum due for goods or services rendered. *arch.* LME. b A certificate authorizing the repayment of import duty on goods which are re-exported. M17. †2 *gen.* An acknowledgement of indebtedness (*lit.* & *fig.*). L16–L17. †3 A certificate of a loan made to the government. E18–E19. 4 A sealed bond issued by a corporation or company in respect of a long-term (esp. fixed-interest) loan, the principal of which, in Britain, constitutes a charge on the assets of the company. M19.

Comb.: **debenture bond** = sense 4 above; **debenture stock** company stock comprising debentures, with only the interest secured.

debentured *a.* having or secured by a debenture. E19.

debile /ˈdiːbʌɪl/ *a. arch.* M16. [Fr. *débile* or L *debilis*.] Weak, debilitated.

debilitate /dɪˈbɪlɪteɪt/ *v.t.* M16. [L *debilitat-* pa. ppl stem of *debilitare* weaken, f. *debilitas*: see DEBILITY, -ATE³.] Weaken, enfeeble.

A. BROOKNER Emerging slowly from some debilitating illness.

debilitative *a.* causing debilitation, tending to debilitate L17.

debilitation /dɪˌbɪlɪˈteɪʃ(ə)n/ *n.* LME. [Fr. *débilitation* or its source L *debilitatio(n-)*, f. as prec.: see -ATION.] The action of debilitating, weakening; a debilitated condition.

debility /dɪˈbɪlɪti/ *n.* LME. [(O)Fr. *débilité* f. L *debilitas*, f. *debilis* weak: see -ITY.] 1 Weakness, infirmity, lack of strength or vitality; feebleness of purpose etc. LME. †2 An instance of weakness. M16–E19.

debit /ˈdɛbɪt/ *n.* LME. [Sense 1 f. L *debitum* DEBT *n.*; sense 2 f. Fr. *débit*.] †1 A debt. LME–E17. 2 The acknowledgement of a sum owing by entry in an account; (a sum entered on) the debit side (see below) of an account. Opp. CREDIT *n.* 10. L18.

2 *direct debit*: see DIRECT *a.*

Comb.: **debit card**: giving the holder access (through a computer terminal) to an account in order to transfer funds to another's account when making a purchase etc.; **debit side** the side or column of an account, conventionally the left-hand side, in which debits are entered.

debit /ˈdɛbɪt/ *v.*¹*t.* L17. [f. the n.] Enter a sum on the debit side of (an account) or of the account of (a person), (foll. by *with* the sum); enter (a sum) on the debit side of an account (foll. by *against* or *to* the account, the person whose account is debited).

debitable *a.* L19.

debit /ˈdɛbɪt/ *v.*²*t.* L19. [Fr. *débiter*: see next.] Put into circulation, spread (news etc.).

debitage /dɛbɪˈtɑːʒ/ *n.* M20. [Fr. *débitage* cutting of stone.] *Archaeol.* Waste material produced in the making of prehistoric stone implements.

debiteuse /dɛbɪˈtjuːz, -ˈtəːz/ *n.* E20. [Fr. *débiteuse* a device that dispenses or discharges some substance, fem. of *débiteur*, f. *débiter* retail, dispense.] *Glass-making.* A troughlike refractory object which floats on the molten glass in the Fourcault process, and has a slit through which the sheet glass is drawn.

†**debitor** *n.* L15. [OFr. (learned var. of *det(t)or*) f. L *debitor*: see DEBTOR.] 1 = DEBTOR 1. L15–L18. 2 = DEBTOR 2. M16–M17.

†**debitrice** *n.* a female debtor LME–E18.

deblazon /dɪˈbleɪz(ə)n/ *v.t.* Long *rare.* E17. [f. DE- 1 + BLAZON *v.*] = BLAZON *v.*

deblur /diːˈbləː/ *v.t.* Infl. **-rr-**. M20. [f. DE- 3 + BLUR *n.*] Clarify (an image), remove blur from, bring into focus.

†**deboise** *v.t.* Pa. pple **deboist**. E17–E18. [By-form.] = DEBAUCH *v.* I. Chiefly as *deboist* pa. ppl a.

debonair /dɛbəˈnɛː/ *a.* & *n.* Also **-nn-**, **-aire**. ME. [OFr. *debonaire* (mod. *débonnaire*), f. *de bon aire* of good disposition.] A *adj.* †1 Of a gentle disposition, meek, gracious, courteous. ME–L17. 2 Pleasant in manner, affable, urbane; cheerful, carefree, unembarrassed. E18.

1 SPENSER Was neuer Prince so meeke and debonaire. 2 F. ASTAIRE The carefree, the best-dressed, the debonair Astaire!

†B *n.* 1 A courteous being or person. Only in LME. 2 Debonair character or disposition. LME–M18.

debonairly *adv.* LME. **debonairness** *n.* LME.

†**debonairty**, **-arity**, *n.* debonair character or disposition ME–L17.

debord /dɪˈbɔːd/ *v.i.* Now *rare* or *obs.* L16. [Fr. *déborder*, f. *dé-* DE- 3 + *bord* edge, border.] Of a body of water: go beyond its margins, overflow.

†**debosh** *v.* var. of DEBAUCH *v.*

deboshed *ppl a.* see DEBAUCHED.

debouch /dɪˈbaʊtʃ, -ˈbuːʃ/ *v.* M18. [Fr. *déboucher*, f. *dé-* DE- 3 + *bouche* mouth, after synon. It. *sboccare*.] 1 *v.i.* (Orig. *Mil.*, of troops etc.) emerge from a narrow or confined place into open ground; issue (as) from a mouth or outlet (*into, on*). M18. 2 *v.t.* Lead into open ground; provide an outlet for; pour forth. M18.

1 A. PRICE The Parliamentary battle-line began to debouch from the trees. M. M. KAYE Here another spring debouched from the rocks above. 2 J. CHEEVER An enormous samovar . . debouched forty men in Cossack uniform singing.

debouchment *n.* E19.

débouché /debuʃe/ *n.* Pl. pronounced same. M18. [Fr., f. as prec.] An opening where troops etc. (may) debouch; *gen.* an outlet.

debouchure /dɪbʊˈʃʊə/ *n.* M19. [Alt. of EMBOUCHURE after DEBOUCH. The sense is not Fr.] The mouth or outlet of a river etc.

Debrett /dɪˈbrɛt/ *n. colloq.* M19. [John *Debrett* (1750–1822), London publisher and compiler of the first edition (1803).] 'Debrett's Peerage of England, Scotland and Ireland'.

debridement /deɪˈbriːdmɑ̃, dɪˈbriːdm(ə)nt/ *n.* Also **dé-**. M19. [Fr. = unbridling.] *Med.* The removal of damaged tissue or foreign matter from a wound etc.

debride *v.t.* [back-form.] subject to debridement M20.

debrief /diːˈbriːf/ *v.t.* M20. [f. DE- 3 + BRIEF *v.* 3.] Question (a person) about a completed mission, undertaking, etc.

Life He went to the debriefing shed and made a routine report on the . . bombing mission.

debris /ˈdɛbriː, ˈdeɪbriː/ *n.* Also **dé-**. E18. [Fr. *débris*, f. †*débriser* break down or up, f. *dé-* DE- 3 + *briser* break.] The remains of anything broken down or destroyed (orig. *fig.*, of institutions, States, etc.); fragments, wreckage, ruins; accumulated waste matter; *Geol.* fragmentary material accumulated from the breakdown of rocks etc.

A. GEIKIE The sandstone cliffs . . are battered down and their debris carried out to sea. C. CONNOLLY A writer has to construct his shell, like the caddis worm, from the débris of the past. R. SUTCLIFF The wells were choked with the debris of thirty autumns.

de Broglie /də ˈbrəʊli, də ˈbrɒgli/ *a. phr.* E20. [Louis Victor *de Broglie* (1892–1987), Fr. physicist.] *Physics.* Designating the wave(length) representing or accounting for the wavelike properties of a material particle in wave mechanics.

debruise /dɪˈbruːz/ *v.t.* ME. [OFr. *debruisier*, *debrisier*, f. *dé-* DE- 3 + *bruisier*, *brisier* (mod. *briser*) break.] †1 Break down, smash in pieces. ME–E17. 2 *Her.* Cross and partially hide (a charge, esp. an animal) with an ordinary which extends over the field. Chiefly as *debruised* ppl a. M16.

debt /dɛt/ *n.* ME. [(O)Fr. *dette* f. Proto-Romance use as fem. n. of pl. of L *debitum* neut. pple of *debere* owe; *-b-* introduced 16 after Fr. †*debte*.] 1 Something owed or due; something (as money, goods, or service) which one person is under an obligation to pay or render to another. ME. b *spec.* In biblical translations and allusions: an offence requiring atonement, a sin. ME. 2 A liability or obligation to pay or render something; the condition of being so liable or obligated. ME. †3 (One's) duty. Chiefly *Sc.* ME–L16.

1 B. T. WASHINGTON It was my greatest ambition . . to save money enough with which to pay this debt. b AV *Matt.* 6:12 And forgiue vs our debts, as we forgiue our debters. 2 AV He hath for euer bound the Church vnto him, in a debt of speciall remembrance and thankefulnesse. C. A. LINDBERGH I left France with a debt of gratitude which . . I shall always remember. T. S. ELIOT She's always in debt. *Proverb*: Out of debt, out of danger.

Phrases: *bad debt*: see BAD *a.* **debt of honour** a debt that is not legally enforceable, *esp.* a gambling debt. **debt of** or **to nature** (the necessity of) death. **floating debt**: payable on demand or at a certain time. *good debt*: see GOOD *a.* **in debt to someone**, **in someone's debt** owing something to someone. **National Debt** the total of all a State's borrowings. **small debt**: of a limited amount, for which summary jurisdiction is provided in a county or (*Sc.*) sheriff's court.

Comb.: **debt-collector** a person whose business it is to collect debts on behalf of creditors; **debt-slave** a person kept in slavery until a debt is paid.

debtless *a.* LME.

†**debt** *a.* ME–E17. [Prob. f. the n.] Owed, owing.

SHAKES. *Haml.* To pay ourselves what to ourselves is debt.

†**debted** *ppl a.* LME–E17. [Perh. aphet. f. INDEBTED.] Owed; (of a person) indebted.

debtee /dɛˈtiː/ *n.* M16. [f. DEBTOR: see -EE¹.] A person to whom a debt is owed; a creditor.

debtor /ˈdɛtə/ *n.* ME. [OFr. *det(t)or*, *-our* f. L *debitor*, f. *debit-* pa. ppl stem of *debere* owe: see -OR.] 1 A person who is indebted to another; one who owes money or an obligation or duty. ME. b In biblical translations and allusions: a person who has offended or sinned against another. ME. 2 (An entry on) the debit side of an account. Cf. earlier DEBITOR 2. E18.

debug /diːˈbʌg/ *v.t.* Infl. **-gg-**. M20. [f. DE- 3 + BUG *n.*²] 1 Delouse. M20. 2 Remove the faults from (a machine, system, computer program, etc.). M20. 3 Remove concealed microphones, wiretaps, etc., from. M20.

debugger *n.* a person who or thing which debugs; *esp.* a computer program which detects, prevents, or corrects programming errors: M20.

debunk /diːˈbʌŋk/ *v.t. colloq.* Orig. *US.* E20. [f. DE- 3 + BUNK *n.*³] Expose the false claims or pretensions of; reduce the inflated reputation of (a person, institution, idea, etc.), esp. by ridicule.

debunker *n.* E20.

†**deburse** *v.t.* Chiefly *Sc.* LME–L18. [Fr. *débourser*: see DISBURSE.] = DISBURSE *v.* I.

debus /diːˈbʌs/ *v.t.* & *i. colloq.* (chiefly *Mil.*). Infl. **-ss-**. E20. [f. DE- 3 + BUS *n.* 3.] Unload or alight from a motor vehicle or vehicles.

Debussyan /dəˈbuːsɪən, -ˈb(j)uːs-/ *a.* & *n.* E20. [f. *Debussy* (see below) + -AN.] A *adj.* Of or pertaining to the French composer Achille-Claude Debussy (1862–1918), his music, or his style of composition. E20. B *n.* An interpreter, student, or admirer of Debussy or his music. M20.

Debussy'esque *a.* resembling the style of Debussy M20.

début /ˈdeɪb(j)uː, ˈdɛb-; deɪˈbjuː, dɛˈbjuː/ *n.* Also **de-**. M18. [Fr., f. *débuter* lead off.] Entry into society; the first appearance in public of a performer etc.

BYRON The début Of embryo actors, to the Drama new. **make one's début** appear or perform in public for the first time.

début /ˈdeɪb(j)uː, ˈdɛb-/ *v.i.* Also **deb-**. L18. [Partly f. Fr. *débuter* lead off, partly f. DÉBUT *n.*] Make one's début; appear or perform in public for the first time.

débutant /ˈdɛbjʊtɒ̃, ˈdeɪ-/ *n.* Also **de-**. E19. [Fr., pres. pple of *débuter* lead off: see -ANT¹.] A male person making his début.

débutante /ˈdɛbjʊtɑːnt, ˈdeɪ-/ *n.* Also **de-**. E19. [Fr., fem. of *débutant*: see prec.] 1 A female performer etc. making her début. E19. 2 A young woman making her social début; *loosely* a young woman in fashionable society. Cf. DEB, DEBBY *n.* E19.

Debye /dəˈbʌɪ/ *n.* In sense 2 usu. **d-**. E20. [Peter J. W. *Debye* (1884–1966), Du. physicist.] *Physics.* I 1 Used *attrib.* and in *comb.* to designate concepts and methods arising out of Debye's work. E20.

1 **Debye-Scherrer method** /ˈʃɛrə/ [Paul H. *Scherrer* (1890–1969), Swiss physicist]: for obtaining X-ray diffraction patterns of powdered crystalline samples. **Debye temperature** a temperature used to characterize crystalline solids in Debye's theory of

specific heats, corresponding to excitation of all lattice vibrations of the maximum allowed frequency.

II 2 A unit of electric dipole moment (esp. used for molecular moments) equal to 3.336×10^{-30} coulomb metre. Also *Debye unit*. M20.

deca- /ˈdɛkə/ *comb. form*. Bef. a vowel **dec-**. [Gk *deka* ten.] Used w. the sense 'having ten, tenfold'; *spec.* in names of units of measurement, used to denote a factor of ten, as *decagram*, *decalitre*, *decametre*, etc. Abbrev. *da*.

decagynous /dɪˈkadʒɪnəs/ *a.* (*Bot.*) having ten pistils M19. **decahydro'naphthalene** *n.* (*Chem.*) a colourless liquid hydrocarbon, $C_{10}H_{18}$, used esp. as a solvent in the paint industry; = DECALIN: L19. **decamer** *n.* (*Chem.*) a compound whose molecule is composed of ten molecules of monomer M20. **deca'meric** *a.* (*Chem.*) of the nature of a decamer, consisting of a decamer or decamers M20. **deca'metric** *a.* (of radio waves) having a wavelength of 10 to 100 metres M20. **decandrous** /dɪˈkandrəs/ *a.* (*Bot.*) having ten stamens E19. **decangular** /dɪˈkaŋgjʊlə/ *a.* having ten angles, decagonal E19. **deca'peptide** *n.* (*Biochem.*) any peptide composed of ten amino-acid residues E20. **deca'phyllous** *a.* (*Bot.*) having ten leaves L18. **decaploid** *a.* [-PLOID] *Biol.* having ten homologous sets of chromosome E20.

decachord /ˈdɛkəkɔːd/ *n.* Also **-cord**. LME. [Late L *decachordus* adj., *decachordus*, *-um* n., f. Gk *dekakhordos* ten-stringed, f. as DECA- + *khordē* string (see CORD *n.*[1]).] A musical instrument, esp. a psaltery, having ten strings.

decad /ˈdɛkad/ *n.*[1] E17. [Late L *decad-*, *-as* f. Gk *dekas*, f. *deka* ten: see -AD[1].] *The* number ten, as the perfect number of the Pythagoreans.

decad *n.*[2] see DECADE.

decadal /ˈdɛkəd(ə)l/ *a.* M18. [f. as DECAD *n.*[1] + -AL[1].] Of or relating to the number ten; belonging to a decade.

decadary /ˈdɛkəd(ə)ri/ *a.* E19. [Alt. of Fr. *décadaire* (f. as next) after -ARY[1].] *Fr. Hist.* Of or pertaining to a decade of ten days.

decade /ˈdɛkeɪd, dɪˈkeɪd/ *n.* Also (now *rare*) **-ad** /ˈdɛkəd/. LME. [(O)Fr. *décade* f. late L *decas*, *decad-*: see DECAD *n.*[1]] 1 Each of ten books or parts of a single literary work. LME. 2 A group or series of ten; *spec.* each of the five divisions of each chapter of the rosary. L16. 3 (The predominant sense.) A period of ten years. E17. b *Fr. Hist.* A period of ten days, substituted for a week in the French Republican calendar of 1793. L18. 4 (A range of quantities spanning) a power of ten. Freq. used *attrib.* to denote sets of resistors or other electrical components providing values of resistance ranging from one to ten times a base value. E20.

1 LD MACAULAY As hopelessly lost as the second decade of Livy. 3 M. L. KING The decade of 1955 to 1965 with its constructive elements misled us.

decadence /ˈdɛkəd(ə)ns/ *n.* M16. [Fr. *décadence* f. med.L *decadentia*, f. *decadent-* pres. ppl stem of Proto-Romance vb whence also DECAY *v.*: see -ENCE.] The process of falling away or declining (from a state of excellence, vitality, prosperity, etc.); decadent condition; decay, deterioration, *spec.* of a particular period in art, literature, etc., after a culmination.

GOLDSMITH Some pathetic exclamation on the decadence of taste and genius. E. M. FORSTER I have no profession. . . It is another example of my decadence.

decadency /ˈdɛkəd(ə)nsi/ *n.* M17. [f. as prec.: see -ENCY.] Decaying condition; decadence.

decadent /ˈdɛkəd(ə)nt/ *a.* & *n.* M19. [Fr. *décadent*, f. as DECADENCE: see -ENT.] A *adj.* 1 Declining, decaying (from a condition of excellence, vitality, prosperity, etc.); characteristic of decadence, self-indulgent. M19. 2 Designating or belonging to a period of (artistic) decadence; *spec.* = AESTHETIC *a.* 4. L19.

1 G. ORWELL Our civilization is decadent, and our language . . must . . share in the general collapse.

B *n.* A decadent person; *spec.* an adherent of a decadent movement in art, literature, etc. L19.

decadentism *n.* the qualities or spirit of a decadent movement in art, literature, etc.; decadent behaviour or characteristics. L19. **decadently** *adv.* L19.

decadic /dɪˈkadɪk/ *a.* M19. [Gk *dekadikos*, f. *dekas*, *dekad-*: see DECAD *n.*[1], -IC.] Belonging to or designating the system of counting by tens; denary.

Decaf /ˈdiːkaf/ *n.* Also **d-**. L20. [Abbrev.] (Proprietary name for) decaffeinated coffee; a drink made with this.

decaffeinate /diːˈkafɪneɪt/ *v.t.* M20. [f. DE- 3 + CAFFEINE + -ATE[3].] Remove the caffeine from, reduce the quantity of caffeine in (coffee etc.). Chiefly as *decaffeinated* ppl a.

decaffeini'zation *n.* the process of decaffeinating coffee etc. E20.

decagon /ˈdɛkəg(ə)n/ *n.* M17. [med.L *decagonum* f. Gk *dekagōnon*, f. *deka-* DECA- + *-gōnos* -GON.] A plane figure with ten straight sides and ten angles.

decagonal /dɪˈkagən(ə)l/ *a.* having the form of a decagon; having ten sides: L16.

decahedron /dɛkəˈhiːdr(ə)n, -ˈhɛd-/ *n.* Pl. **-dra** /-drə/, **-drons**. E19. [f. DECA- + -HEDRON.] *Geom.* A solid figure or object with ten plane faces.

decahedral *a.* having the form of a decahedron; having ten faces: E19.

decal /ˈdiːkal/ *n.* Chiefly *N. Amer.* M20. [Abbrev. of DECALCOMANIA.] A picture etc. prepared on special paper for durable transfer on to glass, china, plastic models, etc.

decalage /ˈdiːkəlɑːʒ/ *n.* E20. [Fr. *décalage* displacement, f. *décaler* displace.] *Aeronaut.* The difference in the angle of incidence between two aerofoils on an aeroplane.

decalcify /diːˈkalsɪfʌɪ/ *v.t.* M19. [f. DE- 3 + CALCIFY.] Deprive (bone etc.) of calcium compounds. Chiefly as *decalcified* ppl a.

decalcifi'cation *n.* M19.

decalcomania /dɪˌkalkəˈmeɪnɪə/ *n.* M19. [Fr. *décalcomanie*, f. *décalquer* transfer a tracing + *-manie* -MANIA.] The process of transferring pictures etc. from specially prepared paper on to surfaces of glass, china, etc.

decalescence /diːkəˈlɛs(ə)ns/ *n.* L19. [f. DE- 3 + CALESCENCE.] *Metall.* The absorption of heat by a metal, without a corresponding increase in temperature, when the metal is heated through a critical point.

decalescent *a.* E20.

decalin /ˈdɛkəlɪn/ *n.* Also **dek-**, (US proprietary name) **D-**. E20. [f. DECA- + *-l-* + -IN[1].] *Chem.* = DECAHYDRONAPHTHALENE.

Decalogue /ˈdɛkəlɒg/ *n.* Also **d-**. LME. [Fr. *décalogue* or eccl.L *decalogus* f. Gk *dekalogos*, orig. fem. adj. (sc. *biblos* book), after *hoi deka logoi* the Ten Commandments (Septuagint), f. *deka* ten + *logos* saying, speech: see -LOGUE.] *The* Ten Commandments collectively as a body of law.

Decalogist /dɪˈkalədʒɪst/ *n.* (*rare*) a person who expounds the Decalogue M17.

†**decalvation** *n.* LME–M18. [L *decalvatio(n-)*, f. *decalvare* make bald, f. *de-* DE- 1 + *calvus* bald: see -ATION.] Removal of hair, making bald.

decamp /dɪˈkamp/ *v.i.* L17. [Fr. *décamper*, f. *dé-* DE- 3 + *camp* CAMP *n.*[2] Cf. earlier DISCAMP.] 1 Orig. *Mil.* Break up or leave a camp; remove from a camping-place. L17. 2 Go away promptly or suddenly; take oneself off. M18.

1 WELLINGTON We found on our arrival that the armies of both chiefs had decamped. 2 O. MANNING The Minister had decamped to Switzerland with the Ministry funds.

decampment *n.* [Fr. *décampement*] the breaking up of a camp; prompt departure: L17.

decan /ˈdɛk(ə)n/ *n.* OE. [Late L *decanus*: see DEAN *n.*[1]] †1 A chief or ruler of ten, = DEAN *n.*[1] 4. OE–M16. †2 = DEAN *n.*[1] I. LME–M16. 3 *Astrol.* Each of the three divisions of a zodiacal sign, extending over ten degrees; the ruler of such a division. L16.

decanal /dɪˈkeɪn(ə)l, ˈdɛk(ə)n(ə)l/ *a.* E18. [med.L *decanalis*, f. as prec.: see -AL[1].] 1 Of or pertaining to a dean or deanery. E18. 2 Designating or pertaining to the south side of the choir of a church, on which the dean usually sits. Cf. CANTORIAL. L18.

decanally *adv.* (*rare*) L19.

decanate /ˈdɛk(ə)neɪt/ *n.* M17. [med.L *decanatus*, f. as DECAN: see -ATE[1].] *Astrol.* Each of the three divisions (of ten degrees) of a zodiacal sign.

decane /ˈdɛkeɪn/ *n.* L18. [f. DECA- + -ANE.] *Chem.* Any of a series of saturated hydrocarbons (alkanes) with the formula $C_{10}H_{22}$; *spec.* (also *n-decane*) the unbranched isomer, $CH_3(CH)_8CH_3$.

decani /dɪˈkeɪnʌɪ/ *a.* M18. [L, genit. of *decanus* DEAN *n.*[1]] = DECANAL 2; *Mus.* to be sung by the decanal side in antiphonal singing (cf. CANTORIS).

decant /dɪˈkant/ *v.t.* M17. [med.L *decanthare* (whence also Fr. *décanter*), f. L *de-* DE- 1 + *canthus* angular lip of a jug f. Gk *kanthos* corner of the eye.] 1 Pour off (a liquid or solution) by gently inclining the vessel so as not to disturb sediment. M17. 2 Pour (wine etc.) from a bottle into a decanter; *loosely* pour into a drinking-vessel. M18. 3 Empty out; move or transfer as if by pouring. *colloq.* M18.

3 F. WELDON The bus broke down and we were all . . decanted into another.

decantation /dɪkanˈteɪʃ(ə)n/ *n.* M17. [Fr. *décantation* or med.L *decanthatio(n-)*, f. as prec.: see -ATION.] The action of decanting, esp. of pouring off liquid from sediment.

decanter /dɪˈkantə/ *n.* E18. [f. DECANT + -ER[1].] 1 A vessel used for decanting or receiving decanted liquors; *spec.* a bottle of clear or cut glass, with a stopper, from which wine etc. is served. E18. 2 A person who decants. Only in Dicts. M18.

1 M. ALLINGHAM He . . shot a hopeless glance at the whisky decanter.

decapacitate /diːkəˈpasɪteɪt/ *v.t.* M20. [f. DE- + CAPACITATE.] *Physiol.* Remove the effect of capicitation from; deprive (a spermatozoon) of the ability to penetrate an ovum. Usu. in *pass.*

decapaci'tation *n.* M20.

decapitalize /diːˈkapɪt(ə)lʌɪz/ *v.t.* Also **-ise**. L19. [f. DE- 3 + CAPITAL *n.*[2] + -IZE.] 1 Reduce from the rank of capital city. *rare*. L19. 2 Reduce the capital assets of. M20.

decapitali'zation *n.* L19.

decapitate /dɪˈkapɪteɪt/ *v.t.* E17. [Late L *decapitat-* pa. ppl stem of *decapitare*, f. *de-* DE- 3 + *caput*, *capit-* head: see -ATE[3].] 1 Cut off the head of, behead; cut the top or end from (a thing). E17. 2 Dismiss abruptly from office. *US*. M19.

1 C. CHAPLIN He had cut his throat, almost decapitating himself. C. CONRAN Skin the tomatoes, then decapitate them with a saw-bladed knife.

decapitator *n.* a person who or thing which decapitates E19.

decapitation /dɪˌkapɪˈteɪʃ(ə)n/ *n.* M17. [Fr. *décapitation* or med.L *decapitatio(n-)*, f. as prec. (see -ATION), or f. prec. on the anal. of similar pairs.] 1 The action of beheading a person or cutting the top or end from a thing; the fact of being so decapitated. M17. 2 Summary dismissal from office. *US*. M19.

decapod /ˈdɛkəpɒd/ *n.* & *a.* E19. [Fr. *décapode* f. mod.L *Decapoda* (see below), use as n. of neut. pl. adj., f. as DECA- + -POD.] A *n.* 1 *Zool.* A crustacean of the order Decapoda, members of which have ten feet or legs, and which includes the lobster, crab, shrimp, etc. Also, a cephalopod of the sub-order Decapoda, members of which have ten tentacles, as the cuttlefish and squid. E19. 2 A steam locomotive with ten driving-wheels. Chiefly *US*. L19. B *adj.* *Zool.* Of or pertaining to the (crustacean or cephalopod) Decapoda. E19.

de'capodan *a.* = DECAPOD *a.* M19.

decapsulate /diːˈkapsjʊleɪt/ *v.t.* E20. [f. DE- 3 + CAPSULE *n.* + -ATE[3].] (Surgically) remove the capsule of.

decapsu'lation *n.* E20.

decarbonate /diːˈkɑːb(ə)neɪt/ *v.t.* M19. [f. DE- 3 + CARBON *n.* + -ATE[3]. Cf. Fr. *décarbonater*.] Remove carbon or carbon compounds from.

decarbonize /diːˈkɑːb(ə)nʌɪz/ *v.t.* Also **-ise**. E19. [f. DE- 3 + CARBON *n.* + -IZE.] Remove carbon or carbon compounds from; *spec.* remove carbon deposits from (an internal-combustion engine).

decarboni'zation *n.* M19.

decarboxylate /diːkɑːˈbɒksɪleɪt/ *v.* E20. [f. DE- 3 + CARBOXYL + -ATE[3].] *Chem.* **1** *v.t.* Remove a carboxyl group from (a molecule). E20. **2** *v.i.* Lose a carboxyl group; undergo decarboxylation. M20.

decarboxyˈlation *n.* the removal of a carboxyl group from a molecule E20.

decarburize /diːˈkɑːbjʊrʌɪz/ *v.t.* Also **-ise**. M19. [f. DE- 3 + CARBURIZE, after Fr. *décarburer.*] Chiefly *Metall.* Remove carbon from.

decarburiˈzation *n.* M19.

decarch /ˈdɛkɑːk/ *n.* Also **dek-**. M17. [Gk *dekarkhēs*, *-os* decurion, f. *deka* ten + *arkhos* leader.] *Gk Hist.* Each of a ruling body of ten.

decarchy /ˈdɛkɑːki/ *n.* Also **dek-**. M17. [Gk *dekarkhia*, f. as prec.: see -Y[3].] *Gk Hist.* A ruling body of ten.

decartelization /diːˌkɑːtɛlʌɪˈzeɪʃ(ə)n/ *n.* Also **-ll-**; **-isation**. M20. [f. DE- 3 + CARTEL(L)IZATION.] Abolition of a system of trade cartels.

decastyle /ˈdɛkəstʌɪl/ *a.* & *n.* E18. [Gk *dekastulos* having ten columns, f. Gk *deka* ten + *stulos* column. Cf. Fr. *décastyle.*] *Archit.* **A** *adj.* Having ten columns (in front). E18. **B** *n.* A building with ten columns in front; a portico etc. of ten columns. E18.

decasualize /diːˈkaʒjʊəlʌɪz, -zj-/ *v.t.* Also **-ise**. L19. [f. DE- 3 + CASUAL *a.* + -IZE.] Do away with the casual employment of (labour) by introducing permanent jobs.

decasualiˈzation *n.* the abolition of casual labour L19.

decasyllabic /dɛkəsɪˈlabɪk/ *a.* & *n.* L18. [f. DECA- + SYLLABIC. Cf. Fr. *décasyllabique.*] *Pros.* **A** *adj.* Consisting of ten syllables. L18. **B** *n.* A line of ten syllables. L19.

Also **ˈdecasyllable** *a.* & *n.* M19.

decathlon /dɪˈkaθlɒn, -lən/ *n.* E20. [f. DECA- + Gk *athlon* contest.] An athletic or sporting contest in which competitors engage in ten different events.

decathlete *n.* a competitor in the decathlon M20.

decatize /ˈdɛkətʌɪz/ *v.t.* Also **-ise**. E20. [f. Fr. *décatir* sponge or steam (cloth) + -IZE.] Give lustre to (cloth) by means of the action of steam.

decaudate /diːˈkɔːdeɪt/ *v.t. rare.* M19. [f. DE- 3 + L *cauda* tail + -ATE[3].] Remove the tail(s) from.

decauˈdation *n.* L19.

Decauville /ˈdəkəʊvɪl/ *a.* & *n.* L19. [P. *Decauville* (1846–1922), French engineer.] (Designating or pertaining to) a type of narrow-gauge railway invented by Decauville.

decay /dɪˈkeɪ/ *n.* LME. [f. the vb.] **1** The process of departing from a thriving condition; progressive decline. Also, the condition of having declined. LME. †**b** Downfall; *poet.* fall, death. LME–E18. **2** Material deterioration, dilapidation, falling apart; ruinous condition. E16. †**b** In *pl.* Ruins, debris. L16–L18. †**3** A cause of decline or deterioration. M16–L17. **4** Mental or physical decline (through illness or old age). L16. †**b** A wasting disease; consumption. E18–E19. **5** The rotting or decomposition of organic tissue; decomposed tissue. L16. **6** Decrease in quantity etc. Now chiefly *Physics*, a gradual decrease in the magnitude of a physical quantity, esp. in the intensity of radioactivity or in the amplitude of an oscillation. Also, the spontaneous change of a substance, nucleus, etc., into another by radioactivity. M17.

1 AV *Lev.* 25:35 If thy brother bee waxen poore, and fallen in decay with thee. R. G. COLLINGWOOD The decay of our civilization, . . a break-down of social structures and . . a drying-up of the emotional springs of life. 2 BACON It is a reverend thing to see an ancient castle or building not in decay. J. STEINBECK Over the whole lot a spirit of decay, of mold and rust. 4 J. FRAME She accepted age with its gradual decay of faculties and energies as an autumnal dignity. 5 J. BRAINE There was a speck of decay on one of her upper incisors. 6 J. A. FLEMING Frictional resistance causes decay in the amplitude of the oscillations by dissipating their energy as heat. J. B. PRIESTLEY These gentlefolk watch the decay of their incomes and keep open house for young male relatives on leave from the East. N. CALDER Decay of uranium produces . . lead.

decay /dɪˈkeɪ/ *v.* L15. [(O)Fr. *decair*, by-form of *decaoir*, var. of *dechaoir*, *decheoir* (mod. *déchoir*) f. Proto-Romance var. of L *decidere*, f. *de-* DE- 1 + *cadere* to fall.] **I** *v.i.* **1** Deteriorate, decline in quality, prosperity, etc. L15. **2** Fall into physical ruin or disrepair; waste away, fall apart; rot. L15. **3** Decrease in quantity or magnitude; dwindle. Now chiefly *Physics*, undergo gradual decrease in the magnitude of a physical quantity. L15. **b** *spec.* Of radioactivity: gradually decrease in intensity. Of a radioactive substance, nucleus, etc.: spontaneously change into one or more different substances, particles, etc. E20. **4** Lose one's health and strength of body or mind; decline through age. M16.

1 SIR W. SCOTT Ancient . . families . . decayed . . into the humble vale of life. JOHN GLOAG Impoverished widows and spinsters of the middle classes . . were officially described as 'decayed gentlewomen'. 2 J. CONRAD His new but already decaying house. C. PRIEST The . . heap that would . . decay into . . compost. 3 C. SAGAN The orbits of artificial satellites are decaying all the time. . . They are . . slowed by collisions with the . . atmosphere. b D. R. HOFSTADTER A photon . . can decay . . into an electron-positron pair. 4 POPE But since, alas! frail beauty must decay.

II *v.t.* **5** Cause to fall off or decline in quality, prosperity, number, etc.; ruin physically, dilapidate. Now *rare.* E16. **b** Destroy by decomposition, make rotten. E17. **6** Cause to fail in health, strength, etc. Now *rare.* M16.

5 M. BERESFORD The Bishop . . faced with an accusation of decaying three houses. 6 ADDISON Almost every thing which corrupts the soul decays the body.

decayable *a.* able or liable to decay E17. **decayer** *n.* a person who or thing which causes decay M16.

decease /dɪˈsiːs/ *n.* ME. [(O)Fr. *décès* f. L *decessus* departure, death, f. pa. ppl stem of *decedere* go away, depart, f. *de-* DE- 1 + *cedere* go.] Departure from life, death. Chiefly *formal* or *Law.*

decease /dɪˈsiːs/ *v.i.* LME. [f. the n.] **1** Depart from life; die. LME. **2** *fig.* Come to an end, perish; cease. M16.

deceased /dɪˈsiːst/ *a.* & *n.* L15. [f. prec. + -ED[1].] **A** *adj.* Dead; *esp.* lately dead; belonging to a dead person. L15. **B** *n.* A (recently) dead person; *collect.* (*rare*) dead persons, *the* dead. E17.

decedent /dɪˈsiːd(ə)nt/ *n.* Chiefly *N. Amer.* L16. [L *decedent-* pres. ppl stem of *decedere* die: see DECEASE *n.*, -ENT.] A deceased person. Formerly also, a person retiring from office.

deceit /dɪˈsiːt/ *n.* ME. [OFr., use as n. of pa. pple (f. L *deceptus*) of *deceveir* DECEIVE.] **1** The action or practice of deceiving; concealment or misrepresentation of the truth in order to mislead; deception, fraud, cheating. ME. **2** An instance of deception; a device intended to deceive; a trick, a wile, a stratagem. ME. **3** Disposition or tendency to deceive or mislead; deceitfulness. ME.

1 MILTON By violence? no . . But by deceit and lies.

deceitful /dɪˈsiːtfʊl, -f(ə)l/ *a.* LME. [f. prec. + -FUL.] Full of deceit; given to deceiving; misleading, false; deceptive.

deceitfully *adv.* LME. **deceitfulness** *n.* LME.

deceivable /dɪˈsiːvəb(ə)l/ *a.* ME. [(O)Fr. *décevable*, f. *décevoir*: see DECEIVE, -ABLE.] **1** Capable of deceiving; tending to deceive. *arch.* ME. **2** Able or liable to be deceived. Now *rare.* M17.

deceivableness *n.* LME. **deceivably** *adv.* (*arch.*) deceitfully, fraudulently, falsely LME.

deceive /dɪˈsiːv/ *v.* ME. [(O)Fr. *deceivre*, *deçoivre* f. L *decipere*, f. *de-* DE- 1 + *capere* take, seize; or f. *deceiv-* tonic stem of *deceveir* (mod. *décevoir*) f. Proto-Romance alt. of L *decipere.*] †**1** *v.t.* Trap or overcome by trickery; take unawares by craft or guile; lead astray. ME–L18. **2** *v.t.* Cause to believe what is false; delude, take in; *refl.* & in *pass.*, allow oneself to be misled, be mistaken, err. ME. **b** *v.i.* Use deceit, act deceitfully. ME. **3** *v.t.* Be or prove false to, betray. Now chiefly *fig.*, disappoint (hopes etc.). ME. †**4** *v.t.* Cheat, defraud; deprive of by deception. (Foll. by *of.*) ME–M18. †**5** *v.t.* Beguile (time etc.). L16–M19.

1 MILTON Th'infernal Serpent . . whose guile . . deceived The mother of mankind. 2 J. CONRAD Cosmopolitan enough not to be deceived by London's topographical mysteries. I. MURDOCH Mor had never deceived his wife, except for . . one or two lies about his health. b SIR W. SCOTT Ah, what a tangled web we weave, When first we practise to deceive! 3 JAS. MILL Never was expectation more completely deceived.

deceiver *n.* a person who or thing which deceives or cheats; a cheat, an impostor: LME. **deceivingly** *adv.* so as to deceive, deceptively LME.

decelerate /diːˈsɛləreɪt/ *v.* L19. [f. DE- 3 + AC)CELERATE.] **1** *v.t.* Diminish the speed of; cause to go slower, retard. L19. **2** *v.i.* Move more slowly, slow down. E20.

deceleˈration *n.* L19. **decelerator** *n.* a device for reducing speed E20. **deceleˈrometer** *n.* an instrument for measuring the deceleration of a moving body E20.

decem- /ˈdɛsəm/ *comb. form.* [L = ten.] Ten, tenfold.

ˌdecemnoveˈnarian *n.* (*rare*) a man or woman of the 19th century M19. **decempedal** /dɪˈsɛmpɪd(ə)l/ *a.* (*rare*) †(*a*) ten feet in length; (*b*) having ten feet: M17.

December /dɪˈsɛmbə/ *n.* ME. [(O)Fr. *décembre* f. L *december*, f. *decem* ten: orig. the tenth month of the Roman year. The meaning of *-ber* is unkn. (cf. *September* etc.).] The twelfth and last month of the year in the Gregorian calendar. Also *fig.*, w. allusion to December's being the month in which the winter solstice occurs in the northern hemisphere.

Comb.: **December moth** a winter-flying lasiocampid moth, *Poecilocampa populi.*

Decembrist /dɪˈsɛmbrɪst/ *n.* L19. [f. prec. + -IST: cf. DEKABRIST.] *Hist.* A participant in an uprising which took place in St Petersburg, Russia, in December 1825, on the accession of Tsar Nicholas I.

decemvir /dɪˈsɛmvə/ *n.* LME. [L, sing. of *decemviri*, orig. *decem viri* ten men.] **1** In *pl.* A council or ruling body of ten. Orig. & *esp.* (*Rom. Hist.*) either of two bodies of magistrates appointed in 451 and 450 BC respectively to draw up a code of laws, who were in the meantime entrusted with the supreme government of Rome. LME. **2** A member of such a body. E18.

decemviral *a.* of or pertaining to decemvirs E17. **decemvirate** *n.* the position or government of decemvirs; a body of decemvirs: E17.

decenary *n.* var. of DECENNARY *n.*[1]

†**decence** *n.* Also **dé-**. L16–M19. [(O)Fr. *décence* f. as next: see -ENCE.] = next.

decency /ˈdiːs(ə)nsi/ *n.* M16. [L *decentia*, f. *decent-*: see DECENT, -Y[3], -ENCY.] **I** †**1** Appropriateness or fitness to the circumstances of the case; seemliness; what is appropriate. M16–M18. †**2** Orderly condition of civil or social life. M17–E18. **3** Propriety of behaviour or demeanour; conformity, behaviour that conforms, to recognized standards of good taste, modesty, or decorum; *esp.* avoidance of impropriety, obscenity, or immorality. M17. **4** Respectability. M18.

1 I. WATTS The great Design of Prudence . . is to determine and manage every Affair with Decency. 3 WORDSWORTH Many . . there are Who live a life of virtuous decency. K. AMIS Why hadn't they had the decency to ask him if he'd like to join in?

II 5 In *pl.* The requirements of decorum or respectable behaviour. M17. **6** An essential of a respectable lifestyle. Usu. in *pl.* L18.

5 LD MACAULAY Careless of the decencies . . expected from a man so highly distinguished. 6 H. SIDGWICK It was not easy to distinguish decencies and comforts on the one hand and luxuries on the other.

decener /ˈdɛs(ə)nə/ *n.* Also **deciner**. LME. [f. as next: see -ER[2]. Cf. DOZENER.] **1** *Hist.* The head of a tithing; a member of a tithing. LME. †**2** A commander of ten soldiers. M16–E17.

decennary /dɪˈsɛn(ə)ri/ *n.*[1] Also **decenary**. M17. [med.L *decenarius*, *decennarius*, f. *decena*, *decenna* tithing: see -ARY[1].] *Hist.* A tithing.

decennary /dɪˈsɛn(ə)ri/ *n.*[2] & *a.* E19. [f. L DECENNIUM + -ARY[1].] **A** *n.* A period of ten years; a decennium. E19. **B** *adj.* Decennial. M19.

decennia *n.pl.* see DECENNIUM.

decenniad /dɪˈsɛnɪad/ *n.* M19. [f. as next + -AD[1].] = DECENNIUM.

decennial /dɪˈsɛnɪəl/ *a.* & *n.* M17. [f. L DECENNIUM + -AL[1].] **A** *adj.* Of or pertaining to a period of ten years; lasting ten years; occurring every ten years; (of a person) holding office for ten years. M17. **B** *n.* (The celebration of) a decennial anniversary. *US.* L19.
†decennal *a.* = DECENNIAL *a.* M17–E18. **decennially** *adv.* L19.

decennium /dɪˈsɛnɪəm/ *n.* Pl. **-ia** /-ɪə/, **-iums.** L17. [L, f. *decennis*, f. *decem* ten + *annus* year.] A period of ten years, a decade.

decent /ˈdiːs(ə)nt/ *a.* M16. [Fr. *décent* or L *decent-* pres. ppl stem of *decere* be fitting: see -ENT.] **1** Suitable or appropriate to the circumstances of the case; fitting. M16. **†b** Appropriate with regard to rank or dignity. M16–L18. **2** Conforming to recognized standards of propriety, good taste, modesty, or decorum; avoiding impropriety, obscenity, or immorality. M16. **b** Sufficiently clothed to see visitors; not in a state of undress. *colloq.* M20. **†3** Handsome, comely. E17–E18. **4** In keeping with one's position or circumstances; respectable. E18. **5** Tolerable, passable, good enough. E18. **6** Of a person: kind, pleasant; obliging, generous; reasonable. *colloq.* E20.
1 A. LURIE A victor must show decent modesty and reserve. 2 S. O'CASEY I always think th' kilts is hardly decent. R. MACAULAY To grow into a decent, civilized young woman. 5 J. KEROUAC If only I had enough money to raise a decent lawyer. 6 R. LEHMANN This is a ripping place, and they're being jolly decent to us.
decentish *a.* E19. **decently** *adv.* M16. **decentness** *n.* (*obs.* exc. *dial.*) decency M16.

decenter *v.* see DECENTRE.

decentralize /diːˈsɛntrəlʌɪz/ *v.t.* Also **-ise.** M19. [f. DE- 3 + CENTRALIZE.] Do away with centralization of; confer local government on; distribute (administrative powers etc.) among local centres.
decentralist *n.* an advocate of decentralization E20. **decentraliˈzation** *n.* M19. **decentralizer** *n.* = DECENTRALIST L19.

decentre /diːˈsɛntə/ *v.t.* Also ***-ter.** L19. [f. DE- 3 + CENTRE *n.* or *v.*] **1** Remove the centre from. L19. **2** Chiefly *Optics.* Place out of centre; render (a lens) eccentric. L19.
decenˈtration *n.* L19.

deceptible /dɪˈsɛptɪb(ə)l/ *a. rare.* M17. [Fr. †*déceptible* or med.L *deceptibilis*, f. *decept-*: see next, -IBLE.] Apt to be deceived.
deceptiˈbility *n.* M17.

deception /dɪˈsɛpʃ(ə)n/ *n.* LME. [(O)Fr. *déception* or late L *deceptio(n-)*, f. L *decept-* pa. ppl stem of *decipere*: see DECEIVE, -ION.] **1** The action of deceiving or cheating; deceived condition. LME. **2** Something which deceives; a piece of trickery. L18.

deceptious /dɪˈsɛpʃəs/ *a.* Now *rare.* E17. [OFr. *decepticus* or late L *deceptiosus*, f. *decept-*: see prec., -IOUS.] That tends to deceive, cheat, or mislead.

deceptive /dɪˈsɛptɪv/ *a.* E17. [OFr. *deceptif, -ive* or late L *deceptivus*, f. *decept-*: see DECEPTION, -IVE.] Apt or tending to deceive; giving a false impression; easily mistaken for something else or as having a different quality.
J. M. MURRY Keats' letters have a deceptive spontaneity which invites the mind to pass over them . . without pausing to penetrate below the surface. N. COWARD It was probably an optical illusion. This half light is very deceptive.
deceptively *adv.* in such a way as to (be apt to) deceive E19. **deceptiveness** *n.* M19.

decerebrate /diːˈsɛrɪbrət/ *a.* L19. [f. DE- 3 + CEREBRUM + -ATE[2].] Having had the cerebrum removed or the brainstem severed below the midbrain; resulting from decerebration.
decereˈbration *n.* the removal of the cerebrum; the cutting of the brainstem below the midbrain: E20.

decern /dɪˈsəːn/ *v.* LME. [(O)Fr. *décerner* f. L *decernere* decide, pronounce a decision, f. *de-* DE- 1 + *cernere* separate, sift. Conf. w. DISCERN.] **I†1** *v.t.* Decide, determine. LME–E17. **2** *v.t.* & *i.* Decree by judicial sentence. Now only *Sc. Law.* LME. **†II** See DISCERN.

decerniture *n.* (*Sc. Law*) the action of decerning; a decree of a Scottish court: M17.

†decernment *n.* var. of DISCERNMENT.

†decerp *v.t.* Pa. t. & pple **decerped, -pt.** M16–L17. [L *decerpere* pluck off, f. *de-* DE- 1 + *carpere* pluck: cf. DISCERP.] Tear or pluck off or out; sever, excerpt, (*from*).

decertify /diːˈsəːtɪfʌɪ/ *v.t.* E20. [f. DE- 3 + CERTIFY.] Remove a certificate or certification (esp. one of insanity) from.
decertifiˈcation *n.* M20.

decession /dɪˈsɛʃ(ə)n/ *n.* Long *rare* or *obs.* LME. [L *decessio(n-)*, f. *decess-* pa. ppl stem of *decedere* depart, f. *de-* DE- 1 + *cedere* go: see -ION. Cf. (O)Fr. *decession.*] Departure, secession; diminution (opp. *accession*).

de-Christianize /diːˈkrɪstʃənʌɪz, -tɪən-/ *v.t.* Also **-ise.** M19. [f. DE- 3 + CHRISTIANIZE.] Deprive of Christian character; make no longer Christian.

deci- /ˈdɛsi/ *comb. form.* [Abbrev. of L *decimus* tenth: see -I-.] Used in names of units of measurement to denote a factor of one-tenth, as *decibel, decigram, decilitre, decimetre*, etc. Abbrev. *d.*

Decian /ˈdiːsɪən/ *a.* L17. [f. *Decius* (see below) + -AN.] Of or pertaining to the Roman Emperor Decius or his reign (249–51); *esp.* designating the persecution of Christians which occurred under Decius.

decibel /ˈdɛsɪbɛl/ *n.* E20. [f. DECI- + BEL *n.*[1]] A logarithmic unit (one-tenth of a bel, abbrev. *dB*) used to express the ratio between two levels of sound intensity, electrical power, etc., one of which is usu. a (stated or understood) reference level; *loosely* a degree of noise.

decidable /dɪˈsʌɪdəb(ə)l/ *a.* L16. [f. next + -ABLE.] **1** Able to be decided. L16. **2** *Math.* & *Logic.* Able to be proved within a formal system of axioms. M20.
decidaˈbility *n.* M20.

decide /dɪˈsʌɪd/ *v.* LME. [Fr. *décider* or L *decidere* cut off, determine, f. *de-* DE- 1 + *caedere* cut.] **1** *v.t.* Settle (a question, dispute, etc.) by finding in favour of one side; bring to a settlement, resolve; influence decisively the outcome of (a contest etc.). LME. **b** *v.i.* Settle a question in dispute, pronounce judgement. (Foll. by *between, in favour of, against.*) M18. **c** *v.t.* Determine on as a settlement, pronounce in judgement. M19. **2** *v.t.* Bring (a person) to a determination or resolution (*against, in favour of, to do*). E18. **3a** *v.t.* Come to a determination or resolution *that, to do, whether.* M19. **b** *v.i.* Come to a determination or resolution (*against, in favour of, (up)on*). M19.
1 POPE Deeds must decide our Fate. CONAN DOYLE The fight [a boxing-match] . . will . . be decided upon points. G. B. SHAW The only evidence that can decide a case of malpractice is expert evidence. b SMOLLETT Let heaven decide Between me and my foes. c F. MARRYAT What you decide shall be irrevocable. 2 E. M. FORSTER Quite a little thing decided me to speak to you. V. S. REID Something which decided him against interfering. 3a I. MURDOCH He wondered if he should call out . . but decided not to. J. WAIN She could not decide whether or not to shorten the skirt. O. MANNING Why had she suddenly decided she must see Flora? b C. S. FORESTER He had already decided on the next move. D. FRASER The Japanese had decided against invasion of Australia.

decided /dɪˈsʌɪdɪd/ *a.* M18. [f. prec. + -ED[1]. Cf. earlier UNDECIDED.] **1** Unhesitating, resolute, determined, = DECISIVE 2. M18. **2** Settled, certain; distinct, pronounced, noticeable; (of an opinion etc.) clearly formed, definite. Cf. DECISIVE 3. M18.
1 A. ALISON He found them vacillating, he left them decided. P. LARKIN She drove them along in an ungainly but decided way. 2 C. DARWIN Habit also has a decided influence. S. UNWIN He . . had decided views about the husbands his daughters ought to accept.
decidedly *adv.* (*a*) definitely, in a manner that precludes all doubt; (*b*) resolutely, unwaveringly: L18. **decidedness** *n.* E19.

decider /dɪˈsʌɪdə/ *n.* L16. [f. DECIDE + -ER[1].] **1** A person who or thing which decides a dispute, question, etc. L16. **2** *spec.* A final match, race, etc., in a series, which will decide the outcome. L19.

decidua /dɪˈsɪdjʊə/ *n.* L18. [mod.L *decidua* (sc. *membrana*), use as n. of fem. sing. of L *deciduus* DECIDUOUS: so called as being discarded at parturition.] *Anat.* The thick layer of modified endometrium which lines the uterus during pregnancy in certain mammals, including humans.
decidual *a.* of or pertaining to the decidua M19. **deciduate** *a.* possessing a decidua; of the nature of a decidua: M19.

deciduoma /dɪˌsɪdjʊˈəʊmə/ *n.* Pl. **-mas, -mata** /-mətə/. L19. [f. prec. + -OMA.] *Med.* An intrauterine tumour composed of retained decidual tissue.
†deciduoma malignum [L = malignant] = *chorionepithelioma* s.v. CHORION.

deciduous /dɪˈsɪdjʊəs/ *a.* M17. [f. L *deciduus*, f. *decidere* fall down or off, f. *de-* DE- 1 + *cadere* fall: see -UOUS.] **†1** Falling down; sinking. *rare.* M17–L18. **2** Of the leaves of a tree or shrub: shed each year at the end of the period of growth. Of a tree or shrub: that sheds its leaves in this way. Opp. EVERGREEN *a.* 1. L17. **3** *gen.* Of a part of a plant or animal: normally discarded at a particular time or stage of growth (opp. PERSISTENT); (of an insect) that sheds its wings after copulation. L17. **b** = DECIDUAL. E19. **4** *fig.* Transitory, fleeting. E19.
3 T. PENNANT Upright branched horns, annually deciduous. **deciduous tooth** = *milk tooth* s.v. MILK *n.*
deciduously *adv.* M19. **deciduousness** *n.* E18.

decile /ˈdɛsʌɪl/ *n.* & *a.* L17. [Corresp. to Fr. *décile*, prob. f. med.L deriv. of L *decem* ten. Cf. Fr. *sextil* SEXTILE, -ILE.] **1** *adj.* & *n. Astrol.* (Designating) the aspect of two planets which are one-tenth of a circle (36 degrees) apart in the sky. L17. **2** *n. Statistics.* Each of the nine values of a variate which divide a frequency distribution into ten equal groups; each of the ten groups thus formed. L19.

decillion /dɪˈsɪljən/ *n.* L18. [f. DECI- after *million, billion*, etc.] Orig. (esp. in the UK), the tenth power of a million (10^{60}). Now usu. (orig. *US*), the eleventh power of a thousand (10^{33}). Also *loosely*, an enormous number.
decillionth *a.* & *n.* M19.

decima /ˈdɛsɪmə/ *n. rare.* M17. [L, for *decima pars* tenth part.] A tenth part; a tax of one-tenth, a tithe.

decimal /ˈdɛsɪm(ə)l/ *a.* & *n.* E17. [mod.L *decimalis*, f. L *decimus* tenth, f. *decem* ten: see -AL[1].] **A** *adj.* **1** Relating to tenth parts or to the number ten; reckoning or proceeding by tens or tenths. E17. **2** Designating, of, or pertaining to a system of coinage or currency, weights and measures, etc., in which the smaller units are related to the principal units as powers of ten. M19.
2 **go decimal** adopt decimal currency.
Special collocations: **decimal arithmetic** (*a*) arithmetic in which arabic numerals are used; (*b*) the arithmetic of decimal fractions. **decimal classification** a library classification using numbers decimally arranged for its notation; *spec.* the Dewey system. **decimal fraction** a fraction in which the denominator (not expressed) is a power of ten and the numerator appears as a series of figures written after a decimal point, which according to their position represent tenths, hundredths, etc. **decimal place** the position of a digit to the right of the decimal point. **decimal point** a dot before the numerator in a decimal fraction. **decimal system** (*a*) the numerical system based on 10, in which numbers are expressed by the digits 0 to 9; (*b*) a system of weights, measures, etc., in which each denomination is 10 times the one before it; (*c*) = *decimal classification* above.
B *n.* A decimal fraction; in *pl.* freq., the arithmetic of such fractions. M17.
recurring decimal: see RECUR *v.*
decimalism *n.* a decimal system or theory M19. **decimalist** *n.* an advocate of a decimal system of coinage or currency, weights and measures, etc. M19. **decimally** *adv.* by tens or tenths; into tenths; as a decimal: L17.

decimalize /ˈdɛsɪm(ə)lʌɪz/ *v.t.* Also **-ise.** M19. [f. prec. + -IZE.] Express as a decimal; convert

to a decimal system (of coinage or currency, weights and measures, etc.).
decimali'zation *n.* M19.

decimate /ˈdɛsɪmeɪt/ *v.t.* L16. [L *decimat-* pa. ppl stem of *decimare*, f. *decimus*: see DECIMAL, -ATE^{3}.] **1** *Hist.* Select by lot and execute one in every ten of, esp. as a punishment in the Roman legions. L16. **2** *gen.* Kill, destroy, or remove one in ten of; *loosely* destroy a large proportion of, cause heavy losses or fatalities in. M17. †**3** Subject to a tithe or tax of one-tenth. M17–M19.
2 R. LEHMANN All my parents' friends, all my friends' brothers were getting killed. Our circle was decimated. V. CRONIN Plague decimated Moscow in 1771.
¶Loose usage prob. stems from a misunderstanding of sense 1 as 'execute nine out of ten of'.
decimator, -ter *n.* †(*a*) a person who exacts tithes; (*b*) a person who or thing which decimates a body of people, etc. L17.

decimation /dɛsɪˈmeɪʃ(ə)n/ *n.* LME. [Late L *decimatio(n-)*, f. as prec.: see -ATION.] **1** *Hist.* (The exaction or payment of) a tithe or tax of one-tenth; *esp.* the tax imposed by Cromwell on Royalists in 1655. LME. **2** *Hist.* The selection by lot and execution of one man in every ten (see DECIMATE *v.* 1). L16. **3** *gen.* The killing or removal of one in ten; *loosely* destruction of a large proportion, infliction of heavy losses or fatalities. L17.

decimetre /ˈdɛsɪmiːtə/ *n.* Also ***-meter**. L18. [f. DECI- + METRE *n.*^{2}] One-tenth of a metre, equal to 3.937 inches.

decimo-sexto /ˌdɛsɪməʊˈsɛkstəʊ/ *n.* Now *rare* or *obs.* Pl. **-os.** L16. [For L *sexto decimo* abl. sing. of *sextus decimus* sixteenth, orig. in phr. *in sexto decimo*.] = SEXTODECIMO.

deciner *n.* var. of DECENER.

decinormal /dɛsɪˈnɔːm(ə)l/ *a.* M19. [f. DECI- + NORMAL *a.*] *Chem.* Of a solution: having a concentration one-tenth of that of a normal solution (i.e. containing one-tenth of a gram-equivalent of solute per litre of solution).

decipher /dɪˈsʌɪfə/ *v.* & *n.* Also **decypher**. E16. [f. DE- 3 + CIPHER *v.*, after Fr. *déchiffrer*.] **A** *v.t.* †**1** Find out, discover; detect, make out. E16–M18. †**2** Reveal, make clear (by signs or actions), give the key to. E16–L18. **3** Convert to plain text (something in cipher); decode. M16. †**4** Portray, describe, delineate. M16–M18. †**5** Express in disguised or symbolic form. L16–E18. **6** *transf.* & *fig.* Succeed in reading or interpreting (hieroglyphics, ill-formed or obliterated characters, etc.); discover the meaning of (something obscure or perplexing). E17.
1 SHAKES. *Tit. A.* You are both decipher'd.. For villains. 2 T. HOLCROFT Each man has his favorite gesture which might decypher his whole character. 4 P. HOLLAND First I will discipher the medicinable vertues of trees. 5 C. COTTON I am the very man deciphered in his book under the name of Venator. 6 N. FRYE Blake's prophecies.. may need interpretation, but not deciphering. A. BRINK The postmark was too indistinct for him to decipher.
B *n.* A deciphered message. M16.
decipherable *a.* E17. **decipherer** *n.* L16. **decipherment** *n.* M19.

decision /dɪˈsɪʒ(ə)n/ *n.* LME. [(O)Fr. *décision* or L *decisio(n-)*, f. *decis-* pa. ppl stem of *decidere* DECIDE: see -ION.] **1** The action of deciding a contest, dispute, etc.; settlement, a final (formal) judgement or verdict. LME. **b** *Boxing.* The awarding of a fight, in the absence of a knockout, to the boxer with the most points. L19. **2** Determined character; firmness, resolve. L18. **3** The action of coming to a determination or resolution with regard to any point or course of action; a resolution or conclusion arrived at. M19.
1 G. B. SHAW The two umpires shall then elect a referee, whose decision shall be final. *New Society* They appealed the juvenile court decision. **b** *split decision*: see SPLIT *a.* 2 R. W. EMERSON On the English face are combined decision and nerve. 3 C. DARWIN I have not been hasty in coming to a decision. S. BELLOW A breath of relief at my decision to surrender. P. FITZGERALD Decision is torment for anyone with imagination. **decision problem** *Math.* & *Logic* the problem of finding a way to decide whether a formula or class of formulas is true or provable within a given system of axioms.
decisional *a.* of or relating to (a) decision L19.

decisive /dɪˈsʌɪsɪv/ *a.* E17. [Fr. *décisif*, *-ive* f. med.L *decisivus*, f. *decis-*: see prec., -IVE.] **1** That finally decides or determines a question, the outcome of a contest, etc.; conclusive. E17. **2** Unhesitating, resolute, determined; = DECIDED 1. M18. **3** Pronounced, unmistakable; undisputed. Cf. DECIDED 2. L18.
1 A. KOESTLER The decisive argument his friends had used to convince him. D. FRASER Midway.. one of the decisive battles of the war. 2 J. C. POWYS The decisive gesture of a strong man showing off before a weak girl. 3 L. STEPHEN A decisive superiority over its rivals. W. S. CHURCHILL A decisive electoral victory.
decisively *adv.* M17. **decisiveness** *n.* E18.

decivilize /diːˈsɪvɪlʌɪz/ *v.t.* Also **-ise**. M19. [f. DE- 3 + CIVILIZE.] Divest of civilization, make uncivilized.
decivili'zation *n.* L19.

deck /dɛk/ *n.*^{1} LME. [MDu. *dec* roof, covering, cloak, f. Gmc base of THATCH *n.* The Naut. sense appears to be an Eng. development.] **I** A covering, surface, or floor. †**1** A material, as canvas, used to form a covering, esp. on a ship; the covering itself. LME–E18. **2** A platform, usu. of wooden planks or metal covered with planks, extending across (part of) a ship, covering in the area below and acting as a floor for the area above. L15. **3** Any surface area used to stand or move on; a floor or platform, e.g. of a pier; a floor or compartment of a bus etc.; a platform for sunbathing. M19. **b** The roof of a railway carriage. *US.* M19. **c** An aeroplane wing, *esp.* a wing of a biplane. *colloq.* M19. **d** The ground; the floor. *slang* (orig. *Aeronaut.*). E20.
2 *boat-deck, flight-deck, half-deck, hurricane-deck, lower deck, main deck, middle deck, orlop deck, poop deck, promenade deck, quarterdeck, upper deck*, etc. **below deck(s)** in(to) the space under the main deck. *between decks*: see BETWEEN *adv. clear the decks*: see CLEAR *v.* 8. **on deck** (*a*) not below deck; (*b*) *fig.* (orig. *US*) on hand, ready for action. 3 *Times* Multi-deck car parks with direct access to the stores. I. SHAW Randolph was sitting on the deck in front of the house. B. BAINBRIDGE When the No. 13 bus came, Ann sat on the top deck at the front. **d** *hit the deck*: see HIT *v.*
II 4 A pack of cards. Now chiefly *N. Amer.* L16. †**b** A pile of things laid flat on each other. Only in 17. **c** A small package of narcotics. *US slang.* E20. **5** A line or group of lines in a newspaper etc. heading differentiated from the others typographically, e.g. by size. E20. **6** A unit comprising the playing and recording mechanisms for sound or video tapes; a similar unit for playing records, compact discs, etc. M20.
4 *cold deck*: see COLD *a. stack the deck*: see STACK *v.* 3. 6 *cassette deck, record deck, tape deck*, etc.
Comb.: **deck-beam** a strong transverse beam supporting the deck of a ship; **deck cargo**: stowed on the deck of a ship; **deck-chair** an adjustable folding chair, used on passenger ships' decks and elsewhere; **deck class** a grade of accommodation on a ship entitling a passenger to deck-space only; **deck-hand** a person employed on the deck of a ship to clean, do odd jobs, etc.; **deck-house** a room erected on the deck of a ship; **deck passenger** a passenger on a ship who has no cabin; **deck quoits** a game played, chiefly on ships, by throwing a rope quoit over a peg; **deck tennis** a game played, esp. on ships, by tossing a quoit etc. to and fro over a net.

deck /dɛk/ *n.*^{2} *colloq.* (orig. *Anglo-Ind.*). M19. [Hind. *dekh* familiar imper. of *dekhnā* see, look at.] = DEKKO *n.*

deck /dɛk/ *v.t.* LME. [(M)Du. *dekken* cover = OE *peććan* cover, roof over, THATCH *v.*, or f. DECK *n.*^{1}] †**1** Cover, clothe; fit out, equip. LME–M17. **2** Cover or clothe in a rich or ornamental style; array, adorn. Freq. foll. by *out*. E16. **3** Provide with a deck; cover (as) with a deck. E17. **4** Knock to the ground, floor. Chiefly *N. Amer.* & *Austral.* M20.
2 J. CLARE Daisies deck the green. A. MOOREHEAD Houses.. decked with garlands and flowers. E. REVELEY Here he was all decked out in.. his Super-suede jacket, his silk shirt and Countess Mara tie. 3 R. GRAVES Fast.. galleys, all decked in as a protection to the oarsmen.

decked /ˈdɛkt/ *a.* L15. [f. DECK *v.*, *n.*^{1}: see -ED^{1}, -ED^{2}.] **1** Arrayed, adorned; that has been decked out. L15. **2** Having a deck or decks; *esp.* as 2nd elem. of comb., having a specified number or kind of decks. M18.
2 *double-decked, single-decked, three-decked, two-decked*, etc.

decker /ˈdɛkə/ *n.*^{1} M16. [f. DECK *v.* + -ER^{1}.] A person who arrays, adorns, or decks out someone or something.

decker /ˈdɛkə/ *n.*^{2} & *a.* L18. [f. DECK *n.*^{1} + -ER^{1}.] **1** *n.* & *adj.* As 2nd elem. of comb.: (a ship, bus, etc.) having a specified number or kind of decks or layers. L18. **2** *n.* A deck-hand; a deck passenger. *Naut. colloq.* E19.
1 *double-decker, single-decker*, etc. (*bus, ship*, etc.); *flush-decker, three-decker, two-decker*, etc. (*ship* etc.).

deckie /ˈdɛki/ *n. Naut. colloq.* Also **-y**. E20. [f. DECK *n.*^{1} + -IE, -Y^{6}.] A deck-hand.

decking /ˈdɛkɪŋ/ *n.* M16. [f. DECK *v.*, *n.*^{1} + -ING^{1}.] **1** The action of DECK *v.*; adornment, ornamentation. M16. **2** The material of the deck(s) of a ship etc. L16.

deckle /ˈdɛk(ə)l/ *n.* M18. [G *Deckel* dim. of *Decke* covering; cf. -LE^{1}.] *Paper-making.* A device which confines the pulp and so limits the size of a sheet of paper, consisting of either a frame on the mould used in hand paper-making, or (in full *deckle strap*) a continuous belt on either side of the wire on a machine.
Comb.: **deckle edge** the rough uncut edge of a sheet of paper, formed by the deckle; **deckle-edged** *a.* having a deckle edge, as handmade paper; *deckle strap*: see above.
deckled *a.* formed by a deckle; deckle-edged: E20.

decky *n.* var. of DECKIE.

declaim /dɪˈkleɪm/ *v.* LME. [Fr. *déclamer* or L *declamare*, f. *de-* DE- 1 + *clamare* CLAIM *v.*] **1** *v.i.* & *t.* Speak aloud or recite with studied rhetorical expression; practise speaking or reciting (a passage). LME. **2** *v.i.* Deliver an impassioned (rather than reasoned) speech; inveigh *against*. L16.
1 R. W. EMERSON Wordsworth.. reciting to me.. like a schoolboy declaiming. E. F. BENSON Declaiming a particularly unchristian psalm which called down many curses on her enemies. 2 L. STERNE Let him declaim as pompously as he chooses upon the subject. R. L. STEVENSON Declaiming.. against the greed and dishonesty of landlords.
declaimer *n.* LME.

declamation /dɛkləˈmeɪʃ(ə)n/ *n.* LME. [Fr. *déclamation* or L *declamatio(n-)*, f. *declamat-* pa. ppl stem of *declamare*: see prec., -ATION.] **1** A rhetorical exercise or address; a set speech. LME. **2** The action or art of speaking or reciting with studied rhetorical emphasis. M16. **3** An impassioned or emotional speech; a harangue. L16. **4** Speaking in an impassioned manner; emotional denunciation. E17.

†**declamator** *n.* LME–E18. [L *declamator*, f. *declamat-*: see prec., -OR.] A declaimer.

declamatory /dɪˈklamət(ə)ri/ *a.* L16. [L *declamatorius*, f. as prec.: see -ORY^{2}.] Of or pertaining to rhetorical declaiming; of the nature of or characterized by declamation.
declamatorily *adv.* L19. **declamatoriness** *n.* M19.

declarable /dɪˈklɛːrəb(ə)l/ *a.* M17. [f. DECLARE + -ABLE.] Able to be declared.

declarant /dɪˈklɛːr(ə)nt/ *n.* L17. [Fr. *déclarant* pres. pple of *déclarer* DECLARE: see -ANT^{1}.] Chiefly *Law.* A person who makes a declaration.

declaration /dɛkləˈreɪʃ(ə)n/ *n.* LME. [L *declaratio(n-)*, f. *declarat-* pa. ppl stem of *declarare* DECLARE: see -ATION.] †**1** The action of explaining or making clear; elucidation. LME–M17. **2** †**a** The setting forth of a topic; exposition. LME–M17. **b** *spec.* A statement or confession of love; a proposal of marriage. *arch.* M18. **3** The action of setting forth, stating, or announcing publicly, formally, or explicitly; a positive statement, an emphatic or solemn assertion. LME. **4** A proclamation or formal public statement, usu. embodied in a document, public act, etc. LME. **5** *Law.* A formal affirmation or statement, usu. made in writing; *esp.* (*a*) a plaintiff's statement of claim; (*b*) an affirmation made in lieu of an oath; (*c*) a formal statement of a party's rights made by a court. L15. 6 *Cards.* An announcement of a score, combination held, trump suit, etc.; *spec.* in *Bridge*, the final bid of the auction, nominating the contract. M19. 7 *Cricket.* The voluntary closing of an innings by the team batting. E20. 8 *Computing.* A definition of a data item etc. to be used in a program. M20.

3 HOBBES If he dye .. without declaration of his Heyre. J. AUSTEN Marianne's declaration that the day would be lastingly fair. 4 LYNDON B. JOHNSON We sought widespread support for a declaration affirming the right of innocent passage through the Gulf of Aqaba. **Declaration of Independence** (the document embodying) the public act by which the American Continental Congress, on 4 July, 1776, declared the N. American colonies to be free and independent of Great Britain. *Declaration of Indulgence*: see INDULGENCE *n.* **declaration of peace** a formal proclamation announcing the end of hostilities. *Declaration of Rights*: see RIGHT *n.*[1] **declaration of the poll** the public official announcement of the numbers of votes for each candidate in an election. **declaration of war** a formal proclamation by one State announcing the commencement of hostilities against another.

declarative /dɪˈklarətɪv/ *n.* & *a.* LME. [(O)Fr. *déclaratif*, *-ive* or L *declarativus* adj., f. *declarat-*: see prec., -ATIVE.] A *n.* A declaratory statement, or act; a declarative sentence. LME. B *adj.* †1 Making clear or evident; (of a person) forthcoming. M16–L18. 2 Characterized by making a declaration; of the nature of a declaration; *Gram.*, (of a sentence) that takes the form of a simple statement. E17. 3 *Computing.* Designating high-level programming languages of a kind that can be used to solve problems without requiring the programmer to specify an exact procedure to be followed. L20.

declaratively *adv.* E17.

declarator /dɪˈklarətə/ *n.* E16. [Repr. Fr. *déclaratoire* adj., f. as next.] *Sc. Law.* An action whereby a legal right or status is declared, but nothing further is done. Also more fully *action of declarator*.

declaratory /dɪˈklarət(ə)ri/ *a.* & *n.* LME. [med.L *declaratorius*, f. L *declarator* declarer, f. *declarat-*: see DECLARATION, -ORY[2].] A *adj.* Having the nature or form of a declaration; explanatory; affirmatory; (of a statute etc.) that explains what the existing law is. LME. †B *n.* A declaration, an explanation. LME–L17.

declare /dɪˈklɛː/ *v.* ME. [L *declarare* make clear, f. *de-* DE- 1 + *clarare*, f. *clarus* clear. Cf. Fr. *déclarer*.] †1a *v.t.* & *i.* w. *of*. Relate, recount (facts, a matter, etc.); tell of. ME–E18. b *v.t.* Explain, make clear, elucidate. LME–L17. 2 *v.t.* Make known or state publicly, formally, or explicitly; affirm, assert; proclaim; (in weakened sense) say, announce. ME. b With compl.: proclaim or assert (a person etc.) to be (something). M16. 3 *v.refl.* Make known one's opinions, intentions, etc.; reveal one's (or *fig.* its own) true nature, identity, etc.; (with compl.) reveal oneself to be. LME. b *v.refl.* & *i.* Announce oneself to be *against*, *for*, *in favour of*, etc., a person, action, etc. M17. †c *v.i.* Announce oneself to be a candidate *for*, make a bid *for*. M17–M18. d *v.refl.* Confess one's love, propose marriage, (*to*). *arch.* M19. 4 *v.t.* Of a thing: manifest, show, prove. (Passing into *fig.* use of sense 2.) LME. 5 *v.i.* Make a legal declaration (see DECLARATION 5). E16. 6 *v.t.* Acknowledge by legal or formal statement; *spec.* acknowledge possession of (goods liable to duty, taxable income, etc.). L17. 7 *v.i.* Foll. by *off*: break off an engagement, practice, etc.; back out, withdraw. *arch. colloq.* M18. 8 *v.i.* & *t.* *Horse-racing.* Withdraw from a race. M19. 9 *v.t.* *Cards.* Announce or nominate by a declaration (see DECLARATION 6). M19. 10 *v.t.* & *i.* *Cricket.* Close (an innings) voluntarily before the usual ten wickets have fallen. L19.

2 E. BOWEN Lewis declared it was hot .. and went out to order Edward a drink. K. VONNEGUT The charter .. declared .. that the presidency .. was to be inherited. **declare war** formally announce the commencement of hostilities (*on*, *against*). **well, I (do) declare** *colloq.*: expr. incredulity, surprise, or vexation. b G. F. KENNAN Men .. who had been declared physically unfit for service. 3 J. CONRAD His vocation for the sea had declared itself. LYNDON B. JOHNSON Wallace .. had declared himself a candidate for President. d M. E. BRADDON He must either declare himself, or .. go away. 4 SIR W. SCOTT Nor track nor pathway might declare That human foot frequented there. 6 A. LOOS I put the unset diamonds in my handbag so I did not have to declare them at the customs.

declared *ppl a.* that has been declared; avowed, made known; (of a person) admitted, professed: LME. **declaredly** /-rɪdli/ *adv.* professedly, avowedly M17. **declarer** *n.* a person who or thing which declares; *spec.* in *Bridge*, the player who first bids the suit of the contract and who therefore plays both his or her own and the exposed hands: LME.

declass /diːˈklɑːs/ *v.t.* L19. [Fr. *déclasser*, f. *dé-* DE- 3 + *classer* CLASS *v.*: cf. next.] Remove or degrade from one's class.

déclassé /deklase (*pl. same*), deɪˈklaseɪ/ *a.* & *n.* Fem. ***-ée***. L19. [Fr., pa. pple of *déclasser*: see prec.] (A person who is) reduced or degraded in social class or status.

declassify /diːˈklasɪfʌɪ/ *v.t.* M19. [f. DE- 3 + CLASSIFY.] Remove from a classification; *spec.* cease to designate (information etc.) as secret.

declassifiable *a.* M20. **declassifiˈcation** *n.* M20.

declension /dɪˈklɛnʃ(ə)n/ *n.* LME. [(O)Fr. *déclinaison*, f. *décliner* DECLINE *v.*, alt. after L *declinatio(n-)* DECLINATION.] 1 *Gram.* The variation of form or inflection of a noun, adjective, or pronoun so as to constitute its different cases; each of the classes into which nouns are divided on the basis of these inflections; the action of declining or of setting out in order the different forms of a noun etc. LME. 2 Inclination from the vertical or horizontal position. Now only *fig.*, moral deviation, falling away from a standard etc., apostasy. Now *arch.* or *literary.* L16. 3 Deterioration, decay; a condition of decline. Now *arch.* or *literary.* E17. 4 The action of declining or refusing politely. *rare.* E19.

declensional *a.* of or belonging to (grammatical) declension M19.

declericalize /diːˈklɛrɪk(ə)lʌɪz/ *v.t.* Also **-ise**. L19. [f. DE- 3 + CLERICAL + -IZE.] Free from clerical influence or character.

declericaliˈzation *n.* L19.

declinable /dɪˈklʌɪnəb(ə)l/ *a.* LME. [(O)Fr. *déclinable* or late L *declinabilis*, f. *declinare* DECLINE *v.*: see -ABLE.] †1 Liable to deteriorate. Only in LME. 2 *Gram.* Able to be declined; having case-inflections. M16.

declinate /ˈdɛklɪnət/ *a.* E19. [L *declinatus* pa. pple of *declinare* DECLINE *v.*: see -ATE[2].] *Bot.* Inclined forwards or downwards.

Also †**declinated** *a.*: only in M18.

declination /dɛklɪˈneɪʃ(ə)n/ *n.* LME. [L *declinatio(n-)*, f. *declinat-* pa. ppl stem of *declinare* DECLINE *v.*: see -ATION.] 1 Inclination from the vertical or horizontal position; downward bend or turn. LME. †b Turning aside, (moral) deviation, falling away from a standard etc. M16–E19. †2 Sinking, descent; *fig.* deterioration, decline, decay. LME–L18. †3 *Gram.* = DECLENSION 1. LME–M18. 4a *Astron.* Angular distance from the celestial equator (corresp. to terrestrial latitude). LME. †b *Surveying.* The deviation of a given vertical plane from the prime vertical or from the meridian. L16–M18. c The angular deviation of a compass needle, orig. from the horizontal (= DIP *n.* 3), now from the true north and south line. Cf. VARIATION 8. M17. 5 Non-acceptance; polite refusal. Now *US.* E17.

Comb.: **declination axis** the axis of an equatorial telescope which is at right angles to the polar axis and about which the telescope is turned in order to alter the declination of the object being viewed; **declination circle** a graduated circle on an equatorial telescope, on which declination is marked.

declinational *a.* L19.

†**declinator** *a.* & *n.* L15–E19. [med.L *declinatorius*: see next, -OR. Cf. DECLINATURE.] *Sc. Law.* (Constituting, in *exception declinator*) a declinature.

declinatory /dɪˈklʌɪnət(ə)ri/ *a.* & *n.* L17. [med.L *declinatorius*, f. *declinat-*: see DECLINATION, -ORY[2]. Cf. (O)Fr. *déclinatoire*.] A *adj.* Expressing refusal. Chiefly *Law* (now *Hist.*), designating a plea claiming exemption from the court's jurisdiction. L17. B *n.* A declinatory plea. Now *Hist.* L17.

declinature /dɪˈklʌɪnətjʊə/ *n.* M17. [Alt. of DECLINATOR: see -URE.] 1 *Sc. Law.* A formal refusal to admit the jurisdiction of a judge or court; refusal of a judge to accept jurisdiction in a case. M17. 2 Courteous refusal. M19.

decline /dɪˈklʌɪn/ *n.* ME. [f. (as) the vb. Cf. (O)Fr. *déclin*.] 1 The process of declining or sinking; (a) gradual loss of vigour or excellence; falling off, decay, diminution, deterioration. ME. b A wasting disease, *esp.* tuberculosis. *arch.* L18. c A fall in price or value. L19. 2 The sinking of the sun towards its setting; the latter part of the course of the day, life, etc. LME. 3 A downward incline, a slope. *rare.* M16.

1 J. ROSENBERG It is only in the .. year of Rembrandt's death that we detect some decline in the artist's expressive power. J. G. FARRELL The Turf, which had fallen into a decline in recent years had revived wonderfully. **on the decline** in a declining state. 2 STEELE A Gentleman who according to his Years should be in the Decline of his Life.

decline /dɪˈklʌɪn/ *v.* LME. [(O)Fr. *décliner* f. L *declinare*, f. *de-* DE- 1 + *clinare* to bend.] I *v.i.* †1 Turn aside; deviate; turn away. LME–M19. †2 Have astronomical or magnetic declination. LME–E18. †3 *fig.* Turn aside in conduct; fall away *from* rectitude, duty, etc. LME–M18. †4 *fig.* Lean or incline *to*. LME–L17. 5 Slope downwards. LME. 6 Bend down, bow down, droop. LME. †7 Descend. *rare.* LME–E17. 8 Of the sun etc.: descend towards setting. Of the day, one's life, etc.: draw towards its close. LME. 9 Fall off in vigour or vitality; decay, diminish; deteriorate. LME. 10 Fall morally or in dignity. Now only *literary* (after Shakes.). LME. 11 (Politely) refuse an invitation, offer, request, etc. (Cf. sense 13b below.) L19.

3 AV *Ps.* 119:157 Yet doe I not decline from thy testimonies. 4 P. HOLLAND That purple luster .. declineth .. to the color of wine. 5 E. J. HOWARD The sloping lawn declined from the house. 6 T. HARDY Declining from his sitting position. 8 R. WOODHOUSE As the Moon, having passed the meridian, declines. 9 R. L. STEVENSON England has already declined, since she has lost the States. J. CONRAD His voice declined to a mere sleepy murmur. H. A. L. FISHER The government which began in a blaze of glory steadily declined in strength. **declining years** old age. 10 SHAKES. *Haml.* What a falling off was there, from me .. to decline Upon a wretch whose natural gifts were poor To those of mine. 11 JOYCE She pressed me to take some cream crackers .. but I declined.

II *v.t.* †12 Avert; deflect, turn aside (*from*, *to*). LME–M18. †13a Turn aside from; avoid, shun. LME–M18. b Turn away from out of unwillingness; not consent to engage in or practise, not agree to *doing*; refuse, esp. politely (an invitation, request, offer, etc., or *to do*). M17. c Give up (a practice). Long *rare.* L17. d *Chess.* Refuse to take a piece or pawn offered in (a gambit). M19. 14 *Sc. Law.* Refuse or formally object to the jurisdiction of (a judge or court). LME. 15 *Gram.* Inflect (a noun, adjective, or pronoun) through its different cases; recite the cases of in order; *loosely* conjugate. LME. †b Recite formally or in a definite order. L16–E17. 16 Bend down, bow down. LME. †17 Lower, degrade. LME–L18. †18 Undervalue, disparage. E16–M17. 19 Cause to slope downwards, incline. L16.

12 S. JOHNSON To decline the pressure of resistless arguments. 13b T. JEFFERSON I decline all newspaper controversy. CARLYLE I declined satisfying his curiosity. A. CARNEGIE He declined an interest in the firm which would have made him a millionaire. P. G. WODEHOUSE I decline to give in to this absurd suggestion. A. GUINNESS She .. offered me a glass of sherry, which I declined. **decline with thanks** refuse graciously; *iron.* reject scornfully. 16 SOUTHEY He sate with folded arms and head declined Upon his breast.

decliner *n.* a person who or thing which declines E17.

declinometer /dɛklɪˈnɒmɪtə/ *n.* M19. [f. DECLINATION + -OMETER.] An instrument for measuring astronomical or magnetic declination.

declive /dɪˈklʌɪv/ *n.* L19. [f. as next.] *Anat.* An area of the upper surface of the vermis of the cerebellum posterior to the culmen.

declive /dɪˈklʌɪv/ *a.* Long *rare* or *obs.* M17. [Fr. *déclive* f. L *declivis* sloping downward, f. *de-* DE- 1 + *clivus* slope.] Sloping downwards.

declivitous /dɪˈklɪvɪtəs/ *a.* L18. [f. next + -OUS.] Having a (considerable) declivity; steep.
declivitously *adv.* L19.

declivity /dɪˈklɪvɪti/ *n.* E17. [L *declivitas*, f. *declivis* sloping down: see DECLIVE *a.*, -ITY.] 1 Downward slope, inclination. E17. 2 A downward slope, sloping ground. L17.

declivous /dɪˈklʌɪvəs/ *a.* L17. [f. L *declivus* rare var. of *declivis*: see DECLIVE *a.*, -OUS.] Sloping downwards, slanting.

declutch /diːˈklʌtʃ/ *v.i.* E20. [f. DE- 3 + CLUTCH *n.*[1]] Disengage the clutch of a motor vehicle.
double-declutch: see DOUBLE *a.* & *adv.*

deco /ˈdɛkəʊ/ *n.* M20. [Abbrev. of Fr. (*art*) *décoratif* decorative (art).] In full *art deco*. A decorative artistic style of the 1920s and 1930s, characterized by modernist and streamlined design.

decoct /dɪˈkɒkt/ *v.t.* Pa. pple **-ed**, (earlier) †**decoct**. LME. [L *decoct-* pa. ppl stem of *decoquere* boil down, f. *de-* DE- 1 + *coquere* COOK *v.*] †1 Prepare (food) by boiling, cook; heat up as in cooking. LME–M17. †2 Mature or prepare (a mineral, metal) by heat (according to old notions). L15–M17. 3 Boil in water etc. so as to concentrate or to extract the essence of; prepare a decoction of. M16. †4 Boil down, concentrate; *fig.* consume. M16–L17. †5 Digest in the stomach. M16–E17.

decoction /dɪˈkɒkʃ(ə)n/ *n.* LME. [(O)Fr. *décoction* or late L *decoctio(n-)*, f. as prec.: see -ION.] 1 Concentration of, or extraction of the essence of, a substance by boiling in water etc. LME. 2 A liquid essence made by boiling; an (esp. medicinal) extract. LME. †3 Maturation or preparation of a mineral or ore by heat (according to old notions). LME–L17. †4 Digestion of food. M16–M17. †5 Reduction, boiling down, (*lit.* & *fig.*). L16–M17.
1 T. THOMSON Catechu . . is . . obtained by decoction and evaporation from a species of mimosa. 2 G. BERKELEY A decoction of briar-roots for the bloody flux.

decode /diːˈkəʊd/ *v.t.* L19. [f. DE- 3 + CODE *n.* or *v.*] Decipher, interpret, translate (a coded message); analyse (a coded audio etc. signal).
decoder *n.* a person who or thing which decodes; *spec.* a device for analysing stereophonic signals and feeding separate amplifier-channels: E20.

decohere /diːkə(ʊ)ˈhɪə/ *v.t.* & *i.* *obs.* exc. *Hist.* E20. [f. DE- 3 + COHERE.] *Electronics.* Restore (a coherer), be restored, to its normal condition of sensitivity.
decoherer *n.* a device for decohering a coherer L19.

decoke /diːˈkəʊk/, *as n. freq.* ˈdiːkəʊk/ *v.* & *n.* *colloq.* E20. [f. DE- 3 + COKE *n.*[1]] A *v.t.* Decarbonize (an internal-combustion engine). E20. B *n.* The action of decarbonizing an engine. M20.

decollate /dɪˈkɒleɪt, ˈdɛkəleɪt/ *v.*[1]*t.* Pa. pple **-ated**, (earlier, long *arch. rare*) **-ate** /-ət/. LME. [Orig. pa. pple, f. L *decollatus* pa. pple of *decollare* behead, f. *de-* DE- 3 + *collum* neck: see -ATE[3].] 1 Behead. LME. 2 *Conchol.* In *pass.* of a shell: be broken off near the apex. Freq. as *decollated* pa. ppl a. M19.
decollator *n.*[1] a person who or thing which decollates; a decapitator: M19.

decollate /diːkəˈleɪt/ *v.*[2]*t.* & *i.* M20. [f. DE- 3 + COLLATE.] Separate (sheets of paper, esp. of continuous stationery) mechanically into different piles.
decollator *n.*[2] a machine for decollating stationery L20.

decollation /dɪkəˈleɪʃ(ə)n/ *n.* LME. [(O)Fr. *décollation* or late L *decollatio(n-)*, f. *decollat-*: see DECOLLATE *v.*[1], -ATION.] The action of beheading; the state of being beheaded; truncation; *Surg.* severance of the head of a foetus.

décollement /deɪˈkɒlmɒ̃, *foreign* dekɔlmɑ̃/ *n.* M19. [Fr., f. *décoller* unstick, disengage: see -MENT.] 1 *Med.* The process of separating organs or tissues from surrounding parts; the state of being thus separated. M19. 2 *Geol.* The sliding (and subsequent deformation) of strata over those beneath; a boundary separating deformed strata from underlying strata which are not (similarly) deformed. E20.

décolletage /dekɔltaːʒ, deɪkɒlˈtɑːʒ/ *n.* L19. [Fr., f. *décolleter*: see next, -AGE.] 1 The low-cut neckline of a woman's garment. L19. 2 Exposure of the neck and shoulders by such a neckline. L19.

décolleté /dekɔlte, deɪˈkɒl(ə)teɪ/ *a.* Also **-ée**. M19. [Fr. (fem. *-ée*), f. *décolleter* expose the neck, f. *dé-* DE- 3 + *collet* collar of a dress etc.] Of a (woman's) garment: having a low-cut neckline. Of a woman: wearing a low-necked garment. Also *fig.*, daring, slightly improper.
Listener Her décolleté dresses and décolleté past.

decolonization /ˌdiːkɒlənʌɪˈzeɪʃ(ə)n/ *n.* Also **-isation**. M20. [f. DE- 3 + COLONIZATION.] The withdrawal of a State from its former colonies, leaving them independent; the acquisition of independence by a former colony.

decolor *v.*, **-ant** *n.* & *a.* see DECOLOUR, -ANT.

decoloration /diːˌkʌləˈreɪʃ(ə)n, ˌdiːkʌl-/ *n.* Also **-lour-**. E17. [Fr. *décoloration* f. L *decoloratio(n-)*, f. *decolorat-* pa. ppl stem of *decolorare* DECOLOUR: see -ATION.] †1 Discoloration, staining. E17–E18. 2 Loss or removal of colour, decolourizing. M17.

decolorise, -ize *vs.* see DECOLOURIZE.

decolour /diːˈkʌlə/ *v.t.* Also *-**or**. LME. [Fr. *décolorer* or L *decolorare*, f. *de-* DE- 3 + *colorare* to colour.] †1 Discolour, stain. LME–M17. 2 = DECOLOURIZE 1. M19.

decolourant /diːˈkʌlər(ə)nt/ *n.* & *a.* Also *-**lor-**. M19. [Fr. *décolorant*, f. *décolorer*: see DECOLOUR, -ANT[1].] A *n.* A decolourizing agent. M19. B *adj.* Able to decolourize, decolourizing. L19.

decolouration *n.* var. of DECOLORATION.

decolourize /diːˈkʌlərʌɪz/ *v.* Also *-**lor-**; **-ise**. M19. [f. DE- 3 + COLOURIZE.] 1 *v.t.* Remove colour from, make colourless or pale. M19. 2 *v.i.* Lose colour, become colourless or pale. E20.
decolouri'zation *n.* M19.

decommission /diːkəˈmɪʃ(ə)n/ *v.t.* E20. [f. DE- 3 + COMMISSION *v.*] Take (a ship, installation, etc.) out of service.

decommunize /diːˈkɒmjʊnʌɪz/ *v.t.* Also **-ise**. L20. [f. DE- 3 + COMMUNIZE.] Remove the features of Communism from; reverse the communization of.
decommuni'zation *n.* L20.

decompensation /ˌdiːkɒmp(ə)nˈseɪʃ(ə)n/ *n.* E20. [f. DE- 3 + COMPENSATION.] *Med.* (A condition of) failure of compensation (COMPENSATION 1b); *esp.* inability of the heart to maintain circulation after a period of compensation.
de'compensated *a.* associated with or exhibiting decompensation M20.

decomplement /diːˈkɒmplɪm(ə)nt/ *v.t.* M20. [f. DE- 3 + COMPLEMENT *n.*] *Immunol.* Inactivate the complement in (blood serum, an animal).
decomplemen'tation *n.* the process or result of inactivating serum complement M20.

decomplex /ˈdiːkɒmplɛks/ *a.* M18. [f. DE- 2 + COMPLEX *a.*] Repeatedly complex; made up of complex parts.

decomposable /diːkəmˈpəʊzəb(ə)l/ *a.* L18. [f. next + -ABLE.] Able to be decomposed or separated into its constituent elements.
decomposa'bility *n.* M19.

decompose /diːkəmˈpəʊz/ *v.* M18. [Fr. *décomposer*, f. *dé-* DE- 3 + *composer* COMPOSE.] 1 *v.t.* Break down or separate into its component elements or simpler constituents. M18. 2 *v.i.* Undergo (esp. chemical) decomposition; break down, decay, rot. L18.
1 D. BREWSTER We have . . by absorption decomposed green light into yellow and blue. 2 T. H. HUXLEY Soon after death the softer parts of organized bodies begin to decompose. *fig.*: S. H. BEER Insofar as deference has collapsed, class has decomposed.

decomposible /diːkəmˈpəʊzɪb(ə)l/ *a.* E19. [f. prec. + -IBLE.] = DECOMPOSABLE.
decomposi'bility *n.* L19.

decomposite /diːˈkɒmpəzɪt/ *n.* & *a.* E17. [Late L *decompositus* (for Gk *parasunthetos*), f. *de-* DE- 2 + *compositus* COMPOSITE *a.* & *n.*] = DECOMPOUND *n.* & *a.*

decomposition /ˌdiːkɒmpəˈzɪʃ(ə)n/ *n.* M17. [Branch I f. as prec. + -ION; branch II f. Fr. *décomposition*, f. as DECOMPOSE + -ITION.] †I 1 Compounding of things already composite, decompounding. M–L17.
II 2 The action or process of separating or resolving something into its component elements or simpler constituents. M18. 3 *spec.* The natural breaking-down of (organic) matter into simpler substances; rotting, decay, disintegration, putrescence; decayed condition. L18.
3 J. LUBBOCK The bones were in such a state of decomposition, that the ribs and vertebrae crumbled into dust. *fig.*: M. MUGGERIDGE The whole decaying social structure, the stench of whose decomposition was so strongly in my nostrils. *double decomposition*: see DOUBLE *a.* & *adv.*

decompound /ˈdiːkɒmpaʊnd/ *n.* & *a.* E17. [f. DE- 2 + COMPOUND *a.* or *n.*[1]] (A word, substance, etc.) made up of elements that are themselves compound; (something) repeatedly compound.

decompound /diːkəmˈpaʊnd/ *v.* LME. [f. DE- 2 (sense 1), 3 (sense 2) + COMPOUND *v.*] 1 *v.t.* Compound further, form by adding to or combining compounds. Freq. as *decompounded* ppl a., consisting of compound constituents. LME. 2 *v.i.* & *t.* Decompose. M18.

decompress /diːkəmˈprɛs/ *v.t.* & *i.* E20. [f. DE- 3 + COMPRESS *v.*] Subject to or undergo decompression.
decompressive *a.* of, pertaining to, or producing decompression E20. **decompressor** *n.* a device for reducing compression E20.

decompression /diːkəmˈprɛʃ(ə)n/ *n.* E20. [f. DE- 3 + COMPRESSION.] The process of relieving or reducing pressure; *spec.* (*a*) the returning of a subject experiencing increased pressure, e.g. a deep-sea diver, to atmospheric pressure, usu. gradually under controlled conditions; (*b*) (sudden) reduction of air pressure in an aircraft etc. to the ambient external pressure; (*c*) surgical relief of excessive internal pressure in a part of the body.
Comb.: **decompression chamber**: in which pressure can be maintained either above atmospheric, esp. in order to decompress a diver etc. gradually, or below atmospheric, e.g. to subject an organism to reduced pressure; **decompression sickness** a condition which results from too rapid decompression (and consequent formation of nitrogen bubbles in the tissues) and may involve pain in the joints (the bends (BEND *n.*[3])), numbness, nausea, paralysis, etc.

deconcentrate /diːˈkɒns(ə)ntreɪt/ *v.t.* L19. [f. DE- 3 + CONCENTRATE *v.*] Reverse or reduce the concentration of; decentralize.
deconcen'tration *n.* L19.

decondition /diːk(ə)nˈdɪʃ(ə)n/ *v.t.* M20. [f. DE- 3 + CONDITION *v.*] Undo the results of conditioning in (a person, animal, etc.); remove or reverse the conditioned reflexes of.

decongest /diːk(ə)nˈdʒɛst/ *v.t.* M20. [Back-form. f. DECONGESTION.] Relieve the congestion of; *esp.* ease the flow of traffic etc. in or through (a place).

decongestant /diːk(ə)nˈdʒɛst(ə)nt/ *n.* & *a.* M20. [f. DE- 3 + CONGEST *v.* + -ANT[1].] A *n.* A decongestive agent; *spec.* a substance which relieves nasal congestion. M20. B *adj.* That relieves (esp. nasal) congestion. M20.

decongestion /diːk(ə)nˈdʒɛstʃ(ə)n/ *n.* E20. [f. DE- 3 + CONGESTION.] The reduction or relief of congestion.

decongestive /diːk(ə)nˈdʒɛstɪv/ *a.* E20. [f. prec. + -IVE.] That reduces or relieves congestion.

deconsecrate /diːˈkɒnsɪkreɪt/ *v.t.* L19. [f. DE- 3

+ CONSECRATE *v.*] Undo the consecration of; transfer (a church etc.) to secular use; secularize.
deconse'cration *n.* M19.

deconstruction /diːk(ə)n'strʌkʃ(ə)n/ *n.* L19. [f. DE- 3 + CONSTRUCTION.] **1** The reverse of construction; taking to pieces. *rare.* L19. **2** A strategy of critical analysis of (esp. philosophical and literary) language and texts which emphasizes features exposing unquestioned assumptions and inconsistencies. L20.
deconstruct *v.t.* subject to deconstruction L19. **deconstructible** *a.* able to be deconstructed, amenable to deconstruction L20. **deconstructionism** *n.* the theory or practice of deconstruction L20. **deconstructionist** *n.* & *a.* (*a*) *n.* an adherent or practitioner of deconstruction; (*b*) *adj.* of or pertaining to deconstruction or deconstructionists: L20. **deconstructor** *n.* a practitioner of deconstruction L20.

decontaminate /diːk(ə)n'tamɪneɪt/ *v.t.* M20. [f. DE- 3 + CONTAMINATE *v.*] Remove contamination from; *esp.* free from (the risk of) contamination by infectious disease, harmful chemicals, radioactivity, etc.
decontami'nation *n.* M20.

decontextualize /diːk(ə)n'tɛkstjʊəlʌɪz/ *v.t.* Also **-ise.** L20. [f. DE- 3 + CONTEXTUALIZE.] Study or treat in isolation from its context.
decontextuali'zation *n.* L20.

decontrol /diːk(ə)n'trəʊl/ *n.* & *v.* E20. [f. DE- 3 + CONTROL *n.* or *v.*] **A** *n.* The removal of (esp. governmental) control or restrictions. E20. **B** *v.t.* Infl. **-ll-.** Release from (esp. governmental) controls; remove restrictions on. E20.

deconvolution /ˌdiːkɒnvə'luːʃ(ə)n/ *n.* L20. [f. DE- 3 + CONVOLUTION.] The action or process of deconvolving something.

deconvolve /diːk(ə)n'vɒlv/ *v.t.* L20. [f. DE- 3 + CONVOLVE.] *Math.* & *Physics.* Resolve (a function) into the functions of which it is a convolution; *gen.* resolve into constituent elements. Also, obtain by resolving thus.

décor /'deɪkɔː/ *n.* Also **de-.** L19. [Fr., f. *décorer* DECORATE *v.*] **1** The scenery and furnishings of a theatre stage; the set. L19. **2** (The overall effect of) the decoration and furnishings of a room, building, etc. E20.
2 N. MAILER Staring at the grey, green and beige décor of their living room.

decorament /'dɛkərəm(ə)nt/ *n. rare.* E18. [Late L *decoramentum*, f. *decorare* DECORATE *v.*: see -MENT.] Decoration, ornament.

decorate /'dɛkərət/ *ppl a.* (orig. *pa. pple*). Long *arch.* LME. [L *decoratus* pa. pple of *decorare*: see next, -ATE[2].] Adorned, decorated; ornate.

decorate /'dɛkəreɪt/ *v.t.* M16. [f. prec. or L *decorat-* pa. ppl stem of *decorare* beautify, f. *decus, decor-* embellishment: see -ATE[3].] **1** Embellish; grace, honour. Now *rare* or *obs.* M16. **2** Provide with adornments, add colour or ornament to; make (a house etc.) more attractive with paint, wallpaper, etc.; serve as adornment to. L18. **3** Invest (a person) with a military or other decoration, medal, etc. Usu. in *pass.* E19.
1 J. A. FROUDE War and plunder were decorated by poetry as the honourable occupation of heroic natures. 2 E. PEACOCK The old armour which decorated its walls. J. H. PARKER The custom of decorating churches with flowers. M. GIROUARD Rooms were decorated in a wide variety of tertiary colours. 3 G. ORWELL So far from being decorated, he had been censured for showing cowardice in the battle.
decorated *a.* (*a*) that has been decorated; (*b*) (**D-**) designating or displaying the architectural style of the second stage of English Gothic (14th cent.), characterized by increasing use of decoration, and geometrical, curvilinear, and reticulated tracery: E17.

decoration /dɛkə'reɪʃ(ə)n/ *n.* LME. [(O)Fr. *décoration* or late L *decoratio(n-)*, f. *decorat-*: see prec., -ATION.] **1** The action of decorating; the fact or condition of being decorated; ornateness. LME. **2** A thing that adorns; an ornament. In *pl.*, temporary ornaments (bunting, lights, paper chains, etc.) put up on festive occasions. L16. **3** A medal, cross, etc., conferred and worn as an honour. E19.
1 S. JOHNSON She.. applied all her care to the decoration of her person. 2 R. HOGGART Pin-ups used to be, and still are, standard decoration for servicemen's billets. E. MANNIN The dress was black and very plain, its sole decoration an Egyptian collarette of gold and coral.
Comb.: **Decoration day** *US* = *Memorial Day* s.v. MEMORIAL *n.*

decorative /'dɛk(ə)rətɪv/ *a.* LME. [Isolated early use f. (O)Fr. *décoratif, -ive*; later (L18) f. DECORATE *v.*: see -ATIVE.] Pertaining to or of the nature of decoration; ornamental.
J. WYNDHAM The finger-nails.. showed a length more decorative than practical. *decorative arts*: see ART *n.*[1]
decoratively *adv.* L19. **decorativeness** *n.* M19.

decorator /'dɛkəreɪtə/ *n.* M18. [f. DECORATE *v.* + -OR.] A person who decorates; *spec.* (freq. more fully *painter and decorator*) one whose business is the decoration of buildings with paint, wallpaper, etc.

decore /dɪ'kɔː/ *v.t.* Long *obs.* exc. *Sc.* LME. [(O)Fr. *décorer* f. L *decorare* DECORATE *v.*] Decorate, adorn, embellish.
decorement *n.* [OFr.] an ornament, an embellishment L16.

decorous /'dɛk(ə)rəs/ *a.* M17. [f. L *decorus* + -OUS.] †**1** Appropriate, seemly. M–L17. **2** Characterized by decorum; not violating good taste or propriety; dignified and decent. L17.
2 J. I. M. STEWART Junior Ministers.. probably keep more.. decorous company than writers do. I. MCEWAN Their greetings were intimate yet restrained, decorous.
¶Pronunc. after L with stress on 2nd syll. was formerly common but is now old-fashioned.
decorously *adv.* in a decorous manner; with decorum: E19. **decorousness** *n.* L17.

decorticate /diː'kɔːtɪkeɪt/ *v.t.* E17. [L *decorticat-* pa. ppl stem of *decorticare*, f. *de-* DE- 3 + *cortex, cortic-* bark: see -ATE[3].] Remove the peel, husk, bark, or outer layer from; subject to decortication. Freq. as *decorticated* ppl a.
decorticator *n.* a person who or thing which decorticates; a device for decorticating: L19.

decortication /dɪˌkɔːtɪ'keɪʃ(ə)n/ *n.* E17. [L *decorticatio(n-)*, f. as prec.: see -ATION.] The removal of the peel, bark, or other outer layer from something; *spec.* surgical removal of the cortex of the brain or other organ, esp. the cutting of the brainstem above the midbrain.

decorum /dɪ'kɔːrəm/ *n.* M16. [L, use as n. of neut. sing. of *decorus* seemly.] **I1** Suitability of artistic or literary style to the subject; congruity, unity. M16. **2** Suitability to the dignity or circumstances of a person or occasion. *arch.* L16. **3** Propriety of behaviour or demeanour; seemliness; etiquette. L16.
1 T. HEARNE Neither is a just Decorum always observ'd, for he sometimes makes Blockheads and Barbarians talk like Philosophers. 2 SHAKES. *Ant. & Cl.* Majesty, to keep decorum, must No less beg than a kingdom. 3 J. AUSTEN His sense of decorum is strict. D. CECIL He could not.. trust himself to behave with proper decorum during the ceremony.
II†**4** Beauty arising from congruity, order, or harmony; orderliness. L16–E18. **5**†**a** An appropriate act. E17–E18. **b** A particular usage required by politeness or decency. Usu. in *pl.* Now *rare.* E17.
5b GOLDSMITH No decorums could restrain the impatience of his blushing mistress to be forgiven.

découpage /dekupaːʒ/ *n.* Pl. pronounced same. M20. [Fr., f. *découper* cut up or out.] **1** The decoration of a surface with cut-out paper patterns or illustrations; an object so decorated. M20. **2** *Cinemat.* The cutting or editing of a film. M20.

decouple /diː'kʌp(ə)l/ *v.* E17. [Orig. f. Fr. *découpler*; later f. DE- 3 + COUPLE *v.*] **1** *v.t.* Uncouple. *rare* in *lit.* sense. E17. **2** *v.t.* Make separate or independent (*from*); *esp.* in *Physics*, make the coupling between oscillators, systems, etc. so weak that there is little transfer of energy between them. M20. **3** *v.i.* Become decoupled; *esp.* in *Physics*, cease to interact (so that thermal equilibrium is no longer maintained), become differentiated. M20.
2 *Times* If we want to bring interest rates down we have to decouple the pound from the dollar.

decoy /'diːkɔɪ, dɪ'kɔɪ/ *n.* E17. [Perh. f. Du. *de kooi* the decoy: see COY *n.*] **1** A pond from which net-covered channels lead, into which ducks or other wildfowl can be enticed for capture. E17. **2** A bird or animal, or an imitation of one, used to attract others. Also *fig.*, a person or thing employed to entice or deceive others into capture, danger, error, etc.; a swindler's confederate; a tempter; a bait, an enticement. Cf. earlier DECOY-DUCK. M17.
2 J. BUCHAN She would be the decoy.. to get Karolides out of the care of his guards.
Comb.: DECOY-DUCK; **decoy ship**: used to decoy enemy vessels.

decoy /'diːkɔɪ, dɪ'kɔɪ/ *v.t.* M16. [Prob. f. the n., but in isolated Sc. use earlier.] Entice (an animal) into a trap, esp. with the aid of another animal. Also *fig.*, lure, tempt, entice, ensnare, (a person etc.). (Foll. by *into, out of, from* a place, situation, action, etc., or adv.)
H. MARTINEAU They would not be decoyed away by a false alarm. W. IRVING A black horse.. being decoyed under a tree by a tame mare.

decoy-duck /'diːkɔɪdʌk, dɪ'kɔɪ-/ *n.* E17. [f. DECOY *n.* + DUCK *n.*[1], tr. Du. *kooieend.*] A tame or imitation duck used to decoy others; *fig.* a person who entices others into danger or mischief. Cf. DECOY *n.* 2.

decrease /'diːkriːs, dɪ'kriːs/ *n.* LME. [OFr. *de(s)creis*, f. stem of *de(s)creistre*: see next.] **1** The process of growing less; diminution; an amount by which something is decreased. LME. †**2** The waning of the moon. E17–M18.

decrease /dɪ'kriːs, 'diːkriːs/ *v.i.* & *t.* LME. [OFr. *de(s)creiss-* pres. stem of *de(s)creistre* (mod. *décroître*) f. Proto-Romance var. of L *decrescere*, f. *de-* DE- 1 + *crescere* grow.] (Cause to) grow less; lessen; diminish.
A. SILLITOE The bruise was still visible.. though the swelling had decreased. J. G. FARRELL Decreasing the chances of his proposal being accepted.
decreasingly *adv.* to a decreasing extent E19.

decreation /diːkrɪ'eɪʃ(ə)n/ *n.* M17. [f. DE- 3 + CREATION.] The undoing of creation; annihilation.
¶Rare bef. 20.

decree /dɪ'kriː/ *n.* ME. [OFr. *decré* var. of *decret* f. L *decretum* use as n. of neut. of *decretus* pa. pple of *decernere* DECERN.] **1** An edict or law of an ecclesiastical council, settling some disputed point of doctrine or discipline; in *pl.* = DECRETAL. ME. **2** An ordinance or edict set forth by the civil or other authority; an authoritative decision having the force of law. LME. **3** A judicial decision; *spec.* (*a*) *Eng. Law* the judgement of a court of equity, divorce, probate, or (*Hist.*) admiralty; (*b*) *Sc. Law* a final judgement or sentence of a civil court, whereby the question at issue is decided (earlier as DECREET *n.* 1b). LME. **4** The will, as shown by events, of God, or of providence, nature, etc., personified. L16.
2 SHAKES. *Merch. V.* There is no force in the decrees of Venice. *Times* In France the matter.. is being decided.. by presidential decree. 3 **decree nisi** /'nʌisʌi/ [NISI] a provisional order for divorce, made absolute unless cause to the contrary is shown within a fixed period. 4 T. KEN Her Conscience tells her God's Decree.. made her free.

decree /dɪ'kriː/ *v.* Pa. t. & pple **decreed.** LME. [f. the n.] **1** *v.t.* Command by decree; order, appoint, or assign authoritatively. LME. **b** Of God, or providence, nature, etc., personified: ordain. L16. **2** *v.t.* & *i.* Decide, determine, or resolve authoritatively (*that*, (arch.) *to do*). LME. **3** *v.t.* & *i. Law.* Pronounce (as) judgement in a cause. Formerly, pronounce judgement on. M16.
1 R. GRAVES The Senate had decreed an arch in Livia's memory. b SHAKES. *Twel. N.* Fate, show thy force:.. What is decreed must be. 2 HOBBES Whatsoever that Assembly shall Decree. H. FIELDING Here we decreed to rest and dine. JO GRIMOND The Organisation and Methods division decreed that every office must have a Budget. 3 M. L. KING The Court decreed an end to the old Plessey decision of 1896.
decreer *n.* a person who or body etc. which decrees E17.

decreet /dɪ'kriːt/ *n. arch.* Long only *Sc.* LME. [(O)Fr. *décret* or L *decretum* DECREE *n.*] **1**†**a** *gen.* A decree. LME–E17. **b** *Sc. Law.* A final judgement or sentence of a civil court, whereby the question at issue is decided. L15. †2 A determination, a resolve. LME–L16.

decreet /dɪˈkriːt/ *v.t.* & *i. arch. obs.* exc. *Sc.* LME. [f. the n. or Fr. *décréter*, f. as the n.] Decree; *esp.* pronounce (as) a legal judgement.

decrement /ˈdɛkrɪm(ə)nt/ *n.* L16. [L *decrementum*, f. *decre-* stem of *decrescere* DECREASE *v.*: see -MENT.] 1 At Oxford University, an amount deducted from a scholar's endowment for college expenses. Long *obs.* exc. *Hist.* L16. 2 The process or fact of growing (gradually) less; an instance of this; decrease, diminution, loss, waste. E17. b Chiefly *Her.* The waning of the moon. E17. 3 A quantity lost by diminution or waste: a negative increment. M17. b In full *decrement of life*. The annual decrease in a given set of people by death. M18. c *Physics*. The ratio (often expressed logarithmically, freq. *logarithmic decrement*) of the amplitudes in successive cycles of a damped oscillation. L19.

decreolize /diːˈkriːə(ʊ)lʌɪz, -ˈkrɪ-/ *v.t.* Also **-ise**. M20. [f. DE- 3 + CREOLIZE.] Cause (a language) to lose creole characteristics. Usu. in *pass*.
decreoliˈzation *n.* L20.

decrepit /dɪˈkrɛpɪt/ *a.* Also †**-id**. LME. [L *decrepitus* (partly through Fr. *décrépit*), f. *de-* DE- 1 + *crepitus* pa. pple of *crepare* to rattle, creak.] Worn out; enfeebled with age and infirmity: dilapidated.
DRYDEN How can you be so good to an old decrepid man? D. MURPHY The dwelling itself was so irreparably decrepit that no modern squatter would stay there overnight.
decrepitly *adv.* M19. †**decrepitness** *n.* = DECREPITUDE E17–E18.

decrepitate /dɪˈkrɛpɪteɪt/ *v.* M17. [f. DE- 1 + L *crepitat-* pa. ppl stem of *crepitare* crackle: see -ATE[3].] 1 *v.t.* Heat (a crystalline substance) until crackling ceases. M17. 2 *v.i.* Crackle and disintegrate on heating. L17.
decrepiˈtation *n.* M17.

decrepitude /dɪˈkrɛpɪtjuːd/ *n.* L16. [(O)Fr. *décrépitude*, f. L *decrepitus*: see DECREPIT, -TUDE.] The state of being decrepit; feebleness and decay, esp. due to old age.
Also †**decrepity** *n.* L16–E17.

decrescendo /diːkrɪˈʃɛndəʊ/ *adv.*, *a.*, *n.*, & *v.i.* Pl. of n. **-os**. E19. [It., pres. pple of *decrescere* DECREASE *v.*] = DIMINUENDO.

decrescent /dɪˈkrɛs(ə)nt/ *a.* & *n.* E17. [L *decrescent-* pres. ppl stem of *decrescere* DECREASE *v.*: see -ENT.] A *adj.* Decreasing; growing gradually less. Esp. of the moon: waning (in *Her.* depicted with the horns directed to the sinister side). Cf. INCRESCENT. E17. B *n.* The waning or decrescent moon. E17.

decreta *n.* pl. of DECRETUM.

decretal /dɪˈkriːt(ə)l/ *n.* & *a.* ME. [Late L *decretale* (whence also (O)Fr. *décrétale*), use as n. of neut. sing. of *decretalis* adj. (whence the Eng. adj.), f. L *decret-* pa. ppl stem of *decernere* DECERN: see -AL[1].] A *n.* 1 *Eccl.* A papal decree or decretal epistle; a document issued by a pope determining some point of doctrine or ecclesiastical law; in *pl.*, the collection of such decrees forming part of the canon law. ME. 2 *gen.* A decree; an ordinance. L16. B *adj.* 1 Pertaining to, of the nature of, or containing, a decree or decrees (esp. papal). L15. †2 Esp. of God's laws: imperative, inviolable. Also, decisive, definitive. Only in 17.
†**decretaline** *a.* of or pertaining to the decretals E17–E18. **decretalist** *n.* (*a*) a holder of the Calvinistic doctrine of the decrees of God; (*b*) = DECRETIST: E18. **decretally** *adv.* in a decretal way; by way of decree: E17.

decretion /dɪˈkriːʃ(ə)n/ *n.* Long *rare.* M17. [f. L *decret-* pa. ppl stem of *decrescere* DECREASE *v.* + -ION. Cf. ACCRETION.] Decrease.

decretist /dɪˈkriːtɪst/ *n.* LME. [med.L *decretista*, f. *decretum* DECREE *n.* + *-ista* -IST.] A person versed in (esp. papal) decretals.

decretive /dɪˈkriːtɪv/ *a.* E17. [f. L *decret-* pa. ppl stem of *decernere* DECERN + -IVE.] Of the nature of, involving, or relating to a decree.

decretorial /diːkrɪˈtɔːrɪəl/ *a.* L16. [f. L *decretorius* DECRETORY + -AL[1].] †1 = DECRETORY 1. L16–M17. 2 = DECRETIVE. L18.

decretory /dɪˈkriːt(ə)ri/ *a.* Now *rare* or *obs.* L16. [L *decretorius*, f. *decret-* pa. ppl stem of *decernere* determine: see DECERN, DECREE *n.*, -ORY[2].] 1 Determinative, critical; *spec.* pertaining to or decisive of the final outcome of a disease etc. L16. †2 = DECRETIVE. M17–E19.

decretum /dɪˈkriːtəm/ *n.* Pl. **-ta** /-tə/. E17. [L.] A decree.

†**decrew** *v.i. rare* (Spenser). Only in L16. [Fr. *décru* pa. pple of *décroître* DECREASE *v.*] Decrease, wane.

decrial /dɪˈkrʌɪəl/ *n. rare.* E18. [f. DECRY + -AL[1].] An act of decrying; open disparagement.

decrier /dɪˈkrʌɪə/ *n.* L17. [f. DECRY + -ER[1].] A person who decries.

decriminalize /diːˈkrɪmɪn(ə)lʌɪz/ *v.t.* Also **-ise**. M20. [f. DE- 3 + CRIMINAL + -IZE.] 1 Reform through psychiatric treatment. *rare.* M20. 2 Make, or treat as, no longer criminal; legalize (esp. a drug, or its possession or use). L20.
decriminaliˈzation *n.* M20.

decrown /diːˈkraʊn/ *v.t.* Now *rare* or *obs.* E17. [f. DE- 3 + CROWN *n.*] Deprive (a monarch etc.) of the crown.

decry /dɪˈkrʌɪ/ *v.* & *n.* E17. [f. DE- 1 + CRY *v.*, after Fr. *décrier* cry down. Cf. DESCRY *v.*[1]] A *v.t.* 1 Chiefly *Hist.* Denounce, suppress, or depreciate (coins etc.) by proclamation. E17. 2 Cry out against; disparage openly; belittle. M17.
1 W. BLACKSTONE The king may . . decry . . any coin of the kingdom, and make it no longer current. 2 O. SITWELL There were some who had even decried Britain's War Effort.
B *n.* The decrying of money etc. *rare.* L17.

decrypt /ˈdiːkrɪpt/ *n.* M20. [f. the vb.] A deciphered cryptogram.

decrypt /diːˈkrɪpt/ *v.t.* M20. [f. DE- 3 + *crypt-* as in *cryptogram* etc.] Decipher (a cryptogram) with or without knowledge of the key.
decryption *n.* M20.

decubitus /dɪˈkjuːbɪtəs/ *n.* L19. [mod.L, f. L *decumbere* lie down, after *accubitus* reclining at table, etc. Earlier in Fr.] *Med.* the manner or posture of lying; the recumbent position.
decubital *a.* pertaining to or resulting from decubitus L19.

decuman /ˈdɛkjʊmən/ *a.* M17. [L *decumanus* var. of *decimanus* of or belonging to the tenth part or tenth cohort, (by metonymy) large, f. *decimus*: see DECIMAL.] 1 Esp. of a wave: very large, immense. M17. 2 *Rom. Hist.* Of or belonging to the tenth cohort. E19.
1 F. W. FARRAR Amid the decuman billows of modern scepticism. 2 **decuman gate** the main gate of the camp where the tenth cohort was quartered.

decumbency /dɪˈkʌmb(ə)nsi/ *n.* M17. [f. next: see -ENCY.] 1 Lying down; decumbent position or posture. M17. 2 The action of taking to one's bed. M17.
Also **decumbence** *n.* M17.

decumbent /dɪˈkʌmb(ə)nt/ *n.* & *a.* E17. [L *decumbent-* pres. ppl stem of *decumbere* lie down, f. *de-* DE- 1 + *-cumbere*: see CUMBENT.] †A *n.* A person lying (ill) in bed. Only in 17. B *adj.* 1 Lying down; reclining. Now *rare* or *obs.* M17. †b Lying in bed through illness. L17–M18. 2a *Bot.* Of a plant, shoot, etc.: lying or trailing on the ground (with the extremity ascending). L18. b *Zool.* Of hairs or bristles: lying flat on the surface of the body. E19.

decumbiture /dɪˈkʌmbɪtʃə/ *n.* Now *rare* or *obs.* M17. [Irreg. f. L *decumbere* (see prec.) + -URE.] 1 The act or time of taking to one's bed in an illness; *Astrol.* a horoscope made for the time at which this happens, affording prognostication of the outcome. M17. 2 Lying down, *spec.* as an invalid in bed. L17.

decuple /ˈdɛkjʊp(ə)l/ *n.* & *a.* LME. [Late L *decuplus* adj., *decuplum* n., f. *decem* ten.] A *n.* A tenfold amount; a number or quantity ten times another. LME. B *adj.* Tenfold. E16.
decuplet *n.* a set of ten things of the same kind L19.

decuple /ˈdɛkjʊp(ə)l/ *v.t.* & *i.* L17. [Late L *decuplare*, f. *decuplus*: see prec.] Multiply or increase tenfold.
Also **decuplate** *v.t.* & *i.* L17.

decurion /dɪˈkjʊərɪən/ *n.* LME. [L *decurio(n-)*, f. *decuria* (see DECURY) after *centurio(n-)* CENTURION.] 1 *Rom. Hist.* A cavalry officer in command of a company of ten horse. Also *gen.*, a captain of ten men. LME. 2 *Rom. Hist.* A member of the senate of a colony or municipal town; a town councillor. LME. 3 A member of the great council in Italian cities and towns. M17.
decurionate *n.* the office of a decurion M19.

decurrence /dɪˈkʌr(ə)ns/ *n.* M17. [f. next + -ENCE.] †1 The state or act of running down; lapse (of time). M–L17. 2 *Bot.* The condition of being decurrent. M19.
decurrency *n.* M17.

decurrent /dɪˈkʌr(ə)nt/ *a.* LME. [L *decurrent-* pres. ppl stem of *decurrere* run down. f. *de-* DE- 1 + *currere* run: see -ENT.] †1 Running down. Only in LME. 2 *Bot.* Of a leaf etc.: extending down the stem below the point of attachment. M18.
decurrently *adv.* E19.

†**decursion** *n.* LME. [L *decursio(n-)*, f. *decurs-* pa. ppl stem of *decurrere*: see prec., -ION.] 1 Downward course; lapse (of time). LME–L17. 2 *Antiq.* A marching of soldiers etc.; a solemn procession around a funeral pyre. E17–E18.

decursive /dɪˈkəːsɪv/ *a.* L18. [mod.L *decursivus*, f. *decurs-*: see prec., -IVE.] *Bot.* = DECURRENT 2.
decursively *adv.* E19.

†**decurtate** *v.t.* Pa. pple & ppl a. **-ate(d)**. L16–M19. [L *decurtat-* pa. ppl stem of *decurtare* cut short, abridge, f. *de-* DE- 1 + *curtare* shorten: see -ATE[3].] Cut short, shorten, abridge.

†**decurtation** *n.* LME–E18. [L *decurtatio(n-)*, f. as prec.: see -ATION.] The action or an act of cutting short, shortening, or abridging.

decurved /dɪˈkəːvd/ *a.* M19. [f. DE- 1 + CURVE *v.* + -ED[1].] Curving or bending downwards.

decury /ˈdɛkjʊri/ *n.* M16. [L *decuria*, f. *decem*, after *centuria* CENTURY.] *Rom. Hist.* A division, company, or body of ten.

decus /ˈdiːkəs/ *n. slang. obs.* exc. *Hist.* L17. [L *decus et tutamen* 'ornament and safeguard', inscribed on the rim.] A crown-piece.

decussate /dɪˈkʌsət/ *a.* E19. [L *decussatus*, f. as next: see -ATE[2].] 1 Having the form of an X; X-shaped. E19. 2 *Bot.* (Bearing leaves etc.) arranged oppositely in pairs, each pair being at right angles to the pair below. M19.
decussately *adv.* M19.

decussate /dɪˈkʌseɪt, ˈdɛkəseɪt/ *v.t.* & *i.* M17. [L *decussat-* pa. ppl stem of *decussare* divide crosswise, f. *decussis* the numeral 10, coin worth 10 asses, intersection of lines crosswise (X), f. *decem* ten: see AS *n.*, -ATE[3].] Arrange or be arranged in decussate form; (cause to) intersect.
decussated *ppl a.* (*a*) formed with crossing lines like an X; intersected; having decussations; (*b*) *Rhet.* = CHIASTIC: M17.

decussation /dɪkəˈseɪʃ(ə)n, dɛkə-/ *n.* M17. [L *decussatio(n-)*, f. *decussat-*: see prec., -ATION.] 1 Crossing of lines, rays, fibres, etc., so as to form a figure like an X; intersection. M17. 2 *Rhet.* = CHIASMUS 2. M19.

decyl /ˈdɪsʌɪl, -sɪl/ *n.* M19. [f. Gk *deka* ten + -YL.] *Chem.* Any of the series of monovalent radicals $C_{10}H_{21}$·, obtained from the decanes. Usu. in *comb.*

decypher *v.* & *n.* see DECIPHER.

dedal *n.*, *a.* vars. of DAEDAL *n.*, *a.*

Dedalean, -ian *a.* var. of DAEDALIAN.

Dedalic *a.* var. of DAEDALIC.

dedans /dəˈdɑ̃/ *n.* E18. [Fr. = inside, interior.] *Real Tennis.* The open gallery at the end of the service side of the court; the spectators watching a match (from this area).

dedecorate /dɪˈdɛkəreɪt/ *v.t.* E17. [Sense 1 f. L *dedecorat-* pa. ppl stem of *dedecorare* dishonour, f. *dedecus*, *dedecor-* disgrace: see -ATE[3]; sense 2 f. DE- 3 + DECORATE *v.*] †1 Dishonour. Only in E17. 2 Disfigure. E19.

dedendum /dɪˈdɛndəm/ *n.* E20. [L *dedendum* neut. gerundive of *dedere* give up, surrender.] *Mech.* The radial distance from the pitch circle of a cog-wheel, worm-wheel, etc., to the bottoms of the tooth spaces or grooves.

dedentition /diːdɛnˈtɪʃ(ə)n/ *n.* M17. [f. DE- 3 + DENTITION.] *Physiol.* The shedding of the (deciduous) teeth.

dedicant /ˈdɛdɪk(ə)nt/ *n.* L19. [L *dedicant-* pres. ppl stem of *dedicare*: see next.] A person who dedicates or is dedicated (*to*).

dedicate /ˈdɛdɪkət, -eɪt/ *a.* (orig. *pa. pple*). *arch.* LME. [L *dedicatus* pa. pple of *dedicare* proclaim, devote, consecrate, f. *de-* DE- 1 + *dic-* weak var. of *dic-* say: see -ATE[2].] Dedicated.

dedicate /ˈdɛdɪkeɪt/ *v.t.* LME. [L *dedicat-* pa. ppl stem of *dedicare*, after prec. or DEDICATION: see -ATE[3].] **1** Devote with solemn rites *to* a god, saint, or sacred use; consecrate, set apart (a church etc.), esp. without certain forms necessary for legally consecrating ground or buildings. LME. **2** Introduce (a book, piece of music, or other artistic work) with words (usu. written therein) addressed *to* a friend, patron, etc., as a mark of honour, regard, or gratitude. E16. †**b** Address (a letter etc.) *to*. L17–L18. **3** Give up earnestly or wholly *to* a special purpose, cause, etc. M16. **4** Formally or legally devote (land) for the use of the general public or for a particular purpose (*spec.* forestry: cf. DEDICATED 1b). M19.

1 A. RIDLER Can we say Mass to dedicate our bombs? K. CLARK The great Romanesque churches were dedicated to the saints whose relics they contained. 2 YEATS A subtle book which I cannot praise as I would, because it has been dedicated to me. 3 I. WALTON When you . . dedicate a day or two to this Recreation. N. MOSLEY She knew he would not force her, since they were both people dedicated to non-violence. E. WELTY Irene . . had dedicated her life to Sylvia, sparing herself nothing.

dedica'tee *n.* a person to whom something is dedicated M18. **dedicative** *a.* having the attribute of dedicating M17. **dedicator** *n.* a person who dedicates, *esp.* one who inscribes a book to a friend, patron, etc. L16.

dedicated /ˈdɛdɪkeɪtɪd/ *a.* L16. [f. prec. + -ED[1].] **1** *gen.* That has been dedicated. L16. **b** Of private woodland: managed for timber production according to an approved plan and with financial assistance from the forestry authority. M20. **2** Of a person: devoted to his or her aims or vocation; single-mindedly loyal and conscientious. M20. **3** Esp. of (part of) a computer: (designed and) used exclusively for a particular purpose or by a particular user. L20.

2 I. MURDOCH One of those dedicated single women on whom society so much depends. J. CHEEVER Francis had been a dedicated boy scout when he was young. 3 *Broadcast* Consumer demand for a dedicated children's television service. *Which Computer?* A 16-bit processor with its own 32 KB of dedicated RAM.

dedication /dɛdɪˈkeɪʃ(ə)n/ *n.* LME. [(O)Fr. *dédication* or L *dedicatio(n-)*, f. as prec.: see -ATION.] **1** The action of dedicating, or the fact of being dedicated, to God, a saint, sacred purposes, etc. LME. **b** A service or form of words by which something is dedicated. LME. **2** The action of dedicating a book, artistic work, etc.; a dedicatory inscription. L16. **3** The action of dedicating oneself to a particular purpose, cause, etc. E17. **b** The quality of being dedicated in aims, vocation, etc. (see DEDICATED 2). M20. **4** Formal or legal giving over of land etc. to public or other use, *spec.* of woodland: see DEDICATED 1b. E19.

dedicatory /ˈdɛdɪkət(ə)ri, ˈdɛdɪkeɪt-, -ˈkeɪt(ə)ri/ *a.* & *n.* M16. [f. late L *dedicator*, f. *dedicat-*: see DEDICATE *v.*, -OR, -ORY[2]. Cf. Fr. *dédicatoire*.] A *adj.* That has the attribute of dedicating; serving to dedicate something. M16. †**B** *n.* A dedicatory inscription or address. L16–L17.

dedicatorily *adv.* E19.

dedifferentiate /ˌdiːdɪfəˈrɛnʃɪeɪt/ *v.i.* E20. [f. DE- 3 + DIFFERENTIATE *v.*] *Biol.* Of a cell, tissue, etc.: undergo a reversal of differentiation, lose specialized characteristics.

dedifferenti'ation *n.* E20.

†**dedignation** *n.* LME–E18. [OFr. f. L *dedignatio(n-)*, f. *dedignat-* pa. ppl stem of *dedignari* DISDAIN *v.*: see -ATION.] Disdain, contempt.

dedimus /ˈdɛdɪməs/ *n.* LME. [L *dedimus potestatem* 'we have given the power', used in the wording of the writ.] *Law.* In full *dedimus potestatem* /pɒtɪˈsteɪtəm, -ˈstɑː-/. A writ empowering a private person to do some act in place of a judge.

dedition /dɪˈdɪʃ(ə)n/ *n.* Now *rare* or *obs.* E16. [OFr. *dedicion* or L *deditio(n-)*, f. *dedit-* pa. ppl stem of *dedere* give up, f. *de-* DE- 1 + *dare* give: see -ION.] Yielding, surrender.

dedolent /ˈdɛdəl(ə)nt/ *a.* Long *rare.* M17. [L *dedolent-* pres. ppl stem of *dedolere*, f. *de-* DE- 3 + *dolere* grieve: see -ENT.] That feels sorrow no more; insensible, callous.

dedolomitization /ˌdiːdɒləmɪtʌɪˈzeɪʃ(ə)n/ *n.* Also **-isation**. E20. [f. DE- 3 + DOLOMITIZATION.] *Geol.* Conversion of dolomite into rock of another kind; *esp.* loss of magnesium from dolomite (leaving calcite).

de'dolomitize *v.t.* cause to undergo dedolomitization E20.

deduce /dɪˈdjuːs/ *v.t.* LME. [L *deducere*, f. *de-* DE- 1 + *ducere* to lead.] **1** Lead, bring, convey. *arch.* LME. †**b** Divert. M16–M17. **c** *Rom. Hist.* Found (a colony). E17. **2** Infer, draw as a logical conclusion (*from* something already known or assumed); derive by a process of reasoning. LME. **3** Draw from its source, derive; trace the origin of, show to be derived (*from*). *arch.* L15. **4** Orig., conduct (a process), deal with (a matter). Later, trace the course of, go through in sequence. *arch.* L15. †**5** Deduct, subtract. L15–E19. †**6** Reduce to a different form. L16–M18.

2 SIR T. MORE Ye case once graunted, ye deduce your conclusion very surelye. N. MARSH From that . . I deduce that you are a painter in oils. S. WEINBERG The existence of the antielectron was first deduced theoretically by . . Dirac. 3 J. USSHER They deduced themselves from the Athenians. F. W. FARRAR The attempt to prove that all languages were deduced from the Hebrew. 4 GIBBON The general design of this work will not permit us . . to deduce the various fortunes of his private life.

†**deducement** *n.* the act of deducing; a deduction: E17–E19.

deducible /dɪˈdjuːsɪb(ə)l/ *a.* & *n.* E17. [f. prec. + -IBLE.] (An inference, conclusion, etc.) able to be deduced.

deduci'bility *n.* M19. **deducibleness** *n.* E18.

deduct /dɪˈdʌkt/ *v.t.* LME. [L *deduct-* pa. ppl stem of *deducere* DEDUCE.] **1** Subtract (*from*), take away (an amount, portion, etc.). LME. †**2** = DEDUCE 3, 4. M16–M17. †**3** = DEDUCE 1. M16–E17. **4** = DEDUCE 2. Now *rare.* M16.

deductable *a.* = DEDUCTIBLE *a.* L19.

deductible /dɪˈdʌktɪb(ə)l/ *a.* & *n.* M19. [f. prec. + -IBLE.] A *adj.* That can or may be deducted; *spec.* (in full *tax-deductible*) that may be deducted from one's tax or taxable income. M19. **B** *n.* A proportion of the risk which must be borne by the holder of an insurance policy. Orig. *US.* E20.

deduction /dɪˈdʌkʃ(ə)n/ *n.* LME. [(O)Fr. *déduction* or L *deductio(n-)*, f. as prec.: see -ION.] **1** Subtraction, taking away; an amount subtracted. LME. **2** An act of leading forth or away. *rare.* LME. **b** *Rom. Hist.* The founding of a colony. L17. **3** The process of deducing a conclusion from what is known or assumed; inference from the general to the particular (cf. *induction*); an inference, a conclusion. L15. †**4** The action of setting down in order; a detailed account. M16–E19. †**5** Derivation. E17–M19.

deductive /dɪˈdʌktɪv/ *a.* M17. [med.L *deductivus*, f. as DEDUCT *v.*: see -IVE.] Of or pertaining to deduction; of the nature of or characterized by deduction; reasoning from the general to the particular (cf. *inductive*).

deductively *adv.* M17. **deductivism** *n.* belief in the superiority of, or preference for, deductive over inductive methods of reasoning E20. **deductivist** *n.* & *a.* (*a*) an adherent of deductivism; (*b*) of or pertaining to deductivists or deductivism: M20.

deductory /dɪˈdʌkt(ə)ri/ *a. rare.* E17. [L *deductorius*, f. *deductor* agent-n. f. *deducere* DEDUCE: see -ORY[2].] †**1** *Law.* Having the effect of bringing a matter before a court. Only in E17. **2** = DEDUCTIVE. M17.

dee /diː/ *n.* & *v.* L18. [Repr. pronunc. of *D, d* as the letter's name.] **A** *n.* **1** The letter D, d; a D-shaped object, *esp.* an iron or steel loop for connecting parts of a harness or for fastening articles to a saddle. L18. **b** *Physics.* Either of two hollow semicircular electrodes used to accelerate particles in a cyclotron. E20. **2** A detective. *slang.* L19. **B** *v.t.* Pa. t. & pple **deed.** *euphem.* = DAMN *v.* 4. Chiefly as *deed*, damned. M19.

deed /diːd/ *n.* & *v.* [OE *dēd*, (WS) *dǣd* = OFris. *dēd(e)*, OS *dād* (Du. *daad*), OHG *tāt* (G *Tat*), ON *dáð*, Goth. *-deþs*, f. Gmc, ult. f. IE base of DO *v.*] **A** *n.* **1** A thing done by a responsible agent; an act. OE. **b** A brave, skilful, or conspicuous act; a feat. OE. †**c** A thing to be done, a contemplated task; duty. ME–L16. **2** Action, performance; actual fact. (Freq. contrasted w. *word.*) OE. **b** *collect.* Doings; ado, to-do. *dial.* E16. **3** *Law.* A written or printed instrument signed (and sealed and delivered) by the disposer, effecting some legal disposition such as the transfer of property or the creation of a contract. ME.

1 SHAKES. *Jul. Caes.* They that have done this deed are honourable. *take the will for the deed*: see WILL *n.*[1] **b** TENNYSON Arthur yet had done no deed of arms. C. CAUDWELL Deeds of outstanding individual heroism. 2 J. RUSKIN The strength of Hercules is for deed not misdeed. **in deed** in action, in practice, in actual fact; earlier also in all senses of INDEED. **in very deed** *arch.* in undoubted effect or fact, in truth. 3 B. TARKINGTON His father had never given Mabel a deed to her house. *deed of association*: see ASSOCIATION 1. *deed of covenant*: see COVENANT *n. deed of gift*: see GIFT *n.* 2. *title-deed*: see TITLE *n.*

Comb.: **deed-box** a strongbox for keeping deeds and other documents; **deed poll** [POLL *a.*] a deed made and executed by one party only (so called because the paper is polled or cut even, not indented).

B *v.t.* Convey or transfer by legal deed. *US.* E19.

deedful *a.* full of deeds, active, effective E17. **deedless** *a.* without action or deeds; performing no deeds, inactive: L16.

deed /diːd/ *adv.* Also **'deed.** Now chiefly *Sc.* M16. [Aphet.] = INDEED.

deedy /ˈdiːdi/ *a.* *dial.* & *colloq.* LME. [f. DEED *n.* + -Y[1].] Active, industrious; effective, handy; earnest, serious.

deedily *adv.* E19.

deejay /diːˈdʒeɪ, ˈdiːdʒeɪ/ *n. slang* (orig. *US*). M20. [Repr. pronunc. of abbrev. DJ.] A disc jockey.

Deely-bobber /ˈdiːlɪbɒbə/ *n.* Also **Deelie-, d-.** M20. [Fanciful.] **1** (US proprietary name for) a construction toy comprising a number of interlinking building blocks. M20. **2** (US proprietary name for) a piece of novelty headgear consisting of a pair of ornaments, e.g. balls, attached like antennae by springs or wires to a headband. L20.

deem /diːm/ *v.* & *n.* [OE *dēman* = OFris. *dēma*, OS *dōmian* (Du. *doemen*), OHG *tuomen*, ON *dœma*, Goth. *domjan*, f. Gmc base of DOOM *n.*[1]] **A** *v.* **1**†**a** *v.t.* & *i.* Act as judge (with respect to); sit in judgement (on), pronounce judgement (on). OE–E17. **b** *v.t.* Administer (law). *arch.* LME. †**2** *v.t.* Sentence, condemn (*to*, *to do*); censure. OE–E17. †**3** *v.t.* Decree; decide; award. OE–E17. †**4** *v.t.* Announce; tell, say. *poet.* OE–M16. **5** *v.t.* & (now *rare*) *i.* Believe, consider, judge, or count to be or *to be*; believe etc. *that*, (a person or thing) *to do*, *to have done*. OE. †**6** Form a judgement or opinion of or *of*; distinguish (between). ME–L16. **7** *v.i.* Expect, hope *to do*. *rare.* ME. **8** *v.i.* Think in a specified way *of*. LME. **9**†**a** *v.t.* Think of as existing; imagine, suspect. LME–L16. **b** *v.i.* Foll. by *of*: think of, imagine. *poet. rare.* E19.

1 J. SKENE Thou Judge be ware, for as ye deme, ze sall be demed. 5 POPE He too, I deem, implores the power divine. T. HARDY When she deemed . . that she had carried the alarm far enough, she . . dragged herself back again. J. G. FARRELL The major had . .

deemed it best to say nothing. J. BARZUN To accomplish what he deemed his mission. 8 SIR W. SCOTT Where the ties of affection were highly deemed of. 9b BYRON Something unearthly which they deem not of.

†**B** *n.* Judgement, opinion, surmise. LME–M17.

deemer *n.* †(*a*) a judge; (*b*) *gen.* a person who deems: OE.

de-emphasis /diːˈɛmfəsɪs/ *n.* M20. [f. DE- 3 + EMPHASIS.] A lessening or removal of emphasis; *spec.* the reversal of pre-emphasis in an audio signal by attenuating higher frequencies, so as to restore tonal balance on reproduction.

de-emphasize /diːˈɛmfəsʌɪz/ *v.t.* Also **-ise**. M20. [f. DE- 3 + EMPHASIZE.] Remove emphasis from, reduce emphasis on.

deemster /ˈdiːmstə/ *n.* ME. [f. DEEM + -STER. Cf. DEMPSTER, DOOMSTER.] **1** *gen.* A judge. *arch.* ME. **2** (The title of) either of the two justices of the Isle of Man. E17.

deener *n.* var. of DEANER.

deep /diːp/ *n.* [OE *dēop* neut. of *dēop* adj.: see next.] †**1** Depth, deepness *rare.* OE–M17. **2** A deep part of the sea, a lake, or river. Freq. in *pl.*, deep water, a deep place. OE. **3** *sing.* & †in *pl. The* ocean; *the* deep sea. *poet.* & *rhet.* OE. **b** *The* depths or abyss of space. L16. **4** A deep place in the earth; a cavity, an abyss, a pit. LME. **5** The remote central part. *rare.* LME. **6** A mysterious region of thought or feeling. *poet.* & *rhet.* LME. **7** The middle *of* winter or night, when the cold, dark, etc., are at their most intense. M16. **8** *Naut.* An estimated fathom on a sounding-line between marked depths. Cf. earlier DIP *n.* 4a. M19. **9** *Cricket.* The deep field. E20.

2 CARLYLE Some silent . . mountain-pool, into whose black deeps you fear to gaze. 3 *Book of Common Prayer* We therefore commit his body to the Deep. POPE The monstrous wonders of the deeps. *rapture(s) of the deep*: see RAPTURE *n.* b SHAKES. *1 Hen. IV* I can call spirits from the vasty deep. 6 K. HULME The rock of desolation, and the deep of despair.

deep /diːp/ *a.* [OE *dēop* = OFris. *diāp*, OS *diop*, *diap* (Du. *diep*), OHG *tiuf* (G *tief*), ON *djúpr*, Goth. *diups* f. Gmc, f. base repr. also by DIP *v.*] **I** *lit.* **1** Having great, or a specified, extension downward from the top. OE. **2** Having great, or a specified, extension inward from the surface or edge. OE. **b** *pred.* After a number: in that number of ranks one behind the other. (Passing into adv.) L17. **3** Going or placed far, or a specified distance, down, back, or, inwards; sunk *in*; (of a ship) low in the water. OE. **b** *spec.* In *Cricket*, distant from the batsman; in *Football, Hockey*, etc., distant from the front line of one's team. M19. †**4** Covered with a depth of mud, sand, etc. LME–E19. **5** Of a physical action etc.: extending to or coming from a depth. L15.

1 I. MURDOCH He feared the deep crevasses down which a man might slide. J. C. OATES It was fairly shallow in parts, and as deep as . . fifteen feet in others. *between the devil and the deep (blue) sea*: see DEVIL *n.* 2 SHELLEY When birds die In the deep forests. D. H. LAWRENCE He had a deep cut across his thumb. b C. THIRLWALL The Thebans . . stood five-and-twenty deep. 3 DRYDEN The frozen Earth lyes buried there . . seven Cubits deep in Snow. J. RHYS Standing knee deep in the river. 4 SMOLLETT Three hundred miles through deep roads. 5 H. S. MERRIMAN She . . swept him a deep curtsey. J. STEINBECK Lee lifted the bottle . . and took a deep hot drink. R. P. WARREN He gulped a full, deep, exquisite breath.

II *fig.* **6** Of an oath, sin, etc.: solemn; grave. Now *rare* or *obs.* OE. **7** Penetrating far into a subject; hard to fathom; profound, not superficial. OE. **8** That affects one profoundly; rooted in one's innermost feelings. ME. **9** Having profound knowledge, learning, or insight. ME. **10** Cunning, subtle, secretive. Now *slang.* ME. **11** Of a condition, quality, state, etc.: intense, profound, extreme. LME. **12** Of colour etc.: intense, vivid. LME. **13** Of sound etc.: low in pitch; full-toned, resonant; not shrill. LME. **14** Of an agent: who does (what is expressed by the n.) profoundly. E16. **15** *pred.* Involved or immersed greatly or to a specified degree (*in*). (Passing into adv.) M16. **16** Of an action etc.: mentally absorbing. L16. **17** Involving heavy expense or liability. Now *rare.* L16. **18** *pred.* After a number: having that number of engagements or obligations. (Passing into adv.) E20.

6 MILTON A deep and serious verity. 7 DAY LEWIS He preaches such deep sermons Lily can't make head or tail of them. 8 I. MURDOCH He felt a deep need to explain this. 9 R. HOLINSHED A deepe clerke, and one that read much. 10 DICKENS You're a deep one, Mr. Pip. 11 T. HARDY Little Abraham was aroused from his deep sleep. J. CONRAD A . . deserted street in deep shadow. 12 R. HOOKE All manner of Blues, from the faintest to the deepest. 13 J. D. SALINGER I made my voice quite deep so that she wouldn't suspect my age. 14 M. ARNOLD Shakspeare was no deep reader. 15 R. KIPLING He was deep in meditation, mechanically clicking his rosary. 16 E. W. LANE He passed the next night in deep study. 17 SWIFT That ruinous practice of deep gaming. 18 H. JAMES Mrs Guy . . was always engaged ten parties deep.

Special collocations & comb. (see also s.v. DEEP *adv.*): **deep-bodied** *a.* (of a fish etc.) having a body which is much deeper dorsoventrally than it is wide. **deep breathing** the act of breathing deeply esp. as a form of physical exercise. **deep-dish pie** (orig. *US*) a pie without pastry on the bottom, baked in a deep dish. **deep end** the deeper end of a swimming pool (*go (in) off* or *at the deep end*, give way to emotion or anger; *in at the deep end*, into a difficult situation without preparation). **deep field** *Cricket* that part of the field near the boundary, esp. behind the bowler. **deep kiss**: involving contact between partners' tongues. **deep litter** a deep layer of litter used in poultry-houses etc. **deep mourning**: expressed by dressing completely in black. **deep-mouthed** *a.* (esp. of a dog) having a deep voice. **deep sea** the deeper parts of the sea, at a distance from the shore (*deep-sea fishing*: involving prolonged periods at sea; *deep-sea lead, line*, a lead and line used for soundings in deep water). †**deep-sinker** *Austral.* (a drink served in) a glass of the largest size. **deep six** *slang* burial, death, esp. at sea; *the* grave. **deep-six** *v.t.* (*slang*) bury or lose at sea or in water, dispose of irretrievably. **Deep South** the southernmost parts of the US, *esp.* those states adjacent to the Gulf of Mexico. **deep space** the regions of space that are either outside the earth's atmosphere or beyond the solar system. **deep structure** *Ling.* in transformational grammar, (the representation of) the fundamental abstract grammatical or semantic relationships of the elements of a phrase or sentence (opp. *surface structure*). **deep tank** a section of a ship's hold used to store liquid. **deep therapy** curative treatment with short-wave X-rays of high penetrating power. **deep water** (or **waters**) *fig.* trouble, difficulty (usu. *in, into, deep water*). **deep X-ray therapy** = *deep therapy* above.

deepish *a.* L19. **deepmost** *a.* (*rare*) deepest E19.

deep /diːp/ *v.* Long *rare.* [OE *dīepan*, *dȳpan* = OFris. *diūpa* (Du. *diepen*), MHG *tiefen*, *tiufen*, Goth. *gadiupjan*, f. as DEEP *a.* Cf. DEEPEN.] †**1** *v.t.* = DEEPEN 1. OE–E17. †**2** *v.t.* Plunge or immerse deeply (*lit.* & *fig.*). LME–L16. **3** *v.i.* = DEEPEN 2. L16.

deep /diːp/ *adv.* [OE *dīope*, *dēope*, f. as DEEP *a.*] **1** Deeply; far down, in, on, or back; *fig.* profoundly, intensely, seriously, heavily. OE. **2** *Cricket.* In the deep field. M19.

1 W. H. DIXON The three men sat up deep into the night. T. WILLIAMS Dusk settles deeper. L. DEIGHTON Her eyes were . . sunk deep into her face. *Proverb*: Still waters run deep. *drink deep*: see DRINK *v.*

Comb.: **deep-down** *a.* & *adv.* far down, very deep(ly); **deep drawing** the process of shaping a sheet or strip of metal by forcing it through a die while cold; **deep-drawn** *a.* (*a*) drawn from the depths; (*b*) produced by or suitable for deep drawing; **deep-etch(ing)** a photo-engraving process in which the lithographic plate is slightly etched; †**deep-fet**, **deep-fetched** *adjs.* from far below the surface; far-fetched; **deep-fried** *a.* (of food) fried in fat or oil of sufficient depth to cover it; **deep-frying** the frying of food in enough fat or oil to cover it completely; **deep-laid** *a.* planned with great cunning; secret and elaborate; **deep-milking** the production of a good yield of milk; **deep-mined** *a.* (of coal etc.) obtained far below the surface of the ground (as opp. *opencast*); **deep-read** *a.* (*arch.*) skilled by extensive reading, erudite; **deep-rooted** *a.* (esp. of a belief etc.) deeply rooted or implanted; **deep-seated** *a.* (esp. of disease, emotion, etc.) sited or originating far below the surface, deeply rooted; **deep-set** *a.* (esp. of the eyes) deeply set.

deepen /ˈdiːp(ə)n/ *v.* L16. [f. DEEP *a.* + -EN[5], superseding DEEP *v.*] **1** *v.t.* Make deep or deeper. L16. **2** *v.i.* Become deep or deeper. L17.

1 J. STOW He . . heightened the ditches, deepened the trenches. S. KING The religious business began to deepen its hold on her. 2 J. GALSWORTHY The sky that had been blue . . deepened . . to the bloom of purple grapes. A. S. BYATT The snow was still deepening and the roads . . were blocked.

deepener *n.* a person who or thing which deepens something E19. **deepeningly** *adv.* so as to become deeper, in a deepening manner M19.

deepest /ˈdiːpɪst/ *n. arch.* & *poet.* LME. [Superl. of DEEP *a.* used absol.: see -EST[1].] *The* deepest part *of.*

deep-freeze /diːpˈfriːz, *as n. also* ˈdiːpfriːz/ *n.* & *v.* In sense A.1 also (US proprietary name) **Deepfreeze**. M20. [f. DEEP *a.* + FREEZE *n.*[1]] **A** *n.* **1** A refrigerator etc. in which food can be quickly frozen and stored for long periods at a very low temperature. M20. **2** Cold storage; *fig.* suspension of activity, suspended animation. M20. **B** *v.t.* Infl. as FREEZE *v.* Freeze and store in a deep-freeze; preserve as by refrigeration. Freq. as *deep-frozen* ppl a. M20.

deep-freezer *n.* = DEEP-FREEZE *n.* 1 M20.

deepie /ˈdiːpi/ *n. colloq.* M20. [f. DEEP *a.* + -IE, after *talkie* etc.] A three-dimensional cinematographic or television film.

deeping /ˈdiːpɪŋ/ *n.* E17. [f. DEEP *v.* or *a.* + -ING[1].] A fathom-deep section of a fishing net.

deeply /ˈdiːpli/ *adv.* OE. [f. DEEP *a.* + -LY[2].] **1** With profound thought, insight, knowledge, etc.; thoroughly. OE. **b** With profound cunning or subtlety. L16. †**2** Solemnly. ME–L17. **3** Gravely, seriously, heavily. LME. **4** With intense feeling, emotion, etc.; in a high degree, extremely. LME. **5** To a great depth; far down, back, or inwards. LME. **6** With complete absorption of the faculties. M17. **7** With deep colour. L17. **8** With a deep voice or sound. L19.

1 B. JOWETT I should like to consider the matter a little more deeply. b SHAKES. *Tam. Shr.* Both dissemble deeply their affections. 3 J. A. FROUDE The archbishop had committed himself so deeply that he could not afford to wait. 4 D. H. LAWRENCE He despised it deeply and bitterly. E. WAUGH Air Force jokes are deeply depressing. 5 J. TYNDALL The glacier was deeply fissured. E. BOWEN Woods . . go back deeply behind the ruin. H. SECOMBE He bowed deeply, a theatrical gesture. 6 G. GREENE In a few minutes he was deeply asleep. 7 J. BUCHAN She . . blushed deeply.

deepness /ˈdiːpnɪs/ *n.* Now *rare.* OE. [f. DEEP *a.* + -NESS. Largely superseded by DEPTH.] **1** Depth of thoughts, feelings, qualities, etc.; profundity, intensity, seriousness. OE. †**2** A deep place; a deep part of the sea. OE–M16. **3** Physical depth; (considerable) extension downwards, inwards, or from front to back. ME.

deepsome /ˈdiːps(ə)m/ *a. poet. rare.* E17. [f. DEEP *a.* or *n.* + -SOME[1].] Having depth; more or less deep.

deer /dɪə/ *n.* Pl. same, (*rare*) **-s**. [OE *dēor* = OFris. *diār*, OS *dior* (Du. *dier*), OHG *tior* (G *Tier*), ON *dýr*, Goth. (dat. pl.) *diuzam*, f. Gmc f. IE, orig. 'breathing creature'.] **1** An animal, a beast, *esp.* a quadruped. Long *obs.* exc. in *small deer* (arch.), small creatures collectively, *fig.* insignificant things. OE. **2** Any ruminant quadruped of the family Cervidae, distinguished in the male by the presence of deciduous branching horns or antlers and in the young by the presence of spots, or of the related families Tragulidae and Moschidae (both lacking horns). OE.

2 *fallow deer, moose-deer, mouse deer, musk deer, red deer, reindeer, roe-deer, rusa deer, sika deer, Virginian deer*, etc.

Comb.: **deer-ball** an underground fruiting body of a fungus of the genus *Elaphomyces*; **deerberry** (the fruit of) any of various N. American shrubs, esp. *Vaccinium caesium* or *V. stamineum*; **deer-brush** a shrub, *Ceanothus integerrimus*, of the south-western US; **deer-coloured** *a.* (now *rare*) tawny red; **deer-culler** *NZ* a professional shooter of deer; **deer-fly** any of various flies which infest deer, *esp.* one of the tabanid genus *Chrysops*; *deer-forest*: see FOREST *n.* 2b; **deer-grass**, **deer-hair** a small moorland club-rush, *Trichophorum cespitosum*; **deer-horn** (*a*) (the material of) a deer's antler; (*b*) *US* a large mussel, *Tritigonia verrucosa*, the shell of which is used to make buttons etc.; **deer-hound** a dog used for hunting deer, a staghound; *esp.*

a large rough-haired greyhound; **deer-lick** a spring or damp spot impregnated with salt etc., where deer come to lick; **deer-mouse** any mouse of the large N. and Central American genus *Peromyscus*; esp. *P. maniculatus*, which is common throughout N. America; **deer-park** a park in which deer are kept; **deer's hair** = *deer-hair* above; **deerskin** *a.* & *n.* (made from) the skin of a deer; **deerstalker** (*a*) a hunter who stalks deer; (*b*) a cloth cap peaked in front and behind, with earflaps which are usually tied up on the top; **deer-stealer** *arch.* a poacher who kills and steals deer; **deer-track** the track of a deer; a path made by deer.

deerlet *n.* a small deer; *spec.* a chevrotain: L19. **deerlike** *a.* resembling (that of) a deer M19.

de-escalate /diːˈɛskəleɪt/ *v.* M20. [f. DE- 3 + ESCALATE.] 1 *v.t.* Reduce the level or intensity of; reverse the escalation of (a crisis, war, etc.). M20. 2 *v.i.* Become less intense. M20.

de-escaˈlation *n.* M20.

deeshy /ˈdiːʃi/ *a. Anglo-Ir.* E19. [Origin unkn.] Tiny; insignificant.

de-ethicize /diːˈɛθɪsʌɪz/ *v.t.* Also **-ise**. L19. [f. DE- 3 + ETHICIZE.] Deprive of its ethical character; separate from ethics.

deevy /ˈdiːvi/ *a. colloq.* Now *rare.* E20. [Affected alt. of DIVVY *a.*[1]] Divine, delightful.

de-excite /diːɪkˈsʌɪt/ *v.t.* M20. [f. DE- 3 + EXCITE *v.*] *Physics.* Cause (an atom etc.) to undergo a transition from an excited state to a lower or ground state.

de-exciˈtation *n.* M20.

deface /dɪˈfeɪs/ *v.t.* ME. [(O)Fr. †*défacer*, earlier *deffacer*, for OFr. *desfacier*, f. *des-* DE- 3 + FACE *n.*] 1 Spoil the surface or appearance of, disfigure, mar. ME. 2 Destroy, demolish. Long *arch.* ME. 3 Blot out, obliterate, efface (writing etc.). ME. †4 Destroy the reputation of, discredit. LME–M17. †5 Outshine, put in the shade. Also, outface, abash. M16–L18.

1 P. BAYNE Every religion . . will be more or less defaced by error. C. PRIEST Walls defaced with spray-can graffiti. 3 M. R. MITFORD The beginning of this letter is irreparably defaced.

defacement *n.* the action of defacing; defaced condition; a disfigurement: M16. **defacer** *n.* a person who or thing which defaces M16.

de facto /deɪ ˈfaktəʊ, diː/ *adv.* & *a. phr.* E17. [L = of fact.] (Existing, held, etc.) in fact, in reality; in actual existence, force, or possession, whether by right or not.

defaecate *ppl a.*, *v.* see DEFECATE *ppl a.*, *v.*

defaecation *n.* var. of DEFECATION.

defaillance /dɪˈfeɪl(ə)ns/ *n.* Also ***défaillance*** /defajɑ̃ːs/. E17. [Fr. *défaillance*, f. (O)Fr. *défaillir* fail f. Proto-Romance, f. as DE- 1 + FAIL *v.*: see -ANCE.] Weakness, shortcoming, failure.

defalcate /ˈdiːfalkeɪt/ *v.* M16. [med.L *defalcat-* pa. ppl stem of *defalcare*, f. *de-* DE- 1 + L *falx*, *falc-* sickle, scythe: see -ATE[3].] †1 *v.t.* Subtract (a part) from a whole, deduct. M16–E19. †2 *v.t.* Reduce, curtail. L17–E19. 3 *v.i.* Commit defalcations, misappropriate property in one's charge. M19.

ˈdefalcator *n.* a person who misappropriates funds etc. E19.

defalcation /diːfalˈkeɪʃ(ə)n/ *n.* LME. [med.L *defalcatio(n-)*, f. as prec.: see -ATION.] †1 The action of cutting off or subtracting; a deduction. LME–M19. †2 Reduction of a whole by taking away a part, *spec.* of an account etc. by an amount set against it. L15–M19. 3 Diminution suffered or sustained. *arch.* M17. 4 Falling away, defection; shortcoming, failure. M18. 5 (An act of) misappropriation of money or other property by a person to whom it is entrusted; *sing.* & (usu.) in *pl.*, an amount misappropriated. M19.

defalk /dɪˈfɔːlk/ *v.* Now *rare* or *obs.* LME. [(O)Fr. *défalquer* or med.L *defalcare*: see DEFALCATE.] †1 *v.t.* Reduce by deductions. LME–M18. 2 *v.t.* Subtract; *spec.* deduct (a sum) from an account etc. LME. †3 *v.i.* Make a deduction; take away *from*. LME–M18.

defamation /dɛfəˈmeɪʃ(ə)n, diː-/ *n.* ME. [(O)Fr. *diffamation* f. late L *diffamatio(n-)*, f. L *diffamat-* pa. ppl stem of *diffamare*: see DEFAME *v.*, -ATION.] †1 The bringing of dishonour upon someone; disgrace, shame. ME–E18. 2 The action, or an act of defaming; the fact of being defamed; *Law* the offence of bringing a person into undeserved disrepute by making false statements (whether written or spoken); libel, slander. LME.

defamatory /dɪˈfamət(ə)ri/ *a.* LME. [med.L *diffamatorius*, f. L *diffamat-*: see prec., -ORY[2]. Cf. (O)Fr. *diffamatoire.*] 1 Of the nature of or characterized by defamation; tending to defame. LME. 2 (Habitually) employing defamation. M18.

defame /dɪˈfeɪm/ *n.* Long *rare.* LME. [OFr. *deffame* (usu. *desfame*, *diff-*), f. *deffamer*, *diffamer*: see next.] Disgrace, infamy; defamation, slander.

defame /dɪˈfeɪm/ *v.t.* ME. [OFr. *diffamer*, also *desf-*, *def(f)-*, f. L *diffamare* spread about as an evil report, f. *dis-* DIF-, DE- 3 + *fama* FAME *n.*] 1 Bring dishonour on; shame, disgrace. *arch.* ME. 2 Attack the good reputation of, speak ill of; slander, libel. ME. †3 Cause to be suspected of an offence; accuse. Usu. foll. by *of*. ME–E19.

1 TENNYSON The grand old name of gentleman, Defamed by every charlatan. 2 MILTON Hypocrites . . Defaming as impure what God declares Pure. 3 SIR W. SCOTT Rebecca . . is, by many . . circumstances, defamed of sorcery.

defamer *n.* ME.

defamed /dɪˈfeɪmd/ *ppl a.* LME. [f. prec. + -ED[1]. Sense 3 after Fr. *diffamé.*] †1 Disgraced, dishonoured, infamous. LME–M17. 2 Attacked in reputation; slandered, libelled. L17. 3 *Her.* Of a lion or other animal: without its tail. M19.

defamiliarize /diːfəˈmɪljərʌɪz/ *v.t.* Also **-ise**. L20. [f. DE- 3 + FAMILIARIZE.] Render unfamiliar, esp. as a formalist technique.

defamiliariˈzation *n.* [tr. Russ. *ostranenie* making strange] L20.

defamous /ˈdɛfəməs/ *a.* Long *rare.* LME. [f. DEFAME *n.* + -OUS.] †1 Infamous, disgraceful. LME–M16. 2 Defamatory. LME.

defang /diːˈfaŋ/ *v.t.* M20. [f. DE- 3 + FANG *n.*] Extract the fangs of (a snake etc.); *fig.* render harmless.

defat /diːˈfat/ *v.t.* Infl. **-tt-**. E20. [f. DE- 3 + FAT *n.*[2]] Remove fat or fats from.

defatigable /dɪˈfatɪgəb(ə)l/ *a.* M17. [Orig. (obs. f. E18) f. DE- 1 + FATIGABLE. Later (M20) back-form. f. INDEFATIGABLE.] Easily wearied, apt to tire.

E. WAUGH Then they lost interest. I did too. I was always the most defatigable of hacks.

defatigation /dɪˌfatɪˈgeɪʃ(ə)n/ *n.* Long *rare.* E16. [L *defatigatio(n-)*, f. *defatigat-* pa. ppl stem of *defatigare* weary, exhaust, f. *de-* DE- 1 + *fatigare*: see FATIGUE *v.*, -ATION.] The action of tiring out; exhaustion; fatigue.

default /dɪˈfɔːlt/ *n.* & *a.* ME. [Partly f. OFr. *défaute*, f. *défaillir* (see DEFAILLANCE) on the model of *faute* FAULT *n.*, *faillir* FAIL *v.*; partly f. (O)Fr. *défaut* back-form. f. *défaute.*] A *n.* 1 Lack; absence or scarcity of. Now only in *in default of* below. ME. 2 An imperfection, a defect, a blemish, (latterly only in character or things immaterial). *arch.* ME. 3 Failure to act or perform adequately (by a person or, formerly, a thing); failure to compete in or finish a contest; failure to fulfil a legal requirement, esp. to appear in court on the appointed day. ME. †b *Hunting.* Failure to follow the scent. ME–M18. †c An error, a mistake. LME–E19. 4 Failure to meet (now esp. financial) obligations; negligence; an instance of this. ME. 5 A preselected option adopted by a computer etc. when no other is specified by the user. M20.

2 SWIFT My own excellencies and other men's defaults. 3 J. AGEE Some failure of the soul or default of the heart. 4 H. FAST The bank took it over on a mortgage default.

Phrases: **by default** because of absence or failure to act. **go by default** incur judgement by default; fail or be overlooked because of negligence etc. **in default** guilty of default. **in default of** if or since (a thing) is lacking. **judgement by default** judgement awarded to the plaintiff on the defendant's failing to plead. **make default** fail to appear in court.

B *attrib.* or as *adj.* 1 Dealing with or relating to a (legal or financial) default. L19. 2 Adopted by a computer etc. if no other command is given. M20.

default /dɪˈfɔːlt/ *v.* ME. [f. the n.; partly suggested by (O)Fr. *défaut* 3 pres. indic. of *défaillir*: see DEFAILLANCE.] 1 *v.i.* Be lacking or deficient. Long *rare.* ME. †2 *v.i.* Fail in strength, faint. LME–E17. 3 *v.t.* Put in default; *Law* declare in default and enter judgement against (a party). LME. 4 *v.i.* Fail to fulfil an obligation (now esp. financial) or engagement (also foll. by *on* an obligation etc.); fail to appear in court or take part in a contest; lose a case etc. by default. L16. 5 *v.t.* Fail to fulfil (an obligation); lose by default; fail to make payment of. M17.

4 J. GROSS When it came to it the other contributors defaulted, so he took on the job single-handed. 5 T. C. WOLFE When her boarders defaulted payments she seized their belongings. *New Yorker* Let's go . . and have a nice beer and default the fourth set.

defaulter /dɪˈfɔːltə/ *n.* M17. [f. prec. + -ER[1].] 1 A person etc. who is guilty of default, *esp.* one who fails to fulfil a legal or financial obligation. M17. 2 A serviceman or servicewoman guilty of a military offence. E19.

defeasance /dɪˈfiːz(ə)ns/ *n.* LME. [OFr. *defesance*, f. *defesant* pres. pple of *de(s)faire* (mod. *défaire*) undo, f. *des-*, *dé-* DE- 3 + *faire* do: see -ANCE.] 1 *Law.* a A condition which, if fulfilled, renders an agreement or instrument null and void; a document setting out such a condition. LME. b Annulment; rendering null and void. L16. †2 Discharge from an obligation. *Sc.* LME–M16. 3 Defeat, undoing. *arch.* L16.

defease /dɪˈfiːz/ *v.t.* L15. [Back-form. f. prec. and next.] †1 Discharge from an obligation; deduct from a charge etc. *Sc.* L15–M17. 2 Undo, destroy. *rare.* E17.

defeasible /dɪˈfiːzɪb(ə)l/ *a.* ME. [AN, f. stem of OFr. *defesant*: see DEFEASANCE, -IBLE, FEASIBLE.] Able to be (legally) defeated or annulled; liable to forfeiture.

defeasiˈbility *n.* L19. **defeasibleness** *n.* (*rare*) E17.

defeat /dɪˈfiːt/ *n.* M16. [f. the vb: cf. Fr. *défaite.*] 1 The action of gaining victory in a battle, competition, vote, etc.; the state or an instance of being vanquished or overcome. M16. †2 Undoing, ruin; an act of destruction. L16–M17. 3 Frustration of plans etc.; the action of bringing to nothing; *Law* annulment. L16.

1 J. R. GREEN The defeat of the Armada. J. HELLER It was check mate, match, and defeat from the opening move. 2 SHAKES. *Much Ado* If you . . Have . . made defeat of her virginity. 3 EVELYN My defeat of correspondence at Rome.

defeat /dɪˈfiːt/ *v.t.* LME. [AN *defeter*, f. *defet*, OFr. *deffait*, *desfait* pa. pple of *desfaire* (mod. *défaire*) f. med.L *disfacere* undo, f. L *dis-* DE- 3 + *facere* make.] †1 Undo, do away with, destroy. LME–M17. 2 *Law.* Annul. LME. †3 Disfigure, deface, spoil. LME–E17. 4 Cause to fail, frustrate (a plan etc.), baffle. L15. 5 Gain victory over in battle, competition, matter decided by voting, etc.; vanquish, overcome. M16. †6 Do out *of*, cheat, disappoint; deprive *of*, dispossess. M16–M19.

1 SHAKES. *Oth.* His unkindness may defeat my life. 4 SHAKES. *Haml.* My stronger guilt defeats my strong intent. 5 J. G. FARRELL England had been defeated in the first test match. *fig.*: SHELLEY She Who loved me did with absent looks defeat Despair.

defeater *n.* M19. †**defeatment** *n.* L16–M18.

defeatism /dɪˈfiːtɪz(ə)m/ *n.* E20. [Fr. *défaitisme*, f. *défaite* DEFEAT *n.*: see -ISM.] Conduct or thinking encouraging the expectation or acceptance of defeat; disposition to accept defeat.

defeatist *n.* & *a.* [Fr. *défaitiste*] (a person) advocating defeatism or tending to accept defeat E20.

defeature /dɪˈfiːtʃə/ *n.* & *v. arch.* L16. [OFr. *deffaiture*, *desfaiture* destruction, disguise, f. *desfaire*: see DEFEAT *v.*, -URE. In sense A.2 assoc. w. FEATURE *n.* (cf. DISFEATURE).] A *n.* †1 a Undoing, ruin. L16–E17. b Defeat. L16–M19. 2 Disfigurement, marring of features. L16.

2 SHAKES. *Com. Err.* Careful hours with time's deformed hand Have written strange defeatures in my face.

B *v.t.* Disfigure. L18.

†**defecate** *a.* Also **-faec-**. LME–M18. [L *defaecatus* pa. pple, f. as next: see -ATE².] Purified from dregs, clear; (esp. spiritually) pure.

defecate /ˈdɛfɪkeɪt, ˈdiːf-/ *v.* Also **-faec-**. L15. [L *defaecat-* pa. ppl stem of *defaecare*, f. *de-* DE- 3 + *faex*, pl. *faeces* dregs: see FAECES, -ATE³.] 1 *v.t.* Clear from dregs or impurities; purify, clarify, refine, (*lit.* & *fig.*). Now *rare.* L15. 2 *v.t.* Remove in purifying; purge away, void as excrement. Now *rare.* L15. 3 *v.i.* Discharge faeces from the bowels. M19.

1 *fig.*: S. JOHNSON To defecate and clear my mind by brisker motions.

defecated *ppl a.* (now *rare*) purified (esp. spiritually), clarified; (of evil) unmitigated: E17. **defecator** *n.* a person who or thing which defecates; *spec.* in sugar manufacture, an apparatus in which sugar solutions are purified: M19.

defecation /dɛfɪˈkeɪʃ(ə)n, diːf-/ *n.* Also **-faec-**. E17. [L *defaecatio(n-)*, f. as prec.: see -ATION.] 1 Purification from dregs; clarification, refinement. Now chiefly *techn.* E17. 2 Discharging of faeces from the bowels. M19.

defect /ˈdiːfɛkt, dɪˈfɛkt/ *n.* LME. [L *defectus*, f. *defect-* pa. ppl stem of *deficere* leave, desert, fail, f. *de-* DE- 3 + *facere* make, do. Partly through OFr. *defect* deficiency.] 1 The absence of something essential to completeness; a lack, a deficiency. LME. 2 A shortcoming, a failing; a fault, an imperfection. (The usual sense.) LME. b *Physics.* An irregularity in a crystal lattice, such as a vacant site, interstitial atom, etc. M20. †3 Imperfection, faultiness. M16–L18. †4 A falling away; defection. M16–L18. †5 Failure of the sun, moon, etc., to shine; an eclipse. Only in 17. 6 A quantity or amount by which something falls short of a given quantity etc. M17.

1 J. MORLEY The excess of scepticism and the defect of enthusiasm. **in defect** wanting, deficient. **in defect of** for want of. 2 H. JAMES She . . accused herself of no end of defects. *Punch* Should any mechanical defect ever occur, we promise to repair or replace your pen. **the defects of a person's qualities** those faults which often accompany a person's particular virtues. 6 *mass defect*: see MASS *n.*² & *a.*

defect /dɪˈfɛkt/ *v.* L16. [L *defect-*: see prec.] †1 *v.i.* Fail, fall short, become deficient. L16–L17. 2 *v.i.* Fall away in allegiance (*from*); desert; *esp.* desert to or *to* a country with an opposing ideology. L16. 3 *v.t.* Cause to desert. Long *rare.* M17.

2 L. DEIGHTON Your wife defected. . . Your wife is working for the bloody Russkies.

defectible /dɪˈfɛktɪb(ə)l/ *a.* Now *rare.* E17. [Late L *defectibilis*, f. as prec.: see -IBLE.] Liable to fail or fall short.

defectiˈbility *n.* E17.

defection /dɪˈfɛkʃ(ə)n/ *n.* M16. [L *defectio(n-)*, f. *defect-*: see DEFECT *n.*, -ION.] 1 The action or fact of failing or becoming defective; a failure. *arch.* M16. b Imperfection, defectiveness; a defect. *obs.* exc. *Sc.* L16. 2 Desertion of one's party, cause, etc., esp. in order to join the opposition; the leaving of one's country to settle in a country with an opposing ideology. M16. 3 A falling away from faith, duty, or principles; backsliding. *arch.* M16.

1 C. BRONTË I underwent . . miserable defections of hope. 2 D. FRASER The defection of her Italian Ally would pose grave problems for Germany. 3 J. PRIESTLEY The times of defection and idolatry.

defective /dɪˈfɛktɪv/ *a.* & *n.* ME. [(O)Fr. *défectif*, *-ive*, or late L *defectivus*, f. *defect-*: see DEFECT *n.*, -IVE.] A *adj.* 1 Having a defect or defects; imperfect, incomplete (in some respect); faulty. ME. b Deficient or lacking *in* (†*of*). LME. c *spec.* Of a person: having a mental handicap. Also more fully *mentally defective.* Now freq. considered *offensive.* L19. †2 At fault; guilty of negligence, error, or wrongdoing. LME–L17. 3 Lacking for completion; missing. *arch.* L15. 4 *Gram.* Lacking one or more of the forms, inflections, or uses normal for the part of speech. L15.

1 J. TYNDALL My defective French pronunciation. G. GREENE A defective gutter which emptied itself like a tap. 3 CARLYLE I wish you had a Fortunatus hat; it is the only thing defective in your outfit.

B *n.* †1 A thing lacking. Only in L15. 2 A person who is inadequate or handicapped; *spec.* (more fully *mental defective*) a person who has a mental handicap. Now freq. considered *offensive.* L16. 3 *Gram.* A word lacking one or more of the forms, inflections, or uses normal for the part of speech. L16.

defectively *adv.* E17. **defectiveness** *n.* E17.

defector /dɪˈfɛktə/ *n.* M17. [L *defector*, f. as DEFECT *n.*: see -OR.] A person who defects; one who changes sides or who deserts (cf. DEFECT *v.* 2).

†**defectuous** *a.* M16–E18. [med.L *defectuosus*, f. *defectus* DEFECT *n.*: see -UOUS. Cf. (O)Fr. *défectueux*.] Defective, faulty, imperfect.

†**defedation** *n.* Also **defoed-**. M17–L18. [Fr. †*défédation* or med.L *defoedatio(n-)*, f. *defoedat-* pa. ppl stem of late L *defoedare* defile, f. *de-* DE- 1 + *foedare*, f. *foedus* foul.] The action of making impure, pollution; a contamination.

defeminize /diːˈfɛmɪnʌɪz/ *v.t.* Also **-ise**. E20. [f. DE- 3 + FEMINIZE.] Deprive of femininity; make less feminine.

defeminiˈzation *n.* E20.

defence /dɪˈfɛns/ *n.* Also ***defense**. ME. [OFr. *defens(e)* (mod. *défense*) f. late L use as ns. of *defensum*, *defensa* neut. and fem. pa. pples of *defendere*: see DEFEND.] I 1 Prohibition. *obs.* exc. as below. ME. †2 The action of warding off. LME–L16.

1 **in defence** (of fish or waters) prohibited from being taken or fished in.

II 3 *gen.* The action of guarding from attack; resistance against attack; protection. ME. †b The faculty or capacity of defending; strength against attack. L15–M17. 4 A means of resisting attack; a defensive force; the military resources of a country; in *pl.*, fortifications, defensive installations. ME. 5 Defending, supporting, or maintaining by argument; justification, vindication; an argument, speech, or writing used to this end. LME. 6 (The science or art of) defending oneself; self-defence. *arch.* E17. 7 *Chess.* A move or series of moves played with the object of countering an opponent's attack. Also, any opening or opening variation initiated by Black. E17. 8 *Sports & Games.* An attempt to resist an opponent's attack; play, moves, or tactics aimed at such resistance; (the function of) those members of a team whose principal responsibility is to resist attacks; *Cricket* batting, the batsmen, (opp. to bowling, the bowlers). E19. b A reigning champion's attempt to retain a title. M20. 9 *Psychoanalysis.* Avoidance of conscious conflict or anxiety by repression, compensation, projection, or other (unconscious) mechanism; a mechanism for this (= *defence mechanism* (b) below). E20.

3 A. RADCLIFFE What are your weapons of defence? *Proverb*: Attack is the best form of defence. *civil defence*: see CIVIL *a.* **defence in depth** a system of defence with successive areas of resistance. **line of defence** (*a*) *Mil.* a line representing the course of a projectile fired from a curtain-wall to defend a bastion; (*b*) a line or series of points at which an enemy is resisted (*lit.* & *fig.*). SELF-DEFENCE. b SPENSER A man of great defence. 4 AV *Ps.* 94:22 The Lord is my defence. C. RYAN His real fear was that German armour . . would break through his meagre defences. *Rolling Stone* His immune system, the body's defense against illness. *attrib.*: C. R. ATTLEE The Government are thinking . . of having a Defence Minister. 5 B. JOWETT Socrates prefaces his defence by resuming the attack. H. JAMES Will you hear me abused without opening your lips in my defence? 7 *French defence*, *Indian defence*, *Nimzowitsch defence*, *Sicilian defence*, etc.

III (Orig. f. branch I, later also f. II.) 10 *Law.* A defendant's denial of the truth of allegations made against him or her; a pleading in answer to a plaintiff's statement of claim; the case against an allegation or claim; an issue of law or fact that could relieve a defendant of liability. Also, the person(s) defending the accused. LME.

10 A. PATON The defence will be that the shot was fired in fear and not to kill. *Rolling Stone* The defense had argued insanity.

Comb.: **defence bond**: issued by a government borrowing money for military defence; **defenceman** in ice hockey and lacrosse, a player in a defensive position; **defence mechanism** (*a*) a process by which an organism reacts against pathogens, predators, etc.; (*b*) *Psychoanalysis* a usu. unconscious mental process avoiding conscious conflict or anxiety.

defenceless *a.* (*a*) without defence; unprotected; †(*b*) affording no defence or protection: M16. **defencelessly** *adv.* E19. **defencelessness** *n.* E18.

defence /dɪˈfɛns/ *v.t.* Also **defense**. LME. [f. the n.] 1 Defend, protect; provide with defences, fortify. Long *rare* in *gen.* sense. LME. 2 *Sports & Games.* Attempt to resist the attack of (an opponent); attempt to resist (an attack). *N. Amer.* M20.

2 *Montreal Star* We did a pretty poor job of defensing him and even when we played good defence against him it didn't seem to help.

defend /dɪˈfɛnd/ *v.* ME. [(O)Fr. *défendre* f. L *defendere* ward off, protect, f. *de-* DE- 1 + *-fendere* (as in *offendere* OFFEND).] I †1 *v.t.* Ward off, avert. ME–E19. †2 *v.t.* Prevent, hinder; keep *from* doing something. ME–M17. 3 *v.t.* Prohibit, forbid. *arch.* ME. II 4 *v.t.* Ward off an attack on; fight for the safety of; protect from or against assault or injury; keep safe. ME. b *Sports & Games.* Protect (a wicket etc.) from the ball; resist an attack on (a goal etc.). M18. 5 *v.t.* Uphold by argument, vindicate; speak or write in favour of. ME. †b Maintain (a contested statement); contend (*that*). L15–E17. 6 *v.i.* Resist an attack; put up a defence. M16.

4 P. HOLLAND Trees . . defended and clad with thick leaued branches. F. FITZGERALD Defending the airport against enemy attack. 5 J. PRIESTLEY I am far from pretending . . to defend this passage of Irenæus. 6 *Toronto Sun* Champion Hulla Hogan defending against Randy (Macho Man) Savage. *Guardian* Mabbutt . . proved his all-round qualities . . by defending well and heading England's first goal.

III (Orig. f. branch I, later also f. II.) 7 *v.t.* & *i.* *Law.* Deny the truth of (an allegation against oneself); present a defence of (oneself, one's cause); represent (a defendant) as legal counsel. LME.

7 L. STEFFENS He was defended by three attorneys of high repute in criminal jurisprudence.

Phrases: **God defend**, **heaven defend** *arch.* may God or heaven forbid or prevent it.

defendable *a.* LME.

defendant /dɪˈfɛnd(ə)nt/ *a.* & *n.* ME. [(O)Fr. *défendant* pres. pple of *défendre*: see prec., -ANT¹.] A *adj.* 1 †a *pres. pple.* Defending. Only in ME. b Defending oneself, or an opinion, cause, etc., against attack; opposing the plaintiff's plea in a suit at law. LME. †2 Defensive. *rare.* Only in L16. B *n.* †1 The challenged party in a wager of battle. LME–E19. 2 A person or body sued or accused in a court of law. LME. 3 A defender against hostile attack; a protector. Now *rare.* LME. †4 = DEFENDER 3. E–M17.

defender /dɪˈfɛndə/ *n.* ME. [AN *defendour*, OFr. *defendeor*, f. as DEFEND + -ER².] 1 A person who defends or wards off an attack; a protector. ME. b *Ir. Hist.* (**D-**.) A member of a society of Roman Catholics formed in the late 18th cent. to resist the Orangemen. L18. 2 Chiefly *Sc. Law.* = DEFENDANT *n.* 2. LME. 3 A person who defends by argument; one who speaks or writes in defence of a person, cause, or opinion. E16. 4 *Sports & Games.* A player who defends, one whose principal responsibility is to resist attacks. Also, a reigning champion who defends a title. M18.

3 **Defender of the Faith**: a title of English monarchs since Henry VIII, who received it from Pope Leo X as a reward for writing against Luther. *public defender*: see PUBLIC *a.* & *n.* 4 *left defender*: see LEFT *a.* *right defender*: see RIGHT *a.*

Defenderism *n.* (*Ir. Hist.*) the principles or policy of the Defenders L18. **defendress** *n.* (now *rare*) [Fr. *défenderesse*] a female defender LME.

defenestration /ˌdiːfɛnɪˈstreɪʃ(ə)n/ *n.* E17. [mod.L *defenestratio(n-)*, f. *de-* DE- 1 + *fenestra* window: see -ATION.] The action of throwing a thing or (usu.) a person out of a window.

¶ Chiefly in *the Defenestration of Prague*, an incident in 1618 which precipitated the Thirty Years War.

deˈfenestrate *v.t.* E17.

†**defensative** *a.* & *n.* Also **-itive**. L16. [Extended form of DEFENSIVE (cf. *preventive*, *-ative*): see -ATIVE.] A *adj.* 1 Able to be defended. Only in L16. 2 Defensive, protective;

of the nature of a defence. E17–E18. **B** *n.* = DEFENSIVE *n.* 1. L16–L18.

defense *n.*, *v.* see DEFENCE *n.*, *v.*

defensible /dɪˈfɛnsɪb(ə)l/ *a.* ME. [Late L *defensibilis*, f. *defens-* pa. ppl stem of *defendere* DEFEND: see -IBLE.] †**1** Of a weapon, armour, fortified place, etc.: (capable of) affording defence; defensive. ME–E19. **2** Able to be defended; easily defended; justifiable. LME. †**3** In a state of defence; secure. L16–L18.

defensiˈbility *n.* M19. **defensibleness** *n.* L17. **defensibly** *adv.* LME.

defension /dɪˈfɛnʃ(ə)n/ *n.* LME. [L *defensio(n-)*, f. *defens-*: see prec., -ION. Cf. OFr. *defension.*] †**1** Protection; vindication. LME–M16. **2** The formal defence of a thesis as an academic exercise, esp. in Roman Catholic colleges. M16.

defensist /dɪˈfɛnsɪst/ *n.* E20. [f. DEFENSE *n.* + -IST.] *Russ. Hist.* A person who advocated a continuation of the 1914–18 war by Russia against Germany, in preference to the conclusion of a separate peace.

†**defensitive** *n.* & *a.* var. of DEFENSATIVE.

defensive /dɪˈfɛnsɪv/ *a.* & *n.* LME. [(O)Fr. *défensif*, *-ive* f. med.L *defensivus*, f. *defens-*: see DEFENSIBLE, -IVE.] **A** *adj.* **1** Serving or intended for defence, protective; having the function of or aimed at resisting an opponent's attack. LME. **b** *Cricket.* Of batting: cautious, having the protection of the wicket as the chief consideration. L19. **2** Of the nature of a defence or vindication (*of*). E17. **3** Of or pertaining to defence. M17.

1 SHAKES. *Rich. II* As a moat defensive to a house. F. BURNEY I was obliged to resolve upon a defensive conduct in future. W. CAMP As a tackler and defensive player . . he was exceptional. J. CONRAD The perfect stillness . . made her raise her eyes . . with a hard, defensive expression. K. CLARK Grim defensive houses strong enough to withstand party feuds. J. LEHANE The primary emphasis in defensive play is to prevent the offensive player from doing what he wants to do. **defensive end** *Amer. Football* (the position of) a defensive winger who lines up close to the tackle. 2 H. BROUGHTON Two little workes defensive of our Redemption. 3 S. AUSTIN Their position was entirely a defensive one.

B *n.* †**1** Something that serves to defend or protect; *esp.* a medicine, dressing, etc., serving to prevent injury or infection. LME–E18. **2** A state or position of defence. Chiefly in *on the defensive.* E17.

2 SWIFT The French army acts now wholly on the defensive.

defensively *adv.* in a defensive manner; as regards defence: M16. **defensiveness** *n.* E17.

defensor /dɪˈfɛnsə/ *n.* LME. [AN *defensour*, OFr. *defensëor* (mod. *-eur*) f. L *defensor*, f. *defens-*: see DEFENSIBLE, -OR.] †**1** A defender. LME–L17. **2** *Rom. Hist.* In the later period of the empire, a provincial magistrate whose duty was to afford protection against oppression by a governor. LME.

defensory /dɪˈfɛns(ə)ri/ *n.* & *a.* LME. [Late L *defensorius* adj., f. *defensor*: see prec., -ORY[1], -ORY[2].] †**A** *n.* A defence. LME–L17. **B** *adj.* Serving or intended for defence, defensive. M16.

defer /dɪˈfəː/ *v.*[1] Infl. **-rr-**. Also †**differ.** LME. [(O)Fr. *différer* defer, differ: see DIFFER *v.*] †**1** *v.t.* Put on one side. Only in LME. **2** *v.t.* Put off (an action or procedure, an event, matter, or question, †a person) to some later time; delay, postpone, (a thing, *doing*, †*to do*). LME. **b** Relegate to a later part of a work. M16. **c** Postpone the date of military call-up of (a person). *US.* M20. †**3** *v.t.* Waste (time etc.) in delay. LME–M17. **4** *v.i.* Procrastinate, delay. LME.

2 AV *Prov.* 13:12 Hope deferred maketh the heart sicke. J. USSHER Neither did he long defer to put those Jews to death. J. LONDON Her first proposal would have to be deferred to a more propitious time. A. J. CRONIN He made up his mind to defer the more exacting examinations until another time. **deferred annuity**: that does not begin immediately. **deferred payment** payment by instalments. **deferred share**: on which no dividend is payable until after a certain lapse of time, or until all the dividend on ordinary and preference shares has been paid. 3 SHAKES. *1 Hen. VI* Defer no time, delays have dangerous ends. 4 E. YOUNG Be wise to-day; 'tis madness to defer.

deferment *n.* a putting off; postponement: E17. **deferral** *n.* = DEFERMENT L19. **deferrer** *n.* M16.

defer /dɪˈfəː/ *v.*[2] Infl. **-rr-**. LME. [(O)Fr. *déférer* f. L *deferre* carry away, refer (a matter), f. *de-* DE- 1 + *ferre* bear, carry.] †**1** *v.i.* Submit oneself *to.* *Sc.* LME–L15. †**2** *v.t.* Submit (a matter *to* a person etc.) for determination or judgement; refer. L15–L17. †**3** *v.t.* Offer, proffer, tender; esp. in *Law*, offer for acceptance. M16–M19. **4** *v.i.* Submit or make concessions in opinion or action (*to* a person etc.); pay deference *to.* L17.

4 V. SACKVILLE-WEST Everybody must defer. She, and she alone, must decide. S. BELLOW He deferred to his brother's opinion.

deference /ˈdɛf(ə)r(ə)ns/ *n.* M17. [Fr. *déférence*, f. as prec.; see -ENCE.] **1** Submission to or compliance with the acknowledged superior claims, skill, judgement, or other qualities, of another. M17. **2** Courteous regard; the manifestation of a disposition to yield to the claims or wishes of another. M17.

1 I. D'ISRAELI Charles often yielded a strange deference to minds inferior to his own. 2 EARL OF CHATHAM Their age and learning . . entitle them to all deference. I. COLEGATE The two footmen standing . . with just the right mixture of deference and shared pleasure in the guests' surprise.

Phrases: **in deference to** out of respect for the authority or wishes of.

deferent /ˈdɛf(ə)r(ə)nt/ *n.* & *a.*[1] LME. [Fr. *déférent* or (Astron.) its source, med.L *deferent-*, *-ens*, use as n. of pres. pple of *deferre*: see DEFER *v.*[2], -ENT.] **A** *n.* **1** *Hist. Sci.* In the Ptolemaic system: the circular orbit of the centre of the epicycle in which a planet was thought to move. LME. **2** A carrying or conducting agent; *spec.* (*Anat.*) a deferent duct (see sense B.2 below). Now *rare* or *obs.* E17. **B** *adj.* †**1** Of or pertaining to the deferent in the Ptolemaic system. Only in LME. **2** Carrying or conveying to a particular destination; *spec.* (*Anat.*) designating or pertaining to a duct for conveying fluids, e.g. the vas deferens. Now *rare* or *obs.* E17.

deferent /ˈdɛf(ə)r(ə)nt/ *a.*[2] E19. [f. DEFER *v.*[2] and DEFERENCE: see -ENT.] Showing deference, deferential.

deferential /dɛfəˈrɛnʃ(ə)l/ *a.*[1] E19. [f. DEFERENCE + -IAL, after *prudence*, *prudential*, etc.] Characterized by or showing deference, respectful.

deferentiˈality *n.* L19. **deferentially** *adv.* M19.

deferential /dɛfəˈrɛnʃ(ə)l/ *a.*[2] Now *rare* or *obs.* L19. [Fr. *déférentiel*, f. *déférent* DEFERENT *a.*[1]] *Anat.* Serving to convey; pertaining to a deferent duct (see DEFERENT *a.*[1] 2).

defervescence /diːfəˈvɛs(ə)ns/ *n.* E18. [f. L *defervescent-* pres. ppl stem of *defervescere* cease boiling, etc., f. *de-* DE- 3 + *fervescere* inceptive vb f. *fervere* be hot: see -ENCE.] **1** Cooling down. Only in Dicts. E18. **2** *Med.* (The period of) the decrease of bodily temperature accompanying the abatement of fever. M19.

Also †**defervescency** *n.* M–L17.

defial /dɪˈfʌɪəl/ *n. rare.* LME. [OFr. *defiaille*, f. *défier* defy; in mod. use directly f. DEFY *v.*: see -AL[1].] = next.

defiance /dɪˈfʌɪəns/ *n.* ME. [(O)Fr. *défiance* (now only = distrust), f. *défier* DEFY *v.*: see -ANCE.] †**1** Renunciation of allegiance or friendship, rejection; (a) declaration of hostility. ME–M17. **2** A challenge to a fight or contest, or to uphold an assertion etc. Now *rare* or *obs.* ME. **3** The act of defying; open or daring resistance to authority or an opposing force. E18.

2 SHAKES. *Rich. II* Shall we . . send Defiance to the traitor, and so die? 3 J. SHARP This open and scandalous violation and defiance of his most sacred fundamental laws. R. MAY When parents say 'Don't' he often must scream defiance at them.

Phrases: †**at defiance** in enmity or hostility. *cartel of defiance*: see CARTEL 1. **in defiance of** with open disregard of.

defiant /dɪˈfʌɪənt/ *a.* L16. [f. Fr. *défiant*, or directly f. prec.: see -ANT[1].] Showing open resistance or defiance.

¶ Rare bef. M19.

defiantly *adv.* M19. **defiantness** *n.* (*rare*) L19.

defibrillation /ˌdiːfɪbrɪˈleɪʃ(ə)n/ *n.* M20. [f. DE- 3 + FIBRILLATION.] *Med.* The stopping of fibrillation of the heart (by administering a controlled electric shock).

deˈfibrillate *v.t.* stop the fibrillation of M20. **deˈfibrillator** *n.* an apparatus used to control heart fibrillation M20.

defibrinate /diːˈfʌɪbrɪneɪt/ *v.t.* M19. [f. DE- 3 + FIBRIN + -ATE[3].] *Med.* Remove fibrin from (blood).

defibriˈnation *n.* the process of removing fibrin from blood; the state of being deficient in fibrin: L19.

†**deficience** *n.* LME–M19. [f. as next: see -ENCE.] = next.

deficiency /dɪˈfɪʃ(ə)nsi/ *n.* M17. [f. next: see -ENCY.] **1** The quality or state of being deficient; (the amount of) a shortfall; something lacking, a defect. M17. **2** *Genetics.* The loss of a segment from a chromosome; the segment lost. E20.

1 J. H. NEWMAN Where art has to supply the deficiencies of nature. H. CECIL Mrs Poulter was very short of gin and had to make up the deficiency with water. P. PARISH In children vitamin C deficiency may delay bone growth. **mental deficiency** the condition of having a mental handicap.

Comb.: **deficiency disease**: caused by the lack of a vitamin or other essential substance in the diet; **deficiency payment**: paid to producers by Government to ensure a guaranteed minimum price.

deficient /dɪˈfɪʃ(ə)nt/ *a.* & *n.* L16. [L *deficient-* pres. ppl stem of *deficere* undo, leave, fail, f. *de-* DE- 3 + *facere* make, do: see -ENT.] **A** *adj.* †**1** Theol. *deficient cause*, that failure or deficiency which causes some result or state. Cf. *efficient cause.* L16–L17. †**2** Failing, fainting. E–M17. **3** Incomplete, lacking (*in*) something, defective. E17. **b** *Math.* Of a number: that exceeds the sum of its divisors. Opp. ABUNDANT *a.* 3. E18. **4** Insufficient in quantity, force, etc.; inadequate. M17.

3 P. G. WODEHOUSE I am not deficient in an appreciation of the humorous. T. HEGGEN A competent metallurgist, but his knowledge of explosives was deficient. **mentally deficient** having a mental handicap. 4 R. W. EMERSON Uniformly polite, but with deficient sympathy.

B *n.* †**1** A deficiency. M–L17. **2**†**a** A deficient thing; a defaulter. M17–E18. **b** A person who has a mental handicap. Now *rare.* E20.

deficiently *adv.* E18.

deficit /ˈdɛfɪsɪt, ˈdiː-/ *n.* L18. [Fr. *déficit*, f. L 3rd person sing. pres. indic. of *deficere*: see prec.] (The amount of) a deficiency, esp. of money; an excess of expenditure or liabilities over income or assets.

Comb.: **deficit financing** the financing of deficit spending; **deficit spending** Government spending, in excess of revenue, of funds raised by borrowing, not by taxation.

de fide /diː ˈfʌɪdi/ *a. phr.* M17. [L = of faith.] To be accepted as an article of faith.

defier /dɪˈfʌɪə/ *n.* L16. [f. DEFY *v.* + -ER[1].] A person who defies.

†**defiguration** *n.* L16–M19. [f. med.L *defigurat-* pa. ppl stem of *defigurare* disfigure, f. *de-* DE- 3 + *figurare* FIGURE *v.*: see -ATION. Cf. Fr. *défiguration.*] Disfigurement.

defilade /dɛfɪˈleɪd/ *v.* & *n.* E19. [f. Fr. *défiler* + -ADE. Cf. ENFILADE.] **A** *v.t.* Shield (a position, troops, etc.) from observation or (enfilading) fire by utilizing natural obstacles or erecting fortifications. E19. **B** *n.* The action of defilading; protection of troops etc. from enemy observation or fire; an obstacle or fortification giving protection. M19.

defile /dɪˈfʌɪl, ˈdiːfʌɪl/ *n.* Also †**defilé(e).** L17. [Fr. *défilé* use as n. of pa. pple of *défiler* DEFILE *v.*[2]] **1** A narrow way through which troops can only march in file; a gorge, a narrow mountain pass. L17. **2** The action of marching in single file or in narrow columns; a march in file. M19.

defile /dɪˈfʌɪl/ *v.*[1] LME. [Alt. of DEFOUL after BEFILE.] **I** *v.t.* **1** Make physically dirty or foul; soil, pollute. LME. **2** Corrupt morally, taint, sully. LME. **3** Violate the chastity of; deflower, debauch. LME. **4** Desecrate, profane; make unfit for ritual or ceremonial use. LME. †**5** Defame, dishonour. LME–E18.

1 H. LATIMER An evyll birde that defiles hys own nest. 2 AV *Mark* 7:20 That which commeth out of the man, that defileth the man. 3 M. PRIOR The husband murder'd, and the wife defil'd. 4 F. M. CRAWFORD It is a criminal offence . . for a non-Hindu person to defile the food of even the lowest caste man. 5 SHAKES. *Mids. N. D.* He is defil'd That draws a sword on thee.

II *v.i.* †6 Cause defilement, drop excrement. M-L16. †7 Become foul. Only in L17.

6 SHAKES. *1 Hen. IV* This pitch, as ancient writers do report, doth defile.

defilement *n.* the act of defiling; the state of being defiled; a thing which defiles: L16. **defiler** *n.* LME.

defile /dɪˈfʌɪl/ *v.*[2]*i.* E18. [Fr. *défiler*, f. *dé-* DE- 3 + *file* FILE *n.*[2]] March in single file or in narrow columns.

definable /dɪˈfʌɪnəb(ə)l/ *a.* M17. [f. next + ABLE *a.*] Able to be defined.

defina'bility *n.* M19. **definably** *adv.* E19.

define /dɪˈfʌɪn/ *v.* LME. [OFr. *definer* f. Proto-Romance var. of L *definire* (whence Fr. *définir*), f. *de-* DE- 1 + *finire* FINISH *v.*] I *v.t.* †1 Bring to an end; settle. LME-L17. 2 Determine or indicate the boundary or extent of. LME. b Delineate, make distinct in outline or form. Freq. *refl.* E19. †3 State precisely; declare. LME-M17. 4 Set out precisely, describe or explain the nature, properties, scope, or essential qualities of (a thing or concept). LME. b Interpret or state precisely the meaning of (a word or phrase). M16. 5 *v.t.* Determine, prescribe, fix precisely, specify. L15. †6 Restrict, confine. E16-M17. 7 Establish the character or essence of, characterize. M17. 8 Separate by definition, distinguish *from*. *rare.* E19.

1 I. BARROW A more ready way to define Controversies. 2 S. HEANEY Machine-gun posts defined a real stockade. b MRS H. WARD The slender figure suddenly defined itself against the road. 4 J. BUCHAN He . . defines the problems which he leaves for later . . philosophers to solve. b BOSWELL A lady once asked him how he came to define *Pastern* 'the *knee* of a horse'. 5 GIBBON Two or three years were loosely defined for the term of my absence. 7 M. AMIS A serious Fauntleroy defined by his frill shirt and pageboy collar.

II *v.i.* †9 Decide, pass judgement. LME-E17. †10 Make a precise statement. LME-E17. 11 Frame a description or definition. L16.

11 BURKE When we define we seem in danger of circumscribing nature within the bounds of our own notions.

Phrases: **define one's position** state one's position clearly.

defined *a.* having a definite or specified outline or form; clearly marked, definite: E18. **definement** *n.* (*rare*) definition, description. E17. **definer** *n.* a person who or thing which defines L16.

definiendum /dɪˌfɪnɪˈɛndəm/ *n.* Pl. **-da** /-də/. L19. [L *definiendum* neut. gerundive of *definire*: see DEFINE.] The word or phrase which is (to be) defined; the word or symbol being introduced by definition into a system.

definiens /dɪˈfɪnɪɛnz/ *n.* Pl. **definientia** /dɪfɪnɪˈɛntɪə/. L19. [med.L *definiens* pres. pple of *definire*: see DEFINE.] The defining part of a definition, the word or phrase that states the meaning; the verbal or symbolic expression to which a definiendum is declared to be equivalent.

definite /ˈdɛfɪnɪt/ *a.* & *n.* M16. [L *definitus* pa. pple of *definire*: see DEFINE *v.*, -ITE[2].] A *adj.* 1 Having fixed limits or form; determinate, certain, precise, specific; (of a person) decided, sure in opinion, statement, etc. M16. 2 *Gram.* Designating the article (demonstrative adjective or similar element) which is principally used to indicate a defined or particularized individual (viz. in English *the*); in German etc., designating an adjective inflection used after such an article, or an adjective with such a form. E18.

1 E. BOWEN The eyebrows were lightly marked but their structure was definite. A. THWAITE He should not begin any translations without some definite promise from a publisher.

Special collocations & phrases: **definite description** *Philos.* a denoting phrase introduced by the definite article or equivalent. **definite inflorescence** *Bot.* = CYME *n.* 2. **definite integral** *Math.* an integral taken between specified upper and lower limits of the independent variable and calculated as the difference between the values of the integral at these limits. *past definite*: see PAST *n.*

B *n.* Something which is definite; *spec.* in *Gram.*, a noun denoting a definite thing or object. M16.

definitely *adv.* (*a*) in a definite manner, with certainty; (*b*) (*colloq.*, as an emphatic affirmative) certainly, yes (*definitely not*, no): L16. **definiteness** *n.* E18.

definition /dɛfɪˈnɪʃ(ə)n/ *n.* Also (earlier) †**diff-**. LME. [(O)Fr. *définition* (OFr. also *diff-*) f. L *definitio(n-)*, f. *definit-* pa. ppl stem of *definire*: see DEFINE, -ITION.] 1 The action of settling a controversy etc., (a) decision; *spec.* a formal decision of an ecclesiastical authority. Now *rare* or *obs.* LME. 2 A precise statement of the nature, properties, scope, or essential qualities of a thing; an explanation of a concept etc.; a statement or formal explanation of the meaning of a word or phrase. LME. 3 The action of defining the nature of a thing or the meaning of a word. E17. 4 Precision, clarity, exactitude. M19. 5 The action of making, or the state of being made, visually clear and distinct; the capacity of a lens etc. to make an image distinct to the eye; the degree of clarity of a photograph, television picture, or other image. M19.

2 S. JOHNSON It has been found hard to describe man by an adequate definition. N. PODHORETZ Cardinal Newman's definition of a gentleman as a person who could be at ease in any company. R. SCRUTON It is a limp definition of conservatism to describe it as the desire to conserve. **contextual definition**, **definition in use**: in which the signification of an expression, symbol, etc., is defined implicitly by its context or use. *nominal definition*: see NOMINAL *a.* 3 R. G. COLLINGWOOD Definition necessarily means defining one thing in terms of something else. **by definition** self-evidently, axiomatically. 4 W. SANSOM That her eyes were shadowed with illness or trouble he could with definition say. 5 S. NEWCOMB The definition of this telescope is very fine. M. INNES Shadows that were losing definition and merging.

definitional *a.* of, pertaining to, or of the nature of a definition M19. **definitionally** *adv.* M20.

definitive /dɪˈfɪnɪtɪv/ *a.* & *n.* Also (earlier) †**diff-**. LME. [(O)Fr. *définitif* (OFr. also *diff-*) f. L *definitivus* pa. pple of *definire*: see DEFINE, -IVE.] A *adj.* 1 Having the function or character of finality; decisive, conclusive, final; definite, fixed, finally settled, unconditional. LME. †b Of a person: definite, decided. E17-M18. c Of a literary or artistic work etc.: setting a standard; authoritative, reliable, complete. L19. †2 *Metaphysics.* Having a definite position but not occupying space. E16-E18. 3 Serving to define or specify; *Gram.* specifying the individual referred to. M18. 4 Serving to define visually. *rare.* E19. 5 *Philately.* Of a postage stamp: forming the regular or standard issue (i.e. not special or commemorative). E20.

1 LD MACAULAY A jury had pronounced: the verdict was definitive. S. NEWCOMB A definitive orbit of the comet. E. BOWEN This evening's fiasco has been definitive: I think it better our acquaintance should close. **definitive host** *Biol.*: of the adult or sexually reproductive form of a parasite. c D. MACDONALD Here is the definitive work, and I hope it will become a model for future scholarly biographies. L. DEIGHTON Some of his performances remained definitive ones. 3 W. TAYLOR To preserve a name of sect, which ought to be simply definitive, from sliding into a term of reproach.

B *n.* †1 A definitive judgement or sentence. L16-E19. †2 *Gram.* A definitive word; an article, a demonstrative. M18-E19. 3 *Philately.* A definitive postage stamp. E20.

definitively *adv.* E16. **definitiveness** *n.* E18.

definitor /dɪˈfɪnɪtə, dɛfɪˈnʌɪtə/ *n.* L15. [Late L *definitor* a person who determines, (in med.L) definitor, f. *definit-*: see DEFINITION, -OR.] 1 *RC Ch.* An officer of the chapter in certain monastic orders responsible for rulings on disciplinary matters. L15. †2 A kind of surveying instrument. M17-L18.

definitory /dɪˈfɪnɪt(ə)ri/ *n.* L17. [f. as prec.: see -ORY[1].] *RC Ch.* A body or council of definitors.

definitory /dɪˈfɪnɪt(ə)ri/ *a.* E20. [f. L *definit-* (see DEFINITION) + -ORY[2].] Relating or belonging to definition.

definitude /dɪˈfɪnɪtjuːd/ *n.* M19. [f. DEFINITE after *infinite*, *infinitude*: see -TUDE. Cf. earlier INDEFINITUDE.] The quality of being definite; precision.

definitum /dɛfɪˈnʌɪtəm/ *n.* Pl. **-ta** /-tə/. E17. [L *definitum* thing defined, neut. of pa. pple of *definire* DEFINE.] *Logic.* The thing or expression which a definition defines.

deflagrate /ˈdɛfləgreɪt/ *v.t.* & *i.* E18. [L *deflagrat-* pa. ppl stem of *deflagrare* burn up, f. *de-* DE- 1 + *flagrare* burn: see -ATE[3].] Chiefly *Chem.* (Cause to) burst into flames and burn away rapidly.

deflagrating spoon a long-handled metal spoon used for holding small quantities of materials that deflagrate.

deflagrator *n.* an apparatus for producing deflagration E19.

deflagration /dɛfləˈgreɪʃ(ə)n/ *n.* E17. [L *deflagratio(n-)*, f. as prec.: see -ATION.] †1 The rapid burning away of anything in a destructive fire. E17-M19. 2 Chiefly *Chem.* The action of deflagrating; rapid combustion accompanied by flame. M17.

deflate /dɪˈfleɪt/ *v.* L19. [f. DE- 3 + *-flate* of INFLATE *v.*] 1 *v.t.* Release the air or gas from (something inflated). L19. b *v.i.* Of an inflated object: go down, become emptied of the inflating air or gas. E20. 2 *v.t.* Reduce the size or importance of; depreciate, debunk; cause to lose conceitedness or confidence. E20. b *v.i.* Lose one's spirit, confidence, etc.; climb down. E20. 3 *v.t.* *Econ.* Reduce the inflation of (a currency). E20. b *v.i.* Pursue a policy of deflation. Also, become reduced by deflation. E20.

1 H. JAMES The train the cyclist takes when his tyre's deflated. 2 H. G. WELLS My disposition to deflate the reputation of Marx. N. COWARD There's nothing more deflating than telling someone some exciting news and discovering that they already know it. E. REVELEY Adrian's bitchiness had entirely deflated her sense of well-being.

deflater, **-or** *n.* a person who or thing which deflates L19.

deflation /dɪˈfleɪʃ(ə)n/ *n.* L16. [Branch I (ult.) f. L *deflat-* ppl stem of *deflare* blow away, f. *de-* DE- 1 + *flare* to blow; sense 2 through G. Branch II f. prec.: see -ATION.] I †1 The loss or release of heat from within an object. Only in L16. 2 *Geogr.* The removal of particles of rock, sand, etc., by the wind. L19. II 3 The release of air from something inflated. L19. 4 *Econ.* A policy or process of reducing economic activity and the inflation of currency. Opp. *inflation.* E20. 5 Reduction in importance, reputation, confidence, etc.; disparagement. M20.

deflationary *a.* of, pertaining to, or tending to (esp. economic) deflation E20. **deflationist** *n.* & *a.* (*a*) *n.* an advocate of a policy of deflation; (*b*) *adj.* of or pertaining to deflationists; deflationary: E20.

deflect /dɪˈflɛkt/ *v.* M16. [L *deflectere* bend aside, f. *de-* DE- 1 + *flectere* to bend.] 1 *v.t.* Bend or turn aside from a straight course; cause to deviate (*from*); change the direction of. (*lit.* & *fig.*) M16. 2 *v.i.* Change direction; deviate from its or one's course. E17. 3 *v.t.* Turn to something other than its natural quality or use. Now *rare* or *obs.* E17. 4 *v.t.* Bend or curve downwards. Chiefly (*Bot.* & *Zool.*) as *deflected* ppl a. = DEFLEXED. M17.

1 H. READ He was deflected from this intention by the unexpected appearance of a figure. O. MANNING Quintin did nothing to deflect or direct enquiries. J. D. SALINGER Almost anything could deflect a marble from going straight to its mark. 2 R. H. ELLIOT Then deflecting a little to their right, they got on a long ridge of grassy hill. C. POTOK It hit the finger section of my glove, deflected off, . . and knocked me down. 3 T. KEN To greatest Good deflected greatest ill.

deflective *a.* having the quality of deflecting E19.

deflection /dɪˈflɛkʃ(ə)n/ *n.* Also **deflexion**. E17. [Late L *deflexio(n-)*, f. L *deflex-* pa. ppl stem of *deflectere* DEFLECT: see -ION. Cf. Fr. *déflexion* (also †*déflection*).] 1 The action of turning, or state of being turned, from a straight line or course; the amount of such deviation; a lateral turn or deviation. E17. 2 The turning of a word or phrase aside from its actual form, application, or use. *arch.* E17. 3 The action of bending something downwards; down-curved condition; a downward bend or curve. M17. 4 (The extent of) the movement of an instrument's pointer away from its zero. M17.

1 BACON A digression and deflexion from the ordinary course of generations. C. MERIVALE The great deflection of the coast southward from Cape Wrath. 3 J. S. FOSTER Excessive deflection of beams and buckling of columns must be avoided.

deflectometer /dɪflɛkˈtɒmɪtə/ *n.* M19. [f. DEFLECT *v.* + -OMETER.] An instrument for measuring the deflection or deformation of an object under stress.

deflector /dɪˈflɛktə/ *n.* M19. [f. DEFLECT + -OR.] A device that deflects; *esp.* a plate or diaphragm that deflects a current of air etc.

deflex /dɪˈflɛks/ *a. rare.* L18. [L *deflexus* pa. pple of *deflectere* DEFLECT.] = next.

deflexed /dɪˈflɛkst/ *a.* E19. [f. prec. + -ED[1].] *Bot. & Zool.* Bent or curving downwards.

deflexion *n.* var. of DEFLECTION.

deflexure /dɪˈflɛkʃə, -sjə/ *n. rare.* M17. [f. L *deflex-*: see DEFLECTION, -URE.] Deflection.

deflocculate /diːˈflɒkjʊleɪt/ *v.t.* & *i.* E20. [f. DE- 3 + FLOCCULATE *v.*] (Cause to) undergo deflocculation.

deflocculant *n.* a deflocculating agent M20. **defloccu'lation** *n.* the process by which floccules in a liquid break up into fine particles, producing a dispersion E20.

defloration /diːflɔːˈreɪʃ(ə)n/ *n.* LME. [(O)Fr. *défloration* or late L *defloratio(n-)*, f. *deflorat-* pa. ppl stem of *deflorare*: see next, -ATION.] 1 The action of deflowering a virgin. LME. 2 A selection of choice passages from a book; the selecting of such passages. LME.

1 *Observer* A rather perfunctory defloration in a Scarborough hotel. 2 T. CARTE The Historia Britonum out of which . . he made those deflorations.

deflower /diːˈflaʊə/ *v.t.* LME. [OFr. *deflourer*, earlier *de(s)flo(u)rer* (mod. *déflorer*) f. Proto-Romance var. of late L *deflorare*, f. *de-* DE- 3 + *flos, flor-* FLOWER *n.*] 1 Deprive (a woman) of her virginity; violate, ravish. LME. b *fig.* Ravage, desecrate, spoil. L15. †2 Select or abstract the finest parts from (a book etc.). LME–L18. 3 Deprive or strip of flowers. M17.

1 S. RUSHDIE The . . headmistress . . refused to concede that the wretch might have been deflowered upon her antiseptic premises. b J. R. LOWELL A sanctuary which telegraph or telephone had not deflowered. 3 KEATS Garlands . . From vales deflower'd.

deflowerer *n.* M16.

defluent /ˈdɛflʊənt/ *a.* & *n. rare.* M17. [L *defluent-* pres. ppl stem of *defluere* flow down, f. *de-* DE- 1 + *fluere* flow: see -ENT.] (A stream etc.) that flows down or away.

defluence *n.* a flowing down or away L17. †**defluency** *n.* = DEFLUENCE: only in M17. †**defluous** *a.* flowing down, falling E18–E19.

defluvium /dɪˈfluːvɪəm/ *n.* E19. [L *defluvium* loss by flowing or falling away.] *Med.* A complete shedding of hair, fingernails, or another part, as a result of disease.

defluvium capillorum /kapɪˈlɔːrəm/ [mod.L = of the hair] shedding of hair, alopecia.

†**deflux** *n.* L16–E18. [L *defluxus*, f. *deflux-* pa. ppl stem of *defluere*: see DEFLUENT.] = next.

defluxion /dɪˈflʌkʃ(ə)n/ *n.* M16. [Fr. *défluxion* or late L *defluxio(n-)*, f. *deflux-*: see prec., -ION.] †1 A flowing or running down; a shedding. M16–M19. b Something that flows or runs down; an emanation. Only in 17. 2 *spec. Med.* A flow or running esp. from the nose or eyes; catarrh, phlegm. *obs.* exc. *Sc.* L16.

defocus /diːˈfəʊkəs/ *v.t.* & *i.* Infl. **-s-**, **-ss-**. M20. [f. DE- 3 + FOCUS *v.*] Put or go out of focus.

†**defoedation** *n.* var. of DEFEDATION.

†**defoil** *v.* var. of DEFOUL.

defoliate /diːˈfəʊlɪeɪt/ *v.t.* L18. [Late L *defoliat-* pa. ppl stem of *defoliare*, f. *de-* DE- 3 + *folium* leaf: see -ATE[3].] Remove the leaves from; cause the defoliation of, esp. as a military tactic.

defoliant *n.* a chemical used to cause defoliation M20. **defoliator** *n.* a thing that defoliates; *spec.* an insect which strips trees of their leaves: L19.

defoliation /dɪˌfəʊlɪˈeɪʃ(ə)n/ *n.* M17. [f. as prec.: see -ATION.] 1 Loss or shedding of leaves. M17. 2 Deliberate destruction of foliage (for military purposes). M20.

deforce /dɪˈfɔːs/ *v.t.* LME. [AN *deforcer*, OFr. *deforcier*, f. *des-* DE- 3 + *forcier*, *forcer* FORCE *v.*[1] Cf. ENFORCE *v.* etc.] 1 *Law.* Keep by force (*from* the rightful owner); withhold wrongfully. LME. b Deprive forcibly (*of* rightful property); deprive wrongfully. LME. 2 *Sc. Law.* Forcibly prevent (a legal officer) from carrying out an official duty. LME. †3 Rape. *Sc.* LME–E17.

deforcement *n.* L15. **deforcer** *n.* LME.

deforciant /dɪˈfɔːsɪənt/ *n.* LME. [AN *deforceant* pres. pple of *deforcer*: see prec., -ANT[1].] *Law.* A person who deforces another of property.

deforest /diːˈfɒrɪst/ *v.t.* M16. [f. DE- 3 + FOREST *n.* Cf. DE-AFFOREST, DISAFFOREST, DISFOREST.] 1 *Hist.* = DISAFFOREST 1. M16. 2 = DISFOREST 2. L19.

defore'station *n.* L19.

deform /dɪˈfɔːm/ *a. arch.* LME. [L *deformis*, f. *de-* DE- 3 + *forma* shape. Cf. DIFFORM.] Deformed; hideous.

MILTON Sight so deform what heart of rock could long Drie-ey'd behold?

†**deformly** *adv.* L17–M18.

deform /dɪˈfɔːm/ *v.* LME. [OFr. *difformer*, *de(s)former* (mod. *difformer*, *déformer*) f. med.L *difformare*, L *deformare*, f. as DIS-, DE- 3 + *forma* FORM *n.*] 1 *v.t.* Mar the beauty or excellence of; disfigure, deface. LME. 2 *v.t.* Spoil the form or shape of; misshape. LME. 3 *v.t.* Chiefly *Sci.* Alter the form or configuration of. LME. 4 *v.i.* Chiefly *Sci.* Undergo deformation. (*rare* bef. M20.) M18.

1 N. HAWTHORNE The square . . had mean little huts, deforming its ample space. 2 SHAKES. *Rich. III* Cheated of feature by dissembling nature, Deform'd, unfinish'd. 3 D. CAMERON A tendency for the wind to deform the balloon. 4 *Which?* If the driver hits the wheel this bracket deforms, absorbing some of the force.

deformer *n.* L15.

deformable /dɪˈfɔːməb(ə)l/ *a.* LME. [f. prec. + -ABLE.] †1 Deformed, disfigured. LME–L17. 2 Able to be deformed. L19.

deforma'bility *n.* L19.

deformation /diːfɔːˈmeɪʃ(ə)n/ *n.* LME. [(O)Fr. *déformation* or L *deformatio(n-)* (med.L *diff-*), f. *deformat-* pa. ppl stem of *deformare*: see DEFORM *v.*, -ATION.] 1 The action or result of marring the appearance, beauty, or excellence of; disfigurement, defacement. LME. 2 Alteration of form for the worse; the action or result of misshaping. M16. b An altered form of a word, used esp. to avoid overt blasphemy or profanity (as *dad*, *od*, etc., for *God*). L19. 3 Chiefly *Sci.* Change in shape, configuration, or structure (*of*); the extent of this; an altered structure etc. M19.

1 I. WATTS The deformations and disgraces of time. 2 R. WHATELY A most extensive ecclesiastical reformation (or deformation, as it may turn out). 3 A. CAYLEY Two skew surfaces . . deformations of each other. *Scientific American* These . . fracture zones resulted from some massive deformation of the earth's crust. ELASTIC *deformation. plastic deformation*: see PLASTIC *a.* & *n.*[3]

deformational *a.* of or pertaining to deformation E20.

deformed /dɪˈfɔːmd/ *a.* LME. [f. DEFORM *v.* + -ED[1].] †1 Marred in appearance, defaced. LME–E18. 2 Misshapen, distorted. Now chiefly of a person: misshapen in body or limb. LME. †3 Shapeless, formless. M16–L17. 4 Perverted; morally repugnant. M16. 5 Chiefly *Sci.* That has undergone deformation. L20.

2 J. MARQUAND His left hand was badly deformed from some wound and was minus three fingers.

deformedly /dɪˈfɔːmɪdli, -mdli/ *adv.* (now *rare*) L16.

deformity /dɪˈfɔːmɪti/ *n.*[1] Also †**diff-**. LME. [OFr. *deformité* (*deff-*, *desf-*) f. L *deformitas*, f. *deformis* misshapen: see DEFORM *a.*, -ITY.] 1 The quality or condition of being deformed; disfigurement; (esp. bodily) misshapenness. LME. 2 An instance or kind of disfigurement or malformation, esp. of the body. LME. b A deformed being or thing. L17. 3 (An instance of) moral disfigurement or crookedness. LME.

1 SHAKES. *Rich. III* To spy my shadow in the sun And descant on mine own deformity. HOR. WALPOLE Beautifull Gothic architecture was engrafted on Saxon deformity. 2 E. P. THOMPSON Tailors had a characteristic deformity of the shoulders and chest. 3 T. NORTON The corruption and deformitie of our nature. LD MACAULAY Cromwell had tried to correct the deformities of the representative system.

†**deformity** *n.*[2] var. of DIFFORMITY *n.*[1]

†**defoul** *v.t.* Also **defoil**. ME. [OFr. *defouler*, *defuler*, f. *dé-* DE- 1 + *fouler* to tread: see FOIL *v.*[1], FULL *v.*[1] Cf. DEFILE *v.*[1]] 1 Trample down; break, crush. ME–L16. b *fig.* Oppress; maltreat, abuse. ME–M16. 2 Deflower, debauch. ME–L16. 3 Violate (a law, holy place, etc.); desecrate. ME–E17. 4 Make filthy or dirty; pollute; *fig.* defile, corrupt. ME–E17.

deframe /diːˈfreɪm/ *v.t.* E20. [f. DE- 3 + FRAME *v.*] Remove the frame from (a picture).

defraud /dɪˈfrɔːd/ *v.* & *n.* LME. [OFr. *defrauder* or L *defraudare*, f. *de-* DE- 1 + *fraudare* to cheat, f. *fraus, fraud-* FRAUD.] A *v.* 1 *v.t.* Take or withhold rightful property, status, etc., from (a person) by fraud; deprive wrongfully, cheat. (Foll. by *of.*) LME. 2 *v.i.* Act with or employ fraud. LME.

1 E. KIRKE We who defraud four million citizens of their rights. E. F. BENSON All three . . considered that they and theirs had been positively defrauded. *Daily Mirror* The scrounger who defrauded the country of £36,000. 2 AV *Mark* 10:19 Doe not beare false witnesse, Defraud not.

†**B** *n.* = DEFRAUDATION. LME–E19.

defrauder *n.* LME. **defraudment** *n.* the action or an act of defrauding M17.

defraudation /dɪfrɔːˈdeɪʃ(ə)n/ *n.* LME. [OFr., or late L *defraudatio(n-)*, f. L *defraudat-* pa. ppl stem of *defraudare*: see prec., -ATION.] (An act of) fraudulent deprivation of property or rights; cheating.

defray /dɪˈfreɪ/ *v.t.* LME. [Fr. *défrayer*, f. *dé-* DE- 3 + †*frai*, †*frait* (usu. pl. *frais*, †*fres*) expenses, cost, f. med.L *fredum*, *-us*, fine for breach of the peace.] †1 Pay out, spend (money). LME–E17. †2 Pay the expenses of (a person), reimburse; entertain free of charge. L16–M19. 3 Pay for; meet the expense of. Now *arch. rare.* L16. 4 Pay (the expense or cost of something); meet, settle. L16.

2 P. SIDNEY Defraying the mariners with a ring bestowed upon them. 3 C. BARKER The estate of the defunct member was not sufficient to defray his funeral. 4 E. A. FREEMAN The payment was defrayed out of the spoils.

defrayable *a.* liable to be defrayed L19. **defrayal** *n.* the action of defraying, defrayment E19. **defrayer** *n.* L16. **defrayment** *n.* the action or fact of defraying; payment (of expenses etc.): M16.

defreeze /diːˈfriːz/ *v.t.* E20. [f. DE- 3 + FREEZE *v.*] = DEFROST.

defrock /diːˈfrɒk/ *v.t.* E17. [Fr. *défroquer*, f. *dé-* DE- 3 + *froc* FROCK.] Deprive of priestly frock or ecclesiastical rank; unfrock.

defrost /diːˈfrɒst/ *v.* L19. [f. DE- 3 + FROST *n.*] 1 *v.t.* Unfreeze, remove the frost from (frozen food, the interior of a refrigerator, a windscreen, etc.). L19. 2 *v.i.* Become unfrozen. M20.

defroster *n.* a device for defrosting, esp. one preventing the formation of ice on a windscreen E20.

deft /dɛft/ *a.* ME. [Var. of DAFT.] †1 = DAFT 1. *rare.* Only in ME. 2 Clever or neat in action; skilful, dexterous. LME. 3 Tidy, trim, neat; pretty. *obs.* exc. *dial.* L16. 4 Quiet; gentle. *obs.* exc. *dial.* M18.

2 M. FRAYN By a deft manoeuvre Riddle got herself appointed to a Procedure Committee. J. G. FARRELL Matthews was deft and experienced at removing ladies' garments.

deftly *adv.* LME. **deftness** *n.* E17.

defterdar /dɛftəˈdɑː/ *n.* Also †**t-** & other vars. L16. [Turk. f. Pers. *daftardār*, f. *daftar* DUFTER + *-dār* holder.] A Turkish finance officer or treasurer; *esp.* a provincial accountant-general.

defunct /dɪˈfʌŋ(k)t/ *a.* & *n.* M16. [L *defunctus* pa. pple of *defungi* discharge, perform, finish, f.

de- DE- 3 + *fungi* perform. Cf. (O)Fr. *défunt*.] A *adj.* 1 Dead, deceased. M16. 2 No longer in use or in existence; out of fashion. M18.

2 A. POWELL A Ninetyish aestheticism . . was by no means defunct in Oxford of those days. A. WEST A reporter from the now defunct *Evening Star*.

B *n. The* deceased, *the* dead. M16.

defunctive *a.* pertaining to dying; becoming defunct: E17. **defunctness** *n.* L19.

defunction /dɪˈfʌŋ(k)ʃ(ə)n/ *n. rare.* L16. [Late L *defunctio(n-)*, f. *defunct-* ppl. stem of *defungi*: see prec., -ION.] Dying, death.

defuse /diːˈfjuːz/ *v.t.* M20. [f. DE- 3 + FUSE *n.*[1]] 1 Remove the fuse from (an explosive). M20. 2 *fig.* Reduce the likelihood of trouble arising from (a crisis etc.). M20.

2 A. T. ELLIS She knocked over a cup in her haste to defuse this touchy situation.

defusion /diˈfjuːʒ(ə)n/ *n.* E20. [f. DE- 3 + FUSION, tr. G *Entmischung* separation.] *Psychiatry.* A reversal of the normal fusion of (*spec.* life and death) instincts.

defy /dɪˈfʌɪ/ *n.* Now chiefly *US.* L16. [Fr. *défi*, f. *défier*: see next. In recent use perh. directly f. the vb.] (A) declaration of defiance; a challenge to fight.

DRYDEN The challenger with fierce defie His trumpet sounds.

defy /dɪˈfʌɪ/ *v.* ME. [(O)Fr. *défier* (earlier *des-*, *def-*) f. Proto-Romance, f. L *dis-* (see DE-) + *fidus* faithful, rel. to *fides* FAITH.] 1 *v.t.* Renounce faith or allegiance to; declare hostilities or war against. *obs.* exc. *Hist.* ME. 2 *v.t.* Challenge to or *to* combat or battle. *arch.* ME. †3 *v.t.* Reject, renounce, disdain, revolt at. ME–E18. †4 *v.i.* Show lack of faith; have distrust *of.* LME–E17. 5 *v.t.* Challenge the power of; resist openly, refuse to obey. LME. b Of a thing: resist completely, present insuperable obstacles to. E18. 6 *v.t.* Challenge *to do* something which the challenger believes cannot be done. L17.

2 MILTON Th' infernal Serpent . . Who durst defie th' Omnipotent to Arms. 3 J. GAY The mastiff . . Whose honest jaws the bribe defy'd. 5 ISAIAH BERLIN Mill likes dissent, . . those who defy the establishment. M. EDWARDES The fear that employees would . . defy union instructions. b C. PATMORE Beauty which defies analysis. E. WAUGH A . . warmth which defied the gathering blizzard. 6 C. DARWIN I defy any one at first sight to be sure that it is not a fish leaping for sport. P. P. READ A hard look, as if defying him to say that he disapproved of her scheme.

dégagé /degaʒe, deɪˈgɑːʒeɪ/ *a.* Fem. **-ée.** L17. [Fr., pa. ppl a. of *dégager* set free, f. *dé-* DE- 3 after *engager* ENGAGE *v.*] Unconstrained, relaxed; detached, unconcerned.

C. CHAPLIN To offset my embarrassment I assumed a dégagé manner.

degas /diːˈgas/ *v.t.* Infl. **-ss-.** E20. [f. DE- 3 + GAS *n.*[1]] Remove unwanted gas from.

degasifiˈcation *n.* the process of degassing E20. **degasify** *v.t.* = DEGAS E20.

de Gaullism *n.*, **-ist** *a.* & *n.* see GAULLISM, -IST.

degauss /diːˈgaʊs/ *v.t.* M20. [f. DE- 3 + GAUSS.] Neutralize the magnetic field of (a ship esp. as a protection against magnetic mines) by encircling it with a conductor carrying electric current; remove unwanted magnetism from (esp. a television receiver) by this or other means.

degeneracy /dɪˈdʒɛn(ə)rəsi/ *n.* M17. [f. next: see -ACY.] 1 The condition, quality, or property of being degenerate. M17. 2 An instance of being degenerate; a degenerate thing or state. *rare* exc. *Physics* (cf. DEGENERATE *a.* 3). L17.

1 ADDISON Nature in its utmost Corruption and Degeneracy. P. W. ATKINS A distortion of the molecule that removes the degeneracy of the electronic states.

degenerate /dɪˈdʒɛn(ə)rət/ *a.* & *n.* L15. [L *degeneratus* pa. pple, f. as next: see -ATE[2].] A *adj.* (orig. *pa. pple*). 1 Degenerated; having lost the qualities that are normal and desirable or proper to the kind; having fallen from excellence; debased, degraded; that has reverted to a lower type; in *Biol.*, having a simpler structure or a lower degree of activity. L15. 2 Characterized by degeneration. M17. 3 *Physics.* Of a quantized or oscillating system: having two or more states with the same energy. Of a state or states: equal in energy (with one or more others). Of particles: occupying degenerate states. E20. b Of matter: so compressed (as in some stars) that electrons or other particles occupy degenerate energy levels and exert pressure (resisting further compression) through quantum effects. Hence, consisting of such matter. M20.

1 J. A. FROUDE The degenerate representatives of a once noble institution. J. RABAN A . . yellow, vulpine bitch—a degenerate descendant of the Saluki family. **degenerate code** *Biochem.* a genetic code in which each amino acid is incoded by several different triplets. 2 POPE Such men as live in these degenerate days. 3 P. W. ATKINS The three *np*-orbitals of any free atom constitute a triply degenerate set of [wave] functions.

B *n.* A degenerate person or animal; *esp.* someone considered to be of debased mentality or character. M16.

W. J. H. SPROTT The deplorable Jukes family, their dismal record of defectives and degenerates.

degenerately *adv.* M17. **degenerateness** *n.* M17.

degenerate /dɪˈdʒɛnəreɪt/ *v.* M16. [L *degenerat-* pa. ppl stem of *degenerare* depart from its race or kind, f. *degener* debased, ignoble, f. *de-* DE- 1 + *genus, gener-* kind: see -ATE[3].] I *v.i.* 1 Lose the qualities that are normal and desirable or appropriate to the kind or type; revert to a lower type; deteriorate physically, mentally, or morally; gradually change *into* something inferior; in *Biol.*, change to a simpler structure or a less active form. M16. 2 Show a decline or degeneration *from* an antecedent or standard. Now *rare* or *obs.* M16. †3 Be or become altered (without implying debasement); change, differ. M16–E17.

1 T. TAYLOR When men degenerate, and by sinne put off the nature of man. J. K. JEROME We never ought to allow our instincts of justice to degenerate into mere vindictiveness. H. G. WELLS A complicated metaphysical digression that began badly and degenerated towards the end. I. MURDOCH A road which degenerated into a farm track. 2 POPE How the son degenerates from the sire. 3 R. HAKLUYT Some . . followed Courses degenerating from the Voyage before pretended.

II *v.t.* 4 Cause to deteriorate; debase, degrade. M17.

4 A. BRONTË How completely his past life has degenerated his once noble constitution.

degeneration /dɪˌdʒɛnəˈreɪʃ(ə)n/ *n.* L15. [Fr. *dégénération* or late L *degeneratio(n-)*, f. as prec.: see -ATION.] 1 The condition of having degenerated or being degenerate; degeneracy. L15. 2 The process of degenerating; change or reversion to an inferior type or state; decay, decline; in *Biol.*, change to a simpler structure or less active form. L16. b *Med.* & *Biol.* (A particular kind of) deterioration in the structure or function of a cell or tissue. M19. †3 That which has degenerated; a degenerate form. M17–M18.

2b *fig.*: *fatty degeneration, hyaline degeneration, Nissl degeneration*, etc.

degenerationism *n.* (*Hist.*) the belief that all humankind was once civilized and that primitive peoples have degenerated from this state M20. **degenerationist** *n.* & *a.* (*Hist.*) (*a*) *n.* an adherent of degenerationism; (*b*) *adj.* of or pertaining to degenerationism or degenerationists: L19.

degenerative /dɪˈdʒɛn(ə)rətɪv/ *a.* M19. [f. as DEGENERATE *v.* + -ATIVE.] Of the nature of, tending to, or associated with degeneration.

degenerative disease: characterized by progressive, often irreversible, deterioration of tissue or loss of function.

degenerescence /dɪˌdʒɛnəˈrɛs(ə)ns/ *n.* M19. [Fr. *dégénérescence*, f. *dégénérer* to degenerate: see -ESCENT, -ENCE.] Tendency to degenerate; the process of degeneration.

†**degenerous** *a.* L16–E19. [f. L *degener* (see DEGENERATE *v.*) + -OUS, after GENEROUS.] Unworthy of one's ancestry or kind; degenerate; characterized by degeneration.

deglaciation /ˌdiːgleɪsɪˈeɪʃ(ə)n, -glas-/ *n.* L19. [f. DE- 3 + GLACIATION.] *Geol.* The disappearance of ice from a previously glaciated region.

deglamorize /diːˈglamərʌɪz/ *v.t.* Also **-our-, -ise.** M20. [f. DE- 3 + GLAMORIZE *v.*] Deprive of glamour.

deglamoriˈzation *n.* M20.

deglaze /diːˈgleɪz/ *v.t.* L19. [f. DE- 3 + GLAZE *n.* In sense 2 after Fr. *déglacer.*] 1 Remove the glaze from, give a dull or matt surface to. L19. 2 Dilute the meat sediments in (a pan) in order to make a gravy or sauce. M20.

deglute /dɪˈgluːt/ *v.t.* & *i. rare.* L16. [L *deglut(t)ire* swallow down, f. *de-* DE- 1 + *glut(t)ire* swallow.] Swallow (food etc.).

deglutinate /dɪˈgluːtɪneɪt/ *v.t.* E17. [L *deglutinat-* pa. ppl stem of *deglutinare* unglue, f. *de-* DE- 3 + *glutinare* to glue: see -ATE[3].] †1 Unglue; loosen or separate (things glued together). E17–E18. 2 Extract the gluten from (a cereal, esp. wheat). L19.

degluti'nation *n.* †(*a*) ungluing; (*b*) removal of gluten: E17.

deglutition /diːgluːˈtɪʃ(ə)n/ *n. arch.* exc. *Med.* M17. [Fr. *déglutition* or mod.L *deglutitio(n-)*, f. *deglutit-* pa. ppl stem of *deglut(t)ire*: see DEGLUTE, -ITION.] The action of swallowing.

deglutitious *a.* (*rare*) of or pertaining to swallowing E19. **deglutitory** *a.* (*rare*) having the function of swallowing; pertaining to swallowing: M19.

†**degorge** *v.t.* E16–E18. [Fr. *dégorger* (OFr. *des-*), f. *dé-* DE- 3 + *gorge* GORGE *n.*[1]] = DISGORGE.

degradation /dɛgrəˈdeɪʃ(ə)n/ *n.*[1] M16. [(O)Fr. *dégradation* or eccl.L *degradatio(n-)*, f. *degradat-* pa. ppl stem of *degradare*: see DEGRADE *v.*, -ATION.] 1 Deposition from some office, rank, or position of honour, as a punishment. M16. 2 Lowering in character or quality; moral or intellectual debasement. L17. 3 (Action leading to) lowering in social position, status, or estimation; humiliation. M18. 4 Reduction in strength, amount, or other measurable property. M18. 5 The wearing down and disintegration of material, esp. *Geol.*, of rock, strata, etc., by erosion etc. L18. 6 Reduction to an inferior type, or to a simpler or more rudimentary structure. M19. b *spec.* (Natural or artificial) conversion of matter to simpler substances; chemical breakdown. L19. c *Physics.* Conversion of energy to a form less able to be transformed. L19.

2 B. C. BRODIE Nothing can tend more to every kind of . . degradation than the vice of gin-drinking. P. H. GIBBS War . . was the degradation of all civilized ideals. 3 H. MARTINEAU They would complain of the degradation of obtaining their food by rendering service. D. WELCH I hated to be fed. It seemed the final degradation. 4 *Engineering* The picture degradation normally experienced between successive generations of facsimile pictures. 5 JOHN PHILLIPS The chalk . . yields rather easily to degradation. 6c F. HOYLE Levelling-up of the energy distribution within a system is often referred to as 'degradation', or more technically as an increase of . . entropy.

degradational *a.* of, pertaining to, or characterized by (esp. structural) degradation M19.

degradation /diːgrəˈdeɪʃ(ə)n/ *n.*[2] E18. [Fr. *dégradation* f. It. *digradazione*, f. *digradare* come down by degrees. Cf. GRADATION.] The gradual lessening in intensity of colour or light in a painting, *esp.* that which gives the effect of distance.

degradative /dɪˈgreɪdətɪv/ *a.* M20. [f. DEGRADE *v.* + -ATIVE.] Causing (esp. structural) degradation.

degrade /dɪˈgreɪd/ *n.* E20. [f. the vb.] A defective piece of timber; the production of defects in timber that lower its quality.

degrade /dɪˈgreɪd/ *v.* LME. [(O)Fr. *dégrader* f. eccl.L *degradare*, f. *de-* DE- 1 + *gradus* rank, degree. Cf. DISGRADE.] I *v.t.* 1 Reduce to lower rank, depose from a position of honour; *spec.* deprive formally of rank, office, degree, or ecclesiastical orders, as a punishment. (Foll. by *from.*) LME. 2 Lower in estimation; bring into dishonour or contempt. LME. 3 Lower in character or quality, debase. M17. 4 Chiefly *Geol.* Wear down and cause to disintegrate. E19. 5 Reduce in strength, amount, or some other measurable property. M19. b *spec.* Reduce or tone down in colour (cf. DEGRADATION *n.*[2]). M19.

6 Reduce to an inferior type; make simpler or more rudimentary in structure. M19. b *Physics.* Reduce (energy) to a less convertible form. L19. c Convert to simpler substances; break down chemically. M20.

1 J. PRIESTLEY A priest could not be degraded but by eight bishops. J. H. NEWMAN The man .. was degraded from his high estate. 2 P. G. WODEHOUSE You're degrading yourself by sponging on him. 3 B. MAGEE They degraded art to the level of entertainment. 5 R. COBDEN He proposed to degrade prices instead of aiming to sustain them. 6 G. ROLLESTON Annelids degraded by the special habit of parasitism.

II *v.i.* 7 Undergo degradation, esp. in type or structure; degenerate; break down chemically. L18. 8 *Oxford* & *Cambridge Univs.* Orig., defer taking one's honours examination for one year beyond the statutory time. Now, take an examination for a degree lower than one's standing or lower than that for which one originally entered. E19.

7 TENNYSON Throned races may degrade. *New Scientist* Atrazine and other herbicides .. are made to degrade quickly.

degrada'bility *n.* susceptibility to (chemical or biological) degradation M20. **degradable** *a.* able to be degraded; *spec.* susceptible to chemical or biological degradation (cf. BIODEGRADABLE): M19. **degrader** *n.* M18. **degrading** *ppl a.* that degrades; *esp.* that lowers in dignity or debases: L17. **degradingly** *adv.* so as to degrade; to a degrading extent: E18.

degraded /dɪ'greɪdɪd/ *a.*[1] L15. [f. prec. + -ED[1].] That has been degraded; showing degradation, debased.

degraded /dɪ'greɪdɪd/ *a.*[2] M16. [f. DE- 1 + L *gradus* step + -ED[2].] *Her.* Of a cross: set on steps or degrees.

†**degraduate** *v.t.* E17–M19. [f. DE- 3 + GRADUATE *v.*] Degrade from a position or dignity.

†**degraduation** *n.* (*rare*): only in L16.

degranulate /diː'granjʊleɪt/ *v.* M20. [f. DE- 3 + GRANULATE *v.*] *Med.* 1 *v.t.* Remove granules or granularity from, cause the degranulation of. M20. 2 *v.i.* Lose granules or granularity, undergo degranulation. M20.

degranu'lation *n.* M20.

degras /'dɛgrəs, *foreign* degrɑ/ *n.* Also **dé-**. L19. [Fr. *dégras*, f. *dégraisser* remove grease from.] 1 A dark wax or grease obtained when fish-oils are rubbed into hides and recovered, used in the dressing of leather; a preparation containing this or synthesized in imitation of it; moellon. L19. 2 Wool-grease, wool-fat; a crude mixture of wax and fats obtained by scouring wool or treating it with organic solvents. *US.* L19.

degrease /diː'griːs/ *v.t.* L19. [f. DE- 3 + GREASE *n.*] Remove grease or fat from.

degree /dɪ'griː/ *n.* ME. [(O)Fr. *degré* f. Proto-Romance, f. L *de-* DE- 1 + *gradus* step, GRADE *n.*] I 1 a A step, *esp.* each of a flight of steps; a rung of a ladder. *obs.* exc. *Her.* ME. b A thing placed like a step in a series; a row, a tier. E17. 2 A step in direct genealogical descent; in *pl.*, the number of steps from a common ancestor by which is determined the closeness of the relation of collateral descendants. ME. 3 A stage or position in a social or official scale; a class, rank, grade, station, etc. ME. 4 Relative state or condition; manner, way, respect. ME. 5 A step or stage in a process or scale. Esp. in *by degrees* below. ME. 6 A stage in intensity or amount; the relative intensity, extent, or amount of a quality, attribute, or action. LME.

1a SHAKES. *Jul. Caes.* Scorning the base degrees By which he did ascend. 2 H. JAMES A .. poor relation, of distant degree. T. H. WHITE I am .. near cousin to Joseph of Arimathea—and you .. are but the eighth degree from .. Jesus Christ. 3 T. GUNN I served / all degrees and both sexes. 4 O. W. HOLMES A simple evening party in the smallest village is just as admirable in its degree. 5 DRYDEN To go unknown is the next degree to going invisible. 6 LONGFELLOW I have the faculty of abstraction to a wonderful degree. W. S. CHURCHILL Pitt was able to bring a degree of order into this chaos. ISAIAH BERLIN The ordinary run of men are blind in varying degrees to that which truly shapes their lives.

II *spec.* & *techn.* senses. 7 A stage of proficiency in an art, craft, course of study, etc.; *spec.* an academic rank conferred by a university or college as a mark of proficiency in scholarship; *Law* (now *rare*) the status of barrister. LME. b Any of the ranks of Freemasonry. LME. 8 *Gram.* Each of the three stages (see POSITIVE, COMPARATIVE, SUPERLATIVE *adjs.*) in the comparison of an adjective or adverb. LME. 9 A unit of measurement of angles or circular arcs, and hence of latitude, longitude, etc., equal to the 90th part of a right angle or the 360th part of the circumference of a circle (symbol °). LME. b A position on the earth's surface as measured by degrees; latitude; longitude. M17. 10 *Mus.* Each of the successive notes of a scale (esp. the diatonic scale); the interval between any two of these; each of the successive lines and spaces on the stave. L17. 11 A legal grade of crime or criminality. L17. 12 *Physics.* A unit in a scale of temperature, hardness, etc., (symbol ° or deg, or omitted where the letter indicating the scale being used serves as the symbol). E18. 13 *Math.* The rank of an equation or expression (or a curve etc. representing it) as determined by the highest power of the unknown or variable quantity, or the highest dimensions of the terms which it contains. M18. 14 Each of a number of grades, usu. three (*first, second, third*), used to classify burns according to their severity. M19.

7 I. MURDOCH Ann was reading for a degree in English. 9 F. HOYLE A plane with a slope of 10 degrees to the horizontal. b S. BUTLER He knew the Seat of Paradise, Could tell in what Degree it lies. 12 J. C. OATES Midday temperatures as high as 105 degrees. *degree absolute, degree Celsius, degree centigrade, degree Fahrenheit, degree Kelvin, degree Rankine*, etc. 13 M. KLINE The methods of solving the second, third, and fourth degree equations were quite different.

Phrases: advanced degree: see ADVANCED 2. **by degrees** by successive stages, little by little, gradually. *degree of comparison*: see COMPARISON 4. *degree of* FREEDOM. *degrees of cold*: see COLD *n. first degree*: see FIRST *a., adv.,* & *n.* **forbidden degrees** = *prohibited degrees* below. **honorary degree** an academic degree awarded as a recognition of distinction or a tribute of honour. *Levitical degrees*: see LEVITICAL *a.* **prohibited degrees** the number of steps of consanguinity or affinity within which marriage is not allowed. *second degree*: see SECOND *a. Song of Degrees*: see SONG *n.*[1] *third degree*: see THIRD *a.* **to a degree** *colloq.* to a considerable extent. **to the last degree** to the utmost measure.

Comb.: **degree day** (*a*) a day on which academic degrees are formally awarded; (*b*) (orig. *US*) a unit used to determine the heating requirements of buildings, representing a fall of one degree below a specified average outdoor temperature for one day.

degreeless *a.* without a degree or degrees E19.

degree /dɪ'griː/ *v.t.* LME. [f. the n.] Chiefly as *degreed* ppl a. †1 Advance or change by degrees. LME–M17. 2 Confer an academic degree on. M16.

2 *Guardian* Much-degreed ladies.

degression /dɪ'grɛʃ(ə)n/ *n.* L15. [L *degressio(n-)* going down, f. *degress-*: see next, -ION.] †1 Stepping down, descent. Only in L15. 2 Stepwise reduction, esp. of taxation. L19.

degressive /dɪ'grɛsɪv/ *a.* E20. [f. L *degress-* pa. ppl stem of *degredi* descend + -IVE.] Characterized by stepwise reduction, esp. (*a*) in levels of taxation, (*b*) in the length of a book's bibliographical description in different contexts.

dégringolade /degrɛ̃gɔlad/ *n.* Pl. pronounced same. L19. [Fr., f. *dégringoler* descend rapidly.] A rapid descent or deterioration; decadence.

degu /'deɪguː/ *n.* M19. [Amer. Sp. f. S. Amer. Indian *deuñ.*] Any of several S. American rodents of the family Octodontidae, *spec.* one of the genus *Octodon*, similar to cavies.

degum /diː'gʌm/ *v.t.* Infl. **-mm-**. L19. [f. DE- 3 + GUM *n.*[2]] Deprive of gum; *spec.* deglutinate (silk) as part of processing.

degust /dɪ'gʌst/ *v.t.* & *i.* E17. [L *degustare*, f. *de-* DE- 1 + *gustare* to taste; in mod. use f. Fr. *déguster*.] Taste, savour, (food etc.).

degustate /dɪ'gʌsteɪt/ *v.t. rare.* L16. [L *degustat-* pa. ppl stem of *degustare*: see prec., -ATE[3].] Taste, savour.

degustation /diːgʌ'steɪʃ(ə)n/ *n.* M17. [L *degustatio(n-)*, f. as prec.: see -ATION.] The action of tasting or savouring.

degut /diː'gʌt/ *v.t.* Infl. **-tt-**. M20. [f. DE- 3 + GUT *n.*] Remove the guts, contents, or essential elements of.

dehair /diː'hɛː/ *v.t.* E20. [f. DE- 3 + HAIR *n.*] Remove the hair from (a skin), unhair.

de haut en bas /də o ɑ̃ bɑ/ *adv. phr.* L17. [Fr. = from above to below.] In a condescending or superior manner.

dehisce /dɪ'hɪs/ *v.i.* M17. [L *dehiscere*, f. *de-* DE- 1 + *hiscere* inceptive of *hiare* to gape. Cf. HIATUS.] Gape, open out (chiefly *Physiol.* & *Anat.*); in *Bot.*, (of a seed-vessel etc.) burst open.

dehiscence /dɪ'hɪs(ə)ns/ *n.* E19. [mod.L *dehiscentia*, f. L *dehiscent-* pres. ppl stem of *dehiscere*: see prec., -ENCE.] Gaping, opening by divergence of parts (chiefly *Physiol.* & *Anat.*); in *Bot.*, the bursting open of seed-vessels etc. in order to discharge their mature contents.

dehiscent *a.* gaping open; *Bot.* (of a seed-vessel etc.) bursting open when ripe: M17.

dehonestate /diː'ɒnɪsteɪt/ *v.t. rare.* M17. [L *dehonestat-* pa. ppl stem of *dehonestare* to dishonour, f. *de-* DE- 3 + *honestus* honest: see -ATE[3].] Dishonour; disparage.

dehone'station *n.* [L *dehonestatio(n-)*] LME.

dehorn /diː'hɔːn/ *v.t.* L19. [f. DE- 3 + HORN *n.*] 1 Deprive (an animal) of horns. L19. 2 Saw off the end or the protruding branches of (a log etc.); prune heavily. E20.

dehorner *n.* a person who dehorns; an instrument for dehorning animals: L19.

dehors /dəɔːr, də'hɔː/ *prep.* E18. [OFr. prep., mod.Fr. adv. and n.] *Law.* Outside of; not within the scope of.

dehort /dɪ'hɔːt/ *v.* Now *rare.* M16. [L *dehortari* dissuade, f. *de-* DE- 1 + *hortari* exhort.] 1 *v.t.* & *i.* Use exhortation to dissuade (a person). Now only foll. by *from* a course of action etc. M16. †2 *v.t.* Advise strongly against (a course of action etc.). M–L17.

1 J. WHITGIFT Christ doth not here dehort from bearing rule .. but from seeking rule. SOUTHEY Croker dehorts me from visiting Ireland. 2 DONNE I am far from dehorting those fixed Devotions.

dehorter *n.* L16.

dehortation /diːhɔː'teɪʃ(ə)n/ *n.* Now *rare.* E16. [L *dehortatio(n-)*, f. *dehortat-* ppl stem of *dehortari*: see prec., -ATION.] Exhortation intended to dissuade, earnest dissuasion (*from*).

dehortative /dɪ'hɔːtətɪv/ *a.* & *n.* (*a*) *adj.* dehortatory; (*b*) *n.* an address or argument designed to dissuade: E17. **dehortatory** /dɪ'hɔːtət(ə)ri/ *a.* characterized by dehortation; intended to dissuade: L16.

Dehua /deɪ'hwɑː/ *a.* & *n.* Also **Tê-hua** /teɪ'hwɑː/. E20. [Place of origin in Fujian province, SE China.] (Designating) a white glazed Chinese porcelain, esp. of the Ming period (= *blanc de chine* s.v. BLANC *n.* 4).

dehumanize /diː'hjuːmənʌɪz/ *v.t.* Also **-ise**. E19. [f. DE- 3 + HUMANIZE.] Deprive of human attributes; make impersonal or machine-like.

dehumani'zation *n.* M19.

dehumidify /diːhjuː'mɪdɪfʌɪ/ *v.t.* M20. [f. DE- 3 + HUMIDIFY.] Reduce the humidity of; remove moisture from.

dehumidifi'cation *n.* M20. **dehumidifier** *n.* a device or substance for dehumidification E20.

dehydr- *comb. form* see DEHYDRO-.

dehydrase /dɪ'hʌɪdreɪz/ *n.* E20. [f. DEHYDRO- + -ASE.] *Biochem.* 1 = DEHYDROGENASE. E20. 2 = next. M20.

dehydratase /diː'hʌɪdrəteɪz/ *n.* M20. [f. next + -ASE.] *Biochem.* Any enzyme catalysing the removal of a molecule of water from a substrate.

dehydrate /diː'hʌɪdreɪt/ *v.* L19. [f. DE- 3 + Gk *hudr-*, *hudōr* water + -ATE[3].] 1 *v.t.* Deprive of water, make dry; make (esp. the body) deficient in water; remove water from (esp. a food, in order to preserve it and reduce its bulk); in *Chem.*, remove the elements of water from. Freq. as *dehydrated* ppl a. L19. 2 *v.i.* Lose water as a constituent. L19.

1 L. GOULD Regular lunches . . instead of dehydrated plastic steaks. *fig.*: *Times* A series of rather dehydrated arguments between . . intellectual types.

¶ In ppl forms freq. stressed on 1st syll.

dehy'dration *n.* the action of dehydrating; the condition of being dehydrated: M19.

dehydro- /diːˈhʌɪdrəʊ/ *comb. form.* Bef. a vowel also **dehydr-**. [f. DE- 3 + HYDRO-.] Used in *Chem.* w. the senses 'that has lost hydrogen', 'that has lost (the elements of) water'.

dehydroa'cetic, dehydra'cetic *adjs.*: *dehydr(o)acetic acid*, a crystalline cyclic compound, $C_8H_8O_4$, obtained especially by heating ethyl acetoacetate L19. **dehydroa'scorbic** *a.*: *dehydroascorbic acid*, a metabolic oxidation product, $C_6H_6O_6$, of ascorbic acid M20. **dehydrocho'lesterol** *n.* a provitamin, $C_{27}H_{44}O$, which on ultraviolet irradiation (in skin tissue) is converted to vitamin D_3 M20.

dehydrogenase /diːhʌɪˈdrɒdʒəneɪz/ *n.* E20. [f. as next + -ASE.] *Biochem.* An enzyme which abstracts a hydrogen atom or hydrogen atoms from a substrate.

dehydrogenate /diːhʌɪˈdrɒdʒəneɪt/ *v.t.* M19. [f. DE- 3 + HYDROGEN + -ATE[3].] *Chem.* Remove one or more hydrogen atoms from (a compound).

dehydroge'nation *n.* M19.

dehydrogenize /diːhʌɪˈdrɒdʒənʌɪz/ *v.t.* Now *rare*. Also **-ise**. M19. [f. as prec. + -IZE.] = prec.

dehydrogeni'zation *n.* L19.

de-ice /diːˈʌɪs/ *v.t.* M20. [f. DE- 3 + ICE *n.*] Remove ice from, prevent the formation of ice on, (an aeroplane, windscreen, etc.).

de-icer *n.* a device or substance for de-icing (esp. windscreens) M20.

deicide /ˈdiːɪsʌɪd, ˈdeɪɪ-/ *n.* E17. [eccl.L *deicida* killer of a god, or directly f. L *deus*, *dei-* god: see -CIDE. Cf. Fr. *déicide*.] 1 The killing of a god. E17. 2 The killer of a god. M17.

deicidal *a.* of or pertaining to deicide; god-killing: M19.

deictic /ˈdʌɪktɪk/ *a.* & *n.* E19. [Gk *deiktikos*, f. *deiktos* vbl adj. of *deiknunai* to show. Cf. DEIXIS.] A *adj.* 1 *Logic.* Designating or pertaining to reasoning which proves directly. Cf. *elenctic*. E19. 2 *Ling.* Serving to relate that which is spoken of to the spatial and temporal context of the utterance; *spec.* demonstrative. L19. B *n. Gram.* A deictic word, form, or expression. M20.

†**deictical** *a.* = DEICTIC *a.* 1: only in M17. **deictically** *adv.* (*a*) with direct indication; (*b*) with regard to deixis: M17.

deid *n.* see DEATH.

deific /diːˈɪfɪk, deɪ-/ *a.* L15. [(O)Fr. *déifique* or eccl.L *deificus*, f. L *deus* god + *-ficus* -FIC.] Deifying, making divine; *loosely* divine, godlike.

deification /ˌdiːɪfɪˈkeɪʃ(ə)n, ˌdeɪɪ-/ *n.* LME. [eccl.L *deificatio(n-)*, f. *deificat-* pa. ppl stem of *deificare*: see DEIFY, -ATION.] 1 The action of deifying; deified condition; a deified embodiment. LME. 2 *Theol.* The action or process of becoming a sharer in the divine nature. L17.

deificatory *a.* (*rare*) serving to deify; pertaining to deification: E17.

deiform /ˈdiːɪfɔːm, ˈdeɪɪ-/ *a.* M17. [med.L *deiformis*, f. L *deus* god: see -FORM.] 1 Having the form of a god. M17. 2 Godlike in nature or character; holy, divine. M17.

dei'formity *n.* M17.

deify /ˈdiːɪfʌɪ, ˈdeɪɪ-/ *v.t.* ME. [(O)Fr. *déifier* f. eccl.L *deificare*, f. L *deus* god: see -FY.] 1 Render godlike in character, spirit, or quality. ME. 2 Make a god of; exalt to the position of a god; enrol among the gods. LME. 3 Treat as a god; worship. L16.

1 T. HERBERT No vertue more deified a Prince then Clemencie. 2 M. L. KING Nontheistic humanism, a philosophy that deifies man by affirming that humanity is God. 3 S. SMILES It is possible to over-estimate success to the extent of almost deifying it.

deifier *n.* (*rare*) M18.

deign /deɪn/ *v.* ME. [OFr. *degnier*, *deigner*, (also mod.) *daigner* f. L *dignare*, *-ari* deem worthy, f. *dignus* worthy.] 1 *v.i.* Think it worthy of oneself, see fit, condescend, *to do*. ME. 2 *v.t.* Condescend to give or grant (an answer etc.). Usu. w. neg. *arch.* L16. †b Condescend to accept or take. L16–M17. †3 Treat as worthy *of*; dignify *with*. L16–M17.

1 H. BELLOC Hardly deigning to reply to your timid sentences. D. ABSE Lunch-time arrived and still no driver deigned to stop for us. 2 M. C. CLARKE The spirit stalks away, deigning no reply. b SHAKES. *Ant. & Cl.* Thy palate then did deign The roughest berry on the rudest hedge.

Dei gratia /deɪɪ ˈgrɑːtɪə, diːʌɪ ˈgreɪʃə/ *adv. phr.* E17. [L.] By the grace of God.

deil /diːl/ *n. Sc.* LME. [Var. of DEVIL *n.*] 1 The Devil, esp. according to popular conception. LME. 2 A mischievously energetic or troublesome person, = DEVIL *n.* 4b. L18.

1 *deil (a)* HAET.

de-index /diːˈɪndɛks/ *v.t.* L20. [f. DE- 3 + INDEX *v.*] Cancel the indexation of (pensions or other benefits).

de-inde'xation *n.* L20.

deindustrialize /diːɪnˈdʌstrɪəlʌɪz/ *v.t.* Also **-ise**. L19. [f. DE- 3 + INDUSTRIALIZE.] Make less or no longer industrial; reduce the industrial capacity of.

deindustriali'zation *n.* M20.

deinothere /ˈdʌɪnə(ʊ)θɪə/ *n.* Also †**dino-**. M19. [f. mod.L *Deinotherium* (see below), f. Gk *deinos* terrible + *thērion* wild animal.] *Palaeont.* An extinct proboscidean mammal of the genus *Deinotherium*, known from fossil remains of Lower Miocene to Upper Pleistocene age.

de-institutionalize /ˌdiːɪnstɪˈtjuːʃ(ə)n(ə)lʌɪz/ *v.t.* Chiefly *N. Amer.* Also **-ise**. M20. [f. DE- 3 + INSTITUTIONALIZE.] Remove from a mental etc. institution; free from the effects of institutional life. Chiefly as *de-institutionalized* ppl a.

de-institutionali'zation *n.* L20.

deionize /diːˈʌɪənʌɪz/ *v.t.* Also **-ise**. E20. [f. DE- 3 + IONIZE.] Remove the ions or ionic constituents from (water etc.).

deioni'zation *n.* E20. **deionizer** *n.* an apparatus for removing ions from water etc. M20.

Deipara /diːˈɪpərə, deɪˈɪp-/ *n. rare.* M17. [Late L, f. *deus* + *-parus*, *-a* bearing (see -PAROUS): a L equiv. of Gk *theotokos*.] Mother of God (as a title of the Virgin Mary).

deiparous *a.* being the mother of God M17.

deipnosophist /dʌɪpˈnɒsəfɪst/ *n.* E17. [Gk *deipnosophistēs*, used in pl. as title of a work by Atheneus (3rd cent. AD), describing long discussions at a banquet, f. *deipnon* dinner + *sophistēs* wise man.] A person skilled in the art of dining and table talk.

deisal *adv.* & *n.* var. of DEASIL.

deism /ˈdiːɪz(ə)m, ˈdeɪɪ-/ *n.* L17. [f. L *deus* god + -ISM, after next. Cf. Fr. *déisme*.] The doctrine or belief of deists; belief in one God who created but does not intervene in the universe; natural religion. Cf. ATHEISM, THEISM *n.*[1]

deist /ˈdiːɪst, ˈdeɪɪ-/ *n.* E17. [Fr. *déiste*, f. L *deus* god + *-iste* -IST.] Orig., a person who believes in God or gods (opp. *atheist*). Now, a person who believes in one God who created but does not intervene in the universe. Cf. THEIST.

de'istic *a.* of the nature of or pertaining to deists or deism L18. **de'istical** *a.* = DEISTIC M18. **de'istically** *adv.* L19.

Deiters /ˈdʌɪtəz/ *n.* M19. [Otto Friedrich Carl *Deiters* (1834–63), Ger. anatomist.] *Anat.* 1 *cells of Deiters*, *Deiters' cells*, supporting cells alternating with the outer hair cells in the organ of Corti. M19. 2 *nucleus of Deiters*, *Deiters' nucleus*, the lateral vestibular nucleus in the brain. L19.

deity /ˈdiːɪti, ˈdeɪɪ-/ *n.* Also **D-**. ME. [(O)Fr. *déité* f. eccl.L *deitas*, rendering Gk *theotēs*, f. *theos* god: see -TY[1].] 1 The divine nature of God; divinity. ME. 2 The estate or rank of a god; divine status; godship. LME. 3 A divine being; a god. LME. 4 Chiefly *Theol.* (Usu. **D-**.) A supreme being as creator of the universe; *the Deity*, the supreme being, God. L16.

1 *Daily Telegraph* The Christian Church must maintain its historic faith in the deity of Christ. 2 E. B. BROWNING All the false gods with a cry Rendered up their deity. 3 W. S. CHURCHILL John Nicholson . . the liberator of Delhi, was even worshipped by some Punjabis as a deity. *fig.*: SHAKES. *L.L.L.* The liver-vein, which makes flesh a deity. 4 E. B. PUSEY Men spoke of 'the Deity' . . and . . had lost sight of the Personal God.

deityship *n.* the status or personality of a deity L17.

deixis /ˈdʌɪksɪs/ *n.* M20. [Gk = reference, f. *deiknunai* to show. Cf. DEICTIC]. The function or use of a deictic word, form, or expression.

déjà entendu /deʒa ɑ̃tɑ̃dy, ˈdeɪʒɑː ɒ̃tɒ̃ˈduː/ *n. phr.* M20. [Fr. = already heard, after DÉJÀ VU.] A feeling (correct or illusory) that one has already heard or understood the words, music, etc., currently under attention.

déjà lu /deʒa ly, ˈdeɪʒɑː luː/ *n. phr.* M20. [Fr. = already read, after next.] A feeling that one may have read the present passage, or one very like it, before.

déjà vu /deʒa vy, deɪʒɑː vuː/ *n. phr.* E20. [Fr. = already seen.] 1 *Psychol.* The illusory feeling of having already experienced the present moment or situation. E20. 2 The (correct) impression that something similar has been previously experienced; tedious familiarity. M20.

1 A. KOESTLER A dream-like feeling that he has had this nightmare before, a feeling that the psychologists term *déjà vu*. 2 S. TOWNSEND My mother is looking for a job. I have got a sense of *déjà vu*.

deject /dɪˈdʒɛkt/ *a.* (orig. *pa. pple*). *arch.* LME. [L *dejectus* pa. pple f. as next.] 1 Cast down, overthrown; lowered in fortune or character; debased. LME. †b *Astrol.* Of a planet: that has lost its influence. LME–L16. 2 Downcast, dispirited. E16.

†**dejectly** *adv.* E17–M18.

deject /dɪˈdʒɛkt/ *v.t.* LME. [L *deject-* pa. ppl stem of *dejicere* throw down, f. *de-* DE- 1 + *jacere* to throw.] 1 Cast down; overthrow. *arch.* LME. b Bend down, allow to droop. *arch.* E17. c Lower (the eyes). *arch.* E17. †2 Cast down from high estate or dignity; humble, abase. LME–L17. 3 Dishearten, dispirit; make sad or gloomy. LME. †4 Dismiss, reject. M16–M17. †5 Weaken; lessen. L16–L17.

3 S. JOHNSON Nothing dejects a trader like the interruption of his profits.

dejected /dɪˈdʒɛktɪd/ *a.* L16. [f. prec. + -ED[1].] 1 Low-spirited, downcast, depressed. L16. 2 Lowered; allowed to droop; cast down, overthrown. *arch.* E17. †3 Abased, humbled, lowly. E17–E18.

1 W. COWPER I am cheerful on paper sometimes, when I am absolutely the most dejected of all creatures. B. BAINBRIDGE His manner still continued dejected and depressed. 2 POPE With humble mien and with dejected eyes. R. HEBER The mute swain . . With . . dejected head. H. JAMES Looking at her dejected pillar. 3 SHAKES. *Lear* The lowest and most dejected thing of fortune.

dejectedly *adv.* E17. **dejectedness** *n.* E17.

dejection /dɪˈdʒɛkʃ(ə)n/ *n.* LME. [L *dejectio(n-)*, f. as DEJECT *v.*: see -ION.] 1 Depression of spirits; a dejected state, low spirits. LME. †2 A lowering in fortunes, condition, quality, etc.; abasement; humiliation. LME–M17. †b *Astrol.* The state (of a planet) of having lost its influence. LME–E18. 3 *lit.* The action of casting down; the fact of being cast down. *arch.* L15. †4 *Med.* Defecation; in *pl.*, faeces. E17–M19. 5 Weakening, diminution, esp. of bodily strength. Now *rare* or *obs.* M17.

1 BOSWELL That miserable dejection of spirits to which he was constitutionally subject. F. PARKMAN A deep dejection fell upon them. A. J. CRONIN That pit of dejection into which . . he would plummet. 3 J. RUSKIN A hole . . for the convenient dejection of hot sand and lead.

†**dejeune** *n.* Also **dejune**. M17–M19. [Fr. dial. *déjun*: see DISJUNE.] = DÉJEUNER 1.

déjeuner /deʒœne (*pl. same*), ˈdeɪʒəneɪ/ *n.* Also †*-né*. L18. [Fr., use as n. of inf. = break one's fast: see DISJUNE.] 1 A morning meal (early or late) in France or elsewhere; breakfast or (usu.) lunch. See also *petit déjeuner* s.v. PETIT *a.*[2] L18. 2 A set of cups, saucers, plates, etc., for serving breakfast, breakfast service. L18.

†**dejune** *n.* var. of DEJEUNE.

de jure /diː ˈdʒʊəri, deɪ ˈjʊəreɪ/ *adv.* & *a. phr.* M16. [L = of law.] (Existing, held, etc.) rightfully, according to law (freq. as opp. to *de facto*).

Dekabrist /ˈdɛkəbrɪst/ *n.* L19. [Russ. *dekabrist*, f. *dekabr'* December.] *Hist.* = DECEMBRIST.

dekalin *n.* var. of DECALIN.

dekarch, -archy *ns.* vars. of DECARCH, -ARCHY.

dekink /diːˈkɪŋk/ *v.t.* M20. [f. DE- 3 + KINK *n.*[2]] Remove kinks from.

dekko /ˈdɛkəʊ/ *n.* & *v. slang* (orig. *Army*). L19. [Hind. *dekho* polite imper. of *dekhnā* to look. Cf. DECK *n.*[2]] **A** *n.* Pl. **-os.** A look. L19.

K. TYNAN Once I'd grabbed hold of the script and taken a good dekko at it, my worst fears were confirmed.

B *v.t.* & *i.* Look (at). L19.

del /dɛl/ *n.* E20. [Abbrev. of DELTA, from the operator's being represented by an inverted capital delta.] *Math.* The symbolic differential operator ∇, defined as $\mathbf{i}\partial/\partial x + \mathbf{j}\partial/\partial y + \mathbf{k}\partial/\partial z$, where **i**, **j**, and **k** are vectors directed respectively along the Cartesian axes *x*, *y*, and *z*. Also called *nabla*.

delabialize /diːˈleɪbɪəlʌɪz/ *v.t.* Also **-ise.** L19. [f. DE- 3 + LABIALIZE.] *Phonet.* Pronounce without lip-rounding; deprive of labial character.

delabiali'zation *n.* E20.

†**delacrimation** *n.* Also **-cry-.** E17–L19. [L *delacrimatio(n-)*, f. as DE- 1 + LACHRYMATION.] (Excessive) lachrymation.

delafossite /dɛləˈfɒsʌɪt/ *n.* L19. [f. Gabriel *Delafosse* (1796–1878), Fr. mineralogist + -ITE[1].] *Min.* A black hexagonal oxide of iron and copper occurring usu. as tabular crystals or as botryoidal crusts.

delaine /dəˈleɪn/ *n.* M19. [Abbrev.] = MOUSSELINE-*de-laine*.

delaminate /diːˈlamɪneɪt/ *v.i.* L19. [f. DE- 1 + L *lamina* thin plate, layer + -ATE[3].] Split into separate layers.

delami'nation *n.* L19.

delapse /dɪˈlaps/ *v.i.* Now *rare* or *obs.* M16. [L *delaps-* pa. ppl stem of *delabi*, f. *de-* DE- 1 + *labi* slip, fall.] Fall or slip down, sink, (*lit.* & *fig.*).

Delasol /diːlɑːˈsɒl/ *n. obs.* exc. *Hist.* Also **D la sol.** E17. [f. as next.] *Medieval Mus.* The note D in Guido d'Arezzo's 6th and 7th hexachords, where it was sung to the syllables *la* or *sol*. Cf. ALAMIRE, BEMI, CESOLFA etc.

Delasolre /ˌdiːlɑːsɒlˈreɪ/ *n. obs.* exc. *Hist.* Also **D la solre.** LME. [f. D as a pitch letter + *la*, *sol*, and *re* designating tones in the solmization of Guido d'Arezzo (*c* 990–1050).] *Medieval Mus.* The note D in Guido d'Arezzo's 3rd, 4th, and 5th hexachords, where it was sung to the syllables *la*, *sol*, or *re*. Cf. ALAMIRE, BEMI, CESOLFA, etc.

délassement /delɑsmɑ̃/ *n.* Pl. pronounced same. E19. [Fr., f. *délasser* relax, f. *dé-* DE- 3 + *las* weary: see -MENT.] Relaxation.

delate /dɪˈleɪt/ *v.t. arch.* L15. [L *delat-* stem of functional pa. pple of *deferre*: see DEFER *v.*[2], -ATE[3].] †**1** Hand down or over; refer (a matter, *to* a person). L15–M19. **2** Relate, report, (esp. an offence). L15. **3** Accuse, impeach; denounce to a tribunal, esp. (*Hist.*) that of the Scottish civil and ecclesiastical courts. E16. †**4** = DEFER *v.*[2] 3. M16–L19. †**5** Carry down or away, convey. L16–E17.

delation /dɪˈleɪʃ(ə)n/ *n. arch.* M16. [L *delatio(n-)*, f. *delat-*: see prec., -ATION.] **1** The action of informing against someone; accusation, denunciation, criminal information. M16. †**2** Conveyance (to a place); transmission. L16–E17. †**3** Handing down, transference. L17–L19.

delator /dɪˈleɪtə/ *n. arch.* LME. [L *delator*, f. *delat-*: see DELATE, -OR.] An informer, a secret or professional accuser.

Delaware /ˈdɛləwɛː/ *n.* & *a.* E18. [River *Delaware* (see below).] **A** *n.* Pl. **-s**, same. **1** A member of a N. American Indian people formerly inhabiting the Delaware river basin in the north-eastern US. E18. **2** Either or both of two Algonquian languages of this people. E19. **B** *attrib.* or as *adj.* Of or pertaining to the Delawares or their languages. E18.

Delawarean /dɛləˈwɛːrɪən/ *n.* E20. [f. *Delaware* (see below) + -AN.] A native or inhabitant of Delaware, a State of the US.

Also **Delawarian** *n.* M20.

delay /dɪˈleɪ/ *n.* ME. [(O)Fr. *délai*, f. as next.] **1** The action or process of delaying; procrastination; lingering; putting off. ME. **2** Hindrance to progress; (a period of) time lost by inaction or inability to proceed. M18. **b** *spec.* The time interval between the propagation of an electrical signal and its reception. M20.

1 SHAKES. *Haml.* For who would bear . . the law's delay. C. S. FORESTER What the hell's all this delay for, Mr Hornblower? D'you want us to miss the tide? **without** (any, **further**, etc.) **delay** immediately, at once. 2 B. JOWETT There will be a delay of a day.

Comb.: **delay line** a device producing a desired delay in the transmission of an electrical signal.

delay /dɪˈleɪ/ *v.*[1] ME. [OFr. *delayer* var. of *deslaier*, presumably f. *des-* DE- 3 + *laier* leave.] **1** *v.t.* Put off to a later time; postpone, defer, (a thing, *doing*, (arch.) *to do*). ME. †**b** Put (a person) off, keep (a person) waiting. LME–M18. **2** *v.t.* Impede the progress of, make late, hinder. LME. **3** *v.i.* Loiter, be late; wait; (now *poet.*) tarry in a place. LME.

1 POPE Th' unprofitable moments . . That . . still delay Life's instant business to a future day. TENNYSON As the tender ash delays To clothe herself, when all the woods are green. A. C. BOULT Mozart had works complete in his head, and delayed writing them down until the last possible minute. 2 STEELE Joy and Grief can hasten and delay Time. R. C. HUTCHINSON I thought the snow might delay the train. I. MURDOCH I had been delayed by the strike. 3 SHAKES. *1 Hen. IV* Advantage feeds him fat while men delay. W. C. BRYANT Wind of the sunny south! oh still delay, in the gay woods. P. KAVANAGH Eusebius was delaying up the road till the priest went away.

delayer *n.* E16.

†**delay** *v.*[2] ME. [Fr. *délayer*, in OFr. *desleier* f. Proto-Romance, f. L *dis-* DIS- 2 + *ligare* bind. Cf. ALLAY *v.*[1]] **1** *v.i.* Of the sight: grow dim. Only in ME. **2** *v.t.* Mitigate, assuage, alleviate LME–E17. **3** *v.t.* Weaken by admixture, dilute, qualify; debase (coin). L15–E17.

delayed /dɪˈleɪd/ *a.* M16. [f. DELAY *v.*[1] + -ED[1].] **1** That has been delayed; retarded, deferred, held back. M16. **2** *spec. Nuclear Physics.* Of a particle: emitted by one of the products of fission or other decay process. Cf. *prompt*. M20.

Comb.: **delayed-action** *a.* operating, designed to operate, after a predetermined interval of time.

del credere /dɛl ˈkreɪdəri, -ˈkrɛd-/ *a.*, *adv.*, & *n. phr.* L18. [It. = of belief, of trust.] *Comm.* (Subject or relating to) a selling agent's guarantee, for which a commission is charged, that the buyer is solvent.

dele /ˈdiːli/ *v.* & *n.* E18. [L *dele* 2nd person sing. pres. imper. act. of *delere* DELETE.] **A** *v.t.* Delete, or mark for deletion, from typeset material. E18.

RICHARD MORRIS The comma after ape should be deled.

B *n.* A proofreaders' sign indicating matter to be deleted. E18.

delect /dɪˈlɛkt/ *v.* Long *rare.* LME. [L *delectare*: see next. Cf. OFr. *delecter*.] †**1** *v.t.* Ease the pain of. Only in LME. **2** *v.t.* & *i.* = DELIGHT *v.* M16.

delectable /dɪˈlɛktəb(ə)l/ *a.* Now *literary* or *affected.* LME. [(O)Fr. *délectable* f. L *delectabilis*, f. *delectare* to delight: see -ABLE.] Enjoyable, pleasing, delightful, delicious.

MILTON Trees of God, Delectable both to behold and taste. W. BOYD Every biting insect saw her as a delectable target.

delecta'bility *n.* LME. **delectableness** *n.* E16. **delectably** *adv.* LME.

delectate /ˈdiːlɛkteɪt, dɪˈlɛkteɪt/ *v.t. literary* or *affected.* Now *rare.* E19. [L *delectat-*: see next, -ATE[3].] Delight.

delectation /diːlɛkˈteɪʃ(ə)n/ *n.* Now *literary* or *affected.* LME. [(O)Fr. *délectation* f. L *delectatio(n-)*, f. *delectat-* pa. ppl stem of *delectare* delight: see -ATION.] The action of delighting; pleasure, entertainment.

J. CAREY Bogus suffering, put on a stage for the delectation of a crowd, offended his reason.

delectus /dɪˈlɛktəs/ *n.* E19. [L, use as n. of pa. pple of *deligere* pick out, select, f. *de-* DE- 1 + *legere* choose.] A selection of (esp. Latin or Greek) passages for translation.

delectus personae /dɪˌlɛktəs pəːˈsəʊniː/ *n. phr.* M18. [L *delectus personae* lit. 'choice of a person'.] *Law* (now *Hist.*). The right of each partner in a firm, party to a contract, etc., to choose or be satisfied with any person subsequently admitted to partnership etc.

delegable /ˈdɛlɪgəb(ə)l/ *a.* M17. [f. L *delegare*: see DELEGATE *v.*, -ABLE.] Able to be delegated.

delegacy /ˈdɛlɪgəsi/ *n.* LME. [f. DELEGATE *n.* after *prelate*, *prelacy*: see -ACY.] **1** The action or system of delegating; the state of being delegated; appointment as a delegate; delegated authority. LME. **2** A body or committee of delegates. L15.

delegant /ˈdɛlɪg(ə)nt/ *n.* E17. [L *delegant-* pres. ppl stem of *delegare*: see DELEGATE *v.*, -ANT[1].] Chiefly *Law* (now *Hist.*). A person who delegates.

delegate /ˈdɛlɪgət/ *n.* LME. [L *delegatus* use as n. of pa. pple of *delegare*: see next, -ATE[2].] **1** A person deputed or authorized to act for or represent another or others; a deputy, a member of a deputation; *esp.* a person chosen or elected to represent others at a meeting, conference, etc. LME. **2** A commissioner appointed by the Crown to hear appeals from ecclesiastical courts. *obs.* exc. *Hist.* M16. **3** At Oxford University, a member of any of various permanent committees entrusted with some branch of University business. E17. **4** A non-voting representative of a territory in the US Congress. L18.

1 E. MELLOR He [the priest] claims simply to stand as delegate of heaven. E. LONGFORD The Paris peace conference had opened . . with Wellington and Castlereagh as British delegates. **House of Delegates** in the US, the lower house of the legislature in Virginia, West Virginia, and Maryland. *walking delegate*: see WALKING *ppl a.*

delegateship *n.* the position or office of a delegate M19.

delegate /ˈdɛlɪgeɪt/ *v.t.* Pa. pple & ppl a. **-ated,** (earliest form, long *arch.*) **-ate** /-ət/. LME. [L *delegat-* pa. ppl stem of *delegare*, f. *de-* DE- 1 + *legare* send on a commission: see -ATE[3].] **1** Send or commission (a person) to act as a deputy or representative; depute. LME. †**2** *loosely.* Assign, deliver, convey. LME–L18. **3** Assign or entrust (a duty, authority, etc.) to another as agent or deputy. L15. **4** *Law.* Assign (a debtor to oneself) to a creditor as debtor in one's place. E19.

1 S. UNWIN It was the elder boy's duty to decide what tools . . were needed and to delegate the small boys to fetch them. 3 BOLINGBROKE The Peers have an inherent, the Commons a delegated Right. T. JEFFERSON Those bodies . . to whom the people have delegated the powers of legislation.

delega'tee *n.* (chiefly *Law*, now *Hist.*) a person to whom something or someone is delegated L19. **delegator** *n.* a person who delegates L19.

delegation /dɛlɪˈgeɪʃ(ə)n/ *n.* E17. [L *delegatio(n-)*, f. as prec.: see -ATION.] **1** The action of delegating, the fact of being delegated; entrusting of authority to a representative. E17. **2** A commission given to a delegate; delegated power. E17. **3** *Law* (now *Hist.*). Assignment of a debtor by his or her creditor to a creditor of the latter. E18. **4** A delegated body; a number of people chosen to act as representatives; a deputation. L18.

1 H. EVANS [Gerald] Long commanded by orderly delegation; he had an acute sense of hierarchy. 2 J. LOCKE When . . others usurp the place, who have no such authority or delegation. 4 R. P. GRAVES Mrs Pankhurst led a delegation to Parliament to present a petition to the Prime Minister.

delegatory /ˈdɛlɪgət(ə)ri/ *a.* L16. [L *delegatorius*, f. *delegat-*: see DELEGATE *v.*, -ORY[2].] †**1** Of a person: holding delegated authority. Only in L16. **2** Of, relating to, or of the nature of delegation or delegated power. E17.

delegitimize /diːlɪˈdʒɪtɪmʌɪz/ *v.t.* Also **-ise.** M20. [f. DE- 3 + LEGITIMIZE.] Withdraw legitimate status from.

delegitimi'zation *n.* L20.

delete /dɪˈliːt/ *v.t.* Pa. pple **-d,** (earlier) †**delete.** LME. [L *delet-* pa. ppl stem of *delere* blot out, efface.] †1 Destroy, annihilate, do away with. LME–M19. 2 Cross out, cancel, remove, or erase (a character, letter, word, passage, etc.); make no longer effective by removal from a printed etc. record. M16. b Remove (an item, esp. a recording) from a catalogue, so that it is no longer offered for sale. M20. 3 *Genetics*. In *pass.* Be lost from a chromosome. E20.

2 H. BEVERIDGE The peerage would be granted if the censure were deleted. H. ARENDT They deleted from Jewish prayerbooks the visions of an ultimate restoration of Zion. *fig.*: T. REID So imprinted as not to be deleted by time.

deleterious /dɛlɪˈtɪərɪəs/ *a.* M17. [f. med.L *deleterius* f. Gk *dēlētērios* noxious: see -OUS.] Injurious to life or health, noxious, harmful; mentally or morally damaging.

BYRON 'Tis pity wine should be so deleterious, For tea and coffee leave us much more serious. R. W. EMERSON Politics is a deleterious profession.

†deleterial *a.* = DELETERIOUS: only in 17. **deleteriously** *adv.* L19. **deleteriousness** *n.* E19. **†deletery** *a.* = DELETERIOUS L16–L17.

deletion /dɪˈliːʃ(ə)n/ *n.* L15. [L *deletio(n-)*, f. *delet-* pa. ppl stem of *delere* DELETE: see -ION.] 1 The action of obliterating or destroying; annihilation, destruction. *arch.* L15. 2 The action of deleting written or printed matter; the fact of being deleted; a deleted passage etc., an erasure. L16. b The action of deleting an item, esp. a recording, from a catalogue; the item deleted. M20. 3 *Genetics*. = DEFICIENCY 2. E20.

delf /dɛlf/ *n.*[1] *obs.* exc. *dial.* Also **-ph**. [OE *dælf*, *(ge)delf*, f. as DELVE *v.*] 1 An excavation; a pit, ditch, quarry, etc.; a drainage canal (in the fens). OE. 2 A cut turf, a sod. *Sc.* E16. 3 A spade-thrust. E17. †4 A bed of earth or a mineral that is or can be dug into. E17–E18.

†delf *n.*[2] & *a.* var. of next.

delft /dɛlft/ *n.* & *a.* Also **†delf, delph** /dɛlf/. L17. [f. *Delf*, now *Delft*, a town in the Netherlands.] (Designating) a kind of tin-glazed earthenware, usu. having blue decoration on a white ground, made in Delft or (in imitation of this) elsewhere.

Delhi belly /dɛli ˈbɛli/ *n. phr. slang.* M20. [*Delhi*, capital of India.] An upset stomach accompanied by diarrhoea, esp. as suffered by visitors to India.

deli /ˈdɛli/ *n. colloq.* (orig. *US*). M20. [Abbrev.] = DELICATESSEN (esp. sense 2); in Australia, a small shop open long hours selling perishable goods, newspapers, etc.

Delian /ˈdiːlɪən/ *a.*[1] L16. [f. L *Delius*, Gk *Dēlios* Delos (see below) + -AN.] Of or pertaining to Delos, a Greek island in the Cyclades, or its inhabitants.

Delian League a confederacy of ancient Greek States under Athens, formed in 478 BC to oppose the Persians. **Delian problem**: of finding geometrically the side of a cube having twice the volume of a given cube (from the Delian oracle's pronouncement that a plague in Athens would cease if the cubical altar to Apollo were doubled in size).

Delian /ˈdiːlɪən/ *a.*[2] & *n.* M20. [f. *Delius* (see below) + -AN.] A *adj.* Of or pertaining to the English composer Frederick Delius (1862–1934), his music, or his style of composition. M20. B *n.* An interpreter, student, or admirer of Delius or his music. M20.

†delibation *n.* M17–L18. [L *delibatio(n-)*, f. *delibare* take a little of, taste, f. *de-* DE- I + *libare* to taste: see -ATION.] A portion extracted; a taste or slight knowledge *of* something.

†deliber *v.* LME. [Fr. *délibérer* or L *deliberare*: see DELIBERATE *v.*] 1 *v.i.* = DELIBERATE *v.* 1. LME–L15. 2 *v.i.* & (in *pass.*) *v.t.* = DELIBERATE *v.* 2. LME–L16. 3 *v.t.* = DELIBERATE *v.* 3. Only in M16.

deliberant /dɪˈlɪb(ə)r(ə)nt/ *n. rare.* L17. [L *deliberant-* pres. ppl stem of *deliberare*: see DELIBERATE *v.*, -ANT[1].] A person who deliberates.

deliberate /dɪˈlɪb(ə)rət/ *a.* LME. [L *deliberatus* pa. pple, f. as next: see -ATE[2].] 1 Carefully thought out, studied; intentional, done on purpose. LME. 2 Firm, unhurried, purposeful; careful, not rash or hasty. L16.

1 L. P. HARTLEY The silence which had become habitual to her, unless she made a deliberate effort to break it. R. D. LAING Contrived, deliberate, cynical lies. 2 J. R. GREEN Striving to be deliberate in speech. J. STEINBECK Abra moved with firm and deliberate steps.

deliberately *adv.* L15. **deliberateness** *n.* E17.

deliberate /dɪˈlɪbəreɪt/ *v.* M16. [L *deliberat-* pa. ppl stem of *deliberare*, f. *de-* DE- I + *librare* weigh, f. *libra* scales: see -ATE[3]. Cf. earlier DELIBER.] 1 *v.i.* Think carefully, pause for consideration, ponder; confer, take counsel together. Foll. by *about*, *on*, *upon*, †*of*. M16. †2 *v.i.* & (in *pass.*) *v.t.* Resolve, determine (*to do*). M16–M17. 3 *v.t.* Think over, confer about, deliberate on. Now usu. w. obj. cl. M16.

1 J. A. FROUDE The future relations of the two countries could now be deliberated on with a hope of settlement. W. S. MAUGHAM I deliberated a long time about buying it. B. PYM He deliberated for a moment then walked into a pew. 3 C. TOURNEUR To deliberate The cause or author of this accident. W. ROBERTSON She deliberated . . how she might overcome the regent's scruples.

deliberator *n.* [L *deliberator*] a person who deliberates. L18.

deliberation /dɪˌlɪbəˈreɪʃ(ə)n/ *n.* LME. [OFr. *deliberacion* (later and mod. *délibération*), f. L *deliberatio(n-)*, f. *deliberat-*: see prec., -ATION.] I 1 The action of deliberating; careful consideration, weighing up with a view to decision. LME. 2 *spec.* Consideration and discussion of a question by a legislative assembly, committee, etc.; debate; an instance of this (freq. in *pl.*). LME. †3 A resolution, a determination; a plan, an intention. M16–E18.

1 J. UPDIKE The answer came after maddening deliberation 'No'. 2 P. LARKIN The chairman of the . . panel . . has risen to announce the result of its deliberations.

II 4 The quality of acting with careful thought; avoidance of precipitancy; deliberateness of action; absence of hurry; slowness in action or movement. LME.

4 S. WILLIAMS The chiefs consulted with great deliberation. F. RAPHAEL Susan served the meal with a slow deliberation which emphasized the trouble she had taken with it. C. PRIEST Raising and lowering my feet with the deliberation of a shackled man.

deliberative /dɪˈlɪb(ə)rətɪv/ *a.* L15. [Fr. *délibératif*, *-ive*, or L *deliberativus*, f. *deliberat-*: see DELIBERATE *v.*, -ATIVE.] 1 Characterized by deliberation. L15. 2 Concerned with or having the function of deliberating. M16. 3 *Gram.* Expressing deliberation or doubt. M19.

deliberatively *adv.* M17. **deliberativeness** *n.* M17.

delible /ˈdɛlɪb(ə)l/ *a.* E17. [L *delebilis*, f. *delere*: see DELETE, -IBLE and cf. INDELIBLE, UNDELIBLE.] Able to be deleted or effaced.

delicacy /ˈdɛlɪkəsi/ *n.* LME. [f. next + -ACY.] I The quality of being delicate. †1 Addiction to pleasure or sensuous delights; voluptuousness, luxuriousness. LME–M18. †2 Luxury, indulgence. LME–E18. †b Gratification, pleasure. LME–M17. †3 The quality of being delightful or delicious; beauty, daintiness, pleasantness. LME–M17. †4 Fastidiousness. LME–L18. 5 Exquisite fineness of texture, substance, finish, etc.; graceful slightness, tender beauty. L16. 6 Weakliness of constitution or health; susceptibility to disease or injury. M17. 7 Fineness of skill, expression, touch, etc. L17. 8 Sensitivity of perception, feeling, observation, etc.; (of an instrument) sensitiveness, precision. E18. 9 Avoidance of what is immodest or offensive; careful regard for the feelings of others. E18. 10 The quality or condition of requiring careful and skilful handling. L18.

5 J. R. GREEN She would play with her rings that her courtiers might note the delicacy of her hands. 8 LD MACAULAY His principles would be relaxed, and the delicacy of his sense of right and wrong impaired. 9 STEELE A false Delicacy is Affectation, not Politeness. S. LEWIS They coughed politely . . they blew their noses with a delicacy altogether optimistic and refined. 10 BURKE Our concerns in India were matters of delicacy. J. GALSWORTHY When June determined on anything, delicacy became a somewhat minor consideration.

II 11 A thing which gives delight. Now *esp.* a choice or dainty item of food. LME. 12 A delicate trait, observance, or attention. E18. 13 A nicety, a refinement. L18.

11 P. PEARCE A tea-table laden with delicacies for him alone. 12 STEELE The . . Delicacies that attend the Passion towards them [women] in elegant Minds. 13 E. A. FREEMAN The grammatical delicacies of the written language.

delicate /ˈdɛlɪkət/ *a.* & *n.* LME. [(O)Fr. *délicat* or L *delicatus*, of unkn. origin: see -ATE[2].] A *adj.* 1 Delightful, pleasant, charming, lovely, nice. Now only of food: dainty and palatable. LME. †2 Characterized by sensuous delight; luxurious, voluptuous; (of a person) given to pleasure or luxury. LME–M18. †3 Self-indulgent, indolent. LME–E17. †4 Fastidious, particular. LME–L18. †5 Not robust; effeminate. LME–L17. 6 Of weakly constitution; liable to illness or injury; not strong. LME. b Fragile; easily spoiled or damaged. M16. 7 Fine in texture, finish, quality, workmanship, etc.; exquisitely shaped or constructed; slight, slender, soft. LME. b Soft or subdued in colour. E19. 8 Having finely-developed perception, feeling, appreciation, etc.; (of a person or instrument) sensitive. M16. 9 Finely skilful. L16. †b Characterized by skilful action. L16–L17. 10 Sensitive to propriety, modesty, or the feelings of others; avoiding what is offensive or immodest. M17. 11 So slight as to be hard to appreciate; subtle. L17. 12 Requiring careful and skilful handling; ticklish. M18.

1 EVELYN Haerlem is a very delicate town. G. WHITE The sun broke out into a warm delicate day. M. PATTISON Not to take delight in delicate meats. 5 SHAKES. *Haml.* Witness this army . . Led by a delicate and tender prince. 6 V. WOOLF I am supposed . . to be too delicate to go with them, since I get so easily tired and am then sick. *in a delicate condition*: see CONDITION *n.* 8. b K. ISHIGURO The teacup . . was of the same delicate material. 7 E. WAUGH A delicate pair of gold manicure scissors. J. HARVEY It was a fine face with delicate edges and corners. b D. H. LAWRENCE Looking at the water, I perceived a delicate flush from the west. 8 T. HEGGEN Ensign Pulver's feet were enormous and he was delicate about them. G. ORWELL You could not control the beating of your heart, and the telescreen was quite delicate enough to pick it up. 9 SHAKES. *Oth.* So delicate with her needle. 10 L. STERNE We were both too delicate to communicate what we felt to each other upon the occasion. 11 A. BAIN Discrimination of the most delicate differences. 12 S. NAIPAUL The subject is a delicate one and I do not pursue it. E. REVELEY The whole thing will take some pretty delicate manoeuvering.

B *n.* †1 A person with luxurious or fastidious tastes. LME–E18. 2 A luxury, a delight; *esp.* a choice item of food. Now *rare* or *obs.* LME.

delicately *adv.* LME. **delicateness** *n.* M16.

délicatesse /delikatɛs/ *n.* L17. [Fr., f. *délicat* delicate.] Delicacy.

delicatessen /ˌdɛlɪkəˈtɛs(ə)n/ *n.* Orig. *US.* L19. [G *Delikatessen* pl. or Du. *delicatessen* pl., f. as prec.] 1 Cooked meats, cheeses, and unusual or foreign prepared foods. L19. 2 A shop, or shop counter or department, selling delicatessen. M20.

†delice *n.* ME. [(O)Fr. *délice* masc., *délices* fem. pl., f. L *delicium* neut. sing., *deliciae* fem. pl.] 1 Delight, pleasure; *esp.* sensual or worldly pleasure. ME–L17. 2 A delight; a delicacy. ME–M19.

delicious /dɪˈlɪʃəs/ *a.* & *n.* ME. [OFr. (mod. *délicieux*) f. late L *deliciosus*, f. L *delicia*, pl. *deliciae*: see prec., -OUS.] A *adj.* 1 Highly delightful; giving great pleasure or enjoyment; intensely amusing. ME. 2 Highly pleasing to the bodily senses, esp. to those of taste or smell. ME. †3 Characterized by or addicted to sensuous indulgence. ME–L17.

1 C. KINGSLEY A delicious joke it would have been. ARNOLD BENNETT A delicious wave of joy and of satisfaction animated him. 2 V. WOOLF These delicious mouthfuls of roast duck. B. PYM The delicious fragrance of shrubs. I. MURDOCH He paraded his delicious fiancée in theatre foyers.

B *n.* (Also **D-**.) A variety of eating apple of N. American origin. E20.

Golden Delicious: see GOLDEN *a*. *Red Delicious*: see RED *a*.
deliciously *adv.* ME. **deliciousness** *n.* LME.

delict /dɪˈlɪkt, ˈdiːlɪkt/ *n. arch.* LME. [L *delictum* use as n. of *delictus* pa. pple of *delinquere*: see DELINQUENT.] A violation of law; an offence.
in flagrant delict = IN FLAGRANTE DELICTO.
deˈlictual *a.* (*rare*) of or belonging to a delict L19.

deligation /dɛlɪˈgeɪʃ(ə)n/ *n.* Now *rare* or *obs.* M17. [f. DE- 1 + LIGATION.] *Med.* †1 Bandaging; a bandage. M17–M19. 2 The tying of an artery etc. with a ligature. M19.

delight /dɪˈlʌɪt/ *n.* ME. [OFr. *delit*, f. stem of *delitier* f. L *delectare* to allure, charm, frequent. of *delicere*. The spelling with *-gh-* on the analogy of native wds like *light* dates from 16.] 1 The fact or condition of being delighted; pleasure, joy, or gratification felt in a high degree. ME. 2 A thing which or person who causes great pleasure or joy, a source of delight. ME. 3 The quality of delighting; delightfulness. Now *poet.* ME. 4 *Turkish delight*, †*lumps of delight*, a sweet made of flavoured gelatinous lumps coated with powdered sugar. M19.
1 COLERIDGE He gazed! he thrilled with deep delight! B. JOWETT The branch of knowledge . . in which he takes the greatest delight. 2 LD MACAULAY The poetry and eloquence of Greece had been the delight of Raleigh. K. A. PORTER She enjoyed Freytag's good looks, he was a delight to her eyes. L. BLUE There are many other delights in a Polish kitchen. *New Scientist* The mammalogist's delight—faecal analysis. *debs'* or *deb's delight*: see DEB. *hell's delight*: see HELL *n.* *lady's delight*: see LADY *n.* & *a.* 3 WORDSWORTH She was a Phantom of delight.
delightless *a.* not giving delight L16.

delight /dɪˈlʌɪt/ *v.* ME. [OFr. *delitier*: see prec.] 1 *v.t.* Give great pleasure or enjoyment to; please highly. Freq. in *pass.* (foll. by *with*, *at*, †*in*, *to do*). ME. b *v.i.* Give great pleasure, cause delight. L19. 2 *v.i.* & (*arch.*) *refl.* Be highly pleased (*to do*, *with*), take great pleasure (*in*). ME. †3 *v.t.* Enjoy greatly, delight in. LME–E17.
1 W. CATHER She laughed as if the idea . . delighted her. A. MASON More than pleased: he had been delighted. b G. F. ATHERTON There had been much to delight and awe. 2 AV *Ps.* 119:16 I will delight my selfe in thy statutes. J. MORLEY The kind of man whom this system delights to honour. G. M. TREVELYAN Ever since the days of Burns . . the English have delighted in Scottish tradition and story.
delighter *n.* a person who takes delight (*in*) L16. **delightingly** *adv.* with delight E17.

delightable /dɪˈlʌɪtəb(ə)l/ *a.* Long *rare*. ME. [Orig. f. OFr. *delitable*, f. *delitier*: see DELIGHT *n.*, -ABLE; later directly f. DELIGHT *n.* or *v.*] Causing delight, delightful.

delighted /dɪˈlʌɪtɪd/ *a.* E17. [f. DELIGHT *n.*, *v.*: see -ED[2], -ED[1].] †1 Causing delight; delightful. E17–M18. 2 Filled with delight, highly pleased or gratified. L17.
1 SHAKES. *Oth.* If virtue no delighted beauty lack. 2 M. SPARK He laughed in a delighted way.
delightedly *adv.* E19.

delightful /dɪˈlʌɪtfʊl, -f(ə)l/ *a.* LME. [f. DELIGHT *n.* + -FUL.] 1 Causing delight; highly pleasing, charming. LME. †2 Experiencing delight; delighted. L16–L17.
delightfully *adv.* L16. **delightfulness** *n.* L16.

delightsome /dɪˈlʌɪts(ə)m/ *a.* Now *literary*. E16. [f. DELIGHT *n.* + -SOME[1].] Delightful.
delightsomely *adv.* L16. **delightsomeness** *n.* L16.

delignification /ˌdiːlɪgnɪfɪˈkeɪʃ(ə)n/ *n.* E20. [f. DE- 3 + LIGNIN + -FICATION.] The removal of lignin from woody tissue.
deˈlignify *v.t.* subject to delignification (chiefly as *delignified* ppl a.) M20.

Delilah /dɪˈlʌɪlə/ *n.* Also †**Dal-**. L16. [The woman who betrayed Samson to the Philistines (*Judges* 16).] A temptress, a seductive and treacherous woman.

delimit /dɪˈlɪmɪt/ *v.t.* M19. [Fr. *délimiter* f. L *delimitare*, f. *de-* DE- 1 + *limitare*: see LIMIT *v.*] Mark or determine the limits of; define the territorial boundary of.
delimitate *v.t.* = DELIMIT L19. **delimitative** *a.* having the function of delimiting L19. **delimiter** *n.* (*Computing*) a character etc. used to indicate the beginning or end of a group of characters or a field M20.

delimitation /dɪˌlɪmɪˈteɪʃ(ə)n/ *n.* M19. [Fr. *délimitation* f. L *delimitatio(n-)*, f. *delimitat-* pa. ppl stem of *delimitare*: see prec., -ATION.] The action of delimiting; determination of a limit or boundary, esp. of the frontier of a territory.

†**deline** *v.t.* L16–M18. [L *delineare*: see DELINEATE *v.*] = DELINEATE *v.*

delineable /dɪˈlɪnɪəb(ə)l/ *a. rare.* M17. [f. as prec. + -ABLE.] Able to be delineated.

delineate /dɪˈlɪnɪət/ *ppl a.* Now *arch.* or *poet.* L16. [L *delineatus* pa. pple, f. as next: see -ATE[2].] Delineated; traced out, portrayed, described.

delineate /dɪˈlɪnɪeɪt/ *v.t.* M16. [L *delineat-* pa. ppl stem of *delineare* outline, sketch out, f. *de-* DE- 1 + *lineare* draw lines, f. *linea* LINE *n.*[2]: see -ATE[3].] 1 Trace out by lines, trace or serve as the outline of. M16. 2 Represent by drawing, portray; draw in fine detail. L16. 3 Sketch out, outline (something to be constructed, a scheme, etc.). E17. 4 *fig.* Describe or portray in words; express. E17.
1 F. R. WILSON The exact position is delineated on the plan. S. SPENDER Straight mouldings delineate tall windows. 2 G. GROTE If . . lions could paint, they would delineate their gods in form like themselves. 3 MARVELL Not willing . . to deliniate his whole proposall. 4 M. FRAYN Every well-formed smile . . seemed to delineate an intolerable sadness. H. ACTON A tendency to identify herself with the characters she delineated.
delineative *a.* pertaining to delineation; serving to delineate: M19. **delineator** *n.* (*a*) a person who delineates; (*b*) an instrument for tracing outlines: L18.

delineation /dɪˌlɪnɪˈeɪʃ(ə)n/ *n.* L16. [Late L *delineatio(n-)*, f. as prec.: see -ATION.] 1 The action of tracing out something by lines; a drawing, a diagram, a figure. L16. 2 The action of outlining something to be constructed or established; a sketch, a plan, a rough draft. L16. 3 Pictorial representation; a drawing, a portrait. L16. 4 The action of portraying in words; description, expression. L16.

†**delinquence** *n.* L17–M19. [f. as next: see -ENCE.] The fact of being a delinquent; culpable failure in duty.

delinquency /dɪˈlɪŋkw(ə)nsi/ *n.* M17. [eccl.L *delinquentia*, f. as next: see -ENCY.] 1 The quality of being a delinquent; failure in or violation of duty; delinquent behaviour. M17. 2 A delinquent act; a failing, a misdeed, an offence. Usu. in *pl.* M17.
1 *juvenile delinquency*: see JUVENILE *a.*

delinquent /dɪˈlɪŋkwənt/ *n.* & *a.* L15. [L *delinquent-* pres. ppl stem of *delinquere* be at fault, offend, f. *de-* DE- 1 + *linquere* leave: see -ENT.] A *n.* 1 A person who fails in duty or obligation; an offender; now *esp.* a young offender. L15. 2 *Hist.* (A name given by the parliamentarians to) a person who helped Charles I and Charles II to make war between 1642 and 1660. M17.
1 STEELE Where Crimes are enormous, the Delinquent deserves little Pity. I. MURDOCH Had he turned out a problem child, perhaps a delinquent. *juvenile delinquent*: see JUVENILE *a.*
B *adj.* 1 Failing in or neglectful of a duty or obligation; guilty of a misdeed or offence. E17. 2 Of or pertaining to a delinquent or delinquents. M17.
1 P. HOLLAND Having offended or being delinquent in any duetie. 2 I. MCEWAN Raymond, in his earlier, delinquent days had fed glass splinters to the pigeons.

†**deliquate** *v.* M17. [f. DE- 3 + LIQUATE *v.*] 1 *v.i.* Deliquesce. M17–E19. 2 *v.t.* Dissolve, melt down. Only in L17.

deliquesce /dɛlɪˈkwɛs/ *v.i.* M18. [L *deliquescere* melt away, dissolve, f. *de-* DE- 1 + *liquescere* inceptive of *liquere* be liquid: see -ESCE.] 1 *Chem.* Become liquid by absorbing moisture from the air, as certain salts do. M18. 2 *Biol.* Esp. of fungi: become liquid after maturity, or in the course of decay. M19. 3 *gen.* Melt away, dissolve. Chiefly *fig.* M19.

deliquescence /dɛlɪˈkwɛs(ə)ns/ *n.* M18. [f. as next: see -ESCENCE.] The process of deliquescing; the property of being deliquescent; liquid produced in deliquescing.
Also **deliquescency** *n.* (*rare*) M18.

deliquescent /dɛlɪˈkwɛs(ə)nt/ *a.* L18. [L *deliquescent-* pres. ppl stem of *deliquescere*: see DELIQUESCE, -ESCENT.] 1 *Chem.* That deliquesces; having the property of dissolving in moisture absorbed from the air. L18. 2 *gen.* Turning to liquid, melting away (chiefly *fig.*); *joc.* dissolving in perspiration. M19. b Esp. of fungi: turning to liquid in the process of maturity or decay. L19. 3 Of a tree, trunk, etc.: dissolving into ramifications, repeatedly branching. M19.
2 J. BRAINE A middle-aged woman . . with black dyed hair and a sort of deliquescent distinction.

†**deliquiate** *v.i.* M18–M19. [Irreg. f. L *deliquare* (= DELIQUATE) or f. DELIQUIUM *n.*[2]] = DELIQUESCE *v.* 1.

deliquium /dɪˈlɪkwɪəm/ *n.*[1] *arch.* E17. [L *deliquium* failure, want, (in med.L) offence, transgression, f. *delinquere*: see DELINQUENT.] 1 Failure of the vital powers, a swoon. E17. †2 A failure of light, an eclipse. M–L17. 3 (Confused w. next.) A melting away; the state of having melted. Chiefly *fig.* E18.

†**deliquium** *n.*[2] E17–E19. [f. DELIQUATE after *effluvium* etc.] *Chem.* = DELIQUESCENCE.

delirament /dɪˈlɪrəm(ə)nt/ *n. rare.* LME. [L *deliramentum*, f. *delirare*: see DELIRIUM, -MENT.] Raving, frenzy; a craze.

†**delirancy** *n.* M17–M18. [f. L *delirare* (see DELIRIUM) + -ANCY.] Raving, madness.

deliration /dɛlɪˈreɪʃ(ə)n/ *n.* E17. [L *deliratio(n-)*, f. *delirat-* pa. ppl stem of *delirare*: see DELIRIUM, -ATION.] Delirium, mental aberration, madness; absurdity.

delire /dɪˈlɪə/ *v.i.* Long *obs.* exc. *Sc.* LME. [L *delirare*: see DELIRIUM. Cf. Fr. *délirer*.] Go astray, err, esp. in reason; wander in mind, go mad, rave.
R. BURNS Gotten fright, An' liv'd an' di'd deleerit.

deliriant /dɪˈlɪrɪənt/ *a.* & *n.* L19. [f. DELIRIUM + -ANT[1].] (A drug) having the power to produce delirium.

deliriate /dɪˈlɪrɪeɪt/ *v.t. rare.* M17. [f. as prec. + -ATE[3].] Make delirious.

delirious /dɪˈlɪrɪəs/ *a.* L16. [f. as next + -OUS.] 1 (Of an action etc.) belonging to or characteristic of delirium; betraying delirium or ecstasy. L16. 2 (Of a person) affected with delirium; temporarily or apparently mad, raving; wildly excited, ecstatic. E18.
1 BYRON How the giant element From rock to rock leaps with delirious bound. W. B. CARPENTER The delirious ravings of Intoxication or of Fever. 2 J. GALSWORTHY The young man seemed quite delirious about her. J. FRAME They thought he was drunk . . until they realized he was delirious with pneumonia.
deliriously *adv.* E19. **deliriousness** *n.* L18.

delirium /dɪˈlɪrɪəm/ *n.* Pl. **-iums**, **-ia** /-ɪə/. M16. [L *delirium*, f. *delirare* deviate, be deranged, f. *de-* DE- 1 + *lira* ridge between furrows.] 1 A disordered state of the mind resulting from disease, intoxication, etc., characterized by incoherent speech, hallucinations, restlessness, and often extreme excitement. M16. 2 Great excitement; ecstasy, rapturous frenzy. M17.
1 **delirium tremens** /ˈtriːmənz, trɛ-/ [L = trembling delirium] delirium with tremors and terrifying delusions, occurring esp. as a withdrawal symptom in chronic alcoholism. 2 W. IRVING He . . danced in a delirium of joy, until he upset the canoe.

†**delirous** *a.* M17–E18. [f. L *delirus*, f. as prec.: see -OUS.] Delirious, raving.

delish /dɪˈlɪʃ/ *a. colloq.* E20. [Abbrev.] Delicious.

delitescent /dɛlɪˈtɛs(ə)nt/ *a.* Now *rare.* L17. [L *delitescent-* pres. ppl stem of *delitescere* hide away, lurk, f. *de-* DE- 1 + *latescere*, inceptive of *latere* lie hid: see -ESCENT.] Lying hidden, concealed; latent.
delitescence *n.* L18. **delitescency** *n.* L17.

deliver /dɪˈlɪvə/ *a.* Long *arch.* ME. [OFr. *de(s)livre*, f. *delivrer*: see next.] Free of encumbrance; agile, nimble, active; mentally quick, lively.
deliverly *adv.* LME. **deliverness** *n.* LME.

deliver /dɪˈlɪvə/ *v.* ME. [(O)Fr. *délivrer* f. Proto-Gallo-Romance, f. L *de-* DE- 1 + *liberare* LIBERATE *v.*] I *v.t.* 1 Save, rescue, set free, (*from*,

†*of*). ME. **b** *Pottery* & *Founding*. Release from the mould. M19. **2** Free, rid, divest, (*of*, *from*). *arch.* ME. **b** Unload (a ship, container, etc.). L18. **3** Assist (a woman, *rarely* a female animal) in giving birth; assist at the birth of (a child, offspring); give birth to. Freq. (earlier) in *pass.*, give birth (foll. by *of* a child, offspring), be born. ME. **4** *refl.* Disburden oneself *of* what is in one's mind; speak, discourse. ME. **5** Give up entirely, give over; surrender, yield, abandon, resign. Freq. foll. by *up*, *over*. ME. **b** *refl.* Devote oneself *to*. *rare*. M16. **6** Hand over to another's possession or keeping, transfer; *esp.* bring and hand over (a letter, a parcel, ordered goods, etc.) to the proper recipient or address; present, render (an account etc.). ME. **b** *Law*. Hand over formally (esp. a sealed deed to the grantee). L16. **7** Give out in words; utter, recite; pronounce (judgement etc.). LME. †**8** Communicate, make known; describe, report, set forth. LME–E19. **9** Launch, aim, send forth (a blow, an attack, etc.); cast, throw, project (a missile, ball, etc.); produce, supply. Also with indirect obj. L16.

1 AV *1 Sam.* 17:37 The Lord .. will deliver me out of the hand of this Philistine. T. HARDY A mood of disgust .. from which he was only delivered by .. abandoning these studies. 2 W. LITHGOW The vertue to deliuer a woman from her paine in child-birth. **deliver a jail** (*Hist.*): clear it of prisoners in order to bring them to trial at the assizes. 3 SHAKES. *Wint. T.* She is, something before her time, deliver'd. S. PLATH Will .. had to deliver eight babies before he could graduate. G. BOURNE The majority of women will deliver their heaviest child when they are about 35. B. TRAPIDO The baby .. could not be delivered without forceps. *fig.*: B. JOWETT I have been delivered of an infinite variety of speeches about virtue before now. 4 L. VAN DER POST Theologians .. delivering themselves of resounding solemnities. 5 SHAKES. *Rich. II* See them delivered over To execution and the hand of death. M. PATTISON When premiers deliver up their portfolios. A. MASON God would deliver their enemies into their hand. **b** M. BRADBURY Howard delivers himself to the task of persuasion. 6 W. H. PRESCOTT A message which he must deliver in person. B. MALAMUD He delivered the prisoner first to Secret Police Headquarters. *fig.*: G. GREER The marriage bargain offers what cannot be delivered if it is thought to offer emotional security. **deliver the goods** *fig.* carry out one's part of an agreement, do what is expected of one. 7 J. AGATE Good criticisms .. tellingly delivered. W. S. CHURCHILL Scarcely literate enough to deliver a decent sermon. M. MCCARTHY They had never heard 'their marriage is not lawful' delivered with such emphasis. 8 SHAKES. *Wint. T.* I .. heard the old shepherd deliver the manner how he found it. 9 T. MEDWIN In delivering his harpoon he lost his balance. I. MURDOCH She .. brought the brush into play, delivering me a sharp jab on the ankle. I. T. BOTHAM You can't decide how you're going to play a ball before it's delivered. *Dirt Bike* The six-speed gearbox .. delivers almost 50 miles per gallon.

II *v.i.* **10** Give birth; hand something over; distribute mail, goods, etc., to the proper recipients or addresses; speak, pronounce; *Cricket* bowl a ball. LME. **b** *spec.* Provide what is expected or what one has promised. (Foll. by *on* a pledge etc.) Orig. *US*. M20. **11** *Pottery* & *Founding*. Come free from the mould. L18.

10 J. ROBINSON They first delivered on civil affairs: afterwards the discourse turned on war. SIR W. SCOTT Are we commanded to stand and deliver on the King's highway? OED The postman who delivers in that part of the town. M. BRADBURY Mrs Macintosh, when she did deliver, delivered in bulk, and had twins. **b** S. BRILL Fitzsimmons was trying to deliver on one of the reforms he had promised the government.

deliverable *a.* able to be delivered M18.

deliverance /dɪˈlɪv(ə)r(ə)ns/ *n.* ME. [(O)Fr. *délivrance*, f. as prec.: see -ANCE.] **1** The act of setting free, the fact of being set free; liberation, release, rescue. ME. **2** The action of giving up, or of handing over or transferring, surrender; = DELIVERY 2, 3. Long *obs.* exc. *Law* (see below). ME. †**3** The bringing forth of offspring; = DELIVERY 4. LME–M17. †**4a** The delivery of words, utterance, enunciation; the action of stating something, declaration, narration. LME–E17. **b** A (formal or authoritative) utterance. M19. **5** *Law* (chiefly *Sc.*). Judgement delivered, verdict; a judicial or administrative order. LME.

1 HOBBES Our deliverance from the bondage of sin. W. C. WILLIAMS A sense of thanksgiving for her miraculous deliverance. 2 **writ of second deliverance** *Law* (now *Hist.*) a writ for re-delivery to the owner of goods distrained or unlawfully taken. 4b J. S. MILL The recorded deliverances of the Founder of Christianity.

deliverer /dɪˈlɪv(ə)rə/ *n.* ME. [OFr. *delivrere*, f. as DELIVER *v.*: see -ER[2].] **1** A person or being who sets free or releases; a rescuer, a saviour. ME. **2** A person who hands over, transfers, or commits something to another; one who delivers letters, parcels, ordered goods, etc. LME. **3** A person or being who utters, enunciates or recites, something; one who pronounces judgement etc. L16.

1 *Great Deliverer*: see GREAT *a.*

deliveress *n.* (*rare*) a female deliverer M17.

delivery /dɪˈlɪv(ə)ri/ *n.* LME. [AN *delivree* use as n. of fem. pa. pple of *deliver*: see DELIVER *v.*, -Y[3]. Sense 6 is assoc. w. DELIVER *a.*] **1a** Hist. *jail-delivery*, the action of clearing a jail of prisoners in order to bring them to trial at an assize; the application of the judicial process to the prisoners in a jail. LME. **b** The action of setting free; deliverance. Now *rare*. L15. **2** The action of giving up possession *of*, surrender. LME. **3** The action of handing over something to another; *esp.* a (scheduled) performance of the action of delivering letters, goods, etc. LME. **b** *Law*. A formal handing over or transfer, esp. of a deed to the grantee or a third party. L16. **4** The act of giving birth, or assisting at a birth; parturition, childbirth. L16. **5** The uttering of words, a speech, a pronouncement; the manner of enunciating speech, song, etc. L16. †**b** Setting forth in words; narration, statement. L16–M17. †**6** (Free) use of the limbs; bodily activity, bearing. L16–E19. **7** The sending forth or delivering of a missile, a blow, etc.; the throwing or bowling of a ball etc.; the action shown in doing this. Also, discharge, provision, supply. E18.

3 DICKENS It [a letter] will be here by the two o'clock delivery. 5 JAS. MILL Four days were occupied in the delivery of the speech. A. POWELL This delivery made his words .. appear to protest. 6 H. WOTTON The duke had the neater limbs, and freer delivery. 7 J. FINGLETON Bailey .. played 'doggo' to 388 deliveries. *Scientific American* Dissatisfaction with the delivery of medical care in the U.S.

Phrases: *cash on delivery*: see CASH *n.*[1] *constructive delivery*: see CONSTRUCTIVE *a.* 1. *special delivery*: see SPECIAL *a.* *symbolic delivery*: see SYMBOLIC *a.* *symbolical delivery*: see SYMBOLICAL *a.* **take delivery of** receive after ordering.

Comb.: **delivery room** a specially-equipped hospital room in which births take place; **delivery van**, **vehicle**, etc.: for making deliveries of goods.

dell /dɛl/ *n.*[1] [OE = MLG, MDu. *delle* (Du. *del*), MHG *telle* (G dial. *Telle*), f. Gmc, f. base also of DALE *n.*[1]] **1** A small valley or natural hollow, usu. wooded. OE. †**2** A deep hole, a pit. LME–L18.

dell /dɛl/ *n.*[2] *arch. slang.* M16. [Origin unkn.] A young woman, a wench.

Della Cruscan /dɛlə ˈkrʌskən/ *a.* & *n. phr.* E19. [f. It. (*Accademia*) *della Crusca* (Academy) of the bran (w. ref. to 'sifting'): see -AN.] **A** *adj. phr.* Of, pertaining to, or characteristic of the Accademia della Crusca, established at Florence in 1582 with the main purpose of purifying the Italian language. Also, designating, belonging to, or characteristic of an artificial school of English poetry of the late 18th cent. E19. **B** *n. phr.* A member of the Accademia della Crusca or of the Della Cruscan school. E19.

Della Cruscanism *n.* (*rare*) the principles or practices of Della Cruscans L18.

Della Robbia /dɛlə ˈrɒbɪə/ *n. phr.* L18. [A family of 15th-cent. It. painters & sculptors.] In full *Della Robbia ware* etc. Enamelled terracotta ware made by Luca Della Robbia and his successors; any similar ware.

delocalize /diːˈləʊk(ə)lʌɪz/ *v.t.* Also **-ise**. M19. [f. DE- 3 + LOCALIZE.] Detach or remove from its place, not limit to a particular location; *Chem.* in *pass.* (of electrons) be shared among more than two atoms in a molecule.

delocaliˈzation *n.* L19.

delope /dɪˈləʊp/ *v.i.* M19. [Origin unkn.] Of a duellist: deliberately fire into the air.

¶ Popularized in the historical novels of Georgette Heyer (1902–74).

delouse /diːˈlaʊs/ *v.t.* E20. [f. DE- 3 + LOUSE *n.*] Rid of lice; *fig.* rid of undesirable things.

delph *n.*[1] var. of DELF *n.*[1]

delph *n.*[2] & *a.* var. of DELFT.

Delphi /ˈdɛlfi, -fʌɪ/ *n.* M20. [f. as DELPHIC.] In full *Delphi method*, *technique*, etc. A technique of using questionnaires to arrive at consensual judgements, decisions, etc.

Delphian /ˈdɛlfɪən/ *a.* L16. [f. as next + -AN.] = next.

Delphic /ˈdɛlfɪk/ *a.* L16. [f. *Delphi* (see below) + -IC.] Of or relating to Delphi, a town of Phocis in ancient Greece, esp. as the site of a sanctuary and oracle of Apollo; resembling or characteristic of the oracle of Delphi; (of an utterance etc.) obscure, ambiguous, enigmatic.

Times Mr Begin maintained a Delphic silence about his intentions.

delphically *adv.* in a manner characteristic of the Delphic oracle; enigmatically, obscurely, prophetically: E20.

delphin /ˈdɛlfɪn/ *n.* & *a.* ME. [L *delphin*, *-inus*: see DOLPHIN. Cf. also DAUPHIN.] †**A** *n.* **1** = DOLPHIN 1. ME–M17. **2** The dauphin. Only in LME. **B** *adj.* (**D-**.) [L phr. *ad usum Delphini*.] Designating or pertaining to an edition of Latin classics prepared 'for the use of the dauphin', son of Louis XIV of France. Cf. earlier DAUPHIN *a.* L18.

delphinidin /dɛlˈfɪnɪdɪn/ *n.* E20. [f. DELPHINIUM + -IDIN.] *Chem.* An anthocyanidin, $C_{15}H_{11}O_7Cl$, found combined as glycosides in many plant pigments.

delphinine /ˈdɛlfɪniːn/ *n.* L19. [f. next + -INE[5].] *Chem.* A poisonous alkaloid obtained from the seeds of stavesacre, *Delphinium staphisagria*.

delphinium /dɛlˈfɪnɪəm/ *n.* E17. [mod.L (see below) f. Gk *delphinion* larkspur, f. DELPHIN (from the shape of the spur).] Any of numerous plants with spurred flowers constituting (or formerly included in) the genus *Delphinium*, of the buttercup family; *esp.* any of certain perennials, hybrids of *D. elatum*, grown for their long spikes of blue, purple, or white flowers (cf. LARKSPUR). Also, a flower or flowering stem of such a plant.

delphinoid /ˈdɛlfɪnɔɪd/ *a.* & *n.* L19. [Gk *delphinoeidēs*, f. *delphin* DOLPHIN: see -OID.] *Zool.* **A** *adj.* Of the nature of a dolphin; related to the dolphins; belonging to the division Delphinoidea, which includes the dolphins, killer whales, and porpoises. L19. **B** *n.* A delphinoid mammal; a member of Delphinoidea. L19.

Delphinus /dɛlˈfʌɪnəs/ *n.* L17. [L *delphinus*: see DOLPHIN.] (The name of) a small constellation of the northern hemisphere near Cygnus; the Dolphin.

delta /ˈdɛltə/ *n.* ME. [L f. Gk.] **1** The fourth letter (Δ, δ) of the Greek alphabet. ME. **2** A tract of alluvial land, often more or less triangular in shape, enclosed or traversed by the diverging mouths of a river; orig. (*the Delta*) *spec.* that of the River Nile. M16. **3** A triangle; a triangular area or formation. Usu. *attrib.*: (*a*) Electr. *delta connection* etc., a closed arrangement (represented by a triangle) of three-phase windings in series, each of the three wires of the circuit being connected to a junction of two windings; (*b*) *delta wing*, a triangular swept-back wing of an aircraft. M17. **4** Denoting the fourth in a numerical sequence: a *attrib. Sci.* Freq. written δ. (*a*) *Astron.* (preceding the genitive of the L name of the constellation): the fourth brightest star in a constellation; (*b*) *delta rays*, rays of low penetrative power consisting of slow electrons released from atoms by other particles (esp. alpha rays); (*c*) *delta rhythm*, *waves*, slow electrical activity of the unconscious brain, consisting of deep oscillations having a frequency of 0.5 to 3 hertz. L18. **b** A fourth-class or poor mark in an examination etc. E20.

4b delta plus, minus rather better, worse, than the average fourth class.

deltaic /dɛlˈteɪk/ *a.* M19. [f. prec. + -IC.] Of, pertaining to, or forming a (river) delta; of the nature of a delta.

deltidium /dɛlˈtɪdɪəm/ *n.* Pl. **-dia** /-dɪə/. M19. [mod.L, dim. of Gk DELTA: see -IDIUM.] *Zool.* A plate covering the triangular space between the beak and the hinge in certain brachiopods.

deltiology /dɛltɪˈɒlədʒi/ *n.* M20. [f. Gk *deltion* dim. of *deltos* writing tablet: see -OLOGY.] The hobby of collecting postcards.

deltiologist *n.* a person who collects postcards M20.

deltoid /ˈdɛltɔɪd/ *a.* & *n.* M18. [Fr. *deltoïde* or mod.L *deltoides* f. Gk *deltoeidēs*, f. DELTA: see -OID.] **A** *adj.* **1** Like the Greek letter delta (Δ) in shape; triangular. M18. **b** *Anat.* Designating or pertaining to the large muscle of triangular shape covering the shoulder joint. M18. **2** Of the nature of a (river) delta. M19. **B** *n.* **1** The deltoid muscle. M18. **2** A deltoid moth. M19.

deltoidal *a.* M19.

delucidate *v.* var. of DILUCIDATE.

delude /dɪˈluːd, -ˈljuːd/ *v.t.* LME. [L *deludere* play false, mock, f. *de-* DE- I + *ludere* play, f. *ludus* play, game.] †**1** Play with under the pretence of seriousness; cheat the hopes of; mock. LME–E18. **2** Cause to accept foolishly a false or mistaken belief; deceive, beguile; impose upon with false impressions. LME. †**3** Frustrate the purpose of; evade, elude. LME–L17.

2 TINDALE *Acts* 8:11 With Sorcery he had deluded their wittes. D. H. LAWRENCE I don't delude myself that I shall find an elixir of life in Dresden. G. M. TREVELYAN This cheerful picture . . must not delude us into imagining that England was already the land of improved agriculture.

deluder *n.* L16.

deluge /ˈdɛljuːdʒ/ *n.* & *v.* LME. [(O)Fr. *déluge*, alt., after pop. formations in *-uge*, of earlier *diluve*, *delouve* f. L DILUVIUM.] **A** *n.* A great flood or inundation (*lit.* & *fig.*); a torrent, a heavy downpour. LME.

J. L. MOTLEY The memorable deluge . . out of which the Zuyder Zee was born. W. BLACK This deluge of rhetoric. C. MCCULLOUGH Not a gentle downpour but a steady, roaring deluge which went on and on. **the Deluge** Noah's flood (*Gen.* 6–8).

B *v.t.* Flood, inundate, (*lit.* & *fig.*). L16.

W. IRVING The kingdom was deluged with pamphlets.

deluginous /dɪˈljuːdʒɪnəs/ *a.* [after *ferruginous* etc.] like a deluge M19.

delusion /dɪˈluːʒ(ə)n, -ˈljuː-/ *n.* LME. [Late L *delusio(n-)*, f. *delus-* pa. ppl stem of *deludere*: see DELUDE, -ION.] **1** The action of deluding or of being deluded; the state of being deluded. LME. **2** A false impression or opinion, esp. as a symptom of mental illness. M16.

1 SIR T. MORE Thinges . . done by the deuill for our delusion. 2 C. GEIKIE The poor fellow was only labouring under a delusion. R. D. LAING A common paranoid delusion is that there is a plot directed against the self. **delusions of grandeur** an exaggerated estimation of one's own status or personality; megalomania.

delusional *a.* of the nature of or characterized by delusion L19.

delusive /dɪˈluːsɪv, -ˈljuː-/ *a.* E17. [f. as prec. + -IVE.] Tending to delude; of the nature of a delusion; deceptive, unreal, disappointing.

delusively *adv.* M17. **delusiveness** *n.* M17.

delusory /dɪˈluːs(ə)ri, -ˈljuː-; -z-/ *a.* L15. [Late L *delusorius*, f. *delus-*: see DELUSION, -ORY².] Delusive.

delustre /diːˈlʌstə/ *v.t.* Also ***-ter**. E20. [f. DE- 3 + LUSTRE *n.*¹] Remove lustre or sheen from (a textile).

de luxe /dɪ ˈlʌks, ˈlʊks, də/ *a. phr.* E19. [Fr. = of luxury.] Luxurious, sumptuous; of a superior kind.

POULE-*de-luxe*.

delve /dɛlv/ *n.* L16. [Partly alt. of DELF *n.*¹, partly f. the vb.] **1** Something that has been delved; an excavation, a pit. Also, a hollow, a wrinkle. Now *literary*. L16. **2** An act of delving. M19.

delve /dɛlv/ *v.* [OE *delfan* = OFris. *delva*, OS *bi-delban* (Du. *delven*), OHG *bi-telban*, f. WGmc.] **I** *v.t.* **1** Dig, turn up with a spade; make by digging, excavate; burrow. Now *literary* exc. *Sc.* & *north.* OE. **2** Dig *up* or *out*, exhume. Also, put in by digging, bury. Now *arch.* & *dial.* OE. **3**†**a** Penetrate (as) by digging. Only in ME. **b** Dent, indent. *dial.* L18.

1 TOLKIEN Dwarves . . had delved for themselves great halls and mansions . . in the . . Ered Luin. *fig.*: SHAKES. *Sonn.* Time . . delves the parallels in beauty's brow. 2 N. HAWTHORNE Minerals, delved . . out of the hearts of the mountains.

II *v.i.* **4** Labour with a spade, dig. Now *literary* exc. *Sc.* & *north.* OE. **b** *transf.* Reach, dig with the hand, *in* or *into* a container etc. M20. **5** *fig.* Search, esp. painstakingly; research in documents etc.; investigate, make enquiry. (Foll. by *in*, *into*.) LME. **6** Work hard, slave. *dial.* & *slang.* M19. **7** Of a slope, road, etc.: make a sudden dip or descent. M19.

4 *Proverb*: When Adam delved and Eve span, who was then the gentleman? **b** A. PRICE Stocker delved into his brief-case. 'There's another cutting here.' 5 G. SAINTSBURY He never delves beneath the surface for hidden wealth of suggestion. 6 L. M. ALCOTT Delve like slaves.

delver *n.* a person who delves OE.

dem /dɛm/ *n.* *colloq.* M20. [Abbrev. of DEMONSTRATION. Cf. DEMO *n.*²] = DEMONSTRATION 3; *esp.* a practical display of a piece of equipment etc.

dem /dɛm/ *pron.* & *demonstr. a.* *Black English.* M19. [Repr. a pronunc.] = THEM.

dem /dɛm/ *v.t.* & *i.* Now *arch.* or *affected.* Infl. **-mm-**. Also (earlier) **demn**. ME. [Repr. alt. pronunc.] = DAMN *v.*, esp. as an imprecation.

BARONESS ORCZY That demmed elusive Pimpernel.

demagnetize /diːˈmagnɪtʌɪz/ *v.t.* Also **-ise**. M19. [f. DE- 3 + MAGNETIZE.] Remove the magnetization of; deprive of magnetic properties.

demagnetiˈzation *n.* M19. **demagnetizer** *n.* L20.

demagnify /diːˈmagnɪfʌɪ/ *v.t.* & *i.* M20. [f. DE- 3 + MAGNIFY.] Reduce the degree of magnification of (the image in an electron microscope etc.).

demagnifiˈcation *n.* M20.

demagogic /dɛməˈgɒgɪk, -ˈgɒdʒɪk/ *a.* M19. [Gk *dēmagōgikos*, f. *dēmagōgos* DEMAGOGUE: see -IC.] Of, pertaining to, or of the nature of a demagogue.

demagogical *a.* M18.

demagogue /ˈdɛməgɒg/ *n.* & *v.* M17. [Gk *dēmagōgos*, f. *dēmos* people + *agōgos* leading, f. *agein* to lead. Cf. Fr. *démagogue*.] **A** *n.* **1** In ancient Greece etc., a leader or orator who espoused the cause of the common people. M17. **2** A leader or orator who appeals to popular desires or prejudices to further personal interests, a rabble-rouser. M17. **B** *v.* Chiefly *US.* **1** *v.i.* Behave like a demagogue. (*rare* bef. M19.) M17. **2** *v.t.* Deal with (a matter) in the manner of a demagogue. L19.

demagogism *n.* = DEMAGOGY 1, 2 E19. **demagoguery** *n.* = DEMAGOGY 1, 2 M19.

demagogy /ˈdɛməgɒgi, -gɒdʒi/ *n.* M17. [Gk *dēmagōgia*, f. as prec.: see -Y³.] **1** The actions, principles, or qualities of a demagogue. M17. **2** The rule of demagogues. M19. **3** A body of demagogues. L19.

demand /dɪˈmɑːnd/ *n.* ME. [(O)Fr. *demande*, f. as next.] **1** An authoritative or peremptory request or claim; *transf.* something demanded. ME. **2** A question, a request. *arch.* ME. **3** *Law.* A legal claim, esp. to property; the action of making a legal claim. LME. **4** The action of demanding; requesting or claiming peremptorily or authoritatively. E17. **5** A call for a commodity or service on the part of consumers; *Econ.* the desire and ability of consumers to purchase goods or services (correl. to *supply*). E18. **6** An urgent or pressing requirement; need actively expressing itself. Freq. in *pl.* L18.

1 W. ROBERTSON Henry's extravagant demands had been received at Madrid with that neglect which they deserved. *fig.*: S. BUTLER Compassion is . . a demand of nature, to relieve the unhappy. 4 SHAKES. *Haml.* He shall . . to England For the demand of our neglected tribute. 5 B. T. WASHINGTON There was a demand for bricks in the general market. J. B. PRIESTLEY A large number of . . excellent skilled workmen . . who might as well be crossbow-men . . for all the demand there is for their services. 6 T. COLLINS His private fortune is fully sufficient for all demands even of good society. M. GORDON One of those women who make impossible demands on everyone.

Phrases: *final demand*: see FINAL *a.* **in demand** sought after, generally desired. **on demand** as soon as or whenever requested. *supply and demand*: see SUPPLY *n.*

Comb.: **demand curve** a graph showing how the demand for a commodity or service varies with some other factor, esp. price; **demand deposit** *US* a bank account from which funds may be drawn on demand; **demand draft** a draft payable on demand; **demand-driven** *a.* (*Econ.*) caused or affected by consumer demand; **demand feeding**: of a baby when it cries, not according to a timetable; **demand-led** *a.* (*Econ.*) determined by consumer demand; **demand note** (*a*) a request for payment; (*b*) *US* = *demand draft* above.

demand /dɪˈmɑːnd/ *v.* LME. [(O)Fr. *demander* f. L *demandare* hand over, entrust, (in med.L) demand, request, f. *de-* DE- I + *mandare* to commission, order.] **I** *v.t.* **1** Ask for (a thing) imperiously, urgently, or authoritatively; ask peremptorily (*that*, *to do*); claim as of right. LME. **2** *Law.* Formally claim (esp. realty) as the rightful owner. LME. †**3** Ask (a person) formally or authoritatively to inform one (*of*, *how*, etc.). LME–E18. **4** Ask authoritatively or brusquely to know; insist on being told. Freq. w. direct speech as obj. L15. †**5** Ask (a person) *for*; require (a person) *to do*. E17–L18. **6** Ask to see (a person); require to appear, summon. M17. **7** Of a thing: require, need. E18.

1 GOLDSMITH Two ruffians . . demanded to speak with the king. L. RITCHIE To demand that the bones . . should be returned to their care. W. S. CHURCHILL The Crown claimed ownership . . and demanded a licence fee. 4 SHAKES. *Lucr.* They . . demanded the cause of her sorrow. J. STEINBECK 'What's funny about it?' George demanded defensively. 7 J. B. PRIESTLEY Fellows capable of working day and night . . when the occasion demanded it. C. S. FORESTER The temperament that demands immediate action in the face of a crisis.

II *v.i.* **8** Ask, inquire, make inquiry *of* (†*at*) a person etc. *arch.* LME. **9** Make a demand (†*for*), ask authoritatively. E16.

8 AV *Luke* 3:14 And the soldiers likewise demanded of him, saying, And what shall we do? 9 SHAKES. *All's Well* Our French lack language to deny, If they demand.

demandable *a.* that may be demanded or claimed LME. **demander** *n.* LME. **demanding** *a.* that demands; hard to satisfy, exacting, difficult: L19.

demandant /dɪˈmɑːnd(ə)nt/ *n.* L15. [AN, use as n. of pres. pple of (O)Fr. *demander*: see prec., -ANT¹.] **1** *Law.* A plaintiff, esp. in a real action. L15. **2** A person who makes a demand or claim. L16. **3** A person who questions or interrogates. M17.

demantoid /dɪˈmantɔɪd/ *n.* L19. [G, f. *Demant* diamond.] A lustrous green gem variety of andradite garnet.

demarcate /ˈdiːmɑːkeɪt/ *v.t.* E19. [Back-form. f. next: see -ATE³.] Mark out or determine the boundaries or limits of; separate or distinguish *from*.

demarcator *n.* L19.

demarcation /diːmɑːˈkeɪʃ(ə)n/ *n.* Also **-k-**. E18. [Sp. *demarcación* (Port. *demarcação*) f. *demarcar* mark out the bounds of, f. *de-* DE- I + *marcar* MARK *v.*: see -ATION.] The action of marking the boundary or limits of something; delimitation, separation; a dividing line (*lit.* & *fig.*). Orig. in *line of demarcation* below.

B. MAGEE Their chief aim was to find a criterion of demarcation between sense and nonsense. **line of demarcation** a dividing line; orig. *spec.* that dividing the New World between the Spanish and the Portuguese, decreed by Pope Alexander VI in 1493.

Comb.: **demarcation dispute** an industrial dispute concerning the separation of kinds of work considered by trade unions to belong to particular trades.

demarcative /dɪˈmɑːkətɪv/ *a.* M20. [f. prec.: see -ATIVE.] Chiefly *Ling.* Of, pertaining to, or characterized by demarcation; serving to demarcate words etc.

demarch /diːmɑːk/ *n.* M17. [L *demarchus* f. Gk *dēmarkhos*, f. *dēmos* people + *arkhos* leader.] In ancient Greece, the chief magistrate of an Attic deme. In modern Greece, the mayor of a commune.

démarche /demarʃ (*pl. same*), deɪˈmɑːʃ/ *n.* M17. [Fr., f. *démarcher* take steps, f. *dé-* DE- 1 + *marcher* MARCH *v.*²] A step, a proceeding; *esp.* a diplomatic action or initiative.

demark /diːˈmɑːk/ *v.t.* M19. [f. DEMARCATION after MARK *v.*] = DEMARCATE.

demarkation *n.* var. of DEMARCATION.

dematerialize /diːməˈtɪərɪəlaɪz/ *v.* Also **-ise.** L19. [f. DE- 3 + MATERIALIZE.] 1 *v.t.* Deprive of material character or qualities. L19. 2 *v.i.* Lose material qualities; cease to have material existence; *fig.* disappear, vanish. L19.

2 *Listener* Nuclear particles behave in embarrassingly paranormal ways, materialising and dematerialising.

dematerialiˈzation *n.* L19.

deme /diːm/ *n.* M19. [Gk *dēmos* DEMOS.] 1 A township of ancient Attica; an administrative division in modern Greece. M19. 2 *Biol.* A group of taxonomically similar animals or plants forming a distinct local population. M20.

†**demean** *n.* LME. [f. DEMEAN *v.*¹] 1 Bearing, behaviour, demeanour. LME–M18. 2 Treatment (of others). *rare* (Spenser). Only in L16.

demean /dɪˈmiːn/ *v.*¹*t.* ME. [(O)Fr. *démener* lead, exercise, practise, *se démener* behave, f. Proto-Romance, f. L *de-* DE- 1 + *minare* drive (animals), (orig.) drive on with threats, f. L *minari* threaten.] †1 Conduct, manage, control, handle. ME–M17. 2 *refl.* Behave, conduct oneself (in a specified way). ME. 3 Deal with (a person) in a particular way; *esp.* treat badly. *obs.* exc. *Sc.* LME. †4 Express, exhibit (an emotion etc.). LME–E17.

2 N. HAWTHORNE The Prince Borghese certainly demeans himself like a kind and liberal gentleman. 3 SPENSER That mighty man did her demeane With all the evill termes . . That he could make.

demean /dɪˈmiːn/ *v.*²*t.* E17. [f. DE- 1 + MEAN *a.*¹, after *debase.*] Lower in dignity or status, humble, (esp. oneself).

W. BLACK Could a girl so far demean herself as to ask for love? M. BRADBURY That demeans them into something trivial.

demeaning *ppl a.* that demeans; beneath one's dignity: L19.

demeanour /dɪˈmiːnə/ *n.* Also *-**or.** L15. [f. DEMEAN *v.*¹, prob. by assoc. w. †*havour* HAVIOUR: see -OUR.] 1 Conduct, way of acting, behaviour, esp. towards others. Formerly also, an action (cf. MISDEMEANOUR). Now *rare.* L15. 2 Bearing, mien, outward manner. L15.

2 E. WAUGH Curiosity and resentment contended for mastery in Troutbeck's demeanour. A. HIGGINS Trying to assume a calmness of demeanour which she did not feel.

démêlé /demele/ *n.* Pl. pronounced same. M17. [Fr. = quarrel, contest.] A debate, a contention, a quarrel.

†**demember** *v.t. Sc.* LME–E18. [Fr. *démembrer* or med.L *demembrare*: see next.] = DISMEMBER.

demembration /diːmɛmˈbreɪʃ(ə)n/ *n. obs.* exc. *Hist.* L16. [med.L *demembratio(n-)*, f. *demembrat-* pa. ppl stem of *demembrare* var. of *dismembrare* dismember: see DISMEMBRATION, -ATION.] Chiefly *Sc. Law.* The cutting off of a limb; dismemberment.

déménagement /demenaʒmɑ̃/ *n.* L19. [Fr.] The removal of household possessions from one place to another; moving house.

demency /ˈdɛm(ə)nsi/ *n.* Long *rare.* E16. [f. as DEMENTIA: see -ENCY.] Madness, dementia, loss of mental faculties.

dement /dɪˈmɛnt/ *a.* & *n.* L15. [Fr. *dément* or L *demens*: see next.] A *adj.* Demented, insane. Long *rare.* L15. B *n.* A person affected with dementia. L19.

dement /dɪˈmɛnt/ *v.t.* M16. [OFr. *dementer* or late L *dementare*, f. *demens*, *-ment-* insane, f. *de-* DE- 3 + *mens*, *ment-* mind.] Send out of one's mind, drive mad.

demenˈtation *n.* [med.L *dementatio(n-)*] the act of dementing; the state or fact of being demented: E17.

dementate /dɪˈmɛnteɪt/ *v.t.* Now *rare* or *obs.* E17. [L *dementat-* pa. ppl stem of *dementare*: see prec., -ATE³.] = prec.

demented /dɪˈmɛntɪd/ *a.* M17. [f. DEMENT *v.* + -ED¹.] 1 Out of one's mind; crazy, mad. M17. 2 *Med.* Suffering from dementia. L19.

dementedly *adv.* L19. **dementedness** *n.* L19.

démenti /demɑ̃ti/ *n.* Pl. pronounced same. L16. [Fr., f. *démentir* contradict, f. *dé-* DE- 3 + *mentir* to lie.] A contradiction, a denial; now *esp.* an official denial of a published statement.

dementia /dɪˈmɛnʃə/ *n.* L18. [L, f. *demens*: see DEMENT *v.*, -IA¹.] 1 *Psychiatry.* Chronic mental and emotional deterioration caused by organic brain disease. L18. 2 Madness, folly. L19.

1 ***dementia praecox*** /ˈpriːkɒks/ *n.* (now *arch.* or *Hist.*) [L *praecox* precocious] = SCHIZOPHRENIA. *senile dementia*: see SENILE *a.* 1.

demerara /dɛməˈrɛːrə, -ˈrɑːrə/ *n.* Also **D-.** M19. [*Demerara* (see below).] In full *demerara sugar.* A light-brown raw cane-sugar orig. and chiefly from the Demerara region of Guyana.

demerger /diːˈməːdʒə/ *n.* M20. [f. DE- 3 + MERGER.] The dissolution of a merger between companies etc.

demerit /diːˈmɛrɪt/ *n.* LME. [OFr. *de(s)merite* or L *demeritum*, f. *demerit-* pa. ppl stem of *demereri* merit, deserve, f. *de-* DE- 1, 3 + *mereri* MERIT *v.*] 1 A quality that deserves reward or gratitude, merit, worth. Freq. in *pl.* Long *arch. rare.* LME. †b A meritorious or deserving act. M16–M17. 2 Quality or conduct deserving censure; lack of merit, a defect. LME. †b A blameworthy act, a sin, an offence. LME–M17. †3 That which is deserved, one's desert; *esp.* punishment. E17–E18. 4 In full *demerit mark.* A mark awarded against an offender, esp. in a school or the armed forces or for traffic offences. Chiefly *N. Amer.* E20.

1 J. GAY Envy not the demerits of those who are most conspicuously distinguished. 2 S. RICHARDSON God teach me humility, and to know my own demerit! J. K. GALBRAITH They . . oppose the expenditure not on the merits of the service but on the demerits of the tax system. 3 A. CADE Ahab . . had quickly his demerits, being destroyed. 4 M. J. BRUCCOLI He accumulated conduct demerits and did poorly in his studies.

demerit /diːˈmɛrɪt/ *v.* LME. [L *demerit-* (see prec); partly after Fr. *démériter.*] I *v.t.* †1 Merit, deserve, be worthy of, earn. LME–E18. †2a Take away the merit of, disparage. L16–M17. b Give a demerit (DEMERIT *n.* 4) to. *US.* L19. 3 Fail to merit; deserve to lose or be without. *arch.* M17. II *v.i.* †4 Incur or deserve disapproval or blame. E17–M18.

demeriˈtorious *a.* blameworthy, sinful LME.

Demerol /ˈdɛmərɒl/ *n.* M20. [Origin unkn.] *Pharm.* (Proprietary name for) pethidine.

demersal /dɪˈməːs(ə)l/ *a.* L19. [f. L *demersus* pa. pple of *demergere* submerge, sink, f. *de-* DE- 1 + *mergere* plunge, dip: see -AL¹.] (Of fish etc.) living near the bottom of the sea; (of fish-eggs) deposited at or sinking to the seabed.

demerse /dɪˈməːs/ *v.t. arch.* LME. [L *demers-* pa. ppl stem of *demergere*: see prec.] Immerse, submerge.

demersion *n.* (now *rare* or *obs.*) [L *demersio(n-)*] L17.

demesmerize /diːˈmɛzməraɪz/ *v.t.* Also **-ise.** M19. [f. DE- 3 + MESMERIZE.] Bring out of a hypnotic state.

demesne /dɪˈmeɪn, dɪˈmiːn/ *n.* & *a.* ME. [AN, OFr. *demeine*, later AN *demesne*, use as n. of adj. = of or belonging to a lord, f. L *dominicus* of a lord or master, f. *dominus* lord. Cf. DOMAIN.] A *n.* 1 *Law* (now *Hist.*). The possession of real property as one's own. ME. †b *gen.* Possession; dominion, power. ME–M18. 2a The land or territory subject to a ruler: sovereign territory; a realm, domain. *arch.* ME. b *sing.* & (freq.) in *pl.* Landed property, estates. L16. 3a *Hist.* Land held and worked by the owner for the maintenance of his or her own household, i.e. not let to a subordinate tenant. LME. b The land immediately adjacent to a manor-house etc. retained by the owner for his or her own use; the park, home farm, etc. M16. 4 *fig.* A district, a region; the territory or sphere *of. arch.* or *poet.* L16.

Phrases: **ancient demesne** (tenure of) land recorded in Domesday Book as belonging to the Crown. **demesne of the Crown** the Crown Lands. **hold in demesne** occupy as the owner, not sublet to a tenant or tenants. **in one's demesne as of fee** in one's possession as an inherited estate. **royal demesne** = *demesne of the Crown* above.

B *attrib.* or as *adj.* Of, pertaining to, or constituting a demesne. LME.

demesnial *a.* = DEMESNE *a.* M19.

demethylate /diːˈmɛθɪleɪt/ *v.t.* M20. [f. DE- 3 + METHYLATE *v.*] *Chem.* Remove a methyl group from (a molecule).

demethyˈlation *n.* E20.

Demetian /dɪˈmiːʃ(ə)n/ *a.* Also **Di-.** M18. [f. *Demetia*, *Dimetia* (see below) + -AN.] Of or pertaining to an area in SW Wales (once the ancient kingdom of Demetia and now the county of Dyfed) its inhabitants, or the dialect of English spoken there.

demi *n.* pl. of DEMOS.

demi *a.* & *n.* see DEMY.

demi- /ˈdɛmi/ *pref.* [f. Fr. *demi* f. med.L *dimedius* half, for L *dimidius.* Cf. DEMY.] Used in wds adopted f. Fr. and in Eng. formations w. the senses 'half, half-sized, partial(ly), curtailed, inferior', forming ns. f. ns., as *demigod*, *demilune*, *demi-monde*, *demisemiquaver*, etc., or, less commonly, adjs. f. adjs. and vbs f. vbs. Prevalent in some subjects w. much vocabulary of Fr. origin, as *Heraldry*, *Costume*, *Armour*, *Fortification*, etc., but as a living prefix almost completely displaced by SEMI-.

demi-ˈbastion *n.* (*Fortif.*) a half-bastion comprising one flank and one front L17. **demi-ˈcannon** *n.* (*Hist.*) a cannon of about 6½ inches (16.5 cm) bore M16. †**demicastor** *n.* (a hat made from) inferior beaver's fur or a mixture of beaver's and other fur M17–E18. **demi-circle** *n.* (now *rare*) a semicircle M17. **demi-ˈculverin** *n.* (*Hist.*) a cannon of about 4½ inches (11.4 cm) bore L16. **demi-devil** *n.* a half-devil E17. **demi-gorge** *n.* (*Fortif.*) the length of half of the gorge or entrance of a bastion, measured from either point where the bastion joins the curtain to the point of intersection of the lines of the adjacent curtains E18. **demi-hag, -hake** *n.* (*Hist.*) a small hackbut M16. †**demi-isle** *n.* a peninsula E17–L18. **demi-lion** *n.* (*Her.*) a figure of a lion cut off below the waist E17. †**demi-puppet** *n.* (*rare*, Shakes.) a half-sized or dwarf puppet: only in E17. †**demi-tint** *n.* (*Painting*) a half tint M18–E19. **demi-toilet(te)** *n.* half evening (or dinner) dress, not full dress E19. **demi-volte** *n.* (*Horsemanship*) a 180-degree turn pivoting on the horse's quarters M17.

demi-caractère /ˌdɛmikarəkˈtɛː, *foreign* dəmikaraktɛːr (*pl. same*)/ *n.* & *a.* L18. [Fr., lit. 'half character'.] *Ballet.* A *n.* A dance retaining the form of the character dance but executed with steps based on the classical technique. Also, a dancer of demi-caractères. L18. B *adj.* Of, pertaining to, or designating dancing of this kind. E19.

demi-glace /ˈdɛmɪglas/ *n.* E20. [Fr., lit. 'half-glaze'.] *Cookery.* In full *demi-glace sauce.* A meat-stock from which the liquid has been partially evaporated.

demigod /ˈdɛmɪgɒd/ *n.* M16. [f. DEMI- + GOD *n.*, tr. L *semideus.*] In *Mythol.*, a partly divine being: the offspring of a god and a mortal, a mortal raised to divine rank, or an inferior deity; *gen.*, a person who has godlike powers. Cf. SEMIGOD.

demigoddess *n.* (*rare*) a female demigod E17.

†**demigration** *n.* E17–M18. [L *demigratio(n-)*, f. *demigrat-* pa. ppl stem of *demigrare*, f. *de* DE- 1 + *migrare* MIGRATE: see -ATION.] Removing oneself to another place; migration.

demijohn /ˈdɛmɪdʒɒn/ *n.* M18. [Prob. alt. of Fr. *dame-jeanne* 'Lady Jane', assim. to DEMI- and JOHN.] A bulging narrow-necked bottle holding from 3 to 10 gallons (13.6 to 45.5 litres), usu. cased in wicker and with one or two wicker handles.

demi-lance /ˈdɛmɪlɑːns/ *n. obs.* exc. *Hist.* L15. [Fr. †*demie lance* lit. 'half lance'.] 1 A lance with a short shaft, chiefly used in the 15th and 16th cents. L15. 2 A light horseman armed with a demi-lance. M16.

demi-lancer *n.* = DEMI-LANCE 2 M16.

demilitarize /diːˈmɪlɪtərʌɪz/ *v.t.* Also **-ise**. L19. [f. DE- 3 + MILITARIZE.] Remove the military organization or forces from (a frontier, zone, etc.); place (a State) under an obligation not to maintain armed forces.

demilitariˈzation *n.* L19.

demilune /ˈdɛmɪluːn/ *n.* & *a.* E18. [Fr. *demi-lune* lit. 'half-moon'. Cf. SEMILUNE.] **A** *n.* 1 *Fortif.* An outwork resembling a bastion, with a crescent-shaped gorge. E18. 2 A half-moon, a crescent; a crescent-shaped body. M18. **B** *adj.* Crescent-shaped, semilunar. L19.

demi-mondaine /dəmimɔ̃dɛn (*pl. same*), ˌdɛmɪmɒnˈdeɪn/ *n.* L19. [Fr., f. as next.] A woman of the *demi-monde*.

demi-monde /dəmimɔ̃d; dɛmɪˈmɒnd, ˈdɛmɪ mɒnd/ *n.* M19. [Fr., lit. 'half world'.] The class of women of doubtful reputation and social standing; the class of kept women or *loosely* of prostitutes; *transf.* any social group regarded as behaving with doubtful propriety or legality.

demineralize /diːˈmɪn(ə)r(ə)lʌɪz/ *v.t.* Also **-ise**. M20. [f. DE- 3 + MINERALIZE.] Remove the salts from (seawater etc.).

demineraliˈzation *n.* (*a*) an abnormal loss of salts from the body; (*b*) the removal of salts from seawater etc.: E20. **demineralizer** *n.* an apparatus or installation for demineralization M20.

demi-ostage /dɛmɪˈɒstɪdʒ/ *n.* Long *obs.* exc. *Hist.* Also **-ostade** /-stəd/. E16. [OFr. *demie ostade*, f. *demi(e)* DEMI- + *ostade* worsted.] A cloth, half-worsted half-linen; linsey-woolsey.

demiourgos *n.* see DEMIURGE.

demi-pension /dəmipɑ̃sjɔ̃/ *n.* M20. [Fr.] In France etc.: (the price of) bed, breakfast, and one other meal at a hotel etc.; half-board.

demi-pique /ˈdɛmɪpiːk/ *n.* & *a.* L17. [f. DEMI- + alt. of PEAK *n.*[1] (Not conn. w. Fr. *demi-pique* half-pike.)] *Hist.* (Designating) a saddle having a peak of about half the height of that of the older war-saddle.

demi-piqued *a.* M18.

demi-rep /ˈdɛmɪrɛp/ *n. arch.* M18. [f. DEMI- + abbrev. of REPUTABLE. Cf. REP *n.*[2]] A woman of doubtful reputation, esp. as regards chastity.

demi-saison /dəmisɛzɔ̃/ *a.* M18. [Fr., lit. 'half season'.] Of a style of fashion: intermediate between that of the past and that of the coming season.

demise /dɪˈmʌɪz/ *n.* & *v.* LME. [AN, use as n. of fem. pa. pple of OFr. *de(s)mettre* (mod. *démettre*) dismiss, (refl.) resign, abdicate.] **A** *n.* 1a *Law.* Conveyance or transfer of an estate by will or lease; an instance of this. LME. b Transference of sovereignty, as by the death or deposition of the sovereign. Chiefly in *demise of the crown*. M17. 2 A death which occasions such transference; *gen.* death; downfall, disappearance, final fate. M16.

2 S. RICHARDSON Her father's considerable estate, on his demise . . went with the name. GLADSTONE The Odyssey does not bring us to the demise of Odusseus. C. BEATON The war of 1914–18 had hastened the demise of the tightly swathed skirt.

B *v.* 1 *v.t. Law.* Convey or grant (an estate) by will or lease. LME. b Transmit (a title etc., esp. sovereignty) by death or abdication. L17. †2 *v.t.* a Let go; dismiss. M16–E17. b Pass on, impart. L16–M17. 3 *v.i.* Decease, die; pass on the crown (by death). *rare*. E18.

1b G. B. SMITH He . . recommended the Convention to declare that James II had voluntarily demised the crown. 2b SHAKES. *Rich. III* What Honour Canst thou demise to any child of mine?

demisable *a.* M17.

demi-sec /dɛmɪˈsɛk; *foreign* dəmisɛk/ *a.* M20. [Fr., lit. 'half-dry'.] Of wine: medium dry.

demi-semi- /ˈdɛmɪsɛmi/ *pref.* Also as adj. **demi-semi**. E19. [f. DEMI- + SEMI-, after next.] Half half-, quarter-. Usu. *derog.*, insignificant, inadequate. Cf. SEMI-DEMI-.

demisemiquaver /ˈdɛmɪsɛmɪˌkweɪvə/ *n.* E18. [f. DEMI- + SEMIQUAVER.] *Mus.* A note of half the value of a semiquaver, represented as a quaver with three hooks.

demiss /dɪˈmɪs/ *a.* L16. [L *demissus* let down, dejected, pa. pple of *demittere* DEMIT *v.*[1]] 1 Submissive, humble; abject, base. *arch.* L16. †2 Hanging down; *esp.* (of the head or countenance) downcast. L16–L17.

†**demissive** *a.* = DEMISS E17–M18. **demissness** *n.* (*arch.*) E17.

demission /dɪˈmɪʃ(ə)n/ *n.*[1] M16. [Fr. *démission*, OFr. *desmission*, corresponding to med.L var. of L *dimissio(n-)* DIMISSION.] 1 Resignation, relinquishment, abdication. M16. 2 Sending away, dismissal. *rare*. E19.

1 T. CARTE Apply to his Majesty for a demission of his charge. G. HUNTINGTON I was sent to a post abroad. But I am at liberty to give my demission.

demission /dɪˈmɪʃ(ə)n/ *n.*[2] M17. [L *demissio(n-)*, f. *demiss-* pa. ppl stem of *demittere*: see DEMIT *v.*[1], -ION.] 1 Abasement, degradation. Now *rare*. M17. †2 Dejection, depression. M17–E18. †3 Lowering; bending down. E–M18.

†**demissory** *n.* & *a.* var. of DIMISSORY.

demist /diːˈmɪst/ *v.t.* M20. [f. DE- 3 + MIST *n.*[1]] Clear the mist from (a windscreen etc.).

demister *n.* a device for demisting a windscreen etc. M20.

demit /dɪˈmɪt/ *v.*[1]*t.* Also †**di-**. Infl. **-tt-**. LME. [L *demittere* let or send down, f. *de-* DE- 1 + *mittere* send.] †1 Abase, humble (oneself). LME–L17. 2 Send, put, or let down; lower. E17.

demit /dɪˈmɪt/ *v.*[2] Chiefly *Sc.* Infl. **-tt-**. E16. [Fr. *démettre*, OFr. *desmettre*, f. *des-*, *dé-* DE- 3 + *mettre*, taking the place of L *dimittere*: see DIMIT *v.*[1], DISMISS *v.*] 1 *v.t.* Let go, send away, dismiss. *arch.* E16. †2 *v.t.* Put away, part with. M16–L17. 3 *v.t.* & *i.* Resign; abdicate. M16. †4 *v.t.* Send out. L17–M18. †5 *v.t.* Convey by lease. Only in L18.

demitasse /ˈdɛmɪtas; *foreign* dəmitɑs (*pl. same*)/ *n.* M19. [Fr., lit. 'half-cup'.] (The contents of) a small coffee-cup.

demiurge /ˈdiːmɪəːdʒ, ˈdɛm-/ *n.* Also in Gk form **demiourgos** /diːmɪˈaʊəgəs/, pl. **-goi** /-gɔɪ/, & (earliest) L form **demiurgus** /diːmɪˈəːgəs/, pl. **-gi** /-dʒʌɪ/. E17. [eccl.L *demiurgus* f. Gk *dēmiourgos* craftsman, artisan, f. *dēmios* public (f. as DEMOS) + *-ergos* working.] 1 *Gk Hist.* A magistrate in certain Greek States and in the Achaean League. E17. 2 (Also **D-**.) In Platonic philosophy, the fashioner of the world. In Gnosticism etc., the being subordinate to the supreme being, who is responsible for the existence of the world. L17.

demiˈurgic *a.* of or pertaining to the demiurge or the work of the demiurge; creative: L17. †**demiurgical** *a.* = DEMIURGIC E17–L18. **demiˈurgically** *adv.* E19.

demi-vierge /dəmivjɛrʒ/ *n.* Pl. pronounced same. E20. [Fr., lit. 'half-virgin', f. *Les demi-vierges* (1874), a novel by M. Prévost.] A woman who behaves licentiously while remaining a virgin.

demn *v.* var. of DEM *v.*

demnition /dɛmˈnɪʃ(ə)n/ *n.*, *a.*, & *adv.* Chiefly *US.* M19. [Repr. alt. pronunc.] = DAMNATION *n.* 3, *a.* & *adv.*

Demo /ˈdɛməʊ/ *n.*[1] *US colloq.* Pl. **-os**. L18. [Abbrev.] = DEMOCRAT *n.* 2.

demo /ˈdɛməʊ/ *n.*[2] *colloq.* Pl. **-os**. M20. [Abbrev. of DEMONSTRATION. Cf. DEM *n.*] **A** *n.* 1 = DEMONSTRATION 6. M20. 2 A practical demonstration of the capabilities of a piece of equipment, computer software, group of musicians, etc.; a piece of equipment, software, a recording, etc., displayed or distributed for this purpose. Freq. *attrib.* M20.

2 attrib.: *demo-disc*, *-tape*, etc.

B *v.t.* Give a practical demonstration of; *esp.* record (a song etc.) or display (an item of esp. computing equipment) for demonstration purposes. L20.

demob /diːˈmɒb/ *v.* & *n. colloq.* E20. [Abbrev.] **A** *v.t.* Infl. **-bb-**. = DEMOBILIZE. E20. **B** *n.* = DEMOBILIZATION. M20.

Comb.: **demob suit** a suit issued to a serviceman on demobilization.

demobilize /diːˈməʊbɪlʌɪz/ *v.t.* Also **-ise**. L19. [Fr. *démobiliser*, f. as DE- 3 + MOBILIZE.] Release from a mobilized state or from service in the armed forces; disband (troops etc.).

demobiliˈzation *n.* the action of demobilizing, the disbanding of troops etc. M19.

democracy /dɪˈmɒkrəsi/ *n.* L16. [(O)Fr. *démocratie* f. late L *democratia* f. Gk *dēmokratia*, f. as DEMOS + -CRACY.] 1 Government by the people; a form of government in which the power resides in the people and is exercised by them either directly or by means of elected representatives; a form of society which favours equal rights, the ignoring of hereditary class distinctions, and tolerance of minority views. L16. 2 A State or community in which the power of government resides in or is exercised by the people. L16. 3 That class of people which has no hereditary or special rank or privilege; the common people. Now *rare*. M17. 4 (**D-**.) The Democratic Party of the US; its principles or members. *US*. E19.

1 G. M. TREVELYAN An age of transition from aristocracy to democracy, from authority to mass-judgement. B. CASTLE The Labour Party . . rank and file were ready to defend the unions to death as a vital expression of democracy. 2 C. S. LEWIS All nations, those we call democracies as well as dictatorships.

democrat /ˈdɛməkrat/ *n.* & *a.* L18. [Fr. *démocrate*, f. as prec. after *aristocrate* ARISTOCRAT.] **A** *n.* 1 An adherent or advocate of democracy; orig. (now *Hist.*), an opponent of the aristocrats in the French Revolution of 1790. L18. 2 (**D-**.) A member of the Democratic Party of the US, or more widely, of any political party styled 'Democratic'. L18. 3 More fully *democrat wagon*. A light wagon seating two or more people and usu. drawn by two horses. *N. Amer.* (now *Hist.*). L19.

1 H. ARENDT A true democrat, he wanted to liberate an oppressed people and not bestow privileges upon individuals. 2 *Christian Democrat*, *Social Democrat*, etc. 3 B. BROOKER There were buggies and democrats drawn up at the stores.

B *adj.* Democratic. *rare*. L18.

democratic /dɛməˈkratɪk/ *a.* & *n.* E17. [(O)Fr. *démocratique* f. med.L *democraticus* f. Gk *dēmokratikos*, f. *dēmokratia* DEMOCRACY: see -IC.] **A** *adj.* 1 Of the nature of or characterized by democracy; advocating or upholding democracy; *gen.* favouring social equality. E17. 2 (**D-**.) Of or pertaining to a political party styled 'Democratic', *spec.* the US Democratic Party (see below). E19.

1 A. S. NEILL Summerhill is a self-governing school, democratic in form. D. BOGARDE He rather wished the General was not so damned democratic, and had not insisted on sharing everyone's discomfort. *fig.*: *Nature* All the . . neutrinos would interact equally, the neutral current being 'democratic' in neutrino types. 2 *Christian Democratic*, *Social Democratic*, etc. **Democratic Party** one of the two main US political parties (the other being *Republican*) which generally supports international commitment and broad social reform.

B *n.* = DEMOCRAT *n. rare*. M17.

democratical *a.* & *n.* (*a*) *adj.* = DEMOCRATIC *a.* 1; †(*b*) *n.* = DEMOCRAT *n.* 1: L16. **democratically** *adv.* E17.

democratise *v.* var. of DEMOCRATIZE.

democratism /dɪˈmɒkrətɪz(ə)m/ *n.* L18. [f. DEMOCRAT + -ISM.] Democracy as a principle or system.

democratize /dɪˈmɒkrətʌɪz/ *v.* Also **-ise**. L18. [Fr. *démocratiser*, f. as DEMOCRAT, DEMOCRACY: see -IZE.] 1 *v.t.* Make democratic; give a democratic character to. L18. 2 *v.i.* Become democratic. *rare*. M19.

democratiˈzation *n.* M19. **democratizer** *n.* L19.

Democritean /dɪˌmɒkrɪˈtiːən/ *a.* M19. [f. L *Democriteus* (Gk *Dēmokriteios*) + -AN.] Of, pertaining to, or after the style of the Greek philosopher Democritus (5th cent. BC), or of his theories.

Also †**Democrital** *a.*: only in E17. **Demoˈcritic** *a.* M17. †**Democritical** *a.* M17–E18.

démodé /demode, deɪˈməʊdeɪ/ *a.* L19. [Fr., pa. pple of *démoder* send or go out of fashion, f. *dé-*

DE- 3 + *mode* fashion.] Out of fashion, unfashionable.

demodectic /diːməˈdɛktɪk/ *a.* Also (earlier) **-decic** /-ˈdiːsɪk/. L19. [f. mod.L *Demodex* (see below) f. Gk *dēmos* fat + *dēx* woodworm, + -IC.] *Vet. Med.* Of, pertaining to, or caused by parasitic mites of the genus *Demodex*.

demoded /diːˈməʊdɪd/ *a.* L19. [f. DÉMODÉ + -ED[1].] = DÉMODÉ.

demodulation /ˌdiːmɒdjʊˈleɪʃ(ə)n/ *n.* E20. [f. DE- 3 + MODULATION.] *Electronics & Physics.* The process of extracting a modulating signal from the carrier wave.

deˈmodulate *v.t.* extract (a modulating signal) from its carrier; separate a modulating signal from: M20. **deˈmodulator** *n.* a device or circuit used to effect demodulation E20.

Demogorgon /diːməˈgɔːg(ə)n/ *n.* L16. [Late L *Demogorgon* of uncertain origin: perh. a disguised oriental name.] *Mythol.* (The name of) a mysterious and terrible infernal god.

demographic /dɛməˈgrafɪk, diː-/ *a.* & *n.* L19. [f. next: see -GRAPHIC.] A *adj.* Of or pertaining to demography. L19. B *n.* In *pl.* Demographic statistics; (usu. treated as *sing.*) the branch of knowledge that deals with these. M20.

demographical *a.* = DEMOGRAPHIC *a.* E20. **demographically** *adv.* E20.

demography /dɪˈmɒgrəfi/ *n.* L19. [f. Gk *dēmos* people + -OGRAPHY.] The branch of knowledge that deals with human populations; *esp.* the statistical analysis of births, deaths, migrations, disease, etc., as illustrating the conditions of life in communities.

demographer *n.* L19.

demoiselle /dɛmwɑːˈzɛl/ *n.* E16. [Fr.: see DAMSEL.] 1 A young lady, a girl. *arch.* E16. 2 A Eurasian and N. African crane, *Anthropoides virgo*, with elongated black breast-feathers and white neck-plumes. Now usu. more fully *demoiselle crane*. L17. 3 A dragonfly or (*esp.*) a damselfly. M19. 4 A damselfish. L19.

demolish /dɪˈmɒlɪʃ/ *v.t.* M16. [(O)Fr. *démoliss-* lengthened stem of *démolir* f. L *demoliri*, f. *de-* DE- 3 + *moliri* construct, f. *moles* mass: see MOLE *n.*[3], -ISH[2].] 1 Destroy (a building etc.) by violent disintegration of its fabric; pull or throw down. M16. 2 Overthrow (an institution); refute (a theory); make an end of. E17. 3 Eat up quickly and entirely. *joc.* M18.

1 G. ORWELL The bomb had demolished a group of houses. A. N. WILSON The City Council wanted to demolish a derelict church . . to make way for . . a Leisure Park. 2 *New Statesman* [The authors] demolish the myth that Labour owed its 1974 victory to public . . approval of its radical promises. 3 J. BEERBOHM He demolished the whole side of a young guanacho at one sitting.

demolishable *a.* L18. **demolisher** *n.* E17. **demolishment** *n.* (now *rare*) = DEMOLITION E17.

demolition /dɛməˈlɪʃ(ə)n, diː-/ *n.* M16. [(O)Fr. *démolition* f. L *demolitio(n-)*, f. *demolit-* pa. ppl stem of *demoliri*: see prec., -ITION.] 1 Destruction, overthrow. Chiefly *fig.* use of sense 2. M16. 2 The action of demolishing a building etc.; the fact or state of being demolished. E17. 3 In *pl.* Demolished remains, ruins. Long *rare*. M17.

Comb.: **demolition ball** a large metal ball which, hung from a crane, may be swung against a building to demolish it; **demolition derby** (orig. *US*) a competition in which cars are driven so as to collide; **demolition order**: issued by a local authority for the pulling down of a building or buildings.

demolitionist *n.* a person who aims at or advocates demolition M19.

demon /ˈdiːmən/ *n.*[1] In senses 2, 3 also **dae-**. ME. [med.L *demon*, L *daemon* f. Gk *daimōn* divinity, genius. Cf. (O)Fr. *démon*. Also (in sense 1) repr. L *daemonium*, Gk dim. *daimonion*. Cf. DAIMON.] 1 An evil spirit; a malignant being of superhuman nature. ME. b Esp. in biblical translations and allusions: an evil or unclean spirit possessing or actuating a demoniac; a heathen god or idol. E18. 2 An attendant or indwelling spirit, one's genius; = DAIMON. LME. 3 *Gk Mythol.* A being of a nature between that of gods and men; an inferior divinity, a spirit; the soul of a deceased person regarded as an inferior divinity. M16. 4 A person, or personified animal or thing, of a malignant or terrible nature or of a hideous appearance. E17. 5 *fig.* An evil passion or agency, now *esp.* alcoholic drink, regarded as a spirit or devil. E18. 6 A person of superhuman or diabolical energy, skill, etc.; an action etc. exhibiting superhuman or diabolical energy, skill, etc. L19. 7 *Cards.* A form of patience (also *demon patience*); *esp.* (also *racing demon*) a competitive version of this using several packs. L19.

1 T. WRIGHT The three special characteristics of mediæval demons were horns, hoofs . . and tails. 2 SHAKES. *Ant. & Cl.* Antony. . . Thy dæmon . . is Noble, courageous, high, unmatchable. 3 J. BRYANT Subordinate daemons, which they supposed to be emanations and derivatives from their chief Deity. 4 CARLYLE The Tartar Khan, with his shaggy demons of the wilderness. 5 JOYCE Had her father only avoided the clutches of the demon drink. 6 **a demon for work** etc. a person who works etc. strenuously. *Maxwell's demon*: see MAXWELL.

Comb.: **demon bowler** *Cricket* a particularly successful bowler in a match or series; *demon patience*: see sense 7 above.

demoness *n.* a female demon M17. **demonish** *a.* (*rare*) demonic M19.

demon /ˈdiːmən/ *n.*[2] *Austral. slang.* L19. [App. f. Van *Diemen*'s Land, an early name for Tasmania, after prec.] 1 A police officer; a detective. L19. 2 A bushranger; a convict. E20.

demonetize /diːˈmʌnɪtʌɪz, -mɒn-/ *v.t.* Also **-ise**. M19. [Fr. *démonétiser*, f. *dé-* DE- 3 + L *moneta* MONEY *n.*: see -IZE. Cf. MONETIZE.] Deprive of standard monetary value; withdraw (gold etc.) from use as money.

demonetiˈzation *n.* M19.

demoniac /dɪˈməʊnɪak/ *a.* & *n.* LME. [(O)Fr. *démoniaque* f. eccl.L *daemoniacus*, f. *daemonium*: see DEMON *n.*[1], -AC.] A *adj.* 1 Possessed by a demon or an evil spirit. LME. b Of or pertaining to possession by evil spirits. L17. 2 Of or pertaining to demons. M17. 3 Befitting a demon, devilish. E19. 4 = DEMONIC 2. M19. B *n.* A person possessed by a demon or evil spirit. LME.

demoniacal /diːməˈnʌɪək(ə)l, dɛm-/ *a.* = DEMONIAC *a.* 1, 2, 3 E17. **demoniacally** /diːməˈnʌɪək(ə)li/ *adv.* E19.

demonian /dɪˈməʊnɪən/ *a.* L17. [f. L *daemonium*: see DEMON *n.*[1], -AN.] Of, relating to, or of the nature of a demon or demons.

demonial *a.* (*rare*) [OFr.] = DEMONIAN L17. **demonianism** *n.* (the doctrine of) demoniacal possession M18.

demonic /dɪˈmɒnɪk/ *a.* Also (esp. in sense 2) **dae-**. M17. [Late L *daemonicus* f. Gk *daimonikos*, f. *daimon*: see DEMON *n.*[1], -IC.] 1 Of, belonging to, or of the nature of an evil spirit; devilish. M17. 2 Relating to, of the nature of, or having supernatural power or genius. L18.

demonical *a.* (*a*) = DEMONIC 1; (*b*) = DEMONIAC *a.* 1: L15. **demonically** *adv.* in a manner befitting a demon; superhumanly: E20.

demonise *v.* var. of DEMONIZE.

demonism /ˈdiːmənɪz(ə)m/ *n.* Also **dae-**. L17. [f. DEMON *n.*[1] + -ISM.] Belief in the evil power of demons; worship of demons; the doctrine of demons.

demonist *n.* a believer in or worshipper of demons M17.

demonize /ˈdiːmənʌɪz/ *v.t.* Also **-ise**. L18. [f. DEMON *n.*[1] + -IZE.] 1 Make into or like a demon; represent as a demon. L18. 2 Subject to demonic influence. M19.

demoniˈzation *n.* the action of making into or like a demon L18.

demono- /ˈdiːmənəʊ/ *comb. form.* [Repr. Gk *daimono-* comb. form of *daimon* DEMON *n.*[1]: see -O-.] Of or relating to demons.

demoˈnocracy *n.* the rule of demons M18. **demoˈnographer** *n.* a writer on demons M18. **demoˈnolatrous** *a.* of, pertaining to, of the nature of, or practising demon-worship M19. **demoˈnolatry** *n.* demon-worship M17. **demonoˈmania** *n.* a mental illness in which the patient believes himself or herself possessed by an evil spirit M19.

demonology /diːməˈnɒlədʒi/ *n.* Also †**dae-**. L16. [f. prec. + -LOGY.] The branch of knowledge that deals with demons or with beliefs about demons; a treatise on demons.

demonoˈlogical *a.* concerned with demonology E19. **demonoˈlogically** *adv.* M19. **demonologist** *n.* a person versed in demonology L17.

demonopolize /diːməˈnɒpəlʌɪz/ *v.t.* Also **-ise**. L19. [f. DE- 3 + MONOPOLIZE.] Destroy the monopoly of; make no longer a monopoly.

demonopoliˈzation *n.* L20.

demonstrable /dɪˈmɒnstrəb(ə)l, ˈdɛmən-/ *a.* LME. [L *demonstrabilis*, f. *demonstrare*: see DEMONSTRATE *v.*, -ABLE.] 1 Able to be shown or made evident. Formerly also occas., evident. LME. 2 Able to be proved conclusively. LME.

demonstraˈbility *n.* the quality or condition of being demonstrable E19. **demonstrableness** *n.* L17. **demonstrably** *adv.* so as to be demonstrable; by demonstration: M17.

†**demonstrance** *n.* LME. [OFr., f. *demonstrer* f. L *demonstrare*: see DEMONSTRATE *v.*, -ANCE.] 1 A pointing out, a sign; indication. LME–E18. 2 Demonstration, proof. LME–M17.

†**demonstrate** *a.* (*pa. pple*). E16. [L *demonstratus* pa. pple, f. as next: see -ATE[2].] 1 Evident. E16–M17. 2 Demonstrated. L16–E18.

demonstrate /ˈdɛmənstreɪt/ *v.* M16. [L *demonstrat-* pa. ppl stem of *demonstrare*, f. *de-* DE- 1 + *monstrare* to show: see -ATE[3].] †1 *v.t.* Point out, indicate; set out. M16–L17. 2 *v.t.* Make known by outward indications; manifest, show; show evidence of (feelings etc.). L16. 3 *v.t.* Establish by logical reasoning or argument, or by practical proof; prove beyond doubt, prove the existence or reality of. L16. 4 *v.t.* Describe and explain with the help of examples or specimens, or by experiments; display, explain, and implement the working functions of (a piece of equipment, etc.). L17. b *v.i.* Teach or act as a demonstrator. M19. 5 *v.i.* Make a military demonstration. E19. 6 *v.i.* Make or take part in a public protest etc. (*against*, *in support of*, etc.). L19.

2 WELLINGTON His Highness has demonstrated the most implicit confidence in the protection of the British power. H. CARPENTER Nobody's appearance actually demonstrates their spiritual character. 3 SIR T. BROWNE Archimedes demonstrates . . that the proportion of the Diameter unto the Circumference is as 7 almost unto 22. S. SASSOON I had been ambitious of winning races because that had seemed a . . way of demonstrating my equality with my contemporaries. D. LESSING She might have deduced it all for herself without waiting to have it demonstrated. 4 C. P. SNOW I demonstrated the principle of the leg-glance. J. KEROUAC The idea was to get invited . . to a dinner party and then leap up and start demonstrating the pressure cooker. 6 A. J. P. TAYLOR Select bands of unemployed . . marched on London, where they demonstrated to little purpose.

demonstration /dɛmənˈstreɪʃ(ə)n/ *n.* LME. [OFr. *demonstracion* (later *-tion*) or L *demonstratio(n-)*, f. as prec.: see -ATION.] 1 †a The action of pointing out, indicating, or making known. Also, a sign, an indication. LME–L17. b A manifestation or outward display of or *of* feeling, a quality, etc. M16. 2 The action or process of making evident by reasoning; establishing beyond doubt by argument, deduction, or practical proof; (with *pl.*) a logical argument which proves an asserted conclusion. LME. b Something which serves as proof or evidence; a proof. LME. 3 A practical exhibition or explanation of something by experiment or example, esp. in scientific instruction, in order to teach or inform; a practical display of a piece of equipment etc. to show how it works and its capacity. E19. 4 *Rom. Law.* The statement of the alleged facts on which the plaintiff's case is founded. M19. 5 A show of military force or of offensive movement. M19. 6 An exhibition of public opinion on a political or other question, usually taking the form of a mass meeting or procession. M19.

1b R. L. STEVENSON He dares not be comical; his fun must escape from him unprepared, and . . be unaccompanied by any physical demonstration. E. TEMPLETON She was not given to demonstrations of motherly fondness in company. 2 L. T. C. ROLT Left to the engineer to prove the theorist wrong by practical demonstration. 3 J. MARQUAND What followed gave me a first hand demonstration .. of how news travels in Peking. R. WARNER Some demonstrations of the latest type of machine-guns. *attrib.*: *Which Micro?* A demonstration tape that explains the MSX system. 5 H. P. BROUGHAM The Barons having, by an armed demonstration, compelled the King to allow the appointment. 6 *Sunday Times* Protest demonstrations against the Government's Industrial Relations Bill. M. RICHLER It was the largest demonstration since the war and many who had come to protest were astonishingly young.

demonstrational *a.* M19. **demonstrationist** *n.* a person who takes part in a demonstration L19.

demonstrative /dɪˈmɒnstrətɪv/ *a.* & *n.* LME. [(O)Fr. *démonstratif*, *-ive* f. L *demonstrativus*, f. as DEMONSTRATE *v.*: see -ATIVE.] **A** *adj.* **1** Having the function or quality of demonstrating; making evident or manifest; illustrative; serving as conclusive evidence (*of*). LME. **2** *Gram.* Esp. of a pronoun or adjective: indicating the person or thing referred to. (Earlier in sense B. below.) E16. **3** *Rhet.* Describing with praise or censure. Now *rare* or *obs.* M16. **4** Provable by demonstration. E17. **5** Given to or characterized by open expression of feelings etc. E19. **6** That teaches or informs by practical display and description. *rare.* E19.

1 G. CHALMERS These military works .. are equally demonstrative of their skill. F. BOWEN Logic, as it proceeds from axiomatic principles, .. is a purely demonstrative science. 2 I. WATT There are 9 'thats'—only two of them demonstrative and the rest relative pronouns. 5 J. SIMMS Sumi had always been a demonstrative child; she sprang at us and hugged us.

B *n. Gram.* A demonstrative pronoun or adjective. LME.

demonstratively *adv.* L16. **demonstrativeness** *n.* M17.

demonstrator /ˈdɛmənstreɪtə/ *n.* E17. [L, f. as DEMONSTRATE *v.*: see -OR. Partly after Fr. *démonstrateur*.] **1** A person who or thing which demonstrates, points out, or proves. E17. **2** *spec.* **a** A person who teaches by demonstration, esp. in a laboratory etc.; one who explains the workings of a piece of equipment etc. to prospective customers. L17. **b** A piece of equipment used for demonstration; a motor vehicle in which a prospective customer may take a test drive. M20. **3** A person who takes part in a public demonstration. L19.

2 C. ISHERWOOD An overalled woman demonstrator was exhibiting the merits of a patent coffee-strainer. 3 H. KISSINGER Antiwar demonstrators had marched against him continually since he became President.

demonstratorship *n.* the position or post of a scientific demonstrator M19. **demonstratory** /dɪˈmɒnstrət(ə)ri/ *a.* that has the property of demonstrating E18.

demoralize /dɪˈmɒrəlʌɪz/ *v.t.* Also **-ise**. L18. [Fr. *démoraliser* (f. *dé-* DE- 3 + *moral* MORAL *a.*), a wd of the French Revolution: see -IZE.] **1** Corrupt the morals or moral principles of; deprave. *arch.* L18. **2** Lower or destroy the morale or confidence of; dishearten. M19.

1 SOUTHEY To debase, demoralize, and debilitate human nature. 2 J. R. GREEN The long series of English victories had .. demoralized the French soldiery.

demoraliˈzation *n.* the action of demoralizing; a demoralized condition: L18. **demoralizer** *n.* L19. **demoralizingly** *adv.* E20.

De Morgan /də ˈmɔːg(ə)n/ *n.* E20. [Augustus *De Morgan* (1806–71), Eng. mathematician.] *Logic* & *Math.* Used in *possess.* to designate two laws of propositional calculus: (*a*) the negation of a conjunction is equivalent to the alternation of the negations of the conjoined expressions; (*b*) the negation of an alternation is equivalent to the conjunction of the negations of the alternated expressions; (symbolically: $\sim(p \wedge q) \equiv \sim p \vee \sim q$; $\sim(p \vee q) \equiv \sim p \wedge \sim q$).

demos /ˈdiːmɒs/ *n.* Pl. **-mi** /-mʌɪ/. L18. [Gk *dēmos*.] **1** A district of ancient Attica, Greece; a deme. *rare.* L18. **2** (**D-**.) The common people of an ancient Greek State; (a personification of) the populace, esp. in a democracy. M19.

Demosthenean /dɪˌmɒsθəˈniːən, dɛmɒs ˈθiːnɪən/ *a.* Also **-ian**. M18. [f. Gk *Dēmosthenēs* (see below): see -EAN, -IAN.] Of, pertaining to, or resembling the Athenian statesman and orator Demosthenes (384–322 BC) or his style of oratory.

Also **Demosthenic** /dɛmɒsˈθɛnɪk/ *a.* E19.

demote /diːˈməʊt/ *v.t.* L19. [f. DE- 3 + PROMOTE *v.*] Reduce to a lower rank or class.

JOHN BROOKE He was first elevated to the leadership of the House of Commons and then summarily demoted to make way for Fox.

demotic /dɪˈmɒtɪk/ *a.* & *n.* E19. [Gk *dēmotikos* popular, f. *dēmotēs* one of the people, f. as DEMOS: see -OT[2], -IC.] **A** *adj.* **1 a** Designating or pertaining to the popular simplified form of Egyptian hieroglyphic script. Opp. *hieratic.* E19. **b** Designating or pertaining to a form of modern Greek based on popular speech. E20. **2** *gen.* Of or pertaining to the common people; popular, vulgar. M19.

2 *Listener* Advertising has .. to use simple, forceful, easily understandable words—'demotic' language. M. STOTT Perhaps .. we shall, like the Chinese, have some kind of demotic English and some kind of Mandarin?

B *n.* Demotic language; demotic script. E20.

demoticist /-sɪst/ *n.* a student of demotic script E20.

demotion /diːˈməʊʃ(ə)n/ *n.* E20. [f. DEMOTE after *promotion*.] The action of demoting; reduction to a lower rank or class.

demotivate /diːˈməʊtɪveɪt/ *v.t.* L20. [f. DE- 3 + MOTIVATE.] Reduce the motivation of; make less strongly motivated.

demotiˈvation *n.* L20.

demount /diːˈmaʊnt/ *v.* M16. [Orig. f. Fr. *démonter* (cf. DISMOUNT *v.*); in recent use f. as next.] **†1** *v.i.* Dismount. Also, admit of unmounting. *Sc.* M–L16. **2** *v.t.* Remove from its mounting; unmount; dismantle (for later reassembly). Cf. next. Orig. *Sc.* L16. **3** *v.i.* Descend. *rare.* M19.

¶In sense 2 not recorded 18–19; reintroduced in 20 after next.

demountable /diːˈmaʊntəb(ə)l/ *a.* E20. [f. DE- 3 + MOUNT *n.*[2] + -ABLE, prob. after Fr. *démontable*.] Able to be dismantled or removed from its mounting (and readily reassembled or repositioned).

demountaˈbility *n.* M20.

dempster /ˈdɛm(p)stə/ *n.* ME. [f. as DEEMSTER w. shortening of vowel of first syll.] **1** A judge. Long *obs.* exc. *Sc.* ME. **2** In Scotland: an officer of the court who pronounced sentence as directed by the judge, and often also acted as public executioner. *obs.* exc. *Hist.* LME.

demulce /dɪˈmʌls/ *v.t.* Now *rare* or *obs.* M16. [L *demulcere*: see next.] Soothe, mollify; soften, make gentle.

demulcent /dɪˈmʌls(ə)nt/ *a.* & *n.* M18. [L *demulcent-* pres. ppl stem of *demulcere* stroke caressingly, f. *de-* DE- 1 + *mulcere* stroke, appease: see -ENT.] **A** *adj.* Soothing, mollifying; allaying irritation. M18. **B** *n. Med.* A substance giving protection from or relieving (physical) irritation. M18.

demur /dɪˈməː/ *n.* ME. [(O)Fr. *demeure*, f. *demeurer*: see next.] **†1** Delay, waiting; procrastination. Also, residence, stay. ME–E18. **2 †a** *Law.* = DEMURRER *n.*[1] 1. M16–E18. **b** The action of demurring or objecting; an objection. Freq. in *without, with no, demur.* M17. **†3** Hesitation, pause; a state of indecision. L16–E19.

2b P. L. FERMOR Warming to the scheme after initial demur.

demur /dɪˈməː/ *v.* Infl. **-rr-**. ME. [OFr. *demo(u)rer*, (also mod.) *demeurer*, delay, linger, wait f. Proto-Romance var. of L *demorari*, f. *de-* DE- 1 + *morari* tarry, delay.] **†1** *v.i.* & *t.* (Cause to) linger, tarry, or delay. ME–L17. **2** *v.i.* **a** *Law.* Enter a demurrer. E17. **b** *gen.* Raise scruples or objections; take exception *to* or *at.* M17. **c** *v.t.* Object to. *rare.* E19. **†3** *v.i.* Hesitate, pause in uncertainty. M17–E19. **†b** *v.t.* Hesitate about. *rare.* M17–M18.

2b A. MACLAREN We can afford to recognise the fact, though we demur to the inference. F. WELDON Butt and Sons at first demurred, but then conceded.

demure /dɪˈmjʊə/ *a.* & *v.* LME. [Perh. f. AN *demuré*, OFr. *demo(u)ré* pa. pple of *demo(u)rer* (see prec.), infl. by OFr. *mur, meür* (mod. *mûr*) grave, f. L *maturus* ripe, MATURE *a.*] **A** *adj.* **†1** Calm, settled, still. Only in LME. **2** Orig., sober, grave, composed. Later also, affectedly or artificially quiet and serious; coy; decorous. LME.

2 MILTON Come, pensive Nun, devout and pure, Sober, steadfast and demure. J. FOWLES Theirs was an age when the favoured feminine look was the demure, the obedient, the shy.

†B *v.* **1** *v.i.* Look demurely. *rare* (Shakes.). Only in E17. **2** *v.t.* Make demure. E–M17.

demurely *adv.* LME. **demureness** *n.* E16. **demurity** *n.* (*rare*) demure quality; (an embodiment of) demureness: L15.

demurrable /dɪˈməːrəb(ə)l/ *a.* E19. [f. DEMUR *v.* or *n.* + -ABLE.] Chiefly *Law.* Able to be demurred to; open to objection.

demurrage /dɪˈmʌrɪdʒ/ *n.* *M17. [OFr. *demo(u)rage*, f. as DEMUR *v.*: see -AGE. In sense 2 f. DEMUR *n.* or *v.* + -AGE.] **†1** Procrastination; delay, waiting; detention. M17–E19. **2** Failure to load or discharge a chartered ship within the time agreed with the owner; the rate or amount payable to the owner by the charterer in respect of such failure. M17. **b** (A charge for) the similar retention of railway trucks or other goods. M19.

demurral /dɪˈməːr(ə)l/ *n. rare.* E19. [f. DEMUR *v.* + -AL[1].] The action of demurring; demur.

demurrant /dɪˈmʌr(ə)nt/ *a.* & *n.* LME. [OFr. *demo(u)rant*, f. as DEMUR *v.*: see -ANT[1].] **A** *adj.* **1** Staying, dwelling, resident. Long *arch. rare.* LME. **†2** Demurring, hesitating, putting off. *rare.* M17–M19. **B** *n.* Chiefly *Law.* A person who demurs or puts in a demurrer. E19.

demurrer /dɪˈmʌrə/ *n.*[1] E16. [AN, use as n. of inf. = OFr. *demo(u)rer*: see DEMUR *v.*, -ER[4].] **1** *Law.* An objection to the relevance of an opponent's point even if granted, which stays the action until relevance is settled. E16. **b** *gen.* An objection. L16. **†2** A state of hesitation, a pause. E16–M17.

demurrer /dɪˈməːrə/ *n.*[2] E18. [f. DEMUR *v.* + -ER[1].] A person who demurs.

demutualize /diːˈmjuːtʃʊəlʌɪz, -tjʊə-/ *v.t.* Also **-ise**. L20. [f. DE- 3 + MUTUALIZE.] Change (a building society etc.) from a mutual organization to one of a different kind.

demutualiˈzation *n.* L20.

demy /ˈdɛmi, *in senses A.2, B.3* dɪˈmʌɪ/ *a.* & *n.* Also (now *rare* or *obs.*) **demi**. LME. [f. DEMI- or its source, Fr. *demi.*] **A** *adj.* **1** Half, half-sized, diminutive. Now *rare* or *obs.* LME. **2** Designating, of, or pertaining to any of various sizes of paper, now *spec.* that measuring 564 × 444 mm (approx. 22.2 × 17.5 inches) or (*Austral.*) 216 × 138 mm (approx. 8.5 × 5.4 inches). M16. **B** *n.* **†1** A Scottish coin of varying value, orig. a half-mark. LME–L16. **2** A foundation scholar at Magdalen College, Oxford (from orig. having an allowance half that of a Fellow). L15. **3** Demy paper. E18.

demyship *n.* a scholarship at Magdalen College, Oxford M16.

demyelinate /diːˈmʌɪəlɪneɪt/ *v.t.* M20. [f. DE- 3 + MYELIN + -ATE[3].] *Med.* Remove or destroy the myelin of (nerve tissue etc.). Chiefly as *demyelinated*, *-ting* ppl adjs.

demyeliˈnation *n.* M20.

demystify /diːˈmɪstɪfʌɪ/ *v.t.* M20. [f. DE- 3 + MYSTIFY.] Remove the mystery from; clarify, simplify, explain.

demystifiˈcation *n.* M20.

demythicize /diːˈmɪθɪsʌɪz/ *v.t.* Also **-ise**. M20. [f. DE- 3 + MYTHICIZE.] Remove the attribution of a mythical character to (a legend, etc.); demythologize.

demythiciˈzation *n.* M20.

demythologize /diːmɪˈθɒlədʒʌɪz/ *v.t.* Also **-ise**. M20. [f. DE- 3 + MYTHOLOGIZE.] Remove the mythical elements from (a legend, cult, etc.); *spec.* in *Theol.*, reinterpret the mythological elements of (the Bible).

demythologiˈzation *n.* M20.

den /dɛn/ *n.*[1] [OE *denn* corresp. to MLG, MDu. *denne* low ground (WFlem. *den* threshing-floor), OHG *tenni* (G *Tenne*) floor, threshing-floor, f. Gmc. Rel. to DENE *n.*[1]] **1** The lair or habitation of a wild animal. OE. **b** A subdivision of a Cub Scout pack. *US.* M20. **2** A place of retreat or concealment; a resort of criminals etc. ME. **b** A small cramped (esp. squalid) room or house; a small private room set aside for a person's work, hobbies, etc. L18. **c** In children's games: a sanctuary, 'home'. L19. **3** A hollow place, a cavern. *obs.* exc. as coinciding w. above. ME. †**b** *Anat.* A cavity. LME–L17. **4** A deep hollow between hills, usu. wooded; a dingle. *Sc.* M16.

1 *beard the lion in his den*: see BEARD *v.* 1. 2 SIR W. SCOTT The Cavern, where .. A giant made his den of old. *Times* A search for the forger's den and printing equipment was continuing. *den of thieves, den of vice, gambling den, opium den*, etc. b E. PEACOCK The filthy den where her mother lived. A. BOYLE A rented house complete with .. a small den .. used as a combined study and photographic darkroom. 3 BUNYAN I lighted on a certain place, Where was a Denn; And I laid me down .. to sleep. 4 R. BURNS Auld Coila's .. dens and dells.

Comb.: **den mother** the woman leader of a Cub Scout den or *transf.* of any group.

¶ Sense 4 may be represented earlier in place-names.

den *n.*[2] var. of DENE *n.*[2]

den /dɛn/ *v.* Infl. **-nn-**. ME. [f. DEN *n.*[1]] **1** *v.t.* Ensconce or hide (oneself) in a den. In *pass.*, be ensconced in a den. ME. **2** *v.i.* Live in, hide oneself in, or retreat into a den. E17.

2 den up *US colloq.* retire into a den for the winter.

denar /ˈdiːnə, dɪˈnɑː, dɪˈnɛː/ *n.* M16. [AN *dener* = (O)Fr. DENIER *n.*[2]] *Hist.* Any of various coins, as the Roman denarius, the Spanish dinero, the Middle Eastern dinar.

denarius /dɪˈnɛːrɪəs, dɪˈnɑːrɪəs/ *n.* Pl. **-rii** /-rɪʌɪ, -rɪiː/. LME. [L (ellipt. for *denarius nummus* coin containing ten [asses]), f. *deni* by tens, distrib. of *decem* ten. Cf DENIER *n.*[2], DENAR.] *Hist.* **1** An ancient Roman silver coin, orig. of the value of ten asses. Also occas., an English or British penny (as the origin of the abbrev. *d.* in *£ s. d.* etc.). LME. **2** A unit of weight equal to that of a Roman silver denarius. LME. **3** More fully *golden denarius.* An ancient Roman gold coin worth 25 silver denarii. M17.

denary /ˈdiːn(ə)ri/ *a.* M19. [L *denarius* containing ten: see prec.] Having ten as the basis of reckoning, decimal.

denatant /diːˈneɪt(ə)nt/ *a.* E20. [f. DE- 1 + NATANT.] Of the migration of fish: in the same direction as the current. Opp. CONTRANATANT.

dena'tation *n.* the act of migrating with the current E20.

denationalize /diːˈnaʃ(ə)n(ə)lʌɪz/ *v.t.* Also **-ise**. E19. [Fr. *dénationaliser* (f. *dé-* DE- 3 + *nationaliser* NATIONALIZE), a wd of the French Revolution: see -IZE.] **1** Deprive (a person etc.) of nationality; deprive (a country, people, etc.) of national identity or characteristics. E19. **2** Make (an institution etc.) no longer national; destroy the association of (an institution etc.) with the whole, or a particular, nation. M19. **3** Transfer (an industry etc.) from national to private ownership. E20.

denationali'zation *n.* E19.

denaturalize /diːˈnatʃərəlʌɪz/ *v.t.* Also **-ise**. E19. [f. DE- 3 + NATURALIZE.] **1** Change the nature or properties of, make unnatural; occas., make (alcohol etc.) unfit for drinking. E19. **2** Deprive (a person, esp. oneself) of citizenship. E19.

denaturali'zation *n.* E19. **denaturalizer** *n.* a person who or thing which denaturalizes M19.

denature /diːˈneɪtʃə/ *v.* L17. [Fr. *dénaturer*, OFr. *des-*, f. *des-*, *dé-* DE- 3 + as NATURE *n.*] **1** *v.t.* Make unnatural. L17. **2** *v.t.* Change the nature or properties of; *esp.* make (alcohol etc.) unfit for consumption. L19. **3** *spec. Biochem.* **a** *v.t.* Cause denaturation (see below) of (a macromolecule), e.g. by heat or acid. E20. **b** *v.i.* Of a macromolecule: undergo denaturation. M20.

1 R. G. COLLINGWOOD Artistic motives are genuinely present, but denatured by subordination to a non-artistic end.

denaturant *n.* a substance added to alcohol etc. as a denaturing agent E20. **denatu'ration** *n.* the action of denaturing; *spec.* (*Biochem.*) alteration of the properties of a macromolecule or macromolecular aggregate by disruption of its conformation: L19.

denaturize /diːˈneɪtʃərʌɪz/ *v.t.* Also **-ise**. L19. [f. DE- 3 + NATURE *n.* + -IZE.] =DENATURE *v.* 2.

denaturi'zation *n.* M20.

†**denay** *n.*, *v.* vars. of DENY *n.*, *v.*

denazify /diːˈnɑːtsɪfʌɪ/ *v.t.* M20. [f. DE- 3 + NAZI + -FY.] Chiefly *Hist.* Remove from, declare (esp. judicially) to be free from, Nazi allegiance or influence; remove Nazis from (official positions etc.).

denazifi'cation *n.* M20.

dendriform /ˈdɛndrɪfɔːm/ *a.* M19. [f. as Gk *dendron* tree + -I- + -FORM.] Of the form of a tree; branching, arborescent.

dendrite /ˈdɛndrʌɪt/ *n.* E18. [Fr., f. Gk *dendritēs* adj., pertaining to a tree, f. *dendron* tree: see -ITE[1].] **1** (A stone, mineral, etc., bearing) a natural treelike or mosslike marking. E18. **2** A branching crystalline growth. L19. **3** *Anat.* Any of the branched processes of a nerve cell, through which impulses are received by the cell. L19.

dendritic /dɛnˈdrɪtɪk/ *a.* L18. [f. prec. + -IC.] **1** Of the nature of or pertaining to a dendrite; of a branching form; arborescent, treelike. L18. **2** Having arborescent markings. E19.

dendritical *a.* = DENDRITIC *a.* E19. **dendritically** *adv.* L19.

dendro- /ˈdɛndrəʊ/ *comb. form* of Gk *dendron* tree: see -O-.

dendrocli'matic *a.* of or pertaining to dendroclimatology M20. **dendroclima'tology** *n.* the branch of science that deals with obtaining information about past climates by examining growth rings in (ancient) timber M20. **dendrogram** *n.* (*Biol.*) a branched diagram representing the relationship between taxa M20. **den'drometer** *n.* an instrument for measuring the size of trees M19. **dendrophil**, **-phile** *n.* a lover of trees L19.

dendrochronology /ˌdɛndrəʊkrəˈnɒlədʒi/ *n.* E20. [f. prec. + CHRONOLOGY.] The science of dating events and environmental variations by means of the comparative study of the growth rings in (ancient) timber.

dendrochrono'logical *a.* pertaining to, involving, or obtained by the use of dendrochronology M20. **dendrochrono'logically** *adv.* M20. **dendrochronologist** *n.* M20.

dendroid /ˈdɛndrɔɪd/ *a.* & *n.* M19. [f. DENDRO- + -OID.] **A** *adj.* Tree-shaped, arborescent, dendritic; *spec.* (*Palaeont.*) designating or pertaining to graptolites of the order Dendroidea, which form much-branched colonies. M19. **B** *n.* *Palaeont.* A dendroid graptolite. E20.

dendrology /dɛnˈdrɒlədʒi/ *n.* E18. [f. DENDRO- + -LOGY.] The branch of science that deals with trees.

dendro'logic *a.* (*rare*) E19. **dendro'logical** *a.* L19. **dendrologist** *n.* E19.

dendron /ˈdɛndrɒn/ *n.* L19. [f. DENDRITE + *-on* as in *axon* etc.] *Anat.* = DENDRITE 3.

dene /diːn/ *n.*[1] Also **dean**. [OE *denu* f. Gmc. Rel. to DEN *n.*[1]] A valley; now usu. *spec.*, the deep narrow wooded valley of a rivulet.

dene /diːn/ *n.*[2] Also **den** /dɛn/. ME. [Perh. rel. to LG (whence G) *düne*, Du. *duin* DUNE.] A bare sandy tract by the sea; a low sand-hill.

denegation /dɛnɪˈɡeɪʃ(ə)n/ *n.* L15. [Fr. *dénégation* f. late L *denegatio(n-)*, f. *de-* DE- 1 + *negare*: see -ATION.] †**1** Refusal of what is asked. L15–M17. **2** Denial, contradiction. M19.

denegatory *a.* (*rare*) contradictory E19.

dene-hole /ˈdiːnhəʊl/ *n.* Also **dane-** /ˈdeɪn-/. M18. [Origin uncertain: perh. f. DANE + HOLE *n.*[1] Assoc. by later archaeologists with DENE *n.*[2] and DEN *n.*[1]] *Archaeol.* An ancient excavation of a kind found in chalk-formations in England and France, consisting of a narrow shaft sunk down to the chalk, and there widening out into one or more chambers.

denervate /diːˈnəːveɪt/ *v.t.* E20. [f. DE- 3 + NERVATE *v.*] *Med.* Remove or cut off the nerve supply from (an organ etc.).

dener'vation *n.* E20.

dengue /ˈdɛŋɡi/ *n.* Also **denga** /ˈdɛŋɡə/. E19. [W. Indian Sp., f. Kiswahili *denga*, *dinga* (in full *kidingapopo*), identified w. Sp. *dengue* fastidiousness, prudery, w. ref. to the stiffness of the neck and shoulders caused by the disease.] A debilitating tropical viral disease which is transmitted to man by the mosquito *Aedes aegypti*, and is characterized by an eruptive fever and severe pain esp. in the joints and muscles. Also *dengue-fever*.

deniable /dɪˈnʌɪəb(ə)l/ *a.* M16. [f. DENY *v.* + -ABLE.] That can be denied.

denia'bility *n.* E19.

denial /dɪˈnʌɪ(ə)l/ *n.* E16. [f. DENY *v.* + -AL[1].] **1** The act of saying 'no'; refusal of something asked or desired. E16. **2** A statement or assertion that something is untrue or untenable; contradiction; refusal to acknowledge the existence or reality of a thing. L16. **3** (A) disavowal, disowning; *esp.* refusal to acknowledge a person as leader etc. L16. **4** *Law.* The opposing by a defendant of a charge etc. made against him or her. E18. **5** A drawback, disadvantage. *dial.* M18. **6** *Bridge.* A bid intended to show weakness in response to one's partner's bid. E20.

1 SHAKES. *Tam. Shr.* Neuer make denial; I must and will have Katherine to my wife. SELF-DENIAL. 2 B. JOWETT The denial of abstract ideas is the destruction of the mind. 3 AV *John* 18 Peters deniall.

denier /dɪˈnʌɪə/ *n.*[1] LME. [f. DENY *v.* + -ER[1].] A person who denies.

denier /ˈdɛnɪə/ *n.*[2] LME. [(O)Fr. f. L DENARIUS.] **1** *Hist.* A French coin of little value (equal to one twelfth of a sou) which was withdrawn from use in the 19th cent.; (the type of) a very small sum. LME. †**2** = DENARIUS 2. M16–E18. †**3** = DENARIUS 1. L16–E17. **4** Orig., a unit of weight used for silk, equal to $1/24$ oz. (1.181 gram). Now, a unit of fineness of yarn equal to the weight in grams of 9000 metres of it. M19.

1 SHAKES. *Rich. III* My dukedom to a beggarly denier.

denigrate /ˈdɛnɪɡreɪt/ *v.t.* LME. [L *denigrat-* pa. ppl stem of *denigrare*, f. *de-* DE- 1 + *nigrare* blacken, f. *niger* black: see -ATE[3].] **1** Make black or dark in colour. Now *rare* or *obs.* LME. **2** Blacken the reputation of (a person etc.); defame, decry. E16.

2 G. F. FIENNES Whether, if I called Judas .. a not too good apostle, I was denigrating the profession of apostle. P. ACKROYD He was not .. happy with his journalistic productions and tended to denigrate them .. to his friends.

denigrator *n.* a person who or thing which denigrates someone or something M17. **denigratory** /dɛnɪˈɡreɪt(ə)ri, ˈdɛnɪɡrət-/*a.* defamatory M20.

denigration /dɛnɪˈɡreɪʃ(ə)n/ *n.* LME. [L *denigratio(n-)*, f. as prec.: see -ATION.] **1** The action or process of blackening or darkening in colour. Now *rare* or *obs.* LME. **2** Blackening of reputation or character; defamation. LME.

dénigrement /denigrəmɑ̃/ *n.* L19. [Fr.] Blackening of character, denigration.

denim /ˈdɛnɪm/ *n.* & *a.* Orig. †**serge denim**. L17. [*serge denim* f. Fr. *serge de Nîmes* serge of Nîmes (a city in southern France).] **A** *n.* Orig., a kind of serge. Now, a twilled hard-wearing cotton fabric (freq. blue) used for overalls, jeans, etc. In *pl.*, overalls or jeans made of denim. L17. **B** *adj.* Made of denim. E18.

denitrate /diːˈnʌɪtreɪt/ *v.t.* M19. [f. DE- 3 + NITRATE.] Remove nitrates from.

deni'tration *n.* E19.

denitrify /diːˈnʌɪtrɪfʌɪ/ *v.t.* L19. [f. DE- 3 + NITRIFY.] Remove nitrates or nitrites from; *esp.* (of bacteria) remove nitrates etc. from (soil) by chemical reduction, ultimately to gaseous nitrogen.

denitrifi'cation *n.* L19.

denizate /ˈdɛnɪzeɪt/ *v.t.* E17. [AL *denizat-* pa. ppl stem of *denizare*, *denizatio(n-)*, f. DENIZEN *n.* & *a.*: see -ATE[3].] *Law.* Make a denizen; naturalize.

deni'zation *n.* E17.

†**denize** *v.t.* L16–E18. [f. next, prob. repr. an AN form.] Make a denizen; naturalize.

denizen /ˈdɛnɪz(ə)n/ *n.* & *a.* LME. [AN *deinzein* (f. OFr. *deinz* within f. late L *de intus* from within + *-ein* f. L *-aneus*), assim. to *citizen*.] **A** *n.* **1** A person who lives within a country, as opp. to a foreigner who lives outside its boundaries; *gen.* an inhabitant, an occupant, a citizen (*of* a place). LME. 2 A person who lives in a country but is not native-born; a foreigner admitted to residence and allowed certain rights. E16. b A person admitted to or given the freedom of a particular group; one who, though not a native, is at home in a particular place. M16. c A foreign word, animal, plant, etc., which has become naturalized. L16.

1 G. P. R. JAMES The towns .. and their laborious denizens. H. CARPENTER Salmon, Lobster, and many smaller denizens of sea and river-bed. 2 I. D'ISRAELI Charles seemed ambitious of making English denizens of every man of genius in Europe. b H. REED He was a denizen .. of Alpine regions, and of Greek and Italian plains.

B *attrib.* or as *adj.* That has the entitlements of or is a denizen. L15.

denizenship *n.* the position or status of a denizen E17.

denizen /ˈdɛnɪz(ə)n/ *v.t.* M16. [f. the n.] Make a denizen; naturalize.

SOUTHEY The cholera is not a passing evil. It is denizened among us.

Denmark /ˈdɛnmɑːk/ *n.* L18. [A country in Scandinavia: see DANE.] 1 *Denmark satin*, a kind of worsted used esp. to make women's shoes. *obs.* exc. *Hist.* L18. 2 *Denmark Street* [a London street], the world of composers and publishers of popular music, Tin Pan Alley. M20.

denn /dɛn/ *n.* M20. [Revival of OE (Kentish), surviving as *-den* in place-names e.g. *Tenterden*, perh. = DEN *n.*[1] Cf. MDu. *dann* forest, haunt of wild beasts.] *Hist.* A woodland pasture (in SE England), esp. for swine.

†**dennage** *n.* see DUNNAGE.

dennebol /ˈdɛnəbɒl/ *n.* *S. Afr.* E20. [Afk., f. *denne* (boom) pine (tree) + *bol* ball, bulb.] A fir cone.

dennet /ˈdɛnɪt/ *n.* E19. [Perh. f. a surname.] Chiefly *Hist.* A light open two-wheeled carriage, similar to a gig, popular in Britain in the early 19th cent.

denominable /dɪˈnɒmɪnəb(ə)l/ *a.* M17. [med.L *denominabilis*, f. L *denominare* DENOMINATE: see -ABLE.] Able to be denominated or named.

denominal /dɪˈnɒmɪn(ə)l/ *n.* & *a.* M20. [f. DE- 2 + NOMINAL.] *Gram.* = DENOMINATIVE *n.*, *a.* 2.

denominate /dɪˈnɒmɪneɪt/ *v.t.* Pa. pple **-ated**, (orig.) †**-ate**. LME. [L *denominat-* pa. ppl stem of *denominare*, f. *de-* DE- 1 + *nominare* to name: see -ATE[3].] 1 Give a name to; name, call, (orig. *from* or *after* something). LME. 2 Of a thing: give (something) its name or character, characterize; make what it is. Now *rare.* L16. †3 Denote. Only in 18.

1 R. H. MOTTRAM That standard compost that .. before nine .. was denominated 'coffee', .. before or after noon 'soup', until the end of the day, when .. it became 'tea'. 2 J. BENTHAM That .. acquaintance with the .. classics which denominates a man a good scholar.

denomination /dɪˌnɒmɪˈneɪʃ(ə)n/ *n.* LME. [OFr. *denominacion* (later & mod. *-tion*) or L *denominatio(n-)*, f. as prec.: see -ATION.] 1 The action of naming (*from* or *after*); giving a name to, calling by a name. LME. 2 A characteristic name given to a thing or class of things; a designation, a title. LME. 3 A class of one kind of unit in any system of numbers, weights, money, etc., distinguished by a specific name. L15. 4 A class, sort, or kind distinguished by a specific name. M17. 5 A body of people classed together under the one name; *spec.* a religious sect or body with distinctive name and organization. M17.

2 SIR W. SCOTT Gypsies, jockies, or cairds .. by all these denominations such banditti were known. 3 M. MCCARTHY Her .. boxes held Stamps of various denominations. D. BAGLEY A bank-note of large denomination. 4 A. HAMILTON Good Cotton Cloth of several Qualities and Denominations. 5 M. L. KING Within American Protestantism there are more than two hundred and fifty denominations.

denominational /dɪˌnɒmɪˈneɪʃ(ə)n(ə)l/ *a.* M19. [f. prec. + -AL[1].] Belonging to or of the nature of a denomination; (esp. of education, a school, etc.) sectarian.

denominationalism *n.* adherence to denominational principles or a denominational system (of education) M19. **denominationalize** *v.t.* make denominational M19. **denominationally** *adv.* M19.

denominative /dɪˈnɒmɪnətɪv/ *n.* & *a.* L16. [Late L *denominativus* adj., f. *denominat-*: see DENOMINATE, -ATIVE.] A *n.* *Gram.* A word formed or derived from a noun. L16. B *adj.* 1 That gives a name to something; *esp.* (of a word or term) having the function of naming or describing. L16. 2 *Gram.* Formed or derived from a noun. L18.

denominatively *adv.* M16.

denominator /dɪˈnɒmɪneɪtə/ *n.* M16. [Fr. *dénominateur* or med.L *denominator*, f. *denominat-*: see DENOMINATE, -OR.] 1 The number written below the line in a vulgar fraction, which gives the denomination or value of the parts into which the integer is divided; the divisor in an algebraic fraction. (Correl. to *numerator.*) M16. 2 A person who or thing which gives a name to something. Now *rare.* L16.

1 **common denominator** a common multiple of the denominators of several fractions; *fig.* something common to or characteristic of a number of things, people, etc.; (*least* or *lowest common denominator*, the lowest such multiple or common characteristic).

de nos jours /də no ʒuːr/ *postpositive a. phr.* E20. [Fr., = of our days.] Of the present time; contemporary.

denotata *n.* pl. of DENOTATUM.

denotation /diːnə(ʊ)ˈteɪʃ(ə)n/ *n.* M16. [Fr. *dénotation* or L *denotatio(n-)*, f. *denotat-* pa. ppl stem of *denotare*: see DENOTE, -ATION.] 1 The action of denoting; expression by marks, signs, or symbols; indication. M16. b A mark etc. denoting a thing; a sign. M17. 2 The meaning or signification of a term, as distinct from its implications or connotations. E17. 3 A term used to describe something; a designation. M17. 4 *Logic.* The object or range of objects which a word denotes; extension. M19.

denotational *a.* M20.

denotative /dɪˈnəʊtətɪv, ˈdiːnə(ʊ)teɪtɪv/ *a.* & *n.* E17. [f. L *denotat-*: see prec., -ATIVE.] A *adj.* Having the quality of denoting; designating, indicative. E17. B *n.* A denotative term. M20.

denotatively *adv.* M19.

denotatum /diːnəʊˈteɪtəm, -ˈtɑːt-/ *n.* Pl. **-tata** /-ˈteɪtə, -ˈtɑːtə/. M20. [L *denotatum* neut. pa. pple of *denotare* DENOTE.] *Philos.* The thing denoted by an expression; *esp.* an existent object of reference. Cf. DESIGNATUM.

denote /dɪˈnəʊt/ *v.t.* L16. [(O)Fr. *dénoter* or L *denotare*, f. *de-* DE- 1 + *notare* NOTE *v.*[1]] 1 Mark out; distinguish by a mark or sign. L16. 2 Indicate; be an outward or visible sign of. L16. b Give to understand; make known. M17. †3 Note down; describe. Only in 17. 4 Signify; be a symbol for or a name of. M17. b Express *by* a symbol. L19. 5 Designate; have as a meaning or name; be predicated of. (Freq. as opp. *connote.*) M19.

2 OED A falling barometer denotes an approaching storm. J. MARQUAND I was reminded again that the smile of a Japanese does not necessarily denote humour. b SMOLLETT Thou hast enough Denoted thy concern. 4 B. RUSSELL No sentence can be made up without at least one word which denotes a universal. b M. KLINE These fields .. have four sides, which we shall denote by *a*, *b*, *c*, *d*. 5 H. SPENCER We can do no more than ignore the connotation of the words, and attend only to the things they avowedly denote. R. FRY Some other word to denote what we now call art.

denotable *a.* able to be denoted or marked L17. **denotement** *n.* (*a*) the fact of denoting; (*b*) a token, a sign: E17. **denotive** *a.* serving to denote M19.

denouement /deɪˈnuːmɒ̃, -mɒŋ/ *n.* Also **dé-**. M18. [Fr., f. *dénouer* (earlier *des-*) untie, f. *des*, *dé-* DE- 3 + *nouer* to knot.] The unravelling of the complications of a plot, or of a confused situation or mystery; the final resolution of a play, novel, or other narrative.

denounce /dɪˈnaʊns/ *v.t.* ME. [OFr. *dénoncier* (mod. *dénoncer*) f. L *denuntiare* give official information, f. *de-* DE- 1 + *nuntiare* make known, report.] 1 Give official information of; proclaim, announce. Now *arch. rare.* ME. †b Of a thing: indicate, portend, presage. L16–M18. 2 Proclaim or pronounce (a person) to be (cursed, a rebel, etc.); publicly declare (a person or thing) to be wicked or evil, accuse publicly, openly inveigh against. ME. †b Proclaim (*as*) *king*, *emperor*, etc. L15–E17. 3 Make known (an offender) to the authorities; inform against. L15. 4 Announce as a threat or warning. *arch.* L16. 5 Give formal notice of the termination of (a treaty, armistice, etc.). M19.

1 AV *Deut.* 30:18 I denounce unto you this day, that ye shall surely perish. J. STRYPE He was solemnly denounced excommunicate. 2 W. S. CHURCHILL General Weyler's policy of herding civilians into concentration camps .. was vehemently denounced. B. MOORE The Bishop .. denounced Hartmann as a false priest. 3 J. AYLIFFE Archdeacons .. shall .. denounce such of them as are negligent .. to the Bishop. 4 W. IRVING Captain Wyeth .. had heard the Crows denounce vengeance on them, for having murdered two of their warriors.

denouncement *n.* the action of denouncing; denunciation: M16. **denouncer** *n.* LME.

de nouveau /də nuvo/ *adv. phr.* L18. [Fr. = from new.] Afresh, starting again from the beginning.

de novo /deɪ ˈnəʊvəʊ, diː/ *adv. phr.* E17. [L = from new.] = prec.

†**densation** *n.* E17–E18. [L *densatio(n-)*, f. *densat-* pa. ppl stem of *densare* make thick, f. *densus*: see next, -ATION.] Thickening, condensation.

dense /dɛns/ *a.* LME. [Fr., or L *densus* thick, dense, crowded.] 1 Closely compacted in substance; thick, compact; having a high density. LME. b With the constituent parts closely crowded together; closely set. L18. 2 *fig.* Profound, intense; impenetrable. M18. b Crass, stupid. E19. 3 *Photogr.* Of high density (DENSITY 4). L19.

1 R. J. SULLIVAN It pervades all bodies, dense as well as rare. H. KELLER A dense fog, when it seemed as if a tangible white darkness shut you in. F. HOYLE Seawater that has lost its heat in melting icebergs is very dense and plunges to the very bottom of the ocean. b F. MARRYAT The crowd .. was so dense that it was hardly possible to move. P. THEROUX The jungle .. was so dense no light showed through it. 2 B. FRANKLIN Six weeks of the densest happiness I have met with. P. SCOTT Such dense blackness of skin. b E. F. BENSON The stuffy girls were not so dense as not to perceive her opinion of them.

densely *adv.* E19. **densen** *v.t.* & *i.* (*rare*) make or become (more) dense M19. **denseness** *n.* M17.

Denshire *n.* & *v.* see DEVONSHIRE.

densify /ˈdɛnsɪfʌɪ/ *v.t.* E19. [f. DENSE + -I- + -FY.] Make (more) dense.

densimeter /dɛnˈsɪmɪtə/ *n.* M19. [f. L *densus* DENSE + -IMETER. Cf. DENSOMETER.] An instrument for measuring density, esp. of liquids.

densitometer /dɛnsɪˈtɒmɪtə/ *n.* E20. [f. next + -OMETER.] An instrument for measuring photographic density.

densitoˈmetric *a.* E20. **densitometry** *n.* E20.

density /ˈdɛnsɪti/ *n.* E17. [Fr. *densité* or L *densitas*, f. *densus*: see DENSE, -ITY.] 1 The quality or condition of being closely compacted in substance; closeness of texture or consistency. E17. 2 *Physics.* The degree of consistency of a body or substance measured by the quantity of mass in unit volume. M17. b Any of various physical properties defined as a quantity (of electric charge, particles, energy, etc.) per unit (physical or mathematical) extent. Usu. w. specifying wd. L19. 3 The degree of aggregation; a crowded state; *spec.* in any population, the average number of individuals per spatial unit. M19. 4 *Photogr.* (A measure of) the opacity of the image produced (i.e. the amount of silver deposited) in a photographic emulsion under given conditions. L19. 5 *fig.* Stupidity, crassness. L19. 6 *Computing.* = *packing density* s.v. PACKING *n.*[1] M20.

1 *fig.*: W. J. BATE In all of these works are the same weight and density of meaning. 2 R. V. JONES This gives a mean density for the rocket of about four times that of water. b H. M. ROSENBERG The density of states will be used to describe the number of atomic oscillators per unit energy .. range. *charge density*, *electron density*, etc. *optical density*: see OPTICAL *a.* *vapour density*: see VAPOUR *n.* 3 N. HAWTHORNE Stems,

supporting a cloud-like density of boughs. E. F. SCHUMACHER The United States could accommodate more than half the world population before it attained a density equal to that of the United Kingdom.

densometer /dɛnˈsɒmɪtə/ *n.* L19. [f. L *densus* DENSE + -OMETER.] = DENSIMETER.

dent /dɛnt/ *n.*[1] ME. [Var. of DINT *n.*; in sense 3 prob. f. DENT *v.* Cf. DUNT *n.*] **1** †**a** A stroke or blow, *esp.* one given with a weapon; = DINT *n.* I. ME–E17. **b** A clap of thunder. Long *obs.* exc. *dial.* ME. †**2** Dealing of blows; vigorous wielding of a weapon; force of attack. LME–L16. **3** A hollow or impression in a surface, as made by a blow with a sharp or edged instrument; an indentation. M16. **b** *fig.* A (detrimental) reducing effect or reduction. M20.

3 GEO. ELIOT Dents and disfigurements in an old family tankard. J. CARY The lower cottages in a dip or dent on the hillside. **b** *Times* There is going to be a dent in our profits.

dent /dɛnt/ *n.*[2] M16. [Fr. = tooth.] **1** A toothlike notch in the edge of something. Now only in *Needlework*, a pointed or square design cut as a decorative edging to the hem of a dress etc. M16. **2** A tooth-shaped projection, esp. in a clothmakers' card, a gearwheel, etc.; *spec.* in weaving, = SPLIT *n.* 2b. E18.

1 DRYDEN His [a cock's] comb . . In dents embattl'd like a castle-wall.

dent /dɛnt/ *a.* & *n.*[3] LME. [Abbrev. of *dented* pa. pple of next.] **A** *adj.* †**1** Embossed. Only in LME. †**2** *Her.* Indented. Only in E17. **3** Designating a variety of Indian corn having a dent or depression in each kernel. *US.* M19. **B** *n.* Dent corn. *US.* M19.

dent /dɛnt/ *v.* LME. [Prob. aphet. f. INDENT *v.*[2]] **1** *v.t.* Make a dent in, as with a blow on a surface; mark with a dent or dents; indent. LME. **b** *fig.* Have an (esp. adverse) effect on; damage. M20. **2** *v.t.* Imprint, impress. LME. **3** *v.i.* Sink *in*, so as to make or dent; become indented. L15.

1 M. E. BRADDON Armour . . battered and dented at Cressy. R. MACAULAY The sun beat hotly on the asphalt, making it soft, so that one could dent it with one's heels. **b** *Listener* Lack of candour . . has further dented public faith in Downing Street statements. 3 K. KESEY The head dented into the pillow.

dental /ˈdɛnt(ə)l/ *a.* & *n.* L16. [Late L *dentalis*, f. L *dens*, *dent-* tooth: see -AL[1].] **A** *adj.* **1** Of or pertaining to a tooth, the teeth, or dentistry; of the nature of a tooth. L16. **2** *Phonet.* Of a consonant: articulated with the tip of the tongue against the upper front teeth as English *th* /θ, ð/, French *d, n, t*; = ALVEOLAR *a.* L16.

Special collocations: *dental floss*: see FLOSS *n.*[2] 3. **dental formula**: expressing the number and kinds of teeth possessed by a mammal (usu. written in the form of a 'fraction' with the upper and lower lines describing the upper and lower jaws respectively). **dental hygienist** an ancillary dental worker specializing in oral hygiene, scaling and polishing of teeth, etc. **dental mechanic** a person who makes and repairs artificial teeth. **dental nurse** a nurse who assists a dentist. *dental* PLAQUE. **dental surgeon** a dentist. **dental technician** = *dental mechanic* above.

B *n.* **1** *Phonet.* A dental consonant. L17. †**2** A tooth shell. L17–E18. †**3** = DENTEX. M18–M19. **4** *Archit.* = DENTIL. M18.

denˈtality *n.* (*Phonet.*) dental quality L19. **dentaliˈzation** *n.* (*Phonet.*) the action of dentalizing; the state of being dentalized: L19. **dentalize** *v.t.* (*Phonet.*) make dental, change into a dental sound M19. **dentally** *adv.* M20.

dentalium /dɛnˈteɪlɪəm/ *n.* Pl. **-lia** /-lɪə/. M19. [mod.L (see below), f. late L *dentalis*: see prec.] A tusk shell (*spec.* of the genus *Dentalium*), freq. used as an ornament or as currency by primitive peoples.

dentaria /dɛnˈtɛːrɪə/ *n.* E19. [mod.L (see below), fem. sing. of late L *dentarius*: see next.] Any cruciferous plant of the genus *Dentaria* (now freq. included in the genus *Cardamine*), characterized by toothlike scales on the roots, e.g. coral-root, pepper-root.

dentary /ˈdɛnt(ə)ri/ *a.* & *n.* M19. [Late L *dentarius*, f. L *dens*, *dent-* tooth: see -ARY[1]. Cf. Fr. *dentaire*.] *Anat.* & *Zool.* **A** *adj.* Of or connected with the teeth. M19.

dentary bone = sense B. below.

B *n.* A bone of the lower jaw in non-mammalian vertebrates, bearing the teeth when these are present. M19.

dentate /ˈdɛnteɪt/ *a.* LME. [L *dentatus*, f. *dens*, *dent-* tooth: see -ATE[2].] Chiefly *Zool.* & *Bot.* Toothed; having toothlike projections or notches along the edge; *spec.* (of a leaf etc.) having sharp outwardly directed teeth.

dentated *a.* = DENTATE M18. **denˈtation** *n.* the condition or fact of being dentate E19.

-dentate /ˈdɛnteɪt/ *suff.* [f. as prec.] Forming adjs. with the senses (*a*) *Zool.* & *Bot.* having teeth or toothlike projections of the specified number or kind, (*b*) *Chem.* forming the specified number of bonds with another atom, esp. as a ligand; as *bidentate*, *curvidentate*, *duplicato-dentate*, *polydentate*.

dented /ˈdɛntɪd/ *a.* LME. [f. DENT *n.*[1], *n.*[2], *v.*: see -ED[2], -ED[1].] **1** Having a dent or dents; bent inward, incurved (now only by a blow etc.). LME. **2** Indented, notched; toothed. LME.

1 A. TYLER They had reached his car, a dented gray Chevy.

dentellated /ˈdɛntɪleɪtɪd/ *a.* Also **-elated**. L18. [f. as next; after Fr. *dentelé*: see -ATE[2], -ED[1].] Having small notches or teeth; finely indented.

dentelle /dɛnˈtɛl; *foreign* dɑ̃tɛl (*pl. same*)/ *n.* M19. [Fr., f. *dent* tooth + *-elle* -EL[2].] **1** (A piece of) lace. M19. **2** *Bookbinding.* An ornamental tooling resembling lace edging. Usu. *attrib.* L19.

†**dentello** *n.* see DENTIL.

dentex /ˈdɛntɛks/ *n.* Pl. same. M19. [mod.L (see below) f. L *dentex*, *-tix* a kind of marine fish.] A sea bream of the genus *Dentex*; spec. *D. dentex* of the Mediterranean and N. African Atlantic coast.

denti- /ˈdɛnti/ *comb. form* of L *dens*, *dent-* tooth, *dentes* teeth: see -I-.

dentiform *a.* of the form of or resembling a tooth; tooth-shaped: E18. **denˈtigerous** *a.* bearing teeth; (of a cyst) surrounding an unerupted tooth: M19. **dentiˈlingual** *a.* & *n.* (*Phonet.*) (a consonant, sound, etc.) formed by the teeth and tongue L19.

Denticare /ˈdɛntɪkɛː/ *n.* Chiefly *N. Amer.* Also **d-**. M20. [f. DENTAL *a.* + CARE *n.*, after MEDICARE.] Dental care; a scheme providing this, esp. sponsored by a State (US proprietary) or province.

denticle /ˈdɛntɪk(ə)l/ *n.* LME. [L *denticulus*: see DENTICULE.] **1** Chiefly *Zool.* A small tooth or toothlike projection. In early use *spec.* a pointer on the rete of the astrolabe. LME. **2** *Archit.* = DENTIL I. Now *rare.* L17.

denticular /dɛnˈtɪkjʊlə/ *a.* M19. [f. as DENTICULE + -AR[1].] **1** *Archit.* Characterized by dentils. M19. **2** Resembling or of the nature of a small tooth. L19.

denticulate /dɛnˈtɪkjʊlət/ *a.* M17. [L *denticulatus*, f. as DENTICULE: see -ATE[2].] Having small teeth or toothlike projections; finely toothed.

denticulated *a.* (*a*) = DENTICULATE; (*b*) *Archit.* = DENTICULAR I: M17. **denticuˈlation** *n.* the condition of being denticulate or finely toothed; an instance of this; a small indentation or projection: L17.

denticule /ˈdɛntɪkjuːl/ *n.* M16. [L *denticulus* dim. of *dens*, *dent-* tooth: see -CULE.] *Archit.* That member of the entablature in which the dentils are cut.

dentifrice /ˈdɛntɪfrɪs/ *n.* LME. [Fr. f. L *dentifricium*, f. *dens*, *dent-* tooth (cf. DENTI-) + *fricare* to rub.] A powder, paste, or other preparation for cleaning the teeth.

dentil /ˈdɛntɪl/ *n.* & *a.* Also (earlier) in It. form †**-tello**, pl. **-telli**. L16. [(It. *dentello* or) Fr. †*dentille* (now *dentelle*) fem. dim. of *dent* tooth, f. L *dens*, *dent-*.] *Archit.* **A** *n.* **1** Each of the small rectangular blocks resembling teeth, under the bed-moulding of the cornice in the Ionic, Corinthian, Composite, and sometimes Doric, orders. L16. †**2** = DENTICULE. E18–E19. **B** *attrib.* or as *adj.* Consisting of or containing dentils; resembling (a series of) dentils. M18.

dentine /ˈdɛntiːn/ *n.* Also ***-tin** /-tɪn/. M19. [f. L *dens*, *dent-* tooth + -INE[4].] The hard dense tissue forming the chief constituent of teeth.

dentinal /-tɪn(ə)l/ *a.* pertaining to or of the nature of dentine M19.

dentiscalp /ˈdɛntɪskalp/ *n.* Now *rare* or *obs.* M17. [L *dentiscalpium* toothpick, f. as DENTI- + *scalpere* scrape.] A toothpick, a tooth-scraper.

dentist /ˈdɛntɪst/ *n.* M18. [Fr. *dentiste*, f. *dent* tooth: see -IST.] A person whose profession it is to diagnose and treat diseases, injuries, and malformations of the teeth, jaws, and mouth, extract teeth, insert artificial ones, etc.

denˈtistical *a.* (*rare*) of, pertaining to, or of the nature of a dentist E19. **dentistry** *n.* the profession or practice of a dentist M19.

dentition /dɛnˈtɪʃ(ə)n/ *n.* L16. [L *dentitio(n-)*, f. *dentit-* pa. ppl stem of *dentire* teethe, f. *dens*, *dent-* tooth: see -ITION.] **1** The production or cutting of teeth; teething. L16. **2** The characteristic arrangement, kind, and number of teeth in a particular species at a particular age. M19.

denture /ˈdɛntʃə/ *n.*[1] Long *obs.* exc. *dial.* LME. [Aphet.] An indenture.

denture /ˈdɛntʃə/ *n.*[2] *rare.* L17. [f. DENT *v.* + -URE.] An indentation, indent.

denture /ˈdɛntʃə/ *n.*[3] L19. [Fr., f. *dent* tooth: see -URE.] *sing.* & (usu.) in *pl.* A set of (esp. artificial) teeth.

denturist *n.* a maker of artificial dentures M20.

denuclearize /diːˈnjuːklɪərʌɪz/ *v.t.* Also **-ise**. M20. [f. DE- 3 + NUCLEAR *a.* + -IZE.] Deprive of nuclear weapons; remove nuclear weapons from.

denucleariˈzation *n.* M20.

denudate /dɪˈnjuːdeɪt/ *v.t.* Pa. pple **-ated**, (orig.) †**-ate**. LME. [L *denudat-* pa. ppl stem of *denudare*: see DENUDE, -ATE[3].] Strip naked or bare; denude.

denudation /diːnjʊˈdeɪʃ(ə)n/ *n.* LME. [Late (eccl.)L *denudatio(n-)* uncovering, laying bare, as prec.: see -ATION.] **1** The action of making bare; a stripping off of clothing or covering; denuded condition. LME. **2** The action of divesting or depriving (*of*). M17. **3** *Geol.* The laying bare of an underlying rock or formation through the erosion of what lies above it. E19.

1 *fig.*: DONNE The Denudation of your Souls and your Sins by a humble confession. 3 C. DARWIN The enormous power of denudation which the sea possesses.

denudational *a.* of or pertaining to (geological) denudation E20. **deˈnudative** *a.* having the property of denuding; causing (geological) denudation: L19.

denude /dɪˈnjuːd/ *v.* LME. [L *denudare*, f. *de-* DE- I + *nudare* to bare, f. *nudus* nude.] **1** *v.t.* Make naked or bare; strip *of* clothing or covering. LME. **b** *fig.* Strip, divest, deprive, (*of* any possession, attribute, etc.). L15. **c** *Geol.* Of a natural agency: expose (a rock or formation) by the removal of overlying material. M19. **2** *v.i.* Divest oneself of a legal right etc. L17.

1 D. H. LAWRENCE The park was denuded of its timber. **b** A. BURGESS That wicked boy has denuded the larder of practically everything. W. S. CHURCHILL The Island he had left denuded of troops. **c** A. R. WALLACE Rapidly denuded by rain and rivers.

denumerable /dɪˈnjuːm(ə)rəb(ə)l/ *a.* E20. [f. late L *denumerare*: see next, -ABLE.] *Math.* Finite or countably infinite, enumerable; *spec.* able to be counted by one-to-one correspondence with the infinite set of all positive integers.

denumeraˈbility *n.* M20. **denumerably** *adv.* M20.

denumeration /dɪˌnjuːməˈreɪʃ(ə)n/ *n.* Now *rare.* E17. [f. late L *denumerare*, f. *de-* DE- I + *numerare* count out, enumerate: see -ATION.] **1** Enumeration; reckoning. E17. **2** *Law* (now *Hist.*). An immediate payment of money. E18.

denunciate /dɪˈnʌnsɪeɪt, -ʃɪ-/ *v.t.* & *i.* L16. [med.L *denunciat-* for L *denuntiat-* pa. ppl stem of *denuntiare*: see DENOUNCE, -ATE[3].] Denounce; inveigh openly (against).

denunciative *a.* denunciatory E17.

denunciation /dɪˌnʌnsɪˈeɪʃ(ə)n/ *n.* LME. [(O)Fr. *dénonciation* or L *denunciatio(n-)*, f. as prec.: see -ATION.] **1** *gen.* (A) public announcement; (a) proclamation, declaration. *arch.* LME. **2** An accusation before a public prosecutor; a charge. LME. **3** (A) warning, (a) threatening announcement. M16. †**4** *Sc. Law.* The action or an act of denouncing a person as a rebel or outlaw. L16–L19. **5** (A) public condemnation, (an) invective. M19. 6 The action or an act of denouncing a treaty. L19.

1 W. BLACKSTONE Why . . a denunciation of war ought always to precede the actual commencement of hostilities. 3 W. WHISTON The prophet . . by the denunciation of miseries, weakened the alacrity of the multitude. 5 M. MEYER Kierkegaard's denunciation of state religion. G. PRIESTLAND Many proposals for action are little more than gestures of denunciation.

denunciator /dɪˈnʌnsɪeɪtə, -ʃɪ-/ *n.* L15. [Fr. *dénonciateur* or L *denunciator*, f. as DENUNCIATE: see -OR.] A person who denounces or utters denunciations. Formerly, in *Civil Law*, one who lodges a charge or complaint against another.

denunciatory *a.* of or pertaining to denunciation; characterized by denouncing: E18.

denutrition /diːnjuˈtrɪʃ(ə)n/ *n.* Now *rare* or *obs.* M19. [f. DE- 3 + NUTRITION.] *Med.* Degeneration of tissue arising from lack of nutrition. Also, treatment by deprivation of nourishment.

†deny *n.* Also **denay**. LME. [Fr. *déni*, OFr. *desni*, f. stem of *dénier* DENY *v.*] 1 Refusal of what is asked, offered, etc. LME–E17. 2 Contradiction of a statement; negation. M16–E17.

deny /dɪˈnʌɪ/ *v.t.* Also **†denay**. ME. [OFr. *deni-* tonic stem of *deneier*, *denoier*, later (also mod.) *dénier*, f. L *denegare*, f. *de-* DE- 1 + *negare* say no, refuse.] 1 Contradict (a statement or allegation); declare to be untrue or untenable. ME. 2 *Logic.* Assert the contradictory of (a proposition). LME. 3 Refuse to admit the truth of (a doctrine etc.); refuse to admit the existence or reality of. LME. 4 Refuse to recognize or acknowledge (a person or thing) as having a certain character or certain claims; disown, disavow, repudiate. LME. 5 Withhold (a thing requested, claimed, or desired); refuse to give or grant. (Foll. by *to* a person, or w. indirect obj.) LME. **b** Refuse access to (a person sought). M17. 6 Refuse the request or demand of (a person). Formerly also, reject (a candidate). LME. **†b** Refuse admittance to (a visitor). L16–M18. 7 Refuse *to be* or *do*. *obs.* exc. *Sc.* LME. 8 Refuse permission to or for; forbid (*to do*, *the doing of*). Now *rare.* LME. †9 Refuse to take or accept. LME–E18. 10 *refl.* Refrain from the gratification of desire; be abstinent. LME.

1 H. FIELDING Jones could not deny the charge. W. CRUISE I beg leave to deny this to be law. S. BELLOW My client denies that he struck him. R. P. JHABVALA We have, I can't deny, had a lot of trouble with him. 3 ROBERT BURTON Many deny Witches at all. G. BERKELEY They who deny the Freedom and Immortality of the soul in effect deny its being. 4 R. L. STEVENSON A man must not deny his manifest abilities, for that is to evade his obligations. 5 I. D'ISRAELI All the consolations of fame were denied him during his life. V. NABOKOV To bring that coffee to her, and then deny it until she had done her morning duty. *fig.*: J. BUTLER The known course of human things . . denies to virtue its full scope. **b** R. B. SHERIDAN He is . . in the house, though the servants are ordered to deny him. 6 T. HARDY Don't refuse me, . . I shall think it hard if you deny me. 8 SHAKES. *Tit. A.* One thing more, That womanhood denies my tongue to tell. 10 W. S. MAUGHAM My mother . . denied herself so that I shouldn't go hungry.

denyingly *adv.* in a way that denies or refuses LME.

deobstruct /diːəbˈstrʌkt/ *v.t.* M17. [f. DE- 3 + OBSTRUCT. Cf. med.L *deobstruere*.] Clear of obstruction; unblock.

†deobstruent *n.* & *a.* L17–M19. [f. DE- 3 + OBSTRUENT.] (A medicine or substance) that clears obstructions by opening the natural passages or pores of the body.

deoch an doris /dɒx (ə)n ˈdɒrɪs, dɒk/ *n. phr.* *Sc.* & *Ir.* Also **doch**. L17. [Gael. *deoch an doruis*, Ir. *deoch an dorais* a drink at the door.] A drink taken at parting, a stirrup-cup.

deoculate /diːˈɒkjʊleɪt/ *v.t.* *rare.* E17. [f. DE- 3 + L *oculus* eye + -ATE[3].] Blind; put out the eyes of. Usu. in *pass.*

deodand /ˈdiːə(ʊ)dand/ *n.* E16. [Law Fr. *deodande* f. AL *deodanda*, *-um*, f. L *Deo dandum* thing to be given to God (*Deus* god, *dare* give).] Something to be given to God; *spec.* (*Law*, now *Hist.*) a thing forfeited to the Crown for a religious or charitable use, as having caused a human death; *loosely* a sum forfeited as the value of a deodand.

deodar /ˈdiːə(ʊ)dɑː/ *n.* E19. [Hind. *deodār* f. Skt *devadāru*.] A cedar, *Cedrus deodara*, native to the Himalayas, which is used as a source of timber in the Indian subcontinent and is also planted as an ornamental elsewhere.

deodorant /dɪˈəʊd(ə)r(ə)nt/ *n.* M19. [f. as next + -ANT[1].] A substance that removes or conceals unwanted odours; *esp.* a preparation applied to the skin to inhibit the odour of perspiration.

deodorize /dɪˈəʊdərʌɪz/ *v.t.* Also **-ise**. M19. [f. DE- 3 + L *odor* ODOUR + -IZE.] Destroy the odour of; remove or conceal the (unpleasant) odour of.

deodoriˈzation *n.* M19. **deodorizer** *n.* something that deodorizes, a deodorant M19.

Deo gratias /deɪəʊ ˈɡrɑːtɪəs, ˈɡrɑːʃɪəs/ *int.* L16. [L = (we give) thanks to God.] Thanks be to God.

deontic /dɪˈɒntɪk/ *n.* & *a.* M19. [f. as next + -IC.] A *n.* *Philos.* In *pl.* (treated as *sing.*). The branch of philosophy that deals with duty or obligations. M19. **B** *adj.* *Philos.* & *Ling.* Of or relating to duty or obligation, or its linguistic expression. M20.

deontology /diːɒnˈtɒlədʒi/ *n.* E19. [f. Gk *deont-* pres. ppl stem of *dei* it is right + -OLOGY.] The science of duty or moral obligation; ethics.

deontoˈlogical *a.* M19. **deontologist** *n.* M19.

deoperculate /diːə(ʊ)ˈpəːkjʊlət/ *a.* M17. [f. DE- 3 + OPERCULATE.] †1 Uncovered. *rare.* Only in M17. 2 *Bot.* Having shed the operculum; having an operculum that does not separate from the capsule. M19.

†deoppilate *v.t.* & *i.* E17–E18. [f. DE- 3 + OPPILATE.] *Med.* Remove an obstruction or obstructions (from).

†deoppilation *n.* the removal of obstructions M17–M19. **†deoppilative** *a.* & *n.* (a medicine or drug) tending to remove obstructions E17–E18.

de-orbit /diːˈɔːbɪt/ *v.* & *n.* M20. [f. DE- 3 + ORBIT *n.* or *v.*] A *v.t.* & *i.* (Cause to) leave or move out of orbit around the earth or other body. M20. **B** *n.* A spacecraft's moving out of orbit. M20.

deordination /dɪˌɔːdɪˈneɪʃ(ə)n/ *n.* Now *rare* or *obs.* L15. [Late L *deordinatio(n-)*, f. L *de-* DE- 3 + *ordinatio(n-)* ORDINATION.] Departure from or violation of (esp. moral) order; disorder.

†deosculation *n.* M17–L18. [f. L *deosculat-* pa. ppl stem of *deosculari* kiss warmly: see DE- 1, OSCULATION.] Kissing.

Deo volente /ˌdeɪəʊ vɒˈlɛnteɪ/ *adv. phr.* M18. [L.] God willing; if nothing prevents it.

deoxidate /diːˈɒksɪdeɪt/ *v.t.* L18. [f. DE- 3 + OXIDATE.] *Chem.* = next.

deoxiˈdation *n.* L18.

deoxidize /diːˈɒksɪdʌɪz/ *v.t.* Also **-ise**. L18. [f. DE- 3 + OXIDIZE.] *Chem.* Remove (esp. combined) oxygen from; reduce. Cf. prec., DEOXYGENATE.

deoxidizer *n.* a deoxidizing agent M19.

deoxy- /diːˈɒksi/ *comb. form.* Also **desoxy-** /dɛˈsɒksi/. [f. DE- 3 + OXY-.] Used in *Chem.* w. the senses 'that has lost oxygen', 'that has fewer oxygen atoms'.

deoxyˌcorticoˈsterone *n.* (*Biochem.*) a corticosteroid hormone, $C_{21}H_{30}O_3$, involved in regulating the salt and water balance M20. **deoxyˈribose** *n.* (*Biochem.*) any of the isomeric sugars ($C_5H_{10}O_4$) derived from ribose by replacement of a hydroxyl group by a hydrogen atom; *spec.* (more fully *2-deoxyribose*) that isomer present in DNA: M20.

deoxygenate /diːˈɒksɪdʒəneɪt/ *v.t.* L19. [f. DE- 3 + OXYGENATE.] Remove (esp. free) oxygen from. Cf. DEOXIDATE, DEOXIDIZE.

deoxygeˈnation *n.* E19.

deoxyribonucleic /dɪˌɒksɪrʌɪbəʊnjuːˈkleɪɪk, -ˈkliːɪk; -ˈnjuː-/ *a.* Also **desoxy-** /dɛˌsɒksɪ-/. M20. [f. *deoxyribose* (s.v. DEOXY-) + NUCLEIC.] Biochem. *deoxyribonucleic acid*, = DNA.

deoxyribonuclease *n.* = DNASE M20. **deoxyribonucleotide** *n.* a nucleotide containing deoxyribose M20.

depaint /dɪˈpeɪnt/ *v.t.* Long *arch.* *rare.* Pa. pple (earlier, *arch.*) **depaint, -ed**. ME. [Orig. pa. pple, f. (O)Fr. *dépeint* pa. pple of *dépeindre* f. L *depingere*: see DE- 1, PAINT *v.* Cf. DEPEINCT, DEPICT.] 1 Represent in colours; paint; depict; delineate. Freq. in *pass.* ME. 2 Paint or decorate (as) with painted figures; paint or colour (a surface). Usu. in *pass.* ME. 3 Portray in words; describe graphically or by comparison. Also foll. by *out*, *forth*. LME. †4 Stain. LME–E17.

depalatalization /diːˌpalət(ə)lʌɪˈzeɪʃ(ə)n/ *n.* Also **-isation**. M20. [f. DE- 3 + PALATALIZATION.] *Phonet.* Loss of palatalization.

depark /diːˈpɑːk/ *v.t.* M16. [f. DE- 3 + PARK *n.* Cf. Fr. *déparquer* (earlier †*des-*).] = DISPARK.

†depart *n.* ME. [Partly f. (O)Fr. *départ*, f. as next; partly f. next.] 1 The act of departing, departure; parting; death. ME–M19. 2 *Chem.* The separation of one substance from another. LME–M18.

depart /dɪˈpɑːt/ *v.* ME. [(O)Fr. *départir* f. Proto-Romance var. of L *dispertire* divide: see DE- 3, PART *v.*] I Divide or part. †1 *v.t.* & *i.* Separate into two or more parts. ME–L18. †2 *v.t.* Divide or part among persons etc.; distribute; occas., impart, bestow. ME–M17. **b** *v.i.* Share or partake (*in* a thing, *with* a person). LME–M16. †3 *v.t.* Sunder; separate *from* another (*lit.* & *fig.*). ME–L17. **b** *v.i.* Separate, make separation. LME–L15. **c** *v.i.* *Chem.* Separate a metal from an alloy or solution. E–M18. †4 *v.t.* Break off or dissolve (a connection etc.). LME–L16. **b** *v.i.* Of a connection etc.: be broken off or dissolved. LME–E16.

3 CAXTON That god hath ioyned man may not departe. 4 MALORY Ye departed the loue bitwene me and my wyf.

II Go apart or away. †5 *v.i.* Part or separate from each other; take leave of each other. ME–M17. 6 *v.i.* Go away (*from*); take one's leave; (esp. of public transport) set out, start, leave, (*for*). Now chiefly *formal* or *literary*. ME. †**b** Go away *to*, *into*; make one's way. LME–E17. **c** Leave this world, decease, die, pass away. Now chiefly as DEPARTED *a.* 3. E16. 7 *v.t.* Go away from, leave, forsake. Now chiefly in *depart this life* below. ME. 8 *v.i.* Diverge, deviate, withdraw, desist, (*from* a course of action etc.). LME. †9 *v.t.* Send away, dismiss. L15–E17.

6 A. E. HOUSMAN And wish them farewell And watch them depart on the way. *Observer* The train about to depart from platform one. **b** AV *Matt.* 2:12 They departed into their owne countrey another way. 7 T. KEIGHTLEY The clergy were ordered to depart the kingdom. 8 HOBBES A design to depart from the worship of God. H. L. MENCKEN Their speculations tend . . to depart from the field of true science. J. ADAMSON One matinee performance at which they had departed from the script.

Phrases: **depart from (this) life, depart this life** (now chiefly *formal* or *literary*) die. **†depart with** part with, give up, give away.

†departable, -ible *a.* LME–M18.

departed /dɪˈpɑːtɪd/ *a.* & *n.* LME. [f. prec. + -ED[1].] A *adj.* †1 Divided into parts. Only in LME. †2 Separated, parted; cut off from the main body, schismatic. LME–M17. 3 That has departed by death; deceased. E16. 4 Past, bygone. M16.

3 ADDISON Magicians, Demons, and departed Spirits. 4 J. SAUNDERS Antiquity and departed greatness.

B *absol.* as *n.* A deceased person; *pl.* deceased people as a class, *the* dead. E18.

E. LONGFORD If the living Albert kept Queen Victoria and Disraeli apart, the dear departed brought them together.

départment *n.* see DEPARTMENT.

departer /dɪˈpɑːtə/ *n.*[1] LME. [f. DEPART *v.* + -ER[1]. In sense 2 perh. f. Fr. †*départeur* (OFr. *departeör*).] †1 A divider, a distributor; a discerner. Only in LME. 2 A person who departs or goes away. Formerly also, a seceder. L16.

†departer *n.*[2] E16–M18. [Use as n. of AN infinitive *departer* = (O)Fr. *départir* DEPART *v.*: see -ER[4].] = DEPARTURE *n.* 2.

department /dɪˈpɑːtm(ə)nt/ *n.* In sense 4 also ***département*** /departəmɑ̃ (*pl. same*)/. LME. [(O)Fr. *département*, f. as DEPART *v.*: see -MENT.] †1 Division, partition, distribution. *rare.*

LME–L17. †2 Departure; separation; leave-taking, withdrawal; decease. L15–L17. 3 A separate part of a complex whole or organized system, a branch, *esp.* of municipal or State administration, of a university, school, or college, or of a shop; *loosely*, an area of (specialist) activity. M18. 4 An administrative district in France and some other countries. L18.

3 C. ISHERWOOD To find my way through departments of underwear, outfitting, .. sport and cutlery. H. BELLOC Lombroso's own department of charlatanry was to attack Christian morals.

Comb.: **department store** a large shop supplying many kinds of goods from various departments.

departmental /diːpɑːtˈmɛnt(ə)l/ *a.* L18. [f. prec. + -AL[1].] Of or pertaining to a department.

departmental store = DEPARTMENT *store*.

departmentalism *n.* adherence to departmental methods or structure M19. **departmentaliˈzation** *n.* division into departments M19. **departmentalize** *v.t.* divide into departments L19. **departmentally** *adv.* L19.

departure /dɪˈpɑːtʃə/ *n.* LME. [OFr. *departeüre*, f. as DEPART *v.*: see -URE.] 1 The action of going away; *arch.* decease, death. LME. 2 *Law.* A change in pleading from the ground taken by the same party in an earlier plea. L15. †3 Separation, severance, parting. Also, a boundary separating two areas, a division. E16–E18. 4 The action of setting out or starting on a journey; *esp.* the (scheduled) starting of a train, aeroplane, or public transport vehicle; the starting or setting out on a course of action or thought. M16. 5 *Naut.* The amount of a ship's change of longitude. Also, the bearing of an object on the coast, taken at the start of a voyage, from which the dead reckoning begins. M17. 6 Withdrawal, divergence, deviation, (*from* a path, course, or standard). L17 7 In full *departure lounge.* An area in an airport in which passengers wait immediately prior to boarding. M20.

1 S. JOHNSON The loss of our friends .. impresses .. upon us the necessity of our own departure. SAKI The farewell dinner .. in honour of her son's departure. 4 OED The Booking Office is open 15 minutes before the departure of each train. J. BARZUN The free public high school of 1900 was a bold departure. **new departure** a fresh start, the beginning of a new course of procedure. 6 H. J. S. MAINE Partial and local departures from the Brehon Law were common all over Ancient Ireland.

depascent /dɪˈpas(ə)nt/ *a. rare.* M17. [L *depascent-* pres. ppl stem of *depascere* eat up, consume, f. *de-* DE- 1 + *pascere* feed, pasture: see -ENT.] Consuming.

depasture /diːˈpɑːstʃə, -tjə/ *v.* E16. [f. DE- 1 + PASTURE *v.*] 1 *v.t.* Of cattle: consume the produce of (land) by grazing on it; use for pasturage. E16. 2 *v.i.* Of cattle: graze. M16. 3 *v.t.* Put (cattle) to graze; pasture, feed, (cattle). E18. 4 *v.t.* Of land: give pasturage to (cattle). E19.

depasturage *n.* the consumption of pasture by grazing animals; the right of pasture: M18.

†**depatriate** *v.i.* L17–L18. [med.L *depatriat-* pa. ppl stem of *depatriare* (also *dis-*) leave home, f. L *de-* DE- 3 + *patria* fatherland: see -ATE[3].] Leave or renounce one's native country; expatriate oneself.

depauperate /dɪˈpɔːp(ə)rət/ *a.* LME. [med.L *depauperatus* pa. pple, f. as next: see -ATE[2].] 1 *gen.* Made poor, impoverished. Long *obs.* exc. *Sc. rare.* LME. 2 Chiefly *Bot.* & *Zool.* Imperfectly developed, stunted; (of a flora or fauna) lacking in numbers or variety of species. M19.

depauperate /dɪˈpɔːpəreɪt/ *v.t.* M16. [med.L *depauperat-* pa. ppl stem of *depauperare*, f. L *de-* DE- 1 + *pauperare* make poor, f. *pauper* poor: see -ATE[3].] Make poor, impoverish; reduce in quality, vigour, or capacity.

depauperated *a.* = DEPAUPERATE *a.* M17. **depaupeˈration** *n.* [med.L *depauperatio(n-)*] M17.

depauperize /diːˈpɔːpərʌɪz/ *v.*[1]*t.* Also **-ise**. M19. [f. DE- 3 + PAUPERIZE.] = DISPAUPERIZE.

depauperize /dɪˈpɔːpərʌɪz/ *v.*[2]*t. rare.* Also **-ise**. L19. [f. DE- 1 + PAUPERIZE, after L *depauperare*: see DEPAUPERATE *v.*] Depauperate, pauperize.

depauperiˈzation *n.* M19.

dépaysé /depeize/ *a.* Fem. **-ée**. E20. [Fr. = (removed) from one's own country.] Removed from one's habitual surroundings.

†**depeinct** *v.t.* Also **depinct**. L16–L17. [Intermediate forms between DEPAINT & DEPICT: cf. OFr. *depeinct*, It. *depinto*.] = DEPICT.

depel /dɪˈpɛl/ *v.t.* Long *rare.* Also **-ll**. Infl. **-ll-**. M16. [L *depellere* drive out, f. *de-* DE- 1 + *pellere* drive.] Drive away, expel.

†**depencil** *v.t.* Infl. **-l(l)-**. L16–M18. [f. DE- 1 + PENCIL *v.*] Write with a pencil or a brush, inscribe, depict.

depend /dɪˈpɛnd/ *v.i.* LME. [(O)Fr. *dépendre* f. Proto-Romance var. of L *dependere*, f. *de-* DE- 1 + *pendere*: cf. PEND *v.*[3]] 1 Hang down, be suspended *from*. Now chiefly *literary.* LME. †2 Wait in suspense or expectation *on*, *upon*. LME–E18. 3 Be in suspense, be undetermined; be waiting for settlement; be pending. Chiefly as *depending* ppl a. LME. 4 Be attached, as a result or consequence is to its condition or cause; be contingent, be conditioned. Foll. by *(up)on*, †*of*, (colloq.) *interrog. cl.*, or *absol.* LME. 5 Foll. by *(up)on*, †*of*: belong to or be connected with as something subordinate; be grammatically dependent on. LME. 6 Rely in mind, reckon, or count confidently *on* or *upon*. E16. b Be sure or confident *that. arch. colloq.* E18. 7 Foll. by *on*, *upon*: rest entirely on for maintenance, support, or other requirement; be obliged to use; be unable to do without. M16. †8 Impend. *rare.* E17–E18.

1 R. LEHMANN From one hand depended a meagre trail of botanical specimens. 2 DRYDEN The hearer on the speaker's mouth depends. 3 T. HUTCHINSON Whilst these disputes .. were depending, the .. Indians made attacks. 4 SLOAN WILSON The broadcasting company's decision might depend on the recommendation Dick gave him. K. LAFFAN Depends how you look at it, sir. R. HAYMAN Depending on whether you viewed it from the plain .. or from the woods, the castle presented different aspects. *Observer* Whether there is inside information .. or not, depends. **that depends** the question can only be answered conditionally. 5 T. FULLER Hereupon a story depends. 6 K. A. PORTER The kind of man a girl may depend on to be a gentleman in whatever circumstances. A. PRICE I'll have a damn good try... You can depend on that. b J. C. MORISON We may depend that a swift blight would have shrivelled his labours. 7 A. E. STEVENSON We depend on our forests for vast and constantly increasing supplies of .. essential timber products. D. BAGLEY I always depend on my intuition and it rarely lets me down. P. FITZGERALD It was quite wrong to come to depend too much upon one's children.

depender *n.* †(*a*) *rare* a protector, a supporter; †(*b*) (chiefly *Sc.*) a dependant; (*c*) *rare* a person who depends or relies *on* something: L15.

dependable /dɪˈpɛndəb(ə)l/ *a.* M18. [f. prec. + -ABLE.] Able to be depended on; trustworthy, reliable.

dependaˈbility *n.* E20. **dependableness** *n.* M19. **dependably** *adv.* M19.

dependance *n.* see DEPENDENCE *n.*

dependancy *n.* see DEPENDENCY.

dependant /dɪˈpɛnd(ə)nt/ *n.* Also ***-ent**. LME. [Fr. *dépendant* pres. pple of *dépendre*: see DEPEND, -ANT[1], -ENT.] †1 Something subordinately attached, belonging to, or connected with, something else; a dependency. LME–M19. 2 A person who depends on another for maintenance or position; a retainer, a servant, a subordinate. L16.

dependant *a.* see DEPENDENT *a.*

dependence /dɪˈpɛnd(ə)ns/ *n.* Also **-ance**. LME. [(O)Fr. *dépendance*, f. as DEPEND: see -ANCE, -ENCE.] †1 The action of hanging down; something that hangs down. *rare.* LME–L17. 2 The relation of having existence hanging upon, or conditioned by, the existence of something else; the fact of depending *on* another thing or person; the state or condition of being dependent. LME. 3 = DEPENDENCY 4. Now *rare.* M16. 4†a A quarrel or affair of honour awaiting settlement. L16–E19. b The condition of waiting for settlement, now esp. for the resolution of a legal action. E17. 5 The condition of a dependant; inability to do without someone or something; subjection, subordination. E17. 6 The condition of waiting in faith or expectation; reliance, confident trust. E17. b An object of confidence or trust; something (to be) relied on. Now *rare* or *obs.* M18.

2 J. TYNDALL The chain of dependence which runs throughout creation. N. CHOMSKY The dependence of the American economy on Third World resources. 3 E. HEMINGWAY It had been a dependence of the Grand Hotel—but now it was its own hotel. 5 J. MORTIMER Sudden freedom, growing up, the end of dependence. 6 B. JOWETT Living .. in dependence on the will of God.

dependency /dɪˈpɛnd(ə)nsi/ *n.* Also ***-ancy**. L16. [f. as prec.: see -ANCY, -ENCY.] 1 = DEPENDENCE 2. L16. 2 = DEPENDENCE 5. L16. †3 = DEPENDENCE 6. L16–E17. 4 A dependent or subordinate thing; *esp.* a country or province controlled by another. Formerly also, a body of dependants, a household establishment. E17. †5 = DEPENDENCE 4a. E17–E19.

1 SHAKES. *Meas. for M.* The oddest frame of sense, such a dependency of thing on thing, As e'er I heard. 2 A. STORR Every child, if it is to become an adult in its own right, has to escape from dependency. *Times* Self-generated and minus any dependency on government gratuities. 4 G. MURRAY An Empire, in which Athens .. dictated the foreign policy, while the dependencies paid tribute for their protection.

dependent *n.* see DEPENDANT *n.*

dependent /dɪˈpɛnd(ə)nt/ *a.* Also **-ant**. LME. [f. as DEPENDANT *n.*] 1 Hanging down, pendent. LME. 2 Contingent on or determined or conditioned by something else. (Foll. by *on*, *upon.*) LME. 3 Resting entirely on someone or something for maintenance, support, or other requirement; obliged to use something; unable to do without someone or something, esp. a drug; maintained at another's cost. (Foll. by *on*, *upon.*) LME. 4 Subordinate, subject; *Gram.* (of a grammatical unit) in a subordinate relation to another grammatical unit. (Foll. by *on*, *upon.*) E17.

1 J. MORSE A regular rock, from the upper part of which are dependent many excrescences. 2 H. POWER Effects dependent upon the same .. Causes. **dependent variable** *Math.*: having a value depending on that of another variable. 3 C. S. LEWIS Trustfully dependent upon the grown-ups. 4 ISAAC TAYLOR The temper of mind which is proper to a dependant and subordinate agent.

dependently *adv.* M17.

depeople /dɪˈpiːp(ə)l/ *v.t. arch.* E17. [Fr. *dépeupler*, f. *dé-* DE- 3 + *peuple* PEOPLE *n.* Cf. DISPEOPLE.] Depopulate.

†**deperdit** *a.* & *n.* Also **-ite**. E17. [L *deperditus* pa. pple of *deperdere* destroy, ruin, f. *de-* DE- 1 + *perdere* destroy, lose.] A *adj.* Lost, abandoned. E–M17. B *n.* Something lost or perished. Only in E19.

deperdition /diːpəːˈdɪʃ(ə)n/ *n.* Now *rare* or *obs.* E17. [Fr. *déperdition*, f. as prec.: see -ITION.] Loss, waste, destruction by wasting away.

deperition /diːpəˈrɪʃ(ə)n/ *n. rare.* L18. [f. DE- 1 + L *perire* perish + -ITION, perh. after prec.] Perishing, complete wasting away.

deperm /diːˈpəːm/ *v.t.* M20. [f. DE- 3 + abbrev. of *permanent* (*magnetism*).] Demagnetize (a ship).

depersonalize /diːˈpəːs(ə)n(ə)lʌɪz/ *v.t.* Also **-ise**. M19. [f. DE- 3 + PERSONALIZE.] Deprive of personality; make impersonal.

depersonaliˈzation *n.* the action of depersonalizing; the fact of being depersonalized; *Psychiatry* a pathological state in which one's thoughts and feelings seem unreal or not to belong to oneself: E20.

depetal /diːˈpɛt(ə)l/ *v.t.* Infl. **-ll-**, ***-l-**. M20. [f. DE- 3 + PETAL.] Remove the petals from.

dephlegmate /dɪˈflɛgmeɪt/ *v.t. obs.* exc. *Hist.* M17. [f. L *de-* DE- 3 + *phlegma* PHLEGM: see -ATE[3].] *Chem.* Free from phlegm or watery matter, rectify.

dephlegˈmation *n.* M17. ˈ**dephlegmator** *n.* an apparatus for dephlegmation E19.

dephlogisticate /diːfləˈdʒɪstɪkeɪt/ *v.t.* L18. [f. DE- 3 + PHLOGISTICATE.] 1 *Chem.* (now *Hist.*). Deprive of 'phlogiston'. L18. †2 Relieve of inflammation. M–L19.

1 **dephlogisticated air** oxygen (orig. so analysed).

dephlogistiˈcation *n.* L18.

dephosphorize /diːˈfɒsfərʌɪz/ *v.t.* Also **-ise.** L19. [f. DE- 3 + PHOSPHORIZE.] Free (esp. steel) from phosphorus.
dephosphoriˈzation *n.* L19.

dephosphorylate /diːfɒsˈfɒrɪleɪt/ *v.t.* E20. [f. DE- 3 + PHOSPHORYLATE *v.*] *Chem.* Remove a phosphate group from (a compound), esp. (*Biochem.*) enzymatically.
dephosphoryˈlation *n.* M20.

depict /dɪˈpɪkt/ *v.t.* LME. [L *depict-* pa. ppl stem of *depingere* portray, f. *de-* DE- 1 + *pingere* paint. Cf. DEPAINT, DEPEINCT.] 1 Portray or represent (as if) in colours or in drawing, painting, or sculpture. LME. 2 Portray or represent in words; describe graphically. M18.
1 D. LODGE The stained-glass windows . . that depict Scenes from the life of Our Lady. B. PYM Faded sepia photographs depicting groups of country people. 2 JOHN BROOKE King George has been depicted as a neurotic and unstable character. M. ESSLIN Plays depicting a . . brutal nightmare world.
depicter, -or *n.* M19. **depiction** *n.* [L *depictio(n-)*] the action of depicting; painted representation; graphic description: L17. **depictive** *a.* having the quality or function of depicting E19.

depicture /dɪˈpɪktʃə/ *n.* E16. [f. as prec. + -URE.] Depiction.

depicture /dɪˈpɪktʃə/ *v.t.* L16. [f. DE- 1 + PICTURE *v.*] 1 = DEPICT. L16. 2 Picture to one's own mind; imagine. L18.
depicturement *n.* M19.

depigment /diːˈpɪgm(ə)nt/ *v.t.* E20. [f. DE- 3 + PIGMENT *n.*] Deprive of pigment; reduce the pigmentation of. Chiefly as *depigmented* ppl a.
ˌ**depigmenˈtation** *n.* loss or deficiency of pigment L19.

depilate /ˈdɛpɪleɪt/ *v.t.* M16. [L *depilat-* pa. ppl stem of *depilare*, f. *de-* DE- 1 + *pilare* deprive of hair, f. *pilus* hair: see -ATE[3].] Remove the hair from.

depilation /dɛpɪˈleɪʃ(ə)n/ *n.* LME. [L *depilatio(n-)*, f. as prec.: see -ATION.] 1 The action of stripping of hair; the condition of being without hair. LME. †2 Pillage. Only in 17.

depilatory /dɪˈpɪlət(ə)ri/ *a.* & *n.* E17. [L *depilatorius*, f. as DEPILATE: see -ORY[2].] A *adj.* Having the property of removing hair. E17. B *n.* A depilatory agent or substance. E17.

depilous /ˈdɛpɪləs/ *a.* M17. [f. L *depilis*, f. *de-* DE- 1 + *pilus* hair: see -OUS.] Deprived of hair; without hair.

†**depinct** *v.* var. of DEPEINCT.

deplace /dɪˈpleɪs/ *v.t. rare.* M19. [Fr. *déplacer*, f. *dé-* DE- 3 + *placer* to place.] = DISPLACE.

deplane /diːˈpleɪn/ *v.* E20. [f. DE- 3 + PLANE *n.*[4]] 1 *v.i.* Disembark from an aeroplane. E20. 2 *v.t.* Remove from an aeroplane. M20.

deplete /dɪˈpliːt/ *a.* L19. [L *depletus* pa. pple of *deplere*: see next.] Emptied out, exhausted (*of* contents).

deplete /dɪˈpliːt/ *v.* E19. [L *deplet-* pa. ppl stem of *deplere* empty out, f. *de-* DE- 3 + base of *plenus* full.] 1 *v.t.* & *i. Med.* (now *rare* or *obs.*). Empty or relieve (the bodily system, blood-vessels) when overcharged, as by bleeding or purgatives. E19. 2 *v.t.* Deprive of contents or stocks; empty out, exhaust; reduce the numbers or quantity of. M19.
2 A. E. STEVENSON As . . higher grade . . mineral resources are depleted, the costs of extraction . . go up. A. FRASER This royal family had recently been depleted by two deaths. V. ACKLAND I was feeling utterly depleted and drained.
depletive, depletory *adjs.* (*Med.*) characterized by or causing depletion M19.

depletion /dɪˈpliːʃ(ə)n/ *n.* M17. [Fr. *déplétion* or late L *depletio(n-)* (earlier *depletura*) blood-letting, f. as prec.: see -ION.] 1 The action of depleting; the condition of being depleted; the emptying of contents; exhaustion. M17. 2 *Med.* (now *rare* or *obs.*). The emptying or relieving of overfilled organs or cavities in the body. M18.
1 J. M. KEYNES The depletion of the surplus stocks will have an offsetting effect on the amount by which investment increases. T. WILLIAMS He holds the bottle to the light to observe its depletion.
Comb.: **depletion allowance** *US* a tax concession allowable to a company whose normal business activities (esp. oil extraction) reduce the value of its own assets.

deplorable /dɪˈplɔːrəb(ə)l/ *a.* E17. [Fr. *déplorable* or late L *deplorabilis*, f. *deplorare*: see DEPLORE, -ABLE.] To be deplored, lamentable, regrettable, wretched. Now usu., objectionable, scandalous, exceedingly bad.
W. ROBERTSON The people beheld the deplorable situation of their sovereign with insensibility. P. G. WODEHOUSE Odd . . how often the noblest girls had these deplorable brothers. L. MACNEICE He often writes badly—most of his verse is deplorable.
deploraˈbility *n.* M19. **deplorableness** *n.* M17. **deplorably** *adv.* M17.

deploration /diːplɔːˈreɪʃ(ə)n/ *n.* Now *rare.* L15. [L *deploratio(n-)*, f. *deplorat-* pa. ppl stem of *deplorare*: see next, -ATION.] The action of deploring; lamentation.

deplore /dɪˈplɔː/ *v.* M16. [(O)Fr. *déplorer* or It. *deplorare* f. L *deplorare*, f. *de-* DE- 1 + *plorare* wail, bewail.] 1 *v.t.* Weep for, bewail, lament; grieve over, regret deeply. Now usu., regard as scandalous, feel or express strong disapproval of. M16. †b Give up as hopeless. *rare.* M16–E18. †c Tell with grief. *rare* (Shakes.). Only in E17. †2 *v.i.* Lament, mourn. M17–L18.
1 H. F. CARY He . . must aye deplore With unavailing penitence his crime. D. MURPHY Twice a week Mrs Mansfield called to drink tea . . and deplore the appalling inroads being made by democracy on good manners. b W. CONGREVE A true Poetick State we had deplor'd.
deplorer *n.* L17. **deploringly** *adv.* in a deploring manner M19.

deploy /dɪˈplɔɪ/ *v.* & *n.* L15. [Fr. *déployer* f. L *displicare* unfold (later also, explain), also late L *deplicare* unfold, explain, f. *de-*, *dis-* (see DE-) + *plicare* fold.] A *v.* †1 *v.t.* Unfold, display. Only in L15. 2 *v.t.* a *Mil.* Spread out (troops etc.) to form an extended line instead of a column; bring (armaments, men, etc.) into position for action. L18. b *gen.* Bring into or position for effective action, make good use of. M19. 3 *v.i.* Chiefly *Mil.* (Of troops etc.) spread out in line; take up positions for action. L18.
2a E. HEATH We . . deployed our guns on the hills close to Caen. D. FRASER The 18th Division was already deployed in Picardy. b E. BOWEN He was an excellent match, and . . the cream of the young lady visitors . . must have been deployed for him. M. HUNTER The form of writing that best deploys his particular talent. H. WILSON The arguments he will be deploying. 3 R. GRAVES John's men . . could not deploy, because of the narrowness of the defile.
B *n. Mil.* The action or process of deploying. L18.
deployment *n.* L18.

deplumate /dɪˈpluːmət/ *a. rare.* LME. [med.L *deplumatus* pa. pple of *deplumare*: see DEPLUME, -ATE[2].] Stripped of feathers, deplumed.
Also **deplumated** *a.* E18.

deplumation /diːpluˈmeɪʃ(ə)n/ *n.* E17. [Fr. *déplumation*, or f. next + -ATION.] The action of depluming; the condition of being deplumed; loss of feathers; *fig.* loss of honour, wealth, etc.

deplume /dɪˈpluːm/ *v.t.* LME. [Fr. *déplumer*, OFr *desplumer* or med.L *deplumare*, f. L *de-* DE- 3 + *plumare* PLUME *v.*] 1 Strip (a bird etc.) of feathers; pluck the feathers off. LME. 2 *fig.* Strip or deprive of honour, ornament, wealth, etc. M17.

depoeticize /diːpəʊˈɛtɪsʌɪz/ *v.t.* Also **-ise.** E19. [f. DE- 3 + POETICIZE.] Deprive of poetic character.
Also **deˈpoetize** *v.t.* M19.

depolarize /diːˈpəʊlərʌɪz/ *v.t.* Also **-ise.** E19. [f. DE- 3 + POLARIZE.] Chiefly *Physics.* Reduce or remove the polarization or polarity of.
depolariˈzation *n.* E19. **depolarizer** *n.* a device for depolarizing light etc. M19.

depolish /diːˈpɒlɪʃ/ *v.t.* L19. [f. DE- 3 + POLISH *v.* or *n.*[1]] Remove the polish from; deprive of polish.

depoliticize /diːpəˈlɪtɪsʌɪz/ *v.t.* Also **-ise.** M20. [f. DE- 3 + POLITICIZE.] Make non-political; remove from political activity or influence.
depoliticiˈzation *n.* E20.

depollute /diːpəˈluːt, -ˈljuːt/ *v.t.* M20. [f. DE- 3 + POLLUTE *v.*] Cleanse of (environmental) pollution.

depolymerize /diːˈpɒlɪmərʌɪz/ *v.t.* & *i.* Also **-ise.** L19. [f. DE- 3 + POLYMERIZE.] *Chem.* (Cause to) break down into monomers or other smaller units.
depolymeriˈzation *n.* L19.

depone /dɪˈpəʊn/ *v.* Chiefly *Sc.* LME. [L *deponere* lay aside, put down, (in med.L) testify, f. *de-* DE- 1 + *ponere* to place.] 1 *v.t.* & *i.* State, declare, or testify on oath in court; depose. (Foll. by *that*, *to*.) LME. †2 *v.t.* Lay down (a burden, an office). M16–M19.
†**deponer** *n.* a person who depones, a deponent (DEPONENT *n.* 2) M16–M18.

deponent /dɪˈpəʊnənt/ *a.* & *n.* LME. [L *deponent-* pres. ppl stem of *deponere*: see prec., -ENT.] A *adj. Gram.* Of a verb: passive (in Latin) or middle (in Greek) in form, but active in sense. LME. B *n.* 1 A deponent verb. M16. 2 A person who makes a deposition under oath; a person who gives written testimony or makes an affidavit for use in court etc. M16.
¶ Deponent verbs were so called from the notion that they had laid aside a passive sense. In fact they were orig. reflexive.

depopularize /diːˈpɒpjʊlərʌɪz/ *v.t.* Also **-ise.** M19. [f. DE- 3 + POPULARIZE.] Deprive of popularity; make unpopular.

depopulate /diːˈpɒpjʊlət/ *ppl a.* (orig. *pa. pple*). Now *arch.* or *poet.* M16. [L *depopulatus* pa. pple, f. as next: see -ATE[2].] Laid waste; deprived (wholly or partly) of inhabitants.

depopulate /diːˈpɒpjʊleɪt/ *v.* M16. [L *depopulat-* pa. ppl stem of *depopulare*, *-ari* ravage, f. *de-* DE- 1 + *populare*, *-ari* (f. *populus* people) lay waste, (in med.L) depopulate: see -ATE[3].] †1 *v.t.* Ravage, plunder, lay waste. M16–L17. †2 *v.t.* Reduce or lessen the number of; thin out. M16–L18. 3 *v.t.* Reduce the population of; deprive (wholly or partially) of inhabitants. L16. b *v.i.* Become less populous. M18. †4 *v.t.* Destroy, cut off. L16–M17.
3 J. CHILD The late Plague, which did much depopulate this Kingdom. F. SPENCE Forests and valleys were . . depopulated of game.
depopulator *n.* [L *depopulator*] †(*a*) a devastator; (*b*) a person or agent that reduces the population of a district etc.: LME.

depopulation /diːˌpɒpjʊˈleɪʃ(ə)n/ *n.* LME. [Late L *depopulatio(n-)*, f. as prec.: see -ATION.] †1 Laying waste, devastation, ravaging. LME–E19. 2 Reduction of population; the action or process of depriving of inhabitants. LME. b Depopulated condition. M17.

†**deport** *n.* L15. [OFr *de(s)port* diversion, pleasure, etc., f. as next or DISPORT *v.*] 1 = DISPORT *n.* Only in L15. 2 Behaviour, deportment. L15–M18.

deport /dɪˈpɔːt/ *v.*[1] L15. [OFr. *deporter*, f. *de-* DE- 1 + *porter* carry, PORT *v.*[1]] †1 *v.t.* Bear with; treat with consideration. *rare.* Only in L15. †2 *v.i.* & *refl.* Abstain, forbear. L15–E17. 3 *refl.* Bear or conduct oneself (in a specified manner). Now *rare.* L16.

deport /dɪˈpɔːt/ *v.*[2]*t.* M17. [Fr. *déporter* f. L *deportare* f. *de-* DE- 1 + *portare* carry.] Carry away, remove; *esp.* remove into exile, banish, expel from a country.
A. BRINK Undesirable immigrant. Promptly deported.
deportable *a.* liable to or punishable by deportation L19. **deportee** /diːpɔːˈtiː/ *n.* a person who is or has been deported L19.

deportation /diːpɔːˈteɪʃ(ə)n/ *n.* L16. [Late L *deportatio(n-)*, f. L *deportat-* pa. ppl stem of *deportare*: see prec., -ATION.] The action of carrying away; *esp.* forcible removal of a person from a country, banishment.

deportment /dɪˈpɔːtm(ə)nt/ *n.* E17. [(O)Fr. *déportement*, f. as DEPORT *v.*[1]: see -MENT.] †1 Manner of conducting oneself; general behaviour. E17–M19. 2 Bearing, demeanour, manners, esp. of a cultivated kind. M17.
2 J. GALSWORTHY Swithin drew his heels together, his deportment ever admirable.

deposal /dɪˈpəʊz(ə)l/ *n.* LME. [Prob. f. AN *deposaille*, f. as next: see -AL[1].] = DEPOSITION 2.

depose /dɪˈpəʊz/ *v.* ME. [(O)Fr. *déposer*, based on L *deponere* (see DEPONE *v.*) but re-formed after L pa. pple *depositus* and (O)Fr. *poser*: see POSE *v.*[1]] **1** *v.t.* Remove from office or authority; *esp.* dethrone. ME. **2** *v.t.* Lay down, put down, deposit. *arch.* LME. †**b** *v.t.* Lay aside, remove, overcome, (a feeling, quality, etc.). LME–L17. †**c** Place for safe keeping; entrust. L16–M18. †**3** *v.t.* Take away, deprive someone of (authority etc.); remove (a burden or obligation). LME–L17. **4** *v.t.* & *i.* Bear witness, testify, (to); affirm; *spec.* attest by or make a written deposition (see DEPOSITION 1). LME. **5** *v.t.* Examine (a deponent) on oath; cite as a witness. M16.

1 P. USTINOV The boyars promptly deposed Vassili, and left the throne empty for a while. 4 BROWNING And what discretion proved, I find deposed At Vire, confirmed by his own words. R. K. NARAYAN The railway staff are going to depose against me. W. GOLDING Augustus deposed before an ecclesiastical court that Miss Chudleigh had never been his wife.

deposable *a.* able or liable to be deposed M17. **deposer** *n.* a person who deposes L16.

deposit /dɪˈpɒzɪt/ *n.* L16. [L *depositum* use as n. of neut pa. pple of *deponere*: see DEPONE.] **1** The state of being deposited or placed in safe-keeping. Freq. in *on, upon,* †*in, deposit.* L16. **2** Something stored or entrusted to a person for safe-keeping. M17. **b** A sum of money placed in an account with a bank, building society, etc., usu. at interest. M18. **c** A sum of money or other security required and laid down as a pledge for the fulfilment of a contract, the return of something hired, etc., or as the first instalment of payment, and often refundable at the end of the transaction. M18. **d** *spec.* A sum paid on nomination by each of the candidates in a parliamentary election in the UK, which is refunded if the candidate receives more than a specified percentage of the votes cast. E20. **3** A depository, a depot. Chiefly *US.* E18. **4** The act of depositing; *Sc. Law* a contract whereby goods are transferred from one person to another for safe-keeping but must be returned on demand. L18. **5** A layer of matter that has collected, a natural accumulation of a substance. L18.

2d *Times* In 1951 no Liberals ran—they probably needed to convalesce after losing deposits. 5 E. M. FORSTER Over everything there lay a deposit of heavy white dust. N. CALDER Rich deposits of metal have accumulated.

Comb.: *deposit account*: see ACCOUNT *n.*

deposit /dɪˈpɒzɪt/ *v.* E17. [Fr. †*dépositer* or med.L *depositare* f. L *depositum*: see prec.] **1** *v.t.* Pay or give (esp. money) to another as a pledge for the fulfilment of a contract etc., or as the first instalment of a payment. E17. **2** *v.t.* Place in a repository or in someone's charge, for safe keeping; *spec.* place (money) in a bank, building society, etc., usu. at interest. M17. †**3** *v.t. fig.* Lay aside, give up. M17–E19. **4** *v.t.* Put, place, or set down; lay (an egg). L17. **5** *v.t.* Of a natural agent: form or lay down as a deposit. Freq. in *pass.* L17. **b** *v.i.* Form a natural deposit, settle. *rare.* M19.

2 B. TRAPIDO He . . deposited one million lire in my bank account. 4 H. JAMES He . . deposited his big tea-cup upon the table. F. TUOHY A taxi was depositing the last drunks outside the doors of the apartment buildings. 5 D. L. SAYERS If a person takes arsenic, a certain proportion . . will be deposited in the skin, nails, and hair. F. TUOHY The stream had deposited centuries of rich dark soil.

depositable *a.* E17. **deposiˈtee** *n.* a person with whom something is deposited L17.

depositary /dɪˈpɒzɪt(ə)ri/ *n.* E17. [Late L *depositarius*, f. L *deposit-* pa. ppl stem of *deponere*: see DEPONE, -ARY[1]. Cf. (O)Fr. *dépositaire.*] **1** A person or body receiving something in trust; a trustee. E17. **2** = DEPOSITORY 2. L18.

1 C. BRONTË I have never been the depositary of her plans and secrets.

depositary /dɪˈpɒzɪt(ə)ri/ *a. rare.* M19. [f. DEPOSIT *n.* + -ARY[1].] **1** Chiefly *Geol.* Belonging to or of the nature of a deposit. M19. **2** Receiving deposits. L19.

†**depositate** *v.t.* E17–L18. [med.L *depositat-* pa. ppl stem of *depositare*: see DEPOSIT *v.*, -ATE[3].] Deposit.

depositation /dɪˌpɒzɪˈteɪʃ(ə)n/ *n.* Chiefly *Sc.* E17. [f. med.L *depositare* (see DEPOSIT *v.*) + -ATION.] = DEPOSIT *n.* 4.

deposition /dɛpəˈzɪʃ(ə)n, diː-/ *n.* LME. [(O)Fr. *déposition* f. L *depositio(n-)*, f. *deposit-* pa. ppl stem of *deponere*: see DEPONE, -ION.] **1** The giving of testimony on oath in court; the testimony so given; *spec.* a sworn written statement that may be read out in court as a substitute for the production of the witness. LME. **2** The action of deposing from a position of power or authority; dethronement; degradation. LME. **3** The action of depositing, laying down, or putting in a position of rest; interment, *spec.* the laying of a saint's body and relics in a new resting-place. LME. **4** (A representation of) the taking down of the body of Jesus from the Cross. M16. †**5** The action of laying aside or giving up something. Chiefly *fig.* L16–M18. **6** The placing of something in a repository, account, etc., or in someone's charge for safe-keeping; a deposit. Now *rare.* L16. **7** The process of depositing by natural agency. L18. **b** A natural deposit or accumulation. L18.

1 *fig.*: T. MALLON Our diaries . . can be our depositions. 2 C. V. WEDGWOOD The removal of King Charles by deposition or by death. 7 D. ATTENBOROUGH Rocks are not built up by deposition but broken down by erosion.

depositional *a.* of, pertaining to, or resulting from (geological) deposition E20.

depositor /dɪˈpɒzɪtə/ *n.* L16. [f. DEPOSIT *v.* + -OR.] †**1** A person who makes a legal deposition. Only in L16. **2** A person who places something in the charge of another; *spec.* a person who places money in an account at a bank, building society, etc. E17.

depository /dɪˈpɒzɪt(ə)ri/ *n.* M17. [med.L *depositorium*, f. L *deposit-* pa. ppl stem of *deponere*: see DEPONE, -ORY[1].] **1** = DEPOSITARY *n.* 1. M17. **2** A storehouse, a repository. M18.

2 H. AINSWORTH The Jewel Tower . . the depository of the Regalia.

†**depositum** *n.* L16. [f. as DEPOSIT *n.*] **1** Something given as a pledge or entrusted to another for safe-keeping; *spec.* (*fig.*) the faith or doctrine which is committed to the keeping of the Church. L16–L18. **2** = DEPOSITORY 2. M17–L18.

depositure /dɪˈpɒzɪtjə/ *n. rare.* M17. [f. L *deposit-* (see DEPOSITION) + -URE.] = DEPOSITION 3.

depot /ˈdɛpəʊ/ *n.* Also (now *rare*) **depôt.** L18. [Fr. *dépôt*, OFr. *depost* f. L *depositum*: see DEPOSIT *n.*] **1** †**a** The action or an act of depositing. *rare.* L18–M19. **b** A deposit, a collection, a store. Now *spec.* (*transf.* f. sense 4 below) a localized accumulation of a substance in the body. M19. **2** A military establishment at which stores are deposited, recruits or other troops assembled, or, formerly, prisoners of war confined; *esp.* a regimental headquarters. L18. **3** A place where goods etc. are deposited or stored, often for later dispatch; a storehouse, an emporium. L18. **b** A place where vehicles, locomotives, etc., are housed and maintained and from which they are dispatched for service; *N. Amer.* a railway or bus station. M19. **4** A site in the body at which a particular substance naturally concentrates or is deposited. E20.

1b P. PARISH It takes several days for the depot of the drug to accumulate, so high starter doses are normally given. 2 T. PARKER The letter . . told me to report to the depot at Bassingbourne. 3 G. G. SCOTT The church was used as the coal depôt for the castle. R. H. TAWNEY The Portuguese Government made it [Antwerp] in 1503 the depôt of the Eastern spice trade. b L. T. C. ROLT Midnight after the last electric train has gone to its depot. 4 *attrib.*: *Lancet* Daily injections . . were replaced by a single intramuscular depot injection.

Comb.: **depot battalion, company**: remaining behind at headquarters when the rest of the regiment is on foreign service; **depot ship**: acting as a depot, for small warships, fishing vessels, naval forces, etc.

†**depravate** *v.t.* Pa. pple **-ated, -ate.** E16–M19. [L *depravat-*: see next, -ATE[3].] = DEPRAVE.

depravation /dɛprəˈveɪʃ(ə)n/ *n.* E16. [L *depravatio(n-)*, f. *depravat-* pa. ppl stem of *depravare*: see next, -ATION.] †**1** Vilification, defamation, detraction. E16–E17. **2** The action or fact of making or becoming depraved; degeneration (esp. moral), corruption. M16. †**b** Vitiation or corruption of a text etc. M16–M19. †**c** Physical degeneration of an organ etc. M17–M19. **3** The condition of being depraved; an instance of depravity. L16.

1 SHAKES. *Tr. & Cr.* Stubborn critics, apt . . For depravation. 2 A. COWLEY The total Loss of Reason is less deplorable than the total Depravation of it. 3 R. TAYLOR A sense of the depravation of our nature, or of original sin which is in us.

deprave /dɪˈpreɪv/ *v.* LME. [(O)Fr. *dépraver* or L *depravare*, f. *de-* DE- 1 + *pravus* crooked, perverse, wrong.] **I 1** *v.t.* & *i.* Vilify, defame, disparage; speak ill (of). Now *rare.* LME. **2** *v.t.* †**a** Misconstrue, misrepresent; pervert the meaning or intention of. LME–E18. **b** Vitiate, corrupt, (a text, word, etc.). Now *rare.* LME. †**c** Debase (coin), fraudulently alter, falsify, (a seal etc.). L16–M18. **3** *v.t.* & *i.* Corrupt in moral character or habits. L15. **4** *v.t. gen.* Make bad, deteriorate, impair. Now *rare.* M16.

1 MILTON Unjustly thou deprav'st it with the name Of Servitude. BYRON Behold the host! delighting to deprave, Who track the steps of Glory to the grave. 3 J. FOWLES Prostitutes . . were explicable as creatures so depraved that they overcame their . . disgust at the carnal in their lust for money. C. HAMPTON Peevishly complaining about the tendency of modern literature to deprave and corrupt. 4 S. JOHNSON The loss of teeth may deprave the voice of a singer.

II [By confusion.] †**5** *v.t.* Deprive. L16–M18.

depravedly /-vɪdli, -vdli/ *adv.* in a depraved manner M17. **depravedness** *n.* E17. **depravement** *n.* depravation; perversion, corruption: M17. **depraver** *n.* M16.

depravity /dɪˈpravɪti/ *n.* M17. [Alt. of PRAVITY after prec.] **1** Moral corruption, wickedness; *Theol.* the innate corruption of human nature due to original sin. M17. †**2** *gen.* Deteriorated quality; a defect. M17–M18. **3** A depraved act or practice. M17.

1 J. MACKINTOSH The winding approaches of temptation, the slippery path to depravity. T. S. ELIOT He's a fiend in feline shape, a monster of depravity. 3 R. L. STEVENSON Combining in one person the depravities of . . two civilisations.

deprecate /ˈdɛprɪkeɪt/ *v.t.* E17. [L *deprecat-* pa. ppl stem of *deprecari*, f. *de-* DE- 1 + *precari* pray: see -ATE[3].] **1** Pray against (evil); try to avert by prayer. *arch.* E17. †**2** Entreat, beseech, (a person). E17–E19. **3** Plead or protest against; express disapproval of or an earnest wish against. M17. †**4** Invoke (evil). M–L18. **5** [By assoc.] = DEPRECIATE 1. L19.

1 H. MARTINEAU The rest of the nation were at church, deprecating God's judgments. 3 F. A. G. OUSELEY Such a method of proceeding is greatly to be deprecated. H. KISSINGER He deprecated an interim settlement, claiming that Egypt would reject it. 5 M. FRAYN Trying to shrink into himself, as if to deprecate . . his authority and to become as other men.

deprecatingly *adv.* so as to deprecate M19. **deprecator** *n.* [L] a person who deprecates something or someone M17.

deprecation /dɛprɪˈkeɪʃ(ə)n/ *n.* LME. [L *deprecatio(n-)*, f. as prec.: see -ATION.] **1** A prayer, *spec.* one to ward off evil, disaster, etc. *arch.* LME. **2** (An) expression of disapproval; (expression of) a wish that something may be averted. E17. †**3** An imprecation. *rare.* M17–E19. **4** [By assoc.] = DEPRECIATION 2. Orig. & chiefly in *self-deprecation.* E20.

2 S. JOHNSON The censures of criticism, which, however, I shall not endeavour to soften by a formal deprecation. DICKENS A tone of gentle deprecation. 4 A. FRASER Rather peculiar-looking, as he himself was the first to admit, with typical self-deprecation.

deprecative /ˈdɛprɪkətɪv/ *a.* LME. [Fr. *déprécatif* f. L *deprecativus*, f. as DEPRECATE: see -ATIVE.] That deprecates, deprecatory; of or pertaining to deprecation.

deprecatively *adv.* M17.

deprecatory /ˈdɛprɪkət(ə)ri, -keɪt-/ *a.* L16. [Late L *deprecatorius*, f. L *deprecator* deprecator, f. as DEPRECATE: see -ORY[2].] 1 Trying to avert evil by prayer. *arch.* L16. 2 Expressing disapproval or a wish that something may be averted; deprecating anticipated unpleasantness or disapproval. E18.

1 DONNE All his Prayer . . is but Deprecatory, he does not pray that God will forbeare him. 2 GEO. ELIOT 'Oh', said Rosamund, with a slight deprecatory laugh, 'I was only going to say that we sometimes have dancing.'

deprecatorily *adv.* L19.

depreciate /dɪˈpriːʃɪeɪt, -sɪeɪt/ *v.* LME. [Late L *depreciat-* pa. ppl stem of *depretiare* (med.L *deprec-*), f. *de-* DE- 1 + *pretium* price: see -ATE[3].] 1 *v.t.* Disparage, belittle, underrate. LME. b *v.i.* Be disparaging; detract *from*. E18. 2 *v.t.* Lower the value of; *esp.* lower the market price of, reduce the purchasing power of (money). M17. 3 *v.i.* Fall in value. M18.

1 R. ELLMANN Before this Wilde depreciated pity as a motive in art; now he embraced it. 2 J. GALSWORTHY A Sanatorium would depreciate the neighbourhood, and he should certainly sign the petition . . against it. 3 E. WILSON The value of the paper money had depreciated almost to zero.

depreciatingly *adv.* disparagingly M19. **depreciative** /dɪˈpriːʃətɪv, -ʃɪətɪv/ *a.* depreciatory M19. **depreciator** *n.* a person who depreciates or causes depreciation L18. **depreciatory** /dɪˈpriːʃət(ə)ri, -ʃɪət(ə)ri/ *a.* tending to depreciate; disparaging: E19.

depreciation /dɪˌpriːʃɪˈeɪʃ(ə)n, -sɪˈeɪ-/ *n.* M18. [f. prec. + -ATION.] 1 The action or process of lowering in value; *esp.* (a) fall in the exchange value of currency etc. M18. b (An allowance made in balance sheets etc. for) loss of value due to wear and tear. M19. 2 The action of speaking slightly of someone or something; disparagement, belittlement. L18.

depredate /ˈdɛprɪdeɪt/ *v.* Now *rare* or *obs.* E17. [L *depraedat-*: see next, -ATE[3].] 1 *v.t.* Prey on, pillage, consume. E17. 2 *v.i.* Make depredations (*on*). L18.

depredation /dɛprɪˈdeɪʃ(ə)n/ *n.* L15. [Fr. *déprédation* f. late L *depraedatio(n-)*, f. *depraedat-* pa. ppl stem of *depraedari*, f. *de-* DE- 1 + *praedari* to plunder: see -ATION.] 1 The action of plundering, pillaging, or despoiling; an instance of robbery or pillage; in *pl.*, ravages. L15. b *Sc. Law.* The (capital) offence of stealing cattle by armed force. *obs.* exc. *Hist.* L18. 2 *fig.* †a Destructive waste, consumption (*of*). E–M17. b In *pl.* Harmful effects of natural agents, destructive operations. M17.

1 A. FRASER The beautiful stained glass . . had not survived the depredations of the Parliamentary troops. A. BROOKNER War and depredation may have raged up and down the coast. 2b A. T. ELLIS Tying up some Michaelmas daisies against the depredations of the wind.

depredator /ˈdɛprɪdeɪtə/ *n.* E17. [Late L *depraedator*, f. as DEPREDATE: see -OR.] A person who or agent which makes depredations; a despoiler, a pillager.

depredatory /dɪˈprɛdət(ə)ri, ˈdɛprɪdeɪt(ə)ri/ *a.* characterized by depredation; plundering, ravaging: M17.

†**deprehend** *v.t.* LME. [L *deprehendere*, f. *de-* DE- 1 + *prehendere* seize.] 1 Take by surprise; catch in the act. LME–L17. b Seize, capture, arrest. M16–M19. 2 Detect, discover; perceive, understand. LME–L17.

depress /dɪˈprɛs/ *v.t.* LME. [OFr. *depresser* f. late L *depressare* frequent. of L *depress-* pa. ppl stem of *deprimere* press down, f. *de-* DE- 1 + *premere* press.] †1 Overcome, subjugate, vanquish. LME–L17. 2 Bring into a lower position physically; press or push down. LME. 3 Bring down in fortune or status; humble, debase. Also, keep down, oppress. Now *rare* or *obs.* LME. †b Depreciate, disparage. M16–L18. 4 Lessen the energy, force, or intensity of; reduce in activity or degree, weaken. LME. b Lower (a musical note, the voice, etc.) in pitch. M16. c Decrease in economic activity; lower in market value or price. L19. 5 Dispirit, deject, sadden; cause to feel depression. LME.

2 C. MILNE The steel balls . . were trapped in grooves until you depressed a . . plunger. F. HOYLE The weight of the ice-age glaciers depressed the whole Scandinavian area. 3 MILTON Depressing . . their King . . to the condition of a Captive. W. PENN Therefore depress Vice and cherish Virtue. 4 STEELE Wine . . raises the Imagination, and depresses Judgment. P. PARISH Any drug which depresses brain function may produce dependence. c *Times* The Falklands news depressed BATs a further 8 p. 5 A. EDEN What depressed me most was that I could see no hope of improvement ahead.

depressible *a.* able to be depressed. M19. **depressing** *a.* that depresses, causing depression; *esp.* dispiriting: L18. **depressingly** *adv.* M19. **depressingness** *n.* E20.

depressant /dɪˈprɛs(ə)nt/ *a.* & *n.* L19. [f. prec. + -ANT[1].] 1 *Med.* (An agent) that lowers functional or nervous activity; (a) sedative. L19. 2 (An influence which is) depressing or dispiriting. L19. 3 In flotation separation of ores etc., (an agent) that causes sinking of certain components. M20.

depressed /dɪˈprɛst/ *ppl a.* LME. [f. DEPRESS + -ED[1].] †1 *Astrol.* Of a planet: in its least influential position. Only in LME. 2 Having a flattened or hollowed form, such as would result from downward pressure. L16. 3 Pressed down; put or kept down by force or pressure. E17. 4 Brought low in fortune or status; oppressed; socially or economically deprived. E17. b Lowered in energy, force, intensity, amount, or degree; weakened. M19. 5 Lowered in physical position, sunken; lower than the general surface. M17. 6 Dejected, dispirited; suffering from depression. L18.

Special collocations: **depressed area** an area of economic depression. **depressed class(es)** (in the Indian subcontinent) the lowest caste(s). **depressed fracture** a fracture of the skull involving displacement of bone inward from the normal cranial contour.

depressedly /dɪˈprɛstli, -ˈprɛsɪdli/ *adv.* M18.

depression /dɪˈprɛʃ(ə)n/ *n.* LME. [(O)Fr. *dépression* or L *depressio(n-)*, f. *depress-*: see DEPRESS, -ION.] 1 *Astron.* etc. Angular distance below the horizon or a horizontal plane. LME. 2 Defeat, suppression; degradation. Now *rare* or *obs.* LME. 3 Dejection, melancholy, low spirits. LME. b *Med.* A pathological state of excessive melancholy, characterized by a mood of hopelessness, with feelings of inadequacy, and sometimes physical symptoms. E20. 4 Lowering in physical position, sinking; the action of pressing down; the fact or condition of being pressed down. M17. 5 A sunken place on the ground or other surface; a hollow. M17. 6 (A) reduction in quality, vigour, amount, activity, etc.; *spec.* (a) severe and prolonged decline in economic activity, a slump. L18. b Lowering of pitch of the voice, a note, etc. M19. 7 An atmospheric region or weather system marked by relatively low barometric pressure; = CYCLONE 1C. L19.

3 GEO. ELIOT In a state of deep depression, overmastered by those distasteful miserable memories. b G. PRIESTLAND Depression . . has little to do with the perfectly normal experience of 'feeling a bit depressed'. 5 D. NOBBS The depression left in the upholstery by her recently-departed bottom. 6 J. D. MACDONALD A whole world on the slide into depression. **the Depression** the financial and industrial slump of 1929 and subsequent years.

depressive /dɪˈprɛsɪv/ *a.* & *n.* E17. [Fr. *dépressif*, *-ive* or med.L *depressivus*, f. *depress-*: see DEPRESS, -IVE.] A *adj.* Tending to produce, involving, or characterized by depression, esp. of the spirits; dispiriting, melancholy; *Med.* involving, marked by, or suffering from pathological depression. E17. B *n. Med.* A person suffering from depression. M20.

manic-depressive: see MANIC.

depressively *adv.* M17. **depressiveness** *n.* M19.

depressor /dɪˈprɛsə/ *n.* E17. [L *depressor*, f. *depress-*: see DEPRESS, -OR.] 1 A person who or thing which depresses. E17. 2 *Anat.* A muscle which pulls down the part to which it is attached. Also *depressor muscle*. E17. 3 A surgical instrument for pressing down some organ etc. L19.

†**depressure** *n.* E17–L18. [f. L *depress-*: see DEPRESS, -URE.] The action or an instance of depressing; (a) depression.

depressurize /diːˈprɛʃərʌɪz/ *v.t.* Also **-ise**. M20. [f. DE- 3 + PRESSURIZE.] Cause an appreciable drop of air or gas pressure in (a container, compartment, etc.), esp. to the pressure prevailing in the surroundings.

depriment /ˈdɛprɪm(ə)nt/ *n.* & *a. rare.* E17. [L *depriment-* pres. pple of *deprimere*: see DEPRESS, -ENT.] (Something) that depresses.

deprival /dɪˈprʌɪv(ə)l/ *n.* E17. [f. DEPRIVE + -AL[1].] The act of depriving, deprivation.

deprivation /dɛprɪˈveɪʃ(ə)n/ *n.* LME. [med.(eccl.)L *deprivatio(n-)*, f. *deprivat-* pa. ppl stem of *deprivare*: see next, -ATION.] 1 Removal from office or position, esp. of a member of the clergy from a benefice or preferment. LME. 2 *gen.* The action of depriving; the fact of being deprived; loss *of* something enjoyed or desired; deprived condition, hardship. M16.

deprivative /dɪˈprɪvətɪv/ *a.* of, pertaining to, or characterized by deprivation. E18.

deprive /dɪˈprʌɪv/ *v.t.* ME. [OFr. *depriver* f. med.(eccl.)L *deprivare*, f. *de-* DE- 1 + *privare* deprive.] I Dispossess, debar. Foll. by *of*, (now *rare*) *from*; also (now *rare*) w. double obj. (cf. branch II below). 1 Divest, strip, dispossess (a person etc.) of a possession. ME. 2 Divest of (esp. ecclesiastical) office; depose. ME. 3 Deny (a person) the future possession or enjoyment of something; debar from a right etc. LME.

1 SLOAN WILSON A fire engine, deprived of its siren. ISAIAH BERLIN To coerce a man is to deprive him of freedom. 2 H. HALLAM Archbishop Bancroft deprived a considerable number of puritan clergymen. 3 AV *Isa.* 38:10 I am depriued of the residue of my yeeres. HOBBES Deprived from all possibility to acquire . . necessaries. R. PRICE Both saving and depriving them further speech.

II †4 Take away, remove (a possession). ME–M17.

deprivable *a.* liable to be deprived L16. **deprived** *a.* subject to deprivation, dispossessed; now *esp.* underprivileged, poor, (of a child) lacking a normal home life: M16. †**deprivement** *n.* deprivation M17–E18. **depriver** *n.* LME.

de profundis /deɪ prəˈfʊndɪs/ *n.* & *adv. phr.* LME. [L = from the depths, the initial wds of *Ps.* 130 (129).] A *n.* A psalm of penitence; *spec.* Psalm 130 (129 in the Vulgate); *gen.* a cry of appeal from the depths (of sorrow, humiliation, etc.). LME. B *adv. phr.* Out of the depths (of sorrow etc.). LME.

deprogramme /diːˈprəʊgram/ *v.t.* Also ***-gram**. L20. [f. DE- 3 + PROGRAMME *v.*] Release (a person) from apparent brainwashing by systematic indoctrination.

deproletarianize /ˌdiːprəʊlɪˈtɛːrɪənʌɪz/ *v.t.* Also **-ise**. M20. [f. DE- 3 + PROLETARIANIZE.] Cause to lose proletarian character or qualities.

deproletariani'zation *n.* M20.

deproteinize /diːˈprəʊtiːnʌɪz/ *v.t.* Also **-ise**. M20. [f. DE- 3 + PROTEIN + -IZE.] Remove the protein from, esp. as a measure in chemical purification.

deproteini'zation *n.* M20.

deprovincialize /diːprəˈvɪnʃ(ə)lʌɪz/ *v.t.* Also **-ise**. M19. [f. DE- 3 + PROVINCIALIZE.] Remove provincial elements or character from; make broader in outlook etc.

depside /ˈdɛpsʌɪd/ *n.* E20. [f. Gk *depsein* make supple, tan + -IDE.] *Chem.* Any of a class of naturally-occurring phenols, found esp. in lichens, which include some tannins and have two or more phenolic groups joined by ester linkages in the molecule.

depsidone /-sɪdəʊn/ *n.* any depside derivative in which the phenolic rings are joined also by ether linkages M20.

Deptford pink /dɛtfəd ˈpɪŋk/ *n. phr.* M17. [*Deptford*, a district of south-east London, formerly a village.] A rare wild pink of dry banks, *Dianthus armeria*, with clusters of rose-red flowers.

depth /dɛpθ/ *n.* LME. [f. DEEP *a.* + -TH[1], after *long*: *length* etc. Largely superseding earlier DEEPNESS.] I 1 Extent or distance from the top downwards, from the surface or edge inwards or from front to back; a particular measurement of this. LME. b *Mil.* The distance from front to rear of a body of soldiers etc., as measured by the number of ranks. M17. 2 Intensity or profundity of a feeling, moral quality, or state. LME. 3 The quality of having considerable extension downwards, inwards, or from front to back. E16. 4a Abstruseness of (subjects of) thought; complexity. L16. b Intellectual penetration, sagacity, insight. E17. 5 Intensity of physical qualities or conditions, as silence, darkness, colour, etc. E17.

1 B. GOOGE Trenches of a cubite in depth. J. UPDIKE They swim in the icy water . . at a depth no greater than their height. 2 J. WESLEY The Depth of sympathetic Woe! 3 TINDALE *Matt.* 13:5 Because it had no depth of earth. 4a C. MARLOWE Settle thy studies, Faustus, and begin To sound the depth of that thou wilt profess. b T. HEARNE A man of extraordinary Depth. A. S. BYATT Boys before the age of self-consciousness . . could give . . depths they were unconscious of to lines they didn't understand. 5 DRYDEN All seeking the noise in the depth of silence. D. LESSING Her smart new coat flaring jade, emerald, dark green, as she moved through varying depths of light.

II 6 A deep body of water; a deep part of the sea, or of any body of water. Usu. in *pl.* LME. †b = DEEP *n.* 3. LME–E17. 7 A deep, remote, or inmost part (*of*). Freq. in *pl.* LME. 8 *fig.* A deep, mysterious, unfathomable, etc., region of or *of* thought, feeling, character, etc. Freq. in *pl.* LME. 9 A deep place in the earth etc.; the lowest part of a pit, cavity, etc. Formerly also, a valley. E16. 10 A vast or unfathomable space (*of*). Usu. in *pl.* E17. 11 The deepest, harshest, or most intense period. E17.

6 E. LANGLEY The blue lake chanted in its blue and white depths. C. SAGAN Organisms now live from the top of Mount Everest to the deepest portions of the abyssal depths. 7 POPE Some safer world, in depth of woods embrac'd. V. WOOLF How did she manage these things in the depths of the country? 8 AV *Ps.* 130:1 Out of the depths have I cried unto thee, O Lord. E. WAUGH Depths of confusion you didn't know existed. B. BAINBRIDGE Nina wasn't the sort to like lovable men. Perhaps Douglas had hidden depths. 9 POPE A monster, horrible and fell, Begot by furies in the depths of hell. J. B. PRIESTLEY Moaning for a doctor from the depths of the armchair into which he'd collapsed. 10 LONGFELLOW Measureless depths of air around. 11 E. BOLTON Though it were the depth of Winter. R. BROOKE Fish (fly-replete, in depth of June . . .).

Phrases: defence in depth: see DEFENCE *n.* 3. *depth of field*: see FIELD *n. depth of focus*: see FOCUS *n.* **in depth** profound(ly), comprehensive(ly); penetrating(ly). **out of one's depth** in water too deep to stand in; *fig.* beyond one's capacities or understanding. *rapture(s) of the depths*: see RAPTURE *n.*

Comb.: **depth-bomb, -charge** a bomb that explodes under water at a pre-set depth, used for attacking a submerged submarine etc.; **depth-finder** a device for measuring the depth of the sea etc., esp. using echo-sounding; **depth psychology** psychology seeking to explain behaviour in terms of the unconscious; psychoanalysis intended to reveal hidden motives etc.; **depth-recorder** a recording depth-finder.

depthen *v.t.* (*rare*) = DEEPEN I L16. **depthless** *a.* (*a*) unfathomable; abyssal; (*b*) shallow, superficial: E17.

depurate /dɪˈpjʊəreɪt, ˈdɛpjʊreɪt/ *v.t.* E17. [med.L *depurat-* pa. ppl stem of *depurare*, f. DE- I + *purare* purify, f. *purus* pure: see -ATE[3].] Make free from impurities; subject to depuration.

depurative *a.* & *n.* [med.L *depurativus*] (an agent) that purifies L17. ˈ**depurator** *n.* an agent or apparatus that purifies M19. **de**ˈ**puratory** *a.* = DEPURATIVE L17.

depuration /dɛpjʊˈreɪʃ(ə)n/ *n.* E17. [f. as prec. + -ATION.] Purification, refining; *esp.* the process of keeping shellfish etc. in clean water for a period so as to free them of undesirable substances.

depure /dɪˈpjʊə/ *v.t.* Long *arch. rare.* LME. [(O)Fr. *dépurer* or med.L *depurare*: see DEPURATE.] = DEPURATE.

deputable /dɪˈpjuːtəb(ə)l, ˈdɛpjʊ-/ *a.* E17. [f. DEPUTE *v.* + -ABLE.] Able to be deputed, suitable for deputing.

deputation /dɛpjʊˈteɪʃ(ə)n/ *n.* LME. [Late L *deputatio(n-)*, f. L *deputat-* pa. ppl stem of *deputare*: see DEPUTE *v.*, -ATION.] †1 *gen.* Appointment, assignment to an office, function, etc. LME–M17. b An appointment by the lord of a manor to the office and rights of a gamekeeper. *obs.* exc. *Hist.* M18. 2 *spec.* Appointment to act on behalf of another or others; delegation. M16. 3 A document conveying an appointment; a commission, a warrant. *obs.* exc. *Hist.* E17. 4 A body of people, or a single person, appointed to represent another or others, usu. on a particular mission. M17.

1b S. WALPOLE Country gentlemen who were desirous of doing a neighbour a good turn were in the habit of giving him a 'deputation' as a gamekeeper. 4 T. STOPPARD Inspecting the toilets like a deputation from the Water Board. P. USTINOV They sent the Tsar a deputation which repeated their demands for urgent constitutional reforms.

deputative /ˈdɛpjʊtətɪv/ *a.* M17. [Late L *deputativus*, f. *deputat-*: see prec., -ATIVE.] Characterized by deputation; of the nature of a deputy or deputation.

deputatively *adv.* M17.

deputator /ˈdɛpjʊteɪtə/ *n. rare.* M17. [f. L *deputat-*: see DEPUTATION, -OR.] A person who deputes another to act for him or her.

depute /ˈdɛpjuːt/ *a.* (orig. *pa. pple*) & *n.* Now only *Sc.* LME. [(O)Fr. *député* pa. pple of *députer* DEPUTE *v.* (repr. late L *deputatus*). Cf. DEPUTY.] A *adj.* †1 *pa. pple.* Deputed; imputed; appointed, assigned. LME–E17. 2 *adj.* Appointed or acting as deputy, *spec.* in certain legal offices. Freq. *postpositive.* LME. B *n.* A person deputed; a deputy. LME.

depute /dɪˈpjuːt/ *v.t.* LME. [Partly f. (O)Fr. *députer* f. L *deputare* destine, assign, f. *de-* DE- I + *putare* consider; partly based on DEPUTE *n.*] †1 Appoint, assign, or ordain to or for a particular office, purpose, or function. LME–L17. 2 Appoint as a substitute, representative, or deputy. LME. †3 Impute, ascribe, attribute. LME–L16. †4 Consign, deliver over. LME–L15. 5 Commit (a task, authority, etc.) to or *to* a deputy or substitute. L15.

2 SHAKS. *Oth.* To depute Cassio in Othello's place. A. JOHN The Princess . . deputing me to see them into their train, sent us off in her car. 5 DEFOE The Devil may depute such and such powers and privileges to his confederates.

deputize /ˈdɛpjʊtʌɪz/ *v.* Also **-ise**. M18. [f. next + -IZE.] 1 *v.t.* Appoint as a deputy. Chiefly *US.* M18. 2 *v.i.* Act as a deputy or understudy (*for*). M19.

deputy /ˈdɛpjʊti/ *n.*, *a.*, & *v.* LME. [Var. of DEPUTE *n.*, w. final syll. of the Fr. retained: see -Y[5].] A *n.* 1 A person appointed or delegated to act or to exercise authority for another or others; a substitute, a lieutenant. LME. b *Law.* A person authorized to exercise disinterestedly the whole or a part of an office on behalf of the office-holder. LME. 2 *spec.* a A person deputed to exercise authority on behalf of the sovereign (power); a Lord or a Deputy Lieutenant (of Ireland), a viceroy, a proconsul. *obs.* exc. *Hist.* LME. b In The City of London, a person who acts instead of an alderman in the absence of the latter. M16. c An overseer responsible for safety in a coalmine. M19. 3 A member of a legislative assembly, *spec.* of a Chamber of Deputies (see below). E17.

1 H. P. BROUGHAM The lesser barons were called to send deputies, instead of attending personally. **by deputy** by another person in one's stead, by proxy. 3 **Chamber of Deputies** the lower house of Parliament of the French Third Republic, of Italy, and some other countries.

B *attrib.* or as *adj.* Deputed; acting or appointed to act instead of another or others. L15.

deputy lieutenant the deputy of the Lord Lieutenant of a county.

C *v.t.* Appoint or send as deputy. *rare.* E17.

deputyship *n.* the position or the term of office of a deputy L16.

deracialize /diːˈreɪʃəlʌɪz/ *v.t.* Also **-ise**. L19. [f. DE- 3 + RACIAL + -IZE.] Remove racial characteristics or features from.

deracialiˈ**zation** *n.* M20.

deracinate /dɪˈrasɪneɪt/ *v.t. literary.* L16. [f. Fr. *déraciner* (OFr. *des-*), f. *dé-* DE- 3 + *racine* root: see -ATE[3].] Tear up by the roots (*lit.* & *fig.*), eradicate.

deraciˈ**nation** *n.* E19.

déraciné /derasine (*pl. same*), deɪˈrasɪneɪ/ *a.* & *n.* Fem. **-ée**. E20. [Fr. = uprooted, pa. ppl a. of *déraciner*: see prec.] A *adj.* Uprooted from one's environment; displaced geographically or socially. E20. B *n.* A *déraciné* person. E20.

deraign /dɪˈreɪn/ *v.*[1]*t. obs.* exc. *Hist.* ME. [AN *derainer, dereiner*, OFr. *deraisnier, dereis-* f. Proto-Romance, f. L *de-* DE- I + *ratio(n-)* account, REASON *n.*[1]] 1 *Law.* Prove, justify, or vindicate (a claim etc.), esp. by wager of battle; dispute (the claim of another) thus. ME. 2 Maintain a claim to; claim the possession of, esp. by wager of battle. ME. 3 Decide (a claim or dispute) by judicial argument or by wager of battle; determine. ME. 4a *deraign battle, combat*, etc., maintain a wager of battle or single combat in vindication of a claim, right, etc. Also (*pseudo-arch.*), do battle; order, arrange a battle. LME. †b Dispose in battle array; order. *pseudo-arch.* L16–E18.

deraign /dɪˈreɪn/ *v.*[2]*t.* E16. [OFr. *desregner* var. of *desrengier* (mod. *déranger*) put out of ranks, DERANGE.] †1 Put into disorder; derange. E16–E18. 2 In *pass.* Be discharged from (religious) orders. *obs.* exc. *Hist.* L16.

deraignment /dɪˈreɪnm(ə)nt/ *n.*[1] *obs.* exc. *Hist.* M16. [OFr. *desrenement*, f. *desregner*: see prec., -MENT.] The action of DERAIGN *v.*[2]; discharge from religious orders.

deraignment /dɪˈreɪnm(ə)nt/ *n.*[2] *obs.* exc. *Hist.* E18. [OFr. *desraisnement, derainement*, f. *desraisnier*: see DERAIGN *v.*[1], -MENT.] The action of DERAIGN *v.*[1]; vindication of a claim etc., esp. by wager of battle.

derail /dɪˈreɪl/ *v.* M19. [Fr. *dérailler*, f. *dé-* DE- 3 + *rail* RAIL *n.*[2]] 1 *v.t.* Cause (a train etc.) to run off the rails. M19. 2 *v.i.* Leave the rails. M19.

1 *fig.*: H. CRANE Passions of this kind completely derail me from anything creative for days.

derailment *n.* the fact or an instance of a train's leaving the rails. M19.

derailleur /dɪˈreɪlə, -ljə/ *n.* M20. [Fr. *dérailleur*, f. as prec. + *-eur* -OR.] A bicycle gear in which the ratio is changed by switching the line of the chain (while pedalling) so that it jumps to a different sprocket.

derange /dɪˈreɪn(d)ʒ/ *v.t.* L18. [Fr. *déranger* (OFr. *desrengier, desregner* DERAIGN *v.*[2]), f. *dé-, des-* DE- 3 + *rang* RANK *n.*] 1 Disturb or destroy the arrangement of; throw into confusion; disorder, disarrange. L18. 2 Disturb the normal state, working, or operation of; cause to act irregularly. L18. 3 Make insane; drive mad. Freq. as *deranged* ppl a. L18. 4 Intrude on, interrupt. M19.

1 LD MACAULAY This letter deranged all the projects of James. 2 B. C. BRODIE Habits . . which tend in any degree to derange the animal functions, should be scrupulously avoided. D. H. LAWRENCE Time was all deranged. 3 E. CALDWELL He had been killed by a deranged person. P. ROSE The eldest child was quite deranged with joy and suffered convulsions. 4 R. L. STEVENSON I am sorry to have deranged you for so small a matter.

derangement /dɪˈreɪn(d)ʒm(ə)nt/ *n.* M18. [Fr. *dérangement*, f. as prec.: see -MENT.] The act of deranging; the fact of being deranged; disorder; insanity.

derate /diːˈreɪt/ *v.t.* & *i.* E20. [f. DE- 3 + RATE *n.*[1]] Diminish or remove part or all of the burden of rates (from).

deration /diːˈraʃ(ə)n/ *v.t.* E20. [f. DE- 3 + RATION.] Free (a commodity) from rationing, make no longer rationed.

derationalize /diːˈraʃ(ə)n(ə)lʌɪz/ *v.t.* Also **-ise**. L19. [f. DE- 3 + RATIONALIZE.] Deprive of reason.

derationaliˈ**zation** *n.* M20.

deratization /diːˌratʌɪˈzeɪʃ(ə)n/ *n.* Also **-isa-**. E20. [f. DE- 3 + RAT *n.*[1] + -IZATION.] The expulsion or extermination of rats from a property, vessel, etc.

deray /dɪ'reɪ/ *n.* Long *obs.* exc. *Sc. arch.* ME. [AN *derai*, OFr. *desrai*, f. AN *deraier*, OFr. *desreer*, f. Proto-Romance, f. L DIS- + Gmc base also in ARRAY *v.*] 1 Disorder, disturbance, tumult, confusion. ME. †2 Violence, molestation. ME–M16. 3 Disorderly mirth and revelry. LME.

Derby /'dɑːbi; *dial.* & *US* 'dəːbi/ *n.* Also (esp. in senses 2b, 3, 4), **d-**. E17. [A city and county (see also next) in the north midlands of England, and an earldom named from the county. See also DARBY.] 1 Used *attrib.* to designate things made in or associated with Derby. E17. b In full *Derby cheese*. A hard pressed cheese made from skimmed milk, chiefly in Derbyshire. E19. c In full *Derby porcelain*. A variety of porcelain made at Derby; *spec.* a soft-paste porcelain made from *c*1750. M19. 2 A flat horse-race (founded in 1780 by the twelfth Earl of Derby) run annually at Epsom, England. Also, any of various equivalent races elsewhere. M19. b An important game or contest; *spec.* (freq. *local derby*) a football etc. match between two teams from the same area. E20. 3 In full *derby hat*. A bowler hat. *N. Amer.* L19. 4 Orig., a kind of sporting boot having no stiffening and a very low heel. Now, a low-heeled shoe. E20. 5 *Derby scheme*, in the war of 1914–18, a recruiting scheme initiated by the seventeenth Earl of Derby. E20.

1b *sage Derby*: see SAGE *n.*[1] c *Crown Derby*: see CROWN *n.* 2 **Derby day**: on which the Derby is run. *donkey derby*: see DONKEY. *Kentucky Derby*: see KENTUCKY. *roller derby*: see ROLLER *n.*[1] b *demolition derby*: see DEMOLITION.

¶ See also *Lord Derby* s.v. LORD *n.*

Derbyshire /'dɑːbɪʃə/ *n.* L18. [An English county: see prec., SHIRE *n.*] 1 *Derbyshire spar*, fluorspar. L18. 2 *Derbyshire neck*, goitre, formerly endemic in parts of Derbyshire. E19. 3 In full *Derbyshire cheese*. = DERBY 1b. E20.

†der-doing *ppl a. pseudo-arch. rare* (Spenser). Only in L16. [App. after DERRING-DO.] Doing daring deeds.

†dere *n.* OE–E19. [OE *daru* = OHG *tara*, f. WGmc; later f. or assim. to the vb.] Harm, injury. Esp. in *do a person dere*.

dere /dɪə/ *v.* Long *obs.* exc. *Sc.* & *north.* [OE *derian* = OFris. *dera*, OS *derian*, f. WGmc, f. base of prec.] †1 *v.t.* Hurt, harm, injure. OE–E17. b *v.i.* Do harm. OE–LME. 2 *v.t.* Trouble, grieve, vex, incommode. ME.

derealize /diː'rɪəlʌɪz/ *v.t.* Also **-ise**. L19. [f. DE- 3 + REALIZE *v.*] *Philos.* Deprive of reality, make unreal.

derecognition /ˌdiːrɛkəg'nɪʃ(ə)n/ *n.* M20. [f. DE- 3 + RECOGNITION.] The withdrawal of official recognition; *esp.* withdrawal of political recognition by one State from another.

de'recognize *v.t.* withdraw recognition from M20.

deregister /diː'rɛdʒɪstə/ *v.t.* E20. [f. DE- 3 + REGISTER *n.*[1]] Remove from a register.

deregis'tration *n.* E20.

deregulate /diː'rɛgjʊleɪt/ *v.t.* M20. [f. DE- 3 + REGULATE.] Free from regulation, esp. tariff restriction; decontrol.

deregu'lation *n.* M20. **deregu'latory** *a.* L20.

derelict /'dɛrəlɪkt/ *a.* & *n.* M17. [L *derelictus* pa. pple of *derelinquere* forsake wholly, abandon, f. *de-* DE- 1 + *relinquere* leave, forsake.] **A** *adj.* 1 Forsaken, abandoned by the owner, occupier, etc.; (of a ship) abandoned at sea; (esp. of property) dilapidated, decrepit, neglected. M17. 2 Remiss or negligent in the performance of one's duty. Chiefly *N. Amer.* M19.

1 J. WYNDHAM A few derelict cars . . stood about on the roads. I. MURDOCH He loved its derelict splendours, the huge ornate neglected mansions of a vanished bourgeoisie. **derelict land** *Law* land left dry by the recession of the sea etc. 2 N. BAWDEN If . . you yourself have been derelict in your duty.

B *n.* 1 A piece of property abandoned by the owner, occupier, etc.; a ship abandoned at sea. L17. 2 A forsaken person; *esp.* a person abandoned or disregarded by society, a vagrant, a social outcast. E18. 3 A person who is negligent or remiss in the performance of his or her duty. *N. Amer.* L19.

2 BROWNING Misuse me, your derelict. A. MILLER Derelicts and old men lounge here to watch the strangers go by.

dereliction /dɛrə'lɪkʃ(ə)n/ *n.* L16. [L *derelictio(n-)*, f. *derelict-* pa. ppl stem of *derelinquere*: see prec., -ION.] 1 The state of being abandoned or forsaken; dilapidation, neglect. L16. 2 The act of deliberate abandonment. Now *rare* exc. *Law*, of a chattel or movable. E17. b *Law.* The leaving behind of dry land by the retreat of the sea; the land thus left. M18. †3 Failure, cessation; *esp.* sudden failure of the bodily or mental powers. M17–L18. 4 Reprehensible abandonment; wilful neglect. Chiefly in *dereliction of duty*. L18. b Failure in duty; shortcoming. E19.

1 J. HARVEY The dereliction of a breakfast-table . . bobbing with orange-peels, ribboned with bacon-rind, cluttered with jams and marmalades. 2 GIBBON This wise dereliction of obsolete, vexatious, and unprofitable claims. 4 BURKE A dereliction of every opinion and principle that I have held. J. GALSWORTHY So grave a dereliction of all duty, both human and divine. b W. STYRON I was guilty of a grave dereliction.

†derelinquish *v.t.* E17–M19. [f. DE- 1 + RELINQUISH, after L *derelinquere*: see DERELICT.] Relinquish utterly, abandon.

derepress /diːrɪ'prɛs/ *v.t.* M20. [f. DE- 3 + REPRESS *v.*] Make no longer repressed or inhibited; activate.

derepression *n.* M20.

derequisition /ˌdiːrɛkwɪ'zɪʃ(ə)n/ *v.t.* M20. [f. DE- 3 + REQUISITION *v.*] Return after requisitioning.

derestrict /diːrɪ'strɪkt/ *v.t.* M20. [f. DE- 3 + RESTRICT *v.*] Remove restrictions from.

derestricted *ppl a.* free from restrictions; *spec.* (of a road) not subject to a special speed limit on traffic: M20. **derestriction** *n.* M20.

deride /dɪ'rʌɪd/ *v.* M16. [L *deridere*, f. *de-* DE- 1 + *ridere* laugh (at).] 1 *v.t.* Laugh contemptuously or scornfully at; treat with scorn; mock. M16. †2 *v.i.* Laugh contemptuously or scornfully. Only in 17.

1 J. K. JEROME They stood there, shouting ribaldry at him, deriding him, mocking him, jeering at him. F. SPALDING The public derided Post-Impressionism.

derider *n.* M16. **deridingly** *adv.* in a deriding manner L16.

de rigueur /də rigœːr, də rɪ'gəː/ *pred. a. phr.* M19. [Fr., lit. 'of strictness'.] Required by custom or etiquette.

derisible /dɪ'rɪzɪb(ə)l/ *a.* M17. [Late L *derisibilis*, f. *deris-*: see next, -IBLE. In mod. use f. DERISION, on the analogy of *vision*, *visible*.] To be derided; worthy of derision.

derision /dɪ'rɪʒ(ə)n/ *n.* LME. [(O)Fr. *dérision* f. late L *derisio(n-)*, f. *deris-* pa. ppl stem of *deridere* DERIDE: see -ION.] 1 The action of deriding; ridicule, mockery. LME. b An instance of this. *rare.* M16. 2 An object of ridicule; a laughing-stock. Now *rare* exc. *Sc.* M16.

1 J. GLASSCO Every attempt I made to write was greeted with derision. **be in derision** (now *rare*) be a laughing-stock. **bring into derision** mock, make a laughing-stock of. **have, hold, in derision** *arch.* mock, treat with scorn.

derisive /dɪ'rʌɪsɪv, -z-/ *a.* M17. [f. (as) prec. + -IVE, after *decision*, *decisive*.] 1 Scoffing, mocking. M17. 2 = DERISORY 2. L19.

1 T. HARDY A low gurgle of derisive laughter followed the words. J. HELLER Curt, derisive tongue and . . knowing, cynical eyes.

derisively *adv.* M17. **derisiveness** *n.* M19.

derisory /dɪ'rʌɪs(ə)ri, -z-/ *a.* E17. [Late L *derisorius*, f. *deris-*: see DERISION, -ORY[2].] 1 = DERISIVE 1. E17. 2 So small or unimportant as to be ridiculous; laughably inadequate. E20.

2 S. UNWIN What would appear to them a derisory sum might be of importance to a poet. *Oxford Times* Both rejected the present rate offer as 'derisory'.

derivable /dɪ'rʌɪvəb(ə)l/ *a.* M17. [f. DERIVE + -ABLE.] Able to be derived (*from*).

deriva'bility *n.* M19.

derival /dɪ'rʌɪv(ə)l/ *n. rare.* L16. [f. DERIVE + -AL[1].] A derived form; derivation.

derivate /'dɛrɪvət, -eɪt/ *ppl a.* & *n.* LME. [L *derivat-* pa. ppl stem of *derivare*: see DERIVE, -ATE[2].] **A** *ppl a.* Derived. Now *rare.* LME. **B** *n.* Something derived, a derivative; *esp.* a product obtained chemically from a raw material. LME.

derivately *adv.* (*rare*) M17.

derivation /dɛrɪ'veɪʃ(ə)n/ *n.* LME. [Fr. *dérivation* or L *derivatio(n-)*, f. as prec.: see -ATION.] †1 The action or process of leading or carrying a current of water etc. *from* a source, *to* another part; diversion; *spec.* in *Med.*, the drawing off of pus, blood, etc., from a diseased part of the body. LME–L19. 2 Formation of a word from an earlier word, base, or root. LME. b The tracing of a word from or back to its root or roots; a statement of this. L16. 3 Extraction, origin, descent. L15. †4 Transmission; communication. L16–L17. 5 The action of obtaining, drawing, or deducing from a source. M17. 6 A derived product; a derivative. Now *rare.* M17.

1 J. RAY Plenty of Vessels for the derivation of Air to all their Parts. 3 SHAKES. *Hen. V* As good a man as yourself, both in the disciplines of war and in the derivation of my birth. 5 E. A. FREEMAN There was no real derivation of English law from Normandy. D. R. HOFSTADTER The derivation of a theorem is an explicit . . demonstration of how to produce that theorem according to the rules of the formal system. 6 MILTON The Father is the whole substance, . . the Son a derivation, and portion of the whole.

derivational *a.* M19. **derivationally** *adv.* L19. **derivationist** *n.* a person concerned with derivation L19.

derivative /dɪ'rɪvətɪv/ *a.* & *n.* LME. [Fr. *dérivatif* f. L *derivativus* pa. pple of *derivare*: see next, -ATIVE.] **A** *adj.* †1 Having the effect of transferring or conveying. Chiefly *Med.*, having the power to draw off fluid from a diseased part of the body. LME–L19. 2 Derived or obtained from another; coming from a source; not original. M16. b Formed or originating from another word, base, or root. M16. c *Law.* Secondary, subordinate. L18. d *Geol.* Derived from older rocks; (of a fossil) occurring at a site other than the one where it was formed. L19.

2 STEELE They can only gain a secondary and derivative kind of Fame. T. GUNN I am . . a rather derivative poet. I learn what I can from whom I can.

B *n.* 1 A word derived from another word, base, or root by a process of word-formation; a word which is not a root. LME. 2 *gen.* Something derived; a thing flowing, proceeding, or originating from another. L16. 3 *Math.* An expression (obtained by differentiation of a function) which represents the instantaneous rate of change of the function with respect to an independent variable. M19. 4 *Chem.* A compound obtained from another by substitution or other simple process. M19. †5 *Med.* A method or agent that produces derivation (DERIVATION 1). Only in M19.

1 J. H. BURTON The use of a Greek derivative gives notice that you are scientific. 2 J. BRYANT Subordinate dæmons, . . emanations and derivatives from their chief Deity. A. STORR Some dreams . . are certainly derivatives of the patient's early childhood. 3 **first, second, third,** etc., **derivative**: obtained by differentiating a function once, twice, three times, etc. *partial derivative*: see PARTIAL *a.*

derivatively *adv.* M17. **derivativeness** *n.* M17.

derive /dɪ'rʌɪv/ *v.* LME. [(O)Fr. *dériver* or L *derivare*, f. *de-* DE- 1 + *rivus* brook, stream.] I *v.t.* †1 Conduct (water or another fluid) *from* a source etc. *to* or *into* a channel etc.; draw or convey through a channel; draw off, drain; *spec.* in *Med.*, divert (pus etc.) to another part of the body. LME–E19. b Carry, lead, (a channel of any kind). M16–L18. †2 Bring, turn, direct; bring down. L15–E19. 3 Obtain, get, draw, (a thing *from* a source). Freq. in *pass.*, arise, be descended, be formed, originate *from*; (of a word) be formed *from* an earlier word, base, or root. E16. b Trace, obtain (ancestry, origin, pedigree, etc.). L16. c *Chem.* Obtain (a compound) from another by substitution or other simple process. M19. 4 Obtain by reasoning; gather, deduce. E16. †5 Pass on, transmit, convey from one to another; hand *down*. M16–M19. 6 Trace or show the origin, derivation, or pedigree of; state (a thing) to have originated *from*; *esp.* trace the origin of (a word) from its etymological source. M16. 7 *refl.* Originate; come or descend *from*. M17.

3 SHAKES. *1 Hen. VI* By my mother I derived am from Lionel Duke of Clarence. J. CONRAD Stevie did not seem to derive any personal gratification from what he had done. R. MACAULAY If they could derive advantage from betraying you, betray you they would. J. BARTH Tambo and Bones .. played the instruments from which their names are derived. **derived fossils** *Geol.*: occurring in rocks other than those to which they are native. b T. HERBERT The Mountains of the Moone .. whence seven-mouthed Nyle, derives his Origen. 4 J. R. GREEN It is difficult .. to derive any knowledge of Shakspere's inner history from the Sonnets. *Scientific American* In order to derive Einstein's result. 6 H. FIELDING An action which malice itself could not have derived from an evil motive. S. JOHNSON That etymologist .. who can seriously derive dream from drama. 7 J. LOCKE Experience; in that all our Knowledge is founded, and from that it ultimately derives itself.

II *v.i.* 8 Flow, come, arise, originate, *from*, (occas.) *out of* (a source). LME. b Of a word: originate, come as a derivative (*from* a root etc.) L18. 9 Descend, pass on, come (*to* a receiver etc.). Now *rare*. M16.

8 A. W. KINGLAKE There was an authority not deriving from the Queen or the Parliament. G. GREENE As a story the American picture derives from Hawthorne not Kingsley. K. VONNEGUT His family's wealth derived from the discovery .. of .. buried pirate treasure. 9 M. PATTISON Puritanism .. derives to this country directly from Geneva.

deriver *n.* E17.

derm /dəːm/ *n.* Now *rare* or *obs.* M19. [f. as next. Cf. Fr. *derme*.] *Anat.* = DERMIS.

derma /'dəːmə/ *n.* Now *rare* or *obs.* E18. [mod.L f. Gk = skin.] = DERMIS.

dermabrasion /dəːmə'breɪʒ(ə)n/ *n.* M20. [f. Gk DERMA + ABRASION.] The surgical removal of superficial layers of skin with a rapidly revolving abrasive tool.

dermal /'dəːm(ə)l/ *a.* E19. [f. as prec. + -AL[1].] 1 Of or pertaining to the skin or (esp.) the dermis. E19. 2 *Bot.* Epidermal. L19.

dermapteran /dəː'maptərən/ *n.* & *a.* L19. [f. mod.L *Dermaptera* (see below), f. Gk DERMA + *pteron* wing.] *Entomol.* A *n.* An insect of the order Dermaptera, comprising the earwigs. L19. B *adj.* Of or belonging to Dermaptera. L19.

Also **dermapterous** *a.* L19.

dermat- *comb. form* see DERMATO-.

dermatitis /dəːmə'tʌɪtɪs/ *n.* L19. [f. as next + -ITIS.] *Med.* Inflammation of the skin, usu. of known or specified causation. Cf. ECZEMA.

dermato- /'dəːmətəʊ/ *comb. form* of Gk *derma*, *-mat-* skin, hide, leather: see -O-. Bef. a vowel also **dermat-**. Cf. DERMO-.

der'matogen *n.* (*Bot.*) in the histogen theory, a supposed outermost layer of the apical meristem, which develops into the epidermis (cf. PERIBLEM, PLEROME) L19. **dermato'graphia** *n.* = DERMOGRAPHISM L19. **derma'tographism** *n.* = DERMOGRAPHISM E20. **dermatomy'cosis** *n.* (*Med.*) ringworm infestation, tinea L19. **dermatomyo'sitis** *n.* (*Med.*) inflammation of the skin and underlying muscles, with erythema and oedema, often associated with internal cancer L19. **dermatoplasty** *n.* (an instance of) the surgical replacement of damaged or destroyed skin, as by plastic surgery or skin grafting L19. **derma'toptic** *a.* (*Zool.*) characterized by or relating to the ability of skin to perceive light L19.

dermatoglyphics /dəːmətəʊ'glɪfɪks/ *n.pl.* (usu. treated as *sing.*). E20. [f. prec. + Gk *gluphikos* GLYPHIC + -S[1].] The branch of science that deals with skin patterns (e.g. fingerprints), esp. of the hands and feet; in *pl.*, superficial features of the skin.

dermatoglyphic *a.* E20. **dermatoglyphically** *adv.* M20.

dermatology /dəːmə'tɒlədʒi/ *n.* E19. [f. as prec. + -LOGY.] The branch of science that deals with the skin, esp. its disorders. Formerly also, a treatise on the skin.

dermato'logical *a.* L19. **dermatologist** *n.* M19.

dermatome /'dəːmətəʊm/ *n.* L19. [f. as prec. + -TOME.] 1 *Surg.* A device for removing an intact layer of skin. L19. 2 *Embryol.* The lateral wall of a somite, regarded as the origin of the connective tissue of the skin. E20. 3 *Anat.* An area of the skin supplied by nerves from a single spinal root. E20.

dermatophyte /'dəːmətə(ʊ)fʌɪt/ *n.* L19. [f. as prec. + -PHYTE.] A pathogenic fungus that grows on skin, mucous membranes, hair, nails, feathers, etc.

dermatophytic /-'fɪtɪk/ *a.* L19. **dermatophy'tosis** *n.*, pl. **-toses** /-'təʊsiːz/, a disease caused by a dermatophyte L19.

dermatosis /dəːmə'təʊsɪs/ *n.* Pl. **-toses** /-'təʊsiːz/. M19. [f. as prec. + -OSIS.] *Med.* Any (esp. non-inflammatory) disease of the skin.

dermestid /dəː'mɛstɪd/ *n.* & *a.* L19. [mod.L *Dermestidae* (see below), f. *Dermestes* genus name, irreg. f. Gk DERMA + *esthiein* eat: see -ID[3].] *Entomol.* A *n.* Any of numerous small beetles of the family Dermestidae, many members of which are destructive (esp. as larvae) to hides, skin, fur, wool, and other animal substances. L19. B *adj.* Of, pertaining to, or designating this family. L19.

dermis /'dəːmɪs/ *n.* M19. [mod.L, after EPIDERMIS.] *Anat.* The skin; *spec.* the layer of leathery collagenous tissue, sometimes referred to as the 'true skin', which lies beneath the epidermis and forms the bulk of the thickness of the skin.

dermo- /'dəːməʊ/ *comb. form.* [Repr. Gk *dermo-* abbrev. of DERMATO-.] = DERMATO- (which has largely replaced *dermo-* as a living formative).

dermo'graphia *n.* = DERMOGRAPHISM E20. **der'mographism** *n.* (*Med.*) an allergic condition of the skin in which applied pressure, as by lines being drawn, produces persistent raised marks or weals L19.

dermoid /'dəːmɔɪd/ *a.* & *n.* E19. [f. DERMA + -OID.] A *adj.* Of the skin; skinlike. E19.

dermoid cyst *Med.* a teratoma containing epidermis, hair follicles, and sebaceous glands, derived from residual embryonic cells.

B *n. Med.* A dermoid cyst. L19.

dermopteran /dəː'mɒptərən/ *n.* & *a.* E20. [f. mod.L *Dermoptera* (see below), f. as DERMO- + Gk *pteron* wing: see -AN.] *Zool.* A *n.* A mammal of the order Dermoptera which comprises the colugos or flying lemurs. E20. B *adj.* Of or belonging to Dermoptera. E20.

dern *n.*[1], *a.*[1], & *adv.* see DARN *n.*[2], *a.*, & *adv.*

dern /dəːn/ *a.*[2] & *n.*[2] *obs.* exc. *Sc.* & *dial.* [OE *derne*, *dierne* = OFris. *dern*, OS *derni*, OHG *tarni*, f. WGmc.] A *adj.* †1 Kept concealed or secret; deceitful, secretive, sly. OE-L16. 2 Of a place: not generally known, private. *arch.* OE. †3 Deep, intense. LME-L16. 4 Dark, dreary, sombre; wild, desolate. *arch.* L15. B *n.* †1 A secret. OE-ME. †2 A secret place. ME-E18. 3 Secrecy, concealment; darkness, obscurity. *arch.* ME.

†**dernly** *adv.* ME-E17.

dern /dəːn/ *v.*[1] *obs.* exc. *Sc.* & *dial.* Also **darn** /dɑːn/. [OE *diernan* = OS *dernian*, OHG *tarnen*, f. WGmc, f. base of DERN *a.*[2] & *n.*[2]] 1 *v.t.* Hide, conceal. OE. 2 *v.i.* & *refl.* Seek concealment, hide oneself. L16. 3 *v.t.* Cause to hide. L16.

dern *v.*[2] see DARN *v.*[2]

dernier /dɛrnje, 'dəːnjeɪ/ *a.* E17. [Fr. f. OFr. *derrenier*, f. *derrein*: see DARREIN.] Last, ultimate, final. Now only as below.

dernier cri /kri, kriː/, ***le dernier cri*** /lə/ [Fr., lit. '(the) last cry'] the very latest fashion. ***dernier mot*** /mo, məʊ/ the last word. ***dernier ressort*** /rəsɔːr, rə'sɔː/, †***resort*** a last refuge; orig., the last court of appeal.

¶Formerly fully naturalized.

derogate /'dɛrəgət/ *ppl a.* (orig. *pa. pple*). Now *rare*. LME. [L *derogatus* pa. pple, f. as next: see -ATE[2].] †1 Abrogated in part, lessened in authority etc. LME-M16. 2 Debased. E17.

†**derogately** *adv.* (*rare*, Shakes.): only in E17.

derogate /'dɛrəgeɪt/ *v.* LME. [L *derogat-* pa. ppl stem of *derogare*, f. *de-* DE- I + *rogare* ask, question, propose (a law): see -ATE[3].] †1 *v.t.* Repeal or abrogate in part (a law etc.); destroy or impair the force, effect, or authority of. LME-L17. 2 *v.t.* Detract from; disparage, depreciate. LME. 3 *v.t.* Take away (something *from* a thing) so as to lessen or impair it. *arch.* E16. 4 *v.i.* Take away something *from*; detract *from*. M16. 5 *v.i.* Degenerate; deviate *from* correct behaviour etc. E17.

2 M. EDELMAN We learn to .. derogate the conventional speech of the working class .. as .. sloppy and impoverished. 4 LD BRAIN It will not .. derogate from Harvey's uniqueness to compare him with .. Sherrington. 5 S. BECKETT Should you .. feel like derogating from the general to the particular, remember I am here.

derogator *n.* L16.

derogation /dɛrə'geɪʃ(ə)n/ *n.* LME. [Fr. *dérogation* or L *derogatio(n-)* (only in sense 'partial abrogation of a law'), f. as prec.: see -ATION.] 1 The lessening or impairment of the power or authority *of*; detraction *from*. LME. 2 The action of lowering in value or estimation; disparagement, depreciation. LME. 3 The partial abrogation or repeal of a law etc. L15. 4 Falling off in rank or character; degeneration, debasement. M19.

1 T. CARTE Papal usurpations, to the derogation of the crown. 2 ADDISON He had heard the Plaintiff speak in derogation of the Portuguese. 4 G. A. SALA Men .. who shudder at the derogation and degradation of the Northern American clergy.

derogative /dɪ'rɒgətɪv/ *a.* L15. [Fr. †*derogatif*, *-ive* or late L *derogativus*, f. as DEROGATE *v.*: see -ATIVE.] Tending to derogation, derogatory.

derogatively *adv.* L19.

derogatory /dɪ'rɒgət(ə)ri/ *a.* E16. [Late L *derogatorius*, f. as DEROGATE *v.*: see -ORY[2].] 1 Tending to detract from authority, rights, etc.; impairing in force or effect. Foll. by *from*, *to*, †*of*. E16. 2 Lowering in honour or estimation; unsuited to one's dignity or position; depreciatory, disrespectful, disparaging. L16.

1 H. COX This Act was annulled as derogatory to the King's just rights. 2 H. G. WELLS In secret she invented derogatory names for him; 'Old Uncle Nose-up ..' for example.

derogatorily *adv.* E17. **derogatoriness** *n.* E18.

derout /dɪ'raʊt/ *n. arch.* M17. [Fr. *déroute*, f. as next.] An utter defeat, a rout.

derout /dɪ'raʊt/ *v.t. arch.* M17. [Fr. *dérouter*, OFr. *des-*, f. *dé-* DE- 3 + *route* ROUT *n.*[3]] Put completely to flight.

derrick /'dɛrɪk/ *n.* E17. [*Derrick*, the surname of a noted London hangman fl. 1600.] †1 (D-.) A hangman; hanging; the gallows. E17-L18. 2 A contrivance for hoisting or moving heavy weights: †a *Naut.* A tackle used at the outer quarter of the mizen-mast. M-L18. b A spar or boom set up obliquely, with its head steadied by guys, and fitted with tackle, orig. used on board ship. M18. c A kind of crane with a jib or adjustable arm pivoted to the foot of the central post, deck, or floor. M19. 3 A framework erected over an oil-well or similar boring, to support the drilling apparatus. M19.

derricking *n.* hoisting or moving heavy weights by a derrick L19. **derricking** *a.* operating as or like a derrick E20.

derrière /dɛrɪ'ɛː; dɛrjɛːr (*pl. same*)/ *n. colloq.* L18. [Fr. = behind.] The buttocks; = BEHIND *n.* 1.

derring-do /dɛrɪŋ'duː/ *n. pseudo-arch.* L16. [Misconstruction (by Spenser and others) of LME *dorryng do(n)* daring to do, orig. in Chaucer, copied by Lydgate & misprinted in 16th-cent. eds. as *derrynge do*.] Daring action or feats, heroic courage.

SIR W. SCOTT Singular .. if there be two who can do a deed of such derring-do.

derring-doer *n.* (*rare*) a performer of daring feats L16.

derringer /'dɛrɪndʒə/ *n. N. Amer.* M19. [Henry *Deringer* (1786-1868), US gunsmith.] A small pistol with large bore.

derris /'dɛrɪs/ *n.* M19. [mod.L (see below) f. Gk = leather covering (referring to the pod).] 1 Any of various tall tropical leguminous climbing plants of the genus *Derris*. Also called *tuba*. M19. 2 The powdered tuberous root of any of such plants (or of other genera containing rotenone), orig. used in Malaya to stupefy fish, now in general use as an insecticide. L19.

derry /ˈdɛri/ *int.* & *n.* M16. [Origin unkn. Sense 3 may be a different wd.] **I** *int.* & *n.* **1** Used as a meaningless word in the refrains of popular songs. Also *derry down*. Cf. DOWN *n.*[3] & *int.* 1a. M16.

II *n.* **2** A ballad, a set of verses. *rare*. M19. **3** [App. f. *derry down*.] A tendency to disapprove of someone or something; a dislike, a prejudice, a grudge; = DOWN *n.*[3] 4. *Austral.* & *NZ*. L19.

3 D. STUART And warfare, that's another thing Peter has a derry on.

dertrum /ˈdəːtrəm/ *n.* L19. [mod.L f. Gk *dertron* beak.] *Ornith.* The extremity of the upper bill of a bird's beak.

derv /dəːv/ *n.* M20. [f. *d*iesel-*e*ngined *r*oad *v*ehicle.] Diesel fuel for road-vehicles.

dervish /ˈdəːvɪʃ/ *n.* L16. [Turk. *derviş* f. Pers. *darvēš* poor, a religious mendicant.] A Muslim (*spec.* Sufi) religious man who has taken vows of poverty and austerity; *spec.* (more fully *dancing, whirling, howling*, etc., *dervish*) one whose order includes the practice of dancing etc. as a spiritual exercise.

J. R. ACKERLEY After.. some genial tail-wagging they instituted fun and games and whirled about together like dervishes.

desacralize /diːˈsakrəlʌɪz/ *v.t.* Also **-ise**. E20. [f. DE- 3 + SACRAL *a.*[2] + -IZE.] Ritually remove a taboo from; make less sacred.

desacraliˈzation *n.* E20.

desai /ˈdɛsʌɪ/ *n.* L17. [Marathi *deśāī*.] *Hist.* In India, a revenue official or petty chief.

desalinate /diːˈsalɪneɪt/ *v.t.* M20. [f. DE- 3 + SALINE *n.* + -ATE[3].] Remove the salt from (esp. seawater).

desaliˈnation *n.* M20.

desalt /diːˈsɔːlt, -ˈsɒlt/ *v.t.* E20. [f. DE- 3 + SALT *n.*[1]] Remove salt or salts from.

desaparecido /ˌdesapareˈsiðo/ *n.* Pl. **-os** /-ɒs/. L20. [Sp. = (one who has) disappeared.] A person who disappeared in Argentina during the period of military rule between 1976 and 1983, presumed killed by members of the armed services or the police.

desaturate /diːˈsatʃʊreɪt, -tjʊr-/ *v.t.* E20. [f. DE- 3 + SATURATE *v.*] Cause to become unsaturated, make less saturated.

desatuˈration *n.* E20.

désaxé /dezakse/ *a.* & *adv.* E20. [Fr.] Of a motor-car crankshaft: (set) out of line with the centre of the cylinder.

descale /diːˈskeɪl/ *v.t.* M20. [f. DE- 3 + SCALE *n.*[3]] Remove scale from.

descaler *n.* a substance or device for removing scale M20.

descamisado /ˌdeskamiˈsaðo, dɛsˌkamɪˈsɑːdəʊ/ *n.* Pl. **-os** /-ɒs, -əʊz/. M19. [Sp. = shirtless. Cf. *sansculotte*.] *Hist.* An extreme liberal in the Spanish Revolutionary War of 1820–3; *transf.* a revolutionary.

descant /ˈdɛskant/ *n.* Also **dis-** /ˈdɪs-/. LME. [OFr. *deschant* (mod. *déchant*) f. med.L *discantus* part-song, refrain, f. as DIS- 1 + *cantus* song.] **I** *Mus.* **1** A melodious accompaniment to a simple theme sung or played above it. LME. **2** The soprano or highest part of the score in part-singing. M16. **3** Musical composition, harmony; a harmonized composition. M16. **4** A melodious song. *arch.* or *poet.* L16. **5** An instrumental prelude consisting of variations on a given theme. M17.

1 E. FIGES Her high voice sounded in a thin piping descant above the rest. 2 M. AMIS I was a *soprano*, a *first* soprano, often taking descants, in the choir. 4 W. C. BRYANT I hear the wood-thrush piping one mellow descant more.

II *transf.* **6** (A) discourse on a theme or subject; an observation, a criticism, a remark. *arch.* L16. †**7** (A) variation from that which is typical or customary. M17–E18.

6 ADDISON After this short descant on the uncertainty of our English weather. 7 T. FULLER Running, Leaping, and Dancing, the descants on the plain song of walking.

descant /dɪˈskant, dɛ-/ *v.i.* Also **dis-**. LME. [Prob. f. the n.: so OFr. *deschanter* (mod. *déchanter*).] **1** Sing harmoniously (*arch.*); play or sing a descant. LME. **2** Make remarks or observations; comment or talk at length *on* or *upon* a theme, esp. in praise. E16.

2 SHAKES. *Rich. III* To spy my shadow in the sun And descant on mine own deformity. J. GALSWORTHY On this theme he descanted for half an hour.

descanter *n.* LME.

descend /dɪˈsɛnd/ *v.* ME. [(O)Fr. *descendre* f. L *descendere*, f. *de-* DE- 1 + *scandere* to climb.] **I** *v.i.* **1** Go down, come down; fall, sink; be lowered. ME. **b** Of a planet, zodiacal sign, etc.: move away from the zenith, *esp.* go below the horizon; move southwards. LME. **c** Alight from a conveyance. L15. †**d** Withdraw *into* oneself for meditation. L16–L17. **2** Proceed or go on to what follows, esp. from the general to the particular. ME. **3** Slope or extend downwards. LME. **4** Of sound: fall in pitch, go down the scale. LME. **b** Come or go down in any scale; proceed from superior to inferior. E17. **5** Condescend, lower oneself, stoop, (*to do*). LME. **6** Fall violently upon, attack. LME. **b** Foll. by *on, upon*: make an inconvenient, unexpected, or unwelcome visit. E20. **7** Come of, derive *from* a progenitor or predecessor; *fig.* derive from, originate. Now usu. in *pass.* LME. **8** Be transmitted by inheritance; pass by heredity, pass to an heir. LME.

1 J. HAYWARD I passed to the Nile descending on it at my leasure to the sea. J. FORBES The shades of evening began to descend. P. KAVANAGH A couple of crows descended from the parched sky and landed in Tarry's plot of turnips. b MILTON The setting Sun Slowly descended. c J. BUCHAN A big.. car, from which a man in a raincoat had descended. 2 LD MACAULAY Historians rarely descend to those details from which alone the real state of a community can be collected. 3 D. H. LAWRENCE A flight of stone steps descended into the depths of the water itself. TOLKIEN He could see the heads of the trees descending in ranks towards the plain. 5 S. JOHNSON I have seldom descended to the arts by which favour is obtained. 6b ALDOUS HUXLEY I have.. staying with me in Balliol young Robert Nichols, who descended on me for a day or two. 7 SHAKES. *A.Y.L.* Thou shouldst have better pleas'd me with this deed, Hadst thou descended from another house. DAY LEWIS Her mother.. was directly descended from Oliver Goldsmith's uncle. 8 W. GOUGE The Crowne and Kingdome by just and unquestionable title descended on her. STEELE The eternal Mark of having had a wicked Ancestor descends to his Posterity.

II *v.t.* †**9** Bring or send down. L15–L17. **10** Go or come down, climb down; move downstream along (a river etc.). E17.

10 T. HARDY He descended the stone stairs to a lower story of the castle.

descendable *a.* see DESCENDIBLE.

descendance /dɪˈsɛnd(ə)ns/ *n.* Now *rare*. Also **-ence**. L16. [(O)Fr., or med.L *descendentia*, *descendent-* pres. ppl stem of *descendere*: see prec., -ANCE, -ENCE.] The action or fact of descending from a particular ancestor or origin.

descendancy, -ency *n.* E17.

descendant /dɪˈsɛnd(ə)nt/ *a.* & *n.* Also (now *rare*) **-ent**. LME. [(O)Fr., pres. pple of *descendre*: see DESCEND, -ANT[1], -ENT.] **A** *adj.* **1a** *Her.* Descending towards the base of the shield. Now *rare* or *obs.* LME. **b** Of a planet etc.: moving away from the zenith; *Astrol.* moving towards or just sinking below the western horizon. L16. **c** *gen.* Descending; coming or going down. *rare*. L16. **2** Deriving or descending from an ancestor. L16.

B *n.* **1** A person, animal, plant, or thing descended or derived from an ancestor or predecessor; issue, offspring. E17. **2** *Astrol.* & †*Astron.* The part of the heavens just descending below the horizon; the point at which the western horizon intersects the ecliptic. L17.

1 C. DARWIN The existing forms of life are the descendants by true generation of pre-existing forms. F. W. FARRAR The Gothic language.. has left no direct descendants. O. MANNING A last descendant of one of the Greek Phanariot families that had ruled and exploited Rumania under the Turks. D. DONOGHUE The IRA's claim to be the only true descendants of our Republican martyrs.

descendence *n.* var. of DESCENDANCE.

descendent *a.* & *n.* see DESCENDANT.

descendental /disɛnˈdɛnt(ə)l/ *a.* *rare*. M19. [f. prec. after *transcendental*.] That descends to matter of fact; realistic.

E. P. WHIPPLE With his brain full of transcendental morality, and his heart full of descendental appetites.

†**descender** *n.*[1] *Law*. LME–M18. [AN, use as n. of infinitive = (O)Fr. *descendre*: see DESCEND, -ER[4].] Descent, right of succession.

descender /dɪˈsɛndə/ *n.*[2] M17. [f. DESCEND + -ER[1].] **1** A person who or thing which descends. M17. **2** *Typogr.* & *Palaeogr.* A descending letter; a part or stroke projecting below letters such as x. E19.

descendible /dɪˈsɛndɪb(ə)l/ *a.* Also **-able**. L15. [OFr. *descendable*, f. as DESCEND: see -ABLE, -IBLE.] **1** Able to be inherited. L15. **2** Able to be descended; down which a person may go. *rare*. M18.

descending /dɪˈsɛndɪŋ/ *vbl n.* LME. [f. DESCEND + -ING[1].] **1** The action of DESCEND; descent, going down. LME. †**2** A downward slope: extension downwards. L15–E17. †**3** Parentage, lineage. *rare* (Shakes.). Only in E17.

Comb.: **descending node** *Astron.* the point at which the moon's or a planet's orbit crosses the ecliptic from north to south.

descending /dɪˈsɛndɪŋ/ *ppl a.* L16. [f. DESCEND + -ING[2].] **1** Moving downwards, coming down; directed or extended downwards. L16. **2** Proceeding to what is lower in position or value, or later in order; falling in pitch, stress, etc. L16.

1 **descending letter** *Typogr.* & *Palaeogr.* a letter with a part or stroke projecting below letters such as x.

descension /dɪˈsɛnʃ(ə)n/ *n.* Now *rare*. LME. [OFr. f. L *descensio(n-)*, f. *descens-* pa. ppl stem of *descendere*: see DESCEND, -ION.] **1** The action of descending, descent. LME. †**2** Descent from an ancestor, lineage. LME–L16. †**3** A fall in dignity or status; condescension. LME–L17. †**4** A method of distillation in which the vapour was made to distil downwards. LME–M17. **5** *Astron.* & *Astrol.* The descending of a celestial object; a measure of this. Long *rare*. M16.

descensional *a.* (*rare*) E18.

descensive /dɪˈsɛnsɪv/ *a.* LME. [f. L *descens-* (see prec.) + -IVE.] Characterized by or producing downward movement, falling.

descent /dɪˈsɛnt/ *n.* ME. [(O)Fr. *descente*, f. *descendre* DESCEND after *attente*, *vente* f. *attendre*, *vendre*.] **1** The fact of descending or being descended from an ancestor or predecessor; derivation, origin. ME. †**2a** A line of descent, lineage, race, stock. ME–E17. †**b** A descendant; offspring, issue. L15–M17. **c** A generation. E16. **3** *Law*. The passing of (real) property by inheritance, esp. in the event of intestacy. ME. **b** The transmission of titles, privileges, etc., or characteristics by inheritance. LME. **4** The action or an act of descending; downward movement. LME. **b** *spec.* The action or an act of climbing or travelling down a mountain, slope, stair, etc. E17. †**c** = DESCENSION 4. M17–E18. **5** A downward slope. L16. †**b** The lowest part. *rare* (Shakes.). Only in E17. **c** A means of descending, a way leading downwards. M17. **6** A fall in any scale; *fig.* a decline to a lower state or condition. L16. †**b** A lower stage; a degree below. L16–E18. **7** A sudden attack or invasion. E17.

1 J. YEOWELL A chieftain of imperial descent. J. FISKE The descent of the genus *equus* from a five-toed mammal not larger than a pig. 2b G. CHAPMAN She went Up to the chamber, where the fair descent Of great Alcinous slept. c J. RAY Such as can prove their Gentility for three or four Descents. 4 J. KEILL The great resistance they met with in their descent through the Air. S. KITZINGER The intense and thrilling sensations of the descent of the baby's head. *Washington Post* The 85-ton Skylab, whose slow descent from orbit threatened to bring it crashing to earth. **the Descent** *spec.* the descent of Christ into hell. 5 *New York Times* The variety of terrain that makes this descent so much fun for skiers. 6 MILTON Oh, foul descent! that I, who erst contended With gods to sit in the highest, am now constrained Into a Beast. *method of steepest descent(s)*: see STEEP *a.* 7 J. R. GREEN A daring descent of the English forces upon Cadiz.

Comb.: **descent group** *Anthropol.* a unit of social organization based on common descent.

descloizite /deɪˈklɔɪzʌɪt/ *n.* M19. [f. Alfred *Des Cloizeaux* (1817–97), Fr. mineralogist + -ITE[1].] *Min.* An orthorhombic basic vanadate of zinc, copper, and lead occurring chiefly as a secondary mineral encrusting ores of its constituent metals.

descramble /diːˈskramb(ə)l/ *v.t.* M20. [f. DE- 3 + SCRAMBLE *v.*] Convert or restore (a signal) to intelligible form by applying the reverse of the scrambling process; recover an original signal from (a scrambled signal). Cf. UNSCRAMBLE.

descrambler *n.* = UNSCRAMBLER L20.

describable /dɪˈskrʌɪbəb(ə)l/ *a.* E19. [f. next + -ABLE.] Able to be described.

¶ Earlier in INDESCRIBABLE.

describe /dɪˈskrʌɪb/ *v.t.* LME. [L *describere* write down, copy, f. *de-* DE- 1 + *scribere* write. Cf. earlier DESCRIVE *v.*] **I 1** Portray in words, recite the characteristics of, give a detailed or graphic account of. Foll. by *as*: assert to be, call. LME. †**2** Enter in a register, enrol. L15–M17. **b** Write down, transcribe, copy out. E–M17. **3** Trace the outline of (a geometrical figure etc.), mark out, draw. L15. **b** Trace by motion; move in (a specified line). M16. **4** Portray visually, make a likeness of, picture. Now *rare* or *obs.* E16. †**b** Of a thing: stand for or represent visually. M17–L18. **5** Mark off, divide. *rare.* M16.

1 G. SAINTSBURY In a much sounder sense than that in which.. Matthew Arnold described it as being so, the eighteenth century was to be the Age of Prose. P. ACKROYD He describes.. the routines of bourgeois life—flannel suits, the cakes and tea. S. NAIPAUL It was impossible for her to describe the beauty of the river;.. to convey its peacefulness. 3 DRYDEN With chalk I first describe a circle here. b J. MCPHEE The sun describes a horseshoe around the margins of the sky.

II After confusion of DESCRIVE, DESCRY *v.*[2] and DESCRY *v.*[1] **6** Descry, perceive. Now *rare.* L16.

6 MILTON I describ'd his way Bent all on speed, and markt his Aerie Gate.

describer *n.* M16.

descrier /dɪˈskrʌɪə/ *n.* L16. [f. DESCRY *v.*[1] + -ER[1].] A person who descries or discovers something.

descript /dɪˈskrɪpt/ *ppl a.* Now *rare* or *obs.* M17. [L *descriptus* pa. pple of *describere* DESCRIBE.] Described, apportioned; inscribed, engraved.

descripta *n.* pl. of DESCRIPTUM.

description /dɪˈskrɪpʃ(ə)n/ *n.* LME. [(O)Fr. f. L *descriptio(n-)*, f. *descript-* pa. ppl stem of *describere*: see DESCRIBE, -ION.] **1** A detailed account of a person, thing, scene, or event; a verbal portrait. LME. **b** The action of describing someone or something verbally; verbal representation or portraiture. LME. **c** *Logic.* A definition by non-essential attributes. E17. †**2** The action of writing down or inscribing; an inscription. LME–L18. **b** Registration, enrolment. LME–E17. **3**†**a** A particular design; individual characteristics. LME–M16. **b** The combination of attributes which defines a particular class or type; the type or variety defined, a sort, a kind, a class. L16. †**4** Pictorial representation. *rare.* E–M17. **5** The action of drawing a geometrical figure. M17. **b** The action of tracing or passing along a particular course. E18.

1 H. JAMES He had been to places that people had written books about, and they were not a bit like the descriptions. *definite description*: see DEFINITE *a.* **b knowledge by description** *Philos.* knowledge or understanding not based on direct experience. 3b D. G. MITCHELL The man must be a roué of the worst description. B. MOORE That's the first flying machine of any description that has ever landed on Muck.

descriptionist *n.* a person who professes to give a description, *spec.* one who avoids evaluation or explanation E19.

descriptive /dɪˈskrɪptɪv/ *a.* M18. [Late L *descriptivus*, f. *descript-*: see prec., -IVE.] **1** Serving or seeking to describe; characterized by description. M18. **2** Consisting of or concerned with description of observable things or qualities; not expressing feelings or valuations. M19. **b** *Ling.* Describing a language as it is, avoiding comparison or prescription. E20. **3** *Gram.* Of an adjective etc.: assigning a quality rather than restricting the application of the expression modified. E20.

1 **descriptive geometry**: concerned with the description of surfaces, figures, solids, etc., esp. by means of projection on to planes.

descriptively *adv.* L18. **descriptiveness** *n.* M19.

descriptivism /dɪˈskrɪptɪvɪz(ə)m/ *n.* M20. [f. prec. + -ISM.] **1** *Philos.* The doctrine that the meanings of ethical or aesthetic terms and statements are purely descriptive rather than prescriptive, evaluative, or emotive. M20. **2** *Ling.* The practice or advocacy of descriptive linguistics. M20.

descriptivist *n.* & *a.* (*a*) *n.* an adherent or advocate of descriptivism; (*b*) *adj.* of or pertaining to descriptivism or descriptivists: M20.

descriptor /dɪˈskrɪptə/ *n.* M20. [L = describer, f. *descript-*: see DESCRIPTION, -OR.] An element or term that has the function of describing, identifying, or indexing.

descriptum /dɪˈskrɪptəm/ *n.* Pl. **-ta** /-tə/. M20. [L *descriptum* neut. pa. pple of *describere* DESCRIBE.] *Philos.* The object of a description; the object to which a descriptor refers.

descrive /dɪˈskrʌɪv/ *v.t. obs.* exc. *Sc.* ME. [OFr. *descrivre* (mod. *décrire*) f. L *describere* DESCRIBE. Through DESCRY *v.*[2] conf. w. DESCRY *v.*[1]] **I 1** = DESCRIBE 1. ME. †**2** = DESCRIBE 2. ME–L15. †**3** = DESCRIBE 3, 4, 5. LME–M16. †**II 4** Descry, perceive. ME–L16.

†**descry** *n.* LME [f. next.] **1** A war cry. Only in LME. **2** Perception from a distance. Only in E17.

descry /dɪˈskrʌɪ/ *v.*[1] *t.* ME. [OFr. *descrier* (mod. *décrier*) cry (down), publish. In branch II assoc. w. DECRY *v.* Cf. DECRY *v.*] †**I 1** Disclose, reveal (a secret); betray. ME–L17. **2** Challenge to fight; taunt. ME–L15. **3** Announce, declare, make known. LME–M17. **4** Denounce, disparage. LME–L17.

II 5 Catch sight of, esp. from a distance; espy. ME. **6** Discover by observation; find out, perceive. LME. †**7** Investigate, explore. L16–M18.

5 JO GRIMOND A detour so that his passengers may descry them [seals] reclining like bananas on the rocks. 6 B. MAGEE One has to go on reading for several pages before beginning to descry.. what it is he is saying. A. STORR Their readiness to descry hostility where none exists.

†**descry** *v.*[2]*t.* ME–E17. [Partly f. OFr. *descrire*, partly phonet. reduction of DESCRIVE.] = DESCRIBE I.

desecrate /ˈdɛsɪkreɪt/ *v.t.* L17. [f. DE- 3 + stem of *con-secrate*. (L *desecrare* or *desacrare* meant 'consecrate').] **1** Remove or violate the sacred nature of, profane; *fig.* spoil or treat with contempt (something venerated or admired). L17. **2** Dismiss from holy orders. *arch.* L17. **3** Dedicate or devote *to* evil. E19.

1 E. B. PUSEY The.. vessels of the Temple.. were desecrated by being employed in idol-worship. P. KAVANAGH He couldn't imagine any person with an artistic sense permitting such gross vulgarity to desecrate the hall of their house. 3 J. STEPHEN Particular spots.. were desecrated to Satan.

deseˈcration *n.* the action of desecrating; a desecrated state: E18. **desecrative** *a.* calculated or tending to desecrate M19. **desecrator** *n.* L19.

deseed /diːˈsiːd/ *v.t.* M20. [f. DE- 3 + SEED *n.*] Remove the seed(s) from.

desegregate /diːˈsɛgrɪgeɪt/ *v.t.* M20. [f. DE- 3 + SEGREGATE *v.*] Remove from segregation; *esp.* (orig. *US*) abolish racial segregation in (schools etc.) or of (persons etc.).

desegreˈgation *n.* M20.

desensitize /diːˈsɛnsɪtʌɪz/ *v.t.* Also **-ise**. E20. [f. DE- 3 + SENSITIZE.] Reduce or eliminate the sensitivity of (*spec.* film, a lithographic plate, etc., to light, a person or animal to an allergen, a person to a neurosis, phobia, etc.).

desensitiˈzation *n.* E20. **desensitizer** *n.* a desensitizing agent M20.

desert /dɪˈzəːt/ *n.*[1] ME. [OFr., f. *deservir* DESERVE.] **1** Deserving, being worthy of reward or punishment. ME. **b** Merit, excellence, worth. LME. **2** An action or quality deserving reward or punishment. Usu. in *pl.* LME. **3** Due reward or punishment, something deserved. Freq. in *get, have, meet with*, etc., *one's deserts.* LME.

desert /ˈdɛzət/ *n.*[2] ME. [(O)Fr. *désert* f. late L (Vulgate) *desertum* use as n. of neut. of *desertus* left waste, pa. pple of *deserere* leave, forsake.] An uncultivated, sparsely inhabited tract of land, a wilderness. Now *spec.* a waterless and treeless region.

SHAKES. *A.Y.L.* In this desert inaccessible, Under the shade of melancholy boughs. R. P. JHABVALA Hot winds whistle columns of dust out of the desert into the town. *fig.*: *Daily Express* Once they move out of a town centre, others will follow, leaving a desert. *New Statesman* Far too many children have died in a desert of apathy. *ship of the desert*: see SHIP *n.* 5.

Comb. (cf. next): **desert boot** a suede etc. boot reaching to or just above the ankle; **desert ironweed** (the wood of) a small leguminous tree, *Olneya tesota*, of arid parts of south-western N. America, with purplish flowers, very tough wood, and seeds formerly eaten locally; also called *palo de hierro*; **desert island** a remote and presumably uninhabited island; **desert lark** any of several larks of the genus *Ammomanes*, found from N. and W. Africa to the Middle East and India; **desert lemon, lime** *Austral.* = KUMQUAT 2; **desert oak** *Austral.* a casuarina, *C. decaisneana*; **desert pavement** *Geol.* in arid regions, a surface layer of closely-packed or cemented pebbles, rock fragments, etc., from which fine material has been removed by the wind; **desert rat** *colloq.* a soldier of the 7th British armoured division (with a jerboa as its badge) in the N. African desert campaign of 1941–2; **desert rose** a flower-like aggregate of tabular crystals of a mineral, occurring in arid areas, a rock rose; **desert varnish** a dark hard film of oxides formed on exposed rock surfaces in arid regions.

desertic /dɪˈzəːtɪk/ *a.* characteristic of a desert; desolate: M20.

desert /ˈdɛzət/ *a.* ME. [(O)Fr. *désert* f. L *desertus* pa. pple: see prec. Now treated as attrib. use DESERT *n.*[2]] **1** Uninhabited, desolate, lonely. ME. **b** Of the nature of a desert; uncultivated, barren. LME. **2** Deserted, forsaken, abandoned. *arch.* LME.

¶ Orig., & archaically in 18 & 19, stressed on 2nd syll.

desertness *n.* barren desolation LME.

desert /dɪˈzəːt/ *v.* LME. [Fr. *déserter* f. late L *desertare*, f. L *desertus*: see DESERT *n.*[2]] **1** *v.t.* Give up, relinquish, leave. LME. **2** *Sc. Law.* **a** *v.t.* Cease to pursue (an action, summons, etc.). Formerly also, adjourn (Parliament). L15. **b** *v.i.* Cease to have legal force; become inoperative. M16. **3** *v.t.* Forsake, abandon, (a person or thing having a claim upon one). M17. **b** Abandon or give up *to* something. *arch.* M17. **c** Of a power or faculty: fail (someone). M17. **4** *v.i.* Run away from or forsake one's duty, post, or party, esp. from service in the armed forces. L17.

1 POPE His slacken'd hand deserts the lance it bore. J. HAWKES St. Kilda,.. where men clung tenaciously for a time, but which.. they have now deserted. 2a **desert the diet** abandon criminal proceedings, finally or temporarily. 3 J. GALSWORTHY Deserting his wife and child and running away with that foreign governess. P. ROTH Louis deserts basic training and.. goes to hide out from the Korean War in a slum somewhere. b W. S. LANDOR Gracious God! Desert me to my sufferings, but sustain My faith in Thee! c C. CHAPLIN Mother obeyed like a child;.. her will seemed to have deserted her. 4 F. FITZGERALD Its soldiers deserted in droves to escape their enemy or to rejoin their families.

deserted *ppl a.* Forsaken, abandoned, left desolate E17. **desertedness** *n.* E19.

deserter /dɪˈzəːtə/ *n.* M17. [f. prec. + -ER[1], after Fr. *déserteur.*] **1** A person who deserts someone or something. M17. **2** *spec.* A member of the armed forces who deserts. M17.

desertification /dɛˌzəːtɪfɪˈkeɪʃ(ə)n/ *n.* L20. [f. DESERT *n.*[2]: see -FICATION.] The process by which fertile land becomes desert.

deˈsertify *v.t.* make desert, cause desertification of L20.

desertion /dɪˈzəːʃ(ə)n/ *n.* LME. [(O)Fr. *désertion* f. late L *desertio(n-)*, f. *desert-* pa. ppl stem of *deserere*: see DESERT *n.*[2], -ION.] **1** The action of deserting, forsaking, or abandoning. LME. **b** *Law.* Wilful abandonment of one's duty or obligations, esp. (*a*) to service in the armed forces, (*b*) to live with one's spouse. E18. **2** The state of being deserted or abandoned. M16.

desertization /dɛzətʌɪˈzeɪʃ(ə)n/ *n.* Also **-isa-**. M20. [f. DESERT *n.*[2] + -IZATION.] = DESERTIFICATION.

desertless /dɪˈzəːtlɪs/ *a.* M16. [f. DESERT *n.*[1] + -LESS.] †**1** Unmerited, undeserved. M16–M17. **2** Without merit, undeserving. E17.

deserve /dɪˈzəːv/ *v.* ME. [OFr. *deservir* (mod. *desservir*), f. L *deservire* serve zealously or well, f. *de-* DE- 1 + *servire* SERVE *v.*[1]] †**1** *v.t.* Earn or become worthy of (reward, punishment, etc.); secure by service or actions, gain, win. ME–L18. **2** *v.t.* Be entitled to, *to do*; be worthy to have; be a justifiable cause of. ME. **3** *v.i.* Be or (formerly) become entitled; be worthy to be *well* or *ill* treated at the hands *of*. ME. †**4** *v.t.* & *i.* foll. by *to*, *for*. Be of service to, treat or serve well. LME–M17. †**5** *v.t.* Give in return for service rendered; requite. LME–E17.

2 P. DEHN We had suffered too little To deserve all the flowers, the kisses, the wine and the thanks. O. MANNING I don't know what I've done to deserve a daughter like you. H. L. MENCKEN They are really citizens of mark, whose opinions . . deserve to be heard and attended to. F. WARNER What crime can so deserve such pain? **3** THACKERAY Deputies who had deserved well of their country. B. JOWETT Slaves ought to be punished as they deserve.

deserver *n.* LME.

deserved /dɪˈzəːvd/ *ppl a.* M16. [f. prec. + -ED[1].] **1** Rightfully earned, merited. M16. †**2** Meritorious, worthy. *rare* (Shakes.). Only in E17.

deservedly /-vɪdli/ *adv.* according to desert or merit; rightfully, worthily: M16. **deservedness** /-vɪdnɪs/ *n.* worthiness, desert; excellence: E17.

deserving /dɪˈzəːvɪŋ/ *vbl n.* ME. [f. as prec. + -ING[1].] The action of DESERVE *v.*; desert, merit.

deserving /dɪˈzəːvɪŋ/ *a.* M16. [f. as prec. + -ING[2].] Meritorious, worthy. Foll. by *of*: showing conduct or qualities which ought to be given (praise, censure, help, etc.).

LD MACAULAY Delinquents . . deserving of exemplary punishment. F. WELDON She was deserving, so would never get what she deserved. R. C. A. WHITE Victorian notions of identifying those who are 'the deserving poor'.

deservingly *adv.* M16. **deservingness** *n.* M17.

de-sex /diːˈsɛks/ *v.t.* E20. [f. DE- 3 + SEX *n.*] Castrate, spay; deprive of distinctive sexual qualities; remove or minimize the sexual appeal of.

desexualize /diːˈsɛksjʊəlʌɪz, -ˈsɛkʃʊəl-/ *v.t.* Also **-ise**. L19. [f. DE- 3 + SEXUAL + -IZE.] Deprive of sex, sexuality, or sexual qualities.

desiccant /ˈdɛsɪk(ə)nt/ *n.* & *a.* L17. [L *desiccant-* pres. ppl stem of *desiccare*: see DESICCATE *v.*, -ANT[1].] **A** *n.* A drying or desiccating agent. L17. **B** *adj.* Serving to desiccate. L18.

desiccate /ˈdɛsɪkeɪt/ *ppl a.* & *n.* LME. [f. L *desiccatus* pa. pple, f. as next: see -ATE[2].] **A** *ppl a.* Desiccated, dried. *arch.* LME. **B** *n.* A desiccated substance or product. E20.

desiccate /ˈdɛsɪkeɪt/ *v.* L16. [L *desiccat-* pa. ppl stem of *desiccare*, f. *de-* DE- 1 + *siccare* make dry, f. *siccus* dry: see -ATE[3].] **1** *v.t.* Remove the moisture from, dry up, (now esp. foodstuffs for preservation); *fig.* deprive of energy or feeling, make impersonal. Freq. as *desiccated* ppl a. L16. **2** *v.i.* Become dry, dry up. *rare.* L17.

1 BACON Wine helpeth to digest and desiccate the moisture. R. H. TAWNEY Piety imprisoned in a shrivelled mass of desiccated formulae. J. GRIGSON Whip the cream and fold it in, with a good tablespoon of desiccated coconut. B. BAINBRIDGE So desiccated by age that a smile might have broken her into little pieces. **2** *Nature* The lake is now desiccating.

¶ Formerly stressed on 2nd syll.

desiccation /dɛsɪˈkeɪʃ(ə)n/ *n.* LME. [L *desiccatio(n-)*, f. as prec.: see -ATION.] The action of desiccating; the condition of being desiccated.

desiccative /ˈdɛsɪkətɪv/ *a.* & *n.* LME. [Late L *desiccativus*, f. as DESICCATE *v.*: see -ATIVE.] **A** *adj.* Having the tendency or quality of drying up. LME. **B** *n.* A drying agent, a desiccant. Now *rare* or *obs.* LME.

desiccator /ˈdɛsɪkeɪtə/ *n.* M19. [f. DESICCATE *v.* + -OR.] An apparatus or device for desiccating a substance; *spec.* (*Chem.*) an apparatus containing a drying agent for removing moisture from specimens.

desiccatory /dɛˈsɪkət(ə)ri/ *a.* L18. [f. as prec. + -ORY[2].] Desiccative, drying.

desiderata *n.* pl. of DESIDERATUM.

desiderate /dɪˈzɪdərət, -ˈsɪd-/ *a.* & *n.* Long *arch. rare.* M17. [L *desideratus* pa. pple, f. as next: see -ATE[2].] **A** *adj.* Desired; desirable. M17. †**B** *n.* Something desired; a desideratum. M–L17.

desiderate /dɪˈzɪdəreɪt, -ˈsɪd-/ *v.t.* M17. [L *desiderat-* pa. ppl stem of *desiderare* desire, perh. f. *de-* DE- 1 + *sider-* star: see -ATE[3].] Feel the lack of, regret the absence of, long for, desire.

desideration /dɪˌzɪdəˈreɪʃ(ə)n, -ˌsɪd-/ *n.* L15. [L *desideratio(n-)*, f. as prec.: see -ATION.] **1** The action of desiderating, desire. L15. **2** A thing desired, a desideratum. *rare.* M19.

desiderative /dɪˈzɪdərətɪv, -ˈsɪd-/ *a.* & *n.* M16. [Late L *desiderativus*, f. as DESIDERATE *v.*: see -ATIVE.] **A** *adj.* **1** *Gram.* Pertaining to or designating a verb formed from another to express a desire of doing the act denoted. M16. **2** *gen.* Having, expressing, or pertaining to desire. M17. **B** *n. Gram.* A desiderative verb, verbal form, or conjugation. M18.

desideratum /dɪˌzɪdəˈrɑːtəm, -ˈreɪtəm; -ˌsɪd-/ *n.* Pl. **-ta** /-tə/. M17. [L *desideratum* use as n. of neut. sing. of pa. pple of *desiderare* DESIDERATE *v.*] A thing for which desire is felt; a thing lacked and wanted, a requirement.

desiderium /dɛzɪˈdɛrɪəm, -sɪ-/ *n.* Pl. ***-ia*** /-ɪə/. E18. [L, f. *desiderare* DESIDERATE *v.*] A desire or longing, esp. for something once possessed; a sense of loss.

†**desidiose** *a.* E18–E19. [L *desidiosus* slothful, f. *desidia* sitting idle, f. *desidere* sit about, sit idle, f. *de-* DE- 1 + *sedere* sit.] Idle, indolent, slothful, sluggish.

desight /dɪˈsʌɪt/ *n.* Now *rare* or *obs.* M19. [Prob. var. of DISSIGHT, alt. after DE-.] An unsightly object, an eyesore.

design /dɪˈzʌɪn/ *n.* M16. [Fr. †*desseing* (now *dessein*, *dessin*), f. *desseigner*, *dessi(g)ner* f. It. *disegnare* f. L *designare* DESIGNATE *v.*] **1** A plan or scheme conceived in the mind; a project. M16. **b** A plan or purpose of attack (*up*)*on* a person or thing. Now freq. in *pl.*, a plot or intention to gain possession of something or to attract someone. L17. **c** The action or fact of planning or plotting; *esp.* hypocritical scheming. E18. **2** A purpose, an intention, an aim. L16. **b** Purpose, intention. Chiefly in *by* (†*up*)*on*) *design*, on purpose, deliberately. E17. **3** An end in view, a goal. E17. **4** A preliminary sketch; a plan or pattern from which a picture, building, machine, etc., may be made. M17. **5** An idea as executed, the combination of elements in the finished work; an artistic device, a pattern. M17. **6** The action or art of planning and creating in accordance with appropriate functional or aesthetic criteria; the selection and arrangement of artistic or functional elements making up a work of art, machine, or other object. M17.

1 LD MACAULAY Grey . . had concurred in the design of insurrection. B. RUBENS She sat on the bench directly in front of his desk, not with any design, but because, unlike the others, it was empty. **b** J. LOCKE A sedate, settled design upon another man's life. H. READ The Klee drawings . . are addressed to an intelligent public; they have a design on us. M. MOORCOCK Esmé clutched my arm so tightly and listened so attentively that I began to suspect she had designs on me. **c** B. TAYLOR 'Twas all deceit and lying, false design. **2** B. HARRIS They who ask relief, have one design: and he who gives it another. C. S. FORESTER It is my design to eliminate all possibility of collusion. **b** J. A. MICHENER The younger braves . . had gone partly by accident, partly by design, well into the mountains. **3** M. W. MONTAGU Happiness is the natural design of all the world. **4** K. CLARK In 1801 Telford did a design of London Bridge, a single span of iron. **5** D. WILSON A silver bracelet of rare and most artistic design. I. COLEGATE Cushions embroidered by his mother in vaguely ecclesiastical designs. **6** TENNYSON What a lovely shell . . With delicate spire and whorl, How exquisitely minute, A miracle of design. R. DAWKINS Like a fashion in women's clothes, or in American car design. *Daily Telegraph* Independent school heads are mainly responsible for the design of a major new examination. **argument from design** *the* argument that the complexity of the universe and the adaptation of means to ends are evidence of an intelligent Creator.

designful *a.* full of design; intentional: L17. **designless** *a.* void of design, purposeless M17.

design /dɪˈzʌɪn/ *v.* LME. [Partly f. L *designare* DESIGNATE *v.*, partly f. Fr. *désigner* f. L.] **I** †**1** *v.t.* = DESIGNATE *v.* 2. LME–M17. **2** *v.t.* = DESIGNATE *v.* 4. *arch.* LME. †**3** *v.t.* = DESIGNATE *v.* 3. L16–M17. **4** *v.t.* (Cf. DESIGNATE *v.* 1.) †**a** Appoint to an office or function; nominate. L16–E18. **b** Devote *to* a fate or purpose. *obs.* exc. as passing into sense 9. L16. †**5** *v.t.* Assign (something *to* a person); grant, give. L16–L19. **6** *v.t.* Set (a thing) apart *for* (†*to*, †*on*) a person. (Passing into sense 9.) M17.

2 SOUTHEY The plains . . ere long to be design'd Castille. **3** T. WARMSTRY Designing forth unto us the place whither hee is ascended. **4b** B. G. GERBIER The Duke . . designed in his Will ten Thousand Gilders . . to . . alter what he had Built amisse.

II 7a *v.t.* Plan and execute (a structure, work of art, etc.); fashion, shape; make a preliminary sketch for (a work of art etc.); make drawings and plans for the construction or production of (a building, machine, garment, etc.). LME. **b** *v.t. gen.* Draw, sketch; outline, delineate. Now *rare* or *obs.* M17. **c** *v.i.* Be a designer of works of art, buildings, machines, garments, etc. M17. **8** *v.t.* Form a plan or scheme of; contrive. M16. **9** *v.t.* Intend, purpose, (something, *as*, *to be*, *to do*, *doing*, *that*); create or intend *for* a specific purpose. E17. **b** *v.t.* in *pass.* & *v.i.* Intend to start on a journey or course, set out or be bound *for*. *arch.* M17. **10** *v.t.* Have in view, contemplate. L17.

7a J. FERGUSSON The Roman bridges were designed on the same grand scale as their aqueducts. G. B. SHAW To snatch moments from his painting and sculpture to design some wonderful dresses for us. D. CARNEGIE The car was so designed that it could be operated entirely by hand. **b** EVELYN The prospect was so tempting that I designed it with my crayon. **c** J. RUSKIN A painter designs when he chooses some things, refuses others, and arranges all. **8** W. FAULKNER We had long ago designed marriage for him. **9** S. BUTLER How does the Devil know What 'twas that I design'd to do? DEFOE I did not design you should have heard. G. ORWELL Political language . . is designed to make lies sound truthful and murder respectable. NEB *Eph.* 2:10 Good deeds for which God has designed us. I. MURDOCH An air of self-righteousness which was clearly designed as a provocation.

designable /ˈdɛzɪgnəb(ə)l/ *a.*[1] M17. [f. L *designare* (see DESIGNATE *v.*) + -ABLE.] Distinguishable, identifiable.

designable /dɪˈzʌɪnəb(ə)l/ *a.*[2] L19. [f. DESIGN *v.* + -ABLE.] Able to be designed.

designata *n.* pl. of DESIGNATUM.

designate /ˈdɛzɪgnət/ *ppl a.* (orig. *pa. pple*). LME. [L *designatus* pa. pple, f. as next: see -ATE[2].] †**1** *pa. pple* Indicated, manifested. Only in LME. **2** *postpositive adj.* Appointed to office but not yet installed. M17.

2 B. WEBB The twenty Ministers designate . . went to Buckingham Palace to be sworn in.

designate /ˈdɛzɪgneɪt/ *v.t.* L18. [L *designat-* pa. ppl stem of *designare*, f. *de-* DE- 1 + *signare* SIGN *v.*: see -ATE[3]. Cf. earlier DESIGN *v.* I.] **1** Appoint to an office or function, nominate; destine or devote to a fate or purpose. (Foll. by *as*, *for*, *to*.) L18. **2** Serve as a name for, stand for, signify, be descriptive of. E19. **3** Point out, indicate, specify. E19. **4** Call by a name or distinctive term; name, identify, describe, characterize (*as*). E19.

1 F. D. MAURICE Josiah . . was designated to his task before his birth. D. FRASER Brooke was . . designated to succeed Wavell as Commander-in-Chief. **2** R. L. STEVENSON It was odd to hear them, throughout the voyage, use shore words to designate portions of the vessel. J. GASKELL The Borough Orphanage . . (Children's Welfare they preferred you to designate it). **3** W. S. LANDOR Her hair flew loosely behind her, designating that she was in haste. J. MARQUAND If you will be so kind as to drop me at the point I designate. *Which Computer?* The word processing keys can be designated as function keys.

designative *a.* serving to designate something E17. **designator** *n.* (*rare*) E18. **designatory** *a.* of or pertaining to a designator or designation, designative E18.

designation /dɛzɪɡˈneɪʃ(ə)n/ *n.* LME. [(O)Fr. *désignation* or L *designatio(n-)*, f. as prec.: see -ATION.] 1 The action of marking or pointing out; indication by words or signs. LME. 2 The action or an act of setting aside for or devoting to a particular purpose; *Sc. Law* the setting apart of manses or glebes for the clergy. Now *arch.* or *Hist.* L16. 3 The action of appointing or nominating a person to office; the fact of being nominated. E17. †b The appointment of a thing; the summoning of an assembly. M17–L18. †4 The quality of being marked out or fitted for a particular employment; a vocation; suitability. M17–L18. †5 Purpose, intention, design. M17–M18. 6 A distinctive mark or indication. M17. 7 A descriptive name, an appellation; *Law* a statement of profession, residence, etc., added for purposes of identification to a person's name. E19.

designatum /dɛsɪɡˈnɑːtəm, -ˈneɪtəm; -z-/ *n.* Pl. **-ta** /-tə/. M20. [L *designatum* neut. pa. pple of *designare* DESIGNATE *v.*] The object or class of objects designated by a sign. Cf. DENOTATUM.

designed /dɪˈzʌɪnd/ *ppl a.* L16. [f. DESIGN *v.* + -ED[1].] 1 Planned, intended. L16. †2 Designated. E17–M18. 3 Fashioned according to a design. L19.

designedly /-nɪdli/ *adv.* On purpose, intentionally M17.

designer /dɪˈzʌɪnə/ *n.* & *a.* M17. [f. DESIGN *v.* + -ER[1].] A *n.* 1 A schemer, an intriguer. M17. 2 A person who prepares designs for a work of art, machine, or other object for construction or manufacture. M17. 3 *gen.* A person who designs or plans. L17.

2 A. ROAD Apart from visualising the architectural settings for a drama, the designer is responsible for furnishing it and finally for providing the props. J. S. FOSTER The separation existing between designer and constructor. *dress-designer, fashion designer, interior designer,* etc.

B *attrib.* or as *adj.* Bearing the name or label of a famous (fashion) designer; designed for a specific purpose, esp. to be fashionable. L20.

E. JONG All gotten up in designer clothes. **designer drug** a drug synthesized to mimic a legally restricted or prohibited drug without being subject to such restriction.

designing /dɪˈzʌɪnɪŋ/ *ppl a.* L17. [f. DESIGN *v.* + -ING[2].] 1 Scheming, crafty, artful. L17. 2 Characterized by constructive forethought. L17.

designingly *adv.* L17.

designment /dɪˈzʌɪnm(ə)nt/ *n.* Long *arch. rare.* L16. [f. DESIGN *v.* + -MENT.] †1 Appointment or nomination to office; consignment to a fate. L16–M18. 2 Planning, designing; an enterprise, an undertaking, a design. L16. †3 Artistic representation; an outline or sketch, an original design. L16–E18. †4 Indication by sign or token. Only in 17.

desilver /diːˈsɪlvə/ *v.t.* M19. [f. DE- 3 + SILVER *n.*] Remove silver from.

desilverize /diːˈsɪlvərʌɪz/ *v.t.* Also **-ise.** M19. [f. DE- 3 + SILVER *n.* & *a.* + -IZE.] Extract the silver from (lead etc.).

desilveriˈzation *n.* L19.

desinence /ˈdɛsɪn(ə)ns/ *n.* L16. [Fr. *désinence* f. med.L *desinentia*, f. *desinent-* pres. ppl stem of *desinere* leave off, close: see -ENCE.] Termination, close; *Gram.* a suffix, an ending of a word.

desiˈnential *a.* pertaining to or of the nature of a desinence E19.

desipience /dɪˈsɪpɪəns/ *n.* M17. [L *desipientia*, f. *desipere* be foolish: see -ENCE.] Folly; silliness.

desipiency *n.* (*rare*) = DESIPIENCE L17. **desipient** *a.* (*rare*) foolish, silly E18.

desirable /dɪˈzʌɪərəb(ə)l/ *a.* & *n.* LME. [(O)Fr. *désirable*, f. *désirer*, after L *desiderabilis*: see DESIRE *v.*, -ABLE.] A *adj.* Worth having or wishing for; causing desire; to be desired. LME.

G. B. SHAW It is not desirable that they should rule the world. C. S. FORESTER The more desirable the man—the richer, the handsomer, the more influential—the fiercer was the competition.

B *n.* A desirable person or thing. M17.

desiraˈbility *n.* (*a*) the quality of being desirable; (*b*) *rare* a desirable thing: E19. **desirableness** *n.* M17. **desirably** *adv.* E19.

desire /dɪˈzʌɪə/ *n.* ME. [(O)Fr. *désir*, f. as next.] 1 The fact or condition of desiring; the feeling that one would derive pleasure or satisfaction from possessing or attaining something; a longing. ME. 2 *spec.* Sexual appetite; lust. ME. 3 An expressed wish, a request. *arch.* LME. 4 Something desired or longed for. LME.

1 E. W. LANE The elder King felt a strong desire to see his brother. J. BARZUN The democrat's conscious desire is philanthropic; he wants love to prevail. V. S. PRITCHETT Frustrated in his desire for larger premises. 2 S. W. BAKER The flesh of the crocodile is.. supposed to promote desire. 3 J. BISCHOFF I.. send, at your desire, a general list of articles. 4 W. DAMPIER We steered off.. expecting a Sea-Breez at E.N.E., and the third day had our desire. STEELE Farewel my Terentia, my Heart's Desire.

desireful *a.* †(*a*) desirable; (*b*) full of desire, desirous: LME. **desireless** *a.* E17. **desirelessness** *n.* M20.

desire /dɪˈzʌɪə/ *v.* ME. [(O)Fr. *désirer* f. L *desiderare* DESIDERATE *v.*] I *v.t.* 1 Long for, want earnestly (a thing, (a person) *to do, that*). ME. b Feel sexual desire for, lust after. LME. c Feel the loss of, miss. Now *rare* or *obs.* M16. †2 Of a thing: require, demand. LME–E17. 3 Express a wish for, ask for, request, (a thing (*of* a person), *to do, that*). LME. †b Request to know or be told. *rare.* L15–E18. †4 Request the presence or attendance of, invite (*to* a place or course of action). LME–M17. 5 Express a wish to (a person), entreat, command. Foll. by *to do, that,* †*of* the thing desired. *arch.* L15.

1 TENNYSON You desire your child to live. S. LEWIS A man who desired to lease a store-building. A. SILLITOE I would like for him only what I desire for myself. *leave something, much,* etc., *to be desired*: see LEAVE *v.*[1] 2 SPENSER A doleful case desires a dolefull song. 3 S. PEPYS My song.. which he has often desired of me. EARL OF CHATHAM If you are forced to desire farther information.. do it with proper apologies. SIR W. SCOTT He alighted at the.. Convent, and desired to see the Duke. 4 SHAKES. *L.L.L.* But shall we dance, if they desire us to't? 5 SHELLEY Go desire Lady Jane She place my lute. E. M. FORSTER Mrs Wilcox had desired her.. to forward the enclosed.

II *v.i.* 6 Feel desire, have a desire. LME.

6 AV *Prov.* 13:4 The soule of the sluggard desireth, and hath nothing.

desired *ppl a.* †(*a*) affected with desire, desirous; (*b*) wished for, longed for: ME. **desiredness** *n.* the condition of being desired M19. **desiringly** *adv.* with desire, longingly L15.

desirous /dɪˈzʌɪərəs/ *a.* ME. [AN = OFr. *desireus* (mod. *désireux*) f. Proto-Romance, f. L *desiderare* DESIDERATE *v.*: see -OUS.] 1 Having desire, wishful, wanting. Usu. foll. by *of, that, to do.* ME. †2 Of the nature of, characterized by, or expressing desire; covetous. LME–M17. †3 Full of (esp. martial) spirit, ardent. LME–L15. †4 Desirable. LME–E18.

1 MILTON From dance to sweet repast they turn Desirous. T. HARDY Each of the lovers was desirous that the marriage should be kept as private as possible. G. B. SHAW Men and women are equally qualified or equally desirous to legislate, to govern. P. ACKROYD Desirous of fame and yet unsure how to claim it.

desirously *adv.* (*a*) with desire, longingly; †(*b*) willingly, readily: LME. **desirousness** *n.* (now *rare*) M16.

desist /dɪˈzɪst, dɪˈsɪst/ *v.* LME. [(O)Fr. *désister* f. L *desistere*, f. *de-* DE- 1 + *sistere* redupl. of *stare* to stand.] 1 *v.i.* Cease (*from,* †*in,* †*to do*); stop, forbear. LME. b Refrain, abstain, (*from*). M20. †2 *v.t.* Discontinue. E16–L18.

1 M. LEITCH He'd had to desist from smashing things because of the noise. b R. SHAW He wanted to cry out.., but desisted because he felt he didn't have the right.

desistance, -ence *n.* cessation, discontinuation M17.

desition /dɪˈsɪʃ(ə)n/ *n. rare.* E17. [Late L *desitio(n-)*, f. *desit-* pa. ppl stem of *desinere* cease: see -ITION.] Termination or cessation of being; ending.

desize /diːˈsʌɪz/ *v.t.* M20. [f. DE- 3 + SIZE *n.*[2]] Remove size from (textiles).

desk /dɛsk/ *n.* LME. [med.L *desca*, prob. based on Prov. *desc(a)* basket or It. *desco* table, butcher's block, f. L DISCUS discus, (Vulgate) dish, disc (of a sundial). Cf. DISH *n.*] 1 An article of furniture (sometimes portable), having a flat or sloping surface serving as a rest for books, paper, etc., for reading or writing at and freq. also as a repository for writing materials etc. LME. 2 In a place of worship, a sloping board or rest on which books used in the service are laid. Hence, a choir-stall; *Sc.* a seat or pew; (chiefly *US*) a minister's stall, a pulpit. LME. †3 A shelf or case for books. M16–E18. 4 The function or office of the occupant(s) of a desk, esp. in a church or office; clerical work. L16. 5 (In full *music desk*) a music stand, esp. as shared by two players in an orchestra; the player(s) at a desk. M19. 6 A (specified) section of an organization; *esp.* a section of a newspaper office dealing with a specified topic or (*US*) with editorial work. E20. 7 A counter for a cashier, hotel receptionist, etc.; the person(s) on duty in reception etc. M20.

1 *copydesk, office desk, reading-desk, roll-top desk, school-desk, writing-desk,* etc. 2 *litany-desk, prayer-desk.* 4 T. DWIGHT He [a professor of divinity] educated between forty and fifty for the desk. 5 *Gramophone* It seems as though only a couple of desks are playing. 6 E. NEWBY The Foreign Office.. I was interviewed by a representative of the Asian Desk. 7 P. BAIR Ask the desk to ring through to Miss Jackson's room.

Comb.: **desk-bound** *a.* obliged to remain working at a desk; **desk diary** a diary of a size and nature suited to use on a desk, esp. in an office for recording engagements etc.; **desk dictionary** a one-volume dictionary of middle size, suited to use on a desk for general reference; **desk job** a job based at a desk, esp. as opp. to one in active military service; **desk lamp** a reading-lamp suited to use on a desk; **desk-man** †(*a*) a clergyman; (*b*) a person who works at a desk, a white-collar worker; *spec.* a journalist who works mainly at a desk; **desk sergeant** *US* a sergeant in administrative charge of a police station;

desktop /ˈdɛsktɒp/ *n.* & *a.* Also **desk-top, desk top.** E20. [f. prec. + TOP *n.*[1]] A *n.* 1 The working surface of a desk. E20. 2 A desktop computer. *colloq.* L20. 3 *Computing.* The working area of a computer screen viewed as a representation of the top of a desk, used with icons resembling familiar office equipment. L20.

B *attrib.* or as *adj.* Of a size and nature suitable for use on a desk; *esp.* designating or pertaining to a microcomputer suitable for use on an ordinary desk. Also, able to be undertaken from a desk. M20.

desktop publishing the production of high-quality printed matter using a desktop computer and a laser printer.

desman /ˈdɛsmən/ *n.* L18. [Fr. & G f. Sw. *desman-råtta* muskrat, f. *desman* musk.] Either of two semi-aquatic insectivorous shrewlike mammals of the mole family Talpidae, *Desmana moschata* of European Russia, and *Galemys pyrenaicus* of the Pyrenees.

desmid /ˈdɛsmɪd/ *n.* M19. [mod.L *Desmidium* genus name, as if f. dim. of Gk *desmos* band, chain: see -IDIUM.] Any member of the family Desmidiaceae of freshwater microscopic unicellular green algae, often found united in chains or masses.

desmo- /ˈdɛsməʊ/ *comb. form* of Gk *desmos* bond, chain: see -O-.

desmognathous /dɛsˈmɒɡnəθəs/ *a.* (*Ornith.*) designating or displaying a palatal structure in which the maxillopalatine bones meet each other in the median line M19. **desmosome** *n.* (*Cytol.*) an area of a cell surface by which it is bound to another cell; a pair of such areas: M20.

desmoid /ˈdɛsmɔɪd/ *a.* M19. [f. Gk *desmos* bond or *desmē* bundle: see -OID.] Fibrous, ligamentous; *esp.* (*Med.*) designating a benign fibromatous and collagenous tumour of (esp. abdominal) muscle.

désoeuvré /dezœvre/ *a.* M18. [Fr.] Unoccupied; languidly idle.

desolate /ˈdɛs(ə)lət/ *a.* & *n.* LME. [L *desolatus* pa. pple, f. as next: see -ATE[2].] A *adj.* 1 Left alone, lonely; destitute of joy or comfort, forlorn, wretched. LME. 2 Uninhabited, deserted; ruinous, neglected; barren, dreary. LME. †3 Destitute or deprived *of*. LME–E18. †4 Lacking virtue; evil; dissolute. LME–L18.

1 V. WOOLF To stand, like a desolate sea-bird, alone. P. P. READ Never in his life before had he felt so desolate—abandoned by everyone who had ever loved him. 2 G. BERKELEY Roads untrodden, fields untilled, houses desolate. A. PATON The red desolate hills, where the earth had torn away like flesh. J. BRAINE It was only a small theatre but suddenly it seemed big and echoing and desolate.

B *n*. A desolate place or person. Long *rare*. LME.

SOUTHEY Travelling the trackless desolate.

desolately *adv*. M16. **desolateness** *n*. E17.

desolate /ˈdɛsəleɪt/ *v.t.* LME. [L *desolat-* pa. ppl stem of *desolare* abandon, f. *de-* DE- 1 + *solus* alone: see -ATE[3].] 1 Deprive of inhabitants, depopulate; devastate, lay waste; make barren; spoil by neglect. LME. 2 Leave alone or friendless, forsake; make wretched; overwhelm with misery. M16.

1 DEFOE Would quite desolate the island, and starve them. C. LYELL As if the city had been desolated by the plague. 2 G. B. SHAW Agreeable surprises instead of desolating disappointments.

desolater *n*. M17. **desolatingly** *adv*. in a manner or to an extent that desolates or saddens L19. **desolative** *a*. (*rare*) tending to desolate L16. **desolator** *n*. L18.

desolation /dɛsəˈleɪʃ(ə)n/ *n*. LME. [Late L *desolatio(n-)*, f. as prec.: see -ATION.] 1 The action or an act of laying waste or rendering uninhabitable a land etc.; devastation. LME. 2 The condition of being naturally or by external agency unfit for habitation; waste or ruined state; dreary barrenness. LME. **b** A desolate place; a dreary waste or ruin. E17. 3 Deprivation of comfort; wretchedness; grief; solitariness, loneliness; a feeling of wretchedness or loneliness. LME.

1 T. PENNANT The general desolation of the place by the Danes. 2 N. MONSARRAT Along the deserted road, under the cruel moonlight which revealed only dust and desolation. 3 SHAKES. *L.L.L.* You have liv'd in desolation here, Unseen, unvisited. W. HOLTBY There was upon his face a desolation so haggard . . she hardly recognised him.

Desolre /diːsɒlˈreɪ/ *n*. *obs*. exc. *Hist*. Also **D sol re**. LME. [f. *D* as a pitch letter + *sol*, *re* designating tones in the solmization of Guido d'Arezzo (*c*990–1050).] *Medieval Mus*. The note D in Guido d'Arezzo's 1st and 2nd hexachords, where it was sung to the syllables *sol* and *re* respectively. Cf. ARE *n*.[1], BEFA, CEFAUT, etc.

de son tort /də sɔ̃ tɔːr/ *postpositive a. phr*. L17. [Fr. = of his wrong.] *Law*. Acting and liable (as executor or trustee) but without authorization.

desophisticate /diːsəˈfɪstɪkeɪt/ *v.t.* M19. [f. DE- 3 + SOPHISTICATE *v*.] Remove sophistication from; render unsophisticated.

desophistiˈcation *n*. M19.

desorb /diːˈsɔːb/ *v*. E20. [Back-form. f. next.] *Physical Chem*. 1 *v.t.* Remove (a substance etc.) from a surface upon which it is adsorbed. E20. 2 *v.i.* Of a substance: leave a surface upon which it is adsorbed. M20.

desorption /diːˈsɔːpʃ(ə)n/ *n*. E20. [f. DE- 3 + ADSORPTION.] *Physical Chem*. The release of a substance from a surface on which it is adsorbed, or from solution in a liquid phase.

desoxy- *comb. form* see DEOXY-.

desoxyribonucleic *a*. see DEOXYRIBONUCLEIC.

despair /dɪˈspɛː/ *n*. ME. [AN var. of OFr. *desespeir* (mod. *désespoir*).] 1 Complete loss or absence of hope; (a feeling of) hopelessness. ME. 2 A cause of hopelessness; a thing about which there is no hope. E17.

1 R. P. WARREN A sadness overcame him, more than sadness, a despair. M. L. KING Revolution, though born of despair, cannot long be sustained by despair. *personified*: W. COWPER Hollow-eyed Abstinence, and lean Despair. *counsel of despair*: see COUNSEL *n*. 1. **in despair** in a despairing state, affected by a feeling of hopelessness. 2 SHAKES. *Macb*. Strangely-visited people, All swoln and ulcerous . . The mere despair of surgery, he cures. SHELLEY Those faultless productions, whose very fragments, are the despair of modern art.

despairful *a*. full of despair, desperate L16. **despairfully** *adv*. E17.

despair /dɪˈspɛː/ *v*. ME. [OFr. *despeir-* tonic stem of *desperer* f. L *desperare* to despair (of), f. *de-* DE- 1 + *sperare* to hope, f. *speres* old pl. of *spes* hope.] 1 *v.i.* & †*refl*. Lose or give up hope; be without hope. (Foll. by *of*, †*to do*.) ME. †2 *v.t.* Deprive of hope, cast into despair. *rare*. LME–E17. †3 *v.t.* Lose or give up hope of, be without hope of. LME L18.

1 M. W. MONTAGU His life was despaired of. L. DURRELL We carried her disease backwards and forwards over Europe . . until I began to despair. M. MOORCOCK Herr Lustgarten was beginning . . to despair of teaching me more.

despaired *ppl a*. (*a*) (long *obs*. exc. *US dial*.) in despair, hopeless, desperate; (*b*) that is despaired *of* (or †of): ME. **despairer** *n*. a person who despairs E17. **despairingly** *adv*. in a despairing manner M17. **despairingness** *n*. (*rare*) the condition of being despairing E18.

despatch *n*., *v*. vars. of DISPATCH *n*., *v*.

despecialize /diːˈspɛʃ(ə)lʌɪz/ *v.t.* Also **-ise**. L19. [f. DE- 3 + SPECIALIZE.] Make less specialized or more general.

despecialiˈzation *n*. L19.

†**despect** *n*. LME–M19. [L *despectus*: see DESPITE *n*.] (A cause of) contempt.

†**desperacy** *n*. E17–E19. [f. DESPERATE *a*.: see -ACY.] Desperation.

desperado /dɛspəˈrɑːdəʊ/ *n*. Pl. **-oes**, ***-os**. E17. [Refash. of DESPERATE *n*. after Sp.: see -ADO 1.] †1 = DESPERATE *n*. 1. E17–E18. 2 A desperate or reckless person, esp. a criminal. M17.

2 D. CARNEGIE The two-gun desperado was one of the most dangerous criminals ever encountered in the history of New York.

desperadoism *n*. the action or qualities of a desperado L19.

desperate /ˈdesp(ə)rət/ *n*. Now *rare*. M16. [f. the adj.] 1 A person in despair; a wretch. M16. †2 = DESPERADO *n*. 2. E17–E18.

desperate /ˈdɛsp(ə)rət/ *a*. & *adv*. LME. [L *desperatus* pa. pple of *desperare*: see DESPAIR *v*.] A *adj*. I 1 In despair, despairing (*of*). *arch*. LME. 2 Given up as hopeless. Now chiefly of a debt: not recoverable. LME. 3 Leaving little or no room for hope; extremely grave or dangerous. L15. †**b** Of an undertaking etc.: hopeless of accomplishment. M17–L19. 4 Expressive or indicative of despair. M16.

1 SHAKES. *Two Gent*. I am desperate of obtaining her. 3 SWIFT Younger brothers of obscure families, and others of desperate fortunes. J. M. MURRY His suffering from Tom's desperate illness. N. MONSARRAT The food situation on the island had now become so desperate that it had overtaken even the bombing as the worst misery of their lives. 4 DISRAELI He was answered only with desperate sobs.

II 5 Driven to desperation, reckless from despair; heedless of danger; violent, lawless. L15. †**b** Utterly careless *of*. *rare*. Only in E17. **c** Having an extreme need or great anxiety *for*, *to do*. M20. 6**a** Outrageous, extravagant; shocking. M16. **b** Extremely bad; extreme, excessive, awful. E17. 7 Characterized by the recklessness, violence, or resolution of despair; undertaken in desperation as a last resort; staking all on a small chance. L16. †**b** Involving serious risk. L16–M17.

5 J. BUCHAN The party who wish to upset the republic are pretty desperate fellows. C. S. FORESTER 'Put it down, d'ye hear?' said Hornblower, desperate with worry. c M. MOORCOCK I was desperate to talk my way clear of this terrible man. *Daily Telegraph* A university graduate so desperate for work that he travels 240 miles a day. 6b POPE Concluding all were desp'rate sots and fools, Who durst depart from Aristotle's rules. DAY LEWIS We did not go in for a desperate amount of washing. M. BINCHY Wasn't it desperate the way things never come singly. 7 MILTON His look denounc'd Desperate revenge, and Battel dangerous To less than Gods. LD MACAULAY A desperate conflict against overwhelming odds.

B *adv*. Desperately. M17.

DICKENS It's a desperate sharp night for a young lady to be out in.

desperate /ˈdɛsp(ə)reɪt/ *v.t.* *rare*. E19. [f. the adj., after vbs in -ATE[3].] Make desperate.

desperately /ˈdɛsp(ə)rətli/ *adv*. L15. [f. DESPERATE *a*. + -LY[2].] 1 In despair or (now esp.) desperation; recklessly; with the energy or violence of despair. L15. 2 To a desperate degree; so as to leave little or no room for hope; extremely, excessively, awfully. L16.

1 W. CATHER A shivering gray kitten, . . clinging desperately to the wood with her claws. JOYCE (Wrings her hands slowly, moaning desperately) O Sacred Heart of Jesus, have mercy on him! 2 AV *Jer*. 17:9 The heart is deceitfull aboue all things, and desperately wicked. G. B. SHAW An enthusiast and a desperately hard worker. E. L. DOCTOROW So desperately in love she could no longer see properly. *Sunday Express* His son Greg, desperately ill with cancer.

desperateness /ˈdɛsp(ə)rətnɪs/ *n*. M16. [f. as prec. + -NESS.] 1 = DESPERATION 2. M16. †2 = DESPERATION 1. L16–M17. 3 The state or quality of leaving little or no room for hope; extreme gravity. L16.

desperation /dɛspəˈreɪʃ(ə)n/ *n*. LME. [OFr. f. L *desperatio(n-)*, f. *desperat-* pa. ppl stem of *desperare*: see DESPAIR *v*., -ATION.] 1 The action of despairing (*of*); the condition of having utterly lost hope; despair. Now *rare*. LME. 2 Despair leading to recklessness, or recklessness arising from despair; extreme need or great anxiety *for*, *to do*. M16.

despicable /dɪˈspɪkəb(ə)l, ˈdɛspɪk-/ *a*. M16. [Late L *despicabilis*, f. *despicari* look down upon, f. *de-* DE- 1 + base cogn. w. *specere* look: see -ABLE.] 1 Deserving to be despised; vile, morally contemptible. M16. †2 Miserable, wretched. M17–E18. †3 Contemptuous. M17–L18.

despicaˈbility *n*. E19. **despicableness** *n*. M17. **despicably** *adv*. M17.

†**despight** *n*., *prep*., *v*. vars. of DESPITE *n*. etc.

†**despightful** *a*. var. of DESPITEFUL.

despin /diːˈspɪn/ *v.t.* Infl. as SPIN *v*. M20. [f. DE- 3 + SPIN *v*.] Counteract the spinning motion of; prevent from spinning.

despiritualize /diːˈspɪrɪtjʊəlʌɪz/ *v.t.* Also **-ise**. M19. [f. DE- 3 + SPIRITUALIZE.] Deprive of spiritual character.

despiritualiˈzation *n*. L19.

despisable /dɪˈspʌɪzəb(ə)l/ *a*. Now *rare*. ME. [OFr., f. *despis-* stem of *despire* DESPISE *v*.: see -ABLE.] Despicable.

despise /dɪˈspʌɪz/ *n*. Long *rare*. LME. [Prob. f. OFr. *despiz*, *-s* nom. of *despit* DESPITE *n*., but taking the form of an Eng. deriv. of DESPISE *v*.] Contempt, scorn.

despise /dɪˈspʌɪz/ *v*. ME. [OFr. *despis-* pres. stem of OFr. *despire*, f. L *despicere*, f. *de-* DE- 1 + *specere* look.] 1 *v.t.* Regard as inferior or worthless; feel contempt for. ME. **b** Scorn or disdain *to do*, *that*. Long *rare*. LME. †2 *v.i.* Look down (*up*)*on*, *up*, *above*. Only in ME. †3 *v.t.* Treat with contempt; disregard. ME–M17.

1 D. RUNYON He hates and despises cheaters at cards, or dice. E. FERBER One of the vaqueros who still despised the jeep or Ford as a means of locomotion. b E. B. WHITE I despise to go anywhere.

despisal *n*. the act of despising; contempt: M17. **despisement** *n*. (*arch*.) contempt, scorn E17. **despiser** *n*. ME. **despisingly** *adv*. scornfully, contemptuously L16.

despite /dɪˈspʌɪt/ *n*. *arch*. Also †**despight**. ME. [OFr. *despit* (mod. *dépit*) f. L *despectus* looking down (on), f. *despect-* pa. ppl stem of *despicere*: see prec.] 1 Contempt, scorn, disdain. ME. 2 Contemptuous treatment or behaviour; outrage, injury. ME. †3 Disregard of opposition, defiance. (Foll. by *to*.) ME–E18. 4 Indignation, anger, *esp*. such as arises from offended pride or vexation; the bearing of a grudge; ill will, spite. ME. 5 An act demonstrating contempt, hatred, or malice; an outrage. Usu. in *pl*. ME.

Phrases: **in despite of** (*arch*. also w. *possess*. of n. or pron.) = DESPITE *prep*.

despite /dɪˈspʌɪt/ *v*. *arch*. Also †**despight**. LME. [OFr. *despiter* (mod. *dépiter*) f. L *despectare* frequent. of *despicere*: see DESPISE *v*.] 1 *v.t.* Show contempt for, treat with contempt. LME. †2 *v.t.* Provoke to anger; spite. M16–M17. †3 *v.i.* Show contempt or ill will. M16–M18.

despite /dɪˈspʌɪt/ *prep*. Also †**despight**. LME. [Abbrev. of *in despite of* s.v. DESPITE *n*.] Notwithstanding, in spite of or (*arch*.) *of*. Formerly also, in contempt of, in defiance of.

KEATS His Voice leapt out, despite of godlike curb. M. ROBERTS Despite the sunshine, the air is chilly.

despiteful /dɪˈspʌɪtfʊl, -f(ə)l/ *a. arch.* Also †**despight-**. LME. [f. DESPITE *n.* + -FUL.] 1 Contemptuous, scornful, disdainful. LME. 2 Malicious, spiteful; cruel. LME.
despitefully *adv.* LME. **despitefulness** *n.* M16.

despiteous /dɪˈspɪtɪəs/ *a.* Orig. †**-itous**. See also DISPITEOUS. ME. [AN *despitous*, OFr. *despitos* (mod. *dépiteux*); alt. of LME after PITEOUS.] 1 Full of contempt, or ill will; opprobrious, insulting. *arch.* ME. 2 = DISPITEOUS 2. ME.
despiteously, †**-itously** *adv.* ME.

despoil /dɪˈspɔɪl/ *n. arch.* L15. [OFr. *despoille*, f. as next.] 1 The action of despoiling. L15. †2 A thing or things plundered, spoil. L15–E17.

despoil /dɪˈspɔɪl/ *v.t.* Now *literary*. ME. [OFr. *despoill(i)er*, *despuillier* (mod. *dépouiller*) f. L *despoliare*, f. *de-* DE- 1 + *spolia* (see SPOIL *n.*).] 1 Strip of some possession(s) by violence; plunder, rob (*lit.* & *fig.*) (Foll. by *of* the possession(s).) ME. †2 *spec.* Strip of clothes or armour; undress (oneself, another). (Foll. by *of* the clothing etc.) ME–E18. †3 Make useless, spoil, destroy. LME–L17. †4 Carry off as spoil, remove forcibly, steal. L15–E17.
1 GIBBON The cities of Greece and Asia were despoiled of their most valuable ornaments. DICKENS The coach . . despoiled by highway-men. H. JAMES Her ruling passion had in a manner despoiled her of her humanity.
despoiler *n.* LME. **despoilment** *n.* = DESPOLIATION E19.

despoliation /dɪˌspəʊlɪˈeɪʃ(ə)n/ *n.* Now *literary*. L16. [Late L *despoliatio(n-)*, f. L *despoliat-* pa. ppl stem of *despoliare*: see prec., -ATION.] The action of despoiling; the condition of being despoiled.

despond /dɪˈspɒnd/ *v.* & *n.* M17. [L *despondere* give up, resign, abandon, f. *de-* DE- 1 + *spondere* promise.] A *v.i.* Lose heart or hope; become dejected. (Foll. by *of*.) M17. B *n.* Despondency. Orig. & chiefly in *Slough of Despond*, (a bog in Bunyan's *Pilgrim's Progress* representing) a state of despondency. *arch.* L17.
desponder *n.* (*rare*) L17. **despondingly** *adv.* in a desponding manner, dejectedly M17.

despondency /dɪˈspɒnd(ə)nsi/ *n.* M17. [f. as prec. + -ENCY.] Dejection resulting from loss of heart or hope.
Also **despondence** *n.* L17.

despondent /dɪˈspɒnd(ə)nt/ *a.* L17. [f. as prec. + -ENT.] 1 Characterized by despondency. L17. 2 Expressive of despondency. M19.
despondently *adv.* L17.

despot /ˈdɛspɒt/ *n.* M16. [Fr. *despote*, earlier †*despot* f. med.L *despota* f. Gk *despotēs* master, lord (orig. applied to a god and to the absolute ruler of a non-free people).] 1 *Hist.* a A petty Christian ruler dependent on or tributary to the Turks after the Turkish conquest of Constantinople. M16. b (Used as a form of address to) a Byzantine emperor or prince of the imperial house. E17. 2 An absolute ruler; a tyrant, an oppressor. L18. 3 A bishop or patriarch of the Eastern Orthodox Church. E19.
despotat, **-ate** *n.* (*Hist.*) the dominion of a Greek despot under the Turks M19. **despotize** *v.i.* rule as a despot, act despotically L18.

despotic /dɛˈspɒtɪk/ *a.* M17. [Fr. *despotique* f. Gk *despotikos*, f. *despotēs*: see prec., -IC.] Of, pertaining to, or of the nature of a despot; arbitrary, tyrannical.
†**despotical** *a.* = DESPOTIC E17–M19. **despotically** *adv.* L17.

despotism /ˈdɛspətɪz(ə)m/ *n.* E18. [Fr. *despotisme*, f. as DESPOT: see -ISM.] 1 The rule of a despot; despotic government; the exercise of absolute political authority. E18. 2 Absolute power or control. L18. 3 A political system under the control of a despot; a despotic State; an arbitrary government. M19.
1 BURKE The simplest form of government is despotism, where all the inferior orbs of government are moved merely by the will of the Supreme. 2 R. SCRUTON The authority, the responsibility, and the despotism of parenthood. 3 V. S. PRITCHETT From despotisms like the Soviet Union the only voices that tell one anything are the voices of private life.
despotist *n.* an advocate of despotism L18.

despumate /dɪˈspjuːmeɪt, ˈdɛspjʊ-/ *v.* M17. [L *despumat-* pa. ppl stem of *despumare* skim (off), f. *de-* DE- 1 + *spuma* foam, froth, scum: see -ATE[3]. Cf. next.] 1 *v.t.* Skim; clarify (a liquid) by removing the scum from its surface. M17. 2 *v.i.* Of a liquid: become clarified by casting off the scum. M18.
despuˈmation *n.* (*a*) the removal of froth or scum from a liquid; the condition of being freed from scum; (*b*) *arch.* the expulsion of impure matter from the fluids of the body; the despumated matter: E17.

†**despume** *v.t.* LME–M18. [f. L *despumare* (see prec.) or Fr. *despumer* f. L.] = DESPUMATE 1.

desquamate /ˈdɛskwəmeɪt/ *v.* E18. [L *desquamat-* pa. ppl stem of *desquamare* scale (off), f. *de-* DE- 1 + *squama* scale: see -ATE[3].] †1 *v.t.* Remove the scales from, take the surface layer off, peel. E–M18. 2 *v.i.* Come off in the form of scales; flake off. E19.
desquamative /dɪˈskwamətɪv/ *a.* characterized by desquamation M19. **desquamatory** /dɪˈskwamət(ə)ri/ *a.* & *n.* (*a*) *adj.* of or pertaining to desquamation; (*b*) *n.* a desquamatory implement: M17.

desquamation /dɛskwəˈmeɪʃ(ə)n/ *n.* M16. [f. as prec.: see -ATION.] 1 A cast-off scale of skin etc.; something which has desquamated. *rare.* M16. 2 The action or fact of desquamating; *spec.* the shedding of the outer layer of the skin. E17.

des res /ˈdɛz rɛz/ *n. phr.* L20. [Abbrev.: cf. RES *n.*[2]] (In advertisements & *iron.*) A desirable residence.

†**dess** *n.* M–L16. [OFr. *deis* DAIS.] A desk.
SPENSER Ne ever once did looke up from her desse.

dessert /dɪˈzəːt/ *n.* M16. [Fr., use as n. of pa. pple of *desservir* clear the table, f. *des-* DIS- 1 + *servir* SERVE *v.*[1]] A course of fruit, nuts, sweets, etc., served at the end of a meal. Also, (orig. *US*) a pudding or sweet course.
Attrib. & *comb.*: In the sense 'for the serving or eating of dessert', as *dessert fork*, *knife*, *plate*, *service*, etc.; in the sense 'suitable for serving for dessert', as *dessert apple*, *pear*, etc. Special combs., as **dessertspoon** (*a*) a spoon intermediate in size between a tablespoon and a teaspoon; (*b*) a dessertspoonful; **dessertspoonful** the amount a dessertspoon will hold (a recognized measure for medicine, culinary ingredients, etc.); **dessert wine** a wine suitable for drinking with dessert, *esp.* a still, sweet, sometimes fortified, wine.

dessiatine /ˈdɛsjətiːn, -ʃj-/ *n.* Also **desyatin** & other vars. L18. [Russ. *desyatina* lit. 'tithe'.] A Russian measure of land, equivalent to about 1.1 hectares or 2.7 acres.

dessous /dəsu/ *n.* M18. [Fr. = lower part, (in pl.) underwear.] 1 *dessous des cartes* /dɛ kart/ ['of the cards'], the underside of playing-cards when dealt face down; *fig.* a secret kept in reserve, an unknown factor. M18. 2 (Women's) underwear. E20.

destabilize /diːˈsteɪbɪlʌɪz, -b(ə)l-/ *v.t.* Also **ise**. E20. [f. DE- 3 + STABILIZE.] Deprive of stability, make unstable; *spec.* make (a country or area) politically unstable, undermine (a foreign government).
destabiliˈzation *n.* L20.

destain /diːˈsteɪn/ *v.t.* M20. [f. DE- 3 + STAIN *n.*] Remove stain from; *spec.* in *Biol.* & *Chem.*, selectively remove stain from (a substrate, specimen for microscopy, etc.) after it has previously been stained.

de-Stalinize /diːˈstɑːlɪnʌɪz/ *v.t.* & *i.* Also **-ise**. M20. [f. DE- 3 + *Stalin*: see STALINISM.] *Soviet Hist.* Remove or counteract the influence of Stalin or Stalinism (on); remove traces of Stalin or Stalinism (from).
de-Staliniˈzation *n.* M20.

De Stijl /də ˈstʌɪl/ *n.* & *a.* M20. [Du. = the style (see below).] (Of, pertaining to, characteristic of, or designating) a movement in art and architecture associated with the Dutch periodical *De Stijl* (1917–32), founded by Theo van Doesburg and Piet Mondrian, and devoted to the principles of neo-plasticism.

destinal /ˈdɛstɪn(ə)l/ *a.* LME. [f. Fr. *destin* (masc.) OFr. *destine* (fem.), f. *destiner* DESTINE: see -AL[1].] Of, pertaining to, or according to destiny or fate.
J. MCQUEEN The planets represent the destinal forces of the universe.
¶In isolated use bef. 20.

destinate /ˈdɛstɪneɪt/ *v.t.* Now *rare*. Pa. pple & ppl a. †**-ate** (earlier), **-ated**. LME. [L *destinat-*: see next, -ATE[3].] = DESTINE.

destination /dɛstɪˈneɪʃ(ə)n/ *n.* LME. [(O)Fr., or L *destinatio(n-)*, f. *destinat-* pa. ppl stem of *destinare*: see DESTINE, -ATION.] I 1 The action of appointing or intending a person or thing for a particular end or purpose; the fact of being so appointed or intended. Now *rare*. LME. 2 The end or purpose for which a person or thing is destined. M17. 3 The fact of being destined or bound for a particular place. Chiefly in *place* etc. *of destination* (= sense 4 below). L18. 4 The place to which a person or thing is going, the intended end of a journey. E19.
4 K. M. E. MURRAY After a much delayed railway journey they reached their destination nearly eleven hours after leaving Oxford.
II 5 *Sc. Law.* The nomination by the testator of successors to heritable or movable property in a certain order; the series of heirs so nominated. E18.

destine /ˈdɛstɪn/ *v.t.* ME. [(O)Fr. *destiner* f. L *destinare* make firm, establish, f. *de-* DE- 1 + causative deriv. of *stare* STAND *v.*] 1 Foreordain, predetermine, decree. Now usu. in *pass.*, be fated, turn out (by hindsight) *to be* or *do*. ME. 2 Ordain, appoint. *obs.* exc. as passing into sense 1. LME. 3 Set apart *for* or devote *to* a particular purpose, activity, etc.; intend *for*, *to do*. Usu. in *pass.* M16. 4 In *pass.* Be bound or intended *for* a place, be going *to* or *from* a place. L18.
1 R. FRY An event . . which was destined to change ultimately the face of things. 3 H. READ He was well educated, and destined for the diplomatic service. 4 S. UNWIN Many cases of books destined for Japan had been detained and opened. *Times* Traffic . . destined to and from the South-east.

destiny /ˈdɛstɪni/ *n.* Also (esp. when personified) **D-**. ME. [(O)Fr. *destinée* f. Proto-Romance use as n. of L *destinata* fem. pa. pple of *destinare*: see prec., -Y[5].] 1 The predetermined course of events; that which is destined to happen; the fate of a particular person, country, etc.; the ultimate condition; a person's lot in life. ME. 2 The power or agency that (supposedly) predetermines events, invincible necessity, (freq. personified or as a goddess); in *pl.*, the three Fates of mythology. LME.
1 H. REED That battle which settled the destiny of Saxon independence. E. O'NEILL You are fully competent to direct the destiny of this company. P. TILLICH In every act of moral self-affirmation man contributes to the fulfilment of his destiny. *Guardian* Secure in their Biblical faith that their deeds are part of a divinely ordained destiny. J. CHEEVER She was the woman life meant him to have; she was his destiny. *manifest destiny*: see MANIFEST *a.* 2 *man of destiny*: see MAN *n.*

destiny /ˈdɛstɪni/ *v.t.* Long *rare*. LME. [f. the n.] Ordain or predict the destiny of.

destitute /ˈdɛstɪtjuːt/ *a.* & *n.* LME. [L *destitutus* forsaken, pa. pple of *destituere*, f. *de-* DE- 1 + *statuere* set up, place.] A *adj.* 1 †a Of a place: abandoned, deserted. LME–L16. b Of a person: left friendless or helpless, forlorn. *obs.* exc. as passing into sense 1c. E16. c Without resources or (formerly) some particular resource; without means of subsistence; in great need of food, shelter, etc. (Bef. 18 often an implication of uses of sense 1b.) E16. 2 †a Deprived or bereft *of* (something formerly possessed). LME–E17. b Devoid *of* (something desirable). L15. B *n.* A destitute person. M18.
destitutely *adv.* (*rare*) M16. **destituteness** *n.* M17.

destitute /ˈdɛstɪtjuːt/ *v.t.* Now *rare*. LME. [Partly f. prec., partly repr. L *destituere* (see prec.).] 1 Deprive or divest *of*; make destitute. LME. †2 Forsake, desert, abandon. M16–L17. 3 Lay waste, ruin. M16. †4 Frustrate, disappoint, defeat. M16–E17. 5 Deprive of office, depose. L16.

destitution /dɛstɪˈtjuːʃ(ə)n/ *n.* LME. [(O)Fr. f. L *destitutio(n-)*, f. *destitut-* pa. ppl stem of *destituere*: see DESTITUTE *a.*, -ION.] 1 The state of being deprived or devoid *of* something;

deprivation, want. LME. **b** *spec.* Extreme poverty, great need of food, shelter, etc. E17. **2** Deprivation of office; discharge, dismissal. Long *rare.* L15.

destock /diːˈstɒk/ *v.i.* M20. [f. DE- 3 + STOCK *n.*[1]] Reduce the quantity or number of stock held. Chiefly as *destocking* vbl n.

destool /diːˈstuːl/ *v.t.* E20. [f. DE- 3 + STOOL *n.*] In W. Africa: remove (a tribal chief) from authority, depose.
destoolment *n.* E20.

destour *n.* var. of DASTUR *n.*[1]

destrier /ˈdɛstrɪə, dɛˈstriːə/ *n.* Now *arch.* or *Hist.* Also **destrer** /ˈdɛstrə/. ME. [AN *destrer*, OFr. *destrier*, f. Proto-Romance, f. L *dext(e)ra*, f. as DEXTER (being led by the right hand of a squire).] A medieval knight's warhorse, a charger.

destroy /dɪˈstrɔɪ/ *v.t.* ME. [OFr. *destruire* (mod. *détruire*) f. Proto-Romance alt. of L *destruere*, f. *de-* DE- 1 + *struere* pile up.] **1** Pull or break down, demolish; smash to pieces, shatter. ME. †**2** Lay waste, ravage; reduce (a person) to poverty. ME–E17. **3** Ruin completely, make utterly useless, spoil. ME. **b** Ruin financially, professionally, or in reputation; deprive of power or prestige; defeat or discredit utterly. L18. **4** Deprive of life, kill; wipe out, annihilate. ME. **b** Kill (a sick or unwanted animal) humanely. M19. **5** Put an end to or do away with (something immaterial, a condition, institution, etc.). ME. **b** *Law.* Nullify, invalidate. E19. **6** Counteract or neutralize the effect of; make ineffective. E18.

1 M. MEYER The castle . . had been largely destroyed by a fire. H. KISSINGER An Egyptian . . missile destroyed an Israeli reconnaissance plane. 3 J. FORBES The long drought and extreme heat have destroyed their vegetables. J. B. PRIESTLEY Building on the old sites, instead of going outside, . . and there destroying a good piece of country. b H. WILSON The great events that ended the careers of Asquith and Lloyd George, and almost destroyed Baldwin. 4 R. J. SULLIVAN A deluge . . covered the whole coasts, and destroyed the greatest part of the inhabitants. J. STEINBECK Maybe Kino has cut off his own head and destroyed himself. b DAY LEWIS The soldiers had been ordered . . to destroy their pets before they sailed away. 5 J. HAWKES The trees drove out the game herds . . and so destroyed the livelihood of the hunters. G. VIDAL The applause came, destroying the silence.

Phrases: **destroying angel** (*a*) = DANITE 2; (*b*) a highly poisonous mushroom of the genus *Amanita*, spec. *A. virosa*.

destroyable *a.* LME. **destroyingly** *adv.* as a destroyer, destructively E19.

destroyer /dɪsˈtrɔɪə/ *n.* LME. [f. prec. + -ER[1].] **1** A person who or thing which destroys. LME. **2** *spec.* A fast warship of a type designed to protect other ships by attacking submarines etc. with guns and torpedoes. L19.

Comb. & phrases: **destroyer-escort** (chiefly *US*) a small destroyer (warship); **destroyer leader** *US* a large destroyer (warship); *torpedo-boat destroyer, torpedo destroyer*: see TORPEDO *n.*

destruct /dɪˈstrʌkt/ *v.* & *n.* M17. [L *destruct-*: see DESTRUCTION.] A *v.t.* †**1** *gen.* Destroy. Only in M17. **2** *spec.* Bring about the deliberate destruction of (one's own rocket, missile, etc.). See also SELF-DESTRUCT *v.* M20. **B** *n.* The action of deliberately destroying one's own rocket, missile, etc. M20.

destructful /dɪˈstrʌktfʊl, -f(ə)l/ *a.* M17. [f. as prec. + -FUL.] Destructive.

destructible /dɪˈstrʌktɪb(ə)l/ *a.* M18. [Fr., or late L *destructibilis*, f. *destruct-*: see next, -IBLE.] Able or liable to be destroyed.
¶Earlier in INDESTRUCTIBLE.
destructiˈbility *n.* M18.

destruction /dɪˈstrʌkʃ(ə)n/ *n.* ME. [(O)Fr. f. L *destructio(n-)*, f. *destruct-* pa. ppl stem of *destruere*: see DESTROY, -ION.] **1** The action of destroying; demolition, devastation, slaughter. ME. **2** The fact or condition of being destroyed; ruin. ME. **3** A means of destroying; a cause of ruin. LME.

1 *Listener* How can we stand by and do nothing to prevent the destruction of the world? 2 M. MITCHELL Despite all Frank had told her about the town burning to the ground, she had never really visualized complete destruction. 3 H. MARTINEAU The deplorable mistake which was likely to prove the destruction of the whole family.

destructional *a.* of or pertaining to destruction; formed by destructive agencies, *spec.* by denudation: E20.

destructionist /dɪˈstrʌkʃ(ə)nɪst/ *n.* E19. [f. prec. + -IST.] **1** *Theol.* A person who believes in the final annihilation of the wicked. E19. **2** An advocate of a policy of destruction, esp. of an existing social system. Chiefly *derog.* M19.

destructive /dɪˈstrʌktɪv/ *a.* & *n.* L15. [(O)Fr. *destructif, -ive* f. late L *destructivus*, f. *destruct-*: see DESTRUCTION, -IVE.] A *adj.* Destroying, tending to destroy; deadly *to*, causing destruction *of*; refuting or disparaging without amending, merely negative, not constructive. L15.

STEELE Vice is in itself destructive of Pleasure. O. MANNING It's the greatest destructive force in the world, poverty. *Financial Times* A rag-bag of constructive and destructive criticism, of praise and outright damnation. *destructive distillation*: see DISTILLATION 2.

B *n.* **1** Something destructive; an agent or means of destruction. M17. **2** = DESTRUCTIONIST 2. Chiefly *derog.* M19.

destructively *adv.* M17. **destructiveness** *n.* M17.

destructor /dɪˈstrʌktə/ *n.* L17. [L *destructor*, f. *destruct-*: see DESTRUCTION, -OR.] **1** A person who or thing which destroys (= DESTROYER 1). L17. **2** *spec.* A furnace for burning refuse, an incinerator. L19.

destructure /diːˈstrʌktʃə/ *v.t.* M20. [f. DE- 3 + STRUCTURE *n.*] Destroy or dismantle the structure of, deprive of structure.
destructuˈration *n.* L20.

desudation /diːsjʊˈdeɪʃ(ə)n/ *n. rare.* LME. [Late L *desudatio(n-)*, f. L *desudat-* pa. ppl stem of *desudare* sweat greatly: see -ATION.] *Med.* Profuse sweating.

desuetude /dɪˈsjuːɪtjuːd, ˈdɛswɪ-/ *n.* E17. [Fr. *désuétude* or its source L *desuetudo*, f. *desuet-* pa. ppl stem of *desuescere* become unaccustomed, f. *de-* DE- 1 + *suescere* be accustomed: see -TUDE. Cf. earlier DISSUETUDE.] †**1** The action of discontinuing something; discontinuance *of*, protracted cessation *from.* E17–E18. **2** A state of disuse. M17. **3** The action of passing into disuse. E19.

2 C. R. ATTLEE Old English words and phrases, long since fallen into desuetude. 3 C. LAMB The gradual desuetude of old observances.

desulfurate, -ize *vs.*, etc.: see DESULPHURATE etc.

desulphurate /diːˈsʌlfəreɪt/ *v.t.* Also *__-sulfur-__. L18. [f. DE- 3 + SULPHURATE.] = next.
desulphuˈration *n.* M18.

desulphurize /diːˈsʌlfərʌɪz/ *v.t.* Also **-ise**, *__-sulfur-__. M19. [f. DE- 3 + SULPHURIZE.] Make free from sulphur; remove sulphur or its compounds from.
desulphuriˈzation *n.* M19. **desulphurizer** *n.* an apparatus for desulphurizing M19.

desultorious /dɛs(ə)lˈtɔːrɪəs/ *a.* Now *rare* or *obs.* M17. [f. as next + -OUS.] = DESULTORY 1.

desultory /ˈdɛs(ə)lt(ə)ri, -z-/ *a.* L16. [L *desultorius* pertaining to a vaulter, superficial, f. *desultor*, f. *desult-* pa. ppl stem of *desilire* leap down, f. *de-* DE- 1 + *salire* leap: see -ORY[2].] **1** Skipping about or jumping from one thing to another (*lit.* & *fig.*); pursuing an irregular or erratic course (*lit.* & *fig.*); going constantly from one subject to another; digressive; lacking a fixed plan or purpose, unmethodical; occurring irregularly, intermittent. L16. **2** Occurring randomly in isolation; occasional, disconnected. E18.

1 R. BENTLEY Persons of a light and desultory temper, that skip about, and are blown with every wind, as Grasshoppers are. G. WHITE I shot at it but it was so desultory that I missed my aim. T. C. WOLFE He found desultory employment as a soda-jerker, or as a delivery boy. I. WALLACE The rest of the short afternoon . . had been lost to . . napping, reading, and desultory chatter about the children, the new position that was in the offing, the utopia that was possible after that. R. TRAVERS The search out west, desultory as it was compared with the scouring of the Blue Mountains. A. GUINNESS He pushed the tagliatelli around his plate in a desultory way, indifferent to the gaieties of the Piazza Navona. 2 R. L'ESTRANGE 'Tis not for a desultory thought to attone for a lewd course of life. J. GALSWORTHY Nothing to stare at but . . desultory Colonials charging up and down.

desultorily *adv.* M17. **desultoriness** *n.* M17.

desuperheat /diːˈsuːpəhiːt/ *v.t.* M20. [f. DE- 3 + SUPERHEAT *v.*] Reduce the degree of superheat of (steam).
desuperheater *n.* an apparatus for desuperheating steam M20.

desyatin *n.* var. of DESSIATINE.

desynchronize /diːˈsɪŋkrənʌɪz/ *v.t.* Also **-ise.** L19. [f. DE- 3 + SYNCHRONIZE.] Remove the synchronization from, put out of step or phase.

desynonymize /diːsɪˈnɒnɪmʌɪz/ *v.* Also **-ise.** E19. [f. DE- 3 + SYNONYM + -IZE.] **1** *v.t.* End the synonymy of, differentiate in meaning (synonymous words). E19. **2** *v.i.* Cease to be synonymous. M19.
desynonymiˈzation *n.* M19.

detach /dɪˈtatʃ/ *v.* L16. [Fr. *détacher*, earlier †*destacher*, f. *des-* DIS- 1 + stem of *attacher* ATTACH.] †**1** *v.t.* Discharge (a gun). Only in L16. **2** Unfasten and remove, disconnect, disunite, separate, (*from*). L17. **3** *v.t. Mil.* Separate and send off (a part from a main body) for a particular purpose, send on a separate mission. L17. **4** *v.i.* Disengage, withdraw, separate oneself. M19.

2 J. AGATE I found I was holding a velvet geranium which . . had become detached from Mrs Pat's headgear. S. KAUFFMANN Russell was able to detach a bit of his mind from what Norris was saying and consider Florence. B. MOORE Three monks detached themselves from the larger group. 4 *Scientific American* As the bubbles form and expand they detach from their moorings and rise to the surface. *Navy News* H.M.S. Herald detached from the survey ground and headed for Bandar Abbas.

detachaˈbility *n.* the quality of being detachable E19. **detachable** *a.* able to be detached E19.

detached /dɪˈtatʃt/ *a.* E18. [f. prec. + -ED[1].] **1** Disconnected, separate(d), standing apart, (*from*); *spec.* (*a*) (of a building, esp. a dwelling-house) not joined to any other (cf. SEMI-DETACHED); (*b*) (of the retina) separated from the sclera (a condition causing partial or total blindness). E18. **2** Characterized by emotional detachment; aloof, objective. E20.

1 A. J. P. TAYLOR A new ministry of fuel and power, detached from the board of trade, was set up. S. HILL He would buy a better house than this, detached perhaps, not a terrace. J. S. FOSTER Freestanding piers have been referred to as isolated or detached piers. 2 J. F. KENNEDY The protection of her Navy had enabled Britain to take a detached view of events in Europe. S. MIDDLETON Now Fisher grew detached, immersed in his own thoughts.

detachedly *adv.* L18. **detachedness** *n.* M18.

detachment /dɪˈtatʃm(ə)nt/ *n.* M17. [Fr. *détachement*, f. as DETACH: see -MENT.] **1** *gen.* The action of detaching; the state of being detached, absence of connection, separation, (*from*). M17. **2** *Mil.* The separation of a number of troops, ships, etc., from the main body for a particular purpose; the action of sending on a separate mission. L17. **3** A part of a military unit dispatched from the main body; *transf.* any portion of a large body separately employed. L17. **4** A condition of spiritual separation from the world; aloofness from or *from* surroundings and circumstances; freedom from or indifference to worldly concerns, emotional commitments, etc.; impartiality, objectivity. L18.

1 R. FRY The complete detachment of the artistic vision from the values imposed on vision by everyday life. 2 DEFOE The army, after so many detachments, was not above nineteen thousand men. 3 J. REED Detachments of the two regiments . . had . . been surrounded by Cossacks. A. JOHN A detachment of American tourists would appear. *Voluntary Aid Detachment*: see VOLUNTARY *a.* 4 B. PYM To observe their joys and sorrows with detachment as if one were watching a film or a play. P. LIVELY One of those medium-sized market towns that give an impression of slight detachment from the present.

detail /ˈdiːteɪl/ *n.* E17. [Fr. *détail*, f. as next.] **1** The treatment of a matter item by item; attention to particulars; small or minor items or events collectively. E17. 2 A meticulous account or description of particulars. *arch.* L17. 3 *Mil.* The distribution of the orders of the day; a written list of orders, a roster. E18. b The assignment of a small party for a particular duty; a small detachment for a particular duty; the duty assigned. L18. 4 A particular; a small part of a whole; a minor or unimportant item or circumstance. L18. 5 *spec.* A small part of a work of art, esp. considered in isolation; a minor feature or decoration in a building, picture, etc.; the items, particulars, or parts of a building or work of art considered collectively; the manner of treating these. E19. b In full *detail drawing*. An architect's or designer's separate large drawing of a small part of a building, machine, etc.; a working drawing. E19.

1 DAY LEWIS The vividness and detail of the author's recollections. L. VAN DER POST Self-contained . . even to such detail as a snake-bite outfit. N. FREELING The characteristic feminine memory for detail. 3b B. MALAMUD Had the cell searched by a detail of five guards. S. BELLOW I didn't often get the toilet detail; he had too many important tasks for me. 4 W. S. MAUGHAM You give the reader broad indications and leave him to fill in the details. R. K. NARAYAN He asked details of our various movements. 5 P. NICHOLSON The detail of both sculpture and masonry on the building.

Phrases: **in detail** (*a*) item by item, minutely, (also *in great* or *much detail*); (*b*) *Mil.* by the engagement of small portions of a force one after the other. **go into detail** deal with a thing in its individual particulars. **war of detail** a war carried on in detail rather than by general engagements.

Comb.: *detail drawing*: see sense 5b above; **detail man** *US* a company's representative whose job is to sell (esp. new) drugs to doctors, pharmacists, etc.

detail /ˈdiːteɪl/ *v.t.* M17. [Fr. *détailler*, f. *dé-* DE- 3 + *tailler* cut in pieces.] 1 Relate or describe minutely; give particulars of, itemize. M17. 2 Orig. *Mil.* Assign to a specific duty. E18.

1 G. W. KNIGHT It is unnecessary to detail more than a few of the numerous references to darkness. J. ARCHER The story of the probable break-up of Nethercote and Company was detailed on the financial pages. 2 B. GUTTERIDGE Sentries were detailed and posted. MALCOLM X Some were detailed as ushers, who seated the people by designated sections. JO GRIMOND My sisters had been detailed to look after me in London.

detailed *ppl a.* having much detail; related or described minutely; paying attention to detail: M18. **detailer** *n.* L18. **detailing** *vbl n.* (*a*) the action of the vb; (*b*) (the treatment of) detail in a work of art, building, design, etc.: M19.

†**detain** *n. rare* (Spenser). Only in L16. [f. the vb.] Detention.

detain /dɪˈteɪn/ *v.t.* LME. [Repr. tonic stem of (O)Fr. *détenir*, f. Proto-Romance var. of L *detinere*, f. *de-* DE- 1 + *tenere* hold.] †1 In *pass.* Be afflicted *with* sickness or infirmity. LME–M17. 2 Place or keep in confinement; keep as a prisoner, esp. without charge. L15. 3 Withhold, retain; *esp.* keep back what is due or claimed. Now *rare* or *obs.* M16. 4 Keep in a certain place or condition; hold. *obs.* exc. as passing into sense 5. M16. 5 Keep from proceeding; hold back, delay, stop. M16. †b Restrain from action. Only in 17.

2 R. MACAULAY They would be conducted to London by the escort, and detained there for questioning. ANTHONY SMITH About twenty thousand people are compulsorily detained in psychiatric and special hospitals. 5 W. COBBETT I was detained . . partly by the rain, and partly by company that I liked very much. S. BELLOW Leventhal did not halt until Allbee detained him, stepping in his way.

detainable *a.* able to be detained E19. **detainingly** *adv.* so as to detain a person M19. **detainment** *n.* detention L16.

detainee /dɪteɪˈniː, diː-/ *n.* E20. [f. prec. + -EE[1].] A person detained in custody, esp. on political grounds.

detainer /dɪˈteɪnə/ *n.*[1] M16. [f. as prec. + -ER[1].] A person who or thing which detains.

detainer /dɪˈteɪnə/ *n.*[2] E17. [AN *detener* use as n. of inf. = (O)Fr. *détenir*: see DETAIN *v.*, -ER[4].] *Law.* 1 The action of withholding or keeping; *spec.* the (wrongful) retention of goods taken from the owner for distraint etc. E17. 2 The detaining of a person, esp. in custody or confinement. Now *arch.* or *Hist.* L17. 3 An order authorizing the continued detention of a person in custody who would otherwise be released. M19.

1 **forcible detainer** the unlawful possession or retention of land by (the threat of) violence.

detant *n.* see DETENT.

detassel /diːˈtas(ə)l/ *v.t. US.* L19. [f. DE- 3 + TASSEL *n.*[1]] Remove the tassels from (Indian corn).

detect /dɪˈtɛkt/ *v.* Pa. pple & ppl a. †**detect, -ed.** LME. [L *detect-* pa. ppl stem of *detegere*, f. *de-* DE- 3 + *tegere* cover.] †1 *v.t.* Uncover, expose, display. LME–M18. †2 *v.t.* Disclose information about; inform against, accuse; give (a person) away. LME–E19. 3 *v.t.* Discover the real (esp. hidden or disguised) character of; discover *in doing*, †*to be*. Formerly also, discover in the act *of*. L16. 4 *v.t.* Discover the presence, existence, or fact of (something apt to elude notice); use an instrument to discover or observe (a signal, radiation, etc.). M18. b Investigate or discover as a detective. E20. 5 *v.i.* Be engaged in detective work; act as a detective. E20.

3 J. BENTHAM You have detected a baker in selling short weight. 4 G. GREENE A new finger-print stunt, . . by which they could detect the print even when the hand had been gloved. I. MURDOCH Through the leaves she detected the flash of a white shirt. B. LOVELL Scientists . . succeeded in detecting the radio emission from the planet.

detectaˈbility *n.* the state of being detectable, ability to be detected E19. **detectable** *a.* able to be detected M17. **detectably** *adv.* in a way that can be detected, to a detectable degree L19. **detectiˈbility** *n.* = DETECTABILITY L20. **detectible** *a.* = DETECTABLE M19.

detecter *n.* see DETECTOR.

detection /dɪˈtɛkʃ(ə)n/ *n.* L15. [Late L *detectio(n-)*, f. as DETECT: see -ION.] †1 Exposure, revelation of what is concealed; accusation. L15–E18. 2 The finding out or discovery of what is unknown, hidden, or disguised; detective work. E17. 3 *Electr.* Extraction of a desired signal; demodulation. E20.

2 S. JOHNSON It is easy for the author of a lie, however malignant, to escape detection. E. RUTHERFORD The detection of a minute quantity of neon. D. L. SAYERS A 'talk' on 'Detection in Fact and Fiction'.

detectional *a.* M20.

detective /dɪˈtɛktɪv/ *a.* & *n.* M19. [f. DETECT + -IVE, after *elect, elective*, etc.] A *adj.* 1 Of, pertaining to, or employed in the investigation of things apt to elude notice or deliberately concealed, esp. of crimes; having the character or function of detection. M19. 2 [attrib. use of the n.] Describing crime and the detection of criminals. L19.

1 GEO. ELIOT Vexed by the detective wisdom of critics. G. B. SHAW Divorces and executions and the detective operations that lead up to them. 2 *detective fiction, novel, novelist, story*, etc.

B *n.* A police officer or other person whose occupation it is to investigate crimes by eliciting evidence, information, etc.; a person engaged in detective work; the position or rank of a police detective. M19.

B. JOWETT The criminal turned detective is wonderfully suspicious and cautious. W. SAFIRE Phrase detectives the world over are searching for the origins of 'the social safety net'. *Daily Telegraph* Detectives in the original investigation protested at meeting 'a wall of silence' from potential witnesses. *private detective*: see PRIVATE *a.*

Comb.: **detective inspector, sergeant**, etc.: a police detective with the specified rank.

detectival *a.* of or pertaining to detective work E20.

detector /dɪˈtɛktə/ *n.* Also (now *rare*) **-er.** M16. [f. DETECT *v.* + -OR, -ER[1].] †1 A person who or thing which discloses information; an accuser, an informer. M16–M18. 2 A person who finds out things which are apt to elude notice. E17. 3 An instrument or device which detects something liable to elude notice or indicates something out of the ordinary; a device for the detection or demodulation of electric signals. M19.

2 J. S. MILL The keenest detector of the errors of his predecessors. 3 N. SHUTE The detector on his periscope head indicated a high level of radioactivity. R. V. JONES Whether I could develop an airborne infra-red detector so that it could be mounted on a nightfighter and thus detect bombers. *lie-detector, metal-detector*, etc.

detemporalize /diːˈtɛmp(ə)r(ə)lʌɪz/ *v.t.* Also **-ise.** E20. [f. DE- 3 + TEMPORALIZE.] Make timeless in character; detach from a particular time.

†**detenebrate** *v.t.* M17–E18. [f. DE- 3 + L *tenebra* darkness + -ATE[3].] Free from darkness or obscurity.

detension /diːˈtɛnʃ(ə)n/ *v.* & *n.* M20. [f. DE- 3 + TENSION *n.*] A *v.t.* Remove or reduce the tension from. M20. B *n.* A removal or reduction of tension or anxiety; a relaxation. M20.

detent /dɪˈtɛnt/ *n.* In sense 3 also **detant** /dɪˈtant/. L17. [Fr. *détente*, OFr. *destente*, f. *destendre* (mod. *détendre*) slacken, f. *des-* DIS- 2 + *tendre* stretch. In Eng. assoc. w. L *detent-* pa. ppl stem of *detinere* DETAIN *v.*, whence branch II.] I 1 In clocks and watches, a catch which regulates striking. L17. 2 Any stop or catch in a machine which prevents a motion until released. M19. 3 In a gunlock, a small piece designed to prevent the sere from catching in the half-cock notch in the tumbler. L19. II 4 Restraint, inhibition. E20.

détente /deɪˈtɑ̃ː(n)t, -tɒ̃(n)t, -tɑːnt, -tɒnt/ *n.* E20. [Fr. = loosening, relaxation: see prec.] The easing of strained relations, esp. between States.

detention /dɪˈtɛnʃ(ə)n/ *n.* LME. [Fr. *détention* or late L *detentio(n-)*, f. *detent-* pa. ppl stem of *detinere* DETAIN *v.*: see -ION.] 1 The retention or withholding of what is due or claimed. LME. 2 Now chiefly *Law.* Holding in one's possession or control; retention. LME. 3 The action of arresting or confining, the state of imprisonment or confinement, now *esp.* of a military or political offender. L16. b At schools: keeping in as a punishment; an instance of this. L19. 4 Hindrance to progress; compulsory delay. E17.

1 SHAKES. *Timon* The detention of long-since-due debts. 3 LYTTON Offering twenty guineas reward for his detention. H. ARENDT In totalitarian countries all places of detention ruled by the police are made to be veritable holes of oblivion.

Attrib. & comb.: In the sense 'where people are held in detention', as *detention barrack, camp*, etc. Special combs., as **detention centre** *spec.* an institution in which young offenders are detained for short periods.

détenu /deɪtəˈnuː; *foreign* detny (*pl. same*)/ *n.* Also **de-.** E19. [Fr., use as n. of pa. pple of *détenir* DETAIN *v.*] A detainee, now esp. in the Indian subcontinent.

deter /dɪˈtəː/ *v.t.* Infl. **-rr-.** M16. [L *deterrere*, f. *de-* DE- 1 + *terrere* frighten.] 1 Restrain or discourage (*from* acting or proceeding) by fear, doubt, dislike of effort or trouble, or consideration of consequences. M16. 2 Inhibit, prevent. M20.

1 J. L. WATEN I wanted to join in the laughter but Father's face deterred me. S. NAIPAUL No threat would deter them from producing it and delivering it free of charge. 2 *Scientific American* This tactic could deter torpedo attack.

determent *n.* the action or fact of deterring; a deterring circumstance: M17. **deterrable** *a.* M20.

deterge /dɪˈtəːdʒ/ *v.t.* E17. [Fr. *déterger* or L *detergere*, f. *de-* DE- 1 + *tergere* wipe.] Cleanse (formerly esp. *Med.*, of pus or other morbid matter); wash off or out.

detergency /dɪˈtəːdʒ(ə)nsi/ *n.* E18. [f. as next: see -ENCY.] 1 Detergent quality. E18. 2 The process of cleansing a solid by means of a liquid; the action of a detergent. M20.

detergent /dɪˈtəːdʒ(ə)nt/ *a.* & *n.* E17. [L *detergent-* pres. ppl stem of *detergere*: see DETERGE, -ENT.] A *adj.* Cleansing; having the properties of a detergent. E17. B *n.* A cleansing agent. Now *esp.* a synthetic substance mixable with water which resembles soap in its cleansing properties but does not combine with the salts present esp. in hard water; also, an oil-soluble substance which holds dirt in suspension in lubricating oils. L17.

deteriorate /dɪˈtɪərɪəreɪt/ *v.* Pa. pple & ppl a. **†-ate** (earlier), **-ated**. L16. [Late L *deteriorat-* pa. ppl stem of *deteriorare*, f. *deterior* worse: see -ATE[3].] **1** *v.t.* Make worse; lower in character or excellence. L16. **2** *v.i.* Become worse; become impaired in quality or value; degenerate. L17.

1 H. L. MENCKEN The accompanying hooey pollutes and deteriorates their mind. 2 D. ADAMS What had started out as excellent entertainment had.. deteriorated into mere abuse. P. ROSE His health deteriorated so badly that the East India Company gave him a medical leave.

deteriorative *a.* causing or tending to deterioration E19. **deteriorator** *n.* M19.

deterioration /dɪˌtɪərɪəˈreɪʃ(ə)n/ *n.* M17. [Fr. *détérioration* f. late L *deterioratio(n-)*, f. as prec.: see -ATION.] The process of growing or making worse; a deteriorated condition.

A. WEST My father was as well aware of his deterioration as anyone, and he did not enjoy the progressive stages of his decline.

deteriorationist *n.* a person who holds that deterioration, not progress, is the order of things E19.

determa /dɪˈtəːmə/ *n.* M18. [Prob. f. Guyanan name.] The hard reddish timber of a tropical American tree of the laurel family, *Ocotea rubra*; = *red* LOURO.

determinable /dɪˈtəːmɪnəb(ə)l/ *a.* & *n.* LME. [Orig. f. OFr. (= fixed, determinate) f. late L *determinabilis* finite, f. *determinare*: see DETERMINE, -ABLE. Later f. DETERMINE + -ABLE.] **A** *adj.* **†1** Fixed, definite. LME–M17. **2** Able to be authoritatively decided, definitely fixed, or definitely ascertained. LME. **3** Liable to come to an end; terminable. Chiefly *Law* (of a lease etc.). L16.

2 R. HOOKER Affairs.. which were not determinable one way or other by the Scripture. G. GROTE Whether Sidon or Tyre was the most ancient, seems not determinable.

B *n. Philos.* Something which can be more precisely specified; *spec.* a general term or concept under which several specific terms or concepts fall. L19.

determinaˈbility *n.* E19. **determinableness** *n.* E18. **determinably** *adv.* in a determinable manner; to a determinable degree: LME.

determinacy /dɪˈtəːmɪnəsi/ *n.* L19. [f. DETERMINATE *a.*: see -ACY. Cf. earlier INDETERMINACY.] Determinateness, definiteness.

determinandum /dɪˌtəːmɪˈnandəm/ *n.* Pl. **-da** /-də/. E20. [L *determinandum* use as n. of neut. gerundive of *determinare* DETERMINE.] *Logic* & *Gram.* A part of a proposition or expression which is to be qualified or limited by thought or by another part of the expression. Cf. next, DETERMINATUM.

determinans /dɪˈtəːmɪnanz/ *n.* Pl. **-nantia** /-ˈnantɪə, -ʃɪə/. E20. [L *determinans* use as n. of pres. pple of *determinare* DETERMINE.] *Logic* & *Gram.* A qualifying or limiting part of a proposition or expression. Cf. prec., DETERMINATUM.

determinant /dɪˈtəːmɪnənt/ *a.* & *n.* E17. [L *determinant-* pres. ppl stem of *determinare*: DETERMINE: see -ANT[1]. As n. partly tr. L *determinans*: see prec.] **A** *adj.* Determining; that determines; determinative. E17.

B *n.* **1** A determining factor or agent; a ruling or conditioning element. L17. **b** *Gram.* A limiting or qualifying word or expression. M19. **c** *Logic.* Each of the elements in a conjunction (CONJUNCTION 7). L19. **2** *Univ. Hist.* = DETERMINER *n.*[2] 2. M19. **3** *Math.* A square matrix (usu. represented with a vertical line at each side) which has a numerical or algebraic value obtained by adding and subtracting products of the elements of the matrix according to certain rules; a quantity obtained from or represented by a square matrix in this way. M19. **4** *Biol.* A gene or other factor which determines the character and development of a cell or group of cells in an organism. L19.

1 G. GORER Area.. seems to be much less of a determinant than age and poverty. A. STORR The events of early childhood as determinants of later personality and problems. 4 **antigenic determinant** = EPITOPE.

determiˈnantal *a.* (*Math.*) relating to, consisting of, or expressed as a determinant M19.

determinantia *n.* pl. of DETERMINANS.

determinata *n.* pl. of DETERMINATUM.

determinate /dɪˈtəːmɪnət/ *a.* LME. [L *determinatus* pa. pple, f. as next: see -ATE[2].] **1** Definitely bounded or limited; clearly defined; distinct; finite. LME. **b** *Math.* Having a fixed value or magnitude. E18. **2** Settled, fixed, established. LME. **3** Finally determined upon or decided; definitive. M16. **4** Fixed in mind or purpose; resolved, resolute. M16. **†5** Intended. L16–E17.

1 G. BERKELEY The clear and determinate meaning of my words. 2 J. S. MILL A determinate order of precedence among them. 3 *Times* One of the determinate reasons for the decision. 4 S. JOHNSON A Tory so ardent and determinate that he did not willingly consort with men of different opinions. 5 SHAKES. *Twel. N.* My determinate voyage is mere extravagancy.

determinately *adv.* L15. **determinateness** *n.* M17.

†determinate *v.t.* & *i.* Pa. pple & ppl a. **-ate** (earlier), **-ated**. LME–L19. [L *determinat-* pa. ppl stem of *determinare* DETERMINE: see -ATE[3].] = DETERMINE.

determination /dɪˌtəːmɪˈneɪʃ(ə)n/ *n.* LME [(O)Fr. *détermination* f. L *determinatio(n-)*, f. as prec.: see -ATION.] **1** The settlement of a suit or controversy by the authoritative decision of a judge or arbiter; a settlement or decision so made, an authoritative opinion. LME. **†b** The settlement of a question by reasoning or argument. LME–L16. **c** The discussion and resolving of a question or the upholding of a thesis in a scholastic disputation; *spec.* in *Univ. Hist.*, (performance in) an exercise consisting of a series of disputations, qualifying a bachelor of arts to proceed to a master's degree. *obs.* exc. *Hist.* M17. **2** A bringing or coming to an end; a termination. *arch.* in *gen.* sense. L15. **b** *Law.* The cessation of an estate or interest of any kind. L15. **3** The action of coming to a decision; the result of this; a fixed intention. L15. **4** The action of definitely locating, identifying, or establishing the nature of something; exact ascertainment (*of*); a fact established, a conclusion or solution reached. L16. **5** The action of determining bounds or fixing limits; delimitation, definition. L16. **b** *Logic.* The process of making a notion more specific by the addition of attributes. Also, a determining attribute. M17. **6** A tendency to move or flow in a fixed direction; a determining bias. *arch.* M17. **7** The definite direction or motivation of the mind or will towards an object or end. Now *rare.* L17. **8** Resoluteness, determinedness; fixity of intention. E19.

1 ADDISON They were neither of them dissatisfied with the Knight's Determination. B. JOWETT In the determination of this question the identity of virtue and knowledge is found to be involved. 2 W. STUBBS The war continued.. seeming year by year further removed from a determination. 3 P. FITZGERALD Her courage.. was only a determination to survive. 4 W. WHEWELL Generally founded on astronomical determinations. 5 HOBBES The Circumscription of a thing, is.. the Determination, or Defining of its Place. 6 R. L. STEVENSON Some determination of blood to the head. 8 DAY LEWIS The set of the lips suggests a certain inward firmness, a quality of determination.

determinative /dɪˈtəːmɪnətɪv/ *a.* & *n.* M17. [Fr. *déterminatif*, *-ive* or late L *determinativus*, f. as DETERMINATE *v.*: see -IVE.] **A** *adj.* Characterized by determining something; serving to determine something; decisive; limiting, distinguishing, identifying. M17. **B** *n.* A thing which determines something; *spec.* a sign (in hieroglyphic writing) or a morpheme indicating the semantic classification of a word. M19.

determinatively *adv.* in a determinative manner, to a determinative degree; definitely, decisively: E17. **determinativeness** *n.* E19.

determinator /dɪˈtəːmɪneɪtə/ *n.* M16. [Late L *determinator*, f. as DETERMINATE *v.*: see -OR.] A person who or thing which determines something; a determiner.

determinatum /dɪˌtəːmɪˈnɑːtəm, -ˈneɪtəm/ *n.* Pl. **-ta** /-tə/. E20. [L *determinatum* use as n. of neut. pa. pple of *determinare* DETERMINE.] *Logic* & *Gram.* A part of a proposition or expression that has been qualified or limited. Cf. DETERMINANDUM, DETERMINANS.

determine /dɪˈtəːmɪn/ *v.* LME. [(O)Fr. *déterminer* f. L *determinare* bound, limit, fix f. *de-* DE- 1 + *terminare* TERMINATE *v.*] **I** Put an end to; come to an end. **1** *v.t.* Now chiefly *Law.* Bring to an end, conclude. LME. **2** *v.i.* Now chiefly *Law.* Come to an end; cease to exist or be. LME. **†b** End *in* (a conclusion, result, etc.). E17–L19. **3** *v.t.* Bound, limit. Now only *spec.* (*a*) *Logic* limit by adding differentia; (*b*) *Gram.* limit the application or reference of (a noun). LME. **†b** Limit *to*, restrict *to*. LME–L17. **4** *v.t.* Settle or decide (a dispute, controversy, etc., or a sentence, conclusion, issue, etc.) as a judge or arbiter. Foll. by simple obj., subord. cl. w. *that*, *what*, *whether*, etc. LME. **b** *v.i.* Discuss and resolve a question or uphold a thesis in a scholastic disputation; *spec.* in *Univ. Hist.*, perform in the exercise of determination (see DETERMINATION 1C). *obs.* exc. *Hist.* L16. **5** *v.i.* Come to a judicial decision; make or give a decision about something. (Formerly foll. by *of*, *on*.) Cf. sense 13 below. LME. **†6** *v.t.* Lay down authoritatively; pronounce, declare. LME–M17. **7** *v.t.* Settle or fix beforehand (now esp. a date); ordain, decree. LME. **†8** *v.t.* Conclude from reasoning or investigation, deduce, (a person or thing *to be*, *that*). L15–E19. **9** *v.t.* Fix or decide causally, condition as a cause or antecedent, be a deciding or the decisive factor in; decide on, select, choose. M17. **10** *v.t.* Definitely locate, identify, or establish the nature of; ascertain exactly. M17. **b** *Geom.* Fix or define the position of. M19.

1 W. STUBBS The death of Edward III determined the crisis. 2 W. CRUISE The estate of Martin did not determine by his death. b R. SOUTH But that which begins in vanity, must needs determine in vexation of spirit. 4 H. H. MILMAN The Dean presided in all causes.., and determined them. B. JOWETT The law will determine all our various duties towards relatives. A. E. STEVENSON Our entire military establishment must be re-examined to determine how we can best build and keep the forces we need for our national security. b **determining bachelor** = DETERMINER *n.*[2] 2. 5 S. JOHNSON The general inability of man to determine rightly concerning his own. 9 H. T. LANE The way the mother deals with the child determines its future character. B. WEBB It was MacDonald who alone determined who should be in his cabinet. C. BLACKWOOD None of her reactions seemed to be determined by external events. 10 C. IVES What it is that inspires an art effort is not easily determined. B. GUEST Middle-class Americans are just as eager as the English to determine one's social position.

II Direct to an end. **11** *v.t.* Give an aim or direction to; direct; impel *to*. *arch.* LME. **b** *v.i.* Take its course, tend *to* (a particular end). *arch.* M17. **†12** *v.refl.* Bring oneself to a decision or resolve (*to do*). LME–E18. **13** *v.i.* Come to a decision *that*; resolve *to do*, *on doing*, *on* a course of action. Cf. sense 5 above. E16. **14** *v.t.* Decide the course of (a person); bring to a decision or resolution (*to do*). L17.

11 W. CULLEN Animals are determined to take in aliment by the appetites of hunger and thirst. T. R. MALTHUS Thus determining a greater quantity of capital to this particular employment. 13 J. A. FROUDE The bishops.. determined on a further appeal to the pope. G. VIDAL I determined to defer my attack on Paul's methods until a safer time. 14 E. DOWDEN Credit.. for having determined Shelley to travel abroad.

determined /dɪˈtəːmɪnd/ *a.* LME. [f. prec. + -ED[1].] **1** *gen.* That has been determined. LME. **2a** Resolved *that*, *to do*, *on doing*, *on* a course of action. E16. **b** Resolute; showing determination; characterized by determination. E17. **3** Decided or resolved on, settled. M16.

2a G. GREENE He was determined that it should have a superficial legality. O. MANNING She's determined to be an independent, wage-earning woman. D. JACOBSON He was already grimly and irrevocably determined on a course of action. b T. HARDY Her determined negative deterred his scrupulous heart. E. O'NEILL A brutal, determined-looking man of forty.

determinedly *adv.* M16. **determinedness** *n.* M18.

determiner /dɪˈtəːmɪnə/ *n.*[1] *obs.* exc. *Hist.* LME. [AN, use as n. of inf. = (O)Fr. *déterminer*: see DETERMINE, -ER[4].] *Law.* The final determining of a judge or court. Chiefly in OYER *and determiner.*

determiner /dɪˈtəːmɪnə/ *n.*[2] M16. [f. DETERMINE *v.* + -ER[1].] **1** *gen.* A person who or thing which determines or decides something. M16. **2** *Univ. Hist.* A (successful) candidate in the exercise of determination (see DETERMINATION 1c). L16. **3** *Biol.* = DETERMINANT *n.* 4. *arch.* E20. **4** *Gram.* A modifying word which limits the application or reference of the noun modified, in English being one of a class including articles and other definite and indefinite adjectives, and demonstrative, quantifying, and possessive adjectives, or in other analyses some subset of these, all of which precede any descriptive adjective. Cf. PREDETERMINER. M20.

determinism /dɪˈtəːmɪnɪz(ə)m/ *n.* L18. [f. DETERMINE + -ISM.] **1** The doctrine that human action is necessarily determined by motives regarded as external forces acting on the will. L18. **2** The doctrine that everything that happens is determined by a necessary chain of causation. L19.

determinist /dɪˈtəːmɪnɪst/ *a.* & *n.* M19. [f. as prec. + -IST.] **A** *adj.* Of or pertaining to determinism; adhering to determinism. M19. **B** *n.* An adherent of determinism. L19.

determiˈnistic *a.* L19. **determiˈnistically** *adv.* L19.

deterrent /dɪˈtɛr(ə)nt/ *a.* & *n.* E19. [L *deterrent-* pres. ppl stem of *deterrere* DETER: see -ENT.] **A** *adj.* That deters; tending to deter. E19.

B *n.* A thing that deters; *esp.* a nuclear weapon the possession of which by a State or alliance is intended to deter any attack from an opposing power. E19.

Observer Britain should also be prepared to give up her independent deterrent and stop the manufacture of nuclear weapons.

deterrence *n.* the action of deterring or preventing by fear M19.

detersion /dɪˈtəːʃ(ə)n/ *n.* Now *rare.* E17. [Late L *detersio(n-)*, f. *deters-* pa. ppl stem of *detergere*: see DETERGE, -ION.] The action or an act of cleansing (formerly esp. *Med*, of pus or other morbid matter).

detersive /dɪˈtəːsɪv/ *a.* & *n.* L16. [Fr. *détersif, -ive*, f. L *deters-*: see prec., -IVE.] **A** *adj.* Cleansing, having the power to cleanse, (formerly esp. *Med.*, of pus or other morbid matter). L16. **B** *n.* A cleansing or detersive agent. M17.

detest /dɪˈtɛst/ *v.* L15. [L *detestari* denounce, renounce, f. *de-* DE- 1 + *testari* bear witness, call to witness, f. *testis* witness. Perh. partly back-form. f. DETESTATION.] **I 1** *v.t.* Hate or dislike intensely; abhor, abominate. L15. **†2** *v.t.* Curse, calling God to witness; denounce, execrate. M16–M18.

1 D. ACHESON Perón was a fascist and a dictator detested by all good men. W. STYRON She detested New York subway trains for their grime and their noise.

†II 3 *v.t.* & *i.* Attest, protest, testify. M16–E17.

detester *n.* E17.

detestable /dɪˈtɛstəb(ə)l/ *a.* LME. [(O)Fr. *détestable* or L *detestabilis*, f. as prec.: see -ABLE.] Intensely hateful or odious; execrable, abominable.

detestaˈbility *n.* M19. **detestableness** *n.* E17. **detestably** *adv.* M16.

detestation /diːtɛˈsteɪʃ(ə)n/ *n.* LME. [(O)Fr. *détestation* f. L *detestatio(n-)*, f. *detestat-* pa. ppl stem of *detestari* DETEST: see -ATION.] **†1** Public or formal execration (*of*). LME–L17. **2** Intense dislike or hatred; abhorrence. LME. **3** A detested person or thing. E18.

dethrone /diːˈθrəʊn, dɪ-/ *v.t.* E17. [f. DE- 3 + THRONE *n.*] Remove from a throne (*lit.* & *fig.*), depose; end the supremacy or dominant influence of.

J. BARZUN Dewey's effect on schooling was to dethrone subject matter and replace it by techniques. *Times* The dethroned world champion.

dethronement *n.* E18. **dethroner** *n.* M17.

detin /diːˈtɪn/ *v.t.* Infl. **-nn-**. E20. [f. DE- 3 + TIN *n.*] Remove the tin from (tin plate).

detinue /ˈdɛtɪnjuː/ *n.* LME. [OFr. *detenue* use as n. of fem. pa. pple of *detenir* DETAIN *v.*, assim. to L *detinere.*] *Law.* The wrongful detention of a personal chattel; (in full *action of detinue*) an action against this.

detonate /ˈdɛtəneɪt/ *v.* E18. [L *detonat-* pa. ppl stem of *detonare*, f. *de-* DE- 1 + *tonare* to thunder: see -ATE[3]. Partly back-form. f. DETONATION.] **1** *v.i.* Undergo detonation. E18. **2** *v.t.* Cause to detonate. E19.

detonative *a.* having the property of detonating L19.

detonation /dɛtəˈneɪʃ(ə)n/ *n.* L17. [Fr. *détonation*, f. *détoner* f. L *detonare*: see prec., -ATION.] **1** (The sudden loud noise accompanying) an explosive chemical reaction whose gaseous products expand supersonically; explosion with loud report. L17. **b** Rapid premature combustion of the fuel in an internal-combustion engine, causing pinking. E20. **2** The action of causing a substance, bomb, etc., to explode. E18. **3** *gen.* A sudden loud noise; *fig.* a sudden outburst of feeling. M19.

detonator /ˈdɛtəneɪtə/ *n.* E19. [f. DETONATE + -OR.] **†1** A gun fired by means of a percussion cap. E–M19. **2** A contrivance for detonating, esp. as part of a bomb, shell, etc. L19. **3** A railway fog-signal consisting of an explosive device designed to be placed on a rail and set off by a train passing over it. L19.

†detonize *v.i.* & *t.* Also **-ise**. M18–E19. [f. Fr. *détoner* (see DETONATION) + -IZE.] = DETONATE.

detorsion /dɪˈtɔːʃ(ə)n/ *n.* In sense 1 also **-tort-**. L16. [f. L *detors-, detort-* pa. ppl stem of *detorquere*, f. *de-* DE- 1 + *torquere* twist: see -ION. Sense 2 perh. f. DE- 3 + TORSION *n.*] **1** Twisting, distortion; *esp.* perversion of meaning. Now *rare* or *obs.* L16. **2** *Zool.* Evolutionary reversion of gastropods to a primitive linear anatomical organization, involving reversal of a 180° torsion displayed by their immediate ancestors. E20.

†detort *v.t.* M16–E19. [L *detort-*: see prec.] Turn aside from its purpose; twist, pervert, esp. in meaning; derive by distortion.

detortion *n.* see DETORSION.

detour /ˈdiːtʊə/ *n.* & *v.* Also **dé-** /ˈdeɪ-/. M18. [Fr. *détour* change of direction, f. *détourner* turn away.] **A** *n.* A deviation from one's route, a roundabout way; a digression. M18.

E. O'NEILL They make wide detours to avoid the spot where he stands. G. SARTON The best anatomists . . did not find the truth except after many detours.

B *v.* **1** *v.i.* Make a detour. M19. **2** *v.t.* Send by a detour. E20. **3** *v.t.* Make a detour round, bypass. M20.

1 D. ALDIS Mary detoured to pick up her bag from the table. 2 LADY BIRD JOHNSON The storm detoured him to Pittsburgh. 3 J. HERSEY A railroad line that detoured the city in a wide semi-circle.

detox /ˈdiːtɒks/ *n. colloq.* (chiefly *US*). L20. [Abbrev.] = DETOXIFICATION. Also, a detoxification centre.

detox /diːˈtɒks/ *v.t. colloq.* L20. [Abbrev. of DETOXIFY.] **1** Modify (a motor vehicle or engine) to remove or limit the emission of toxic fumes. L20. **2** Subject (an alcoholic, drug addict, etc.) to detoxification. Chiefly *US.* L20.

detoxicate /diːˈtɒksɪkeɪt/ *v.t.* M19. [f. DE- 3 + L *toxicum* poison, after *intoxicate.*] = DETOXIFY.

detoxiˈcation *n.* = DETOXIFICATION E20.

detoxification /diːˌtɒksɪfɪˈkeɪʃ(ə)n/ *n.* E20. [f. as prec.: see -FICATION.] The action of detoxifying, esp. an alcoholic or drug addict; the state of being detoxified.

Comb.: **detoxification centre** a (usu. residential) centre for the treatment of alcoholism or drug addiction.

detoxify /diːˈtɒksɪfʌɪ/ *v.t.* E20. [f. as prec. + -FY.] Remove poison from; free from poisonous qualities.

detract /dɪˈtrakt/ *v.* LME. [L *detract-* pa. ppl stem of *detrahere*, f. *de-* DE- 1 + *trahere* draw.] **I 1** *v.t.* Take away, subtract, deduct, (now esp. much, something, or other indef. obj.). (Foll. by *from* a whole, †*a* possessor). LME. **2** *v.t.* Take away from the reputation or estimation of, disparage, belittle. Now *rare.* LME. **3** *v.i.* Foll. by *from*: take something away from, diminish; reduce the credit due to; disparage, belittle, (something immaterial or abstract, †something material). L16. **†b** *v.i.* Speak disparagingly. L16–L18.

1 SHAKES. *1 Hen. VI* Shall I . . Detract so much from that prerogative As to be call'd but viceroy of the whole. 3 E. J. HOWARD Her eyes were her only good feature, said her mother, and proceeded to dress her in every shade of inferior blue which detracted from them. M. MEYER The follies of Hedin's age do not detract from the achievements of his saner years. B. PYM The view of the neglected garden next door would detract from the elegance of the occasion.

†II 4 *v.t.* & *i.* Draw away or aside, withdraw, divert. M16–E19. **5** *v.t.* & *i.* Protract (time); delay. M16–M17.

†III 6 *v.t.* Draw back from, refuse; relinquish. L16–E17.

detracˈtation *n.* (*rare*) = DETRACTION LME. **detractingly** *adv.* so as to detract, disparagingly L16.

detracter *n.* see DETRACTOR.

detraction /dɪˈtrakʃ(ə)n/ *n.* ME. [(O)Fr. *détraction* f. L *detractio(n-)*, f. as DETRACT: see -ION.] **1** The action of detracting from a person's merit or reputation; disparagement, belittlement; calumny, slander. ME. **2** *gen.* A taking away, subtraction, deduction. Also, a part to be detracted. Now only *from* merit, reputation, etc. E16. **†3** Prolonging, delay. L16–M17.

1 ADDISON Females addicted to Censoriousness and Detraction. 2 N. PINKNEY There is one heavy detraction . . from the excellence of the . . climate.

detractive /dɪˈtraktɪv/ *a.* L15. [OFr. *detractif, -ive* or med.L. *detractivus*, f. as DETRACT: see -IVE.] **1** Conveying, of the nature of, or given to, detraction. L15. **2** Tending to detract *from.* M17.

detractively *adv.* L19. **detractiveness** *n.* E18.

detractor /dɪˈtraktə/ *n.* Also **-er**. LME. [AN *detractour*, (O)Fr. *détracteur* or L *detractor*, f. as DETRACT, -OR.] A person who detracts from another's merit or reputation; a disparager, a belittler.

detractory *a.* [L *detractorius*] = DETRACTIVE L16. **detractress** *n.* (*rare*) a female detractor E18.

detrain /diːˈtreɪn/ *v.t.* & *i.* L19. [f. DE- 3 + TRAIN *n.*[1]] Discharge or alight from a railway train.

detrainment *n.* L19.

détraqué /detrake/ *a.* & *n.* Fem. **-ée**. E20. [Fr., pa. ppl a. of *détraquer* put out of order, derange.] **A** *adj.* Deranged; crazy; psychopathic. E20. **B** *n.* Pl. pronounced same. A deranged person, a psychopath. E20.

detribalize /diːˈtrʌɪb(ə)lʌɪz/ *v.t.* Also **-ise**. E20. [f. DE- 3 + TRIBAL + -IZE.] Make (a person) no longer a member of a tribe; remove the tribal social structure from.

detribaliˈzation *n.* E20.

detriment /ˈdɛtrɪm(ə)nt/ *n.* & *v.* LME. [(O)Fr. *détriment* or L *detrimentum*, f. *detri-* preterite stem of *deterere* wear away, f. *de-* DE- 1 + *terere* rub: see -MENT.] **A** *n.* **1** Loss sustained by or damage done to a person or thing; an instance of this. LME. **2** A cause of loss or damage; something detrimental. E16. **3** *Her.* Eclipse, esp. of the moon. E17. **4** *Astrol.* The position or (weak) condition of a planet when in the sign opposite its house. E17. **5** In *pl.* Charges made by certain colleges or societies on their members. L17.

1 J. S. MILL The luxury of doing as they like without detriment to their estimation. E. JONES Overpraising young girls, to the detriment of their later character.

B *v.t.* Cause loss or damage to. Now *rare.* E17.

detrimental /dɛtrɪˈmɛnt(ə)l/ *a.* & *n.* L16. [f. prec. + -AL[1].] **A** *adj.* Causing loss or damage; prejudicial, harmful. (Foll. by *to.*) L16. **B** *n.* A person who or thing which is prejudicial or damaging; *esp.* (*arch. slang*) a younger son of the aristocracy, an ineligible suitor. M19.

detrimentally *adv.* L19.

detrital /dɪˈtrʌɪt(ə)l/ *a.* M19. [f. DETRITUS + -AL[1].] Of, pertaining to, or of the nature of detritus.

detrited /dɪˈtrʌɪtɪd/ *a.* L17. [f. L *detritus* DETRITUS + -ED[1].] Worn down; formed as detritus.

detrition /dɪˈtrɪʃ(ə)n/ *n.* L17. [med.L *detritio(n-)*, f. *detri-*: see DETRIMENT, -ITION.] The action of wearing away by rubbing.

detritus /dɪˈtrʌɪtəs/ *n.* L18. [L *detritus* rubbing away, f. *detri-*: see DETRIMENT. In sense 2 after Fr. *détritus*.] †1 Wearing away by rubbing; disintegration. L18–E19. 2 Matter produced by detrition; *esp.* material eroded or washed away, as gravel, sand, silt, etc. E19. 3 Debris of any kind. M19.

3 S. BRETT The detritus of coffee-cups, publicity photographs and handouts that littered her desk.

detritic /dɪˈtrɪtɪk/ *a.* (*rare*) = DETRITAL M19.

de trop /də tro, ˈtrəʊ/ *a. phr.* M18. [Fr., lit. 'excessive'.] Not wanted, unwelcome, in the way.

detrude /dɪˈtruːd/ *v.t.* LME. [L *detrudere*, f. *de-* DE- 1 + *trudere* thrust.] 1 Thrust or push down; formerly also, subdue, defeat. LME. 2 Thrust out or away, expel. M16.

detruncate /diːˈtrʌŋkeɪt/ *v.t.* E17. [L *detruncat-* pa. ppl stem of *detruncare*, f. *de-* DE- 1 + *truncare*: see TRUNCATE *v.*] Shorten by lopping off a part; cut short.

detrunˈcation *n.* [L *detruncatio(n-)*] the action of cutting off or short; the state of being cut short: E17.

detrusion /dɪˈtruːʒ(ə)n/ *n.* E17. [Late L *detrusio(n-)*, f. *detrus-* pa. ppl stem of *detrudere* DETRUDE: see -ION.] The action of thrusting down or away.

detrusor /dɪˈtruːsə/ *n.* M18. [mod.L, f. L *detrus-*: see prec., -OR.] *Anat.* In full *detrusor muscle*. The muscular layer of the wall of the bladder.

detumescence /diːtjʊˈmɛs(ə)ns/ *n.* L17. [f. L *detumescere* subside from swelling, f. *de-* DE- 3 + *tumescere* swell: see -ENCE.] Subsidence from swelling, or (*fig.*) from tumult; subsidence of the penis or clitoris from erection.

detune /diːˈtjuːn/ *v.t.* E20. [f. DE- 3 + TUNE *v.*] 1 Alter or adjust (an oscillatory system) so that its resonant frequency no longer coincides with the frequency of some other oscillation with which it interacts. E20. 2 Reduce the performance or efficiency of (a motor vehicle or engine) by adjustment. M20.

detur /ˈdiːtə/ *n.* L18. [L *detur* let there be given, the first wd of the accompanying inscription.] Any of several prizes of books given annually at Harvard University.

†**deturn** *v.t.* LME–M18. [Fr. *détourner* (OFr. *destorner*), f. *dé-*, *des-* DE- 3 + *tourner* TURN *v.*] Turn away or aside.

deturpate /dɪˈtəːpeɪt/ *v.t.* & *i.* Now *rare.* E17. [L *deturpat-* pa. ppl stem of *deturpare* make unsightly: see -ATE[3].] Make or become vile or base.

deturˈpation *n.* debasement, defilement L15.

deuce /djuːs/ *n.*[1] L15. [OFr. *deus* (mod. *deux*) f. L *duos* two.] 1 The two on a die or in a pack of cards; a throw of two at dice. L15. 2 *Tennis.* The state of the score (40 points all, or, in real tennis, five or more games all) at which either side must gain two consecutive points or games to win. L16. 3 (A sum of) twopence (*arch.*), two pounds, or two dollars; a two-dollar bill. *slang.* L17.

Comb.: **deuce-ace** *arch.* a throw of two and one at dice; a poor throw, bad luck; **deuce set** in real tennis, a set in which the score reaches five games all; **deuce game** (*a*) in real tennis, a game which levels the score at more than five games each side; (*b*) in lawn tennis, a game in which the score reaches 40 points all.

deuce /djuːs/ *n.*[2] *colloq.* M17. [LG *duus* = G *Daus*, prob. ult. identical w. prec., a throw of two (aces) at dice being the worst possible.] Misfortune, mischief; the Devil. Freq. in exclamatory or imprecatory phrs. (in which *devil* can always be substituted) expr. surprise, incredulity, impatience, displeasure, dismay, or negation, or merely emphatic.

SWIFT The deuce he is! married to that vengeance! R. BURNS The deuce of the matter is this: .. his salary is reduced. P. V. WHITE Dear me, if these educated young ladies are not the deuce. G. HEYER Why the deuce does she want to make Evelyn's acquaintance? **a** (or **the**) **deuce of a —** a very bad or very remarkable —. **the deuce to pay** trouble to be expected.

deuced /ˈdjuːsɪd, djuːst/ *a.* & *adv. arch. colloq.* L18. [f. prec. + -ED[2].] Damned, devilish(ly).

deucedly /ˈdjuːsɪdli/ *adv.* E19.

deus absconditus /ˌdeɪəs abˈskɒndɪtəs, ˌdiːəs/ *n. phr.* M20. [L = hidden god: cf. *Isaiah* 45:15.] A god who is hidden from human perception.

†**deusan** *n.* Also **-z-**. L16–L19. [Fr. *deux ans* two years: so called from its lasting quality.] = *apple-john* s.v. APPLE.

deus ex machina /ˌdeɪəs ɛks ˈmakɪnə, ˌdiːəs/ *n. phr.* L17. [mod.L, tr. Gk *theos ek mēkhanēs* lit. 'god from the machinery' (by which gods were suspended above the stage in Gk theatre).] A power, event, or person arriving in the nick of time to solve a difficulty; a providential (often rather contrived) interposition, esp. in a novel or play.

deut- *comb. form* see DEUTO-.

deutan /ˈdjuːtan/ *n.* & *a.* M20. [f. *deut(er)an* in DEUTERANOMALY, DEUTERANOPIA.] *Ophthalm.* (A person) exhibiting deuteranomaly or deuteranopia.

deuter- *comb. form* see DEUTERO-.

deuteragonist /djuːtəˈragənɪst/ *n.* M19. [Gk *deuteragōnistēs*, f. as DEUTERO-, AGONIST.] The person of next importance to the protagonist in a drama.

deuteranomaly /djuːt(ə)rəˈnɒməli/ *n.* M20. [f. DEUTERO- (green being regarded as the 2nd component of colour vision) + ANOMALY.] *Ophthalm.* Anamolous trichromatism involving reduced sensitivity to green; partial deuteranopia. Cf. next, PROTANOMALY.

deuteranomal *n.* a person exhibiting deuteranomaly E20. **deuteranomalous** *a.* of, pertaining to, or exhibiting deuteranomaly M20.

deuteranopia /djuːt(ə)rəˈnəʊpɪə/ *n.* E20. [f. as prec. + AN-[5] + -OPIA.] *Ophthalm.* Colour-blindness (esp. dichromatism) involving insensitivity to green; green-blindness. Cf. prec., PROTANOPIA.

ˈdeuteranope *n.* a deuteranopic individual E20. **deuteranopic** *a.* of, pertaining to, or exhibiting deuteranopia M20.

deuterate /ˈdjuːtəreɪt/ *v.t.* Also **deuteriate** /djuːˈtɪərɪeɪt/. M20. [f. DEUTERIUM + -ATE[3].] *Chem.* Replace ordinary hydrogen in (a substance) by deuterium. Freq. as *deuterated* ppl a.

deuteˈration *n.* M20.

deuteric /ˈdjuːtərɪk/ *a.* E20. [f. DEUTERO- + -IC.] *Geol.* Designating, pertaining to, or resulting from alteration of the minerals of an igneous rock during the later stages of consolidation.

deuterium /djuːˈtɪərɪəm/ *n.* M20. [f. Gk *deuteros* second + -IUM.] *Chem.* A naturally-occurring isotope of hydrogen with about double the mass of the commonest isotope, differing from it in having a neutron as well as a proton in the nucleus (symbol ^{2}H or D). Also called *heavy hydrogen*.

ˈdeuteride *n.* a binary compound of deuterium with a metal or radical M20.

deutero- /ˈdjuːtərəʊ/ *comb. form.* Bef. a vowel also **deuter-**. [Gk, f. *deuteros* second: see -O-.] Forming wds w. the sense 'second, secondary'. Also (*Chem.*), forming names of deuterated compounds.

deuterocaˈnonical *a.* of, pertaining to, or constituting a second or secondary canon (of sacred books) L17. **deuteroˈchloroform** *n.* deuterated chloroform, $CDCl_3$, used as a solvent in NMR spectroscopy M20. **Deutero-Iˈsaiah** *n.* the supposed later author of *Isaiah* 40–55 M19. **deuteˈromerite** *n.* (*Zool.*) = DEUTOMERITE L19. **deuterostome** *n.* (*Zool.*) a metazoan organism whose mouth develops from a secondary embryonic opening, as a vertebrate, an echinoderm M20.

deuterogamy /djuːtəˈrɒgəmi/ *n.* M17. [Gk *deuterogamia*, f. as DEUTERO- + -GAMY.] 1 Marriage after the death or divorce of a first spouse. M17. 2 *Bot.* Fertilization occurring other than by simple fusion of gametes. L19.

deuterogamist *n.* a person who practises or upholds deuterogamy M18.

deuteron /ˈdjuːtərɒn/ *n.* M20. [f. Gk *deuteros* second + -ON, after PROTON.] *Physics.* The nucleus of an atom of deuterium.

deuto- /ˈdjuːtəʊ/ *comb. form.* Bef. a vowel **deut-**. [Abbrev. of DEUTERO-.] Forming wds w. the sense 'second, secondary'.

deuˈtomerite *n.* (*Zool.*) the posterior division of the body in gregarine protozoans, which contains the nucleus (cf. PROTOMERITE) E20. **deuˈtoxide** *n.* (*Chem.*, *arch.*) the second in a series of oxides of an element E19.

Deutschmark /ˈdɔɪtʃmɑːk/ *n.* Also **Deutschemark**. M20. [G = German mark (MARK *n.*[2]).] The basic monetary unit of Germany (until 1990, of the Federal Republic of Germany), equal to 100 pfennigs; a coin of this value. Abbrev. *DM*, *D-mark*.

deutzia /ˈdjuːtsɪə, ˈdɔɪt-/ *n.* M19. [mod.L, f. Johann van der *Deutz*, 18th-cent. Du. patron of botany: see -IA[1].] Any shrub of the Asian and Central American genus *Deutzia*, which belongs to the saxifrage family and includes many ornamentals, usu. with white flowers.

†**deuzan** *n.* var. of DEUSAN.

deva /ˈdeɪvə/ *n.* E19. [Skt = a god, (orig.) a shining one.] Any of a class of deities in Vedic mythology; any of the lower-level gods in Hinduism and Buddhism.

devadasi /deɪvəˈdɑːsi/ *n.* E19. [Skt *devadāsī* lit. 'female servant of a god' (cf. prec.).] A hereditary female dancer in a Hindu temple.

devall /dɪˈvɔːl/ *v.* & *n.* LME. [(O)Fr. *dévaler* descend. f. Proto-Romance, f. L *de-* DE- 1 down + *vallis* valley. Cf. AVALE.] A *v.i.* †1 Move or slope downwards. LME–M17. 2 Cease, leave off. *Sc.* & *north.* M16. B *n.* 1 A slope. *Sc.* L17. 2 A stop, a cessation. *Sc.* E19.

devalorize /diːˈvalərʌɪz/ *v.t.* Also **-ise**. E20. [Fr. *dévaloriser*, f. *dé-* DE- 3 + *valoriser* VALORIZE.] = DEVALUE.

devaloriˈzation *n.* E20.

devaluate /diːˈvaljʊeɪt/ *v.t.* L19. [f. DE- 3 + VALUE *n.* + -ATE[3].] = DEVALUE.

devaluation /diːˌvaljʊˈeɪʃ(ə)n/ *n.* E20. [f. prec. or next: see -ATION.] The action or an act of devaluing something or someone; the fact of being devalued.

devaluationist *n.* an advocate or supporter of devaluation (of a currency) M20.

devalue /diːˈvaljuː/ *v.t.* E20. [f. DE- 3 + VALUE *n.*] Reduce or annul the value of; deprive of value; *spec.* reduce the official value of (a currency) relative to gold or another currency.

LYNDON B. JOHNSON The British government had decided to devalue the pound from $2.80 to $2.40. M. SARTON Men still do rather consistently undervalue or devalue women's powers. W. BOYD The reek of corn beer on his breath tended to devalue his protestations of innocence.

Devanagari /deɪvəˈnɑːg(ə)ri, dɛv-/ *a.* & *n.* L18. [Skt, f. *deva* god + *nāgarī* NAGARI (an earlier name of the script).] (Designating) the principal script used for Sanskrit, Hindi, and other Indian languages.

devance /dɪˈvɑːns/ *v.t. arch.* L15. [(O)Fr. *devancer*, f. *devant* before, in front.] Anticipate, forestall, outstrip.

¶ Became obs. in 17 but reused in 19.

devast /dɪˈvɑːst, ˈdɛvəst/ *v.t.* M16. [Fr. *dévaster* f. L *devastare*: see next.] Devastate.

devaster *n.* (*rare*) L18.

devastate /ˈdɛvəsteɪt/ *v.t.* M17. [L *devastat-* pa. ppl stem of *devastare*, f. *de-* DE- 1 + *vastare* lay waste: see -ATE[3].] Lay waste, ravage; make desolate or wretched.

P. H. GIBBS France would have to rebuild all the areas devastated by war. P. ROSE She probably died of heart disease. Dickens was devastated.

¶ Rare bef. 19.

devastating *ppl a.* that devastates; very effective, overwhelming: M17. **devastatingly** *adv.* E20. **devastative** *a.* having the quality of devastating, ravaging E19. **devastator** *n.* E19.

devastation /dɛvəˈsteɪʃ(ə)n/ *n.* LME. [Fr. *dévastation* or late L *devastatio(n-)*, f. as prec.: see -ATION.] 1 The action of devastating; the fact or state of being devastated. LME. 2 *Law.* (An instance of) waste of the property of a deceased person by an executor or administrator. L17.

devastavit /diːvəˈsteɪvɪt/ *n.* M17. [L = he has wasted.] *Law.* A writ against an executor or administrator for devastation (see DEVASTATION 2); the offence of devastation.

devein /diːˈveɪn/ *v.t.* M20. [f. DE- 3 + VEIN *n.*] Remove the vein(s) of; *spec.* remove the dorsal vein of (a shrimp or prawn).

devel /ˈdɛv(ə)l/ *n.* & *v. Sc.* L18. [Origin unkn.] A *n.* A stunning blow. L18. B *v.t.* Infl. **-ll-**. Strike with a stunning blow. E19.

develop /dɪˈvɛləp/ *v.* Also (now *rare*) **-ope**. M17. [(O)Fr. *développer* (also *desveloper* DISVELOP) f. Proto-Romance, f. L DIS- + base repr. also by OFr. *voloper* envelop, Prov. *volopar*, It. *viluppare* wrap up: ult. origin unkn.] I *v.t.* 1 Unfold, unroll; unfurl (a banner). Now *arch.* exc. *Her.* M17. b *Math.* Convert (a curved surface) conceptually into a plane figure, as if by unrolling. M19. 2 Uncover, reveal, (something immaterial or †material); make known, bring to light; discover, detect, find out. Now *US.* M18. 3 Unfold more fully; bring out all that is potentially contained in; bring out from a latent to an active or visible state; make fuller, more elaborate or systematic, or bigger; cause to grow or mature, evolve, (*from, out of*); cause to come into existence or operation; display in operation; begin to exhibit or suffer from. M18. b *Chess.* Bring (a piece) into position for effective use. M19. c *Math.* Expand (a function etc.) in the form of a series. Cf. earlier DEVELOPABLE 1a, DEVELOPMENT 4. L19. d *Mus.* Subject (a theme etc.) to development (DEVELOPMENT 7). L19. e Convert (land) to new use, so as to realize its potentialities; construct buildings etc. on (land). L19. 4 *refl.* Come gradually into existence, operation, or a visible state. L18. 5 Process (photographic film etc.) chemically so as to make visible the image(s) contained in it; convert (a photographic image) into visible form by processing. M19.

3 A. HENFREY In the Banyan tree adventitious roots are frequently developed on the outstretched woody branches. R. G. COLLINGWOOD Expounding and developing the doctrines in a series of books. D. CUSACK Teach them whatever you like, so long as it develops their character. G. VIDAL She had in recent years developed a most alarming habit. L. DEIGHTON The thick muscular legs were developed in his teens by sixty-eight-kilometre weekend cycle rides. R. L. FOX The Greeks had been slow to develop advanced siege equipment. R. P. JHABVALA In Kashmir the girl had developed dysentery. G. BOYCOTT You have to . . develop the skill through constant practice.

II *v.i.* 6 Grow, mature, (*into*); make progress; come gradually into existence or operation; exhibit itself; become fuller, more elaborate or systematic, or bigger. M19. 7 Come to light, become known. *US.* M19.

6 H. T. LANE As the child develops so the complication and variety of its toys should increase. L. A. G. STRONG A small seaside town which had neither expanded nor developed for close on fifty years. S. SPENDER He wrote his novels without in the least knowing how the story would develop. R. K. NARAYAN A smirk developed into a chuckle.

developable /dɪˈvɛləpəb(ə)l/ *a.* E19. [f. prec. + -ABLE.] 1 *Math.* a Able to be expanded as a series. E19. b Of a curved surface: able to be (conceptually) unrolled into a plane. M19. 2 *gen.* Able to be developed. E19. 3 Able to be developed photographically. L19.

developed /dɪˈvɛləpt/ *ppl a.* M17. [f. as prec. + -ED[1].] That has been developed; grown, mature; (of a country etc.) economically advanced, industrialized.

W. S. CHURCHILL The far more fruitful and developed land in the West. A. GRAY She . . was called Big June to distinguish her from the less developed girls she sat among. *Marxism Today* The harsh conflict of interests between the developed and developing world.

developement *n.* see DEVELOPMENT.

developer /dɪˈvɛləpə/ *n.* M19. [f. DEVELOP + -ER[1].] 1 A person who or thing which develops something. M19. b *spec.* A chemical agent for developing photographs. M19. c A person who develops land; a speculative builder. E20. 2 A person who develops or matures at a specified time or speed, as *late, slow,* etc., *developer.* M20.

1 F. D. MAURICE Developers of a certain set of theories about gods, men, and nature. *Woman* The world's most successful bustline developer. 2 F. J. SCHONELL The doctrine that dull children are frequently slow developers.

developing /dɪˈvɛləpɪŋ/ *ppl a.* L19. [f. as prec. + -ING[2].] In the process of development; (of a country etc.) becoming economically more advanced, becoming industrialized.

Which? A lot of clothing and some textiles can be made much more cheaply in developing countries than in Western Europe and North America.

development /dɪˈvɛləpm(ə)nt/ *n.* Also (now *rare*) **develope-**. M18. [f. as prec. + -MENT, after Fr. *développement.*] I *gen.* 1 The action or process of developing; evolution, growth, maturation; an instance of this; a gradual unfolding, a fuller working-out. M18. 2 A developed form or product; a result of developing; a change in a course of action or events or in conditions; a stage of advancement; an addition, an elaboration. M18. 3 The state of being developed; a developed condition, a full-grown state. M19.

1 GLADSTONE Essential to the entire development of my case. E. B. TYLOR Stages of development or evolution, each the outcome of previous history. G. B. SHAW The scarcity of labor in America . . has led to a development of machinery there. JOYCE An arrest of embryonic development at some stage antecedent to the human. B. RUSSELL Organic life, we are told, has developed gradually from the protozoon to the philosopher, and this development, we are assured, is indubitably an advance. A. J. P. TAYLOR Their hope was for the recovery of old industries, not the development of new ones. *research and development*: see RESEARCH *n.*[1] 3. 2 L. STERNE A map . . with many other pieces and developements of this work will be added to the end of the twentieth volume. J. H. NEWMAN The butterfly is the development . . of the grub. E. F. SCHUMACHER Many of these small units . . provide society with most of the really fruitful new developments. D. FRASER The next development which dominated military thinking was the threat from the considerable increases made in air power. 3 H. L. MANSEL His disciple . . has carried the doctrine to its fullest development.

II *spec.* 4 The action of unrolling something. *obs.* exc. *Math.*, the action of developing (DEVELOP 1b) a curved surface. E19. 5 The action of developing a photograph. M19. 6 *Chess.* The action or an act of bringing pieces into a position for effective use; the disposition of pieces at an early stage of a game. M19. 7 *Mus.* Elaboration of a theme by modification of melody, harmony, rhythm, etc., esp. in the second section of a sonata movement; a passage or section with such elaboration. L19. 8 The action of developing land etc. so as to realize its potentialities; speculative building; a developed site, *esp.* a new housing estate. L19. 9 Economic advancement or industrialization of a country etc. not previously developed. E20.

8 P. NASH All those courageous enemies of 'development' to whom we owe what is left of England. *Home Finder* The small development—of just 23 detached homes—is attractively laid out to give a 'village' atmosphere. *ribbon development*: see RIBBON *n.* 9 *Daedalus* All African countries lack sufficient managerial, administrative, and technical skills to undertake the massive task of development contemplated at independence. *separate development*: see SEPARATE *a.*

Comb.: **development area**: where new industries etc. are actively encouraged in order to counteract unemployment.

developmental /dɪˌvɛləpˈmɛnt(ə)l/ *a.* M19. [f. prec. + -AL[1].] Of or pertaining to development; incidental to growth; evolutionary; subject to or in process of development.

P. LEACH Your child's developmental clock has told him that it is time to stop being a baby. T. KENEALLY The munitions section was so far developmental. E. C. MINKOFF One of the central problems of the field known as *developmental biology* is the discovery of the processes that control the transcription and subsequent expression of genes in the various types of body cells.

developmentalism *n.* belief in a theory of development; evolutionism: M20. **developmentalist** *n.* a believer in a theory of development; an evolutionist: M19. **developmentally** *adv.* in relation or reference to development M19.

développé /devlɔpe/ *n.* Pl. pronounced same. E20. [Fr., use as n. of pa. pple of *développer* DEVELOP.] A ballet movement in which one leg is raised and then fully extended.

Devensian /dɪˈvɛnzɪən/ *a.* & *n.* M20. [f. L *Devenses* dwellers near the River Dee (*Deva*), on the border between England and Wales, + -IAN.] *Geol.* (Designating or pertaining to) the most recent Pleistocene glaciation in Britain, identified with the Weichselian of northern Europe (and perhaps the Würm of the Alps).

deverbal /diːˈvəːb(ə)l/ *n.* & *a.* M20. [f. DE- 2 + VERB + -AL[1].] *Gram.* (A word) formed on or derived from a verb.

deverbative /diːˈvəːbətɪv/ *n.* & *a.* E20. [f. DE- 2 + VERB + -ATIVE, after *denominative.*] *Gram.* = prec.

devest /dɪˈvɛst/ *v.t. arch.* M16. [OFr. *de(s)vester*, *devestir*, f. *des-* DIS- 1 + L *vestire* clothe, f. *vestis* garment.] †1 = DIVEST 1, 2. M16–E19. 2 *Law.* = DIVEST 3. L16. †b Dispossess (a person) of some right, authority, etc., with which he or she has been invested. M17–E19.

devesture *n.* (*rare*) the action of devesting M17.

deviable /ˈdiːvɪəb(ə)l/ *a.* E20. [f. late L *deviare* (see DEVIATE *v.*): see -ABLE.] Able to be deviated, deflectable.

deviaˈbility *n.* E20.

deviance /ˈdiːvɪəns/ *n.* M20. [f. DEVIANT *a.*: see -ANCE.] The state or quality of being deviant; deviant behaviour or characteristics.

deviancy *n.* M20.

deviant /ˈdiːvɪənt/ *a.* & *n.* LME. [Late L *deviant-* pres. ppl stem of *deviare*: see DEVIATE *v.*, -ANT[1].] A *adj.* Deviating, divergent, esp. from normal social or sexual standards or behaviour. LME. B *n.* A person who or thing which deviates from the normal, esp. from normal social or sexual standards or behaviour. E20.

¶Rare bef. 20.

deviate /ˈdiːvɪət/ *a.* & *n.* M16. [Late L *deviatus* pa. pple, f. as next: see -ATE[2]. In mod. use after the vb.] A *adj.* †1 Turned out of the way, remote. M16–M17. 2 = DEVIANT *a.* M20. B *n.* 1 = DEVIANT *n.* E20. 2 *Statistics.* The value of a variate measured from some standard point of distribution, usu. the mean, and usu. expressed in terms of the standard deviation of the distribution. E20.

deviate /ˈdiːvɪeɪt/ *v.* M17. [Late L *deviat-* pa. ppl stem of *deviare*, f. L *de-* DE- 1 + *via* way: see -ATE[3].] 1 *v.i.* Turn out of the way, turn aside, swerve, (*lit.* & *fig.*); diverge, digress, differ. (Foll. by *from.*) M17. 2 *v.t.* Cause to turn aside or swerve, deflect, change the direction of, (*lit.* & *fig.*). (Foll. by *from.*) Now chiefly as *deviated* ppl a., not straight, oblique, deviant. M17.

1 T. HARDY He has not . . deviated one hair's breadth from the course he laid down. N. SHUTE He deviated fifty yards towards it. A. POWELL A most devoted wife . . never deviating in admiration of her husband. C. P. SNOW The summer weather . . hadn't deviated for four months.

deviative /-ətɪv/ *a.* causing deviation, tending to deviate L19.

deviation /diːvɪˈeɪʃ(ə)n/ *n.* LME. [(O)Fr. *déviation* f. med.L *deviatio(n-)*, f. as prec.: see -ATION.] 1 Divergence from a course, method, rule, or norm; an instance of this. (Foll. by *from.*) LME. b *spec.* (An instance of) divergence from a moral or sexual norm. E17. c (An instance of) divergence from the political doctrine or practices of a government or party, esp. a Communist party. M20. 2 The action or an act of swerving or changing direction. M17. 3 Divergence from the straight line, mean, or standard; variation; the amount of this. L17. b *spec.* (The amount of) deflection of the needle of a compass due to local magnetism, esp. of the iron etc. in a ship. E19. c *Statistics.* The amount by which a single measurement differs from the mean. M19.

3 *conjugate deviation*: see CONJUGATE *a.* **c mean deviation** the mean of the absolute deviations. **standard deviation** the square root of the mean of the squares of the deviations.

deviationism *n.* political deviation, a tendency to depart from (esp. Communist) party doctrine or practices: M20. **deviationist** *n.* & *a.* (*a*) *n.* a person who departs from (esp. Communist) party doctrine or practices; (*b*) *adj.* of or pertaining to deviationism or deviationists: M20.

deviator /ˈdiːvɪeɪtə/ *n.* M17. [f. DEVIATE *v.* + -OR.] **1** A person who or thing which deviates. M17. **2** *Math.* The non-isotropic component of a tensor, esp. a stress tensor. M20.

deviatoric /diːvɪəˈtɒrɪk/ *a.* (*Math.*) of, associated with, or represented by a deviator M20.

device /dɪˈvʌɪs/ *n.* Also †**devise**. See also DEVISE *n.* ME. [OFr. *devis* (masc.), *-ise* (fem.) f. Proto-Romance derivs. of L *divis-* pa. ppl stem of *dividere* DIVIDE *v.*] **I 1** Intent, desire; will, pleasure; an inclination, a fancy. Long only in *leave* etc. *to one's own devices* (passing into sense 2). ME. †**b** An order, a request. ME–M16. †**c** Opinion, notion; advice. LME–L16. **2** An arrangement, a plan, a scheme; an (ingenious) expedient; a stratagem, a trick. ME. **3** A thing designed for a particular function or adapted for a purpose; an invention, a contrivance, *esp.* a (simple) mechanical contrivance. LME. **b** An explosive contrivance, *esp.* a nuclear bomb. M20. **4** A literary composition; *esp.* a dramatic entertainment, a masque. *arch.* LME. **b** A conceit, a witticism; a witty composition. *arch.* L16. **5** An artistic design, a drawing, a figure. LME. **b** *spec.* An emblematic or heraldic design, a cognizance, an emblem; a motto. LME. **6a** The action of devising or planning; inventive faculty, ingenuity. Now *arch. rare.* LME. **b** The manner in which a thing is devised; make, look. *arch.* LME. †**7** Familiar conversation, chat. L15–E17.

2 B. TRAPIDO Aggression is the device I have for surviving the pain of Roger's presence. J. BARNES As for coincidences in books—there's something cheap and sentimental about the device. 3 K. CLARK The architect has used the device known as flying buttresses. G. VIDAL Various offices, equipped with all the latest communication devices. *Daily Express* America had exploded 18 devices since last August. **5b** LONGFELLOW A banner with the strange device, 'Excelsior!' W. H. AUDEN The tyrant's device: *Whatever Is Possible Is Necessary.* **6b** H. ALLEN The tweaking nose of the largest rabbit was a miracle of rare device.

†**II** See DEVISE *n.*

deviceful *a.* (now *rare*) full of or characterized by invention, ingenious L16. **deviceless** *a.* M19.

devil /ˈdɛv(ə)l/ *n.* Also (esp. in sense 1) **D-**. See also DEIL. [OE *dēofol* = OFris. *diovel*, OS *diubul*, *-al* (Du. *duivel*), OHG *tiufal* (G *Teufel*), ON *djǫfull*, f. Chr.L *diabolus* f. Gk *diabolos* (in the Septuagint rendering Heb. *Śāṭān* SATAN) lit. 'accuser, slanderer', f. *diaballein* slander, traduce, f. *dia-* across + *ballein* throw.] **1** In Jewish and Christian theology, *the* supreme spirit of evil, the tempter and spiritual enemy of humankind, the adversary of God, popularly believed to appear in various forms, esp. in that of a man with horns, cloven hoofs, and a forked tail; Satan. Freq. in exclamatory or imprecatory phrs. expr. surprise, incredulity, impatience, displeasure, dismay, or negation, or merely emphatic (cf. DEUCE *n.*², DIABLE *int.*). OE. **2** A demon; *esp.* (in biblical translations and allusions) a heathen god or idol; an evil or unclean spirit supposed to possess a demoniac. OE. **3** A malignant being of angelic or superhuman nature or powers; *esp.* a follower of Satan, one of the fallen spirits described as rebelling against God and having the chief function of tormenting and tempting humankind, a fiend. Also, a malignant god. OE. **4** A human being of diabolical character or qualities; an exceptionally cruel or wicked person. OE. **b** A provoking or troublesome person; a mischievously energetic, clever, self-willed, or reckless person. E17. **c** A luckless or wretched person. Chiefly in *poor devil*. L17. **d** A vicious or unmanageable animal. M19. **5** Any of various animals or birds associated in character or appearance with the Devil; *spec.* †(*a*) the coot; (*b*) *sea devil*, = *devilfish* below; (*c*) (more fully *Tasmanian devil*) a carnivorous nocturnal marsupial, *Sarcophilus harrisi*, native to Australia (now only Tasmania); (*d*) *Indian devil* (N. Amer.), the puma; also, the wolverine; (*e*) *dial.* the swift. Usu. w. specifying wd. L16. **6** The personification of evil and undesirable qualities by which a human being may be possessed or actuated. E17. **b** Fighting spirit; dash or energy in attack; 'go'. L18. **7** A person employed in a subordinate position to work under the direction of or for a particular person; *spec.* (*a*) *Hist.* (more fully *printer's devil*) an errand-boy or junior assistant in a printing office; (*b*) a junior legal counsel working for a principal; (*c*) a literary hack doing what his or her employer takes the credit and payment for. L17. **8** *pred. The* worst that can happen, *the* worst possible person or thing. L17. **9** A kind of exploding firework; a squib, a cracker. M18. **10** A highly seasoned, peppery dish of broiled or fried meat; peppery seasoning for meat. L18. **11** Any of various instruments or mechanical devices associated (more or less obviously) with the Devil, esp. one fitted with sharp teeth or spikes, or for tearing or other destructive work. M19. **12** A moving sand-spout, a sand-storm; (in full *dust devil*) a dust-storm, a whirlwind. M19. **13** *Naut.* The seam in the upper deck planking next to a ship's waterways. Also, the seam between the garboard strake and the keel. Now *arch.* or *Hist.* L19.

1 T. HERBERT Black as the devill, and as treacherous. BYRON And wonders why the devil he got heirs. BROWNING The devil appears himself, Armed and accoutred, horns and hoofs and tail! R. W. EMERSON 'That is W,' said the teacher. 'The Devil!' exclaimed the boy, 'is that W?' J. E. HOPKINS Wesley could not see why the devil should have all the good tunes. NEB *Matt.* 4:1 Jesus was then led away . . into the wilderness, to be tempted by the devil. J. GORES Who the devil do you think gave it to me? *Devil take the hindmost* (a motto of selfish competition), *Give the Devil his due*, *Needs must when the Devil drives*, *Talk of the Devil* (*and he is bound to appear*) (said when someone arrives just after being mentioned), *The Devil can quote Scripture for his own ends*, *The Devil finds work for idle hands to do*, *The Devil is not so black as he is painted*, *The Devil looks after his own*, & other proverbs. 2 MILTON Devils to adore for deities. A. MASON A celebrated exorcist was several times accused of casting out devils by the power of Beelzebub. 3 C. S. LEWIS Screaming out that devils were tearing him and that he was . . falling down into Hell. 4 SHAKES. *Oth.* Thou dost belie her, and thou art a devil. AV *John* 6:70 Haue not I chosen you twelue, and one of you is a deuill? b R. B. SHERIDAN An ill-tempered little devil! She'll be in a passion all her life. S. MIDDLETON He was a devil for pushing his nose into an argument. c G. GREENE The poor devils are burnt alive. d T. MEDWIN He was the fastest trotter in the cantonment, but a restless devil. 6 H. BROADHURST The devil of short-sighted greed is powerful enough if left alone. b BARONESS ORCZY He seemed to have the very devil in his fingers, and the coach seemed to fly along the road. 8 SIR W. SCOTT To be cross-examined by those who have seen the true thing is the devil. V. WOOLF Audiences were the devil O to write a play without an audience.

Phrases: **a devil of a —** an extreme —, a terrible —, a very difficult or unusual —. **between the devil and the deep (blue) sea** in a dilemma, forced to choose one of two unwelcome possibilities. *blue devil*: see BLUE *a.* *Cartesian devil*: see CARTESIAN *a.* **devil a bit, devil a one**, etc., not at all, not even one, etc. *devil's own luck*: see LUCK *n.* *dust devil*: see sense 12 above. **go to the devil** be damned, take a ruinous course; freq. *imper.*, go away at once. *hold a candle to the devil*: see HOLD *v.* *Indian devil*: see sense 5 above. *limb. of the devil*: see LIMB *n.*¹ **play the devil with** cause severe damage to or trouble for. *printer's devil*: see sense 7 above. *raise the devil*: see RAISE *v.* *red devil*: see RED *a.* *sea devil*: see sense 5 above. *sell one's soul, oneself*, etc., *to the devil*: see SELL *v.* *Tasmanian devil*: see sense 5 above. **the devil (and all) to do** *arch.* much ado, much trouble and turmoil. †**the devil on two sticks** = DIABOLO. **the devil's own —** an exceptional or extreme instance of —. *the devil's* (*own*) *job*: see JOB *n.*¹ **the devil to pay** extreme trouble or difficulty concerning a particular circumstance or obligation. *the world, the flesh, and the devil*: see FLESH *n.* *thorny devil*: see THORNY 1.

Comb.: **devil bird** (*a*) *dial.* the swift; (*b*) in Sri Lanka (Ceylon), the brown wood owl, *Strix leptogrammatica*; **devil dance** a ritual dance performed for the invocation, propitiation, or exorcism of spirits; **devil dancer** a performer of a devil dance; **devil-devil** *Austral.* (*a*) in folk-lore, a devil, an evil spirit; (*b*) = GILGAI; **devil-dodger** *arch. joc.* a preacher, a ranter; a person who tries to secure salvation by attending the services of more than one religious denomination; **devilfish** any of various fishes of supposedly devilish appearance or reputation, *spec.* (*a*) the angler-fish; (*b*) *N. Amer.* the manta; **devil-in-a-bush** love-in-a-mist, *Nigella damascena*; **devil-may-care** *a.* & *n.* (*a*) *adj.* reckless, rollicking; (*b*) *n.* a reckless or rollicking person or attitude; **devil-on-the-coals** *Austral. slang* a small damper hastily baked in hot ashes; **devil's advocate** [tr. L *advocatus diaboli*] the official whose function is to put the case against beatification or canonization by the Roman Catholic Church; *transf.* a person who provokes argument or discussion by supporting the opposite side or by pointing out the weaknesses of his or her own case; **devil's bit** [from the supposedly 'bitten-off' root shape] (*a*) (more fully *devil's bit scabious*) a bluish-flowered scabious, *Succisa pratensis*, of damp pastures; (*b*) *US* a plant of the lily family, *Chamaelirium luteum*, bearing spikelike racemes of white flowers; also called *blazing star*; **devil's bones** *arch.* dice; **devil's books** *arch.* playing-cards (= *devil's picture-books* below); **devil's club** *N. Amer.* a prickly shrub of the aralia family, *Oplopanax horridus* of western N. America; **devil's coach-horse** a large predatory rove-beetle, *Ocypus olens*, which habitually raises its tail when alarmed; **devil's darning-needle** a dragonfly or damselfly; **devil's dirt** asafoetida (= *devil's dung* below); *devil's dozen*: see DOZEN *n.*; **devil's dung** asafoetida (= *devil's dirt* above); **devil's dust** the flock to which old cloth is reduced by a mechanical devil, shoddy; **devil's grip** *colloq.* pleurodynia, esp. as a symptom of Bornholm disease; **devil's guts** (*a*) *dial.* dodder; (*b*) *Austral.* any parasitic climbing plant of the genus *Cassytha* of the laurel family; *devil's limb*: see LIMB *n.*¹; *devil's matins*: see MATIN *n.* 2; **devil's milk** *dial.* any of various plants, esp. spurges, with acrid milky juice; **devils-on-horseback** (*a*) = *angels on horseback* s.v. ANGEL; (*b*) a similar dish of prune or plum in bacon; **devil's needle** = *devil's darning-needle* above; **devil's paintbrush** *N. Amer.* a naturalized European hawkweed, *Pilosella aurantiaca*, with orange flower-heads and black-haired involucres; *devil's paternoster*: see PATERNOSTER 1c; **devil's picture-books** *arch.* playing-cards (= *devil's books* above); *devil's tattoo*: see TATTOO *n.*¹ 2; **devil's twine** = *devil's guts* (b) above; **devil-wood** *US* a tree of the olive family, *Osmanthus americanus*, a native of US swamps (also called *American olive*); the hard wood of this tree; **devil-worship** the worship or cult of a devil or the Devil, Satanism; **devil-worshipper** a person who practises devil-worship.

devildom *n.* (*a*) the dominion or rule of a devil or the Devil, exercise of diabolic power; (*b*) the domain of the Devil, the condition of devils: L17. **deviless** *n.* (now *rare*) a female devil L17. **devilet** *n.* (*a*) a little devil; (*b*) *dial.* the swift: L18. **devilhead** *n.* (long *arch. rare*) devilhood ME. **devilhood** *n.* the condition and estate of a devil or the Devil E17. **deviling** *n.* (*a*) a young devil, an imp, a mischievous little creature; (*b*) *dial.* the swift, the pied wagtail: L16. **devilism** *n.* a system of action or conduct appropriate to a devil, devilish quality M17. **devilize** *v.* (*a*) *v.t.* make a devil of, make devilish in character; †(*b*) *v.i.* play the devil, act as a devil: E17. **devilkin** *n.* a little devil, an imp M18. **devil-like** *a.* & *adv.* diabolical(ly) L15. **devilship** *n.* (*a*) (chiefly *joc.* as a title) a person having the status of a devil; (*b*) the condition or quality of a devil; the position or office of devil: ME.

devil /ˈdɛv(ə)l/ *v.* Infl. **-ll-**, ***-l-**. L16. [f. the n.] †**1** *v.t.* (Foll. by *it*) play the devil; play the devil with. L16–M17. **2** *v.t.* Cook with peppery condiments. E19. **3** *v.t.* Worry (a person) excessively; harass, annoy, tease. *colloq.* (chiefly *US*). E19. **4** *v.i.* Work as a lawyer's or author's devil (*for* a principal). M19. **5** Tear to pieces, break up, score, scratch, esp. with a devil (DEVIL *n.* 11). L19.

devilish /ˈdɛv(ə)lɪʃ/ *a.* & *adv.* LME. [f. as prec. + -ISH¹.] **A** *adj.* **1** Like the Devil or a devil; wicked, fiendish. LME. **2** Characteristic or worthy of the Devil; diabolical; damnable; execrable. LME. **3** Of or belonging to the Devil. E16. **4** Violent, terrible; extremely bad; enormous, excessive. *arch. colloq.* M17.

1 BROWNING We pronounce Count Guido devilish and damnable. 2 W. GOUGE The matchlesse, mercilesse, devilish, and damnable gun-powder-treason. 3 J. H. BURTON So skilled in devilish arts of

magic. 4 THACKERAY She has a devilish deal more than ten thousand pounds.

B *adv.* Excessively, exceedingly; very. *arch. colloq.* E17.

P. H. GIBBS I'm devilish glad to be home again.

devilishly *adv.* in a devilish manner; *arch. colloq.* excessively, exceedingly, very: E16. **devilishness** *n.* M16.

devilment /ˈdɛv(ə)lm(ə)nt/ *n.* L18. [f. as prec. + -MENT.] 1 Action befitting a devil; mischief, wild spirits, reckless daring. L18. 2 A devilled dish of food. *rare.* L18. 3 A devilish device or invention, a devilish or strange phenomenon. L19.

devilry /ˈdɛv(ə)lri/ *n.* LME. [f. as prec. + -RY.] †1 A demon; a demoniacal possession. LME–L15. 2 Black magic; dealing with the Devil; diabolical art. LME. 3 Devilish action or conduct; (an act of) extreme wickedness, cruelty, or perversity; wicked mischief. L15. b Reckless mischief, daring, or hilarity. M19. 4 The Devil and his works. M16. 5 A system of devils, demonology. M19. 6 *collect.* A company of devils. M19.

deviltry /ˈdɛv(ə)ltri/ *n.* L18. [f. prec. after *harlotry* etc.] = DEVILRY.

devious /ˈdiːvɪəs/ *a.* & *adv.* L16. [f. L *devius*, f. *de-* DE- 1 + *via* way: see -OUS.] A *adj.* 1 Lying out of the way; remote, sequestered. Now *rare.* L16. 2 Pursuing an indirect or winding course; circuitous, rambling; deviating from the straight way, erring; subtly cunning, wily, unscrupulous, dishonest. E17.

1 E. K. KANE These devious and untrodden ice-fields. 2 J. R. LOWELL A shoal of devious minnows wheel from where a pike Lurks balanced. C. V. WEDGWOOD To evade them they had travelled . . by devious ways, thus greatly lengthening the journey. W. GOLDING I should . . have to be subtle, devious, diplomatic. P. LARKIN The devious ways of practical politics.

B *adv.* With an indirect or winding course, circuitously. Now *rare.* L18.

C. BRONTË I sought the Continent, and went devious through all its lands.

deviously *adv.* M18. **deviousness** *n.* E18.

devirginate /diːˈvəːdʒɪneɪt/ *v.t.* Long *rare.* Pa. pple & ppl a. †-**ate** (earlier), -**ated**. LME. [Orig. pa. pple, f. L *devirginatus* pa. pple of *devirginare*, f. *de-* DE- 3 + *virgo*, *virgin-* virgin: see -ATE[2], -ATE[3].] Deprive of virginity.

devirgiˈnation *n.* E17.

devisable /dɪˈvʌɪzəb(ə)l/ *a.* LME. [AN (in OFr. = dividable), f. as DEVISE *v.*; in sense 2 f. DEVISE *v.*: see -ABLE.] 1 *Law.* That can be devised by will. LME. 2 Contrivable. E17.

devise /dɪˈvʌɪz/ *n.* Also †**device**. ME. [Var. of DEVICE, f. OFr. *devise* fem.] †I1 See DEVICE I. ME. II2 *Law.* The action of devising real estate by will; (a clause containing) a testamentary disposition of real property. Formerly more widely, the action of bequeathing, a bequest. LME.

devise /dɪˈvʌɪz/ *v.* ME. [(O)Fr. *deviser* f. Proto-Romance, f. L *divis-* pa. ppl stem of *dividere* DIVIDE *v.*] †1 *v.t.* Divide; distribute; distinguish. ME–L15. †2 *v.t.* Consider, look at attentively, examine; meditate on; decide; conceive, imagine, guess. Foll. by simple obj. or obj. cl. ME–E19. 3 *v.t.* Plan, contrive, (something (now usu. immaterial), *how*, †*that*, †*to do*); invent, create. ME. b *v.t.* Plan in a secret, underhand, or artful way, plot, (something, †*to do*); feign (something, †*that*); forge. *arch.* ME. c *v.i.* Make plans, scheme. Formerly also, pretend. LME. †4 *v.t.* Accomplish, achieve, manage (something, *to do*). ME–L16. †5 *v.t.* Recount, relate, describe. ME–L16. b *v.i.* Give an account; confer, talk, (*of*). LME–L19. †6 *v.t.* Appoint, direct. LME–E17. 7 *v.t. Law.* Assign (real estate) by will. Formerly more widely, bequeath. LME.

3 MILTON How suttly to detain thee I devise. W. S. MAUGHAM She could devise some means to persuade him. F. L. WRIGHT A foundation for that particular soil had to be devised to bear the load of any building we wanted to build. K. MOORE He and Roberta would devise adventure stories. b W. COWPER Devising . . calamity to Troy.

devisement *n.* (*rare*) †(*a*) a description, an account; (*b*) the action of devising; a device: LME.

devisee /dɪvʌɪˈziː/ *n.* M16. [f. prec. + -EE[1].] *Law.* A person to whom property is devised by will.

deviser /dɪˈvʌɪzə/ *n.* L15. [Alt. of next: see -ER[1].] A person who devises; a contriver, a planner, an inventor.

devisor /dɪˈvʌɪzɔː, dɪvʌɪˈzɔː/ *n.* LME. [AN *devisour*, OFr. *deviseor*, f. as DEVISE *v.*] 1 = DEVISER. Now *rare.* LME. 2 *Law.* A person who devises property by will. M16.

devitalize /diːˈvʌɪt(ə)lʌɪz/ *v.t.* Also -**ise**. E19. [f. DE- 3 + VITALIZE.] Deprive of vitality or vital qualities; reduce the vitality of.

devitaliˈzation *n.* L19.

devitrify /diːˈvɪtrɪfʌɪ/ *v.t.* M19. [f. DE- 3 + VITRIFY.] Deprive of vitreous qualities; make (glass or vitreous rock) hard, opaque, and crystalline.

devitrifiˈcation *n.* M19.

devocalize /diːˈvəʊk(ə)lʌɪz/ *v.t.* Also -**ise**. L19. [f. DE- 3 + VOCALIZE.] *Phonet.* = DEVOICE.

devoice /diːˈvɔɪs/ *v.t.* M20. [f. DE- 3 + VOICE *v.*] *Phonet.* Make (a vowel or voiced consonant) voiceless.

devoid /dɪˈvɔɪd/ *a.* LME. [Orig. pa. pple of next.] 1 Foll. by *of*: quite lacking or free from, empty of, destitute of. LME. †2 *absol.* Void, empty. *rare.* Only in L16.

1 W. G. PALGRAVE A very simple style of dress, devoid of ornament or pretension. E. WAUGH The room, though spacious, was almost devoid of furniture. I. WALLACE Her . . face was devoid of any makeup except at the lips. 2 SPENSER When I awoke, and found her place devoyd.

devoid /dɪˈvɔɪd/ *v.t.* Long *rare.* Pa. pple & ppl a. †**devoid** (cf. prec.), **devoided**. ME. [OFr. *devoidier*, *devuidier* (mod. *dévider*), f. *de-* DE- 3 + *voider*, *vuider* VOID *v.* In isolated mod. use back-form. f. prec.] †1 Cast out, expel, discharge; withdraw *oneself*. ME–M16. †2 Vacate, leave. LME–M16. 3 Empty *of*, free *of*, divest *of*. LME. †4 Avoid, shun. LME–M16. †5 Make ineffective or invalid. *rare.* Only in E17.

devoir /dəˈvwɑː/ *n. arch.* ME. [AN *dever*, OFr. *deveir* (mod. *devoir*) f. L *debere* owe. Cf. ENDEAVOUR.] 1 Duty; a dutiful act. Chiefly in *do one's devoir*. ME. †2 One's best or utmost, an effort. LME–L17. †3 (A) service due or rendered. LME–M18. 4 An act of civility. Usu. in *pl.*, courteous or formal attentions. LME. †5 In *pl.* Moneys due, dues. LME–M17.

2 **put oneself in devoir** [after Fr. *ce mettre en devoir* do one's utmost.] 4 A. SEAGER He paid his devoirs to his hostess and went . . into the dining room.

¶The mod.Fr. spelling was introduced in 15 and the pronunc. was subsequently conformed to it.

devolatilize /diːˈvɒlətɪlʌɪz/ *v.t.* Also -**ise**. M19. [f. DE- 3 + VOLATILIZE.] Remove volatile components from, make no longer volatile.

devolatiliˈzation *n.* E20.

devolute /ˈdiːvəluːt, ˈdɛv-/ *v.t.* M16. [L *devolut-* pa. ppl stem of *devolvere* DEVOLVE.] Transfer by devolution.

devolution /diːvəˈluːʃ(ə)n, dɛv-/ *n.* L15. [Late L *devolutio(n-)* (in med.L sense), f. as prec.: see -ION.] 1 The transference of an unexercised right to the ultimate owner; transference by default. L15. †b The passing of jurisdiction on appeal. L16–E18. 2a Descent by natural, legal, or due succession; the action of passing something on to a successor. M16. b The deputing or delegation of work or authority; *esp.* the transfer of some powers by the British or UK House of Parliament to bodies appointed by and responsible to it, or by central government to a local or regional administration, esp. in Scotland and Wales. M18. 3a The action of rolling down; descent with a rolling motion. *arch.* E17. b The rolling or passing of time; descent through a series of stages. M17. c (In contrast to *evolution*.) Degeneration. *rare.* L19.

2a DONNE Now for the riches themselves . . he may have them by devolution from his parents. b B. RUSSELL There should be devolution of the powers of the State to various kinds of bodies. *Guardian* The demand for devolution . . was conceded . . to stem the threatening tide of nationalism. 3b C. N. MANLOVE Devolution into ignorance and slavedom. c *Daily Telegraph* Instead of the survival of the fittest, we encourage the survival of the stupidest: devolution.

devolutionary *a.* of, pertaining to, or characterized by devolution L19. **devolutionist** *n.* & *a.* (*a*) *n.* a believer in or advocate of (political) devolution; (*b*) *adj.* of or pertaining to devolutionists; tending towards devolution: E20.

devolve /dɪˈvɒlv/ *v.* LME. [L *devolvere*, f. *de-* DE- 1 + *volvere* to roll.] I *v.t.* 1 Cause to descend with a rolling motion, roll down. Also, unroll, unfurl. *arch.* LME. †b Overturn, overthrow. LME–M17. c Cause to pass down by the revolution of time (*into* a state or condition); cause to descend through a series of stages. *arch.* M16. 2†a Transfer (a right) to the ultimate owner, esp. through the failure or forfeiture of the holder. (Foll. by *to*, *unto*.) L15–M19. b Cause to descend by natural, legal, or due succession; pass on by inheritance. (Foll. by *to*, (arch.) *unto*.) M16. †c Cause to fall or alight *on* or *upon* an object; throw *on* or *upon* a resource. E17–E18. d Cause (a charge or responsibility) to fall *on* or *upon* a deputy; delegate (work, authority). M17.

1 DE QUINCEY Where little England . . now devolves so quietly to the sea her sweet pastoral rivulets. 2b S. JOHNSON Students . . can seldom add more than some small particle of knowledge, to the hereditary stock devolved to them from ancient times. d H. A. L. FISHER The territorial lord, upon whom . . the exercise of political power is in fact devolved. *Marxism Today* 50% of Scots favouring a devolved assembly and 30% of Scots wanting a separate parliament.

II *v.i.* 3a Pass or fall *to* another, esp. through the failure or forfeiture of the holder; pass by default *to*. M16. b Pass by natural, legal, or due succession (*to*). E17. c Fall as a charge or responsibility *on* or *upon*. M18. 4a Pass by the revolution of time *to* or *into* a state or condition; descend through a series of stages, degenerate, (*into*). L16. b Roll or flow down (*from*); unroll, unfurl. *arch.* M17.

3b M. HUNTER Succession to the ruling rights devolved through the eldest daughter of a line. J. BARNES It was brought back . . by a roving cousin, and has devolved to me from my sister. c E. BOWEN So few having this gift, she felt it devolved on her to use it. T. BENN The peerage that devolved on me as his heir when Father died. 4a DE QUINCEY Four separate movements through which this impassioned tale devolves. J. BEE A gentleman and scholar devolving into the buffoon . . is an unseemly sight. b SMOLLETT Devolving from thy parent lake, A charming maze thy waters make. E. BLUNDEN The earth heaved up to a great height in solid crags and clods, with devolving clouds of dust.

devolvement *n.* M19.

Devon /ˈdɛv(ə)n/ *n.* M19. [A county in SW England: see DEVONSHIRE.] 1 Used *attrib.* to designate things found in, originating from, or associated with Devon. M19. 2 (An animal of) a breed of red beef cattle. M19. 3 *Angling.* A type of artificial lure. E20.

Devonian /dɛˈvəʊnɪən, dɪ-/ *a.* & *n.* E17. [f. med.L *Devonia*, f. *Devon(shire)*: see DEVONSHIRE, -AN, -IAN.] A *adj.* 1 Of or pertaining to Devon(shire). E17. 2 *Geol.* Designating or pertaining to the fourth period of the Palaeozoic era, following the Silurian and preceding the Carboniferous. M19. B *n.* 1 The dialect of Devon(shire). *rare.* M17. 2 A native or inhabitant of Devon(shire). L19. 3 *Geol.* The Devonian period; the system of rocks dating from this time. L19.

devonport *n.* var. of DAVENPORT *n.*[1]

Devonshire /ˈdɛv(ə)nʃə/ *n.* & *v.* Also (repr. local pronunc.) **Denshire** /ˈdɛnʃə/; (as vb) **d-**. E17. [A county (OE *Defenascīr*) in SW England: cf. DEVON.] A *n.* 1 Used *attrib.* to designate things found in, originating from, or associated with Devonshire (now Devon). E17. 2 The dialect of Devonshire; = DEVONIAN *n.* 1. M19.

1 **Devonshire cream** clotted cream. **Devonshire slipper** a type of stirrup-iron.

B *v.t.* & *i.* Clear or improve (land) by burning turf, stubble, etc. Now *arch.* or *Hist.* E17.

dévot /devo (*pl. same*), deɪˈvəʊ/ *n.* Fem. -***ote*** /-ɔt (*pl. same*), -ɒt/. E18. [Fr., use as n. of adj.: see DEVOUT.] A devotee; a devout person.

†devota *n.* see DEVOTO.

devote /dɪˈvəʊt/ *a.* & *n. arch.* ME. [Partly var. of DEVOUT, partly directly f. L *devotus*.] **A** *adj.* **1** = DEVOUT *a.* 1. ME. **2** Devoted, dedicated, (*to*). LME. **†B** *n.* A devotee. M17–E18.

devote /dɪˈvəʊt/ *v.t.* L16. [L *devot-* pa. ppl stem of *devovere*, f. *de-* DE- 1 + *vovere* vow.] **1** Dedicate formally, consecrate, (*to*). L16. **2** Apply or give up zealously or exclusively *to*. E17. **3** Consign to destruction; invoke a curse on. (Earlier as DEVOTED 3.) *arch.* M17.

1 W. LAW All Christians are by their Baptism devoted to God. 2 L. M. MONTGOMERY Jane says she will devote her whole life to teaching, and never, never, marry. R. G. COLLINGWOOD I learnt to devote my time more and more to music. H. L. MENCKEN Even more than Cato the Censor he devoted himself wholeheartedly to arousing fears and fomenting hatred. G. F. KENNAN *Pravda* devoted the first four and a half pages of its six-page issue exclusively to a single document. E. ROOSEVELT The begum had devoted herself to trying to carry out his plans. 3 GIBBON The hostile army was devoted with dire execrations to the gods of war and . . thunder.

devotement *n.* an act of devoting; devotion, dedication: E17.

dévote *n.* see DÉVOT.

†devoté *n.* E18–E19. [Pseudo-Fr. alt. of DEVOTE *n.* or DEVOTEE.] A devotee.

devoted /dɪˈvəʊtɪd/ *a.* L16. [f. prec. + -ED[1].] **1** Vowed; dedicated; consecrated. L16. **2** Characterized by devotion; zealously or exclusively attached (*to*); given up *to*. L16. **3** Consigned to evil or destruction; cursed; doomed. *arch.* E17.

2 V. BRITTAIN Several wards exclusively devoted to head wounds and eye cases. R. PARK The girl was selflessly devoted to her father. K. A. PORTER The most devoted married pair. S. NAIPAUL Together with about one hundred and fifty of his most devoted disciples, he had migrated West.

devotedly *adv.* E19. **devotedness** *n.* M17.

devotee /dɛvəʊˈtiː/ *n.* M17. [f. DEVOTE *v.* + -EE[1].] **1** *gen.* A person who is zealously devoted *to* a cause, pursuit, etc.; a votary (*of*), an enthusiast (*of*). M17. **2** *spec.* A person characterized by religious devotion esp. of an extreme or superstitious kind. L17.

1 R. F. BURTON As fanatical a devotee of vegetarianism. 2 S. ANDERSON The devotee going swiftly through decade after decade of his rosary.

devotion /dɪˈvəʊʃ(ə)n/ *n.* ME. [(O)Fr. *dévotion* or L *devotio(n-)*, f. as DEVOTE *v.*: see -ION.] **1** The fact or quality of being devoted to divine worship or service; reverence, devoutness. (Foll. by *to*, *towards* a god etc.) ME. **†b** A devout feeling or impulse. ME–E17. **2** Religious observance, divine worship; a form of prayer or worship directed to a special object or for private use; in *pl.* & *†sing.*, prayers (and meditation), private worship. ME. **3a** The fact or quality of being devoted to a person, cause, pursuit, etc.; earnest application; zealous or exclusive attachment. ME. **b** Zealous or exclusive application *to* a use or purpose. M19. **4** The action of setting apart for a sacred purpose; solemn dedication, consecration. E16. **†5** An oblation; alms. M16–M17. **†6** Devoted service, personal disposal. Chiefly in *at the devotion of*, entirely devoted to (a person). M16–M19. **†7** An end to which someone or something is devoted; a purpose, an intent. L16–M17.

1 LD MACAULAY The austere devotion which . . gave to his court the aspect of a monastery. 2 JOYCE She believed steadily in the Sacred Heart as the most generally useful of all Catholic devotions. G. SANTAYANA Modest and scattered worshippers . . intent each on his own devotions. 3a R. L. STEVENSON Perpetual devotion to what a man calls his business, is only to be sustained by perpetual neglect of many other things. H. ACTON Her family loyalty was too intense to be hidden, and strong political dissent could not weaken her devotion. b J. W. KRUTCH The devotion of every foot of ground to immediately productive purposes. 4 W. J. LOFTIE The inscription records the devotion of some town or place to a divinity.

devotionary *a.* (now *rare*) = DEVOTIONAL M17. **devotionist** *n.* (now *rare*) a person who professes or practises devotion M17.

devotional /dɪˈvəʊʃ(ə)n(ə)l/ *a.* M17. [f. prec. + -AL[1].] Pertaining to, of the nature of, or characterized by (esp. religious) devotion.

devotionalism *n.* devotional behaviour or belief M19. **devotionalist** *n.* a person given to devotion M18. **devotionally** *adv.* M17.

†devoto *n.* Pl. **-o(e)s**. Fem. **-ta**. L16–E18. [It. & Sp. f. L *devotus*: see DEVOUT.] A devotee.

devour /dɪˈvaʊə/ *v.t.* ME. [OFr. *devour-* tonic stem of *devorer* f. L *devorare*, f. *de-* DE- 1 + *vorare* swallow.] **1** Swallow or eat up greedily or voraciously, eat like a beast. ME. **2** Of an inanimate agency or, formerly, a person: consume destructively; waste, destroy; engulf. ME. **3** Absorb the attention of, engross. Usu. in *pass.* E16. **4** Take in greedily the sense or appearance of; study or look at avidly. L16. **5** Traverse (a distance, road, etc.) rapidly. L16.

1 J. G. FARRELL There was no sign of the dead mouse. Presumably it had been devoured by the cats. K. CROSSLEY-HOLLAND Thor felt hungry. He devoured an entire ox, and . . eight salmon. 2 G. CRABBE The ocean roar Whose greedy waves devour the lessening shore. W. STUBBS Whom the sword spared famine and pestilence devoured. R. H. MORRIESON We heard the . . crackle of flame devouring the ancient timber. M. SARTON A day of small agitations . . that devoured my peace. 3 L. M. MONTGOMERY Anne was devoured by secret regret. 4 C. MCKAY The . . bold-eyed boys . . Devoured her shape with eager, passionate gaze. I. MURDOCH He . . had been devouring books of every kind in an insatiable hunger for knowledge. 5 SHAKES. *2 Hen. IV* He seem'd in running to devour the way, Staying no longer question. P. CAREY The Cadillac devoured the miles.

devourable *a.* E17. **devourer** *n.* LME. **devouringly** *adv.* voraciously, so as to devour M16. **devourment** *n.* the action of devouring E19.

devout /dɪˈvaʊt/ *a.* & *n.* ME. [(O)Fr. *dévot* f. L *devotus* pa. pple of *devovere* DEVOTE *v.* See also DEVOTE *a.* & *n.* and cf. DÉVOT, DEVOTO.] **A** *adj.* **1** Devoted to divine worship or service, earnestly religious, pious; showing religious devotion, reverential. ME. **2** Deeply respectful; devoted, dedicated, (*to*). Formerly also, eager *to*. *arch.* LME. **3** *gen.* Earnest, sincere, hearty, genuine. (Earlier as DEVOUTLY 3.) E19.

1 M. SPARK The devout Moslems . . who surge in their thousands to Mecca. I. MURDOCH He . . formed a strong attachment to Saint Brigid . . and went on devout pilgrimages upon her tracks. 2 HUGH WALPOLE Young, handsome, . . and the most devout of lovers. 3 L. M. MONTGOMERY 'Thanks be to goodness . . ,' breathed Marilla in devout relief.

†B *n.* A devotee. E17–E18.

devoutness *n.* LME.

devoutly /dɪˈvaʊtli/ *adv.* ME. [f. prec. + -LY[2].] **1** With religious devotion, piously, reverentially. ME. **†2** Intently, carefully. LME–L15. **3** *gen.* Earnestly, sincerely, heartily, genuinely. E17.

†devove *v.t.* M16–E19. [L *devovere*: see DEVOTE *v.*] Devote.

dew /ˈdjuː/ *n.* [OE *dēaw* = OFris *dāw*, OS *dau* (Du. *dauw*) OHG *tou* (G *Tau*), ON *dǫgg* (genit. *dǫggvar*), f. Gmc.] **1** The moisture deposited in minute drops on any cool surface by the condensation of atmospheric vapour between evening and morning. OE. **2** *fig.* Something likened to dew as coming with refreshing power or with gentleness, or as characteristic of the morning. ME. **3** Moisture, a liquid, esp. when formed in minute drops or glistening; *esp.* (*a*) tears; (*b*) sweat. ME. **4** An exudation or surface deposit on a plant etc. (Earlier in MILDEW.) Now *rare* exc. in HONEYDEW, MILDEW. M16.

1 WORDSWORTH The dew was falling fast, the stars began to blink. LYTTON Arch and blooming faces bowed down to bathe in the May dew. M. SHADBOLT The paddocks glittered with dew under the cool early sun. 2 SHELLEY Sleep, that healing dew of heaven. LONGFELLOW Having the dew of his youth, and the beauty thereof. 3 SOUTHEY The dews of death Stood on his livid cheek. SIR W. SCOTT Those poor eyes that stream'd with dew. *mountain dew*: see MOUNTAIN.

Comb.: **†dew-beater** (*a*) an early pioneer; (*b*) in *pl.* (*slang*), feet; **dewberry** (*a*) (the fruit of) a trailing European bramble, *Rubus caesius*, the berries of which are covered with a bluish bloom; any of several low-growing N. American brambles, esp. *Rubus flagellaris*; (*b*) *obs.* exc. *dial.* a gooseberry; **dewbow** an arch resembling a rainbow, occurring on a dew-covered surface; **dew-cup** *Sc.* the plant lady's mantle; **dewdrop** a drop of dew; something resembling a drop of dew; **dewdropped** *a.* covered or glistening with dew; **dewfall** the deposition of dew; the time when this begins; **dew point** *Meteorol.* the atmospheric temperature (dependent on pressure and humidity) below which dew is deposited, i.e., at which the pressure of atmospheric water vapour becomes equal to saturation vapour pressure; **dew-pond** a shallow (usu. artificial) pond (maintained largely by precipitation) situated on downs where there is no adequate groundwater supply; **dew-rake** a rake for removing grass or stubble; **dew-ret** *v.t.* ret or macerate (flax, hemp, etc.) by prolonged exposure to atmospheric moisture instead of by steeping in water (opp. *water-ret*); **dew-snail** (now *dial.*) a slug; **dew-worm** †(*a*) ringworm; (*b*) an earthworm.

dewless *a.* E17.

dew /djuː/ *v.* ME. [Corresp. to OHG *touwōn* (G *tauen*), ON *dǫggva*, f. Gmc, f. base of prec. Prob. already in OE.] **†1** *v.i.* Give or produce dew; *impers.* in *it dews, it is dewing*, etc., dew falls, dew is falling, etc. ME–E18. **2** *v.t.* Wet with or as with dew; moisten; steep. ME.

2 SIR W. SCOTT Fairy strains of music fall, Every sense in slumber dewing. J. G. COZZENS Heat and whisky had dewed his face with sweat.

Dewali *n.* var. of DIWALI.

dewan /dɪˈwɑːn/ *n.* Also **di-**. L17. [Urdu f. Pers. *dīwān* DIVAN, in sense 'fiscal register'. Cf. DOUANE.] *Hist.* A chief treasury official, finance minister, or prime minister in some Indian States.

dewani /dɪˈwɑːni/ *n.* Also **di-**. L18. [Urdu f. Pers. *dīwānī* f. *dīwān*: see prec.] *Hist.* The function or office of dewan; the right of revenue collection in some Indian States.

Dewar /ˈdjuːə/ *n.* L19. [Sir James *Dewar* (1842–1923), Brit. physicist & chemist.] **1** (Also **d-**.) In full *Dewar vessel, flask*, etc. A double-walled flask with an evacuated interspace for preventing the transfer of heat into or from the inner container. L19. **2** *Chem.* Used *attrib.* of structures for the benzene molecule which were postulated by Dewar and are of higher energy and lower symmetry than the Kekulé structure. E20.

dewater /diːˈwɔːtə/ *v.t.* E20. [f. DE- 3 + WATER *n.*] Remove water from.

dew-claw /ˈdjuːklɔː/ *n.* L16. [App. f. DEW *n.* + CLAW *n.*[1]] **1** The rudimentary inner toe or hallux sometimes present in dogs. L16. **2** Either of the side toes forming the false hoof of even-toed ungulates, e.g. deer. L16.

dew-clawed *a.* having dew-claws L16.

Dewey /ˈdjuːɪ/ *n.* L19. [f. Melvil *Dewey* (1851–1931), US librarian.] Used *attrib.* to designate a library classification using three-figure numbers from 000 to 999 to cover the major branches of knowledge, any further subdivisions being made by adding figures after the decimal point.

De-Witt /dəˈwɪt/ *v.t.* Long *obs.* exc. *Hist.* L17. [f. John and Cornelius *De Witt*, Du. statesmen murdered by a mob in 1672.] Lynch.

dewlap /ˈdjuːlap/ *n.* ME. [f. DEW *n.* + LAP *n.*[1], perh. after ON (ODa. *doglæp*).] The fold of loose skin hanging from the neck of cattle; *transf.* a similar feature of another animal, bird, or man.

dewlapped *a.* having a dewlap LME.

deworm /diːˈwəːm/ *v.t.* M20. [f. DE- 3 + WORM *n.*] Rid (an animal etc.) of worms.

†dewtry *n.* L16–E18. [f. cognates of Hind. *dhatūrā* DATURA, as Marathi *dhutrā*, *dhotrā*.] Any of several Indian plants of the genus *Datura* (family Solanaceae), esp. the thorn-apple, *D. stramonium*; a stupefying drug or drink prepared from such a plant.

dewy /ˈdjuːɪ/ *a.* OE. [f. DEW *n.* + -Y[1].] **1** Characterized by the presence of dew; covered or wet with dew. OE. **b** Affected by the presence of dew. Chiefly *poet.* E18. **c** Consisting of dew. *poet.* E19. **2** Of the nature or quality of dew, moist; resembling dew; *poet.* suggestive of dew in gentleness, refreshing power, etc. OE. **b**

Moistened as with dew. L16. **c** Innocently trusting, naively sentimental. M20.

1 MILTON From Noon to dewy Eve. b SOUTHEY O'er the landscape spread The dewy light. c T. HOOD The buds were hung with dewy beads. 2 SHAKES. *Rich. III* These dewy tears. W. COWPER Awaking from thy dewy slumbers. c *Times* The dewy ingenue from *Stage Struck*.

Comb.: **dewy-eyed** *a.* (*a*) with moist eyes, affected to tears; (*b*) = sense 2c above.

dewily *adv.* after the manner of dew E19. **dewiness** *n.* E17.

dexamethasone /dɛksəˈmɛθəsəʊn, -zəʊn/ *n.* M20. [f. *dexa-* (blend of HEXA- and DECA-) + METHYL + *-a-* + CORTISONE.] *Pharm.* A synthetic corticosteroid, $C_{22}H_{29}FO_5$, which is used esp. as an anti-inflammatory agent.

dexamphetamine /dɛksamˈfɛtəmiːn, -ɪn/ *n.* M20. [f. DEXTRO- + AMPHETAMINE.] *Pharm.* The pharmacologically more active dextrorotatory isomer of amphetamine.

Dexedrine /ˈdɛksədriːn, -ɪn/ *n.* Also **d-**. M20. [Prob. f. DEXTRO- after *Benzedrine*.] (Proprietary name for) dexamphetamine sulphate; a tablet of this.

dexie *n.* var. of DEXY.

Dexter /ˈdɛkstə/ *n.* Also **d-**. L19. [Said to be f. a Mr *Dexter*, credited with establishing the breed.] In full *Dexter Kerry*. (An animal of) a small hardy breed of Irish cattle originating from the Kerry breed.

dexter /ˈdɛkstə/ *a.* M16. [L, f. base repr. also by Gk *dexios*.] **1** Of or on the right-hand side of a person or thing, esp. (*Her.*, opp. *sinister*) of a shield etc., (i.e. to an observer's left). M16. †**b** Of an omen: seen or heard on the right-hand side, hence auspicious. M17–E18. †**2** Dexterous. E–M17.

†**dexterious** *a.* L16–M17. [f. L DEXTER + -IOUS.] = DEXTEROUS.

†**dexteriously** *adv.* E–M17.

dexterity /dɛkˈstɛrɪti/ *n.* E16. [Fr. *dextérité* f. L *dexteritas*, f. as DEXTER *a.*: see -ITY.] **1** Mental adroitness or skill, cleverness. E16. **2** Manual or manipulative skill or adroitness; good physical coordination. M16. **3** A skilful, adroit, or clever act. Usu. in *pl.* L16. **4** Right-handedness, the using of the right hand. *rare.* L19.

1 A. POWELL Stringham's dexterity at imitating the manner. Q. BELL Not the slightest dexterity in the use of language. 2 R. L. STEVENSON Under the left shoulder he carried a crutch, which he managed with wonderful dexterity. M. BARING A famous pianist played some elaborate fantasies which showed off the dexterity of his fingers. A. CARTER The manual dexterity of an assembler of precision instruments. 3 C. BURT A consistent tendency . . to undertake new dexterities with the left hand.

dexterous /ˈdɛkst(ə)rəs/ *a.* Also **dextrous** /ˈdɛkstrəs/. E17. [f. L DEXTER + -OUS. Cf. earlier DEXTERIOUS.] **I** Of a person. **1** Having mental adroitness or skill, clever; contriving. E17. **2** Having manual or manipulative skill or adroitness, deft of hand; having good physical coordination. M17. **3** = DEXTRAL *a.* 3. L19.

1 SOUTHEY She was devout in religion, . . dextrous in business. 2 A. WILSON Marie-Hélène, so dexterous with her needle as a rule, pricked her finger.

II Of a thing or action. **4** Done with or characterized by dexterity. E17.

4 W. H. AUDEN His dextrous handling of a wrap.

dexterously *adv.* E17. **dexterousness** *n.* E17.

dextral /ˈdɛkstr(ə)l/ *a.* & *n.* M17. [med.L. *dextralis* f. L *dextra* right hand: see -AL[1].] **A** *adj.* **1** Situated on the right-hand side; of or pertaining to the right hand or the right-hand side. M17. **2** *Conchol.* Of a spiral shell: having the whorls ascending from left to right (of the observer). M19. **3** Of a person: (predominantly) right-handed. E20. **4** *Geol.* Of, pertaining to, or designating a strike-slip fault in which the motion of the block on the further side of the fault from an observer is towards the left. M20. **B** *n.* A (predominantly) right-handed person. E20.

¶Opp. SINISTRAL.

dextrality /dɛkˈstralɪti/ *n.* right-handedness, use by preference of the right hand M17. **dextrally** *adv.* in a dextral manner or direction, to the right L19.

dextran /ˈdɛkstran/ *n.* L19. [f. DEXTRO- + -AN.] **1** *Chem.* A carbohydrate gum produced by the fermentation of some sugars and other organic materials. L19. **2** *Med.* A solution containing degraded, partially hydrolysed dextran, used as a substitute for blood plasma. M20.

dextrin /ˈdɛkstrɪn/ *n.* M19. [f. DEXTRO- + -IN[1].] A carbohydrate gum formed by enzymic or other hydrolysis of starch and used as an adhesive, thickening agent, etc.

dextro- /ˈdɛkstrəʊ/ *comb. form.* [f. L *dexter*, *dextra* right + -O-.] Turning or turned to the right; *Chem.* dextrorotatory. Opp. LAEVO-.

dextroˈcardia *n.* a congenital abnormality in which the disposition of the heart is reversed so that it occupies a mirror image of its normal position L19. **dextrotartaric** *a.*: *dextrotartaric acid*, the dextrorotatory (and predominant naturally-occurring) form of tartaric acid L19. **dextroˈtartrate** *n.* a dextrorotatory tartrate M19.

dextrorotatory /dɛkstrəʊˈrəʊtət(ə)ri/ *a.* L19. [f. prec. + ROTATORY.] *Chem.* Having or relating to the property (possessed by some compounds) of rotating the plane of polarized light to the right, i.e. clockwise when viewed in the opposite direction to that of propagation. Opp. LAEVOROTATORY.

dextroroˈtation *n.* (the property of) rotating the plane of polarized light in this direction L19.

dextrorse /ˈdɛkstrɔːs/ *a.* M19. [L *dextrorsum*, *dextrorsus*.] Turned or spiralling upwards towards the right; dextral.

Also **dexˈtrorsal** *a.* E19.

dextrose /ˈdɛkstrəʊz, -s/ *n.* M19. [f. as DEXTRO- + -OSE[2].] *Chem.* The dextrorotatory (and predominant naturally-occurring) form of glucose. Cf. LAEVULOSE.

dextrous *a.* var. of DEXTEROUS.

dexy /ˈdɛksi/ *n. slang.* Also **dexie**. M20. [Abbrev.] (A tablet of) Dexedrine.

dey /deɪ/ *n.*[1] *obs.* exc. *dial.* [OE *dǣġe* = ON *deigja* female servant, f. base meaning 'kneader'. Cf. DAIRY, LADY *n.*] A woman or (occas.) a man in charge of a dairy. Formerly also *gen.*, a female servant.

Comb.: **dey-house** a dairy; **dey-woman** a dairymaid, a woman in charge of a dairy.

dey /deɪ/ *n.*[2] Also (esp. in titles) **D-**. M17. [Fr. f. Turk. *dayı* maternal uncle, used also as a courtesy title.] *Hist.* (The title of) any of the supreme rulers of Algiers, 1710–1830, orig. the commanding officers of the janizaries of Algiers under the Ottoman Empire. Also, (the title of) the local ruler of Tunis or Tripoli under nominal Ottoman suzerainty.

deyship *n.* the position or dignity of a dey E18.

dezincification /diːˌzɪŋkɪfɪˈkeɪʃ(ə)n/ *n.* L19. [f. DE- 3 + ZINC *n.* + -FICATION.] *Metall.* Removal or loss of zinc from an alloy.

deˈzincify *v.t.* L19.

dghaisa /ˈdʌɪsə/ *n.* Also **-ajsa**. L19. [Maltese.] A boat resembling a gondola, used in Malta.

dha /dɑː/ *n.* Also **dhar**. E19. [Burm.] A Myanmar (Burmese) unit of length, between 3.5 and 4 m (approx. 10 ft 8 inches and 12 ft 2 inches).

dhak /dɑːk/ *n.* E19. [Hind. *dhāk*, *ḍhāk*.] A leguminous tree of eastern India and Myanmar (Burma), *Butea monosperma*, with showy orange or red flowers. Also *dhak tree*.

dhal /dɑːl/ *n.* Also **dal**. L17. [Hind. *dāl*.] Split pulses (esp. the seed of the pigeon-pea, *Cajanus cajan*), a common foodstuff in the Indian subcontinent.

dhaman /ˈdɑːmən/ *n.* Also **-min**. L19. [Hind. *dhāman*, *dhāmin*.] **1** An Indian rat-snake, *Ptyas mucosus*. L19. **2** (The tough elastic wood of) an Indian tree of the genus *Grewia* (family Tiliaceae), esp. *G. tiliifolia*. L19.

dhamma /ˈdɑːmə, ˈdʌmə/ *n.* E20. [Pali f. as DHARMA.] Esp. among Theravada Buddhists, = DHARMA.

dhan /dɑːn/ *n.* E19. [Hind. *dhān* rice plant, unhusked rice f. Skt *dhānya*.] In the Indian subcontinent: rice in the husk.

dhand /dand/ *n.* M19. [Sindhi.] A lake or swamp in the province of Sind in Pakistan.

dhania /ˈdanɪə/ *n.* E20. [Hindi *dhaniyā*.] In Indian cookery: coriander.

dhar *n.* var. of DHA *n.*

dharma /ˈdɑːmə, ˈdəːmə/ *n.* L18. [Skt = something established, decree, custom. Cf. DHAMMA.] In *Hinduism*: social or caste custom, right behaviour, law; justice, virtue; natural or essential state or function, nature. In *Buddhism*: universal truth or law, esp. as proclaimed by Buddha.

Comb.: **dharmashastra** a Hindu lawbook; **dharmasutra** an early Vedic collection of rules of life for priests.

dharmsala /ˈdɑːmsɑːlə, ˈdəːmʃɑːlɑː/ *n.* Also ***dharma-*** /ˈdɑːmə-, ˈdəːmə-/. E19. [Repr. Hind. pronunc. of Skt *dharmaśālā*, f. *dharma* (see prec.) + *śālā* house.] In the Indian subcontinent: a building devoted to religious or charitable purposes, *esp.* a rest-house for travellers.

dharna /ˈdəːnə, -ɑː/ *n.* Also **dhurna**. L18. [Hind. *dharnā* placing, act of sitting in restraint.] In the Indian subcontinent: a mode of compelling payment or compliance, by sitting at the debtor's or offender's door without eating until the demand is complied with. Chiefly in *sit (in) dharna*.

dhobey *n.* var. of DOBEY.

dhobi /ˈdəʊbi/ *n.* Also **-by**, **-bie**. M19. [Hind. *dhobī*, f. *dhob* washing.] A washerman or washerwoman in the Indian subcontinent.

Comb.: **dhobi itch** *colloq.* ringworm infestation of the groin or armpit, or contagious dermatitis, in tropical climates.

dhol /dəʊl/ *n.* M19. [Hind. pronunc. of Skt *dhola*.] A large barrel-shaped or cylindrical drum, usu. with two heads, used in the Indian subcontinent.

dholak /ˈdəʊlək/ *n.* Also **-uk**. M19. [Hind. *ḍholak*, f. as prec. + dim. suff. *-ak*.] A medium-sized barrel-shaped or cylindrical drum, usu. with two heads, used in the Indian subcontinent.

dhole /dəʊl/ *n.* Pl. **-s**, same E19. [Origin unkn.] The Asiatic wild dog, *Cuon alpinus*, native to the Indian subcontinent, China, and SE Asia.

dholuk *n.* var. of DHOLAK.

dhoney /ˈdəʊni/ *n.* Also **doney**. L16. [Telugu *doni*; cf. Pers. *dōnī* a yacht, and TONI.] A small sailing vessel of southern India.

dhoon *n.* var. of DUN *n.*[4]

dhoti /ˈdəʊti/ *n.* Also **dhootie** /ˈduːti/. E17. [Hind. *dhotī*.] A cloth worn by male Hindus, the ends being passed through the legs and tucked in at the waist.

dhow /daʊ/ *n.* Also **dow**. L18. [Arab. *dāwa*, prob. rel. to Marathi *dāw*.] A lateen-rigged sailing vessel of the Arabian Sea, with one or two masts. Formerly also *loosely*, an Arab slaver or other vessel.

dhrupad /ˈdruːpəd/ *n.* L19. [Skt *dhrupada* kind of dance.] A classical form of northern Indian vocal music, usu. sung in a slow tempo, consisting of a prelude and four sections developing various parts of the raga.

dhurna *n.* var. of DHARNA.

dhurra *n.* var. of DURRA.

dhurrie /ˈdʌri/ *n.* Also **dhurry**, **du-**. L19. [Hind. *darī*.] A large piece of heavy cotton cloth used, orig. in the Indian subcontinent, as a carpet and also as a sofa-cover, curtain, etc.

dhu stone /ˈdjuː stəʊn, ˈdʒuː/ *n. phr.* L19. [f. Welsh *du* black + STONE *n.*] A type of dolerite found in the Clee Hills, Shropshire.

dhyal /dʌɪˈɑːl/ *n.* M19. [Hind. *dahiyal*, *dahel*. Cf. earlier DIAL-BIRD.] In the Indian subcontinent, = MAGPIE-*robin*.

dhyana /dɪˈɑːnə/ *n.* M19. [Skt *dhyāna*.] *Hinduism & Buddhism.* Profound meditation; the penultimate stage of yoga.

di- /dɪ, dʌɪ/ *pref.*[1] (not productive). Repr. L *di-* the reduced form of *dis-* DIS- used bef. *b*, *d*, *g* (usually), *j* (sometimes), *l, m, n, r, s* + consonant, and *v*. In late L *di-* was sometimes changed back to the full form *dis-*: hence *dismiss, disrupt*.

di- /dʌɪ, dɪ/ *pref.*[2] [Gk, f. *dis* (adv.) twice.] Used (*a*) in wds of Gk origin or in Eng. formations modelled on them, w. the sense 'twice, doubly', as *dilemma, diphthong, dicotyledon*; (*b*) as a productive suff. used in chemical names to indicate the presence of two atoms of an element or two similar radicals, as *dioxide, dichromate*, sometimes replacing two atoms of hydrogen, as *dinitrobenzene*.

di- /dʌɪ/ *pref.*[3] The form of DIA-[1] used bef. a vowel or (sometimes) an aspirate.

dia- /dʌɪə/ *pref.*[1] See also DI-[3]. [Gk f. *dia* (prep.) through.] Used in wds of Gk origin, and in Eng. formations modelled on them, w. the senses 'through', as *diaphanous*, 'across', as *diameter*, 'transversely' as *diaheliotropic*, 'apart' as *diaeresis*.

dia- /dʌɪə/ *pref.*[2] [Repr. Gk *dia* (see DIA-[1]) in phrases such as *dia kōdeiōn, dia tessarōn*, treated in L as single wds (*diacodion, diatessaron*), sometimes with Latinized ending (*diachylum*).] Used in names, mostly *obs.*, of compound medicines, w. the sense 'made or consisting of'.

diabase /ˈdʌɪəbeɪs/ *n.* M19. [Fr., irreg. as if for *di-* (DI-[2]) + *base* 'rock with two bases'; later perh. assoc. w. Gk *diabasis* transition.] *Petrogr.* Orig. = DIORITE. Later (in the UK), an altered or (formerly) pre-Tertiary dolerite; (in the US) any dolerite.
diaˈbasic *a.* pertaining to or of the nature of diabase L19.

diabetes /dʌɪəˈbiːtiːz/ *n.* M16. [L f. Gk *diabētēs*, lit. 'siphon' (f. *diabainō* go through).] Either of two metabolic disorders marked by the production of excessive quantities of urine: (*a*) (more fully *diabetes mellitus* /mɪˈlʌɪtəs/ [L *mellitus* sweet]) one in which the pancreas secretes insufficient insulin and the body in consequence fails to metabolize glucose, leading to loss of energy and accumulation of glucose in the blood and urine; (*b*) *diabetes insipidus* /ɪnˈsɪpɪdəs/ [L *insipidus* INSIPID], a rare disorder of the pituitary gland caused by deficiency of vasopressin.
bronze(d) diabetes: see BRONZE *n.* & *a.*, *v.*
†**diabete** *n.* = DIABETES LME–M17. ˌ**diabetoˈgenic** *a.* producing or produced by diabetes (mellitus) E20.

diabetic /dʌɪəˈbɛtɪk/ *a.* & *n.* L18. [Fr. *diabétique*, f. *diabète* DIABETES + *-ique* -IC.] **A** *adj.* Of, pertaining to, or suffering from diabetes (mellitus); (of a food product) made with a low sugar content for the benefit of diabetics. L18. **B** *n.* A person affected with diabetes (mellitus). M19.
Also **diabetical** *a.* (long *rare*) E17.

diable /djɑːbl/ *int.* & *n.* L16. [Fr. f. eccl.L *diabolus* DEVIL *n.*] **A** *int.* Expr. impatience, amazement, dismay, etc. L16. **B** *n. le diable*, = DIABOLO. Now *rare* or *obs.* M19.

diable au corps /djɑːbl o kɔːr/ *n. phr.* Pl. ***diables au corps*** (pronounced same). L19. [Fr., lit. 'devil in the body'.] Restless energy; a spirit of devilry.

diablerie /dɪˈɑːbləri/ *n.* Also **-ery**. M18. [Fr., f. DIABLE: see -ERY.] **1** Dealings with the Devil; sorcery, witchcraft. M18. **b** *fig.* Mischievous fun, devilment. M19. **2** The mythology or lore of devils; a description or representation of devils. E19. **3** The realm of devils. M19.

diables au corps *n. phr.* pl. of DIABLE AU CORPS.

diablotin /dɪˈablə(ʊ)tɪn; *foreign* djɑblotɛ̃ (*pl. same*)/ *n.* E19. [Fr., dim. of DIABLE.] **1** A little devil, an imp. E19. **2** In Trinidad, the oil-bird, *Steatornis caripensis*. E19. **3** The black-capped petrel, *Pterodroma hasitata*, a rare bird which breeds in the mountains of several W. Indian islands. L19.

diabolic /dʌɪəˈbɒlɪk/ *a.* & *n.* LME. [(O)Fr. *diabolique* f.) eccl.L *diabolicus*, f. *diabolus* DEVIL *n.*: see -IC.] **A** *adj.* **1** Of, pertaining to, or deriving from the Devil or devils; of or pertaining to witchcraft. LME. **2** Having the qualities of the Devil or a devil; inhumanly cruel or wicked, fiendish. L15. **3** Resembling a devil in appearance. M19. †**B** *n.* An agent or follower of the Devil. E16–M17.

diabolical /dʌɪəˈbɒlɪk(ə)l/ *a.* & *n.* E16. [f. as prec. + -AL[1].] **A** *adj.* **1** = DIABOLIC *a.* 1. E16. **2** = DIABOLIC *a.* 2. M16. **b** (In weakened sense.) Outrageous, disgraceful; disgracefully bad or defective. *slang.* M20. **3** = DIABOLIC *a.* 3. M18.
1 HOBBES Hee was commonly thought a Magician, and his Art Diabolicall. **2** R. A. FREEMAN This crime was planned with the most diabolical cleverness. **b** *Listener* A parody piece . . which took diabolical liberties with Eurovision song contests. S. TOWNSEND Asked our postman about communications between Tunisia and England. He said they were 'diabolical'.
†**B** *n.* = DIABOLIC *n.* M16–E19.
diabolically *adv.* (*a*) fiendishly, very wickedly; (*b*) *slang* shockingly, excruciatingly; exceedingly: L16. **diabolicalness** *n.* E18.

diabolify /dʌɪəˈbɒlɪfʌɪ/ *v.t.* M17. [f. eccl.L *diabolus* or Gk *diabolos* DEVIL *n.* + -I- + -FY.] Make a devil of, represent as a devil.

diabolise *v.* var. of DIABOLIZE.

diabolism /dʌɪˈabəlɪz(ə)m/ *n.* E17. [f. eccl.L *diabolus* or Gk *diabolos* DEVIL *n.* + -ISM.] **1** Dealings with the Devil or evil spirits; witchcraft, sorcery. E17. **2** Belief in or worship of the Devil. M17. **3** Devilish or atrociously wicked conduct. L17. **4** The character or nature of a devil. M18.
diabolist *n.* a person who believes in or seeks to deal with the Devil L19.

diabolize /dʌɪˈabəlʌɪz/ *v.t.* Also **-ise**. E18. [f. as prec. + -IZE.] **1** Convert into a devil, render diabolical, represent as a devil. E18. **2** Subject to demonic influence. E19.
diaboliˈzation *n.* L19.

diabolo /dɪˈabələʊ, dʌɪ-/ *n.* Pl. **-os**. E20. [It. f. eccl.L *diabolus* DEVIL *n.*] A game in which a two-headed top is thrown up and caught on a string stretched between two sticks; the top used in this game.
¶Earlier called *le diable* (see DIABLE *n.*); also *the devil on two sticks*.

Diabolonian /dʌɪˌabəˈləʊnɪən/ *n.* Also **d-**. L17. [f. eccl.L *diabolus* DEVIL *n.* after *Babylonian* etc.] A member of the host of Diabolus (the Devil) in Bunyan's *Holy War*; a follower of the Devil.

diacatholicon /dʌɪəkəˈθɒlɪkən/ *n.* Long *rare*. LME. [OFr. & med.L, repr. Gk *dia katholikōn* made of general ingredients: see DIA-[2].] Orig., a kind of laxative electuary. Hence, a universal remedy.

diacaustic /dʌɪəˈkɔːstɪk/ *a.* & *n.* E18. [f. DIA-[1] + Gk *kaustikos* burning: see CAUSTIC.] *Physics.* **A** *adj.* Of a curve or surface: formed by the intersection of rays of light refracted from a curved surface. E18. **B** *n.* A diacaustic curve or surface. Cf. CATACAUSTIC. E18.

diacetate /dʌɪˈasɪteɪt/ *n.* E19. [f. DI-[2] + ACETATE.] *Chem.* A salt or ester containing two acetic acid radicals, $CH_3COO·$.

diacetic /dʌɪəˈsiːtɪk/ *a.* L19. [f. DI-[2] + ACETIC.] Chem. *diacetic acid*, = ACETOACETIC *acid.*

diacetylmorphine /dʌɪˌasɪtʌɪlˈmɔːfiːn/ *n.* L19. [f. DI-[2] + ACETYL + MORPHINE *n.*] *Chem.* An acetyl derivative of morphine, more commonly called heroin. Cf. DIAMORPHINE.

diachronic /dʌɪəˈkrɒnɪk/ *a.* M19. [f. DIA-[1] + Gk *khronos* time + -IC.] †**1** Lasting through existing time. *rare*. Only in M19. **2** Concerned with or pertaining to the historical development of a language, culture, etc. Opp. *synchronic*. E20.
diachronically *adv.* in a diachronic manner, with regard to historical development M20. **diachroˈnistic** *a.* = DIACHRONIC 2 M20. **diachroˈnistically** *adv.* = DIACHRONICALLY M20. **diˈachrony** *n.* the historical development of a language etc. M20.

diachronism /dʌɪˈakrənɪz(ə)m/ *n.* E20. [f. as prec. + -ISM.] *Geol.* The occurrence of a geological feature in different palaeontological zones; the property of being diachronous.

diachronous /dʌɪˈakrənəs/ *a.* E20. [f. as prec. + -OUS.] **1** *Geol.* Not of a uniform geological age throughout; exhibiting diachronism. E20. **2** = DIACHRONIC 2. M20.

diachylon /dʌɪˈakɪlɒn/ *n. obs.* exc. *Hist.* Also **-chylum** /-kɪləm/, **-culum** /-kjʊləm/. ME. [OFr. *diaculon, -chilon* f. late L *diachylon* f. L *diachylon* repr. Gk *dia khulōn* composed of juices: see DIA-[2], CHYLE.] Orig., an ointment or salve made of vegetable juices. Later, a plaster with a medication made by boiling together litharge (lead oxide), olive oil, and water.

diacid /dʌɪˈasɪd/ *a.* M19. [f. DI-[2] + ACID *n.*] *Chem.* Of a base etc.: (composed of molecules) able to combine with two monovalent acid radicals.

diaclinal /dʌɪəˈklʌɪn(ə)l/ *a.* L19. [f. DIA-[1] + Gk *klinein* to lean, slope + -AL[1].] *Geol.* Of a valley, river, etc.: crossing a fold; passing through an anticline or syncline.

†**diacodium** *n.* Also **-ion**. LME–E19. [med.L, repr. Gk *dia kōdeiōn* (a preparation) made from poppy-heads: see DIA-[2].] A syrup prepared from poppy-heads, used as an opiate.

diaconal /dʌɪˈakən(ə)l/ *a.* E17. [eccl.L *diaconalis*, f. *diaconus* DEACON *n.*: see -AL[1].] Of or pertaining to a deacon.

diaconate /dʌɪˈakəneɪt, -ət/ *n.* E18. [eccl.L *diaconatus*, f. *diaconus*: see prec., -ATE[1].] **1** The position or office of deacon. E18. **2** The period during which a person is a deacon. L19. **3** A body of deacons. L19.

diaconicon /dʌɪəˈkɒnɪkɒn/ *n.* Also in L form **-cum** /-kəm/. E18. [Gk *diakonikon* neut. adj., f. *diakonos* DEACON *n.*: see -IC.] *Chr. Ch.* The part of an Orthodox church south of the sanctuary where vestments and sacred vessels are kept.

diacoustics /dʌɪəˈkuːstɪks/ *n.pl.* (usu. treated as *sing.*). Now *rare* or *obs.* L17. [f. DI-[3] + ACOUSTICS.] The science of refracted sound. Cf. CATACOUSTICS.

diacritic /dʌɪəˈkrɪtɪk/ *a.* & *n.* L17. [Gk *diakritikos*, f. *diakrinein* distinguish, f. *krinein* separate: see DIA-[1].] **A** *adj.* Of a mark or sign: serving to distinguish different values or sounds of the same letter, as in é, è, ë, ē, etc. L17. **B** *n.* A diacritic mark. M19.

diacritical /dʌɪəˈkrɪtɪk(ə)l/ *n.* & *a.* L17. [f. as prec. + -AL[1].] †**A** *n.* = DIACRITIC *n.* Only in L17. **B** *adj.* **1** = DIACRITIC *a.* M18. **2** Having the ability to distinguish, discerning. M19.

diacritically /dʌɪəˈkrɪtɪk(ə)li/ *adv.* E19. [f. DIACRITIC *a.* or DIACRITICAL *a.*: see -ICALLY.] With diacritic marks.

diactinic /dʌɪakˈtɪnɪk/ *a.* M19. [f. DI-[3] + ACTINIC.] Transparent to actinic light.

diaculum *n.* see DIACHYLON.

diadelphous /dʌɪəˈdɛlfəs/ *a.* E19. [f. DI-[2] + Gk *adelphos* brother + -OUS.] *Bot.* Of stamens: united by the filaments so as to form two groups. Of a plant: having the stamens so united.

diadem /ˈdʌɪədɛm/ *n.* & *v.* ME. [(O)Fr. *diadème* f. L *diadema* f. Gk = regal headband of the Persian kings, f. *diadein* bind round.] **A** *n.* **1** Something worn on the head as a symbol of honour, esp. royalty; a crown. Now chiefly *poet.* & *rhet.* ME. **b** *spec.* A wreath of leaves or flowers worn round the head. M16. **c** *spec.* A headband, plain or jewelled, worn by or in imitation of oriental monarchs. L16. **2** Royal or imperial power, sovereignty. ME. **3** Something that confers dignity; a crowning glory. E16. **4** An adornment on the top of something. L18.
1 E. PERRONET Bring forth the royal diadem And crown him Lord of all. **3** J. NEAL The name of Yankee was a reproach here; it was a diadem there. **4** BYRON Mont Blanc is the monarch of mountains . . With a diadem of snow.
Comb.: **diadem monkey** = SAMANGO; **diadem spider** the garden spider, *Araneus diadematus*, which spins orb webs.
B *v.t.* Adorn (as) with a diadem. LME.
W. JONES Every stalk is diadem'd with flowers.
diademed monkey = SAMANGO.
diademated *a.* (now *rare* or *obs.*) wearing a diadem E18.

diadic *a.* & *n.* var. of DYADIC.

diaeresis /dʌɪˈɪərɪsɪs, -ˈɛr-/ *n.* Also ***dieresis**. Pl. **-eses** /-ɪsiːz/. L16. [L f. Gk *diairesis* n. of action f. *diairein* take apart, divide, f. as DIA-[1] +

hairein take.] 1 The division of one syllable into two, esp. by the resolution of a diphthong into two simple vowels. L16. 2 The sign ¨ placed over a vowel to indicate that it is pronounced separately, as in *Brontë*, *naïve*. E17. 3 *Pros.* A break in a line where the end of a foot coincides with the end of a word. M19.

diaeretic /dʌɪəˈrɛtɪk/ *a.* (now *rare*) of or pertaining to diaeresis M17.

diagenesis /dʌɪəˈdʒɛnɪsɪs/ *n.* L19. [f. DIA-[1] + -GENESIS.] *Geol.* The physical and chemical changes (other than metamorphism) undergone by a sediment after deposition; the recombination of the constituents of a mineral to form a new mineral.

diageˈnetic *a.* involving or of the nature of diagenesis; produced by diagenesis: L19. **diageˈnetically** *adv.* M20.

diageotropic /ˌdʌɪədʒiːəˈtrɒpɪk, -ˈtrəʊp-/ *a.* L19. [f. DIA-[1] + GEOTROPIC.] *Bot.* Pertaining to or characterized by a tendency to grow horizontally.

diageotropism *n.* L19.

diaglyphic /dʌɪəˈglɪfɪk/ *a. rare.* M19. [f. Gk *diagluphein* carve in intaglio + -IC.] Of the nature of an intaglio; engraved.

diagnose /ˈdʌɪəgnəʊz, -ˈnəʊz/ *v.* M19. [Back-form. f. next.] 1 *v.t.* & *i.* Make a diagnosis of, infer the presence of (a particular disease etc.) from symptoms. M19. 2 *v.t.* Ascertain the condition of (a person etc.) by diagnosis. E20.

diagˈnosable *a.* L19.

diagnosis /dʌɪəgˈnəʊsɪs/ *n.* Pl. **-noses** /-ˈnəʊsiːz/. L17. [mod.L *diagnosis* f. Gk, f. *diagignōskein* distinguish, discern, f. as DIA-[1] + *gignōskein* KNOW *v.*] 1 The process of determining the nature of a disease etc.; the identification of a disease from a patient's symptoms etc.; a formal statement of this. L17. b *transf.* & *fig.* (A conclusion from) analysis; the ascertainment of the cause of a mechanical fault etc. M19. 2 *Taxon.* The distinctive characterization of a species etc. M19.

1 *differential diagnosis*: see DIFFERENTIAL *a.* 2.

diagnostic /dʌɪəgˈnɒstɪk/ *a.* & *n.* E17. [Gk *diagnōstikos* able to distinguish, *hē diagnōstikē* (sc. *tekhnē*) the art of distinguishing diseases: see prec., -IC.] A *adj.* 1 Of or pertaining to diagnosis. E17. 2 Of use in diagnosis; characteristic, distinctive. M17. 3 *Computing.* Of a program or a routine within one: designed to identify program errors or system faults and to give information about them. M20.

2 D. ATTENBOROUGH The diagnostic character of having not one but two pairs of antennae.

B *n.* 1 A diagnosis. Now *rare* exc. in *pl.*, the art of diagnosis. E17. 2 A distinctive symptom or characteristic; a specific trait. M17. 3 *Computing.* An output that helps a user to identify an error or malfunction; a facility or routine for producing such an output. Usu. in *pl.* M20.

1 PLASMA *diagnostics.*

diagnostically *adv.* M17. **diagnosticate** *v.t.* diagnose M19. **diagnoˈstician** *n.* a person skilled in diagnosis; a person who makes a diagnosis: M19.

diagonal /dʌɪˈagən(ə)l/ *a.* & *n.* M16. [L *diagonalis* f. Gk *diagōnios* from angle to angle, f. as DIA-[1] + *gōnia* angle: see -AL[1]. Cf. (O)Fr. *diagonal.*] A *adj.* 1 (Of a line) joining two non-adjacent vertices of a figure or solid; extending between opposite corners or edges of something. M16. 2 Having an oblique direction; slanting. M16. 3 Marked with diagonal or oblique lines; having some part situated obliquely. L17.

2 J. ROSENBERG The diagonal shadow cast by the nose. 3 H. N. MOSELEY A wide patch of diagonal ornamentation upon the abdomen. **diagonal cloth** = DIAGONAL *n.* 3. **diagonal matrix** *Math.*: having non-zero elements only in the diagonal running from the upper left to the lower right.

B *n.* 1 A diagonal line. L16. 2 An oblique part of something. M19. 3 A twilled fabric with the ridges running diagonally. M19.

diagonalizable *a.* (*Math.*) able to be diagonalized M20. **diagonaliˈzation** *n.* (*Math.*) the process of diagonalizing M20. **diagonalize** *v.* (*a*) *v.i.* (*rare*) move obliquely; (*b*) *v.t.* (*Math.*) transform into a diagonal matrix: L19. **diagonally** *adv.* in a diagonal direction; obliquely, slantwise: LME.

diagram /ˈdʌɪəgram/ *n.* & *v.* E17. [L *diagramma* f. Gk, f. *diagraphein* mark out by lines, f. as DIA-[1] + *graphein* write: see -GRAM.] A *n.* 1 A sketch or figure showing the features of an object needed for exposition, rather than its actual appearance. E17. 2 A figure composed of lines serving to illustrate or prove a theorem etc. in geometry or logic. M17. 3 A figure (e.g. a graph or a histogram) representing a series of related numerical quantities. M19.

1 *floral diagram*: see FLORAL *a.* *tree diagram*: see TREE *n.* 5b. *vowel diagram*: see VOWEL *n.* 3 INDICATOR *diagram.*

B *v.t.* Infl. **-mm-**, ***-m-**. Represent by or in a diagram; *fig.* give an outline or summary of. Chiefly *US.* M19.

diagraˈmmatic *a.* M19. **diagraˈmmatically** *adv.* M19.

diagrammatize /dʌɪəˈgramətʌɪz/ *v.t.* Also **-ise**. L19. [f. Gk *diagrammat-* stem of *diagramma* DIAGRAM + -IZE.] Put into diagrammatic form; represent by a diagram.

diagraph /ˈdʌɪəgrɑːf/ *n.* E18. [Branch I f. Gk *diagraphē*, f. as DIA-[1], -GRAPH. Branch II f. Fr. *diagraphe*, f. stem of Gk *diagraphein* (see DIAGRAM).] I†1 A description. *rare.* Only in E18. 2 A diagram in logic. *rare.* M19. II 3 An instrument for mechanically drawing projections or making copies, consisting of a pen governed by cords and pulleys which in turn are controlled by a pointer. Now *rare.* M19. 4 A combined protractor and scale for plotting. L19.

diaˈgraphic *a.* (now *rare*) of or pertaining to drawing or graphic representation M17. †**diagraphical** *a.* = DIAGRAPHIC: only in E17.

diagrid /ˈdʌɪəgrɪd/ *n.* M20. [f. DIAGONAL *a.* + GRID *n.*] A supporting structure of diagonally intersecting ribs of metal, concrete, etc.

diagrydium /dʌɪəˈgrɪdɪəm/ *n.* LME. [Late L, alt. of Gk *dakrudion* a kind of scammony, dim. of *dakru* a tear.] A preparation of scammony, formerly used in pharmacy.

diaheliotropic /ˌdʌɪəhiːlɪəˈtrɒpɪk, -ˈtrəʊp-/ *a.* L19. [f. DIA-[1] + HELIOTROPIC.] *Bot.* Pertaining to or characterized by a tendency to grow transversely to incident light.

diaheliotropism *n.* L19.

diakinesis /dʌɪəkʌɪˈniːsɪs/ *n.* E20. [f. DIA-[1] + Gk *kinēsis* motion.] *Cytol.* The last stage of the prophase of the first meiotic division, just before the disappearance of the nuclear membrane.

dial /dʌɪ(ə)l/ *n.*[1] & *v.* ME. [med.L *diale* dial of a clock, use as n. of neut. of adj. implied by *dialiter* daily, f. L *dies* day: see -AL[1]. Cf. OFr. *dial* wheel in a clock that completes one turn daily.] A *n.* 1†a A mariner's compass. ME–M17. b A miner's compass for underground surveying. M17. 2 An instrument for telling the time of day by means of the shadow cast by a pointer on a graduated surface; *esp.* a sundial. LME. †3 A timepiece or chronometer of any kind; a clock, a watch. LME–L17. 4 The face of a clock or watch, marked to show the hours etc. LME. 5 A circular plate or face with numbered markings on it from which can be read a measurement etc. indicated by a pointer; any device in which a moving element shows the numerical value of something, *esp.* one on a radio showing the frequency to which it is tuned. M18. b A circular plate on a telephone with numbers etc. and a disc with finger-holes which is rotated for each digit of a number being called. L19. 6 A person's face. *slang.* E19. 7 A lapidary's instrument for holding a gem during cutting and polishing. L19.

2 *horizontal dial, nocturnal dial, vertical dial*, etc. *moon-dial*: see MOON *n.* *sundial*: see SUN *n.*[1] 5 M. LOWRY Hugh . . turned the radio dial back and forth, trying to get San Antonio. J. HAWKES Rows of knobs, dials with needles all set at zero.

B *v.* Infl. **-ll-**, ***-l-**. 1 *v.i.* & *t.* Survey using a miner's dial. M17. 2 *v.t.* Measure or indicate (as) with a dial. E19. 3 *v.i.* & *t.* Operate the dial (or the keys) of a telephone; do this for (a digit or series of digits); call (a number, a person, etc.) by this means to establish telephonic connection. E20.

2 *fig.*: P. J. BAILEY To teach us how to dial bliss. 3 G. GREENE I was just going to dial Inquiries. W. DE LA MARE Dial 999, and gain . . Safety from fire, police and ambulance. **dial-a-**: used to prefix a n. to form adjs. and ns. denoting something that can be provided or ordered by telephone. **dial up** operate a telephone dial or keypad; gain access to (a computer etc.) over a telephone line in this way; ring up.

Comb. (mainly f. the n.): **dial-plate** the face-plate of a dial; *esp.* that of a clock or watch, marked with the hours; **dial telephone**: operated by means of a dial; **dial tone** *N. Amer.* = DIALLING *tone*; **dial-up** *a.* pertaining to or designating a data transmission link that uses the public telephone system, access to it being gained by dialling.

dial /ˈdʌɪəl/ *n.*[2] E20. [f. *dial*lylbarbituric acid.] *Pharm.* A preparation of diallylbarbituric acid, used as a sedative.

dial-bird /ˈdʌɪəlbəːd/ *n.* M18. [f. Hind. *dahiyal*, *dahel* (see DHYAL) after DIAL *n.*[1]: see BIRD *n.*] In the Indian subcontinent, = MAGPIE-*robin*.

dialect /ˈdʌɪəlɛkt/ *n.* M16. [Fr. *dialecte* or L *dialectus*, f. Gk *dialektos* discourse, way of speaking, f. *dialegesthai* converse with, discourse, f. as DIA-[1] + *legein* speak.] †1 = DIALECTIC *n.* 1. M16–M18. 2 A manner of speaking, language, speech; *esp.* one peculiar to or characteristic of a particular person or class; idiom. L16. 3 A form of speech peculiar to a district; a variety of a language with non-standard vocabulary, pronunciation, or idioms; any language in relation to the language family to which it belongs. L16. 4 *Computing.* A particular version of a programming language. M20.

2 J. CLARKE The Lawyer's Dialect. J. FOSTER The theological dialect. G. ORWELL The political dialects to be found in pamphlets, leading articles, . . and the speeches of Under-Secretaries. 3 DAY LEWIS Hardly understanding a word he said because of his thick East-Anglian dialect. *eye-dialect*: see EYE *n.*

Comb.: **dialect geography** the study of local differences within a speech area.

diaˈlectal *a.* belonging to or of the nature of a dialect M19. **diaˈlectally** *adv.* M19.

dialectic /dʌɪəˈlɛktɪk/ *n.* LME. [(O)Fr. *dialectique* or its source L *dialectica* f. Gk *dialektikē* use as n. (sc. *tekhnē* art) of fem. of *dialektikos* pertaining to discourse, f. *dialektos*: see prec., -IC. Pl. after L *dialectica* treated as neut. pl.] I *sing.* or in *pl.* (treated as *sing.* or *pl.*). 1 The art of critically investigating the truth of opinions; logical disputation or argument. Formerly, logic as applied to rhetorical reasoning. LME. 2 The philosophy of metaphysical contradictions and their solutions, esp. in the thought of Kant and Hegel; the world process seen as a continuing unification of opposites; the existence or action of opposing forces or tendencies in society etc. L18.

2 *Listener* Dialectics is indeed the grammar of Marxist thinking.

II 3 A dialectic philosopher; a critical enquirer after truth; a logical disputant. M17.

dialectic /dʌɪəˈlɛktɪk/ *a.* M17. [L *dialecticus* f. Gk *dialektikos*: see prec. In branch II f. DIALECT + -IC.] I 1 Of, pertaining to, or of the nature of logical disputation. M17. 2 Fond of or practising logical disputation. M19. II 3 = DIALECTAL. Now *rare.* E19.

dialecticism /-sɪz(ə)m/ *n.* (*a*) *rare* the tendency or influence of dialects; (*b*) dialectic philosophy or practice: L19.

dialectical /dʌɪəˈlɛktɪk(ə)l/ *n.* & *a.* E16. [f. as prec. + -ICAL.] †A *n.* = DIALECTIC *n.* 1. Only in E16.

B *adj.* I 1 = DIALECTIC *a.* 1. M16. 2 Of or pertaining to dialectic as a philosophy. L18.

1 J. C. RANSOM His understanding is intuitive rather than dialectical. 2 **dialectical materialism** the Marxist theory of political and historical events as due to the conflict of social forces caused by man's material needs and interpretable as a series of contradictions and their solutions.

II 3 = DIALECTAL. M18.

dialectically *adv.* (*a*) by means of dialectic, logically; (*b*) as regards dialect, dialectally: L16.

dialectician /dʌɪəlɛkˈtɪʃ(ə)n/ *n.* M16. [Fr. *dialecticien*, f. as DIALECTIC *a.*: see -ICIAN.] 1 A person skilled in disputation; a logician. M16. 2 A student of dialects. M19.

dialectology /dʌɪəlɛk'tɒlədʒi/ *n.* L19. [f. DIALECT + -OLOGY.] The branch of linguistics that deals with dialects.
ˌ**dialecto'logical** *a.* L19. **dialectologist** *n.* L19.

dialer *n.* see DIALLER.

dialing *vbl n.* see DIALLING.

dialist /'dʌɪəlɪst/ *n.* Also **-ll-**. M17. [f. DIAL *n.*[1] + -IST.] A maker of dials; a person who uses a dial.

diallage /*in sense 1* dʌɪ'alədʒi -dʒi, *in sense 2* 'dʌɪəlɪdʒ/ *n.* E18. [Gk *diallagē* interchange, f. *diallassein* to interchange, f. as DIA-[1] + *allassein* to change, f. *allos* other.] **1** A rhetorical figure by means of which arguments, after being considered from various points of view, are all brought to bear upon one point. E18. **2** *Min.* A green, brown, or grey monoclinic pyroxene (usu. a variety of augite or diopside) with a metallic lustre and occurring in lamellar or foliated masses. E19.

dialler /'dʌɪələ/ *n.* Also ***dialer**. M18. [f. DIAL *n.*[1] & *v.* + -ER[1].] **1** A person who surveys mines etc. by using a dial. M18. **2** A device for dialling telephone numbers automatically. M20.

dialling /'dʌɪəlɪŋ/ *vbl n.* Also ***dialing**. L16. [f. DIAL *n.*[1] & *v.* + -ING[1].] **1** The art of constructing dials. L16. **2** The use of a compass in underground surveying. L17. **3** The action of using the dial (or keys) of a telephone. M20.
3 *direct dialling*: see DIRECT *a.*
Comb.: **dialling code** the sequence of numbers dialled to connect a telephone to the exchange of the telephone being called; **dialling tone**: produced by a telephone when a caller may start to dial.

diallist *n.* var. of DIALIST.

diallyl /dʌɪ'alʌɪl, -lɪl/ *a.* & *n.* M19. [f. DI-[2] + ALLYL.] *Chem.* **A** *adj.* (Composed of molecules) containing two allyl groups. M19. **B** *n.* A liquid diallyl compound, $(CH_2CHCH_2\cdot)_2$; hexa-1,5-diene. L19.

dialog *n.* & *v.* see DIALOGUE.

dialogical /dʌɪə'lɒdʒɪk(ə)l/ *a.* E17. [Late L *dialogicos* f. Gk *dialogikos*, f. *dialogos*: see DIALOGUE, -ICAL.] Of, pertaining to, or of the nature of dialogue.
dialogic *a.* = DIALOGICAL M19. **dialogically** *adv.* M18. **dialo'gician** *n.* = DIALOGIST 1 M20.

dialogise *v.* var. of DIALOGIZE.

dialogism /dʌɪ'alədʒɪz(ə)m/ *n.* M16. [Late L *dialogismos* f. Gk, f. *dialogizesthai* DIALOGIZE: see -ISM.] **1** *Rhet.* The discussion of a subject under the form of a dialogue. M16. **2** A conversational phrase or speech; a spoken or written dialogue. E17.

dialogist /dʌɪ'alədʒɪst/ *n.* M17. [Late L *dialogista* f. Gk *dialogistēs*, f. *dialogos*: see DIALOGUE, -IST.] **1** A writer of dialogue(s). M17. **2** A participant in a dialogue. L17.
dialo'gistic *a.* having the nature or form of dialogue; taking part in a dialogue, argumentative: L17. **dialo'gistical** *a.* (*rare*) dialogistic E18. **dialo'gistically** *adv.* M17.

dialogize /dʌɪ'alədʒʌɪz/ *v.i.* Also **-ise**. E17. [Gk *dialogizesthai* converse, debate, f. *dialogos*: see next, -IZE. Cf. earlier DIALOGUIZE.] Converse, carry on a dialogue (*with*).

dialogue /'dʌɪəlɒg/ *n.* & *v.* ME. [OFr. *dialoge* (mod. *dialogue*) f. L *dialogus* f. Gk *dialogos* conversation, discourse, f. *dialegesthai*: see DIALECT.] **A** *n.* Also ***-log**. **1** A literary work in conversational form; this kind of composition; the conversational part of a novel etc. ME. **2** A conversation between two or more people; verbal interchange of thought, discussion. LME. **3** Discussion or diplomatic contact between representatives of two nations or blocs; the exchange of proposals, valuable or constructive communication between different groups. M20.
1 M. H. ABRAMS The philosopher in the Platonic dialogues . . operates with three categories. A. ROAD A script writer has to tell his story through dialogue. 2 J. FRAME He . . conducted a dialogue with his reason. 3 H. KISSINGER In the nuclear age we cannot be without dialogue with Moscow.
Phrases: **dialogue of the deaf** a discussion in which the parties are unresponsive to what the others say.
B *v.* **1** *v.t.* Express in the form of a dialogue; provide (a story etc.) with dialogue. L16. **2** *v.i.* Take part in a dialogue (*with*). E17.
dialoguer *n.* = DIALOGIST L19. **dialoguist** *n.* = DIALOGIST 1 M18. **dialoguize** *v.i.* (long *rare*) = DIALOGIZE L16.

dialysate /dʌɪ'alɪzeɪt/ *n.* Also ***-lyz-**. L19. [f. DIALYSIS, DIALYSE + -ATE[2].] The part of a mixture which passes through the membrane in dialysis; the solution so obtained. Formerly, the part that does not pass through the membrane.

dialyse /'dʌɪəlʌɪz/ *v.* Also ***-lyze**. M19. [f. DIALYSIS after *analyse*.] **1** *v.t.* Subject to dialysis; obtain by means of dialysis. M19. **2** *v.i.* Pass through a membrane in dialysis. E20.
dialysable *a.* able to dialyse or to be separated by dialysis L19. **dialyser** *n.* an apparatus for carrying out dialysis, *esp.* an artificial kidney M19.

dialysis /dʌɪ'alɪsɪs/ *n.* Pl. **-lyses** /-lɪsiːz/. M16. [L f. Gk *dialusis*, f. *dialuein* part asunder, f. as DIA-[1] + *luein* set free.] †**1** *Rhet.* A statement of disjunctive propositions. M–L16. †**2** = DIAERESIS 1, 2. E18–E19. **3** A process in which solutes are selectively removed from a solution as a result of their different abilities to pass through a semipermeable membrane; the use of such a process to purify the blood, e.g. of a person without adequately functioning kidneys; an occasion of undergoing this. M19.
3 *renal dialysis*: see RENAL *a.*
dia'lytic *a.* M19.

dialyzate *n.* see DIALYSATE.

dialyze *v.* see DIALYSE.

diamagnet /dʌɪə'magnɪt/ *n.* M19. [Back-f. from next.] = DIAMAGNETIC *n.*

diamagnetic /dʌɪəmag'nɛtɪk/ *n.* & *a.* M19. [f. DIA-[1] + MAGNETIC.] **A** *n.* A body or substance that exhibits diamagnetism. M19. **B** *adj.* **1** Of a substance or object: having a small negative magnetic susceptibility; magnetizing in a direction opposite to that of an applied magnetic field and repelled by a magnetic. M19. **2** Of or pertaining to diamagnetism or diamagnetic substances. M19.
diamagnetically *adv.* in a diamagnetic manner; as regards diamagnetism: M19.

diamagnetism /dʌɪə'magnɪtɪz(ə)m/ *n.* M19. [f. DIA-[1] + MAGNETISM, after prec.] Diamagnetic phenomena; the property of being diamagnetic.

diamanté /dɪə'mɒnteɪ; *foreign* djamɑ̃te (*pl. of n. same*)/ *a.* & *n.* E20. [Fr., pa. pple of *diamanter* set with diamonds, f. *diamant* DIAMOND *n.*] (Material) given a sparkling effect by means of artificial gems, powdered crystal, etc.

diamantiferous /dʌɪəmən'tɪf(ə)rəs/ *a.* L19. [Fr. *diamantifère*, f. *diamant* DIAMOND *n.*: see -I-, -FEROUS.] = DIAMONDIFEROUS.

diamantine /dʌɪə'mantɪn, -iːn/ *a.* & *n.* M16. [Fr. *diamantin*, f. *diamant* DIAMOND *n.*: see -INE[1].] **A** *adj.* †**1** Hard as diamond, adamantine. M16–M17. **2** Consisting of or of the nature of diamond; containing diamonds. E17. **B** *n.* Powdered boron used as an abrasive. L19.

diameter /dʌɪ'amɪtə/ *n.* LME. [(O)Fr. *diamètre* f. L *diametrus*, -*os* f. Gk *diametros* (sc. *grammē* line) diagonal, diameter, f. as DIA-[1] + *metron* measure: see -METER.] **1** A straight line passing through the centre of a circle or sphere and ending at the circumference or surface; *Math.* a similar line through the centre of a conic or a quadric surface; a straight line joining the midpoints of a set of parallel chords of any curve. LME. **2** The transverse measurement of any geometrical figure or body, esp. of a circle, cylinder, or sphere; *Archit.* the transverse measurement of a column at its base, taken as a unit of measurement for the proportions of an order. LME. **b** A unit used in expressing the number of times a linear dimension is enlarged by a microscope, in a photograph, etc. M19. †**3** The diametrical or direct opposite; contrariety, contradiction. L16–M17. **4** The whole extent *of* any region, from one side or end to the other. E17.
1 *conjugate diameter*: see CONJUGATE *a.* **2 in diameter** as measured along a diameter. **b** F. O'BRIEN The castor of a bed-leg, magnified to roughly 118 diameters.

diametral /dʌɪ'amɪtr(ə)l/ *a.* LME. [(O)Fr. *diamétral* f. late L *diametralis*, f. *diametrus*: see prec., -AL[1].] **1** Of or pertaining to a diameter; containing or being a diameter. LME. †**b** Forming, or situated in, a straight line. LME–M17. †**2** = DIAMETRICAL 2. E17–M18.
diametrally *adv.* (*a*) = DIAMETRICALLY (b); †(*b*) = DIAMETRICALLY (a): LME.

diametrical /dʌɪə'mɛtrɪk(ə)l/ *a.* M16. [f. Gk *diametrikos*, f. *diametros* DIAMETER: see -IC.] **1** = DIAMETRAL 1. M16. **2** Of opposition, difference, etc.: entire, complete. E17. †**3** Completely opposed in nature or result. M17–M18.
diametric *a.* = DIAMETRICAL E19. **diametrically** *adv.* (*a*) in the way of direct or complete opposition; directly, completely; (*b*) in the manner or direction of a diameter: M17.

diamide /dʌɪ'eɪmʌɪd, -'am-; 'dʌɪəmʌɪd/ *n.* M19. [f. DI-[2] + AMIDE.] *Chem.* A compound whose molecule contains two amido groups.

diamidine /dʌɪ'amɪdiːn/ *n.* M20. [f. DI-[2] + AMIDINE *n.*[2]] *Chem.* A compound having a structure based on two amidine groups (usu. joined by a chain of carbon atoms and/or two benzene rings).

diamine /dʌɪ'eɪmiːn, -'am-; 'dʌɪəmiːn/ *n.* M19. [f. DI-[2] + AMINE.] *Chem.* A compound whose molecule contains two amino groups, esp. when joined to radicals other than acid radicals.

diamond /'dʌɪəmənd/ *n.* & *a.* ME. [(O)Fr. *diamant* f. med.L *diamas*, *diamant-* alt. of L *adamas* ADAMANT. In sense A.7 f. Du. *diamant*.] **A** *n.* **1** A usu. colourless or lightly tinted precious stone of great brilliance, hardness, and value, occurring chiefly in alluvial deposits; the allotrope of carbon of which it consists (the hardest naturally occurring substance), used also for cutting and abrading. ME. **b** Any crystal or crystalline mineral resembling the diamond in brilliance, *esp.* rock crystal. Usu. w. name etc. denoting place of origin. L16. †**2** Any substance of extreme hardness; adamant. LME–M17. **3** A thing or person of great worth; a person of brilliant attainments etc. LME. **4** A rhombus placed with its diagonals horizontal and vertical. Formerly, a solid of octahedral or rhombohedral form. L15. **b** *Cards.* A red rhombus on the face of a playing-card. In *pl.* (occas. treated as *sing.*), one of the four suits into which a pack of playing-cards is divided, distinguished by such markings; *sing.* a card of this suit. L16. **c** *Baseball.* The area formed by the four bases; the entire field. L19. **5** *Her.* The tincture gules in the fanciful blazon of arms of peers. Long *obs.* exc. *Hist.* L16. **6** A tool with a small diamond for cutting glass. L17. **7** A former small size of type equal to about 4½ points. L18. **8** A glittering particle or point. E19. **9** In *pl.* Shares in companies that mine diamonds. E20. **10** (The emblem of) one of the highest international awards for gliding. M20.
1b *Bristol diamond*, *Cornish diamond*, *Quebec diamond*, etc. 4b E. LINKLATER Four hearts and a diamond in her hand. 8 E. THOMAS The great diamonds Of rain on the grassblades.
Phrases: **black diamond** (*a*) a dark-coloured diamond; (*b*) in *pl.*, coal. **diamond cut diamond** (a situation in which) wit or cunning meets its match. **diamond in the rough** = *rough diamond* s.v. ROUGH *a. rose diamond*: see ROSE *n. rough diamond*: see ROUGH *a. table diamond*: see TABLE *n.*
B *attrib.* or as *adj.* **1** Made or consisting of diamond. M16. †**b** Hard as diamond; adamantine. L16–M17. **2** Of the shape of a diamond, rhombic; forming a design consisting of diamonds. L16. **b** Having a surface cut into facets. E18. **3** Set or furnished with a diamond or diamonds. E17.
Comb. & special collocations: **diamond-bird** *Austral.* a pardalote; **diamond-cement**: used in setting diamonds; **diamond crossing** a place where two railway lines cross obliquely without communicating; **diamond-cut** *a.* (*a*) cut into the shape of a diamond; (*b*) cut with facets like a diamond; **diamond-drill**: set with diamonds for boring any hard substance; **diamond-field** a tract of land yielding diamonds; **diamond frame** a bicycle frame having a diamond shape; **diamond jubilee** the 60th (or 75th) anniversary of a monarch's accession, etc.; **diamond pane** a small diamond-shaped window-pane set in

lead (usu. in *pl.*); **diamond-point** (*a*) a diamond-tipped stylus used in engraving; (*b*) a point at a diamond crossing (usu. in *pl.*); **diamond rattlesnake** = DIAMONDBACK *rattlesnake*; **diamond ring effect** *Astron.* a phenomenon visible at the edge of a total solar eclipse, when the reappearing edge of the sun resembles a diamond ring; **diamond-shaped** *a.* of the shape of a diamond, rhombic; **diamond snake** any of various snakes with diamond-shaped markings, *esp.* a variety of the Australian python, *Python spilotes*, with yellow markings; **Diamond State** *US* Delaware; **diamond stitch** an embroidery stitch producing a diamond pattern; **diamond wedding** the sixtieth (or seventy-fifth) anniversary of a wedding; **diamond willow** *N. Amer.* (timber from) a willow with a diaper pattern in the bark and wood from leaf-scars.

diamondize *v.t.* bedeck (as) with diamonds L16. **diamondlike** *a.* resembling (that of) a diamond M16. **diamondwise** *adv.* in the manner or form of a diamond M16.

diamond /ˈdʌɪəmənd/ *v.t.* M18. [f. the n.] Furnish or adorn (as) with diamonds.

diamondback /ˈdʌɪəməndbak/ *n.* & *a.* E19. [f. DIAMOND *n.* & *a.* + BACK *n.*[1]] A *n.* A diamondback terrapin, rattlesnake, etc. (see below). E19.

B *adj.* Having a back with diamond-shaped markings on it. L19.

diamondback moth a small grey plutellid moth, *Plutella maculipennis*, which is a pest of vegetables and ornamental plants. **diamondback rattlesnake, rattler** either of two N. American rattlesnakes, *Crotalus adamanteus* or *C. atrox*. *diamondback terrapin*: see TERRAPIN *n.*[1] 1.

diamondbacked *a.* L19.

diamonded /ˈdʌɪəməndɪd/ *a.* M17. [f. DIAMOND *n.*, *v.*: see -ED[2], -ED[1].] 1 Marked or covered with diamond shapes; having such a shape. M17. 2 Adorned (as) with diamonds; wearing diamonds. M19.

diamondiferous /dʌɪəmənˈdɪf(ə)rəs/ *a.* L19. [f. DIAMOND *n.* + -I- + -FEROUS.] Yielding diamonds.

diamorphine /dʌɪəˈmɔːfiːn/ *n.* E20. [Abbrev.] = DIACETYLMORPHINE.

†**dian** *n.*[1] Also **diana**. L16–L17. [Fr. *diane* f. Sp. *diana* reveille, f. *dia* day.] A trumpet-call or drum roll at early morning, reveille.

MARVELL The bee through these known allies hums Beating the dian with its drums.

Dian *n.*[2] see next.

Diana /dʌɪˈanə/ *n.*[1] Also **Dian** /ˈdʌɪən/; (sense 3) **diana**. LME. [L *Diana* Roman moon goddess and patron of virginity and hunting, whence also (O)Fr. *diane*.] 1 The moon. *poet.* LME. 2 A young woman with the chastity or hunting skill of the goddess Diana. L18. 3 More fully *diana monkey*. A tropical W. African tree monkey, *Cercopithecus diana*, with a crescentic white mark on its forehead. E19.

Phrases: *tree of Diana*: see TREE *n.*

†**diana** *n.*[2] var. of DIAN *n.*[1]

diandrous /dʌɪˈandrəs/ *a.* L18. [f. DI-[2] + Gk *anēr*, *andr-* man + -OUS.] 1 *Bot.* Having two stamens. L18. 2 *Zool.* Having two male mates. L19.

diandry *n.* (*Biol.*) fertilization in which two sets of chromosomes are contributed by a sperm or sperms M20.

Dianetics /dʌɪəˈnɛtɪks/ *n.* Also **d-**. M20. [f. as next: see -ICS.] A system developed by the American writer L. Ron Hubbard (1911–86) which has as its aim the relief of psychosomatic disorder by a process of cleansing the mind of harmful mental images.

dianetic *a.* M20.

dianoetic /dʌɪənəʊˈɛtɪk/ *a.* L17. [Gk *dianoētikos*, f. *dianoeisthai* think, f. as DIA-[1] + *noein* think, suppose: see NOETIC.] *Philos.* Of or pertaining to thought; intellectual.

†**dianoetical** *a.* = DIANOETIC L16–L17. **dianoetically** *adv.* E19.

dianthus /dʌɪˈanθəs/ *n.* L18. [f. Gk *Dios* of Zeus + *anthos* flower.] A plant of the genus *Dianthus*, of the pink family, which besides pinks includes other fragrant plants with pink or reddish flowers.

diapalma /dʌɪəˈpalmə/ *n.* Now *rare* or *obs.* M17. [med.L, f. as DIA-[2] + L *palma* PALM *n.*[1]] A desiccating plaster composed originally of palm oil, litharge, and zinc sulphate.

diapase *n.* see DIAPASON.

diapasm /ˈdʌɪəpaz(ə)m/ *n.* *arch.* L16. [L *diapasma* f. Gk, f. *diapassein* sprinkle over.] A scented powder for sprinkling over the person.

diapason /dʌɪəˈpeɪs(ə)n, -z-/ *n.* & *v.* Also (*poet.*) **diapase** /ˈdʌɪəpeɪz/. LME. [L *diapason* f. Gk *diapasōn*, i.e. *dia pasōn* (*khordōn*) through all (notes).] A *n.* 1 The interval of an octave; the consonance of two notes an octave apart; a part in music producing such a consonance. Now *rare* & chiefly *Hist.* LME. †b *fig.* Complete harmony or agreement. L16–L18. 2a The combination of notes or parts in a harmonious whole; a melody; *esp.* a swelling sound; a grand burst of harmony; a rich, deep burst of sound. E16. b The whole range of notes in the scale; the compass of a voice or musical instrument. L17. c Range, spectrum, scope. M19. 3 Either of two foundation stops in an organ (*open* and *stopped diapason*), of which the open diapason gives the sound most characteristic of an organ; any of various other stops with flue pipes giving a similar quality of tone. E16. 4 A fixed standard of musical pitch, *spec.* 435 Hz (now superseded). M19.

1 BACON The true Coincidence of Tones into Diapasons. 2a H. M. STANLEY A deep and melodious diapason of musical voices. R. H. BARHAM Full many an Aldermanic nose Rolled its loud diapason after dinner. c A. HELPS In marriage the whole diapason of joy and sorrow is sounded.

B *v.t.* & *i.* Resound sonorously. E17.

diapause /ˈdʌɪəpɔːz/ *n.* & *v.* L19. [f. DIA-[1] + PAUSE *n.*] *Biol.* A *n.* A period of retarded or suspended development. L19. B *v.i.* Undergo or be in diapause. Chiefly as *diapausing* ppl a. M20.

diapedesis /dʌɪəpəˈdiːsɪs/ *n.* E17. [mod.L *diapedesis* f. Gk, ult. f. as DIA-[1] + *pēdan* leap, throb.] *Med.* The passage of red blood cells through the apparently intact walls of the capillaries, as in acute inflammation.

diapente /dʌɪəˈpɛnti/ *n.* Now *rare* & chiefly *Hist.* LME. [OFr. f. late L, f. Gk *dia pente* composed of five: see DIA-[2]. Cf. DIAPASON.] 1 *Mus.* The interval of a fifth. LME. 2a A medicine composed of five ingredients. E17. †b A beverage made of five ingredients; punch. L17–M18.

diaper /ˈdʌɪəpə/ *n.* & *a.* ME. [OFr. *dia(s)pre* f. med.L *diasprum* f. med.Gk *diaspros* adj., f. as DIA-[1] + *aspros* white.] A *n.* 1 A kind of textile; since the 15th cent. a linen or cotton material woven so that it consists of a pattern of small diamonds, each filled with some device. ME. 2 A towel, napkin, etc., of this material; (now chiefly *N. Amer.*) a baby's nappy (orig. made of diaper). L16. 3 A geometrical or ornamental design in which a panel, shield, etc., is covered by diamonds; any space-filling geometrical pattern. M17. B *adj.* 1 (Made) of diaper. LME. 2 Having a pattern of diamonds, diapered. LME.

diapery *n.* (*rare*) †(*a*) = DIAPER *n.* 1; (*b*) = DIAPERING (b): LME.

diaper /ˈdʌɪəpə/ *v.t.* LME. [f. prec.: cf. (O)Fr. *diaprer*, *diapré* diapered.] I 1 Decorate with a small uniform pattern, esp. of diamonds. LME. 2 Adorn with diversely coloured details; variegate. L16. II 3 Change the nappy of (a baby). *N. Amer.* M20.

diapering *vbl n.* (*a*) the action of the vb; (*b*) diapered decoration or patterns: LME.

diaphane /ˈdʌɪəfeɪn/ *a.* & *n.* M16. [(O)Fr., f. med.L *diaphanus* DIAPHANOUS.] †A *adj.* Transparent; diaphanous. M16–E19. B *n.* 1 A transparent body or substance. M19. 2 A light figured silk fabric. L19.

diaphaˈneity *n.* transparency M17. †**diaphanity** *n.* = DIAPHANEITY L15–M17.

diaphanie /dɪˈafəni/ *n.* M19. [Fr., f. as prec.] A process for imitating painted or stained glass by means of coloured paper.

diaphanous /dʌɪˈaf(ə)nəs/ *a.* E17. [med.L *diaphanus* f. Gk *diaphanēs*, f. as DIA-[1] + *phainein*, *phan-* to show: see -OUS.] Transparent; translucent; *esp.* (of a fabric etc.) so light and insubstantial as to be almost transparent.

J. CONRAD Mist.. draping the.. shores in diaphanous folds.

diaphanously *adv.* L17.

diaphone /ˈdʌɪəfəʊn/ *n.* E20. [f. DIA-[1] + -PHONE, PHONE *n.*[1]] 1 A low-pitched fog signal operated by compressed air, characterized by the 'grunt' which ends each note. E20. 2 *Ling.* = next. M20.

diaphoneme /dʌɪəˈfəʊniːm/ *n.* M20. [f. DIA-[1] + PHONEME.] *Ling.* A phonemic unit of a language comprising a set of systematically corresponding forms from all its dialects. Also, each dialectal variant of such a set.

diaphoˈnemic *a.* M20. **diaphoˈnemically** *adv.* M20.

diaphonic /dʌɪəˈfɒnɪk/ *a.*[1] L18. [In sense 1 f. next: see -IC. In sense 2 f. as DIAPHONY. In sense 3 f. DIAPHONE.] †1 Of or pertaining to diaphonics. *rare.* L18–M19. 2 Of or pertaining to diaphony. E19. 3 *Ling.* Of or pertaining to a diaphone. M20.

diaphonically *adv.* (*Ling.*) M20.

†**diaphonics** *n.pl.* L17–E18. [f. DIA-[1] + Gk *phōnē* sound + -ICS.] = DIACOUSTICS.

diaphony /dʌɪˈaf(ə)ni/ *n.* M17. [Late L *diaphonia* dissonance f. Gk, f. *diaphōnos* dissonant, f. as DIA-[1]: see -PHONY.] 1 (A) dissonance. *rare.* M17. 2 *Early Mus.* Two-part polyphony. M19.

diaphorase /dʌɪˈafəreɪz/ *n.* M20. [f. Gk *diaphoros* different + -ASE.] *Biochem.* A flavoprotein enzyme able to oxidize a reduced form of NAD.

diaphoresis /dʌɪəfəˈriːsɪs/ *n.* L17. [Late L *diaphoresis* f. Gk, f. *diaphorein* carry away, dissipate by sweating, f. as DIA-[1] + *phorein* carry.] *Med.* Sweating, *esp.* artificially induced sweating.

diaphoretic /-ˈrɛtɪk/ *a.* & *n.* (an agent) that induces or promotes sweating LME.

diaphototropic /ˌdʌɪəfəʊtəˈtrɒpɪk, -trəʊp-/ *a.* E20. [f. DIA-[1] + PHOTOTROPIC *a.*] *Bot.* = DIAHELIOTROPIC.

diaphototropism *n.* E20.

diaphragm /ˈdʌɪəfram/ *n.* & *v.* LME. [Late L *diaphragma* f. Gk, f. as DIA-[1] + *phragma* fence.] A *n.* 1 The muscular sheet which in mammals separates the thoracic and abdominal cavities and whose contraction leads to expansion of the lungs in respiration. LME. 2 *Zool.* A septum separating successive chambers of a shell. M17. 3 *Bot.* A layer of cells forming a partition in plant tissue. M17. 4 An opaque disc or plate with a central hole for restricting the light entering an optical instrument; *esp.* one in a camera that enables the effective aperture to be varied. M17. 5 A taut flexible membrane, esp. in various mechanical and acoustic devices. M19. 6 A thin bowl-shaped piece of rubber or plastic made to be inserted into the vagina and over the cervix as a contraceptive. M20.

4 *iris diaphragm*. 5 G. J. KING Microphones.. must have some sort of diaphragm or element which responds to the sound wave.

B *v.t.* Provide (esp. a lens) with a diaphragm; subject (light) to the effect of a diaphragm. M17.

diaphragm down reduce the aperture of (a lens) with a diaphragm.

diaphragmatic /-fragˈmatɪk/ *a.* of or pertaining to a diaphragm, of the nature of a diaphragm M17. **diaphragˈmatically** *adv.* by means of the diaphragm or a diaphragm L19.

diaphthoresis /dʌɪəfθəˈriːsɪs/ *n.* Pl **-reses** /-ˈriːsiːz/. M20. [f. Gk *diaphtheirein* destroy utterly, after ns. in *-oresis*.] *Petrogr.* Retrograde metamorphism.

diaphysis /dʌɪˈafɪsɪs/ *n.* Pl. **-physes** /-fɪsiːz/. M19. [Gk *diaphusis* growing through, f. as DIA-[1] + *phusis* growth.] *Anat.* The shaft or central part of a long bone; *spec.* the part ossified from the main centre of ossification.

diapir /ˈdʌɪəpɪə/ *n.* E20. [f. Gk *diapeirainein* pierce through, f. as DIA-[1] + *peirainein*, f. *peran* pierce.] *Geol.* An anticline in which a core of rock has moved upward to pierce the overlying strata.

diapiric /-ˈpɪrɪk/ *a.* of or pertaining to a diapir; having a structure characterized by an upward protruding body of rock, sediment, etc.: M20. **diaˈpirically** *adv.* in the manner of a diapir, with local upwelling M20. **diapirism** *n.* diapiric activity; a localized upward motion of rock, sediment, etc.: M20.

diapophysis /dʌɪəˈpɒfɪsɪs/ *n.* Pl. **-physes** /-fɪsiːz/. M19. [f. DIA-[1] + APOPHYSIS.] *Anat.* & *Zool.* Each of a pair of transverse processes on the superior or dorsal side of a vertebra.

diaporesis /dʌɪəpəˈriːsɪs/ *n.* L17. [mod.L *diaporesis* f. Gk = being at a loss.] A rhetorical figure in which the speaker professes to be uncertain which of two or more courses, statements, etc., to adopt.

diapositive /dʌɪəˈpɒzɪtɪv/ *n.* L19. [f. DIA-[1] + POSITIVE *n.*] A positive photographic slide or transparency.

†diapre *a.* M16–E18. [Fr. *diapré* pa. pple of *diaprer* to diaper, f. OFr. *diapre* DIAPER *n.*] *Her.* Diapered.

diapsid /dʌɪˈapsɪd/ *a.* & *n.* E20. [mod.L *Diapsida*, f. DI-[2] + Gk (*h*)*apsid-*, (*h*)*apsis* arch.] *Zool.* (Pertaining to or designating) a reptile whose skull has two pairs of temporal arches.

diarch /ˈdʌɪɑːk/ *a.* L19. [f. DI-[2] + Gk *arkhē* origin.] *Bot.* Of the primary xylem of the root: arising from two distinct points of origin. Of a root: having such xylem.

diarchy /ˈdʌɪɑːki/ *n.* Also **dy-**. M19. [f. DI-[2] after *monarchy*.] A mode of joint government by two; government by two independent authorities; *spec.* the system of provincial government in India from 1921 to 1937.
diˈarchal, diˈarchial, diˈarchic *adjs.* E20.

diarial /dʌɪˈɛːrɪəl/ *a.* M19. [f. L *diarium* DIARY *n.* + -AL[1] or f. DIARY *n.* + -IAL.] Of, pertaining to, or of the nature of a diary or journal.

diarian /dʌɪˈɛːrɪən/ *a.* Now *rare* or *obs.* L18. [f. as prec. + -AN, -IAN.] = prec. Formerly also, journalistic.

diarise *v.* var. of DIARIZE.

diarist /ˈdʌɪərɪst/ *n.* E19. [f. DIARY *n.* + -IST.] The author of a diary; a person who keeps a diary.
diaˈristic *a.* of the style of a diarist; of the nature of a diary: L19.

diarize /ˈdʌɪərʌɪz/ *v.* Also **-ise**. L18. [f. DIARY *n.* + -IZE.] 1 *v.i.* Keep a diary, write in a diary. L18. 2 *v.t.* Record in a diary. L19.

diarrhoea /dʌɪəˈrɪə/ *n.* Also ***-rrhea**. LME. [Late L f. Gk *diarrhoia*, f. *diarrhein* flow through, f. as DIA-[1]: see -RRHOEA.] A condition of excessively frequent and loose bowel movements. Also, watery or semi-liquid faeces characteristic of this condition.
fig.: HOR. WALPOLE He . . was troubled with a diarrhoea of words. *verbal diarrhoea*: see VERBAL *a.* 2.
diarrhoeal *a.* of, pertaining to, or affected with diarrhoea; of the nature of or characterized by diarrhoea: M17. **diarrhoeic** *a.* = DIARRHOEAL L19.

diarthrosis /dʌɪɑːˈθrəʊsɪs/ *n.* Pl. **-throses** /-ˈθrəʊsiːz/. L16. [Gk *diarthrōsis*, f. as DI-[3], ARTHROSIS.] *Anat.* Any articulation that allows one bone to move freely against another; a freely movable joint.
diarthrodial *a.* M19.

diary /ˈdʌɪəri/ *n.* L16. [L *diarium* journal, diary, (in pl.) daily allowance, f. *dies* day: see -ARY[1]. In sense 3 ellipt. for *diary fever.*] 1 A daily record of events, transactions, thoughts, etc., esp. ones involving the writer. L16. 2 A book in which to keep such a record, usu. having dates printed in it; a book or calendar with daily memoranda, esp. for people with a particular interest; a person's list of forthcoming engagements. E17. †3 A fever or other illness lasting only for a day. M–L17.
1 D. FRASER He began to keep . . a private diary of his thoughts and experiences. 2 DESK *diary*.

diary /ˈdʌɪəri/ *a.* Now *rare* or *obs.* L16. [med.L *diarius* daily, f. L *dies* day: see -ARY[1].] †1 Daily. L16–E17. 2 Lasting for one day; short-lived. Esp. in *diary fever.* E17.

disceuast, -scevast *ns.* vars. of DIASKEUAST.

diascope /ˈdʌɪəskəʊp/ *n.* M20. [f. DIA-[1] + -SCOPE.] A projector for use with transparencies.
diaˈscopic *a.* E20.

†diascordium *n.* E17–E19. [mod.L, f. Gk *dia scordiōn*: see DIA-[2], SCORDIUM.] A medicine made from the dried leaves of various herbs.

diaskeuast /dʌɪəˈskjuːast/ *n.* Also **-sceuast, -scevast** /-ˈsiːvast/. E19. [Gk *diaskeuastēs* reviser of a poem, interpolator, f. *diaskeuazein* edit, f. as DIA-[1] + *skeuazein* make ready.] A reviser; *esp.* a person who made one of the old recensions of Greek writings.

Diaspora /dʌɪˈasp(ə)rə/ *n.* Also **d-**. L19. [Gk, f. *diaspeirein* disperse, f. as DIA-[1] + *speirein* sow, scatter.] *The* dispersion of Jews among the Gentile nations; all those Jews who live outside the biblical land of Israel; (the situation of) any body of people living outside their traditional homeland.
Observer The famine, the diaspora and the long hatred of Irish Americans for Britain.
¶The term originated in *Deut.* 28:25 (Septuagint).

diaspore /ˈdʌɪəspɔː/ *n.* E19. [Gk *diaspora* (so named because of its decrepitation): see prec.] *Min.* Native aluminium hydrogen oxide, $HAlO_2$, occurring esp. in bauxite and clay as transparent or translucent orthorhombic crystals of various colours.

diastaltic /dʌɪəˈstaltɪk/ *a.* L17. [Gk *diastaltikos* serving to distinguish or expand, f. *diastellein*: see DIASTOLE *n.*] 1 Of ancient Greek music: tending to exhalt the mind, exhilarating; contrasted w. SYSTALTIC *a.* 2. *rare.* L17. 2 *Physiol.* Reflex. Now *rare.* M19.

diastase /ˈdʌɪəsteɪz/ *n.* M19. [f. as next. Cf. -ASE.] *Biochem.* An amylase, *esp.* one that hydrolyses starch to maltose and is present in seeds and the pancreas.
diaˈstatic *a.* pertaining to or of the nature of diastase L19. **diaˈstatically** *adv.* as diastase L19.

diastasis /dʌɪəˈsteɪsɪs/ *n.* Pl. **-ases** /-eɪsiːz/. Now *rare.* E18. [mod.L f. Gk = separation, f. as DIA-[1] + *stasis* placing.] *Med.* Separation of two parts of a bone without fracture, esp. of an epiphysis from a long bone.

diastem /ˈdʌɪəstɛm/ *n.* L17. [Gk *diastēma*: see next.] 1 In ancient Greek music, an interval, *esp.* one forming a single degree of the scale. L17. 2 *Geol.* A period when there was a temporary halt to deposition; a non-sequence. E20.

diastema /dʌɪəˈstiːmə/ *n.* Pl. **-mata** /-mətə/. LME. [Late L *diastema* f. Gk, = space between.] 1 = DIASTEM 1. LME. 2 *Zool.* & *Anat.* A gap separating teeth of one kind from those of another, found in most mammals except man. M19.
diasteˈmatic *a.* M17.

diaster /dʌɪˈastə/ *n.* L19. [f. DI-[2] + ASTER.] *Cytol.* The stage in mitosis when the chromosomes are in two groups near the poles of the spindle, prior to forming daughter nuclei. Formerly, the pattern of the chromosomes at this stage.
diastral *a.* L19.

diastereoisomer /ˌdʌɪəstɛrɪəʊˈʌɪsəmə/ *n.* M20. [f. DIA-[1] + STEREOISOMER.] *Chem.* Either of a pair of stereoisomeric compounds that are not mirror images of one another.
diaˌstereoisoˈmeric *a.* E20.

diastole /dʌɪˈastəli/ *n.* L16. [Late L *diastole* f. Gk = separation, expansion, dilatation, f. *diastellein*, f. as DIA-[1] + *stellein* put, place.] 1 *Physiol.* The phase of the heartbeat when the heart relaxes, dilates, and fills with blood. Formerly also, the expansion of the lungs in breathing. Opp. SYSTOLE. L16. 2 *Class. Pros.* The lengthening of a naturally short syllable. L16. 3 *Gk Gram.* A mark (originally semicircular) used to indicate the separation of words, still occas. used in the form of a comma to distinguish a few confusable words. E18.
1 *fig.*: GEO. ELIOT There must be a systole and diastole in all inquiry.
diaˈstolic *a.* L17.

diastrophism /dʌɪˈastrəfɪz(ə)m/ *n.* L19. [f. Gk *diastrophē* distortion, dislocation, ult. f. as DIA-[1] + *strephein* to turn: see -ISM.] The disturbances and dislocations of the earth's crust which have produced the major inequalities of its surface.
diastrophic /-ˈstrəʊfɪk, -ˈstrɒfɪk/ *a.* L19.

diastyle /ˈdʌɪəstʌɪl/ *a.* & *n.* Also (earlier) **†-stylos**. M16. [Partly f. L *diastylos* f. Gk *diastulos* having a space between the columns; partly f. Gk *diastulion* intercolumnar space; both ult. f. as DIA-[1] + *stulos* column.] *Archit.* (A colonnade etc.) having a distance between columns equal to three (or four) diameters (in the Doric order 2¾); (a distance between columns) equal to this number of diameters.

diasyrm /ˈdʌɪəsəːm/ *n.* Also (earlier) **†-syrmus**. M16. [Late L *diasyrmus* f. Gk *diasurmos* disparagement.] A rhetorical figure expressing disparagement or ridicule.

diasystem /ˈdʌɪəsɪstəm/ *n.* M20. [f. DIA-[1] + SYSTEM.] *Ling.* A linguistic macro-system constructed by treating phonological variants between dialects as part of a continuum of variation.
diasyˈstemic *a.* L20.

diatessaron /dʌɪəˈtɛsərən/ *n.* LME. [Late L, f. Gk *dia tessarōn* composed of four: see DIA-[2].] 1 *Mus.* The interval of a fourth. Now *rare* & chiefly *Hist.* LME. 2 A medicine composed of four ingredients. Now *rare* & chiefly *Hist.* LME. 3 An arrangement of the four Gospels as one narrative. L16.

diathermacy /dʌɪəˈθəːməsi/ *n.* M19. [Fr. *diathermasie* f. Gk *diathermasia* a warming through, f. as DIA-[1] + *thermasia* heat, w. assim. to -ACY.] = DIATHERMANCY 2.

diathermal /dʌɪəˈθəːm(ə)l/ *a.* M19. [f. DIA-[1] + THERMAL *a.*] = DIATHERMANOUS.

diathermancy /dʌɪəˈθəːm(ə)nsi/ *n.* M19. [Fr. *diathermansie*, f. as DIA-[1] + Gk *thermansis* heating, w. assim. to -ANCY.] †1 The property of radiant heat of comprising radiation with different wavelengths and refrangibilities. Only in M19. 2 The property of being diathermanous. M19.

diathermaneity /ˌdʌɪəθəːməˈniːəti/ *n.* *rare.* M19. [Fr. *diathermanéité*, f. *diathermane* (see DIATHERMOUS) after *diaphanéité* DIAPHANEITY.] = DIATHERMANCY 2.

diathermanous /dʌɪəˈθəːmənəs/ *a.* M19. [Fr. *diathermane*, f. as DIA-[1] + Gk *thermē*, *thermon* heat after DIAPHANE: see -OUS.] Transparent to infrared radiation.

diathermic /dʌɪəˈθəːmɪk/ *a.* M19. [Fr. *diathermique*, f. as DIA-[1] + Gk *thermē*, *thermon* heat: see -IC.] 1 = DIATHERMANOUS. M19. 2 Of or pertaining to diathermy. E20.
diathermically *adv.* by means of a diathermic current E20. **diathermous** *a.* = DIATHERMANOUS M19.

diathermy /ˈdʌɪəθəːmi/ *n.* E20. [f. DIA-[1] + Gk *thermos* heat + -Y[3].] *Med.* The generation of heat inside the body by passing high-frequency electric currents through it using external electrodes.
medical diathermy: in which the tissues are merely warmed. **surgical diathermy**: in which there is local cauterization etc.

diathesis /dʌɪˈaθəsɪs/ *n.* Pl. **-eses** /-əsiːz/. M17. [mod.L f. Gk = disposition, f. *diatithenai* arrange.] 1 *Med.* A constitutional predisposition to a particular disease or condition; constitution. M17. 2 *Ling.* The voice of a verb. M20.
1 *fig.*: H. J. S. MAINE The intellectual diathesis of the modern world.
diaˈthetic *a.* M19. **diaˈthetically** *adv.* L19.

diatom /ˈdʌɪətəm/ *n.* M19. [mod.L *Diatoma* genus name, f. Gk *diatomos* (adj.) cut in two, f. *diatemnein* to cut through.] A microscopic unicellular alga that has a rigid siliceous cell wall and occurs esp. as plankton and as a fossil in diatomaceous earth.
diatomaceous /-ˈmeɪʃəs/ *a.* (*a*) of or pertaining to diatoms; (*b*) consisting of or formed from the fossil remains of diatoms (*diatomaceous earth*, a soft friable porous material used esp. for filters and insulation): M19.

diatomic /dʌɪəˈtɒmɪk/ *a.* & *n.* M19. [f. DI-[2] + ATOMIC.] *Chem.* A *adj.* Consisting of two atoms. Also, dibasic, divalent. M19. B *n.* A diatomic compound. M20.

diatomite /dʌɪˈatəmʌɪt/ *n.* L19. [f. DIATOM + -ITE[1].] Diatomaceous earth; a sedimentary rock resembling chert, formed by the consolidation of this.

diatonic /dʌɪəˈtɒnɪk/ *a.* E17. [(O)Fr. *diatonique* or late L *diatonicus*, f. Gk *diatonikos* at intervals of a tone, f. as DIA-¹ + *tonos* TONE *n.*: see -IC.] *Mus.* **1** *Hist.* Designating (ancient Greek music based on) a tetrachord divided into two tones and a lower semitone. E17. **2** Using only the notes proper to one key without chromatic alteration; based on a scale with five tones and two separated semitones. L17.

2 G. MEREDITH Crossjay's voice ran up and down a diatonic scale. A. HOPKINS Diatonic notes are those which 'belong' to a particular scale. C. IVES The first movement . . is primarily diatonic.

diatonically *adv.* E18. **diatonicism** /-sɪz(ə)m/ *n.* (an instance of) the use of diatonic tonality M20. **di'atonism** *n.* = DIATONICISM E20.

diatreme /ˈdʌɪətriːm/ *n.* E20. [f. DIA-¹ + Gk *trēma* perforation.] *Geol.* A long vertical pipe or plug formed when gas-filled magma forced its way up through rock.

diatribe /ˈdʌɪətrʌɪb/ *n.* L16. [Fr. f. L *diatriba* learned discussion f. Gk *diatribē* spending of time, discourse, f. as DIA-¹ + *tribein* rub.] **1** A discourse, a disquisition. *arch.* L16. **2** A dissertation or discourse directed against a particular person or work; a piece of bitter criticism; scolding, denunciation. E19.

2 C. KINGSLEY A rambling, bitter diatribe on the wrongs and sufferings of the labourers. H. JAMES Diatribes against the British middle-class.

diatribist *n.* a person who writes or utters a diatribe M17.

diaulos /dʌɪˈɔːlɒs/ *n.* E18. [Gk, f. as DI-² + *aulos* pipe.] *Gk Antiq.* A double course in which the racers rounded a goal and returned to the starting-point.

diazepam /dʌɪˈazɪpam, -ˈeɪz-/ *n.* M20. [f. BENZO)DIAZEP(INE + AM(IDE).] *Pharm.* A tranquillizer of the benzodiazepine group, $C_{16}H_{13}N_2OCl$, used esp. as an anti-anxiety agent, hypnotic, and muscle relaxant.

¶A proprietary name for this drug is VALIUM.

diazeuctic /dʌɪəˈzjuːktɪk/ *a.* L17. [Gk *diazeuktikos* disjunctive, ult. f. *zeugnunai* to join: see DIA-¹.] In ancient Greek music, designating a tone separating two tetrachords, and tetrachords so separated.

diazine /ˈdʌɪəziːn/ *n.* E20. [f. DI-² + AZINE.] *Chem.* Any compound whose molecule contains a six-membered ring of four carbon and two nitrogen atoms; *spec.* each of the three simplest such compounds (pyrazine, pyridazine, and pyrimidine).

diazinon /dʌɪˈazɪnɒn/ *n.* M20. [f. prec. + *-on* of unkn. origin.] An organophosphorus insecticide derived from pyrimidine.

diazo /dʌɪˈazəʊ, -ˈeɪzəʊ/ *a.* & *n.* M20. [Abbrev. of DIAZOTYPE.] **A** *adj.* Designating or pertaining to a process which employs the effect of light on material sensitized with a diazonium compound. M20. **B** *n.* Pl. **-os.** (A copy made by) the diazo process. M20.

diazo- /dʌɪˈazəʊ, -ˈeɪzəʊ/ *comb. form.* Also as attrib. adj. **diazo** (cf. prec.). [f. DI-² + AZO-.] *Chem.* Indicating the presence of two nitrogen atoms, now *spec.* the group ·N=N· joined to one carbon atom. Cf. AZO-, DIAZONIUM.

diazo'methane *n.* a poisonous yellow gas, CH_2N_2, used as a methylating agent L19.

diazoma /dʌɪəˈzəʊmə/ *n.* E18. [L *diazoma* f. Gk = girdle, partition, etc.] **1** A semicircular passage in the auditorium of an ancient Greek theatre, parallel to its outer border and about halfway up the tiers of steps. E18. †**2** *Anat.* The diaphragm. E18–L19.

diazonium /dʌɪəˈzəʊnɪəm/ *n.* L19. [f. DIAZO- + -ONIUM.] *Chem.* The monovalent ion $·N_2^+$ when attached to a carbon atom in an organic (usu. aromatic) compound. Usu. in *comb.*

diazotize /dʌɪˈazətʌɪz, -ˈeɪz-/ *v.t.* Also **-ise.** L19. [f. DIAZO- + -IZE, after AZOTE.] *Chem.* Convert (esp. an aromatic amine) into a diazo or diazonium compound or group, e.g. in dye manufacture.

diazotizable *a.* L19. **diazoti'zation** *n.* L19.

diazotype /dʌɪˈazəʊtʌɪp, -ˈeɪz-/ *n.* L19. [f. DIAZO- + -TYPE.] A diazo copying or colouring process.

dib *n.* var. of DUB *n.*¹

dib /dɪb/ *v.* Infl. **-bb-.** E17. [Alt. of DAB *v.*] **1** *v.t.* & *i.* Dab lightly, tap. E17. **2** *v.i.* Dap for fish. L17. **3** *v.t.* & *i.* = DIBBLE *v.*¹ 1, 2. *dial.* M18.

dibber *n.* = DIBBLE *n.* M18.

dibasic /dʌɪˈbeɪsɪk/ *a.* M19. [f. DI-² + BASIC *a.*] *Chem.* Of an acid: having two replaceable hydrogen atoms. Formerly also, divalent.

dibasicity /dʌɪbeɪˈsɪsɪti/ *n.* dibasic quality L19.

dibatag /ˈdɪbətag/ *n.* L19. [Somali.] An antelope, *Ammodorcas clarkei*, with recurved horns, found in Somalia and eastern Ethiopia.

dibble /ˈdɪb(ə)l/ *n.* & *v.*¹ LME. [App. conn. w. DIB *v.*: see -LE¹.] **A** *n.* A pointed instrument for making holes in the ground for bulbs etc. LME. **B** *v.* **1** *v.t.* Make a hole in (the soil) with or as with a dibble; sow or plant by this means. (Foll. by *in.*) M16. **2** *v.i.* Use a dibble; make holes in the soil. L18.

dibbler *n.* (*a*) a person who dibbles; (*b*) an agricultural implement for dibbling; (*c*) a marsupial mouse, *Antechinus apicalis*, of Australia: E19.

dibble /ˈdɪb(ə)l/ *v.*²*i.* E17. [Perh. alt. of DABBLE *v.* or f. DIB *v.* + -LE³.] †**1** = DABBLE *v.* 2. Only in E17. **2** = DIB *v.* 2. M17.

dibbuk *n.* var. of DYBBUK.

dibenzanthracene /dʌɪbɛnˈzanθrəsiːn/ *n.* E20. [f. DI-² + BENZ- + ANTHRACENE.] *Chem.* Any of various isomeric anthracene derivatives with five fused rings in the molecule and the formula $C_{22}H_{14}$; *spec.* one that occurs in coal tar and tobacco smoke and is carcinogenic.

diborane /dʌɪˈbɔːreɪn/ *n.* E20. [f. DI-² + BORANE.] *Chem.* A borane containing two boron atoms; *spec.* B_2H_6, a poisonous gas.

dibranchiate /dʌɪˈbraŋkɪət/ *a.* & *n.* M19. [mod.L *dibranchiata*, f. DI-² + Gk *bragkhia* gills: see -ATE².] (Designating or pertaining to) a cephalopod with one pair of gills, sometimes placed in a group Dibranchiata comprising all living cephalopods except the pearly nautilus.

dibs /dɪbz/ *n.*¹*pl.* M18. [Prob. f. DIBSTONES.] **1** A children's game played with pebbles or sheep's knuckle-bones; the pebbles or bones so used. Cf. JACK *n.*¹ 15b. M18. **2** Money. *slang.* E19.

dibs /dɪbz/ *n.*² M18. [Arab., prob. rel. to Heb. *dĕbaš* honey.] A thick sweet syrup made in Middle Eastern countries by boiling down the juice of ripe grapes.

dibs /dɪbz/ *int.* & *n.*³ *N. Amer.* M20. [Prob. rel. to DUBS *int.* & *n.*¹] (Demanding) a first claim or option. (Foll. by *on.*)

E. EAGER You always get dibs on first 'cause you're the oldest.

dibstones /ˈdɪbstəʊnz/ *n.pl.* L17. [f. DIB *v.* (prob.) + STONE *n.* + -S¹.] = DIBS *n.*¹ 1.

dicacity /dɪˈkasɪti/ *n. literary.* L16. [L *dicacitas* raillery, f. *dicac-*, *dicax* sarcastic, f. *dic-* stem of *dicere* speak: see -ITY.] Raillery, banter; talkativeness.

dicarboxylic /ˌdʌɪkɑːbɒkˈsɪlɪk/ *a.* L19. [f. DI-² + CARBOXYLIC.] *Chem.* Having two carboxyl groups in the molecule.

dicast /ˈdɪkast/ *n.* Also **dik-.** E19. [Gk *dikastēs* judge, juryman, f. *dikazein* judge, f. *dikē* judgement.] *Gk Hist.* Each of the 6000 citizens selected annually in ancient Athens to try cases in the courts.

dicasterion /dɪkaˈstɪərɪən/ *n.*, pl. **-ria** /-rɪə/, = DICASTERY M17. **di'castery** *n.* any of the courts in which the dicasts sat; the court or body of dicasts: M19. **di'castic** *a.* of or pertaining to a dicast or dicasts M19.

dicatalectic /ˌdʌɪkatəˈlɛktɪk/ *a.* L19. [f. DI-² + CATALECTIC *a.*] *Pros.* A metrical line lacking a syllable both in the middle and at the end.

dice /dʌɪs/ *n.* ME. [(O)Fr. *dés*: see DIE *n.*¹] **I** *pl.* **1** Pl. of DIE *n.*¹ ME. **2** A game or games played with dice. ME.

II *sing.* Pl. **dices.** **3** = DIE *n.*¹ 1. *colloq.* LME. †**4** = DIE *n.*¹ 2. LME–M16.

3 E. HAYWOOD Never to touch a card or throw a dice again. *fig.*: T. D'URFEY The uncertain Dice of Fate thus far runs well.

Phrases: **in the dice** liable or destined to be. LIAR *dice*. **no dice** *colloq.* (there is) no chance of success, cooperation, etc. *poker-dice*: see POKER *n.*³

Comb.: **dice-box** a box from which dice are thrown.

dice /dʌɪs/ *v.* LME. [f. prec.] **I 1** *v.t. Cookery.* Cut into small cubes. LME. **2** *v.t.* Chequer, mark with squares. M17. **II 3** *v.i.* Play or gamble with dice. LME. **4** *v.t.* Gamble *away* at dice. M16. **5** *v.t.* Reject, throw away; leave alone. *Austral. slang.* M20. **6** *v.i.* Drive (as if) in a race (*with*). M20.

3 **dice with death** take great risks. 5 F. HARDY No bastard puts my daughter in the family way then dices her . . and gets away with it. 6 A. ALVAREZ Two cars in a hurry, he thought, young fools dicing home after a party.

dicer *n.* a person who plays or gambles with dice LME.

dicentra /dʌɪˈsɛntrə/ *n.* M19. [mod.L f. Gk *dikentros*, f. as DI-² + *kentron* (see CENTRE *n.*).] Any plant of the genus *Dicentra*, of the fumitory family, which includes herbaceous perennials with drooping racemose flowers, e.g. bleeding heart.

dicentric /dʌɪˈsɛntrɪk/ *a.* & *n.* M20. [f. DI-² + -CENTRIC.] (A chromosome etc.) having two centromeres.

dicey /ˈdʌɪsi/ *a. slang.* M20. [f. DICE *n.* + -Y¹.] Risky; unreliable, uncertain.

A. BLOND Fishermen and canners whose tenure is extremely dicey.

dich- *comb. form* see DICHO-.

dichasium /dʌɪˈkeɪzɪəm/ *n.* Pl. **-sia** /-zɪə/. L19. [f. Gk *dikhasis* division, f. *dikhazein* divide, f. *dikha* apart, + -IUM.] *Bot.* A cyme in which each flowering branch gives rise to two more branches symmetrically placed, so that there is symmetry about a median plane.

dichlamydeous /dʌɪkləˈmɪdɪəs/ *a.* M19. [f. DI-² + Gk *khlamus*, *khlamud-* cloak + -EOUS.] Of a flower: having both a calyx and a corolla.

dichloride /dʌɪˈklɔːrʌɪd/ *n.* E19. [f. DI-² + CHLORIDE.] A compound with two chlorine atoms in its molecule. Formerly, a compound with one chlorine atom and two of another element.

dichlorodifluoromethane /dʌɪˌklɔːrəʊdʌɪˌflʊərəʊˈmiːθeɪn/ *n.* M20. [f. DI-² + CHLORO-² + DI-² + FLUORO- + METHANE.] An easily liquefied gas, CCl_2F_2, used as an aerosol propellant and a refrigerant.

dichlorvos /dʌɪˈklɔːvɒs/ *n.* M20. [f. DI-², CHLOR-¹, V(INYL, PH)OS(PHATE *n.*, elems. of the systematic name (see below).] A pale yellow liquid organophosphorus compound used as an insecticide and veterinary anthelmintic: 2,2-dichlorovinyl dimethyl phosphate, $(CH_3O)_2PO_2CHCCl_2$.

dicho- /ˈdʌɪkəʊ/ *comb. form.* Bef. a vowel also **dich-.** [Gk *dikho-*, f. *dikha* in two, apart.] Apart, in two; separately.

dichogamous /dʌɪˈkɒgəməs/ *a.* [Gk *gamos* marriage] designating a flower in which male and female reproductive organs mature at different times, so that self-fertilization is prevented (cf. HOMOGAMOUS 2) M19. **di'chogamy** *n.* the condition of being dichogamous M19.

dichoptic /dʌɪˈkɒptɪk/ *a.* L19. [f. DICHO- + OPTIC *a.*] **1** *Entomol.* Of the eyes: widely separated. Of an insect: having such eyes. L19. **2** Involving or pertaining to the presentation of different (not merely stereoscopic) images to the two eyes. M20.

dichoptically *adv.* M20.

dichoree /dʌɪkəˈriː/ *n.* E19. [Fr. *dichorée* f. L *dichoreus* f. Gk *dikhoreios*, f. as DI-² + *khoreios* CHOREE.] *Pros.* A foot consisting of two trochees.

dichotic /dʌɪˈkɒtɪk/ *a.* M20. [f. DICHO- + Gk *ous*, *ōt-* ear + -IC.] Involving or pertaining to the presentation of different auditory signals to the two ears.

†**dichotomia** *n.* see DICHOTOMY.

dichotomic /dʌɪkɒˈtɒmɪk/ *a.* L19. [f.

DICHOTOMY + -IC.] Involving dichotomy, dichotomous.
dichotomically *adv.* L19.

dichotomise *v.* var. of DICHOTOMIZE.

dichotomist /dʌɪˈkɒtəmɪst, dɪ-/ *n.* L16. [f. as next + -IST.] A person who dichotomizes something.

dichotomize /dʌɪˈkɒtəmʌɪz, dɪ-/ *v.* Also **-ise.** E17. [f. DICHOTOMY + -IZE.] 1 *v.t.* Divide into two (esp. sharply defined) parts, esp. in a classification. E17. 2 *v.i.* Divide or branch successively into two, esp. sharply. M19.
dichotomiˈzation *n.* M20. **dichotomized** *ppl a.* divided into two; *spec.* (of the moon) with exactly half the disc illuminated: E18.

dichotomous /dʌɪˈkɒtəməs, dɪ-/ *a.* L17. [f. late L *dichotomos* f. Gk *dikhotomos*, f. as DICHO- + *temnein* to cut: see -OUS.] Exhibiting or characterized by dichotomy; *spec.* in *Bot.*, (of branching) in which the axis is divided into two branches (cf. POLYTOMOUS).
dichotomously *adv.* E19.

dichotomy /dʌɪˈkɒtəmi, dɪ-/ *n.* Also (earlier) in L form †**-tomia.** L16. [mod.L *dichotomia* f. Gk *dikhotomia* division in two: see DICHO-, -TOMY.] 1 Division (esp. sharply defined) into two classes, parts, etc. L16. b A sharp or paradoxical contrast. M20. 2 *Astron.* The phase of the moon etc. at which exactly half the disc appears illuminated. M17. 3 *Bot.* & *Zool.* Repeated bifurcation of a plant etc. Cf. POLYTOMY. E18.
1b M. AMIS The coffee-table featured.. Shakespeare texts and a copy of *Time Out*—an intriguing dichotomy.

dichroiscope *n.* var. of DICHROSCOPE.

dichroism /dʌɪˈkrəʊɪz(ə)m/ *n.* E19. [f. Gk *dikhroos* two-coloured, f. as DI-² + *khrōs* colour: see -ISM.] The property of certain substances of absorbing light to a different extent according to the direction from which it comes or its direction or state of polarization; the property of having a different colour when viewed from a different direction.
dichroic *a.* exhibiting or pertaining to dichroism M19.

dichroite /dʌɪˈkrəʊʌɪt/ *n.* E19. [f. as prec. + -ITE¹.] *Min.* = CORDIERITE.
dichroˈitic *a.* = DICHROIC M19.

dichromasy /dʌɪˈkrəʊməsi/ *n.* E20. [f. DI-² + -CHROMASY.] Dichromatic colour vision.

dichromat /ˈdʌɪkrəmat/ *n.* Also **-ate** /-eɪt/. E20. [Back-form. f. DICHROMATIC.] A person with dichromatism.

dichromate /dʌɪˈkrəʊmeɪt/ *n.*¹ M19. [f. DI-² + CHROMATE.] *Chem.* A usu. red or orange salt containing the ion $Cr_2O_7^{2-}$.

dichromate *n.*² var. of DICHROMAT.

dichromatic /dʌɪkrə(ʊ)ˈmatɪk/ *a.* & *n.* M19. [f. DI-² + CHROMATIC.] A *adj.* 1 Having two colours; *spec.* (of an animal etc.) occurring with two different kinds of colouring, independently of age or sex. M19. 2 Having or designating a form of colour-blindness in which the range of colours seen is limited to those produced by two primary colours, rather than the usual three. L19. B *n.* = DICHROMAT *n.* L19.
diˈchromatism *n.* the quality or fact of being dichromatic L19.

dichromic /dʌɪˈkrəʊmɪk/ *a.* M19. [f. Gk *dikhrōmos*, f. as DI-² + *khrōma* colour: see -IC.] = DICHROMATIC *a.* 2.

dichroscope /ˈdʌɪkrəskəʊp/ *n.* Also **dichroi-** /dʌɪˈkrəʊɪ-/. M19. [f. DICHROISM + -SCOPE.] An instrument for observing or measuring dichroism.

Dick /dɪk/ *n.*¹ In sense 2 **d-**. M16. [Male forename, playful alt. of *Ric-* f. AN *Ricard*, L *Ricardus*, whence *Richard* (of which it is used as a familiar abbrev.).] 1 A man, a fellow; a lad. Freq. w. qualifying adj. M16. 2 The penis. *coarse slang.* L18.
1 *Tom, Dick, and Harry*: see TOM *n.*¹
Comb.: **dickhead** *slang* a stupid person.
¶ See also *clever Dick* s.v. CLEVER *a.*, *Spotted Dick* s.v. SPOTTED.

dick /dɪk/ *n.*² *slang.* M19. [Abbrev. of DECLARATION.] *take one's dick*, declare solemnly, affirm, (*that*).

dick /dɪk/ *n.*³ *slang.* E20. [Perh. abbrev. of DETECTIVE or f. obs. slang *dick* look, f. Romany.] A detective; a police officer.

dickcissel /dɪkˈsɪs(ə)l, ˈdɪks-/ *n.* L19. [Imit. of its cry.] A migratory songbird, *Spiza americana*, of N. and Central America, like a house sparrow but with a yellow breast.

dicken /ˈdɪk(ə)n/ *int. Austral.* & *NZ slang.* Also **-in, -on.** L19. [Alt. of next.] Expr. disgust or disbelief. (Foll. by *on.*)
D. M. DAVIN Dicken on that for a joke.

dickens /ˈdɪkɪnz/ *n. colloq.* L16. [Prob. f. the surname *Dickens*.] The Devil, the deuce. Chiefly in exclamatory phrases.
L. ARMSTRONG Everybody..was frantic as the dickens. **play the dickens** cause mischief. (**what** etc.) **the dickens!** expr. astonishment, irritation, etc.

Dickensian /dɪˈkɛnzɪən/ *a.* & *n.* L19. [f. *Dickens* (see below) + -IAN.] A *adj.* Of or pertaining to the English novelist Charles Dickens (1812–70) or his writing; similar to or suggestive of the situations or social conditions portrayed in his novels. L19.
Economist Employees busy making school satchels in allegedly Dickensian conditions.
B *n.* An admirer or student of Dickens or his writing. E20.
Dickensiˈana *n.pl.* [-ANA] publications or other items concerning or associated with Dickens L19. **Dickensianly** *adv.* L20. **ˈDickensy** *a.* = DICKENSIAN *a.* M19.

dicker /ˈdɪkə/ *n.*¹ ME. [Corresp. to MLG *dēker*, MHG *techer*, (also mod.) *decher*, f. WGmc f. L *decuria* group of ten, f. *decem* ten + *vir* man. Prob. already in OE.] 1 *Hist.* A quantity, esp. of hides, numbering ten. (Foll. by *of.*) ME. †2 A considerable number, a lot. L16–L17.

dicker /ˈdɪkə/ *n.*² Orig. *US.* E19. [f. the vb.] Barter; articles exchanged in barter; a deal.

dicker /ˈdɪkə/ *v.* Orig. *US.* E19. [Origin uncertain: perh. f. DICKER *n.*¹] 1 *v.i.* Trade by barter; haggle. E19. 2 *v.t.* Barter, exchange. M19. 3 *v.i.* Vacillate, dither; hesitate. M20.
1 S. BELLOW She..dickered with the photographer, ..trying to beat down his price. 3 B. PEARSON Henderson, though he dickered, usually came round to the majority opinion.

dickey, dickie *ns.* vars. of DICKY *n.*

dickin, dickon *ints.* vars. of DICKEN.

dicky /ˈdɪki/ *n.* Also **-ey, -ie.** M18. [Prob. several different wds: app. partly f. name *Dicky*, f. as DICK *n.*¹ + -Y⁶.] 1 An under petticoat. *obs.* exc. *dial.* M18. 2 A donkey; *spec.* a he-ass. *colloq.* L18. 3 In full *dicky-bird*: a A small bird. *colloq.* L18. b A word. (*rhyming*) *slang.* E20. 4a A false shirt-front. *colloq.* E19. b A shirt collar. *US colloq.* M19. 5 Also *dicky seat*. a Chiefly *Hist.* A seat at the front of a horse-drawn carriage for the driver; a seat at the rear for servants or a guard. E19. b An outside folding seat at the back of a motor vehicle. E20.
Comb.: *dicky-bird*: see sense 3 above; **dicky bow** *colloq.* a bow-tie; *dicky seat*: see sense 5 above.

dicky /ˈdɪki/ *a.* L18. [Origin uncertain: perh. f. *Dick* (see DICK *n.*¹) in proverbial phr. *as queer* etc. *as Dick's hatband.*] 1 Almost over; near death, defeat etc. Chiefly in (*all*) *dicky with*, *dicky up with*, all up with (a person etc.). *dial.* L18. 2 Unsound, shaky. *slang.* E19.
2 D. STOREY A doctor's note about a dicky heart.

diclinous /dʌɪˈklʌɪnəs, ˈdʌɪklɪnəs/ *a.* E19. [f. mod.L *Diclines* n.pl., f. as DI-² + Gk *klinē* bed: see -OUS.] *Bot.* Of a flower or flowering plant: having stamens and pistils in separate flowers.
diclinism *n.* diclinous condition L19.

dicondylian /dʌɪkɒnˈdɪlɪən/ *a.* L19. [f. Gk *dicondulos*, f. as DI-² + *condulos*: see CONDYLE, -IAN.] *Zool.* Of a skull: having two occipital condyles.

dicot /ˈdʌɪkɒt/ *n.* L19. [Abbrev.] = next.

dicotyledon /ˌdʌɪkɒtɪˈliːd(ə)n/ *n.* E18. [mod.L *dicotyledones* pl., f. as DI-² + COTYLEDON.] *Bot.* A flowering plant having two cotyledons; a member of either of the two groups (Dicotyledoneae or Dicotyledones) into which flowering plants are classified. Cf. MONOCOTYLEDON.
dicotyledonous *a.* L18.

dicoumarin /dʌɪˈkuːmərɪn/ *n.* L19. [f. DI-² + COUMARIN.] *Chem.* Orig., any compound with a basic structure of two joined coumarin molecules. Now *spec.* = next.

dicoumarol /dʌɪˈkuːmərɒl/ *n.* M20. [f. prec. + -OL.] *Chem.* & *Pharm.* A derivative, $C_{19}H_{12}O_6$, of coumarin used as an anti-coagulant. Cf. prec.

dicrotic /dʌɪˈkrɒtɪk/ *a.* E19. [f. Gk *dikrotos* double-beating + -IC.] 1 Of the pulse: having a detectable double beat owing to an exaggerated dicrotic wave (see sense 2). E19. 2 Designating a usu. small transient increase in pressure during the overall decreasing pressure of a heartbeat, and a notch representing this in a sphygmogram. M19.
ˈdicrotism *n.* M19.

dict /dɪkt/ *n.* Now *rare* or *obs.* LME. [OFr. (mod. *dit*) or its source L *dictum* use as n. of neut. pa. pple of *dicere* say.] A saying, a maxim.

dict /dɪkt/ *v.t.* Now *rare* or *obs.* E17. [L *dictare* DICTATE *v.*] Put into words; dictate.

dicta *n.pl.* see DICTUM.

dictamen /dɪkˈteɪmɛn/ *n.* Now *rare* or *obs.* Pl. **-mina** /-mɪnə/. L15. [Late L *dictamen*, f. *dictare* DICTATE *v.*] A dictate, a pronouncement.

dictamnus /dɪkˈtamnəs/ *n.* M16. [L: see DITTANY.] = FRAXINELLA. Also = DITTANY 1.

Dictaphone /ˈdɪktəfəʊn/ *n.* Also **d-.** E20. [f. DICTATE *v.*, DICTATION + -PHONE.] (Proprietary name for) a machine that records speech and will subsequently reproduce it for transcription etc.

dictate /ˈdɪkteɪt/ *n.* L16. [L *dictatum* use as n. of neut. pa. pple of *dictare* DICTATE *v.*] 1 An authoritative instruction (esp. of reason, conscience, nature, etc.). Usu. in *pl.* L16. 2 A dictated utterance. Now *rare* or *obs.* E17. †3 An authoritative pronouncement, a dictum. E17–E18. †4 A current saying, a maxim. M–L17.
1 S. JOHNSON I could not receive such dictates without horror. P. G. WODEHOUSE Follow the dictates of your heart. V. S. REID The dictates of His Gracious Majesty, King George III.

dictate /dɪkˈteɪt/ *v.* L16. [L *dictat-* pa. ppl stem of *dictare* frequent. of *dicere* say: see -ATE³.] 1 *v.t.* & *i.* Express in words which are to be written down; say or read aloud (matter to be transcribed, *to* a writer or recording machine). L16. 2 *v.t.* Prescribe, lay down authoritatively (terms, things to be done, etc.); require as an imperative. E17. 3 *v.i.* Lay down the law, give orders. M17.
2 R. TRAVERS Prudence should have dictated a quiet and withdrawn residence.
ˈdictative *a.* of the nature of prescription or command L18.

dictation /dɪkˈteɪʃ(ə)n/ *n.* M17. [Late L *dictatio(n-)*, f. as prec.: see -ATION.] 1 Authoritative utterance or prescription. M17. b The exercise of dictatorship. M19. 2 The act of dictating (for transcription). E18. 3 A dictated utterance. M19.
1 DISRAELI The terms were at his own dictation. 3 R. LOWELL Taking Ford's dictation on Samuel Butler in longhand.
Comb.: **dictation speed** a rate of speech suitable for dictation.

dictator /dɪkˈteɪtə/ *n.* LME. [L *dictator*, f. as. DICTATE *v.*: see -OR.] 1 *Rom. Hist.* A chief magistrate with absolute power who was appointed in an emergency. LME. 2 An absolute ruler, usu. temporary or irregular, of a State; *esp.* one who suppresses or succeeds a democratic government. L16. 3 A person exercising absolute authority of any kind or in any sphere; a domineering person. E17. 4 A person who gives dictation to a writer or recording machine. E17.
2 LYNDON B. JOHNSON The Dominicans had lived for thirty years under the iron-fisted rule of dictator Leonidas Trujillo. 3 SWIFT The dictators of behaviour, dress, and politeness.
dictatorate *n.* the position of a dictator M19. **dictatorship** *n.* the position of a dictator; a State ruled by a dictator; absolute authority in any sphere: M16.

dictatorial /dɪktəˈtɔːrɪəl/ *a.* E18. [f. L *dictatorius*, f. as prec. + -AL[1].] Of, pertaining to, or proper to a dictator; imperious, overbearing.

R. L. STEVENSON He rose . . to almost dictatorial authority in the State.

dictatorially *adv.* L18. **dictatorialness** *n.* L19. †**dictatorian** *a.* = DICTATORIAL M17–E18. ˈ**dictatory** *a.* = DICTATORIAL M17. ˈ**dictatorily** *adv.* = DICTATORIALLY L18.

dictatress /dɪkˈteɪtrɪs/ *n.* L18. [f. DICTATOR + -ESS[1].] A female dictator.

Also **dictatrix** /-trɪks/ *n.*, pl. **-trices** /-trɪsiːz/, E17.

dictature /dɪkˈteɪtʃə/ *n.* M16. [L *dictatura*, f. as DICTATE *v.*: see -URE.] 1 = DICTATORSHIP. M16. 2 A collective body of dictators. M18.

diction /ˈdɪkʃ(ə)n/ *n.* M16. [(O)Fr., or L *dictio(n-)* saying, mode of expression, (later) word, f. *dict-* pa. ppl stem of *dicere* say.] †1 A word. M16–L17. †2 A phrase; a locution. M16–E18. †3 Speech; verbal description. L16–E17. 4 The choice of words and phrases in speech or writing; the manner of enunciation in speaking, singing, etc. L17.

4 W. H. AUDEN To clothe my fiction in up-to-date diction, The contemporary jargon of Pride. *Wardour-street diction*: see WARDOUR STREET 1.

dictionary /ˈdɪkʃ(ə)n(ə)ri/ *n.* E16. [med.L *dictionarium* (sc. *manuale* MANUAL *n.*) and *dictionarius* (sc. *liber* book), f. L *dictio(n-)*: see prec., -ARY[1].] I 1 a A book explaining or translating, usu. in alphabetical order, words of a language or languages, giving their pronunciation, spelling, meaning, part of speech, and etymology, or one or some of these. E16. †b The vocabulary or whole list of words used or admitted by someone. L16–E18. c An ordered list stored in and used by a computer; *esp.* a list of words acceptable to a word processor. M20. 2 A book of information or reference on any subject in which the entries are arranged alphabetically. M17.

1a *abridged dictionary, children's dictionary, dictionary of Americanisms, pronouncing dictionary, slang dictionary, unabridged dictionary*, etc. **have swallowed the dictionary** use long and recondite words. 2 *biographical dictionary, dictionary of the Bible, dictionary of proverbs*, etc.

II *fig.* 3 A person or thing regarded as a repository of knowledge, convenient for consultation. E17.

Dictograph /ˈdɪktəgrɑːf/ *n.* Also **d-**. E20. [f. as DICTAPHONE + -O- + -GRAPH, after *phonograph*.] (Proprietary name for) a telephonic instrument which reproduces in one room the sounds made in another.

dictum /ˈdɪktəm/ *n.* Pl. **-ta** /-tə/, **-tums**. L16. [L: see DICT *n.*] 1 A saying, an utterance; *esp.* one that claims some authority, a pronouncement. L16. 2 *Law.* An expression of opinion by a judge which is not essential to the decision and so has no binding authority as precedent. See also OBITER DICTUM. L18. 3 A common saying; a maxim. E19.

1 P. ACKROYD A lover of allusive quotation (particularly from the *dicta* of Sherlock Holmes). 3 J. S. MILL The *dictum* that truth always triumphs.

dicty /ˈdɪkti/ *a.* *US slang.* E20. [Origin unkn.] Conceited, snobbish; elegant, stylish, high-class.

dictyosome /ˈdɪktɪə(ʊ)səʊm/ *n.* L19. [f. Gk *diktuon* net + -SOME[3].] *Biol.* Any of the discrete bodies forming the Golgi apparatus in some cells.

dictyostele /ˈdɪktɪə(ʊ)stiːl/ *n.* E20. [f. Gk *diktuon* net + STELE.] *Bot.* A stele, typical of many ferns, in which the vascular tissue is in separate strands; *esp.* one in which the phloem and xylem are arranged concentrically in each strand.

dictyoˈstelic *a.* M20.

dicynodont /dʌɪˈsɪnədɒnt/ *n.* & *a.* M19. [mod.L *Dicynodontia* (see below), f. DI-[2] + CYNO- + -ODONT.] *Palaeont.* A *n.* A fossil reptile with no teeth except for two in the upper jaw; a member of the suborder Dicynodontia of mammal-like therapsid reptiles. M19. B *adj.* Designating or pertaining to a dicynodont. L19.

did *v.* see DO *v.*

didache /ˈdɪdəkiː/ *n.* In sense 1 **D-**. L19. [Gk *didakhē* teaching.] 1 *the Didache*, a short early Christian manual. L19. 2 The instructional element in early Christianity, as contrasted with the kerygma. M20.

didactic /dɪˈdaktɪk, dʌɪ-/ *a.* & *n.* M17. [Gk *didaktikos*, f. *didak-* stem of *didaskein* teach: see -IC. In Eng. perh. after Fr. *didactique*.] A *adj.* Having the character or manner of a teacher; intended to instruct; having instruction as an ulterior purpose. M17.

T. F. DIBDIN The dullest of all possible didactic and moral poetry. A. HAILEY Letting Harry London get to the point in his own didactic way.

B *n.* †1 A didactic author or treatise. M17–M19. 2 In *pl.* (treated as *sing.* or *pl.*). The art of teaching. M19.

didactical *a.* (*rare*) = DIDACTIC *a.* E17. **didactically** *adv.* E17. **didacticism** /-sɪz(ə)m/ *n.* the practice or quality of being didactic M19. **didactive** *a.* = DIDACTIC *a.* E18.

didactyl /dʌɪˈdaktɪl/ *a.* E19. [f. DI-[2] + Gk *daktulos* finger.] *Zool.* Characterized by or having two fingers or toes.

Also **didactylous** *a.* E19.

didakai *n.* var. of DIDICOI.

didapper /ˈdʌɪdapə/ *n.* LME. [Prob. f. as DIVE-DAP.] A small diving bird; a little grebe.

fig.: R. CARPENTER Thou art a Didapper peering vp and downe in a moment.

didascalic /dɪdəˈskalɪk/ *a.* E17. [L *didascalicus* f. Gk *didaskalikos* instructive, f. *didaskalos* teacher, f. *didaskein* teach: see -IC.] Pertaining to a teacher; didactic.

didder /ˈdɪdə/ *v.i. obs.* exc. *dial.* See also DITHER *v.* LME. [Rel. to DADDER, DODDER *v.*] Tremble, shake, shiver.

diddery *a.* M19.

diddicoy *n.* var. of DIDICOI.

diddle /ˈdɪd(ə)l/ *v.*[1] M17. [App. parallel to DIDDER: cf. DADDLE *v.*] †1 *v.i.* = DADDLE *v.* Only in M17. 2 *v.i.* Jerk from side to side; play the violin; dance a jig. *Sc.* & *dial.* E18. 3 *v.t.* & *i.* Copulate (with); masturbate. *slang.* L19.

diddle /ˈdɪd(ə)l/ *v.*[2] *colloq.* E19. [Origin uncertain: perh. back-form. f. DIDDLER, or identical with prec.] 1 *v.t.* Cheat, swindle (*out of*). E19. 2 *v.t.* Ruin; kill. Now *rare* or *obs.* E19. 3a *v.t.* Pass (time) idly, trifle *away*. E19. b *v.i.* Idle, potter, loaf (*about, around*); play *around*. E19.

3b H. NICOLSON I rather diddle about in the morning.

diddle- /ˈdɪd(ə)l/ *comb. form* of DIDDLE *v.*[1] or *v.*[2]

diddle-diddle *n.* & *int.* (repr.) the sound of a fiddle; the action of playing a fiddle: E16. **diddledum** *n.* a trifling thing L16.

diddler /ˈdɪdlə/ *n.* *colloq.* E19. [f. DIDDLE *v.*[2] + -ER[1] or f. the name of Jeremy *Diddler* in J. Kenney's play *Raising the Wind* (1803).] A mean swindler, a cheat.

diddums /ˈdɪdəmz/ *int.* & *n.* L19. [f. *did 'em*, i.e. 'did they' (sc. 'tease you' etc.) + -S[1].] (A form of address to young children and *joc.* to adults) expr. commiseration or endearment.

J. ELLIOT She's quite happy. Aren't you, diddums?

diddy /ˈdɪdi/ *n.* *slang* & *dial.* L18. [Alt. of TITTY *n.*[2]] A woman's breast or nipple; an animal's teat.

didelphid /dʌɪˈdɛlfɪd/ *n.* & *a.* L19. [mod.L *Didelphidae* (see below), f. DI-[2] + Gk *delphus* womb: see -ID[3].] *Zool.* (Of, pertaining to, or designating) a marsupial of the family Didelphidae, containing the opossums, or (formerly) any marsupial.

didgeridoo /dɪdʒ(ə)rɪˈduː/ *n.* Also **-dj-**, **-du**. E20. [Aborig., of imit. origin.] A long tubular wooden musical instrument of the Australian Aborigines which is blown to produce a resonant sound.

didicoi /ˈdɪdɪkɔɪ/ *n.* *slang* & *dial.* Also **didakai**, **diddicoy**, & other vars. M19. [Perh. alt. of Romany *dik akei* look here.] A Gypsy; an itinerant tinker.

didjeridoo, **-du** *n.* vars. of DIDGERIDOO.

didn't *v.* see DO *v.*

dido /ˈdʌɪdəʊ/ *n.* *dial.* & *US slang.* Pl. **-o(e)s**. E19. [Origin unkn.] A prank, an antic; a disturbance, a row. Freq. in *to cut didoes*.

didrachm /ˈdʌɪdram/ *n.* M16. [Late L *didrachma, didrachmon* f. Gk *didrakhmon*, f. as DI-[2] + DRACHMA.] An ancient Greek silver coin worth two drachmas.

didric, **-ik** *ns.* vars. of DIEDERIK.

didst *v.* see DO *v.*

didy /ˈdʌɪdi/ *n.* *US colloq.* E20. [Childish form of DIAPER *n.*: see -Y[6].] A baby's nappy.

didymis /ˈdɪdɪmɪs/ *n.* Long *rare.* Pl. **-mes** /-miːz/. Also (earlier) †**dyndym(e)**, **-my**. LME. [Abbrev. of Gk *epididumis* EPIDIDYMIS.] = EPIDIDYMIS.

didymium /dɪˈdɪmɪəm/ *n.* M19. [f. Gk *didumos* twin (adj.) + -IUM.] A naturally occurring mixture of neodymium and praseodymium, used to colour glass for optical filters.

¶ Orig. regarded as an element.

didymous /ˈdɪdɪməs/ *a.* L18. [f. Fr. *didyme* (f. as prec.) + -OUS.] *Bot.* & *Zool.* Growing in pairs, twin.

didynamous /dʌɪˈdɪnəməs, dɪ-/ *a.* L18. [f. DI-[2] + Gk *dunamis* power + -OUS.] *Bot.* Having or designating stamens arranged in two pairs, each of unequal length.

die /dʌɪ/ *n.*[1] Pl. in branch I **dice** /dʌɪs/ (see also DICE *n.*); in branch II **dies**. ME. [(O)Fr. *dé*, pl. *dés*, f. L DATUM.] I 1 A small cube whose six faces are marked with from one to six spots, used in games of chance by being thrown from a box, the hand, etc., the score being decided from the uppermost face; a cube with different markings, or a solid with a different number of faces, used in the same way. ME. b *fig.* Chance, luck. L16. 2 A small cubical segment, esp. of meat etc. for cooking. Usu. in *pl.* LME.

1 HAZLITT Dependent on the turn of a die, on the tossing up of a halfpenny. E. O'NEILL It is not gambling when I know the dice are loaded in my favor. b SPENSER His harder fortune was to fall Under my speare; such is the dye of warre. 2 E. RAFFALD Turnips and carrots cut in dice.

II 3 A cubical block; *Archit.* = DADO 1. M17. 4 An engraved stamp for impressing a design on some softer material as in coining, striking a medal, embossing paper, etc. L17. 5 Any of various devices for shaping bulk material; *esp.* (*a*) an internally threaded hollow tool for cutting a screw thread; (*b*) a part into which a punch is driven; (*c*) a block with a hole through which material is extruded; (*d*) a hollow mould into which material is forced prior to solidification. E19. 6 A toy. *Sc.* E19.

Phrases: **as straight** or **true as a die** (of a person) entirely honest or loyal. **the die is cast** the decisive or irrevocable step is taken.

Comb.: **die-cast** *v.t.* cast in a mould; **die-casting** the casting of hot metal or plastic in a mould; an article so made; **die-link** *Numism.* the relationship established between coins struck from the same die; **die-sinker** an engraver of dies; **die-stamping** embossing paper etc. with a die.

†**die** *n.*[2] var. of DYE *n.*

die /dʌɪ/ *v.*[1]*i.* Pa. t. & pple **died** /dʌɪd/; pres. pple **dying** /ˈdʌɪɪŋ/. ME. [ON *deyja* (= OS *dōian*, OHG *touwen*), f. Gmc base also of DEAD *a.* & *adv.* Corresp. vb perh. already in OE, reinforced f. ON.] I Of animate or sentient things. 1 Of a person or animal: lose life, cease to live, suffer death; expire. Freq. w. prep. phr. denoting the cause or manner of death. ME. b *Theol.* Suffer spiritual death; perish everlastingly. ME. 2 Of a plant, living tissue, etc.: lose the vital force; cease to be alive. LME. 3 Suffer the pains or dangers of death; face death. LME. 4 Experience great suffering; languish; be consumed with longing *for*, desire greatly *to do*. L16. 5 Become exhausted *with* laughing; be overcome with embarrassment, boredom, etc. (Also foll. by *of*.) L16. 6 Have an orgasm. (Freq. a secondary sense in fig. uses of sense 1.) L16. 7 Of a person's heart: apparently stop beating, as in a faint. E17.

1 R. CAMPBELL She died only the other day at the age of about a hundred and ten. J. FOWLES Four sons, two of whom died in the First World War. *die of illness*

or *hunger, by violence, the sword,* or *one's own hand, from a wound, through neglect, on the scaffold, at the stake, in battle, for a friend* or *a cause, in poverty.* b NEB *John* 11:26 No one who is alive and has faith shall ever die. 2 SHELLEY The pale flowers are dying. *Nature* After death of the brain, other organs and tissues die at different times. 3 AV *1 Cor.* 15:31 I protest by your rejoicing which I have in Christ Jesus our Lord, I die daily. 4 G. ALLEN The pretty American's dying to see you. 5 M. WILMOT I thought I should have died, when Lady Grace told him *audibly* he had turned over *two leaves.* P. SCOTT I am dying of thirst. 6 POPE Who only hoped upon his foe to die.

II *transf.* 8 Come to an end, cease to exist; pass out of memory or knowledge. Of a flame etc.: go out. Of an engine: stop running. ME. 9 Of a substance: lose its characteristic quality; become inactive or flat. E17. 10 Pass by dying *into* something else; change *into* something at death or termination; *Archit.* merge *into,* terminate gradually *in* or *against.* M17. 11 Pass gradually away, esp. out of hearing or sight; fade away. E18

8 C. A. LINDBERGH The engine sputtered and died. E. WAUGH The secret had died with him. 10 TENNYSON The twilight died into the dark. 11 S. BECKETT A single confused sound, .. swelling, dying. P. BARKER Elaine .. started to say something else, but the words died on her lips.

Phrases etc.: **die a (specified) death** meet (a particular kind of) death. **die game** die fighting, not yielding to weakness or cowardice. **die hard** die painfully or after a struggle. **die in harness** die while in a job, die before retirement. **die in one's bed** die of natural causes. **die in one's boots** or (*arch.*) **shoes** = *die with one's boots on* below. **die in the last ditch** die desperately defending something, die fighting to the last extremity. *die like a dog*: see DOG *n.* **die on someone** (*a*) die in the presence or charge of someone; (*b*) cease to be of use or interest to someone. **die the death** (*arch.* or *joc.*) be put to death; (of a performer, performance, etc.) be received very badly, be a failure. **die with one's boots** or **shoes on** die a violent death. *do or die*: see DO *v.* **hope** or **wish I may die, hope to die** *colloq.*: said to vouch for the truth of an assertion. *lie down and die*: see LIE *v.*[1] **never say die** refuse to give in, keep your courage up. *the tune the (old) cow died of*: see TUNE *n. wish I may die*: see *hope I may die* above. *wish to curl up and die*: see CURL *v.*

With advs. in specialized senses: **die away** (*a*) diminish gradually in force, activity, etc., cease or disappear by degrees; (*b*) (*arch.* or *poet.*) pass slowly from life, swoon; (*c*) *Archit.* merge gradually into an adjacent structure. **die back** (of the shoot of a plant etc.) die from the tip towards the root. **die down** (*a*) subside by natural degrees into a quieter state; (*b*) (of a plant) die above ground but stay alive below, as an annual occurrence. **die off** (*a*) be removed one by one by death, lose members by successive deaths; (*b*) (of a sound etc.) = *die away* (a) above. **die out** become extinct, gradually cease to be.

Comb.: **die-away** *a.* having a languishing or affectedly feeble manner; **die-back** the progressive dying back of a shrub or tree shoot owing to disease or unfavourable conditions; **die-in** *colloq.* a demonstration in which people lie down as if dead.

die /dʌɪ/ *v.*[2]*t.* E18. [f. DIE *n.*[1]] Provide with a die; shape using a die.

†die *v.*[3] var. of DYE *v.*

diecious *a.* see DIOECIOUS.

diederik /ˈdiːdərɪk/ *n. S. Afr.* Also **didric, -ik,** /ˈdɪdrɪk/, **diedrik** /ˈdiːdrɪk/. L18. [Imit.] A small African cuckoo, *Chrysococcyx caprius.*

diegesis /dʌɪəˈdʒiːsɪs/ *n.* Pl. **-geses** /-ˈdʒiːsiːz/. E19. [Gk *diēgēsis* narrative. In mod. use partly f. Fr. *diégèse* f. Gk.] A narrative, a report of action, a plot, now esp. in a cinema or television film.

diegetic /dʌɪˈdʒɛtɪk/ *a.* L20.

†Diego *n.* E17. [Sp. = James (name of the patron saint of Spain).] 1 A Spaniard. Cf. DAGO 1. Only in 17. 2 A Spanish sword; a sword of the Spanish type. E18–M19.

die-hard /ˈdʌɪhɑːd/ *n.* & *a.* Also **diehard.** M19. [f. *die hard* s.v. DIE *v.*[1]] **A** *n.* 1 A person who resists to the last. M19. 2 A resolute opponent of change; a very conservative person. E20. 3 A Scotch terrier. E20.

1 **The Die-hards** *slang* (in the British army) the 4th Battalion The Queen's Regiment (orig. the 57th Regiment of Foot).

B *adj.* Resisting to the last; staunchly opposing change. L19.

die-hardism *n.* E20.

dieldrin /ˈdiːldrɪn/ *n.* M20. [f. O. *Diels* (1876–1954), Ger. chemist + ALDRIN.] An insecticide consisting of an epoxide, $C_{12}H_8Cl_6O$, of aldrin.

dielectric /dʌɪɪˈlɛktrɪk/ *n.* & *a.* M19. [f. DI-[3] + ELECTRIC.] *Physics.* **A** *n.* A substance which does not allow the passage of an electric current through it. M19.

B *adj.* 1 Pertaining to or involving a dielectric, or the transmission of electric force without an electric current. M19. 2 That is a dielectric; non-conducting. L19.

1 **dielectric constant** permittivity. **dielectric heating**: by means of a high-frequency electric field which produces heating throughout the substance of a dielectric.

dielectrically *adv.* L19.

dielectrophoresis /dʌɪˌɪlɛktrəfəˈriːsɪs/ *n.* M20. [Blend of DIELECTRIC *n.* and ELECTROPHORESIS.] The migration of uncharged particles towards a maximum of the electric field.

Diels–Alder reaction /diːlzˈɔːldə rɪˌakʃ(ə)n/ *n. phr.* M20. [f. as DIELDRIN + K. *Alder* (1902–58), Ger. chemist.] *Chem.* The addition of a conjugated diene to a compound with a double or triple bond so as to form a six-membered ring.

dielytra /dʌɪˈɛlɪtrə/ *n.* Now *rare.* M19. [mod.L, f. DI-[2] + Gk *elutron* sheath.] A plant of a former genus called *Dielytra*, now included in *Dicentra* (see DICENTRA).

diencephalon /dʌɪɛnˈsɛf(ə)lɒn/ *n.* L19. [f. DI-[3] + Gk *egkephalos* brain.] *Anat.* The caudal part of the forebrain, consisting of the epithalamus, thalamus, hypothalamus, and ventral thalamus and the third ventricle. Cf. TELENCEPHALON.

ˌdienceˈphalic *a.* L19.

diene /ˈdʌɪiːn/ *n.* E20. [f. DI-[2] + -ENE.] *Chem.* Any organic compound containing two double bonds between carbon atoms.

dieresis *n.* see DIAERESIS.

diervilla /ˈdɪəvɪlə/ *n.* E19. [mod.L, f. *Dierville,* Fr. surgeon and discoverer of the plant, *c* 1700 + -A[1].] Any of various deciduous flowering shrubs of the honeysuckle family, most of which are now placed in the genus *Weigela* leaving a few in *Diervilla.*

dies /ˈdiːeɪz, *Law* ˈdʌɪiːz/ *n.* Pl. same. L17. [L.] A day. Only in (chiefly legal) phrs.: see below.

Dies irae /ˌdiːeɪz ˈɪərʌɪ, ˈɪəreɪ/ [L = day of wrath] a 13th-cent. Latin sequence formerly obligatory in a requiem mass in the Roman Catholic Church. ***dies non*** /dʌɪiːz ˈnɒn/ *Law* = *dies non juridicus* below. ***dies non juridicus*** /ˌdʌɪiːz nɒn dʒʊəˈrɪdɪkəs/, pl. ***juridici*** /-dɪsʌɪ/, [lit. 'day not (judicial)'] *Law* a day on which no legal business is done; a day that does not count or cannot be used for a particular purpose.

diesel /ˈdiːz(ə)l/ *n.* Also **D-.** L19. [R. *Diesel* (1858–1913), Ger. engineer.] 1 In full *diesel engine.* An internal-combustion engine in which indrawn air is compressed so as to heat it sufficiently to ignite the fuel that subsequently enters the cylinder. L19. 2 A vehicle with a diesel engine. E20. 3 Fuel for diesel engines; diesel oil. L20.

Comb.: **diesel-electric** *a.* & *n.* (an engine, locomotive, etc.) driven by electric motors powered by current from a generator which is driven by a diesel engine; *diesel engine*: see sense 1 above; **diesel oil** a petroleum fraction used as fuel in diesel engines.

dieseliˈzation *n.* the process of dieselizing M20. **dieselize** *v.t.* equip with a diesel engine or with diesel-electric locomotives M20.

diesis /ˈdʌɪɪsɪs/ *n.* Pl. **-eses** /-ɪsiːz/. LME. [L f. Gk = quarter-tone, f. *diienai* send through, f. as DI-[3] + *ienai* send.] 1 *Mus.* An interval equal to the difference between an octave and four minor thirds (*greater diesis*) or three major thirds (*lesser diesis*); *Hist.* any of various intervals smaller than a tone, *esp.* a quarter-tone. LME. 2 *Typogr.* The double dagger. E18.

diestrum, -us *ns.* see DIOESTRUS.

diet /ˈdʌɪət/ *n.*[1] ME. [(O)Fr. *diète* f. L *diaeta* f. Gk *diaita* course of life.] 1 Food; *esp.* one's habitual food. Freq. w. specifying wd. ME. †2 A manner of life; a way of living or thinking. LME–M17. 3 A manner of sustenance, as regards the kind of food eaten. LME. 4 A prescribed course of food, restricted in kind or limited in quantity, *esp.* one used to control one's weight; (a) restricted provision or intake of food. LME. 5 Board. Formerly also, an allowance or provision of food. *obs.* exc. *Hist. dial.* LME. 6 An allowance for the expenses of living. Long *obs.* exc. *Hist.* L15.

1 M. W. MONTAGU Herbs or roots .. and plain dry bread. That is their lenten diet. 3 M. PYKE Agricultural people living on a mainly vegetarian diet. R. HOGGART A balanced diet. 4 S. JOHNSON To preach diet and abstinence to his patients. A. POWELL His wife kept him on a diet. *fig.*: *Guardian* It will provide a diet of feature films, sport, serials, talk shows and quizzes. 5 SHAKES. *1 Hen. IV* You owe money here .. for your diet and by-drinkings.

Comb.: **diet-bread** special bread prepared for invalids etc.; **diet-drink**: prescribed and prepared for medicinal etc. purposes; **diet-sheet** a paper showing the daily diet prescribed for an individual patient etc.

diet /ˈdʌɪət/ *n.*[2] LME [med.L *dieta* day's journey, allowance, work, wages, assoc. w. L *dies* day. In senses 1 & 2 cf. (O)Fr. *journée.*] †1 A day's journey; an excursion. Chiefly *Sc.* LME–M17. 2 A meeting formally arranged for discussion or transaction of national or international business; a conference, a congress. LME. b *spec.* The regular meeting of the estates of a realm or confederation; *esp.* any of various foreign legislative assemblies, e.g. the former German *Reichstag.* M16. 3 A session or sitting of a court etc. on an appointed day; a single session of any assembly occupying (a part of) one day. *Sc.* L15. 4 An appointed date or time; *spec.* the day on which a party in a legal case is cited to appear in court. *Sc.* M16. 5 The metal scraped or cut from gold and silver assayed day by day at the Mint, and retained for the purpose of trial. E18.

2b H. A. L. FISHER Luther was summoned to Worms to attend upon the young Emperor and his first Diet. 3 *desert the diet*: see DESERT *v.* 2a.

diet /ˈdʌɪət/ *v.* LME. [f. DIET *n.*[1], after OFr. *dieter,* med.L *diaetare.*] **I** *v.t.* 1 Feed, esp. in a particular way or with specified food. LME. 2 Regulate or restrict the habitual food of (a person) in nature and quantity for a particular purpose, esp. treatment or punishment. LME. 3 Provide with daily meals; board. Now *rare* or *obs.* M17.

1 *fig.*: SHAKES. *Cymb.* Thou art all the comfort The gods will diet me with. 2 R. LOWELL His newly dieted figure was vitally trim.

II *v.i.* 4 Take one's habitual food, meals, etc.; feed *on. arch.* M16. 5 Board (*with* a person, *at, in* a house etc.). Now *rare* or *obs.* L16. 6 Eat according to set rules; restrict the amount or kind of food one eats, now esp. to control one's weight. M17.

6 A. NEWMAN My wife used to diet.

dieter *n.* L16.

dietary /ˈdʌɪət(ə)ri/ *n.* & *a.* LME. [med.L *dietarium,* f. L *diaeta, dieta*: see DIET *n.*[1], -ARY[1].] **A** *n.* 1 A diet; a book etc. prescribing a diet. LME. 2 A regulated allowance of food in a hospital, prison, etc. M19.

1 L. MUMFORD New food crops .. enriched the dietary of Europe.

B *adj.* Of or pertaining to (a) diet or a dietary. E17.

dietetic /dʌɪəˈtɛtɪk/ *n.* & *a.* M16. [L *diaeteticus* f. Gk *diaitētikos,* f. *diaita*: see DIET *n.*[1], -IC.] **A** *n. Med. sing.* & (usu.) in *pl.* (treated as *sing.* or *pl.*). The application of the principles of nutrition to the choice and use of diet. M16. **B** *adj.* Of or pertaining to diet or dietetics. L16.

†dietetical *a.* = DIETETIC *a.* E17–E19. **dietetically** *adv.* M19.

diether /dʌɪˈiːθə/ *n.* M20. [f. DI-[2] + ETHER *n.*[1]] *Chem.* Any compound whose molecule contains two oxygen atoms each linked as in an ether.

diethyl /dʌɪˈiːθʌɪl, -ˈɛθɪl/ *a.* M19. [f. DI-[2] + ETHYL.] *Chem.* Having two ethyl groups in the molecule.

diethyl ether = ETHER *n.*[1] 4a.

diethylamide /-ˈɛmʌɪd/ *n.* a compound in which the group $\cdot N(C_2H_5)_2$ replaces a hydrogen atom or a hydroxyl group M20; **diethylstil'boestrol, -bes-** *n.* = STILBOESTROL 2 M20.

dietic /dʌɪ'ɛtɪk/ *n.* & *a.* M17. [f. DIET *n.*[1] + -IC.] †A *n.* A dietetic article or application. Only in M17. B *adj.* = DIETETIC *a.* E18.
Also †**dietical** *a.*: only in M17.

dietine /'dʌɪətiːn/ *n.* M17. [Fr. *diétine* dim. of *diète* DIET *n.*[2]: see -INE[4].] A subordinate diet (DIET *n.*[2]); *spec.* (*Hist.*) a Polish provincial diet which elected deputies for the national diet.

dietist /'dʌɪətɪst/ *n.* E17. [f. DIET *n.*[1] + -IST.] A dietitian.

dietitian /dʌɪə'tɪʃ(ə)n/ *n.* Also **-ician**. M19. [f. DIET *n.*[1] + *-itian* irreg. form of -ICIAN.] A person who is skilled in or practises dietetics.

Dietl's crisis /'diːt(ə)lz krʌɪsɪs/ *n. phr.* L19. [f. J. *Dietl* (1804–78), physician of Kraków, Poland + CRISIS.] *Med.* An acute renal pain often accompanied by vomiting and abdominal distension. Freq. in *pl.*

dif *n.* & *a.* see DIFF.

dif- /dɪf/ *pref.* (not productive). Assim. form of L DIS- bef. *f.*

diff /dɪf/ *n.* & *a. colloq.* In senses A.1, B. also **dif.** L19. [Abbrev.] A *n.* 1 = DIFFERENCE *n.* L19. 2 = DIFFERENTIAL *n.* 3. M20. B *adj.* = DIFFERENT *a.* E20.

diffarreation /dɪ,farɪ'eɪʃ(ə)n/ *n.* E17. [L *diffareatio(n-)*, f. as DIF- + *farreum* spelt-cake: see -ATION.] *Rom. Hist.* The dissolution of a marriage solemnized by confarreation.

differ /'dɪfə/ *n. Sc.* & *north.* M16. [f. next.] = DIFFERENCE *n.*

differ /'dɪfə/ *v.* See also DEFER *v.*[1] LME. [(O)Fr. *différer* differ, (also) defer, f. L *differre*, f. DIF- + *ferre* carry.] †I 1 See DEFER *v.*[1] LME.
II 2 *v.t.* Separate from each other in qualities; make dissimilar, different, or distinct; cause to vary; differentiate (one thing *from* another). Now *rare.* LME. 3 *v.i.* Be of a variant or contrasting nature or inclination; be unlike, distinct, or various. (Foll. by *from.*) LME. 4 *v.i.* Be at variance; hold opposed or contrasting views on a subject; disagree. (Foll. by *from, with.*) M16. †5 *v.i.* Express disagreement; dispute; quarrel (*with*). E17–M18.
2 W. FAULKNER That thin clear quenchless lucidity which alone differed him from this bear. 3 G. GREENE If we had believed in sin, our behaviour would hardly have differed. H. L. MENCKEN If they differ from the rest it is only in the superior impudence and shamelessness of their false pretenses. I. ASIMOV The varying patterns in wall and floor covering and the differing designs in tableware. 4 J. H. NEWMAN She may . . differ from me in opinion. C. IVES Geniuses . . differ as to *what* is beautiful and *what* is ugly . . but they all agree that beauty is better than ugliness. *agree to differ*: see AGREE *v.* 10.

difference /'dɪf(ə)r(ə)ns/ *n.* & *v.* ME. [(O)Fr. *différence* f. L *differentia*, f. *different-*: see DIFFERENT, -ENCE.] A *n.* 1 The condition, quality, or fact of being not the same in quality or nature; dissimilarity; non-identity. ME. 2 An instance of unlikeness; a respect in which things differ. LME. 3 The quantity by which amounts differ; the remainder left after subtraction. LME. b *spec.* The amount of increase or decrease in the price of stocks or shares between certain dates. E18. 4 A divergence or disagreement in opinion; a dispute; a quarrel. LME. 5 A mark, device, or characteristic feature. Now *rare* or *obs.* exc. *Her.*, an alteration made in a coat of arms to distinguish branches or members of the same family. LME. b *Logic.* A characteristic distinguishing a species from others of the same genus. M16. 6 A distinction regarded as conceived by a person rather than existing in the objects. Now only in *make a difference between* below. LME. †7 A division, a class, a kind. M16–L17.
1 G. BURNET In all this Diversity there is no real difference. J. BARZUN The difference between a scientist and an inventor. 2 S. SPENDER The differences between us remained more striking than the resemblances. J. B. PRIESTLEY The chief difference in the congregation was that there were fewer young people in it. 4 K. AMIS Buckmaster and the chauffeur were having a little difference about something. 5 SHAKES. *Haml.* An absolute gentleman, full of most excellent differences. 6 E. STILLINGFLEET To make them more capable of putting a difference between truth and falsehood.
Phrases: *a distinction without a difference*: see DISTINCTION 2. †**at difference** at variance. **make a difference between** treat differently. **make all the difference** be the deciding factor; be very significant. *same difference*: see SAME *a.* **split the difference** take the average of two proposed amounts. **with a difference** in a special way.
B *v.* †1 *v.i.* Be different, differ. *rare.* Only in L15. 2 *v.t.* †a *gen.* Make different, alter, vary. L15–L17. b *Her.* Make an alteration in or addition to (a coat of arms) in order to distinguish branches or members of the same family. E18. 3 *v.t.* Cause or constitute a difference in; differentiate, distinguish (one thing *from* another). Freq. in *pass.* L16. 4 *v.t.* Perceive or mark the difference in or between; make a distinction between. (Foll. by *from.*) Now *rare.* L16. †5 *v.i.* Perceive or mark the difference (*between*). M–L17. 6 *Math.* Find the difference or (formerly) the derivative of. Now *rare* or *obs.* L17.
3 E. B. TYLOR Theologic change which differences the Jew of the Rabbinical books from the Jew of the Pentateuch. 4 G. CHAPMAN I have remov'd those erring mists . . That thou may'st difference Gods from men.

†**differency** *n.* E17–E19. [L *differentia*: see DIFFERENT, -ENCY.] = DIFFERENCE *n.*

different /'dɪf(ə)r(ə)nt/ *a.*, *n.*, & *adv.* LME. [(O)Fr. *différent* f. L *different-* pres. ppl stem of *differre*: see DIFFER *v.*, -ENT.] A *adj.* 1 Having divergent characters or qualities; having dissimilar or distinguishing attributes; unlike; of other form, nature, or quality. (Foll. by *from, to, than,* †*against,* †*with.*) LME. 2 Distinct, separate, other. M17. 3 Out of the ordinary, unusual, special. *colloq.* E20.
1 I. MCEWAN A resigned smile of welcome, markedly different from his usual boisterous style. J. BRAINE Each wall was in a different shade of green. *same but different*: see SAME *a.* 2 TOLKIEN He poured them out two full bowls from a stone jar; but from a different jar.
B *n.* †1 = DIFFERENCE *n.* 4. L15–E17. 2 Something different; a contrary, an opposite. *rare.* L16.
C *adv.* Differently. Chiefly *joc.* or *dial.* M18.
¶ *different than*, *different to* are often regarded as incorrect, though used by many well-known writers since the 17th cent.; *different than* is commoner in American than in British English.
differently *adv.* in a different manner, to a different degree; diversely: LME. **differentness** *n.* the quality of being different E18.

differentia /dɪfə'rɛnʃɪə/ *n.* Pl. **-iae** /-iiː/. L17. [L: see DIFFERENCE *n.*] A distinguishing mark or characteristic, *esp.* (*Logic*) that distinguishing a species from others of the same genus.

differentiable /dɪfə'rɛnʃɪəb(ə)l/ *a.* M19. [f. DIFFERENTIATE *v.* + -ABLE, after *deprecate, deprecable, depreciate, depreciable,* etc.] Able to be differentiated.
differentia'bility *n.* E20.

differential /dɪfə'rɛnʃ(ə)l/ *a.* & *n.* M17. [med.L *differentialis*, f. L DIFFERENTIA: see -AL[1].] A *adj.* 1 Of or relating to difference or diversity; exhibiting or depending on a difference; varying according to circumstances. M17. 2 Constituting or pertaining to a specific difference; distinctive, special. M17. 3 *Math.* Relating to infinitesimal differences. E18. 4 *Physics* & *Mech.* Pertaining to, exhibiting, or involving the difference between two or more physical quantities. M18.
1 J. E. T. ROGERS Differential duties in favour of colonial timber. 2 DE QUINCEY Every case in the law courts . . presents some one differential feature peculiar to itself. **differential diagnosis** the process of differentiating between two similar diseases etc. 3 *differential calculus*: see CALCULUS 1. **differential coefficient** = DERIVATIVE *n.* 3. **differential equation**: involving derivatives. 4 **differential gear**: enabling power to be divided between two axles in line with one another and able to rotate at different speeds, as when a vehicle corners.
B *n.* 1 *Math.* a The infinitesimal difference between two successive values of a variable; either of the two quantities whose ratio constitutes a differential coefficient. E18. †b A logarithmic tangent. E18–M19. 2 An amount by which a basic charge or payment is varied; a difference between the wages of different categories of worker or between the prices of similar products etc. from different companies. L19. 3 A differential gear. E20.
differentially *adv.* (*a*) distinctively, specially; (*b*) in relation to the difference between two measurable quantities; in two different directions: M17.

differentiate /dɪfə'rɛnʃɪeɪt/ *v.* & *n.* E19. [med.L *differentiat-* pa. ppl stem of *differentiare*, f. L DIFFERENTIA: see -ATE[3].] A *v.* 1 *v.t. Math.* Obtain the derivative or differential of. E19. 2 *v.t.* Constitute a difference in, of, or between; serve to make different *from.* M19. 3 *v.t.* Make different in the process of growth or development. Usu. in *pass.* M19. 4 *v.i.* Become differentiated or specialized. L19. 5 *v.t.* & *i.* Observe, ascertain, or recognize the difference (in or between); distinguish, discriminate, (between). L19.
2 A. WILSON The famous private life that's supposed to differentiate him from other public servants. 3 W. B. CARPENTER 'Protoplasm' or living jelly, which is not yet differentiated into 'organs'. M. K. POPE In Late Latin it was the tonic vowel that was differentiated if juxtaposed to a final flexional vowel that was homophonous. 5 J. JASTROW One important use of child study is to differentiate between functions that in the adult have become merged. T. E. HULME They first began to be differentiated by the German writers on aesthetics in the eighteenth century.
B *n.* A rock produced by the differentiation of a magma. E20.
differentiatedness *n.* the property of being differentiated M20. **differentiator** *n.* a person who or thing which differentiates L19.

differentiation /,dɪfərɛnʃɪ'eɪʃ(ə)n/ *n.* E19. [f. prec.: see -ATION.] The action or process of differentiating.
R. BARTHOLOW A careful differentiation of the causes. A. R. WALLACE Long continued isolation would often lead to the differentiation of the species. P. TILLICH Not conformity but differentiation is the end of the ways of God.

difficile /'dɪfɪsiːl, *foreign* difisil/ *a.* LME. [Fr. f. L *difficilis*, f. DIF- + *facilis* easy.] †1 = DIFFICULT *a.* 1. LME–L17. †2 = DIFFICULT *a.* 3. L15–M17. 3 = DIFFICULT *a.* 2. M16.
3 R. BROOKE These Oxford people are so damn difficile.
diffi'cileness *n.* E17.

difficilior lectio /dɪfɪ'kɪlɪɔː ,lɛktɪəʊ/ *n. phr.* Pl. **difficiliores lectiones** /dɪfɪkɪlɪ'ɔːreɪz lɛktɪ,əʊneɪz/. E20. [L, from the maxim *difficilior lectio potior* the harder reading is to be preferred. See also LECTIO DIFFICILIOR.] *Textual Criticism.* The more difficult or unexpected of two variant readings and therefore the one that is less likely to be a copyist's error; (the principle of) giving preference to such a reading.

difficult /'dɪfɪk(ə)lt/ *a.* LME. [Back-form. f. DIFFICULTY *n.* Cf. prec.] 1 Requiring physical or mental effort or skill; occasioning or attended with trouble. (Foll. by *to do, of, in.*) LME. 2 Of a person: not easy to get on with; unaccommodating, stubborn, argumentative; *arch.* hard to satisfy, fastidious. E16. 3 Hard to understand; puzzling, obscure. M16.
1 WORDSWORTH Knowledge . . is difficult to gain. J. L. MOTLEY It is difficult to imagine a more universal disaster. J. CONRAD Some harbours . . are made difficult of access by . . sunken rocks. *Daily Mirror* Help to see him through the difficult weeks ahead. 2 S. BELLOW He . . became quarrelsome once again, difficult, touchy, exaggerating, illogical, overly familiar. 3 H. T. BUCKLE One of the most difficult of our poets.
difficultly *adv.* with difficulty; obscurely: M16. **difficultness** *n.* difficulty; perversity: M16.

difficult /'dɪfɪk(ə)lt/ *v.t.* LME. [Fr. †*difficulter* f. med.L *difficultare*, f. as DIFFICULTY *n.*] †1 Impede, render difficult to accomplish. LME–E19. 2 Put in a difficulty, perplex, embarrass (a person). Usu. in *pass.* Chiefly *Sc.* L17.
†**difficultate** *v.t.* (*rare*) = DIFFICULT *v.* 1 E17–E19.

difficulty /'dɪfɪk(ə)lti/ *n.* LME. [L *difficultas*, f. as DIF- + *facultas*: see FACULTY *n.* Also infl. by

Fr. *difficulté*.] 1 The quality, fact, or condition of requiring effort or skill. LME. 2 Reluctance, unwillingness; an objection. *obs.* exc. in *make a difficulty* etc. below. LME. 3 Something difficult; a hindrance; an obscure point. LME. 4 Perplexing character, obscurity. E16. 5 *sing.* or in *pl.* A condition in which action or progress is difficult, *esp.* a shortage of money. E18.

1 J. THURBER Peifer twisted around on the sofa, slowly and with difficulty. 2 F. VERE Her Majesty . . with some difficulty (as her manner was) granted the men to be levied. 3 R. MACAULAY The jeep . . solved all our transport difficulties. 4 YEATS A book whose difficulty had offended indolence. 5 S. SMILES A serious difficulty occurred between him and his wife on this very point. *Times* One of America's biggest banks . . was in difficulties.

Phrases: **make a difficulty** or **difficulties, †make difficulty** show reluctance, be unaccommodating.

diffidation /dɪfɪˈdeɪʃ(ə)n/ *n. arch.* M18. [med.L *diffidatio(n-)*, f. *diffidare* renounce an alliance, f. Proto-Romance, whence also DEFY *v.*: see -ATION.] The dissolution of a relationship of trust or allegiance; declaration of hostilities.

diffide /dɪˈfʌɪd/ *v.i.* Now *rare.* M16. [L *diffidere*, f. as DIF- + *fidere* trust.] Lack confidence (*in*).

diffidence /ˈdɪfɪd(ə)ns/ *n.* LME. [Fr. †*diffidence* or its source L *diffidentia*, f. as next: see -ENCE.] 1 Lack of confidence; distrust, (a) doubt. Now *rare* or *obs.* LME. 2 Lack of confidence in one's abilities or worth; self-mistrust; (a feeling of) shyness. E17.

2 W. C. WILLIAMS I feel a certain diffidence about attempting to speak of the book at all.

Also **diffidency** *n.* (long *rare*) E17.

diffident /ˈdɪfɪd(ə)nt/ *a.* LME. [L *diffident-* pres. ppl stem of *diffidere*: see DIFFIDE *v.*, -ENT.] 1 Lacking confidence or trust (*in*); distrustful, mistrustful (*of*). Now *rare.* LME. 2 Lacking self-confidence; timid in one's dealings with others. E18.

diffidently *adv.* E17.

†diffinition *n.* see DEFINITION.

†diffinitive *a.* & *n.*: see DEFINITIVE.

†difflation *n.* M16–M18. [L *difflat-* pa. ppl stem of *difflare*, f. as DIF- + *flare* blow: see -ATION.] Dispersion by blowing.

diffluence /ˈdɪflʊəns/ *n.* M17. [f. (as) next: see -ENCE.] 1 The action or fact of flowing apart; dispersion by flowing. M17. 2 Dissolution into a liquid state; deliquescence. M19.

1 G. E. HUTCHINSON The western end of Windermere suggests glacial diffluence.

diffluent /ˈdɪflʊənt/ *a.* E17. [L *diffluent-* pres. ppl stem of *diffluere* flow apart or away, f. as DIF- + *fluere* flow: see -ENT.] Characterized by or exhibiting diffluence.

†difform *a.* M16. [(O)Fr. *difforme* or med.L *difformis* f. L *deformis*: see DIF-, DEFORM *a.*] 1 Of diverse forms; differing in shape. M16–L17. 2 Irregular in shape; without regularity of parts. E17–M19.

†difformity *n.*[1] Also **deform-**. M16. [Fr. *difformité* or med.L *difformitas*, f. *difformis*: see prec., -ITY.] 1 Difference or diversity of form; absence of uniformity between things. M16–M19. 2 Divergence in form (*from*); lack of conformity (*with* or *to* a standard). M16–L17.

†difformity *n.*[2] var. of DEFORMITY *n.*[1]

diffract /dɪˈfrakt/ *v.t.* E19. [L *diffract-*: see next.] Cause (light etc.) to undergo diffraction.

fig.: CARLYLE Some obscure distorted image of right . . diffracted, exaggerated, in the wonderfullest way.

diffractive *a.* tending to diffract E19. **diffractively** *adv.* by diffraction L19. **diffractogram** *n.* a photograph etc. of a diffraction pattern M20. **diffracˈtometer** *n.* an instrument for measuring diffraction, esp. of X-rays in crystallography E20. **diffracˈtometry** *n.* the measurement of diffraction; the use of a diffractometer: M20.

diffraction /dɪˈfrakʃ(ə)n/ *n.* L17. [Fr., or mod.L *diffractio(n-)*, f. L *diffract-* pa. ppl stem of *diffringere* break in pieces, f. as DIF- + *frangere* break: see -ION.] The breaking up of a beam of light into a transverse series of dark and light bands or coloured spectra by the edge of an opaque body or a narrow aperture; an analogous phenomenon with other waves; the spreading of waves of any kind by the edge of an obstacle.

Comb.: **diffraction grating** a plate of glass or polished metal ruled with very close equidistant parallel lines, producing a spectrum by diffraction and subsequent interference of the transmitted or reflected light. **diffraction pattern** the pattern formed by light, X-rays, etc., after diffraction, esp. by a crystal.

diffusable /dɪˈfjuːzəb(ə)l/ *a.* L18. [f. as next + -ABLE.] = DIFFUSIBLE.

diffusant /dɪˈfjuːz(ə)nt/ *n.* M20. [f. as next + -ANT[1].] A substance which diffuses through another.

diffusate /dɪˈfjuːzeɪt/ *n.* M19. [f. DIFFUSE *v.* + -ATE[1].] A substance which has diffused through a membrane or barrier; a dialysate.

diffuse /dɪˈfjuːs/ *a.* LME. [Fr. *diffus* or L *diffusus* extensive, pa. pple of *diffundere* pour out, f. as DIF- + *fundere* pour.] †1 Confused, perplexed; vague, obscure, doubtful. LME–E17. 2 Of style, a writer, etc.: not concise; wordy, verbose. LME. 3 Widespread, dispersed; *spec.* (of light, disease, etc.) not localized or concentrated. L15.

3 S. JOHNSON The pomp of wide margin and diffuse typography.

diffusely *adv.* LME. **diffuseness** *n.* the quality of being diffuse, esp. in speech or writing L15.

diffuse /dɪˈfjuːz/ *v.* LME. [L *diffus-* pa. ppl stem of *diffundere*: see prec.] I 1 *v.t.* & *i.* Spread abroad or pour forth as from a centre of dispersion; spread widely over an area or through a region. LME. †2 *v.t.* Pour out like a fluid, shed. L16–M18. 3 *v.t.* Extend or stretch out (the body, limbs, etc.) freely. *arch.* or *poet.* L17. 4 *Sci.* a *v.t.* Cause to pass or intermingle by diffusion. E19. b *v.i.* Of a fluid or individual atoms etc.: undergo diffusion, pass by diffusion. M19.

1 T. KEN Love . . will all diffuse in Extacy. D. MASSON A heartless man does not diffuse geniality and kindness around him. L. DEIGHTON The moonlight . . was diffused by the thin cloud. 2 SHAKES. *Temp.* Who, with thy saffron wings, upon my flow'rs Diffusest honey drops. 4a D. ATTENBOROUGH Species appeared which could fill their air-bags by diffusing gas into them from the blood.

†II 5 *v.t.* Make confused, obscure, or indistinct. Chiefly as *diffused* ppl a. M16–E17.

diffusedly *adv.* †(*a*) confusedly, obscurely; (*b*) with diffusion, interpenetration, etc.; †(*c*) with prolixity of language: M16. **diffusedness** *n.* the quality of being widely dispersed E17. **diffuser** *n.* a person who or thing which diffuses; *esp.* (*a*) a device for diffusing light; (*b*) a duct for broadening an airflow and reducing its speed: L17.

diffusible /dɪˈfjuːzɪb(ə)l/ *a.* L18. [f. prec. + -IBLE. Cf. DIFFUSABLE.] Capable of diffusing or of being diffused; *spec.* (of fluids etc.) able to intermingle by diffusion.

diffusiˈbility *n.* E19.

diffusion /dɪˈfjuːʒ(ə)n/ *n.* LME. [L *diffusio(n-)*, f. *diffus-*: see DIFFUSE *v.*, -ION.] †1 The action of pouring out or forth; outpouring, effusion. Chiefly *fig.* LME–M17. 2 The action or result of spreading abroad; wide and general distribution; the state of not being localized. L16. 3 *fig.* Dispersion, dissemination, (of knowledge, fame, etc.); *Anthropol.* the spread of elements of culture etc. from one region or people to another. M18. 4 Copiousness of language; prolixity. L18. 5 *Sci.* The spontaneous intermingling of fluids by the natural random motion of their particles; the spread of a single fluid in this way. E19.

2 H. E. BATES The coppery diffusion of light filtering down through crowds of turning leaves. 3 B. C. BRODIE The effect which the general diffusion of knowledge produces on society.

diffusional *a.* pertaining to or involving diffusion M20. **diffusionism** *n.* the theory that all or most cultural similarities are due to diffusion E20. **diffusionist** *a.* & *n.* (*a*) *adj.* of or pertaining to diffusionism; (*b*) *n.* an advocate of diffusionism: L19.

diffusive /dɪˈfjuːsɪv/ *a.* E17. [med.L *diffusivus*, f. as DIFFUSE *v.*: see -IVE.] 1 Having the quality of diffusing; characterized by diffusion (*lit.* & *fig.*). E17. †2 Of a body of people: consisting of members in their individual capacity rather than a collective or representative one. M17–E18. 3 = DIFFUSE *a.* 2. L17.

diffusively *adv.* E17. **diffusiveness** *n.* M17.

diffusivity /dɪfjuːˈsɪvɪti/ *n.* L19. [f. prec. + -ITY.] Diffusibility; *spec.* = *thermal diffusivity* s.v. THERMAL *a.*

dig /dɪg/ *n.*[1] L17. [f. DIG *v.*] 1 A tool for digging. *dial.* L17. 2 A thrust, a sharp poke, as with the elbow etc. E19. b *fig.* A remark directed against a person. M19. 3 A diligent or plodding student. *US slang.* M19. 4 An act or spell of digging; a depth or quantity to be dug. L19. b (An expedition for the purpose of) an archaeological excavation. *colloq.* L19. 5 In *pl.* Lodgings. *colloq.* L19.

dig /dɪg/ *n.*[2] *Austral.* & *NZ colloq.* E20. [Abbrev.] = DIGGER 4.

dig /dɪg/ *v.* Infl. **-gg-**. Pa. t. & pple **dug** /dʌg/, (*arch.* & *dial.*) **digged**. ME. [Perh. f. OE *dīc* DITCH *n.* & already in OE.] 1 *v.i.* Make a hole in, excavate, or turn up the ground etc. with a spade, pick, hands, claws, snout, etc. ME. b *v.i.* Make archaeological investigations. E20. 2 *v.t.* Penetrate and turn (the ground etc.) with a spade etc.; *esp.* break up and turn (the soil) to prepare it for cultivation. LME. b *v.t.* Excavate archaeologically. M18. 3 *v.t.* Make (a hole, mine, etc.) by digging. LME. 4a *v.t.* Obtain or extract by digging. (Foll. by *from*, *out of*.) LME. b *v.i.* Study a subject closely. Chiefly *US.* E19. c *v.i.* Understand. *slang.* M20. d *v.t.* Appreciate, enjoy; understand; look at or listen to (something to be enjoyed). *slang.* M20. †5 *v.t.* Put *in* or *into* the ground by digging; bury. M16–M17. 6 *v.t.* Thrust or force *in* or *into*. M16. 7 *v.i.* Penetrate or make one's way *into* or *through* (as) by digging; make an excavation *under*. M16. 8 *v.t.* Spur (a horse) vigorously; give (a person) a sharp thrust or nudge. M16. 9 *v.i.* Have lodgings. *colloq.* E20.

1 J. BUCHAN An old stationmaster was digging in his garden. b T. E. LAWRENCE I would like to dig in the Persian gulf. 2 D. LESSING Ground . . was being dug for new gardens. 3 **dig a pit for** *fig.* try to entrap. *dig the grave of*: see GRAVE *n.*[1] 4a DAY LEWIS Keyes, the gardener, was digging potatoes. b L. M. ALCOTT Laurie 'dug' to some purpose that year. d D. MACDONALD The women's magazine is such an ancient and essential form of journalism that even the English dig it. 5 J. PALSGRAVE I wyll dygge this dogge in to the grounde somewhere for feare of stynkyng. 6 D. WELCH He grasped me tightly and dug his fingers into my flesh.

With advs. in specialized senses: **dig down** (*a*) cause to fall by digging; (*b*) lower or remove by digging; (*c*) *N. Amer. colloq.* pay money from one's own pocket. **dig in** (*a*) mix (something) with the soil by digging; (*b*) cause to penetrate, drive in deeply, (*dig in one's heels, toes*, etc., keep resolutely or obstinately to one's decision, opinion, etc.); (*c*) establish one's position; prepare a defensive trench or pit; *Cricket* consolidate one's position as a batsman; (*d*) *dial.* & *N. Amer. colloq.* set to work earnestly and energetically; (*e*) *colloq.* begin eating, esp. heartily. **dig out** (*a*) extract or remove by digging; *fig.* obtain or get out by search or effort; (*b*) form by excavation; (*c*) *US colloq.* depart. **dig up** (*a*) take or get out of the ground by digging; (now *colloq.*) obtain, find, search out; (*dig up the tomahawk*: see TOMAHAWK *n.*); (*b*) break up or open by digging, excavate; (*c*) break up and loosen the soil of (fallow land).

Digambara /diːˈgʌmbərə/ *n.* E19. [Skt *Digāmbara*, lit. 'sky-clad'.] A member of one of the two principal sects of Jainism, which enjoins nakedness and the renunciation of all property. Cf. SVETAMBARA.

digamma /dʌɪˈgamə/ *n.* L17. [L f. Gk, f. *di-* DI-[2], GAMMA (from the shape of the letter).] The sixth letter (Ϝ, ϝ) of the original Greek alphabet, probably equivalent to W, later disused.

digammated *a.* spelt with or having the digamma E19.

digamy /ˈdɪgəmi/ *n.* E17. [Late L *digamia* f. Gk, f. *digamos* married to two people, f. as DI-[2] + -GAMY.] 1 The state of having married again after the death or divorce of the first spouse. E17. †2 = BIGAMY 1. M17–M18.

digamist *n.* a person who has entered into digamy M17. **digamous** *a.* M19.

digastric /dʌɪˈgastrɪk/ *n.* & *a.* L17. [mod.L *digastricus*, f. as DI-[2] + Gk *gastēr* belly: see -IC.] *Anat.* A *n.* A mandibular muscle that assists in opening the jaw. L17. B *adj.* 1 Of a muscle: having two thick fleshy parts with a tendon between. E18. 2 Of or pertaining to the digastric muscle of the jaw. M19.

Digby /ˈdɪgbi/ *n.* E19. [See below.] In full *Digby chick(en)*. A dried or cured herring of a type caught at Digby, Nova Scotia.

digenean /dʌɪdʒɪˈniːən, dʌɪˈdʒɛnɪən/ *n.* & *a.* M20. [f. mod.L *Digenea* (see below), f. as DI-[2] + Gk *genea* race, generation: see -AN.] *Zool.* A *n.* A trematode fluke of the subclass Digenea, which comprises endoparasitic species with a complex life cycle involving two to four hosts; a digenetic fluke. M20. B *adj.* Of or pertaining to the digeneans. M20.

digenesis /dʌɪˈdʒɛnɪsɪs/ *n.* L19. [f. DI-[2] + -GENESIS.] = ALTERNATION *of generations*.

dige'netic *a.* (*a*) pertaining to or characterized by digenesis; (*b*) designating a parasite which has a life cycle involving more than one host; digenean: L19.

digenite /ˈdɪdʒənʌɪt/ *n.* M19. [f. Gk *digenēs* of doubtful kind + -ITE[1].] *Min.* A blue to black cubic copper sulphide occurring in copper ores.

†**digerent** *a.* & *n. rare.* L15. [L *digerent-*, pres. ppl stem of *digerere*: see DIGEST *v.*, -ENT.] A *adj.* Digesting. L15–M18. B *n.* A medicine etc. that promotes suppuration. M18–M19.

digest /ˈdʌɪdʒɛst/ *n.* LME. [L *digesta* matters methodically arranged, neut. pl. of *digestus* pa. pple of *digerere* divide, distribute, dissolve, digest, f. *di-* DI-[1] + *gerere* bear, carry.] †1 = DIGESTION 1, 2. LME–M18. 2 *Law.* a The writings of Roman jurists collected and condensed by order of Justinian. Usu. *the Digest.* LME. b An abstract of some body of law, systematically arranged. L16. 3 A digested collection of statements; a methodically arranged compendium or summary of information. M16. b *spec.* A periodical composed chiefly of condensed versions of pieces previously published elsewhere. E20. 4 A substance obtained by digestion with heat etc. E20.

3 H. G. WELLS We have to make a digest now of all that stuff and keep it up-to-date. b J. CANNAN Mad ideas they'd got from medical articles in Digests.

digest /dɪˈdʒɛst, dʌɪ-/ *v.* LME. [L *digest-* ppl stem of *digerere*: see prec.] 1 *v.t.* & *i.* Assimilate (food) in the stomach and bowels or otherwise into the bodily system. LME. b *v.t.* Cause or promote the digestion of (food). L15. c *v.i.* Of food: undergo digestion. L16. 2 *v.t.* a Settle and arrange methodically in the mind; consider, ponder. LME. b Comprehend and assimilate mentally; obtain mental nourishment from. M16. 3 *v.t.* Arrange methodically; reduce to a systematic or convenient form; classify. L15. †4 *v.t.* a Disperse; dissipate. E16–E18. b Divide and dispose, distribute. L16–L17. 5 *v.t.* Bear without resistance; brook; endure. M16. b Get over the effects of. *arch.* L16. †6 *v.t.* & *i.* Mature (a tumour); (cause to) suppurate. M16–M18. 7 *v.i.* & *t.* Treat (a substance) with heat and usu. moisture or chemicals in order to decompose it, extract soluble constituents, etc. L16. †8 *v.t.* Mature or bring to a state of perfection, esp. by the action of heat. E17–E18.

1 C. DARWIN Several leaves caught successively three insects each, but most of them were not able to digest the third fly. 2a JOSEPH HALL When the kyng had long digested and studied on this matter. b D. BOGARDE There shouldn't, he reasoned, having digested his Intelligence Reports, be much . . opposition. 3 SWIFT I have had no manner of Time to digest it into Order, or correct the Stile. 5 W. IRVING This wanton attack . . is too much even for me to digest!

digestant *n.* something taken to promote digestion L19. **digestedly** *adv.* in a digested or well-arranged manner E17. **digester** *n.* a person who or thing which digests; *esp.* (*a*) a person or organism that digests food in a specified manner; (*b*) a vessel in which substances are digested: L15.

digestible /dɪˈdʒɛstɪb(ə)l, dʌɪ-/ *a.* LME. [(O)Fr. f. L *digestibilis*, f. as prec.: see -IBLE.] Able to be digested; easily digested.

digesti'bility *n.* M18. **digestibleness** *n.* M17. **digestibly** *adv.* L19.

digestif /diʒɛstif (*pl. same*), dʌɪˈdʒɛstɪf/ *n.* E20. [Fr.: see DIGESTIVE.] Something which promotes good digestion, esp. a drink taken after a meal.

digestion /dɪˈdʒɛstʃ(ə)n, dʌɪ-/ *n.* LME. [(O)Fr. f. L *digestio(n-)*, f. as DIGEST *v.*: see -ION.] 1 The process by which ingested food is broken down in the body into forms that may be readily assimilated. Also (*Med.*), the enzymic breakdown of bodily tissue in various disease states. LME. 2 The power or faculty of digesting food; the ability to assimilate food without discomfort. LME. †3 The process of maturing an ulcer or wound; disposition to healthy suppuration. LME–M19. 4 The process of digesting a substance by heat, solvent, etc. Formerly also, susceptibility to the action of heat; a product of (gentle) heating. LME. †5 The action of methodizing and reducing to order; the result of this, a digest. M16–L18. 6 Mental assimilation or absorption of concepts etc. E17. 7 The action of bearing without resistance; endurance. Now *rare* or *obs.* M17.

1 SHAKES. *Rich. II* Things sweet to taste prove in digestion sour. 2 ARNOLD BENNETT The children feared goose for their father, whose digestion was usually unequal to this particular bird. 6 T. FULLER He had a great appetite to learning, and a quick digestion. 7 L. STERNE The silent digestion of one wrong provokes a second.

digestive /dɪˈdʒɛstɪv, dʌɪ-/ *a.* & *n.* LME. [(O)Fr. *digestif*, *-ive* or its source L *digestivus*, f. as DIGEST *v.*: see -IVE.] A *adj.* 1 Having the function of digesting food; engaged in or pertaining to the digestion of food. LME. 2 (Supposedly) promoting or aiding the digestion of food; digestible. LME. b *spec.* Designating a type of semi-sweet wholemeal biscuit. L19. 3 Pertaining to or promoting chemical digestion. M17.

1 **digestive gland** *Zool.* = HEPATOPANCREAS.

B *n.* 1 Something which promotes good digestion. LME. b *spec.* A digestive biscuit. M20. 2 An ointment etc. which promotes healthy suppuration in an ulcer or wound. Now *rare* or *obs.* M16.

digestively *adv.* in a way that promotes digestion; with regard to digestion: E17. **digestiveness** *n.* E18.

†**digestory** *a.* & *n.* E17. [Late L *digestorius*, f. as DIGEST *v.*: see -ORY[2].] A *adj.* = DIGESTIVE *a.* 3. Only in E17. B *n.* A vessel or organ of digestion. L17–M18.

digger /ˈdɪgə/ *n.* LME. [f. DIG *v.* + -ER[1].] 1 *gen.* A person who or animal which digs. LME. b A miner, *esp.* one who searches for gold. M16. c *Eng. Hist.* A member of a short-lived 17th-cent. radical Puritan group which believed in communal ownership of land and began cultivating commons. M17. d A N. American Indian of any of several tribes who subsisted chiefly on roots. M19. e A person who digs for archaeological purposes. E20. 2 (A part of) a tool or machine for digging. L17. 3 More fully *digger wasp*. A wasp that burrows in the soil; *esp.* any of several usu. solitary wasps of the superfamily Sphecoidea. M19. 4 An Australian or New Zealander, esp. a private soldier. Freq. as a form of address: mate, pal. *colloq.* E20.

Comb.: **digger's delight** *Austral.* a speedwell, *Veronica perfoliata*, supposed to indicate the presence of gold; *digger wasp*: see sense 3 above.

digging /ˈdɪgɪŋ/ *vbl n.* LME. [f. DIG *v.* + -ING[1].] 1 The action of DIG *v.*; an instance of this. LME. 2 In *pl.* Materials dug out. M16. 3 *sing.* & (usu.) in *pl.* (treated as *sing.* or *pl.*). A place where digging is carried on; *esp.* a mine, a gold-field. M16. b *sing.* & (usu.) in *pl.* Archaeological excavation; the site of such an excavation. E20. 4 In *pl.* Lodgings. *colloq.* M19.

1 *double digging*: see DOUBLE *a.* & *adv.* 3 POOR MAN'*s diggings*.

Comb. **digging-stick** a primitive digging implement consisting of a pointed stick, sometimes weighted by a stone.

dight /dʌɪt/ *v.t.* Pa. pple **dight**. [OE *dihtan* = MLG, MDu. *dichten* compose, contrive (Du. *dichten* invent, compose), OHG *tihtōn*, *dihtōn* (G *dichten*) write, compose verses, ON *dikta* compose in Latin, invent, contrive, f. L *dictare* appoint, prescribe, dictate, (in med.L) write, compose.] I Direct, ordain, dispose of, deal with. †1 Direct, give directions to. Only in OE. †2 Appoint, ordain, (a fate etc.). OE–M16. †3 Keep in order, manage, govern. ME–E16. †4 Deal with, use, (in some manner); *esp.* maltreat. ME–M17. b Have sexual relations with. Only in LME. †5 Place, put; remove. ME–M16. b Put into a specified state, esp. to death; cause (death). ME–E19.

II Compose, make. †6 Compose (with words); set down in writing. OE–LME. †7 Construct, make. ME–E17. †8 Perform, do. ME–L16.

III Put in order, make ready. †9 Put in order, arrange. ME–L15. 10 Equip, furnish, (*with*). Now usu. in *pass. arch.* ME. 11 Clothe, array, adorn. Now usu. in *pass. arch.* & *poet.* ME. †b Dress (a wound). LME–M16. c Put on (armour etc.). L16. d Dirty, befoul. *dial.* M17. †12 Make (a person, esp. oneself) ready (*to do*). ME–L16. b Direct (oneself), make (one's way); go. ME–L16. 13 Make ready for use or a purpose; prepare. *poet.* ME. b Winnow (corn). *Sc.* & *north.* L15. c Wipe clean or dry. *Sc.* & *north.* E16. 14 Repair, put right. Now *dial.* ME. †15 Cultivate, dress, (crops, land, etc.). LME–M16.

11 MILTON Storied windows richly dight, Casting a dim religious light. H. MACDIARMID All the changes in which the hawthorn is dight. 13 W. MORRIS This Queen of the many wooers dights the wedding for us.

†IV 16 Lift. *rare* (Spenser). Only in L16.

dighter *n.* (now *dial.*) OE.

digit /ˈdɪdʒɪt/ *n.* LME. [L *digitus* finger, toe.] 1 *Math.* Each of the ten arabic numerals from 0 to 9, esp. when part of a number. LME. 2 *Astron.* The twelfth part of the diameter of the sun or moon, esp. as a measure of the magnitude of an eclipse. L16. 3 A finger, a toe, (now *joc.* exc. *Anat.*). Also *Zool.*, an analogous structure at the end of the limbs of many higher vertebrates. M17. 4 A finger's breadth as a unit of length; ¾ inch. M17.

1 M. AMIS I dialled seven digits. BINARY *digit. parity digit*: see PARITY *n.*[1] *significant digit*: see SIGNIFICANT *a.* 1C.

digital /ˈdɪdʒɪt(ə)l/ *n.* & *a.* LME. [L *digitalis*, f. as prec.: see -AL[1].] A *n.* †1 = DIGIT 1. Only in LME. 2 A finger. *joc.* M19.

B *adj.* 1a Of, pertaining to, using, or being a digit (DIGIT 1) or digits; *spec.* designating a computer which operates on data in the form of digits or similar discrete elements. (*rare* bef. M20.) L15. b Designating or pertaining to a recording in which the original signal is represented by the spacing between pulses rather than by a wave, to make it less susceptible to degradation. M20. 2 Of or pertaining to a finger or fingers. M17. 3 *Anat.* Resembling a finger or the hollow impression made by one. M19.

1a **digital clock, watch**: showing the time by means of displayed digits rather than hands on a dial. *digital root*: see ROOT *n.*[1]

digitally *adv.* (*a*) by means of or with respect to the fingers; (*b*) by means of digits; in digital form: M17.

digitalis /dɪdʒɪˈteɪlɪs/ *n.* E17. [mod.L use as n. (sc. *herba* plant) of L *digitalis* pertaining to the finger, after G *Fingerhut* thimble, foxglove.] 1 The foxglove. E17. 2 A preparation of dried foxglove leaves used as a drug, esp. to stimulate the heart; a glycoside or mixture of glycosides present in this. L18.

digitalin *n.* the pharmacologically active constituent(s) of the foxglove M19.

digitalize /ˈdɪdʒɪt(ə)lʌɪz/ *v.*[1]*t.* Also **-ise**. E20. [f. prec. + -IZE.] *Med.* Administer digitalis to; produce a physiological response in (a subject) by this means.

digitali'zation *n.*[1] L19.

digitalize /ˈdɪdʒɪt(ə)lʌɪz/ *v.*[2]*t.* Also **-ise**. M20. [f. DIGITAL + -IZE.] = DIGITIZE 2.

digitali'zation *n.*[2] M20.

digitate /ˈdɪdʒɪtət, -eɪt/ *a.* M17. [L *digitatus*, f. as DIGIT: see -ATE[2].] 1 *Zool.* Having separate fingers or toes. M17. 2 *Bot.* & *Zool.* Divided into parts resembling fingers; having deep radiating divisions. M18.

digitately *adv.* M19.

digitate /ˈdɪdʒɪteɪt/ *v.* M17. [med.L *digitat-* pa. ppl stem of *digitare* point at, indicate, f. as DIGIT: see -ATE[3].] †1 *v.t.* Indicate. *rare.* Only in M17. 2 *v.i.* Become divided into finger-like parts. M18.
digiˈtation *n.* †(*a*) the action of touching or pointing with the finger; (*b*) the condition of being digitate; (*c*) a finger-like process or division: M17.

digitated /ˈdɪdʒɪteɪtɪd/ *a.* M17. [f. as DIGITATE *a.* + -ED[1].] *Bot.* & *Zool.* = DIGITATE *a.*

digiti- /ˈdɪdʒɪti/ *comb. form* of L *digitus* DIGIT: see -I-.
digitiform *a.* like a finger M19. **digitigrade** *a.* & *n.* [L *-gradus* walking] *Zool.* (*a*) *adj.* walking on the digits, the heels not touching the ground, like a dog or cat; designating or adapted for such a manner of walking; not plantigrade; (*b*) *n.* a digitigrade animal: M19.

digitize /ˈdɪdʒɪtʌɪz/ *v.t.* Also **-ise**. L17. [f. DIGIT *n.* + -IZE.] 1 Manipulate, point at, or count with the fingers. *rare.* L17. 2 Convert (a varying quantity) into a sequence of digits; represent in digital form. M20.
digitiˈzation *n.* M20. **digitizer** *n.* (*a*) *rare* a person who digitizes; (*b*) a device that converts analogue signals etc. to digital ones: M18.

digitorium /dɪdʒɪˈtɔːrɪəm/ *n.* L19. [f. as prec. + -ORIUM.] A small portable silent keyboard on which a pianist etc. can exercise the fingers.

digitoxin /dɪdʒɪˈtɒksɪn/ *n.* L19. [f. DIGITALIS + TOXIN.] A potentially poisonous steroid glycoside, $C_{41}H_{64}O_{13}$, that is present in the foxglove etc. and is used like digoxin.

digladiation /dʌɪˌgladɪˈeɪʃ(ə)n/ *n.* Now *rare* or *obs.* L16. [f. L *digladiat-* pa. ppl stem of *digladiari* contend fiercely, f. as DI-[1] + *gladius* sword: see -ATION.] 1 Hand-to-hand fighting, esp. with swords. L16. 2 *fig.* Bickering; argument. L16.

diglossia /dʌɪˈglɒsɪə/ *n.* M20. [f. Gk *diglōssos* bilingual (f. as DI-[2] + *glōssa* tongue) + -IA[1], after Fr. *diglossie.*] *Ling.* The systematic use by a community of two different languages or varieties or dialects of a language in different situations.
diglossic *a.* M20.

diglot /ˈdʌɪglɒt/ *a.* & *n.* Also **-tt**. L19. [Gk *diglōttos*, f. as DI-[2] + *glōtta* tongue.] A *adj.* Using two languages; containing a text in two languages. L19. B *n.* A diglot book. L19.
diˈglottic *a.* speaking two languages M19. **diglottism** *n.* the use of (words derived from) two languages L19.

diglyph /ˈdʌɪglɪf/ *n.* E18. [Gk *digluphos* doubly indented, f. as DI-[2] + *gluphein* carve.] *Archit.* An ornamental projecting face or tablet with two vertical grooves.

†**dignation** *n.* LME–M18. [L *dignatio(n-)*, f. *dignat-* pa. ppl stem of *dignare, -ari* think worthy, DEIGN: see -ATION.] The act of treating someone as worthy; favour shown, honour conferred.

dignified /ˈdɪgnɪfʌɪd/ *a.* L17. [f. next + -ED[1].] †1 Ranking as a dignitary, esp. an ecclesiastical one. L17–M19. 2 Invested with dignity; exalted. M18. 3 Marked by dignity; having self-respect without haughtiness; stately. E19.
3 L. M. MONTGOMERY Mrs. Allan is too old to dance and sing and . . it wouldn't be dignified in a minister's wife.
dignifiedly *adv.* E19.

dignify /ˈdɪgnɪfʌɪ/ *v.t.* LME. [Fr. †*dignifier* (OFr. *dignefier*) f. late L *dignificare*, f. L *dignus* worthy: see -FY.] 1 Add dignity or honour to; render illustrious or majestic. LME. b Represent as worthy; give a high-sounding name to. E17. †2 Confer a title or honour upon. L16–E18.
1 POPE No Turbots dignify my boards. R. GRAVES A Royal Duke, with no campaigning medals To dignify his orders. b P. G. WODEHOUSE He made his way to the small apartment dignified by the name of library.
dignifier *n.* E17.

dignitary /ˈdɪgnɪt(ə)ri/ *n.* & *a.* L17. [f. next after *propriety*, *proprietary*: see -ARY[1].] A *n.* A person holding an official position of some status, esp. in the Church. L17.
E. HEATH The Governor's garden party . . the military band playing, local dignitaries there to meet us.
B *adj.* Pertaining to or invested with a dignity, esp. an ecclesiastical one. E18.

dignity /ˈdɪgnɪti/ *n.* ME. [OFr. *digneté*, (also mod.) *dignité* f. L *dignitas*, f. *dignus* worthy: see -ITY.] I 1 The quality of being worthy or honourable; true worth, excellence. ME. 2 Honourable or high estate; degree of estimation, rank. ME. b *collect.* Persons of high rank. M16. 3 An honourable office, rank, or title; an official position. ME. 4 A person who holds a high or official position, a dignitary. ME. 5 Elevated manner; fit stateliness. M17.
1 T. JEFFERSON I recollect no work of any dignity which has been lately published. *Economist* Steel workers . . prayed with the Pope . . while he spoke of the dignity of labour. 2 A. STORR Concepts . . which cannot yet be awarded the dignity of a scientific hypothesis. **beneath one's dignity** unfitting for one to do. 3 GIBBON He . . distributed the civil and military dignities among his favourites and followers. 5 J. H. NEWMAN He preserved in his domestic arrangements the dignity of a literary and public man. G. A. BIRMINGHAM Tommy is a very lovable dog . . entirely lacking in dignity of figure or pose. **stand on one's dignity** insist on respectful treatment.
II 6 *Astrol.* A situation in which a planet's influence is heightened, either by its zodiacal position or by its aspects with other planets. LME.

digonal /ˈdɪgən(ə)l, dʌɪˈgəʊn(ə)l/ *a.* L19. [f. DI-[2] + Gk *gōnia* angle + -AL[1].] *Cryst.* Designating an axis of twofold symmetry.

digoxin /dɪˈdʒɒksɪn/ *n.* M20. [Contr. of DIG(IT)OXIN.] A potentially poisonous steroid glycoside, $C_{41}H_{64}O_{14}$, that is present in the foxglove etc. and is used as a cardiac stimulant.

digram /ˈdʌɪgram/ *n.* M17. [f. DI-[2] + -GRAM.] A group or word of two letters.

digraph /ˈdʌɪgrɑːf/ *n.*[1] L18. [f. DI-[2] + -GRAPH.] A group of two letters representing one sound.
diˈgraphic *a.* (*a*) pertaining to or of the nature of a digraph; (*b*) written in two different characters or alphabets: L19.

digraph /ˈdʌɪgrɑːf/ *n.*[2] M20. [f. *directed graph*: see DIRECT *v.*, GRAPH *n.*[1]] *Math.* A network of lines in which each line has a direction; a set of elements together with ordered pairs of the elements.

digress /dʌɪˈgrɛs/ *v.i.* E16. [L *digress-* pa. ppl stem of *digredi*, f. *di-* DI-[1] + *gradi* proceed, step, f. *gradus* a step.] †1 Deviate *from* an allegiance, standard, course of action, etc. E16–E17. 2 Depart from the main or the intended subject in speech or writing, esp. temporarily. E16. 3 Go aside from or *from* one's course; deviate; stray. M16. †4 Infringe a law or moral standard. M16–M17.
2 P. ACKROYD But I digress into matters which no longer concern me. 3 C. LAMB I digress into Soho, to explore a bookstall.
digresser *n.* M17. **digressingly** *adv.* by way of digression M19.

digression /dʌɪˈgrɛʃ(ə)n/ *n.* LME. [(O)Fr., or its source L *digressio(n-)*, f. as prec.: see -ION.] 1 Deviation from the main or intended subject in speech or writing, esp. temporarily; an instance of this. LME. 2 The action of turning aside from a course. Now *rare.* LME. †3 Infringement of a law or moral standard. E16–E17. 4 *Astron.* etc. Deviation from a particular line or a mean position. M17.
1 D. JACOBSON I was speaking, then, before that last digression, about the rheumy frustrations and resentments that afflicted me. 2 J. RAY We made a digression to S. Marino. 3 SHAKES. *Lucr.* Then my digression is so vile, so base, That it will live engraven in my face.
digressional *a.* pertaining to or characterized by digression. L18. **digressionary** *a.* of the nature of a digression M18.

digressive /dʌɪˈgrɛsɪv/ *a.* E17. [Late L *digressivus*, f. as DIGRESS: see -IVE.] Characterized by or given to digression; of the nature of (a) digression.
digressively *adv.* M18. **digressiveness** *n.* L19.

diguanide /dʌɪˈgwɑːnʌɪd/ *n.* E20. [f. DI-[2] + GUANID(IN)E.] *Chem.* = BIGUANIDE, DIGUANIDINE.

diguanidine /dʌɪˈgwɑːnɪdiːn/ *n.* L19. [f. DI-[2] + GUANIDINE.] *Chem.* Any compound containing two guanidine radicals, $\cdot NH\cdot C(NH)(NH_2)$. Formerly also, the compound biguanide.

digue /dig (*pl. same*), diːg/ *n.* E16. [Fr. f. OFr. (also *dique*) f. Flem., Du. *dijk* DYKE *n.*[1]] A dyke (DYKE *n.*[1] 8) in the Netherlands, Flanders, or France.

digyny /dʌɪˈdʒʌɪni/ *n.* M20. [f. DI-[2] + Gk *gunē* woman + -Y[3].] *Biol.* Fertilization in which two sets of chromosomes are contributed by an ovum or ova.
digynic *a.* L20.

dihedral /dʌɪˈhiːdr(ə)l/ *a.* & *n.* L18. [f. DI-[2] + -HEDRAL.] A *adj.* 1 Having or contained by two planes or plane faces (e.g. of a crystal). L18. 2 Having or being an angle made by aircraft wings with one another, esp. when less than 180°. E20. B *n.* A dihedral angle or inclination. E20.

dihexagonal /dʌɪhɛkˈsag(ə)n(ə)l/ *a.* M19. [f. DI-[2] + HEXAGONAL.] *Cryst.* (Of a prism or pyramid of the hexagonal system) such that a horizontal cross-section has 12 angles, alternate ones being equal; of or pertaining to a crystal of this kind.

dihybrid /dʌɪˈhʌɪbrɪd/ *n.* & *a.* E20. [f. DI-[2] + HYBRID.] *Genetics.* A *n.* A hybrid that is heterozygous at two genetic loci. E20. B *adj.* Of, pertaining to, or being a dihybrid. E20.
dihybridism *n.* E20.

dihydr- *pref.* see DIHYDRO-.

dihydrate /dʌɪˈhʌɪdreɪt/ *n.* E20. [f. DI-[2] + HYDRATE *n.*] *Chem.* A hydrate containing two moles of water per mole of the compound.

dihydric /dʌɪˈhʌɪdrɪk/ *a.* L19. [f. DI-[2] + HYDRIC *a.*[1]] *Chem.* Containing two hydroxyl groups or (formerly) two hydrogen atoms in the molecule.

dihydro- /dʌɪˈhʌɪdrəʊ/ *pref.* Bef. a vowel also **dihydr-**. [f. DI-[2] + HYDRO-.] *Chem.* Containing two atoms of hydrogen in the molecule.
dihydrotesˈtosterone *n.* the compound into which testosterone is converted in tissue where it exerts its hormonal effect M20.

dihydroxy- /dʌɪhʌɪˈdrɒksi/ *comb. form.* [f. DI-[2] + HYDROXY-.] *Chem.* Containing two hydroxyl groups in the molecule.
ˌdihydroxyˈacetone *n.* a strongly reducing isomer, $(CH_2OH)CO$, of glyceraldehyde used in lotions for colouring the skin in sunlight L19.

diiamb /dʌɪˈʌɪam(b)/ *n.* M18. [Late L *diiambus* f. Gk *diambos*, f. *di-* DI-[2] + *iambos* IAMBUS.] *Pros.* A metrical foot consisting of two iambs.

dijudicate /dʌɪˈdʒuːdɪkeɪt/ *v.i.* & *t.* Now *rare.* E17. [L *dijudicat-*: see next, -ATE[3].] Pass judgement (on or between).

dijudication /ˌdʌɪdʒuːdɪˈkeɪʃ(ə)n/ *n.* Now *rare.* M16. [L *dijudicatio(n-)*, f. *dijudicat-* pa. ppl stem of *dijudicare* judge, determine, f. *di-* DI-[1] + *judicare* to judge: see -ATION.] 1 The action or faculty of judging between matters; discernment, discrimination. M16. 2 The pronouncing of a judgement. E17.

dika /ˈdiːkə/ *n.* M19. [Mpongwe *odika* condiment.] (The fruit or seed of) the wild mango, *Irvingia gabonensis*, a W. African tree. Also, dika bread.
Comb.: **dika bread** a paste prepared from dika seeds, which is a staple of some African peoples; **dika fat, oil** a fatty substance expressed from dika seeds.

dikaryon /dʌɪˈkarɪən/ *n.* E20. [f. DI-[2] + Gk *karuon* nut.] *Biol.* A pair of unfused haploid nuclei of opposite mating type in a cell or spore which divide simultaneously when the cell divides; a dikaryotic cell, mycelium, etc.
dikaryˈotic *a.* containing a dikaryon; composed of dikaryons: M20.

dik-dik /ˈdɪkdɪk/ *n.* L19. [E. Afr. name, of imit. origin.] Any of several very small African antelopes constituting the genus *Madoqua*.

dike *ns.*, *v.* vars. of DYKE *n.*[1], *n.*[2], *v.*

dike /dʌɪk/ *v.*[2]*i.* *US colloq.* M19. [Origin uncertain: perh. alt. of DECK *v.*] Dress stylishly or with elegance. Usu. foll. by *out.*

dike-grave *n.* var. of DYKE-GRAVE.

diketone /dʌɪˈkiːtəʊn/ *n.* L19. [f. DI-[2] + KETONE.] *Chem.* Any compound with two carbonyl groups each attached to two carbon atoms.

dikh /dɪk/ *n. Anglo-Ind.* L19. [Urdu *dikk* troubled, vexed.] Trouble, worry, vexation.

dikkop /ˈdɪkəp/ *n. S. Afr.* M19. [Afk., f. *dik* thick + *kop* head.] 1 Any of certain African stone curlews, esp. *Burhinus vermiculatus* or *B. capensis.* M19. 2 A form of the disease bluetongue. L19.

diktat /ˈdɪktat/ *n.* M20. [G, f. as DICTATE *n.*] 1 A severe settlement, esp. one imposed by a victorious nation on a defeated one. M20. 2 A dictate; a categorical assertion. M20.

dilacerate /dɪˈlasəreɪt, dʌɪ-/ *v.t.* Pa. pple & ppl a. **-ated**, (earlier) †**-ate**. LME. [Orig. pa. pple, f. L *dilaceratus* pa. pple of *dilacerare*, f. *di-* DI-[1] + *lacerare* tear, lacerate: see -ATE[2], -ATE[3].] Tear apart; tear in pieces.

dilaceˈration *n.* LME.

dilambdodont /dʌɪˈlamdədɒnt/ *a.* L19. [f. DI-[2] + LAMBDA + -ODONT.] *Zool.* Having molar teeth with two transverse pointed ridges.

Dilantin /dʌɪˈlantɪn/ *n.* M20. [f. DI-[2] + *-l-* + HYD)ANT(O)IN *n.*] (US proprietary name for) phenytoin.

dilapidate /dɪˈlapɪdeɪt/ *v.* Pa. pple & ppl a. **-ated**, †**-ate**. E16. [L *dilapidat-* pa. ppl stem of *dilapidare*, f. *di-* DI-[1] + *lapis, lapid-* stone: see -ATE[3].] 1 *v.t.* Waste, squander, (a benefice or estate). E16. 2 *v.t.* Bring (a building etc.) into a state of decay, disrepair, or partial ruin. Chiefly as *dilapidated* ppl a. L16. 3 *v.i.* Become dilapidated; fall into ruin, decay, or disrepair. E18.

2 J. RUSKIN A large and dilapidated pair of woman's shoes. J. STEINBECK The sagging dilapidated porch. E. MANNIN Dilapidated taxis. *Practical Householder* You can bring new life to dilapidated and neglected woods. 3 S. JOHNSON The church of Elgin . . was . . shamefully suffered to dilapidate by deliberate robbery and frigid indifference.

dilapidator *n.* L16.

dilapidation /dɪˌlapɪˈdeɪʃ(ə)n/ *n.* LME. [Late L *dilapidatio(n-)*, f. as prec.: see -ATION.] 1 Squandering; wasteful expenditure. LME. 2 The action of pulling down, allowing to decay, or in any way impairing (orig. *spec.* ecclesiastical) property. LME. b In *pl.* A sum charged to an incumbent or tenant against wear and tear during occupation of premises. M16. 3 The process of falling into decay; the condition of being in ruins or disrepair. LME. 4 The falling of stones or masses of rock from mountains or cliffs by natural agency. L18.

1 T. R. MALTHUS The dilapidation of the national resources. 3 F. WELDON The neighbours complained about the dilapidation and the weeds in the garden.

dilatant /dʌɪˈleɪt(ə)nt, dɪ-/ *a.* M19. [f. DILATE *v.*[2] + -ANT[1].] Dilating; expansive; *esp.* exhibiting dilatancy.

dilatancy *n.* the property of increasing in volume when subjected to pressure or deformed L19.

dilatate /ˈdʌɪlətət/ *a. rare.* LME. [L *dilatatus* pa. pple of *dilatare*: see DILATE *v.*[2], -ATE[2].] Dilated.

dilatation /dʌɪleɪˈteɪʃ(ə)n, dɪ-, -lə-/ *n.* LME. [OFr. f. late L *dilatatio(n-)*, f. L *dilatat-* pa. ppl stem of *dilatare*: see DILATE *v.*[2], -ATION.] 1 Chiefly *Sci.* a The action or process of dilating; the condition of being dilated; expansion, enlargement. LME. b A dilated form; a dilated part of any structure. M19. 2 The action or practice of dilating on a subject; expatiation, enlargement. LME. 3 The spreading abroad (of abstract things); dissemination. *arch.* LME.

1 **dilatation and curettage** *Med.* an operation involving dilatation of the cervix and curettage of the uterus, carried out to arrest irregular menstrual bleeding, to terminate a pregnancy, to diagnose certain uterine diseases, etc.; abbrev. *d. and c.*

dilatational *a.* of or pertaining to dilatation L19. **ˈdilatative** *a.* (now *rare*) of the nature of or tending to dilatation E18.

dilatator /ˈdʌɪləteɪtə/ *n.* Now *rare.* E17. [Late L, f. L *dilatat-*: see prec., -OR.] = DILATOR.

dilate /dʌɪˈleɪt/ *a. arch.* L15. [L *dilatus* pa. pple of *differre* DEFER *v.*[1], but used in sense of *dilatatus* DILATATE *a.*: see -ATE[2].] Dilated; widely extended or expanded.

†**dilate** *v.*[1]*t.* LME–M17. [OFr. *dilater* f. late L *dilatare* frequent. of L *differre* DEFER *v.*[1] Cf. DILATORY.] Delay, defer; protract, prolong.

¶During currency prob. identified w. DILATE *v.*[2]

dilate /dʌɪˈleɪt, dɪ-/ *v.*[2] LME. [(O)Fr. *dilater* f. L *dilatare* spread out, f. *di-* DI-[1] + *latus* wide.] 1 *v.t.* Make wider or larger; expand, amplify, enlarge. LME. †2 *v.t.* Spread abroad; extend, disseminate, disperse. LME–E18. †3 *v.t.* Relate at length; enlarge upon. LME–E19. 4 *v.i.* Discourse or write at large (*on, upon*). M16. 5 *v.i.* Become wider or larger; spread out, expand. M17.

4 E. CRISPIN The Major dilated on Sal's unusual competence as a watchdog. 5 E. FIGES Her eyes . . dilated with some deep, dark, inward vision.

dilatable *a.* able to be dilated, expandable E17. **dilataˈbility** *n.* the ability to be dilated, expansibility L17. **dilative** *a.* †(*a*) serving to diffuse or disperse food; (*b*) having the property of dilating or expanding: E16.

dilater /dʌɪˈleɪtə, dɪ-/ *n.* Now *rare.* E17. [f. prec. + -ER[1].] 1 *gen.* A person who or thing which dilates something. E17. 2 *Surg.* = DILATOR 1. M17. 3 *Anat.* = DILATOR 2. L17.

†**dilation** *n.*[1] LME–M17. [OFr. *dilacion* (later †*dilation*) f. L *dilatio(n)-*, f. *dilat-*: see DILATORY, -ION.] Delay, postponement, procrastination.

dilation /dʌɪˈleɪʃ(ə)n/ *n.*[2] LME. [Irreg. f. DILATE *v.*[2] as if containing -ATE[3]: see -ATION.] = DILATATION.

dilatometer /dʌɪləˈtɒmɪtə/ *n.* L19. [f. DILATE *v.*[2] + -OMETER.] An instrument for measuring the expansion of a liquid.

dilatoˈmetric *a.* L19. **dilatometry** *n.* E20.

dilator /dʌɪˈleɪtə, dɪ-/ *n.* L17. [f. DILATE *v.*[2] + -OR. Cf. earlier DILATER.] 1 *Surg.* An instrument for dilating an opening or cavity in the body. L17. 2 *Anat.* A muscle that dilates an organ. M18.

dilatory /ˈdɪlət(ə)ri/ *a.* & *n.* LME. [Late L *dilatorius* delaying, f. L *dilator* delayer, f. *dilat-* pa. ppl stem of *differre* DEFER *v.*[1]: see -ORY[2].] A *adj.* 1 Tending to cause delay; having the purpose of gaining time. LME. 2 Given to or characterized by delay; slow, tardy. E17.

1 **dilatory plea** *Law*: put in for the sake of delay. 2 J. A. FROUDE His political advisers were impatient of these dilatory movements. C. C. TRENCH His ruling passion was . . the bustle of business, but he was as dilatory in despatching it as he was eager to engage in it.

B *n. Law.* A dilatory plea. LME.

dilatorily *adv.* E18. **dilatoriness** *n.* L17.

dildo /ˈdɪldəʊ/ *n.* Pl. **-o(e)s**. L16. [Origin unkn.] 1 A penis; *esp.* an artificial erect penis used for sexual pleasure. Also (*slang*), a stupid or despicable person. L16. 2 Used in refrains as a meaningless wd. E17. 3 More fully *dildo tree*. Any of several W. Indian cacti with tall ribbed cylindrical stems, esp. *Cereus peruvianus* and *Lemaireocereus hystrix.* L17.

†**dilection** *n.* LME. [(O)Fr., or eccl.L *dilectio(n-)* (Christian) love, f. L *dilect-* pa. ppl stem of *diligere* esteem highly, love: cf. DILIGENT.] 1 Love, affection; *esp.* spiritual or Christian love. LME–L17. 2 Choice, esp. (*Theol.*) as exercised by God, election. LME–M17. 3 Beloved (as an honorific title). E18–M19.

dilemma /dɪˈlɛmə, dʌɪ-/ *n.* & *v.* E16. [L f. Gk *dilēmma*, f. as DI-[2] + *lēmma* assumption, premiss.] A *n.* 1 In *Rhet.*, a form of argument involving an opponent in choice between two (or more) alternatives, both equally unfavourable. In *Logic*, a syllogism with two conditional major premisses and a disjunctive minor premiss. E16. 2 A choice between two (or several) alternatives which are equally unfavourable; a position of doubt or perplexity; a difficult situation. L16.

2 B. BAINBRIDGE He walked thoughtfully back . . , pondering on how he would extricate himself from this dilemma in a dignified manner. D. BOGARDE Three corridors. . . 'Dilemma Left, right or center?' *on the horn(s) of a dilemma*: see HORN *n.* PRISONER'*s dilemma.*

B *v.t.* Place in a dilemma. *rare.* M17.

dileˈmmatic *a.* M19. †**dilemmatical** *a.* M–L17. **dileˈmmatically** *adv.* M17.

dilettante /dɪlɪˈtanti/ *n.* & *a.* Pl. **-ti** /-ti/, **-tes**. M18. [It., use as n. of vbl adj. f. *dilettare* f. L *delectare* DELIGHT *n.*] A *n.* A lover of the fine arts; a person who cultivates the arts as an amateur; a person who takes an interest in a subject merely as a pastime and without serious study, a dabbler. M18.

T. BALOGH Mr. Churchill . . refused to trust the dilettantes at the Treasury.

B *adj.* Of, pertaining to, or characteristic of a dilettante; amateur. M18.

dilettant /ˈdɪlɪtɑːnt/ *a.* & *n.* = DILETTANTE M19. **dilettantish** *a.* L19. **dilettantism** *n.* the practice or action of a dilettante, amateur dabbling; the character of dilettanti: E19. **dilettantist** *a.* characterized by dilettantism M19.

diligence /ˈdɪlɪdʒ(ə)ns/ *n.*[1] ME. [(O)Fr. f. L *diligentia*, f. *diligent-*: see DILIGENT, -ENCE.] †1 Careful attention; heedfulness, caution. ME–L18. 2 The quality of being diligent; industry, assiduity. LME. †b An act of diligence; in *pl.*, labours, exertions. LME–M17. †c A diligent person. *rare* (Shakes.) Only in E17. †3 Speed, dispatch, haste. L15–L18. 4 *Sc. Law.* The legal process by which payments are enforced, debts recovered, etc. Also, a warrant issued by a court to enforce the attendance of witnesses or the production of documents. M16. 5 *Law.* The attention and care required in a given situation. E17.

diligence /ˈdɪlɪdʒ(ə)ns; *foreign* diliʒɑ̃ːs (*pl. same*)/ *n.*[2] L17. [Fr., abbrev. of *carrosse de diligence* 'coach of speed'.] *Hist.* A public stagecoach, esp. in France.

diligent /ˈdɪlɪdʒ(ə)nt/ *a.* & *adv.* ME. [(O)Fr. f. L *diligent-, -ens* assiduous, attentive, pres. pple of *diligere* esteem highly, love, choose, take delight in, f. as DI-[1] + *legere* choose: see -ENT.] A *adj.* 1 Of a person: steady in application; assiduous, industrious; attentive to one's duties. ME. 2 Of an action: steadily applied; prosecuted with activity and perseverance. LME. †3 Attentive; heedful, careful. LME–M18.

1 F. TUOHY Although he complains of his courses he is a very diligent boy.

†B *adv.* Diligently. L15–L16.

diligently *adv.* ME.

dill /dɪl/ *n.*[1] [OE *dile* & *dyle*, respectively = OS *dilli* (Du. *dille*), OHG *tilli, dilli* (G *Dill* f. LG), & MDu. *dulle*, MHG *tülle*, ON *dylla*: ult. origin unkn.] An umbelliferous annual plant, *Anethum graveolens*, with scented seeds and leaves and small yellow flowers; the seeds or leaves of this plant used as a flavouring.

Comb.: **dill pickle** a pickled cucumber, gherkin, etc., flavoured with dill; **dill-water**: prepared from dill as a carminative.

dill /dɪl/ *n.*[2] *Austral.* & *NZ slang.* M20. [App. back-form. f. DILLY *a.*[1]] A fool, a simpleton; *esp.* a person who is duped by a trickster.

dilligrout /ˈdɪlɪgraʊt/ *n.* M17. [Origin unkn.] *Hist.* A kind of pottage which was offered to the British monarch on coronation day by the lord of the manor of Addington, Surrey (now part of London).

dilling /ˈdɪlɪŋ/ *n.* Now *dial.* L16. [Origin unkn.] Formerly, as a term of endearment: darling; the youngest of a family. Now *dial.*, the weakling of a litter.

dilly /ˈdɪli/ *n.*[1] L18. [Abbrev. of DILIGENCE *n.*[2]] †1 = DILIGENCE *n.*[2] *colloq.* L18–L19. 2 Any of various carts, trucks, etc., used in agriculture and industrial operations. *dial.* M19.

dilly /ˈdɪli/ *n.*[2] *Austral.* M19. [Aborig. *dili.*] In full *dilly-bag*. A small bag or basket (formerly of plaited grass etc.) for carrying food etc.

dilly /ˈdɪli/ *n.*[3] *slang* (orig. *US*). M20. [f. DILLY *a.*[2]] A delightful or remarkable person or thing; an outstanding example (*of*). Freq. *iron.*

dilly /ˈdɪli/ *a.*[1] *dial.* & *colloq.* (chiefly *Austral.*). L19. [Perh. f. DAFT *a.* + SILLY *a.*] Foolish, stupid; eccentric, queer.

dilly /ˈdɪli/ *a.*[2] *colloq.* L19. [f. 1st syll. of DELIGHTFUL, DELICIOUS + -Y[6].] Delightful, delicious.

dilly /ˈdɪli/ *int.* & *n.*[4] *colloq.* & *dial.* M19. [Origin unkn.] (Used as a call to) a duck.

dilly-dally /ˈdɪlɪdali/ *n.* & *v. colloq.* E17. [Redupl. of DALLY.] †A *n.* Trifling hesitancy, dilly-dallying. Only in 17. B *v.i.* Vacillate; dawdle, loiter. M18.

dilly-ˈdallier *n.* L19.

dilogy /ˈdɪlədʒi, ˈdʌɪ-/ *n.* M17. [L *dilogia* f Gk, f. *dilogos*, f. as DI-[2] + *logos* saying, speech: see -LOGY.] *Rhet.* (An) ambiguity.

dilruba /dɪlˈruːbə/ *n.* E20 [Hind. *dilrubā* = robber of the heart.] An Indian musical instrument with a long neck, three or four strings played with a bow, and several sympathetic strings.

dilse *n.* see DULSE.

dilucid /dʌɪˈluːsɪd/ *a. obs.* exc. *poet.* M17. [L *dilucidus* clear, bright, f. *dilucere*, f. *di-* DI-[1] + *lucere* shine.] Clear to the sight; lucid, plain.

†**dilucidity** *n.* lucidity: only in E17.

dilucidate /dɪˈluːsɪdeɪt/ *v.t.* Long *rare.* Also **de-**. M16. [Late L *dilucidat-* pa. ppl stem of *dilucidare* make clear, f. as prec.: see -ATE[3].] Elucidate.

†**dilucidation** *n.* E17–M18.

diluent /ˈdɪljʊənt/ *n.* & *a.* E18. [L *diluent-* pres. ppl stem of *diluere*: see DILUTE *v.*, -ENT.] A *n.* 1 A medicine used to increase the proportion of water in the blood and other body fluids. Now *rare* or *obs.* E18. 2 *gen.* Something which dilutes, dissolves, or makes more fluid. L18. B *adj.* Diluting; serving to attenuate or weaken by the addition of water etc. M18.

dilute /dʌɪˈl(j)uːt, dɪ-/ *a.* E17. [L *dilutus* pa. pple, f. as next.] 1 Weak, paltry. *obs.* exc. as *fig.* use of sense 2. E17. 2 Watered down; (of a solution) containing a high proportion of solvent. M17.

diluteness *n.* M17.

dilute /dʌɪˈl(j)uːt, dɪ-/ *v.t.* M16. [L *dilut-* pa. ppl stem of *diluere* wash away, dissolve f. *di-* DI-[1] + *-luere* comb. form of *lavare* to wash.] 1 Weaken; take away the strength or force of, esp. by addition. M16. 2 Diminish the brilliancy or strength of (colour). M17. 3 Make (a liquid) thinner, weaker, or less concentrated by adding water or other solvent; make (a gas) less concentrated by admixture. L17.

1 E. BOWEN Sunset mists diluted the moon. R. CONQUEST Diluting brilliant essence With seepage of other minds.

dilutable *a.* able to be diluted; intended to be diluted before use: L20. **dilutedly** *adv.* in a diluted or weakened manner M19. **diluˈtee** *n.* an unskilled or semi-skilled worker who takes a place hitherto occupied by a skilled worker E20. **diluter** *n.* something which or someone who dilutes; *spec.* (*a*) a diluent; (*b*) a device for automatically obtaining any desired dilution of a sample: E18. **dilutive** *a.* tending to dilute; characterized by dilution: E17.

dilution /dʌɪˈl(j)uːʃ(ə)n, dɪ-/ *n.* M17. [f. prec. + -ION.] 1 The action of diluting. M17. b The substitution of unskilled or semi-skilled workers for skilled ones. E20. 2 Dilute condition; the degree to which a solution has been diluted. E19. 3 Something in a dilute condition. M19.

2 ANTHONY HUXLEY This eelworm-killer is effective at a dilution of one part in five million.

dilutional *a.* involving or characterized by dilution, esp. (*Med.*) as a result of increased blood plasma M20.

diluvial /dʌɪˈl(j)uːvɪəl, dɪ-/ *a.* M17. [Late L *diluvialis*, f. *diluvium*: see DILUVIUM, -AL[1].] 1 Of or pertaining to a deluge, esp. Noah's Flood. M17. 2 *Geol.* Produced by or resulting from a supposed general deluge, or periods of catastrophic action of water; of, pertaining to, or being diluvium. E19.

2 **diluvial theory** etc.: postulating a general deluge or catastrophic flood as an explanation of geological features.

diluvialist *n.* an advocate of a diluvial theory E19.

diluvian /dʌɪˈl(j)uːvɪən, dɪ-/ *a.* M17. [f. as prec. + -AN.] = DILUVIAL 1.

diluvianism *n.* belief in a past universal deluge; belief in a diluvial theory: E19.

diluvium /dʌɪˈl(j)uːvɪəm, dɪ-/ *n.* Pl. **-ia** /-ɪə/. E19. [L *diluvium*, f. *diluere*: see DILUTE *v.*] *Geol.* (A deposit of) superficial material formerly attributed to a universal deluge but now to glacial action; drift.

dim /dɪm/ *a.*, *n.*, & *adv.* [OE *dim(m)* = OFris. *dim*, ON *dimmr* rel. to synon. OHG *timbar* (MHG, mod. dial. *timmer*), OSw. *dimber*, OIr. *dem* black, dark.] A *adj.* Compar. & superl. **-mm-**. 1 Of a light or illuminated object: faintly luminous, not shining brightly or clearly; somewhat dark, shadowy. OE. 2 Not clear to the sight; obscured by distance etc., scarcely visible; misty, indistinct. OE. b *fig.* Not clear to the understanding; indistinctly apprehended; obscure. ME. 3 Of colour, or an object in respect of its colour: not bright; dull, lustreless. ME. 4 Of a person or eyes: not seeing clearly. Of sight: poor. ME. b *fig.* Dull of apprehension; *colloq.* not intellectually bright, somewhat stupid. ME. 5 Of sound, esp. the voice: indistinct, muffled. ME.

1 J. RHYS Her room was dim, with a shaded candle by the bed. W. GOLDING Even in that dim light I could see she was shivering. 2 D. H. LAWRENCE The dim smoke wavering up the chimney. R. BROOKE That fills The soul with longing for dim hills And faint horizons. b A. EDEN The Boer war . . was a dim memory. SIAN EVANS He felt a dim desire, which, as his thoughts lingered, grew in urgency. 3 R. L. STEVENSON All retired and shady spots Where prosper dim forget-me-nots. 4 **take a dim view of** *colloq.* regard with disfavour or pessimism.

Comb.: **dim-sighted** *a.* having dim sight; unperceptive; **dim-wit** *colloq.* a stupid person; **dim-witted** *a.* (*colloq.*) stupid, dull; **dim-wittedness** the fact or quality of being a dim-wit.

B *n.* Dimness; obscurity; dusk. LME.

C *adv.* Compar. & superl. **-mm-**. Dimly. LME.

dimly *adv.* in a dim manner; obscurely; faintly: ME. **dimmish** *a.* L15. **dimmy** *a.* (somewhat) dim LME. **dimness** *n.* OE.

dim /dɪm/ *v.* Infl. **-mm-**. OE. [f. the adj.] 1 *v.t.* Make (more) dim, obscure; render indistinct; becloud (the eyes). OE. 2 *v.i.* Become (more) dim; lose brightness, clarity, or distinctness. ME.

1 J. BUCHAN Memories of which time has not dimmed the rapture. R. CHURCH This drab khaki which had dimmed the British army since the Boer War. **dim out** reduce the brightness of (lights); subject to a dim-out (see below).

Comb.: **dim-out** a reduction in the brightness or use of lights, esp. in wartime; a gradual dimming of lights in a theatre, cinema, etc.

Dimaris /ˈdɪmərɪs/ *n.* E19. [A mnemonic of scholastic philosophers first used in med.L, I indicating a particular affirmative proposition and A a universal affirmative proposition.] *Logic.* The third mood of the fourth syllogistic figure, in which a particular affirmative conclusion is drawn from a particular affirmative major and a universal affirmative minor premiss.

dimble /ˈdɪmb(ə)l/ *n. obs.* exc. *dial.* L16. [Perh. conn. w. DIM *a.* or DINGLE *n.*] A deep and shady dell, a dingle.

dime /dʌɪm/ *n.* Also †**disme**. LME. [(O)Fr. *dime*, †*disme*, f. L *decima* use as n. (sc. *pars* part) of fem. of *decimus* tenth.] 1 A tenth part; a tithe. *obs.* exc. *Hist.* LME. 2 A coin worth a tenth of a dollar (10 cents); in *pl.* also (*colloq.*), money. *N. Amer.* L18.

2a **dime a dozen** commonplace.

Comb.: **dime novel** *N. Amer.* a cheap sensational novel; **dime-store** *N. Amer.* (*a*) a shop selling cheap merchandise (orig. one where the maximum price was a dime); (*b*) *attrib.* cheap and inferior.

dimension /dɪˈmɛnʃ(ə)n, dʌɪ-/ *n.* & *v.* LME. [Fr. f. L *dimensio(n-)*, f. *dimens-* pa. ppl stem of *dimetiri* measure out, f. *di-* DI-[1] + *metiri* measure.] A *n.* 1 Measurable spatial extent of any kind, as length, breadth, area, volume. Now usu. in *pl.* LME. †b Duration. LME–L17. c The magnitude or scale of an abstract thing. M17. 2 A mode of linear extension of which there are three in space, two on a flat surface, etc., and which corresponds to one of a set of coordinates specifying the position of a point; *Math.* such a coordinate. LME. b *Math.* Any of a number of quantities in a product, esp. of unknowns. M16. c *Sci.* The power to which any fundamental quantity or unit is raised in a product defining a derived quantity or unit; in *pl.*, the product itself. M19. d An attribute or status that may be seen as inhering in or characterizing an abstract thing; an aspect. E20. †3 The action of measuring, measurement. M16–L18. b *Mus.* The division of a longer note into shorter ones; in *pl.*, measured strains. L16–M17. †4 Measurable form; in *pl.*, material parts, as of the body. L16–M17.

1 K. TYNAN Shrinking before our eyes to the dimensions of a pickled walnut. **of large** etc. **dimensions** of large etc. size. c G. F. KENNAN Soviet trade never quite achieved, . . between the two wars, the dimensions of prewar Russian trade. 2 R. A. KNOX How do we get our notion of solid objects, when we can only see in two dimensions? FOURTH *dimension.* b OED x^3, x^2y, xyz are each of three dimensions. d A. O. J. COCKSHUT The religious dimension . . would have given coherence and deeper meaning to the . . scraps of virtue displayed by Flora. *Listener* Atomic bombs . . brought a new dimension of destruction and horror to warfare.

Comb.: **dimension line**: showing, usu. with arrowheads, the parts or lines to which the figured dimensions refer in a plan etc.

B *v.t.* 1 Measure, reduce to measurement. *rare.* M18. 2 Mark the dimensions on (a plan etc.). Cf. earlier DIMENSIONED 3. E20.

dimensional /dɪˈmɛnʃ(ə)n(ə)l, dʌɪ-/ *a.* E19. [f. prec. + -AL[1].] 1 Of or pertaining to dimension or magnitude. E19. b Of, pertaining to, or involving dimensions of units or physical qualities. L19. 2 Having a specified number of dimensions. L19.

1b **dimensional analysis**: using the fact that quantities added to or equated with each other must have the same dimensions to make inferences about the relations between quantities and units. 2 H. MOORE The child learning to see, first distinguishes only two-dimensional shape.

dimensioˈnality *n.* dimensional quality; the fact of having (so many) dimensions: M16. **dimensionally** *adv.* as regards dimensions L19.

dimensioned /dɪˈmɛnʃ(ə)nd, dʌɪ-/ *a.* M16. [f. DIMENSION *n.*, *v.*: see -ED[2], -ED[1].] †1 Having material extent. Only in M16. 2 Having a particular size or set of measurements. E18. 3 Of a plan etc.: having dimensions and distances marked on it. L19. 4 Having a specified number of dimensions. Usu. in *comb.* L19.

2 BETTY SMITH An aircraft dimensioned like a coffin.

dimensionless /dɪˈmɛnʃ(ə)nləs, dʌɪ-/ *a.* M17. [f. DIMENSION *n.* + -LESS.] 1 Having no spatial extent; extremely minute. M17. 2 Measureless, immense. E19. 3 Having none of the three dimensions of space. M19. b Of a physical quantity or its unit: having no dimensions; of the nature of a pure number, with a value independent of the choice of other units. E20.

dimensive /dɪˈmɛnsɪv, dʌɪ-/ *a.* M16. [med.L *dimensivus*, f. L *dimens-*: see DIMENSION, -IVE.] †1 Having or related to spatial extension. M16–L17. †2 Serving to measure or trace out the dimensions of something. L16–E17. 3 Of or pertaining to dimension or magnitude. *rare.* M19.

dimensurator /dɪˈmɛnsjʊreɪtə, dʌɪ-/ *n. obs.* exc. *Hist.* L17. [f. DI-[1] + MENSURATE *v.* + -OR.] A surveyor's measuring instrument.

dimer /ˈdʌɪmə/ *n.* E20. [f. DI-[2] + -MER.] *Chem.* A compound having twice the number of each atom in its molecule as another compound; *esp.* one in which two identical molecules or radicals are joined together.

dimeriˈzation *n.* formation of or conversion into a dimer M20. **dimerize** *v.t.* & *i.* (cause to) be converted into a dimer M19.

dimeric /dʌɪˈmɛrɪk/ *a.* L19. [In sense 1 f. Gk *dimerēs* bipartite, in sense 2 f. prec.: see -IC.] 1 *Zool.* Having a right and a left side. *rare.* L19. 2 *Chem.* Of the nature of a dimer, consisting of a dimer or dimers. E20.

dimerous /ˈdɪm(ə)rəs/ *a.* E19. [f. mod.L *dimerus* f. Gk *dimerēs*: see prec., -OUS.] *Bot.* & *Entomol.* Having two parts or members, *spec.* in a whorl.

dimeter /ˈdɪmɪtə/ *n.* L16. [Late L *dimeter*, n., *dimetrus* adj. & n., f. Gk *dimetros* of two measures, f. as DI-² + *metron* measure.] *Pros.* A line of two measures.

Dimetian *a.* var. of DEMETIAN.

†**dimetient** *n.* & *a.* L16. [L *dimetient-* pres. ppl stem of *dimetiri*: see DIMENSION, -ENT.] A *n.* A diameter. L16–E18. B *adj.* 1 *dimetient line*, a diameter. E17–E18. 2 Expressing the dimension. Only in M19.

dimication /dɪmɪˈkeɪʃ(ə)n/ *n.* Now *rare.* E17. [L *dimicatio(n-)*, f. *dimicat-* pa. ppl stem of *dimicare* fight: see -ATION.] Fighting; contention.

dimidiate /dɪˈmɪdɪət/ *a.* M18. [L *dimidiatus* pa. pple, f. as next: see -ATE².] Divided into two; *Bot.* & *Zool.* having one half different from the other, esp. in size or sex.

dimidiately *adv.* M19.

dimidiate /dɪˈmɪdɪeɪt/ *v.t.* L16. [L *dimidiat-* pa. ppl stem of *dimidiare* halve, f. *dimidium* half, f. *di-* DI-¹ + MEDIUM: see -ATE³.] 1 *Her.* Represent only half of (a bearing or coat of arms), esp. in one half of a shield divided per pale; combine (one coat) *with* another in this way. L16. 2 *gen.* Divide in half, reduce to a half. E17

dimidiˈation *n.* the action of halving, the condition of being halved; *spec.* (*Her.*) the combination of two coats of arms by juxtaposing the dexter half of one and the sinister half of the other: LME.

diminish /dɪˈmɪnɪʃ/ *v.* LME. [Blend of DIMINUE and MINISH.] I *v.t.* 1 Make smaller or less (in fact or in appearance). LME. 2 Lessen the power, reputation, or self-esteem of (a person); belittle, depreciate. LME. †3 Subtract, remove, (*from*). E16–E17. †4 Deprive in part *of*. Usu. in *pass.* M16–M18. 5 *Archit.* Make (a column etc.) taper. M16.

1 L. DURRELL Nor were our follies diminished by these warnings. 2 MILTON Impiously they thought Thee to diminish.

II *v.i.* 6 Become less or smaller; decrease. E16. †7 Foll. by *from*: make less; detract from. M17–E19.

6 G. GREENE They climbed up .. and the sound of the others diminished below them.

Phrases: **diminishing glass** an instrument through which an object appears smaller than when viewed by the naked eye. **diminishing mirror** a convex mirror giving a smaller image. **law of diminishing returns** *Econ.* the principle that as expenditure etc. increases each further increase produces a proportionately smaller return.

diminishable *a.* able to be diminished (earlier in UNDIMINISHABLE) L18. **diminishableness** *n.* the property of being diminishable L19. **diminisher** *n.* (*rare*) a person who or thing which diminishes E17. **diminishingly** *adv.* †(*a*) disparagingly; (*b*) decreasingly: L17. **diminishment** *n.* diminution, lessening M16.

diminished /dɪˈmɪnɪʃt/ *ppl a.* E17. [f. prec. + -ED¹.] 1 That has been diminished; reduced. E17. 2 *Mus.* Of an interval: less by a semitone than the corresponding minor or perfect interval. Of a chord: containing such an interval. Opp. AUGMENTED 2. E18.

1 MILTON O thou [sun] .. at whose sight all the Starrs Hide their diminisht heads. ALDOUS HUXLEY Bernard had to slink back, diminished, to his rooms. **diminished responsibility** *Law* mental weakness or disturbance not classifiable as insanity but recognized as ground for reducing the charge of murder to that of manslaughter.

†**diminue** *v.t.* & *i.* LME–M16. [(O)Fr. *diminuer* f. med.L *diminuere* f. L *deminuere* lessen, *diminuere* break up small, f. *de-* DE- 1, *di-* DI-¹ + *minuere*: see MINUTE *a.*] Diminish; speak disparagingly (of).

diminuendo /dɪˌmɪnjʊˈɛndəʊ/ *n.*, *v.*, *adv.*, & *a.* L18. [It. = diminishing, pres. pple of *diminuire* f. L *deminuere*: see DIMINUE.] *Mus.* A *n.* Pl. **-dos, -di** /-di/. A gradual decrease in loudness; a passage (to be) played or sung with such a decrease. L18. B *v.i.* Become quieter; grow less. L18. C *adv.* & *adj.* (A direction:) with a gradual decrease in loudness. E19.

†**diminute** *a.* LME–M18. [L *diminutus* pa. pple, f. as next.] Diminished; incomplete.

†**diminutely** *adv.* LME–M19.

diminute /dɪˈmɪnjuːt/ *v.t.* *rare.* LME. [L *diminut-* pa. ppl stem of *diminuere*: see DIMINUE.] = DIMINISH 2.

diminution /dɪmɪˈnjuːʃ(ə)n/ *n.* ME. [(O)Fr. f. L *diminutio(n-)*, f. as prec.: see -ION.] †1 Representation of something as less than it is. ME–M17. 2 The action of making or becoming less; reduction; lessening. LME. †3 Partial deprivation, curtailment. LME–L17. †4 Lessening of honour or reputation. L16–M18. 5 *Mus.* The repetition of a subject (esp. in fugues) in notes half or a quarter of the length of those of the original. L16. 6 *Law* (now *Hist.*). The absence of a correct certification of a record sent up from a lower court to a higher one. M17. 7 *Archit.* The tapering of a column etc.; the extent of this. E18. 8 *Cytol.* The loss or expulsion of chromosomal elements from the nuclei of embryonic cells that develop into somatic cells. E20.

diminutive /dɪˈmɪnjʊtɪv/ *a.* & *n.* LME. [(O)Fr. *diminutif, -ive* f. late L *diminutivus*, f. as DIMINUTE *v.*: see -IVE.] A *adj.* 1 *Gram.* Expressing diminution in size or status; (of a word) denoting something small of its kind, hence something regarded with affection, familiarity, or contempt (as English *lassie, ringlet, princeling*); (of an affix, esp. a suffix) added to the radical to form a diminutive word. LME. 2 Small; remarkably small, tiny. L16. †3 Disparaging, depreciative. M17–L18. †4 Making less or smaller. L17–E18.

1 L. BLOOMFIELD Some have the diminutive suffix [-ij], as *Peggy, Maggie* for *Margaret, Fanny* for *Frances.* 2 SHAKES. *Lear* The poor wren, (the most diminutive of birds).

B *n.* 1 A diminutive word or affix. LME. 2 *Her.* One of the smaller ordinaries corresponding in form and position to the larger, but of less width. L16. 3 A diminutive thing or person; a small form *of* something. E17.

diminutival /dɪˌmɪnjʊˈtʌɪv(ə)l/ *a.* & *n.* (*Gram.*) = DIMINUTIVE *a.* 1, *n.* 1 M19. **diminutively** *adv.* E17. **diminutiveness** *n.* E18.

†**dimiss** *v.* LME–E18. [L *dimiss-*: see DISMISS *v.*] = DISMISS *v.*

†**dimission** *n.* LME. [L *dimissio(n-)*, f. as prec.: see -ION.] 1 = DEMISSION *n.*¹ 1. LME–M16. 2 = DEMISSION *n.*¹ 2. LME–E19.

dimissory /ˈdɪmɪs(ə)ri/ *n.* & *a.* Also †**dem-**. LME. [Late L *dimissorius* (in *litterae dimissoriae*), f. as DIMISS, -ORY².] †A *n.* In *pl.* = *letters dimissory*. LME–E18. B *adj.* 1 Pertaining to leave-taking; valedictory. Long *rare.* L16. 2 *letters dimissory, dimissory letter*, a letter or licence from a bishop etc. authorizing the bearer as a candidate for ordination by another bishop. L16.

†**dimit** *v.*¹*t.* Infl. **-tt-**. LME. [L *dimittere*: see DISMISS *v.* Cf. DEMIT *v.*²] 1 Send away, dismiss. LME–E18. 2 Convey by lease. L15–E17. 3 Lay aside, give up, resign. M16–L17.

†**dimit** *v.*² var. of DEMIT *v.*¹

dimity /ˈdɪmɪti/ *n.* LME. [It. *dimito* or med.L *dimitum* f. Gk *dimitos*, f. as DI-² + *mitos* thread of the warp; the origin of the final *-y* is unkn.] A stout cotton fabric woven with raised stripes or motifs.

dimmer /ˈdɪmə/ *n.* E19. [f. DIM *v.* + -ER¹.] A person who or thing which makes something dim; *esp.* a control for reducing the brightness of a light.

dimmer /ˈdɪmə/ *v.i.* L19. [f. DIM *v.* + -ER⁵.] Appear dimly, faintly, or indistinctly. (Foll. by *up.*)

dimorphemic /dʌɪmɔːˈfiːmɪk/ *a.* M20. [f. DI-² + MORPHEMIC.] *Ling.* = BIMORPHEMIC.

dimorphic /dʌɪˈmɔːfɪk/ *a.* M19. [f. Gk *dimorphos*, f. as DI-² + *morphē* form: see -IC.] Existing or occurring in two distinct forms, *spec.* (*a*) (*Bot.* & *Zool.*) in the same plant or species, (*b*) (*Min.*) of the same crystalline substance.

dimorphism *n.* M19. **dimorphous** *a.* = DIMORPHIC M19.

dimorphotheca /ˌdʌɪmɔːfəˈθiːkə/ *n.* M19. [mod.L, f. as prec. + THECA.] A southern African plant of the genus *Dimorphotheca*, of the composite family, grown elsewhere as a half-hardy garden annual.

dimple /ˈdɪmp(ə)l/ *n.* & *v.* LME. [Corresp. to OHG *tumphilo* (MHG *tümpfel*, G *Tümpel*) deep place in water, f. Gmc, perh. a nasalized form of base of DEEP *a.*; prob. already in OE. Cf. DUMP *n.*³] A *n.* 1 A small hollow or dent in the surface of part of the human body, esp. in the cheeks or chin. LME. 2 Any slight depression in the surface of something. M17.

2 SOUTHEY The gentle waters gently part In dimples round the prow. S. B. FLEXNER The modern golf ball has 360 dimples.

B *v.* 1 *v.t.* Mark (as) with dimples. L16. 2 *v.i.* Break into or form dimples or ripples. E17.

1 B. HARTE Leaden rain .. dimpling like shot the sluggish pools. 2 TENNYSON Low knolls That dimpling died into each other. K. MANSFIELD Suddenly his face dimpled; it broke into a wide, toothless smile.

dimpled *a.* marked (as) with dimples L16. **dimply** *a.* full of or characterized by dimples E18.

dimps /dɪmps/ *n.* *dial.* L17. [Perh. f. DIM *n.*, or dial. var. of *dumps* pl. of DUMP *n.*¹] Dusk, twilight.

dimpsey *n.*, *a.* vars. of DIMPSY *n.*, *a.*

dimpsy /ˈdɪmpsi/ *n.* *dial.* & *colloq.* Also **-ey.** L19. [f. prec. + -Y⁶.] Dusk, twilight; = prec.

dimpsy /ˈdɪmpsi/ *a.* *dial.* & *colloq.* Also **-ey.** L19. [f. as prec. + -Y¹.] Dusky, dim.

dim sum /dɪm ˈsʌm/ *n. phr.* Also **dim sim** /dɪm ˈsɪm/ & other vars. Pl. **sum(s)** etc. M20. [Chin. (Cantonese) *tím sam*, f. *tím* dot + *sam* heart.] A Chinese snack consisting of different hot savoury pastries.

din /dɪn/ *n.* [OE *dyne, dynn* = OHG *tuni*, ON *dynr*, f. Gmc.] A loud noise; *esp.* a continuous confused distracting noise.

G. HUNTINGTON The muffled din of the station grew acuter whenever the door was opened.

dinful *a.* noisy L19.

din /dɪn/ *v.* Infl. **-nn-**. [OE *dynian* = OS *dunian*, MHG *tünen* roar, rumble, ON *dynja* come rumbling down, f. Gmc base of prec.] I *v.i.* †1 Of a place etc.: resound with noise. OE–E16. 2 Make a din; give out or be a loud confused sound. ME.

2 V. WOOLF A familiar sound shook and trembled—increased—fairly dinned in their ears.

II *v.t.* 3 Assail with clamour or persistent noise. L17. 4 Repeat continually so as to weary; *esp.* get (a lesson etc.) *into* a person by continual repetition. Cf. DING *v.*² 1a. E18.

3 R. C. SINGLETON With never-ceasing words On this and that side is the hero dinned. 4 R. RENDELL Ever since I was eighteen I've had it dinned into me I mustn't drink.

dinanderie /dinɑ̃dri/ *n.* M19. [Fr., f. *Dinant* (formerly *Dinand*), a town near Liège, Belgium + *-erie* -ERY.] Domestic and other utensils of brass (freq. embossed) made in late medieval times in and around Dinant; ornamental brassware from other parts, including India and the eastern Mediterranean region.

Dinantian /dɪˈnanʃɪən/ *a.* & *n.* E20. [Fr. *dinantien*, f. *Dinant* (see prec.) + -IAN.] *Geol.* (Of, pertaining to, or designating) the Lower Carboniferous in Europe or the rocks dating from this time.

dinar /ˈdiːnɑː/ *n.* M17. [Arab., Pers. *dīnār*, Turk., Serbo-Croat *dinar* f. late Gk *dēnarion* f. L DENARIUS.] 1 Any of various coins formerly used in the East, *esp.* a gold mohur. M17. 2 The basic monetary unit of Serbia and neighbouring States (and formerly of Yugoslavia), equal to 100 paras. L19. 3 The basic monetary unit of Algeria, Bahrain, Iraq, Jordan, Kuwait, Libya, Tunisia, and (formerly) South Yemen, equal to 100 centimes in Algeria, 1,000 fils in Bahrain, Iraq, Jordan, Kuwait, and (formerly) South Yemen, 1,000 dirhams in Libya, and 1,000 millimes in Tunisia; a monetary unit of Iran, equal to one-hundredth of a rial. M20.

Dinaric /dɪˈnarɪk/ *a.* M19. [f. *Dinara*, a mountain in Dalmatia + -IC.] Pertaining to or designating a mountain range extending south-easterly along the eastern side of the Adriatic.

din-din /ˈdɪndɪn/ *n.* *colloq.* Also **-dins** /-dɪnz/. L19. [Childish or joc. redupl. of DINNER *n.*] Dinner.

dindle /ˈdɪnd(ə)l/ *v.* & *n.* Now *Sc.* & *north.* LME. [Prob. imit.: cf. DINGLE *v.*, TINGLE *v.*, TINKLE *v.*] A *v.* 1 *v.i.* Make a ringing sound or one that causes vibration. LME. 2 *v.i.* & *t.* (Cause to) tremble or vibrate, esp. with sound. LME. 3 *v.i.* Tingle as with cold or pain. L15.

2 W. H. AUDEN While war-horns dindled the heavens.

B *n.* A vibration; a tingling sensation. E19.

dine /dʌɪn/ *n. obs.* exc. *dial.* LME. [f. the vb.] Dinner; dinner-time.

dine /dʌɪn/ *v.* ME. [OFr. *disner* (mod. *dîner*) prob. f. *desjuner, desjëuner* break fast: see DISJUNE.] 1 *v.i.* Have dinner. Foll. by *on* (what is eaten), *off* (a stock or supply). ME. 2 *v.t.* Give dinner to. Of a room etc.: accommodate for dining purposes. LME.

1 J. BETJEMAN Lunching with poets, dining late with peers.

Phrases: **dine out** dine away from home. **dine out on** be invited to dinner on the strength of (one's knowledge of an interesting event, etc.). **dine with Duke Humphrey** *arch.* go without dinner. *wine and dine*: see WINE *v.*

diner /ˈdʌɪnə/ *n.* E19. [f. prec. + -ER[1].] 1 A person who dines; a dinner-guest. E19. 2 A railway dining-car. Orig. *US.* M19. 3 A cheap roadside restaurant, orig. one built to resemble a railway dining-car. *N. Amer.* M20. 4 A dining-room, *esp.* a small one. M20.

4 *kitchen-diner*: see KITCHEN *n.*

Comb.: **diner-out** (pl. **diners-out**) a person who often dines out, *esp.* one much in demand as a dinner-guest for his or her social qualities.

dinero /dɪˈnɛːrəʊ/ *n.* Pl. **-os.** L17. [Sp. = coin, money f. L *denarius* DENARIUS.] 1 *Hist.* A monetary unit in Spain and Peru, now disused. L17. 2 Money. *US slang.* M19.

dinette /dʌɪˈnɛt/ *n.* M20. [Irreg. f. DINE *v.* + -ETTE.] 1 A small room or area of a room set aside for meals, as in a kitchen or caravan. M20. 2 A set of furniture for a dinette. M20.

ding /dɪŋ/ *n.*[1] ME. [f. DING *v.*[1]] 1 A blow, a knock; a push. Now *Sc.* & *dial.* ME. 2 A dent; a small damaged area. *colloq.* M20.

ding /dɪŋ/ *n.*[2] M18. [f. the int.] A ringing metallic sound; *gen.* a din.

ding /dɪŋ/ *n.*[3] *Austral. slang. derog.* M20. [Abbrev. of DINGBAT.] An Italian; a Chinese; any foreigner.

ding /dɪŋ/ *n.*[4] *Austral. slang.* M20. [Prob. f. WINGDING.] A wild party, a celebration.

ding /dɪŋ/ *v.*[1] Pa. t. **dinged,** (*Sc.* & *north.*) **dang** /daŋ/; pa. pple **dinged,** (*Sc.* & *north.*) **dung** /dʌŋ/. ME. [Prob. of Scand. origin: cf. ON *dengja* to hammer, whet a scythe, OSw *dängia,* Da. *dænge* beat, bang.] 1 *v.i.* Deal heavy blows; knock, hammer. Usu. foll. by *on, at. arch.* ME. 2 *v.t.* Strike with heavy blows; beat, thrash. Now *Sc.* ME. b *fig.* Overcome or surpass, beat. Now *Sc.* E18. 3 *v.t.* Knock, throw, or drive with violence in some direction. *arch.* ME. 4 *v.i.* †a Propel oneself forcefully, press, drive; fling oneself about; throw oneself or fall (*down*) heavily. LME–E18. b Of rain, snow, etc.: beat down heavily and without intermission. Usu. foll. by *down, on. Sc.* E16. 5 *v.t.* Throw away, discard; *spec.* get rid of (something incriminating). *slang.* M18. b Give up, abandon, (an enterprise). Esp. in *ding it. Austral. slang.* L19. 6 In mild imprecations, freq. in imper. or optative form: damn. *dial.* & *US.* E19.

1 JOYCE Costello dinged with his fist upon the board. 2 HENRY MORE The rider fiercely dings His horse with iron heel. 3 **ding down** overthrow, demolish. 6 GEO. ELIOT Ding me if I remember a sample to match her.

ding /dɪŋ/ *v.*[2] M16. [Imit., but in sense 1 infl. by prec. and DIN *v.*] 1 a *v.t.* Din *into* a person. M16. b *v.i.* Speak with wearisome persistence, esp. reprovingly. L16. 2 *v.i.* Make a sound like metal heavily struck; ring like a bell struck once. Also redupl. E19.

2 DICKENS Sledge hammers were dinging upon iron all day long. J. HERRIOT The bell ding-dinged and the tram began to move.

ding /dɪŋ/ *int.* L16. [Imit.: cf. DING *v.*[2]] Repr. the ringing sound of a heavy bell, or of metal when struck.

ding-a-ling /ˈdɪŋəlɪŋ/ *n.* & *a.* Also **dingaling.** L19. [Imit.: cf. DING *int., n.*[2]] A *n.* 1 The sound of a bell. L19. 2 A person who acts strangely, orig. as a result of long imprisonment; an eccentric; a fool. *N. Amer. slang.* M20. B *adj.* Foolish, stupid. *N. Amer. slang.* L20.

Ding an sich /dɪŋ an zɪç/ *n. phr.* M19. [G = thing in itself.] *Philos.* A thing as it really is, apart from human observation or experience of it; = NOUMENON.

dingbat /ˈdɪŋbat/ *n. slang.* M19. [Origin uncertain: perh. f. DING *v.*[1] + BAT *n.*[1]; cf. also DINGUS. In sense 4 prob. assoc. w. BAT *n.*[3], BATS *a.*] 1 Any of various vaguely specified objects, *esp.* (*a*) anything used as a missile; (*b*) (a piece of) money; (*c*) a gadget, a contraption; a thingummy. *US.* M19. 2 A vagabond, a tramp. *US.* E20. 3 A stupid or foolish person. *N. Amer.* E20. 4 Madness; a drunken delusion. *Austral.* & *NZ.* E20. 5 An army batman. *Austral.* E20. 6 A typographical device other than a letter or numeral (e.g. an asterisk), used for ornament etc. *US.* E20.

4 **give a person the dingbats** make a person nervous. **have the dingbats** be crazy, be suffering from delirium tremens.

dingbats /ˈdɪŋbats/ *pred. a. Austral.* & *NZ slang.* M20. [f. pl. of prec.] Crazy, eccentric; suffering from delirium tremens.

ding-dong /ˈdɪŋdɒŋ, dɪŋˈdɒŋ/ *int., adv., n., a.,* & *v.* Also **dingdong.** M16. [Imit.] A *int.* & *adv.* 1 Repr. the sound of a bell. M16. 2 *adv.* With zeal and vigour. L17.

2 M. R. MITFORD I shall set to work at the 'Heiress' ding-dong.

B *n.* 1 The sound of a bell when individual strokes are heard rather than a continuous ring; a bell etc. that gives such a sound, *esp.* a device for sounding the quarter hours by a single stroke on either of two bells of different pitch; a jingle of rhyme. M16. 2 A heated argument, a quarrel. *colloq.* E20. 3 A noisy party. *colloq.* M20.

2 H. BELLOC A ding-dong of assertion and counter-assertion.

C *adj.* 1 Of or pertaining to the sound of bells or the jingle of rhyme. E17. 2 Of a fight or dispute: in which prospective victory swings between one side and the other; hotly contested. *colloq.* M19.

D *v.i.* Ring as or like a bell; *fig.* speak with wearying repetition. M17.

dinge /dɪn(d)ʒ/ *n.*[1] E17. [Origin unkn.: rel. to DINGE *v.*[1]] A depression in the surface of something, caused by a blow; a dint.

dinge /dɪn(d)ʒ/ *n.*[2] *dial.* & *colloq.* E19. [f. DINGE *v.*[2] or back-form. f. DINGY *a.*] Dinginess, drabness; darkness. Formerly, a dark night.

J. R. ACKERLEY The dust and dinge of the cluttered house.

dinge /dɪn(d)ʒ/ *n.*[3] & *a. US slang. derog.* M19. [f. DINGY *a.*] A *n.* A Black. M19. B *adj.* Of or pertaining to Blacks or their jazz-playing. M19.

dinge /dɪn(d)ʒ/ *v.*[1]*t.* Orig. *dial.* E17. [Origin unkn.: goes with DINGE *n.*[1]] Make an impression in the surface of; dent, dint; damage.

dinge /dɪn(d)ʒ/ *v.*[2]*t. dial.* & *colloq.* E19. [f. DINGY *a.*] Make dingy.

dinger /ˈdɪŋə/ *n.* L18. [f. DING *v.*[1] + -ER[1].] 1 A thief who throws away identifiable objects to avoid detection (cf. DING *v.*[1] 5). *Criminals' slang.* Now *rare* or *obs.* L18. 2 Something outstanding of its kind; a 'humdinger'. *slang* (chiefly *US*) & *dial.* L19.

2 J. STEINBECK Been a dinger of a crop.

dinges *n.* var. of DINGUS.

dinghy /ˈdɪŋgi/ *n.* E19. [Hindi *ḍiṅgī, ḍẽgī.* Spelt *-gh-* in Eng. to indicate the hard *g.*] 1 A rowing boat used on the rivers of the Indian subcontinent. E19. 2 Any small boat; *spec.* (*a*) one carried on a warship or merchant vessel; the tender of a yacht; (*b*) a small pleasure-boat or racing-boat; (*c*) an inflatable life-raft, esp. one carried on an aircraft. E19.

dingle /ˈdɪŋg(ə)l/ *n.* ME. [Origin uncertain: perh. a doublet of DIMBLE.] †1 A deep abyss. Only in ME. 2 A deep hollow or dell, *esp.* (chiefly *literary*) one shaded by trees. Also (*dial.*) a cleft between hills. M17.

2 SOUTHEY Seek some sequestered dingle's coolest shade.

Comb.: **dingle-bird** = *bell-miner* s.v. BELL *n.*[1]

dingly *a.* of the nature of a dingle, having many dingles M19.

dingle /ˈdɪŋg(ə)l/ *v.* L16. [Prob. imit.: cf. DINDLE *v.*, TINGLE *v.*, TINKLE *v.*] 1 *v.i.* & *t.* (Cause to) tingle. L16. 2 *v.i.* Ring like a bell, tinkle. E19. 3 *v.i.* Vibrate with sound. M19.

dingleberry /ˈdɪŋg(ə)lbɛri/ *n. US.* M20. [f. unkn. 1st elem. + BERRY *n.*[1]] 1 A deciduous cranberry, *Vaccinium erythrocarpum,* of the south-eastern US. M20. 2 A particle of faecal matter attached to anal hair. Usu. in *pl. slang.* M20. 3 A foolish or stupid person. *colloq.* M20.

dingle-dangle /dɪŋg(ə)lˈdaŋg(ə)l/ *adv., n., v.,* & *a.* L16. [Redupl. of DANGLE *a.* & *n., v.*] A *adv.* In a dangling fashion; hanging loosely. L16. B *n.* A swinging to and fro; an ornament etc. that dangles. E17. C *v.i.* Dangle loosely. M17. D *adj.* Swinging loosely to and fro, dangling. L17.

dingo /ˈdɪŋgəʊ/ *n.* & *v.* L18. [Aborig. *dingu.*] A *n.* Pl. **-oes.** 1 The wild or semi-domesticated dog of mainland Australia, *Canis dingo.* L18. 2 A treacherous, cowardly, or despicable person. *Austral. slang.* E20.

2 V. PALMER I'd be a hell of a dingo .. if I didn't help you now.

B *v. Austral. slang.* 1 *v.i.* Behave in a contemptible way. M20. 2 *v.t.* Shirk, back out of. M20.

1 **dingo on a person** let a person down.

dingus /ˈdɪŋgəs/ *n. colloq.* Also **dinges.** L19. [f. Du. *ding* thing.] A gadget, a contraption; a 'thingummy'.

dingy /ˈdɪn(d)ʒi/ *a.* M18. [Perh. ult. referrable to OE *dynge* dung, manured land, f. DUNG *n.*: see -Y[1].] 1 Dirty, soiled. *dial.* M18. 2 Disagreeably devoid of brightness or freshness of colour, esp. from grime or neglect; drab, dirty-looking. In *Bot.* & *Zool.* (formerly *gen.*), of a naturally sombre colour. M18.

2 DISRAELI Its plumage of a dingy, yellowish white. W. GERHARDIE A bare and dingy room in a .. shabby hostel. *fig.*: H. JAMES She's not for a dingy little man of letters; she's for .. the bright rich world. **dingy skipper** a Eurasian skipper, *Erynnis tages,* which has grey-brown wings with dark markings.

dingily *adv.* E19. **dinginess** *n.* E19.

dining /ˈdʌɪnɪŋ/ *vbl n.* LME. [f. DINE *v.* + -ING[1].] The action of DINE *v.*; a dinner.

Comb.: **dining-car** a railway carriage in which meals are served on the journey; **dining-chair** an upright chair used at a dining-table; **dining-room** a room in a house etc. set aside for the principal meals; **dining-table** a table on which meals are served in a dining-room etc.

dink /dɪŋk/ *n.*[1] *Austral. slang.* M20. [Origin unkn.] A ride on the handlebar of a bicycle.

dink /dɪŋk/ *n.*[2] *US.* M20. [Imit.] A drop-shot in tennis.

dink /dɪŋk/ *n.*[3] *US slang. derog.* M20. [Origin unkn.] A Vietnamese.

dink /dɪŋk/ *n.*[4] *colloq.* Also **DINK.** L20. [Acronym, f. *d*ouble *i*ncome, *n*o *k*ids.] Either partner of a (usu. professional) married couple without children, both of whom have an income from work.

dink /dɪŋk/ *a.*[1] *Sc.* & *north.* E16. [Origin unkn.] Finely dressed, trim, spruce.

dinkly *adv.* L18.

dink /dɪŋk/ *a.*[2] & *adv. Austral.* & *NZ colloq.* E20. [Abbrev.] = DINKUM *a.* & *adv.* Esp. in *fair dink.*

dink /dɪŋk/ *v.*[1]*t. Sc.* E19. [f. DINK *a.*[2]] Dress (esp. oneself) finely, adorn.

dink /dɪŋk/ *v.*[2]*t. Austral. slang.* M20. [f. DINK *n.*[1]] Give a ride on the handlebar of a bicycle to.

dink /dɪŋk/ *v.*[3]*i.* Chiefly *US.* M20. [f. DINK *n.*[2]] In tennis, volleyball, and other games with a net: execute a drop-shot that falls just beyond the net.

Dinka /ˈdɪŋkə/ *n.* & *a.* M19. [Afr. name *Jieng* people.] A *n.* Pl. **-s,** same. 1 A member of a Sudanese people of the Nile basin. M19. 2 The language of this people. L19. B *adj.* Of or pertaining to the Dinkas or Dinka. M19.

dinkel /ˈdɪŋk(ə)l/ *n.* Also **D-.** M19. [G.] = SPELT *n.*[1]

dinkey *n.* var. of DINKY *n.*[1]

dinki-di *a.* var. of DINKY-DIE.

dinkie *n.* var. of DINKY *n.*[2]

dinkie *a.* var. of DINKY *a.*

dinkum /ˈdɪŋkəm/ *n.*, *a.*, & *adv.* L19. [Origin unkn.] A *n.* 1 (Hard) work; one's due share of a task. *dial.* & *obs. Austral. colloq.* L19. 2 = *dinkum oil* below. *Austral.* & *NZ colloq.* E20. †3 (**D-**) An Australian or New Zealander, *esp.* one who fought in the war of 1914–18. *Austral.* & *NZ colloq.* Only in E20.

1 R. BOLDREWOOD It took us an hour's hard dinkum to get near the peak.

B *adj.* & *adv.* In full *fair dinkum* (also *square, straight, dinkum*). Genuine(ly), authentic(ally); honest(ly), straightforward(ly); *interrog.* really? you aren't having me on? *Austral.* & *NZ colloq.* L19.

Weekly Dispatch Real dinkum Australians . . knew . . that wombats can't fly. N. MARSH Give you a pain in the neck, dinkum, she would. F. CLUNE The Simpson Desert . . is the only fair-dinkum desert in Australia. A. WRIGHT It's like a story out of a book . . but it's dinkum. **dinkum oil** the honest truth, reliable information.

dinky /ˈdɪŋki/ *n.*[1] Also **-key**. M19. [f. DINKY *a.* In sense 'small boat' perh. alt. of DINGHY.] A small contrivance; *spec.* a small boat or locomotive.

dinky /ˈdɪŋki/ *n.*[2] *colloq.* Also **-ie**. L20. [f. (as) DINK *n.*[4] + -Y[6], -IE.] = DINK *n.*[4]

dinky /ˈdɪŋki/ *a.* Also **-kie**. L18. [f. DINK *a.*[2] + -Y[1].] 1 Small and neat; dainty, cute. *dial.* & *colloq.* (esp. *Sc.* & *N. Amer.*). L18. 2 Trifling, insignificant, unimpressive. *N. Amer. colloq.* L19.

1 W. H. AUDEN In a dinky straw hat. D. WELCH Dinky lattice panes. **Dinky car, Toy** (proprietary name for) a die-cast miniature motor vehicle. 2 H. CRANE In a dinky stuffy apartment.

dinky-die /dɪŋkɪˈdʌɪ/ *a. Austral.* & *NZ slang.* Also **dinki-, -di**. E20. [f. DINKUM + -Y[1] with a nonsensical addition.] = DINKUM *a.*

dinmont /ˈdɪnm(ə)nt/ *n. Sc.* & *north.* ME. [Origin uncertain: 2nd elem. perh. Sc. form of MONTH.] A wether between the first and second shearing.

dinna *v.* see DO *v.*

dinner /ˈdɪnə/ *n.* ME. [OFr. *di(s)ner* (mod. *dîner*) use as n. of inf.: see DINE *v.*] The main meal of the day, eaten either about midday or in the evening; a formal meal of several courses, *spec.* one held publicly to honour a person, mark an occasion, etc.

DAY LEWIS Sunday dinner was a joint, two veg. and pudding affair, far superior to our weekday lunches or evening meals. G. B. SHAW Speeches made by my uncle at charitable dinners. **done like a dinner** *Austral. slang* utterly defeated. *eat dinners*: see EAT *v.* **have had more — than a person has had hot dinners** *colloq.*: used hyperbol. to indicate a person's wide experience of a given activity or phenomenon. (*like a*) *dog's dinner*: see DOG *n.* WORKING *dinner.*

Comb.: **dinner-bell**: rung to announce dinner; **dinner-dance** a dinner followed by dancing; **dinner-horn** *US* a horn blown to call workers on a farm etc. to dinner; **dinner jacket** a man's short usu. black dress-coat without tails, worn with a black tie for evening functions; **dinner lady** a woman employed to serve midday meals in a school; **dinner-pail** *US* a pail in which a labourer's or schoolchild's dinner is carried and kept warm (*hand, pass,* or *turn in one's dinner-pail* (slang), die); **dinner service** a set of matching plates, dishes, etc., for serving dinner; **dinner-table** a dining-table; **dinner theatre** *N. Amer.* a theatre in which a meal is included in the price of a ticket; **dinner-time**: when dinner is customarily eaten; **dinner wagon** a trolley with tiers for holding dishes etc., for service in a dining-room.

dinnerless *a.* not provided with a dinner M17. **dinnery** *a.* characterized by or suggestive of dinners M19.

dinner /ˈdɪnə/ *v.* M18. [f. the n.] 1 *v.i.* & *t.* (w. *it*). Have dinner, dine. M18. 2 *v.t.* Entertain to dinner; provide with dinner. E19.

dinoflagellate /dʌɪnə(ʊ)ˈfladʒəleɪt/ *a.* & *n.* L19. [mod.L *Dinoflagellata*, f. Gk *dinos* a whirling + L FLAGELLUM: see -ATE[2].] *Biol.* A *adj.* Designating or pertaining to a dinoflagellate. L19. B *n.* Any of a group of unicellular mostly pigmented aquatic (esp. marine) organisms with two flagella, variously classed as algae and as protozoa. E20.

dinosaur /ˈdʌɪnəsɔː/ *n.* M19. [mod.L *dinosaurus*, f. Gk *deinos* fearsome + -SAUR.] An extinct terrestrial reptile, freq. of gigantic size, of a group which was dominant in Mesozoic times, some having pelvic girdles like lizards (order Saurischia) and others like birds (order Ornithischia); *fig.* something that has not adapted to changing circumstances, a clumsy survival from earlier times.

dinoˈsaurian *a.* & *n.* (*a*) *adj.* of or pertaining to a dinosaur or the dinosaurs; (*b*) *n.* a dinosaur: M19.

†dinothere *n.* var. of DEINOTHERE.

dinsome /ˈdɪns(ə)m/ *a. Sc.* E18. [f. DIN *n.* + -SOME[1].] Full of din, noisy.

dint /dɪnt/ *n.* [OE *dynt*, reinforced in ME by related ON *dyntr* (*dyttr*), *dynta*: cf. DENT *n.*[1], DUNT.] †1 A stroke or blow; *esp.* one given with a weapon. OE–M19. †b A stroke of thunder. ME–E19. 2 The dealing of blows; force of attack or impact (*lit.* & *fig.*); violence, attack, force. Now *rare* or *obs.* exc. in *by dint of*, through (constant) application of (a remedy etc.), by means of, by force of. ME. 3 An impression made in a surface (as) by a blow or by pressure; an indentation; *fig.* an effect, an impression produced. L16.

2 SHAKES. *Jul. Caes.* You weep, and I perceive you feel The dint of pity. SMOLLETT By dint of cross-examination, I found he was not at all satisfied. J. MCPHEE Do the Alaskan natives, by dint of aboriginal use . . have special claim to Alaskan land . . ? †**by dint of sword** by force of arms. †**under, within** etc. **the dint of** within the range of (something harmful). 3 V. WOOLF A little dint sharpened between his brows. W. S. CHURCHILL A hardy . . race which . . had . . made a deep dint upon the politics of England.

dintless *a.* producing or showing no dint M16.

dint /dɪnt/ *v.* ME. [f. the n.] †1 *v.t.* Strike, beat. ME–M17. 2 *v.†i.* & *t.* Make a dint or impression in (or †*in*). LME. 3 *v.t.* Drive in (as) with pressure. (Foll. by *into*.) L16.

2 J. M. NEALE In his master's steps he trod, Where the snow lay dinted. 3 DRYDEN Deep dinted wrinkles.

diocesan /dʌɪˈɒsɪs(ə)n/ *a.* & *n.* LME. [Fr. *diocésain* f. med.L *diocesanus*, late L *dioecesanus*, f. L *dioecesis* DIOCESE: see -AN.] *Eccl.* A *adj.* Of or pertaining to a diocese. LME. B *n.* 1 The bishop of a diocese. LME. 2 One of the clergy or people of a diocese. Now *rare.* E16.

diocese /ˈdʌɪəsɪs/ *n.* ME. [OFr. *diocise* (mod. *diocèse*) f. late L *diocesis* for L *dioecesis* governor's jurisdiction, district, (Eccl.) diocese, f. Gk *dioikēsis* administration, government, (Eccl.) diocese, f. *dioikein* keep house, administer, f. as DI-[3] + *oikos* house.] 1 *Eccl.* The region over which a bishop has jurisdiction and pastoral charge subject only to an archbishop or metropolitan. ME. 2 A division of a country under a governor; *spec.* each of the twelve units (consisting of several provinces) into which the Roman Empire was divided from the time of Diocletian. *obs.* exc. *Hist.* L15.

†diocesian *a.* & *n.* E17–E18. [med.L *diocesianus*, f. late L *diocesis* DIOCESE: see -IAN.] = DIOCESAN *a.* & *n.*

dioch /ˈdʌɪɒk/ *n.* Also **diock**. L19. [Perh. f. Afr. name.] Any of various African weaver-birds of the genus *Quelea*.

dioctahedral /ˌdʌɪɒktəˈhiːdr(ə)l/ *a.* E19. [f. DI-[2] + OCTAHEDRAL.] 1 *Cryst.* Bounded by sixteen planes, i.e. in the form of an octahedral prism with tetrahedral summits. *rare.* E19. 2 *Min.* Having or designating a crystal structure in which there are two metal ions for each octahedron of hydroxyl or oxygen ions. M20.

diode /ˈdʌɪəʊd/ *a.* & *n.* L19. [f. DI-[2] + Gk *hodos* way.] †A *adj.* Of a telegraph system: in which two messages can be transmitted simultaneously along one line, either in the same or in opposite directions. Only in L19. B *n. Electronics.* 1 A thermionic valve with two electrodes (a cathode and an anode). E20. 2 A semiconductor rectifier with two terminals. M20.

2 *Gunn diode, junction diode, photodiode, Schottky diode*, etc.

diodon /ˈdʌɪədɒn/ *n.* L18. [f. DI-[2] + -ODON.] A tropical globe-fish of the genus *Diodon*, in which each jaw has, instead of teeth, an undivided enamel beak.

dioecious /dʌɪˈiːʃəs/ *a.* Also ***diec-**. M18. [f. mod.L *Dioecia*, a class in Linnaeus's sexual system (f. as DI-[2] + Gk *oikos* house) + -OUS.] 1 *Bot.* Bearing male and female flowers on different plants. Also, (of a cryptogam) having male and female organs in different plants. M18. 2 *Zool.* Having male and female reproductive organs in separate individuals. E19.

dioeciously *adv.* L19. **dioeciousness** *n.* L19. **dioecism** /-sɪz(ə)m/ *n.* dioecious state L19. **dioecy** /-si/ *n.* dioecism M20.

dioestrus /dʌɪˈiːstrəs/ *n.* Also **-trum** /-trəm/, ***diest-** /dʌɪˈɛst-/. E20. [f. DI-[2] + OESTRUS.] A relatively short interval of sexual quiescence or inactivity in an animal between recurrent periods of oestrus.

dioestrous *a.* E20.

Diogenes /dʌɪˈɒdʒɪniːz/ *n.* L16. [See below.] A person, esp. one of pointedly ascetic or unsociable behaviour, who is likened to Diogenes (*c*400–*c*325 BC), a Greek Cynic philosopher reputed to have shown his contempt for the comforts of civilization by living in a tub.

Comb.: **Diogenes-crab** a W. Indian hermit crab, *Coenobita diogenes*, which lives in the empty shell of a snail.

Diogenic /-ˈdʒɛnɪk/ *a.* pertaining to or resembling Diogenes M19. **Diogenical** /-ˈdʒɛnɪk(ə)l/ *a.* = DIOGENIC L16.

diogenite /dʌɪˈɒdʒɪnʌɪt/ *n.* L19. [f. Gk *Diogenēs* descended from Zeus + -ITE[1].] Any of a group of achondritic meteorites consisting largely of hypersthene and bronzite.

diol /ˈdʌɪɒl/ *n.* E20. [f. DI-[2] + -OL.] *Chem.* A compound whose molecule contains two hydroxyl groups, esp. attached to different carbon atoms.

-dione /ˈdɪəʊn/ *suff.* [f. DI-[2] + -ONE.] *Chem.* Forming the names of compounds containing two carbonyl groups, as *menadione*.

†dionise *n.* Also in med.L form **dionysia**. LME–M19. [OFr. f. med.L *dionysia* f. L *dionysias* f. Gk *dionūsias*, f. *Dionūsos*: see DIONYSIAN.] A precious stone credited by medieval writers with warding off drunkenness when ground and added to water.

Dionysiac /dʌɪəˈnɪzɪak/ *n.* & *a.* Also **d-**. E19. [Late L *Dionysiacus* f. Gk *Dionūsiakos*, f. *Dionūsos*: see next, -AC.] A *n.* In *pl.* The festivals of Dionysus held at various times of the year in ancient Greece. E19.

B *adj.* = DIONYSIAN *a.* I. M19.

W. A. PERCY The gowns . . insist on hanging from the . . shoulders with something of a dionysiac abandon.

Dionysiacal /dʌɪənɪˈzʌɪək(ə)l/ *a.* = DIONYSIAC *a.* M19. **Dionysiacally** /-ˈzʌɪək-/ *adv.* E19. **Dionysic** /-ˈnʌɪsɪk/ *a.* = DIONYSIAC *a.* M19.

Dionysian /dʌɪəˈnɪzɪən/ *a.* & *n.* E17. [f. L *Dionysius* f. Gk *Dionūsios* adj., also as pers. name, f. *Dionūsos* Dionysus (see below): see -AN, -IAN.] A *adj.* 1 Of or pertaining to Dionysus, the Greek god of fruitful vegetation, wine, etc., whose cult was frequently marked by ecstatic rites; sensual, abandoned; (of character, literary work, etc.) inspired by instinct and emotion (opp. *Apollonian*). E17. 2 Pertaining to or characteristic of the Elder or Younger Dionysius, tyrants of Syracuse notorious for cruelty. E17. 3 Pertaining to the abbot Dionysius the Little (fl. 6th cent.) or the system of dating events from the birth of Jesus which he suggested. M17.

3 **Dionysian period** [said to have been introduced by Dionysius for calculating the date of Easter] = LUNISOLAR *period*.

B *n.* A worshipper or follower of Dionysus; a person of Dionysian character. E20.

Diophantine /dʌɪəˈfantʌɪn/ *a.* E18. [f. *Diophantus* of Alexandria (fl. 3rd cent. AD), mathematician + -INE[1].] *Math.* Pertaining to the solution of indeterminate equations and the restriction of variables to integral values; designating a polynomial equation with integral coefficients for which integral solutions are required.

diopside /dʌɪˈɒpsʌɪd/ *n.* E19. [Fr., irreg. f. as DI-[2] + Gk *opsis* aspect; later interpreted as f. Gk *diopsis* a view through.] *Min.* A monoclinic silicate of calcium and magnesium of the pyroxene group, occurring as white to pale green transparent to translucent crystals.

diop'sidic *a.* M20.

dioptase /dʌɪˈɒpteɪz/ *n.* E19. [Fr., irreg. f. Gk *dioptos* transparent, f. as DI-[3] + *optos* visible.] *Min.* A hexagonal hydrated silicate of copper occurring as green transparent to translucent crystals.

diopter /dʌɪˈɒptə/ *n.* Also **-tra** /-trə/. In sense 3 also **dioptre**. L16. [Fr. *dioptre* f. L *dioptra* f. Gk.] 1 = ALIDADE. L16. 2 An ancient optical instrument for measuring angles, altitudes, etc. E17. 3 A unit for expressing the power of a lens, equal to the reciprocal of its focal length in metres. L19.

dioptric /dʌɪˈɒptrɪk/ *a.* & *n.* M17. [Gk *dioptrikos* relating to the use of the dioptra: see DIOPTER, -IC.] A *adj.* †1 Pertaining to or being a diopter. M–L17. 2 Of a lens etc.: serving as a medium for sight; assisting vision by refraction. M17. 3 Pertaining to or employing refraction. L17. †4 Able to be seen through. E–M19. B *n.* In *pl.* (treated as *sing.*). The branch of optics that deals with refraction. M17.

dioptrical *a.* E17. **dioptrically** *adv.* by means of refraction M18.

diorama /dʌɪəˈrɑːmə/ *n.* E19. [Fr., f. as DIA-[1] after PANORAMA.] 1 A scenic painting, viewed through a peephole, in which changes in lighting, colour, etc., are used to suggest different times of day, changes in weather, etc.; a building in which such paintings are exhibited. E19. 2 A small-scale tableau in which three-dimensional figures are shown against a painted background; a museum display of an animal etc. in its natural setting; a scale model of an architectural project in its surroundings. E20. 3 *Cinemat.* A small-scale set used in place of a full-scale one for special effects, animation, etc. M20.

1 *fig.*: R. C. HUTCHINSON This continuous twilight, the diorama of roofs and gables ranging on livid smoke.

dioramic /-ˈramɪk/ *a.* M19.

diorite /ˈdʌɪərʌɪt/ *n.* E19. [Fr., irreg. f. Gk *diorizein* distinguish, f. as DI-[3] + *orizein* limit: see -ITE[1].] *Geol.* Any of a class of coarse-grained intermediate plutonic rocks consisting essentially of plagioclase feldspar and hornblende or other mafic minerals.

dioritic /-ˈrɪtɪk/ *a.* M19.

diorthosis /dʌɪɔːˈθəʊsɪs/ *n.* Pl. **-thoses** /-ˈθəʊsiːz/. *arch.* E18. [Gk *diorthōsis*, f. as DI-[3] + *orthos* straight: see -OSIS.] The act of putting straight or in order; an agent that accomplishes this.

diorthotic /-ˈθɒtɪk/ *a.* M19.

Dioscuric /dʌɪəˈskjʊərɪk/ *a.* Also **d-**. E20. [f. Gk *Dioskouroi* (f. *Dios* genit. of *Zeus* + *kouros*, *koros* boy, son) + -IC.] Pertaining to or resembling the legend of the twin sons of Zeus, Castor and Pollux.

diosgenin /dʌɪˈɒsdʒənɪn/ *n.* M20. [G, f. mod.L *Dios(corea* type genus of the yam family (f. *Dioscorides* 1st-cent. AD Gk physician) + GENIN.] *Chem.* A sapogenin, $C_{27}H_{42}O_3$, obtained from Mexican yams of the genus *Dioscorea* and used in the preparation of steroid hormones.

diosma /dʌɪˈɒzmə/ *n.* E19. [mod.L, f. Gk *dios* divine + *osmē* odour.] *Bot.* Any of various heathlike shrubs of the rue family belonging to the Southern African genus *Diosma* or formerly included in it, noted for their strong balsamic smell.

diota /dʌɪˈəʊtə/ *n.* M19. [L *diota* f. Gk *diōtē* two-eared, f. as DI-[2] + *ous*, *ōt-* ear.] *Class. Antiq.* A two-handled vessel; *spec.* an amphora.

†**dioti** *n.* M17–M18. [Gk, f. *dia* (*touto*) *hoti* for the reason that.] A 'wherefore', a reason. Cf. HOTI.

diotic /dʌɪˈɒtɪk/ *a.* M20. [f. DI-[2] + Gk *ous*, *ōt-* ear + -IC.] Involving or pertaining to the presentation of the same auditory signal to both ears.

diotically *adv.* M20.

Diotrephes /dʌɪˈɒtrəfiːz/ *n.* M17. [A man named in *3 John* 9.] A person who loves pre-eminence among others, esp. in a congregation.

Diotrephesian /-ˈfiːzjən, -ʒ(ə)n/, **Diotrephian** /-ˈtrɛf-/, **Diotrephic** /-ˈtrɛf-/ *adjs.* of the nature of a Diotrephes M19.

dioxan /dʌɪˈɒksan/ *n.* Also ***-ane** /-eɪn/. E20. [f. DI-[2] + OX- + -AN, -ANE.] A saturated cyclic diether, $C_4H_8O_2$, that is a toxic flammable liquid used as a solvent; any derivative of this.

dioxide /dʌɪˈɒksʌɪd/ *n.* M19. [f. DI-[2] + OXIDE.] *Chem.* Any oxide containing two atoms of oxygen in its molecule or empirical formula.

dioxin /dʌɪˈɒksɪn/ *n.* E20. [f. DI-[2] + OX- + -IN[1].] 1 *Chem.* Each of three unsaturated cyclic compounds, $C_4H_6O_2$ and $C_4H_4O_2$. *rare.* E20. 2 Any derivative of such a compound, *esp.* tetrachlorodibenzoparadioxin. L20.

dip /dɪp/ *n.* L16. [f. the vb.] 1 An act of dipping; *spec.* (*colloq.*) a bathe in the sea etc. L16. b A minor fall in value or magnitude. L19. 2 A downward slope of a surface; *esp.* in *Mining* & *Geol.*, the angle made by a stratum etc. with the horizontal. L17. b *Mining.* In full *dip-head*. A passage driven downwards, esp. in the direction of dip. L19. 3 The angle made with the horizontal at any point by the earth's magnetic field. E18. †4a = DEEP *n.* 8. M18–M19. b Depth or amount of submergence, e.g. of a vessel. L18. 5 *Astron.* & *Surveying.* The apparent depression of the horizon due to the observer's elevation and the curvature of the earth. L18. 6 A hollow to which the surrounding high ground dips. L18. 7 In full *dip candle*. A candle made by repeatedly dipping a wick into tallow. E19. 8a A substance into which food may be dipped before eating, *esp.* (*a*) fat and juice left after the cooking of meat; (*b*) a savoury sauce. E19. b A boiled dumpling. Usu. in *pl. Austral. slang.* M19. 9 A quantity of liquid taken up by dipping. M19. 10 Crude turpentine. M19. 11 A pickpocket. *slang.* M19. 12 *Pros.* An unstressed element in a line of alliterative verse. L19. 13 A liquid into which something is dipped for treatment, *esp.* one for killing vermin on sheep, horses, etc.; a vat or tank for this purpose. L19. 14 A receptacle from which a hidden prize may be obtained by dipping. E20.

1 JAS. GRANT A half-hour's 'dip' into some circulating-library book. TENNYSON Ev'n to the last dip of the vanishing sail She watch'd it. R. BRAUTIGAN She caught twenty fish with one dip. H. CARPENTER They take an early morning dip in an icy stream. b *Daily Telegraph* A £122 million dip in profits from Imperial Chemical Industries. 6 S. HILL You can't see our farmhouse, it lies in the dip beyond the beeches there. 8a M. BRADBURY A bowl of tomatoes and a cheese dip, into which they started popping the tomatoes. 9 S. WARREN His pen . . with a fresh dip of ink in it. 13 *sheep-dip* etc. 14 *lucky dip*: see LUCKY *a.*

Comb. (partly f. the vb stem): *dip candle*: see sense 7 above; *dip-head*: see sense 2b above; **dip circle** a graduated vertical circle with a dipping-needle; **dip needle** = *dipping-needle* s.v. DIP *v.* 9; **dip-net** *n.* & *v.* (*a*) *n.* a small fishing net with a long handle; (*b*) *v.t.* catch using a dip-net; **dip pen**: that has to be dipped in ink; **dip slope** a usu. gentle slope of the land that approximately follows that of the underlying strata; **dipstick** (*a*) a rod for dipping into liquid, esp. oil in a motor vehicle, to find its depth; (*b*) *coarse slang* the penis; (*c*) *slang* a stupid or contemptible person; **dip-switch**: for dipping headlights.

dip /dɪp/ *v.* Infl. **-pp-**. Pa. t. & pple **dipped**, †**dipt**. [OE *dyppan* f. Gmc base repr. also by DEEP *a.*] I *v.t.* 1 Put or let down for a moment *in* or *into* (a liquid); immerse partially and briefly. OE. b Immerse in a colouring solution, dye; imbue something with (a colour) by dipping. *poet.* M17. c Make (a candle) by repeatedly immersing a wick in hot tallow. E18. d Immerse (a sheep, horse, etc.) in a bath of vermin-killing liquid. E19. 2 Baptize by dipping or immersing. Now usu. *contempt.* OE. 3 Take (liquid, grain, etc.) out of a body of it by dipping with a scoop etc. (Foll. by *up*.) E17. b Take (snuff) by dipping something into it and rubbing it on the gums. *US.* M19. c Pick the pocket of. *slang.* E20. 4 *fig.* †a Implicate, involve, (*in* any affair). E17–L18. b Involve in debt; mortgage; pawn. *colloq.* M17. 5 Suffuse with moisture. *arch.* M17. 6 Lower or let down for a moment, as if dipping in a liquid; *spec.* lower and then raise (a flag, an aircraft's wing in flight, etc.) in salute or (a sail) in tacking. L18. b Lower (headlight beams), lower beams of (headlights), to avoid dazzling oncoming motorists. E20.

1 H. READ He dipped his hand into the stream, right up to his sensitive wrist. b MILTON With . . colours dipt in Heav'n. 3 P. S. BUCK This cauldron he filled partly full of water, dipping it with a half-gourd from an earthen jar. 4a HOR. WALPOLE Having been deeply dipped in the iniquities of the South Sea. b DRYDEN Never dip thy Lands. 5 MILTON A cold shuddering dew Dips me all o'er.

II *v.i.* 7 Plunge down a little into water or other liquid and quickly emerge. Foll. by *in*, *into*, *under*. LME. 8 Sink or drop as if into water; extend downward a little way. LME. b Fall a little in value or magnitude, esp. temporarily. M20. 9 Have a downward inclination, slope downwards. M17. 10 Put one's hand, a ladle, etc., into water, a receptacle, etc., to take something out. (Foll. by *into*.) L17. b Pick pockets. *slang.* E19. c Dip snuff. *US.* M19. d Dip the headlights of a vehicle. E20. 11 Look cursorily *into* a subject, book, etc. L17. 12 Go deeply *into* a matter. M18. 13 = DAP *v.* I. L18.

7 W. C. SMITH Slowly the muffled oars dip in the tide. 8 E. BOWEN Gulls dipped over the lawn in a series of white flashes. TOLKIEN The Sun dipped and vanished. b *Broadcast* This week's figures . . show . . its audience share dipping to just under 41%. 9 W. SCORESBY In this hemisphere, the north end of the [magnetic] needle dips. E. GARRETT You have no idea how the road dips. **dipping-needle** a magnetic needle mounted so as to be capable of moving in a vertical plane about its centre of gravity, and thus indicating by its dip the direction of the earth's magnetic field; 10 A. HIGGINS She had a shiny black reticule . . into which she was continually dipping for cigarettes. 11 J. AGATE The only book of Proust's into which I have not dipped at one time or another.

Phrases: **dip into savings, reserves**, etc.: spend part of them. **dip one's wick** *coarse slang* (of a man) have sexual intercourse. **dip out** *Austral. slang* lose an opportunity or advantage, be unsuccessful.

dipping *n.* (*a*) the action of the vb; (*b*) a liquid into which things are dipped, *esp.* = DIP *n.* 8a(a): LME.

dipeptide /dʌɪˈpɛptʌɪd/ *n.* E20. [f. DI-[2] + PEPTONE + -IDE.] *Chem.* Any peptide containing two amino-acid residues in its molecule.

dipeptidase /-ɪdeɪz/ *n.* an enzyme which hydrolyses a dipeptide but not higher peptides E20.

diphasic /dʌɪˈfeɪzɪk/ *a.* L19. [f. DI-[2] + PHASIC.] Characterized by having two phases; occurring in or consisting of two phases.

diphen- /ˈdʌɪfɛn/ *comb. form.* [f. DI-[2] + PHEN-.] *Chem.* & *Pharm.* Denoting the presence of two phenyl groups.

diphen'hydramine *n.* an antihistamine compound used for the symptomatic relief of allergies M20. **diphe'noxylate** *n.* a pethidine derivative used to treat diarrhoea and colitis M20.

diphenyl /dʌɪˈfiːnʌɪl, -ˈfɛnɪl/ *n.* L19. [f. DI-[2] + PHENYL.] = BIPHENYL.

diphenyl- /dʌɪˈfiːnʌɪl, -ˈfɛnɪl/ *comb. form.* [f. prec.] *Chem.* = DIPHEN-.

dipheny'lamine *n.* a crystalline compound, $(C_6H_5)_2NH$, used in making azo dyes and as an insecticide and larvicide M19. **diphenylhy'dantoin** *n.* = PHENYTOIN M20.

diphonemic /dʌɪfə(ʊ)ˈniːmɪk/ *a.* M20. [f. DI-[2] + PHONEMIC.] Of a speech sound: able to be assigned to either of two phonemes.

diphosphopyridine nucleotide /dʌɪˌfɒsfəˈpɪrɪdiːn ˈnjuːklɪətʌɪd/ *n. phr.* M20. [f. DI-[2] + PHOSPHO- + PYRIDINE + NUCLEOTIDE.] *Biochem.* The coenzyme NAD.

diphtheria /dɪfˈθɪərɪə/ *n.* M19. [mod.L, f. Fr. *diphthérie*, substituted by P. Bretonneau for his earlier *diphthérite*: see DIPHTHERITIS, -IA[1].] An acute contagious bacterial disease characterized by the inflammation of a mucous membrane, esp. in the throat, the formation of a false membrane, and the production of potentially fatal toxins affecting the heart and nerves.

diphtherial, diphtherian (now *rare*), **diphtheric** /-ˈθɛrɪk/ *adjs.* L19.

diphtheritic /dɪfθə'rɪtɪk/ *a.* M19. [f. next: see -ITIC.] Of the nature of or pertaining to diphtheria; affected with diphtheria.

diphtheritis /dɪfθə'rʌɪtɪs/ *n.* Now *rare* or *obs.* E19. [Fr. *diphthérite* (now *diphthérie*: see DIPHTHERIA), f. Gk *diphthera* or *diphtheris* skin, hide + *-ite* -ITIS.] = DIPHTHERIA.

diphtheroid /'dɪfθərɔɪd/ *a.* & *n.* M19. [f. DIPHTHERIA, DIPHTHERITIS + -OID.] A *adj.* Resembling diphtheria or the bacterium that causes it. M19. B *n.* A bacterium which resembles the one causing diphtheria but is not pathogenic, *esp.* one of the genus *Corynebacterium.* E20.

diphthong /'dɪfθɒŋ/ *n.* & *v.* LME. [Fr. *diphtongue* f. L *diphthongus* f. Gk *diphthoggos*, f. as DI-[2] + *phthoggos* voice, sound.] A *n.* 1 A union of two vowels pronounced in one syllable. LME. 2 A sequence of two vowel characters representing a single sound or a diphthong (sense 1), a vocalic digraph. M16. 3 A ligature of the Roman alphabet. L16.

1 **falling diphthong**: with more stress on the first vowel than on the second. **rising diphthong**: with more stress on the second vowel than on the first.

B *v.t.* Sound as or make into a diphthong. M19.

diph'thongal *a.* of, pertaining to, or of the nature of a diphthong M18. **diph'thongally** *adv.* M19. **diph'thongic** *a.* = DIPHTHONGAL M19. **diphthongi'zation** *n.* the changing of a simple vowel into a diphthong L19. **diphthongize** *v.t.* & *i.* turn into or form a diphthong M19.

diphy- /'dɪfi/ *comb. form.* [Gk *diphu-* f. *diphuēs*, f. DI-[2] + *phuein* generate.] Of double form, double, bipartite.

diphycercal /-'səːk(ə)l/ *a.* [Gk *kerkos* tail] designating a fish's tail in which the vertebral column continues straight to the tip and the dorsal and ventral parts are approximately alike; having such a tail: M19. **diphyodont** *a.* & *n.* [Gk *odont-* tooth] (pertaining to or designating) an animal in which one set of teeth is replaced by another in the course of its development (cf. MONOPHYODONT) M19.

diphyletic /dʌɪfʌɪ'lɛtɪk/ *a.* E20. [f. DI-[2] + PHYLETIC *a.*] *Taxon.* Having evolved from two sets of ancestors; (of a classification) implying such an origin.

diphyllous /dʌɪ'fɪləs/ *a.* L18. [mod.L *diphyllus* (f. Gk DI-[2] + *phullon* leaf) + -OUS.] *Bot.* Having two leaves (or sepals).

dipl- *comb. form* see DIPLO-.

diplegia /dʌɪ'pliːdʒə/ *n.* L19. [f. DI-[2] after HEMIPLEGIA, PARAPLEGIA.] *Med.* Paralysis of corresponding parts on both sides of the body, usu. affecting the legs more severely than the arms.

dipleidoscope /dɪ'plʌɪdəskəʊp/ *n.* M19. [f. Gk *diploos* double + *eidos* form, image + -SCOPE.] An optical instrument for determining the meridian transit of a celestial object from the coincidence of two images formed by reflection in a hollow triangular prism.

diplex /'dʌɪplɛks/ *a.* L19. [Alt. of DUPLEX *a.* after DI-[2].] *Telecommunications.* Pertaining to or designating the transmission or reception of two signals simultaneously in the same direction over one channel or with one aerial. Cf. DUPLEX *a.* 2.

diplexer *n.* a device which enables two transmitters to operate simultaneously using the same aerial M20.

diplo- /'dɪpləʊ/ *comb. form.* Bef. a vowel **dipl-**. [Gk, f. *diploos*, *diplous* double; also repr. DIPLOID: see -O-.] Double; diploidal.

dipla'cusis *n.* [Gk *akousis* hearing] the hearing of two different notes when only one is sounded L19. **diploba'cillus** *n.*, pl. **-cilli**, a bacillus that occurs predominantly in pairs E20. **diplo'blastic** *a.* [-BLAST] *Zool.* having ectoderm and endoderm but no mesoderm, as in coelenterates L19. **diplo'coccal** *a.* (*Bacteriol.*) of, pertaining to, or caused by a diplococcus E20. **diplo'coccus** *n.*, pl. **-cocci**, *Bacteriol.* a coccus that occurs predominantly in pairs, as a pneumococcus L19. **diplograph** *n.* an instrument for writing with two pens etc. simultaneously L19. **diplo'graphic** *a.* of or pertaining to writing double E19. **diplo'graphical** *a.* = DIPLOGRAPHIC M18. **diplo'hedral** *a.* = DIPLOIDAL L19. **diplo'hedron** *n.* [-HEDRON] *Cryst.* = DIPLOID *n.* 1 L19. **diplo'nema** *n.* [-NEMA] *Cytol.* = DIPLOTENE E20. **diplophase** *n.* (*Biol.*) the phase in a life cycle when cell nuclei are diploid E20. **diplopod** *n.* & *a.* (*Zool.*) (*a*) *n.* any animal of the arthropod class (or subclass or order) Diplopoda, characterized by two pairs of legs on each segment; a millipede; (*b*) *adj.* of, pertaining to, or designating a diplopod or the Diplopoda: M19. **diplo'stemonous** *a.* [Gk *stēmōn* warp (for *stēma* stamen)] *Bot.* having the stamens in two series (the outer opposite the sepals, the inner opposite the petals) or (formerly) twice as many as the petals M19. **diplo'stemony** *n.* (*Bot.*) diplostemonous condition L19. **diplotene** *n.* [-TENE] *Cytol.* the stage of the prophase of the first meiotic division that follows pachytene, when the tetrads begin to separate into two pairs of chromatids E20.

diplodocus /dɪ'plɒdəkəs/ *n.* Also **D-**. L19. [mod.L, f. Gk DIPLO- + *dokos* beam.] Any Jurassic sauropod dinosaur of the genus *Diplodocus*, which comprises gigantic herbivorous animals with long necks.

diploe /'dɪpləʊiː/ *n.* L16. [Gk *diploē* doubling, f. *diploos* double.] Light cancellous bony tissue between the hard dense inner and outer layers of the skull.

diploid /'dɪplɔɪd/ *n.* & *a.* L19. [f. DIPLO- + -OID, (senses A.2, B.) ID *n.*[1]] A *n.* 1 *Cryst.* A cubic form with twelve pairs of similar quadrilateral faces. L19. 2 *Biol.* A diploid cell or organism. E20.

B *adj. Biol.* (Of a cell) containing two homologous sets of chromosomes, one from each parent; (of an individual) composed of diploid cells. E20.

diploid number the number of chromosomes in the body cells of an organism.

di'ploidal *a.* (*Cryst.*) of, pertaining to, or designating a cubic crystal class containing the diploid and the pyritohedron M20. **diploidy** *n.* (*Biol.*) diploid condition E20.

diploidion /dɪpləʊ'ɪdɪən/ *n.* M19. [Gk., dim. of *diplois*, *diploid-* double cloak.] A chiton or tunic worn by women in ancient Greece, with the part above the waist double and the outer fold hanging loose.

diploma /dɪ'pləʊmə/ *n.* & *v.* M17. [L *diploma*, *diplomat-* f. Gk = folded paper, f. *diploun* make double, fold, f. *diploos* double.] A *n.* Pl. **-mas**, (*rare*) **-mata** /-mətə/. 1 A State paper, an official document; a charter; in *pl.*, historical or literary muniments. M17. 2 A document conferring some honour, privilege, or licence; a certificate of a university, college, or (*N. Amer.*) school degree or qualification; such a degree or qualification. M17. B *v.t.* Award a diploma to. Chiefly as *diplomaed*, *-a'd* ppl a. M19.

'diplomate *n.* [-ATE[1]] a person who holds a diploma L19. †**diplomate** *v.t.* [-ATE[3]] invest with a degree, privilege, or title by diploma M17–M18.

diplomacy /dɪ'pləʊməsi/ *n.* L18. [Fr. *diplomatie*, f. *diplomatique* DIPLOMATIC after *aristocratie* ARISTOCRACY: see -ACY.] 1 The management of international relations by negotiation; the method by which these relations are managed by ambassadors etc.; skill in such affairs. L18. †2 The diplomatic body. L18–M19. 3 Adroitness in personal relations; tact. M19.

diplomat /'dɪpləmat/ *n.* E19. [Fr. *diplomate* back-form. f. *diplomatique* DIPLOMATIC after *aristocrate* ARISTOCRAT.] A person engaged in diplomacy, esp. accredited to a court or seat of government; an adroit negotiator.

diploma'tese *n.* (*colloq.*) language regarded as typical of diplomats L20.

diplomatic /dɪplə'matɪk/ *a.* & *n.* E18. [(Fr. *diplomatique* based on) mod.L *diplomaticus*, f. L *diploma* DIPLOMA: see -IC.] A *adj.* 1 Of or pertaining to official or original documents, charters, or manuscripts; textual. E18. 2 Of or pertaining to the management of international relations; of or belonging to diplomacy. L18. 3 Skilled in negotiations or relations of any kind; tactful; (of a statement etc.) uncandid, subtle. E19.

1 **diplomatic copy, edition**: exactly reproducing an original. 2 H. MACMILLAN Diplomatic relations were re-established at the level of chargé d'affaires. **diplomatic bag**: that contains official mail from an embassy etc. **diplomatic corps** the body of ambassadors and their staff attached to a court or seat of government. **diplomatic immunity** immunity from legal action possessed by virtue of belonging to the diplomatic mission of a foreign State. **diplomatic service** the branch of the public service which is concerned with the official representation of a country abroad. 3 H. JAMES I'm diplomatic and calculating—I don't show him how bad I am.

B *n.* 1 A diplomat. L18. 2 *sing.* & in *pl.* (treated as *sing.*). The diplomatic art; diplomacy. L18. 3 *sing.* & in *pl.* The palaeographic and critical study of old documents. E19.

2 W. TAYLOR Our ministers are not great in diplomatics. 3 W. A. PANTIN These administrative records . . have an archaeology or a diplomatic of their own.

diplomatical *a.* = DIPLOMATIC *a.* 1, 2 L18. **diplomatically** *adv.* M19.

diplomatise *v.* var. of DIPLOMATIZE.

diplomatist /dɪ'pləʊmətɪst/ *n.* E19. [f. Fr. *diplomate* DIPLOMAT or L *diplomat-* (see DIPLOMA) + -IST.] A diplomat.

diplomatize /dɪ'pləʊmətʌɪz/ *v.* Also **-ise**. L17. [In branch I f. L *diplomat-* (see DIPLOMA), in branch II f. DIPLOMAT: see -IZE.] I 1 *v.t.* Invest with a diploma. *rare.* L17. II 2 *v.i.* Act or serve as a diplomat; use diplomatic arts or skill. E19. 3 *v.t.* Act as a diplomat towards or in connection with. M19.

diplont /'dɪplɒnt/ *n.* E20. [f. DIPL- + -ONT.] *Biol.* An organism which is diploid throughout its life cycle except for the gametes.

diplopia /dɪ'pləʊpɪə/ *n.* E19. [f. DIPLO- + -OPIA.] *Med.* Double vision.

diplopic /-'plɒp-/ *a.* L19.

dipnoan /'dɪpnəʊən/ *n.* & *a.* L19. [f. mod.L *Dipnoi* pl. (see below), f. Gk *dipnoos* with two breathing apertures, f. as DI-[2] + *pnoē* breathing: see -AN.] A *n.* A fish of the (mostly extinct) order or subclass Dipnoi, characterized by a lung or lungs as well as gills; a lungfish. L19. B *adj.* Of, pertaining to, or designating a dipnoan. L19.

Also **dipnoid** *n.* & *a.* L19.

dipody /'dɪpədi/ *n.* M19. [Late L *dipodia* f. Gk, f. *dipous*, *dipod-* two-footed, f. as DI-[2] + *pous* foot: see -Y[3].] *Pros.* A double foot; two feet making one measure.

Also **dipodia** /dʌɪ'pəʊdɪə/ *n.* E19.

dipolar /dʌɪ'pəʊlə/ *a.* M19. [f. DI-[2] + POLAR *a.*] *Sci.* Of or pertaining to two poles; having two poles.

dipole /'dʌɪpəʊl/ *n.* E20. [f. DI-[2] + POLE *n.*[2]] 1 *Sci.* A pair of equal and opposite electric charges or magnetic poles, esp. close together; a molecule etc. with such a pair. E20. 2 An aerial composed of two equal straight rods mounted in line with one another and having an electrical connection to its centre; *spec.* such an aerial half a wavelength long overall. E20.

Comb.: **dipole moment** the product of the separation of the charges etc. of a dipole and the magnitude of each.

Dippel's oil /'dɪp(ə)lz ɔɪl/ *n. phr* E19. [J. C. *Dippel* (1672–1734), Ger. alchemist.] More fully *Dippel's animal oil.* Bone-oil.

dipper /'dɪpə/ *n.* LME. [f. DIP *v.* + -ER[1].] 1 Any of several stocky short-tailed songbirds constituting the genus *Cinclus* and family Cinclidae, which habitually bob up and down, frequent fast-flowing streams, and swim and walk under water to feed; *esp.* the Eurasian *C. cinclus* and the N. American *C. mexicanus*; also called *water ouzel.* Formerly also, any of several freshwater diving birds. LME. 2 A person who dips; *spec.* one who immerses something in a fluid. E17. b A pickpocket. *slang.* L19. 3 A person who uses immersion in baptism, *esp.* an Anabaptist or Baptist. E17. 4a A utensil for dipping up water etc.; *spec.* a pan with a long handle. L18. b In full *dipper dredge.* A dredging-boat with a single bucket at the end of an arm. L19. c (The scoop of) an excavator. E20. 5a [From the similarity of its shape to the utensil.] (**D-**.) (In full *Big* or *Great Dipper*) the Plough, in Ursa Major. *Little Dipper*, a pattern of stars in Ursa Minor. *N. Amer.* M19. b *big dipper*, a switchback in a fairground or place of amusement. M20. 6 A receptacle for oil, varnish, etc., attached to a palette. M19. 7 A vat or tank in which sheep dip is used. L19. 8 A means of dipping a vehicle's headlights. E20.

1 W. IRVING A lounger in the Bodleian library, and a great dipper into books.

Comb.: **dipper gourd** a gourd used as a dipper; a form of the Old World tropical vine *Lagenaria siceraria* which bears such gourds.

dipperful *n.* (*US*) as much as a dipper will hold M19.

dippy /ˈdɪpi/ *a. slang.* E20. [Origin unkn.] Crazy (*about, over*); mad.

diprotodont /dʌɪˈprəʊtə(ʊ)dɒnt/ *n.* & *a.* L19. [f. DI-² + PROTO- + -ODONT.] **A** *n.* A huge extinct Australian marsupial with two incisors in the lower jaw. L19. **B** *adj.* Of, pertaining to, or designating such an animal. L19.

Also **diprotodon** *n.* M19.

dipsas /ˈdɪpsas/ *n.* Pl. **dipsades** /ˈdɪpsədiːz/. LME. [L f. Gk, orig. adj. = causing thirst, f. *dipsa* thirst.] A mythical serpent whose bite produced a raging thirst.

dipso /ˈdɪpsəʊ/ *a.* & *n. colloq.* L19. [Abbrev.] **A** *adj.* = DIPSOMANIACAL. L19. **B** *n.* Pl. **-os.** = DIPSOMANIAC. E20.

dipsomania /dɪpsə(ʊ)ˈmeɪnɪə/ *n.* Also **dyp-**. M19. [f. Gk *dipso-* comb. form (see -O-) of *dipsa* thirst + -MANIA.] A morbid paroxysmal craving for alcohol; alcoholism. Also, persistent drunkenness.

dipsomaniac *n.* a person with dipsomania M19. **dipsomaˈniacal** *a.* pertaining to or suffering from dipsomania M19.

Diptera /ˈdɪpt(ə)rə/ *n.pl.* M18. [mod.L f. Gk, f. *dipteros* two-winged, f. as DI-² + *pteron* wing: see -A³.] (Members of) a large order of two-winged insects including flies, gnats, mosquitoes, etc.

dipterist *n.* a person who studies Diptera L19. **dipteroˈlogical** *a.* of or pertaining to the study of Diptera L19. **dipteˈrologist** *n.* = DIPTERIST L19.

dipteral /ˈdɪpt(ə)r(ə)l/ *a.* E19. [f. L *dipteros*, f. Gk (see DIPTERA), + -AL¹.] *Archit.* Having a double peristyle.

dipteran /ˈdɪpt(ə)r(ə)n/ *n.* & *a.* M19. [f. DIPTERA + -AN.] **A** *n.* An insect belonging to the Diptera. M19. **B** *adj.* Of or pertaining to the Diptera. M20.

dipterocarp /ˈdɪpt(ə)rə(ʊ)kɑːp/ *n.* & *a.* Also **D-**. L19. [mod.L *Dipterocarpus*, f. Gk *dipteros* (see DIPTERA) + *karpos* fruit.] **A** *n.* A tree of the mostly SE Asian family Dipterocarpaceae, comprising resinous timber trees such as teak. L19. **B** *adj.* = DIPTEROCARPOUS. E20.

dipteroˈcarpous *a.* pertaining to or designating the dipterocarps L19.

dipterous /ˈdɪpt(ə)rəs/ *a.* L18. [f. DIPTERA + -OUS.] *Entomol.* Having two wings; of or pertaining to the Diptera.

diptote /ˈdɪptəʊt/ *n.* & *a.* E17. [Late L *diptota* f. Gk, neut. pl. of *diptōtos*, f. as DI-² + *ptōtos* falling (*ptōsis* case). Cf. TRIPTOTE.] *Gram.* (A noun) having only two cases.

diptych /ˈdɪptɪk/ *n.* E17. [Late L *diptycha* f. late Gk *diptukha* pair of writing-tablets, neut. pl. of Gk *diptukhos* folded in two, f. as DI-² + *ptukhē* fold.] 1 Something folded so as to have two leaves, *esp.* an ancient hinged writing-tablet, with waxed inner surfaces for writing on with a stylus. E17. 2 *Eccl. Hist.* In *pl.* Tablets recording a list of the living and the dead who were prayed for at the Eucharist; the names themselves; the intercessions in the course of which they were introduced. M17. 3 An altarpiece or painting composed of two leaves which close like a book. M19.

diptychous *a.* of, pertaining to, or of the nature of a diptych L19.

dipylon /ˈdɪpɪlɒn/ *n.* & *a.* Also (earlier) †**-lum.** M19. [(L f.) Gk *dipulon* neut. of *dipulos* double-gated, f. as DI-² + *pulē* gate.] *Gk Archaeol.* **A** *n.* A double gateway in which the two gates are placed side by side; *spec.* (**D-**) a gateway on the north-west side of Athens. M19. **B** *adj.* Designating or pertaining to the Dipylon of Athens; *spec.* designating or pertaining to a style of Greek pottery found during excavations near this site, or the designs found on such pottery. L19.

dipyramidal /dʌɪpɪˈramɪd(ə)l/ *a.* M20. [f. DI-² + PYRAMIDAL.] = BIPYRAMIDAL.

diˈpyramid *n.* = BIPYRAMID M20.

dipyridamole /dʌɪpɪˈrɪdəməʊl/ *n.* M20. [f. DI-² + PYR(IMIDINE + PIPER)ID(INE + AM(INO- + -OL.] A drug used as a coronary vasodilator in angina pectoris and to reduce platelet aggregation and hence the chance of thrombosis.

diquark /ˈdʌɪkwɔːk, -kwɑːk/ *n.* M20. [f. DI-² + QUARK *n.*².] *Physics.* A pair of quarks bound together.

diquat /ˈdʌɪkwɒt/ *n.* M20. [f. DI-² + QUATERNARY.] (The cation of) a quaternary compound, $C_{12}H_{12}N_2Br_2$, used as a contact herbicide and desiccant.

dir- /dɪr/ *pref.* (not productive). Var. of L DIS- bef. vowels.

Dircaean /dəːˈsiːən/ *a.* E17. [f. L *Dircaeus* f. *Dirce*, Gk *Dirkē* + -AN.] Of or pertaining to the fountain of Dirce in Boeotia, ancient Greece; *fig.* poetic, Pindaric.

the Dircaean swan [tr. L *Dircaeus cygnus* (Horace)] the Greek poet Pindar.

dirdum /ˈdəːdəm/ *n. Sc.* & *north.* LME. [Origin uncertain: cf. Gael. *d(i)urdan* anger, snarling, Ir. *deardan* storm, tempest.] 1 Uproar; a tumultuous noise or din. LME. 2 An outcry; a strong rebuke; blame. E18.

dire /ˈdʌɪə/ *a.* M16. [L *dirus* fearful, threatening evil.] 1 Dreadful, calamitous, terrible; ominous; *colloq.* urgent, desperate. M16. 2 Very bad, awful; unpleasant. E20.

1 MILTON All monstrous, all prodigious things.. Gorgons and Hydra's and Chimera's dire. C. BRONTË Forced by dire necessity. 2 B. PYM The dire state of fiction publishing. E. O'NEILL I didn't say anything so dire, did I.

direly *adv.* E17. **direness** *n.* E17.

direct /dɪˈrɛkt, dʌɪ-/ *n.* E17. [App. f. DIRECT *v.*] 1 A direction, an instruction. Long *rare.* E17. 2 *Mus.* A sign placed on the stave at the end of a page or line to indicate the position of the next note. L17.

direct /dɪˈrɛkt, dʌɪ-/ *a.* & *adv.* LME. [f. as next.] **A** *adj.* 1 Straight, undeviating in course, not circuitous or crooked. LME. **b** Of ancestry or a descendant: proceeding in or derived from a continuous succession from parent to offspring. M16. **c** *Logic.* Proceeding immediately from consequent to antecedent, from cause to effect, etc. E19. 2a *Astron.* Of (the motion of) a planet etc.: proceeding from west to east, not retrograde. LME. **b** *Math.* & *Mus.* Following the simple or natural order; not inverse or inverted. L16. 3 Going straight to the point; without circumlocution or ambiguity; straightforward, esp. in manner or conduct; frank. M16. 4 Perpendicular to a given surface; not oblique. M16. 5 Existing or occurring without intermediaries or intervention; immediate, uninterrupted. L16. 6 Of an electric current: that flows in one direction only, without reversal of polarity. Hence, associated with or producing such a current. Cf. ALTERNATING 2. L19.

1 M. MITCHELL Instead of continuing the direct assault, he swung his army in a wide circle. 3 R. KIPLING This was at once a gross insult and a direct lie. J. IRVING A flat, direct introduction explaining why he had not tried to put the epic in verse. 5 T. HARDY Almost every.. effect in that woodland place had hitherto been the direct result of the regular terrestrial roll. A. BEVAN Before the Industrial Revolution, man's relations with physical nature were immediate and direct. L. DURRELL This gave him direct access to the affections and understanding of our.. friends.

Special collocations: **direct action**: done as the most immediately effective way of achieving an object. **direct address** *Computing*: specifying the location of data to be used as an operand. **direct debit** the automatic debiting of a bank account at the request of a creditor. **direct dialling**: of a telephone number by the caller, without making use of an operator. **direct drilling** *Agric.*: of seed into unprepared soil. **direct-drive** *a.* (of a turntable etc.) driven directly by the motor, without an intervening belt. **direct dye**: not needing a mordant. **direct grant**: of money paid directly to a school by the Government as opp. to a local authority (*direct-grant school*, a school which observes agreed conditions regarding the admission of pupils etc. while in receipt of such a grant). **direct hit** striking the target directly (not as the result of a ricochet etc.). **direct labour**: (*a*) involved in production rather than administration, maintenance, etc.; (*b*) employed by the authority commissioning the work, not by a contractor. **direct mail** advertising sent unsolicited through the post to prospective customers. **direct mailing** the sending of direct mail. **direct method** the teaching of a foreign language in that tongue, without the use of the student's native language or the study of formal grammar. **direct object** *Gram.* the primary object of the action of a verb. **direct opposite** that which is entirely or exactly opposite. **direct oration** *Gram.* = *direct speech* below. **direct proportion** the relation between quantities whose ratio is constant. **direct question** a question on a specific matter requiring a definite answer; *Gram.* a question in direct speech, a question that is a main clause. **direct ray** a ray of light proceeding without reflection or refraction. **direct rule** rule by a central government without devolution. **direct speech** *Gram.* words quoted as actually spoken, not modified in person, tense, etc., by being reported (= ORATIO RECTA). **direct tax**: levied on the person who bears the ultimate burden of the tax, e.g. income tax,but not value added tax. **direct taxation**: by a direct tax.

B *adv.* Directly. LME.

W. S. MAUGHAM I'm not going to Bertha, I'm going to Craddock direct.

directness *n.* L16.

direct /dɪˈrɛkt, dʌɪ-/ *v.* Pa. pple **directed**, (earlier) †**direct**. LME. [L *directus* pa. pple of *dirigere, derigere* straighten, direct, guide f. *di-* DI-¹, DE- I + *regere* put straight, rule.] 1 *v.t.* Formerly, send (a letter etc.) especially *to* someone. Now, write on the outside of (a letter etc.) a name and address for delivery (*to* a recipient). LME. †**b** *v.t.* Dedicate (a book etc.) *to*. LME–E17. **c** *v.i.* Write *to* a person (*at* an address). E18. 2 *v.t.* Address (spoken words) *to* someone. *arch.* LME. †**b** Give (an injunction, command, etc.) *to*. LME–M17. 3 *v.t.* Cause to move in or take a specified direction; turn towards a specified destination or target; aim (a missile, a remark, etc.) *at* or *against*; turn *to* an aim or purpose. LME. **b** Inform or guide (a person) as to the way; show or tell (a person) the way (*to*). E17. 4 *v.t.* Regulate the course of; guide with advice. LME. **b** *v.t.* Conduct (a musical performance). L19. **c** *v.t.* & *i.* Supervise and control the acting of (a film, play, etc.); guide and train (an actor) in performing a role. E20. 5 *v.t.* Keep in proper order; control, govern the actions or movements of. E16. 6a *v.t.* Give authoritative instructions to; order (a person) *to do*, (a thing) *to be done*; order the performance of. M16. **b** *v.i.* Give instructions; command *that*. M17.

1 LD HOUGHTON Lady Ellesmere's letter missed me altogether, although directed as I desired. **c** DICKENS You may direct to me.. at 18 York Place. 2 HOBBES To whom the Speech is directed. 3 J. R. GREEN The efforts of the French monarchy had been directed to the conquest of Italy. B. JOWETT Everybody's eyes were directed towards him. G. GREENE He directed at her his whole technique of appeasement. D. BARNES The doctor.. directed his steps back to the café. **b** J. B. PRIESTLEY A turning at the bottom of this main street directed me to the Playhouse. J. RATHBONE Rubin now directed me firmly up the wide stairs. 4 SHAKES. *Merch. V.* Some god direct my judgment! 5 D. DU MAURIER Something other than blind emotion directed her actions. F. ASTAIRE A lone M.P. in the middle of the cross streets, directing traffic. 6a W. LITHGOW He made fast the door as he was directed. **b** H. WILSON The ability of the prime minister to direct that such and such an issue shall go straight to Cabinet.

directable *a.* able to be directed L19. **directedness** *n.* the quality of being directed E20. **direcˈtee** *n.* a person who is directed or under direction E20.

direction /dɪˈrɛkʃ(ə)n, dʌɪ-/ *n.* LME. [Fr., or its source L *directio(n-)*, f. *direct-* pa. ppl stem of *dirigere*: see DIRECT *v.*, -ION.] 1 The action or function of directing; guidance, instruction; management. LME. †2 Arrangement, order. LME–M16. 3 An instruction on what to do, how to proceed, or where to go. Usu. in *pl.* LME. 4 The action of addressing a letter, parcel, etc.; the (name and) address on an envelope etc. Formerly also, the dedication of a book etc. E16. †5 Capacity for directing; administrative faculty. L16–M17. 6 The course taken by something in relation to the point towards which it is moving; the line towards anything in its relation to a given line; a point to or from which a person moves, turns, etc. M17. **b** *fig.* The course of development of thought, effort, or action; a distinct tendency or trend; linear or consistent progress. M18. **7** = DIRECTORATE. *arch.* E18.

1 SHAKES. *Oth.* A soldier fit to stand by Caesar And give direction. GEO. ELIOT She felt the need of direction even in small things. D. FRASER The Chiefs of Staff Committee was concerned with the overall direction of war. 3 GOLDSMITH Provide him with proper directions for finding me in London. 5 SHAKES. *Rich. III* Call for some men of sound direction. 6 J. BUCHAN Making farther from London in the direction of some western port. N. MOSLEY She appeared to be seen from two directions at once. b B. JOWETT New directions of enquiry. *Times* Gold shares lacked direction with the bullion price virtually unchanged.

Phrases: **sense of direction** the ability to know without guidance towards which place one is walking etc. *stage direction*: see STAGE *n.*

Comb.: **direction-finder** a device for direction-finding; **direction-finding** the process of finding the direction from which radio waves are coming; **direction-indicator** a device showing the direction in which the driver is about to turn a motor vehicle.

directional *a.* (*a*) pertaining to the giving or taking of directions; (*b*) of or pertaining to direction in space, esp. of radio transmission within a narrow angle; (of a well) drilled at an angle to the vertical: E17. **directio'nality** *n.* directional quality; maintenance of direction: M20. **directionally** *adv.* L19. **directionless** *a.* lacking aim or direction M19. **directionlessness** *n.* M20.

directive /dɪˈrɛktɪv, dʌɪ-/ *n.* M17. [med.L *directivum* use as n. of neut. of *directivus*: see next.] Something which directs; *spec.* a general instruction for procedure or action given to a subordinate.

H. KISSINGER The ABM directive went the way of many other Presidential instructions to the Defense Department.

¶ Rare bef. E20.

directive /dɪˈrɛktɪv, dʌɪ-/ *a.* LME. [med.L *directivus*, f. L *direct-* pa. ppl stem of *dirigere*: see DIRECT *v.*, -IVE. Cf. (O)Fr. *directif*, *-ive*.] **1** Having the quality, function, or power of directing; serving to direct. LME. †**2** Subject to direction. *rare* (Shakes.). Only in E17.

1 J. S. MILL Utility or Happiness, considered as the directive rule of human conduct. J. C. MAXWELL The directive action of the earth's magnetism on the compass needle. A. STORR Those who are directive by nature.

directively *adv.* in a directive manner; so as to direct or guide: M17. **directiveness** *n.* E18. **direc'tivity** *n.* (*a*) the quality or state of being directed by a vital force or by God; (*b*) the property or degree of being directional: E20.

directly /dɪˈrɛktli, dʌɪ-/ *adv.* & *conj.* LME. [f. DIRECT *a.* + -LY².] **A** *adv.* **1** In a straight line; without deviation; *Math.* linearly. LME. **2** Straightforwardly; plainly; pointedly. LME. **3** Completely, absolutely; exactly. LME. **4** Without an intermediary; by a direct process. E16. **5** At right angles to a surface, not obliquely. M16. **6** At once, immediately; presently, in a little while. E17.

1 L. HELLMAN I went directly to Paris. DAY LEWIS Her mother . . was directly descended from Oliver Goldsmith's uncle. 2 BURKE I asked him his opinion directly, and without management. 3 J. M. COETZEE A clap burst directly over him and it began to pour. 4 B. PYM She did not like to approach me directly. 5 V. WOOLF The rain poured down more directly and powerfully as the wind fell. 6 V. WOOLF She went off directly after tea. I. MURDOCH I'll be back directly.

B *conj.* As soon as, the moment after. L18.

G. GREENE He realized how childish he sounded directly he had spoken.

Directoire /dɪˈrɛktwɑː; *foreign* dirɛktwaːr (*pl. of n. same*)/ *n.* & *a.* L18. [Fr, f. as DIRECTORY *n.*] **A** *n. Hist.* The French Directory. L18.

B *adj.* Also **d-**. Of, pertaining to, or resembling an extravagant style of fashion, decorative art, etc., prevalent at the time of the Directory and characterized esp. by an imitation of Greek and Roman modes. L19.

Directoire knickers women's knee-length knickers with elastic or bands at the waist and knee.

director /dɪˈrɛktə, dʌɪ-/ *n.* LME. [AN *directour* f. late L *director*, f. L *direct-* pa. ppl stem of *dirigere*: see DIRECT *v.*, -OR.] **I 1** A person who or thing which directs, governs, or guides; a manager, a superintendent. LME. **2** A member of the board that manages the affairs of a company. M17. **3** *Eccl.* A spiritual adviser. M17. **4** A person who directs a theatre or cinema production. E20.

1 **director-general** the chief administrator of a project etc. *Director of Public Prosecutions*: see PROSECUTION *n.* 5.

II 5 A person who or thing which causes something to take a particular direction; *Surg.* an instrument for guiding the course of the knife etc. when an incision is made. M17.

directorate *n.* (*a*) = DIRECTORSHIP; (*b*) management by directors; (*c*) a board of directors: M19. **direc'torial** *a.* (*a*) of, pertaining to, or of the nature of a director or direction; (*b*) of or pertaining to a body of directors; (also **D-**) belonging to the French Directory: L18. **direc'torially** *adv.* M19. **directorship** *n.* the position or office of a director E18.

directory /dɪˈrɛkt(ə)ri, dʌɪ-/ *n.* LME. [Late L *directorium* use as n. of neut. sing. of *directorius*: see next, -ORY¹.] **1** Something that serves to direct; a guide; a book of rules or directions, *esp.* one for the conduct of public or private worship, an ordinal. LME. **b** A book containing an alphabetical or classified list of the people in some category, e.g. telephone subscribers or clergy, with information about them. M18. **c** A computer file listing information about a set of other files or of programs etc. M20. †**2** A surgical director. L17–M18. **3** A body of directors; *spec.* in *Hist.* (also **D-**) the executive of five people in power in revolutionary France, 1795–9. L18.

1b *telephone directory* etc.

Comb.: **directory enquiries** a service which telephone callers may ring to find the number of a subscriber.

directory /dɪˈrɛkt(ə)ri, dʌɪ-/ *a.* LME. [Late L *directorius*, f. *director* DIRECTOR: see -ORY².] Serving or tending to direct; guiding; *spec.* designating (any part of) a statute which is advisory rather than mandatory in effect.

directress /dɪˈrɛktrəs, dʌɪ-/ *n.* E17. [f. DIRECTOR + -ESS¹.] A female director. Formerly also, a governess.

directrice /dɪˈrɛktriːs/ *n.* M17. [Fr., f. as next.] = DIRECTRESS.

directrix /dɪˈrɛktrɪks, dʌɪ-/ *n.* Pl. **-trices** /-trɪsiːz/. E16. [med.L, fem. of late L DIRECTOR: see -TRIX.] **1** = DIRECTRESS. E16. **2** *Geom.* A fixed line with reference to which a curve or surface is defined; *spec.* the straight line the distance of which from any point on a conic bears a constant ratio to the distance of the same point from the focus. E18.

direful /ˈdʌɪəf(ə)l, -fʊl/ *a. literary.* L16. [Irreg. f. DIRE *a.* + -FUL.] Presaging dire consequences; dreadful, terrible.

direfully *adv.* L18. **direfulness** *n.* M17.

dirempt /dɪˈrɛm(p)t/ *v.t.* Long *rare*. Pa. t. & pple †**dirempt**, **dirempted**. M16. [L *dirempt-* pa. ppl stem of *dirimere*, f. *dir-* DIS- 1 + *emere* take.] Separate, divide; break off.

diremption *n.* (now *rare*) forcible separation, esp. of man and wife; removal: L16.

†**direption** *n.* L15. [L *direptio(n-)*, f. *dirept-* pa. ppl stem of *diripere* tear asunder, lay waste, f. *di-* DI-¹ + *rapere* tear away: see -ION.] **1** The action of snatching away or dragging apart violently. L15–L17. **2** The sacking or pillaging of a town etc. E16–E19.

dirge /dəːdʒ/ *n.* & *v.* Also (n., earlier) †**dirige**. ME. [L *dirige* imper. of. *dirigere* DIRECT *v.*, first wd of the antiphon *Dirige, Domine, Deus meus, in conspectu tuo viam meam* (Ps. 5:8) formerly in the Office of the Dead.] **A** *n.* **1** *RC Ch.* The Office of the Dead, *esp.* the morning office. *arch.* ME. **2** A song of mourning sung at a funeral etc. or in commemoration of the dead; a slow mournful song; a lament. E16. **3** A funeral feast, a wake. *Sc.* M17. **B** *v.* **1** *v.t.* Sing a dirge over, commit with a dirge. *rare.* M19. **2** *v.t.* & *i.* Sing (as) a dirge. L19.

dirgeful *a.* full of lamentation, mournful L18.

dirham /ˈdɪərəm/ *n.* Also **-hem**. L18. [Arab. f. Gk *drachmē* (see DRACHMA).] A monetary unit of Morocco (now the basic unit), Libya, the United Arab Emirates (the basic unit), Qatar, and formerly some other Middle Eastern countries, equal to 100 centimes in Morocco, one-thousandth of a dinar in Libya, 100 fils in the United Arab Emirates, and one-hundredth of a riyal in Qatar. Formerly also, an Arabian unit of weight.

†**dirige** *n.* see DIRGE.

†**dirigent** *a.* & *n.* E17–M19. [L *dirigent-* pres. ppl stem of *dirigere* DIRECT *v.*: see -ENT.] (Something) that directs or guides.

dirigible /ˈdɪrɪdʒɪb(ə)l/ *a.* & *n.* L16. [f. L *dirigere* DIRECT *v.* + -IBLE.] **A** *adj.* Able to be directed, *spec.* in respect of motion. L16. **B** *n.* A dirigible balloon or airship. L19.

dirigi'bility *n.* the quality of being dirigible, controllability L19.

dirigisme /diriʒism/ *n.* Also ***dirigism*** /ˈdɪrɪdʒɪz(ə)m/. M20. [Fr., f. *diriger* f. L *dirigere* DIRECT *v.*: see -ISM.] The policy of State direction and control in economic and social matters.

dirigiste /diriʒist/ *a.* of or pertaining to *dirigisme* M20.

diriment /ˈdɪrɪm(ə)nt/ *a.* M19. [L *diriment-* pres. ppl stem of *dirimere*: see DIREMPT *v.*, -ENT.] That renders absolutely void; nullifying.

diriment impediment: making a marriage null and void from the first.

dirk /dəːk/ *n.* & *v.* Also (earlier) †**durk**. M16. [Origin unkn.] **A** *n.* A kind of short dagger, *esp.* that of a Scottish Highlander. M16. **B** *v.t.* Stab with a dirk. L16.

dirl /dəːl/ *v.* & *n. Sc.* & *north.* E16. [Alt. of THIRL *v.*¹] **A** *v.* **1** *v.t.* Pierce, thrill; cause to tingle, esp. by a sharp blow. E16. **2** *v.i.* Vibrate, esp. in response to a blow, a sound, etc.; tingle. E18. **3** *v.i.* Produce a vibrating sound; ring. E19. **B** *n.* A thrill, a vibration; a tremulous sound. L18.

dirndl /ˈdəːnd(ə)l/ *n.* M20. [G dial., dim. of *Dirne* girl.] **1** A dress in the style of Alpine peasant costume with a bodice and full skirt. M20. **2** More fully *dirndl skirt*. A full skirt with a tight waistband. M20.

dirt /dəːt/ *n.* & *v.* ME. [ON *drit* excrement, corresp. to MDu. *drēte* (Du. *dreet*), rel. to the vbs OE *ġedrītan* = ON *drita*, MDu. *drīten* (Du. *drijten*).] **A** *n.* **1** Excrement, faeces. ME. **2** Unclean matter that soils, filth; *esp.* mud, mire. ME. **3** *fig.* Something worthless or (*US*, *Austral.*, & *NZ slang*) mean; scurrilous information, scandal; a despicable person. ME. **4** Dirtiness, foulness, uncleanness, (*lit.* & *fig.*); meanness, sordidness. E17. **5** Earth, soil. L17. **6** *Mining* etc. Useless material, *esp.* that from which an ore or other useful substance is separated. L18. **7** Bad weather. *dial.* M19. **8** Firedamp. M19.

3 SHAKES. *Haml.* Spacious in the possession of dirt. L. G. GIBBON The dirt of gentry sat and ate up your rents but you were as good as they were. L. ALTHER What's the point of having grown children if they won't tell you the dirt?

Phrases: **do dirt to** *slang* harm or injure maliciously. **eat dirt** (*a*) accept insults or humiliation; (*b*) *US* make a humiliating confession. *kiss the dirt*: see KISS *v.* *pay-dirt*: see PAY-. **treat like dirt**: as worthless or contemptible.

Comb.: **dirt bike** a motorcycle designed for unmade roads and scrambling across difficult terrain; **dirt cheap** *a.* & *adv.* very cheap; **dirt-eating** a disease characterized by a morbid craving to eat earth; **dirt farmer** *US*: who farms his own land himself; **dirt money**: paid to workmen handling dirty materials or working in dirty conditions; **dirt-pie** a mud-pie; **dirt road** *N. Amer.* an unmade road, with only the natural surface; **dirt-track** a course made of rolled cinders, brick-dust, etc., for motorcycle racing etc., or of earth for flat-racing; **dirt-wagon** *US* a dustcart.

B *v.t.* Make dirty, soil. *arch.* L16.

dirtless *a.* E17.

dirty /ˈdəːti/ *a.*, *n.*, & *adv.* LME. [f. DIRT *n.* + -Y¹.] **A** *adj.* **1** Soiled with dirt, unclean. LME. **b** That makes a person or thing dirty or unclean. L18. **c** Of a nuclear weapon: producing a lot of fallout. *colloq.* M20. **2a** Morally unclean or impure; obscene, pornographic; titillating; pertaining to or characterized by illicit sexual pleasure. E16. **b** Bringing dishonour, base, corrupt; (of money etc.) earned by dishonourable or corrupt means. L17. **3** Containing or mixed with dirt. M16. **4** Disgusting, repulsive, hateful. E17. **5** (Of weather) rough, squally, wet and windy; marked by such weather. M17. **6** Of colour: tinged with what destroys purity or clearness; inclining to a brownish or greyish colour. M17. **7** Of a shape or movement: not smooth, irregular. *colloq.* E20. **8** Of jazz or popular music: having a slurred, rasping, or distorted tone. E20.

1 H. JOLLY His nappy may be dirty at every feed. b *Daedalus* Every economy has 'dirty-work' jobs that have to be done. 3a A. SILLITOE Sniping was a dirty weapon like poison gas or liquid fire. P. MOYES You and Veronica were going off for . . a dirty week-end. b A. F. DOUGLAS-HOME Politics was a dirty business. 4 D. H. LAWRENCE You are only dirty foreigners. 5 J. RABAN Just another sort of reef to steer one's way round on dirty nights. 7 C. GASKIN They said it was a very *dirty* fracture.

Special collocations & phrases: **dirty Allan** *Sc.* the Arctic skua, *Stercorarius parasiticus*. **dirty dog** *slang* a despicable or untrustworthy person. **dirty end of the stick** *colloq.* the difficult or unpleasant part in a situation. **dirty look** *colloq.* a look of disapproval, anger, or disgust. **dirty money** = *dirt money* s.v. DIRT *n.* (see also sense 3b above). **dirty old man** *colloq.* a man who is regarded as having sexual interests inappropriate to his advanced years. **dirty trick** a mean or despicable act; in *pl.* (*slang*), intelligence operations, underhand activity aimed at discrediting a political opponent. **dirty word** an obscene word; *fig.* a word denoting a concept regarded as discreditable. **dirty work (at the crossroads)** dishonourable, illicit, or underhand behaviour.

B *absol.* as *n. do the dirty*, play a mean trick (*on* a person). *colloq.* E20.

C *adv.* Very, exceedingly. *slang.* E20.

K. AMIS A dirty great Baronial doorway.

dirtily *adv.* L16. **dirtiness** *n.* M16. **dirtyish** *a.* E19.

dirty /ˈdəːti/ *v.* L16. [f. the adj.] **1** *v.t.* Make dirty, soil. (Foll. by *up*.) L16. **2** *v.i.* Become dirty. M19.

2 J. CARLYLE Dark blue morocco . . which won't dirty in a hurry.

dis /dɪs/ *a.* & *v.*[2] *colloq.* Also **diss.** E20. [Abbrev. of DISCONNECTED.] **A** *adj.* Broken, not working; *fig.* weak in the head. E20. **B** *v.t.* Infl. **-ss-**. Break, damage. M20.

dis /dɪs/ *v.*[1] & *n. slang.* L19. [Abbrev.] *Printing.* **A** *v.t.* Infl. **-ss-**. = DISTRIBUTE 5. L19. **B** *n.* Type that is ready for distribution. L19.

dis- /dɪs/ *pref.* [Repr. OFr. *des-*, *dis-* (mod. *dés-*, *dé-*, *dis-*) or its source L *dis-* 'two ways, in two', rel. to BIS-, BI- (= Gk *dis-*, DI-[2]), f. L *duo* two, appearing bef. *p*, *t*, *c*, *q*, and *s* (see also DI-[1], DIF-, DIR-). Occas. repr. late L *dis-* for L *de-* DE- I.] **1** In wds adopted f. Fr. and L w. the sense 'apart, away, asunder, abroad,' as *discern*, *disperse*, *disquisition*, *dissident*, *distant*, *distinguish*, *distraction*, etc. **b** Occas. in wds w. the senses 'between' and 'separate, singly', as *discept* etc. **2** In wds adopted f. Fr. and L w. privative force, as *disadvantage*, *disagree*, *disease*, *disgrace*, *displease*, *dissuade*, etc. Also as a freely productive pref. w. privative force (occas. replacing earlier *mis-*, as in *dislike*) forming (*a*) vbs f. vbs (w. their derivative ns., adjs., etc.) w. the sense 'reverse, undo', as *disestablish*, *disown*, etc.; (*b*) vbs f. ns. w. the senses 'strip of, free, rid of', as *disfrock*, *dispeople*, etc., 'deprive of the character, title, etc. of', as *disbishop*, *dischurch*, etc., 'expel from', as *disbar*, *disbench*, etc., 'undo, spoil', as *discomplexion*; (*c*) vbs f. adjs. w. the sense 'undo, reverse the quality denoted', as *disable* etc.; (*d*) ns. f. ns. w. the sense 'the absence or opposite of the state, quality, etc., in question', as in *dishonour* etc.; (*e*) adjs. f. adjs. w. negative force, as *dishonest* etc. **3** In wds adopted f. Fr. and L w. intensive force 'utterly' with wds already implying reversal or removal, as *disannul*, *disturb*, etc., and occas. in wds formed in Eng. after these, as *disembowel*, *disgruntled*, etc.

disac'cept *v.t.* (*rare*) refuse acceptance to M17. **†disacceptance** *n.* refusal to accept, non-acceptance M17–E18. **disa'ccommodate** *v.t.* (now *rare* or *obs.*) put to inconvenience, incommode E17. **disaccommo'dation** *n.* (now *rare* or *obs.*) the action of inconveniencing; lack of suitability or agreement: E17. **†disadjust** *v.t.* (*rare*) unsettle, disturb E17–M18. **†disadorn** *v.t.* (*rare*) deprive of adornment: L16–E18. **disa'ffiliate** *v.t.* & *i.* cancel affiliation (of) L19. **disaffili'ation** *n.* the action of disaffiliating E20. **disa'llegiance** *n.* (*rare*) absence or withdrawal of allegiance M17. **disa'lly** *v.t.* (*poet. rare*) free from alliance or union L17. **disa'menity** *n.* a disadvantage, an unpleasant feature, (of a place etc.) E20. **disa'nalogy** *n.* lack of analogy, dissimilarity E17. **†disangelical** *a.* not angelical, the reverse of angelical: L17–M18. **disa'noint** *v.t.* annul the anointing or consecration of M17. **†disappendant, -ent** *a.* (*Law*) not appendant M17–M18. **disappli'cation** *n.* the act or result of making inapplicable L20. **disa'pply** *v.t.* treat (a condition etc.) as not applying L20. **disappro'bation** *n.* disapproval M17. **dis'approbative** *a.* = DISAPPROBATORY E19. **disappro'batory** *a.* characterized by or expressing disapproval E19. **disa'rrange** *v.t.* bring into disorder, make untidy M18. **disa'rrangement** *n.* the action or result of disarranging M18. **disar'ticulate** *v.* (*a*) *v.t.* separate joint from joint, make disjointed; (*b*) *v.i.* become disjointed, lose structural cohesion: M19. **disarticu'lation** *n.* the action or result of disarticulating M19. **†disattention** *n.* lack of attention, neglect E17–M18. **dis'balance** *n.* & *v.* (*a*) *n.* an imbalance; (*b*) *v.t.* disturb the balance of: M19. **dis'benefit** *n.* a drawback, an undesirable feature or consequence L20. **dis'body** *v.t.* = DISEMBODY M17. **dis'brain** *v.t.* remove the brain from M17. **dis'bud** *v.t.* remove the buds of; deprive of (superfluous) buds: E18. **dis'cage** *v.t.* let out as from a cage M17. **†discamp** *v.* [after It. *scampare*] (*a*) *v.i.* decamp; (*b*) *v.t.* decamp from; force to decamp: L16–L17. **dis'candy** *v.i.* (*arch.*) melt; *fig.* melt away E17. **dis'canonize** *v.t.* †(*a*) exclude from the canon; (*b*) cancel the canonization of: E17. **disca'pacitate** *v.t.* (*rare*) deprive of capacity, incapacitate M17. **dis'case** *v.* (*arch.*) (*a*) *v.t.* unsheathe; (*b*) *v.t.* & *i.* undress; divest *of*: L16. **dis'class** *v.t.* cut off from a social class L19. **dis'climax** *n.* (*Ecol.*) a climax community in which the natural climax is modified by human interference, grazing, or other disturbances M20. **dis'cloister** *v.t.* release from seclusion M17. **disco'here** *v.i.* cease to cohere L19. **dis'commonize** *v.t.* = DISCOMMON 2 L19. **†disconfidence** *n.* (*rare*) lack or absence of confidence E17–L18. **discon'firm** *v.t.* (tend to) disprove (a hypothesis etc.); suggest the falsity of: M20. **discon'firmable** *a.* able to be shown to be false or unlikely M20. **disconfir'mation** *n.* the process or result of disconfirming M20. **discon'firmatory** *a.* serving to disconfirm M20. **discon'gruity** *n.* (now *rare* or *obs.*) lack of congruity; disagreement, inconsistency: E17. **discon'sider** *v.t.* (*rare*) bring into disrepute, discredit L19. **disconside'ration** *n.* (*rare*) the action of discrediting; the fact of being discredited, disrepute: L19. **†disconsonant** *a.* not consonant, out of agreement; discordant: M17–E19. **†discourt** *v.t.* dismiss from court L16–M19. **†discovenant** *v.t.* break covenant with, exclude from a covenant M17–M19. **discredence** *n.* (*rare*) disbelief LME. **discredibility** *n.* (*rare*) lack or absence of credibility E19. **dise'conomy** *n.* (a factor causing) a disproportionately large increase in costs arising from an increase in the size of an organization M20. **dis'edge** *v.t.* take the edge off, blunt E17. **dis'educate** *v.t.* undo or pervert the education of L19. **†dis-element** *v.t.* put (something) out of its element E17–E18. **disem'bed** *v.t.* free from being embedded L19. **disem'bellish** *v.t.* deprive of embellishment or adornment E17. **disem'bosom** *v.* (*a*) *v.t.* cast out or separate from the bosom; reveal; (*b*) *v.refl.* & *i.* disclose what is in one's inmost thoughts, unburden oneself: M18. **†disembrace** *v.t.* refrain or withdraw from embracing; undo the embraces of: M17–L18. **disem'ploy** *v.t.* cease to employ, dismiss from employment E17. **disem'ployment** *n.* (*rare*) absence or withdrawal of employment M17. **disem'power** *v.t.* deprive of power conferred M18. **dise'nable** *v.t.* make unable or incapable; disable: E17. **disen'joy** *v.t.* get no enjoyment from, dislike E20. **dise'nnoble** *v.t.* deprive of nobility; make ignoble: M17. **†disenrol** *v.t.* (*rare*) remove (a name) from a roll or list M17–M19. **disen'slave** *v.t.* (now *rare*) set free from enslavement M17. **disen'trammel** *v.t.* free from entanglement M19. **disen'trance** *v.t.* bring out of or wake from a trance M17. **disen'twine** *v.t.* free from being entwined, disentangle E19. **dise'quality** *n.* (long *rare*) inequality; disparity: E17. **†disespouse** *v.t.* (*rare*, Milton) undo the marriage or betrothal of: only in M17. **dis'faith** *n.* lack of faith; unfaithfulness: L19. **dis'flesh** *v.t.* (*arch.*) deprive of or free from the flesh E17. **dis'frock** *v.t.* unfrock M19. **dis'garland** *v.t.* divest of a garland or garlands E17. **dis'garrison** *v.t.* (*arch.*) deprive of a garrison L16. **†disgout** *v.t.* (*rare*) free or relieve from gout E17–M18. **dis'gulf** *v.t.* eject or discharge (as) from a gulf M17. **disha'bilitate** *v.t.* (now *rare* or *obs.*) make incapable; *spec.* (*Sc. Law*, now *Hist.*) subject to dishabilitation: M17. **dishabili'tation** *n.* (*Sc. Law*, now *Hist.*) disqualification from the inheritance, possession, or transmission of land M17. **disha'bituate** *v.t.* make unaccustomed M19. **dishalluci'nation** *n.* a freeing from hallucination, disillusion L19. **†dishaunt** *v.t.* (chiefly *Sc.*) cease to attend (esp. a church or church service) L16–E19. **dis'hoard** *v.t.* release from a hoard E20. **dis'home** *v.t.* deprive of or eject from a home L19. **dis'horn** *v.t.* remove the horns from L16. **dis'horse** *v.t.* cause to dismount from a horse M19. **dis'humanize** *v.t.* deprive of human attributes, dehumanize M19. **†dishumour** *n.* ill humour: only in 18. **disi'magine** *v.t.* cease to imagine; imagine not to exist: M17. **disi'mmure** *v.t.* set free from confining walls; liberate: E17. **disim'pale** *v.t.* disengage from a spike E20. **disim'passioned** *a.* freed from passion; dispassionate: M19. **disim'perialism** *n.* renunciation of imperial possessions M20. **†disimplicate** *v.t.* free from implication or involvement M17–M18. **disim'prison** *v.t.* release from imprisonment E17. **disim'prisonment** *n.* the action of disimprisoning M17. **disim'prove** *v.t.* & (*rare*) *i.* make or become worse M17. **disim'provement** *n.* (a) deterioration, worsening M17. **disin'carcerate** *v.t.* = DISIMPRISON M17. **disincarce'ration** *n.* = DISIMPRISONMENT M19. **disin'carnate** *a.* disembodied, not incarnate L19. **disin'carnate** *v.t.* = DISEMBODY 1 L19. **disin'corporate** *v.t.* make no longer a corporate body L17. **disincorpo'ration** *n.* the action of disincorporating a town etc. L18. **disindi'vidualize** *v.t.* divest of individuality M19. **disin'fest** *v.t.* rid of infesting insects, vermin, etc. E20. **disinfes'tation** *n.* the process of disinfesting E20. **†disinhabit** *v.t.* rid of inhabitants M16–E19. **disin'hibit** *v.* (*a*) *v.i.* (*rare*) reduce or remove inhibition; (*b*) *v.t.* release from inhibition; make less inhibited: E20. **disinhi'bition** *n.* the suppression of an inhibition; the state of not being inhibited: E20. **disin'hibitory** *a.* tending to cause, or characterized by, disinhibition M20. **disin'hume** *v.t.* exhume E19. **disinsecti'zation** *n.* the removal of insects M20. **disin'sectize** *v.t.* remove insects from (esp. an aircraft) M20. **disin'tegrity** *n.* (now *rare*) lack of entireness; disintegrated condition: L18. **disintermedi'ation** *n.* (*Econ.*) a reduction in the use or role of banks and savings institutions as intermediaries between lenders and borrowers; transfer of savings and borrowings away from banks etc.: M20. **disin'vent** *v.t.* undo the invention of M19. **disin'volve** *v.t.* free from an involved condition, disentangle E17. **†diskindness** *n.* (an) unkindness; unfriendliness: L16–M18. **dis'leaf, -'leave** *v.t.* strip of leaves L16. **dis'likelihood** *n.* (*rare*) improbability E19. **dis'limb** *v.t.* cut off the limbs of; tear limb from limb: M17. **dis'link** *v.t.* unlink, uncouple, separate, (things that are linked) E17. **dis'load** *v.t.* & *i.* unload, disburden M16. **dis'lustre** *v.* (*a*) *v.t.* deprive of lustre; dim, sully; (*b*) *v.i.* lose its lustre: M17. **dis'marble** *v.t.* free from marble or the appearance of marble M19. **dis'mast** *v.t.* deprive of masts, break the mast(s) of M18. **dis'nest** *v.t.* (*rare*) remove (as) from a nest; empty (a nest) *of*: L16. **disob'struct** *v.t.* (now *rare*) free from obstruction E17. **disoccu'pation** *n.* lack of occupation M19. **dis'occupy** *v.t.* cease to occupy, vacate L19. **disor'ganic** *a.* having no organization or systematic arrangement M19. **†disoxidate** *v.t.* deoxygenate: only in E19. **†disoxygenate** *v.t.* deoxygenate E–M19. **dis'parish** *v.t.* (*a*) deprive of the status of a parish; (*b*) deprive of a parish; eject from a parish: L16. **dis'pauper** *v.t.* (*Hist.*) deprive of the legal status of a pauper M17. **dis'pauperize** *v.t.* free from a state of pauperism; *Hist.* relieve (a community etc.) of responsibility for paupers: M19. **dis'peace** *n.* (chiefly *Sc.*) the absence or reverse of peace; disquiet; dissension: E19. **dis'petal** *v.t.* strip of petals M19. **displume** *v.* †(*a*) *v.i.* (of a bird) moult; (*b*) *v.t.* = DEPLUME: L15. **dis'pope** *v.t.* deprive of the popedom M17. **dis'privilege** *v.t.* deprive of privilege E17. **†disprofess** *v.t.* (*rare*, Spenser) renounce the profession of: only in L16. **†disproperty** *v.t.* (*rare*, Shakes.) deprive of property, dispossess: only in E17. **dis'realize** *v.t.* (*rare*) divest of reality, idealize L19. **disreco'mmend** *v.t.* (*rare*) cause to be unfavourably regarded, give a recommendation against L17. **disrecommen'dation** *n.* something that causes a person or thing to be unfavourably regarded M18. **disre'late** *v.t.* remove the connection between M17. **†disrest** *n.* disquiet, unrest M16–E18. **†disrest** *v.t.* (*a*) remove from a place of rest; (*b*) deprive of rest, disturb: L17–M18. **dis'reverence** *v.t.* (*arch.*) treat with irreverence; deprive of reverence: E16. **dis'roof** *v.t.* unroof M19. **dis'save** *v.i.* spend more than one's income, by drawing on savings or realizing capital

For other words beginning with *dis-* see the main alphabetic sequence of entries

M20. **dis'sceptre** *v.t.* deprive of the sceptre or of kingly authority L16. **dis'seat** *v.t.* unseat; remove from where it is situated: E17. **dis'sepulchred** *a.* (*rare*) disentombed M17. **dis'shadow** *v.t.* (*rare*) free from shadow or shade E17. **dis'sheathe** *v.t.* & †*i.* (*rare*) draw or (formerly) be drawn out of a sheath E17. †**disshiver** *v.* (*a*) *v.t.* shiver in pieces, shatter; (*b*) *v.i.* become shattered: L16–M17. **dis'shroud** *v.t.* (*rare*) strip of a shroud; *fig.* reveal, expose: L16. **dis'sight** *n.* an unsightly object, an eyesore E18. **dis'sightly** *a.* (*rare*) unsightly L18. **dis'soul** *v.t.* (*rare*) take away the soul from E17. **dis'sunder** *v.t.* (*arch.*) sever, divide L16. **dis'sympathy** *n.* (*rare*) absence of sympathy M19. **dis'tenant** *v.t.* (*rare*) deprive of a tenant L16. **dis'tune** *v.t.* put out of tune LME. **dis'turnpike** *v.t.* free (a road) of turnpikes L19. **dis'uniform** *a.* without uniformity L17. **disuni'formity** *n.* absence of uniformity E18. **dis'unify** *v.t.* undo or prevent the unity of L19. **disu'tility** *n.* injuriousness, harmfulness; a factor that tends to nullify the utility of something; a drawback: L19. †**disveil** *v.t.* remove a veil from; unveil, unmask: L16–M19. †**disvest** *v.t.* divest, strip; undress: E17–M18. †**disvouch** *v.t.* (*rare*) = DISAVOW L15–E17. **disvulnera'bility** *n.* the faculty of recovering from injuries exceptionally quickly L19. **dis'warren** *v.t.* deprive of the character of a warren; make no longer a warren: M17. **dis'wig** *v.t.* deprive of a wig L18. **dis'wood** *v.t.* deprive of wood or trees E17.

disa /'dʌɪsə/ *n.* M19. [mod.L, ult. origin unkn.] Any of various terrestrial orchids of the genus *Disa*, native to southern Africa and Madagascar and with dark green leaves.

disability /dɪsə'bɪlɪti/ *n.* L16. [f. DIS- 2 + ABILITY.] 1 Lack of ability (*to do* something); inability, incapacity. Now *rare*. L16. 2 Shortage of money. E17. 3 An instance of lacking ability; now *spec.* a physical or mental condition (usu. permanent) that limits a person's activities or senses, esp. the ability to work. E17. 4 Incapacity recognized or created by the law; legal disqualification. M17.

disable /dɪs'eɪb(ə)l/ *v.t.* LME. [f. DIS- 2 + ABLE *a.*] 1 Disqualify legally; pronounce legally incapable. (Foll. by *from doing*, †*to do*.) LME. 2 Make incapable of action or use; deprive of physical or mental ability, esp. through injury or disease. L15. 3 Pronounce incapable; disparage, belittle. Now *rare* or *obs.* E16. †4 Make or pronounce of no validity. M16–L17.

2 R. D. HAMPDEN Men are disabled from understanding what they have been taught to condemn. *Scientific American* A car that is disabled or illegally parked. 3 SHAKES. *A.Y.L.* Farewell, Monsieur Traveller.., disable all the benefits of your own country, be out of love with your nativity.

disablement *n.* the action of disabling; the state or fact of being disabled: L15. **disableness** *n.* (*arch.*) inability, incapacity; disabled state: E17.

disabled /dɪs'eɪb(ə)ld/ *a.* & *n.* LME. [f. prec. + -ED[1].] A *adj.* 1 Legally disqualified. Now *rare* or *obs.* LME. 2 Made incapable of action or use; *esp.* (of a person) possessing a disability. M17. 3 For the use of people with physical disabilities. L20. B *absol.* as *n.pl. The* disabled people as a class. E20.

disablist /dɪs'eɪblɪst/ *a.* L20. [f. prec. + -IST, after *racist*.] Practising or displaying discrimination against the disabled.

disabuse /dɪsə'bjuːz/ *v.* & *n.* E17. [f. DIS- 2 + ABUSE *n.*] A *v.t.* 1 Rid *of* illusion, a mistaken conception, etc.; undeceive, disillusion. E17. 2 Mar, spoil, misuse. *Sc.* E17.

1 H. A. L. FISHER If Justinian expected to extend to the north African littoral a Roman peace he was soon disabused. P. ACKROYD I do not disabuse them of this charming notion.

†B *n.* The act of disabusing; the fact of being disabused. E17–E18.

disaccharide /dʌɪ'sakərʌɪd/ *n.* L19. [f. DI-[2] + SACCHARIDE.] *Chem.* Any sugar that consists of two monosaccharide residues linked together.

disaccharase, disaccharidase *ns.* an enzyme which hydrolyses a disaccharide M20.

disaccord /dɪsə'kɔːd/ *n.* M16. [f. DIS- 2 + ACCORD *n.*: cf. (O)Fr. *désaccord*.] Disagreement, variance; lack of accord.

disaccord /dɪsə'kɔːd/ *v.i.* LME. [Fr. *désaccorder*, f. as DIS- 2, ACCORD *v.*] Disagree; be at variance.

disaccordance *n.* (*rare*) disagreement, variance LME. **disaccordant** *a.* (*rare*) discordant, at variance L15.

disaccustom /dɪsə'kʌstəm/ *v.t.* L15. [OFr. *desaco(u)stumer* (mod. *désaccoutumer*), f. as DIS- 2, ACCUSTOM *v.*] 1 Cause (a thing) to cease to be customary; break off (a habit or practice). *arch.* L15. 2 Cause (a person) to lose a habit; make unaccustomed (*to*, †*from*). M16.

disacknowledge /dɪsək'nɒlɪdʒ/ *v.t.* L16. [f. DIS- 2 + ACKNOWLEDGE *v.*] Refuse to acknowledge, disown.

disacknowledgement *n.* M17.

disacquaint /dɪsə'kweɪnt/ *v.t.* Now *rare* or *obs.* M16. [f. DIS- 2 + ACQUAINT *v.*] Estrange, make unfamiliar.

disa'cquaintance *n.* lack of acquaintance L16.

†**disadvance** *v.t.* LME–M17. [OFr. *desavancer* repel, push back, f. as DIS- 2, ADVANCE *v.*] Check the advance of; draw back, lower; *fig.* hinder from progress, lower the status of.

SPENSER That forced him his shield to disadvaunce.

disadvantage /dɪsəd'vɑːntɪdʒ/ *n.* & *v.* LME. [(O)Fr. *désavantage*, f. DIS- 2, ADVANTAGE *n.*] A *n.* 1 Lack of advantage; an unfavourable condition or circumstance. LME. 2 Loss of or injury to credit, reputation, or interest. LME.

1 R. ELLMANN Lewes must have appeared to disadvantage beside this taller, handsomer.., younger banker. 2 STEELE I..never speak Things to any Man's Disadvantage.

B *v.t.* Place at a disadvantage; affect unfavourably. M16.

Daily Telegraph His colour, always disadvantaging him, has damaged his native spontaneity.

disadvantaged *ppl a.* & *n.* (*the* people who are) placed at a disadvantage, now esp. in relation to social opportunities E17.

disadvantageous /ˌdɪsadv(ə)n'teɪdʒəs/ *a.* E17. [f. DIS- 2 + ADVANTAGEOUS, perh. after Fr. *désavantageux*.] 1 Involving disadvantage; unfavourable, prejudicious. E17. 2 Tending to the discredit of a person or thing; disparaging, derogatory. M17.

disadvantageously *adv.* E17. **disadvantageousness** *n.* E18.

†**disadventure** *n.* LME–M17. [OFr. *desaventure*, f. as DIS- 2, ADVENTURE *n.*] Mishap, misfortune.

†**disadventurous** *a.* unfortunate, disastrous L16–E18.

disadvise /dɪsəd'vʌɪz/ *v.t.* M17. [f. DIS- 2 + ADVISE.] 1 Advise against (an action, course, etc.). M17. 2 Dissuade (a person) *from*. L17.

disaffect /dɪsə'fɛkt/ *v.t.* E17. [f. DIS- 2 + AFFECT *v.*[1]] 1 Have no affection for; dislike, regard with aversion. *arch.* E17. 2 Alienate, estrange; make unfriendly or less friendly; *spec.* make discontented with a constituted authority, as the Government, one's employer, etc. M17.

1 J. SHIRLEY Unless you disaffect his person. 2 G. F. KENNAN The Communists..set about trying to disaffect these men from their loyalty to their own governments.

disaffected *ppl a.* that has been disaffected; unfriendly; discontent, *spec.* with a constituted authority, as the Government, one's employer, etc.: M17.

disaffection /dɪsə'fɛkʃ(ə)n/ *n.* E17. [Partly f. DIS- 2 + AFFECTION *n.*; partly f. DISAFFECT *v.* after AFFECTION *n.*: see -ION.] 1 Lack or alienation of affection; estrangement; dissatisfaction; *spec.* discontentment with a constituted authority, as the Government, one's employer, etc. E17. †2 Bodily disorder or indisposition. M17–M18.

disaffirm /dɪsə'fəːm/ *v.t.* M16. [f. DIS- 2 + AFFIRM.] Contradict, deny; *spec.* in *Law*, reverse (a previous decision), repudiate (a settlement).

disaffirmance *n.* the action of disaffirming; annulment, repudiation: E17. **disaffir'mation** *n.* = DISAFFIRMANCE M19.

disafforest /dɪsə'fɒrɪst/ *v.t.* LME. [AL *disafforestare*, f. as DIS- 2, AFFOREST. Cf. DEAFFOREST, DEFOREST, DISFOREST.] 1 *Hist.* Free from the operation of forest laws; reduce from the legal status of forest to that of ordinary land. LME. 2 = DISFOREST 2. *rare.* M19.

disaffore'station *n.* the action or result of disafforesting land etc. L16. **disafforestment** *n.* = DISAFFORESTATION L19.

disaggregate /dɪs'agrɪgeɪt/ *v.t.* E19. [f. DIS- 2 + AGGREGATE *v.*] Separate into component parts; cease to treat as aggregated.

disaggre'gation *n.* E19.

disagree /dɪsə'griː/ *v.i.* Pa. t. & pple **-reed**. L15. [(O)Fr. *désagréer*, f. as DIS- 2, AGREE.] 1 Differ in nature, be unlike; not correspond. (Foll. by *with*, †*to*, †*from*.) L15. 2 Refuse to accord or agree (to a proposal etc.); withhold assent. (Foll. by *to*, *with*, †*from*.) L15. 3 Differ in opinion. (Foll. by *with*, (now *rare*) *from*.) M16. 4 Be at variance, quarrel, fall out. M16. 5 Of food, climate, etc.: be unsuited to a person's constitution, cause discomfort or illness. Foll. by *with*. M16.

1 A. B. DAVIDSON The other numerals are nouns, and disagree in gender with the words they enumerate. 2 GLADSTONE I beg now to move that the House disagree with the Lords' amendment. 3 POPE Who shall decide when Doctors disagree? AGREE *to disagree*. 4 S. HAYWARD Children of the same family ought not to disagree.

disagreer *n.* (*rare*) E17.

disagreeable /dɪsə'griːəb(ə)l/ *a.* & *n.* LME. [(O)Fr. *désagréable*, f. as DIS- 2, AGREEABLE *a.*] A *adj.* †1 Not in agreement; characterized by difference; incongruous; discordant. (Foll. by *to*, *with*.) LME–M18. 2 Not to one's taste or liking; unpleasant, offensive. L17. 3 Bad-tempered, unamiable, surly. E18. 4 Feeling discomfort, uneasy. Chiefly *US*. E19.

2 J. JOHNSTON Pale mauve, a colour I normally find quite disagreeable.

B *n.* A disagreeable thing or experience. Usu. in *pl.* L18.

D. CECIL Hankering after life on earth, even after its disagreeables.

disagreea'bility *n.* L18. **disagreeableness** *n.* L16. **disagreeably** *adv.* L17.

disagreement /dɪsə'griːm(ə)nt/ *n.* L15. [f. DISAGREE after AGREEMENT.] 1 (A) refusal to accord or agree; the withholding of assent. L15. 2 (A) difference of opinion. L16. 3 A quarrel; dissension. L16. 4 (A) difference in nature, (an) unlikeness, (a) lack of correspondence. L16. 5 Unsuitableness to a person's constitution. E18.

disallow /dɪsə'laʊ/ *v.* LME. [OFr. *desalouer*, f. as DIS- 2, ALLOW *v.*] †1 *v.t.* Blame; refuse to praise. LME–M17. †2 *v.t.* & *i.* foll. by *of*. Disown. LME–M17. 3 *v.t.* Treat as invalid; refuse to accept (a claim, suggestion, etc.). LME. 4 *v.t.* & †*i.* foll. by *of*. Refuse to permit or sanction; prohibit; prevent. L15.

3 E. WAUGH No. 13..cut across country...This lap has therefore been disallowed by the judges. 4 O. SACKS Violent stiffness..disallowed even passive movement.

disallowable *a.* not to be permitted or sanctioned LME. **disallowance** *n.* (*a*) the action or result of disallowing; †(*b*) *Mus.* an irregularity: M16.

disambiguate /dɪsam'bɪgjʊeɪt/ *v.t.* M20. [f. DIS- 2 + AMBIGU(OUS + -ATE[3].] Remove ambiguity from.

ˌdisambigu'ation *n.* (the result of) the removal of ambiguity E19.

Disamis /'dɪsəmɪs/ *n.* M16. [A mnemonic of scholastic philosophers first used in med.L, A indicating a universal affirmative proposition and I a particular affirmative proposition.] *Logic.* The second mood of the third syllogistic figure, in which a particular affirmative conclusion is drawn from a particular affirmative major and a universal affirmative minor premiss.

disanchor /dɪs'aŋkə/ *v.* LME. [OFr. *desancrer*, f. as DIS- 2, ANCHOR *v.*] 1 *v.i.* Weigh anchor, leave an anchorage. LME. 2 *v.t.* Release (a ship) from anchorage; weigh the anchor of. L15.

disanimate /dɪs'anɪmeɪt/ *v.t.* L16. [f. DIS- 2 + ANIMATE *v.*, prob. after Fr. *désanimer*.] Deprive of life, spirit, vigour, or animation.

disani'mation *n.* M17.

disannex /dɪsə'nɛks/ *v.t.* LME. [OFr. *desannexer*, f. as DIS- 2, ANNEX *v.*] End the annexation of (land etc.); disjoin.

ˌdisanne'xation *n.* L19.

disannul /dɪsə'nʌl/ *v.t.* Infl. **-ll-**. L15. [f. DIS- 3 + ANNUL.] 1 Cancel, annul. L15. †2 Deprive (a person) *of* an attribute etc. by annulment; *fig.* do out *of*. Also foll. by *from*. M16–E17.

disannulment *n.* E17.

For other words beginning with *dis-* see the main alphabetic sequence of entries

disapparel /dɪsəˈpar(ə)l/ *v.t.* & †*i.* Now *rare*. L16. [f. DIS- 2 + APPAREL *v.*] Undress.

disappear /dɪsəˈpɪə/ *v.* LME. [f. DIS- 2 + APPEAR *v.* after Fr. *disparaître*.] 1 *v.i.* Cease to appear or be visible; pass from sight, vanish; gradually cease to be distinguishable. LME. 2 *v.i.* Cease to be present, go away; pass from existence; go, leaving no trace; be lost. M17. 3 *v.t.* Cause to disappear. L19.

1 JOYCE He disappears into . . the pork butcher's. L. DEIGHTON The giant planes climbed into the darkness and disappeared. 2 J. BUCHAN I would disappear early on the Sunday morning and return late at night. H. L. MENCKEN The idea of restitution seems to have disappeared from our criminal law.

Phrases: **do a** (or **the**) **disappearing trick, act** *colloq.* disappear suddenly or unexpectedly.

disappearance *n.* the action or an act of disappearing E18. **disappearer** *n.* a person who disappears L19.

disappoint /dɪsəˈpɔɪnt/ *v.* & *n.* LME. [(O)Fr. *désappointer*, f. as DIS- 2, APPOINT *v.*] A *v.* 1 *v.t.* Reverse the appointment of; deprive of an office, position, or possession. Now *rare*. LME. 2 *v.t.* Frustrate or fail to fulfil the desire or expectation of (a person). Freq. in *pass.* (foll. by *in*, *with*, †*of*). L15. b *v.i.* Cause disappointment, be disappointing. M19. †3 *v.t.* Break off (what has been appointed); fail to keep (an engagement). M16–M17. 4 *v.t.* Prevent the realization or fulfilment of (a plan, purpose, etc.); frustrate (a hope). L16. †5 *v.t.* Equip or prepare improperly. L16–M17. †6 *v.t.* Undo, destroy, overthrow. E17–E18.

1 BYRON He would keep it Till duly disappointed or dismiss'd. 2 J. P. HENNESSY Trollope . . had been disappointed in his expectations of promotion. **agreeably** etc. **disappointed** agreeably etc. surprised by something better than one expected it to be. b G. GREENE One knows what to expect and Mr Cagney seldom disappoints. 3 JOSEPH HALL So as to put off and disappoint the day which he had set. 4 G. B. SHAW It would certainly disappoint the main hope of its advocates. 5 SHAKES. *Haml.* Cut off even in the blossoms of my sin, Unhous'led, disappointed, unanel'd. 6 STEELE They endeavour to disappoint the good works of the most learned . . of men.

†B *n.* = DISAPPOINTMENT. M17–M19.

disappointedly *adv.* in a disappointed way or tone L19. **disappointingly** *adv.* (*a*) in a disappointing way; (*b*) (modifying a sentence) it is disappointing that: L19.

disappointment /dɪsəˈpɔɪntm(ə)nt/ *n.* E17. [f. prec. + -MENT.] 1 (An instance of) the frustration or non-fulfilment of desire or expectation. E17. 2 Dejection or distress caused by this. M18. 3 A person who or thing which disappoints. M18.

1 J. TYNDALL Severe labour and frequent disappointment. M. MEYER It was a bitter disappointment to Strindberg . . to find himself treated . . as a servant. 2 SCOTT FITZGERALD 'It's not exactly a *police* dog,' said the man with disappointment in his voice. 3 W. COWPER One who has been a disappointment and a vexation to them.

disappropriate /dɪsəˈprəʊprɪeɪt/ *v.t.* Pa. pple & ppl a. **-ated**, (earlier) †**-ate**. E17. [med.L *disappropriat-* pa. ppl stem of *disappropriare*, f. as DIS- 2 + L *appropriare* APPROPRIATE *v.*] Dissolve the appropriation of (a property etc.).

ˌ**disappropriˈation** *n.* the action of disappropriating M17.

disapprove /dɪsəˈpruːv/ *v.* L15. [f. DIS- 2 + APPROVE *v.*[2]] †1 *v.t.* Prove to be untrue or wrong; disprove. L15–L18. 2 *v.t.* Have or express an unfavourable opinion of. M17. 3 *v.i.* Have or express an unfavourable opinion (*of*). E18.

2 M. TREVOR He disapproved this impatience. 3 H. JAMES She disapproved of clamorous children. C. P. SNOW He disapproved intensely.

disapprovable *a.* deserving disapproval M17. **disapproval** *n.* the act or fact of disapproving, possession or expression of an unfavourable opinion (*of*) M17. **disapprover** *n.* L18. **disapprovingly** *adv.* in a disapproving manner M19.

disard *n.* var. of DIZZARD.

disarm /dɪsˈɑːm/ *v.* & *n.* LME. [(O)Fr. *désarmer*, f. as DIS- 2, ARM *v.*[1]] A *v.* I *v.t.* 1 Deprive (a person) of a weapon or (*arch.*) armour; force a weapon from the hand of (an opponent). (Foll. by *of*.) LME. 2 *fig.* Deprive (anger etc.) of the power to injure or intimidate; allay the hostility or suspicions of (a person). LME. 3 Remove or dismantle the defences of (a city, ship, etc.); deprive (an animal) of its organs of attack and defence; remove the fuse of (a bomb). E17.

1 G. GREENE Unless you give me your revolver I shall call the crew to disarm you. 2 J. G. COZZENS Accustomed to disarm some of their critics by cheerfully agreeing with them. M. KEANE Her unquestioning confidence in love . . had disarmed him of any unkindness towards her. H. GUNTRIP His aggression was disarmed when he discovered that she really understood him.

II *v.i.* 4 Divest oneself of weapons or (*arch.*) armour. L16. 5 Of a nation etc.: reduce or abandon its state of military preparedness for war; renounce the use of (esp. nuclear) weapons. M18.

5 A. J. AUGARDE Most governments refuse to disarm until their 'enemies' disarm.

B *n.* Chiefly *Fencing*. The action of disarming or forcing a weapon from the hand of an opponent. E19.

disarmer *n.* (*a*) a person who disarms; (*b*) a person who advocates or campaigns for (esp. nuclear) disarmament: M17. **disarming** *ppl a.* that disarms a person; charmingly persuasive, winsome: M19. **disarmingly** *adv.* E20.

disarmament /dɪsˈɑːməm(ə)nt/ *n.* L18. [f. prec. + -MENT, after ARMAMENT and Fr. *désarmement*.] The action of disarming; *esp.* the reduction or abandonment of a state of military preparedness for war; the renunciation of specified weapons, by a nation.

NUCLEAR *disarmament*. *unilateral disarmament*: see UNILATERAL 2a.

disarray /dɪsəˈreɪ/ *n.* LME. [AN *dissairay*, OFr. *desaroi* (mod. *désarroi*), f. as DIS- 2, ARRAY *n.*] 1 The state of being out of any regular order; disorder, confusion. LME. 2 Imperfect or incorrect dress. *arch.* L16.

1 E. FIGES Sitting . . with her hair in disarray. *Times* This is the second year that the meeting has ended in disarray.

disarray /dɪsəˈreɪ/ *v.t.* LME. [f. DIS- 2 + ARRAY *v.*, perh. after OFr. *desare(i)er*, *desaroier*, f. *desaroi*: see prec.] 1 Throw into disorder or confusion; make untidy. LME. 2 Undress; strip (*of* clothing, any adjunct). L15.

2 SHELLEY My song, its pinions disarrayed of might, drooped.

disassemble /dɪsəˈsɛmb(ə)l/ *v.* E17. [f. DIS- 2 + ASSEMBLE.] †1 *v.t.* Separate, scatter, disperse. *rare*. Only in E17. 2 *v.t.* Take (a machine etc.) to pieces, dismantle. E20. 3 *v.i.* Undergo disassembly; separate into constituent elements. M20.

disassemblage *n.* = DISASSEMBLY L20. **disassembler** *n.* (*Computing*) a program for converting machine code into assembly language L20. **disassembly** *n.* the action of disassembling M20.

disassociate /dɪsəˈsəʊʃɪeɪt, -sɪ-/ *v.t.* E17. [f. DIS- 2 + ASSOCIATE *v.*] = DISSOCIATE 1. (Foll. by *from*.)

Times Efforts to disassociate their country from the attempt to murder the Pope.

ˌ**disassociˈation** *n.* the action of disassociating; the fact of being disassociated; dissociation: L19.

disaster /dɪˈzɑːstə/ *n.* & *v.* L16. [Fr. *désastre* or its source It. *disastro*, f. *dis-* DIS- 2 + *astro* star (f. L *astrum*). Cf. *ill-starred*.] A *n.* 1 (A) sudden or great misfortune; an event of ruinous or distressing nature, a calamity; complete failure. L16. †2 An unfavourable aspect of a star or planet. E–M17.

1 D. FRASER Disaster always brought out the best in Churchill. *Daily Telegraph* The Houghton Main colliery disaster in which five miners died.

Comb.: **disaster area**: in which a major disaster has recently occurred; **disaster movie** *colloq.* a film whose plot centres on a major disaster such as a flood, fire, aircrash, etc.

B *v.t.* Bring disaster on; ruin; cause serious injury to. Usu. in *pass.* Now *rare*. L16.

disastrous /dɪˈzɑːstrəs/ *a.* L16. [Fr. *désastreux* f. It. *disastroso*, f. *disastro* DISASTER: see -OUS.] †1 Struck by or subject to disaster; ill-fated; unlucky. L16–E19. 2 Presaging disaster, ill-omened; unpropitious. *arch.* E17. 3 Of the nature of a disaster, calamitous; attended with disaster. E17.

1 J. MARSTON He prov'd alwaies desastrous in love. 3 M. EDWARDES A mass exodus of dealers would have been as disastrous as a major strike.

disastrously *adv.* E17.

disattire /dɪsəˈtaɪə/ *v.t.* Long *rare*. L15. [f. DIS- 2 + ATTIRE *v.*] Undress.

disauthorize /dɪsˈɔːθəraɪz/ *v.t.* Long *rare*. Also **-ise**. M16. [f. DIS- 2 + AUTHORIZE.] Strip of authority; make or treat as of no authority.

disavail /dɪsəˈveɪl/ *v.t.* & †*i.* Now *rare* or *obs.* LME. [f. DIS- 2 + AVAIL *v.*] Be disadvantageous or harmful (to).

disavow /dɪsəˈvaʊ/ *v.t.* LME. [(O)Fr. *désavouer*, f. as DIS- 2 + AVOW *v.*[1]] 1 Disclaim knowledge of, responsibility for, or approval of; disown, repudiate. LME. †2 Refuse to admit or acknowledge as true or valid; deny. E–M17. †3 Refuse to accept or *to do*. E–M17.

1 P. ACKROYD He was later to disavow the book, and never allowed any part to be reprinted.

disavowable *a.* liable or able to be disavowed L19. **disavowal** *n.* the action of disavowing, repudiation, denial M18.

disband /dɪsˈband/ *v.* L16. [Fr. †*desbander* (now *dé-*), f. *des-* DIS- 2, BAND *n.*[3]] I *v.t.* 1 Break up the organization of (a band or company); dissolve and dismiss from service (a military force etc.). L16. †b Discharge from a band or company. Only in 17. †2 Let loose; turn out; send away. E17–L18. †3 Break up the coherence of, disintegrate. L17–L18.

II *v.i.* 4 Break up as a body of soldiers or an organization; cease to be a band or company; break rank, disperse; leave military service. L16. †5 Disintegrate; separate *from* a group. M–L17.

4 J. SPEED The rest disbanded, turned their backes, and fled toward the desert.

disbandment *n.* E18.

disbar /dɪsˈbɑː/ *v.*[1]*t.* Infl. **-rr-**. M16. [f. DIS- 1 + BAR *v.*] Exclude; prevent; = DEBAR.

¶ Recorded again M20 after being obs. since L16.

disbar /dɪsˈbɑː/ *v.*[2]*t.* Infl. **-rr-**. M17. [f. DIS- 2 + BAR *n.*[1]] Expel from the bar; deprive (a lawyer) of legal status and privileges.

disbarment *n.* M19.

†**disbark** *v.*[1]*t.* & *i.* M16–M19. [Fr. †*desbarquer* (now *dé-*: cf. DEBARK *v.*[1]), f. as DIS- 2 + *barque* BARK *n.*[3]] = DISEMBARK.

disbark /dɪsˈbɑːk/ *v.*[2]*t.* L16. [f. DIS- 2 + BARK *n.*[2]] = DEBARK *v.*[2]

disbelief /dɪsbɪˈliːf/ *n.* L17. [f. DIS- 2 + BELIEF. Superseded *misbelief*.] The action or an act of disbelieving; mental rejection of a statement; positive unbelief.

W. E. H. LECKY A disbelief in ghosts. A. MACLEAN I stared at Judith Haynes in disbelief. *suspend disbelief*: see SUSPEND 4.

disbelieve /dɪsbɪˈliːv/ *v.* M17. [f. DIS- 2 + BELIEVE. Superseded *misbelieve*.] 1 *v.t.* Refuse to believe (a person, statement, etc.). M17. 2 *v.i.* Be a sceptic; have no belief or faith *in*. M18.

1 H. HALLAM To disbelieve such a contemporary witness as Sir Thomas More. W. S. CHURCHILL His warning was disbelieved. 2 SOUTHEY It is not possible to hear and disbelieve. G. B. SHAW To disbelieve in marriage is easy.

disbeliever *n.* M17.

disbench /dɪsˈbɛn(t)ʃ/ *v.t.* E17. [f. DIS- 2 + BENCH *n.*] †1 Unseat. *rare* (Shakes.). Only in E17. 2 Deprive of the status of a bencher. L19.

disboard /dɪsˈbɔːd/ *v.i.* *rare*. E17. [OFr. *desborder* (mod. *dé-*), f. *des-* DIS- 2 + *bord* BOARD *n.*] = DISEMBARK.

disbowel /dɪsˈbaʊəl/ *v.t.* Infl. **-ll-**, ***-l-**. LME. [f. DIS- 2 + BOWEL *n.*] = DISEMBOWEL.

disbranch /dɪsˈbrɑːn(t)ʃ/ *v.t.* L16. [f. DIS- 2 + BRANCH *n.*] 1 Cut or break off the branches of. L16. 2 Cut or break off; sever. E17.

disburden /dɪsˈbɔːd(ə)n/ *v.* Also (*arch.*) **-burthen** /-ˈbɔːð(ə)n/. M16. [f. DIS- 2 + BURDEN *n.*] 1 *v.t.* Remove a burden from; relieve of a burden. M16. 2 *v.t.* Get rid of (a burden); discharge, unload. L16. 3 *v.i.* Discharge its load. M17.

1 GEO. ELIOT The need . . to disburden her mind. P. DE VRIES A case I simply could not seem to close,

drop, resolve, or otherwise disburden myself of. 2 J. PORY This small river . . disburdeneth it selfe into the sea not farre from the city. ADDISON Lucia, disburden all thy cares on me.

disburdenment *n.* E19.

disburse /dɪsˈbəːs/ *v.* & *n.* M16. [OFr. *desbourser* (mod. *débourser*), f. as DIS- 2, BURSE. Cf. DEBURSE.] A *v.* 1 *v.t.* Pay out (money). M16. 2 *v.t.* Pay money to meet (an expense or cost), defray. M16. †3 *v.t.* Give out or away. L16–L17. 4 *v.i.* Pay money. E17. †B *n.* = DISBURSEMENT. E17–L18.

disbursal *n.* = DISBURSEMENT L16. **disbursement** *n.* the action of disbursing; money paid out: L16. **disburser** *n.* E17.

disburthen *v.* see DISBURDEN.

disc /dɪsk/ *n.* Also (*US* & *Computing* now the usual form) **disk.** M17. [Fr. *disque* or its source L DISCUS.] 1 The seemingly flat round form that the sun, moon, and other celestial objects present to the eye; any similar round luminous shape. M17. 2 = DISCUS 1. *obs.* exc. *Hist.* E18. 3 A flat circular object thin in relation to its diameter. E18. b A sound or video recording in the form of a disc; a gramophone record, a compact disc. L19. c *Computing.* A data storage device in the form of a disc with a prepared, usu. magnetizable, surface. M20. 4 *Bot.* & *Zool.* A roundish flattened part in a plant or animal; *spec.* (in a composite flower-head with two types of floret) the inner, closely packed, tubular florets round which the outer, ligulate florets (ray) are arranged. E18. b *Anat.* The layer of cartilage and pulp between successive vertebrae. L19.

3 G. GROTE Whether the earth was a disk or a sphere. B. MALAMUD A peephole at eye level covered by a metal disc.

Phrases etc.: *black disc*: see BLACK *a.* *compact disc*: see COMPACT *a.* 1. FLOPPY *disc. hard disc*: see HARD *a.* *optic disc*: see OPTIC *a.* *optical disc*: see OPTICAL *a.* **slipped disc** an intervertebral disc that has become displaced or prolapsed and can cause pain, weakness, or paralysis by pressure on nerves or the spinal cord. *videodisc*: see VIDEO *a.* & *n.*

Comb.: **disc brake**: that uses disc-shaped friction surfaces; **disc camera**: in which the images are formed on a disc, not on a roll of film; **disc drive** *Computing* a device with a read/write head and means for rotating a disc or disc pack; **disc emulator** *Computing* a program that enables part of a memory to be used as if it were a disc; **disc floret** any of the tubular florets forming the disc in certain composite plants (see sense 4 above); **disc harrow**: with concave cutting discs at an oblique angle; **disc jockey** a person who introduces and plays recorded music on a radio programme etc.; **disc pack** *Computing* an assembly of discs on a common spindle inside a removable protective cover; **disc parking** a system in which parked vehicles must display a disc showing time of arrival or latest permitted time of departure.

discless *a.* M19. **disclike** *a.* resembling a disc, disc-shaped L19.

disc /dɪsk/ *v.t.* & *i.* Chiefly *US* & *NZ.* Also **disk.** L19. [f. the n.] Cultivate with a disc harrow or similar implement.

discal /ˈdɪsk(ə)l/ *a.* M19. [f. L DISCUS + -AL[1].] Of, pertaining to, or of the nature of, a disc; discoid.

discalceate /dɪsˈkalsɪət/ *a.* & *n.* M17. [L *discalceatus*, f. as DIS- 2 + *calceatus* pa. pple of *calceare* to shoe, f. *calceus* shoe: see -ATE[2].] A *adj.* Barefoot; wearing sandals as the only footwear. M17. B *n.* A discalceate friar or nun. Now *rare* or *obs.* M17.

discalceate /dɪsˈkalsɪeɪt/ *v.t.* & *i.* E17. [Late L *discalceat-* pa. ppl stem of *discalceare*, f. as DIS- 2 + L *calceare*: see prec., -ATE[3].] Take off the shoes (of). Chiefly as *discalceated* ppl a.

discalced /dɪsˈkalst/ *a.* M17. [f. *discalceated* (see prec.) after Fr. *déchaux*.] = DISCALCEATE *a.*

discant *n.*, *v.* vars. of DESCANT *n.*, *v.*

discard /ˈdɪskɑːd/ *n.* M18. [f. the vb.] 1 *Cards.* The action or an act of discarding a card; a discarded card. M18. 2 *gen.* a The act of rejecting, abandoning, or discharging. L18. b A rejected, abandoned, or discharged person or thing. L19.

1 *ruff and discard*: see RUFF *n.*[2] 3. 2a **(in)to the discard** into oblivion or disuse.

discard /dɪˈskɑːd/ *v.* L16. [f. DIS- 2 + CARD *n.*[2], after Fr. †*de(s)carter*.] 1 *v.t.* & *i. Cards.* Throw out or reject (a card) from a hand. Also, play (a card) from a remaining suit when not following suit or trumping. L16. 2 *v.t.* Cast aside; reject; abandon; give up. L16. 3 *v.t.* Dismiss from employment, service, or office; discharge. L16.

2 E. TAYLOR Things she had eagerly collected not very long ago and would soon discard. 3 SWIFT My man . . is a sad dog; and the minute I come to Ireland I will discard him.

discardable *a.* L20. **discarder** *n.* L19. **discardment** *n.* (*rare*) abandonment M19.

discarnate /dɪsˈkɑːnət/ *a.* LME. [f. DIS- 2 + L *caro*, *carn-* flesh, or late L *carnatus* fleshy: see -ATE[2].] †1 Stripped of flesh. *rare.* LME–M17. 2 Separated from the flesh or the body; disembodied. L19.

discarˈnation *n.* E20.

discectomy /dɪsˈkɛktəmi/ *n.* Also ***disk-.** L20. [f. DISC *n.* + -ECTOMY.] Surgical removal of (part of) an intervertebral disc; an instance of this.

discept /dɪˈsɛpt/ *v.i. rare.* M17. [L *disceptare*, f. as DIS- 1 + *captare* try to catch.] Dispute, debate; express disagreement.

disceptation /dɪsɛpˈteɪʃ(ə)n/ *n. arch.* LME. [OFr., or its source L *disceptatio(n-)*, f. *disceptat-* pa. ppl stem of *disceptare*: see prec., -ATION.] Disputation, debate.

discern /dɪˈsəːn/ *v.* Also †**decern.** LME. [(O)Fr. *discerner* f. L *discernere*, f. as DIS- 1 + *cernere* to separate. Conf. w. DECERN.] †1 *v.t.* Mark as separate or distinct; distinguish. LME–M17. 2 *v.i.* Perceive or recognize the difference or distinction *between*. *arch.* LME. 3 *v.t.* & (now *rare*) *i.* Distinguish (one thing or fact) by the intellect; recognize or perceive distinctly. LME. b *v.i.* Have cognizance, judge *of*. Now *rare* or *obs.* E17. 4 *v.t.* & (*rare*) *i.* Distinguish by the sight (or another sense); make out by looking. LME. 5 *v.t.* Recognize as distinct; separate mentally. *arch.* L15.

3 S. BELLOW I had learned to discern the real Kitty. A. N. WILSON Fiona had instantly discerned that he had been lying to her. 4 A. WILSON Meg, as November fogs thickened . . could not discern the outlines of the Cathedral. 5 J. RUSKIN Not having yet the taste to discern good Gothic from bad.

discerner *n.* E16. **discerning** *a.* that discerns; showing discernment, *esp.* having quick or true insight: L16. **discerningly** *adv.* with discernment M17.

discernible /dɪˈsəːnɪb(ə)l/ *a.* Also (earlier) **-able.** M16. [f. prec. + -ABLE; later conformed to L *discernibilis*: see -IBLE.] 1 Able to be discerned; perceptible. M16. †2 Distinguishable (*from* something else). Only in 17.

discernibleness *n.* E18. **discernibly** *adv.* M17.

discernment /dɪˈsəːnm(ə)nt/ *n.* Also †**decern-.** L16. [f. DISCERN + -MENT.] †1 The act of distinguishing; a distinction. L16–M17. 2 The faculty of discerning, discrimination; keenness of intellectual perception; insight. L16. 3 The act of discerning; intellectual perception. L17.

3 B. JOWETT The savage . . has a quicker discernment of the track than the civilized man.

discerp /dɪˈsəːp/ *v.t.* Now *rare.* Pa. t. & pple **discerped, -pt.** LME. [L *discerpere*, f. as DIS- 1 + *carpere* pick, pluck, etc.] 1 Tear or pluck to pieces. LME. 2 Tear or pluck off or out; sever (*from*). Cf. earlier DECERP. M17.

†**discerpible** *a.* M17–E18. [f. prec. + -IBLE.] = DISCERPTIBLE.

¶ Survived longer (-M19) in INDISCERPIBLE.

†**discerpibility** *n.* L17–E18.

discerptible /dɪˈsəːptɪb(ə)l/ *a. literary.* M18. [f. L *discerpt-* pa. ppl stem of *discerpere* (see prec.) + -IBLE.] Able to be plucked apart or divided into parts; not indestructibly one.

discerptiˈbility *n.* M18.

discerption /dɪˈsəːpʃ(ə)n/ *n.* Now *rare.* M17. [Late L *discerptio(n-)*, f. as prec.: see -ION.] 1 The action of pulling to pieces; fragmentation. M17. 2 The action of tearing off, severance; a portion torn off or severed. L17.

discette *n.* var. of DISKETTE.

discharge /ˈdɪstʃɑːdʒ, dɪsˈtʃɑːdʒ/ *n.* LME. [f. the vb.] 1 The act of freeing from obligation, liability, or restraint; exoneration from accusation or blame; release from a responsibility or position, or from service; release from custody; dismissal from office or employment. LME. b Something that frees from obligation; a certificate of this; a receipt. LME. 2 The act of freeing from or removing a load; unloading (*of* a ship etc.); removal (*of* a cargo etc.). L16. 3 The act of firing a weapon or missile, letting fly an arrow, etc. L16. 4 Fulfilment, execution, (of an obligation, duty, etc.). L16. 5 The act of settling a monetary liability; payment. E17. 6 The act of sending or pouring out; ejection; (the rate or amount of) emission. E17. b That which is emitted, esp. from a wound etc. L17. c The release of a quantity of electricity from a charged object; a flow of electricity through the air or other gas, esp. when accompanied by luminosity. M18. d The place where a river enters the sea or a lake. L18. 7 Formerly, the act of sending away. Now only in *Law*, dismissal or reversal of a court order. L17. 8 *Archit.* The relieving of some part of weight or pressure; a structure for effecting this. E18. 9 The process of removing the colour from a fabric; a mixture used for this. M19.

1 DISHONOURABLE *discharge.* HONOURABLE *discharge.* *undesirable discharge*: see UNDESIRABLE *a.* b DEFOE I sent for a notary, and caused him to draw up a general release or discharge. 4 L. TRILLING He charges women not to interfere with men in the discharge of their cultural duty. 5 T. JEFFERSON The discharge of the debt . . is vital to the destinies of our government. 6 SHAKES. *A.Y.L.* The wretched animal heav'd forth such groans That their discharge did stretch his leathern coat Almost to bursting. d *fig.*: A. STORR Whether there is, in animals or humans, an internal accumulation of aggressive tension which needs periodic discharge. TOWNSEND *discharge.*

Comb.: **discharge lamp, tube**: producing light by means of an electric discharge.

discharge /dɪsˈtʃɑːdʒ/ *v.* ME. [OFr. *descharger* (mod. *dé-*) f. late L *discar(r)icare* unload, f. L DIS- 2 + late L *car(ri)care*: see CHARGE *v.*] I With the person or thing relieved as (notional) obj. 1 *v.t.* Relieve *of* (an obligation etc.); exonerate; release *from*; relieve (a bankrupt) of residual liability. ME. †b Relieve (oneself) of an obligation by fulfilling it. L16–E18. 2a *v.t.* & *i.* Unload (a ship etc.); relieve of a load; disburden. LME. b *v.t.* Rid, deprive, (*of*). Now *rare.* LME. c *v.t.* Disburden (oneself) by speech. E16. d *v.t.* & *i.* Eject a projectile from (a weapon), fire (a weapon). M16. e *v.t.* & *i.* Release an electric charge (from). M18. 3 *v.t.* Command not to do something; prohibit, forbid. *obs.* exc. *dial.* LME. 4 *v.t.* Relieve of a responsibility or position; release from service; dismiss from office or employment. LME. †5 *v.t.* Clear of a charge or accusation; acquit. LME–M18. 6 *v.t.* Dismiss (a person charged with an offence); release from custody. M16. b Send away; let go. M16. 7 *v.t. Archit.* Relieve (some part) of pressure by distributing it over adjacent parts. M17.

1 SHAKES. *Much Ado* I discharge thee of thy prisoner. 2c E. BOWEN He could not discharge himself of what he had come out to say. 4 EVELYN Being . . discovered to be a rampant Socinian, he was discharged of employment. 6 A. PATON The guilt of the second and third accused is not established, and they will be accordingly discharged. b B. BAINBRIDGE Pamela was discharged from hospital.

II With the thing removed as (notional) obj. 8 *v.t.* Acquit oneself of (an obligation) by fulfilment or performance; pay (a debt etc.). LME. †b Pay for (an item); settle with (a creditor). M16–M19. †c Account for, explain. *rare* (Spenser). Only in L16. 9 *v.t.* Remove or have removed (a cargo or load). L15. b *v.t.* & *i.* Let fly (a missile, blow, etc.); fire (a shot). E16. c *v.t.* & *i.* (Allow to) escape or flow out; pour forth, emit; (of a river) empty (itself), flow *into*. E17. 10 *v.t.* †a Remove, abolish, (an obligation, institution, liability, etc.). E16–L18. b *Law.* Cancel, annul, (a court order). L18. 11 *v.t.* Acquit oneself of, perform, (an obligation, office, function, etc.). M16. 12a *v.t.* Remove (dye) *from* a textile etc.; pattern (a textile) by removing parts of the ground colour. E18. **b** *v.i.* Of ink, dye, etc.: be washed out, run when wet. L19.

9c SHAKES. *Macb.* Infected minds To their deaf pillows will discharge their secrets. ANTHONY HUXLEY Oil is discharged all over the oceans . . by ships cleaning out tanks.

dischargeable *a.* LME. **dischar'gee** *n.* a person who has been discharged L19. **discharger** *n.* a person who or thing which discharges; *spec.* an apparatus for producing an electric discharge: M16.

discharm /dɪs'tʃɑːm/ *v.i.* & *t. rare.* L15. [OFr. *de(s)charmer*, f. *des-* DIS- 2 + *charmer* CHARM *v.*[1]] Undo, or free from the influence of, a charm.

†**dischurch** *v.t.* E17. [f. DIS- 2 + CHURCH *n.*] **1** Deprive of the character of a church. E17–L19. **2** Exclude from the Church. M–L17.

disci- /'dɪsi, 'dɪski/ *comb. form* of L DISCUS: see -I-.

disciform *a.* disc-shaped, discoidal M19. **di'scigerous** *a.* (*Bot.*) bearing a disc or discs L19.

†**discide** *v.t.* L15–L17. [L *discidere*, f. as DIS- 1 + *caedere* to cut.] Cut in pieces; cut off or away.

SPENSER Her lying tongue was in two parts divided . . And as her tongue so was her hart discided.

discinct /dɪ'sɪŋkt/ *a. rare.* M17. [L *discinctus* pa. pple of *discingere* undo the belt or girdle of.] Not (tightly) girt; *fig.* unconfined.

disciple /dɪ'sʌɪp(ə)l/ *n.* OE. [L *discipulus* learner, f. *discere* learn; reinforced in ME by OFr *deciple.*] **1** One of the personal followers of Jesus during his life; *spec.* one of the twelve Apostles. OE. **b** In the New Testament, any early believer in Christ. Hence, in later religious use, a professed Christian. LME. **2** *gen.* A personal follower of a religious or other teacher. OE. **3** A follower of another person's example or doctrine; an adherent of a leader in thought, art, or conduct. ME. **4** A student, a pupil. Now *arch.*, *affected*, or *joc.* ME.

1 AV *John* 20:20 Then were the disciples glad, when they saw the Lord. **b** **Disciples (of Christ)** a Protestant denomination, found chiefly in the US, which rejects creeds and regards the Bible as the only basis of faith. 2 L. TRILLING Alfred Adler was . . an early disciple of Freud's who broke away from his master. 3 P. H. GIBBS She became a disciple of his liberal creed. G. S. FRASER In his clear, direct way of writing more a disciple of Jonson than of Donne.

disciplehood *n.* (now *rare*) = DISCIPLESHIP LME. **discipleship** *n.* the status of being a disciple M16.

disciple /dɪ'sʌɪp(ə)l/ *v.t.* L16. [f. the n.] **1** Train, educate. Long *rare.* L16. **2** Make a disciple of; *spec.* convert to Christianity. *arch.* E17. †**3** Subject to discipline or chastisement. E17–E19.

1 SPENSER Fraile youth is oft to follie led . . That better were in vertues discipled.

disciplinable /'dɪsɪplɪnəb(ə)l, dɪsɪ'plɪn-/ *a.* LME. [Late L *disciplinabilis* to be learned by teaching, f. *disciplinare* instruct: see DISCIPLINE *v.*, -ABLE.] **1** Amenable to instruction or training. LME. **2** Subject or liable to disciplinary action. L19.

disciplinal /'dɪsɪplɪn(ə)l, dɪsɪ'plʌɪn(ə)l/ *a.* E17. [In sense 1, f. late L *disciplinalis*; in sense 2, f. DISCIPLINE *n.* + -AL[1].] †**1** = DISCIPLINABLE 1. Only in E17. **2** Belonging to or of the nature of discipline. M19.

2 J. G. FITCH Disciplinal problems of a boarding-school.

disciplinant /'dɪsɪplɪnənt/ *n.* E17. [Sp. *disciplinantes* (pl.) or It. *disciplinanti* (pl.), f. med.L *disciplinare* DISCIPLINE *v.*: see -ANT[1].] *Eccl. Hist.* A member of a Spanish order of flagellants.

disciplinarian /ˌdɪsɪplɪ'nɛːrɪən/ *n.* & *a.* In *Eccl. Hist.* **D-**. L16. [f. as next + -AN: see -ARIAN.] **A** *n.* **1** *Eccl. Hist.* An Elizabethan Puritan who supported the Genevan or Presbyterian ecclesiastical polity. L16. **2** A person who maintains or advocates (strict) discipline in an army, school, etc. M17.

2 H. MELVILLE Three of these officers . . were strict disciplinarians.

B *adj.* **1** *Eccl. Hist.* Of or belonging to the Disciplinarians (see sense A.1 above). L16. **2** Pertaining to discipline; disciplinary. M17.

disciplinarianism *n.* the principles and practice of a disciplinarian M19.

disciplinary /'dɪsɪplɪn(ə)ri, dɪsɪ'plɪn-/ *a.* L15. [med.L *disciplinarius*, f. L *disciplina*: see DISCIPLINE *n.*, -ARY[1].] **1** Relating to ecclesiastical discipline (DISCIPLINE *n.* 6); formerly *spec.*, = DISCIPLINARIAN *a.* 1. L15. **2** Pertaining to the acquisition of learning. L15. **3** Pertaining to, promoting, or enforcing disciplined behaviour. L16.

3 G. B. SHAW He [a private soldier] is taught his proper place by appropriate disciplinary measures. *Daily Mirror* The Test and County Cricket Board's disciplinary committee.

disciplinarily *adv.* (*rare*) E18.

disciplinatory /'dɪsɪplɪˌneɪt(ə)ri, dɪsɪ'plɪnət(ə)ri/ *a.* M19. [med.L *disciplinatorius*, f. L *disciplinat-* pa. ppl stem of *disciplinare* DISCIPLINE *v.*: see -ORY[2].] Tending to promote discipline.

discipline /'dɪsɪplɪn/ *n.* ME. [(O)Fr. f. L *disciplina*, f. *discipulus* DISCIPLE *n.*] **1** Chastisement or correction undergone as a penance, self-mortification. Also, a beating or similar punishment. ME. **b** A scourge or whip, esp. as an instrument of penance. E17. **2**†**a** Instruction given to pupils or disciples; teaching, education. LME–E17. **b** A particular course of discipleship or corpus of doctrines. *rare.* M17. **3** A branch of learning or scholarly instruction. LME. **4** Instruction fitting one to perform an activity; training. Freq. *fig.*, moral progress brought about by adversity etc. LME. **b** *spec.* Training in military exercises etc.; drill. Formerly, knowledge of military tactics; the art of war. LME. †**c** Medical treatment, regimen. *rare.* M18–E19. **5** Controlled and orderly behaviour resulting from training. E16. **b** The system of order and strict obedience to rules enforced among pupils, soldiers, or others under authority; a particular instance of this. M17. **6** The system by which a Church maintains order and exercises control over its members. M16. **b** The system by which the practices of a Church (as opp. to its doctrines) are regulated; *spec.* (*Eccl. Hist.*) the Calvinist polity, adopted by the Presbyterians and Puritans. M16.

1 J. SERGEANT If any be found unchast, she receives three Disciplines or scourgings. **2b** **Discipline of the Secret** the practice ascribed to the early Church of excluding catechumens and pagans from certain doctrines and rites. 3 *Lancet* Disciplines such as biochemistry and immunology. 5 H. H. KITCHENER It will be your duty . . to set an example of discipline and perfect steadiness under fire. **b** F. MARRYAT A flagrant . . violation of discipline. M. PATTISON The inmates . . were submitted to an almost monastic discipline. M. EDWARDES Taking the company as a whole discipline was lax.

discipline /'dɪsɪplɪn/ *v.t.* ME. [(O)Fr. *discipliner* or late L *disciplinare*, f. L *disciplina* DISCIPLINE *n.*] **1** Scourge or flog as a penance or in self-mortification; *gen.* thrash, chastise. ME. **2** Give instruction to, educate, train. Now *rare.* LME. **3** Train in habits of obedience, bring under control; *spec.* drill (troops). L16. **4** Subject (esp. a member of a Church or other organization) to formal rebuke, loss of privileges, etc., for an offence. E19.

1 SHAKES. *Coriol.* Has he disciplin'd Aufidius soundly? 3 C. BRONTË Suppose you were no longer a girl well reared and disciplined, but a boy indulged from childhood. A. J. P. TAYLOR An alliance of men with widely differing views, not a disciplined army. 4 *New York Times* If McEnroe was not harshly disciplined by tennis officials for his disruptive antics.

discipliner *n.* LME.

discipular /dɪ'sɪpjʊlə/ *a.* M19. [f. L *discipulus* DISCIPLE *n.* + -AR[1].] Of, belonging to, or of the nature of a disciple.

discission /dɪ'sɪʃ(ə)n/ *n.* M17. [Late L *discissio(n-)*, f. L *disciss-* pa. ppl stem of *discindere* split in two, f. as DIS- 1 + *scindere* cleave, tear.] An act of tearing or cutting apart. Now only *Surg.*, an incision, esp. into the lens of the eye in a case of cataract.

disclaim /dɪs'kleɪm/ *n.* Now *rare.* LME. [AN *disclaime*, f. *disclamer*: see next.] A (formal) denial or repudiation of a claim.

disclaim /dɪs'kleɪm/ *v.* LME. [AN *desclaim-* tonic stem of *desclamer*, *dis-* (AL *disclamare*), f. *des-* DIS- 1 + *clamer* CLAIM *v.*] **I** *v.i.* **1** *Law.* Renounce one's claim to something; repudiate another's claim; make a formal disclaimer. (Foll. by †*in* the thing disclaimed, †*from* or †*out of* the claim of the other party.) LME. †**2** Renounce all part *in*; express one's withdrawal or dissent *from.* M16–M17. †**3** Cry out or declaim *against.* E17–M18.

2 JONSON The sourer sort Of shepherds now disclaim in all such sport.

II *v.t.* **4** Renounce all (legal) claim to. LME. **b** Relinquish (part of a patent) by a disclaimer (DISCLAIMER *n.*[1] 1b). M19. **5** Deny one's possession of or connection with; disown, disavow. L16. †**b** Refuse to acknowledge (a person) to be (so and so). L16–L17. †**6** Attack the pretensions of. L16–M17. †**7** Decline, refuse, *to do.* L16–E19. **8** Refuse to admit (something claimed by another); reject the authority of. M17. **b** *Her.* Declare to have no right to bear a coat of arms. M17.

5 T. HEYWOOD Sir, shee's yours, Or I disclaime her ever. I. D'ISRAELI The real author . . obliged him afterwards to disclaim the work in print. D. HAMMETT He . . disclaimed any knowledge of his client's whereabouts. **b** I. WALTON To perswade him . . to disclaim himself a Member of the Church of England. 8 GIBBON The troops . . disclaimed the command of their superiors.

disclaimant *n.* (*Law*) a person who disclaims (esp. part of a patent specification) L19.

disclaimer /dɪs'kleɪmə/ *n.*[1] LME. [AN *disclaimer* inf. used as n.: see prec., -ER[4].] **1** *Law.* The action or an act of repudiating another's claim or renouncing one's own; refusal to accept a trust etc. LME. **b** An alteration by which a patentee amends specification so as to relinquish part of his or her claim to an invention. M19. **2** *gen.* A denial of a claim, pretension, etc.; a disavowal. L18. **3** *Her.* An announcement by heralds of people not entitled to armorial bearings. M19.

2 E. WAUGH The Bishop . . believes I am a secret envoy from the Pope and laughs away all my disclaimers as modesty and guile.

disclaimer /dɪs'kleɪmə/ *n.*[2] E18. [f. DISCLAIM *v.* + -ER[1].] A person who disclaims or renounces something.

disclamation /dɪsklə'meɪʃ(ə)n/ *n.* M16. [med.L *disclamatio(n-)*, f. *disclamat-* pa. ppl stem of *disclamare*: see DISCLAIM *v.*, -ATION.] **1** *Sc. Law.* A feudal tenant's disavowal of a person as a superior. M16. **2** *gen.* Repudiation; a disclaimer. E17.

†**disclose** *n.* M16–M18. [f. the vb.] The act of disclosing; (a) disclosure.

disclose /dɪs'kləʊz/ *v.* LME. [OFr. *desclos-* pres. stem of *desclore* f. Proto-Gallo-Romance, f. L DIS- 2 + *claudere* CLOSE *v.*] †**1** *v.t.* & *i.* Open up (something closed or folded up); unclose, unfold. LME–E18. **2** *v.t.* Remove the cover from; expose to view. LME. **b** Hatch (a young bird etc., *fig.* mischief). Now *rare* or *obs.* LME. **3** *v.t.* Make known, reveal. LME. †**4** *v.i.* Come to light. L15–M18.

1 B. GOOGE It [a rosebud] discloseth it selfe and spreadeth abroad. 2 H. JAMES The . . portal remained ajar, disclosing possible vistas. W. BOYD Small sharp teeth disclosed by a mouth continually parted in a smile. 3 H. ADAMS The Normans . . disclose most unexpected qualities. E. WAUGH Inquiries . . disclosed that a young lady . . had appeared in the booking office early that afternoon.

disclosed *ppl a.* (*a*) that has been disclosed; (*b*) *Her.* (of a non-predacious bird) depicted with wings outspread: L15. **discloser** *n.* M16. **disclosing** *ppl a.* (*a*) that discloses; (*b*) *Dentistry* (of a tablet, solution, etc.) revealing, by means of a special dye, any plaque on the teeth: E17.

disclosure /dɪs'kləʊʒə/ *n.* L16. [f. DISCLOSE *v.* + -URE, after *closure.*] **1** The action or an act of making known or visible. L16. **2** The hatching of young from the egg; the liberation of an insect from the pupa. Now *rare* or *obs.* M17. **3** That which is disclosed; a revelation. E19.

1 J. I. M. STEWART There had still been no public disclosure of the state of the tower.

disco /ˈdɪskəʊ/ *n.* & *v.* M20. [Abbrev. of DISCOTHÈQUE.] A *n.* Pl. **-os.** 1 A place or event at which recorded pop music is played for dancing. M20. 2 More fully *disco music.* Pop music of the kind played at discos, with a heavy bass beat. L20. B *v.i.* Dance at a disco or in the style characteristic of discos. L20.

discobolus /dɪˈskɒbələs/ *n.* Pl. **-li** /-lʌɪ, -liː/. E18. [L f. Gk *diskobolos*, f. as DISCUS + *-bolos* throwing, f. *ballein* to throw.] *Class. Hist.* A discus-thrower; a statue representing one in action.

discography /dɪˈskɒɡrəfi/ *n.* M20. [f. DISC *n.* + -OGRAPHY.] A catalogue of sound recordings; *esp.* a compilation of the recordings of a particular artist or composer.
discographer *n.* M20. **discoˈgraphical** *a.* M20.

discoid /ˈdɪskɔɪd/ *a.* & *n.* L18. [Gk *diskoeidēs*, f. *diskos*: see DISCUS, -OID.] A *adj.* Disc-shaped; *Bot.* (of a plant of the composite family) bearing flowers consisting of a disc without rays. L18. B *n.* A disc-shaped structure. E19.
diˈscoidal *a.* discoid E18.

discolor *n.*, *v.* see DISCOLOUR *n.*, *v.*

discolorate /dɪsˈkʌləreɪt/ *v.t. rare.* Also **-lour-**. M17. [med.L *discolorat-*: see next, -ATE³.] = DISCOLOUR *v.* 1.

discoloration /dɪsˌkʌləˈreɪʃ(ə)n, ˌdɪsk-/ *n.* Also **-lour-**. M17. [Fr. (now *décoloration*), or med.L *discoloratio(n-)*, f. *discolorat-* pa. ppl stem of *discolorare* DISCOLOUR *v.*: see -ATION.] 1 The action of discolouring; the state of being discoloured; alteration or loss of colour. M17. 2 A discoloured marking etc., a stain. L17.

discolour /dɪsˈkʌlə/ *n.* Now *rare.* Also ***-color**. LME. [f. DIS- 2 + COLOUR *n.*] = DISCOLORATION.

discolour /dɪsˈkʌlə/ *v.* Also ***-color**. LME. [In senses 1 & 2 f. OFr. *descolorer* or med.L *discolorare*, f. L *colorare* COLOUR *v.*; in sense 3 f. L *discolor* adj., f. *color* COLOUR *n.*: see DIS- 2.] 1 *v.t.* Change or spoil the colour of; *esp.* make duller or dingier; stain, tarnish. LME. 2 *v.i.* Become discoloured; lose or change colour. LME. †3 *v.t.* Cause to be of various colours. Chiefly as *discoloured* ppl a. L15–M17.
1 *fig.*: R. L. STEVENSON We had each of us some whimsy . . which discoloured all experience to its own shade.
discolourment *n.* the action or result of discolouring, discoloration. E19.

discolourate *v.* **-ation** *n.* vars. of DISCOLORATE, -ATION.

discombobulate /dɪskəmˈbɒbjʊleɪt/ *v.t. N. Amer. slang.* Also **-boberate** /-ˈbɒbəreɪt/ & other vars. M19. [Prob. alt. of *discompose* or *discomfit.*] Disturb, upset, disconcert.
ˌdiscombobuˈlation *n.* M19.

discomfit /dɪsˈkʌmfɪt/ *v.* & *n.* ME. [OFr. *desconfit* pa. pple of *desconfire* (mod. *déconfire*) f. Proto-Romance, f. L DIS- 2 + *conficere* put together, destroy, consume, f. as CON- + *facere* do.] A *v.t.* 1 Defeat in battle; beat, rout. *arch.* ME. 2 Baffle, thwart, defeat the plans, hopes, or purposes of; throw into confusion, disconcert, embarrass. LME.
2 R. SHARROCK Not impeded by those wants that usually discomfit private persons in such enquiries. W. STYRON He seemed flustered, discomfited.
†**B** *n.* Discomfiture. ME–M19.
discomfiter *n.* E16.

discomfiture /dɪsˈkʌmfɪtʃə/ *n.* ME. [OFr. *desconfiture* (mod. *déconfiture*), f. as prec.; see -URE.] 1 Complete defeat in battle, rout. *arch.* ME. 2 Defeat or frustration of plans, hopes, or purposes; utter disappointment; confusion, embarrassment. LME.
1 SHAKES. *1 Hen. VI* Sad tidings . . Of loss, of slaughter, and discomfiture. 2 D. WELCH Laughing to cover up my discomfiture.

discomfort /dɪsˈkʌmfət/ *n.* LME. [OFr. *desconfort* (mod. *dé-*), f. as next.] †1 Loss or deprivation of courage; discouragement, disheartenment. LME–M16. †2 Absence or deprivation of comfort, pleasure, or gladness; distress, grief, sorrow; annoyance. Also, something that causes this. LME–M19. 3 Uneasiness of body or mind; lack of comfort (*lit.* & *fig.*). Also, something which makes one uncomfortable, an inconvenience, a hardship. M19.
2 LONGFELLOW Thus did that poor soul wander in want and cheerless discomfort. 3 E. BAKKER Her towering over him added to his discomfort. P. THEROUX The journey was not worth this discomfort.

discomfort /dɪsˈkʌmfət/ *v.t.* ME. [OFr. *desconforter* (mod. *dé-*), f. as DIS- 2, COMFORT *v.*] I†1 Deprive of courage or strength of mind; dishearten, dismay. ME–E18. 2 Deprive of comfort, pleasure, or gladness; distress, sadden; make unhappy. *arch.* ME. 3 Make uneasy or uncomfortable in mind or body. M19. II 4 = DISCOMFIT *v.* LME.
discomforter *n.* a person who or thing which discomforts E19.

discomfortable /dɪsˈkʌmf(ə)təb(ə)l/ *a.* Now *rare.* LME. [OFr. *desconfortable*, f. as prec.: see -ABLE.] 1 Causing discouragement, distress, annoyance, etc.; destructive of comfort, pleasure, or happiness. LME. †2 Marked by an absence of comfort or happiness; miserable. E16–E17. 3 Lacking in material comfort; causing physical discomfort. E17. 4 Of a person: feeling uncomfortable, uneasy. *rare.* M19.
1 R. L. STEVENSON Singing was their refuge from discomfortable thoughts.
discomfortableness *n.* L16. **discomfortably** *adv.* E17.

discomforture /dɪsˈkʌmfətʃə/ *n. rare.* LME. [f. DISCOMFORT *v.* + -URE, after DISCOMFITURE.] Distress; (a) discomfort. Also, discomfiture.

discommend /dɪskəˈmɛnd/ *v.* LME. [f. DIS- 2 + COMMEND *v.*] 1 *v.t.* & *i.* Find fault (with), express disapproval (of). LME. 2 *v.t.* Speak dissuasively of; advise against the use etc. of. M16. 3 *v.t.* Cause to be received or looked on unfavourably. Now *rare* or *obs.* L16.
discommendable *a.* (*a*) worthy of censure; †(*b*) not to be recommended: E16. **disˌcommenˈdation** *n.* the action or an act of discommending L16.

discommodate /dɪsˈkɒmədeɪt/ *v.t.* Long *rare.* E17. [Prob. alt. of INCOMMODATE.] Inconvenience, incommode.

discommode /dɪskəˈməʊd/ *v.t.* E18. [Fr. †*discommoder* var. of *incommoder* INCOMMODE *v.*: see DIS- 2.] Put to inconvenience; disturb, trouble.

discommodious /dɪskəˈməʊdɪəs/ *a.* Long *rare.* M16. [f. DIS- 2 + COMMODIOUS.] Causing trouble or inconvenience; disadvantageous, troublesome.
discommodiously *adv.* M17. **discommodiousness** *n.* L16.

discommodity /dɪskəˈmɒdɪti/ *n.* E16. [f. DIS- 2 + COMMODITY, perh. infl. by INCOMMODITY.] 1 The quality of being unsuitable or inconvenient. E16. 2 A disadvantage, an inconvenience. M16.

discommon /dɪsˈkɒmən/ *v.t.* LME. [f. DIS- 2 + COMMON *n.*, *a.*: cf. also COMMON *v.*] †1 Cut off from membership of a community; disfranchise; excommunicate. LME–M17. 2 In the universities of Oxford and Cambridge: deprive (a tradesman) of the right to deal with undergraduates. Now *Hist.* M16. 3 Deprive of the right of common; deprive (land) of the status of a common, enclose. L16.

discommons /dɪsˈkɒmənz/ *v.t.* Now *Hist.* M19. [f. DIS- 2 + COMMONS *n.pl.*] 1 Deprive (an undergraduate) of commons. M19. 2 = DISCOMMON 2. M19.

discommune /dɪsˈkɒmjuːn/ *v.t.* L16. [f. DIS- 2 + COMMUNE *v.* or *n.*¹, after med.L *discommunicare.*] 1 = DISCOMMON 1. Long *rare.* L16. 2 = DISCOMMON 2. Now *Hist.* L17.

discompose /dɪskəmˈpəʊz/ *v.t.* L15. [f. DIS- 2 + COMPOSE.] 1 Disturb the composure of; ruffle, agitate. L15. 2 Disturb the order or arrangement of; throw into confusion. Now *rare* or *obs.* E17. †3 Make ill or indisposed. Chiefly as *discomposed* ppl a. L17–E18.
1 J. SMEATON Not a breath of wind discomposed the surface of the water. 2 MILTON Unwak'ned Eve With Tresses discompos'd.
discomposedly /-zɪdli/ *adv.* in a discomposed manner E17. **discomposedness** /-zɪdnɪs/ *n.* disturbed state, disquietude L17. **discomposingly** *adv.* in a way that discomposes L19.

discomposure /dɪskəmˈpəʊʒə/ *n.* E17. [f. prec. after COMPOSURE.] 1 Disorder, confusion; disarrangement. Now *rare* or *obs.* E17. †2 Indisposition, ill health. M17–M18. 3 Disturbance of mind or feelings; agitation, perturbation. M17.
1 MILTON The Prelates . . put all things into a foule discomposure. 3 LD MACAULAY A series of sermons was preached . . by Popish divines, to the great discomposure of zealous churchmen.

†**disconcert** *n. rare.* M17–M19. [f. DIS- 2 + CONCERT *n.*] Lack of agreement or concerted action, disunity in action.

disconcert /dɪskənˈsəːt/ *v.* L17. [Fr. *desconcerter* (now *dé-*), f. as DIS- 2, CONCERT *v.*] 1 *v.t.* Upset the progress or action of; spoil plans for, defeat expectations of. L17. 2 *v.t.* Disturb the self-possession of; ruffle, fluster. E18. b *v.i.* Disturb self-possession, be upsetting. Chiefly as *disconcerting* ppl a. E19.
1 LD MACAULAY The scheme was . . completely disconcerted by the course which the civil war took. 2 B. PYM He was disconcerted to find that he had lost his place. b *Smart Set* A baffling reserve, a poise that disconcerted. Q. BELL She could do disconcerting things—calmly throw a pair of scissors into the fire.
disconcertedly *adv.* in a disconcerted manner M19. **disconcertingly** *adv.* in a manner that disconcerts one L19. **disconcertion** *n.* = DISCONCERTMENT L18. **disconcertment** *n.* the action of disconcerting; the state of being disconcerted: M19.

disconformable /dɪskənˈfɔːməb(ə)l/ *a.* L16. [f. DIS- 2 + CONFORMABLE.] †1 *gen.* Not conformable. L16–E19. 2 *Geol.* Containing or constituting a disconformity. E20.

disconformity /dɪskənˈfɔːmɪti/ *n.* L16. [f. DIS- 2 + CONFORMITY.] 1 Complete lack of agreement or correspondence; nonconformity. (Foll. by *to*, *with.*) L16. 2 *Geol.* An unconformity in which the strata above and below are more or less parallel, the lower set having been eroded but not deformed. E20.

disconnect /dɪskəˈnɛkt/ *v.t.* L18. [f. DIS- 2 + CONNECT.] 1 Break the connection of or between; *spec.* terminate the connection of (a device, household, etc.) to an electricity etc. supply or a telephone network. (Foll. by *from*, †*with.*) L18. †2 Separate into individual components, fragment. (Cf. DISCONNECTED *a.* 2.) L18–E19.
1 T. HOOD It was impossible to disconnect him with old clothes and oranges. G. SWIFT I disconnect the television, carry it out to the car.
disconnectable *a.* M20. **disconnecter**, **-or** *n.* a device for breaking a connection L19.

disconnected /dɪskəˈnɛktɪd/ *ppl a.* L18. [f. prec. + -ED¹.] 1 Having no connection (*with*); detached (*from*); separated. L18. 2 Having constituent parts badly connected; (of speech, a speaker, etc.) incoherent, rambling. L19.
1 HANNAH MORE The chronology being reduced to disconnected dates, instead of presenting an unbroken series.
disconnectedly *adv.* M19. **disconnectedness** *n.* L19.

disconnection /dɪskəˈnɛkʃ(ə)n/ *n.* Also (earlier) **-connexion**. M18. [f. DISCONNECT after *connection.*] The state or fact of being disconnected; lack of connection, disconnectedness; the action of disconnecting.

disconsolate /dɪsˈkɒns(ə)lət/ *a.* & *v.* LME. [med.L *disconsolatus*, f. L DIS- 2 + *consolatus* pa. pple of *consolari* CONSOLE *v.*] A *adj.* 1 Without consolation or comfort; forlorn, inconsolable; unhappy, disappointed. LME. 2 Of a place, thing, etc.: causing or showing a complete lack of comfort; cheerless, miserable. LME.
1 C. C. TRENCH The death of the Queen . . was a sad blow to Caroline, who had to return disconsolate to Anspach. 2 DEFOE A desolate, disconsolate wilderness. O. MANNING She made a disconsolate little gesture.
†**B** *v.t.* Make disconsolate; deprive of consolation. M16–M18.
disconsolately *adv.* M17. **disconsolateness** *n.* M17. **disconsoˈlation** *n.* disconsolate condition L16. †**disconsolatory** *a.* (*rare*) that makes disconsolate, saddening M17–E19.

discontent /dɪskən'tɛnt/ *n.*[1] L16. [f. DIS- 2 + CONTENT *n.*[1]] 1 Lack of content; dissatisfaction. L16. †b Annoyance, displeasure. Only in 17. 2 A feeling of discontent. L16. †3 A cause of discontent, a grievance. E–M17.

discontentful *a.* (*arch.*) E17.

discontent /dɪskən'tɛnt/ *a.* & *n.*[2] Now *rare.* LME. [f. DIS- 2 + CONTENT *a.*: cf. Fr. †*descontent.*] A *adj.* 1 Discontented; dissatisfied. LME. †2 Displeased, annoyed. L15–M17.

1 *Times* Non-Christian groups in Britain which are discontent with state schooling.

B *n.*[2] A discontented person, a malcontent. L16.

discontent /dɪskən'tɛnt/ *v.t.* L15. [f. DIS- 2 + CONTENT *v.*: cf. Fr. †*descontenter.*] 1 Displease, annoy. Now *rare.* L15. 2 Deprive of contentment; make dissatisfied; unsettle through frustration, disappointment, etc. Chiefly as *discontented* ppl a. E16.

†**discontentation** *n.* = DISCONTENT *n.*[1] 1, 3 M16–M18. **discontentedly** *adv.* in a discontented manner L16. **discontentedness** *n.* discontent, dissatisfaction L16. **discontentment** *n.* (*a*) = DISCONTENT *n.*[1] 1, 2; †(*b*) = DISCONTENT *n.*[1] 3: L16.

discontinuance /dɪskən'tɪnjʊəns/ *n.* LME. [AN *discontinuaunce*, OFr. *-ance*, f. as DISCONTINUE: see -ANCE.] 1 The action of discontinuing; temporary or permanent interruption; cessation. LME. b The interruption or cessation of a lawsuit by the plaintiff. M16. 2 *Law.* The loss of the right of possession or entry by an heir to an estate following its wrongful alienation by a deceased tenant. Now *Hist.* LME. †3 Temporary absence from a place, *spec.* one's home. Only in 17.

discontinuation /ˌdɪskəntɪnjʊ'eɪʃ(ə)n/ *n.* E17. [(O)Fr. f. med.L *discontinuatio(n-)*, f. *discontinuat-* pa. ppl stem of *discontinuare*: see next, -ATION.] = DISCONTINUANCE 1.

discontinue /dɪskən'tɪnjuː/ *v.* LME. [(O)Fr. *discontinuer* f. med.L *discontinuare*, f. L DIS- 2 + *continuare* CONTINUE *v.*] I *v.t.* †1 Break the continuity of; interrupt, disrupt, sunder. LME–L18. 2 Cause to cease existing or being done, put a stop to; cease from (an action or habit); stop taking (a periodical) or paying (a subscription); *Law* †dismiss or abandon (a suit). LME. †3 *Law.* Alienate (land etc.) so as to cause discontinuance. LME–E19. †4 Cease to frequent, occupy, or inhabit. L15–M17.

1 J. RAY This bank of earth . . is discontinued by seven . . breaks or apertures. 2 M. SPARK Freddy decided to discontinue the lessons with Abdul. 4 SHAKES. *Much Ado* I must discontinue your company.

II *v.i.* 5 Cease to continue; cease, stop. LME. †6 Be absent (*from*); cease to reside. Only in 17.

5 J. BARET To discontinue a while from labour. 6 AV *Jer.* 17:4 Thou . . shalt discontinue from thine heritage that I gave thee.

discontinu'ee *n.* (*Hist.*) a person to whom an estate was alienated in a case of discontinuance L16. **discontinuer** *n.* (*a*) a person who discontinues something; (*b*) *spec.* an absentee: L16. **discontinuor** *n.* (*Hist.*) the tenant whose alienation of an estate caused a discontinuance L18.

discontinuity /ˌdɪskɒntɪ'njuːɪti/ *n.* L16. [med.L *discontinuitas*, f. as next: see -ITY.] 1 The quality or state of being discontinuous; lack of continuity; interrupted condition. L16. 2 A break in continuity; an abrupt change in value; *Math.* a point at which a function is discontinuous or undefined. L18.

2 **discontinuity layer** a layer of seawater etc. in which the temperature changes rapidly with depth.

discontinuous /dɪskən'tɪnjʊəs/ *a.* M17. [med.L *discontinuus*, f. as DIS- 2, CONTINUOUS: cf. Fr. *discontinu.*] †1 Producing discontinuity; breaking continuity between parts; gaping. M17–E18. 2 Not continuous in space or time; characterized by lack of continuity; having interstices or breaks; interrupted, intermittent. E18.

1 MILTON The griding sword with discontinuous wound Pass'd through him. 2 A. LURIE Are we persuading our readers to divide their lives into ever smaller, discontinuous bits? **discontinuous function** *Math.* that has one or more discontinuities (cf. *continuous*).

discontinuously *adv.* in a discontinuous manner, without continuity M19. **discontinuousness** *n.* discontinuous condition, lack of continuity M19.

disconvenience /dɪskən'viːnɪəns/ *n.* & *v.* Now *dial.* LME. [f. DIS- 2 + CONVENIENCE *n.*, or alt. of INCONVENIENCE *n.*] A *n.* †1 Lack of agreement or correspondence; incongruity, inconsistency. LME. †2 Unfitness, unsuitability, impropriety. LME–L16. 3 (A) disadvantage; (an) inconvenience. M16. B *v.t.* Inconvenience. E19.

disconvenient /dɪskən'viːnɪənt/ *a.* Now *dial.* LME. [f. DIS- 2 + CONVENIENT, or alt. of INCONVENIENT.] †1 Not in accordance (*with*); incongruous; unsuitable. LME–M17. 2 Inconvenient, disadvantageous. LME.

discophile /'dɪskəfʌɪl/ *n.* Also **-phil** /-fɪl/. M20. [f. DISC *n.* + -O- + -PHILE.] A person who collects or is interested in gramophone records or compact discs.

discord /'dɪskɔːd/ *n.* ME. [OFr. *descord*, *dis-* (mod. *discord(e)*), f. as next.] 1 Disagreement between persons; dissension, strife. ME. 2 Lack of agreement between things; difference, incongruity. LME. 3 *Mus.* Lack of harmony between notes sounded together, dissonance; a chord, interval, or note producing this, *spec.* any interval except the unison, octave, perfect fifth and fourth, major and minor third and sixth, and their octave. Cf. CONCORD *n.*[1] 2b. LME. 4 A clashing of sounds, a confused noise; a harsh or unpleasing sound. L16.

1 SHAKES. *1 Hen. VI* An age of discord and continual strife. APPLE *of discord.* 2 R. MACAULAY This makes a discord in the mind, the happiness and the guilt . . pulling in opposite directions.

di'scordful *a.* (*rare*) full of discord, quarrelsome L16. **discordous** *a.* (long *rare*) discordant L16.

discord /dɪ'skɔːd/ *v.i.* ME. [OFr. *descorder*, (also mod.) *dis-*, f. L *discordare* be at variance, f. *discors*, *discord-* discordant, f. as DIS- 2 + *cor*, *cord-* heart.] 1 Be in disagreement, quarrel, (*with*); dissent (*from*). ME. 2 Of sounds: be discordant, clash. Now *rare.* ME. 3 Be different (*from*), be inconsistent (*with*). LME.

1 CARLYLE We discorded commonly on two points. 3 R. FABYAN Thyse two nacions discorde in maners, but nat in clothing and in fayth. S. HIERON Not because it accordeth or discordeth with the original.

discordance /dɪ'skɔːd(ə)ns/ *n.* ME. [OFr. *descordance*, (also mod.) *dis-*, f. med.L *discordantia*, f. L *discordare*: see prec., -ANCE.] 1 Lack of agreement or conformity. ME. 2 Discord of sounds. LME.

Also **discordancy** *n.* E17.

discordant /dɪ'skɔːd(ə)nt/ *a.* & *n.* LME. [OFr. *descordant*, (also mod.) *dis-* pres. pple of *discorder*: see DISCORD *v.*, -ANT[1].] A *adj.* 1 Not in accord; at variance; disagreeing, differing; incongruous. (Foll. by *from*, *with*, †*to*.) LME. 2 *spec.* Of a sound or musical instrument: inharmonious, dissonant; jarring. LME. 3 Living in discord, quarrelsome. M16. 4 *Geol.* Having a direction that cuts across that of adjacent or underlying strata. E20.

1 GLADSTONE Testimony . . in no case discordant with that of the Iliad. 2 J. C. POWYS A series of shrill discordant screams. 3 WELLINGTON He united that discordant and turbulent race.

†B *n.* In *pl.* Discordant things, attributes, or propositions. LME–M16.

discordantly *adv.* LME.

discothèque /'dɪskətɛk/ *n.* Also **-theque**. M20. [Fr., orig. = record-library, after *bibliothèque*: cf. DISC *n.* 3b.] = DISCO *n.* 1.

discounsel /dɪs'kaʊns(ə)l/ *v.t.* Long *rare.* Infl. **-ll-**, ***-l-**. L15. [OFr. *desconseillier* (mod. *déconseiller*), f. as DIS- 2, COUNSEL *v.*] †1 Dissuade (*from* a course of action). L15–E17. 2 Advise against (an action or undertaking). L16.

discount /'dɪskaʊnt/ *n.* E17. [Fr. †*descompte* (earlier *desconte*, now *décompte*), f. *descompter*: see next.] †1 *gen.* A reduction in the amount or in the gross value of something. E17–L18. 2 *spec.* A deduction (usu. a certain percentage) made from an amount due or a price in return for prompt or early payment, or offered to special customers; any deduction made from a nominal value or price. L17. 3a The percentage (representing the interest on the payment) deducted from the face value of a bill of exchange or promissory note when it changes hands before the due date. L17. b *Stock Exch.* The amount by which the price of a stock falls short of its issue price or the value of the assets it represents; *gen.* the amount by which an actual price falls short of a nominal one. E18. 4 The action or an act of discounting a bill, note, etc. M19.

Phrases: **at a discount** at less than the nominal value or price; *fig.* in low esteem: opp. *at a premium. trade discount*: see TRADE *n.*

Attrib. & *comb.*: In the sense 'regularly offering goods at less than the standard price', as *discount shop*, *store*, etc. Special combs., as **discount-broker** a person who procures the discounting of bills of exchange, usu. by acting as intermediary; a dealer in bills; **discount house** (*a*) in Britain, a firm specializing in buying and selling bills of exchange; (*b*) (chiefly *US*) a discount shop (see above).

discount /dɪs'kaʊnt, 'dɪskaʊnt/ *v.t.* E17. [Fr. †*descompter* (mod. *décompter*), in commercial senses prob. f. It. (*di*)*scontare*, both f. med.L *discomputare*, f. L DIS- 2 + *computare* COMPUTE *v.*] I†1 Deduct or regard as deducted, esp. from a sum due. E17–E19. 2 Buy or sell (a bill of exchange) at a discount (DISCOUNT *n.* 3). L17. 3 Reduce (a price); reduce in price; *esp.* sell (goods) at a discount. M20.

II *fig.* 4 Leave out of account as unimportant or irrelevant; allow for falsehood or exaggeration in (statements). E18. 5 Reduce the effect of (a possible future event or sensation) by taking it into account beforehand. Also, part with (a future good) for some present consideration. M19.

4 C. J. WILLS One learns to mentally discount the statements made by the natives. G. GREENE He gave me . . good advice which I was unwise enough to discount. W. GOLDING That was the least of the dangers . . and one almost to be discounted. 5 G. BRIMLEY Discounting immortality for pottage.

di'scountable *a.* that may be discounted; (of a period) within which a bill may be discounted: E19. **di'scounter** *n.* (*a*) a person who discounts a bill; (*b*) a person engaged in discount trading: M18.

discountenance /dɪ'skaʊntɪnəns/ *n. arch.* L16. [Partly f. OFr. *descontenance*; partly f. DIS- 2 + COUNTENANCE *n.*, after next.] The fact or an act of discountenancing; disfavour or disapprobation shown.

SHELLEY The discountenance which Government will show to such an association.

discountenance /dɪs'kaʊnt(ə)nəns, -tɪn-/ *v.t.* L16. [f. DIS- 2 + COUNTENANCE *n.*, partly after Fr. †*descontenancer.*] 1 Put out of countenance, abash, embarrass. Chiefly as *discountenanced* ppl a. L16. 2 Discourage with cold looks, express disfavour of, (esp. an activity, practice, etc.); refuse to sanction or allow. L16.

2 G. ORWELL 'Mrs.' was a word somewhat discountenanced by the Party.

discountenancer *n.* E17.

discouple /dɪs'kʌp(ə)l/ *v.t.* Now *rare.* L15. [OFr. *descupler* (mod. *découpler*), f. as DIS- 2, COUPLE *v.*] End the pairing of, uncouple.

discourage /dɪs'kʌrɪdʒ/ *v.t.* LME. [OFr. *descouragier* (mod. *décourager*), f. as DIS- 2, COURAGE.] 1 Deprive of courage, confidence, hope, or the will to proceed; dishearten, deject. LME. 2 Dissuade or deter *from* (†*for*, †*to do*). LME. 3 Inhibit or seek to prevent (an action etc.) by expressing disapproval. M17.

1 J. CONRAD This discouraged Schomberg, who had looked up hopefully. A. J. CRONIN It must be dreadfully discouraging, to meet always with abuse. 3 J. YEATS Laws were made to discourage usury.

discourager *n.* M17. **discouragingly** *adv.* in a discouraging manner L17.

discouragement /dɪs'kʌrɪdʒm(ə)nt/ *n.* M16. [OFr. *descouragement* (mod. *dé-*), f. as prec.: see -MENT.] 1 The state of being discouraged; lack of inclination to act or make an attempt. M16. 2 The action or fact of discouraging. E17. 3 A discouraging thing, event, or influence. E17.

3 E. WAUGH Too hasty publication would be a discouragement to you now.

discourse /'dɪskɔːs/ *n.* LME. [L *discursus* running to and fro, (in late L) intercourse, (in

For other words beginning with *dis-* see the entry for **dis-**

med.L) argument, f. *discurs-* pa. ppl stem of *discurrere*, f. as DIS- 1 + *currere* run; form assim. to COURSE *n.*[1]] 1 The process or faculty of reasoning. Also *discourse of reason*. Now *rare* or *obs.* LME. †2 Onward course (in space or time). M16–E17. 3a (An) exchange of words; (a) conversation, (a) talk. Now *literary* or *arch.* M16. †b Conversational power. L16–M17. †c Familiar intercourse; familiarity. *rare* (Shakes.). Only in E17. †4 An account, a narrative. L16–M17. 5 A formal discussion of a topic in speech or writing; a treatise, homily, etc.; a treatise, a homily. L16. 6 *Ling.* A connected series of utterances, forming a unit for analysis etc. M20.

1 W. RALEIGH The Dog.. we see is plentifully furnished with inward discourse. 3a DEFOE I have had a long discourse with my father. C. C. TRENCH A blue-stocking who engaged in learned discourse with .. Leibnitz. b SHAKES. *Com. Err.* I know a wench of excellent discourse, Pretty and witty. c SHAKES. *Haml.* If you be honest and fair, your honesty should admit no discourse to your beauty.

Phrases: *universe of discourse*: see UNIVERSE 4.

discourse /dɪsˈkɔːs/ *v.* M16. [f. the n., partly after Fr. *discourir.*] I 1 *v.i.* Hold discourse; converse, confer. M16. 2 *v.i.* Speak or write at length on a topic. M16. 3 *v.t.* Go through in speech or writing, tell, relate; confer about, discuss. *arch.* M16. †b Utter, say; speak or write formally. E17–M18. c Give out (music). *arch.* E17. 4 *v.t.* Address words to; converse with; harangue. Now *arch.* & *dial.* L16. 5 *v.t.* While *away* (time) in conversation. E17.

1 L. M. MONTGOMERY You needn't stop to discourse with sympathetic listeners. 2 A. POWELL Mr. Templar.. discoursed.. of redemption dates. A. MASON He discoursed with erudition.. on whatever subject they cared to raise. 3 R. WHITLOCK Alcibiades cut of his Dogs Taile.. that so the talkative people might lesse discourse his other Actions. b JAS. HARRIS The Joy.. in recollecting what we have discoursed on these Subjects.

†II 6 *v.t.* Turn over in the mind. M16–M17. 7 *v.i.* Pass from premisses to conclusions; reason. L16–L17.

discourser *n.* M16.

†**discoursive** *a.* L16. [f. DISCOURSE *v.* + -IVE: cf. DISCURSIVE.] 1 Having the faculty of reason. L16–L17. 2 Proceeding by reason or argument. L16–M18. 3 Passing from one thing to another; discursive. L16–E18. 4 Fond of conversation, talkative; of the nature of dialogue, conversational. L16–M17.

discourteous /dɪsˈkəːtjəs/ *a.* L16. [f. DIS- 2 + COURTEOUS.] Lacking in courtesy; uncivil, rude.

discourteously *adv.* L16. **discourteousness** *n.* (*rare*) E18.

discourtesy /dɪsˈkəːtəsi/ *n.* M16. [f. DIS- 2 + COURTESY *n.*] Impoliteness, lack of courtesy; an instance of this, a discourteous act.

†**discous** *a.* Only in 18. [mod.L *discosus*, f. L DISCUS: see -OUS.] Having a disc; discoid.

discover /dɪˈskʌvə/ *v.* ME. [OFr. *descovrir* (mod. *découvrir*) f. late L *discooperire*, f. L DIS- 2 + *cooperire* COVER *v.*[2]] I 1 *v.t.* Make known, divulge, disclose, (a secret etc.). *arch.* ME. †b *v.i.* Reveal one's secrets, confess. LME–L17. 2 *v.t.* Disclose the identity of (a person); betray. *arch.* ME. 3 *v.t.* Expose to view, allow to be seen. *arch.* in *gen.* sense. LME. b *Chess.* Give (check) by removing a piece which stands between the checking piece and the king. L15. c *Theatr.* Present (a character) in a given position on the stage when the curtain rises. Usu. in *pass.* L18. 4 *v.t.* Exhibit, display, (a quality, feeling, etc.), esp. in action. *arch.* LME. †5 *v.t.* & *i.* Orig. *Mil.*, reconnoitre. Later *gen.*, explore (territory). LME–M19. 6 *v.t.* Become aware of for the first time (a thing or person previously unknown or overlooked); find. Freq., be the first to observe (a new country, a scientific phenomenon, etc.). M16. b Catch sight of, espy. *arch.* L16. c *v.t.* Perceive for the first time the attractions or merits of; *esp.* be the first to recognize the potential of (a film star etc.). E20. †7 *v.i.* Have or obtain a view; look, see. L16–E18. †8 *v.t.* & *i.* Discern; distinguish (*between, from*). E17–L18.

1 SHAKES. *Much Ado* The Prince discovered to Claudio that he loved my niece. J. DAVIES They contain some secrets which Time will discover. 2 C. KINGSLEY He was on the point of discovering himself to them. 3 POPE We stand discover'd by the rising fires. H. ALLEN A bowl of soup, .. white rolls, and a bottle of wine discovered themselves. c E. O'NEILL At the rise of the curtain Ruth is discovered sitting by the stove. 4 POPE A lofty gentleman Whose.. gait discovered when he had published a new book. H. BELLOC The greatness of the English soul is best discovered in that strong rebuke of excesses. 5 W. H. PRESCOTT He was empowered to discover and occupy the country for the distance of two hundred leagues. 6 H. BLAIR Harvey discovered the circulation of the blood. W. S. MAUGHAM Though the police had looked with care, they had discovered no fingerprints. R. LYND We shall, perhaps, discover that freedom is better when we cease to possess it. b F. BROOKE From the top of the hill you discover Aden. c R. CHURCH I spent the time reading an author whom I had newly discovered—Charles Dickens.

†II 9 *v.t.* Remove the covering from; *esp.* uncover (the head), unroof (a building). LME–M19. 10 Take off (a covering). M16–M19.

10 AV *Jer.* 13:22 For the greatnesse of thine iniquitie are thy skirts discouered.

discovera'bility *n.* discoverable quality M19. **discoverable** *a.* able to be discovered L16. **discoverably** *adv.* M17. **discoverer** *n.* †(*a*) a person who discloses secrets, an informer; †(*b*) a military scout or spy; (*c*) a person who finds out or discovers something previously unknown: ME.

discovert /dɪsˈkʌvət/ *a.* & *n.* LME. [OFr. *descovert* (mod. *découvert*) pa. pple of *descovrir*: see prec.] A *adj.* †1 Uncovered, exposed, unprotected. LME–E16. 2 *Law.* Of a woman: without a husband, not covert (COVERT *a.* 5). M18. †B *n.* An exposed state. Chiefly in *at discovert*, off one's guard. LME–L16.

discoverture *n.* †(*a*) *rare* an indication, a manifestation; (*b*) *Law* the state of being discovert: L16.

discovery /dɪˈskʌv(ə)ri/ *n.* M16. [f. DISCOVER + -Y[3], after *recover, recovery.*] 1 The action or an act of revealing something secret or not generally known; disclosure. Now *rare* exc. *Law*, (a) compulsory disclosure by a party to an action of relevant facts or documents in the possession of an opponent. M16. †b (A) display, (a) manifestation, (of a feeling or quality). L16–M18. 2 The action or an act of finding or becoming aware of for the first time; *esp.* the first bringing to light of a scientific phenomenon, etc. Also, detection of a person. M16. 3 (An) exploration, (a) reconnaissance. Now *rare* or *obs.* E17. 4 Something discovered or brought to light. E17. b A person whose talents are recognized and made known for the first time. M20. †5 Information or evidence that bring something to light. M17–E18.

1 W. BLACKSTONE The bankrupt.. is bound upon pain of death to make a full discovery of all his estate. b S. JOHNSON His companions.. could make no discovery of their ignorance or surprise. 2 W. S. LANDOR Shew me.. a discoverer who has not suffered for his discovery.. whether a Columbus or a Galileo. C. BRONTË Anxious.. to avoid discovery, I had.. resolved to assume an alias. D. H. LAWRENCE She had made a strange discovery. 3 DEFOE I had a great desire to make a more perfect discovery of the island. 4 C. DARWIN The principle is a modern discovery.

Comb.: **discovery method** a method of education in which pupils are encouraged to acquire knowledge by their own investigations rather than by listening and reading; **discovery well** the first successful oil well in a new field.

discreate /dɪskrɪˈeɪt/ *v.t.* L16. [f. DIS- 2 + CREATE *v.*] Reduce (something created) to nothing or chaos.

discre'ation *n.* E17.

discredit /dɪsˈkrɛdɪt/ *n.* M16. [f. DIS- 2 + CREDIT *n.*, after It. (*di*)*scredito*, Fr. *discrédit.*] 1 Loss or lack of credit; impaired reputation; disrepute, disgrace; an instance of this. M16. 2 Loss or lack of belief or confidence; disbelief, distrust. M17. 3 Loss or lack of commercial credit. M18.

1 B. JOWETT Such conduct brings discredit on the name of Athens. 2 GEO. ELIOT There were obvious facts that at once threw discredit on the printed document.

discredit /dɪsˈkrɛdɪt/ *v.t.* M16. [f. DIS- 2 + CREDIT *v.*, after It. (*di*)*screditare*, Fr. *discréditer.*] 1 Refuse to credit, disbelieve. M16. 2 Take away the credibility of; destroy confidence in; cause to be disbelieved. M16. 3 Injure the reputation of; bring into disrepute. L16.

2 R. LYND This explanation.. has been discredited in recent years.

discreditable /dɪsˈkrɛdɪtəb(ə)l/ *a.* M17. [f. DIS- 2 + CREDITABLE.] Bringing discredit to; shameful, disgraceful.

discredita'bility *n.* L19. **discreditably** *adv.* M19.

discreet /dɪˈskriːt/ *a.* ME. [(O)Fr. *discret, -ète* f. L *discretus* pa. pple of *discernere* DISCERN, w. late L & Proto-Romance sense f. its deriv. *discretio(n-)* DISCRETION. Cf. DISCRETE *a.*] 1 Showing discernment or judgement in speech or action; judicious, prudent; intentionally unobtrusive. ME. 2 Civil, polite, courteous. Chiefly *Sc.* ME.

1 T. HARDY You should be more discreet in your bearing towards this soldier. F. FORSYTH Offering to the investor a highly discreet and even secretive service in banking.

discreetly *adv.* ME. **discreetness** *n.* the quality of being discreet, discretion LME.

discrepance /dɪsˈkrɛp(ə)ns/ *n.* LME. [OFr., f. as next: see -ANCE.] 1 = DISCREPANCY. Now *rare*. LME. †2 Distinction, difference. E16–E17.

discrepancy /dɪsˈkrɛp(ə)nsi/ *n.* E17. [L *discrepantia*, f. as next: see -ANCY.] The quality of being discrepant; lack of correspondence, disagreement; an instance of this; an inconsistency.

E. A. FREEMAN There is little or no discrepancy as to the facts. R. TRAVERS He remarked on the numerous discrepancies in Butler's stories. E. FROMM The discrepancy between behaviour and character.

discrepant /dɪsˈkrɛp(ə)nt/ *a.* LME. [L *discrepant-* pres. ppl stem of *discrepare* be discordant, f. as DIS- 1 + *crepare* to creak: see -ANT[1].] 1 Exhibiting difference, dissimilarity, or lack of agreement; discordant, inconsistent. (Foll. by *from*, †*to*.) LME. †2 Apart or separate in space. *rare*. L16–E19.

1 A. STORR Basic social assumptions may be so widely discrepant that communication becomes impossible.

discrepate /dɪsˈkrɛpeɪt/ *v. rare.* L16. [L *discrepat-* pa. ppl stem of *discrepare*: see prec., -ATE[3].] †1 *v.i.* Differ (*from*), be discrepant. L16–M17. 2 *v.t.* & *i.* Distinguish (one *from* another, *between*). M19.

discre'pation *n.* †(*a*) difference; (*b*) discrimination: LME.

discrete /dɪˈskriːt/ *a.* & *n.* LME. [L *discretus*: see DISCREET.] A *adj.* 1 Separate, detached from others; individually distinct; not continuous or coalescent. LME. 2 Consisting of or pertaining to distinct or individual parts; (of a magnitude or quantity) not continuously variable, taking only certain values. L16. †3 *Gram.* & *Logic.* Of a conjunction: adversative. Of a proposition: disjunctive. E–M17. 4 Not concrete or material, abstract. M19.

1 W. J. ONG If we wish to take each poem individually as a discrete object existing in its own right. V. GLENDINNING The Anglo-Irish do not even constitute a discrete nationality. 2 H. HALLAM Dealing with continuous or geometrical, not merely with discrete or arithmetical quantity. H. M. ROSENBERG The energy of the particle can only have certain special discrete values.

B *n.* A separate part or item. L19.

discretely *adv.* E18. **discreteness** *n.* M19.

†**discrete** *v.t.* M17–M19. [L *discret-*: see next.] Divide into discrete parts; separate completely.

discretion /dɪˈskrɛʃ(ə)n/ *n.* ME. [(O)Fr. *discrétion* f. L *discretio(n-)* separation, (in late L & Proto-Romance) discernment, f. *discret-* pa. ppl stem of *discernere* DISCERN: see -ION.] †1 The faculty of discerning. ME–M17. 2a Ability to discern what is right, fitting, or advisable, esp. as regards one's own conduct; the quality of being discreet; prudence, sound judgement. ME. b Propriety of behaviour; civility, courtesy. *Sc.* L18. 3 The action of discerning or judging; judgement; decision, discrimination. *obs.* exc. in phrs. and as passing into sense 4. LME. 4

Freedom to decide or act as one thinks fit, absolutely or within limits; having one's own judgement as sole arbiter. LME. b *Law*. A court's degree of freedom to decide a sentence, costs, procedures, etc. LME. †5 With possess. adj., (as *your* etc. *discretion*): a title of respect to a bishop (or nobleman). LME–E16. 6 The action or result of separating or distinguishing; separation, disjunction, distinction. LME.

1 HOBBES The Discretion of times, places, and persons necessary to a good Fancy. 2a CONAN DOYLE Dr. Watson is the very soul of discretion. A. STORR Professional discretion means that the therapist is virtually unable to discuss his work with his family. 3 C. WHITEHEAD She put it to Myte's discretion whether he would continue to harbour a young knave. 4 S. RAVEN It is at our discretion to make exceptions to the general rule.

Phrases: **age of discretion** the age at which one is considered fit to manage one's affairs or take responsibility for one's actions. **at the discretion of** (to be settled or disposed of) according to the judgement or choice of. **use one's discretion** exercise one's judgement (rather than follow a prescribed rule etc.). **years of discretion** = *age of discretion* above.

discretional *a.* discretionary M17. **discretionally** *adv.* M17. **discretionarily** *adv.* at one's discretion L17. **discretionary** *a.* (*a*) pertaining to discretion, left to discretion; †(*b*) discreet: L17.

discretive /dɪˈskriːtɪv/ *n.* & *a.* L15. [Late L *discretivus* serving to distinguish, f. *discret-*: see prec., -IVE. Cf. OFr. *discretif, -ive.*] †**A** *n.* Something discretive; *spec.* a disjunctive conjunction or proposition. L15–E18. **B** *adj.* 1 = DISJUNCTIVE *a.* L16. †2 Serving to distinguish or discriminate. E17–E19.

discretively *adv.* M17. **discretiveness** *n.* M19.

discretization /dɪˌskriːtʌɪˈzeɪʃ(ə)n/ *n.* Also **-isation**. M20. [f. DISCRETE *a.* + -IZATION.] The process of making or the state of being discrete; *spec.* (*Math.*), (a) representation or approximation by means of a discrete quantity.

diˈscretize *v.t.* M20.

discriminable /dɪˈskrɪmɪnəb(ə)l/ *a.* M18. [f. DISCRIMINATE *v.* + -ABLE, after *separate* vb, *separable*.] Able to be discriminated; distinguishable.

discriminaˈbility *n.* E20. **discriminably** *adv.* M20.

discriminal /dɪˈskrɪmɪn(ə)l/ *a. rare.* L17. [Late L *discriminalis* serving to divide or separate, f. L *discrimen, -min-*: see DISCRIMINATE *v.*, -AL[1].] *Palmistry*. Designating the line on the palm between the hand and the arm.

discriminant /dɪˈskrɪmɪnənt/ *a.* & *n.* M19. [L *discriminant-* pres. ppl stem of *discriminare* DISCRIMINATE *v.*: see -ANT[1].] **A** *adj.* 1 Discriminating; showing discrimination or discernment. M19. 2 *Statistics*. Designating a function of several variates that is used to give the best classification of items for which values of the variates are available. M20. **B** *n.* 1 *Math.* A function derived from another function and providing information about its behaviour. M19. 2 *gen.* That which enables discrimination; a distinguishing feature, *spec.* a discriminant function. E20.

discriminate /dɪˈskrɪmɪnət/ *a.* E17. [L *discriminatus* pa. pple, f. as next: see -ATE[2]. Cf. earlier INDISCRIMINATE.] 1 Distinct, distinguished. *arch.* E17. 2 Marked by discrimination or discernment; making careful or exact distinctions. E19.

2 T. R. MALTHUS Much may be done by discriminate charity.

discriminately *adv.* L18. **discriminateness** *n.* E18.

discriminate /dɪˈskrɪmɪneɪt/ *v.* E17. [L *discriminat-* pa. ppl stem of *discriminare*, f. *discrimen, -min-* division, distinction, f. *discernere* DISCERN: see -ATE[3].] 1 *v.t.* Make or constitute a difference in or between; distinguish, differentiate. E17. 2 *v.t.* Distinguish with the mind; perceive the difference in or between. M17. 3 *v.i.* Make or recognize a distinction, esp. a fine one; provide or serve as a distinction; exercise discernment. L18. 4 *v.i.* Make a distinction in the treatment of different categories of people or things, esp. unjustly or prejudicially *against* people on grounds of race, colour, sex, social status, age, etc. L19.

1 G. GROTE Capacities which discriminate one individual from another. 2 I. BARROW We take upon us . . to discriminate the goats from the sheep. *Nature* Hearing in insects may discriminate the frequency, the intensity and the direction of the sound. 3 H. T. BUCKLE It is by reason, and not by faith, that we must discriminate in religious matters. *Scientific American* A simple energy measurement serves to discriminate between the two kinds of event. 4 M. TWAIN To be discriminated against on account of my nationality. R. NIEBUHR Educational suffrage tests . . would discriminate in favour of the educated Negro against the servile, old-time Negro. L. P. HARTLEY We asked everyone we could, . . we didn't discriminate.

discriminating *ppl a.* (*a*) constituting a distinction, affording ground for distinction; (*b*) perceiving or making distinctions with sensitivity, discerning: M17. **discriminatingly** *adv.* M19. **discriminatory** *a.* discriminative; *esp.* practising or evincing racial, sexual, or similar discrimination: E19.

discrimination /dɪˌskrɪmɪˈneɪʃ(ə)n/ *n.* M17. [Late L *discriminatio(n-)*, f. as prec.: see -ATION.] 1 The action or an act of discriminating or distinguishing; the fact or condition of being discriminated or distinguished; a distinction made. M17. b *spec.* The practice or an instance of discriminating against people on grounds of race, colour, sex, social status, age, etc.; an unjust or prejudicial distinction. L19. c *Psychol.* The perception of a difference between two stimuli, esp. as evidenced by a different reaction to each. L19. 2 Something which serves to distinguish; a difference, a distinguishing mark. Now *rare* or *obs.* M17. †3 A recrimination. *rare.* M–L17. 4 The faculty of discriminating; the ability to observe accurately and make fine distinctions; perceptiveness, acuity, good judgement or taste. E19.

1 G. STANHOPE A perfect Discrimination shall then be made between the Good and Bad. I. MURDOCH He loves trouble, his own or other people's without discrimination. b A. G. GARDINER No people which tolerates titles, and so deliberately sets up social discriminations in its midst. B. SCHWARTZ A profound change . . in the attitude of that tribunal [the US Supreme Court] toward racial discrimination. M. L. KING The personal torment of discrimination cannot be measured. *Times* Employers who have cheated women of equal pay by job-grading schemes . . may be taken to court for sex discrimination. G. CLARE Officially there was no discrimination against Jews. *positive discrimination*: see POSITIVE *a.* *reverse discrimination*: see REVERSE *a.* 2 S. JOHNSON Where we see . . the whole at once, we readily note the discriminations.

discriminative /dɪˈskrɪmɪnətɪv/ *a.* M17. [f. DISCRIMINATE *v.* + -IVE.] 1 Having the quality or character of observing or making distinctions with accuracy; showing discrimination, discerning. M17. 2 Serving to discriminate or distinguish; distinctive, distinguishing. L17.

1 SOUTHEY Bombs and rockets are not discriminative. 2 S. JOHNSON The discriminative excellence of Homer is elevation and comprehension of thought.

discriminatively *adv.* M17. **discriminativeness** *n.* M19.

discriminator /dɪˈskrɪmɪneɪtə/ *n.* M19. [f. as prec. + -OR.] 1 A person who discriminates. M19. 2 An electric circuit whose output depends on how some property of the input departs from a fixed value; *spec.* one for converting a frequency-modulated signal to an amplitude-modulated one. M20. 3 A quality or feature that enables distinctions to be made. M20.

discrown /dɪsˈkraʊn/ *v.t.* L16. [f. DIS- 2 + CROWN *n.*, *v.*[1]] Deprive of a crown or royal status; *fig.* deprive of supremacy, dignity, or adornment.

†**discruciate** *v.t.* E17–L18. [L *discruciat-* pa. ppl stem of *discruciare*, f. as DIS- 3 + *cruciare* to torment: see EXCRUCIATE *v.*, -ATE[3].] Torture, excruciate, (chiefly *fig.*).

†**disculp** *v.t. rare.* E17–M18. [med.L *disculpare*: see next.] = next.

disculpate /dɪsˈkʌlpeɪt/ *v.t.* L17. [med.L *disculpat-* pa. ppl stem of *disculpare*, f. L DIS- 1 + *culpare* to blame, f. *culpa* fault, blame: see -ATE[3]. Cf. EXCULPATE.] Clear of blame or accusation; exculpate.

disculˈpation *n.* M18.

†**discumbent** *n.* & *a.* M16. [L *discumbent-* pres. ppl stem of *discumbere* lie down, f. as DIS- 3 + *-cumbere*: see CUMBENT.] **A** *n.* 1 A person reclining at table, a guest at a feast. M16–E17. 2 A person confined to bed. Only in M18. **B** *adj.* Reclining. E–M18.

†**discumbency** *n.* reclining posture at meals M17–M18.

discumber /dɪsˈkʌmbə/ *v.t.* E18. [f. DIS- 2 + CUMBER *v.*: cf. OFr. *descombrer* (mod. *décombrer*).] Relieve of a burden, disencumber.

discursion /dɪsˈkəːʃ(ə)n/ *n.* M16. [OFr., or late L *discursio(n-)*, f. L *discurs-*: see DISCOURSE *n.*, -ION.] †1 The action of running or moving to and fro. *rare.* M16–L17. 2 Reasoning. *rare.* E17. 3 The action of moving away from the subject under discussion; digression. M19.

discursive /dɪsˈkəːsɪv/ *a.* L16. [med.L *discursivus*, f. *discurs-*: see DISCOURSE *n.*, -IVE.] 1 Passing rapidly or indiscriminately from subject to subject; rambling, digressive; extending over or dealing with a wide range of topics. L16. 2 Proceeding by argument or reasoning; ratiocinative; not intuitive. L16. 3 Running hither and thither. E17.

1 H. G. WELLS My reading has been rather discursive. 2 F. FERGUSSON The needs of the discursive intellect.

discursively *adv.* L17. **discursiveness** *n.* L17. **discurˈsivity** *n.* M20.

discursory /dɪsˈkəːs(ə)ri/ *a. rare.* L16. [med.L *discursorius*, f. *discurs-*: see DISCOURSE *n.*, -ORY[2].] †1 Of the nature of discourse or reasoning. L16–E17. 2 Discursive, digressive. L19.

discus /ˈdɪskəs/ *n.* M17. [L f. Gk *diskos*.] 1 A heavy thick-centred disc or plate thrown in ancient and modern athletic sports; the sporting event in which it is thrown. M17. †2 Any disc or disc-shaped body. L17–E18.

discuss /dɪˈskʌs/ *v.* & *n.* LME. [L *discuss-* pa. ppl stem of *discutere* dash to pieces, disperse, (in Proto-Romance) investigate, f. as DIS- 1 + *quatere* shake.] **A** *v.t.* †1a Drive away, dispel, disperse, (*lit.* & *fig.*); *spec.* (*Med.*) disperse (a swelling, obstruction, etc.). LME–E19. b Shake off; set free. M–L16. †2 Examine or investigate (a matter); try judicially. LME–E17. †3 Give judgement on (a matter). LME–L18. †4 Make known, declare. LME–M17. 5 Investigate or examine by argument; debate; talk about (a topic) to, with, or *with* another person. LME. 6 *Law* (chiefly *Sc.*). Exhaust legal proceedings against (a debtor), esp. against the person primarily liable before proceeding against a surety. L16. 7 Consume (food etc.), esp. with leisurely enjoyment. Chiefly *joc.* E19.

4 SHAKES. *Hen. V* Art thou a gentleman? What is thy name? Discuss. 5 R. L. STEVENSON I could see the pair discussing what they ought to do. H. BELLOC In a further paper I shall discuss the much-disputed point of authorship.

†**B** *n.* = DISCUSSION 1, 2. M16–M17.

discussant *n.* a person who takes part in a discussion, esp. a prearranged one E20. **discusser** *n.* L16. **discussible** *a.* M17.

discussion /dɪˈskʌʃ(ə)n/ *n.* ME. [(O)Fr. f. L *discussio(n-)*, f. as prec.: see -ION.] †1 Judicial examination or decision. ME–E16. 2 Examination (*of* a point) by argument etc.; debate; an exchange of views; a conversation. M16. †3 *Med.* The dissipation or dispersal of swellings, a tumour, etc. E17–M18. 4 *Law* (chiefly *Sc.*). The exhaustion of legal proceedings against a debtor (see DISCUSS *v.* 6). L17. 5 The consumption *of* food etc., esp. with leisurely enjoyment. Chiefly *joc.* M19.

2 H. J. LASKI A discussion group to thrash out the problems of governmental re-organisation. P. TILLICH One of the earliest philosophical discussions of courage, in Plato's dialogue Laches.

discussional *a.* of the nature or pertaining to discussion M19. **discussionist** *n.* a debater M19.

discussive /dɪˈskʌsɪv/ *a.* & *n.* L16. [med.L *discussivus*, f. as DISCUSS: see -IVE.] **A** *adj.* †1 Having the property of dissipating swellings etc. L16–E18. †2 Able to settle a point in question; decisive. E–M17. 3 Of or pertaining to discussion or debate. *arch.* M17. †**B** *n.* A preparation having the property of dissipating swellings etc. Only in 17.

discussively *adv.* (*rare*) E17.

discutient /dɪ'skjuːʃ(ə)nt/ *a.* & *n.* Now *rare* or *obs.* E17. [L *discutient-* pres. ppl stem of *discutere*: see DISCUSS *v.*, -ENT.] (A preparation) having the property of dissipating swellings etc.

disdain /dɪs'deɪn, -z-/ *n.* ME. [AN *dedeigne*, OFr. *desdeign* (mod. *dédain*), f. as next.] **1** a The feeling that is entertained towards something unworthy of notice or beneath one's dignity; scorn, contempt. ME. b A feeling of this kind. *rare.* M17. †**2** Anger or annoyance arising from offended dignity. ME–L17. †**3** Loathsomeness; aversion. L16–M17.

1 A. STORR Some schizoid patients . . may proclaim their disdain for convention by eccentricity in dress.

disdain /dɪs'deɪn, -z-/ *v.* LME. [OFr. *desdeignier* f. Proto-Romance alt. of late L *dedignare*, cl.L *dedignari*, f. *de-* DE- 1 + *dignare*, *-ari* DEIGN.] **1** *v.t.* Consider to be unworthy of oneself or of one's notice; regard with disdain; scorn (*to do*, *doing*). LME. †**2** *v.t.* Be angry or offended at. LME–L17. †**3** *v.i.* Be moved with indignation; be indignant (*at*, *that*); take offence. LME–L18. †**4** *v.t.* Move to indignation or scorn; offend, displease. LME–E19.

1 J. BARNES He wanted all writers to live obscurely in the provinces, . . disdain reputation. 3 W. TAYLOR Disdaining that the enemies of Christ should abound in wealth.

disdainable *a.* (*rare*) worthy of disdain E17. **disdainer** *n.* L16.

disdainful /dɪs'deɪnfʊl, -f(ə)l/ *a.* M16. [f. DISDAIN *n.* + -FUL.] **1** Full of or showing disdain; scornful, contemptuous. (Foll. by *of*, *to do*.) M16. †**2** Hateful. M–L16.

disdainfully *adv.* M16. **disdainfulness** *n.* M16.

disdar /'diːzdɑː/ *n.* M18. [Turk. *dizdar* f. Pers. *dizdār*, f. *diz* castle + *dār* holder.] *Hist.* The warden of a castle or fort in Turkey, Persia, etc.

†**disdiapason** *n.* E17–L18. [L *disdiapason* f. Gk *dis dia pasōn*, f. *dis* twice: see DIAPASON.] *Mus.* The interval of a double octave; a fifteenth.

disease /dɪ'ziːz/ *n.* In sense 1 also (now usu.) **dis-ease** /dɪs'iːz/. ME. [AN *desease*, *dis-*, OFr. *desaise*, f. *des-* DIS- 2 + *aise* EASE *n.* In sense 1 reformed in E20 f. DIS- 2 + EASE *n.*] **1** Absence of ease; inconvenience; trouble. ME. †b A cause of discomfort; an annoyance. LME–E18. **2** (A) disorder of structure or function in an animal or plant of such a degree as to produce or threaten to produce detectable illness or disorder; a definable variety of such a disorder, usu. with specific signs or symptoms or affecting a specific location; (an) illness, (a) sickness. LME. **3** *fig.* A bad quality, habit, or disposition regarded as affecting or having a hold on a person etc. E16.

2 GIBBON The legions of Augustus melted away in disease and lassitude. *Scientific American* Trichinosis . . is obviously a common infection but a rare disease. *Alzheimer's disease*, *coeliac disease*, *deficiency disease*, *Dutch elm disease*, *foot-and-mouth disease*, *industrial disease*, *Parkinson's disease*, *slimmers' disease*, etc. 3 T. FULLER Bad Latin was a catching disease in that age. S. BRETT The artistic temperament is a disease which afflicts amateurs. *British disease*, *English disease*, etc.

diseaseful *a.* (now *rare*) †(*a*) troublesome; (*b*) full of or affected with disease; †(*c*) unwholesome: LME.

disease /dɪ'ziːz/ *v.t.* ME. [AN var. of OFr. *desaaisier*, f. *desaise* n. (see prec.) after *aaisier*, *aiser* EASE *v.*] †**1** Deprive of ease, disturb; put to inconvenience; annoy. ME–L17. **2** Cause illness in; affect with disease. (Earlier in DISEASED 1.) L15.

1 J. KNOX He wold not disease hymself to heare a sermon. 2 *fig.*: E. HICKERINGILL Evil Ministers Disease the Common-wealth.

diseased /dɪ'ziːzd/ *ppl a.* LME. [f. prec. + -ED[1].] **1** Affected with disease. LME. **2** Characterized by or symptomatic of disease. L16.

diseasedly /-zɪdli/ *adv.* L17. **diseasedness** /-zɪdnɪs/ *n.* E17.

disedify /dɪs'ɛdɪfʌɪ/ *v.t.* E16. [f. DIS- 2 + EDIFY.] Shock or weaken spiritually or morally.

disedifi'cation *n.* M17.

disembark /dɪsɪm'bɑːk/ *v.t.* & *i.* L16. [Fr. *désembarquer*, Sp. *desembarcar*, or It. *disimbarcare*, f. Proto-Romance, f. as DIS- 2, Fr. *embarquer*, EMBARK *v.*[1]] Put or go ashore from a ship; remove from or leave an aircraft, train, etc.

disembar'kation *n.* L18.

disembarrass /dɪsɪm'barəs/ *v.t.* E18. [f. DIS- 2 + EMBARRASS *v.*, prob. after Fr. †*désembarrasser* (now *débarrasser*).] **1** Free *from* an embarrassment, encumbrance, or complication; rid or relieve (oneself) *of.* E18. **2** Disentangle (one thing *from* another). M18.

disembarrassment *n.* E19.

disembody /dɪsɪm'bɒdi/ *v.t.* E18. [f. DIS- 2 + EMBODY.] **1** Separate (the soul) from the body; free (anything) from that in which it is embodied. Freq. as *disembodied* ppl a. E18. **2** Disband (a military corps etc.). *arch.* M18.

1 J. A. SYMONDS Disembodying the sentiments which were incarnated in simple images.

disembodiment *n.* M19.

disembogue /dɪsɪm'bəʊg/ *v.* & *n.* L16. [Sp. *desembocar*, f. *des-* DIS- 2 + *embocar* run into a creek or strait, f. *en-* IN-[1] + *boca* mouth.] **A** *v.* †**1** *v.i.* Of a sailor or vessel: come out of the mouth of a river, strait, etc., into the open sea. L16–E19. **2** *v.i.* & *t.* Of a river, lake, etc.: flow or empty *into*; discharge into the sea etc. L16. **3** *v.i.* & *t.* Pour out; emerge or discharge in quantity. E17.

2 POPE The deep roar of disemboguing Nile. SOUTHEY Where wild Parana disembogues A sea-like stream. 3 CARLYLE Paris disembogues itself . . to witness, with grim looks, the *Séance Royale*.

†**B** *n.* The mouth of a river. Only in 17.

disemboguement *n.* the action or place of disemboguing L17.

disembowel /dɪsɪm'baʊəl/ *v.t.* Infl. **-ll-**, ***-l-**. E17. [f. DIS- 3 + EMBOWEL: cf. DISBOWEL.] Remove the bowels or entrails of, eviscerate; rip up so as to cause the bowels to protrude.

fig.: Y. MENUHIN A cottage upright, disembowelled, its inner workings exposed on the floor.

disembowelment *n.* L19.

disembroil /dɪsɪm'brɔɪl/ *v.t.* E17. [f. DIS- 2 + EMBROIL *v.*[1] Cf. Sp. *desembrollar*.] Extricate from confusion or entanglement.

disemburden /dɪsɪm'bəːd(ə)n/ *v.t.* & *i.* Also (*arch.*) **-burthen** /-'bəːð(ə)n/. E19. [f. DIS- 2 + EM-[1] + BURDEN *v.*] = DISBURDEN.

¶ There is no evidence for a vb *emburden*.

disenact /dɪsɪn'akt/ *v.t. rare.* M16. [f. DIS- 2 + ENACT *v.*] Repeal.

dise'nactment *n.* M19.

disenamour /dɪsɪn'amə/ *v.t.* L16. [f. DIS- 2 + ENAMOUR.] Free from being enamoured.

Nature He later became very much disenamoured with Marxism.

disenchant /dɪsɪn'tʃɑːnt, dɪsɛn-/ *v.t.* L16. [(O)Fr. *désenchanter*, f. as DIS- 2, ENCHANT *v.*] Free from enchantment or illusion.

DRYDEN A noble stroke or two Ends all the charms, And disenchants the grove. Q. BELL Virginia, who had been delighted by her first sight of the Italians, was becoming disenchanted.

disenchanter *n.* a person who removes enchantment M17. **disenchantment** *n.* the action of disenchanting; a disenchanted state: E17.

disencourage /dɪsɪn'kʌrɪdʒ, dɪsɛn-/ *v.t.* Now *rare* or *obs.* M17. [f. DIS- 2 + ENCOURAGE.] Deprive of encouragement, discourage.

†**disencouragement** *n.* L16–E18.

disencumber /dɪsɪn'kʌmbə, dɪsɛn-/ *v.t.* L16. [f. DIS- 2 + ENCUMBER *v.*, prob. after (O)Fr. *désencombrer*. Cf. DISCUMBER.] Relieve of or free from encumbrance.

disencumbrance *n.* (now *rare*) deliverance or freedom from encumbrance E18.

disendow /dɪsɪn'daʊ, dɪsɛn-/ *v.t.* M19. [f. DIS- 2 + ENDOW.] Deprive or strip (esp. a Church) of endowments.

disendower *n.* M19. **disendowment** *n.* M19.

disenfranchise /dɪsɪn'frantʃʌɪz/ *v.t.* E17. [f. DIS- 2, 3 + ENFRANCHISE.] †**1** Set free, enfranchise. *rare.* E–M17. **2** Deprive of civil privileges or of voting rights; disfranchise. M17.

disenfranchisement /-ɪz-/ *n.* E18.

disengage /dɪsɪn'geɪdʒ/ *v.* & *n.* E17. [f. DIS- 2 + ENGAGE *v.*, prob. after Fr. *désengager*.] **A** *v.* **1** *v.t.* Free from engagement, promise, obligation, etc. *obs.* exc. in DISENGAGED. E17. **2** *v.t.* Loosen or free from something adhering, entangling, or interlocking; loosen (a bond). E17. **3** *v.i.* Detach oneself; get loose. M17. **4** *v.i.* *Fencing.* Pass the point of one's sword over or under the opponent's blade to change the line of attack. L17.

2 E. LANGLEY Gently we disengaged ourselves from the company and strolled off. R. COBB The priest eventually disengaged his hand from my friend's avid embrace.

B *n.* A fencer's movement to disengage. L18.

disengaged /dɪsɪn'geɪdʒd, dɪsɛn-/ *ppl a.* E17. [f. prec. + -ED[1].] Free of engagement or obligation; not engaged; detached; *esp.* at leisure to attend to any visitor, business, etc.

disengagedness *n.* L17.

disengagement /dɪsɪn'geɪdʒm(ə)nt/ *n.* M17. [f. as prec. + -MENT, after ENGAGEMENT or Fr. *désengagement*.] **1** Absence of engagement or involvement; the action of disengaging or of freeing from involvement. (Foll. by *from*.) M17. b Liberation *of* gas, heat, etc. L18. **2** Freedom from (mental) occupation; detachment; ease of manner or behaviour. E18. **3** The breaking of an engagement to be married. L18. **4** *Fencing.* = DISENGAGE *n.* L18. **5** A withdrawal of military forces; a renunciation of military or political influence in a specified area. M20.

1 W. J. M. RANKINE Effecting . . disengagement by wheels in rolling contact. R. GARNETT That disengagement from all traditional and conventional influences . . which characterises younger men.

disentail /dɪsɪn'teɪl/ *v.* & *n.* M17. [f. DIS- 2 + ENTAIL *v.*[2]] **A** *v.t.* †**1** Divest, deprive, *of.* Only in M17. **2** *Law.* Free from entail; break the entail of (an estate). M19. **B** *n.* The act of breaking an entail. M19.

disentailment *n.* = DISENTAIL *n.* M19.

disentangle /dɪsɪn'taŋg(ə)l/ *v.* L16. [f. DIS- 2 + ENTANGLE.] **I** *v.t.* **1** Free (something) from that in or with which it is entangled; extricate; free *from* complications, difficulties, etc. L16. **2** Bring out of a tangled state; unravel, untwist. M17.

1 G. BERKELEY To disentangle our minds from . . prejudices. E. BOWEN To disentangle her parasol from a long spray of creeper. 2 E. K. KANE Patience to disentangle the knots of my harness.

II *v.i.* **3** Be or become disentangled. E17.

disentanglement *n.* M18.

disenthral /dɪsɪn'θrɔːl/ *v.t.* Also ***-ll**. Infl. **-ll-**. M17. [f. DIS- 2 + ENTHRAL.] Free from enthralment.

disenthralment, ***-all-** *n.* E19.

disenthrone /dɪsɪn'θrəʊn/ *v.t.* E17. [f. DIS- 2 + ENTHRONE.] = DETHRONE.

disenthronement *n.* L19.

disentitle /dɪsɪn'tʌɪt(ə)l/ *v.t.* M17. [f. DIS- 2 + ENTITLE *v.*] Deprive of a rightful claim (*to*).

disentomb /dɪsɪn'tuːm/ *v.t.* E17. [f. DIS- 2 + ENTOMB.] Remove from a tomb; disinter, unearth, (*lit.* & *fig.*).

disentombment *n.* M19.

disentrail /dɪs'ɛntreɪl/ *v.t.* Long *rare.* LME. [f. DIS- 2 + ENTRAIL *n.*[1]] Remove the entrails of, disembowel; draw forth from the entrails.

disenvelop /dɪsɪn'vɛləp, dɪsɛn-/ *v.t.* Also (now *rare*) **-ope**. M17. [f. DIS- 2 + ENVELOP or ENVELOPE.] Free from a wrapping or covering; *fig.* unfold, develop, (a meaning etc.).

disepalous /dʌɪ'sɛp(ə)ləs/ *a.* M19. [f. DI-[2] + SEPAL + -OUS.] *Bot.* Having or consisting of two sepals.

disequilibrate /dɪsɪ'kwɪlɪbreɪt, -iːkwɪ'lʌɪbreɪt/ *v.t.* L19. [f. DIS- 2 + EQUILIBRATE.] Destroy the equilibrium of, throw out of balance.

disequilibrium /ˌdɪsiːkwɪ'lɪbrɪəm, dɪsɛ-/ *n.* Pl. **-bria** /-brɪə/, **-briums**. M19. [f. DIS- 2 + EQUILIBRIUM.] Lack or loss of equilibrium, instability; an imbalance.

J. M. KEYNES A most rapid and powerful corrective of real disequilibria in the balance of international payments.

†**disert** *a.* LME–L17. [L *dis(s)ertus* pa. pple of *disserere* discuss, discourse, f. as DIS- 1, 1b + *serere* interweave, connect, compose.] Fluent; well-spoken, eloquent.

For other words beginning with *dis-* see the entry for **dis-**

†**disertly** *adv.* clearly, eloquently, in plain terms LME–L18.

disestablish /dɪsɪˈstablɪʃ/ *v.t.* L16. [f. DIS- 2 + ESTABLISH.] Terminate the establishment of, depose from an official position; *spec.* deprive (a Church) of a special State connection and support, remove from a position as the national or State Church.

disestablisher *n.* M19. **dises'tablishment** *n.* the action or process of disestablishing, esp. a Church E19. **dise,stablishmen'tarian** *n.* an advocate of disestablishment L19. **dise,stablishmen'tarianism** *n.* (usu. as a factitious long word) L19.

disesteem /dɪsɪˈstiːm/ *n.* E17. [f. DIS- 2 + ESTEEM *n.* Cf. Fr. †*désestime*, next.] The action of disesteeming; the fact of being disesteemed; low estimation or regard.

disesteem /dɪsɪˈstiːm/ *v.t.* & †*i.* w. *of.* L16. [f. DIS- 2 + ESTEEM *v.*, perh. after Fr. †*désestimer.*] Have a poor opinion of, regard lightly; despise.

P. GOODMAN A commercially debauched popular culture makes learning disesteemed.

dise'steemer *n.* E17.

disestimation /ˌdɪsɛstɪˈmeɪʃ(ə)n/ *n.* Long *rare.* L16. [f. DIS- 2 + ESTIMATION *n.*, after prec.] = DISESTEEM *n.*

diseuse /diːˈzəːz, *foreign* dizøːz/ *n.* Pl. pronounced same. L19. [Fr. = talker, fem. of *diseur*, f. *dire* say.] A female artiste who specializes in monologue.

disfame /dɪsˈfeɪm/ *n. arch. rare.* LME. [Orig. f. OFr. *desfame*, *dis-*, f. *desfamer* DEFAME *v.*; later f. DIS- 2 + FAME *n.*] Disrepute; defamation.

disfashion /dɪsˈfaʃ(ə)n/ *v.t.* M16. [f. DIS- 2 + FASHION *v.*] Spoil the fashion or shape of, disfigure.

disfavour /dɪsˈfeɪvə/ *n.* Also *-**or**. M16. [f. DIS- 2 + FAVOUR *n.*, prob. after Fr. †*desfaveur.*] 1 Unfavourable regard, dislike, disapproval. M16. †2 An act or expression of dislike or ill will. M16–M17. 3 The condition of being disliked or disapproved of. L16.

1 J. GALSWORTHY He noticed with sour disfavour that June had left her wine-glass full of wine. 3 CARLYLE The poor young Prince . . had fallen into open disfavour.

disfavour /dɪsˈfeɪvə/ *v.t.* Also *-**or**. M16. [f. DIS- 2 + FAVOUR *v.*] †1 Spoil the looks or appearance of; disfigure. M16–E17. 2 Regard or treat with disfavour. L16. †3 Dislike. L16–M18.

disfavourable /dɪsˈfeɪv(ə)rəb(ə)l/ *a.* Long *rare.* Also *-**or-**. M16. [f. DIS- 2 + FAVOURABLE.] Unfavourable.

disfavourably *adv.* M17.

disfeature /dɪsˈfiːtʃə/ *v.t.* M17. [f. DIS- 2 + FEATURE *n.* Cf. DEFEATURE *v.*] Disfigure, deface.

disfellowship /dɪsˈfɛlə(ʊ)ʃɪp/ *n.* & *v.* E17. [f. DIS- 2 + FELLOWSHIP *n.*] **A** *n.* Lack of or exclusion from fellowship. E17. **B** *v.t.* Exclude from (esp. religious) fellowship; excommunicate. Chiefly *US.* M19.

disfiguration /dɪsˌfɪgjʊˈreɪʃ(ə)n, -ˌfɪgə-/ *n.* M17. [f. DISFIGURE *v.* + -ATION. Cf. OFr. *desfiguration.*] = DISFIGUREMENT.

disfigure /dɪsˈfɪgə/ *v.t.* LME. [OFr. *desfigurer* (mod. *dé-*) f. Proto-Romance, f. L DIS- 2 + *figura* FIGURE *n.*] 1 Spoil the appearance or beauty of; deform, deface. LME. †2 Alter the figure or appearance of, disguise. LME–E18. †3 Carve (a peacock) at table. L15–E18.

1 LD MACAULAY Their diction was disfigured by foreign idioms. D. M. THOMAS Rather an ugly baby, disfigured by a hare lip.

disfigurer *n.* L18. **disfiguringly** *adv.* in a disfiguring manner; so as to disfigure: E20.

disfigurement /dɪsˈfɪgəm(ə)nt/ *n.* M17. [f. prec. + -MENT.] 1 The action of disfiguring; the fact of being disfigured. M17. 2 Something that disfigures; a deformity, a blemish. M17.

disflower /dɪsˈflaʊə/ *v.t.* E17. [f. DIS- 2 + FLOWER *n.*] 1 Deprive or strip of flowers; *fig.* rob of its beauty or excellence, spoil. E17. †2 Make to be no longer a flower. Only in E17.

disforest /dɪsˈfɒrɪst/ *v.t.* E16. [AL (cf. *disforestatio(n-)*), f. as DIS- 2 + FOREST *n.* Cf. DEAFFOREST, DEFOREST, DISAFFOREST.] 1 *Hist.* = DISAFFOREST *v.* 1. E16. 2 Clear (land etc.) of forests or trees. M17.

ˌdisfore'station *n.* E17.

disform /dɪsˈfɔːm/ *v.* LME. [f. DIS- 2 + FORM *v.*^{1} Cf. DEFORM *v.*] 1 *v.t.* Deform, disfigure, deface. *obs.* exc. *dial.* LME. 2 *v.i.* Change form, lose form or arrangement. *rare.* M19.

disfranchise /dɪsˈfran(t)ʃʌɪz/ *v.t.* LME. [f. DIS- 2 + FRANCHISE *v.*] 1 Deprive of the rights and privileges of a free inhabitant of a borough, city, country, etc.; deprive of a right or privilege formerly held. LME. 2 *spec.* Deprive (a place) of the right of returning an elected representative, or (a person) of the right of voting in an election. E18.

disfranchisement /-ɪz-/ *n.* E17. **disfranchiser** *n.* M19.

disfunction *n.* var. of DYSFUNCTION.

disfurnish /dɪsˈfəːnɪʃ/ *v.t.* M16. [OFr. *desfournir*, f. as DIS- 2, FURNISH *v.*] Deprive of or *of* appurtenances or belongings; make destitute *of.*

disfurnishment *n.* E17.

disgarnish /dɪsˈgɑːnɪʃ/ *v.t.* LME. [OFr. *desgarnir* (mod. *dé-*), f. as DIS- 2 + *garnir*: see GARNISH *v.*] Deprive of something that garnishes or furnishes; disfurnish, despoil.

disgavel /dɪsˈgav(ə)l/ *v.t.* Infl. **-ll-**. L17. [f. DIS- 2 + GAVEL(KIND).] *Hist.* Relieve or exempt from the tenure of gavelkind.

disglorify /dɪsˈglɔːrɪfʌɪ/ *v.t. rare.* L16. [f. DIS- 2 + GLORIFY.] Deprive of glory; treat with dishonour. Usu. in *pass.*

disgorge /dɪsˈgɔːdʒ/ *v.* L15. [OFr. *desgorger* (mod. *dé-*), f. as DIS- 2, GORGE *n.*^{1}] 1 *v.t.* & *i.* Eject (matter) from or as from the throat; yield up, cease to hold on to, (esp. what has been wrongly appropriated). L15. 2 *v.t.* Discharge the contents of, empty. L16.

1 J. BUCHAN He . . was entitled to his share in the profits . . and he was determined to make Haraldsen disgorge. S. MIDDLETON A bus . . disgorged its complement of old-age pensioners. 2 J. HEYWOOD Their stomacks some disgorg'd. ADDISON The four Rivers which disgorge themselves into the Sea of Fire.

disgorgement *n.* the action of disgorging L15. **disgorger** *n.* a thing which disgorges; *spec.* a device for extracting a hook from a fish's throat: M19.

disgown /dɪsˈgaʊn/ *v. arch.* M18. [f. DIS- 2 + GOWN *n.*] 1 *v.i.* Take off one's gown. M18. 2 *v.t.* Deprive of a gown; unfrock. L19.

disgrace /dɪsˈgreɪs/ *n.* L16. [Fr. *disgrâce* f. It. *disgrazia*, f. *dis-* DIS- 2 + *grazia* f. L *gratia* GRACE *n.*] 1 Loss of high favour or respect, downfall from a position of honour; the state of being no longer held in honour. Formerly also, the disfavour shown to a person in such a state. L16. 2 Loss of general or public respect; ignominy, shame. L16. †3 A disfavour; a dishonour; an affront. L16–M18. †4 (A) misfortune. L16–M18. †5 The expression of dishonour and reprobation; opprobrium, reproach; an expression or term of reprobation. L16–L17. 6 A thing or person involving dishonour; a cause of shame or reproach. L16. 7 Lack of grace. *rare.* L16.

1 LD MACAULAY The King . . had determined that the disgrace of the Hydes should be complete. 2 J. A. FROUDE The disgrace which the queen's conduct had brought upon her family. E. NESBIT Resistance was useless. There is no disgrace in yielding. E. TEMPLETON She was in disgrace at school. 3 BACON The interchange continually of favours and disgraces. 5 HOBBES Then Hector him with terms of great disgrace Reproved. 6 G. STEIN He would be sure to turn out no good and be a disgrace to a German family.

disgrace /dɪsˈgreɪs/ *v.t.* M16. [Fr. *disgracier* f. It. *disgraziare*, f. *disgrazia*: see prec.] †1 Spoil the (esp. outward) grace of; disfigure M16–L18. †2 Put out of countenance; discomfit, dismay. M16–E17. 3 Dismiss from favour; degrade from a position of honour, rank, etc. M16. †4 Bring intentionally into disfavour or disgrace (*with* another); put to shame. M16–E18. 5 Bring shame or discredit on; be a disgrace to. M16. †6 Speak of so as to dishonour; revile; speak slightingly of. M16–E19.

1 W. COWPER Withered stumps disgrace the sylvan scene. 3 LD MACAULAY Queensberry was disgraced for refusing to betray the interests of the Protestant religion. 4 SHAKES. *Much Ado* As I wooed for thee to obtain her, I will join with thee to disgrace her. 5 R. GRAVES I made the plea without stammering or forgetting my words or otherwise disgracing myself.

disgracer *n.* L16.

disgraceful /dɪsˈgreɪsfʊl, -f(ə)l/ *a.* L16. [f. DISGRACE *n.* + -FUL.] †1 Lacking in grace; unbecoming, unpleasing. L16–E18. 2 Full of or involving disgrace; shameful, dishonourable. L16. 3 Inflicting disgrace, degrading. Formerly also, opprobrious. E17.

2 L. M. MONTGOMERY Mr. Phillips said my spelling was disgraceful. 3 J. REYNOLDS These . . disgraceful epithets with which the poor imitators are so often loaded. H. COLERIDGE It does not appear that Sir Samuel . . ever submitted to this disgraceful punishment.

disgracefully *adv.* E17. **disgracefulness** *n.* L16.

disgracious /dɪsˈgreɪʃəs/ *a.* L16. [Fr. *disgracieux*, f. as DIS- 2, GRACIOUS.] 1 Ungracious, unfavourable, unkind. Now *rare* or *obs.* L16. †2 Out of favour; disliked. L16–E17. 3 Graceless, inelegant; unbecoming. L19.

disgrade /dɪsˈgreɪd/ *v.t.* LME. [OFr. *desgrader* var. of *degrader* DEGRADE *v.*] = DEGRADE *v.* 1.

disgra'dation *n.* = DEGRADATION *n.*^{1} 1 E18.

disgregate /ˈdɪsgrɪgeɪt/ *v.t.* Now *rare.* LME. [Late L *disgregat-* pa. ppl stem of *disgregare*, f. L DIS- 1 + *gregare* collect into a flock, back-form. f. *congregare* CONGREGATE *v.*: see -ATE^3.] †1 Dissipate, dispel. Only in LME. †2 Separate, sever, *from.* Only in L16. 3 Separate into individual parts, disintegrate. E17.

disgre'gation *n.* disintegration, dispersal E17.

†**disgross** *v.t.* M16–E19. [OFr. *desgrosser*, *-grossir* (mod. *dégrosser*, *-grossir*), f. as DIS- 2, GROSS *a.*] Make finer; *spec.* reduce the thickness of (metal bars) in wire-making.

disgruntle /dɪsˈgrʌnt(ə)l/ *v.t.* M17. [f. DIS- 3 + GRUNTLE *v.*^{1}] Make discontented; put into a sulky humour. Chiefly as *disgruntled* ppl a.

disgruntlement *n.* moody discontent L19.

disguisal /dɪsˈgʌɪz(ə)l/ *n. rare.* M17. [f. DISGUISE *v.* + -AL^1.] The action or an act of disguising.

disguise /dɪsˈgʌɪz/ *n.* ME. [f. the vb.] †1 Alteration of a customary style of dress; a new or strange fashion. ME–L16. 2 Alteration of dress, appearance, etc., to conceal identity; the state of being disguised in order to deceive. LME. 3 A garment, style, manner, etc., assumed for concealment or deception; a means of concealment or deception; a false appearance. L16. 4 The act or practice of disguising; concealment of reality under a false appearance. E17. †5 A masque. E–M17. 6 Intoxication. Now *rare* or *obs.* E17.

2 B. HARRIS In this extremity he left that City in disguise. BLESSING *in disguise.* 3 W. BELSHAM This high-sounding language is merely the disguise of ignorance. G. MEREDITH Perfect candour can do more for us than a dark disguise. L. DEIGHTON The 'bookcase' . . proved to be an artful disguise for the doors of a cocktail cabinet. 4 T. MEDWIN Friend . . to whom I communicate without disguise the inmost secrets of my breast.

disguiseless *a.* M19.

disguise /dɪsˈgʌɪz/ *v.t.* ME. [OFr. *desguis(i)er* (mod. *déguiser*), f. as DIS- 2, GUISE *n.*] **I**†1 Alter the usual style or fashion of dress of (a person); deck out. ME–L16. †2 Make different in appearance (*from* others, the proper or natural form, etc.); transform; disfigure. ME–L17. b Alter or assume (clothing, a name) to conceal a person's identity. Only as *disguised* ppl a. LME–M17. 3 Change the dress or personal appearance of (a person) to conceal his or her identity; conceal the identity of by dressing *as* a particular (type of) person, *in* a particular garb, or *with* a particular feature. ME. 4 Deliberately alter the appearance of (a thing) so as to mislead or deceive; exhibit in a false light; misrepresent. LME. 5 Conceal the nature or existence of (anything) by a counterfeit show or appearance. L16. 6 Hide (a material object), cover up. L16. 7 Conceal the identity of under a different name or title. M17.

For other words beginning with *dis-* see the entry for **dis-**

2 DRYDEN Faces . . disguised in death. 3 AV *1 Kings* 20:38 The prophet . . disguised himselfe with ashes vpon his face. G. B. SHAW The fugitive . . , disguised in an old coat. H. ADAMS She disguised herself as a squire. 4 T. GALE Plato's custome to desguise the Traditions he received from the Jews. 5 E. ROOSEVELT The low, gentle voice disguised a determination that could be as hard as steel. G. VIDAL Cave did not bother to disguise his boredom. 6 F. HERBERT Here in his quarters . . the ship's harsh metal was disguised with draperies.

II 8 Intoxicate, make drunk or tipsy. Chiefly as *disguised* ppl a. *arch. slang.* M16.

disguisedly /-zɪdli/ *adv.* in a disguised manner, in disguise L16. **disguisedness** /-zɪdnɪs/ *n.* the state of being disguised E17. **disguiser** *n.* †(*a*) *rare* a person who makes or wears newfangled or elaborate garments; †(*b*) a guiser, a mummer; (*c*) a person who or thing which disguises: LME. **disguising** *n.* (*a*) the action of the vb; (*b*) (*obs.* exc. *Hist.*) a masquerade, a performance by mummers etc.: LME.

disguisement /dɪsˈɡʌɪzm(ə)nt/ *n.* L16. [f. prec. + -MENT. Cf. OFr. *desguisement* (mod. *déguisement*).] 1 The fact of disguising or of being disguised. L16. 2 Something which disguises or is used for disguise. L16. 3 In *pl.* Additions or accessories that alter the appearance; adornments. L16.

disgust /dɪsˈɡʌst/ *n.* L16. [Fr. *desgoust* (now *dégoût*), f. *desgouster* (mod. *dégoûter*), or f. It. *disgusto*, f. *disgustare*: see next.] 1 (An instance of) repugnance or strong aversion; profound instinctive dissatisfaction; strong indignation. L16. 2 Strong distaste for (some item of) food, drink, medicine, etc.; nausea. E17. †3 An outbreak of mutual ill feeling; a difference, a quarrel. E17–M18. 4 Something that causes strong dislike or repugnance; an annoyance, a vexation. Now *rare* or *obs.* M17.

1 S. AUSTIN He soon retreated in disgust across the Alps. R. L. STEVENSON So many dead bodies lying all around, that I took a disgust of the place . . almost as strong as fear. A. S. NEILL They cannot overcome a sense of sin and shame and disgust.

disgust /dɪsˈɡʌst/ *v.* E17. [Fr. *desgouster* or It. *disgustare*, ult. f. as DIS- 2 + L *gustus* taste.] †1 *v.t.* Have a strong distaste for or repugnance to; loathe. E17–L19. 2 *v.t.* & *i.* Offend the senses or sensibilities (of); cause disgust (in). E17. 3 *v.t.* Arouse such disgust in (a person) as deters him or her from a proposed purpose. Foll. by *from*, *of*, *against*. E18.

2 M. O. W. OLIPHANT He was disgusted with Phoebe for bringing the message. I. MURDOCH Drunkenness disgusts me. 3 J. O. JUSTAMOND The Monarch was ever soon disgusted of gratifications that were merely sensual.

disgustedly *adv.* in or with disgust M19. **disgusting** *ppl a.* that disgusts, distasteful, sickening, repulsive M18. **disgustingly** *adv.* in a disgusting manner, so as to cause disgust; *colloq.* annoyingly: M18. **disgustingness** *n.* M19.

disgustful /dɪsˈɡʌstfʊl, -f(ə)l/ *a.* E17. [f. DISGUST *n.* + -FUL.] 1 Causing disgust; sickening; offensive; repulsive; shocking. E17. 2 Causing dislike; distasteful, displeasing. *arch.* E17. 3 Associated with or characterized by disgust. M19.

3 ALDOUS HUXLEY Studying Mr. Boldero with a close and disgustful attention.

disgustfully *adv.* M18. **disgustfulness** *n.* M19.

dish /dɪʃ/ *n.* [OE *disċ* corresp. to OS *disk* (Du. *disch*) table, OHG *tisc* plate (G *Tisch* table), ON *diskr*, all f. L DISCUS discus, (Vulgate) dish, disc (of a sundial). Cf. DESK.] 1 A broad shallow flat-bottomed vessel for holding food to be cooked or served, now esp. one with a shape other than circular and having some depth; a glass vessel with a stem or base for holding an individual portion of food; in *pl.* also, table vessels collectively after use. OE. 2 A hollow vessel used for drinking or as a beggar's receptacle for alms; a cup. *arch.* LME. 3a The food served in a dish; a particular form of prepared food. LME. b An attractive person, esp. a woman. *slang.* E20. c *one's dish*, something exactly suited to one's taste. *slang.* E20. 4 A dish or (*arch.*) cup with its contents; as much as a dish will hold. LME. b *Mining.* A gallon of tin ore ready for the smelter; a measuring box for lead ore, by statute fixed to contain 15 pints. Also, the proportion of tin or lead ore paid as royalty to the owner of the mine. M16. 5 Any shallow concave vessel or receptacle. M17. 6 A depression or concavity shaped like a dish, esp. in the side of a spoked wheel; the degree of such concavity; the condition of a wheel with such concavity. E19. 7 A microwave reflector or aerial with a shallow concave surface. Also *dish aerial*, (US) *antenna*. M20.

1 J. STEINBECK Supper was over and the dishes dipped and wiped. D. WELCH The Boys moved about, serving . . vegetables from silver dishes. *Leicester Chronicle* A shallow ovenproof dish. *butter dish, chafing-dish, fruit dish*, etc. †**cast, lay, throw something in a person's dish** reproach him or her with it. 2 *clap-dish*: see CLAP *v.*[1] 3a E. DAVID Interesting potato dishes invented by French cooks. **dish of the day** a dish specially featured on a day's menu. *made dish*: see MADE *ppl a. side dish*: see SIDE *n.* **standing dish** a dish that appears daily or at every meal. 4 BYRON He sate him pensive o'er a dish of tea. V. WOOLF I must now pick a dish of raspberries for dinner. 5 *evaporating dish*. 7 *satellite dish*: see SATELLITE *n.*

Comb.: *dish aerial, antenna*: see sense 7 above. **dishcloth** a cloth used for washing dishes (*dishcloth gourd*, any gourd of the genus *Luffa*, the fruit of which yields loofahs); **dish-clout** (*arch.* & *dial.*) = *dishcloth* above; **dish-cover** a cover put over a dish to keep food warm; **dish-faced** *a.* having a concave face; *spec.* (of a dog) having the face concave from the indentation below the forehead to the nose; *dish-mop*: see MOP *n.*[2] 1; **dish-pan** *N. Amer.*: in which dishes are washed up (*dish-pan hands*: roughened by much washing up or use of detergents); **dishrag** = *dishcloth* above; **dishtowel** *Sc.* & *N. Amer.* a tea towel; **dishwasher** (*a*) a servant who washes dishes; a machine that does this automatically; (*b*) = WASHER *n.*[1] 1a; (*c*) *Austral.* the restless flycatcher, *Myiagra inquieta*, which has a repetitive call; **dishwater** the dirty water in which dishes have been washed; **dishwatery** *a.* resembling dishwater.

dishful *n.* the contents of a dish, the quantity held by a dish ME.

dish /dɪʃ/ *v.* LME. [f. the n.] 1 *v.t.* & *i.* Put (food) into a dish ready for the table. Freq. foll. by *out*, *up*. LME. 2 *v.t.* a Present attractively for acceptance. Usu. foll. by *up*, †*out*. E17. b Give *out* carelessly or indiscriminately. *slang.* M20. 3a *v.i.* Be or become dish-shaped or concave. M17. b *v.t.* Make concave; *spec.* incline the spokes of (a wheel) towards the centre. Chiefly as *dished* pa. pple. M18. 4 *v.t.* Defeat or swindle completely; ruin, spoil the chances of. *slang.* L17. 5 *v.i.* Of a horse: move its forefeet with a semicircular or scooping motion. M19.

1 E. ACTON They [turnips] may be dished in the centre of . . mutton cutlets. 2a O. WELLES Gossip columnists who must daily dish up a ration of rumours, jokes, slanders. b **dish it out** *N. Amer. colloq.* deal out punishment; fight hard. 4 *Listener* Politicians love to dream of allying themselves with erstwhile enemies to dish their friends.

dishing *vbl n.* (*a*) the action of the vb; (*b*) oblique positioning of the spokes of a wheel: L17.

dishabille /dɪsəˈbiːl/ *n.* Also **des-**, **dés-** /deɪz-/, ***déshabillé*** /dezabije (*pl. same*), deɪzaˈbiːjeɪ/. L17. [Fr. *déshabillé* use as n. of pa. pple of *déshabiller* undress, f. *des-* DIS- 2 + *habiller* to dress.] 1 The state of being casually or only partially dressed. Chiefly in *in dishabille*, EN DÉSHABILLÉ. L17. 2 A garment or costume of a casual or informal style. L17.

1 M. MITCHELL He was . . unshaven and without a cravat but somehow jaunty despite his dishabille. L. EDEL The actress in her state of confused déshabille backstage. 2 R. FIRBANK She wore a dishabille of mignonette-green silk.

†**dishabit** *v.t. rare* (Shakes.). Only in L16. [f. DIS- 2 + HABIT *v.*] Remove from its resting-place; dislodge.

dishallow /dɪsˈhaləʊ/ *v.t.* M16. [f. DIS- 2 + HALLOW *v.*[1]] Destroy the sanctity of.

disharmonic /dɪshɑːˈmɒnɪk/ *a.* L19. [f. DIS- 2 + HARMONIC.] Not harmonic; anharmonic; disharmonious.

disharmonious /dɪshɑːˈməʊnɪəs/ *a.* M17. [f. DIS- 2 + HARMONIOUS.] 1 Not in harmony or agreement. M17. 2 Of sounds: discordant. L17.

disharmoniously *adv.* M17.

disharmonize /dɪsˈhɑːmənʌɪz/ *v.t.* & *i.* Also **-ise**. E19. [f. DIS- 2 + HARMONIZE after next.] Put or be out of harmony.

disharmony /dɪsˈhɑːməni/ *n.* E17. [f. DIS- 2 + HARMONY, prob. after *discord*.] 1 Lack of harmony or agreement, discord; dissonance. E17. 2 Something discordant. M19.

1 CARLYLE Disharmony of mind and tongue. 2 *Church Times* This . . organist was really frightful in playing false notes and disharmonies.

†**disheart** *v.t.* L16–E17. [f. DIS- 2 + HEART *n.*] = next.

dishearten /dɪsˈhɑːt(ə)n/ *v.t.* L16. [f. DIS- 2 + HEARTEN, or f. prec. + -EN[5], after *hearten*.] Cause to lose heart; make despondent.

G. ORWELL He had become much disheartened after losing money in a lawsuit.

disheartenedness *n.* dispirited condition L17. **dishearteningly** *adv.* in a way that disheartens M18. **disheartenment** *n.* the act of disheartening; the state of being disheartened, dejection: M19.

dishelm /dɪsˈhɛlm/ *v.*[1] L15. [f. DIS- 2 + HELM *n.*[1], after OFr. *desheaulmer*.] †1 *v.i.* Take off one's helmet. Only in L15. 2 *v.t.* Strip of a helmet. E16.

dishelm /dɪsˈhɛlm/ *v.*[2]*t.* M19. [f. DIS- 2 + HELM *n.*[2]] Deprive of the helm or rudder.

disher /ˈdɪʃə/ *n.* ME. [f. DISH *n.*, *v.* + -ER[1].] 1 A person who makes or sells dishes. Now *rare* or *obs.* ME. 2 A person who serves food. L16.

disherison /dɪsˈhɛrɪz(ə)n/ *n.* Also (earlier) †**disheriteson**. ME. [OFr. *des(h)ereteisun*, *-eison*, f. *des(h)eriter*: see next, -ISON.] The act of disinheriting; disinheritance.

†**disherit** *v.t.* ME–L18. [OFr. *des(h)eriter* (mod. *déshériter*) f. Proto-Romance, f. L DIS- 2 + *hereditare* inherit. Superseded by DISINHERIT.] Dispossess of or bar from an inheritance or (*fig.*) other possession or advantage; disinherit. (Foll. by *of*, (rare) *from*.)

†**disheritment** *n.* (*rare*) LME. †**disheritor** *n.* E17.

†**disheriteson** *n.* see DISHERISON.

†**dishevel** *a.* see DISHEVELY.

dishevel /dɪˈʃɛv(ə)l/ *v.t.* Infl. **-ll-**, ***-l-**. L16. [Prob. chiefly back-form. f. DISHEVELLED: cf. Fr. †*descheveler* (now *décheveler*).] Loosen and throw about in disorder (hair etc.), make dishevelled.

dishevelment *n.* dishevelled or untidy state M19.

†**dishevelee** *a.* see DISHEVELY.

dishevelled /dɪˈʃɛv(ə)ld/ *a.* Also ***-eled**. LME. [f. next + -ED[1].] †1 Bare-headed; having one's hair hanging loose. LME–M17. 2 Of the hair: unconfined, hanging loose; (now usu.) disordered, unkempt. L16. 3 Having one's clothes etc. in disarray. E17. 4 *gen.* Untidy, disorderly. M17.

3 CONAN DOYLE Ian Murdoch staggered into the room, pallid, dishevelled, his clothes in wild disorder. 4 JAN MORRIS His house . . was . . stacked with books, and . . gloriously dishevelled.

†**dishevely** *a.* Also **-elee**, **-el**. LME–L15. [OFr. *deschevelé* pa. pple of *descheveler*, f. *des-* DIS- 2 + *chevel* hair.] = DISHEVELLED 1.

dishonest /dɪsˈɒnɪst/ *a.* LME. [OFr. *deshoneste* (mod. *déshonnête*) f. Proto-Romance alt. of L *dehonestus*, f. *honestus* HONEST *a.*: see DE-, DIS-.] †1 Bringing dishonour; shameful, discreditable. LME–M18. †2 Unchaste, lewd. LME–M18. 3a Of conduct, a statement, etc.: not straightforward or honourable; (now chiefly) fraudulent, of the nature of or involving theft, lying, or cheating. E17. b Of a person: lacking in probity or integrity, untrustworthy; (now chiefly) apt to steal, cheat, lie, or act fraudulently. M18. †4 Ugly, unsightly. M17–E18.

1 MILTON That dishonest victory At Chaeronéa, fatal to liberty. 3a LD MACAULAY A most dishonest and inaccurate French translation. J. LE CARRÉ It didn't appeal to Liz much, the secrecy, it seemed dishonest. b *Economist* 'Shrinkage' due to dishonest staff and shoplifters cost them £650m last year.

dishonestly *adv.* LME.

dishonest /dɪsˈɒnɪst/ *v.t.* Long *rare*. LME. [OFr. *deshonester* f. Proto-Romance alt. of L *dehonestare*, f. *honestare* honour, adorn: see DE-, DIS-.] †1 Bring shame on. LME–M17. †2 Defame, calumniate. M16–E17. 3 Violate the chastity of; cause (a woman) to be sexually unfaithful. L16. †4 Make ugly, deform. L16–M17.

dishonesty /dɪsˈɒnɪsti/ *n.* LME. [OFr. *desho(n)nesté* f. Proto-Romance, f. (after L *honestas*, *-tat-* HONESTY) L *dehonestus*: see DISHONEST *a.*] †1 Dishonour, shame; a dishonourable act. LME–L16. †2 Sexual misconduct, unchastity; a lewd act. LME–M17. †3 Foul or unsightly appearance; ugliness. LME–M16. 4 Lack of integrity or straightforwardness; *spec.* willingness to steal, cheat, lie, or act fraudulently. Also, a dishonest or fraudulent act. L16.

4 R. L. STEVENSON They could see no dishonesty where a man who is paid for an hour's work gives half an hour's . . idling in its place.

dishonor *n.*, *v.*, **-orable** *a.* see DISHONOUR *n.* etc.

dishonour /dɪsˈɒnə/ *n.* Also ***-honor**. ME. [OFr. *deshonor* (mod. *déshonneur*) f. Proto-Romance, f. L DIS- 2 + *honor* HONOUR *n.*] 1 The reverse of honour or respect; a state of shame or ignominy. Also, a piece of ignominious treatment, an indignity. ME. 2 A source or occasion of dishonour; a disgrace. M16. 3 Failure to honour a cheque or other financial obligation. M19.

1 SHAKES. *Hen. VIII* So good a lady that no tongue could ever Pronounce dishonour of her. **do (a) dishonour to** treat with indignity, insult. **to the dishonour of** so as to bring into discredit. 2 R. EDEN They toke it for a dishonour, to . . forsake theyr Captayne.

dishonour /dɪsˈɒnə/ *v.t.* Also ***-honor**. ME. [(O)Fr. *déshonorer* f. med.L *dishonorare*, f. L DIS- 2 + *honorare* HONOUR *v.*] 1 Treat with dishonour or indignity; behave irreverently towards. ME. 2 Bring dishonour or shame on by one's actions; disgrace. ME. 3 Violate the chastity of, cause (a woman) to be sexually unfaithful. *arch.* LME. 4 (Of a bank) decline to accept or pay (a cheque etc.); default on (one's debts). E19.

2 W. K. KELLY America . . dishonours herself by tolerating slavery. 3 M. AYRTON Theseus . . deserted Ariadne, dishonoured the queen of the Amazons. 4 *Business Week* 90% of the institutions surveyed showed no increase in losses as a result of dishonored checks.

dishonourer *n.* L17.

dishonourable /dɪsˈɒn(ə)rəb(ə)l/ *a.* Also ***-honor-**. LME. [Orig. f. prec. + -ABLE; in part f. DIS- 2 + HONOURABLE.] 1 Entailing dishonour, ignominious. Of an action: base, discreditable. LME. †2 Of a person: held in low esteem. *rare.* E17–M18. 3 Of a person: having no sense of honour; unprincipled. L17.

1 SHAKES. *Jul. Caes.* We petty men . . peep about To find ourselves dishonourable graves. G. B. SHAW It would have been dishonorable to betray her. **dishonourable discharge** *US* discharge from the armed forces for dishonourable actions, such as theft or desertion, usu. by sentence of court martial.

dishonourableness *n.* E18. **dishonourably** *adv.* L16.

dishouse /dɪsˈhaʊs/ *v.t.* L16. [f. DIS- 2 + HOUSE *n.*[1], *v.*[1]] 1 Oust from or deprive of a house. L16. 2 Clear (land) of houses. M17.

dishy /ˈdɪʃi/ *a. slang.* M20. [f. DISH *n.* + -Y[1].] Very good-looking or attractive.

J. GARDNER Mm, is *that* him? . . He's dishy. B. W. ALDISS Singapore is the dishiest workshop ever invented.

disillusion /dɪsɪˈluːʒ(ə)n, -ˈljuː-/ *n.* L16. [f. DIS- 3 (sense 1) & 2 (sense 2) + ILLUSION.] †1 Illusion, delusion. L16–E17. 2 Disillusionment, disenchantment. M19.

2 H. ACTON The general climate was one of war weariness and disillusion after the elation of victory.

disillusionary *a.* pertaining to or of the nature of disillusion L19.

disillusion /dɪsɪˈluːʒ(ə)n, -ˈljuː-/ *v.t.* M19. [f. the n.] Deprive of belief in an illusion or ideal; disenchant, undeceive.

C. S. FORESTER Randall could not believe in victory: he had been disillusioned too often.

disillusioner, **disillusionist** *ns.* L19. **disillusionment** *n.* the action or an act of disillusioning; the state of being disillusioned; (a) disenchantment: M19.

disillusionize /dɪsɪˈluːʒ(ə)nʌɪz, -ˈljuː-/ *v.t.* Also **-ise**. M19. [f. DISILLUSION *n.* + -IZE.] = prec.

disillusionizer *n.* L19.

disillusive /dɪsɪˈluːsɪv, -ˈljuː-/ *a.* L19. [f. DIS- 2 after *illusive*.] Tending to disillusion.

disincentive /dɪsɪnˈsɛntɪv/ *n.* & *a.* M20. [f. DIS- 2 + INCENTIVE *n.*] (Constituting) a source of discouragement, esp. in an economic or commercial matter.

disincline /dɪsɪnˈklʌɪn/ *v.t.* M17. [f. DIS- 2 + INCLINE *v.*] Make unwilling or averse. (Foll. by *for*, *to*, *from*, *to do*.)

D. CECIL A . . changeable temperament . . disinclined him to stick to any course of life for long.

disincliˈnation *n.* M17. **disinclined** *a.* unwilling, averse M17.

disincommodate /dɪsɪnˈkɒmədeɪt/ *v.t. rare.* M17. [Blend of DISCOMMODATE and INCOMMODATE.] Inconvenience, incommode.

disinfect /dɪsɪnˈfɛkt/ *v.t.* L16. [Fr. *désinfecter*, f. *dés-* DIS- 2 + *infecter* INFECT *v.*] †1 Rid (a person or place) of an infection. *rare.* L16–E18. 2 Cleanse (a room, clothes, etc.) from infection by destroying infecting micro-organisms, esp. by chemical means. M17.

2 N. MAILER The pills they kept to disinfect their drinking water. *Time* Phenols . . are employed by many plants and primitive animals to heal and disinfect wounds.

disinfecter *n.* M19. **disinfection** *n.* E19. **disinfector** *n.* M19.

disinfectant /dɪsɪnˈfɛkt(ə)nt/ *n.* & *a.* M19. [Fr. *désinfectant* pres. pple of *désinfecter*: see prec., -ANT[1].] A *n.* An agent (usu. chemical) used for disinfection. M19. B *adj.* Having the property of disinfecting. L19.

disinflation /dɪsɪnˈfleɪʃ(ə)n/ *n.* L19. [f. DIS- 2 + INFLATION.] 1 = DEFLATION 3. L19. 2 *Econ.* The reversal of monetary inflation; the return to a state of equilibrium from an inflationary state. M20.

disinflationary *a.* M20.

disinformation /ˌdɪsɪnfəˈmeɪʃ(ə)n/ *n.* M20. [f. DIS- 2 + INFORMATION after Russ. *dezinformatsiya*.] (The dissemination of) deliberately false information, esp. as supplied by one government to another or to the public.

disinˈform *v.t.* L20.

disingenuity /ˌdɪsɪndʒɪˈnjuːɪti/ *n.* M17. [f. next after INGENUITY.] 1 Disingenuousness. M17. 2 A piece of unfair treatment or underhand dealing. L17.

disingenuous /dɪsɪnˈdʒɛnjʊəs/ *a.* M17. [f. DIS- 2 + INGENUOUS.] Insincere, lacking in frankness or honesty; fraudulent.

W. GOLDING I should be disingenuous if I pretended not to be flattered.

disingenuously *adv.* M17. **disingenuousness** *n.* L17.

disinherison /dɪsɪnˈhɛrɪz(ə)n/ *n.* M16. [Alt. of DISHERISON after next.] Disinheritance.

disinherit /dɪsɪnˈhɛrɪt/ *v.t.* LME. [f. DIS- 2 + INHERIT, superseding DISHERIT.] Dispossess of or bar from an inheritance.

fig.: E. B. BROWNING Earth, methinks, Will disinherit thy philosophy.

disinheritance *n.* dispossession from an inheritance M16.

disintegrable /dɪsˈɪntɪgrəb(ə)l/ *a.* L18. [f. DISINTEGRATE + -ABLE.] Able to be disintegrated.

disintegrant /dɪsˈɪntɪgr(ə)nt/ *a.* & *n.* M19. [f. next + -ANT[1].] A *adj.* Disintegrating; becoming disintegrated. M19. B *n.* An agent that causes disintegration. L19.

disintegrate /dɪsˈɪntɪgreɪt/ *v.* L18. [f. DIS- 2 + INTEGRATE *v.*] I *v.t.* 1 Separate into its component parts or particles; reduce to fragments, break up, destroy the cohesion or integrity of. L18. b *Physics.* Produce the disintegration of (an atomic nucleus etc.). E20. 2 Separate or break off as particles *from* the whole mass. L19.

1 R. KIRWAN Marlites . . are not disintegrated by exposure to the atmosphere. G. MEREDITH We cannot modify our class distinctions without risk of disintegrating the social structure.

II *v.i.* 3 Undergo disintegration. M19.

3 R. P. WARREN The old stonework disintegrating into a heap of rubble.

disintegrative *a.* tending to cause disintegration M19. **disintegratively** *adv.* L19. **disintegrator** *n.* M19.

disintegration /dɪsˌɪntɪˈgreɪʃ(ə)n/ *n.* L18. [f. prec. + -ATION.] 1 The action or process of disintegrating; the condition of being disintegrated. L18. 2 *Physics.* The process in which an atomic nucleus changes into another nuclide by emitting one or more particles or splitting into smaller nuclei; the decay of a subatomic particle. E20.

1 A. C. RAMSAY The constant atmospheric disintegration of cliffs. R. SCRUTON The disintegration of authority means the collapse of justice. 2 *Nature* The disintegration-rate . . correctly specifies the strength of a radioactive source.

disintegrationist *n.* an advocate of disintegration L19.

disinter /dɪsɪnˈtəː/ *v.t.* E17. [Fr. *désenterrer*, f. *dés-* DIS- 2 + *enterrer* INTER *v.*] 1 Remove (a buried object) from the ground; exhume. E17. 2 Take out as if from a tomb; bring out of concealment. E18.

1 SIR T. BROWNE To disenterre the bodies of the deceased. 2 G. GREENE How can I disinter the human character from the heavy scene?

†**disinteress** *v.* E17–M17. [Fr. *désintéresser*, f. *dés* DIS- 2 + *intéresser* INTERESS *v.*] = DISINTEREST *v.*

†**disinteressed** *a.* E17. [f. prec. + -ED[1] or f. DIS- 2 + *interessed* pa. ppl a. of INTERESS *v.*] 1 = DISINTERESTED 1. Only in 17. 2 = DISINTERESTED 2. E17–E18.

†**disinteressment** *n.* M17–E18. [Fr. *désintéressement*, f. as prec. + -MENT.] Impartiality, disinterestedness.

disinterest /dɪsˈɪnt(ə)rɪst/ *n.* M17. [f. DIS- 2 + INTEREST *n.*] 1 Impartiality, disinterestedness. M17. 2 That which is contrary to interest or advantage; disadvantage, prejudice, injury. M17. 3 Absence of interest (*in*), unconcern. L19.

2 J. NORRIS Whatever . . tends to the Disinterest of the Public, is Evil.

disinterest /dɪsˈɪnt(ə)rɛst/ *v.t.* Now *rare* exc. as next. E17. [f. DIS- 2 + INTEREST *v.* Cf. DISINTERESS.] Rid of interest or concern; detach from an interest or party. (Foll. by *in*, *of*, *from*.)

disinterested /dɪsˈɪnt(ə)rɪstɪd/ *a.* E17. [f. prec. + -ED[1], or f. DIS- 2 + INTERESTED.] 1 Not interested, unconcerned. E17. 2 Not influenced by one's own advantage; impartial, free from personal interest. M17.

1 P. ACKROYD He asked me with all the curiosity of a thoroughly disinterested person. 2 M. BEERBOHM May I assume that your love for me has been entirely disinterested?

¶ Sense 1 is now often regarded as incorrect.

disinterestedly *adv.* E18. **disinterestedness** *n.* L17.

disinteresting /dɪsˈɪnt(ə)rɪstɪŋ/ *a.* M18. [f. DIS- 2 + INTERESTING.] Uninteresting, arousing no interest.

disintermediation /ˌdɪsɪntəmiːdɪˈeɪʃ(ə)n/ *n.* M20. [f. DIS- 2 + INTERMEDIATION.] *Econ.* Investment or borrowing of moneys without the mediation of a bank or other controlled institution; disinvestment from banks etc. in favour of direct investment in the securities market.

disinterment /dɪsɪnˈtəːm(ə)nt/ *n.* L18. [f. DISINTER + -MENT.] 1 Exhumation. L18. 2 Something disinterred. E19.

disintoxicate /dɪsɪnˈtɒksɪkeɪt/ *v.t.* L17. [f. DIS- 2 + INTOXICATE *v.*] Free from intoxication or (*fig.*) enchantment.

¶ Rare bef. M20.

ˌdisintoxiˈcation *n.* E20.

disintricate /dɪsˈɪntrɪkeɪt/ *v.t.* Now *rare.* L16. [f. DIS- 2 + INTRICATE *v.*] Free from intricacy; disentangle, extricate.

disinvest /dɪsɪnˈvɛst/ *v.* M17. [f. DIS- 2 + INVEST.] 1 *v.t.* Deprive *of* that with which one is invested; divest. M17. 2 *v.i.* Remove financial investment. L20.

disinvestment /dɪsɪnˈvɛs(t)m(ə)nt/ *n.* M20. [f. DIS- 2 + INVESTMENT.] *Econ.* Withdrawal or

For other words beginning with *dis-* see the entry for **dis-**

realization of investments or assets; the process of disinvesting.

disinvitation /,dɪsɪnvɪ'teɪʃ(ə)n/ *n. rare.* L17. [f. DIS- 2 + INVITATION.] The withdrawal or cancellation of an invitation.

disinvite /dɪsɪn'vʌɪt/ *v.t.* L16. [f. DIS- 2 + INVITE *v.*] Withdraw or cancel an invitation to.
P. WYLIE Not being disinvited I tagged along.
¶ Obs. after L17; recorded again L19.

disinvoltura /disinvɔl'tu:ra/ *n.* M19. [It., f. *disinvolto* unembarrassed, f. *disinvolgere* unwind.] Self-assurance; lack of constraint.
F. A. KEMBLE A woman, who moves with more complete *disinvoltura* in her men's clothes than most men do.

disjaskit /dɪs'dʒɑːskɪt/ *a. Sc.* Also **-ket, -ked.** E19. [Perh. alt. of *dejected.*] Dilapidated; dejected; exhausted.

disject /dɪs'dʒɛkt/ *v.t.* L16. [L *disject-* pa. ppl stem of *disicere*, f. as DIS- 1 + *jacere* to throw.] Scatter, disperse; break up, dismember.
disjection *n.* M18.

disjecta membra /dɪs,jɛktə 'mɛmbrə/ *n. phr. pl.* E18. [Alt. of L *disjecti membra poetae* limbs of a dismembered poet (Horace).] Scattered remains. Cf. MEMBRA DISJECTA.
R. G. COLLINGWOOD A world full of shattered ideas, *disjecta membra* of old systems of life and thought.

disjoin /dɪs'dʒɔɪn/ *v.* LME. [OFr. *desjoign-* pres. stem of *desjoindre* (mod. *dé-*) f. L *disjungere*, f. as DIS- 2 + *jungere* JOIN *v.*] 1 *v.t.* Put or keep apart; separate, sever. LME. 2 *v.t.* Dissolve, break up; unfasten; separate into parts. Now *rare* or *obs.* L16. 3 *v.i.* Separate oneself (*from*); part, become separate. L16.

disjoint /dɪs'dʒɔɪnt/ *a.* & *adv.* LME. [OFr. *desjoint* pa. pple of *desjoindre*: see prec.] A *adj.* †1 Disjointed, out of joint, disconnected. LME–E18. 2 Separate, separated; *spec.* (*Logic*, of two or more sets) having no elements in common. L16. †B *adv.* Apart, asunder. Only in LME.
disjointly *adv.* (*a*) separately, apart; (*b*) *rare* disjointedly, disconnectedly: E17.

disjoint /dɪs'dʒɔɪnt/ *v.* LME. [Orig. f. prec., later partly f. DIS- 2 + JOINT *n.*] 1 *v.t.* Destroy the connection and arrangement of; dislocate, disturb. LME. 2 *v.t.* = DISJOIN 1. L16. 3 *v.t.* Take to pieces. L16. 4 *v.i.* Be disjointed; suffer dislocation, come apart. E17.
1 *fig.*: GIBBON A lyric writer of taste . . disjointing the order of his ideas. 2 T. JEFFERSON Great Britain, disjointed from her colonies. 3 R. LOVELACE Like watches by unskilfull men Disjoynted, and set ill againe. 4 SHAKES. *Macb.* Let the frame of things disjoint.
disjointure *n.* the fact of being disjointed; disconnection, separation: M18.

disjointed /dɪs'dʒɔɪntɪd/ *ppl a.* L16. [f. prec. + -ED[1].] 1 Of speech, writing, etc.: not properly connected; incoherent, rambling. L16. 2 Separated joint from joint, disconnected; consisting of separated or poorly connected parts. E17.
1 J. GALSWORTHY In the fourth carriage a disjointed conversation was carried on. 2 C. THIRLWALL The huge frame of the Persian empire was disjointed and unwieldy.
disjointedly *adv.* L19. **disjointedness** *n.* M17.

disjunct /'dɪsdʒʌŋkt/ *a.* & *n.* LME. [L *disjunctus* pa. pple of *disjungere*: see DISJOIN.] A *adj.* 1 Disjoined, separate, distinct. Now *rare* exc. *techn.* LME. 2 *Logic.* †a = DISJUNCTIVE *a.* 2. L16–M17. b Designating each term of a disjunctive proposition. M19. 3 *Mus.* Designating motion by leaps of more than one degree of a scale (i.e. by intervals of more than a second); proceeding by or involving such leaps. Opp. CONJUNCT *a.* 4. L17.
1 *Scientific American* Two disjunct areas in Malaya support a single species of tree.
B *n. Logic.* Each of the terms of a disjunctive proposition. E20.
†**disjunctly** *adv.* M17–E18.

disjunction /dɪs'dʒʌŋkʃ(ə)n/ *n.* LME. [OFr. *disjunction* (mod. *-jonction*) or its source L *disjunctio(n-)*, f. *disjunct-* pa. ppl stem of *disjungere*: see DISJOIN, -ION.] 1 The action of disjoining; the condition of being disjoined; separation. LME. 2 *Logic.* (A statement expressing) the relation between statements of which the truth of one and only one is asserted (exclusive 'or'). Also = ALTERNATION 4 (inclusive 'or'). L16.
1 R. D. LAING The disjunction between his concept of her and her experience of herself.

disjunctive /dɪs'dʒʌŋktɪv/ *n.* & *a.* LME. [L *disjunctivus*, f. *disjunct-*: see prec., -IVE.] A *adj.* 1 *Gram.* Of a conjunction: expressing an alternative, or implying an adversative relation between the clauses it connects (opp. *copulative*). LME. 2 *Logic.* Asserting the truth of one or other of two or more statements; involving a premiss of this kind; of the nature of a disjunction. L16. 3 Having the property of disjoining; characterized by separation. L16.
3 G. STEINER The syntax and structure of the Indo-Germanic languages are strongly disjunctive.
B *n.* 1 *Gram.* A disjunctive conjunction. M16. 2 *Logic.* A disjunctive proposition or statement. M16.
disjunctively *adv.* in a disjunctive manner; alternatively, not jointly; adversatively L16.

disjuncture /dɪs'dʒʌŋktʃə/ *n.* LME. [med.L *disjunctura*, f. *disjunct-*: see DISJUNCTION, -URE. Cf. OFr. *desjointure.*] Separation, disconnection; a breach, a hiatus; a disjointed state.
T. GOODWIN Disjunctures, or brokenness of bones. *Scientific American* Allegations . . of a disjuncture between academic medicine and the effective delivery of medical care.

disjune /dɪs'dʒuːn/ *n.* Chiefly *Sc. arch.* L15. [OFr. *desjeün* (mod. dial. *déjun*), f. *desjeüner* (mod. *déjeuner*) to break fast, breakfast (n.), f. *des-* DIS- 2 + *jeün* fasting f. L *jejunus.*] Breakfast.

disk *n., v.*, **diskectomy** *n.* see DISC *n., v.*, DISCECTOMY.

diskette /dɪ'skɛt/ *n.* Also **discette.** L20. [f. DISK *n.* + -ETTE.] *Computing.* A small flexible plastic disc with a magnetic coating used as an inexpensive data storage device of moderate capacity; a floppy disc; such a disc together with its protective envelope.

†**disleal** *a. rare* (Spenser). Only in L16. [It. *disleale.*] Disloyal.

dislikable *a.* var. of DISLIKEABLE.

dislike /dɪs'lʌɪk; *contrasted w. like* 'dɪslʌɪk/ *n.* L16. [f. the vb.] †1 Displeasure, disapproval, (as directed at some object). L16–M18. 2 The feeling that something is distasteful, unpleasant, unattractive, or objectionable. L16. b A particular aversion, something disliked. E17. †3 Disagreement, discord. L16–M17.
1 W. PENN A letter from the government, in dislike of such proceedings. 2 P. G. WODEHOUSE His dislike amounted to positive loathing. A. LURIE The look of cool dislike on Steve's face. b G. L. HARDING Likes and dislikes in the way of scenery are so very personal. W. GASS Pa took a dislike to Hans and said I shouldn't go with Hans so much.
†**dislikeful** *a.* (*a*) unpleasant; (*b*) characterized by dislike: only in L16.

†**dislike** *a.* L16–M17. [f. DIS- 2 + LIKE *a.*] Unlike, dissimilar.
†**dislikeness** *n.*: only in 17.

dislike /dɪs'lʌɪk/ *v.* M16. [f. DIS- 2 + LIKE *v.*[1]: superseded MISLIKE.] †1 *v.i.* Be displeased, offended, or dissatisfied (*with*); disapprove (*of*). M16–L17. †2 *v.t.* Displease, annoy, offend. Only in 3rd person. L16–E19. 3 *v.t.* Not like; have a distaste for, have an aversion or objection to. L16. 4 *v.t.* Show or express aversion to. *obs.* exc. in *disliking* ppl a. E17.
2 SHAKES. *Oth.* I'll do't; but it dislikes me. 3 J. CONRAD A crowd, which disliked to be disturbed by sounds of distress. E. F. BENSON No young man dislikes being treated intimately by a woman. C. P. SNOW I disliked the sound of the job—I felt it was nothing like good enough.
disliker *n.* L16.

dislikeable /dɪs'lʌɪkəb(ə)l/ *a.* Also **-likable.** M19. [f. prec. + -ABLE.] Able to be disliked; producing dislike, easy to dislike.

†**disliken** *v.t. rare* (Shakes.). Only in E17. [f. DISLIKE *a.* + -EN[5].] Make unlike, disguise.

dislimn /dɪs'lɪm/ *v.* E17. [f. DIS- 2 + LIMN.] 1 *v.t.* Obliterate the outlines of; efface, blot out. E17. 2 *v.i.* Become effaced; vanish. M19.

dislocate /'dɪslə(ʊ)kət/ *ppl a.* Now *rare* or *obs.* LME. [med.L *dislocatus* pa. pple of *dislocare*: see DISLOCATION, -ATE[2].] Dislocated.

dislocate /'dɪslə(ʊ)keɪt/ *v.t.* L16. [Prob. back-form. f. DISLOCATION, but perh. f. prec.: see -ATE[3].] 1 Destroy or disturb the normal connection of (a joint or limb); displace (a bone) from its proper position. L16. 2 *gen.* Put out of a proper (or former) place; displace, shift. Now *rare.* E17. 3 Put out of proper position or orientation in relation to adjoining parts. M17. 4 Put (affairs, the working of something) out of order or out of the normal course; upset, disrupt. M17.
2 G. MEREDITH No sooner was he comfortably established than she wished to dislocate him. 3 R. L. STEVENSON Something, flood or earthquake, had dislocated the whole structure at one joint, so that it hung two ways. 4 M. L. KING To dislocate the functioning of a city without destroying it.
dislocative *a.* (*rare*) serving to dislocate, causing dislocation. E19. **dislo'catory** *a.* causing dislocation. L19.

dislocation /dɪslə(ʊ)'keɪʃ(ə)n/ *n.* LME. [OFr., or med.L *dislocatio(n-)*, f. *dislocat-* pa. ppl stem of *dislocare*, f. L DIS- 1 + *locare* place: see -ATION.] 1 Displacement of a bone from its natural position in a joint; luxation. LME. 2 *gen.* Displacement; removal from a proper (or former) position. E17. b *Geol.* The fracture of strata with upheaval or subsidence; a result of this, a fault. L17. c *Cryst.* A displacement of the lattice structure of a crystal. M20. 3 Disarrangement of parts; a disordered state. M17. 4 *Mil.* The distribution of troops to a number of garrisons or stations. E19.
2 *New Republic* The prevailing mood of Kafkaesque dislocation. 3 E. B. PUSEY The utter dislocation of society. V. WOOLF Something's wrong, he thought; there's a gap, a dislocation, between the word and the reality. *Adweek* (*US*) Recessions create dislocations in the labor force—furloughs, layoffs, all manner of unpleasantness.

dislodge /dɪs'lɒdʒ/ *v.* LME. [OFr. *dislog(i)er*, f. *des-* DIS- 2 + *logier*, (also mod.) *loger* LODGE *v.*] 1 *v.t.* Remove or turn out of a settled or established position; displace. LME. b *Mil.* Drive (an enemy) from a lodgement or other established position. LME. †c *Mil.* Shift the position of (a force, one's quarters). L15–L17. d *Hunting.* Drive (an animal) out of its lair. E17. †2 *v.i. Mil.* Leave a place of encampment. L15–M18. 3 *v.i.* Leave the place where one lives or is staying; (of a thing) leave the place where it has been settled. Now *rare.* E16.
1 M. SHADBOLT It was as if a falling pebble had dislodged stones, and stones boulders. 3 H. COGAN Proclaimed, that all persons . . should upon pain of death dislodge speedily out of the Island.

dislodgement /dɪs'lɒdʒm(ə)nt/ *n.* Also **-dgm-.** E18. [f. prec. + -MENT.] The action or an act of dislodging; displacement.

dislodgment *n.* var. of DISLODGEMENT.

†**disloign** *v.t. rare* (Spenser). Only in L16. [OFr. *desloignier*, f. *des-* DIS- 1 + *loin* far.] Remove to a distance.

dislove /dɪs'lʌv/ *n. rare.* M16. [f. DIS- 2 + LOVE *n.*] Disappearance of love; unfriendliness; hatred.

dislove /dɪs'lʌv/ *v.t.* Now *rare.* M16. [f. DIS- 2 + LOVE *v.*] Not love; hate; cease loving.

disloyal /dɪs'lɔɪ(ə)l/ *a.* & *n.* L15. [OFr. *desloial* (mod. *déloyal*), f. *des-* DIS- 2 + *loial* LOYAL.] A *adj.* 1 Unfaithful to personal ties of duty or affection, as friendship, marriage, etc. L15. 2 Untrue to a political allegiance, lacking loyalty to a government or other constituted authority. L16.
1 SHAKES. *Rich. II* Thou dost suspect That I have been disloyal to thy bed. E. B. BROWNING Without a thought disloyal.
B *n.* A disloyal person; a traitor; a rebel. Now *rare.* E17.
disloyalist *n.* M19. **disloyally** *adv.* LME.

For other words beginning with *dis-* see the entry for **dis-**

disloyalty /dɪsˈlɔɪ(ə)lti/ *n.* LME. [f. prec. + -TY[1], or f. DIS- 2 + LOYALTY: cf. OFr. *desloyau(l)té* (mod. *déloyauté*).] The quality of being disloyal; lack of loyalty; violation of allegiance or duty to one's country etc.

dismail /dɪsˈmeɪl/ *v.t. arch.* LME. [OFr. *desmailler*, f. *des-* DIS- 2 + *maille* MAIL *n.*[2]] Divest of mail; break the mail off.

dismal /ˈdɪzm(ə)l/ *n.* ME. [AN *dis mal* f. med.L *dies mali* evil days; in branch II f. the adj.] **I** †**1** *The* 24 evil or unlucky days (2 in each month) in the medieval calendar; *gen.* evil days; the time of old age. Only in ME. **II** †**2** The devil. L15–L16. †**3a** A funeral mute. Only in E18. **b** In *pl.* Mourning garments. M–L18. **4** One of the dreary tracts of swampy land on the eastern seaboard of the US. E18. **5** *the dismals*, low spirits, the 'dumps'. M18. **b** In *pl.* Depressing circumstances, miseries. E19.

dismal /ˈdɪzm(ə)l/ *a.* LME. [f. DISMAL *n.* I.] **1** Designating each of the 24 evil or unlucky days of the medieval calendar. *obs.* exc. *Hist.* LME. †**2** *gen.* Boding or bringing misfortune and disaster; malign. L16–M17. **3** Of the nature of misfortune or disaster; calamitous. Now *rare.* L16. **4** Orig., causing dismay, dreadful. Now, causing gloom, depressing; sombre, dreary, cheerless. L16. **5** Exhibiting or expressing gloom. E18. **6** Feeble; inept. *colloq.* M20.

1 SPENSER An ugly feend, more fowle than dismall day. 4 W. IRVING The sight of this wreck . . gave rise to many dismal anecdotes. E. F. BENSON Minorca . . had been a dismal failure. H. KELLER The weather has been awfully dismal. D. H. LAWRENCE The sea was grey and shaggy and dismal. **dismal Desmond** a toy dog with drooping ears; *colloq.* a gloomy person. **dismal Jimmy** *colloq.* a gloomy person. **dismal science** (*colloq.* & *joc.*) economics. 5 G. BURNET Wrote dismal letters to the Court. W. IRVING The warriors returned, in dismal procession. 6 *Economist* Galsworthy's dismal efforts at working-class descriptions.

disˈmality *n.* dismal quality or state; an instance of this: E18. **dismalize** *v.t.* make (more) dismal M18. **dismally** *adv.* L16. **dismalness** *n.* E17.

disman /dɪsˈman/ *v.t.* Infl. **-nn-**. E17. [f. DIS- 2 + MAN *n.*] †**1** Deprive of personal existence or manhood. E–M17. **2** Deprive (a country etc.) of men. M19.

dismantle /dɪsˈmant(ə)l/ *v.t.* L16. [OFr. *desmanteler* (mod. *démanteler* in mil. sense), f. *des-* DIS- 2 + *manteler* fortify.] **1** Destroy the defensive capability of (a fortification etc.); raze; pull down, take to pieces, disassemble. L16. **2** Strip (something) of necessary equipment, covering, furniture, or apparatus; *esp.* strip (a fortress) of its defences, strip (a vessel) of its rigging. (Foll. by *of* the equipment, covering, etc.). E17. †**3** Divest of a mantle or cloak; uncloak (*lit.* & *fig.*). Only in 17. †**4** Strip off or remove (a covering). E–M17.

1 H. COGAN Causing all the walls of it to be dismantelled, he razed the place quite to the ground. A. BROOKNER Watching tents being put up and dismantled. *Observer* When Great Britain dismantled the British Empire it gave the land back to the original owners. 2 J. SULLIVAN When Greece was dismantled by the Romans.

dismantlement *n.* L19. **dismantler** *n.* M18.

dismark /dɪsˈmɑːk/ *v.t. rare.* E17. [Fr. †*desmarquer* (now *dé-*) remove a mark from.] Remove a (distinguishing) mark from.

dismarry /dɪsˈmari/ *v.t. rare.* E16. [OFr. *desmarier* (mod. *dé-*), f. *des-* DIS- 2 + *marier* MARRY *v.*] Annul the marriage of; divorce.

†**dismask** *v.t.* L16–M17. [Fr. †*desmasquer* (now *dé-*), f. *des-* DIS- 2 + *masquer* MASK *v.*[2]] Divest of a mask or covering; unmask.

dismay /dɪsˈmeɪ/ *n.* ME. [f. the vb.] **1** Loss of moral courage or resolution in the face of difficulty or danger; faintness of heart from terror or inability to cope with a situation; consternation, discouragement; keenly felt disappointment. ME. †**2** Dismaying influence or operation. *rare* (Spenser). Only in L16.

1 G. B. SHAW My amusement at this soon changed to dismay. TOLKIEN 'Your news is all of woe!' cried Éomer in dismay.

dismayful *a.* appalling L16. **dismayfully** *adv.* in dismay L16.

dismay /dɪsˈmeɪ/ *v.* ME. [f. assumed OFr. vb f. Proto-Romance, f. L DIS- 2 + Gmc base of MAY *v.*[1]] **1** *v.t.* Fill with dismay; reduce to despair. Formerly also (*rare*), defeat or rout by sudden onslaught. ME. †**2** *v.i.* Become utterly discouraged or faint-hearted. LME–L16.

1 J. G. FARRELL She hugged him tightly with tears in her eyes, dismayed at how much he had changed.

dismayedness *n.* dismayed condition L16. **dismayer** *n.* L16. **dismayingly** *adv.* so as to cause dismay (*rare* bef. E20) M18.

†**disme** *n.* var. of DIME.

dismember /dɪsˈmɛmbə/ *v.t.* ME. [OFr. *desmembrer* (mod. *dé-*) f. Proto-Romance (cf. med.L *dismembrare*) f. L DIS- 2 + *membrum* MEMBER *n.* In sense 4 directly f. DIS- 2 + MEMBER *n.* 2. Cf. DEMEMBER.] **1** Cut off the limbs of; tear or divide limb from limb. ME. **b** Carve (a heron or certain other birds). *obs.* exc. *Hist.* LME. **2** *fig.* Break up into smaller units, esp. so as to mutilate; *spec.* partition (an empire or other territory). ME. **3** Sever (a limb) from or *from* the body; *fig.* separate (a part) from or *from* the main body. Now *rare.* L16. **4** Deprive of membership. M17.

dismembered *ppl a.* that has been dismembered; *spec.* (*Her.*) having the limbs narrowly separated from the body: M16. **dismemberer** *n.* L16.

dismemberment /dɪsˈmɛmbəm(ə)nt/ *n.* M17. [f. prec. + -MENT.] **I 1** Expulsion from membership. *rare.* M17. **II 2** The action or an act of dismembering; a dismembered condition. M18. **3** A detached part formed by separation from the main body. M19.

†**dismembration** *n.* M17–E19. [med.L *dismembratio(n-)*, f. *dismembrare*, f. L DIS- 2 + *membrum* MEMBER *n.*: see -ATION.] = DEMEMBRATION.

dismiss /dɪsˈmɪs/ *n.* Long *rare.* L16. [f. the vb.] An act of dismissing; a dismissal.

dismiss /dɪsˈmɪs/ *v.* Pa. t. & pple **dismissed**, †**dismist**. LME. [med.L *dismiss-* var. of L *dimiss-* pa. ppl stem of *dimittere*, f. *di-* DI-[1] + *mittere* send: see DIS- 1. Cf. DIMISS, DIMIT *v.*[1]] **I** *v.t.* **1** Free from custody or confinement. LME. †**2** Release from a legal liability; exclude from a legal advantage. (Foll. by *of*.) LME–M17. **3** Remove, esp. with dishonour, from a post or employment; discharge, expel. (Foll. by *from*, †*of*, or double obj.) LME. **b** Pay off (a hired vehicle etc.). E17. **c** *Cricket.* Put (a batsman or side) out, esp. *for* a given score. L19. †**4** Deprive or disappoint of an advantage. Foll. by *of*, *from*. L15–M17. **5** Permit or direct (a person) to go from one's presence; send away. M16. **b** Let go, send away, (a thing); give egress to. E17. **6** Send away in various directions, disperse, (an assembly etc.); disband (an army etc.). L16. **7** Banish from the mind (a thought, feeling, etc.); treat as unworthy of consideration. L16. †**b** Allow to be forgotten; overlook (an offence, a promise made). E17–L18. **8** Send out of court; deny further hearing to (a legal action or claim). E17. **9** Reject (a person) as unsuitable; *spec.* put away, divorce, (a wife). E17. **10** Lay aside, get rid of. Now chiefly w. immaterial obj. L17. **11** Pass from the consideration of, bring (a subject) to an end; treat summarily. L17.

1 *transf.*: J. SYLVESTER Blushing Aurora had yet scarce dismist Mount Libanus from the Nights gloomy Mist. 3 J. R. GREEN The King dismissed those of his ministers who still opposed a Spanish policy. *Listener* He was dismissed the service and sent back to England. 5 G. VIDAL My father dismissed me with an awkward pat. b J. HAWKESWORTH As a slinger whirls a stone that he would dismiss with all his strength. 7 A. BLEASDALE He inspects the cigarette end and dismisses, reluctantly, the chances of smoking it. *Times* We trust that this unfounded . . allegation will be dismissed. L. HUDSON Lacan . . would certainly dismiss the present text as part of a cowardly Anglo-Saxon plot. 10 HOBBES [Gods] can their form dismiss, And when they will, put on a new disguise. 11 ADDISON I shall dismiss this Paper with a Story out of Josephus.

II *v.i.* **12** Of a body of people: disperse from ordered assembly; (*Mil.*, in *imper.*) used as a word of command at the end of drilling. E19.

12 A. S. NEILL The class refused to dismiss, they crowded round Dorothy.

dismissable *a.* = DISMISSIBLE E19. **dismissible** *a.* liable to be dismissed from office M19.

dismissal /dɪsˈmɪs(ə)l/ *n.* E19. [f. prec. + -AL[1], repl. next.] The action or an act of dismissing, esp. from employment, one's presence, or one's thoughts.

Z. GREY Sampson had told me to clear out, and although I did not take that as a dismissal I considered I would be wise to leave the ranch at once. T. E. LAWRENCE The Drill-Adjutant, approaching . . to learn why one squad was delayed in dismissal. K. AMIS His dismissal of the captain of the Eleven off the first ball of the innings.

dismission /dɪsˈmɪʃ(ə)n/ *n.* Now *rare.* M16. [f. DISMISS *v.* + -ION, after Fr. †*desmission* (now *démission*): see DEMISSION *n.*[1]] **1** Removal from office or employment; discharge. Also, a notice of discharge. M16. **2** Release from confinement; liberation. E17. **3** The action of sending a person away; permission to go. Formerly freq., an official send-off. E17. **b** The action of sending assembled persons away in various directions; dispersal; disbandment. M17. **4** Rejection, discarding; *spec.* repudiation of a wife. E17. **5** The action of dispelling or banishing from the mind. M18.

dismissive /dɪsˈmɪsɪv/ *a.* M17. [f. DISMISS *v.* + -IVE.] Of the nature of or characterized by dismissal; tending to dismiss; suggesting unworthiness of any (further) consideration; disdainful.

Encounter Their dicta Relegated to dismissive footnotes.

dismissively *adv.* E20. **dismissiveness** *n.* L20.

dismissory /dɪsˈmɪs(ə)ri/ *a.* & *n.* Long *rare.* M17. [Alt. of DIMISSORY after DISMISS *v.*] **A** *adj.* = DIMISSORY *a.* M17. †**B** *n.* In *pl.* Letters dimissory. Only in E18.

dismoded /dɪsˈməʊdɪd/ *a.* L19. [Alt. of DEMODED (cf. DÉMODÉ): see DIS- 2.] Unfashionable.

dismount /dɪsˈmaʊnt/ *n.* M17. [f. the vb.] An act or method of dismounting (from a horse etc.).

dismount /dɪsˈmaʊnt/ *v.* M16. [f. DIS- 2 + MOUNT *v.*, prob. after OFr. *desmonter*, med.L *dismontare*: cf. DEMOUNT *v.*] **I** *v.t.* **1** Take down (a thing) from that on which it is mounted; *esp.* remove (a gun) from its carriage. M16. **2**†**a** Come down from (a height). L16–M19. **b** Get off (a horse). E17. **3** Throw (a person) down from a horse; unseat. Also, deprive (a cavalry unit) of mounts. L16. †**4** Lower from a high position; *fig.* reduce in rank or esteem. L16–M18. **5** Remove (a gem etc.) from its setting or mount; take (a mechanism) from its framework, take apart. E17.

4 G. HERBERT His eyes dismount the highest Starre. W. PENN Drunkenness . . spoils Health, dismounts the Mind.

II *v.i.* **6** Come down from or *from* a height. *arch.* L16. **7** Get off a horse etc. or a bicycle or motorcycle; alight from a vehicle. (Foll. by *from*.) L16.

6 T. HARDY Somerset dismounted from the stile. 7 GIBBON He . . dismounted to present the pilgrim with his camel. I. MURDOCH Mor dismounted at the drive, as the coarse gravel was not pleasant for cycling on. J. LE CARRÉ The bus . . was held up in a traffic jam near a tube station; he dismounted and caught a tube.

dismountable *a.* able to be dismounted; (of a gun or cannon) that can be removed from its carriage for transport: E18.

dismutation /dɪsmjuːˈteɪʃ(ə)n/ *n.* E20. [f. DIS- 3 + MUTATION.] *Chem.* Disproportionation, esp. involving both oxidation and reduction of a (usu. biological) compound.

disˈmutase *n.* an enzyme which catalyses a dismutation, esp. of superoxide ions into oxygen M20. **disˈmute** *v.i.* & *t.* (cause to) undergo dismutation M20.

disna *v.* see DO *v.*

disnaturalize /dɪsˈnatʃ(ə)r(ə)lʌɪz/ *v.t.* Also **-ise**. E18. [f. DIS- 2 + NATURALIZE.] = DENATURALIZE *v.*

disnature /dɪsˈneɪtʃə/ *v.t.* LME. [OFr. *desnaturer* (mod. *dé-*), f. *des-* DIS- 2 + *naturer* to form, shape f. med.L *naturare*, f. *natura* NATURE *n.*] Deprive of natural quality, character, appearance, etc.

Disneyesque /dɪznɪˈɛsk/ *a.* M20. [f. Walt(er Elias) *Disney* (1901–66), US cartoonist + -ESQUE. Cf. WALT DISNEY.] Having the characteristics or in the style of the animated cartoons of Walt Disney or the company he founded.

ˌ**Disneyfiˈcation** *n.* the action or process of making Disneyesque; Disneyesque state: M20. ˈ**Disneyfy** *v.t.* make Disneyesque L20. ˈ**Disneyland** [a large amusement park near Los Angeles] a fantastic or fanciful place, a never-never land M20.

disobedience /dɪsəˈbiːdɪəns/ *n.* LME. [OFr. *desobedience* f. Proto-Romance alt. of eccl.L *inoboedientia*, f. L *oboedientia* OBEDIENCE: see DIS- 2.] The fact or condition of being disobedient; neglect or refusal to obey; an instance of this.

civil disobedience: see CIVIL *a.*

†**disobediency** *n.* L16–E18.

disobedient /dɪsəˈbiːdɪənt/ *a.* LME. [OFr. *desobedient* f. Proto-Romance alt. of eccl.L *inoboedient-*, f. L *oboedient-* OBEDIENT: see DIS- 2.] **1** Refusing or failing to obey; neglectful or not observant of what is laid down as a command or duty; refractory, rebellious; insubordinate. LME. **2** *transf.* Not yielding to treatment. L16.

1 SIR W. SCOTT These are not loving subjects, but disobedient rebels. 2 E. DARWIN Medicines.. rendering.. parts of the system disobedient to stimuli.

disobediently *adv.* M16.

disobey /dɪsəˈbeɪ/ *v.* LME. [(O)Fr. *désobéir* f. Proto-Romance alt. of eccl.L *inoboedire*, f. L *oboedire* OBEY: see DIS- 2.] **1** *v.i.* Be disobedient; show disobedience (†*to* an authority). LME. **2** *v.t.* Act in violation of the orders of (a person, a law, etc.); refuse or neglect to obey. LME.

disobeyer *n.* (*a*) *gen.* a person who disobeys; †(*b*) *spec.* a recusant, a rebel: LME.

†**disobligation** *n.* E17. [f. DIS- 2 + OBLIGATION after next.] **1** Freedom from obligation. E17–L18. **2** A disobliging act; an affront, a slight. M17–L18. **3** The feeling of being disobliged; a grudge. M17–M18.

2 C. CIBBER Mrs. Oldfield receiv'd it rather as a favour than a disobligation. 3 STEELE I.. shall never give a Vote out of Peevishness or personal Disobligation.

disoblige /dɪsəˈblʌɪdʒ/ *v.t.* L16. [(O)Fr. *désobliger* f. Proto-Romance, f. DIS- 2 + L *obligare* OBLIGE.] †**1** Release, set free, esp. from obligation or duty. L16–L17. **b** Detach from an allegiance. M–L17. **2** Refuse to consider the wishes or convenience of; offend, affront. M17. **3** Incommode, trouble. *obs.* exc. *dial.* M17.

3 S. JUDD I.. hope my presence, Madam, will not disoblige you.

disobligement *n.* (long *rare*) †(*a*) = DISOBLIGATION 1, 2; (*b*) = DISOBLIGATION 3: M17. **disobliging** *ppl a.* (*a*) not disposed to consider another's wishes, unaccommodating; †(*b*) inconvenient: M17. **disobligingly** *adv.* M17. **disobligingness** *n.* M17.

disomic /dʌɪˈsəʊmɪk/ *a.* & *n.* E20. [f. DI-[2] + -SOME[3] + -IC.] *Biol.* **A** *adj.* Of, pertaining to, or having a chromosome represented twice in a chromosomal complement. E20. **B** *n.* A disomic individual etc. M20.

ˈ**disome** *n.* a pair of homologous chromosomes E20.

†**disopinion** *n.* L16. [f. DIS- 2 + OPINION *n.*] **1** A difference of opinion; dissent. *rare.* L16–M17. **2** An adverse or low opinion (*of*); disesteem. E17–E18.

disorb /dɪsˈɔːb/ *v.t.* E17. [f. DIS- 2 + ORB *n.*[1]] **1** Remove (a star etc.) from its sphere. E17. **2** Deprive of an orb as a symbol of sovereignty. M19.

†**disordain** *v.t.* ME. [OFr. *desordener* (mod. *désordonner*) f. Proto-Romance, f. L DIS- 2 + *ordinare* ORDAIN.] **1** = DISORDER *v.* 5. Only in ME. **2** = DISORDER *v.* 1. Only in LME.

disorder /dɪsˈɔːdə/ *n.* M16. [f. the vb, after Fr. *désordre.*] **1** Lack of order or regular arrangement; disarray, a confused state. M16. **2** (A) disturbance, (a) commotion; *esp.* (a) breach of public order. M16. **3** A breach of discipline or orderly conduct, an irregularity. Formerly *spec.*, an irregularity of conduct, a misdemeanour. L16. †**4** Agitation of mind, discomposure. L16–M19. **5** A disturbance of the normal state of the body or mind. L17.

1 E. FERBER Books leaning.. against each other or fallen flat in zigzag disorder. H. M. ROSENBERG The presence of all types of defect increases the disorder of the crystal. 2 A. J. P. TAYLOR There were fresh disorders [in India]... Gandhi, Nehru, and many other Congress leaders were again imprisoned. *Didcot Herald* Police report an increase in public disorder and violence due to drunkenness. 3 G. BURNET The king had another mistress.. she fell into many scandalous disorders. 5 J. K. JEROME We caught colds, and whooping cough, and all kinds of disorders. A. CLARE The prevalence of particular psychiatric disorders.

disorder /dɪsˈɔːdə/ *v.* L15. [App. an assim. to ORDER *v.* of earlier DISORDAIN. In sense 6 f. DIS- 2 + ORDER *v.*] **I** *v.t.* **1** Upset the order or arrangement of; throw into confusion. L15. **2** Upset the health or function of (the body etc.). M16. †**3** Disturb the mind or feelings of; discompose, agitate. Also, confuse (the features) with signs of mental agitation. L16–E19. †**4** *refl.* Violate moral order or rule; behave in a riotous or unrestrained manner. L16–M17. †**5** Remove from holy orders, defrock. L16–L17. **6** Rescind an order for; countermand. M17.

1 E. BLUNDEN Even getting out of the narrow steep trenches with heavy equipment.. threatened to disorder the assault. 2 G. BERKELEY The east wind.. never fails to disorder my head. 3 DEFOE I looked very earnestly at her; so that it a little disordered her.

II *v.i.* †**7** Become disordered, fall into disarray. E16–M17.

disordered *ppl a.* (*a*) that has been disordered; in a state of disorder; †(*b*) irregular, contrary to rule or law; †(*c*) riotous, disorderly: L15.

disorderly /dɪsˈɔːdəli/ *a.* & *n.* L16. [f. DISORDER *n.* + -LY[1].] **A** *adj.* **1** Opposed to or violating public order or morality or constitutional authority; *esp.* unruly, turbulent, riotous. L16. **2** Marked by lack of order or regularity; confused, irregular, untidy. M17.

1 G. B. SHAW A gay, disorderly, anarchic spoilt child. **disorderly conduct** *Law* unruly or offensive behaviour constituting a minor offence. **disorderly house** *Law* a building in which disorderly conduct takes place, *spec.* a brothel. *drunk and disorderly*: see DRUNK *a.* 1. 2 G. BERKELEY A disorderly and confused chaos. D. H. LAWRENCE The long white locks fell unbraided and disorderly on either side of the.. face.

B *n.* A disorderly person. E19.

disorderliness *n.* L16.

disorderly /dɪsˈɔːdəli/ *adv.* M16. [f. as prec. + -LY[2].] **1** Not in accordance with order or rule; in an unruly or riotous manner. M16. **2** Without order or regular arrangement; confusedly, irregularly. M16.

disordinate /dɪsˈɔːdɪnət/ *a.* Long *rare.* LME. [med.L *disordinatus* inordinate, for cl.L *inordinatus*, f. *ordinatus* ORDINATE *a.*: see DIS- 2.] Transgressing the bounds of what is fitting or reasonable; unrestrained, inordinate.

disordinately *adv.* L15.

disordination /ˌdɪsɔːdɪˈneɪʃ(ə)n/ *n.* Long *rare.* E17. [med.L *disordinatio(n-)* disarrangement, f. *disordinat-* pa. ppl stem of *disordinare*, f. L DIS- 2 + *ordinare* ORDAIN: see -ATION.] The action of disarranging or putting out of order; disordered or uncoordinated condition.

disorganize /dɪsˈɔːgənʌɪz/ *v.t.* Also **-ise.** L18. [Fr. *désorganiser* f. *des-* DIS- 2 + *organiser* ORGANIZE. This and related wds date in Eng. from the French Revolution.] Destroy the organization, systematic arrangement, or orderly connection of; throw into confusion. Chiefly as *disorganized* ppl a.

J. RUSKIN A vast and disorganized mob, scrambling each for what he can get.

disorganiˈzation *n.* L18. **disorganizer** *n.* L18.

disorient /dɪsˈɔːrɪɛnt/ *v.t.* M17. [Fr. *désorienter*, f. *des-* DIS- 2 + *orienter* ORIENT *v.*] Cause (a person) to lose his or her sense of direction; make confused as to what is true or correct.

disorientate /dɪsˈɔːrɪənteɪt/ *v.t.* E18. [f. DIS- 2 + ORIENTATE.] **1** Turn from the east, give an alignment other than eastern; change or vary the alignment of. E18. **2** = DISORIENT. E18.

1 R. F. CHAPMAN The membrane is usually.. made up.. of disoriented fibres in an amorphous matrix.

disˌorienˈtation *n.* (*a*) deviation from an eastern alignment; (*b*) the condition of having lost one's bearings; a confused mental state (sometimes caused by disease) in which a person's sense of time, place, or personal identity is disturbed: M19.

disour /ˈdɪzʊə, dɪˈzʊə/ *n. obs.* exc. *Hist.* ME. [OFr. (mod. *diseur*), f. *dire* say: see -OUR. Cf. DISEUSE.] A professional storyteller, a minstrel; a jester.

disown /dɪsˈəʊn/ *v.t.* E17. [f. DIS- 2 + OWN *v.*] †**1** Cease to own; renounce possession of. Only in E17. **2** Refuse to acknowledge as one's own; disclaim, repudiate. M17. **b** Refuse to acknowledge the authority of. L17. †**3** Refuse to acknowledge or admit (something asserted); deny. M17–E18. **4** In the Society of Friends: expel, repudiate from membership. E18.

2 R. G. COLLINGWOOD Bad art arises when instead of expressing these emotions we disown them. L. DURRELL Her family had disowned her and turned her out.

disowner *n.* L19. **disownment** *n.* the action or an act of disowning; *spec.* expulsion from the Society of Friends: E19.

†**dispaint** *v.t. rare* (Spenser). Only in L16. [f. DIS- 1 + PAINT *v.*] Paint with various colours.

†**dispair** *v.t.* L16–M18. [f. DIS- 2 + PAIR *n.*[1]] End the pairing of, separate (things forming a pair).

†**disparage** *n.* ME. [OFr. *desparage* unsuitable marriage, f. *des-* DIS- 2 + *parage* equality of rank f. Proto-Romance, f. L *par* equal: see -AGE.] **1** Inequality of rank in marriage; an unequal match; disgrace resulting from this. ME–L16. **2** Disparagement, dishonour. LME–E17.

1 SPENSER Her friends.. Dissuaded her from such a disparage.

disparage /dɪˈsparɪdʒ/ *v.t.* LME. [OFr. *desparagier*, f. as prec.] †**1** Marry (oneself or another) to someone of unequal rank; degrade by such a match. LME–L18. **2** Bring discredit or reproach upon; dishonour; lower in esteem. LME. †**3** Degrade, lower in position or dignity; cast down in spirit. LME–E18. **4** Speak of or treat slightingly or critically; vilify; undervalue, depreciate. E16.

3 POPE I am disparaged and disheartened by your commendations. ADDISON I'll not disparage myself to be a Servant in a House that is haunted. 4 W. PLOMER Too loyal and fond a parent to say anything disparaging about him. P. MEDAWAR To express dissatisfaction with psychoanalysis is not to disparage psychological medicine as a whole.

disparager *n.* a person who disparages, a detractor E17. **disparagingly** *adv.* in a disparaging manner E18.

disparagement /dɪˈsparɪdʒm(ə)nt/ *n.* L15. [OFr., f. as prec.: see -MENT.] **1** Lowering of value, honour, or estimation; dishonour, disgrace, indignity, discredit; something that causes this. L15. **2** Marriage to a person of inferior rank; disgrace or dishonour incurred by this. *obs.* exc. *Hist.* E16. **3** The action or an act of referring to or treating in a slighting or depreciatory way; depreciation, detraction; undervaluing. L16.

1 MILTON The learnedest of England thought it no disparagement to sit at his feet.

disparate /ˈdɪsp(ə)rət/ *a.* & *n.* LME. [L *disparatus* pa. pple of *disparare* separate, f. as DIS- 1 + *parare* prepare. In use often assoc. w. L *dispar* unequal (cf. DISPARITY).] **A** *adj.* **1** Essentially different or diverse in kind, unlike; incommensurable, without comparison or relation; composed of elements of this kind. LME. **2** Unequal. M18.

1 E. JONES I can perceive a connexion between these apparently disparate topics. M. EDWARDES These problems faced a disparate group of people. 2 F. W. FARRAR His authority was in no way disparate with theirs.

B *n.* A disparate thing or person; *esp.* in *pl.*, things so unlike that there is no basis for their comparison. L16.

disparately *adv.* L19. **disparateness** *n.* M17.

disparition /dɪspəˈrɪʃ(ə)n/ *n.* Now *literary.* L16. [Fr., f. *disparaître* disappear, after *apparition.*] Disappearance.

disparity /dɪˈsparɪti/ *n.* M16. [Fr. *disparité* f. late L *disparitas*, f. *paritas* PARITY *n.*[1]: see DIS- 2.] **1**

For other words beginning with *dis-* see the entry for **dis-**

The quality of being unlike or different; dissimilarity, difference, incongruity; an instance of this. M16. 2 Inequality (of age, rank, strength, etc.); an instance of this. L16.

1 H. L. MENCKEN The disparity between the glorious .. passing imagined by the young soldier and the messy finish that is normally in store. 2 W. S. CHURCHILL He watched vigilantly for the chance of a battle, even at a disparity in odds.

dispark /dɪsˈpɑːk/ *v.t.* M16. [f. DIS- 2 + PARK *n.* Cf. Fr. †*desparquer* (now *dé-*).] Deprive of the status of a park; convert (parkland) to other uses.

dispart /dɪsˈpɑːt/ *n.* L16. [Origin uncertain: perh. f. DISPART *v.*[1]] 1 The difference between the semi-diameter of a gun at the base ring and at the swell of the muzzle. L16. 2 A sight-mark placed on the muzzle of a gun, to make the line of sight parallel to the bore. Also *dispart-sight.* L16.

dispart /dɪsˈpɑːt/ *v.*[1] *arch.* L16. [It. (*di*)*spartire* divide, part, or L *dispartire* distribute, divide, f. as DIS- 1 + *partire* PART *v.*] 1 *v.t.* & *i.* Part asunder, split in two. L16. 2 *v.t.* Divide into parts or shares; distribute. E17. 3 *v.t.* Separate, sever; dissolve (a union). M17.

1 J. WESLEY The Sea .. fled, Disparted by the wondrous Rod. 2 F. ROBERTS The Old Testament .. is disparted by the Holy Ghost himself into two general heads.

dispartment *n.* (*rare*) a separation, a split L17.

dispart /dɪsˈpɑːt/ *v.*[2]*t.* L16. [f. DISPART *n.*] 1 Ascertain the dispart of (a gun); make allowance for the dispart in aiming (a gun). L16. 2 Provide (a gun) with a dispart-sight. M17.

dispassion /dɪsˈpaʃ(ə)n/ *v.* & *n.* E17. [f. DIS- 2 + PASSION *n.*] †A *v.t.* Free from passion. Chiefly as *dispassioned* ppl a. E17–M18. B *n.* Freedom from passion; calmness. Formerly also, apathy. L17.

dispassionate /dɪsˈpaʃ(ə)nət/ *a.* L16. [f. DIS- 2 + PASSIONATE *a.*] Free from the influence or effect of strong emotion; calm; impartial.

J. R. GREEN A dispassionate fairness towards older faiths. E. BOWEN Matchett's voice was flat and dispassionate.

dispassionately *adv.* M17. **dispassionateness** *n.* M19.

dispatch /dɪˈspatʃ/ *n.* Also **des-**. M16. [f. next, or It. *dispaccio*, Sp. *despacho*.] I An act or quality. †1 Dismissal of a person after settlement of business; *spec.* official dismissal given to an ambassador on completion of his errand. M16–L17. 2 Killing; death by violence. L16. 3 Settlement of business, accomplishment of a task; (prompt or speedy) performance. L16. †b Conduct, management. *rare* (Shakes.). Only in E17. 4 Prompt settlement or accomplishment; promptitude; speed, efficiency, rapidity of progress. L16. 5 The sending of a messenger, letter, etc. to a destination or for a purpose. E17. †6 The act of getting rid or disposing of something, esp. hastily. E–M17.

2 **happy dispatch** *joc.* hara-kiri. *hatches, matches and dispatches*: see HATCH *n.*[2] 3 H. MARTINEAU Three members of the Committee sat daily for the dispatch of common business. A. WILSON Sonia's voice was as cool .. as the quick despatch with which she wound the bandage round the little boy's arm. b SHAKES. *Macb.* You shall put This night's great business into my dispatch. 4 CARLYLE All turns on dispatch; loiter a little, and Friedrich himself will be here again! R. BRADBURY She worked with energy and dispatch. 5 S. PEPYS To Woolwich to give order for the dispatch of a ship.

II A thing. 7 A written message given or requiring fast delivery, *esp.* an official one on State or military matters; a piece sent in by a reporter. M16. 8 An agency for the quick transmission of goods etc.; a conveyance by which goods or mail are dispatched. L17. 9 A false die with some faces bearing the wrong number of spots. *arch. slang.* E19.

7 **mentioned in dispatches** distinguished by having one's actions commended in an official military dispatch. 8 *pneumatic dispatch*: see PNEUMATIC *a.*

Comb.: **dispatch-boat** a fast vessel for carrying dispatches; **dispatch-box**, **-case** a container for carrying official (esp. State) and other documents; an attaché case. **dispatch-rider** a rider, esp. a motorcyclist or horseman, who carries (esp. military) dispatches.

dispatchful *a.* †(*a*) having the quality of doing away with expeditiously; (*b*) *arch.* characterized by dispatch, expeditious, hasty: E17.

dispatch /dɪˈspatʃ/ *v.* Also **des-**. E16. [It. *dispacciare* or Sp. *despachar* expedite, f. as DIS- 2 + base (of unkn. origin) of It. *impacciare* hinder, stop, Sp., Port. *empachar* impede, embarrass.] I *v.t.* 1 Send off to a particular destination or recipient or for a particular purpose. E16. †2 Send away from one's presence or employment; dismiss, discharge. M16–M17. 3 Dismiss (a person) after settling his or her business; deal with and send away. Now *rare*. M16. 4 Get rid or dispose of (a person) by putting to death; execute, kill. Formerly also, get rid of or banish (anything), dispel. M16. †b End (a person's life). L16–M17. 5 Get (a task or piece of business) promptly done; accomplish, finish off, conclude. M16. b Eat (food, a meal) quickly; consume, devour. *colloq.* E18. †6 Rid (esp. a person) of an encumbrance or hindrance; deliver, relieve; deprive. Foll. by *of*, *from*. M16–M17.

1 R. DAVENPORT Embassadors were dispatch'd to Bergamo. H. MACMILLAN I despatched a message to the new Prime Minister. A. TOFFLER The maintenance supervisor would dispatch a crew to repair the damage. 4 HENRY MILLER Like mopping up a battlefield: all those who are hopelessly disabled .. you dispatch with one swift blow. 5 J. PRIESTLEY Dominic easily dispatched this task in six days.

II *v.i.* †7 Start promptly for a destination, hurry away. L16–E18. 8 Make haste (*to do*), be quick. *arch.* L16. †9 Conclude or settle one's business; get through, have done (*with*). E–M17.

Phrases: **dispatch out of life, the world**, etc. (now *rare* or *obs.*) kill.

dispatcher *n.* (*a*) a person who or thing which dispatches, *esp.* a person who gives orders for the departure of goods or vehicles; (*b*) *arch. slang* = DISPATCH *n.* 9: M16.

†**dispeed** *v.t.* E17–E19. [App. f. It. †*dispedire*, f. *dis-* DIS- 1 + *spedire* dispatch f. L *expedire* (see EXPEDITE *v.*): infl. in sp. by SPEED *v.*] Dispatch, send off; *refl.* go away quickly.

dispel /dɪˈspɛl/ *v.* Infl. **-ll-**. LME. [L *dispellere*, f. as DIS- 1 + *pellere* to drive.] 1 *v.t.* Drive away, banish, dissipate, (now, something immaterial or vaporous). LME. 2 *v.i.* Be dispelled. M17.

1 M. MITCHELL The fresh air could do little toward dispelling the sickening odours. *New York Law Journal* The court first dispelled any shareholder's liability under the restrictive covenant. J. CHEEVER Any sense of obligation .. was dispelled by their knowing that they were useful to their hostess. N. SAHGAL Cupboard doors were open to dispel monsoon damp.

dispeller *n.* E18.

dispend /dɪˈspɛnd/ *v.t.* Pa. t. & pple **dispended, dispent** /dɪˈspɛnt/. ME. [OFr. *despendre* expend f. L *dispendere* weigh out, pay out, f. as DIS- 1 + *pendere* weigh.] 1 Pay out (money), expend (resources etc.). Now *rare* or *obs.* ME. †2 Employ, consume, or occupy (time). ME–L16. †3 Waste, squander. ME–L15. †4 Distribute, dispense, esp. in charity to the poor. ME–M17. †5 Bring to an end; exhaust, use up. Usu. in *pass.* LME–E16.

dispendious /dɪˈspɛndɪəs/ *a.* M16. [f. L *dispendiosus* hurtful, f. as next: see -OUS. In sense 2 through Fr. *dispendieux* expensive.] †1 Injurious. Only in M16. 2 Expensive; extravagant. E18.

†**dispendium** *n.* Pl. **-iums, -ia**. M17–E18. [L, f. *dispendere*: see DISPEND.] Loss, waste; expenditure, expense.

dispensable /dɪˈspɛnsəb(ə)l/ *a.* In senses 1 & 2 also **-ible**. E16. [med.L *dispensabilis*, f. L *dispensare* DISPENSE *v.*: see -ABLE, -IBLE.] 1 *Eccl.* Subject to dispensation; *spec.* (of action normally prohibited) able to be permitted or condoned in special circumstances; (of a law, vow, etc.) able to be relaxed in special cases. E16. 2 Allowable, excusable. Now *rare* or *obs.* L16. 3 Able to be dispensed with or done without; not necessary, inessential; unimportant. M17.

dispensaˈbility, dispensableness *ns.* the quality of being dispensable M17.

dispensary /dɪˈspɛns(ə)ri/ *n.* L17. [med.L *dispensarium* use as n. of neut. of *dispensarius*, f. L *dispensare*: see DISPENSE *v.*, -ARY[1].] 1 A place, esp. a room in a doctor's surgery or a chemist's shop, in which medicines are dispensed; a public or charitable institution for dispensing medicines or giving medical advice. L17. †2 A collection of different drugs. E–M18.

dispensate /dɪˈspɛnseɪt/ *v.t.* *rare.* E18. [L *dispensat-* pa. ppl stem of *dispensare*: see DISPENSE *v.*, -ATE[3].] Dispense; distribute.

dispensation /dɪspɛnˈseɪʃ(ə)n/ *n.* LME. [(O)Fr. f. L *dispensatio(n-)* (in branch II as tr. Gk *oikonomia* in New Testament and patristic writers), f. as prec.: see -ATION.] I Dealing out, distribution. 1 The action or an act of dispensing or dealing out; distribution; disbursement; economical use or disposal. LME. 2 The process of dispensing a medicine or prescription. M17.

1 I. D'ISRAELI Elizabeth, a queen well known for her penurious dispensations. J. TULLOCH Changes in the dispensation of the Lord's Supper.

II (A mode of) ordering, management. 3 The orderly administration of affairs committed to one's charge; stewardship. *arch.* LME. 4 The ordering of events by divine Providence. Formerly also *gen.*, ordering, management; (an) arrangement. LME. b An arrangement made by providence or nature; a special dealing of providence with a community, family, or person; a judgement, (esp.) a blessing. M17. 5 A religious system regarded as divinely ordained for a particular nation or period (freq. w. specifying wd); the age characterized by such a system; any established or prevailing system under which one lives or works. M17.

4b R. HOOKE So infinitely wise and provident do we find all the Dispensations in Nature. SIR W. SCOTT A humbling dispensation on the house of Peveril. 1 I. A. RICHARDS There are some who, by a natural dispensation, acquire the 'Open Sesame!' to poetry without labour. 5 W. BRUCE The Israelitish dispensation was abolished by the First Coming of Christ. J. BRAINE The last evening under the old dispensation I remember as one remembers the party on the eve of the mutiny.

III Dispensing with a requirement. 6 *Eccl.* (The granting of) a licence permitting in special circumstances the exemption of a person from a penalty or obligation of canon law. LME. 7 The action of dispensing *with* something or doing without. L16. 8 The relaxation or suspension of a statute in a particular case. E17. 9 An exemption, a release from an obligation or requirement; a concession. E17.

6 C. MCCULLOUGH Once your final vows are taken and you are ordained, .. there can be no going back, no dispensation. *transf.*: DRYDEN 'Tis a crime past dispensation. 9 S. JOHNSON Our intimacy was regarded by me as a dispensation from ceremonial visits. W. STYRON Moore gave us five days of absence—a fairly common dispensation during August.

dispenˈsational *a.* L19. **dispensationalism** *n.* (*Chr. Theol.*) belief in a system of historical progression as revealed in the Bible, consisting of a series of (*spec.* seven) stages in God's self-revelation and plan of salvation E20. **dispensationalist** *n.* (*Chr. Theol.*) an adherent of dispensationalism M20.

dispensative /dɪˈspɛnsətɪv/ *a.* Long *rare.* E16. [Late L *dispensativus*, f. L *dispensat-*: see DISPENSATE, -IVE. Cf. (O)Fr. *dispensatif*, *-ive*.] †1 = DISPENSATORY *a.* 1. E16–M17. 2 = DISPENSATORY *a.* 2. E17.

dispensatively *adv.* L16.

dispensator /ˈdɪspɛnseɪtə/ *n.* Now *rare.* LME. [AN *dispensatour*, OFr. *dispensateur* f. L *dispensator*, f. *dispensat-*: see DISPENSATE, -OR 2.] A person who dispenses. Formerly, a steward.

dispensatory /dɪˈspɛnsət(ə)ri/ *n.* M16. [med.L *dispensatorium* storeroom, pantry, pharmacopoeia, use as n. of neut. of late L *dispensatorius*: see next.] 1 A book containing a list of medicines with directions for their use and sometimes their composition and preparation; a pharmacopoeia. M16. 2 A dispensary; *gen.* a place where something is dispensed or given out. Now *rare* or *obs.* L16. †3 = DISPENSARY 2. M17–M18.

dispensatory /dɪˈspɛnsət(ə)ri/ *a.* M17. [Late L *dispensatorius*, f. L *dispensator* DISPENSATOR: see -ORY[1]. In sense 2 f. med.L eccl. use.] †**1** (Of power) exercised by virtue of office; of or pertaining to an administrator or administration. M–L17. **2** That gives dispensations; able to dispense with laws or rules. M17.

dispensatorily *adv.* by dispensation M17.

dispensatrix /dɪspɛnˈseɪtrɪks/ *n.* Pl. **-trices** /-trɪsiːz/. M19. [L, fem. of DISPENSATOR: see -TRIX.] A female dispenser.

dispense /dɪˈspɛns/ *n.* ME. [OFr. *despense* f. med.L *dispensa* use as n. of fem. sing. of pa. pple of *dispendere*: see DISPEND. In senses 3 and 6 prob. f. the vb.] †**1** The act of spending; expenditure; in *pl.*, expenses, costs. ME–E18. †**2** Means of meeting expenditure, money to spend; in *pl.*, supplies. LME–M17. †**3** *Eccl.* = DISPENSATION 6. L15–L18. †**4** The act of dispensing or bestowing liberally. *rare* (Spenser). Only in L16. †**5** A pantry, a buttery. Only in E17. **6** In full *dispense bar*. A bar in a club or hotel for the use of the staff. M20.

dispense /dɪˈspɛns/ *v.* LME. [OFr. *despenser* f. L *dispensare* weigh out, disburse, frequent. of *dispendere*: see DISPEND.] **I** *v.t.* f. cl.L. **1** Distribute, deal out; give out as a share from a general stock. LME. †**b** Spend, employ, (time or talents). E–M17. **2** Administer (a sacrament, justice, authority). LME. **3** Make up (medicine) according to a prescription, give out (a prescribed medicine); carry out (a prescription). M16.

1 S. BRETT The hostess . . dispensed cold tea. I. MCEWAN Patricians dispensing to their son or nephew . . the fruits of their sagacity and wealth. **2** J. A. MICHENER He dispensed an impartial justice which protected men in their ownership of . . property. **3** *fig.*: W. H. AUDEN Panic, shock, are dispensed in measured doses/by fool-proof engines.

II *v.i.* & *t.* f. med.L in eccl. use. **4** *v.i.* Use a power of granting dispensations; grant a dispensation (*in* a special case). LME. †**5** *v.t.* Relax the law in reference to (some thing or person); permit (a person or act) by dispensation; condone. LME–M17. †**6** *v.t.* Do without, forgo. LME–M17. **7** *v.t.* Grant (a person) a dispensation (*from* an obligation or promise). Formerly also, dissolve the obligation of (a vow) by ecclesiastical authority. M16. †**8** *v.i.* Make amends or compensation *for*. *rare* (Spenser). Only in L16.

4 C. O'CONOR The Pope could not dispense in the allegiance due by Catholics to their Sovereigns. **7** J. G. COZZENS He was even dispensed from Lenten abstinence so he could dine with the worldly.

III *v.i.* Foll. by *with* (f. sense 4). †**9** Arrange to grant (a person) dispensation from a law, penalty, or duty; exempt or excuse (oneself) *from* doing something. LME–L18. †**b** Compound with to gain exemption for an offence or a penalty. M16–M17. **10** Arrange to relax or remit the penalty or obligation of (a law or rule), esp. in a special case; give special exemption or relief from. LME. **11** Relax the obligation of (a vow or promise); dissolve the binding force of (an oath), esp. in special circumstances. M16. †**12** Disregard (a duty); fail to heed (one's religious faith). M16–M18. †**13** Deal with (a breach of law) so as to condone it; permit or condone (something illegal or irregular) by dispensation. M16–E18. †**14** Deal with tolerantly; cope with; put up with. L16–L18. **15** Do away with (a requirement or necessity); make unnecessary or superfluous. L16. **16** Excuse or put up with the absence of (a thing or person); forgo, do without. E17.

9 H. LATIMER God had dispensed wyth theym to have manye wyues. **b** SHAKES. *2 Hen. VI* Canst thou dispense with heaven for such an oath? **10** R. BOLT The Pope dispensed with the Christian law forbidding a man to marry his brother's widow. **13** ADDISON His religion dispenses with the violation of the most sacred engagements. **15** F. HALL Familiar facts dispense with all need to draw on the imagination. **16** DICKENS Let us dispense with compliments. P. G. WODEHOUSE Suppose we dispense with coffee and go round and see him.

dispenser /dɪˈspɛnsə/ *n.* LME. [Partly f. OFr. *despenseor*, *-eur* f. L *dispensator* DISPENSATOR; partly f. AN *despens(i)er*, OFr. *despensier*, *dis-* = med.L *dispensarius*, f. med.L *dispensa* DISPENSE *n.*: see -ER[2].] **1 a** A steward of a household. *arch.* LME. **b** An administrator of the law, authority, etc. M17. **2** A person who dispenses or deals out; a spender. LME. **3** A person who dispenses medicines. M19. **4** A container designed to release a predetermined amount; (more fully *cash dispenser*) a machine from which an authorized person can withdraw cash and have a bank account automatically debited. M20.

dispensible *a.* see DISPENSABLE.

dispensive /dɪˈspɛnsɪv/ *a.* Now *rare* or *obs.* L16. [L *dispens-* pa. ppl stem of *dispendere*: see DISPEND *v.*, -IVE. Assoc. w. DISPENSE *v.*] †**1** Subject to dispensation. Only in L16. †**2** Characterized by or given to spending or disbursing. M–L17. **3** = DISPENSATORY *a.* 2. E19.

dispeople /dɪsˈpiːp(ə)l/ *v.t.* LME. [OFr. *despeupler* (mod. *dé-*) f. Proto-Romance, f. L DIS- 2 + *populus* PEOPLE *n.* Cf. DEPEOPLE.] **1** Empty of people; depopulate. LME. †**2** Exterminate (people). Also, make no longer a distinct people. L16–L17. **3** Remove all living creatures from. M17.

dispeopler *n.* E17.

dispermous /dʌɪˈspəːməs/ *a.* M18. [f. DI-[2] + Gk *sperma* seed + -OUS.] *Bot.* Having two seeds.

dispermy /ˈdʌɪspəːmi/ *n.* L19. [f. as prec. + -Y[3].] *Biol.* The entrance of two sperms into a single egg.

diˈspermic *a.* E20.

dispersal /dɪˈspəːs(ə)l/ *n.* E16. [f. DISPERSE *v.* + -AL[1].] **1** The action of dispersing; the condition or state of being dispersed; = DISPERSION 1. E16. **2** In full *dispersal area*, *point*. Any of several separated areas on an airfield where aircraft are parked to minimize their combined vulnerability to attack. M20.

disperse /dɪˈspəːs/ *a.* LME. [In sense 1 f. OFr. *dispers*, in sense 2 f. G *dispers*, both f. L *dispersus* pa. pple of *dispergere*: see next.] †**1** Dispersed. LME–E16. **2** *Chem.* Of a phase: dispersed in another. Of a system: consisting of one phase dispersed in another, continuous, phase. E20.

disperse /dɪˈspəːs/ *v.* LME. [L *dispers-* pa. ppl stem of *dispergere* scatter, f. as DIS- 1 + *spargere* strew.] **1** *v.t.* Drive, throw, or send in different directions; scatter, rout. LME. **2** *v.t.* Distribute from a main source or centre; put (books, currency, or commodities) in circulation; spread around, disseminate. LME. **3** *v.t.* Place or station at widely separated points. Freq. in *pass.* E16. †**4** *v.t.* Separate into parts; divide. M16–E17. †**5** *v.t.* Make known; publish. M16–E17. **6** *v.t.* Cause (esp. something unpleasant) to disappear; dispel, dissipate. M16. **7** *v.i.* Become dispelled or dissipated. L16. **8** *v.i.* (Of people) separate and go different ways; (of a crowd or gathering) break up. M17. **9** *v.t.* *Physics.* Separate (light) into its constituent wavelengths. M17. **10** *v.t.* *Sci.* Distribute (a substance) as small particles throughout another, continuous, one, e.g. in a solution. E20.

1 WORDSWORTH Her feet disperse the powdery snow. P. L. FERMOR The heralds were dispersed, the regiments disbanded . . long ago. **2** C. BURNEY A practice . . thence dispersed into all parts of the Christian world. **3** N. MAILER The regiment was dispersed over an area twenty miles wide and more than ten miles deep. **6** G. W. KNIGHT A clear daylight now disperses the imaginative dark that has eclipsed Scotland. **7** R. L. STEVENSON The dust . . dispersed like the smoke of battle. **8** E. HUXLEY Not only have Jews dispersed first from the Leylands, then to Chapeltown and now to other parts of the city.

dispersaˈbility *n.* M20. **dispersable** *a.* E19. **dispersant** *n.* an agent which causes or maintains a state of dispersion in a surrounding medium; a dispersing agent: M20. **dispersedly** *adv.* in a dispersed or scattered manner M16. **dispersedness** *n.* the condition or state of being dispersed or scattered L16. **disperser** *n.* L16. **dispersiˈbility** *n.* M20. **dispersible** *a.* M20.

dispersion /dɪˈspəːʃ(ə)n/ *n.* LME. [Late L *dispersio(n-)* scattering, f. as prec.: see -ION.] **1** The action of dispersing or scattering abroad; diffusion, dissemination; the condition or state of being dispersed. LME. **b** (Also **D-**.) = DIASPORA. LME. **2** *Physics.* The phenomenon by which light of different wavelengths is spread out by a prism etc. into a spectrum; a variation of speed of propagation of light, sound, etc., with wavelength; the degree of this. E18. **3** *Med.* The removal of inflammation, suppuration, etc., from a part. Now *rare* or *obs.* M18. **4** *Statistics.* The degree to which a set of observed values are spread over a range. L19. **5** *Chem.* A mixture of one substance dispersed throughout another, continuous, one; an emulsion, aerosol, etc.; the state of being so dispersed. E20.

1b H. A. L. FISHER The Dutch settlers in Cape Colony were not imperialists, still less were the Dutch dispersion in the interior.

Comb.: **dispersion hardening** hardening of an alloy by heating at high temperatures followed by rapid cooling, causing the dispersion of one constituent.

dispersive /dɪˈspəːsɪv/ *a.* E17. [f. DISPERSE *v.* + -IVE. Cf. (O)Fr. *dispersif*, *-ive*.] Having the character or quality of dispersing, serving or tending to disperse something; *Physics* causing dispersion (of light etc.).

dispersiveness *n.* M19. **disperˈsivity** *n.* the degree to which the refractive index of a substance varies with wavelength E20.

dispersoid /dɪˈspəːsɔɪd/ *n.* E20. [f. DISPERSE *a.* + -OID.] *Chem.* A disperse system.

dispersonalize /dɪsˈpəːs(ə)n(ə)lʌɪz/ *v.t.* Also **-ise**. L19. [f. DIS- 2 + PERSONALIZE.] = DISPERSONATE 2.

dispersonate /dɪsˈpəːsəneɪt/ *v.t.* E17. [f. DIS- 2 + L *persona* mask + -ATE[3].] †**1** Strip of an assumed character, unmask. Only in E17. **2** Destroy or remove the personality of. Chiefly *refl.* E18.

dispersonify /dɪspəˈsɒnɪfʌɪ/ *v.t.* M19. [f. DIS- 2 + PERSONIFY.] Represent or regard as impersonal.

ˌdispersonifiˈcation *n.* L19.

disphenoid /dʌɪˈsfiːnɔɪd/ *n.* L19. [f. DI-[2] + SPHENOID.] *Cryst.* A solid formed by eight similar scalene triangles, a tetragonal scalenohedron. Also, a crystal form like a double wedge formed by two pairs of scalene or isosceles triangles and having two planes of symmetry.

dispiece /dɪsˈpiːs/ *v.t.* Now *rare.* L15. [OFr. *despiecer* (mod. *dépiécer*), f. *des-* DIS- 1 + PIECE *n.*] Divide into pieces.

dispirit /dɪˈspɪrɪt/ *v.t.* M17. [f. DIS- 2 + SPIRIT *n.*] †**1** Deprive of essential quality or force; deprive of vigour, weaken; deprive (liquor) of its spirit. M17–M18. **2** Lower the morale of, make despondent; dishearten. M17.

2 C. P. SNOW He was dispirited because his triumph . . had not been as intoxicating as he had imagined. T. GUNN I was trying to write novels and poetry, but the results were . . dispiriting.

dispiritedly *adv.* in a dispirited way M19. **dispiritedness** *n.* a dispirited state M17. **dispiritingly** *adv.* in a dispiriting manner L19. **dispiritment** *n.* dispiritedness, disheartenment E19.

dispiteous /dɪsˈpɪtɪəs/ *a.* LME. [Orig. var. of DESPITEOUS; later f. DIS- 2 + PITEOUS.] **1** = DESPITEOUS 1. Now *arch. rare.* LME. **2** Orig., spiteful, malevolent, cruel. Later, pitiless, merciless. E16.

dispiteously *adv.* LME. **dispiteousness** *n.* M19.

displace /dɪsˈpleɪs/ *v.t.* M16. [Partly f. DIS- 2 + PLACE *n.*[1]; partly after Fr. †*desplacer* (now *dé-*), f. *des-* DIS- 1, 2 + PLACE *n.*[1], *placer* vb to place. Cf. DEPLACE.] **1** Move from its proper or usual place. M16. †**b** *fig.* Remove, banish. L16–L17. **2** Remove from office. M16. **3** Replace with something else; take the place of, supplant. L18.

1 displaced person: removed from his or her home country by military events or political pressure. **3** A. CHRISTIE She displaced Midge from the sofa, settled Gerda there. J. BARZUN The notion of helping a child has . . displaced that of teaching him.

displaceaˈbility *n.* L19. **displaceable** *a.* L17. **displacer** *n.* L16.

displacement /dɪsˈpleɪsm(ə)nt/ *n.* E17. [f. prec. + -MENT; in sense 1 perh. f. Fr. †*desplacement*.] **1** Removal from office. *rare.* E17. **2** The moving of something from its place or position; the extent of such a movement; the difference or relation between an initial position of a body and a subsequent position. E19. **3** The removal of something by something else which takes its place; *spec.* the fact of a submerged or partly submerged body occupying a volume which would otherwise be occupied by the fluid; the amount or weight of fluid that would fill this volume in the case of a floating ship etc. E19. **b** *Mech.* The volume swept by a reciprocating system, as in a pump or engine. L19. **4** *Electr.* More fully *electric displacement*. Orig., the polarized state of a dielectric in an electric field. Now, (a vector representing) the component of an electric field due to free separated charges, regardless of any polarization effects; the flux density of such a field. L19. **5** *Psychoanalysis.* The unconscious transfer of an emotion from its original object to something else; the unconscious substitution of an inoffensive concept or activity for one that is disturbing or unacceptable; an instance of such a transfer. E20.

2 S. HAUGHTON A vertical displacement of the strata. 3 W. H. G. KINGSTON Her total length is 320 feet.. with a displacement of 11,407 tons. 5 H. SEGAL She considers an interest in the world to be a displacement from the basic interest in one's own and the parents' bodies.

Phrases & comb.: **displacement activity** (an) animal or human activity that seems irrelevant to the situation in which it occurs. **displacement current** a notional electric current associated with a changing electric field not produced by an actual current, and proportional to the rate of change of displacement with time. **displacement pump** any pump in which liquid is moved out of the pump chamber by a moving surface or by the introduction of compressed air or gas. *displacement ton*: see TON *n.*[1] 2. *displacement tonnage*: see TONNAGE *n.* VIRTUAL *displacement*.

displacency /dɪsˈpleɪs(ə)nsi/ *n.* Now *rare* or *obs.* M17. [med.L *displacentia* for L *displicentia* DISPLICENCY, or alt. of DISPLICENCY.] = DISPLICENCY.

displant /dɪsˈplɑːnt/ *v.t.* L15. [Fr. †*desplanter* (now *déplanter*) f. Proto-Romance, f. L DIS- 1 + *plantare* plant.] **1** Uproot (a plant). L15. †**2** Remove from a town or country of settlement; undo the settlement of (a town, colony, etc.). L16–M17. †**3** *fig.* Eradicate; supplant. E–M17.

display /dɪˈspleɪ/ *n.* L16. [f. the vb.] †**1** Presentation in writing; a description. L16–E18. **2** Something intended for people to look at; an exhibition, a show. M17. **b** A visual presentation of data or signals on the screen of a cathode-ray tube etc.; a device or system used for this. Also more fully *visual display*. M20. **3** The action or an act of displaying or exhibiting to view; (a) manifestation; exhibition, show. L17. **b** The presentation of printed matter in such a way as to make it visually prominent. E19. **c** A specialized pattern of behaviour used by a bird as visual communication. E20. **4** Showiness, ostentation. E19.

2 M. MOORCOCK The better shops were filled with light and wonderful displays. **b** *visual display unit*: see VISUAL *a.* *video display terminal* or *unit*: see VIDEO *a.* & *n.* 3 *Economist* Mrs Marcos's famous collection of shoes now on display in Manila. A. CHRISTIE This display of Edward's unerring and fastidious taste. **b** attrib.: *New Zealand Listener* The display size of the type used makes the distinctive form of the 'long s' self-evident. **c** A. MANNING Some birds have evolved elaborate mutual courtship displays. 4 BYRON As erring man should die, Without display, without parade.

Comb.: **display cabinet, -case**: for displaying items for observation or inspection; **display type**: used for displaying printed matter.

display /dɪˈspleɪ/ *v.* ME. [OFr. *despleier* (mod. *déployer* DEPLOY *v.*) f. L *displicare* scatter, disperse, (in med.L) unfold, f. as DIS- 1, 2 + *plicare* fold.] **I** *v.t.* **1** Unfurl, unfold to view. *obs.* exc. w. implication of sense 3. ME. **2** Lay or place with the limbs extended; to extend (a limb, wing, etc.); *spec.* in *Her.*, extend the wings of (a bird of prey) (chiefly as *displayed* ppl a.). ME. †**b** Carve (a crane) for the table. L15–E19. **3** Expose to view, make visible; show, exhibit. ME. **b** *Typogr.* Make (matter) more prominent by using larger type, open layout, etc. L19. †**4** Describe in words, unfold in narrative; expound, explain. LME–E19. **5** Show (a quality) to be possessed by the subject; reveal; allow to be perceived, give evidence of, make manifest. L15. †**6** Get sight of. L16–E17. †**7** Give voice to, utter. L16–M17. **8** Exhibit ostentatiously; make a show of. E17.

1 POPE See.. her sable flag display'd. 2 SPENSER Thou.. Thy careles limbs in loose sleep dost display. 3 J. BERGER A dress displayed in a shop window. 5 G. SAINTSBURY They often display much more real critical power than later writers. S. NAIPAUL To bring the subject up was to display bad manners. 6 SPENSER They.. did at last display That wanton Lady, with her lover. 8 J. CONRAD The.. forecastle.. where he could display his talents.

II *v.i.* †**9** Show off, behave ostentatiously. *rare* (Shakes.). Only in E17. **10** Of a bird: engage in or use display as visual communication. E20.

10 D. A. BANNERMAN A male gold-crest displaying to the lady of his choice.

displayable *a.* (*rare*) M19. **displayer** *n.* E17.

†**disple** *v.t.* L15–M17. [App. f. DISCIPLINE *n.* or *v.*] Subject to discipline, penance, or punishment, esp. as a religious practice.

SPENSER Bitter Penaunce, with an yron whip, Was wont him once to disple every day.

displeasance /dɪsˈplɛz(ə)ns/ *n.* Long *arch. rare.* ME. [OFr. *desplaisance* (mod. *déplaisance*), f. as next: see -ANCE.] Displeasure. Formerly also, a grievance.

displeasant /dɪsˈplɛz(ə)nt/ *a.* Long *arch. rare.* LME. [OFr. *desplaisant* pres. pple of *desplaisir*: see next, -ANT[1].] **1** Unpleasant; displeasing. LME. †**2** Displeased. L15–E18.

†**displeasantly** *adv.* M16–E18.

displease /dɪsˈpliːz/ *v.* LME. [OFr. *desplais-* pres. stem of *desplaisir, desplaire* (mod. *déplaire*), f. *des-* DIS- 2 + *plaisir* PLEASE *v.*] **1** *v.i.* Cause dislike, be disagreeable, be offensive. LME. **2** *v.t.* Be disagreeable to; offend, annoy; make indignant or angry. LME. **3** *v.t.* In *pass.* Be dissatisfied or indignant. (Foll. by *with, at, to do, that*; †*of*, †*against*.) LME.

displeasedly *adv.* in a displeased manner, with displeasure E17. †**displeasedness** *n.* displeased state, discontent M16–E18. **displeasingly** *adv.* disagreeably, offensively M18. **displeasingness** *n.* the property of causing displeasure M17.

displeasure /dɪsˈplɛʒə/ *n.* & *v.* LME. [OFr. *desplaisir* use as n. of inf.: see prec. Later assim. to PLEASURE *n.*] **A** *n.* **1** The fact or condition of being displeased; dissatisfaction, disapproval; indignation, anger. LME. **2** Something causing offence or trouble; injury, harm; an offence, a wrong. *arch.* LME. †**3** Discomfort, unhappiness; sorrow, trouble; an instance of this, a pain. L15–L19. †**4** A state of unfriendly relations; a disagreement. M–L16.

1 J. P. DONLEAVY The most despicable letter I have ever had the displeasure to receive.

Phrases: †**take (a) displeasure** take offence, be displeased.

B *v.t.* = DISPLEASE 2. *arch.* M16.

displeasurable *a.* (*rare*) L19. **displeasurably** *adv.* (*rare*) M17.

displicency /ˈdɪsplɪs(ə)nsi/ *n.* M17. [L *displicentia*, f. *displicere* displease, f. as DIS- 2 + *placere* PLEASE *v.*: see -ENCY.] The fact or condition of being displeased or dissatisfied.

†**displicence** *n.* E17–M18.

displode /dɪˈspləʊd/ *v. arch.* M17. [L *displodere* burst asunder, f. as DIS- 1 + *plaudere* clap.] †**1** *v.t.* Discharge with an explosion. M17–E18. **2** *v.i.* Explode. M18.

†**displosion** *n.* M17–L18.

dispondee /dʌɪˈspɒndiː/ *n.* L16. [Late L *dispondeus* f. Gk *dispondeios*, f. as DI-[2] + *spondeios* SPONDEE.] *Pros.* A double spondee.

dispon'daic *a.* L19.

dispone /dɪˈspəʊn/ *v.* Chiefly *Sc.* LME. [L *disponere* arrange, dispose, f. as DIS- 1 + *ponere* to place. Cf. DISPOSE *v.*] †**1** *v.t.* Arrange, dispose. LME–E17. †**2** *v.t.* Dispose *to, for*; incline. LME–E17. †**3** *v.t.* Dispose of; give away. LME–M17. **4** *v.t. Sc. Law* Make over, convey, assign, grant. LME. †**5** *v.i.* Foll. by *of*, (*up*)*on*: deal with, dispose of. LME–E19. †**6** *v.i.* Order matters, make arrangements. LME–E18.

dispo'nee *Sc. Law* a person to whom property is conveyed M18. **disponer**, **-or** *n.* †(*a*) a person who disposes or arranges; (*b*) *Law* a person who conveys property to another, a settlor: L15.

disponent /dɪˈspəʊnənt/ *a.* E17. [L *disponent-* pres. ppl stem of *disponere*: see prec., -ENT.] Disposing; inclining in a particular direction, or towards a particular end.

disponge *v.* see DISPUNGE.

disponible /dɪˈspəʊnɪb(ə)l, *foreign* dispɔnibl/ *a.* L19. [f. (as) DISPONE + -IBLE or Fr. *disponible*.] Able to be assigned; at a person's disposal; amenable.

¶ Freq. treated as Fr.

disponi'bility *n.* M19.

disport /dɪˈspɔːt/ *n. arch.* ME. [AN *desport*, f. as next. Cf. DEPORT *n.*] **1** Diversion; relaxation; amusement. ME. **2** A pastime; a game; a sport. LME. †**3** Merriment, fun. LME–E19.

disport /dɪˈspɔːt/ *v.* LME. [AN, OFr. *desporter* (Fr. *déporter* DEPORT *v.*[2]), f. *des-* DIS- 1 + *porter* carry, PORT *v.*[1]] †**1** *v.t.* Divert (from sadness etc.); amuse, entertain. LME–L17. **2** *v.i.* & *refl.* Amuse or divert oneself; occupy oneself pleasurably. Now *esp.* play unrestrainedly, frolic, make a show of oneself. LME.

1 T. HERBERT All the way we sail'd.. we were disported by Whales. 2 P. P. READ Eager to disport herself in her new clothes. H. L. MENCKEN Savage tribes who permit their children to disport freely.

disportment *n.* (an) amusement, (an) entertainment M17.

disposable /dɪˈspəʊzəb(ə)l/ *a.* & *n.* M17. [f. DISPOSE *v.* + -ABLE.] **A** *adj.* **1** Able to be disposed or inclined; inclinable (*to* something). *rare.* M17. **2** Able to be disposed of or dealt with; able to be used, available; at a person's disposal. M17. **3** Designed to be thrown away after being used once, not to be laundered or refilled. M20.

2 D. MASSON They were more disposable as literary ware. T. H. MARSHALL Those whose disposable income and capital do not exceed £420 and £500 respectively. 3 *Sunday Times* Bed pans and bottles.. made of papier maché, to be disposable.

B *n.* An article designed to be thrown away after being used once. M20.

P. LEACH Your basic choice is between washable nappies and disposables.

disposa'bility *n.* M19.

disposal /dɪˈspəʊz(ə)l/ *n.* M17. [f. DISPOSE *v.* + -AL[1].] **1** Power or right to dispose of or deal with as one pleases. Usu. in *at one's disposal* below. M17. †**2** = DISPOSITION 3. M17–E18. **3** The action of disposing of or getting rid of; the action of settling or dealing with. M17. **4** The action of bestowing, giving, or making over; bestowal, assignment; sale. M17. **5** Arrangement, disposition. E19. **6** A waste disposal unit. *N. Amer.* M20.

1 W. BLACKSTONE The lords, who had the disposal of these female heiresses in marriage. **at one's disposal** available for one's use, subject to one's orders or decisions. 2 MILTON Tax not divine disposal. 3 E. A. PARKES The disposal of the dead is always a question of difficulty. *Howard Journal* Children's hearings.. are concerned only with the disposal of the child. *garbage disposal unit*: see GARBAGE *n.* *waste disposal unit*: see WASTE *n.* 4 E. FROMM Via the legal power of the last will the disposal of our property is determined.

dispose /dɪˈspəʊz/ *n.* Now *rare* or *obs.* L16. [f. the vb.] †**1** = DISPOSAL *n.* 1. L16–M18. †**2** = DISPOSAL *n.* 4. L16–L17. †**3** = DISPOSAL *n.* 2, DISPOSITION 3. Only in 17. †**4** = DISPOSITION 7. Only in E17. **5** A person's manner; an air. *rare.* E17.

5 SHAKES. *Oth.* He hath a person and a smooth dispose To be suspected.

dispose /dɪˈspəʊz/ *v.* LME. [(O)Fr. *disposer* based on L *disponere* (see DISPONE) but re-formed after L pa. pple *dispositus* and (O)Fr. *poser*: see POSE *v.*[1]] **I** *v.t.* **1** Place suitably, at intervals, or in order; adjust; arrange in a particular way. LME. **b** Put away or in its proper place. Now *rare.* LME. †**2** = sense 10 below. LME–L17. †**3** Bestow, make over; deal out, dispense, distribute. LME–E19. †**4** Formally assign or hand over. LME–M16. **5** Make fit or ready; prepare (*to do*; *for* something). *arch.* LME. 6 Bring into a mood or frame of mind favourable for something; incline *to* something; make willing *to do*; give (something) a tendency *to*. LME.

1 C. HAMPTON The Indians . . dispose themselves on either side of the stage. 5 W. TAYLOR Those missionaries who are disposing themselves to visit the Syrian churches. 6 D. CECIL Prejudices . . disposed them to be cheerfully opposed to anything . . far-fetched or newfangled. M. SINCLAIR Knitting disposed her to long silences.

II *v.i.* 7 Make arrangements; determine the course of events. LME. †8 Settle matters, make terms. *rare* (Shakes.). Only in E17. †9 Foll. by (*up*)*on*: = senses 11, 12 below. *Sc.* M17–L18.

7 *Proverb*: Man proposes, God disposes.

III *v.i.* Foll. by *of*. †10 Make a disposition of; control, regulate, govern. M16–E19. 11 Get rid of; deal conclusively with, settle; *colloq.* kill. E17. b Show (a claim, argument, or opponent) to be incorrect. L19. c Consume (food or drink). *colloq.* L19. 12 Transfer into the hands of another by sale or bequest. L17.

11 A. J. CRONIN Searching for . . a remark which might tactfully dispose of the past and . . open out the future. J. FRAME A notice . . requesting that lunch wrappers be disposed of in the receptacle provided. G. GREENE It was always his first question and he was glad when he had disposed of it. 12 C. BLACKWOOD I would . . like you to be there when all my possessions are disposed of.

disposer *n.* E16.

disposed /dɪˈspəʊzd/ *ppl a.* LME. [f. prec. + -ED[1].] 1 Arranged, appointed, prepared; suitably placed or situated. LME. †2 In a (specified) condition of body or health. Also, in good health, not indisposed. LME–L17. 3 Having a (specified) disposition or turn of mind; in a (specified) mood. Formerly also, well-disposed, having a favourable disposition. LME. 4 Inclined, in the mood, prepared, (*to do, to, for*). LME. †b Inclined to merriment; in a cheerful mood. L16–E17. 5 Having a physical inclination or tendency (*to do, to*); subject, liable. LME.

1 E. BOWEN She sat well back . . with knees jutting forward, disposed in this attitude almost in spite of herself. 3 ISAIAH BERLIN Humanitarian prophets . . generously disposed towards all mankind. *ill-disposed*: see ILL *adv.* *well-disposed*: see WELL *adv.* 4 I. D'ISRAELI The French Cabinet was strongly disposed for a Spanish war. A. MOOREHEAD Nobody was disposed to listen to him. 5 J. GALSWORTHY Hereditarily disposed to myopia.

disposedly /-zɪdli/ *adv.* with a (good or dignified) bearing E17. **disposedness** /-zɪdnɪs/ *n.* L16.

disposition /dɪspəˈzɪʃ(ə)n/ *n.* LME. [(O)Fr. f. L *dispositio(n-)*, f. *disposit-* pa. ppl stem of *disponere* DISPONE: see -ITION. Later assoc. with DISPOSE *v.*] 1 The action of getting rid of or making over; bestowal by deed or will; = DISPOSAL 3, 4. LME. 2 Power of disposing, control; = DISPOSAL 1. LME. 3 The action of ordering or regulating by (esp. divine) right or power; dispensation, direction, control. *arch.* LME. 4 Arrangement of affairs, esp. for a particular purpose; condition of affairs; in *pl.*, preparations, plans. LME. b *Mil.* The stationing of troops ready for attack or defence; their distribution and allocation; in *pl.*, military measures or preparations. E17. †5 *Astrol.* The situation of a planet in a horoscope, as supposedly affecting events; *spec.* the state of being in the house of another planet. LME–M17. 6 Temperament or character, esp. as displayed in dealings with others; turn of mind. LME. 7 The state or quality of being disposed (*to, to do*); inclination (*for*); the condition of being (favourably or unfavourably) disposed *towards*. LME. †b A frame of mind; a mood. E–M18. 8 A tendency of anything physical (*to, to do*). LME. †b An aptitude, a skill. *rare.* E17–M18. †9 Physical constitution of anything; physical condition of the body, state of health. LME–E19. 10 The fact of being set in order; spatial arrangement; relative position, esp. of constituent parts. L15.

1 STEELE The wanton disposition of the favours of the powerful. 2 GIBBON The choice of action or of repose is no longer in our disposition. 3 DEFOE This seemed to me to be a disposition of Providence. 4 H. WILSON I . . would make dispositions for the work of the day. 6 V. CRONIN Uncle Georg had a cheerful disposition and Sophie found it fun to be with him. J. P. STERN A disposition of mind aiming at the subjugation of any object outside myself. 7 JOHN BROOKE He did not want a wife with a disposition to meddle in politics. 8 W. HAMILTON The different dispositions of wool, silk, etc. to unite with the colouring particles. 10 A. GEIKIE Looking at the disposition of the Highland glens and straths.

dispositional *a.* M19. **dispositionally** *adv.* E20. **dispositioned** *a.* having a (specified) disposition or turn of mind M17.

dispositive /dɪsˈpɒzətɪv/ *a.* LME. [(O)Fr. *dispositif, -ive* or med.L *dispositivus*, f. L *disposit-*: see prec., -IVE.] 1 That has the quality of disposing or inclining; contributory, conducive. LME. 2 Having the quality or function of directing or controlling; relating to control; *Sc.* & *US Law* dealing with disposition by deed or will; effecting disposition of an issue etc. E17. †3 Of or pertaining to a person's natural disposition or inclination. M–L17.

dispositively *adv.* (long *rare*) LME.

dispositor /dɪˈspɒzɪtə/ *n.* L16. [L = disposer, (in med.L) dispositor, f. *disposit-*: see DISPOSITION, -OR.] *Astrol.* The planet in whose house a given planet is situated.

dispository /dɪˈspɒzɪt(ə)ri/ *a.* *rare.* E17. [f. L *disposit-* (see DISPOSITION) + -ORY[2].] †1 = DISPOSITIVE 1. E–M17. 2 = DISPOSITIVE 2. M20.

dispossess /dɪspəˈzɛs/ *v.* & *n.* L15. [OFr. *despossesser*, f. as DIS- 2, POSSESS *v.*] A *v.t.* 1 Put out of possession; strip of possessions; oust, dislodge; deprive *of*. L15. †b Expel or banish *from*; drive *out of*. E17–L18. †c Foll. by double obj.: deprive (a person) of (a possession). *rare* (Shakes.). Only in E17. 2 Free (a possessed person) *of* an evil spirit by exorcism. Formerly also, exorcize (an evil spirit). L16.

1 J. F. W. HERSCHEL Two kinds of prejudices, which . . differ exceedingly in the difficulty of dispossessing them. A. BROOKNER A veteran, dispossessed of all his belongings, returning from the wars. c SHAKES. *Timon* I will choose Mine heir from forth the beggars of the world, and dispossess her all.

B *n.* Eviction of a tenant or squatter. *US.* L19.

attrib.: *dispossess proceedings, warrant*, etc.

dispossessed *ppl a.* & *n.* (*a*) *ppl a.* that has been dispossessed or deprived, esp. of a home; (*b*) *n.pl. the* people who are dispossessed: L16. **dispossession** *n.* the action of dispossessing; deprivation of or ejection from a possession, *spec.* exorcism; the fact of being dispossessed: L16. **dispossessor** *n.* a person who dispossesses L16.

dispost /dɪsˈpəʊst/ *v.t.* Now *rare* or *obs.* L16. [f. DIS- 2 + POST *n.*[4]: cf. Fr. †*desposter* dispossess, *déposter* dismiss from service.] Deprive of a post, dismiss from service.

disposure /dɪˈspəʊʒə/ *n.* M16. [f. DISPOSE *v.* + -URE.] †1 = DISPOSITION 3. M16–L17. 2 Arrangement, order. Now *rare.* E17. †3 = DISPOSAL *n.* 1. Only in 17. 4 = DISPOSAL *n.* 3, 4 *arch.* M17.

dispraise /dɪsˈpreɪz/ *n.* LME. [f. DIS- 2 + PRAISE *n.* or f. the vb.] †1 Contempt. *rare.* Only in LME. 2 The action or fact of dispraising; disparagement; blame, censure. E16. 3 An instance or act of dispraising; a cause of blame, discredit, or disgrace. M16.

2 C. M. YONGE Charles VI would not hear a word in his dispraise.

dispraise /dɪsˈpreɪz/ *v.* ME. [OFr. *despreisier* f. Proto-Romance f. L *depretiare* DEPRECIATE. Cf. DISPRIZE *v.*] 1 a *v.t.* Express disapproval of; find fault with; blame, censure. ME. b *v.i.* Express disapproval or blame. L15. †2 *v.t.* Despise, belittle. LME–E16.

dispraiser *n.* LME. **dispraisingly** *adv.* disparagingly E17.

dispread /dɪˈsprɛd/ *v.t.* & (*rare*) *i.* *arch.* Also **disspread**. Pa. t. & pple **-spread**. L16. [f. DIS- 1 + SPREAD *v.*] Spread out or through; extend, expand, open out.

J. THOMSON Tyrant heat, dispreading through the sky. H. WILLIAMSON He saw, in hut after hut, figures dispread and inert on wet floors.

disprize /dɪsˈprʌɪz/ *n.* Long *rare.* M16. [f. the vb, or f. OFr. *despris*, f. as next.] Disparagement, contempt; belittlement.

disprize /dɪsˈprʌɪz/ *v.t.* LME. [OFr. *desprisier* var. of *despreisier* DISPRAISE *v.*] Despise; disparage, decry, belittle.

disprofit /dɪsˈprɒfɪt/ *n.* *arch.* L15. [f. DIS- 2 + PROFIT *n.*] 1 Detriment, disadvantage. L15. †2 A disadvantage. M16–L17.

disprofit /dɪsˈprɒfɪt/ *v.t.* *arch.* L15. [f. DIS- 2 + PROFIT *v.*] Bring disadvantage to; inconvenience.

disproof /dɪsˈpruːf/ *n.* LME. [f. DIS- 2 + PROOF *n.*] The action or an act of disproving an assertion, claim, etc.; refutation; a disproving fact or piece of evidence.

disproportion /dɪsprəˈpɔːʃ(ə)n/ *n.* M16. [f. DIS- 2 + PROPORTION *n.*, after Fr. *disproportion.*] 1 Lack of proportion; the condition of being out of proportion. M16. 2 An instance of this; something out of proportion. L16.

1 S. KITZINGER The baby cannot pass through the bones of the pelvis; this is called *disproportion.* 2 B. JOWETT A leg too long, or some other disproportion. R. NIEBUHR Inequalities of privilege are due chiefly to disproportion of power.

disproportion /dɪsprəˈpɔːʃ(ə)n/ *v.t.* L16. [f. the n., after Fr. *disproportionner.*] Make or shape out of proportion; make disproportionate *to*.

SHAKES. *3 Hen. VI* To shape my legs of an unequal size; To disproportion me in every part. LYTTON Statutes that disproportion punishment to crime.

disproportionable *a.* out of due proportion, disproportionate L16. **disproportionableness** *n.* M17. **disproportionably** *adv.* E17. **disproportioned** *ppl a.* (*a*) disproportionate; †(*b*) *rare* (Shakes.), inconsistent: L16.

disproportional /dɪsprəˈpɔːʃ(ə)n(ə)l/ *a.* Long *rare.* E17. [f. DISPROPORTION *n.* + -AL[1].] = DISPROPORTIONATE *a.*

disproportionally *adv.* M18.

disproportionality /ˌdɪsprəpɔːʃəˈnalɪti/ *n.* M17. [f. prec. + -ITY.] The quality of being disproportional.

disproportionate /dɪsprəˈpɔːʃ(ə)nət/ *a.* M16. [f. DIS- 2 + PROPORTIONATE *a.*, after Fr. *disproportionné.*] Lacking proportion, poorly proportioned; out of proportion (*to*); relatively too large or too small.

C. S. LEWIS His tiny, child-like snore, so disproportionate to his bulk. D. MURPHY The socially crippling effects of unmarried motherhood constituted an altogether disproportionate punishment for a momentary loss of control.

disproportionately *adv.* L17. **disproportionateness** *n.* M17.

disproportionate /dɪsprəˈpɔːʃ(ə)neɪt/ *v.i.* M20. [Back-form. f. next.] *Chem.* Undergo disproportionation.

disproportionation /ˌdɪsprəpɔːʃəˈneɪʃ(ə)n/ *n.* E20. [f. DISPROPORTION *n.* or *v.* + -ATION.] *Chem.* A transfer of atoms or valency electrons between identical atoms or ions so as to give dissimilar products; decomposition in which a compound is both oxidized and reduced.

disprove /dɪsˈpruːv/ *v.t.* Pa. pple **-proved**, (*arch.*) **-proven** /-ˈprəʊv(ə)n, -ˈpruːv(ə)n/. LME. [OFr. *desprover*, f. as DIS- 2, PROVE *v.*] 1 Prove (an assertion, claim, etc.) to be false or erroneous; show the fallacy or non-validity of. LME. 2 Disapprove of. *obs.* exc. *dial.* LME. 3 Prove the falsity or error of the statement(s) of (a person). Now *rare* or *obs.* L16.

disprovable *a.* †(*a*) reprehensible; (*b*) able to be disproved, refutable: M16. **disproval** *n.* (*rare*) an act of disproving, a disproof E17. **disprovement** *n.* (*rare*) the action or fact of disproving, (a) disproof L16.

disprovide /dɪsprəˈvʌɪd/ *v.t.* *arch.* E16. [f. DIS- 2 + PROVIDE.] Fail to provide for; leave unprovided.

dispunct /dɪsˈpʌŋkt/ *v.t.* *rare.* L16. [L *dispunct-* pa. ppl stem of *dispungere* prick here and there, f. as DIS- 1 + *pungere* to prick.] Mark (as) with a pen for omission or distinction; erase; distinguish, make prominent.

dispunge /dɪˈspʌndʒ/ *v.t.* *arch.* In sense 1 also **disponge**. E17. [Partly f. SPONGE *v.*, partly f. EXPUNGE *v.* by substitution: see DIS- 1.] 1

For other words beginning with *dis-* see the entry for **dis-**

Discharge or release as from a squeezed sponge. E17. †2 Delete, expunge. E–M17.

dispunishable /dɪsˈpʌnɪʃəb(ə)l/ *a.* L16. [f. DIS- 2 + PUNISHABLE. Cf. AN *dispunishable*.] *Law.* Free from liability to punishment or penalty; not punishable.

†dispurse *v.t.* L16–E18. [Alt.] = DISBURSE *v.*

†dispurvey *v.t.* LME–E17. [OFr. *desporveeir*, f. as DIS- 2 + *porveeir*: see PURVEY *v.*] Rob or strip of provisions; make destitute. Usu. in *pass.*

†dispurveyance *n.* (*rare*) lack of provisions, destitution L15–L16.

disputable /dɪˈspjuːtəb(ə)l, ˈdɪspjʊtəb(ə)l/ *a.* L15. [Fr., or L *disputabilis*, f. as DISPUTE *v.*: see -ABLE.] 1 Liable to be disputed; open to question; contentious. L15. †2 Disputatious. *rare* (Shakes.). Only in L16.

1 *Church Times* His highly disputable approach to the New Testament.

diˈsputableness *n.* M17. **disputably** *adv.* M19.

†disputacity *n.* M17–E18. [Irreg. f. DISPUTATIOUS *a.*: see -ACITY.] Disputatiousness.

disputant /dɪˈspjuːt(ə)nt, ˈdɪspjʊt(ə)nt/ *n.* & *a.* L16. [L *disputant-* pres. ppl stem of *disputare*: see DISPUTE *v.*, -ANT[1].] A *n.* A person who disputes or argues; *esp.* one who engages in public debate or disputation. L16. B *adj.* That disputes; engaged in debate or controversy. L17.

disputation /dɪspjuːˈteɪʃ(ə)n, -pjʊˈt-/ *n.* LME. [Fr. f. L *disputatio(n-)*, f. *disputat-* pa. ppl stem of *disputare*: see DISPUTE *v.*, -ATION.] 1 The action of disputing or debating; argument, controversy; debate, discussion. Also, an instance of this. LME. b *spec.* An exercise in which parties formally propose, attack, and defend a set question or thesis. M16. †2 Written discussion or treatment of a subject; a dissertation. M16–E17. †3 Doubtful or disputable condition; doubt. M16–L17. †4 Interchange of ideas; discourse, conversation. *rare* (Shakes.). Only in L16.

disputatious /dɪspjuːˈteɪʃəs, -pjʊˈt-/ *a.* M17. [f. prec.: see -OUS.] Characterized by or given to disputation; prone to argue; fond of argument.

SIR W. SCOTT The wine rendered me loquacious, disputatious, and quarrelsome.

disputatiously *adv.* M19. **disputatiousness** *n.* L17.

disputative /dɪˈspjuːtətɪv/ *a.* L16. [Late L *disputativus*, f. L *disputat-*: see DISPUTATION, -ATIVE.] 1 Disputatious. L16. †2 That is the subject of disputation or dispute; controversial. L16–E18. 3 Of or pertaining to disputation. M17.

disputatively *adv.* L16. **disputativeness** *n.* M19.

disputator /ˈdɪspjʊteɪtə/ *n.* *rare.* L16. [L *disputator*, f. *disputat-*: see DISPUTATION, -ATOR.] A disputant.

dispute /dɪˈspjuːt, ˈdɪspjuːt/ *n.* L16. [f. the vb.] †1 a A logical argument. *rare.* Only in L16. b An oral or written discussion of a subject in which arguments for and against are put forward and examined. E17–M19. 2 An instance of disputing or arguing against something or someone, an argument, a controversy; *esp.* a heated contention, a disagreement in which opposing views are strongly held. E17. 3 The act of disputing or arguing against something or someone; controversy, debate. M17. †4 Strife, contest; a fight, a struggle. M17–M18.

1b T. STANLEY He was the first that committed the disputes of Socrates his Master to writing. 2 *Financial Times* El Al, Israel's national airline, . . has been grounded for more than a month because of a labour dispute. 3 J. WESLEY That once was in the Heat of Dispute. H. CECIL There was no dispute that this was the law, but Martin raised various defences. **beyond, past, without dispute** certainly, indisputably, without question; *be beyond* (etc.) *dispute*, be indisputable (*that*). **in dispute** being argued about.

dispute /dɪˈspjuːt/ *v.* ME. [OFr. *desputer*, (also mod.) *disputer* f. L *disputare* estimate, (in late L) dispute, f. as DIS- 1 + *putare* reckon.] I *v.i.* 1 Contend with opposing arguments or assertions; argue; debate hotly, quarrel, have an altercation. (Foll. by *about*, *on*, *over*, †*against*, †*of*, a subject; *against*, *with*, an opponent.) ME. †2 Contend physically, esp. by force of arms; struggle. M17–E19.

1 R. W. EMERSON He disputed like a devil on these two points. QUILLER-COUCH Four children . . are disputing over a box of wooden soldiers. J. BUCHAN Always very ready to dispute about philosophy.

II *v.t.* 3 Discuss, debate, or argue (a question or point), esp. heatedly. Foll. by direct obj. or subord. cl. ME. 4 Maintain or defend (an assertion, claim, etc.) by argument or disputation; contend (that something is so). Now *rare* or *obs.* LME. 5 Question the correctness or validity of (a statement or an alleged fact); argue with (a person). E16. 6 Contest, strive against, or resist (an action). E17. 7 Move or influence by disputation, argue or persuade (a person) *into* or *out of*. Now *rare* or *obs.* M17. 8 Contend or compete for the possession of; strive to gain against opposition. L17.

3 J. RAY I will not dispute what Gravity is. H. MARTINEAU Disputing whether luxury be a virtue or a crime. B. WEBB One of the most hotly disputed questions within the Labour Party. 4 SWIFT And these, she offer'd to dispute, Alone distinguish'd man from brute. 5 E. WAUGH They were disputing the bill. HARPER LEE A Cunningham disputed a Coningham over land titles and took to the law. 8 F. HOYLE They and their men disputed the possession of caves with bears and mountain lions.

disputer *n.* a person who disputes or is given to disputation LME.

disqualification /dɪsˌkwɒlɪfɪˈkeɪʃ(ə)n/ *n.* E18. [f. DISQUALIFY *v.*: see -FICATION.] 1 Something which disqualifies; a ground or cause of incapacity. E18. 2 The action of disqualifying; the fact or condition of being disqualified. L18.

1 DICKENS I hope you don't think good looks a disqualification for the business. 2 *Times* A driver . . appealed successfully, against the disqualification order.

disqualify /dɪsˈkwɒlɪfʌɪ/ *v.t.* E18. [f. DIS- 2 + QUALIFY.] 1 Deprive of the qualities required (*for* a situation, purpose, etc.); make unfit or unsuited; prevent by lack of qualification *from* doing. E18. 2 Incapacitate legally, pronounce unqualified; debar from a competition because of an infringement of the rules; prohibit from driving. E18.

1 L. STEPHEN Strong passions and keen sensibilities may easily disqualify a man for domestic tranquillity. 2 D. HUME It is usual for the Speaker to disqualify himself for the office. *Times* He also pleaded guilty to driving a bus while disqualified.

disquantity /dɪsˈkwɒntɪti/ *v.t.* *rare.* E17. [f. DIS- 2 + QUANTITY *n.*] Make smaller, reduce; deprive of metrical quantity.

disquiet /dɪsˈkwʌɪət/ *n.* M16. [f. DISQUIET *a.*, *v.*] 1 Absence of calmness or peace; disturbance; uneasiness, anxiety; unrest. M16. †2 A disturbance; a disquieting feeling or circumstance. L16–M18.

1 S. AUSTIN The States of the Church and Naples were still in a state of universal disquiet and ferment. DAY LEWIS My father's moodiness was . . not a source of much disquiet or grievance.

disquiet /dɪsˈkwʌɪət/ *a.* Now *rare.* L16. [f. DIS- 2 + QUIET *a.*] Restless, uneasy; disturbed.

T. UNDERDOWN A sea, which . . was very disquiet. THACKERAY His mind was disquiet.

disquietly *adv.* †(*a*) disquietingly; (*b*) in a disquiet or uneasy manner: E17. **disquietness** *n.* M16.

disquiet /dɪsˈkwʌɪət/ *v.t.* E16. [f. DIS- 2 + QUIET *v.*] Deprive of quietness, peace, or rest; trouble, alarm, worry; make uneasy or restless.

R. D. LAING This . . was profoundly disquieting. It baffled me. It *scared* me. H. KISSINGER What worried Paris could also disquiet Moscow and Damascus.

disquietedly *adv.* in a disquieted manner M19. **disquietedness** *n.* the state of being disquiet L17. **disquieter** *n.* M16. **disquietingly** *adv.* in a disquieting manner, disturbingly, worryingly E20.

disquieten /dɪsˈkwʌɪət(ə)n/ *v.t.* E20. [f. DIS- 2 + QUIETEN *v.*] = DISQUIET *v.*

†disquietment *n.* E17–L18. [f. DISQUIET *v.* + -MENT.] Disquiet; the action of disquieting; a disquieting circumstance.

disquietude /dɪsˈkwʌɪətjuːd/ *n.* E18. [f. DISQUIET *a.* + -TUDE, after *quietude*.] 1 Disquieted condition or state; disquiet. E18. 2 A feeling, occasion, or cause of disquiet; a disquieting circumstance. E18.

disquisition /dɪskwɪˈzɪʃ(ə)n/ *n.* L15. [(O)Fr. f. L *disquisitio(n-)*, f. *disquisit-* pa. ppl stem of *disquirere*, f. as DIS- 1 + *quaerere* seek: see -ITION.] †1 A subject or topic for investigation. L15–M17. 2 Diligent or systematic search; investigation, examination. L16. 3 A treatise or discourse in which a subject is investigated and discussed; a long or elaborate treatise or discourse. M17.

3 J. COLVILLE The P.M.'s lengthy disquisitions in Cabinet on papers which he has not read.

disquisitional *a.* of the nature of a disquisition E19. **disquisitionist** *n.* a person who writes or gives a disquisition M19.

disquisitive /dɪˈskwɪzɪtɪv/ *a.* M17. [f. L *disquisit-*: see prec., -IVE.] Characterized by or given to research or investigation; inquiring.

disquisitor /dɪˈskwɪzɪtə/ *n.* M18. [med.L, f. as prec.: see -OR.] A person who makes disquisition, an inquirer; a person who writes or gives a disquisition.

Disraelian /dɪzˈreɪlɪən/ *a.* L19. [f. *Disraeli* (see below) + -AN.] Pertaining to, characteristic of, or resembling the Conservative statesman and writer Benjamin Disraeli (1804–81).

Daily Telegraph Seeking to give the Disraelian One Nation ideal more concrete expression.

†disrange *v.* LME. [OFr. *desrangier*, *-rengier*, f. *des-* DIS- 2 + *ranc*, *renc* (mod. *rang*) RANK *n.* Cf. RANGE *v.*[1]] 1 *v.i.* & *refl.* Start out; fall out of rank. LME–E17. 2 *v.t.* Throw out of order; disarrange. Only in L18.

disrank /dɪsˈraŋk/ *v.t.* L16. [f. DIS- 2 + RANK *n.*] †1 Throw out of rank or into disorder; confuse. L16–M17. 2 Deprive of rank, reduce to a lower rank; degrade. L16.

disrate /dɪsˈreɪt/ *v.t.* E19. [f. DIS- 2 + RATE *n.*[1]] Chiefly *Naut.* Reduce to a lower rating or rank, demote; remove from a rank or class.

disregard /dɪsrɪˈɡɑːd/ *n.* M17. [f. DIS- 2 + REGARD *n.*] 1 Lack of regard or respect; neglect. Now *esp.* the action of ignoring or treating as of no importance. (Foll. by *of*, *for*, †*to*.) M17. 2 Part of a person's income not to be considered in the assessment of a State benefit. M20.

1 D. NEAL The Bishops fell under a general disregard. J. ROSENBERG A complete disregard for social convention.

disregard /dɪsrɪˈɡɑːd/ *v.t.* M17. [f. DIS- 2 + REGARD *v.*] Pay no regard to; *esp.* ignore, treat as of no importance. Formerly, neglect unduly, slight.

disregardable *a.* M17. **disregardant** *a.* disregarding, neglectful E19. **disregarder** *n.* M17.

disregardful /dɪsrɪˈɡɑːdfʊl, -f(ə)l/ *a.* M17. [f. DIS- 2 + REGARDFUL.] Neglectful, careless.

disregardfully *adv.* M17. **disregardfulness** *n.* (*rare*) M18.

disrelish /dɪsˈrɛlɪʃ/ *n.* E17. [f. the vb or f. DIS- 2 + RELISH *n.*] Distaste, aversion. (Foll. by *for*, †*of*.)

disrelish /dɪsˈrɛlɪʃ/ *v.* M16. [f. DIS- 2 + RELISH *v.* or *n.*] †1 *v.t.* Destroy the relish or flavour of; make distasteful. M16–M18. 2 *v.t.* Have a distaste for; dislike. E17. 3 *v.i.* Be distasteful. M17. †4 *v.t.* Be distasteful to; disgust. M17–E18.

2 R. L. STEVENSON He so much disrelished some expressions of mine that . . he showed me to the door.

disremember /dɪsrɪˈmɛmbə/ *v.t.* & *i.* Chiefly *dial.* M17. [f. DIS- 2 + REMEMBER.] Fail to remember; forget.

disrepair /dɪsrɪˈpɛː/ *n.* L18. [f. DIS- 2 + REPAIR *n.*[2]] The state of being out of repair, or in bad condition for lack of repairs.

E. WAUGH Carpet, curtains and upholstery were inspected for signs of disrepair. J. A. MICHENER A building fallen into sad disrepair.

disreputable /dɪsˈrɛpjʊtəb(ə)l/ *a.* & *n.* L18. [f. DIS- 2 + REPUTABLE, after *disrepute*.] A *adj.* 1 Such as to bring something into disrepute; discreditable. L18. 2 Having a bad reputation; not respectable in character or appearance. E19. B *n.* A disreputable person. M19.

disreputaˈbility *n.* M19. **disreputableness** *n.* E18. **disreputably** *adv.* L18.

disreputation /ˌdɪsrɛpjʊˈteɪʃ(ə)n/ *n.* *arch.* E17. [f. DIS- 2 + REPUTATION.] 1 Loss of reputation; the action of bringing into disrepute; dishonour.

For other words beginning with *dis-* see the entry for **dis-**

E17. †**b** A discrediting circumstance. E17–M18. **2** Lack of reputation, bad reputation; the condition of being in disrepute. M17.

disrepute /dɪsrɪˈpjuːt/ *n.* M17. [f. DIS- 2 + REPUTE *n.*] Loss or absence of reputation; bad repute, dishonour, discredit.
H. T. BUCKLE It brings the administration of justice into disrepute.

disrespect /dɪsrɪˈspɛkt/ *n.* E17. [f. DIS- 2 + RESPECT *n.*; or perh. f. the vb.] **1** Lack of respect or courtesy; discourtesy. E17. †**2** An act that shows disrespect. E17–E18.
1 I. MURDOCH Finn has very little inner life. I mean no disrespect to him in saying this.

disrespect /dɪsrɪˈspɛkt/ *v.t.* E17. [f. DIS- 2 + RESPECT *v.*] Have or show no respect or reverence for; treat with disrespect.
disrespecter *n.* (*rare*) M17.

disrespectable /dɪsrɪˈspɛktəb(ə)l/ *a.* E19. [f. DIS- 2 + RESPECTABLE.] Not worthy of respect, not respectable.
ˌ**disrespectaˈbility** *n.* M19.

disrespectful /dɪsrɪˈspɛktfʊl, -f(ə)l/ *a.* L17. [f. DIS- 2 + RESPECTFUL, after *disrespect*.] Showing disrespect.
disrespectfully *adv.* L17. **disrespectfulness** *n.* L17.

†**disrespective** *a.* E17–M18. [f. DIS- 2 + RESPECTIVE *a.*, after *disrespect*.] Disrespectful.

disrobe /dɪsˈrəʊb/ *v.* LME. [f. DIS- 2 + ROBE *v.* or *n.*[1], perh. after OFr. *desrober*.] **1** *v.t.* Divest of a garment; remove clothing or covering or some possession or quality from. (Foll. by *of*.) LME. **2** *v.i.* Undress; take off clerical robes. E18.
disrobement *n.* M18. **disrober** *n.* M17.

disroot /dɪsˈruːt/ *v.t.* E17. [f. DIS- 2 + ROOT *v.*[1]] **1** Dislodge (something) from the place where it is fixed. E17. **2** Uproot (a plant). E19.

disrump /dɪsˈrʌmp/ *v.t.* & *i.* L16. [L *disrumpere*, f. as DIS- 1 + *rumpere* break.] Break up; = DISRUPT.

disrupt /dɪsˈrʌpt/ *v.* Pa. pple & ppl a. **disrupted,** (earlier, now *poet.*) **disrupt**. LME. [L *disrupt-* pa. ppl stem of *disrumpere*: see prec.] **1** *v.t.* Break apart, burst, shatter; separate forcibly; *esp.* interrupt the normal continuity of (an activity etc.); throw into disorder. LME. **2** *v.i.* Burst open; be disrupted. *rare*. M17.
1 G. MEREDITH Leaving them .. disrupt, as by earthquake. E. FIGES The household routine had been totally disrupted. *Times* War veterans disrupt Senate hearings.
¶In sense 1 rare bef. 18 & only as pa. pple bef. 19.
disrupter, disruptor *ns.* L19.

disruption /dɪsˈrʌpʃ(ə)n/ *n.* LME. [L *disruptio(n-)*, f. as prec.: see -ION.] **1** Disrupted condition, disorder; a disrupted part; a rent, a tear. LME. **2** The action or an act of disrupting something. M17.
1 *Times* Further disruption will be caused by a half-day strike tomorrow morning. 2 T. BURNET Great earthquakes and disruptions. **the Disruption** the great split (of 1843) in the Established Church of Scotland, from which arose the Free Church of Scotland.
disruptionist *n.* a person who favours disruption. L19.

disruptive /dɪsˈrʌptɪv/ *a.* M19. [f. DISRUPT *v.* + -IVE.] Causing or tending to cause disruption or disorder.
A. WEST A student they had come to look on as a disruptive nuisance. *Guardian* A commitment by returning miners to ensure the survival of their own pits will preclude disruptive action.
disruptively *adv.* L19. **disruptiveness** *n.* L19.

disrupture /dɪsˈrʌptʃə/ *n.* & *v.* L18. [f. DISRUPT *v.* after *rupture*.] **A** *n.* The action of disrupting; (a) disruption. L18. **B** *v.t.* Break apart or off; divide by a rupture. E19.

diss /dɪs/ *n.* M19. [Algerian Arab. *dīs*.] In Algeria, a Mediterranean grass, *Ampelodesmos mauritanica*, used for making cordage etc.

diss *a.* & *v.* var. of DIS *a.* & *v.*[2]

dissatisfaction /ˌdɪ(s)satɪsˈfakʃ(ə)n, dɪˌsat-/ *n.* M17. [f. DIS- 2 + SATISFACTION.] **1** The fact or condition of being dissatisfied. M17. **2** In *pl.* Feelings or expressions of discontent. M17.

dissatisfactory /ˌdɪ(s)satɪsˈfakt(ə)ri/ *a.* E17. [f. DIS- 2 + SATISFACTORY.] Not satisfactory; causing dissatisfaction.

dissatisfied /dɪ(s)ˈsatɪsfʌɪd/ *ppl a.* M17. [f. next + -ED[1].] **1** Not satisfied; displeased; left with a feeling of dissatisfaction by the deficiency or inadequacy of something. M17. **2** Showing or expressing dissatisfaction. E19.
dissatisfiedly *adv.* E19. **dissatisfiedness** *n.* E18.

dissatisfy /dɪ(s)ˈsatɪsfʌɪ/ *v.t.* M17. [f. DIS- 2 + SATISFY.] Deprive of satisfaction; fail to satisfy, displease; disquiet.

dissava /dɪˈsɑːvə/ *n.* L17. [Sinhalese *disāva*.] *Hist.* A governor of an administrative district in Ceylon (Sri Lanka).

dissect /dɪˈsɛkt/ *v.* L16. [L *dissect-* pa. ppl stem of *dissecare*, f. as DIS- 1 + *secare* to cut.] **1** *v.t.* Cut in pieces. L16. **2** *v.t. spec.* Methodically cut up (an animal, plant, etc.) in order to show or examine the internal parts. L16. **b** Take *out* an organ etc. without disturbing adjoining tissue. M19. **3** *v.t.* Examine minutely, part by part; analyse, criticize in detail. M17. **4** *v.i.* Perform dissection. L17.
1 **dissecting aneurysm** an annular blood-filled cavity in the wall of an artery where it has split. 2 Attrib.: *dissecting knife, room*, etc. 4 WORDSWORTH Our meddling intellect Misshapes the beauteous forms of things:—We murder to dissect.
dissectible *a.* (*rare*) E19. **dissective** *a.* having the quality of dissecting; serving to dissect: M19.

dissected /dɪˈsɛktɪd/ *ppl a.* L16. [f. prec. + -ED[1].] **1** Divided into pieces; cut up for anatomical study. L16. **2** Having a divided form or structure; *Bot.* (of a leaf) divided into many deep lobes. M17. **b** *Physical Geogr.* Formed by the dissection of a once flat plateau or plain. E20.
1 **dissected map, picture**: that can be reassembled as an exercise or puzzle.

dissection /dɪˈsɛkʃ(ə)n/ *n.* L16. [f. DISSECT + -ION; perh. partly f. Fr. *dissection*, med.L *dissectio(n-)*, f. as DISSECT.] **1** The action or process of dissecting. L16. **b** *Physical Geogr.* The breaking up by erosion of a flat surface such as a plateau or plain into hills, or flat uplands, and valleys. E20. **2** Something which is the result or product of dissecting. L16. **3** Detailed analysis, minute examination. Formerly *spec.*, chemical analysis. E17.

dissector /dɪˈsɛktə/ *n.* L16. [mod.L, f. L *dissect-*: see DISSECT, -OR.] **1** A person who dissects, esp. anatomically. L16. **2** A dissecting instrument. M19.

disseise /dɪsˈsiːz/ *v.t.* Also **-ze**. ME. [AN *disseisir*, OFr. *dessaisir* dispossess, f. as DIS- 2, SEIZE *v.*] **1** *Law* (now *Hist.*). Put out of actual seisin or possession; dispossess (a person) of estates etc., usually wrongfully or by force; oust. (Foll. by *of*, †*from*.) ME. **2** *gen.* Deprive, rob, rid, *of*. ME.
disseiˈsee *n.* a person who is disseised of an estate E16. **disseisor** *n.* a person who disseises LME. **disseisoress** *n.* a female disseisor L16. †**disseisure** *n.* = DISSEISIN 1 L16–E18.

disseisin /dɪsˈsiːzɪn/ *n.* Also **-zin**. LME. [AN *disseisine*, OFr. *dessaisine*, f. as DIS- 2, SEISIN.] **1** *Law* (now *Hist.*). The act or fact of disseising; privation of seisin; *esp.* the wrongful appropriation of the lands or (formerly) the goods of another. LME. **2** *gen.* Dispossession. *arch.* L16.
1 **novel, new, fresh disseisin** disseisin of recent date. 2 M. BEERBOHM Why should the disseizin of his soul have seemed shameful to him? .. He was in love.

disseize *v.*, **disseizin** *n.* vars. of DISSEISE, DISSEISIN.

disselboom /ˈdɪs(ə)lbuːm, *foreign* ˈdɪsəlbʊəm/ *n.* *S. Afr.* E19. [Du., f. *dissel* shaft + *boom* beam, boom.] The pole of a wagon.

dissemblable /dɪˈsɛmbləb(ə)l/ *a.* & *n.* LME. [OFr. *dessemblable*, f. *dessembler*: see next, -ABLE.] **A** *adj.* Dissimilar; various. Now *rare* or *obs.* LME. **B** *n.* In *pl.* Dissimilar things. *rare*. E20.

dissemblance /dɪˈsɛmbl(ə)ns/ *n.* LME. [In sense 1 f. OFr. *dessemblance* (mod. *dissemblance*), f. *dessembler* be unlike, f. *des-* DIS- 2 + *sembler* resemble, seem: see -ANCE. In sense 2 alt. of DISSIMULANCE after *dissemble*.] **1** Dissimilarity, lack of resemblance. LME. **2** The action of dissembling, dissimulation. E17.

dissemble /dɪˈsɛmb(ə)l/ *v.*[1] LME. [Alt. of DISSIMULE, assoc. w. SEMBLANCE.] **1** *v.t.* & *i.* Conceal (one's character, a feeling, an intention, etc.) by feigning a different one. LME. **2** *v.t.* Assume a false appearance of; feign, simulate; pretend (*that*, *to do*). Now only as *dissembled* ppl a. LME. **3** *v.t.* Conceal the identity of, disguise. *arch.* L15. **4** *v.t.* Pretend not to notice, turn a blind eye to; ignore (the fact *that*). E16.
1 A. T. ELLIS None of them knew how unhappy she was, so she would have either to dissemble or explain. M. DRABBLE She had .. dissembled what gifts she had once had.
dissembler *n.* a person who dissembles; a deceiver, a hypocrite: E16. **dissemblingly** *adv.* in a way that disguises one's real character or purpose M16.

dissemble /dɪˈsɛmb(ə)l/ *v.*[2] LME. [OFr. *dessembler*, f. *des-* DIS- 2 + *a-sembler* ASSEMBLE.] †**1** *v.i.* = DISASSEMBLE 1. *rare*. LME. **2** *v.t.* = DISASSEMBLE 2. L20.

†**dissembly** *n.* L16–L17. [Alt.] Assembly.
SHAKES. *Much Ado* Is our whole dissembly appear'd?

disseminate /dɪˈsɛmɪneɪt/ *v.t.* Pa. pple & ppl a. **-ated,** (earlier) **-ate** /-ət/. LME. [L *disseminat-* pa. ppl stem of *disseminare*, f. as DIS- 1 + *semen*, *semin-* seed: see -ATE[3].] Scatter in different directions, as in sowing seed; spread, disperse; diffuse, promulgate, (opinions, knowledge, etc.); *spec.* (*Med.*, chiefly as *disseminated* ppl a.) spread throughout an organ or the body.
C. G. SELIGMAN The mass of the Fulani population .. is disseminated among diverse Negro populations. Q. BELL She collected and disseminated bad news. **disseminated sclerosis** multiple sclerosis.
¶In isolated use bef. 17.
disseminator *n.* E17.

dissemination /dɪˌsɛmɪˈneɪʃ(ə)n/ *n.* E17. [L *disseminatio(n-)*, f. as prec.: see -ATION.] The action of disseminating; the fact or condition of being disseminated; dispersion, diffusion; promulgation.

disseminule /dɪˈsɛmɪnjuːl/ *n.* E20. [Irreg. f. prec. + -ULE.] *Bot.* Any part of a plant that serves to propagate it, e.g. a seed or a fruit.

dissension /dɪˈsɛnʃ(ə)n/ *n.* Also (now *rare*) **-ntion**. ME. [(O)Fr. f. L *dissensio(n-)*, f. *dissens-* pa. ppl stem of *dissentire*: see DISSENT *v.*, -ION.] **1** (A) disagreement of opinion, esp. such as leads to contention or strife. ME. †**2** *Med.* (A) disturbance of the body producing illness. L16–E18. †**3** Disagreement in matters of religion; = DISSENT *n.* 3. E18–E19.
1 M. MITCHELL There were dissensions within the Confederate cabinet, disagreements between President Davis and his generals.

†**dissensious** *a.* var. of DISSENTIOUS.

dissensus /dɪˈsɛnsəs/ *n.* M20. [f. DIS- 2 + CONSENSUS, or L *dissensus* disagreement, f. *dissens-* pa. ppl stem of *dissentire*: see next.] Widespread dissent; the reverse of consensus.
Encounter Differing viewpoints .. erupting into dissensus and minority positions.

dissent /dɪˈsɛnt/ *n.* LME. [f. the vb.] **1** Opposition to a proposal or resolution; an instance of this. LME. **2** (A) difference of opinion, (a) disagreement. Formerly also, a quarrel. L16. **3** *spec.* Difference of opinion on questions of religious doctrine or practice. L16. **b** The state of being separated from a prevailing or established Church, esp. the Church of England; *spec.* Protestant Nonconformism. Also, the Nonconformist community. L18. †**4** Difference in meaning, character, etc. E–M17.
1 H. WILSON It was traditional for any minister who disagreed deeply with the decision to ask for his dissent to be recorded. 2 T. SPENCER I finde no dissent betweene any parties touching this precept. 3b LD MACAULAY The Church of Rome unites in herself all the strength of establishment and all the strength of dissent.

dissent /dɪˈsɛnt/ *v.i.* LME. [L *dissentire* differ in sentiment, f. as DIS- 1 + *sentire* feel. Cf. Fr. *dissentir* (15).] **1** Withhold assent or consent from a proposal etc.; express opposition. (Foll. by *from*, (now *rare*) *to*.) LME. **2** Think

For other words beginning with *dis-* see the entry for **dis-**

differently; have a different opinion, disagree. (Foll. by *from*, *in* a subject; *from*, †*with* a person.) M16. 3 *spec.* Differ in religious doctrine or practice, esp. from a prevailing or established Church. M16. †4 Be at loggerheads; quarrel. M16–M18. †5 Differ in meaning, nature, form, etc., (*from*). M16–M17.

1 B. CASTLE When he talked about freedom to dissent he hadn't meant that we should . . organize an anti-Government campaign. 2 G. GROTE If the public dissent from our views, we say that they ought to concur with us.

dissenting *ppl a.* (*a*) that dissents, esp. from the majority view; (*b*) differing in opinion on religious matters; *spec.* (**D-**) Nonconformist: M16. **dissentingly** *adv.* in a manner expressive of dissent E17. **dissentment** *n.* (*rare*) dissent L17.

dissentaneous /dɪs(ə)n'teɪnɪəs/ *a. arch.* E17. [f. L *dissentaneus* (f. *dissentire* DISSENT *v.*) + -OUS.] Not harmonizing, contradictory, discordant. (Foll. by *to*, *with*.)

dissenter /dɪ'sɛntə/ *n.* M17. [f. DISSENT *v.* + -ER[1].] 1 A person who disagrees with an opinion, resolution, or proposal; a dissentient. M17. 2 A person who dissents in matters of religious belief or practice; *esp.* one who dissociates himself or herself from or *from* a prevailing or established Church. M17. b *spec.* (Now usu. **D-**.) In England, a member of a Protestant Church or sect other than the Church of England; *Hist.* (in Britain and Ireland) a member of any Church or sect, Protestant or Catholic, not established in the area concerned. Now somewhat *derog.* L17.

dissenterism, **D-** *n.* the principles and practice of Dissenters E19.

dissentient /dɪ'sɛnʃɪənt, -ʃ(ə)nt/ *n.* & *a.* E17. [L *dissentient-* pres. ppl stem of *dissentire*: see DISSENT *v.*, -ENT.] (A person) dissenting or expressing dissent, esp. from the majority or official view.

JO GRIMOND If dissentients could be persuaded to abstain instead of actually voting in a different lobby. A. BURGESS There will be no dissentient voices raised to this proposal.

dissentience *n.* (*rare*) M19.

dissention *n.* see DISSENSION.

dissentious /dɪ'sɛnʃəs/ *a.* Now *rare.* Also †**-nsious**. M16. [f. DISSENSION: see -IOUS. Cf. Fr. †*dissentieux*, *-cieux*.] Of, pertaining to, or marked by dissension; given to dissension, quarrelsome. Formerly also, inclined to dissent in matters of religion.

dissepiment /dɪ'sɛpɪm(ə)nt/ *n.* E18. [L *dissaepimentum*, f. *dissaepire* make separate, f. as DIS- 1 + *saepire* divide off by a hedge, f. *saepes* hedge: see -MENT.] *Zool.* & *Bot.* A partition in some part or organ; a septum; *esp.* (*a*) a wall separating the cells of a syncarpous ovary or fruit; (*b*) one of the horizontal plates connecting the vertical septa in corals.

dissepi'mental *a.* M19.

dissert /dɪ'səːt/ *v.* E17. [L *dissert-* pa. ppl stem of *disserere* treat of, discourse, f. as DIS- 1 + *serere* connect, join words in composition.] †1 *v.t.* Discuss, examine. E17–E18. 2 *v.i.* Discourse, expatiate, (*on* a subject). Now *affected.* M17.

dissertate /'dɪsəteɪt/ *v.i.* Now *affected.* M18. [L *dissertat-*: see next, -ATE[3].] = DISSERT 2.

Times I am no scholar to dissertate on the innumerable versions of the *Pervigilium Veneris*.

dissertation /dɪsə'teɪʃ(ə)n/ *n.* E17. [L *dissertatio(n-)*, f. *dissertat-* pa. ppl stem of *dissertare* argue, debate, frequent. of *disserere*: see -ATION.] †1 Discussion, debate. E17–E18. 2 A spoken or written discourse on a subject, in which it is treated at length. M17. b An extended scholarly essay submitted for a degree or other academic qualification. L19.

dissertational *a.* pertaining to or of the nature of a dissertation or long discourse M19.

dissertative /'dɪsəteɪtɪv/ *a.* E19. [f. L *dissertat-*: see DISSERTATION, -IVE.] Marked by or given to dissertations.

dissertator /'dɪsəteɪtə/ *n.* L17. [Late L = disputant, f. as prec.: see -OR.] A person who gives a dissertation.

disserve /dɪ(s)'səːv/ *v.t.* & *i.* E17. [f. DIS- 2 + SERVE *v.*[1], prob. after (O)Fr. *desservir*.] Do a disservice (to), esp. when trying to help; serve badly or imperfectly.

M. SCHORER We can speak of good and bad technique, . . of technique which serves the novel's purpose, or disserves.

disservice /dɪ(s)'səːvɪs/ *n.* L16. [f. DIS- 2 + SERVICE *n.*[1] Cf. Fr. *desservice*.] Detriment, injury; an unhelpful or injurious act.

P. GOODMAN You do a disservice to the . . poor by giving them money, because they will get into trouble.

disserviceable *a.* tending to disserve; unhelpful, detrimental: M17.

†**dissettle** *v.t.* M17–M18. [f. DIS- 2 + SETTLE *v.*] Make unsettled, disturb.

dissettlement /dɪ(s)'sɛt(ə)lm(ə)nt/ *n.* M17. [f. DIS- 2 + SETTLEMENT.] †1 The action of unsettling; unsettled or disturbed condition. Only in M17. 2 Expulsion from a settled place of residence. *rare.* L19.

dissever /dɪ(s)'sɛvə/ *v.* ME. [AN *des(c)everer*, OFr. *des(s)evrer* (mod., techn. *desseuvrer*) f. late L *disseparare*, f. as DIS- 1 + L *separare* SEPARATE *v.*] 1 *v.t.* Separate, sunder, (a person or thing *from* another, two or more people or things from each other). ME. 2 *v.t.* Divide into parts, cut up. LME. †3 *v.t.* Break up, disperse, (a company or combination). LME–E17. 4 *v.i.* Become parted, break up. LME.

1 F. TUOHY Some people, whose anxieties have almost dissevered them from the corporeal world. 4 L. MACNEICE Drifting cloud and gauzy mist Brighten and dissever.

disseverance *n.* the action or an act of dissevering LME. **dissevé'ration** *n.* = DISSEVERANCE L17. **disseverment** *n.* = DISSEVERANCE E17.

dissidence /'dɪsɪd(ə)ns/ *n.* M17. [Fr., or L *dissidentia*, f. *dissident-*: see next, -ENCE.] The state or fact of being dissident; disagreement in opinion, dissent; difference in character.

dissident /'dɪsɪd(ə)nt/ *a.* & *n.* M16. [Fr., or L *dissident-* pres. ppl stem of *dissidere* sit apart, disagree, f. as DIS- 1 + *sedere* sit: see -ENT.] A *adj.* 1 Differing in opinion, character, etc.; disagreeing. (Foll. by *from*.) M16. 2 Dissenting in matters of religion. M19. 3 Voicing political dissent, usu. in a totalitarian (esp. Communist) State. M20.

1 J. R. LOWELL Men . . dissident . . in other respects, were agreed in resenting these impediments.

B *n.* 1 *Hist.* In Poland: a non-Catholic (esp. Orthodox) Christian. M18. 2 A person who disagrees, a dissentient. L18. 3 *spec.* A person who dissents from a prevailing or established form of religion; a dissenter. L18. 4 A person who openly opposes the policies of a totalitarian (esp. Communist) régime. M20.

dissilient /dɪ'sɪlɪənt/ *a. rare.* M17. [L *dissilient-* pres. ppl stem of *dissilire* spring apart, f. as DIS- 1 + *salire* leap.] Springing or tending to spring apart.

dissimilar /dɪ'sɪmɪlə/ *a.* & *n.* L16. [f. DIS- 2 + SIMILAR, after L *dissimilis*, Fr. *dissimilaire*.] A *adj.* Not similar; different in appearance, properties, or nature; unlike. (Foll. by *to*; also *from*, †*with*.) L16.

C. DARWIN We see countries closely corresponding in all their physical conditions, but with their inhabitants utterly dissimilar.

B *n.* A dissimilar thing. Usu. in *pl.* M17.

dissimi'larity *n.* (an instance of) dissimilar character; (a) difference: E18. **dissimilarly** *adv.* M18.

dissimilate /dɪ'sɪmɪleɪt/ *v.t.* & *i.* M19. [f. DIS- 2 + L *similis* similar, after ASSIMILATE *v.*] Make or become different; *esp.* (*Ling.*) subject to or undergo dissimilation.

dissimilatory *a.* (*Philol.*) pertaining to or produced by dissimilation E20.

dissimilation /ˌdɪsɪmɪ'leɪʃ(ə)n/ *n.* M19. [f. prec. after ASSIMILATION.] 1 The action of making dissimilar; the process of becoming dissimilar. M19. 2 *spec.* (*Ling.*) The differentiation of two identical sounds occurring near each other in a word by the change of one of them, as *purple* from OE *purpuran*. L19. 3 *Biol.* Destructive metabolism, catabolism. L19.

dissimile /dɪ'sɪmɪli/ *n.* L17. [L, neut. of *dissimilis* (see next) after SIMILE.] *Rhet.* A comparison or illustration by contrast.

dissimilitude /dɪsɪ'mɪlɪtjuːd/ *n.* LME. [L *dissimilitudo*, f. *dissimilis* unlike, f. as DIS- 2 + *similis* alike: see -TUDE.] 1 Dissimilarity, diversity; an instance of this. LME. †2 *Rhet.* = DISSIMILE. L16–M18.

†**dissimulance** *n.* LME–E18. [L *dissimulantia*, f. *dissimulare*: see next, -ANCE.] = DISSIMULATION 1.

dissimulate /dɪ'sɪmjʊleɪt/ *v.* LME. [L *dissimulat-* pa. ppl stem of *dissimulare*, f. as DIS- 2, SIMULATE *v.*] 1 *v.t.* & *i.* = DISSEMBLE *v.*[1] 1. LME. †2 *v.t.* Combine with, neutralize, (an electric charge, electricity). M–L19.

1 ST G. J. MIVART The long dissimulated Atheism of Mill is now avowed. W. GOLDING The nearer he had come to dissimulating his bile the higher it had risen in his throat. V. GLENDINNING Most people conceal a good deal of what they feel; Edith did not dissimulate.

¶Rare bef. L18.

dissimulation /dɪˌsɪmjʊ'leɪʃ(ə)n/ *n.* LME. [(O)Fr. f. L *dissimulatio(n-)*, f. as prec.: see -ATION.] 1 The action of dissembling; concealment of one's true nature, feelings, etc.; pretence, hypocrisy. Formerly also, an instance of this. LME. †b Disguised form. *rare* (Milton). Only in L17. †2 A flock *of* (small) birds. L15–L17.

1 STEELE Simulation is a Pretence of what is not, and Dissimulation a Concealment of what is. A. G. GARDINER I may . . only be truthful because I haven't courage enough for dissimulation. b MILTON Satan, bowing low His gray dissimulation, disappeared.

dissimulator /dɪ'sɪmjʊleɪtə/ *n.* E16. [L *dissimulator*, f. *dissimulare*: see DISSIMULATE, -OR.] A person who dissimulates; a dissembler.

†**dissimule** *v.t.* & *i.* LME–M17. [(O)Fr. *dissimuler* f. L *dissimulare*: see DISSIMULATE.] = DISSEMBLE *v.*[1]

¶DISSEMBLE *v.*[1] developed from this wd.

†**dissipable** *a.* E17–E18. [L *dissipabilis*, f. *dissipare*: see next, -ABLE.] Able to be dissipated.

dissipate /'dɪsɪpeɪt/ *v.* Pa. pple & ppl a. **-ated**, †**-ate**. LME. [L *dissipat-* pa. ppl stem of *dissipare*, f. as DIS- 1 + *supare* throw: see -ATE[3].] I *v.t.* 1 Drive or cause to go in different directions; disperse (what has been concentrated). Formerly, spread out (troops). *arch.* LME. †b Disperse in flight; rout. E17–L18. 2 Cause (an immaterial thing) to disappear; *esp.* dispel (a feeling etc.) from the mind. LME. 3 Reduce to dust, smoke, or impalpable form; destroy completely (material or immaterial things). L15. 4 Cause to disappear into the atmosphere; disperse (vapour, a cloud, etc.); (of an electrical device etc.) lose (heat), convert (energy) into heat that is lost. M16. 5 Consume wastefully, squander, (money, resources, etc.). L17. 6 Divide (attention, mental activity, etc.) between a variety of objects. L17.

1 C. LAMB To pick up her wandering fruit, which some unlucky dray has just dissipated. C. SAGAN The outer layers of red giants are slowly dissipated into interstellar space. 2 I. D'ISRAELI Cool shades and exquisite viands in a moment dissipated heat and hunger. 3 T. R. MALTHUS Violent hurricanes, by which whole harvests are dissipated. 4 C. MCCULLOUGH The room . . reeked so of roses that open windows could not dissipate their heavy perfume. 6 K. M. E. MURRAY He should . . do one big thing well, rather than dissipate his energies on a number of minor works.

II *v.i.* 7 Become dispersed; melt away, disappear; be reduced to dust or impalpable fragments. E17. 8 Indulge in frivolous or dissolute pleasures; practise dissipation. M19.

7 F. KING A plume of smoke . . which uncurls and then slowly dissipates. A. T. ELLIS Claudia's anxiety dissipated. 8 T. HOOK I was rather out of spirits, so I dissipated in a glass of negus.

dissipated *a.* (*a*) that has been dissipated; (*b*) given to or marked by dissipation, dissolute: E17. **dissipater** *n.* L18. **dissipator** *n.* M16. **dissipative** *a.* tending to dissipate; characterized by dissipation, esp. of energy as waste heat: L17. **dissipa'tivity** *n.* L19.

dissipation /dɪsɪ'peɪʃ(ə)n/ *n.* LME. [(O)Fr., or L *dissipatio(n-)*, f. as prec.: see -ATION.] 1 Reduction to an impalpable form; complete disintegration, dissolution. LME. 2 The action or an act of dispersing; dispersal; *spec.* (*Optics*) the spreading out of a beam of light. Also, dispersed condition. Now *rare* or *obs.* M16. 3 The continuous loss of energy or (formerly) substance, esp. from an electrical device, by its conversion into heat. E17. 4 Wasteful consumption of money, resources, etc.; squandering. M17. 5 (A source of) distraction of the mind from serious matters; (a) diversion, (an) amusement, now esp. of a frivolous or dissolute nature. M18. 6 Immoderate indulgence in physical pleasures; intemperate or dissolute living. L18.

5 S. JOHNSON Change of place . . inevitably produces dissipation of mind. M. HOLROYD After the dissipations of London, both painters tried hard to discipline themselves. 6 DICKENS Tupman was not in a condition to rise, after the unwonted dissipation of the previous night.

dissipationless *a.* L20.

dissociable /*in sense 1* dɪˈsəʊʃəb(ə)l, *in sense 2* dɪˈsəʊʃɪəb(ə)l, -sɪ-/ *a.* E17. [In sense 1, f. DIS- 2 + SOCIABLE *a.* In sense 2, f. Fr. f. L *dissociabilis*, f. *dissociare*: see DISSOCIATE *v.*, -ABLE.] 1 Not sociable, uncompanionable; not well associated, ill-assorted. E17. 2 Able to be dissociated; separable. M19.

dissociaˈbility *n.* †(*a*) *rare* unsociableness; (*b*) dissociable character: M18. **dissociableness** *n.* unsociableness M19.

dissocial /dɪˈsəʊʃ(ə)l/ *a.* M18. [f. DIS- 2 + SOCIAL *a.*] Disinclined or unsuitable for society; unsocial.

dissociˈality *n.* E19. **dissocialize** *v.t.* make dissocial E19.

dissociate /dɪˈsəʊʃɪeɪt, -sɪ-/ *v.* Pa. pple & ppl a. **-ated,** (*rare*) **-ate** /-ət/. M16. [L *dissociat-* pa. ppl stem of *dissociare*, f. as DIS- 1 + *sociare* join together, f. *socius* companion: see -ATE[3].] I *v.t.* 1 Cut off or free from association with something else; separate in fact or thought; disassociate. (Foll. by *from*.) M16. 2 *Sci.* Cause the dissociation of (a compound etc.). M19. 3 *Psychiatry.* Cause (the personality, ideas, etc.) to undergo dissociation (DISSOCIATION *n.* 4). Chiefly as *dissociated* ppl a. L19.

1 A. TUCKER Our very . . desires, which first bring us together, have a tendency likewise to dissociate us. V. BRITTAIN The whole subject of child-birth was completely dissociated in my mind from that of sex. **dissociate oneself from** declare oneself unconnected with. 2 S. WEINBERG The universe was so hot and dense that atoms were dissociated into their nuclei and electrons. 3 **dissociated personality** a pathological state of mind in which two or more distinct personalities coexist in the same person.

II *v.i.* 4 Become dissociated; *spec.* (*Sci.*) undergo dissociation. M19.

dissociative *a.* tending to dissociate; causing dissociation: L19.

dissociation /dɪˌsəʊʃɪˈeɪʃ(ə)n, -sɪ-/ *n.* E17. [Fr., or L *dissociatio(n-)*, f. as prec.: see -ATION.] 1 The action of dissociating; the condition of being dissociated; disassociation. E17. 2 *spec.* in *Sci.* The usu. reversible breaking up of a compound into simpler substances, esp. by the action of heat on a gas or a solvent on a solute; the analogous breaking up of a molecule; the ionization of an atom. M19. 3 *Psychol.* The process or result of breaking up an association of ideas. L19. 4 *Psychiatry.* A process, or the resulting condition, in which certain concepts or mental processes are separated from the conscious personality; *spec.* the state of a person suffering from dissociated personality. L19.

2 **dissociation constant** the product of the concentrations of dissolved ions in a solution, at equilibrium, divided by the concentration of the undissociated molecule.

dissogeny /dɪˈsɒdʒəni/ *n.* M20. [Alt. of next: see -GENY.] *Zool.* The condition, found esp. among certain ctenophores, in which an individual has two periods of sexual maturity, one in the larval and one in the adult stage.

dissogony /dɪˈsɒgəni/ *n.* L19. [f. Gk *dissos* twofold + -GONY.] *Zool.* = prec.

dissoluble /dɪˈsɒljʊb(ə)l/ *a.* M16. [OFr., or L *dissolubilis*, f. *dissolvere*, f. as DIS- 1, SOLVE: see -UBLE. Cf. earlier INDISSOLUBLE.] 1 Able to be broken down into elements or atoms; decomposable. M16. 2 Of a physical connection or (*fig.*) a bond or tie: able to be undone or broken. E17. 3 Able to be dissolved in a liquid; soluble. Now *rare.* M17.

dissoluˈbility *n.* E17.

dissolute /ˈdɪsəluːt/ *a.* & *n.* LME. [L *dissolutus* loose, disconnected, pa. pple of *dissolvere* DISSOLVE *v.*] A *adj.* †1 Having the connection dissolved; disconnected, disunited. LME–M17. †2 Relaxed, enfeebled; lacking firmness of texture or of temperament. LME–E19. †3 Having one's energies or attention relaxed; careless, negligent. LME–M18. 4†a Unrestrained in behaviour; unruly, unbridled; lavish, wasteful. LME–E18. b Undisciplined in style. Now *rare.* M16. 5 Lax in sexual matters, loose-living; abandoned, profligate. LME.

5 J. BUTLER Untimely deaths occasioned by a dissolute course of life. L. HUDSON A grossly dissolute and unprincipled young man.

B *n.* A dissolute person. *rare.* E17.

dissolutely *adv.* LME. **dissoluteness** *n.* M16.

†**dissolute** *v.t. rare.* E17–M18. [f. the adj.] Dissolve, break up, loosen. Chiefly as *dissoluted* ppl a.

dissolution /dɪsəˈluːʃ(ə)n/ *n.* LME. [(O)Fr., or L *dissolutio(n-)*, f. *dissolut-* pa. ppl stem of *dissolvere* DISSOLVE *v.*: see -ION.] 1 Reduction of a body or mass to its constituent elements; disintegration, decomposition. LME. †2 Injurious relaxation or softening; enfeeblement. LME–L17. 3 Unrestrained or dissolute conduct; laxity of morals. Formerly also, (an) extravagance; a dissolute practice. LME. 4 The undoing or severance of something that fastens or joins; *esp.* the dissolving of a partnership, union, etc. LME. 5 The action of bringing to an end; the state of being ended; destruction or ruin of an organized system etc. LME. 6 Extinction of life in a person; decease. E16. 7 The dismissal or dispersal of an assembly, esp. of Parliament for new elections; termination of the existence of a constituted body or association. M16. 8 The process of dissolving or the state of being dissolved in liquid. Formerly, a solution. M16. 9 The melting of a substance at ambient temperature or (formerly) with the application of heat. L16.

3 JER. TAYLOR His youthful aptnesses to dissolution. 6 L. STRACHEY Minute descriptions of her mother's last hours, her dissolution, her corpse. 7 H. P. BROUGHAM The dissolution of the monasteries in Henry VIII's reign. W. S. CHURCHILL The normal period between a Dissolution and the poll is seventeen days.

dissolutive /dɪˈsɒljʊtɪv, ˈdɪsəljuːtɪv, ˈdɪsəljuːtɪv/ *a.* Now *rare.* LME. [med.L *dissolutivus*, f. *dissolut-*: see prec., -IVE.] †1 Having the property of causing to dissolve. LME–L17. 2 Pertaining to disintegration or dissolution. L19.

dissolvable /dɪˈzɒlvəb(ə)l/ *a.* M16. [f. DISSOLVE *v.* + -ABLE; repl. (in part) DISSOLUBLE.] 1 Able to be broken down into its constituent elements; decomposable. M16. 2 Able to be dissolved or (formerly) melted. M17. 3 Of a partnership, ordinance, etc.: able to be broken or annulled. L17.

dissolve /dɪˈzɒlv/ *n.* E20. [f. the vb.] *Cinemat.*, *Television.* A transition between scenes in which one gradually disappears from view at the same time as the following scene gradually appears. Also called *mix.*

match dissolve: see MATCH *a.*

dissolve /dɪˈzɒlv/ *v.* LME. [L *dissolvere*, f. as DIS- 1 + *solvere* loosen, SOLVE.] I *v.t.* 1 Break down (an object or substance) into its component parts; destroy the cohesion of, cause to disintegrate. Now *rare* or *obs.* exc. as assoc. with other senses. LME. 2 Melt, esp. by the application of heat. Now *rare* or *obs.* LME. 3 Cause (a solid or gas) to be incorporated into a liquid so as to be indistinguishable from it; make a solution of. LME. †4 Make weak or languid; relax, enfeeble. LME–M16. 5 Loosen from what holds fast; unfasten, release. *arch.* LME. †6 Release from life. Usu. in *pass.*, die. LME–M18. 7 Cause to disappear gradually from sight or from existence; *Cinemat.*, *Television* cause (a scene) to fade as the following scene gradually appears. LME. †8 *Med.* Disperse (morbid humours); reduce (a swelling); remove or assuage (a pain or ailment). LME–E18. 9 Dismiss, disperse, (an assembly); terminate the existence of (a constituted body or association, esp. Parliament). LME. 10a Undo (a knot, a bond); *fig.* bring to an end (a partnership, union, marriage, etc.). LME. †b Part, divide, (persons united to each other). L16–E17. 11a Destroy the binding force or influence of; *spec.* (*Law*) annul, abrogate, (an injunction). LME. †b Reject the authority of. LME–M17. †c Dispose of (an assertion etc.) as false or erroneous; refute. E16–M19. 12 Solve, clear up, (a problem, doubt, etc.). *arch.* LME. 13 *fig.* Overwhelm emotionally; cause to melt (*into* tears etc.); immerse *in* pleasure or absorbing activity. E16.

1 J. PRIESTLEY Animal substances dissolved by putrefaction . . emit phlogiston. 3 T. H. HUXLEY All natural water . . contains such dissolved salts. E. O'NEILL Is it a powder you dissolve in wine? **dissolve away, off, out** remove or extract by dissolving. 7 J. TYNDALL That promise is a dream dissolved by the experience of eighteen centuries. G. GREENE The photographer had tried to dissolve in mist the rocky outline of the jaw. 9 J. REED The Second . . Congress of Soviets was dissolved, so that the members might hurry to their homes. 10b SHAKES. *Merry W.* She and I, long since contracted, are now so sure that nothing can dissolve us. 11a S. HAZZARD Caro lifted her hands and dissolved the spell. 13 MILTON Anthems clear, As may . . Dissolve me into ecstasies. I. D'ISRAELI Henry Rantzall . . whose days were dissolved in the pleasures of reading.

II *v.i.* 14 Lose solidity or cohesion; disintegrate; vanish or fade away gradually. Now usu. taken as *fig.* from sense 18. LME. 15 Melt. Now *rare.* LME. b *fig.* Give way to unrestrained expression of feeling; melt (*into* tears etc.); faint, swoon. E17. 16 Of an assembly or collective body: disperse, break up, disband. M16. 17 Lose its binding force or influence. E17. 18 Of a solid or gas: become incorporated in a liquid to form a solution. M17. 19 *Cinemat.*, *Television.* Pass *to* or *into* a new scene by means of a dissolve. E20.

14 J. L. WATEN I watched them get smaller in the distance and dissolve into the darkness. I. MURDOCH The painful concentration of her face increased and then dissolved as she . . began suddenly to weep. 15 A. WINCHELL The dissolving ice of the glacier. b B. PYM The young men dissolved into helpless laughter. 16 F. O'BRIEN Groups would form . . and dissolve again quickly. 18 B. NILSON Stir until the sugar dissolves.

dissolver *n.* a person who or thing which dissolves; *spec.* an apparatus for dissolving film or television shots: LME. **dissolvingly** *adv.* in a dissolving manner E19.

dissolvent /dɪˈzɒlv(ə)nt/ *a.* & *n.* M17. [L *dissolvent-* pres. ppl stem of *dissolvere*: see DISSOLVE *v.*, -ENT.] A *adj.* Having the property of causing something to dissolve or of becoming dissolved. M17.

B *n.* An agent which dissolves something; a solvent. M17.

J. RAY Fire—the only Catholic Dissolvent. F. MAHONY Wine is the great dissolvent of mistrust.

dissolvible /dɪˈzɒlvɪb(ə)l/ *a.* Now *rare* or *obs.* L17. [f. DISSOLVE *v.* + -IBLE, or alt. of DISSOLVABLE.] = DISSOLVABLE.

dissonance /ˈdɪs(ə)nəns/ *n.* LME. [(O)Fr., or late L *dissonantia*, f. as next: see -ANCE.] 1 Lack of agreement between things; discordance, discrepancy. LME. 2 (An) unpleasant or jarring combination of sounds. L16. 3 *Mus.* (The quality of) a combination of notes producing beats or sounding as if it needs resolution; a note whose presence causes this. M17.

dissonancy *n.* (now *rare*) = DISSONANCE L16.

dissonant /ˈdɪs(ə)nənt/ *a.* & *n.* LME. [(O)Fr., or L *dissonant-* pres. ppl stem of *dissonare* disagree in sound, f. as DIS- 1 + *sonare* SOUND *v.*[1]] A *adj.* 1 Not in agreement or accord in any respect; at variance, conflicting. (Foll. by *from*, *to*, (rare) *with.*) LME. 2 Discordant in sound, jarring, inharmonious; *Mus.* forming or of the nature of a dissonance. L16.

1 BURKE The interests . . before that time jarring and dissonant, were . . adjusted. 2 J. BRYANT If the name

was dissonant, and disagreeable to their ear, it was rejected as barbarous.

B *n.* A dissonant element; a harsh speech sound. M16.

disso'nantal *a.* employing or characterized by dissonance M20. **dissonantly** *adv.* L18.

†dissonate *a.* M16–L18. [L *dissonatus* pa. pple, f. as next: see -ATE[2].] = DISSONANT 1.

dissonate /ˈdɪs(ə)neɪt/ *v. rare.* L19. [L *dissonat-* pa. ppl stem of *dissonare*: see DISSONANT, -ATE[3].] 1 *v.i.* Of sounds: be dissonant. Chiefly as *dissonating* ppl a. L19. 2 *v.t.* Make dissonant. M20.

disspread *v.* var. of DISPREAD.

dissuade /dɪˈsweɪd/ *v.* L15. [L *dissuadere*, f. as DIS- 2 + *suadere* advise, persuade. Cf. Fr. *dissuader*.] 1 *v.t.* & *i.* Advise or urge (a person) against. (Foll. by *from* (an action etc., *doing*).) Now *rare.* L15. 2 *v.t.* Give advice against, discourage, (an action etc.). Now *rare.* E16. 3 *v.t.* Deflect (a person) by persuasion or influence (*from* (an action etc., *doing*)). L16.

1 V. WOOLF The more she dissuaded, the more he was determined to go. 2 J. STEPHEN His.. friends anxiously dissuaded a journey so full of peril. 3 A. HOPKINS A crowd of anxious nannies trying to dissuade a capricious child from going too far.

dissuader *n.* a person who or thing which dissuades M16.

dissuasion /dɪˈsweɪʒ(ə)n/ *n.* LME. [(O)Fr., or L *dissuasio(n-)*, f. *dissuas-* pa. ppl stem of *dissuadere*: see prec., -ION.] The action or an act of dissuading; (an) exhortation against something.

dissuasive /dɪˈsweɪsɪv/ *a.* & *n.* E16. [f. L *dissuas-*: see prec., -IVE.] A *adj.* Tending to dissuade. E16. B *n.* A dissuasive speech or argument. E17.

dissuasively *adv.* M19. **dissuasiveness** *n.* E18.

†dissuetude *n. rare.* LME. [Late L *dissuetudo*, f. *dissuet-* pa. ppl stem of *dissuescere* = cl.L *desuescere*: see DESUETUDE.] 1 = DESUETUDE 1. LME–M18. 2 = DESUETUDE 2. Only in L16.

dissyllabic *a.* & *n.*, **dissyllabize** *v.*, **dissyllable** *n.* & *a.*, etc.: see DISYLLABIC etc.

dissymmetry /dɪˈsɪmɪtri/ *n.* M19. [f. DIS- 2 + SYMMETRY.] 1 Lack of symmetry, asymmetry. M19. 2 Symmetry between two things related to each other in the way that an object is related to its image in a mirror. L19.

dissy'mmetric *a.* = DISSYMMETRICAL L19. **dissy'mmetrical** *a.* exhibiting dissymmetry; enantiomorphic: M19. **dissy'mmetrically** *adv.* L19.

distad /ˈdɪstad/ *adv.* E19. [f. as DISTAL + -AD[3].] *Anat.* In the direction of the distal part of a limb etc.

distaff /ˈdɪstɑːf/ *n.* & *a.* [OE *distæf*, app. f. the base of MLG *dise*, *disene* distaff, bunch of flax (LG *diesse*) rel. to DIZEN + STAFF *n.*[1]] A *n.* Pl. **-staffs**, **†-staves**. 1 A cleft stick for holding wool or flax wound round for spinning by hand; the corresponding part of a spinning-wheel. (Used as a symbol of women and women's work.) OE. 2 A female heir; *the* female line; *the* female sex. L15.

1 SIR W. SCOTT Serving wenches.. sate plying their distaffs. *have tow on one's distaff*: see TOW *n.*[1] 1. 2 B. HARRIS The Kingdom.. for want of an heir male.. falls to the Distaff.

Phrases: JUPITER's *distaff*. **St Distaff's day** *arch.* 7 January, the day after Twelfth Day, on which women resumed their housework.

B *attrib.* or as *adj.* Female; of or pertaining to women. L16.

S. T. WARNER A great-great uncle.. on the distaff side. *Rolling Stone* All her distaff classmates mooning nightly by their phones for a call.

distain /dɪˈsteɪn/ *v.t. arch.* LME. [OFr. *desteign-* pres. stem of *desteindre* (mod. *déteindre*), f. Proto-Romance, f. as DIS- 1, TINGE *v.*] 1 Imbue or stain with a colour different from the natural one; discolour, stain, tinge. LME. 2 Defile; bring a blot or stain on; sully, dishonour. LME. †3 Deprive of colour, brightness, or splendour, esp. by comparison; outshine. LME–M17.

1 C. MARLOWE The tears that so distain my cheeks. 2 R. BURNS May coward shame distain his name, The wretch that dare not die!

distal /ˈdɪst(ə)l/ *a.* E19. [Irreg. f. DIST(ANT + -AL[1], after *dorsal* etc.] *Sci.* Situated away from the centre of the body or the point of attachment; further, more distant; *spec.* in *Geol.*, designating or characteristic of an area far from but influenced by an area of activity, as a sedimentation zone, a volcanic vent, etc.

distally *adv.* L19.

Distalgesic /dɪst(ə)lˈdʒiːzɪk/ *n.* Also **d-**. M20. [f. *Distillers'* Co. Ltd. + ANALGESIC.] (Proprietary name for) a brand of painkiller containing paracetamol and propoxyphene in tablet form.

distance /ˈdɪst(ə)ns/ *n.* ME. [OFr. *destance*, (also mod.) *distance* or L *distantia*, f. *distant-*: see DISTANT *a.*, -ANCE.] I [OFr. *destance*.] †1 The condition of being at variance; discord, dissension; dispute, debate. ME–M18. †2 A disagreement, a quarrel; an estrangement. ME–M17.

II [L *distantia*.] †3 Difference of quality or nature; diversity. LME–M16.

III [L *distantia*, (O)Fr. *distance*.] 4 The fact or condition of being apart or far off in space; remoteness. LME. 5 The extent of space lying between two points; the space to be passed over before reaching an object; an intervening space. LME. b *Fencing.* A definite interval of space to be kept between two combatants. L16. c *Mil.* The space between adjacent individuals when standing in rank; the space between the ranks. M17. d *Horse-racing.* A distance of 240 yards (220 metres) or thereabouts; orig. (now *US*), the distance from the winning-post which a horse must have reached when the winner finishes in order to qualify for a subsequent heat. L17. e The range within which a boxer can strike his opponent. E19. 6 The length of time between two events; an interval, an intervening period. Now only in *distance of time.* LME. b The scheduled length of a boxing-match. Esp. in *go the distance* below. M20. 7 *Mus.* An interval. M16–L18. 8 (The part of a picture representing) the distant part of a landscape; the more remote part of what the eye can see; a point or region a long way away. M16. 9 Remoteness in personal relations; lack or avoidance of intimacy or familiarity; aloofness, reserve. Formerly also, deference. L16. 10 *fig.* Remoteness or lack of closeness in likeness, relationship, allusion, degree, etc. M17.

4 SHELLEY Afar the Contadino's song is heard.. made sweet by distance. C. H. SISSON A bench some distance from the bed. 5 W. S. MAUGHAM Excursions to places of interest within convenient distance. A. PATON He.. began to walk across the bare fields, measuring the distance with his strides. 6 S. FOOTE Take.. three times a day, at two hours distance. LD MACAULAY An apprehension not to be mentioned, even at this distance of time, without shame and indignation. 8 J. WILLOCK I was unable to walk to any distance. C. DARWIN The rocks.. appear from a distance of a brilliantly white colour. DAY LEWIS A bicycle-bell rings in the distance. 9 SHAKES. *Oth.* He shall in strangeness stand no further off Than in a politic distance. E. REVELEY A certain distance had to be maintained and he kept his own voice deliberately cool.

Phrases: **at a distance**, (*arch.*) **at distance** far off, not very near (*action at a distance*: see ACTION *n.* 1). **go the distance** *Boxing* complete the scheduled duration of a fight. **keep one's distance** remain a certain way away (*from*); avoid closeness; *fig.* avoid undue familiarity. **know one's distance** *arch.* recognize what degree of familiarity is appropriate. LONG-DISTANCE. *lunar distance*: see LUNAR *a. middle distance*: see MIDDLE *a. polar distance*: see POLAR *a. social distance*: see SOCIAL *a. within a measurable distance of*: see MEASURABLE 1. **within hailing**, **walking**, etc., **distance** near enough to reach easily by the specified means (cf. *striking distance* s.v. STRIKING *n.*).

Comb.: **distance learning**: in which lessons are given by post, radio, etc., rather than in person; **distance-post** *Horse-racing*: marking a distance (sense 5d) before the winning-post; **distance runner**: who competes in long- or middle-distance races.

distance /ˈdɪst(ə)ns/ *v.* L16. [f. the n.] 1 *v.t.* Place far off or not very near; separate by a space; dissociate (*from*). L16. 2 *v.t.* Leave far behind in a race etc.; outstrip (*lit.* & *fig.*). M17. b *Horse-racing.* Beat by a distance (see DISTANCE *n.* 5d). L17. c Keep far off from. Now *rare* or *obs.* E18. 3 *v.t.* Make to seem far off. L17.

1 T. FULLER The friendly Sea conveniently distanced from London. L. P. HARTLEY She had.. interests outside his range, interests which.. distanced her from him.

distancy /ˈdɪst(ə)nsi/ *n. rare.* E17. [L *distantia* DISTANCE *n.*: see -ANCY.] †1 Disagreement, difference. Only in E17. †2 The condition of being far off in space. Only in M17. 3 Avoidance of familiarity or intimacy; aloofness; reserve. M19.

distant /ˈdɪst(ə)nt/ *a.* LME. [(O)Fr., or L *distant-* pres. ppl stem of *distare* stand apart, f. as DIS- 1 + *stare* stand.] 1 Separate or apart in space by a specified interval. (Foll. by *from.*) LME. 2 Separated by an unspecified but considerable space; far apart, not close together. LME. 3 Remote or not close in likeness, allusion, degree, etc.; *spec.* remotely related in kinship. M16. †b Different in character or quality; various. M17–E18. 4 Standing, lying, or occurring far off; not close at hand, remote. L16. b Of the eyes or an expression: focused on a distant point; giving an appearance of inattention to immediate surroundings. L19. 5 Far apart or remote in time. E17. 6 Reserved in personal relations; aloof; avoiding intimacy or familiarity. E18.

1 AV *Exod.* 36:22 One board had two tenons, equally distant one from another. E. WAUGH Quarter of a mile distant lay the low sea-front. 3 ADDISON I could still discover a distant Resemblance of my old friend. 4 T. HARDY As they approached.. distant shouts and rattles reached their ears. R. CAMPBELL The distant outline of peaks and bluffs far inland. 5 J. WAIN Revenge was three years distant. 6 A. N. WILSON Towards Sam, formerly his favourite, Fred was now distant, moody, cold.

Special collocations: **distant early warning** *a. phr.* designating a radar system in N. America for giving early warning of a missile attack. **distant signal** a railway signal in advance of the home signal to give warning of the latter's setting.

distantly *adv.* LME. **distantness** *n.* (*rare*) M18.

†distantial *a.* M17–E18. [f. as next + -AL[1].] Distant; diverse.

distantiate /dɪˈstanʃɪeɪt/ *v.t.* E17. [f. L *distantia* DISTANCE *n.* + -ATE[3].] †1 Find the distance of. Only in E17. 2 Put or keep at a distance. M20.

distanti'ation *n.* the action of distantiating M20.

distaste /dɪsˈteɪst/ *n.* L16. [f. DIS- 2 + TASTE *n.*[1], after OFr. *desgoust* (mod. *dégoût*), It. *disgusto* DISGUST *n.*] 1 (A) dislike; (a) mild aversion; (a) preference for the absence or avoidance of something; repugnance. L16. b *spec.* Dislike of food or drink; nausea; a bad taste in the mouth. Now *rare* or *obs.* L16. †2 Unpleasantness; annoyance, discomfort. E17–E18. †3 Offence given or taken. E17–M18. †4 Mutual aversion, estrangement; a disagreement, a quarrel. Only in 17.

1 J. C. POWYS He experienced.. a vague, humorous distaste for his plump, unathletic body. J. L. WATEN Mother.. looked with distaste on the extravagant clothes of the dancers.

distaste /dɪsˈteɪst/ *v.* Now *rare.* L16. [f. DIS- 2 + TASTE *v.*, after OFr. *desgouster* (mod. *dégoûter*), It. (*di*)*sgustare* DISGUST *v.*] 1 *v.t.* Have or conceive distaste for; regard with aversion; dislike mentally. L16. †b *spec.* Dislike the taste of. L16–M17. 2a *v.t.* Excite the dislike or aversion of; displease, offend. Freq. in *pass.* (foll. by *with*, *at*). L16. †b *v.i.* Cause displeasure or offence; be distasteful. E–M17. †3 *v.t.* & *i.* Produce a nasty taste in the mouth (of); nauseate. Only in 17. †4 *v.t.* Spoil the taste or savour of. E–M17.

1 R. L. STEVENSON A man.. whom I distasted at the first look, as we distaste a ferret or an earwig. 2 ADDISON I have.. been very much distasted at this way of writing. 3 SHAKES. *Oth.* Poisons Which at the first are scarce found to distaste.

distasteful /dɪsˈteɪstfʊl, -f(ə)l/ *a.* E17. [f. DISTASTE *n.* + -FUL.] 1 Disagreeable (formerly esp. to the taste); causing dislike or disgust; unpleasant, offensive. E17. †2 Full of or exhibiting dislike or aversion; malevolent. E–M17.

1 DRYDEN Why shou'd you pluck the green distasteful fruit. J. AMBROSE His work must not be

made distasteful to him through too much drudgery. 2 SHAKES. *Timon* After distasteful looks .. They froze me into silence.

distastefully *adv.* (*a*) in a manner causing distaste, unpleasantly; (*b*) (long *rare*) with dislike or aversion: E17. **distastefulness** *n.* (*a*) the quality of causing distaste, offensiveness; †(*b*) dislike, repugnance: E17.

distemper /dɪˈstɛmpə/ *n.*[1] M16. [Partly f. DISTEMPER *v.*[1], partly f. DIS- 2 + TEMPER *n.*] 1 Ill humour, bad temper; uneasiness; disaffection; *Hist.* disturbance of the bodily humours. M16. 2 Disturbed condition of the body or mind; ill health, illness; a mental or physical disorder, a disease, an ailment. L16. †b Intoxication. L16–M17. c (A) disturbed or disordered condition, esp. of society or (formerly) the weather. *arch.* E17. d An often fatal virus disease of dogs characterized by catarrh, cough, and weakness; any of various other animal diseases. M18. †3 A disproportionate mixture of parts; the state of having elements mixed in the wrong proportions. E–M17.

1 W. TAYLOR Let us talk of these things .. without distemper and without eloquence. 2 BROWNING Eccentricity Nowise amounting to distemper. R. C. HUTCHINSON It was .. the slight distemper from pregnancy which made me speak so brusquely. N. MITFORD Having suffered, or enjoyed, most of the distempers in the medical dictionary.

distemper /dɪˈstɛmpə/ *n.*[2] M17. [f. DISTEMPER *v.*[2], after Fr. †*destrempe* (now *détrempe*).] 1 A method of painting in which powder colours are mixed with some glutinous substance dissolved in water, used esp. for scene-painting and interior walls. M17. 2 A liquid prepared for and used in this process; *spec.* whiting mixed with size and water, formerly used for ceilings etc. M19.

distemper /dɪˈstɛmpə/ *v.*[1]*t.* *arch.* ME. [Late L *distemperare* soak, mix, affect by disproportionate mixture, f. as DIS- 2, TEMPER *v.*[1]] †1 Temper incorrectly by mixing elements in the wrong proportions; disturb the due proportion of. Only in ME. 2 Disturb the temper or feelings of; make ill-humoured or ill at ease; trouble, vex, upset. Now *rare* or *obs.* LME. 3 Disorder the health of; make diseased or insane; affect with an illness. LME. †b Intoxicate, make drunk. L15–L17. 4 Disorder or spoil the condition of. Formerly, disturb the weather, air, etc., (usu. in *pass.*) of. LME.

2 JOSEPH HALL Vainely distempering himselfe about idle and frivolous questions. 3 *fig.*: *Listener* The ITV companies are as distempered as parrots about the cash they have to shell out for Channel 4. 4 MILTON Sin, that first Distemper'd all things.

distemper /dɪˈstɛmpə/ *v.*[2]*t.* LME. [OFr. *destremper* or late L *distemperare* soak, macerate, f. as DIS- 1, 3, TEMPER *v.*[1]] 1 Treat with water etc. or other liquid; mix with a liquid to dissolve wholly or partly; dilute; steep. LME–M17. 2 *fig.* Lessen the strength of by dilution; allay. *arch.* L16. 3 Paint or colour in distemper. L19.

1 E. TOPSELL Give the Horse .. the quantity of a Hasel-nut distempered in a quart of Wine. 2 N. HAWTHORNE The May sunshine was .. distempered with a very bitter east-wind.

distemperer *n.* a person who paints in distemper L19.

distemperate /dɪˈstɛmp(ə)rət/ *a.* Now *rare* or *obs.* LME. [Late L *distemperatus*, f. as DIS- 2, TEMPERATE *a.*] †1 Of the air, weather, etc.: not temperate; disturbed; inclement. LME–M17. †2 (Of the bodily humours) not properly tempered, disordered by excess or deficiency of some constituent; diseased; in bad health or poor condition. M16–M17. 3 Immoderate, excessive; intemperate. M16.

distemperature /dɪˈstɛmp(ə)rətʃə/ *n.* M16. [f. DIS- 2 + TEMPERATURE.] 1 Disturbance of the weather; unhealthiness of the air; inclemency. *arch.* M16. 2 = DISTEMPER *n.*[1] 1, 2. *arch.* M16. 3 (A) disturbed or disordered condition of society, the world, etc. Now *rare* or *obs.* L16. 4 Immoderation, excess; intemperance. *arch.* L16.

1 T. HERBERT This distemperature by storms of Wind and Rain turns Summer into Winter. 2 LYTTON The distemperature of an over-laboured brain. SIR W. SCOTT Durward .. found the latter in a state of choleric distemperature.

distempered /dɪˈstɛmpəd/ *ppl a.*[1] LME. [f. DISTEMPER *v.*[1] + -ED[1], perh. immed. after OFr. *destempré* immoderate, deranged, or late L *distemperatus* DISTEMPERATE.] 1 Diseased; affected by a mental or physical disorder; now *esp.* (of feelings, ideas, etc.), disordered, disturbed. LME. †2 = DISTEMPERATE 1. L15–E17. †3 (Of the bodily humours) = DISTEMPERATE 2; disturbed in temper or feelings; ill-humoured, troubled, vexed. L16–M18. †4 = DISTEMPERATE 3. L16–M17. 5 Disordered, spoiled, out of joint. E17.

1 SHAKES. *Sonn.* I, sick withal .. thither hied, a sad distemper'd guest, But found no cure. SWIFT His books, which his distempered imagination represented to him as alive. 4 W. LAUD He must answer for his own distempered language. 5 E. REYNOLDS The .. difficulties under which this distempered Kingdom is now groaning.

distemperedly *adv.* M17. **distemperedness** *n.* M17.

distempered /dɪˈstɛmpəd/ *ppl a.*[2] E17. [f. DISTEMPER *v.*[2] + -ED[1].] †1 Diluted; weakened by dilution. E17–M18. 2 Painted in or with distemper. L18.

distend /dɪˈstɛnd/ *v.t.* & *i.* LME. [L *distendere*, f. as DIS- 1 + *tendere* stretch. Cf. DISTENT.] †1 Stretch out, extend; spread out at full length or breadth; overstretch, overextend. LME–M19. 2 Swell out or enlarge by pressure from within; expand or dilate by stretching. LME.

1 DRYDEN On engines they distend their tortur'd joints. 2 W. IRVING I could see his .. nostrils distend with indignation. P. ACKROYD The meal .. distended my stomach.

distendedly *adv.* in a distended manner M18. †**distendible** *a.* = DISTENSIBLE L17–M18.

distensible /dɪˈstɛnsɪb(ə)l/ *a.* E19. [f. as next + -IBLE.] Able to be distended.

distensiˈbility *n.* M18.

distensile /dɪˈstɛnsʌɪl/ *a.* M18. [f. L *distens-* (see next) + -ILE.] Distensible; capable of distending or causing distension.

distension /dɪˈstɛnʃ(ə)n/ *n.* Also †**-tention**. LME. [L *distensio(n-)*, later var. of *distentio(n-)*, f. *distent-*, *distens-* pa. ppl stem of *distendere* DISTEND: see -ION.] 1 The action of extending or straightening something; extension; straining. Now *rare* or *obs.* LME. 2 The action of distending; the condition of being distended; swelling beyond the normal or usual size. E17.

distent /dɪˈstɛnt/ *pa. pple* & *ppl a.* L16. [L *distentus* pa. pple of *distendere* DISTEND.] †1 Extended. L16–L18. 2 Distended, swollen. E17.

†**distention** *n.* var. of DISTENSION.

disthrone /dɪsˈθrəʊn/ *v.t.* L16. [f. DIS- 2 + THRONE *n.*] Remove from a throne; dethrone (*lit.* & *fig.*).

disthronement *n.* dethronement L19.

distich /ˈdɪstɪk/ *n.* Orig. in L form †**distichon**. E16. [L *distichon* f. Gk *distikhon*, use as n. (sc. *metron* metre) of neut. of *distikhos* of two rows or verses, f. as DI-[2] + *stikhos* row, line of verse.] *Pros.* A pair of verse lines, a couplet.

distichal *a.* L18.

distichous /ˈdɪstɪkəs/ *a.* M18. [f. L *distichus* (f. Gk *distikhos*: see DISTICH) + -OUS.] (Having parts) arranged in two opposite rows; *Bot.* arranged alternately in two vertical rows. Formerly also, dichotomous.

distichously *adv.* M19.

distil /dɪˈstɪl/ *v.* & *n.* Also ***-ll**. LME. [(Partly through (O)Fr. *distiller*) f. L *distillare* alt. of *destillare*, f. *de-* DE- 1 + *stillare*, f. *stilla* a drop.] A *v.* Infl. **-ll-**. 1 *v.i.* Trickle down or fall in minute drops; issue in drops or as a fine moisture; ooze out. LME. b *fig.* Come or be manifested gently or gradually. E17. c Drip or be wet *with*. E18. 2 *v.t.* Let fall or exude in minute drops, or in a vapour that condenses into drops. LME. 3 *v.t.* Give out or impart (a quality, principle, etc.) in minute quantities, infuse. Formerly also, instil. (Foll. by *into*.) LME. 4 *v.t.* Subject to the process of distillation; convert (*into*), or drive (a volatile constituent) *off* or *out*, by this means. LME. 5 *v.t.* Obtain, extract, produce, or make by distillation (*lit.* & *fig.*); *esp.* make (whisky etc.) by distilling raw materials. LME. 6 *v.t.* Extract the essence of (a plant etc. by distillation, a doctrine etc.); concentrate, purify. LME. 7 *v.i.* Undergo distillation; vaporize and then condense; pass *over* as a vapour. LME. †8 *v.t.* Melt, dissolve, (*lit.* & *fig.*). L15–E18. 9 *v.i.* Perform distillation. E17.

1 POPE Soft showers distill'd, and suns grew warm in vain. b R. GRANT Thy bountiful care .. sweetly distils in the dew and the rain. 2 MILTON His dewie locks distill'd Ambrosia. 3 I. WALTON There was distilled into the minds of the common people .. venomous and turbulent principles. 4 R. KIRWAN Brisson dissolved 2 oz. of the purest common salt in 16 oz. of distilled water. J. BELKNAP Molasses to be distilled into rum. 5 E. TEMPLETON Wondering how far her mother distilled her knowledge from actual experience. P. L. FERMOR A liqueur distilled from Tokay grapes. 6 L. EDEL He distilled from the elaborate theorizing of the French poets the essence of symbolist doctrine. 7 H. DAVY The acid .. distills unaltered at 248° Fahrenheit.

†B *n.* A vessel used in distillation; a still. E18–E19.

distillable *a.* E17.

distillate /ˈdɪstɪleɪt/ *n.* M19. [L *distillatus* pa. pple of *distillare*: see prec., -ATE[2].] A liquid formed by condensation of distilled vapour.

distillation /dɪstɪˈleɪʃ(ə)n/ *n.* LME. [L *destillatio(n-)* catarrh, (in late L) a dripping down, f. *destillat-* pa. ppl stem of *destillare*: see DISTIL, -ATION.] 1 The action of trickling or falling down drop by drop. LME. 2 The action or process of vaporizing (some constituent of) a substance by heat, condensing it by cold in a special vessel, and re-collecting the liquid, esp. to free it of dissolved impurities or to separate it from a liquid with a different boiling point; the extraction of a volatile constituent by this means; the separation of volatile from non-volatile constituents by heating in a closed vessel. LME. 3 A product of distilling; something which distils or forms by distilling; a distillate; *fig.* the essence; an extract, an abstract. LME. †4 *Med.* Catarrh. M16–M18.

2 **destructive** or **dry distillation** decomposition of a solid by heating it in a closed vessel and collecting the volatile constituents given off. FRACTIONAL *distillation*.

†**distillatory** *n.* L15–M18. [med.L *distillatorium*, f. L *distillat-*: see next, -ORY[1].] An apparatus for distillation.

distillatory /dɪˈstɪlət(ə)ri/ *a.* L16. [med.L *distillatorius*, f. L *distillat-* alt. of *destillat-*: see DISTILLATION, -ORY[2].] Pertaining to or used in distillation.

distiller /dɪˈstɪlə/ *n.* L16. [f. DISTIL *v.* + -ER[1].] 1 A person who or thing which distils something; *spec.* a person who manufactures alcoholic liquor by distillation. L16. 2 An apparatus for distilling salt water at sea. L19.

distillery /dɪˈstɪləri/ *n.* L17. [f. prec.: see -ERY.] †1 The action of distilling, distillation. L17–E19. 2 A place for distilling something; *spec.* an establishment for distilling alcoholic liquor. M18.

distilment /dɪˈstɪlm(ə)nt/ *n.* Also ***-ll-**. E17. [f. DISTIL *v.* + -MENT.] A distilled essence (*lit.* & *fig.*); something produced by distillation.

distinct /dɪˈstɪŋkt/ *a.* & *n.* LME. [L *distinctus* pa. pple of *distinguere* DISTINGUISH. Cf. (O)Fr. *distinct* (14).] A *adj.* (orig. †*pa. pple*). 1 Distinguished, differentiated. Now *spec.* distinguished as not being the same; separate, individual. (Foll. by *from*.) LME. b Separate from the rest; retaining its own identity. L16. 2 Readily distinguishable by the senses, esp. the sight or hearing, or by the mind; clear, plain, clearly perceptible; well-defined, unambiguous. LME. b That is recognizably or perceptibly such; definite, unmistakable; pronounced, positive. E19. 3 Separated from others by distinguishing characters; recognizably different in nature or qualities (*from*). Also *emphatic*, having well-marked differences. E16. 4 *pred.* Distinctively marked or adorned *with*. *arch.* L16. 5 Of sensory or mental perception: receiving or able to receive clear impressions. Formerly also, able to distinguish clearly; discriminating. E17.

1 Milton No place Is yet distinct by name. G. M. Trevelyan To write the social as distinct from the political history of a nation. G. Gordon Human beings have approximately 200 distinct bones. b E. Huxley The segments of an orange, each distinct and yet wrapped in one skin. A. J. P. Taylor He assumed .. that he could keep his private life entirely distinct from his public image. 2 S. Johnson When common words .. were less distinct in their signification. T. Hardy A face was bending over her, veiled, but still distinct. E. Bowen Lots here could only be purchased on the distinct condition that houses of a fixed value were to be put up. J. le Carré He had the distinct feeling that something was wrong. b G. B. Shaw There is a distinct attempt to increase the feminine interest all through. E. F. Benson She saw his eyes fixed on her in distinct disapproval. 3 Ld Macaulay The firelock of the Highlander was quite distinct from the weapon which he used in close fight. C. Darwin No two marine faunas are more distinct, with hardly a fish, shell, or crab in common. 4 Tennyson The deep sphere overhead, Distinct with vivid stars. 5 R. W. Emerson The droll disguises [of dreams] .. enhancing a real element, and forcing it on our distinct notice.

†**B** *n.* A separate person or thing. *rare.* (Shakes.) Only in E17.

distinctly *adv.* †(*a*) separately, individually; (*b*) clearly, without obscurity; (*c*) (chiefly with adjs. or adj. phrs.) decidedly, markedly: LME. **distinctness** *n.* distinct nature or quality L16.

distinction /dɪˈstɪŋkʃ(ə)n/ *n.* ME. [(O)Fr. f. L *distinctio(n-)*, f. *distinct-* pa. ppl stem of *distinguere*: see DISTINGUISH, -ION.] 1 Each of the parts into which a whole is divided; a subdivision; a category. *obs.* exc. *Hist.* ME. †b Rank, social class. E–M18. 2 The action of distinguishing or discriminating; the noting or making of a difference between things; the result of such action, a difference so made or appreciated. ME. †3 The action of dividing; the fact of being divided; division, partition. LME–E18. b Punctuation of a sentence; a punctuation mark. M16–M17. 4 The condition of being different or distinct; an instance of this, a difference. LME. 5 Something that differentiates; a distinguishing feature or property. LME. †6 The ability to perceive differences; discernment, discrimination. LME–M18. 7 The quality of being clearly perceptible; clarity of perception. Formerly also, the process of making clear to the senses. Now *rare.* LME. 8 (An instance of) excellence that sets a person or thing apart from others; (a) distinctive merit or good quality. Also, pre-eminent rank or position. L17. b In certain examinations: an outstandingly good mark or grade. M20. 9 The showing of special honour or preferential regard. Also, an instance of this; a mark of honour. E18.

2 E. A. Freeman A distinction is drawn between the rule of William himself and the rule of his oppressive lieutenants. C. Geikie Jesus .. teaches universal love without distinction of race, merit, or rank. **a distinction without a difference** an artificially created distinction, where no real difference exists. 3 Dryden The distinction of tragedy into acts. 4 R. Macaulay He has a keen .. insight into the distinction between essentials and non-essentials. A. Moorehead The social distinctions remained: Burke and Wills were officers .., Gray and King were men. 5 J. Butler It may be spoken of as .. the distinction of the present [age] to profess a contracted spirit. 7 Steele All the several Voices lost their Distinction, and rose up in a confused Humming. V. Woolf I see you with extreme distinction. 8 Burke The chase of honours and distinction. L. Strachey He had served with distinction in the war against Napoleon. W. S. Maugham Thick waving hair only sufficiently greying to add to the distinction of his appearance. A. J. P. Taylor New plays of distinction. 9 Jas. Harris For grammatical knowledge, we ought to mention with distinction the learned prelate, Dr. Lowth. W. S. Churchill The new distinctions which have been created by His Majesty for service in the war.

distinctive /dɪˈstɪŋktɪv/ *a.* & *n.* LME. [Late L *distinctivus*, f. L *distinct-*: see prec., -IVE.] A *adj.* 1 Serving to differentiate or distinguish; peculiar to one person or thing as distinct from others, characteristic; having well-marked properties; easily recognized. LME. 2 Having the faculty of perceiving differences; discriminating. *rare.* M17. 3 Having a separate or distinct character or status. *rare.* M19. 4 *Heb. Gram.* Of an accent: used in place of a stop to separate clauses. L19.

1 I. D'Israeli Papist and Protestant now became distinctive names. C. N. Robinson A military organization, wearing a distinctive dress. C. G. Seligman Their products are sufficiently well characterized to be distinctive. W. Boyd He saw the distinctive baldheaded .. figure of his father-in-law. **distinctive feature** *Phonol.* a minimal feature (e.g. voice, labiality) distinguishing one phoneme from another. 3 S. Smiles The refugees .. ceased to exist as a distinctive people.

B *n.* 1 A distinguishing mark; a characteristic. E19. 2 *Heb. Gram.* A distinctive accent. L19.

1 M. B. Keatinge The red umbrella, the distinctive of royalty here.

distinctively *adv.* (*a*) with distinction of treatment; separately, individually; (*b*) characteristically: E17. **distinctiveness** *n.* †(*a*) power of distinguishing; (*b*) distinctive character, force, tendency, etc.: M17.

distingué /dɪˈstaŋgeɪ, *foreign* distɛ̃ge/ *a.* Fem. **-ée**. E19. [Fr.] Having an air of distinction; having a distinguished appearance or manner.

distinguish /dɪˈstɪŋgwɪʃ/ *v.* L16. [Irreg. f. Fr. *distinguer* or L *distinguere* + -ISH[2]: cf. EXTINGUISH.] I *v.t.* †1 Divide, separate; punctuate (writing). L16–E18. 2 Mentally divide *into* different kinds; classify. L16. 3 Serve to make different (*from*); constitute a difference between, differentiate. L16. b Be a distinctive feature of; characterize. E17. 4 Recognize or treat as different (*from*), differentiate. L16. b Separate as a distinct item. M19. 5 Make a distinction in respect of; *esp.* draw distinctions between the meanings of (a word or statement). Also, put *away* or *out of*, or bring *into*, by making fine distinctions. Now *rare.* L16. 6 Perceive distinctly by sight, hearing, or other sense; discern, pick out, esp. with difficulty. L16. 7 Treat with special honour or attention. *arch.* E17. 8 Make noteworthy or outstanding in some respect. Now usu. *refl.* or *pass.* E17.

3 B. Russell Self-consciousness is one of the things that distinguish men from animals. b Ld Macaulay He .. was distinguished by many both of the good and of the bad qualities which belong to aristocrats. 4 Isaiah Berlin Those quasi-aesthetic .. judgments which distinguish essential from inessential. W. Golding It was easy to distinguish him from the scattering of other figures by the strangeness of his dress. b J. E. T. Rogers Items which used to be distinguished are lumped in one general sum. 5 Milton That Proverbial Sentence .. which also the Peripatetics do rather distinguish than deny. 6 B. Pym Voices were heard .. and a few broken sentences could be distinguished. 8 C. Lamb A peculiar sort of sweet pudding .. distinguished the days of his coming. J. Russell Robert Haig distinguished himself in the battle by taking Lord Evers a prisoner.

II *v.i.* 9 Perceive or mark the difference between things; discriminate, make a mental distinction, *between.* L16.

9 R. Macaulay If he had known enough about Anglicanism to distinguish between one kind and another. C. Hampton We .. laid them on the ground, the corpses to one side and the living to another, although it was by no means easy to distinguish. †**distinguish of** or **upon** make distinctions between or in respect of.

distinguisher *n.* L16. **distinguishingly** *adv.* by way of distinction; markedly, pre-eminently: M17. **distinguishment** *n.* (now *rare* or *obs.*) the action of distinguishing; the fact of being distinguished; (a) distinction: L16.

distinguishable /dɪˈstɪŋgwɪʃəb(ə)l/ *a.* L16. [f. prec. + -ABLE.] 1 Able to be differentiated; recognizable as different. L16. 2 Discernible by the senses or the mind. E17. 3 Divisible into different kinds. M17. †4 Worthy of distinction; eminent, remarkable. E18–E19.

distinguishaˈbility *n.* ability to be differentiated or distinguished E20. **distinguishableness** *n.* = DISTINGUISHABILITY M18. **distinguishably** *adv.* E18.

distinguished /dɪˈstɪŋgwɪʃt/ *a.* E17. [f. DISTINGUISH + -ED[1].] †1 Separate, individually distinct. E17–E19. †2 Clearly perceptible; distinct, pronounced. Only in 18. 3 Marked by outstanding excellence or eminence; remarkable (*for*). Now also of people: illustrious, of high social or professional standing. E18. 4 Having an air of distinction; stylish, distingué. M18. 5 Special, distinctive. Now *rare.* M18.

3 Jas. Mill The making of a new Nabob, the most distinguished of all occasions for presents. J. Galsworthy He cherished .. the secret theory that there was something distinguished somewhere in his ancestry. G. Vidal Sooner or later, just about every distinguished man of state is exiled. **Distinguished Conduct Medal**: awarded to warrant and non-commissioned officers and men in the British army and the Royal Air Force for distinguished conduct in action. **Distinguished Flying Cross**: awarded to commissioned and warrant officers in the Royal Air Force for distinguished conduct while flying in action. **Distinguished Flying Medal**: awarded to non-commissioned officers and men in the Royal Air Force for distinguished conduct while flying (other than in action). **Distinguished Service Medal**: the equivalent in the Royal Navy to the Distinguished Conduct Medal. **Distinguished Service Order**: a decoration awarded to British military, naval, and air force commissioned officers for distinguished conduct in action. 4 S. Gibbons She looked distinguished, elegant, and interesting.

distinguishedly *adv.* L17.

distinguo /dɪˈstɪŋgwəʊ/ *n.* Pl. **-os.** L19. [L = I distinguish.] A distinction in thought or reasoning.

distomiasis /dɪstə(ʊ)ˈmʌɪəsɪs/ *n.* Pl. **-ases** /-əsiːz/. L19. [mod.L f. Fr. *distomiase*, f. *Distoma*, a former genus of two-suckered trematode worms, the members of which are now referred to *Fasciola*, *Fasciolopsis*, etc.: see -IASIS.] *Med.* & *Vet. Med.* Infestation of the alimentary tract by flukes or parasitic trematode worms; *spec.* liver-rot.

Also **distomatosis** /ˌdɪstə(ʊ)məˈtəʊsɪs, -stɒm-/ *n.*, pl. **-toses** /-ˈtəʊsiːz/, L19.

†**distort** *a.* L16–M17. [L *distortus* pa. pple, f. as next.] Distorted, awry.

Spenser Her face was ugly, and her mouth distort.

distort /dɪˈstɔːt/ *v.* L15. [L *distort-* pa. ppl stem of *distorquere*, f. as DIS- 1 + *torquere* to twist.] †1 *v.t.* Twist or wrench to one side. L15–E18. 2 *v.t.* *fig.* Give an erroneous turn to, bias, (a person's thoughts, judgements, etc.); present a false account or interpretation of; alter so as to appear other than as it is; misrepresent. L16. b *Electr.* Charge the form of (a signal) during transmission or amplification, thus causing misrepresentation. L19. 3 *v.t.* & *i.* Alter to an unnatural shape by twisting; make or become misshapen; contort (the features). M17.

2 I. D'Israeli To establish a pre-conceived theory .. the historian sometimes distorted facts. H. Spencer Passion distorts judgment. G. Greene His mother had deliberately distorted his age. 3 S. Johnson Any .. posture, long continued, will distort .. the limbs. J. Galsworthy Her face was distorted with anger. G. Greene Those distorting mirrors at fairs. *Which?* On the hill, the jack mounting points distorted slightly.

distortedly *adv.* in a distorted manner L17. **distortedness** *n.* the quality or state of being distorted L17. **distortive** *a.* tending to distort; constituting distortion: E19.

distortion /dɪˈstɔːʃ(ə)n/ *n.* L16. [L *distortio(n-)*, f. as prec.: see -ION.] 1 The action or an act of distorting or twisting out of shape (permanently or temporarily); (a) distorted condition; *spec.* a condition of the body or a limb in which it is twisted out of its natural shape. L16. b (An) alteration of the shape of an image by a lens or mirror. M18. c *Electr.* Unwanted alteration of a waveform, esp. in an electronic device or in its passage through a medium, with consequent impairment of quality. L19. 2 *fig.* The action of perverting words, facts, etc., from their natural interpretation or intent; misconstruction, misrepresentation. M17. 3 A distorted form or image. E19. 4 *Psychoanalysis.* The process of converting repressed elements to an acceptable form before they are presented to the conscious or dreaming mind. E20.

1 T. Medwin That .. distortion generally known by the appellation of club-foot. C. Brontë A .. marked expression of disgust, horror, hatred warped his countenance almost to distortion. b J. Thurber All the mirrors in the house were made of wavy glass and reflected images in fantastic distortions. 2 J. Wesley What a frightful Distortion of my Words is this? L. Stephen He will be amused at the distortion of history. 3 A. Barry Some remains of the objectionable distortion at the entrance from S. Stephen's Hall.

distortional *a.* of or pertaining to distortion L19. **distortionist** *n.* a person who practises distortion, e.g. in drawing caricatures M19. **distortionless** *a.* (*Electr.*) not producing or accompanied by any distortion L19.

distract /dɪˈstrakt/ *ppl a.* Long *arch.* ME. [L *distractus* pa. pple of *distrahere*, f. as DIS- 1 + *trahere* draw, drag. Cf. DISTRACTED, DISTRAUGHT *a.*] 1 = DISTRACTED 5, 3. ME. †2 = DISTRACTED 1. LME–L16. †3 Drawn away, diverted; having the attention diverted. LME–M16. 4 = DISTRACTED 2. L15.

distract /dɪˈstrakt/ *v.t.* Pa. pple **-ed**, †**distract**, (*arch.*) **distraught** /dɪˈstrɔːt/. LME. [L *distract-* pa. ppl stem of *distrahere*: see prec. For origin of arch. pa. pple see DISTRAUGHT *a.*] †1 Draw in different directions; draw away or apart; separate, divide, (*lit.* & *fig.*). LME–M17. b Disperse. E–M17. 2 Divide, break up, esp. so as to produce disorder or disintegration. Formerly also *fig.*, undo, spoil. Long *rare* or *obs.* LME. 3 Orig., turn away from a purpose, destination, or position. Now, divert (the attention, a person) from or *from* something, esp. an intention or preoccupation; stop (a person) from attending fully to something. LME. 4 Throw into a state of mind in which one does not know how to act; greatly perplex, bewilder; trouble, agitate. Usu. in *pass.* LME. †5 Derange; make mad. Usu. in *pass.* LME–L18. 6 Confuse by divergent aims or interests; cause dissension or disorder in; divide the inclination etc. *between* different objects. L16.

1 HOBBES Being distracted in opinions. 2 J. FRYER The Power was distracted among the Captains of the Conqueror. 3 SIR T. BROWNE The needle . . being distracted, driveth that way where the . . powerfuller part of the earth is placed. J. HERSEY The motherless . . children were inconsolable. Father Cieslik worked hard to distract them. A. KOESTLER He wanted to avoid . . anything which might distract him from his task. G. GREENE Next day a number of things distracted me from the fate of Jones. R. HAYMAN He was easily distracted by noises through the wall. 4 SOUTHEY Have fanatic dreams distraught his sense? 6 LD MACAULAY He was distracted between the fear of losing his ears and the fear of injuring his patron.

distractaˈbility *n.* = DISTRACTIBILITY M20. †**distractful** *a.* full of or fraught with distraction M17–M18. **distractible** *a.* able to be distracted M18. **distractiˈbility** *n.* the condition of being distractible; inability to maintain prolonged attention: E20. **distractingly** *adv.* in a manner that distracts; bewilderingly, maddeningly: M19. **distractive** *a.* of distracting quality or tendency E17. **distractively** *adv.* M19. **distractor** *n.* (*US*) an incorrect option in a multiple-choice question M20.

distracted /dɪˈstraktɪd/ *ppl a.* L16. [f. prec. + -ED[1]. Cf. DISTRACT *a.*, DISTRAUGHT *a.*] 1 Drawn apart; torn asunder; separated, divided. Long *rare.* L16. 2 Deranged; out of one's mind; crazed, insane. *arch.* L16. 3 Mentally drawn in different directions; confused by divergent aims or interests; affected by disorder or dissension. L16. 4 So confused or troubled that one hardly knows how to act; unable to settle because of worry, distress, etc.; troubled, disturbed. E17. †5 In a condition of disorder or disintegration; driven hither and thither; in irregular motion, agitated. M17–M19.

1 T. FULLER By putting together distracted syllables. 4 DRYDEN Where shall a Maid's distracted Heart find Rest? G. VIDAL I had never seen him so distracted. 5 T. HOOD The vapours fly Over the dark distracted sky.

distractedly *adv.* L16. **distractedness** *n.* (long *rare*) E17.

†**distractile** *a.* E18–M19. [f. as DISTRACT *v.* + -ILE.] Able to be stretched, extensible.

distraction /dɪˈstrakʃ(ə)n/ *n.* LME. [(O)Fr., or L *distractio(n-)*, f. as DISTRACT *v.*: see -ION.] 1 The action of drawing or forcing apart; forcible disruption, severance; division, separation; removal, dispersal. Now *rare* or *obs.* LME. †b A severed or divided form, drawn apart from others. *rare* (Shakes.). Only in E17. 2 Diversion of the mind, attention, etc., from a particular object or course; the fact of having one's attention or concentration disturbed by something; amusement, relaxation. LME. b An instance or occasion of this; something that distracts or diverts the mind or attention; distracting sounds, events, etc. E17. 3 The fact or condition of being physically or mentally drawn in different directions by conflicting forces or emotions. L16. b Disorder or confusion of affairs, resulting from internal conflict or dissension; the condition of a community torn by conflict or dissension. M17. †4 Mental derangement; insanity. L16–L18. 5 Extreme perturbation of mind or feelings; frenzy. E17.

1 W. HAMILTON The parts which, by the distraction of the whole, come into view. 2 AV *1 Cor.* 7:35 That you may attend vpon the Lord without distraction. b F. W. ROBERTSON The cares of this world—its petty trifling distractions. H. ACTON It was a distraction and a relief to write letters. J. MASTERS There was work to do, and continual distraction outside. 3b STEELE My little affairs are in such distraction till I can come to an hearing in Chancery. 4 C. MATHER A distempered melancholy at last issued in an incurable distraction. 5 **to distraction** almost to a state of madness, distractedly.

Comb.: **distraction-behaviour**, **-flight**, etc.: exhibited by a bird attempting to divert the attention of a possible predator.

distrain /dɪˈstreɪn/ *v.* ME. [OFr. *destreign-* pres. stem of *destreindre* f. L *distringere* draw asunder, f. as DI-[1] + *stringere* draw tight.] I *Law.* 1 *v.t.* Constrain or force (a person), by seizure of a chattel, to meet an obligation; punish in this way for failure to meet an obligation; levy a distress on (a person) so that payment of money owed to one may be obtained. (Foll. by *to do.*) Now *rare* or *obs.* ME. 2 *v.i.* Impose a distress (*for* goods, *on* or *upon* a person or thing). ME. 3 *v.t.* Seize (a chattel) by way of distress; levy a distress on. LME.

1 N. BACON All such as ought to be Knights and are not, shall be distrained to undertake the weapons of Knighthood. A. TUCKER When Squire Peremptory distrained his tenant for rent. 2 MILTON Any seven or more of them . . may distrain and imprison. A. J. AYER When the authorities distrained on his effects, his friends raised the money . . for the first of his books to be put up for auction.

†II *gen.* 4 *v.t.* Press or grasp tightly; squeeze; confine, restrain. LME–E16. 5 *v.t.* Of a circumstance or event: have in its hold; distress, oppress, afflict. LME–E17. 6 *v.t.* Control by force, restrain, subdue. LME–M16. 7 *v.t.* Force or compel (a person) *to do.* Only in LME. 8 *v.t.* Strain out; extract by pressing or straining. LME–M17. 9 *v.t.* Pull or tear off; tear apart. LME–L16. 10 *v.t.* Seize, confiscate, annex. Also (*rare*), deprive (a person) *of.* M16–E18.

distrainable *a.* liable to distraint; able to be distrained for: L16. **distraiˈnee** *n.* a person who is distrained L19. **distrainer** *n.* = DISTRAINOR E17. **distrainment** *n.* the action or fact of distraining, distraint LME. **distrainor** *n.* a person who distrains M16.

distraint /dɪˈstreɪnt/ *n.* M18. [f. prec. after *constraint.*] *Law.* = DISTRESS *n.* 3.

distrait /dɪˈstreɪ, ˈdɪstreɪ, *foreign* distrɛ/ *a.* Fem. **-aite** /-eɪt, *foreign* -ɛt/. LME. [Fr. f. OFr. *destrait* pa. pple of *destraire* f. L *distrahere* DISTRACT *v.*] †1 Distracted in mind; excessively perplexed or troubled. Only in LME. †2 Divided, separated. LME–L16. 3 Absent-minded, not paying attention; distraught. M18.

3 W. A. PERCY In a distrait moment she would sew crimson next to shrimp pink.

¶ Borrowed again from Fr. in 18 after having become obs. in 16.

distraught /dɪˈstrɔːt/ *a.* LME. [Alt. of DISTRACT *ppl a.* by assim. to †*straught* pa. pple: see STRETCH *v.* Cf. also DISTRACTED.] 1 = DISTRACTED 4. Formerly also, mentally drawn or driven in diverse directions or by conflicting emotions (cf. DISTRACTED 3). LME. 2 = DISTRACTED 2. LME. †3 Pulled apart or in different directions. L16–M17.

1 SPENSER I in minde remained . . Distraught twixt feare and pitie. E. WAUGH There came two distraught orphans to ask what arrangements their parents had made. R. ADAMS One of the boys . . began jabbering in a voice distraught with fear. 3 SPENSER His greedy throte . . in two distraught.

distraughtly *adv.* E20. **distraughtness** *n.* (*rare*) L16.

distraught *v.* pa. pple: see DISTRACT *v.*

†**distream** *v.i. poet. rare.* M17–M18. [Irreg. f. DIS- 1 + STREAM *v.*] Flow away in a stream, stream down or away.

distress /dɪˈstrɛs/ *n.* ME. [OFr. *destres(c)e*, *-esse* (mod. *détresse*) f. Proto-Gallo-Romance, f. L *district-* pa. ppl stem of *distringere*: see DISTRAIN.] I *gen.* 1 Severe pressure of trouble, pain, sickness, or sorrow; anguish, affliction; hardship, privation, lack of money or necessities. Also, an instance of this, a misfortune, a calamity; in *pl.*, difficult circumstances. ME. b The state of a ship or aircraft when it needs help from threatened damage or danger. M17. c A state of physical exhaustion or collapse; breathlessness; *Med.* the state of an organ etc. that is not functioning normally or adequately. E19. 2 The action or fact of straining or pressing tightly; pressure, stress; pressure applied to produce or (occas.) prevent action (*lit.* & *fig.*). *obs.* exc. *dial.* ME. †b The overpowering pressure *of* an adverse force, weather, etc. L15–L18.

1 JOSEPH HALL Being in great distress of Conscience. J. H. NEWMAN This event . . filled him with the utmost distress and despondency. DICKENS There is great distress here among the poor. L. STRACHEY The meagre grant . . had by no means put an end to his financial distresses. b LONGFELLOW Some ship in distress, that cannot live In such an angry sea. c FOETAL *distress.* 2b J. SMEATON Driven westward, by distress of weather.

II *Law.* 3 The action of distraining; the lawful seizure of another's chattel in order to make him or her meet an obligation or to obtain payment of money owed from the proceeds of their sale. ME. 4 A chattel seized in such an action. LME.

Comb.: **distress-gun**: used to fire a distress-rocket; **distress-rocket**: fired as a distress-signal; **distress-signal**: from a ship or aircraft in distress; **distress-warrant**: *Law* authorizing a distress.

distress /dɪˈstrɛs/ *v.t.* LME. [AN *destresser*, OFr. *destrecier*, f. as prec.] 1 Subject to severe strain or pressure; exhaust, esp. by extreme physical exertion; afflict. LME. †2 Crush in battle, overwhelm, coerce; harass in war. LME–L18. 3 Constrain by force or the infliction of pain etc. (*to do, into, out of*). Now *rare.* LME. 4 Cause trouble, pain, anguish, or hardship to; vex, make unhappy. Now chiefly *refl.* or *pass.* LME. 5 Steal (belongings); plunder (a person). Long *rare* or *obs.* LME. 6 *Law.* Levy a distress on; distrain on. LME. 7 Damage (a piece of furniture, fabric, etc.) deliberately to simulate the effects of age and wear. M20.

1 GOLDSMITH The . . servants of the crown . . distressed their private fortunes to gratify their sovereign. QUILLER-COUCH Their horses began to be distressed in the heavy sand. 3 A. HAMILTON Men who can neither be distressed nor won into a sacrifice of duty. 4 OED Do not distress yourself about the child, he is safe. J. C. POWYS Henry's crying . . rose to a pitch that was distressing to hear.

distressingly *adv.* in a distressing manner, painfully L18.

distressed /dɪˈstrɛst/ *ppl a.* L16. [f. prec. + -ED[1].] 1 Exhibiting or pertaining to distress; afflicted with pain or trouble; *spec.* living in impoverished circumstances. L16. 2 Of furniture, fabric, etc.: with simulated marks or other features of age and wear. M20.

1 J. TRUSLER Their poverty and distressed situation. **distressed area** a region of high unemployment. 2 *Times* Distressed leathers give new interest to the uppers.

distressedly *adv.* L19. **distressedness** *n.* L16.

distressful /dɪˈstrɛsfʊl, -f(ə)l/ *a. literary* & *poet.* L16. [f. DISTRESS *n.* + -FUL.] 1 Fraught with, causing, or involving distress; distressing, painful. L16. †b Gained by severe exertion. *rare* (Shakes.). Only in L16. 2 = DISTRESSED 1. E17.

distressfully *adv.* L16. **distressfulness** *n.* L19.

distributary /dɪˈstrɪbjʊt(ə)ri/ *a.* & *n.* M16. [f. as next + -ARY[1].] A *adj.* †1 Distinct, several. Only in M16. 2 That distributes; *spec.* designating a distributary of a canal, river, etc. M19. B *n.* Something that distributes; *spec.* a branch of a river etc. which does not return to its parent branch after leaving it (as in a delta). L19.

For other words beginning with *dis-* see the entry for **dis-**

distribute /dɪˈstrɪbjuːt, ˈdɪstrɪbjuːt/ *v.t.* Pa. pple **-ed**, (long *rare*, *obs.* exc. *Sc.*) **distribute**. LME. [L *distribut-* pa. ppl stem of *distribuere*, f. as DIS- 1 + *tribuere* grant, assign.] **1** Deal out in portions or shares among a number of recipients; give a share of to each of a number of people. LME. †**b** Deal out, administer, (justice etc.). E17–M18. **2** Spread or disperse throughout a region; put at different points over an area; spread generally, scatter. LME. **3** Divide (a whole or collective body) into parts with distinct characters and functions. L15. **4** Divide mentally into classes, classify. Formerly also (*Math.*), divide. L16. **5** *Printing* (chiefly *Hist.*). Separate (type that has been set up) and return each character to its proper place in the case. E17. **6** *Logic.* Use (a term) in its full extension so that it refers to every individual of the class it designates. E19.

1 T. HOOD Pray distribute my kindest regards amongst all friends. I. WALLACE She distributed memorandum pads, pencils, ashtrays. 2 A. R. WALLACE Mammalia may be said to be universally distributed over the globe. *Times* The paper is not yet distributed in Scotland. *Which Computer?* A distributed intelligence network of POS VDU's. 3 GIBBON That great peninsula . . was distributed by Augustus into three provinces.

distributable *a.* M17. **distribuˈtee** *n.* (*US Law*) a person to whom a share falls in the distribution of the estate of a deceased person L19. **distributism** *n.* the theory or practice of an equal division of property; agrarianism: E20. **distributist** *a.* & *n.* (*a*) *adj.* of or pertaining to distributism; (*b*) *n.* an advocate of distributism: E20.

distribution /dɪstrɪˈbjuːʃ(ə)n/ *n.* LME. [(O)Fr., or L *distributio(n-)*, f. as prec.: see -ION.] **1** The action of dealing out in portions or shares among a number of recipients; apportionment, allotment; *Econ.* the dispersal of commodities among consumers effected by commerce. LME. **b** *Econ.* The way in which individuals or classes share in the aggregate products of a community. L17. **2** The action of spreading or dispersing throughout a region; the state or manner of being located in different places all over a region. LME. **b** *Statistics.* The way in which a particular characteristic is spread over the members of a class. M19. **c** *Ling.* The range of positions or contexts in which a linguistic element can occur. M20. **3** The division of a whole or collective body into parts, esp. with distinctive characters or functions; division and arrangement; classification. M16. **4** *Archit.* The arrangement of the various parts of a building, esp. of the interior divisions or rooms. E18. **5** *Printing* (chiefly *Hist.*). The action or process of distributing type. E18. **6** *Logic.* The use of a term in its full extension to refer to every individual of the class it designates. E19.

1 J. BUTLER All shall be set right at the final distribution of things. *Truck & Driver* The distribution of horticultural produce throughout the entire south and west of England. b J. S. MILL Diversities in the distribution of wealth. 2 B. LOVELL The distribution of the stars in the Milky Way. *Times* Weaknesses in distribution were blamed for the newspaper's non-arrival in areas of England and Wales. b FREQUENCY *distribution.* c *complementary distribution*: see COMPLEMENTARY 2. 3 R. W. EMERSON The distribution of land into parishes.

Comb.: **distribution board** a panel carrying the fuses etc. of a number of subsidiary electric circuits; **distribution function** *Statistics* a function whose value is either the frequency with which a variable has a value less than or equal to the argument of the function, or the probability that it has such a value; **distribution map**: showing the distribution of rainfall, population, crops, etc.

distributional *a.* of or pertaining to distribution M19. **distributionally** *adv.* M20.

distributive /dɪˈstrɪbjʊtɪv/ *a.* & *n.* LME. [(O)Fr. *distributif, -ive* or late L *distributivus*, f. as prec.: see -IVE.] **A** *adj.* **1** Having the property of distributing; characterized by dealing out in portions or by spreading; given to or engaged in distribution. LME. **2** Expressing distribution; *Gram.* & *Logic* referring to each individual of a class, not to the class collectively. LME. **3** Of, concerned with, or produced by distribution; *spec.* pertaining to or designating a political system etc. under which property is owned by the largest possible number of people. M16. **4** *Math.* Governed by or stating the condition that when an operation is performed on two or more quantities already combined by a second operation, the result is the same as when it is performed on each quantity individually and the products then combined, e.g. that $a \times (b + c) = (a \times b) + (a \times c)$. M19.

1 **distributive fault** *Geol.*: affecting several parallel planes each close to its neighbour. 2 **distributive adjective, pronoun**: denoting one or more individuals of a class, not the class collectively, e.g. *each, either, every.* 3 **distributive justice** justice consisting in the distribution of something in shares proportionate to each recipient's deserts; *esp.* justice concerned with the distribution of rights, duties, etc., among individuals and groups in society. 4 B. RUSSELL The associative, commutative, and distributive laws. A. G. HOWSON The binary operation $\cup$ is distributive over $\cap$.

B *n. Gram.* A distributive word. M16.

distributively *adv.* L16. **distributiveness** *n.* M17. **distribuˈtivity** *n.* (esp. *Math.*) M20.

distributor /dɪˈstrɪbjʊtə/ *n.* LME. [f. DISTRIBUTE + -OR.] **1** A person who distributes something; *spec.* an agent who markets goods, esp. a wholesaler. LME. **2** A thing that distributes a substance, power, etc. M19. **b** A device in an internal-combustion engine for passing the current to each sparking plug in turn. E20.

distributorship *n.* the position of being a distributor, esp. of goods E19.

distributress /dɪˈstrɪbjʊtrɪs/ *n.* M17. [f. prec. + -ESS[1].] A female distributor.

district /ˈdɪstrɪkt/ *n.* & *v.* E17. [Fr. f. med.L *districtus* (territory of) jurisdiction, f. L *district-* pa. ppl stem of *distringere*: see DISTRAIN. Cf. STRICT.] **A** *n.* †**1** The territory under the jurisdiction of a feudal lord. Only in 17. **2** An area of country marked off for a special administrative or electoral purpose, or forming the responsibility of a particular officer or administrative body. M17. **b** *Hist.* A division of an Indian province or presidency under British rule, formerly the major unit of civil administration. L18. **c** A subdivision of a county or (since 1974) of a Scottish region. Orig. *US.* E19. **d** A division of an Anglican parish with its own church or chapel and member of the clergy. E19. **e** In Methodist Churches, a territorial division comprising a number of circuits. M19. **f** An area assigned as the sphere of operation of a person or organization, esp. a midwife or a maternity hospital. M19. **3** An area with a recognizable identity or common characteristics; a locality, a region. E18.

2 *London postal district, Metropolitan district, police district*, etc. c FEDERAL *district.* RURAL *district.* URBAN *district.* 3 OED A manufacturing district; a purely agricultural district. E. BLISHEN The miserable greyness of the district. DAY LEWIS He was much sought after in the district as a 'healer'. *Lake District*: see LAKE *n.*[2] *red-light district*: see RED *a.*

Comb.: **district attorney** *US* the prosecuting officer of a district; **district auditor** a civil servant responsible for auditing the accounts of local authorities; **district court** (*a*) *US* a Federal court of first instance; (*b*) *NZ* a court where all but the most serious civil and criminal cases are heard; **district heating**: of a district or group of buildings from a single central source of heat; **district nurse** a nurse who visits and treats patients in their homes, operating in an assigned area; **district visitor** a person appointed to work in a particular section of a parish under the direction of the parish clergy.

B *v.t.* Divide into districts. Chiefly *US.* L18.

†**district** *a.* M16–E18. [L *districtus* strict, severe, pa. pple of *distringere*: see prec.] Strict, severe, exact.

distringas /dɪˈstrɪŋgas/ *n.* LME. [L *distringas* you shall distrain (the opening wd(s) of the writ), subjunct. of *distringere* (in med.L) DISTRAIN *v.*] *Law* (chiefly *Hist.*). A writ directing the sheriff to distrain upon a person or body.

†**distrouble** *v.t.* ME–E19. [OFr. *destro(u)bler*, f. as DIS- 3, TROUBLE *v.*] Disturb, trouble greatly.

distrust /dɪsˈtrʌst/ *n.* M16. [f. DIS- 2 + TRUST *n.*: cf. next.] **1** Lack of trust or confidence; doubt, suspicion. M16. †**2** The fact of being distrusted; loss of credit. *rare* (Milton). Only in M17. †**3** Breach of trust. *rare* (Milton). Only in M17.

†**distrustless** *a.* without distrust; confident, unsuspecting: E17–M18.

distrust /dɪsˈtrʌst/ *v.* LME. [f. DIS- 2 + TRUST *v.* after Fr. *défier* (cf. DEFY *v.*) or L *diffidere.*] †**1** *v.i.* **a** Foll. by *of*: have a doubt or dread of, suspect. *rare.* Only in LME. **b** Foll. by *of, in, to*: be without confidence in. L16–L17. **2** *v.t.* Put no trust in, have no confidence in; have doubts about the reality, validity, or genuineness of. M16. †**3** *v.t.* Suspect *that* or (a person) *to be.* E17–E18.

2 A. G. GARDINER Johnson . . loved liberty in its social meanings, but distrusted it as a political ideal. L. DURRELL My feeling of unreality had grown to such a pitch that at times I distrusted my own memory. T. CAPOTE Neighbours and old friends had suddenly to endure the unique experience of distrusting each other.

distruster *n.* M17.

distrustful /dɪsˈtrʌs(t)fʊl, -f(ə)l/ *a.* L16. [f. DISTRUST *n.* + -FUL.] **1** Full of or marked by distrust; doubtful, suspicious; lacking confidence; diffident. (Foll. by *of.*) L16. **2** Causing or giving rise to distrust. E17.

1 E. K. KANE I became . . distrustful as to the chance of our ever living to gain the open water. 2 DICKENS Places that had shown ugly and distrustful all night long, now wore a smile.

distrustfully *adv.* E17. **distrustfulness** *n.* L16.

†**disturb** *n.* L16–M17. [f. the vb.] An act of disturbing; (a) disturbance.

MILTON Instant without disturb they took Allarm.

disturb /dɪˈstəːb/ *v.t.* ME. [OFr. *desto(u)rber* f. L *disturbare*, f. as DIS- 3 + *turbare* disturb, f. *turba* tumult, crowd. Cf. STURB.] **1** Agitate and destroy (quiet, peace, etc.); break up the tranquillity or calmness of; distract the attention of, intrude upon. ME. **b** Physically agitate; move from a settled condition or position. L16. **c** *refl.* Get up to greet or accommodate another person. Usu. in neg. contexts. L19. **2** Worry, cause anxiety to. ME. **3** Interfere with the settled course or operation of; put out of its course; frustrate, interrupt. ME. **4** †**a** Deprive *of*; turn or draw away *from* by disturbance. ME–M17. **b** *Law.* Deprive of the peaceful enjoyment or possession *of.* M16.

1 A. HALEY He'd have to arrest him for disturbing the peace. G. VIDAL The slightest sound in the night disturbs me. D. M. THOMAS It was a strict rule not to disturb adults when they were resting. b H. BUTTES Mulberries . . disturbe the stomacke. T. HARDY A plough has never disturbed the turf. c T. L. PEACOCK The stranger was rising up, when Mr. Crotchet begged him not to disturb himself. 2 P. H. GIBBS Halliwell had a strained look, as though this signal . . had disturbed or distressed him. E. O'NEILL As though he were throwing off some disturbing thought. 3 B. JOWETT An error in the original number disturbs the whole calculation. G. B. SHAW It should . . be made an offence to disturb a performance which the Committee has not condemned.

disturbed *ppl a.* that has been disturbed; *Psychiatry* emotionally or mentally unstable or abnormal: L16. **disturbedly** /-bɪdli/ *adv.* M18. **disturbingly** *adv.* to a disturbing degree L19.

disturbance /dɪˈstəːb(ə)ns/ *n.* ME. [OFr. *desto(u)rbance*, f. as prec.: see -ANCE.] **1** The interruption and breaking up of a settled condition or of proper functioning; agitation (physical or social); an instance of this, *spec.* a breach of the public peace. ME. **2** Interference with the continuance of any action or process. ME. **3** Mental discomposure or excitement. LME. **4** *Law.* Interference with a right. L16.

1 E. JONES Complicated disturbances of sight and speech. 2 ADDISON That he may let the ship sail on without disturbance.

disturbancy /dɪˈstəːb(ə)nsi/ *n. rare.* L16. [f. prec. or next + -ANCY.] Disturbance.

disturbant /dɪˈstəːb(ə)nt/ *a.* & *n.* E17. [L *disturbant-* pres. ppl stem of *disturbare*: see DISTURB *v.*, -ANT[1].] **A** *adj.* That disturbs; disquieting. E17. **B** *n.* A disturber. M19.

disturbative /dɪˈstəːbətɪv/ *a. rare.* L17. [f. L *disturbat-* pa. ppl stem of *disturbare* DISTURB *v.*: see -IVE.] Of disturbing tendency or character.

disturber /dɪˈstəːbə/ *n.* In sense 2 also **-or**. ME. [AN *destourbour* (OFr. *destorbëor*), f. as DISTURB *v.*: see -ER[2].] **1** A person who or thing which disturbs peace or quiet or causes disturbance. ME. **2** *Law* (chiefly *Hist.*). A person who hinders another in the lawful enjoyment of a right. L15.

distyle /ˈdʌɪstʌɪl/ *n.* & *a.* M19. [f. DI-[2] + Gk *stulos* column.] *Archit.* (A structure) having or consisting of two columns.

disubstituted /dʌɪˈsʌbstɪtjuːtɪd/ *a.* E20. [f. DI-[2] + *substituted* pa. pple of SUBSTITUTE *v.*: see -ED[1].] *Chem.* Having two substituents in the molecule.

disulfide *n.* see DISULPHIDE.

disulfiram /dʌɪˈsʌlfɪram/ *n.* M20. [f. prec. + THIURAM.] A white powder used esp. in the treatment of alcoholics to make drinking alcohol produce unpleasant after-effects; tetraethylthiuram disulphide, $(C_2H_5)_2NCSSCN(C_2H_5)_2$.

¶A proprietary name for this substance is ANTABUSE.

disulphide /dʌɪˈsʌlfʌɪd/ *n.* Also ***-fide**. M19. [f. DI-[2] + SULPHIDE *n.*] A compound in which two sulphur atoms are joined to another atom or group; an organic compound in which the group —S—S— is joined to different atoms. Formerly also, a compound in which a sulphur atom is joined to two other atoms.

Comb.: **disulphide bond**: joining two sulphur atoms.

disunion /dɪsˈjuːnɪən/ *n.* L15. [f. DIS- 2 + UNION *n.*[2]] **1** Breaking of union; separation, severance. L15. **2** Lack of union or unity; separated condition; dissension, disharmony. L16.

disunionism *n.* the doctrine of disunionists L19. **disunionist** *n.* a person who favours or works for the dissolution of a political union, *spec.* that of the US (before or during the Civil War) or that of Britain and Ireland M19.

disunite /dɪsjuːˈnʌɪt/ *v.* M16. [f. DIS- 2 + UNITE *v.*] **1** *v.t.* Undo the union of; *esp.* cause dissension among, set at variance, alienate. (Foll. by *from*.) M16. **2** *v.i.* Separate; part; fall apart. M17.

1 *Time* Chirac fears that the left, even disunited, could still win.

disunity /dɪsˈjuːnɪti/ *n.* M17. [f. DIS- 2 + UNITY *n.*[1]] Lack of unity; a state of separation; dissension, discord.

†**disusage** *n.* LME–E18. [f. DISUSE *v.* after *usage*. Cf. Fr. †*désusage*.] = DISUSE *n.* 2.

disusance /dɪsˈjuːz(ə)ns/ *n.* *rare.* LME. [f. as prec. after *usance*.] = DISUSE *n.* 2.

disuse /dɪsˈjuːs/ *n.* LME. [f. DIS- 2 + USE *n.*] †**1** The state of being or becoming unaccustomed (*to* something). LME–L18. **2** Discontinuance or prolonged suspension of use, practice, or exercise. M16. **3** The state of being no longer in use. L17.

2 S. T. WARNER The field-path to it is vanishing from disuse. 3 P. H. JOHNSON The wireless, with its earphones, fell into disuse since nobody cared to listen to it.

disuse /dɪsˈjuːz/ *v.t.* LME. [OFr. *desuser*, f. *des-* DIS- 2 + *user* USE *v.*] **1** Make (a person) unaccustomed to something; cause to lose a habit. Usu. in *pass.* *obs.* exc. *dial.* LME. †**2** Misuse, use wrongly. Only in LME. **3** Cease to use. Chiefly as *disused* ppl a. L15.

3 CONAN DOYLE This house is older than the water-pipes. There must be a disused well somewhere.

disvalue /dɪsˈvaljuː/ *n.* E17. [f. DIS- 2 + VALUE *n.*] †**1** Depreciation, disparagement. Only in 17. **2** Negative value or worth; a quality by virtue of which the absence of something is valued more than its presence. E20.

disvalue /dɪsˈvaljuː/ *v.t.* E17. [f. DIS- 2 + VALUE *v.*] Place too little value on, undervalue. Formerly, devalue (*lit.* & *fig.*), disparage.

disvaluable *a.* having negative value; bad: M20. **disvaluˈation** *n.* the action of disvaluing E17.

†**disvelop** *v.t.* L16–M18. [OFr. *desveloper* (mod. *développer*): see DEVELOP.] Unfold, unfurl; display heraldically.

†**disventure** *n.* E17–M18. [Sp. *desventura*, f. *des-* DIS- 2 + *ventura* VENTURE *n.*] A foolish or ill-starred venture.

disvisage /dɪsˈvɪzɪdʒ/ *v.t.* *rare.* E17. [OFr. *desvisager* (mod. *dévisager*), f. *des-* DIS- 2 + *visage* VISAGE *n.*] Disfigure.

disyllabic /dʌɪsɪˈlabɪk, dɪ-/ *a.* & *n.* Also **dissyll-**. M17. [Fr. *dissyllabique*, f. L *disyllabus*: see DISYLLABLE, -IC.] **A** *adj.* Having two syllables. M17. **B** *n.* A disyllabic word. M20.

disyllabically *adv.* L19.

disyllabize /dʌɪˈsɪləbʌɪz, dɪ-/ *v.t.* Also **dissyll-**, **-ise**. L19. [f. L *disyllabus* (see next) + -IZE.] Make disyllabic.

disyllable /dʌɪˈsɪləb(ə)l, dɪ-, ˈdʌɪsɪl-/ *n.* & *a.* Also **dissyll-**. L16. [Alt. (after SYLLABLE *n.*) Fr. *disyllabe*, f. L *disyllabus* adj. f. Gk *disullabos* of two syllables, f. as DI-[2] + *sullabē* SYLLABLE *n.*] **A** *n.* A disyllabic word or metrical foot. L16. **B** *adj.* = DISYLLABIC *a.* M18.

dit /dɪt/ *n.*[1] *arch.* L16. [App. alt. of obs. form of DITE *n.*[1] with substitution of short vowel.] A poetical composition; a ditty.

dit /dɪt/ *n.*[2] M20. [Imit.] In Morse telegraphy: a dot, *esp.* one spoken at the end of a character group.

dit *n.*[3] see DITE *n.*[2]

dit /dɪt/ *v.t.* Now *Sc.* & *dial.* [OE *dyttan*, prob. rel. to DOT *n.*[1]] **1** Stop up, shut, (an opening); fill *up* (a hole or gap). OE. **2** Obstruct the course or way of. ME.

dita /ˈdiːtə/ *n.* L19. [Tagalog *ditâ*.] A tall evergreen tree of the Old World tropics, *Alstonia scholaris* (family Apocynaceae); (more fully *dita bark*) the bark of this, which yields an antimalarial substance.

dital /ˈdʌɪt(ə)l/ *n.* E19. [f. It. *dito* finger, after *pedal*.] A thumb-key by which the pitch of a guitar- or lute-string can be raised a semitone.

ditch /dɪtʃ/ *n.* [OE *dīc*, corresp. to OFris., OS *dīk* ditch, dyke (Du. *dijk*), MHG *tīch* (G *Teich* pond, pool), ON *díki* ditch, DYKE *n.*[1]] **1** A long narrow hollow dug in the ground; a trench, a fosse. OE. **b** *spec.* Such a hollow dug out to hold or conduct water; *rhet.* any watercourse or channel. ME. **c** The trench or piece of ground immediately surrounding a bowling-green. M19. **d** The sea; *spec.* the English Channel; the North Sea. *slang.* E20. †**2** Any hollow dug in the ground; a pit, cave, etc. Only in ME. **3** An embankment; a bank or mound of earth. Now *dial.* L15.

Comb. & *phrases*: **ditch-water**: stagnant in a ditch (freq. in (*as*) *dull as ditch-water*); **last ditch** a place of final desperate defence (*die in the last ditch*: see DIE *v.*[1]). *last-ditch*: see LAST *a.*

ditchless *a.* without a ditch L19.

ditch /dɪtʃ/ *v.* LME. [f. the n.] **1** *v.i.* Make a ditch or ditches. LME. **2** *v.t.* Surround with a ditch; make a ditch for. Also foll. by *around* etc. LME. **3** *v.t.* Dig ditches or furrows in for the purpose of drainage etc.; provide with ditches. LME. **4** *v.t.* Clean out or repair (a ditch). L16. **5** *v.t.* Throw into a ditch; drive (a vehicle) into a ditch; *US* derail (a train). E19. **6** *v.t.* Put (a person) off a train. Usu. in *pass.* *US slang.* L19. **7** *v.t.* Abandon, discard; leave in the lurch. *colloq.* E20. **8** *v.t.* & *i.* Bring (an aircraft) down into the sea in an emergency. *slang.* M20.

7 A. BURGESS He ditches her after a night of love. M. AMIS I ditched the car and walked the last mile. *Dumfries Courier* Even some projects described as 'important' . . may be ditched as the Council draw up their priority lists.

ditcher /ˈdɪtʃə/ *n.* LME. [f. DITCH *n.*, *v.* + -ER[1].] **1** A person who makes and repairs ditches. LME. **2** A machine for making ditches. M19. **3** *Bowls.* A bowl which runs or is driven off the green. L19. **4** [With reference to the Mahratta Ditch, a local fortification.] A resident of Calcutta. *slang.* L19.

ditchy /ˈdɪtʃi/ *a.* L18. [f. DITCH *n.* + -Y[1].] Resembling a ditch; having many ditches or deep furrows.

†**dite** *n.*[1] ME. [(O)Fr. *dit* saying, maxim (f. L DICTUM), use as n. of pa. pple of *dire* say, f. L *dicere*. Cf. DIT *n.*[1]] **1** Something composed and written down; a composition, a letter, a written message. ME–L16. **2** A composition in poetic form, or intended to be set to music; a song, a ditty. ME–M16. **3** Manner or mode of composition; form of speech; diction, language. *Sc.* LME–M16.

dite /dʌɪt/ *n.*[2] Also **dit** /dɪt/. E20. [Origin unkn. Cf. DOIT *n.*] A very little, a jot. Only in *not to care a dite*, i.e. at all.

†**dite** *v.t.* ME. [OFr. *dit(i)er* f. L *dictare* frequent. of *dicere* say. Partly aphet. f. INDICT *v.*[1]] **1** Compose, put in words; indite. ME–M19. **2** Dictate (what is to be written or done). LME–M19. **3** Summon, indict. LME–L18.

ditement /ˈdʌɪtm(ə)nt/ *n.* *obs.* exc. *dial.* ME. [f. prec. + -MENT.] **1** A summons, an indictment. ME. †**2** A written or spoken composition. *Sc.* M16–E17.

diterpene /dʌɪˈtəːpiːn/ *n.* E20. [f. DI-[2] + TERPENE.] *Chem.* Any terpene with the formula $C_{20}H_{32}$; a diterpenoid.

diterpenoid *n.* & *a.* (of or pertaining to) any simple derivative of a $C_{20}H_{32}$ diterpene M20.

ditetragonal /dʌɪtɛˈtragən(ə)l/ *a.* L19. [f. DI-[2] + TETRAGONAL.] *Cryst.* (Of a prism or pyramid of the tetragonal system) such that a horizontal cross-section has eight angles, alternate ones being equal; of or pertaining to such a crystal form.

ditheism /ˈdʌɪθiːɪz(ə)m/ *n.* L17. [f. DI-[2] + THEISM *n.*[1]] Belief in two supreme gods; religious dualism; *esp.* (*a*) the belief in two independent antagonistic principles of good and evil; (*b*) a form of belief which implies that Christ is not of one substance with God the Father.

ditheist *n.* a person who holds the doctrine of ditheism L17. **ditheˈistic** *a.* L17. **ditheˈistical** *a.* M18.

dithematic /dʌɪθɪˈmatɪk/ *a.* & *n.* L19. [f. DI-[2] + THEMATIC.] *Philol.* (A word) containing two significant thematic elements or stems.

dither /ˈdɪðə/ *n.* *colloq.* or *dial.* E19. [f. the vb.] **1** A state of tremulous excitement or apprehension (chiefly in *all of a dither*); vacillation; a state of confusion. E19. **2** The action of trembling or quivering; vibration, esp. (*Engin.*) when caused deliberately for some purpose. L19.

dither /ˈdɪðə/ *v.* M17. [Var. of DIDDER.] **1** *v.i.* Tremble, quiver, thrill. *dial.* M17. **2** *v.i.* Act hesitantly, vacillate, be undecided. *colloq.* E20. **3** *v.t.* Confuse, make nervous or (*Austral.*) drunk. Chiefly as *dithered* ppl a. E20.

1 J. CLARE How have I joy'd, with dithering hands, to find Each fading flower. 2 G. GREENE He stood and dithered awkwardly while I got my drinks. E. LONGFORD For several years Kitty dithered between encouraging and checking their secret romance. G. SWIFT If we don't decide now we might dither for ever.

ditherer *n.* M20.

dithery /ˈdɪð(ə)ri/ *a.* *colloq.* L19. [f. prec. + -Y[1].] Dithering, trembling.

dithio- /dʌɪˈθʌɪəʊ/ *comb. form.* [f. DI-[2] + THIO-.] Containing two sulphur atoms in the molecule, esp. in place of two oxygen atoms or joined together, as *dithio-acid*.

dithionic /dʌɪθʌɪˈɒnɪk/ *a.* M19. [f. DI-[2] + Gk *theion* sulphur + -IC.] Chem. *dithionic acid*, a strong dibasic acid, $H_2S_2O_6$, known only in solution and as crystalline salts.

dithionate *n.* a salt of dithionic acid M19.

dithionous /dʌɪˈθʌɪənəs/ *a.* M20. [f. as prec. + -IC.] *Chem.* = HYDROSULPHUROUS.

dithionite *n.* = HYDROSULPHITE M20.

dithizone /dʌɪˈθʌɪzəʊn/ *n.* E20. [G *Dithizon*, f. as DI-[2], THIO-, AZO-, -ONE, elems. of the systematic name (see below).] *Chem.* A reagent used for the estimation and separation of lead and other metals; diphenylthiocarbazone, $C_{13}H_{12}N_4S$.

dithying /ˈdɪðɪɪŋ/ *a.* *poet.* E20. [Alt. of *dithering* ppl a. of DITHER *v.*] Quivering, trembling.

dithyramb /ˈdɪθɪram(b)/ *n.* Also in L form **dithyrambus** /dɪθɪˈrambəs/, pl. **-bi** /-bʌɪ/. E17. [L *dithyrambus* f. Gk *dithurambos*.] **1** An ancient Greek choric hymn, vehement and wild in character; a Bacchanalian song. E17. **2** A passionate or inflated poem, speech, or writing. M17.

dithyˈrambist *n.* a composer or declaimer of dithyrambs L19.

For other words beginning with *dis-* see the entry for **dis-**

dithyrambic /dɪθɪˈrambɪk/ *a.* & *n.* E17. [L *dithyrambicus* f. Gk *dithurambikos*, f. *dithurambos*: see prec., -IC.] A *adj.* 1 Pertaining to or of the nature of a dithyramb; composing dithyrambs. E17. 2 Resembling a dithyramb in style; wild, vehement, boisterous. E17.

2 E. JONES A dithyrambic letter to the woman he felt so much nearer winning.

B *n.* A dithyramb; a dithyrambic verse etc.; a writer of a dithyramb. M17.

dithyrambically *adv.* L19.

ditone /ˈdʌɪtəʊn/ *n.* E17. [Late L *ditonum* f. Gk *ditonon* ancient major third, neut. of *ditonos*, f. as DI-² + *tonos* TONE *n.* Cf. TRIHEMITONE.] *Mus.* An interval containing two whole tones; *esp.* the Pythagorean major third.

ditransitive /dʌɪˈtransɪtɪv, -ˈtrɑː-, -nz-/ *a.* M20. [f. DI-² + TRANSITIVE.] *Ling.* Of a verb: able to take an indirect object as well as a direct object.

ditriglyph /dʌɪˈtrʌɪglɪf/ *n.* E18. [Fr. *ditriglyphe*, f. as DI-² + *triglyphe* TRIGLYPH.] *Archit.* 1 The space between two triglyphs. *rare.* E18. 2 A spacing between columns of the Doric order which allows the use of two triglyphs in the frieze, between those over the columns; a horizontal distance in Doric architecture regarded as containing two triglyphs. L18.

ditriˈglyphic *a.* M19.

ditrigonal /dʌɪˈtrɪgən(ə)l/ *a.* L19. [f. DI-² + TRIGONAL.] *Cryst.* (Of a prism or pyramid of the hexagonal system) such that a horizontal cross-section has six angles, alternate ones being equal; of or pertaining to such a crystal form.

ditrigonally *adv.* L19.

ditrochee /dʌɪˈtrəʊkiː/ *n.* Also in L form **ditrochaeus** /dʌɪtrə(ʊ)ˈkiːəs/, pl. **-aei** /-iːʌɪ/. E18. [Late L *ditrochaeus* f. Gk *ditrokhaios*, f. as DI-² + *trokhaios* TROCHEE.] *Pros.* A foot consisting of two trochees; a double trochee.

ditroˈchean *a.* containing two trochees M19.

ditsy /ˈdɪtsi/ *a.* *N. Amer. slang.* L20. [Origin unkn.] Conceited, snobbish; stupid; cute; (of a thing) intricate.

dittander /dɪˈtandə/ *n.* ME. [f. as next, w. ending perh. after (O)Fr. *coriandre* CORIANDER.] 1 Pepperwort, *Lepidium latifolium.* ME. †2 = DITTANY I. E–M17.

dittany /ˈdɪtəni/ *n.* LME. [OFr. *dita(i)n* (f. med.L *dictamus*) & med.L *ditaneum* (f. late L *dictamnium*) f. L *dictamnus*, *-um* f. Gk *diktamnon*, perh. f. *Diktē* mountain in Crete where it grows.] 1 A dwarf shrub, *Origanum dictamnus*, of the mint family with pink flowers and white woolly leaves, native to Crete and Greece and cultivated for window-boxes etc.; formerly supposed to have the power to expel weapons. LME. 2 Orig., any of various plants resembling dittany, *spec.* = DITTANDER I. Now (*US*), any plant of the genus *Cunila* of the mint family, sometimes grown as culinary herbs; spec. *C. origanoides.* M16. 3 The plant *Dictamnus albus*, fraxinella. E17.

1 *fig.*: T. BRUGIS But this newes . . was a forcible dittany to drive this arrow out of the wound.

dittay /ˈdɪteɪ, ˈdɪti/ *n.* LME. [OFr. *dit(t)é*: see DITTY.] *Sc. Law* (now *Hist.*). The ground of indictment against a person for a criminal offence; the indictment itself.

ditto /ˈdɪtəʊ/ *a.*, *adv.*, *n.*, & *v.* E17. [It. dial. (Tuscan) var. of *detto* said f. L *dictus* pa. pple of *dicere* say.] A *adj.*, *adv.*, & *n.* (pl. **-os**). †1 In or of the month already named; the aforesaid month. Only in 17. 2 In the same way, similar(ly); the same; (the) aforesaid; (the same as, another of) what was mentioned above or previously. *colloq.* exc. in lists etc. (where usu. repr. by dots or commas under the matter repeated). L17. b *n.* A symbol representing the word 'ditto'. Also *ditto mark.* L19. 3 *n.* Cloth of the same material. Chiefly in *suit of dittos*, a suit of clothes of the same material and colour throughout. *arch.* M18. 4 *n.* Something identical or similar; an exact resemblance; a repetition. L18. 5 (Also **D-**.) (Proprietary name for) a duplicator, a small offset press for copying. E20.

2 S. THEMERSON Four Long Petticoats . . . Three Cambric ditto. R. ADAMS A great iron frying-pan and six ditto spoons. P. ACKROYD He blows up easy and down again ditto. A. BLOND Clauses requiring the author to return an advance are rarely invoked, ditto penalties for late delivery. **say ditto to** express agreement with what has been said by (another). 4 L. OLIPHANT The upper fragment . . the ditto of which is to be found at Irbid.

B *v.* Pa. t. & pple **dittoed** /ˈdɪtəʊd/. 1 *v.t.* Produce (mechanically or otherwise) a duplicate of; match, equal. M19. 2 *v.i.* Say or do the same as another person; agree, echo. L19.

1 T. C. HALIBURTON Where will you ditto our fall? It whips English weather by a long chalk. *Canadian Journal of Linguistics* Papers which are privately circulated in dittoed form.

dittography /dɪˈtɒgrəfi/ *n.* L19. [f. Gk *dittos* double + -GRAPHY.] *Palaeogr.* Unintentional repetition of a letter, word, etc., by a copyist.

ˈdittogram *n.* a dittograph L19. **ˈdittograph** *n.* & *v.* (*a*) *n.* textual matter thus repeated; (*b*) *v.t.* repeat by dittography: L19. **dittoˈgraphic** *a.* L19.

dittology /dɪˈtɒlədʒi/ *n.* L17. [Gk *dittologia* repetition of words, f. as prec.: see -LOGY.] A twofold reading or interpretation.

ditty /ˈdɪti/ *n.* & *v.* ME. [OFr. *dité* composition, treaty f. L *dictatum* use as n. of neut. pa. pple of *dictare* DICTATE *v.*: see -Y⁵. Cf. DICTATE *n.*, DITE *n.*¹] A *n.* 1 Orig., a song, a lay. Now, a short simple song; a bird's song. ME. 2 Any composition in verse. LME. †3 The words or leading theme of a song; a subject, a theme. M16–L17. †B *v.* 1 *v.t.* Sing as a ditty; sing about (something); fit words to (music). L16–L18. 2 *v.i.* Sing a ditty. Only in M17.

ditty-bag /ˈdɪtɪbag/ *n.* M19. [f. unkn. 1st elem. + BAG *n.*] A small bag used by sailors etc. to hold odds and ends.

ditty-box /ˈdɪtɪbɒks/ *n.* L19. [f. as prec. + BOX *n.*²] A box used in the same way as a ditty-bag.

diuresis /dʌɪjʊ(ə)ˈriːsɪs/ *n.* L17. [mod.L, f. as DI-³ + Gk *ourēsis* urination.] Increased excretion of urine, esp. of a temporary nature. Formerly, urination.

diuretic /dʌɪjʊ(ə)ˈrɛtɪk/ *a.* & *n.* LME. [(O)Fr. *diurétique* or late L *diureticus* f. Gk *diourētikos*, f. *diourein* urinate, f. as DI-³ + *ouron* urine: see -IC.] A *adj.* 1 Causing diuresis. LME. †2 Of a person: urinating excessively. M18–E19. B *n.* A diuretic agent. LME.

†diuretical *a.* & *n.* = DIURETIC only in 17. **diuretically** *adv.* M17.

diurnal /dʌɪˈəːn(ə)l/ *a.* & *n.* LME. [Late L *diurnalis*, f. L *diurnus* daily, f. *dies* day: see -AL¹. Cf. JOURNAL *n.* & *a.*] A *adj.* 1 Chiefly *Astron.* Performed in or occupying one day. LME. 2 Belonging to each day; occurring or (*arch.*) published every day; daily; *Sci.* varying with a period of one day. L16. 3 Of the day rather than the night (opp. *nocturnal*); *spec.* (of an animal etc.) active only during the day. L19.

1 *diurnal arc*: see ARC *n.* I. *diurnal circle*: see CIRCLE *n.* D. ADAMS The Earth moved slowly in its diurnal course. 2 T. HARDY The diurnal setting of the sun. J. C. POWYS His diurnal relaxation was his mid-day dinner at the Pilgrims'.

B *n.* 1 *Eccl.* A book containing the daytime canonical hours. Formerly also, any book of devotion. M16. 2 A daybook, a diary. *arch.* E17. 3 A newspaper published daily; *loosely* any newspaper or periodical. *obs.* exc. *Hist.* M17.

diurnalist *n.* (now *rare* or *obs.*) a writer of a journal; a journalist: M17. **diurnally** *adv.* E16.

diurnation /dʌɪəːˈneɪʃ(ə)n/ *n.* M19. [f. L *diurnus* DIURNAL + -ATION, after *hibernation.*] The habit in some animals of sleeping or remaining quiescent during the day.

diuturnal /dʌɪjʊˈtəːn(ə)l/ *a.* Now *rare.* L16. [med.L *diuturnalis*, f. L *diuturnus* of long duration, f. *diu* long, for a long time: see -AL¹.] Of long duration, lasting.

Also **†diuturn** *a.* LME–M17.

diuturnity /dʌɪjʊˈtəːnɪti/ *n.* Now *rare.* LME. [L *diuturnitas*, f. *diuturnus*: see prec., -ITY.] Long duration or continuance.

div /diːv/ *n.*¹ L18. [Pers. *dīv*, f. OPers. *daiva* (Avest. *daēva*) = Skt DEVA.] In Iranian (esp. Zoroastrian) mythology: a demonic power.

div /dɪv/ *n.*² L19. [Abbrev.] *Math.* Divergence (DIVERGENCE 3) (of).

diva /ˈdiːvə/ *n.* L19. [It. f. L *diva* goddess.] A distinguished female (esp. operatic) singer; a prima donna.

divagate /ˈdʌɪvəgeɪt/ *v.i.* *literary.* L16. [L *divagat-* pa. ppl stem of *divagari* wander about, f. as DI-¹ + *vagari* wander: see -ATE³.] Wander about; stray from one place or subject to another; digress.

divaˈgation *n.* the action of divagating; (*a*) deviation, (*a*) digression: M16.

divalent /dʌɪˈveɪl(ə)nt/ *a.* M19. [f. DI-² + -VALENT.] *Chem.* & *Immunol.* Having a valency of two.

divalence *n.* E20. **divalency** *n.* L19.

Divali *n.* var. of DIWALI.

divan /dɪˈvan, dɪˈvan, ˈdʌɪvan/ *n.* L16. [Fr., or It. *divano*, f. Turk. *dīvān* f. Pers. *dīvān* brochure, anthology, register, court, bench. Cf. DEWAN, DOUANE.] 1 An oriental council of State; *spec.* (*Hist.*) the privy council of the Ottoman Empire, presided over by the Sultan or the grand vizier. L16. b Any council. *arch.* E17. 2 The hall where the Ottoman divan was held; an oriental court of justice or council-chamber. L16. 3 In oriental countries, a room entirely open at one side towards a court, garden, river, etc. L17. 4 (Now the usual sense.) A couch or bed without a head- or footboard. Orig., a low bench or a raised part of a floor forming a long seat against the wall of a room. E18. 5 (A smoking-room attached to) a cigar-shop. *arch.* E19. 6 An anthology of poems in Persian or other oriental language; *spec.* a series of poems by one author, with rhymes usually running through the alphabet. E19.

divaricate /dʌɪˈvarɪkət, dɪ-/ *a.* L18. [L *divaricatus*, f. as next, -ATE².] Chiefly *Bot.* & *Zool.* Widely divergent; *esp.* (of a branch) having the stem almost at a right angle.

divaricately *adv.* M19.

divaricate /dʌɪˈvarɪkeɪt, dɪ-/ *v.* E17. [L *divaricat-* pa. ppl stem of *divaricare*, f. as DI-¹ + *varicare* stretch (the legs) apart, f. *varicus* straddling: see -ATE³.] 1 *v.i.* Stretch or spread apart; branch off, diverge; ramify. E17. b *Bot.* & *Zool.* Diverge widely from a stem or main body. Chiefly as *divaricated*, *-ing* ppl adjs. M17. 2 *v.t.* Stretch or open wide apart. L17. 3 *v.t.* Cause to spread or branch out in different directions. Now *rare* or *obs.* L17.

1 G. P. R. JAMES Where these two [roads] divaricated, the horseman stopped. 2 MARVELL I took my compasses, and divaricating them . . I drew the circular line.

divaricatingly *adv.* in a divaricating manner L19. **divaricator** *n.* something which divaricates; *esp.* (*Surg.*) a hinged instrument for holding portions of tissue apart; (*Zool.*, more fully *divaricator muscle*) a muscle that separates parts, e.g. opens a brachiopod shell: L19.

divarication /dʌɪˌvarɪˈkeɪʃ(ə)n, dɪ-/ *n.* L16. [med.L *divaricatio(n-)*, f. as prec.: see -ATION.] 1 The action of divaricating, divergence; straddling of the legs; the state of spreading out or ramifying. L16. 2 A place where something branches off; something which branches off, a ramification. M17. 3 Divergence of opinion; disagreement. M17.

dive /dʌɪv/ *n.* E18. [f. the vb.] 1 An act of diving; a swift descent (esp. head first) into or through water etc.; *spec.* one performed by projecting oneself upwards and inverting the body or somersaulting to keep the head first, esp. as a sport. E18. 2 A sudden darting movement, esp. so as to disappear. L19. 3 A drinking-den; a disreputable place of resort. *colloq.* L19. 4 In boxing, football, etc., a feigned fall intended to deceive an opponent or referee. Freq. in *take a dive.* M20.

1 *nosedive*: see NOSE *n.* *swallow dive*: see SWALLOW *n.*¹ 2 OED He made a dive into the nearest shop.

dive /dʌɪv/ *v.* Pa. t. **dived**, (*N. Amer.* & *dial.*) **dove** /dəʊv/. [OE str. intrans. vb *dūfan* (pa. t. *dēaf*, pl. *dufon*), obs. bef. 14, & wk trans. vb *dȳfan*, *dȳfde*, both f. Gmc, cogn. w. DEEP *a.*, DIP *v.* (Pa. t. *dove* app. after *drive*, *drove*, etc.)] I *v.i.*

1 Descend or plunge, esp. head first, into or through water etc.; execute a dive. OE. b Of a submarine: descend so as to be entirely under water. L19. c Of an aircraft: plunge steeply downwards at increasing or high speed. E20. d In boxing, football, etc.: feign a fall to deceive an opponent or referee. M20. 2 Of a thing: sink deeply into water etc.; penetrate into a body. Long *rare*. ME. 3 Penetrate or search mentally *into* a matter. L16. 4 Put one's hand *into* water, a receptacle, etc., esp. in order to take something out; *arch. slang* pick pockets. L17. 5 Go suddenly or eagerly, esp. into or towards a place or thing. Foll. by prep. M18.

1 P. H. JOHNSON He climbed onto a groin, stretched his arms and dived cleanly into the sparkling sea. 2 SHAKES. *John* To dive like buckets in concealed wells. J. DICKEY I .. saw him kill a quail .., the arrow diving into the black feathers. *transf.*: POPE The fierce soul to darkness dived and hell. 5 QUILLER-COUCH A straight pathway dived between hazel-bushes and appeared again twenty feet above. G. B. SHAW A man of sense would have dived into the nearest cellar.

II *v.t.* 6 Dip, submerge, or plunge (a person or thing) *in* or *into* water etc. *arch.* OE. 7 Thrust (the hand or something held) *into*. L16. 8 Penetrate or traverse by diving; dive into or through. Now *rare*. E17.

7 E. WAUGH Corker began .. to dive his hand into his bosom and scratch his chest. 8 R. W. EMERSON He dives the hollow, climbs the steep.

Comb.: **dive-bomb** *v.t.* (of an aircraft) attack by releasing a bomb while diving towards the target; *slang* (of a bird) swoop down on and away again; release droppings over; **dive-bomber** an aircraft designed for dive-bombing.

¶ As v.t., obs. after 13, a new construction in 16.

dive-dap /ˈdʌɪvdap/ *n.* Now *dial.* Also **-dop** /-dɒp/. [OE *dūfedoppa*, f. as DIVE *v.* + *doppa* agent-n. f. ablaut stem *dēop-*, *dup-* (*dop-*) dip. Cf. DABCHICK, DIDAPPER, next.] = DIDAPPER.

dive-dapper /ˈdʌɪvdapə/ *n.* Now *dial.* M16. [f. prec.: assim. to agent-ns. in -ER[1].] = DIDAPPER.

dive-dop *n.* var. of DIVE-DAP.

†**divell** *v.t.* E17–E19. [L *divellere* tear apart, f. as DI-[1] + *vellere* tear.] Tear or pull apart.

divellent /dɪˈvɛl(ə)nt, dʌɪ-/ *a.* Now *rare.* L18. [L *divellent-* pres. ppl stem of *divellere*: see prec., -ENT.] Tending to cause separation or decomposition.

divellicate /dʌɪˈvɛlɪkeɪt/ *v.t.* Now *rare.* M17. [f. DI-[1] + L *vellicat-* pa. ppl stem of *vellicare* pluck, pinch, f. *vellere* tear: see -ATE[3].] Tear apart, pull to pieces, (*lit.* & *fig.*).

diver /ˈdʌɪvə/ *n.* L15. [f. DIVE *v.* + -ER[1].] 1 Any of various diving birds, *esp.* one of the family Gaviidae, comprising large water-birds with straight sharply pointed bills. Cf. LOON *n.*[2] 1. L15. 2 A person who dives, esp. as an occupation or a sport; an animal good at diving. E16. 3 A pickpocket. *arch. slang.* L16. 4 A thing made to plunge under water. L18.

1 **great northern diver** a large diver, *Gavia immer*, which breeds chiefly in forest lakes in N. America and visits the westernmost parts of Europe in winter. *red-throated diver*: see RED *a.* 2 *pearl-diver, scuba-diver*, etc. 4 *Cartesian diver*: see CARTESIAN *a.*

diverless *a.* L20.

diverge /dʌɪˈvəːdʒ, dɪ-/ *v.* M17. [med.L *divergere*, f. as DI-[1] + L *vergere* bend, turn, incline.] 1 *v.i.* Proceed in different directions from a point; take different courses, turn aside *from* a track or course, (*lit.* & *fig.*); differ. M17. 2 *v.t.* Cause to diverge; deflect. M18. 3 *v.i. Math.* Of an infinite series: not converge (CONVERGE 2). L18.

1 E. M. FORSTER A footpath diverged from the highroad. E. JONES As they grew up their interests diverged. M. M. KAYE Her unusual looks .. diverged too widely from the Indian ideal. 2 **diverging lens**: causing light rays to diverge.

divergement *n.* divergence M18. **diverger** *n.* a person whose thought is divergent (DIVERGENT 2) M20. **divergingly** *adv.* in a diverging manner, with divergence: L18.

divergence /dʌɪˈvəːdʒ(ə)ns, dɪ-/ *n.* M17. [f. prec. + -ENCE, perh. after Fr. *divergence*.] 1 The action, fact, or property of diverging; movement in different directions from the same point so that the intervening distance continually increases; departure from a path or course (*lit.* & *fig.*). M17. 2 A difference or conflict between opinions, interests, wishes, etc. L19. 3 *Math.* The scalar product of the operator ∇ (see DEL) and any given vector. L19. 4 *Meteorol.* & *Oceanogr.* A place where airflows or ocean currents diverge, characteristically marked by downwelling (of air) or upwelling (of water). M20.

1 GLADSTONE The natural divergence of the two traditions. D. LINDSAY By making a long divergence they eventually got round to the other side. 2 L. STEPHEN There was the widest divergence of opinion as to our probable fate. W. S. CHURCHILL A divergence grew between the King and Marlborough.

divergenceless *a.* (*Math.*) having a divergence of zero M20. **divergency** *n.* divergent quality or state; (amount or degree of) divergence: E18.

divergent /dʌɪˈvəːdʒ(ə)nt, dɪ-/ *a.* L17. [f. as prec. + -ENT, perh. after Fr. *divergent*.] 1 Diverging; of or pertaining to divergence; *Math.* (of an infinite series) not convergent. L17. 2 *Psychol.* Of thought: tending to produce a variety of unusual answers or responses; not habitually given to deductive reasoning. Cf. CONVERGENT 3. M20.

1 C. DARWIN The Siamese have small noses, with divergent nostrils. H. MACMILLAN There seemed little likelihood of reconciling the divergent interests.

divergently *adv.* E19.

divers /ˈdʌɪvəz/ *a.*, *pron.*, & *adv. arch.* ME. [(O)Fr. (fem. *diverse*) f. L *diversus* pa. pple of *divertere* DIVERT. See also next.] A *adj.* †1 = DIVERSE *a.* 1. ME–E18. †2 Differing from what is right, good, or profitable; perverse, cruel; adverse, unfavourable. ME–E17. 3 Various, sundry, several; more than one; some number of. ME.

3 G. SAINTSBURY Divers interpretations may be put on that story. R. H. MORRIESON Through divers landing windows, we saw *her*.

B *pron.* Several, some number, (*of*). (Earlier as DIVERSE *pron.*) E16.

HOBBES He subdued divers of the islands.

†C *adv.* Diversely. L16–E18.

diversly *adv.* ME.

diverse /dʌɪˈvəːs, ˈdʌɪvəːs/ *a.*, *pron.*, & *adv.* ME. [Var. of prec., later infl. by *adverse*, *perverse*, etc.] A *adj.* 1 Different in character or quality; not of the same kind; unlike in nature or qualities. (Foll. by *from*, †*to*.) ME. †2 = DIVERS *a.* 3. ME–E18. †3 = DIVERS *a.* 2. LME–L15. 4 Differing from itself in different circumstances, at different times, or in different parts; varied; changeful. M16. †5 Distracting. *rare* (Spenser). Only in L16.

1 H. ARENDT They were a mixture of diverse elements: men as far apart as Zola and Péguy. 4 B. JOWETT The diverse and multiform nature of pleasure.

†B *pron.* = DIVERS *pron.* LME–E18.

†C *adv.* Diversely. LME–E18.

diversely *adv.* ME. **diverseness** *n.* (now *rare*) the quality or state of being diverse; diversity: LME.

†**diverse** *v.* ME. [OFr. *diverser* f. med.L *diversare* frequent. of L *divertere* DIVERT.] 1 *v.t.* Make diverse or different; vary, change. ME–M17. 2 *v.i.* Be or grow diverse or different; vary; differ. Only in ME. 3 *v.t.* & *i.* Turn aside. *rare*. LME–L16.

3 SPENSER The Redcrosse Knight diverst, but forth rode Britomart.

diversification /dʌɪˌvəːsɪfɪˈkeɪʃ(ə)n, dɪ-/ *n.* E17. [med.L *diversificatio(n-)*, f. *diversificat-* pa. ppl stem of *diversificare*: see DIVERSIFY, -ATION.] 1 The action of diversifying; the process of becoming diversified; the fact of being diversified. E17. 2 A diversified condition, form, or structure. Now *rare*. L17.

diversiform /dʌɪˈvəːsɪfɔːm, dɪ-/ *a.* E18. [f. late L *diversi-* comb. form of *diversus* DIVERS + -FORM.] Of various forms; differing in form.

diversify /dʌɪˈvəːsɪfʌɪ, dɪ-/ *v.* LME. [OFr. *diversifier* f. med.L *diversificare* make unlike, f. *diversus* DIVERS: see -FY.] 1 *v.i.* †a Exhibit or produce diversity; vary. LME–E19. b Of a company etc.: enlarge or vary its range of products, field of operation, etc., esp. to reduce its dependence on a particular market etc.; engage in diversification *into*. M20. 2 *v.t.* Make diverse, different, or varied; give variety or diversity to; vary, modify, variegate. L15. †b Differentiate, make different, *from*. L16–E18.

1b *Daily Telegraph* His gallery has ambitious ideas for diversifying into publishing. 2 POPE Swift trouts, diversify'd with crimson stains. J. ROBERTSON That charming lake and .. the diversified scenery around its wooded banks. L. STRACHEY Sometimes the solemnity of the evening was diversified by a concert.

diversifier *n.* (*rare*) L19.

diversion /dʌɪˈvəːʃ(ə)n, dɪ-/ *n.* LME. [Late L *diversio(n-)* turning away, f. L *divers-* pa. ppl stem of *divertere* DIVERT: see -ION.] 1 The action or an act of diverting or turning aside from an expected or usual course, purpose, etc. LME. 2 Something that diverts the mind from preoccupation or boredom; a pleasant mental distraction; an amusement, an entertainment, a pastime. E17. 3 The turning away of the attention, thoughts, etc., esp. in a pleasurable way; distraction, recreation, amusement. M17. 4 Something intended to distract someone else's attention, *spec.* (*Mil.*) a manoeuvre with this purpose. M17. †5 Something that diverts a person from a regular occupation. M–L17. 6 An alternative route; *spec.* one to be taken when a road is temporarily closed. M20.

1 DONNE A diversion .. from this rectitude, this uprightness. E. BOWEN The diversion of traffic out of blocked main thoroughfares into by-ways. H. KISSINGER The ABM .. was attacked as a wasteful diversion of resources from domestic priorities. 2 W. TREVOR A seaside resort of limited diversions. 3 J. AUSTEN All were finding .. diversion in the playful conceits they suggested. 4 WELLINGTON To make the most powerful diversion which may be practicable on the coasts of the Red Sea. *New York Times* One frantic author, worried about a scene to be played on stage, knocked over an ashtray to create a diversion.

diversionary *a.* tending to a diversion, of the nature of a diversion M19. **diversionism** *n.* the activity of a diversionist M20. **diversionist** *n.* & *a.* (*a*) *n.* (esp. in Communist usage) a saboteur, a conspirator against the State; (*b*) *adj.* of the nature of diversionism: M20.

diversity /dʌɪˈvəːsɪti, dɪ-/ *n.* & *a.* ME. [(O)Fr. *diversité* f. L *diversitas*, f. *diversus* DIVERS: see -ITY.] A *n.* 1 The condition or quality of being diverse, different, or varied; variety, unlikeness. ME. 2 An instance of this; a distinction; a different kind, a variety (of a thing etc.). ME. †3 Various kinds, variety (of things etc.). LME–E17. †4 Contrariety to what is agreeable, good, or right; perversity, evil, mischief. LME–E16.

1 C. SAGAN Despite the apparent diversity of terrestrial life forms, they are identical in the deepest sense. 2 J. S. MILL People have diversities of taste. 3 SHAKES. *Temp.* Roaring, shrieking, .. And moe diversity of sounds, all horrible.

B *attrib.* or as *adj.* Designating radio reception in which a signal is received on several channels and the one least affected by fading etc. is automatically used. M20.

diversive /dʌɪˈvəːsɪv, dɪ-/ *a.* Long *rare*. LME. [f. L *divers-*: see DIVERSION, -IVE.] Tending to divert or cause diversion; divertive.

divert /dʌɪˈvəːt, dɪ-/ *v.* LME. [Fr. *divertir* f. L *divertere*, f. as DI-[1] + *vertere* to turn.] 1 *v.t.* Turn aside from a direction or course; cause (esp. traffic) to take a different route; alter (a course); turn *from* one destination or object *to* another. LME. 2 *v.t.* Turn (a purpose, feeling, etc.) elsewhere; interrupt the progress of (an action); avert, ward off. LME. 3 *v.i.* Turn aside from a route, purpose, etc.; deviate, digress, (*lit.* & *fig.*). Now *arch.* or *formal*. LME. †4 *v.i.* & *refl.* Separate *from*; part. M16–E18. †5 *v.t.* Turn awry or out of true. *rare* (Shakes.). Only in E17. 6 *v.t.* Draw (a person etc.) away *from* a particular course, design, etc.; draw (the attention etc.) away *from* one thing *to* another; distract. E17. 7 *v.t.* Draw away from tedious or serious occupations; entertain, amuse. M17. 8 *v.t.* Cause (time) to pass pleasantly; while away. Now *rare*. E18.

1 T. ARNOLD Some of the reinforcements .. were afterwards diverted to other services. E. FIGES I had to get planning permission to divert the stream. 2 MILTON Which Omen .. God hath not diverted. E. M. FORSTER An opportunity of diverting the conversation

while she recovered her composure. 3 W. MUNK He . . was bred to physic, but he diverted to the diplomatic life. 6 O. MANNING She diverted him by taking a small parcel from her handbag. 7 P. WARNER The higher ranks would divert themselves with hunting, drinking.

diverter *n.* E17. **diverti'bility** *n.* (*rare*) ability to be diverted L19. **divertible** *a.* (*rare*) able to be diverted L19. **diverting** *ppl a.* that diverts; *esp.* amusing, entertaining: M17. **divertingly** *adv.* E18. **divertingness** *n.* L17. **divertive** *a.* (now *rare*) tending to divert; amusing, entertaining: L16. **divertor** *n.* a device or apparatus that diverts electricity, impurities, etc. L19.

†diverticle *n.* LME. [f. as next.] 1 A byway, a side-road; a turning out of the main or direct way (*lit.* & *fig.*). LME–L18. 2 = DIVERTICULUM 2. Only in M19.

diverticulum /daɪvəˈtɪkjʊləm/ *n.* Pl. **-la** /-lə/. M17. [med.L *diverticulum* byway, var. of L *deverticulum*, f. *devertere* turn down or aside, f. *de* DE- I + *vertere* to turn: see -CULE.] †1 A byway; a way out, a means of exit. M17–E18. 2 *Med.* A blind tube or sac forming a side-branch of a cavity or passage, *esp.* an abnormal one in the colon etc. E19.

2 *Meckel's diverticulum*: see MECKEL I. *Zenker('s) (pulsion) diverticulum*: see ZENKER *n.*[1]

diverticular *a.* pertaining to, affecting, or of the nature of a diverticulum M19. **diverticulate** *a.* having a diverticulum L19. **ˌdiverticu'lectomy** *n.* (an instance of) surgical removal of an abnormal diverticulum E20. **ˌdiverticu'litis** *n.* (*Med.*) inflammation of an abnormal diverticulum, esp. in the intestine E20. **ˌdiverticu'losis** *n.* (*Med.*) the presence of abnormal diverticula, esp. in the intestine E20.

divertimento /dɪˌvəːtɪˈmɛntəʊ, -ˌvɛːt-/ *n.* Pl. **-ti** /-ti/, **-tos**. M18. [It. = diversion.] 1 A diversion, an amusement. Long *rare*. M18. 2 *Mus.* A composition primarily for entertainment, *esp.* a suite for a small group of instruments or a single instrument; a light orchestral piece. E19.

divertisement /dɪˈvəːtɪzm(ə)nt/ *n.* M17. [Fr. DIVERTISSEMENT.] 1 (An) entertainment, (an) amusement; = DIVERSION 2, 3. M17. 2 = DIVERTISSEMENT I. *arch.* M17.

divertissement /diːvɛːˈtiːsmɒ̃; *foreign* divertismɑ̃ (*pl. same*)/ *n.* E18. [Fr., f. *divertiss-* stem of *divertir* DIVERT: see -MENT.] 1 a A short ballet or other entertainment between acts or longer pieces. E18. b = DIVERTIMENTO 2. L19. 2 An entertainment; = DIVERSION 2. E19.

Dives /ˈdaɪviːz/ *n.* In sense 2 **d-**. LME. [Late L (Vulgate *Luke* 16) = rich man, use as n. of L *dives* rich.] 1 (The type of) a rich man. LME. 2 Hist. *dives costs*, legal costs on the ordinary rather than the reduced scale formerly allowed in certain cases. M19.

divest /daɪˈvɛst, dɪ-/ *v.* E17. [Alt. of DEVEST on L models in *di-*. Cf. med.L *disvestire*, *di-*, *de-*.] 1 *v.t.* Strip *of* a possession, right, or attribute; dispossess, deprive, *of*; free, rid, (esp. oneself) *of*. E17. 2 *v.t.* a Take off (a garment etc.); lay aside, abandon. Now *rare*. E17. b Strip *of* a garment, covering, etc.; strip, undress. E19. 3 *v.t. Law.* Take away (property etc. vested in someone); alienate. L18. 4 *v.t.* & *i.* Sell off (a subsidiary company); get rid of, cease to hold, (an investment). M20.

1 J. GALSWORTHY She could never divest herself of the feeling that the world was the most ungrateful place. B. RUSSELL As soon as we are able to divest our thoughts of irrelevant particularity. 2a BROWNING I will divest all fear. b N. PODHORETZ The . . young gentleman was forthwith divested of his . . red satin jacket.

divestment *n.* the action of divesting; the state of being divested: M18. **divesture** *n.* & *v.* (*a*) *n.* = DIVESTITURE 2; (*b*) *v.t.* undress: M17.

divestitive /daɪˈvɛstɪtɪv, dɪ-/ *a.* E19. [f. as next + -IVE.] Having the property of divesting.

divestiture /daɪˈvɛstɪtʃə, dɪ-/ *n.* E17. [f. med.L *divestit-* pa. ppl stem of *divestire*: DIVEST: see -URE. Cf. med.L *divestitura*.] 1 Deprivation of a possession or right; dispossession; alienation. E17. 2 The action of stripping off clothing or getting rid of something. E19. 3 The process of breaking up a large company by selling off or forcing the sale of subsidiaries; withdrawal of investment. *US.* M20.

divi *n.* & *v.* var. of DIVVY *n.*[1] & *v.*

dividant *a.* see DIVIDENT.

divide /dɪˈvaɪd/ *n.* M17. [f. the vb.] 1 The act of dividing, esp. among a number of people. Formerly also, separation. M17. 2 A ridge or line of high ground forming the division between two valleys or river systems; a watershed; a dividing line, a boundary, (*lit.* & *fig.*). E19.

2 **the Great Divide**: *spec.* between life and death.

divide /dɪˈvaɪd/ *v.* ME. [L *dividere* force apart, separate, remove. Cf. DEVISE *v.*] I *v.t.* 1 Separate into or *into* parts or smaller groups; split up; break or cut apart. ME. b Penetrate by motion through; pass through or across. *arch.* L16. 2 Separate into branches, cause to fork. Usu. in *pass.* LME. 3 Mark out into parts, in fact or thought; cause to consist of parts or distinct areas. Freq. in *pass.* (Foll. by *into*.) LME. 4 Separate into categories; classify. Formerly also, make distinctions with regard to. Usu. foll. by *into*. LME. 5 Separate *from* another person or thing, or an adjacent part; cut off, isolate; be a boundary between; part, sunder. LME. 6 Separate (people) in opinion, feeling, or interest; cause to disagree; set at variance. LME. 7 Distribute or share out *between* or *among* two or more parties, objects of thought, etc., deal out (†*to*). Now also *divide up*. LME. b Take or have a portion of (something) along with another or others; share (*with*). E16. 8 *Math.* a Find how many times (one quantity) contains another. Foll. by *by* the latter quantity. LME. b Of a quantity: be contained in (another quantity) without a remainder. E18. †9 *Mus.* Perform with divisions. Only in L16. 10 Cause (a legislative assembly etc.) to divide (see sense 14 below). E17.

1 I. MURDOCH Julius contented himself with dividing it into four pieces. H. NICOLSON I start dividing the primroses. **divide the hoof** *arch.* (of an animal) have cloven hoofs. 3 L. DEIGHTON The wire roof divided the . . sky into a hundred rectangles. G. GREENE The house was divided into flats. J. HAWKES Walls dividing the rich pastures of the valley. 4 R. W. HAMILTON We commonly divide the people into agricultural and manufacturing. 5 POPE What thin partitions Sense from Thought divide. G. GREENE The breadth of Lake Mälaren divided him from the workmen's quarters on the other bank. 6 H. MACMILLAN Two great sources of dispute divided the successor states to the old Indian Empire. 7 K. VONNEGUT The government ought to divide up the wealth of the country equally. T. CAPOTE They divided between them the household chores, taking turns at the stove and the sink. b DRYDEN Let old Timotheus yield the prize, Or both divide the crown.

II *v.i.* 11 Become divided, undergo division; become separated into parts, or from something else or each other; admit of division; branch, ramify. LME. b Of a Cambridge University term: reach its midpoint. L18. 12 Make a separation or distinction; distinguish (*between*). Now chiefly in *divide and rule* below. LME. 13 *Math.* Perform division. E16. 14 Of a legislative assembly etc.: separate into two groups according to which way a vote is cast, so that those for and those against may be counted. M16. †15 *Mus.* Perform or execute divisions. Only in E17. †16 Have a share. *rare* (Shakes.). Only in E17.

11 SHAKES. *Lear* Love cools, friendship falls off, brothers divide. O. MANNING The street divided into smaller streets. *Nature* The scholarly reading population divides naturally into two types. 12 **divide and rule** [tr. L *divide et impera*] maintain supremacy over subjects or prospective antagonists by preventing them from making common cause.

dividable *a.* (*a*) able to be divided, divisible; †(*b*) *rare* having the function of dividing: L16.

divided /dɪˈvaɪdɪd/ *ppl a.* M16. [f. prec. + -ED[1].] That has been divided; separated into parts; (of a verdict) not unanimous; discordant, at variance.

D. HALBERSTAM Not everyone loved her, people in that community were fiercely divided over her. E. BOWEN Emmeline gave them the best she could of her now divided attention. **divided against itself** consisting of opposing factions. **divided highway** *N. Amer.* a dual carriageway. **divided skirt**: hanging like an ordinary skirt but with separate legs, as in trousers.

dividedly *adv.* E17. **dividedness** *n.* M17.

dividend /ˈdɪvɪdɛnd/ *n.* L15. [AN *dividende* f. L *dividendum* use as n. of neut. gerundive of *dividere* DIVIDE *v.*: see -END.] 1 A portion or share of anything divided, *esp.* the share that falls to each party. *obs.* exc. as *fig.* use of sense b. L15. b A sum received periodically by a shareholder or creditor (cf. sense 4 below). L17. 2 *Math.* A quantity which is to be divided by another (the divisor). M16. †3 The action or an act of dividing or sharing; (a) distribution. M16–E18. 4 A sum of money to be divided among a number of people, e.g. the creditors of an insolvent estate; *esp.* the payment made periodically by a company to its shareholders, usu. expressed as an amount per share; a similar payment made to members or customers of a cooperative in proportion to the amount spent; a payment made to a winner in a football pool. E17.

1 S. JOHNSON A very liberal dividend of praise. b *fig.*: M. M. KAYE Those two hard years in the mountains . . had paid dividends at last, for they had toughened him. *cum dividend*: see CUM 2. *ex dividend*: see EX *prep.*

Comb.: **dividend-stripping** the practice of buying securities ex-dividend and selling them cum-dividend before the next dividend is due in order to avoid the tax payable on dividends; **dividend warrant** the document by which a shareholder receives a dividend.

dividendless *a.* L19.

†divident *n.* & *a.* In sense B.I also **-ant**. LME. [L *divident-* pres. ppl stem of *dividere* DIVIDE *v.*: see -ENT.] A *n.* A person who or thing which divides or separates; something that forms the boundary between two regions etc., *Math.* a divisor. LME–M17. B *adj.* 1 Divided, separate. *rare* (Shakes.). Only in E17. 2 Distributive. Only in M17.

divider /dɪˈvaɪdə/ *n.* E16. [f. DIVIDE *v.* + -ER[1].] 1 A person who distributes or shares something. E16. 2 A person who or thing which divides a whole into parts or portions. M16. b A partition or screen; *spec.* (in full *room-divider*) a screen, piece of furniture, etc., to divide a room into different areas. M20. †3 A person who makes philosophical distinctions. L16–E17. 4 A cause of dissension or discord. M17. 5 In *pl.* Measuring compasses worked by means of a screw fastened to one leg and passing through the other, esp. for setting to small intervals; a simple pair of compasses with steel points. E18.

divi-divi /ˈdɪvɪˌdɪvi/ *n.* M19. [Amer. Sp. f. Carib.] A flowering tree, *Caesalpinia coriaria*, of tropical America (also *divi-divi tree*); its curled pods, used in tanning.

dividual /dɪˈvɪdjʊəl/ *a.* & *n.* *arch.* L16. [f. L *dividuus* (f. as DIVIDE *v.*) + -AL[1].] A *adj.* 1 That is or may be divided or separated from something else; separate, distinct. L16. 2 Divided or divisible into parts; fragmentary. E17. 3 Divided between a number; shared, held in common. M17. B *n.* †1 Something (able to be) divided. Only in M17. †2 *Math.* In division, each of the several parts of the dividend, yielding successively one figure or term of the quotient. E18–E19.

dividually *adv.* separately M17.

dividuality /dɪˌvɪdjʊˈalɪti/ *n.* *rare.* E19. [Back-form. f. INDIVIDUALITY.] The state of not being individual; lack of individuality.

dividuity /dɪvɪˈdjuːɪti/ *n.* *rare.* M17. [L *dividuitatem*, f. as DIVIDUAL: see -ITY.] Divisible or divided quality or state.

dividuous /dɪˈvɪdjʊəs/ *a.* *rare.* M18. [f. as DIVIDUAL + -OUS.] 1 = DIVIDUAL *a.* 2. M18. 2 = DIVIDUAL *a.* I. E19.

divination /dɪvɪˈneɪʃ(ə)n/ *n.* LME. [OFr., or L *divinatio(n-)*, f. *divinat-* pa. ppl stem of *divinare*: see DIVINE *v.*, -ATION.] 1 The action or practice of divining; an act of divining; insight into or discovery of the unknown or the future by supernatural or magical means; (an) augury, (a) prophecy. LME. 2 Guessing by happy instinct or unusual insight; successful conjecture; an inspired insight, a skilful forecast, a good guess. LME.

1 L. DURRELL The Grand Tarot for amateur divination. C. G. SELIGMAN Divination is performed by inspection of the stomach of a slaughtered cow,

and interpretation of the flight of birds. 2 R. HUGHES She had not Rachel's clear divination: she never knew when she might offend. A. NIN At times I have intuitions, swift divinations.

divinator /ˈdɪvɪneɪtə/ *n.* L15. [L *divinator*, f. *divinat-*: see prec., -OR.] A person who practises divination; a diviner, a soothsayer.

diˈvinatory *a.* pertaining to a diviner or to divination, prophetic; conjectural: M16.

divine /dɪˈvʌɪn/ *n.*[1] & *a.* ME. [OFr. *devin*, fem. *-ine*, later (by assim. to L) *divin*, f. L *divinus*, f. *divus* godlike, god, rel. to *deus* god.] **A** *n.* †1 Theology, divinity. Only in ME. †2 Divination. Only in ME. 3 Divine nature, divinity. Now only as *the divine*. *rare.* LME. †4 Divine service. L15–E17.

B *adj.* 1 Of or pertaining to God or a god. LME. 2 Given by or proceeding from God; sanctioned or inspired by God. LME. 3 Addressed or devoted to God; religious, sacred. LME. 4 Partaking of the nature of God or a god; godlike; heavenly. LME. †**b** Immortal, beatified. L16–M17. 5 Superhumanly gifted, or beautiful; of surpassing excellence; *colloq.* excellent, delightful; as good as one could wish for. LME. 6 Connected or dealing with divinity or sacred things; sacred. *arch.* LME. †7 Foreboding, prophetic. E–M17.

1 R. W. EMERSON Accept the place divine providence has found for you. 2 J. WATERWORTH Did this unrivalled Biblist acknowledge any writings as divine, which the Jews did not receive as canonical? **divine right (of kings)** *Hist.* (the right deriving from) the doctrine that monarchs have authority from God alone, independently of their subjects' will. 3 I. WATTS Divine songs, attempted in easy language, for the use of children. *divine office*: see OFFICE *n.* 4. **divine service** the public worship of God. 4 R. A. KNOX They were not to think of Christ after a human fashion. His nature was Divine. R. G. COLLINGWOOD Some divine or at least spiritual being. 5 WORDSWORTH That mighty orb of song, The divine Milton. J. GRENFELL Isn't he divine? He is the best White Russian butler in the whole of New York. **divine proportion**: that of the golden section. 7 MILTON Yet oft his heart, divine of somthing ill, Misgave him.

divineness *n.* (now *rare*) LME.

divine /dɪˈvʌɪn/ *n.*[2] ME. [OFr. *devin* soothsayer, (later) *divin* theologian, f. L *divinus* soothsayer, (in med.L) theologian, use as n. of *divinus* adj.: see prec.] †1 A soothsayer; a prophet, a seer. ME–L16. 2 A person, usu. a cleric, skilled in divinity; a theologian. Formerly, any clergyman. LME. †3 A writer on the theology of a religious system other than Christianity; a priest or religious teacher of a religion other than Christianity. LME–E17.

divine /dɪˈvʌɪn/ *v.* LME. [(O)Fr. *deviner*, f. as prec. after L *divinare* foretell, predict.] **I** *v.t.* †1 Make out or interpret by supernatural or magical insight; disclose, make known. LME–E17. 2 Make out by sagacity, intuition, or fortunate conjecture; conjecture successfully; guess. LME. 3 Have supernatural or magic insight into (things to come); have a presentiment of; predict or prophesy by some special intuition. LME. †4 Conceive of, devise, or contrive by special inspiration or extraordinary sagacity. LME–L16. †5 Of a thing: foreshadow, prognosticate, portend; point out. L16–M19. †6 Make divine; canonize; divinize. L16–E17.

2 L. STRACHEY He alone among public men had divined her feelings at Albert's death. R. H. MOTTRAM He has written to us, you will never divine from whence! Q. BELL Each divined that the other could become a formidable rival. 3 S. BUTLER None . . could divine To which side Conquest would incline. 5 SWIFT A certain magick rod . . divines Whene'er the soil has golden mines. R. W. EMERSON All things wait for and divine him.

II *v.i.* 7 Practise divination; obtain insight into or discovery of the unknown or the future by supernatural or magical means. LME. 8 Foretell the future by divine or superhuman power; prophesy. *arch.* LME. 9 Make an inference by sagacity, intuition, or fortunate conjecture; conjecture, guess. LME. †**b** Foll. by *of*, *on*, *upon*: make conjectures about, augur from. LME–E18.

7 **divining-rod** = *dowsing-rod* s.v. DOWSE *v.*[1] 9 SHAKES. *Oth.* Something from Cyprus, as I may divine.

divinely /dɪˈvʌɪnli/ *adv.* LME. [f. DIVINE *a.* + -LY[2].] 1 With a superhuman excellence or perfection; *colloq.* excellently, delightfully, as well as one could wish. LME. 2 (As) by the agency or power of God or a god. L16. †3 In a holy or pious manner. L16–L17.

1 W. IRVING An elegant young man . . who danced a minuet divinely. 2 G. W. KNIGHT They might be divinely inspired.

diviner /dɪˈvʌɪnə/ *n.* ME. [AN *devinour*, *di-* = OFr. *devineör* etc. (corresp. to L *divinator*), f. *deviner*: see DIVINE *v.*, -ER[2]. In sense 2, after OFr. *divin* DIVINE *n.*[2]] 1 A person who practises divination; *spec.* a dowser. ME. **b** A successful conjecturer, a good guesser. L17. †2 A divine, a theologian; a wise man. LME–M16.

divineˈress *n.* (*arch.*) a female diviner LME.

diving /ˈdʌɪvɪŋ/ *vbl n.* LME. [f. DIVE *v.* + -ING[1].] The action of DIVE *v.*

Comb.: **diving-bell** (*a*) a vessel open at the bottom and with a supply of air in which a person can be let down into deep water; (*b*) the air-filled web in which the water-spider lives under water; **diving-board** an elevated board, projecting over water, for diving from; **diving-suit** a watertight suit, usu. with a helmet and air supply, for wearing when working under water.

diving /ˈdʌɪvɪŋ/ *ppl a.* L16. [f. DIVE *v.* + -ING[2].] That dives.

diving beetle any of various predatory water beetles of the family Dytiscidae, which are enabled to dive by the air stored under their elytra. **diving duck** a duck that habitually dives under water for food; *spec.* any of a tribe of mostly freshwater ducks exemplified by the pochard, scaup, tufted duck, etc. **diving petrel** a petrel of the family Pelecanoididae.

divinify /dɪˈvɪnɪfʌɪ/ *v.t.* M17. [f. L *divinus* DIVINE *a.* + -FY, after *deify*.] Make or regard as divine. Usu. in *pass.*

divinise *v.* var. of DIVINIZE.

divinitize /dɪˈvɪnɪtʌɪz/ *v.t. rare.* Also **-ise**. M17. [Irreg. f. next + -IZE.] = DIVINIZE.

divinity /dɪˈvɪnɪti/ *n.* ME. [(O)Fr. *divinité* f. L *divinitat-* (in Vulgate tr. Gk *theiotēs* and *theotēs*), f. *divinus* DIVINE *a.*: see -ITY.] 1 The organized body of knowledge dealing with the nature, attributes, and governance of God or *transf.* gods; theology. ME. 2 The character or quality of being God or sharing the nature of God; godhood; divine nature; deity, godhead. LME. 3 A divine or celestial being; a god, a goddess; *the* Deity. LME. †4 = DIVINATION 1. *rare.* LME–E17. 5 Quality, virtue, or power characteristic of or appropriate to God. E16. 6 More fully *divinity fudge*. A kind of fudge made with beaten white of egg and nuts. *N. Amer.* E20.

1 H. H. MILMAN He . . was versed in all the divinity of the Greeks. D. ATTENBOROUGH Darwin was far from being an atheist—he had . . taken a degree in divinity. 2 DAY LEWIS I grew up with certain assumptions . . : the divinity of Christ, the assurance of eternal life. 3 *fig.*: THACKERAY Composing a most flaming and conceited copy of verses to his divinity. 5 SHAKES. *Merry W.* There is divinity in odd numbers, either in nativity, chance, or death.

Comb.: **divinity calf** a dark brown calf leather with blind tooling, traditionally used for binding theological works; *divinity fudge*: see sense 6 above.

divinityship *n.* (*a*) the status or personality of a divinity, godship; (*b*) *rare* skill in or knowledge of divinity: L16.

divinize /ˈdɪvɪnʌɪz/ *v.t.* Also **-ise**. M17. [Fr. *diviniser*, f. *divin* DIVINE *a.*: see -IZE.] Make divine; deify.

diviniˈzation *n.* M19.

divisa /diˈvisa/ *n.* M20. [Sp. = device, emblem, ult. f. L *divis-*: see DEVICE, DIVISION.] *Bullfighting.* A bunch of coloured ribbons worn by a bull and denoting its breeder.

divisi /diˈviːsi/ *adv.*, *a.*, & *n.* M18. [It. = divided, pl. pa. ppl a. of *dividere* divide.] *Mus.* **A** *adv.* & *adj.* (A direction:) with a section of players divided into two or more groups each playing a different part. M18. **B** *n.* (The use of) *divisi* playing or scoring. M20.

divisible /dɪˈvɪzɪb(ə)l/ *a.* LME. [(O)Fr., or late L *divisibilis*, f. L *divis-*: see next, -IBLE.] 1 Able to be divided (actually or in thought); distributable; distinguishable. LME. 2 *Math.* Of a quantity: able to be divided without remainder *by* another quantity. Formerly, that is to be divided, forming the dividend. L16.

1 J. PRIESTLEY Every particle of matter is infinitely divisible. T. DREISER Giving her the half of his property, stocks, ready money, and anything else that might be divisible.

divisiˈbility *n.* M17. **divisibleness** *n.* (*rare*) divisibility M17. **divisibly** *adv.* M16.

division /dɪˈvɪʒ(ə)n/ *n.* LME. [OFr. *devisiun*, *di-* (mod. *division*) f. L *divisio(n-)*, f. *divis-* pa. ppl stem of *dividere* DIVIDE *v.*: see -ION.] **I** An action or condition. 1 The action of dividing or state of being divided into parts or branches; separation, partition; severance; an instance of this. LME. **b** (Also **D-**.) The separation of the members of a legislative body etc. into two groups in voting. M16. **c** The splitting of the roots of a perennial plant into parts to be replanted separately, as a means of propagation. E19. 2 The action of distributing among a number; distribution, sharing; an instance of this. LME. †3 The action or an act of distinguishing, or of perceiving or making a difference; (a) distinction. LME–E17. 4 The fact of being divided in opinion, sentiment, or interest; dissension, discord; an instance of this, a disagreement. LME. 5 *Math.* The action or process of dividing one quantity by another; a method of doing this. LME. 6 *Logic.* The action of dividing a wider class into two or more kinds or classes; enumeration of the parts of a whole or of the meanings of a term. M16. 7 *Mus.* The execution of a rapid melodic passage, esp. by dividing each of a succession of long notes into several short ones; a florid phrase or melody; *spec.* a variation (usu. improvised) on an accompanying melody. Now *Hist.* L16. †**b** *fig.* Variation. *rare* (Shakes.). Only in E17. †8 Disposition, arrangement. *rare* (Shakes.). Only in E17.

1 C. CAUDWELL The very division of industrial capitalism from agricultural capitalism has . . separated the country from the town. R. HOGGART There is a rough division of material into three themes. M. L. KING The . . division of India and Pakistan shattered his heart's desire for a united nation. 2 **division of labour** the assigning of different parts of a job or manufacturing process etc. to different people. 4 A. F. DOUGLAS-HOME Not to allow any division in the Cabinet which could be represented as a split on . . policy. 5 **long division** a method of division in which intermediate stages of the calculation are written down as it is made (used with divisors greater than 12). **short division** a method of division in which the quotient is written down directly (used with divisors up to 12). 7b SHAKES. *Macb.* The king-becoming graces, . . I have no relish of them; but abound In the division of each several crime, Acting it many ways.

II A cause or result of dividing. 9 Something that divides or marks separation; a dividing line or mark; a boundary; a partition. LME. **b** At Cambridge University, the date that divides the term into two halves. E19. 10 Each of the parts into which something is or may be divided; a portion, a section. LME. **b** Any of several major parts into which an organization, esp. an army, is divided; *spec.* a group of Army brigades or regiments; a portion of a ship's company assigned to a particular service (in *pl.*, the parade of a ship's company according to its divisions); a group of (esp. soccer) teams within a league between which fixtures are arranged. L16. **c** A portion of a country, county, etc., marked off for some political, administrative, judicial, etc., purpose; *spec.* a part of a county or borough returning a Member of Parliament. M17. **d** *Biol.* A section of a taxonomic grouping; *Bot.* a basic taxonomic grouping ranking above class and below kingdom, equivalent to a phylum; *Zool.* a subsidiary category between major levels of classification. M19. **e** *Hist.* Either of the two or three categories of imprisonment without hard labour or penal servitude to which an offender could be sentenced. M19.

9 E. RUTHERFORD The maximum excursion of the needle . . being not more than three scale divisions. 10 F. SMYTH Over the years, more divisions of blood type

. . have been discovered. *Practical Gardening* Divide and transplant border perennials, . . only replanting the strongest, healthiest divisions. **b** *Family Division*: see FAMILY. **e** ALDOUS HUXLEY The appeal . . won't . . do any good except perhaps to change his six months from second to first division.

Comb. **division-bell**: rung to announce an imminent parliamentary division; *division lobby*: see LOBBY *n.* 3a; **division sign** the sign ÷, placed between two quantities to denote that the one preceding the sign is to be divided by the one following it.

divisionary *a.* (*rare*) divisional M17.

divisional /dɪˈvɪʒ(ə)n(ə)l/ *a.* M17. [f. prec. + -AL¹.] **1** Of the nature of division; pertaining to or characterized by division. M17. **2** Of or pertaining to a division. M19.

2 Divisional Court: consisting of two or three judges from a Division of the High Court.

divisionaliˈzation *n.* (the introduction of) a divisional organization or structure M20. **divisionalize** *v.t.* organize (esp. a company) on a divisional basis L20 **divisionally** *adv.* L18.

divisionism /dɪˈvɪʒ(ə)nɪz(ə)m/ *n.* E20. [f. as prec. + -ISM.] *Art.* The practice of painting with pure colours, using the juxtaposition of contrasting unmixed colours in place of mixed colours.

divisionist *a.* & *n.* (*a*) *adj.* of or pertaining to divisionism; (*b*) *n.* a practitioner or adherent of divisionism: E20.

divisive /dɪˈvʌɪsɪv/ *n.* & *a.* M16. [Late L *divisivus*, f. L *divis-*: see DIVISION, -IVE.] †**A** *n.* Something which divides or separates. *rare.* Only in M16. **B** *adj.* **1** Having the quality or function of dividing; causing or expressing division or distribution; making or perceiving distinctions, analytical. L16. **2** Producing or tending to division of opinion, discord, or disunion. M17.

1 CARLYLE As the one spirit was intuitive, all-embracing . . so the other was scholastic, divisive. **2** A. WEST The class of explosively divisive happenings that cause men and women to think *Enough!* and walk out on their lovers.

divisively *adv.* L15. **divisiveness** *n.* M19.

divisor /dɪˈvʌɪzə/ *n.* LME. [Fr. *diviseur* or L *divisor*, f. *divis-*: see DIVISION, -OR.] *Math.* **1** A quantity by which another (the *dividend*) is to be divided. LME. **2** A quantity that divides another exactly without a remainder; a factor. M16.

divisory /dɪˈvʌɪz(ə)ri/ *a.* E17. [med.L *divisorius*, f. L *divis-*: see DIVISION, -ORY².] Pertaining to division or distribution among a number.

divorce /dɪˈvɔːs/ *n.* LME. [(O)Fr. f. L *divortium* separation, divorce, f. *divortere*, *divertere* DIVERT.] **1** Legal dissolution of marriage by a court or other competent body, or according to recognized forms; a decree dissolving a marriage. LME. **2** Severance, complete separation, esp. of what ought to be or have been united. LME. †**3** Something which causes divorce or separation. *rare* (Shakes.). L16–E17.

1 G. GORER The people who would end the marriage legally, by divorce or separation. Attrib.: *divorce case, court, law*, etc. **2** B. RUSSELL Slavery began the divorce between the purpose of the work and the purposes of the worker.

divorceless *a.* not practising or liable to divorce L16.

divorce /dɪˈvɔːs/ *v.* LME. [(O)Fr. *divorcer* f. late L *divortiare*, f. *divortium*: see DIVORCE *n.*] **1** *v.t.* Legally dissolve the marriage of (a husband and wife); separate (a spouse) by divorce *from*. Freq. in *pass.* LME. **2** *v.t.* Obtain a divorce from (a husband or wife). LME. **3** *v.t. fig.* Separate, sever, detach, (*from*). LME. **4** *v.t.* Dissolve (a marriage or union). *arch.* L16. **5** *v.t. fig.* Put away, remove, dispel; repudiate. *arch.* L16. **6** *v.i.* Legally dissolve one's marriage, obtain a divorce. M17.

1 SHAKES. *3 Hen. VI* I here divorce myself Both from thy table, Henry, and thy bed. **2** O. MANNING Quintin is married already and his wife won't divorce him. **3** R. NIEBUHR If a socialist commonwealth should succeed in divorcing privilege from power. **5** SHAKES. *Rich. II* The man That would divorce this terror from my heart. **6** J. CHEEVER She had left me twice before—the second time, we divorced and then remarried.

divorceable *a.* M17. **divorcement** *n.* the action of divorcing; the fact of being divorced; complete separation: E16. **divorcer** *n.* E17.

divorcé *n.* see DIVORCEE.

divorcee /dɪvɔːˈsiː/ *n.* Also (earlier) ***divorcé***, (fem.) ***-ée***, /divɔrse (*pl. same*), dɪvɔːˈseɪ/. E19. [Partly f. Fr. *divorcé(e)* use as n. of pa. ppl a. of *divorcer* DIVORCE *v.*, partly f. DIVORCE *v.* + -EE¹ after the Fr.] A divorced person.

divot /ˈdɪvət/ *n.* & *v.* E16. [Origin unkn.] **A** *n.* **1** A slice of earth with the grass growing on it, a sod, esp. as formerly used for roofing cottages etc.; such sods collectively. *Sc.* & *north.* E16. **2** *Golf.* A piece of turf cut out by the club-head when a stroke is made. L19.

1 *fail and divot*: see FAIL *n.*¹

B *v. Sc.* **1** *v.t.* Roof (a building) with divots. L17. **2** *v.i.* Cut divots. L18.

divulgate /dʌɪˈvʌlgeɪt, dɪ-/ *v.t.* Now *rare*. Pa. pple & ppl a. †**-ate** (earlier), **-ated**. LME. [L *divulgat-* pa. ppl stem of *divulgare*: see next, -ATE³.] Make commonly known.

divulˈgation *n.* †(*a*) publication; (*b*) disclosure: M16.

divulge /dʌɪˈvʌldʒ, dɪ-/ *v.* LME. [L *divulgare*, f. as DIS- 1 + *vulgare* publish, propagate, f. *vulgus* common people.] †**1** *v.t.* Make publicly known; publish (a statement, book, etc.). LME–L18. †**b** Make a public announcement about (a person). L16–L17. **2** *v.t.* Declare or tell openly (something private or secret); disclose, reveal. E17. **3** *v.i.* Become publicly known. *rare.* E17. †**4** *v.t.* Make common, impart generally. *rare* (Milton). Only in M17.

1b SHAKES. *Merry W.* I will . . divulge Page himself for a secure and wilful Actæon. **2** M. LAVIN Plans which . . he would shortly have to divulge to the family. G. SWIFT Freddie . . was a great blabber-mouth and divulged everything.

divulgement *n.* †(*a*) *rare* something that is divulged; (*b*) divulgence: M17. **divulgence** *n.* the action of divulging, disclosure M19. **divulger** *n.* E17.

divulsion /dʌɪˈvʌlʃ(ə)n, dɪ-/ *n.* Now *rare.* E17. [Fr., or L *divulsio(n-)*, f. *divuls-*: see next, -ION.] The action of tearing or pulling apart; violent separation.

divulsive /dʌɪˈvʌlsɪv, dɪ-/ *a.* Now *rare.* E17. [f. L *divuls-* pa. ppl stem of *divellere* (see DIVELL) + -IVE.] Tending to tear apart.

Divvers /ˈdɪvəz/ *n.* *Oxford Univ. slang.* Now *Hist.* L19. [f. DIVINITY: see -ER⁶.] Divinity moderations (the first public examination in divinity).

divvy /ˈdɪvi/ *n.*¹ & *v.* *colloq.* Also **divi**. L19. [Abbrev. of DIVIDEND.] **A** *n.* A dividend; a share, a portion. L19. **B** *v.t.* & *i.* foll. by *up.* Divide (*up*), share. L19.

divvy /ˈdɪvi/ *a.*¹ *slang.* Now *rare.* E20. [f. DIVINE *a.* + -Y¹. Cf. DEEVY.] Delightful, 'divine', 'heavenly'.

divvy /ˈdɪvi/ *a.*² & *n.*² *dial.* & *slang.* L20. [Origin unkn.] **A** *adj.* Foolish, idiotic. L20. **B** *n.* A fool, an idiot. L20.

Diwali /dɪˈwɑːliː/ *n.* Also **Dewali, Divali**. L17. [Hindi *diwālī* f. Skt *dīpāvalī*, *dīpālī* row of lights, f. *dīpa* light, lamp.] A Hindu festival with lights, held over three nights in the period October to November, to celebrate the new season at the end of the monsoon.

diwan(i) *ns.* vars. of DEWAN(I).

dix /diːs/ *n.* L19. [Fr. = ten, f. L *decem*.] The lowest trump in bezique and related card-games, entitling a player to a score of ten points.

dix-huitième /dizɥitjɛm/ *a.* & *n.* E20. [Fr. = eighteenth.] (Of or pertaining to) the eighteenth century.

Dixie /ˈdɪksi/ *n.*¹ *US.* M19. [Origin unkn.] The southern States of the US, the South.

Comb.: **Dixieland** (*a*) Dixie; (*b*) a kind of jazz characterized by a rhythm strongly accenting the second and fourth beats and by collective improvisation.

Dixiecrat *n.* (*colloq.*) any of the southern Democrats who seceded from the party in 1948 in opposition to its policy of extending civil rights; any dissident or right-wing Democrat: M20.

dixie /ˈdɪksi/ *n.*² E20. [Hind. *degcī* cooking-pot f. Pers. *degča* dim. of *deg* iron pot.] A large iron kettle or pot in which stew, tea, etc., is made or carried by soldiers etc.

dixit /ˈdɪksɪt/ *n.* L16. [L = he has said: see IPSE DIXIT.] An utterance or statement (quoted as) already made.

diz /dɪz/ *v.* & *n.* Now *rare.* Also **dizz**. M17. [Back-form. f. DIZZY *a.* after *craze*, *crazy*, etc.] **A** *v.t.* Infl. **-zz-**. Make dizzy or giddy. M17. **B** *n.* The action of making dizzy or giddy. *rare.* E19.

dizen /ˈdʌɪz(ə)n, ˈdɪ-/ *v.t.* Now *arch.* & *poet.* M16. [f. base repr. by the 1st syll. of DISTAFF and in MDu. *disen* (perh. the immediate source): see -EN⁵.] †**1** Dress (a distaff) with flax etc. for spinning. M–L16. **2** Dress, esp. with finery; deck *out*, bedizen. Also foll. by *up*. E17.

dizygotic /dʌɪzʌɪˈgɒtɪk/ *a.* M20. [f. DI-² + ZYGOTE + -IC] Of twins: derived from two separate ova, and so not identical.

dizygous /dʌɪˈzʌɪgəs/ *a.* M20. [f. DI-² + Gk *zugon* yoke + -OUS.] = prec.

dizz *v.* & *n.* var. of DIZ.

dizzard /ˈdɪzɑːd/ *n.* Now *rare* or *obs.* Also **disard**. E16. [Origin uncertain: perh. modified f. DISOUR; in sense 2 app. assoc. w. DIZZY *a.*] †**1** = DISOUR. E16–E17. **2** A fool, a blockhead. M16.

dizzy /ˈdɪzi/ *a.* [OE *dysiġ* = OFris. *dusig*, MDu. *dosech*, *dösech*, LG *dusig*, *dösig* giddy, OHG *tusic* foolish, weak, f. WGmc: see -Y¹.] **1** Foolish, stupid. Long *obs.* exc. *dial.* OE. **2** Having a sensation of whirling in the head with one's sense of balance disordered and a consequent tendency to fall; giddy. ME. **3** Mentally or morally unsteady or in a whirl; lacking mental or moral stability; *colloq.* scatterbrained. E16. **4** Accompanied by or producing dizziness; making dizzy; *spec.* (of a mountain, tower, etc.) very high. E17. **5** Arising from or caused by giddiness; reeling, tottering. E18. **6** Whirling rapidly (*lit.* & *fig.*). L18. **7** Startling, astonishing. *slang.* L19.

3 B. JOWETT My head is dizzy with thinking of the argument. D. HAMMETT A dizzy blonde that likes men and fun and hasn't got much sense. **5** GEO. ELIOT Thought gave way to a dizzy horror, as if the earth were slipping away from under him.

dizzily *adv.* ME. **dizziness** *n.* OE.

dizzy /ˈdɪzi/ *v.* [OE *dysiġan* = OFris. *dusia*; branch II re-formed f. the adj.] †**I** *v.i.* **1** Act foolishly or stupidly. OE–ME.

II *v.t.* **2** Make dizzy. E16. **3** Bewilder, confuse mentally. E17.

3 J. BARZUN World trade was increasing at a dizzying rate.

dizzyingly *adv.* in a dizzying manner, amazingly, bewilderingly E20.

Dizzyite /ˈdɪzɪʌɪt/ *n.* L19. [f. *Dizzy*, nickname of Benjamin Disraeli (see below) + -ITE¹.] A follower or admirer of the Conservative statesman and writer Benjamin Disraeli (1804–81).

djellaba(h) *n.* var. of JELLABA.

djibba(h) *n.* var. of JIBBA.

djinn *n.* see JINNEE.

DNA /diːɛnˈeɪ/ *n.* M20. [Abbrev. of DEOXYRIBONUCLEIC *acid*.] A nucleic acid in which the sugar component is deoxyribose; a self-replicating material present in nearly all living organisms, esp. in chromosomes, as the carrier of genetic information and the determiner of protein synthesis, usu. occurring as a molecular double helix in which a phosphate group alternates with a deoxyribose sugar linked to a base. Cf. RNA.

Comb.: **DNA polymerase** any of several enzymes which synthesize DNA and are responsible for its repair and replication; **DNA virus** a virus in which the genetic information is stored in the form of DNA.

DNase /diːɛnˈeɪz/ *n.* an enzyme which breaks DNA up into smaller molecules, a deoxyribonuclease M20.

do /duː/ *n.*¹ Pl. **dos, do's**. L16. [f. DO *v.*] **1 a** The action of doing; that which is done; business, concern; in *pl.*, affairs. Now *rare* or *obs.* L16. **b** Something done in a set or elaborate manner; an entertainment; a party, a social function; a military engagement. *colloq.* E19. **c** *sing.* & (usu.) in *pl.* Behaviour towards someone, treatment. Chiefly in *fair dos*, equitable treatment, fair shares. *colloq.* M19. **2** Commotion, trouble; a fuss, an ado. *obs.* exc. *dial.* L16. **3** A swindle; an imposture; a hoax. *slang.* E19. **4** A success. Only in *make a do of*. *Austral.* & *NZ colloq.* E20. **5** An instruction; an injunction to do something. Usu. in *pl.* in *dos and don'ts*. E20. **6** = *hairdo* s.v. HAIR *n. colloq.* E20. **7** Excrement. *nursery* or *slang*. L20.

1a O. CROMWELL It's probable the Kirk has done their doo. **b** B. BAINBRIDGE Met him at a masonic do last year. *poor do*: see POOR *a.*

do *n.*[2] var. of DOH.

do /duː, *unstressed* dʊ/ *v.* Pres. indic.: 1, 2, *pl.*, & (*dial.*) 3 **do**; 3 **does** /dʌz, d(ə)z/; 2 (*arch.*) **doest** /ˈduːɪst/ (now confined to the principal vb), **dost** /dʌst, dəst/ (now usu. aux.); 3 (*arch.* & *poet.*) **doth** /dʌθ, dəθ/ or **doeth** /ˈduːɪθ/. Past indic.: **did** /dɪd/; also (*colloq.*, *dial.*, & *non-standard US*) **done** /dʌn/, 2 (*arch.*) **didst** /dɪdst/. Pres. subjunct.: **do**. Past subjunct.: **did**. Imper. **do**. Pres. pple **doing** /ˈduːɪŋ/. Pa. pple **done**. Informal abbrev. forms: **didn't** /ˈdɪd(ə)nt/ = *did not*; **doesn't** /ˈdʌz(ə)nt/ = *does not*; **don't** /dəʊnt/ = *do not*, (*non-standard*) *does not*; **'s** /s/ = *does* (interrog.). Sc. forms: **dae** /deɪ/ = *do*; **dinna** /ˈdɪnə/ = *do not*, **disna** /ˈdɪznə/ = *does not*. See also DUNNO. [OE *dōn* corresp. to OFris. *duā*, OS *dōn* (Du. *doen*), OHG *tuon* (G *tun*), f. WGmc f. IE stem repr. also by Skt *dadhāmi* put, lay, Gk *tithēmi* I place, L *facere* make, do. Cf. DEED *n.*, DOOM *n.*[1]] **I** *v.t.* as full vb. **1 a** Put, place, (*lit.* & *fig.*). *obs.* exc. *dial.*, with preps. (see *do off* etc. below), & in *do to* DEATH. OE. **†b** *refl.* Put or set oneself; proceed, go. Only in ME. **†c** Use, disburse, (money) for a particular purpose. LME–E16. **2** Confer on, impart to, (a person etc.); cause (a person etc.) to receive (something abstract, usu. good). Also foll. by *to* the recipient. OE. **3** Perform, effect, engage in, be the agent of, (an action, good, work, etc.); carry out (a function, duty, etc.); carry out, obey, (a command, wish, etc.); follow (advice, a bidding); perform duly (a ritual, esp. penance); *arch.* commit (a crime). OE. **b** In an interrog. or indef. cl. introduced by *what*: follow as an occupation, work at for a living. E20. **4 a** As pa. pple (*done*), esp. in perf. tenses. Accomplished, finished, brought to a conclusion; (of a wager etc.) accepted, agreed, (freq. *absol.* as *int.*). ME. **b** Exhaust; ruin, be the downfall of, (a person); *slang* beat up, kill, defeat. LME. **c** In *pass.* Have nothing more to say or to do; have finished; (foll. by *with*) give up concern or lose interest in. M18. **5** Exert or use (one's best, one's diligence, etc.) in effecting something. ME. **†6** Deliver (a message). E16–E18. **7** Deal with, do things to, perform actions on, (the nature of the action being usu. inferable from the obj. or subj.); *esp.* arrange (hair, flowers); decorate or clean (a room); cook (food), esp. to the right degree (usu. in *pass.*); wash (crockery); tend (a garden); attend to (a person), subject (a person) to immunization, a test, etc.; neuter or spay (an animal). E16. **8** Produce, bring into existence by one's action. L16. **b** Of a public house, hotel, etc.: provide (meals, accommodation). L20. **9** Act (a play); play the part of. L16. **10** Work at, study; take (a course of instruction); (of an artist, reviewer, etc.) take as one's subject; translate (*into*). M17. **11** Hoax, cheat, swindle. *slang*. M17. **12** Traverse (a distance); attain, travel at, (a speed). L18. **13** Break into, steal from, (a place). *slang*. L18. **14** Arrest; charge with an offence; convict. *slang*. L18. **15** Visit, see the sights of, (a place); attend (an entertainment). *colloq.* E19. **16** Spend (a time) as a prisoner, serve. *slang*. M19. **17** Be sufficient for, satisfy, (a person). Cf. sense 27 below. *colloq.* M19. **18** Orig., drink (an alcoholic liquor). Now, take or smoke (a drug) otherwise than therapeutically. *slang*. M19. **19** Provide food or lodgings for; treat or entertain *well*. *colloq.* L19. **20** Look after and manage (a horse); *dial.* & *NZ* look after, provide food for, (sheep). L19. **21** Have sexual intercourse with. L19. **22** Spend all of. Also foll. by *in*. *Austral.* & *NZ slang*. L19.

1a J. FOXE If I would not tell where I had done him. W. STEWART He did him in his will. **2** LD BERNERS The which dyd them great trouble. F. MARRYAT I did a gipsy a good turn once. S. WALPOLE A day's sport which would have done credit to these modern days. M. KEANE A brisk walk would do you good. W. GOLDING To call them 'assistants' does their memory scant justice. **3** AV *Matt.* 6:10 Thy will be done. DEFOE We knew not what to do with this poor girl. R. H. MOTTRAM Powerful, docile servants of a younger age, that could do the work of ten men. V. WOOLF As the whole thing is a bad joke, let us, at any rate, do our part. IRVING BERLIN Anything you can do, I can do better. E. WAUGH A smartly dressed young man was doing a brisk trade in bogus tickets. C. P. SNOW It doesn't do any harm to touch wood. **b** J. BETJEMAN You ask me what it is I do... I'm partly a liaison man and partly P.R.O. **4a** SWIFT When dinner is done. DICKENS 'Dine with me to-morrow.'.. 'Done!' RIDER HAGGARD By the time that the horses had done their forage. D. L. SAYERS Mr. Bunter congratulated himself on a number of things attempted and done. S. BECKETT Have you not done tormenting me? **c** F. MARRYAT One little bit more, and then I am done. E. REVELEY Heidi was soon done with literature. **5** DEFOE They bade the Swedes do their worst. P. H. JOHNSON I do my best for her. **7** M. DRABBLE The spaghetti was not quite done. J. WINTERSON She played *Lead Kindly Light*. Her doing the keys, and me doing the pedals. **8** C. HOLLYBAND We have done five or six copies in the same paper. E. NESBIT It's the pipe we did bubbles with in the summer. **b** W. J. BURLEY The Marina doesn't do meals other than breakfast. **9** E. BOWEN Colonel Duperrier asked her to pour out tea and do hostess. *Times* Institutions under threat of closure.. are saying 'They're doing a Beeching on us.' **10** R. BUCHANAN There Amos often sat and did his accounts. O. W. HOLMES Life is painting a picture, not doing a sum. I. MURDOCH She'll.. do a secretarial course next year. G. SWIFT Children, do you remember when we did the French Revolution? **12** T. MOORE Did the four miles in less than twenty minutes. G. B. SHAW The old cars only do twelve miles to the gallon. J. MASTERS Patrick passed us on his Norton, doing about seventy. **14** S. TOWNSEND If he's not careful he will get done by the police for obscene language. **17** M. GEE Will fish and chips do you? **19** J. K. JEROME He said they would do him for the whole week at two pounds five.

II *v.i.* as full vb. **23** Act or behave in a specified way; perform some activity. OE. **b** Perform deeds; be active. LME. **24** Proceed in an emergency or difficulty; manage, get by. ME. **25** Fare, get on, make progress, *spec.* as regards health. Foll. by adv., esp. *well*. ME. **26** In perf. tenses (*have* etc. *done*). Make an end, conclude; cease to have dealings *with*. ME. **27** Serve a purpose, suffice; be adequate; be suitable, acceptable, or appropriate. Cf. sense 17 above. L16.

23 J. SELDEN Preachers say, Do as I say, not as I do. A. RADCLIFFE He had done imprudently to elect her for the companion of his whole life. N. MITFORD When in Rome.. we do as the Romans do. **b** LONGFELLOW Let us.. be up and doing. G. K. CHESTERTON At Trafalgar.. We did and died like lions. *Times* Younger people, with no money and no showrooms but ready to do for themselves. **24** SHAKES. *Rich. II* How shall we do for money for these wars? R. MACAULAY They could just do on it.. with what she herself earned. **25** SHAKES. *2 Hen. IV* May I ask how my lady his wife doth? E. B. BROWNING She was ill only three hours and is doing excellently now. M. DRABBLE Mrs Maugham had done well at school. J. GRENFELL Say how-do-you-do to Mr Hindhorst. C. CAUSLEY Telling him How the lobelias are doing. **26** CARLYLE There is endless merit in a man's knowing when to have done. W. GOLDING Let us have done with her for a moment. **27** CHESTERFIELD Adieu, my dear! I find you will do. E. A. FREEMAN It would hardly have done to send him. I. MURDOCH Would the same time on Sunday morning do for Miles? P. CAMPBELL I had one fairly good dark suit.. that would do for the evenings.

III As aux. vb (see also sense 35 below). **28** Causative uses. **†a** Cause *that* a person or thing should do something; produce the effect *that*. OE–LME. **b** With obj. & inf.: cause (a person etc.) to or *to* (do something, esp. know, or be done). Now *arch. rare*. OE. **†c** With inf. only: cause to or *to* (do or be done). ME–M16. **29** As a substitute for a vb just used. **a** *v.i.* Repl. a vb & its obj. (if any) in affirmatives, and in imperatives conveying assent to a request or suggestion. OE. **b** *v.i.* & *t.* (w. *it*). Repl. a vb, with *as*, *it*, *so*, or *which* referring to the earlier vb or cl. OE. **c** *v.t.* & *i.* Repl. a vb and taking its construction(s). ME. **d** *v.i.* Repl. a vb in an emphatic repetition. L16. **e** *v.i.* Ellipt. for periphrastic aux. (sense 30 below). E17. **30** As periphrastic aux. in past and pres. tenses. **a** In simple affirmative sentences. Now *arch.* & *dial.* exc. *Law*. OE. **b** In affirmative sentences w. inverted wd order. OE. **c** In questions and negations; the now usual foll. by exc. w. *dare*, *ought*; not used w. *be*, *can*, *may*, or *must*, nor w. *have* as aux. (nor, formerly, w. *have* as v.t.). LME. **d** In affirmative sentences, used to give emphasis, esp. in contrast w. what precedes or follows. L16. **31** As periphrastic aux. in imperatives. **a** Adding emphasis or urgency to an exhortation or command. OE. **b** Used w. *not* (colloq. jointly contr. to *don't*) as the now normal form of the neg. imper. L16. **32** In progressive active tense (*be doing*): **a** Happen, go on; (of an activity or, formerly, an object) be being done. Cf. *nothing doing* below. ME. **b** In an interrog. or indef. cl. introduced by *what*: have as an explanation or reason for being (in a place). M18.

28b SPENSER Sometimes, to do him laugh, she would assay To laugh. SIR W. SCOTT We.. do thee, Sir Patrick Charteris.. to know, that [etc.]. **29a** J. COLLINS We pay double the price we formerly did. G. B. SHAW *Lady Farwaters*. May I try to explain? *The Clergyman*. Please do. D. ABSE I feel much better now than I did a month ago. **b** W. CRUISE Whoever wanted to surrender must.. do it in person. S. T. WARNER He told them to go away, he even begged them to do so. A. T. ELLIS The churches are closing, as the cinemas did. **c** GOLDSMITH I.. chose my wife, as she did her wedding-gown. **d** P. BEER He rang me up In a dream, My brother did. D. L. SAYERS 'Ev another crumpet, do, Mr. Bunter. **e** J. CONRAD Everybody supposed Haldin was in the provinces... Didn't you? E. BOWEN 'I cleared out.' 'So you did.' **30a** *Book of Common Prayer* O Lord, who.. didst fast fourty days and fourty nights. **b** J. CONRAD More than any other event does 'stranding' bring to the sailor a sense of.. failure. **c** H. HUNTER Do we not see there.. talents distracted? J. FISKE The popular histories do not have much to say about these eighteen days. ANTHONY SMITH Do you like water-melon? **d** T. HARDY At last a packet did indeed arrive at the village. S. SPENDER The Dents du Midi do look incredibly like teeth. R. P. JHABVALA For all she was so thin and white, she did look tough. **31a** T. HARDY Do you hop up here. M. KEANE Oh Mother, do let them come. **b** J. CONRAD And don't you forget it. DYLAN THOMAS Do not go gentle into that good night. **32** S. PEPYS My closett is doing by upholsters. M. W. MONTAGU What is doing among my acquaintance at London. L. MANN He had invited her so that he might ascertain whether there was anything doing. **b** J. JOHNSTON What's that fellow doing here? I. MURDOCH She lay awake wondering what that.. hairy body was doing in her bed.

IV *spec.* uses of parts of the vb (see also senses 4, 26, 32 above). **33** *to do* inf., after *be* (in 3rd person) or a n.: proper or necessary to be done; (formerly also) the thing to be done. Cf. TO-DO. ME. **†34** *do* imper.: go on! (as a wd of encouragement or incitement). LME–E17. **35** *done* pa. pple: used as a perfective aux., and as adv. in senses 'already', 'completely'. *US dial.* E19. **36** *don't*: used in 3rd person neg. imperatives after *let's*, in place of simple *not*. *US slang*. M20.

33 P. A. MOTTEUX There was the Devil and all to do. **35** J. H. BEADLE People have done forgot they had any Injun blood in 'em. E. T. WALLACE I don't know what you need with another boy. You done got four. F. O'CONNOR He done gone off with a woman. **36** *New Yorker* Let's don't go yet.

Phrases: **do a —** *colloq.* behave like, do an impersonation of, (a specified person). *do a guy*: see GUY *n.*[2] *do a hand's turn*: see HAND *n.* *do a line with*: see LINE *n.*[2] *do a number on*: see NUMBER *n.* *do (any) good*: see GOOD *n.* *do a person in the eye*: see EYE *n.* **do (a person) proud** *colloq.* give (a person, oneself) reason for being proud, treat with honour or great generosity. *do a person wrong*: see WRONG *n.*[2] *do a* or *the ton*: see TON *n.*[1] *do battle*: see BATTLE *n.* *do brown*: see BROWN *a.* 3. *do dirt to*: see DIRT *n.* *do good*: see *do any good* above. *do homage*: see HOMAGE *v.* 1. **do it** (*a*) *colloq.* have sexual intercourse; (*b*) *slang* urinate; defecate; (*c*) succeed in a task etc. *done to a turn*: see TURN *n.* **don't — me** *colloq.* do not use the word — or mention the name of — to me. *do one's bit*: see BIT *n.*[2] *do one's block*: see BLOCK *n.* 6b. **do oneself well** *colloq.* make liberal provision for one's creature comforts (cf. sense 17 above). **do one's head** or **nut** *slang* become very worried or angry. *do one's (own) thing*: see THING *n.*[1] *do one's scone*: see SCONE 3. *do one's stuff*: see STUFF *n.* *do* *one's utmost*: see UTMOST *n.* 2b. **do or die** perform deeds in the face of great danger. *do right by*: see RIGHT *n.*[1] **do something for** or to *colloq.* enhance the appearance or quality of. **do the —** *colloq.* do what is (proper etc.), be (amiable etc.); (*do the dirty*: see DIRTY *n.*). *do the other thing*: see OTHER *a. do the ton*: see TON *n.*[1] *do the trick*: see TRICK *n. do things to*: see THING *n.*[1] *do to* DEATH. *do violence to* or *unto*: see VIOLENCE. **do well for oneself** prosper. **do well out of** profit by, benefit from. *do wonders*: see WONDER *n. do wrong to*: see WRONG *n.*[2] *do your worst*: see WORST *a., adv.,* & *n. get done with*: see GET *v.* **have done it** *colloq.* have made a mess of something, incur disaster (see also *do it* above); *that's done it*, (*a*) (expr. dismay or exasperation) the limit of tolerance has been reached, that is the last straw; (*b*) (expr. delight) that achieves the desired end, that has brought success. **have to do** (*a*) *arch.* & *dial.* have business or concern (freq. *interrog.*); (*b*) be connected *with*, have business *with*, (freq. as *have nothing*, or *not have anything, to do*). *how do (you do)?*: see HOW *adv. I* NEVER *did!* **it is not** (usu. **isn't**) **done** *colloq.* it contravenes custom, opinion, or propriety. *make do*: see MAKE *v.* **nothing doing** nothing is happening, there is no business; *colloq.* there is no chance of success; I will not comply or accept. **not know what to do with oneself** be embarrassed, be bored. **no you don't** *colloq.* I will prevent you (from doing what you were about to do or have just begun). *over and done with*: see OVER *adv. tell a person what to do with —*: see TELL *v.* **that will** (or **that'll**) **do** (*a*) that is sufficient; (*b*) (as exclam.) stop that! **what did you, shall I,** etc., **do with it?** where did you, shall I, etc., put it? *when all is said and done*: see SAY *v.*[1]

With advs. in specialized senses: **do away** †(*a*) *v.phr.t.* dismiss, remove; (*b*) *v.phr.t.*, & (now usu.) *i.* w. *with* put an end to, abolish. **do down** †(*a*) put down (*lit.* & *fig.*); (*b*) *colloq.* overcome; cheat, swindle. **do in** *slang* damage greatly, ruin; murder; (see also sense 21 above, DONE *ppl a.* 3). **do off** *arch.* take off, remove. **do on** *arch.* put on, don. **do out** †(*a*) put out (*of*), remove, extinguish; (*b*) clean, redecorate, refurbish, (a room); (*c*) *do a person out of*, deprive of, esp. fraudulently or unfairly. **do over** (*a*) overlay, cover, *with*; (*b*) *slang* = sense 11 above; (*c*) *colloq.* wear out, tire out, (usu. in *pass.*); (*d*) *Austral.* & *NZ slang* handle (a person) roughly; (*e*) *slang* = sense 21 above; (*f*) = *do out* (b) above; (*g*) *N. Amer.* do again. **do up** †(*a*) put up, raise, open; (*b*) repair, renovate; (*c*) wrap up (a parcel), make into a parcel; (*d*) dress up, adorn; (*e*) *slang* ruin; get the better of; beat up; (see also DONE *ppl a.* 3).

With preps. in specialized senses: **do by** act towards or deal with (a person) in a specified way. **do for** (*a*) (now *colloq.*) act for, manage; provide for, attend to; *esp.* act as housekeeper for; (*b*) *colloq.* ruin, seriously damage or injure, destroy, kill; (see also sense 27 above). **do to** or (*arch.*) **unto** = *do by* above; (see also sense 2 above). **do with** (*a*) deal with, have to do with; (*b*) put up with, tolerate, accept; manage with, find sufficient; *could do with* (colloq.), would find useful or should like to have; (see also senses 4,26 and in Phrases above). **do without** manage without (something specified or (*absol.*) understood contextually); complete a task without.

doab /ˈdəʊab/ *n.* Also **duab** /ˈduːab/. E19. [Urdu f. Pers. *dō-āb*, f. *dō* two + *āb* water.] A tongue or tract of land between two confluent rivers, esp. in the Punjab.

doable /ˈduːəb(ə)l/ *a.* LME. [f. DO *v.* + -ABLE.] Able to be done; practicable.

do-all /ˈduːɔːl/ *n.* Now *rare.* M17. [f. DO *v.* + ALL.] A factotum.

doat *v.* var. of DOTE *v.*[1]

doater *n.* var. of DOTER.

doatish *a.* var. of DOTISH.

doaty *n.* var. of DOTEY.

doaty *a.* var. of DOTY *a.*

dob /dɒb/ *v.* E19. [Var. of DAB *v.*] **1** *v.t.* Put down with an abrupt movement. *dial.* E19. **2** *v.t.* & *i.* Throw (a stone etc.) at a target. *dial.* M19. **3** *v.t.* Foll. by *in*: betray, inform against. *slang* (chiefly *Austral.*). M20.

dobber /ˈdɒbə/ *n.*[1] *US local.* E19. [Du.] The float of a fishing-line.

dobber /ˈdɒbə/ *n.*[2] M19. [Prob. f. DOB *v.* + -ER[1].] **1** A lump; something unusually large. *dial.* M19. **2** A large marble. Chiefly *dial.* L19.

dobbie *n.* var. of DOBBY.

dobbin /ˈdɒbɪn/ *n.* L16. [The pers. name *Dobbin* (dim. of *Dob*), altered forms of *Robin*, *Rob.* Sense 2 is perh. a distinct wd.] **1** (A pet name for) a draught horse or farm horse. Sometimes *contempt.*, an old horse. L16. **2** A small drinking-vessel; *esp.* a short thick glass tumbler. L18.

dobby /ˈdɒbi/ *n.* Also **dobbie.** L17. [Perh. a playful application of pers. name *Dobbie*, f. *Dob* (see prec.) + -IE.] **1** A stupid fellow; a booby, a dunce. *dial.* L17. **2** A spirit or apparition attached to a particular house or locality; *esp.* a household brownie. *dial.* L18. **3** A mechanism attached to a loom for weaving small devices similar to but simpler than those produced by a Jacquard loom. L19. **4** In full *dobby-horse.* A wooden figure of a horse, used in folk-plays or fairgrounds. Cf. HOBBY-HORSE *n.* L19.

Comb.: **dobby-weave** a patterned weave consisting of small geometric devices repeated frequently.

dobchick *n.* see DABCHICK.

dobe /ˈdəʊbi/ *n. US colloq.* Also **'dobe, dobie, doby.** M19. [Aphet.] = ADOBE.

Dobermann /ˈdəʊbəmən/ *n.* Also **-man.** E20. [Ludwig *Dobermann*, 19th-cent. Ger. dog-breeder.] In full *Dobermann pinscher.* (An animal of) a medium-sized breed of dog with a smooth coat, freq. used as a guard dog.

dobey /ˈdəʊbi/ *v.t. Naut. slang.* Also **dhob-.** E20. [f. DHOBI.] Wash (clothes). Chiefly as *dobeying* vbl n.

dobie *n.* var. of DOBE.

dobla /ˈdəʊblə/ *n. obs.* exc. *Hist.* L16. [Sp. Cf. *doble* double.] An obsolete Spanish gold coin.

Dobos Torte /ˈdɒbɒʃ ˌtɔːtə/ *n. phr.* Also **Dobos Torta, d- t-.** Pl. **Dobos Torten** /ˈtɔːt(ə)n/. E20. [G *Dobostorte*, f. J. C. *Dobós* (1847–1924), Hungarian pastry-cook + *Torte* tart, pastry, cake (cf. TORTE). Cf. Hungarian *dobostorta.*] A rich cake made of alternate layers of sponge and chocolate or mocha cream, with a crisp caramel topping.

dobro /ˈdɒbrəʊ/ *n.* Orig. *US.* M20. [f. the *Do*(*pěra*) *Bro*(*thers*, its Czech-American inventors.] (US proprietary name for) a type of acoustic guitar with steel resonating discs inside the body under the bridge, popular for playing country and western music.

dobson /ˈdɒbs(ə)n/ *n. US.* L19. [Origin unkn.] A larva of a dobsonfly, esp. *Corydalus cornutus*, used as fish bait.

Comb.: **dobsonfly** a large neuropterous insect (family Corydalidae) of continents other than Europe, the larva of which is predatory and aquatic.

Dobsonian /dɒbˈsəʊnɪən/ *a.* & *n.* L20. [f. John *Dobson*, 20th-cent. US amateur astronomer: see -IAN.] *Astron.* **A** *adj.* Designating or pertaining to a large aperture, short focal length, low-cost Newtonian reflecting telescope, or the simple altazimuth mount used for it. L20. **B** *n.* A Dobsonian telescope. L20.

doby *n.* var. of DOBE.

doc /dɒk/ *n.*[1] *colloq.* M19. [Abbrev. of DOCTOR *n.*] A person who is a doctor or has the title 'Doctor', *esp.* a medical practitioner.

doc /dɒk/ *n.*[2] *slang.* L20. [Abbrev.] A documentary.

Doccia /ˈdɒtʃɪə/ *n.* M19. [See below.] In full *Doccia porcelain, china*, etc. A type of porcelain made at Doccia, an Italian town near Florence.

docent /ˈdəʊs(ə)nt, *foreign* doˈtsɛnt/ *n.* L19. [G *Docent*, *Dozent*, f. L *docent-*: see next, and cf. PRIVATDOZENT.] **1** Orig. = PRIVATDOZENT. Now, in certain US universities and colleges, a member of the teaching staff below professorial rank. L19. **2** A (usu. voluntary) guide in a museum, art gallery, or zoo. Chiefly *US.* E20.

docent /ˈdəʊs(ə)nt/ *a.* M17. [L *docent-* pres. ppl stem of *docere* teach: see -ENT.] That teaches or instructs.

Docete /ˈdəʊsiːt/ *n.* Pl. **Docetes,** also in L form **Docetae** /dəʊˈsiːtiː/. L18. [med.L *Docetae* f. patristic Gk *Dokētai*, f. Gk *dokein* seem, appear.] *Eccl. Hist.* A Docetist. Usu. in *pl.*

Docetism /dəʊˈsiːtɪz(ə)m/ *n.* Also **Doket-** /dəʊˈkiːt-/. M19. [f. prec. + -ISM.] *Chr. Ch.* The belief or doctrine, held as a heresy by some early Christians, that Christ's body was either a phantasm or of real but celestial substance, and his sufferings only apparent.

docetic, D- *a.* of or pertaining to Docetism or Docetists M19. **docetically** *adv.* L19. **Docetist** *n.* a follower of docetic teaching L19.

doch an doris *n. phr.* var. of DEOCH AN DORIS.

dochmius /ˈdɒkmɪəs/ *n.* Pl. **-mii** /-mɪʌɪ/. E19. [L f. Gk *dokhmios* lit. 'slanted, oblique'.] *Class. Pros.* A metrical foot having the basic form of an iambus followed by a cretic.

dochmiac *a.* & *n.* (*a*) *adj.* of the nature of a dochmius; composed of dochmii; (*b*) *n.* a dochmiac foot or verse: L18.

docible /ˈdɒsɪb(ə)l/ *a. obs.* exc. *dial.* LME. [Fr., or late L *docibilis*, f. *docere* teach: see -IBLE.] **1** Capable of learning, teachable; docile, tractable. LME. **2** Able to be imparted by teaching. Now *rare.* M17.

dociˈbility *n.* E17.

docile /ˈdəʊsʌɪl/ *a.* L15. [L *docilis*, f. *docere* teach. Cf. Fr. *docile* (16).] **1** Apt or willing to learn; teachable. Now *rare.* L15. **2** Submissive to training or direction, not assertive; easily managed, tractable. L18. **3** Of a thing: submitting readily to treatment. L18.

1 S. AUSTIN His docile and intelligent pupil. **2** A. LEWIS The milk-white oxen waited Docile at the yoke. D. MURPHY I sat beside my mother like the most docile of Victorian daughters.

docilely *adv.* M19.

docility /də(ʊ)ˈsɪlɪti/ *n.* M16. [L *docilitas*, f. as prec.: see -ITY. Cf. Fr. *docilité* (15).] The quality of being docile. Now *esp.* amenability to training or direction, lack of assertiveness, tractability.

docimastic /dɒsɪˈmastɪk/ *a.* M18. [Gk *dokimastikos*, f. *dokimazein* test, scrutinize: see -IC.] Of or pertaining to the assay of metals.

docimasy /ˈdɒsɪməsi/ *n.* Now *rare.* E19. [Gk *dokimasia*, f. *dokimazein*: see prec., -Y[3].] Subjection of something to experimental tests; *esp.* the assaying of metallic ores.

docity /ˈdɒsɪti/ *n. colloq.* & *dial.* L17. [App. alt. of DOCILITY.] Quickness of comprehension; gumption.

dock /dɒk/ *n.*[1] [OE *docce*, corresp. to MDu. *docke-blaederen* (whence G *Dockenblätter*), ODa. *ådokke* (= OE *ēadocce* water-dock).] Any of several coarse weeds of the genus *Rumex*, of the knotgrass family, with sheathing stipules, whorls of inconspicuous usu. greenish flowers, and large leaves popularly used to relieve nettle-stings; esp. *R. obtusifolius* and *R. crispus.* Also, any of various unrelated coarse plants of similar habit, *esp.* burdock.

in dock, out nettle: a charm uttered in applying dock-leaves to nettle-stings; formerly also, a proverbial expression for changeableness and inconstancy. *patience-dock*: see PATIENCE *n. sour dock*: see SOUR *a.*

dock /dɒk/ *n.*[2] LME. [Perh. identical w. 2nd elem. of OE *fingerdoccan* finger muscles, and corresp. to Fris. *dok* bunch, ball (of twine etc.), (M)LG *dokke* bundle of straw, OHG *tocka* (southern G *Docke*) doll. In sense 6 f. DOCK *v.*[1]] **1** The solid fleshy or bony part of an animal's tail. LME. **2** A person's buttocks. Long *obs.* exc. *Sc.* and in *strong-docked* (see STRONG *a.*). E16. †**3** The skirts of a garment. E–M16. **4** The stump left after a tail is docked; *gen.* (now *dial.*), a cut end of anything, a stump. L16. **5** Part of a crupper in the form of a ring through which a horse's tail is inserted; a crupper; a covering for a horse's tail. E17. **6** The action or an act of docking or cutting short. Now only *spec.* (*Sc.*), a haircut. M17.

dock /dɒk/ *n.*[3] LME. [MLG, MDu. *docke* (mod. *dok*), of unkn. origin.] **1** An artificial basin, usu. with floodgates to control the water-level, in which ships can be repaired, built, or loaded and unloaded. LME. **b** The body of water between adjacent wharves. E19. †**2** The bed (in the sand or mud) in which a vessel lies dry at low water; the hollow made by a vessel lying in the sand. L15–M17. †**3** A creek in which ships may lie on the mud or ride at anchor, according to the tide. M–L16. †**4** A trench or canal to admit a boat. M17–E18. **5** *sing.* & (usu.) in *pl.* A range of docks (sense 1 above) together with the adjoining wharves, warehouses, and offices (*commercial docks*); a dockyard (*naval docks*). E18. **6** A wharf, a pier. Orig. *US.* E19. **7** An enclosure in a platform into which a single railway line runs and terminates. L19. 8 *Theatr.* More fully *scene-dock.* A storage space for scenes at the side or back of a stage. L19. 9 A raised platform from which lorries or railway trucks are loaded and unloaded. *N. Amer.* E20.

Phrases: *dry dock*: see DRY *a.* **floating dock** a floating structure serving as a dry dock. **graving dock** a dry dock. **in dock** *colloq.* in or into hospital; in or into a garage for repair etc. *wet dock*: see WET *a.*

Comb.: **dock-glass** a large wineglass of a type orig. used by excisemen for wine-tasting; **dockland, D-** the area about a city's docks, esp. those of London; **dockside** *n.* & *a.* (situated in) the area immediately adjacent to a dock; **docksman** a man employed at a dock; *spec.* one who opens and shuts dock gates; **dock-warrant** a certificate given to the owner of goods warehoused at a dock.

dock /dɒk/ *n.*[4] L16. [Prob. orig. a cant wd and identical w. Flem. *dok* fowl-pen, rabbit-hutch.] The enclosure in a courtroom in which the prisoner is placed during a criminal trial. Orig., one filled with prisoners whose trial was scheduled for the day (see *bail-dock* s.v. BAIL *n.*[2]).

in the dock *fig.* under scrutiny or interrogation for some suspected misdeed.

Comb.: **dock brief** a brief handed in court directly to a barrister selected from those present by a prisoner in the dock (instead of through the agency of a solicitor).

¶Hardly known bef. E19 exc. in *bail-dock*.

dock /dɒk/ *v.*[1]*t.* LME. [f. DOCK *n.*[2]] 1 Cut short (a tail, hair, etc.); cut short the tail of (an animal). Formerly also, cut short the hair of (a person). LME. 2 Abridge or reduce by taking away a part; curtail; deprive *of*; *esp.* (*colloq.*) make a deduction from the pay of (a person) or from (pay) as a fine, subscription, etc. Also, deduct (something) *from* pay. LME. 3 Put an end to (an entail) by breaking the line of succession to the estate. E17.

2 E. A. BARTLETT Her creditors have been docked of three-fourths of their due. A. J. CRONIN He's afraid to ask the Council for anything in case they dock his wretched salary to pay for it. A. S. NEILL He is docked of all his pocket money until the debt is paid. *Accountant* The . . company suddenly finds its contribution to group profits has been docked.

Comb.: **dock-tailed** *a.* with a tail cut short.

dock /dɒk/ *v.*[2] E16. [f. DOCK *n.*[3]] †1 *v.t.* Put (a vessel) into anchorage in a roadstead etc. E16–E17. †2 Bring or put (a vessel) ashore to rest in the mud, or in a trench or creek. L16–M18. 3a *v.t.* Bring or put (a vessel) into dock. E17. b *v.i.* Of a vessel or those aboard: come into dock; enter port. L19. 4 *v.t.* Provide (a port etc.) with docks. M18. 5a *v.t.* Join (a spacecraft) to another in space. M20. b *v.i.* Join spacecraft in space; be joined to another spacecraft in space. M20.

2 SHAKES. *Merch. V.* I should . . see my wealthy Andrew dock'd in sand. 3a S. PEPYS We . . saw the manner and trouble of docking such a ship. b C. PRIEST The ship was always expected, whether we docked at noon or midnight. 5 *New Scientist* Soviet designers are now providing their manned spacecraft with a docking tunnel.

dockage /ˈdɒkɪdʒ/ *n.*[1] M17. [f. DOCK *n.*[3] + -AGE.] (The charges for) docking facilities; docks collectively; the berthing of a vessel in a dock.

dockage /ˈdɒkɪdʒ/ *n.*[2] L19. [f. DOCK *v.*[1] + -AGE.] The action of docking an amount; deduction.

docken /ˈdɒk(ə)n/ *n. Sc. & north.* LME. [App. f. OE *doccan* pl. & infl. sing. of *docce* DOCK *n.*[1]] = DOCK *n.*[1]

docker /ˈdɒkə/ *n.*[1] M18. [f. DOCK *n.*[3] + -ER[1].] 1 A person who lives in or near a dock; (**D-**) *spec.* a native or inhabitant of Devonport, formerly called Plymouth Dock. M18. 2 A labourer in a dock. L19.

docker /ˈdɒkə/ *n.*[2] E19. [f. DOCK *v.*[1] + -ER[1].] A person who docks tails.

docker /ˈdɒkə/ *n.*[3] *colloq.* (now *Hist.*). L19. [f. DOCK *n.*[4] + -ER[1].] A dock brief.

docket /ˈdɒkɪt/ *n.* Also †**docquet(t)**, †**dogget(t)**. L15. [Origin uncertain: perh. f. DOCK *v.*[1] + -ET[1].] 1 An abridged account, a summary; an abstract. *obs.* exc. *Hist.* L15. b An abstract of the contents of proposed letters patent, written on the monarch's bill which authorized their preparation and copied into a register. M16. c *Law.* An abridged account of judicial proceedings, esp. of a case in Chancery; a register of judicial decisions or cases. M17. 2 A list of law cases due to be heard or tried; *transf.* a list of matters for discussion or things to be done; an agenda. Freq. in *on the docket*. *US.* E18. 3 A document or inscription giving particulars, esp. of something attached; *spec.* a label attached to goods to indicate their destination, nature, value, etc.; a customs warrant certifying that duty has been paid on goods entering; a warrant or voucher entitling the holder to obtain or receive something. Cf. DUCAT 3. E18. 4 A workman's record of jobs done during the day or week. M20. 5 A set of papers on a given topic; a file. M20.

1c †**strike a docket** enter a bond with the Lord Chancellor to show that a debtor is a bankrupt. 2 B. TARKINGTON The court had cleared up the docket by sitting to unseemly hours of the night. 3 T. HOOD Tourists . . Provided with passport, that requisite docket. JOYCE The box of pawn-tickets . . had just been rifled and he took up idly . . the blue and white dockets.

docket /ˈdɒkɪt/ *v.t.* Also †**docquet(t)**, †**dogget(t)**. E17. [f. the n.] †1 Furnish (letters patent etc.) with a docket. E17–M19. 2 *Law.* Enter a summary of (a judgement etc.) in a register. L17. 3 Annotate (a letter or document) with a brief note of its contents etc. M18. 4 *Law.* Enter (a case or suit) on the list of those due to be heard. *US.* E19. 5 *fig.* Assign to a category; classify. M19.

5 D. WELCH He only looked at things in the room that he could date and docket Other things were quite missed.

dockominium /dɒkəˈmɪnɪəm/ *n. US.* L20. [f. DOCK *n.*[3] + CONDOMINIUM.] A privately owned landing-stage at a marina etc.; a waterfront condominium with a private landing-stage.

dockyard /ˈdɒkjɑːd/ *n.* E18. [f. DOCK *n.*[3] + YARD *n.*[1]] An area with docks and workshops for the building, outfit, and repair of ships; *esp.* a Government establishment of this kind for the use of the Royal Navy.

Comb.: **dockyard man**, (*colloq.*) **dockyard matey** a male employee in a Government dockyard.

Doc Martens *n. phr.* see DOCTOR MARTENS.

†**docquet(t)** *n.*, *v.* vars. of DOCKET *n.*, *v.*

doct /dɒkt/ *a. rare.* E18. [L *doctus* pa. pple of *docere* teach.] Learned.

doctor /ˈdɒktə/ *n.* ME. [OFr. *doctour* f. L *doctor* teacher, f. *doct-* pa. ppl stem of *docere* teach: see -OR.] 1 A person skilled in, and therefore entitled to teach or speak authoritatively on, any branch of knowledge; an eminently learned person. *arch.* ME. 2 *Chr. Ch.* a Any of certain theologians (orig. four each in the Western and the Eastern Church) whose canonization as saints is due esp. to their outstanding learning and influence. ME. b A leading medieval schoolman. E17. 3 A person who gives instruction in some branch of knowledge, or inculcates opinions or principles; a teacher. (Foll. by *of*.) Now *rare.* LME. †b An assistant schoolmaster. *Sc.* M17–L18. 4 A holder of the highest degree awarded in a university faculty or (now) by some other competent body. Now usu. used as a title preceding a name (freq. abbrev. *Dr*); formerly also used as a form of address. LME. 5 A person who is learned in theology or law. *arch.* LME. 6 Orig., an authority on medicine or surgery; a doctor of medicine. Now, any medical practitioner, *esp.* one who is qualified or registered and (in Britain and Ireland) is not a surgeon; *spec.* a general practitioner; (chiefly as an official designation) a dentist; *N. Amer.* also (only as a title preceding a name), an ophthalmic optician, a veterinarian. Also used as a title preceding a name (freq. abbrev. *Dr*) and used as a form of address. LME. b *fig.* A thing that improves health or promotes well-being; *spec.* (*a*) *colloq.* a reviving drink; (*b*) *colloq.* in the W. Indies, southern Africa, and western Australia, a cool sea breeze which usually blows for part of the day in summer. M17. c A person who mends or repairs things of a certain kind. L19. 7 A false or loaded die. *arch. slang.* L17. 8 = *surgeon fish* s.v. SURGEON *n.* M18. 9 A blade for removing surplus ink, fibres, etc., in printing and paper-making machines. Also *doctor blade.* L18. 10 An added ingredient used to adulterate food or drink. L18. 11 A cook on board ship or (*US, Austral.*, & *NZ*) in a camp. *slang.* E19. 12 *Angling.* A kind of hackled dry fly. M19.

1 POPE Who shall decide, when Doctors disagree? 2b *the Angelic Doctor*: see ANGELIC *a.*[1] 2. *the Seraphic Doctor*: see SERAPHIC *a.* 3 BURKE These new Doctors of the Rights of men. 4 *Doctor of Civil Law*, *Doctor of Divinity*, *Doctor of Philosophy*, etc. 6 G. GREENE Doctor Castle's study . . had been left unchanged after the doctor's death. **go for the doctor** *Austral. slang* make every effort; bet heavily. (**just**) **what the doctor ordered** *colloq.* something beneficial or desirable, esp. in a given situation. **you're the doctor** *colloq.* the decision is up to you. c *play-doctor*, *saw doctor*, *tree doctor*, etc. 12 *silver doctor*: see SILVER *n.* & *a.*

Comb.: **doctor bird** *W. Indies* a hummingbird; **doctor blade** = sense 9 above; **doctor-fish** (*a*) = sense 8 above; (*b*) the tench; **Doctors' Commons** *Hist.* (the site of) a London building occupied by the former College of Doctors of Laws, in which legal business relating to wills, marriage licences, divorce proceedings, etc., was transacted; *doctor's mandate*: see MANDATE *n.*; *doctor's orders*: see ORDER *n.*; **doctor's stuff, doctor-stuff** *derog. colloq.* medicine.

doctorhood *n.* the status or rank of a doctor L19. **doctorism** *n.* (*a*) the principles or practices of doctors; (*b*) a saying characteristic of doctors: M17. **doctorize** *v.t.* (*rare*) = DOCTOR *v.* 1 E17. **doctorly** *a.* like, characteristic of, or befitting a doctor L16.

doctor /ˈdɒktə/ *v. colloq.* M16. [Partly f. prec. n., partly (in sense 2) f. med.L *doctorare* (see DOCTORATE *v.*).] 1 *v.i.* Cite learned persons. Only as *doctoring* vbl n. *rare.* Only in M16. 2 *v.t.* Confer the degree or title of doctor on; make a doctor; address as 'doctor'. L16. 3 *v.t.* Treat, as a doctor; give medical treatment to. E18. b Repair, patch up, set to rights, (machinery etc.); take steps to improve or make acceptable. E19. c Castrate or spay (an animal). E20. 4 *v.t.* Alter or disguise the appearance, flavour, or character of; falsify, tamper with, adulterate; 'cook'. L18. 5 *v.i.* Practise as a physician. Chiefly as *doctoring* vbl n. M19. 6 *v.i.* Receive treatment by a doctor. L19.

2 J. R. LOWELL I have been over to Oxford to be doctored. 3 S. BELLOW I doctored myself with tranquillizers. b A. BLOND A writer, gaining his main income . . from doctoring film scripts. 4 P. V. PRICE As wine got old in cask . . it would be doctored . . with honey . . or fruit juices that might make it palatable. M. RICHLER He wasn't awfully good at school, and so . . he would doctor his report card. 5 A. D. T. WHITNEY Preaching ran in the King family, as politics or doctoring . . run in some others.

doctorer *n.* L19.

doctoral /ˈdɒkt(ə)r(ə)l/ *a.* L16. [f. DOCTOR *n.* + -AL[1].] Of or pertaining to an eminently learned person or a teacher. Now *spec.* of or pertaining to (the holder of) a doctorate.

doctorally *adv.* L16.

doctorand /ˈdɒktərand/ *n.* Also in L form **doctorandus** /dɒktəˈrandəs/, pl. **-di** /-dʌɪ/. E20. [G f. med.L *doctorandus.*] A candidate for a doctor's degree.

doctorate /ˈdɒkt(ə)rət/ *n.* M17. [Partly f. as next; partly f. med.L *doctoratus* = sense 2 below, f. L DOCTOR *n.*: see -ATE[1].] 1 A person who has a doctor's degree. *rare.* M17. 2 The highest degree awarded in a university faculty or (now) by some other competent body; a doctor's degree. L17.

doctorate /ˈdɒktəreɪt/ *v.t.* Now *rare.* Pa. pple **-ated**, (earlier) †**-ate**. L16. [med.L *doctorat-* pa. ppl stem of *doctorare*, f. L DOCTOR *n.*: see -ATE[3].] = DOCTOR *v.* 2.

doctoress *n.* var. of DOCTRESS.

doctorial /dɒkˈtɔːrɪəl/ *a.* E18. [f. DOCTOR *n.* + -IAL.] = DOCTORAL.

doctorially *adv.* M19.

Doctor Martens /dɒktə ˈmɑːtɪnz/ *n. phr.* Also **Doctor Marten's, Doc M-, Dr M-.** L20. [Klaus *Maertens*, Ger. inventor of the sole.] (Proprietary name for) a type of heavy (esp. laced) boot or shoe with a cushioned sole.

doctorship /ˈdɒktəʃɪp/ *n.* L16. [f. DOCTOR *n.* + -SHIP.] 1 = DOCTORATE *n.* 2. L16. 2 The position, character, or function of a teacher or learned person; teaching; learning, scholarship. L16. 3 The personality or dignity of a doctor. Chiefly *joc.* or *iron.* as a title. E17. 4 The function or practice of a medical doctor; medical skill or attendance. M17.

doctress /ˈdɒktrɪs/ *n.* Also **doctoress** /ˈdɒkt(ə)rɪs, -ɛs/. M16. [f. DOCTOR *n.* + -ESS[1], after Fr. †*doctoresse*.] 1 A female teacher; a learned woman; a female holder of a doctor's degree. Now *rare* or *obs.* M16. 2 A female medical doctor, a lady doctor. L16. 3 A doctor's wife or daughter. *joc.* M18.

doctrinaire /dɒktrɪˈnɛː/ *n.* & *a.* E19. [Fr., f. DOCTRINE + *-aire* -ARY[1].] A *n.* 1 *Hist.* In early 19th-cent. France, a member of a political movement which supported constitutional government and the reconciliation of the principles of authority and liberty. E19. 2 A person who tries to apply principle without allowance for circumstance; a pedantic theorist. M19. B *adj.* Pertaining to or of the character of a doctrinaire; seeking to apply a doctrine in all circumstances; theoretical and unpractical. M19.

doctrinairism *n.* M19.

doctrinal /dɒkˈtrʌɪn(ə)l, ˈdɒktrɪn-/ *n.* LME. [OFr., f. med.L *doctrinale* use as n. of neut. of late L *doctrinalis*: see next.] †1 A textbook; a book of instruction on any subject. Orig. the title of a particular textbook on grammar. LME–M17. 2 In *pl.* Matters or points of doctrine or instruction. E17.

doctrinal /dɒkˈtrʌɪn(ə)l, ˈdɒktrɪn-/ *a.* LME. [Late L *doctrinalis*, f. *doctrina* DOCTRINE: see -AL[1].] 1 Of or pertaining to doctrine; dealing with or concerned with inculcating doctrine or doctrines. LME. †2 Serving to teach or instruct; instructive, didactic. L16–M17.

1 D. NEAL Doctrinal Puritans. J. A. FROUDE Doctrinal conservatism.

doctrinalism *n.* the laying of stress on, or rigid adherence to, doctrinal matters L19. **doctrinalist** *n.* M19. **doctrinally** *adv.* in a doctrinal way; as doctrine; as regards doctrine: LME.

doctrinarian /dɒktrɪˈnɛːrɪən/ *n.* & *a.* M18. [f. med.L *doctrinare* (see DOCTRINATE) + -ARIAN.] A *n.* †1 A member of the Brothers of Christian Doctrine, or Christian Brothers, a lay teaching order instituted at Rheims in 1680. M–L18. 2 = DOCTRINAIRE *n.* 2. M19. B *adj.* = DOCTRINAIRE *a.* L19.

doctrinarianism *n.* L19.

doctrinary /ˈdɒktrɪn(ə)ri/ *a.* M19. [Fr. DOCTRINAIRE: see -ARY[1].] = DOCTRINAIRE *a.*

doctriˈnarity *n.* doctrinaire quality M19.

doctrinate /ˈdɒktrɪneɪt/ *v. arch.* M17. [med.L *doctrinat-* pa. ppl stem of *doctrinare* teach, f. *doctrina* DOCTRINE: see -ATE[3].] †1 *v.t.* Teach, instruct. Only in M17. 2 *v.i.* Give instruction *on* a subject. *rare.* M19.

doctrine /ˈdɒktrɪn/ *n.* LME. [(O)Fr. f. L *doctrina* teaching, learning, f. DOCTOR *n.*: see -INE[4].] †1 The action of teaching or instructing; a lesson; a precept. LME–E18. †b Preaching. M16–E17. 2 That which is taught; instruction; a body of teaching, *esp.* that concerning a particular subject or set of beliefs; a dogma, a tenet; a political or ethical principle. LME. 3 A body of principles or tenets, a system of beliefs; a theory; a branch of knowledge. Now *rare* or *obs.* LME. †4 Learning, knowledge. LME–E17. †5 Discipline. *rare.* L15–M16.

1 AV *Mark* 4:2 And he.. said vnto them in his doctrine, Hearken. 2 BURKE The doctrine of the equality of all men. C. HILL The Laudians rejected the Calvinist doctrine of predestination. MONROE DOCTRINE. 3 EARL OF CHATHAM A.. notion of.. the solar system: together with the doctrine of comets.

doctrinism *n.* adherence to or propounding of doctrine L19. **doctrinist** *n.* M19.

†doctrix *n.* E17–M18. [L, fem. of DOCTOR *n.*] A female doctor.

docudrama /ˈdɒkjʊdrɑːmə/ *n.* M20. [f. DOCUMENTARY + DRAMA.] = DRAMA-*documentary.*

document /ˈdɒkjʊm(ə)nt/ *n.* LME. [(O)Fr. f. L *documentum* lesson, proof, instance, (in med.L) written instruction, official paper, f. *docere* teach: see -MENT.] †1 Teaching; (a piece of) instruction, a lesson; (a) warning. LME–E19. †2 Evidence, proof. Usu. foll. by *of*, *that*. LME–M19. 3 Something written, inscribed, engraved, etc., which provides evidence or information or serves as a record; *esp.* an official paper. LME.

3 A. E. STEVENSON Our great documents, from the Declaration of Independence to the Atlantic Charter. S. NAIPAUL His testament, a rambling document some forty pages long. *social document*: see SOCIAL *a.*

Comb.: **document case** a lightweight usu. flexible case for carrying papers.

document /ˈdɒkjʊmɛnt/ *v.t.* M17. [f. prec.] †1 Teach, instruct. M17–M18. †b Instruct or admonish authoritatively; rebuke. L17–E19. 2 Prove or support by documentary evidence; record in documents. Freq. in *pass.* E18. 3 Provide with documents, esp. legally required papers. Usu. in *pass.* E19. 4 Provide (a person) with evidence or information, keep informed. E19.

1 BUNYAN That they might be documented in all good and wholesome things. b DRYDEN I am finely documented by my own daughter! 2 A. POWELL Like many Welsh families my father's had been documented from an early period. 3 J. ARNOULD By sailing his ship imperfectly or improperly documented, he forfeits his rights to protection under the policy.

docuˈmentable *a.* L16. **docuˈmentably** *adv.* L20.

documental /dɒkjʊˈmɛnt(ə)l/ *a.* L16. [f. DOCUMENT *n.* + -AL[1].] †1 Instructive; didactic. L16–E17. 2 Of or pertaining to documents; documentary. E19.

docuˈmentalist *n.* a person engaged in documentation M20.

documentary /dɒkjʊˈmɛnt(ə)ri/ *a.* & *n.* E19. [f. as prec. + -ARY[1].] A *adj.* 1 Of, pertaining to, or consisting of a document or documents. E19. 2 Affording evidence, evidential. *rare.* M19. 3 Relating to teaching or instruction. *rare.* L19. 4 Factual, realistic; *esp.* (of a film etc.) based on real events, places, or circumstances and usu. intended primarily to record or inform. E20.

1 LD MACAULAY They were in possession of documentary evidence which would confound the guilty. 4 *Punch* Most documentary films seem to hinge upon the exposition of some staple industry.

B *n.* A documentary film or programme. M20.

D. ADAMS One of our film producers is already making a fascinating documentary about the indigenous cavemen.

ˌ**documenˈtarian** *n.* = DOCUMENTARIST M20. **documentarily** *adv.* M19. **documentarist** *n.* a person who makes documentaries M20.

documentation /ˌdɒkjʊmɛnˈteɪʃ(ə)n/ *n.* M18. [f. DOCUMENT *v.* + -ATION.] †1 Instruction, admonition. M18–M19. 2 The provision of documents. L19. 3 Preparation or use of documentary evidence or authorities. L19. 4 The process or speciality of accumulating and classifying documents and making them available to others. E20. 5 Documents collectively; the documents accompanying or belonging to something. E20.

5 *Which Micro?* The BBC Micro has.. excellent documentation.

documentative /dɒkjʊˈmɛntətɪv/ *a.* L20. [f. as prec. + -IVE.] Of the nature of a documentary; employing or providing documentation.

documentize /ˈdɒkjʊm(ə)ntʌɪz/ *v.t.* Now *dial.* Also **-ise**. L16. [f. DOCUMENT *n.* + -IZE.] 1 Preach, moralize. Formerly, teach, instruct. L16. †2 Provide with evidence. Only in M18.

docutainment /dɒkjʊˈteɪnm(ə)nt/ *n. N. Amer.* L20. [f. DOCU(MENTARY + ENTER)TAINMENT.] (A) documentary film or programme designed as entertainment.

dod /dɒd/ *n.*[1] *Sc.* & *north.* ME. [Rel. to DOD *v.*[1]] A rounded summit or eminence, *esp.* one that is a lower summit or shoulder of a hill.

dod /dɒd/ *n.*[2] M17. [Cogn. w. Du. *dodde* in same sense.] The greater reed-mace, *Typha latifolia.*

dod /dɒd/ *n.*[3] & *int.* Chiefly *dial.* L17. [Alt. Cf. DAD *n.*[2]] God: used in oaths and exclamations, and (*US*) as an intensive w. vbs and pa. pples.

C. E. CRADDOCK Dod-rot that critter.

Comb.: **dod-rotted** *a.* (*US*) damned, dratted.

dod /dɒd/ *n.*[4] *Sc.* L18. [Gael. = peevishness.] A fit of ill humour; usu. in *pl.*, sulks, esp. in *take the dods.*

dod /dɒd/ *v.*[1]*t. obs.* exc. *dial.* Infl. **-dd-**. ME. [Rel. to DOD *n.*[1]: ult. origin unkn. Cf. DODDY *n.*[2]] Make the top of (something) blunt, rounded, or bare; shave the head of; lop (a tree); dehorn (an animal).

dod /dɒd/ *v.*[2]*t. obs.* exc. *dial.* Infl. **-dd-**. M17. [Imit.: cf. DAD *v.*] Beat, knock.

†doddard *n. rare.* L17–L18. [App. f. DOD *v.*[1] + -ARD: cf. *pollard*, DODDERED *a.*[1]] = DOTARD *n.*[2]

dodder /ˈdɒdə/ *n.* ME. [Corresp. to MLG *dod(d)er*, MHG *toter* (G *Dotter*).] 1 Any plant of the genus *Cuscuta*, related to the bindweeds, comprising leafless threadlike twining plants with parasitic suckers. ME. 2 Any of various choking or climbing weeds. *dial.* L19.

dodder /ˈdɒdə/ *v.i.* E17. [Alt. of or parallel to DADDER.] 1 Tremble or shake owing to frailty or illness. E17. 2 Walk unsteadily or falteringly, totter; be feeble. E19.

dodderer *n.* an infirm, feeble, or inept person E20. **doddering** *ppl a.* that dodders; feeble in body or mind; inept, footling: M18. **dodderingness** *n.* E20. **doddery** *a.* apt to tremble or totter, esp. from age or infirmity; faltering, shaky: M19.

doddered /ˈdɒdəd/ *a.*[1] L17. [App. orig. f. DOD *v.*[1] (cf. DODDARD, DODDLE *n.*[1], DOTTER *v.*); later also assoc. w. DODDER *n.*] Of a tree, esp. an oak: having lost the top or branches, esp. through age and decay.

doddered /ˈdɒdəd/ *a.*[2] Chiefly *dial.* M19. [f. DODDER *v.* + -ED[1].] Infirm, doddery; doddering; dilapidated.

dodderel /ˈdɒd(ə)r(ə)l/ *n. dial.* E18. [f. DOD *v.*[1]: cf. DODDERED *a.*[1], DOTTEREL.] A doddered tree; a pollard.

doddie *n.* var. of DODDY *n.*[1], *n.*[2]

doddle /ˈdɒd(ə)l/ *n.*[1] & *a. obs.* exc. *dial.* E17. [f. DOD *v.*[1]: cf. DODDARD.] (Designating) a pollard.

doddle /ˈdɒd(ə)l/ *n.*[2] *colloq.* M20. [Origin uncertain: perh. f. DODDLE *v.*] An easy task; something requiring little effort or skill; a walk-over.

J. KELMAN It is never a doddle to beg from acquaintances.

doddle /ˈdɒd(ə)l/ *v.i.* L16. [f. obscure 1st elem. + -LE[3]. Cf. DADDLE *v.*, DAWDLE *v.*, DODDER *v.*, TODDLE *v.*] Walk with short, faltering, or unsteady steps; toddle; totter; dawdle.

doddy /ˈdɒdi/ *n.*[1] Now *Sc.* Also **-ie**. L16. [Abbrev.] = DODDYPOLL.

doddy /ˈdɒdi/ *n.*[2] *Sc.* Also **-ie**. L18. [f. DOD *v.*[1] + -Y[6], -IE.] A hornless cow or bull.

doddypoll /ˈdɒdɪpəʊl/ *n. arch.* Also (earlier) **†dot(t)y-**. LME. [App. f. DOTE *v.*[1], later referred to DOD *v.*[1] + POLL *n.*[1]: cf. *roundhead.*] A stupid person; a dolt, a blockhead.

dodeca- /ˈdəʊdɛkə/ *comb. form* of Gk *dōdeka* twelve. Bef. a vowel **dodec-**.

doˈdecamer *n.* (*Chem.*) a compound whose molecule is composed of twelve molecules of monomer M20. **dodecaˈmeric** *a.* (*Chem.*) of the nature of a decamer, consisting of a dodecamer or dodecamers M20. **dodecandrous** /dəʊdɪˈkandrəs/ *a.* (*Bot.*) having twelve stamens E19. **dodecaˈphonic** *a.* (*Mus.*) pertaining to, using, or designating the twelve-note system M20. **dodecaphonist** /dəʊˈdɛkəf(ə)nɪst, dəʊdɪˈkaf(ə)nɪst/ *n.* (*Mus.*) a composer of dodecaphonic music M20. **dodecaphony** /dəʊˈdɛkəf(ə)ni, dəʊdɪˈkaf(ə)ni/ *n.* (*Mus.*) the twelve-note system M20. **dodecarchy** *n.* (government by) a ruling body of twelve M17. **dodecastyle** *n.* a portico or colonnade of twelve columns E19. **dodecasyˈllabic** *a.* (*Pros.*) composed of dodecasyllables L19. **dodecaˈsyllable** *n.* (*Pros.*) a word or line of twelve syllables M18.

dodecad /ˈdəʊdɪkad, dəʊˈdɛkad/ *n.* Also **-ade** /-eɪd/. L17. [f. Gk *dōdeka* twelve, after *decade.*] A group or set of twelve items.

Also **†dodecady** *n.*: only in E17.

dodecagon /dəʊˈdɛkəg(ə)n/ *n.* M17. [Gk *dōdekagōnon*, f. *dōdeka* twelve + *-gōnos* -GON.]

Geom. A plane figure with twelve straight sides and twelve angles.

dodecahedrane /dəʊdɛkəˈhiːdreɪn/ *n.* M20. [f. next + -ANE.] *Chem.* A crystalline hydrocarbon, $(CH)_{20}$, in which the carbon atoms of each molecule lie at the vertices of a regular dodecahedron.

dodecahedron /ˌdəʊdɛkəˈhiːdr(ə)n, -ˈhɛd-/ *n.* Pl. **-dra** /-drə/, **-drons**. L16. [Gk *dōdekaedron* neut. of *dōdekaedros*, f. *dōdeka* twelve + *hedra* seat, face.] *Geom.* & *Cryst.* A solid figure or object with twelve plane faces; *esp.* (more fully *regular dodecahedron*) one with twelve equal regular pentagonal faces.

dodecahedral *a.* having the form of a dodecahedron; having twelve faces: L18. **dodecahedric** *a.* = DODECAHEDRAL L19.

dodecane /ˈdəʊdɪkeɪn/ *n.* L19. [f. DODECA- + -ANE.] *Chem.* Any of a series of saturated hydrocarbons (alkanes) with the formula $C_{12}H_{26}$; *spec.* (also n-*dodecane*) the unbranched isomer, $CH_3(CH_2)_{10}CH_3$.

dodecaˈnoic *a.* = LAURIC M20.

†dodecatemory *n.* E17–E18. [Gk *dōdekatēmorion*, f. *dōdekaton*, fem. *-tē*, twelfth + *morion* a part.] A twelfth part; *esp.* (*Astrol.*) each of the twelve houses of the zodiac; a twelfth part of a sign, 2½ degrees.

dodecyl /ˈdəʊdɪsʌɪl, -sɪl, dəʊˈdiːs-/ *n.* L19. [f. DODECANE + -YL.] *Chem.* A radical $C_{12}H_{25}$·, derived from a dodecane. Usu. in *comb.*

dodgast /ˈdɒdgɑːst/ *v.t.* *US dial.* L19. [f. DOD *n.*[3] + *gast*, prob. f. BLAST *v.*] Confound, curse: used in oaths and exclamations. Chiefly as *dodgasted* ppl a.

dodge /dɒdʒ/ *n.* L16. [f. the vb.] **1** An act of dodging; a quick sideways movement. Formerly, *the* slip. L16. **2** A trick; an artifice, esp. as a means of eluding or cheating someone. E17. **3** A clever or adroit expedient or stratagem; *colloq.* something showing ingenuity or shrewdness. M19.

1 L. PARR He was forced to avoid him by giving a sudden dodge to one side. 2 DICKENS 'It was all false, of course?' 'All, sir . . , reg'lar do, sir; artful dodge'. V. WOOLF His little dodges deceived nobody. **on the dodge** engaged in crooked or dishonest proceedings. 3 F. C. BURNAND This is a queer sort of dodge for lighting the streets. H. A. VACHELL He had other dodges to capture trade.

dodge /dɒdʒ/ *v.* M16. [Origin unkn.] **†1** *v.i.* Go this way and that in one's speech or behaviour; negotiate, haggle; dither. M16–M18. **2** *v.i.* Play fast and loose (esp. *with* a person); prevaricate. L16. **3** *v.t.* Play fast and loose with; frustrate or impede by shifts and pretexts; trifle with. L16. **4†a** *v.i.* Use changes of position *with* a person to evade or catch him or her. M17–E18. **b** *v.i.* Move to and fro, change position, esp. quickly; move quickly to evade a pursuer, blow, etc., or to gain an advantage. (Foll. by various preps., advs., and advb. phrs.) L17. **c** *v.t.* Move up and down or to and fro (*lit.* & *fig.*); move suddenly, jerk; question or address at random rather than sequentially. E19. **5** *v.t.* Evade (a pursuer) by sudden changes of direction or (a blow) by sudden movement; evade, escape, esp. by cleverness or trickery. L17. **6** *v.i.* Of a bell in change-ringing: move one place contrary to the normal sequence, and then back again in the following round. L17. **7** *v.t.* Follow stealthily and with subterfuges to avoid discovery; dog (a person's steps). Now *rare* or *obs.* E18. **8** *v.i.* (also foll. by *on*) & *t.* Jog. *Sc.* & *north.* E18.

4a W. HUBBARD He began to dodge with his pursuers. b A. SILLITOE He dodged between tall green buses. J. B. PRIESTLEY It was . . easier too to dodge out of sight if we caught a glimpse of people who might be looking for us. J. OSBORNE I used to have to dodge downstairs for the post. c R. MARSH He made a snatch at it. . . Sydney dodged it out of his reach. 5 J. GALSWORTHY Haven't you attorneys invented a way yet of dodging this damned income tax? D. ABSE We crossed the road, dodging the traffic. D. ADAMS You can't dodge your responsibilities by saying they don't exist!

Phrases: **dodge Pompey** (*a*) *Naut. slang* shirk work; (*b*) *Austral. slang* steal grass. *dodge the column*: see COLUMN *n.* 4.

Dodgem /ˈdɒdʒ(ə)m/ *n.* Also **Dodg'em**, **dodgem**. E20. [f. DODGE *v.* + 'EM.] A small electrically powered car at a funfair, driven in an enclosure with the aim of bumping other cars and avoiding bumps from them. Also *Dodgem car*.

¶Proprietary name in the US.

dodger /ˈdɒdʒə/ *n.* M16. [f. DODGE *v.* + -ER[1].] **1** A person who dodges; *esp.* an artful or elusive person. M16. **2a** A maize-flour cake. *US.* M19. **b** A sandwich; bread; food. *Austral.* & *Mil. slang.* E20. **3** A small handbill or circular. *US.* L19. **4** A screen on a ship's bridge etc. giving protection from spray. L19.

dodger /ˈdɒdʒə/ *a.* *Austral. slang.* M20. [Origin unkn.] Good, excellent.

dodgery /ˈdɒdʒəri/ *n.* M17. [f. DODGE *n.* or *v.* + -ERY.] The employment of dodges; trickery.

dodging /ˈdɒdʒɪŋ/ *vbl n.* L16. [f. DODGE *v.* + -ING[1].] The action of DODGE *v.*; an instance of this; *Photogr.* the deliberate modification of the intensity of a particular part of a photograph during processing or enlarging.

dodgy /ˈdɒdʒi/ *a.* M19. [f. DODGE *v.* + -Y[1].] **1** Full of trickery; cunning, artful. M19. **2** Difficult, awkward, unreliable; tricky, risky. *colloq.* L19.

2 H. PINTER It'd be a bit dodgy driving tonight.

dodgily *adv.* L19. **dodginess** *n.* L19.

dodkin /ˈdɒdkɪn/ *n.* *obs.* exc. *Hist.* Also **dot-**, **†doit-**. LME. [MDu. *doytkin* dim. of *duit*, *deuyt* DOIT *n.*: see -KIN.] A doit; any coin of very low value.

dodman /ˈdɒdmən/ *n.* Now *dial.* M16. [Origin unkn.: cf. HODMANDOD.] A snail.

dodo /ˈdəʊdəʊ/ *n.* Pl. **-o(e)s**. E17. [Port. *doudo* simpleton, fool.] **1** A large flightless bird, *Raphus cucullatus*, with stumpy wings, which inhabited Mauritius until it became extinct in the 17th cent. E17. **2** An old-fashioned, stupid, or inactive person or institution. *colloq.* L19.

1 *dead as the* (or *a*) *dodo*: see DEAD *a.* *solitary dodo*: see SOLITARY *a.*

Dodonean /dəʊdəˈniːən/ *a.* Also **-ian**. M16. [f. L *Dodonaeus* f. Gk *Dōdōnaios*, f. *Dōdōnē* Dodona: see -EAN, -IAN.] Of or pertaining to Dodona in ancient Epirus, where there was an oracle of Zeus in an oak grove.

doe /dəʊ/ *n.* [OE *dā*: ult. origin unkn.] **A** *n.* **1** The female of British deer, *spec.* the fallow deer and roe-deer. OE. **b** The female of certain other kinds of deer, as the reindeer. L17. **2** A female hare, rabbit, ferret, or rat. E17. **3** A (large) female kangaroo. *Austral.* M19.

Comb.: **doe-eyed** *a.* (esp. of a woman) having large gentle dark eyes; **doeskin** (*a*) (leather of) the skin of a doe; (*b*) a smooth closely-cut woollen or twilled cloth.

B *attrib.* or as *adj.* (Of an animal) female; of or from a doe. LME.

¶The corresponding male animal is usu. called *buck*.

doegling /ˈdəːglɪŋ/ *n.* Also **dog-**. M19. [Faeroese.] A bottlenose whale, *Hyperoodon ampullatus*, of the N. Atlantic.

doek /dʊk/ *n.* *S. Afr.* L18. [Afk. = cloth: cf. DUCK *n.*[3]] A cloth, *esp.* a head-scarf.

doer /ˈduːə/ *n.* ME. [f. DO *v.* + -ER[1].] **1** A person who does something; a person who acts rather than merely talking or thinking. ME. **2** A person who acts on behalf of another; an agent; a lawyer. Now *Sc.* LME. **3** A cheat. *slang.* M19. **4** An animal or plant that thrives (in a specified way). M19. **5** A person of character; an eccentric person. *Austral.* & *NZ.* E20.

4 F. D. DAVISON Piebald was a good doer; . . that pony's head would go down to the food through it all. 5 **good doer** a warm-hearted person. **hard doer** a tough character; an eccentric person.

does, doest, doeth *vs.* see DO *v.*

doff /dɒf/ *v.* See also DAFF *v.*[2] LME. [Contr. of *do off*: see DO *v.*] **1a** *v.t.* Put or take off (a garment etc.); take off or raise (a hat), esp. in respect or greeting; *fig.* throw off, get rid of, (a mood etc.). Now *arch.* or *literary.* LME. **b** *v.i.* Raise one's hat (*to* a person). *arch. rare.* L17. **†2** *v.t.* Put (a person) *off* (with an excuse etc.). L16–M17. **3** *v.t.* **a** Automatically remove (cotton etc.) from the carding-cylinder during its progress through a carding-machine. E19. **b** Remove (empty bobbins or spindles) from a textile machine. M19.

1 K. TYNAN The royal courtesan doffs her baser attributes.

doffer *n.* a person who or thing which doffs, esp. in textile manufacture E19.

dog /dɒg/ *n.* & *a.* [Late OE *docga* (once), of unkn. origin.] **A** *n.* **1** A carnivorous mammal, *Canis familiaris*, long domesticated for hunting or guarding, as a pet, etc., and existing in many diverse breeds. LOE. **b** *spec.* A dog used for hunting; a hound. ME. **c** A watchdog; *School slang* a child who keeps watch. LME. **d** Any of various wild animals related to the dog or thought to resemble it; *spec.* (*a*) *US colloq.* a prairie dog; (*b*) *Austral.* a dingo. Usu. w. specifying wd or in *comb.* L18. **e** In full *tinned dog*. Tinned meat. *Austral.* L19. **f** In *pl.* *The* greyhound races. *colloq.* E20. **2** As a term of abuse: a worthless or contemptible person; a wretch, a cur. ME. **b** A person who betrays his or her associates; an informer. Chiefly in *turn dog* (*on*). *US* & *Austral. slang.* M19. **3** A male dog. Also, a male fox or wolf. LME. **4** Any of various mechanical devices, usu. with a tooth or claw, for gripping or holding; *esp.*: (*a*) a clamp for supporting something (e.g. part of a building) or holding something in place; (*b*) (in a firearm) = *dog-head* below; (*c*) a grappling-iron for gripping a log or other heavy object which has to be hoisted or held in position; (*d*) a projection or tooth acting as a detent; a catch which engages the teeth of a ratchet-wheel. LME. **5** (Usu. **D-**.) *The* star Sirius (see *dog-star* below); (more fully *Great Dog*) *the* constellation Canis Major, containing Sirius; (more fully *Lesser* or *Little Dog*) *the* constellation Canis Minor. M16. **†6** A kind of gun or cannon. M16–M17. **7** An andiron; an analogous support for a dog-grate. Also *firedog*, *dog-iron*. L16. **†8** An adept *at* something. Also *old dog*. L16–E18. **9** A lively or rakish young man; (usu. w. prec. adj., in playful reproof or commiseration) a fellow, a chap. E17. **10** Any of various atmospheric phenomena. Usu. as 2nd elem. of comb. (Earliest in *sun-dog* s.v. SUN *n.*[1]) M17. **11** *ellipt.* A dogfish. L17. **12** Any of several sorts of coin; *esp.* a copper coin formerly used in the W. Indies. Earliest in *black dog* s.v. BLACK *a.* E18. **13** Display, stylishness; pretentious airs, affected dignity; esp. *put on* (*the*) *dog*. *colloq.* (chiefly *N. Amer.*). L19. **14** A sausage. Usu. in *pl. slang.* L19. **b** = HOT DOG *n. phr.* 2. M20. **15** In *pl.* [Abbrev. of *dog's meat.*] Feet. *rhyming slang.* E20. **16** Something that is or turns out worthless; a failure, a dud. *slang* (chiefly *N. Amer.*). M20. **17** A horse that is slow or difficult to handle. *slang.* M20.

1 *bulldog*, *German shepherd dog*, *guide-dog*, *gun dog*, *lap-dog*, *long dog*, *sheepdog*, *watchdog*, etc. d *hyena-dog*, *native dog*, *prairie dog*, etc. 2 SIR W. SCOTT Dog of an unbeliever . . darest thou press upon a Christian? b R. BOLDREWOOD Are you going to turn dog, now that you know the way in? 9 T. C. WOLFE That dull dog, Cicero. S. SASSOON He posed as a gay dog, chaffing the nurses. B. MASON He had enough wry stories . . to elicit the great New Zealand tribute, 'ah: a proper dag.' 10 WATER-DOG. 13 W. STEVENS Sweeney is completely without side or dog. 16 *New Yorker* The enormous Cadillac . . turned out to be a dog and had to be junked.

Phrases: *bottom dog*: see BOTTOM *a.* *Danish dog*: see DANISH *a.* **die like a dog, die a dog's death** die shamefully. *dirty dog*: see DIRTY *a.* **dog and bone** *rhyming slang* a telephone. **dog in the manger** a person who selfishly refuses to let others enjoy benefits for which he or she personally has no use. *dog on* (*it*): see DOGGONE. **dogs of war** *fig.* the havoc accompanying war. *Great Dog*: see sense 5 above. *hair of the dog* (*that bit one*): see HAIR *n.* **help a lame dog over a stile** come to the aid of a person in need. **keep a dog and bark oneself** do the work for which one employs others. *lazy dog*: see LAZY *a.* *Lesser Dog*: see sense 5 above. **let sleeping dogs lie** & vars., refrain from intervening in a situation which is safest left alone. **like a dog with two tails** in a state of great delight. *Little Dog*: see sense 5 above. *Negro dog*: see NEGRO. **not a dog's chance** no chance whatever. *rain cats and dogs*: see CAT *n.*[1] *running dog*: see RUNNING *ppl a.* *see a man about a dog*: see SEE *v.* *shock-dog*: see SHOCK *n.*[4] 1. *short dog*: see SHORT *a.*

SPOTTED *dog*. *tinned dog*: see sense 1e above. *top dog*: see TOP *a.* **to the dogs** to ruin or destruction; *go to the dogs*, deteriorate shockingly; *send* or *throw to the dogs*, discard as worthless. *try it on the dog*: see TRY *v. turn dog*: see sense 2b above. *upper dog*: see UPPER *a. yellow dog*: see YELLOW *a.*

B *attrib.* or as *adj.* **1** Of or pertaining to dogs; canine. M16. **2** Of certain animals, esp. ones related to the dog: male. M16. **3** Of a language etc.: debased, corrupt, mongrel. E17.

2 *dog fox, dog hyena, dog otter*, etc. **3** *dog Latin* etc.

Comb.: With certain adjs. in sense 'as — as a dog, thoroughly, extremely', as *dog-poor, dog-sick*, etc. Special combs., as **†dog-ape** a cynocephalus; **dogbane, dog's-bane** any of various plants reputedly poisonous to dogs; *esp.* any of various members of the genus *Apocynum* (family Apocynaceae); **dog-biscuit** a hard dry savoury biscuit fed to dogs; *Mil. slang* an army mattress; **dog-box** *(a)* a box or compartment for a dog or dogs to lie in; *in the dog-box* (NZ slang), in disfavour; *(b) Austral. slang* a compartment in a railway carriage without a corridor; a railway goods wagon; **dog-bramble** any of several thorny shrubs, *esp.* a N. American wild gooseberry, *Ribes cynosbati*; **dogcart** *(a)* a small cart drawn by dogs; *(b)* a two-wheeled open carriage with two cross-seats back to back, the rear one orig. made to shut up so as to form a box for sportsmen's dogs; **dog-cheap** *a.* & *adv.* (*arch.*) costing very little; dirt cheap; **dog-clutch** a (mechanical) clutch with the teeth of one part engaging in slots in the other; **dog-collar** a collar for a dog's neck; *fig.* a close-fitting collar; *spec.* a clerical collar; also, a jewelled band worn by women, a choker; **dog-daisy** the ox-eye daisy, *Leucanthemum vulgare*; *north.* the common daisy, *Bellis perennis*; **dog-days** the days about the time of the heliacal (or cosmical) rising of the dog-star, traditionally regarded as the hottest and unhealthiest time of the year; *fig.* a period in which malignant influences prevail; **dog-eat-dog** *a.* marked by mutually destructive competition; **dog-end** *slang* a cigarette-end; **dogface** *US slang* a US soldier, esp. an infantryman; **dog-faced** *a.* having a face like a dog; *spec.* designating baboons of the genus *Papio*, from their prognathous jaws; **dog-fennel** the weed stinking camomile, *Anthemis cotula*; **dog-fall** *Wrestling*: in which both wrestlers touch the ground together; **dog fence** *Austral.*: designed to exclude dingoes from a range; **dogfight** *n.* & *v.* *(a) n.* a fight between dogs; *fig.* a violent and confused fight; a fight between aircraft at close quarters; *(b) v.i.* take part in a dogfight; **dogfish** *(a)* any of various small sharks of the families Squalidae, Scyliorhinidae, and Triakidae; *esp.* the nurse hound or large spotted dogfish (*Scyliorhinus stellaris*), the lesser spotted dogfish (*S. canicula*), and the spur-dog or spiny or piked dogfish (*Squalus acanthias*); **†***(b) fig.* a person held in contempt; **dog-fly** [tr. Gk *kunamuia*] any of various flies troublesome to dogs; now *esp.* (*US*) = *stable-fly* s.v. STABLE *n.*[1]; **dog-grass** *(a)* couch grass, *Leymus repens*; *(b) dial.* = *dog's-tail* below; **dog-grate** a detached grate for a fireplace; **dog-handler** a person, esp. a police officer, in charge of a dog or dogs; **doghead** the hammer of a gunlock; **dog-headed** *a.* having a dog's head or a head like a dog's; **dog-hole** a hole fit for a dog; *contempt.* a mean or cramped dwelling; **dog-hook** an iron bar with a bent prong for securing or hoisting a log etc.; **doghouse** *(a)* (now *N. Amer.*) a kennel; *(b) in the doghouse* (fig., colloq.), in disgrace; *(c) colloq.* any small structure likened to a kennel, *esp.* a hut, a shelter; *(d) slang* a double bass; **dog-hutch** = *dog-hole* above; **dog-in-the-manger** *a.* characteristic of a dog in the manger (see Phrases above); *dog-iron*: see DOG *n.* 7; **dog-leech** *(a) arch.* a veterinary surgeon who treats dogs; **†***(b)* an ignorant medical practitioner; **dogleg** *Golf* a fairway which turns to left or right; **dog-leg(ged)** *a.* bent like a dog's hind leg; *dog-leg(ged) fence* (Austral. & NZ), a fence made of logs or trees laid horizontally on crossing supports; *dog-leg(ged) stair*, a staircase without a well; **dog-lichen** a large prostrate leaflike lichen, *Peltigera canina*, with apothecia produced on upward-pointing narrow lobes; **dogman** *Austral.* a man who gives directional signals to a crane-operator on a building-site, often riding on the goods lifted by the crane; **dog-meat** prepared horse-flesh or offal sold as food for dogs; **dog-nail** a nail with a solid and slightly countersunk head; a large nail with a head projecting sideways; **dog-nap** a short sleep, a catnap; **dog-paddle** *n.* & *v.* (*colloq.*) *(a) n.* an elementary form of swimming stroke; *(b) v.i.* swim using this stroke; **dog-race** a race between greyhounds; in *pl.* also, a meeting for such races; **dog-robber** *slang (a)* in *pl.*, civilian clothes worn by a naval officer on shore leave; *(b)* an army or navy officer's orderly; **dogrose** any of various related wild roses with faintly scented, usu. pale pink flowers, esp. *Rosa canina*; **dog's age** *slang* a very long time; *dog's-bane*: see *dogbane* above; **dog's breakfast** *slang* a mess; **dog's-cabbage** a fleshy plant, *Theligonum cynocrambe*, grown as a pot-herb in Mediterranean regions; **dog's dinner** *slang (a) dressed* etc. *like a dog's dinner*, dressed etc. ostentatiously or overelaborately; *(b)* = *dog's breakfast* above; **dog-shore** a temporary wooden support for a ship just before launching; **dogskin** (leather from or imitating) a dog's skin; **†dog's-leather**: made from the skin of dogs; **dog-sleep** a light, fitful, or (formerly) feigned sleep; **dog's letter** [tr. L *litera canina*] the letter R (from its resemblance in sound to the snarl of a dog); **dog's life** a life of constant harassment or drudgery; a miserable life; **dog's-meat** *(a)* = *dog-meat* above; *fig.* carrion; *(b) rhyming slang* feet (cf. sense 15 above); *dog's mercury*: see MERCURY *n.*; **dog's-nose** a mixture of beer and gin or rum; *dog's onion*: see ONION *n.* 1b; **dog's-tail** a grass of the genus *Cynosurus*, with flowers in spikelike panicles, *esp.* (more fully *crested dog's-tail*) a common pasture grass, *C. cristatus*; **dog-star, D-.** *(a)* the star Sirius, in the constellation of the Great Dog, the brightest of the fixed stars; *(b)* (in full *Lesser Dog-star*) Procyon, a star of the first magnitude in the Little Dog; **dog-stone** *(a)* a stone used for a millstone; *(b)* in *pl.* (now *rare* or *obs.*) [tr. med.L *testiculus canis*], any of various British orchids; **dog's-tongue** = *hound's-tongue* s.v. HOUND *n.*[1]; **dog-stove** = *dog-grate* above; *dog's trick*: see *dog-trick* below; **dog-tag** *(a)* a tag attached to a dog's collar, giving the owner's address, the dog's name, etc.; *(b) N. Amer. slang* a soldier's metal identity tag; **dog-tent** a small tent shaped like a kennel; **dog-tired** *a.* as tired as a dog after a long chase; utterly exhausted; **dog-town** *US* an area occupied by a colony of prairie dogs; **dog-trials** *Austral.* & *NZ* sheepdog trials; **dog-trick** (now *rare* or *obs.*), **dog's trick** a mean low-down trick; **dogtrot** an easy trot like that of a dog; **dog tucker** *Austral.* & *NZ* mutton used as food for working dogs; **dog-vane** *Naut.* a small improvised vane placed on a gunwale or shroud to show the direction of the wind; **dog violet** any of various related scentless violets, esp. *Viola riviniana*, common in woods and hedges; **dogwatch** *(a) Naut.* either of the two shorter (two-hour) watches (4–6, 6–8 p.m.); *(b) US slang* a night shift, esp. in a newspaper office; **dog-weary** *a.* = *dog-tired* above; **dog-whelk** *(a)* any of various carnivorous marine gastropods of the family Nassariidae; *(b)* = *dog-winkle* below; **dog-whipper** *Hist.* an official formerly employed to whip dogs out of a church; a sexton, a beadle; **dog-winkle** a carnivorous marine gastropod, *Nucella* (*Thais*) *lapillus*.

¶Perh. orig. applied to a particular breed, a mastiff or other powerful dog; adopted in this sense into Continental langs., at first usu. with the attribute 'English'. In Gmc langs. the generic name was *hund*: see HOUND *n.*

doglike *a.* *(a)* resembling (that of) a dog; *(b) fig.* excessively submissive or devoted: E16.

dog /dɒg/ *v.* Infl. **-gg-**. E16. [f. the n. In sense 8 back-form. f. DOGGER *n.*[3]] **1** *v.t.* Follow on the heels of; pursue closely (a person, a person's footsteps, etc.); *fig.* beset continually. E16. **2** *v.i.* Follow in close pursuit. E16. **3** *v.t.* Drive or chase (esp. *out*) with a dog or dogs. L16. **4** *v.t.* Fasten or secure by means of a (mechanical) dog. L16. **5** *v.t.* In imprecations: damn. Chiefly in (*be*) *dogged if. US slang.* M19. **6** *v.i.* Go grouse-shooting using dogs to rouse the birds. Chiefly as *dogging* vbl n. L19. **7** *v.i.* Betray someone; turn dog *on* (DOG *n.* 2b). *Austral. slang.* L19. **8** *v.i.* Hunt dingoes. Chiefly as *dogging* vbl n. Cf. DOGGER *n.*[3] *Austral.* E20. **9** *v.t.* (esp. w. *it*). Not try hard (at) or make an effort (over). *US slang.* E20.

1 S. NAIPAUL I went out into the lobby, dogged at a discreet distance by my spy. H. MOORE Insults and misunderstanding . . dogged him all his life.

dogan /ˈdəʊgən/ *n. Canad. slang.* M19. [Origin uncertain: perh. f. *Dogan*, an Irish surname.] An Irish Roman Catholic.

dogana /də(ʊ)ˈgɑːnə/ *n.* M17. [It.: see DOUANE.] In Italy (and Spain): a custom-house; the customs.

dogaressa /dəʊgəˈrɛsə/ *n.* E19. [It., irreg. fem. of DOGE.] *Hist.* The wife of a doge.

dogate /ˈdəʊgeɪt/ *n.* Also **dogeate** /-dʒ-/. E18. [Fr. *dogat* f. It. *dogato*, f. DOGE: see -ATE[1].] The position or status of a doge.

dogberry /ˈdɒgb(ə)ri, -bɛri/ *n.*[1] Also **†dog's berry.** E16. [f. DOG *n.* + BERRY *n.*[1]] The fruit of the wild cornel or dogwood, *Cornus sanguinea*; (in full *dogberry tree*) the shrub itself. Also, (the fruit of) any of various other shrubs or small trees with fruit of poor eating quality, as the N. American rowan, *Sorbus americana*.

Dogberry /ˈdɒgbɛri, -b(ə)ri/ *n.*[2] M19. [A foolish constable in Shakespeare's *Much Ado*.] An ignorant self-important petty official.

dogbolt /ˈdɒgbəʊlt/ *n.* LME. [Prob. f. DOG *n.* + BOLT *n.*[1], but only readily so explained in sense 3.] **†1** A butt for ridicule; a fool; a contemptible wretch. LME–E19. **†2** A kind of bolt or blunt-headed arrow. L16–E17. **3** Any of various kinds of mechanical fastener. E19.

dogdom /ˈdɒgdəm/ *n. joc.* M19. [f. DOG *n.* + -DOM.] The world of dogs or dog-fanciers; dogs collectively.

doge /dəʊdʒ/ *n.* M16. [Fr. (monosyllabic) f. It. (disyllabic) f. Venetian It. *doze* ult. f. L DUX, *duc-* leader.] *Hist.* The chief magistrate in the former republics of Venice and Genoa.

dogeship *n.* the status, position, or personality of a doge L17.

dog-ear /ˈdɒgɪə/ *v.* & *n.* Also (earlier) **dog's-** /ˈdɒgz-/. M17. [f. DOG *n.* (+ -'S[1]) + EAR *n.*[1]] **A** *v.t.* Disfigure (a book etc.) by turning down the corners of the pages; make worn or grubby by repeated or careless use. Chiefly as *dog-eared* ppl a. M17. **B** *n.* **I** Now usu. **dog-.** **1** The corner of the page of a book turned over or creased by repeated or careless use, or to keep a place. M18. **II dog's-** only. **2** *Naut.* A loop formed by a leech rope when a sail is reefed. M19. **3** *Naut.* A corner of a shark's-mouth in an awning. L19.

dogeate *n.* var. of DOGATE.

dogged /ˈdɒgɪd/ *a.* & *adv.* ME. [f. DOG *n.* + -ED[2]. Cf. CRABBED.] **A** *adj.* **†1** Having the bad qualities of a dog; vicious, mean, spiteful; (of a thing) difficult to deal with, intractable. ME–L17. **2a** Ill-tempered, surly, morose. Now always with mixture of sense 2b: displaying sullen obstinacy. LME. **b** Having the tenacity or persistence of a dog; stubborn, unyielding. L18. **3** *gen.* Having some other characteristic or habit of a dog; of or pertaining to a dog or dogs. Now *rare* or *obs.* LME.

2a S. PEPYS My wife in a dogged humour for my not dining at home. G. GISSING He had not spoken angrily but in a curiously dogged tone, with awkward emphasis. **b** C. STEAD I won't have this cussed obstinacy. I'll break that miserable dogged spirit of yours. D. ACHESON The dogged, unbeatable courage of the British. *Proverb*: It's dogged as does it. **3** SHAKES. *John* Now for the bare-pick'd bone of majesty Doth dogged war bristle his angry crest.

B *adv.* **†1** Viciously, spitefully. Only in LME. **2** Excessively, thoroughly. *colloq.* & *dial.* E19.

doggedly *adv.* LME. **doggedness** *n.* M16.

dogger /ˈdɒgə/ *n.*[1] ME. [MDu. = trawler, fishing boat.] *Hist.* A kind of two-masted fishing boat with bluff bows formerly used in the North Sea. Also *dogger boat*.

dogger /ˈdɒgə/ *n.*[2] In sense 2 **D-.** L17. [Perh. a deriv. of DOG *n.*] **1a** A kind of ironstone found in globular concretions; a concretion of this. *dial.* L17. **b** *Geol.* A large roughly spherical mass of sandstone. L19. **2** *Geol.* The lowest division of the Middle Jurassic in Yorkshire, composed of marine sandstones and oolites; the Middle Jurassic system and period in Europe. E19.

dogger /ˈdɒgə/ *n.*[3] *Austral.* L19. [f. DOG *n.* + -ER[1].] A person who hunts dingoes. Cf. DOG *v.* 8.

doggerel /ˈdɒg(ə)r(ə)l/ *a.* & *n.* Also **doggrel** /ˈdɒgr(ə)l/. LME. [App. f. DOG *n.* & *a.* (with contempt. force as in *dog Latin*): see -REL.] **A** *adj.* Of verse: burlesque and composed in irregular rhythm; trivial, paltry; undignified. LME.

BARONESS ORCZY His doggerel verse, 'We seek him here, we seek him there,' etc.

B *n.* Burlesque verse in irregular rhythm; (a specimen of) trivial or pedestrian verse. M17.

doggerelize *v.t.* turn into doggerel E19. **doggerelizer** *n.* a writer of doggerel E19.

doggery /ˈdɒg(ə)ri/ *n.* E17. [f. DOG *n.* + -ERY.] **1** Foul or abusive language. *rare.* E17. **2** Doglike behaviour; *esp.* dishonest or knavish behaviour. M19. **3** Dogs collectively; *fig.* [tr. Fr. *canaille*] a rabble. M19. 4 A cheap or disreputable saloon. *US slang*. M19.

doggess /ˈdɒɡɪs/ *n. joc.* M18. [f. DOG *n.* + -ESS[1].] A female dog, a bitch.

†dogget, -ett *ns., vs.* vars. of DOCKET *n., v.*

doggie *n.* var. of DOGGY *n.*

doggish /ˈdɒɡɪʃ/ *a.* LME. [f. DOG *n.* + -ISH[1].] **1** Pertaining to or resembling (that of) a dog. LME. **2** *spec.* Having the bad qualities of a dog; malicious; surly, ill-tempered; snappish; spiteful. Now *rare*. LME.

doggishly *adv.* L16. **doggishness** *n.* L16.

doggo /ˈdɒɡəʊ/ *adv. slang.* L19. [App. f. DOG *n.* + -O.] Without moving or making a sound; without doing anything that would draw attention to one's presence. Chiefly in *lie doggo*.

doggone /ˈdɒɡɒn/ *v., a., adv.,* & *n. colloq.* (chiefly *N. Amer.*). Also **dog-gone, dog-on,** & (esp. as vb) **dog gone**. E19. [Prob. alt. of *God damn*.] **A** *v.t.* (esp. w. *it*). Damn, confound. E19.

R. H. MORRIESON Doggone it, .. she *was* pretty.

B *adj.* Damned, confounded; (esp. w. *I'm*) astonished, blowed. M19.

S. LEWIS By golly, here they go and use up all the towels, every doggone one of 'em.

C *adv.* Confoundedly, damnably. L19.

R. D. SAUNDERS You was so dog-gone proud of the blue coat.

D *n.* A damn. M20.

E. CALDWELL That will be my ship coming in, and I don't give a dog-gone for the name you call it.

dog-goned /ˈdɒɡɒnd/ *a. colloq.* (chiefly *N. Amer.*). M19. [Prob. alt. of *God-damned*.] = DOGGONE *a.*

C. E. MULFORD Well, I'll be dog-goned if here ain't Hopalong!

doggrel *a.* & *n.* var. of DOGGEREL.

doggy /ˈdɒɡi/ *n.* Also **-ie**. L17. [f. DOG *n.* + -Y[6], -IE.] **1** A little dog; (a pet name for) a dog. L17. **2** *Mining.* = DEPUTY *n.* 2c. Orig., a subordinate to a butty (BUTTY *n.*[1] 2). *dial.* M19. **3** An officer's servant or assistant. Cf. *dog-robber* (b) s.v. DOG *n. slang.* E20.

Comb.: **doggy-bag** a bag in which a diner may take away leftovers, *esp.* one provided by a restaurant.

doggy /ˈdɒɡi/ *a.* LME. [f. DOG *n.* + -Y[1]. Cf. HORSY.] **†1** = DOGGISH 2. LME–L16. **2** = DOGGISH 1. M19. **3** Of a person: devoted to or concerned with dogs. M19. **4** Stylish, smart, dashing. Cf. DOG *n.* 13. *slang.* L19.

2 A. BURGESS They looked up at me with eyes that would soon grow doggy and pleading.

dogie /ˈdəʊɡi/ *n. N. Amer.* Also **dogy**. L19. [Origin unkn.] A neglected or undernourished calf on a range, *esp.* one without a mother.

dogless /dɒɡlɪs/ *a.* M19. [f. DOG *n.* + -LESS.] Having no dog.

dogling *n.* var. of DOEGLING.

dogma /ˈdɒɡmə/ *n.* Pl. **-mas, -mata** /-mətə/. M16. [Late L f. Gk *dogma, dogmat-* opinion, decree, f. *dokein* seem good, think.] **1** An opinion, a belief; *spec.* a tenet or doctrine authoritatively laid down, esp. by a Church or sect; an arrogant declaration of opinion. M16. **2** Doctrines or opinions, esp. on religious matters, laid down authoritatively or assertively. L18.

1 R. NIEBUHR The idea of the class struggle is a dogma which creates .. the conflict experience of the worker. R. LOWELL The year when Pius XII defined the dogma of Mary's bodily assumption. 2 J. MORLEY It places character on the pedestal where Puritanism places dogma. G. BROWN What he didn't have was dogma—he accepted that there could be more than one way of accomplishing a purpose.

dogmatic /dɒɡˈmatɪk/ *n.* & *a.* E17. [L *dogmaticus* f. Gk *dogmatikos*, f. DOGMA: see -ATIC.] **A** *n.* **1** = DOGMATIST *n.* 1. *obs.* exc. *Hist.* E17. **2** *sing.* & (now usu.) in *pl.* (treated as *sing.*). A system of dogma; *spec.* dogmatic theology. M19.

B *adj.* **1** Of philosophy or medicine: based on a priori assumptions rather than empirical evidence. L17. **2** Concerned with propounding opinions; *esp.* (of a person, writing, etc.) asserting doctrines or views in an opinionated or arbitrary manner. L17. **3** Of, pertaining to, or of the nature of a (religious) dogma or dogmas; doctrinal. L17.

2 G. MURRAY He lays down .. lots of rules, .. some of them hopelessly dogmatic and inhuman. J. K. GALBRAITH When people are least sure, they are often most dogmatic. 3 J. S. MILL A .. Christian in all but the dogmatic sense of the word. *dogmatic* THEOLOGY.

dogmatician /-ˈtɪʃ(ə)n/ *n.* an expert on or student of dogmatics M19.

dogmatical /dɒɡˈmatɪk(ə)l/ *a.* & *n.* E17. [f. as prec. + -AL[1].] **A** *adj.* = DOGMATIC *a.* E17. **†B** *n.* In *pl.* Dogmatics. E17–E18.

dogmaticalness *n.* L17.

dogmatically /dɒɡˈmatɪk(ə)li/ *adv.* M17. [f. DOGMATIC *a.* or DOGMATICAL *a.*: see -ICALLY.] In a dogmatic manner.

dogmatise *v.* var. of DOGMATIZE.

dogmatism /ˈdɒɡmətɪz(ə)m/ *n.* E17. [Fr. *dogmatisme* or late L *dogmatismus*, f. L DOGMA: see -ISM.] **1** Positive assertion of dogmas or opinions; dogmatic character. Formerly also, the propounding of new doctrines. E17. **b** A dogmatic tenet or system. *rare*. E19. **2** A system of philosophy with principles based on reasoning alone, not experience. L18.

dogmatist /ˈdɒɡmətɪst/ *n.* E16. [Fr. *dogmatiste* or late L *dogmatistes* f. Gk, f. *dogmatizein*: see next, -IST.] **1** A philosopher or physician of a dogmatic school (see DOGMATIC *a.* 1). E16. **†2** A person who propounds new doctrines. L16–L18. **3** A person who dogmatizes; *esp.* one who asserts his or her opinions forcefully or in a doctrinaire manner. M17.

dogmatize /ˈdɒɡmətaɪz/ *v.* Also **-ise**. E17. [(O)Fr. *dogmatiser* or late L *dogmatizare* f. Gk *dogmatizein* lay down as one's opinion, f. DOGMA: see -IZE.] **1** *v.i.* Speak or write authoritatively or imperiously without giving arguments or evidence in support of one's assertions. E17. **2** *v.t.* Formulate into a dogma; assert dogmatically. E17. **†3** *v.i.* Teach new doctrines. Only in 17.

1 A. S. NEILL I should not dare dogmatize about girls who never go to lessons. 2 *Daily Telegraph* I find the views expressed .. dogmatised to the point of polemic absurdity.

dogmatiˈzation *n.* (*rare*) L19. **dogmatizer** *n.* E17.

dognapping /ˈdɒɡnapɪŋ/ *n. colloq.* M20. [f. DOG *n.* after *kidnapping*.] The stealing of dogs in order to get a ransom or reward from the owners, or to sell them.

dognapper *n.* M20.

do-good /ˈduːɡʊd/ *n.* & *a.* M17. [f. *do good*: see GOOD *n.*] **A** *n.* **1** A person who or thing which does good or is of use. *obs.* exc. as in sense 2. M17. **2** *spec.* = DO-GOODER. E20. **B** *adj.* Designating or typical of a 'do-good'. M20.

do-gooder /duːˈɡʊdə/ *n. colloq.* E20. [f. as prec. + -ER[1].] A person who actively tries to help other people, *esp.* one regarded as unrealistic or officious.

do-goodery *n.* the activities or attitudes of do-gooders M20. **do-gooding** *a.* & *n.* (*a*) *adj.* behaving as a do-gooder; (*b*) *n.* the activities of a do-gooder: M20. **do-goodism** = DO-GOODERY M20.

Dogra /ˈdəʊɡrə/ *n.* & *a.* Also (see senses A2,B below) **-ri** /-ri/. M19. [Dogri *ḍogrā*.] **A** *n.* **1** Pl. **-s**, same. A member of a mainly Hindu people predominating in the Jammu district of the Indian State of Jammu and Kashmir. M19. **2** Usu. **-ri**. The Indo-Aryan language of this people. M20. **B** *adj.* Of or pertaining to the Dogras or (usu. **-ri**) their language. L19.

Dogrib /ˈdɒɡrɪb/ *n.* & *a.* L19. [f. DOG *n.* + RIB *n.*, as tr. Dogrib *Thlingchadinne* dog's flank (f. their legend that they are descended from a dog).] **A** *n.* **1** A member of an Athapaskan people of NW Canada. L19. **2** The language of this people, belonging to the Na-Dene family. E20. **B** *adj.* Of or pertaining to the Dogribs. M20.

dogsbody /ˈdɒɡzbɒdi/ *n.* Also **dog's body, dog's-body**. E19. [f. DOG *n.* + -'S[1] + BODY *n.*] **1** Peas boiled in a cloth. Also, sea-biscuits soaked to a pulp with water and sugar. *Naut. slang.* E19. **2** A person given a variety of menial tasks; *Naut. slang* a junior officer. E20.

dog's-ear *v.* & *n.* see DOG-EAR.

dog's tooth /ˈdɒɡz tuːθ/ *n. phr.* L16. [f. DOG *n.* + -'S[1] + TOOTH *n.*] **1** Now more fully *dog's tooth violet*. Any of various spring-flowering plants of the genus *Erythronium* of the lily family, so called from the toothed perianth segments; esp. *E. dens-canis*, with mottled leaves and purplish flowers. L16. **2** More fully *dog's tooth grass*. A creeping grass, *Cynodon dactylon*, common in warmer parts of the world and used for lawns and fodder. E17. **3** (A fabric in) a broken check pattern; = *houndstooth* s.v. HOUND *n.*[1] M20.

dog-tooth /ˈdɒɡtuːθ/ *n.* & *v.* LME. [f. DOG *n.* + TOOTH *n.*] **A** *n.* Pl. **-teeth**. **1** An eye-tooth. LME. **2** A stone ornament with four leaves radiating from a raised central point, much used in Norman and Early English architecture. Also *dog-tooth moulding*. M19. **3** = DOG'S TOOTH 3. M20.

Comb.: **dog-tooth spar** a form of calcite with pointed scalenohedral crystals; **dog-tooth violet** = DOG'S TOOTH 1.

B *v.t.* Decorate with dog-tooth moulding. M19.

dogwood /ˈdɒɡwʊd/ *n.* L16. [f. DOG *n.* + WOOD *n.*[1] Cf. DOGBERRY *n.*[1]] **1** Any of various shrubs and small trees of the genus *Cornus* (family Cornaceae); their hard horny wood; *esp.* (*a*) the wild cornel, *C. sanguinea*, a shrub with dark red twigs and clusters of small white flowers; (*b*) *N. Amer.* (also *flowering dogwood*) the flowering cornel, *C. florida*, a deciduous tree in which the flowers are surrounded by large petal-like bracts. L16. **2** (The wood of) any of various shrubs and trees suggesting the wild cornel in appearance or by the hardness of their wood; *esp.* (*W. Indies*) the leguminous tree *Piscidia piscipula*; *Austral.* the leguminous shrub *Jacksonia scoparia*. L17.

dogy *n.* var. of DOGIE.

doh /dəʊ/ *n.* Also **do**. M18. [It. *do* arbitrary syllable repl. UT.] *Mus.* In solmization: the keynote of a major diatonic scale (also *movable doh*); the note C (also *fixed doh*).

dohickey *n.* var. of DOOHICKEY.

doigté /dwate/ *n.* L19. [Fr., f. *doigt* finger f. L *digitus* DIGIT.] *Fencing.* The use of the fingers and thumb in manipulating the sword.

doiled /dɔɪld/ *a. Sc.* Also **doilt, doylt,** /dɔɪlt/. E16. [Origin unkn.] Stupid, foolish; confused, affected in mind; wearied.

doily /ˈdɔɪli/ *a.* & *n.* Also **doyl(e)y**. L17. [*Doiley* or *Doyley*, 17th-cent. London draper.] **†A** *adj.* Designating a woollen material used esp. for summer wear; made of this material. L17–E18.

doily napkin = sense B.1 below.

B *n.* **1** [Ellipt. for *doily napkin* above.] A small ornamental napkin used at dessert. *arch.* L18. **2** A small light ornamental mat of paper or cloth, used on a plate beneath sandwiches, cakes, etc. M19.

doing /ˈduːɪŋ/ *n.* ME. [f. DO *v.* + -ING[1].] **1** The action of DO *v.*; action, conduct; performance, execution, (*of* something). Freq. w. possess., attributing responsibility to a specified agent. ME. **b** Sexual intercourse. E17. **c** Effort put into accomplishing something. *colloq.* M20. **2** A deed, an action; an activity. Usu. (now always, exc. *Sc.*) in *pl.* LME. **b** A scolding; a thrashing; a defeating. *colloq.* & *dial.* E19. **3** In *pl.* Ingredients for a dish; a prepared or fancy dish; food, victuals; drink. *US dial.* & *Austral. slang.* M19. **4** In *pl.* Trimmings, ornaments, etc., for a dress. *US colloq.* M19. **5** In *pl.* (treated as *sing.* or *pl.*). A thing needed; requisites; something referred to without being named. *slang.* E20. **6** In *pl.* Excrement. *slang.* M20.

1 SHAKES. *Tr. & Cr.* Things won are done; joy's soul lies in the doing. *Book of Common Prayer* This is the Lords doing: and it is marvellous in our eyes. R. LAWLER I'm not blamin' him. This is Barney's doin', he cooked this up. c L. NKOSI Took a bit of doing, but .. we pulled it off. 2 BARONESS ORCZY Feelings .. ran very high .. against the French and their doings. J. GALSWORTHY It was a habit with him to tell her the doings of his day. 5 J. FOWLES There were all the doings to make tea with. P. LIVELY If either of you need the doings it's first right at the end of the passage.

doing /ˈduːɪŋ/ *ppl a.* L16. [f. DO *v.* + -ING[2].]

That does, acts, or performs; *spec.* busy; energetic.
up and doing: see UP *adv.*[2] & *a.*[2]

doit /dɔɪt/ *n.* Now *arch.* or *Hist.* L16. [MLG *doyt* = MDu. *duit, deuyt.* Cf. DODKIN.] 1 A small Dutch coin formerly in use, the eighth part of a stiver; any very small coin or sum. L16. 2 *fig.* A very small part *of* anything; a bit, a jot. Esp. in *not care a doit.* M17.

doit /dɔɪt/ *v.* *Sc.* & *north.* M16. [Origin uncertain: perh. alt. of DOTE *v.*[1] Cf. next.] 1 *v.i.* Behave stupidly; be confused or enfeebled, esp. through old age or drink. M16. 2 *v.t.* Make confused, befuddle; puzzle. Cf. earlier DOITED. M18. 3 *v.i.* Walk unsteadily. L18.

doited /ˈdɔɪtɪd/ *a.* *Sc.* & *north.* LME. [Origin uncertain: perh. alt. of *doted* pa. pple of DOTE *v.*[1]] Having the faculties impaired, esp. by age.

doitkin *n.* see DODKIN.

do-it-yourself /ˌduːɪtjəˈsɛlf, -jə-/ *n.* & *a.* M20. [f. *do it yourself* (DO *v.* 3).] A *n.* The action or practice of doing practical work, esp. one's household repairs and maintenance, oneself, rather than paying to have it done. M20. B *adj.* Pertaining to do-it-yourself; suitable or intended for use by a do-it-yourselfer or amateur; interested in do-it-yourself. M20.
do-it-yourselfer *n.* a person who practises do-it-yourself M20.

dojo /ˈdəʊdʒəʊ/ *n.* Pl. **-os**. M20. [Jap., f. *dō* way, pursuit + *-jō* a place.] A room or hall in which judo or other martial arts are practised; an area of padded mats for the same purpose.

doke /dəʊk/ *n.* Now *dial.* E17. [Origin uncertain: cf. EFris. *dölke* small hollow, dimple. See also DOLK.] A hollow; a dent; a dimple.

Doketism *n.* var. of DOCETISM.

dol /dəʊl/ *n.* M20. [L *dolor* pain.] A unit of intensity of pain.

dolabriform /də(ʊ)ˈlabrɪfɔːm/ *a.* M18. [f. L *dolabra* pickaxe + -I- + -FORM.] *Bot.* & *Entomol.* Axe-shaped.

Dolby /ˈdɒlbi, ˈdəʊl-/ *n.* & *a.* M20. [R. M. *Dolby* (b. 1933), US engineer.] (Proprietary name designating) a kind of electronic noise-reduction system used esp. to reduce tape hiss.
Dolbyed *a.* (UK proprietary) provided with a Dolby L20. **Dolbyized** *a.* (US proprietary) = DOLBYED L20.

dolcan /ˈdɒlkən/ *n.* M19. [f. It. *dolce* sweet: cf. It. *dolciano.*] A kind of soft-toned organ-stop, wider at the top than at the bottom.

dolce far niente /ˌdoltʃe far niˈɛnte/ *n. phr.* E19. [It. = sweet doing nothing.] Delightful idleness. Cf. FAR NIENTE.

dolce vita /doltʃe ˈviːta, dəʊltʃeɪ ˈviːtə/ *n. phr.* M20. [It. = sweet life.] A life of luxury, pleasure, and self-indulgence. Freq. preceded by *the* or *la* /la/.

doldrum /ˈdɒldrəm/ *n.* L18. [Perh. f. DULL *a.* after *tantrum.*] I *sing.* †1 A dull, sluggish, or stupid person. L18–E19.
II In *pl.* (usu. w. *the*). 2 A condition of dullness or drowsiness; low spirits, despondency. E19. 3 The condition of a ship which makes no headway. E19. 4 A region of calms, sudden storms, and light unpredictable winds near the Equator. M19. 5 *fig.* A state or period of little activity or progress in affairs. L19.
5 J. BARZUN Fiction languishes and the theater is in the doldrums.

dole /dəʊl/ *n.*[1] *Sc.* & *north.* **dale** /deɪl/. [OE *dāl* f. Gmc base also of DEAL *n.*[1]] †1 The state of being divided; division. OE–ME. 2†a A part or division of a whole. OE–L16. b A portion of an area of land, esp. a common field. Chiefly *Sc.* & *north.* *obs.* exc. *Hist.* ME. c A portion for sale; *Sc.* a former measure in which coal was sold. E18. d *Mining.* A portion of ore. E19. 3 One's share, one's portion. *arch.* ME. 4 Fate, destiny; lot in life. Chiefly in *happy man be his dole* (proverbial) *arch.* ME. †5 Dealing, intercourse. ME–M16. 6 Dealing out, distribution, esp. of charitable gifts. ME. 7 That which is doled out, *esp.* a gift of food or money made in charity. LME. †b A reward given to hounds. L16–L17. c State relief paid to the unemployed. Usu. *the dole. colloq.* E20. 8 = DEAL *n.*[1] 3. *Sc.* E18.
7c R. HOGGART A man out of work and drawing the dole. **on the dole** in receipt of unemployment benefit.
Comb.: **dole bludger** *Austral.* a person who draws unemployment benefit in preference to getting or seeking work; **dole queue** a queue of people waiting to collect unemployment benefit (*lit.* & *fig.*).

dole /dəʊl/ *n.*[2] *arch.* & *dial.* Also **dool, dule**, /duːl/. ME. [OFr. *dol, doel, duel* (mod. *deuil*) mourning f. pop.L *dolus*, f. L *dolere* grieve.] 1 Grief, sorrow; distress of mind. ME. 2 Mourning, lamentation. Chiefly in *make dole.* ME. 3 A cause of grief; a grievous or piteous thing; a sorrow. ME. †4 Clothes etc. worn as a sign of mourning. E16–M18. 5 A funeral. *obs.* exc. *dial.* M16.

dole /dəʊl/ *n.*[3] LME. [L *dolus* deceit f. Gk *dolos.*] †1 Guile, deceit, fraud. LME–M19. 2 *Sc. Law* (now *Hist.*). The wrongful intention necessary to make an act a crime. M17.

dole *n.*[4] var. of DOOL *n.*[1]

dole /dəʊl/ *v.*[1] ME. [OFr. *doleir, doloir* (mod. (*se*) *douloir*) f. L *dolere* grieve.] †1 *v.i.* Sorrow, lament. ME–L18. 2 *v.t.* Mourn, bewail. *obs.* exc. *Sc. dial.* M16. 3 *v.i.* Of a bird: coo. M19.

dole /dəʊl/ *v.*[2]*t.* LME. [f. DOLE *n.*[1]] 1 Give as a dole; distribute as charity. LME. †2 Spread *about, around*; distribute. E–M18. 3 Give *out* in small quantities; deal *out* sparingly. M18.
3 A. MOOREHEAD At each meal he carefully doled out the food.
doler *n.* a person who doles something (usu. foll. by *out*) L16.

doleful /ˈdəʊlfʊl, -f(ə)l/ *a.* & *n.* ME. [f. DOLE *n.*[2] + -FUL.] A *adj.* 1 Fraught with or causing sorrow, distressing; gloomy, dismal. ME. 2 Of a person etc.: full of pain, grief, or suffering; sorrowful; melancholy, discontented. ME. 3 Expressive of grief, suffering, or sad regret. ME.
1 MILTON Regions of sorrow, doleful shades. 3 DAY LEWIS Her pure, rather doleful voice.
B *n.* †1 In *pl.* Mourning clothes. *rare.* Only in M18. 2 In *pl.* A doleful state, *the* dumps. *colloq.* L18.
dolefully *adv.* ME. **dolefulness** *n.* LME.

dolent /ˈdəʊl(ə)nt/ *a.* *arch.* LME. [(O)Fr. f. Proto-Gallo-Romance, f. L *dolent-* pres. ppl stem of *dolere* grieve: see -ENT.] 1 = DOLEFUL *a.* 2. LME. 2 = DOLEFUL *a.* 3. L15. †3 = DOLEFUL *a.* 1. L15–L16.

dolerite /ˈdɒlərʌɪt/ *n.* M19. [Fr. *dolérite*, f. Gk *doleros* deceptive (because it was difficult to distinguish from diorite): see -ITE[1].] An igneous rock chemically the same as basalt and gabbro but medium-grained with a usu. ophitic texture.
dole'ritic *a.* M19.

dolesome /ˈdəʊls(ə)m/ *a.* Now *rare.* M16. [f. DOLE *n.*[2] + -SOME[1].] = DOLEFUL *a.* 1, 3.
dolesomely *adv.* L16. **dolesomeness** *n.* E17.

doless /ˈduːlɪs/ *a.* *dial.* & *colloq.* (chiefly *Sc.* & *US*). Also **do-less**. M18. [f. DO *v.* + -LESS.] Lazy, good-for-nothing; lacking energy.
M. MEAD Too lazy, too do-less, to make an effort.

dolia *n.* pl. of DOLIUM.

doli capax /dɒlɪ ˈkapaks/ *a. phr.* L17. [f. L *doli* genit. sing. of *dolus* (see DOLE *n.*[3], DOLUS) + *capax* capable.] *Law.* Capable of having the wrongful intention to commit a crime.

dolicho- /ˈdɒlɪkəʊ/ *comb. form* of Gk *dolikhos* narrow: see -O-. Cf. BRACHY-, PLATY-.
dolicho'pellic *a.* [Gk *pella* bowl] having or designating a pelvis whose anteroposterior diameter is nearly as great as its transverse diameter L19.

dolichocephalic /ˌdɒlɪkəʊsɪˈfalɪk, -kɛˈfalɪk/ *a.* Also †**-keph-**. M19. [f. prec. + -CEPHALIC.] Long-headed; *spec.* having a cranial index of less than 75.
'dolichocephal *a.* & *n.* (pl. **-s**) [back-form. f. mod.L pl.] †(*a*) *adj.* dolichocephalic; (*b*) *n.* a dolichocephalic person: L19. **dolicho'cephali** *n.pl.* (now *rare* or *obs.*) [mod.L] dolichocephals M19. **dolicho'cephalism** *n.* dolichocephalic condition M19. **dolicho'cephalous** *a.* dolichocephalic M19. **dolicho'cephaly** *n.* dolichocephalism M19.

dolichos /ˈdɒlɪkɒs/ *n.* L18. [mod.L f. Gk = long, w. allus. to the length of the pods.] Any of several tropical leguminous plants of the genus *Dolichos*, grown for food or fodder.

doli incapax /ˌdɒlɪ ɪnˈkapaks/ *a. phr.* L17. [f. as DOLI CAPAX: see IN-[2].] *Law.* Not *doli capax*, esp. because under 14 years old.

†**doliman** *n.* see DOLMAN.

doline /dɒˈliːnə, -ˈliːn/ *n.* Also **-ina** /-iːnə/. L19. [G, f. Slovene *dolina* valley.] A typically funnel-shaped basin in a karstic region.

do-little /ˈduːlɪt(ə)l/ *n.* & *a.* L16. [f. DO *v.* + LITTLE *n.*] A *n.* A person who does little; a lazy person. L16. B *adj.* Lazy. L17.

dolium /ˈdəʊlɪəm/ *n.* Pl. **-ia** /-ɪə/. L15. [L *dolium.*] *Rom. Antiq.* A large earthenware vessel for storing grain, wine, etc.

dolk /dɒlk/ *n.* *obs.* exc. *dial.* ME. [Origin uncertain: for sense 1 cf. OFris. *dolch*, OHG *tolg* wound; for sense 3 cf. DOKE.] †1 A wound; a scar. Only in ME. 2 = DOKE. E19. 3 A dab, a light blow. M19.

doll /dɒl/ *n.*[1] M16. [Pet-form of female forename *Dorothy*, with *l* for *r* as in *Hal, Sal, Moll*, for *Harry, Sarah, Mary.*] †1 A female favourite, a mistress. M16–E17. 2 A small model of a human figure, usu. a child or woman, for use as a toy. L17. b A ventriloquist's or puppeteer's dummy. L19. c A hit or score in the game of Aunt Sally. L20. 3 A woman who is pretty but unintelligent or frivolous. L18. b Any woman or girl, *esp.* an attractive one; occas., a pleasant or attractive man. *slang.* M19.
2 C. MCCULLOUGH The doll had jointed arms and legs which could be moved anywhere. *Dutch doll, peg doll, rag doll, Russian doll, walking doll*, etc. 3b R. LARDNER Betsy is some doll when she is all fixed up.
Comb.: **doll-baby** *US* = sense 2 above; **doll hospital** *US* = *doll's hospital* below; **dollhouse** *N. Amer.* = *doll's house* below; **doll's hospital** an establishment that repairs dolls and sells materials for making them; **doll's house** a miniature toy house for dolls; a very small house.
dolldom *n.* the world of dolls M19. **dollhood** *n.* the state or condition of a doll, or of being like a doll L19. **dollship** *n.* (with possess. adj., as *her* etc. *dollship*) a mock title of respect given to a doll M18.

doll /dɒl/ *n.*[2] M20. [Perh. var. of DOOL *n.*[1]] *Horse-racing.* A hurdle used as a barrier.

†**doll** *v.*[1]*t.* LME. [Origin unkn.] 1 Warm moderately; mull. LME–M17. 2 Make (drink) stale or vapid. LME–M19.

doll /dɒl/ *v.*[2]*t.* & *i.* *colloq.* E20. [f. DOLL *n.*[1]] Foll. by *up*: dress up finely or elaborately; make (esp. oneself) smart.
H. L. WILSON Jeff said he'd also doll up in his dress suit and get shaved. F. ASTAIRE The Globe Theatre was all dolled up with fresh paint. J. KEROUAC Old Mr. Burke dolled himself up for a date.

dollar /ˈdɒlə/ *n.* M16. [Early Flem., LG *daler* (Du. *daalder*) f. G *Taler* (formerly also *thaler*), abbrev. of *Joachimst(h)aler* coin from the silver mine of *Joachimst(h)al*, i.e. Joachim's valley, now Jáchymov in the Czech Republic. Cf. THALER.] 1 *Hist.* A German thaler; any of various northern European coins bearing an equivalent name. M16. 2 *Hist.* A Spanish or Spanish-American peso or piece of eight (also largely used in the British N. American colonies at the time of the War of Independence). L16. 3 The basic monetary unit of the United States, equal to 100 cents; a basic monetary unit in Canada, Australia, New Zealand, and numerous other countries; a note or coin of the value of one dollar. L18. 4 A five-shilling piece, a crown. *slang. obs.* exc. *Hist.* E19.
Phrases: **be dollars to doughnuts** (or **buttons** etc.) *US* be a certainty (*that*). *bottom dollar*: see BOTTOM *a.* (*like*) *a* MILLION *dollars*. *top dollar*: see TOP *a.*
Comb.: **dollar area** those countries which have a currency linked to the US dollar; **dollarbird** the broad-billed roller, *Eurystomus orientalis*, a brown and blue-green bird of parts of Asia and Australia that has a round white patch on each wing; **dollar day** *N. Amer.*: when a shop makes special price reductions, usu. including some to a dollar; **dollar diplomacy**: which seeks to advance a country's financial and commercial interests abroad and hence its international influence; **dollar gap** the excess of a country's import trade with the dollar area over the corresponding export trade; **dollar-mark**, **-sign** the

symbol $, placed before a number to denote that many dollars; **dollar spot** a discoloured area caused by disease, esp. on a lawn; a fungal disease that affects lawns in this way.

Dollardom *n.* (now *rare*) (the inhabitants of) a place where the people's main aim is seen as amassing dollars; rich Americans collectively: M19. **dollari'zation** *n.* the action or process of aligning a currency with the US dollar L20.

dollop /'dɒləp/ *n.* & *v.* L16. [Perh. of Scand. origin (cf. Norw. dial. *dolp* lump).] A *n.* 1 A clump of grass, weeds, etc., in a field. *obs.* exc. *dial.* L16. 2 A shapeless, usu. large, lump or portion. *colloq.* E19. 3 A slovenly woman; a trollop. *dial.* E19.

2 L. CHAMBERLAIN Serve with a dollop of sour cream.

B *v.t.* 1 Tumble about. *dial.* E19. 2 Serve *out* or put *on* in substantial quantities. *colloq.* M19.

dolly /'dɒli/ *n.*[1] E17. [f. DOLL *n.*[1] + -Y[6].] †1 a = DOLL *n.*[1] 1 *slang.* E17–M19. b A slattern, a useless woman. *dial.* E19. 2 a (A name, esp. in voc., for) a child's doll. See also *corn dolly* s.v. CORN *n.*[1] L18. b A girl, a woman, *esp.* a young attractive one. *colloq.* E20. 3 A short wooden pole with projecting pieces at one end and a handle at the other, used for stirring clothes in a washtub. Formerly also, a washtub; a machine for washing clothes. L18. 4 Something placed between a ram and a pile; a punch, *esp.* one for shaping the head of a rivet. M19. 5 A simple device for crushing auriferous quartz by repeated blows. *Austral.* & *S. Afr.* M19. 6 A small platform on wheels used as a conveyance; *spec.* one used as a mobile base for a film or television camera. E20. 7 In ball games, a ball that is easily caught or hit; *Cricket* a donkey-drop. *colloq.* E20. 8 The pivoted lever of a tumbler switch. M20. 9 A weighted barbless hook with a lure, used in fishing for snoek. *S. Afr.* M20.

2b *Daily Mirror* Always falling wildly in and out of love with dishy dollies.

Comb.: **dolly-bag** = DOROTHY BAG; **dolly-bird** *colloq.* an attractive and stylish young woman; **dolly mixture** a mixture of tiny sweets of various shapes and colours; a sweet from such a mixture; **dolly mop** *slang* a slattern; a prostitute; **dolly peg** = sense 3 above; **dolly pot** *Austral.* in a dolly, the vessel in which quartz is crushed; **dolly-tub** (*a*) a washtub; (*b*) *Mining* a vessel in which ore is washed.

dolly /'dɒli/ *n.*[2] M19. [Hind. *ḍālī.*] In the Indian subcontinent, an offering of fruit or flowers etc., presented usu. on a tray.

dolly /'dɒli/ *a.*[1] M19. [f. DOLL *n.*[1] + -Y[1].] 1 Resembling (that of) a doll. M19. 2 Stupid, foolish. L19. 3 Designating a very easy catch, shot, etc., in a ball game, esp. cricket. *colloq.* L19. 4 Of a person: attractive, stylish. Cf. *dolly-bird* s.v. DOLLY *n.*[1] *colloq.* M20.

2 JOYCE Grinning all over his big Dolly face.

†dolly *a.*[2] var. of DOWIE.

dolly /'dɒli/ *v.* M19. [f. DOLLY *n.*[1]] 1 *v.t.* & *i.* Beat or crush (esp. quartz) using a dolly; extract (gold) in this way. M19. 2 *v.t.* Wash or stir (clothes) in a dolly-tub. M19. 3 a *v.i.* Of a camera or its operator: travel on a dolly, esp. *in* towards the subject or *out* away from it. M20. b *v.t.* Move (esp. a camera) on a dolly. M20. 4 *v.t.* Doll or smarten *up*. *colloq.* M20.

3a M. AYRTON The camera dollies about all over the acres of smooth marble. *fig.*: G. MACBETH Someone dollied in to kill. b R. B. PARKER He was getting awkward to handle. . . They dollied him out.

Dolly Varden /dɒlı 'vɑːd(ə)n/ *n.* & *a.* L19. [A character in Dickens's *Barnaby Rudge*.] 1 (Designating) a print dress with a large flower pattern, worn with the skirt gathered up in loops. L19. 2 (Designating) a large hat, formerly worn by women, trimmed with flowers and with one side bent downwards. L19. 3 (Designating) a brightly spotted char, *Salvelinus malma*, that is a sporting fish of western N. America. L19.

dolman /'dɒlmən/ *n.* In sense 1 also (earlier) **†doliman**. L16. [In sense 1 f. Fr. *doliman*; in sense 2 f. Fr. *dolman* f. G f. Hungarian *dolmány*; both ult. f. Turk. *dolama(n)*.] 1 A long Turkish robe open in front and with narrow sleeves. L16. 2 A hussar's jacket worn with the sleeves hanging loose. L19. 3 A woman's mantle with dolman sleeves. L19. 4 In full *dolman sleeve*. A loose sleeve made in one piece with the body of a coat etc. M20.

dolmas /'dɒlməs/ *n.* Pl. **dolmades** /dɒl'mɑːðez/. Also **dolma**, pl. **-s**. L17. [mod.Gk *ntolmas* f. Turk. *dolma*, f. *dolmak* fill, be filled.] In the cookery of Greece, Turkey, and other East European countries: a dish of seasoned chopped meat and rice enclosed in a vine leaf, cabbage, pepper, etc.

dolmen /'dɒlmɛn/ *n.* M19. [Fr., perh. f. Corn. *tolmen* hole stone.] A megalithic structure found esp. in Britain and France, consisting of a large flat stone supported on stone slabs set vertically in the ground forming a burial chamber, probably orig. covered by an earth mound.

dol'menic *a.* L19.

dolmus /'dɒlmʊʃ/ *n.* M20. [Turk. *dolmuş* filled, (as n.) dolmus.] In Turkey, a shared taxi.

dolomite /'dɒləmʌɪt/ *n.* L18. [Fr. *dolomi(t)e*, f. D. *Dolomieu* (1750–1801), Fr. geologist: see -ITE[1].] A rock-forming mineral that is a hexagonal carbonate of calcium, magnesium, and usu. iron etc. and occurs as translucent crystals of various colours; a sedimentary rock composed chiefly of this mineral, alone or with calcite.

dolomitic /dɒlə'mɪtɪk/ *a.* of the nature of or containing dolomite E19. **dolomitization** /ˌdɒləmɪtʌɪ'zeɪʃ(ə)n/ *n.* conversion into dolomite M19. **dolomitize** /'dɒləmɪtʌɪz/ *v.t.* convert into dolomite (chiefly as *dolomitized* ppl a.) L19.

Dolophine /'dɒləfiːn/ *n.* *US.* M20. [f. *dolo-* of unkn. origin + MOR)PHINE.] Methadone.

¶ Proprietary name in the US.

dolor *n.* see DOLOUR.

dolorific /dɒlə'rɪfɪk/ *a.* Now *rare.* M17. [med.L *dolorificus*, f. L *dolor*: see DOLOUR, -FIC.] Causing pain.

dolorifuge /'dɒlərɪfjuː(d)ʒ/ *n.* L19. [f. L *dolor* (see DOLOUR) + -FUGE.] Something that drives away pain.

dolorimeter /dɒlə'rɪmɪtə/ *n.* M20. [f. L *dolor* (see DOLOUR) + -IMETER.] An instrument for measuring (sensitivity to) pain.

doloroso /dɒlə'rəʊzəʊ/ *a.*, *adv.*, & *n.* E19. [It. = dolorous.] *Mus.* (In) a plaintive or pathetic style.

dolorous /'dɒl(ə)rəs/ *a.* Now chiefly *literary* & *joc.* LME. [OFr. *doleros* (mod. *douloureux*) f. late L *dolorosus*, f. L *dolor*: see DOLOUR, -OUS.] 1 Causing or accompanied by physical pain; painful. LME. 2 Causing or giving rise to grief or sorrow; distressing; dismal. LME. 3 Full of sorrow; expressing sorrow. LME.

1 W. ROBERTS The dolorous sensations . . which constantly torment diabetic patients. 2 W. BLACK We had a dolorous day of rain. 3 MILTON A dolorous groan.

dolorously *adv.* LME. **dolorousness** *n.* M16.

dolos /'dɒlɒs/ *n.* *S. Afr.* Pl. **dolosse** /'dɒlɒsə/, (in sense 2) **dolossies** /'dɒlɒsɪz/. L19. [Afk., of unkn. origin.] 1 An animal bone, esp. a knuckle-bone, used for divination. Usu. in *pl.* L19. 2 In *pl.* Children's playthings; a game played with dolosse. E20. 3 Each of a series of interlocking concrete blocks used to guard against erosion by the sea. L20.

dolose /dəʊ'ləʊs/ *a.* Now *rare.* M17. [L *dolosus*, f. *dolus*: see DOLE *n.*[3], -OSE[1].] *Law.* Characterized by criminal intention; deceitful. Cf. DOLOUS.

dolosse, dolossies *ns.* pls. of DOLOS.

dolostone /'dɒləstəʊn/ *n.* M20. [f. DOLOMITE + STONE *n.*] *Geol.* (A) rock consisting of dolomite.

dolour /'dɒlə/ *n.* Now *literary.* Also ***-or.** ME. [OFr. *dolo(u)r* (mod. *douleur*) f. L *dolor* pain, grief: see -OUR, -OR.] †1 Physical suffering, pain; a pain, a painful affliction. ME–E18. 2 Mental pain or suffering; sorrow, distress; in *pl.* (now *rare*), griefs, sorrows. ME. †3 The outward expression of grief; lamentation, mourning. ME–M17. †4 Indignation. E–M17.

2 V. NABOKOV I spend my doleful days in dumps and dolours. T. ROETHKE I'm full of dolor and gloom about . . human existence.

dolous /'dəʊləs/ *a.* Now *rare.* E20. [f. L *dolus* (see DOLE *n.*[3]) + -OUS.] *Law* (chiefly *Sc.*) = DOLOSE.

dolphin /'dɒlfɪn/ *n.* LME. [OFr. *daulphin* f. Prov. *dalfin* f. med.L *dalphinus* for L *delphinus* f. Gk *delphin* (earlier *delphis*). Cf. DAUPHIN, (earlier) DELPHIN.] I 1 A toothed whale of the family Delphinidae, similar to a porpoise but longer and with a beaklike snout; *spec.* (more fully *common dolphin*), *Delphinus delphis*; (in full *river dolphin*) a similar toothed whale of the family Platanistidae, found only in some tropical rivers of S. America and southern Asia and without the social behaviour of true dolphins. In early use also, a fabulous fish of the R. Nile. LME. b = DORADO 1. Cf. *dolphinfish* below. E17. 2 A figure of a dolphin in heraldry, sculpture, etc., usu. represented with a curved body and formerly symbolizing love, diligence, or swiftness. LME. 3 (Usu. **D-**.) *The* constellation Delphinus. LME. 4 a *Hist.* Either of two handles cast solid with a cannon, nearly over the trunnions. E18. b *Naut.* A strap of plaited rope, fastened round the mast of a square-rigged ship (*dolphin of the mast*) or hung below the gunwale as a fender. M18. c *Gk Antiq.* A heavy weight suspended from a ship's mast, to be dropped into an enemy ship at close quarters. L18. d *Naut.* A pile or group of piles in the seabed used as a mooring for ships, to mark a channel, or to protect the pier of a bridge; a mooring post or buoy. M19. 5 A black aphid, *Aphis fabae*, that attacks beans. L18. †II 6 = DAUPHIN *n.* 1. LME–E18.

Comb.: **dolphinfish** either of the two tropical marine fishes forming the family Coryphaenidae, marked by a long dorsal fin and a deeply forked tail (cf. DORADO 1); **dolphin-striker** *Naut.* a short gaff spar fixed vertically under the bowsprit.

†dolphinate *n.* = DAUPHINATE: only in M17. **dolphined** *a.* (*literary*) having, associated with, or containing dolphins E20. **†dolphiness** *n.* = DAUPHINESS M16–E17.

dolphinarium /dɒlfɪ'nɛːrɪəm/ *n.* Pl. **-ia** /-ɪə/, **-iums**. M20. [f. prec. + AQU)ARIUM, after *oceanarium*.] A large aquarium in which dolphins are kept and trained, usu. for public entertainment.

dolt /dəʊlt/ *n.* & *v.* M16. [Perh. ult. var. of *dulled* pa. pple & ppl a. of DULL *v.*] A *n.* A dull stupid person, a fool, a blockhead. M16. †B *v.t.* Make foolish; call a dolt; make a fool of. M16–L19.

doltish *a.* somewhat dull and stupid, rather foolish M16. **doltishly** *adv.* L16. **doltishness** *n.* M16.

dolus /'dɒləs/ *n.* E17. [L: see DOLE *n.*[3]] *Law.* Deceit; intentional damage.

dolus bonus /'bɒnəs/ [L = good] deceit not intended to cause damage. **dolus malus** /'maləs/ [L = bad] deceit with malicious intention to harm.

Dom /dɒm/ *n.*[1] L17. [In sense 1 abbrev. of L *dominus* lord, master; in sense 2 Port. *dom* f. L *dominus*. Cf. DAN *n.*[1], DON *n.*[1], DAME.] 1 Master: used as a title preceding the names of some Roman Catholic ecclesiastical and monastic dignitaries, esp. of Benedictine and Carthusian monks. L17. 2 In Portugal and Brazil, used as a title of respect preceding male forenames, esp. of men of the royal family or the Church hierarchy. E18.

Dom /dəʊm/ *n.*[2] & *a.* E19. [Hindi *Ḍom* f. Skt *Ḍom(b)a*.] In the Indian subcontinent: (pertaining to or designating) a member of a very low caste.

dom /dəʊm/ *n.*[3] M19. [G f. L *domus* house. Cf. DOME *n.*] A cathedral church in Germany, Austria, and other German-speaking areas. Cf. DOME *n.* 2.

-dom /dəm/ *suff.* [OE *-dōm* = OS *-dōm* (Du. *-dom*), OHG *-tuom* (G *-tum*), use as suff. of OE *dōm* DOOM *n.*[1], OHG *tuom* position, condition, dignity.] 1 Forming ns. f. ns. and adjs. w. the senses 'rank, condition', 'domain', as in *earldom*, *freedom*, *kingdom*. 2 Forming ns. f. ns. as collect. pl. or w. the sense 'the ways of —s' as in *officialdom*.

domain /də(ʊ)'meɪn/ *n.* LME. [Fr. *domaine* alt. (by assoc. w. L *dominus* lord, master) of OFr. *demaine, demeine* DEMESNE.] †1 = DEMESNE *n.* 1.

rare. LME–M17. **2** (A) heritable property; (an) estate or territory held in possession; lands, dominions. LME. **b** An area under rule or influence; the area of activity of a person, institution, etc. M18. **c** A public park, a recreation-ground; *the Domain*, a park in Sydney popular for speech-making. *Austral.* & *NZ.* L19. **d** *Physics.* In a ferromagnetic material, a region in which all the atoms or ions are magnetically aligned in the same direction. E20. **3** A sphere of thought or operation; the situations where a particular science, law, etc., is applicable. M18. **4** *Math.* A set with two binary operations defined by postulates stronger than those for a ring but weaker than those for a field. L19. **5** *Math.* The set of values that the independent variable of a function can take. E20. **6** *Logic.* The class of all terms bearing a given relation to a given term. E20.

2 W. S. CHURCHILL The Electoral Prince of Bavaria, heir to prodigious domains. A. J. TOYNBEE The traveller.. is entering the former domain of the Inca Empire. b P. NORMAN Nanny Belmayne's domain begins at the top of the first flight of stairs. 3 J. MACKINTOSH Contracting.. the domain of brutal force and of arbitrary will. G. B. SHAW An astronomer whose mental domain is the universe. 6 B. RUSSELL If paternity be the relation, fathers form its domain.

Phrases: **eminent domain** *Law* superiority of the sovereign power over all property in a State, with constitutional right of expropriation in the public interest. *in the public domain*: see PUBLIC *a.*

Comb.: **Domain orator** *Austral.* a person who makes public speeches in the Domain.

domainal *a.* M19.

domaine /də'meɪn/ *n.* M20. [Fr.: see prec.] A vineyard. Usu. in *domaine-bottled* below.

Comb.: **domaine-bottled** *a.* (of a wine) bottled at the vineyard where the grapes of which it is made were grown.

domal /'dəʊm(ə)l/ *a.* & *n.* E18. [In branch A.I f. L *domus* house, (in med.L) planetary house, in branch A.II f. DOME *n.*: see -AL^{1}.] **A** *adj.* **I 1** Of or pertaining to a house or houses; domestic. E18. **2** *Astrol.* Of or pertaining to a house of the zodiac. E18. **II 3** Of, pertaining to, or shaped like a dome. E20. **4** *Phonet.* Of a speech sound: articulated with the tip of the tongue against the highest part (or dome) of the palate; cacuminal. E20. **B** *n. Phonet.* A domal speech sound. E20.

domanial /də(ʊ)'meɪnɪəl/ *a.* E19. [Fr. f. med.L *domanialis*, f. *domanium* lordship, domain: see -IAL.] Of or pertaining to (a) domain.

Domdaniel /dɒm'danɪəl/ *n. literary.* E19. [Fr., app. f. Gk *dōma Daniēl* or L *domus Danielis* hall or house of Daniel.] (The name of) a fabled submarine hall where a magician or sorcerer met with his disciples; *transf.* a den of iniquity, a hell.

dome /dəʊm/ *n.* & *v.* E16. [In sense A.1 directly f. L *domus* house; in other senses f. Fr. *dôme* f. It. DUOMO (dial. *domo*) house, house of God, cathedral, cupola, f. L *domus*.] **A** *n.* **I** A house. **1** A house, a home; a stately building, a mansion. Now chiefly *literary.* E16. †**2** A cathedral church. Cf. DOM *n.*^{3} L17–M18.

1 SWIFT Sad charnel-house! a dismal dome, For which all mortals leave their home.

II A hemispherical surface. **3** A rounded vault forming (the chief part of) the roof of a building, and having an elliptical or polygonal base; a large cupola. M17. **b** The revolving openable hemispherical roof of an astronomical observatory. M19. **c** A stadium with a domed roof. Cf. ASTRODOME (b). *N. Amer.* M20. **4** The vaulted roof of a cavern or natural hollow; the concave vault of the sky; a natural canopy of trees etc. E18. **5** A dome-shaped part of anything; a convex lid or cover. E18. **b** The rounded summit of a natural object, as a mountain, hill, wave, etc. M19. **c** In full *dome fastener.* A press-stud consisting of a rounded portion which clips into a socket, used esp. as a fastener for gloves. E20. **6** The head. *slang.* L19. **7** *Geol.* A dome-shaped landform or underground structure. E20.

3 M. GIROUARD A tower capped by a green copper dome. 4 J. L. WATEN The high dome of light-blue sky. 5 T. S. ELIOT The egg's well-rounded dome. 7 N. CALDER Salt domes are favourite targets for oil prospectors.

Phrases: **Dome of Silence** (proprietary name for) a type of castor fitted to furniture.

Comb.: *dome fastener*: see sense 5c above; **dome-headed** *a.* having a large rounded head; **dome-light**: with a dome-shaped cover or shade.

B *v.* **1** *v.t.* Cover (as) with a dome. L19. **2** *v.t.* Make dome-shaped. L19. **3** *v.i.* Be or become dome-shaped. L19.

2 MRS H. WARD The roof had been raised and domed. 3 *Scientific American* A caldera whose floor has slowly domed upward in the millenniums since the eruption. *Nature* Towards the end of the Carboniferous period uplift.. and doming of the region took place.

domed /dəʊmd/ *a.* L18. [f. DOME + -ED^{1}, -ED^{2}.] **1** Dome-shaped, vaulted. L18. **2** Having a dome or domes. M19.

domelet /'dəʊmlɪt/ *n.* L19. [f. DOME *n.* + -LET.] A miniature dome.

doment /'duːm(ə)nt/ *n. dial.* & *colloq.* E19. [f. DO *v.* + -MENT.] A fuss, a performance; a to-do.

Domesday /'duːmzdeɪ/ *n.* ME. [Var. of DOOMSDAY.] More fully *Domesday Book.* A comprehensive record of the extent, value, ownership, and liabilities of lands in England, made in 1086 by order of William the Conqueror.

transf.: E. A. FREEMAN A Domesday of the conquerors was.. drawn up.., a forerunner of the great Domesday of the conquered.

¶App. a pop. name alluding to *doomsday* 'Day of Judgement', applied during 12 to the book as a final authority on matters about which it was referred to.

domestic /də'mɛstɪk/ *a.* & *n.* LME. [(O)Fr. *domestique* f. L *domesticus*, f. *domus* house, after *rusticus* RUSTIC *a.* etc.] **A** *adj.* **1** Of or pertaining to the home, house, or household; pertaining to one's home or family affairs. LME. **2** Not wild; (of an animal) kept by or living with humans, tame; (of a plant) cultivated. L15. †**3** Having the character or position of the inmate of a house, housed. Also, intimate, familiar, at home. (Foll. by *with.*) E16–M18. **4** Of or pertaining to one's own country or nation; not foreign or international; indigenous; made in one's own country, not imported. M16. **5** Attached to home; fond of home life or duties. M17.

1 K. CLARK Ivory mirror cases and other domestic objects. A. THWAITE The two friends, the baby and the cat offered a picture of domestic bliss. **domestic bursar** a person in charge of the administrative or financial affairs of a college or university. **domestic science** cookery and other household activities, as subjects to be taught. **domestic service** the position or occupation of a household servant. 2 T. HARDY A panting fox.. trotted past them tamely as a domestic cat. **domestic fowl** a bird reared for meat, eggs, or feathers; in *pl.* poultry; *spec.* the widely domesticated form of the SE Asian jungle fowl, *Gallus gallus*, a cock, a hen, a chicken. 3 CHESTERFIELD Domestic in the best company and the best families. 4 W. S. CHURCHILL The domestic law of England was outraged by the arrogance.. of the French despot. *domestic trade*: see TRADE *n.* *gross domestic product*: see GROSS *a.* 5 J. H. NEWMAN It is praiseworthy and right to be domestic.

B *n.* †**1** A member of a household; someone living in the same house as another person; a member of the family (*lit.* & *fig.*). M16–M18. **2** A household servant. E17. †**b** A domestic animal. *rare.* E–M18. †**3** An inhabitant of the same country; a native, a compatriot. Only in 17. **4** An article of home manufacture (usu. in *pl.*); *US* a plain cotton fabric. E17. **5** A kind of cigar. *US colloq.* (now *rare*). M19.

domestical *a.* & *n.* (now *rare* or *obs.*) (*a*) *adj.* domestic; (*b*) *n.* a domestic; a member of a household: LME. **domestically** *adv.* in a domestic way; as regards domestic matters or home life; familiarly: L16. **domesticism** /-sɪz(ə)m/ *n.* devotion to home life L18. **domesticize** /-saɪz/ *v.t.* domesticate M17. †**domesticly** *adv.* M17–M18.

domesticable /də'mɛstɪkəb(ə)l/ *a.* E19. [f. DOMESTICATE *v.* + -ABLE.] Able to be domesticated or tamed.

domesticate /də'mɛstɪkət/ *n.* M20. [f. next: see -ATE^{2}.] A domesticated animal.

domesticate /də'mɛstɪkeɪt/ *v.* M17. [med.L *domesticat-* pa. ppl stem of *domesticare*, f. L *domesticus*: see DOMESTIC, -ATE^{3}.] **1** *v.t.* Settle as a member of a household; cause to feel at home; naturalize (esp. a plant or animal). M17. **2** *v.t.* Accustom (an animal) to being kept by or to living with humans; bring under control, tame. M17. **3** *v.t.* Attach (a person) to home life and household matters; make domestic. M18. †**4** *v.i.* Live on familiar terms or at home *with*; take up residence, settle down. M18–M19.

1 GLADSTONE An element in the Greek nation originally foreign, but now domesticated. 2 C. G. SELIGMAN They possess no domesticated animals except the dog. 3 G. GREENE The domesticated man with a devoted wife and six children to support. M. BRADBURY Henry has domesticated the space, and filled it with potted plants.

domesti'cation *n.* the action of domesticating; the fact of being domesticated: L18. **domesticator** *n.* L19.

domesticity /dɒmɛ'stɪsɪti, dəʊm-/ *n.* E18. [f. DOMESTIC + -ITY. Cf. Fr. *domesticité*, late L *domesticitas.*] **1** The quality or state of being domestic; *esp.* (attachment to) home life. E18. **b** The state in an animal of being domesticated. M19. **2** In *pl.* Domestic affairs, arrangements, or concerns. E19.

1 L. STEPHEN A masculine woman with no talent for domesticity.

domett /'dɒmɪt, də'mɛt/ *n.* & *a.* Also **domette** /də'mɛt/. E19. [Perh. f. a proper name.] (Made of) a kind of plain cheap cloth with a cotton warp and a woollen weft (later cotton only).

domical /'dəʊmɪk(ə)l/ *a.* M19. [f. DOME *n.* + -ICAL.] **1** = DOMED 1. M19. **2** = DOMED 2. M19.

†**domic** *a.* = DOMICAL: only in E19. **domically** *adv.* L19.

domicile /'dɒmɪsʌɪl, -sɪl/ *n.* & *v.* Also **-cil** /-sɪl/. LME. [(O)Fr. f. L *domicilium*, f. *domus* house.] **A** *n.* **1** A place of residence or customary habitation; a dwelling-place; a home. LME. **2** *Law.* The place of a person's permanent residence, which he or she leaves only temporarily. L17. **3** The fact of being resident; residence. M19. **4** The place at which a bill of exchange is made payable. L19. **B** *v.* **1** *v.t.* Establish in a fixed residence; settle in a home. Usu. in *pass.* LME. **2** *v.t.* Make (a bill of exchange) payable at a place specified by the acceptor. E19. **3** *v.i.* Have one's home, live. M19.

†**domiciliar** *a.* & *n. rare.* M17. [med.L *domiciliarius*: see next, -AR^{1}.] **A** *adj.* Of or pertaining to one's domicile. Only in M17. **B** *n.* A canon of a minor order having no voice in a chapter. Only in M18.

domiciliary /dɒmɪ'sɪlɪəri/ *a.* L19. [Fr. *domiciliaire* f. med.L *domiciliarius*, f. L *domicilium* DOMICILE: see -ARY^{1}.] Of or pertaining to a person's home; occurring at home.

S. KITZINGER Her first domiciliary delivery. **domiciliary visit** a visit by an official to a person's home, *esp.* one made by a doctor, midwife, etc., to see a patient.

domiciliate /dɒmɪ'sɪlɪeɪt/ *v.* L18. [f. L *domicilium* DOMICILE + -ATE^{3}, after Fr. *domicilier.*] **1** *v.t.* = DOMICILE *v.* 1. L18. †**2** *v.t.* Accustom to a house or permanent dwelling-place; domesticate (an animal). *rare.* L18–E19. **3** *v.i.* = DOMICILE *v.* 3. E19.

ˌ**domicili'ation** *n.* L18.

†**domify** *v.t.* LME–E18. [Fr. *domifier* f. med.L *domificare* build houses, f. L *domus* house: see -FY.] *Astrol.* Divide (the heavens) into twelve houses; locate (the planets) in their respective houses.

†**domification** *n.* E17–E18.

domina /'dɒmɪnə/ *n.* Now *rare.* E18. [L = mistress, lady.] A lady of rank; the superior of a nunnery.

dominance /'dɒmɪnəns/ *n.* E19. [f. next: see -ANCE.] **1** The fact or position of being dominant; paramount influence, ascendancy, dominion, sway. E19. **2** *Genetics.* The phenomenon whereby, in an individual containing two allelic forms of a gene, one is expressed to the exclusion of the other. E20. **3** *Ecol.* The predominance of one or more species in a plant or animal community. E20.

1 D. ACHESON Two German bids for dominance in Europe. A. STORR Male therapists are often put off by dominance and assertiveness in women.

dominancy *n.* dominant quality, position, or condition M19.

dominant /ˈdɒmɪnənt/ *a.* & *n.* LME. [(O)Fr., f. L *dominant-* pres. ppl stem of *dominari* DOMINATE: see -ANT[1].] A *adj.* 1 Exercising chief authority or rule; ruling, prevailing; most influential. LME. 2 *Law.* Designating (tenement of) land whose owner has an easement over someone else's land. E18. 3 *Mus.* Based on or pertaining to the dominant. M18. 4 Occupying a commanding position; overtopping its surroundings; *spec.* (of a forest tree) having its crown free to light on all sides. M19. 5 *Genetics.* Of a gene or allele: expressed even when inherited from only one parent. Of a hereditary trait: controlled by such a gene; appearing in an individual to the exclusion of its allelic counterpart, when alleles for both are present. Opp. *recessive.* (Foll. by *to, over.*) E20. 6 *Ecol.* Designating the predominant species in a plant or animal community. E20.

1 W. S. CHURCHILL His dominant theme was that conscience and the moral law must govern political decisions. J. F. LEHMANN My will remained dominant . . over my senses and emotions. C. P. SNOW How China could avoid becoming the dominant power on earth. 3 *Music Teacher* Harmonizing a melody, employing inversions and the dominant seventh. 4 J. TYNDALL A bay, sheltered by dominant hills.

B *n.* †1 = DOMINATION 3. Only in LME. 2 *Mus.* The fifth note of the diatonic scale of a key; the reciting note in a church mode, usu. a fifth or a third above the final. E19. 3 *Genetics.* A dominant gene or trait (see sense A.5 above). E20. 4 *Ecol.* A predominant species of a plant or animal community. E20.

2 *fig.*: M. TRIPP If the keynote was tolerance, the dominant was fidelity.

dominantly *adv.* so as to be dominant or to prevail; predominantly; *Genetics* as a dominant trait: M19.

dominate /ˈdɒmɪneɪt/ *v.* E17. [L *dominat-* pa. ppl stem of *dominari* rule, govern, f. *dominus* lord, master: see -ATE[3].] 1 *v.t.* Rule over, govern; control, master; have a commanding influence over; be the most influential or conspicuous thing in. E17. 2 *v.i.* Predominate, prevail; have a commanding influence (*over*); be the most influential or conspicuous person or thing present. E19. 3 *v.i.* Of something high or tall: occupy a commanding position (*over*). E19. 4 *v.t.* Overlook (*lit.* & *fig.*). M19.

1 T. H. HUXLEY The Germans dominate the intellectual world. W. BRONK Death dominates my mind. S. BRETT Bill and Carla's bedroom . . was dominated by an enormous circular bed. 2 ALDOUS HUXLEY She only wanted to dominate, to be the leader and make him do what she wanted. P. CAREY The distinctive odour of a mental hospital. Floor polish, methylated spirits and chlorine seemed to dominate. 4 BOSW. SMITH This hill . . dominates the plain.

domination /dɒmɪˈneɪʃ(ə)n/ *n.* LME. [(O)Fr. f. L *dominatio(n-)*, f. as prec.: see -ATION.] 1 The action of dominating; ascendancy, sway, control; the state of being dominated. LME. †2 A territory under rule; a dominion. LME–M17. 3 In Christian theology, a member of the fourth order of the ninefold celestial hierarchy, ranking directly below the thrones and above the virtues (usu. in *pl.*). Also, a conventional representation of such a being. LME.

1 G. VIDAL He was used to domination . . but it made him uneasy . . to feel that his own will was so easily bent by others. J. BERGER To liberate the Southern Slavs . . from the domination of the Hapsburgs.

dominative /ˈdɒmɪnətɪv/ *a.* L16. [(O)Fr. *dominatif, -ive* or med.L *dominativus*, f. as DOMINATE: see -ATIVE.] Having the quality of ruling or dominating; of lordly authority.

dominator /ˈdɒmɪneɪtə/ *n.* LME. [Orig. f. (O)Fr. *dominateur*, later f., or assim. to, L *dominator*, f. as prec: see -OR.] 1 A person who or thing which dominates; a ruler, a lord. LME. †2 *spec. Astrol.* A planet or sign that dominates a particular person or region. L16–M17.

dominatrix /dɒmɪˈneɪtrɪks/ *n.* Pl. **-trices** /-trɪsiːz/. M16. [L *dominatrix* fem. of *dominator*: see prec., -TRIX.] A female dominator or ruler.

¶ Rare bef. L20.

domine /ˈduːmɪni, ˈdʊə-/ *n.* Also (esp. as a title) **D-**. M16. [L, voc. of *dominus* lord, master. Cf. DOMINEE, DOMINIE.] †1 Lord, master; sir: used in respectful address to a clergyman or a member of one of the professions. M16–L17. 2 = DOMINIE I. Now *rare* or *obs.* E17. 3 A member of the clergy, a pastor; *esp.* a pastor of the Dutch Reformed Church. (Cf. DOMINEE, DOMINIE 2). *arch.* M17.

dominee /ˈduːmɪni, ˈdʊə-/ *n. S. Afr.* Also (esp. as a title) **D-**. M20. [Afk. & Du. f. L DOMINE.] A pastor of the Dutch Reformed Church.

domineer /dɒmɪˈnɪə/ *v.* & *n.* L16. [Du. *domineren* f. (O)Fr. *dominer* f. L *dominari* DOMINATE: see -EER.] A *v.* I *v.i.* 1 Rule arbitrarily or despotically; act imperiously; tyrannize; be overbearing. (Foll. by *over.*) L16. †b Assume lordly airs, swagger. E17–M18. †2 Revel; feast riotously. L16–L17. †3 Predominate, prevail. E17–E19. 4 Of something high or tall: tower (*over, above*); occupy a commanding position. M17.

1 ADAM SMITH The mercantile company which domineers in the East Indies. H. KELLER It pleased me to domineer over her, and she generally submitted to my tyranny. 2 SHAKES. *Tam. Shr.* Go to the feast, revel and domineer.

II *v.t.* 5 *v.t.* Govern imperiously, tyrannize over, dominate absolutely. M18. 6 *v.t.* Of something high or tall: tower over, command. E19.

B *n.* A domineering manner or air; imperious swaggering. Now *rare.* E19.

domineerer *n.* (now *rare*) a person who domineers, a tyrant, a despot M17. **domineering** *a.* (*a*) tyrannical; overbearing, offensively assertive or dictatorial; †(*b*) predominating, prevailing: L16. **domineeringly** *adv.* L17. **domineeringness** *n.* L19.

dominial /dəˈmɪnɪəl/ *a.* M18. [f. DOMINION + -AL[1].] Of or pertaining to ownership.

dominical /dəˈmɪnɪk(ə)l/ *n.* & *a.* ME. [(O)Fr., or late L *dominicalis*, f. L *dominicus*, f. *dominus* lord, master: see -ICAL.] A *n. Chr. Ch.* 1 A book, garment, or other item intended for use on Sundays; *spec.* a veil formerly worn by women when receiving the Eucharist. Now *rare.* ME. †2 The Lord's day, Sunday. M16–L17. †3 = *dominical letter* (see sense B.2 below). L16–L17. 4 A person who observes the Christian Sunday but does not treat it strictly as representing the sabbath of the Israelites. M19.

B *adj.* I *Chr. Ch.* Also **D-**. 1 Of or pertaining to the Lord (Christ); Lord's. ME. 2 Of or pertaining to Sunday. LME.

1 R. HARRIES The Church is not now regarded as a profession in which a career may be advanced. This is . . a return to more Dominical standards. **dominical day** Sunday. **dominical year** the year of Our Lord (numbered from an assumed year of the birth of Jesus). 2 **dominical letter** the one of the seven letters A–G used to indicate the dates of Sundays in a particular year (sometimes printed in red, or distinctive type, in the calendar).

II Other uses. †3 Belonging or pertaining to a demesne or domain; domanial. M16–L18.

Dominican /dəˈmɪnɪk(ə)n/ *n.*[1] & *a.*[1] L16. [med.L *Dominicanus*, f. *Dominicus* L name of St Dominic (Sp. *Domingo* de Guzmán): see below, -AN.] A member of, designating or pertaining to, the Order of Friars Preachers (Black Friars), founded in 1215 by the Spanish priest St Dominic (*c*1170–1221) as a mendicant order devoted to preaching and the study of theology.

†**Dominic** *n.* & *a.* = DOMINICAN *n.*[1] & *a.*[1] LME–L17. **Dominica'ness** *n.* a Dominican nun M19.

Dominican /dɒmɪˈniːk(ə)n, dəˈmɪnɪk(ə)n/ *n.*[2] & *a.*[2] E19. [f. *Dominica* (see below), so called because discovered on a Sunday (L *dies dominica*) in 1493 + -AN.] A native or inhabitant of, of or pertaining to, the island of Dominica in the Lesser Antilles.

Dominican /dəˈmɪnɪk(ə)n/ *n.*[3] & *a.*[3] M19. [Sp. *Dominicana*, f. as DOMINICAN *a.*[1] & *n.*[1] after *Santo Domingo* one of the earliest settlements and subsequently the capital of the Dominican Republic.] A native or inhabitant of, designating or pertaining to, the Dominican Republic, which occupies the eastern half of the island of Hispaniola in the Greater Antilles.

Dominicker /ˈdɒmɪnɪkə/ *n.* & *a. US.* Also **d-**. E19. [Alt. of *Dominica* (see DOMINICAN *n.*[2] & *a.*[2]).] (Designating) a hen of an American breed characterized by barred plumage and yellow legs.

dominie /*in sense 1* ˈdɒmɪni, *in senses 2 & 3* ˈdəʊmɪni, ˈdɒmɪni/ *n.* L17. [Alt. of DOMINE.] 1 A schoolmaster; a teacher. Now chiefly *Sc.* L17. 2 A pastor of the Dutch Reformed Church; *dial.* any minister. *US.* L17. 3 More fully *dominie apple.* A variety of large apple. *US.* E19.

dominion /dəˈmɪnjən/ *n.* ME. [OFr. f. med.L *dominio(n-)*, f. *dominium* property, f. *dominus* lord, master.] 1 A domain, a territory; *esp.* (*sing.* & in *pl.*) the land of a feudal lord; the territory of a particular ruler or government. ME. b *Hist.* (Also **D-**.) A country outside Great Britain or (in early use) England under the sovereignty of or owing allegiance to the Crown; *esp.* (the title of) any of the larger self-governing nations that belong or once belonged to the British Commonwealth. E17. 2 The power or right of governing; sovereign authority, lordship; dominance, influence, control. LME. 3 *Chr. Ch.* = DOMINATION 3. Usu. in *pl.* E17. 4 *Law.* Ownership, property; right of possession. M17.

1 LD MACAULAY The wide dominion of the Franks was severed into a thousand pieces. b *attrib.*: A. F. DOUGLAS-HOME Her leaders could . . make a good case for Dominion status (i.e. complete independence within the Commonwealth) on the country's record and prospects. **the Dominion** *colloq.* (now *rare*) Canada. **the Old Dominion** *US colloq.* Virginia. 2 B. JOWETT For ages physicians have been under the dominion of prejudices. P. ACKROYD Neither tears nor hollow laughter hold dominion. J. C. OATES The dominion of men over beasts. 4 T. JEFFERSON Our Saxon ancestors held their lands . . in absolute dominion, unencumbered with any superior.

Comb.: **Dominion day** *Hist.* = *Canada Day* s.v. CANADA I.

Dominique /ˈdɒmɪnɪk, dɒmɪˈniːk/ *n.* & *a. US.* Also **d-**. E20. [Fr. name for *Dominica* (see DOMINICAN *n.*[2] & *a.*[2]).] = DOMINICKER.

dominium /dəˈmɪnɪəm/ *n.* M18. [L: see DOMINION.] *Law.* Lordship, ownership, dominion. Chiefly as below.

dominium directum /dɪˈrɛktəm/ [L = direct ownership] the rights reserved to a lord or superior. ***dominium utile*** /ˈjuːtɪli/ [L = ownership of use] the rights (e.g. of possession or use) reserved to a tenant or vassal.

domino /ˈdɒmɪnəʊ/ *n.* & *int.* L17. [Fr. = hood worn by priests in winter (also in Sp., = a masquerade garment), prob. ult. f. L *dominus* lord, master, but unexpl.] A *n.* Pl. **-o(e)s.** 1 A garment worn to cover the head and shoulders; *spec.* a loose cloak with a mask for the upper part of the face, worn to conceal the identity at masquerades etc. L17. 2 A person wearing a domino. M18. 3 Each of a set of small oblong pieces, usu. 28 in number and marked with 0 to 6 pips in each half, used in various matching and trick-taking games; in *pl.* (treated as *sing.*) or †*sing.*, the game played with such pieces, in which matching halves are placed in contact. L18. b In *pl.* The teeth. *arch. slang.* E19. c In *pl.* The keys of a piano. *arch. slang.* L19. 4 [f. the int.] The end, the finish. Chiefly in *be all domino*, be all up (*with*). *slang.* M19. 5 In full *domino paper.* Paper printed with a design from a woodblock and coloured, used as wallpaper etc. M19.

1 *fig.*: DISRAELI As for Pantheism, it is Atheism in domino. 3 **make the domino** *colloq.* go out first in the game of dominoes; finish first.

Comb.: **domino effect**: by which one event triggers a succession of other, often similar, events, like a falling domino at the beginning of a line of up-ended dominoes; *domino paper*: see sense 5 above; **domino theory** the theory that a domino effect will occur, *spec.* (*Polit.*) that when one county in SE Asia becomes Communist-controlled the same thing will happen to its neighbours.

B *int.* Notifying that one has matched up all

one's dominoes; *transf.* notifying or registering the end of something. M19.

dominoed *a.* wearing a domino L19.

domitable /'dɒmɪtəb(ə)l/ *a. rare.* L17. [f. L *domitare* frequent. of *domare* to tame: see -ABLE. Cf. earlier INDOMITABLE.] Tameable.

domite /'dəʊmʌɪt/ *n.* E19. [G *Domit*, f. Puy de *Dôme* peak in the Massif Central, France: see -ITE[1].] *Petrogr.* A trachyte containing biotite and oligoclase, *esp.* one containing tridymite.

domitic /də'mɪtɪk/ *a.* L19.

†**domo** *n.* see DUOMO.

Dom Pedro /dɒm 'pedrəʊ/ *n. phr. US.* Also **Don Pedro** /dɒn/. L19. [Prob. f. DOM *n.*[1], DON *n.*[1] + male forename *Pedro.*] A card-game like Sancho Pedro but in which the joker is used.

dompt /dɒm(p)t/ *v.t. rare.* L15. [Fr. *dompter*: see DAUNT *v.*] Tame, subdue; daunt.

domus /'dəʊməs/ *n.* M18. [L = house.] (The fellows of) an Oxford or Cambridge college with regard to its domestic affairs.

domy /'dəʊmi/ *a.* M19. [f. DOME + -Y[1].] = DOMED.

don /dɒn/ *n.*[1] E16. [Sp. (in sense 1c It.) f. L *dominus* lord, master. Cf. DAME, DAN *n.*[1], DOM *n.*[1]] **1 a** (**D-**.) Used as a title of respect preceding the forename of a Spanish man (orig. one of high rank) or (formerly, *joc.*) preceding the name or designation of any man. E16. **b** A Spanish lord or gentleman. E17. **c** A high-ranking or powerful member of the Mafia. *N. Amer. slang.* M20. **2** A distinguished or skilled man; a man who is outstanding in some way. *arch.* L16. **3** At British universities, esp. Oxford and Cambridge: a head, fellow, or tutor of a college; a member of the teaching staff. M17.

2 DRYDEN The great dons of wit.

don /dɒn/ *n.*[2] Long *obs.* exc. *dial.* L15. [Fr. f. L *donum* gift.] A donation, a gift.

don /dɒn/ *v.* Infl. **-nn-**. LME. [Contr. of *do on*: see DO *v.*] **1** *v.t.* Put on (a garment etc.). LME. **2** *v.refl.* & *i.* Dress oneself. Chiefly *north.* E19. **3** Dress (a person) *in* a garment. Chiefly *north.* M19.

¶Became largely obs. in 17; revived in 19.

dona /'dəʊnə/ *n.* In sense 1 also ***doña*** /'dɒnja/; in sense 2 also **donah, doner**. E17. [Port. *dona*, Sp. *doña*, f. L *domina* fem. of *dominus*: see DON *n.*[1] Cf. DONNA.] **1** (Used as a courtesy title preceding the name of) a Spanish or Portuguese lady. E17. **2** A woman; a girlfriend. *slang.* Now *rare.* M19.

Donald Duck /dɒn(ə)ld 'dʌk/ *a. phr.* M20. [See below.] Designating or pertaining to the high-pitched nasal quality of the voice of the character Donald Duck in Walt Disney cartoon films.

Daily Telegraph The 'Donald Duck effect' results from divers having to breathe an oxy-helium mixture in depths greater than 600 ft.

donary /'dəʊn(ə)ri/ *n.* L16. [L *donarium*, f. *donum* gift: see -ARY[1].] A votive offering; a gift, a donation.

†**donatar** *n.* var. of DONATOR *n.*[2]

donatary *n.* var. of DONATORY.

donate /'dəʊneɪt/ *n.* Also **-at** /-at/ E19. [med.L *donatus* pa. pple of *donare* give.] A member or associate of any of certain religious orders.

donate /də(ʊ)'neɪt/ *v.* L18. [Back-form. f. DONATION.] **1** *v.t.* & *i.* Make a donation (of), esp. to a charity or institution. L18. **2** *v.t.* Present *with. rare.* M19. **3** *v.t. Chem.* & *Physics.* Of an atom etc.: lose (an electron) by partial transfer to a neighbouring atom, with formation of a bond. M20.

1 C. STEAD She loved to donate things made by herself to their festivals . . and sales of work.

donatee /dəʊnə'tiː/ *n.* E18. [f. prec. + -EE[1].] A recipient of a donation.

†**Donatian** *n.* E17–E19. [f. *Donatus* (see DONATIST) + -IAN.] A Donatist.

donatio mortis causa /də,neɪʃɪəʊ ,mɔːtɪs 'kɔːzə/ *n. phr.* Pl. ***donationes mortis causa*** /dəneɪʃɪ,əʊniːz/. M17. [L = gift by reason of death.] *Law.* A (revocable) gift of personal property made in expectation of the donor's imminent death and taking effect thereafter.

donation /də(ʊ)'neɪʃ(ə)n/ *n.* LME. [(O)Fr. f. L *donatio(n-)*, f. *donat-* pa. ppl stem of *donare* give, f. *donum* gift: see -ATION.] **1** The action or an act of donating; *spec.* (*Law*) the transfer of ownership as a free gift. LME. **2** The right of bestowing or conferring a benefice; gift. Now *rare.* M16. **3** A thing which is donated; a gift or contribution to a charity, fund, etc. L16.

1 J. HELLER The donation of all his organs and tissues for medical use. R. FULLER Far back it gave us life, although We now may look askance at the donation. *Chemistry in Britain* The donation of a lone pair of electrons from BCl into the empty 2*p* orbital of the trichloride. 2 W. PALEY Offices in the donation of the king. 3 B. T. WASHINGTON Small donations from persons of moderate means.

donationes mortis causa *n. phr.* pl. of DONATIO MORTIS CAUSA.

Donatism /'dəʊnətɪz(ə)m/ *n.* L16. [f. next + -ISM.] *Eccl. Hist.* The doctrine or principles of the Donatists.

Donatist /'dəʊnətɪst/ *n.* & *a.* ME. [Late L *Donatista*, f. *Donatus* 2nd Bishop of Carthage after Caecilian: see -IST.] *Eccl. Hist.* **A** *n.* A member of a schismatic body of N. African Christians which originated when they declared invalid the consecration of Caecilian as Bishop of Carthage in 311. ME. **B** *adj.* Of or pertaining to Donatism or the Donatists. E18.

¶Rare bef. L19.

Dona'tistic *a.* E19.

donative /'dəʊnətɪv/ *n.* & *a.* LME. [L *donativum* largesse, f. *donat-*: see DONATION, -IVE.] **A** *n.* **1** A donation, a gift, a bounty, esp. given formally or officially. LME. **2** *Eccl. Hist.* A benefice which is not presentative but given directly. M16. **B** *adj.* Of the nature of a donative; *esp.* (*Eccl. Hist.*) (of a benefice) vesting or vested by donation (opp. PRESENTATIVE *a.* 2). M16.

donator /də(ʊ)'neɪtə/ *n.*[1] LME. [Orig. f. (O)Fr. *donateur* or L *donator*, f. *donat-*: see DONATION, -OR. In mod. use f. DONATE *v.* + -OR.] A person who makes a donation, a donor.

donator /'də(ʊ)nətə/ *n.*[2] *Sc.* Also †**-ar**. E16. [OFr. *donatoire*, Fr. *donataire*, or med.L *donatorius*, *-arius*: see DONATORY, -OR, -AR[2].] = next.

donatory /'dəʊnət(ə)ri/ *n.* Also **-ary**. E17. [med.L *donatorius*, f. *donat-*: see DONATION, -ORY[1]; *donatary* by alt. (cf. med.L *donatarius*, -ARY[1]).] A person who receives a donation, esp. (*Law*) from the Crown in the event of a forfeiture, a failure of succession, etc.

donatrix /də(ʊ)'neɪtrɪks/ *n.* Pl. **-trixes, -trices** /-trɪsiːz/. M16. [L, fem. of *donator*: see DONATOR *n.*[1], -TRIX.] A female donor.

Donau /'dɒnaʊ/ *a.* & *n.* M20. [G = the river Danube.] *Geol.* (Designating or pertaining to) a series of Lower Pleistocene glaciations in the Alps, preceding the Günz.

doncher /'dəʊntʃə/ *v.* (*2 sing. pres.*). *colloq.* Also **doncha, dontcha, dontcher**. L19. [Repr. an informal pronunc.] Don't you. Esp. in *doncher know.*

done /dʌn/ *ppl a.* & *n.* ME. [pa. pple of DO *v.*] **A** *ppl a.* **1** *gen.* That has been done. Also foll. by adv. Cf. esp. DO *v.* 4. ME. **2** Socially acceptable; customary. Usu. in neg. w. *be*, & in *the done thing. colloq.* M19. **3** Tired, exhausted; worn out. Usu. *pred.* foll. by *for*, *in*, *up. colloq.* E20.

1 J. CANNAN The Colonel Blimps from the done-up cottages. *New Yorker* A done deal. *hard-done-by*: see HARD *a., adv.,* & *n.* 2 T. HEALD Some people consider it 'not done' to wear one club tie in another club's premises. 3 A. MOOREHEAD We and our camels being just done up, and scarcely able to reach the depot. *What Video?* Throwing a done-for VCR into the bin? **done to the wide** or **the world** *colloq.* absolutely worn out or defeated.

B *n.* A thing that is done. M19.

doneness *n.* the degree to which food is done or cooked; the state of being sufficiently cooked: M20.

done *v.* see DO *v.*

donee /dəʊ'niː/ *n.* E16. [f. DONOR: see -EE[1].] **1** A person to whom something is given or conveyed, esp. legally. E16. **2** A person who receives a blood transfusion. E20.

Donegal /dɒnɪ'gɔːl, dʌn-, 'dɒnɪgɔːl, 'dʌn-/ *n.* E20. [A county in NW Ireland.] **1** In full *Donegal tweed.* A tweed characterized by bright flecks randomly distributed on a usu. light grey background, orig. woven in Co. Donegal. E20. **2** In full *Donegal carpet.* A coarse knotted carpet of a kind orig. made in Co. Donegal. E20.

doner /'dʌnə/ *n.*[1] *dial.* M19. [Prob. f. DONE *ppl a.* + -ER[1].] A person or animal past hope or fated to die.

doner /'dɒnə, dəʊ-/ *n.*[2] L20. [Abbrev.] = DONER KEBAB.

doner *n.*[3] see DONA.

doner kebab /'dɒnə kɪ'bab, 'dəʊ-, kə-, 'bɑːb/ *n. phr.* M20. [Turk. *döner kebap*, f. *döner* rotating + *kebap* KEBAB.] A Turkish dish consisting of spiced lamb roasted on a vertical rotating spit and sliced thinly.

doney *n.* var. of DHONEY.

dong /dɒŋ/ *n.*[1] Pl. same. E19. [Vietnamese.] A monetary unit (now the basic unit) of Vietnam, now equal to 10 hào or 100 xu.

dong /dɒŋ/ *n.*[2] L19. [Coined by E. Lear.] A fabulous creature represented as having a luminous nose.

dong /dɒŋ/ *n.*[3] L19. [f. the vb.] **1** A deep resonant sound (as) of a large bell. L19. **2** A heavy blow, a punch. *Austral.* & *NZ colloq.* M20.

dong /dɒŋ/ *n.*[4] *slang* (chiefly *N. Amer.*). M20. [Origin uncertain: perh. f. prec.] The penis.

dong /dɒŋ/ *v.* L16. [Imit.] **1** *v.i.* (Of a large bell) sound resonantly; make a deep resonant sound like that of a large bell. L16. **2** *v.t.* Hit, punch. *colloq.* (esp. *Austral.* & *NZ*). L19.

donga /'dɒŋgə/ *n.* L19. [Nguni.] **1** A ravine or watercourse with steep sides. *S. Afr.* L19. **2** A broad shallow depression in the ground. *Austral.* E20. **3** A makeshift shelter; a temporary dwelling. *Austral.* E20.

dongle /'dɒŋg(ə)l/ *n.* L20. [Arbitrary]. *Computing.* A software protection device which must be plugged into a computer to enable the protected software to be used on it.

Dongola /'dɒŋgələ, dɒn'gəʊlə/ *n.* & *a.*[1] Also **d-**. L19. [A district of Sudan.] (Designating) a type of leather resembling kid, made from goat, sheep, or calf skin.

dongola /'dɒŋgələ, dɒn'gəʊlə/ *a.*[2] Also **D-**. L19. [Origin unkn.: cf. prec., *gondola.*] Designating a race or racing in which punts are paddled by teams of people.

Donizettian /dɒnɪ'zɛtɪən, -'tsɛ-/ *a.* & *n.* M19. [f. *Donizetti* (see below) + -AN.] **A** *adj.* Of, pertaining to, or characteristic of the Italian operatic composer Gaetano Donizetti (1797–1848) or his music. M19. **B** *n.* An interpreter, student, or admirer of Donizetti or his music. M20.

donjon /'dɒndʒ(ə)n, 'dʌn-/ *n.* Also (now *rare*) **dungeon** /'dʌndʒ(ə)n/. See also DUNGEON *n.* ME. [See DUNGEON *n.*] **1** The great tower or keep of a castle, in the innermost court or bailey. ME. **2** See DUNGEON *n.* 1.

Don Juan /dɒn 'dʒʊən, 'wɑːn/ *n. phr.* M19. [A legendary Sp. nobleman famous for his seductions. Cf. DON *n.*[1]] A man with a reputation for seducing women; a rake, a libertine.

Don Juanism *n. phr.* L19.

donk /dɒŋk/ *n. colloq.* E20. [Abbrev. of DONKEY.] **1** = DONKEY 1, 2. E20. **2** A donkey engine. M20.

1 A. RANSOME Roger's being a donk and starting some silly game.

donkey /'dɒŋki/ *n.* L18. [Origin unkn.: in early use pronounced to rhyme with *monkey*, whence the proposed derivations f. DUN *n.*[1] and the male pers. name *Duncan* (cf. DICKY *n.*, NEDDY).] **1** = ASS *n.*[1] L18. **2** A stupid or silly person. M19. **3 a** In full *donkey engine.* A small or auxiliary engine, esp. on a ship. M19. **b** In full *donkey pump.* A small or auxiliary pump. M19. **4** A simple card-game often played with special cards. E20. 5 A low stool used by an artist at an easel. M20.

Phrases: (**a penny** etc. **more and**) **up goes the donkey** *colloq.*: used w. allusion to the cry of a travelling showman inviting contributions to complete a sum of money. **talk the hind leg(s) off a donkey** *colloq.* talk at very great length; talk persuasively.

Comb.: **donkey deep** *NZ slang* much involved; **donkey derby** a race in which competitors are mounted on donkeys; a meeting for such races; **donkey drop** *colloq.* in cricket etc., a slow ball bowled or hit so that it travels in a high curve; **donkey jacket** a thick weatherproof jacket worn esp. by workmen; **donkey-lick** *v.t.* (*Austral. slang*) defeat easily or thoroughly; **donkeyman** a man in charge of a donkey engine; a man with responsibilities in a ship's engine-room; **donkey's breakfast** *slang* a straw mattress; **donkey-stone** *n.* & *v.* = *hearthstone* s.v. HEARTH; **donkey stool** = sense 5 above; **donkey's years** *colloq.* a very long time; **donkey vote** *Austral. colloq.*: in which a voter or voters allocate their preferences simply by going down the list of candidates on the voting paper; **donkey-work** the hard or unattractive part of an undertaking.

donkeydom *n.* folly, stupidity M19. **donkeyish** *a.* asinine, rather stupid or silly M19.

donna /ˈdɔnna, ˈdɒnə/ *n.* E17. [It. f. L *domina*: see DONA.] (Used as a courtesy title preceding the name of) an Italian, or a Spanish or Portuguese, lady. See also PRIMA DONNA, SECONDA DONNA.

Donnan equilibrium /ˌdɒnən iːkwɪˈlɪbrɪəm, ɛkwɪ-/ *n. phr.* E20. [f. G. *Donnan* (1870–1956), Brit. physical chemist.] *Physical Chem.* The equilibrium that exists between two ionic solutions when one or more of the ionic species cannot pass from one solution to the other, producing a difference in osmotic pressure and electrical potential between the solutions.

donnard *v.* pa. pple: see DONNER.

donnée /dɔne, ˈdɒneɪ/ *n.* Also ***donné***. L19. [Fr., fem. pa. ppl a. of *donner* give.] 1 A subject, theme, or motif of a literary work. L19. 2 A datum, a given fact; a basic assumption. L19.

1 J. CAREY Those vague economic données that we come to expect in a Dickens novel. 2 J. P. STERN Leaving . . the question of how such a reverence is possible, we may accept it as a metaphysical donnée.

donner /ˈdɒnə/ *v.t. Sc.* & *north.* Pa. pple **donnered, donnard.** E18. [Origin unkn.] Daze, stun, stupefy. Chiefly as *donnered* ppl a.

donnish /ˈdɒnɪʃ/ *a.* E19. [f. DON *n.*[1] + -ISH[1].] Resembling or characteristic of a college don; having a pedantic stiffness or gravity of manner.

donnishly *adv.* E20. **donnishness** *n.* M19.

donnot *n.* var. of DO-NOUGHT.

Donnybrook /ˈdɒnɪbrʊk/ *n.* Also **d-**. M19. [A suburb of Dublin, Ireland, once famous for its annual fair.] A scene of uproar and disorder; an uproarious meeting; a heated argument.

donor /ˈdəʊnə, -nɔː/ *n.* LME. [AN *don(o)ur*, AN & OFr. *doneur*, f. L *donator*: see DONATOR *n.*[1], -OR.] 1 A person who gives or (*Law*) conveys something. LME. 2 A person or animal, or a corpse, that is used as a source of tissue for transplantation; a blood donor; a man who contributes semen for artificial insemination. E20. 3a *Chem.* An atom, molecule, etc., that loses part of itself in combining with another; *esp.* an atom that gives up two valency electrons in forming a coordinate bond. E20. b *Physics.* An impurity atom in a semiconductor which has more valency electrons than the majority of atoms and effectively contributes a conducting electron to the material. M20.

2 *universal donor*: see UNIVERSAL *a.*

Comb.: **donor card** a card which a person carries to authorize the use of his or her body for transplant surgery after death; **donor country**: which gives economic aid to another country.

donorship *n.* M20.

do-nothing /ˈduːnʌθɪŋ/ *n.* & *a.* L16. [f. DO *v.* + NOTHING.] A *n.* A person who does nothing; an idler. L16. B *adj.* That does nothing; characterized by doing nothing; indolent, idle. M19.

do'nothingism *n.* M19. **do'nothingness** *n.* E19.

do-nought /ˈduːnɔːt/ *n.* Now chiefly *dial.* Also **donnot** /ˈdɒnət/ L16. [App. f. *do nought.*] A do-nothing; a good-for-nothing.

Donovan body /ˈdɒnəvən bɒdi/ *n. phr.* E20. [C. *Donovan* (1863–1951), Ir. physician.] *Med.* The intracellular body characteristic of the lesions of donovanosis, identified as due to an anaerobic rod-shaped bacterium, *Calymmatobacterium granulomatosis*.

donova'nosis *n.*, pl. **-noses** /-ˈnəʊsiːz/, a chronic granulomatous skin disease of the inguinal and genital regions, endemic in southern India and the Caribbean and thought to be caused by the bacteria that form Donovan bodies; also called *granuloma inguinale*: M20.

Don Pedro *n. phr.* var. of DOM PEDRO.

Don Quixote *n.* see QUIXOTE.

donship /ˈdɒnʃɪp/ *n.* E17. [f. DON *n.*[1] + -SHIP.] 1 With possess. adj. (as *his* etc. *donship*): a title of respect given to a don (DON *n.*[1] 1). E17. 2 The status of being a don; possession of the title 'don'. L18.

donsie /ˈdɒnsi/ *a. Sc.* Also **-sy**. See also DAUNCY. E18. [f. Gael. *donas* bad luck (f. *dona* bad) + -IE. Cf. SONSY.] 1 Unlucky. E18. 2 Dejected, glum. E18. 3 Neat, tidy, esp. affectedly so. *Sc.* & *north.* Now *rare* or *obs.* E18. 4 Sickly; delicate, feeble. L18. 5 Ill-behaved; bad-tempered. Now *rare* or *obs.* L18. 6 Stupid. E19.

don't /dəʊnt/ *n.* L19. [f. *don't*: see DO *v.*] A prohibition; an injunction not to do something. Usu. in *pl.* in *dos and don'ts*.

don't *v.* see DO *v.*

don't-care /ˈdəʊntkɛː/ *a.* & *n.* L19. [f. *don't* (see DO *v.*) + CARE *v.*] A *adj.* Careless, indifferent; reckless. L19. B *n.* A careless or indifferent person. E20.

don't-'carish *a.* M19. **don't-'carishness** *n.* M19.

dontcha, dontcher *vs.* vars. of DONCHER.

don't-know /dəʊntˈnəʊ/ *n.* L19. [f. *don't* (see DO *v.*) + KNOW *v.*] A person who does not know or disclaims knowledge; *esp.* one who is undecided when replying to an opinion poll or questionnaire.

donut *n.* see DOUGHNUT.

donzel /ˈdɒnz(ə)l/ *n.* Now *arch.* or *Hist.* L16. [It. *donzello* f. Proto-Romance dim. of L *dominus* lord, master: see -EL[2]. Cf. DON *n.*[1], DAMSEL.] A young gentleman not yet knighted; a squire, a page.

donzella /donˈdzella, dɒntˈsɛlə/ *n.* Pl. ***-lle*** /-lle/, ***-llas*** /-ləz/. M19. [It., fem. of *donzello*: see prec.] A young Italian or Provençal woman.

doo *n.* see DOVE *n.*

doob /duːb/ *n.* E19. [Hind. *dūb* = Skt *dūrvā*.] In the Indian subcontinent, = DOG'S TOOTH 2.

doocot /ˈduːkət/ *n.* Orig. & chiefly *Sc.* LME. [f. DOO + COT *n.*[1]] A dovecot; *Sc. Antiq.* a type of large stone dovecot characteristic of the Scottish Lowlands.

doodad /ˈduːdad/ *n.* Chiefly *N. Amer.* E20. [Origin unkn.] Something not readily nameable; a thingummy; *esp.* a fancy ornament of an unnecessary kind.

R. DAVIES Full of marquetry woodwork . . and filigree doodads around the ceiling.

doodah /ˈduːdɑː/ *n. slang.* E20. [The refrain *doo-da(h)* of the plantation song 'Camptown Races'.] 1 *all of a doodah*, in a state of excitement; in a flap. E20. 2 = prec. E20.

doodle /ˈduːd(ə)l/ *n.* E17. [LG *dudel-* in *dudeltopf*, *-ldopp* simple fellow.] 1 A foolish person; a dolt, a ninny. *colloq.* E17. 2 = DOODLEBUG 1. *US colloq.* L19. 3 An idle scrawl or figure drawn absent-mindedly or to while away the time. M20.

doodle /ˈduːd(ə)l/ *v.*[1] E19. [f. DOODLE *n.*] 1 *v.t.* Make a fool of; cheat. *dial.* E19. 2 *v.i.* & *t.* Scrawl or draw absent-mindedly or to while away the time. M20.

doodler *n.* a person who draws doodles M20.

doodle /ˈduːd(ə)l/ *v.*[2]*t.* Chiefly *Sc.* E19. [G *dudeln*: cf. *Dudelsack* bagpipe.] Play (a bagpipe).

Comb.: **doodle-sack** a bagpipe.

doodlebug /ˈduːd(ə)lbʌg/ *n.* M19. [f. DOODLE *n.* + BUG *n.*[2]] 1 The larva of the ant-lion; any of various similar insects. *US.* M19. 2 A divining rod for finding oil etc.; any device used for the same purpose. *US colloq.* E20. 3 A prospector for oil etc. *US colloq.* M20. 4 Any of various kinds of small vehicle. *US colloq.* M20. 5 A flying bomb of the 1939–45 war. *colloq.* M20.

doodlebugger *n.* (*US*) = sense 3 above M20.

doodle-doo /duːd(ə)lˈduː/ *n. nursery* or *joc.* L18. [Abbrev. of COCK-A-DOODLE-DOO.] A cockerel.

doofer /ˈduːfə/ *n. slang.* Also **-fah**; **-vah, -ver,** /-və/. M20. [Prob. alt. of *do for* in phrs. like *that will do for now.*] An unspecified object or device; a thingummy.

doohickey /ˈduːhɪki/ *n. colloq.* (chiefly *N. Amer.*). Also **dohickey, doohicky.** E20. [f. DOO(DAD + HICKEY.] An unspecified object or device, *esp.* a mechanical one.

doojigger /ˈduːdʒɪgə/ *n. US colloq.* M20. [f. DOO(DAD + JIGGER *n.*[1]] A small object, a gadget, a thingummy.

dool /duːl/ *n.*[1] Also **dole** /dəʊl/. LME. [Corresp. to OFris. *dōl* (Du. *doel*) aim, mark.] 1 A boundary or landmark in the form of a post, stone, or unploughed strip. LME. 2 The goal in a game. *Sc.* M16.

2 **hail the dool** score a goal.

dool *n.*[2] var. of DOLE *n.*[2]

doolally /duːˈlali/ *a. slang* (orig. *Mil.*). E20. [*Deolali*, a town near Bombay.] Orig. (now less usual) *doolally tap* [Urdu f. Pers. *tap* fever]. Temporarily insane; deranged; feeble-minded, simple, foolish.

Doolan /ˈduːlən/ *n. NZ slang.* Also **d-**. M20. [Prob. the Irish surname.] A Roman Catholic, *spec.* an Irish one.

doolie /ˈduːli/ *n.* Also **-ly.** E17. [Hind. *ḍolī* dim. of *ḍolā* cradle, swing, litter, f. Skt *dolā*, *ḍolā* to swing.] A simple litter, formerly used in the Indian subcontinent for transporting the wounded.

doom /duːm/ *n.*[1] [OE *dōm* = OFris., OS *dōm*, OHG *tuom*, ON *dómr*, Goth. *dōms*, f. Gmc, f. a base meaning 'to place', 'to set', repr. also by DO *v.* For the sense-development cf. Gk *themis* law (*the-* to place), L *statutum* STATUTE *n.*] 1 A statute, a law; *gen.* an ordinance, a decree. *obs.* exc. *Hist.* OE. 2 A judicial decision, *esp.* one formally pronounced; *spec.* a sentence of punishment. OE. 3 The process of judging, as in a court of law; a trial. *arch.* OE. †4 Justice, equity. Chiefly in versions of Scripture or in scriptural allusions. OE–L16. †5 Right to judge; *gen.* power, authority. OE–LME. 6 The Last Judgement; a pictorial representation of this. Now chiefly in *crack of doom*. *arch.* ME. †7 Personal opinion or judgement. ME–E17. †8 Faculty of judging; discernment. LME–L17. 9 Irrevocable lot, fate, destiny, (esp. evil). LME. 10 The fated ending to a person's life, career, or course of action; impending ruin or disaster. L16.

1 J. LINGARD He revised the whole code of Anglo-Saxon law, and compiled a new book of dooms. 2 S. BECKETT To record the doom, don the black cap. 3 C. KINGSLEY The Judge is set, the doom begun! 6 MILTON The wakefull trump of doom. J. T. MICKLETHWAITE The . . hobgoblins of mediaeval dooms. **Day of Doom** (*a*) the Day of Judgement; †(*b*) *transf.* the last day of one's life. 8 DRYDEN With . . unerring Doom, He sees what is, and was, and is to come. 9 D. H. LAWRENCE She knew her life would be unhappy. . . Yet it was her doom She had to come back to him. T. H. WHITE It will be your glorious doom . . to enjoy the nobility of your proper title. 10 J. R. GREEN The minister's doom was sealed. V. GLENDINNING The atmosphere of impending doom . . lay heavily on them all.

Comb.: **doombook** *Hist.* a code of Germanic or Anglo-Saxon laws, *spec.* that ascribed to Alfred the Great; **doom-laden** *a.* portending, suggesting, or predicting doom; **doom-ring** *Archaeol.* a ring of stones forming the boundary of the old Norse courts of judgement; **doomsayer** = DOOMSTER 3; **doom-tree** *Hist.*: on which condemned persons were hanged; **doomwatch** a watch for signs of impending disaster, esp. of environmental destruction; **doomwatcher** a person who takes part in a doomwatch or who predicts environmental disaster.

doomful *a.* (*arch.*) fraught with impending disaster; fateful: L16. **doomfully** *adv.* M20.

doom *n.*[2] var. of DOUM.

doom /du:m/ *v.* LME. [f. DOOM *n.*[1]] **I** *v.t.* **1** Pass judgement on. *obs.* exc. as in sense 2. LME. **2** Give judgement against; sentence, condemn, (*to* a punishment). L16. **3** Pronounce or fix as a sentence or fate; decree. *arch.* L16. **4** Destine inexorably *to* a (usu. unwelcome) fate or *to do*. Also *absol.*, consign to certain misfortune or destruction. Chiefly as *doomed* ppl a. E17.

1 P. FLETCHER There the equall Judge . . dooms each voice aright. 2 MILTON He dooms it as contrary to Truth. LD MACAULAY An act was passed which doomed him to perpetual exile. 3 SHAKES. *Tit. A.* The Emperor in his rage will doom her death. 4 G. F. KENNAN They thought Kornilov's venture doomed to failure. F. WELDON I . . cannot afford to throw anything away, and am doomed to wear it for ever.

II *v.i.* **5** Give judgement; decide. Now *rare* or *obs.* L16.

doomer /'du:mə/ *n. arch.* OE. [f. DOOM *n.*[1] + -ER[1]; later f. DOOM *v.*] A person who tries a case or pronounces a sentence, *esp.* a judge.

dooms /du:mz/ *adv. Sc. & north.* E19. [Origin uncertain: perh. alt. of †*doon(s)* in same sense, f. *doon* var. of DOWN *adv.*] Extremely, very; (with imprecatory force) deucedly.

doomsday /'du:mzdeɪ/ *n.* In sense 2 **D-**. See also DOMESDAY. OE. [f. genit. of DOOM *n.*[1] + DAY *n.*] **1** The day when God is expected to judge the world, the Day of Judgement; any day of decisive judgement or final dissolution. OE. **2** = DOMESDAY. L16.

1 till doomsday to the end of the world; for ever.

Comb.: **doomsday machine, bomb** a hypothetical bomb capable of annihilating the world.

doomsman /'du:mzmən/ *n. arch.* Pl. **-men**. ME. [f. DOOM *n.*[1] + -'S[1] + MAN *n.*] = DOOMSTER 1, DEEMSTER 1.

doomster /'du:mstə/ *n.* LME. [Var. of DEEMSTER after DOOM *n.*[1], *v.*] **1** = DEEMSTER 1. *arch.* LME. **2** *Sc.* = DEMPSTER 2. *obs.* exc. *Hist.* E17. **3** A person who predicts disaster, esp. of a political or economic nature; a doomsayer. L20.

doomy /'du:mi/ *a.* M20. [f. DOOM *n.*[1] + -Y[1].] Portending, suggesting, or predicting doom; ominous; gloomy, weird.

New Society Anyone who is less than doomy about Britain's population 'problem'. CLIVE JAMES 'Come with us', boomed a doomy tape, 'into the Mesozoic age.'

doomily *adv.* L20. **doominess** *n.* L20.

Doona /'du:nə/ *n. Austral.* Also **d-**. L20. [Perh. f. Sw. *dun* down.] (Proprietary name for) a quilted eiderdown or duvet.

doonga /'du:ŋgə/ *n.* Also **dunga**. E20. [Hind. *dõgā*.] In the Indian subcontinent, a flat-bottomed dugout with a square sail.

door /dɔ:/ *n.* [OE *duru* (fem. *u*-stem) = OFris. *dure*, OS *duru* & OE *dor* (neut. *a*- stem) = OS *dor*, (O)HG *tor* gate, Goth. *daur* both f. Gmc, f. IE base repr. also by L *foris*, Gk *thura*, Skt *dur*, *dvār*.] **I 1** A hinged or sliding barrier of wood, metal, etc., serving to open or close the entrance to a building, room, cupboard, vehicle, or other enclosure. OE. **b** Indicating the room, house, etc., in a row or series, to which the door belongs. M17. **2** An opening that can be closed by a door, a doorway. LME. **3** Something resembling a door in its movement or function; a lid, a valve, a cover; an opening. LME. **4** Either of the two boards or metal plates attached to the ends of a trawl-net. E20.

1 SIR W. SCOTT She stood before her lover's door and knocked for admittance. *back door, French door, front door, side door, patio door*, etc. *double door, folding door, glass door, sliding door*, etc. b J. MASTERS His office . . was three doors from the Collector's.

II *fig.* **5** A means of access, admission, or exit; a means to a specified end; a suitable occasion, an opportunity. Chiefly in phrs. below. OE.

5 A. W. KINGLAKE Which left open a door to future negotiation. H. KELLER I did not dream that that interview would be the door through which I should pass . . from isolation to friendship. M. L. KING A democratic educational system requires multiple doors.

Phrases: *at* DEATH*'s door. a toe in the door*: see TOE *n.* **be at a person's door** = *lie at a person's door* below. *behind* CLOSED *doors*. **close the door on** or **to** make impossible, preclude. DARKEN *a person's door(s)*. *folding door(s)*: see FOLDING *ppl a. foot in the door*: see FOOT *n. in doors*: see INDOORS *adv.* **†is the wind in that door?** is the wind in that quarter? is that how matters are going? *keep the wolf from the door*: see WOLF *n.* **lay something at a person's door** impute something reprehensible etc. to a person. LEDGED *door*. **lie at a person's door** be the fault or responsibility of a person. *nail to the barn door*: see NAIL *v. next door*: see NEXT *a.* **open a door to** or **for** provide an opportunity for, make possible. *open door*: see OPEN *a.* **out of doors** (*a*) outside the house, in or into the open air; †(*b*) *fig.* out of place, irrelevant: see OUT-OF-DOORS. **show a person the door** dismiss a person unceremoniously from one's presence. **shut the door on** or **to** = *close the door on* above. *shut the stable door when the horse has bolted*: see STABLE *n.*[1] *Venetian door*: see VENETIAN *a.* **within door(s)** *arch.* in or into a building, indoors. WITHOUT DOOR. WITHOUT DOORS.

Comb.: **doorbell** a bell inside a building that can be rung from outside to indicate that someone is at the door; **door-case** = *door-frame* below; **door-cheek** (now *north.*) = *doorpost* below; **door-frame** the frame inside a doorway, in which the door is hung; **door-head** the horizontal upper part of a door-frame; **doorkeeper** a person who guards a door; a janitor; **door-knob**: for turning to release the catch of a door; *door-knocker*: see KNOCKER 2; **doorman** an attendant at the entrance to a shop, office, or place of entertainment; a doorkeeper; **doormat** a mat for wiping mud etc. from the shoes on entering a building; *fig.* a passive subservient person; **doornail** a large-headed nail with which doors were formerly studded for strength or ornament; now esp. in *dead as a doornail* (see DEAD *a.*); **door-plate** a plate on or by a front door of a building, bearing the name of the occupant(s) or the nature of the business conducted there; **doorpost** either of the two uprights in a door-frame; a jamb; **door-sill** = SILL *n.*[1] 3a; **doorsman** *arch.* = *doorman* above; **door-stead** (now *dial.*) = *doorway* below; **door-stone** a flagstone situated in front of a door; **doorstop** a device fixed to the ground or the wall to prevent a door from opening too widely or from striking the wall; a weight or wedge that can be used to keep a door open; **door-to-door** *a.* (of selling, canvassing, etc.) carried on systematically from house to house; **doorward** *arch.* a doorkeeper, a janitor; *Sc. Hist.* a warder of the royal palace; **doorway** the opening filled by a door; **dooryard** *N. Amer.* a yard or garden in front of the door of a house.

doored *a.* having a door or doors LME. **doorless** *a.* ME.

doorstep /'dɔ:stɛp/ *n.*, *a.*, & *v.* E19. [f. DOOR + STEP *n.*[1]] **A** *n.* **1** A step outside a (usu. outer) door, by which the threshold is raised above the level of the ground. E19. **2** A thick slice of bread. *slang.* L19.

1 on the or **one's doorstep** *fig.* very close to one.

B *attrib.* or as *adj.* Door-to-door; brought or made to people in their own homes. E20.

Modern Law Review He had foolishly signed a three-year magazine subscription contract with a doorstep salesman. *Times Lit. Suppl.* Doorstep jobs like delivering milk and selling insurance. *Times* Doorstep deliveries are losing ground to shop sales.

C *v.* Infl. **-pp-**. **1** *v.i.* Go from door to door selling, canvassing, etc. Earliest as *door-stepping* vbl n. E20. **2** *v.t.* Leave (a child) in the care of someone else. M20. **3** *v.t.* & *i.* Call on or wait on the doorstep for (a person) without invitation or arrangement. L20.

3 *Guardian* The 'frightful men' from that newspaper who doorstepped her.

doorstepper *n.* a person who doorsteps L20.

doovah, -ver *ns.* vars. of DOOFER.

doo-wop /'du:wɒp/ *n.* Also **doowhop, doowop**, & other vars. M20. [App. imit.] A style of pop music marked by the use of nonsense phrases as the main line or as harmony, which originated in the US in the 1950s.

doozer /'du:zə/ *n. slang* (chiefly *N. Amer.*). M20. [Origin uncertain: see next, -ER[1].] = DOOZY *n.*

doozy /'du:zi/ *a.* & *n. slang* (chiefly *N. Amer.* & *Austral.*). Also **-ie**. E20. [Origin uncertain: perh. rel. to DOUSE *v.*[1]] **A** *adj.* Excellent, stunning. E20. **B** *n.* A thing of surpassing size or excellence; a stunner. E20.

dop /dɒp/ *n.*[1] *obs.* exc. *dial.* L16. [f. DOP *v.*] A quick bob or curtsy.

dop /dɒp/ *n.*[2] E18. [Du. & Afk. = shell, husk. In senses 3 & 4 perh. a different wd.] **†1** The pupa-case of an insect. *rare.* Only in E18. **2** A small copper cup into which a diamond is cemented while it is being cut or polished. M18. **3** In full *dop brandy*. Brandy, esp. of a cheap or inferior kind. *S. Afr.* L19. **4** A tot of liquor, esp. of wine as given to farm labourers in the Cape Province. *S. Afr.* M20.

dop /dɒp/ *v. obs.* exc. *dial.* LME. [f. base of OE *doppettan* immerse, baptize, f. Gmc: see DIP *v.*, DEEP *a.* Cf. also DAP *v.*] **†1** *v.i.* Plunge or sink suddenly into water etc.; dive, plop. LME–L17. **2** *v.i.* Make a quick bob or curtsy. M16. **†3** *v.t.* Dip or immerse quickly, as in baptism. M16–M17.

dopa /'dəʊpə/ *n.* E20. [G, f. initial letters of DI-[2] + OXY- + PHENYL + ALANINE.] An amino acid formed from tyrosine in the nerves and adrenal medulla as a precursor of dopamine, and given (as L-dopa) in the treatment of Parkinsonism; dihydroxyphenylalanine, $C_9H_{11}NO_4$.

L-dopa the laevorotary form of dopa, levodopa.

dopamine /'dəʊpəmi:n/ *n.* M20. [f. prec. + AMINE.] *Biochem.* An amine that occurs esp. in nervous and peripheral tissue as a neurotransmitter and a precursor of noradrenaline, adrenalin, and melanin; 3,4-dihydroxyphenylethylamine, $C_8H_{11}NO_2$.

dopami'nergic *n.* releasing or involving dopamine as a neurotransmitter M20.

dopant /'dəʊp(ə)nt/ *n.* M20. [f. DOPE *v.* + -ANT[1].] A substance used to dope a semiconductor.

dopchick *n.* see DABCHICK.

dope /dəʊp/ *n.* E19. [Du. *doop* sauce, f. *doopen* dip, mix, adulterate. In branch II prob. orig. a distinct wd.] **I** Senses orig. *US.* **1** A thick liquid, *esp.* one used as a lubricant. Also, a thick gravy. *US.* E19. **2** An absorbent material used to hold a lubricant or a high explosive. L19. **3** Orig., opium, *esp.* the thick treacly preparation used in opium-smoking. Now *gen.*, any narcotic or stupefying drug. Also, alcoholic drink. *slang.* L19. **4** A preparation, mixture, or medicinal drug not more precisely defined; 'stuff'. *slang.* L19. **b** A drug etc. administered to a racehorse or greyhound to interfere with its performance, or to an athlete as a stimulus. L19. **c** A varnish applied to the cloth surface of aeroplane parts to keep them taut and airtight. E20. **d** A substance added to a fuel to increase its efficiency. M20. **5** (A drink of) Coca-Cola or other carbonated beverage. *US slang.* E20. **6** Information, esp. on a particular topic or of a kind not generally divulged; essential facts or details. Also, statements designed to gloss over the truth; misleading talk. *slang.* E20.

4 A. D. GILLESPIE The hay fever is better now, more because the season is passing than by reason of the doctor's 'dopes'. 6 *Chicago Daily News* What does the average layman think, upon getting all this reassuring dope? M. LEITCH If you want the inside story, names, dates, places, all the dope on . . the Brotherhood, I can supply it.

II 7 A foolish or silly person. *colloq.* (orig. *dial.*). M19. **8** A person under the influence of drugs or drink; a drug addict. *US slang.* E20.

7 T. ROETHKE He's a dope in some ways, but very honest.

Comb.: **dope-fiend** *slang* a drug addict; **dope-ring** *slang* a group of people engaged in buying, selling, and using illicit drugs; **dope-runner** *slang* a person who smuggles or traffics in illicit drugs; **dope-sheet** *N. Amer. slang* a sheet of paper giving information or instructions; *spec.* one containing details of the horses entered for a race, with their past form.

dope /dəʊp/ *v.* Orig. *US.* M19. [f. the n.] **1** *v.t.* Smear, daub; *spec.* apply dope to (the outer fabric of an aeroplane etc). M19. **2** *v.t.* Treat with an adulterant; doctor. L19. **b** Add an impurity to (a semiconductor) to produce a desired electrical characteristic. M20. **3** *v.t.* Administer stimulating or stupefying drugs to (a horse, a person). L19. **4** *v.i.* Indulge in drug-taking. E20. **5** *v.t.* Foll. by *out*: work out; infer or find out by surmising; reckon (*that*). *US.* E20.

5 R. H. DAVIS We would study the morning papers and . . from them try to dope out the winners. B. SCHULBERG I'm going to sell it to Hollywood. I even got the title all doped out. *Village Voice* She started

reading the media .. to dope out the treatment of women.

doper *n.* a person who administers or (now chiefly) habitually takes drugs E20. **dopester** *n.* (*slang*) (*a*) a person who collects information on, and forecasts the results of, sporting events, elections, etc.; (*b*) a drug addict: E20.

dopey /ˈdəʊpi/ *a. slang* (orig. *US*). Also **dopy**. L19. [f. DOPE *n.* + -Y¹.] 1 Sluggish or stupefied (as) with a drug. L19. 2 Foolish, silly. L19.

1 G. ORWELL I was dopey from morphia but still in great pain. 2 R. JAFFE She decided that she would never talk about her dopey ambitions again.

dopily *a.* M20. **dopiness** *n.* dopey quality; *spec.* (*NZ*) a deficiency disease in sheep: M20.

doppelgänger /ˈdɒpəlɡɛŋə; ˈdɒp(ə)lɡɛŋə, -ɡaŋə/ *n.* Also ***-ganger***. M19. [G, lit. 'double-goer'. Cf. DOUBLE-GANGER.] A supposed spectral likeness or double of a living person.

Dopper /ˈdɒpə/ *n. S. Afr.* Also **d-**. M19. [Afk., of unkn. origin.] A member of a strictly Calvinistic sect of the Dutch Reformed Church, proverbial for ultra-conservatism in ideas, manners, and dress.

doppie /ˈdɒpi/ *n. S. Afr.* L19. [Afk., dim. of *dop* (DOP *n.*²).] 1 An empty cartridge case, a percussion cap. *colloq.* L19. 2 A grapeskin. M20.

doppione /dɒpˈpjoːne, dɒpɪˈəʊni/ *n.* Pl. ***-ni*** /-ni/. M20. [It., f. *doppio* double.] *Early Mus.* A double-bore woodwind instrument of the Italian Renaissance.

Doppler /ˈdɒplə/ *n.* Also **d-**. L19. [C. J. *Doppler* (1803–53), Austrian mathematician and physicist.] Used *attrib.* and (formerly) in *possess.* with ref. to the effect explained by him (see below).

Doppler broadening: of spectral lines as a result of the different velocities of the emitting atoms giving rise to different Doppler shifts; **Doppler effect** the observed increase (or decrease) in the pitch or frequency of sound, light, and other waves when the source and observer are getting closer (or further away); **Doppler radar**: using the Doppler effect to ascertain the radial velocity of a detected object; **Doppler shift** the change in frequency caused by the Doppler effect; **Doppler width**: of spectral lines, due to Doppler broadening.

dopy *a.* var. of DOPEY.

dor /dɔː/ *n.*¹ Also **dorr**. OE. [Prob. imit. Cf. MLG *dorte* drone.] †1 Any of various kinds of bee or buzzing fly. Also *dor-bee*, *-fly*, etc. OE–L17. 2 More fully *dor-beetle*. Any of various coleopterous insects that make a buzzing sound, *esp.* a dung-beetle of the genus *Geotrupes*. LME.

Comb.: *dor-bee*: see sense 1 above; *dor-beetle*: see sense 2 above; **dor-bug** *US* any insect that makes a buzzing sound; *dor-fly*: see sense 1 above; **dor-hawk** the nightjar.

†**dor** *n.*² M16–M19. [Rel. to DOR *v.*: perh. f. ON *dár* scoff, in phr. *draga dár at* make game of.] Mockery. Chiefly in *give someone the dor*, *receive the dor*, etc.

dor /dɔː/ *v.t.* Long *obs.* exc. *dial.* L16. [Rel. to DOR *n.*²: perh. f. ON *dára* mock, make sport of.] Mock, make game of; confound, stupefy.

dor the dotterel cajole or hoax a simpleton.

dorado /dəˈrɑːdəʊ/ *n.* Pl. **-os**. E17. [Sp. = gilded, f. late L *deauratus* pa. pple of *deaurare* gild over: see DORY *n.*¹] 1 A dolphinfish, *Coryphaena hippurus*, noted for its splendid blue-green and silver colours and fast speed and caught as a sporting and food fish; = DOLPHIN 1b. E17. 2 (Usu. **D-**.) (The name of) a small constellation of the southern hemisphere, between Pictor and Reticulum; the Swordfish. L17. 3 A carplike game-fish, *Salminus maxillosus*, of the characin family, found in S. American rivers and of a golden colour. L19.

Dorcas /ˈdɔːkəs/ *n.*¹ E19. [mod.L, f. *Gazella dorcas* (see below), f. Gk *dorkas* deer, gazelle.] More fully *Dorcas gazelle*. A small gazelle, *Gazella dorcas*, found in N. Africa and western Asia.

Dorcas /ˈdɔːkəs/ *n.*² M19. [A woman in *Acts* 9:36.] (A meeting of) a society of women in a church, whose aim is to make and provide clothing for the poor. Also *Dorcas meeting*, *society*.

Comb.: **Dorcas basket**: of needlework for charitable purposes.

doré /*n.* ˈdɔːreɪ, -riː; *adj.* ˈdɔːreɪ, ˈdɒr-/ *n.* & *a.* L18. [Fr., pa. pple of *dorer* gild f. late L *deaurare*: see DORY *n.*¹] A *n.* The wall-eye, *Stizostedion vitreum*. *Canad.* L18. B *n. Metall.* Containing gold. L19.

doria /ˈdɔːrɪə/ *n.* Also **dorea**. L17. [Hind. *ḍoriyā* striped cloth.] A kind of striped Indian muslin, sometimes flowered between the stripes.

Dorian /ˈdɔːrɪən/ *n.* & *a.* M16. [f. L *Dorius* (f. Gk *Dōrios* of Doris) + -IAN.] A *n. Hist.* A native or inhabitant of Doris (Doria), a division of ancient Greece. M16.

B *adj.* Of or pertaining to Doris (Doria). L16.

Dorian mode *Mus.* (*a*) an ancient Greek mode, reputedly simple and solemn in character; (*b*) a church mode with D as the final and A as the dominant.

Doric /ˈdɒrɪk/ *a.* & *n.* In *Archit.* orig. †**-ica**. M16. [L *Doricus* f. Gk *Dōrikos*, f. *Dōrios*: see prec., -IC.] A *adj.* 1 Of or pertaining to Doris or the Dorians. M16. b Of a dialect: broad; rustic. E17. 2 *Archit.* Designating the simplest and sturdiest of the three Greek orders, and its Roman adaptation, characterized by a capital consisting of a thick square abacus resting on an echinus and (in the case of Greek Doric) no base to the column. M16.

B *n.* 1 *Archit.* The Doric order. E17. 2 A broad or rustic dialect; *spec.* (*a*) the Doric dialect of ancient Greek; (*b*) a Scottish or northern form of English. M17. 3 *Typogr.* (The name of) a kind of sanserif type. M19.

2 C. GIBBON The good doctor dropped into the broadest Doric.

Dorise *v.* var. of DORIZE.

Dorism /ˈdɔːrɪz(ə)m/ *n.* L17. [Gk *Dōrismos* speaking Doric, f. *Dōrizein*: see next, -ISM.] 1 A Doric form of expression. L17. 2 Culture of a Dorian character. L19.

Dorize /ˈdɔːrʌɪz/ *v.* Now *rare*. Also **-ise**. L17. [Gk *Dōrizein*: see -IZE.] 1 *v.i.* Behave like the Dorians; speak or write in Doric. L17. 2 *v.t.* Make Dorian. M19.

dorje /ˈdɔːdʒeɪ/ *n.* M19. [Tib.] A representation of a thunderbolt in the form of a short double trident or sceptre, held by lamas during prayers.

dork /dɔːk/ *n.*¹ *slang*. M20. [Perh. var. of DIRK *n.*, infl. by DICK *n.*¹ 2.] 1 The penis. M20. 2 A stupid or contemptible person. L20.

Dorking /ˈdɔːkɪŋ/ *a.* & *n.* L18. [A town in Surrey, England.] A *adj.* (Designating a bird) of a breed of large white fowl with five toes. L18. B *n.* (A fowl of) this breed. L18.

dorlach /ˈdɔːləx/ *n. Sc.* L16. [Gael. Cf. DOURLACH.] †1 A quiver. L16–E19. 2 A bundle formerly carried on the person by Highland troops; a kitbag; a portmanteau. M17.

dorm /dɔːm/ *n. colloq.* E20. [Abbrev.] = DORMITORY *n.* 1.

dormancy /ˈdɔːm(ə)nsi/ *n.* L18. [f. next: see -ANCY.] Dormant condition, esp. of a plant or seed.

dormant /ˈdɔːm(ə)nt/ *a.* & *n.* LME. [(O)Fr., pres. pple of *dormir* f. L *dormire* to sleep: see -ANT¹.] A *adj.* 1 Fixed in position. Chiefly in *dormant table*, *tree*. LME. 2 In a state of rest; not in operation; in abeyance; latent. LME. b Of an animal: with animation suspended. Of a plant or seed: with development suspended. L18. 3 *Her.* Of an animal: lying with its head resting on its paws and its eyes closed. Usu. *postpositive*. E16. 4 Sleeping; lying as in sleep; intellectually inactive. E17. 5 *dormant window*, a dormer window. M17.

1 **dormant tree** a fixed horizontal beam; a sleeper. 2 T. H. HUXLEY Many volcanoes .. are merely dormant. *Times* The main clearing banks will not disclose how much is lying in dormant accounts. A. BROOKNER That fear that lies dormant even in the strongest heart. **dormant partner** = *sleeping partner* s.v. SLEEPING *ppl a.* *warrant dormant*: see WARRANT *n.*¹ 8.

B *n.* †1 = *dormant tree* above. LME–M17. 2 = *dormant window* above. E18.

dormer /ˈdɔːmə/ *n.* L16. [OFr. *dormëor*, f. *dormir* (see DORMANT) + *-ëor* -ER².] 1 A vertical window that projects from a sloping roof. Formerly, the window of a dormitory or bedroom. Also *dormer window*. L16. 2 A room for sleeping in; a dormitory. *obs.* exc. *Hist.* E17. †3 = *dormant tree* s.v. DORMANT *a.* 1. E17–M19.

Comb.: **dormer bungalow**: having an upper storey with a dormer window in the roof-space; **dormer room**: in the roof-space of a house etc., lit by a dormer window.

dormered *a.* M19.

dormeuse /dɔrmøːz (*pl. same*), dɔːˈməːz/ *n.* M18. [Fr., fem. of *dormeur* lit. 'sleeper', f. *dormir*: see DORMANT.] †1 A cap or hood worn in bed. Only in M18. 2 A travelling-carriage adapted for sleeping in. *obs.* exc. *Hist.* E19. 3 A kind of couch or settee. M19.

dormice *n.* pl. of DORMOUSE.

dormie *adv.* & *pred. a.* var. of DORMY.

dormient /ˈdɔːmɪənt/ *a.* Now *rare*. M17. [L *dormient-* pres. ppl stem of *dormire* to sleep: see -ENT.] Sleeping; dormant, latent.

dormition /dɔːˈmɪʃ(ə)n/ *n.* L15. [Fr. f. L *dormitio(n-)*, f. *dormit-* pa. ppl stem of *dormire* to sleep: see -ION.] The act of sleeping; falling asleep; *fig.* death (of a holy person); in the Orthodox Church, (a feast commemorating) the passing of the Virgin Mary from earthly life.

dormitive /ˈdɔːmɪtɪv/ *a.* & *n.* L16. [Fr. *dormitif*, *-ive*, f. L *dormit-*: see prec., -IVE.] A *adj.* Causing sleep, soporific. L16. B *n.* A soporific medicine. Now *rare*. E17.

dormitory /ˈdɔːmɪt(ə)ri/ *n.* LME. [L *dormitorium* use as n. of neut. of *dormitorius*, f. *dormit-*: see DORMITION, -ORY¹.] 1 A room for sleeping in; *spec.* a room or building in a school, monastery, or other institution containing beds, and sometimes divided into separate chambers. LME. b A university or college hall of residence or hostel. *US*. M19. c A town, village, or suburb where people live whose work is elsewhere in a neighbouring city or city centre. Also *dormitory town* etc. E20. 2 *fig.* A resting-place. M17. †3 A cemetery; a grave, a vault. M17–L19.

†**dormitory** *a.* E17–M19. [L *dormitorius*: see prec.] Causing sleep.

Dormobile /ˈdɔːmə(ʊ)biːl/ *n.* Also **d-**. M20. [f. DOR(MITORY *n.* + AUTO)MOBILE *n.* or MOBILE *a.*] (Proprietary name for) a kind of van whose rear compartment has windows and can be used for sleeping and eating in.

dormouse /ˈdɔːmaʊs/ *n.* & *a.* LME. [Origin unkn.; from 16 assoc. w. Fr. *dormir*, L *dormire*: see DORMANT.] A *n.* Pl. **-mice** /-mʌɪs/. 1 Any rodent of the family Gliridae, comprising small, nocturnal, mostly arboreal animals of Europe, Asia, and N. Africa with soft fur and a sometimes bushy tail; *esp.* the British species, *Muscardinus avellanarius*, noted for its long period of hibernation. Also (usu. w. specifying wd), either of two similar rodents, *Platacanthomys lasiurus* of India and *Typhlomys cinereus* of China. LME. 2 A sleepy or dozing person. M16.

1 *edible dormouse*: see EDIBLE *a.* *fat dormouse*: see FAT *a.*

B *attrib.* or as *adj.* Resembling (that of) a dormouse; sleepy, dozy. E17.

SHAKES. To awake your dormouse valour. *Listener* When some dormouse economist wakes up the whole monetary system will vanish like Alice's pack of cards.

dormy /ˈdɔːmi/ *adv.* & *pred. a.* Also **dormie**. M19. [Origin unkn.] Of a golfer: as many holes ahead of an opponent as there are holes to play. attrib.: *dormy one*, *two*, etc.

dornick /ˈdɔːnɪk/ *n.*¹ Now *rare* or *obs.* Also (*Sc.*) **-ock**. LME. [*Doornik*, Flemish name for Tournai.] Any of various fabrics orig. manufactured at Doornik (Tournai) in SW Belgium; *esp.* (*a*) a silk or wool fabric formerly used for hangings, carpets, vestments, etc.; (*b*) a linen fabric used in Scotland for tablecloths, napkins, etc. Also, a cloth or covering made of such a fabric.

dornick /ˈdɔːnɪk/ *n.*² *US dial.* Also **dar-** /ˈdɑː-/. M19. [Cf. Ir. *dornóg* handful, small stone.] A stone, a pebble; a small boulder.

dornock *n.* see DORNICK *n.*¹

doronicum /dəˈrɒnɪkəm/ *n.* M16. [mod.L f. mod.Gk *dōronikon* f. Pers. *darūnak*.] Any of various yellow-rayed plants of the genus *Doronicum*, of the composite family, esp. the early-flowering kinds grown in gardens.

Dorothy bag /ˈdɒrəθi bag/ *n. phr.* E20. [f. female forename *Dorothy*.] A bag gathered at the top by a drawstring; *esp.* a woman's handbag of this form slung by loops from the wrist.

dorp /dɔːp/ *n.* Now *S. Afr.* L15. [Du.: see THORP.] A village, a small town, esp. in the Netherlands or (now) South Africa.

dorr *n.* var. of DOR *n.*[1]

dorsad /ˈdɔːsad/ *adv.* E19. [f. L *dorsum* back + -AD[3].] *Anat.* & *Zool.* Towards the dorsal side.

dorsal /ˈdɔːs(ə)l/ *a.* & *n.* LME. [(O)Fr., or late L *dorsalis* f. L *dorsualis*, f. as DORSUM: see -AL[1]. Cf. DOSSAL.] A *adj.* †1 Of a knife: having one cutting edge. LME–M16. 2 Of or pertaining to the back of a person or animal; situated on or near the back; shaped like the back, in the form of a ridge. LME. 3 *Anat.*, *Zool.*, etc. Pertaining to, situated on, or designating the part of any organ or structure that faces to the rear or the upper side, or is the upper, outer, or convex part; *Bot.* relating to or designating the abaxial or outer surface of a carpel etc. or the surface of a thallus furthest from the substrate (i.e. the upper side). E19. b *Phonet.* Of a speech sound: made with the back of the tongue. E20.

2 T. PENNANT The dorsal and anal fins. QUILLER-COUCH A dorsal ridge of slate-coloured rock. S. KITZINGER Midwives sometimes prefer to have women in a dorsal or modified lithotomy position for examination. 3 S. H. VINES The dorsal surface of ordinary leaves. R. F. CHAPMAN Immature insects nearly always have a line along the dorsal midline of the head.

B *n.* 1 A dorsal fin; a dorsal (thoracic) vertebra. M19. 2 *Eccl.* = DOSSAL 2. L19. 3 *Phonet.* A dorsal sound. M20.

dorˈsality *n.* (*Phonet.*) dorsal quality M20. **dorsalmost** *a.* nearest to the back L19. **dorsally** *adv.* in a dorsal position or direction; on or towards the back: M19.

dorse /dɔːs/ *n.*[1] E16. [L DORSUM back, (in med.L also) back of document (cf. ENDORSE *v.*).] †1 = DOSSAL. Only in E16. 2 The reverse side of a parchment or document; the cover of a book. M17.

dorse /dɔːs/ *n.*[2] E17. [LG *dorsch* = ON *torskr* codfish.] A young cod.

dorsel *n.* var. of DOSSEL *n.*[1]

dorser *n.* var. of DOSSER *n.*[1]

Dorset /ˈdɔːsɪt/ *a.* & *n.* M18. [See sense 1 below.] 1 *gen.* Used *attrib.* to designate things, esp. produce, from or characteristic of Dorset, a county in SW England. M18. 2 (Designating) either of two breeds of short-woolled sheep bred for meat: (*a*) (more fully *Dorset Down*) a Down sheep with brown face and legs; (*b*) (more fully *Dorset Horn* or *Horned*) a sheep with a white face, and horns on the ewe and the ram; a sheep of either breed. E19. 3 (Designating) an extinct breed of pig; a pig of this breed, red with black markings. Also *Dorset Gold Tip*. E20. 4 *Dorset cheese*, blue vinny cheese. E20.

dorsi- /ˈdɔːsi/ *comb. form.* E18. [f. as DORSUM + -I-.] Of, to, or on the back. Also = DORSO-.

dorˈsiferous *a.* (of a fern etc.) bearing seeds on the underside of a frond or leaf E18. **dorsifixed** *a.* (*Bot.*, of an anther) attached along its dorsal edge to the filament L19. **dorsiflex** *v.t.* & *i.* bend (esp. the hand or foot) dorsally or towards its upper surface E20. **dorsiˈflexion** *n.* (*a*) *rare* a bow, a bending of the back; (*b*) the action of dorsiflexing: E19. **dorsiflexor** *n.* a muscle that dorsiflexes the hand or foot M20. **dorsiˈventral** *a.* (*a*) *Bot.* (of a leaf etc.) having unlike dorsal and ventral surfaces; (*b*) = DORSOVENTRAL: L19.

dorso- /ˈdɔːsəʊ/ *comb. form.* M19. [f. as next + -O-.] The back and (what is denoted by the 2nd elem.).

dorsoˈlateral *a.* of, pertaining to, or involving the dorsal and lateral surfaces M19. **dorsoˈventral** *a.* extending along or designating an axis joining the dorsal and ventral surfaces; of, pertaining to, or involving these surfaces: L19. **dorsoˈventrally** *adv.* in a dorsoventral direction L19.

dorsum /ˈdɔːsəm/ *n.* L18. [L = back.] 1 A ridge, a long hill. L18. 2 *Zool.* & *Anat.* The dorsal surface of a part, e.g. the hand or tongue. M19.

dort /dɔːt/ *n. Sc.* M17. [Rel. to next, DORTY: ult. origin unkn.] *sing.* & (usu.) in *pl.* Sulkiness, ill humour, sulks. Chiefly in *the dorts*.

Meg Dorts a peevish woman.

dort /dɔːt/ *v.i. Sc.* E17. [Rel. to prec., DORTY: ult. origin unkn.] Sulk.

dorter /ˈdɔːtə/ *n.* Also **-tour** /-tʊə/, **-toir** /-twɑː/. ME. [OFr. *dortour* (mod. *dortoir*) f. L *dormitorium* DORMITORY *n.*] Chiefly *Hist.* A bedroom, a dormitory, esp. in a monastery.

dorty /ˈdɔːti/ *a. Sc.* E16. [Rel. to DORT *n.*, *v.*: ult. origin unkn.] 1 Sulky, pettish; haughty; saucy. E16. 2 Fastidious. L18. 3 Sluggish. E19. 4 Delicate, feeble; (of an animal or plant) difficult to rear. E20. 5 Of the weather: dry. Of rain: holding off. E20.

dory /ˈdɔːri/ *n.*[1] ME. [Fr. *dorée* use as n. of fem. pa. pple of *dorer* gild f. late L *deaurare*, f. L *de-* DE- I + *aurare* gild, f. *aurum* gold.] Any of several marine fishes constituting the family Zeidae, characterized by thin deep bodies; *esp.* = JOHN DORY.

dory /ˈdɔːri/ *n.*[2] *N. Amer.* & *W. Indies.* Also **dorey**. E18. [Origin uncertain; perh. f. Miskito *dóri* dugout.] A skiff, *esp.* a flat-bottomed one.

doryphore /ˈdɒrɪfɔː/ *n.* M20. [Fr. = Colorado beetle, f. Gk *doruphoros* spear-carrier; coined by Sir Harold Nicolson.] A self-righteously pedantic critic.

dos-à-dos /dozado, dəʊzəˈdəʊ/ *adv.*, *n.*, & *a.* M19. [Fr., f. *dos* back: see DOSSIER. Cf. DO-SE-DO.] A *adv.* Back to back. M19. B *n.* Pl. same. A seat, carriage, etc., so constructed that the occupants sit back to back. *arch.* M19. C *adj.* Designating binding or books in which two volumes are bound together facing in opposite directions and sharing a central board. M20.

dosage /ˈdəʊsɪdʒ/ *n.* M19. [f. DOSE *v.*, *n.* + -AGE. Cf. Fr. *dosage*.] 1 The operation of dosing; the addition or giving of a dose or doses. M19. 2 The size or frequency of a dose or doses. L19. 3 A dose; *spec.* a small amount of sugar added to some wines before the final corking, to make them sweet. L19.

1 *Nature* Feeding tryptophan after dosage with monoamine oxidase inhibitors leads to an exacerbation of psychotic symptoms. 2 O. SACKS In the first week of medication . . the dosage was being slowly increased. J. R. S. FINCHAM The roentgen unit, in terms of which X-ray dosage is expressed. 3 P. MATTHIESSEN The doctor thinks he has dysentery, . . and has pressed preventive dosages on all the rest of us. *Which?* The bottle is topped up with more of the same wine, plus the 'dosage'.

dose /dəʊs/ *n.* LME. [Fr. f. late L *dosis* f. Gk = giving, gift, portion of medicine (Galen), f. *didonai* give.] 1 A definite quantity of a medicine or drug (prescribed to be) given or taken at any one time. LME. b An amount of ionizing radiation to which a person etc. is exposed. E20. 2 A definite quantity of something regarded as analogous in some respect to medicine. E17. 3 An unpleasant experience; a bout *of* influenza etc. M19. 4 (An infection with) venereal disease. *slang.* E20.

1 I. MURDOCH With a large dose of sleeping pills and alcohol in his body. R. MACAULAY I went and saw the camel, and gave it a dose of its sedative. M. MOORCOCK I was using cocaine in stronger and stronger doses. *a dose of one's own medicine*: see MEDICINE *n.*[1] **a dose of salts** a dose of laxative salts (*like a dose of salts*, very rapidly). 2 C. MERIVALE To repeat and daily increase the dose of flattery. L. BLUE Occasional doses of solitude increase my pleasure. 3 *Washington Post* A badly sprained wrist and a heavy dose of the flu have kept him out of uniform.

Comb.: **dosemeter** = DOSIMETER.

dose /dəʊs/ *v.t.* M17. [f. prec.: cf. Fr. *doser*.] 1 Give doses or medicine to; add a dose to. M17. 2 Divide into, or administer in, doses. E18. 3 Infect with venereal disease. *slang.* M20.

1 V. S. REID Mother boils castor oil to dose him. R. TRAVERS Trying to poison his wife with dosed lemon syrup.

doser *n.* a person who gives a dose; *contempt.* a physician: L19.

do-se-do /dəʊzɪˈdəʊ, -sɪ-/ *n.* & *v.* Also **-si-**. E20. [Alt. of DOS-À-DOS.] A *n.* A figure in square dancing in which a facing couple pass round each other back to back, without turning, to finish in the same position they started from. E20. B *v.i.* Perform a do-se-do. E20.

dosh /dɒʃ/ *n. slang.* M20. [Origin unkn.] Money.

do-si-do *n.* & *v.* var. of DO-SE-DO.

dosimeter /dəʊˈsɪmɪtə/ *n.* Also †**doso-**. L19. [f. DOSE *n.* + -IMETER, -OMETER.] A device for measuring doses, esp. of ionizing radiation. Also called *dosemeter*.

dosiˈmetric *a.* L19. **dosimetry** *n.* L19.

doss /dɒs/ *n. slang.* L18. [Origin unkn. Cf. DOSS *v.*[2]] 1 A place for sleeping in; a bed; *esp.* a bed in a common lodging-house. Also *doss-down*. L18. 2 Sleep. M19.

Comb.: **doss-house** a common lodging-house.

doss /dɒs/ *v.*[1] L16. [Perh. rel. to MDu. *dossen*: see DOUSE *v.*[1]] 1 *v.t.* & †*i.* Butt, toss, or gore (a person) with the horns. Now *dial.* L16. 2 *v.t.* Toss (the horns). Now *dial.* L16. 3 *v.t.* Throw or toss (something or oneself) *down* with force. *Sc.* M18.

doss /dɒs/ *v.*[2]*i. slang.* L18. [Rel. to DOSS *n.*] Sleep or bed *down*, esp. at a common lodging-house or in improvised accommodation.

P. L. FERMOR Humble travellers in Holland could doss down in police stations.

dossal /ˈdɒs(ə)l/ *n.* Also **-el.** M17. [med.L *dossale* neut. of *dossalis* for late L *dorsalis* DORSAL. Cf. OFr. *dossal*, *-el*; DOSSER *n.*[1]] 1 An ornamental cloth forming a cover for the back of a seat. *arch.* M17. 2 *Eccl.* An ornamental cloth hung at the back of an altar or at the sides of the chancel. M19.

dossel /ˈdɒs(ə)l/ *n.*[1] *obs.* exc. *dial.* Also **dorsel** /ˈdɔːs(ə)l/. M18. [App. var. of DOSSER *n.*[1], with substitution of *-el* for -ER[2].] A pannier or other basket borne by an animal. Cf. DOSSER *n.*[1] 2.

dossel *n.*[2] var. of DOSSAL.

dosser /ˈdɒsə/ *n.*[1] *obs.* exc. *Hist.* Also **dorser** /ˈdɔːsə/. ME. [OFr. DOSSIER: cf. med.L *dorsarium*, *dossarium*, f. L DORSUM, pop.L *dossum*, & see -ER[2].] 1 An ornamental cloth used to cover the back of a seat, esp. a throne or chair of State, or as a wall-hanging. Cf. DOSSAL. Long *rare*. ME. 2 A basket carried on the back; a pannier borne by an animal. Cf. DOSSEL *n.*[1] LME.

dosser /ˈdɒsə/ *n.*[2] *slang.* M19. [f. DOSS *v.*[2] + -ER[1].] A person who 'dosses'; a vagrant.

dosseret /ˈdɒsərɛt/ *n.* M19. [Fr., dim. of DOSSIER: see -ET[1].] *Archit.* An additional block of stone placed above an abacus in the columns of many Byzantine and some Romanesque arcades.

dossier /ˈdɒsɪə, -ɪeɪ, -jeɪ/ *n.* L19. [Fr. = bundle of papers in a wrapper having a label on the back, (in OFr. = DOSSER *n.*[1]), f. *dos* back (f. pop.L *dossum* for L DORSUM) + *-ier* -ARY[1].] A collection of papers or information about a particular person or matter.

K. VONNEGUT Fred's dossier in the law firm's confidential files.

dossil /ˈdɒsɪl/ *n.* Now *rare.* ME. [OFr. *do(i)sil* f. Proto-Gallo-Romance (med.L) *duciculus*, f. L *ducere* lead, conduct.] †1 A plug for a barrel; a spigot. Cf. DOTTLE *n.*[2] I. ME–L15. 2 A wad of lint or rag for stopping a wound etc. L16.

dost *v.* see DO *v.*

Dostoevskian /dɒstɔɪˈɛfskɪən/ *a.* Also **Dostoiev-**, **Dostoyev-**. E20. [f. *Dostoevsky* (see below) + -AN.] Pertaining to or characteristic of the Russian novelist Fedor Mikhailovich Dostoevsky (1821–81), or his works.

dot /dɒt/ *n.*[1] [OE *dott* (once); sense 2 may be f. Du. *dot* knot.] †1 The head of a boil. Only in OE. †2 A small lump, a clot. L16–M19. 3 A minute spot, speck, or mark; *esp.* a minute roundish mark written or printed. M17. 4 *spec.* a A point used in punctuation, as or as part of a punctuation mark, or to form part of or modify a letter or character. M18. b *Mus.* A point placed after a note or rest to lengthen it by half as much again, or over a note to indicate that it is to be performed staccato. E19. c The shorter of the two signals (the other being the dash) which in various combinations make up the letters of the Morse alphabet. M19. d In *pl.* (The notes of) written or printed music. *slang.* E20. e A pointlike element of a television picture; an area of phosphor on the inside of a television tube corresponding to this. E20. 5 A little child; a small creature. *colloq.* M19.

Phrases: *double dot*: see DOUBLE *a.* & *adv.* **off one's dot** *slang* & *dial.* out of one's senses (cf. DOTTY *a.*[2] 2). **on the dot** punctually, at the precise moment. *the year dot*: see YEAR *n.*[1] **to a dot** exactly, precisely.

Comb.: **dot-map** a statistical map using dots as indicators of numbers or frequency; **dot matrix** a regular array of positions which are filled selectively to create a character (on a screen or on paper); also (in full *dot matrix printer*) = *matrix printer* s.v. MATRIX *n.*; **dot plant** a garden plant that is planted singly to stand out against the surrounding plants; **dot-stitch**: used in making dots in embroidery; **dot product** *Math.* = *scalar product* s.v. SCALAR *a.* 2.

dot /dɒt/ *n.*[2] M19. [(O)Fr. f. L *dos*, *dot-*: see DOWER.] A dowry only the income from which is at the husband's disposal. Cf. DOTE *n.*[2]

dot /dɒt/ *v.t.* Infl. **-tt-**. M18. [f. DOT *n.*[1]] 1 Mark with a dot or dots; fill *in* with dots. M18. b Add the dot to (a letter *i* or *j*). Chiefly in *dot the i's (and cross the t's)* below. M19. 2 Jot *down*; write (*down*) compendiously. L18. 3 Occur singly throughout (an area etc.) or over (a surface). Usu. as DOTTED *a.* 2. L18. 4 Disperse or scatter (*about*) like dots. Usu. as DOTTED *a.* 3. E19. 5 Hit, strike. Esp. in *dot (a person) one*. *slang.* L19.

1b H. JAMES It dots every i, it places every comma. 3 T. C. WOLFE Small houses dotted the land. 4 *Cookery Year* Cut.. fat into small flakes and dot them evenly over two-thirds of the pastry.

Phrases & comb.: **dot and carry (one)** = *dot and go one* below. **dot-and-carry(-one)** *n.* & *a.* (*a*) *n.* (a teacher of) elementary arithmetic; (*b*) *adj.* = *dot-and-go-one* adj. below. **dot and go one** like a lame person, limpingly. **dot-and-go-one** *n.* & *a.* (*a*) *n.* (the limp of) a person who is lame in one leg or has an artificial leg; (*b*) *adj.* limping, halting in gait. **dot the i's (and cross the t's)** *fig.* particularize minutely, complete in detail.

dottable *a.* M19.

dotage /ˈdəʊtɪdʒ/ *n.* LME. [f. DOTE *n.*[1] or *v.*[1] + -AGE. Cf. Fr. *radotage*, f. *radoter* talk idly or nonsensically.] 1a The state of having the intellect impaired, esp. through old age; senility; imbecility; stupidity, folly; *one's second childhood*. LME. b A stupid or foolish thought, word, or action. E16. 2a The action of doting on someone; foolish or excessive love or affection. LME. b An object doted upon. M17.

1a LD MACAULAY Now fast sinking into dotage. E. GLASGOW Wait until I'm a hundred... Don't hurry me into my dotage.

dotaku /ˈdəʊtakuː/ *n.pl.* Also **dō-**. E20. [Jap.] Prehistoric Japanese bronze objects, shaped like bells and usu. decorated with geometric designs or scenes from life.

dotal /ˈdəʊt(ə)l/ *n.* & *a.* LME. [L *dotalis*, f. *dos* DOT *n.*[2]: see -AL[1]. Perh. through OFr. or (as adj.) Fr. *dotal*, f. as DOT *n.*[2]] †A *n.* A dowry. Only in LME. B *adj.* Pertaining to or designating a dowry or dower. E16.

†**dotant** *n. rare* (Shakes.). Only in E17. [f. DOTE *v.*[1] + -ANT[1]. Cf. Fr. *radotant*.] = DOTARD *n.*[1]

dotard /ˈdəʊtəd/ *n.*[1] & *a.*[1] LME. [f. DOTE *v.*[1] + -ARD. Cf. DOTTERED.] A *n.* A person in his or her dotage; a stupid or foolish person. LME. B *adj.* Senile; in one's second childhood; stupid, foolish. LME.

dotard /ˈdəʊtəd/ *n.*[2] & *a.*[2] Also †**-tt-**. L16. [Origin unkn. Cf. DODDARD, DOTTERED; also DOTE *n.*[3], *v.*[2]] (Designating) a tree that has lost its branches, esp. through age or decay.

dotate /dəʊˈteɪt/ *v.t.* Now *rare*. Pa. pple **-ated**, †**-ate**. M16. [L *dotat-* pa. ppl stem of *dotare*: see next, -ATE[3].] Endow.

dotation /dəʊˈteɪʃ(ə)n/ *n.* LME. [(O)Fr., or med.L *dotatio(n-)*, f. *dotare* endow, f. *dos*, *dot-* DOT *n.*[2]: see -ATION.] The action of endowing; (an) endowment.

dotchin /ˈdɒtʃɪn/ *n.* L17. [Chin. *dù ching*, f. *dù* measure + *ching* steelyard.] A small hand-steelyard used in southern China.

†**dote** *n.*[1] ME–M19. [App. based on MDu. *dote* folly.] A foolish or weak-minded person; a dotard.

dote /dəʊt/ *n.*[2] *arch.* E16. [Fr., obs. var. of DOT *n.*[2]] 1 = DOT *n.*[2] E16. †2 A natural gift or endowment. Usu. in *pl.* M16–M17.

dote /dəʊt/ *n.*[3] L19. [Origin unkn. Cf. DOTE *v.*[2], DOTARD *n.*[2] & *a.*[2]] Decay in wood.

dote /dəʊt/ *v.*[1] Also **doat**. ME. [Corresp. to MDu. *doten* be silly (whence OFr. *redoter*, mod. *radoter*). Cf. DOIT *v.*] I *v.i.* 1 Be silly or deranged; act or talk foolishly or stupidly. ME. 2 Have the intellect impaired through old age. ME. 3 Be infatuated; have or show excessive affection. (Foll. by *on*, *upon*, †*of*.) L15.

1 COLERIDGE Others.. dote with a mad idolatry. 2 G. CRABBE We grow unfitted for that world and dote. 3 J. A. MICHENER He doted upon her and was enraptured when she presented him with two strong sons. J. BARNES Perhaps those who forgive and dote are more irritating than they ever suspect.

II *v.t.* †4 Drive mad; make foolish; infatuate. L15–E17. †5 Have excessive affection for, dote on. L15–L17. †6 Say or think foolishly. M16–E17.

dotingly *adv.* in a doting manner or degree; infatuatedly; fondly: M16.

dote /dəʊt/ *v.*[2]*i. obs.* exc. *dial.* & *US*. LME. [Origin unkn. Cf. DOTE *n.*[3], DOTARD *n.*[2] & *a.*[2]] Of a tree, timber, a seed, etc.: decay. Chiefly as *doted*, *doting* ppl adjs.

doter /ˈdəʊtə/ *n.* Also **doater**. M16. [f. DOTE *v.*[1] + -ER[1].] 1 A person who is foolishly affectionate; a person who dotes. M16. 2 = DOTARD *n.*[1] E17.

dotey /ˈdəʊti/ *n.* Chiefly *Anglo-Ir.* Also **do(a)ty**. M17. [Rel. to DOTE *v.*[1]] A person, esp. a child, of whom one is fond. Usu. as a form of address.

doth *v.* see DO *v.*

dotish /ˈdəʊtɪʃ/ *a. arch.* Also **doat-**. E16. [f. DOTE *n.*[1] + -ISH[1].] Silly, stupid, childish.

dotishness *n.* L16.

dotkin *n.* var. of DODKIN.

†**dottard** *n.* & *a.* var. of DOTARD *n.*[2] & *a.*[2]

dotted /ˈdɒtɪd/ *a.* L18. [f. DOT *n.*[1], *v.*: see -ED[2], -ED[1].] 1 Formed of dots. L18. b Of (an) engraving: executed by dots instead of lines; stippled. E19. 2 Irregularly marked with or occupied by dots or things occurring singly. L18. b *spec.* Designating moths marked thus. M19. 3 Scattered (*about* etc.) like dots; occurring or situated singly here and there. E19. 4 Of a musical note, a symbol, etc.: having an added dot. M19.

2 W. GOLDING The beach.. was dotted with groups of boys. W. TREVOR He pulls the dotted handkerchief from his pocket. 3 P. SCOTT There were chairs dotted here and there on the lawn. M. SINCLAIR A tiny Dutch landscape... Trees dotted about. 4 F. A. G. OUSELEY One dotted semibreve in the canto fermo.

Special collocations: **dotted line** a line of dots or small dashes, *esp.* one on a document to indicate the space left for a signature and therefore acceptance of its terms; (*dotted-line responsibility*, indirect responsibility to another in an organizational structure; *sign on the dotted line*, agree fully or formally). **dotted rhythm** *Mus.*: in which long notes alternate with short notes.

dottel *n.* var. of DOTTLE *n.*[2]

dotter /ˈdɒtə/ *n.* M19. [f. DOT *v.* + -ER[1].] A person who or thing which marks something with dots; an instrument for making dots.

dotter /ˈdɒtə/ *v.i.* Now *Sc.* LME. [Rel. to DODDER *v.*, TOTTER *v.*] Move unsteadily; totter; fall.

dottered /ˈdɒtəd/ *a.* Now *Sc.* L16. [Perh. alt. of DOTARD *a.*[1] or *a.*[2]] Worn out or enfeebled with age.

dotterel /ˈdɒt(ə)r(ə)l/ *n.* & *a.* Also **dottrel** /ˈdɒtr(ə)l/. LME. [f. DOTE *v.*[1] + -REL.] A *n.* 1 A small, exceptionally tame plover, *Eudromias morinellus*, found on open ground in northern Europe and northern Asia and migrating to the Mediterranean. Also (usu. w. specifying wd), any of several other plovers of Australia, New Zealand, and S. America of the genera *Eudromias*, *Charadrius*, and *Peltohyas*. LME. 2 A silly or deranged person; a dotard. Now *dial.* LME. 3 A doddered tree; a pollard. Now *dial.* E17. B *attrib.* or as *adj.* 1 *dotterel tree* = sense A.3 above. Now *dial.* M16. 2 Foolish, doting. Now *rare* or *obs.* L16.

dottle /ˈdɒt(ə)l/ *n.*[1] & *a.* LME. [f. DOTE *v.*[1] or *n.*[1] + -LE[1].] A *n.* A fool, a silly person; a dotard. Now *Sc.* LME. B *adj.* In a state of dotage; deranged; silly. *Sc.* E19.

Also **dottled** *a.* (*Sc.*) E19.

dottle /ˈdɒt(ə)l/ *n.*[2] Also **dottel**. LME. [f. DOT *n.*[1] + -LE[1].] †1 A plug for a barrel or other vessel. Cf. DOSSIL *n.* 1. LME–M18. 2 (A plug of) tobacco left at the bottom of a pipe after smoking. E19.

dottrel *n.* & *a.* var. of DOTTEREL.

dottrified /ˈdɒtrɪfʌɪd/ *a.* Chiefly *Sc.* & *dial.* E19. [f. DOTE *v.*[1] + -ERY + -FY + -ED[1].] Having the intellect impaired; stupefied, dazed.

dotty /ˈdɒti/ *a.*[1] E19. [f. DOT *n.*[1] + -Y[1].] Consisting of or characterized by dots; resembling a dot.

dotty /ˈdɒti/ *a.*[2] L19. [Perh. f. DOTE *n.*[1] (cf. earlier DOTTYPOLL) or rel. to DOTTER *v.*] 1 Having an unsteady or feeble gait. Now *rare*. L19. 2 Feeble-minded, insane; harmlessly eccentric; silly; absurd, crazy; absurdly enthusiastic *about*. *colloq.* L19.

1 D. ABSE Dotty, shifty points of glitterings. 2 H. L. WILSON Mr. Jackson had chosen the part of Oswald, a youth who goes quite dotty. *Daily Telegraph* It was 'dotty' for the nation to spend £2 million trying to save a picture. B. BAINBRIDGE All foreigners are dotty about their mothers.

dottily *adv.* in an eccentric or absurd manner, to an eccentric or absurd degree M20. **dottiness** *n.* dotty quality, *esp.* insanity, eccentricity L19.

†**dottypoll** *n.* see DODDYPOLL.

doty *n.* var. of DOTEY.

doty /ˈdəʊti/ *a.* Also **doaty**. M19. [Rel. to DOTE *n.*[3], DOTARD *n.*[2] & *a.*[2]] Of wood: decayed, rotten.

dotiness *n.* L19.

†**dotypoll** *n.* see DODDYPOLL.

Douai *n.* var. of DOUAY.

douane /duːˈɑːn/ *n.* M17. [Fr. f. It. *do(g)ana* f. Arab. *dīwān* office f. OPers. *dīwān* DIVAN. Cf. DEWAN.] A custom-house in France or other Mediterranean country.

douanier /duːˈɑːnɪeɪ/ *n.* a customs officer, *esp.* one at a douane M18.

douar /ˈduːɑː, dwɑː/ *n.* Also **dowar, duar**. E18. [Colloq. Arab. form of Arab. *dawwār* circling, after Fr. *douar*.] In Arab countries, an encampment of tents, a village.

Douay /ˈdaʊeɪ, ˈduːeɪ/ *n.* Also **Douai**. M19. [A town (now *Douai*) in France (see below).] In full *Douay version*, *Bible*. An English translation of the Vulgate formerly used in the Roman Catholic Church, begun at Douai and completed there in 1609.

double /ˈdʌb(ə)l/ *n.* ME. [Partly (in branch I) f. next, partly (in branch II) f. DOUBLE *v.*] I 1 A double quantity; twice as much or as many. ME. 2 *Hist.* Any of various coins formerly current in France or Guernsey. ME. †3a A duplicate or copy of a document. LME–M18. †b In *pl.* Twins. Only in L15. c An exact counterpart; a person who is very like another; a wraith. L18. 4 A double person or thing identified contextually, as a double victory, a double century, a double event, etc. L16. b *RC Ch.* (now *Hist.*). [Ellipt. for *double feast*.] Any of the higher ranking feasts. L17. c *Mil.* A double pace. Chiefly in *at the double* below. M19. d A double measure of spirits. E20. e A double room. *colloq.* M20. 5 *Campanol.* A change in which two pairs of bells change places. L17. 6 *Printing.* An accidental duplication of a word or passage. Cf. DOUBLET 4b. E18. 7 *Mus.* A variation (usu. the theme with ornamentation) in 17th- and 18th-cent. music. E19. 8 An actor who takes two parts in the same performance. Also, an understudy. E19. 9 In *pl.* A game of tennis, badminton, etc., between two pairs of players rather than one. L19. 10 A bet on two horses in different races in which winnings from the first are placed on the later one. L19. 11 *Cards* (esp. *Bridge*). A call that doubles the value of the points to be won or lost on an opponent's bid. E20. **12** (A throw on B) the narrow ring enclosed by the two outer circles of a dartboard, scoring double. M20.

1 B. JOWETT Ten, which is the double of five. **3c** P. V. WHITE Her reflection is a double that she has grown to hate. **4b** C. MACKENZIE We are going . . to keep the feast as the Feast of the Immaculate Conception, a double of the first class with octave. **c at the double** in double time; *transf.* as fast as possible. **9** MIXED *doubles*. **10** *twin double*: see TWIN *a.* & *n.*

II 13 A sharp turn made in running by a hunted animal; a sharp alteration in the course of a river; *fig.* an evasive turn or shift in action, argument, etc. L16. **14** A fold; a folded piece of material. Now *rare* or *obs.* L16.

double /ˈdʌb(ə)l/ *a.* & *adv.* ME. [OFr. *doble*, *duble* (mod. *double*) f. L *duplus* DUPLE.] **A** *adj.* **1** Consisting of two members, things, layers, sets, etc.; twofold, forming a pair; occurring twice, repeated. ME. **b** Folded, doubled; bent, stooping forward, doubled up. LME. **c** Having some essential part or feature present twice; (of a flower) having more than the usual number of petals, often owing to the conversion of stamens and sometimes carpels into petals; (of a domino) having the same number of pips in each half. LME. **2** Having a twofold relation or application; dual; ambiguous. ME. **3** Twice as much or as many; of twice the, or twice *the*, measure, amount, or capacity. (Formerly foll. by *of, over, to*.) ME. **4** Characterized by duplicity; false, deceitful. ME. **5** Of two or more times the usual size, value, strength, etc. LME. **b** *Mus.* Lower in pitch by an octave. L17.

1 SHAKES. *Mids. N. D.* Like to a double cherry . . , Two lovely berries moulded on one stem. STEELE Is Dimpple spelt with a single or double P? DICKENS Nickleby gave a double knock. L. DURRELL The double burden of her own poor circumstances and illness. **b** W. OWEN Bent double, like old beggars under sacks. **2** T. HERBERT The word . . admitting a double construction, sheep and apple. F. MARRYAT He . . is a double traitor. **3** A. DE MORGAN The average error of the first . . is double of that of the second. LD MACAULAY His army . . might easily have been increased to double the number. **4** G. BURNET He was . . either very double or very inconstant. **5** V. SCANNELL Ten new pennies For a pint and a double gin.

B *adv.* †**1** After a numeral: times, -fold. ME–L17. **2** To twice the amount or extent; in two ways or respects; doubly. LME. **b** In a pair or couple; two together; two at once. L16. **3** With duplicity, deceitfully. *rare.* L16.

2 KEATS Bright eyes were double bright. **b** R. B. SHERIDAN Content to ride double, behind the butler.

Phrases: **double or quits** *colloq.* the next game, throw, etc., will decide whether the stake is to be doubled or cancelled. **see double** (seem to) perceive two images of one object.

Special collocations & comb.: *double acrostic*: see ACROSTIC *n.* 1. **double-acting** *a.* acting in two ways or directions; *spec.* (of an engine) in which pistons are pushed from both sides alternately. **double agent** a person who purports to spy for one country or organization while actually working for a hostile or rival one. **double album** two long-playing records or two cassettes packaged together and sold as a set. **double axe** an axe with two blades. **double-bank** *v.* (*a*) *v.t.* provide or work with two sets of rowers, horses, etc., side by side; (*b*) *v.i.* & *t.* (*Austral.* & *NZ*) ride two on (a horse or bicycle); carry (a second person) thus; cf. DOUBLE *v.* 17; (*c*) *v.t.* & *i.* = *double-park* below. **double-banked** *a.* & *adv.* designating, having, or with two (sets of) things side by side. **double bar** *Mus.* a pair of closely spaced bar-lines marking the end of a work or of a section of one. **double-bar** an Australian waxbill, *Poephila bichenovii*. **double-barrel** *a.* & *n.* (*a*) *adj.* double-barrelled; (*b*) *n.* a double-barrelled gun; (a person with) a double-barrelled name. **double-barrelled** *a.* (*a*) (of a gun) having two barrels; (*b*) serving a double purpose, twofold; (*c*) (of a surname) having two (usu. hyphenated) elements. *double bassoon*: see BASSOON 1. **double bed** a bed for two people. **double bill** a cinema or theatre show with two principal items. **double bind** (*a*) *Psychol.* a situation in which contradictory attitudes are expressed towards a child or other person, or contradictory demands are made of him or her, so that he or she cannot avoid being at fault; (*b*) *gen.* a situation in which either of two possible courses will be wrong; a dilemma. **double-bitted** *a.*[1] having two bits. **double-bitted** *a.*[2] (*Naut.*) (of a cable) wound twice round the bitts or round two pairs of bitts. *double blank*: see BLANK *n.* 11. **double-blind** *a.* & *n.* (designating) a test etc. in which neither tester nor subject has knowledge of identities or other factors that might lead to bias. **double bluff** a bluff in which a person deliberately emphasizes one course of action etc. to suggest that a contradictory course will be taken, and then takes the first course. **double bogey** *Golf* a score of two strokes over par. **double-bogey** *v.t.* & *i.* (*Golf*) complete (a hole) in two strokes over par. **double boiler** a saucepan with a detachable upper compartment heated by boiling water in the lower. **double bond** *Chem.* two covalent bonds between the same two atoms. **double-book** *v.t.* & *i.* accept two mutually exclusive bookings for (the same room, seat, etc.); book (a person) into a room, seat, etc., also assigned to another. **double-breasted** *a.* (of a jacket etc.) having a substantial overlap of material at the front, freq. fastened with two rows of buttons. **double bridle** a bridle comprising both curb and snaffle bits, each with its own set of reins. **double century** a score of 200, esp. in cricket; (a cycle ride of) 200 miles. **double-check** *v.t.* verify twice or in two ways. **double chin** a chin with a fold of flesh under it. **double-chinned** *a.* having a double chin. **double-clutch** *v.i.* (*US*) = *double-declutch* below. *double coconut*: see COCONUT 4. *double* CONCERTO. **double cream** thick cream containing a high proportion of fat. **double-crop** *v.t.* cultivate (land) under a system of double cropping. **double cropping** the cultivation of two crops from the same land in a single season. **double cube** *Archit.* a room of which the breadth is equal to the height and the length is double it. *double dagger*: see DAGGER *n.*[1] **double date** *colloq.* a social engagement involving two couples. **double-date** *v.i. colloq.*) go on a double date. **double-dealer** a cheat, a deceiver. **double-dealing** deceit, treachery. **double-dealing** *a.* deceitful, treacherous. **double-deck(ed)** *adjs.* having two decks or layers. **double-decker** *n.* & *a.* (designating) something with two decks or layers; *spec.* (designating) a bus, ship, etc., with an upper and a lower deck for passengers. **double-declutch** *v.i.* release and re-engage the clutch twice when changing gear in a motor vehicle. **double decomposition** *Chem.* the simultaneous decomposition of two compounds in a reaction with the formation of two new ones. **double-dig** *v.t.* dig two spits deep, as in double digging. **double digging** digging in which one spit of soil is taken off and the underlying second spit broken up before being covered again. **double-digit** *a.* = *double-figure* below. **double digits** = *double figures* below. **double-dink** *v.i.* & *t.* (*Austral.* & *NZ slang*) carry (a person) as a second rider on a bicycle or horse. **double dip** *N. Amer.* an ice-cream cone with two scoops of ice-cream. **double-dipper** *N. Amer.* & *Austral.* a person who practises double-dipping. **double-dipping** *N. Amer.* & *Austral.* the practice of commuting an occupational pension to a lump sum and then drawing a State pension that would not otherwise be due, or of receiving an income from two jobs, esp. a pension from a former job and a salary from a current one. **double door(s)** (*a*) a pair of doors side by side in one opening, meeting in the middle; (*b*) two doors situated one close behind the other. **double dot** *Mus.* two dots placed side by side after a note to lengthen it by three-quarters of its value. **double-dot** *v.t.* & *i.* (*Mus.*) mark with or employ double dots (chiefly as *double-dotted* ppl a., *double-dotting* vbl n.). **double dummy** whist or bridge with two hands exposed, allowing every card to be located by the players. *double Dutch*: see DUTCH *n.*[1] **double-dye** *v.t.* dye twice; *fig.* imbue or stain deeply with guilt; (chiefly as *double-dyed* ppl a.). **double eagle** (*a*) a figure of an eagle with two heads; (*b*) *Golf* = ALBATROSS 3; (*c*) a former US coin worth twenty dollars. **double-edged** *a.* having two cutting edges; *fig.* acting both ways; damaging to the user as well as an opponent. **double-ender** something with both ends alike. **double entry** a method of bookkeeping in which each transaction is entered twice, once to the credit of one account and once to the debit of another. **double event** the winning of two events at the same meeting or in the same season; a dual success or occurrence. **double exposure** *Photogr.* the action or result of exposing the same frame, plate, etc., on two occasions, either accidentally or deliberately. **double fault** *Tennis* two consecutive faults in serving, together resulting in the loss of a point. **double-fault** *v.i.* commit a double fault. **double feast** *RC Ch.* = DOUBLE *n.* 4b. **double feature** a cinema programme with two full-length films. **double fertilization** *Bot.* the mode of fertilization in angiosperms, in which one sperm nucleus fuses with an egg nucleus to produce the embryo and the other fuses with the two polar nuclei to produce the endosperm. **double-figure** *a.* equal in quantity, rate, etc., to a number, esp. a percentage, between 10 and 99 inclusive. **double figures** (a quantity, score, etc., equal to) a number between 10 and 99 inclusive. **double first** (a person gaining) first-class honours in two subjects or examinations at university. **double flat** *Mus.* a sign (𝄫) placed before a note to indicate that it is to be lowered two semitones; a note so marked or lowered. **double fleece** *Austral.* & *NZ* a fleece from a sheep that has missed a shearing. **double-fronted** *a.* having two fronts or faces; (of a house) having the principal windows on either side of the front door. *double* FUGUE. **double glazing** (the provision of) two sheets of glass fixed one behind the other in a window to reduce heat loss, noise, etc. **double Gloucester (cheese)** [made at Berkeley, Gloucestershire] a firm cheese similar to Cheddar but milder. **double-handed** *a.* (*a*) made to be lifted or held with two hands, two-handled; (*b*) capable of a double use, application, or action (*lit.* & *fig.*). **double harness** harness for two horses etc.; *fig.* matrimony, close partnership. *double harp*: see HARP *n.* **double-head** *v.* (*a*) *v.i.* (of a train) be pulled by two locomotives; (*b*) *v.t.* (of two locomotives) jointly pull (a train) (usu. in *pass.*). **double-headed** *a.* having a double head or two heads; double-ended; (of a train) pulled by two locomotives. **double header** (*a*) *US* (*rare*) a kind of firework; (*b*) a train pulled by two locomotives; (*c*) *N. Amer.* two games or matches in succession between the same opponents. **double-hearted** *a.* (*arch.*) deceitful, dissembling. **double-heartedness** *n.* (*arch.*) double-hearted nature. **double helix** a pair of helices intertwined about a common axis, esp. in the structure of the DNA molecule. **double hyphen** a mark consisting of one hyphen above another, sometimes used at the end of a line to show that a hyphen would be there even if it were not a line-end. **double image** (*a*) duplicate images of an object seen simultaneously, as when the eyes fail to focus; (*b*) *Art* an image, representation, etc., which allows two irreconcilable interpretations simultaneously. **double indemnity** *US* the provision for payment of double the face amount of an insurance policy when death occurs as a result of an accident. **double jeopardy** (the immunity which prevents) the prosecution of a person twice for the same offence. **double-jointed** *a.* having joints that allow an unusual bending and flexibility of fingers, limbs, etc. **double-jointedness** double-jointed condition. **double knitting** (*a*) knitting that is tubular, for ties, belts, etc.; (*b*) knitting with yarn of double thickness; (more fully *double knitting wool, yarn*) yarn for knitting that is double the usual thickness. **double life** a life in which two different characters (and careers) are sustained simultaneously, of which usu. one is virtuous and one not. **double-lock** *v.t.* lock by a double turn of the key. **double meaning** (possession of) two meanings; (use of) an ambiguous expression; *spec.* = DOUBLE ENTENDRE. **double-meaning** *a.* having or employing a double meaning. **double-minded** *a.* (*a*) in two minds, uncertain, wavering; †(*b*) having two meanings. **double-mindedness** double-minded quality or state. **double negative** *Gram.* a construction containing two negative elements (esp. where one is redundant, now considered ungrammatical in standard English); *loosely*, either of the two negatives in such a construction. *double nelson*: see NELSON *n.*[2] *double obelisk*: see OBELISK *n.* 2. *double* OXER. **double paddle** a paddle with a blade at each end. **double-park** *v.t.* & *i.* park (a vehicle) alongside another vehicle already parked at the roadside etc. **double play** *Baseball* a play in which two runners are put out. *double* PNEUMONIA. **double precision** *Computing* the use of twice the usual number of bits or words to represent a number. **double-precision** *a.* (*Computing*) having double precision. **double-queued** *a.* (*Her.*) (of an animal) having two tails. **double-quick** *a., adv., n.,* & *v.* (*a*) *adj.* (*Mil.*) designating the fastest marching time next to the run; (*b*) *adv.* in double-quick time; very quickly, smartly; (*c*) *n.* double-quick time; (*d*) *v.i.* (*Mil.*) march in double-quick time. **double reed** a wind instrument reed with two slightly separated blades, as in the oboe and bassoon. **double-reef** *v.t.* (*Naut.*) reduce the spread of (a sail) by two reefs. **double refraction** the refraction of unpolarized light into two rays or beams going in different directions, producing a double image of an object; the property of causing this, exhibited by some crystals. **double rhyme** rhyme involving two syllables in each rhyming line. **double room** a bedroom for two people. **double salt** *Chem.* a salt which when crystalline is composed of two simple salts (which it usu. yields in solution) and has different properties from either. **double saucepan** = *double boiler* above. **double sharp** *Mus.* a sign (𝄪) placed before a note to indicate that it is to be raised two semitones; a note so marked or raised. **double shuffle** a dance in which each foot in turn makes two shuffles.

double-shuffle *v.i.* dance a double shuffle. **double-shot** *v.t.* load (a gun) with a double quantity of shot. **double-space** *v.t.* lay out (a text) with double spacing. **double spacing** spacing in which a line is left empty between successive lines of a (esp. typewritten) text. **double-speak** language or talk that is (usu. deliberately) ambiguous or obscure. **double standard** (*a*) bimetallism; (*b*) (the application of) a standard, principle, etc., applied more strictly to some people or situations than others. **double star** a pair of stars that appear as one until viewed in a telescope, *esp.* a binary star. **double steal** *Baseball* a play in which two base-runners each steal a base. **double-stopping** *Mus.* the sounding of two strings at once on an instrument to give an interval. **double summertime** daylight saving in which clocks are two hours ahead of standard winter time. **double take** a delayed and usu. contradictory reaction to an occurrence or situation immediately after one's first reaction. **double-talk** = *double-speak* above. *double team*: see TEAM *n.* 5a. **double-team** *v.* (*US*) (*a*) *v.i.* combine two teams into one; (*b*) *v.i.* bring double pressure to bear *on* a person; (*c*) *v.t.* block (an opposing player) with two players. *double tertian*: see TERTIAN *n.* 1. **doublethink** the mental capacity to accept as equally valid two entirely contradictory opinions or beliefs; the practice of doing this. **double tides** *advb. phr.* twice as long or as hard, as hard or as much as possible; (chiefly in *work double tides*). **double time** (*a*) *Mil.* a marching pace in which approximately twice as many steps per minute are made as in slow time; (*b*) *Mus.* a rhythm made twice as fast as an earlier rhythm; (*c*) a rate of pay equal to twice the standard rate (given for working extra on holidays etc.). **double-time** *v.i.* march or play in double time. **double-tongued** *a.* saying contradictory or inconsistent things; deceitful or insincere in speech. **double tonguing** *Mus.* tonguing in which two alternating movements of the tongue are made (usually as in sounding *t* and *k*), to facilitate rapid playing of a wind instrument. **double top** *Darts* (a throw into) the double-scoring segment of the top (20) space of a dartboard, worth 40 points. **doubletree** [after *singletree* s.v. SINGLE *a.* & *adv.*] a crossbar of a wagon with a swingletree at each end, enabling two horses to draw. **double vision** the simultaneous perception of two images of one object. **double wedding** a wedding of two couples at the same time. **double-wide** *n.* & *a.* (*US*) (designating) a semi-permanent mobile home consisting of two separate units connected on site. *double yellow*: see YELLOW *n.* *double yellow line*: see YELLOW *a.*

doublefold *a.* & *adv.* twofold ME. **doubleness** *n.* the quality or state of being double; duplicity, deceitfulness: LME.

double /ˈdʌb(ə)l/ *v.* ME. [OFr. *dobler, dubler* (mod. *doubler*) f. late L *duplare*, f. L *duplus* DUPLE.] **1** *v.t.* Make double; increase twofold; put two in the place of one; multiply by two; *arch.* amount to twice as much as. ME. **b** *Mus.* Add the same note in a higher or lower octave to. M18. **c** *Chess.* Place a pawn or rook on the same file behind (another piece of the same kind and colour); place (two pawns or two rooks) thus. M18. **2** *v.i.* Become twice as much or as many as before; increase twofold. ME. †**3** *v.t.* Repeat, reiterate; *Sc.* make a copy or duplicate of. LME–E19. **b** Speak with repetition of sounds; stammer. *rare.* LME–E17. **4** *v.t.* (Now chiefly *Her.*) add a second layer of material to, line, (a garment); cover (a ship) with an additional layer of planking. LME. **5a** *v.t.* Fold (a cloth, paper, etc.) so as to bring the two parts into contact, parallel; bend (the body), esp. into a stooping or curled-up posture (also foll. by *up*); clench or close (the hand). LME. **b** *v.i.* Become folded together or bent over; (of a person or limbs) bend double, stoop, curl up, (also foll. by *up*). M17. **c** *v.t.* Lay together and compress into one (two or more textile filaments or slivers). Freq. as *doubling* vbl n. M19. **6a** *v.t.* Sail round or to the other side of (a cape or headland). M16. **b** *v.i.* Foll. by *upon*: enclose (an enemy fleet) from two sides. M18. **7** *v.i.* Make evasive turns or shifts; use duplicity, act deceitfully. Now *rare* or *obs.* M16. **8a** *v.i.* Turn suddenly and sharply in running, like a hunted animal; turn (*back*) in one's course; pursue a winding or tortuous course. L16. **b** *v.t.* Avoid or escape by so doubling; give the slip to. E19. **9a** *v.t. Mil.* Make double the length of (a rank or file) by bringing up another rank or file; bring up (a rank or file) in this way. L16. **b** *v.i. Mil.* Of a rank or file: march into position behind another so as to make it double. M17. **10** *v.i.* & *t.* (Cause to) share a room or quarters with or *with* another, esp. where the accommodation is intended for one only. Usu. foll. by *up*. L18. **11a** *v.t. Theatr.* Perform (a part) in place of another player; stand in for (a player); combine the performance of (two parts) in a play etc. E19. **b** *v.i.* Perform two parts or an additional part in a play etc.; perform or function in an additional capacity *as*. E20. **12** *v.i.* March in double time; go at the double. L19. **13** *v.i.* & *t. Billiards, Snooker*, etc. Of a ball: rebound from a cushion; *spec.* (of an object-ball) rebound from one cushion and enter a pocket. Of a player: cause (a ball) to do this. L19. **14** *v.t.* & *i. Bridge.* Counter (a bid) by declaring a double. L19. **15** *v.t.* & *i. Mus.* Play on or *on* a second instrument in addition to a main one. E20. **16** *v.i.* Foll. by *up*: increase a stake in betting twofold. E20. **17** *v.t.* Carry (a person) as a second rider on a bicycle. Cf. *double-bank* s.v. DOUBLE *a.* & *adv. NZ.* M20.

1 SHAKES. *Lear* Thy fifty yet doth double five and twenty. B. JOWETT Ignorance doubled by conceit of knowledge. O. HENRY If I doubled the number of trips I would see her twice as often. G. GREENE He doubled the tip. 2 C. PEBODY The circulation doubled. A. ALVAREZ Whenever he relaxed everything doubled: two brandy glasses, . . two professors. 5a DRYDEN The page is doubled down. YEATS He is all doubled up with age. R. CARVER She doubled her legs under her. J. G. COZZENS A slow involuntary spasm doubled her. b OED The leaf has been folded, and tends to double over. 8a DRYDEN See how he doubles, like a hunted hare. P. WARNER They were completely fooled when he doubled on his tracks. 11b C. P. SNOW The governor of Kate's hospital also doubled as a trustee of the Opera. B. MOORE The tobacconist's shop . . , which doubled as the post office. 15 L. FEATHER A clarinetist would double on tenor sax. *Gramophone* An arrangement for flute (doubling piccolo), two violas . . and piano.

doublé /duble/ *a.* M19. [Fr., pa. pple of *doubler* line, DOUBLE *v.*] Covered or lined *with*; (of a book) having a doublure; plated *with* precious metal.

double-bass /dʌb(ə)lˈbeɪs/ *n.* M18. [f. DOUBLE *a.* + BASS *n.*[2], after It. *contrabasso*: see CONTRABASS.] The largest and deepest-toned instrument of the violin family, played with one end resting on the floor.

double-cross /dʌb(ə)lˈkrɒs/ *n.* & *v.* Also **doublecross**. E19. [f. DOUBLE *a.* + CROSS *n.*] **A** *n.* **1** In gaming, the cheating of two parties by trying to win a game or match after promising to lose it; *gen.* betrayal of a collaborator or partner in a dishonest or secret transaction. E19. **2** A plant variety that is a cross between two hybrids that are themselves crosses between separate inbred lines. E20. **3** An embroidery stitch consisting of a one cross-stitch superimposed on another. M20. **B** *v.t.* Betray in a double-cross; cheat. E20.

double-crosser *n.* E20.

double entendre /ˌduːb(ə)l ɒ̃ːˈtɒ̃ːdr(ə), *foreign* dubl ɑ̃tɑ̃ːdr/ *n. phr.* Pl. **double entendres** (pronounced same). L17. [Obs. Fr. (now *double entente*) = double understanding.] A double meaning; an ambiguous expression; a phrase with two meanings, one usually indecent. Also, the use of such a meaning or phrase.

double entente /dubl ɑ̃tɑ̃ːt/ *n. phr.* Pl. **-s -s** (pronounced same). L19. [Fr.: see prec.] = prec.

double-face /ˈdʌb(ə)lfeɪs/ *n.* & *a.* E19. [f. DOUBLE *a.* + FACE *n.*, or back-form. f. next.] **A** *n.* **1** Duplicity. *rare.* E19. **2** A double-faced person. L19. **3** Double-faced fabric. M20. **B** *adj.* = DOUBLE-FACED 2b. L19.

double-faced /dʌb(ə)lˈfeɪst/ *a.* M16. [f. DOUBLE *a.* + FACE *n.* + -ED[2].] **1** Of a person: insincere, two-faced. M16. **2** Having two faces, sides, or aspects (*lit.* & *fig.*). L16. **b** Of a fabric: finished on both sides. L19.

2 O. JESPERSEN Some phrases are . . double-faced. J. GALSWORTHY The double-faced stove in the centre.

double-facedness *n.* M19.

double-ganger /ˈdʌb(ə)lgaŋə/ *n.* M19. [Partial tr.] = DOPPELGÄNGER.

double-gee /ˈdʌb(ə)ldʒiː/ *n. Austral.* L19. [Alt., after DOUBLE *a.* & *adv.*] = DUBBELTJIE 2.

doubler /ˈdʌblə/ *n.*[1] *obs.* exc. *dial.* LME. [AN *dobler, dubler* = OFr. *do(u)blier* f. med. L *duplarium*, f. L *duplus* DUPLE + *-arium* -ARY[1].] A large plate or dish.

doubler /ˈdʌblə/ *n.*[2] M16. [f. DOUBLE *v.* + -ER[1].] A person who or thing which doubles something; *spec.* a device for doubling the voltage or frequency of a signal.

doubles ententes *n. phr.* pl. of DOUBLE ENTENTE.

doublet /ˈdʌblɪt/ *n.* ME. [OFr., f. *double*: see DOUBLE *a.*, -ET[1].] **1** *Hist.* A close-fitting body garment formerly worn by men, with or without sleeves and a short skirt. ME. **2** In *pl.* The same number on two dice thrown at once. LME. †**b** A form of backgammon. Only in 17. **3** A counterfeit or simulated jewel composed of two pieces of crystal or glass cemented together with a layer of colour between them, or of a thin slice of a gem cemented on a piece of glass or inferior stone. LME. **4** Either of two things precisely alike or in some way identical; either of a pair; *esp.* either of two words in a language that have the same ultimate derivation. M16. **b** *Printing.* = DOUBLE *n.* 6. M19. **c** A story, episode, or saying occurring in two different biblical contexts and so regarded as derived from distinct sources. L19. **5** A pair, a couple; *spec.* a lens composed of two simple lenses; a magnifying glass consisting of this. E19. **b** *Physics.* A pair of related lines occurring close together in a spectrum; a pair of related atomic states or energy levels with slightly different energies. L19. **c** A pair of words of equal length that have to be changed into each other in a word-ladder; in *pl.*, the pastime of doing this. L19.

1 **doublet and hose** (the type of) masculine attire; *arch.* light or informal attire (without a cloak or gown). 4 *Verbatim* The members of a doublet may have moved apart very little in meaning (as *frail*: *fragile*). 5b H. M. ROSENBERG The state is split by the crystalline electric field into two degenerate doublets.

doubleton /ˈdʌb(ə)lt(ə)n/ *n.* E20. [f. DOUBLE *a.* after SINGLETON.] *Cards.* A suit of which a hand contains only two cards; a pair of cards of such a suit; each card of such a pair.

doubling /ˈdʌblɪŋ/ *vbl n.* LME. [f. DOUBLE *v.* + -ING[1].] **1** The action of DOUBLE *v.* Also foll. by *up*. LME. **2** *Her.* The lining of a garment. L16. **3** A sudden change of direction; *fig.* an evasion, a deceitful action. E17. **4** The state of being folded; a fold. M17.

1 R. W. EMERSON The rapid doubling of the population. A. GARVE Intourist had given some of our booked rooms to a delegation from Mongolia, which meant a lot of doubling up. *Melody Maker* A violinist anxious to learn a 'doubling instrument'.

doubloon /dʌˈbluːn/ *n.* E17. [Fr. *doublon* or its source Sp. *doblón*, f. *doble* DOUBLE *a.*: see -OON.] **1** *Hist.* A Spanish gold coin, a pistole of double value. E17. **2** In *pl.* Money. *slang.* E20.

doublure /dəˈblʊə, duː-; *foreign* dublyːr (*pl. same*)/ *n.* L19. [Fr. = lining, f. *doubler* to line: see -URE.] An ornamental lining, usu. of leather, on the inside of a book-cover.

doubly /ˈdʌbli/ *adv.* LME. [f. DOUBLE *a.* + -LY[2].] **1** In a double or twofold manner; in two ways; to a double degree, twice as much. LME. †**2** Deceitfully. LME–M18.

1 SHAKES. *Rich. II* Thy blows, doubly redoubled. T. HARDY The duty of breaking the news was made doubly painful. **doubly incontinent** unable to control urination and defecation.

doubt /daʊt/ *n.* ME. [OFr. *dote, dute* (mod. *doute*), f. *douter*: see next.] **1a** Uncertainty as to the truth or reality of something or as to the wisdom of a course of action; occasion or room for uncertainty. ME. **b** A feeling of uncertainty; an inclination to disbelieve or hesitate; a reason to disbelieve or hesitate, a reservation. Usu. in *pl.* LME. †**2a** Apprehension, fear. ME–M17. **b** A cause for fear; a risk, a danger. ME–L16. †**3** A matter surrounded in uncertainty; a doubtful point. LME–L17.

1a G. B. SHAW There can be no doubt of that: everybody knows it. J. CONRAD He had little doubt . . of his power to get hold of the girl. M. EDWARDES The Committee . . casts doubt on the value of the Ryder report. b C. DARWIN One great authority . . entertains grave doubts on this subject. *Daily Telegraph* 3 per cent. of church-goers have doubts. D. LODGE I had my doubts but dutifully plied him with questions. JAN MORRIS He had doubts about the saint. 2 LD BERNERS They dare not, for dought of Kyng Charlemayne. 3 AV *Dan.* 5:16 I haue heard of thee, that thou canst make interpretations, and dissolue doubts.

Phrases: *benefit of the doubt*: see BENEFIT *n.* **beyond (all) doubt, beyond (the shadow of) a doubt** = *without (a) doubt* below. **make doubt** be uncertain, doubt, (*that, whether*). **in doubt** (*a*) in a state of mental uncertainty or indecision; (*b*) not certainly known or decided. **no doubt** in all likelihood, doubtless; orig. in stronger sense = *without (a) doubt* below. †**out of doubt** = *without (a) doubt* below. **without (a) doubt** certainly, unquestionably.

doubt /daʊt/ *v.* ME. [OFr. *doter, duter* (mod. *douter*) f. L *dubitare* waver, hesitate, f. *dubius* DUBIOUS. The Latinized sp. appeared in 15, following Fr. †*doubter*.] I Be uncertain. 1 *v.i.* Be undecided in opinion or belief; be in doubt. (Foll. by *of*.) ME. 2 *v.t.* Hesitate to believe or trust; feel uncertain of, call in question, have reservations about. ME. 3 *v.t.* With clauses: feel uncertain *whether, if*; hesitate to believe, think it unlikely, that or *that* (chiefly *US* exc. as follows). After neg. or interrog. main cl. foll. by *that, but that, but*. ME. †4 *v.t.* Hesitate, scruple, *to do*. ME–M18. 5 Of a thing: cause to doubt; make undecided. M19.

1 AV *Matt.* 14:31 O thou of little faith, wherefore didst thou doubt? 2 DRYDEN He . . The beauty doubted, but believ'd the wife. A. RADCLIFFE My lord, you have never yet doubted my word. R. W. EMERSON They doubt a man's sound judgment if he does not eat with appetite. 3 W. SELWYN It never was doubted, but that one partner might bind the rest. D. MAHON Death is near, . . I doubt if I shall survive another . . winter. W. GOLDING I doubt he'll bother to come. 5 J. G. WHITTIER This . . somewhat doubted him at first, as the book was not canonical.

II Fear, be in fear. 6 *v.t.* †a Dread, be afraid of. ME–E18. b Fear, be afraid, *that* or *lest*; fear that. *arch.* exc. *Sc.* & *dial.* LME. 7 *v.refl.* [= OFr. *se douter*.] Be afraid (that). Now *rare* or *obs.* ME. †8 *v.i.* Be in fear; be afraid (*of*). ME–L16. 9 *v.t.* In weakened sense (app. infl. by branch I): anticipate (with fear) the possibility of; expect (esp. something unwelcome), suspect. Freq. foll. by *that*. *arch.* exc. *Sc.* & *dial.* E16.

6a JAS. KELLY Do well and doubt no man. 7 SIR W. SCOTT I doubt me his wits have gone a bell-wavering by the road. 9 W. H. PRESCOTT They doubted some sinister motive . . in the conduct of the French king. A. TROLLOPE I doubt that Thackeray did not write the Latin epitaph. D. L. SAYERS 'Hech, my lord,' said he, cheerfully. 'I dooted ye'd be here before verra long.' L. G. GIBBON Man, it's a fair tough case, I doubt I'll need your help.

doubtable *a.* (*a*) uncertain, open to doubt; †(*b*) redoubtable: LME. **doubter** *n.* E17.

doubtful /ˈdaʊtfʊl, -f(ə)l/ *a.* & *n.* LME. [f. DOUBT *n.* + -FUL.] A *adj.* 1 Causing or subject to doubt; uncertain, questionable, ambiguous; that is only questionably, or is not unequivocally, such. LME. b Unpredictable in result. LME. c Of dubious character; not to be counted on in some capacity. M19. 2 Feeling doubt or uncertainty; divided or unsettled in opinion. LME. †3 To be feared; dreadful, terrible. LME–M16. 4 Such as gives cause for apprehension. *arch.* LME. †5 Full of fear; apprehensive (*that*). M16–L18.

1 ADDISON A doubtful Passage in a Latin Poet. C. DARWIN The question whether certain doubtful forms should be ranked as species or varieties. SCOTT FITZGERALD It was doubtful if he knew who Andrew Jackson was. E. F. SCHUMACHER A change which is not an unquestionable improvement is a doubtful blessing. b SOUTHEY The fight Hung doubtful. c R. MACAULAY She and that boy mix with some pretty doubtful company. T. E. LAWRENCE Don't put yourself about expecting me, for I'm a doubtful starter. 2 J. A. FROUDE He was doubtful of the prospects of the rebellion. B. JOWETT He was doubtful . . whether the ideal . . state could be realized. 4 GIBBON The consul . . reported the doubtful and dangerous situation of the empire.

B *n.* A doubtful person or thing; *esp.* a person who has not made up his or her mind on an issue. L16.

doubtfully *adv.* L15. **doubtfulness** *n.* LME.

doubting /ˈdaʊtɪŋ/ *ppl a.* LME. [f. DOUBT *v.* + -ING².] That doubts; sceptical. Formerly also, fearful.

doubting Thomas: see THOMAS *n.*¹ 1.

doubtingly *adv.* in a hesitant or doubting manner E16. **doubtingness** *n.* (*rare*) L18.

doubtless /ˈdaʊtlɪs/ *adv.* & *a.* LME. [f. DOUBT *n.* + -LESS.] A *adv.* 1 Without doubt; certainly, unquestionably. Now chiefly expressing concession of a statement. LME. 2 In all likelihood; probably; no doubt. M17.

1 AV *Ps.* 126:6 He that goeth forth and weeping, bearing precious seed, shall doubtless come again with rejoicing. 2 W. S. MAUGHAM He would marry again. . . Next time doubtless he would choose a different sort of woman.

B *adj.* Free from doubt; certain, indubitable. Formerly also, free from apprehension. LME.

SHAKES. *John* Pretty child, sleep doubtless and secure.

doubtlessly *adv.* = DOUBTLESS *adv.* LME. **doubtlessness** *n.* L19.

douc /duːk/ *n.* L18. [Fr. f. Vietnamese *douc, dok*.] A langur, *Pygathrix nemaeus*, found in the forests of Vietnam. Also *douc langur*.

douçaine /duːˈseɪn/ *n.* M20. [Fr., f. *douce*: see next.] *Early Mus.* A soft-toned reed instrument. Cf. DOUCET *n.* 2.

douce /duːs/ *a.* ME. [OFr. *dous* (mod. *doux*), fem. *douce* f. L *dulcis* sweet. Cf. DULCE *a.*] 1 Pleasant, sweet. (Formerly a stock epithet of France.) Now *Sc.* & *north.* ME. 2 Quiet, sober, sedate. *Sc.* & *north.* E18.

doucely *adv.* E17. **douceness** *n.* E17.

doucepere *n.* var. of DOUZEPER.

doucet /ˈduːsɪt/ *n.* Also **dowset** /ˈdaʊsɪt/. LME. [OFr., use as n. of *doucet, doucette* dim. of *doux*, DOUCE. Cf. DULCET *n., a.*] 1 *Cookery.* A sweet or sweetened dish. *obs.* exc. *dial.* (in comb. *doucet-pie*). LME. †2 A wind instrument resembling a flute. Cf. DOUÇAINE. Only in LME. 3 *Hunting.* In *pl.* The testicles of a deer. M16.

†**doucet** *a.* see DULCET *a.*

douceur /dusœːr, duːˈsəː/ *n.* LME. [Fr. f. Proto-Romance var. of L *dulcor* sweetness.] 1 Orig., sweetness of manner, amiability, (of a person). Now, agreeableness, charm (chiefly in *douceur de vivre* etc. below). LME. †2 A complimentary speech or turn of phrase. L17–E19. 3 A conciliatory present; a gratuity, a bribe. M18. 4 A tax benefit available to a person who sells a work of art by private treaty to a public collection rather than on the open market. L20.

1 F. BURNEY He . . answered with all his accustomed douceur and politeness. I. MURDOCH A curious relationship grew up between Michael and Dora, something . . which had for Michael a certain ease and *douceur*. ***douceur de (la) vie*** /də la vi/, ***douceur de vivre*** /də viːvr/ [Fr. *vie* life, *vivre* live] the pleasure or amenities of life. 3 N. GULBENKIAN When I have a bet, a winning one, . . all my servants get a little *douceur*.

douche /duːʃ/ *n.* & *v.* M18. [Fr. f. It. *doccia* conduit pipe, f. *docciare* pour by drops f. Proto-Romance, f. L *ductus* DUCT *n.*] A *n.* (The application of) a jet of (esp. cold) liquid or air to a part of the body, as a form of bathing or for medicinal purposes; *spec.* the flushing of the vagina, as a contraceptive measure. Also, a syringe or similar device for producing such a jet. M18.

fig.: P. BROOK From the fanatical chastity of Isabella and the mystery of the Duke we are plunged back to Pompey and Barnadine for douches of normality.

Comb.: **douche-bag** a small syringe for douching the vagina, esp. as a contraceptive measure.

B *v.* 1 *v.t.* Administer a douche to. M19. 2 *v.i.* Take a douche; *spec.* take a vaginal douche, esp. as a contraceptive measure. M19.

doucin /ˈduːsɪn, *foreign* dusɛ̃/ *n.* L16. [Fr., f. as DOUCE.] A sweet variety of wild apple, used as a stock.

dough /dəʊ/ *n.* [OE *dāg* = MLG *dēch* (Du. *deeg*), OHG *teic* (G *Teig*), ON *deig*, Goth. *daigs*, f. Gmc, f. IE base meaning 'smear, knead'. Cf. DUFF *n.*²] 1 A mass of flour that has been moistened and kneaded for making into bread, pastry, cakes, etc. OE. 2 Any soft pasty mass. M16. 3 Money. *slang* (chiefly *N. Amer.*). M19.

1 **(my) cake is dough** my project has failed. 3 M. PUZO Twenty million bucks is a lot of dough.

Comb.: **dough-baked** *a.* imperfectly baked, so as to remain doughy; *fig.* deficient in reason or sense; **doughboy** (*a*) a boiled flour dumpling; (*b*) *US colloq.* an infantryman; **dough-face** (*a*) a mask made of dough; (*b*) *US Hist.* a northern congressman who supported the South, esp. on the question of slavery; **dough-trough** a trough or vessel in which dough is placed to rise.

dough /dəʊ/ *v. rare.* M17. [f. the n.] †1 *v.i.* Work with dough; be a baker. Only in M17. 2 *v.t.* Make into dough; mix *in* with dough. L19.

doughnut /ˈdəʊnʌt/ *n.* Also ***donut**. L18. [f. DOUGH *n.* + NUT *n.*] 1 A small spongy cake of sweetened and fried dough, freq. ring-shaped, or spherical with a jam or cream filling. L18. 2 Any of various circular objects with a hole in the middle, *esp.* a motor-car or aeroplane tyre. *colloq.* E20. b A toroidal vacuum chamber in some particle accelerators. M20.

dought /daʊt/ *n.* Now *Sc. rare.* ME. [Orig. perh. repr. OE *duguþ* worth, virtue, manhood, f. *dugan*: see DOW *v.*¹ Later, back-form. f. next.] Power, strength, ability.

doughty /ˈdaʊti/ *a.* Now *arch.* or *joc.* [Late OE *dohtiġ*, earlier *dyhtiġ* = MLG, MDu. *duchtich* (Du. *duchtig*), MHG *tühtic* (G *tüchtig*), f. Gmc: see DOW *v.*¹] Fearless and resolute; stout-hearted.

SIR W. SCOTT After this doughty resolution, I went doggedly to work. R. COBB A . . doughty fighter against bureaucracy.

doughtily *adv.* ME. **doughtiness** *n.* ME.

doughy /ˈdəʊi/ *a.* E17. [f. DOUGH *n.* + -Y¹.] Resembling dough in appearance or consistency; (of bread etc.) imperfectly baked.

J. M. GOOD A pallid doughy countenance. *fig.*: SHAKES. *All's Well* All the unbak'd and doughy youth of a nation.

doughiness *n.* E17.

Douglas /ˈdʌgləs/ *n.*¹ M19. [David *Douglas* (1798–1834), Sc. botanical explorer.] 1 *Douglas fir, spruce*, or *pine*, a very tall coniferous timber tree, *Pseudotsuga menziesii*, native to western N. America. M19. 2 *Douglas squirrel*, a chickaree, *Tamiasciurus douglasi*. *N. Amer.* L19.

Douglas /ˈdʌgləs/ *n.*² M19. [James *Douglas* (1675–1742), Sc. physician.] *Anat.* Used in *possess.* or after *of* to designate anatomical structures described by or named after Douglas.

Douglas's pouch = RECTO-UTERINE *pouch*.

Douglas /ˈdʌgləs/ *n.*³ *Austral. slang.* E20. [The *Douglas* Axe Manufacturing Co., orig. of East *Douglas*, Massachusetts, US.] An axe.

swing Douglas: see SWING *v.*

Douglasite /ˈdʌgləsʌɪt/ *n.* & *a.* M20. [f. *Douglas* (see below) + -ITE¹.] *Hist.* A *n.* A supporter of the economic theories of social credit of Major C. H. Douglas (1879–1952). M20. B *adj.* Pertaining to or characteristic of Douglasites. M20.

Doukhobor *n.* var. of DUKHOBOR.

doulocracy *n.* var. of DULOCRACY.

Doulton /ˈdəʊlt(ə)n/ *a.* & *n.* L19. [John *Doulton* (1793–1873), Eng. potter.] (Proprietary name designating) pottery or porcelain made at the factories of John Doulton or his successors.

doum /duːm/ *n.* Also **doom**. E18. [Arab. *dawm, dūm*.] More fully *doum-palm*. An Egyptian palm, *Hyphaene thebaica*, usu. with a dichotomously branched trunk, bearing an edible fruit the size of an apple.

doup /duːp/ *n.* *Sc.* E16. [Cf. ON *daup*.] 1 A hollow bottom; *esp.* the bottom of an eggshell. *obs.* exc. *dial.* E16. 2 The buttocks. M17. 3 The end or last part of anything, as a candle. E18.

douppion *n.* var. of DUPION.

dour /ˈdʊə/ *a.* Orig. *Sc.* LME. [Prob. f. Gael. *dùr* dull, stupid, obstinate = (M)Ir. *dúr*, perh. f. L *durus* hard.] 1 Severe, stern, relentless; fierce, bold. *Sc.* & *north.* LME. 2 Obstinate, stubborn.

Sc. & *north.* LME. 3 Gloomily taciturn; sullen. L15.

1 J. DALRYMPLE He led a dour and hard lyfe. LYTTON Tostig is a man . . dour and haughty. F. ORMSBY Never again would dour fields lie Quite so forbidding, stones be so bare. 2 J. BUCHAN I know the ways of those London journalists, and they're a dour crop to shift. 3 P. THEROUX These Indians are habitually dour—their faces wrinkled into frowns. J. STEINBECK She had a dour Presbyterian mind.

dourly *adv.* L15. **dourness** *n.* LME.

dourine /ˈdʊəriːn/ *n.* L19. [Fr.] A chronic, usu. fatal, venereal disease of horses caused by a trypanosome.

†dourlach *n. Sc.* Only in 19. [App. var. of DORLACH.] A short sword; a dagger.

douro *n.* var. of DURO.

douroucouli /dʊərʊˈkuːli/ *n.* Also **-coli** /-ˈkɒli/. M19. [Prob. a S. American Indian name.] = *night monkey* s.v. NIGHT *n.*

dourra *n.* var. of DURRA.

douse /daʊs/ *n.* M16. [f. DOUSE *v.*[1] Cf. DOUST.] A dull heavy blow.

douse /daʊs/ *v.*[1]*t.* Also **dowse**. M16. [Perh. rel. to similar and partly synon. MDu., LG *dossen*, Du. *doesen*, G dial. *dusen* beat, strike. Cf. DOSS *v.*[1]] 1 Strike, knock, punch. Now *dial.* M16. 2 *Naut.* Lower (a sail etc.) or slacken (a rope) suddenly or in haste; close (a porthole). E17. 3 Throw *down* with force; *fig.* put down or pay out (money). Chiefly *dial.* L18. 4 Take off, doff, (clothes, esp. a hat). L18.

2 E. JONG 'Dowse your Topsail and salute her!' I cried.

douser *n.*[1] a heavy blow L18.

douse /daʊs/ *v.*[2] E17. [Prob. imit. (cf. *souse*), but perh. identical w. prec.] 1 *v.t.* Plunge vigorously into water or other liquid; immerse (*in*). E17. 2 *v.t.* Wet thoroughly with a liquid, drench. Usu. foll. by *with*, *in*.) E17. 3 *v.i.* Plunge or be plunged into water. E17. 4 Put out, extinguish, (a light, fire, etc.). Also *fig.*, suppress (a feeling), put an end to (an activity). L18.

1 *fig.*: L. MACNEICE When we were children Spring was easy, Dousing our heads in suds of hawthorn. 2 B. CHATWIN He had doused himself once a week in the wash-house. T. KENEALLY The pyre . . was doused in fuel and lit. 4 T. E. LAWRENCE I see the Corporal's cigarette doused. L. GARFIELD With the moon now doused in a creeping sea of cloud. T. CAPOTE Dick doused the flashlight. E. BIRNEY His spirits, never easy to douse, were sustained by his . . winnings at black jack.

douser *n.*[2] (*a*) someone who drenches another person; (*b*) a screen in a projector which cuts off the light before it reaches the film: L19.

†doust *n.* E17–E18. [Perh. alt. of DOUSE *n.*] A firm blow; a punch.

dout /daʊt/ *v.* & *n.* Also (now only as n.) **dowt**. E16. [Fused f. *do out*: see DO *v.*] A *v.t.* Extinguish, put out, (a fire or light). *obs.* exc. *dial.* E16. B *n.* 1 A thing which extinguishes something. *obs.* exc. *dial.* L16. 2 A cigarette-end. *Sc. colloq.* M20.

douter *n.* (*obs.* exc. *dial.*) a person who or thing which extinguishes something E17.

douzaine /duːˈzeɪn/ *n.* L18. [Fr. = DOZEN *n.*] In Guernsey and Alderney, a body of twelve people elected to represent a parish.

douzainier, **-zenier** /duːzəˈnɪə/ *n.* a member of a douzaine L17.

douzeper /ˈduːzəpɛː/ *n. arch.* Also **doucepere** /ˈduːs-/. ME. [Orig. in pl. form *douzepers* f. OFr. *douze pers* (mod. *douze pairs*) twelve peers.] Each of the twelve paladins of Charlemagne, the bravest of his knights; any of the twelve chief peers of France, temporal and spiritual, regarded as their symbolic heirs; *fig.* any illustrious person. Usu. in *pl.*

dove /dʌv/ *n.* Also (*Sc.*) **doo** /duː/. ME. [ON *dúfa* = OFris. *dūve*, OS *duba* (Du. *duif*), OHG *tūba* (G *Taube*), Goth. *dūbo*, f. Gmc base taken to be imit. of the bird's cry.] 1 Any bird of the family Columbidae; a pigeon; *esp.* a turtle-dove or similar small pigeon. Formerly (now *dial.*), any of the native British pigeons. (In Christian symbolism typifying gentleness and harmlessness.) ME. b *Greenland dove*, the black guillemot. Cf. DOVEKIE. *dial.* L17. 2 A person, esp. a woman, for whom one feels tender affection. Chiefly in *my dove*. LME. 3 An image of a dove as a symbol of innocence, harmlessness, or peace. Also (*Chr. Ch.*), a vessel formerly used to enclose the pyx. E16. 4 a In full *dove-colour*. A warm grey with a tone of pink or purple. L16. b A dove-coloured marble. E19. 5 A gentle or innocent person. Formerly, a simpleton. L16. 6 *Chr. Ch.* [Cf. *Luke* 3:22 etc.] The Holy Spirit, esp. in his outward manifestation. E18. 7 (Usu. **D-**.) *The* constellation Columba. Also *Noah's Dove*, *the Dove of Noah*. L18. 8 *Polit.* A person who believes in a policy of negotiation and conciliation rather than warfare or confrontation. Opp. *hawk*. M20.

1 *collared dove*, *ring-dove*, *rock-dove*, *stock dove*, *turtle-dove*, etc. 2 TENNYSON She is coming, my dove, my dear. 5 *soiled dove*: see SOILED *a.*[1] 8 S. BRILL Gibbons . . had gone to North Vietnam . . with some fellow doves in search of peace feelers.

Comb.: *dove-colour*: see sense 4a above; **dove-eyed** *a.* having mild or gentle eyes like a dove's; **dove-flower** an orchid, *Peristeria elata*, native to Central America and northern S. America; **dove-hawk** *dial.* the hen-harrier; **dovehouse** a dovecot; **dove-marble** = sense 4b above; **dove orchid** = *dove-flower* above; **dove's-foot** (**cranesbill**) a cranesbill, *Geranium molle*, with small pink flowers and round, softly hairy, deeply divided leaves; **dove tree** a deciduous tree, *Davidia involucrata*, native to China, with heads of small petalless flowers subtended by huge white bracts.

dovelet *n.* a young or small dove E19. **dovelike** *a.* resembling (that of) a dove; *esp.* gentle, peace-loving: L16. **doveling** *n.* = DOVELET; also, (a term of endearment for) a small child: E17.

dove /dəʊv/ *v.*[1]*i. Sc.* & *north.* L18. [Rel. to OE *dofung* dotage; ON *dofna*, Goth. *daubnan* become heavy, flat, or dead. Cf. earlier DOVER.] 1 Doze, become drowsy. L18. 2 Be stupid. *Sc.* E19.

dove *v.*[2] pa. t.: see DIVE *v.*

dovecot /ˈdʌvkɒt/ *n.* Also **-cote** /-kəʊt/ See also DOOCOT. LME. [f. DOVE *n.* + COT *n.*[1]] A structure housing doves or pigeons, usu. placed at a height above the ground and with entrances for the birds to fly in by.

flutter, or **cause a flutter among**, **the dovecots** startle or perturb a sedate or conventionally-minded community.

dovekie /ˈdʌvki/ *n.* E19. [Sc. dim. of DOVE *n.*] Orig., the black guillemot, *Cepphus grylle* (cf. DOVE *n.* 1b). Now usu. the little auk, *Alle alle*.

dover /ˈdəʊvə/ *v.* & *n. Sc.* & *north.* E16. [App. f. (as) DOVE *v.*[1]: see -ER[5].] A *v.* 1 *v.i.* & *t.* (Cause to) doze or be unconscious. E16. 2 *v.i.* Wander aimlessly or confusedly; walk unsteadily. *Sc.* E19. B *n.* A light or fitful sleep; a doze. E19.

Dover's powder /ˈdəʊvəz paʊdə/ *n. phr.* E19. [Thomas Dover (1660–1742), Eng. physician.] *Pharm.* A mixture of opium and ipecacuanha, formerly much used as an anodyne and diaphoretic.

dovetail /ˈdʌvteɪl/ *n.* & *v.* M16. [f. DOVE *n.* + TAIL *n.*[1]] A *n.* 1 A joint formed by one or more tenons in the shape of a dove's tail, i.e. a reversed wedge, fitting into mortises of corresponding shape. M16. 2 A tenon or mortise of such a joint. L17. 3 *Her.* A dovetailed line of partition. L17.

Comb.: **dovetail joint** = sense 1 above; **dovetail moulding** *Archit.*: composed of alternating triangles and reversed triangles.

B *v.* 1 *v.t.* Fit together or join with a dovetail. M16. 2 *v.t.* & *i.* (*fig.*) Fit together or become adjusted perfectly, so as to form a compact or harmonious whole. (Foll. by *with*, *into*.) E19.

2 A. GEIKIE The readiness with which Forbes had begun to dovetail zoology and geology. C. S. LEWIS Every problem of conduct was dovetailed into a complex and rigid moral theology. P. L. FERMOR Meals within meals dovetailing so closely . . that there is hardly an interprandial moment.

dovetailed *a.* (*a*) joined by means of a dovetail; (*b*) (having an end) shaped like a dove's tail or inverted triangle; (*c*) *Her.* (of a line of partition) forming a row of inverted triangles with open apices, as in a dovetail joint: M17. **dovetailer** *n.* a machine for making dovetails; a person who dovetails: E19.

dovey /ˈdʌvi/ *n.* Also **dovie**. M18. [Dim. or pet-form of DOVE *n.*: see -Y[6], -IE.] Used as a term of endearment: little dove. Cf. LOVEY, LOVEY-DOVEY.

dovish /ˈdʌvɪʃ/ *a.* M16. [f. DOVE *n.* + -ISH[1].] †1 Of simplicity etc.: like that of a dove. Only in M16. 2 Chiefly *Polit.* Inclined to advocate negotiation and conciliation (cf. DOVE *n.* 8); conciliatory. Opp. *hawkish*. M20.

dovishness *n.* M20.

dow /daʊ/ *n.*[1] *slang.* E19. [Abbrev.] A dowager.

Dow /daʊ/ *n.*[2] M20. [Abbrev.] *The* Dow-Jones average.

dow *n.*[3] var. of DHOW.

dow /daʊ/ *v.*[1]*i.* Now *Sc.* & *north.* [OE *dugan* corresp. to OS *dugan*, OHG *tugan* (G *taugen*), ON *duga*: a Gmc preterite-present vb rel. to DOUGHTY.] †1 Be good, strong, vigorous, virtuous, valiant, or manly. Only in OE. †2 Be of use or profit to a person, avail. Usu. *impers.* in (*it*) *dows* etc. OE–L16. †3 Be valid or of value; be worth or good for something. ME–L18. †4 Be good, fitting, or proper for someone; become, befit, behove. Usu. *impers.* in *it dows* etc. Only in ME. 5 Have the strength or ability, be able (to do something). Usu. in neg. contexts. Now *rare* exc. *poet.* ME. 6 Do well, thrive, prosper. ME.

†dow *v.*[2] see DUE *v.*

dowable /ˈdaʊəb(ə)l/ *a.* Now *rare.* LME. [AN, f. (O)Fr. *douer* endow: see next, -ABLE.] *Law.* Entitled to dower; able to be endowed.

dowager /ˈdaʊədʒə/ *n.* M16. [OFr. *douag(i)ere*, f. *douage* dower, f. *douer* portion out, endow, f. L *dotare*: see DOWER, -ER[2].] 1 A widow holding title or rank, or property, derived from her late husband. Freq. appositive, as *queen dowager*, *princess dowager*, *countess dowager* or *dowager countess*, etc. M16. 2 A dignified elderly lady. *colloq.* E19.

1 D. HUME He espoused Eleanor, dowager of William Earl of Pembroke. E. A. FREEMAN A marriage with their dowager aunt. J. GRENFELL The Dowager Duchess cuts the cake.

dowagerly *a.* (*rare*) M19.

dowar *n.* var. of DOUAR.

dowd /daʊd/ *n.*[1] ME. [Origin unkn. In mod. use partly back-form. f. DOWDY *a.*] A person, usu. a woman, of dull unfashionable appearance; a dowdy woman.

dowd /daʊd/ *n.*[2] *obs.* exc. *dial.* M18. [Origin unkn.: cf. DOWDY *n.*[2]] A woman's cap or night-cap.

dowdy /ˈdaʊdi/ *n.*[1] & *a.* L16. [f. DOWD *n.*[1] + -Y[6].] A *n.* A woman who is shabbily, unfashionably, or unattractively dressed. L16.

B *adj.* (Of a person, esp. a woman) shabbily, badly, or unattractively dressed; (of a garment) lacking smartness and freshness, shabby, unattractively dull. L17.

R. WEST I can't stand by and see my sister turning into a dowdy, middle-aged frump.

dowdily *adv.* L19. **dowdiness** *n.* M19. **dowdyish** *a.* E19. **dowdyism** *n.* dowdy character or quality M19.

dowdy /ˈdaʊdi/ *n.*[2] *obs.* exc. *dial.* L18. [Origin unkn.: cf. DOWD *n.*[2]] = DOWD *n.*[2]

dowel /ˈdaʊəl/ *n.* & *v.* ME. [Perh. f. MLG *dovel*, corresp. to OHG *tubili* (MHG *tübel*: G *Döbel* after LG) f. Gmc f. IE, whence Gk *tuphos* wedge.] A *n.* A short round rod that projects from one (usu. wooden) surface and fits into a matching hole in another, so as to hold the two together without showing; a headless wooden pin used similarly. Also *dowel pin*. ME. B *v.t.* Infl. **-ll-**, ***-l-**. Fasten with a dowel or dowels. L17.

dowelled *a.* E19. **dowelling** *n.* (*a*) the action of the vb; (*b*) wood in cylindrical form suitable for cutting into dowels: L19.

do-well /ˈduːwɛl/ *n.* LME. [f. DO *v.* + WELL *adv.*] 1 The action of doing well. Freq. personified. *obs.* exc. *dial.* LME. 2 A prosperous person. *rare.* M19.

dower /ˈdaʊə/ *n.* & *v.* LME. [OFr. *douaire* f. med. L *dotarium*, f. L *dotare* endow, f. *dos*, *dot-* dowry, DOT *n.*[2], rel. to *dare* give: see -ARY[1].] A *n.* 1 *Law* (now *Hist.*). The share of a dead man's estate that was formerly allowed to his widow for life. LME. 2 = DOWRY 2. Now *arch.* & *poet.* LME. 3 An endowment or gift of nature; a talent. LME.

Comb.: **dower chest** (*a*) a wedding-chest; (*b*) *US* a hope chest; **dower house** a smaller house on the estate of a large one, forming part of a widow's dower and intended as her place of residence; **dower land**: forming part of a widow's dower.

B *v.* 1 *v.t.* Give a dowry to; endow *with* a dowry. L15. 2 *v.t.* Endow or furnish *with* an attribute, talent, or gift. L18.

1 E. BOWEN The daughters should be well dowered with Bland money. 2 E. M. FORSTER A man dowered with coarse kindliness, and rustic strength.

†**doweress** *n.* a widow holding a dower; a dowager: E16–E19. **dowerless** *a.* E17.

dowf /daʊf/ *n.*, *a.*, & *v.* *Sc.* (now *dial.*) & *north.* LME. [Origin uncertain: perh. f. ON *daufr* deaf.] A *n.* 1 A spiritless, stupid, or gloomy person. LME. 2 A dull blow. E18. B *adj.* 1 Of a person, a sound, or (formerly) the weather: dull. Of a person: lacking spirit or energy; gloomy. E16. †2 Of an excuse: unconvincing, feeble. L18–M19. 3 Of wood or vegetation: decayed. Of ground: unfertile. E19. C *v.* 1 *v.i.* & *t.* Be or make dull or sluggish. E19. 2 *v.t.* Hit with something soft; thump. E19. 3 *v.t.* Bounce (a ball). Now *rare.* E19.

dowfness *n.* lack of spirit E16.

dowfart /ˈdaʊfət/ *n.* & *a.* *Sc. arch.* E18. [f. prec. + *-art* -ARD. Cf. DUFFER *n.*[2]] A *n.* A dull or stupid person. E18. B *adj.* Dull, stupid. L18.

dowie /ˈdaʊi/ *a.* *Sc.* & *north.* Also †**dolly**. E16. [Origin uncertain: perh. ult. f. DULL *a.* + -Y[1].] Dull and lonely; dreary; dismal.

dowitcher /ˈdaʊɪtʃə/ *n.* M19. [Iroquoian: cf. Mohawk *tawistawis* snipe.] Either of two wading birds of the genus *Limnodromus* (family Scolopacidae), related to the sandpiper and breeding in Arctic and subarctic regions, *L. griseus* or *L. scolopaceus*, the short- and long-billed dowitchers of N. America.

Dow-Jones /daʊˈdʒəʊnz/ *n.* Also **Dow Jones**. E20. [f. *Dow Jones & Co.*, Inc., US financial news agency, f. C. H. *Dow* (1851–1902) & E. D. *Jones* (*c*1855–1920).] In full *Dow-Jones (industrial) average*. An index of the average level of share prices on the New York Stock Exchange at any time, based on the daily price of a selection of representative stocks. Cf. Dow *n.*[2]

dowl /daʊl/ *n.* Now *dial.* LME. [Perh. rel. to DOWN *n.*[2]] A barb of a feather; down, fluff.

dowlas /ˈdaʊləs/ *n.* & *a.* ME. [*Daoulas*, a village in Brittany.] A *n.* Orig., a coarse kind of linen. Now, a strong calico made in imitation of it. ME. B *attrib.* or as *adj.* Made of dowlas. M16.

dowless /ˈdaʊlɪs/ *a.* *Sc.* L18. [f. DOW *v.*[1] + -LESS.] Without strength or energy; feeble; infirm.

dowly /ˈdauli/ *a.* *north.* LME. [Origin uncertain: perh. rel. to DOWIE.] Doleful, miserable, gloomy, lonely.

down /daʊn/ *n.*[1] [OE *dūn* = OFris. *dūne*, OS *dūna* (Du. *duin*, cf. DUNE), perh. ult. f. a Celt. wd whence also (O)Ir. *dún*, Welsh †*din*, fort, cogn. w. OE *tūn* TOWN *n.*] 1 A hill. *obs.* exc. as passing into sense 2. OE. 2 An open tract of high ground; *spec.* in *pl.*, (*the*) treeless undulating chalk uplands of S. and SE England and elsewhere, traditionally a major source of pasturage. ME. 3 A sand-hill, a dune. Now *rare.* E16. 4 (**D-**.) (A sheep of) any of several short-woolled hornless breeds originally raised on the English downs, or bred from such a breed. (Earliest in SOUTHDOWN.) L18.

2 R. KIPLING Little, lost, Down churches praise The Lord who made the hills. **dale and down** (now *arch.* & *poet.*) lowland and upland. **North Downs** *the* hills forming a ridge across Kent and Surrey. **South Downs** *the* hills forming a ridge across Sussex and Hampshire. **The Downs** (*a*) see sense 2 above; (*b*) part of the sea (opposite the North Downs) off east Kent. 4 *Dorset Down, Hampshire Down, Oxford Down*, etc.

Comb.: **downland** land forming downs.

downlike *a.* resembling downland or a down L17.

down /daʊn/ *n.*[2] ME. [ON *dúnn*, whence LG *dune*, G *Daune*.] 1 Soft loose fluffy feathers, as on young birds (used in cushions, quilts, etc.). ME. 2 Fine short soft hairs on some plants, fruits, and seeds. LME. 3 (A mass of) short soft hair on the skin, *spec.* that which appears on a boy's face at puberty. L16. 4 Any material of a soft fluffy nature. E17.

1 L. MACNEICE Baby pigeons covered with yellow down. 2 *thistledown*: see THISTLE. 3 DRYDEN The callow down began To shade my chin, and call me first a man. D. LESSING A tiny down on his bare forearm gleamed gold. D. JACOBSON There was no down on . . her cheeks or upper lip. 4 A. REID Nitre . . effloresces . . on their surface, in the form of a crystalline down.

downless *a.* L16.

down /daʊn/ *n.*[3] & *int.* L16. [f. DOWN *adv.* or ellipt. for 'downward motion'.] 1 a *n.* & *int.* Used as a meaningless word in the refrains of popular songs. Also *derry down*. Cf. DERRY I. L16. †b The burden or refrain of a song. E–M17. 2 A descent (*lit.* & *fig.*); a reverse of fortune. Chiefly in *ups and downs* (see UP *n.*). E18. b An act of throwing or putting something down; *spec.* in American and Canadian football, (*a*) a play to advance the ball; (*b*) each of a fixed number of attempts to advance the ball 10 yards. M19. c A feeling or period of depression or low spirits or lack of vigour. *colloq.* M20. †3 A suspicion; a suggestion of illegality. *slang.* E–M19. 4 A tendency to view with suspicion and disapproval; a prejudice, a grudge, a resentment. Chiefly in *have a down on*. *colloq.* M19. 5 *Dominoes.* The play of the first piece. L19. 6 The position or action of a dog lying down in response to a command. M20.

2 *Times* The index spent most of the morning on the down. 4 *Abingdon Herald* One of the men . . had a particular down on drugs because a member of his family had got into serious trouble with them. M. BINCHY You've always had a down on her.

down /daʊn/ *v.*[1]*t.* *rare.* E17. [f. DOWN *n.*[2]] Cover or line with down, make downy.

down /daʊn/ *v.*[2] L17. [f. DOWN *adv.*] I *v.i.* Now *rare.* 1 Foll. by *with*: put or throw down; have done with. L17. 2 Come or go down, descend. E19. 3 Foll. by *on*, *upon*: come down on, attack (*lit.* & *fig.*). M19.

II *v.t.* †4 w. *it.* Move downwards, descend. Only in M18. 5 Bring, put, throw, or knock down; get the better of. L18. 6 Drink, esp. all of. *colloq.* E20.

5 S. JOHNSON He talked of one whom he did not know, but I *downed* him with the King of Prussia. R. S. SURTEES His horse . . had downed him three times. *Sun* (*Baltimore*) The American fighters reported downing 110 of the Nazi interceptors. *Globe & Mail* (*Toronto*) London Lords downed Kitchener Oaks 31–14 yesterday. *New Yorker* Downed trees with their roots . . sticking high in the air. **down tools** stop work, esp. as a form of industrial action. 6 W. SOYINKA A waiter refills his glass; he downs it.

down /daʊn/ *adv.* & *a.* Superl. DOWNMOST. OE. [Aphet. f. ADOWN.] A *adv.* & (after *be* or other copula) *pred. a.* I Denoting motion or direction in space. 1 In a descending direction; from above, to the ground, to a lower place. OE. 2 To a place regarded as lower in position; e.g. in the direction of a current; with the wind; from the capital to the country; away from university; from the House of Lords to the House of Commons. ME.

1 O. MANNING The bamboo blinds were pulled down. C. P. SNOW She looked down at her plate. M. ROBERTS I go up and down like a seesaw. 2 GOLDSMITH We caught him up accidentally in our journey down. N. MARSH Twenty years ago this month I came down from Cambridge.

II Denoting position in space. 3 In a low or lowered situation or position; on the ground or floor. ME. 4 At a place or in a situation regarded as lower in position; e.g. at a distance from the capital, not at one's university. M19. b = DOWN-STAGE *adv.* L19.

3 M. EDGEWORTH The new carpet is down in the two drawing rooms. 4 F. MARRYAT A gentleman who lived down in Hampshire. R. DAVIES A smile that would have melted . . a lad down from Cambridge.

III Of posture, position, attitude, etc. 5 In or into a fallen, sitting, or overturned posture or position. ME. 6 So as to bring down, reach, or overtake by the action of the vb. M17. 7 Prostrate from illness, esp. *with* (formerly *in*) a specified ailment; ill. E18.

5 D. H. LAWRENCE The minister flushed with confusion and sat down again. E. M. FORSTER All the flats . . might be pulled down, and new buildings . . arise. 6 *pull down, ride down, run down, throw down*, etc. 7 WOODES ROGERS We have now about 50 men down. DAY LEWIS Struck down by some obscure glandular disease.

IV Particular varieties of direction or position. 8 Of the sun, moon, etc.: below the horizon, set. ME. 9 In ref. to (the payment of) a sum of money: (laid) on the table or counter; (paid) on the spot or on the instant. LME. 10 Downstairs; to the ground-floor, basement, etc., from an upper floor or room, *esp.* from one's bedroom or to the dining-room; on a lower floor after getting up and leaving an upstairs bedroom. L16. 11 Down the throat, into the stomach. L16. 12 On paper or other surface used for writing; in writing, in print; in a programme or schedule. L16. 13 Below the surface or to the bottom of the water; into the depths of the sea. Usu. w. *go*. E17. 14 (Filling or to fill spaces) along a vertical line of a crossword puzzle. Usu. following the number of the word or clue (passing into *adj.*). E20.

8 L. BINYON At the going down of the sun and in the morning. 9 P. PORTER A suit . . easily got for two pounds down. 10 D. H. LAWRENCE Presently he came down dressed. D. HALLIDAY Anne-Marie had got breakfast, but no one was down. 11 M. B. KEATINGE Which homely fare they wash down with a spoonful of light wine. 12 T. HARDY When he had jotted down something he went to the telescope again. *Guardian* Angus Wilson . . was down to chair Saturday's session. 13 W. COWPER When Kempenfelt went down With twice four hundred men. 14 R. RENDELL How many letters in fifteen down.

V Of order, time, condition, quality, or value. 15 In or into a position regarded as lower or inferior, a state of subjection, discomfiture, etc. ME. b So as to make silent, submissive, etc., by the action of the vb. L16. c Behind one's opponent or opponents in a game or competition by a stated number of points. L19. 16 From an earlier to a later time. LME. 17 To or at a value, price, or rate that is lower than or no higher than previously. L16. 18 From a roused, excited, distressed, or violent state; in or into a state of calm or quiescence. L16. 19 In or into a state of depression or low spirits or lack of vigour. *colloq.* E17. 20 To a smaller size or bulk, finer particles, or a thinner consistency. M17. 21 In or into a state weaker, milder, or less pronounced in quality. E19. 22 Aware, alert; wise *to*. *arch. slang.* E19. 23 Chiefly *Computing*. Out of action; in or into a state of being unavailable for use. M20.

15 H. REED If the spirit of a nation goes down, its poetry will go down with it. b A. BIRRELL He was immediately frowned down by Mrs. Snagsby. *howl down, shout down*, etc. c H. H. HILTON At the fourteenth hole he was one down. 16 G. BERKELEY Throughout all ages down to our own. O. HENRY They hand it down from one generation to another. 17 W. LONGMAN Employers . . combined to keep down wages. J. STEINBECK Wages went down and prices went up. P. LARKIN His temperature was down this morning nearly a whole point. 18 COLERIDGE Down dropt the breeze. W. S. MAUGHAM Women felt a little irritable at times, but . . they'd calm down after a bit. 19 H. D. THOREAU The Captain is rather down about it, but I tell him to cheer up. L. K. JOHNSON Don't let problems get you down. *Sunday Times* She was looking a little down because she had had . . gastro-enteritis. 20 M. B. KEATINGE Ground down into dust. *boil down, melt down, thin down, water down*, etc. 21 A. GILBERT 'Can't you keep that radio down?' the landlady would implore. *soften down, tone down*, etc. 23 *Times* The computer's down again.

VI 24 With ellipsis of vb of action (esp. *sit*, *lie*), *imper.*, & after aux. vbs. LME.

24 SHAKES. *Coriol.* Down, ladies, let us shame him with our knees. SHELLEY Long live Iona! down with Swellfoot! F. MARRYAT Down, Smoker, good dog! W. H. SMYTH Down oars! . . Down with the helm. R.

BRIDGES That house.. That blocks the way must down.

Phrases: **be down on** (*a*) *arch. slang* understand, be wise to; (*b*) assail, fall upon; (*c*) disapprove of. **cash down** money paid at once, (as though) laid on a counter. *do down*: see DO *v.* **down along** *dial.* & *colloq.* in or to the West Country of England. **down and out** [w. allus. to a boxer who is knocked out] beaten in the struggle of life, completely without resources or means of livelihood. *down at heel*: see HEEL *n.*[1] **down east, Down East** *N. Amer.* (in or into) the north-eastern coastal part of the US (esp. Maine) or the Maritime Provinces of Canada. *down in the dumps*: see DUMP *n.*[1] 2. **down in the mouth** *colloq.* dejected, miserable. *down on one's luck*: see LUCK *n.* **down south** (in or into) the southern part of a country. **down to** (*a*) as far as (the lowest, smallest, least, or last item or member); (*b*) attributable to; (*c*) the responsibility of, up to. *down to earth, down-to-earth*: see EARTH *n.*[1] *down to the ground*: see GROUND *n.* **down under, Down Under** *colloq.* (in or to) the antipodes, Australia or New Zealand. *eyes down*: see EYE *n.* *hands down*: see HAND *n.* *hull down*: see HULL *n.*[2] *let one's hair down*: see HAIR *n.* *thumbs down*: see THUMB *n.* *two-up (and) two-down*: see TWO *n.* 4. *with one's* PANTS *down*. *with one's* TROUSERS *down*.

B *attrib. adj.* **1** Directed downwards; descending. M16. **b** Of a train or coach: travelling away from the capital or principal terminus. Of a line or platform: used by such a train. M19. †**2** Downright, positive. Only in E17. **3** That is in low spirits or poor health; lacking vigour. Now *rare* or *obs.* exc. as *pred. a.* (see DOWN *adv.* 19 above). M17. **b** Causing or characterized by depression or low spirits or lack of vigour. *slang.* M20. **4** Of a crossword clue or answer: that fills or is intended to fill the spaces along a vertical line of the puzzle. Cf. sense A.14 above. E20. **5** *Particle Physics.* Designating a *d* quark. Cf. UP *a.*[1] 6. L20.

3b T. LEARY Alcohol is a 'down' experience. It narrows consciousness and makes you rather sloppy. S. TUROW A down week with a couple of lighter spots.

Special collocations: **down lead** a wire connecting an elevated aerial to a receiver or transmitter. **down payment** an initial payment made at the time that something is bought on credit. **down timber** *N. Amer.* (timber from) fallen trees brought down by wind, storm, or other natural agency. See also DOWN-.

¶In *Particle Physics*, the symbols *d* and *u* (M20) appeared in print earlier than the descriptions *down* and *up* (cf. sense B.5 above).

down /daʊn/ *prep.* LME. [f. DOWN *adv.* Cf. ADOWN *prep.*] **1** In a descending direction along, through, or into; from the top to the bottom of; from a higher to a lower part of. LME. **b** At or in a lower part of. M18. **2** To or at a place regarded as lower than or as a lower part of; along the course or extent of. LME. **3** (Down) to; (down) at. *colloq.* L19.

1 E. BOWEN For two-and-a-half hours, up hill, down dale, they had been rushing through cold scenery. M. AMIS I came down the steps. **b** M. B. KEATINGE In the timbered parts of France, down the Loire. **2** N. COX Some Hares will go up one side of the Hedge, and come down the other. V. WOOLF Endless avenues down which.. he might wander. A. PRICE Paris is only about seventy miles down the road. M. BRADBURY The Kirks.. believe in dividing all tasks equally down the middle, half for you, half for me. **3** A. BUZO Been down the pub for lunch? W. FAULKNER When you are relieved, go down your dugout and stay there. R. RENDELL We've got more.. than they've got down the library.

Phrases: **down cellar** *N. Amer.* in or into the cellar. **down home** *N. Amer.* at or to one's home; see also DOWN-HOME. *down one's street*: see STREET *n.* **down the course** (of a horse) trailing some way behind the leaders in a race; **down the drain, down the pan** *colloq.* lost, wasted. **down the road** *N. Amer. colloq.* in the future, later on. **down the track** *Austral. slang* in the future, later on. **down the tube**(**s**) *colloq.* lost; wasted. **down town** into a town from a higher or outlying part (see also DOWNTOWN). *right down one's street*: see STREET *n.*

down- /daʊn/ *pref.* [Repr. DOWN *adv.*, *prep.*] Prefixed to ns., adjs., and vbs in various relations and in various senses, esp. indicating (*a*) position below, at a lower level (of), or further from the interior or source (of), as *downhole, downrange, downside*; (*b*) motion or direction down, downwards, to a lower level (of), or further away from the interior or source (of), as *down-curved, downpipe, downrate.*

downbow *n.* (*Mus.*) a stroke in which a bow is drawn across a string from the heel to the tip L19. **down-calving** *a.* (of a cow or heifer) near the time of calving L19. **down-'channel** *adv.* & *a.* (moving, leading, etc.) towards the lower end of a channel M19. **downcoast** *a.* & *adv.* (situated, extending, etc.) further down the coast L19. **downcurrent** *n.* a descending current of air or water M19. **down-curved** *a.* curved downwards M20. **down-dip** *a.* & *adv* (situated or occurring) in a direction downwards along the dip E20. **down-draught** *n.* (*a*) *Sc.* a ne'er-do-well, a profligate; a depressing influence; (*b*) a descending current of air, esp. down a chimney into a room: M19. **down-'easter** *n.* (*N. Amer.*) a person who lives or was born Down East E19. **downface** *v.t.* contradict, controvert; browbeat; outwit: E20. **downfault** *v.t.* (*Geol.*) move downwards in faulting M20. **downfold** *n.* (*Geol.*) a syncline E20. **downglide** *n.* (*Phonet.*) a glide from a relatively high tone to a lower one M20. †**down-gyved** *a.* (*rare*, Shakes.) hanging down like fetters: only in E17. **downhaul** *n.* (*Naut.*) a rope by which a sail, spar, or flag is hauled down; a rope that stops the end of a spinnaker boom from lifting: M17. **down-'home** *a.* (chiefly *US*) pertaining to, or reminiscent of, one's home; unaffected, unpretentious: E20. **downlight(er)** *ns.* a light placed or designed to throw illumination downwards M20. **downlink** *n.* a telecommunications link for signals coming from a spacecraft to earth L20. **download** *v.* & *n.* (*Computing*) (*a*) *v.t.* transfer (software or data) to a smaller machine; (*b*) *n.* the action or process of downloading software or data: L20. **downloadable** *a.* (*Computing*) able to be downloaded L20. †**downlooked** *a.* having downward or downcast looks, guilty-looking; demure: M17–E19. **downlooking** *a.* that looks down L18. **downpipe** *n.* a pipe leading downwards, *esp.* one to carry rainwater from a roof to a drain M19. **downplay** *v.t.* play down, make little of M20. **downrange** *adv.* & *a.* (situated or occurring) at a point along the course of a missile, spacecraft, etc., or beyond the (intended) landing-place M20. **down-river** *adv.* & *a.* (*a*) *adv.* at or towards a point nearer the mouth of a river; (*b*) *adj.* situated or occurring down-river: M19. **downset** *n.* †(*a*) *rare* a going down or setting (as) of the sun; (*b*) *Sc.* an establishment, a settlement; (*c*) *rare* a rebuke: E17. **downshift** *n.* & *v.* (*a*) *n.* a movement downwards, *esp.* a change to a lower gear in a motor vehicle; (*b*) *v.i.* make a downshift: M19. **downsize** *v.t.* (chiefly *US*) reduce in size, make in a smaller size L20. **downspout** *n.* (chiefly *US*) a downpipe from a roof L19. **down-'stage** *adv.*, *a.*, & (after preps.) *n.* (at or towards, of or pertaining to) the front of a theatre stage L19. **downstart** *n.* [after *upstart*] a person who has descended to, or falsely claims to originate from, a humble social position L19. **down-street** *adv.* (*colloq.* & *dial.*) down the street; in, into, or towards the lower part of a town: E19. **down-stroke** *n.* a downward stroke, esp. of a pen etc. on paper M19. **downsun** *adv.* & *a.* in a direction away from the sun M20. **down-the-line** *a.* & *n.* (*a*) *adj.* thorough, out and out; (*b*) *a.* & *n.* (designating) trap-shooting in which shooters stand at fixed firing positions along a straight line, and move to the next position on the line after a certain number of shots: M20. **downtime** *n.* (*a*) time, or an occasion, when a machine, computer, or vehicle is out of action or not available for use; (*b*) (an opportunity for) time off; a rest: M20. **down-to-date** *a.* up-to-date L19. **downtoner** *n.* (*Ling.*) an adjective or adverb which reduces the force of what it qualifies, or constitutes a weak or partial denial of it M20. **downturn** *n.* a downward turn, esp. in economic conditions E20. **downwarp** *n.* & *v.* (*Geol.*) (*a*) *n.* a gentle extensive depression of the earth's surface; (*b*) *v.t.* & *i.* (cause to) undergo downwarping: E20. **downwarping** *n.* (*Geol.*) the local sinking of the earth's surface to form a downwarp E20. **downwash** *n.* (*Aeronaut.*) the downward deflection of an air-stream by a wing etc. E20. **down'weigh** *v.t.* weigh down, depress, (*lit.* & *fig.*); outweigh: E17. **downzone** *v.t.* (*US*) rezone (land, property) to a lower, more restrictive zoning grade M20.

down-and-out /ˈdaʊnən(d)aʊt/ *n. colloq.* E20. [f. *down and out* s.v. DOWN *adv.*] A person completely without resources or means of livelihood; a vagrant, a tramp.

HUGH WALPOLE A down-and-out with holes in his boots. R. HARRIES Someone mentally holding her nose whilst coldly dishing out soup to a down-and-out.

Also **down-and-outer** *n.* E20.

downbear /daʊnˈbɛː/ *v.t.* Now *rare.* Pa. t. & pple as BEAR *v.*[1] ME. [f. DOWN- + BEAR *v.*[1]] Bear or press down, cause to sink, (*lit.* & *fig.*).

downbeat /ˈdaʊnbiːt/ *n.* & *a.* L19. [f. DOWN- + BEAT *n.*[2]] **A** *n.* A downward beat; *Mus.* the first or most heavily accented beat of a measure (indicated by a conductor's downward beat). L19. **B** *adj.* Pessimistic, gloomy; relaxed, unemphatic. M20.

downcast /ˈdaʊnkɑːst/ *n.* ME. [f. DOWN- + CAST *n.*[1]] **1** The action of casting down (*lit.* & *fig.*); destruction, ruin; the downward direction of a look; *Geol.* = DOWNTHROW *n.* 2. ME. **2** The introduction of fresh air down a shaft into a mine; a shaft by which this is done (also *downcast shaft*). M19.

downcast /ˈdaʊnkɑːst/ *a.* E17. [Partly f. DOWN- + CAST *ppl a.*, partly as pa. pple of DOWNCAST *v.*] **1** Cast down, destroyed. Chiefly *fig.*, dispirited, depressed. E17. **2** Of a look, the eyes, etc.: directed downwards, lowered. E17.

1 S. T. WARNER He'll get over it..; but just now he's dreadfully downcast. D. LODGE She was a bit downcast by this chilly reception. **2** L. P. HARTLEY Her downcast eyes were bent in an ecstasy of maternal devotion on the doll.

downcast /daʊnˈkɑːst/ *v.t.* Now only *poet.* Pa. t. & pple **downcast**. ME. [f. DOWN- + CAST *v.*] Cast down (*lit.* & *fig.*); destroy, ruin; make dispirited, depress.

downcome /ˈdaʊnkʌm/ *n.* LME. [f. DOWN- + COME *v.*; cf. *income.*] (A) downcoming; a downward swoop by a hawk or falcon.

downcomer /ˈdaʊnkʌmə/ *n.* M19. [f. DOWN- + COMER.] A pipe for conveying gas, steam, etc., down from the top of a furnace or boiler; a downpipe.

downcoming /ˈdaʊnkʌmɪŋ/ *ppl a.* M19. [f. DOWN- + COMING *a.*] That comes down or onwards.

down-coming /ˈdaʊnkʌmɪŋ/ *n.* ME. [f. DOWN- + COMING *n.*] The action or an act of coming down (*lit.* & *fig.*); (a) descent; (a) downfall.

downconverter /ˈdaʊnkənvəːtə/ *n.* M20. [f. DOWN- + CONVERTER.] *Electronics.* A device that downconverts a signal.

downconversion *n.* conversion (of a signal) to a lower frequency, esp. in television reception M20. **downconvert** *v.t.* subject to downconversion M20.

down-country /ˈdaʊnkʌntri, *as adj.* & *adv. also* daʊnˈkʌntri/ *n.*, *a.*, & *adv.* E19. [f. DOWN- + COUNTRY.] **A** *n.* In N. America, Australia, New Zealand, and other countries: *the* flat or low-lying part of the country as opp. to the hilly regions; *the* more densely settled regions. E19. **B** *adj.* Situated in or pertaining to the down-country; (of a person) from the down-country. L19. **C** *adv.* In, into, or towards the down-country. L19.

downed /daʊnd/ *a.* E20. [f. DOWN *v.*[1], *n.*[2]: see -ED[1], -ED[2].] Covered or lined with down.

downer /ˈdaʊnə/ *n.*[1] *colloq.* E20. [f. DOWN *n.*[3] + -ER[6].] = DOWN *n.*[3] 4.

downer /ˈdaʊnə/ *n.*[2] *slang.* M20. [f. DOWN *v.*[2] or *adv.* + -ER[1].] **1** A drug, esp. a barbiturate pill, with a depressant or tranquillizing effect. M20. **2** A depressing person or event; a failure. L20.

downfall /ˈdaʊnfɔːl/ *n.* ME. [f. DOWN- + FALL *n.*[1]] **1** (The cause of) a fall from prosperity, high estate, etc.; a person's ruin. ME. **2** The action of falling down; sudden descent. Now *rare.* LME. **b** A great fall of water; a downpour. E17. **3** A steep descent, a precipice; an abyss, a gulf, a pit. *obs.* exc. *Sc.* M16.

1 W. IRVING The downfall of his great expectations. R. P. GRAVES The.. intellectual arrogance which led to his downfall in Greats. **2** TENNYSON 'Tween the spring and downfall of the light.

downfall /ˈdaʊnfɔːl/ *v.i.* Now chiefly *literary.* Infl. as FALL *v.* ME. [f. DOWN *adv.* + FALL *v.*] Fall down; have a downfall. Chiefly as *downfallen* ppl a., *downfalling* vbl n. & ppl a.

downfield /*as adv.* daʊnˈfiːld, *as adj.* ˈdaʊnfiːld/ *adv.* & *a.* E20. [f. DOWN- + FIELD *n.*] **A** *adv.* **1** *Sport.* = UPFIELD *adv.* 1. E20. **2** *Chem.* & *Physics.* In a direction corresponding to a smaller field strength. M20. **B** *adj.* **1** *Sport.* = UPFIELD *a.* M20. **2** *Chem.* & *Physics.* Situated of occurring in the direction of smaller field strengths. M20.

downgrade /ˈdaʊŋgreɪd/ *n.* Orig. *US.* M19. [f. DOWN- + GRADE *n.*] A downward gradient, esp. on a railway or road; a downward course (*lit.* & *fig.*).

M. RENAULT A steep downgrade for which he had put the car in second. *Sun* (*Baltimore*) Profits are on the downgrade.

downgrade /ˈdaʊŋgreɪd, daʊnˈgreɪd/ *v.t.* M20. [f. the n.] Lower in rank, grade, status, or estimation; demote; belittle.

A. LURIE Kenneth's odd lack of sympathy with people's love affairs.., his tendency to rather downgrade that side of things. *Times* Brokers Laing & Cruickshank.. has now downgraded its estimate for the year from £18m to £15m.

downhearted /daʊnˈhɑːtɪd/ *a.* M17. [f. DOWN *a.* + HEART *n.* + -ED[2].] In low spirits, discouraged, dejected.

downheartedly *adv.* M17. **downheartedness** *n.* E19.

downhill /*as n. & attrib. adj.* ˈdaʊnhɪl; *as adv. & pred. adj.* daʊnˈhɪl/ *n., adv., & a.* M16. [f. DOWN- + HILL *n.*] A *n.* 1 The downward slope of a hill; a decline, a descent, (*lit.* & *fig.*). M16. †2 In *pl.* False dice which give low numbers. *slang.* L17–E19. 3 *Skiing.* A downhill race. M20.

1 **downhill of life** the later half of life.

B *adv.* & *adj.* 1 *adv.* & (after *be* or other copula) *pred. a.* Down a slope, esp. of a hill; in a descending direction; on a decline, downwards, (*lit.* & *fig.*); in a worsening situation; in a situation free of difficulty or impediments. E17. 2 *attrib. a.* Sloping or descending downwards; declining (*lit.* & *fig.*); occurring down a slope, esp. of a hill. E18.

1 E. BOWEN The road coming downhill from the north-west turned south. R. ADAMS A stone rolled downhill. *Gay News* From this point it is downhill all the way: a host of deprivations and disasters. *Guardian* It was downhill from then on, though it actually took a year to secure the country completely. **go downhill** *fig.* deteriorate. 2 J. A. FROUDE The monks had travelled swiftly on the downhill road of human corruption. *Globe & Mail* (*Toronto*) The dangerous downhill pistes of Europe.

downˈhiller *n.* a skier who takes part in downhill races M20.

downhole /*as adj.* ˈdaʊnhəʊl, *as adv.* daʊnˈhəʊl/ *a.* & *adv.* M20. [f. DOWN- + HOLE *n.*[1]] Chiefly *Oil Industry.* A *adj.* Used, occurring, or performed down or in a well or hole drilled in the earth's surface. M20. B *adv.* Down or in a drilled hole or well. M20.

Downing Street /ˈdaʊnɪŋ striːt/ *n. phr.* L18. [A street in London containing the official residence of the Prime Minister and the Foreign and Commonwealth Office, f. Sir George *Downing* (*c*1624–84), Eng. diplomat and owner of the site.] The British Government; the Prime Minister; the Foreign and Commonwealth Office.

downish /ˈdaʊnɪʃ/ *a.* L17. [f. DOWN *a.* + -ISH[1].] Somewhat downcast.

down-lie /daʊnˈlʌɪ/ *v.i.* Now *rare* exc. *north.* E16. [f. DOWN- + LIE *v.*[1]] Lie down, go to bed. Also, be in labour, give birth. Chiefly as *down-lying* vbl n. & ppl a.

down-market /*as adj.* ˈdaʊnmɑːkɪt, *as adv.* daʊnˈmɑːkɪt/ *a.* & *adv.* L20. [f. DOWN- + MARKET *n.*] A *adj.* Of or relating to the cheaper end of the market; cheap, with popular appeal. L20. B *adv.* Towards the cheaper end of the market. L20.

downmost /ˈdaʊnməʊst/ *adv.* & *a.* L18. [f. DOWN *adv.* & *a.* + -MOST.] Furthest down.

downpour /ˈdaʊnpɔː/ *n.* E19. [f. (as) next.] A pouring down; *esp.* a heavy fall of rain.

downpour /daʊnˈpɔː/ *v.i.* & *t.* L18. [f. DOWN- + POUR *v.*] Pour downwards.

J. CARROLL Colman let his hand wind through her downpouring hair.

downrate /daʊnˈreɪt/ *v.t.* M20. [f. DOWN- + RATE *v.*[1]] Reduce the rating of, downgrade; decrease the size, value, or performance of.

downright /ˈdaʊnrʌɪt; *also* (*as following adv.*) daʊnˈrʌɪt/ *adv., a., & n.* ME. [Aphet. f. ADOWNRIGHT.] A *adv.* †1 Straight down; vertically downwards. ME–M18. 2 Thoroughly, absolutely, positively. Usu. foll. by adj. or ppl a. ME. †3 In a direct or straightforward manner; plainly, definitely. Only in 17. †4 At once, immediately. M17–E18.

1 POPE He.. Shot to the black abyss, and plung'd downright. 2 R. FALCONER Killed four downright. D. PIPER When one compromises in art, the results are often artistically mediocre if not downright bad. 3 SHAKES. *A.Y.L.* You have heard him swear downright he was.

B *adj.* 1 Directed straight downwards; vertical; directly descending. M16. 2 That is thoroughly or entirely the thing specified; out-and-out, positive; nothing less than. M16. 3 Plain, definite, straightforward; not circuitous; (of a person's speech or behaviour) so direct as to be blunt. E17.

1 BUNYAN He gave him again a down-right blow, and brought him upon his knees. 2 B. JOWETT He is a downright atheist. B. BETTELHEIM The number of inadequacies and downright errors in the translations is enormous. 3 R. G. COLLINGWOOD Hobbes accepted the same position and stated it, with his usual trenchancy, in a more downright form. H. E. BATES A true downright Evensford character who.. did not care a damn for her or anyone else.

C *n.* †1 A vertical line, a perpendicular. Only in L17. 2 In *pl.* A grade of wool next above seconds in some classifications. L18.

downrightly *adv.* M17. **downrightness** *n.* E17.

down-river /*as adv.* daʊnˈrɪvə, *as adj.* ˈdaʊnrɪvə/ *adv.* & *a.* M19. [f. DOWN- + RIVER *n.*[1]] A *adv.* Away from the source of a river. M19. B *adj.* Situated or occurring further down a river; leading or directed away from the source of a river. L19.

downrush /ˈdaʊnrʌʃ/ *n.* M19. [f. DOWN- + RUSH *n.*[2]] A downward rush; a rapid descent.

Down's /daʊnz/ *n. colloq.* exc. *attrib.* L20. [Abbrev.] = DOWN'S SYNDROME.

downscale /ˈdaʊnskeɪl/ *a.* & *v. US.* M20. [f. DOWN- + SCALE *n.*[4], *v.*[2]] A *adj.* At the lower end of the social scale; of low quality; down-market. M20. B *v.t.* Reduce the scale of, scale down. M20.

downside /ˈdaʊnsʌɪd/ *n., adv., & a.* L17. [f. DOWN- + SIDE *n.*] A *n.* 1 The underside. Only in *downside up.* L17. 2 A risk of falling in value; a downward trend or movement; a negative aspect of something; a drawback. M20.

2 *Times* There is little downside in the shares. *Daily Express* The political downside.. exceeds anything positive that could come out of it. **on the downside** falling in value.

B *adv.* Upside down, downwards. M19.

C *adj.* (At risk of) falling in value; negative in aspect; constituting a drawback. M20.

National Observer (*US*) What is the upside potential contrasted with the downside risk?

downslope /ˈdaʊnsləʊp/ *n., adv., & a.* E20. [f. DOWN- + SLOPE *n.*[1]] A *n.* A downward slope. E20. B *adv.* At or towards a lower point on a slope. E20. C *adj.* Caused by, occurring, or acting on a downward slope; descending. M20.

Downsman /ˈdaʊnzmən/ *n.* Pl. **-men.** E20. [f. DOWN *n.*[1] + -S[1] + MAN *n.*] A man who lives on or is a native of the Sussex Downs.

Down's syndrome /ˈdaʊnz sɪndrəʊm/ *n. phr.* Also **Down syndrome.** /ˈdaʊn sɪndrəʊm/. M20. [J. H. L. *Down*, Eng. physician (1828–96). See also DOWN'S.] A congenital condition (usu. due to an extra chromosome) marked by diminished intelligence, short stature, and a flattened facial profile.

¶The term is much preferred in medical circles to the older *mongolism*, which is now increasingly considered *offensive.*

downstairs /ˈdaʊnstɛːz/ *a.* Also **-stair** /-stɛː/. E19. [f. next.] Situated or occurring downstairs or below stairs.

M. R. MITFORD Her down-stair life was less happy. W. FAULKNER He looked through a downstairs window.

downstairs /daʊnˈstɛːz; *as n. also* ˈdaʊnstɛːz/ *adv.* & *n.* L16. [f. DOWN *prep.* + STAIR + -S[1].] A *adv.* Down the stairs; to, on, or of the ground floor or lower floors of a house etc. L16.

E. WAUGH All I possess.. is downstairs in your hall. E. J. HOWARD To stay downstairs after the others had all gone up to bed.

B *n.* The ground floor or lower floors of a house etc. M19.

New Yorker When the children grew up they would often be given the downstairs to live in.

downstate /ˈdaʊnsteɪt/ *n., adv., & a. US.* E20. [f. DOWN- + STATE *n.*] A *n.* The region of a State remote from large cities, a rural area. E20. B *adv.* In or to the part of a State remote from large cities, esp. the southern part. M20. C *adj.* Of, pertaining to, or characteristic of an area downstate; situated downstate. M20.

downstater *n.* a person from downstate E20.

downstream /*as adv.* daʊnˈstriːm; *as adj.* ˈdaʊnstriːm/ *adv.* & *a.* L18. [f. DOWN- + STREAM *n.*] A *adv.* 1 In the direction in which a stream or river flows. L18. 2 *Biol.* Towards the part of a sequence of genetic material where transcription takes place later than at a given point. Opp. UPSTREAM *adv.* 3. L20. B *adj.* 1 Situated or occurring downstream. M19. 2 *Oil Industry.* Pertaining to, involved in, or designating activities other than exploration and extraction. M20.

down-swept /ˈdaʊnswɛpt/ *a.* E20. [f. DOWN- + SWEPT *ppl a.*] Having a downward sweep, curved downwards.

downswing /ˈdaʊnswɪŋ/ *n.* L19. [f. DOWN- + SWING *n.*[1]] 1 *Golf.* The descending movement of the club when a player is about to hit the ball. L19. 2 (A period marked by) a downward trend, esp. in economic conditions. M20.

Down syndrome *n. phr.* var. of DOWN'S SYNDROME.

downthrow /ˈdaʊnθrəʊ/ *n.* E17. [f. DOWN- + THROW *n.*[2]] 1 A throwing or being thrown down; an overthrow, a downfall. *rare.* E17. 2 *Geol.* The downward movement of strata on one side of a fault; the extent of this. M19.

downthrow /daʊnˈθrəʊ/ *v.* Infl. as THROW *v.* L16. [f. DOWN- + THROW *v.*] 1 *v.t.* Throw down, overthrow; *Geol.* cause to sink in relation to adjacent rocks. L16. 2 *v.i. Geol.* Give rise to a downthrow; sink. L20.

downtown /*as adv.* daʊnˈtaʊn; *as adj. or n.* ˈdaʊntaʊn/ *adv., a., & n.* Chiefly *N. Amer.* E19. [f. DOWN- + TOWN *n.*] A *adv.* In or into the lower or more central part or the business part of a town or city. E19.

R. JAFFE Let's go downtown to the doughnut shop.

B *adj.* Situated or occurring downtown; pertaining to or characteristic of such an area. M19.

B. ULANOV Squalid little towns in downtown New York. M. HOWARD My father.., neat widower in dark downtown suits.

C *n.* The downtown part of a town or city; a downtown area. M19.

Globe & Mail (*Toronto*) A 500 ft. treed property just 18 minutes to downtown. *Billings* (*Montana*) *Gazette* Designers.. have long warned the downtowns were doomed.

downˈtowner *n.* an inhabitant or frequenter of a downtown area M19.

downtrodden /ˈdaʊntrɒd(ə)n/ *a.* & *pa. pple.* M16. [f. DOWN- + TRODDEN.] 1 Trampled down; beaten down (as) by treading. M16. 2 Crushed by oppression or tyranny; oppressed, kept under. L16.

1 LONGFELLOW The flowers, downtrodden by the wind. 2 J. MARTINEAU The downtrodden serfs of Franconia. R. P. GRAVES Although quiet and studious, Alfred was not downtrodden by any of the boys for long.

Also **ˈdowntrod** *a.* & *pa. pple* M16.

downward /ˈdaʊnwəd/ *adv., a., & prep.* ME. [Aphet. f. ADOWNWARD.] A *adv.* 1 = DOWNWARDS 1. ME. 2 = DOWNWARDS 2. ME. 3 = DOWNWARDS 3. E17.

B *adj.* 1 Lying or situated below; lower. *rare.* ME. 2 Directed, moving, extending, pointing, leading, etc., towards what is lower; inclined downward. M16.

1 DRYDEN Aurora.. lights the downward Heav'n. 2 E. A. FREEMAN Steps in a downward scale. T. H. HUXLEY The downward current of the river. *National Observer* (*US*) With our new downward mobility,

the quasi marriage is apt to be a . . college-bred phenomenon.

†C *prep.* = DOWN *prep.* I. *rare.* Only in LME.

downwardly *adv.* (*downwardly*: see MOBILE *a.* 4) M19. **downwardness** *n.* M19.

downwards /ˈdaʊnwədz/ *adv.* LME. [f. prec.: see -WARDS.] **1** Towards a lower place or position; towards what is below; with a descending motion or tendency. LME. **2** Towards something which is lower in order, inferior, or less important. M17. **3** Onward from an earlier to a later time. L19.

1 R. LEHMANN Small, thick writing, . . running downwards on the page. V. WOOLF She ferreted in her bag; then held it up mouth downwards. M. SINCLAIR From his nose and cheek-bones downwards his beard hung straight. 2 *Television* Teletext improvements have to be downwards compatible so that older decoders will receive something recognisable. 3 L. O. PIKE From the time of Glanville downwards.

downwell /*as adj.* ˈdaʊnwɛl, *as adv.* daʊnˈwɛl/ *a.* & *adv.* M20. [f. DOWN- + WELL *n.*[1]] *Oil Industry.* A *adj.* = DOWNHOLE *a.* M20. B *adv.* = DOWNHOLE *adv.* L20.

downwell /daʊnˈwɛl/ *v.i.* M20. [f. DOWN- after *upwell.*] Of seawater etc.: sink in a downward current.

downwelling *n.* downward movement of fluid in the sea or the atmosphere; a downward current: M20.

downwind /daʊnˈwɪnd/ *adv.* & *a.* Also as two wds. E19. [f. DOWN- + WIND *n.*[1]] A *adv.* In the direction of the wind. E19. B *adj.* Occurring or situated downwind. L19.

downy /ˈdaʊni/ *n. slang.* E19. [f. DOWNY *a.*[1]] †**1** A shrewd, sharp, or knowing person. Only in E19. **2** A bed. M19.

2 **do the downy** lie in bed.

downy /ˈdaʊni/ *a.*[1] M16. [f. DOWN *n.*[2] + -Y[1]. In sense 5 also infl. by DOWN *adv.* 22.] **1** Covered with down, esp. as a distinguishing epithet of plants and animals or as connoting youth, immaturity, or innocence. M16. **2** Of the nature of or like down; feathery; fluffy. L16. **3** Made of or containing down. L16. **4** Soft and yielding as down. E17. **5** Shrewd, sharp, knowing. *slang.* E19.

1 H. KELLER Large, downy peaches. R. KIPLING It brought not the faintest flush to Stalky's downy cheek. *downy birch*: see BIRCH *n.* **downy woodpecker** a small black and white woodpecker, *Picoides pubescens*, of N. America. 2 R. H. DANA Thick downy feathers, taken from the breasts of various birds. S. ANDERSON His eyebrows, and the downy beard . . were pale. **downy mildew** mildew marked by a whitish down composed of fungal sporangiophores or conidiophores and penetrating more deeply into the plant than powdery mildew; a lower fungus of the family Peronosporaceae which causes this. 3 POPE Belinda still her downy pillow prest. 4 E. YOUNG Time steals on with downy Feet. 5 M. E. BRADDON You're the downiest bird—I beg your pardon, the cleverest woman I ever met with.

downily *adv.* (*rare*) M19. **downiness** *n.* L17.

downy /ˈdaʊni/ *a.*[2] L17. [f. DOWN *n.*[1] + -Y[1].] Of the nature of a down or downland; characterized by downs.

J. L. MOTLEY A rolling, downy country.

dowry /ˈdaʊ(ə)ri/ *n.* ME. [AN *dowarie* = (O)Fr. *douaire* DOWER.] †**1** = DOWER *n.* I. ME–M19. **2** Property or money brought by a bride to her husband; the portion given with the bride. LME. **3** A present made by a man to the father of his prospective bride as a condition of her being allowed to marry. Formerly, a present given by one spouse to the other. LME. **4** = DOWER *n.* 3. LME. †**5** The property or endowment of a church. LME–L15.

dowryless *a.* E20.

Dowsabel /ˈdaʊsəbɛl/ *n.* Long *arch.* L16. [Alt. (through Fr.) of female forename *Dulcibella.*] A sweetheart, a pet. Freq. as a form of address.

dowse /daʊz/ *v.*[1]*i.* L17. [Origin unkn.] Search for hidden water, mineral deposits, etc., by passing a forked stick or rod over the surface of the ground under which it is hoped to find them, so that it might dip suddenly when brought over the right spot.

Comb.: **dowsing-rod** a forked stick or rod which is held in the hands and passed over the surface of the ground in dowsing; also called *divining-rod.*

dowser *n.* a person who dowses, or has the gift of dowsing M19.

dowse *v.*[2] var. of DOUSE *v.*[1]

dowset *n.* var. of DOUCET *n.*

dowt *v.* & *n.* see DOUT.

doxographer /dɒkˈsɒɡrəfə/ *n.* L19. [f. Gk *doxa* opinion + -O- + -GRAPHER.] A writer who collected and recorded the opinions of the ancient Greek philosophers.

doxoˈgraphic *a.* of or pertaining to (the work of) a doxographer or the doxographers M20. **doxoˈgraphical** *a.* = DOXOGRAPHIC L19. **doxography** *n.* the branch of knowledge that deals with doxographic writings; a collection of doxographic writings: M20.

doxology /dɒkˈsɒlədʒi/ *n.* Also **D-**. M17. [med. L *doxologia* f. Gk, f. *doxa* expectation, opinion, repute, glory, f. *dokein*: see DOCETIC, -OLOGY.] *Chr. Ch.* †**1** The utterance of praise to God, thanksgiving. Only in M17. **2** A liturgical formula of praise to God. M17.

2 *Daily Telegraph* The doxology which has been commonly added to the Lord's Prayer since the second century. **Greater Doxology** the *Gloria in excelsis*. **Lesser Doxology** the *Gloria Patri.*

doxoˈlogical *a.* pertaining to or of the nature of a doxology M17. **doxoˈlogically** *adv.* L19. **doxologize** *v.* (*a*) *v.i.* say a doxology; (*b*) *v.t.* address a doxology to: E18.

doxorubicin /dɒksəʊˈruːbɪsɪn/ *n.* L20. [f. D(E)OX(Y- + -O- + L *rubus* red + -I- + -MY)CIN.] An antibiotic produced by a streptomycete and used to treat leukaemia and various tumours, including cancer.

doxy /ˈdɒksi/ *n.*[1] *literary* or *joc.* (orig. *slang*). M16. [Origin unkn.] Orig., a beggar's wench. Now, a mistress; a prostitute; a promiscuous woman; *dial.* a girlfriend.

doxy /ˈdɒksi/ *n.*[2] *arch. joc.* M18. [f. *orthodoxy*, *heterodoxy*, etc.] Opinion, esp. on theological matters.

doxycycline /dɒksɪˈsʌɪkliːn/ *n.* M20. [f. D(E)OXY- + TETRA)CYCLINE.] A broad-spectrum antibiotic of the tetracycline group which has a long half-life in the body.

doyen /ˈdɔɪən, ˈdwɑːjã/ *n.* LME. [Fr.: see DEAN *n.*[1]] †**1** A leader or commander of ten. *rare.* Only in LME. **2** The most senior or most prominent of a particular category or body of people. L17.

2 C. R. ATTLEE Smuts was the doyen and the only one of us who had taken part in the conduct of the First World War. J. GROSS Saintsbury had become generally accepted as the doyen of academic critics, the nearest thing to a Critic Laureate.

Doyenne /dwɑːˈjɛn/ *n.*[1] Also **Doyenné** /dwɑːˈjɛneɪ/. M18. [Fr. (*poire de*) *doyenné* deanery (pear), f. as prec.] Any of several varieties of dessert pear.

Doyenne du Comice /duː kɒˈmiːs/ [Fr.: see COMICE] a large yellow late-fruiting variety of dessert pear that is a favourite for cultivation.

doyenne /ˈdɔɪɛn, dɔɪˈɛn, dwɑːˈjɛn/ *n.*[2] M19. [Fr., fem. of DOYEN.] A female doyen.

doyley *n.* var. of DOILY.

doylt *a.* var. of DOILED.

doyly *n.* var. of DOILY.

doz. /dʌz/ *n.* L19. [Abbrev.] = DOZEN *n.*

doze /dəʊz/ *v.*[1] & *n.* M17. [Origin unkn.: perh. earlier in dial. Cf. Da. *døse* make drowsy.] A *v.* **1** *v.t.* Stupefy, muddle; make drowsy or dull; bewilder, perplex. *obs.* exc. *Sc. dial.* M17. **2** *v.i.* Sleep drowsily, be half asleep; fall into a light sleep. L17. **3** *v.t.* Foll. by *away*, *out*: pass or spend (time) in dozing. L17.

1 DEFOE The tobacco had . . dozed my head. 2 R. B. SHERIDAN I have been dozing over a stupid book. M. SHADBOLT He dozed uneasily, in fits and starts. **doze off** fall lightly asleep.

B *n.* A spell of dozing; a short light sleep. M18.

dozed *ppl a.* (*a*) stupefied, drowsy; (*b*) (of timber) decayed inside: M17. **dozedness** *n.* (now *rare*) drowsiness, sleepiness M17.

doze /dəʊz/ *v.*[2]*t. colloq.* M20. [Back-form. f. DOZER *n.*[2]] Clear, level, or move, with a bulldozer; use a bulldozer on.

dozen /ˈdʌz(ə)n/ *n.* & *a.* (in mod. usage functioning like a *determiner*). ME. [OFr. *dozeine*, *-aine* (mod. *douzaine*) f. Proto-Romance, ult. f. L *duodecim* twelve.] A *n.* Pl. same (after a numeral or quantifier), **-s.** **1** A group or set of twelve or *colloq.* approximately twelve (*of* a particular class). ME. **b** In *pl.* As many as might number a few dozen; a lot *of. colloq.* M18. **c** A dozen lashes of the whip. M19. **d** *the dozens*, an exchange of insults, usu. about the other person's mother or family, engaged in as a game or ritual among US Blacks. Freq. in *play the dozens.* E20. †**2** A kind of kersey. Usu. in *pl.* LME–E18. †**3** The town council of a borough. *Sc.* LME–L16.

1 D. L. SAYERS And another dozen of Bass while it settles. G. B. SHAW She wants him to buy her another dozen. W. FAULKNER A face, then three, then a dozen, turned to look at him. *a dime a dozen*: see DIME 2. *baker's dozen*: see BAKER. **by the dozen** in large quantities. **daily dozen** *colloq.* physical exercises done daily on rising. **devil's dozen** thirteen. *half a dozen*: see HALF *a.* *half-dozen*: see HALF-. **long dozen** thirteen. *rump and dozen*: see RUMP *n.* *talk nineteen to the dozen*: see TALK *v.* **b** D. H. LAWRENCE Dozens of men were lounging round the cart.

B *adj.* After an article, numeral, or quantifier: twelve. LME.

M. AYRTON There are a dozen small bronzes.

dozenth *a.* twelfth E18.

dozen /ˈdəʊz(ə)n/ *v.i.* *Sc.* & *north.* E18. [Back-form. f. next.] Become torpid, numb, or stiff with cold.

dozened /ˈdəʊz(ə)nd/ *a.* *Sc.* & *north.* LME. [Origin unkn.] **1** Stupefied, dazed. LME. **2** Torpid; numb; stiff with cold. L16.

dozener /ˈdʌz(ə)nə/ *n.* M16. [Prob. f. AN *doseyner* f. *dizeiner*, OFr. *disenier* (mod. *dizenier*) leader of ten (cf. DECENER), f. (O)Fr. DIX + *-ain* f. L *-eni*: see -ER[2].] *Hist.* The constable or other officer of a borough in some localities.

dozer /ˈdəʊzə/ *n.*[1] E18. [f. DOZE *v.*[1] + -ER[1].] A person who dozes.

dozer /ˈdəʊzə/ *n.*[2] *colloq.* M20. [Abbrev.] = BULLDOZER.

dozy /ˈdəʊzi/ *a.* & *n.* L17. [f. DOZE *v.*[1] + -Y[1].] A *adj.* **1** Sleepy, drowsy; *colloq.* slow on the uptake, stupid, lazy. L17. **2** Of timber or fruit: in a state of incipient decay. L19. B *n.* A dozy person. *colloq.* M19.

dozily *adv.* M19. **doziness** *n.* L17.

dozzle /ˈdɒz(ə)l/ *n.* M20. [Origin unkn.] A hollow refractory brick fitted to the top of an ingot-mould to provide a reservoir of molten metal, which flows downward to fill cavities in the ingot.

Also **dozzler** *n.* E20.

dozzle /ˈdɒz(ə)l/ *v.t.* Long *obs.* exc. *dial.* M17. [Frequent. of DOZE *v.*[1]: see -LE[3].] Make stupid; stupefy.

drab /drab/ *n.*[1] E16. [Perh. f. Du. or LG; cf. Du. *drab* dregs, LG *drabbe* thick dirty liquid, *drabbig* muddy. Cf. DRABBLE.] **1** A dirty untidy woman; a slut, a slattern. E16. **2** A prostitute. *arch.* M16.

1 BETTY SMITH He was so handsome that Francie felt like a dark drab alongside of him.

drabbish *a.*[1] (*rare*) sluttish M16. **drabby** *a.*[1] pertaining to or of the nature of a drab; frequented by drabs: E17.

drab /drab/ *n.*[2] & *a.* M16. [Prob. alt. of OFr. *drap* cloth: see DRAPE *v.* Cf. DRAP-DE-BERRY.] A *n.* I **1** Any of various undyed cloths of a dull neutral colour. M16.

II [absol. use of the adj.] **2** A dull light brown colour; cloth or clothing, *esp.* (in *pl.*) breeches, of this colour. E19. **3** Any of various dull-coloured moths. E19. **4** In *pl.* The long wing-feathers of a female ostrich near the junction with the body. *S. Afr.* L19. **5** A dull or lifeless character or appearance; monotony. E20.

2 M. R. MITFORD Woe to white gowns! Woe to black! Drab was your only wear. 5 *Westminster Gazette* The one sustained note of colour in the dreary drab of Irish life.

B *adj.* Compar. & superl. **-bb-**. **1** Of a dull light brown colour. L18. **2** Dull, monotonous; lacking brightness or colour. L19.

1 G. DOWNES The cottages . . were of a deep drab hue. 2 J. BUCHAN Sansculottes who sought to . . reduce the great to a drab level of mediocrity. A. EDEN

In the cold and rain of mid-winter the prospect was drab and dour.

drabbiness *n.* the state or quality of being drabby L19. **drabbish** *a.*[2] somewhat drab in colour or appearance M19. **drabby** *a.*[2] rather drab, drabbish M19. **drably** *adv.* L19. **drabness** *n.* L19.

drab /drab/ *n.*[3] Long *rare.* M18. [Origin unkn.] A wooden case with a sloping bottom in which the remaining liquid was separated from salt after boiling.

drab /drab/ *n.*[4] E19. [Perh. redupl. of DRIB *n.*] A small or petty amount. Chiefly in *dribs and drabs* (see DRIB *n.*).

drab /drab/ *v.i. arch.* Infl. **-bb-**. L16. [f. DRAB *n.*[1]] Associate with prostitutes, whore.

draba /'dreɪbə/ *n.* Also **D-**. E17. [mod.L f. Gk *drabē* kind of cress.] Any cruciferous plant of the genus *Draba*, comprising spring-flowering alpines.

drabant /drə'bant/ *n. obs.* exc. *Hist.* E18. [Sw. (= G *Trabant*, It. *trabante*, Fr. *traban*, *draban*, Czech & Pol. *drabant*, Hungarian *darabont*, Romanian *dorobant*) ult. f. Turk. *derban* f. Pers. *darbān* porter, guard. Cf. TRABANT.] A halberdier; a member of the Swedish monarch's bodyguard.

drabbet /'drabɪt, drə'bɛt/ *n.* E19. [f. DRAB *n.*[2] + -ET[1].] A coarse drab linen formerly used for workmen's clothes.

drabble /'drab(ə)l/ *v.i.* & *t.* LME. [LG *drabbelen* walk or paddle in water or mire: cf. DRAB *n.*[1], -LE[3].] Become or make dirty and wet by contact with water or mud.

R. KIPLING The sad valleys all drabbled with rain.

drabbler /'drablə/ *n.* Also **drabler**. L16. [f. DRABBLE *v.*: see -ER[1].] *Naut.* An additional length of canvas laced to the foot of a bonnet to give even greater area of sail.

†**drab-de-Berry** *n.* var. of DRAP-DE-BERRY.

drabi /'drabi/ *n.* E20. [Alt. of DRIVER.] In the Indian subcontinent: a muleteer.

drabler *n.* var. of DRABBLER.

drac *n.* var. of DRACH.

dracaena /drə'siːnə/ *n.* E19. [mod.L f. Gk *drakaina* fem. of *drakōn* DRAGON.] Any of numerous shrubs and trees of the agave family that belong to the genera *Dracaena* and *Cordyline* and are grown for their ornamental foliage.

drach /drak/ *n. colloq.* Also **drac(k)**. M20. [Abbrev.] = DRACHMA 4.

drachm /dram/ *n. arch.* LME. [OFr. *dragme* or late L *dragma* var. of L DRACHMA. Cf. DRAM *n.*[1]] 1 = DRACHMA 2. Now *rare* or *obs.* LME. b = DIRHAM. Now *rare* or *obs.* M16. 2 A unit of weight orig. equal to the weight of a drachma; an apothecaries' weight of ⅛ ounce (60 grains); an avoirdupois weight of $^1/_{16}$ ounce (approx. 27.344 grains). Also = *fluid drachm* s.v. FLUID *a.* LME. 3 *fig.* A small quantity. LME.

3 T. HARDY 'Now do you see the truth?' she whispered . . without a drachm of feeling.

drachma /'drakmə/ *n.* Pl. **-mas**, **-mae** /-miː/. E16. [L f. Gk *drakhmē* an Attic weight and coin. Cf. prec., DRAM *n.*[1]] 1 = DRACHM 2. Now *rare* or *obs.* E16. 2 *Hist.* The principal silver coin of ancient Greece. L16. 3 *Hist.* The ancient Jewish quarter-shekel. L16. 4 The basic monetary unit of modern Greece, equal to 100 lepta; a coin of this value. L19.

drack *n.* var. of DRACH.

drack /drak/ *a. Austral. slang.* M20. [Perh. f. (as) DRACULA, but cf. DRECK.] Unattractive, uninteresting, inferior.

drackly /'drakli/ *adv. dial.* L19. [Alt. of DIRECTLY.] *drackly minute*, at once; *the* or *this* very minute (*that*).

Draco /'dreɪkəʊ/ *n.* L17. [L: see DRAGON.] (The name of) a constellation of the northern hemisphere between Ursa Minor and Hercules.

dracocephalum /drakə'sɛf(ə)ləm/ *n.* M19. [mod.L, f. Gk *drakōn* DRAGON + *kephalē* head.] Any plant of the genus *Dracocephalum* of the mint family, comprising annual and perennial plants with spikes or racemes of flowers.

dracone /'drakəʊn/ *n.* M20. [Gk *drakōn* DRAGON.] A large flexible sausage-shaped container for liquids, to be towed on the surface of the sea.

draconian /drə'kəʊnɪən, dreɪ-/ *a.* Also **D-**. L19. [f. Gk *Drakōn* Draco (see below) + -IAN.] Of, pertaining to, or characteristic of the supposed Athenian legislator Draco (fl. *c*620 BC) or the severe penal code attributed to him; harsh, cruel; severe, strict.

S. RUSHDIE The threat . . could never be eliminated unless he . . were empowered to take draconian punitive measures. R. C. A. WHITE Failure to respond has draconian consequences.

draconic /drə'kɒnɪk, dreɪ-/ *a.* L17. [Partly f. Gk *drakōn* DRAGON, partly f. as prec.: see -IC.] 1 Of, pertaining to, or of the nature of, a dragon. L17. 2 (Also **D-**.) = DRACONIAN. E18. 3 *Astron.* [Cf. DRAGON *n.* 7.] *draconic month*, *period*, the period of 27.2122 days between successive passages of the moon through the ascending or the descending node. L19.

draconically *adv.* in a draconian manner, rigorously, severely M17.

Draconid /'dreɪkənɪd/ *n.* & *a.* E20. [f. L DRACO (see also DRAGON) + -ID[3].] *Astron.* (Designating) any of a shower of meteors seeming to radiate from the constellation Draco in October in some years, associated with Comet Giacobini–Zinner. Also called *Giacobinid*.

draconites /drakə'nʌɪtiːz/ *n.* L15. [L *draconitis*, f. as prec.] A fabled precious stone supposed to have been formed in the brain of a dragon.

dracontiasis /drakɒn'tʌɪəsɪs/ *n.* Pl. **-ases** /-əsiːz/. L19. [f. Gk *drakontion* Guinea worm + -IASIS.] *Med.* The condition of having a Guinea worm or its larvae inside the body.

dracontine /drə'kɒntʌɪn/ *a. rare.* E19. [f. as prec. + -INE[1].] = DRACONIC 1.

Dracula /'drakjʊlə/ *n.* M20. [Count *Dracula*, a Transylvanian vampire king depicted in Bram Stoker's novel *Dracula* of 1897.] A person of grotesque, terrifying, and savage character.

dracunculus /drə'kʌŋkjʊləs/ *n.* Pl. **-li** /-lʌɪ, -liː/. E17. [L, f. as DRACONID + *-culus* -CULE.] 1 = DRAGON 10. *rare.* E17. 2 The Guinea worm. E18. 3 = DRAGONET 2. M18.

dracunculiasis /-'lʌɪəsɪs/ *n.*, pl. **-ases** /-əsiːz/, = DRACONTIASIS M20. **dracuncu'losis** *n.*, pl. **-loses** /-'ləʊsiːz/, = DRACONTIASIS M20.

draegerman /'dreɪgəmən/ *n. N. Amer.* Pl. **-men**. E20. [f. A. B. Dräger (1870–1928), Ger. inventor of a type of breathing apparatus, + MAN *n.*] A member of a crew trained for underground rescue work.

draff /draf/ *n.* ME. [Perh. repr. an OE wd = MLG, MDu. *draf*, OHG pl. *trebir* (G *Treber*, *Träber* husks, grains), also rel. to ON *draf* draff, husks, Norw. *drav* mash. Perh. rel. to DRIVEL *v.*] Dregs, lees; refuse; *esp.* the grains of malt left after brewing or distilling.

fig.: MILTON The brood of Belial, the draffe of men.

Comb.: **draffsack** (now *dial.*) a sack of draff; *fig.* a big paunch; a lazy glutton.

draffy *a.* full of dregs or draff; worthless: E17.

draft /drɑːft/ *n.* & *a.* M16. [Repr. mod. pronunc. of DRAUGHT *n.*] A *n.* I 1 *gen.* = DRAUGHT *n.* Now chiefly *N. Amer.* M16.

II *spec.* 2 A plan, a drawing, *esp.* one showing work to be executed. Formerly also, a chart. (Earlier as DRAUGHT *n.* 26 and in DRAFTSMAN 1.) L17. 3 A preliminary version or rough form of something to be written or printed, esp. an official document. (Earlier as DRAUGHT *n.* 25.) M18. 4 The turn of a balance as the lighter side becomes the heavier; a deduction from gross weight allowed for this. (Earlier as DRAUGHT *n.* 12.) Now *rare.* M18. 5 The drawing off or selection of a detachment (esp. of livestock or troops) from a larger group for a special duty or purpose; *US* selective conscription. Also, a group or individual selected in this way; a contingent, a reinforcement. (Earlier as DRAUGHT *n.* 16.) L18. b In full *draft ewe*. A ewe selected from a flock. M19. 6 The drawing of money by a written order; a bill or cheque drawn, esp. by one branch of a bank on another. (Earlier as DRAUGHT *n.* 15.) L18. b *fig.* A demand or claim made *on* a person's friendship, confidence, etc. M19. 7 A groove near the edge of a stone to serve as a guide for a stone-cutter. (Earlier as DRAUGHT *n.* 28.) L19.

3 R. WEST An ordinary swan or goose quill for the rough draft, and for his fair copy the crow quill. B. CASTLE The original draft of the industrial policy White Paper had been pretty unsatisfactory. 5 WELLINGTON If the bullocks are not occasionally recruited by drafts of fresh calves. J. T. ADAMS There was no draft, there were only . . volunteers. *attrib.*: *Listener* Students . . were protesting against the war by turning in their draft cards. 6 G. J. GOSCHEN Teas shipped from China . . are generally paid for by a draft . . on a London merchant.

B *attrib.* or as *adj.* 1 = DRAUGHT *a.* 1, 2. Now chiefly *US.* E17. 2 Prepared as a draft. L19.

draft /drɑːft/ *v.t.* E18. [Partly f. the n., partly repr. pronunc. of DRAUGHT *v.*] 1 Remove or select (esp. livestock or troops) from a larger body for a special purpose; *US* conscript (*lit.* & *fig.*); persuade or force (a reluctant person) to stand for office. E18. 2 Make a draft of (something to be written etc.); draw up in a preliminary form. (Earlier as DRAUGHT *v.* 1.) E19. 3 Cut a draft on (a stone). Chiefly as *drafted* pa. pple. (Earlier as DRAUGHT *v.* 3.) L19.

1 E. J. HOWARD I volunteered for the army and got drafted into the Royal Corps of Signals. G. BOYCOTT A practice match . . with local builders drafted in as reinforcements. N. PODHORETZ With conscription still in effect . . I was certain to be drafted. 2 V. CRONIN She drafted ukases, directives, projects, memoranda. . . A secretary . . corrected misspellings. P. THEROUX A Patagonian lawyer who had helped to draft the legal aspects of the treaty.

draf'tee *n.* (*US*) a conscript M19. **drafter** *n.* (*a*) a person employed in drafting livestock; (*b*) a person who prepares preliminary drafts; a draftsman; (*c*) a draught horse; a horse used in drafting livestock: E19.

draftsman /'drɑːf(t)smən/ *n.* Pl. **-men**. M17. [f. DRAFT *n.* + -'S[1] + MAN *n.* Cf. DRAUGHTSMAN.] 1 = DRAUGHTSMAN 1. Now chiefly *N. Amer.* M17. 2 A person who drafts or draws up a document, esp. a legal clause or a parliamentary bill. M18.

draftsmanship *n.* the function, quality, or art of a draftsman; skill in drafting documents etc.; (cf. DRAUGHTSMANSHIP): L19.

†**drafty** *a.*[1] L16–E19. [Origin unkn.] Rubbishy, filthy, (*lit.* & *fig.*).

drafty *a.*[2] see DRAUGHTY *a.*

drag /drag/ *n.* ME. [Partly f. the vb, partly f. MLG *dragge* grapnel. See also DRUG *n.*[2]] 1 *Agric.* a A heavy harrow used for breaking up the surface of land. ME. b Any of several implements with prongs or claws. L18. 2 A drag-net; an apparatus for dragging a river etc. or for dredging. ME. 3†a A raft. LME–E17. b A sledge. L16. c Any wheeled vehicle. Now *spec.* (*a*) *Hist.* a private horse-drawn coach like a stagecoach; (*b*) *slang* a motor car. M18. d More fully *drag race*. A motor race run over a straight ¼ mile as a test of acceleration, usu. between two cars at a time. M20. 4 A hook with which something is dragged. *obs.* exc. *dial.* L15. 5 Something that impedes movement; *spec.* an iron shoe that can be applied to a wheel as a brake. E18. b The force resisting the motion of a body through a liquid or gas. E20. 6 *Hunting.* a The scent left by a fox or other hunted animal; a strong-smelling lure for hounds in place of this. M18. b A hunt following an artificial drag; a club that organizes such hunts. Also *drag hunt*. E19. 7†a The robbery of a vehicle. *slang.* L18–E19. b A prison sentence of three months. *slang.* M19. 8 The action or fact of dragging; forcible motion or progress against resistance. E19. 9 A boring or dreary person or event. E19. 10 The slow-moving part of a herd on a cattle-drive. M19. 11 A street, *esp.* (also *main drag*) the principal street of a town. *slang.* M19. 12 Women's clothes as worn by a man; (less commonly) men's clothes as worn by a woman; a party at which such clothes are worn; *gen.* clothes. Freq. in *in drag*. L19. 13 A relationship where a person has influence over someone; influence. *US slang.* L19. 14 An inhalation of smoke from a cigarette etc.; a spell of smoking a cigarette etc. *slang.*

E20. **15** *Mus.* A drum-stroke consisting of two or more grace-notes preceding a beat. E20. **16** (Music for) a kind of slow dance. *US.* E20.

5 *fig.*: I. ZANGWILL She was a drag on his career. 6 LD RAVENSWORTH His bloodhounds sniff the drag Of . . antlered stag. 8 H. ALLEN The ship . . began to drift down the river, . . gathering way as the drag of the ebb became heavier. 9 J. DIDION Doris Jeanne thought California was strictly a drag. 12 *Listener* Laurence Olivier, doing his Othello voice and attired . . in Arab drag. A. BEATTIE He . . acted in a porn film about the war, in drag. 13 G. ADE He knows I've got a drag in the precinct. J. T. FARRELL He grew up with guys who got plenty of drag in this town. 14 D. LODGE Another joint was circulating, and this time Philip took a drag or two.

Comb.: **drag act** an act by a drag artist or drag artists; **drag anchor** = SEA *anchor*; **drag artist** a performer in a variety show etc. who appears in drag; **drag-chain** (*a*) a chain used to retard the motion of a vehicle; *fig.* a check, a hindrance; (*b*) a strong chain for coupling railway vehicles; **drag-hook** (*a*) a hook used for dragging; (*b*) a hook on the end of a drag-chain; **drag-hound** a hound used for drag-hunting; *drag-hunt*: see sense 6b above; **drag-hunting** the sport of following with hounds the trail supplied by an artificial drag; **drag-line** a rope by which a bucket or grab is drawn towards an excavator; (also *drag-line excavator*) an excavator with this; **drag queen** *slang* a male homosexual transvestite; *drag race*: see sense 3d above; **drag-racing** the holding of or participation in drag races; **drag-rope** a rope used for haulage; **drag saw**: with which the effective stroke is given by the pull rather than by the thrust; **drag-staff** *Hist.* a trailing pole hinged to the rear of a coach etc. to check backward movement when stopped on a steep slope; **drag-strut** *Aeronaut.* a strut used to strengthen a wing against forces arising from drag.

drag /drag/ *v.* Infl. **-gg-**. LME. [ON *draga* or obscurely developed f. OE *dragan*: see DRAW *v.*] **I 1** *v.t.* Draw or pull along with force, difficulty, or friction; allow (the feet, a tail, etc.) to trail along the ground. LME. **b** Of a ship: trail (an anchor) along the seabed after it has come adrift. L17. **c** Foll. by adv. or prep.: take or escort (a person) to or away from a place or event despite his or her reluctance. *colloq.* L18. **2** *v.i.* Hang back with a retarding tendency; lag behind, esp. in singing or playing. E16. **3** *v.i.* Trail or hang under its own weight while being moved; (of a door) catch on the ground. M17. **4** *v.t.* Protract, prolong, or continue tediously. Now usu. foll. by *out.* L17. **5** *v.i.* Advance or progress slowly and painfully; be tediously prolonged; become tedious by protraction. Freq. foll. by *on.* M18. **6** *v.i.* Suck *on* or *at* a cigarette etc. to draw in the smoke. *colloq.* E20.

1 T. WILLIAMS She has dragged her wardrobe trunk into the centre of the bedroom. *fig.*: J. T. STORY All this is going to be dragged through a coroner's court. *drag ass*: see ARSE *n.* 1. **drag one's feet** or **heels** *fig.* be deliberately slow or reluctant in accomplishing or proceeding with something. **drag the chain** *Austral.* & *NZ slang* work slowly or lazily, lag behind others. **drag through the mud** publish unpleasant information or allegations about. c J. BENTHAM I have to regret being the cause . . of dragging you out thus early. J. CANNAN I was dragged to an Old Tyme Dance in the Town Hall. 2 OED The quartet was not sung in time, the tenor dragged. 3 W. GOLDING He . . limped forward, left foot dragging a little. 5 G. GISSING Winter dragged to its end. ANNE STEVENSON Schoolgirls dragging in crocodile/through the damp lanes.

II 7 *v.t.* Catch by means of a drag-net or dredging. LME. **8** *v.t.* & *i.* Draw a drag-net, grapnel, etc., along the bed of (a river etc.) to clear it or free objects; search in this way for a body. M16. **9** *v.t.* Break up the surface of (land) with a drag or heavy harrow. E18. **10** *v.t.* Put a drag on (a wheel or vehicle); impede in this way. E19. **11** *v.t.* Rob (a vehicle). *slang.* E19. **12** *v.i.* Race a motor vehicle, take part in a drag race. *N. Amer.* M20.

8 J. FOWLES The police were going to drag the ponds.

With advs. in specialized senses: **drag in** introduce (a topic) in a forced manner or needlessly. **drag up** *colloq.* (*a*) rear (a child) roughly and without proper training (freq. in *pass*); (*b*) deliberately mention (a subject or event, usu. unpleasant, that is generally forgotten or ignored).

dragger *n.* L15. **draggingly** *adv.* slowly and with difficulty L19.

†dragant *n.* Also **dragagant**. ME–E18. [OFr. f. L *tragacantha*: see TRAGACANTH. Cf. ADRAGANT.] Tragacanth.

dragée /ˈdrɑːʒeɪ; *foreign* draʒe (*pl. same*)/ *n.* L17. [Fr.: see DREDGE *n.*[1]] A sweet consisting of a centre covered with some coating, *esp.* a sugared almond etc. or a chocolate; a small silver-coated sugar ball for use in cake decoration; a sweet used as a vehicle for a medicine or drug. Formerly also, a mixture of spices etc. Cf. DREDGE *n.*[1] 1.

drageoir /draʒwaːr/ *n.* Pl. pronounced same. M19. [Fr., f. as prec.] A box for holding sweets.

draggle /ˈdrag(ə)l/ *v.* E16. [Dim. & frequent. of DRAG *v.*: see -LE[3].] **1** *v.t.* Make dirty, untidy, and usu. wet, esp. by trailing through something. E16. **2** *v.i.* Trail on the ground; hang trailing or untidily. L16. **3** *v.i.* Come on or follow slowly; lag; straggle in the rear. L16.

1 CARLYLE The wet day draggles the tricolor. T. HARDY Lifting her skirts to avoid draggling them in the white dust. S. LEACOCK All draggled with the mud and rain he stood. R. MACAULAY Her draggled hair drooping like dark seaweed round her face.

draggle-tail /ˈdrag(ə)lteɪl/ *n.* & *a.* L16. [f. prec. + TAIL *n.*[1]] **A** *n.* **1** A bedraggled person or animal; *esp.* (*arch.*) a woman with draggled or untidily trailing skirts, a slut. L16. **2** In *pl.* Skirts that trail on the ground. *arch.* M19.

1 SWIFT What a draggletail she will be before she gets to Dublin.

B *attrib.* or as *adj.* Draggle-tailed; draggled. E17.

A. CARTER In the long, rank, soaking grass among draggletail dog-daisies.

draggle-tailed *a.* that is a draggle-tail; *arch.* sluttish: M17. **draggle-tailedness** *n.* L19.

draggly /ˈdragli/ *a.* M19. [f. DRAGGLE *v.* + -Y[1].] Inclined to draggle.

draggy /ˈdragi/ *a.* L19. [f. DRAG *v.* + -Y[1].] **1** Inclined to drag or cause dragging; heavy; slow; lacking liveliness. L19. **2** Tedious; boring. *colloq.* E20.

dragginess *n.* L19.

drag-net /ˈdragnet/ *n.* M16. [f. DRAG *n.* + NET *n.*[1] Cf. OE *drægnet*, Sw. *draggnot*; also DRAY *n.*[1]] A net drawn through a river or across ground to trap fish or game; *fig.* a means of systematically discovering criminals or criminal activity.

dragoman /ˈdragə(ʊ)mən/ *n.* Pl. **-mans, -men**. LME. [Obs. Fr. (now *drogman*) f. It. *dragomanno* f. med.Gk *dragoumanos* f. Arab. *tarjumān* (formerly w. *-g-*), f. *tarjama* interpret: rel. to Aram. *targěm* interpret, Akkadian *targumannu* interpreter. Cf. TARGUM, TRUCHMAN.] An interpreter, a guide; *esp.* a person employed as a guide or courier in countries where Arabic, Turkish, or Persian is spoken.

dragon /ˈdrag(ə)n/ *n.* & *a.* ME. [(O)Fr. f. L *draco, dracon-* f. Gk *drakōn* serpent.] **A** *n.* **†1** A huge serpent or snake; a python. ME–E18. **2** A mythical monster like a huge reptile, combining ophidian and crocodilian structure, usu. with wings and claws and often breathing fire. ME. **b** A creature or person represented in a role like that of some dragon of legend, e.g. as a watchful guardian of treasure. L16. **3** A representation or figure of a dragon. Formerly, an ensign or standard depicting a dragon. ME. **b** (Usu. **D-**.) *The* constellation Draco. M16. **c** In full *dragon china*. A kind of porcelain decorated with designs of dragons. L18. **d** Any of twelve tiles so designated which make up one of the suits in mah-jong. E20. **4** In biblical translations: (*a*) a large sea creature; †(*b*) a jackal. ME. **5** More fully *the* (*old*) *Dragon*. Satan. *arch.* ME. **6a** A devilish or wicked person. LME. **b** A fierce person; *esp.* an aggressively watchful or protective woman, a duenna. M18. **†7** *Astron.* The part of the moon's apparent path which lies south of the ecliptic. LME–E16. **†8** A shooting star with a luminous tail. LME–L18. **9** Death. *arch.* E16. **10** More fully *dragon arum*. A Mediterranean arum, *Dracunculus vulgaris*, having a large spathe that is dark purple on the inside and a dark purple spadix. Also *green dragon*. Cf. DRAGONS. M16. **†11** = DRAGOON *n.* 1, 2. E17–M19. **12** = DRAGONET 2. Formerly, any of various other fishes, *esp.* an angler-fish (*Lophius*). E17. **†13** A small cataract in a horse's eye. E17–E18. **14** = *flying lizard* s.v. FLYING *ppl a.* E19. **15** = DRAGOON *n.* 4. M19.

2 SHAKES. *John* Saint George, that swing'd the dragon. SIR W. SCOTT They . . faced the dragon's breath of fire. 4 AV *Ps.* 74:13 Thou brakest the heads of the dragons in the waters. 6b R. CHURCH The headmistress, a formidable dragon . . , terror of the slum mothers.

Phrases: **chase the dragon** *slang* take heroin etc. by heating it in tinfoil and inhaling the fumes through a tube or roll of paper. *flying dragon*: see FLYING *ppl a.* KOMODO *dragon*. *Rouge Dragon*: see ROUGE *a.* SEA *dragon*.

B *attrib.* or as *adj.* Of a dragon; like (that of) a dragon. E17.

Comb. & special collocations: **dragon arum** an arum, *Dracunculus vulgaris*, native to the eastern Mediterranean, with a deep purple spathe and spadix; *dragon china*: see sense A.3c above; **dragonfish** †(*a*) = DRAGONET 2; (*b*) any of various long slender marine fishes of the order Stomiiformes; (*c*) a fish of Antarctic seas of the family Bathydraconidae; (*d*) = SEA-*moth*; **dragonfly** any insect of the suborder Anisoptera (order Odonata), comprising predatory insects with a long slender body, a large head, and two unequal pairs of large transparent wings that are spread while resting; any other odonate insect; **dragon root** either of two stemless tuberous hardy plants of the lily family, *Arisaema dracontium* and *A. triphyllum*, native to N. America; **dragon's blood** any of various red plant resins; *esp.* that which exudes from the fruit of some palms of the genus *Daemonorops*, used as a colouring for varnishes; **dragon's head** (*a*) *arch.* [cf. sense 7 above] the ascending node of the moon's orbit; (*b*) *arch.* the heraldic tincture tenné when blazoning is by the heavenly bodies; (*c*) *Bot.* = DRACOCEPHALUM; **dragon ship** *Hist.* a Viking long ship, esp. one ornamented with a beaked prow; **dragon's tail** (*a*) *arch.* [cf. sense 7 above] the descending node of the moon's orbit; (*b*) *arch.* the heraldic tincture sanguine when blazoning is by the heavenly bodies; **dragon's teeth** (*a*) (something likened to) the teeth of the dragon killed by Cadmus in Greek legend, which when he sowed them turned into armed men; (*b*) *colloq.* upward-pointing obstacles laid in the ground to stop tanks etc. passing or to slow traffic down; **dragon-tree** a tall tree, *Dracaena draco* (cf. DRACAENA), of the Canary Islands that has orange berries and panicles of greenish flowers and whose stem is a source of dragon's blood; **Dragon variation** *Chess* a form of the Sicilian defence involving a fianchetto of the Black king's bishop.

drago'ness *n.* a female dragon; a woman who is a dragon: M17. **dragonish** *a.* (*a*) of the nature or character of a dragon; fierce, severe; (*b*) somewhat like a dragon in shape: M16. **dragonism** *n.* (*rare*) †(*a*) dragonish nature; devilry; (*b*) jealous and watchful guardianship: L16. **dragonize** *v.* (*a*) *v.t.* turn into a dragon; (*b*) *v.t.* & *i.* guard or watch (over) like a dragon: M19.

dragonet /ˈdragənɪt/ *n.* ME. [(O)Fr., dim. of DRAGON: see -ET[1].] **1** A young or small dragon. ME. **2** Any of various perciform marine fishes of the family Callionymidae, which tend to lie partly buried in the seabed and in the case of males are brilliantly coloured, esp. *Callionymus lyra* of the NE Atlantic. M18.

dragonnade /dragəˈneɪd/ *n.* & *v.* Orig. **†dragoonade**. E18. [Fr., f. as DRAGOON *n.*: see -ADE.] **A** *n.sing.* & (usu.) in *pl.* A persecution conducted by Louis XIV against French Protestants in the 1680s, in which dragoons were quartered on them; any persecution conducted with the aid of troops. E18. **B** *v.t.* Subject to dragonnades. L19.

†dragons *n.* LME–M18. [OFr. *dragance* var. of *dragonce* f. late L *dracontia* f. Gk *drakontion*, f. *drakōn* DRAGON.] = DRAGON *n.* 10.

dragoon /drəˈguːn/ *n.* E17. [Fr. *dragon*: see -OON.] **†1** A kind of carbine or musket. E–M17. **2** Orig., a mounted infantryman. Now, a member of any of several cavalry regiments in the household troops of the British army. E17. **3** A rough fierce man. E18. **4** A pigeon that is a cross between a horseman and a tumbler. E18.

dragoon /drə'guːn/ *v.t.* L17. [f. the n. after Fr. *dragonner.*] 1 Set dragoons upon; force or drive with the aid of dragoons; persecute, oppress. L17. 2 Force *into* a course of action etc. by rigorous or harassing measures. L17.

1 D. NEAL His brother of France . . was dragooning his Protestant subjects out of his kingdom. J. COLVILLE He . . dragooned the Chiefs of Staff and Ismay in the War Room. 2 E. BOWEN Dragooning the lower classes into healthy activities.

†**dragoonade** *n.* see DRAGONNADE.

†**dragooner** *n.* M17. [In senses 1 perh. f. G *Dragoner* f. as DRAGOON *n.* In sense 2 f. DRAGOON *v.* + -ER[1].] 1 = DRAGOON *n.* 2. M17–E18. 2 A person who dragoons or takes part in dragonnades; a rigid persecutor. L17–E19.

dragsman /'dragzmən/ *n.* E19. [f. DRAG *n.* + -'S[1] + MAN *n.*] 1 The driver of a drag (see DRAG *n.* 3c). E19. 2 A person who steals from vehicles. *slang.* E19.

dragster /'dragstə/ *n.* M20. [f. DRAG *n.* + -STER.] A car built or modified for use in drag races.

drail /dreɪl/ *v.* & *n.* L16. [App. alt. of TRAIL *v.*] A *v.* 1 *v.t.* & *i.* (Cause to) trail, draggle. *obs.* exc. *dial.* L16. 2 *v.i.* Fish with a drail. *N. Amer.* M17. B *n.* 1 A ring etc. to which a tie may be secured; *spec.* (*Hist.*) a metal ring on a horse-drawn plough to which a trace was attached. L16. 2 A fish-hook weighted to enable it to be dragged through water at a depth; a line with such a hook. *N. Amer.* M17.

drain /dreɪn/ *n.* ME. [f. the vb.] 1 A channel or pipe along which liquid drains away; *esp.* (*a*) a pipe for leading away rainwater etc.; (*b*) an open channel made to drain an area of land; an artificial river. ME. b *Med.* A tube or wick for draining a wound or abscess. M19. c *Electronics.* (The material forming) the part of a field-effect transistor to which the current-carriers flow after passing the gate. Opp. SOURCE *n.* 5c. M20. 2 The action or an act of draining; drainage. Now only *fig.*, a continual loss, demand, or expenditure. E18. 3 A small (remaining) quantity of liquid; in *pl.*, dregs; *slang* a drink. E19.

1 L. LEE We found the drain blocked already and the yard full of water. *down the drain*: see DOWN *prep.* *French drain*: see FRENCH *a.* **laugh like a drain** *colloq.* laugh loudly, guffaw. 2 A. WILSON At fifty-seven he could not afford . . such exacting drains upon his creative energies. M. FONTEYN The drain of top dancers and choreographers leaving the country. *brain drain*: see BRAIN *n.*

Comb.: **drainboard** *N. Amer.* = *draining-board* s.v. DRAIN *v.*; **draincock**: for draining the water out of a boiler etc; **drainpipe** a pipe for carrying off surplus water or liquid refuse from a building; *attrib.* (of trousers etc.) very narrow; in *pl.*, narrow tight-fitting trousers.

drain /dreɪn/ *v.* [OE *drēahnian*, *drēhnian*, prob. f. Gmc base repr. also by DRY *a.*] †1 *v.t.* Strain (liquid) through any porous medium. OE–M17. 2 *v.t.* Drink (liquid, a drink) to the last drops. LME. 3 *v.t.* Empty by drinking, drink dry. LME. 4 *v.t.* Cause (a liquid) to come out of or leave something gradually or in small quantities, esp. by means of a pipe, channel, etc.; carry *off* or *away* thus; *fig.* cause gradually to disappear or go to waste. M16. †5 Let fall in drops. *rare* (Shakes.). Only in L16. 6 *v.t.* Cause water etc. to flow from or out of; make (a marsh etc.) dry by providing an outflow for water; (of a river) receive water from (a specified area); remove purulent matter from (an abscess). L16. b Deprive of strength, resources, vitality, etc.; exhaust emotionally. M17. 7 *v.i.* Of liquid: flow away or out. Usu. foll. by *away*, *off*. L16. 8 *v.i.* Become dry or drier as a result of water draining away. L17.

2 W. BOYD The little boys were noisily draining soft drinks. *drain* (*to*) *the* LEES. 3 DICKENS They had drained the cup of life to the dregs. E. CRISPIN Widger picked up his glass, drained it at a gulp, and put it down. 4 M. FRAYN Held upside down to drain the water out of its works. 6 *fig.*: E. BOWEN Lounge and drawing-room had been drained of their usual occupants. b *Daily Telegraph* We are thoroughly exasperated and drained by the whole thing. 7 *fig.*: P. BARKER A rush of colour to her face . . drained away as quickly as it came, leaving her even whiter. SLOAN WILSON Suddenly the tension drained out of him, and he felt relaxed. 8 *Practical Photography* Pick up the print with tongs, allow it to drain and then transfer to the stop bath.

Comb.: **draining-board** a sloping, usu. grooved, board on which washed dishes etc. are put to drain into an adjacent sink.

drainable *a.* E17.

drainage /'dreɪnɪdʒ/ *n.* M17. [f. DRAIN *v.* + -AGE.] 1 The action of draining something; the manner in which something is drained. M17. 2 Water etc. carried away by a drain. M19. 3 A system of drains; a means of draining. L19. 4 An area drained; a river valley, a drainage basin. Chiefly *US*. L19.

1 *fig.*: W. IRVING This constant drainage of the purse.

Comb.: **drainage basin** = BASIN 6(a); **drainage tube** *Med.* a tube, usu. with lateral perforations, for draining a wound etc.

drainer /'dreɪnə/ *n.* L16. [f. DRAIN *v.* + -ER[1].] 1 A thing that acts as a means of draining something; *esp.* a container in which wet things are put to drain. L16. b = *draining-board* s.v. DRAIN *v.* M20. 2 A person who drains, *esp.* one who makes field-drains. E17.

drainless /'dreɪnlɪs/ *a.* E19. [f. DRAIN *n.* + -LESS.] 1 Inexhaustible. *poet.* E19. 2 Not provided with drains. E20.

drake /dreɪk/ *n.*[1] [OE *draca* = OFris., MLG, MDu. *drake* (Du. *draak*), OHG *trahho* (G *Drache*), f. WGmc f. L *draco* DRAGON.] 1 A dragon (cf. FIRE-DRAKE 1); an ensign or standard depicting a dragon. *arch.* OE. †2 A fiery meteor. (Surviving longer in FIRE-DRAKE 2.) ME–E17. 3 [f. LG.] A kind of small cannon. *obs.* exc. *Hist.* E17. 4 *Angling.* (An artificial fly imitating) a mayfly, esp. (*green drake*) a subimago or (*grey drake*) a gravid female of *Ephemera*. Also *drake-fly*. M17.

drake /dreɪk/ *n.*[2] & *a.* ME. [Corresp. to LG *drake*, *drache* f. WGmc base repr. also by 2nd elem. of OHG *antrahho*, *antrehho* (G *Enterich*).] A *n.* A male duck. ME.

drake's tail an unruly tuft or curl of hair at the back of the head. *ducks and drakes*, *duck and drake*: see DUCK *n.*[1]

B *attrib.* or as *adj.* Designating a duck that is male. L19.

Dralon /'dreɪlɒn/ *n.* Also **d-**. M20. [After NYLON.] (Proprietary name for) an acrylic textile fibre; (of) fabric made from this.

S. TOWNSEND This . . reduced me to silent sobs into the Dralon cushions.

dram /dram/ *n.*[1] & *v.* LME. [OFr. *drame* or med.L *drama*, vars. of OFr. *dragme*, late L *dragma*: see DRACHM.] A *n.* †1 = DRACHMA 2. LME–M16. 2 = DRACHM 2. Now chiefly *US*. LME. 3 *fig.* = DRACHM 3. M16. 4 A small drink of spirits etc. E18.

2 *fluid dram*: see FLUID *a.* 4 A. S. NEILL He always brought a flask of whisky and gave each one a dram.

Comb.: **dram-drinker** a tippler; **dram-shop** *US* (*arch.*) an establishment where spirits are sold, a bar-room.

B *v.t.* & *i.* Infl. **-mm-**. (Cause to) drink drams, tipple. Now *rare* or *obs.* E18.

dram /dram/ *n.*[2] & *a.* M17. [Abbrev. of *Drammen* (see below).] (Designating) timber from the town of Drammen in Norway.

drama /'drɑːmə/ *n.* Orig. †**drame**. E16. [(Fr. *drame* f.) late L *drama* f. Gk *drama(t-)*, f. *dran* do, act, perform.] 1 A play for acting on stage, radio, etc., esp. one with high emotional content. E16. 2 The dramatic art; the composition and presentation of plays. Formerly usu. *the drama*. E17. 3 A situation in which there is conflict; *esp.* a dramatic series of events leading up to a particular outcome. E18. 4 Dramatic quality; interest, excitement. M20.

1 *lyric drama*: see LYRIC *a.* 1. *music drama*: see MUSIC *n.* 2 L. C. KNIGHTS Restoration drama—tragedy as well as comedy— . . is insufferably dull. 3 R. V. JONES After the drama of Dunkirk the next few days were surprisingly quiet. 4 L. MACNEICE The hills to-day were monotonous, lacking in drama.

Comb.: **drama-doc** *slang*, **drama-documentary** a film (esp. for television) dramatizing or based on real events.

¶ Cf. MELODRAMA.

Dramamine /'draməmiːn/ *n.* Also **d-**. M20. [f. *dram-*, of unkn. origin + AMINE.] *Pharm.* (Proprietary name for) an antihistamine used to counter nausea, esp. travel sickness.

dramatic /drə'matɪk/ *a.* & *n.* L16. [Late L *dramaticus* f. Gk *dramatikos*, f. *dramat-* DRAMA: see -IC.] A *adj.* 1 Of or pertaining to drama; dealing with or employing the forms of drama. L16. 2 Characteristic of drama or a play-actor, theatrical; fit for representation in a drama, striking, impressive; sudden. E18.

1 M. SPARK Jenny was already showing her dramatic talent. **dramatic irony** = TRAGIC *irony*. 2 M. PEAKE He took a dramatic step towards Lady Cora. I. SMITH There are going to be no dramatic changes in Rhodesia. O. MANNING A dramatic range of high ridges could be seen on the horizon.

B *n.* †1 A dramatic poet; a dramatist. M17–M18. 2 In *pl.* Dramatic compositions or presentations (now chiefly in *amateur dramatics*); dramatic behaviour. L17.

2 A. BROOKNER Monica's face dropped. . . No dramatics, please, thought Edith.

dramatical *a.* (now *rare*) = DRAMATIC *a.* 1 M17. **dramatically** *adv.* in a dramatic manner; with dramatic or theatrical effect: M17. **dramaticism** /-sɪz(ə)m/ *n.* dramatic quality M19. **dramaticule** *n.* (*rare*) a minor or insignificant drama E19.

dramatise *v.* var. of DRAMATIZE.

dramatism /'dramətɪz(ə)m/ *n.* M19. [f. Gk *dramat-* DRAMA + -ISM.] 1 Dramatization. *rare.* M19. 2 Dramatic quality. *rare.* L19. 3 A theory of social action that analyses behaviour in terms of dramatic forms and convention. L20.

dramatis personae /ˌdramətɪs pəː'səʊnʌɪ, -niː/ *n.pl.* (freq. treated as *sing.*). M18. [L *dramatis personae* persons of the drama.] The (list of) characters in a play; *fig.* the participants in an event etc.

dramatist /'dramətɪst/ *n.* L17. [f. Gk *dramat-* DRAMA + -IST.] A person who writes dramas or (formerly) dramatic poetry; a playwright.

dramatistic /dramə'tɪstɪk/ *a.* M20. [f. as prec. + -IC.] *Sociol.* Of or pertaining to dramatism.

dramatistically *adv.* M20.

dramatize /'dramətʌɪz/ *v.* Also **-ise**. L18. [f. Gk *dramat-* DRAMA + -IZE.] 1 *v.t.* Put into dramatic form; adapt (a novel etc.) as a play. L18. b *v.i.* Write plays. E19. 2a *v.t.* Describe or represent dramatically; make dramatic. E19. b *v.i.* & *refl.* Behave dramatically or theatrically. L19. 3 *v.i.* Be adaptable as a play. E19.

1 SIR W. SCOTT They are busy dramatizing the Lady of the Lake here. 2a A. WESKER She manages to dramatize the smallest piece of gossip into something significant. b G. VIDAL Enid's dramatizing herself, that's all.

dramati'zation *n.* the action of dramatizing; a dramatized version: L18.

dramaturge /'dramətəːdʒ/ *n.* Also **-g**; ***Dramaturg*** /dramə'tʊrk/, pl. **-gen** /-gən/. M19. [Fr. *dramaturge*, G *Dramaturg*, f. Gk *dramatourgos*, f. *dramat-*, DRAMA + *-ergos* worker.] A dramatist; *spec.* a reader and literary editor etc. to a permanent theatrical company.

dramaturgy /'dramətəːdʒi/ *n.* E19. [Gk *dramatourgia* composition of dramas (f. *dramatourgos* DRAMATURGE: see -Y[3]), prob. after G *Dramaturgie.*] 1 Dramatic composition; the dramatic art. E19. 2 Dramatic or theatrical acting. Now *rare*. M19. 3 *Sociol.* A theory which interprets individual behaviour as the dramatic projection of a chosen self. M20.

drama'turgic(al) *adjs.* M19. **drama'turgically** *adv.* M20. **dramaturgist** *n.* a dramatist E19.

Drambuie /dram'buːi, -'bjʊi/ *n.* Also **d-**. L19. [f. Gael. *dram buidheach* satisfying drink.] (Proprietary name for) a Scotch whisky liqueur; a drink of this.

†**drame** *n.* see DRAMA.

drammock /'dramək/ *n.* *Sc. arch.* M17. [Gael. *dramag.*] Oatmeal mixed with cold water.

Drang /draŋ/ *n.*[1] M19. [G.] Strong tendency, pressure; urge, strong desire. Chiefly in phrs.

Drang nach Osten /nax 'ɔstən/ [lit. 'drive towards the east'] *Hist.* a German imperialistic policy of eastward expansion. STURM UND DRANG.

drang *n.*[2] var. of DRONG.

drank *v.* pa. t. & pple: see DRINK *v.*

drant /drant/ *n.* & *v. Sc.* & *dial.* Also **draunt** /drɔːnt/. E18. [App. onomatopoeic after DRAWL or DRONE *n.*, *v.* and RANT.] A *n.* A drone; a drawl. E18. B *v.i.* Speak with a drawl. E18.

drap *n.* see DROP *n.*

drápa /'drɑːpə, 'draʊpə/ *n.* Pl. ***-pur*** /-pʊə/. M19. [ON, prob. f. *drepa* to strike.] An old Icelandic heroic and laudatory poem.

†**drap-de-Berry** *n.* Also **drab-**, **-du-**; **D-**. E17–E19. [Fr. = cloth of Berry.] A type of woollen cloth from Berry in France.

drape /dreɪp/ *n.* M17. [Partly f. Fr. *drap* (see next), partly f. next.] **1** Cloth; (a piece of) drapery. M17. **2** A curtain. Usu. in *pl. N. Amer.* E20. **3** *sing.* & (usu.) in *pl.* A man's suit, *esp.* one comprising a long jacket and narrow trousers. *slang.* M20. **4** The way a garment or fabric hangs. M20. **5** *Surg.* A sterilized covering for use in an operation. M20.

Comb.: **drape jacket** *slang* the jacket of a drape suit; **drape suit** *slang* = sense 3 above.

drape /dreɪp/ *v.* LME. [In sense 1 f. (O)Fr. *draper*, f. *drap* cloth f. late L *drappus*, perh. of Celt. origin: cf. DRAB *n.*[2] In other senses back-form. from DRAPERY suggested by mod.Fr. *draper*.] †**1** *v.t.* & *i.* Weave; make by weaving. LME–L17. **2** *v.t.* Cover, hang, or adorn (as) with cloth or drapery; cover with a sterilized drape. M19. **3** *v.t.* Arrange or place (clothing etc.) *around* something, esp. in graceful folds. Also foll. by *about*, *over*. M19. **4** *v.i.* Of fabric or a garment: admit of being (readily) draped. M20. **5** *v.refl.* Place (oneself) on or against something for support, esp. in drunken unsteadiness. *colloq.* M20.

2 D. LODGE Another girl whose blonde head is becomingly draped with a black lace mantilla. G. SWIFT The body on the stretcher.. was entirely draped by the red blanket. 3 I. MCEWAN Mary appeared.., a cardigan draped around her shoulders. *fig.*: J. T. FARRELL Clouds.. draping shadows over the park.

drap(e)a'bility *n.* drapeable quality L20. **drap(e)able** *a.* (of fabric etc.) that hangs easily, without stiffness M20. **draping** *ppl a.* hanging in graceful folds or sheets L19.

draper /'dreɪpə/ *n.* LME. [AN, & (O)Fr. *drapier*, f. *drap* cloth: see prec., -ER[2].] Orig., a maker of (woollen) cloth. Now, a dealer in cloth.

drapery /'dreɪp(ə)ri/ *n.* & *v.* ME. [(O)Fr. *draperie*, f. *drap* cloth (see DRAPE *v.*), *drapier* DRAPER: see -ERY.] A *n.* **1** Cloth, fabrics. ME. †**2** The place where a draper works. LME–E17. **3** The trade of a draper. L15. **4** The artistic arranging of clothing in painting and sculpture. E17. **5** Cloth with which something is draped; hangings; clothing, *esp.* clothing that hangs; in *pl.*, curtains. L17.

5 W. HOLTBY The flying drapery of her lilac tunic. O. MANNING The monstrous catafalque appeared, black and blackly ornamented with fringed draperies. *fig.*: W. HOWITT Nature is stripped of all her summer drapery.

Comb.: **drapery artist**, **drudge**: employed by another artist to paint in the drapery.

B *v.t.* Cover with drapery; drape. E19.

†**drapet** *n. rare.* L16–L18. [It. *drappetto* dim. of *drappo* cloth f. late L *drappus*.] A cloth, a covering.

drappie /'drapi/ *n. Sc.* Also **-ppy**. L18. [f. DRAP *n.* + -IE, -Y[6].] A little drop, *spec.* of spirits.

drápur *n.* pl. of DRÁPA.

drastic /'drastɪk, 'drɑː-/ *a.* & *n.* L17. [Gk *drastikos* active, effective, f. *dran* do: see -IC.] A *adj.* **1** Of a medicine: acting strongly or violently. L17. **2** *gen.* Vigorous and decisive; having violent effects; severe. E19.

2 W. S. CHURCHILL Drastic measures were necessary to protect the emancipated Negro. A. BRINK If you don't put an end to it soon something drastic will happen.

B *n.* A drastic medicine; *esp.* a strong laxative. L18.

drastically *adv.* M19.

drat /drat/ *v.t.* & *i.* Infl. **-tt-**. E19. [Aphet. f. *od-rat*, f. OD *n.*[1] + RAT *v.*[2]] Damn, confound: used in exclamations of angry annoyance.

A. TROLLOPE Drat their impudence. J. HARTLEY It's that dratted dog after th' cat. *People* 'Oh drat it!' said Mrs. Fairbanks. B. CLEARY 'Drat!' said Mitchell, kicking the fence and wishing he knew what to do.

dratch /dratʃ/ *v.i.* Now *Sc.* & *dial.* Also **dretch** /drɛtʃ/. ME. [Origin unkn.] Delay, linger; dawdle.

dratchell /'dratʃ(ə)l/ *n. Sc.* & *dial.* Also **drotchell** /'drɒtʃ(ə)l/. M18. [Origin uncertain: perh. rel. to prec.] A slut.

draught /drɑːft/ *n.* & *a.* See also DRAFT *n.* ME. [ON *dráttr* = MDu. *dragt*, OHG *traht* (G *Tracht*), f. Gmc base of DRAW *v.*] A *n.* **I** Senses in which the dominant idea is of an action. **1** The action or an act of pulling something along, esp. a vehicle or farm implement; traction. ME. **b** *fig.* Attraction; tendency, inclination; impulse. (Foll. by *to*, *towards*.) *arch.* ME. **2** The action or an act of drawing a net for fish etc. ME. **b** A site where a net is customarily drawn. LME. **3** A single act of drinking or of inhaling tobacco smoke etc.; (long *obs.* exc. *Sc.*) breathing; an amount drunk or inhaled at one go. ME. **b** *fig.* The taking in by the senses or the mind of something that affects one deeply; something experienced deeply. LME. **c** A dose of medicine; a potion. M17. †**4** The action of drawing a bow; a bowshot. ME–E17. **5** A stroke with a weapon. Long *obs.* exc. *dial.* ME. †**6** The action of drawing a brush, pencil, etc., across a surface; a mark so made. ME–M17. **b** Drawing (as an art). M16–M18. †**7** A course followed, a way; *fig.* a way of behaving. Only in ME. **8** †**a** A move in chess etc. LME–M17. **b** In *pl.* (usu. treated as *sing.*). A game in which two players each start with 12 (or occas. 20) pieces of equal value on opposite sides of a chequered board, the pieces being moved diagonally with the aim of capturing those of the opponent. LME. **c** Each of the pieces used in the game of draughts. L19. **9** The action of drawing a saw through a block of wood or stone; a measure of timber etc. so cut. LME. **10** The action of drawing out to a greater length, stretching; something drawn out or spun, a thread. LME. **11** The action of drawing liquor from a cask etc.; the condition of being (ready to be) so drawn. LME. **12** = DRAFT *n.* 4. Now *rare* or *obs.* L15. †**13** (An) extraction, (a) derivation; an act of drawing a lot. Long *rare* or *obs.* L15. **14** The depth of water needed to float a ship. E17. **15** The drawing of money by a written order (cf. DRAFT *n.* 6). Formerly also, the order itself. M17. **16** (The selection of) a detachment drawn from a larger group (see DRAFT *n.* 5). E18.

1 *Daily Telegraph* Horses.. were far too valuable to use for draught. 3 A. WILSON She stood by the open window, drawing in great draughts of.. air. A. UTTLEY He drained the cup at a draught. **b** S. JOHNSON Make the draught of life sweet or bitter. **c** **black draught** *Hist.* a purgative medicine (*lit.* & *fig.*). 8b *Polish draughts*: see POLISH *a.* 11 **on draught** (of beer etc.) ready to be drawn from a cask, not bottled or canned etc.

II Senses in which the dominant idea is that of something drawn. **17** An amount or thing that is pulled or carried, esp. as a measure; a load. Now *rare* exc. *techn.* ME. **18** The quantity of fish taken in one drawing of the net; a catch. LME. **b** A unit of weight of eels, equal to 20 lb (approx. 9.1 kg). M19. †**19** More fully *draught-bridge*. A drawbridge. LME–M16. **20** The entrails of an animal removed prior to cooking. Now *obs.* or *dial.* LME. †**21** A passage of writing; an extract. LME–E17. **22** A thing drawn up or devised; a scheme, a plan, a design; a plot. Now *rare* or *obs.* LME. **23** A thing which is drawn on paper etc.; a drawing, a sketch. Now *rare* or *obs.* in *gen.* sense. LME. **b** Representation in sculpture; a sculptured figure. M–L17. **24** A sketch in words; a brief account; an outline, an abstract. Now *rare.* E16. **25** = DRAFT *n.* 3. Also, an artist's initial or preparatory sketch etc. E16. **26** = DRAFT *n.* 2. L16. **27** *Weaving.* The succession in which the threads of the warp are inserted into the heddles of the loom to produce the required pattern. E19. **28** = DRAFT *n.* 7. M19.

18 TINDALE *Luke* 5:9 He was vtterly astonyed.. at the draught of fisshe. 23 S. JOHNSON He.. embellished [his pages] with elegant draughts and illuminations. 24 J. LOCKE Thus I have, in a short draught, given a view of our original Ideas.

III A thing that draws or is used in drawing; a current. **29 a** A thing used in pulling; *esp.* a harness for horses to draw with. LME. **b** A team of horses etc. used for draught together with the vehicle drawn. Now *dial.* E16. **30** A flow, esp. of liquid. LME. **b** The course of a stream; a narrow valley. M17. **31** More fully *draught-house*. A privy, a lavatory. Now *rare* or *obs.* LME. †**32** A cesspool, a sewer; a drainage channel. E16–E18. **33** A current of air in a room, chimney, or other confined space. L18.

30 P. LEACH Sometimes the draught reflex makes the second breast leak milk while the baby sucks from the first. 33 DICKENS A sore throat, from sitting in constant draughts. *feel the draught*: see FEEL *v.*

B *attrib.* or as *adj.* **1** Of an animal: used for pulling a cart, plough, etc.; of a breed suitable for this. LME. **2** Of beer etc.: on draught (see sense 11 above). M19. **3** = DRAFT *a.* 2. L19.

Comb. & *special collocations*: **draughtboard** a chequered board (identical to a chessboard) used for the game of draughts; *draught-bridge*: see sense 19 above; **draught ewe** = DRAFT *n.* 5b; **draught-excluder** a device or material for excluding draughts, esp. from doors or windows; †**draught-hound**: used for tracking by scent; **draught horse** a strong horse used for or of a breed suitable for draught; *draught-house*: see sense 31 above; **draught-net** a net that is drawn for fish; **draught-proof** *a.* & *v.* (*a*) *adj.* proof against draughts; (*b*) *v.t.* make draught-proof (usu. in *pass.*); **draught-screen**: for shelter against draughts; **draught-tree** (now *rare* or *obs.*) the pole of a wagon etc. to which the drawing gear is attached.

draught /drɑːft/ *v.t.* M17. [f. the n. Cf. DRAFT *v.*] **1** = DRAFT *v.* 2. M17. **2** = DRAFT *v.* 1. E18. **3** = DRAFT *v.* 3. M19.

draughtman /'drɑːftmən/ *n. rare.* Pl. **-men**. E18. [f. DRAUGHT *n.* + MAN *n.*] †**1** *morning's draughtman-man*, a man who indulges in a morning draught of liquor; a tippler. Only in E18. **2** A draughtsman; *spec.* = DRAUGHTSMAN 3. M19.

draughtmanship *n.* = DRAUGHTSMANSHIP L19.

draughtsman /'drɑːf(t)smən/ *n.* Pl. **-men**. E18. [f. DRAUGHT *n.* + -'S[1] + MAN *n.* Cf. earlier DRAFTSMAN.] **1** A person whose profession is to make drawings, plans, or sketches; a person skilled in drawing or designing. E18. **2** = DRAFTSMAN 2. E19. **3** = DRAUGHT *n.* 8c. Cf. DRAUGHTMAN 2. L19.

1 J. W. BURGON Though he was no draughtsman, he was the author of a large portfolio of portraits.

draughtsmanship *n.* the function, quality, or art of a draughtsman; skill in draughting or drawing; (cf. DRAFTSMANSHIP): M19.

draughtsperson /'drɑːf(t)spəːs(ə)n/ *n.* L20. [f. as prec. + PERSON *n.*] = DRAUGHTSMAN 1.

draughtswoman /'drɑːf(t)swʊmən/ *n.* Pl. **-women** /-wɪmɪn/. M19. [f. as prec. + WOMAN *n.*] A female draughtsman.

draughty /'drɑːfti/ *a.* Also ***drafty**. E19. [f. DRAUGHT *n.* + -Y[1].] **1** Artful, crafty. *Sc.* E19. **2** Letting in draughts, subject to draughts. M19.

draughtiness *n.* L19.

draunt *n.* & *v.* var. of DRANT.

drave /dreɪv/ *n. Sc.* & *north.* L16. [f. as DROVE *n.*] A communal fishing expedition in which each participant supplies a net and takes a share of the profit; a haul of fish; a shoal.

drave *v.* pa. t.: see DRIVE *v.*

Dravidian /drə'vɪdɪən/ *a.* & *n.* M19. [f. Skt *drāvida* pertaining to the Tamils f. *Dravida* Tamil: see -IAN.] **1** (Of, pertaining to, or designating) any of a group of languages spoken chiefly in southern India and Sri Lanka (Ceylon), including Tamil, Telugu, and Brahui. M19. **2** (Of, pertaining to, or designating) a member of a dark-skinned people of southern

India and Sri Lanka that mostly speak a Dravidian language, including Tamils and Kanarese. M19.

Dravidic /drəˈvɪdɪk/ *a.* M19. [f. as prec.: see -IC.] Dravidian.

draw /drɔː/ *n.* LME. [f. the vb.] **1** The action or an act of drawing. LME. **b** *The* action of drawing a revolver from its holster in order to shoot. M19. **c** A suck at a pipe, cigarette, etc.; a smoke. Chiefly *dial.* & *N. Amer.* L19. **2a** A drawer of a cabinet. *US.* L17. **b** (The movable part of) a drawbridge. *US.* L18. **3** An event in which lots are drawn, a raffle; an order of contestants etc. decided in this way; a lot drawn. M18. **4** Attractive power or effect; a person or thing drawing or able to draw custom, attention, etc. *colloq.* E19. **5** Something or someone used to elicit a person's knowledge or intentions; a person from whom such information may be extracted. *arch. slang.* E19. **6** Orig. †*draw game, race*, etc. A game etc. which has ended without an outright winner; a drawn game. E19. **7** An amount drawn or drawn out etc. E19. **8** *Hist.* In cricket, a stroke to the leg side (no longer used) in which the batsman deflected the ball so that it passed between the wicket and his legs; a player positioned to field balls so hit. M19. **9a** More fully *draw poker*. The standard form of the game of poker. M19. **b** The deal in poker after discarding. L19. **10** A shallow valley. *US.* L19. **11** A cavity inside cast metal resulting from shrinkage during solidification. E20.

1 *Abingdon Herald* The first draw of the day was in Flamborough, where a fox was killed. 3 *luck of the draw*: see LUCK *n.* 4 A. WILSON His name would still be a great draw for bourgeois audiences. 6 *hold to a draw*: see HOLD *v.*

draw /drɔː/ *v.* Pa. t. **drew** /druː/; pa. pple **drawn** /drɔːn/. [OE *dragan* = ON *draga*, OFris. *draga*, OS *dragan* (Du. *dragen*), OHG *tragan* (G *tragen*), Goth. *(ga)dragan*.] **I** Cause to move, pull. **1a** *v.t.* Cause (something) to move towards, or past a part of, oneself by the application of force; pull. OE. **b** *v.t.* & *i.* Pull (something, esp. a vehicle or its load) so as to make it follow along behind; *Hist.* drag (a criminal) on a hurdle etc. to the place of execution. Formerly also *fig.*, agree (*with*); be in a like situation *with*. ME. **c** *v.i.* Be drawn; admit of being drawn. M17. †**2** *v.t.* Tear apart; pull *in pieces, asunder*. ME–E18. **3a** *v.t.* & *i.* Pull back the string of (a bow) ready to shoot; pull back (the arrow) on the string; hoist (a sail); pull up (a drawbridge); pull out (a bolt, an organ-stop); haul in (a net). ME. **b** *v.t.* Pull (a veil etc.) over something so as to conceal it; pull (a curtain, blinds) open or shut. LME. **4** *v.t.* Cause to come, move, or go (from or to some place, position, or condition); lead, bring, take, convey, put. *obs.* exc. as assoc. with other senses. ME. †**5** *v.t.* Render into another style of writing; translate. ME–M16. †**6** *v.t. fig.* Adduce, appeal to for confirmation; assign, attribute; turn aside to a purpose, pervert. ME–E18. **7** *v.t.* & *i.* Contract, shrink; pull or become out of shape or place. Usu. as DRAWN *a.* LME. †**8** *v.t.* Construct (a ditch, canal, wall) from one point to another. LME–L18. †**9** *v.t.* Pass (food) through or *through* a strainer; bring to the required consistency thus. LME–L18. †**10** Operate on (a number) with one of the processes of arithmetic: add *to, together*; multiply *into*; subtract *out of*. LME–E19. **11** *v.t. Naut.* Of a ship: require (a specified depth of water) for floating. M16. †**12** *v.t.* Bring (the edges of a tear etc.) together by sewing; mend (a rent). L16–E17. **13** *v.t.* In various games, direct or divert (a ball) in some way; *spec.* in *Cricket* (now *rare*), divert (the ball) to the on side of the wicket with the bat; *Golf* drive (the ball) purposely to the left of a right-handed player or vice versa; *Bowls* cause (the bowl) to travel in a curve to the desired point. M19.

1a ADDISON He drew a Paper of Verses out of his Pocket. F. BURNEY I . . drew my hat over my face. G. GREENE Josef . . drew the string on which the revolver dangled a couple of inches higher. I. MCEWAN He took her wrist and drew her into the street. *refl.*: W. C. RUSSELL Wilfrid . . drew himself erect. b SHAKES. *Oth.* Think every bearded fellow that's but yok'd May draw with you. D. BAGLEY There were carts pushed by hand or drawn by donkey. 3a AV *1 Kings* 22:34 A certain man drew a bow at a venture. W. LONGMAN He then drew the bolt, the door was opened. T. H. WHITE Boys . . are inclined to catch hold of the nock of the arrow when they draw. 4 T. HERBERT Hee . . drawes his forces against Rantas. W. IRVING He hastened to draw him from the seductions of the garden. 11 J. CONRAD She drew too much water to cross the bar.

II Come; go. **14** *v.i.* Come *together*; move or make one's way *towards*; also w. advs. in specialized senses (see below). Formerly without adv. or advb. phr.: move, come, go. OE. †**15** *v.refl.* Go *towards* or *to*; withdraw *from*. ME–E17. †**16** *v.i.* Tend, approach, *to* or *towards* some condition, state, etc. ME–E17. **17** *v.i.* Move in time *to* or *towards* an event, a particular time, etc. ME. **18** *v.i. Hunting.* Of a hound etc.: track game by its scent; move slowly towards the game after pointing. (Foll. by *after, on, upon.*) L16. **19** *v.i.* Gradually get further *away from* or gain *on* an antagonist or competitor in a race etc. E19.

15 W. RALEIGH As their people increased, they drew themselves more westerly towards the Red sea. 16 R. KNOLLES Of a darke colour, somewhat drawing toward a violet. 17 B. JOWETT The days of Socrates are drawing to a close.

III Take in; attract. **20a** *v.t.* Take (a breath); take (air etc.) into the lungs. See also *draw breath* s.v. BREATH. ME. **b** *v.i.* Of a chimney, pipe, etc.: promote or allow a current of air through it. Of a smoker: suck *at* a pipe etc. M18. **21** *v.t.* Attract by physical force, as a magnet; tend to become covered or affected with (rust etc.). ME. **22a** *v.t.* Attract (a person) by affecting his or her inclination, sympathies, etc.; cause (the mind, eyes, etc.) to become directed *to, from*, etc., or attracted; lead (a person) into, from, etc. (a course of action, condition, etc.). ME. **b** *v.i.* Exercise allurement or attraction; prove an attraction; attract crowds. L16. **23** *v.i.* & †*t.* Gather together, collect, assemble. ME. **24** *v.t.* Cause (an enemy etc.) to fall *on* or *upon* a person; bring (disaster etc.) *on* or *upon*; bring about as a result, bring on. ME. **25** *v.t.* Induce (a person) *to do*. M16.

20b F. MARRYAT The fire does not draw well. R. CHANDLER I finished filling the pipe, put a match to it, got it drawing. 21 E. KIRKE The rod draws the electricity from the air. *fig.*: J. TILLOTSON The blessings it will draw down upon us. 22a ADDISON To draw the Eyes of the World upon her. THOMAS HUGHES It is wonderful . . how you feel drawn to a man who feeds you well. L. J. JENNINGS A great bereavement . . drew his mind from public affairs. G. GREENE I feel an enormous desire to draw attention to myself. S. BELLOW He did not want to be drawn into a quarrel. b J. R. LOWELL Mr. Emerson always draws. 23 A. RADCLIFFE Our desolate party drew round it. 24 T. MARTIN Rage drew on Thyestes the vengeance of heaven. 25 M. LASKI One of the things that had drawn him to ask her to dance.

IV Take out; deprive. **26a** *v.t.* Remove or extract (an object) from what it is fixed or embedded in; *esp.* take (a playing-card or suit) from a pack. (Foll. by *from.*) ME. **b** *v.t.* & *i.* Take (a weapon) from a sheath or holster in readiness for immediate use. ME. **27a** *v.t.* & *i.* Pull or take (one thing) from a number in order to decide something by chance; obtain or win (something) in this way. ME. **b** *v.t.* Set apart (sheep) from a flock; separate (seeds) from the husks. L15. **28a** *v.t.* & †*i.* Raise (water) from a well etc. by hauling or pumping; obtain (beer etc.) from a cask or (water) from a tap; run (a bath); cause (blood) to flow from an incision etc. ME. **b** *v.t.* Extract (liquor, juice, etc.) by suction, pressure, infusion, or distillation. M16. **c** *v.i.* Of tea: infuse. E19. **29a** *v.t.* Take or obtain *from* a source; derive; deduce, infer, (a conclusion). ME. **b** *v.t.* Take, receive, or obtain (money) from a source of supply. L16. **c** *v.i.* Obtain information, resources, etc., *from*. E19. **30** *v.t.* Cause to come out or appear; elicit, evoke; *spec.* cause (a particular playing-card) to be played by another player. ME. **31** *v.t.* Extract something from; empty, drain, exhaust, deplete; *spec.* disembowel (a fowl etc., *Hist.* a criminal after hanging). ME. **b** Remove coals from (a fire, furnace, etc.). E19. **32** *v.t.* Drag or pull a net through or along (a river etc.) for fish; search (a wood etc.) for game. LME. **33** *v.t.* & *i.* Cause a flow of (blood, matter, etc.) to a particular part of the body; promote suppuration. LME. **b** Drain off or away, esp. by means of a channel. E17. †**34** *v.t.* Withdraw (stakes, a racehorse, etc.). L16–M19. **35** *v.t.* Force (a badger or fox) from its hole. M19. **36** *v.t.* Elicit information or conversation from (a person). *colloq.* M19. **37** *v.t.* Rouse (a person) to action, speech, or anger; irritate, exasperate. *colloq.* M19. **38** *v.t.* & *i.* Finish (a game etc.) with no one a winner or scores equal. (Earlier as DRAWN *ppl a.* 2.) M19.

26 T. HARDY He drew the corks of the mineral waters. H. ROTH He would draw several of her teeth. E. BOWEN He kept drawing long black horsehairs from the seat of his chair. b R. JARRELL He drew a big revolver and he shot me. 27a STEELE Neither of them had drawn the Thousand Pound. W. MORRIS We . . shared the spoil by drawing short and long. TOLKIEN They now drew lots for the watches. 28a H. ROBBINS He . . walked over to the sink, and drew a glass of water. c F. TUOHY The two women . . waited for the Indian tea to draw. 29a A. FLEMING The stocke from whence he draweth his descent. *Daily Telegraph* Gilt-edged investors were looking a bit happier . . , drawing comfort from the improving pound. b B. PYM Letty had been retired for a week and had drawn the first payment of her pension. 32 A. EDEN Hounds were drawing the home coverts. 33 R. D. BLACKMORE His poultice began to draw. 36 J. SIMMS I tried to involve him in a political discussion, . . but he refused to be drawn.

V Extend. **39** *v.t.* Pull out to a greater length; extend, lengthen; prolong, protract. Usu. foll. by *out*. ME. **b** Make (wire) by drawing metal through successively smaller holes; elongate and attenuate (a sliver of cotton etc.) by passage through pairs of rollers revolving at successively greater speeds. E16. †**40** *v.t.* & *i.* Amount to or *to*. LME–M16. **41** *v.i. Naut.* Of a sail: swell out tightly with the wind. E17.

39 T. ELLWOOD I Prayed often, and drew out my Prayers to a great length. P. THEROUX A man melting tubes of glass and drawing them thin.

VI Make, depict. **42a** *v.t.* Trace (a line or figure), make (a picture), by drawing a pen, pencil, etc., across a surface; cut (a furrow) with a ploughshare. ME. **b** *v.i.* Draw pictures, practise the art of drawing. M16. **c** *v.t.* Represent by a drawing, depict; *fig.* represent in words, describe. L16. **43** = *draw up* (b) below. Formerly also, write (a story), compose (a song). ME. †**44** *v.t.* Devise, contrive; set in order, arrange. M16–M17. **45** *v.t.* Shape or carve (stone, wood, etc.) by shaving thin slices off it. M17. **46** *v.t.* Write out (a cheque etc.) in due form to authorize payment. (Foll. by *on, upon* the person etc. that has to pay.) M17. **47** *v.i.* Draw a cheque etc. *on* or *upon* a person etc.; call *on* or *upon* a person for or *for* funds, or any source for or *for* something. L17. **48** *v.t.* Make, formulate, (a comparison, contrast, distinction, etc.). L18.

42a J. RHYS She took a sharp stick and drew lines and circles on the earth under the tree. 43 L. STEPHEN Langton had employed Chambers . . to draw his will. 44 F. HAWKINS The matter of any Book or Science, drawn into Indexes or Tables. 47 P. ACKROYD There were few intellectual models upon which to draw. V. GLENDINNING Edith was drawing deeply on her childhood memories for this poetry.

Phrases: *draw a bead on*: see BEAD *n.* 4c. **draw a blank** fail in a search; elicit no response. *draw a veil (over)*: see VEIL *n.* 5. **draw bit, bridle, rein** check one's horse or (*fig.*) oneself. *draw breath*: see BREATH. *draw bridle*: see *draw bit* above. *draw in one's horns*: see HORN *n.* **draw it mild** *fig.* [f. drawing beer] be moderate, not exaggerate. **draw level (with)** come from behind to a position alongside in a race etc. *draw (one's) steel*: see STEEL *n.*[1] **draw one's sword against** take up arms against, attack (*lit.* & *fig.*). *draw rein*: see *draw bit* above. *draw straws*: see STRAW *n.* *draw stumps*: see STUMP *n.*[1] *draw the badger*: see BADGER *n.*[2] 1. **draw the cloth** *arch.* remove the tablecloth after a meal, clear away. *draw the line at*: see LINE *n.*[2] *draw the longbow*: see LONG *a.*[1] *draw the short straw*: see STRAW *n.* *draw the stumps*: see STUMP *n.*[1]

With advs. in specialized senses: **draw back** move backwards from one's position, *fig.* withdraw from an undertaking. **draw down** (*a*) make (metal, plastic) thinner by hammering, stretching, etc.; (*b*) make a drawing of (a loan), borrow. **draw forth** evoke. **draw in** (*a*) entice (*to do*); deceive, take in; persuade to take part; make to include in a conversation; (*b*) draw tight, cause to shrink; (*c*) (of a day) approach its end, (of night) approach, (of successive evenings) become shorter; (*d*) (of a train etc.) enter a station; (of a vehicle) move towards the side of the road; (*e*) = sense 20a above. **draw near (to)** approach (*lit.* & *fig.*). **draw off** (*a*) withdraw (troops); move off; (*b*) drain away by a tap etc., esp. without disturbing the bottom or sediment of the liquid. **draw on** (*a*) come near; (*b*) bring on, involve as a consequence; (*c*) entice, allure; (*d*) pull on (a garment etc.). **draw out** (*a*) = *draw up* (b) below; (*b*) elicit, evoke; (*c*) lead out, detach, or array (troops); (of troops) move out of camp etc.; (*d*) induce to talk; (*e*) (of successive days) grow longer; (*f*) (of a train etc.) leave a station; (of a vehicle) move away from the side of the road. **draw up** (*a*) bring (esp. troops) or come into regular order; (*b*) compose (a document), esp. in a formally correct way; write out in due form; (*c*) come up *with*, come close *to*; gain on or overtake an antagonist in a race; (*d*) bring or come to a halt, pull up; (*e*) make *oneself* stiffly erect; (*f*) take up *with* (a person).

draw- /drɔː/ *comb. form.* [Repr. DRAW *n.*, *v.*] In combs. in various relations and with various senses, as 'that is drawn', 'that draws', 'involving drawing'.

drawbench *n.* a machine with a bed along which wire etc. can be reduced in cross-section by being drawn through a restricting aperture M19. **draw-boy** *n.* (*Hist.*) the boy who pulled the strings of a draw-loom; the device by which this was later effected: M18. **drawcard** *n.* something that attracts attention or custom M20. **draw-gate** *n.* a sluice-gate L18. **draw-glove(s)** *n.* (*Hist.*) a parlour-game which consisted in a race at drawing off gloves when certain words were spoken M17. **draw-hoe** *n.* a hoe used with a pulling action E19. **draw-in** *n.* (*a*) *rare* something that draws things in; (*b*) a lay-by: M19. **draw-kiln** *n.* a limekiln from which the burned lime is drawn out at the bottom E19. **draw-knife** *n.* (*a*) a blade with a handle at each end at right angles to it, drawn towards the user to remove wood from a surface; (*b*) = *drawing-knife* (a) s.v. DRAWING *vbl n.*: E18. **draw-leaf** *n.* an extending leaf of a draw-table M20. **draw-loom** *n.* (*Hist.*) a loom used for figure weaving, in which the warp threads passed through loops in strings which were pulled in a particular order to produce a pattern M19. **draw-net** *n.* a drag-net E17. **draw-off** *a.* designating a tap by which liquid may be drawn from a vessel E20. **draw-plate** *n.* a plate with a number of graduated apertures through which wire or metal strip can be drawn to make it thinner M19. *draw-poker*: see DRAW *n.* 9a. **draw-shave** *n.* a draw-knife for shaving spokes etc. E19. **draw-sheet** *n.* a sheet so placed that it can be taken from under a patient without remaking the whole bed L19. **drawstop** *n.* an organ-stop which is pulled out to admit air to a rank of pipes L19. **draw-string** *n.* a string, cord, etc., that can be pulled to tighten the mouth of a bag, the waist of a garment, etc. M19. **draw-table** *n.* a table with parts that can be pulled out to make it larger E20. **draw-well** *n.* a deep well from which water is drawn by a bucket suspended on a rope LME. **draw-works** *n.pl.* the machinery in an oil derrick for raising and lowering the drill pipe and providing the power for turning it E20.

drawable /ˈdrɔː(r)əb(ə)l/ *a.* LME. [f. DRAW *v.* + -ABLE.] Able to be drawn.

drawback /ˈdrɔːbak/ *n.* & *a.* E17. [f. *draw back* s.v. DRAW *v.*] A *n.* †1 A person who draws back or hesitates. Only in E17. 2 A refund of excise or import duty when the imported item is subsequently exported or used in producing an export. Formerly, the action of getting such a refund. L17. b A deduction, a diminution. Foll. by *from*. M18. 3 Something that hinders progress or impairs satisfaction; a hindrance, a disadvantage. E18. 4 In iron-founding, a removable part of a mould. M19. 5 The inhalation of smoke from a cigarette etc. *Austral.* & *NZ*. M20.

3 P. WARNER The greatest drawback to armour was its suffocating effect. D. M. THOMAS Except for the major drawback of being apart from her husband, she was busy and contented.

B *attrib.* or as *adj.* (Having a part) that can be drawn back. E18.

drawbar /ˈdrɔːbɑː/ *n.* M16. [f. DRAW- + BAR *n.*[1]] 1 A bar that can be removed, esp. in a fence to allow passage. M16. 2 A bar on a vehicle to which something can be attached to pull it or be pulled. M19. 3 A submerged fireclay block used in glass-making to stabilize the position of sheet glass during drawing. M20. 4 Any of a number of bars that may be pulled out to control harmonics on an electric organ. M20.

drawbridge /ˈdrɔːbrɪdʒ/ *n.* ME. [f. DRAW- + BRIDGE *n.*[1]] 1 A bridge or section of a bridge hinged at one end for drawing up and lowering to prevent or permit passage across it or to open or close a channel spanned by it. ME. 2 A movable bridge or gangway on a ship etc. M19.

Drawcansir /ˈdrɔːkansə, drɔːˈkansə/ *n.* L17. [A blustering braggart in Villiers's 'The Rehearsal' (1672), who in the last scene enters a battle and kills all the combatants, f. burlesque alt. of *Almanzor* in Dryden's 'Conquest of Granada' (1670–2), perh. intended to suggest *draw a can* (of liquor).] A person formidable to both friend and enemy; a fierce swashbuckler.

drawdown /ˈdrɔːdaʊn/ *n.* L18. [f. *draw down* s.v. DRAW *v.*] †1 Something that is drawn down. *rare*. Only in L18. 2 (A) lowering of the water level in a lake etc.; a withdrawal of water or oil from a reservoir etc. M20. 3 An act of raising money through loans; borrowing. L20.

drawee /drɔː(r)ˈiː/ *n.* M18. [f. DRAW *v.* + -EE[1].] The person, bank, etc., on whom a bill of exchange is drawn.

drawer /*in branch I* ˈdrɔː(r)ə; *in branches II, III* drɔː/ *n.* ME. [f. DRAW *v.* + -ER[1], in branch II after (O)Fr. *tiroir*, f. *tirer* draw.] I 1 A person who or thing which draws. ME. b A tapster. *arch.* M16. c A person who makes a drawing; a draughtsman. L16. d A person who draws a bill of exchange. L17. e A legal draftsman. L18. 2 An instrument, tool, etc., for drawing out or extracting. Long *rare*. M16.

II 3 In *pl.* Knickers, underpants, briefs. Formerly also, any garment worn next to the body below the waist; stockings. M16.

3 DROOPY *drawers*.

III 4 A box-shaped receptacle made to slide horizontally in and out of a frame or a table for access. L16. 5 In *pl.* = *chest of drawers* s.v. CHEST *n.* L17.

4 *bottom drawer*: see BOTTOM *a.* *top drawer*: see TOP *a.*

drawing /ˈdrɔː(r)ɪŋ/ *n.* ME. [f. DRAW *v.* + -ING[1]. In branch II abbrev. of WITHDRAWING.] I 1 *gen.* The action of DRAW *v.*; an instance of this, *esp.* a raffle. ME. 2 *spec.* The action of drawing a line on paper etc.; the art of representing or figuring by means of lines, esp. in monochrome; representation in which delineation of form is primary. LME. 3 A picture, diagram, or representation of something drawn in monochrome or in which delineation of form is primary. L17. b The arrangement of the lines in a drawing which determine form. M18. 4 Something which is drawn out or obtained by drawing; in *pl.*, money drawn out of a business or account. M19.

1 JER. TAYLOR Little drawings aside of the curtains of peace. B. WEBB There has been a rapid drawing together . . of Liberals and Conservatives against Labour. *deep drawing*: see DEEP *adv.* 2 J. REYNOLDS Painting comprises both drawing and colouring. **out of drawing** incorrectly drawn, esp. as regards perspective. *technical drawing*: see TECHNICAL *a.* 3 W. S. MAUGHAM On the walls were drawings by the great French masters. *detail drawing*, *exploded drawing*, *working drawing*, etc. 4 **drawing of tea** an amount of tea leaves taken to make a pot of tea.

II 5 = WITHDRAWING. Only in †*drawing-chamber*, DRAWING-ROOM. LME.

Comb.: **drawing account** an account from which money can be drawn, esp. against credited future earnings or an allowance of expenses; **drawing-block** a pad of drawing-paper; **drawing-board**: on which paper may be spread for drawing plans etc. on; *back to the drawing-board* (colloq.), back to begin afresh (after the failure of an enterprise); **drawing-book** a book for drawing in or containing designs to be copied; †**drawing-chamber** a private room; a drawing-room; **drawing-knife** (*a*) a farrier's knife for trimming hoofs; (*b*) = *draw-knife* (a) s.v. DRAW-; **drawing-master** a teacher of drawing; **drawing-paper** stout paper for drawing on; **drawing-pin**: with a round flat head for fastening paper to a drawing-board etc.; **drawing-string** = DRAWSTRING.

drawing /ˈdrɔː(r)ɪŋ/ *ppl a.* LME. [f. DRAW *v.* + -ING[2].] That draws, esp. a vehicle, matter from a wound, or an audience.

drawing card = DRAWCARD.

drawing-room /ˈdrɔː(r)ɪŋruːm, -rʊm/ *n.* & *a.* M17. [Abbrev. of WITHDRAWING-*room*.] A *n.* 1 Orig., a private room attached to a more public one. Now, a room where guests can be formally received and to which they can retire after dinner; a sitting-room. M17. b The company assembled in a drawing-room. M19. c A private compartment in a train. *US*. M19. 2 *Hist.* A levee; a formal reception, esp. at court. E18. B *attrib.* or as *adj.* Suitable for or characteristic of a drawing-room; *esp.* (of a story, song, play, etc.) distinguished by an observance of social proprieties; polite, restrained. M19.

drawing-roomy *a.* E20.

drawish /ˈdrɔː(r)ɪʃ/ *a.* E20. [f. DRAW *n.* + -ISH[1].] Of a game of chess: likely to lead to a draw.

drawk /drɔːk/ *n.* Now *dial.* ME. [med.L *drauca*.] Any of several weeds that grow in corn, *esp.* brome, darnel, or wild oats.

drawl /drɔːl/ *v.* & *n.* L16. [Prob. orig. slang f. EFris., LG, Du. *dralen* delay, linger. Cf. DRAIL.] A *v.* 1 *v.i.* & *t.* (usu. foll. by *out*). Speak or utter with indolence or deliberate slowness; speak or utter with vowels more prolonged than is usual. L16. 2 *v.i.* Move slowly and loiteringly, crawl; trail. Now *rare*. L16. 3 *v.t.* Pull slowly or with effort, drag; drag *on* or *out* in time; cause to pass slowly *away*. L16.

2 W. OWEN The blind-cord drawls across the window sill.

B *n.* The action of drawling; a slow indolent utterance; speech or an accent with vowels more prolonged than is usual. M18.

R. LEHMANN 'No, I can't imagine,' said Madeleine in a thoughtful drawl.

drawler *n.* M19. **drawlingly** *adv.* in a drawling manner M18.

drawlatch /ˈdrɔːlatʃ/ *n.* & *v.* ME. [f. DRAW *v.* + LATCH *n.*[1]] A *n.* 1 A sneak-thief. *obs.* exc. *dial.* ME. 2 A lazy or worthless person. *derog. arch.* M16. B *v.i.* Act in a sneaky way; dawdle, waste time. *obs.* exc. *dial.* L16.

drawly /ˈdrɔːli/ *a.* E19. [f. DRAWL *n.* + -Y[1].] Of the nature of a drawl; characterized by drawling.

drawn /drɔːn/ *a.* ME. [pa. pple of DRAW *v.*] 1 That has been drawn; *spec.* (of a gun etc.) taken out ready for immediate use; (of a line, picture, etc.) formed on paper etc.; (of wire, glass, etc.) made by drawing. ME. 2 Of a battle, game, etc.: ended without an outright winner; resulting in a draw. Of a position in chess: resulting in a draw if both players make the best moves. E17. 3 Of fabric, a garment, etc.: gathered. M19. 4 Of a face, expression, etc.: distorted or lined by pain, anxiety, or fear. L19. 5 Of a shoot or plant: thin and elongated, spindly. L19.

1 A. K. GREEN A long drawn-out tale. *deep-drawn*: see DEEP *adv.*

Special collocations: **drawn butter** melted butter. **drawn-(thread)work** ornamental work on a fabric done by drawing out threads, usu. with additional needlework.

dray /dreɪ/ *n.*[1] & *v.* LME. [Corresp. formally to OE *dræge* (also *drægnet*) drag-net, f. base of *dragan* DRAW *v.* & AL *dreia*. Cf. MLG *drage* bier, litter (G *Trage* hand-barrow, litter).] A *n.* 1 A cart without wheels, a sledge. Now *dial.* & *US*. LME. 2 A low cart without sides used esp. by brewers for carrying heavy loads. (Earliest in *drayman*.) L16. 3 A two-wheeled cart. *Austral.* & *NZ*. M19.

Comb.: **dray-cart** = senses 1, 2 above; **dray-horse** a large strong horse used for pulling a dray; **drayman** the driver of a dray, *esp.* a brewer's driver; **dray-road, -track** (chiefly *Austral.* & *NZ*) a road or track used chiefly by drays, a narrow track.

B *v.t.* Convey by dray; bring *up* or *in* by dray. M19.

drayage *n.* (*a*) conveyance by dray; (*b*) the charge for this: L18.

dray *n.*[2] var. of DREY.

dread /drɛd/ *n.* ME. [f. DREAD *v.*] **1** Extreme fear or apprehension; great awe. ME. †**2** Doubt; risk of something being otherwise. ME–M16. **3** An object or cause of dread. ME. **4** A sudden take-off and flight by a colony of gulls or other birds. M20. **5** A Rastafarian; a person who wears dreadlocks. L20.

1 C. CONNOLLY The dread of loneliness being keener than the fear of bondage, we get married. 3 MILTON Shouting to behold Their once great dread, captive and blind before them.

Comb.: **dreadlock** a tight ringlet or braid in a hairstyle, characteristic of Rastafarians, in which the head is covered with such ringlets that hang down loose (usu. in *pl.*).

†**dread** *a.*[1] Only in ME. [Aphet. f. ADRAD w. assim. to prec.] Afraid, terrified.

¶ Survives in derivs. DREADLY, DREADNESS.

dread /drɛd/ *a.*[2] LME. [pa. pple of next.] **1** Feared greatly; dreadful, awful. LME. **2** Held in awe, revered. *arch.* LME.

1 F. W. FABER A bondage dreader far than death. R. ELLISON The dread possibility.. of being expelled. 2 SHAKES. *2 Hen. VI* A messenger from Henry, our dread liege.

dread /drɛd/ *v.* Earlier †**a-**. [OE *adrǣdan* late form of *ondrǣdan* = OS *antdrādan*, OHG *intrātan*, f. *ond-*, *and-* (as in ANSWER *n.*) + a WGmc base of unkn. origin. Aphet. in ME after which *adread* is not recorded. See also YDRED.] **1** *v.t.* Fear greatly; regard with awe. OE. **2** *v.t.* Have a shrinking apprehension of; look forward to with anxiety or fear; be afraid *that*, *to do*. OE. †**b** Fear for. *rare.* M–L16. †**3** *v.i.* Be greatly afraid. OE–M19. **4** *v.refl.* Fear, be afraid. Now only foll. by subord. cl. Long *arch.* OE. **5** *v.t.* Cause to fear; terrify. Long *obs.* exc. *Sc. arch.* ME.

2 T. MOORE I sometimes dread that all is not right at home. J. BUCHAN The thing I hoped for and had dreaded to miss. P. ROSE Mrs Ruskin hated Scotland and.. dreaded going there. 3 AV *1 Chron.* 22:13 Dread not, nor be dismayed.

dreaded *ppl a.* regarded with dread; *colloq.* & *joc.* regarded with mock fear or light-hearted contempt: M16. **dreader** *n.* (now *rare*) M16. **dreadingly** *adv.* (*rare*) with dread L16.

dreadful /ˈdrɛdfʊl, -f(ə)l/ *a.*, *adv.*, & *n.* ME. [f. DREAD *n.* + -FUL.] **A** *adj.* †**1** Full of dread; terrified; awed. ME–M17. **2** Inspiring dread or awe; formidable; terrible. ME. **3** Exceedingly bad, long, or boring; troublesome, disagreeable, horrid. *colloq.* E18.

2 H. JAMES He was haunted.. with dreadful visions of what might have befallen her. 3 G. VIDAL The acoustics of the Odeon are dreadful.

B *adv.* Dreadfully. Now *non-standard.* L17.

C *n.* A story in a crudely sensational style; a cheap book or magazine of such stories. L19.

penny dreadful: see PENNY *a.*

dreadfully *adv.* †(*a*) with fear or awe; (*b*) terribly, fearfully; *colloq.* exceedingly: ME. **dreadfulness** *n.* †(*a*) the state of having fear or dread; (*b*) the quality of being dreadful or fearsome: LME.

dreadless /ˈdrɛdlɪs/ *a.* & *adv.* Now *rare.* LME. [f. DREAD *n.* + -LESS.] **A** *adj.* Without dread; fearless; without danger, secure. LME. †**B** *adv.* Without doubt or fear of mistake. LME–M16.

dreadlessly *adv.* E17. **dreadlessness** *n.* L16.

dreadly /ˈdrɛdli/ *adv. arch.* ME. [f. DREAD *a.*[1] + -LY[2].] **1** In a manner that inspires dread. ME. **2** With dread or awe. *rare.* L17.

dreadness /ˈdrɛdnɪs/ *n.* Long *arch. rare.* ME. [f. DREAD *a.*[1] + -NESS.] Dreadfulness.

dreadnought /ˈdrɛdnɔːt/ *n.* & *a.* Also **-naught**, (in sense 3) **D-**. E19. [f. DREAD *v.* + NOUGHT *n.* In sense A.3 f. the name of a particular British battleship.] **A** *n.* **1** A heavy overcoat; a type of thick woollen cloth used for such overcoats. Cf. FEARNOUGHT. *arch.* E19. **2** A fearless person. E19. **3** *Hist.* Any of a class of battleships (orig. superior to all their predecessors) whose main armament was entirely big guns of the same calibre. E20. **B** *adj.* Fearless. *rare.* M19.

dream /driːm/ *n.*[1] Long *obs.* exc. perh. in DREAM-HOLE. [OE *drēam* corresp. to OS *drōm* joy, music (also dream).] †**1** Joy, gladness, mirth. OE–ME. **2** Music, melody; sound, noise. OE.

dream /driːm/ *n.*[2] & *a.* ME. [Corresp. in sense to OFris. *drām*, OS *drōm* (Du. *droom*), OHG *troum* (G *Traum*), ON *draumr*. Perh. rel. to prec.] **A** *n.* **1** A series of thoughts, images, sensations, or emotions occurring in the mind during sleep. ME. **2** A vision of the imagination indulged in when awake, *esp.* one prompted by desire, hope, or ambition; a flight of fancy; a state of mind in which awareness of immediate reality is temporarily shut out, a reverie. See also DAYDREAM *n.* LME. **3** Something seen in a dream; a vision. M17. **4** An exceptionally enjoyable or attractive person or thing. L19. **5** An enduring hope or aspiration; an ideal. E20.

1 S. JOHNSON Striving, as is usual in dreams, without ability to move. 2 W. DAMPIER These may seem to the Reader but Golden Dreams. G. GREENE He stood in a dream, fingering his long grey moustache. 3 MILTON Suddenly stood at my Head a dream. 4 K. TENNANT I picked up a dress in Innes thats a dream. 5 L. M. MONTGOMERY It's always been one of my dreams to live near a brook. M. MITCHELL He was still a young girl's dream of the Perfect Knight.

Phrases: *American dream*: see AMERICAN *a.* **like a dream** *colloq.* easily, effortlessly. *loves' young dream*: see LOVE *n.* OPIUM *dream. sweet dreams*: see SWEET *a.* & *adv.* **waking dream** an involuntary dream occurring when awake. *wet dream*: see WET *a.*

B *attrib.* or as *adj.* Such as one dreams of or longs for; ideal; perfect. Cf. DREAMY 4. L19.

P. G. WODEHOUSE I wasn't everybody's dream girl. D. EDEN She planned her dream home.

Comb. & *special collocations*: **dreamboat** *colloq.* a very attractive thing or person (esp. of the opposite sex); **dream-book**: containing interpretations of dreams; **dreamland** an ideal or imaginary land; **dream ticket** (the conjunction of) an ideal pair of candidates standing together for political office; **dream-time** *Austral.* = ALCHERINGA; **dream vision** (a poem in) a form freq. used by medieval poets, in which the poet recounts an alleged dream often open to allegorical interpretation; **dreamworld** a state of mind distanced from reality.

dreamery *n.* (*a*) a place conducive to dreaming; (*b*) dreaminess; the material of dreams: E19. **dreamful** *a.* full of dreams; dreamy: M16. **dreamfully** *adv.* L19. **dreamfulness** *n.* E20. **dreamish** *a.* (*rare*) rather dreamy L16. **dreamless** *a.* E17. **dreamlessly** *adv.* L19. **dreamlessness** *n.* E20. **dreamlike** *a.* appearing unreal, vague, or shadowy, as in a dream E19.

dream /driːm/ *v.* Pa. t. **dreamed** /drɛmt, driːmd/, **dreamt** /drɛmt/. ME. [f. (as) DREAM *n.*[2]] **1** *v.i.* Experience dreams during sleep (*of*, *about*, †*on*). ME. **2** *v.t.* See, hear, or feel in a dream; experience or imagine (a dream, vision, etc.) in sleep. Foll. by simple obj., *that*. ME. **3** *v.t.* Imagine as in a dream; picture to oneself; believe possible (*that*). Usu. in neg. contexts. LME. **4** *v.i.* Think *of* as at all possible or appropriate; have any conception *of*. Usu. in neg. contexts. M16. **5** *v.i.* Fall into reverie; indulge in daydreams. (Foll. by *of*.) Cf. DAYDREAM *v.* M16. **6** *v.i.* **a** Act dreamily, procrastinate. Only in M16. **b** Hover or hang dreamily or lightly. M19. **7** *v.t.* Bring (esp. oneself) in a dream to a specified state or place. E18.

2 HOBBES He dreamed that God spake to him. TENNYSON Last night.. I dream'd a vision of the dead. 3 J. BUCHAN He did not dream that it would be his fate to fall.. under the walls of Arras. T. GUNN Dreaming the flower I have never seen. 4 SHAKES. *Haml.* There are more things in heaven and earth, Horatio, Than are dreamt of in your philosophy. K. AMIS I wouldn't dream of doing anything behind his back. 5 R. LEHMANN Dinah.. had dreamed always of living in the country. P. KAVANAGH He walked slowly, dreaming, along the narrow path. 6b N. HAWTHORNE Mist.. dreamed along the hills. 7 R. H. FROUDE I may dream myself among lakes and mountains.

With advs. in specialized senses: **dream away** spend or lose (time etc.) dreamily or unpractically. **dream up** think up, devise, invent.

dreamer *n.* a person who dreams; a visionary; *esp.* an idle or unpractical person: ME. **dreamingly** *adv.* in a dreaming or dreamlike manner M16.

dream-hole /ˈdriːmhəʊl/ *n.* Now *rare.* M16. [Perh. f. DREAM *n.*[1] (as referring to holes by which the sound of bells escaped) + HOLE *n.*[1]] An opening in an outside wall of a church tower, barn, etc.

dreamy /ˈdriːmi/ *a.* M16. [f. DREAM *n.*[2] + -Y[1].] **1** Full of dreams; characterized by dreaming; causing dreams. M16. **2** Given or pertaining to reverie; fanciful; unpractical. E19. **3** Such as might occur in a dream, dreamlike; vague, indistinct; misty, cloudy. M19. **4** Perfect, ideal; delightful. Cf. DREAM *a. colloq.* L19.

1 TENNYSON Within the dreamy house, The doors upon their hinges creak'd. E. K. KANE A dreamy but intense slumber. 2 G. STEIN She was always sort of dreamy and not there. 3 B. JOWETT He has a dreamy recollection of hearing [it]. D. H. LAWRENCE He lay there.., his face all dreamy and boyish, very unusual. 4 N. BLAKE The water's absolutely dreamy And I bet you're a super swimmer.

dreamily *adv.* M19. **dreaminess** *n.* L18.

drear /drɪə/ *n.* M16. [Back-form. f. DREARY.] †**1** Dreariness, sadness, gloom. M16–M19. **2** A dreary person. *colloq.* M20.

drear /drɪə/ *a.* Chiefly *poet.* E17. [Abbrev.] = DREARY *a.* 3.

dreary /ˈdrɪəri/ *a.* & *n.* [OE *drēoriġ*, f. *drēor* gore f. Gmc, f. base of OE *drēosan* drop, fall, OS *driosan*, Goth. *driusan*, and OS *drōr*, OHG *trōr*, ON *dreyri* gore, blood, MHG *trūrec* (G *traurig* sorrowful): see -Y[1].] **A** *adj.* †**1** Gory, bloody; cruel; dreadful. OE–E17. **2** Of a person etc: sad, melancholy. Now *rare* or *obs.* OE. **3** Dismal, gloomy; dull, tediously uninteresting. M17.

3 OED A dreary speech by a dreary orator. D. M. THOMAS The dreary yard with its rubbish heaps, and the backs of more slums.

B *n.* A dreary person. *colloq.* E20.

drearihead *n.* (*arch.*) [-HEAD] (*a*) sadness; (*b*) gloominess, dreariness: ME. **drearihood** *n.* (*arch.*) = DREARIHEAD M17. **drearily** *adv.* OE. **dreariment** *n.* (*arch.*) (the expression of) dreary condition L16. **dreariness** *n.* †(*a*) sadness, sorrowfulness; (*b*) dismal or gloomy character, tedious dulness: OE. **drearisome** *a.* (chiefly *dial.*) [-SOME[1]] dreary, desolate M17.

dreck /drɛk/ *n. slang.* Also **drek.** E20. [f. Yiddish *drek* (G *Dreck*) filth, dregs, dung f. MHG *drec* f. Gmc base repr. also by OE *þreax* rubbish, rottenness, ON *þrekkr*, OFris *threkk*, prob. conn. with Gk *skatos* dung, *sterganos* privy, lavatory, L *stercus* excrement.] Rubbish, trash.

dredge /drɛdʒ/ *n.*[1] ME. [OFr. *dragie*, (also mod.) DRAGÉE, in med.L *drageia*, *dragetum*, *-ata* perh. f. L *tragemata* spices f. Gk.] †**1** A comfit, a sweet consisting of a coated seed or grain of spice, a dragée. Also, a mixture of spices etc. ME–E17. **2** A mixture of grains, esp. oats and barley, sown together. Also *dredge corn.* ME.

dredge /drɛdʒ/ *n.*[2] L15. [Perh. f. MDu *dregghe* grappling-hook, but the final consonant of the Eng. wd suggests a native origin. Perh. rel. to DRAG *n.* Earliest in *dredge-boat.*] An apparatus for collecting and bringing up objects or material from the bed of a river etc. by dragging or scooping; a drag-net; a boat or machine for dredging.

Comb.: **dredge-boat** a boat used for dredging.

dredge /drɛdʒ/ *v.*[1] E16. [f. DREDGE *n.*[2]] **1** *v.t.* Bring *up* or collect, clear *out* or *away*, using a dredge. E16. **2** *v.i.* Use a dredge. L17. **3** *v.t.* Clean out the bed of (a river etc.) using a dredge; search in this way. M19.

1 *fig.*: C. S. FORESTER Randall raked back in his memory, trying to dredge up the schoolboy geography he had once learned. 3 V. WOOLF The pool had been dredged and a thigh bone recovered.

dredge /drɛdʒ/ *v.*[2]*t.* Also †**drudge.** L16. [f. DREDGE *n.*[1]] **1** Sprinkle with a powdered substance, esp. flour, sugar, or (orig.) a mixture of spices. L16. **2** Sprinkle (a powdered substance) *over.* M17.

1 *fig.*: D. W. JERROLD His.. hair was dredged with grey.

Comb.: **dredging-box** = DREDGER *n.*[2]

dredger /ˈdrɛdʒə/ *n.*[1] E16. [f. DREDGE *v.*[1] + -ER[1].] **1** A person who uses a dredge-boat or dredging apparatus, esp. for collecting oysters. E16. **2** A boat or machine used for dredging. E17.

dredger /ˈdrɛdʒə/ *n.*[2] Also †**drudger.** M17. [f. DREDGE *v.*[2] + -ER[1].] A container with a perforated lid for sprinkling a powdered substance, esp. sugar or flour.

dree /driː/ *n.* Chiefly as *literary archaism*. LME. [f. the vb.] Suffering, grief, trouble.

¶In isolated use bef. L19.

dree *a.* & *adv.* see DREICH.

dree /driː/ *v.* Long *obs.* exc. *Sc.* & *north.* exc. as *literary archaism*. Also **drie**. Pa. t. & pple **dreed**. [OE *drēogan* f. Gmc base repr. also by Goth. *driugan* do military service, ON *drýgja* perpetrate, practise.] **1** *v.t.* †**a** Perform (service); do (a person's will); commit (sin). OE–ME. **b** Do, perform, (penance). ME. **2** *v.t.* Endure, undergo, (something burdensome, painful, etc.). OE. **3** *v.i.* Endure, continue, last. ME. **4** *v.t.* Pass, spend, (time, one's life). Also foll. by *forth*, *out*. ME.

2 E. GASKELL To dree all the cruel slander they'll put upon him. **dree one's weird** submit to one's fate.

¶As an archaism, following use by Sir Walter Scott.

dreep /driːp/ *v.* & *n.* Now chiefly *dial.* [OE *drēopan* = OS *driopan*, OHG *triofan*, ON *drjúpa*, f. Gmc base of DROP *v.*: cf. DRIP *n.*, *v.*. In Sc. a dial. var. of DRIP *v.*] **A** *v.i.* **1** Fall in drops; drip. OE. **2** Droop; *fig.* lose courage; walk very slowly; act lethargically. LME.

2 L. A. G. STRONG A shuffling, dreeping old crone.

B *n.* **1** A wet, dripping, condition. M19. **2** An ineffective, spiritless, or mournful person; a 'drip'. E20.

dreepy *a.* droopy, spiritless L19.

dreg /drɛg/ *n.* & *v.* ME. [Prob. of Scand. origin: cf. ON pl. *dreggjar*, MSw. *drägg*, Sw. pl. *drägg*.] **A** *n.sing.* & (usu.) in *pl.* **1** The sediment of a liquor; grounds, lees. ME. †**2** Excrement; rubbish; corrupt matter. ME–M17. **3** The most worthless part or parts; the refuse. M16. **4** The last remains or traces; *sing.* a small remnant, a small quantity or drop. L16.

1 DICKENS He flings the dregs of his wine at Edwin. 3 W. STYRON *You* must be part of the bottomless dregs of this loathsome city. 4 E. BOWEN At first, in those dregs of daylight, he saw nobody there.

†**B** *v.t.* Make dreggy. *rare*. E17–E19.

dreggish *a.* (now *rare*) of the nature of dregs or refuse; affected by dregs; *fig.* base, vile: M16. **dreggy** *a.* containing dregs; of the nature of dregs; turbid, polluted; impure: LME.

dreich /driːx/ *a.* & *adv.* Long *obs.* exc. *Sc.* & *north.* Also **dreigh**, **driech**, **driegh**; (*obs.* in *Sc.*) **dree** /driː/. ME. [f. as DREE *v.*, corresp. to ON *drjúgr* enduring, lasting.] **A** *adj.* †**1** Patient, long-suffering. Only in ME. †**2** Heavy, mighty, great; fierce. Only in LME. **3** Long; tedious, persistent; slow, tardy; dreary, miserable, gloomy, bleak. LME.

3 R. L. STEVENSON My life is a bit driegh.. I see little company. D. H. LAWRENCE A grey, dree afternoon.

B *adv.* = DREICHLY. ME.

dreichly *adv.* †(*a*) heavily, mightily, vehemently; in a dreich manner; (*b*) slowly, persistently: LME.

dreidel /ˈdreɪd(ə)l/ *n.* Chiefly *N. Amer.* Also **dreidl**. M20. [Yiddish *dreydl*, f. MHG *dræ(je)n* (G *drehen*) turn.] A four-sided spinning-top with a Hebrew letter on each side; a game of put-and-take played with this, esp. at Hanukkah.

dreigh *a.* & *adv.* var. of DREICH.

dreikanter /ˈdrʌɪkɑːntə, -kan-/ *n.* Pl. same, **-s**. E20. [G, lit. 'three-edged thing', f. *drei* three + *Kante* edge: see CANT *n.*[1], -ER[1].] An angular faceted pebble whose surface has been cut by wind-blown sand, *esp.* one with three facets.

drek *n.* var. of DRECK.

drench /drɛn(t)ʃ/ *n.* [OE *drenċ* f. Gmc, f. var. of base of DRINK *v.*; corresp. to OS *dranc*, OHG *tranc(h)* (G *Trank*), ON *drekka*, Goth. *dragk*.] †**1** *gen.* A drink, a draught. OE–ME. **2** A medicinal or poisonous draught; a potion. *arch.* OE. **3** A drink or dose of medicine given to an animal. M16. **4** The act of drenching or soaking; a soaking, a downpour. E19.

4 F. NORRIS The horse, restive under the drench of the rain, moved uneasily. *fig.*: A. THWAITE Sun's incessant drench.

drench /drɛn(t)ʃ/ *v.* [OE *drenċan* = OFris. *drenza*, OS *drenkian* (Du. *drenken*), OHG *trenchen* (G *tränken*), ON *drekkja*, Goth. *dragkjan*, f. Gmc.] **1** *v.t.* Force (an animal) to take a draught of medicine; *arch.* force (a person) to drink. OE. †**2** *v.t.* & *i.* Drown; (cause to) sink in water. ME–M17. **3** *v.t.* **a** Wet thoroughly (as) by immersion; soak, steep. ME. **b** Wet thoroughly with falling or thrown liquid. M16. **4** *v.t. fig.* Overwhelm; saturate as in a liquid, cover thoroughly all over. Formerly also, plunge *in* or *into* despair, sin, etc. ME.

1 **drenching-gun** a device for giving a medicinal drench to an animal. 3a A. DAVIS Sweat drenched my clothes before I had hardly gotten started. A. T. ELLIS I fell in that bloody stream and I'm drenched. **b** R. L. STEVENSON A drenching rain. 4 W. GOLDING Half the plain and the mountains.. were drenched in milky light. A. COOKE His unique popularity in being drenched by a continuous blizzard of invitations.

drencher *n.* a person who or thing which drenches; *esp.* a drenching shower; a drenching-gun: ME.

dreng /drɛŋ/ *n.* OE. [ON *drengr* young man, lad, fellow (Sw. *dräng* man, servant, Da. *dreng* boy, apprentice).] *Eng. Hist.* A free tenant, esp. in ancient Northumbria, holding by a tenure partly military, partly servile.

drengage *n.* the tenure or service of a dreng L17.

Dresden /ˈdrɛzd(ə)n/ *a.* & *n.* M18. [See below.] **A** *adj.* **1** Designating (a piece of) china made at Meissen, near Dresden, Germany, with elaborate decoration and delicate colouring. M18. **2** Having a delicate or frail prettiness. E20. **B** *n.* Dresden china. M18.

Dresdener *n.* a person who lives in or comes from Dresden L19.

dress /drɛs/ *n.* M16. [f. the vb.] **1** The action or an act of dressing. Now *rare* or *obs.* M16. **2** Clothing, *esp.* outer clothing; clothing belonging to a particular occupation, country, or (esp. formal or ceremonial) occasion. M16. **3** *transf.* External covering, *esp.* the plumage of a bird; outward form. E17. **4** Orig., a suit of clothes, an outfit, an article of clothing. Now, a woman's or girl's garment consisting of a skirt and a bodice; (w. qualifying n.) a garment for a specified occasion or part of the body. M17. †**5** A dressing for a wound. L17–L18. **6** A finish put on something to set off its appearance. L19.

2 DICKENS Your black silk frock will be quite dress enough. J. CONRAD The dress I wore was.. that of a sailor come ashore from some coaster. J. RABAN He'd lost his head-dress.. and was wearing Western dress. A. LURIE Fashion, as opposed to mere dress, is.. sprinkled with foreign terms. *battledress*, *evening dress*, *fancy dress*, *full dress*, *morning dress*, etc. 3 H. J. LASKI The *Letter Concerning Toleration* was published in its Latin dress, and four years afterwards an English translation appeared. 4 DAY LEWIS She wears a long dress with a dark band above the hem. *cocktail-dress*, *head-dress*, *nightdress*, etc.

Attrib. & *comb.*: In the sense 'constituting or worn (as part of) full dress', as *dress-shirt*, *dress shoes*, *sword*, *uniform*, etc. Special combs., as **dress agency** an agency, shop, etc., that buys used clothes privately and resells them; **dress-carriage**: reserved for state or semi-state occasions; **dress circle** the lowest and most expensive gallery of seats in a theatre etc., in which evening dress was at one time required; **dress coat** a man's swallow-tailed coat used for formal dress; **dress-conscious** *a.* aware of what is fashionable in dress, particular about clothes; **dress house** (now *rare*) a brothel; **dress-improver** *Hist.* = BUSTLE *n.*[2]; **dress length** a piece of material sufficient to make a dress; **dressmake** *v.i.* make dresses, do dressmaking; **dressmaker** a person, usu. a woman, who makes dresses (*dressmaker's dummy*: see DUMMY *n.* 5b); **dressmaking** the action or occupation of making dresses; **dress parade** (*a*) a display of clothes by mannequins; (*b*) a military parade in full-dress uniforms; **dress-preserver** = *dress-shield* below; **dress rehearsal** a rehearsal in full costume, *esp.* a final such rehearsal; *transf.* a (final) practice session; **dress sense** a feel for the appropriateness of certain garments to a certain person (esp. oneself) or occasion; **dress-shield** a piece of waterproof or other material fastened under the armpit of a dress to protect it from perspiration; **dress-shirt** a shirt for wearing with evening dress; **dress weight** (*a*) a small weight placed in the hem of a dress etc.; (*b*) cloth of a suitable weight for making into dresses.

dress /drɛs/ *v.* Pa. t. & pple **dressed** /drɛst/, (*arch.* & *poet.*) **drest** /drɛst/. ME. [(O)Fr. *dresser* f. Proto-Romance, f. L *directus* DIRECT *a.*] **I** Make straight; order; make ready. †**1** *v.t.* Put to rights, set in order, put straight. ME–L17. **b** Place or set in position. LME–E16. †**2a** *v.t.* Erect, set *up*, make straight. LME–L16. **b** *v.refl.* & *i.* Raise oneself, rise. LME–L15. **3** *v.t.* †**a** *gen.* Make ready, prepare; arrange, draw up. LME–M18. **b** Treat or prepare (something) in a way proper to its character or purpose; smooth (stone, a line of cast type); prepare and finish (a skin, leather, fabric, etc.); prepare (ore) for further processing by removing waste. L15. **c** Cleanse (corn) from chaff etc. M17. **d** Remove (something) in the process of preparing, purifying, or cleansing. E18. **e** *Angling.* Prepare (a fly) for use on a fish-hook. M19. **4** *v.t.* Prepare (esp. an animal carcass) for use as food. LME. **b** Add a sauce or other mixture to (food, esp. a salad). L18. †**5** *v.refl.* & *i.* Prepare (oneself). (Foll. by *for*, *to do*.) LME–L16. **6a** *v.t.* Attire in suitable or fine clothing; array; adorn with apparel. Now often simply, put clothes on, clothe; LME. **b** *v.refl.* & *i.* Put on one's clothes; wear clothes in a specified way; *spec.* put on clothes appropriate to a formal or ceremonial occasion. M17. **c** *v.i.* Of a male: have the genitals habitually on one or other side of the fork of the trousers. M20. **7** *v.t.* Equip; adorn, deck; *spec.* adorn (a ship) with flags etc.; display goods in (a shop window) in an artistic or attractive way. LME. **b** Equip (a play etc.) with appropriate costumes. M18. **c** Fill (a theatre etc.) by means of complimentary tickets. L19. **8** *v.t.* Treat (a person) with deserved firmness or severity; thrash; scold. Now usu. foll. by *down*. LME. †**9** *v.t.* Train or break in (a horse etc.). LME–L18. **10** *v.t.* Treat (a wound, a wounded person) with remedies; apply a dressing to. L15. **11** Cultivate, tend, (a field, garden, plant, etc.); treat with manure, compost, or other fertilizer or food. E16. **12** Comb, brush, or arrange (the hair). E16. **b** Groom (a horse etc.). M16. **13** *Mil.* **a** *v.t.* Draw up (troops, a body of men, etc.) in proper alignment; correct the alignment of. M18. **b** *v.i.* Come into the correct place in line etc. L18. **14** *v.t.* Make (an artificial fly) for use in fishing. E19. **15** *v.i.* Of food: turn out (well etc.) when dressed. Of stone, etc.: be (easily etc.) dressed. E19.

3b R. GRAVES The dressed stones of the rampart. 4 B. MACDONALD I could dress chickens.. in about two minutes without once tearing the skin. **b** J. AUSTEN These two girls had been.. dressing a sallad and cucumber. 6a M. R. MITFORD Good Mr. Norris.. dressed his little daughter's doll. J. STEINBECK He himself was dressed in new white clothes. **dressed to kill** dressed to create a striking impression, often in very smart or sophisticated clothes. *dressed up to the nines*: see NINE *n.* 2. *mutton dressed as lamb*: see MUTTON. **b** S. JOHNSON He was come back to dress himself for a ball. F. A. KEMBLE It is close upon time to dress for dinner. J. RHYS Get up and dress yourself, and come downstairs. N. SHUTE She dressed in the red shirt and slacks that she had worn when she had met Dwight first. H. ROTH Even when you go to the market, you dress like a lady. 7 T. GAGE The Chamber was richly dressed and hung with many pictures, and with hangings. J. CLAVELL A high matted roof dressed with white silk. 10 R. L. STEVENSON He had recently been wounded, and still more recently dressed. S. SASSOON The little doctor.. would soon be dressing the wounds of moaning men. 13a A. W. KINGLAKE The battalion dressed its ranks with precision.

†**II** Direct. **16** *v.t.* Straighten the course of (*lit.* & *fig.*); direct, guide; turn or send in a given direction. ME–L16. **17** *v.refl.* & *i.* Go, set off, proceed. LME–L16. **18** *v.t.* Address (words) *to*. LME–M17.

With advs. in specialized senses: **dress down** dress informally or less formally than would be expected. **dress out** attire conspicuously. **dress up** dress elaborately or in masquerade; put on or wear one's best clothes or clothes for a formal occasion; *fig.* disguise by embellishment; (esp. of a child) dress oneself in a costume or in special clothes as an entertainment.

Comb.: **dress-up** *n.* & *a.* (*a*) *n.* the action of dressing up, esp. in one's best clothes; an occasion or gathering which requires formal dress; (*b*) *adj.* requiring or designating formal dress.

dressage /ˈdrɛsɑːʒ, -ɑːdʒ/ *n.* M20. [Fr., lit. 'training', f. *dresser* to train, drill.] The training of a horse in obedience and deportment; the execution by a horse of precise movements in response to its rider.

dresser /ˈdrɛsə/ *n.*[1] ME. [f. DRESS *v.* + -ER[1].] 1 A person who prepares, treats, finishes, or otherwise dresses some material or piece of equipment. ME. 2 A person who dresses another. E17. b *spec.* A person whose job is to look after theatrical costumes and help actors to dress. M19. 3 A tool or machine used in the operation of dressing. E17. 4 A person who dresses elegantly or in a specified way. L17. 5 A surgeon's assistant who helps in hospital operations. M18. 6 *Mil.* A person from whom a parading body of troops takes its alignment. L18.

4 LYTTON The most perfect dresser that even France could exhibit.

dresser /ˈdrɛsə/ *n.*[2] LME. [OFr. *dresseur, dreçor* (mod. *dressoir*), f. *dresser* prepare: see -ER[2].] 1 *Hist.* A sideboard or table in a kitchen on which food could be prepared; a table in a dining-room or hall from which dishes were served or on which plate was displayed. LME. 2 A kind of sideboard surmounted by shelves for storing and displaying dishes, plates, kitchen utensils, etc. M16. 3 A dressing-table; a bureau. *N. Amer.* L19.

2 *Welsh dresser*: see WELSH *a.*

dressing /ˈdrɛsɪŋ/ *n.* LME. [f. DRESS *v.* + -ING[1].] 1 *gen.* The action of DRESS *v.*; an instance of this. LME. 2 *spec.* a The action of preparing or finishing various materials. LME. b A beating, a thrashing; a scolding, an upbraiding. Now usu. *dressing down.* M18. c *Mil.* The proper alignment of troops. L18. d *dressing up*, the action or practice of dressing in masquerade or in special clothes as an entertainment, or of dressing in one's best clothes or clothes for a formal occasion. M19. 3 (A) sauce or other mixture added to food, esp. a salad; a seasoning; stuffing. E16. 4 *sing.* & (usu.) in *pl.* (Decorative) clothing. Now *rare.* E17. 5 A piece of material placed directly on to a wound or diseased area. E18. 6 Manure, compost, or other fertilizer spread over or ploughed into land to improve it. M18. 7 A glaze, stiffening, or other preparation used in the finishing of fabrics. E19.

1 J. K. JEROME As a girl, she never understood dressing. *window-dressing*: see WINDOW *n.* 2a *mineral dressing, ore dressing*, etc. d *attrib.*: A. WILSON Strange old hats and frocks in the dressing-up box in the nursery. 3 *French dressing, salad-dressing, thousand island dressing, vinaigrette dressing*, etc. 6 *Practical Gardening* A dressing of bonemeal during the late autumn is usually productive.

Comb.: **dressing-box** (now *rare*) a dressing-case; **dressing-case**: used for holding toilet articles; **dressing-chest** a piece of bedroom furniture with a flat top and storage facilities, for use while dressing (*duchesse dressing-chest*: see DUCHESSE 2); **dressing-comb**: used for dressing the hair; **dressing forceps**: used in applying and removing surgical dressings; **dressing-gown** a loose robe worn while one is not fully dressed, while resting, etc.; *Hist.* any loose informal gown; **dressing-room** a place for dressing or for changing one's clothes, esp. in a theatre, a sports centre, or attached to a bedroom; **dressing-station** a place for giving emergency treatment to the wounded; **dressing-table** a piece of bedroom furniture with a flat top, an upright mirror, and usu. drawers underneath for use while dressing, arranging one's hair, applying make-up, etc. (*duchesse dressing-table*: see DUCHESSE 2).

dressy /ˈdrɛsi/ *a.* M18. [f. DRESS *n.* + -Y[1].] 1 Attentive to dress; given to elaborate or noticeably smart dressing. M18. b *fig.* Excessively elaborate. M19. 2 Of a garment or accessory: suitable for a formal occasion, stylish. Of an occasion or function: requiring formal dress or one's best clothes. L18.

1 DAY LEWIS He was a dressy man, keeping his trousers in a press and trees in his shoes. 2 M. GEE Why do you always wear those earrings? They're much too dressy.

dressiness *n.* E19.

dretch *v.* var. of DRATCH.

drew /druː/ *n. obs.* exc. *dial.* LME. [Origin unkn.] A drop, a very small amount of liquid.

drew *v.* pa. t.: see DRAW *v.*

drey /dreɪ/ *n.* Also **dray**. E17. [Origin unkn.] A squirrel's nest.

Dreyfusard /ˈdreɪfʊsɑː, -ɑːd/ *n.* L19. [Fr., f. *Dreyfus* (see below) + -ARD.] *Hist.* A defender or supporter of Alfred Dreyfus (1859–1935), a Jewish Frenchman convicted of treason in 1894 and declared innocent in 1906.

drib /drɪb/ *n.* Chiefly *Sc.* & *dial.* exc. in phr. below. E18. [f. the vb or DRIBBLE *n.*, DRIBLET.] An insignificant quantity; a driblet.

dribs and drabs *colloq.* [DRAB *n.*[4]] small and intermittent sums or amounts.

drib /drɪb/ *v.* E16. [Alt. of DRIP *v.*] †1 *v.i.* Fall in drops; *fig.* go on little by little. Only in E16. 2 *v.t.* Let fall in drops; *fig.* utter as in driblets. Now *rare.* M16. †3 *v.t.* Shoot (an arrow) so that it falls short or wide of the mark. Cf. DRIBBLE *v.* 1. M–L16.

dribble /ˈdrɪb(ə)l/ *n.* L17. [f. the vb.] 1 A small barely continuous stream, a trickle; a small amount of liquid; a small stream of saliva. L17. 2 A field drain of broken stones, between which the water trickles. *local.* M19. 3 In football etc., an act of dribbling. L19.

dribbly *a.* given to or marked by dribbling E20.

dribble /ˈdrɪb(ə)l/ *v.* M16. [Frequent. of DRIB *v.*: see -LE[3]. In sense 4 perh. infl. by DRIVEL *v.* With sense 5 (perh. a different wd) cf. Du. *dribbelen* toddle, trip.] †1 *v.t.* & *i.* Shoot (an arrow), be shot, short or wide of the mark. Cf. DRIB *v.* 3. M16–E17. 2 *v.t.* Allow to flow in a trickle or in slow drops; give out in driblets. (Foll. by *out, away, forth.*) L16. 3 *v.i.* Flow or run out in a trickle or in slow drops. E17. 4 *v.i.* Let saliva trickle from the mouth. L17. 5 *v.t.* & *i.* In football, hockey, basketball, and other games: keep (the ball or puck) moving in front of one by a succession of pushes or taps. M19.

2 W. S. CHURCHILL It is a perilous policy to dribble out reinforcements and to fritter away armies. 3 S. RAVEN The scraps of paper dribbled through his fingers like confetti. *fig.*: C. P. SNOW Margaret.. did not let the chit-chat dribble on. 4 E. M. BRENT-DYER Mamma says.. Geoff must be starting to teethe because he dribbles so much. 5 J. LEHANE The player dribbles with his right hand,.. using proper fingertip control to keep the ball below knee level. M. ROBERTS Her eyes on the ball which she dribbled expertly.

dribbler *n.* a person who dribbles, esp. at football etc. M19. **dribbling** *vbl n.* (*a*) *rare* a quantity given out in driblets; (*b*) the action of the vb: L16. **dribbling** *ppl a.* that dribbles; *fig.* insignificant, made up of petty items: L16.

dribblet *n.* var. of DRIBLET.

driblet /ˈdrɪblɪt/ *n.* Also **-bb-**. L16. [f. DRIB *v.* + -LET.] 1 A small sum of money. Formerly *spec.*, a small debt. L16. 2 A small or insignificant quantity or part. L17. 3 A thin stream or small quantity of liquid. M19.

2 V. SACKVILLE-WEST These bits of information were imparted.. in driblets and with caution. 3 R. K. NARAYAN The river trickling away in minute driblets.

Comb.: **driblet cone**: produced by successive ejections of small amounts of lava.

†**dricksie** *a.* see DRUXY.

driddle /ˈdrɪd(ə)l/ *v.* & *n. Sc.* E17. [Imit., infl. by *dribble, diddle* & perh. Norw. dial. *dritla* walk slowly trailing something.] A *v.* 1 *v.i.* Walk slowly or uncertainly; work in a dilatory way; waste one's time. E17. 2 *v.i.* & *t.* Spill, dribble, trickle. E19. 3 *v.i.* Play the fiddle. M19. B *n.* 1 A dawdler; an idler; an awkward person. E19. 2 = DRIBLET 3. M19.

drie *v.* var. of DREE *v.*

driech *a.* & *adv.* var. of DREICH.

dried /drʌɪd/ *ppl a.* ME. [f. DRY *v.* + -ED[1].] 1 Deprived of moisture, desiccated. Also *dried-off, -out, -up.* ME. 2 *spec.* Of food: preserved by the removal of its natural moisture. LME.

1 *cut and dried*: see CUT *ppl a.* 1.

dried *v.* pa. t. & pple of DRY *v.*

driedoring /ˈdrɪdʊərɪŋ/ *n. S. Afr.* Also **-doorn** /-dʊər(ə)n/. E19. [Afk., f. Du. *drie* THREE + *doorn* THORN *n.*] Any of several thorny flowering shrubs and small trees of the dry plains of southern and tropical Africa, esp. *Rhigozum trichotomum.*

driegh *a.* & *adv.* var. of DREICH.

drier /ˈdrʌɪə/ *n.* Also **dryer**. ME. [f. DRY *v.* + -ER[1].] 1 A person engaged in drying. ME. 2 A natural agency that removes moisture. E16. 3 A substance mixed with oil-paint, oil, ink, etc., to make it dry more quickly. M19. 4 A machine or appliance for drying laundry, hair, etc. L19. 5 A substance that dries (quickly or slowly). L19.

4 *hair-drier, spin-drier, tumble-drier*, etc.

Comb.: **drier-up** a person who does the drying when dishes etc. are washed.

drieth *n.* var. of DRYTH.

drift /drɪft/ *n.* ME. [Orig. f. ON *drift* snowdrift; later f. MDu. *drift* drove, course, current = OFris. (*ur*)*drift* expulsion, MHG, G *Trift* passage for or of cattle, pasturage, drove, f. Gmc base of DRIVE *v.*] I Something driven. 1 An accumulation of snow, sand, etc., driven together by the wind. ME. 2 A driving mass of rain, dust, etc. LME. 3 A body of animals (rarely, persons) driven or moving along together. Formerly also, a flock of birds. Now *dial.* LME. 4 A tool for driving or ramming in piles etc. Also = *drift-pin* below. M16. 5 A floating log or mass of wood driven by the current. E17. 6 *Geol.* Material originally deposited by a current of ice, water, or air; *spec.* Pleistocene glacial and fluvioglacial deposits left when the ice sheet retreated. M19. 7 A set of fishing nets. Also = *drift-net* below. M19. 8 A large irregular mass of flowering plants, *esp.* ones planted in a garden. E20. 9 *Astron.* Either of two groups of stars that appear to have some motion towards one or other vertex in the sky. E20.

1 T. HERBERT The sands by the fury of Tempests lie in great drifts. M. ARNOLD The field Strewn with.. yellow drifts Of wither'd leaves. *snowdrift*: see SNOW *n.*[1] 2 TENNYSON Thro' scudding drifts the rainy Hyades Vext the dim sea. 3 J. M. SYNGE You'll lose my drift of heifers and my blue bull. 8 W. BRONK Great drifts of purple flowers hold / the roadside.

II The action of driving. 10 The action of driving or impelling; *esp.* (*Hist.*) the driving of all the cattle within a forest to a particular place on a fixed day, with a view to establishing ownership, levying fines, etc. LME. 11 The fact or state of being driven (as) by a current; any slow steady movement in some direction. LME. b *Motor Racing.* A controlled skid, used in taking bends. M20. c *fig.* The practice of waiting on events; inaction. Chiefly in *policy of drift.* M20. 12 The aim or purpose of an activity. Now chiefly, the tenor or purport of speech or writing. LME. †13 A scheme, a plot. E16–L17. 14 The natural course or tendency of events, actions, etc.; a trend. M16. †15 Delay, procrastination. *Sc.* M16–M17. 16 (The amount of) deviation from a course (e.g. of an aircraft, projectile, migrating bird), esp. as a result of a current. L17. 17 A slow variation in the characteristics or operation of an electric circuit or device. L19. †18 *Aeronaut.* Drag, air resistance. L19–E20. 19 *Ling.* Gradual modification of a language, as brought about by internal changes rather than external influences. E20.

10 R. SOUTH A man being under the drift of any passion, will still follow the impulse of it. 11 M. WEBB The night was full of the smell of.. moss, with a drift of primrose scent now and again. *Listener* The drift [of the population] away from the big cities continues. CONTINENTAL *drift. urban drift*: see URBAN *a.* c W. S. CHURCHILL Resolved to be irresolute, adamant for drift. 12 W. COWPER My sole drift is to be useful. A. BURGESS I do not quite understand the drift of your statement. D. LODGE Philip was able to follow his drift pretty well. 14 H. J. LASKI The drift of opinion in.. Europe was towards benevolent despotism. *wage drift*: see WAGE *n.*

III A course along which something is driven. 20 A horizontal passage in a mine, *esp.* one following a mineral vein; an inclined tunnel dug from the surface to a seam of coal etc. Also *driftway.* E17. 21 More fully *driftway.* A lane along which animals are driven. *local.* E17. 22 A ford. *S. Afr.* L18. 23 Each of the rows in which underwood is laid when felled. E19.

Comb.: **drift-anchor** = SEA *anchor*; **drift-bottle**: thrown into the sea to determine currents; **drift-ice** detached pieces of ice drifting with the wind or ocean currents; **drift-indicator** an instrument for showing the drift of an aircraft; **drift mine**: to which access is gained by a drift; **drift mining**: by means of drifts (rather than shafts or open working); **drift-net** a large net for herrings etc., kept upright by weights at the bottom and floats at the top and allowed to drift with the tide; **drift-pin** a steel pin driven into a hole in a piece of metal to enlarge or shape it; **drift sight** = *drift-indicator* above; *driftway*: see senses 20, 21 above; **driftweed** (*a*) seaweed driven ashore by the waves; (*b*) either of two kinds of seaweed, gulfweed, *Sargassum bacciferum*, and tangle, *Laminaria digitata*; **driftwood** wood floating about on, or cast ashore by, the water.

drift /drɪft/ *v.* M16. [f. the n.] †1 *v.t.* Subject (a person, a legal action, etc.) to delays. *Sc.* M16–M17. 2 *v.t.* Of a current of water or air: drive or carry along. E17. b Allow (a fishing net) to be borne by the current. M19. 3 *v.t.* & *i.* Blow or be blown into heaps. M18. b Cover or become covered with snowdrifts. M19. 4 *v.i.* Be driven along (occas., off course) by a current of water or air; move with the stream or wind; gradually deviate from a position or course. M18. b *transf.* & *fig.* Move passively or aimlessly; be brought involuntarily or imperceptibly *into* a condition, a way of life, etc. E19. 5 *v.i.* Come, go, or move in a casual or aimless manner. Also, depart. *colloq.* M19. 6 *v.t. Mech.* Enlarge (a hole) with a drift-pin. M19. 7 *v.t.* & *i. Mining.* Excavate a drift (in), tunnel (through). M19. 8 *v.t.* Drive (animals) slowly, allowing them to feed as they go. *US.* L19.

2 J. CONRAD The light winds and strong currents . . had drifted the boat about. 3 J. STEINBECK The wind . . drifted the sand of the country like snow. E. SHANKS The withered leaves that drift in Russell Square. b R. W. EMERSON Struggling through the drifted roads. 4 J. BARTH The boat wouldn't be moored, but would drift up and down the river on the tide. S. KING A little snow began to drift down from the sky. *Nature* The satellite tends to drift slowly in longitude. b A. MACLEAN His eyes closed and I thought he was drifting off into sleep. A. HAILEY It was uncharacteristic . . for him merely to 'go along' and let things drift. 5 M. TWAIN Some . . will have to drift around to two or three hotels . . before they find accommodations. V. WOOLF He had left Cambridge after two terms . . and then travelled and drifted. E. BOWEN The children . . drifted amiably into the informal classrooms. **drift apart** (of partners in a marriage or other relationship) suffer a gradual loss of affection or contact.

driftage *n.* the process or extent of drifting; drifted material: M18. **drifting** *vbl n.* (*a*) the action of the vb; (*b*) in *pl.*, that which is drifted: E17. **driftingly** *adv.* †(*a*) dilatorily; (*b*) in a drifting way: L16.

drifter /ˈdrɪftə/ *n.* M19. [f. DRIFT *v.* + -ER[1].] 1 *Mining.* a A person who excavates drifts. M19. b A percussion drill driven by compressed air used in drifting. E20. 2 A boat or person engaged in fishing with a drift-net; a fishing vessel etc. used by the Royal Navy, esp. in wartime, for patrolling, conveying stores, etc. L19. 3 = *drift-bottle* s.v. DRIFT *n.* L19. 4 A person leading an aimless or vagrant way of life. L19. 5 A wind causing snow to drift. E20.

driftless /ˈdrɪftlɪs/ *a.* E19. [f. DRIFT *n.* + -LESS.] 1 Aimless, without a purpose. E19. 2 *Geol.* Free from drift. L19.

drifty /ˈdrɪfti/ *a.* L16. [f. DRIFT *n.* + -Y[1].] †1 Full of secret aims; wily. Only in L16. 2 Containing much driving snow or many snowdrifts. M18. 3 Of a garment: flowing. L19.

drill /drɪl/ *n.*[1] Now *rare* or *obs.* LME. [Rel. to DRILL *v.*[2] Sense 1 is perh. a different wd.] †1 A small amount of liquid imbibed. Only in LME. 2 A small stream; a rill. E17.

drill /drɪl/ *n.*[2] E17. [f. DRILL *v.*[3] In sense 1 prob. f. Du. *dril, drille.*] 1 A tool or machine for making holes in bulk material, or sinking wells, by using a rotating cutting tip or a reciprocating hammer or chisel; *spec.* a dentist's rotary tool for cutting away part of a tooth etc. E17. b A univalve mollusc, *Urosalpinx cinerea*, which bores into the shells of young oysters. Also *oyster drill.* L19. 2 (Repeated) training or instruction in military exercises; a form or instance of this. M17. b *transf.* Intensive instruction or training in a subject. E19. 3 A person who drills soldiers. E19. 4 *The* correct or recognized procedure. *colloq.* M20.

1 *Archimedean drill, diamond drill, hammer drill, percussion drill,* etc. 2 T. HEGGEN Loading drill on the five-inch gun. S. HILL The days were taken up with a succession of drills and parades and inspections. b *Tennis* Enormous benefit to tennis fitness can be gained by pressure training and high quality drills. SWEDISH *drill.* 4 D. O'GRADY Angle parking was the drill, front to kerb.

Comb.: **drill-book** a manual of instruction in military drill; **drill pipe** *Oil Industry* piping which carries and rotates the bit during drilling and conveys the circulating mud; **drill-sergeant** a non-commissioned officer who trains soldiers in military exercises; **drill-ship**: used to support a drilling rig; **drill stem** *Oil Industry* in percussion drilling, a heavy metal rod added above the bit to give weight; in rotary drilling, = KELLY *n.* 4; also, the whole drill-string; *drill-stem test*, a test of potential made by sampling from a partly drilled well; *drill string*: see STRING *n.* 22b.

drill /drɪl/ *n.*[3] M17. [Prob. of Afr. origin: cf. MANDRILL.] A W. African baboon, *Mandrillus leucophaeus*, allied to the mandrill.

drill /drɪl/ *n.*[4] E18. [Perh. a use of DRILL *n.*[1]] 1 A small furrow in which seed is sown; a ridge with such a furrow on its top; a row of seeds so sown. E18. 2 A machine which makes drills, sows seed in them, and covers the seed sown. M18.

1 C. S. LEWIS Just ordinary drills of cabbages.

drill /drɪl/ *n.*[5] & *a.* E18. [Abbrev. of DRILLING *n.*] (Made of) a tough twilled cotton or linen fabric.

W. HOLTBY Farmers' wives in white drill overalls.

†**drill** *v.*[1] ME. [Origin unkn.] 1 *v.t.* & *i.* Make postponement or delay (of). Only in ME. 2 *v.t.* Foll. by *away, on, out*: protract; fritter (time) away, fill (time) aimlessly. M17–M18. 3 *v.t.* Lead (a person) *on*; entice (a person) *in, into,* or *out of* something. Also foll. by *along.* M17–M18.

2 J. USSHER Purposely drilling out the time, hoping to encline the Senate to favour his designe. 3 R. HEAD [He] was pickt up by a pack of Rogues in the streets and drilled into a Tavern. T. GRAY He drilled him on with various pretences.

†**drill** *v.*[2]*i.* E17–L18. [App. var. of TRILL *v.*[1]: rel. to DRILL *n.*[1]] Flow in a small stream or in drops; trickle.

drill /drɪl/ *v.*[3] E17. [MDu. *drillen* bore, turn in a circle, brandish = MLG *drillen* roll, turn, whence (M)HG *drillen* turn, round off, bore, drill soldiers.] I Make a hole (in). 1 *v.t.* Make a hole or passage in (something), esp. with a drill. E17. b Shoot (a person etc.). *colloq.* E19. 2 *v.t.* Produce (a hole) or sink (an oil well) by or as by drilling. M17. 3 *v.i.* Drill a hole or well. L17. †4 *v.t.* Turn round and round; churn (butter). L17–M19.

1 R. JEFFERIES Rabbit-holes drill the bank everywhere. 2 J. HIGGINS The bullet drilled a neat hole through the windscreen. 3 N. CALDER Equipped for drilling into the bed of the deep ocean. *Economist* Five rigs are now drilling. *drilling mud*: see MUD *n.*[1] **drilling rig** a structure above an oil well etc. containing the machinery needed to drill it. *drilling string*: see STRING *n.* 22b.

II Military & derived senses. 5 *v.t.* & *i.* Train or be trained in military exercises and the use of arms. E17. 6 *v.t.* & *i.* Instruct or be instructed (*in* a subject) by repeated exercises. Also, regulate (affairs) exactly. E17. 7 *v.t.* Inculcate (knowledge etc.) *into* a person by strict methods. M19.

5 E. LINKLATER The whole army would be paraded and drilled in a variety of movements. C. MILNE We drilled on the Square, marching and counter-marching. 6 E. K. KANE We had drilled with knapsacks and sledge till we were almost martinets in our evolutions on the ice. H. KELLER I had been well drilled in English by Miss Sullivan. N. PODHORETZ I needed repeated drilling before the lesson of those negotiations could . . sink in. 7 A. KOESTLER The necessity to drill every sentence into the masses by . . endless repetition.

drillable *a.* L19. **driller** *n.*[1] (*a*) a person who teaches or practises military drill; (*b*) a person who or a machine which drills holes or wells: M17.

drill /drɪl/ *v.*[4]*t.* M18. [f. DRILL *n.*[4]] 1 Sow (seed) in drills, rather than broadcast; raise (a crop) in drills. M18. 2 Sow or plant (ground) in drills. L18.

1 *direct drilling*: see DIRECT *a.*

driller *n.*[2] L18.

drilling /ˈdrɪlɪŋ/ *n.* M17. [Alt. of G *Drillich*, earlier †*drilich* f. L *trilix, trilic-* triple-twilled, f. *tri-* three + *licium* thread.] = DRILL *n.*[5]

drily /ˈdrʌɪli/ *adv.* Also **dryly**. LME. [f. DRY *a.* + -LY[2].] In a dry manner, with dryness, (chiefly *fig.*).

GOLDSMITH The poet either drily didactive . . or triflingly volatile. T. HARDY He said drily that he could manage to do that, not without some contempt for the state of her knowledge. A. KOESTLER He finished a shade more drily, without warmth in his voice. J. M. COETZEE Before he could chew his stomach began to retch drily.

Drinamyl /ˈdrɪnəmɪl/ *n.* Also **d-**. M20. [f. D(EXT)R(O- + AMPHETAM)IN(E + AMYL.] *Pharm.* (Proprietary name for) a stimulant drug prepared from dexamphetamine and amylobarbitone.

dring *n.*, *v.* vars. of THRING *n.*[1], *v.*

drink /drɪŋk/ *n.* OE. [f. the vb.] 1 Liquid swallowed or suitable for swallowing, esp. to quench thirst or as refreshment or nourishment. OE. b *transf.* Liquid absorbed or taken in by anything. E17. 2 A particular kind of liquid for drinking; a beverage. OE. 3 *spec.* Intoxicating drink, alcohol; (excessive or habitual) indulgence in this. OE. 4 A glass or portion of (*spec.* alcoholic) liquid for drinking. Also, a quantity of liquid swallowed at one draught. OE. b A medicinal potion. ME. 5 *the drink*, the sea; some large body of water. *colloq.* M19.

1 AV *Matt.* 25:42 I was thirstie, and ye gaue me no drinke. LD MACAULAY The crews had better food and drink than they had ever had before. b EVELYN If they [plants] shrivel and fold up, give them Drink. 2 D. LODGE A small kiosk that sold tea, fizzy drinks, . . bread. 3 J. B. GOUGH Who ever saw me the worse for drink? CONAN DOYLE A rough, uncouth man, with . . a perpetual smell of drink. R. TRAVERS Drink was the reason of his downfall. 4 G. B. SHAW He goes to the sideboard for a drink of lemonade. J. WAIN He took a long drink of gin . . and put down his empty glass. B. GELDOF Daphne and I were engaged in a bout of spontaneous nobbing. . . We went for a drink afterwards.

Phrases: *be meat and drink to*: see MEAT *n.* **in drink** inebriated, drunk. *long drink*: see LONG *a.*[1] *mix one's drinks*: see MIX *v.* **on the drink** *colloq.* indulging in alcohol (to excess). *short drink*: see SHORT *a. soft drink*: see SOFT *a. strong drink*: see STRONG *a. tall drink*: see TALL *a.* **the Big Drink** (*a*) the Mississippi; (*b*) the Atlantic.

Attrib. & *comb.*: Esp. (freq. in *pl.*) with ref. to alcoholic drinks, as *drink(s) party, table, tray*, etc. Special combs., as **drink-money** [cf. Fr. *pourboire*] a gratuity to be spent on drinks; **drink-offering** a libation of wine or other liquid to a god. **drink-taken** *a.* [misunderstanding of Anglo-Ir. *have drink taken* = have taken drink] suffering from the effects of alcohol.

drinkless *a.* ME.

drink /drɪŋk/ *v.* Pa. t. **drank** /draŋk/, (now *non-standard*) **drunk** /drʌŋk/. Pa. pple **drunk**, (now *non-standard*) **drank**, (*arch.*) **drunken** /ˈdrʌŋkən/. See also DRUNK, DRUNKEN *adjs.* [OE *drincan* = OFris. *drinka*, OS *drinkan* (Du. *drinken*), OHG *trinkan* (G *trinken*), ON *drekka*, Goth. *drigkan*, f. Gmc.] 1 *v.t.* Swallow and take (liquid), or the liquid in (a vessel), into the stomach, esp. to quench thirst or as refreshment or nourishment; swallow (something solid) in a liquid. OE. 2 *v.i.* Swallow a liquid, take a drink. (Foll. by *from, out of*, †*in* a vessel, *of* the liquid or source.) OE. 3 *v.i. spec.* Take or be in the habit of taking alcoholic drink, esp. to excess. ME. 4 a *v.i.* Foll. by *to*: drink in honour of, toast; take a ceremonial drink from one's glass to express one's hopes for (a person's health, the success of an enterprise, etc.) or the health, success, etc., of (a person etc.). Formerly, offer a drink to (a person) after first taking a sip from it. ME. b *v.t.* Toast, drink to, (a person's health or (*arch.*) a person); wish (health, success, etc.) to or *to* a person etc. by drinking. Also, respond to or mark (a toast) by drinking. LME. †5 *v.t.* & *i. fig.* Suffer, have painful experience (of). ME–L17. 6 *v.t. fig.* Take eagerly into the mind or consciousness, esp. through the senses; look at or listen to with delight or agreement. Usu. foll. by *in.* ME. 7 *v.t. transf.* Of a porous substance, a plant, etc.: absorb (moisture). Freq. foll. by *in*, *up*. LME. **8** *v.i.* Of wine etc.: have a specified flavour or character when drunk. LME. **9** *v.t.* Spend or waste (money) on liquor. Also foll. by *away*, *up*. LME. **10** *v.t.* w. compl. Reduce to a specified state by drinking. L16. †**11** *v.t.* Inhale (tobacco smoke); smoke (tobacco etc.). L16–L18.

1 H. ROTH He drank the water in breathless . . gulps. B. PYM She drank two glasses of gin. **2** J. STEINBECK Kino drank long and thirstily at the pool. **3** OED Poor woman! her husband drinks. S. KING Sometimes when he drank he turned mean. **4a** SHAKES. *2 Hen. VI* Here, neighbour Horner, I drink to you in a cup of sack. R. V. JONES We still drink at the annual dinner to the memory of the Old Boys who fell. **b** BURKE We drank the man we were so much obliged to. JOHN MAYNE 'The King' and other loyal toasts . . Were drank aloud. E. WAUGH Miss Runcible's health was widely drunk in the refreshment tent. T. S. ELIOT I'll have a glass of sherry, To drink success to the flat. **5** AV *Job* 21:20 His eyes shall see his destruction, and he shall drinke of the wrath of the Almightie. **6** SHAKES. *Rom. & Jul.* My ears have not yet drunk a hundred words Of thy tongue's uttering. J. BUCHAN We halted on the top of the Lammer Law to drink in the view. **8** C. RAY A vintage which was (as the wine merchants say) 'drinking very nicely now'. **10** P. HAWKER We having nearly drunk the landlord out of . . his . . wine. J. CONRAD Her skipper drank himself to death.

Phrases & comb.: **drink and drive** drive a motor vehicle soon after drinking alcohol or with too much alcohol in one's blood. **drink-and-drive** *a.* = *drink-drive* adj. below. **drink deep** take a copious draught or draughts. **drink-drive** *a.* pertaining to (the laws relating to) drink-driving. **drink-driving** driving a motor vehicle with the proportion of alcohol in one's blood greater than the legal limit. **drink hail** *imper.* (*Hist.*) drink health, drink good luck (the customary reply to a pledge in drinking in early English times: cf. WASSAIL). *drink like a fish*: see FISH *n.*[1] *drink one's fill*: see FILL *n.*[1] 1. *drink the three outs*: see OUT *n.* 2. *drink the waters*: see WATER *n.* 5. *drink with the flies*: see FLY *n.*[1] **drink under the table** surpass (a drinking companion) in ability to stay sober.

With advs. in specialized senses: **drink down** (*a*) swallow straight off; (*b*) extinguish the thought of (something) by taking an alcoholic drink; (*c*) = *drink under the table* above. **drink in** welcome in (an occasion) with festive drinking; see also senses 6, 7 above. **drink off**, (now *dial.*) **out** consume the whole of (a drink) at one go. **drink up** drink the whole of; drink what remains (of); see also senses 7, 9 above.

drinkable /ˈdrɪŋkəb(ə)l/ *a.* & *n.* LME. [f. DRINK *v.* + -ABLE.] **A** *adj.* Able to be drunk, suitable for drinking. LME. **B** *n.* A drinkable substance, an item of drink. Usu. in *pl.* E18.

drinkaˈbility *n.* M19. **drinkably** *adv.* sufficiently to be drinkable, so as to be drinkable M17.

drinker /ˈdrɪŋkə/ *n.* OE. [f. DRINK *v.* + -ER[1].] **1** A person who drinks; *spec.* one who takes alcoholic drinks, esp. to excess. OE. **2** (In full *drinker caterpillar*) the caterpillar of a large brownish European moth, *Euthrix* (*Philudoria*) *potatoria*, which shows a predilection for taking up water; (in full *drinker moth*) the moth itself. L17. **3** A vessel or device from which an animal can drink. M20.

1 OED His father was a hard drinker. A. PRICE The pub's early evening drinkers. *social drinker*: see SOCIAL *a.*

drinkery /ˈdrɪŋk(ə)ri/ *n.* M19. [f. DRINK *n.* + -ERY.] A place where alcoholic drink is supplied.

drinkie /ˈdrɪŋki/ *n. nursery* or *joc.* Also **drinky**. M20. [Dim. of DRINK *n.*: see -IE, -Y[6].] *sing.* & in *pl.* A drink.

ALAN BENNETT Come along now let's give you a drinkie. N. BAWDEN Nearly feeding time, isn't it? Anyone ready for drinkies?

drinking /ˈdrɪŋkɪŋ/ *vbl n.* ME. [f. DRINK *v.* + -ING[1].] **1** The action of DRINK *v.*; *spec.* the taking of alcoholic drink, esp. to excess. ME. **2** An occasion of convivial drinking. Now *rare* or *obs.* LME.

Phrases & comb.: **drinking-bout** a spell of hard drinking. **drinking fountain** a device that can be made to produce a little jet of water for drinking from. **drinking-horn** *Hist.* a drinking-vessel carved from an animal's horn. **drinking problem** *euphem.* an addiction to alcohol. **drinking-song** a hearty song about (and usu. sung at the time of) convivial drinking. **drinking up** the finishing of a drink (*drinking-up time*, a short period legally allowed for the consumption of drinks bought before closing-time in a public house). **drinking-water** water reserved, or pure enough, for drinking. *social drinking*: see SOCIAL *a.*

drinky *n.* var. of DRINKIE.

drinky /ˈdrɪŋki/ *a. colloq.* & *dial.* M19. [f. DRINK *n.* + -Y[1].] (Somewhat) drunk.

drip /drɪp/ *n.* LME. [f. the vb.] **1** †**a** A falling drop. LME–M16. **b** *sing.* & in *pl.* Liquid which drips or falls in drops. E18. **2a** A projection on a cornice, sill, etc., designed to deflect rainwater from the wall below. M17. **b** Each of a series of steps on a gently sloping roof. E18. **3** The act or fact of dripping; the sound made by falling drops. L17. **b** *Med.* The continuous slow introduction of fluid into the body, usu. intravenously; fluid so introduced; an apparatus used for this purpose, having a chamber through which the fluid can be seen to drip. M20. **4** The angle made by a stratum with the horizontal; dip; (cf. DRIP *v.* 4). Now *rare* or *obs.* M19. **5** A receptacle for waste or overflow. L19. **6** *fig.* **a** Nonsense, flattery; sentimental drivel. *slang.* E20. **b** A stupid, feeble, or dull person. *slang.* M20. **c** A grumble, a complaint. *slang.* M20.

1b V. L. CAMERON An awning . . to keep the drips off. **3** BYRON On the ear Drops the light drip of the suspended oar.

Phrases: **in a drip** in a dripping condition; saturated.

Comb.: **drip coffee** *N. Amer.*: made by allowing boiling water to percolate through ground coffee; **drip culture** hydroponic growth of plants using a drip-feed; **drip-drip** (the sound of) continuous dripping; **drip-feed** a method of feeding, lubrication, etc., in which liquid is supplied drop by drop; **drip joint** an overlapping joint in metal roofing designed to keep out rainwater; **drip mat** a small mat placed under a glass etc. to catch drips; **drip painting** a method of painting by which the colour is dripped on to the surface, not applied directly; a painting so produced; **drip pan**: to catch drops of liquid; **dripstone** (*a*) a moulding or cornice over a door, window, etc., to deflect the rain; (*b*) a porous stone used as a filter; (*c*) a stone structure produced by dripping water; a stalactite, a stalagmite; **drip tray** = *drip pan* above.

drip /drɪp/ *v.* Infl. **-pp-**. [OE *dryppan*, *drȳpan*, f. Gmc base also of DROP *n.*, MDa. *drippe* vb (Da. *dryppe*). Cf. DREEP.] **1** *v.t.* Let (a liquid) fall in drops; let (drops) fall. OE. **2** *v.i.* Be so wet (*with* liquid) as to shed drops. OE. **3** *v.i.* Fall in drops. OE. †**4** *v.i.* Slope, slant, dip. Cf. DRIP *n.* 4. E–M18. **5** *v.i.* Complain, grumble. *slang.* M20.

1 G. GREENE He dripped the heavy black oil into the well of each machine. J. STEINBECK His head still dripped water from the scrubbing and dousing. **2** H. MARTINEAU Girls wrung out their dripping hair. D. DUNN Underwear Drips from sagging clothes lines. *fig.*: A. PRICE Great-great-grandmother, dripping with jewels. **dripping wet** very wet. **3** J. TYNDALL The rain . . came through the roof, and dripped from the ceiling.

drip-drop /ˈdrɪpdrɒp/ *n.* & *v.* M19. [f. DRIP *n.*, *v.* + DROP *n.*, *v.*] **A** *n.* Continuous dripping with alternation of sound. M19. **B** *v.i. fig.* Pass very slowly, like dripping water. L19.

drip-dry /*as vb* drɪpˈdrʌɪ; *as adj.* & *n.* ˈdrɪpdrʌɪ/ *v.*, *a.*, & *n.* M20. [f. DRIP *v.* + DRY *a.*] **A** *v.* **1** *v.i.* Of a garment or fabric: dry without creases when hung up to drip after being washed. M20. **2** *v.t.* & *i.* Dry (a garment etc.) by hanging up to drip. M20. **B** *adj.* & *n.* (A garment or fabric) that will drip-dry. M20.

dripping /ˈdrɪpɪŋ/ *vbl n.* LME. [f. DRIP *v.* + -ING[1].] **1** The fall of liquid in drops; *sing.* & (usu.) in *pl.*, liquid so falling. LME. **2** *spec.* Fat melted from roasting meat and eaten cold or used in cooking. LME.

Comb.: **dripping crust** a pastry crust made with dripping; **dripping-pan**: used to catch the dripping from roasting meat; **dripping toast**: spread with dripping.

dripple /ˈdrɪp(ə)l/ *v.i.* E19. [Blend of DRIP *v.* and DRIBBLE *v.*] **1** Trickle; flow in a small stream. E19. **2** Drip with moisture. E19.

drisheen /drɪˈʃiːn/ *n.* E20. [Ir. *drisín* intestine.] A sausage made from sheep's blood, oatmeal, milk, and seasoning.

drive /drʌɪv/ *n.* L17. [f. the vb.] **1** The action or an act of driving, esp. game or livestock; *US* a round-up of cattle. L17. **b** *spec.* A journey or ride in a vehicle under one's direction. L18. **c** A forceful stroke made by driving the ball in various games; *colloq.* a hard punch. M19. **2** A road for vehicles; (in proper names) a road represented as pleasant to drive along or with fine views; *esp.* a private road leading to a house. E19. **b** A broad track in a wood. L19. **3** A quantity of timber (to be) floated downstream. *N. Amer.* M19. **4** Pressure exerted on or by a person. M19. **5** *Mining.* = DRIFT *n.* 20. M19. **6** An organized effort to gain a particular end; an intensive campaign. L19. **b** *Mil.* A forceful advance or attack. E20. **7** An occasion at which several sets of people play a progressive card- or table game. E20. **8** *Psychol.* & *Zool.* An inner urge to satisfy some basic need or motivation; persistent behaviour directed towards a goal. E20. **9** Determination to achieve one's purpose; energy, initiative, persistence. E20. **10a** A mechanism for transmitting (esp. rotary) motion to the wheels of a vehicle, a turntable, etc. E20. **b** The position of the driving controls of a motor vehicle, specified as on the left- or the right-hand side. M20. **c** In a motor vehicle with automatic transmission: the position of the selector lever in which the gears are automatically changed as required. M20. **d** *Computing.* = *disc drive* s.v. DISC *n.* M20. **11** *Electr.* The signal supplied as the input to a transistor, amplifier, etc. M20. **12** A thrill, a feeling of exhilaration, *esp.* one induced by drugs. *US slang.* M20.

1 S. W. BAKER After the tiger has killed a buffalo, there is much art required in the conduct of the drive. J. M. HUNTER Cowboys returning home after the drives. C. MAIR When it is mainly saw-logs that are cut, the fully improved streams make the drive easy. **b** R. LOWELL I was . . taken on Sunday afternoon drives through the suburbs. **c** M. FRAYN He selected a club from the golf bag . . and began practising drives from a tee. B. C. PELTON The forehand drive [in badminton] . . is flat, hard, and hit from a sidearm position. **2** S. MIDDLETON He parked in the street, though he knew there would be room on the drive. J. MCCLURE 'Did Zondi give you Sally's address . . ?' 'It's 39 Woodland Drive, Parktown.' **4** W. ARTHUR The constant drive of work has . . driven a postponable duty out of the way. **6** *Times Weekly* The export drive of the motor industry. *QuarterBack* The 80-yard, 13-play drive . . has its place in pro football lore. ECONOMY *drive*. **7** *beetle drive*, *domino drive*, *whist drive*, etc. **8** R. FINE The individual finds it difficult to recognize his unconscious emotional drives. N. TINBERGEN When an animal's fighting drive is aroused. **9** M. MCCARTHY I have the drive but lack the talent. LD BRAIN With characteristic drive and organizing ability Cairns built up the neurosurgical department. **10a** N. SHUTE A big four-wheel-drive truck. *belt drive*, *chain drive*, etc. **b** P. P. READ A white Jaguar . . with French registration plates and a left-hand drive. **c** *Times* The coroner said the selector lever must have been in 'drive'.

Phrases etc.: *direct-drive*: see DIRECT *a.* *final drive*: see FINAL *a.* **full drive** (now *rare* or *obs.*) at full speed, with maximum impetus.

drive /drʌɪv/ *v.* Pa. t. **drove** /drəʊv/, (*arch.*) **drave** /dreɪv/; pa. pple **driven** /ˈdrɪv(ə)n/. [OE *drīfan* = OFris. *drīva*, OS *drīban* (Du. *drijven*), OHG *trīban* (G *treiben*), ON *drífa*, Goth. *dreiban*, f. Gmc.] **I** Force (a living being, a vehicle, etc.) to move on. **1** *v.t.* Urge (animals, people) in some (usu. specified) direction by blows, shouts, etc. OE. **2a** *v.t.* & *i.* Cause (animals, an enemy) to flee before one, esp. into an area where they can be captured or killed; cause (bees) to enter a new hive; *Hist.* impound a tenant's cattle in lieu of unpaid rent. ME. **b** *v.t.* Search (an area) for game, cattle, etc.; clear (an area) of animals etc. LME. **3** *v.t.* Compel to leave or go (*out*; *to*, *from*, *out of* a place). ME. **4** *v.t.* Impel (a person etc.) powerfully and irresistibly; bring forcibly into or out of some state, or into the state of being (mad etc.). (Foll. by *to do*; *to*, *into* an action; *into*, *out of*, etc., a state.) ME. **b** Urge on; force to work, *esp.* overwork. M17. †**5** *v.i.* Ride hard on horseback. ME–L15. **6a** *v.t.* Orig., control and guide (a draught animal or the vehicle drawn). Now usu., operate and control the course of (a motor vehicle, locomotive, etc.). LME. **b** *v.i.* (Be competent to) drive a vehicle; drive a draught animal; travel in a vehicle under one's control or direction; (of a vehicle) travel under a driver's control. L16. c *v.t.* Convey or carry in a vehicle. M17. 7 *v.t. fig.* Direct (guilt, blame, etc.) *on* or *upon* a person. Now *rare* or *obs.* LME.

1 J. BUCHAN I helped to drive sheep to the local market. 2a SIR W. SCOTT Drive the fleet deer the forest through. J. FORBES To encircle the herd, and to await his signal to commence driving. J. INGLIS The Indian jackal . . can fight in an ugly way when driven into a corner. G. L. HARDING The Muslims were driven back and their three great leaders . . were killed. 3 G. B. SHAW I am sent . . to drive the English away from Orleans and from France. J. STEINBECK The sun . . drove the fog headlong from the sky. 4 O. HENRY Driven by hunger, he had committed an onslaught upon a bottle of . . infant's food. QUILLER-COUCH His isolation . . drove him to return the men's friendship. W. S. CHURCHILL His foreign policy had driven the Scots into alliance with France. P. TILLICH His anxiety does not drive him to the construction of imaginary worlds. R. TRAVERS The death of his wife had driven Weller into a deep melancholia. G. PALEY This place drives me nuts. b A. WILSON Young people need leading, not driving. 6 P. GOODMAN Kids of other periods drove the horses at an early age; in rural places they drive cars at fourteen. b *Sunday Express* We drove back to her home. M. DRABBLE She drives quite well. *Times* The security van was . . driving north in the inside lane. c M. AMIS I offered to drive her home in my powerful green car.

II Impel (matter) by physical force. 8 *v.t.* Cause (an object) to move by applying force to it; propel, carry or send along; *N. Amer.* & *NZ* guide the course of (timber floating downstream). OE. b Supply motive power for (machinery etc.), electrical power to (a device), or chemical power for (a reaction or phenomenon). L16. 9a *v.t.* Impel forcibly; throw, hit; hit (a ball) hard; *Cricket* hit (the ball) with the bat swung freely downwards; hit a ball delivered by (a bowler) in this way; *Tennis, Badminton*, etc., hit (the ball, the shuttlecock) with a freely swung racket; *Golf* hit (the ball) with a powerful stroke, esp. from a tee using a driver. OE. b *v.i.* Drive a ball (in golf etc.); make a driving shot; (of a cricket bat) be suited to doing this. E19. 10a *v.t.* Force by a blow or thrust (*into, through*, etc.); *spec.* force (a nail, stake, etc.) into or *into* a solid body by repeated blows. ME. b *v.i.* Of a nail etc.: go when driven. E18. 11 *v.i.* & *t.* Aim (a blow or missile), strike, (*at*). Also *let drive.* LME. 12 *v.t.* & *i.* Cause (a tunnel, cavity, etc.) to penetrate solid material; *spec.* bore (a tunnel) horizontally or nearly so. L15. 13 *v.t.* Spread, or (formerly) beat, out thinly. Now only of colour painting. L15. 14 *v.t.* Separate (feathers or down) by a current of air so that the lightest are driven off and may be collected. (Earlier as DRIVEN *ppl a.* 2.) L17.

8 C. M. YONGE Alice and I used to drive hoops. J. CONRAD A ship may be 'driven ashore' by stress of weather. b N. NICHOLSON Every wagon of cold coal Is fire to drive a turbine wheel. *Which?* You will normally need a more powerful amplifier to drive a less efficient speaker. *Scientific American* The bioluminescence of fireflies . . is driven by a sequence of chemical reactions. 9b M. MCCORMACK He missed from four feet after driving into the rough. 10a A. RANSOME She . . grabbed one of the big spades and drove it as hard as she could into the ground. J. STEINBECK His father set another nail and drove it in. A. GRAY He . . drove his fist hard into her stomach. 11 SWIFT [He] let drive at us with a large folio. E. O'NEILL He lets drive a terrific swing, his fist landing full on the . . face.

III Maintain (a course). 15 *v.t.* Carry on vigorously, engage in, practise, (a custom, trade, etc.); carry through, perform; bring to a conclusion, conclude, (a transaction). Also foll. by *on, through. arch.* exc. in *drive a hard bargain* below. OE. 16 *v.i.* Advance quickly; come with violence; rush, hasten; work hard (*at*). OE. b Play music energetically or with a strong rhythm. *colloq.* M20. 17a *v.t.* Move along, esp. with force, under the action of wind, a current, etc.; float along, drift. ME. b *v.i. fig.* Proceed in a course; tend. LME.

15 SWIFT We drove on the war at a prodigious disadvantage. LD AUCKLAND The Portuguese princess spoke French sufficient to drive a conversation. 16 W. CLUBBE In swarms again they seek the Hive As fast as ever they can drive. T. GRAY I have been driving away at the 'Flora', of late, very hard. b J. LENNON I was rhythm guitarist. . . I can make a band drive. 17a LONGFELLOW A mist was driving down the British Channel. C. FRANCIS Often ships would drive straight up on to the rocks.

IV Other uses. 18 *v.t.* & *i.* Protract, prolong, (time or occupation); put off, defer. Also foll. by *off, out, on.* ME. †19 *v.t.* Live out, endure, (one's days, fate); experience (hardship, grief, etc.). Only in ME. †20a *v.t.* & *i.* While *away*, pass, spend, (time). (Foll. by *off, over*, etc.) ME–E19. b *v.i.* Of time: pass away. LME–L18. †21 *v.t.* a Conclude, infer, deduce. (Foll. by *out.*) LME–L17. b Derive *from* a source. M–L16. 22 *v.t.* Fish with a drift-net. L17.

Phrases: †**drive a buck (of clothes** etc.) carry out buck-washing. *drive a coach and horses* etc. *through*: see COACH *n.* 1. **drive a hard bargain** be severe or uncompromising in making a bargain, settlement, etc. **drive a quill** or **pen** write; work in an office. **drive the centre**, **cross**, or **nail** *US* make a perfect shot, hit the centre of a target. **drive the green** *Golf* hit the ball from a tee on to the green. *drive to the wall, drive up the wall*: see WALL *n.*[1] *needs must when the devil drives*: see DEVIL *n.*

With advs. & preps. in specialized senses: **drive at** have as one's meaning or purpose (now usu. in rel. or interrog. cl. with *what*). **drive off** (*a*) cause (liquid) to leave a solution as vapour, by heating; (*b*) leave in a vehicle; (*c*) *Golf* drive a ball from the tee. **drive out** (*a*) oust, take the place of, (a person); (*b*) *Typogr.* respace (type) to cover a larger area, move (type) forward to accommodate an insertion etc.; (*c*) see also senses 3, 22a above. **drive over** = *drive out* (b) above.

Comb.: **drive-belt**: that transmits torque; **drive-by** *a.* & *n.* (designating) an action, esp. a shooting or murder, carried out from a passing vehicle; **drive-in** *a.* & *n.* (designating) a cinema, bank, restaurant, etc., that can be visited without getting out of one's car; **drive-on** *a.* (of a ship) on to which a motor vehicle may be driven from land; **drive shaft**: that transmits torque; **drive system** *Austral.* a method of felling trees in hilly country by making one at the top of a hill topple on to others partly cut through; **drive-through** *n.* & *a.* (chiefly *N. Amer.*) (*a*) *n.* a restaurant, shop, etc., with a window to which customers drive to be served; (*b*) *adj.* designating the window of a drive-through; (of a place) suitable for driving through; **drive-yourself** *a.* & *n.* (designating) a motor vehicle hired out and driven by the hirer.

driva'bility *n.* the capacity of a motor vehicle for being driven, esp. easily or economically L20. **drivable** *a.* able to be driven, suitable for driving M19.

†**drivel** *n.*[1] ME–L16. [App. f. LG: cf. MDu. *drevel* scullion, turnspit f. *drivan* to drive.] 1 A driving tool or implement; a carpenter's punch. ME–L16. 2 A servant doing menial work; a drudge. ME–L16. 3 A fool, an imbecile. L15. 4 A dirty slovenly person. M16.

drivel /ˈdrɪv(ə)l/ *n.*[2] ME. [f. the vb.] 1 Spittle trickling from the mouth, slaver. Now *rare.* ME. 2 Silly nonsense, twaddle. M19.

drivel /ˈdrɪv(ə)l/ *v.* Infl. **-ll-**, * **-l-**. [OE *dreflian* (in pres. pple glossing med.L *reumaticus* rheumy), perh. rel. to DRAFF: cf. -LE[3].] I 1 *v.i.* Let saliva or mucus trickle from the mouth or nose; dribble, slobber. OE. †2 *v.t.* Let (saliva etc.) trickle from the mouth or nose; allow to flow *out* through a crack. L16–E18. †3 *v.i.* (Of saliva etc.) escape from the mouth or nose; trickle. E17–L18. †4 *v.t.* Make wet with saliva; slobber on. E–M17. II Transf. use. 5a *v.i.* Talk in a childish or idiotic way. Also foll. by *on.* LME. b *v.t.* Say in a childish or idiotic way. Now *rare.* M18. 6 *v.t.* Fritter *away* or drag *out* in a childish or idiotic way. M18.

driveller *n.* a person who drivels M16. **drivelling** *ppl a.* (*a*) childish, idiotic; (*b*) slavering, dribbling: LME. **drivellingly** *adv.* M18.

driven /ˈdrɪv(ə)n/ *ppl a.* L15. [pa. pple of DRIVE *v.*] 1 Of snow: piled into drifts or made smooth by the wind. Chiefly in *white* or *pure as* (*the*) *driven snow.* L15. 2 Of feathers or down: selected by driving so as to get only the lightest. (Cf. DRIVE *v.* 14.) E17. 3 Urged onward, impelled; forced; powered; (of a person) showing intensity or compulsion in his or her behaviour; having as the chief reason or determinant the thing specified. Freq. as 2nd elem. of comb. M17.

2 SHAKES. *Oth.* My thrice-driven bed of down. 3 B. FRIEDAN One, after five years of therapy, was no longer a driven woman. *consumer-driven, market-driven, receipt-driven*, etc. **driven well** *US* a tube-well.

driven *v.* pa. pple: see DRIVE *v.*

driver /ˈdrʌɪvə/ *n.* LME. [f. DRIVE *v.* + -ER[1].] 1 A person who drives a vehicle, cattle, etc. LME. b The overseer of a gang of slaves; *slang* a hard or exacting supervisor or manager. M18. c *Cricket.* A batsman skilled at driving. E20. 2 A boat used in fishing with a drift-net. M17. 3 A tool or instrument for driving, as a punch or tamping-iron. L17. b *Golf.* A wooden-headed club (now always straight-faced) for driving off. M19. 4 *Naut.* Orig., an additional sail set square on the mizen-mast to take advantage of a following wind. Now, a spanker, *esp.* a small one. M18. 5 Part of a machine or electrical device which transmits or provides power to another part. M19. 6 In full *driver ant.* Any of various blind tropical ants of the subfamily Dorylinae, esp. of the genera *Eciton* (in America) and *Anomma* (in Africa), which migrate in large columns that prey mainly on insects and spiders. Also called *army ant, visiting ant.* M19. 7 A horse trained to be driven in harness. *US.* L19. 8 A leather strap on sheep-shearers' hand shears to prevent the hand from slipping on to the blades. *Austral.* & *NZ.* M20.

1 *bus-driver, cab-driver, engine-driver, taxi-driver*, etc. **in the driver's seat** in control.

driverless *a.* L19.

driveway /ˈdrʌɪvweɪ/ *n.* Chiefly *N. Amer.* M19. [f. DRIVE *v.* + WAY *n.*] 1 A passageway by which hay, grain, etc., can be taken into a barn. M19. 2 A course along which game is driven in hunting. L19. 3 A road along which animals or vehicles are driven; *spec.* a private road leading to a house, a drive. L19. 4 A scenic highway. *Canada.* E20.

driving /ˈdrʌɪvɪŋ/ *vbl n.* LME. [f. DRIVE *v.* + -ING[1].] The action of DRIVE *v.*

Attrib. & comb.: Esp. in the senses 'relating to driving a horse or a vehicle', as *driving gloves, school, whip*, 'relating to or used for the transmission of power', as *driving axle, gear.* Special combs., as **driving band** (*a*) = *driving belt* below; (*b*) a band of soft metal on a projectile with which the rifling of a gun barrel engages to impart rotary motion; **driving belt** a broad flat strap passing round two wheels or shafts to transmit motion from one to the other; **driving box** the seat on which the driver of a horse-drawn carriage sits; **driving iron** *Golf* = DRIVER 3b; formerly, any of various iron clubs; **driving licence** an official document authorizing a person to drive a motor vehicle; **driving range** *Golf* an area equipped for practising driving; **driving seat** the seat on which the driver of a vehicle sits; *in the driving seat*, in control; **driving test** a test of a person's competence to drive which has to be passed before he or she is allowed to drive without individual restriction; **driving-wheel** each of the wheels by which the power of a motor vehicle, locomotive, etc., is conveyed to the road or track.

driving /ˈdrʌɪvɪŋ/ *ppl a.* ME. [f. DRIVE *v.* + -ING[2].] 1 Setting in motion; impelling, actuating. ME. 2 Moving along rapidly, esp. before the wind. E17. 3 Energetic, dynamic, forceful. Chiefly *US.* M19.

1 **driving force, power** the force or power by which a machine or vehicle is driven; *fig.* a source of energy, a person who or thing which strongly motivates. 2 DRYDEN Perpetual Sleet, and driving Snow. 3 D. NORDEN A driving up-tempo version of 'I met her on the Beach.'

drizzle /ˈdrɪz(ə)l/ *n.* & *v.* M16. [Prob. f. OE *drēosan* to fall = OS *driusan*, Goth. *driusan*: see DREARY, -LE[1].] A *n.* 1 Rain that falls in fine spraylike droplets; an example of this. M16. 2 A tiny trickle. E18.

1 P. THEROUX The rain was not a brisk purifying downpour, but a dark tedious drizzle. 2 *Listener* They have also produced a drizzle of mediocre sit-coms.

B *v.* 1 *v.i.* Rain or fall in fine spraylike droplets. Usu. *impers.* in *it drizzles, it is drizzling*, etc. M16. 2 *v.t.* Shed in fine drops; sprinkle (a liquid), let fall in a thin trickle. M16. 3 *v.t.* & *i.* Sprinkle or wet (esp. food) with liquid in fine drops or a thin trickle. E19. 4 *v.i.* Pick the gold thread out of discarded tassels, embroideries, etc., into which it was woven. L19.

1 R. MACAULAY Rain had begun to drizzle. J. BUCHAN The following morning it still drizzled. *transf.*: *Nature* Magnetospheric electrons constantly drizzle

down into the stratosphere. 2 SHAKES. *Jul. Caes.* Fierce fiery warriors fight upon the clouds . . Which drizzled blood upon the Capitol. C. MCCULLOUGH Meggie beat green food coloring into a bowl of runny icing and began to drizzle it over already baked fir trees. 3 *Freetime* Fill it with . . ice cream, drizzle with hot chocolate.

drizzling *ppl a.* that drizzles; drizzly: M16. **drizzly** *a.* of the nature of drizzle; marked by drizzling rain: L17.

Dr Martens *n. phr.* var. of DOCTOR MARTENS.

drog /drəʊg/ *v.t.* Also **drogue**. L17. [Origin uncertain: perh. back-form. f. or f. as next.] Carry in a drogher.

drogher /ˈdrəʊgə/ *n.* Also **drog(g)er, droguer**. M17. [Fr. †*drogueur* a ship that fished and dried herring and mackerel f. Du. *droger* drier, f. *droogen* to dry.] A W. Indian coasting vessel; any slow coasting vessel.

drogue /drəʊg/ *n.* E18. [Origin unkn.] 1 A board, tub, etc., attached to the end of a harpoon line to check a whale's progress. E18. 2 A canvas cone open at both ends or other device towed behind a sailing vessel to slow it down. L19. 3 A fabric cone or cylinder open at both ends and towed behind an aircraft to serve as a brake or target; a similar device used as a wind-sock or an auxiliary parachute. E20. 4 A funnel-shaped device at the end of the supply line from a tanker aircraft, which receives the probe from an aircraft to be refuelled in flight. M20.

3 attrib.: *drogue parachute*.

drogue *v.* var. of DROG.

droguer *n.* var. of DROGHER.

droit /drɔɪt, *foreign* drwa/ *n.*[1] LME. [(O)Fr. f. Proto-Romance use as n. of var. of L *directum* neut. of *directus* DIRECT *a.*] 1 A right; a legal claim; something to which one has a legal claim; a due. LME. †2 Law, right, justice; a law. L15–M16.

1 **droit of Admiralty** a right by which proceeds arising from wrecks, the seizure of enemy ships, etc., could be claimed by the Court of Admiralty and are now paid into the Exchequer. **droit(s) du** (or **de**) **seigneur** /drwɑː duː, də, senˈjəː; *foreign* drwa dy, də, seɲœːr/ an alleged custom by which a medieval feudal lord might have sexual intercourse with a vassal's bride on the wedding-night.

†**droit** *n.*[2] M16–M19. [Origin unkn.] A very small unit of weight, equal to 1/480 grain (about 0.135 mg).

droitural /ˈdrɔɪtjər(ə)l/ *a.* M18. [f. Fr. *droiture* straightness, rightness (f. med.L *drectura* f. L *directura*, f. *direct-* pa. ppl stem of *dirigere* DIRECT *v.*: see -URE) + -AL[1].] *Law* (now *Hist.*). Relating to a right to property, as distinguished from possession.

droke /drəʊk/ *n. dial.* & *Canad.* L18. [Origin unkn.] 1 A groove, a furrow; a ditch; a narrow usu. steep passageway; a valley. L18. 2 A clump or belt of trees. E19.

droll /drəʊl/ *n. arch.* M17. [Fr. *drôle*, perh. f. MDu. *drolle* (mod. *drol*) imp, goblin.] 1 A humorist, a jester; a buffoon. M17. †2 A comedy, a farce; an enacted piece of buffoonery; a puppet-show. M17–E19. †3 The action of jesting; burlesque writing or style. L17–M19.

droll /drəʊl/ *a.* E17. [Fr. *drôle*, earlier *drolle*, f. as prec.] Amusing, now esp. in a dry or whimsical way; queer, odd, surprising.

SIR W. SCOTT A droll sort of house . . a pretty, somewhat fantastical residence. P. G. WODEHOUSE His sudden grab at the hair of any adult . . within reach was very droll. E. WAUGH A pretty, droll girl. C. SANDBURG He enjoyed droll stories.

drollish *a.* L17. **drollness** *n.* E19. **drolly** /ˈdrəʊl-li/ *adv.* M17.

droll /drəʊl/ *v. arch.* M17. [Fr. †*drôler* play the wag, f. as DROLL *n.*] 1 *v.i.* Make fun; jest, joke; lark about. (Foll. by *with*, *at*, *on*, *upon*.) M17. 2 *v.t.* Send *away* or *off* by laughter or mockery; bring *forth* like a jester or buffoon. Formerly also, laugh (a person) *out of* or *into* something. M17.

drollery /ˈdrəʊləri/ *n.* L16. [Fr. *drôlerie*, f. as DROLL *n.*; see -ERY.] †1 A comic picture; a caricature. L16–L19. †2 = DROLL *n.* 2. E17–M19. 3 A joke; a funny story. M17. 4 Joking, buffoonery. M17. 5 The quality of being droll; droll humour. M18.

3 H. CARPENTER The rather feeble drolleries of the early limerick books. 4 G. MAXWELL There seems no end to its fun, its energy, its drollery. 5 C. S. LEWIS Drollery, whimsicality, the kind of humour that borders on the fantastic, was my line.

drome /drəʊm/ *n. colloq.* Also **'drome**. E20. [Abbrev.] 1 = AERODROME 1. E20. 2 = AERODROME 2. E20.

-drome /drəʊm/ *suff.* [Repr. Gk *dromos* course, running, avenue, rel. to *dramein* run.] Forming ns. denoting (*a*) a place for running, a course, etc., as in AERODROME 2, HIPPODROME; (*b*) a thing that runs, as in AERODROME 1, PALINDROME. Cf. also SYNDROME.

dromedary /ˈdrɒmɪd(ə)ri, ˈdrʌm-/ *n.* ME. [OFr. *dromedaire* (mod. *dromadaire*) or late L *dromedarius* adj. (sc. *camelus*), f. L *dromas*, *dromad-* dromedary (f. Gk = runner) + *-arius* -ARY[1].] 1 A camel of a swift and light breed (usu. the Arabian or one-humped camel) specially reared and trained for riding. ME. †2 = DROMOND. L15–M16. 3 A stupid bungling person. Now *dial.* M16.

dromic /ˈdrɒmɪk/ *a.* M19. [Gk *dromikos*, f. *dromos*: see -DROME, -IC.] Suitable for racing; pertaining to or of the form of a racecourse; *spec.* designating the basilican type of Orthodox church.

Also **dromical** *a.* M17.

dromoi *n.* pl. of DROMOS.

dromomania /drɒməˈmeɪnɪə/ *n.* E20. [f. Gk *dromos* (see -DROME, -O-) + -MANIA.] A mania for roaming or running.

dromomaniac *n.* a person who has such a mania; (*joc.* or *slang*) an athlete: M20.

dromond /ˈdrɒmənd, ˈdrʌm-/ *n.* ME. [AN *dromond*, OFr. *dromon(t)*, f. late L *dromo*, *dromon-*, f. late Gk *dromōn*, f. Gk *dromos*: see -DROME.] *Hist.* A very large medieval ship formerly used in war and trade.

dromos /ˈdrɒmɒs/ *n.* Pl. **-moi** /-mɔɪ/. M19. [Gk: see -DROME.] *Gk Antiq.* An avenue or entrance-passage to an ancient temple, tomb, etc., often between rows of columns or statues.

drone /drəʊn/ *n.* [OE *drān*, *drǣn*, corresp. to OS *drān*, *dreno*, MLG *drāne*, *drōne* (LG *drōne*), OHG *treno* (MHG *tren(e)*, G dial. *Dräne*), prob. f. WGmc wd meaning 'to boom'. In branch II partly f. the vb.] I 1 A male bee in a colony of bees, which does no work but can fertilize the queen. OE. 2 An indolent person; an idler. E16. 3 A pilotless aircraft or missile directed by remote control. M20. II 4 A continuous steady deep humming or buzzing sound; *spec.* a continuous low note produced by a musical instrument. E16. 5 A bagpipe or other musical instrument that produces a continuous low tone. E16. 6 a A bass pipe of a bagpipe, which emits only one continuous tone. L16. b On a stringed instrument, a string used to produce a continuous droning sound. L18. 7 A monotonous tone of speech. L18. 8 A monotonous speaker. L18.

4 P. H. GIBBS The drone of German aeroplanes. A. BURGESS The power-house drone of the refrigerator.

Comb.: **drone-bee** = sense 1 above; *drone-beetle*: see DOR *n.*[1] 2; **drone-fly** a flower-fly, *Eristalis tenax*, similar to the honeybee in appearance and behaviour.

dronage *n.* the condition of a drone or male bee M19.

drone /drəʊn/ *v.* E16. [f. the n.] I 1 *v.i.* Act in a sluggish or indolent manner. E16. 2 *v.t.* Pass *away*, drag *out*, (life, time) sluggishly and indolently. M18.

II 3 *v.i.* Emit a drone; hum on one note; talk monotonously; fly or travel with a droning sound. E16. †4 *v.t.* Play (a bagpipe); smoke (a pipe). M16–E17. 5 *v.t.* Utter, give *out*, in a drone. E17.

3 DAY LEWIS On and on droned the voices. G. GREENE A mosquito droned to the attack. 5 THACKERAY Penitents . . droning their dirges.

droner *n.* M16. **droningly** *adv.* in a droning way, boringly L19.

drong /drɒŋ/ *n. dial.* Also **drang** /draŋ/. L18. [f. ablaut var. of base of DRING *v.*, THRING *v.*] A narrow lane or passage.

drongo /ˈdrɒŋgəʊ/ *n.* Pl. **-o(e)s**. M19. [Madagascan name.] 1 Any of several black birds with long forked tails that belong to the passerine family Dicruridae and occur in Africa, southern Asia, and Australia. M19. 2 A stupid, foolish, or incompetent person. *Austral.* & *NZ slang.* M20.

2 J. CLEARY You're just a bloody drongo who doesn't know any better.

dronish /ˈdrəʊnɪʃ/ *a.* L16. [f. DRONE *n.* + -ISH[1].] Of the nature of a drone or male bee; living on another's labour; indolent, sluggish.

drony /ˈdrəʊni/ *a.* L18. [f. DRONE *n.* + -Y[1].] 1 Resembling a drone or male bee; sluggish. L18. 2 Characterized by a monotonous tone, boring to listen to. E19.

droob /druːb/ *n. Austral. slang.* M20. [Origin uncertain: perh. alt. of DROOP *n.*] An unprepossessing or contemptible person, esp. a man.

drooby *a.* L20.

droog /druːg/ *n. slang.* M20. [Alt. of Russ. *drug* friend.] A member of a gang; a young ruffian.

drook *v.* var. of DROUK.

drool /druːl/ *n.* E19. [Cf. DROOL *v.*[2]] 1 A slow or slothful person. *Sc.* E19. 2 Spittle; = DRIVEL *n.*[2] 1. *US colloq.* M19. 3 = DRIVEL *n.*[2] 2. *colloq.* E20.

drool /druːl/ *v.*[1] *i.* & *t. obs.* exc. *Sc.* (now *rare*). M17. [Origin unkn.] Make a mournful sound; utter mournfully.

drool /druːl/ *v.*[2] E19. [Contr. of DRIVEL *v.*] 1 *v.i.* & (*rare*) *t.* Dribble; salivate in anticipation. E19. 2 *v.i.* Talk foolishly or nonsensically; ramble (*on*). L19. 3 *v.i.* Express or feel inordinate sentimentality or enthusiasm. (Foll. by *over*.) M20.

1 A. HAMILTON There may be drooling of saliva. T. HARDY The glebe cow drooled. K. TENNANT Cooking . . of such a quality that the boarders were . . drooling impatiently long before the bell went. 2 J. CAREY He had tried nursing his wife, and soon got sick of her drooling inanities. 3 W. STYRON Those stacks of records of yours make me drool. A. COOKE When Brando came out with one sweat shirt, the town drooled over him.

drooler *n.* L19.

droop /druːp/ *n.* M17. [f. as next.] 1 The act or fact of drooping; a drooping attitude; a loss of energy or spirit. M17. 2 A fool; an ineffectual languid person. M20.

1 A. TYLER A slump in his posture, a little droop to his shoulders. *Hi-Fi News* Some power supply droop.

Comb.: **droop-snoot, -snooter** *colloq.* (an aircraft with) a nose that can be lowered to increase visibility.

droop /druːp/ *a.* E16. [f. the vb.] Drooping. Chiefly in parasynthetic combs., as *droop-wristed*.

droop /druːp/ *v.* ME. [ON *drúpa* hover, hang the head for sorrow, f. Gmc base also of DROP *n.*] 1 *v.i.* Hang or sink down, as from weariness; bend or slope downwards; (of the eyes) look downwards; (of the eyelids) fall. ME. 2 *v.i.* a Flag in spirit or courage, lose heart. ME. b Lose energy, flag, languish; become less in size, quantity, value or importance. LME. 3 *v.i.* Sink; decline, draw to a close. Now only *poet.* (of the sun, day, etc.). LME. †4 *v.i.* Sink or crouch out of sight; lie hidden. LME–L15. 5 *v.t.* Allow to hang or sink down; bend downwards; cast down (the eyes or face). L16.

1 V. WOOLF Two cracked vases, from which red flowers drooped. 2b *Daily Telegraph* The exchange rate has begun to droop. 5 T. C. WOLFE The honeysuckle drooped its heavy mass upon the fence.

drooper *n.* L16. **droopingly** *adv.* in a drooping or dejected manner LME. **droopingness** *n.* a drooping state or condition M17.

droopy /ˈdruːpi/ *a.* ME. [f. prec. or ON *drúpr* drooping spirits: see -Y[1].] Dejected, gloomy; drooping.

droopy drawers *slang* an untidy, sloppy, or depressing person.

droopiness *n.* E19.

drop /drɒp/ *n.* Also (*Sc.*) **drap** /drap/. [OE *dropa* corresp. to OS *dropo*, ON *dropi*, with var. corresp. to OHG *tropfo* (G *Tropfen*), f. Gmc, f.

wk grade of base also of DROOP *v.*: cf. DRIP *n.* In branch II f. the vb.] **I 1** A small round pear-shaped or hemispherical mass of liquid that hangs or falls separately or adheres to a surface; a liquid globule; (*ellipt.* or contextually) a tear-drop, a drop of blood, etc. OE. **b** In dispensing medicine: the smallest separable quantity of a liquid; *sing.* & (usu.) in *pl.*, a medicinal solution applied in drops. LME. †**2** A disease (supposedly) characterized by drops; *esp.* gout. OE–M16. **3** Any minute quantity of liquid; *fig.* a particle or minute amount of something immaterial. ME. **b** *spec.* A small portion or quantity of alcoholic drink. *colloq.* L17. **4** A spot of colour on a surface; *fig.* a stain, a spot. Now *rare* or *obs.* LME. **5** Something resembling a drop of liquid in size, shape, or pendulous quality; *spec.* a (pendent) ornament or bead of glass, metal, etc., as in an earring or chandelier. E16. **b** A piece of small shot. *Sc.* E17. **c** A small chiefly round sweet, lozenge, or other confection. L17. **d** *Archit.* = GUTTA *n.*[1] 2. L17. †**6** In full *drop weight*. An old Scottish weight equal to 1/16 ounce. M16–E19.

1 DRYDEN On his . . Ears . . Sweat in clammy Drops appears. DEFOE They would be faithful to him to the last drop. J. C. POWYS A faint trickle of water . . fell down drop by drop into the ditch. R. HUGHES The moisture from the mist collected on my hair, and two drops rolled over . . my cheek. *dewdrop, raindrop, tear-drop*, etc. *drop serene*: see SERENE *a.* *hanging drop*: see HANGING *a.* **b** *ear-drops, eye-drops*, etc. **3** S. O'CASEY I just come in for a drop o' milk for a cup o' tea. D. CUSACK To add one more drop of bitterness to the sorrow she is already experiencing. **a drop in the bucket** or **ocean** a negligibly small amount in proportion to the whole or to what is needed. **b** E. O'NEILL He never touched a drop till he was forty. **have a drop in one's eye** show slight signs of intoxication. **have had a drop too much** *colloq.* be drunk. **4** *rosy drop*: see ROSY *a.* **5** *ear-drops*: see EAR *n.*[1] **(Prince) Rupert's drop** a tadpole-shaped bubble of glass which bursts explosively when the tail is broken in any part. **c** *acid drop, chocolate drop, cough drop, pear-drop*, etc.

II 7 The action or an act of falling or letting fall abruptly or in drops; (a) dropping. Formerly, a drip, a shower. LME. **b** *fig.* A decrease in something that can be measured or quantified. M19. **c** *Sport.* = DROP-KICK, DROP-STROKE. M19. **d** An act of dropping men, supplies, etc., by parachute; the landing of an aircraft. M20. **8** Something that drops; *dial.* a windfall. E18. **b** *Theatr.* A painted curtain or piece of scenery lowered on to the stage. M19. **c** (The number of) the young produced at a birth. L19. **9** A small platform or trapdoor which is withdrawn from under the feet of a person being hanged; *the* gallows. L18. **10** The depth to which something sinks, falls, or is below the general level. L18. **11** A descent of sufficient size and steepness for a person to be able to fall down it; the distance of the bottom below the top. E19. **12** *The* advantage over someone; *spec.* the fact of having someone covered with a firearm. Chiefly in *get* or *have the drop* (*on*). *colloq.* M19. **13** A letterbox. *US.* L19. **14** A receiver of stolen goods; a fence. *Criminals' slang.* E20. **15** A hiding place for stolen or illicit goods; in espionage, a place where items may be collected by a confederate. M20. **16** A delivery of goods from a lorry. M20. **17** *Cards.* A situation in which a card is dropped (DROP *v.* 29). M20. **18** Money given as alms or a bribe; the action of so giving money. *slang.* M20.

7 BROWNING The drop of the woodland fruit's begun. H. JAMES His expectation had had a drop. **at the drop of a hat** *colloq.* promptly, without hesitation. **b** J. C. OATES Despite the drop in temperature she left her French doors open. *New York Times* You get a significant drop in voting if you have a light mist on election day. **8b** *act-drop*: see ACT *n.* *backdrop*: see BACK-. **11** M. LOWRY Trees . . grew down into the gulch, their foliage partly obscuring the terrific drop. G. ORWELL A sheer drop of ten or twenty metres, with boulders at the bottom. **15** *New Yorker* One of the nearby stores is a heroin drop.

dropless *a.* LME. **droplike** *a.* resembling (that of) a drop of liquid L19. **dropwise** *adv.* in drops L17.

drop /drɒp/ *v.* Infl. **-pp-**. Pa. t. & pple **dropped,** (*arch.*) **dropt**. [OE *drop(p)ian*, f. as the n.] **I** *v.i.* **1** Of a liquid: fall in drops; drip. OE. **2** Give off moisture in drops; drip (*with*). ME. **3** Allow or cause drops to fall; weep. LME. **4** Descend freely under the action of gravity; reach the ground after doing this. LME. **b** Of ground etc.: incline or fall steeply to a lower level. Of a sail: have a specified vertical depth. M18. **5** Of a person or animal: sink to the ground, allow oneself to fall, esp. because exhausted, wounded, or dead. LME. **b** Die. M17. **c** Of a dog: crouch down abruptly at the sight of game. M19. **6** Call *in* or *by* as a casual or unexpected visitor; come or go *back, over, into*, etc., in a casual or undesigned way; come *across* or *upon* a person or thing. M17. **7** Pass easily or imperceptibly *into* a condition; fall *asleep*. M17. **8** Drop anchor. M17. **9** Come to an end through not being kept up; lapse. L17. **10** Fall in amount, degree, or pitch. Of the face: become downcast. E18. **11** Be carried gently downstream by the wind or current. Usu. foll. by *down*. L18. **12** Fall *behind, to the rear*, etc., through allowing others to pass one. E19. **13** Spend or lose money; give a tip. *slang.* L19. **14** Of a playing-card: be dropped (see sense 29 below). M20.

1 OED Sweat dropped from his brow. **2** LD MACAULAY The rabble of Comus . . dropping with wine. **4** W. COWPER His apples might hang till they dropt from the tree. E. HEMINGWAY It was snowing and the flakes were dropping diagonally through the pines. R. MACAULAY Barbary swung herself through the window, dropped lightly on her feet. **b** R. L. STEVENSON Mountain forests, dropping thousands of feet toward the far sea-level. **5** C. P. SNOW They would be working till they dropped. I. WALLACE Edna Foster dropped into her . . chair with a sigh of relief. **6** CONAN DOYLE We could drop in on each other in the evenings without an invitation. L. HUGHES Drop by Sunday and lemme know for sure. J. GARDNER I'll drop back later to see how you're doing. SLOAN WILSON If you would care to drop into my office . . we can work something out. **7** A. B. EDWARDS We soon dropped back into the old life of sight-seeing and shopping. **9** J. GALSWORTHY George yawning, the conversation dropped. **10** H. JAMES The storm of the night . . had dropped. SCOTT FITZGERALD Her voice, dropping an octave lower, filled the room with . . scorn. M. EDWARDES The British market for trucks had dropped alarmingly. *Financial Times* MTD (Mangula) dropped 16 to 54p.

II *v.t.* **15** Let (a liquid) fall in drops; shed (tears). ME. **16** Allow (something) to fall by relaxing one's hold or ceasing to give support; allow or cause to drop; *spec.* allow (esp. troops, supplies) to fall by parachute. In early use also *fig.*, perpetrate (a trick etc.). ME. **b** Bring to the ground by a blow or shot. E18. **17** Sprinkle with drops; *transf.* dot with spots of colour. *arch.* LME. **18** Utter or mention casually or as if unconsciously; let fall (a hint etc.). E17. **19** Abandon, cease to continue or pursue, (an activity, practice, study, etc.); give up association with (a person). E17. **b** Discard from a team; *gen.* (chiefly *US*) dismiss from employment. *colloq.* M19. **c** Lose (a game etc.) unexpectedly. Chiefly *US.* M20. **20** Give birth to; lay (an egg). M17. **21** Lose, give, or part with (money). *slang.* L17. **22** Bend the knees and lower the body to make (a curtsy). L17. **23** Send (a note etc.) in a casual manner. M18. **24** Set down (a passenger) from a vehicle or ship, esp. on the way to another destination; leave (a packet) at a house etc. L18. **25** Omit (a letter or syllable) in reading or pronunciation. M19. **26** Lower (the eyes), esp. from modesty or shame. M19. **27** Lower the level or position of; *transf.* reduce the pitch or loudness of (the voice). M19. **28** In football, score (a goal) by a drop-kick. L19. **29** Play (a lower card) in the same trick as a higher one, esp. because of the need to follow suit. M20. **30** Put into circulation (counterfeit money, forged cheques). *slang.* M20. **31** Take (a drug) orally. *slang.* M20.

16 *Times* The first atomic bomb had been dropped . . on Hiroshima. J. ORTON He takes it off, kicks away his shoes and drops his trousers. ROBERT ANDERSON Laura stoops and picks up the raincoat which Tom has dropped. **b** J. W. SCHULTZ He fired his Henry rifle . . dropping two of the enemy. **17** S. ROGERS Fish . . dropt with crimson and gold. **18** J. BETJEMAN His womenfolk . . smooth their . . twinsets And drop the names of earls. *name-drop*: see NAME *n.* **19** R. TRAVERS When the jury failed to agree the prosecution was dropped. J. CHEEVER I've never liked her parties, and I'm glad she's dropped us. W. MARCH When you get this letter, drop everything . . and come back to me. M. ROBERTS Helen is glad to drop the subject. **b** G. BOYCOTT He was dropped by England after a couple of Test matches. **23** T. SHARPE I was about to drop you a line asking if I could see you. **24** A. BURGESS Drop me outside the town. I can pick up a trishaw. N. MAILER The newspapers were already being dropped at the early morning stands. **27** C. BEATON Nor did the new fashion permit women simply to drop their skirts. E. WAUGH Anthony dropped his voice to a . . whisper.

Phrases: *drop a brick*: see BRICK *n.* *drop anchor*: see ANCHOR *n.*[1] **drop astern** outdistance (a boat), leave in the rear. *drop a* CLANGER. *drop a stitch*: see STITCH *n.*[1] **drop dead!** *slang* an exclam. expressing intense scorn of the person addressed. **drop-eared** *a.* (of a dog) having ears that hang down; opp. PRICK-EARED 1. **drop it!** stop that! have done! stop talking or arguing about that! *drop one's aitches*: see AITCH. *drop one's bundle*: see BUNDLE *n.* **drop short** fall short (*of*). **fit** or **ready to drop** worn out, exhausted. *let (it) drop*: see LET *v.*[1] *the bottom drops out of*: see BOTTOM *n.* *the penny drops*: see PENNY *n.*

With advs. & preps. in specialized senses: **drop away** fall away or be lost gradually. **drop down to** = *drop to* below. **drop in** come in one by one or at intervals; (see also sense 6 above). **drop into** *colloq.* attack fiercely. **drop off** (*a*) *v.phr.i.* gradually withdraw or cease to come, diminish; (*b*) *v.phr.i.* die; fall asleep; (*c*) *v.phr.t.* = sense 24 above. **drop on** come down heavily on; reprimand, punish; (usu. in *pass.*). **drop on to** = *drop to* below. **drop out** (*a*) cease to appear or participate in an activity; *spec.* abandon one's studies from deliberate choice; withdraw from conventional society; (*b*) remove dots from (an area of a halftone picture or plate). **drop to** *slang* (chiefly *US* & *Austral.*) become aware of, recognize, realize.

drop- /drɒp/ *comb. form.* [Repr. DROP *v.*, *n.*] Prefixed to wds, esp. ns., in various senses, as 'that drops', 'involving a drop', 'shaped like a drop'.

drop-black *n.* bone-black ground into water, formed into drops, and dried L19. **drop-curtain** *n.* (*Theatr.*) = *act-drop* s.v. ACT *n.* M19. **drop-dead** *a.* (*slang*) (*a*) designating the latest date or time by which something can be done; (*b*) that surprises one, *esp.* outstandingly attractive, stunning: M20. **drop-fly** *n.* = DROPPER *n.* 3 L19. **drop-forge** *v.t.* make by drop-forging L19. **drop-'forging** *vbl n.* forging in which a drop-hammer falls repeatedly on to heated metal, forcing it into a die; a forging made in this way: L19. **drop-hammer** *n.* a heavy weight raised mechanically and allowed to drop, as used in drop-forging and pile-driving; a drop-forging machine: M19. **drop-handle** *n.* a handle that hangs down when not held L19. **drop-'handlebar(s)** *n.* a bicycle handlebar, bicycle handlebars, in which the handles are bent below the rest of the bar M20. **drop-head** *a.* & *n.* (*a*) (designating) a sewing-machine, typewriter, etc., that can be lowered into a table etc. so as to leave a flat top; (*b*) (having) a car-roof that can be folded down or removed; (*c*) (designating) a chapter-heading lower down the page than the first line of ordinary pages: L19. **drop initial** *n. phr.* (*Typogr.*) = *drop-letter* (*b*) below M20. *drop-keel*: see KEEL *n.*[1] **drop-kick** *n.* (*Rugby Football*) a kick made by dropping the ball and kicking it as it drops: M19. **drop-leaf** *n.* & *a.* (having) a hinged flap on a table or desk which can be raised to increase the surface area: L19. **drop-letter** *n.* (*a*) *N. Amer.* a letter posted at a post office for local delivery or collection from that office; (*b*) *Typogr.* a large letter at the beginning of a section of text, occupying more than the depth of one line: M19. **drop-light** *n.* (*a*) *US* a portable gas-lamp attached to the gas pipe by a flexible tube; (*b*) an electric light suspended from the ceiling: L19. **drop-line** *n.* a weighted fishing-line for fishing near the bottom of a river etc. M19. **drop-press** *n.*: in which metal is formed using a drop-hammer M19. **drop-ripe** *a.* (of fruit) ripe enough to drop: E18. **drop-scene** *n.* a drop-curtain; the final scene of a drama, a denouement: E19. **drop-scone** *n.* a small pancake formed by dropping spoonfuls of batter on a hot surface; a griddle-cake: L19. **drop-seed** *n.* a grass that readily drops its seed, esp. *Muhlenbergia diffusa* M19. **drop-shot** *n.* (*a*) small gunshot; (*b*) = *drop-stroke* below: L17. **dropside** *n.* & *a.* (having) a side of a cot or lorry that drops down E20. **dropstone** *n.* †(*a*) a stalactite, a stalagmite; (*b*) *Geol.* a stone embedded in a sedimentary deposit and believed to have got there after being released from a melting glacier: L17. **drop-stroke** *n.* a soft stroke or shot in tennis, squash, etc., causing the ball to drop abruptly after crossing the net or hitting the wall L19. **drop-tank** *n.* an aircraft fuel tank that can be dropped when empty M20. **drop test** *n. phr.* a test of the strength of an object, in which it is dropped from a height under controlled conditions, or a set weight is dropped on it from a given height L19. **drop-testing** *vbl n.* the performance of a drop test E20.

drop-in /ˈdrɒpɪn/ *n.* & *a.* E19. [f. *drop in*: see DROP *v.* 6.] A *n.* 1 An unexpected or informal visitor or visit. *colloq.* E19. 2 A place or function at which one can turn up informally, without prior appointment or referral. *colloq.* (chiefly *N. Amer.*). M20. B *adj.* 1 Designed to drop into position. E20. 2 Of a place or function: at which one may turn up informally, without prior appointment or referral. M20.

droplet /ˈdrɒplɪt/ *n.* E17. [f. DROP *n.* + -LET.] A minute drop.

Comb.: **droplet infection**: conveyed by droplets of mucus sprayed into the air when a person coughs etc.

†**dropling** *n.* E17–L18. [f. DROP *n.* + -LING[1].] A little drop.

drop-off /ˈdrɒpɒf/ *a.* & *n.* E20. [f. *drop off* s.v. DROP *v.*] A *adj.* Of or pertaining to dropping off; (of a place) where things or people can be dropped off or set down. E20.

B *n.* 1 An act or instance of dropping off; *spec.* a diminution, a decrease; a slowing down. E20. 2 A declivity; a steep drop; a cliff. *N. Amer.* M20.

1 *National Observer (US)* There is a small extra charge . . for drop offs and pickups in Lincoln. *Nature* A reflectance spectrum showing a steep dropoff in the UV.

drop-out /ˈdrɒpaʊt/ *n.* L19. [f. *drop out* s.v. DROP *v.*] 1 *Rugby Football.* A drop-kick made from within the defending team's 22-metre (formerly 25-yard) line in order to restart play after the ball has gone dead. L19. 2 On a bicycle, a small U-shaped end to a fork or stay, made to receive the axle. E20. 3 A person who drops out of a course of activity or study, or who abandons conventional society in favour of an alternative lifestyle. *colloq.* M20. 4 On a halftone picture or plate, a highlight area from which the tiny dots produced by the screen have been removed; a halftone with such an area. Also *drop-out halftone.* M20. 5 A flaw or loss of coating on magnetic tape or disc; a momentary loss of recorded signal due to this; an error in data caused by the failure to read a bit or sequence of bits. M20.

5 *What Video?* A high grade chrome tape . . with improved signal-to-noise ratio and less dropout.

droppable /ˈdrɒpəb(ə)l/ *a.* E20. [f. DROP *v.* + -ABLE.] Able to be dropped or (esp.) discarded.

dropped /drɒpt/ *ppl a.* Also (*arch.*) **dropt**. L15. [f. DROP *v.* + -ED[1].] †1 Marked with specks or spots. L15–E17. 2 That has been dropped; lowered; having a lower position than usual. L16. 3 Of an egg: poached. *Sc.* & *US.* E19. 4 *Rugby Football.* Of a goal: scored from a drop-kick. L19.

2 **dropped handlebar(s)** = DROP-HANDLEBAR(S). **dropped scone** = DROP-SCONE.

dropper /ˈdrɒpə/ *n.* M17. [f. DROP *v.* + -ER[1].] 1 A person who drops or lets something fall in drops. Formerly (*slang*), a distiller. M17. b A person who passes forged cheques, counterfeit money, etc. *slang.* M20. c A person who delivers goods, liquor, etc., from a market or store to a retailer. *Austral.* & *NZ colloq.* M20. 2 *dropper-in*, a casual caller. E19. 3 In fly-fishing, an artificial fly attached to a leader above the tail-fly. Also *dropper-fly.* M19. 4 *Mining.* A vein branching off a main lode. M19. 5 A short glass tube with a rubber bulb at one end and a narrow opening at the other end, for administering a liquid in drops. L19. 6 *Hort.* A shoot growing downwards from the base of a bulb and itself developing a bulb at the apex. L19. 7 A vertical part of a fence etc.; *esp.* a light vertical lath used between the main uprights to keep the wires spaced. Chiefly *Austral.*, *NZ*, & *S. Afr.* E20.

dropping /ˈdrɒpɪŋ/ *vbl n.* OE. [f. DROP *v.* + -ING[1].] 1 The action of DROP *v.*; an instance of this. OE. 2 That which falls or is shed in drops, as rain or melted wax. Usu. in *pl.* LME. 3 *spec.* The excrement of animals, birds, etc.; a lump of this. Usu. in *pl.* L15. †4 *sing.* & in *pl.* The eaves from which water drops. L16–E18. 5 In *pl.* Waste material cast off from a machine in certain processes of textile manufacture. E20.

2 T. TROLLOPE Collecting the droppings from the great wax candles.

Comb.: **dropping-bottle**: used to supply fluid in small quantities; **dropping-field**, **-point** a place prepared for the dropping of troops, supplies, bombs, etc., from an aircraft; **dropping-well**: formed by the dropping of water from above; **dropping-zone** = *dropping-field* above.

dropping /ˈdrɒpɪŋ/ *ppl a.* LME. [f. DROP *v.* + -ING[2].] 1 Falling in drops; having moisture falling off in drops, dripping; rainy. LME. 2 *gen.* Falling; decreasing. E18. 3 Of gunfire or a shot: desultory, not continuous. E18.

droppingly *adv.* drop by drop; *fig.* one by one: LME.

droppy /ˈdrɒpi/ *a.* Now *dial.* M17. [f. DROP *n.* + -Y[1].] Dripping, rainy.

dropsical /ˈdrɒpsɪk(ə)l/ *a.* L17. [f. DROPSY + -ICAL, after *hydropical.*] 1 Of, pertaining to, or resembling dropsy. L17. 2 Affected with or subject to dropsy. L17. 3 Enlarged, swollen; saturated with water. E18.

3 L. WHISTLER The swollen populations, wretched in the dropsical cities.

dropsically *adv.* L18.

dropsied /ˈdrɒpsɪd/ *a.* E17. [f. next + -ED[2].] Swollen (as) with water; turgid; watery.

dropsy /ˈdrɒpsi/ *n.* & *a.* ME. [Aphet. f. HYDROPSY.] A *n.* 1 A condition marked by an excess of watery fluid in the tissues or cavities of the body. ME. †2 An insatiable thirst or craving. M16–E18. 3 Money, esp. paid as a tip or bribe. *slang.* M20. †B *adj.* = DROPSICAL 2, 3. L15–L17.

dropt *v.* pa. t. & pple: see DROP *v.*

dropwort /ˈdrɒpwəːt/ *n.* LME. [f. DROP *n.* + WORT *n.*[1], on account of the tuberous root-fibres.] 1 A plant of calcareous grassland, *Filipendula vulgaris*, allied to meadowsweet. LME. 2 Now only more fully *water-dropwort*. Any of several aquatic or marsh-loving umbellifers of the genus *Oenanthe*. L16.

2 *hemlock water-dropwort*: see HEMLOCK *n.*

drosera /ˈdrɒs(ə)rə/ *n.* E19. [mod.L f. Gk *droseros* dewy.] Any plant of the genus *Drosera*, sundew; a powder prepared from this, formerly used against respiratory ailments.

droshky /ˈdrɒʃki/ *n.* Also **-sky** /-ski/. E19. [Russ. *drozhki* pl., dim. of *drogi* wagon, hearse, pl. of *droga* centre pole of a carriage.] A low open horse-drawn carriage used esp. in Russia; any horse-drawn passenger vehicle.

drosometer /drɒˈsɒmɪtə/ *n.* E19. [f. Gk *drosos* dew + -OMETER.] An instrument for measuring the amount of dew deposited.

drosophila /drɒˈsɒfɪlə/ *n.* E19. [mod.L, f. Gk *drosos* dew + *philos* loving.] A fruit fly of the genus *Drosophila*, much used as an experimental subject in genetics.

drosophilist *n.* a person who studies or uses drosophilas M20.

drosophyllum /drɒˈsɒfɪləm/ *n.* L19. [mod.L, f. Gk *drosos* dew + *phullon* leaf.] A subshrub, *Drosophyllum lusitanicum*, of the sundew family, native to SW Europe and NW Africa and with leaves that secrete drops of glutinous fluid by which insects are captured.

dross /drɒs/ *n.* & *v.* [OE *drōs* = MDu. *droes(e)* dregs. Cf. MLG *drōsem*, MDu. *droesen(e)* (Du. *droesem*), OHG *truosana* (G *Drusen*) dregs, lees, corresp. to OE genit. pl. *drōsna.*] A *n.* 1 Impurities separated from metal by melting; the scum which forms on the surface of molten metal. OE. 2 Foreign matter mixed with anything; dregs of wine, chaff of corn, etc. LME. b *Mining.* Iron pyrites in coal; waste from the sorting of coal. E19. 3 *gen.* Refuse, rubbish, worthless matter, esp. as contrasted with or separated from something of value. LME.

3 J. LONDON His face was transfigured, purged of all earthly dross, and pure and holy. L. DEIGHTON He asked me what I thought about the crowd she was running around with. I told him they were absolute dross.

B *v.t.* †1 Make impure; corrupt. Only in M17. †2 Sift *out* as dross. Only in M17. 3 Free from dross. L19. 4 Convert (an impurity in metal) into dross that can be removed. L19.

drossiness *n.* the quality or condition of being drossy M17. **drossy** *a.* characterized by or containing dross, impure LME.

drostdy /ˈdrɒsti, drɒs(t)ˈdeɪ/ *n. S. Afr.* Pl. **-dies**. L18. [Afk. f. Du. *drost* bailiff.] 1 *Hist.* The district under a landdrost. L18. 2 A building that was formerly the official residence of a landdrost. L18.

drotchell *n.* var. of DRATCHELL.

dróttkvætt /ˈdrəʊtkvʌɪt/ *n.* Also ***dróttkvæði*** /ˈdrəʊtkvʌɪði/. L18. [ON = court poem.] A complex verse-form used by the skaldic poets of early Scandinavia.

drought /draʊt/ *n.* Also (now *poet.*, *Sc.*, *Anglo-Ir.*, *US*, & *dial.*) **drouth** /draʊθ, *Sc.* druːθ/. [Late OE *drūgaþ*, f. Gmc base of DRY *a.* Cf. (M)LG *drogede*, (M)Du. *droogte*, f. *droog* dry. For *drouth* cf. *highth* HEIGHT *n.* and see -TH[1].] 1 Dryness, aridity, lack of moisture. *arch.* & *poet.* LOE. †2 Dry country; a desert. *rare.* LOE–L17. 3 (A spell of) continuous dry weather; (a) prolonged absence of rain. ME. 4 Thirst. *arch.*, *poet.*, & *dial.* LME. 5 *fig.* Absence or shortage of anything necessary or desirable; a prolonged deficiency. E17.

1 TENNYSON The burning drouth Of that long desert to the south. 3 W. STYRON What began as a simple dry spell developed into a searing drought. *Times* In times of drought, many Africans do not survive. 5 T. MIDDLETON A drouth of virtue, And dearth of all repentence.

droughted *a.* affected by drought M20.

droughty /ˈdraʊti/ *a.* Also (now *poet.*, *Sc.*, *Anglo-Ir.*, *US*, & *dial.*) **drouthy** /ˈdraʊθi, *Sc.* ˈdruːθi/. L15. [f. prec. + -Y[1].] 1 Dry, arid; lacking rain. L15. 2 Thirsty; fond of (alcoholic) drink. E17.

droughtily *adv.* without drink M20. **droughtiness** *n.* E18.

drouk /druːk/ *v.t. Sc.* & *north.* Also **drook**. E16. [Origin unkn. Cf. ON *drukna* be drowned, *drukkit* drunk.] Drench, as with heavy rain.

drouth *n.*, **drouthy** *a.* see DROUGHT, DROUGHTY.

drove /drəʊv/ *n.* [OE *drāf*, f. ablaut var. of base of DRIVE *v.*] †1 The action of driving. Only in OE. 2 A number of cattle, horses, sheep, or goats being driven in a body or moving together; a herd, a flock. OE. 3 *transf.* A (moving) crowd or group of other animals or of people; a horde, a shoal, a multitude; *sing.* & (esp.) in *pl.*, a large number. OE. 4 A channel for drainage or irrigation. OE. 5 An unenclosed road or track, chiefly for cattle, esp. in the Fens. M17. 6 A broad chisel for use by stonemasons. E19.

2 S. LEACOCK Droves of young lambs with their shepherds, proceeding to market. 3 S. MIDDLETON One needs no brains to pass, but candidates fail in droves.

Comb.: **drove-road** an ancient unmetalled road for cattle.

drove /drəʊv/ *v.*[1] M17. [f. DROVE *n.*, or (in sense 1) back-form. f. DROVER.] 1 *v.i.* & *t.* Drive (cattle etc.); be a drover. M17. 2 *v.t.* Dress (stone) in parallel lines using a drove. E19.

drove *v.*[2] pa. t.: see DRIVE *v.*

drover /ˈdrəʊvə/ *n.* LME. [f. DROVE *n.* + -ER[1].] 1 A person who drives cattle or other livestock to market; a dealer in livestock. LME. 2 A boat used for fishing with a drift-net. L16.

drow /draʊ, drəʊ/ *n.*[1] *Sc.* L16. [Perh. f. ablaut var. of base of DREE *v.*] A fit of illness, a fainting fit, a qualm.

drow /draʊ, drəʊ/ *n.*[2] *Sc.* E17. [Origin unkn.] A cold wet mist; a drizzling shower.

drowk /draʊk/ *v.i. obs.* exc. *dial.* E16. [Origin unkn.] Droop.

drown /draʊn/ *v.* Pa. t. & pple **drowned** /draʊnd/, (*arch.* & *dial.*) **drownded** /ˈdraʊndɪd/. ME. [Rel. to ON *drukkna* be drowned, f. Gmc base of DRINK *v.* Prob. already in OE.] 1 *v.i.* Suffer death by suffocation in liquid. ME. 2 *v.t.* Kill by suffocation in liquid. Of a liquid: kill by suffocation. ME. †3 *v.i.* & *t.* (Cause to) sink; go or send to the bottom of the sea etc. ME–E17. 4 *v.t.* Submerge, inundate, flood; drench; add a lot of or too much water to. ME. **b** Foll. by *out*: drive out (people etc.), prevent (work), by flooding. L17. **5** *v.t.* Make inaudible, ineffective, or unidentifiable by being louder, stronger, etc.; overwhelm, swamp, dilute excessively. Also foll. by *out*. ME. **b** Stupefy (oneself) with alcoholic drink; deaden (sorrow etc.) with drink. (Foll. by *in* drink.) LME. †**6** *v.t. Law.* Nullify by merging in something greater. M17–E19.

1 E. HEMINGWAY I thought..I would drown because of my boots, but I thrashed and fought through the water. **2** SHAKES. *3 Hen. VI* I'll drown more sailors than the mermaid slay. G. B. SHAW Someday you'll walk into the river and drown yourself. **like a drowned rat** very wet and bedraggled. **4** C. BOYLE Once they drowned a whole village To make a reservoir. P. FITZGERALD The sea had drowned the woodlands in salt. **drowned valley**: wholly or partly submerged by a change in sea level. **5** *Scientific American* The orchestra's much stronger sounds would drown out the singer's. *Photography* An incredibly tedious press release..drowns the disturbing message of this exhibition. **b** J. M. SYNGE And I swamped and drownded with the weight of drink. E. O'NEILL I might as well forget her..and drown my sorrows.

drowner *n.* (*a*) a person who or thing which drowns; (*b*) a manager of water-meadows: M16. **drowningly** *adv.* so as to drown E19.

drowse /draʊz/ *n.* L17. [f. the vb.] The action or an act of drowsing; the state of being half asleep.

drowse /draʊz/ *v.* [OE *drūsian* f. Gmc base also of *drēosan* fall: see DREARY. Later back-form. f. DROWSY.] †**1** *v.i.* Sink, droop; become slow. Only in OE. **2** *v.i.* Be drowsy or half asleep; doze (*off*). L16. **3** *v.i.* Be or become inactive, dull, or sluggish. *arch.* L16. **4** *v.t.* Make drowsy; *arch.* make dull or lethargic. E17. **5** *v.t.* Pass *away* (time) drowsily or in drowsing. M19.

2 D. JACOBSON I would fall into a doze, wake.., drowse again. **3** TENNYSON Let not your prudence.. drowse. **4** A. S. BYATT Marcus, drowsed by the fire,.. nodded and jerked awake. **5** M. M. KAYE Men and animals..drowsed away the slow hours until the sun was low.

drowsy /ˈdraʊzi/ *a.* L15. [Prob. f. stem of OE *drūsian*: see prec.] **1** Inclined to sleep; heavy with sleep, sleepy; half asleep. L15. **2** Caused or characterized by sleepiness or inactivity. E16. **3** Inducing sleepiness; soporific. L16. **4** Heavy, dull; sluggish, lethargic. *arch.* L16.

Comb.: **drowsy-head** a sleepy or sluggish person.

drowsihead *n.* (*arch.*) drowsiness L16. **drowsily** *adv.* L15. **drowsiness** *n.* (*a*) sleepiness, the state of being drowsy; (*b*) *arch.* lethargy, sloth: M16.

drub /drʌb/ *n.* & *v.* E17. [Prob. ult. f. Arab. *daraba* beat, (pronounced *dreb* or similarly in NW Africa).] **A** *n.* A blow, a thump. Formerly *spec.*, a bastinado. E17.

B *v.* Infl. **-bb-**. **1** *v.t.* Beat with a stick; cudgel, flog, thump; beat in a fight or contest. Formerly *spec.*, bastinado. M17. **2** *v.t.* Drive (an idea etc.) *into* or *out of* a person, drive (a person) *into* or *out of* a habit etc., by drubbing. L17. **3** *v.t.* Abuse or criticize roundly. E19. **4** *v.t.* & *i.* Beat, beat *on*, (a drum etc.), hit repeatedly; stamp (one's foot). M19. **5** *v.i.* Give out a sound of being beaten. M19.

1 W. BESANT He drubbed and belaboured his servants every day. S. KINGSLEY We must drub the enemy and drub him soundly. *Toronto Star* It was no contest last night as the Islanders drubbed the Habs, 7–0. **4** W. D. HOWELLS Teaching the young..how to drub the piano. C. RAINE Thugs who drub The helpless air with clubs. **5** S. MIDDLETON The signal drubbed on unanswered.

drubber *n.* E18. **drubbing** *vbl n.* (*a*) the action of the vb; (*b*) a beating, a thrashing: M17.

†**drubly** *a.* OE–E16. [OE *drōflic*, prob. infl. by obs. ME *trouble* adj. disturbed, f. OFr. f. base of TROUBLE *v.* Cf. DRUMLY.] Stirred up, turbid, (*lit.* & *fig.*).

drucken *a.* see DRUNKEN *a.*

drudge /drʌdʒ/ *n.*[1] L15. [f. or rel. to DRUDGE *v.*] A person who does heavy, unpleasant, or servile work; a dogsbody, a hack.

A. WOOD He was the common drudge..to make, correct, or review the Latine Sermons. M. DRABBLE All I am is a servant,..a household drudge.

†**drudge** *n.*[2] var. of DREDGE *n.*[2]

drudge /drʌdʒ/ *v.* ME. [Perh. f. stem of OE *drēogan* DREE *v.* or var. of DRUG *v.*[1]] **1** *v.i.* Work hard at heavy, unpleasant, or servile tasks; toil. In early use, carry a heavy burden. ME. **2** *v.t.* Pass (time) *away* in drudgery; (foll. by *out*) perform as drudgery; (foll. by *down*) repress with drudgery. M17. **3** *v.t.* Subject to drudgery. *rare.* E19.

1 E. BLISHEN My father had been out..enjoying himself while she drudged at home. R. CHURCH Drudging sullenly at subjects I despised.

¶Some or all apparent early examples may in fact belong to DRUG *v.*[1]

drudgingly *adv.* in a drudging manner L17.

drudger /ˈdrʌdʒə/ *n.*[1] M18. [f. prec. + -ER[1].] A person who drudges.

†**drudger** *n.*[2] var. of DREDGER *n.*[2]

drudgery /ˈdrʌdʒ(ə)ri/ *n.* M16. [f. DRUDGE *n.*[1] + -ERY.] The work of a drudge; heavy, unpleasant, or servile work; wearisome toil.

drug /drʌg/ *n.*[1] LME. [(O)Fr. *drogue*, of unkn. origin.] **1** Any substance that affects the physical or mental functioning of a living organism; *esp.* one used for the treatment or prevention of an ailment or disease. Formerly also, any substance used in chemistry, dyeing, or any technical process. Orig. in *pl.* LME. **b** A stimulant or narcotic taken otherwise than medicinally, *esp.* one that is addictive or subject to legal restriction. L19. **2** A commodity no longer in demand and so unsaleable. Now usu. *a drug on* (or *in*) *the market*. M17.

1 T. CORYAT Women..annoint their haire with oyle, or some other drugs. J. H. BURN A healthy person ought to fall asleep without needing a drug. *controlled drug*: see CONTROL *v.* 2a. *miracle drug*: see MIRACLE *n.* *orphan drug*: see ORPHAN *a.* **b** M. AMIS The drugs I like are cocaine and mandrax. D. SHANNON That psychiatrist, after I'd listened to him half an hour I thought he was on drugs himself. *dangerous drug*: see DANGEROUS *a.* 2.

Comb.: **drug abuse** the non-medicinal or excessive use of drugs; **drug addict** a person with an addiction to a drug; **drug addiction** addiction to a drug or drugs; **drug bust** a seizure of illegal drugs by the police or other law enforcement agency; **drug buster** *colloq.* a member of a drug squad; **drug-peddler, -pusher** a person who sells (addictive) drugs illegally; **drug(s) squad** a division of a police force appointed to investigate crimes involving illegal drugs; **drugstore** *N. Amer.* a chemist's shop also selling miscellaneous articles and often light refreshment (*drugstore cowboy*, a braggart, a loafer; a person who is not a cowboy but dresses like one); **drug traffic** illegal dealing in (addictive) drugs.

drugless *a.* L19.

drug /drʌg/ *n.*[2] *obs.* exc. *dial.* M17. [f. or rel. to DRUG *v.*[1]] A low truck for carrying timber etc.

drug /drʌg/ *v.*[1]*i.* & *t.* Long *obs.* exc. *dial.* Infl. **-gg-**. L15. [Perh. rel. to DRAG *v.*] Pull, drag.

¶See note s.v. DRUDGE *v.*

drug /drʌg/ *v.*[2] Infl. **-gg-**. E17. [f. DRUG *n.*[1]] **1** *v.t.* Mix or adulterate (food or drink) with a drug, esp. a narcotic or poison. E17. **2** *v.t.* Administer a drug to (a person etc.), esp. in order to stupefy or poison; *fig.* stupefy; (now *arch.*) nauseate, cloy. M17. **3** *v.i.* Take drugs; *esp.* habitually indulge in narcotics etc. L19.

1 SHAKES. *Macb.* I have drugg'd their possets. **2** W. COWPER Some baneful herb Which cast into our cup shall drug us all. V. BRITTAIN The..music of the Mass drugged my senses with anodyne sweetness. T. KENEALLY Farmers..kept drugging him from flasks of rum. **3** H. C. BAILEY I don't drink and I don't drug.

drugger /ˈdrʌgə/ *n.* L16. [f. DRUG *n.*[1], *v.*[2] + -ER[1].] †**1** = DRUGGIST. L16–M18. **2** A person who administers a drug. M19. **3** A user of (addictive or narcotic) drugs; a drug addict. *colloq.* M20.

druggery /ˈdrʌg(ə)ri/ *n.* Now *rare.* E16. [Fr. *droguerie*, f. as DRUG *n.*[1]: see -ERY.] **1** Drugs collectively; the subject of medicine. E16. **2** A place where drugs are kept. M19.

drugget /ˈdrʌgɪt/ *n.* & *a.* M16. [Fr. *droguet*, of unkn. origin.] **A** *n.* A coarse woven fabric used for floor and table coverings; such a covering. Formerly, (a garment made of) cloth made of wool (alone or with silk or linen) and used for clothing. M16. **B** *attrib.* or as *adj.* Made of drugget. L16.

druggie *n.* var. of DRUGGY *n.*

druggist /ˈdrʌgɪst/ *n.* Now *N. Amer.* E17. [Fr. *droguiste*, f. as DRUG *n.*[1]: see -IST.] A dealer in medicinal drugs; *spec.* = CHEMIST 4.

druggister /ˈdrʌgɪstə/ *n.* *obs.* exc. *dial.* M17. [f. prec. + -ER[1].] = prec.

druggy /ˈdrʌgi/ *n.* *slang.* Also **-gie**. M20. [f. DRUG *n.*[1] + -Y[6], -IE.] = DRUGGER 3.

druggy /ˈdrʌgi/ *a.* L16. [f. DRUG *n.*[1] + -Y[1].] **1** Of, pertaining to, or of the nature of a medicinal drug. L16. **2** Of, pertaining to, or characteristic of narcotic etc. drugs or users of such drugs. *colloq.* M20.

1 H. JAMES The druggy aroma. **2** *Times* I was enmeshed in a very druggy crowd at the time.

†**drugster** *n.* E17–E18. [f. DRUG *n.*[1] + -STER.] = DRUGGIST.

Druid /ˈdruːɪd/ *n.* & *a.* Also **d-**. M16. [Fr. *druide* or L *druidae*, *druides* pl. f. Gk *druidai* f. Gaulish *druides*.] **A** *n.* **1** A member of an order of priests and teachers among the Celts of ancient Gaul, Britain, and Ireland, later reputed to be magicians and soothsayers. M16. **2** A philosophic bard or poet; a priest, a chaplain. M17. **3** A member of any of various groups that are held to be present-day representatives of ancient Druidism or to be derived from it; (a title of) any of certain officers of the Welsh Gorsedd. M19.

B *adj.* Of or pertaining to Druids. L17.

T. WARTON Here Poesy..In druid songs her solemn spirit breath'd. **Druid stone**: of which the megalithic monument Stonehenge on Salisbury Plain in Wiltshire is made.

Drui'dess *n.* (now *rare*) a female Druid M18. **Dru'idic** *a.* = DRUID *a.* L18. **Dru'idical** *a.* = DRUID *a.* M18. **Druidism** *n.* the religious and philosophical system of Druids E18. **Druidry** *n.* (*rare*) = DRUIDISM M19.

drum /drʌm/ *n.*[1] LME. [Prob. f. MDu., LG *tromme* of imit. origin. Cf. DRUMSLADE.] **I 1** An instrument of music or communication sounded by striking and made of a pliable membrane stretched taut over the open end of a hollow cylinder or hemisphere or over a thin hoop; a percussion instrument consisting of some form of hollow body but without a membrane. LME. **b** The body of a banjo. L19. **2a** *Mil.* A drummer. Formerly also, a man or a small party sent with a drum as a messenger to an enemy. E16. **b** In *pl.* The percussion section or drum kit of a pop, rock, or jazz group. E20. **3** The sound of the instrument; a noise like that of a drum. M17. **b** Any fish of the percoid family Sciaenidae, found mainly in shallow sea and able to make a drumming noise; a croaker. M17. **4** *Hist.* Orig., an evening party or assembly. Later, a tea party, esp. when joined by more guests after the meal. M18. **5** *the drum*, the facts; reliable or inside information. *Austral. slang.* M20.

1 LONGFELLOW Our hearts.., like muffled drums, are beating Funeral marches to the grave. *Scientific American* Such percussion instruments as steel drums and hollow-log drums. *bass drum*, *kettledrum*, *side drum*, *snare drum*, *tenor drum*, etc. **beat** or **thump the (big) drum(s)** make loud or ostentatious advertisement or protest. **3** O. HENRY The soft drum of the ponies' hoofs. **b** *red drum*: see RED *a.*

II Something likened to a drum in shape or function. **6** The tympanic membrane, the eardrum. Formerly also, the middle ear. E17. **7** A cylindrical appliance or part of a machine; *spec.* a cylinder round which a rope, belt, etc., passes. E18. **b** (The contents of) the cartridge-holding part of a machine-gun. L19. **c** *Computing.* More fully *magnetic drum*. A data storage device in the form of a rotatable cylinder with a magnetizable outer surface. M20. **8** *Archit.* The solid part of a Corinthian or Composite capital; one of the cylindrical blocks forming the shaft of a column; the vertical wall supporting a dome. E18. **9** A cylindrical container for packing dried fruit, holding oil, etc. L18. **b** The bundle of a tramp, miner, etc., a swag. *Austral.* & *NZ slang.* M19. **c** A tin in which tea etc. is made, a billycan. *slang.* M20. **10** *Zool.* An organ which produces or amplifies the natural sound of certain animals. E19. **11** A cylinder hoisted (together with a cone) by coastguards etc. to give warning of a strong gale. M19.

7 *brake drum*: see BRAKE *n.*[7]

Comb.: *drum-and-trumpet history*: see HISTORY *n.*; **drumbeat** a beat on a drum; **drum brake**: in which brake shoes on the vehicle press against a brake drum on the wheel; **drumfire** heavy continuous rapid artillery fire; *fig.* a barrage of criticism etc.; **drum-fish** *n.* & *v.* (*a*) *n.* = sense 3b above; (*b*) *v.i.* (*US*) fish for drum-fish; *drum-kit*: see KIT *n.*[1] 2d; **drum-machine** an electronic device that imitates the sound of percussion instruments; **drum major** †(*a*) the chief drummer of a regimental band; (*b*) *arch.* an NCO in command of the drummers of a regimental band; (*c*) the leader of a marching band; **drum majorette** (orig. *US*) a female leader of a marching band; a girl who leads or takes part in a parade etc. twirling a baton; **drum printer**: in which the paper is hammered against a drum with as many circular bands of types on it as there are printing positions on a line; **drum roll** a rapid succession of notes sounded on a drum; **drum tower**: of cylindrical, usu. squat form, as at the angle of a castle wall.

drummy *a.* like the sound of a drum; characterized by a drum: M19. †**drumster** *n.* (*rare*) a drummer L16–M19.

drum /drʌm/ *n.*[2] *Sc.* & *Anglo-Ir.* E18. [Gael. & Ir. *druim* back, ridge.] A long narrow hill often separating two parallel valleys; a drumlin.

drum /drʌm/ *n.*[3] *slang.* L18. [Origin uncertain: perh. f. Romany. Cf. Romanian *drum*, Gk *dromos* street.] †**1** A street. L18–L19. **2** A house, a lodging; a room, a flat; a low dive, a brothel; *US* a saloon, a nightclub. M19.

drum /drʌm/ *v.* Infl. **-mm-**. L16. [f. DRUM *n.*[1]] **I** *v.i.* **1** Beat or play (as) on a drum; make a continuous noise by rapidly repeated blows. L16. **2** Sound like a drum; resound. E17. **3** Of a bird, insect, etc.: make a loud reverberating noise, as by the quivering of the wings. E19. **4** Solicit orders, canvass, (*for*). *US.* M19. **5** Foll. by *up*: make tea etc. in a billycan; prepare a rough-and-ready outdoor meal. *slang.* E20. **6** Steal from unoccupied premises. Cf. sense 12b below. *slang.* E20.

1 DRYDEN Heart . . take thy rest . . ; For thou shalt drum no more. E. BOWEN Rain . . still drummed through the leaves. J. STEINBECK Lennie drummed on the table with his fingers. T. C. WOLFE A woodpecker drummed on . . a . . chestnut-tree. 3 J. E. TAYLOR Flies and gnats drum around you.

II *v.t.* **7** Summon (as) by the beat of a drum; *esp.* attempt to obtain (custom etc.) by canvassing or soliciting. (Foll. by *up.*) E17. **8** Cashier with drums beaten to heighten disgrace; expel or dismiss with ignominy. (Foll. by *out.*) M18. **9** Drive (a person etc. *into* a state, or a lesson, idea, etc. *into* a person) by constant repetition. E19. **10** Beat (one's fingers etc.) repeatedly on a surface, as if drumming. (Foll. by *on, upon.*) M19. **11** Play (a tune) on or as on a drum. M19. **12** Hit repeatedly; *dial.* thrash, beat, (a person). L19. **b** Knock at (a house) to check whether it is unoccupied before attempting a robbery; reconnoitre with a view to robbery. Cf. sense 6 above. *slang.* M20. **13** Inform, warn; give (a person) 'the drum' (DRUM *n.*[1] 5). *Austral. slang.* E20.

7 E. BLISHEN The paralysis of conventional training during the war years had made it necessary to drum up new teachers in a hurry. CLIVE JAMES I finally drummed up the courage to take a look. *Times* It was difficult to drum business in the money markets yesterday. 8 T. AMORY They . . ought to be drummed out of society. 9 H. BUSHNELL Small children are . . drummed into apathy by dogmatic catechisms. M. MEYER Continually drumming into him the importance of duty. 13 S. L. ELLIOTT Someone musta drummed him Vic had extra razor blades.

drumble /ˈdrʌmb(ə)l/ *n.* M16. [f. the vb.] An inert or sluggish person, a drone.

drumble /drʌmb(ə)l/ *v.i.* Now *dial.* ME. [Imit.] **1** Drone; mumble. ME. **2** Be sluggish; move sluggishly. L16.

Comb.: **drumbledore** a bumble-bee; a dor; *fig.* a heavy stupid person; **drumbledrone** a drone-bee; a bumble-bee.

drumhead /ˈdrʌmhɛd/ *n.* & *a.* E17. [f. DRUM *n.*[1] + HEAD *n.*] **A** *n.* **1** The stretched skin or membrane of a drum. E17. **2** The eardrum. Cf. DRUM *n.*[1] 6. M17. **3** The top of a capstan or a mechanical drum. L17. **4** More fully *drumhead cabbage.* A flat-topped variety of cabbage. L18.

B *attrib.* or as *adj.* Held or done during military operations or with men in battledress; resembling or characteristic of a summary court martial so held. M19.

J. R. LOWELL There was more reason in the drumhead religious discipline . . than he may have thought. D. ACHESON Resistance groups hunting out and executing, after drumhead trials, collaborators. *Daily Telegraph* Servicemen . . have the freedom of the town and were planning . . a drumhead service in the market square.

drumlin /ˈdrʌmlɪn/ *n.* M19. [App. f. DRUM *n.*[2] + *-lin* repr. -LING[1].] A long low oval mound of compacted boulder clay rounded and smoothed by past glacial action.

drumlinized *a.* formed into or covered with drumlins E20. **drumlinoid** *a.* & *n.* (a hill, rock mass, etc.) resembling a drumlin in shape L19.

drumly /ˈdrʌmli/ *a.* Orig. *Sc.* Also **-lie**. E16. [App. nasalized var. of DRUBLY.] (Of the sky, a person's looks, etc.) gloomy, cloudy, troubled; (of water) turbid, not clear; *fig.* muddled, confused, obscure; giddy.

drummer /ˈdrʌmə/ *n.* L16. [f. DRUM *v.* + -ER[1].] **1** A person who beats a drum. L16. **2** Any animal which makes a drumming noise or action. E18. **3** A person who solicits custom or orders; a commercial traveller; a salesman. *colloq.* E19. **4** A thief; a housebreaker. *slang.* M19. **5** The slowest shearer in a shed. *Austral.* & *NZ slang.* L19. **6** A swagman, a tramp. *Austral.* & *NZ slang.* M20.

drumming /ˈdrʌmɪŋ/ *vbl n.* L16. [f. DRUM *v.* + -ING[1].] The action of DRUM *v.*; an instance of this; a sound like a drum.

Drummond light /ˈdrʌmənd lʌɪt/ *n. phr.* M19. [T. *Drummond* (1797–1840), Sc. engineer.] A powerful lamp producing limelight.

†**drumslade** *n.* E16. [Alt. of LG *trommelslag* drum beat, f. *trommel* drum (f. as DRUM *n.*[1]) + *slag* beat.] **1** A drum. E16–M17. **2** A drummer. E16–L18.

drumstick /ˈdrʌmstɪk/ *n.* L16. [f. DRUM *n.*[1] + STICK *n.*[1]] **1** A stick for beating a drum. L16. **2** The lower joint of the leg of a cooked or dressed fowl. M18. **3** In full *drumstick tree*. Either of two trees, *Cassia sieberana*, an African shower tree valued for its timber, and *Moringa oleifera*, the Indian horseradish tree. M19. **4** *Cytol.* An appendage of the nucleus of a polymorphonuclear leucocyte, characteristic of females. M20.

Comb.: **drumstick primula** a primula, *Primula denticulata*, with a globular head of usu. purplish flowers on an erect stem; *drumstick tree*: see sense 3 above.

drungar /ˈdrʌŋgə/ *n.* E17. [med.L *drungarius*, f. late L *drungus* body of soldiers: see -AR[2].] *Hist.* *drungar of the fleet*, a Byzantine admiral.

drunk /drʌŋk/ *a.* & *n.* ME. [pa. pple of DRINK *v.*, shortened f. DRUNKEN *v.* Cf. DRUNKEN *a.*] **A** *adj.* (now usu. *pred.*). **1** Affected by alcohol in the body to such an extent that one is without full or proper control of one's faculties or behaviour; inebriated; intoxicated; *fig.* overcome *with* emotion etc. ME. †**2** = DRUNKEN *a.* 3. LME–L17. **3** = DRUNKEN *a.* 4. M19.

1 J. R. GREEN Napoleon was drunk with success. W. OWEN Many had lost their boots But limped on . . Drunk with fatigue. I. WALLACE She wondered why three drinks had not made her drunk. **appeal from Philip drunk to Philip sober** suggest that an opinion etc. represents a passing mood only. *blind drunk*: see BLIND *adv.* *dead drunk*: see DEAD *adv.* **drunk and disorderly** (committing the offence of) creating a public disturbance under the influence of alcohol. **drunk as a fiddler, lord,** & vars., very drunk.

Comb.: **drunk-driving** *N. Amer.* = *drink-driving* s.v. DRINK *v.*

B *n.* **1** A drinking-bout; a period or state of drunkenness. *slang.* L18. **2** A person who is drunk or is frequently drunk. M19.

Comb.: **drunk tank** *N. Amer. slang* a large prison cell for the detention of drunks.

drunkery *n.* (*contempt.*) a place to get drunk in; a public house, a bar: E19. **drunkish** *a.* E18. **drun'kometer** *n.* (*US*) an instrument for determining the level of alcohol in the breath (cf. BREATHALYSER) M20.

drunk *v.* pa. t. & pple: see DRINK *v.*

drunkard /ˈdrʌŋkəd/ *n.* ME. [Prob. f. MLG *drunkert*, f. *drunken*; cf. MDu. *dronker*, Du. *dronkaard*, whence early mod.Fr. *dronquart*: see -ARD.] **1** A person inordinately fond of drinking alcohol, esp. to excess; a person who is habitually drunk. ME. **2** The marsh marigold. L19.

drunken /ˈdrʌŋk(ə)n/ *a.* (now usu. *attrib.*). Also (*Sc.*) **drucken** /ˈdrʌk(ə)n/. OE. [pa. pple of DRINK *v.*: cf. DRUNK *a.* Sc. form f. ON.] **1** **a** = DRUNK *a.* 1. OE. **b** Habitually or frequently drunk. M16. **2** Proceeding from or pertaining to drink or drunkenness. LME. **3** Of a thing: drenched, saturated with moisture. Now *rare* or *obs.* LME. **4** Uneven, unsteady; reeling in motion or course. L18.

1a V. WOOLF He lurches back to his seat like a drunken sailor. *fig.*: E. K. KANE We were so drunken with cold that we strode on steadily. b E. E. NAPIER Drunken, lazy, good-for-nothing fellows. 2 S. JOHNSON Men who . . destroy in a drunken frolick the happiness of families. BURKE The delirium of a low, drunken alehouse.

drunkenly *adv.* L16. **drunkenness** /-n-n-/ *n.* the state of being drunk (*lit.* & *fig.*); intoxication; the habit of drinking to excess: OE. †**drunkensome** *a.* = DRUNKEN 1b ME–M19.

drunken *v.* pa. pple: see DRINK *v.*

†**drunkness** *n.* ME–E18. [Syncopated f. DRUNKENNESS.] = DRUNKENNESS.

drupe /druːp/ *n.* M18. [L *drupa*, *druppa* overripe olive (in mod.L, drupe) f. Gk *druppa* olive.] A fleshy indehiscent fruit with an outer skin and a central stone enclosing the seed (e.g. a cherry, a plum).

dru'paceous *a.* of the nature of a drupe; bearing drupes: E19. **drupelet** /ˈdruːplɪt/ *n.* a little drupe forming part of a compound fruit like a blackberry L19. **drupel** /ˈdruːp(ə)l/ *n.* [mod.L *drupella*] = DRUPELET M19.

Druse /druːz/ *n.*[1] & *a.* Also **-ze**. L18. [(Fr. f.) Arab. *Durūz* pl. of *Durzī* var. of *Darazī*, f. the name of Muḥammad ibn Ismāʿīl ad-*Darazī* (d. 1019), one of the founders.] **A** *n.* Pl. same, **-s**. A member of a small religious and political sect, orig. an offshoot of the Ismaili Shiite Muslims, that lives chiefly in Syria and Lebanon and believes in the divinity of the 6th Fatimid caliph of Egypt (d. AD 1020). L18. **B** *adj.* Of, pertaining to, or designating the Druse. L18.

Also **Drusian** †*n.* & *a.* L16.

druse /druːz/ *n.*[2] E19. [Fr. f. G, = MLG *drūse*, *drose*, Du. *droes*.] (A cavity in a rock lined with) a crust of small projecting crystals.

drusy *a.* covered or lined with a druse; containing druses, of the nature of a druse: L18.

druther /ˈdrʌðə/ *adv.* & *n.* *N. Amer.* L19. [f. a US dial. pronunc. of *would rather*. Cf. RUTHER, RATHER *n.*] **A** *adv.* Rather, by preference. L19.

D. BAKER Would you druther I wouldn't go?

B *n.* In *pl.* Preference, choice; one's way in a matter. L19.

Globe & Mail (*Toronto*) If Robert Stanfield had his druthers, he would announce his retirement about May.

druxy /ˈdrʌksi/ *a.* Also (earlier) †**dricksie**. L16. [Origin unkn.] Of timber: having decayed spots hidden by healthy wood.

Druze *n.* & *a.* var. of DRUSE *n.*[1] & *a.*

druzhina /ˈdrʊʒiːnə/ *n.* Pl. **-nas, -ny** /-ni/. L19. [Russ., f. *drug* friend + *-ina* group suff.] *Hist.* **1** The retinue or bodyguards of a Russian prince. L19. **2** In the USSR: a military or police unit; *spec.* a detachment of volunteers assuming police powers. M20.

druzhinnik /ˈdrʊʒiːnɪk/ *n.* pl. **-i** /-i/, a member of a druzhina M20.

dry /drʌɪ/ *n.* Pl. **dries, drys**. ME. [f. the adj.] **1** Dryness, esp. of the atmosphere; drought. ME. **b** *The* dry season. Chiefly *Austral. colloq.* L19. **2** *The* land (as opp. to the sea). ME. **3** A place for drying things. L19. **4** A person who opposes the sale and consumption of alcohol; a prohibitionist. *colloq.* L19. **5** A desert, a waterless area. *Austral.* E20. **6** A dry wine, cocktail, or other drink. M20. **7** The process or an act of drying. M20. **8** *Theatr.* An act of forgetting one's lines on the stage. M20. **9** A Conservative politician who is uncompromisingly opposed to high Government spending. *slang.* L20.

dry /drʌɪ/ *a.* & *adv.* [OE *drȳġe* rel. to (M)LG *dröge, dreuge*, MDu. *drōghe* (Du. *droog*), f. Gmc.] **A** *adj.* **I** As a physical quality. **1** Lacking or free from moisture. OE. **b** *Hist.* Designating a quality associated with dryness and regarded in medieval and later times as one of four qualities inherent in all things; having a preponderance of this quality. Cf. *moist, hot, cold.* OE. **c** Lacking or free from rain; having scanty or deficient rainfall. ME. **d** Free of tears; not accompanied by weeping. LME. **2** Having lost its natural moisture; desiccated, parched. OE. **b** Of a watercourse, pond, etc., or moisture on a surface: having disappeared by evaporation, draining, wiping, etc.; dried up. LME. **3** Not in, on, or under water; (of a boat, fish, etc.) beached, stranded. ME. **4** Of bread, toast, etc.: served without butter or other spread. ME. **5** Of a person: wanting drink, thirsty. Of a thing or condition: causing thirst. LME. **b** Not accompanied by or associated with (alcoholic) drink; *spec.* (of a person) favouring the prohibition of the liquor trade; (of a place) where alcoholic drink is banned. L15. **c** Abstaining from alcohol, esp. after overindulging; having stopped taking an addictive drug. M20. **6** Not or no longer yielding water or other liquid; (of a cow etc.) not yielding milk. LME. **7** *Med.* Not accompanied by a discharge; (of a cough) without phlegm; (of a wound) not discharging blood or pus. LME. †**b** Occurring without bloodshed. Of a blow: bruising rather than breaking the skin; *loosely* hard, severe. M16–L18. **8** Solid, not liquid; of or pertaining to solid substances or commodities. L17. **9** Of a wall: made without using mortar. See also *drywall* below. E18. **10** Designating a process or apparatus in which no liquid is used. L18. **11** Of a young child: continent of urine. M20.

1 N. GORDIMER You had no dry clothes to replace wet ones. P. S. BUCK With this dry wind the wheat seed . . could not sprout. **c** H. QUICK The pedestrian made his way over earth paths in dry and through puddles of mud in wet weather. **2** C. FREEMAN His mouth was dry. A. N. WILSON He nibbled his dry little bit of seed cake. **b** I. WATTS Let our songs abound, And ev'ry tear be dry. E. HEMINGWAY A . . bridge across what was usually a dry river-bed. **5** T. HARDY I am sometimes that dry in the dog days that I could drink a quarter-barrel. OED Better have a pint; it's dry work. **b** T. H. WHITE Bottles of wine were opened so that it should not be a dry meeting. **6** H. FAST The well is good, and it's never gone dry. **8** G. OGLE Neither the Wine nor dry Provisions were come. **10** J. BOWYER Warm air heating, the only dry central heating system.

II *fig.* **12** Orig., lacking religious ardour. Now, unemotional, impassive; without sympathy or cordiality. ME. †**b** Of a person: miserly; unresponsive, reserved. M16–L17. **13** Giving no satisfaction or result; barren, unproductive. ME. **14** Expressed in or marked by a matter-of-fact tone with feigned unawareness of humour. M16. **15** Of rent, fees, etc.: paid in cash. Now *rare* or *obs.* L16. **16** Not enlarged upon; plain, bare, matter-of-fact. E17. **17** Uninteresting, unattractive, dull. E17. **18** *Art.* Characterized by stiff and formal outlines, construction, etc. E18. **19** Of wine etc.: having all or most of the sugar fermented into alcohol; not sweet (formerly, not tasting sweet or fruity). E18. **20** Of a sound: harsh, rasping. Of a sound, an acoustic, a room, etc.: lacking warmth or resonance. L18.

12 A. F. DOUGLAS-HOME A dry, tight-lipped, meticulous character, with little or no sense of humour. **14** R. C. HUTCHINSON He talked with dry appreciation of eccentrics he had travelled with. **16** M. W. MONTAGU I would willingly return . . something more . . than dry thanks impertinently expressed. **17** M. PATTISON Annals . . valuable to the antiquary, but dry and profitless to others. **18** T. E. HULME A poem which is all dry and hard, a properly classical poem. **19** J. ASHBY-STERRY In Mrs. Williams' driest sherry He toasts the Lass of Bolney Ferry! **20** *Sunday Times* The house has become a bit too dry It needs another half second of resonance.

Phrases: (*as*) *dry as a chip, whistle*: see CHIP *n.*, WHISTLE *n.* (**as**) **dry as dust** extremely dry; *spec.* extremely dull and uninteresting, arid, unrewarding (cf. DRYASDUST). *extra dry*: see EXTRA *adv. high and dry*: see HIGH *a. home and dry*: see HOME *adv. keep one's powder dry*: see POWDER *n.*[1] *milk dry*: see MILK *v. run dry*: see RUN *v. suck dry*: see SUCK *v.*

Special collocations & comb.: **dry battery** a battery consisting of dry cells; a dry cell. **dry-blow** *v.* (*Austral.*) (*a*) *v.i.* perform dry-blowing; (*b*) *v.t.* seek for gold in (a material or place) by dry-blowing; (*c*) *v.t.* attempt to clean without using water. **dry-blower** *Austral.* (*a*) a person who performs dry-blowing; a gold-miner; (*b*) a sieve etc. used in dry-blowing. **dry-blowing** *Austral.* the separation of gold from the soil etc. in which it is found by means of an air current. *dry-bob*: see BOB *n.*[5] **dry-bulb** *a.* designating (the temperature as measured with) a thermometer with an ordinary exposed bulb, usu. used along with a wet-bulb one. *dry canteen*: see CANTEEN I. **dry cell** a voltaic cell in which the electrolyte is in the form of a paste or is otherwise prevented from spilling. **dry-clean** *v.* (*a*) *v.t.* clean (a garment, textile, etc.) using an organic solvent, without water; (*b*) *v.i.* (of a garment etc.) have the property that it can be dry-cleaned. **dry-cleaner** an establishment that carries out dry-cleaning. **dry-cure** *v.t.* preserve (meat etc.) by salting and drying, rather than pickling. **dry death** (*a*) death without bloodshed; (*b*) (*rare* Shakes.) death other than by drowning. **dry diggings** gold diggings away from a river or stream. **dry dock** a narrow basin into which a vessel may be floated and the water then pumped out so that repairs can be carried out on the hull. **dry-dock** *v.t.* place (a vessel) in dry dock for repairs. *dry distillation*: see DISTILLATION 2. **dry farming** (chiefly *N. Amer.*) a method of farming in semi-arid areas without the aid of irrigation; dry-land farming. **dry fly** *Angling* an artificial fly which floats lightly on the water. **dry-fly** *v.i.* fish with a dry fly. **dry-foot** *adv.* without wetting the feet (†*draw* or *hunt dry-foot*, track game by the mere scent of the feet). **dry fuck** *US coarse slang* an act of sexual intercourse that is simulated or unsatisfactory. *dry* GANGRENE. **dry goods** (chiefly *N. Amer.*) drapery and haberdashery. **dry hole** a well drilled for oil or gas but yielding none. **dry ice** carbon dioxide in the form of a solid block, which sublimes at −78°C and is used as a refrigerant. **dry joint** a soldered joint with faulty electrical continuity. DRY LAND. **dry light**: in which one sees things without prejudice, uninfluenced by personal predilection. *dry Martini*: see MARTINI *n.*[2] *dry mass*: see MASS *n.*[1] **dry matter** *NZ* feedstuff for farm animals. **dry measure** a measure of capacity for corn etc. **dry milk** *US* dried milk. **dry mounting**: in which paper impregnated with shellac, or a coating of shellac, is placed between the print etc. and the mount, the whole then being pressed between hot plates to produce bonding. DRY-NURSE. **dry-point** a needle for engraving without acid on bare copper plate; engraving by this means; (a print made from) an engraving so produced. *dry prune*: see PRUNE *n.* 2. **dry rot** a type of decay of wood in poorly ventilated or humid conditions, in which the cellulose is attacked and the wood readily reduced to a powder; the fungus *Serpula lacrymans*, which causes this; *fig.* unsuspected moral or social decay. **dry-rotten** *a.* decayed with dry rot. **dry run** (*a*) *US* a stream bed which is filled only after rain; (*b*) *colloq.* a rehearsal, a try-out. **dry-salt** *v.t.* = *dry-cure* above. **dry-salter** *Hist.* a dealer in drugs, dyestuffs, gums, oils, tinned or pickled foodstuffs, etc. **dry saltery** a dry-salter's store; *sing.* & in *pl.*, the commodities sold at such a store. *dry scall*: see SCALL *n.* **dry season** a period of a month or more each year in tropical and subtropical regions when there is little or no rainfall. **dry shampoo** a cleaner for the hair, upholstery, etc., which does not need water. **dry shave** (*a*) a shave without water, soap, or other lubricant; (*b*) *Austral.* & *NZ* a teasing caress in which an unshaven cheek is rubbed against a woman's face. **dry shaver** an electric or other razor for use without water. **dry-shod** *adv.* without wetting one's shoes. **dry sink** *N. Amer.* an antique (usu. wooden) kitchen-cabinet with an inset sink, now usu. used as a plant-holder or for some other purpose. **dry-ski** *a.* designating a school etc. for indoor training in skiing. **dry slope** an artificial slope on which to ski. **dry spell** a period of dry weather. *dry steam*: see STEAM *n.* **dry-stone** *a.* designating a stone wall built without using mortar. **dry suit** a diving suit under which warm clothing can be worn. **dry valley**: in which the original river or stream has disappeared. **drywall** plasterboard (see also sense 9 above). *dry-wash*: see WASH *n.* 5c. *dry way*: see WAY *n.* **dry well** = *dry hole* above.

B *adv.* In a dry way; without the use of liquid; without drawing blood. L15.

dry /drʌɪ/ *v.* Pa. t. & pple **dried** /drʌɪd/. See also DRIED *ppl a.* [OE *drȳġan* v.t., *drūgian* v.i., f. as DRY *a.*] **I** *lit.* **1** *v.t.* Remove the moisture from by wiping, evaporation, draining, etc. (freq. foll. by *off, out, up*); preserve (food etc.) by the removal of its natural moisture. OE. **b** Stop the flow of milk of (a cow or other mammal). Also foll. by *off, up.* M16. **2** *v.i.* Lose moisture by wiping, evaporation, drainage, etc. Also foll. by *off, out.* OE. **b** Of a well, spring, etc.: cease to give water. Usu. foll. by *up.* ME. **c** Of a cow etc.: cease to give milk. E19. **3** *v.t.* Remove (water, moisture) by evaporation, drainage, etc. (also foll. by *up*); wipe away (tears). ME. **4** *v.i.* Of water etc.: disappear by evaporation etc. Freq. foll. by *up.* ME. **5** *v.i.* Dry crockery, cutlery, etc., after it has been washed. Also foll. by *up.* M20.

1 E. O'NEILL She dries her eyes and regains her composure. E. HEMINGWAY Make a fire in the kitchen and dry your things. **2** G. B. SHAW His clothes are drying in the sun. J. BUCHAN Acres of spongy ground which . . dried up at the first frosts. **dry straight** *fig.* come right eventually. *hang* (*one's bat*) *out to dry*: see HANG *v.* **b** *fig.*: M. DE LA ROCHE The fount of his gratitude must dry up from the unceasing flow. **4** SHAKES. *All's Well* Great floods have flown From simple sources, and great seas have dried. TENNYSON The sap dries up: the plant declines.

II *fig.* **6** *v.i.* Foll. by *up*: stop, cease; come to an end; *spec.* stop talking. *colloq.* M19. **7a** *v.i.* Forget one's lines on stage. Also foll. by *up.* L19. **b** *v.t.* Foll. by *up*: cause (a performer) to forget lines. E20. **8** *v.i.* & *t.* Foll. by *out*: (cause to) undergo treatment for drug or alcohol addiction. M20.

6 SCOTT FITZGERALD 'Oh, dry up!' retorted Basil. *New York Times* As selling dried up, the glamours gained on new buying. **7** L. A. G. STRONG A colleague of mine once dried in the middle of a scene.

dryad /ˈdrʌɪəd, -ad/ *n.* Also **D-**. Pl. **-ads, -ades** /-ədiːz/. LME. [(O)Fr. *dryade* f. L *Dryades* pl. of *Dryas* f. Gk *Druas, Druadēs*, f. *drus* tree: see -AD[1].] *Class. Mythol.* A nymph supposed to inhabit trees, a wood nymph.

transf.: BYRON The palm, the loftiest dryad of the woods.

dry'adic *a.* L19.

dryas /ˈdrʌɪəs/ *n.* L18. [L: see prec.] **1** Any of several creeping alpines of the genus *Dryas*, belonging to the rose family and having white or yellowish flowers. L18. **2** (**D-**.) *Geol.* A type of clay or a subarctic phase characterized by the growth of dryases. E20.

Dryasdust /ˈdrʌɪəzdʌst/ *n.* M19. [Dr *Dryasdust*, a fictitious character (f. (*as*) *dry as dust* s.v. DRY *a.*) to whom Sir Walter Scott dedicated novels.] A laborious dull antiquarian or historian; a scholar occupied with uninteresting details.

Drydenian /drʌɪˈdiːnɪən/ *a.* L17. [f. *Dryden* (see below) + -IAN.] Of, pertaining to, or resembling the English poet, dramatist, and critic John Dryden (1631–1700), his works, or his style.

Also **Drydenish** /ˈdrʌɪd(ə)nɪʃ/ *a.* L17.

dryer *n.* var. of DRIER.

drying /ˈdrʌɪɪŋ/ *vbl n.* LME. [f. DRY *v.* + -ING[1].] The action of DRY *v.* Also *drying-off, -out, -up.*

H. OLDENBURG The too hasty drying thereof spoils it. I. SHAW Jean was spending more and more time in drying-out clinics.

Attrib. & *comb.*: in the sense 'used in or for drying something', as *drying-closet, -floor, -green, -rack*, etc. Special combs., as **drying-day** a specified (good etc.) type of day for the drying of washing outdoors.

drying /ˈdrʌɪɪŋ/ *ppl a.* LME. [f. DRY *v.* + -ING[2].] That dries; causing drying; in the process of drying. *spec.* that dries quickly.

W. B. CARPENTER A cold drying wind. W. FAULKNER His boots and puttees not caked with the drying mud of trenches. **drying oil**: that thickens or hardens on exposure to air.

dryish /ˈdrʌɪɪʃ/ *a.* E18. [f. DRY *a.* + -ISH[1].] Somewhat dry.

dry land /*n. phr.* drʌɪ ˈland; *adj.* ˈdrʌɪland/ *n. phr.* & *a.* ME. [f. DRY *a.* + LAND *n.*[1]] **A** *n. phr.* **1** Land as opp. to the sea, a river, etc.; land that is dry, not swampy or under water. ME. **2** *sing.* &

(usu.) in *pl.* An area, or land, where rainfall is low, esp. when farmed without irrigation. Chiefly *N. Amer.* E20. B *attrib.* or as *adj.* (usu. w. hyphen). 1 Living or occurring on the land. L17. 2 Established or (able to be) grown or bred on dry lands; (of farming) practised on dry lands without irrigation. Chiefly *N. Amer.* L19.

dry'lander *n.* (*N. Amer.*) a person who has settled on or who farms dry lands E20.

dryly *adv.* var. of DRILY.

dryness /'drʌɪnɪs/ *n.* LME. [f. DRY *a.* + -NESS.] The state or condition of being dry (*lit.* & *fig.*); absence or deficiency of moisture; prohibition of alcohol; absence of emotion or cordiality; dullness, lack of interest.

dry-nurse /'drʌɪnəːs/ *n.* & *v.* M16. [f. DRY *a.* + NURSE *n.*[1]] A *n.* 1 A woman who looks after a baby but does not breast-feed it. Opp. *wet-nurse.* M16. 2 *fig.* A person who coaches another (esp. a superior) in his or her duties. *arch.* E17.

B *v.t.* Look after without breast-feeding (another person's baby); be a dry-nurse to (*lit.* & *fig.*). L16.

G. J. W. WOLSELEY Some regular officers who had been selected . . for the purpose of dry-nursing their inexperienced colonels.

Dryopithecus /drʌɪəʊ'pɪθɪkəs/ *n.* M19. [mod.L, f. Gk *drus* tree + *pithēkos* ape.] A member of the fossil genus *Dryopithecus* of partly tree-dwelling Old World anthropoid apes of Miocene times, ancestral to present-day African pongids.

dryopithecine /-siːn/ *a.* & *n.* (*a*) *adj.* of, pertaining to, or designating the Dryopithecinae, a subfamily of the Pongidae including Dryopithecus and believed to be ancestral to man; designating a five-cusped tooth pattern found in Dryopithecus and in the lower molars of man and other hominoids; (*b*) *n.* a dryopithecine individual: M20.

dryster /'drʌɪstə/ *n.* Now *arch.* or *Hist.* ME. [f. DRY *v.* + -STER.] A person employed in drying something.

dryth /drʌɪθ/ *n. obs.* exc. *dial.* Also **drieth**. M16. [f. DRY *a.* + -TH[1], after *warmth.*] 1 Dryness, dry condition. M16. 2 Thirst. M16. 3 Dry weather, drought. L16.

dry-up /'drʌɪʌp/ *n.* L19. [f. *dry up*: see DRY *v.*] An act or instance of drying up.

duab *n.* var. of DOAB.

duad /'djuːad/ *n.* M17. [Gk *duas*, *duad-* the number two (see -AD[1]), prob. infl. by L *duo*. Cf. DYAD.] A combination of two; a couple, a pair.

du'adic *a.* of, pertaining to, or consisting of a duad or duads L19.

dual /'djuːəl/ *n.* & *a.* LME. [L *dualis*, f. *duo* two: see -AL[1].] A *n.* †1 Either of the two middle incisor teeth in each jaw. LME–M16. 2 *Gram.* A form of nouns, verbs, etc., denoting two people or things (in addition to singular and plural); a word in this number. M17. 3 In a chess problem, an alternative second or later move by White that fulfils the stipulations in a manner not intended by the composer. L19.

B *adj.* 1 Of or pertaining to two; shared by two, joint; *spec.* (*Gram.*) denoting two people or things. E17. 2 Composed or consisting of two parts; twofold, double. M17.

2 F. O'BRIEN His laugh had a dual function, partly to applaud his jest, partly to cloak his anger. S. SONTAG Everyone . . holds dual citizenship in the kingdom of the well and in the kingdom of the sick.

Special collocations & *comb.*: **dual carriageway** a road with a dividing strip between traffic going in opposite directions. **dual control** (*a*) control exercised by two parties jointly; (*b*) in *pl.*, duplicated controls in an aircraft, motor vehicle, etc., for instructor and learner. **dual-control** *a.* (of a vehicle or aircraft) controllable by both instructor and learner. **dual number** *Gram.* = sense A.2 above. **dual personality** two distinct personalities in one individual. **dual-purpose** *a.* serving two purposes; *spec.* (of a car) usable for passengers and goods. **dual-standard** *a.* (of equipment etc.) capable of working to either of two specifications.

dually *adv.* in a dual manner; *Gram.* in the dual number: M17.

dual /'djuːəl/ *v.t.* Infl. **-ll-**, ***-l-**. E20. [f. the adj.] 1 *Chess.* In *pass.*, admit of a dual (see DUAL *n.* 3). E20. 2 Convert into dual form; *spec.* make (a road) into a dual carriageway. M20.

dualise *v.* var. of DUALIZE.

dualism /'djuːəlɪz(ə)m/ *n.* L18. [f. DUAL *a.* + -ISM, after Fr. *dualisme.*] 1 A theory or system of thought which recognizes two independent principles (cf. MONISM, PLURALISM 2); *spec.* (*a*) the theory that mind and matter exist as separate entities; (*b*) the doctrine that there are two conflicting powers, good and evil, in the universe; (*c*) the doctrine that Christ had two natures, human and divine. L18. 2 The state of being dual; twofold division, duality. M19. 3 *Gram.* The fact of expressing two in number. L19.

1 D. R. HOFSTADTER Dualism is the conceptual division of the world into categories. 2 R. W. EMERSON An inevitable dualism bisects nature, so that each thing is a half, and suggests another thing to make it whole. M. S. LIVINGSTON Wave-particle dualism in the properties of light.

dualist /'djuːəlɪst/ *n.* M17. [f. DUAL *a.* + -IST. In sense 1 after PLURALIST, in sense 2 after Fr. *dualiste.*] †1 A holder of two benefices. Only in M17. 2 A person who holds any of the doctrines of dualism. E19.

dualistic /djuːə'lɪstɪk/ *a.* L18. [f. prec. + -IC, after Fr. *dualistique.*] 1 Of or pertaining to dualism; of the nature of dualism. L18. 2 Dual. M19.

dualistically *adv.* M19.

duality /djuː'alɪti/ *n.* LME. [Late L *dualitas* dual nature, f. L *dualis* DUAL *a.*: see -ITY. In sense 2 app. after PLURALITY: cf. DUALIST.] 1 The state or condition of being dual or having two parts or natures; twofold condition, dualism. LME. †2 The simultaneous holding of two benefices. E–M17.

1 *principle of duality*: see PRINCIPLE *n.*

dualize /'djuːəlʌɪz/ *v.t.* Also **-ise**. M19. [f. DUAL *a.* + -IZE.] Make or regard as dual.

duan /'duːən/ *n.* M18. [Gael. & Ir.] A (Gaelic or Irish) poem, song, or canto.

duar *n.* var. of DOUAR.

duarchy /'djuːɑːki/ *n.* L16. [f. L (or irreg. f. Gk) *duo* two, after *monarchy* etc.] Government by two joint rulers; a diarchy.

dub /dʌb/ *n.*[1] *Sc.* & *north.* Also **dib** /dɪb/. LME. [Origin unkn. Cf. MLG, LG, WFris. *dobbe.*] 1 A muddy or stagnant pool, a puddle. LME. 2 A deep dark pool in a river or stream. M16.

Comb.: **dub-skelper** a person who splashes through puddles; *fig.* an idle person, a vagrant.

dub /dʌb/ *n.*[2] L16. [Imit.: cf. DUB-A-DUB, RUB-A-DUB.] 1 The beat or the sound of a drum. L16. 2 A tap, a blow (resembling a drum beat). M17.

2 N. HAWTHORNE Jotting down each dull footstep with a melancholy dub of his staff.

dub /dʌb/ *n.*[3] *Criminals' slang.* In sense 2 also **dubs**. L17. [Rel. to DUB *v.*[3]] 1 A key, a picklock. L17. 2 A turnkey, a jailer. E19.

dub /dʌb/ *n.*[4] *obs.* exc. *Hist.* L18. [Telugu *dabbu.*] A small copper coin formerly used in parts of India.

dub /dʌb/ *n.*[5] *slang* (orig. *US*). L19. [Perh. f. DUB *v.*[1] 10.] An inexperienced or unskilful person; a fool, a duffer.

dub /dʌb/ *n.*[6] L20. [f. DUB *v.*[5]] 1 A remixed version of a piece of recorded (esp. Black) music, usu. with the melodic line removed and special effects added. L20. 2 A kind of Black performance poetry, orig. accompanied by dub music. L20.

dub /dʌb/ *v.*[1]*t.* Infl. **-bb-**. LOE. [AN *duber*, aphet. f. *aduber*, OFr. *adober* (mod. *adouber*) equip with armour, repair, mend: ult. origin unkn.] I Give (a title) to. With obj. & compl., or (now *rare*) simple obj. 1 Confer knighthood on by ceremonially touching on the shoulder with a sword; make (a person) a knight. LOE. 2 Invest with a dignity or title; give a name, description, or nickname to. Now freq. *joc.* ME.

1 C. KINGSLEY Thou wast dubbed knight in this church. O. NEUBECKER It was the custom to dub new knights before the beginning of the fighting. 2 POPE A Man of wealth is dubb'd a Man of worth. T. HARDY She was light and slight, of the type dubbed elegant. A. J. TOYNBEE The officiants are medicine men, though, to save appearances, they are dubbed 'sacristans'. M. EDWARDES The media dubbed it the 'tea break strike'.

II Dress; trim. †3 Equip, clothe, adorn. ME–E18. 4 *Angling.* Make up (an artificial fly); dress (a hook) *with* a fly. LME. †5 Disguise (inferior goods); adulterate (wine). Only in LME. 6 Cut off the comb and wattles of (a cock). L16. 7 Smear or rub (now *spec.* hide, leather) with grease. Cf. DUBBING 4, DUBBIN. E17. 8 Trim or crop (trees, hedges, etc.). *obs.* exc. *dial.* M17. 9 Trim or make smooth with an adze. E18. 10 Make blunt; beat flat. M18. 11 Dress (cloth); *spec.* beat with teazels in order to raise nap. *obs.* exc. *dial.* E19.

dub /dʌb/ *v.*[2] Infl. **-bb-**. L15. [Imit. Cf. EFris. *dubben* butt, beat, strike.] 1 *v.t.* Thrust, poke, prod. Formerly also, strike, hit. L15. b *v.i.* Make a thrust; poke *at.* M19. 2 *v.i.* & *t.* Beat (a drum); (of a drum) beat, sound. Cf. DUB-A-DUB, RUB-A-DUB. L16.

dub /dʌb/ *v.*[3]*t. slang.* Infl. **-bb-**. L17. [Perh. f. DUP *v.* = do up. Cf. DUB *n.*[3]] †1 Unlock, open (a door). L17–L18. 2 Shut or lock *up.* M18.

dub /dʌb/ *v.*[4]*i. slang.* Infl. **-bb-**. E19. [Origin unkn.] Foll. by *up*, *in*: give money, make a contribution, pay up, chip in.

dub /dʌb/ *v.*[5]*t.* Infl. **-bb-**. E20. [Abbrev. of DOUBLE *v.*] Add (sounds or music) to a film, recording, or broadcast; provide (a film etc.) with an alternative soundtrack, esp. in a different language; transfer or combine (recorded sound-tracks). Freq. as *dubbed* ppl a., *dubbing* vbl n.

F. ASTAIRE The foot sounds had to be dubbed in, due to the difficulty of picking them up . . on the set during shooting. J. D. WATSON Dubbed voices uttered words of uncontrolled passion.

dub-a-dub /'dʌbədʌb, dʌbə'dʌb/ *n.*, *a.*, *adv.*, & *v.* M16. [Imit. Cf. DUB *n.*[2], RUB-A-DUB.] A *n.*, *a.*, & *adv.* (With, like) the sound made in beating a drum. M16. B *v.t.* & *i.* Beat (a drum); drum. L16.

dubash /duː'bɑːʃ/ *n.* L17. [Hind. *dubhāṣī*, f. *du-* two + Skt *bhāṣā* language.] In the Indian subcontinent: an interpreter, an intermediary, a mercantile broker.

dubba /'dʌbə/ *n.* Also **dubber**. L17. [Hind. *ḍabbā*, Urdu *dabbah.*] In the Indian subcontinent: a leather bottle or skin bag, used chiefly for holding oil, ghee, etc.

dubbeltjie /'dœbəlki, -tʃi/ *n. S. Afr.* L17. [Sense 1 f. Afk. f. Du. *dubbeltje* double stiver, two-penny piece. Sense 2 is prob. a different wd. See also DOUBLE-GEE.] 1 A Dutch two-stiver coin or an English penny, both formerly current in South Africa; in *pl.*, money. *obs.* exc. *Hist.* L17. 2 Any of various trailing weeds with spiny burs, esp. *Tribulus terrestris* or *Emex australis*; one of these burs. L18.

dubber *n.* var. of DUBBA.

dubbin /'dʌbɪn/ *n.* & *v.* E19. [Alt. of DUBBING 4.] A *n.* A preparation of grease for softening and waterproofing leather. E19. B *v.t.* Apply dubbin or a similar substance to. L19.

dubbing /'dʌbɪŋ/ *n.* ME. [f. DUB *v.*[1] + -ING[1].] 1 The action of DUB *v.*[1] I; the conferring of knighthood, the giving of a name or title. ME. †2 Attire, dress, array. Only in ME. 3 *Angling.* The preparation of an artificial fly; the materials used in this. L17. 4 = DUBBIN *n.* Now *rare* or *obs.* L18. 5 Trimming with an adze etc.; smoothing, levelling. E19.

dubby /'dʌbi/ *a. colloq.* & *dial.* E19. [f. DUB *v.*[1] + -Y[1].] Blunt; short, dumpy.

duberous /'djuːb(ə)rəs/ *a. joc.* & *dial.* L18. [Alt. of DUBIOUS.] Dubious, doubtful, unsure.

dubiety /djuː'bʌɪɪti/ *n.* M18. [Late L *dubietas*, f. *dubium*: see DUBIOUS, -ITY.] The state or quality of being dubious; uncertainty; an instance of this.

dubiosity /djuːbɪ'ɒsɪti/ *n.* M17. [f. as next + -ITY.] 1 A doubtful matter, an uncertainty. M17. 2 Doubt, uncertainty. M19.

dubious /ˈdjuːbɪəs/ *a.* M16. [f. L *dubiosus*, f. *dubium* doubt: see -OUS.] 1 Giving rise to doubt; of questionable value or truth; uncertain, vague. M16. b Of uncertain outcome. M17. c Of questionable character; suspect, untrustworthy. M19. 2 Wavering in opinion, hesitant, inclined to doubt; expressing uncertainty. M17.

1 T. HEGGEN The islands began to grow dubious on the horizon. J. F. LEHMANN I had the dubious satisfaction of knowing that I had been 'put on their files'. b MILTON His utmost power.. oppos'd In dubious Battel on the Plains of Heav'n. c W. S. CHURCHILL He resorted to dubious methods of raising money. J. ROSENBERG The quack.. equipped with all the paraphernalia of his dubious profession. 2 A. HELPS I followed them, dubious as to whether I should ultimately interfere. CONAN DOYLE The Inspector rubbed his chin and looked at me with dubious eyes.

dubiously *adv.* M17. **dubiousness** *n.* M17.

dubitable /ˈdjuːbɪtəb(ə)l/ *a.* E17. [L *dubitabilis*, f. *dubitare* to doubt: see -ABLE. Cf. earlier INDUBITABLE.] Open to doubt or question, able to be doubted.

dubitably *adv.* M19.

dubitant /ˈdjuːbɪt(ə)nt/ *a.* E19. [L *dubitant-* pres. ppl stem of *dubitare* to doubt: see -ANT[1].] Doubting, having doubts, hesitant.

dubitate /ˈdjuːbɪteɪt/ *v.i.* E19. [L *dubitat-* pa. ppl stem of *dubitare* to doubt: see -ATE[3].] Doubt, hesitate, waver.

dubitation /djuːbɪˈteɪʃ(ə)n/ *n.* LME. [(O)Fr. f. L *dubitatio(n-)*, f. as prec.: see -ATION.] The action of doubting; (a) doubt.

dubitative /ˈdjuːbɪtətɪv/ *a.* E18. [(O)Fr. *dubitatif*, *-ive* or late L *dubitativus*, f. as DUBITATE: see -ATIVE.] Inclined to doubt; expressing doubt or hesitation.

dubitatively *adv.* E17.

Dublin Bay prawn /ˌdʌblɪn beɪ ˈprɔːn/ *n. phr.* M20. [*Dublin*: see next.] = NORWAY *lobster*. In *pl.*, scampi.

Also **Dublin prawn** *n. phr.* E20.

Dubliner /ˈdʌblɪnə/ *n.* E20. [f. *Dublin* (see below) + -ER[1].] A native or inhabitant of Dublin, capital city of the Republic of Ireland.

Dubonnet /duːˈbɒneɪ; *foreign* dybɔnɛ (*pl. same*)/ *n.* E20. [Name of a family of French wine merchants.] Proprietary name for a sweet French flavoured wine drunk as an aperitif: a drink of this.

dubs *n.*[2] see DUB *n.*[3]

dubs /dʌbz/ *int.* & *n.*[1] *local.* E19. [Abbrev. of *doubles*. Cf. DIBS *int.* & *n.*[3]] (A situation provoking) a cry used in games of marbles; a marble used in certain games.

ducal /ˈdjuːk(ə)l/ *a.* L15. [Fr., f. *duc* DUKE *n.*: see -AL[1].] 1 Of or pertaining to a duke or dukedom; characteristic of or like a duke. Also, of a doge. L15. 2 Of the rank of duke. L18.

ducally *adv.* in a ducal manner; as a duke: E19.

ducape /ˈdjuːkeɪp/ *n.* M17. [Origin unkn.] A heavy silk dress fabric.

ducat /ˈdʌkət/ *n.* Also (esp. in sense 3) **ducket(t)**. LME. [It. *ducato* or its source, med.L *ducatus* DUCHY.] 1 *Hist.* Orig., a silver coin minted by Robert II of Sicily, as Duke of Apulia, in 1140. Later, any of various gold or silver coins formerly current in most European countries. LME. 2 A piece of money. In *pl.*, money, cash. *arch. colloq.* L18. 3 A ticket; *esp.* a railway or admission ticket. Cf. DOCKET *n.* 3. *slang.* L19.

ducatoon /dʌkəˈtuːn/ *n.* E17. [Fr. *ducaton* f. It. *ducatone*, f. as prec.: see -OON.] *Hist.* A silver coin formerly current in some European countries.

duce /ˈduːtʃeɪ/ *n.* Also **D-**. E20. [It. = leader.] A leader; *spec. il* (It. = the) or *the Duce*, the title assumed by Benito Mussolini (1883–1945), creator and leader of the Fascist State in Italy.

duces *n.*[1] pl. of prec.

duces *n.*[2]*pl.* see DUX.

duces tecum /djuːsiːz ˈtiːkəm/ *n. phr.* E17. [L (*sub poena*) *duces tecum* (under penalty) you shall bring with you.] *Law.* A writ commanding a person to produce documentary evidence in court or at a deposition. Also *subpoena duces tecum*.

Duchenne /duːˈʃɛn/ *n.* L19. [G. B. A. *Duchenne* (1806–75), Fr. neurologist.] *Med.* Used *attrib.* and in *possess.* to designate a severe form of muscular dystrophy described by Duchenne.

duchess /ˈdʌtʃɪs, -ɛs/ *n.* Also (esp. in titles) **D-**. Also †**dutchess**. LME. [(O)Fr. *duchesse* f. med.L *ducissa*, f. L *dux*, *duc-*: see DUKE *n.*, -ESS[1].] I 1 A lady of nobility: *spec.* (*a*) the wife or widow of a duke; (*b*) a woman holding a title equivalent to duke in her own right. LME. 2 A woman of imposing or showy appearance. *slang.* L17. 3 A girl or woman, *spec.* one's wife or mother; a costermonger's wife. Also used as a familiar form of address. Cf. DUTCH *n.*[2] *slang.* E20.

1 *grand duchess*: see GRAND *a.*[1]

II 4 A roofing-slate of a large size. Cf. COUNTESS 2, LADY *n.* 11. E19. 5 A size of writing paper. E20.

III Cf. DUCHESSE. 6 = DUCHESSE 1. E19.

Comb.: **duchess potatoes** = DUCHESSE *potatoes*; **duchess sleeve** = DUCHESSE *sleeve*.

duchesse /duːˈʃɛs; ˈdʌtʃɪs, -ɛs; *foreign* dyʃɛs (*pl. same*)/. *n.* Also **D-**. L18. [Fr.: see prec.] 1 A chaise longue consisting of two facing armchairs connected by a detachable footstool. L18. 2 More fully *duchesse dressing-chest*, (*dressing*)-*table*. A dressing-table with a pivoting mirror. M19. 3 More fully *duchesse satin*, *satin duchesse*. A soft heavy kind of satin. L19.

Comb.: *duchesse dressing-chest*, *dressing-table*: see sense 2 above; **duchesse lace** a kind of Brussels pillow-lace, worked with fine thread in large sprays; **duchesse potatoes** mashed potatoes mixed with egg, baked or fried in small cakes or used as garnish; *duchesse satin*: see sense 3 above; **duchesse set** a set of fabric or lace mats for a dressing-table; **duchesse sleeve** an ornately trimmed sleeve covering two-thirds of the arm; *duchesse-table*: see sense 2 above; **duchesse toilet cover** a fabric or lace mat for a dressing-table.

duchy /ˈdʌtʃi/ *n.* LME. [Partly f. OFr. *duché* fem., later form of *duchée* f. Proto-Romance, f. L *dux*, *duc-*, partly f. (O)Fr. *duché* masc. f. med.L *ducatus* territory of a duke, f. L *dux*, *duc-*: see DUKE *n.*, -Y[5].] 1 The territory ruled by a duke or duchess. LME. 2 *spec.* (**D-**.) Each of the royal dukedoms of Cornwall and Lancaster, having certain estates, revenues, and jurisdiction of their own. L15.

1 *grand duchy*: see GRAND *a.*[1]

duck /dʌk/ *n.*[1] Pl. **-s**, (in sense 1, also) same. [OE *duce* or *dūce*, f. Gmc base of DUCK *v.*] 1 Any of numerous swimming-birds belonging to the family Anatidae, distinguished from the swans and geese (also Anatidae) esp. by their generally smaller size. Also *spec.*, any of the domesticated forms of the mallard or wild duck *Anas platyrhynchos*. OE. b *spec.* The female of this fowl, (the male being the *drake*). LME. c The flesh of this fowl as food. L18. 2a As a term of familiarity or endearment: darling, dear; an attractive thing. Cf. DUCKS, DUCKY *n. colloq.* L16. b A fellow, a chap; an individual. *slang* (chiefly *US*). M19. 3 A British soldier of the Bombay Presidency. *colloq.* (now *Hist.*). E19. 4 A children's game in which a small stone is placed on a larger and the players throw stones to try to dislodge it; the target stone used in this. E19. 5 *Cricket.* Orig. *duck('s) egg*. A score of nought by a batsman. M19. 6 A savoury meatball, a faggot. L19.

1 *dabbling duck*, *diving duck*, *eider duck*, *ferruginous duck*, *harlequin duck*, *long-tailed duck*, *mandarin duck*, *Muscovy duck*, *ruddy duck*, *shelduck*, *swallow-tailed duck*, *tree duck*, *tufted duck*, *velvet duck*, *wood duck*, etc. 2a C. H. SPURGEON Her child.. was so much her 'duck' that he grew up to be a goose. *Sun* Nutty Nottingham Council has banned workers calling each other 'love' or 'duck' under new anti-sexism laws. b M. TWAIN Are you the duck that runs the gospel-mill next door? 5 F. RAPHAEL Julia clean-bowled him for a duck.

Phrases: **a duck of a —** a dear, sweet, pretty, or desirable —. BOMBAY DUCK. *break one's duck*: see BREAK *v.* **dead duck** *slang* (orig. *US*) a useless person or thing, a failure, a bankrupt. **ducks and drakes**, **duck and drake** a pastime in which a flat stone is bounced across the surface of water; idle play (*make ducks and drakes of*, *play ducks and drakes with*, trifle with, use recklessly, squander). **fine weather for ducks** wet, rainy weather. **lame duck** a disabled or powerless person or thing; *spec.* a person or company who cannot meet financial obligations. **like a duck in thunder**, **like a (dying) duck in a thunderstorm** with upturned eyes, looking flabbergasted or distressed. **like water off a duck's back** producing no effect. *Lord love a duck*: see LOVE *v.* 1. *ruptured duck*: see RUPTURE *v.* 1. **sitting duck** a target that one cannot (or should not) miss. **take to something like a duck to water** take to something very readily.

Comb.: **duck ant** a termite; **duck** or **duck's arse**, (*US*) **ass** a hairstyle with the back hair tapered like a duck's tail; abbrev. *d.a.*; **duckbill** (*a*) = PLATYPUS; (*b*) *duckbill wheat*, red wheat or rivet-wheat; (*c*) = *duck's bill* below; *duck-billed* PLATYPUS; **duckboard** a (slatted) board laid to facilitate movement over soft ground or fragile surfaces; **duck decoy** = DECOY *n.* 1; **duck-dive** *n.* & *v.* (make) a vertical dive down into the water; **duck** or **duck's egg** (*a*) the egg of a duck; (*b*) see sense 5 above; (*c*) a pale greenish-blue colour (freq. *attrib.*); **duck hawk** (*a*) *N. Amer.* the peregrine; (*b*) *dial.* the marsh harrier; **duckmeat**, **duck's meat** = *duckweed* below; **duck-mole** *Austral.* = PLATYPUS; **duckpin** *US* a short squat bowling pin; *duck's egg*: see *duck egg* above; **duck-shot**: of a size suitable for shooting wild ducks; **duck-shove** *v.i.* & *t.* (*Austral.* & *NZ slang*) jump a queue (orig. of a taxi not waiting on the rank); engage in sharp practice, evade responsibility (for). *duck's meat*: see *duckmeat* above; **duck soup** *slang* (orig. & chiefly *US*) an easy task, a pushover; *duck's arse*, *ass*: see *duck arse* above; **duck's bill** (an object having the spatulate shape of) the bill of a duck (freq. *attrib.*); **duck's disease** *joc.* short legs; **duckstone** = sense 4 above; **ducktail** (*a*) *S. Afr.* a young hooligan; (*b*) = *duck('s) arse* above; **duck-walk** (*a*) a duckboard track; (*b*) a waddle; a walk in a squatting position; **duckweed** any of various tiny aquatic plants belonging to the genus *Lemna* and related genera of the family Lemnaceae, which freq. carpet the surface of stagnant water and which consist of a flattened or gibbous frond bearing a minute flower in a lateral pocket; *collect.* a mass of such plants.

duck /dʌk/ *n.*[2] M16. [f. DUCK *v.*] 1 A rapid jerky lowering of the head or body; a rapid evasive movement. M16. 2 A quick plunge in water, a dip. M19.

duck /dʌk/ *n.*[3] & *a.* M17. [(M)Du. *doek* linen, linen cloth = OFris., OS *dōk*, OHG *tuoh* (G *Tuch*), of unkn. origin.] A *n.* 1 A strong untwilled linen or cotton fabric used for outer clothing (esp. by sailors), small sails, etc. M17. 2 In *pl.* Trousers of this material. E19. B *adj.* Made of duck. M19.

duck /dʌk/ *n.*[4] *colloq.* Also **DUKW**, **dukw**. M20. [Alt. (after DUCK *n.*[1]) of *DUKW*, a combination of factory serial letters designating features of the vehicle.] An amphibious lorry, a landing-craft.

duck /dʌk/ *v.* ME. [Corresp. to OFris. *dūka*, MLG, MDu. *dûken* (Du. *duiken*), OHG *tūhhan* (G *tauchen*), f. Gmc. Prob. already in OE: cf. DUCK *n.*[1]] I *v.i.* 1 Suddenly go under water and emerge; dip the head rapidly under water; plunge, dive; descend rapidly. ME. 2 Bend or stoop quickly; bob, lower the head suddenly, esp. as an evasive measure; move quickly and unobtrusively. M16. 3 Back *out*, withdraw, abscond. *colloq.* L19. b *Bridge.* Play a low card to a trick rather than attempt to win with a high card. E20.

1 W. GOLDING She.. stepped down into cooler water, ducked, then got out. 2 J. KOSINSKI Someone threw an apple-core; I ducked and it hit the principal. J. ARCHER Charles ducked into a nearby phone booth and rang Clive. *fig.*: BROWNING Law ducks to Gospel here. 3 D. ABSE I had ducked out from a lecture. H. CARPENTER His third novel.. ducked out of contemporary social issues entirely.

II *v.t.* 4 Submerge or dip (a person or thing) briefly (*in*, *into*, *under* water etc.). ME. 5 Lower (esp. the head) momentarily; jerk down. L16. 6 Get away from, avoid, dodge. *colloq.* L19. b *Bridge.* Deliberately lose (a trick) or fail to beat (a card) by playing a low card. E20.

4 SIR W. SCOTT Duck her in the loch, and then we will see whether she is witch or not. 5 T. HEGGEN He ducked his head below the level of the rail and crouched there. **duck up** *Naut.* haul up (the foot of a sail etc.) to allow the steersman a view forward. 6 R. HYDE Soldiers who had ducked the church parades. G. SWIFT I'm not trying to duck your questions. I'll answer them.

ducker *n.* (*a*) a person who ducks or dives under water; (*b*) (*obs.* exc. *dial.*) a diving bird: L15.

ducket(t) *n.* see DUCAT.

duckie *n.* var. of DUCKY *n.*

ducking /ˈdʌkɪŋ/ *vbl n.*[1] M16. [f. DUCK *v.* + -ING[1].] The action of DUCK *v.*

Comb.: **ducking-pond** *n.*[1] *Hist.* a pond into which offenders were ducked; **ducking-stool** *Hist.* a chair at the end of a rising and falling pole, formerly used to duck scolds and other offenders in water.

ducking /ˈdʌkɪŋ/ *n.*[2] L16. [f. DUCK *n.*[1] + -ING[1].] The catching, hunting, or shooting of wild ducks.

Comb.: **ducking-pond** *n.*[2] a pond on which ducks may be hunted or shot.

ducking /ˈdʌkɪŋ/ *n.*[3] E19. [f. DUCK *n.*[3] + -ING[3].] = DUCK *n.*[3]

duckling /ˈdʌklɪŋ/ *n.* LME. [f. DUCK *n.*[1] + -LING[1].] A young duck.

ugly duckling: see UGLY *a.*

ducks /dʌks/ *n. colloq.* M20. [f. DUCK *n.*[1] + -S[4].] = next. Cf. DUCK *n.*[1] 2a.

ducky /ˈdʌki/ *n. colloq.* Also **duckie**. M16. [f. DUCK *n.*[1] + -Y[6].] †1 A woman's breast. M16–M19. 2 As a term of familiarity or endearment: darling, dear. Cf. DUCK *n.*[1] 2a, DUCKS. E19.

ducky /ˈdʌki/ *a. colloq.* L19. [f. DUCK *n.*[1] + -Y[1].] Sweet, pretty; fine, splendid.

duct /dʌkt/ *n.* M17. [L *ductus* leading, (in med.L) aqueduct, f. *duct-* pa. ppl stem of *ducere* to lead. Cf. DUCTUS.] I†1 The action of leading; guidance. M–L17. †2 Course, direction. M17–E18. 3 A stroke drawn or traced as part of a letter; the manner of making such a stroke. M18. II4 *Anat.* & *Zool.* A tube or passage in the body for conveying fluids (now usu. lymph or glandular secretions). Cf. earlier DUCTUS 2. L17. b *Bot.* Any of the vessels of the vascular tissue of plants, containing air, water, etc. M19. 5 A channel or tube made for conveying liquid, gas, air, electric cable, etc.; *spec.* a trough in a printing machine which holds the ink and controls its flow to the rollers. E18.

4 *ejaculatory duct*, *Müllerian duct*, *parotid duct*, *vitelline duct*, *Wolffian duct*, etc.

Comb.: **ductwork** a system of ducts for conveying gases, liquids, etc.

ducting *n.* a system of ducts; tubing, piping: M20.

duct /dʌkt/ *v.t.* M20. [f. the n.] Convey through a duct; provide with a duct or ducts (chiefly as *ducted* ppl a.).

ducted fan, propeller (in a turbine) a multibladed fan, propeller, rotating inside a coaxial duct which prevents radial flow at the blade tips.

ductible /ˈdʌktɪb(ə)l/ *a.* Long *rare.* LME. [Fr. (obs.), f. L *duct-*: see DUCT *n.*, -IBLE.] = DUCTILE.

ductile /ˈdʌktʌɪl/ *a.* ME. [OFr., or L *ductilis*, f. as DUCT *n.*: see -ILE.] 1 Flexible, pliant, malleable. ME. b *spec.* Of a material, esp. metal: able to be drawn out into wire, tough. E17. c Of liquid: (able to be) conducted through channels. E18. 2 (Of a person etc.) able to be led or drawn, docile; tractable, open to persuasion. E17.

1 J. H. BURTON The Roman law . . has proved extremely ductile and accommodating. b J. S. FOSTER Ductile materials which allow them to yield rather than break. 2 MRS H. WARD The man . . was in truth childishly soft and ductile.

ductility /dʌkˈtɪlɪti/ *n.* M17. [f. prec. + -ITY.] 1 Ability of a material to be drawn out into wire, extended, or worked upon; malleability, pliableness. M17. 2 Tractableness, docility. M17.

ductless /ˈdʌktlɪs/ *a.* M19. [f. DUCT *n.* + -LESS.] *Anat.* Having no duct; *spec.* (of a gland) that secretes directly into the bloodstream, endocrine.

ductor /ˈdʌktə/ *n. rare.* LME. [L = leader, f. *duct-*: see DUCT *n.*, -OR.] †1 A leader; an officer. LME–E17. †2 A line running in some direction. Only in M17. 3 A roller forming part of the ink duct of a printing machine from which other rollers derive ink. M19.

ductule /ˈdʌktjuːl/ *n.* L19. [L, dim. of *ductus*: see DUCT *n.*] *Anat.* A minute duct.

†ducture *n.* E17. [f. L *duct-* (see DUCT *n.*) + -URE, after *fracture* etc.] 1 A stroke drawn or traced. Only in E17. 2 Leading, guidance. E17–E18. 3 Extension or movement in some direction; an instance of this. Only in L17. 4 A channel. Only in L17.

ductus /ˈdʌktəs/ *n.* M17. [L: see DUCT *n.*] †1 = DUCT *n.* 2. Only in M17. 2 *Anat.* = DUCT *n.* 4. Now only in mod.L names of particular vessels. M17. 3 = DUCT *n.* 3. L19.

ductus litterarum /ˌdʌktəs lɪtəˈrɑːrəm/ *n. phr.* L19. [mod.L, f. L *ductus* (see prec.) + *litterarum* genit. pl. of *littera* letter.] The general shape and formation of letters and their combinations in manuscripts, the study of which may enable the restoration of true readings in a corrupt text.

dud /dʌd/ *n.* & *a. slang* & *dial.* ME. [Origin unkn.] A *n.* 1 An article of clothing. Now only in *pl.*, clothes; effects, things. ME. b In *pl.* Rags, ragged clothes. E16. 2 A useless or ineffective person. E19. 3 A counterfeit, useless, futile, or unsatisfactory thing; *esp.* (*a*) a bomb, firework, etc., that fails to go off; (*b*) a dishonoured cheque. L19.

1 S. L. ELLIOTT These are me clean duds for meetin' Rosebud at the station. *lag of duds*: see LAG *n.*[1] 3. 2 J. GALSWORTHY It's when you don't understand that you feel such a dud. R. GRAVES An expert on shell-fish, otherwise a dud.

B *adj.* Counterfeit; bad, useless, worn out, ineffective, unsatisfactory. E20.

H. ROSHER As luck would have it, the weather was dud. E. HEATH The dud engine would have to be changed.

duddery *n.* (*dial.*) a place where woollen cloth is sold or manufactured M16. **duddy** *a.* (*Sc.*) ragged E18.

dude /duːd, djuːd/ *n.* & *v. slang* (orig. *US*). L19. [Prob. f. G dial. = fool (cf. LG *dudenkop* 'stupid head').] A *n.* 1 A fastidious, aesthetic person; a dandy, a fop. *slang.* L19. 2 A holiday-maker in the western US, *esp.* one who holidays on a ranch; a tenderfoot. L19. 3 A fellow, a guy. E20.

Comb.: **dude ranch** a ranch which provides entertainment for tourists etc.

B *v.i.* & *refl.* Dress oneself (*up*) as or like a dude. L19.

dudess, dudine /duːˈdiːn, djuː-/ *ns.* a female dude L19. **dudish** *a.* characteristic of a dude; foppish: L19.

dudeen /duːˈdiːn/ *n. Anglo-Ir.* Also **dudheen**. M19. [Ir. *dúidín* dim. of *dúd* pipe: see -EEN[2].] A short clay tobacco-pipe.

dudgeon /ˈdʌdʒ(ə)n/ *n.*[1] LME. [Origin uncertain: cf. AN *digeon* (14th cent.).] 1 A kind of wood used esp. for the handles of knives, daggers, etc. *obs.* exc. *Hist.* LME. 2a In full *dudgeon-dagger*. A dagger with a hilt made of dudgeon. Also, a butcher's steel for sharpening knives. *arch.* L16. †b The hilt of a dagger, made of dudgeon. *rare* (Shakes.). Only in E17.

dudgeon /ˈdʌdʒ(ə)n/ *n.*[2] L16. [Origin unkn.] Resentment; a feeling of anger or offence. Chiefly in *in* (*high*, *great*, etc.) *dudgeon*, in angry resentment, having taken offence.

SIR W. SCOTT They often parted in deep dudgeon. R. L. STEVENSON I was old and spiteful . . and retired to pour forth my dudgeon to Fanny. D. M. DAVIN He would construe some jest as an insult, and withdraw in a dudgeon.

dudheen *n.* var. of DUDEEN.

due /djuː/ *n.* LME. [Fr. *du* (now *dû*) use as n. of pa. pple of *devoir* owe f. L *debere*: see next.] †1 Something which is due; a debt. LME–L17. 2 With possess. of the person owed: something which is due to a person legally or morally; one's rights, one's deserts; one's due share or quantity *of*. LME. 3a *sing.* & (usu.) in *pl.* An obligatory payment; a fee, a tribute, a toll; a legal charge; *spec.* the membership fee for a college, club, etc. LME. b *gen.* In *pl.* With possess. of the person owing: something which is owed by a person; one's debts; *fig.* one's obligations, one's responsibilities. M18. †4 Something which is due to be done; (a) duty. LME–L17. †5 Right, just title. L16–M17. 6 *Naut.* Something duly or thoroughly done. M19.

2 JOHN BROOKE The second monarch . . has received less than his due from historians. D. L. SAYERS He had . . missed the promotion he felt to be his due. J. OSBORNE Even from other young women . . she receives her due of respect and admiration. **give a person his** or **her due** treat a person fairly or with justice. **give the Devil his due** treat even a bad or undeserving character with justice. 3a P. SCOTT It was like belonging to a Union without having to pay the dues. **pay one's dues** *fig.* fulfil one's obligations; undergo hardships to succeed or gain experience. 6 **for a full due** thoroughly, so that it will not need to be done again.

due /djuː/ *a.* & *adv.* ME. [OFr. *dëu* (mod. *dû*, fem. *due*) f. Proto-Romance var. of L *debitus* (cf. DEBIT *n.*) pa. pple of *debere* owe.] A *adj.* 1 That is owing or payable as an obligation or debt. ME. 2 That ought to be or to be done; fitting, proper, rightful, appropriate. ME. †3 *pred.* Foll. by *to*: belonging to or incumbent upon by right or as a duty or necessity. LME–M17. 4 *pred.* That ought to be given, granted, or administered *to*. LME. 5 Merited, deserved. LME. 6 Adequate, sufficient. LME. 7 *due to*: a *adj. phr.* Attributable to, ascribable to. M17. b *prep. phr.* (Often considered *erron.*, though widely used.) Because of, on account of, owing to. L19. 8 *pred.* Expected, intended, or under engagement to arrive or appear, or *to do* something, at a specified time or *absol.* now; scheduled or in line *for* something at a specified time or *absol.* now. M19.

1 J. R. GREEN The amount of service due from the serf had become limited by custom. **fall** or **become due** become immediately payable. 2 H. GREEN Everything must proceed, and in due order. I. WATT His . . sense that due decorums must also be attended to. **in due course, time** etc., after a suitable interval, at the proper time. *with all due respect*: see RESPECT *n.* 4 STEELE The first Place among our English Poets is due to Milton. 5 JOSEPH HALL The Lord . . shall execute due vengeance upon Satan. H. ADAMS Somewhat more than her due share of conventional moral reproof. 6 J. WESLEY A due Degree of Exercise. 7a E. M. FORSTER Death . . was due to heart disease. B. BAINBRIDGE He liked touching people—it was due to him being a foreigner. b J. D. MACDONALD The beach dwindled due to erosion. 8 F. M. FORD He advised me to buy Caledonian Deferred, since they were due to rise. L. MACNEICE My boat to Lochboisdale—due at 5.30. K. AMIS They were due back the day before yesterday. A. PRICE He was due for a CID transfer in a few months' time. F. WELDON Susan enquires when the baby is due.

Special collocations: **due date**: on which payment of a bill etc. falls due.

B *adv.* 1 = DULY. *arch.* L16. 2 Of a compass point, or a direction: exactly, directly. L16.

1 SHAKES. *2 Hen. IV* Every third word a lie, duer paid to the hearer than the Turk's tribute. 2 M. INNES There is a . . mission station about eighty miles due north. G. L. HARDING From Karak the road runs almost due south.

dueful *a.* (*arch.*) due, appropriate L16. **dueness** *n.* LME.

†due *v.t.* Also (earlier) **dow**. ME–L16. [(O)Fr. *douer*: see ENDOW. Later form after ENDUE.] Endow.

duel /ˈdjuːəl/ *n.* L15. [It. *duello* or L *duellum*, arch. form of *bellum* war, used in med.L for judicial single combat.] 1a A judicial single combat. *obs.* exc. *Hist.* L15. b Chiefly *Hist.* A private fight between two people, prearranged and fought with deadly weapons, usually in the presence of two seconds, in order to settle a quarrel. E17. 2 Any contest between two people, parties, animals, or forces. L16. 3 Duelling as a practice. *rare.* E17.

duel /ˈdjuːəl/ *v.* Infl. **-ll-**, ***-l-**. M17. [f. the n.] 1 *v.i.* Fight a duel or duels. M17. †2 *v.t.* Encounter or overcome in a duel. M17–E18.

1 **duelling pistol** a long-barrelled pistol of a type made in identical pairs and used for duelling.

dueller *n.* a duellist E17.

duellist /ˈdjuːəlɪst/ *n.* Also ***duelist**. L16. [f. DUEL *n.* + -IST, after Fr. *duelliste* or It. *duellista*.] A person who fights a duel or duels.

duello /djuːˈɛləʊ/ *n.* Pl. **-os**. L16. [It. = duel.] 1 Duelling, as a custom; the established code of duellists. L16. 2 A duel. Now *rare* or *obs.* E17.

duende /duːˈɛndeɪ, *foreign* ˈdwende/ *n.* E20. [Sp.] 1 A ghost, an evil spirit. E20. 2 Inspiration, magic. M20.

duenna /djuːˈɛnə/ *n.* M17. [Sp. *dueña*, †*duenna* f. L *domina* lady, mistress.] **1** An older woman acting as governess and companion to one or more girls, esp. within a Spanish family. M17. **2** A chaperon. E18.

duet /djuːˈɛt/ *n.* & *v.* M18. [G *Duett* or It. *duetto*, f. *duo* two: see DUO, -ET[1].] **A** *n. Mus.* (A composition for) two voices or two performers. M18.

fig.: S. MIDDLETON The conversation became a duet between the Hollies and Terry.

B *v.i.* Infl. **-tt-**. Perform a duet (*with*). E19.

duettist *n.* a person who takes part in a duet L19.

duettino /djuːɛˈtiːnəʊ/ *n.* Pl. **-os.** M19. [It., dim. of next.] A short duet.

duetto /djuːˈɛtəʊ/ *n.* Pl. **-os.** E18. [It., dim. of *duo* duet: see DUO.] = DUET *n.*

duff /dʌf/ *n.*[1] L18. [Origin unkn.: cf. DUFF *v.*[2], DUFFER *n.*[1]] **1** Something worthless; counterfeit money; smuggled goods; the passing or selling of such things. *slang.* L18. **2** Decaying vegetable matter covering forest ground. *Sc.* & *US.* E19. **3** Coal dust; dross. M19.

duff /dʌf/ *n.*[2] M19. [North. var. of DOUGH *n.* Cf. *enough*.] **1** Dough, paste. *dial.* M19. **2** A boiled pudding; a dumpling. M19.

2 R. H. DANA Christmas . . . The only change was that we had a 'plum duff' for dinner.

duff /dʌf/ *a. colloq.* L19. [Perh. f. DUFF *n.*[1], but cf. DUFFER *n.*[2]] Worthless, false, bad, defective, dud.

J. LYMINGTON I went down to the pub because the play was so duff. *Which?* To find the duff bulb you'll have to test each bulb in turn.

duff /dʌf/ *v.*[1]*t.* & *i.* E19. [Back-form. f. DUFFER *n.*[2]] In golf, mishit (a shot or a ball); *gen.* make a mess of (something), bungle.

duff /dʌf/ *v.*[2] *slang.* M19. [Perh. back-form. f. DUFFER *n.*[1]] **1** *v.t.* Falsify, make (a thing) appear to be something which it is not; pass off (a worthless article) as valuable. M19. **2** *v.t.* Alter the brands on (stolen cattle); rustle (cattle); graze (stock) illicitly on another's land. *Austral.* M19. **3** *v.t.* Cheat (a person). M19. **4** *v.i.* With *up*: become foggy or hazy. L19. **5** *v.t.* With *up*: beat up, thrash. M20.

duffing *a.* (*a*) that duffs something; (*b*) counterfeit, worthless but passed off as valuable: M19.

duffadar *n.* var. of DAFADAR.

duffel *n.* var. of DUFFLE.

duffer /ˈdʌfə/ *n.*[1] M18. [Origin unkn.: cf. DUFF *n.*[1]] **1** A person who sells worthless articles as valuable, on false pretences. M18. **2** A pedlar, a hawker. L18. **3** A person who duffs cattle. *Austral.* M19.

duffer /ˈdʌfə/ *n.*[2] & *v. colloq.* M19. [Perh. alt. of DOWFART.] **A** *n.* **1** A useless, incompetent, or stupid person. M19. **2** A useless or defective article; *esp.* a counterfeit coin. M19. **3** An unproductive mine or claim. *Austral.* & *NZ.* M19.

1 M. E. BRADDON I was always a duffer at dancing.

B *v.i.* Of a mine: prove no good, give *out*. *Austral.* & *NZ.* L19.

duffle /ˈdʌf(ə)l/ *n.* & *a.* Also **duffel**. M17. [f. *Duffel*, a town in Belgium.] **A** *n.* **1** A coarse woollen cloth with a thick nap. M17. **2** Sporting or camping equipment; food and clothing. Chiefly *US.* M19. **3** = *duffle-coat* below. M20. **B** *attrib.* or as *adj.* Made of duffle. L17.

Special collocations & comb.: **duffle bag** a cylindrical canvas bag closed by a drawstring. **duffle-coat** a coat made of duffle; *spec.* a warm coat with a hood, fastened at the front with toggles.

dufrenite /duːˈfreɪnʌɪt, djuː-/ *n.* M19. [f. Pierre *Dufrenoy* (1792–1857), Fr. mineralogist + -ITE[1].] *Min.* A monoclinic hydrated basic phosphate of ferrous and ferric iron, usu. occurring as dark-green to brown botryoidal masses or crusts.

dufrenoysite /duːfrɪˈnɔɪzʌɪt, djuː-/ *n.* M19. [f. as prec. + *-s-* + -ITE[1].] *Min.* A monoclinic sulphide of lead and arsenic usu. occurring as grey prisms with a metallic lustre.

dufter /ˈdʌftə/ *n.* L18. [Urdu f. Arab., Pers. *daftar* register f. Gk *diphthera* hide. Cf. DEFTERDAR.] In the Indian subcontinent: an official register or record; also, a business office.

dug /dʌg/ *n.* M16. [Origin unkn.] The udder of a female mammal, *derog.* a woman's breast; a teat, a nipple.

duggy *a.* (*rare*) having large dugs E17.

dug *v.* pa. t. & pple: see DIG *v.*

dugong /ˈduːgɒŋ, ˈdjuː-/ *n.* Pl. **-s**, same. E19. [Ult. f. Malay *duyung*.] A sirenian, *Dugong dugon*, inhabiting coastal waters of the Indian Ocean, the SW Pacific, and adjacent seas.

dugout /ˈdʌgaʊt/ *ppl a.* & *n.* E18. [f. *dug* pa. pple of DIG *v.* + OUT *adv.* Cf. *dig out* s.v. DIG *v.*] **A** *ppl a.* Hollowed out by digging; excavated; *esp.* (of a canoe) made from a hollowed out tree-trunk. E18. **B** *n.* **1** A dugout canoe. E19. **2a** A rough dwelling hollowed out in a bank or hillside and roofed with turf, canvas, etc. Chiefly *US.* M19. **b** A hollowed out roofed shelter used in trench warfare; an underground shelter for protection from air raids or nuclear attack. E20. **c** A low shelter at the side of a baseball, football, etc., pitch, with seating for the team manager, trainer, players, etc. Orig. *US.* E20. **3** A person of outdated appearance or ideas; *spec.* a retired officer recalled to service. *slang.* M19.

duiker /ˈdʌɪkə, *foreign* dœɪkər/ *n. S. Afr.* Also **duyker**. Pl. **-s**, same. L18. [Du. = diver f. MDu. *dūker*, f. *dūken* dive, DUCK *v.*; sense 1 from the animal's habit of plunging through bushes when alarmed.] **1** Any of various small African antelopes of the genera *Cephalophus* and *Silvicapra*; spec. *S. grimmia*, widespread in southern African savannah and bush. L18. **2** A cormorant. M19.

duka /ˈduːkə/ *n.* E20. [Kiswahili f. Arab. *dukkān* shop, store, business.] In Kenya, a shop, a store.

duk-duk /ˈdʌkdʌk/ *n.* L19. [Local name.] (A member of) a secret society in New Britain (Papua New Guinea) which executes justice and practises sorcery.

duke /djuːk/ *n.* Also (esp. in titles) **D-**. OE. [(O)Fr. *duc* f. L DUX, *duc-* leader, rel. to *ducere* to lead.] **1** In some European countries: a sovereign prince, the ruler of a duchy. OE. †**b** = DOGE. M16–E19. **2**†**a** A leader; a captain, a general; a chief, a ruler. ME–L16. **b** *Rom. Hist.* [L DUX.] A provincial military commander under the later emperors. M17. **3** In Britain and some other countries: a male holding the highest hereditary title of nobility (ranking next below a prince). LME. **4** More fully *duke cherry*. A hybrid between the sweet cherry, *Prunus avium*, and sour cherry, *P. cerasus*; the fruit of such a tree. M17. **5** [f. *Duke of Yorks* below.] A hand, a fist, a finger. Usu. in *pl. slang.* L19. **b** The verdict in a boxing-match (from the practice of raising the victor's arm). *slang.* M20.

5 J. MITFORD Always ready with dukes up to go to the offensive. **b** D. RUNYON Ledoux gets the duke by unanimous vote of the officials.

Phrases: *dine with Duke Humphrey*: see DINE *v.* 1. *duke cherry*: see sense 4 above. *Duke of Argyll's tea plant*: see *tea plant* s.v. TEA *n.* *Duke of Argyll's tea-tree*: see TEA-TREE 3. *Duke of Exeter's* DAUGHTER. **Duke of Yorks** *rhyming slang* 'forks', i.e. fingers, hands, fists. *Iron Duke*: see IRON *n.* & *a.* *grand duke*: see GRAND *a.*[1] **royal duke** a duke who is also a royal prince.

dukeling *n.* (*a*) a petty duke; (*b*) *arch.* a duke's child: E17. **dukely** *a.* (*rare*) belonging to or befitting a duke L16. **dukeship** *n.* the office of a duke; (a humorous title for) a duke: M16.

duke /djuːk/ *v.* LME. [f. the n.] **1** *v.t.* Confer dukedom on. LME. **2** *v.i.* & *t.* (w. *it*). Act as a duke. E17. **3** *v.t. slang.* Shake hands with. M19. **4** *v.t.* & *i.* Fight with the fists, box, punch. Also *duke it out*. *US slang.* M20.

dukedom /ˈdjuːkdəm/ *n.* LME. [f. DUKE *n.* + -DOM.] **1** The territory ruled by a duke; a duchy. LME. **2** The dignity or office of a duke. L15.

dukery /ˈdjuːkəri/ *n.* M16. [f. DUKE *n.*: see -ERY, -RY.] **1**†**a** The dignity or office of a duke. M–L16. **b** A duchy. *rare.* M19. **2** The residence or estate of a duke; *spec.* (*the Dukeries*) an area of N. Nottinghamshire containing several ducal estates. E19.

Dukhobor /ˈduːkəbɔː/ *n.* Also **Doukh-**. L19. [Russ., f. *dukh* spirit + *borets* wrestler.] A member of a Russian Christian sect similar to the Society of Friends, many members of which migrated to Canada in 1899 after persecution for refusing military service.

dukw *n.* var. of DUCK *n.*[4]

dulcamara /dʌlkəˈmɛːrə/ *n.* L16. [med.L *dulcamara*, f. L *dulcis* sweet + *amara* bitter.] (A medicinal extract from) woody nightshade or bittersweet, *Solanum dulcamara*.

dulce /ˈduːlseɪ/ *n.* M17. [Sense 1 f. the adj.; sense 2 f. Sp.] †**1** Sweetness, gentleness. M17–E18. **2** A sweet substance; a sweet wine. M19.

†**dulce** *a.* L15–E18. [L *dulcis* or a refash. of DOUCE after the L.] Sweet (to the senses); agreeable; soothing.

dulcet /ˈdʌlsɪt/ *n.* LME. [f. (as) next. Cf. DOUCET *n.*] †**1** = DOUCET *n.* 2. Only in LME. **b** A dulcet note or tone. Only in L16. †**2** = DOUCET *n.* 3. L16–M17. **3** *Mus.* A soft organ-stop of 4-ft length and pitch. L19.

dulcet /ˈdʌlsɪt/ *a.* Also †**doucet**. LME. [(O)Fr. *doucet* dim. of *doux*, fem. *douce*, refash. after L *dulcis*: see -ET[1].] **1** Sweet to the taste or smell. *arch.* LME. **2** Sweet to the eye, (now esp.) ear, or feelings; pleasing to hear; soothing, mild. LME.

1 LONGFELLOW Catawba wine Has a taste more divine, More dulcet, delicious, and dreamy. 2 C. BAX The climate there is so dulcet that they are immune from all disease. K. CROSSLEY-HOLLAND Light-headed with desire, wholly taken in by her dulcet tones.

dulcetly *adv.* M19. **dulcetness** *n.* E16.

dulcian /ˈdʌlsɪən/ *n.* M19. [G *Dulzian*, or f. next. Cf. OFr. *doulçaine* etc., a kind of flute.] **1** *Hist.* An early one-piece bassoon. M19. **2** = BASSOON 2. Also = next. M19.

dulciana /dʌlsɪˈɑːnə/ *n.* L18. [med.L, f. L *dulcis* sweet.] *Mus.* A small-scaled, soft, open metal diapason usu. of 8-ft length and pitch.

dulcifluous /dʌlˈsɪflʊəs/ *a. rare.* E18. [f. L *dulcis* sweet + *-fluus* flowing + -OUS.] Sweetly or softly flowing.

dulcify /ˈdʌlsɪfʌɪ/ *v.t.* L16. [L *dulcificare*, f. *dulcis* sweet: see -FY.] **1** Make sweet to the taste, sweeten; *fig.* sweeten in temper, mollify. L16. †**2** *Chem.* Wash the soluble salts out of; neutralize the acidity of. E17–E19.

dulcification *n.* E17.

dulciloquent /dʌlˈsɪləkwənt/ *a.* M17. [f. L *dulcis* sweet + *loquens* pres. pple of *loqui* speak: see -ENT.] Speaking sweetly.

dulcimer /ˈdʌlsɪmə/ *n.* L15. [OFr. *doulcemer*, *-mele* corresp. to Sp. †*dulcemele*, It. *dolcemelle*, presumably f. L = sweet song.] **1** A musical instrument with metal strings of graduated length over a trapezoidal soundbox, struck with hammers. L15. **2** More fully *Appalachian dulcimer*. An American folk instrument, a kind of zither. M20.

dulcin /ˈdʌlsɪn/ *n.* Also **-ine**. M19. [f. L *dulcis* sweet + -IN[1].] *Chem.* †**1** = DULCITOL. M19–E20. **2** A synthetic compound, *p*-ethoxyphenylurea, $C_9H_{12}N_2O_2$, formerly used as a sweetening agent. L19.

dulcinea /dʌlsɪˈniːə, -ˈsɪnɪə/ *n.* M17. [*Dulcinea*, object of Don Quixote's devotion in the book by M. Cervantes.] An idolized and idealized woman; a sweetheart.

dulcite /ˈdʌlsʌɪt/ *n.* Now *rare* or *obs.* M19. [f. L *dulcis* sweet + -ITE[1].] *Chem.* = next.

dulcitol /ˈdʌlsɪtɒl/ *n.* L19. [f. prec. + -OL.] *Chem.* A hexahydric alcohol, $C_6H_{14}O_6$, which is a reduced counterpart of galactose and occurs in certain plants.

dulcitone /ˈdʌlsɪtəʊn/ *n.* L19. [f. L *dulcis* sweet + TONE *n.*] *Mus.* A keyboard instrument with steel forks struck by hammers.

dulcitude /ˈdʌlsɪtjuːd/ *n.* Now *rare.* E17. [L *dulcitudo*, f. *dulcis* sweet: see -TUDE.] Sweetness.

dulcorous /ˈdʌlk(ə)rəs/ *a. rare.* L17. [f. L *dulcor* sweetness + -OUS.] Sweet.

dule *n.* var. of DOLE *n.*[2]

dulia /djʊˈlʌɪə/ *n.* LME. [med.L f. Gk *douleia* servitude, f. *doulos* slave.] *RC Ch.* The veneration properly given to saints and angels. Cf. HYPERDULIA, LATRIA.

dull /dʌl/ *a.* [OE *dol* = OS (Du.) *dol*, OHG *tol* (G *toll*); superseded in ME by forms f. cognate MLG, MDu. *dul.*] 1 Slow of understanding, not quick-witted; obtuse, stupid. In early use also occas., fatuous, foolish. OE. 2 Of an edge or weapon: blunt. ME. 3 Without keen sensation; insensible, inanimate, benumbed; *dial.* hard of hearing, deaf. LME. b Of pain etc.: indistinctly felt, not acute. E18. 4 Slow-moving, sluggish; inactive; drowsy. LME. b Of trade: slow, stagnant, not brisk. Of goods etc.: not easily saleable. E18. 5 Of a person, a mood, etc.: depressed, listless, not lively or cheerful. LME. 6 Uninteresting; uneventful: unexciting, tedious, boring. LME. 7 Of colour, sound, taste, etc.: not bright, vivid, or keen; dim, indistinct, insipid. LME. b Of weather: overcast, cloudy; gloomy. L16.

1 H. JAMES Her quick perception . . made him feel irretrievably dull. 2 SHAKES. *Rich. III* The murd'rous knife was dull . . Till it was whetted on thy stone-hard heart. 3 TENNYSON You never would hear it; your ears are so dull. b OED A sharp pain, followed by a dull ache. 4 R. CHANDLER About four in the morning, when . . the crew were all dull with fatigue. A. SILLITOE Coal to bank up the dull fire. 5 DICKENS When other people were merry, Mrs. Varden was dull. 6 A. S. NEILL There is always something happening . . there isn't a dull day in the whole year. 7 J. CONRAD The sun sank low, and from glowing white changed to a dull red. b J. TYNDALL Dawn was dull, but the sky cleared as the day advanced.

Comb. & *special collocations*: **dull emitter** a thermionic valve filament which operates at a relatively low temperature; a valve with such a filament; **dull-head** a stupid person, a blockhead; **dull-headed** *a.* stupid, slow-witted; †**dull-pate** = *dull-head* above; **dull-witted** *a.* = *dull-headed* above.

dullify *v.t.* (*colloq.*, now *rare*) make dull M17. **dullish** *a.* rather dull LME.

dull /dʌl/ *v.* ME. [f. the adj.] 1 *v.t.* Make sluggish or inert; make stupid or unresponsive. ME. 2 *v.t.* Make blunt. ME. †3 *v.t.* Make listless, depressed, or gloomy. LME–E17. 4 *v.t.* Make less sensitive; blunt the keenness of (senses, feelings, etc.). LME. 5 *v.t.* Take away the brightness, clearness, or intensity of; make indistinct; tarnish. LME. 6 *v.i.* Become dull(er); become sluggish or stupid; become blunt; grow dim or tarnished. LME.

1 R. LEHMANN Dancing dulls the brain a bit. 2 B. CORNWALL Your sword is dulled With carnage. **dull the edge of** *fig.* make less sensitive, interesting, or effective. 4 TENNYSON Weeping dulls the inward pain. B. MALAMUD His hearing is dulled in the right ear since Berezhinsky hit him. 5 M. SINCLAIR Smears of damp dulled the polished lid of the piano. 6 G. P. SCROPE Lava . . at a white heat, gradually dulling to a faint red.

dullard /ˈdʌləd/ *n.* & *a.* ME. [Prob. f. MDu. *dull-*, *dollaert*, f. *dul* DULL *a.*: see -ARD.] A *n.* A dull or stupid person; a dolt, a dunce. ME. B *adj.* Dull, stupid. L16.

dullness /ˈdʌlnɪs/ *n.* Also **dulness**. LME. [f. DULL *a.* + -NESS.] The quality or state of being dull.

dullsville /ˈdʌlzvɪl/ *n. N. Amer. slang.* Also **D-**. M20. [f. DULL *a.* + *-s-* + -VILLE.] A town, place, or situation of extreme dullness or boredom.

dully /ˈdʌli/ *a.* Long *rare.* L15. [f. DULL *a.* + -Y[1].] 1 Gloomy, dreary, miserable. L15. 2 Faint, indistinct. M19.

dully /ˈdʌl-li/ *adv.* LME. [f. DULL *a.* + -LY[2].] In a dull manner.

dulness *n.* var. of DULLNESS.

dulocracy /djuːˈlɒkrəsi/ *n. rare.* Also **doul-** /duː-/. M17. [Gk *doulokratia*, f. *doulos* slave: see -CRACY.] Government by slaves.

dulosis /djuːˈləʊsɪs/ *n.* E20. [Gk *doulōsis* slavery, f. *douloun* enslave, f. *doulos* slave.] *Entomol.* The enslavement by certain kinds of ant of worker ants of other species.

dulotic /-ˈlɒtɪk/ *a.* E20.

dulse /dʌls/ *n.* Also (*Sc.*) **dilse** /dɪls/. E17. [Ir., Gael. *duileasg* = Welsh *delysg*, *dylusg*.] An edible seaweed, *Rhodymenia palmata*, with dark red, palmately divided fronds.

dulsome /ˈdʌlsəm/ *a. obs.* exc. *dial.* E17. [f. DULL *a.* + -SOME[1].] Dull, dreary, dismal.

duly /ˈdjuːli/ *adv.* LME. [f. DUE *a.* + -LY[2].] In due manner, order, form, or season; correctly, properly, fitly; punctually; sufficiently.

E. YOUNG The Man Is yet unborn, who duly weighs an Hour. J. BUCHAN The altar was being duly prepared for the victim. D. CECIL At . . the correct age for first love, he duly fell in love with her.

duma /ˈduːmə, ˈdjuː-/ *n.* L19. [Russ.] *Hist.* A Russian elective municipal council; *spec.* the elective legislative council of state of 1905–17.

dumb /dʌm/ *a.* & *n.* [OE *dumb* = OFris, OS *dumb* (Du. *dom*) stupid, OHG *tumb* stupid, deaf (G *dumm* stupid), ON *dumbr*, Goth. *dumbs* mute. In sense 4 prob. reinforced by G *dumm*, Du. *dom.*] A *adj.* 1 Lacking the faculty of speech, either abnormally (in humans) or normally (in other animals and things). OE. b Temporarily deprived of speech by surprise, shock, grief, or fear. Chiefly in *strike dumb*. ME. c Inarticulate; having no voice in government etc. M19. 2 Not emitting or accompanied by sound; silent, mute; drowned out. OE. b Of an action, an expression, etc.: performed or made without speech. M16. 3 Persistently silent; taciturn; reticent. ME. 4 Stupid, ignorant, foolish. ME. b Of a computer terminal: not having independent data-processing capability. Opp. INTELLIGENT *a.* L20. 5 Meaningless, senseless. Now *rare.* M16. 6 Lacking some expected quality, feature, or accessory. Usu. *attrib.* (as in some special collocations below). L16.

1 *dumb as a beetle, a stone*, etc. 2 SHELLEY Its thunder made the cataracts dumb. TENNYSON The streets are dumb with snow. b DICKENS Pleasant answered with a short dumb nod. G. GREENE He was aware . . of her dumb approval. 3 SHAKES. *Haml.* This spirit, dumb to us, will speak to him. 4 D. HAMMETT I'm not dumb enough to fall for that. 5 TINDALE The byshop of Rome . . with his domme traditions.

B *absol.* as *n.* A dumb person. Long chiefly *collect. pl.*, *the* dumb people as a class. OE.

Special collocations & comb.: *deaf and dumb*: see DEAF *a.* & *n.* **dumb ague** *arch.* malarial fever without clearly-defined episodic attacks. **dumb animal** an animal regarded pityingly or contemptuously as without speech. **dumb barge**: without means of propulsion. **dumb blonde** a pretty but stupid blonde person (usu. female). **dumb cane** a W. Indian plant, *Dieffenbachia seguine*, of the arum family, with an acrid juice which swells the tongue and destroys the power of speech. **dumb chum** *joc.* = *dumb friend* below. **dumb cluck** *slang* a stupid person, a blockhead. *dumb crambo*: see CRAMBO 2. **dumb friend** *joc.* a domestic animal. **dumbhead** *slang* a stupid person, a blockhead. **dumb-iron** either of a pair of curved side-members of a motor-vehicle chassis, joining it to the front springs. **dumb nettle** = *dead-nettle* s.v. DEAD *a.* **dumb ox** *colloq.* a stupid, awkward, or taciturn person (*the dumb ox* St Thomas Aquinas). **dumb peal** a muffled peal of bells. **dumb piano** a set of piano keys for exercising the fingers. **dumb play** = *dumb show* (b) below. **dumb sheave** *Naut.* a sheaveless block having a hole for a rope to be rove through. **dumb show** (*a*) in early drama, a part of a play acted without words, exhibiting additional action or simply emblematical; (*b*) significant action without speech; an instance of this. **dumbstricken, dumbstruck** *adjs.* rendered temporarily speechless. **dumb waiter** a movable table, esp. with revolving shelves, for use in a dining-room; a small lift for conveying food, tableware, etc.

dumbly *adv.* M16. **dumbness** *n.* the quality or condition of being dumb, inability to speak (*deaf-dumbness*: see DEAF *a.* & *n.*) LME.

dumb /dʌm/ *v.* ME. [f. the adj.] †1 *v.i.* Become dumb or silent. Only in ME. 2 *v.t.* Make dumb or silent. E17.

dumb-bell /ˈdʌmbɛl/ *n.* Also **dumbell**. E18. [f. DUMB *a.* + BELL *n.*[1]] 1 Formerly, an apparatus like that for ringing a church bell, used for exercise. Now, a short bar weighted at each end with a ball or disc, used usu. in pairs for exercising the muscles. E18. 2 An object shaped like a dumb-bell, with two rounded masses connected by a narrow bar. M19. 3 A stupid person, a blockhead. *slang.* E20.

dumb-dumb /ˈdʌmdʌm/ *n. slang* (orig. *US*). Also **dum-dum**. L20. [Redupl. of DUMB *a.*] A stupid person, a blockhead.

dumbell *n.* var. of DUMB-BELL.

dumbfound /dʌmˈfaʊnd/ *v.t.* Also **dumfound**. M17. [App. f. DUMB *a.* + (CON)FOUND.] Strike dumb; confound, nonplus. Chiefly as *dumbfounded* ppl a.

dumbfounder /dʌmˈfaʊndə/ *v.t.* Also **dumfounder**. E18. [f. prec., assim. to FOUNDER *v.*] = prec. Chiefly as *dumbfoundered* ppl a.

dumble /ˈdʌmb(ə)l/ *n. dial.* L16. [App. f. as DUMMEL. Cf. DRUMBLE *n.*] A bumble-bee. Also *dumble-bee*.

Comb.: **dumbledore** a loud buzzing insect, a bumble-bee.

dumbo /ˈdʌmbəʊ/ *n. slang.* Pl. **-os**. M20. [f. DUMB *a.* + -O, w. pronunc. infl. by JUMBO.] A stupid person, a blockhead.

†**dumby** *n.* & *a.* var. of DUMMY *n.* & *a.*

dum casta /dʌm ˈkastə/ *n.* & *a. phr.* L19. [Abbrev. of L *dum sola et casta vixerit* as long as she shall live alone and chaste.] *Law.* (Designating) a clause conferring on a woman a benefit which is to cease should she (re)marry or cease to lead a chaste life.

dumdum /ˈdʌmdʌm/ *n.* Also **dum-dum**. L19. [*DumDum*, a town and arsenal near Calcutta, India, where the bullets were first produced.] In full *dumdum bullet*. A kind of soft-nosed bullet that expands on impact to inflict extensive injuries.

dum-dum *n.*[1] see prec.

dum-dum *n.*[2] var. of DUMB-DUMB.

dumfound, -founder *v.s.* vars. of DUMBFOUND, -FOUNDER.

dumka /ˈdʊmkə/ *n.* Pl. **-kas, -ky** /-ki/. L19. [Czech & Pol. f. Ukrainian.] An alternately melancholy and gay piece of Slavonic music.

dummel /ˈdʌm(ə)l/ *n.* & *a. dial.* L16. [App. f. as DUMBLE. Cf. DRUMBLE *n.*] A *n.* A stupid person. L16. B *adj.* Stupid; sluggish. L19.

dummerer /ˈdʌmərə/ *n. slang. obs.* exc. *Hist.* M16. [f. DUMB *a.*] A beggar pretending to be dumb.

dummkopf /ˈdʊmkɒpf/ *n. slang* (orig. *US*). Also †**domcop**. E19. [G, f. *dumm* (see DUMB *a.*) + *Kopf* head. Var. f. Du.] A stupid person, a blockhead.

dummy /ˈdʌmi/ *n.* & *a.* Also †**dumby**. L16. [f. DUMB *a.* + -Y[6].] A *n.* 1 A person who cannot speak. *colloq.* L16. b (A beggar who pretends to be) a deaf-mute. L19. 2a *Whist.* A hand dealt to an imaginary fourth player which is turned up and played by one of the other players as partner; (a game played with) this imaginary player. M18. b *Bridge.* The partner of the declarer, whose cards are exposed after the first lead; this player's hand. L19. 3 A stupid person, a blockhead. L18. 4 A person taking no real part or present only for appearances, a figurehead; a person who is merely a tool of another; *Austral. Hist.* one who buys land on behalf of another (not entitled to buy it). M19. 5 An object serving to replace the genuine or usual one; a substitute, an imitation; a counterfeit. M19. b *spec.* A model of a human body to hang or display clothes on; a (usu. adjustable) model of a human torso to fit clothes on. Also *dress-maker's dummy*, *tailor's dummy*. M19. c A set of sheets of paper made up to resemble a book etc.; a mock-up of a newspaper etc. M19. d A model of a human body used as a target in shooting or bayonet practice or in safety tests for vehicles etc. L19. e A teat of rubber, plastic, etc., given to a baby to suck as a comforter. E20. f In football and other games, a feigned pass or kick intended to deceive an opponent. E20. g A model of a person or animal made by a ventriloquist to appear to talk etc. Also *ventriloquist's dummy*. M20. h *Computing.* An instruction or sequence of data that merely occupies space. M20. 6 A barge, vehicle, etc., with no means of propulsion. M19.

3 *New Yorker* You've just been had, dummy. 4 D. BAGLEY Our . . corporation might have caught a tiger by the tail—Favel is no one's dummy. 5 R. V. JONES The warhead was a dummy made of concrete. P. PARISH Half the patients are given the true drug, half are given the dummy.

Phrases: *double dummy*: see DOUBLE *a.* & *adv.* **in dummy** in dummy form. **sell a** or **the dummy (to)** in football and other games, deceive (an opponent) by a feigned pass or kick.

B *attrib.* or as *adj.* That is a dummy, of the nature of a dummy; counterfeit, sham. M19.

Special collocations & *comb.*: **dummy run** a practice, a trial run, a rehearsal. **dummy teat, tit** a baby's dummy (see sense A.5e above).

dummy /ˈdʌmi/ *v.* L19. [f. the n.] **1** *v.t.* & *i.* *Austral. Hist.* Acquire (land) by acting as a dummy (see DUMMY *n.* 4). L19. **2** *v.t.* Make a dummy or imitation of. E20. **3** *v.i.* Foll. by *up*: refuse to talk, keep quiet. *US slang.* E20. **4** *v.t.* & *i.* *Football* etc. Sell a dummy (to); feign (a pass); make (one's way) by selling a dummy or dummies. M20.

dumortierite /djuˈmɔːtjərʌɪt/ *n.* L19. [f. V.-E. *Dumortier* (1802–76), Fr. geologist + -ITE[1].] *Min.* An orthorhombic borosilicate of aluminium occurring as small violet or blue needles or fibrous masses esp. in gneisses and schists.

dumosity /djuːˈmɒsɪti/ *n.* *rare.* M17. [f. L *dumosus* bushy, f. *dumus* thorn-bush, bramble: see -ITY.] Dense bushy growth; a mass of bushes or brambles.

dump /dʌmp/ *n.*[1] E16. [Prob. of LG or Du. origin and a fig. use of MDu. *domp* exhalation, mist, rel. to DAMP *n.*] †**1** A reverie; *sing.* & in *pl.* perplexity, absence of mind. E16–L17. **2** A fit of depression. Now only in *the dumps*, a state of depression, low spirits. *colloq.* E16. †**3** A melancholy tune or song. M16–M19.

2 (**down**) **in the dumps** depressed, low spirited.

dump /dʌmp/ *n.*[2] L18. [App. identical w. 1st elem. of DUMPLING.] **1** An object of a dumpy shape; a dumpy person. L18. **2** A small coin; a trivial sum; a jot; *spec.* (*Austral. Hist.*) a circular piece removed from the centre of a (holey) dollar and issued as currency. E19.

1 CARLYLE A .. vulgar little dump of an old man. **2** G. K. CHESTERTON I do not care a dump whether they know the alphabet.

dump /dʌmp/ *n.*[3] *dial.* L18. [Perh. f. Norse: cf. Norw. *dump* pit, pool.] A deep hole in the bed of a river or pond.

dump /dʌmp/ *n.*[4] L18. [f. DUMP *v.*[1]] **1** A heap or pile of refuse or waste material; a place where refuse etc., is deposited; *esp.* (*US* & *S. Afr.*) a pile of earth, ore, etc., from mining operations, or the place where this is deposited. L18. **b** (The site of) a store of provisions, ammunition, equipment, etc., deposited for later use. E20. **2** A dull abrupt thud; a bump. E19. **b** *Surfing.* = DUMPER 2. M20. **3** An act or the practice of dumping. L19. **b** An act of defecation. Chiefly *N. Amer.* M20. **c** *Computing.* The process or result of dumping data; a printout or listing of stored data, esp. of the complete contents of a computer's memory. M20. **4** An unpleasant, shabby, or dreary place. *colloq.* L19.

1 *mine dump.* **b** J. HILTON Cans of petrol were fetched from a dump close by. **2** B. M. CROKER Mrs. Brande .. was now let down with a dump. **3b** W. H. AUDEN To start the morning With a satisfactory Dump. **4** G. PALEY You could have a decent place on a decent street instead of this dump.

Comb.: **dump tank**: into which liquid can be rapidly discharged; **dump truck** etc. (chiefly *N. Amer.*) = DUMPER *truck* etc.; **dump valve**: allowing the rapid discharge of a liquid.

dump /dʌmp/ *v.*[1] ME. [Perh. f. ON; cf. Da. *dumpe*, Norw. *dumpa* fall suddenly, fall plump. In mod. use partly imit: cf. THUMP *v.*] †**1** *v.i.* & *t.* Fall or drop with sudden force; plunge. Only in ME. **2** *v.t.* Strike heavily, thump. *Sc.* L16. **3** *v.t.* Throw down in a lump; deposit unceremoniously; tip out (rubbish etc.); drop, esp. with a bump. Orig. *US.* L18. **b** Put (goods) on the market in large quantities and at low prices; *spec.* send (goods unsaleable at high price in the home market) to a foreign market for sale at a lower price. M19. **c** Discard; abandon; get rid of. *colloq.* E20. **d** *v.t.* & *i.* Void (as) excrement, defecate. Chiefly *N. Amer.* E20. **e** Of a wave: hurl (a swimmer or surfer) down with great force. Chiefly *Austral.* M20. **f** *Computing.* Copy (stored data) to a different location (esp. an external storage medium); list (stored data). M20. **4** *v.t.* Compress (a wool bale) (as) by hydraulic pressure. *Austral.* & *NZ.* M19.

3 J. B. PRIESTLEY Oakroyd's reply .. was to fetch his bag of tools and dump it down at the other's feet. A. TOFFLER Industrial waste dumped into a river can turn up .. thousands of miles away in the ocean. *fig.*: E. REVELEY He .. decided to dump the whole thing .. into the laps of his superiors. **b** P. CAREY There was a surfeit and .. talk of dumping grain on the world market. **c** D. STIVENS You've dumped plenty of fellows before. **d dumping syndrome** *Med.* a group of symptoms, including abdominal discomfort and distension and sometimes abnormally rapid bowel evacuation, occurring after meals in some patients who have undergone gastric surgery. **dump on** *colloq.* criticize severely, treat with scorn or contempt, defeat heavily.

†**dump** *v.*[2]*i.* & *t.* M16–M19. [f. DUMP *n.*[1]] Fall or cast into depression, gloom, or abstraction.

dumper /ˈdʌmpə/ *n.* L19. [f. DUMP *v.*[1] + -ER[1].] **1** A person who or thing which dumps; *esp.* (in full *dumper truck* etc.) a truck etc. with a body that tilts or opens at the back for unloading. L19. **2** A large wave which hurls a swimmer or surfer down with great force. Chiefly *Austral.* E20.

dumpish /ˈdʌmpɪʃ/ *a.* E16. [f. DUMP *n.*[1] + -ISH[1].] †**1** Dull, slow-witted; abstracted. E16–L17. **2** Dejected, melancholy; down in the dumps. M16.

dumpishly *adv.* E17. **dumpishness** *n.* M16.

dumpling /ˈdʌmplɪŋ/ *n.* E17. [Origin uncertain: cf. DUMP *n.*[2], -LING[1].] **1** A (usu. globular) mass of dough boiled or baked either plain or enclosing fruit etc. E17. **2** A small fat person or animal. E17.

1 NORFOLK *dumpling.* **2** DICKENS A nice little dumpling of a wife.

dumpoked /ˈdʌmpəʊkt/ *a.* L17. [Urdu *dampukt*, f. Pers. *dam* breath, vapour + *puktah* cooked.] *Indian Cookery.* (Of meat, esp. fowl) boned, steamed, and stuffed.

dumpoke *n.* a dish of dumpoked meat L17.

dumpster /ˈdʌm(p)stə/ *n.* *N. Amer.* M20. [f. DUMP *v.*[1] + -STER.] A very large container for rubbish, a skip.

dumpty /ˈdʌm(p)ti/ *n.* & *a.* E19. [Var. of DUMPY *a.*[2] & *n.* Cf. HUMPTY-DUMPTY.] = DUMPY *a.*[2] & *n.*

dumpy /ˈdʌmpi/ *a.*[1] E17. [f. DUMP *n.*[1] + -Y[1].] Dejected; melancholy; down in the dumps.

dumpy /ˈdʌmpi/ *a.*[2] & *n.* M18. [f. 1st elem. of DUMPLING (cf. DUMP *n.*[2]) + -Y[1].] **A** *adj.* Short and stout; rounded. M18.

dumpy level a spirit level used in surveying, having a short telescope with a large aperture.

B *n.* A dumpy person, animal, or thing. E19.

dumpily *adv.* L19. **dumpiness** *n.* E19.

dun /dʌn/ *n.*[1] LME. [f. DUN *a.*] **1** (A name for) a horse. Now *spec.* a dun horse. LME. **2** Dun colour; a dun hue. M16. **3** *Angling.* (An artificial fly imitating) any of various dusky-coloured flies, esp. mayflies in the subimago stage. L17.

2 T. HARDY When beeches drip in browns and duns.

dun /dʌn/ *n.*[2] E17. [Abbrev. of DUNKIRK privateer.] **1** A person who duns; an importunate creditor; a debt-collector. E17. **2** A demand for money, esp. in payment of a debt. L17.

1 R. GRAVES Creditors dog my steps, duns rap perpetually at my door.

dun /dʌn/ *n.*[3] L18. [Ir. *dún*, Gael. *dùn* hill, hill-fort, Welsh †*din.*] A prehistoric hill-fort or fortified eminence, esp. in Scotland or Ireland.

dun /duːn/ *n.*[4] Also **dhoon**, & other vars. E19. [Hind. *dūn.*] Any of the wide flat valleys in the Siwalik hills, lying parallel to the base of the Himalayas; *spec. the* valley of Dehra in Uttar Pradesh, India.

dun /dʌn/ *a.* [OE *dun(n)* = OS *dun* date-brown, nut-brown, prob. rel. to OS *dosan*, OHG *tusin* (cf. DUSK *a.*).] **1** Of a dull or dingy brown colour, dull greyish-brown; *spec.* (of a horse) of a sandy grey colour with black legs, mane, and tail, and usu. a dark dorsal stripe. OE. **2** Dark, dusky; murky; gloomy. *poet.* ME.

1 SHAKES. *Sonn.* If snow be white, why then her breasts are dun. **2** WILLIAM COLLINS Dun Night has veil'd the solemn view.

Special collocations & *comb.*: **dun-bar** a noctuid moth, *Cosmia trapezina*, with two grey-brown bands on the forewing. **dun-bird** the pochard. **dun-diver** a female or immature goosander or merganser.

dunness /-n-n-/ *n.* E17. **dunnish** *a.* rather dun or dusky E16.

dun /dʌn/ *v.*[1]*t.* Infl. **-nn-**. OE. [f. the adj.] Make dun or dingy; darken or dull the colour of.

dun /dʌn/ *v.*[2]*t.* Infl. **-nn-**. M17. [f. DUN *n.*[2]] Make repeated and persistent demands upon, esp. for money owed; pester, plague, assail constantly.

J. A. MICHENER The bank was dunning them to repay a small loan.

dunam /ˈdʊnəm/ *n.* E20. [mod.Heb. *dûnām*, Arab. *dūnum* f. Ottoman Turk. *dūnum*, Turk. *dönüm*, f. *dönmek* go round.] A variable measure of land used in the Ottoman Empire and its successor States, including Israel (where it is equal to about 900 sq. metres).

dunce /dʌns/ *n.* & *v.* E16. [f. John *Duns* Scotus (*c*1266–1308), scholastic theologian, whose followers were a predominating scholastic sect until discredited by humanists and reformers in the 16th cent.] **A** *n.* †**1** An adherent of Duns Scotus, a Scotist; a hair-splitter, a sophist. Freq. *attrib.*, as *dunce man*, *prelate.* E16–M17. †**2** A copy of the works of Duns Scotus; a book embodying his teaching on theology or logic. M16–M17. †**3** A dull book-learned pedant. L16–M18. **4** A person who shows no capacity for learning; a dullard, a blockhead. L16.

3 T. FULLER A dunce, void of learning but full of books. **4** R. W. DALE Some boys remain dunces though they are sent to the best schools. **dunce's cap** a paper cone formerly put on the head of a dunce at school as a mark of disgrace.

B *v.t.* Puzzle; make a dunce of. Now *rare.* L16.

duncedom *n.* dunces collectively; a dunce's condition or character: E19. **duncehood** *n.* the condition or character of a dunce; stupidity: E19. **duncery** *n.* †(*a*) the practice or character of a Scotist; (*b*) the state, practice, or character of a dunce; stupidity: L16. **duncical** *a.* †(*a*) of or pertaining to the Scotists; (*b*) of or pertaining to a dunce; stupid: M16. **duncify** *v.t.* (*rare*) make a dunce of L16.

dunch /dʌn(t)ʃ/ *a.* Long *dial.* L16. [Origin unkn.: cf. DUNNY *a.*[2]] **1** Deaf. L16. **2** Blind. L17. **3** Of bread etc.: heavy, doughy. M19. **4** Stupid; dull. M19.

dunch /dʌn(t)ʃ/ *v.* & *n.* Chiefly *dial.* ME. [Origin unkn.] **A** *v.t.* Strike with a short rapid blow. Now *esp.* jog with the elbow. ME. **B** *n.* A jog with the elbow; a sharp shock. LME.

duncish /ˈdʌnsɪʃ/ *a.* M19. [f. DUNCE + -ISH[1].] Of the nature of or characteristic of a dunce; stupid.

duncishly *adv.* M19. **duncishness** *n.* E19.

Dundee /dʌnˈdiː, ˈdʌndiː/ *n.* M19. [A Scottish city on the Firth of Tay.] **1** *Dundee rambler*, a variety of rambling rose. M19. **2** *Dundee marmalade*, (proprietary name for) a kind of marmalade orig. made in Dundee. M19. **3** *Dundee cake*, a kind of rich fruit cake usu. decorated with split almonds. L19.

dunder /ˈdʌndə/ *n.*[1] L18. [f. Sp. *redundar* overflow.] The lees or dregs of cane-juice, used in rum distillation.

dunder *n.*[2] & *v.* var. of DUNNER *n.*[2] & *v.*

dunderhead /ˈdʌndəhɛd/ *n.* E17. [Perh. f. DUNDER *n.*[2] + HEAD *n.*] A ponderously stupid person, a numskull.

dunderheaded *a.* stupid, thickheaded E19.

dunderpate /ˈdʌndəpeɪt/ *n.* *arch.* L17. [f. as prec. + PATE *n.*[1]] = prec.

Dundonian /dʌnˈdəʊnɪən/ *n.* L19. [f. DUNDEE after *Aberdonian.*] A native or inhabitant of the Scottish city of Dundee.

Dundreary /dʌnˈdrɪəri/ *n.* *arch.* Pl. **-ries, -rys.** M19. [Lord *Dundreary*, a character in T. Taylor's comedy *Our American Cousin* (1858).] In *pl.*, or *sing.* in *Dundreary weepers*, *Dundreary whiskers.* Long side-whiskers worn without a beard. Cf. PICCADILLY I.

dunducketty /dʌnˈdʌkəti/ *a. colloq.* & *dial.* E19. [App. f. DUN *a.* + DUCK *n.*[1]] Of a dull, drab, muddy colour.

dune /djuːn/ *n.* L18. [(O)Fr. f. MDu. *dūne* (Du. *duin*) = OE *dūn* DOWN *n.*[1]] A mound or ridge of loose sand, or other sediment, formed by the wind, esp. on the sea-coast.
Comb.: *dune buggy*: see BUGGY *n.*

dung /dʌŋ/ *n.* [OE *dung* = OFris., MDu. *dung(e)*, OHG *tunga* manuring (G *Dung* manure): cf. Sw. *dynga* muck, dung, Da. *dynge* heap, Icel. *dyngja* heap, dung: ult. origin unkn.] 1 Manure; the faeces of an animal or occas. a person. OE. 2 Something morally filthy or defiling; something vile. ME. 3 A journeyman tailor who submits to terms of employment rejected by his fellows. *slang. obs.* exc. *Hist.* M18.
2 AV *Phil.* 3:8 I have suffered the losse of all things, and doe count them but doung, that I may win Christ.
Comb.: **dung-beetle** any of various beetles which lay their eggs in dung or roll up balls of dung for their larvae to feed on; **dung-cart**: for conveying manure; **dung-fly** a dipteran insect of the family Scatophagidae, laying its eggs in fresh dung; *esp.* the yellow-brown *Scatophaga stercoraria*; **dung-fork**: for spreading manure; **dung-heap** a dunghill; **dung-pot** (*dial.* exc. *Hist.*) a horse-drawn tub etc. for carrying manure; **dung-worm** an earthworm found in cow-dung, *esp.* one used as bait.
dungy *a.* resembling (that of) dung; foul; containing much dung: E17.

dung /dʌŋ/ *v.*[1] [OE *dyngian*, f. as prec. In ME assim. to, or formed anew from, the n.] 1 *v.t.* Manure with dung. OE. 2 *v.i.* Excrete dung. LME. 3 *v.t.* Immerse (calico) in a preparation containing cow-dung or equivalent chemicals, to remove superfluous mordant. *obs.* exc. *Hist.* M19.

dung *v.*[2] pa. pple: see DING *v.*[1]

dunga *n.* var. of DOONGA.

dungaree /dʌŋɡəˈriː/ *n.* L17. [Hind. *duṅgrī*.] A coarse Indian calico; in *pl.*, overalls or trousers of dungaree or a similar material, *esp.* trousers with a bib.

dungeon /ˈdʌndʒ(ə)n/ *n.* Also (*arch.*) **donjon** /ˈdɒndʒ(ə)n, ˈdʌn-/. See also DONJON. ME. [(O)Fr. *donjon* f. Proto-Gallo-Romance = 'lord's tower' or 'mistress tower' (in med.L *dangio(n-)*, *dunjo(n-)*, *donjo(n-)*), f. L *dominus* master, lord.] 1 A strong subterranean cell for prisoners; a deep dark vault. ME. 2 See DONJON 1.
1 A. CARTER Dungeons . . had been converted into cellars for his wines. *fig.*: G. R. PORTER Palissy . . confined within the dungeon of his own breast, those feelings of bitterness.

dungeon /ˈdʌndʒ(ə)n/ *v.t.* E17. [f. the n.] Put or keep in a dungeon; imprison.

dunghill /ˈdʌŋhɪl/ *n.* & *a.* ME. [f. DUNG *n.* + HILL *n.*] A *n.* 1 A heap of dung or refuse in a farmyard etc. ME. 2 *transf.* & *fig.* a A mass of filth; a disgusting place or situation. E16. b A vile or base person. M16. c [f. *dunghill cock* below.] A coward. *arch.* M18.
Comb.: **dunghill cock, fowl**, etc. (*arch.*) a common barnyard fowl as opp. to a gamecock.
B *attrib.* or as *adj.* Vile as a dunghill; base; cowardly. *arch.* LME.

dunite /ˈdʌnʌɪt/ *n.* M19. [f. *Dun* Mountain, New Zealand (where first described) + -ITE[1].] *Geol.* A coarse-grained igneous rock consisting essentially of olivine, with chromite xenoliths.

duniwassal /ˈduːnɪwas(ə)l/ *n. Sc.* Now *arch.* or *Hist.* M16. [f. Gael. *duine* man + *uasal* noble, of gentle birth.] A (Highland) gentleman of secondary rank.

dunk /dʌŋk/ *n.* M20. [f. the vb.] *Basketball.* In full *dunk shot.* A shot made by jumping and pushing the ball down through the basket from above.

dunk /dʌŋk/ *v.t.* Orig. *US.* E20. [Pennsylvanian G *dunke* to dip, f. G *tunken* (OHG *dunkōn*, MHG *tunken, dunken*). Cf. DUNKER.] 1 Dip (bread, a biscuit, etc.) in a drink or soup while eating; immerse (*lit.* & *fig.*). E20. 2 *Basketball.* Shoot (the ball) down through the basket by jumping so that the hands are above the ring. M20.

Dunkard /ˈdʌŋkəd/ *n. US.* M18. [f. as next: see -ARD.] = next.

Dunker /ˈdʌŋkə/ *n.*[1] Also **T-** /t-/. E18. [Pennsylvanian G, f. as DUNK *v.*: see -ER[1].] A member of a US religious sect deriving orig. from German Baptists, who administer baptism by triple immersion.

dunker /ˈdʌŋkə/ *n.*[2] Orig. *US.* E20. [f. DUNK *v.* + -ER[1].] A person who dunks bread, biscuit, etc.; a basketball player who dunks the ball.

Dunkirk /dʌnˈkəːk, dʌŋˈk-/ *n.* L16. [Seaport of France (Fr. *Dunkerque*). Cf. DUN *n.*[2]] 1 A privateer (from Dunkirk). Long *obs.* exc. *Hist.* L16. 2 (The scene of) a withdrawal under fire such as or comparable with the evacuation of British forces in France from Dunkirk between 29 May and 3 June, 1940; a momentous crisis. M20.
Comb.: **Dunkirk spirit** refusal to surrender or despair in a time of crisis.
Dunkirker *n.* (*a*) a native or inhabitant of Dunkirk; (*b*) (*obs.* exc. *Hist.*) = DUNKIRK 1: L16.

dunlin /ˈdʌnlɪn/ *n.* Pl. **-s**, same. M16. [Prob. f. as DUN *a.* + -LING[1], f. its greyish-brown upperparts (in winter).] A sandpiper, *Calidris alpina*, occurring throughout the holarctic region.

Dunlop /ˈdʌnlɒp/ *n.* E19. [A parish near Ayr in Strathclyde, Scotland.] In full *Dunlop cheese.* A full-cream hard cheese originally made in Dunlop.

dunnage /ˈdʌnɪdʒ/ *n.* & *v.* Also (earlier) †**denn-**. ME. [Origin unkn.] Chiefly *Naut.* A *n.* Mats, brushwood, gratings, etc., stowed among a cargo to prevent wetting or chafing; *colloq.* miscellaneous baggage, a sailor's belongings. ME.
Comb.: **dunnage bag** a kitbag.
B *v.t.* Stow with dunnage. M19.

dunnakin *n.* var. of DUNNIKEN.

dunnamany /ˈdʌnəmɛni/ *v.i. colloq.* M19. [Repr. informal pronunc.] Chiefly as 1st person sing.: don't know how many.

dunnart /ˈdʌnɑːt/ *n.* E20. [Aborig.] Any of various small insectivorous marsupials of the genus *Sminthopsis*, of Australia and New Guinea.

dunner /ˈdʌnə/ *n.*[1] L17. [f. DUN *v.*[2] + -ER[1].] = DUN *n.*[2] 1.

dunner /ˈdʌnə/ *n.*[2] & *v. Sc.* Also **dunder** /ˈdʌndə/. L18. [Perh. imit., or frequent. rel. to DIN *n.*, *v.* Perh. earlier in DUNDERHEAD.] A *n.* A resounding noise; a jarring blow. L18. B *v.i.* Resound; fall or strike with a reverberating noise. E19.

dunniken /ˈdʌnɪkɪn/ *n. dial.* & *slang.* Also **dunnakin** & other vars. L18. [Origin uncertain: perh. f. as DUNNY *n.* + KEN *n.*[2]] An earth-closet; a lavatory, *esp.* an outside one.

dunno /ˈdʌnəʊ, dəˈnəʊ/ *v.t.* & *i. colloq.* M19. [Repr. informal pronunc.] Chiefly as 1st person sing.: do not know.
C. MORGAN Well, I dunno. P'raps I'm wrong.

dunnock /ˈdʌnək/ *n.* L15. [App. f. DUN *a.* + -OCK.] A small brown woodland or garden bird, *Prunella modularis*, with dark grey head and breast. Also called *hedge sparrow.*

dunny /ˈdʌni/ *n.* In sense 1 also †**danna**. E19. [Origin uncertain: perh. f. DUNG *n.* May be earlier in DUNNIKEN, of which sense 3 is an abbrev.] 1 Dung, faeces. Usu. *attrib. slang.* E19. 2 An underground passage or cellar, esp. in a tenement. *Sc.* E20. 3 An earth-closet; a lavatory, *esp.* an outdoor one. *slang* (chiefly *Austral.* & *NZ*). M20.

dunny /ˈdʌni/ *a.*[1] E16. [f. DUN *a.* + -Y[1].] Somewhat dun or greyish-brown; dunnish.

dunny /ˈdʌni/ *a.*[2] *dial.* E18. [Origin unkn.: cf. DUNCH *a.*] Dull of hearing, deaf; dull-witted, stupid.

Dunstable /ˈdʌnstəb(ə)l/ *a.* & *n.* M16. [A town in Bedfordshire, England.] A *adj.* 1 Connected with or made in Dunstable. M16. b *spec.* Designating a kind of straw plait, or the method of plaiting it. *obs.* exc. *Hist.* L18. 2 [f. *Dunstable way* below.] Direct, straightforward, downright. *arch.* L16.
1 **Dunstable way** *arch.* the road from London to Dunstable (part of the Roman Watling Street), regarded as the type of a direct route or straightforward course.
B *n. plain* or *downright Dunstable*, something direct or simple, *esp.* plain language, the simple facts. *arch.* L16.
V. WOOLF The plain Dunstable of the matter is, I'm not in the mood . . to-night.

dunster /ˈdʌnstə/ *n. obs.* exc. *Hist.* E17. [*Dunster* (see below).] A woollen cloth made in or near the town of Dunster in Somerset, England.

dunstone /ˈdʌnstəʊn/ *n. local.* L18. [f. DUN *a.* + STONE *n.*] Any of various kinds of stone of a dun or dull brown colour, *esp.* dolerite or magnesian limestone.

dunt /dʌnt/ *n.* & *v. Sc.* & *dial.* LME. [Perh. var. of DINT *n.* Cf. DENT *n.*[1]] A *n.* 1 A firm dull-sounding blow. LME. 2 A beat or palpitation of the heart. M18. 3 A wound made by a firm blow. L19. B *v.* 1 *v.t.* Hit or knock firmly with a dull sound; drive *out* by so knocking. L15. 2 *v.i.* Of the heart: beat violently. M16.

dunter /ˈdʌntə/ *n. local.* L17. [f. prec. + -ER[1].] The eider.

duo /ˈdjuːəʊ/ *n.* Pl. **-os**. L16. [It. (whence also Fr.) f. L = two.] 1 *Mus.* A duet. L16. 2 Two people; a couple; *esp.* a pair of entertainers. L19.

duo- /ˈdjuːəʊ/ *comb. form.* [f. L *duo* two. Corresp. to Gk *duo*.] Prefixed to other L roots to form composite numerals (*duodecimal*), and irreg. used w. other words as equivalent to BI- or DI-[2] (*duopoly*, *duotone*).

duodecad /djuːə(ʊ)ˈdɛkad/ *n.* Also **-ade** /-eɪd/. E17. [Late L *duodecas*, *-cad-* twelve: cf. DECADE.] A group of twelve; a period of twelve years.

duodecennial /ˌdjuːə(ʊ)dɪˈsɛnɪəl/ *a.* M17. [f. L *duodecennium* period of twelve years, f. *duodecim* twelve + *annus* year: see -AL[1].] Of twelve years.

duodecimal /djuːə(ʊ)ˈdɛsɪm(ə)l/ *a.* & *n.* L17. [f. L *duodecimus* twelfth + -AL[1]: cf. DECIMAL.] A *adj.* Of twelfths or twelve; reckoning or reckoned by twelve. L17. B *n.* In *pl.* (treated as *sing.*) = CROSS-MULTIPLICATION. E18.
duodecimally *adv.* E19.

duodecimo /djuːəʊˈdɛsɪməʊ/ *n.* & *a.* M17. [L (*in*) *duodecimo* in a twelfth (*sc.* of a sheet), f. as prec.] A *n.* Pl. **-os**. A size of book or paper in which each leaf is one-twelfth of a standard printing-sheet. (Abbrev. *12mo.*) M17. B *attrib.* or as *adj.* Of this size, in duodecimo; *fig.* diminutive. L18.

duoden- *comb. form* see DUODENO-.

duodenal /djuːəˈdiːn(ə)l/ *a.* M19. [f. DUODENUM + -AL[1].] Of or pertaining to the duodenum.

duodenary /djuːəˈdiːnəri/ *a.* M19. [L *duodenarius* containing twelve, f. *duodeni* distrib. of *duodecim* twelve: see -ARY[1].] = DUODECIMAL *a.*

duodeno- /djuːəˈdiːnəʊ/ *comb. form* of next: see -O-. Bef. a vowel also **duoden-**.
duodeˈnectomy *n.* (an instance of) surgical removal of all or part of the duodenum E20. **duodeˈnitis** *n.* inflammation of the duodenum M19. **duodeno-jeˈjunal** *a.* of or pertaining to the duodenum and jejunum L19. **duodeˈnostomy** *n.* (an instance of) surgical opening of the duodenum, usu. for the purpose of introducing food L19.

duodenum /djuːəˈdiːnəm/ *n.* LME. [med.L *duodenum* (so called from its length = twelve fingers' breadth), f. L *duodeni*: see DUODENARY.] *Anat.* The first portion of the small intestine immediately beyond the stomach, leading to the jejunum.

duologue /ˈdjʊəlɒɡ/ *n.* M18. [f. DUO- after *monologue*.] A conversation between two people; a dramatic piece with two actors.

duomo /ˈdwəʊməʊ, *foreign* ˈdwɔmo/ *n.* Also (earlier) †**domo**. Pl. **-mos** /-məʊz/, **-mi** /-mi/. M16. [It.: see DOME *n.*] An Italian cathedral.

duopoly /djʊˈɒpəli/ *n.* E20. [f. DUO- after *monopoly*.] A condition in which there are only two suppliers of a certain commodity, service, etc.; the domination of a particular market by two firms; control or domination by two people or groups; two suppliers, firms, etc., controlling a particular market.

duopolist *n.* a firm etc. operating in a duopoly M20. **duopo'listic** *a.* M20.

duotone /'djuːətəʊn/ *n.* & *a.* E20. [f. DUO- + TONE *n.*] A *n.* (The process of making) a halftone illustration in two colours from the same original using different screen angles. E20. B *attrib.* or as *adj.* Made by this process; *gen.* of or in two tones or colours. E20.

dup /dʌp/ *v.t. dial.* or *arch.* Infl. **-pp-**. M16. [Contr. of *do up* s.v. DO *v.*] Open (a door, gate, etc.).

dupable /'djuːpəb(ə)l/ *a.* Also **dupeable**. M19. [f. DUPE *v.*^{1} + -ABLE.] Able to be duped; gullible.

dupa'bility *n.* M19.

dupe /djuːp/ *n.*^{1} L17. [Fr., joc. application of dial. *dupe* hoopoe, from the bird's supposedly stupid appearance.] A person who allows himself or herself to be deluded; a victim of deception.

SIR W. SCOTT The ready dupe of astrologers and soothsayers. R. P. WARREN He had been the dupe in the game which the senator was playing.

dupe /djuːp/ *n.*^{2} & *a. colloq.* E20. [Abbrev. of DUPLICATE *a.* & *n.*] Chiefly *Cinemat.* A *n.* A duplicate; *spec.* a duplicate negative made from a positive print. E20. B *adj.* Duplicate. M20.

dupe /djuːp/ *v.*^{1}*t.* M17. [f. as DUPE *n.*^{1}, after Fr. *duper.*] Deceive, mislead, make a dupe of; cheat.

duper *n.* L18. **dupery** *n.* the action of duping, deception; the condition of a person who is duped: M18.

dupe /djuːp/ *v.*^{2}*t. colloq.* E20. [f. DUPE *n.*^{2}] *Cinemat.* Make a dupe of (see DUPE *n.*^{2}).

dupeable *a.* var. of DUPABLE.

dupion /'djuːpɪən/ *n.* Also **douppion** /'duːp-/, **dupp-** /'dʌp-/. E19. [Fr. *doupion* = It. *doppione*, f. *doppio* double.] 1 A double cocoon made by two silkworms. E19. 2 (A rough irregular silk made from) the thread of double cocoons; an imitation of this made from other fibres. E20.

duplation /djuː'pleɪʃ(ə)n/ *n.* LME. [Late L *duplatio(n-)*, f. L *duplat-* pa. ppl stem of *duplare* to double: see -ATION.] The process of doubling; multiplication by two.

duple /'djuːp(ə)l/ *a.* & *n.* M16. [L *duplus*, f. *duo* two.] A *adj.* Double, twofold. Now *rare* exc. as below. M16.

duple proportion, ratio: that of 2 to 1. **duple rhythm, time** *Mus.*: in which there are two beats in a bar.

†B *n.* = DOUBLE *n.* 1. E17–L18.

duplet /'djuːplɪt/ *n.* M17. [f. prec., after DOUBLET: see -ET^{1}.] †1 In *pl.* = DOUBLET 2. *rare*. Only in M17. 2 *Mus.* A group of two equal notes, *spec.* occurring in music with an odd number of beats in a bar. E20.

duplex /'djuːplɛks/ *n.* E20. [f. the adj.] 1 A two-family house; an apartment occupying two storeys. *N. Amer.* E20. 2 *Biochem.* A double-stranded polynucleotide molecule. M20.

duplex /'djuːplɛks/ *a.* M16. [L *duplex*, f. *duo* two + *plic-* base of *plicare* to fold.] 1 Having two parts, twofold, dual; combining two elements esp. with similar functions. M16. b *Metall.* Designating or made by a steel-making process employing successive treatment in two furnaces or by two methods. E20. c Designating paper or board made from two differently coloured layers of paper, or coloured differently on either side. E20. d *Genetics*. Of a polyploid individual: having the dominant allele of a particular gene represented twice (either homozygously or heterozygously). E20. e *Biochem.* Of a molecule or structure: having two polynucleotide strands linked side by side. M20. 2 *Telecommunications.* Pertaining to or designating the transmission or reception of two signals simultaneously in opposite directions over one channel or with one aerial. Cf. DIPLEX. L19.

1 **duplex escapement** in a clock or watch, an escapement in which the escape-wheel has both spur and crown teeth.

du'plexity *n.* (*rare*) duplex quality E19.

duplex /'djuːplɛks/ *v.* L19. [f. the adj.] 1 *v.t. Telecommunications.* Make (a cable, system, etc.) duplex (DUPLEX *a.* 2). L19. 2 *v.i. Metall.* Make steel by a duplex process. Chiefly as *duplexing* vbl n. E20.

duplexer *n.* (*Telecommunications*) a device enabling duplex transmission or reception of radio signals M20.

duplex querela /ˌdjuːplɛks kwɪ'riːlə, -'reɪlə/ *n.* E18. [Law L, lit. 'double complaint'.] *Eccl. Law.* The procedure in the Anglican Church by which a priest may challenge a bishop who refuses to institute him to a benefice to which he has been presented; a court's direction to a bishop to proceed with the institution.

duplicable /'djuːplɪkəb(ə)l/ *a.* E20. [f. DUPLIC(ATE *v.* + -ABLE.] Able to be duplicated.

duplica'bility *n.* E20.

duplicate /'djuːplɪkət/ *a.* & *n.* LME. [L *duplicatus* pa. pple, f. as next: see -ATE^{2}.] A *adj.* 1 Double, consisting of two corresponding parts, existing in two examples. LME. 2 Doubled, consisting of twice the number or quantity. M16. 3 Exactly like some other thing (with any number of copies or specimens). E19. 4 *Genetics.* Of genes: indistinguishable in effect. E20.

3 R. W. EMERSON The duplicate copy of Florio, which the British Museum purchased.

Special collocations: **duplicate bridge, whist**: in which the same hands are played successively by different players. **duplicate proportion, ratio**: of the squares of two numbers. *duplicate whist*: see *duplicate bridge* above.

B *n.* 1 Each of two things exactly alike; *esp.* the one which is made from or after the other; a second copy, with equal legal force, of an original letter or document. M16. b A pawnbroker's ticket. *arch.* M19. 2 Either of two or more specimens of a thing exactly or virtually alike; a thing which is the exact counterpart of another, regarded as the original; an additional specimen of a stamp or other item in a collection. L17. 3 = *duplicate bridge* or *whist* above. L19.

1 W. STUBBS The rolls of the treasurer and chancellor were duplicates. B. PLAIN He wanted to have a picture of you . . so I had a duplicate made of the one on my night table. **in duplicate** in two exactly corresponding copies. 2 C. LAMB As if a man should suddenly encounter his own duplicate.

duplicate /'djuːplɪkeɪt/ *v.* L15. [L *duplicat-* pa. ppl stem of *duplicare*, to double, f. as DUPLE: see -ATE^{3}.] 1 *v.t.* Make or be a double or exact copy of; repeat; provide in duplicate or multiple. L15. 2 *v.t.* Double; multiply by two; redouble. L16. 3 *v.i. Eccl.* Celebrate the Eucharist twice in one day. L18.

1 C. BEATON She never ordered one thing of a kind, but duplicated each item by the dozens. J. RABAN The formation . . more exactly duplicated the geological structure of Saudi Arabia's richest oil field. *Dirt Bike* Do not attempt to duplicate any stunts that are beyond your own capabilities. **duplicating machine** a machine for making copies of documents, drawings, etc., from a stencil sheet.

duplicative *a.* & *n.* (*a*) *adj.* having the quality of doubling or producing double; (*b*) *n.* an addition that constitutes a duplicate: L19.

duplication /djuːplɪ'keɪʃ(ə)n/ *n.* LME. [(O)Fr., or L *duplicatio(n-)*, f. as prec.: see -ATION.] 1 *Math.* Multiplication by two. Now *rare* or *obs.* LME. 2 *gen.* The action of doubling or duplicating; repetition of an action or thing; division into two by natural growth or spontaneous division. L16. b *Genetics.* The existence in a chromosome set of two copies of a particular segment; the duplicated segment itself; the process by which it arises. E20. †3 *Anat.* A folding, a doubling; a fold. L16–M18. 4 *Law* (now *Hist.*). A pleading on the part of a defendant in reply to a replication. E17. 5 *Eccl.* The celebration of the Eucharist twice in one day by the same priest. M19. 6 A duplicate copy; a counterpart. L19.

1 **duplication of a cube** *Math.* the problem of finding the side of a cube having twice the volume of a given cube; the Delian problem.

duplicato- /djuːplɪ'keɪtəʊ/ *comb. form.* M18. [f. L *duplicatus*: see DUPLICATE *a.* & *n.*, -O-.] *Bot.* Doubly.

duplicato-'dentate *a.* doubly dentate M19.

duplicator /'djuːplɪkeɪtə/ *n.* L19. [f. DUPLICATE *v.* + -OR.] A person who or thing which duplicates; *spec.* = *duplicating machine* s.v. DUPLICATE *v.* 1.

duplicature /'djuːplɪkeɪtʃə, -kətjʊə/ *n.* L17. [Fr., f. as DUPLICATE *v.*: see -URE.] Chiefly *Anat.* A doubling; a fold.

duplicitous /djuː'plɪsɪtəs, djʊ-/ *a.* L19. [f. next: see -OUS.] Characterized by or displaying duplicity; *esp.* deceitful, two-faced.

duplicitousness *n.* M20.

duplicity /djuː'plɪsɪti, djʊ-/ *n.* LME. [(O)Fr. *duplicité* or late L *duplicitas*, f. as DUPLEX *a.*, *duplic-*: see -ITY.] 1 The quality of being deceitful in manner or conduct; the practice of being two-faced, of dishonestly acting in two opposing ways; deceitfulness; double-dealing. LME. 2 The state of being numerically or physically double; doubleness. *arch.* L16. 3 *Law.* The coupling of two or more matters in one plea or charge. M19.

1 S. KAUFFMANN Now he lay there stroking her hair and thinking of his wife, hating his duplicity. 2 G. F. CHAMBERS The duplicity of Saturn's ring.

duply /djʊ'plʌɪ/ *v.* & *n. Sc. obs.* exc. *Hist.* E16. [med.L *duplica*: cf. Fr. *duplique*, and REPLY *n.* = Fr. *réplique*.] *Law.* A *v.i.* Make a duply. E16.

B *n.* (usu. in *pl.*). 1 *Law.* A rejoinder that was formerly given to a pursuer's reply; a second reply. L16. 2 In a debate, the rejoinder that comes fourth after the original assertion. M17.

2 SIR W. SCOTT Answers, replies, duplies, triplies, quadruplies, followed thick upon each other.

dupondius /djuː'pɒndɪəs/. *n.* Pl. **-ii** /-ɪʌɪ/. E17. [L.] *Rom. Antiq.* A bronze or brass coin of the value of two asses.

duppion *n.* var. of DUPION.

duppy /'dʌpi/ *n. W. Indies.* L18. [Origin uncertain: perh. W. Afr.] A ghost or spirit, usu. a malevolent one but occas. a good-natured one.

Dupuytren /djʊ'pwiːtrɒ̃, -trən/ *n.* L19. [Baron Guillaume *Dupuytren* (1777–1835), Fr. surgeon.] *Med.* 1 *Dupuytren's contraction* or *contracture*, fixed forward curvature of one or more fingers due to fixation of the finger tendons and their sheaths to the skin of the palm. L19. 2 *Dupuytren's fracture*, a fracture of the fibula just above the malleolus. L19.

dura /'djʊərə/ *n.*^{1} L19. [Abbrev.] = DURA MATER.

dura *n.*^{2} var. of DURRA.

durability /djʊərə'bɪlɪti/ *n.* LME. [(O)Fr. †*durabilité* f. late L *durabilitas*, f. *durabilis*: see next, -ITY.] The quality of being durable.

durable /'djʊərəb(ə)l/ *a.* & *n.* ME. [(O)Fr. f. L *durabilis*, f. *durare* see DURE *v.*, -ABLE.] A *adj.* 1 Steadfast, unyielding; able to endure fatigue or discomfort. *obs.* exc. *dial.* ME. 2 Capable of lasting; persistent; permanent, not transitory. LME. 3 Able to withstand change, decay, or wear. LME. b *spec.* Designating goods which remain useful over a period of time, as distinguished from those produced for immediate consumption. M20.

2 E. POUND Prose of permanent or durable interest. 3 R. L. STEVENSON The sandy peninsula of San Francisco . . shaken . . by frequent earthquakes, seems in itself no very durable foundation.

B *n.* A durable manufactured article. Usu. in *pl.* M20.

CONSUMER *durable*.

durableness *n.* (now *rare*) durability L16. **durably** *adv.* L15.

durain /'djʊəreɪn/ *n.* E20. [f. L *durus* hard, after FUSAIN.] *Geol.* One of the lithotypes of coal, being a hard, compact material of dull grey-black appearance.

dural /'djʊər(ə)l/ *a.* L19. [f. DURA *n.*^{1} + -AL^{1}.] Of or pertaining to the dura mater.

Duralumin /djʊ'raljʊmɪn/ *n.* E20. [Origin uncertain: perh. f. *Düren*, a town in Germany, or f. L *durus* hard; (see ALUMINIUM).] (Proprietary name for) any of a series of aluminium alloys which contain copper and other elements and combine strength and hardness with lightness.

dura mater /djʊərə 'meɪtə/ *n. phr.* LME. [med.L *dura mater* 'hard mother', inexact tr. Arab. *al-'umm al-jāfiya* 'coarse mother' (*al-'umm* 'mother' indicating a relationship between parts). Cf. PIA MATER.] *Anat.* The dense, tough, fibrous lining of the cranial cavity and spinal canal, serving as the outermost envelope of the brain and spinal cord. Abbrev. DURA *n.*[1]

duramen /djʊˈreɪmɛn/ *n.* M19. [L *duramen* hardness, f. *durare*: see DURE *v.*] *Bot.* The heartwood of a tree or other woody plant.

durance /ˈdjʊər(ə)ns/ *n. arch.* LME. [OFr., f. as DURE *v.*: see -ANCE.] †1 Continuance, duration. LME–L17. b Lasting quality, durability. L16–M19. 2 Imprisonment or forced confinement. Now esp. in *in durance vile*. Cf. DURESS 4. E16. †3 A hard-wearing woollen or worsted cloth, in appearance like buff leather. Cf. DURANT *n.* L16–E18. 4 Endurance (of fatigue etc.). *arch.* L16.

durant /ˈdjʊər(ə)nt/ *a.* & *n.* LME. [(O)Fr., pres. pple of *durer*: see DURE *v.*, -ANT[1].] †A *adj.* Lasting, continuous; current. LME–M17. B *n.* A hard-wearing woollen cloth; a variety of tammy. (Cf. DURANCE 3.) *obs.* exc. *Hist.* E18.

durante /djʊəˈranti/ *pres. pple* & *prep.* LME. [L, abl. sing. of *durans* enduring.] During. *obs.* exc. in L phrs.

durante beneplacito /bɛnɪˈplasɪtəʊ/ during pleasure. ***durante vita, vita durante*** /ˈviːtə/ while life continues.

duration /djʊəˈreɪʃ(ə)n/ *n.* LME. [OFr. f. med.L *duratio(n-)*, f. L *durat-* pa. ppl stem of *durare*: see DURE *v.*, -ATION.] 1 The continuance or length of time; the time during which anything continues. LME. †b Durability, permanence. M17–M18. c *Phonet.* The length of a sound. L19. †2 Hardening. E–M17.

1 R. L. STEVENSON We discussed the probable duration of the voyage. H. READ There was no permanency in his life, no sense of duration. H. KISSINGER A campaign of eight weeks' duration. **for the duration** until the end of the (current) war; for a long or an unconscionably long time. b J. HANWAY The brick.. appears to be ill prepared for duration.

durational *a.* L19. **durationless** *a.* having no duration E20.

durative /ˈdjʊərətɪv/ *a.* & *n.* L19. [f. prec. + -IVE.] A *adj.* Continuing; *spec.* in *Gram.*, denoting continuing action. L19. B *n. Gram.* A verb in the durative aspect. E20.

duratively *adv.* E20. **duraˈtivity** *n.* E20.

durbar /ˈdəːbɑː/ *n.* E17. [Urdu f. Pers. *darbār* court.] 1 A public levee held by an Indian ruler or by a British ruler in India. Also, the court of an Indian ruler. E17. 2 A hall or place of audience where durbars were held. E17.

durchkomponiert /ˈdʊrçkɔmponiːrt/ *a.* L19. [G, f. *durch* through + *komponiert* composed.] *Mus.* (Of composition) having a formal design which does not rely on repeated sections; *esp.* (of song) having different music for each stanza; through-composed.

dure /djʊə/ *a. arch.* LME. [(O)Fr. *dur* f. L *durus* hard.] Hard (*lit.* & *fig.*).

dure /djʊə/ *v.* ME. [(O)Fr. *durer* f. L *durare* harden, endure, f. *durus* hard.] 1 *v.i.* Last, continue in existence. *arch.* & *dial.* ME. †2 *v.i.* Hold out, persist, survive; continue in a certain state or condition. ME–L16. †3 *v.i.* Extend, stretch out into space. ME–E16. †4 *v.t.* Sustain, undergo, endure. ME–L16. 5 *v.i.* Harden. Now *rare* or *obs.* LME.

†**dureful** *a.* lasting, durable L16–E17.

Düreresque /djʊərəˈrɛsk/ *a.* M19. [f. *Dürer* (see below) + -ESQUE.] In the style or manner of the German painter and engraver Albrecht Dürer (1471–1528).

duress /djʊ(ə)ˈrɛs, ˈdjʊərɛs/ *n.* Also †**-esse**. ME. [OFr. *duresse* f. L *duritia*, f. *durus* hard: see -ESS[2].] †1 Harsh treatment; oppression, cruelty; harm, injury. ME–L17. †2 Hardness; roughness, violence; endurance, firmness. LME–M17. 3 Constraint, compulsion, esp. through imprisonment, threats, or violence; *spec.* in *Law*, constraint illegally exercised to force a person to perform an act. LME. 4 Forced confinement, imprisonment. Cf. DURANCE 2. LME.

3 J. L. AUSTIN Voidable for duress or undue influence. A. FRASER A laborious composition, no doubt written under duress. 4 J. MCCARTHY Some of the missionaries had been four years in duresse.

du reste /dy rɛst/ *adv. phr.* E19. [Fr., lit. 'of the rest'.] Besides, moreover.

Durex /ˈdjʊərɛks/ *n.* Also **d-**. Pl. same. M20. [Invented wd.] (Proprietary name for) a contraceptive sheath, a condom.

durgah /ˈdəːgə/ *n.* L18. [Pers. *dargāh* royal court.] In the Indian subcontinent: the tomb and shrine of a Muslim holy man.

Durham /ˈdʌrəm/ *n.* L18. [See below.] Used *attrib.* to designate things originating in or associated with the city of Durham in NE England.

Durham mustard *Hist.* ground mustard orig. produced in Durham in the 18th cent. *Durham shorthorn*: see *shorthorn* s.v. SHORT *a.*

durian /ˈdʊərɪən/ *n.* L16. [Malay *durian* f. *duri* thorn, prickle.] A Malayan tree, *Durio zibethinus*, of the bombax family, widely grown in tropical Asia; the spinous fruit of this, the pulp of which is foul-smelling but palatable.

duricrust /ˈdjʊərɪkrʌst/ *n.* E20. [f. L *durus* hard + -I- + CRUST *n.*] *Geol.* A hard crust formed at or near the ground surface in semi-arid climates by the deposition of minerals from groundwater which rises by capillary action and evaporates.

during /ˈdjʊərɪŋ/ *prep.* & *conj.* LME. [pres. pple of DURE *v.* (see -ING[2]), after OFr. *durant* & L abl. absol., as DURANTE *vita, vita durante.*] A *prep.* Throughout the duration of; in the course of, in the time of. LME.

J. CONRAD Some time during the night the crew came on board. M. AMIS During the early months of the year, the air was like cold washing-up. A. N. WILSON Hilaire Belloc was born during a thunderstorm.

†B *conj.* While (*that*); until (*that*). L16–L17.

†**durity** *n.* LME–L19. [L *duritas*, f. *durus* hard: see -ITY.] Hardness (*lit.* & *fig.*).

†**durk** *n.* & *v.* see DIRK.

Durkheimian /dəːkˈhʌɪmɪən/ *a.* & *n.* E20. [f. Émile *Durkheim* (see below) + -IAN.] A *adj.* Of or characteristic of the French sociologist Émile Durkheim (1858–1917) or his sociological theories. E20. B *n.* A follower or adherent of Durkheim. M20.

durmast /ˈdəːmɑːst/ *n.* L18. [Perh. orig. erron. for *dunmast*, f. DUN *a.* + MAST *n.*[2]] More fully *durmast oak*. A Eurasian oak, *Quercus petraea*, which bears sessile acorns and grows chiefly on acid soils.

durn /dəːn/ *n.*[1] Now *dial.* ME. [Origin uncertain: perh. f. Norse. Cf. in same sense OSw. *dyrni*, Norw. *dyrn*, Sw. dial. *dörne*, ult. f. Gmc base of DOOR *n.*] 1 A solid wood doorpost; *sing.* & (usu.) in *pl.*, the framework of a doorway. ME. 2 *Mining.* In *pl.* (treated as *sing.*). A frame of timbering. L18.

durn *n.*[2], *a.*, *adv.*, & *v.*: see DARN *n.*[2] etc., DARN *v.*[2]

duro /ˈdʊərəʊ/ *n.* Also **douro**. Pl. **-os**. L18. [f. Sp. *peso duro* hard or solid piastre.] In Spanish America and (formerly) Spain: a peso or dollar coin (as opp. to a note).

Duroc /ˈdjʊərɒk/ *n.* L19. [Name of a stallion owned by Isaac Frink, sheriff of Saratoga Co., N.Y., and said to have been bought on the same day (in 1823) as the pigs from which he developed the breed.] Orig., (a pig of) a breed developed in New York State. Now (also *Duroc-Jersey*), (a pig of) a breed derived by crossing the original breed with the Jersey Red. Also *Duroc pig*.

duroy /djʊˈrɔɪ/ *n. obs.* exc. *Hist.* E17. [Origin unkn. Cf. CORDUROY *n.*] A kind of lightweight worsted material formerly made in western England, used for men's clothing.

durra /ˈdʊrə, ˈdʊərə/ *n.* Also **dhurra, dourra, dura**, & other vars. L18. [Arab. *dura*.] A variety of grain sorghum, *Sorghum bicolor* var. *durra*, grown esp. in N. Africa and the Indian subcontinent.

durrie, -y *ns.* vars. of DHURRIE.

durst *v.* pa. t.: see DARE *v.*[1]

durum /ˈdjʊərəm/ *n.* E20. [L *durum* neut. of *durus* hard.] In full *durum wheat*. A type of wheat grown in arid regions, *Triticum durum*, marked by hard seeds rich in gluten, which are used in the manufacture of pasta.

durwan /dəːˈwɑːn/ *n.* L18. [Urdu *darwān* f. Pers.] In the Indian subcontinent: a porter, a doorkeeper.

durzi /ˈdəːzi/ *n.* E19. [Urdu f. Pers. *darzī*.] In the Indian subcontinent: a tailor.

†**dush** *v.* & *n. Sc.* & *north.* ME. [Perh. alt. of DASH *v.*[1]: cf. CRUSH *v.*, CRASH *v.*] A *v.* 1 *v.i.* Rush; strike against something; fall heavily. ME–E19. 2 *v.t.* Rush or throw down violently. LME–E19. B *n.* A violent blow or impact; the sound of violent collision. LME–E20.

dusk /dʌsk/ *a.* & *n.* [OE *dox* rel. to OS *dosan*, OHG *tusin* darkish (of colour), dull, f. Gmc base repr. also by L *fuscus* dark, dusky. Metathesized in ME. Cf. DUN *a.*] A *adj.* 1 Dark, shadowy; dusky. Now *poet.* OE. †2 Obscure, veiled from perception. ME–L16.

B *n.* 1 The darker stage of twilight; the time of this. E17. 2 Shade, shadow; gloom; duskiness. E18.

1 R. L. STEVENSON The mail picked us up about dusk at the Royal George. J. WAIN The long golden evening gradually yielded first to twilight and then to a deep dusk, through which we could barely discern each other's faces. 2 TENNYSON In the dusk of thee [Old Yew], the clock Beats out the little lives of men.

dusken *v.t.* & *i.* (*rare*, now *poet.*) make or become dusky or obscure M16. **duskly** *adv.* (*poet.*) M19. **duskness** *n.* (now *poet.*) LME.

dusk /dʌsk/ *v.* Now chiefly *poet.* [OE *doxian*, f. as prec. Metathesized or re-formed in ME.] 1 *v.i.* Become dusk or dim; grow dark; be dusky. OE. 2 *v.t.* Make dusky; darken, dim, obscure. LME.

1 TENNYSON Little breezes dusk and shiver. G. GISSING When it began to dusk.. supper was prepared. 2 *fig.*: LD BERNERS Vnderstandyng, which is dusked in errours.

duskish /ˈdʌskɪʃ/ *a.* M16. [f. DUSK *a.* & *n.* + -ISH[1].] Rather dusky; somewhat dark.

duskishly *adv.* L16. **duskishness** *n.* M16.

dusky /ˈdʌski/ *a.* M16. [f. DUSK *a.* & *n.* + -Y[1].] 1 Somewhat black or dark in colour; darkish. M16. b *euphem.* Of a person: Black. Esp. *Austral.*, Aboriginal. E19. 2 Shady or shadowy; deficient in light; dim, obscure. L16. 3 *fig.* Gloomy, melancholy. Now *rare* or *obs.* E17.

1 R. T. PETERSON The immature Blue-faced Booby is dusky-brown with a white belly. **dusky cranesbill** a European cranesbill, *Geranium phaeum*, with usu. dark purple flowers. *dusky perch*: see PERCH *n.*[1] **dusky titi** a mainly grey-brown cebid monkey, *Callicebus moloch*, occurring in the forests of tropical America. 2 SHAKES. *1 Hen. VI* Here dies the dusky torch of Mortimer, Chok'd with ambition of the meaner sort. H. JAMES Dusky with the shade of magnificent elms. 3 W. FALCONER Here no dusky frown prevails.

duskily *adv.* E17. **duskiness** *n.* E17.

Dussehra /ˈdʌʃərə, -ʃ-/ *n.* Also **Dashera, Dassera**, & other vars. L18. [Hind. *dasahrā* f. Skt *daśaharā*.] The tenth (final) day of the Hindu autumn festival of Navaratri.

dust /dʌst/ *n.* [OE *dūst* = OFris. *dūst*, MDu. *donst*, *dūst* (LG *dust*, Du. *duist* meal-dust, bran), ON *dust*. Cf. OHG *tun(i)st* wind, breeze, LG *dunst* vapour.] 1 Finely powdered earth or other matter lying on the ground or on surfaces, or carried about by the wind; any substance pulverized; fine particles of matter; an example of this. OE. b This and other household refuse. Usu. in *comb.*, as *dustbin*, *dustman*, etc. E18. c Pollen; spores. L18. 2 *fig.* a (The material of) the human frame. (Cf. *Gen.* 2:7, 3:19.) *arch.* OE. b A dead person's remains. OE. c As the type of that which is worthless or contemptible, or occupies the lowest position. ME. 3 A particle of matter, a pinch of something. Now *rare.* L16. 4 A cloud of finely powdered earth or of other fine particles floating in the air; *fig.* confusion, turmoil, disturbance; *slang* a row, an uproar. L16. 5 Money; cash. *arch. slang.* E17. 6 An act of cleaning by wiping off dust. L20.

1 J. BRAINE There wasn't one chip, one scratch, one speck of dust anywhere. E. WELTY The peppering of red road dust on the old man's hat. U. LE GUIN Drought had.. dried the soil to a fine grey dust, that now rose up on every wind. *brick-dust, coal-dust, gold-*

dust, sawdust, stardust, etc. **2a** R. GRANT Frail children of dust. **b** SHAKES. *Haml.* May not imagination trace the noble dust of Alexander till 'a find it stopping a bung-hole? **c** C. N. ROBINSON The Navy that.. humbled to the dust the pride of France. **3** SHAKES. *John* A grain, a dust, a gnat, a wandering hair. **4** T. BROWN Quarrel and raise a Dust about nothing. R. CARSON Drifting arsenic dusts.. spread over neighbouring farms.

Phrases (chiefly *fig.*): *bite the dust*: see BITE *v. bull-dust*: see BULL *n.*[1] & *a. cosmic dust*: see COSMIC 3. *dry as dust*: see DRY *a.* **dust and ashes** something very disappointing or disillusioning. *happy dust*: see HAPPY *a.* **in the dust** dead and buried. *kiss the dust*: see KISS *v.* **not see a person for dust** find a person hastily departed. **shake the dust off one's feet** depart indignantly or disdainfully (cf. *Matt.* 10:14). **throw dust in a person's eyes** mislead a person by misrepresentation or by diverting attention from a point. **wait until the dust settles** wait until a situation calms down.

Comb.: **dust-bath** a bird's rolling in or sprinkling itself with dust to clean its feathers; **dustbin** a container for household refuse; **dustbinman** a dustman; **dust bowl** an area of land made unproductive by wind erosion of soil, esp. following loss of vegetation through drought, inappropriate farming practices, etc.; **dust-box** (*a*) *arch.* a box from which a fine powder is sprinkled on wet ink to dry it; (*b*) (chiefly *Austral.*) a dustbin; **dust-cap** a cap to protect something from dust; **dustcart** a vehicle for collecting household refuse; **dust-cloth**: put over things as a protection from dust; **dust-coat**: worn as a protection against dust; **dust-colour** dull light brown; **dust cover** a removable cover to protect furniture etc. from dust; a dust-jacket; *dust devil*: see DEVIL *n.* 12; **dust disease** *colloq.* pneumoconiosis; **dustheap** a heap of household refuse; *dust-jacket*: see JACKET *n.* 3b; **dustman** (*a*) a man employed to remove refuse from dustbins; (*b*) a sandman; **dustpan** a hand-held receptacle into which dust can be brushed from the floor; **dust-sheet** a cover to protect furniture etc. from dust; **dust-shot** the smallest size of gunshot; **dust-storm** a dry storm in which clouds of dust or sand are raised and carried along; **dust-trap** something in or on or under which dust readily collects; **dust-up** *colloq.* a fight, a disturbance; **dust-wrapper** a dust-jacket.

dustless *a.* E17.

dust /dʌst/ *v.* ME. [f. the n. Cf. ON *dusta.*] †**1** *v.i.* Be dusty. Only in ME. †**2** *v.t.* & *i.* (Cause to) crumble into dust. LME–L17. **3** *v.t.* Make dusty. M16. **4** *v.t.* Free from dust; wipe, brush, or beat the dust from. M16. **b** Brush, shake, or rub off as dust. L18. **5** *v.t.* Sprinkle with dust or powder; sprinkle powdered insecticide etc. on (a crop), esp. from the air. L16. **b** Strew or sprinkle as dust or powder. L18. **c** *v.refl.* & *i.* Of a bird: take a dust-bath. L18. **6** *v.t.* Beat; strike. Now *colloq.* & *dial.* E17. **7** *v.i.* Ride or go quickly; hurry. *slang* (chiefly *US*). M17.

3 J. A. FROUDE We go out.. and dust our feet along its thoroughfares. **4** A. PATON He dusted his feet on the frayed mat outside Kumalo's door. N. MONSARRAT The rooms were.. cleaned, dusted, polished, and set to rights. **dust a person's jacket** *colloq.* thrash a person. **b** S. LEWIS He dusted the cigar-ash off his vest. **5** W. CATHER Marie took out.. rolls, and began to dust them over with powdered sugar. **b** B. SPOCK It should be dusted on your hand first.. and then rubbed gently on his [the baby's] skin. **6** M. TWAIN So she.. dusted us both with the hickry.

With advs. in specialized senses: **dust down** wipe or brush the dust from. **dust off** (*a*) = *dust down* above; (*b*) *US slang* = sense 7 above; (*c*) *US slang* defeat, kill, get rid of.

dustak /ˈdʌstək/ *n. obs.* exc. *Hist.* Also **-stu(c)k**. M18. [Urdu *dastak* f. Pers.] In the Indian subcontinent: a pass, a permit.

duster /ˈdʌstə/ *n.* L16. [f. DUST *n.* or *v.* + -ER[1].] **1** A cloth, (less usu.) brush or other article for dusting surfaces. L16. **b** A person who dusts. M19. **2** A device for sifting or applying dust; a sieve. M17. **3** A dust-coat. Now usu. a woman's loose casual full-length coat. Also *duster-coat*. M19. **4** *Naut.* An ensign, a flag. *slang*. E20.

1 *feather duster*: see FEATHER *n. linen duster*: see LINEN *a.* & *n.* **4** *red duster*: see RED *a.*

dusting /ˈdʌstɪŋ/ *vbl n.* E17. [f. DUST *v.* + -ING[1].] **1** The action of DUST *v.*; *esp.* (*a*) the removal of dust from furniture etc. by wiping or brushing; (*b*) the action or result of sprinkling with dust or powder; a quantity of dust or powder sprinkled over something. E17. **2** A thrashing; a fight. *colloq.* L18.

1 DICKENS Mrs. Bardell resumed her dusting. L. BLUE Scatter liberally with sugar and a dusting of cinnamon. *fig.*: B. BAINBRIDGE He had a nice chest.. with only a dusting of freckles between his shoulders. *crop-dusting*: see CROP *n.*

Comb.: **dusting-powder** a powder for dusting, *esp.* talcum powder.

dustoor, -oory *ns.* vars. of DASTUR *n.*[2], DASTURI.

dustu(c)k *n.* var. of DUSTAK.

dusty /ˈdʌsti/ *a.* OE. [f. DUST *n.* + -Y[1].] **1** Full of, abounding with, or strewn with dust. OE. **2** Of the nature of or pertaining to dust; finely powdered like dust. LME. **3** Of colour: appearing as though sprinkled with dust, dull. E17. **4** *fig.* Mean, worthless; uninteresting, 'dry as dust'; vague, unsatisfactory. E17.

Special collocations & *phrases*: **dusty answer** an unsatisfactory answer; a rebuff. **dusty miller** (*a*) any of several plants grown for their ornamental greyish or whitish foliage, *esp.* silver ragwort, *Senecio cineraria*, snow in summer, *Cerastium tomentosum*, and a N. American mugwort, *Artemisia stellerana*; (*b*) a kind of artificial fishing-fly; (*c*) *US* any of various speckled noctuid moths. **not** (or **none**) **so dusty** *colloq.* not so bad, fairly good.

dustily *adv.* L16. **dustiness** *n.* L16.

Dusun /ˈduːs(ə)n/ *n.* & *a.* L18. [Malay *dusun* orchard, village.] **A** *n.*Pl. same, **-s**. **1** (**d-**.) In Malaysia: a village, a cultivated area. L18. **2** A member of a Dyak people inhabiting the Malaysian state of Sabah (N. Borneo); the Indonesian language of this people. M19. **B** *attrib.* or as *adj.* Of or pertaining to the Dusun or their language. M19.

Dutch /dʌtʃ/ *n.*[1] LME. [f. the adj.] **I 1** The West Germanic language of the area of north and central Europe now largely comprising Germany, Austria, Switzerland, and the Low Countries; any dialect of this language. Without specifying wd (as *High, Low*) *obs.* exc. *Hist.*. LME. **2** *spec.* The language of the Netherlands (spoken also in what is now N. Belgium: cf. *Flemish*). E18. **b** Afrikaans. *S. Afr.* M18. **3** The German language as spoken by American immigrants from Germany or by Americans of German descent. Now *spec.* Pennsylvania Dutch. *US.* M18.

II 4 *collect. pl.* Formerly *gen.*, the people of the area of north and central Europe in which German or Dutch is spoken. Now *spec.* (*a*) the people of the Netherlands; (*b*) *S. Afr.*, *derog.* the Afrikaans-speakers, the South Africans of Dutch descent; (*c*) *US* the American immigrants from Germany or the Americans of German descent, *esp.* the Pennsylvania Dutch. L16.

4 beat the Dutch *US* be or do something extraordinary or startling (chiefly in *that beats the Dutch*).

III 5 Desertion, escape, suicide. Chiefly in *do a* (or *the*) *Dutch*. *slang*, orig. *US*. E20. **6** *in Dutch*, in disgrace, in trouble. *slang* (orig. *US*). E20.

Phrases: *Cape Dutch*: see CAPE *n.*[1] **double Dutch** gibberish, completely incomprehensible language. **High Dutch** (*a*) *arch.* High German; (*b*) *S. Afr.* Netherlands Dutch as opp. to Afrikaans. **Low Dutch** (*a*) Low German (in the wider sense: see GERMAN *n.*[1] & *a.*[1]); (*b*) *arch.* Netherlands Dutch; (*c*) *rare* Afrikaans; (*d*) (in this dictionary) Dutch and Low German (Middle and Modern). PENNSYLVANIA *Dutch*. *South African Dutch*: see SOUTH.

Dutch /dʌtʃ/ *n.*[2] *slang*. L19. [Abbrev.] = DUCHESS *n.* 3.

Dutch /dʌtʃ/ *a.* & *adv.* ME. [MDu. *dutsch* Dutch, Netherlandish, German (Du. *duitsch* German) = OE *þēodisc* Gentile, OS *thiudisc*, f. Gmc, f. as OE *þeod* people, -ISH[1]. Cf. OHG *diutisc* national, popular, vulgar. In spec. US uses tr. G *deutsch, Deutsche.*] **A** *adj.* **1** Of, pertaining to, or designating the Germanic people of the area of north and central Europe now largely comprising Germany, Austria, Switzerland, and the Low Countries, or of any part of this area; of, pertaining to, or designating the West Germanic language of this people or any of its dialects; Teutonic. Without specifying wd (as *High, Low*) *obs.* exc. *Hist.* ME. **2** *spec.* Of, pertaining to, or designating the people of the Netherlands (Holland) or their language (spoken also in what is now N. Belgium: cf. *Flemish*); native to or originating in the Netherlands; characteristic of or attributed (often casually, usu. derogatorily) to the people of the Netherlands. E17. **b** Of, pertaining to, or designating South Africans of Dutch descent; Afrikaans-speaking; of Afrikaans. *S. Afr.*, *derog.* M18. **3** Of, pertaining to, or designating American immigrants from Germany or Americans of German descent, or the German language as spoken by them. Now *spec.* Pennsylvania Dutch. *US.* M18.

Phrases: As for DUTCH *n.*[1]

Special collocations: **Dutch act** *US slang* = DUTCH *n.*[1] 5 (chiefly in *do a* (or *the*) *Dutch act*). *Dutch auction*: see AUCTION *n.* 1. **Dutch bargain**: concluded by drinking together. **Dutch barn** a roof, supported on poles, over hay etc. **Dutch cap** (*a*) a woman's lace cap with a triangular piece turned back on each side; (*b*) a contraceptive diaphragm. **Dutch cheese** a cheese from the Netherlands, characteristically spherical in shape. *Dutch clover*: see CLOVER *n. Dutch courage*: see COURAGE *n.* 4. **Dutch defence** *Chess* a defence replying to the queen's pawn opening with a two-square move of the king's bishop's pawn. **Dutch doll** a jointed wooden doll. **Dutch elm disease** a destructive disease of elms (first found in the Netherlands) caused by infestation with the fungus *Ceratocystis ulmi* and spread by bark beetles. **Dutch feast**: at which the host gets drunk before the guests. **Dutch hoe** a hoe used with a pushing action. **Dutch interior** a painting of the interior of a Dutch room or house, by or in the style of Pieter de Hooch (1629–83). **Dutch light** a cold frame in which the glass is a single large pane. **Dutch lunch**: at which each person pays for his or her own share. **Dutch metal** an alloy of copper and zinc imitating gold leaf. *Dutch nightingale*: see NIGHTINGALE *n.*[1] 3. *Dutch oven*: see OVEN *n.* 2. **Dutch pink** a yellow lake pigment. **Dutch reckoning** *slang* faulty reckoning. **Dutch roll** *Aeronaut.* a short-period lateral oscillation of an aircraft. **Dutch rush** the rough horsetail, *Equisetum hyemale*. **Dutch tile** a kind of glazed tile painted in colours. **Dutch treat** a party, or outing, meal, etc., at which each person pays his or her own share of the expenses. **Dutch uncle** a well-disposed, authoritative person (*talk to like a Dutch uncle*, lecture with kindly severity). **Dutch wife** (*a*) a frame of cane etc. used for resting the limbs in bed; (*b*) an artificial sexual partner.

Comb.: **Dutchland** †(*a*) [f. G *Deutschland*] Germany; (*b*) *rare* the Netherlands.

B *adv.* In a Dutch fashion. Now chiefly in *go Dutch*, pay for one's own share, share the expense, of food, drink, entertainment, etc. E17.

¶Although some early uses refer to the area which is now the Netherlands, the restriction of *Dutch* to this (to the exclusion of Germany etc.) took place in the 17th cent. with the country's independence and increasing contact with Britain.

†**Dutcher** *n.* (*rare*) one of the Dutch (see DUTCH *n.*[1] 4) L17–E19. **Dutchify** *v.t.* make Dutch, give a Dutch character to L17. **Dutchy** *n.* (*slang, derog.*) a Dutchman, a German M19.

Dutch /dʌtʃ/ *v.t. obs.* exc. *Hist.* M18. [f. the adj.] Clarify and harden (quills) in hot sand or flames.

†**dutchess** *n.* var. of DUCHESS.

Dutchman /ˈdʌtʃmən/ *n.* Pl. **-men**. LME. [f. DUTCH *a.* + MAN *n.*] **1** *gen.* A man who is a member of a Teutonic nation; a German. Long *obs.* exc. as below. LME. **2** An adult male native or inhabitant of the Netherlands. L16. **3** A Dutch ship. M17. **4** An adult male American immigrant from Germany or American of German descent, *spec.* a Pennsylvania Dutchman (see PENNSYLVANIA); *slang* any adult male German. *US.* L18. **5** An adult male European or foreigner. *slang* (chiefly *US*). M19. **6** A piece of wood or stone used to repair a flaw or fault or to patch up bad workmanship. Chiefly *US.* M19.

Phrases: **Dutchman's breeches** (*a*) a plant of the fumitory family, *Dicentra cucullaria*, which is native to eastern N. America and bears white, spurred flowers (from the shape of which the name is derived) and finely divided leaves; (*b*) *slang* (orig. *Naut.*) a small patch of blue sky. **Dutchman's pipe** a climbing vine of the birthwort family, *Aristolochia durior*, which is native to eastern N. America and bears hook-shaped tubular flowers. **Flying Dutchman** (the captain of) a spectral ship supposedly doomed to sail the seas forever. **or I'm a Dutchman, I'm a Dutchman if**: expr. asseveration.

Dutchwoman *n.*, pl. **-women**, †(*a*) a woman of a Teutonic nation, a German woman; (*b*) a woman of the Netherlands: L18.

duteous /ˈdjuːtɪəs/ *a.* L16. [f. DUTY + -OUS. Cf. BEAUTEOUS.] Characterized by the performance of duty to a superior; dutiful; obedient, subservient.

duteously *adv.* E19. **duteousness** *n.* M17.

dutiable /ˈdjuːtɪəb(ə)l/ *a.* L18. [f. DUTY + -ABLE.] Liable to customs or other duties.

dutied /ˈdjuːtɪd/ *a. US.* L18. [f. DUTY + -ED[2].] Dutiable.

dutiful /ˈdjuːtɪfʊl, -f(ə)l/ *a.* M16. [f. DUTY *n.* + -FUL.] Regular or willing in obedience or service; conscientious.

dutifully *adv.* M16. **dutifulness** *n.* L16.

dutiless /ˈdjuːtɪlɪs/ *a.* Long *arch. rare.* L16. [f. DUTY + -LESS.] Not dutiful.

du tout /dy tu/ *adv. phr.* E19. [Fr., abbrev. of *pas du tout.*] Not at all; by no means.

duty /ˈdjuːti/ *n.* & *a.* LME. [AN *deweté*, *dueté*, f. *du(e)* DUE *a.*: see -TY[1].] **A** *n.* **1** That which is owed; what one owes; one's due; a debt of money, goods, or service. Long *obs.* exc. as below. LME. **2** A payment due and enforced by law or custom; now *esp.* the payment to the public revenue levied on the import, export, manufacture, or sale of goods, on the transfer of property, for licences etc., for legal recognition of documents, etc. Freq. in *pl.* LME. †**b** Payment for the services of the Church. Usu. in *pl.* LME–M16. **c** *Sc. Law.* A payment made by a vassal to a superior in recognition of feudal authority. M16. **3** The behaviour due to a superior; homage; deference; an expression of respect. LME. **4** The action or behaviour due by moral or legal obligation; an obligation; the binding force of what is morally right. LME. **5** (An) action required by one's business, occupation, or function; the performance of or engagement in the activities required by one's business, occupation, or function. LME. **b** *Eccl.* Performance of the prescribed services or offices of the Church; *RC Ch.* attendance at services and confession. E16. **6** A measure of an engine's effectiveness expressed in units of work done per unit of fuel. E19.

1 TINDALE *Matt.* 20:14 Take that which is thy duty. E. COKE If *A.* be accountable to *B.* and *B.* releaseth him all his duties. **2** *customs duty, death duty, excise duty, probate duty, stamp duty*, etc. *countervailing duty*: see COUNTERVAIL *v.* 5. *umboth duty*: see UMBOTH 2. **3** N. ROWE What Duty, what Submission shall they not pay to that Authority? T. H. WHITE Hob made a duty to Merlyn, who returned it courteously. **4** P. G. WODEHOUSE With your magnificent physique . . it is your duty to the future of the race to marry. A. S. NEILL Women . . compelled by a sense of duty to . . look after elderly parents. D. MURPHY It was a parental duty to try to persuade me to rethink. *personified*: WORDSWORTH Stern Daughter of the Voice of God! O Duty! **5** V. BRITTAIN He was transferred to the Somerset Light Infantry for temporary duty. E. LONGFORD His duties were to supervise the various harbour works, lifeboats and salvage. **do duty as, for** serve as or pass for (something else). **do one's duty** *euphem.* defecate, urinate. *heavy-duty*: see HEAVY *a.* **off duty** not on duty, not engaged in one's duties; spent, engaged in, etc., when not on duty. **on duty** engaged in one's business or occupation or in performing one's function.

Comb.: **duty-bound** *a.* obliged by duty; **duty cycle** the cycle of operation of a device acting intermittently; the time occupied by this esp. as a fraction of available time; **duty-free** *a.*, *adv.*, & *n.* (*a*) *adj.* & *adv.* exempt from payment of customs and excise duty, esp. as a small personal allowance on (re-)entering a country; (*duty-free shop*: at which duty-free goods are sold); (*b*) *n.* a duty-free article; **duty-paid** *a.* (of goods) on which customs or excise duty has been paid.

B *attrib.* or as *adj.* **1** Of a visit, call, or other undertaking: done as a duty rather than as a pleasure. E19. **2** Of a person: having specific duties; being on duty. L19.

1 C. ISHERWOOD A duty-party, given once a year, to all the relatives, friends and dependents of the family. A. CHRISTIE We had him to lunch with some other Duty people. **2** P. LAURIE The Duty Officer, an elderly inspector.

duumvir /djuːˈʌmvə/ *n.* Pl. **-virs**, in L form **-viri** /-VIrAI/. E17. [L, sing. f. *duum virum* genit. pl. of *duo viri* two men.] In *Rom. Hist.*, of a pair of coequal magistrates or officials; *gen.* either of two people with joint authority, a coalition of two people.

duumvirate *n.* [L *duumviratus*] (*a*) the position or office of duumvirs; the joint authority of two people; (*b*) two people with joint authority, the members of a coalition of people: M17.

duvet /ˈdjuːveɪ, ˈduː-/ *n.* M18. [Fr. = DOWN *n.*[2]] A thick soft quilt used instead of other bedclothes. Also called *continental quilt.*

Duvetyn /ˈdjuːvɪtɪn, ˈdʌvtɪn/ *n.* Also **d-**. E20. [f. as prec.] (Proprietary name for) a soft worsted and silk material.

dux /dʌks/ *n.* Pl. **duces** /ˈdjuːsiːz/, **duxes**. M18. [L = leader.] **1** *Mus.* The subject of a fugue or canon; the leading voice or instrument in a fugue or canon. Opp. COMES. M18. **2** The top pupil in a class or school. Chiefly *Sc.*, *NZ*, & *S. Afr.* L18.

duxelles /ˈdʌks(ə)lz, *foreign* dyksɛl/ *n.* L19. [Marquis *d'Uxelles*, 17th-cent. Fr. nobleman.] A seasoning or sauce of shallots, parsley, onions, and mushrooms.

duyker *n.* var. of DUIKER *n.*

dvandva /ˈdvandvə/ *n.* M19. [Skt *dvandva* f. *dva* two.] *Ling.* More fully *dvandva compound.* A compound word containing two elements as if joined by *and*, as *whisky-soda.*

Dvořákian /(d)vɔːˈʒakɪən/ *a.* & *n.* L19. [f. *Dvořák* (see below) + -IAN.] **A** *adj.* Of, pertaining to, or characteristic of the Czech composer Antonin Leopold Dvořák (1841–1904) or his music. L19. **B** *n.* An interpreter, student, or admirer of Dvořák or his music. L20.

dwale /dweɪl/ *n.* ME. [Prob. of Scand. origin: cf. Da. *dvale* dead sleep, stupor, *dvaledrik* sleeping draught.] †**1** A stupefying or soporific drink, *esp.* the juice or infusion of belladonna. ME–E17. **2** Belladonna, deadly nightshade. Formerly also, any of various other plants yielding similar narcotic preparations. LME. **3** *Her.* The tincture sable in the fanciful blazon of arms of peers. Long *obs.* exc. *Hist.* M16.

dwalm /dwɑːm/ *n.* & *v. Sc.*, *N. Ir.*, & *north.* Also **dwam**. E16. [f. Gmc base of DWELL *v.* Cf. OE *dwolma* confusion, chaos, OHG *twalm*, MDu. *dwelm* stupefaction, giddiness, OS *dwalm* delusion.] **A** *n.* A fainting fit; dizziness, giddiness. E16. **B** *v.i.* Faint, swoon; fail in health. E16.

dwang /dwaŋ/ *n.* Chiefly *Sc.* L15. [Cf. Du. *dwang* force, compulsion, constraint.] A short piece of timber used for any of various purposes; *esp.* one inserted between floor joists to prevent distortion. Also, a crowbar, a wrench.

dwarf /dwɔːf/ *n.* & *a.* [OE *dweorg*, *dweorh* = OFris. *dwirg*, MDu. *dwerch* (Du. *dwerg*), OHG *twerg* (G *Zwerg*), ON *dvergr*, f. Gmc.] **A** *n.* Pl. **dwarfs, dwarves** /dwɔːvz/. **1** An abnormally undersized person. OE. **b** Any of a mythical race of diminutive beings, typically skilled in mining and metalworking and often possessing magical powers, figuring esp. in Scandinavian folklore. ME. **2** An animal or plant of much smaller size than the average of its kind or species. M17. **3** *Astron.* A small dense star. Freq., a main-sequence star as opp. to a superdense star or to a giant or supergiant. E20.

1 *fig.*: H. BELLOC Many troubles that seem giants at evening are but dwarfs at sunrise. **b** C. S. LEWIS The old bright-hooded, snowy-bearded dwarfs we had in those days before . . Walt Disney vulgarised the earthmen. **3** *red dwarf*: see RED *a.* *white dwarf*: see WHITE *a.*

B *adj.* Of or pertaining to a dwarf, dwarfish; of unusually small stature or size, diminutive; puny, stunted (naturally or deliberately); *esp.* designating species or varieties of plants and animals which are much smaller than the average of their kind. L16.

1 M. ATWOOD Even the dwarf swing is there . . perhaps they expected grandchildren, visiting here. **dwarf wall** a low wall; *spec.* one forming the base of a palisade or railing, or supporting the joists under a floor.

dwarfism *n.* the condition or character of being a dwarf; abnormally short stature: M19. **dwarfling** *n.* a small dwarf E17. **dwarfness** *n.* M17. **dwarfy** *a.* of the nature of a dwarf, dwarfish E17.

dwarf /dwɔːf/ *v.* E17. [f. the n.] **1** *v.t.* Stunt, restrict the growth of; stunt the development or extent of (*lit.* & *fig.*). E17. **2** *v.t.* Cause to look or seem small by contrast or by distance (*lit.* & *fig.*). M19. **3** *v.i.* Become dwarf or (relatively) undersized. M19.

1 R. W. EMERSON The incessant repetition of the same hand-work dwarfs the man, robs him of his strength, wit, and versatility. *Which?* Commercial growers . . often dwarf the plants with chemicals. **2** B. WEBB Our close comradeship . . the ideal marriage—dwarfs all other human relationships. J. LE CARRÉ The wharf . . dwarfed by the decks of cargo ships. **3** TENNYSON By him [Mark Antony] great Pompey dwarfs.

dwarfish /ˈdwɔːfɪʃ/ *a.* M16. [f. DWARF *n.* & *a.* + -ISH[1].] Approaching the size of a dwarf; resembling (that of) a dwarf; of below average size or stature, diminutive, puny.

dwarfishly *adv.* M18. **dwarfishness** *n.* M17.

dwarves *n.pl.* see DWARF *n.*

dweeb /dwiːb/ *n. US slang.* L20. [Origin unkn.] A person who is boringly conventional, puny, or studious.

dweeby *a.* L20.

dwell /dwɛl/ *n.* ME. [f. the vb. Cf. also ON *dvǫl* stay, delay.] †**1** Delay, stay, stoppage; continuance in a state or place. ME–M16. **2** A slight regular pause in the motion of (a part of) a machine, allowing time for its own or another part's operation. M19.

dwell /dwɛl/ *v.* Pa. t. & pple **dwelt** /-t/, (now *rare*) **dwelled**. [OE *dwellan* corresp. to OS *bidwellian* hinder, MDu. *dwellen* stun, perplex, OHG, MHG *twellen* delay, harass, ON *dvelja* (v.t.) delay, (v.i. & refl.) tarry, stay, f. Gmc.] †**1** *v.t.* Mislead, delude; stun, stupefy. OE–ME. †**2** *v.t.* Hinder, delay. Only in OE. †**3** *v.i.* Tarry, delay; discontinue an action. ME–L15. †**4** *v.i.* Continue in existence, last, persist; remain. Only in ME. **5** *v.i.* Continue for a time in a place, state, or condition. ME. **b** Of a horse: be slow in raising the feet, pause before taking a jump. M18. **c** Of (part of) a machine: pause slightly during its working (cf. DWELL *n.* 2). M19. **6** *v.i.* Reside, live, have one's home. *literary.* ME. †**b** *v.t.* Inhabit. E16–L18. †**c** *v.t.* Cause to reside *in. rare* (Milton). Only in M17. **7** *v.i.* Foll. by *on*, *upon*, †*in*: keep one's attention fixed on (an object); ponder, consider (a matter) at length; write or speak at length on (a subject). ME.

5 SHAKES. *Merch. V.* I'll rather dwell in my necessity. *Horse & Hound* Here hounds dwelt round the buildings for a while. **6** R. L. STEVENSON I see . . men dwell in contentment with noisy scullions. W. GASS Living in a city, among so many, dwelling in the heat and tumult of incessant movement. **7** B. PYM She preferred not to dwell on how it might work, not to speculate. A. WILSON The speech dwelt mainly on defeat and the saving power of evil.

dweller *n.* LME.

dwelling /ˈdwɛlɪŋ/ *n.* ME. [f. prec. + -ING[1].] **1** The action of DWELL *v.* ME. **2** A place of residence; a habitation, a house. LME.

Comb.: **dwelling-house**: used as a residence, not for business purposes; **dwelling-place** a place of residence, an abode, a house.

dwelt *v.* pa. t. & pple: see DWELL *v.*

dwile /dwʌɪl/ *n. dial.* E19. [Cf. Du. *dweil* mop.] A floorcloth, a mop, a flannel.

dwindle /ˈdwɪnd(ə)l/ *v.* & *n.* L16. [Frequent. of next: see -LE[3].] **A** *v.* **1** *v.i.* Become reduced in size or quantity; shrink; waste away. L16. **b** *fig.* Diminish in quality, value, or importance; decline, degenerate. L17. **2** *v.t.* Cause to shrink, reduce gradually in size. *rare.* M17.

1 J. B. PRIESTLEY The sun came struggling through again and the rain dwindled to a few glittering drops. R. C. HUTCHINSON The uproar had dwindled to silence. **b** G. MURRAY The great hope had dwindled to be very like despair.

B *n.* The process of dwindling. Also, a dwindled object. *rare.* M18.

dwine /dwʌɪn/ *v.* Now *Sc.*, *dial.*, & *arch.* [OE *dwīnan* = (M)LG, MDu. *dwīnen*, ON *dvína*. Cf.

prec.] 1 *v.i.* Waste or pine away; fade, wither. OE. 2 *v.t.* Cause to pine or waste away. *rare.* L16.

dy /dʌɪ/ *n.* M20. [Sw. = mire, ooze f. ON *dý*: perh. f. Gmc base of DUNG *n.*] A sediment rich in allochthonous organic matter deposited in nutrient-poor lakes. Cf. GYTTJA.

dyad /ˈdʌɪad/ *n.* L17. [Late L *dyad-*, *dyas* f. Gk *duad-*, *duas*, f. *duo* two: see -AD[1]. Cf. DUAD.] A *n.* 1 The number two; a group of two, a pair; a twofold entity. L17. b *Pros.* A group of two lines with different rhythms. L19. c *Math.* An operator which is a combination of two vectors. Now *rare.* L19. †2 *Chem.* A divalent atom or radical. M–L19. B *attrib.* or as *adj.* = DYADIC *a.* M19.

dyadic /dʌɪˈadɪk/ *a.* & *n.* Also **diadic.** E18. [Gk *duadikos*, f. *duad-*, *duas*: see prec., -IC.] A *adj.* 1 Of, pertaining to, or of the nature of a dyad; double, twofold. E18. 2 *Philos.* Designating or pertaining to a relationship between exactly two entities, or a predicate expressing such a relationship. L19. b *Math.* & *Computing.* Designating an expression, operator, etc., which requires or acts on two arguments. M20. B *n.* *Math.* A vector dyad or combination of dyads. Now *rare.* L19.

Dyak /ˈdʌɪak/ *n.* & *a.* Also **Dayak.** M19. [Malay = up-country.] A *n.* A member of a group of aboriginal peoples inhabiting parts of Borneo and Sarawak; the language of these peoples. M19. B *attrib.* or as *adj.* Of or pertaining to these peoples or their language. M19.

Sea Dyak = IBAN.

dyarchy *n.* var. of DIARCHY.

dybbuk /ˈdɪbʊk/ *n.* Also **dibbuk.** Pl. **-im** /-ɪm/, **-s.** E20. [Yiddish *dibek* f. Heb. *dibbūq*, f. *dāḇaq* cling, cleave.] In Jewish folklore, a malevolent wandering spirit that enters and possesses the body of a living person until exorcized.

dye /dʌɪ/ *n.* Also **†die.** [OE *dēah*, *dēag* f. Gmc. Obs. after ME until re-formed f. the vb in L16.] 1 Colour produced by or as by dyeing; shade, hue, tinge. Now chiefly *fig.* OE. 2 A (natural or synthetic) substance used for dyeing; *esp.* a colouring matter used in solution. OE.

1 J. WILSON Wings and crests of rainbow dyes. C. STEAD Not a householder in Annapolis but considered Eastport a civic disgrace of deep dye. 2 *New Scientist* Whereas dyes react with material at a molecular level, pigments are generally macromolecular. *adjective dye*: see ADJECTIVE *a.* 2. *basic dye*: see BASIC *a.* 2. *direct dye*: see DIRECT *a.*

Comb.: **dye-house** a building in which a dyer works; **dye laser** a tunable laser using the fluorescence of an organic dye; **dye-line** (a print made by) the diazo process; **dyestuff, dyeware** (a substance yielding) a dye; **dye-wood**: yielding a dye.

dye /dʌɪ/ *v.* Also **†die.** Pa. t. & pple **dyed**; pres. pple **dyeing.** [OE *dēagian* perh. of Gmc origin. Not recorded again until LME.] 1 *v.t.* Colour, stain, tinge, suffuse; *esp.* impregnate with colouring matter, change the colour of by means of a (natural or synthetic) colouring material in solution. With compl.: make (a thing) a specified colour (thus), or *of*, *into*, *to* a colour. OE. b *v.i.* or w. compl. only: (have the ability to) impart colour to a thing. LME. 2 *v.i.* Take a colour (well or badly) in the process of dyeing. L19.

1 J. GALSWORTHY Swithin stared at her; a dusky orange dyed his cheeks. DYLAN THOMAS Mrs Beynon's new mauve jumper, it's her old grey jumper dyed. F. WELDON Colleen dyed her white . . shirt bright red. **dyed-in-(the-)grain** (*a*) dyed in kermes; dyed in any fast colour; dyed in the fibre or thoroughly; (*b*) *fig.* = *dyed-in-(the-)wool* (b). **dyed-in-(the-)wool** (*a*) *lit.* (now *rare*) dyed while the material is in a raw state, and hence more thoroughly and permanently; (*b*) *fig.* unchangeable, inveterate. b J. LINDLEY Genista tinctoria . . Dyes yellow.

dyeable /ˈdʌɪəb(ə)l/ *a.* M20. [f. prec. + -ABLE.] Able to be dyed.

dyea'bility *n.* M20.

dyer /ˈdʌɪə/ *n.* LME. [f. DYE *v.* + -ER[1].] A person whose occupation is the dyeing of cloth etc.

In *possess.* in names of plants yielding dyes: **dyer's broom** = *dyer's greenweed* below. *dyer's greenweed*: see *greenweed* s.v. GREEN *a.* **dyer's rocket** the plant weld, *Reseda luteola.* **dyer's weed** (*a*) = *dyer's greenweed* above; (*b*) = *dyer's rocket* above.

dyery *n.* a place or building where dyeing is carried out M18.

dyester /ˈdʌɪstə/ *n.* Now *Sc. arch.* LME. [f. DYE *v.* + -STER.] = prec.

dying /ˈdʌɪɪŋ/ *vbl n.*[1] & *a.*[1] ME. [f. DIE *v.*[1] + -ING[1].] A *n.* The action of DIE *v.*[1] ME.

B *attrib.* or as *adj.* [freq. identified w. next]. Of or connected with death or dying; done, occurring, or (of words, a wish, etc.) expressed at the time of death. L16.

dying oath made at, or with the solemnity proper to, death. **to** or **until one's dying day** for the rest of one's life.

dying /ˈdʌɪɪŋ/ *ppl a.*[2] & *n.*[2] LME. [f. DIE *v.*[1] + -ING[2].] A *ppl a.* That dies; at the point of death; mortal; *fig.* that ends, ceases, fades. LME.

dying god: whose death is commemorated annually, typifying the seasonal death of vegetation.

B *absol.* as *n.pl.* The people who are dying. L18.

dyingly *adv.* in a dying manner, in dying LME. **dyingness** *n.* dying or languishing quality E18.

dyke /dʌɪk/ *n.*[1] Also **dike.** ME. [ON *dík*, *díki* or (branch II) MLG *dīk* dam, MDu. *dijc* ditch, pool, mound, dam (Du. *dijk* dam): see DITCH *n.*] I Something dug out. †1 A long narrow excavation, a ditch (as a boundary-marker, defensive measure, etc.). ME–L16. †2 Any hollow dug in the ground; a pit, cave, etc. ME–L15. 3 A hollow dug out to hold or conduct water; a drainage ditch; any watercourse or channel. LME. 4 A lavatory. *slang.* E20.

3 POPE Thames, The King of dykes!

II Something built up. 5†a The wall of a city; a fortification. ME–M16. b A low wall of turf or stone serving as a division or enclosure. LME. 6 A bank formed by throwing up the earth from a ditch. L15. 7 A (raised) causeway. L15. 8 An embankment, long ridge, or dam against flooding, esp. as built in the Netherlands against the sea. M17. 9 *fig.* A barrier, an obstacle, a defence. L18. 10a *Mining.* A fissure filled with rock; a fault. *dial.* L18. b *Geol.* A sheet of rock filling a fissure; *esp.* a mass of igneous rock that has intruded upwards through strata, sometimes showing as a ridge at the surface. E19.

5b R. SIBBALD The Ruins of a dry-stone dyke. 8 J. A. MICHENER He might by building a dyke hold back the wadi and prevent it from washing away the fields. 9 BYRON He there builds up a formidable dyke Between his own and others' intellect.

Comb.: **dyke-reeve** [perh. alt. of DYKE-GRAVE] *Hist.* an officer who had charge of the drains and sea banks in fenland counties.

dyke /dʌɪk/ *n.*[2] *slang. derog.* Also **dike.** M20. [Origin unkn.: cf. BULL-DIKE, earlier BULL-DIKER.] A (masculine) lesbian; a masculine woman.

dykey *a.* having the appearance or characteristics of a lesbian M20.

dyke /dʌɪk/ *v.* Also **dike.** ME. [f. DYKE *n.*[1]: cf. DITCH *v.*] 1 *v.i.* Make a dyke, ditch, or excavation; dig. ME. 2 *v.t.* Provide with a dyke or dykes, for defence or (later) as a protection against flooding or to improve drainage. ME. 3 *v.t.* Clean out (a ditch or watercourse). Now *rare* or *obs.* E16.

dyker *n.* a person who constructs or works at dykes OE.

dyke-grave /ˈdʌɪkgreɪv/ *n.* Also **dike-.** M16. [MDu. *dijcgrave*, f. *dijc* (see DYKE *n.*[1]) + *grave* (mod. *graaf*) GRAVE *n.*[2]] *Hist.* A dyke-reeve; an officer in the Netherlands with similar duties.

dynameter /dʌɪˈnamɪtə/ *n.* E19. [f. Gk *dunamis*: see next, -METER.] = DYNAMOMETER 2.

dynamic /dʌɪˈnamɪk/ *a.* & *n.* E19. [Fr. *dynamique* f. Gk *dunamikos*, f. *dunamis* force, power: see -IC.] A *adj.* 1 Of or relating to force producing motion (opp. *static*). E19. b Of or pertaining to the science of dynamics. M19. 2 *Philos.* Of or relating to dynamism (DYNAMISM 1). E19. 3 Active, potent, energetic, forceful; characterized by action or change. M19. 4 *Med.* Affecting bodily function, as opp. to causing pathological organic change. M19. 5 *Mus.*, *Electronics*, etc. Of or relating to the volume of sound produced by a voice, instrument, or sound recording equipment. L19. 6 *Computing.* Of a memory or store: orig., having a moving component; now usu., depending on an applied voltage to refresh it periodically. M20.

1 J. TYNDALL According to the dynamic view . . heat is regarded as a motion. 3 C. P. MASON The adjective is a static attribute, the verb is a dynamic attribute. M. MCCARTHY Kay and Harald were too busy and dynamic to let convention cramp their style. J. BARNES Adolescence is a dynamic period, the mind and body thrusting forward to new discoveries all the time. 5 A. HOPKINS Dynamic marks . . . the technical term for *f*, *p*, *ff*, *mf*, etc. *Gramophone* It sounds . . wider in dynamic range . . than most broadcasts of that period.

Special collocations: **dynamic equilibrium** a state of balance between continuing processes. **dynamic friction**: between surfaces in relative motion. **dynamic metamorphism** *Geol.*: produced by mechanical forces. **dynamic pressure**: due to the motion of a fluid. **dynamic range** the difference between the softest and loudest levels of recorded sound etc. *dynamic viscosity*: see VISCOSITY 2.

B *n.* †1 = DYNAMICS 1. Only in L19. 2 An energizing or a motive force. L19. 3 = DYNAMICS 3. M20.

2 H. KISSINGER It could no longer conquer the world. . . The dynamic had gone. T. O'BRIEN Sarah . . understood the dynamic of our age. It was all escalation.

dynamical /dʌɪˈnamɪk(ə)l/ *a.* E19. [f. as prec. + -ICAL.] 1 = DYNAMIC *a.* 1. E19. 2 *Theol.* Of or relating to inspiration as endowing with divine power rather than promoting mechanical action. M19. 3 *Philos.* = DYNAMIC *a.* 2. M19. 4 *Med.* = DYNAMIC *a.* 4. *rare.* M19.

dynamically /dʌɪˈnamɪk(ə)li/ *adv.* M19. [f. DYNAMIC *a.* or prec.: see -ICALLY.] In a dynamic or dynamical manner; as regards dynamics.

dynamicist /dʌɪˈnamɪsɪst/ *n.* M20. [f. next + -IST.] An expert in or student of the science of dynamics.

dynamics /dʌɪˈnamɪks/ *n.pl.* L18. [f. as DYNAMIC: see -ICS.] 1 (Treated as *sing.*) The branch of mechanics that treats of motion in itself, and of the motion of bodies or matter under the influence of forces (including *kinematics* and *kinetics*: opp. *statics*). L18. b That branch of any science in which forces or changes are considered. M19. 2 The motive forces, physical or moral, in any sphere; the dynamic properties of a system. M19. 3 *Mus.*, *Electronics*, etc. The variation or amount of volume of sound in a musical performance, sound recording, etc. L19.

1b J. S. MILL Social Dynamics is the theory of society considered in a state of progressive movement. C. LYELL Those . . conversant with dynamics of glacier motion. 2 G. GORER This absence of overt aggression, calls for an explanation if the dynamics of English character are to be . . described. T. BARR Every scene should have some changes and dynamics in it. 3 A. COPLAND Merely by changing the dynamics . . one can transform the emotional feeling of the very same . . notes.

dynamise *v.* var. of DYNAMIZE.

dynamism /ˈdʌɪnəmɪz(ə)m/ *n.* M19. [f. Gk *dunamis* force, power + -ISM.] 1 *Philos.* Any system or theory which holds that the phenomena of matter or mind are due merely to the action of forces. M19. 2 Dynamic character, the operation of force; energizing action or power; energy, drive. M19.

dynamist *n.* (*a*) = DYNAMICIST; (*b*) an adherent of philosophical dynamism: M19. **dyna'mistic** *a.* L19.

dynamitard /dʌɪnəmɪˈtɑːd/ *n.* Now *rare.* L19. [f. DYNAMITE after *communard*, prob. after Fr. (obs., rare).] = DYNAMITER (b).

dynamite /ˈdʌɪnəmʌɪt/ *n.*, *v.*, & *a.* M19. [f. Gk *dunamis* force, power + -ITE[1].] A *n.* 1 A high explosive consisting of nitroglycerine absorbed in an inert material such as kieselguhr. M19. 2 *fig.* Something or someone potentially dangerous, disruptive, or devastating to an opponent etc. E20. 3 Heroin or a similar drug. *slang.* E20.

2 *Guardian* Withdrawal may be political dynamite. J. DIDION We've got a new Arabian at the ranch. . . Pereira blue mare, dynamite.

B *v.t.* Blow up, wreck, or charge with dynamite or a similar explosive. L19.

C *adj.* Powerful; explosive; extraordinarily good. *slang.* M20.

dynamiter *n.* (*a*) a person who employs dynamite or a similar explosive; (*b*) *spec.* a person who causes explosions as a means of attacking a government or political system: L19.

dynamize /ˈdʌɪnəmʌɪz/ *v.t.* Also **-ise**. M19. [f. DYNAMIC + -IZE.] Endow with power; make (more) dynamic. Orig. *spec.* in *Homoeopathy*, make (a medicine) more active by pulverizing or shaking.

dynamiˈzation *n.* M19.

dynamo /ˈdʌɪnəməʊ/ *n.* Pl. **-os**. L19. [Abbrev. of *dynamo-electric machine* (see next).] 1 A machine which converts mechanical energy into electric energy by electric induction, usu. by a rotating conductor in a magnetic field. L19. 2 *fig.* & *transf.* Something or someone very energetic or active; a source of power energizing a system; *esp.* the postulated system of circulating electric currents within the earth's core which is believed to generate the earth's magnetic field. L19.

2 D. OGILVY I have to rely on .. empirical techniques for spotting creative dynamos. E. J. KORMONDY The turnover of phosphorus may be .. sufficient to turn the ecosystem dynamo.

dynamo- /ˈdʌɪnəməʊ/ *comb. form* of Gk *dunamis* force, power: see -O-.

dynamo-eˈlectric *a.* of or pertaining to the conversion of mechanical to electric energy; *dynamo-electric machine* (now *Hist.*) = DYNAMO 1: L19. **dynamoˈgenesis**, **dynaˈmogeny** *ns.* the generation of (increased) nervous or mental activity L19. **dynamometaˈmorphism** *n.* (*Geol.*) = *dynamic metamorphism* s.v. DYNAMIC *a.* L19.

dynamometer /dʌɪnəˈmɒmɪtə/ *n.* E19. [Fr. *dynamomètre*, f. as prec. + -METER.] 1 An instrument for measuring the mechanical energy exerted by an animal, engine, etc., or by the action of a force. E19. 2 An instrument for measuring the magnifying power of a telescope. M19.

Comb.: **dynamometer car** a railway vehicle containing equipment for measuring and recording the performance of a locomotive pulling the vehicle.

dynamoˈmetric(al) *adjs.* of or pertaining to the measurement of force or the use of a dynamometer M19. **dynamometry** *n.* L19.

dynamotor /ˈdʌɪnəməʊtə/ *n.* E20. [f. Gk *dunamis* force, power + MOTOR *n.*] A form of rotary converter combining an electric motor and a generator.

dynast /ˈdɪnəst, ˈdʌɪnəst, -ast/ *n.* M17. [L *dynastes* f. Gk *dunastēs*, f. *dunasthai* be able, be powerful.] A person in (esp. hereditary) power, a ruler; a member or founder of a dynasty.

dynastic /dɪˈnastɪk, dʌɪ-/ *n.* & *a.* E17. [Gk *dunastikos*, f. *dunastēs*: see prec., -IC.] †A *n.* = prec. Only in E17. B *adj.* Of, pertaining to, or connected with a dynasty or dynasties. E19.

dynastical *a.* = DYNASTIC M18. **dynastically** *adv.* M19. **dynasticism** /-sɪz(ə)m/ *n.* the dynastic principle, the system of ruling dynasties L19.

dynasty /ˈdɪnəsti/ *n.* LME. [Fr. *dynastie* or late L *dynastia* f. Gk *dunasteia* power, domination, f. *dunastēs*: see DYNAST, -Y[3].] †1 Lordship, sovereignty, power; régime. LME–M19. 2 A succession of hereditary rulers; a line or family of monarchs. LME. 3 A succession of leaders in any sphere; a prominent family spanning a number of generations. E19.

dyne /dʌɪn/ *n.* L19. [Fr., f. Gk *dunamis* force, power.] *Physics.* The unit of force in the centimetre-gram-second system, equal to 10^{-5} newton; the force that, acting on a mass of one gram, gives the mass an acceleration of one centimetre per second per second.

dynode /ˈdʌɪnəʊd/ *n.* M20. [f. as prec. + -ODE[2].] *Physics.* An electrode which emits secondary electrons, used in electron multipliers etc.

Dyophysite /dʌɪˈɒfɪsʌɪt/ *n.* M19. [Late Gk *duophusitai*, f. *duo* two + *phusis* nature.] *Theol.* A person who holds the doctrine of the coexistence of two natures, divine and human, in Christ. Cf. MONOPHYSITE.

Dyothelite /dʌɪˈɒθɪlʌɪt/ *n.* Also **-lete** /-liːt/. M19. [f. Gk *duo* two + *thelētēs* agent-n. f. *thelein* to will + -ITE[1], after MONOTHELITE.] *Theol.* A person who holds the (orthodox) doctrine that Jesus had two wills, divine and human. Cf. MONOTHELITE.

dypsomania *n.* var. of DIPSOMANIA.

dys- /dɪs/ *pref.* [Gk *dus-*, cogn. w. Skt *dus-*, OHG *zūr-* (G *zer-*), ON *tor-*, OE TO-[2].] Forming ns. and adjs. w. the sense 'bad, difficult, unfavourable, abnormal, impaired' (opp. EU-). In *Med.*, often w. counterparts of related meaning in A-[10].

dyˈsarthria *n.* difficult or unclear articulation of (otherwise normal) speech L19. **dyscalˈculia** *n.* severe difficulty in calculation, as a result of cerebral disorder M20. **dyschezia** /dɪsˈkiːzɪə/ *n.* [Gk *khezein* defecate] difficult or painful defecation M19. **dyskiˈnesia** *n.* an abnormality or impairment of voluntary movement E18. **dysˈlalia** *n.* a speech disorder, *esp.* one in which a person uses words or sounds peculiar to himself or herself M19. **dysˈphonia** *n.* difficulty in speaking due to a disorder of the throat, mouth, or vocal organs E18. **dysˈphotic** *a.* (of ocean depths etc.) receiving insufficient light to bring about photosynthesis E20. **dysˈprosody** *n.* abnormality of speech inflection, stress, and rhythm, occurring in aphasia M20. **dysˈrhythmia** *n.* an abnormality of physiological rhythm, esp. in the electrical activity of the brain E20. **dysˈrhythmic** *a.* of or pertaining to dysrhythmia M20. **dysteleoˈlogical** *a.* of, pertaining to, or marked by dysteleology M19. **dysteleˈology** *n.* the denial of final causes or purpose in natural phenomena (opp. TELEOLOGY); biological study conforming to this viewpoint: M19. **dysˈthymia** *n.* [Gk *dusthumia*] *Psychiatry* depression, despondency M19. **dysˈthymic** *a.* (*Psychiatry*) of, pertaining to, or suffering from dysthymia M20.

dysaesthesia /dɪsɪsˈθiːzɪə/ *n.* Also *__dysesth-__. Pl. **-iae** /-iiː/. E18. [mod.L f. Gk *dusaisthēsia*, f. *dus-* DYS- + *anaisthēsia* ANAESTHESIA.] *Med.* An abnormal (unpleasant) sensation felt when touched, caused by disease or dysfunction of sensory tracts or peripheral nerves; the state of having sensations of this kind. Cf. PARAESTHESIA.

dyscrasia /dɪsˈkreɪsɪə, -zɪə/ *n.* LME. [Late L f. Gk *duskrasia* bad temperament or mixture, f. *dus-* DYS- + *krasis* CRASIS: see -IA[1]. Cf. DYSCRASY.] *Med.* Orig., an imbalance of humours, a distemper. Now, any abnormal or disordered state of the body or bodily part.

dyscrasic *a.* of the nature of, pertaining to, or affected by dyscrasia L19.

dyscrasite /ˈdɪskrəsʌɪt/ *n.* M19. [f. Gk *duskrasia*: see prec., -ITE[1].] *Min.* A native alloy of antimony and silver belonging to the orthorhombic system and usu. occurring as masses of pyramidal crystals.

†**dyscrasy** *n.* LME–M19. [Partly f. as DYSCRASIA, partly f. OFr. *dyscrasie*: see -Y[3].] = DYSCRASIA.

dysenteric /dɪsɛnˈtɛrɪk/ *n.* & *a.* LME. [L *dysentericus* f. Gk *dusenterikos*, f. *dusenteria*: see next, -IC.] †A *n.* Dysentery, or a disorder associated with it. Only in LME. B *adj.* Of, pertaining to, or of the nature of dysentery; affected with or suffering from dysentery. E18.

†**dysenterical** *a.*: only in 17.

dysentery /ˈdɪs(ə)nt(ə)ri/ *n.* LME. [OFr. *dissenterie* or L *dysenteria* f. Gk *dusenteria*, f. *dusenteros* afflicted in the bowels, f. *dus-* DYS- + *entera* bowels: see -Y[3].] Inflammation of the mucous membranes of the large intestine, with griping pains, diarrhoea, and evacuation of mucus and blood. Now *spec.* this condition as a result of bacterial or amoebic infection.

dysesthesia *n.* see DYSAESTHESIA.

dysfunction /dɪsˈfʌŋkʃ(ə)n/ *n.* Also **dis-**. E20. [f. DYS- + FUNCTION *n.*] Orig. & chiefly *Med.* An abnormality or impairment of function.

A. KOESTLER I have never had any glandular disfunction. A. BURGESS The heating was in a state of dysfunction.

dysfunctional *a.* M20. **dysfunctionally** *adv.* M20.

dysgenic /dɪsˈdʒɛnɪk/ *a.* E20. [f. DYS- + -GENIC.] Exerting a detrimental effect on later generations; tending to racial degeneration. Opp. EUGENIC.

dysgenically *adv.* M20. **dysgenics** *n.* (the branch of knowledge that deals with) racial degeneration E20.

dysgraphia /dɪsˈgrafɪə/ *n.* M20. [f. DYS- + Gk *graphia* writing.] Difficulty in writing coherently, as a symptom of cerebral disease or damage. Cf. AGRAPHIA.

dysgraphic *a.* & *n.* (*a*) *adj.* of, pertaining to, or affected with dysgraphia; (*b*) *n.* a person affected with dysgraphia: M20.

dyslexia /dɪsˈlɛksɪə/ *n.* L19. [f. DYS- + Gk *lexis* speech (conf. w. L *legere* read) + -IA[1].] A developmental disorder marked by extreme difficulty in reading, or in understanding written words; word-blindness. Cf. ALEXIA.

dyslectic *a.* & *n.* = DYSLEXIC M20. **dyslexic** *a.* & *n.* (*a*) *adj.* of, pertaining to, or affected with dyslexia; (*b*) *n.* a person affected with dyslexia: M20.

dyslogistic /dɪsləˈdʒɪstɪk/ *a.* E19. [f. DYS- + EULOGISTIC.] Expressing disapproval, having a bad connotation, opprobrious.

dyslogistically *adv.* M19. **ˈdyslogy** *n.* (*rare*) censure, disparagement M19.

dysmenorrhoea /ˌdɪsmɛnəˈriːə/ *n.* Also *__-rrhea__. E19. [f. DYS- + MENORRHOEA.] *Med.* Painful menstruation.

dysmenorrhoeal *a.* = DYSMENORRHOEIC M19. **dysmenorrhoeic** *a.* of, pertaining to, or affected with dysmenorrhoea L19.

dyspareunia /dɪspəˈruːnɪə/ *n.* L19. [f. DYS- + Gk *pareunos* lying with, f. *para* beside + *eunē* bed: see -IA[1].] *Med.* Difficult or painful sexual intercourse.

dyspathy /ˈdɪspəθi/ *n.* M16. [Fr. †*dispathie*, taken as the opposite of Gk *sumpatheia* SYMPATHY.] †1 *Med.* Non-susceptibility to a disease. Only in M16. 2 Antipathy, dislike; disagreement of feeling. Opp. *sympathy.* E17.

dyspepsia /dɪsˈpɛpsɪə/ *n.* E18. [L f. Gk *duspepsia*, f. *duspeptos* difficult of digestion, f. *dus-* DYS- + *peptos* cooked, digested: see -IA[1].] Indigestion; abdominal pain or discomfort associated with taking food.

Also **dyspepsy** *n.* (now *rare*) M17.

dyspeptic /dɪsˈpɛptɪk/ *a.* & *n.* L17. [f. Gk *duspeptos*: see prec., -IC.] A *adj.* †1 Indigestible; causing dyspepsia. *rare.* Only in L17. 2 Of or pertaining to dyspepsia; subject to or suffering from dyspepsia; despondent (as) through dyspepsia. E19. B *n.* A person subject to or suffering from dyspepsia. E19.

dyspeptical *a.* (*rare*) = DYSPEPTIC *a.* 2 E19. **dyspeptically** *adv.* M19.

dysphagia /dɪsˈfeɪdʒɪə, -dʒə/ *n.* L18. [mod.L, f. Gk *dus-* DYS- + -PHAGIA.] *Med.* Difficulty in swallowing, as a symptom of disease.

dysphemia /dɪsˈfiːmɪə/ *n.* L19. [Gk *dusphēmia* evil language, f. *dus-* DYS- + *phēmē* speaking: see -IA[1].] *Med.* Stammering.

dysphemism /ˈdɪsfɪmɪz(ə)m/ *n.* L19. [f. DYS- after *euphemism*.] The substitution of a derogatory or unpleasant term for a pleasant or neutral one; a term so used. Opp. EUPHEMISM.

dyspheˈmistic *a.* M20.

dysphoria /dɪsˈfɔːrɪə/ *n.* M19. [Gk *dusphoria* malaise, discomfort, f. *dusphoros* hard to bear, f. *dus-* DYS- + *pherein* to bear: see -IA[1].] A state of unease or discomfort; *esp.* an unpleasant state of mind marked by malaise, depression, or anxiety. Opp. EUPHORIA.

dysphoric *a.* M20.

dysplasia /dɪsˈpleɪzɪə/ *n.* E20. [f. DYS- + -PLASIA.] *Med.* Abnormal growth or development of body tissue.

dysˈplastic *a.* of, pertaining to, or characterized by dysplasia E20.

dyspnoea /dɪspˈniːə/ *n.* Also *__-pnea__. M17. [L f. Gk *duspnoia*, f. *dus-* DYS- + *pnoē* breathing: see -A[1].] *Med.* Difficulty in breathing or shortness of breath, as a symptom of disease.

dyspnoeal *a.* = DYSPNOEIC L19. **dyspnoeic** *a.* of, pertaining to, or affected with dyspnoea M19.

dysprosium /dɪsˈprəʊzɪəm/ *n.* L19. [f. Gk *dusprositos* difficult of access + -IUM.] *Chem.* A metallic chemical element, atomic no. 66, of the lanthanide series. (Symbol Dy.)

dyss /dɪs/ *n.* Also **dysse**. Pl. **dysser** /'dɪsə/. M20. [Da. *dysse.*] *Archaeol.* A megalithic chambered tomb of a kind found in Denmark.

dystocia /dɪs'təʊsɪə/ *n.* Also **-ch-** /-k-/. E18. [Gk *dustokia.*] *Med.* Difficult or abnormally painful childbirth.
dystocial *a.* E19.

dystonia /dɪs'təʊnɪə/ *n.* E20. [f. DYS- + TONE *n.* + -IA[1].] *Med.* A state of abnormal muscle tone; *esp.* a postural disorder marked by spasm of the trunk, neck, shoulders or limbs and due to disease of the basal ganglia of the brain.
dystonic *a.* E20.

dystopia /dɪs'təʊpɪə/ *n.* L18. [f. DYS- + UTOPIA.] An imaginary place or condition in which everything is as bad as possible. Opp. UTOPIA.
¶In isolated nonce uses bef. M20.
dystopian *a.* & *n.* M19.

dystrophia /dɪs'trəʊfɪə/ *n.* L19. [f. Gk *dus-* DYS- + *-trophia* nourishment.] *Med.* Impaired nourishment of a bodily part; any unexplained abnormality of tissue. Cf. DYSTROPHY.
dystrophia myotonica /mʌɪə'tɒnɪkə/ a form of dominantly inherited muscular dystrophy accompanied by myotonia.

dystrophic /dɪs'trɒfɪk, -'trəʊf-/ *a.* L19. [f. as prec. + -IC. In sense 2 f. G *dystroph.*] **1** *Med.* Of, pertaining to, or affected with dystrophia or (muscular) dystrophy. L19. **2** Of a lake: having brown water due to the presence of much dissolved organic matter and little oxygen. M20.

dystrophy /'dɪstrəfi/ *n.* L19. [f. as DYSTROPHIA: see -TROPHY.] *Med.* = DYSTROPHIA. Chiefly in *muscular dystrophy*, any of a group of hereditary diseases marked by progressive wasting of certain muscles.

dysuria /dɪs'jʊərɪə/ *n.* LME. [Late L *dysuria* f. Gk *dusouria*, f. *dus-* DYS- + *ouron* urine: see -IA[1]. Cf. next.] *Med.* Painful or difficult urination.
dysuric *a.* of, pertaining to, or affected with dysuria M19.

†**dysury** *n.* E16–M19. [Partly f. as prec., partly f. OFr. *dissurie*: see -Y[3].] = prec.

dytiscid /dɪ'tɪskɪd, -sɪd/ *n.* & *a.* M19. [f. as next: see -ID[3].] *Entomol.* **A** *n.* Pl. **-ids, -ides** /-ɪdiːz/. A member of the family Dytiscidae, which includes most water-beetles (including *Dytiscus*). M19. **B** *adj.* Of, pertaining to, or designating this family. L19.

dytiscus /dɪ'tɪskəs/ *n.* M19. [mod.L (see below), irreg. f. Gk *dutikos* able to dive, f. *duein* to dive.] *Entomol.* A member of the genus *Dytiscus* of large carnivorous water-beetles; *esp.* the great diving beetle, *D. marginalis.*

dyvour /'dʌɪvə/ *n. Sc.* L15. [Origin unkn.] A bankrupt; a debtor; a beggar.

dzho *n.* var. of DZO.

dziggetai /'dzɪgətʌɪ, 'dʒɪg-/ *n.* L18. [Mongolian *chikitei*, having ears, eared, f. *chiki* ear.] = KYANG.

dzo /ʒəʊ, zəʊ/ *n.* Also **dzho, zho, zo**. Pl. **-os**, same. M19. [Tib. *mdso.*] A hybrid between a yak and a domestic cow.

dzong *n.* var. of JONG *n.*[2]

Dzongkha /'dzɒŋkə/ *n.* E20. [Tib.] A form of Tibetan used as the official language of Bhutan.

E

E, e /iː/, the fifth letter of the modern Eng. alphabet and of the ancient Roman one, repr. the Semitic ∃ (= *h*), but adopted by the Greeks (and from them by the Romans) as a vowel. The sound orig. represented by the letter probably varied from a mid-front to a low front vowel. For its principal mod. sounds see the Key to the Pronunciation. Pl. **ees, E's, Es.**

I 1 The letter and its sound. **2** The shape of the letter.

2 E-shaped *a.* having a shape or a cross-section like the capital letter E.

II Symbolical uses. **3** Used to denote serial order; applied e.g. to the fifth group or section, sheet of a book, etc. **4** *Mus.* (Cap. E.) The third note of the diatonic scale of C major. Also, the scale of a composition with E as its keynote. **5** *Logic.* (Cap. E.) A proposition which is universal and negative. **6** The fifth hypothetical person or example. **7** *Math.* (Italic *e.*) The irrational number 2.71828..., equal to the limit of $(1 + 1/n)^n$ as *n* tends to infinity; the sum $1 + 1/1! + 1/2! + 1/3! + 1/4! + \ldots$, where ! denotes a factorial. **8** (Usu. cap. E.) Designating the fifth highest class (of academic marks, etc.). **9** *E-layer*, a stratum of the ionosphere between the lowest (D-) and highest (F-) layers, able to reflect long radio waves. Also called *Heaviside layer, Kennelly(-Heaviside) layer*.

III 10 Abbrevs.: (A small selection only is given here. Those all in caps. or small caps. also occur with a full stop after each letter; some of those all in caps. also occur (i) with initial cap. only, (ii) in small caps.) **E.** = east(ern); *slang* ecstasy (the drug); Egyptian; Engineering; European (as *e* or *E*, printed on packets to denote that the weight is one that complies with a relevant European Community directive; in *E number*, (a code number preceded by the letter E, assigned to) an additive that accords with EC Food Additive directives); (as *pref.*) exa-. **E, e** (*Physics*) = energy. **ea.** = each. **E. & O.E.** = errors and omissions excepted. **EBCDIC** /ˈɛbsɪdɪk/ = Extended Binary Coded Decimal Interchange Code, a standard 8-bit character code used in computing and data transmission. **EC** = East Central; European Commission; European Community; Executive Committee. **Eccles.** = Ecclesiastes (in the Bible). **Ecclus** = Ecclesiasticus (Apocrypha). **ECG** = electrocardiogram. **E. coli** = *Escherichia coli* (see COLI). **Econ.** = Economics. **ECT** = electroconvulsive therapy. **ed.** /ɛd/ = edited (by); edition; editor; educated (at); education. **EDD** = English Dialect Dictionary. **EDP** = electronic data processing. **EDT** (*US*) = Eastern Daylight Time. **EDTA** (*Chem.*) = ethylenediamine tetra-acetic acid, a crystalline acid, $(CH_2COOH)_2NCH_2CH_2N(CH_2COOH)_2$, widely used as a chelating agent, esp. in the form of its salts. **Edw.** = Edward. **EE** = Early English. **EEC** = European Economic Community. **EEG** = electroencephalogram. **EETPU** = Electrical, Electronic, Telecommunications, and Plumbing Union. **EFL** = English as a foreign language. **EFTA** /ˈɛftə/ = European Free Trade Association. **EFTPOS** = electronic funds transfer at point-of-sale. **e.g.** = [L] *exempli gratia* for example. **EGA** (*Computing*) = enhanced graphics adapter. **ELT** = English language teaching. **EMF, emf** = electromotive force. **EMG** = electromyogram. **EMS** = European Monetary System. **EMU** = Economic and (or European) Monetary Union. **e.m.u.** = electromagnetic unit(s). **encl.** = enclosed; enclosure. **ENE** = east-north-east. **ENG** = electronic news-gathering. **Eng. Tech.** = Engineering Technician. **ENSA** /ˈɛnsə/ (*Hist.*) = Entertainments National Service Association, an organization which served to arrange entertainments for the British armed services during the war of 1939–45. **ENT** = ear, nose, and throat. **EOC** = Equal Opportunities Commission. **EOG** = electro-oculogram. **EOKA** /eɪˈəʊkə/ (*Hist.*) = [Gk] *Ethnikē Organōsis Kupriakou Agōnos* National Organization of Cypriot Struggle, an underground movement for furthering the Greek cause in Cyprus in the 1950s. **EP** = electroplate(d); extended-play (record). **Ep.** = Epistle. **e.p.** (*Chess*) = en passant. **EPA** (*US*) = Environmental Protection Agency. **Eph.** = Ephesians (New Testament). **EPNS** = electroplated nickel silver. **EPOS** = electronic point-of-sale. **ER** = [L] *Edwardus Rex* King Edward; [L] *Elizabetha Regina* Queen Elizabeth. **Er** (*Chem.*) = erbium. **ERA** (*US*) = (*Baseball*) earned run average; Equal Rights Amendment. **ERM** = Exchange Rate Mechanism. **ERNIE** /ˈəːni/ = electronic random number indicator equipment, the device used for drawing the prize-winning numbers of premium bonds. **Es** (*Chem.*) = einsteinium. **ESA** = environmentally sensitive area; European Space Agency. **Esd.** = Esdras (Apocrypha). **ESE** = east-south-east. **ESN** = educationally subnormal. **ESP** = extrasensory perception; English for special purposes. **Esq.** = Esquire. **ESR** (*Physics*) = electron spin resonance. **EST** = (*US*) Eastern Standard Time; electro-shock (or electric shock) treatment. **Esth.** = Esther (in the Bible & Apocrypha). **e.s.u.** = electrostatic unit(s). **ET** = extraterrestrial (being). **ETA** = estimated time of arrival; /ˈɛtə/ = [Basque] *Euzkadi ta Azkatasuna* Basque Homeland and Liberty, a Basque separatist organization active in Spain from the 1960s. **etc.** = et cetera. **ETD** = estimated time of departure. **Eu** (*Chem.*) = europium. **eV** = electronvolt. **EVA** (*Astronaut.*) = extravehicular activity. **ex div.** (*Comm.*) = ex dividend. **Exod.** = Exodus (in the Bible). **exor.** = executor. **ext.** = exterior; external. **Ezek.** = Ezekiel (in the Bible).

e- /ɪ, ɛ/ *pref.* Repr. L *e-* var. of EX-[1] bef. consonants exc. *c, f, h, p, q, s, t*. Also used (in preference to *ex-*) to form adjs. (chiefly in -ATE[2]) with non-Latin sense 'not having, deprived of', as *ecaudate*.

ea /iːə/ *n.* Long *obs.* exc. *dial.* Also **eau** /əʊ/. [OE *ēa*. Var. as if f. Fr. *eau* water.] A stream, a watercourse; a drainage canal, a sewer.

each /iːtʃ/ *a.* (in mod. usage also classed as a *determiner*) & *pron.* [OE *ǣlċ* = OFris. *ellik, elk, ek*, MLG *ellik*, MDu. *elic, ellic*, (M)LG, (M)Du. *elk*, OHG *eogilīh* (G *jeglich*), f. WGmc phr. = ever alike, f. as AYE *adv.*[1] + ALIKE *a.*] **A** *adj.* Used bef. a sing. n. to give the same sense in relation to individuals as does *both* or *all* bef. the pl. n. in relation to the category or aggregate of them (almost = EVERY, but with reference rather to the separate members). (Preceding the n. and adjs., but bef. the def. article or possess. adjs. Formerly also w. *a(n)* interposed bef. the n.) OE.

E. YOUNG Each night we die, Each morn are born anew. J. CONRAD Each day of the ship's life. W. FAULKNER Creeping up toward the collar . . and across toward each armpit. **each and every** — every single —. **each way** *Betting* to win or to be placed.

B *pron.* **1** Each one, each person: referring individually to things or people previously specified or implied, or following (after *of*). OE. **2** Distributed or in relation to each member of an aggregate. Freq. with ref. to price: apiece, for each one. OE.

1 J. COULTER They each have long spades. S. T. WARNER He gave each of the islanders a ginger-bread nut. SCOTT FITZGERALD They were sitting at different ends of the room, each wearing a green eye-shade. J. BUCHAN Wood, sea and hill . . have never lost their spell for me. But the spell of each was different. T. S. ELIOT I have heard the mermaids singing, each to each. G. GREENE Long tables with an urn at the end of each. C. P. SNOW Each thought the other a master of his trade. **all and each** (*arch.*), **each and all** all collectively and individually. **each other** (used as a compound reciprocal pron.) one another (in accus., dat., or genit.), each . . . the other, each . . . another. 2 DRYDEN Studious of Honey, each in his Degree. SHAFTESBURY We have each of us a daemon. OED I paid sixpence each for them. E. BAKER At every intersection old men held out eight arms each, pointing the ways to heaven. **each to each** with exact correspondence of members or parts.

¶Cf. EVERY, ILK *a.*[2] & *pron.*[2]

eager /ˈiːgə/ *a.* ME. [AN *egre*, (O)Fr. *aigre* f. Proto-Romance f. L *acer, acr-*.] **1** Sharply perceived by the taste or other senses; pungent, acrid; sharp, biting; sour, tart; (of air etc.) cold. Now *rare* or *obs.* ME. **2** Ardent, impetuous; fierce. *obs.* exc. *dial.* ME. **3** Of a person, an action, etc.: full of or manifesting keen desire or appetite; impatiently longing. ME. †**4** Hungry; hungry-looking. L15–M18. †**5** Of metal: brittle. L16–M18.

1 SHAKES. *Haml.* It is a nipping and an eager air. 3 G. BERKELEY Those gentlemen who are called men of pleasure, from their eager pursuit of it. TOLKIEN An eager light was in their eyes. W. GOLDING He was poor, hard-working, eager to improve himself. H. CARPENTER The greedy populace, eager for gold and jewels. *eager beaver*: see BEAVER *n.*[1]

eagerly *adv.* ME. **eagerness** *n.* LME.

eagle /ˈiːg(ə)l/ *n.* ME. [AN *egle*, (O)Fr. *aigle* f. L *aquila*.] **1** Any of various large diurnal birds of prey belonging to the family Accipitridae, renowned for keen vision and powerful flight. ME. **2** A representation or figure of an eagle, esp. as an ensign in the Roman or French imperial armies, or as an armorial bearing. ME. **b** *spec.* A figure of the bald eagle as the emblem of the United States; *the Eagle*, the US. L18. **3** An object, esp. a lectern, made in the form of an eagle. LME. **4** (Usu. **E-**.) *The* constellation Aquila. LME. **5** A coin bearing the image of an eagle; *esp.* a US gold coin worth ten dollars. M18. **6** *Golf.* A hole played in two strokes under par or bogey. E20.

1 *bateleur eagle, fish eagle, golden eagle, harpy eagle, sea-eagle*, etc. *bald eagle*: see BALD *a. legal eagle*: see LEGAL *a.* 2 *double eagle*: see DOUBLE *a.* & *adv.*

Comb.: **eagle-eye(d)** keen sight(ed); **eagle-hawk** *Austral. colloq.* the wedge-tailed eagle, *Aquila audax*; **eagle owl** any of several very large owls of the genus *Bubo*, with ear-tufts, esp. *B. bubo* of Eurasia and N. Africa; **eagle ray** any of various large rays which constitute the family Myliobatidae, with long pointed pectoral fins; spec. *Myliobatis aquila*, of the Mediterranean and eastern Atlantic; **eagle-stone** = AETITES.

eaglet *n.* a young eagle L16.

eagle /ˈiːg(ə)l/ *v.* M17. [f. the n.] **1** *v.i.* & *t.* (w. *it*). Fly like an eagle. *rare.* M17. **2** *v.t. Golf.* Play (a hole) in two strokes under par or bogey. M20.

eagle-wood /ˈiːg(ə)lwʊd/ *n.* E18. [tr. Port. *pao de aguila* wood of AGILA, confused w. L *aquila* eagle. Cf. Fr. *bois d'aigle*.] Aloes wood.

eagre /ˈeɪgə, ˈiː-/ *n.* E17. [Origin unkn.] A tidal bore in a river; now *esp.* that in the River Trent.

ealdorman *n.* see ALDERMAN.

Eames chair /ˈiːmz tʃɛː/ *n. phr.* M20. [f. *Eames* (see below) + CHAIR *n.*[1]] A chair designed by the US architect and designer Charles Eames (1907–78), or in the functional style popularized by him; *esp.* an office chair of moulded plastic and plywood. (Proprietary name.)

ean /iːn/ *v.t.* & *i.* [OE *ēanian* f. Gmc.] = YEAN. **eanling** *n.* a young lamb L16.

-ean /ˈiːən, ɪən/ *suff.* [f. L or Gk ending (see below) + -AN.] Forming adjs. (often used as ns.) w. the sense 'of, belonging to, characteristic of', chiefly Anglicizations of L adjs. in *-aeus, -eus,* and Gk adjs. in *-aios, -eios,* as *empyrean, Epicurean, Euclidean, European, Herculean, Jacobean, subterranean,* only rarely in Eng. formations (as *Caribbean, Tyrolean*) exc. where the root itself provides *-e-* (-IAN being more usual), as *Carlylean.* Often with parallel forms in -IAN.

ear /ɪə/ *n.*[1] [OE *ēare* = OFris. *āre,* OS, OHG *ōra* (Du. *oor,* G *Ohr*), ON *eyra,* Goth. *ausō,* f. Gmc, f. IE base also of L *auris,* Gk *ous, ōs.*] **I 1** The organ of hearing in humans and animals, considered with regard to its function or to its structure (in mammals divisible generally into the *external ear, middle ear,* and *inner ear:* see below). OE. **b** The imagined organ of hearing of the mind, the heart, or other quasi-personified object. LME. **2** *spec.* The external ear. OE. **3** Voluntary hearing, listening, attention. ME. **4** *sing.* & in *pl.* The sense of hearing; auditory perception. ME. **5** The faculty of discriminating sounds; esp. the ability to recognize musical intervals (more fully *ear for music, musical ear*). E16.

1 H. C. JACKSON Rumours have come to my ears. W. N. HODGSON The summons in our ears was shrill. *fig.:* T. H. WHITE He listened to their difficulties with an impatient ear. **b** *Proverb:* Walls have ears (i.e. there may be listeners anywhere). J. H. BURTON The illustrious Eastern conqueror, whose name fills the ear of fame. **2** J. T. FARRELL Plunked in here all afternoon without even room to wriggle my ears. **3** C. CHAPLIN Mother . . kept an alert ear on the way we talked, correcting our grammar. **4** CHESTERFIELD Most people have ears, but few have judgement. **5** P. H. NEWBY I understand Arabic. I've an ear for languages.

II An object resembling the external ear in appearance, shape, position, or function. **6** An atrium of the heart. LME–L17. **7** The handle of a drinking-vessel, bottle, etc. LME. **8** A projection on the side of a tool or a piece of machinery, serving as a support, handle, etc. L16. **9** *Zool.* & *Bot.* = AURICLE 3. L17. **10** In *pl.* A citizens'-band radio; its aerial. Chiefly in *have one's ears on. US slang.* L20.

Phrases: **about one's ears** down upon oneself. **all ears** eagerly attentive. *a word in a person's ear:* see WORD *n.* BELIEVE *one's ear(s). bend someone's ear:* see BEND *v. cauliflower ear:* see CAULIFLOWER *n.* **close one's ears** refuse to listen. CLOTH *ears. cock one's* (or *the*) *ears:* see COCK *v.*[1] 6. **dry behind the ears** mature, experienced. *ear for music:* see sense 5 above. **external ear** the pinna, with or without the meatus leading to the eardrum. *fall on deaf ears:* see DEAF *a.* 3. **fall on someone's ear(s)** be heard by someone. **gain the ear of** obtain the favourable attention of. *get the right* (or *wrong*) *sow by the ear:* see SOW *n.*[1] **give ear** listen. **go in (at) one ear and out (at) the other** be heard but leave no impression. **have a person's ear** have his or her favourable attention. *have a wolf by the ears:* see WOLF *n.* **have by the ears** keep or obtain a secure hold on. **have** etc. **one's ear to the ground** be on the alert regarding rumours or trend of opinion. **have the ear of** have the favourable attention of. *have the right* (or *wrong*) *sow by the ear:* see SOW *n.*[1] *head over ears:* see *over head and ears* below. *hold a wolf by the ears:* see WOLF *n.* **inner** (or **internal**) **ear** the labyrinth of the temporal bone, containing the semicircular canals and the cochlea. **lead by the ears** keep in abject dependence. *lend an ear, lend one's ears:* see LEND *v. long ear:* see LONG *a.*[1] **middle ear** the eardrum and the space (containing the ossicles) between the eardrum and the inner ear. *musical ear:* see sense 5 above. *music to one's ears:* see MUSIC *n.* **on one's ear** (*a*) roused, indignant; (*b*) drunk. *one's ears burn:* see BURN *v.* 4. **open one's ears** listen. **outer ear** = *external ear* above. **out on one's ear** dismissed ignominiously. **over (head and) ears, head over ears** deeply immersed (*lit.* & *fig.*). *pin a person's, one's ears back:* see PIN *v. play (it) by ear:* see PLAY *v. prick (up) the* (or *one's*) *ears:* see PRICK *v. sea-ear:* see SEA. **set by the ears** put at variance, cause to quarrel. *speak in a person's ear:* see SPEAK *v. stop one's ears:* see STOP *v. talk a person's ear off:* see TALK *v. thick ear:* see THICK *a. third ear:* see THIRD *a.* & *n. tin ear:* see TIN *n.* & *a. turn a deaf ear (to):* see DEAF *a.* 3. **up to the ears** *colloq.* very deeply involved (*in*). **wet behind the ears** immature, inexperienced. *with a flea in one's ear:* see FLEA *n. would give one's ears:* see GIVE *v.*

Comb.: **earache** pain in the (middle) ear; **ear-bash** *v.i.* & *t.* (*slang*) talk inordinately (to); **ear-basher** *slang* a chatterer, a bore; **ear-biter** *slang* a habitual borrower of money; **ear-clip** an earring, esp. one that clips on; **ear covert** = AURICULAR *n.* 2; **ear-defenders** (a pair of) plugs or ear-muffs which protect the eardrums from loud or persistent noise; **ear-drops** (*a*) medicinal drops for the ear; (*b*) hanging earrings; **eardrum** the membrane of the middle ear, closing the inner end of the external auditory meatus and serving to transmit sound to the ossicles; also, the entire hollow part of the middle ear; **†ear finger** the little finger (as most easily inserted into the ear); **ear-flap** (*a*) = *ear lobe* below; (*b*) a flap of material covering the ear; **earhole** the orifice of the ear; **ear-lap, ear lobe** the lower soft pendulous part of the external ear; **ear-lock** a lock of hair over or above the ear; **earmuff** a covering for the ear to protect it from cold, noise, etc.; **earphone** a device worn on the ear to aid hearing or to listen to radio, telephone, etc., communication; **ear-pick, -picker** an instrument for clearing the ear of wax etc.; **earpiece** (*a*) a part of a helmet covering the ear; (*b*) an apparatus designed to be applied to the ear, as part of a telephone, radio receiver, etc.; **ear-piercing** *a.* shrill; **earplug** (*a*) an ornament worn in the lobe of the ear; (*b*) a wad of cotton wool, wax, etc., placed in the ear to keep out cold air, water, or excessive noise; **earring** an ornament, orig. always a ring, now often a drop, stud, etc., worn on the lobe of the ear; **earringed** *a.* wearing earrings; **ear-shell** (the shell of) an edible mollusc of the genus *Haliotis,* an abalone; **ear-splitting** *a.* excessively loud; *ear-stud:* see STUD *n.*[1] 5d; **ear-trumpet** a conical tube (formerly) used by the partially deaf as an aid to hearing; **ear-tuft** either of a pair of tufts of longer feathers on the top of the head of a bird, esp. of some owls; **earwax** a yellow waxy secretion which collects in the external ear; **ear-witness:** whose testimony is based on his or her own hearing.

earful *n.* (*colloq.*) a large quantity of talk; a strong reprimand: E20. **earlike** *a.* resembling an ear in shape E19.

ear /ɪə/ *n.*[2] [OE *ēar* = OFris. *ār,* OS *ahar* (Du. *aar*), OHG *ahir, ehir* (G *Ähre*), ON *ax,* Goth. *ahs,* f. Gmc base rel. to L *acus, acer-* husk, chaff. See also ICKER.] A spike or head of corn; the part of a cereal plant which contains its flowers or seeds; *N. Amer.* a head of maize.

R. GRAVES The little corn that had been planted withered before it came to an ear. **in the ear** at the stage when ears are borne.

ear /ɪə/ *v.*[1]*t.* Now *arch.* & *dial.* [OE *erian* = OFris. *era,* OS *erian,* OHG *erren,* ON *erja,* Goth. *arjan,* f. IE base repr. also by L *arare.*] Plough, till (the ground); turn *up* by ploughing.

fig.: SHAKES. *Ant. & Cl.* The Sea . . which they ear and wound With keels.

ear /ɪə/ *v.*[2]*i.* LME. [f. EAR *n.*[2]] Of corn or maize: produce ears, come into ear.

ear *adv., prep.,* & *conj.* see ERE.

eared /ɪəd/ *a.*[1] LME. [f. EAR *n.*[1] + -ED[2].] Furnished with ears or earlike appendages; (with specifying wd) having ears of a specified kind.

eared seal any of various seals of the family Otariidae, comprising the fur seals and sea lions.

eared /ɪəd/ *a.*[2] LME. [f. EAR *n.*[2] or *v.*[2]: see -ED[2], -ED[1].] Of corn etc.: having ears, that has come into ear.

earing /ˈɪərɪŋ/ *n.* Also **-rr-**. E17. [f. EAR *n.*[1] + -ING[1] or RING *n.*[1]] *Naut.* Any of a number of small ropes used to fasten the upper corners of a square sail to its yard.

earl /əːl/ *n.* Also (esp. in titles) **E-**. [OE *eorl* = OS, OHG *erl,* ON *jarl,* of unkn. origin. Cf. JARL.] **1** *Hist.* In the OE constitution: a man of noble rank, as distinguished from a churl (see CHURL *n.* 2); a hereditary nobleman ranking directly above a thane (THANE 3). OE. **†b** A warrior, a (brave) man. *poet.* Only in OE. **2** *Hist.* A Danish under-king, a jarl; (under Cnut and his successors), a governor of one of the great divisions of England, as Wessex, Mercia, etc. OE. **3** A British or Irish nobleman ranking below a marquess and above a viscount, corresponding to the European *count.* Cf. COUNTESS. OE. **†b** = COUNT *n.*[2] OE–L18.

Comb. & *phrases:* **Earl Grey** a superior type of tea flavoured with bergamot; **Earl Marshal** a high officer of State in Britain (now hereditary in the line of the Dukes of Norfolk), orig. deputizing for the Constable of England as judge of the court of chivalry, now presiding over the College of Arms and having ceremonial duties on various Royal occasions; *earl palatine:* see PALATINE *a.*[1]

earldom *n.* (*a*) (*obs.* exc. *Hist.*) the territory governed by an earl; (*b*) the rank or dignity of an earl: OE. **earlship** *n.* (*a*) = EARLDOM (b); †(*b*) nobility, manliness: OE.

earless /ˈɪəlɪs/ *a.* E17. [f. EAR *n.*[1] + -LESS.] **1** Having no ears. E17. **2** Without a sense of hearing; without an ear for music; *poet.* where nothing is heard. E19.

2 WORDSWORTH In some deep dungeon's earless den.

earlet /ˈɪəlɪt/ *n.* E17. [f. EAR *n.*[1] + -LET.] **†1** An earring. Only in E17. **2** Something resembling a small ear; (formerly) an atrium of the heart. M17. **b** A tragus, esp. when largely developed as in some bats. M19.

early /ˈəːli/ *a.* & *n.* ME. [f. the adv., after ON *árligr.*] **A** *adj.* **1** Designating, belonging to, or existing, occurring, etc., near to the beginning of a period of time, as the morning, the day, the evening, the year, a lifetime. ME. **2** Designating, belonging, or relating to the initial stage of an epoch, of a person's development, of the history of a people, of the world, of a science etc.; ancient. L17. **3** Near the beginning in serial order. E18. **4** Connected with the initial part of any division of time, continuous action, etc.; occurring before it is too late; arriving, occurring, etc., before the usual or expected time. In *compar.* and *superl.,* former, foremost, first (in time). M18. **b** Of a future date or event: not remote, near at hand. M19.

1 W. COWPER Our most important are our earliest years. H. JAMES She had come up . . by an early train. DAY LEWIS My earliest memory is a smell of bacon. I. MURDOCH Women pick up these conventions at such an early age. U. BENTLEY In the early hours of the next morning. **2** J. BONNYCASTLE Astronomy is a science of the earliest antiquity. LD MACAULAY Early fathers of the Church. P. G. WODEHOUSE The gruesome Early Victorianness of it all. **3** OED The early chapters of the book. L. HELLMAN Mr. Goldwyn was in his early fifties when we first met. **4** B. GOOCH This consideration shou'd engage our earliest . . attention. LD MACAULAY Henry Wharton . . whose early death was soon after deplored by men of all parties. A. CHRISTIE The train couldn't have been ten minutes early. J. F. LEHMANN An elation I had not known since the early days at The Hogarth Press. I. MURDOCH Dark . . clumps of green betokened the early tulips. *Financial Times* It is still too early to predict how far they will get. **b** D. LIVINGSTONE There being no prospect of an early peace.

Phrases & special collocations: **early closing** orig. (usu. *attrib.*), the reduction of the daily hours in certain trades; now, the closing of business premises at the end of the morning on a certain day of the week. **early days** early in time for something (to happen etc.). **Early English** *Archit.* the first stage of English Gothic (13th cent.) with pointed arches, lancet windows, and simple tracery. **early grave** an untimely or premature death. **early hours** *the* hours immediately after midnight. **early leaver** a pupil who leaves school without completing the session or the full course of study. **early music:** of the earliest times up to and including the Renaissance. **early night** a night when one goes to bed before the usual time. **early purple orchid, orchis** a common spring-flowering woodland orchid, *Orchis mascula,* with purple flowers. **early retirement:** from one's occupation before the statutory age, esp. in return for a financial consideration. **early riser** a person who habitually gets up early from bed. *early spider orchid:* see *spider orchid* s.v. SPIDER *n. early* STIRRER. **early warning:** esp. of missile attacks. **early wood** the less dense inner part of the annual ring of a tree. **keep early hours** rise and retire early. *the early bird:* see BIRD *n.*

B *ellipt.* as *n.* **1** Early morning; an early occasion. Usu. in *superl.:* *at the earliest,* in the earliest possible eventuality. LME. **2** An early fruit or vegetable. Usu. in *pl.* M19. **3** In *pl.* Early years or days. E20.

1 SHAKES. *Oth.* To-morrow with your earliest Let me have speech with you.

†earlily *adv.* M17–E18. **earliness** *n.* L16. **earlyish** *a.* & *adv.* somewhat early; early on: M19.

early /ˈəːli/ *adv.* OE. [f. ERE + -LY[2], after ON *árliga*.] **1** Near the beginning of a period of time, esp. of the morning, the day, the year, a lifetime. OE. **2** Far back in date, anciently. ME. **3** At a time before something else; in good time; before the usual time, prematurely; in *compar.*, beforehand, previously. ME. **4** Near the beginning of a sequence. L19.

1 J. MORLEY Voltaire perceived very early in life that to be needy was to be dependent. S. LEACOCK We got out early, just after sunrise. K. AMIS One clear, bright morning early in April. **early and late** at all hours, incessantly. 2 LD MACAULAY As early as the reign of Elizabeth. 3 W. WOTTON This Abuse was early redrest. G. GREENE Winter had fallen early on the House of Stare. J. MITCHELL Her husband had died two years earlier. **early on** at an early stage. 4 OED His name appears very early in the list.

earmark /ˈɪəmɑːk/ *n.* & *v.* LME. [f. EAR *n.*[1] + MARK *n.*[1]] **A** *n.* **1** A mark in the ear of a sheep or other animal, indicating ownership or identity. LME. **2** *transf.* & *fig.* A mark of ownership or identification. L16. **B** *v.t.* **1** Mark (an animal) in the ear as a sign of ownership or identity; *gen.* mark as one's own by means of an identifying sign. L16. **2** Set aside (money etc.) for a particular purpose. L19.

earn /əːn/ *v.*[1]*t.* [OE *earnian* = MLG *arnen*, OHG *arnēn*, *arnōn* reap, f. WGmc, f. base rel. to OE *esne* labourer, man, OHG *esni*, Goth. *asneis* hired labourer.] **1** Receive or be entitled to (money, wages, etc.) in return for work done or services rendered; bring in as income; obtain or deserve in return for efforts or merit. OE. **b** Of money etc. invested, an asset: gain as interest or profit. L19. **2** Of a quality, an action, etc.: acquire for a person (a name, reputation, reproach, etc.), incur. L16. **3** *Baseball.* Score (a run) without any error by the fielding side. M19.

1 E. WAUGH Twenty pounds! Why, it takes me half a term to earn that. L. HELLMAN I earn a living as a carpenter. M. GORDON A child didn't have to earn its mother's love. *absol.*: C. HAMPTON If the public stop wanting me, I stop earning. *earn an honest penny*: see HONEST *a.* **earned income**: from work or services; cf. UNEARNED 2. *earn one's keep*: see KEEP *n.* *pay-as-you-earn*: see PAY-. *save-as-you-earn*: see SAVE *v.* 12. 2 E. WAUGH His comparative old age had earned him the sobriquet of 'uncle'.

earner *n.* a person who or thing which earns; a profitable activity, *esp.* (*colloq.*) an easy means of making money: E17.

earn /əːn/ *v.*[2]*t.* & *i.* *dial.* Also (*Sc.* & *north.*) **yearn** /jəːn/. [OE *ġeirnan*, f. as Y- + metath. alt. of *rinnan* RUN *v.* See also EARNING *n.*[2] Cf. RENNET *n.*[1]] Coagulate, curdle.

†**earn** *v.*[3]*i.* L16. [App. var. of YEARN *v.*[1]] **1** Desire strongly, long. L16–M17. **2** Grieve. L16–E18.

earnest /ˈəːnɪst/ *n.*[1] [OE *eornust*, *-ost* = MLG *ernest*, OHG *ernust* (G *Ernst*), f. base repr. also by ON *ern* brisk, vigorous, Goth. *arniba* safely, of unkn. origin.] **1** Seriousness, as opp. to jest. Now only in *in* (*real* etc.) *earnest*, serious(ly), intense(ly), sincere(ly). OE. †**2** Ardour in battle; intense passion. Only in ME.

1 J. WESLEY I am in great Earnest when I declare . . that I have a deep conviction. L. GARFIELD The snow . . began again in earnest.

earnest /ˈəːnɪst/ *n.*[2] ME. [Prob. ult. f. OFr. *erres* ARLES, assim. first to -NESS, then to prec.] (A sum of) money given in part-payment, esp. for the purpose of binding a bargain; *fig.* a foretaste, token, or pledge of one's intention or of what is to come.

R. MACAULAY Destruction, savagery; an earnest . . of the universal doom. J. RATHBONE What earnest can you give me that you will perform what you promised?

Comb.: **earnest money**, **penny** a small sum of money paid to secure a bargain.

earnest /ˈəːnɪst/ *a.* & *adv.* [OE *eornost(e)* = OFris. *ernst*, MLG *ernest*, f. as EARNEST *n.*[1]] **A** *adj.* **1** Serious in intention, not trifling; zealous, intense, ardent; resulting from or displaying sincere conviction. OE. **2** Weighty, important. *rare.* M16.

1 I. D'ISRAELI There was a good deal of earnest impetuosity in his temper. H. KELLER The thought of going to college took root in my heart and became an earnest desire. E. M. FORSTER The chapel was . . filled with an earnest congregation. 2 S. RICHARDSON Sir Charles had earnest business in town.

†**B** *adv.* In an earnest manner, earnestly. E17–L18.

earnestly *adv.* OE. **earnestness** *n.* M16.

earnful /ˈəːnfʊl, -f(ə)l/ *a.* *obs.* exc. *dial.* E16. [Alt. of YEARNFUL. Cf. EARN *v.*[3]] Full of longing desire; sorrowful.

earning /ˈəːnɪŋ/ *n.*[1] OE. [f. EARN *v.*[1] + -ING[1].] †**1** The fact of deserving, merit; one's desert. OE–ME. †**2** In *pl.* Gain, profit. ME–E18. **3** In *pl.* The amount of money earned; income from work etc. M18. **4** The action of becoming entitled to payment in return for work carried out. L19.

3 **immoral earnings**: from prostitution. *invisible earnings*: see INVISIBLE *a.*

Comb.: **earnings-related** *a.* (of a pension, benefit, etc.) proportionate to a person's earned income over a specified period.

earning /ˈəːnɪŋ/ *n.*[2] *obs.* exc. *Sc.* & *dial.* In sense 1 also (*Sc.* & *north.*) **yearn-** /ˈjəːn-/. ME. [f. EARN *v.*[2] + -ING[1].] **1** A means of curdling milk; rennet. ME. **2** The curdling of milk for cheese. L18.

earring *ns.* see EAR *n.*[1], EARING.

earshot /ˈɪəʃɒt/ *n.* E17. [f. EAR *n.*[1] + SHOT *n.*[1], after *bowshot* etc.] The distance over which something may be heard; hearing. Chiefly in *within*, *out of*, *earshot*.

earth /əːθ/ *n.*[1] [OE *eorþe* = OFris. *erthe*, OS *erþa* (Du. *aarde*), OHG *erda* (G *Erde*), ON *jǫrð*, Goth. *airþa*, f. Gmc.] **I** (The material of) the ground. **1** The ground considered as a surface, a solid stratum, or a place of burial. OE. **2** The soil as suitable for cultivation. OE. **3** The material which makes up the earth's surface; soil, mould, dust, clay. OE. **b** *Hist.* This as one of the four elements of the ancients. ME. †**c** Clay as a material for pottery. (Cf. EARTHEN *a.* 1b, EARTHENWARE.) ME–M17. **4** A particular substance having properties of stability, dryness, non-volatility, lack of taste or smell, etc., associated with the material of the ground; *spec.* in *Chem.*, a metallic oxide with these properties. Usu. w. specifying wd. ME. **5** (The material of) the human body. ME. **6** The lair of a burrowing animal, esp. a fox. LME. **7** The ground regarded as having zero electrical potential; electrical connection with the ground, whether intentional or otherwise; an electrical terminal to which such a connection should be made; a conductor kept at zero potential (by making direct or indirect contact with the ground). Freq. *attrib.* M19.

3 *attrib.*: J. STEINBECK He threw it down and beat it into the earth floor with his fist. 5 SHELLEY The indignant spirit cast its mortal garment Among the slain—dead earth. 7 *earth connection*, *leakage*, *wire*, etc.

II The world. **8** The land and the sea, as distinguished from the sky; (also **E-**) the planet on which humankind lives; the present abode of humankind as distinguished from heaven or hell as places of future existence. OE. **b** The inhabitants of the world collectively. LME. **c** A world resembling the earth; a (habitable) planet. L17. **9** The dry land as distinguished from the sea. OE. **10** A country, a territory. *arch.* OE. **11** *the earth*, a great or excessive amount, esp. of money. *colloq.* E20.

8 J. SCOTT Spreading . . even to the utmost ends of the earth. R. C. TRENCH Earth is not a shadow of heaven, but heaven . . a dream of earth. C. SAGAN Tiny intrepid unmanned spacecraft from the world called Earth. b AV *Gen.* 11:1 And the whole earth was of one language, and one speech. 11 A. CHRISTIE Would it be terribly expensive? . . She'd heard they charged the earth.

Phrases etc.: ALKALINE *earth*. **back to earth** = *down to earth* below. *brown earth*: see BROWN *a.* **down to earth** back to reality from fantasy. **down-to-earth** *a.* plain-spoken, unpretentious; practical, realistic. *fruits of the earth*: see FRUIT *n.* 1. *fuller's earth*: see FULLER *n.*[1] *go the way of all the earth*: see GO *v.* **go to earth** (of a hunted animal) hide itself in a burrow; *fig.* go into hiding. *green earth*: see GREEN *a.* **lay in the earth** bury (a person). *like nothing on earth*: see NOTHING *pron.* & *n.* *mother earth*: see MOTHER *n.*[1] *move heaven and earth*: see HEAVEN *n.* **on earth** existing anywhere; (*no person*, *place*, etc., *on earth* no person, place, etc., at all; as an intensive: *who*, *what*, *where*, etc., *on earth?*). *rare earth*: see RARE *a.*[1] *red earth*: see RED *a.* **run to earth** chase (a fox etc.) to its lair; *fig.* find after long searching. *scorched earth policy*: see SCORCH *v.*[1] **spaceship earth** the world considered as a planet with finite resources common to all humankind. *the end(s) of the earth*: see END *n.* 1. *the salt of the earth*: see SALT *n.*[1] *white earth*: see WHITE *a.* *yellow earth*: see YELLOW *a.*

Comb.: **earth almond** = CHUFA; **earth-ball** a fungus, *Scleroderma aurantium*, forming spherical fruiting bodies on the ground beneath esp. birch trees; **earth-born** *a.* (*poet.* & *rhet.*) (*a*) born by emerging from the earth; (*b*) born on earth, of earthly or mortal race; (*c*) (of a thing) arising from or produced by the earth; **earth closet** a lavatory in which earth is used to cover excreta; **earth colour** a pigment obtained from the earth, as an ochre or umber; **earthfast** *a.* fixed in the ground; **earth god**, **goddess**: of the earth, concerned with fertility and usu. the underworld; **earth house** an underground dwelling; *fig.* the grave; **earth hunger** a strong desire to own or control land; **earth-light** = *earth-shine* below; **earth-man** (*a*) a man whose interest lies in the material rather than the spiritual world; (*b*) (chiefly *Sci. Fiction*) a man living on or native to the planet Earth; **earth mother** a spirit or being symbolizing the earth; *fig.* a sensual and maternal woman; **earth-mover** a vehicle or machine designed for earth-moving; **earth-moving** the excavation of large quantities of soil; **earth-nut** (any of various plants bearing) an edible roundish tuber or other underground body; *spec.* (*a*) = *pignut* (a) s.v. PIG *n.*[1]; (*b*) = PEANUT *n.* 1; **earth pig** = AARDVARK; **earth pillar** *Geol.* a free-standing column of earth, usu. one capped by a stone protecting the top from erosion; **earthquake** a (violent) movement or shaking of the earth's surface usu. due to geological forces or volcanic action; *fig.* a major social etc. disturbance; **earth-rise** the apparent rise of the earth over the moon's horizon as seen from the moon; **earth science(s)**: dealing with the various aspects of the physical constitution of the earth, as geology, geophysics, oceanography, meteorology, etc.; **earth-shaking**, **-shattering** *adjs.* (*fig.*) extremely important, momentous; having a devastating effect; **earthshine** the sun's light reflected from the earth, *esp.* that which illuminates the moon; **earth-soul** the supposed collective consciousness of the earth or humankind; **earth-star** any fungus of the genus *Geastrum*, the fruiting bodies of which grow on the ground and split into lobes which fold back giving a star-shaped structure; esp. *G. triplex*, found in woodland; **earth station** a transmitting station which retransmits signals received from satellites; an aerial for receiving such signals; *earth tremor*: see TREMOR *n.* 3; **earth-wax** = OZOCERITE; **earth-woman** (chiefly *Sci. Fiction*) a woman living on or native to the planet Earth; **earthwork** an embankment, fortification, etc., made of earth; the process of excavation or building in earth; **earthworm** (*a*) an oligochaete worm which burrows in the soil and has a soft moist reddish body; (*b*) *fig.* an abject or contemptible person.

earthlike *a.* (*a*) resembling (that of) the planet earth; (*b*) resembling earth or soil: L19.

earth /əːθ/ *n.*[2] *obs.* exc. *dial.* [OE (WS) *ierþ* f. Gmc, f. IE base also of EAR *v.*[1]: see -TH[1].] The action or an act of ploughing.

earth /əːθ/ *v.* ME. [f. EARTH *n.*[1]] **1** *v.t.* Bury (a corpse). *obs.* exc. *dial.* ME. **2** *v.t.* Drive (a fox etc.) to its earth. L16. **3** *v.refl.* & *i.* Hide oneself underground; go into an earth. E17. **4** *v.t.* Plunge or hide underground; cover with earth. *poet.* M17. **5** *v.t.* Cover (the roots and stems of plants) with heaped-up earth. Usu. foll. by *up*. M17. **6** *v.t.* Connect electrically with (an) earth. L19.

earth-board /ˈəːθbɔːd/ *n.* M17. [f. EARTH *n.*[1] or *n.*[2] + BOARD *n.*] The mould-board of a plough.

earthbound /ˈəːθbaʊnd/ *ppl a.*[1] E17. [f. EARTH *n.*[1] + *bound* pa. pple of BIND *v.*] Fixed on or in the earth's surface; restricted to the planet Earth or to worldly concerns.

SHAKES. *Macb.* Who can impress the forest, bid the tree Unfix his earthbound root? DAY LEWIS Earth's first faint tug at the earthbound soul.

earthbound /ˈəːθbaʊnd/ *ppl a.*[2] M20. [f. EARTH *n.*[1] + BOUND *ppl a.*[2]] Moving towards the earth.

earthen /ˈəːθ(ə)n/ *a.* ME. [f. EARTH *n.*[1] + -EN[4].] **1** Made of earth. ME. **b** Made of baked clay. LME. **2** Characteristic of the earth, esp. as opp. to heaven; materialistic, earthly. L16.

earthenware /ˈəːθ(ə)nwɛː/ *n.* & *a.* M17. [f. prec. + WARE *n.*[2]] **A** *n.* (Vessels or other objects made of) baked clay, esp. the opaque usu.

porous kind baked at a relatively low temperature. M17. **B** *attrib.* or as *adj.* Made of earthenware. E19.

earthiness /ˈəːθɪnɪs/ *n.* LME. [f. EARTHY *a.* + -NESS.] **1** The quality of resembling earth as a substance or (*Hist.*) as one of the four elements. LME. †**b** Earthy matter. E16–L17. **2** Earthliness, worldliness; the condition of being earthy or coarse. L17.

earthliness /ˈəːθlɪnɪs/ *n.* M16. [f. EARTHLY *a.* + -NESS.] †**1** = EARTHINESS 1. M16–M17. **2** The quality or state of being earthly or terrestrial; worldliness, materialism. L16.

earthling /ˈəːθlɪŋ/ *n.* L16. [f. EARTH *n.*[1] + -LING[1].] **1** An inhabitant of the earth. L16. **2** A worldly or materialistic person. E17.

earthly /ˈəːθli/ *a.*, *adv.*, & *n.* OE. [f. EARTH *n.*[1] + -LY[1].] **A** *adj.* **1** Of or pertaining to the earth, terrestrial; worldly, material. Opp. *celestial*, *heavenly*, *spiritual.* OE. **2** Pertaining to or resembling earth as a substance; earthy. *arch.* LME. †**b** Pale or lifeless as earth. *rare* (Shakes.). Only in L16. †**3** Existing or living in or on the ground. L16–M17. **4** On earth, at all. Only in neg. & interrog. contexts. *colloq.* M18.

1 I. MURDOCH This earthly joy was being .. transformed into a heavenly joy. *earthly paradise*: see PARADISE *n.* 1. **4** ARNOLD BENNETT There's no earthly reason why you should not go back. G. GREENE What earthly difference does it make?

B *adv.* On earth, in any way, at all. *rare.* LME.

SIR W. SCOTT I do not know earthly where to go or what to do.

C *ellipt.* as *n.* An earthly chance, use, hope, difference, etc.; any chance etc. whatever. Only in neg. contexts. *colloq.* L19.

K. MANSFIELD He hadn't a ghost of a chance, he hadn't an earthly.

earthward /ˈəːθwəd/ *adv.* & *a.* LME. [f. EARTH *n.*[1] + -WARD.] **A** *adv.* Orig. *to the earthward.* Towards the earth. LME. **B** *adj.* Moving or directed towards the earth. M19.

Also **earthwards** *adv.* M19.

earthy /ˈəːθi/ *a.* LME. [f. EARTH *n.*[1] + -Y[1].] **1** Resembling or suggestive of earth as a substance; having the physical qualities characteristic of earth; (of a mineral) lustreless, friable, and rough to the touch. LME. **b** Made of earth; soiled with earth. LME. **2** Pertaining to the earth, living or existing on earth; worldly, concerned with material rather than spiritual matters. *arch.* LME. †**3** Pertaining to or having the qualities of earth as one of the four elements; heavy, gross, dull. LME–L17. **4** *fig.* (orig. from 3). Coarse, unrefined, crude; grossly material. L16. **5** Pertaining to the ground or what is below the ground; subterranean. M17. **6** Of the nature of or pertaining to a substance of the kind called an earth. E18. **7** Electrically connected to earth; at zero electrical potential. L19.

1 E. FIGES Strong earthy smells which come from out of doors. **b** G. DURRELL Andraia now emerged, scratched and earthy. **2** SHAKES. *John* What earthy name to interrogatories Can task the free breath of a sacred king? **4** B. MACDONALD She was a very kind neighbour .. but she was earthy and to the point. L. VAN DER POST His language .. could be just as earthy as it was poetic. T. C. WOLFE It amused her .. to listen to Mary's obscene earthy conversation. **5** DRYDEN Those earthy spirits black and envious are.

earwig /ˈɪəwɪɡ/ *n.* & *v.* [OE *ēarwicga*, f. *ēare* EAR *n.*[1] + *wicga* earwig, prob. rel. to WIGGLE *v.*: the insect was formerly believed to crawl into the human ear.] **A** *n.* **1** An insect of the order Dermaptera, esp. the common *Forficula auricularia*, characterized by an elongated, flattened body with large terminal forceps. OE. **b** A small centipede. *US.* L19. †**2** A whisperer; a flatterer; an insincere follower. LME–L18. **B** *v.t.* Infl. **-gg-**. Pester with private importunities; influence by secret communications. *arch.* M19.

ease /iːz/ *n.* ME. [AN *ese*, OFr. *eise*, (also mod.) *aise* †elbow room, †favourable occasion, convenience, f. Proto-Romance alt. of L *adjacens* use as n. of pres. pple of *adjacere*: see ADJACENT.] †**1** Opportunity, means or ability to do something. ME–L15. **2** Comfort, convenience; formerly also, advantage, enjoyment. ME. †**b** A convenience, a luxury. LME–M17. **3** Absence of pain or discomfort; freedom from annoyance. ME. **b** *spec.* Freedom from embarrassment or awkwardness in social behaviour. M18. **4** Relief of pain, discomfort, or annoyance. Usu. foll. by *from.* LME. **b** Alleviation of a constraint, burden, or obligation. Now *rare.* LME. †**c** An act or means of relieving pain, discomfort, an obligation, etc. LME–M18. **5** Freedom from toil; leisure; idleness, sloth. LME. **b** Indifference, unconcern. *rare.* E19. **6** Absence of awkwardness or difficulty; dexterity. Chiefly in *with ease*, easily. E17.

2 HOBBES The ease, and benefit the Subjects may enjoy. T. JEFFERSON The portion which came .. to Mrs. Jefferson .. doubled the ease of our circumstances. **3** S. JOHNSON Ease, a neutral state between pain & pleasure. **b** F. TUOHY A lack of ease, something ponderous and embarrassing in his manner. **4** E. W. LANE Liberate him, said the King, and give us ease. CONAN DOYLE It was half a sleep and half a faint, but at least it was ease from pain. **5** R. ELLIS Ease hath entomb'd princes of old renown. J. BUCHAN The position of a judge was the most honourable .. —ease without idleness, an absorbing intellectual pursuit. **b** J. BENTHAM It is a matter of ease to me not to know. **6** L. C. KNIGHTS The sinewy ease of Dryden's satires. M. KEANE He jumped up and settled himself with neat ease in the saddle.

Phrases: **at (one's) ease** (*a*) comfortable, relaxed; without annoyance or embarrassment; †(*b*) well-to-do. *chapel of ease*: see CHAPEL *n.* *ill at ease*: see ILL *a.* & *adv.* **put, set, a person at (his, her) ease** avoid embarrassing a person by undue formality. **set at ease** reassure, relieve from anxiety. **stand at ease** *Mil.* stand on parade in a relaxed attitude with the feet apart. **take one's ease** make oneself comfortable, relax. *with ease*: see sense 6 above.

easeless *a.* without ease; *esp.* without relief (from pain etc.): L16.

ease /iːz/ *v.* ME. [Orig. f. OFr. *aisier*, *aaisier*, f. phr. *a aise* at ease; later directly f. the n.] **I** *v.t.* **1** Make more comfortable, relieve from physical pain or discomfort. ME. †**b** Refresh with rest or food; show hospitality to. ME–L17. **2** Relieve (a person who is oppressed, troubled, etc.) of a burden, pain, or anxiety; give relief to; help, assist. Also foll. by *of*, †*from.* ME. **b** Rob, deprive *of. joc.* E17. **3** Give mental relief to; comfort, relieve (the mind or heart). LME. **4** Relieve (pain, distress, etc.); lighten (a burden etc.). LME. **5** Make easy or easier, facilitate. LME. **6** Slacken, make less tight; cause to work more freely, esp. by altering or loosening. Freq. *Naut.*, slacken (a rope, sail, etc.). E17. **b** Reduce the engine speed of (a ship etc.). M19. **7** Move gently or gradually *down*, *into*, *out of*, etc., L17. **b** *Dressmaking.* Join by edges of unequal length, distributing the excess of one evenly along the join. Also foll. by *in.* M20.

1 E. M. FORSTER The driver .. had got out to ease the horses. **ease nature, oneself** urinate or (*esp.*) defecate. **2** T. URQUHART He .. gave unto each .. a horse to ease them on their way. G. BORROW A powerful priest .. has .. eased me of my sins. **3** CONAN DOYLE It would ease my mind if someone knew the truth before I died. **4** P. H. GIBBS The food was hardly enough to ease the pangs of hunger. **5** A. G. GARDINER Otmar eased the passage up the slope by zigzagging. **6** G. S. NARES The earings are eased down. OED Tell the carpenter to ease the door a little. K. WARREN The first timetable was clearly much too tight, being eased by 14 minutes on 7 August. **ease the helm** reduce the angle of the helm in a steamship to slow down the rate of swing. **7** I. FLEMING He eased the cylinder out of his pocket. J. CHEEVER The conductor .. eased her down the steps. **ease in, into** break in gently to (work etc.); manoeuvre into (a place, appointment, etc.). **ease out** manoeuvre out of a place, appointment, etc.

II *v.i.* †**8** Take one's ease, rest. Only in LME. **9** Slacken, cease; become less burdensome; relax or cease one's efforts, *spec.* in rowing. Freq. w. advs. L16. **b** Of shares: become easier, fall a little in value. E20. **10a** Move oneself gently or effortlessly. Chiefly *N. Amer.* E20. **b** Pass gently or easily, drift; seep. L20.

9 M. TWAIN When .. approaching the shoalest part of the reef, the command is given to 'Ease all!' E. F. NORTON The slope began to ease off. K. ISHIGURO The rain had eased to a drizzle. **10a** R. CARVER He eased in behind the steering wheel.

easer *n.* L16.

easeful /ˈiːzfʊl, -f(ə)l/ *a.* LME. [f. EASE *n.* or *v.* + -FUL.] **1** That gives ease, comfort, or relief; soothing. LME. **2** Unoccupied, at rest; indolent, slothful. E17.

easefully *adv.* E17. **easefulness** *n.* M17.

easel /ˈiːz(ə)l/ *n.* L16. [Du. *ezel* = G *Esel* ass. Cf. HORSE *n.* 8.] A (usu. wooden) frame used to support a picture, a blackboard, etc.

Comb.: **easel-picture**: painted at an easel or small enough to stand on one.

easement /ˈiːzm(ə)nt/ *n.* LME. [OFr. *aisement*, f. *aisier* EASE *v.*: see -MENT.] **1** Relief from pain, discomfort, or any burden; alleviation. LME. †**b** *spec.* The relieving of the body by defecation or urination. LME–E18. †**c** *spec.* Refreshment by food and rest; accommodation, hospitality. LME–E19. **2** (An) advantage, convenience, comfort; formerly also, gratification, enjoyment. LME. **3** A (supplementary) building, room, shed, etc., provided for the sake of convenience. *arch.* LME. **4** The right or privilege of using something not one's own; *spec.* in *Law*, an entitlement to rights (e.g. right of way) over another's land. LME.

1 W. S. CHURCHILL An easement in the drastic petrol rationing system. **2** R. V. JONES I had no easements such as a staff car.

easily /ˈiːzɪli/ *adv.* Formerly compared †**-lier**, †**-liest.** ME. [f. EASY *a.* + -LY[2].] **1** Comfortably; in a relaxed fashion; without pain or anxiety; self-indulgently. ME. **2** With little labour or difficulty. ME. **3** Smoothly, freely. LME. **4** Without hurry, gradually; calmly, quietly. *obs.* exc. *dial.* LME. †**5** *but easily*, only indifferently, only poorly. LME–M16. **6** With little resistance or reluctance. M17. **7** At least; without doubt; by a comfortable margin. *colloq.* M20.

1 J. KOSINSKI Four men entered the room, talking and smiling easily. **2** J. BUCHAN He would have beaten me easily if the course had been longer. E. BOWEN Anna could remember being a child more easily .. than she could remember being Portia's age. **3** M. KEANE She .. shut the drawer, then tried it again to see if it slid and ran easily. **6** DAY LEWIS The small fatalists accept more easily than most philosophers the knowledge that what is is. **7** C. P. SNOW She was easily the most attractive woman there.

easiness /ˈiːzɪnɪs/ *n.* LME. [f. EASY *a.* + -NESS.] **1** Tranquillity, (spiritual) comfort. *rare.* LME. **2** The quality of not being difficult; facility. LME. **3** Gentleness, indulgence. LME. **4** The quality of being relaxed in manner, style, etc. M16. **5** Indifference; indolence. L16. †**6** The quality of being easily influenced; lack of firmness. E17–L18.

eassel /ˈiːs(ə)l/ *adv. Sc.* L18. [Obscurely f. next.] Eastward, easterly.

east /iːst/ *adv.*, *a.*, & *n.* [OE *ēast-* = OFris. *āst*, OS, OHG *ōst* (Du. *oost*, G *ost*) repr. of Gmc base (with suff. in OE *ēastan*, OS, OHG *ōstana*, ON *austan* from the east), f. IE, whence also L *aurora* dawn, Gk *auōs* dawn, *aurion* tomorrow (cf. Skt *uṣas* morning, dawn); as simple adv. = OS, OHG *ōstar*, ON *austr* toward the east, f. Gmc.] **A** *adv.* †**1** From the east. OE–ME. **2** In the direction of that part of the horizon where the sun rises, in the direction of the earth's diurnal rotation about the polar axis; towards the cardinal point which is 90° clockwise from the north point. OE. **b** Foll. by *of*: further in this direction than. L18.

B *adj.* **1** (Also **E-**.) Designating (a person or the people of) the eastern part of a country, region, city, etc. OE. **2** Situated in or lying towards the east or eastern part of something; on the easterly side. ME. **b** Facing east. M17. **c** *spec.* Designating or situated in the end of a Christian church that contains the (high) altar, traditionally but not necessarily the geographical east. E18. **3** Of or pertaining to the east; (of a wind) coming from the east. LME.

1 *East Africa*, *East London*, *East Midlands*, *East Sussex*, etc. **2** G. GREENE The wind's east, and I'm damned if it hasn't begun to rain.

C *n.* In senses 1, 2, 3 usu. w. *the.* **1** (The direction of) that part of the horizon or the sky where the sun rises; *spec.* the cardinal point which is 90° clockwise from the north point. ME. 2 (Freq. **E-**.) The eastern part of the world relative to another part, or of a (specified) country, region, town, etc.; *spec.* (*a*) that part of the world which lies to the east of Europe, the culture and civilization of that part; (*b*) *Hist.* = *Eastern Empire* s.v. EASTERN; (*c*) *Hist.* the Communist States of eastern Europe. Also (*transf.*), the inhabitants of such a part of the world, such a region, country, etc. ME. 3 The east wind. Chiefly *poet.* M18. 4 (**E-**.) In bridge, (formerly) whist, or other four-handed partnership game: the player who occupies the position so designated, and who sits opposite 'West'. In mah-jong, = *east wind* (a) below. E20.

1 SHAKES. *Much Ado* The gentle day . . Dapples the drowsy east with spots of grey.

Special collocations, comb., & phrases: **eastabout** *adv.* (*Naut.*) by an easterly route; eastwards. **East African** (a native or inhabitant) of eastern Africa. **east and west** lengthwise along a line from east to west. *East* ANGLIAN. **eastbound** *a.* & *n.* (*a*) *adj.* travelling or heading eastwards; (*b*) *n.* (chiefly *N. Amer.*) an eastbound train. **east-by-north, east-by-south** (in the direction of) the compass point 11¼° or one point north, south, of the east point. **East Coaster** a native or inhabitant of the east coast of a country. **East Coast fever** a severe form of theileriasis affecting cattle esp. in Africa. **†East Country** the Baltic countries. **east end** the eastern part of something, esp. a church; *spec.* (*East End*) the eastern part of London, including the docks. **East Ender** a native or inhabitant of London's East End. **East India** *Hist.* the whole of SE Asia to the east of and including India; *East India Company*, a company formed to trade with East India, esp. the English company incorporated in 1600 and dissolved in 1874; *East India mahogany*, a leguminous tree, *Pterocarpus dalbergioides*. *East* INDIAMAN. **East Indies** †(*a*) = *East India* above; (*b*) the region of the Malay archipelago. **east-north-east** (in the direction) midway between east and north-east. **East Side** *US* the eastern part of Manhattan. **East Sider** *US* a native or inhabitant of Manhattan's East Side. **east-south-east** (in the direction) midway between east and south-east. **east wind** (*a*) (usu. w. cap. initials) one of the four players in mah-jong, the player who throws the highest score and draws the first four tiles at the outset of the game, preceding South Wind; (*b*) each of four tiles so designated, which with north, south, and west winds make up the suit of winds in mah-jong; (see also sense B.3 above). *Far East*: see FAR *a.* *Middle East*: see MIDDLE *a.* *Near East*: see NEAR *a.* **to the east (of)** in an easterly direction (from).

eastmost *a.* (chiefly *Sc.*) easternmost ME.

Easter /ˈiːstə/ *n.* [OE *ēastre*, pl. *ēastron* (also *ēastro*, -*a*) = OFris. *āsteron*, OHG *ōstarūn* (G *Ostern* pl.) app. f. *Ēostre* Northumb. var. of *Ēastre*, a goddess whose feast was celebrated at the vernal equinox, f. Gmc, cogn. w. Skt *usrā* dawn. Cf. EAST.] 1 The most important of the Christian festivals, commemorating the resurrection of Christ and observed annually on the Sunday which follows the first full moon after the vernal equinox; *colloq.* Easter week or the weekend from Friday to Monday including Easter Sunday (see below). OE. †2 The Jewish passover. OE–E17.

Comb.: **Easter bunny** (a representation of) a rabbit popularly said to bring gifts to children at Easter; **Easter Day** = *Easter Sunday* below; **Easter-dues** money payable at Easter to the incumbent of a parish by the parishioners; **Easter egg**: presented as a gift at Easter (orig. a hard-boiled egg brightly painted, now usu. a confectionery egg); **Easter lily** (chiefly *N. Amer.*) any of various spring-flowering lilies or similar plants; *spec.* a tall cultivated variety of *Lilium longiflorum*, a white-flowered lily native to Japan; **Easter Monday** the Monday after Easter Sunday; **Easter-offering(s)** orig. = *Easter-dues* above; now usu. the proceeds of the Easter Sunday collection; **Easter Parade** a parade or pageant held at Eastertime, esp. of people in new or striking clothes. **Easter sitting(s)** = *Easter term* (a) below; **Easter Sunday**: on which the festival of Easter is observed; **Easter term** (*a*) a term in the courts of law, formerly movable and occurring between Easter and Whitsuntide, but now fixed within a certain period; (*b*) in the older universities, a term formerly occurring between Easter and Whitsuntide and now included in the Trinity term; in some universities and schools, the term between Christmas and Easter; **Eastertide** the period from Easter Sunday until Pentecost (formerly until Ascension Day); **Eastertime** Easter Sunday and the following days up to Ascensiontide; **Easter week**: beginning with Easter Sunday.

easter /ˈiːstə/ *a. obs.* exc. *Sc.* & *dial.* LME. [Perh. repr. OE compar. *ēasterra* (cf. ON *austarr* more to the east), f. as EAST + -ER³.] Lying towards or nearest the east; eastern.

Easterling /ˈiːstəlɪŋ/ *n.* Also **e-**. LME. [App. f. EASTER *a.* + -LING¹, prob. after Du. *oosterling*.] 1 A native or inhabitant of eastern Germany or the Baltic coasts, *esp.* a citizen of the Hanse towns. *obs.* exc. *Hist.* LME. 2 *gen.* A native or inhabitant of an eastern country or district; a member of the Orthodox Church. *arch.* M16.

easterly /ˈiːstəli/ *adv.*, *a.*, & *n.* LME. [Prob. f. EASTER *a.* + -LY², -LY¹.] A *adv.* 1 In an eastward position or direction, towards the east. LME. 2 Esp. of a wind: (nearly) from the east. L16.

1 R. GRAVES The full moon easterly rising, furious, Against a winter sky ragged with red.

B *adj.* 1 Situated towards or facing the east; directed towards the east. M16. 2 Esp. of a wind: coming (nearly) from the east. M16.

1 E. DUNKIN The most easterly part of this constellation.

C *n.* An easterly wind. Usu. in *pl.* E20.

R. FRAME Aldeburgh with its biting easterlies and . . flat leaden skies.

easterliness *n.* (*rare*) E20.

†eastermost *a.* M16–M19. [f. EASTER *a.* + -MOST.] = EASTERNMOST.

eastern /ˈiːst(ə)n/ *a.* & *n.* [OE *ēasterne* = OS, OHG *ōstroni*, ON *austrœnn*, f. Gmc, f. base of EAST.] A *adj.* 1 Of, pertaining to, or characteristic of the east or its inhabitants, *esp.* of or pertaining to the part of the world east of Europe; living in or originating from the east; oriental. OE. b *spec.* Situated or living in the (north-)east of the US, esp. New England; of, from, or relating to this region. L18. 2 Of a wind: blowing from the east. *poet.* OE. 3 Situated in the east; directed, facing, or lying towards the east; having a position relatively east. LME.

1 SHAKES. *Ant. & Cl.* Oh Eastern star! J. CONRAD Easy enough to dispose of a Malay woman, a slave after all, to his Eastern mind. **Eastern Church** the Orthodox Church. **Eastern Empire** the more easterly of the two parts into which the Roman Empire was divided in AD 395. *Eastern* HEMISPHERE. **Eastern (Standard) Time** the standard time used in the eastern parts of Canada and the US, or in eastern Australia. *Far Eastern*: see FAR *a.* *Middle Eastern*: see MIDDLE *a.* *Near Eastern*: see NEAR *a.* 3 ADDISON The eastern end of the isle rises up in precipices. J. TYNDALL A pale light now overspread the eastern sky.

B *n.* 1 A native or inhabitant of the east; an oriental. *rare.* OE. 2 A member of the Orthodox Church. M19.

easterner *n.* (*a*) a native or inhabitant of the eastern part of a country, esp. the eastern States of the US; (*b*) *Hist.* an opponent of the concentration of forces on the Western Front in the war of 1914–18 (cf. WESTERNER (b)): M19. **easternmost** *a.* situated furthest to the east; most easterly: L18.

East Indian /iːst ˈɪndɪən/ *a.* & *n. phr.* M16. [f. *East India* s.v. EAST + -AN.] A *adj. phr.* Chiefly *Hist.* Of or pertaining to the region of the Malay archipelago or (formerly) the whole of SE Asia and India. M16.

East Indian walnut = KOKKO 1.

B *n. phr.* 1 = EURASIAN *n. obs.* exc. *Hist.* E19. 2 A resident of the West Indies descended from the indigenous peoples of the Indian subcontinent. M20.

easting /ˈiːstɪŋ/ *n.* E17. [f. EAST + -ING¹.] 1 Chiefly *Naut.* Distance travelled or measured eastward. E17. 2 *Cartography.* Distance eastward from a point of origin (freq. from the south-west corner of a map); a figure representing this, expressed by convention as the first part of a grid reference (usu. in *pl.* or more fully *easting coordinate*). Cf. NORTHING 2. M18. 3 Easterly tendency; a running or shifting eastward. M19.

Eastlake /ˈiːstleɪk/ *a.* & *n.* L19. [See below.] (Designating) furniture associated with the English designer Charles Locke Eastlake (1836–1906) and his book *Hints on Household Taste* (1878).

eastland /ˈiːstlənd/ *n. obs.* exc. *Hist.* or *poet.* OE. [f. EAST + LAND *n.*¹] An eastern country or district; *spec.* (**E-**) the Baltic countries (= *East Country* s.v. EAST).

eastward /ˈiːstwəd/ *adv.*, *a.*, & *n.* OE. [f. EAST + -WARD.] A *adv.* Towards the east (*of*); in an easterly direction. OE.

AV *1 Kings* 17:3 Get thee hence, and turne thee Eastward.

B *adj.* Situated or directed towards the east; moving or facing towards the east. LME.

eastward position: of the celebrant standing in front of and facing the altar (and so facing east) in the Eucharist.

C *n.* The direction or area lying to the east or east *of* a place etc.; *US* the eastern side or part, esp. of the US. M17.

eastwardly *adv.* & *a.* (*a*) *adv.* in or from an easterly direction; (*b*) *adj.* moving, lying, or facing towards the east; (of a wind) blowing (nearly) from the east: M17. **eastwards** *adv.* = EASTWARD *adv.* E16.

easy /ˈiːzi/ *a.*, *adv.*, & *n.* ME. [AN *aisé*, OFr. *aisié* (mod. *aisé*), pa. pple of *aisier* put at ease: see EASE *v.*, -Y⁵.] A *adj.* 1 Characterized by ease or rest; comfortable, quiet, tranquil. ME. b Conducive to ease or comfort. LME. 2 Presenting few difficulties; offering little resistance; (of an action, task, object, etc.) that can be accomplished with little effort. ME. †3 Of a person: lenient, gentle. ME–E18. 4 Of motion etc.: unhurried, gentle, slow, not hard-pressed. LME. 5 Free from anxiety or care. LME. 6 Esp. of manner, movement, etc.: free from constraint or awkwardness, smooth. LME. b Of literary composition etc.: showing no trace of effort, fluent. E18. 7 Of a condition, penalty, etc.: moderate, not oppressive or burdensome. LME. 8 Moved without difficulty to action or belief; compliant, yielding; (esp. of a woman) promiscuous. LME. 9 That is obtained with little effort or sacrifice. LME. †10 Insignificant, of little importance; not very good. LME–M17. 11 Loosely fitting; not tight. L16. 12 = *easy-going* (a) below. M17. 13 Well off, comfortable. E18. 14 *Stock Exch.* etc. Not much in demand; not showing eager demand. M19.

1 DEFOE My Condition began now to be . . much easier to my mind. H. BELLOC The River Sarthe . . runs . . through easy meadow-land. *make life easy* (*for*): see LIFE *n.* b **easy on the eye(s)**, **easy to look at** *colloq.* pleasant to look upon. 2 W. CATHER It's awfully easy to rush into a profession you don't really like. G. GREENE We were an easy target in the light of the flames. M. AMIS People are easy to frighten. (*as*) *easy as ABC*, *falling off a log*, *kiss my hand*, *pie*, *winking*, etc. **easy of access** easily reached. 3 R. BENTLEY Pisistratus . . a generous and easie Governour. 4 E. TOPSELL They have a very slow and easie pace. 5 J. M. COETZEE There is nothing special about you, you can rest easy about that. M. ROBERTS Smiling, easy, with not a care in the world. 6 ROBERT ANDERSON They are easy with each other, casual. A. THWAITE Ibsen was never an easy man. *free and easy*: see FREE *a.* 7 S. PEPYS Secure it for me on the easiest terms you can. *at an easy rate*: see RATE *n.*¹ 8 LD MACAULAY Juries were no longer so easy of belief. S. BELLOW Mimi, isn't that her name? She looks like an easy broad. **I'm easy** (*colloq.*) I'm agreeable (to whatever is proposed), I don't mind. **of easy virtue** of a woman: promiscuous. 9 DRYDEN The Swain . . Receives his easy Food from Nature's Hand. 11 SHAKES. *All's Well* This woman's an easy glove, my lord; she goes off and on at pleasure. 12 DRYDEN Easy Sloath. W. SANSOM We're easy folk in these parts, we leave doors unlocked. 13 G. BERKELEY Men easy in their fortunes, and unprovoked by hardships of any sort.

B *adv.* (Now chiefly *colloq.*) 1 Without difficulty. LME. 2 Not tightly; with freedom of movement. E18. 3 At a leisurely pace, without exertion; in a relaxed manner; comfortably, calmly. L18.

1 BYRON A wavering spirit may be easier wreck'd. H. REED You can do it quite easy. **come easy to** present little difficulty to. **easy come easy go** what is easily acquired is soon lost or spent. 2 KEATS The bolts full easy slide. 3 T. FORREST Which kept the vessel's head to the sea, and made her lie easy. **easy does it** go carefully, take your time. **easy on** do not be alarmed. **go easy** act or proceed cautiously (*go easy with* or *on*, use sparingly). **take it easy** proceed comfortably or carefully; do no more than one has to; relax. In commands: **easy!** (move) gently. **easy all!** stop (rowing). **stand easy!** *Mil.*: with greater freedom or informality than 'at ease'.

Special collocations & comb.: **easy-care** *a.* (of esp. man-made fabrics) serviceable, simple to wash, dry, etc. **easy chair** an upholstered chair, usu. with arms, designed for comfort. **easy circumstances** affluence. **easy game** *colloq.* someone or something overcome, outwitted, or persuaded without difficulty. **easy-going** (*a*) fond of comfort, indolent, not strict, taking things as they come; (*b*) (of a horse) having an easy gait. **easy listening** (recorded) popular music that is tuneful and undemanding. **easy meat** = *easy game* above. **easy money** money obtained without effort (and often illegally) or (*Stock Exch.* etc.) at low interest. **easy-paced** *a.* (of a cricket pitch or golf course) allowing the ball to come at an easy pace off or along it. **easy-peasy** *slang* [redupl.] very simple. **easy rider** *US slang* (*a*) a sexually satisfying lover; (*b*) a guitar. **Easy Street** *colloq.* comfortable circumstances, affluence. *easy touch*: see TOUCH *n. easy virtue*: see sense 8 above.

C *n.* A rest, a breather. *colloq.* L19.

G. R. LOWNDES We took a day's easy . . by the salmon pool.

easy /ˈiːzi/ *v.* M16. [f. the adj.] †1 *v.t.* Facilitate; assist. Only in M16. 2 *v.t.* & *i. Rowing.* (Cause to) cease rowing. M19.

eat /iːt/ *n.* Now *colloq.* [OE *ǣt* = OFris. *ēt*, OS *āt*, OHG *āz*; in mod. use f. the vb.] 1 Food. Now only in *pl.*, things to eat. OE. 2 An act of eating, a meal. OE.

1 J. P. DONLEAVY On the table were eats the like of which . . have never been seen on this isle. 2 J. FRAME Goodbye and thank you for the little eat.

eat /iːt/ *v.* Pa. t. **ate** /eɪt, ɛt/, (*obs.* exc. *Sc.* & *dial.*) **eat**. Pa. pple **eaten** /ˈiːt(ə)n/, †**eat**. [OE *etan* = OFris. *eta*, OS *etan* (Du *eten*), OHG *ezzan* (G *essen*), ON *eta*, Goth. *itan*, f. Gmc, f. IE base of L *edere*, Gk *edein*.] I Consume for nutriment. 1 *v.t.* Have as food; take into the mouth, masticate if necessary, and swallow (solid food; also fluid, e.g. soup, for which a spoon is used). OE. †b *fig.* Submit to, accept meekly (an insult, an injury, etc.). LME–E17. c *fig.* Receive (esp. a stage performance) with vigorous enjoyment; acclaim. (Foll. by *up*.) *colloq.* E20. d Perform fellatio or cunnilingus on (a person). *US slang.* E20. 2 *v.i.* Consume food, take a meal; feed (†*on*, †*upon*); *arch.* eat some *of* a food. OE. 3 *v.t.* Leave (grain, grass, etc.) to animals to be eaten. Foll. by *with*. E16. 4 *v.i.* Have a certain consistency or flavour when eaten. L16. 5 *v.t.* Provide with food. *US slang.* M19.

1 J. M. SYNGE He eat the insides of a clock and died after. D. ATTENBOROUGH Some caterpillars have made themselves unpleasant to eat. M. AMIS They found out he was eating his diet *and* his normal food. c N. MITFORD London society . . simply ate Cedric up. 2 AV *Exod.* 34:15 Lest . . thou eate of his sacrifice. POPE Yet on plain pudding deign'd at home to eat. G. VIDAL You lovely ones must have dinner with me this evening, otherwise I must eat alone. **eat Chinese, Indian**, etc. have a meal of Chinese, Indian, etc., food. 3 *Perthshire Journal* The pasture . . he intended to eat with sheep. 4 SHAKES. *All's Well* Like one of our French wither'd pears: . . it eats drily. 5 J. T. TROWBRIDGE I might hide ye; but I can't eat ye.

II Destroy by devouring. 6 *v.t.* Devour, consume; feed destructively on (crops, vegetation, etc.). OE. b Bother, vex; make anxious. *colloq.* (orig. *US*). L19. 7 *v.t.* Gnaw, wear away by gnawing; destroy gradually or insidiously by corrosion, erosion, disease, etc. ME. 8 *v.i.* Make a way (*into*, *through*) by gnawing, corrosion, etc. E17. 9 *v.t.* Make (a hole, a passage, one's way) by gnawing, corrosion, etc. L17.

6 AV *Exod.* 10:12 Stretch out thine hand . . for the locusts, that they may . . eate euery herbe of the land. OED He went to Africa, and got eaten by a lion. *fig.*: SHAKES. *Rich. III* Or, earth, gape open wide and eat him quick. A. S. NEILL If you throw any nutshells on that floor Mrs. Findlay will eat you. b A. MILLER He thinks I've been spiting him all these years and it's eating him up. 7 AV *Acts* 12:23 Hee was eaten of wormes and gaue up the ghost. COLERIDGE His limbs The silent frost had eat, scathing like fire. J. HODGSON The cliffs chalky and stratified, . . eaten into caves. 8 *fig.*: E. BIRNEY Night's dissolvent eats into the west / browning the stippled mauve. 9 DRYDEN The slow creeping Evil eats his way . . and makes the Life his Prey. T. H. HUXLEY Little water-courses may be eaten out of solid rock by a running stream.

Other phrases, & with advs. in specialized senses: **eat away** destroy gradually (*lit.* & *fig.*). **eat crow** *N. Amer.* submit to humiliation. **eat dinners** = *eat one's terms* below. *eat dirt*: see DIRT *n. eat humble pie*: see HUMBLE *a.*[1] **eat its head off** (of an animal) cost more for food than it will sell for. *eat like a horse*: see HORSE *n.* **eat off** clear off (a crop) by feeding it to animals. *eat one's cake and have it*: see CAKE *n.* **eat one's heart** (**out**) brood or suffer with grief or longing. **eat one's terms** be studying for the Bar, and therefore having to dine a certain number of times in the Hall of an Inn of Court. **eat one's words** retract, usu. in a humiliated manner, something one has said. **eat oneself sick** eat until one vomits or feels ill. **eat out** (*a*) *v.phr.t.* destroy parasitically or corrosively; (*b*) *v.phr.t.* encroach upon (space; formerly also, time); (*c*) *v.phr.i.* take a meal elsewhere than at one's residence. **eat (a person) out of house and home** (usu. *hyperbol.*) ruin (a person) by eating all he or she has. **eat out of a person's hand** be entirely submissive or obedient to a person. *eat the bread of*: see BREAD *n.*[1] **eat the wind out of** *Naut.* sail to windward of (another vessel). **eat up** (*a*) consume completely or wastefully; (*b*) consume all the resources of; (*c*) annex rapaciously; (*d*) assimilate the ideas of; (*e*) absorb; (*f*) wear out the life of (*with* remorse etc.); (*g*) traverse (a distance) rapidly; (*h*) finish eating; (see also sense 1c above). *have one's cake and eat it* etc.: see CAKE *n.* **he** etc. **won't eat you** he etc. will not injure or harm you.

Comb.: **eat-in** *a.* (*N. Amer.*) designating a kitchen designed for eating in as well as cooking.

eatery *n.* (*colloq.*, chiefly *N. Amer.*) a restaurant, a café E20.

eatable /ˈiːtəb(ə)l/ *a.* & *n.* LME. [f. prec. + -ABLE.] A *adj.* Able to be eaten; edible; palatable. LME. B *n.* An article of food. Usu. in *pl.* L17.

eatage /ˈiːtɪdʒ/ *n. north.* M17. [f. EAT *v.* + -AGE.] 1 Grass available (only) for grazing, esp. the aftermath. M17. 2 The right of using for pasture. M19.

eaten *v.* pa. pple: see EAT *v.*

eater /ˈiːtə/ *n.* OE. [f. EAT *v.* + -ER[1].] 1 A person, animal, or thing that eats (*lit.* & *fig.*); a person who or animal which eats a specified food, or in a specified way. OE. 2 A fruit suitable for eating raw. E20.

1 COVERDALE *Ezek.* 36:13 Thou art an eater vp of men, and a waister of thy people. J. L. WATEN Ginger was a slow eater. ANTEATER. *bee-eater*: see BEE *n.*[1] **big eater** a person with a large appetite. 2 P. LOVESEY She offered apples, but . . her eaters had gone soft.

eath /iːθ/ *a.* & *adv.* Now *dial.* & *Sc.* Also (*Sc.*) **eith**. [OE *ēaþe*, *ȳþe* adj. = OS *ōþi*, OHG *ōdi*; OE *ēaþe* adv. = OS *ōþo*, OHG *ōdo*, ON *auð-*; both f. Gmc.] A *adj.* Easy, presenting little difficulty. OE. B *adv.* Easily. OE.

Also **eathly** *adv.* & †*a.* OE.

eating /ˈiːtɪŋ/ *vbl n.* ME. [f. EAT *v.* + -ING[1].] The action or habit of taking food.

Comb.: **eating apple** etc.: suitable for eating raw; **eating-house** (*a*) a restaurant; †(*b*) a refectory; *eating irons*: see IRON *n.* 16.

eau /əʊ; *foreign* o/ *n.*[1] [Fr.] The Fr. for 'water', occurring in various phrases used in Eng.

eau-de-Cologne /əʊdəkəˈləʊn/ a lightly-scented perfume made orig. at Cologne E19. **eau de Javel(le)** /əʊ də ʒaˈvɛl/ Javelle water E19. **eau-de-Luce** /əʊdəˈluːs/ (*obs.* exc. *Hist.*) a medicinal preparation of alcohol, oil of amber, oil of lavender, and ammonia M18. **eau-de-Nil** /əʊdəˈniːl, *foreign* odnil/ [lit. 'water of (the) Nile'] a pale greenish colour (supposedly resembling Nile water) L19. **eau de toilette** /əʊ də twɑːˈlɛt, *foreign* o də twalɛt/ toilet water E20. **eau-de-vie** /əʊdəˈviː, *foreign* odvi/ [lit. 'water of life'] brandy M18. **eau sucreé** /əʊ ˈsuːkreɪ, *foreign* o sykre/ water with sugar in it E19. SALLE *d'eau*.

eau *n.*[2] see EA.

eave /iːv/ *n.sing.* E17. [f. next, with *-s* taken as pl. suff. -S[1].] = next.

eaved *a.* provided with eaves M19. **eaving** *n.* = next L16.

eaves /iːvz/ *n.pl.* (orig. †*sing.*). [OE *efes*, corresp. to OFris. *ose*, MLG *ovese*, Flem. *oose*, MDu. *ovese*, *ose*, OHG *obasa*, *-isa*, MHG *ob(e)se* (G dial. *Obsen*) eaves, porch, ON *ups*, Goth. *ubizwa* porch, f. Gmc, prob. f. base of OVER *adv.* See also prec.] 1 The projecting edge of a roof or thatch, which overhangs the side of the building. OE. b The edge or margin of a wood or forest. Long *arch. rare.* OE. 2 *transf.* Something that projects or overhangs slightly. ME.

1 MILTON Ushered with a shower still . . With minute-drops from off the eaves. N. GORDIMER A rim of shady light where the mud walls did not meet the eaves. b TOLKIEN They had reached the eaves of Mirkwood. 2 G. BORROW A leather hat . . with the side eaves turned up.

Comb.: **eaves-board, -catch** a horizontal board fixed under the eaves, making the lowest tile course(s) incline less steeply than the rest of the roof; **eaves-trough** a rainwater gutter under the eaves.

eavesdrop /ˈiːvzdrɒp/ *n.* LME. [Prob. f. ON *upsardropi*, f. *ups* EAVES + *dropi* DROP *n.* Cf. OE *yfæsdrypæ* 'eaves-drip', WFris. *œsdrip*, *-drup*, Flem. *oosdrup* eaves.] The dripping of water from the eaves of a house; the ground on which such water falls.

eavesdrop /ˈiːvzdrɒp/ *v.t.* & *i.* Infl. **-pp-**. E17. [Back-form. f. next.] Listen secretly to (a person, private conversation), orig. by standing beneath the eaves of a house. Formerly also, stand beneath the eaves of (a building) in order to overhear conversation within.

J. SHIRLEY It is not civil to eavesdrop him. C. ISHERWOOD George eavesdrops on their conversation. A. HAILEY Yvette started to eavesdrop by making tape recordings.

eavesdropper /ˈiːvzdrɒpə/ *n.* LME. [f. EAVESDROP *n.* + -ER[1].] A person who eavesdrops (formerly an indictable public nuisance).

ébauche /eboːʃ/ *n.* Pl. pronounced same. E18. [Fr.] 1 A sketch; a rough-hewn sculpture; a first draft. E18. 2 A partly finished watch movement. E20.

ebb /ɛb/ *n.* & *a.* [OE *ebba* = (M)LG, (M)Du. *ebbe* (Du. *eb*), f. WGmc, f. base of OF *prep.*, as if meaning 'a running off or away'.] A *n.* 1 The outward movement of the tide; the return of tidewater towards the sea. Opp. *flow*. OE. 2 *gen.* A flowing away, a subsiding; *fig.* decline, decay; a change to a less favourable state. LME. b A point or state of decline or depression; esp. in *at a low ebb*. L16. †3 In *pl.* Shallows. L16–E19.

1 S. BECKETT I didn't have to row, the ebb was carrying me out. 2 JOSEPH HALL This . . was the Ebbe of his greatnesse. A. C. SWINBURNE Her ebbs and flows of passion. b F. MUIR The scene where Eliza . . at her lowest ebb, had decided to run for it.

Comb.: **ebb-tide** = sense 1 above.

B *adj.* 1 (Of water, a well, a furrow, etc.) shallow, not deep; having a short supply. *obs.* exc. *dial.* LME. 2 Near the surface. *obs.* exc. *dial.* E17.

1 R. LEIGHTON This Apostle . . drew from too full a spring to be ebb of matter. 2 R. PLOT Sometimes it lyes so ebb . . that they plow up the head of it.

ebb /ɛb/ *v.* [OE *ebbian* (f. EBB *n.*) = (M)LG, (M)Du. *ebben*.] 1 *v.i.* Of the sea, tidal water, etc.: flow back, recede. Freq. in *ebb and flow*. Cf. FLOW *v.* 10. OE. 2 *v.i. gen.* Flow out or away; sink lower, subside; *fig.* decline, decay; fade or waste away. ME. 3 *v.t.* Prevent (fish etc.) from returning to sea with the ebb-tide. L15.

1 SHAKES. *L.L.L.* The sea will ebb and flow. R. HUGHES The water of the bay began to ebb away. 2 DEFOE As my money declined, their respect would ebb with it. H. JAMES The flood of summer light had begun to ebb. B. CHATWIN Her strength ebbed away on a diet of corned beef and packet potato.

†**ebdomadary** *n.* see HEBDOMADARY *n.*

Ebenezer /ɛbɪˈniːzə/ *n.* L17. [Heb. *'eḇen hā-'ezer* lit. 'stone of the help', name of the memorial stone set up by Samuel after the victory of Mizpeh (1 *Sam.* 7:12).] 1 *raise, set up*, etc., *one's Ebenezer*, express gratitude for divine help in reaching one's present circumstances. L17. 2 [Evidently by a misunderstanding of 'raise'.] Temper, anger. *US slang.* M19. 3 A Nonconformist chapel. M19.

ébéniste /ebenist/ *n.* Pl. pronounced same. E20. [Fr., f. *ébène* ebony.] An ebonist; *spec.* a French cabinet-maker who veneers furniture (orig. with ebony).

Ebionite /ˈiːbjənʌɪt/ *n.* & *a.* LME. [med.L *ebionita*, f. Heb. *'eḇyōn* poor: see -ITE[1].] Of or pertaining to, a member of, a Christian sect of the 1st to 3rd cents. which held that Jesus was a mere man, and that the Mosaic law was binding on Christians.

Ebio'nitic *a.* pertaining to the Ebionites or their beliefs M19. **Ebionitism** *n.* (tendency towards) the beliefs or practices of the Ebionites L18.

Eblaite /'ɛbləʌɪt, 'iːb-/ *n.* & *a.* L20. [f. *Ebla*, ancient name of the city of Tell Mardikh in northern Syria + -ITE[1].] A *n.* 1 An inhabitant of ancient Ebla. L20. 2 A Semitic language known from tablets of *c* 2400 BC discovered at the site of Ebla. L20. B *adj.* Of or pertaining to ancient Ebla, its inhabitants, or this language. L20.

Eblis /'ɛbliːs/ *n.* Also **I-** /'ɪ-/. L18. [Arab. *Iblīs* prob. contr. of Gk *diabolos* DEVIL *n.*] The Devil in Islam.

Ebo *n.* & *a.* var. of IGBO.

E-boat /'iːbəʊt/ *n.* Now *Hist.* M20. [f. *e*nemy + BOAT *n.*] A German torpedo boat during the war of 1939–45.

ebon /'ɛb(ə)n/ *n.* & *a.* Now only *poet.* LME. [OFr. *eban* (mod. *ébène*) = med.L *ebanus*, var. of L *ebenus* f. Gk *ebenos* ebony tree.] A *n.* 1 The wood ebony. Also *ebon-wood*. LME. †2 An ebony tree. Also *ebon tree*. LME–E17.

B *adj.* Made of ebony; black as ebony. L16.

fig.: SHAKES. *Ven. & Ad.* Death's ebon dart.

ebonite /'ɛbənʌɪt/ *n.* M19. [f. next + -ITE[1].] = VULCANITE 2.

ebony /'ɛb(ə)ni/ *n.* & *a.* LME. [f. EBON, perh. after IVORY.] A *n.* 1 The hard, heavy, black or very dark timber of any of various tropical trees, esp. of the genus *Diospyros* (family Ebenaceae), native to W. Africa, India, Sri Lanka (Ceylon), and SE Asia. Also *ebony-wood*. LME. 2 A tree yielding this wood. Also *ebony tree*. M18. 3 A very dark brown or black colour. E19. b A Black. *US. arch.* M19. B *adj.* Made of ebony; of the colour of ebony. M17.

ebonist *n.* a worker or dealer in ebony or other ornamental woods E18. **ebonize** *v.t.* make (furniture etc.) look like ebony M19.

éboulement /ebulmɑ̃/ *n.* Pl. pronounced same. E19. [Fr., f. *ébouler* crumble.] A crumbling and falling of rock etc.; a landslide.

ebracteate /ɪ'braktɪət, -eɪt/ *a.* M19. [mod.L *ebracteatus*, f. L *e-* E- + *bractea* BRACT: see -ATE[2].] *Bot.* Having no bracts.

ebriety /ɪ'brʌɪəti/ *n. literary.* LME. [Fr. *ébriété* or L *ebrietas*, f. *ebrius* drunk: see -ITY.] Drunkenness, the state or habit of intoxication; *fig.* excitement; formerly also, an instance of drunkenness.

ebriosity /iːbrɪ'ɒsɪti/ *n. rare.* M17. [L *ebriositas*, f. *ebriosus* habitually drunk: see -OSITY.] (Habitual) intoxication; excitement.

ebrious /'iːbrɪəs/ *a.* Now *rare.* M16. [f. L *ebrius* + -OUS.] Drunken; characteristic of intoxication.

Also **ebriose** *a.* (*joc.*) L19.

†ebullate *v.i.* E17–M18. [Late L *ebullare*, var. of *ebullire*: see EBULLIENT, -ATE[3].] Boil.

ebulliate /ɪ'bʌlɪeɪt/ *v.i.* & *t. rare.* L16. [Irreg. f. L *ebullire*: see EBULLIENT, -ATE[3].] Boil.

ebullience /ɪ'bʌlj(ə)ns, -'bʊl-/ *n.* M18. [f. next: see -ENCE.] Ebullient quality; enthusiasm, exuberance; a boiling up as of liquid (chiefly *fig.*).

Also **ebulliency** *n.* M17.

ebullient /ɪ'bʌljənt, -'bʊl-/ *a.* L16. [L *ebullient-* pres. ppl stem of *ebullire* boil up, f. *e-* E- + *bullire* BOIL *v.*: see -ENT.] 1 Boiling; agitated as if boiling. L16. †2 Of the bodily humours: hot, effervescent, agitated. E17–M18. 3 (The usual sense.) Bubbling over with enthusiasm or excitement; exuberant. M17.

1 G. P. SCROPE Lava in a liquid and ebullient state. 2 E. YOUNG They scarce can swallow their ebullient spleen. 3 W. HOLTBY Leaping, slavering, wild, restless, beautiful, ebullient dog. S. NAIPAUL The atmosphere . . was as ebullient and as joyous as a Civil Rights rally in the early 1960s.

ebulliently *adv.* L19.

ebulliometer /ɪˌbʌlɪ'ɒmɪtə, -ˌbʊl-/ *n.* M20. [Fr. *ébulliomètre*, f. L *ebullire*: see prec., -OMETER.] = next.

ebullioscope /ɪ'bʌlɪə(ʊ)skəʊp, -'bʊl-/ *n.* M19. [Fr. *ébullioscope*, f. L *ebullire*: see EBULLIENT, -O-, -SCOPE.] An instrument for the precise measurement of boiling points.

ebullio'scopic *a.* of or pertaining to ebullioscopy or an ebullioscope E20. **ebullioscopy** /-'ɒskəpi/ *n.* the precise measurement of boiling points, *spec.* (*Chem.*) as a means of determining the molecular weight of a compound from the rise in the boiling point of a liquid when the compound is dissolved in the liquid E20.

ebullism /'ɛbʌlɪz(ə)m/ *n.* M20. [f. L *ebullire*: see EBULLIENT, -ISM.] The formation of bubbles in body fluids owing to reduced ambient pressure.

ebullition /ɛbə'lɪʃ(ə)n, -bʊ-/ *n.* LME. [Late L *ebullitio(n-)*, f. *ebullit-* pa. ppl stem of *ebullire*: see EBULLIENT, -ITION.] †1 *Med.* A state of agitation of the bodily humours, ascribed to heat. LME–M18. 2 *fig.* (now taken as from sense 3). Agitation, commotion; a sudden outburst of war, emotion, etc. M16. 3 *lit.* Boiling; the bubbling and agitation of a heated liquid. L16. b The action of overflowing or rushing out in a state of turbulence; rapid bubbling, effervescence. L16.

2 S. JOHNSON Such faults may be said to be ebullitions of genius. W. S. CHURCHILL We expected a certain amount of local ebullition while matters readjusted themselves. 3 D. BREWSTER Fluids of easy ebullition. b C. LYELL A great ebullition of gas.

†ebulum *n.* OE–M18. [L.] Danewort. In later use, elderberry wine.

eburnation /ɪbəː'neɪʃ(ə)n/ *n.* M19. [f. L *eburnus* made of ivory, f. *ebur*: see IVORY, -ATION.] *Med.* The exposure of a hard dense surface on a bone due to the wearing down of cartilage, esp. in osteoarthritis.

eburnean /ɪ'bəːnɪən/ *a.* Also **-ian**. M17. [f. L *eburneus* made of ivory, f. *ebur*: see IVORY, -AN, -IAN.] Made of or resembling ivory.

ecad /'iːkad/ *n.* E20. [f. Gk *oikos* house + -AD[1].] *Ecol.* An organism modified by its environment.

écarté /eɪ'kɑːteɪ, *foreign* ekarte/ *n.* E19. [Fr., pa. pple of *écarter* discard, f. *é-* (f. as ES-) + *carte* CARD *n.*[2]] 1 A card-game for two people in which cards may be exchanged for others and those from the two to the six are excluded. E19. 2 *Ballet.* A pose with one arm and one leg extended, the body being at an oblique angle to the audience. E20.

ecaudate /ɪ'kɔːdeɪt/ *a.* M19. [mod.L *ecaudatus*, f. L E- + CAUDA: see -ATE[2].] *Zool.* Tailless, or having only a very short tail.

ecbatic /ɛk'batɪk/ *a.* M19. [Gk *ekbatikos*, f. *ekbasis* digression, f. stem of *ekbainein* go out, digress: see -IC.] *Gk Gram.* Of a clause or conjunction: denoting a result or consequence as distinct from a purpose or intention.

ecbolic /ɛk'bɒlɪk/ *n.* & *a.* M18. [f. Gk *ekbolē* expulsion + -IC.] *Med.* (An agent) that induces expulsion of the foetus.

ecce /'ɛki, 'ɛtʃeɪ, 'ɛksi/ *int.* LME. [L.] Lo!; behold.

Ecce Homo /'həʊməʊ/ behold the Man (*John* 19:5); (as *n. phr.*) a portrayal of Jesus wearing the crown of thorns. **ecce signum** /'sɪgnəm/ behold the sign.

†ecceity *n.* [med.L *ecceitas*: see -ITY] the quality of being present M16–E18.

eccentric /ɪk'sɛntrɪk, ɛk-/ *n.* & *a.* Also (chiefly in sense B.3) **exc-**. LME. [Late L *eccentricus* adj., f. Gk *ekkentros*, f. *ek-* EX-[2] + *kentron*: see CENTRE *n.*, -IC.] A *n.* 1 *Astron.* A circle or orbit not having the earth precisely in its centre. Now *Hist.* LME. 2 A disc or wheel mounted eccentrically on a revolving shaft so as to transmit a backward-and-forward motion (esp. to the slide-valve of a steam engine) through a linkage consisting of a ring (or strap) and connecting rod. E19. 3 A person whose behaviour is habitually unusual or whimsical. M19.

B *adj.* 1 Of a circle: not concentric with another (foll. by *to*). Of two or more circles: not mutually concentric. M16. †b *fig.* Having little in common. Only in 17. 2 Of orbital motion: not referrable to a fixed centre; not circular. Of a curve or orbit: deviating from a circular form. E17. 3 That has its axis, point of support, etc., not centrally placed. Of an axis etc.: not passing through the centre, not central. M17. b (*attrib.* use of the *n.*) Worked by or connected with an eccentric (sense A.2 above). E19. 4 *fig.* Irregular, anomalous, capricious; (of a person) habitually unusual, odd, whimsical. M17.

3 *eccentric projection*: see PROJECTION 7. 4 V. S. PRITCHETT His eccentric interpretation of the Christian ethic. A. CARTER Eccentric boots that laced up to her knee but left her toes bare. A. CLARE Society becomes unable to tolerate the eccentric . . behaviour of one of its members and the psychiatrist . . designates him 'ill'.

eccentrical *a.* †(*a*) = ECCENTRIC *a.* 1, 2; (*b*) = ECCENTRIC *a.* 4: M16. **eccentrically** *adv.* in an eccentric manner L17.

eccentricity /ɛksɛn'trɪsɪti/ *n.* In sense 1 also **exc-**. M16. [f. prec. + -ITY.] 1 The quality of being abnormally centred or of not being concentric. M16. b Deviation of a curve, orbit, etc., from circularity; the extent of such deviation (for an ellipse, equal to the distance between the foci divided by the length of the major axis). L17. †c Distance from the centre. E–M19. 2 The quality or habit of deviating from what is usual or customary; oddity, whimsicality; an instance of eccentric behaviour, etc. L17.

2 E. WAUGH Mrs M's latest eccentricity is to put bricks in the lavatory cisterns to save water. H. ACTON She was able to laugh at his foibles with a secret admiration for the vigorous eccentricity of his character.

ecchondroma /ɛkɒn'drəʊmə/ *n.* Pl. **-mas**, **-mata** /-mətə/. L19. [mod.L, f. Gk *ek* out + CHONDROMA.] *Med.* A chondroma growing outwards from the surface of a bone or cartilage. Cf. ENCHONDROMA.

ecchymoma /ɛkɪ'məʊmə/ *n.* Now *rare* or *obs.* Pl. **-mas**, **-mata** /-mətə/. M16. [mod.L f. Gk *ekkhumōma*, f. *ekkhumonathai* extravasate blood: see -OMA.] *Med.* A swelling caused by bleeding beneath the skin. Cf. next.

ecchymosis /ɛkɪ'məʊsɪs/ *n.* Pl. **-moses** /-'məʊsiːz/. M16. [mod.L f. Gk *ekkhumōsis*, f. *ekkhumonathai*: see prec., -OSIS.] *Med.* An area of discoloration and occas. swelling due to bleeding beneath the skin, whether through injury (bruising) or other cause.

ecchymosed *a.* [f. Fr. *ecchymosé*] affected with ecchymosis M19.

Eccles cake /'ɛk(ə)lz keɪk/ *n. phr.* L19. [*Eccles*, a town in Greater Manchester, England.] A round cake of pastry filled with currants etc.

ecclesia /ɪ'kliːzjə/ *n.* L16. [eccl.L f. Gk *ekklēsia* assembly, (eccl.) church, f. *ekklētos* pa. ppl a. of *ekkalein*, f. *ek-* EX-[2] + *kalein* call, summon.] *Hist.* A regularly convoked assembly; *esp.* the general assembly of Athenian citizens. Also, later, the Christian Church.

ecclesial /ɪ'kliːzj(ə)l/ *a.* M17. [OFr. *ecclésial*, f. as prec. + -AL[1].] Ecclesiastical.

¶Rare bef. M20.

ecclesiarch /ɪk'liːzɪɑːk/ *n.* L18. [f. Gk *ekklēsia* church + -ARCH.] A ruler of the Christian Church.

ecclesiast /ɪ'kliːzɪast/ *n.* LME. [eccl.L *ecclesiastes* f. Gk *ekklēsiastēs* member of an assembly, f. *ekklēsia*: see ECCLESIA. In the Septuagint rendering Heb. *qōheleṯ*.] 1 (**E-**) *The* author of the biblical book Ecclesiastes: Solomon. LME. 2 A functionary or administrator of the Christian Church. LME. 3 *Hist.* A member of the Athenian ecclesia. M19.

ecclesiastic /ɪˌkliːzɪ'astɪk/ *a.* & *n.* LME. [Fr. *ecclésiastique* or eccl.L *ecclesiasticus* f. Gk *ekklēsiastikos*, f. *ekklēsiastēs*: see prec., -IC.] A *adj.* 1 = ECCLESIASTICAL *a.* 1. LME. 2 = ECCLESIASTICAL *a.* 2. E17. B *n.* †1 In *pl.* = ECCLESIASTICAL *n.* 1. E17–M18. 2 A member of the clergy, a priest. M17.

ecclesiasticism /-sɪz(ə)m/ *n.* ecclesiastical spirit or principles; attention, esp. overattention, to details of ecclesiastical practice or administration: M19. **ecclesiasticize** /-sʌɪz/ *v.t.* make ecclesiastical M19.

ecclesiastical /ɪˌkliːzɪ'astɪk(ə)l/ *a.* & *n.* LME. [f. prec. + -AL[1].] A *adj.* 1 Of or pertaining to the Christian Church. Opp. *civil* or *secular*. LME. 2 Of or pertaining to the Christian clergy; clerical. M16.

Special collocations: **Ecclesiastical Commission(ers)** *Hist.* a body, subordinate to the Privy Council, which managed the estates and revenues of the Church of England from 1835 to 1948. **ecclesiastical courts**: for maintaining the discipline of the Church of England and administering ecclesiastical law. **ecclesiastical law**: derived from canon and civil law, administered in ecclesiastical courts. *ecclesiastical year*: see YEAR *n.*[1]

B *n.* **1** In *pl.* Matters concerning the Christian Church. M17. **2** = ECCLESIASTIC *n.* 2. *rare.* L19.

ecclesiastically *adv.* L16.

ecclesiastico- /ɪˌkliːzɪˈastɪkəʊ/ *comb. form.* L17. [f. as prec. + -O-.] Used chiefly to form adjs. f. adjs. w. the sense 'ecclesiastical and, ecclesiastically', as *ecclesiastico-conservative*, *-military*.

ecclesiolatry /ɪˌkliːzɪˈɒlətri/ *n.* M19. [f. ECCLESIA + -O- + -LATRY.] Excessive reverence for the Christian Church or church traditions.

ecclesiology /ɪˌkliːzɪˈɒlədʒi/ *n.* M19. [f. as prec. + -OLOGY.] **1** The branch of knowledge that deals with the Christian Church or churches, esp. church building and decoration. M19. **2** Theology as applied to the nature and structure of the Christian Church. M20.

eˌcclesioˈlogic *a.* L19. **eˌcclesioˈlogical** *a.* M19. **eˌcclesioˈlogically** *adv.* L19. **ecclesiologist** *n.* M19.

†eccoprotic *a.* & *n.* M17–E19. [Gk *ekkoprōtikos*, f. *ekkoproun* evacuate (the bowels), f. *ek-* EX-[2] + *kopros* dung: see -IC.] (A drug) having a mildly laxative effect.

eccrine /ˈɛkrʌɪn, -krɪn/ *a.* M20. [f. Gk *ekkrinein* secrete, f. *ek-* EX-[2] + *krinein* to separate: see INE[1].] *Physiol.* Designating or pertaining to those sweat glands which lose none of their cytoplasm during secretion. Cf. APOCRINE.

ecdysiast /ɛkˈdɪzɪast/ *n.* M20. [f. as next after *enthusiast*.] A striptease artist.

ecdysiasm *n.* the art or occupation of striptease M20.

ecdysis /ˈɛkdɪsɪs, ɛkˈdʌɪsɪs/ *n.* Pl. **-dyses** /-dɪsiːz, -ˈdʌɪsiːz/. M19. [Gk *ekdusis*, f. *ekduein* put off, shed, f. *ek-* EX-[2] + *duein* put.] The action or process of shedding an outer skin or integument, as in insects, reptiles, etc.

ecdysial /-ˈdɪz-/ *a.* E20. **ecdysone** *n.* (*Biochem.*) a steroid hormone that controls moulting in insects and other arthropods M20.

ecgonine /ˈɛkgəʊniːn, -nɪn/ *n.* M19. [f. Gk *ekgonos*, f. *ek* out of + *gon-*, *gen-* to produce: see -INE[5].] *Chem.* An alkaloid, $C_9H_{15}NO_3$, obtained by the hydrolysis of cocaine.

†eche *v.* var. of EKE *v.*

echelle /eɪˈʃɛl/ *n. obs.* exc. *Hist.* L17. [Fr. *échelle*: see next.] An arrangement of ribbons in the form of a ladder, decorating the front of the stomacher of a dress, etc.

echelon /ˈɛʃəlɒn, ˈeɪʃ-/ *n.* Also **†-ll-**. L18. [Fr. *échelon*, f. *échelle* ladder f. L *scala*: see SCALE *n.*[4], -OON.] **1** An arrangement of troops or equipment in parallel lines such that the end of each line is stepped somewhat sideways from that in front; *gen.* a formation of people or things arranged, individually or in groups, in a similar stepwise fashion. Also *echelon arrangement*, *formation*, etc. L18. **2** Each of the divisions of an echelon formation. E19. **b** Each of the subdivisions of the main supply service for troops in warfare. E19. **3** (A group of people occupying) a particular level in any organization. M20.

1 in echelon arranged in an echelon; cf. EN ÉCHELON. **2b** *rear echelon*: see REAR *a.*[1] **3** *Times* The higher echelons of the law and politics have become almost an Oxford preserve.

echelon /ˈɛʃəlɒn, ˈeɪʃ-/ *v.t.* M19. [f. the n. or Fr. *échelonner*.] Arrange in an echelon formation. Freq. as *echeloned* ppl a.

†echeneis *n. rare.* L16–L18. [Gk *ekhenēis*, f. *ekhein* to hold + *naus* (dat. *nēi*) ship, from its supposed power to hold back a ship.] = REMORA 1.

echeveria /ɛtʃɪˈvɪərɪə/ *n.* M19. [mod.L *Echeveria* (see below), f. Anastasio *Echeverría* or *Echeveri*, 19th-cent. Mexican botanical illustrator: see -IA[1].] Any of various succulent plants of the genus *Echeveria* (family Crassulaceae) native to S. and Central America.

échevin /ˈeɪʃəvɛ̃/ *n.* Pl. pronounced same. L17. [Fr.] In France, a municipal magistrate. In Belgium, a civic dignitary next in rank to the mayor.

echidna /ɪˈkɪdnə/ *n.* M19. [mod.L *Echidna* former genus name f. Gk *ekhidna* viper.] Either of two spiny insectivorous monotreme mammals, *Tachyglossus aculeatus* (the short-nosed echidna), native to Australia and New Guinea, and *Zaglossus bruijni* (the long-nosed echidna), native to New Guinea. Also called *spiny anteater*.

echinate /ˈɛkɪneɪt/ *a.* L17. [L *echinatus*, f. ECHINUS: see -ATE[2].] *Bot.* Covered with rigid bristles or prickles.

echinate /ˈɛkɪneɪt/ *v.* M17. [f. as prec.: see -ATE[3].] **1** *v.t. Bot.* As *echinated* ppl a. = prec. M17. **2** *v.t.* & *i. Zool.* Of a sponge spicule: project from (the fibrous skeleton) at an acute angle. L19.

echini *n.* pl. of ECHINUS.

echinite /ˈɛkɪnʌɪt/ *n.* M18. [f. ECHINUS + -ITE[1].] *Palaeont.* A fossil echinoderm.

echino- /ɪˈkʌɪnəʊ, ˈɛkɪnəʊ/ *comb. form* of Gk *ekhinos* hedgehog, sea urchin: see -O-.

echinoˈpluteus *n.* (*Zool.*) the free-swimming larval form of a sea urchin E20.

echinococcus /ɪˌkʌɪnə(ʊ)ˈkɒkəs/ *n.* Pl. **-cocci** /-ˈkɒk(s)ʌɪ, -ˈkɒk(s)iː/. M19. [mod.L *Echinococcus* (see below), f. as prec. + Gk *kokkos* seed, grain.] A tapeworm (formerly *spec.*, an encysted larval form) of the genus *Echinococcus*, members of which occur as adults in the intestines of dogs, wolves, etc., and as larval hydatid cysts in sheep and other animals, and sometimes humans.

echinococcosis /-kəˈkəʊsɪs/ *n.* (*Med.*) hydatid disease caused by echinococci E20.

echinoderm /ɪˈkʌɪnə(ʊ)dəːm, ˈɛkɪn-/ *n.* M19. [f. as ECHINO- + Gk *derma*, *-mat-* skin.] *Zool.* Any member of the phylum Echinodermata of coelomate, radially symmetric animals including the starfishes, brittle-stars, sea urchins, sea cucumbers, and crinoids.

echinoˈdermal, **-ˈdermatous** *adjs.* of, pertaining to, or characteristic of the echinoderms M19.

echinoid /ˈɛkɪnɔɪd/ *n.* & *a.* M19. [f. ECHINUS + -OID.] *Zool.* **A** *n.* An echinoderm of the class Echinoidea: a sea urchin. M19. **B** *adj.* Of, belonging to, or characteristic of the class Echinoidea or sea urchins. M19.

echinulate /ɪˈkɪnjʊlət/ *a.* M19. [f. as next + -ULE + -ATE[2], after AURICULATE etc.] Having or covered with small prickles.

echinus /ɪˈkʌɪnəs/ *n.* Pl. **-ni** /-nʌɪ/. LME. [L f. Gk *ekhinos* hedgehog, sea urchin. The origin of sense 2 (also in L & Gk) is unkn.] **1** A sea urchin. Now *spec.* a member of the genus *Echinus*, which includes the common edible sea urchin *E. esculentus*. LME. **2** *Archit.* An ovolo moulding next below the abacus of a capital. M16.

echites /ɪˈkʌɪtiːz/ *n.* Pl. same. LME. [Gk *ekhitēs*, f. *ekhis* viper.] **†1** = AETITES. LME–M18. **2** A climbing plant of the neotropical genus *Echites*, of the dogbane family. M18.

echium /ˈɛkɪəm/ *n.* L19. [mod.L (see below) f. Gk *ekhion*, f. *ekhis* viper, w. allus. to the spotted stem.] A plant or shrub of the Eurasian genus *Echium*, of the borage family, e.g. viper's bugloss, *E. vulgare*.

echiuroid /ˈɛkɪjʊ(ə)rɔɪd, ɛkɪˈjʊərɔɪd/ *n.* & *a.* L19. [f. mod.L *Echiuroidea* phylum name (see below), f. *Echiurus* genus name, f. Gk *ekhis* viper + *oura* tail: see -OID.] *Zool.* **A** *n.* Any member of the phylum Echiura (formerly Echiuroidea) of unsegmented marine worms, which have an anterior flattened unretractable proboscis; a spoonworm. L19. **B** *adj.* Of, belonging to, or characteristic of this phylum. L19.

echo /ˈɛkəʊ/ *n.* Pl. **-oes**, (*rare*) **-os**. ME. [(O)Fr. *écho* or L *echo* f. Gk *ēkhō* rel. to *ēkhē* sound.] **1** A repetition of a sound or sounds due to the reflection of the sound waves; the secondary sound(s) so produced. ME. **b** The cause of such repetition of sound personified; in Greek mythology (**E-**), the name of an oread. LME. **c** The reflection of a radio wave, ultrasonic signal, etc.; a reflected radio etc. signal. E20. **2** A person who reflects or imitates the language or opinions of others; a person who assents merely to flatter. Freq. in titles of newspapers. ME. **3** In verse, the repetition of the concluding syllables of a line to form the next line. L16. **4** A repetition or close imitation of an idea, a style, effect, etc.; a weakened reproduction. E17. **5** *Mus.* A section of an organ, or occas. a separate instrument, located away from the main instrument or enclosed, and used to produce softer and seemingly more distant sounds. Also *echo organ*. E18. **6** *Bridge* & *Whist.* A conventional play of a higher card in a suit followed by a lower, used to request a further lead of that suit by one's partner or to indicate the number of cards held in that suit. Also called *peter*. M19.

1 A. GRAY What seemed like echoes were the footsteps of someone behind. **to the echo** so strongly as to produce echoes. **b** SHAKES. *Rom. & Jul.* The cave where Echo lies. P. G. WODEHOUSE Don't repeat everything I say, as if you were an echo in the Swiss mountains. **c** R. V. JONES Detecting aircraft by echoes arising from reflected radio waves. **2** M. L. KING How often the church has been an echo rather than a voice. **4** FRANCIS THOMPSON No man can admire . . that of which he has no echo in himself. R. G. COLLINGWOOD Thus . . the sound of his groans, produces in us an echo of his pain.

Comb.: **echocardiogram** a tracing or image obtained by echocardiography; **echocardiographer** a person who uses echocardiography; **echocardiography** examination of the heart by means of ultrasound; **echo chamber**: for producing reverberation of sounds; **echoencephalogram** a tracing or image obtained by echoencephalography; **echoencephalography** examination of the inside or contents of the skull by means of ultrasound; **echolocate** *v.t.* locate by echolocation; **echolocation** location of objects by means of reflected sound (usu. ultrasound); **echometer** †(*a*) a device for measuring the duration of sounds; (*b*) an echo-sounder; *echo organ*: see sense 5 above; **echo-sounder** an apparatus for echo-sounding; **echo-sounding** the action or process of ascertaining depths or other distances by means of the time taken to receive an echo from a distant object, e.g. the seabed; **echo verse**: using the technique of the echo (sense 3).

echogram *n.* a record made by an echo-sounder M20. **echograph** *n.* a recording echo-sounder M20. **echoless** *a.* E18.

echo /ˈɛkəʊ/ *v.* M16. [f. the n.] **1** *v.i.* Of a sound: be repeated as an echo, reverberate. M16. **2** *v.i.* Of a place: resound with an echo, give rise to echoes. L16. **3** *v.t.* Repeat (a sound, voice, etc.) by reflection or as if by reflection; repeat the words of, imitate or resemble the style, effect, etc., of; flatter by servile assent. L16. **†4** *v.i.* Act as an echo *to*. M17–M18. **5** *v.i. Bridge* & *Whist.* Play an echo. L19.

1 K. MANSFIELD His long swinging steps echoed over the bare floor. **2** W. STYRON The cavernous room echoed with a tomblike roar to my sudden sneeze. **3** CONAN DOYLE Ugly rumours which . . agitated the University and were echoed in the learned societies. N. O. BROWN Murry, echoing . . D. H. Lawrence, adopts a stance of moral superiority.

echoer *n.* E19. **echoingly** *adv.* with an echo M19.

echoey /ˈɛkəʊi/ *a.* Also **echoy**. M19. [f. ECHO *n.* + -Y[1].] Of the nature of or like an echo; liable to resound with echoes.

echoic /ɛˈkəʊɪk/ *a.* L19. [f. ECHO *n.* + -IC.] Onomatopoeic; imitative of a sound.

echoism /ˈɛkəʊɪz(ə)m/ *n.* L19. [f. ECHO *n.* + -ISM.] Onomatopoeia.

echolalia /ɛkəʊˈleɪlɪə/ *n.* L19. [mod.L, f. Gk *ēkhō* echo + -LALIA.] The meaningless repetition of words and phrases, esp. as a sign of schizophrenia; repetition of speech by a child learning to talk.

echolalic *a.* M20.

echopraxia /ɛkəʊˈpraksɪə/ *n.* E20. [mod.L, f. Gk *ēkhō* echo + *praxis* action: see -IA[1].] The meaningless repetition or imitation of the movements of others, as a psychological disorder.

echopractic *a.* E20.

echo-virus /ˈɛkəʊvʌɪrəs/ *n.* Also **ECHO virus.** M20. [f. *e*nteric *c*ytopathogenic *h*uman *o*rphan + VIRUS.] *Med.* Any of a group of enteroviruses which are often asymptomatic but may cause mild meningitis, respiratory symptoms like those of a cold, etc.

echoy *a.* var. of ECHOEY.

echt /ɛçt/ *a.* & *adv.* E20. [G.] Authentic(ally), genuine(ly), typical(ly).

C. LAMBERT England has never produced an artist so 'echt-English' as Mussorgsky is 'echt-Russian'. N. FREELING Are you married? . . I see your ring, but is that camouflage or *echt*?

éclair /eɪˈklɛː, ɪ-/ *n.* M19. [Fr., lit. 'lightning'.] A small finger-shaped cake of choux pastry, filled with cream and iced, esp. with chocolate icing.

eclaircise /ɪˈklɛːsʌɪz/ *v.t. rare* (chiefly *US*). M18. [Back-form. f. next, assim. to *-ise*, -IZE.] Make clear, elucidate.

éclaircissement /eklɛrsismɑ̃/ *n.* Pl. pronounced same. M17. [Fr., f. *éclairciss*- lengthened stem of *éclaircir* clear up f. as EX-[1], *clair* clear: see CLEAR *a.*, -MENT.] A clarification of what is obscure or misunderstood; an explanation.

eclampsia /ɪˈklam(p)sɪə/ *n.* M19. [mod.L f. Fr. *éclampsie* irreg. f. Gk *eklampsis* sudden development, f. *eklampein* shine out.] *Med.* A dangerous disorder of late pregnancy characterized by high blood pressure, albuminuria, and fits. (See also PRE-ECLAMPSIA.)

eclamptic *a.* M19.

éclat /ɛˈklɑː, ˈeɪklɑː, *foreign* ekla/ *n.* & *v.* L17. [Fr., f. *éclater* burst out.] **A** *n.* **1** Radiance, dazzling effect (now only *fig.*); brilliant display. L17. †**2** Ostentation, publicity; public exposure, scandal; a sensation. L17–L19. **3** Social distinction; celebrity, renown. M18. **4** Conspicuous success; universal acclamation. Chiefly as *with* (*great* etc.) *éclat*. M18.

1 G. ETHEREGE The Eclat of so much beauty . . ought To have charm'd me sooner.

B *v.t.* & *i.* Make or become known or notorious. *rare*. M18.

eclectic /ɪˈklɛktɪk/ *a.* & *n.* L17. [Gk *eklektikos*, f. *eklegein* to select, f. *ek*- EX-[2] + *legein* choose.] **A** *adj.* **1** *Hist.* Designating, of, or belonging to a class of ancient philosophers who selected from various schools of thought such doctrines as pleased them. L17. **2** Made up of selections. *rare*. E19. **3** *gen.* That borrows freely or is derived from various sources or systems; broad rather than exclusive in matters of opinion, taste, etc. M19.

3 DISRAELI With . . an eclectic turn of mind, Mr. Vavasour saw something good in everybody. A. TATE The eclectic miscellany of easy speculations and solutions to which his more sensitive contemporaries succumbed.

B *n.* A person who is eclectic in method or outlook; *Hist.* an eclectic philosopher. E19.

eclectical *a.* = ECLECTIC *a.* M19. **eclectically** *adv.* M19. **eclecticism** *n.* eclectic philosophy; an eclectic outlook or method: L18. **eclectism** *n.* = ECLECTICISM M19.

†**eclegme** *n.* E17–E18. [med.L *eclegma* alt. of L *ecligma* f. Gk *ekleigma*, f. *ekleikhein* lick out.] *Med.* A linctus or syrupy medicine which is licked off the spoon.

eclipse /ɪˈklɪps/ *n.* ME. [(O)Fr. *e(s)clipse* (mod. *éclipse*) f. L *eclipsis* f. Gk *ekleipsis*, f. *ekleipein* be eclipsed, leave its place, fail to appear, f. *ek*- EX-[2] + *leipein* leave.] **1** The interception of the light of a celestial object by the intervention of another object between that object and the observer, or between that object and what illuminates it (as when a satellite enters the shadow of its primary). ME. **b** A temporary or permanent deprivation of light. E16. **2** *fig.* Obscuration, obscurity; dimness; loss of brilliance or splendour. LME. **3** *Ornith.* A plumage-phase of a bird (esp. of a male duck) during a post-nuptial moult when distinctive marking or coloration tends to become obscured. M19.

1 JAS. HARRIS Often had mankind seen the sun in eclipse. *annular eclipse*: see ANNULAR I. **eclipse of the moon, lunar eclipse**: caused by the interposition of the earth between the sun and moon, such that the moon is darkened. **eclipse of the sun, solar eclipse**: caused by the interposition of the moon between the sun and earth, covering all or part of the sun's disk as seen from the earth. *lunar eclipse*: see *eclipse of the moon* above. *solar eclipse*: see *eclipse of the sun* above. *total eclipse*: see TOTAL *a.* **b** MILTON Blind among enemies . . Irrecoverably dark, total eclipse. 2 G. HUNTINGTON His interest in a subject could undergo an eclipse and disappear altogether. W. S. CHURCHILL Jackson, from whom so much had been hoped, appeared in physical eclipse. 3 D. A. BANNERMAN The male [mallard] in eclipse resembles the female closely.

eclipse /ɪˈklɪps/ *v.* ME. [(O)Fr. *éclipser*, f. as prec.] **1** *v.t.* Of a celestial object: intervene so as to cause the eclipse of (another object). Also *gen.*, intercept light so as to obscure. ME. **2** *v.t.* Cast a shadow on, obscure, deprive of lustre. LME. †**b** Put out of sight; extinguish (life). L16–M17. **3** *v.t.* Make dim by comparison; surpass in brilliance etc., outshine. LME. †**4** *v.i.* Suffer an eclipse. LME–M18. **5** *v.t.* Orig., elide or omit (a sound) in pronunciation. Now *spec.* (in Irish and Welsh) cause the eclipsis of (a sound). L16.

1 L. DEIGHTON The . . fog that eclipsed his forward vision. 2 E. REVELEY It was all beginning to sound horribly plausible, and George felt his humour quickly eclipsed. **b** SHAKES. *1 Hen. VI* Born to eclipse thy life this afternoon. 3 DISRAELI One must sing in a room or the nightingales would eclipse us. A. GRAY He had . . expected it to eclipse the work of everyone else. 4 MILTON The night-hag . . comes . . to dance With Lapland witches while the . . moon Eclipses at their charms.

Phrases: **eclipsing binary** or **variable** *Astron.* a binary star system whose brightness varies periodically as the dimmer component passes in its orbit in front of the brighter and vice versa.

eclipsable *a.* able to undergo eclipsis M19. **eclipser** *n.* L16.

eclipsis /ɪˈklɪpsɪs/ *n.* Pl. **eclipses** /ɪˈklɪpsiːz/. M16. [Gk *ekleipsis*: see ECLIPSE *n.* In sense 1 perh. confused w. ELLIPSIS.] †**1** (An) ellipsis; a mark indicating this. M16–E18. **2** In Irish and Welsh, a change in an initial consonantal sound under the (historical) influence of a preceding nasal. M19.

ecliptic /ɪˈklɪptɪk/ *n.* & *a.* LME. [L *eclipticus* adj. f. Gk *ekleiptikos*, f. *ekleipein*: see ECLIPSE *n.*, -IC.] **A** *n.* The great circle of the celestial sphere representing the sun's apparent path during a year (so called because eclipses of the sun or moon can occur only when the moon is close to this circle). LME. **B** *adj.* Of or pertaining to an eclipse, eclipses, or the ecliptic. LME.

ecliptical *a.* (*rare*) = ECLIPTIC *a.* M16.

eclogite /ˈɛklɒdʒʌɪt/ *n.* M19. [Fr., f Gk *eklogē*, w. allus. to its selective content: see next, -ITE[1].] *Geol.* Any of a class of dense, granulose, metamorphic rocks consisting largely of garnet and a pyroxene together with other distinctive minerals.

eclogue /ˈɛklɒg/ *n.* Also †**eg-**. LME. [L *ecloga* f. Gk *eklogē* selection, esp. of poems, f. *eklegein*: see ECLECTIC.] A short poem, *esp.* a pastoral dialogue such as those of Virgil.

eclosion /ɪˈkləʊʒ(ə)n/ *n.* L19. [Fr. *éclosion*, f. *éclore* to hatch, ult. f. as EX-[1] 1 + L *claudere* to close.] Emergence from concealment; *esp.* the emergence of an insect from the pupa, or a larva from the egg.

eco- /ˈiːkəʊ, ˈɛkəʊ/ *comb. form.* [Extracted f. ECOLOGY.] Of or pertaining to ecology, ecological; environmental.

ecoca'tastrophe *n.* (an occurrence of) major damage to the natural environment, esp. where caused by human activity M20. **eco'cidal** *a.* designed or tending to damage the natural environment L20. **ecocide** *n.* (esp. wilful) destruction of the natural environment M20. **ecoclimate** *n.* the climate of a particular habitat M20. **eco-friendly** *a.* (*colloq.*) avoiding harm to the natural environment L20. **eco-geo'graphic(al)** *adjs.* pertaining to location and environment M20. **eco-label** *n.* a label identifying manufactured products that satisfy certain conditions of environmental significance L20. **ecophene** /-fiːn/ *n.* [PHEN(OTYP)E] any of the range of phenotypes produced by one genotype in reaction to extremes of habitat E20. **eco-raider** *n.* (*US*) a person who makes violent attacks in order to protect the natural environment L20. **ecosphere** *n.* (*a*) the region of space (around the sun or a star) within which conditions compatible with the existence of life (esp. on planets) may theoretically occur; (*b*) = BIOSPHERE: M20. **ecosystem** *n.* a system of organisms occupying a habitat, together with those aspects of the physical environment with which they interact M20. **ecotone** *n.* [Gk *tonos* tension] a region of transition between two ecological communities E20. **Eco'topia** *n.* [after *Utopia*] an ecologically ideal region or form of society L20. **ecotype** *n.* a subspecies occupying a particular habitat E20.

†**ecod** *int.* M18–M19. [f. as AGAD.] = EGAD.

ecological /iːkəˈlɒdʒɪk(ə)l, ɛk-/ *a.* Also †**oe-**. L19. [f. next + -ICAL.] Of, belonging to, or concerned with ecology.

ecologic *a.* = ECOLOGICAL L19. **ecologically** *adv.* E20.

ecology /ɪˈkɒlədʒi, ɛ-/ *n.* Also †**oe-**. L19. [f. Gk *oikos* house: see -OLOGY.] **1** The branch of biology that deals with organisms' relations to one another and to the physical environment in which they live; (the study of) such relations as they pertain to a particular habitat or a particular species. Also *spec.*, = *human ecology* below. L19. **2** (Also **E-**.) The political movement that seeks to protect the environment, esp. from pollution. Usu. *attrib.* L20.

1 *Nature* The ecology of a glacial lake. *fig.*: *Church Times* The finely balanced ecology of public-service broadcasting. **human ecology** the branch of knowledge that deals with the interaction of humans with their environment.

ecologist *n.* M20.

econometric /ɪˌkɒnəˈmɛtrɪk/ *a.* M20. [f. ECONOMY + -METRIC.] Of, pertaining to, or concerned with econometrics.

econometrical *a.* = ECONOMETRIC L20. **econometrically** *adv.* L20. **econometrician** /-məˈtrɪʃ(ə)n/ *n.* a student of or specialist in econometrics M20. **econometrist** *n.* = ECONOMETRICIAN L20.

econometrics /ɪˌkɒnəˈmɛtrɪks/ *n.* M20. [f. as prec.: see -ICS.] The branch of economics that deals with the application of mathematics, esp. statistics, to economic data.

economic /iːkəˈnɒmɪk, ɛk-/ *n.* & *a.* Also (earlier) †**oe-**. LME. [(O)Fr. *économique* or L *oeconomicus* f. Gk *oikonomikos*, f. *oikonomos*: see ECONOMY, -IC.] †**A** *n.sing.* (see also ECONOMICS). Household management, housekeeping; a person versed in this. LME–M17.

B *adj.* †**1a** Of or relating to household management. L16–L18. **b** Relating to the management of private, domestic, etc., finances; *gen.* (passing into sense 4), relating to monetary considerations, financial. M19. **2** = ECONOMICAL 4. Now *rare*. M18. **3** *Theol.* Pertaining to or marked by economy in doctrine or divine government. E19. **4** Of, pertaining to, or concerned with economics; relating to the wealth of a community or nation. M19. **b** Maintained for profit, on a business footing; paying (at least) the expenses of its operation or use. M19. **c** Of a subject: studied from a utilitarian or material standpoint. M19.

1a W. COWPER That I in wisdom œconomic aught Pass other women. **b** J. BRAINE It hadn't the remotest connection with . . economic necessity, it was . . self-indulgence. *Which?* The main economic drawback of the diesel car—its price—remains. 2 M. EDGEWORTH I never saw any one so economic of her smiles. 4 A. J. P. TAYLOR The British government had developed a conscious economic policy . . during the first World war. **c** *economic geology*, *economic history*, etc.

Special collocations: *economic* GEOGRAPHY. *economic growth*: see GROWTH *n.* 1C. **economic man** a (hypothetical) man who manages his finances strictly according to his own material interests. **economic rent** (*a*) a rent that brings a fair return on capital and current expenditure; (*b*) *Econ.* the amount by which what is paid to a particular economic factor, e.g. a worker, land, etc., exceeds the minimum payment necessary to keep that factor in its present use or employment. **economic warfare** the use by a State of measures (e.g. blockade) whose primary effect is to harm the economy of another State.

economical /iːkəˈnɒmɪk(ə)l, ɛk-/ *a.* Also (earlier) †**oe-**. L15. [f. as prec. + -AL[1].] †**1** = ECONOMIC *a.* 1a. L15–M18. **2** *Theol.* = ECONOMIC *a.* 3. L16. 3 = ECONOMIC *a.* 1b, 4. L18. 4 (The usual sense.) Characterized by or tending to economy; careful of resources, not wasteful; sparing, thrifty. L18.

4 R. KIPLING She's economical (I call it mean) in her coal. T. S. ELIOT Then we can share a taxi, and be economical. *Minicomputer Forum* An economical way of providing online computer services. **economical with the truth** discreditably reticent.

economically *adv.* (*a*) *Theol.* according to divine economy; (*b*) with economy, not wastefully; (*c*) as regards economics: L17.

economics /iːkəˈnɒmɪks, ɛk-/ *n.pl.* (usu. treated as *sing.*). Also (earlier) †**oe-**. L16. [f. ECONOMIC + -S¹, orig. after L *oeconomica*, Gk *ta oikonomika*, a treatise by Aristotle.] †1a (A treatise on) household management. Cf. ECONOMIC *n.* L16–L18. b The management of private or domestic finances; pecuniary position, monetary matters. M19. 2 The branch of knowledge that deals with the production and distribution of wealth in theory and practice; the application of this discipline to a particular sphere; the condition of a State etc. as regards material prosperity; the financial considerations attaching to a particular activity, commodity, etc. L18.

1b CARLYLE The family economics getting yearly more propitious. 2 M. PYKE One of the principles of economics unfortunately is, that in times of scarcity prices rise. J. S. FOSTER His choices must be made in terms of . . the economics of the end result.

economise *v.* var. of ECONOMIZE.

economism /ɪˈkɒnəmɪz(ə)m/ *n.* E20. [Fr. *économisme*, f. as ECONOMY: see -ISM.] Belief in the primacy of economic causes or factors.

economist /ɪˈkɒnəmɪst/ *n.* Also (earlier) †**oe-**. L16. [f. Gk *oikonomos*: see ECONOMY, -IST.] †1 A person who manages a household. L16–M19. 2 A person who attends to the effective use of resources, esp. money; an advocate or practitioner of economy, a thrifty person. E18. 3a [Fr. *économiste.*] *Hist.* A member of an 18th-cent. French philosophical school which advocated adherence to a supposed natural order of social institutions. M18. b A believer in or advocate of economism. M20. 4 An expert in or student of economics. E19.

Phrases: **political economist** an expert in or student of political economy.

economize /ɪˈkɒnəmaɪz/ *v.* Also **-ise**, (earlier) †**oe-**. M17. [f. as prec. + -IZE.] †1 *v.i.* Manage a household. Only in M17. †2 *v.t.* Manage, organize. Only in L17. 3 *v.i.* Practise economy; reduce expenses; make savings *in* or *on* a commodity etc. L18. 4 *v.t.* Use sparingly; make a saving in. E19. 5 *v.t.* Make (productive) use of; turn to the best account. *arch.* M19.

3 J. W. CARLYLE Light is one of the things I do not like to economise in. P. H. GIBBS Your father wants us to economize He's getting worried about the new taxes. 4 G. GREENE Stooped . . under a single globe, economising fuel. 5 ALLAN RAMSAY Who knows . . what motive powers may . . be economised.

economiˈzation *n.* M19. **economizer** *n.* (*a*) a person who economizes; (*b*) a device intended to effect a saving in the use of fuel etc.: M19.

economy /ɪˈkɒnəmi/ *n.* & *a.* Also (earlier) †**oe-**. L15. [(O)Fr. *économie* or L *oeconomia* f. Gk *oikonomia*, f. *oikonomos* manager of a household, steward, f. *oikos* house: see -NOMY.] A *n.* I Management. 1 The management or administration of the resources (freq. *spec.* financial resources) of a community or establishment; the art or science of managing material resources. L15. 2†a Household management. M16–L17. b The manner of ordering a household or domestic etc. finances. *arch.* E18. 3 The careful or sparing use of resources; frugality; the effecting of saving *in* a commodity etc. L17. b An instance or a means of reducing expenditure or saving. L18. c The cheapest class of some service or product, *esp.* of air travel. M20.

1 T. PENNANT Rural œconomy is but at a low ebb here. E. F. BENSON It is better economy . . to pay three-halfpence for an egg you can eat than a penny for one you can't. *black economy*: see BLACK *a.* **political economy** the branch of economics that deals with the economic problems of government; *arch.* = ECONOMICS 2. 2b J. PRIESTLEY Impertinence . . to watch over the œconomy of private people. 3 C. DARWIN The economy shown by nature in her resources. J. KOSINSKI Splitting each match in halves for economy. **economy of scale**: resulting from the greater efficiency of large-scale processes. b J. O'HARA What a foolish economy it is to save money on an orchestra. H. MACMILLAN Among the Government economies . . was a further cut . . in staff to Government Departments. *false economy*: see FALSE *a.*

II Constitution; economic system. 4 The constitution, organization, or structure of something; an ordered system. *arch.* (exc. as in sense 5 below). L16. †b Physical arrangement or structure; layout. L17–M18. 5 The organization or ordered state of a community or nation as regards its (esp. material) resources and concerns; the (economic) condition of a State etc. M17.

4 D. HUME With regard to the œconomy of the mind . . all vice is indeed pernicious. H. DAVY Water is absolutely necessary to the economy of vegetation. b MILTON Such œconomy or disposition of the fable as may stand best with . . decorum. 5 A. J. P. TAYLOR It seems that statesmen can do nothing right when the economy is going wrong. J. W. KRUTCH A pastoral or even a hunting economy capable of supporting the very small remaining population. *mature economy*: see MATURE *a.* MIXED *economy*. PLANNED *economy*. *wage economy*: see WAGE *n.*

III *Theol.* 6 The method of divine government of (an aspect or part of) the world; a system of this suited to particular circumstances. M17. 7 The presentation of doctrine or, by extension, 'truth', in such a way as to suit particular circumstances. Occas. in a bad sense (infl. by sense 3 etc.): discreditable reticence. L18.

6 F. MYERS Egyptian influence in the Mosaic Economy. 7 *transf.*: OED I do not impute falsehood . . , but I think there has been considerable economy of truth.

B *attrib.* or as *adj.* (Of a product) offering the customer the best value for money; of economy class, economy-sized (see below); designed to be economical to use. E19.

A. THIRKELL She . . licked the so-called economy label that was to take the envelope back to its sender.

Comb. & *special collocations*: **economy class** the cheapest class of air travel, hotel accommodation, etc.; **economy drive** a campaign to make savings by reducing expenses; **economy-size(d)** (of) a size (usu. the largest in a range) in which goods are sold that offers the customer the best value for money.

¶Adj. rare bef. 20.

écorché /ˈɛkɔːʃeɪ; *foreign* ekɔrʃe (*pl. same*)/ *n.* M19. [Fr., pa. pple of *écorcher* flay.] *Art.* An anatomical subject treated so as to display the musculature.

écossaise /ɛkɒˈseɪz, *foreign* ekɔsɛːz/ *n.* Pl. pronounced same. M19. [Fr., fem. of *écossais* Scottish.] (A dance to) a lively tune in duple time.

ecotage /ˈiːkətɑːʒ, ˈɛ-/ *n.* L20. [f. ECO- after *sabotage.*] Sabotage carried out for ecological reasons.

ecoteur /iːkəˈtəː, ɛ-/ *n.* [after *saboteur*] a person who carries out ecotage L20.

ecphonesis /ɛkfəˈniːsɪs/ *n.* Now *rare* or *obs.* Pl. **-neses** /-ˈniːsiːz/. L16. [Gk *ekphōnēsis*, f. *ekphōnein* cry out, f. *ek-* EX-² + *phōnein* speak.] *Rhet.* An exclamation.

†**ecphractic** *a.* M17–L19. [Gk *ekphraktikos*, f. *ekphrassein* remove obstructions: see -IC.] *Med.* Laxative.

ecphrasis /ˈɛkfrəsɪs/ *n.* Also **ek-**. Pl. **-ases** /-əsiːz/. E18. [Gk *ekphrasis*, f. *ekphrazein*, f. *ek-* EX-² + *phrazein* speak.] *Rhet.* A lucid, self-contained explanation or description.

écrevisse /ekrəvis/ *n.* Pl. pronounced same. M18. [Fr.] A crayfish.

ecru /ˈeɪkruː, ˈɛkruː/ *a.* & *n.* M19. [Fr. *écru* raw, unbleached.] (Of) the colour of unbleached linen; light fawn.

†**ecstacy** *n.* & *v.* var. of ECSTASY.

ecstasiate /ɛkˈsteɪzɪeɪt/ *v.t.* & *i.* E19. [f. ECSTASY + -ATE³.] = ECSTASIZE.

ecstasis /ˈɛkstəsɪs/ *n.* L16. [mod.L f. Gk *ekstasis*: see ECSTASY.] Ecstasy.

ecstasize /ˈɛkstəsaɪz/ *v.t.* & *i.* Also **-ise**. M19. [f. next + -IZE.] Throw into an ecstasy: go into ecstasies.

ecstasy /ˈɛkstəsi/ *n.* & *v.* Also †**ex(s)t-**, †**-acy**. LME. [OFr. *extasie* f. late L *extasis* f. Gk *ekstasis*, f. *eksta-* stem of *existanai* put out of place, f. as EX-² + *histanai* to place: see -Y³.] A *n.* 1 The state of being distracted by some emotion; a frenzy, a stupor; (now the usual sense) an exalted state of feeling (freq. in *pl.*), rapture (esp. of delight). LME. †2 Orig., a swoon, a trance. Later (*Med.*), a pathological state of absorption and unresponsiveness. L16–L19. 3 A state of trance or rapture such as is supposed to accompany religious, prophetic, or mystical inspiration; poetic frenzy. M17. 4 (Freq. **E-**.) A hallucinogenic drug, = *MDMA* s.v. M, M. L20.

1 SHAKES. *Macb.* On the torture of the mind to lie In restless ecstasy. W. OWEN Gas! Gas! Quick, boys!—An ecstasy of fumbling, Fitting the clumsy helmets just in time. D. H. LAWRENCE His presence . . touched her with an ecstasy, a thrill of pure intoxication. *an ecstasy* (or *ecstasies*) *of woe, joy, rage, despair*, etc. **in ecstasies** extremely delighted, filled with pleasure. 3 MILTON Certaine women in a kind of ecstasie foretold of calamities to come. T. GRAY He that rode sublime Upon the seraph wings of ecstacy.

B *v.t.* Send into a state of ecstasy; enrapture. Now *rare.* E17.

D. H. LAWRENCE Obscenely ecstasied Sucking live blood.

ecstatic /ɪkˈstatɪk, ɛk-/ *a.* & *n.* Also †**ex(s)t-**. L16. [Fr. *extatique* f. Gk *ekstatikos*, f. *eksta-*: see prec., -IC.] A *adj.* Of the nature of, characterized by, or producing ecstasy; enraptured, extremely delighted. L16.

POPE In trance extatic may thy pangs be drowned. M. LASKI Ecstatic with happiness Margaret fox-trotted in her father's arms. R. WEST An ecstatic sense of ease.

B *n.* 1 A person who is subject to spells of (esp. mystical etc.) ecstasy. M17. 2 In *pl.* Transports of ecstasy (usu. *iron.*). E19.

ecstatical *a.* (*arch.*) = ECSTATIC *a.* E17. **ecstatically** *adv.* M17.

ectasia /ɛkˈteɪzɪə/ *n.* L19. [mod.L, f. as next with irreg. substitution of -IA¹.] *Med.* Dilatation of a blood-vessel or vessels, esp. when congenital and extensive. Cf. ANEURYSM.

ectasis /ˈɛktəsɪs/ *n. rare* (only in Dicts.) or *obs.* Pl. **-ases** /-əsiːz/. M16. [mod.L f. Gk *ektasis*, f. *ekteinein* stretch out, f. *ek-* EX-² + *teinein* stretch.] The extension of a short syllable. Also, = prec.

ectene /ˈɛktɪni/ *n.* Also **ek-**. M19. [eccl.Gk, f. *ektenēs* extended.] *Gk Orthodox Ch.* A litany recited by a deacon and choir.

Ecthesis /ˈɛkθɪsɪs/ *n.* E18. [Gk *ekthesis* exposition, f. as EX-² + THESIS.] *Theol.* An edict of the Emperor Heraclius of 638 maintaining the Monothelite doctrine that Jesus had only one (divine) will.

ecthlipsis /ɛkˈθlɪpsɪs/ *n.* Pl. **-pses** /-psiːz/. L16. [mod.L f. Gk *ekthlipsis*, f. *ekthlibein* squeeze out.] *Class. Pros.* The removal of a syllable ending in *m* before a vowel.

ecthyma /ɛkˈθʌɪmə/ *n.* M19. [mod.L f. Gk *ekthuma*, f. *ekthnein* break out as heat or bodily humours.] *Med.* An ulcerative impetigo affecting also lower layers of the skin.

ecto- /ˈɛktəʊ/ *comb. form.* [Repr. Gk *ekto-* stem of *ektos* adv.: see -O-.] Outside, external.

ectocrine /-krʌɪn, -krɪn/ *n.* (*Biol.*) any metabolite that is released into an organism's environment and influences the vital processes of other organisms M20. **ectoloph** *n.* (*Zool.*) the outer ridge on the crown of a lophodont tooth E20. **ectoˈparasite** *n.* a parasite that inhabits the outer surface of the body (as skin, fur, feathers, etc.) of its host M19. **ectoˈpterygoid** *a.* & *n.* (*Zool.*) (designating or pertaining to) a palatal bone of most reptiles and some amphibians, lateral to the pterygoid L19. **ectoˈthermic** *a.* (*Zool.*) dependent on external sources of body heat (cf. POIKILOTHERMIC): M20. **ectotrophic** /-ˈtrəʊfɪk, -ˈtrɒfɪk/ *a.* (*Bot.*) (of a mycorrhiza) forming tissue on the surface of roots L19.

ectoblast /ˈɛktə(ʊ)blast/ *n.* M19. [f. prec. + -BLAST.] *Biol.* = EPIBLAST.

ectoˈblastic *a.* L19.

ectoderm /ˈɛktə(ʊ)dəːm/ *n.* M19. [f. ECTO- + Gk *derma* skin.] *Biol.* The outer germ layer of the embryo in early development, giving rise to epidermis and neural tissue; cells or tissue derived from this; such cells as forming the outer layer of the body of a coelenterate etc.

ectodermal *a.* of, pertaining to, or derived from the ectoderm L19.

ectogenesis /ɛktə(ʊ)'dʒɛnɪsɪs/ *n.* E20. [f. ECTO- + -GENESIS.] *Biol.* Reproduction occurring outside the body.

ectoge'netic, -genic *adjs.* E20.

ectomorph /'ɛktə(ʊ)mɔːf/ *n.* M20. [f. ECTO- + -MORPH.] A person of lean build (with noticeable development of tissue derived from the embryonic ectoderm, as the skin and nervous system).

ecto'morphic *a.* of, pertaining to, or characteristic of an ectomorph; of the nature of an ectomorph: M20. **ectomorphy** *n.* the state or property of being an ectomorph M20.

-ectomy /'ɛktəmi/ *suff.* [f. Gk *ektomē* excision, f. *ek-* EX-[2] + *temnein* to cut: cf. -TOMY.] Forming ns. denoting surgical operations in which some part is removed, as *appendicectomy, hysterectomy, tonsillectomy*, etc.

ectopia /ɛk'təʊpɪə/ *n.* M19. [mod.L, f. Gk *ektopos* out of place f. *ek-* EX-[2] + *topos* place: see -IA[1].] *Med.* The presence of an organ, cells, or tissue at an abnormal site.

ectopic /ɛk'tɒpɪk/ *a.* L19. [f. prec. + -IC.] *Med.* Occurring in an abnormal position or place; *esp.* (of pregnancy) characterized by development of the foetus elsewhere than in the uterus.

ectopic beat = EXTRASYSTOLE.

ectopically *adv.* M20.

ectoplasm /'ɛktə(ʊ)plaz(ə)m/ *n.* L19. [f. ECTO- + -PLASM.] **1** *Biol.* The outer, clear, non-granular part of the cytoplasm in some cells (e.g. amoeba). Now *rare.* L19. **2** A viscous substance supposed to exude from the body of a medium during a spiritualistic trance. E20.

ecto'plasmic *a.* of, pertaining to, of the nature of, or resembling ectoplasm L19. **ecto'plasmically** *adv.* in the manner of ectoplasm M20. **ecto'plastic** *a.* = ECTOPLASMIC E20.

ectoproct /'ɛktə(ʊ)prɒkt/ *n.* & *a.* E20. [f. mod.L *Ectoprocta* (see below), f. as ECTO- + Gk *prōktos* anus.] *Zool.* **A** *n.* A bryozoan of the coelomate phylum Ectoprocta, having the anus opening outside the lophophore. Cf. ENTOPROCT. E20. **B** *adj.* Of, belonging to, or characteristic of Ectoprocta. E20.

ecto'proctan *a.* & *n.* = ECTOPROCT M20. **ecto'proctous** *a.* = ECTOPROCT *a.* L19.

ectrodactyly /ɛktrə(ʊ)'daktɪli/ *n.* L19. [f. Gk *ektrōma* or *ektrōsis* miscarriage, abortion (f. *ek-* EX-[2] + *trō-* to damage) + *daktulos* finger: see -Y[3].] *Med.* Congenital absence of digits.

ectrodac'tylia *n.* (*rare*) = ECTRODACTYLY M19. **ectrodactylism** *n.* = ECTRODACTYLY L19.

ectromelia /ɛktrə(ʊ)'miːlɪə/ *n.* E20. [f. as prec. + Gk *melos* limb + -IA[1].] *Med.* **1** Congenital absence of a limb or limbs. E20. **2** A viral disease of mice which may cause the loss of limbs. M20.

ectropion /ɛk'trəʊpɪən/ *n.* L17. [mod.L *ectropium*, Gk *ektropion*, f. Gk *ek-* EX-[2] + *trepein* to turn.] *Med.* Eversion of the eyelid.

ectype /'ɛktʌɪp/ *n.* M17. [Gk *ektupon* neut. of *ektupos* worked in relief, f. *ek-* EX-[2] + *tupos* figure: see TYPE *n.*] A replica or copy of an original, a reproduction. Formerly also, an impression in wax etc.

ectypal *a.* of, pertaining to, or of the nature of, an ectype M17.

ecu /'ɛkjuː, 'iː-, 'eɪ-; -kuː/ *n.* Pl. same, **-s.** L20. [Abbrev.] = *European Currency Unit* s.v. EUROPEAN *a.* 3.

écu /'ɛkuː, *foreign* eky (*pl. same*)/ *n.* L16. [Fr. f. L *scutum* shield.] A French gold or silver coin orig. bearing three fleurs-de-lis on a shield, differing in value at different periods (usu. three or five francs).

Ecuadorian /ɛkwə'dɔːrɪən/ *a.* & *n.* Also **-rean.** M19. [f. *Ecuador* (see below) + -IAN.] **A** *adj.* Of, belonging to, or characteristic of Ecuador, an equatorial country in S. America. M19. **B** *n.* A native or inhabitant of Ecuador. M19.

ecuelle /ɛ'kwɛl/ *n.* Also **é-.** M19. [Fr. *écuelle* ult. f. L *scutella*.] **1** A two-handled soup bowl. M19. **2** The process or apparatus by which oils are extracted from the peel of citrus fruit. L19.

ecumaniac /iːkjʊ'meɪnɪak, ɛk-/ *n. colloq.* M20. [f. next + -MANIAC.] A zealous or overzealous supporter of ecumenism.

ecumenical /iːkjʊ'mɛnɪk(ə)l, ɛ-/ *a.* Also (earlier) **oe-** /iː-/. L16. [f. late L *oecumenicus* f. Gk *oikoumenikos* of or belonging to *hē oikoumenē* the (inhabited) earth, the whole world: see -AL[1].] **1** Of or belonging to the whole Christian world or the universal Church. In recent use freq.: marked by ecumenism, seeking (worldwide) Christian unity that transcends doctrinal differences; of or representing Christians of several denominations; interdenominational. L16. **2** Universal, general, worldwide. E17.

1 ecumenical council any of various representative councils of the church worldwide (since the 9th cent., of the Roman Catholic church alone) whose decisions are considered authoritative. **Ecumenical Patriarch** (a title of) the Patriarch of Constantinople.

¶The spelling with *e-* is not recorded bef. M19.

ecumenic *a.* = ECUMENICAL L16. **ecumenicalism** *n.* ecumenicity; (esp.) ecumenism: L19. **ecumenicality** *n.* = ECUMENICITY M19. **ecumenically** *adv.* M18. **ecume'nicity** *n.* [eccl.L *oecumenicitas*] ecumenical character; (Christian) universality; ecumenism: M19. **ecumenics** *n.* (*a*) the branch of knowledge that deals with the Christian Church as a unity; (*b*) ecumenism: M20.

ecumenism /ɪ'kjuːmənɪz(ə)m/ *n.* M20. [f. prec. + -ISM.] Belief in or striving for the worldwide unity of Christians, transcending differences of doctrine.

ecumenist *n.* an adherent of ecumenism M20.

eczema /'ɛksɪmə, 'ɛkzɪmə/ *n.* M18. [mod.L f. Gk *ekzema, -mat-*, f. *ekzein* boil over, (of disease) break out, f. *ek-* EX-[2] + *zein* to boil.] Non-infective superficial inflammation of the skin, usu. with itching and vesicular discharge. Cf. DERMATITIS.

eczematous /ɛk'sɛ-, ɛk'zɛ-/ *a.* of or pertaining to eczema; characterized by eczema: M19.

-ed /d, ɪd, t, (*see below*)/ *suff.*[1] Also **-d, -'d,** (see below). See also -T[3]. [OE *-ed, -ad, -od* (*-ud*), *-d* repr. Gmc ppl suff. f. IE.] Forming the pa. t. & pple of weak vbs; also ppl adjs. having the same form as such pa. pples, with senses (of v.t.) 'that has been subject to the vbl action, that expresses subjection to the vbl action', (of v.i.) 'that has performed the vbl action, that habitually performs the vbl action in the stated manner.' In 15–17, often added without change of meaning to adapted forms of L pa. pples and ppl adjs. in -ATE[2]. Cf. -EN[6].

¶Mod. Eng. usage is as follows: (i) Pronunciation /ɪd/ after /t/, /d/, and after other consonants in some ppl adjs. and derived advs. in general use, more widely in arch. and poet. use. Orthographic representation *-ed*, in arch. and poet. use sometimes *-èd*. Examples: *folded, listed, blessed* (ppl a.), *learned* (ppl a.), *advisedly, markedly, hornèd* (arch. & poet.). (ii) Pronunciation /t/ after voiceless consonants other than /t/, except in some ppl adjs. etc. (see (i) above). Orthographic representation *-d* after *-e*, otherwise *-ed*; after a shortened vowel, in some irreg. forms, and in arch. and poet. use also *-t*. Cf. -T[3]. Examples: *baked, peeped, pushed, crept, slept, bought* (irreg.), *blest* (arch. & poet.), *wrapt* (arch. & poet.). (iii) Pronunciation /d/ after voiced consonants other than /d/, except in some ppl adjs. etc. (see (i) above), and after vowels. Orthographic representation *-d* after *-e* and after *-l* in some irreg. forms, otherwise *-ed*, also *'d* after *-a* and more widely in arch. and poet. use. Examples: *inclined, refereed, carried, cried, sold* (irreg.), *absorbed, rigged, seemed, hallowed, huzzaed* or *huzza'd, climb'd* (arch. & poet.).

-ed /d, ɪd, t (*as prec.*)/ *suff.*[2] Also **-d, 'd,** (as prec.). [OE *-ede* = OS *-ôdi*, f. Gmc.] Forming adjs. f. ns. w. the senses 'possessing, provided with, characterized by', as *bearded, moneyed, jaundiced*, 'having the character of', as *bigoted, dogged*. Used freely to form adjs. f. collocation of adj. & n., as *quick-witted, three-cornered, good-humoured*.

edacious /ɪ'deɪʃəs/ *a.* Now *literary* or *joc.* E19. [f. L *edac-, edax* (f. *edere* eat) + -OUS: see -ACIOUS.] Of or relating to eating; voracious; *fig.* greedy.

J. R. LOWELL The edacious tooth of Time.

edacity *n.* the quality of being edacious; capacity for eating: E17.

Edam /'iːdam/ *n.* E19. [A town near Amsterdam, in the Netherlands.] In full *Edam cheese*. A mild spherical pressed Dutch cheese, usu. yellow with a red rind.

edaphic /ɪ'dafɪk/ *a.* L19. [f. Gk *edaphos* floor + -IC.] *Biol.* Of the soil; produced or influenced by the soil.

edaphically *adv.* M20.

Edda /'ɛdə/ *n.* L17. [Either from the name of the great-grandmother in the ON poem *Rigsþul* or f. ON *óðr* poetry.] Either of two Icelandic books, (*a*) the *Elder* or *Poetic Edda*, a collection, made *c* 1200, of ancient Old Norse poems on mythical and traditional subjects; (*b*) the *Younger* or *Prose Edda*, a miscellaneous handbook to Old Norse poetry, written *c* 1230.

Eddaic /ɛ'deɪɪk/ *a.* of, pertaining to, or resembling the contents of, the Eddas L19. **Eddic** *a.* = EDDAIC M19.

edder /'ɛdə/ *v.* & *n.* Now *dial.* Also **ether** /'ɛðə/. E16. [Doubtfully identified w. OE *eodor, eder* enclosure. Cf. YEDDER.] **A** *v.t.* Interlace or bind (a hedge etc.) at the top with osiers, withes, etc. E16. **B** *n.* Osiers etc. used for this purpose. L16.

eddish /'ɛdɪʃ/ *n.* Now *dial.* OE. [Origin unkn. Sense 2 perh. a different wd, but cf. OE *edisċhenn* quail, perh. 'stubble-hen'.] †**1** A park or enclosed pasture for cattle. Only in OE. **2** Grass, clover, etc., which grows again; an aftermath; stubble, a stubble-field. LME.

eddo /'ɛdəʊ/ *n.* Chiefly *W. Indies.* Pl. **-oes.** L17. [Of W. African origin: cf. Fante *edwó(w)* yam, *ndwo(w)* root.] **1** A tuber of (a variety of) taro; a similar edible tuber. Usu. in *pl.* L17. **2** A plant bearing such tubers. M18.

eddy /'ɛdi/ *n.* & *v.* LME. [Prob. f. base of OE *ed-* again, back. Cf. ON *iða* eddy.] **A** *n.* A circular or contrary motion in water, esp. at the side of the main current; a similar motion in air, fog, smoke, etc.; a small whirlpool or vortex. LME.

G. ORWELL Little eddies of wind were whirling dust and torn paper into spirals. *fig.*: P. ACKROYD Eddies of loud, barking laughter swept across the room.

Comb.: **eddy current** a localized circulating current induced within the body of an electrical conductor by magnetic field variation; **eddy-wind**: that moves in an eddy.

B *v.t.* & *i.* (Cause to) move in an eddy or eddies. M18.

L. LEE This fearful spice, eddying up from its box. R. GRAVES Not enough breeze to eddy a puff of smoke.

eddyless *a.* E17.

edelweiss /'eɪd(ə)lvʌɪs/ *n.* M19. [G, f. *edel* noble + *weiss* white.] A plant of the composite family, *Leontopodium alpinum*, of the Alps and other European mountains, bearing small heads surrounded by conspicuous white woolly bracts spreading like a star.

edema *n.* see OEDEMA.

Eden /'iːd(ə)n/ *n.* ME. [Late L (Vulgate), Gk (Septuagint) *Ēdēn*, Heb. *'ēden*, perh. f. Akkadian *edinu* f. Sumerian *eden* plain, steppe, assoc. w. Heb. *'ēden* delight.] The abode of Adam and Eve in the biblical account of creation; a delightful abode, a paradise, a state of supreme happiness. Also *garden of Eden*

SHAKES. *Rich. II* This scept'red isle, . . This other Eden, demi-paradise.

Edenic /ɪ'dɛnɪk/ *a.* of, pertaining to, or resembling Eden M19.

edenite /'iːd(ə)nʌɪt/ *n.* M19. [f. *Edenville*, Orange County, New York + -ITE[1].] *Min.* A light-coloured variety of hornblende containing relatively little iron.

edentate /ɪ'dɛnteɪt/ *a.* & *n.* E19. [L *edentatus* pa. pple of *edentare* render toothless, f. *e-* E- + *dent-, dens* tooth: see -ATE[2].] **A** *adj.* Having few or no teeth; *spec.* (*Zool.*) of or pertaining to the mammalian order Edentata, members of which (anteaters, sloths, and armadillos) lack incisor and canine teeth. E19. **B** *n.* An edentate mammal. M19.

edentulous /ɪˈdɛntjʊləs/ *a.* E18. [f. L *edentulus*, f. *e-* E- + *dent-*, *dens* tooth: see -ULOUS.] Having no teeth, toothless.

edestin /ɪˈdɛstɪn/ *n.* L19. [f. Gk *edestos* eatable + -IN[1].] *Biochem.* A globulin found in wheat, hempseed, etc.

edge /ɛdʒ/ *n.* [OE *eċġ* = OFris. *egg*, OS *eggia* (Du. *egge*), OHG *ekka* (G *Ecke*), ON *egg*, f. Gmc, f. IE base meaning 'be sharp or pointed', as in L *acies* edge, Gk *akis* point.] **I** Something that cuts. **1** The sharpened side of the blade of a cutting instrument or weapon. OE. **b** A cutting weapon or tool. *poet.* OE. **c** The sharpness given to a blade by whetting. LME. **2** *fig.* Effectiveness; trenchant force; keenness. L16. **†b** Ardour; in a weaker sense: inclination. L16–M19. **c** An advantage, superiority. Chiefly as *have* etc. *the edge* (*on*, *over*). *colloq.* E20. **d** A state of intoxication. *US colloq.* E20.

1 A. DUGGAN He carried a curved scimitar, so that in his fencing he relied on the edge and neglected the point. *knife-edge*: see KNIFE *n.* *razor-edge*, *razor's edge*: see RAZOR. b SHAKES. *Coriol.* Men and lads, Stain all your edges on me. c T. HARDY A sword that has no edge. *fig.*: A. N. WILSON What gives Belloc's fiction its cutting edge. 2 K. GRAHAME The edge of their hunger was somewhat dulled. E. GLASGOW The March wind had a biting edge. S. HILL His voice had taken on an edge of sarcasm. M. HUNTER The tension in our household took on an unbearable edge. c *Listener* Labour's special relationship with the working classes . . was supposed to give it an edge over the tories. P. ROTH In the shoulders and chest I had the edge.

II Something sharp or narrow. **3** The crest of a narrow ridge; a perilous path on a ridge. LME. **4** The narrow surface or side of a thin object; in *Bookbinding*, each of the three surfaces (*top edge*, *bottom edge*, and *fore-edge*) not protected by the binding. M17. **5** A line along which two surfaces of a solid intersect. In *Skating*, the inner or outer side of the blade of a skate. L18.

3 *fig.*: POPE Each . . Greek . . Stands on the sharpest edge of death or life. 4 L. STERNE Laying the edge of her finger across her two lips.

III A boundary, a margin. **6** The boundary line of a surface or region, a border; the region adjacent to this, a margin. LME. **b** The edging of a garment, curtain, etc. E16. **7** The brink or verge of a bank or precipice; the area close to a steep drop. LME. **8** *fig.* The beginning *of* a portion of time, *of* a season; the limit *of* a quality or emotion; (*colloq.*) *the* limit of what is reasonable or decent. E17.

6 E. HEMINGWAY Whitewashed stones that marked the edge of the road. G. GREENE A table at the edge of the dance floor. 7 R. POLLOK Toppling upon the perilous edge of Hell. DAY LEWIS Leaning so far over the edge of it [a pulpit] . . that he all but pitched head first into the congregation. 8 S. JOHNSON I made a journey to Staffordshire on the edge of winter. E. BOWEN He would go over the edge, quite mad. J. BUCHAN I came to the edge of fear.

Phrases: **†back and edge** adjoining, close by. **edge to edge** with edges adjacent. **give an edge to** sharpen, make keener, stimulate. *have* etc. *the edge* (*on*, *over*): see sense 2c above. *leading edge*: see LEADING *a.* *not put too fine an edge (up)on it*: see FINE *a.* **on edge** nervously irritable, excited, keyed up. **on the edge of** on the point of (an action); almost involved in or affected by. *on the ragged edge*: see RAGGED *a.* 2. **set an edge (up)on** = *give an edge to* above. **set a person's teeth on edge** cause a person acute irritation or discomfort, as if from eating sour fruit. **take the edge off** blunt, weaken, dull (a person's appetite, argument, tone of voice, etc.). **the edge of the sword** *rhet.* the instrument of slaughter or conquest. **the rough** (or **sharp**) **edge of one's tongue** abusiveness, reviling. *trailing edge*: see TRAILING *a.*

Comb.: **edge connector** *Electronics* a connector with a row of contacts, fitted to the edge of a printed circuit board to facilitate connection to external circuits; **edge-on** with the edge foremost; **edge-rail** a railway rail which bears the wheels on its edge; **edge-runner** an apparatus for crushing stone, fibres, or other material; **edge-tool** (*a*) any implement with a sharp cutting edge (now chiefly *fig.*); (*b*) a hand-worked or machine-operated cutting tool; **edge well**: located at or near the edge of an oilfield or gas field.

edgeless *a.* L16.

edge /ɛdʒ/ *v.* ME. [f. the n.: see also EGG *v.*[1]] **1** *v.t.* Give an edge, impart sharpness, to (a weapon, tool, etc.). ME. **b** *fig.* Give keenness or incisive force to (appetite, wit, endeavour, etc.). L16. **c** Urge on, incite, encourage. Now only w. *on*. Cf. EGG *v.*[1] L16. **2** *v.t.* Set (the teeth) on edge. *obs.* exc. *dial.* ME. **3** *v.t.* Provide with or *with* an edging; form a border to. M16. **b** Enclose, surround; go round the edge of. M17. **4** *v.i.* Move edgeways; advance, esp. gradually and obliquely. Orig. chiefly *Naut.* E17. **b** *v.t.* Insinuate *into* a place; push by imperceptible degrees (*away*, *in*, *off*, *out*, etc.); make (one's way) thus. L17. **5** *v.t.* *Cricket.* Deflect (the ball) with the edge of the bat. E20. **6** Defeat by a small margin. *N. Amer.* M20.

1 POPE Thy sure divinity shall . . edge thy sword to reap the glorious field. b G. BRIMLEY The piercing cold of the night-wind edged with sea-salt. 3 J. STEINBECK The concrete highway was edged with a mat of tangled, broken, dry grass. O. MANNING The single rusted rail that edged the quay. b POPE A bay there lies, Edg'd round with cliffs. A. TYLER She edged puddles . . and hopped across flowing gutters. 4 F. MARRYAT The . . admiral edged away with his squadron. M. AMIS I stayed where I was while Rachel edged forward with the queue. b S. CENTLIVRE A Son of One and Twenty, who wants . . to edge himself into the Estate! W. IRVING Every one edging his chair a little nearer. S. O'FAOLÁIN I . . edged my bicycle through the creaking gate. 5 *Times* Fortunate . . to edge Wilson only just wide of . . gully. 6 *Globe & Mail* (*Toronto*) The Jays edged the Royals 6–5.

edged *a.* (*a*) having a cutting edge; (*b*) having an edge or border (of a specified kind): ME. **edger** *n.* (*a*) a person whose job is to make or otherwise work on the edge of an article; (*b*) a tool for making or trimming an edge: L16. **edging** *n.* (*a*) the action of the vb (*edging-shears*: for trimming the edges of a lawn); (*b*) something forming an edge; a border, fringe, etc., sewn on the edge of a garment, curtain, etc.; a border surrounding a flower-bed: LME.

edgeways /ˈɛdʒweɪz/ *adv.* Also (*rare*) **-way** /-weɪ/. M16. [f. EDGE *n.* + -WAYS.] With the edge foremost, uppermost, or towards the spectator.

get a word in edgeways: see WORD *n.*

edgewise /ˈɛdʒwʌɪz/ *adv.* E18. [f. EDGE *n.* + -WISE.] **1** = EDGEWAYS. E18. **2** Edge to edge. M19.

edgy /ˈɛdʒi/ *a.* L18. [f. EDGE *n.* + -Y[1].] **1** Having an edge or edges; sharp-edged. L18. **2** Of a painting; having the contours too hard. E19. **3** *fig.* Having one's nerves on edge; irritable, testy. M19. **b** Eager; alert, sharp. *Sc.* & *dial.* M19.

edgily *adv.* M19. **edginess** *n.* E19.

edh *n.* var. of ETH.

edible /ˈɛdɪb(ə)l/ *a.* L16. [Late L *edibilis*, f. *edere* eat: see -IBLE.] **A** *adj.* Eatable, fit to be eaten. L16.

edible crab a large European crab, *Cancer pagurus*, caught for food. **edible dormouse** a nocturnal dormouse, *Glis glis*, of western Eurasia, resembling a squirrel, valued as food in some countries. **edible frog** a green frog, *Rana esculenta*, native to Continental Europe and introduced in Britain. **edible snail** a large European snail, *Helix pomatia*, valued as a delicacy.

B *n.* A thing that is edible, an article of food. Usu. in *pl.* M17.

edi'bility *n.* M19. **edibleness** *n.* L18.

edict /ˈiːdɪkt/ *n.* ME. [L *edictum* use as n. of neut. pa. pple of *edicere* proclaim, f. *e-* E- + *dicere* say, tell.] **1** An order proclaimed by authority; an ordinance or proclamation having the force of law; *esp.* (*Hist.*) any of those issued by the Roman praetors and emperors, or the French monarchs. ME. **2** *Sc. Hist.* A proclamation made in some public place whereby all concerned were summoned to appear before the courts. E18.

1 W. STYRON I got to read it and you got to sign it. That's the edict of the court. *fig.*: R. HOOKER The generall Edicts of nature. **Edict of Nantes** an edict issued by Henry IV of France in 1598, granting toleration to the Protestants (revoked by Louis XIV in 1685).

edictal /ɪˈdɪkt(ə)l/ *a.* L17. [Late L *edictalis*, f. as prec.: see -AL[1].] **1** *Sc. Hist.* Done by means of public proclamation (see EDICT 2). L17. **2** Of or pertaining to an edict or edicts; consisting of edicts. M19.

edictally *adv.* (chiefly *Sc.*) by means of an edict or edicts L17.

edicule *n.* var. of AEDICULE.

edification /ˌɛdɪfɪˈkeɪʃ(ə)n/ *n.* LME. [L *aedificatio(n-)*, f. *aedificat-* pa. ppl stem of *aedificare* build: see EDIFY, -ATION.] **1** Building, construction. *arch.* LME. **†b** A building. LME–M17. **2** The building up of the church, or the soul, in faith and holiness; the imparting of moral and spiritual stability and strength by suitable instruction and exhortation. LME. **3** Mental or moral improvement, enlightenment, or instruction. LME.

2 J. H. NEWMAN In providing for the religious necessities of posterity, they were directly serving their own edification. 3 B. JOWETT Kindly answer, for the edification of the company and myself. A. SCHLEE He had been distributing tracts for the edification of their fellow passengers.

edificatory /ˌɛdɪfɪˈkeɪt(ə)ri/ *a.* M17. [Late L *aedificatorius*, f. *aedificat-*: see prec., -ORY[2].] Intended or suitable for (esp. religious) edification.

edifice /ˈɛdɪfɪs/ *n.* LME. [(O)Fr. *édifice* f. L *aedificium*, f. *aedis*, *aedes* (see next) + *-fic-* var. of *fac-* stem of *facere* make.] **1** A building, esp. a large and stately one; *fig.* a large and complex construction (freq. abstract). LME. **†2** The process of building; architectural style. L16–M17.

1 H. JAMES He had been living . . in an edifice of red brick, with granite copings and an enormous fan-light over the door. R. M. PIRSIG One logical slip and an entire scientific edifice comes tumbling down.

edificial /ɛdɪˈfɪʃ(ə)l/ *a.* [late L *aedificialis*] *rare* (*a*) of the nature of an edifice; (*b*) architectural: M17.

edify /ˈɛdɪfʌɪ/ *v.* ME. [(O)Fr. *édifier* f. L *aedificare*, f. *aedis*, *aedes* dwelling, temple, (orig.) hearth + *-ficare*: see -FY.] **1** *v.t.* & **†***i.* Construct (a building), build. *arch.* ME. **†b** *v.t.* Provide with buildings. LME–L16. **2** *v.t.* *gen.* Construct, make, set up, establish; build up, strengthen. *arch.* ME. **†b** *v.i.* Take form, grow; *fig.* prosper, achieve success. LME–M17. **3** *v.t.* **a** Build up (the church, the soul) in faith and holiness; benefit or strengthen spiritually. ME. **b** Improve in a moral sense; inform, instruct. LME. **†4** *v.i.* Profit spiritually or morally; gain instruction. E17–M19.

1 LONGFELLOW The names of all who had died in the convent since it was edified. 2 SIR T. BROWNE Edified out of the Rib of Adam. SWIFT To edify a name and reputation. 3a E. A. FREEMAN He was much edified by the king's prayers and almsdeeds. b J. BUCHAN He was a preacher at heart, as every young Scotsman is, since we have all a craving to edify our fellows.

edifier *n.* LME. **edifying** *a.* that edifies; that tends to moral or spiritual improvement; instructive: E16. **edifyingly** *adv.* M17.

Edipal *a.* see OEDIPAL.

edit /ˈɛdɪt/ *n.* M20. [f. the vb.] An act or spell of editing a recording etc.; the action or process of editing; a feature or facility that allows for or performs editing.

edit /ˈɛdɪt/ *v.t.* L18. [Partly f. Fr. *éditer* publish, edit (based on *édition*: see next); partly back-form. f. EDITOR *n.*] **†1** Publish (a literary work previously existing in manuscript). Only in L18. **2** Prepare an edition of (a work or works by an earlier author); bring into order for publication, after compilation by others or oneself; act as editor of (a newspaper etc.); reword for a purpose. L18. **b** Prepare (a film, tape, etc.) by rearrangement, cutting, or collation of recorded material to form a unified sequence. E20.

2 K. AMIS He gave a compressed, but otherwise only slightly edited, account of his past relations with Margaret. **edit out** remove from the final version of a book, account, film, etc.

edition /ɪˈdɪʃ(ə)n/ *n.* LME. [(O)Fr. *édition* f. L *editio(n-)*, f. *edit-* pa. ppl stem of *edere* put forth, f. *e-* E- + *dare* put.] **1** A form or version of a literary work at its first publication, and after each revision, enlargement, abridgement, or change of format; one copy in such a form; the entire number of similar copies of a book, newspaper, etc., issued at one time; the entire number of any product issued at one time. LME. **†2** The action of putting forth; publication. M16–M17. **†3** The action of producing or bringing into existence; birth, creation (of orders of knighthood, etc.), extraction, origin. L16–L17. **4** Any of several forms or versions resembling another in which a thing or person appears at different times; the whole number of any product issued at one time. E17.

1 *facsimile edition, first edition, limited edition, paperback edition, pocket edition, revised edition, special edition, variorum edition,* etc. R. TRAVERS Butler composed another notice .. taking it to the newspaper office in time to catch .. Saturday's edition. D. MURPHY He chanced to notice the ten-volume 1840 edition of Sismondi's *Histoire.* 4 DONNE All the vertuous Actions they expresse, Are but a new, and worse edition Of her some one thought. M. ALLINGHAM A larger-than-life edition of his stage self. H. MOORE Of a very small piece [of sculpture] one doesn't mind if the edition goes to ten.

editionize *v.t.* produce (a newspaper) in several editions L20.

editio princeps /ɪˌdɪʃɪəʊ ˈprɪnsɛps/ *n. phr.* Pl. ***editiones principes*** /ɪdɪʃɪˌəʊniːz ˈprɪnsɪpiːz/. E19. [mod.L, f. L *editio* (see prec.) + PRINCEPS.] The first printed edition of a book.

editor /ˈɛdɪtə/ *n.* & *v.* M17. [L = producer, exhibitor, f. *edit-*: see EDITION, -OR.] A *n.* †1 The publisher of a book. Only in M17. 2 A person who edits material for publication, broadcasting, etc.; a person who prepares an edition of a literary work; a person who selects or commissions material for publication. E18. 3 A person who has charge of the running and contents of a newspaper, periodical, etc., or of a particular section of the publication; a person who is responsible for the style and content of a reference book. L18. b The head of a department of a publishing house. E20. 4 A person who cuts and edits films or tapes. E20. 5 *Computing.* A program enabling the user to alter programs or to alter or rearrange textual or other information held in a computer. M20.

3 *city editor, financial editor, sports editor,* etc.

Phrases & comb.: *copy editor*: see COPY *n.*[1] **editor-in-chief** the chief editor of a publication, in a publishing house, etc. *literary editor*: see LITERARY *a.*

B *v.t.* Edit. *rare.* M20.

editorship *n.* the duties, functions, and office of an editor L18. **editress** *n.* a female editor L18.

editorial /ɛdɪˈtɔːrɪəl/ *a.* & *n.* M18. [f. prec. + -IAL.] A *adj.* Of or pertaining to an editor or editing; written by or as by the editor, distinguished from news and advertising matter; of or pertaining to an editorial. M18. B *n.* A newspaper article written by, or under the direct responsibility of, the editor. M19.

editorialist *n.* a person who writes editorials, or makes editorial comment E20. **editorialize** *v.* (*a*) *v.i.* write editorials; comment editorially (*b*) *v.t.* add editorial comment to: M19. **editorially** *adv.* in an editorial manner or capacity E19.

Edo /ˈɛdəʊ/ *n.* & *a.* Pl. of n. **-os**, same. L19. [Edo name of Benin City.] (Of, pertaining to, or designating) a people inhabiting the district of Benin in Nigeria; (of) the Kwa language of this people.

educable /ˈɛdjʊkəb(ə)l, ˈɛdʒʊ-/ *a.* M19. [f. as next.] Able to be educated.

educaˈbility *n.* M19.

educatable /ˈɛdjʊkeɪtəb(ə)l/ *a.* M19. [f. next + -ABLE.] = prec.

educataˈbility *n.* L19.

educate /ˈɛdjʊkeɪt/ *v.t.* Pa. pple **-ated**, (*obs.* exc. *Sc.*) **-ate**. LME. [L *educat-* pa. ppl stem of *educare* rel. to *educere* EDUCE: see -ATE[3].] 1 Bring up (children) so as to form their habits, manners, intellectual aptitudes, etc.; *spec.* instruct, provide schooling for. LME. †b Rear by attention to physical needs. Only in 17. 2 Train so as to develop intellectual or moral powers generally, or in a particular mental or physical faculty; instruct, discipline. M19.

1 B. JOWETT The youth of a people should be educated in forms .. of virtue. O. MANNING He had been educated at an English public school. 2 T. S. ELIOT The multiplication of critical books .. may supply opinion instead of educating taste. A. LOOS I ought .. to educate Piggie how to act with a girl like American gentlemen. **educated guess**: based on experience.

educator *n.* [L] M16. **educatory** *a.* that has an educating influence M19.

education /ɛdjʊˈkeɪʃ(ə)n/ *n.* M16. [(O)Fr. *éducation* or L *educatio(n-)*, f. as prec.: see -ATION.] †1 The process of nourishing or rearing. M16–M17. 2 The process of bringing up children in particular manners, habits, or ways of life. *obs.* exc. with the notion of 3. M16. b The training of animals. M16. 3 The systematic instruction, schooling, or training of children and young people, or, by extension, instruction obtained in adult life; the whole course of such instruction received by a person. Also, provision of this, as an aspect of public policy. E17. 4 The development of mental or physical powers; moulding of (some aspect of) character. M19.

1 R. LOVELL They delight in woods, and places of their first education. 2 SHAKES. *Tam. Shr.* Christopher Sly, .. by education a cardmaker. 3 S. GIBBONS The education bestowed on Flora Poste by her parents had been expensive, athletic and prolonged. H. KELLER The next important step in my education was learning to read. A. J. P. TAYLOR The committee recommended economies in education and public health. *primary, secondary, tertiary education. adult education*: see ADULT *a.* 2. COLLEGE *of education.* ELEMENTARY *education. further education*: see FURTHER *a.* 2. *higher education*: see HIGH *a. physical education*: see PHYSICAL *a. public education*: see PUBLIC *a.* & *n.* 4 H. E. MANNING Education is the formation of the whole man—intellect .. character, mind, and soul. DAY LEWIS Monart did more than any other place for my sensuous education.

educatioˈnese *n.* (*derog.*) jargon-ridden language supposedly characteristic of educationalists and educational administrators M20. **educationist** *n.* = EDUCATIONALIST E19.

educational /ɛdjʊˈkeɪʃ(ə)n(ə)l/ *a.* M17. [f. prec. + -AL[1].] †1 Due to or arising from education. M17–E19. 2 Of, pertaining to, or concerned with education. Also, educative. E19.

educationalist *n.* a student of the methods of education; an advocate of education: M19. **educationally** *adv.* with reference to education; *educationally subnormal* (of a child) retarded in mental development and unable to be taught in ordinary schools: M19.

educative /ˈɛdjʊkətɪv/ *a.* M19. [f. as EDUCATE + -IVE.] Of or pertaining to education; conducive to education, having the power of educating.

educe /ɪˈdjuːs/ *v.t.* LME. [L *educere*, f. *e-* E- + *ducere* to lead.] †1 Lead or draw out; *Med.* remove by drawing out. LME–M17. 2 Bring out or develop from latent or rudimentary existence; elicit; evoke. E17. 3 Infer (a principle etc.) *from* a set of data. M19.

2 T. GALE Chaos was that ancient slime, out of which al things were educed. 3 J. BARZUN In most subjects few attempts are made to educe principles from ever larger masses of facts.

educible *a.* L17.

educrat /ˈɛdjʊkrat, ˈɛdʒʊ-/ *n. N. Amer.* (*derog.*). M20. [f. EDU(CATION + -CRAT.] An educational administrator or theorist.

educt /ˈiːdʌkt/ *n.* L17. [L *eductum* neut. pa. pple of *educere* EDUCE.] †1 That which is brought forth as young. Only in L17. †2 *Chem.* A component of a substance, which is released by the substance's decomposition. L18–L19. 3 That which is educed; a result of inference or development. E19.

eduction /ɪˈdʌkʃ(ə)n/ *n.* LME. [L *eductio(n-)*, f. *educt-* ppl stem of *educere*: see EDUCE, -ION.] †1 A leading or putting out; *Med.* a removal by drawing out. LME–E18. 2 The action or result of educing. Also, an educt, an inference. M17. †3 The exhaust of steam from a cylinder in a steam engine. L18–M19.

eductive *a.* [med.L *eductivus*] tending to educe LME.

edulcorate /ɪˈdʌlkəreɪt/ *v.t.* M17. [med.L *edulcorat-* pa. ppl stem of *edulcorare*, f. *e-* E- + late L *dulcor* sweetness, f. L *dulcis* sweet: see -ATE[3].] †1 Sweeten, make sweet. M17–E18. 2 Purify or soften by removing acid properties. M17. 3 Free from soluble impurities by washing or filtration. M17.

edulcoˈration *n.* M18.

Edward /ˈɛdwəd/ *n.* L16. [Male forename.] Any of various coins issued in the reign of any of the Kings of England or Great Britain called Edward.

¶ See also *King Edward* (*VII potato*) s.v. KING *n.*

Edwardian /ɛdˈwɔːdɪən/ *a.* & *n.* M19. [f. prec. + -IAN.] A *adj.* Belonging to or characteristic of the reign of any of the King Edwards of England or Great Britain; *spec.* of Edward VII or his reign (1901–10). M19. B *n.* 1 A past or present member of a school named after a King, or Saint, Edward. L19. 2 A person of the period of Edward VII. E20.

Edwardiˈana *n.pl.* [-ANA] publications or other items concerning or associated with a school named after King, or Saint, Edward or the reign of Edward VII E20. **Edwardianism** *n.* the collective characteristics, or a sentiment or expression, of the reign of Edward VII M20. **Edwardine** *a.* belonging to or characteristic of the reign of Edward VI or VII M19.

'ee *pers. pron.* see YE *pron.*

-ee /iː/ *suff.*[1] [f. or after AN *-é* pa. ppl suff. f. L *-atus* -ATE[2].] 1 Used orig. in legal terms (w. corresp. agent-ns. in *-or*) to form ns. f. vbs (occas. L ppl stems), w. the sense 'person affected directly or indirectly by the vbl action', as *appellee, legatee, lessee, vendee.* Now used more widely (without corresp. terms in *-or*) to form ns. (*a*) f. vbs, w. the sense 'person subject to an action or involved in an action', as *employee, payee, devotee, escapee, conferee, standee*; (*b*) f. ns., w. the sense 'person having to do with', as *bargee, patentee*; (*c*) f. adjs., w. the sense 'person described as', as *absentee.* 2 Used to Anglicize mod.Fr. ns. in *-é* (f. pples), as *debauchee, refugee.*

-ee /iː/ *suff.*[2] [Origin unkn.] Forming diminutives, as *bootee, coatee*, or with vague or fanciful sense, as *goatee, settee.*

eejit /ˈiːdʒɪt/ *n. dial.* (chiefly *Anglo-Ir.* & *Sc.*). L19. [Repr. a pronunc.] = IDIOT *n.* 1.

eejity *a.* idiotic M20.

eel /iːl/ *n.* & *v.* [OE *ǣl* = OFris. *ēl*, OS, OHG *āl* (Du. *aal*, G *Aal*), ON *áll*, f. Gmc, of unkn. origin.] A *n.* 1 Any of various snakelike fishes of the genus *Anguilla*, members of which spend most of their lives in fresh water but breed in warm deep oceans. Also (usu. w. specifying wd), any of numerous slender, elongated fishes belonging to the order Anguilliformes (which includes *Anguilla*) or (*loosely*) other orders. OE. 2 The eel as the proverbial type of something slippery or evasive; a slippery or evasive person or thing. E16. 3 A microscopic nematode worm, as found in fermented flour paste, vinegar, etc. *arch. colloq.* M17.

1 *conger eel, moray eel, sand eel, snipe eel*, etc. *electric eel*: see ELECTRIC *a.* **jellied eels** cooked eels set in jelly. *silver eel*: see SILVER *n.* & *a.* SPINY *eel.*

Comb.: **eel-fare** the passage of young eels upriver; (in *pl.*) a brood of young eels (cf. ELVER); **eel-grass** (*a*) = ZOSTERA; (*b*) *US* = *tape-grass* s.v. TAPE *n.*; **eelpout** †(*a*) a burbot; (*b*) any small thick-lipped fish of the family Zoarcidae, *esp.* the viviparous blenny, *Zoarces viviparus*; **eelskin** (material similar to) the skin of an eel; **eel-spear** a pronged instrument for transfixing eels; **eelworm** a nematode worm, *esp.* one parasitic on plants.

B *v.* 1 *v.i.* Fish for eels. Chiefly as *eeling* vbl n. L18. 2 *v.t.* & *i.* Move like an eel. Also *eel one's way.* E20.

eelery *n.* a place where eels are caught M19. **eel-like** *a.* resembling (that of) an eel L17. **eely** *a.* eel-like M17.

Eem /iːm/ *a.* & *n.* L19. [A river in the Netherlands.] *Geol.* (Designating or pertaining to) the last interglacial stage of the Pleistocene in northern Europe, preceding the Weichsel glaciation.

Also **ˈEemian** *a.* & *n.* E20.

e'en *adv.* see EVEN *adv.*

-een /iːn/ *suff.*[1] [Repr. Fr. *-ine.*] Forming names of fabrics, usu. of an inferior or coarser quality than that denoted by the root wd, as *sateen, velveteen.*

-een /iːn/ *suff.*[2] [Repr. Ir. *-in* dim. suff.] Used in adoptions of Ir. diminutives, as *colleen, dudeen, poteen, spalpeen*, and in (orig. Ir.) formations on Eng. wds, as *buckeen, squireen.*

e'er *adv.* see EVER.

-eer /ɪə/ *suff.* [Repr. Fr. *-ier* f. L *-arius*: cf. -IER, -ARY[1].] 1 Forming ns. f. ns., w. the sense 'person concerned with', as *auctioneer*, *mountaineer*, occas. w. derog. implication, as *profiteer*, *sonneteer*; occas. w. ref. to things, as *gazetteer*, *muffineer*. 2 Forming vbs f. these ns., freq. as back-forms. f. derivs. in *-eering*, w. the sense 'be concerned with', as *electioneer*, *profiteer*.

eerie /ˈɪəri/ *a.* Orig. *Sc.* & *north.* ME. [Prob. repr. OE *earg* cowardly.] 1 Fearful, usu. superstitiously. Now *rare*. ME. 2 Inspiring unease or fear; spine-tingling; strange, weird, gloomy. L18.

1 R. TANNAHILL The watch-dog's howling . . makes the nightly wanderer eerie. 2 J. G. FARRELL There was something eerie about this vast shadowy cavern and the Major . . felt a shiver of apprehension. A. PRICE His eerie faculty for total recall of every fact.

¶Not in general use bef. 19.

eerily *adv.* M19. **eeriness** *n.* LME.

ef- /ɪf, *stressed* ɛf/ *pref.* Assim. form of OFr. ES- and EX-[1] bef. *f*.

eff /ɛf/ *v. slang.* M20. [f. name of letter F, F, euphem. abbrev. of FUCK *v.*] 1 *v.t.* & *i.* = FUCK *v.* (used as an expletive on its own account, as a milder alternative to *fuck*, or as a euphemistic report of the use of the full word). M20. 2 *v.i.* Utter *fuck* or an equivalent word. Esp. in *eff and blind*, use strong expletives, swear continuously. M20.

effer *n.* M20. **effing** *ppl a.* & *adv.* = FUCKING M20.

effable /ˈɛfəb(ə)l/ *a.* E17. [Obs. Fr., or L *effabilis*, f. *effari* to utter, f. EF- + *fari* speak: see -ABLE. Cf. earlier INEFFABLE.] That can or may be expressed or described in words. Now only in antithesis to *ineffable*.

Observer Trying to take on the ineffable, philosophers are always running the risk of making the eminently effable (chairs, tables and so on) entirely mysterious.

efface /ɪˈfeɪs/ *v.t.* L15. [(O)Fr. *effacer*, f. *es-* (see ES-, EF-) + *face* FACE *n.*] †1 Pardon or obtain absolution for (an offence). L15–M18. 2 Rub out or obliterate (writing, marks, painted or sculptured figures, etc.) from a surface. E17. b Erase (words or sentences) from a document. Now only *fig.* M18. 3 *gen.* Cause to disappear entirely, remove all trace of; *fig.* wipe out or obliterate (a memory or mental impression). E17. 4 Outshine, eclipse, utterly surpass. E18. b *refl.* Treat or regard oneself as insignificant; allow oneself to be overlooked or ignored. L19.

1 J. WESLEY In tender Mercy Look on me, And all my Sins efface. 2 A. NIN Inscriptions on the walls, half effaced by time. b LD MACAULAY To efface the penal laws from the statute book. 3 H. A. L. FISHER The strong provincial feelings of Burgundy and Aquitaine . . were not allowed altogether to efface the historic image of Rome. SLOAN WILSON Before daylight, they had effaced all signs of the struggle and dragged the bodies into the woods. 4 M. W. MONTAGU Her beauty effaced everything I have seen. b C. P. SNOW Orbell, who had been quiet all the evening, was effacing himself and listening.

effaceable *a.* M19. **effacement** *n.* L18.

†effatum *n.* Pl. **-ta**. Also Anglicized as **effate**. M17–L18. [L, use as n. of neut. pa. pple of *effari*: see EFFABLE.] A saying, dictum, or maxim.

effect /ɪˈfɛkt/ *n.* LME. [OFr. (mod. *effet*), or L *effectus*, f. *effect-* pa. ppl stem of *efficere* accomplish, f. EF- + *facere*, *fic-* make, do.] 1 Something accomplished, caused or produced; a result, a consequence. LME. b Results in general; the quality of producing a result, efficacy. LME. c A particular phenomenon (chiefly in physical science), usu. named after its discoverer or describer. M19. †2 A contemplated result, a purpose. LME–M17. 3 Accomplishment, fulfilment; *obs.* exc. in *bring to effect* etc. below. LME. †4 An outward sign, an appearance; a phenomenon. LME–M17. †5 Reality, fact, as opp. to appearance. LME–L17. 6 Operative influence. LME. 7†a Something attained or acquired as the result of an action. *rare* (Shakes.). Only in E17. b In *pl.* Property (excluding real property); goods, belongings. E18. 8 The impression produced on a spectator or listener by a work of art or literature, a performance, etc. M18. b A (pleasing or remarkable) combination of colour or form in a picture, landscape, etc. L19. c Lighting, sound, etc., used to enhance a play, film, broadcast, etc.; the means of producing this. Freq. in *pl.* L19.

1 H. H. WILSON The beneficial effects of their interposition had given shelter and security to private trade. D. DAVIE Always the overt intention is to exalt poetry; and always the effect is to emasculate it. b MILTON This Tree . . is of Divine effect To open Eyes. J. PRIESTLEY A law was made . . but it had little effect. c *Auger effect*, *Compton effect*, *Doppler effect*, *Faraday effect*, *Hall effect*, *night effect*, *Peltier effect*, *Raman effect*, *shot effect*, *surface effect*, *Wallace effect*, *Weissenberg effect*, *Zeeman effect*, etc. 6 A. KOESTLER Liquor did not seem to have a stimulating effect on him. DAY LEWIS The full effect of my mother's death . . did not show itself until my adolescence. 7b S. SONTAG To burn the clothes and other effects of someone who died of TB. 8 J. AGATE William Devlin . . has already played Clemenceau with magnificent effect. R. DAVIES People are always charmed by clever mechanisms that give an effect of life. b H. READ Certain effects which he obtained—the representation of mist, of foam, of swirling water—still baffle our analysis. c T. BARR When the filmed sequences are assembled . . sound effects and music are added. A. ROAD The technical tricks—the visual and electronic effects which are so much a part of *Doctor Who*.

Phrases: **bring to effect** accomplish, realize. **bring** or **carry into effect** realize, make operative. *cause and effect*: see CAUSE *n.* **for effect** for the sake of making an impression on an audience. **give effect to** make operative, put into force. *ill effect*: see ILL *a.* & *adv.* **in effect** (*a*) in fact, in reality; (*b*) virtually, for all practical purposes. **law of effect** (*Psychol.*): that a response to a stimulus will be more probably learned if it proves to be accompanied or followed by an event satisfying to the organism. **leave no effects** leave nothing for one's heirs. **no effects** no or insufficient funds (written by a banker on a dishonoured cheque). **of no (†none) effect** having no result, unsuccessful. **personal effects** one's own movable property, personal belongings. **put into effect** accomplish, realize, make operative. *spot effect*: see SPOT *n.* & *a.* **take effect** prove successful; become operative, come into force (*from* a certain date). **to the effect that** to that end, with that significance. **to this, that, effect** having this, that, result or implication. **with effect from** coming into operation at (a certain time).

effectless *n.* L16.

effect /ɪˈfɛkt/ *v.* L16. [f. the n.] 1 *v.t.* & †*i.* Bring about (an event or result); accomplish (an intention or desire). L16. †b Produce (a state or condition). L16–M17. c Make, construct, build. Now *rare* or *obs.* L18. †2 *v.t.* Give effect to (an intention); fulfil (a promise). L16–M17.

1 G. M. TREVELYAN Corn Law Repeal . . effected no immediate economic or social revolution. R. C. A. WHITE A police officer may use reasonable force . . to effect the arrest.

effecter *n.* a person who or thing which brings about an event, accomplishes a purpose, etc. E17. **effectible** *a.* M17. **effector** *n.* (*a*) = EFFECTER; (*b*) (*Biol.*, freq. *attrib.*) an organ or cell acting in response to a stimulus: E17.

effective /ɪˈfɛktɪv/ *a.* & *n.* LME. [L *effectivus*, f. *effect-*: see EFFECT *n.*, -IVE.] A *adj.* †1 Concerned with or having the function of accomplishing or executing. LME–E17. 2 Powerful in effect; effectual; efficient, efficacious. LME. b Making a strong impression; striking, vivid. M19. †3 That is concerned in the production *of* an event or condition; having the power of acting on objects. L16–L17. 4 Fit for work or (esp. military) service. L17. 5 Having an effect or result. M18. b Actually usable or brought to bear; equivalent in its effect. L18. c *Gram.* = PERFECTIVE *a.* 3. M20. 6 Actual, *de facto*, in effect; (of an order etc.) operative, in force. L18.

2 C. S. FORESTER He judged that . . silence would be more effective than speech. *Which Micro?* Four effective, if not brilliant, items of software. b J. CONRAD The white stairs, the deep crimson of the carpet, and the light blue of the dress made an effective combination of colour. 5 J. H. BURTON The honour of the first effective shot. b **effective temperature** *Physics* the temperature of an object calculated from the radiation emitted by the object, assuming it to behave as a black body. 6 J. C. RANSOM Classical and medieval philosophies and sciences which have passed from our effective knowledge. C. V. WEDGWOOD The King would remain as the respected figurehead, but effective power . . would be exercised by the gentry, the lawyers, and the merchants.

B *n.* †1 An efficient cause. Only in 17. 2 An effective serviceman or other person. Usu. in *pl.* E18. 3 *Gram.* = PERFECTIVE *n.* 2. M20.

effectively *adv.* LME. **effectiveness** *n.* the quality of being effective E17. **effecˈtivity** *n.* (the degree of) effectiveness M19.

effectual /ɪˈfɛktʃʊəl/ *a.* LME. [med.L *effectualis*, f. L *effectus*: see EFFECT *n.*, -AL[1].] 1 Efficacious, producing the intended result, effective. LME. b Of a legal document etc.: valid, binding. LME. †2 Of a prayer or plea: earnest, zealous, urgent. LME–E17. †3 Real, actual, in existence. LME–M17. †4 Pertinent, to the point; conclusive. L16–L17.

Special collocations: **effectual calling** *Theol.* the action of the Holy Spirit in instilling Christian faith. **effectual grace** *Theol.* the special grace given to those elected to salvation.

effectuˈality *n.* effectual quality M17. **effectually** *adv.* LME. **effectualness** *n.* (now *rare*) M16.

effectuate /ɪˈfɛktʃʊeɪt/ *v.t.* L16. [med.L *effectuat-* pa. ppl stem of *effectuare*, f. *effectus*: see EFFECT *n.*, -ATE[3].] Cause to happen, put into effect, accomplish.

effectuˈation *n.* E17.

effeir /ɪˈfɪə/ *n.* & *v. Sc.* LME. [Alt. of AFFAIR.] A *n.* †1 A concern, a cause, an important matter. LME–E17. 2 Appearance, array; show, pomp, ceremony. Long *obs.* exc. (*Hist.*) in *effeir of war*. LME. B *v.i. obs.* exc. *Sc. Law.* 1 Appertain, fall by right. Esp. in *as effeirs*, in the proper way, as appropriate. LME. 2 Be appropriate, pertain, relate *to*. M16.

effeminacy /ɪˈfɛmɪnəsi/ *n.* E17. [f. next + -ACY.] 1 The presence of feminine characteristics in a man; unmanly weakness or delicacy. E17. †2 Addiction to womanizing. M–L17.

effeminate /ɪˈfɛmɪnət/ *a.* & *n.* LME. [L *effeminatus* pa. pple of *effeminare* make feminine, f. EF- + *femina* woman: see -ATE[2].] A *adj.* 1 (Of a man) having characteristics regarded as feminine or unmanly; delicate, feeble, self-indulgent. LME. b Characterized by or proceeding from unmanly weakness, softness, or delicacy. L16. †c Gentle, tender, compassionate. Only in L16. †2 Excessively amorous; addicted to womanizing. L15–L16.

1 J. BRAINE Despite the manicure and the diamond ring he didn't look effeminate. b GIBBON Rome was . . humbled beneath the effeminate luxury of Oriental despotism. c SHAKES. *Rich. III* Your tenderness of heart And gentle, kind, effeminate remorse.

B *n.* An effeminate man. L16.

effeminately *adv.* E16. **effeminateness** *n.* L16.

effeminate /ɪˈfɛmɪneɪt/ *v.* Now *rare* or *obs.* LME. [L *effeminat-* pa. ppl stem of *effeminare*: see prec., -ATE[3].] †1 *v.i.* Become womanish or unmanly; grow weak. LME–E17. 2 *v.t.* Make womanish or unmanly; enervate, enfeeble. M16. †3 *v.t.* Make into or represent as a woman. L17–M18.

effeminize /ɪˈfɛmɪnʌɪz/ *v.t.* Now *rare*. Also **-ise**. E17. [f. EFFEMINATE *a.* + -IZE.] Make effeminate.

effendi /ɛˈfɛndi/ *n.* E17. [Turk. *efendı* f. mod.Gk *aphentē* voc. of *aphentēs* f. Gk *authentēs* lord, master.] A man of education or social standing in an eastern Mediterranean or Arab country. Freq. (usu. *Hist.*) as a title of respect or courtesy in Turkey or (former) Turkish territory.

efferent /ˈɛf(ə)r(ə)nt/ *a.* M19. [L *efferent-* pres. ppl stem of *efferre*, f. EF- + *ferre* bring, carry: see -ENT.] *Anat.* Conducting outwards (of a nerve: away from the central nervous system; of a blood-vessel: away from an organ). Opp. AFFERENT.

effervesce /ɛfəˈvɛs/ *v.i.* E18. [L *effervescere*, f. EF- + *fervescere* inceptive of *fervere* be hot, boil: see -ESCE.] †1 Break into violent chemical action. E–M18. 2 Give off bubbles of gas, *esp.* as a result of chemical action; bubble. L18. b Of a gas: issue in bubbles. M19. 3 *fig.* Show great excitement or enthusiasm; become lively or vivacious. M19.

effervescence /ɛfəˈvɛs(ə)ns/ *n.* E17. [f. as next: see -ESCENCE.] †1 The action of boiling up. E17–E18. 2 The action of bubbling up as if boiling; the vigorous rise of bubbles of gas from a liquid, *esp.* as a result of chemical action. L17. 3 *fig.* Vigorous action, exuberance, vivacity. M18.

effervescency *n.* effervescent condition, effervescence L17.

effervescent /ɛfəˈvɛs(ə)nt/ *a.* L17. [L *effervescent-* pres. ppl stem of *effervescere*: see EFFERVESCE, -ESCENT.] †1 Boiling, bubbling with heat. Only in L17. 2 Having the property of effervescing; bubbly, fizzy; *fig.* exuberant. M19.

effete /ɪˈfiːt/ *a.* E17. [L *effetus* exhausted as by bearing young, f. EF- + *fetus* breeding: see FOETUS.] †1 No longer fertile; past producing offspring. E17–M19. †2 Of a substance or object: that has lost its special virtue or quality, exhausted, worn out. M17–M19. 3 No longer vigorous or capable of effective action; decadent, degenerate. L18. b Weak, ineffectual; effeminate. E20.

1 CARLYLE Nature . . was as if effete now; could not any longer produce Great Men. 2 EVELYN That imprison'd and Effœte Air, within the Green-house. 3 R. FRY The worn-out rags of an effete classical tradition long ago emptied of all meaning. b A. BROOKNER Next to her, Frederick appears effete, decorative, luxurious.

effeteness *n.* M19.

†**efficace** *n.* ME–E18. [OFr. f. L *efficacia*: see EFFICACY.] Efficacy, effect.

efficacious /ɛfɪˈkeɪʃəs/ *a.* E16. [f. L *efficac-*, *efficax*, f. *efficere*: see EFFECT *n.*, -ACIOUS.] That does or is certain to produce the intended effect; effective.

P. MEDAWAR At present there is no convincing evidence that psychoanalytic treatment as such is efficacious.

efficaciously *adv.* M17. **efficaciousness** *n.* M17.

efficacity /ɛfɪˈkasɪti/ *n.* LME. [(O)Fr. *efficacité* f. L *efficacitas*, f. *efficax*: see prec., -ACITY.] = next.

efficacy /ˈɛfɪkəsi/ *n.* E16. [L *efficacia*, f. *efficax*: see EFFICACIOUS, -Y[3].] 1 Power or capacity to produce effects; ability to bring about the intended result. E16. †2 An effect. M16–M17.

efficience /ɪˈfɪʃ(ə)ns/ *n.* Now *rare* or *obs.* M17. [f. as next: see -ENCE.] Causative or productive activity. Also, efficacy.

efficiency /ɪˈfɪʃ(ə)nsi/ *n.* L16. [L *efficientia* f. as next: see -ENCY.] 1 The fact of being an efficient cause. Now *rare* or *obs.* L16. †b The action of an efficient cause; production. M–L17. 2 The quality of being efficient; the ability to accomplish or fulfil what is intended; effectiveness, competence. M17. 3 *Physics.* †a The work done by a force in operating a machine; the total energy expended by a machine. E–M19. b The ratio of useful work performed by a device or system to the total energy input. M19. 4 In full *efficiency apartment*. A room or small flat with limited washing and cooking facilities. *N. Amer.* M20.

2 R. WHATELY The penalty annexed to any law is an instance, not of its efficiency, but . . of its failure. F. TUOHY He conducted his course at the University with an efficiency which shone beside the amateurish efforts of his colleagues. 3b *thermal efficiency*: see THERMAL *a.*

Comb.: *efficiency apartment*: see sense 4 above; **efficiency audit** an examination of a business etc. to ascertain the efficiency of its procedures; **efficiency bar** a point on a salary scale which may not be passed until the employee's efficiency is proved; **efficiency engineer, expert**: who advises on the efficiency of an organization or production process.

efficient /ɪˈfɪʃ(ə)nt/ *a.* & *n.* LME. [L *efficient-* pres. ppl stem of *efficere*: see EFFECT *n.*, -ENT.] A *adj.* 1 Making, causing; that makes a thing what it is. Usu. with *cause*. Cf. DEFICIENT *a.* 1. LME. 2 Effective, producing the desired result with the minimum wasted effort; (of a person) capable, competent; *Physics* characterized by high (or specified) efficiency. L18.

2 H. B. STOWE He was an expert and efficient workman. G. GREENE The appeal to sentiment was heartlessly efficient; it had struck him in the place where he was most vulnerable and at the hour when he was most alone.

†B *n.* 1 That which makes a thing what it is; the cause of an effect. L16–E19. 2 A trained soldier, *esp.* one volunteering for service. M–L19.

efficiently *adv.* †(*a*) as by an efficient cause; (*b*) in an efficient manner, effectively: E17.

†**effierce** *v.t. rare* (Spenser). Only in L16. [f. EF- + FIERCE.] Make fierce, madden.

effigial /ɪˈfɪdʒɪəl/ *a. rare.* E18. [f. L *effigies* EFFIGY + -AL[1].] Of the nature of an effigy.

effigiate /ɪˈfɪdʒɪeɪt/ *v.t.* Now *rare.* E17. [Late L *effigiat-* pa. ppl stem of *effigiare*, f. *effigies*: see next, -ATE[3].] Present a likeness of, portray.

effigiˈation *n.* the action of representing; a likeness: M16.

effigy /ˈɛfɪdʒi (*pl. same*)/ *n.* Also (*arch.*) **effigies** /ɪˈfɪdʒiːz/. M16. [L *effigies*, f. *effig-* stem of *effingere*, f. EF- + *fingere* fashion, shape.] A representation of (usu.) a person in the form of a sculptured figure or a dummy. Also, a portrait on a coin.

C. V. WEDGWOOD The validity of the seal . . , which bore the name and effigy of King Charles. C. THUBRON Some Russians suspect this is not Lenin's body at all, but an effigy. **burn, hang**, etc., **in effigy** subject an image of (a person) to a semblance of a punishment desired for the original (formerly also done in the case of a criminal who had fled from justice).

Comb.: **effigy mound** a prehistoric earth mound in the shape of an animal.

¶The sing. *effigy* is not recorded bef. M17. Earlier examples are either pl. or in Latin forms.

efflation /ɪˈfleɪʃ(ə)n/ *n.* Now *rare.* L16. [Late L *efflatio(n-)*, f. *efflat-* pa. ppl stem of *efflare*, f. EF- + *flare* to blow: see -ATION.] Blowing out, expulsion of breath; a breath, an emanation.

effleurage /ɛfləːˈrɑːʒ/ *n.* & *v.* L19. [Fr., f. *effleurer* stroke lightly.] A *n.* The technique or process of massaging with a circular stroking movement of the flat or heel of the hand. L19. B *v.i.* Perform this kind of massage. L19.

effloresce /ɛfləˈrɛs/ *v.i.* L18. [L *efflorescere*, f. EF- + *florescere* inceptive of *florere* to blossom, f. *flor-*, *flos* flower: see -ESCE.] 1 Bloom, burst out into or as into flower. L18. 2a *Chem.* Of a crystalline substance: turn to fine powder through loss of water or exposure to air. L18. b Of a salt: be carried in solution to the surface of the ground etc. and crystallize there. Of the ground, a wall, or other surface: become covered with particles of a salt. E19. 3 *fig.* Blossom out; become manifest. M19.

efflorescence /ɛfləˈrɛs(ə)ns/ *n.* E17. [f. L *efflorescent-* pres. ppl stem of *efflorescere*, partly through Fr.: see prec., -ENCE.] 1 The process, or period, of flowering. Chiefly *fig.* E17. †2 Colour developed on the skin; *Med.* a pathological redness or rash. M17–L19. 3 The process of efflorescing of a salt; a powdery deposit resulting from this. M17.

1 R. FRY The change in art is merely the efflorescence of certain long prepared . . effects.

efflorescent *a.* that effloresces; resembling or forming an efflorescence E19.

effluence /ˈɛflʊəns/ *n.* LME. [(O)Fr., or med.L *effluentia*, f. as next: see -ENCE.] 1 A flowing out (esp. of light, electricity, etc., or *fig.*). LME. 2 That which flows out; an emanation. E17.

effluent /ˈɛflʊənt/ *a.* & *n.* LME. [L *effluent-* pres. ppl stem of *effluere*: see next, -ENT.] A *adj.* That flows forth or out. LME. B *n.* A stream or liquid flowing out; *esp.* waste discharged from an industrial process, sewage tank, etc. M19.

effluvium /ɪˈfluːvɪəm/ *n.* Pl. **-ia** /-ɪə/, †**-iums**. M17. [L, f. *effluere*, f. EF- + *fluere* to flow: see -IUM.] †1 A flowing out. M17–E18. 2 Chiefly *Hist.* An outflow or stream of imperceptible particles, esp. as supposedly transmitting electrical or magnetic influence etc. M17. 3 An (esp. unpleasant) exhalation affecting the lungs or the sense of smell. M17.

2 R. BOYLE The Effluvia of the Load-stone. W. COWPER Attracted by the effluvia of my genius. 3 ADDISON The miraculous Powers which the Effluviums of cheese have. C. DARWIN The whole air tainted with the effluvium.

¶Pl. *effluvia* sometimes treated as *sing.*.

efflux /ˈɛflʌks/ *n.* M16. [med.L *effluxus*, f. *efflux-* pa. ppl stem of *effluere*: see prec.] 1 A flowing out (of liquid, gas, etc., or *fig.*). M16. 2 The lapse of time; passing away, expiry. M17. 3 That which flows out; an emanation. M17.

1 J. M. KEYNES An influx of money into one country means an efflux from another. 2 T. MANTON That efflux of time . . between Christ's ascension and his second coming. 3 GLADSTONE The Established Church of Scotland . . was the efflux of the mind of the people.

effluxion /ɪˈflʌkʃ(ə)n/ *n.* E17. [(O)Fr., or late L *effluxio(n-)*, f. *efflux-*: see prec., -ION.] = prec.

efforce /ɪˈfɔːs/ *v.t.* Long *rare* or *obs.* E16. [Fr. *efforcer*: see EFFORT.] Force; compel; force open or out.

efform /ɪˈfɔːm/ *v.t.* Now *rare.* L16. [Late L *efformare* f. L *formare*: see EF-, FORM *v.*[1]] Shape, mould.

effort /ˈɛfət/ *n.* L15. [(O)Fr., earlier nom. *esforz*, f. *esforcier* (now *efforcer*) f. Proto-Romance, f. L EF- + *fortis* strong.] †1 Power; (in *pl.*) properties. L15–L17. 2 Exertion or striving, physical or mental; a vigorous attempt (*at*, *to do*). L15. b The result of any concentrated or special activity; *colloq.* an achievement, a product, anything made. M19. 3 *Physics.* Force applied to a thing in motion along the direction of motion. M19.

2 A. KOESTLER With a considerable effort of will he rose . . and shuffled to the bathroom. J. RHYS I make no effort to save myself. M. KEANE Praising just a little, demanding always more effort, a higher standard of perfection. b A. D. SEDGWICK The Venus is an effort of Ruth's. J. D. WATSON Stepped back from the lab bench and surveyed the afternoon's effort.

effortful *a.* exhibiting, full of, or requiring effort E20. **effortfully** *adv.* M20.

effortless /ˈɛfətlɪs/ *a.* E19. [f. prec. + -LESS.] 1 Making no effort; passive. *arch.* E19. 2 Not involving or requiring effort; easy. M19.

effortlessly *adv.* M19. **effortlessness** *n.* L19.

effraction /ɪˈfrakʃ(ə)n/ *n. rare.* M19. [Fr. f. med.L *effractio(n-)*, f. L *effract-* pa. ppl stem of *effringere*, f. EF- + *frangere* break: see -ION.] Breaking and entering, burglary.

†**effray** *v.t.* Chiefly *Sc.* LME. [Fr. *effrayer*: see AFFRAY *v.*] 1 Frighten; alarm. LME–E19. b Scare off. L16–E17. 2 Be afraid of. L15–E16.

†**effronted** *a.* L16–L17. [f. Fr. *effronté*: see next, -ED[1].] Shameless, barefaced, insolent.

effrontery /ɪˈfrʌnt(ə)ri/ *n.* L17. [Fr. *effronterie*, f. *effronté* f. Proto-Romance, f. late L *effrons* barefaced, f. EF- + *front-*, *frons* forehead: see -ERY.] Shameless audacity; insolence; cheek.

effulge /ɪˈfʌldʒ/ *v. poet.* (now *rare*). E18. [L *effulgere*: see EFFULGENT.] 1 *v.t.* Flash out (light). E18. 2 *v.i.* Shine out brilliantly. M18.

effulgence /ɪˈfʌldʒ(ə)ns/ *n.* M17. [Late L *effulgentia*, f. as next: see -ENCE.] Effulgent quality; splendid radiance.

MILTON On thee Impresst the effulgence of his Glorie abides.

effulgent /ɪˈfʌldʒ(ə)nt/ *a.* M18. [L *effulgent-* pres. ppl stem of *effulgere* shine brightly, f. EF- + *fulgere* shine: see -ENT.] Shining out brilliantly; radiant; resplendent. Freq. *fig.*

effund /ɪˈfʌnd/ *v.t.* Now *rare.* LME. [L *effundere*, f. EF- + *fundere* pour.] Pour out (*lit.* & *fig.*).

†**effuse** *n. rare.* L16–M17. [f. the vb.] Effusion (of blood).

effuse /ɪˈfjuːs/ *a.* M16. [L *effusus* pa. pple of *effundere* EFFUND.] †1 Poured out freely; overflowing; unrestrained. M16–M18. 2 *Conchol.* Of a shell: having lips separated by a groove. *rare.* M19. 3 *Bot.* Of an inflorescence: spreading loosely. L19.

effuse /ɪˈfjuːz/ *v.t.* LME. [L *effus-* pa. ppl stem of *effundere* EFFUND.] Pour forth or out (liquid, air, light, smell, or *fig.*); in *pass.*, be extravasated.

SHAKES. *1 Hen. VI* Maiden blood, thus rigorously effus'd Will cry for vengeance.

effusion /ɪˈfjuːʒ(ə)n/ *n.* LME. [(O)Fr., or L *effusio(n-)*, f. as prec.: see -ION.] 1 A pouring forth (*lit.* & *fig.*); shedding; unrestrained utterance; effusiveness. LME. b *Med.* Escape of fluid (as blood or pus) into a body cavity; accumulation of fluid in a body cavity. M18. †2 Dispersion; confused downfall. LME–E18. 3 Something poured out (*lit.* & *fig.*); *esp.* (usu.

derog.) a literary composition or speech regarded as an outpouring of emotion etc. E17.

1 J. F. W. HERSCHEL The effusion of lava. F. W. FARRAR The fulfilment of Christ's promise in the effusion of His Spirit. P. CAREY He was hurt . . by Harry's lack of effusion in the greeting. 3 V. GLENDINNING Would-be poets who bothered her with their worthless effusions.

effusive /ɪˈfjuːsɪv/ *a.* M17. [f. as EFFUSE *v.* + -IVE.] 1 Pouring out, overflowing. Chiefly *fig.* (of speech, emotion, etc.): exuberant, demonstrative. M17. †2 That proceeds from an outpouring. Only in 18. 3 *Geol.* Of rock: poured out when molten and later solidified. Also, marked by outpouring of igneous rock. L19.

1 J. MCCARTHY Peel . . was not effusive; he did not pour out his emotions. 2 POPE The floor Washed with th' effusive wave.

effusively *adv.* L19. **effusiveness** *n.* L19.

Efik /ˈɛfɪk/ *a.* & *n.* M19. [Efik.] A *adj.* Of, pertaining to, or designating a people of southern Nigeria closely related to the Ibibio, or their Niger-Congo language. M19. B *n.* Pl. same. A member of the Efik people; the Efik language. M19.

efreet *n.* var. of AFREET.

eft /ɛft/ *n.* Also †**ewt**. [OE *efeta*, of unkn. origin. Cf. NEWT.] A newt. Formerly also, a lizard.

eft /ɛft/ *adv.* Long *arch.* & *dial.* [OE *eft* = OFris., OS *eft*, MLG, MDu. *echt*, ON *ept*, *eft*, f. Gmc base of AFTER *adv.*] A second time, again; moreover; afterwards.

eftsoons /ɛftˈsuːnz/ *adv.* Also (earlier) **-soon**. [OE *eftsōna*, f. as prec. + *sōna* SOON *adv.*: see -S[3].] †1 A second time, again; moreover. OE–M17. 2 (Soon) afterwards. *arch.* & *joc.* ME. †3 Occasionally; repeatedly. LME–E18.

egad /ɪˈgad/ *int. arch.* L17. [f. as AGAD.] Expr. amazement or emphasis.

egalitarian /ɪˌgalɪˈtɛːrɪən/ *a.* & *n.* L19. [f. Fr. *égalitaire*, f. as next: see -ARIAN.] A *adj.* That asserts the equality of all humankind; of, relating to, or holding the principle of equal treatment for all persons. L19. B *n.* A person who holds egalitarian views. E20.

egalitarianism *n.* E20.

égalité /egalite/ *n.* L18. [Fr., f. *égal* f. L *aequalis* EQUAL *a.*: see -ITY.] = EQUALITY 2.

egality /ɪˈgalɪti/ *n.* Long *rare.* LME. [Fr. *égalité*: see prec., -ITY.] = EQUALITY.

egall /ˈɛgal/ *a. obs.* exc. *dial.* LME. [(O)Fr. *égal* f. L *aequalis* EQUAL *a.*] = EQUAL *a.*

egally *adv.* LME.

Egeria /ɪˈdʒɪərɪə/ *n.* E17. [A Roman goddess said to have instructed Numa Pompilius.] A tutelary divinity; a patroness and adviser.

egest /ɪˈdʒɛst/ *v.t.* L15. [L *egest-* pa. ppl stem of *egerere*, f. *e-* E- + *gerere* bear, carry.] Excrete; expel from the body.

egesta /ɪˈdʒɛstə/ *n.pl.* E18. [L, use as n. of neut. pl. of *egestus* pa. pple of *egerere*: see prec.] Egested matter; excreta.

egestion /ɪˈdʒɛstʃ(ə)n/ *n.* LME. [L *egestio(n-)*, f. as EGEST: see -ION.] 1 The action of discharging or excreting from the body (opp. *ingestion*). Formerly *spec.*, defecation. LME. †2 Egested matter; excreta. LME–L17.

egestive *a.* of or pertaining to egestion L17.

egg /ɛg/ *n.* ME. [ON: superseding cognate EY *n.*] 1 A (more or less) spheroidal body produced by the female of birds and other animal species, containing the germ of a new individual enclosed in a shell or firm membrane. ME. b *spec.* The egg of the domestic fowl (as an article of food). ME. c Material from inside an egg, esp. as used in or as food. LME. 2 Something resembling an egg in shape or appearance. L16. b A bomb, a mine. *slang.* E20. 3 A person, usu. of a specified character. *colloq.* E17. 4 More fully *egg cell*. The female gamete or reproductive cell in animals or plants; an ovum. L19.

1b SHAKES. *1 Hen. IV* They are up already and call for eggs and butter. c *coddled egg*, *devilled egg*, *fried egg*, *poached egg*, *scrambled egg(s)*, etc. 3 C. MACKENZIE Oxford was divided into Bad Men and Good Eggs. *Punch* Cheerio, old egg.

Phrases: *ant eggs*, *ants'-eggs*: see ANT *n.* **as sure as eggs is** (or **are**) **eggs** *colloq.* undoubtedly. *bad egg*: see BAD *a.* **boiled egg**: cooked by being kept in boiling water for a few minutes. *cock's egg*: see COCK *n.*[1] 1. *curate's egg*: see CURATE *n.* *duck('s) egg*: see DUCK *n.*[1] **egg and anchor, dart, tongue** *Archit.* types of moulding with alternating egg-shaped and triangular figures. **egg-and-spoon race**: in which runners carry an egg in a spoon. **egg on one's face** *colloq.* a condition of looking foolish or being embarrassed or humiliated by the turn of events. **eggs and bacon** *dial.* any of several plants combining shades of yellow and orange or red in the corolla, *esp.* bird's-foot trefoil, *Lotus corniculatus*, and yellow toadflax, *Linaria vulgaris*. **have all one's eggs in one basket** risk everything on a single venture. *lay an egg*: see LAY *v.*[1] *nest egg*: see NEST *n.* *Orphic egg*: see ORPHIC *a.* 1. *Scotch egg*: see SCOTCH *a.* *teach one's* GRANDMOTHER *to suck eggs*. **tread on eggs** walk warily, proceed cautiously.

Comb.: **egg-beater** (*a*) = *egg-whisk* below; (*b*) *US slang* a helicopter; **egg-bound** *a.* (of a hen) unable through weakness or disease to expel its eggs; **egg-box, -carton, -crate**: containing individual spaces for the safe carriage of eggs; **eggbutt snaffle**: with a pair of rings that are joined to the mouthpiece of the bit by a hinge (instead of rings that pass through a hole at each end of the mouthpiece); *egg-carton*: see *egg-box* above; **egg-case** a hollow usu. rigid protective structure secreted by various invertebrates, in which eggs develop; *egg cell*: see sense 4 above; **egg-coddler** an a device for lightly cooking an egg; *egg cosy*: see COSY *n.* 1; *egg-crate*: see *egg-box* above; **egg cream** *US* a drink composed of milk and soda water, with syrup for added flavour; **eggcup** a small cup-shaped receptacle for holding a boiled egg while it is eaten; **egg-custard** a baked usu. sweetened mixture of eggs and milk; a portion of this, as a dessert; **egg-dance** a dance blindfold among eggs; *fig.* an intricate or delicate activity; **egg-eater** a southern African snake of the genus *Dasypeltis* that eats eggs; **egg-drop (soup)** a Chinese soup made by trailing beaten egg into a simmering meat broth; **egg-flip** = *egg-nog* below; **egg flower soup** = *egg-drop (soup)* above; **egg-nog** a hot or cold alcoholic drink with added egg and usu. milk; **eggplant** (now chiefly *N. Amer.*) the aubergine plant (orig. the form bearing white fruit); its fruit, an aubergine; **egg-plum** a small egg-shaped yellow plum; **egg roll** a spring roll; **Egg Saturday** the Saturday before Shrove Tuesday; **egg sauce** a savoury milk-based sauce to which boiled egg has been added; **eggs Benedict** a dish consisting of poached eggs on a slice of ham on toast, with a covering of hollandaise sauce; **egg-shaped** *a.* elongated and rounded with one end broader than the other; **egg-slice** a kitchen utensil with a flat metal blade for lifting cooked eggs out of a pan; **egg-slicer** a kitchen utensil with parallel wires on a hinged frame for slicing hard-boiled eggs; **egg-spoon** a spoon for eating boiled egg, smaller than a teaspoon; **egg tempera** a medium for painting consisting of tempera colours mixed with egg-yolk; **egg-timer** a device for timing the cooking of eggs; *spec.* a sealed glass vessel with a narrow neck in the middle and containing some sand, the fall of which when the vessel is inverted occupies a known time; **egg-tooth** a hard white protuberance on the beak or jaw of an embryonic bird or reptile which is used to crack the egg and is discarded after hatching; **egg-whisk**: for beating eggs to a froth; **egg-white** = WHITE *n.* 1; *egg-yolk*: see YOLK *n.*[1]

eggery *n.* (*a*) a collection of eggs; (*b*) an establishment for the production of eggs: M19. **eggler** *n.* (*dial.*) [perh. after *pedlar*] an egg-dealer L18. **eggless** *a.* E20.

egg /ɛg/ *v.*[1]*t.* ME. [ON *eggja* (Da. *egge*) = EDGE *v.*] Incite, urge; provoke, tempt. Now always foll. by *on* (*to do*, *to* an act).

B. BAINBRIDGE I egged him on. . . It wasn't his fault.

egg /ɛg/ *v.*[2] L18. [f. the n.] 1 *v.i.* Collect or go looking for birds' eggs. L18. 2 *v.t.* Add egg to; cover with egg. M19. 3 *v.t.* Pelt with eggs. M19.

eggar /ˈɛgə/ *n.* Also **egger**. E18. [Prob. f. EGG *n.* + -ER[1].] Any of several large brown lasiocampid moths, *esp.* (more fully *oak eggar*) *Lasiocampa quercus*, which makes egg-shaped cocoons. Also more fully *eggar moth*.

egger /ˈɛgə/ *n.*[1] M19. [f. EGG *v.*[2] or *n.* + -ER[1].] A collector of birds' eggs.

egger *n.*[2] var. of EGGAR.

egghead /ˈɛghɛd/ *n. colloq.* E20. [f. EGG *n.* + HEAD *n.*] A person regarded as intellectual or highbrow.

eggheaded *a.* (*a*) having an egg-shaped head; (*b*) *colloq.* intellectual, highbrow: E20. **eggheadedness** *n.* M20.

eggshell /ˈɛgʃɛl/ *n.* & *a.* LME. [f. EGG *n.* + SHELL *n.*] A *n.* The thin shell or external covering of a bird's egg. LME.

walk on eggshells = *tread on eggs* s.v. EGG *n.*

B *adj.* Having the delicacy of an eggshell; (of a paint or finish) having the slight sheen or the pale colour of a bird's egg. LME.

DAY LEWIS A sky of egg-shell blue. **eggshell china**: of extreme thinness and delicacy.

eggshell-ful *n.* as much as the shell of a hen's egg could hold LME.

eggy /ˈɛgi/ *a.*[1] E18. [f. EGG *n.* + -Y[1].] Containing an egg or eggs; rich in eggs. Also, stained with egg.

eggy /ˈɛgi/ *a.*[2] *colloq.* & *dial.* M20. [f. EGG *v.*[1] + -Y[1].] Annoyed, irritated.

†**eglantere** *n.* var. of EGLATERE.

eglantine /ˈɛgləntʌɪn/ *n.* LME. [Fr. *églantine* f. OFr. *aiglent* f. Proto-Romance, f. (after L *spinulentus* thorny) L *acus* needle, *aculeus* prickle, sting: see -INE[1].] Any of several hedge shrubs; *spec.* the sweet-brier, *Rosa rubiginosa*. Also occas. (chiefly *dial.*), the dogrose *Rosa canina*; the honeysuckle *Lonicera periclymenum*.

†**eglatere** *n.* Also (earlier) **eglantere, eglent-**. LME–M19. [AN *eglanter*, OFr. *aiglentier*, (also mod.) *églantier*, f. *aiglent* (see prec.) + *-ier* -ER[2].] Eglantine, sweet-brier.

†**eglogue** *n.* var. of ECLOGUE.

églomisé /eglɔmize/ *a.* & *n.* Pl. of n. pronounced same. L19. [Fr., f. *Glomy*, 18th-cent. Parisian picture-framer.] A *adj.* Of glass: decorated on the back with engraved gold or silver leaf or paint. Freq. in *verre églomisé* /vɛːr/ [= glass]. L19. B *n.* (A panel of) *verre églomisé*. L19.

†**egma** *n. rare* (Shakes.). Only in L16. [Alt.] An enigma.

ego /ˈiːgəʊ, ˈɛ-/ *n.* Pl. **-os**. E19. [L = I *pron.*] 1 *Metaphysics.* Oneself, the conscious thinking subject. Also *joc.* E19. 2 *Psychoanalysis.* That part of the mind which has a sense of individuality and is most conscious of self; *spec.* according to Freud, the part which mediates between the id and the superego and deals with external reality. L19. 3 Self-esteem, self-importance; a person's sense of this in himself or herself. L19.

3 D. CARNEGIE Bores intoxicated with their own egos, drunk with a sense of their own importance.

Comb.: **ego-ideal** (*a*) *Psychol.* a part of the mind that is evolved from the ego by awareness of parental and social standards and tries to impose upon it concepts of ideal behaviour; the superego; (*b*) a person's ideal conception of himself or herself; **ego-identity** *Psychol.* a person's sense of identity as gained from self-perception and others' perception of him or her; **ego-psychology** a form of psychoanalysis dealing mainly with the ego, esp. as regards its control of libidinal impulses and its understanding of the external environment; **ego trip** *colloq.* an activity etc. devoted to increasing one's self-esteem; **ego-trip** *v.i.* (*colloq.*) indulge in an ego trip.

egoless *a.* M20. **egolessness** *n.* L20.

egocentric /ɛgə(ʊ)ˈsɛntrɪk, iː-/ *a.* & *n.* E20. [f. EGO + -CENTRIC.] A *adj.* Centred in the ego; self-centred, egotistical. E20. B *n.* An egocentric person. M20.

egocentrically *adv.* M20. ˌ**egocenˈtricity** *n.* E20. **egocentrism** *n.* E20.

egoism /ˈɛgəʊɪz(ə)m, ˈiː-/ *n.* L18. [Fr. *égoïsme* f. mod.L *egoismus*, f. L EGO: see -ISM.] 1 Solipsism. *obs.* exc. *Hist.* L18. 2a A selfish aim or act. L18. b The ethical theory which regards self-interest as the foundation of morality (opp. TUISM); systematic selfishness. E19. 3 = EGOTISM 1. E19. 4 The habit of seeing matters chiefly as they concern oneself, self-centredness; self-opinionatedness. M19.

2b H. SPENCER The promptings of egoism are duly restrained by regard for others.

egoist /ˈɛgəʊɪst, ˈiː-/ *n.* L18. [Fr. *égoïste*, f. as EGO: see -IST.] 1 A solipsist. *obs.* exc. *Hist.* L18. 2 A systematically selfish person; a self-centred or self-opinionated person. E19.

egoˈistic *a.* M19. **egoˈistical** *a.* M19. **egoˈistically** *adv.* L19.

egoity /ɪˈgəʊɪti/ *n.* Now *rare.* M17. [f. as EGO +

-ITY.] That which forms the essence of personal identity; selfhood.

egomania /ɛgə(ʊ)'meɪnɪə, iː-/ *n.* E19. [f. EGO + -MANIA.] Morbid egotism; obsessive self-love or self-centredness.

egomaniac *n.* & *a.* (*a*) *n.* a person with egomania; (*b*) *adj.* = EGOMANIACAL: L19. **,egoma'niacal** *a.* characteristic of or affected with egomania M20.

egotise *v.* var. of EGOTIZE.

egotism /'ɛgətɪz(ə)m, 'iː-/ *n.* E18. [f. as EGO + -ISM, w. euphonic *t*.] 1 Too frequent use of first person pronouns; the practice of continually talking about oneself. E18. 2 Self-conceit; selfishness. L18.

egotist /'ɛgətɪst, 'iː-/ *n.* E18. [f. prec. + -IST.] A person characterized by egotism.

ego'tistic *a.* M19. **ego'tistical** *a.* E19. **ego'tistically** *adv.* E19.

egotize /'ɛgətʌɪz, 'iː-/ *v.i.* Also **-ise**. L18. [f. EGOT(ISM + -IZE.] Talk or write in an egotistic way.

egregious /ɪ'griːdʒəs/ *a.* M16. [f. L *egregius* surpassing, illustrious, f. *e-* E- + *greg-*, *grex* flock: see -IOUS.] 1 Remarkably good; outstanding, striking; distinguished, excellent. Now *rare*. M16. 2 Remarkable in a bad sense; gross, flagrant; shocking. L16. 3 Prominent, protruding. *rare*. L16.

2 N. PEVSNER Pages 122–3 are a masterpiece of egregious diddling. C. P. SNOW The most egregious man who had ever been awarded fifteen honorary degrees.

egregiously *adv.* M16. **egregiousness** *n.* E17.

egress /'iːgrɛs/ *n.* M16. [L *egressus*, f. *egress-* pa. ppl stem of *egredi* go out, f. *e-* E- + *gradi* proceed, step.] 1 The action of going out or coming out; the right or freedom to do this. M16. 2 *Astron.* The end of an eclipse, occultation, or transit; emersion. M17. 3 A way out; an outlet (*lit.* & *fig.*). L17.

1 R. RENDELL Lodged in the .. skull, egress stopped by the frontal bone, was a bullet. 3 R. WEST A position from which there seemed no egress save by way of someone's pain.

egress /ɪ'grɛs/ *v.i.* L16. [f. the n.] Go out; issue forth.

egressive *a.* (*a*) tending to egress; characterized by egression; (*b*) *Phonet.* (of a speech sound) made with expulsion of air; (of an airflow) outward: L17.

egression /iː'grɛʃ(ə)n, ɪ-/ *n.* LME. [L *egressio(n-)*, f. *egress-*: see EGRESS *n.*, -ION.] 1 = EGRESS *n.* 1. LME. †2 Emergence *from* a specified condition; a departure from the norm; an outburst. E16–M18.

egret /'iːgrɪt, 'ɛ-/ *n.* LME. [AN *egrette*, (O)Fr. *aigrette* f. Prov. *aigreta*, f. stem of *aigron* corresp. to OFr. HERON: see -ET[1].] 1 Any of several kinds of heron, mostly of the genus *Egretta*, white, and with long plumes in the breeding season. LME. †2 = AIGRETTE. Only in M17. 3 The feathery pappus of the seed of the dandelion, thistle, etc. L18.

1 CATTLE-*egret*. *great egret*: see GREAT *a*. *snowy egret*: see SNOWY *a*.

†**egriot** *n.* var. of AGRIOT.

egromancy /'ɛgrəmansi/ *n.* *arch.* LME. [Alt.] Necromancy.

egurgitate /ɪ'gəːdʒɪteɪt/ *v.t.* *rare*. M17. [f. REGURGITATE, with substitution of pref.: see E-.] Vomit; *fig.* eject, utter.

egusi /ɛ'gʌsi/ *n.* E20. [Yoruba.] Watermelon seeds, as an item of food.

Egyptian /ɪ'dʒɪpʃ(ə)n/ *a.* & *n.* ME. [f. *Egypt* (see below) + -IAN.] A *adj.* 1 Of, pertaining to, or native to Egypt, a country in NE Africa. ME. 2 Gypsy. *joc. rare*. M18. 3 Designating a style of lettering with no serifs and minimal variation of thickness in the strokes. Also, designating a typeface with large block serifs. E19.

Special collocations: **Egyptian bean** = LABLAB. **Egyptian black** stoneware made by Wedgwood and his successors from clay stained black by added iron oxide or manganese oxide. **Egyptian days** (*obs.* exc. *Hist.*) the 24 evil or unlucky days of the medieval calendar. **Egyptian goose** an African sheldgoose, *Alopochen aegyptiacus*, that has been introduced into Britain. **Egyptian lily** the arum lily, *Zantedeschia aethiopica*. **Egyptian lotus** either of two water lilies, the blue-flowered *Nymphaea caerulea* and the white-flowered *N. lotus*, regarded as sacred in ancient Egypt. **Egyptian onion** a form of tree onion; **Egyptian plover** = *crocodile bird* s.v. CROCODILE *n.* **Egyptian vulture** a black and white vulture, *Neophron percnopterus*. **Egyptian wheel** = NORIA.

B *n.* 1 A native or inhabitant of Egypt. ME. 2 A Gypsy. E16. 3 The Hamito-Semitic language used in Egypt until the 3rd cent. AD. M16. 4 Egyptian lettering or type. M19. 5 An Egyptian cigarette. L19.

Egyptianism *n.* Egyptian characteristics, inclination to Egyptian ways E19. **Egyptiani'zation** *n.* the action of Egyptianizing something M20. **Egyptianize** *v.* †(*a*) *v.i.* behave like an Egyptian; (*b*) *v.t.* make like Egypt or an Egyptian; *spec.* (*Hist.*, of the Egyptian Government) transfer into Egyptian hands (property or interests in the hands of non-Egyptians): M17.

Egypticity /iːdʒɪp'tɪsɪti/ *n.* L19. [f. *Egypt* (see prec.) + -ICITY.] The character or quality of being Egyptian.

Egyptizing /'iːdʒɪptʌɪzɪŋ/ *ppl a.* Also **-ising**. M19. [f. *Egypt* (see EGYPTIAN) + -IZE + -ING[2].] Becoming Egyptian in character.

Egypto- /ɪ'dʒɪptəʊ/ *comb. form.* M19. [f. Gk *Aiguptos* Egypt: see -O-.] Used in senses 'Egyptian and', as *Egypto-Arabic* etc.; 'Egypt', as *Egyptomania* etc.

Egyptology /iːdʒɪp'tɒlədʒi/ *n.* M19. [f. *Egypt* (see EGYPTIAN) + -OLOGY.] The branch of archaeology that deals with Egyptian antiquities.

E,gypto'logical *a.* M19. **Egyptologist** *n.* M19.

eh /eɪ/ *int.* M16. [Natural exclam. Cf. EIGH, earlier AY *int.*[2]] †1 Expr. sorrow. Only in M16. 2 *interrog.* Inviting assent or conveying emphasis. *colloq.* L18. 3 *interrog.* Expr. a request for the repetition or clarification of something just said. *colloq.* M19.

2 J. M. SYNGE You want someone to look after you eh? 3 T. BACON Eh? What's that, Sackville?

eicos- /'ʌɪkɒs/ *comb. form.* Also **eicosa-** /'ʌɪkɒsə/, **eicosi-** /'ʌɪkɒsi/. [f. as ICOS-.] Orig. = ICOS-. Now *spec.* in *Chem.*, forming names of compounds or radicals containing twenty atoms of an element, usu. carbon.

eicosapent(a)e'noic *a.*: *eicosapent(a)enoic acid*, a polyunsaturated fatty acid, $C_{19}H_{29}COOH$, which is present in fish oils and is a metabolic precursor of prostaglandins in humans M20. **eicose'noic** *a.*: *eicosenoic acid*, an unsaturated fatty acid, $C_{19}H_{37}COOH$, which is present in fish oils and the wax of some plant seeds M20.

†**eicosahedron** *n.* var. of ICOSAHEDRON.

eicosane /'ʌɪkɒseɪn/ *n.* Also **icos-**. L19. [f. EICOS- + -ANE.] *Chem.* Any saturated hydrocarbon having the formula $C_{20}H_{42}$, of which there are many isomers; *spec.* the normal straight-chain isomer.

eicosa'noic *a.* = ARACHIDIC E20. **ei'cosanoid** *n.* any of a group of biologically active compounds with the same carbon skeleton as eicosane, *esp.* one of those occurring as metabolites of certain fatty acids L20.

eid /iːd/ *n.* Also **id**. L17. [Arab. *'īd* festival f. Aram.] A Muslim feast-day; *spec.* that of breaking the fast at the end of Ramadan (also called *id ul-fitr*).

eident /'ʌɪd(ə)nt/ *a.* *Sc.* Also **-ant**, **id-**. ME. [ON *iðinn* with assim. to pres. pples in *-and*.] 1 Industrious, diligent; conscientious, attentive. ME. 2 Continual, persistent. ME.

eidently *adv.* ME.

eider /'ʌɪdə/ *n.* L17. [Icel. *æður* genit. *æðar* in *æðarfugl* eider duck f. ON *æðr*. See also next.] 1 Any large northern sea-duck of the genera *Somateria* and *Polysticta*; spec. *S. mollissima*, the male of which is largely black and white and the female dull brown, and which is the source of eider-down. Also *eider duck*. L17. 2 = EIDERDOWN 1. M18.

1 **king-eider** an Arctic eider, *Somateria spectabilis*, distinguished by the orange bill and frontal shield of the male.

eiderdown /'ʌɪdədaʊn/ *n.* Also **eider-down** (the usual form in sense 1). M18. [Icel. *æðardúnn*, f. as prec., DOWN *n.*[2]] 1 The soft feathers from the breast of the eider *Somateria mollissima*, with which it lines its nest. M18. 2 A quilt filled with this or with another soft material. L19. 3 A thick soft heavily-napped fabric. L19.

eidetic /ʌɪ'dɛtɪk/ *a.* & *n.* E20. [f. Gk *eidētikos*, f. *eidos* form: see -ETIC.] *Psychol.* A *adj.* Of, pertaining to, or designating a recollected mental image having unusual vividness and detail, as if actually visible; (of a person) capable of perceiving such images. E20. B *n.* A person able to perceive eidetic images. E20.

eidetically *adv.* E20. **eidetiker** /ʌɪ'dɛtɪkə/ *n.* [G] a person with the faculty of seeing eidetic images L20.

eidolon /ʌɪ'dəʊlɒn/ *n.* Pl. **-la** /-lə/, **-lons**. M17. [Gk *eidōlon*: see IDOL.] †1 An emanation considered by atomic philosophers to constitute the visible image of an object. *rare*. Only in M17. 2 A spectre, a phantom. Also, an idealized image. E19.

2 E. A. POE An Eidolon named Night On a black throne. M. RENAULT She was the perennial *eidolon*, the clean pampered harlot.

Eidophusikon /ʌɪdə(ʊ)'fjuːzɪkɒn/ *n.* *obs.* exc. *Hist.* Also **-con**. L18. [f. Gk *eidos* form + *phusikon* neut. of *phusikos* natural, f. *phusis* nature.] A kind of lantern depicting natural scenes and phenomena.

†**eidouranion** *n.* L18–E19. [f. as prec. + *ouranos* heaven.] A mechanical device that represented the motions of celestial objects.

eigen- /'ʌɪgən/ *comb. form.* [G *eigen* OWN *a.*] Used in *Math.* & *Physics* w. general sense 'characteristic, proper', orig. in compounds adopted from G with tr. of the second elem. only.

eigenfrequency *n.* any of the resonant frequencies of a system M20. **eigenfunction** *n.* each of a set of independent functions which are the solutions to a given differential equation E20. **eigenstate** *n.* a quantum-mechanical state corresponding to an eigenvalue of a wave equation M20. **eigentone** *n.* a frequency at which acoustic resonance occurs in a given enclosed space M20. **eigenvalue** *n.* (*a*) each of a set of values of a parameter for which a differential equation has a non-zero solution (an eigenfunction) under given conditions; (*b*) any of the numbers such that a given matrix minus that number times the identity matrix has zero determinant: E20. **eigenvector** *n.* a vector which when operated on by a given operator gives a scalar multiple of that vector M20.

eigh /eɪ/ *int.* *dial.* M18. [Natural exclam.: cf. EH.] Expr. surprise or asseveration.

eight /eɪt/ *a.* & *n.* (*cardinal numeral*). [OE *ehta* (*eahta*, *ahta*) = OFris. *achta*, *acht(e)*, OS, OHG *ahto* (Du., G *acht*), ON *átta*, Goth. *ahtau*, f. Gmc f. IE, whence also L *octo*, Gk *oktō*, Skt *aṣṭā*.] A *adj.* One more than seven (a cardinal numeral represented by 8 in arabic numerals, viii, VIII in roman). OE.

E. O'NEILL A small, square compartment about eight feet high. A. J. P. TAYLOR Trade union membership reached a peak of over eight million. W. BOYD One of eight hotels in Nairobi. *Financial Times* The amendment .. gives shareholders a majority (eight-fifteenths) of the seats. **(an) eight days** *arch.* a week.

B *n.* 1 Eight persons or things identified contextually, as parts or divisions, years of age, points, runs, etc., in a game, chances (in giving odds), minutes, inches, shillings (now *Hist.*), pence, etc. OE. 2 One more than seven as an abstract number; the symbol(s) or figure(s) representing this (8 in arabic numerals, viii, VIII in roman); (more fully *figure of eight*) a figure shaped like 8, esp. in ice-skating. OE. 3 The time of day eight hours after midnight or midday (on a clock, watch, etc., indicated by the numeral eight displayed or pointed to). Also *eight o'clock*. LME. 4 The eighth of a set or series with numbered members, the one designated eight, (usu. *number eight*, or with specification, as *book eight*, *chapter eight*, etc.); a size etc. denoted by eight, a shoe, glove, garment, etc., of such a size, (also *size eight*). E16. 5 A set of eight; a thing having a set of eight as an essential or distinguishing feature; *spec.* (*a*) a playing-card marked with eight pips or spots; (*b*) a crew of eight in a rowing boat; in *pl.*, boat races (esp. at Oxford) between such crews; (*c*) an eight-oared boat; (*d*) in *pl.*, eight leaves to the sheet in a printed book, octavo; (*e*) a line or verse with eight syllables; (*f*) an engine or motor vehicle with eight cylinders. L16. 6 Each of a set of eight; *spec.* a large plant-pot of which eight are formed from one cast of clay. E19.

1 TENNYSON Eight that were left to make a purer world. DAY LEWIS I had had diphtheria at the age of eight or nine. **piece of eight** [*sc.* reals], **real of eight** *Hist.* a Spanish dollar. 2 *lazy eight*: see LAZY *a.* 3 R. MAUGHAM I'm at work from eight in the morning. 4 A. AYCKBOURN My slippers are eights. *factor eight*: see FACTOR *n.* 7c. **one over the eight** *slang* (*a*) *n.* one alcoholic drink too many; (*b*) *adj.* slightly drunk. 5 *middle eight*: see MIDDLE *a.* *V-eight*: see V, V 2.

Comb.: Forming compound cardinal numerals with multiples of ten from twenty to ninety, as *thirty-eight*, (arch.) *eight-and-thirty*, etc., and (*arch.*) their corresponding ordinals, as *eight-and-thirtieth* etc., and with multiples of a hundred, as *208* (read *two hundred and eight*, US also *two hundred eight*), *5008* (read *five thousand and eight*, US also *five thousand eight*), etc. With ns. + -ER[1] forming ns. w. the sense 'something (identified contextually) being of or having eight —s', as *eight-seater*, *-wheeler*, etc. Special combs., as **eight ball** *N. Amer.* (the black ball, numbered eight, in) a variety of the game of pool; *behind the eight ball*, at a disadvantage, baffled; **eight-day clock** a clock that goes for eight days without being wound up; **eightpence** eight pence, esp. of the old British currency before decimalization; **eightpenny** *a.* worth or costing eightpence; **eight-pounder** a gun throwing a shot that weighs eight pounds; **eight-square** *a.* & *adv.* [after *four-square*] in the form of a regular octagon, with eight equal sides.

eightfold *a.* & *adv.* (*a*) *adj.* eight times as great or as numerous; having eight parts, divisions, elements, or units; (*Eightfold Path*, the Buddhist path to nirvana, comprising eight aspects in which an aspirant must become practised; *eightfold way* (Physics), the grouping of hadrons into supermultiplets by means of SU(3)); (*b*) *adv.* to eight times the number or quantity: OE.

eighteen /eɪˈtiːn, ˈeɪtiːn/ *a.* & *n.* (*cardinal numeral*). [OE *e(a)htatēne* = OFris. *achatīne*, OS *ahtotian* (Du. *achttien*), OHG *ahtozehan* (G *achtzehn*), ON *átján*, f. Gmc base of EIGHT, -TEEN.] A *adj.* One more than seventeen (a cardinal numeral represented by 18 in arabic numerals, xviii, XVIII in roman). OE.

SIR W. SCOTT About eighteen years since.

B *n.* 1 Eighteen persons or things identified contextually, as years of age, chances (in giving odds), minutes, shillings (now *Hist.*), pence, etc. OE. 2 One more than seventeen as an abstract number; the symbols or figures representing this (18 in arabic numerals, xviii, XVIII in roman). LME. 3 The eighteenth of a set or series with numbered members, the one designated eighteen, (usu. *number eighteen*, or with specification, as *book eighteen*, *chapter eighteen*, etc.); a size etc. denoted by eighteen, a garment etc. of such a size, (also *size eighteen*). E16. 4 A set of eighteen; a thing having a set of eighteen as an essential or distinguishing feature; *spec.* (*a*) in *pl.*, eighteen leaves to the sheet in a printed book, octodecimo; (*b*) a team of eighteen in Australian Rules football. L17.

1 D. H. LAWRENCE Our boys must stay at school till they are eighteen. A. J. P. TAYLOR Though 140 Labour M.P.s elected in 1929 belonged to the I.L.P., only eighteen pledged themselves to support its policy.

Comb.: Forming compound numerals with multiples of a hundred, as *518* (read *five hundred and eighteen*, US also *five hundred eighteen*), *5018* (read *five thousand and eighteen*, US also *five thousand eighteen*), etc. In dates used for one thousand eight hundred, as *1812* (read *eighteen twelve*), *eighteen-nineties*, etc. With ns. + -ER[1] forming ns. w. the sense 'something (identified contextually) being of or having eighteen —s', as *eighteen-tonner*, *-wheeler*, etc. Special combs., as **eighteen-pounder** a gun throwing a shot that weighs eighteen pounds.

eighteenmo *n.*, pl. **-os**, octodecimo E19.

eighteenth /eɪˈtiːnθ, ˈeɪtiːnθ/ *a.* & *n.* (*ordinal numeral*). [OE *e(a)htotēoþa*, repl. in ME by forms f. EIGHTEEN + -TH[2]. Cf. OFris. *ahtatīnda*, *ahtendesta*, *achtiensta*, ON *átjándi*.] A *adj.* Next in order after the seventeenth, that is number eighteen in a series, (represented by 18th). OE.

ALDOUS HUXLEY In the eighteenth century, when logic and science were the fashion. W. FAULKNER His eighteenth birthday and legal age for joining up.

B *n.* 1 The eighteenth person or thing of a category, series, etc., identified contextually, as day of the month, (following a proper name) person, esp. monarch or pope, of the specified name, etc. OE. 2 *Mus.* An interval embracing eighteen notes on the diatonic scale; a note an eighteenth above another given note; a chord of two notes an eighteenth apart. L19.

1 LONGFELLOW On the eighteenth of April, in Seventy-five.

Comb.: Forming compound ordinal numerals with multiples of a hundred, as *three-hundred-and-eighteenth* (*318th*), *five-thousand-and-eighteenth* (*5018th*), etc.

eighteenthly *adv.* in the eighteenth place L17.

eighth /eɪtθ/ *a.* & *n.* (*ordinal numeral*). [OE *e(a)htoþa* = OFris. *achte*, OHG *ahtodo* (G *achte*), f. Gmc, f. base of EIGHT, -TH[2].] A *adj.* Next in order after the seventh, that is number eight in a series, (represented by 8th). OE.

S. KUNITZ Doomsday is the eighth day of the week. **eighth note** *Mus.* (*N. Amer.*) a quaver. **eighth part** *arch.* = sense B.3 below. *eighth wonder of the world*: see WONDER *n.*

B *n.* 1 The eighth person or thing of a category, series, etc., identified contextually, as day of the month, (following a proper name) person, esp. monarch or pope, of the specified name, etc. OE. †2 *Mus.* An octave; a note an octave above another given note. LME–E18. 3 Each of eight equal parts into which something is or may be divided, a fraction which when multiplied by eight gives one, (= *eighth part* above). M16.

1 JOYCE An animated altercation . . as to whether the eighth or the ninth of March was the correct date of the birth of Ireland's patron saint. R. BOLT Our Sovereign Lord, Harry, . . The Eighth of that name. 3 *Economist* Five-eighths of our income is going to be spent for us by the state.

Comb.: Forming compound ordinal numerals with multiples of ten, as *forty-eighth* (*48th*), *five-thousand-and-eighth* (*5008th*), etc.

eighthly *adv.* in the eighth place L16.

eightieth /ˈeɪtɪɪθ/ *a.* & *n.* (*ordinal numeral*). LME. [f. EIGHTY + -TH[2].] 1 *adj.* & *n.* (The person or thing) next in order after the seventy-ninth, that is number eighty in a series, (represented by 80th). LME. 2 *n.* Each of eighty equal parts into which something is or may be divided, a fraction which when multiplied by eighty gives one. M19.

Comb.: Forming compound numerals with multiples of a hundred, as *two-hundred-and-eightieth* (*280th*), *five-thousand-and-eightieth* (*5080th*), etc., and (*arch.*) with numerals below ten, as *five-and-eightieth* etc.

eightsome /ˈeɪts(ə)m/ *pron.*, *n.*, & *a.* ME. [f. EIGHT + -SOME[2].] A *pron.* & *n.* 1 Formerly, eight in all. Now, a group of eight. Chiefly *Sc.* ME. †2 One of eight. LME–M16. 3 *ellipt.* An eightsome reel. E20. B *attrib.* or as *adj.* For eight; *esp.* (of a dance) performed by eight people together. M16.

eighty /ˈeɪti/ *a.* & *n.* (*cardinal numeral*). [OE *hunde(a)htatiġ*, f. *hund* of uncertain origin + *e(a)hta* EIGHT + *-tiġ* -TY[2]. 1st elem. lost early in ME (cf. SEVENTY).] A *adj.* Eight times ten (a cardinal numeral represented by 80 in arabic numerals, lxxx, LXXX in roman). OE.

B *n.* 1 Eighty persons or things identified contextually, as years of age, points, runs, etc., in a game, chances (in giving odds), etc. OE. 2 Eight times ten as an abstract number; the symbols or figures representing this (80 in arabic numerals, lxxx, LXXX in roman). LME. 3 The eightieth of a set or series with numbered members, the one designated eighty, (usu. *number eighty*, or with specification, as *chapter eighty*, *verse eighty*, etc.); a size etc. denoted by eighty (also *size eighty*). E16. 4 Any of a set of eighty; *spec.* a small plant-pot of which eighty are formed from one cast of clay. E19. 5 In *pl.* The numbers from 80 to 89 inclusive, esp. denoting years of a century or units of a scale of temperature; *one's* years of life between the ages of 80 and 89. L19.

1 SCOTT FITZGERALD A . . bungalow at eighty a month. W. FAULKNER He would live to be eighty. 5 E. O'NEILL The rural taste for grandeur in the eighties.

Comb.: Forming compound numerals (cardinal or ordinal) with numerals below ten, as *eighty-nine*, (arch.) *nine-and-eighty*, (*89*), *eighty-first* (*81st*), etc., and (cardinals) with multiples of a hundred, as *380* (read *three hundred and eighty*, US also *three hundred eighty*), *5080* (*five thousand and eighty*, US also *five thousand eighty*), etc. Special combs., as **eighty-six** *n.* & *v.* (*fig.*, *US slang*) (*a*) *n.* an item on a menu that is not available; a customer who is not to be served; (*b*) *v.t.* bar or eject (a person) from a place; reject, abandon.

eigne /eɪn/ *n.* & *a.* Formerly also †**ayne**. LME. [OFr. *ainz né* (mod. *aîné*) earlier born.] †A *n.* In *pl.* Elders. Only in LME. B *adj.* *Law* (now *Hist.*). First-born, eldest. Usu. *postpositive.* L15.

eik *n.*, *v.* see EKE *n.*, *v.*

eikonal /ˈʌɪkən(ə)l, ʌɪˈkəʊn(ə)l/ *n.* & *a.* E20. [f. Gk *eikōn* image + -AL[1].] *Physics.* A *n.* The optical path length of a ray between specified points. Also, the time taken for a wavefront to reach a specified point. E20. B *adj.* 1 Designating an expression that gives the eikonal in terms of the wave velocity. M20. 2 Designating a method of approximately representing the behaviour of particles by means of eikonals. M20.

eild /iːld/ *a.* *Sc.* E18. [Prob. var. of YELD *a.*] Of a cow or other animal: not yielding milk; barren.

-ein /ɪɪn, ɪn/ *suff.* Var. of -IN[1], used in names of some chemical compounds, as *fluorescein*, *phenolphthalein*.

-eine /iːn, iːn/ *suff.* Var. of -INE[5], used in names of some chemical compounds, as *cysteine*.

Einfühlung /ˈaɪnfyːlʊŋ, ˈʌɪnfuːlʊŋ/ *n.* E20. [G, f. *ein-* into + *Fühlung* feeling, f. *fühlen* FEEL *v.*] Empathy.

einkorn /ˈʌɪnkɔːn/ *n.* E20. [G, f. *ein* one + *Korn* CORN *n.*[1], seed.] An inferior kind of diploid wheat, *Triticum monococcum*, with one-grained spikelets that was eaten in prehistoric times but is now grown only as fodder, in parts of Europe.

Einstein /ˈʌɪnstʌɪn/ *n.* E20. [See next.] 1 *Einstein effect* or *shift*, the lengthening of the wavelength of radiation as a result of its passage through a strong gravitational field. E20. 2 (**e-**.) A unit of quantity of light, equal to Avogadro's number of photons. M20.

Comb.: **Einstein-Bose statistics** = BOSE-EINSTEIN STATISTICS.

Einsteinian /ʌɪnˈstʌɪnɪən/ *a.* E20. [f. *Einstein* (see below) + -IAN.] Of, pertaining to, or characteristic of the German-born US physicist Albert Einstein (1879–1955) or his theories.

einsteinium /ʌɪnˈstʌɪnɪəm/ *n.* M20. [f. as prec. + -IUM.] A radioactive metallic chemical element of the actinide series, atomic no. 99, which is produced artificially. (Symbol Es.)

eirenic, **-ical** *adjs.* vars. of IRENIC, -ICAL.

eirenicon /ʌɪˈriːnɪkɒn/ *n.* Also (earlier) **iren-**. E17. [Gk *eirēnikon* neut. sing. of *eirēnikos* IRENIC.] A conciliatory proposal, an attempt to make peace, esp. in a Church or between Churches.

eisegesis /ʌɪsɪˈdʒiːsɪs/ *n.* L19. [Gk *eisēgēsis* a bringing in, f. *eisēgeisthai* introduce, f. *eis* in + *ēgeisthai* to guide.] The interpretation of a (scriptural) text in a way that is biased by one's own ideas.

eisegetical *a.* L19.

†**eisel** *n.* ME–M17. [OFr. *aisil* f. L *acetum*, w. unexpl. ending.] Vinegar.

Eisenhower jacket /ˈʌɪz(ə)nhaʊə ˌdʒakɪt/ *n. phr.* M20. [Dwight D. *Eisenhower* (1890–1969), US soldier and President.] A US military uniform jacket; a short jacket resembling this.

eisteddfod /ʌɪˈstɛðvɒd, ʌɪˈstɛdʌəd/ *n.* Pl. **-fods**, **-fodau** /-vɒdʌɪ/. E19. [Welsh = session, f. *eistedd* sit.] A congress of Welsh bards; a national or local gathering (in Wales, or in other places with a strong Welsh influence) for competitions of literature, music, folk-dance, etc.; *spec.* (**E-**, in full *Royal National Eisteddfod*) an annual national gathering of this kind.

Eisteddfodic /ʌɪstɛðˈvɒdɪk/ *a.* L19.

Eiswein /ˈaɪsvaɪn/ *n.* M20. [G, f. *Eis* ICE *n.* + *Wein* WINE *n.*] Wine made from ripe grapes picked while covered with frost.

eis wool /ˈʌɪʃ wʊl/ *n.* L19. [f. G *Eis* ICE *n.* + WOOL *n.*] A fine glossy type of wool used for scarfs, shawls, etc. Also called *ice-wool*.

eith *a.* & *adv.* see EATH.

either /ˈʌɪðə, ˈiː-/ *a.* (in mod. usage also classed as a *determiner*), *pron.*, *adv.*, & *conj.* [OE *ǣġþer* contr. form of *ǣġ(e)hwæþer* = OFris. *ēider*, MLG, MDu. *ed(d)er* (as adv.), OHG *eogihwedar* (MHG *iegeweder*), f. Gmc phr. f. bases of AYE *adv.*[1], WHETHER *a.*, etc.] A *adj.* 1 Each — of two. Occas., each — of more than two. OE. †b Both. Also *either both*. M16–E17. 2 One or other — of two. Occas., any one — of more than two. ME.
1 E. WAUGH Dame Mildred and Miss Tin sat on either side of the Emperor. S. BELLOW He had a cup of coffee in either hand. B. BAINBRIDGE He had lived in Dublin and Paris and London and had been equally at home in either capital. 2 J. S. LE FANU Her watch .. being seldom more than twenty minutes wrong, either way. J. STEINBECK In either case it was none of their business.
B *pron.* 1 Each of two. (Foll. by *of*: with sing. & †pl. concord.) OE. b Each of more than two. (Foll. by *of*.) L16. 2 One or other of two. (Foll. by *of*: with sing. & (*colloq.*) pl. concord.) M16. b Any one of more than two. (Foll. by *of*.) E17.
1 SPENSER So parted they, as eithers way them led. G. GREENE If an English election is less complex than an American, a Haitian is simpler than either. b W. D. HOWELLS Just above the feet, at either of the three corners. 2 J. RUSKIN I don't mean that either of the writers I name are absolutely thus narrow in their own views. H. JAMES It was impossible to make out from the countenance of either whether a sound had passed between them. SCOTT FITZGERALD Either of them had only to mention the word 'mortifying' to send them both into riotous gasps. b T. HARDY 'Did you walk in through Giant's Ear, or Goblin's Cellar, or Grim Billy?' 'We did not enter by either of these.'
C *adv.* & *conj.* †1 Both — *and*. OE–ME. 2 Followed by coordinate *or*, †*other*, †*either*, (in neg. contexts, *colloq.*) *nor*: as one supposition or equally possible alternative; as one of mutually exclusive possibilities. LME. †3 Or. LME–E17. 4 Following *or*: as an alternative; in addition. *arch.* LME. 5 In neg. & interrog. contexts: any more than the other; likewise; moreover. In hypothet. & condit. contexts: for that matter. E19.
2 B. JOWETT A narration of events, either past, present, or to come. J. MITCHELL The signatories hoped that the Ngulu would not suffer, either directly or indirectly, by the withdrawal of British rule. J. BERGER She .. either had to lean back .., or else stare at his watch-chain. *New York Times* Personally I don't think either Moscow or Washington are going to play any major role. N. ALGREN Without either taking the hand nor lowering his left. 5 J. CONRAD She was a good ship .. and not old either. E. WAUGH He can't bear it and he's not much use at it either. M. AMIS You don't agree? I don't agree either.
Comb.: **either-or** *n.* & *a.* (involving) an unavoidable choice between alternatives.

eiusdem generis *adv.* & *a. phr.* var. of EJUSDEM GENERIS.

ejaculate /ɪˈdʒakjʊlət/ *n.* E20. [f. the vb: see -ATE[2].] Ejaculated semen; a quantity of semen ejaculated at one time.

ejaculate /ɪˈdʒakjʊleɪt/ *v.* L16. [L *ejaculat-* pa. ppl stem of *ejaculari*, f. *e-* E- + *jaculari* to dart, f. *jaculum* dart, javelin, f. *jacere* to throw: see -ATE[3].] 1 *v.t.* Forcefully eject (semen) on achieving orgasm; suddenly eject (any matter) from the human, animal, or plant body. L16. †b *gen.* Throw or shoot out suddenly and quickly. E17–M18. †2 *v.t.* Give off, emit. M17–M19. 3 *v.t.* Say suddenly or quickly, esp. with feeling. M17. 4 *v.i.* Ejaculate semen on achieving orgasm. L19.
ejaculative /-lətɪv/ *a.* of the nature of an ejaculation; pertaining to ejaculation: M17. **ejaculator** *n.* a muscle that brings about ejaculation of semen; a person who ejaculates: E18.

ejaculation /ɪˌdʒakjʊˈleɪʃ(ə)n/ *n.* E17. [Fr. *éjaculation*, f. *éjaculer* f. L *ejaculari*: see prec., -ATION.] 1 The action or an act of ejaculating matter from the body etc.; *spec.* the discharge of semen during orgasm. E17. †2 The action or an act of throwing, throwing up, or shooting out; emission of radiation. E17–E19. 3 Something that is ejaculated; *esp.* a short prayer hastily made; a sudden expression of emotion. E17. 4 The action of saying something suddenly and with feeling. M17.
1 J. L. HARPER Where a seed is dispersed by ejaculation from a capsule. **premature ejaculation** ejaculation of semen during sexual intercourse before penetration or immediately after it. 3 CONAN DOYLE Cunning questions and ejaculations of wonder.

ejaculatio praecox /ɪdʒakjʊˌleɪʃɪəʊ ˈpriːkɒks/ *n. phr.* L19. [mod.L, f. L *ejaculat-* (see EJACULATE *v.*) + *praecox* premature: see PRECOCIOUS.] Premature ejaculation.

ejaculatory /ɪˈdʒakjʊlət(ə)ri/ *a.* M17. [f. EJACULATE *v.* + -ORY[2].] 1 Of the nature of or resembling a spoken ejaculation. M17. 2 Involved with ejaculation, esp. of semen. M17.
2 **ejaculatory duct**: carrying semen to the urethra from where the vas deferens joins the excretory duct of the seminal vesicle.

eject /ˈiːdʒɛkt/ *n.* L19. [L *ejectum* neut. pa. pple of *e(j)icere* (see next), after *subject*, *object*.] A mental state or a sensation that cannot be an object of one's own consciousness but is inferred to exist.

eject /ɪˈdʒɛkt/ *v.* LME. [L *eject-* pa. ppl stem of *e(j)icere*, f. *e-* E- + *jacere* to throw.] 1 *v.t.* Throw out (material, an object) from within; cause to be thrown out; discharge forcefully or violently. LME. 2 *v.t.* Drive out from or *from* a place by force or with indignity. LME. 3 *v.t.* Expel (a person) from or *from* a position or office; dispossess (an occupier) by legal means. LME. 4 *v.t. fig.* Emit, give out. L16. 5 *v.i.* Leave an aircraft or spacecraft as an emergency procedure; bale out. M20.
1 C. LYELL If stones are thrown into the Crater they are instantly ejected. J. WYNDHAM I ejected the two spent cartridge cases, and reloaded. 2 M. MEYER The little kingdoms .. had risen against and ejected their tyrants. D. M. DAVIN I had to eject from the pub a drunk and troublesome Canadian soldier.
Comb.: **eject button**: that is pressed in order to eject a cassette or disc from a machine.

ejecta /ɪˈdʒɛktə/ *n.pl.* (treated as *pl.* or *sing.*). L19. [L, neut. pl. of pa. pple of *e(j)icere* EJECT *v.*] 1 Matter that is thrown out of a volcano or a star. L19. 2 Material discharged from the body, *esp.* vomit. L19.

ejectamenta /ɪˌdʒɛktəˈmɛntə/ *n.pl.* M19. [L, pl. of *ejectamentum*, f. *ejectare* frequent. of *e(j)icere* EJECT *v.*: see -MENT.] = EJECTA I.

ejection /ɪˈdʒɛkʃ(ə)n/ *n.* LME. [(O)Fr. *éjection* or L *ejectio(n-)*, f. as EJECT *v.*: see -ION.] 1 The action or an act of ejecting something or someone. LME. b An emergency procedure in which a pilot is catapulted out of and away from an aircraft. M20. 2 Something that has been ejected. M17.
Comb.: **ejection seat** an aircraft pilot's seat that can be caused to eject its occupant.

ejective /ɪˈdʒɛktɪv/ *a.* & *n.* M17. [f. EJECT *v.* + -IVE.] A *adj.* 1 Having the function or power of ejecting. M17. 2 *Phonet.* Of a consonant: not pulmonic, but articulated by closing the glottis, so as to produce a compression of air which is then forcefully released. M20. B *n. Phonet.* An ejective consonant. M20.

ejectment /ɪˈdʒɛktm(ə)nt/ *n.* E16. [Law Fr. *ejectement*, f. Fr. *éjecter* f. as EJECT *v.*: see -MENT.] 1 (An) ejection of a person from a place or office, *spec.* (*Law*) of a tenant or occupier from property. E16. 2 *Law.* An action in which a person ejected from property seeks to recover possession and damages. L17.

ejector /ɪˈdʒɛktə/ *n.* M17. [f. EJECT *v.* + -OR.] 1 A person who ejects someone, *spec.* (*Law*) a tenant or occupier from property. M17. 2 An appliance or part that serves to eject something, e.g. a cartridge from a gun. L19.
Comb.: **ejector seat** = EJECTION *seat*.

ejido /eˈxiðo, eɪˈhiːdəʊ/ *n.* Pl. **-os** /-ɔs, -əʊz/. L19. [Mex. Sp. f. Sp. = common land (on the road leading out of a village) f. L EXITUS.] In Mexico: a cooperative farm; a piece of land farmed communally.
ejidal *a.* /exiˈðal, eɪˈhiːd(ə)l/ M20.

†**ejulation** *n.* E17–E18. [L *ejulatio(n-)*, f. *ejulat-* pa. ppl stem of *ejulare* wail: see -ATION.] Lamentation.

ejusdem generis /eɪˌ(j)ʊsdɛm ˈdʒɛnərɪs/ *adv.* & *a. phr.* Also **eius-**. M17. [L.] *Law.* A *adv. phr.* As of the same kind. (Foll. by *with*.) M17.
Daily Telegraph 'Other records' .. had to be construed *eiusdem generis* with 'ledgers, day books, cash books and account books'.
B *adj. phr.* Designating the rule of interpretation that general words following an enumeration of particulars are to be understood as limited to the same general category as is jointly implied by the particulars. L19.

eka- /ˈeɪkə/ *comb. form.* L19. [Skt = one.] Prefixed to the name of an element to denote the element expected or postulated to occupy the next lower position in the same group or subgroup of the periodic table, as *eka-bismuth*.

ek dum /eɪk ˈdʌm/ *adv. phr.* Also ***ek dam***. L19. [Hind., f. *ek* one + Urdu *dam* breath.] At once, immediately.

eke /iːk/ *n.* Now chiefly *Sc.* Also (the usual *Sc.* form) **eik** /ɪk, eɪk/. [OE *ēaca* = OFris. *āka*, ON *auki*, f. base also of EKE *v.*] I *gen.* 1 An addition, an increase; an extension. OE. II *spec.* 2 A tag at the end of a bell-rope. Now *rare* or *obs.* E16. 3 *Law.* An appendix or supplement to a document; a codicil; *esp.* one added to include property not covered by the original document. M16. 4 A ring on which a beehive is stood to increase the capacity. Now *dial.* E18. 5 A patch or gusset on a garment. L18. 6 An additional drink, an extra tot. Now *dial.* M19.

eke /iːk/ *v.* Also †**eche**; (the usual *Sc.* form) **eik** /ɪk, eɪk/. [OE *ēacan*, *-ian* (v.i.), *ēcan* (v.t.), = OFris. *āka*, OS *ōkian*, ON *auka*, Goth. *aukan* rel. to L *augere* increase, Gk *aukhein*. Partly f. the n.] 1 *v.t.* & †*i.* Increase, lengthen. Now chiefly *Sc.* OE. b *v.t.* Add to by way of repair, patch. *Sc.* E18. 2 *v.t.* Add (*to*). Now *Sc.* OE. 3 *v.t.* Foll. by *out*: cause to last longer by economical use or by expedients; make up for deficiencies in, supplement, (*with*). L16. 4 *v.t.* Contrive to make (a living) or to support (an existence) by makeshifts. Usu. foll. by *out*. E19.
3 J. K. JEROME His German was easy to understand and he knew a little English with which to eke it out. G. GREENE Spending a little love at a time, eking it out here and there, on this man and that. A. BLOND Bookshops .. eke out their turnover with stationery. 4 *Discovery* The settlers eked out a bare existence from such poor land.

eke /iːk/ *adv. arch.* [OE *ē(a)c* = OFris. *āk*, OS *ōk* (Du. *ook*), OHG *ouh* (G *auch*), ON, Goth. *auk*, perh. f. IE (cf. Gk *au ge* again) or rel. to EKE *v.*] Also; in addition.

eke-name /ˈiːkneɪm/ *n.* Now *rare.* ME. [f. EKE *n.* + NAME *n.*: cf. ON *aukanafn*. See NICKNAME.] An additional name; a nickname.

eking /ˈiːkɪŋ/ *n.* LME. [f. EKE *v.* + -ING[1].] 1 The action of increasing or adding something. Now chiefly *Sc.* LME. 2 An increase. Now *rare.* LME. †3 A protuberance, a projection. Only in LME. 4 *Naut.* A piece of wood inserted to make good a deficiency. Also, the carving under the lower part of a quarter-piece. E19.

ekistics /ɪˈkɪstɪks/ *n.* M20. [f. Gk *oikistikos* relating to settlement, f. *oikizein* settle (a colony), f. *oikos* house: see -ICS.] The branch of knowledge that deals with human settlements and the way they develop and adapt.
ekistic *a.* M20. **eki'stician** *n.* an expert in or student of ekistics M20.

ekka /ˈɛkə/ *n.*[1] E19. [Hind. *ikkā* lit. 'single', f. Skt *eka* one.] In the Indian subcontinent: a small one-horse vehicle.

Ekka /ˈɛkə/ *n.*[2] *Austral. colloq.* M20. [Alt. of *exhibition*.] The Queensland Royal Show ('Brisbane Exhibition'), held each August.

ekker /ˈɛkə/ *n. Univ.* & *School slang.* L19. [f. initial sounds of EXERCISE *n.* + -ER[6].] (Physical) exercise.

ekphrasis *n.* var. of ECPHRASIS.

ektene *n.* var. of ECTENE.

el /ɛl/ *n. US colloq.* E20. [Abbrev. of *elevated*.] An elevated railway.

-el /əl, (ə)l/ *suff.*[1] (not productive). Var. of -LE[1] retained after *ch*, soft *g*, *n*, *r*, *s*, *sh*, *th*, and *v*, as in *kernel*, *swivel*, *teasel*.

-el /ɛl, (ə)l/ *suff.*² (not productive). [(O)Fr.: cf. -LE².] Occurring in ns. and (occas.) adjs. 1 Repr. OFr. *-el* masc. (mod. *-eau*), *-elle* fem., f. L *-ellus*, *-ella*, *-ellum* dim. suff., as in *bowel*, *chapel*, *novel*, *tunnel*. 2 Repr. OFr. *-el* f. L *-ali-* (see -AL¹) adj. suff., as in *vowel*.

Ela /ˈiːlɑː/ *n. obs.* exc. *Hist.* Also **E la**. LME. [f. *E* as a pitch letter + *la*: see ELAMI.] *Medieval Mus.* The note E in the 7th hexachord of Guido d'Arezzo (*c* 990–1050), where it was sung to the syllable *la*, the highest note in Guido's scale; *fig.* as a type of something high or extravagant. Cf. ALAMIRE, ARE *n.*¹ BEFA, CEFAUT, ELAMI, etc.

elaborate /ɪˈlab(ə)rət/ *a.* L16. [L *elaboratus* pa. pple of *elaborare*: see next, -ATE².] †1 Produced by labour. L16–E19. 2 Worked out or accomplished in great detail; full of detail, intricate, complicated; minutely careful, painstaking. E17.

1 S. JOHNSON He has no elegances either lucky or elaborate. 2 J. MORLEY He read Shakespeare, and made an elaborate study of his method. S. LEWIS The rites of preparing for bed were elaborate. R. P. GRAVES Adams had fitted Perry Hall with elaborate precautions against burglary. G. VIDAL A kind of skirt . . tied at the waist with an elaborate belt.

elaborately *adv.* L16. **elaborateness** *n.* M17.

elaborate /ɪˈlabəreɪt/ *v.* Pa. pple **-ated**, (earlier) †**-ate**. L16. [L *elaborat-* pa. ppl stem of *elaborare*, f. *e-* E- + *labor* LABOUR *n.*: see -ATE³.] 1 *v.t.* Produce by effort or labour; make from raw material or simpler constituents; work out in more detail, develop. L16. 2 *v.i.* Become elaborate. L19. 3 *v.i.* Explain something in detail. (Foll. by *on*.) M20.

1 R. BOYLE Honey . . is elaborated by the Bee. W. STYRON He was going to continue, to elaborate and embellish this idea. A. LURIE I began jabbering, elaborating excuses. E. H. GOMBRICH He went out . . to make sketches from nature, and then elaborated them in his studio. 3 N. CHOMSKY This is . . a familiar observation, and I need not elaborate on it.

elaborative *a.* M19. **elaborator** *n.* L19.

elaboration /ɪˌlabəˈreɪʃ(ə)n/ *n.* LME. [L *elaboratio(n-)*, f. as prec.: see -ATION.] 1 The production of chemical substances by natural agencies, esp. in the body. Now *rare*. LME. 2 *gen.* The action or process of elaborating. E17. 3 Something produced by or consisting in this. M18. 4 The state of being elaborated; elaborateness. E19.

2 A. PRICE 'You know Master Charlie well, do you?' . . Audley waited for elaboration, but none came. 3 J. BUCHAN His taste was fastidious, his courtesy of an old-fashioned elaboration. 4 M. O. W. OLIPHANT Copies exist in various stages of elaboration.

elaboratory /ɪˈlab(ə)rət(ə)ri/ *n.* M17. [f. ELABORATE *v.* + -ORY¹, after *laboratory*.] 1 A laboratory. *obs.* exc. *Hist.* M17. 2 An organ or part where a natural product is formed. Now *rare* or *obs.* M17.

elaeolite /ɪˈliːəlʌɪt/ *n.* Also **eleo-**. E19. [f. Gk *elaion* oil + -LITE.] *Geol.* Nepheline, *esp.* a coarse-grained translucent variety with a greasy lustre.

elaidic /ɛləˈɪdɪk/ *a.* M19. [f. Gk *elaion* oil + -ID(E + -IC.] Chem. *elaidic acid*, a solid acid isomeric with oleic acid, of which it is the *trans* analogue.

elain /ɪˈleɪɪn/ *n.* Now *rare* or *obs.* E19. [f. as prec. + -IN¹.] *Chem.* = OLEIN.

Elami /iːlɑːˈmiː/ *n. obs.* exc. *Hist.* Also **E la mi**. LME. [f. *E* as a pitch letter + *la*, *mi*, designating tones in the solmization of Guido d'Arezzo (*c* 990–1050).] *Medieval Mus.* The note E in Guido d'Arezzo's 1st, 2nd, 4th, and 5th hexachords, where it was sung to the syllable *la* or *mi*. Cf. ALAMIRE, ARE *n.*¹, BEFA, CEFAUT, ELA, etc.

Elamite /ˈiːləmʌɪt/ *n.* & *a.* LME. [f. *Elam* (see below) + -ITE¹.] *Hist.* A *n.* A native or inhabitant of Elam, an ancient country in the south-west of present-day Iran; the language of this country (also called *Susian*). LME. B *adj.* Of, pertaining to, or designating the Elamites, their language, or their country. L19.

élan /eɪˈlɒ̃, eɪˈlan, *foreign* elɑ̃/ *n.* M19. [Fr., f. as next.] Vivacity; energy arising from enthusiasm.

élan vital /vital, viːˈtɑːl/ an intuitively perceived life-force in Bergson's philosophy; any mysterious life-force, *esp.* one supposed to have caused the variations from which new species have emerged.

elance /ɪˈlɑːns/ *v.t. arch.* E18. [Fr. *élancer*, f. *é-* (f. as ES-) + *lancer* LANCE *v.*] Cast or throw (a lance, dart, etc.); launch.

eland /ˈiːlənd/ *n.* L18. [Afk. f. Du. = elk f. obs. G *Elend* (now *Elen*) f. Lith. *élnis*.] Either of two large African antelopes of the genus *Tragelaphus*, with spiral horns, *T. oryx* (more fully *common eland*) and *T. derbianus* (more fully *giant eland*).

elanguescence /iːlaŋˈgwɛs(ə)ns/ *n.* M19. [f. L *elanguescent-* pres. ppl stem of *elanguescere* lose strength, f. *e-* E- + *languescere* become weak, f. *languere* be weak, LANGUISH: see -ESCENCE.] The process of gradually fading away into non-existence.

elapid /ˈɛləpɪd/ *n.* & *a.* L19. [mod.L *Elapidae* (see below), f. *Elaps* genus name, f. Gk *elaps* alt. of ELLOPS: see -ID³.] (A snake) of the family Elapidae, the members of which are highly poisonous and include the cobras and usu. the sea-snakes.

elapse /ɪˈlaps/ *n.* L17. [f. the vb.] 1 A flowing out or away; chiefly *fig.*, an emanation, an effluence. Now *rare* or *obs.* L17. 2 A passage of time. L18.

elapse /ɪˈlaps/ *v.* L16. [L *elaps-* pa. ppl stem of *elabi* slip away, f. *e-* E- + *labi*: see LAPSE *n.*] †1 *v.i.* Slip away (from a place, from memory), leave unobtrusively; lapse *into* a condition. L16–M18. 2 *v.i.* Of time or a period of time: pass by, pass. M17. †3 *v.t.* Allow (time) to pass, pass (time). M17–E18.

2 C. CHAPLIN Six weeks had elapsed and still Sydney had not returned.

†**elapsion** *n.* (*rare*) the action of elapsing; also, subsidence: M17–L18.

elasipod /ɪˈlasɪpɒd/ *n.* & *a.* L19. [mod.L *Elasipoda* (see below), f. Gk *elasmos* beaten metal + -I- + Gk *pod-*, *pous* foot.] *Zool.* (Of or designating) a holothurian of the order Elasipoda, found mainly in deep water and with shield-shaped buccal tentacles and no respiratory tree.

elasmobranch /ɪˈlazməbraŋk/ *n.* & *a.* L19. [mod.L *Elasmobranchii* pl., f. Gk *elasmos* beaten metal + *bragkhia* gills.] (Designating) any fish of the larger of the two groups of cartilaginous fishes, comprising sharks, rays, and skates.

elasmosaur /ɪˈlazməsɔː/ *n.* Also in mod.L form **elasmosaurus** /ɪˌlazməˈsɔːrəs/, pl. **-ruses**, **-ri** /-rʌɪ/. L19. [mod.L (see below), f. Gk *elasmos* beaten metal + -SAUR.] A plesiosaur of the genus *Elasmosaurus* with a long neck shaped like that of a swan.

elasmotherium /ɪˌlazməˈθɪərɪəm/ *n.* Also Anglicized as **elasmothere** /ɪˈlazməθɪə/. L19. [mod.L (see below), f. Gk *elasmos* beaten metal + *thērion* wild animal.] *Palaeont.* A large extinct animal of the genus *Elasmotherium*, resembling a rhinoceros.

elastance /ɪˈlast(ə)ns/ *n.* L19. [f. ELASTIC + -ANCE.] 1 *Electr.* The reciprocal of capacitance. L19. 2 *Physiol.* The reciprocal of compliance. M20.

elastase /ɪˈlasteɪz/ *n.* M20. [f. ELASTIN + -ASE.] A pancreatic enzyme which digests elastin.

elastic /ɪˈlastɪk/ *a.* & *n.* M17. [mod.L *elasticus* f. Gk *elastikos*, f. *ela-* stem of *elaunein* to drive.] A *adj.* †1 (Of a gas) having the property of expanding spontaneously to fill whatever space is available; pertaining to or causing this expansion. M17–M18. 2 That spontaneously resumes its normal bulk or shape after contraction, expansion, or distortion by an external force; of or pertaining to this property or phenomenon. L17. b *fig.* Of a person or feeling: not permanently or easily depressed; buoyant. L18. c *Physics.* Of a collision, or scattering of subatomic particles: not involving any loss of kinetic energy. M19. 3 Able to be stretched without permanent alteration of size or shape; made of or containing material of this kind. L18. b *fig.* Flexible, springy; accommodating; loose. M19. c *Econ.* Of demand or supply: sensitive to changes in price or income. L19.

2 J. MILNE An earthquake consists of elastic waves of compression and distortion. b LD MACAULAY Those elastic spirits . . had borne up against defeat. 3b CONAN DOYLE Even the rigid British law becomes human and elastic. E. BLISHEN Many of the contributors had an elastic sense of time.

B *n.* Elastic cord or fabric, usu. woven with strips of rubber. M19.

Special collocations & comb.: *elastic band*: see BAND *n.*² 2. **elastic cartilage** a yellowish kind of cartilage containing elastic fibres, present in the ear and larynx. **elastic deformation** in a metal or other elastic material, distortion under stress that is followed by a full recovery of the original size and shape (cf. *plastic deformation* s.v. PLASTIC *a.* 4b). **elastic fibre** *Anat.* a yellowish fibre composed chiefly of elastin and occurring in networks or sheets in elastic tissue, to which it imparts elasticity. **elastic limit** the extent to which a body may be stretched without permanent alteration of size or shape. *elastic* MODULUS. **elastic-side** *Austral.* a boot without laces and with a piece of elastic at each side (usu. in *pl.*). *elastic stocking*: see STOCKING *n.*¹ 2. **elastic tissue** *Anat.* connective tissue of the kind that occurs in the dermis and the walls of arteries, composed chiefly of elastic fibres.

elastically *adv.* M19. **elasticated** *a.* (of a cloth or garment) made elastic by incorporating elastic thread or fabric E20. **elastician** /iːlaˈstɪʃ(ə)n, ɛ-/ *n.* an expert in or student of elasticity, as a physical phenomenon or property L19. **elasticized** *a.* = ELASTICATED E20.

elasticity /ɛlaˈstɪsɪti, iː-, ɪ-/ *n.* M17. [f. prec. + -ITY.] 1 The state or quality of being elastic (*lit.* & *fig.*). M17. 2 *Econ.* Sensitivity of demand or supply to changes in price or income; *spec.* the ratio of the proportionate change in the former to the proportionate change in the latter. L19.

1 MODULUS *of elasticity*.

elastin /ɪˈlastɪn/ *n.* L19. [f. ELASTIC + -IN¹.] *Biochem.* An elastic fibrous protein that is the chief constituent of elastic fibres and elastic tissue.

elastohydrodynamic /ɪˌlastəʊhʌɪdrə(ʊ)dʌɪˈnamɪk/ *a.* M20. [f. ELASTIC + -O- + HYDRODYNAMIC.] Pertaining to or involving the elastic properties of a liquid or situations where these become significant.

elastomer /ɪˈlastəmə/ *n.* M20. [f. ELASTIC + -O- + -MER.] A polymer possessing the elastic properties of rubber.

elastoˈmeric *a.* M20.

Elastoplast /ɪˈlastəplɑːst/ *n.* E20. [f. ELASTIC + -O- + PLASTER *n.*] (Proprietary name for) a sticking plaster.

†**elatcha** *n.* E17–E19. [Turk. *alaca* particoloured.] A patterned silk fabric from Turkestan.

elate /ɪˈleɪt/ *a.* Now *rare*. LME. [OFr. *elat* proud, and (later) its source L *elatus* pa. pple of *efferre*: see next, -ATE².] Exalted, lofty, proud; in high spirits, exultant.

elate /ɪˈleɪt/ *v.t.* L16. [L *elat-* pa. ppl stem of *efferre*, f. EF- + *ferre* BEAR *v.*¹: see -ATE³.] †1 Raise, elevate. L16–L18. 2 Lift the spirits of, fill with elation; inspire with pride. Chiefly as *elated* ppl a. E17.

2 R. L. STEVENSON I was greatly elated with my new command.

elatedly *adv.* M17. **elatedness** *n.* M18. **elatement** *n.* = ELATION M18.

elater /ˈɛlətə/ *n.* M17. [Gk *elatēr* driver, f. *ela-* stem of *elaunein* to drive.] †1 The elastic property of gases; elasticity, spring; tone. M17–M18. 2 A click-beetle. E19. 3 *Bot.* An elongated appendage in the spore-case of a liverwort, or attached to the spore of a horsetail, which uncoils as it dries and aids in the dispersal of spores. M19.

elaterite /ɪˈlatərʌɪt/ *n.* E19. [f. as prec. + -ITE¹.] An asphaltic pyrobitumen that is soft and elastic when freshly cut and becomes hard and brittle in air.

elaterium /ɛləˈtɪərɪəm/ *n.* M16. [L f. Gk *elatērion*, f. *ela-*: see ELATER, -IUM.] A precipitate from the juice of the squirting cucumber (*Ecballium elaterium*), formerly used as a drastic purgative and emetic.

elation /ɪˈleɪʃ(ə)n/ *n.* LME. [OFr. *elacion*, and (later) its source L *elatio(n-)*, f. *elat-*: see ELATE *v.*, -ATION.] **1 a** Elevation of mind due to success; pride, vainglory. Now *rare*. LME. **b** Elevation of spirits; a feeling of pleasurable self-satisfaction and self-assurance. M18. †**2** Lifting, elevation; carrying out. L15–L17.

1b M. MEYER His moods varied from elation to the blackest depression. A. SILLITOE He walked back . . with a tremendous feeling of elation and freedom, hardly able to believe it belonged to him.

elative /ɪˈleɪtɪv/ *a.* & *n.* L16. [f. ELATE *v.* + -IVE.] **A** *adj.* **1** That elates. *rare*. L16. **2** *Gram.* **a** Designating, being in, or pertaining to a case in some languages that expresses motion away from. M19. **b** Having a superlative and intensive force. E20. **B** *n. Gram. The* elative case; a word, form, etc., in the elative case. E20.

elbow /ˈɛlbəʊ/ *n.* [OE *el(n)boga* = MDu. *elleboghe* (Du *elleboog*), OHG *elinbogo* (G *Ellenbogen*), ON *ǫllnbogi*, f. Gmc, f. bases of ELL *n.*[1] and BOW *n.*[1]] **1** The outer, bony part of the arm at the place where it bends; the part of a garment that covers this. Also, the elbow-joint. OE. **b** The analogous part in the shoulder or hock of a quadruped. E17. **c** A (usu. temporary) loss of dexterity and accuracy in a tennis player's racket arm. Usu. preceded by *the*. L20. **2** Something resembling an elbow; *spec.* (*a*) a sharp bend in a road, river, etc.; (*b*) a projecting corner; (*c*) *Mech.* a piece of piping etc. bent through an angle. L16. **3** An arm of a chair, made to rest the elbow on. *obs.* exc. in *elbow chair* below. E17.

Phrases: **at one's elbow** close at hand. *bend one's elbow*: see BEND *v.* *crook one's elbow*: see CROOK *v.* I. **give a person the (big) elbow** *colloq.* send away, dismiss, or reject a person. *lift one's elbow*: see LIFT *v.* *more power to your* etc. *elbow*: see POWER *n.* **out at elbows** worn out, threadbare; scruffy; poor. *not know one's arse from one's elbow*: see ARSE *n.* I. *rub elbows*: see RUB *v.* †**rub the elbow** show oneself pleased. *shake one's elbow*: see SHAKE *v.* *tennis elbow*: see TENNIS *n.* **up to the elbows** *colloq.* busily engaged *in*.

Comb.: **elbow chair** (*Hist.* exc. *US*): with supports for the arms; **elbow-grease** *joc.* vigorous rubbing; hard manual work or physical effort; **elbow-joint**: between the humerus in the upper arm and the radius and ulna in the forearm; **elbow-length** *a.* (of a sleeve or garment) reaching to the elbow; **elbow-pad**: for protecting the elbow of a garment against wear or the elbow of a person against injury; **elbow-room** *colloq.* (adequate) space to move or work in; **elbow-sleeve**: reaching only to the elbow.

elbow /ˈɛlbəʊ/ *v.* E17. [f. the n.] **1** *v.t.* Thrust with the elbow, nudge. E17. **b** Move aside using the elbow. Chiefly *fig.* & foll. by prep. or adv. E18. †**2** *v.i.* Use the elbows in pushing. M17–L19. **3** *v.t.* Make (one's way), esp. through a throng, by pushing with the arms. L18. **4** *v.i.* Make a detour; follow an indirect or erratic route. E19.

1 R. COOVER Passengers protested at the shoving. . . A woman complained about getting elbowed. **b** J. CARY Yells . . like the shrieks of monkeys elbowed off their perch.

elbowing *n.* the action of thrusting with the elbow; a thrust with the elbow, a nudge: E19.

el cheapo /ɛl ˈtʃiːpəʊ/ *a.* & *n. phr. N. Amer.* & *Austral. slang.* L20. [f. CHEAP *a.* after Sp. such as *El Dorado*, *El Greco*.] **A** *adj. phr.* Cheap; of inferior quality. L20. **B** *n. phr.* Pl. **-os**. Something cheap or inferior. L20.

elchee /ˈɛltʃi/ *n.* L16. [Turk. *elçi*, f. *el* (the representative of) an independent political unit.] An ambassador, esp. in the Middle East.

eld /ɛld/ *n.* [OE (Anglian) *eldu*, (WS) *ieldu* = OFris. *elde*, OS *eldi*, OHG *elti*, ON *elli*, f. Gmc: cf. OLD *n.*[1], *n.*[2]] **1** The age or time of life which a person has reached. *obs.* exc. *dial.* OE. †**2** An age of the world, an era. OE–E16. **3** Old age. *arch.* & *poet.* OE. †**b** Old people; old men; senate, aristocracy. OE–L16. **c** An old person; an old man. *poet.* L18. †**4** Conventional or legal age; a person's majority. ME–E16. †**5** Duration of existence; time as a wearing or destroying agency. LME–M18. **6** The old days, antiquity; people of former times. *arch.* & *poet.* LME.

3 C. KINGSLEY His beard was white with eld. **6** SHAKES. *Merry W.* The superstitious idle-headed eld Receiv'd, and did deliver to our age, This tale of Herne the Hunter.

eld /ɛld/ *a. arch.* & *poet.* E17. [f. the n.: see OLD *a.*] Old, aged.

eld /ɛld/ *v.i.* Long *obs.* exc. *dial.* [OE (WS) *ealdian*, f. *eald* OLD *a.*; cf. OFris. *aldia*, OHG *altēn*, Goth. *us)alþan*.] Grow old.

elder /ˈɛldə/ *n.*[1] [OE *ellærn*, corresp. to MLG *ellern*, *elderne*, *elhorn*, *alhorn*, prob. orig. an adj. formation like (O)HG *ahorn* maple, corresp. to L *acernus* of maple.] **1** A common British shrub or low-growing tree, *Sambucus nigra*, of the honeysuckle family, with cymes of creamy-white flowers, small black berries, and pinnate leaves; any of various other trees of the genus *Sambucus*. Also *elder tree*. OE. **2** Any of several unrelated plants resembling the elder in leaf or flower. L16.

1 dwarf elder = *danewort* s.v. DANE *n.* **2** *box elder*, *ground elder*, *marsh elder*, *water elder*, etc.

Comb.: **elderberry** the black fleshy fruit of the elder; *elder tree*: see sense I above.

elder /ˈɛldə/ *a.* & *n.*[2] [OE *eldra*, *-re* (*ieldra*, *-re*) = OFris. *alder*, *elder*, OS *aldira*, OHG *altiro*, *eltiro* (G *älter*), ON *ellri*, Goth. *alþiza*: see -ER[3]. Rel. to ELD *n.*, OLD *a.*] **A** *adj.* **1** Earlier-born (of two related or indicated persons, esp. children or siblings). Freq. after possess. pron. OE. **2** *gen.* Older. Now only *attrib.*, without *than*. *arch.* OE. **3** Ancient; of or pertaining to ancient or earlier times. LME. †**4** Of or pertaining to the later period of a person's life. L16–M18. †**5** (Of an obligation, right, or title) of longer standing, prior; (of an official etc.) of longer service, senior. M17–M18.

1 I. MURDOCH He turned to her . . as to a mother or an elder sister. J. GROSS The elder Gosse was a naturalist. **2** SHAKES. *Merch. V.* How much more elder art thou than thy looks? **3** SOUTHEY Huge as the giant race of elder times.

Special collocations & *comb.*: **Elder Brother**, pl. **Brethren**, each of thirteen senior members of Trinity House. **elder-brotherly** *a.* pertaining to or appropriate to an elder brother. **elder hand** the person in a card-game for two who is first to be dealt to and therefore begins the play. **elder-sisterly** *a.* pertaining to or appropriate to an elder sister. **elder statesman** (*a*) any of the Japanese statesmen who mainly directed the evolution of Japan in the late 19th cent.; (*b*) a person of ripe years and experience whose opinions are respected.

B *n.* **1** The elder person (of two), *esp.* the elder child or sibling. Usu. after *the* or possess. pron. OE. †**2** A parent; an ancestor; a predecessor. Usu. in *pl.* OE–E17. **3** A person who is older than another who is indicated. Usu. in *pl.* after possess. pron. LME. **b** An old person. L16. **4** A (usu. male) person having authority because of advanced age; a member of a governing body or class consisting of men chosen for their age and experience. Chiefly *Hist.* LME. **5** *Eccl.* An official or minister in the early Church and in various Protestant, esp. Presbyterian, denominations; *US dial.* a minister of any denomination. LME. **b** A member of the Society of Friends responsible for the organization and conduct of meetings for worship. E18.

1 E. B. BROWNING My cousin . . ; My elder by a few years. D. H. LAWRENCE They were pale mites, the elder about ten years old. **3** W. BRONK Children . . are shocked by things their elders do unthinking. **4** P. GALLICO A sweet and gentle people presided over by a tall, stately elder. T. KENEALLY Tribal elders, who . . knew where the soul-stones of each man were hidden. **5** *lay elder*: see LAY *a.* PRESIDING *elder*. *Ruling Elder*: see RULING *a.*

elderhood *n.* the position of an elder, seniority; a body of elders: L16.

elder /ˈɛldə/ *v.* M19. [f. prec.] †**1** *v.t.* w. *it*. Play the elder. *rare*. Only in M19. **2** *v.i.* Become older; begin to show signs of age. *colloq.* & *poet.* L19. **3** *v.t.* Make a request to or admonish (a person) in one's capacity as an elder in a meeting of the Society of Friends. E20.

elderly /ˈɛldəli/ *a.* & *n.* E17. [f. ELDER *a.* + -LY[1].] **A** *adj.* **1** Somewhat old; (of a person) past middle age; (of a thing) not new or recent, showing signs of age. E17. **2** Of or pertaining to a person in later life. L17.

1 LD MACAULAY The elderly inhabitants could still remember the time when the first brick house . . was built.

B *absol.* as *n.pl. The* class of elderly people. Also *sing.* (*rare*), an elderly person. M19.

Observer The House of Lords is a model of how to care for the elderly.

elderliness *n.* L19.

eldern /ˈɛld(ə)n/ *a.* ME. [f. ELDER *a.* + -EN[4], added exceptionally to an adj. (cf. OLDEN *a.*).] **1** Elderly. *obs.* exc. *Sc.* ME. **2** = ELDER *a.* 3. *arch.* ME.

eldership /ˈɛldəʃɪp/ *n.* M16. [f. ELDER *a.* & *n.*[2] + -SHIP.] **1** The position of being the elder; seniority of age. M16. **2** *Eccl.* **a** A body of elders, elders collectively. M16. **b** The office or position of church elder. L16.

eldest /ˈɛldɪst/ *a.* & *n.* [OE *eldest* (*ieldest*) = OFris. *eldest*, OHG *altist* (G *ältest*), ON *ellztr*, Goth. *altista*: see -EST[1]. Rel. to ELDER *a.*] **A** *adj.* **1** First-born, oldest surviving, (of a group of siblings or a family). OE. †**2** *gen.* Oldest, of the greatest age. OE–L19. **3** Earliest, first produced; most ancient. *arch.* OE.

1 R. GARNETT Carlyle was the eldest of nine children. D. H. LAWRENCE Mr. Leivers and Edgar, the eldest son, were in the kitchen. **3** DRYDEN Self-defence is Nature's Eldest Law.

Special collocations: **eldest hand** the person in a card-game for three or more who is first to be dealt to and therefore begins the play.

B *n.* The eldest person, esp. of children or siblings. OE.

G. B. SHAW I shouldnt know my two eldest if I met them. E. O'NEILL The eldest is about fourteen, the two others thirteen and twelve.

elding /ˈɛldɪŋ/ *n. obs.* exc. *dial.* ME. [ON, f. *eldr* fire.] Fuel.

Eldonian /ɛlˈdəʊnɪən/ *a.* L19. [f. *Eldon* (see below) + -IAN.] Of, pertaining to, or characteristic of John Scott, Lord Eldon (1751–1838), regarded as typical of die-hard toryism, or his political beliefs.

Also **Eldonine** /ˈɛldənʌɪn/ *a.* M19.

El Dorado /ɛl dəˈrɑːdəʊ/ *n.* Also **Eldorado**. Pl. **-os**. E19. [Sp., name of a non-existent country or city having much gold, once believed to exist on the Amazon, f. *el* the + DORADO.] A place of fabulous wealth or opportunity.

eldress /ˈɛldrɪs/ *n.* M17. [f. ELDER *n.*[2] + -ESS[1].] A female church elder.

eldritch /ˈɛl(d)rɪtʃ/ *a.* Orig. *Sc.* E16. [Origin uncertain: perh. conn. w. ELF *n.*[1]] Weird, ghostly, unnatural; hideous.

A. T. ELLIS Lydia gave a screech of eldritch mirth.

†**ele** *n.* see AISLE.

Eleatic /ɛlɪˈatɪk/ *a.* & *n.* L17. [L *Eleaticus*, f. *Elea*: see below and -ATIC.] **A** *adj.* Of or pertaining to Elea, an ancient Greek city in SW Italy, or *spec.* the monistic school of philosophy that flourished there in the 6th and 5th cents. BC, propounded by Parmenides, Zeno, and others. L17. **B** *n.* An Eleatic philosopher. M19.

Eleaticism /-sɪz(ə)m/ *n.* Eleatic philosophy or doctrines M19.

elecampane /ˌɛlɪkamˈpeɪn/ *n.* LME. [Ult. f. med.L *enula campana* (*enula* f. L *inula* f. Gk *helenion* elecampane; *campana* prob. 'of the fields', fem. adj. f. L *campus*: see CAMP *n.*[2]] **1** A tall perennial yellow-rayed plant of the composite family, *Inula helenium*, with a bitter root formerly much used to treat pulmonary complaints. LME. **2** The candied root of this plant, formerly eaten as a sweet. E19.

elect /ɪˈlɛkt/ *a.* & *n.* LME. [L *electus* pa. pple of *eligere*, f. *e-* E- + *legere* choose.] **A** *adj.* **1** Chosen for an office or position; *esp.* chosen but not yet installed. Usu. *postpositive*. LME. **2** *gen.* Picked out, chosen; select, choice. L15. **3** *Theol.* Chosen by God for salvation. E16.

1 C. WILMOT The Bride elect dissolved in tears. T. HEGGEN He went down to take among the crew his rightful place as hero-elect of a legend in the making. **3** R. HOOKER The elect Angels are without possibilitie of falling.

B *n.* †**1** A choice. Only in LME. †**2** A person chosen for an office or position, esp. a bishopric. LME–E18. **3** *Theol.* †**a** A person chosen by God, esp. for salvation. LME–M17. **b** *the elect*, those chosen by God for salvation. M16. **4** *Hist.* In the Royal College of Physicians, each of the eight officers who formerly granted licences and elected the President. E16. **5** A specially chosen group of people; an élite. E17.

elect /ɪˈlɛkt/ *v.* LME. [L *elect-* pa. ppl stem of *eligere*: see prec.] †**1 a** *v.t.* Pick out, select (a person or thing), usu. for a particular purpose. LME–E19. **b** *v.t.* & *i. Theol.* Of God: choose (a person) in preference to others for salvation or the receipt of some blessing. M16. **2** *v.t.* Choose (a person) by vote for an office or position. Also foll. by *to* the office & w. the title of the office as 2nd or only obj. LME. **3** *v.t.* & *i.* Choose (a thing, *to do* an action) in preference to an alternative. E16.

2 H. COX Each Town Council elected a delegate. E. WAUGH I have been elected chairman of the Parish Council. 3 R. C. A. WHITE Anyone could elect to be tried by jury. Y. MENUHIN Except for electing the violin . . I scarcely disturbed the family pattern.

electaˈbility *n.* the property of being electable, eligibility for election L20. **electable** *a.* able or qualified to be elected L19.

election /ɪˈlɛkʃ(ə)n/ *n.* ME. [(O)Fr. *élection* f. L *electio(n-)*, f. *elect-*: see ELECT *v.*, -ION.] **1** The formal choosing of a person for an office or position, usu. by vote; the fact of being chosen. ME. **b** *spec.* The choice of a person to fill a vacancy in a representative body by a vote among those represented; an occasion of such choice; the accompanying proceedings. M17. **2** The exercise of deliberate choice or preference, esp. in relation to conduct; *Law* the right, opportunity, or duty of choosing. LME. †**b** Judicious selection, discrimination. M16–E17. **3** *Theol.* The choosing by God of some persons but not others for salvation, or for the receipt of some blessing LME. **4** *Astrol.* The choosing of a propitious time for an undertaking; the time chosen. *obs.* exc. *Hist.* LME. †**5** The selecting of a thing, esp. a medicinal herb, for a particular purpose. E17–E18.

1 S. AUSTIN The empire . . had waived the right . . to interfere in the election of the pope. J. GALSWORTHY He was not seeking election. H. FAST Her election to that very select body was no problem. b *Daily Telegraph* If Mrs Thatcher wins the next election, Labour will have lost four in a row. *election address, manifesto*, etc. BY-ELECTION. **general election**: in which voting, usu. for a government, takes place in all the constituencies of a State. 2 *Daily Telegraph* Thompson . . was committed to Southwark Crown Court for trial . . at his own election.

Comb.: **election bun, cake** *US*: varieties of fancy bread; **election commissioner** any of a body of men appointed to inquire into corruption at an election or (*US*) to take charge of an election; **election petition**: calling for an inquiry into the validity of the election of a Member of Parliament.

electional *a.* (*Astrol.*) M17.

electioneer /ɪˌlɛkʃəˈnɪə/ *v.* & *n.* M18. [f. ELECTION + -EER.] **A** *v.i.* Be active or campaign in a (political) election. M18. **B** *n.* A person who electioneers or has expertise in electioneering. M19.

electioneerer *n.* E19.

elective /ɪˈlɛktɪv/ *a.* & *n.* LME. [(O)Fr. *électif*, *-ive*, f. late L *electivus*, f. as ELECT *v.*: see -IVE.] **A** *adj.* **1** Pertaining to or proceeding from choice; voluntary, optional. *obs.* exc. as below. LME. **b** (Of a course or subject at college or high school) taken at the choice of the student, optional; of, pertaining to, or containing such courses etc. Orig. *US.* M19. **c** *Med.* Of an operation: at the option of the doctor or patient, not urgently necessary. M20. **2** Appointed by election; derived from or dependent on election. L15. †**b** Subject to election at specified intervals. M17–M18. **3** Having the power to elect. M17. **4** Pertaining to election; based on the principle of election. M17. **5** Orig. *Chem.* Having a tendency to act on or be concerned with some things rather than others; preferential; sympathetic. M18.

2 E. A. FREEMAN The hereditary prince may be exchanged for an elective chief magistrate. *New York Times* You have to know when to get into politics in terms of elective office. 4 C. MERIVALE A preference of the elective to the hereditary principle in every department of government. 5 J. TYNDALL Light . . which has been sifted . . by elective absorption. P. ANDERSON Traditional British culture has an elective affinity with certain types of expatriate.

B *n.* †**1** An elected representative. Only in E18. **2** An elective subject or course of study. Orig. *US.* M19.

electively *adv.* LME. **electiveness** *n.* (*rare*) M19.

elector /ɪˈlɛktə/ *n.* LME. [((O)Fr. *électeur* f.) L *elector*, f. as ELECT *v.*: see -OR.] **1** A person who has the right to vote in an election; *spec.* one who has the parliamentary vote; *US* a member of the Electoral College. LME. **2** *Hist.* (Also **E-**.) Each of the Princes of Germany entitled to elect the Holy Roman Emperor. More fully *prince-elector*. E16.

electoral /ɪˈlɛkt(ə)r(ə)l/ *a.* M17. [f. prec. + -AL[1].] **1** Relating to or composed of electors. M17. **2** *Hist.* (Also **E-**.) Holding rank as, or belonging to, a German elector. L17.

1 **electoral college** a body of electors to a particular office, *esp.* one chosen or appointed from a larger group; *spec.* (*a*) the princes who elected the Holy Roman Emperor; (*b*) *US* the group of electors from within each state chosen to elect the President and Vice-President. 2 HOR. WALPOLE George the first, while electoral prince, had married his cousin.

electorally *adv.* with reference to electors or elections L18.

electorate /ɪˈlɛkt(ə)rət/ *n.* E17. [f. ELECTOR + -ATE[1].] **1** *Hist.* The rank or territory of a German elector. E17. **2** The area represented by an elected Member of Parliament in Australia or New Zealand. M19. **3** A body of electors; (the number of) all those entitled to vote in a country or constituency. L19.

†**electoress** *n.* var. of ELECTRESS.

electorial /ɪlɛkˈtɔːrɪəl/ *a.* L18. [f. ELECTOR + -IAL.] = ELECTORAL.

electorship /ɪˈlɛktəʃɪp/ *n.* L16. [f. ELECTOR + -SHIP.] **1** The state or condition of an elector or a member of an electoral college. L16. **2** *Hist.* The position of being a German elector; the dominions of an elector. E17.

Electra /ɪˈlɛktrə/ *n.* E20. [In Gk tragedy, the daughter of Agamemnon and Clytemnestra who caused the death of the latter in revenge for the murder of the former.] Psychol. *Electra complex*, a daughter's subconscious sexual attraction to her father and hostility to her mother. Cf. OEDIPUS.

†**electral** *a.* L17–M18. [f. L *electrum* amber + -AL[1].] Electrical.

electress /ɪˈlɛktrɪs/ *n.* Also †**-oress**; **E-**. E17. [f. ELECTOR + -ESS[1].] *Hist.* The wife of a German elector.

electret /ɪˈlɛktrɪt/ *n.* L19. [f. ELECTR(ICITY + MAGN)ET.] *Physics.* A permanently polarized piece of dielectric material, analogous to a permanent magnet.

electric /ɪˈlɛktrɪk/ *a.* & *n.* M17. [mod.L *electricus*, f. L *electrum* amber f. Gk *ēlektron* (because rubbing amber produces electrostatic phenomena): see -IC.] **A** *adj.* **1** Of a substance or object: capable of developing electricity when rubbed. M17. **2** Operating by means of electricity; caused or produced by electricity; (capable of) producing electricity; = ELECTRICAL *a.* 2. L17. **3** *fig.* Suddenly exciting or thrilling, as if caused by electricity; stimulating; full of tension. E19.

2 *electric battery, cooker, generator*, etc. 3 *Gramophone* The electric urgency of the performance. Y. MENUHIN Bucharest was bustling, . . the air electric with life and enterprise. G. GREENE The strange electric beauty of Miss Elsa Lanchester as Frankenstein's second monster.

Special collocations: **electric arc** = ARC *n.* 4. *electric blanket*: see BLANKET *n.* **electric blue** a steely or brilliant light blue. **electric chair**: in which a criminal is placed to be judicially electrocuted. **electric charge** the quantity whose presence or flow constitutes electricity and which is associated with certain subatomic particles; an amount of this on or in a body. **electric circuit** = CIRCUIT *n.* 9. **electric eel** an elongated S. American freshwater fish, *Electrophorus electricus*, which possesses electric organs and can give a severe electric shock. **electric eye** (*a*) a photoelectric cell that operates a relay when a beam of light illuminating it is interrupted; (*b*) a miniature cathode-ray tube used as a tuning indicator. **electric fence** a fence (often of a single strand of wire) maintained at a low voltage to give a mild shock to an animal touching it. **electric field** a field of force which is electrical in nature. **electric fire** a space heater, usu. a portable one for domestic use, in which the heat is produced by the passage of an electric current. **electric guitar**: in which the vibrations of the strings are not amplified by the body of the instrument but are converted by a pick-up into electrical signals and amplified by an independent amplifier and speaker. **electric organ** (*a*) a part of the body surface in certain fishes which develops an external electric field or voltage; (*b*) an organ operated electrically, *esp.* one in which the sound is produced by electro-acoustic or electromechanical means. **electric ray** any ray of the family Torpedinidae, as the Atlantic torpedo ray, *Torpedo nobiliana*, which possess electric organs and can give an electric shock. **electric shock** the effect on a person or animal of a sudden flow of electric current through the body, usu. causing stimulation of the nerves and contraction of muscles. **electric storm** a violent disturbance of the electric field in the atmosphere; a thunderstorm. *electric telegraph*: see TELEGRAPH *n.* 1. *electric torch*: see TORCH *n.* 1.

B *n.* **1** A substance that can be given an electrostatic charge by friction. *arch.* M17. **2** A thing operated by electricity rather than by other means; *esp.* an electric vehicle, an electric light. L19. **3** An electric wire; an electric circuit; an electrical device. Usu. in *pl.* E20. **4** In *pl.* Shares in electric or electrical engineering companies. M20.

2 *Sunday Express* Petrol mowers . . need more attention than electrics. 3 G. B. SHAW All the drains and telephones and electrics torn up.

electrical /ɪˈlɛktrɪk(ə)l/ *a.* & *n.* M17. [f. prec. + -AL[1].] **A** *adj.* **1** = ELECTRIC *a.* 1. M17–M18. **2** Of or pertaining to electricity; of the nature of electricity; = ELECTRIC *a.* 2. M17. **3** *fig.* = ELECTRIC *a.* 3. L18. **4** Charged with electricity. E19.

2 M. SHELLEY He constructed a small electrical machine.

Special collocations: **electrical conductivity** a measure of the rate at which electricity can pass through a body, the reciprocal of resistivity. **electrical engineer** an expert in electrical engineering. **electrical engineering**: that deals with the utilization of electricity, esp. electric power. **electrical storm** = *electric storm* s.v. ELECTRIC *a.*

B *n.* **1** In *pl.* = ELECTRIC *n.* 4. L20. **2** In *pl.* Electrical products; *esp.* domestic electrical appliances. L20.

electrically /ɪˈlɛktrɪk(ə)li/ *adv.* E19. [f. ELECTRIC *a.* or ELECTRICAL *a.*: see -ICALLY.] **1** By means of electricity; as regards electricity. E19. **2** *fig.* With suddenness, rapidity, or force suggestive of electricity. M19.

electrician /ɪlɛkˈtrɪʃ(ə)n, ɛl-/ *n.* M18. [f. ELECTRIC + -IAN: see -ICIAN.] A person who works with electrical equipment, e.g. instals it, repairs it, or sells it; an expert in or student of electricity.

electrician's tape = *insulating tape* s.v. INSULATE *v.*

electricise *v.* var. of ELECTRICIZE.

electricity /ɪlɛkˈtrɪsɪti, ɛl-, iːl-/ *n.* M17. [f. ELECTRIC + -ITY.] **1** A property of matter or a phenomenon which manifests itself when substances such as glass and amber are rubbed, when a metal wire is moved through a magnetic field, and in other circumstances, and which is now regarded as a form of energy occurring in two modes (positive and negative) as an intrinsic property of electrons and some other subatomic particles; a flow of this energy, an electric current, esp. as a source of power. M17. **b** A supply of electric current laid on in a building or room. M20. **2** The branch of science that deals with electricity. M18.

1 S. LEWIS Throughout, electricity took the place of candles and . . hearth-fires. attrib.: *electricity meter, pole*, etc. *static electricity*: see STATIC *a.* b J. D. WATSON Their host . . kept his house free of gas and electricity. R. JEFFRIES Electricity cuts, roads blocked by snow.

electricize /ɪˈlɛktrɪsʌɪz/ *v.t. rare.* Also **-ise**. L19. [f. as prec. + -IZE.] = ELECTRIFY 1.

electride /ɪˈlɛktrʌɪd/ *n.* L20. [f. ELECTRON *n.*[2] + -IDE.] An ionic solid whose crystal lattice consists of cations and electrons, rather than cations and anions as in a salt.

electrification /ɪˌlɛktrɪfɪˈkeɪʃ(ə)n/ *n.* M18. [f. next: see -FICATION.] 1 The action or process, or an act, of electrifying. M18. 2 The state of being electrified (*lit.* & *fig.*). L18.

1 P. D. JAMES With the electrification of the north-east suburban line, Wrentham Green had increasingly become a commuter town.

electrify /ɪˈlɛktrɪfʌɪ/ *v.t.* M18. [f. ELECTR(IC + -I- + -FY.] 1 Charge with electricity; pass an electric current through, *esp.* give (a person) an electric shock. M18. 2 *fig.* Cause sudden or dramatic excitement in. M18. 3 Convert to electric operation. E20.

1 P. CAREY The tenfoot high electrified fence. 2 M. L. KING He electrified the public with his description of . . the spiritual emptiness of contemporary society. DAY LEWIS The effect . . was electrifying.

electrifier *n.* M19.

electrize /ɪˈlɛktrʌɪz/ *v.t.* Now *rare* or *obs.* Also **-ise.** M18. [f. ELECTR(IC + -IZE.] = ELECTRIFY 1.

electriˈzation *n.* M18.

electro /ɪˈlɛktrəʊ/ *n.* Pl. **-os.** M19. [f. next.] 1 An electroplated coating; electroplate. M19. 2 An electrotype. L19. 3 A style of dance music with a fast electronic beat backed by a synthesizer. L20.

electro- /ɪˈlɛktrəʊ/ *comb. form* of ELECTRIC, ELECTRICITY: see -O-. 1 As a formative elem. of many scientific and techn. wds. 2 Forming combs. denoting (styles of) pop music performed using electronic equipment, as *electro-bop*, *-funk*, etc. L20.

electro-aˈcoustic(al) *adjs.* involving the direct conversion of electrical into acoustic energy or vice versa; (of music) performed or composed with the creative use of electronic equipment: M20. **electro-aˈcoustics** *n.* the branch of science that deals with electro-acoustic phenomena and devices E20. **electro-ˈacupuncture** *n.* acupuncture in which the needles used carry an electric current L20. **electro-aˈnalysis** *n.* chemical analysis by means of electrolytic techniques E20. **electro-anaˈlytical** *a.* of or pertaining to electro-analysis E20. **electrobioˈlogical** *a.* of or pertaining to electrobiology M19. **electrobiˈologist** *n.* an expert in electrobiology; a student or practitioner of electrobiology: M19. **electrobiˈology** *n.* (*a*) the branch of science that deals with the electrical phenomena of living organisms; (*b*) *Hist.* a particular method of hypnotism: M19. **electroˈcardiogram** *n.* (*Med.*) a chart or record produced by an electrocardiograph E20. **electroˈcardiograph** *n.* (*Med.*) an instrument that records or displays the electrical activity of the heart by means of electrodes attached to the skin E20. **electrocardioˈgraphic** *a.* (*Med.*) involving or pertaining to electrocardiography E20. **electrocardioˈgraphically** *adv.* (*Med.*) by means of electrocardiography E20. **electrocardiˈography** *n.* (*Med.*) the practice or technique of using an electrocardiograph or electrocardiograms E20. **electroˈcautery** *n.* cautery by means of an electrically heated instrument L19. **electroˈchemical** *a.* involving electricity as applied to or occurring in chemistry; of or pertaining to electrochemistry; *electrochemical series*, a list of chemical elements in order of the electrical potentials generated by immersion in a standard solution: M19. **electroˈchemically** *adv.* in accordance with the laws of electrochemistry M19. **electroˈchemist** *n.* an expert or worker in, or a student of, electrochemistry M19. **electroˈchemistry** *n.* the branch of science that deals with the relation between electrical and chemical phenomena and the interconversion of these forms of energy E19. **electroˈchromic** *a.* of or pertaining to electrochromism, esp. as used in the construction of displays M20. **electroˈchromism** *n.* a reversible change in the colour of a dye, caused by an electric field M20. **electrocoaguˈlation** *n.* the use of electrical means to destroy or harden tissue or to control bleeding E20. **electrocoat, -coating** *ns.* a process in which an object to be coated is made an electrode in a colloidal suspension of coating particles M20. **electroconˈvulsive** *a.* designating a method of treating certain mental illnesses in which an electric current is passed through the brain so as to produce a convulsion (cf. *ECT* s.v. E, E 10); designating a shock given in this way: M20. **electroˈcorticogram** *n.* (*Med.*) a chart or record of the electrical activity of the brain made using electrodes in contact with it M20. **electrocyte** *n.* a cell generating electricity in the electric organ of a fish L20. **electrodeˈposit** *v.t.* deposit in the course of electrodeposition M19. **electrodepoˈsition** *n.* the deposition of a substance, esp. a metal coating, at an electrode by means of electrolysis M19. **electroˈdermal** *a.* of or pertaining to measurement of the electrical conductivity of the skin, esp. as a guide to a person's emotion M20. **electrodiˈalysis** *n.* dialysis in which the movement of ions is aided by an electric field applied across a membrane by electrodes on either side E20. **electroenˈcephalogram** *n.* (*Med.*) a chart or record produced by an electroencephalograph M20. **electroenˈcephalograph** *n.* (*Med.*) an instrument that records or displays the electrical activity of the brain, using electrodes attached to the scalp M20. **electroencephaˈlographer** *n.* (*Med.*) a person who uses an electroencephalograph M20. **electroencephaloˈgraphic** *a.* (*Med.*) involving or pertaining to electroencephalography M20. **electroencephaloˈgraphically** *adv.* (*Med.*) by means of electroencephalography M20. **electroencephaˈlography** *n.* (*Med.*) the practice or technique of using an electroencephalograph or electroencephalograms M20. **electrofish** *v.t.* fish (a stretch of water) using electrocution or a weak electric field M20. **electroˈfocusing** *n.* = *isoelectric focusing* s.v. ISOELECTRIC *a.* 2b M20. **electroform** *v.* & *n.* (*a*) *v.t.* make by electrodeposition on to a mould; (*b*) *n.* an article made by electroforming: M20. **electrogasdyˈnamic** *a.* pertaining to or involving the transport of charged particles through an electric field by a current of gas, or the generation of electricity by this means M20. **electrogasdyˈnamics** *n.* the branch of technology dealing with electrogasdynamic phenomena and devices M20. **electroˈgenesis** *n.* the production of electricity, esp. by organic tissue L19. **electroglow** *n.* (*Astron.*) an emission of ultraviolet light from the upper atmospheres of Jupiter, Saturn, and Uranus on the side facing the sun L20. **electro-hyˈdraulic** *a.* (*a*) pertaining to or designating a hydraulic system that is powered or controlled electrically; (*b*) involving or employing a high-voltage electrical discharge produced in a liquid: E20. **electro-hyˈdraulically** *adv.* by means of an electro-hydraulic system M20. **electro-hyˈdraulics** *n.* the branch of science that deals with electro-hydraulic phenomena M20. **electrojet** *n.* an intense electric current occurring in a narrow belt in the lower ionosphere near the magnetic equator and where there are strong auroral displays M20. **electrokiˈnetic** *a.* (*a*) of or pertaining to the flow of electricity; (*b*) of or pertaining to motion of particles in a fluid, or of a fluid over a surface, that is associated with a difference of electric potential: L19. **electroless** *a.* of, pertaining to, or designating a method of plating by chemical and not electrical means M20. **elecˈtrologist** *n.* a person who practises electrology M20. **elecˈtrology** *n.* †(*a*) *rare* the branch of science that deals with electricity; (*b*) the removal of hair and skin blemishes electrically by means of pointed electrodes: M19. **electrolumiˈnescence** *n.* luminescence produced electrically, esp. in a phosphor by the application of a voltage L19. **electrolumiˈnescent** *a.* of, pertaining to, or exhibiting electroluminescence; (capable of) producing light by electroluminescence: E20. **electroˈmatic** *a.* [after *automatic*] designating various kinds of electrical, often automatic, equipment E20. **electromeˈchanical** *a.* designating a mechanical device which is electrically operated; of, pertaining to, or involving such a device: L19. **electromeˈchanically** *adv.* by electromechanical means M20. **electroˈmedical** *a.* designating an electrical device used for medical purposes; pertaining to the use of such devices: L19. **electrometaˈllurgic(al)** *adjs.* of or pertaining to electrometallurgy M19. **electromeˈtallurgy** *n.* metallurgy that involves the use of electricity, esp. in electrolytic methods of winning or purifying metals M19. **elecˈtrometer** *n.* any instrument for measuring small voltages while taking negligible current M18. **electroˈmetric** *a.* = ELECTROMETRICAL L19. **electroˈmetrical** *a.* of or pertaining to an electrometer; involving or employing the measurement of voltage: L18. **elecˈtrometry** *n.* the practice or technique of using an electrometer M19. **electromiˈgration** *n.* the migration of particles in an electric field M20. **electroˈmyogram** *n.* (*Med.*) a chart or record produced by an electromyograph E20. **electroˈmyograph** *n.* (*Med.*) an instrument that records, displays, or converts into sound the electrical activity of muscle, using electrodes attached to the skin or inserted into the muscle M20. **electromyoˈgraphic** *a.* (*Med.*) involving or pertaining to electromyography E20. **electromyoˈgraphically** *adv.* (*Med.*) by means of electromyography E20. **electromyˈography** *n.* (*Med.*) the practice or technique of using an electromyograph or electromyograms E20. **electroˈnegative** *a.* †(*a*) electrically negative; (*b*) *Chem.* going to the positive electrode in electrolysis; having a tendency to attract electrons: E19. **electroˈnegatively** *adv.* (*Chem.*) as an electronegative substance E20. **electronegaˈtivity** *n.* (*Chem.*) the degree to which an atom etc. attracts electrons; the state of being electronegative: E20. **electroˈneutral** *a.* (*Chem.*) electrically neutral M20. **electroneuˈtrality** *n.* (*Chem.*) the state of being electrically neutral M20. **electronyˈstagmogram** *n.* (*Med.*) a chart or record produced by an electronystagmograph L20. **electronyˈstagmograph** *n.* (*Med.*) an electro-oculograph used in electronystagmography M20. **electronystagmoˈgraphic** *a.* (*Med.*) of or pertaining to electronystagmography M20. **electronystagmoˈgraphically** *adv.* (*Med.*) by means of electronystagmography L20. **electronystagˈmography** *n.* the investigation of nystagmus by electro-oculographic means E20. **electro-ˈoculogram** *n.* (*Med.*) (*a*) a chart or record produced by an electro-oculograph; (*b*) = ELECTRO-OCULOGRAPH: M20. **electro-ˈoculograph** *n.* (*Med.*) an instrument that records the varying electric potentials of points near the eye as a guide to eye movement M20. **electro-oculoˈgraphic** *a.* (*Med.*) of or pertaining to electro-oculography M20. **electro-oculoˈgraphically** *adv.* (*Med.*) by means of electro-oculography M20. **electro-ocuˈlography** *n.* (*Med.*) the use of an electro-oculograph or electro-oculograms M20. **electro-ˈoptic** *a.* pertaining to or involving the effect of an electric field on light; of or pertaining to electro-optics: L19. **electro-ˈoptical** *a.* = ELECTRO-OPTIC E20. **electro-ˈoptically** *adv.* by means of an electro-optic device or effect E20. **electro-ˈoptics** *n.* the branch of science that deals with the effect of electric fields on light and the optical properties of substances L19. **electro-osˈmosis** *n.* osmosis under the influence of an electric field E20. **electro-osˈmotic** *a.* of, pertaining to, or involving electro-osmosis E20. **electro-osˈmotically** *adv.* by means of or as regards electro-osmosis E20. **electropaint, -painting** *ns.* the application of paint by electrocoating M20. **electrophile** *n.* (*Chem.*) an electrophilic substance or molecule E20. **electroˈphilic** *a.* (*Chem.*) having or involving an affinity for electrons M20. **electrophotoˈgraphic** *a.* of, pertaining to, or produced by electrophotography M20. **electrophoˈtography** *n.* any of various techniques in which fixed images are obtained by means of electricity; *esp.* one that makes use of the photoconductive properties of certain materials, as in xerography: L19. **electrophysioˈlogical** *a.* of or pertaining to electrophysiology or its subject matter M20. **electrophysioˈlogically** *adv.* by means of or as regards electrophysiology M20. **electrophysiˈologist** *n.* an expert in or student of electrophysiology L19. **electrophysiˈology** *n.* the branch of physiology that deals with the electrical phenomena associated with nervous and other bodily activity; the electrical phenomena *of* a bodily process or organ: M19. **electroplaque** *n.* (*Zool.*) a flattened electrocyte L20. **electroplax** *n.* (*Zool.*) = ELECTROPLAQUE E20. **electroplexy** *n.* [(APO)PLEXY] electroconvulsive therapy M20. **electropneuˈmatic** *a.* involving both electric and pneumatic power or operation L19. **electroˈpolish** *v.t.* polish (metal) by electrolysis M20. **electroˈpositive** *a.* †(*a*) electrically positive; (*b*) *Chem.* going to the negative electrode in electrolysis; having valence electrons that are readily removed: E19. **electroˈpositively** *adv.* (*Chem.*) as an electropositive substance E20. **electropoˈsiˈtivity** *n.* the degree to which an atom etc. tends to form a positive ion; the state of being electropositive: M20. **electroreˈception** *n.* (*Zool.*) the detection of electric fields or currents by an animal L20. **eˈlectroreˌceptor** *n.* (*Zool.*) a sensory receptor that responds to an electric field or current M20. **electroreˈduction** *n.* chemical reduction by electrolytic means E20. **electroˈretinogram** *n.* (*Med.*) a chart or record of the electrical activity of the retina M20. **electroˈretinograph** *n.* (*Med.*) an instrument that records or displays the electrical activity of the retina L20. **electroretinoˈgraphic** *a.* (*Med.*) involving or pertaining to electroretinography M20. **electroretiˈnography** *n.* (*Med.*) the practice or technique of using electroretinograms M20. **electroscope** *n.* an electrostatic instrument for detecting the presence and sign of electric charge, used also to ascertain the degree of ionization of the air E19. **electroˈscopic** *a.* of, pertaining to, or involving an electroscope M19. **electro-shock** *n.* (*Med.*) an electric shock; the therapeutic use of electric shocks: M19. **electro-ˈsilver** *n.* articles electroplated with silver L19. **electro-slag** *a.* designating a process for welding or refining metal in which an electric current is passed into the metal through a layer of slag lying on top of it M20. **electroˈstriction** *n.* the elastic deformation of a dielectric in an electric field when independent of the reversal of the field and proportional to the square of the field strength E20.

electro'strictive *a.* of, pertaining to, or employing electrostriction M20. **electro'surgery** *n.* surgery using (esp. high-frequency) electricity L19. **electro'surgical** *a.* by means of or using electrosurgery E20. **electro'synthesis** *n.* chemical synthesis effected by electricity L19. **electro'technical** *a.* of or pertaining to electrotechnics L19. **electrotech'nician** *n.* an expert in or student of electrotechnics E20. **electro'technics** *n.* electrical technology, electrical engineering L19. **electrothera'peutic(al)** *adjs.* of or pertaining to electrotherapy E20. **electrothera'peutics** *n.* = ELECTROTHERAPY M19. **electro'therapy** *n.* medical treatment by means of electricity, as in diathermy and electroconvulsive therapy L19. **electro'therapist** *n.* a person who employs electrotherapy E20. **electro'thermal, -'thermic** *adjs.* using or involving the conversion of electricity into heat L19. **electro'tin** *v.t.* coat with tin electrolytically L19. **electro'valence, -'valency** *ns.* (*Chem.*) valency, or a bond, in which oppositely charged ions are bound together by the electrostatic attraction between them E20. **electro'valent** *a.* (*Chem.*) of, pertaining to, or designating (an) electrovalency E20. **electrovi'scosity** *n.* the property of being electroviscous; the component of the viscosity of a substance that is due to the electroviscous effect: M20. **electro'viscous** *a.* having a viscosity that depends on any electric field that is present; of or pertaining to electroviscosity: M20. **electro'weak** *a.* (*Physics*) pertaining to or designating the weak and electromagnetic interactions regarded as different low-energy manifestations of a single interaction L20.

electrocute /ɪˈlɛktrəkjuːt/ *v.t.* L19. [f. ELECTRO- after *execute*.] 1 Put to death by a strong electric current as a means of capital punishment. L19. 2 Cause death of by electric shock. E20.

electro'cution *n.* execution by electricity; death caused by electricity: L19.

electrode /ɪˈlɛktrəʊd/ *n.* M19. [f. ELECTRIC + Gk *hodos* way, after *anode*, *cathode*.] A conductor by which electricity enters or leaves an object, substance, or region.

A. CLARE Two electrodes . . are applied to the anterior temporal areas of the scalp.

electrodeless *a.* L19.

electrodynamic /ɪˌlɛktrə(ʊ)dʌɪˈnamɪk/ *a.* E19. [f. ELECTRO- + DYNAMIC.] Of or pertaining to the interactions of electric currents with magnetic fields or with other electric currents; (of a device) employing the effects of such an interaction.

electrodynamical *a.* = ELECTRODYNAMIC E20. **electrodynamics** *n.* the branch of physics that deals with electrodynamic phenomena E19.

electrogenic /ɪˌlɛktrə(ʊ)ˈdʒɛnɪk/ *a.* L19. [f. ELECTRO- + -GENIC.] That produces electricity; *spec.* (*Physiol.*) tending to produce a change in electric potential.

electrogenic pump: that transfers ions through a cell membrane and alters the potential across the membrane.

eˌlectroge'nicity *n.* M20.

electrolier /ɪˌlɛktrəˈlɪə/ *n.* L19. [f. ELECTRO- after *chandelier*.] A chandelier in which the lights are electric.

electrolyse /ɪˈlɛktrəlʌɪz/ *v.t.* Also ***-lyze**. M19. [f. next after *analyse*.] Subject to electrolysis; pass an electric current through (a liquid) so as to cause decomposition.

electrolyser *n.* L20. **electroly'sation** *n.* the process of electrolysing M19.

electrolysis /ɪˌlɛkˈtrɒlɪsɪs, ˌɛlɛkˈtrɒlɪsɪs/ *n.* M19. [f. ELECTRO- + -LYSIS.] 1 Chemical decomposition produced by the passage of an electric current through a liquid; the process of passing a current through a liquid to produce a chemical reaction at the electrodes. M19. 2 *Med.* The destruction of tumours and calculi by passing an electric current through them. Now *rare*. M19. 3 The removal of body hair by passing an electric current through the root. E20.

electrolyte /ɪˈlɛktrəlʌɪt/ *n.* M19. [f. ELECTRO- + Gk *lutos* released, f. *luein* to release.] A liquid which contains ions and can be decomposed by electrolysis; *spec.* one used as battery fluid. Also, a substance which gives rise to ions when dissolved, usu. in water, or fused; the ionized or ionizable constituents of a living cell, blood, or other tissue.

electrolytic /ɪˌlɛktrəˈlɪtɪk/ *a.* & *n.* M19. [f. prec. + -IC.] A *adj.* Of, pertaining to, or produced by electrolysis; employing or involving electrolysis. M19. B *n.* Copper that has been refined by electrolysis. E20.

electrolytical *a.* = ELECTROLYTIC *a.* M19. **electrolytically** *adv.* by means of electrolysis; as regards electrolysis: L19.

electrolyze *v.* see ELECTROLYSE.

electromagnet /ɪˌlɛktrə(ʊ)ˈmagnɪt/ *n.* M19. [f. ELECTRO- + MAGNET.] A piece of soft iron surrounded by a coil of wire so that it can be made temporarily magnetic by passing an electric current through the wire.

electromagnetic /ɪˌlɛktrə(ʊ)magˈnɛtɪk/ *a.* E19. [f. ELECTRO- + MAGNETIC.] Of or pertaining to the interrelation of electric currents or fields and magnetic fields; having both electric and magnetic aspects or properties.

electromagnetic radiation: consisting of electromagnetic waves (e.g. light, radio waves, X-rays). **electromagnetic spectrum** the range of wavelengths or frequencies over which electromagnetic radiation extends. **electromagnetic units** a largely disused system of electrical units based on the force between two magnetic poles, assuming the permeability of the vacuum to be 1. **electromagnetic wave** a wave consisting of a travelling periodic fluctuation in both an electric and a magnetic field, these fields being at right angles to each other and to the direction of propagation of the wave.

electromagnetically *adv.* by means of electromagnetism L19. **eˌlectro'magnetism** *n.* electromagnetic phenomena and properties; the branch of physics that deals with these: E19.

electromeric /ɪˌlɛktrə(ʊ)ˈmɛrɪk/ *a.* E20. [f. ELECTRO- after ISOMERIC.] *Chem.* Of, pertaining to, or designating a postulated displacement of electrons in a molecule during a reaction.

electromotive /ɪˌlɛktrəˈməʊtɪv/ *a.* E19. [f. ELECTRO- + MOTIVE *a.*] Pertaining to the flow of an electric current. Chiefly in *electromotive force* below.

electromotive force a force or difference in potential that tends to give rise to an electric current; abbrev. *emf*, *EMF*.

electromotor /ɪˈlɛktrə(ʊ)məʊtə/ *n.* E19. [f. ELECTRO- + MOTOR *n.*] Orig., a metal serving as an element of a voltaic cell. Now, an electric motor.

electron /ɪˈlɛktrɒn/ *n.*[1] M19. [Gk *ēlektron*.] = ELECTRUM 1.

electron /ɪˈlɛktrɒn/ *n.*[2] L19. [f. ELECTRIC + -ON.] A stable subatomic particle which has a constant charge of negative electricity, is a constituent of all atoms, and is the primary carrier of electric current in solids. Cf. LEPTON *n.*[2]

Auger electron: see AUGER *n.*[2] 2. *planetary electron*: see PLANETARY *a.* **positive electron** = POSITRON.

Comb.: **electron diffraction** the diffraction of a beam of electrons by atoms and molecules (used to investigate crystal structure); **electron gun** a device in which electrons from a heated cathode are emitted as a narrow beam, e.g. in a cathode-ray tube; **electron lens** a device for focusing a beam of electrons by means of a magnetic or electric field; **electron micrograph** a magnified image obtained with an electron microscope; **electron microscope**: using a beam of electrons focused by electron lenses in order to achieve much greater magnification and resolution than is possible with light; **electron multiplier** a device for amplifying a current of electrons by utilizing secondary emission of electrons at a succession of anodes; **electron optics** the branch of physics that deals with the behaviour of electrons and electron beams in magnetic and electric fields; **electron pair** (*a*) *Chem.* two electrons of opposite spin occupying the same orbital in an atom or molecule; (*b*) *Physics* an electron and a positron produced together by a high-energy reaction; *electron shell*: see SHELL *n.* 23; **electron spin resonance** resonance in which the transition involved is that of electrons between states of different spin (used to investigate molecular structure etc.); **electron tube** an evacuated or gas-filled tube in which a current of electrons flows from one electrode to another; **electronvolt** a unit of energy equal to that gained or lost by an electron moving through a potential difference of 1 volt, equal to 1.602×10^{-19} joule (symbol eV).

electronic /ɪlɛkˈtrɒnɪk, ɛl-/ *a.* E20. [f. prec. + -IC.] 1 Of or pertaining to the electron or electrons. E20. 2 Designating a device that operates according to the principles or methods of electronics, such as a transistor microchip, or electron tube; operating by means of or employing such devices; (of a musical instrument) generating sound by such devices rather than by mechanical vibration; (of music) using sounds generated or modified electronically and usu. recorded on tape. E20. 3 Of or pertaining to electronics; (of a person) expert in electronics. M20. 4 Using the electronic transmission or storage of information, as by television or computer. L20.

1 C. P. SNOW The electronic structure of the specific atoms. P. W. ATKINS Electronic transitions, when electrons are shifted from one region of an atom or molecule to another. 2 *Times* The largest dollar order for electronic equipment . . yet received in this country. 3 M. MCLUHAN The new electronic and organic age. *Physics Bulletin* The central part to be played by the electronics industry, and the electronic technician in particular. 4 *Daily Telegraph* Evangelists who have made the Electronic Church of the airwaves a power in the . . life of the United States. *British Medical Journal* The launch of an electronic journal, Clinical Notes On-line.

Special collocations: **electronic flash** a very brief but bright flash of light obtained by discharging a capacitor through a gas-discharge tube; a flash-gun that produces such a flash. **electronic mail** the sending of non-spoken information between individuals over a telecommunication network to a location where it is stored for subsequent retrieval, usu. in a computer; information sent in this way. **electronic publishing**: in which texts are made available in magnetic or electronic form. *electronic tag*: see TAG *n.*[1] 10g. *electronic tagging*: see TAGGING *n.* 1(a). **electronic typewriter**: in which solid-state circuitry is used to provide facilities such as the storage of typed characters.

electronically *adv.* by electronic means; as regards an electron or electrons: E20.

electronics /ɪlɛkˈtrɒnɪks, ɛl-/ *n.* E20. [f. as prec. + -ICS.] The branch of physics and technology that deals with the behaviour and flow of electrons, esp. in devices and circuits in which the flow is controlled and utilized.

electronographic /ɪˌlɛktrɒnəˈgrafɪk/ *a.* M20. [f. ELECTRON *n.*[2] + -O- + -GRAPHIC.] 1 Employing or designating a printing process in which ink is transferred without pressure by utilizing electrostatic attraction. M20. 2 Pertaining to or designating an image tube in which photoelectrons are accelerated and focused on a sensitive emulsion to form an image. M20.

e'lectronograph *n.* an image obtained by electronography L20. **eˌlectro'nography** *n.* (the use of) electronographic techniques M20.

electrophone /ɪˈlɛktrəfəʊn/ *n.* M19. [f. ELECTRO- + -PHONE.] 1 *Hist.* An instrument which produced sounds in response to an electric current, e.g. from an induction coil or telephone. M19. 2 Any musical instrument in which the sound is electronically generated or amplified. M20.

electrophonic /ɪˌlɛktrə(ʊ)ˈfɒnɪk/ *a.* M19. [f. prec. + -IC.] 1 Of, pertaining to, or designating an electrophone; (of music) electronic. M19. 2 Of, pertaining to, or designating a sensation of sound produced by the passage of an alternating current or electromagnetic waves through a person. M20.

electrophoresis /ɪˌlɛktrə(ʊ)fəˈriːsɪs/ *n.* E20. [f. ELECTRO- + Gk *phorēsis* being carried.] 1 The migration of molecules or colloidal particles through a liquid or gel under the influence of an applied electric field; a technique employing this to separate, identify, or measure the components of protein mixtures etc. E20. 2 *Med.* = CATAPHORESIS 1. L20.

electrophorese /-ˈriːz/ *v.t.* subject to electrophoresis L20. **electrophoretic** *a.* E20. **electrophoretically** *adv.* M20.

electrophorus /ɪlɛkˈtrɒf(ə)rəs, ɛl-/ *n.* Also Anglicized as **electrophore** /ɪˈlɛktrəfɔː/. L18. [f. ELECTRO-: see -PHORE.] A simple device for building up a static charge, consisting of a dielectric disc that is given a negative charge by friction, and a metal plate that is placed on the disc and then earthed, so that it acquires a positive charge when it is removed.

electroplate /ɪˈlɛktrə(ʊ)pleɪt, ɪˌlɛktrə(ʊ)ˈpleɪt/ *v.* & *n.* M19. [f. ELECTRO- + PLATE *v.*, *n.*] **A** *v.t.* Give (a metal article) a coating of silver, chromium, or other metal by use as the cathode, with the coating metal as the anode, in an electrolytic bath. M19. **B** *n.* **1** Electroplated articles. M19. **2** *Biol.* = ELECTROPLAQUE. M20.
electroplater *n.* M19.

electrostatic /ɪˌlɛktrə(ʊ)ˈstatɪk/ *a.* M19. [f. ELECTRO- + STATIC, after *hydrostatic.*] Of or pertaining to stationary electric charges or electrostatics; employing or designating a steady electric field.
H. M. ROSENBERG Electrons can be focussed into narrow beams by electrostatic or magnetic lenses. **electrostatic units** a system of electrical units based on the force between two electric charges, assuming the permittivity of the vacuum to be 1.
electrostatical *a.* = ELECTROSTATIC M19. **electrostatically** *adv.* L19.

electrostatics /ɪˌlɛktrə(ʊ)ˈstatɪks/ *n.* E19. [f. ELECTRO- + STATICS.] The branch of physics that deals with electrostatic phenomena and properties.

electrotonic /ɪˌlɛktrə(ʊ)ˈtɒnɪk/ *a.* M19. [f. ELECTRO- + TONIC *a.*] **1** Designating the state of an electric conductor in the vicinity of another conductor through which an electric current is flowing. Now *rare* or *obs.* M19. **2** *Biol.* Characterized by electrotonus; of, pertaining to, or designating the steady flow of electric charge in a cell or tissue in the absence of action potentials. M19.

electrotonus /ɪlɛkˈtrɒtənəs, ɛl-/ *n.* M19. [f. ELECTRO- + TONE *n.*, TONUS.] The altered state of a nerve due to the passage of a steady electric current through it.

electrotype /ɪˈlɛktrə(ʊ)tʌɪp/ *n.*, *a.*, & *v.* M19. [f. ELECTRO- + -TYPE.] **A** *n.* A duplicate made by electroplating an object or a mould of it; a relief printing block made in this way. M19.
B *adj.* Pertaining to or designating an electrotype. M19.
Antiquaries Journal The ring . . has been restored to its original form, though an electrotype copy exists of its distorted form as found.
C *v.t.* Make an electrotype of. M19.
electrotyper *n.* L19.

electrum /ɪˈlɛktrəm/ *n.* LME. [L f. Gk *ēlektron.*] **1** A native mixture of gold with 20 per cent or more of silver; a pale yellow alloy with the same composition, used in jewellery. LME. †**2** Amber. LME–L18. **3** An alloy of copper, nickel, and zinc. L19.

electuary /ɪˈlɛktjʊ(ə)ri/ *n. arch.* LME. [Late L *elect(u)arium*, prob. f. Gk *ekleikton*, f. *ekleikhein* lick up.] **1** A medicinal substance mixed with honey or syrup. LME. †**2** = ELECTRUM 1, 2. M16–M17.

eledone /ɛlɪˈdəʊni/ *n.* M19. [mod.L (see below) f. Gk *eledōnē* a kind of polypus.] An eight-armed bottom-dwelling cephalopod of the genus *Eledone*, related to the octopus.

eleemosynary /ˌɛliːˈmɒsɪnəri, -ˈmɒz-/ *n.* & *a.* L16. [med.L *eleemosynarius*, (in sense A.1) *-synarium*, f. eccl.L *eleemosyna* alms f. Gk *eleēmosunē* compassionateness, f. *eleēmōn* compassionate, f. *eleos* mercy: see -ARY[1]. Cf. ALMS.] †**A** *n.* **1** = ALMONRY. L16–L17. **2** = ALMONER. *rare.* M17–E19. **3** A person who is dependent on alms. M–L17.
B *adj.* **1** Of, pertaining to, or of the nature of, alms or almsgiving; charitable. E17. **2** Dependent on or supported by alms. M17.
1 C. BRONTË Eleemosynary relief never yet tranquillized the working classes. 2 N. HAWTHORNE Threw forth . . food, for the flock of eleemosynary doves.

elegance /ˈɛlɪg(ə)ns/ *n.* E16. [Fr. *élégance* f. L *elegantia*, f. *elegant-*: see ELEGANT, -ANCE.] **1** The state or quality of being elegant; refined luxury; tasteful correctness; ingenious simplicity. E16. **2** Something that is elegant; a refinement. L17.

elegancy /ˈɛlɪg(ə)nsi/ *n.* M16. [L *elegantia*: see prec., -ANCY.] **1** = ELEGANCE 1. Now *rare.* M16. **2** = ELEGANCE 2. L16.

elegant /ˈɛlɪg(ə)nt/ *a.* L15. [(O)Fr. *élégant* or L *elegant-*, *elegans* rel. to *eligere* to select: see ELECT *v.*, -ANT[1].] **1** Of a person: that dresses tastefully. L15. **2** Characterized by grace of form, style, or movement; refined; graceful, free from awkwardness, coarseness, or clumsiness. E16. **3** Of a person: correct and delicate in taste. Now only in *elegant scholar.* E17. **b** Refined in manners and habits (formerly also in feeling). E18. **4** Characterized by refined luxury. L17. **5** Of interests, activities, etc.: appropriate to people of refinement and cultivated taste. E18. **6** Ingeniously simple and effective. E18. **7** Excellent, first-rate. *US.* M18.
2 I. MURDOCH The long loose robes, too elegant to be called dressing-gowns, which she . . put on in the evenings. R. CONQUEST A statesmanlike speech in very elegant French. **elegant variation** *iron.* the stylistic fault of deliberately avoiding repetition by using different words for the same thing. 4 WILKIE COLLINS He felt languid pulses in elegant bedrooms. 5 W. M. CRAIG A high state of the elegant arts . . is indicative of great advancement in civilization. 6 W. MEID An elegant solution of this long-standing riddle.
elegantly *adv.* E16.

élégante /elegɑ̃ːt/ *n.* Pl. pronounced same. L18. [Fr., fem. of *élégant* ELEGANT.] A fashionable woman.

elegiac /ɛlɪˈdʒʌɪək/ *a.* & *n.* L16. [Fr. *élégiaque* or late L *elegiacus* f. Gk *elegeiakos*, f. *elegeia*, *elegeion* ELEGY: see -AC.] **A** *adj.* **1 a** *Pros.* Used in or appropriate to elegies. L16. **b** Of a poet: that writes in an elegiac metre, or in a mournful or pensive style. L16. **2** Pertaining to or of the nature of an elegy; mournful, melancholy. E17.
1a SIR W. SCOTT Hast thou no elegiac verse For Brunswick's venerable hearse? **elegiac couplet, distich**: composed of a dactylic hexameter followed by a dactylic pentameter. **elegiac stanza** a quatrain of iambic pentameters rhyming *abab.* 2 L. LEE Mother's lamentations reach elegiac proportions.
B *n.* In *pl.* Elegiac verses. L18.
elegiacal *a.* (*arch.*) = ELEGIAC *a.* LME. **elegiacally** *adv.* L20.

elegiast /ɪˈliːdʒɪast/ *n. rare.* M18. [f. ELEGY after *ecclesiast.*] A writer of elegies.

elegit /ɪˈliːdʒɪt/ *n.* E16. [L 3rd person sing. perf. of *eligere* choose, a wd occurring in the writ.] *Law* (now *Hist.*). A writ of execution by which a judgement creditor was put in possession of all or (earlier) half the goods and lands of a debtor, until the claim was satisfied; the right secured by such a writ.

elegy /ˈɛlɪdʒi/ *n.* E16. [Fr. *élégie* or L *elegia* f. Gk *elegeia*, f. *elegos* mournful poem: see -Y[3].] **1** A song of lamentation, esp. for the dead; a poem written in an elegiac metre. E16. **2** A poem, or poetry, written in elegiac metre, or for which this metre would have been used in classical times. L16.
elegize *v.i.* & *t.* compose an elegy (on); write in a mournful style: E18.

eleme /ˈɛlɪmi/ *n.* & *a.* L19. [Turk. = something selected.] (Designating) a kind of dried fig from Turkey.

element /ˈɛlɪmənt/ *n.* ME. [(O)Fr. *élément* f. L *elementum* (esp. in pl.) principle, rudiment, letter of the alphabet, used as tr. Gk *stoikheion* step, component part.] **I** The four elements. **1** Earth, air, fire, or water (these being collectively regarded as the constituents of the material world by ancient and medieval philosophers). ME. **2** In *pl.* Atmospheric agencies, *esp.* wind and storm. Chiefly as *the elements.* ME. **3** †**a** Any of the celestial spheres of ancient cosmology; a celestial object. ME–E17. **b** The sky. *obs.* exc. *dial.* L15. **4** One of the four elements that is the natural abode of a person etc.; *gen.* one's natural surroundings, one's appropriate or favourite sphere of operation. L16. **5** A primordial principle, a source, an origin. *rare.* E17.
4 G. GISSING Clifford was never so much in his element as when conversing of art. *Truth* Early nineteenth century in character, he was . . out of his element in this neo-Georgian era. *British Journal of Aesthetics* We do not inhabit the same element as the Greeks.
II Component part. **6** Any of the relatively simple substances of which a complex substance or material body is compounded; in *pl.*, the raw material of anything. Orig. *spec.* as in branch I. LME. **b** *spec.* in *Sci.* Any of the substances (numbering more than 100) that cannot be resolved by chemical means into simpler substances and are now known to have a uniform nuclear charge for each such substance and to make up jointly in all matter. M17. **7** In *pl.* Orig., the letters of the alphabet. Now, the rudiments of learning; the first principles of a subject. LME. **b** (Usu. **E-**.) In *pl.* (The name of) a class in a Roman Catholic school, college, or seminary, now only *spec.* the first and most junior class, immediately below Figures, in certain Jesuit schools. M19. **8** *Chr. Ch.* The bread or the wine used in the Eucharist. Usu. in *pl.* M16. **9** A constituent part of an immaterial whole; a usu. small amount *of* some quality or characteristic present in something, a hint. L16. **b** = PARAMETER 2. Usu. in *pl.* L18. **10** *Math.* **a** An infinitesimal portion *of* length, mass, etc. E18. **b** Each of the symbols or quantities that constitute a matrix or determinant. M19. **c** Each of the entities of which a set is composed. M19. **11** Each of the facts or conditions which enter into a process, deliberation, etc.; a contributory factor. E19. **12** A component part of a structure or device; *spec.* the resistance wire that provides the heat in an electric fire, cooker, etc. M19. **b** A definite small part of an animal or plant structure. M19.
6 SHAKES. *Temp.* The elements Of whom your swords are temper'd. b *Practical Gardening* The principal elements obtained from the soil are nitrogen, potassium, phosphorus, calcium and magnesium. **the elements of** the elements that are present in (a compound), in the proportion in which they are present. *trace element*: see TRACE *a.* 7 J. GLASSCO We learned the elements of cookery. **The Elements** Euclid's fundamental treatise on geometry. 9 T. COLLINS Rory's character was made up of two fine elements, the poetic and the prosaic. *Annual Register* The Communist-led elements among the workers. B. WEBB A meeting ground for all elements in the Party. D. LODGE A certain immunity from assault, though an element of risk remained. 11 H. KISSINGER In that relationship the central element would have to be Anglo-French understanding and cooperation. 12 *SLR Camera* The new lens . . has 10 elements in 9 groups. b *sieve element, tracheary element*, etc.

element /ˈɛlɪmənt/ *v.t.* LME. [f. the n.] Make or compound from elements. Now only *fig.*, compose, constitute.

elemental /ɛlɪˈmɛnt(ə)l/ *a.* & *n.* L15. [med.L *elementalis*, f. L *elementum*: see ELEMENT *n.*, -AL[1].] **A** *adj.* **1** Of or pertaining to any or all of the four elements. L15. **b** Of or pertaining to the powers of nature; personifying a phenomenon or aspect of nature; *fig.* comparable to or suggestive of the great forces of nature. E19. †**2** Pertaining to the sky; governed by celestial influences. E16–E17. †**3** Composed of or produced by the four elements; material, not formal; inorganic, not vital. Of fire: physical, actual, not spiritual or figurative; in its hypothetical pure condition rather than the impure form known by experience. M16–M18. **4** Of the nature of an ultimate constituent; basic, primary; *Sci.* (of a chemical element) not combined with another element; of or pertaining to the elements. M16. **5** = ELEMENTARY 3. Now *rare.* L16. **6** That is an essential or constituent part. M17.
1b GLADSTONE Amphitrite appears in the Odyssey only as an elemental power. E. BOWEN For all her . . tentative cosmetics she was suddenly elemental and heroic. 4 E. V. NEALE The primitive elemental operations of thought. J. BARZUN Intent upon a few elemental goals . . —food, shelter, love, survival. *Scientific American* Graphite, the commonest form of elemental carbon. *Times Lit. Suppl.* Three laboratories analysed the elemental composition of the torc.
B *n.* A supernatural entity or force regarded by occultists as capable of producing physical manifestations. L19.
elementally *adv.* M17.

elementalism /ɛlɪˈmɛnt(ə)lɪz(ə)m/ *n.* M19. [f. prec. + -ISM.] 1 The identification of divinities with the powers of nature. M19. 2 An elemental quality or state. E20. 3 The semantic separation of things which are empirically or physically inseparable. M20.

2 *Dance Theatre Journal* The passionate, motivated elementalism of Modern Dance.

elementary /ɛlɪˈmɛnt(ə)ri/ *a.* LME. [L *elementarius*, f. *elementum*: see ELEMENT *n.*, -ARY[1].] †1 = ELEMENTAL *a.* 3. LME–L18. 2 = ELEMENTAL *a.* 1. Now *rare.* M16. 3 Of the nature of elements or rudiments; introductory; fundamental; relating to the first principles of learning; simple, easy. M16. 4 = ELEMENTAL *a.* 4. E17. 5 *Math.* That is an element of length, mass, etc. L19.

3 J. S. MILL Elementary maxims of prudence. CONAN DOYLE 'Excellent!' I cried. 'Elementary,' said he.

Special collocations: **elementary education** formal education at an elementary level in basic subjects. **elementary particle** *Physics* a subatomic particle, *esp.* one not known to be decomposable into other particles. **elementary school** a school providing elementary education; *spec.* (*a*) *Hist.* a school intended for children between the ages of 5 and 13; (*b*) *N. Amer.* a primary school. **elementary teacher** a teacher in an elementary school.

elementarily *adv.* L16. **elementariness** *n.* M17. **elemenˈtarity** *n.* the property of being elementary M17.

elemi /ˈɛlɪmi/ *n.* M16. [mod.L f. Arab. *al-lāmī*.] Any of various oleoresins obtained from tropical trees of the family Burseraceae and used in varnishes and ointments; *esp.* (more fully *American elemi*) that from the gumbo-limbo tree, *Bursera simaruba*, and (more fully *Manila elemi*) that from *Canarium luzanicum* of the Philippines. Also more fully *gum elemi*.

†elench *n.* LME. [L ELENCHUS.] *Logic.* 1 = ELENCHUS. LME–M17. 2 A sophistical argument, a fallacy. LME–L17.

elenchtic *a.* var. of ELENCTIC.

elenchus /ɪˈlɛŋkəs/ *n.* Pl. **-chi** /-kʌɪ/. M17. [L f. Gk *elegkhos* argument of refutation.] *Logic.* A syllogism in refutation of a syllogistic conclusion; a logical refutation.

Socratic elenchus: see SOCRATIC *a.*

elenctic /ɪˈlɛŋktɪk/ *a.* Also **-ch-**. E19. [Gk *elegktikos*, f. *elegkhein* refute: see -IC.] Pertaining to or designating reasoning which proves indirectly, esp. refutation by question and answer. Cf. DEICTIC.

†elenctical *a.* L16–L17.

elenge /ˈɛlɪndʒ/ *a. obs.* exc. *dial.* [OE *ǣlenge*, f. *ǣ*-stressed var. of A-[1] + *lenge* f. var. of Gmc base of LONG *a.*[1]] 1 Long, protracted; tedious. OE. 2 Solitary, remote; dreary, miserable; unhappy. ME. †3 Strange, unusual; foreign. LME–L18.

eleolite *n.* var. of ELAEOLITE.

Eleonora /ɛlɪəˈnɔːrə/ *n.* M19. [*Eleonora* of Arborea (*c*1350–1404), a princess of Sardinia.] *Eleonora('s) falcon*, a long-winged migratory falcon, *Falco eleonorae*, similar to but larger than the hobby, which occurs on islands and cliffs in the Mediterranean area.

elephant /ˈɛlɪf(ə)nt/ *n.* Also (*arch.*) **oli-** /ˈɒlɪ-/. ME. [OFr. *olifant*, *elefant* (mod. *éléphant*) f. Proto-Romance alt. of L *elephantus*, *elepha(n)s* f. Gk *elephas*, *elephant-* ivory, elephant, prob. of alien origin; Eng. *el-* by assim. to L.] 1 The largest living land mammal, with a prehensile trunk used for taking up food and water, a hairless body, and usu. a pair of long curved tusks, of which two species remain in existence. ME. 2 Ivory; a horn or trumpet of ivory. *arch.* ME. †3 = ELEPHANTA. E17–E18. 4 In full *elephant paper*. A former large size of drawing paper, typically 28 × 23 inches (approx. 711 × 584 mm). E18. 5 A shade of grey. L19. 6 (The emblem of) the Republican Party. *US colloq.* L19. 7 A corrugated iron dugout or Nissen hut. Also *elephant dugout, hut. Army slang.* E20.

Phrases: **African elephant** the larger of the two species of elephant, *Loxodonta africana*, with large ears. **Indian elephant** the smaller of the two species of elephant, *Elephas maximus*, with proportionately smaller ears. **Order of the Elephant** a Danish order of knighthood. *pink elephant*: see PINK *a.*[2] **see the elephant** *US* see the sights; see the world, get experience of life. *white elephant*: see WHITE *a.*

Comb.: **elephant-bird** = AEPYORNIS; *elephant dugout*: see sense 7 above; **elephant fish** (*a*) a large silvery chimaeroid fish, *Callorhinchus milii*, of Australia and New Zealand, with a long flexible snout bent sharply downwards at the tip; (*b*) = *elephant-snout fish* below; **elephant grass** any of various tall robust tropical grasses and grasslike plants, *esp.* the African *Pennisetum purpureum*; *elephant hut*: see sense 7 above; **elephant joke** a child's nonsense riddle with an elephant as the subject; *elephant paper*: see sense 4 above; **elephant seal** either of two very large seals of the genus *Mirounga*, of which the males have inflatable snouts; **elephant's ear** any of various ornamental plants, esp. species of begonia, with large heart-shaped leaves; **elephant's foot** either of two southern African yams, *Dioscorea elephantipes* and *D. sylvatica*, with large woody edible tubers projecting above the ground; **elephant shrew** any mammal of the African order Macroscelidea, comprising small insectivorous creatures with a long snout and small hind limbs; **elephant-snout fish** any of various mormyrids with an elongated snout that resembles an elephant's trunk; **elephant's teeth** ivory; **elephant trunk snake** the wart snake of Java, *Acrochordus javanicus*, which has flabby skin.

elephanta /ɛlɪˈfantə/ *n.* Also **-ter** /-tə/. E18. [Port. *elephante*, fem. *-ta* f. Proto-Romance: see ELEPHANT.] A violent storm at the end (or the beginning) of a monsoon.

elephantiasis /ˌɛlɪf(ə)nˈtʌɪəsɪs/ *n.* Pl. **-ases** /-əsiːz/. M16. [L f. Gk, f. *elephas*: see ELEPHANT, -IASIS.] 1 *Med.* A condition in which a part of the body, usu. a limb, is grossly enlarged, esp. when due to obstruction of the lymphatics by filarial worms. Formerly also, any of various diseases characterized by swelling or by alteration of the skin, *esp.* lepromatous leprosy. M16. 2 *fig.* A great or undue expansion or enlargement. M19.

elephantic /ɛlɪˈfantɪk/ *n.* & *a. rare.* L15. [Late L *elephanticus*, f. L *elephantus* ELEPHANT: see -IC.] †A *n.* Leprosy. Only in L15. B *adj.* Elephantine. L16.

elephantine /ɛlɪˈfantʌɪn/ *n.* & *a.* E16. [L *elephantinus* f. Gk *elephantinos*, f. *elephant-*: see ELEPHANT, -INE[1].] †A *n.* Ivory. Only in E16. B *adj.* 1a Resembling an elephant in size or strength; (of a task) requiring the strength of an elephant. E17. b Resembling an elephant in manner; clumsy, unwieldy. M19. 2 Of or pertaining to an elephant or elephants. L17. 3 *Rom. Antiq.* Made of ivory. Only in *elephantine book.* L17.

elephantoid /ɛlɪˈfantɔɪd/ *a.* M19. [f. ELEPHANT + -OID.] = ELEPHANTINE *a.* 1, 2.

elephantry /ˈɛlɪf(ə)ntri/ *n.* M18. [f. ELEPHANT after *cavalry*.] Troops mounted on elephants.

Elers ware /ˈɛləz wɛː/ *n. phr.* M19. [David (1656–1742) and John Philip (1664–1738) *Elers*.] Red stoneware made in Staffordshire in the 17th cent., *esp.* that made by the Elers brothers.

eleusine /ɛljʊˈsʌɪni/ *n.* E19. [mod.L, f. Gk *Eleusin-*, *Eleusis*: see next.] Any of several kinds of millet of the genus *Eleusine* with fingered spikes, much grown as cereals in dry areas of India, Africa, etc.

Eleusinian /ɛljʊˈsɪnɪən/ *a.* M17. [f. L *Eleusinius* adj. (f. Gk *Eleusinios*) + -AN.] Belonging to Eleusis, a village near Athens which in classical times was a town famous for its cult of the corn goddess Demeter.

Eleusinian mysteries the ritual celebrations that were held annually at Eleusis in honour of Demeter.

eleutherian /ɛljʊˈθɪərɪən/ *n.* & *a. rare.* E17. [f. Gk *eleutherios* (f. *eleutheros* free) + -AN.] A *n.* A deliverer. E17. B *adj.* Designating Zeus as protector of political freedom. E19.

eleuthero- /ɪˈljuːθərəʊ/ *comb. form* of Gk *eleutheros* free: see -O-.

eleutheroˈmania *n.* a frantic desire for freedom M19. **eleutheroˈmaniac** *n.* & *a.* (a person) possessed by eleutheromania M19.

elevate /ˈɛlɪveɪt/ *v.t.* Pa. pple **-ated**, (earlier, now *poet.*) **-ate**. LME. [L *elevat-* pa. ppl stem of *elevare*, f. *e-* E- + *levare* lighten, raise: see -ATE[3].] I 1 Raise above the usual position or level, or above the level of surrounding objects. LME. b Orig., hold up to view. Now only *spec.* (*Chr. Ch.*), hold up (the host, the chalice) after speaking the words of institution over it in the Eucharist. E17. †2 Raise in the form of vapour; evaporate. LME–E18. †3 Erect, build. LME–L18. 4 Raise the spirits of; elate, exhilarate. Formerly also, inflate with pride. Now chiefly *joc.*, inebriate. LME. 5 Raise in status, rank, or importance; exalt; promote. L15. 6 Raise the pitch of (the voice). E17. 7 Turn or direct upwards (one's eyes, a glance, a gun); *fig.* lift up (one's hopes or thoughts). *arch.* E17. 8 Raise the moral, intellectual, or cultural level of. E17.

†II 9 Reduce in status or importance, depreciate. M16–L18.

1 D. LARDNER The rope by which the bucket is elevated. J. ROSENBERG Rembrandt . . introduced steps in the background to elevate the rear group. 4 C. RAYNER Fenton was elevated tonight by the splendour of the house, the elegance of the company. 5 CONAN DOYLE He could elevate my simple art . . into a prodigy. C. RYAN He had been elevated to the rank of Field Marshal too quickly. 8 H. T. BUCKLE There is hardly any virtue which so elevates our character as moral courage. *absol.*: M. GRAY The kind of sorrow that purifies and elevates.

elevated /ˈɛlɪveɪtɪd/ *a.* & *n.* M16. [f. ELEVATE + -ED[1].] A *adj.* That has been elevated; raised (*lit.* & *fig.*); exalted, lofty; *joc.* inebriated. M16.

elevated railway, road, etc.: running above ground level on columns etc.

B *ellipt.* as *n.* An elevated railway; a train running on this. *US.* L19.

elevatedly *adv.* L16. **elevatedness** *n.* M18.

elevation /ɛlɪˈveɪʃ(ə)n/ *n.* LME. [(O)Fr. *élévation* or L *elevatio(n-)*, f. as ELEVATE: see -ATION.] 1 The action or process, or an act, of elevating; the state or fact of being elevated. LME. b *Chr. Ch.* The holding up of the host in the Eucharist. L16. c *Ballet.* A dancer's leap; the ability to attain height and perform movements while in the air. Also, the action of tightening the muscles and achieving an erect posture. M19. 2 A raised area, esp. of the ground; a swelling on the skin. LME. 3a The angular height of a body or point in the sky, esp. the celestial pole. Formerly also, the pole's height at any one place, the latitude of a place. LME. b The angle at which a gun or any line of direction is inclined to the horizontal. L17. c Altitude above sea level; height above ground level. M18. 4 Loftiness; grandeur, dignity. M17. 5 A drawing or diagram made by projection on a vertical plane; a frontal or side view, esp. of a building. Cf. PLAN *n.* 3a. M18.

1 J. WOODWARD The disruption of the strata, the elevation of some, and depression of others. L. STRACHEY His sudden elevation to the throne. S. O'FAOLÁIN The glow of spiritual elevation died from his face. 2 C. SAGAN Measurements concerning the mountains and elevations of Mars. 3c J. TYNDALL What was snow at the higher elevations changed to rain lower down. 4 J. MORLEY The classic form, its dignity, elevation, and severity.

elevational *a.* (*Archit.*) of or pertaining to an elevation E20.

elevator /ˈɛlɪveɪtə/ *n.* M17. [mod.L, f. as ELEVATE: see -OR. In mod. use directly f. ELEVATE.] 1 *Anat.* = LEVATOR 1. Now *rare.* M17. 2 A machine for raising corn or grain; a hoist in the form of an endless belt or chain with scoops or the like. L18. b A building for the storage of grain and equipped with a grain elevator. *N. Amer.* M19. c = LIFT *n.*[2] 8. *N. Amer.* L19. 3 *Surg.* An instrument for lifting depressed broken bone, esp. of the skull; an instrument for stripping periosteum from bone; a dental instrument for easing a tooth from a socket. E19. 4 Either of a pair of hinged flaps on the stabilizing wings or tailplane of an aircraft, used to vary the angle of pitch. E20. 5 (**E-**.) In *pl.* (Proprietary name for) shoes with a raised insole intended to make a person appear taller. Also (in *sing.* or *pl.*) *elevator shoe. N. Amer.* M20.

elevatory /ɛlɪˈveɪt(ə)ri/ *n.* & *a.* LME. [med.L *elevatorium*, f. as ELEVATE: see -ORY[2]; as adj. directly f. ELEVATE.] A *n.* = ELEVATOR 3. Now *rare* or *obs.* LME. **B** *adj.* Of or pertaining to elevation; that tends to elevate (*lit.* & *fig.*). E19.

élève /elɛːv/ *n.* Pl. pronounced same. Also **eleve** /ɛˈlɛv/. M18. [Fr. *élève*, f. *élever* raise, bring up, f. *é-* (f. as ES-) + *lever* lift f. L *levare*.] A pupil, a scholar.

eleven /ɪˈlɛv(ə)n/ *a.* & *n.* (*cardinal numeral*). [OE *endleofon*, *-lufon*, *ellefne* = OFris. *andlova*, *elleva*, *al-*, *elvene*, OS *elleban*, OHG *einlif*, (Du., G *elf*), ON *ellifu*, Goth. *ainlif*, f. Gmc, f. base of ONE *a.* + base repr. also by TWELVE.] **A** *adj.* One more than ten (a cardinal numeral represented by 11 in arabic numerals, xi, XI in roman). OE.

New York Times Eleven thousand Palestinian guerrillas . . left West Beirut. *Washington Post* Eleven-twelfths of both amounts would be taxable.

B *n.* **1** Eleven persons or things identified contextually, as years of age, points, runs, etc., in a game, chances (in giving odds), minutes, inches, shillings (now *Hist.*), pence, etc. OE. **2** One more than ten as an abstract number; the symbols or figures representing this (11 in arabic numerals, xi, XI in roman). LME. **3** The eleventh of a set or series with numbered members, the one designated eleven, (usu. *number eleven*, or with specification, as *book eleven*, *chapter eleven*, etc.); a size etc. denoted by eleven, a shoe etc. of such a size, (also *size eleven*). LME. **4** The time of day eleven hours after midnight or midday (on a clock, watch, etc., indicated by the numeral eleven displayed or pointed to). Also *eleven o'clock*. M16. **5** A set of eleven; a thing having a set of eleven as an essential or distinguishing feature; *spec.* a team of eleven at soccer, hockey, or cricket. M18.

1 W. S. GILBERT He's a bit undersized, and you don't feel surprised / when he tells you he's only eleven. A. J. P. TAYLOR Eleven of the Liberals who voted against Lloyd George. **the Eleven** the Apostles, without Judas. **3** J. LE CARRÉ An eleven bus will take me to Hammersmith. **4** G. B. SHAW It enables Parliament to do things at eleven at night that no sane person would do at eleven in the morning. **5** S. RAVEN Give the first eleven a little practice.

Comb. Forming compound numerals with multiples of a hundred, as *611* (read *six hundred and eleven*, US also *six hundred eleven*), etc. In dates used for one thousand one hundred, as *1150* (read *eleven fifty*), *eleven-eighties*, etc. Special combs., as **elevenpence** eleven pence, esp. of the old British currency before decimalization; **elevenpenny** *a.* worth or costing elevenpence; **eleven-plus** *n.* & *a.* (designating) an examination formerly taken by schoolchildren to determine what kind of school they should go to for their secondary education (beginning in their twelfth year).

elevener *n.* *dial.* a drink or light meal taken at about 11 a.m. E19. **elevenfold** *a.* & *adv.* (*a*) *adj.* eleven times as great or as numerous; having eleven parts, divisions, elements, or units; (*b*) *adv.* to eleven times the number or quantity: OE.

elevenses /ɪˈlɛv(ə)nzɪz/ *n.pl.* *colloq.* Also (earlier, *dial.*) **elevens**. L18. [f. prec. + -S¹ + *-es* var. of -S¹.] Light refreshment taken at about 11 a.m.

eleventh /ɪˈlɛv(ə)nθ/ *a.* & *n.* (*ordinal numeral*). [OE *endleofeþa*, f. as ELEVEN (superseding *endlyfta*, *ællefta* = OFris. *andlofta*, *ellefta*, OS *ellifto*, OHG *einlifto*, (Du. *elfde*, G *elfte*), ON *ellifti*, f. Gmc), repl. in ME by forms f. ELEVEN + -TH².] **A** *adj.* Next in order after the tenth, that is number eleven in a series, (represented by 11th). OE.

A. THWAITE The eleventh child of William Grosse. A. J. P. TAYLOR Cotton fell from third to eleventh place among British industries. **at the eleventh hour**, **eleventh-hour** *a.* at the latest possible moment. **eleventh commandment** *joc.* & *iron.* a rule to be observed as strictly as the ten commandments; *spec.* (*a*) one should avoid being found out; (*b*) *US* a Republican should not speak ill of another Republican. **eleventh part** *arch.* = sense B.2 below.

B *n.* **1** The eleventh person or thing of a category, series, etc., identified contextually, as day of the month, (following a proper name) person, esp. monarch or pope, of the specified name, etc. OE. **2** Each of eleven equal parts into which something is or may be divided, a fraction which when multiplied by eleven gives one, (= *eleventh part* above). M16. **3** *Mus.* An interval embracing eleven consecutive notes in the diatonic scale, equivalent to an octave and a fourth; a note an eleventh above another note; a chord of two notes an eleventh apart, or based around the eleventh of a note. L16.

1 G. B. SHAW Even Louis the Eleventh had to tolerate his confessor, standing for the eternal against the temporal throne. W. FAULKNER 10:00 P.M. March eleventh. **2** *Washington Post* One-eleventh of the eligible vehicle owners.

Comb.: Forming compound ordinal numerals with multiples of a hundred, as *two-hundred-and-eleventh* (*211th*) etc.

eleventhly *adv.* in the eleventh place L16.

elevon /ˈɛlɪvɒn/ *n.* M20. [f. ELEV(ATOR + AILER)ON.] A hinged flap on the trailing edge of a delta wing, taking the place of both aileron and elevator in a conventional aircraft.

elf /ɛlf/ *n.*¹ Pl. **elves** /ɛlvz/. [OE, non-WS var. of earlier form of *ylf* = MDu. *elf* f. base also of OE *ælf* = OS, MLG *alf*, MHG *alp* (G *Alp* nightmare), ON *álfr*.] **1** A supernatural, usu. small being of Germanic mythology with magical powers for good or evil; a fairy (sometimes distinguished from a fairy as being male, or, formerly, inferior or more malignant). OE. **2** A mischievous or spiteful creature. M16. **3** A dwarf. M16. **4** A child, *esp.* one that is wilful; a small animal. L16.

Comb.: **elf-arrow** *arch.* a flint arrowhead (regarded as an elves' weapon); **elf-bolt** = *elf-arrow* above; **elf-dock** elecampane; **elf-lock** a tangled mass of hair; **elf-locked** *a.* having elf-locks; **elf-shoot** *v.t.* (*dial.*) shoot with an elf-arrow; **elf-shot** (*a*) a disease, esp. of livestock, attributed to the agency of elves; (*b*) *Sc.* = *elf-arrow* above.

elf /ɛlf/ *n.*² *S. Afr.* Also **elft**. M18. [Afk. f. Du. *elft* shad.] = *bluefish* (a) s.v. BLUE *a.*

†**elf** *v.t.* *rare.* E17–L18. [f. ELF *n.*¹] Tangle or twist (hair) as an elf might.

elfin /ˈɛlfɪn/ *a.* & *n.* L16. [f. ELF *n.*¹, prob. suggested by ME *elvene* genit. pl., and infl. by *Elphin* a character of Arthurian romance.] **A** *adj.* **1** Of, pertaining to, or produced by an elf or elves; of the nature of an elf. L16. **2** Diminutive; full of strange charm; suggestive of an elf. L18.

Special collocations: **elfin-tree** a dwarf, crooked tree such as is found in alpine regions; **elfin-wood** a wood composed of elfin-trees.

B *n.* **1** An elf. L16. **2** The land or realm of the elves. *Sc.* L16. **3** A child. M18.

elfish /ˈɛlfɪʃ/ *a.* M16. [f. ELF *n.*¹ + -ISH¹.] Elvish. Formerly also (of a thing), unmanageable.

G. GREENE A little Robin Goodfellow of a man, full of elfish tricks.

elft *n.* var. of ELF *n.*²

Elgarian /ɛlˈɡɑːrɪən, -ˈɡɛː-/ *a.* & *n.* E20. [f. *Elgar* (see below) + -IAN.] **A** *adj.* Of, pertaining to, or characteristic of the English composer Sir Edward Elgar (1857–1934) or his music, known for its noble pageantry and romantic fervour. E20. **B** *n.* A devotee or interpreter of Elgar's music. L20.

elhi /ˈɛlhʌɪ/ *a.* *N. Amer.* M20. [f. *el*(*ementary school* + *hi*(*gh school*.] Of publishing or educational material: aimed at students of elementary to high school level. Also designating such a student.

Elian /ˈiːlɪən/ *a.* & *n.* E20. [f. *Elia* (see below) + -AN.] **A** *adj.* Of or pertaining to the pseudonymous *Essays of Elia* (1823), or their author Charles Lamb (1775–1834). E20. **B** *n.* An admirer or student of 'Elia'. E20.

†**elicit** *a.* E17–M18. [L *elicitus* pa. pple of *elicere*: see next.] *Philos.* Of an act: evolved immediately from an active power or quality.

elicit /ɪˈlɪsɪt/ *v.t.* M17. [L *elicit-* pa. ppl stem of *elicere* draw forth by trickery or magic, f. *e-* E- + *lacere* deceive.] **1** Draw forth, bring out, from being only latent or potential. M17. **2** Bring out (truths etc.) from being only implied; draw out (information) from a person; evoke, stimulate, (a response, a reaction). (Foll. by *from*.) L17.

1 G. J. ADLER Having elicited sparks from two flints he lighted a large fire. **2** G. GREENE I was unable to elicit from any of the waiters . . the identity of the gentleman. A. BRINK Two more letters . . failed to elicit even an acknowledgement of receipt. L. HUDSON The smell of scent . . elicited a dream in which he was in a perfume shop. E. H. GOMBRICH As so often happens, the demand elicited a supply.

eliciˈtation *n.* M17. **elicitor** *n.* a person who or thing which elicits M19.

†**elicitate** *v.t.* *rare.* M17–M19. [Orig. f. as prec. + -ATE³; later perh. back-form. f. ELICITATION.] Elicit.

elide /ɪˈlʌɪd/ *v.t.* M16. [L *elidere* crush out, f. *e-* E- + *laedere* to dash.] †**1 a** Annul, quash, do away with. Chiefly *Sc. Law.* M16–L19. **b** Make of no account, weaken or destroy, (the force of evidence). L16–L17. **2** Omit (a sound, syllable, etc.) by elision. L18. **3** Pass over in silence; suppress, strike out, or omit, often by running several items together. M19.

2 A. S. BYATT He had a mannered Oxford voice, elided words, and used the pronoun 'one' frequently. **3** F. PALGRAVE Gibbon and Sismondi have elided these monarchs.

eligible /ˈɛlɪdʒɪb(ə)l/ *a.* & *n.* LME. [Fr. *éligible* f. late L *eligibilis*, f. *eligere* choose: see -IBLE.] **A** *adj.* **1** Fit or entitled to be chosen for a position, award, etc. LME. †**2** Subject to appointment by election. M17–M18. **3** That is a matter of choice or preference. *rare.* M18. **4** Desirable, suitable, esp. as a partner in marriage. M18.

1 G. GORER Never more than half the families eligible for membership were actually members at any one time. **4** O. MANNING Edwina was unmarried and reputed to be the most eligible girl in Cairo.

B *n.* An eligible person or thing; *spec.* a desirable marriage partner. M19.

eligiˈbility *n.* M17. **eligibleness** *n.* eligibility L17. **eligibly** *adv.* E19.

eliminable /ɪˈlɪmɪnəb(ə)l/ *a.* M19. [f. ELIMINATE + -ABLE.] Able to be eliminated.

eliminaˈbility *n.* the property or quality of being eliminable M20.

eliminant /ɪˈlɪmɪnənt/ *a.* & *n.* L19. [L *eliminant-* pres. ppl stem of *eliminare*: see next, -ANT¹.] **A** *adj.* Causing or promoting excretion, esp. of harmful substances. L19. **B** *n.* **1** *Math.* A function obtained by eliminating variables from a set of homogeneous polynomial equations. L19. **2** *Med.* An eliminant agent. L19.

eliminate /ɪˈlɪmɪneɪt/ *v.t.* M16. [L *eliminat-* pa. ppl stem of *eliminare* thrust out of doors, expel, f. *e-* E- + *limin-*, *limen* threshold: see -ATE³.] **1** Drive out, expel. Now *rare* or *obs.* M16. †**b** Divulge (a secret); set at liberty. E17–M18. **2** Remove, get rid of, do away with; cause to exist no longer; *spec.* (*a*) exclude from further participation in a competition etc. by defeat; (*b*) murder. E18. **3 a** *Physiol.* Expel (waste matter etc.) from the body. L18. **b** *Chem.* Remove (a simpler substance) from a compound. L19. **4** *Math.* Get rid of (a quantity in an equation) by combining equations. M19. **5** Ignore as irrelevant to an argument or idea. M19. **6** Extract, isolate, disentangle (a fact, principle, etc.) from a mass of details; elicit, deduce. *colloq.* M19.

2 *Times Lit. Suppl.* The result of the late war has been to eliminate Germany from the map. T. BENN We aim to eliminate poverty. M. MCCARTHY Modern machinery and factory processes . . had eliminated all danger of bacteria.

elimiˈnation *n.* the action or process of eliminating E17. **eliminative** *a.* that eliminates or tends to eliminate M19. **eliminator** *n.* a person who or thing which eliminates L19. **eliminatory** *a.* (*rare*) of or pertaining to elimination M19.

elint /ˈɪlɪnt/ *n.* M20. [f. *el*(*ectronic int*(*elligence*.] Covert intelligence-gathering by electronic means. Freq. *attrib.*

elinvar /ˈɛlɪnvɑː/ *n.* E20. [Fr. *élinvar*, f. *élasticité invariable* invariable elasticity.] An alloy, mainly of iron and nickel, whose modulus of elasticity is relatively independent of temperature changes.

eliotropus *n.* see HELIOTROPE.

eliquate /ˈɛlɪkweɪt/ *v.* LME. [L *eliquat-* pa. ppl stem of *eliquare* (in late L) liquefy, dissolve, f. *e-* E- + *liquare* melt, dissolve, liquefy: see -ATE³.] †**1** *v.t.* Melt; liquefy; cause to dissolve or flow freely. LME–E18. **2** *v.t.* & *i.* Separate by partial fusion. *rare.* M19.

eliquation /ɛlɪˈkweɪʃ(ə)n/ *n.* E17. [Late L *eliquatio*(*n-*), f. as prec.: see -ATION.] †**1** Liquefaction. E17–M18. **2** = LIQUATION 1. M18.

elision /ɪˈlɪʒ(ə)n/ *n.* L16. [Late L *elisio*(*n-*), f. L *elis-* pa. ppl stem of *elidere*: see ELIDE, -ION.] **1**

(An) omission of a sound, syllable, etc., running together the sounds on either side of it; (an) omission of a passage in a book etc. L16. 2 A mechanical breaking or disruption. Now *rare* or *obs.* E17.

1 STEELE The.. Elisions, by which Consonants of most obdurate Sound are joined together. 2 †**elision of the air**: formerly assigned as the cause of sound.

elisor /ˈɛlɪzə/ *n.* LME. [OFr. *esliseor* (later *elisour*), f. *e(s)lis-* stem of *esliser* choose, elect.] †1 = ELECTOR 1, 2. LME–E16. 2 *Law.* Either of two people appointed in certain cases to select a jury. Now chiefly *US.* E17.

élite /eɪˈliːt, ɪ-/ *n.* & *a.* Also **elite**. L18. [Fr., use as n. of fem. of obs. pa. pple of *élire*, †*eslire* f. Proto-Romance var. of L *eligere* ELECT *v.*] A *n.* 1 The choice part, the best, (of society, a group of people, etc.); a select group or class. L18. 2 (Usu. **elite.**) A size of type used on typewriters, having twelve characters to the inch. E20.

1 K. M. E. MURRAY Oxford still catered.. for the social elite, who could afford to go to the University as a.. luxury. R. RENDELL She.. spoke of her family and its immediate circle as of an élite. *social élite*: see SOCIAL *a.*

B *attrib. adj.* Of or belonging to an élite; exclusive. M19.

A. MACLEAN They were élite soldiers.. ruthless men.. ruthlessly trained.

élitism *n.* advocacy of or reliance on the leadership or dominance of a select group M20. **élitist** *a.* & *n.* (a person) practising élitism M20.

elixate /ɪˈlɪkseɪt/ *v.t.* LME. [L *elixat-* pa. ppl stem of *elixare* boil thoroughly: see -ATE[3].] 1 Boil; obtain an extract of by boiling. Now *rare* or *obs.* LME. 2 Steep (in water); macerate. Now *rare.* M17.

eliˈxation *n.* (now *rare*) (*a*) the action of boiling; †(*b*) digestion: E17.

elixir /ɪˈlɪksə, -sɪə/ *n.* LME. [med.L f. Arab. *al-ʾiksīr*, f. *al-* AL-[2] + Gk *xērion* desiccative powder for wounds, f. *xēros* dry.] 1 *Alch.* A preparation by means of which it was hoped to change metals into gold; spec. *the* philosopher's stone. LME. 2 More fully *elixir of life* [med.L *elixir vitae*]. A supposed drug or essence capable of prolonging life indefinitely. L15. †3 A strong extract or tincture. L15–E19. 4 The quintessence or kernel of a thing. E17. 5 A sovereign remedy; an aromatic solution used as a medicine or a flavouring (foll. by *of*). M17.

4 W. CHILLINGWORTH The.. Elixir of all that can be said in defence of your church and doctrine. 5 P. FLETCHER The best Elixar for souls drooping pain.

†**elixirate** *v.t.* & *i.* distil, refine by distillation; purify: E17–M18.

†**elixiviate** *v.t. rare.* L17–M18. [f. *e-* E- + LIXIVIATE.] Clear from lixivium or lye; refine thoroughly.

Elizabethan /ɪˌlɪzəˈbiːθ(ə)n/ *a.* & *n.* E19. [f. *Elizabeth*, the name of two queens, the 1st of England and the 2nd of the UK + -AN.] A *adj.* 1 Of, belonging to, or characteristic of the period of Elizabeth I (reigned 1558–1603), Queen of England. E19. 2 Of or belonging to the period of Elizabeth II (reigned from 1952), Queen of the United Kingdom. M20.

1 T. HOOD A large Elizabethan ruff.

B *n.* 1 A person, esp. a poet or dramatist, of the reign of Elizabeth I. Usu. in *pl.* E19. 2 A person of the reign of Elizabeth II. M20.

Elizabethanism *n.* (*a*) a work of literature of the period of Elizabeth I; (*b*) a manner or style characteristic or imitative of that of her reign: L19.

elk /ɛlk/ *n.*[1] Pl. same, **-s**. L15. [Prob. repr. OE *elh*, *eolh* with k for h /x/ as in dial. *dwerk* (OE *dweorh*) DWARF *n.*, *fark* (OE *færh*) FARROW *n.*, *selk* (OE *seolh*) SEAL *n.*[1]] 1 The largest living deer, *Alces alces*, found in northern parts of Europe, Asia, and N. America, and having a growth of skin hanging from the neck and (in males) very large horns. Also (*N. Amer.*) called *moose.* L15. †2 = ELAND. *S. Afr.* Only in 18. 3 = WAPITI. Also more fully *American elk. N. Amer.* L19. 4 The sambar, *Cervus unicolor. Anglo-Ind.* L19. 5 A member of the Benevolent and Protective Order of Elks, a US social and charitable organization. Usu. in *pl.* L19.

Phrases & comb.: *American elk*: see sense 3 above. *Irish elk*: see IRISH *a.* **elk-hound** a large thick-coated hunting dog of Scandinavian origin.

elk /ɛlk/ *n.*[2] *obs.* exc. *dial.* M16. [Origin unkn.] A wild swan. Also, a wild goose.

ell /ɛl/ *n.*[1] [OE *eln* = OFris. *(i)elne*, OS *elina*, MDu. *elne*, *elle* (Du. *el*), OHG *elina* (G *Elle*), ON *ǫln* (*aln-*), Goth. *aleina*, orig. arm, forearm, cogn. w. L ULNA, Gk. *ōlenē* elbow. For loss of final *n* cf. MILL *n.*[1]] 1 *Hist.* A measure of length, varying in different countries: in England equal to 45 inches; in Scotland equal to 37.2 inches; in the Low Countries equal to 27 inches. OE. †2 A measuring rod; = ELL-WAND 2. ME–M18. †3 = ULNA. Cf. ELL-WAND 1. E–M17.

ell /ɛl/ *n.*[2] *dial.* & *US.* L18. [Repr. pronunc. of *L*, *l* as the letter's name.] The letter L, l; *spec.* an extension of a building etc. which is at right angles to the main part; a lean-to.

T. BERGER The dining ell off the living room.

-ella /ˈɛlə/ *suff.* Repr. It. or L dim. suff., as *mozzarella*, *nassella*; *spec.* in *Biol.* in names of genera of bacteria, as *Legionella*, *Salmonella*.

ellagic /ɛˈladʒɪk/ *a.* E19. [Fr. *ellagique*, f. anagram of *galle* gall-nut (*gallique* GALLIC *a.*[2] being already in use): see -IC.] *ellagic acid*, a tetracyclic phenolic compound, $C_{14}H_6O_8$, found in oak-bark and galls and in bezoars and used as a local haemostatic.

ellagiˈtannin *n.* (*Chem.*) any tannin that on hydrolysis gives ellagic acid and a sugar L19.

Ellingtonian /ɛlɪŋˈtəʊnɪən/ *a.* & *n.* M20. [f. *Ellington* (see below) + -IAN.] A *adj.* Of, pertaining to, or characteristic of the distinctively brilliant and atmospheric music of Edward ('Duke') Ellington (1899–1974), US jazz musician. M20. B *n.* A devotee or follower of Duke Ellington or his music. M20.

ellipse /ɪˈlɪps/ *n.* L17. [Fr. f. L *ellipsis*: see next.] 1 One of the conic sections, a symmetrical closed curve traced by a point moving in a plane so that the sum of its distances from two other points is constant; the cross-section of a cone that is cut by a plane making a smaller angle with the base of the cone than the side of the cone makes. L17. 2 *Gram.* = ELLIPSIS 1. *rare.* M19.

1 A. KOESTLER Comets were shown to move either in very elongated ellipses or in parabolas.

ellipsograph *n.* an instrument for drawing ellipses L19.

ellipsis /ɪˈlɪpsɪs/ *n.* Pl. **ellipses** /ɪˈlɪpsiːz/. M16. [L f. Gk *elleipsis* defect, ellipse, grammatical ellipsis f. *elleipein* leave out, fall short, fail, f. *en* in + *leipein* leave.] 1 *Gram.* (An) omission from a sentence of one or more words which would be needed to complete the sense or construction or which occur in the original; the omission of a sentence at the end of a paragraph; a set of dots etc. used to indicate such omission. Formerly, elision of a vowel. M16. 2 = ELLIPSE 1. Now *rare* or *obs.* L16.

ellipsoid /ɪˈlɪpsɔɪd/ *n.* & *a.* E18. [f. ELLIPSE + -OID.] A *n.* A solid or surface of which at least one set of parallel cross-sections are ellipses and the rest circles. E18.

ellipsoid of revolution: obtained by rotating an ellipse about one of its axes.

B *adj.* = ELLIPSOIDAL. M19.

ellipˈsoidal *a.* having the nature or shape of an ellipsoid M19. **ellipˈsoidally** *adv.* L19.

elliptic /ɪˈlɪptɪk/ *a.* E18. [Gk *elleiptikos* defective, f. *elleipein*: see ELLIPSIS, -IC.] That has the form of an ellipse; pertaining to ellipses.

elliptic geometry a non-Euclidean geometry defined so that all straight lines converge.

ellipticity /ɛlɪpˈtɪsɪti/ *n.* elliptic form; degree of deviation from circularity (or sphericity), *spec.* the difference in length of the major and minor axes divided by that of the major (or minor) axis: M18.

elliptical /ɪˈlɪptɪk(ə)l/ *a.* & *n.* M17. [f. prec. + -AL[1].] A *adj.* 1 = prec. M17. 2 *Gram.* Characterized by ellipsis; *spec.* (of sentences etc.) defective, lacking a word or words needed to complete the sense. L18. B *n.* An elliptical galaxy. M20.

elliptically *adv.* in an elliptical manner; *elliptically polarized*, (of light) having a rotating plane of polarization and an electric field vector whose amplitude varies along an elliptic curve: E19. **ellipticalness** *n.* (*rare*) L17.

†**ellops** *n.* E17. [Gk *el(l)ops.*] 1 A kind of fish mentioned by the ancients. E17–L19. 2 A kind of snake. *rare* (Milton). Only in M17.

-ellum /ˈɛləm/ *suff.* [L: see -LE[2].] Forming dim. ns., as *capitellum*, *flagellum*.

ell-wand /ˈɛlwɒnd/ *n.* Chiefly *Sc.* & *north.* LME. [f. ELL *n.*[1] + WAND *n.*] †1 = ULNA. Cf. ELL *n.*[1] 3. Only in LME. 2 An ell-measure: a yard-measure. L15. 3 The group of stars forming the belt in the constellation Orion. E16.

elm /ɛlm/ *n.* [OE *elm* corresp. to MLG, OHG *elm(boum*, *elmo* (MHG *elme*, *ilme*, G dial. *Ilm*) and, with vowel variation, ON *álmr* (Sw., Norw. *alm*), L *ulmus*.] 1 Any of various deciduous trees with serrate leaves, of the genus *Ulmus* and other genera of the family Ulmaceae; *esp.* (*a*) (more fully *English elm*) the European *U. procera*, once common as a hedge tree in central and southern England; (*b*) (more fully *American elm* or *white elm*) *U. americana*, a tree with pale bark of eastern N. America; (*c*) = WYCH ELM. Also more fully *elm tree.* OE. 2 The wood of the elm. L16.

1 *red elm*, *slippery elm*, *Spanish elm*, *water elm*, etc.

elmen *a.* (now *arch.* & *dial.*) (*a*) made of elm; (*b*) of or pertaining to the elm; *elmen tree*, an elm: LME. **elmy** *a.* containing many elms, consisting of elms M18.

El Niño /ɛl ˈniːnjəʊ/ *n. phr.* L19. [Sp. *El Niño* (*de Navidad*) the (Christmas) child, w. ref. to beginning in late December.] Formerly, an annual warm southward current off northern Peru. Now, an irregularly occurring southward current in the equatorial Pacific Ocean, associated with weather changes and ecological damage; these associated phenomena.

elocution /ɛləˈkjuːʃ(ə)n/ *n.* LME. [L *elocutio(n-)*, f. *elocut-* pa. ppl stem of *eloqui*: see ELOQUENT, -ION.] †1 Oratorical or literary expression; literary style as distinguished from matter; the art of appropriate and effective expression. LME–M19. †2 Eloquence, oratory. L16–L18. 3 The art of (public) speaking, esp. of pronunciation, delivery, gesture, and voice production. E17. 4 Manner or style of speaking. E17.

1 H. NEVILLE A Person of good Learning and Elocution. 2 POPE When he speaks, what elocution flows! 3 C. CIBBER True theatrical elocution. 4 BURKE You have a natural, fluent, and unforced elocution.

elocute *v.i.* (*joc.*) [back-form. after *execute* etc.] practise elocution; declaim in an elocutionary manner: L19. **elocutional** *a.* = ELOCUTIONARY M20. **elocutionally** *adv.* M20. **elocutionary** *a.* of or pertaining to elocution M19. **elocutionist** *n.* a person proficient in elocution M19. **elocutionize** *v.i.* (*a*) use florid or eloquent language; (*b*) speak or read in public: M19.

elocutory /ɛləˈkjuːt(ə)ri/ *a. rare.* E19. [f. L *elocut-*: see prec., -ORY[2].] = ELOCUTIONARY.

elodea /ɛləˈdiːə, ɪˈləʊdɪə/ *n.* L19. [mod.L, f. Gk *helōdēs* marshy.] Any of various aquatic plants of the N. and S. American genus *Elodea*, of the frogbit family, with whorled leaves and small white or lilac flowers arising from axillary spathes; esp. *E. canadensis* (Canadian waterweed), widely naturalized in Europe.

éloge /elɔːʒ/ *n.* Pl. pronounced same. M16. [Fr., f. L *elogium* short saying or epitaph, altered f. Gk *elegeia* ELEGY: app. confused w. EULOGIUM, EULOGY.] †1 A commendation; an encomium. M16–E19. 2 A discourse in honour of a deceased person; *esp.* that pronounced on a member of the French Academy by his successor. E18.

¶Treated as alien in recent use, but formerly naturalized.

†**elogium** *n.* L16–L18. [L: see prec.] = next.

†**elogy** *n.* L16. [Anglicized f. prec.: see -Y[4].] 1 A saying, an expression; an explanatory inscription. L16–M17. 2 A brief summary of a person's character, *esp.* a eulogy. E17–M18. 3 A biographical notice. Only in M17. 4 A funeral oration. Only in L17.

Elohim /ɛˈləʊhɪm, ɛləʊˈhiːm/ *n.* L16. [Heb. *ʾĕlōhīm*. Cf. JEHOVAH, YAHWEH] In the Old

Testament and Hebrew Scriptures: God. Cf. JEHOVAH, YAHWEH.

Elohist *n. the* author(s) of the Elohistic parts of the Pentateuch (cf. JEHOVIST 2) M19. **Elo'histic** *a.* of, pertaining to, or designating the parts of the Pentateuch in which *Elohim* is used as the name of God M19.

eloign /ɪ'lɔɪn/ *v.t.* Also †**eloin**. L15. [OFr. *esloignier* (mod. *éloigner*) f. Proto-Romance, for late L *elongare*: see ELONGATE *v.*] **1** †**a** Remove, set at a distance (*from*). L15–L17. **b** *refl.* Retire to a distance, go away. Now *rare*. M16. **2** Remove out of legal jurisdiction. *arch.* M16. **3** Take or send away (property). M17.

†**eloignment** *n.* (*a*) removal; (*b*) distance, separation: L17–M18.

elongate /'iːlɒŋgeɪt/ *a.* E19. [Late L *elongatus* pa. pple of *elongare*: see next, -ATE².] Chiefly *Bot.* & *Zool.* Having a slender form; long in relation to its width.

elongate /'iːlɒŋgeɪt/ *v.* Pa. pple **-ated**, †**-ate**. LME. [Late L *elongat-* pa. ppl stem of *elongare*, f. L *e-* E- + *longe* far off, *longus* long: see -ATE³.] †**1** *v.t.* Remove, set at a distance (*from*). LME–M16. **2** *v.t.* Make longer (esp. relative to the width), draw out; prolong. L16. **3** *v.i.* Recede; *obs.* exc. *Astron.*, (of a celestial object) move so as to increase its angular distance from the sun or a particular point on the celestial sphere. M17. **4** *v.i. Bot.* Grow, become longer; have a slender or tapering form. E19.

elongated /'iːlɒŋgeɪtɪd/ *a.* M18. [f. ELONGATE *v.* + -ED¹.] **1** That has been elongated; made longer. M18. **2** Long in relation to its width. M19.

elongation /iːlɒŋ'geɪʃ(ə)n/ *n.* LME. [Late L *elongatio(n-)*, f. as ELONGATE *v.*: see -ATION.] **1** The action or process, or an act, of elongating. LME. **2** *Astron.* Orig., the angular distance of a celestial object from a particular point on the celestial sphere. Now, the difference in celestial longitude between a planet and the sun or between a moon and its planet. LME. †**3** Removal to a distance; departure; remoteness. L15–L18. **4** The state of being elongated; an extension, a continuation. M18. **5** The amount of extension of something under stress, usu. expressed as a percentage of the original length. L19.

1 D. BREWSTER The figure will undergo most curious elongations and contractions.

elongational *a.* L20.

†**elonge** *n.* see ALLONGE.

elope /ɪ'ləʊp/ *v.i.* L16. [AN *aloper*, perh. f. a ME wd rel. to LEAP *v.*] **1** Run away, abscond. Now *rare*. L16. **2** Orig. in *Law*, run away from one's husband with a lover. Now, run away with a lover, or together, esp. to get married. E17.

1 DICKENS The . . valet . . eloped with all the cash and moveables.

elopement *n.* L16. **eloper** *n.* M18.

eloquence /'ɛləkwəns/ *n.* LME. [(O)Fr. *éloquence* f. L *eloquentia*, f. *eloquent-*: see next, -ENCE.] **1** *sing.* & (*arch.*) in *pl.* The fluent, forcible, and apt use of language, so as to appeal to reason or emotion; the quality of being eloquent; eloquent language. LME. †**2** Speech in general. LME–M17. **3** The art of rhetoric. E17.

1 LYTTON Her father's eloquence had descended to her. R. GRAVES The loud, persistent eloquence of an auctioneer in the slave-market. *fig.*: L. HUDSON His musical eloquence left wild beasts spellbound.

eloquent /'ɛləkwənt/ *a.* LME. [(O)Fr. *éloquent* f. L *eloquent-* pres. ppl stem of *eloqui* speak out, f. *e-* E- + *loqui* speak: see -ENT.] Possessing, exercising, or characterized by eloquence; expressive, persuasive. Also foll. by *of*.

A. FORBES His whole attitude eloquent of discouragement. L. DURRELL Pursewarden . . behind an armchair . . was making eloquent gestures at everyone.

elo'quential *a.* (*rare*) of or pertaining to eloquence LME. **eloquently** *adv.* LME.

elpee /ɛl'piː/ *n.* L20. [Repr. pronunc. of *LP* = *long-player*.] A long-playing record.

Elsan /'ɛlsan/ *n.* M20. [App. f. *E. L.* Jackson, manufacturer + SANITATION.] (Proprietary name for) a transportable lavatory employing chemicals to render wastes inoffensive.

else /ɛls/ *adv.* & *n.* [OE *elles* = OFris. *elles*, *-is*, MDu. *els*, OHG *elles*, *alles*, OSw. *äljes* (Sw. *eljest*), genit. sing. (corresp. to Goth. *aljis*) of Gmc wd rel. to L *alius*, Gk *allos*.] **A** *adv.* **1** In addition to, or in place of, the person or thing just mentioned or alluded to; besides; instead. Used after (formerly also bef.) an indef., rel., or interrog. pron. and certain other wds (as *nothing*, *everybody*, *someone*; *much*, *little*). OE. **b** Used after an indef., rel., or interrog. adj., with a n. interposed or (formerly) following. *arch.* OE. **c** In (some, any, what, etc.) other manner, time, or place. Used after advs. or advb. phrs. correl. w. the prons. mentioned in sense 1. ME. **2**†**a** In a different manner; in a different direction. OE–L16. **b** At another time, at other times; on a previous occasion; already. Now *Sc.* LME. **3** In another case; otherwise; if not, (after a neg.) if so. Now usu. (exc. *colloq.* & *literary*) w. prec. *or*. OE. **b** If it is not believed; for confirmation. Now *rare* exc. *dial.* L16. **c** Bef. an adj.: in other respects, otherwise. *rhet.* E19.

1 V. WOOLF We have done little else and thought of little else all day. W. HOLTBY There's no one else who can run the company. D. CUSACK Someone else will take your classes for the day. R. OWEN Girls . . wearing bikinis . . and not much else. A. BROOKNER Edith, what else will you do? *something else*: see SOMETHING *pron.* & *n.* **b** G. CHAPMAN She kept his person from all else recourse. E. GELLNER Sure of his daily bread, and a good deal else besides. R. ADAMS The din obliterated every noise else. **c** R. POLLOK Sinks—where could he else?—to endless woe. G. GREENE Can't we have dinner somewhere else? **3** J. H. NEWMAN Else how should anyone be saved? I. MURDOCH I will succeed in art, or else in business. D. WELCH Don't squirm, else I'll cut you. **or else** (*a*) or if not, or otherwise; (*b*) *colloq.* a warning or threat of the consequences should a previously expressed order, expectation, etc., not be carried out or realized. **c** N. HAWTHORNE To wander with her through places else so desolate.

Comb.: **elsehow** *adv.* (now *dial.*) in some other way, in other ways; **elsewhen** *adv.* (now *rare*) at or in another time, at other times; **elsewhence** *adv.* (*arch.*) from some other place; **elsewhither** *adv.* (*arch.*) (*a*) to some other place; †(*b*) to whatever place.

†**B** *n. ellipt.* Something else; anything else. OE–L16.

SHAKES. *John* Bastards and else.

¶After *nobody*, *somebody*, *anybody*, *everybody* (also *someone* etc.), *what*, & *who*, the possess. is formed by inflecting *else*, e.g. *nobody else's*.

elsewhere /ɛls'wɛː, 'ɛlswɛː/ *adv.* & *n.* OE. [f. ELSE + WHERE.] **A** *adv.* **1** At or in some other place or other places. OE. **2** To some other place. E16.

1 O. MANNING You'd be better off elsewhere. *Gramophone* Financial restrictions in Britain and elsewhere. 2 GOLDSMITH If used ill in our dealings with one man we . . go elsewhere.

B *n.* Another place. L20.

elsewise /'ɛlswʌɪz/ *adv.* M16. [f. ELSE + -WISE.] In some other manner; otherwise.

elsin /'ɛlsɪn/ *n.* Now *Sc.* & *north.* ME. [App. f. MDu. *elsen(e* (Du. *els*) f. Gmc, f. base also of AWL.] An awl.

Elster /'ɛlstə/ *a.* & *n.* M20. [Tributary of the River Elbe in Germany.] *Geol.* (Designating or pertaining to) a Pleistocene glaciation in northern Europe.

Also **Elsterian** /ɛl'stɪərɪən/ *a.* & *n.* M20.

eluant *n.* var. of ELUENT.

eluate /'ɛljuːət, -eɪt/ *n.* M20. [f. L *eluere*: see ELUTE, -ATE³.] *Chem.* The solution obtained by eluting something.

elucidate /ɪ'luːsɪdeɪt, ɪ'ljuː-/ *v.t.* M16. [Late L *elucidat-* pa. ppl stem of *elucidare*, f. *e-* E- + *lucidus* LUCID: see -ATE³.] Make lucid or clear. Now only *fig.*, throw light upon, explain, clarify.

LD MACAULAY His notes have the rare merit of really elucidating the text.

elucidative *a.* = ELUCIDATORY E19. **elucidator** *n.* M17. **elucidatory** *a.* that elucidates something L18.

elucidation /ɪˌluːsɪ'deɪʃ(ə)n, ɪˌljuː-/ *n.* L16. [med.L *elucidatio(n-)*, f. as prec.: see -ATION.] **1** The action or process of elucidating something. L16. **2** Something that elucidates another thing; an explanation. M17.

elucubrate /ɪ'luːkjʊbreɪt, ɪ'ljuː-/ *v.t.* Now *rare*. M16. [L *elucubrat-* pa. ppl stem of *elucubrare* compose by lamplight: see -ATE³.] Compose by working at night; *gen.* study.

elucubration /ɪˌluːkjʊ'breɪʃ(ə)n, ɪ'ljuː-/ *n.* Now *rare*. M17. [Late L *elucubratio(n-)*, f. as prec.: see -ATION.] **1** The action or an act of studying or composing, esp. at night or with great application. M17. **2** The result of this; a literary composition. M17.

elude /ɪ'luːd, ɪ'ljuːd/ *v.t.* M16. [L *eludere*, f. *e-* E- + *ludere* to play.] †**1** Delude; baffle; disappoint. M16–E18. **2** Evade the force of (an argument). E17. **3** Escape adroitly from, evade, (danger, difficulty, a person's grasp, etc.); slip away from (a pursuer); fail to be caught or grasped by (*lit.* & *fig.*). M17. **b** Fail to be discovered or explained by. L18. **4** Evade compliance with or fulfilment of (a law, request, obligation, etc.). M17.

3 P. G. WODEHOUSE Quite a simple and obvious idea, but till now it had eluded her. J. THURBER Zigzagging across the North Atlantic, to elude the last submarines of the war. F. WELDON Praxis would elude her escort . . and slip off home. **b** R. L. STEVENSON He eluded the notice of the officials.

eluder *n.* M17.

eludible /ɪ'luːdɪb(ə)l, ɪ'ljuː-/ *a. rare.* E18. [f. ELUDE *v.* + -IBLE.] Able to be eluded, avoidable, escapable.

¶INELUDIBLE is recorded earlier.

eluent /'ɛljʊənt/ *n.* Also **-ant**. M20. [L *eluent-* pres. ppl stem of *eluere*: see ELUTE, -ENT, -ANT¹.] *Chem.* A solvent used to elute adsorbed material, esp. in chromatography.

Elul /'iːlʌl, 'ɛ-/ *n.* M16. [Heb. *'ĕlūl*.] In the Jewish calendar, the twelfth month of the civil and sixth of the religious year, usu. coinciding with parts of August and September.

elumbated /ɪ'lʌmbeɪtɪd/ *a.* Now *joc. rare.* L18. [f. L *elumbis* having a dislocated hip (f. *e* out + *lumbus* loin) + -ATE³ + -ED¹.] Weakened in the loins.

elusion /ɪ'luːʒ(ə)n, ɪ'ljuː-/ *n.* M16. [Late L *elusio(n-)* deception, trickery, f. L *elus-* pa. ppl stem of *eludere*: see ELUDE, -ION.] †**1** The action of deluding someone; an illusion. M16–L17. **2** (An) escape; (an) evasion. Now *rare*. E17.

elusive /ɪ'luːsɪv, ɪ'ljuː-/ *a.* E18. [f. L *elus-*: see prec., -IVE.] **1** That fails or refuses to be caught by someone or something. Foll. by *of*. E18. **2** Of an argument or answer: evasive. E18. **3** Difficult to catch or grasp (*lit.* & *fig.*); eluding distinct perception or precise definition; difficult to find, remember, or attain. M18.

1 R. SAVAGE The grot, elusive of the noontide ray. 3 M. L. KING Since emancipation, Negroes had searched for the elusive path to freedom. E. F. BENSON Her ideal life . . hitherto had seemed distant and elusive. A. JOHN His deer . . were too elusive; no hit was scored.

elusively *adv.* L19. **elusiveness** *n.* L19.

elusory /ɪ'luːs(ə)ri, ɪ'ljuː-/ *a.* E17. [med.L *elusorius*, f. L *elus-*: see ELUSION, -ORY².] Tending to elude; evasive.

elute /ɪ'luːt, ɪ'ljuːt/ *v.* M18. [L *elut-* pa. ppl stem of *eluere* wash out, f. *e-* E- + *luere* wash.] †**1** *v.t.* Wash out, cleanse. *rare.* Only in M18. **2** *v.t.* Remove (adsorbed material) by washing the adsorbent with a solvent, esp. as a chromatographic technique. M20. **3** *v.i.* Of adsorbed material: be eluted. L20.

elution /ɪ'luːʃ(ə)n, ɪ'ljuː-/ *n.* E17. [Late L *elutio(n-)*, f. as prec.: see -ION.] **1** Washing to remove impurity. Now *rare* or *obs.* E17. **2** The action or process of eluting; removal of adsorbed material. E20.

elutriate /ɪ'luːtrɪeɪt, ɪ'ljuː-/ *v.t.* M18. [L *elutriat-* pa. ppl stem of *elutriare* wash out, f. *e-* E- + *lutriare* wash.] Decant; purify by straining; *techn.* separate (lighter and heavier particles) using a flow of liquid or gas.

elutri'ation *n.* M17. **elutriator** *n.* an apparatus used for elutriating something E20.

eluvial /ɪ'luːvɪəl, ɪ'ljuː-/ *a.* M19. [f. *e-* E- after *alluvial*.] **1** Of, pertaining to, or of the nature of eluvium. M19. 2 Designating soil and soil horizons that have been subject to eluviation. E20.

eluviate /ɪˈluːvɪeɪt, ɪˈljuː-/ *v.t.* E20. [f. L *eluvio* washing away (f. *eluere*: see ELUTE) + -ATION.] Subject (soil) to eluviation. Usu. in *pass.* & as *eluviated* ppl a.

eluviˈation *n.* the movement of esp. colloidal material in suspension or solution through the soil E20.

eluvium /ɪˈluːvɪəm, ɪˈljuː-/ *n.* L19. [mod.L, f. *e-* E- after *alluvium*.] *Physical Geogr.* Debris formed *in situ* by erosion or deposited by the wind.

elvan /ˈɛlv(ə)n/ *n.* E18. [Origin uncertain: perh. f. Corn. f. Welsh *elfen* element.] In Cornwall: hard intrusive igneous rock.

elven /ˈɛlv(ə)n/ *n.* & *a.* [OE *ælfen*, *elfen*, repr. Gmc fem. of ELF *n.*[1]] †**A** *n.* An elf; orig. *spec.* a female elf. OE–ME. **B** *adj.* (*attrib.*) Of or pertaining to elves; that is an elf. Long *arch. rare.* ME.

elver /ˈɛlvə/ *n.* M17. [Alt. of dial. form of EEL *fare*.] A young eel.

elves *n.* pl. of ELF *n.*[1]

elvish /ˈɛlvɪʃ/ *a.* ME. [f. ELF *n.*[1], *elv-* + -ISH[1].] Of or pertaining to an elf or elves; of the nature of or resembling an elf; supernatural, weird; mischievous. Formerly also, spiteful, peevish; (of an illness) troublesome.

Elysian /ɪˈlɪzɪən/ *a.* M16. [f. next + -AN.] Of, pertaining to, or resembling Elysium; paradisal, glorious.

Elysian fields = ELYSIUM I.

Elysium /ɪˈlɪzɪəm/ *n.* & *a.* L16. [L f. Gk *Elusion* (sc. *pedion* plain).] **A** *n.* **1** The home of the blessed after death, *spec.* in *Gk Mythol.* L16. **2** A place or state of perfect happiness. L16. †**B** *adj.* = ELYSIAN. E17–M18.

elytro- /ˈɛlɪtrəʊ/ *comb. form* (now *rare*) of Gk *elutron* sheath: see -O-. Used chiefly in *Med.*, w. sense 'of the vagina'. Cf COLPO-.

elytron /ˈɛlɪtrɒn/ *n.* Pl. **-tra** /-trə/. M18. [Gk *elutron* sheath.] **1** A sheath, a covering, *spec.* that of the spinal cord. Now *rare* or *obs.* M18. **2** Each of the horny forewings of a coleopterous insect, which form protective sheaths for the hind wings. Cf. TEGMEN. L18. **3** Any of a number of plates or scales on the parapodia of some polychaete worms. M19.

elytral *a.* L19.

Elzevir /ˈɛlzɪvɪə/ *a.* & *n.* Also **-vier**. E18. [Du. *Elsevier*, mod.L *Elzevirius*: see below.] **1** (Designating) a book printed in Elzevir type (see sense 2 below) or by a member of the Elsevier family, who were printers in the Netherlands, 1583–1712, and famous for their editions of the classics. E18. **2** (Designating) type or a typeface adopted by the Elseviers or based on theirs. E18.

Elzeˈvirian *a.* & *n.* (*a*) *adj.* of, pertaining to, or in the style of the Elseviers; (*b*) *n.* a collector of Elzevir editions: E19.

em /ɛm/ *n.* ME. [Repr. pronunc. of *M*, *m* as the letter's name; in sense 2 w. ref. to this letter as having a width equal to the body. Cf. EN.] **1** The letter M, m. ME. **2** *Typogr.* A unit of horizontal measurement in typesetting, equal to the body of any size of metal type or the nominal type-size in photosetting, used for calculating the extent of a line or text; *loosely* a length of 12 points. L18.

Comb.: **em dash** an em rule; **em quad, quadrat** a square spacing unit; **em rule** a rule an em long, a dash (used to indicate pauses and parentheses in a text).

'em /əm/ *pron.* Now *colloq.* ME. [Orig. alt. of HEM *pron.* Now regarded as abbrev. of THEM.] Them.

em- /ɪm, ɛm/ *pref.*[1] [Repr. (O)Fr. assim. form of EN-[1] bef. *b*, *p*, and (occas.) *m*.] Used in wds adopted f. Fr. and in Eng. wds modelled on these as a freely productive pref., forming vbs, as *embark*, *embed*, *embitter*, *embrighten*, *empower*, *empurple*. Often with parallel forms in IM-[1].

em- /ɪm, ɛm/ *pref.*[2] (not productive). Repr. Gk assim. form of EN-[2] bef. *b*, *m*, *p*, *ph*.

†**emacerate** *v.t.* E16–E18. [L *emaceratus*, f. *e-* E- + *maceratus* pa. pple of *macerare*: see MACERATE *v.*, -ATE[3].] Emaciate; impoverish (soil).

emaciate /ɪˈmeɪsɪeɪt, ɪˈmeɪʃ-/ *v.t.* & (*rare*) *i.* Pa. pple **-ated**, (now *rare* or *obs.*) **-ate** /-ət/. E17. [L *emaciat-* pa. ppl stem of *emaciare*, f. *e-* E- + *macies* leanness: see -ATE[3].] Make or become abnormally thin or wasted. Chiefly as *emaciated* pa. pple.

emaciation /ɪˌmeɪsɪˈeɪʃ(ə)n, ɪˌmeɪʃ-/ *n.* M17. [L *emaciatio(n-)*, f. as prec.: see -ATION.] The action or process of emaciating someone; the state of being emaciated.

emacity /ɪˈmasɪti/ *n. rare.* M17. [L *emacitas*, f. *emac-*, *emax* fond of buying, f. *emere* buy: see -ACITY.] Fondness for buying.

email /ˈiːmeɪl/ *n.* Also **e-mail**. L20. [Abbrev.] = ELECTRONIC *mail*.

email ombrant /ɛmeɪl ˈɒmbrənt, *foreign* emaːj ɔ̃brɑ̃/ *n. phr.* Also **é-**. Pl. **email ombrants**, ***émaux ombrants*** /emo ɔ̃brɑ̃/. L19. [Fr. *émail ombrant*, f. *émail* enamel + *ombrer* to shade: see -ANT[1].] A form of decoration in which a coloured glaze is laid over intagliated earthenware or porcelain to give a monochrome picture.

emakimono /iˌmakiˈmoːno, ɪmakɪˈməʊnəʊ/ *n.* Pl. same. M20. [Jap., f. *e* painting, picture + MAKIMONO.] A Japanese scroll containing pictures representing a narrative; a pictorial *makimono*.

emalangeni *n.* pl. of LILANGENI.

emanant /ˈɛmənənt/ *a. arch.* E17. [L *emanant-* pres. ppl stem of *emanare*: see next, -ANT[1].] That emanates from a source.

emanate /ˈɛməneɪt/ *v.* M18. [L *emanat-* pa. ppl stem of *emanare*, f. *e-* E- + *manare* to flow.] **1** *v.i.* Come (as) from a source; issue, proceed, (*from*). M18. **2** *v.t.* Cause (esp. something immaterial or intangible) to emanate. L18.

1 E. B. TYLOR Sparks emanating from the flint and steel. 2 W. FAULKNER Bookcases .. emanating an atmosphere of .. meditation.

ˈemanatist *n.* & *a.* (*Theol.*) (*a*) *n.* a person who believes in a theory of emanation; (*b*) *adj.* = EMANATIONIST: M19. **ˈemanative** *a.* tending to emanate or to emit something; resembling or due to emanation; pertaining to a theory of emanation: M17. **ˈemanatory** *a.* (*a*) resembling an emanation, derivative; (*b*) = EMANATIONIST: M17.

emanation /ɛməˈneɪʃ(ə)n/ *n.* L16. [Late L *emanatio(n-)*, f. as prec.: see -ATION.] **I 1** The process of coming from a source; *Theol.* the generation of the Son, or the procession of the Holy Spirit, from the Father. L16. **2** The action of emitting or evolving something. M18. **II 3** A virtue, power, or other abstract quality (regarded as) emanating from something. L16. **b** A necessary consequence. (Foll. by *of*, *from*.) E18. **4** A person who or thing which emanates from God. M17. **5** Something that emanates from a material object, *esp.* something intangible; *spec.* a flash or beam of light. M17. **b** *Sci.* A radioactive gas emitted by a solid as a product of its radioactive decay; *spec.* the element radon. E20.

5 J. GALSWORTHY The savour, like nothing but the emanation of a refined cheese.

emanational *a.* M19. **emanationism** *n.* the doctrine that the (spiritual) universe derives its existence from the essence of God and not from an act of creation out of nothing L19. **emanationist** *a.* of or pertaining to a theory of emanation M20.

emancipate /ɪˈmansɪpeɪt/ *v.t.* Pa. pple **-ated**, (now *poet.*) **-ate** /-ət/. E17. [L *emancipat-* pa. ppl stem of *emancipare*, f. *e-* E- + *mancipium* slave: see -ATE[3]. In sense 3 because emancipation in Roman Law was effected by a fictitious sale.] **I 1** Release from control or restraint, esp. a legal or political one. E17. **b** *Rom.* & *Civil Law.* Set free (a child) from the power of the father or parents, orig. of the Roman *paterfamilias*. M17. **c** *Austral. Hist.* Discharge (a convict) following a pardon, or after he or she has completed a sentence. L18. **2** Cause to be less bound by social conventions, moral restraints, intellectual prejudices, etc. Freq. as *emancipated* ppl a. Cf. LIBERATE *v.* 4. M17.

1 ADAM SMITH A parcel of emancipated slaves. *refl.*: A. STORR Growing up, a child gradually emancipates itself from dependence. 2 J. CONRAD Antonia .. offered him her hand (in her emancipated way).

†**II 3** Enslave. *rare.* E17–M18.

emancipative *a.* = EMANCIPATORY M19. **emancipator** *n.* L18. **emancipatory** /ɪˈmansɪpət(ə)ri, ɪˌmansɪˈpeɪt(ə)ri/ *a.* that has the function or effect of emancipating M17.

emancipation /ɪˌmansɪˈpeɪʃ(ə)n/ *n.* M17. [L *emancipatio(n-)*, f. as prec.: see -ATION.] The action or process of emancipating.

Catholic Emancipation *Hist.* the freeing of Roman Catholics from the civil disabilities imposed by English law until 1829.

emancipationist *n.* an advocate of the emancipation of any section of society, esp. (*Hist.*) slaves E19.

emancipist /ɪˈmansɪpɪst/ *n.* E19. [f. L *emancipare* (see EMANCIPATE) + -IST.] *Austral. Hist.* An ex-convict who had been pardoned or had completed his or her sentence.

†**emane** *v.i.* & *t.* M17. [(O)Fr. *émaner* or L *emanare*: see EMANATE.] **1** *v.i.* = EMANATE 1. M17–E19. **2** *v.t.* = EMANATE 2. *rare.* E18–E19.

emarginate /ɪˈmɑːdʒɪnət/ *a.* L18. [L *emarginatus* pa. pple of *emarginare*: see next, -ATE[2].] *Bot.* & *Zool.* Notched at the edge.

emarginate /ɪˈmɑːdʒɪneɪt/ *v.t.* E17. [L *emarginat-* pa. ppl stem of *emarginare* remove the edge of, f. *e-* E- + *margin-*, *margo* edge: see -ATE[3].] †**1** Remove dead or diseased material from the edge of (a wound or sore). E–M17. **2** *Bot.* & *Zool.* Make emarginate. Chiefly as *emarginated* ppl a. M18.

emargiˈnation *n.* L17.

emasculate /ɪˈmaskjʊlət/ *a.* E17. [L *emasculatus* pa. pple of *emasculare*: see next, -ATE[2].] Emasculated.

emasculate /ɪˈmaskjʊleɪt/ *v.t.* E17. [L *emasculat-* pa. ppl stem of *emasculare* castrate, f. *e-* E- + *masculus* male: see -ATE[3].] **1** Castrate; *Med.* remove the penis of. E17. **2** Deprive of force and vigour; weaken, make effeminate; *esp.* take the force out of (literary work, legislation, etc.) by alterations. E17.

emascuˈlation *n.* E17. **emasculative** *a.* that tends to emasculate L19. **emasculator** *n.* L19. **emasculatory** *a.* = EMASCULATIVE L19.

émaux ombrants *n. phr.* see EMAIL OMBRANT.

embale /ɪmˈbeɪl/ *v.t.* E18. [f. EM-[1] + BALE *n.*[3]] Wrap up in packages.

emball /ɪmˈbɔːl, ɛm-/ *v.t.* L16. [f. EM-[1] + BALL *n.*[1]] **1** Encompass with a sphere. L16. †**2** Invest with an orb as the emblem of royalty. *rare* (Shakes.). Only in E17.

†**emballage** *n. rare.* E18–E19. [Fr., f. *emballer* pack or wrap up, f. as EM-[1] + *balle* BALE *n.*[3]: see -AGE.] **1** Wrappings, packaging. Only in E18. **2** The action of wrapping or packing up. Only in E19.

embalm /ɪmˈbɑːm, ɛm-/ *v.t.* Also †**im-**. ME. [(O)Fr. *embaumer*, f. as EM-[1] + *baume* BALM *n.*[1]] **1** Preserve (a corpse) from decay, orig. by applying spices, now usu. by arterial injection of a preservative. ME. **2** Endow with balmy fragrance. Formerly, anoint with aromatic spices or oil. LME. **3** *fig.* Preserve from oblivion; keep in (usu. honoured) remembrance. E17.

2 MILTON The buxom air, imbalm'd with odours. L. LEE I was daily embalmed with camphorated oils. 3 TENNYSON Embalm in dying songs a dead regret.

embalmer *n.* L16. **embalmment** *n.* (*a*) a preparation used in embalming; (*b*) the process of embalming: E17.

embank /ɪmˈbaŋk, ɛm-/ *v.t.* Also †**im-**. L16. [f. EM-[1], IM-[1] + earlier synon. BANK *v.*[1]] Enclose or confine (a river etc.) by banks, dykes, etc.

embanker *n.* a person who builds embankments M19.

embankment /ɪmˈbaŋkm(ə)nt, ɛm-/ *n.* L18. [f. prec. + -MENT.] **1** A long bank or mound for confining a river etc. within fixed limits or for carrying a road, railway, or canal. L18. **2** The action or process of embanking. L19.

Comb.: **embankment wall** *Austral.* a retaining wall.

embar /ɪmˈbɑː, ɛm-/ *v.t.* Also †**im-**. Infl. **-rr-**. L15. [(O)Fr. *embarrer*, f. as EM-[1] + *barrer* BAR *v.*]

†1 Break inward the bars of (a helmet). Only in L15. †2 Exclude or debar (a person) from something. Also foll. by *to do*. E16–E17. †3 Oppose a barrier to, obstruct; impede (trade) by an embargo; *Law* prohibit or bar by legal enactment. M16–M17. 4 Enclose within bars; cage, imprison. Freq. *fig.* L16.

embarcadero /ɛm,bɑːkəˈdɛːrəʊ/ *n. US.* Pl. **-os.** M19. [Sp., f. *embarcar* embark.] A wharf, a quay.

embarcation *n.* var. of EMBARKATION.

†**embarge** *n.* & *v.* Also **im-**. L16–M17. [f. as next.] = EMBARGO *n.* & *v.*

†**embargement** *n.* L16–E17.

embargo /ɛmˈbɑːgəʊ, ɪm-/ *n.* & *v.* Also †**im-**. See also EMBARGE. E17. [Sp., f. *embargar* arrest, impede, f. Proto-Romance, f. L *in-* IM-[1] + *barra* BAR *n.*[1]] **A** *n.* Pl. **-oes.** 1 An order prohibiting ships from entering or leaving a country's ports, usu. issued in anticipation of war. E17. 2 An official, usu. temporary, prohibition of a particular commercial activity, or of trade in general, with another country. M17. 3 *gen.* A prohibition, an impediment. L17.

2 DEFOE Trade was .. under a general Embargo. 3 J. AUSTEN She wanted to talk, but there seemed an embargo on every subject. *Daily Telegraph* Blamed newspapers for having ignored his embargo—journalists usually receive copies .. a day or two beforehand.

B *v.t.* 1 Seize, confiscate; *spec.* seize, requisition, or impound (ships, goods, etc.) for the service of the State. M17. 2 Place (ships, trade, etc.) under an embargo. M18.

embark /ɪmˈbɑːk, ɛm-/ *v.*[1] Also †**im-**, †**-barque.** M16. [Fr. *embarquer*, f. as EM-[1] + *barque* BARK *n.*[3]] **I** 1 *v.t.* Put or take on board a ship or aircraft. M16. 2 *v.i.* Go on board a ship or aircraft. (Foll. by *on* the ship etc., *for* the destination.) M16. 3 *v.i.* Set out *on* an activity or enterprise, make a start. Also foll. by *upon, in.* M17.

1 E. J. HOWARD The destroyer .. had embarked all the men off the transports. 2 V. CRONIN They embarked on a galley and two small pleasure ships. JANET MORGAN Archie's squadron .. was to move to Southampton to embark for France. 3 J. HERRIOT Once you embark on a life of crime it gets easier all the time.

II 4 *v.t.* Invest (money) in an undertaking; involve (a person) in an activity or enterprise. (Foll. by *in, on.*) L16.

4 E. H. HUTTEN This failure may embark us on two different courses of action.

embarkment *n.* (now *rare*) = EMBARKATION I L16.

†**embark** *v.*[2] var. of IMBARK *v.*[1]

embarkation /ɛmbɑːˈkeɪʃ(ə)n/ *n.* Also **-cation,** †**im-**. M17. [f. EMBARK *v.*[1] + -ATION. In sense 2 f. Fr. *embarcation* f. Sp. *embarcación.*] 1 The action or process of embarking. M17. †2 A ship, a boat. L17–L19. †3 A body of troops on board ship. E–M18.

1 *attrib.*: R. KIPLING Every one was new to embarkation-duty.

Comb.: **embarkation leave**: taken by a member of the armed forces prior to being sent abroad.

†**embarn** *v.* var. of IMBARN.

†**embarque** *v.* var. of EMBARK *v.*[1]

embarras /ɑ̃bara/ *n.* Pl. pronounced same. M17. [Fr., f. as next.] 1 Embarrassment. Now only in phrs. below. M17. 2 An accumulation of driftwood (partially) blocking a waterway. *N. Amer.* Now *rare* or *obs.* L18.

1 ***embarras de choix, de richesse(s)*** /də ʃwa, də riʃɛs/ [Fr. = of choice, of riches] more choices, more resources, than one knows what to do with.

embarrass /ɪmˈbarəs, ɛm-/ *v.t.* E17. [Fr. *embarrasser* f. Sp. *embarazar* prob. f. Port. *embaraçar*, f. *baraço* halter.] 1 Hamper, impede, (a person, movement, or action). E17. 2 Perplex, throw into doubt or difficulty. L17. 3 Make difficult, complicate, (a question, subject, etc.). M18. 4 Cause (a person) to feel awkward, self-conscious, or ashamed. E19.

2 H. H. MILMAN Frederick .. embarrassed them with the choice among five prelates. 4 F. TUOHY He embarrassed everyone by bursting into tears.

embarrassingly *adv.* in an embarrassing manner or degree L19.

embarrassed /ɪmˈbarəst, ɛm-/ *a.* L17. [f. prec. + -ED[1].] 1 Perplexed, confused; having or expressing a feeling of awkwardness or self-consciousness. L17. 2 Of a route: obstructed. Now only *fig.* E18. **b** Having difficulty in meeting financial obligations; short of money. L19. 3 Of a sentence, narrative, etc.: involved, confused. Now *rare* or *obs.* M18.

1 O. MANNING Arnold gave an embarrassed grunt and excused his emotions. 2 W. S. GILBERT Whose middle-class lives are embarrassed by wives who long to parade as 'My Lady'.

embarrassedly *adv.* L19.

embarrassment /ɪmˈbarəsm(ə)nt, ɛm-/ *n.* L17. [f. EMBARRASS + -MENT.] 1 An embarrassed state or condition; *esp.* a feeling of awkward confusion or self-consciousness. L17. **b** A state of financial difficulty; shortage of money. M19. 2 A thing which embarrasses; in *pl.*, financial difficulties. E18.

Phrases: **embarrassment of riches** = EMBARRAS *de richesse(s)*.

†**embarren** *v.t.* L15–E19. [f. EM-[1] + BARREN *a.*] Make barren.

†**embase** *v.t.* Also **im-**. M16. [Alt. of ABASE, DEBASE, by substitution of EM-[1], IM-[1].] 1 Make lower (*lit.* & *fig.*); reduce in rank or dignity; humiliate; degrade. M16–M19. 2 Debase (coin); *fig.* impair, corrupt. M16–M18. 3 Devalue (coinage); reduce the price of (goods); *fig.* depreciate, discredit. L16–L17.

†**embasement** *n.* L16–E18.

embassade, -ador, -adress *ns.* see AMBASSADE, -ADOR, -ADRESS.

embassage /ˈɛmbəsɪdʒ/ *n.* Also (earlier) **am-** /am-/. L15. [f. OFr. *ambasse* message, embassy + -AGE.] 1 = EMBASSY I. *arch.* L15. 2 The business or message of an ambassador. E16. 3 A body of people sent as a deputation to a head of State; an ambassador and his or her retinue or staff. M16.

embassy /ˈɛmbəsi/ *n.* Also (now *rare*) **am-** /am-/. L16. [OFr. *ambassé, -axée, -asée*, corresp. to Prov. *ambaissada*, OSp. *ambaxada*, It. *ambasciata*, med.L *ambasc(i)ata*, all f. Proto-Romance: see AMBASSADOR, -Y[5].] 1 The position or function of an ambassador. Also, the sending of ambassadors. L16. †2 = EMBASSAGE 2. L16–M18. 3 The official residence or offices of an ambassador. Also = EMBASSAGE 3. L16.

1 SHAKES. *L.L.L.* Here comes in embassy The French king's daughter. SAKI Scuttering footsteps and hurried embassies for outside help. 3 LYTTON A brilliant ball at the Palazzo of the Austrian embassy at Naples. R. GRAVES Send an embassy to the Great King.

embathe /ɪmˈbeɪð, ɛm-/ *v.t. poet.* Also †**im-**. L15. [f. EM-[1], IM-[1] + BATHE *v.*] Bathe; immerse; wet.

embattle /ɪmˈbat(ə)l, ɛm-/ *v.*[1] Also †**im-** ME. [OFr. *embataillier*, f. as EM-[1], BATTLE *n.*] 1 *v.t.* Set in battle array; make ready or arm for battle. ME. 2 *v.refl.* & †*i.* Take up a battle position. LME. 3 *v.t.* Fortify (a building, town, etc.). LME.

¶In sense 3 not always distinguishable from EMBATTLE *v.*[2]

embattled *ppl a.*[1] (*a*) that has been embattled; armed; fortified; (*b*) that is under attack, threat, or pressure; subject to conflict or controversy. L15. **embattlement** *n.*[1] the state of being embattled L20.

embattle /ɪmˈbat(ə)l, ɛm-/ *v.*[2]*t.* LME. [f. EM-[1] + OFr. *bataillier*, f. as BATTLE *n.*: cf. BATTLEMENT.] Provide with battlements. Cf. EMBATTLE *v.*[1]

embattled *ppl a.*[2] (*a*) having battlements; (*b*) (esp. *Her.*) having an edge shaped like battlements: LME. **embattlement** *n.*[2] = BATTLEMENT LME. **embattling** *n.* (*Her.*) a battlement or crenellation M18.

embay /ɪmˈbeɪ, ɛm-/ *v.*[1]*t.* L16. [f. EM-[1] + BAY *n.*[3]] 1 Enclose (as) in a bay, recess; shut in; surround. L16. 2 Put or force (a boat) into a bay. E17. 3 In *pass.* Be formed into bays. M19.

1 W. C. WILLIAMS Beds for the poor and sick embayed into the wall. 2 C. FRANCIS Ships were embayed between two headlands and tacked back and forth for days. 3 G. E. HUTCHINSON Embayed coast lines.

embayment *n.* a bay; a recess in a coastline forming a bay; a recess like a bay: E19.

†**embay** *v.*[2]*t. poet.* L16–M18. [f. EM-[1] + BAY *v.*[3]] Bathe; drench, steep.

embed /ɪmˈbɛd, ɛm-/ *v.t.* Also **im-** /ɪm-/. Infl. **-dd-**. L18. [f. EM-[1], IM-[1] + BED *n.*] 1 Fix firmly in a surrounding mass of solid or semi-solid material. L18. 2 Of a surrounding mass: enclose firmly. M19. 3**a** Place or secure within something else, esp. within a larger or firmer entity; cause to be wholly contained within. M19. **b** *Ling.* Place (a clause etc.) within a larger unit of meaning, e.g. another clause, a sentence, etc. Freq. as *embedded* ppl a. M20. **c** *Math.* Incorporate (a structured set) into a larger structure while preserving the main features; *spec.* represent (a graph) *in* a given surface so that no two edges intersect. M20.

1 H. READ The colour and shape of every stone embedded in the footpath. 3a J. R. LOWELL The winged seeds of his thought embed themselves in the memory. H. KISSINGER He embedded his main observations in easy banter. c *Personal Computer World* You can .. embed validation rules within the program that defines the screen layout.

embeddable *a.* M20. **embeddedness** *n.* the state or property of being embedded E20. **embedment** *n.* (*a*) the action of embedding; (*b*) a thing which contains something else embedded in it: E19.

embellish /ɪmˈbɛlɪʃ, ɛm-/ *v.t.* Also †**im-**. LME. [(O)Fr. *embelliss-* lengthened stem of *embellir*, f. as EM-[1] + *bel* beautiful: see -ISH[2].] Orig., beautify. Now *spec.*, adorn, ornament, decorate; heighten (a narrative) with elaborate or fictitious additions.

S. HAZZARD Brushes and hand-mirrors .., each embellished with a crest. R. COBB A very personal account .. often embellished by my own imagination.

embellisher *n.* L15.

embellishment /ɪmˈbɛlɪʃm(ə)nt, ɛm-/ *n.* Also †**im-**. L16. [f. prec. + -MENT. Cf. (O)Fr. *embellissement.*] 1 The action of embellishing. L16. 2 A thing which embellishes; an ornament, a decoration, an adornment; also, an exaggeration. M17.

ember /ˈɛmbə/ *n.*[1] [OE *ǣmyrġe, ǣmerġe* = MLG *ēmere*, OHG *eimuria* pyre (MHG *eimere*), ON *eimyrje* (Da. *emmer*, Sw. *mörja*) embers, f. Gmc base. For the intrusive *b* cf. *slumber.*] 1 A hot fragment left in a dying fire, or cast out of a fire. Usu. in *pl.* OE. 2 In *pl. fig.* The fading traces of a passing activity, state, etc. E16.

2 J. BENTHAM Success does not .. arise out of the embers of ill-success.

embered *a.* strewn with or burnt to embers L16.

ember /ˈɛmbə/ *n.*[2] *dial.* Also **emmer** /ˈɛmə/, **immer** /ˈɪmə/, & other vars. L17. [Norw. *immer, imbre.*] The great northern diver, *Gavia immer.* Also more fully *ember goose.*

Ember /ˈɛmbə/ *a.* & *n.*[3] Also **e-**. [OE *ymbren*: perh. alt. of *ymbryne* period, revolution of time, f. *ymb* about, around + *ryne* course; perh. based partly on eccl.L *quatuor tempora* (cf. G *Quatember*).] *Chr. Ch.* **A** *adj.* Designating each of four periods, one in each season of the year, which were times of fasting but in Anglican Churches are now associated with ordinations. Chiefly in *Ember day(s)* below. OE.

Ember day a Wednesday, Friday, or Saturday immediately after (1) the first Sunday in Lent, (2) Pentecost, (3) Holy Cross Day (14 September), or (4) St Lucy's Day (13 December), which traditionally have been fast days. **Ember eve** *rare* (Shakes.) the vigil of an Ember day. **Embertide** one of the seasons or times of Ember days. **Ember week** a week in which Ember days occur.

†**B** *n.* An Ember day. OE–L16.

embetter /ɪmˈbɛtə, ɛm-/ *v.t.* Now *rare.* Also †**im-**. M16. [f. EM-[1], IM-[1] + BETTER *a.*] Make better.

embezzle /ɪmˈbɛz(ə)l, ɛm-/ *v.t.* LME. [AN *embesiler*, f. as EM-[1] + *besiler* in same sense (whence BEZZLE *v.*) = OFr. *besillier* maltreat, ravage, destroy; of unkn. origin.] †1 Make off with (provisions, money, etc.); steal. LME–M18. **b** Steal or fraudulently destroy (a legal document); tamper with (any document). LME–L17. †2 Weaken, impair. M16–L17. **b** Squander, dissipate. L16–L18. 3 Esp. of an employee or servant: misappropriate or steal (money, goods, etc.) belonging to or on their way to an employer or master, in violation of trust or duty. L16.

3 G. GREENE A sense of guilt.. as though he had embezzled the company's money.

embezzlement *n.* the action or an act of embezzling; misappropriation of entrusted money etc.: M16. **embezzler** *n.* M17.

embind /ɪmˈbʌɪnd, ɛm-/ *v.t. rare.* Also †**im-**. Pa. t. & pple **-bound** /-ˈbaʊnd/. E17. [f. EM-[1], IM-[1] + BIND *v.*] Confine, hold fast.

embitter /ɪmˈbɪtə, ɛm-/ *v.t.* Also †**im-**. L15. [f. EM-[1], IM-[1] + BITTER *a.*] **I 1** Make (a person or feeling) intensely hostile, bitter, or discontented; exacerbate (a quarrel). L15. **2** Increase the bitterness or pain of. M17. **3** Spoil the sweetness of, sour, (existence, pursuits, etc.). L17.

1 R. LINDNER A soured woman.. embittered for life by her illegitimacy. 2 J. R. GREEN His failure was embittered by heavier disasters elsewhere.

II 4 Make bitter to the taste. Now *rare.* E17.

embitterer *n.* M18. **embitterment** *n.* the action of embittering; the state of being embittered: M17.

emblaze /ɪmˈbleɪz, ɛm-/ *v.*[1]*t.* Also **im-** /ɪm-/. L15. [f. EM-[1], IM-[1] + BLAZE *n.*[1]] **1** Light up, cause to glow. L15. **2** Fill with flames, set ablaze. E18.

emblazer *n.* L18.

emblaze /ɪmˈbleɪz, ɛm-/ *v.*[2]*t.* Now *rare* or *obs.* E16. [f. EM-[1] + BLAZE *v.*[2]] **1** Adorn with heraldic devices; (infl. by EMBLAZE *v.*[1]) make resplendent. E16. †**2** Describe in heraldic terms; represent heraldically; depict or paint in colour. L16–L18. **3** Inscribe or portray conspicuously. L16. **4** Make famous or notorious. L16.

¶Largely superseded by EMBLAZON *v.*

†**emblazon** *n.* M16–M17. [App. f. the vb.] The heraldic depiction of armorial bearings.

emblazon /ɪmˈbleɪz(ə)n, ɛm-/ *v.t.* L16. [f. EM-[1] + BLAZON *v.*] **1** Inscribe or portray conspicuously, (as) on a heraldic shield; adorn with heraldic devices or conspicuously; depict or paint (armorial bearings) in colour; inscribe with words. L16. **2** Celebrate, extol; make illustrious. L16.

1 J. MORLEY He emblazoned it on a banner. J. MARQUAND The lantern carriers.. bearing lights emblazoned with the master's name. 2 J. BARZUN The .. word 'education',.. which we now find emblazoned in all the mansions of life.

¶Cf. BLAZON *v.*

emblazoner *n.* L16. **emblazonment** *n.* the action of emblazoning; a heraldic device or decoration: L18.

emblazonry /ɪmˈbleɪz(ə)nri, ɛm-/ *n.* M17. [f. prec. + -RY.] **1** = BLAZONRY 1; symbolic ornamentation. M17. **2** = BLAZONRY 2; brilliant representation or embellishment (visual or verbal). E19.

emblem /ˈɛmbləm/ *n.* E17. [L *emblema* inlaid work, raised ornament f. Gk *emblēma* insertion, f. *emballein* throw in, insert, f. as EM-[2] + *ballein* throw.] **1** An object, or a picture of one, serving as a symbolic representation of a quality, action, type of person, etc. E17. **2** A heraldic device or symbolic object used as the distinctive badge of a family, nation, organization, etc. E17. **3** A symbol or token *of* something; a typical instance; a person who exemplifies a specified quality. E17. **4** A drawing or picture expressing a moral fable or allegory; a fable or allegory which may be so expressed. E17. †**5** An ornament of inlaid work. E17–L18.

1 K. CLARK Those two emblems of lust and ferocity, the unicorn and the lion. D. STOREY A row of banners .. each bearing the emblem of a saint or an apostle. 2 TOLKIEN A small shield.. bore the running horse.. that was the emblem of the House of Eorl. 3 P. ACKROYD Their first encounter.. had become an emblem of the way things were.

Comb.: **emblem book**: containing drawings accompanied by allegorical interpretations.

emblemize *v.t.* = EMBLEMATIZE M17.

emblem /ˈɛmbləm/ *v.t.* L16. [f. (as) prec.] Be the emblem of; express by means of an emblem, symbolize; provide with an emblem.

emblema /ɛmˈbliːmə/ *n.* Pl. **-mata** /-mətə/. M19. [L *emblema*: see EMBLEM *n.*] *Class. Art.* A carved or mounted ornament in relief.

emblematic /ɛmbləˈmatɪk/ *a.* M17. [f. Gk *emblēmat-, -ma* (see EMBLEM *n.*) + -IC, after Fr. *emblématique*: see -ATIC.] Pertaining to, of the nature of, or serving as an emblem; symbolic, typical, (*of*).

emblematical *a.* = EMBLEMATIC M17. **emblematically** *adv.* E17.

emblematise *v.* var. of EMBLEMATIZE.

emblematist /ɛmˈblɛmətɪst/ *n.* M17. [f. as EMBLEMATIC: see -IST.] A person who invents or uses emblems; a composer of allegories.

emblematize /ɛmˈblɛmətʌɪz/ *v.t.* Also **-ise**. E17. [f. as prec. + -IZE.] **1** Serve as an emblem of; represent mystically, allusively, or allegorically. E17. **2** Of a person: represent using an emblem. M18.

emblements /ˈɛmblɪm(ə)nts/ *n.pl.* L15. [OFr. *emblaement*, f. *emblaer*, *emblaier*, (also mod.) *emblaver* sow with corn, f. *blé* corn.] *Law.* The profits of sown land; *spec.* annually produced plant crops, deemed personal property even when still attached to the soil, and even after unexpected loss of the land before the harvest.

emblic /ˈɛmblɪk/ *n.* M16. [med.L *emblicus* f. Arab. *amlaj* f. OPers. (Pers. *ām(u)la*): cf. Skt *āmalaka*.] (The fruit of) a deciduous tree, *Phyllanthus emblica*, of the euphorbia family, native to tropical Asia.

†**embliss** *v.t. rare.* LME–L18. [f. EM-[1] + BLISS *n.*] Make happy.

embloom /ɪmˈbluːm, ɛm-/ *v.t.* Now *rare* or *obs.* E16. [f. EM-[1] + BLOOM *n.*[1]] Give a bloom to.

emblossom /ɪmˈblɒsəm, ɛm-/ *v.t.* Also **im-** /ɪm-/. M18. [f. EM-[1], IM-[1] + BLOSSOM *n.*] Load or cover with blossoms.

embodiment /ɪmˈbɒdɪm(ə)nt, ɛm-/ *n.* Also (now *rare*) **im-** /ɪm-/. E19. [f. EMBODY + -MENT.] **1** A material or actual thing or person in which an abstract principle, concept, etc., is realized or concretely expressed; a person who is a typical expression *of* a quality, sentiment, etc. E19. **b** The corporeal habitation of a soul. M19. **2** The action of embodying; the process or state of embodying. M19.

1 H. KELLER I thought the professors were the embodiment of wisdom. J. RABAN The city has always been an embodiment of hope. 2 F. HALL Souls.. condemned, by reason of sin, to repeated embodiment.

embody /ɪmˈbɒdi, ɛm-/ *v.* Also (now *rare*) **im-** /ɪm-/. M16. [f. EM-[1], IM-[1] + BODY *n.*, after L *incorporare*.] **1** *v.t.* Provide (a spirit) with a bodily form. M16. **2** *v.t.* Unite into one body or mass; incorporate in a larger whole. M16. **b** Include as a constituent part. M19. **3** *v.t.* Give a material or corporeal character to (what is spiritual). *rare.* M17. **4** *v.t.* Give a material or discernible form to (an abstract principle, concept, etc.); express (such a principle etc.) *in* such a form. M17. **b** Of a material or actual thing or person: be an embodiment of (an abstract concept, quality, etc.). L19. **5a** *v.t.* Form (people) into a body, esp. for military purposes. M17. **b** *v.i.* Form or join a (military) body. M17. †**6** *v.i.* & *refl.* Coalesce, form a homogeneous mass. M17–E18.

2 J. MACKINTOSH Much of these treaties has been embodied into the general law of Europe. *New Scientist* When emulsion paints dry, the individual polymer particles must coalesce and embody the pigment. b H. MACMILLAN The various documents embodying the various agreements. 4 J. E. T. ROGERS A popular notion, embodied in a rhyming couplet. W. S. CHURCHILL The Covenant.. embodied the.. resolve of a whole people to perish rather than submit. b G. BROWN Nobody embodied.. the whole outlook, attitude of the Communist machine bureaucrat as did Kruschev.

embodier *n.* M17.

embog /ɪmˈbɒg, ɛm-/ *v.t.* Also †**im-**. Infl. **-gg-**. E17. [f. EM-[1], IM-[1] + BOG *n.*[1]] Plunge into a bog; hamper (as) in a bog.

†**emboil** *v.t.* & *i. rare* (Spenser). Only in L16. [f. EM-[1] + BOIL *v.*] (Cause to) boil with rage.

†**embold** *v.t.* Also **im-**. LME–E17. [f. EM-[1], IM-[1] + BOLD *a.*] Make bold, embolden.

embolden /ɪmˈbəʊld(ə)n, ɛm-/ *v.* Also **im-** /ɪm-/. L16. [f. EM-[1], IM-[1] + BOLDEN.] **1** *v.t.* Make bold or bolder; encourage, incite. L16. **2** *v.i.* Use or change to a bold typeface. L20.

1 SAKI You embolden one to make daring requests.

emboldener *n.* M19.

embolectomy /ɛmbəˈlɛktəmi/ *n.* E20. [f. EMBOL(US + -ECTOMY.] Surgical removal of an embolus; an instance of this.

emboli *n.* pl. of EMBOLUS.

embolic /ɪmˈbɒlɪk, ɛm-/ *a.* M19. [f. EMBOLUS, EMBOLY + -IC.] **1** *Med.* Pertaining to or caused by an embolus. M19. **2** *Biol.* Characterized by emboly. L19.

embolisation *n.*, **embolise** *v.* vars. of EMBOLIZATION, EMBOLIZE.

embolism /ˈɛmbəlɪz(ə)m/ *n.* LME. [Late L *embolismus* f. Gk *embolismos*, f. *emballein* throw in, f. as EM-[2] + *ballein* throw: see -ISM.] **1** The periodic intercalation of days or a month in a calendar based on a non-solar year to correct the accumulating discrepancy between the calendar year and the solar year; the intercalated period. LME. **2** *Chr. Ch.* In some Eucharistic liturgies, a prayer following and based on the final petition of the Lord's Prayer. E18. **3** *Med.* The blocking of a blood-vessel by something carried into it by the bloodstream (usu. a blood clot but sometimes a tumour, air, fat, etc.). M19. **b** = EMBOLUS 2. E20.

emboˈlismic *a.* of or pertaining to intercalation; intercalary: M18.

embolismus /ɛmbəˈlɪzməs/ *n.* LME. [L: see prec.] †**1** = EMBOLISM 1. *rare.* LME–L18. **2** = EMBOLISM 2. L19.

embolium /ɪmˈbɒlɪəm, ɛm-/ *n.* M19. [L f. Gk *embolion* insertion, f. *emballein*: see EMBOLISM, -IUM.] The marginal part of the corium in some heteropteran insects.

embolization /ɛmbəlʌɪˈzeɪʃ(ə)n/ *n.* Also **-isation**. L17. [f. EMBOLISM, EMBOLIZE: see -IZATION.] †**1** Intercalation, embolism. *rare.* Only in L17. **2** *Med.* The introduction or occurrence of an embolus; the process of embolizing. M20.

embolize /ˈɛmbəlʌɪz/ *v.* Also **-ise**. E20. [f. EMBOLUS, EMBOLISM + -IZE.] *Med.* **1** *v.t.* Introduce an embolus artificially into; cause embolism in. E20. **2** *v.i.* Develop into or form an embolus. M20.

embolus /ˈɛmbələs/ *n.* Pl. **-li** /-lʌɪ, -liː/. M17. [L = piston of a pump, f. Gk *embolos* peg, stopper.] †**1** *Mech.* Something inserted or moving in another; *esp.* the piston of a syringe. M17–M18. **2** *Med.* The blood clot or other object or substance which causes embolism. M19.

emboly /ˈɛmbəli/ *n.* L19. [Gk *embolē* w. assim. to -Y[3].] *Biol.* Formation of a gastrula by invagination of the blastula. Cf. EPIBOLY.

embonpoint /ɑ̃bɔ̃pwɛ̃/ *n.* & *a.* L17. [Fr. phr. *en bon point* in good condition.] **A** *n.* Plumpness. L17.

G. CLARE A good paunch, or.. a bit of embonpoint, added dignity to a man.

B *adj.* Plump. E19.

†**emborder** *v.t.* Also **im-**. M16–M17. [f. EM-[1], IM-[1] + BORDER *n.*] Provide *with* a border; place or set as a border.

embosom /ɪmˈbʊz(ə)m, ɛm-/ *v.t.* Also **im-** /ɪm-/. L16. [f. EM-[1], IM-[1] + BOSOM *n.*] **1** Take to or cherish in one's bosom; embrace. Now *rare.* L16. **2** Enclose, conceal, shelter; envelop, surround. (Foll. by *in*, *with*.) Freq. in *pass.* E17.

2 P. EGAN A small snug country village embosomed in trees.

emboss /ɪmˈbɒs, ɛm-/ *v.*[1] Also †**im-**. LME. [f. OFr. base of Fr. †*imbocer*, *embosser*, f. as EM-[1] + *boce* (mod. *bosse*) BOSS *n.*[1]] **I 1** *v.t.* Cause to bulge or swell out; cover with protuberances. LME. †**b** *fig.* Foll. by *out*: inflate (style, language). M16–M17. **2** Carve, mould, or decorate with figures in relief; (of figures) stand out as ornaments upon. Also, represent (a subject) in relief. LME. **3** Ornament (as) with bosses; decorate sumptuously. L16.

1 SOUTHEY Its fretted roots Embossed the bank. 2 R. SUTCLIFF Look at the pattern embossed here on your dagger-sheath. V. AUSTIN The work is held face down .. and embossed with domed punches. 3 W. COWPER Studs.. emboss his iron door. W. S. LANDOR Did we not.. Emboss our bosoms with the daffodils.

II *v.i.* †**4** Bulge, be convex. *rare.* LME–L16.

embosser *n.* E17. **embossing** *n.* (*a*) the action of the vb; (*b*) embossed ornamentation or lettering; †(*c*) a swelling, a protuberance: LME.

emboss /ɪmˈbɒs, ɛm-/ *v.*[2] Also †**im-**. LME. [OFr. *emboscher* var. of *embuschier* AMBUSH *v.*] †**1** *v.i.* Of a hunted animal: plunge into a wood or thicket. LME–L17. **b** *v.t.* Drive (a hunted animal) to extremity. L16–M18. **2** *v.t.* In *pass.* Be exhausted; foam at the mouth. Now *rare.* L15. **3** *v.t.* Cover with foam. *arch.* M16.

†**emboss** *v.*[3]*t.* L16–E17. [Origin uncertain: perh. f. EM-[1] + as BOSS *n.*[2]] Encase *in* armour; plunge (a weapon) in an enemy's body. Also *fig.*, in *pass.*, be wrapped *in* ease.

embossed /ɪmˈbɒst, ɛm-/ *ppl a.* Also †**im-**. LME. [f. EMBOSS *v.*[1] + -ED[1].] †**1** Humpbacked. Only in LME. **2** Carved or moulded in relief; decorated or ornamented in relief; (of figures, lettering, etc.) standing out in relief. M16. **3** Covered with bosses; richly decorated. *rare.* L16. †**4** Bulging, swollen; inflated (*lit.* & *fig.*). L16–M17.

2 R. COBB Lined notepaper headed with an embossed harp.

embossment /ɪmˈbɒsm(ə)nt, ɛm-/ *n.* Also †**im-**. E17. [f. EMBOSS *v.*[1] + -MENT.] **1** A swelling, a protuberance. Now *rare.* E17. **2** An embossed figure; embossed ornamentation. E17. **3** The action or process of embossing. *rare.* E19.

embosture /ɪmˈbɒstjʊə, ɛm-/ *n. arch. rare.* Also †**im-**. E17. [f. EMBOSS *v.*[1] after *sculpture.*] = EMBOSSMENT.

embothrium /ɪmˈbɒθrɪəm, ɛm-/ *n.* L19. [mod.L, f. EM-[2] + Gk *bothrion* small pit, w. ref. to the anthers.] Any of various S. American evergreen shrubs of the genus *Embothrium* of the protea family, esp. *E. coccineum*, grown for its conspicuous scarlet flowers.

embouchement /ɑ̃buʃmɑ̃/ *n. rare.* M19. [Fr., f. *emboucher*: see next, -MENT.] **1** The mouth of a river. M19. **2** *Anat.* The point at which one vessel leads into another. *rare.* L19.

embouchure /ɑ̃bufyːr, ɒmbʊˈʃʊə/ *n.* M18. [Fr., f. *s'emboucher* refl., discharge itself by a mouth, f. *emboucher* put in or to the mouth, f. as EM-[1] + *bouche* mouth: see -URE.] **1** *Mus.* The manner in which a player's mouth and lips are placed when playing a woodwind or brass instrument. M18. **b** The mouthpiece of a musical instrument, esp. of a flute. M19. **2** The mouth of a river; the opening of a valley on to a plain. L18.

embound /ɪmˈbaʊnd, ɛm-/ *v.t. poet. arch.* Also **im-** /ɪm-/. LME. [f. EM-[1], IM-[1] + BOUND *n.*[1]] Set bounds to; confine.

embourgeoisé /ɑ̃burʒwaze/ *a.* M20. [Fr., pa. pple of *embourgeoiser* make or become bourgeois, f. as EM-[1], BOURGEOIS *a.* & *n.*[2]] That has been bourgeoisified.

embourgeoisement /ɑ̃burʒwazmɑ̃/ *n.* M20. [Fr., f. *embourgeoiser*: see prec., -MENT.] = BOURGEOISIFICATION.

embourgeoisification /ɒmˌbʊəʒwɑːzɪfɪˈkeɪʃ(ə)n/ *n.* L20. [Blend of EMBOURGEOISEMENT and BOURGEOISIFICATION.] = BOURGEOISIFICATION.

embow /ɪmˈbəʊ, ɛm-/ *v.t. arch.* Also †**im-**. LME. [f. EM-[1], IM-[1] + BOW *n.*[1]] **1** Bend into a bow. *rare. obs.* exc. in EMBOWED 2. LME. **2** *Archit.* Arch, vault, (a roof). (Earlier as EMBOWED 1.) L15. †**3** Enclose as in a sphere; encircle. E–M17.

embowment *n.* (*rare*) E17.

embowed /ɪmˈbəʊd, ɛm-/ *ppl a.* Also **im-** /ɪm-/. LME. [f. EMBOW + -ED[1].] **1** *Archit.* Arched, vaulted; curved outwards. LME. **2** Bent into the form of a bow; convex. L16. **3** *Her.* Bent, *esp.* (*a*) (of an arm) bent at the elbow; (*b*) (of a dolphin) with the body arched. E17.

embowel /ɪmˈbaʊ(ə)l, ɛm-/ *v.t.* Now *rare.* Also †**im-**. E16. [In sense 1 f. OFr. *emboweler* alt. of *esboueler*, f. *es-* EX-[1] + *bouel* BOWEL. In sense 2 f. EM-[1], IM-[1] + BOWEL.] **1** = DISEMBOWEL. E16. †**2** Put or convey into the bowels or the depths. L16–M17.

emboweller *n.* (*rare*) L16.

embowelled /ɪmˈbaʊ(ə)ld, ɛm-/ *ppl a.* L15. [f. prec. + -ED[1].] †**1** That has the bowels full. Only in L15. **2** Disembowelled. Now *rare* or *obs.* L16. **3** Concealed in the bowels or heart of something. E17.

embower /ɪmˈbaʊə, ɛm-/ *v.* Also (*arch.*) **im-** /ɪm-/. L16. [f. EM-[1], IM-[1] + BOWER *n.*[1]] **1** *v.t.* Shelter or enclose (as) in a bower; surround with foliage. L16. †**2** *v.i.* Take shelter, lodge as in a bower. L16–E17.

1 B. TARKINGTON George .. stood .. embowered in the big red and gold drawing room.

embowerment *n.* the action of embowering M19.

†**embowl** *v.t.* & *i. rare.* L16–L19. [f. EM-[1] + BOWL *n.*[1]] Make or grow into the form of a globe.

embox /ɪmˈbɒks, ɛm-/ *v.t.* E17. [f. EM-[1] + BOX *n.*[2]] Set (as) in a box.

embrace /ɪmˈbreɪs, ɛm-/ *v.*[1] & *n.* Also †**im-**. ME. [OFr. *embracer* (mod. *embrasser*) f. Proto-Romance base, f. L IM-[1] + *bracchium* arm (cf. BRACE *n.*[1]).] **A** *v.* **1** *v.t.* Encircle, surround; enclose. ME. **2** *v.t.* & (usu. w. pl. subj.) *i.* Hold (a person, each other) closely in the arms, usu. as a sign of affection; *euphem.* have sexual intercourse with. LME. **b** *v.t.* Kiss, esp. on the cheek. M20. †**3** *v.t.* Cultivate (a virtue, disposition, etc.). LME–E17. **4** *v.t.* Take in with the eye or mind; perceive, comprehend. LME. **5** *v.t.* Accept readily or with good grace; avail oneself of (an offer, an opportunity, etc.). LME. †**b** Accept as a friend; welcome the services of (a person). M16–M17. †**6** *v.t.* Take (a matter) in hand, undertake. LME–E19. **7** *v.t.* Take up, adopt, (a doctrine, opinions, a course of action, a profession, etc.). M16. **8** *v.t.* Include, contain; comprise. L16.

1 SHAKES. *Coriol.* You'll see your Rome embrac'd with fire. J. CONRAD The great waters which embrace the continents of this globe. 2 D. H. LAWRENCE Then the two men embraced. C. JACKSON She .. put her arms around him and embraced him passionately. 4 E. R. CONDER The infinite .. the intellect can seize though not embrace. 5 H. JAMES I don't embrace all my mother's quarrels. 7 E. A. FREEMAN The .. home of those .. who embraced the monastic life. W. LIPPMANN They turned away from liberalism and embraced collectivism as a method of ordering affairs. 8 E. WILSON A system of law which should embrace all the different moral systems and thus be universally acceptable. C. C. TRENCH His military interests embraced a passion for uniforms, tactics, weapons and armies.

B *n.* An act of embracing; a clasp, a hug; *euphem.* an act of sexual intercourse. LME.

MILTON In embraces forcible and foule Ingendring with me. A. WILSON He put his arms around her and held her for a moment in a close embrace.

embraceable *a.* able to be embraced; inviting an embrace: M19. **embracingly** *adv.* (*a*) in the manner of a person who embraces; (*b*) comprehensively: M17. **embracingness** *n.* comprehensiveness L19.

embrace /ɪmˈbreɪs, ɛm-/ *v.*[2]*t.* & *i.* Now *rare* or *obs.* LME. [App. back-form. f. EMBRACER *n.*[2]] *Law.* Attempt to influence (a jury or juror) corruptly.

†**embrace** *v.*[3] L15–L16. [f. EM-[1] + BRACE *n.*[1]] Fasten with a brace or buckle. (Foll. by *to.*)

embracement /ɪmˈbreɪsm(ə)nt, ɛm-/ *n.* Also †**im-**. L15. [OFr., f. *embracer*: see EMBRACE *v.*[1], -MENT.] **1** An embrace. *arch.* L15. †**2** An undertaking. L15–M17. **3** A willing acceptance of a doctrine, something offered, etc. M16. **4** The action or an act of perceiving or comprehending. L16. **5** The action of clasping or encircling; the state of being clasped or encircled. E17.

embraceor *n.* var. of EMBRACER *n.*[2]

embracer /ɪmˈbreɪsə, ɛm-/ *n.*[1] Also †**im-**. LME. [f. EMBRACE *v.*[1] + -ER[1].] A person who embraces someone or something.

embracer /ɪmˈbreɪsə, ɛm-/ *n.*[2] Also **-ceor**. LME. [AN, OFr. *embraseor* instigator, f. (O)Fr. *embraser* set on fire, f. as EM-[1] + *braise* live coals. For sense-development cf. ENTICE.] *Law.* A person who attempts to influence a jury or juror corruptly.

embracery *n.* the offence of an embracer; corruption of a jury or juror: LME.

embracive /ɪmˈbreɪsɪv, ɛm-/ *a.* M19. [f. EMBRACE *v.*[1] + -IVE.] **1** Given to or fond of embracing. *rare.* M19. **2** Embracing or tending to embrace all; inclusive. L19.

embracively *adv.* L19.

†**embraid** *v.t.* Also **-bread.** L15–L16. [f. EM-[1] + BRAID *v.*[1]] Plait, braid; interlace, intertwine.

embranchment /ɪmˈbrɑːn(t)ʃm(ə)nt, ɛm-/ *n.* M19. [Fr. *embranchement*, f. as EM-[1], BRANCH *n.*, -MENT.] A branching off or out, as of an arm of a river; a branch, an offshoot.

embrangle /ɪmˈbraŋg(ə)l, ɛm-/ *v.t.* Also **im-** /ɪm-/. M17. [f. EM-[1], IM-[1] + BRANGLE.] Entangle, perplex, confuse.

COLERIDGE The perplexities with which .. I have been thorned and embrangled.

embranglement *n.* E19.

†**embrasure** *n.*[1] *rare* (Shakes.). Only in E17. [f. EMBRACE *v.*[1] + -URE.] = EMBRACE *n.*

embrasure /ɪmˈbreɪʒə, ɛm-/ *n.*[2] & *v.* Also **-zure.** E18. [Fr., f. †*embraser* (now *ébraser*) widen (a door or window opening), of unkn. origin: see -URE.] **A** *n.* **1** *Mil.* An opening in a parapet that widens towards the outside, made to fire a gun through. E18. **2** A slanting or bevelling of the wall on each side of a door or window opening so as to form a recess; the area contained between such walls. M18. **3** *Dentistry.* The angle between adjacent teeth where their two surfaces curve inwards towards the line of contact. M20.

2 A. GUINNESS We were ushered to a round table in a window embrasure.

B *v.t.* Provide with an embrasure. E19.

embrave /ɛmˈbreɪv/ *v.t.* L16. [f. EM-[1] + BRAVE *a.*] †**1** Adorn, embellish. L16–M18. **2** Inspire with courage, make brave. M17.

embrazure *n.* & *v.* var. of EMBRASURE *n.*[2] & *v.*

†**embread** *v.* var. of EMBRAID.

embreathe *v.* var. of IMBREATHE.

embrigade /ˌɛmbrɪˈgeɪd/ *v.t. rare.* L19. [f. EM-[1] + BRIGADE.] Form into a brigade or into any organized body.

embrighten /ɪmˈbrʌɪt(ə)n, ɛm-/ *v.t.* E17. [f. EM-[1] + BRIGHTEN.] Make bright, brighten.

Also †**embright** *v.t.* E17–M18.

embrittle /ɪmˈbrɪt(ə)l, ɛm-/ *v.t.* & *i.* E20. [f. EM-[1] + BRITTLE *a.*] Make or become brittle.

embrittlement *n.* the action or result of embrittling; loss of ductility: E20.

embrocado, embroccata *ns.* vars. of IMBROCCATA.

embrocate /ˈɛmbrəkeɪt/ *v.t.* Now *rare* or *obs.* E17. [med.L *embrocat-* pa. ppl stem of *embrocare*: see next, -ATE[3].] *Med.* Bathe (a diseased or painful part of the body) with liquid.

embrocation /ɛmbrəˈkeɪʃ(ə)n/ *n.* LME. [(O)Fr., or med.L *embrocatio(n-)*, f. *embrocat-* pa. ppl stem of *embrocare*, f. late L *embroc(h)a* f. Gk *embrokhē* lotion: see -ATION.] †**1** The bathing of a diseased or painful part of the body. LME–M17. **2** A liquid applied to a diseased or painful part of the body, now usu. by rubbing; a liniment. LME.

†**embroglio** *n.* var. of IMBROGLIO.

embroider /ɪmˈbrɔɪdə, ɛm-/ *v.* LME. [AN *enbrouder*, f. as EM-[1] + OFr. *brouder*, *broisder* (mod. *broder*) f. Gmc. The form *broid-* is partly due to blending with BROID *v.*] **1** *v.t.* & *i.* Decorate (cloth etc.) with needlework; produce (a design or motif) on cloth in this way. LME. †**b** *gen.* Decorate, variegate; *iron.* smear with dirt, blood, etc. LME–M18. **2** *fig.* †**a** Make splendid, dignify; describe extravagantly. E–M17. **b** Embellish (a narrative etc.) with rhetoric, exaggeration, or fictitious additions. E17.

1 J. BERGER A folded handkerchief with his monogram embroidered upon it. G. VIDAL Xerxes .. dried his lips with the back of an embroidered sleeve. 2b HOR. WALPOLE He had embroidered his own story with some marvellous legends.

embroiderer *n.* LME. **embroideress** *n.* a female embroiderer E18. **embroidering** *n.* (*a*) the action of the vb; (*b*) embroidered decoration: L15.

embroidery /ɪmˈbrɔɪd(ə)ri, ɛm-/ *n.* LME. [AN *enbrouderie*, f. as prec.: see -ERY.] **1** The art of embroidering. LME. **2** Embroidered work or material. L16. 3 Any decoration likened in appearance to needlework; *spec.* (now *poet.*) the natural adornment of the ground by flowers; an adornment consisting of flowers. E17. 4 *fig.* Elaboration; inessential decoration or embellishment. M17.

2 M. PEAKE Laying down her embroidery on a table.

embroil /ɪmˈbrɔɪl, ɛm-/ *v.*[1] & *n.* Also †**im-**. E17. [Fr. *embrouiller*, f. as EM-[1], BROIL *v.*[2]] A *v.t.* 1 Bring (affairs, a narrative, etc.) into a state of confusion. E17. 2 Involve in dissension or hostility (*with* someone); involve in or *in* difficulties, conflict, or intrigue. E17. 3 Throw into uproar or tumult. E17.

2 M. MEYER Although he enjoyed . . making speeches on controversial subjects, he disliked embroiling himself. J. M. COETZEE I did not mean to get embroiled in this.

B *n.* A state of dissension, perplexity, or confusion; an uproar. Now *rare* or *obs.* M17.

embroiler *n.* M17.

†**embroil** *v.*[2]*t. rare.* M17–E18. [f. EM-[1] + BROIL *v.*[1]] Burn up, set fire to.

embroilment /ɪmˈbrɔɪlm(ə)nt, ɛm-/ *n.* E17. [f. EMBROIL *v.*[1] + -MENT.] 1 (An) uproar, (a) tumult. E17. 2 A state of conflict; a quarrel. M17. 3 The action or process of embroiling. M17. 4 A state of complication or confusion; a confused mixture. L17.

embrown /ɪmˈbraʊn, ɛm-/ *v.t.* Also **im-** /ɪm-/. M17. [f. EM-[1], IM-[1] + BROWN *a.*] 1 Darken, make dusky. *poet.* M17. 2 Make brown. E18.

embrue, embrute *vs.* vars. of IMBRUE, IMBRUTE.

embrya *n.pl.* see EMBRYON.

embryo /ˈɛmbrɪəʊ/ *n.* & *a.* LME. [Late L *embryo, embrio*, mistaken form arising from taking Gk *embruon* as a n. in *-ōn, -ōnis*; *embruon* f. as EM-[2] + *bruein* swell, grow.] A *n.* Pl. **-os.** 1 a The entity which develops in a woman's womb until it is born as a baby (if not aborted etc.). Now *esp.*, this entity prior to the time at which all the organs are developed, at about the eighth week after conception (cf. FOETUS); in *Med.* sometimes also distinguished from the conceptus or pre-embryo. LME. b The unborn or unhatched offspring of an animal. M17. 2 *fig.* A thing in a rudimentary stage; a thing as yet no more than an idea. E17. †3 *Chem.* A metal or compound prior to isolation from its natural state or matrix. M17–M18. 4 *Bot.* The part of the inside of a seed which develops into a plant, comprising in higher plants, when mature, a radicle, a plumule, and one or two cotyledons. E18.

Phrases: **in embryo** not yet developed or fully the thing specified.

Comb.: **embryo sac** the cell inside the ovule of a seed plant within which fertilization occurs and which becomes the female gametophyte, containing the zygote and the endosperm nucleus.

B *adj.* = EMBRYONIC 2. M17.

embryo- /ˈɛmbrɪəʊ/ *comb. form* of EMBRYO: see -O-.

embryoˈgenesis *n.* the formation and development of the embryo M19. **embryogeˈnetic** *a.* of or pertaining to embryogenesis L19. **embryogeˈnetically** *adv.* as regards embryogenesis E20. **embryoˈgenic** *a.* = EMBRYOGENETIC M19. **embryˈogeny** *n.* = EMBRYOGENESIS M19. **embryˈoma** *n.*, pl. **-mas, -mata** /-mətə/, *Med.* a tumour (esp. a malignant one of childhood) composed of tissues resembling, or thought to arise from, those of the foetus or foetal remnants E20. **embryˈotomy** *n.* (an instance of) surgical dissection of a foetus in order to remove it from the womb E18. **embryoˈtoxic** *a.* poisonous to an embryo M20. **embryotoˈxicity** *n.* the property of being embryotoxic; the degree to which something is embryotoxic: L20.

embryoid /ˈɛmbrɪɔɪd/ *a.* & *n.* M20. [f. EMBRYO + -OID.] A *adj.* Resembling an embryo. Chiefly in *embryoid body* below. M20.

embryoid body an aggregate of cells resembling an embryo, which develops when certain mouse tumours are injected into the peritoneal cavity of a mouse or grown in culture.

B *n.* An embryonic plant developed in a culture medium from a single cell. M20.

embryology /ɛmbrɪˈɒlədʒi/ *n.* M19. [f. EMBRYO- + -OLOGY.] The branch of science that deals with the development of an organism up to the time of birth or hatching.

embryoˈlogic *a.* = EMBRYOLOGICAL L19. **embryoˈlogical** *a.* of or pertaining to embryology M19. **embryoˈlogically** *adv.* as regards embryology or embryonic development M19. **embryˈologist** *n.* an expert in or student of embryology M19.

embryon /ˈɛmbrɪɒn/ *n.* & *a.* Now *rare* or *obs.* LME. [med.L f. Gk *embruon*: see EMBRYO.] A *n.* Pl. **-brya** /-brɪə/, **-ons.** †1 a = EMBRYO *n.* 1a. LME–E19. b = EMBRYO *n.* 1b. M17. †2 *fig.* = EMBRYO *n.* 2. L16–E19. †3 = EMBRYO *n.* 4. L18–L19. †B *adj.* = EMBRYO *a.* E17–M19.

embryonal /ɪmˈbrʌɪən(ə)l, ɛm-/ *a.* M17. [f. late L *embryon-, embryo*, Eng. EMBRYON + -AL[1].] = EMBRYONIC 1.

embryonary /ɪmˈbrʌɪən(ə)ri, ɛm-/ *a.* M19. [f. as EMBRYONIC + -ARY[1].] Embryonic.

embryonate /ˈɛmbrɪəneɪt/ *a.* L19. [f. EMBRYON(IC + -ATE[2], after next.] = EMBRYONATED 2.

embryonated /ˈɛmbrɪəneɪtɪd/ *a.* M17. [f. as EMBRYONAL + -ATE[3] + -ED[1].] †1 Of a mineral or chemical compound: occurring combined with or embedded in another material. M–L17. 2 Of an egg: containing an embryo. M18.

embryonic /ɛmbrɪˈɒnɪk/ *a.* M19. [f. late L *embryon-*, EMBRYO *n.* + -IC.] 1 Of, pertaining to, or of the nature of an embryo. M19. 2 *fig.* Undeveloped, rudimentary; incipient. M19.

embryonically *adv.* in the embryo; as an embryo; as regards the embryo: L19.

embryoniferous /ˌɛmbrɪəˈnɪf(ə)rəs/ *a.* E19. [f. as prec. + -I- + -FEROUS.] *Bot.* Producing or bearing an embryo.

embryotic /ɛmbrɪˈɒtɪk/ *a.* M18. [f. EMBRYO after *exotic, patriotic*, etc.] 1 = EMBRYONIC 2. M18. 2 = EMBRYONIC 1. M19.

embus /ɪmˈbʌs, ɛm-/ *v.* Infl. **-ss-**. E20. [f. EM-[1] + BUS *n.*, after *embark*.] Chiefly *Mil.* 1 *v.i.* Board a bus or other motor vehicle. E20. 2 *v.t.* Transport by, or put on to, a bus etc. E20.

embusqué /ɑ̃byske/ *n.* Pl. pronounced same. E20. [Fr., pa. pple of *embusquer* f. OFr. *embuschier* AMBUSH *v.*] A person who avoids military service by obtaining a post in a government office or the like.

emcee /ɛmˈsiː/ *n.* & *v.* *slang.* M20. [Repr. pronunc. of the letters *MC*.] A *n.* A master of ceremonies, a compère. M20. B *v.t.* & *i.* Act as master of ceremonies (for). M20.

eme /iːm/ *n.*[1] *obs.* exc. *dial.* [OE *ēam* = OFris. *ēm*, MDu. *oem* (Du. *oom*), OHG *ōheim* (G *Oheim*).] A friend. Formerly, an uncle.

eme *n.*[2] see EMU.

-eme /iːm/ *suff.* [Extracted f. PHONEME.] Used in *Ling.* to form ns. denoting units of structure, as *grapheme, morpheme*.

emend /ɪˈmɛnd/ *v.t.* LME. [L *emendare*, f. *e-* E- + *menda* fault. Cf. AMEND *v.*] Alter (a text) to remove errors and corruptions; *gen.* free from faults, correct, rectify.

E. BOWEN Miss Smith . . considered what she had said, but did not emend it.

emender *n.* L19.

emendate /ˈiːmɛndeɪt/ *v.t.* L19. [f. L *emendat-* (see EMENDATOR) or back-form. f. EMENDATION, EMENDATOR.] = EMEND.

emendation /iːmɛnˈdeɪʃ(ə)n/ *n.* LME. [L *emendatio(n-)*, f. as prec.: see -ATION.] †1 Reformation, improvement. LME–L17. 2 (An) improvement by alteration and correction; *esp.* (an) alteration of a text where it is presumed to be corrupt. L16.

†**emendative** *a.* *rare.* M17–E19. [f. L *emendat-*: see next, -IVE.] Tending to emend.

emendator /ˈiːmɛndeɪtə/ *n.* L17. [L *emendator*, f. *emendat-* pa. ppl stem of *emendare* EMEND: see -ATE[3], -OR.] A person who emends something; a corrector.

emendatory /ɪˈmɛndət(ə)ri/ *a.* M17. [L *emendatorius* corrective, f. as EMENDATE: see -ORY[2].] †1 Disciplinary. Only in M17. 2 Of or pertaining to emendation(s). L18.

emerald /ˈɛm(ə)r(ə)ld/ *n.* & *a.* Also †**-raude**. ME. [OFr. *e(s)meraude* (mod. *émeraude*), f. Proto-Romance alt. of L SMARAGDUS.] A *n.* 1 A bright green precious stone; now *spec.* one consisting of a particular variety of beryl. ME. 2 *Her.* The tincture gules in the fanciful blazon of arms of peers. Now *Hist.* L16. 3 The colour of an emerald, emerald green. E18. 4 Type of a size (6½ points) larger than nonpareil and smaller than minion. L19.

B *adj.* 1 Bright green, like an emerald. E16. 2 Made of or containing an emerald. L19.

2 W. JONES An emerald ring was thought to ensure purity.

Special collocations & comb.: **emerald cuckoo** an African cuckoo, *Chrysococcyx cupreus*, with green and gold plumage. **emerald green** *n.* & *a. phr.* (*a*) *n. phr.* a bright green like that of an emerald; also, the pigment Paris green; the pigment viridian; (*b*) *a. phr.* = EMERALD *a.* 1. **the Emerald Isle** *literary* Ireland. **emerald moth** any of various green geometrid moths of the family Geometridae.

emeraldine /-ɪn, -ʌɪn/ *a.* & *n.* (*a*) *adj.* = EMERALD *a.* 1; (*b*) *n.* a green aniline dye: M19.

†**emeras** *n.* M17–L19. [Origin unkn.] *Her.* An escutcheon on the shoulder of an armed knight.

†**emeraude** *n.* & *a.* var. of EMERALD.

emerge /ɪˈməːdʒ/ *v.i.* L16. [L *emergere*, f. *e-* E- + *mergere* to dip, plunge.] 1 Of a fact, result, etc.: become known as the result of a discussion etc.; come into being with the passage of events. Of a problem: arise, esp. suddenly. L16. 2 Come up out of a liquid after being immersed. M17. 3 Come into view from a place of darkness, concealment, confinement, etc. M17. 4 *fig.* Come out of a situation in a specified state; pass from a state of ignorance, obscurity, etc.; become publicly recognized or noticed. (Foll. by *from* the earlier state, *in* or *into* the later one.) M17.

1 I. MURDOCH After a few more exchanges about country life . . it emerged that Dora had never heard the cuckoo. W. S. CHURCHILL From the Restoration there emerged no national settlement. 2 T. BURNET The mountains emerged, and became dry land again. 3 E. TEMPLETON They saw Mr Parker emerge from the shadowy passage. 4 J. R. GREEN Florence emerged into communal greatness. A. PRICE He'll emerge whiter than white from Colonel Butler's enquiries. G. F. FIENNES Decisions are not made; they emerge.

emergence /ɪˈməːdʒ(ə)ns/ *n.* M17. [med.L *emergentia*, f. L *emergent-* pres. ppl stem of *emergere*: see EMERGE *v.*, -ENCE.] †1 An unforeseen occurrence; an emergency. M17–M19. 2 The process of emerging. E18. 3 *Bot.* An outgrowth from a stem or leaf composed of epidermal and subepidermal tissue. L19.

emergency /ɪˈməːdʒ(ə)nsi/ *n.* & *a.* M17. [f. as prec.: see -ENCY.] A *n.* 1 A situation, esp. of danger or conflict, that arises unexpectedly and requires urgent action; (a person with) a condition requiring immediate treatment. M17. b Pressing need. E18. c *Sport.* A substitute player. Now *Austral.* M19. d A condition of danger or disaster throughout a region. L19. †2 The fact of happening or occurring suddenly or unexpectedly. M17–L18. 3 The action of rising out of the water. Now *rare* or *obs.* M17. †4 The process of emerging into view. M17–M18.

1 J. T. STORY The distant clanging of an ambulance bell racing to an emergency. b DAY LEWIS A certain fund of calm within myself . . which I am able to draw upon in emergency. J. FLEMING Hose pipes to be used in case of emergency. d **state of emergency**: in which a government suspends normal constitutional procedures.

B *attrib.* or as *adj.* Used, issued, called upon, or arising in an emergency. L19.

D. LODGE The airport was on full emergency alert. *emergency exit, landing, service*, etc.

emergent /ɪˈməːdʒ(ə)nt/ *a.* & *n.* LME. [L *emergent-* pres. ppl stem of *emergere*: see EMERGE *v.*, -ENT. In sense 1 tr. med.L *emergens*.] A *adj.* †1 Designating a Jewish year beginning in May in commemoration of the Exodus. Only in LME. 2 Occurring unexpectedly; not specially provided for. *arch.* LME. b Urgent, pressing. E18. 3 Occurring as a consequence of something. E17. 4 That is rising or has risen out of a surrounding medium. E17. 5 In the process of coming out; emerging. M17. 6 Becoming noticed; coming into being; (of a nation) newly formed or independent. M17.

4 W. D. THORNBURY An emergent shore line with offshore bar and lagoon. 5 J. STRUTHERS The sun emergent smiled. **emergent evolution**: in which new traits are regarded as emergents (see sense B.3 below) rather than as resultants. 6 *Amateur Photographer* The original Vogue contract.. made of him a cardinal amongst the emergent cockneys of the era.

B *n.* 1 A person who or thing which emerges; an outcome, a result. Now *rare.* E16. †2 An emergency. E16–E19. 3 An effect produced by a combination of causes but unable to be seen as the sum of their individual effects. Opp. *resultant.* L19.

emergently *adv.* (*rare*) M17.

Emergicenter /ɪˈməːdʒɪsɛntə/ *n. US.* L20. [f. EMERGENCY after SURGICENTER.] (Proprietary name for) a clinic offering emergency treatment for minor illness or injury.

emerited /ɪˈmɛrɪtɪd, iː-/ *a. arch.* L17. [f. as next + -ED¹.] Retired from active service; skilled through long experience.

emeritus /ɪˈmɛrɪtəs, iː-/ *a.* M18. [L *emeritus* pa. pple of *emereri* earn (one's discharge) by service, f. *e-* E- + *mereri* deserve: see MERIT *n.*] Honourably discharged from service; (of a former office-holder, esp. a professor) retired but allowed to retain his or her title as an honour.

emerods /ˈɛmərɒdz/ *n.pl. arch.* LME. [Alt. of HAEMORRHOID + -S¹.] Haemorrhoids.

emersed /ɪˈməːst/ *a. rare.* L17. [f. L *emersus* pa. pple of *emergere* EMERGE + -ED¹.] Standing out from or above a medium; (of part of a plant) raised above the water.

emersion /ɪˈməːʃ(ə)n, iː-/ *n.* M17. [Late L *emersio(n-)*, f. L *emers-* pa. ppl stem of *emergere* EMERGE: see -ION.] 1 *Astron.* The reappearance of a celestial object after its eclipse or occultation. M17. 2 The process of appearing above the surface of water that previously hid the object. M17. 3 *gen.* The action of emerging from concealment or confinement. *rare.* M18.

Emersonian /ɛməˈsəʊnɪən/ *a.* & *n.* M19. [f. *Emerson* (see below) + -IAN.] A *adj.* Of, pertaining to, or characteristic of the US author Ralph Waldo Emerson (1803–82) or his work. M19. B *n.* An admirer or student of Emerson. M19.

Emersonianism *n.* M19.

emery /ˈɛm(ə)ri/ *n.* & *v.* L15. [Fr. *émeri* f. OFr. *esmeri(l)* f. It. *smeriglio* f. Proto-Romance, f. med.Gk *smēri*, cl.Gk *smiris*, *smuris* polishing powder. Cf. SMEAR *n.*] A *n.* 1 A naturally occurring mixture of corundum with an iron oxide or iron spinel, used as an abrasive and polishing material for metal, glass, and stone. L15. 2 In full *emery bag.* A case containing emery, used for keeping needles bright. *US.* M19.

Comb.: *emery bag*: see sense 2 above; **emery board** a thin strip of emery-coated card or wood, used as a nail file; **emery-cloth**, **-paper**: coated with emery powder; **emery powder** ground emery; **emery wheel** an emery-coated grinding or polishing wheel.

B *v.t.* Polish with emery; coat with emery. *rare.* M19.

emesis /ˈɛmɪsɪs/ *n.* L19. [Gk, f. *emein* to vomit.] *Med.* Vomiting.

emetic /ɪˈmɛtɪk/ *n.* & *a.* M17. [Gk *emetikos*, f. *emetos* vomiting f. *emein* to vomit: see -IC.] A *n.* A substance that causes vomiting when ingested, *esp.* one given for this purpose. M17. B *adj.* Causing vomiting; *fig.* sickening, revoltingly sentimental. L17.

emetic tartar = *tartar emetic* s.v. TARTAR *n.*¹

emetical *a.* = EMETIC *a.* L17. **emetically** *adv.* (*rare*) M17.

emetine /ˈɛmɪtiːn/ *n.* E19. [f. Gk *emetos*: see prec., -INE⁵.] An alkaloid, $C_{29}H_{40}N_2O_4$, obtained from the roots of the ipecacuanha plant, *Cephaelis ipecacuanha*, and formerly used as an amoebicide.

†emeu *n.* var. of EMU.

émeute /emøːt/ *n.* L18. [Fr. f. OFr. *esmote*, f. *esmeu* (mod. *ému*) pa. pple of *esmovoir* (mod. *émouvoir*: see EMOTION), after *meute* crowd, uprising.] A popular rising or disturbance.

-emia *suff.* see -AEMIA.

emic /ˈiːmɪk/ *a.* M20. [f. PHONEMIC *a.*] Describing the structure of a particular language or culture in terms of its internal elements and their functioning, rather than in terms of any existing external scheme. Cf. ETIC *a.*

emiction /ɪˈmɪkʃ(ə)n/ *n.* M17. [med.L *emict-* pa. ppl stem of *emingere*, f. *e-* E- + *mingere* urinate: see -ION.] Urine.

emigrant /ˈɛmɪgr(ə)nt/ *n.* & *a.* M18. [L *emigrant-* pres. ppl stem of *emigrare*: see EMIGRATE *v.*, -ANT¹.] A *n.* A person who emigrates; *spec.* (*Hist.*) an emigré from the French Revolution. M18.

B *adj.* 1 That emigrates or has emigrated. L18. 2 Used by emigrants. Only *attrib.* M19.

2 : *emigrant road, ship, train*, etc.

†emigrate *a.* Only in M17. [L *emigratus* pa. pple of *emigrare*: see next, -ATE².] That has migrated.

emigrate /ˈɛmɪgreɪt/ *v.* L18. [L *emigrat-* pa. ppl stem of *emigrare*, f. *e-* E- + *migrare* migrate: see -ATE³.] 1 *v.i.* Leave one's country to settle in another. L18. 2 *v.t.* Cause or assist to do this. L19.

emigratory *a.* that is emigrating; pertaining to emigration: M19.

emigration /ɛmɪˈgreɪʃ(ə)n/ *n.* M17. [Late L *emigratio(n-)*, f. as prec.: see -ATION.] 1 The action or an act of leaving a particular place or environment, permanently or temporarily. Now *rare* exc. as in sense 2. M17. 2 The action or an act of emigrating. L17. 3 The group of people who emigrate from or to a particular place. E19.

1 JER. TAYLOR Frequent Aspirations and Emigrations of his Soul after God. 2 L. T. C. ROLT A sudden wave of emigration to what seemed a new promised land.

emigré /ˈɛmɪgreɪ/ *n.* & *a.* Also **é-**. L18. [Fr. *émigré*, pa. pple of *émigrer* f. L *emigrare*: see EMIGRATE *v.*] A *n.* Orig., a French emigrant, *esp.* one from the Revolution of 1789–99. Now, any emigrant, *esp.* a political exile. L18.

B *adj.* That is an emigré; composed of emigrés. E20.

V. NABOKOV Speeches she heard at émigré political meetings.

Emilian /ɪˈmɪlɪən/ *a.* & *n.* M17. [f. *Emilia* (see below) + -AN.] A *adj.* Of or pertaining to Emilia, a district of northern Italy now part of the region of Emilia-Romagna, its inhabitants, or their dialect of Italian. M17. B *n.* A native or inhabitant of Emilia; the Italian dialect of Emilia. L19.

†emina *n.* see HEMINA.

émincé /emɛ̃se/ *n.* E20. [Fr., use as n. of pa. pple of *émincer* slice thinly, f. *é-* EX-¹ + *mincer*, f. as MINCE *v.*] A dish consisting of thinly sliced meat in sauce.

eminence /ˈɛmɪnəns/ *n.* ME. [L *eminentia*, f. as EMINENT: see -ENCE.] I *lit.* 1 An elevated or lofty position. ME. 2 *Anat.* A (rounded) projection on an organ or part, esp. on a bone. ME. 3 A piece of rising ground; a hill. L17.

1 H. K. WHITE Draw the fix'd stars from their eminence. 3 W. S. CHURCHILL A large wooded eminence known.. as Hussar Hill.

II *fig.* 4 Distinguished superiority in position, attainments, character, or the possession of any quality. ME. †b Mastery, the upper hand. Only in E16. †5 Acknowledgement of superiority. *rare* (Shakes.). Only in E17. 6 An excellence; a distinction, an honour; superiority in degree, outstanding degree. *obs.* exc. in *by* (*way of*) *eminence* below. E17. 7 (Usu. **E-**.) A title of respect given to a cardinal or (formerly) any important person. Chiefly w. possess. adj. M17. b An important or eminent person. M20.

4 B. RUSSELL The rise of men of science to great eminence in the State. b SHAKES. *Tr. & Cr.* You should not have the eminence of him. 6 J. PEARSON There must be.. some great eminence in the object worshipped. **by (way of) eminence** (now *rare*) *par excellence*; especially.

éminence grise /eminɑ̃ːs griz/ *n. phr.* Pl. ***éminences grises*** (pronounced same). M20. [Fr., lit. 'grey eminence', orig. applied to the Capuchin Père Joseph, confidential agent of Cardinal Richelieu (1585–1642). Cf. EMINENCE 7.] A person who exercises power or influence though holding no official position. Also, a confidential adviser.

eminency /ˈɛmɪnənsi/ *n.* E17. [f. as EMINENCE: see -Y³.] †1 = EMINENCE. E17–M18. †2 Importance (of a place or requirement). Only in 17. 3 Prominence or relative importance in one's thoughts. M19.

eminent /ˈɛmɪnənt/ *a.* LME. [L *eminent-* pres. ppl stem of *eminere* project: see -ENT.] 1 High, lofty; towering above the surroundings. *arch.* LME. b Protruding, projecting. *arch.* M16. 2 Remarkable in degree; important, noteworthy. LME. 3 Of a person: exalted, important; distinguished in position, attainments, or character. L16. †4 Of a thing or place: principal, important; valuable. E17–M18. †5 [By confusion.] Imminent. E17–E18.

2 H. P. BROUGHAM The reputation justly acquired by his eminent services. 3 D. M. THOMAS The voice of such an eminent statesman earned instant respect. D. LESSING He.. early became eminent in his field.

Phrases: *eminent* DOMAIN.

eminently /ˈɛmɪnəntli/ *adv.* LME. [f. prec. + -LY².] 1 In or to a remarkable degree; notably, exceptionally. LME. †2 In a high or lofty position. Only in 17. †3 Conspicuously. M17–L18. 4 *Philos.* In a superior manner (esp. of containment of an effect by a cause). M17. †5 [After EMINENT 5.] Imminently, urgently. M–L17.

1 G. W. KNIGHT Cynicism is eminently logical to the modern.. mind. J. GALSWORTHY A task for which she was eminently qualified.

emir /ɛˈmɪə/ *n.* L16. [Fr. *émir* f. Arab. *'amīr*: see AMIR.] 1 A male descendant of Muhammad. Now *rare.* L16. 2 A title of certain Muslim rulers; an Arab prince, governor, or commander. M17.

emirate /ˈɛmərət, ˈɛmɪərət, ɛˈmɪə-/ *n.* (*a*) the rank or position of an emir; (*b*) the region governed or ruled by an emir: M19.

emissary /ˈɛmɪs(ə)ri/ *n.*¹ & *a.* E17. [L *emissarius*, f. *emiss-* pa. ppl stem of *emittere* EMIT: see -ARY¹.] A *n.* A person sent on a special mission, esp. to gain information, promote a cause, etc. Orig. usu. *derog.* E17.

H. JAMES Even if.. you are not Mr Cumnor.. they may still suspect you of being his emissary. H. KISSINGER If.. the Chinese accepted our proposal to send an emissary to Peking or receive theirs in Washington.

B *adj.* †1 Emitted. Only in M17. †2 Sent on a special mission. L17–M19. 3 *Anat.* Of a blood-vessel: branching from a larger one; *spec.* designating veins that pass through the cranial wall and drain venous sinuses inside the skull into veins outside it. M19.

emissary /ˈɛmɪs(ə)ri/ *n.*² E17. [L *emissarium*, f. *emiss-*: see prec., -ARY¹.] 1 An outlet, a channel. *obs.* exc. *Hist.* E17. †2 A duct of the body. M17–M18.

emissile /ɪˈmɪsɪl, -ʌɪl/ *a.* M18. [f. L *emiss-*: see EMISSARY *n.*¹ & *a.*, -ILE.] *Zool.* Able to be protruded.

emission /ɪˈmɪʃ(ə)n/ *n.* LME. [L *emissio(n-)*, f. *emiss-*: see EMISSARY *n.*¹ & *a.*, -ION.] 1 Something emitted; an emanation. LME. 2 The action or an act of emitting. Formerly also, the release of the soul at death; *fig.* the pouring out of affection. E17. b Ejaculation of semen. M17. †3 *gen.* The action of sending out something or someone. E17–E19.

1 *City Limits* Experts monitor sea creatures for nuclear emissions. 2 LD RUTHERFORD The emission of these radiations from radioactive substances. b *nocturnal emission*: see NOCTURNAL *a.* 1. 3 HOBBES The emission of preachers to the infidels.

Comb.: **emission nebula** *Astron.*: that shines with its own rather than reflected light; **emission spectrum**: showing the radiation from an emitting source; **emission theory** *Hist. Sci.* = CORPUSCULAR *theory*.

emissive /ɪˈmɪsɪv/ *a.* M17. [f. L *emiss-*: see EMISSARY *n.*¹ & *a.*, -IVE.] †1 That is emitted. M17–M18. 2 Of or pertaining to emission; *spec.* (*Hist. Sci.*) designating the emission theory of light. M19. 3 That emits or is capable of emitting. L19.

2 R. JAKOBSON The classical distinction between . . emissive (or expressive) aphasia . . and receptive (or sensory) aphasia.

emissivity /ɪmɪˈsɪvɪti-, iːm-/ *n.* (*Physics*) the relative ability of a surface to radiate heat; *spec.* the ratio of the rate at which it radiates heat to the rate at which a black body at the same temperature would radiate heat: L19.

emit /ɪˈmɪt/ *v.t.* Infl. **-tt-**. E17. [L *emittere*, f. *e-* E- + *mittere* send.] 1 Give off, send out from oneself or itself, (something imponderable, as light, sound, scent, flames, etc.); discharge, exude, (a fluid). E17. †2 Send out as an offshoot. M17–M18. †3a Publish (a book or notice). M17–M19. b Issue formally and with authority; *esp.* put (currency) into circulation. L17. †4 Discharge (a missile). Only in E18. 5 Utter, express, (an opinion etc.). M18.

1 I. MURDOCH Gorse bushes . . emitted their strong coconut perfume. P. ACKROYD The strip lighting . . emitted a vague hum. *fig.*: A. POWELL She enjoyed emitting an impression of Cambridge severity. 5 JAS. MILL Complaints were . . emitted of the scarcity of money.

emitter *n.* a thing or substance which emits; *spec.* the part of a transistor where the charge-carriers originate and from where they flow into the base: L19.

emma /ˈɛmə/. L19. Used for the letter m in spoken telephone communications and in the oral spelling of messages.

ack emma, *pip emma*, *toc emma*.

emmarble *v.* see ENMARBLE.

emmarvel /ɪˈmɑːv(ə)l/ *v.t.* Now *rare*. Also (earlier) †**en-**. M18. [f. EN-[1], EM-[1] + MARVEL *n.*[1] or *v.*] Fill with wonder.

emmenagogue /ɪˈmiːnəgɒg, ɛ-/ *a.* & *n.* E18. [f. Gk *emmēna* menses (f. *em-* EM-[2] + *mēn-* month) + *agōgos* leading, eliciting, f. *agein* to lead.] *Med.* †A *adj.* = EMMENAGOGIC. E18–M19. B *n.* An emmenagogic agent. M18.

emmenagogic /ɪˌmiːnəˈgɒdʒɪk/ *a.* promoting or increasing menstrual flow L17.

Emmental /ˈɛməntɑːl/ *n.* Also **-thal**, **-t(h)aler** /-tɑːlə/. E20. [G *Emmentaler* (formerly *-thaler*), f. *Emmental* a region in Switzerland.] A type of hard Swiss cheese with many holes, similar to Gruyère. Also *Emmental cheese*.

emmer /ˈɛmə/ *n.*[1] E20. [G f. OHG *amer.*] A kind of tetraploid wheat, *Triticum dicoccon*, with two-grained spikelets that was eaten in prehistoric times and is now grown for fodder and breakfast cereals.

emmer *n.*[2] var. of EMBER *n.*[2]

emmet /ˈɛmɪt/ *n.* Chiefly *dial.* [OE *ǣmete* wk fem. of *æmet(t)e*: see ANT.] 1 = ANT 1. OE. 2 In Cornwall: a holiday-maker, a tourist. L20.

emmetropia /ɛməˈtrəʊpɪə/ *n.* M19. [f. Gk *emmetros* in measure (f. as EM-[2] + *metron* measure) + *ōp-*, *ōps* eye + -IA[1].] The state of refraction of the normal eye, in which parallel light rays are focused on the retina when the eye is relaxed.

emmetropic /-ˈtrəʊpɪk, -ˈtrɒpɪk/ *a.* L19.

Emmy /ˈɛmi/ *n.* M20. [Origin uncertain: perh. f. *Immy*, f. *image* (*orthicon tube*) + -Y[6].] Any of the statuettes awarded annually by the American Academy of Television Arts and Sciences to an outstanding television programme or performer. Also *Emmy award*.

emodin /ˈɛmədɪn/ *n.* M19. [f. mod.L *emodi* former specific epithet of *Rheum australe* an Asian species of rhubarb, f. Gk *Ēmōdos* Himalayas: see -IN[1].] An orange anthraquinone, $C_{15}H_{10}O_5$, obtained from rhubarb, cascara, and some other plants and having cathartic properties.

emolliate /ɪˈmɒlɪeɪt/ *v.t.* E19. [Irreg. f. L *emollire* (see next) + -ATE[3], after *emaciate* etc.] Soften, make effeminate.

†**emolliative** *a.* (*rare*) that tends to soften: only in E17.

emollient /ɪˈmɒlɪənt/ *a.* & *n.* M17. [L *emollient-* pres. ppl stem of *emollire* make soft, f. *e-* E- + *mollis* soft: see -ENT.] A *adj.* That makes the skin soft or supple; *fig.* soothing; that makes more acceptable. M17.

R. HOGGART Working-class speech and manners . . are more abrupt, less provided with emollient phrases.

B *n.* An emollient agent. M17.

emollience *n.* M20.

†**emollition** *n.* E17–M18. [f. L *emollit-* pa. ppl stem of *emollire*: see prec., -ITION.] The action of making soft.

emolument /ɪˈmɒljʊm(ə)nt, ɛ-/ *n.* LME. [(O)Fr. *émolument* or L *emolumentum*, *emoli-gain*, orig. prob. payment to a miller for the grinding of corn, f. *emolere* grind up, f. *e-* E- + *molere* grind: see -MENT.] 1 *sing.* & (usu.) in *pl.* Profit or gain arising from office or employment; reward, remuneration. LME. †2 Benefit, comfort. M16–M18.

1 N. FREELING A recommendation that you should have the rank and emoluments of a principal commissaire.

emoluˈmentary *a.* profitable, beneficial L18.

†**emong** *prep.* & *adv.* var. of AMONG.

emony /ˈɛməni/ *n.* M16. [Aphet. f. *anemone* (taken as *an emony*).] = ANEMONE *n.* 1.

emote /ɪˈməʊt/ *v.i.* E20. [Back-form. f. next.] Dramatize emotion; act emotionally or theatrically.

emoter *n.* M20.

emotion /ɪˈməʊʃ(ə)n/ *n.* & *v.* M16. [Fr. *émotion*, f. *émouvoir* excite, move the feelings of (after *mouvoir*, *motion*), ult. f. L *emovere*, f. *e-* E- + *movere* move.] A *n.* †1 A public disturbance; a commotion. M16–M18. †2 A migration; a change of position. Only in 17. b A physical agitation or disturbance. L17–E19. 3 Agitation of mind; strong mental feeling. M17. 4 Any of the natural instinctive affections of the mind (e.g. love, horror, pity) which come and go according to one's personality, experiences, and bodily state; a mental feeling. Also, mental feeling as distinguished from knowledge and from will. E19.

2b SHELLEY The winds of heaven mix forever With a sweet emotion. 3 G. HUNTINGTON The colonel announced with emotion that this was the happiest day of his life. 4 A. STORR Those who . . have had a relationship in which their emotions have not been deeply involved. M. AMIS Without a trace of hatred or anger or surprise or any emotion I have felt myself. J. HILTON He had shown so little emotion about anything.

B *v.t.* Make emotional; imbue with emotion. L18.

emotionless *a.* M19. **emotionlessly** *adv.* E20. **emotionlessness** *n.* E20.

emotional /ɪˈməʊʃ(ə)n(ə)l/ *a.* M19. [f. prec. + -AL[1].] 1 Of or pertaining to the emotions; based on or appealing to the emotions. M19. 2 Having the capacity for emotion; *esp.* easily affected by emotion. Also, full of emotion, showing strong emotion. M19.

1 J. ROSENBERG A wide range of emotional expressions, from joy and surprise to horror and pain. F. WARNER My Mother . . forces herself on me by emotional blackmail. DAY LEWIS A woman . . capable of bitter resistance against domestic bullying or emotional exploitation. 2 T. HARDY The singer himself grew emotional, till she could imagine a tear in his eye. *Observer* It was assumed that women were too emotional to broadcast news bulletins. TIRED *and emotional*.

emotioˈnality *n.* emotional character or temperament; the ability to feel or express emotion: M19. **emotionalize** *v.t.* imbue with emotion; deal with emotionally: L19. **emotionally** *adv.* M19.

emotionalism /ɪˈməʊʃ(ə)n(ə)lɪz(ə)m/ *n.* M19. [f. EMOTIONAL + -ISM.] Emotional character; *esp.* a tendency to cultivate or give in weakly to emotion.

emotionalist /ɪˈməʊʃ(ə)n(ə)lɪst/ *n.* M19. [f. EMOTIONAL + -IST.] A *n.* 1 A person who bases a theory of conduct on the emotions. M19. 2 A person given to emotionalism. L19.

B *adj.* Based on or expressed in terms of the emotions. M20.

E. E. EVANS-PRITCHARD Emotionalist interpretations of religion.

emotive /ɪˈməʊtɪv/ *a.* M18. [f. L *emot-* pa. ppl stem of *emovere*: see EMOTION, -IVE.] 1 Arousing or able to arouse feeling or emotion; *spec.* in *Philos.* & *Literary Criticism* expressing emotion, rather than descriptive. M18. 2 Having the capacity for (strong) emotion; of or pertaining to emotion. M19.

1 H. M. KENNEDY The emotive passionate quality of epic diction. C. S. LEWIS We use the highly emotive word 'stagnation' . . for what other ages would have called 'permanence'. K. CLARK The poet and painter . . both drew practically the whole of their emotive power from . . their boyhood. **emotive theory**: that ethical and value judgements are expressions of feeling, not statements. 2 H. SPENCER Actions . . at once conscious, rational, and emotive.

emotively *adv.* L19. **emotiveness** *n.* L19. **emotivism** *n.* (adherence to) the emotive theory M20. **emoˈtivity** *n.* (*a*) the capacity for emotion; (*b*) emotional rather than descriptive quality or expression: M19.

emove /ɪˈmuːv/ *v.t. rare.* E17. [L *emovere*: see EMOTION.] Affect with emotion.

empacket /ɪmˈpakɪt, ɛm-/ *v.t. rare.* E19. [f. EM-[1] + PACKET *n.*] Pack up; put into packets.

†**empair** *v.* var. of IMPAIR *v.*

empale *v.*, **empalement** *n.* vars. of IMPALE, IMPALEMENT.

empanada /ɛmpəˈnɑːdə, *foreign* empaˈnaða/ *n.* M20. [Sp., use as n. of fem. pa. pple of *empanar* bake or roll in pastry, f. as EM-[1] + *pan* bread f. L *panis*.] *Cookery.* A turnover with a filling of meat, cheese, or vegetables.

empanel /ɪmˈpan(ə)l, ɛm-/ *v.* & *n.* Also **im-** /ɪm-/. Infl. **-ll-**, * **-l-**. LME. [AN *empaneller*, f. as EM-[1], IM-[1], PANEL *n.*[1]] A *v.t.* Enter (the names of a jury) on a panel or official list; enrol or constitute (a body of jurors). LME. †B *n.* A list or panel of jurors. E16–L18.

empanelment *n.* the action of empanelling L19.

†**empannel** *v.t. rare.* Infl. **-ll-**. E17–L19. [f. EM-[1] + PANEL *n.*[1]] Put a pack-saddle on.

emparadise *v.* var. of IMPARADISE.

†**emparl** *v.*, †**emparlance** *n.* vars. of IMPARL, IMPARLANCE.

†**empassion** *v.*, **-ed** *ppl a.* vars. of IMPASSION etc.

empathetic /ɛmpəˈθɛtɪk/ *a.* M20. [f. EMPATHY + *-etic*, after *sympathy*, *sympathetic*.] = EMPATHIC *a.*

empathetically *adv.* M20.

empathize /ˈɛmpəθʌɪz/ *v.i.* & (*rare*) *t.* Also **-ise**. E20. [f. next + -IZE.] Exercise or experience empathy *with* or with; sympathize.

empathy /ˈɛmpəθi/ *n.* E20. [Gk *empatheia*, f. as EM-[2] + *pathos* feeling: see -Y[3]; tr. G *Einfühlung*.] The power of mentally identifying oneself with (and so fully comprehending) a person or object of contemplation; = EINFÜHLUNG.

M. L. KING Pity is feeling sorry for someone; empathy is feeling sorry with someone.

emˈpathic *a.* involving empathy; having empathy *to* or *with* a person, feeling, etc.: E20. **emˈpathically** *adv.* E20. **empathist** *n.* an adherent of a theory involving empathy E20.

†**empatron** *v.t. rare* (Shakes.). Only in L16. [f. EM-[1] + PATRON *n.*] Act as patron to.

†**empeach** *v.* & *n.*, †**empeachment** *n.* vars. of IMPEACH *n.* & *v.*, IMPEACHMENT.

empearl *v.* var. of IMPEARL.

empennage /ɛmˈpɛnɪdʒ/ *n.* E20. [Fr. = feathering (of an arrow), empennage, f. *empenner* feather (an arrow), f. as EM-[1] + *penne* feather f. L *penna*: see -AGE.] The group of stabilizing and control surfaces at the tail of an aircraft.

†**empeople** *v.* Also **im-**. L16–M19. [f. EM-[1] + PEOPLE *n.*] Fill with people, populate.

†**emperial** *a.* & *n.* var. of IMPERIAL *a.* & *n.*

†**emperil** *v.* var. of IMPERIL.

emperor /ˈɛmp(ə)rə/ *n.* ME. [OFr. *emperere*, *emperour* (mod. *empereur*), f. L *imperator*, f. *imperare* command, f. as IM-[1] + *parare* prepare, contrive: see -OR.] 1 The male monarch of an empire; orig., the title given to the monarch or head of the Roman Empire (in its various forms). ME. 2 *gen.* A title of sovereignty considered superior to that of king. LME. †3 A military leader or commander. LME–M18. 4 In full *emperor penguin*. The largest kind of penguin, *Aptenodytes forsteri*, found only in the Antarctic. L19. 5 In full *emperor* (*angel-*)*fish*. A golden brown angelfish with yellow stripes, *Pomacanthus imperator*, found in parts of the Indian and Pacific Oceans. L19.

Phrases: *purple emperor*: see PURPLE *a.* *red emperor*: see RED *a.*

Comb.: **emperor goose** a goose, *Anser canagica*, with variegated plumage, found in Alaska and NE Siberia; **emperor moth** any of several large Old World saturniid silk moths; *esp.* the European *Pavonia pavonia*, with prominent eyespots on all four wings.

emperorship *n.* the office, dignity, or reign of an emperor L16.

empery /ˈɛmp(ə)ri/ *n. obs.* exc. *poet.* ME. [OFr. *emperie*, *empirie* f. L *imperium* EMPIRE.] **1** †**a** The status or dominion of an emperor. ME–L16. **b** Absolute dominion. M16. †**2** The legitimate authority of an officer or magistrate; legitimate government. LME–M17. **3** The territory of an emperor or a powerful ruler. LME.

empest *v.* var. of IMPEST.

emphasis /ˈɛmfəsɪs/ *n.* Pl. **-ases** /-əsiːz/. L16. [L f. Gk, orig. = (mere) appearance, f. *emphainein* to exhibit, f. as EM-[2] + *phainein* to show.] †**1** A figure of speech in which more is implied than is actually said; a meaning conveyed by implication. (The sense in Gk & L.) L16–M18. **2** Vigour or intensity of statement or expression. L16. †**b** An intense expression. *rare* (Shakes.). Only in E17. **3** Intensity or force of feeling, action, etc. L16. **4** Stress of voice laid on a word or phrase to indicate an implied extra meaning or to mark its importance. E17. **5** *transf.* Stress laid upon, or importance assigned to, a fact or idea. L17. **6** Visual prominence, sharpness or clarity of contour, colouring, etc. L19.

2 J. MORLEY There is not a sentence of strained emphasis or overwrought antithesis. 4 CONAN DOYLE 'If you think —' 'I *do* think,' said Holmes, with emphasis. 5 L. VAN DER POST The emphasis . . was on skill rather than violence. 6 F. HERBERT Dark hair swept back . . throwing emphasis on sharp cheekbones.

emphasize /ˈɛmfəsʌɪz/ *v.t.* Also **-ise**. E19. [f. prec. + -IZE.] Lay stress on (a word, phrase, etc.); add force to (an argument, action, etc.); bring (a fact, feature, etc.) into special prominence.

P. V. WHITE The slammed door emphasized the silence of the house. L. DEIGHTON He emphasized the lines of his cheek muscles by drawing his fingers down them. B. EMECHETA He . . banged at the kitchen table, just to emphasize his point.

emphasizer *n.* L19.

emphatic /ɪmˈfatɪk, ɛm-/ *a.* & *n.* E18. [Late L *emphaticus* f. Gk *emphatikos*, f. Gk EMPHASIS: see -IC.] **A** *adj.* **1** Of language, tone, gesture, etc.: forcibly expressive. E18. **b** Of a word or syllable: bearing the stress. E19. **c** *Gram.* Imparting emphasis. L19. **2** Of a person: expressing himself or herself with force or emphasis. M18. **3** Of an action or its result, or a state: forcible, pronounced; strongly marked. M19.

1 A. BROOKNER All her gestures were vigorous and all her interventions emphatic. 2 GEO. ELIOT Mr. Lingon was equally emphatic. 3 E. BOWEN Writing had dug through; the sheets were thin, her mother's pencil emphatic. N. SAHGAL The emphatic fullness of her bosom.

B *n.* A letter, word, phrase, etc., that is expressive or indicative of emphasis; *joc.* an expletive. Usu. in *pl.* E19.

emphaticness *n.* L20.

emphatical /ɪmˈfatɪk(ə)l, ɛm-/ *a.* Now *rare*. M16. [f. as prec.: see -ICAL.] †**1** Allusive, suggestive. M16–L18. **2** = EMPHATIC *a.* L16. †**3** That is emphatically designated (such). M17–M18. †**4** Of colour: illusory. M17–E18.

emphatically /ɪmˈfatɪk(ə)li, ɛm-/ *adv.* L16. [f. EMPHATIC *a.* or prec.: see -ICALLY.] **1** In an emphatic way, with emphasis. L16. †**2** In or as (mere) appearance. M–L17. †**3** Allusively, suggestively. M–L17.

emphysema /ɛmfɪˈsiːmə/ *n.* M17. [Late L f. Gk *emphusēma*, f. *emphusan* puff up.] *Med.* **1** Swelling caused by the abnormal presence of air in tissue. M17. **2** More fully *pulmonary* or *vesicular emphysema*. The enlargement and partial amalgamation of the air sacs of the lungs, resulting in breathlessness and wheezing. M19.

emphysematous *a.* of the nature of or pertaining to emphysema M18.

emphyteusis /ɛmfɪˈtjuːsɪs/ *n.* Pl. **-teuses** /-ˈtjuːsiːz/. L16. [Late L f. Gk *emphuteusis* lit. 'implanting', f. *emphuteuein* to implant, f. as EM-[2] + *phuteuein* to plant, f. *phuton* plant: see -PHYTE.] In Roman law and many civil law jurisdictions: a long-term or perpetual lease, heritable and alienable; tenure under such a lease.

emphyteutic *a.* of the nature of or held by emphyteusis M17.

emphyteuta /ɛmfɪˈtjuːtə/ *n.* E18. [Late L f. Gk *emphuteutēs*, f. *emphuteuein*: see prec.] A tenant holding land under emphyteusis.

empicture *v.* var. of IMPICTURE.

empiecement /ɪmˈpiːsm(ə)nt, ɛm-/ *n.* L19. [Fr. *empiècement*, f. as EM-[1], PIECE *n.*: see -MENT.] A piece of material inserted in a garment for decoration.

empierce /ɪmˈpɪəs, ɛm-/ *v.t.* Now *rare*. Also **im-** /ɪm-/. L15. [f. EM-[1], IM-[1] + PIERCE *v.*] Pierce through; transfix.

†**empight** *v.* Also **im-**. Pa. pple same. LME. [f. EM-[1], IM-[1] + *pight* (see PITCH *v.*[2]).] **1** *v.t.* Implant, fix in. Only as *empight* pa. pple. LME–M18. **2** *v.i.* Become fixed. Only in L16.

empire /ˈɛmpʌɪə/ *n.* & *a.* ME. [(O)Fr., earlier *emperie*, f. L *imperium* rel. to *imperator* EMPEROR.] **A** *n.* **I** Something under rule. **1** An extensive territory, esp. an aggregate of many States, under the ultimate authority of one person (an emperor or empress) or one sovereign State; *colloq.* a large group of companies controlled or owned by one company; a person's power or authority in an organization, esp. as represented by the number of his or her subordinates. ME. **2** A sovereign State. Now *rare* or *obs.* M16.

1 F. FITZGERALD Siam was . . building an empire out of the territories of Laos and Cambodia. *Mail on Sunday* His multi-million dollar empire all began in Uncle Robert's garage in Kansas City. *Daily Telegraph* The management appears to be top heavy, . . caused by people reluctant to give up carefully nurtured empires. *fig.*: SHELLEY Scorn and despair—these are mine empire.

II Rulership. **3** Supreme and extensive political dominion, *esp.* that exercised by an emperor. LME. **b** Absolute control; paramount influence. LME. **4** The position or dignity of an emperor. Now *rare*. E16. **5** A government in which the head of State is called an emperor or empress. Freq. as *the Empire* below. E19.

3 *Spectator* We have clung to the rhetoric of empire long after we have lost . . the ability to maintain its reality. b R. L. STEVENSON Long after that death yell was still ringing in my brain, silence had re-established its empire.

B *attrib.* or as *adj.* (Of furniture, dress, etc.) of the style fashionable in France during the Empire (or the Second Empire); (of wine) from the British Commonwealth. M19.

O. LOGAN Your new but ugly little Empire bonnet.

Comb. & *phrases*: **empire-builder** (*a*) *Hist.* a person who added to the territory of the British Empire; a British overseas administrator; (*b*) a person who seeks to increase his or her authority or staff in an organization; **empire-building** the activity of an empire-builder; **Empire City** *US* New York; **Empire Day** *Hist.* the original name of Commonwealth Day; **empire-line** *a.* (of a dress) having a high waist and a low neckline; **Empire State** *US* New York State; **Empire State of the South** *US colloq.* the American State of Georgia; (*Holy*) *Roman Empire*: see ROMAN *a.*; **Second Empire** the (period of) rule of Napoleon III as Emperor of the French, 1852–70; **the Empire** *Hist.* (*a*) the Holy Roman Empire; (*b*) the British Empire; (*c*) the (period of) rule of Napoleon Bonaparte as Emperor of the French, 1804–15.

empiric /ɛmˈpɪrɪk, ɪm-/ *a.* & *n.* LME. [L *empiricus* n. f. Gk *empeirikos*, f. *empeiria* experience, f. *empeiros* skilled, f. as EM-[2] + *peira* trial, experiment: see -IC.] **A** *adj.* = EMPIRICAL. Now chiefly *US*. LME. **B** *n.* **1** *Hist.* Any of a sect of ancient physicians who drew their rules of practice only from experience. LME. **b** *gen.* A scientist who relies solely on observation and experiment. *arch.* L16. **2** A person who practises medicine without scientific knowledge; a quack; a charlatan. *arch.* M16.

empirical /ɛmˈpɪrɪk(ə)l, ɪm-/ *a.* M16. [f. prec. + -AL[1].] **1** Based on, guided by, or employing observation and experiment rather than theory; (of a remedy, rule, etc.) used because it works, or is believed to. M16. †**b** That practises medicine without scientific knowledge. L17–M19. **2** Derived from or verifiable by experience, esp. sense-experience. M17.

1 J. BARNES A co-operative farming venture . . left him with some empirical knowledge, but little understanding of horticultural principle. M. H. ABRAMS By setting out from and terminating in an appeal to the facts, any good aesthetic theory is, indeed, empirical in method. 2 J. S. MILL An empirical law . . is an observed uniformity . . resolvable into simpler laws, but not yet resolved into them.

Special collocations: **empirical formula** *Chem.*: giving the proportions of the various elements present in a molecule, not the actual number of atoms or their arrangement. **empirical psychologist** an exponent or adherent of empirical psychology.

empirically *adv.* M17. †**empiricalness** *n.*: only in M17.

empiricism /ɛmˈpɪrɪsɪz(ə)m, ɪm-/ *n.* M17. [f. EMPIRIC + -ISM.] **1** Practice based on experiment and observation. Formerly, ignorant or unscientific practice, quackery. M17. **2** *Philos.* The doctrine or theory that all knowledge is derived from sense-experience; the doctrine or theory that concepts and statements have meaning only in relation to sense-experience. Opp. RATIONALISM 3. Cf. SENSATIONALISM 1. L18. **3** An assertion made on empirical grounds. M19.

2 *logical empiricism*: see LOGICAL *a.*

empiricist *n.* & *a.* (*a*) *n.* an exponent or adherent of empiricism; (*b*) *adj.* of, pertaining to, or characterized by philosophical empiricism: E18.

empirico- /ɛmˈpɪrɪkəʊ, ɪm-/ *comb. form.* L19. [f. EMPIRICAL, EMPIRICISM + -O-.] Used in sense 'empirical (and)', as *empirico-formalism*, *empirico-psychological*.

†**empiricutic** *a. rare* (Shakes.). Only in E17. [f. EMPIRIC after *pharmaceutic*.] Empirical.

empirio- /ɛmˈpɪrɪəʊ, ɪm-/ *comb. form.* [Alt.] = EMPIRICO-.

empirio-ˈcritical *a.* (*Philos.*) of, pertaining to, or characterized by empirio-criticism E20. **empirio-ˈcriticism** *n. Philos.* a form of positivism rejecting mind–body dualism and restricting knowledge to critically-treated experience L19.

†**empirism** *n.* E18–M19. [Fr. *empirisme*, f. *empirique*, f. as EMPIRIC: see -ISM.] Philosophical empiricism.

emplacement /ɪmˈpleɪsm(ə)nt, ɛm-/ *n.* E19. [Fr., f. as EM-[1] + *place* PLACE *n.*[1]: see -MENT.] **1** *Mil.* A defended or protected position where a gun or missile is placed ready for firing. E19. **2** Situation, position; *spec.* that of a building. E19. **3** The action of putting or settling into place. M19.

emplace *v.t.* [back-form.] put into a specified position or (*Mil.*) an emplacement; situate: M19.

emplane /ɪmˈpleɪn, ɛm-/ *v.t.* & *i.* E20. [f. EM-[1] + PLANE *n.*[4]] Take, put, or go on board an aircraft. (Foll. by *for* a destination.)

†**emplaster** *n.* LME–E19. [OFr. *emplastre* (mod. *emplâtre*) f. L *emplastrum* PLASTER *n.*] A plaster.

†**emplaster** *v.t.* LME–M17. [OFr. *emplastrer* (mod. *emplâtrer*), f. as prec.] Cover with a plaster. Also, apply as a plaster.

†**emplastic** *a.* & *n.* LME. [Late L *emplasticus* f. Gk *emplastikos*, f. *emplastron* PLASTER *n.*: see -IC.] **A** *adj.* Suitable for use as a plaster; adhesive, glutinous. Also, that stops the pores. LME–M18. **B** *n.* An adhesive or glutinous substance. M17–M18.

†**emplastration** *n.* LME. [L *emplastratio(n-)*, f. *emplastrat-* pa. ppl stem of *emplastrare*, f. *emplastrum* PLASTER *n.*: see -ATION.] **1** *Hort.* A way of budding with a piece of bark surrounding the bud and attached like a plaster to a tree. LME–M18. **2** The application of a plaster. M16–M17.

emplastrum /ɪmˈplastrəm, -plɑːs-, ɛm-/ *n. rare.* M16. [L: see PLASTER *n.*] A plaster.

†**empleach** *v.* var. of IMPLEACH.

†**emplead** *v.* var. of IMPLEAD.

†**empledge** *v.* var. of IMPLEDGE.

empleomania /ˌɛmplɪəˈmeɪnɪə/ *n.* L19. [Sp., f. *empleo* employment + -MANIA.] A mania for holding public office.

employ /ɪmˈplɔɪ, ɛm-/ *n.* Also †**im-**. M17. [f. the vb.] †1 The action of employing a person or using a thing. M17–E19. 2 = EMPLOYMENT 2. Now *poet.* & *arch.* L17. †3 = EMPLOYMENT 2b. L17–L18. †4 An official position in public service. L17–E19. 5 The state or fact of being employed, esp. for payment. E18.

5 **in the employ of** employed by (an employer).

employ /ɪmˈplɔɪ, ɛm-/ *v.t.* Also †**im-**. LME. [(O)Fr. *employer* f. Proto-Romance *implicare* for L *implicari* be involved (in) or attached (to), pass. of *implicare* enfold, involve: see IMPLICATE *v.* Cf IMPLY.] 1 Use for a particular purpose, make use of. (Foll. by *for, in, on, †to.*) LME. †2 = IMPLY 1, 2, 4. E16–E17. 3 Use or retain the services of (a person), esp. in return for payment; pay (a person) to work for oneself or one's organization. L16. 4 Keep (a person, a person's senses or powers) occupied or busy; in *pass.*, be engaged *in*, be at work *on* (also foll. by *about*). L16.

1 SHAKES. *Merch. V.* Employ your chiefest thoughts to courtship. J. G. COZZENS She employed frequently all the improper words she knew. C. S. FORESTER They were going to take a leaf out of the Germans' book and employ poison gas. A. WILSON A complicated puzzle on which to employ his wit. 3 A. BLOND If Thomas Chatterton had employed an agent he might not have starved to death. 4 SWIFT He was imploy'd in drinking. G. BERKELEY Speculations to employ our curiosity. *refl.*: T. REID Castle-builders employ themselves . . in romance.

employaˈbility *n.* the character or quality of being employable E20. **employable** *a.* L16.

employe /ɛmplɔɪˈiː, ɛmˈplɔɪiː, ɪm-/ *n.* *US.* E20. [Alt. of EMPLOYÉ, EMPLOYEE.] = EMPLOYEE. Cf. next.

employé /ɒmˈplɔɪeɪ, *foreign* ɑ̃plwaje (*pl. same*)/ *n.* Fem. **-ée**. E19. [Fr., pa. ppl a. of *employer* EMPLOY *v.*] = next. Cf. prec.

employee /ɛmplɔɪˈiː, ɛmˈplɔɪiː, ɪm-/ *n.* M19. [f. EMPLOY *v.* + -EE[1].] A person who works for an employer. Cf. prec., EMPLOYE.

employée *n.* fem. of EMPLOYÉ.

employer /ɪmˈplɔɪə, ɛm-/ *n.* Also †**im-**. L16. [f. EMPLOY *v.* + -ER[1].] A person who employs or who makes use (*of*); *esp.* a person or organization that pays someone to do work on a regular or contractual basis.

employment /ɪmˈplɔɪm(ə)nt, ɛm-/ *n.* Also †**im-**. LME. [f. EMPLOY *v.* + -MENT.] 1 The action of employing; the state of being employed. LME. †b The service of another person. L16–E17. 2 Occupation, business; paid work; an activity in which a person is engaged; *arch.* a special errand or task. L16. b A person's trade, profession, or occupation. M17. †c = EMPLOY *n.* 4. M17–M18. †3 The use or purpose to which something is put. L16–M17.

1 J. GALSWORTHY That public Museum of Art . . had given so much employment to officials. **full employment** a situation in which all persons who wish to have a job can obtain one. **in the employment of** employed by (an employer). b SHAKES. *John* At your employment, at your service, sir! 2 GOLDSMITH I . . went from town to town, working when I could get employment. F. PALGRAVE The character acquired for me by my employments. H. T. LANE He completed the destruction of the book, and then turned to some other employment. 3 SHAKES. *Rich. II* Eight thousand nobles . . The which he hath detain'd for lewd employments.

Comb.: **employment agency** a business that finds employers or employees for those seeking them; **employment exchange** or **office** a State-run employment agency.

emplume /ɛmˈpluːm, ɪm-/ *v.t.* Now *poet.* Also **im-** /ɪm-/. E17. [(O)Fr. *emplumer*, f. as EM-[1], PLUME *n.*] Adorn with or as with plumes.

†**emplunge** *v.* var. of IMPLUNGE.

†**emply** *v.* var. of IMPLY.

empocket *v.* var. of IMPOCKET.

empoison /ɪmˈpɔɪz(ə)n, ɛm-/ *v.* *arch.* Also †**im-**. LME. [OFr. *empoisoner* (mod. *-nn-*), f. as EM-[1], POISON *n.*] I†1 *v.t.* & *i.* Administer poison (to); *esp.* kill by poisoning. LME–L17. 2 *v.t.* Put poison in (food or drink); affect (the body etc.) with poison; dip (a weapon) in poison, envenom. LME.

2 J. PARKER The serpent . . shows its empoisoned fang.

II *fig.* 3 *v.t.* Taint with sin or error; corrupt, spoil. LME. 4 *v.t.* Make (a person's mind or feelings) bitter or virulent; destroy all pleasure in. L16.

4 J. HAWTHORNE His soul had been empoisoned against them and all the world.

empoisoner *n.* LME. **empoisonment** *n.* the action or act of empoisoning; the fact of being poisoned: M16.

empolder *v.* var. of IMPOLDER.

emporium /ɛmˈpɔːrɪəm, ɪm-/ *n.* Pl. **-iums, -ia** /-ɪə/. L16. [L f. Gk *emporion*, f. *emporos* merchant, f. as EM-[2] + vbl stem *por-, per-* to journey.] 1 A centre of commerce; a market. L16. 2 A shop, *esp.* one that sells unusual or fancy goods. Chiefly *joc.* M19.

2 M. MOORCOCK Kircheim's Café, a famous emporium of coffee and cream-cakes.

emporial *a.* of or pertaining to an emporium; of the nature of an emporium: E17.

†**empory** *n.* E17–L18. [f. prec.: see -Y[3].] = EMPORIUM 1.

†**empose** *v.* var. of IMPOSE *v.*

†**empound** *v.* var. of IMPOUND.

†**empoverish** *v.*, **empoverishment** *n.* vars. of IMPOVERISH, IMPOVERISHMENT.

empower /ɪmˈpaʊə, ɛm-/ *v.t.* Also †**im-**. M17. [f. EM-[1], IM-[1] + POWER *n.*] 1 Invest formally with power; authorize, license (a person *to do*). M17. 2 Endow with the ability or power required for a purpose or task; enable, permit. (Foll. by *to do.*) M17.

1 *City Limits* It did not secure the necessary two-thirds that would have empowered the WI executive to campaign actively for it. 2 DEFOE Some have doubted whether the Devil is empowered to take up any human shape.

empowerment *n.* the action of empowering someone; the state of being empowered: M17.

empress /ˈɛmprɪs/ *n.* ME. [OFr. *emperesse*, f. *emperere* EMPEROR: see -ESS[1].] 1 The wife of an emperor; a woman with the power or rank of an emperor. ME. 2 A woman exercising absolute power. ME.

2 SHAKES. *Tit. A.* Tamora, the empress of my soul.

†**empress** *v.t.* LME–E19. [(O)Fr. *empresser*: see next.] Press (*lit.* & *fig.*); oppress.

empressé /ɑ̃prɛse/ *a.* Fem. **-ée**. M19. [Fr., pa. ppl a. of *empresser* urge, (refl.) be eager, (in OFr.) press, crowd in, f. as EM-[1], PRESS *v.*[1]: cf. IMPRESS *v.*[1]] Eager, zealous; showing *empressement.*

empressement /ɑ̃prɛsmɑ̃/ *n.* E18. [Fr., f. *empresser*: see prec., -MENT.] Eagerness; effusive friendliness.

†**emprime** *v.* & *n.* var. of IMPRIME.

†**emprint** *n.*, *v.* see IMPRINT *n.*, *v.*

emprise /ɪmˈpraɪz, ɛm-/ *n.* & *v.* ME. [(O)Fr., use as n. of fem. pa. pple of OFr. *emprendre* f. Proto-Romance, f. L EM-[1] + *prehendere, prendere* take. Cf. ENTERPRISE *n.*] A *n.* 1 An undertaking, *esp.* one of an adventurous or chivalrous nature. *arch.* ME. 2 Chivalry; martial prowess. *arch.* ME. †B *v.t.* Undertake (a deed; *to do*). LME–M19.

†**emprison** *v.* see IMPRISON.

emprosthotonos /ɛmprɒsˈθɒtənɒs/ *n.* Now *rare.* LME. [Gk, f. *emprosthen* before + *tonos* a stretching.] Tetanic spasm in which the head is drawn forwards on to the chest.

†**emprove** *v.*, †**emprovement** *n.* see IMPROVE *v.*[2], IMPROVEMENT.

Empsonian /ɛm(p)ˈsəʊnɪən/ *a.* & *n.* M20. [f. *Empson* (see below) + -IAN.] A *adj.* Resembling or characteristic of the style of Sir William Empson (1906–84), Eng. poet and critic. M20.

Times Lit. Suppl. Sonnets marked by a somewhat Empsonian obscurity.

B *n.* A devotee of Empson or his work. M20.

empt /ɛm(p)t/ *v.* *obs.* exc. *dial.* [OE *ǣmtian*, f. *ǣmta, ǣmetta* leisure: see EMPTY *a.* & *n.*] †1 *v.i.* & *refl.* Be at leisure. Only in OE. 2 *v.t.* Make empty, drain, exhaust. ME. †3 *v.t.* Pour or clear out. Only in E17.

emptin *n.* see EMPTING.

emptiness /ˈɛm(p)tɪnɪs/ *n.* LME. [f. EMPTY *a.* + -NESS.] 1 The condition of being empty. LME. b The condition of being empty *of* specified contents or a particular quality. L16. 2 (An) unoccupied space; a void, a vacuum. L16. 3 In *pl.* Trivialities. M19.

1 L. DURRELL Behind lay the desert, its emptiness echoing like a seashell. D. ATHILL The area of emptiness in the emotional life of any childless woman.

empting /ˈɛm(p)tɪŋ/ *n.* In sense 2 also **-in** /-ɪn/. LME. [f. EMPT *v.* + -ING[1]. In sense 2 partly alt. of EMPTYING.] 1 The action of making empty. *obs.* exc. *dial.* LME. 2 In *pl.* Yeast; the yeasty lees of beer or cider. Cf. EMPTYING 2b. *US.* M17.

emption /ˈɛm(p)ʃ(ə)n/ *n.* LME. [L *emptio(n-)*, f. *empt-* pa. ppl stem of *emere* buy: see -ION.] †1 A tax on the sale of plate and bullion in the King's Exchange. LME–L15. 2 In *Rom. Law* (now *Hist.*), purchase in a contract of sale (correl. to VENDITION); *gen.* the action of buying. M16.

empty /ˈɛm(p)ti/ *a.* & *n.* [OE *ǣmtig, ǣmet(t)ig*, f. *ǣmta, ǣmetta* leisure, perh. f. neg. *ā-* + *mōt* meeting (see MOOT *n.*[1]).] A *adj.* †1 At leisure, unoccupied. Also, unmarried. Only in OE. 2 Of a receptacle: containing nothing. Opp. *full.* OE. b Foll. by *of*, †*in*: lacking, devoid of, (specified contents or a specified quality). L15. 3 Of space, a place, a building, etc.: unoccupied, vacant; containing no furniture or occupants; uninhabited. OE. b *Math.* & *Logic.* Of a class or set: containing no members or elements. M20. 4 Having no load or cargo; unladen. ME. b Of the hand: not bringing or taking away anything. Of a person: empty-handed. E16. 5a Of a thing: lacking substance; meaningless, ineffectual; insincere. ME. b Of a person: lacking knowledge and sense; frivolous, foolish. E17. 6†a Of the body: shrunken, emaciated, weak. LME–E18. †b Without money, destitute. L16–E18. c Hungry. Now *colloq.* L16. d Of a cow or other farm animal: not pregnant. E20.

2 A. NEWMAN Vicky put the empty suitcase on top of the wardrobe. *on an empty stomach*: see STOMACH *n.* b G. GREENE The air was empty of planes. 3 S. HAZZARD He lifted the folded mackintosh . . he had dumped on the empty seat alongside. S. NAIPAUL The office . . is empty and looks as if it has not been used for a long time. 4 **return empty** *arch.* (of a sword) come back without having been used in killing someone. b AV *Luke* 1:53 He hath filled the hungry with good things; and the rich he hath sent empty away. 5a ISAIAH BERLIN Progress and reaction, however much these words have been abused, are not empty concepts.

Special collocations & comb.: **empty calories**: from food containing no nutrients. **empty-handed** *a.* having or bearing nothing (*come empty-handed*, bring nothing, esp. no gift: *go empty-handed*, leave having gained nothing). **empty-headed** lacking common sense or intelligence, frivolous. **empty nest** *fig.* a household where the parents alone remain after the children have grown up and left home. **empty nester** *colloq.* a person whose children have grown up and left home. **Empty Quarter** the Rubʻ al-Ḳālī, a desert region in the south of the Arabian peninsula. **empty word** *Gram.*: having no meaning in itself but having a grammatical function.

B *n.* An empty vehicle, container, etc.; *esp.* one from which the contents have been removed. M19.

Time Out One can actually imagine him taking back the tavern empties.

empty /ˈɛm(p)ti/ *v.* E16. [f. EMPTY *a.*: cf. OE *geǣmtigian.*] 1 *v.t.* Make empty; remove or clear out the contents of; deprive *of* specified contents or a specified quality. E16. b Transfer the contents of (one receptacle) *into* another. L16. c Remove (contents) from what contains them; transfer (contents) from one receptacle *into* another. Also foll. by *out* (*into*). L16. 2 *v.refl.* & (chiefly *N. Amer.*) *i.* Of a river etc.: discharge itself *into* another river, the sea, etc.; flow *into*. M16. 3 *v.refl.* Chiefly *Theol.*, of Christ: drain oneself of resources or *of* a particular attribute; efface oneself utterly. L16. 4 *v.i.* Become empty. M17.

1 D. HAMMETT Spade . . emptied his lungs with a long sighing exhalation. E. BOWEN The greengrocer's crates had been emptied of all but earth. b I. MCEWAN A second bar-hand came by to empty the ashtray into a bucket. c H. ROTH She . . emptied out the peelings that cluttered the sink into the garbage can. 2 T. O'BRIEN Eisenhower Avenue emptied into a huge traffic circle. 4 J. BUCHAN The carriage had emptied, and I was left alone.

emptying /ˈɛm(p)tɪɪŋ/ *n.* L16. [f. EMPTY *v.* + -ING[1].] 1 The action of making empty. L16. 2 What is emptied out of something. M17. b In *pl.* = EMPTING 2. *US.* M19.

empurple /ɪmˈpəːp(ə)l, ɛm-/ *v.* Also †**im-**. L16. [f. EM-[1], IM-[1] + PURPLE *a.* & *n.*] 1 *v.t.* Make purple; *rare* clothe in purple. L16. 2 *v.i.* Become purple. L18.

Empusa /ɛmˈpjuːzə/ *n.* Also †**Empuse, e-**. E17. [Gk *Empousa.*] 1 *Class. Mythol.* A hobgoblin supposed to be sent by Hecate. E17. †2 A spectre, a bogey. Only in 17.

empyema /ɛmpʌɪˈiːmə/ *n.* LME. [Late L f. Gk *empuēma*, f. *empuein* suppurate, f. as EM-[2] + *puon* pus.] *Med.* A condition characterized by an accumulation of pus in a body cavity, esp. the pleural cavity.

empyreal /ɛmpʌɪˈriːəl, -pɪ-, ɛmˈpɪrɪəl/ *a. arch.* & *poet.* LME. [med.L *empyreus* (late L *empyrius*), f. Gk *empurios*, f. as EM-[2] + *pur* fire: see -AL[1].] 1 = EMPYREAN *a.*; *fig.* sublime, exalted. LME. b Of or pertaining to the sky or heavens; celestial. M18. 2 Fiery; composed of or resembling the pure element fire. E17. †3 *Chem.* Of a gas: able to support combustion. L18–E19.

empyrean /ɛmpʌɪˈriːən, -pɪ-, ɛmˈpɪrɪən/ *a.* & *n. arch.* & *poet.* LME. [f. as prec.: see -EAN.] A *adj.* Of or pertaining to the empyrean. LME.

B *n.* 1 The highest heaven, thought by the ancients to be the realm of pure fire and by early Christians to be the abode of God and the angels; *fig.* an exalted region, realm, or group. M17. 2 The heavens, the sky; cosmic space. E19.

1 P. ZIEGLER Both men were members of that conjurors' empyrean, the Magic Circle.

†**empyreum** *n.* E17–L18. [med.L *empyreum* (sc. *caelum*) neut. of *empyreus*: see EMPYREAL.] The empyrean.

empyreuma /ɛmpɪˈruːmə/ *n.* M17. [Gk *empureuma* live coal covered with ashes, f. *empureuein* set on fire, f. as EM-[2] + *pur* fire.] An empyreumatic smell or taste.

empyreumatic /ɛmˌpɪrʊˈmatɪk/ *a.* M17. [Gk *empureumat-* stem of *empureuma*: see prec., -IC.] Having or designating a foul smell or taste produced when organic matter is heated but prevented from burning.

empyreumatical *a.* (*arch.*) M17.

emu /ˈiːmjuː/ *n.* Also †**emeu**, (orig.) †**eme**. E17. [Port. *ema.*] †1 A cassowary. E17–E18. †2 The greater rhea, *Rhea americana*. Only in L18. 3 A large shaggy flightless fast-running Australian bird, *Dromaius novaehollandiae*, related to the cassowary and ostrich. E19.

Comb.: **emu-apple** (the succulent fruit of) an Australian tree, *Owenia acidula*, of the mahogany family; also called *native peach*; **emu-bob** *v.i.* & *t.* (*Austral.*) pick up small pieces of timber from (an area) after clearing or burning; **emu-bush** any of several Australian shrubs, esp. of the genus *Eremophila* (family Myoporaceae), the fruits of which are eaten by the emu; **emu-wren** any of three very small Australian songbirds of the genus *Stipiturus* (family Maluridae), which have very long tail feathers with the sparse open structure seen in emu feathers.

†**emulate** *a. rare* (Shakes.). Only in E17. [L *aemulatus* pa. pple of *aemulari*: see next, -ATE[2].] Ambitious.

emulate /ˈɛmjʊleɪt/ *v.* L16. [L *aemulat-* pa. ppl stem of *aemulari*, f. *aemulus* rival: see -ATE[3].] 1 *v.t.* Compete with; rival or equal in some respect. L16. †2 *v.i.* Strive in a spirit of rivalry *to be* or *to do*. L16–M17. 3 *v.t.* Imitate zealously; try to equal or excel. L16. †4 *v.t.* Wish to rival (a person); be envious or jealous of. E–M17. 5 *v.t.* (Of a computer etc. or its user) reproduce the action of (a different computer or software system) with the aid of hardware or software designed to effect this; run (a program etc.) on a computer other than that for which it was written. M20.

1 SHAKES. *Merry W.* I see how thine eye would emulate the diamond. SIR W. SCOTT My royal nephew will soon emulate his father's wisdom. 3 K. A. PORTER They were . . ideal characters and the first the children had ever admired and longed to emulate.

emulation /ɛmjʊˈleɪʃ(ə)n/ *n.* M16. [L *aemulatio(n-)*, f. as prec.: see -ATION.] 1 The desire or endeavour to equal or surpass others in some achievement or quality. M16. †2 Ambitious rivalry; contention or ill will between rivals. M16–E18. †3 Envy; resentment or disparagement of one's superiors. M16–L18. 4 The technique by which a computer or software system is enabled to execute programs written for a different type of computer, by means of special hardware or software. M20.

emulative /ˈɛmjʊlətɪv/ *a.* L16. [f. EMULATE *v.* + -IVE.] 1 Resulting from or characterized by emulation. L16. 2 Tending or disposed to emulate; imitative *of*. M18.

1 J. HOOLE Emulative zeal. 2 S. RICHARDSON Noble minds, emulative of perfection.

emulatively *adv.* (*rare*) M18. **emulativeness** *n.* (*rare*) L19.

emulator /ˈɛmjʊleɪtə/ *n.* L16. [L *aemulator*, f. as EMULATE *v.*: see -OR.] 1 A person who emulates. L16. 2 A piece of computer hardware or software used with one device to enable it to emulate another. M20.

†**emulatress** *n.* (*rare*) a female emulator E17–M18.

emulge /ɪˈmʌldʒ/ *v.t.* Now *rare* or *obs.* L17. [L *emulgere* milk out: see EMULSION.] Drain (a bodily duct or secretory organ).

emulgent /ɪˈmʌldʒ(ə)nt/ *a.* Now *rare.* L16. [L *emulgent-* pres. ppl stem of *emulgere*: see EMULSION, -ENT.] A *adj.* That strains or purifies; *spec.* designating a renal artery or vein. L16. B *n.* A renal artery or vein. E17.

emulgence *n.* (*rare*) the action or an act of draining something of goodness or substance L17.

emulous /ˈɛmjʊləs/ *a.* LME. [L *aemulus*: see -ULOUS.] †1a Of a thing: closely resembling, imitative *of*. Only in LME. b Seeking to imitate or rival someone or something. (Foll. by *of*.) M17. 2 Characterized or actuated by a spirit of rivalry. Formerly also, zealous; rival. M16. †3 Covetous of praise or power; envious. E–M17.

1b D. M. DAVIN She was . . always emulous of the title and status of Professor. 2 LONGFELLOW Where every emulous scholar hears . . The rustling of another's laurels!

emulously *adv.* M17.

emulsify /ɪˈmʌlsɪfʌɪ/ *v.t.* M19. [f. L *emuls-* + (see EMULSION) + -I- + -FY.] Convert into an emulsion.

emulsifia'bility *n.* the property of being emulsifiable M20. **emulsifiable** *a.* M20. **emulsifi'cation** *n.* L19. **emulsifier** *n.* an apparatus which emulsifies oils etc.; a substance which promotes the emulsification of two liquids: L19.

emulsion /ɪˈmʌlʃ(ə)n/ *n.* & *v.* E17. [Fr. *émulsion* or mod.L *emulsio(n-)*, f. L *emuls-* pa. ppl stem of *emulgere* milk out, f. *e-* E- + *mulgere* to milk (cf. MILK *n.*): see -ION.] A *n.* 1 Orig., a milky liquid obtained by crushing almonds in water. Later, any mixture of two immiscible liquids (e.g. oil and water) in which one is dispersed throughout the other in small droplets (though not as small as in a colloid). E17. b In full *emulsion paint.* A paint consisting of an emulsion of resin in water. M20. 2 A light-sensitive coating on photographic films and plates, consisting of crystals of a silver halide dispersed in a medium such as gelatin. E17.

2 *nuclear emulsion*: see NUCLEAR *a.*

B *v.t.* 1 = EMULSIFY. Now *rare* or *obs.* M18. 2 Paint with emulsion paint. M20.

emulsive /ɪˈmʌlsɪv/ *a.* M19. [f. L *emuls-* (see prec.) + -IVE.] Of the nature of an emulsion.

emulsoid /ɪˈmʌlsɔɪd/ *n.* E20. [f. EMULSION + -OID.] A colloidal system consisting of one liquid dispersed in another; a lyophilic sol.

emunctory /ɪˈmʌŋkt(ə)ri/ *n.* & *a.* LME. [med.L *emunctorius* adj., *-ium* n., f. L *emunct-* pa. ppl stem of *emungere* wipe or blow the nose: see -ORY[2], -ORY[1].] A *n.* A part of the body that serves to cleanse it or get rid of waste products. LME. B *adj.* 1 What is an emunctory. M16. 2 Pertaining to the blowing of the nose. M19.

†**emunge** *v.t.* M17–M19. [L *emungere*: see prec.] Wipe, clean out; *fig.* cheat.

en /ɛn/ *n.* L18. [Repr. pronunc. of *N*, *n* as the letter's name: cf. EM.] 1 The letter N, n. L18. 2 *Typogr.* A unit of horizontal measurement in typesetting, equal to half the body of any size of metal type or half the nominal type-size in photosetting, used for calculating the extent of a line or text; half an em. L18.

Comb.: **en dash** an en rule; **en quad, quadrat** a spacing unit half as wide as an em quadrat; **en rule** a rule an en long, a short dash (as in *1914–18*).

en- /ɪn, ɛn/ *pref.*[1] [Repr. (O)Fr. *en-* f. L IN-[2]. See also EM-[1].] Used in wds adopted f. Fr. and in Eng. wds modelled on these as a freely productive pref., forming vbs (*a*) f. ns., w. the sense 'put into or on', as *enamour, encurtain, engulf, enshroud, entrust*; (*b*) f. ns. or adjs., w. the sense 'bring into the condition or state denoted', as *enrapture, enslave*, sometimes combined w. suff. -EN[5], as *enlighten, enliven*; (*c*) f. vbs, w. the sense 'in, into, on', as *enfold*, or intensive, as *entangle*. Often with parallel forms in IN-[2].

en'centre *v.t.* place in the centre E17. †**endart** *v.t.* (*rare*, Shakes.) direct swiftly, dart, (one's eye): only in L16. †**enfierce** *v.t.* (*rare*, Spenser) make fierce: only in L16. †**enfree** *v.t.* set free L16–E17. **en'freedom** *v.t.* give freedom to L16. **en'guard** *v.t.* guard (carefully) E17. **en'saffron** *v.t.* tinge with saffron-yellow colour M17. **en'sulphur** *v.t.* make sulphurous E17. **en'verdure** *v.t.* make verdurous, cover with verdure L15. †**enwallow** *v.i.* (*rare*, Spenser) wallow: only in L16. **en'wood** *v.t.* cover with trees E17.

en- /ɪn, ɛn/ *pref.*[2] (not productive). Repr. Gk *en-* in, inside, as in *energy, enthusiasm*. See also EM-[2].

-en /ɪn, (ə)n/ *suff.*[1] (not productive). [OE f. Gmc neut. of base of -EN[4].] Forming dims. of ns., as *chicken, maiden*.

-en /(ə)n/ *suff.*[2] (not productive). [OE f. Gmc.] Forming fem. ns., as *vixen*, and abstract ns., as *burden*.

-en /(ə)n/ *suff.*[3] (not productive). [OE *-an*, orig. part of the stem of weak ns.] The termination of the pl. of weak ns., surviving in *oxen*; later forming pl. ns., as *kine*, esp. added to other pls., as in *brethren, children*.

-en /(ə)n/ *suff.*[4] (not productive). After *r* in unstressed syllables **-n.** [OE f. Gmc, = Gk *-inos*, L *-inus* -INE[1], -INE[2].] Forming adjs. f. ns., with senses 'pertaining to, of the nature of, (*esp.*) made of', as *earthen, wheaten, wooden, woollen*. In other wds now chiefly *arch.*, as *silvern*, or metaphorical, as *golden*, having been superseded in general by attrib. use of the n.

-en /(ə)n/ *suff.*[5] (rarely productive). [OE *-nian* f. Gmc. Most wds are later and on the anal. of OE vbs.] 1 Forming vbs w. the sense 'make or become', f. adjs., as *deepen, fasten, moisten*, or f. ns., as *listen*, (later, on the anal. of vbs f. adjs.) *happen, hearten, strengthen*. 2 Occas. repr. Gmc formative of pres. stem in some strong vbs, as in *waken*.

-en /(ə)n/ *suff.*[6] (not productive). After *r* & (*arch.*) *-l* **-n.** [OE *-en* = OS, OHG *-an*, ON *-inn*, *-enn*, Goth. *-ans*, f. Gmc.] Forming the pa. pple of strong vbs, also ppl adjs. f. such pples (senses as for those in -ED[1]), as *mistaken, torn, outspoken*, freq. now in restricted use, as *bounden, cloven, drunken, gotten, proven*. Cf. -ED[1].

enable /ɪnˈeɪb(ə)l, ɛn-/ *v.* Also †**in-**. LME. [f. EN-[1], IN-[2] + ABLE *a.*: cf. ABLE *v.*] 1 *v.t.* a Give power to; strengthen; make adequate or competent. (Foll. by *for, to*.) Now *rare*. LME. b Make able, give the means, *to be* or *to do* something. M16. †2 *v.i.* Become able, gain strength or power. LME–M17. †3 *v.t.* Invest with legal status. L15–E18. 4 *v.t.* Give legal power to; authorize, sanction. L15. †5 *v.t.* Regard as competent. M–L16. 6 *v.t.* Make (an action) possible or effective; make (a device) operational, turn on. E17.

1a *Church Times* The clergy are like joints in the Body of Christ, enabling the Church in its life and mission. b J. BUCHAN Oxford . . enabled me to discover what talents I had. 4 LD MACAULAY An act was . . passed enabling beneficed clergymen . . to hold preferment in England. **enabling act** (*a*) a statute empowering a person or body to take certain action; (*b*) (chiefly *US*) a statute legalizing something otherwise unlawful. 6 P. CASEMENT Psychoanalysis has the potential for enabling a re-birth of the . . personality.

enablement *n.* the action or a means of enabling L15. **enabler** *n.* a person who enables someone; *esp.* a person who helps others to achieve their potential or develop skills: E17.

enact /ɪˈnakt, ɛ-/ *v.t.* Pa. pple **-ed**, (*rare*) **enact**. LME. [f. EN-[1] + ACT *n.*, *v.*, after med.L *inactare*, *inactitare*.] †1 Enter in a public record; chronicle. LME–M17. 2 Make (a bill etc.) into an act; establish (a law, legal penalty, etc.); decree (a thing, *that*). LME. †b Declare officially; appoint. E17–E18. 3 Represent (a scene, play, etc.) on or as on a stage; play (a part); take part in (a drama or scene in real life). LME. †4 Accomplish (a deed). L16–E17. †5 Actuate, influence; inspire; implant (a feeling etc.) *into* a person. E17–M19.

2 ADAM SMITH In 1463 it was enacted that no wheat should be imported. A. STORR There is little point in enacting savage penalties even for savage crime. 3 H. JAMES The scene enacted in the great awe-stricken house. P. ROSE Marriages . . in which the two partners agree on the scenario they are enacting.

¶ Cf. ACT *n.*, *v.*

enactable *a.* L19. **enaction** *n.* (an) enactment M17. **enactive** *a.* pertaining to or concerned with the enactment of law M17. **enactor** *n.* a person who enacts something E17. **enactory** *n.* = ENACTIVE M19. †**enacture** *n.* (*rare*, Shakes.) performance, fulfilment: only in E17.

enactment /ɪˈnaktm(ə)nt, ɛ-/ *n.* E19. [f. ENACT + -MENT, superseding ENACTION.] 1 The action of enacting a law; the state or fact of being enacted. E19. 2 A thing which is enacted; an ordinance, a statute. E19. b In *pl.* The provisions of a law. M19.

enaliosaur /ɪˈnalɪəsɔː/ *n.* Now *rare* or *obs.* M19. [f. Gk *enalios* of the sea, f. as EN-[2] + *hali-* comb. form of *halo-*, *hals* sea: see -SAUR.] Any of various extinct marine reptiles of Mesozoic times, such as a plesiosaur or an ichthyosaur.

enalio'saurian *a.* & *n.* M19.

enallage /ɪˈnalədʒi, ɛ-/ *n.* Now *rare.* E16. [Late L f. Gk *enallagē*, f. base of *enallassein* to exchange, f. as EN-[2] + *allassein* to change, f. *allos* other.] The substitution of one grammatical form for another, as of singular for plural, present for past tense, etc.

†**enaluron** *n.* M16–M18. [Origin uncertain: perh. f. AN.] *Her.* A bordure charged with birds, usu eight in number.

enam /ɪˈnɑːm/ *n.* E19. [Urdu (Pers.) f. Arab. *'in'ām* favour, grant, vbl n. of *'an'ama* bestow a favour.] In the Indian subcontinent: a grant of land free of the land-tax due to the State; land so held.

enamdar /ɪˈnɑːmdɑː/ *n.* [Pers. *-dār* holder] a person who holds an *enam* M19.

enamel /ɪˈnam(ə)l/ *n.* Also †**in-**. LME. [f. the vb.: cf. AMEL *n.*] 1 A glassy opaque or semi-transparent coating applied by fusion to metallic or other hard surfaces, either as ornamentation or as a protective coating. LME. 2 Smooth bright surface-colouring; verdure. Chiefly *poet.* E17. 3 The very hard calcareous substance that occurs as a glossy coating on the crowns of teeth; any of several similar substances forming the outer layer of fish scales. E18. 4 A painting or other artistic work done in enamel. M18. 5 In full *enamel paint*. A kind of paint which flows freely and gives a very smooth glossy finish. M19. 6 A cosmetic giving a smooth glossy appearance. M20.

1 A. URE The enamel of these saucepans is quite free from lead. *fig.*: JER. TAYLOR Those Truths . . are the enamel and beauty of our Churches. 2 W. GOLDING Not a crack in the sky, not a blemish on the dense blue enamel.

Comb.: *enamel paint*: see sense 5 above; **enamel painting** the production of a picture by coating a hard surface with different colours of enamel; **enamelware** enamelled kitchenware; **enamelwork** a product made with the use of enamel.

enamel /ɪˈnam(ə)l/ *v.t.* Also †**in-**. Infl. **-ll-**, ***-l-**. LME. [AN *enameler*, *enamailler*, f. as EN-[1], IN-[2] + *amail*: see AMEL.] 1 Inlay, encrust, or coat (esp. metal) with enamel or a substance resembling enamel; apply a smooth hard coating to. LME. b Apply make-up to (the face) to give an appearance of smoothness; apply nail polish to (a fingernail). E19. 2 Portray (figures etc.) with enamel. L15. †3 *fig.* Adorn magnificently; embellish superficially. L16–L17. 4 Variegate like enamelled work; adorn with rich and varied colours. *arch.* M17.

4 T. PRINGLE Millions of flowers of the most brilliant hues enamel the earth.

enameller *n.* a person who enamels something E17. **enamellist** *n.* an artist who works in enamel L19. **enamelling** *n.* (*a*) the action or technique of the vb; (*b*) enamel coating: LME.

enamelled /ɪˈnam(ə)ld/ *a.* Also †**in-**, ***-eled**. E16. [f. ENAMEL *v.* + -ED[1].] †1 a Of literary style, a speaker, etc.: ornate, florid. E16–M17. b Adorned with varied colours. E17. 2 Having naturally a hard polished surface, like enamel. L16. 3 Ornamented or coated with enamel; given a glossy coating. E17.

3 *Punch* An engraved invitation on enamelled paper. *Discovery* Enamelled kitchen stoves. G. VIDAL The walls . . are covered with enamelled tiles depicting lions.

enamor *v.* see ENAMOUR.

†**enamorado** *n.* E17–M18. [Sp. use as n. of pa. pple of *enamorar* win the love of (cf. ENAMOUR).] A lover.

†**enamorata** *n.* var. of INAMORATA.

†**enamorate** *v.* see INAMORATE *v.*

†**enamorato** *n.* var. of INAMORATO.

enamour /ɪˈnamə, ɛ-/ *v.t.* Also †**in-**, ***enamor**. ME. [(O)Fr. *enamourer* (cf. It. *innamorare*, Sp. *enamorar*), f. as EN-[1], IN-[2] + AMOUR.] 1 Inspire or inflame with love. Usu. in *pass.* Foll. by *of*, *with*, †*on*. ME. 2 Charm, delight, please. Usu. in *pass.* Foll. by *of*, †*on*, †*with*. L16.

1 WELLINGTON He was much enamored of one of the Koorg Rajah's sisters. 2 N. SHUTE I take it that you aren't enamoured of the navy.

enamouredness *n.* (*rare*) = ENAMOURMENT L17. **enamourment** *n.* the state of being enamoured E18.

enanthema /ɛnənˈθiːmə/ *n.* Also Anglicized as **enanthem** /ɪˈnanθɪm/. M19. [f. EN-[2] + EX)ANTHEMA.] *Med.* An eruption occurring on a mucus-secreting surface (e.g. the inside of the mouth).

enanthic *a.* var. of OENANTHIC.

enantio- /ɪˈnantɪəʊ, ɛ-/ *comb. form* of Gk *enantios* opposite: see -O-.

enantio'pathic *a.* (now *rare*) allopathic M19. **enanti'opathy** *n.* (now *rare*) allopathy M19.

enantiodromia /ɪˌnantɪə(ʊ)ˈdrəʊmɪə, ɛ-/ *n.* E20. [Gk = running in contrary ways, f. as ENANTIO- + *dromos* running: see -IA[1].] The process by which something becomes its opposite, and the effects of this; *esp.* the adoption of a set of beliefs which are opposed to those previously held.

eˌnantiodro'miacal, **enantiodromic** *adjs.* M20.

enantiomer /ɪˈnantɪə(ʊ)mə, ɛ-/ *n.* M20. [f. ENANTIO- + -MER.] *Chem.* An enantiomorphous molecule or substance; an optical isomer.

enantio'meric *a.* M20. **enanti'omerism** *n.* the fact or condition of being enantiomeric M20.

enantiomorph /ɪˈnantɪə(ʊ)mɔːf, ɛ-/ *n.* L19. [f. ENANTIO- + -MORPH.] A form (*esp.* a crystal or molecule) related to another as an object is to its image in a mirror; a non-superposable mirror image.

enantio'morphic *a.* = ENANTIOMORPHOUS E20. **enantio'morphically** *adv.* E20. **enantio'morphism** *n.* the fact or condition of being enantiomorphic; the occurrence of two enantiomorphic crystalline forms of a substance: L19. **enantio'morphous** *a.* of or pertaining to an enantiomorph; of the nature of an enantiomorph or enantiomorphs: L19. **enantio'morphously** *adv.* L19.

enantiotropy /ɪˌnantɪˈɒtrəpi, ɛ-/ *n.* E20. [f. ENANTIO- + -TROPY.] *Chem.* The existence of two forms of a substance, one stable above a certain transition temperature at which they are interconverted, the other stable below it.

enantiotropic /-ˈtrəʊpɪk, -ˈtrɒpɪk, ɛ-/ *a.* E20.

enarch /ɛnˈɑːtʃ/ *v.*[1]*t.* Now *rare.* Also **inarch** /ɪn-/. LME. [f. as EN-[1], IN-[2] + ARCH *n.*[1]; perh. orig. f. OFr. *enarchier*.] 1 Build or draw in the form of an arch. LME. 2 Arch in, set or draw an arch over. M16.

†**enarch** *v.*[2] var. of INARCH *v.*[1]

enargite /ˈɛnɑːgʌɪt/ *n.* M19. [f. Gk *enargēs* clear (w. ref. to its cleavage being evident) + -ITE[1].] A sulphide of copper and arsenic that is an important copper ore and occurs as dark grey orthorhombic, usu. prismatic, crystals.

enarm /ɪnˈɑːm, ɛn-/ *v.*[1]*t.* Now *rare* or *obs.* LME. [OFr. *enarmer* arm, equip, f. as EN-[1] + *armer* ARM *v.*[1]] 1 Equip with weapons. *obs.* exc. *Sc.* LME. 2 *gen.* Equip, provide *with*, adorn *with*. LME.

enarm *v.*[2] var. of INARM.

†**enarration** *n.* L16. [L *enarratio(n-)*, f. *e-* E- + *narratio(n-)*: see NARRATION.] 1 An exposition, a commentary. L16–M17. 2 A description, a detailed narrative. L16–E19.

enarthrodial /ɛnɑːˈθrəʊdɪəl/ *a.* Now *rare.* M19. [f. EN-[1] + ARTHRODIA + -AL[1].] *Anat.* Pertaining to or being an enarthrosis.

enarthrosis /ɛnɑːˈθrəʊsɪs/ *n.* Pl. **-throses** /-ˈθrəʊsiːz/. L16. [Gk *enarthrōsis*, f. *enarthros* jointed: see -OSIS. Cf. EN-[2], ARTHROSIS.] *Anat.* A ball-and-socket joint; *esp.* one where the socket covers more than half of the ball.

enascent /ɪˈnas(ə)nt/ *a. rare.* M18. [L *enascent-* pres. ppl stem of *enasci*: see next, -ENT.] That is just coming into being.

enation /ɪˈneɪʃ(ə)n/ *n.* M19. [L *enatio(n-)*, f. *enasci* issue forth, be born, f. *e-* E- + *nasci* be born: see -ATION.] *Biol.* An outgrowth from the surface of an organ (e.g. from a leaf).

en attendant /ɑ̃n atɑ̃dɑ̃/ *adv. phr.* M18. [Fr.] In the meantime, while waiting.

†**enaunter** *conj.* Also **in-**. LME–E17. [Var. of *an*, *in*, *on aunter*, Fr. *en aventure*: see ADVENTURE *n.*] In case, lest by chance.

en avant /ɑ̃n avɑ̃/ *adv.* & *int. phr.* E19. [Fr.] Forward, onwards.

BYRON But never mind—*en avant!* live while you can.

en beau /ɑ̃ bo/ *adv. phr.* E19. [Fr.] In a favourable manner; in the best light.

en bloc /ɑ̃ blɔk, ɒ̃ ˈblɒk/ *adv.* & *a. phr.* M19. [Fr.] A *adv. phr.* As a whole; collectively, all together. M19.

B. BEAUMONT We would go en bloc to a film.

B *a. phr.* Performed or made *en bloc*. E20.

en brosse /ɑ̃ brɔs/ *adv. phr.* E20. [Fr.] Of hair: cut short and bristly.

en cabochon /ɑ̃ kabɔʃɔ̃/ *adv. phr.* E19. [Fr.] With ref. to gem-cutting: as a cabochon; with curved surfaces rather than facets.

Encaenia /ɛnˈsiːnɪə/ *n.* LME. [L f. Gk *egkainia* dedication festival, f. as EN-[2] + *kainos* new, recent.] †1 A renewal; a dedicatory festival. Only in LME. 2 The anniversary festival of the dedication of a place of worship, esp. (in Judaism) of the Temple at Jerusalem. Now *rare* or *obs.* LME. 3 The annual Commemoration of founders and benefactors at Oxford University. L17.

encage /ɪnˈkeɪdʒ, ɛn-/ *v.t.* Also †**in-**. L16. [f. EN-[1], IN-[2] + CAGE *v.*] Confine (as) in a cage.

encamp /ɪnˈkamp, ɛn-/ *v.* Also †**in-**. M16. [f. EN-[1], IN-[2] + CAMP *n.*[2]] 1 *v.t.* & *i.* Lodge (soldiers) in a camp; establish a settled or fortified camp. M16. 2 *v.i.* Make camp; lodge in the open or in a temporary shelter. E18.

encampment /ɪnˈkampm(ə)nt, ɛn-/ *n.* Also †**in-**. L16. [f. prec. + -MENT.] 1 A place where troops are encamped; the temporary quarters of nomads, travellers, etc. L16. 2 The action or an act of encamping; the state of being encamped. L17. 3 A Masonic meeting. L18.

For other words beginning with *en-* see the entry for **en-**[1]

encapsidate /ɪn'kapsɪdeɪt, ɛn-/ *v.t.* L20. [f. EN-[1] + CAPSID *n.*[2] + -ATE[3].] *Microbiol.* Enclose in a capsid.
encapsi'dation *n.* L20.

encapsulate /ɪn'kapsjʊleɪt, ɛn-/ *v.t.* Also **in-** /ɪn-/ L19. [f. EN-[1], IN-[2] + CAPSULE *n.* + -ATE[3].] **1** Enclose in or as in a capsule. L19. **2** *fig.* Exemplify the essential features of; epitomize, typify. M20.
2 V. GLENDINNING A story that encapsulates the confusion of social change.
encapsu'lation *n.* M19.

encapsule /ɪn'kapsjuːl, ɛn-/ *v.t.* L19. [f. EN-[1] + CAPSULE *n.*] = ENCAPSULATE.

encaptivate /ɪn'kaptɪveɪt, ɛn-/ *v.t. rare.* Also †**in-**. E17. [f. EN-[1], IN-[2] + CAPTIVATE *v.*] Make captive, ensnare, (*lit.* & *fig.*); captivate.

encarnadine *v.* var. of INCARNADINE *v.*

encarnalize /ɪn'kɑːn(ə)lʌɪz, ɛn-/ *v.t.* Also **in-** /ɪn-/, **-ise**. M19. [f. EN-[1], IN-[2] + CARNALIZE.] Embody (a spirit, *fig.* an idea); make carnal or sensual.

encase /ɪn'keɪs, ɛn-/ *v.t.* Also †**in-**. M17. [f. EN-[1], IN-[2] + CASE *n.*[2]] **1** Cover or surround like a case; in *pass.*, clad *in*. M17. **2** Put into or enclose within a case or receptacle. E18.
1 P. CAMPBELL The feet were encased in red woollen socks. G. VIDAL Clouds and smog encased Manhattan Island like a celluloid bell. **encased knot** a knot of dead wood surrounded by, but not connected to, the living wood. 2 E. K. KANE The body was encased in a decent pine coffin.

encasement /ɪn'keɪsm(ə)nt, ɛn-/ *n.* Also (*arch.*) **in-** /ɪn-/. M18. [f. ENCASE + -MENT.] **1** A thing that encases; a receptacle, a covering. M18. **2** The act of encasing; the state of being encased; *spec.* in *Bee-keeping*, the surrounding of a queen by worker bees; the mass of bees so produced. E19.

encash /ɪn'kaʃ, ɛn-/ *v.t.* M19. [f. EN-[1] + CASH *n.*[1]] Convert (a draft, bill, cheque, etc.) into cash; obtain in the form of cash payments, realize.
encashable *a.* E20. **encashment** *n.* the action of encashing; the amount of cash receipts: M19.

encaustic /ɛn'kɔːstɪk/ *a.* & *n.* L16. [L *encausticus* f. Gk *egkaustikos*, f. *egkaiein* burn in, f. as EN-[2] + *kaiein* to burn: see -IC.] **A** *adj.* **1** Employing or involving strong heat to fix colours, *spec.* using pigments mixed with wax which is burnt in; (of a painting) produced in this way. L16. **2** Of a brick or tile: decorated with differently coloured clays that are inlaid and burnt in. M19. **B** *n.* **1** [repr. Gk *egkaustikē tekhnē*.] The art or process of encaustic painting. E17. **2** Encaustic work. M18.

encave /ɪn'keɪv, ɛn-/ *v.t.* Also †**in-**. E17. [f. EN-[1], IN-[2] + CAVE *n.*[1]] Enclose or shut up (as) in a cave.

encavern /ɪn'kav(ə)n, ɛn-/ *v.t. rare.* E17. [f. EN-[1] + CAVERN *n.*] Enclose or shut up (as) in a cavern.

-ence /(ə)ns/ *suff.* [Fr. f. L (i) *-entia*, f. pres. ppl stems in *-ent-* -ENT, (ii) *-antia*: see -ANCE.] Forming ns. of quality (or instances of it), as *congruence*, *impertinence*, *sapience*, or of action, as *reference*, *reminiscence*. Since 16 many wds ending in *-ance* f. Fr. have been altered back to *-ence* after L, and more recent wds have taken *-ance* or *-ence* according to the L vowel (hence much inconsistency, as *dependence*, *-ance*, *resistance*, *subsistence*). Cf. -ENCY.

enceinte /ɑ̃sɛ̃ːt, ɒ'sãt/ *n.* Pl. pronounced same. E18. [Fr. f. L *incincta* fem. pa. pple of *incingere* gird in f. IN-[2] + *cingere* gird.] The main enclosure or enclosing wall of a fortified place.

enceinte /ɑ̃sɛ̃t, ɒ'sãt/ *a. arch.* Also †***enseint***. See also ENSIENT. E17. [Fr. f. med.L *incincta* ungirded, f. L IN-[3] + *cincta* fem. pa. pple of *cingere* gird.] Of a woman: pregnant.

encell /ɪn'sɛl, ɛn-/ *v.t.* M17. [f. EN-[1] + CELL *n.*[1]] Place in or as in a cell.

†**encense** *n.*, *v.* see INCENSE *n.*, *v.*[1], *v.*[2]

encentre /ɪn'sɛntə, ɛn-/ *v.t. rare.* E17. [f. EN-[1] + CENTRE *n.*] Centre *in* something, place in the centre.

encephal- *comb. form* see ENCEPHALO-.

encephalic /ɛnsɪ'falɪk, ɛn'kɛf(ə)lɪk/ *a.* M19. [f. Gk *egkephalos* brain (see ENCEPHALO-) + -IC.] Of, pertaining to, or affecting the brain.

encephalisation *n.* var. of ENCEPHALIZATION.

encephalitis /ɛn,sɛfə'lʌɪtɪs, -kɛf-/ *n.* Pl. **-litides** /-'lɪtɪdiːz/. M19. [f. ENCEPHALO- + -ITIS.] Inflammation of the brain, esp. sufficient to impair its function; a condition in which this is a dominant symptom.
encephalitis C = ST LOUIS ENCEPHALITIS.
encephalitic /-'lɪtɪk/ *a.* L19. ,**encepha'litogen** *n.* an encephalitogenic agent M20. **en,cephalito'genic** *a.* capable of causing encephalitis E20. **en,cephalitoge'nicity** *n.* the property of being encephalitogenic M20.

encephalization /ɛn,sɛf(ə)lʌɪ'zeɪʃ(ə)n/ *n.* Also **-isation**. M20. [f. ENCEPHALO- + -IZATION.] An evolutionary increase in the complexity or relative size of the brain; a shift of function from non-cortical parts of the brain to the cortex.

encephalo- /ɛn'sɛf(ə)ləʊ, ɛn'kɛf-/ *comb. form* of Gk *egkephalos* brain, f. as EN-[2] + *kephalē* head: see -O-. Bef. a vowel **encephal-**.
encephalocele *n.* a congenital protrusion of part of the brain through a defect in the skull M19. **encephalogram** *n.* an X-ray photograph of the brain E20. **encephalograph** *n.* (*a*) = ENCEPHALOGRAM; (*b*) = ELECTROENCEPHALOGRAPH: M20. **encephalo'graphic** *a.* of or pertaining to encephalography E20. **encepha'lography** *n.* the radiological investigation of the brain E20. **encephalomye'litis** *n.* inflammation of the brain and the spinal cord; any of several virus diseases (e.g. rabies) so characterized: E20. **encephalo'pathic** *a.* of, pertaining to, or causing encephalopathy L19. **encepha'lopathy** *n.* (a) degenerative disease of the brain (*bovine spongiform encephalopathy*: see BOVINE *a.* 1, *spongiform encephalopathy*: see SPONGIFORM 1) L19.

encephaloid /ɛn'sɛf(ə)lɔɪd/ *a.* M19. [Fr. *encéphaloïde*, f. as ENCEPHALO-: see -OID.] Of a cancerous tumour: having the soft consistency of brain tissue.

encephalon /ɛn'sɛfəlɒn, -'kɛf-/ *n.* M18. [Gk *egkephalon* what is inside the head, f. as EN-[2] + *kephalē* head.] *Anat.* The brain.
Also **encephalos** *n.* (*rare*) E18.

enchafe /ɪn'tʃeɪf, ɛn-/ *v.* Now *rare* or *obs.* LME. [Alt. of ESCHAUFE.] **1** *v.t.* Make hot; *fig.* excite, anger. LME. †**2** *v.i.* Grow hot. Only in LME.

enchain /ɪn'tʃeɪn, ɛn-/ *v.t.* LME. [(O)Fr. *enchaîner* f. Proto-Gallo-Romance, f. as EN-[1] + L *catena* chain.] †**1** Link together as in a chain. LME–M18. **2** Bind with chains; *fig.* restrain, impede the action of. LME. **3** Engage, hold, (the attention, one's emotions, etc.). M17.
2 R. KNOX Ointments.. that stupefy and enchain our senses. 3 C. BRONTË Rachel's acting.. enchained me with interest.
enchainment *n.* the action of enchaining; the state of being enchained: M18.

enchaînement /ɑ̃ʃɛnmɑ̃/ *n.* Pl. pronounced same. M19. [Fr., lit. = a chaining up, a concatenation.] A sequence of steps in ballet.

enchant /ɪn'tʃɑːnt, ɛn-/ *v.t.* Also †**in-**. LME. [(O)Fr. *enchanter* f. L *incantare*, f. as IN-[2] + *cantare* sing: see CHANT *v.*] **1** Put under a spell, bewitch. LME. **b** Endow with magical powers or properties. L16. †**2** Influence powerfully; delude; induce or compel *to do*. LME–L17. **3** Charm, delight, enrapture. Freq. in *pass.* L16.
1b SHAKES. *Macb.* And now about the cauldron sing, .. Enchanting all that you put in. 3 J. A. MICHENER Factories produced glassware that would enchant all subsequent generations who loved beauty. R. CHURCH I was enchanted by the river and its activities.
enchantedly *adv.* in an enchanted manner L20. **enchanting** *a.* (*a*) charming, delightful; (*b*) (now *rare* or *obs.*) that puts someone under a spell: M16. **enchantingly** *adv.* L16.

enchanter /ɪn'tʃɑːntə, ɛn-/ *n.* Also †**in-**. ME. [OFr. *enchanteor*, *-our* (mod. *-eur*) f. late L *incantator* f. L *incantat-*: see INCANTATION, -ER[2].] A person who uses magic, a sorcerer. Formerly also, a conjuror.
enchanter's NIGHTSHADE.

enchantment /ɪn'tʃɑːntm(ə)nt, ɛn-/ *n.* Also †**in-**. ME. [(O)Fr. *enchantement*, f. as ENCHANT: see -MENT.] **1** The use of magic or sorcery; an instance of this; the state of being under a spell. ME. **2** Great charm or fascination; the property of delighting; an enraptured condition. L17.
2 T. CAMPBELL Distance lends enchantment to the view.

enchantress /ɪn'tʃɑːntrɪs, ɛn-/ *n.* LME. [(O)Fr. *enchanteresse*, f. as ENCHANTER: see -ESS[1].] **1** A witch, a sorceress. LME. **2** *fig.* A charming or fascinating woman. E18.

encharge /ɪn'tʃɑːdʒ, ɛn-/ *v.t.* LME. [OFr. *enchargier* (mod. †*encharger*), f. as EN-[1], CHARGE *n.*] †**1** Impose as a duty or responsibility; give (a thing) in charge. (Foll. by a person as indirect obj., *to*.) LME–E19. †**2** Instruct or commission (a person) *to do* something. LME–L18. **3** Burden, entrust, or commission *with*. M17.

encharm /ɪn'tʃɑːm, ɛn-/ *v.t.* LME. [OFr. *encharmer*, f. as EN-[1], CHARM *n.*[1]] Put under a spell, enchant; *fig.* delight. *obs.* exc. *fig.*

†**enchase** *v.*[1]*t.* LME–M18. [OFr. *enchacier*, f. as EN-[1], CHASE *v.*[1]] Drive away, hunt, pursue.

enchase /ɪn'tʃeɪs, ɛn-/ *v.*[2]*t.* LME. [(O)Fr. *enchasser* enshrine, set (gems), encase, f. as EN-[1], *chasse*: see CASE *n.*[2]] **I** Ornament, adorn. **1** Adorn with figures in relief. Also, engrave; adorn (as) with engraved figures. LME. **b** Engrave (figures) *on* or *in* a surface; portray by engraved figures. L16. **2** Set *in* gold or the like. Also (*fig.*), act as a setting for. M16. **3** Set (gold etc.) *with*, (as) with gems. L16. **4** Inlay or variegate *with* gold etc. M17.
II Enclose. †**5** Shut in, enclose. L16–E18. **6** Enshrine *in*, like a relic. E17. **7** Fit or place (a thing) into a space designed to receive it. E17.
6 *fig.*: T. KEN Thy bright Idea in my Heart Enchase.
†**enchasement** *n.* a frame, a setting M17–L18. **enchaser** *n.* a person who enchases or engraves metal. M19.

encheer /ɪn'tʃɪə, ɛn-/ *v.t.* Also †**in-**. L16. [f. EN-[1], IN-[2] + CHEER *v.*] Gladden, make cheerful.

enchilada /ɛntʃɪ'lɑːdə/ *n.* M19. [Amer. Sp., fem. of *enchilado* pa. pple of *enchilar* season with chili, f. as EN-[1] + CHILLI.] A usu. meat-filled tortilla served with chilli sauce.

enchiridion /ɛnkʌɪ'rɪdɪən/ *n.* LME. [Late L f. Gk *egkheiridion*, f. as EN-[2] + *kheir* hand + *-idion* dim. suff.] A handbook, a manual.

enchondroma /ɛnkɒn'drəʊmə/ *n.* Pl. **-mas**, **-mata** /-mətə/. M19. [mod.L, f. as EN-[2] + Gk *khondros* cartilage: see -OMA.] Orig., a chondroma. Now *spec.*, one that arises inside a bone (cf. ECCHONDROMA), usu. in the hand or foot.
enchondromatous *a.* M19. **enchondrosis** *n.*, pl. **-droses** /-'drəʊsiːz/, a chondroma arising from cartilage L19.

enchorial /ɪn'kɔːrɪəl, ɛn-/ *a.* Now *rare* or *obs.* E19. [f. Gk *egkhōrios* in or of the country, f. as EN-[2] + *khōra* country: see -AL[1].] **1** = DEMOTIC *a.* 1. E19. **2** Belonging to or used in a particular country. M19.

encierro /ɛn'θjɛrro/ *n.* Pl. **-os** /-ɒs/. M19. [Sp., lit. shutting in, f. *en-* (f. as IN-[2]) + *cierre* shutting.] The driving of bulls through the streets of a Spanish town from a corral to the bullring.

encincture /ɪn'sɪŋ(k)tʃə, ɛn-/ *v.* & *n.* Chiefly *poet.* E19. [f. EN-[1] + CINCTURE *n.*] **A** *v.t.* = ENGIRDLE. E19. **B** *n.* The fact of being surrounded; an enclosure. *rare.* M19.

encipher /ɪn'sʌɪfə, ɛn-/ *v.t.* Also **-cypher**, (earlier) †**in-**. L16. [f. EN-[1], IN-[2] + CIPHER *n.*] **1 a** Write (a message) in cipher. L16. **b** Convert into coded form using a cipher; encrypt. L19. **2** Combine in a monogram *with*. M17.
encipherment *n.* the action of enciphering something M20.

encircle /ɪn'sɜːk(ə)l, ɛn-/ *v.t.* Also †**in-**. L16. [f. EN-[1], IN-[2] + CIRCLE *n.*] **1** Enclose in a circle; surround, encompass, (*with*). L16. **2** Move in a ring around. Now *rare.* L16.
1 E. WAUGH Immense trees.. encircled Boot Magna Hall. B. HINES Latecomers climbed on to the dustbins,.. encircling each other's bodies with their arms.
encirclement *n.* the act of encircling something; the fact or state of being encircled, esp. by hostile countries: E20. **encircler** *n.* (*rare*) M17.

For other words beginning with *en-* see the entry for **en-**[1]

en clair /ɑ̃ klɛːr/ *adv.* & *a. phr.* L19. [Fr.] (Transmitted, written, etc.) in ordinary language, not in code or cipher.

enclasp /ɪnˈklɑːsp, ɛn-/ *v.t.* Also †**in-**. L16. [f. EN-[1], IN-[2] + CLASP *n.*] Hold (as) in a clasp or embrace.

enclave /ˈɛnkleɪv/ *n.* M19. [Fr., f. (O)Fr. *enclaver* enclose, dovetail f. pop.L, f. *in-* EN-[1] + *clavis* key.] 1 A region belonging to a country but surrounded by another country, as viewed by the latter (cf. EXCLAVE). M19. 2 A culturally or socially distinct minority group in a society or place. M20.

enclave *a.* see ENCLAVÉ.

enclave /ɪnˈkleɪv, ɛn-/ *v.t.* LME. [(O)Fr. *enclaver*: see ENCLAVE *n.* In mod. use f. ENCLAVE *n.*] Surround and isolate; make an enclave of.

¶Rare bef. L19.

enclavé /ɛnˈklɑːvi, ɛn-/ *a.* Also (earlier) **enclave, inclave**, /ɪnˈkleɪv, ɛn-/. M17. [Fr. pa. ppl a. of *enclaver*: see ENCLAVE *n.*] *Her.* Of the border of an ordinary: shaped like a dovetail joint.

†**enclinable** *a.*, †**encline** *v.*, †**enclined** *ppl a.*, see INCLINABLE etc.

enclisis /ˈɛnklɪsɪs/ *n.* L19. [mod.L f. Gk *egklisis*, f. *egklinein* (see next).] *Gram.* Pronunciation as an enclitic; the transfer of accentuation to a previous word.

enclitic /ɪnˈklɪtɪk, ɛn-/ *a.* & *n.* M17. [Late L *encliticus* f. Gk *egklitikos*, f. *egklinein* lean on, f. as EN-[2] + *klinein* to lean, slope: see -IC.] *Gram.* A *adj.* Designating a word so unemphatic as to be pronounced as if part of the preceding word, and sometimes attached to it (as Eng. *of* in *piece of*, *not* in *cannot*, L *-que* and). M17. B *n.* An enclitic word. M17.

†**enclitical** *a.* (*a*) = ENCLITIC *a.*; (*b*) *rare* that leans against something: E17–L18. **enclitically** *adv.* M19.

encloistered /ɪnˈklɔɪstəd, ɛn-/ *a.* Also (earlier) †**in-**. M16. [f. EN-[1], IN-[2] + CLOISTER *n.* + -ED[1].] 1 Shut up in a cloister; *fig.* imprisoned; isolated; sheltered. M16. 2 Surrounded by or provided with cloisters. E17.

enclose /ɪnˈkləʊz, ɛn-/ *v.t.* Also **in-** /ɪn-/. ME. [(O)Fr. *enclos(e)*, pa. pple of *enclore* f. pop.L f. L *includere* INCLUDE.] 1 Orig., shut up in or *in* a room or building; imprison. Now only, seclude in a religious community from the outside world (chiefly as *enclosed* pa. pple). ME. 2 Of things: surround; envelop; contain; *Math.* (of two lines) form (an angle) at their intersection. ME. 3 Surround with or *with* a wall, fence, etc., to prevent free passage in and out. LME. b Put hedges, walls, etc., on (waste or common land) for the purpose of cultivation or allocation to individual owners. LME. c Of an army, a body of people, etc.: surround; hem in. Now *rare*. LME. 4 Insert in or *in* (a container etc.); cover completely; *esp.* place (a document) in the same envelope as a letter. LME.

1 C. MARLOWE In the strongest tower Enclose him fast. O. SHIPLEY The nuns live in community, but are not enclosed. 2 R. L. STEVENSON A house with lawns enclosing it. G. GREENE The darkness had long enclosed them both. 3 E. F. BENSON Parallel brick walls enclosing strips of garden belonging to neighbouring houses. b H. MARTINEAU An Act of Parliament is to be obtained for enclosing Brook common. c H. PHILLIPS Endeavor to enclose the British army and navy in the Delaware bay. 4 P. MORTIMER Dear Mrs. Evans, I enclose a cheque for £10.

enclosed *ppl a.* & *n.* (*a*) *ppl a.* that is enclosed; (*b*) *n.* a thing that is enclosed with a letter (usu. preceded by *the*): L16. **encloser** *n.* †(*a*) a jeweller; (*b*) a person who encloses something, esp. common land: LME.

enclosure /ɪnˈkləʊʒə, ɛn-/ *n.* Also **in-** /ɪn-/. LME. [Legal AN, OFr., f. as prec., -URE.] 1 The action of enclosing, *esp.* the enclosing of waste or common land. LME. 2 A thing that encloses; an encompassing barrier. M16. 3 A thing that is enclosed; a space marked off by boundaries, *spec.* at a racecourse; a document enclosed in the same envelope as a letter. L16. 4 The state of being enclosed, esp. in a religious community. E19.

1 E. P. THOMPSON Wholesale enclosure, in which.. common rights are lost. 3 *members' enclosure, Royal Enclosure, winners' enclosure*, etc. 4 O. SHIPLEY The nuns keep strict enclosure, and lead the contemplative life. T. KENEALLY Enclosure in the ghetto would be compulsory for all Jews.

enclothe /ɪnˈkləʊð, ɛn-/ *v.t. rare.* L15. [f. EN-[1] + CLOTHE *v.*] Clothe, cover.

encloud /ɪnˈklaʊd, ɛn-/ *v.t.* Also †**in-**. L16. [f. EN-[1], IN-[2] + CLOUD *n.*] Envelop in a cloud; overshadow.

†**encluse** *a.* & *n.* var. of INCLUSE.

encode /ɪnˈkəʊd, ɛn-/ *v.t.* E20. [f. EN-[1] + CODE *n.*] Write or represent in code or cipher; convert (information) into another form.

encoder *n.* a person who or thing which encodes something; *esp.* part of a computer that encodes data M20.

encoffin /ɪnˈkɒfɪn, ɛn-/ *v.t.* Also †**in-**. L16. [f. EN-[1], IN-[2] + COFFIN *n.*] Put in or as in a coffin.

encoignure /ɑ̃kwaɲyːr/ *n.* Pl. pronounced same. M19. [Fr., f. as EN-[1] + *coin* corner: see COIN *n.*] A piece of usu. ornamental furniture made with an angle to fit into a corner.

encolour /ɪnˈkʌlə, ɛn-/ *v.t.* Also *-**or**. M17. [f. EN-[1] + COLOUR *n.*] Tinge with colour.

encomia *n.pl.* see ENCOMIUM.

encomiast /ɛnˈkəʊmɪast/ *n.* E17. [Gk *egkōmiastēs*, f. *egkōmiazein* to praise, f. *egkōmion* ENCOMIUM.] A composer or deliverer of an encomium; a flatterer, a eulogizer.

encomiastic /ɛnˌkəʊmɪˈastɪk/ *a.* & *n.* Now *rare*. L16. [Gk *egkōmiastikos*, f. *egkōmiazein*: see prec., -IC.] A *adj.* Commendatory, eulogistic. L16. †B *n.* An encomium. M17–E19.

encomiastical *a.* (now *rare* or *obs.*) = ENCOMIASTIC *a.* L16. **encomiastically** *adv.* (*rare*) M17.

encomienda /ɛnˌkəʊmɪˈɛndə/ *n.* E19. [Sp. = commission, charge, f. *encomendar* commit, charge, f. *en-* (f. as IN-[2]) + *comendar* f. as COMMEND *v.*] *Hist.* An estate granted to a Spaniard in America with powers of taxation and corvée over the Indian inhabitants; (the system derived from) such authority.

encomendero /-mɛnˈdɛːrəʊ/ *n.*, pl. **-os** the holder of an encomienda E19.

encomium /ɛnˈkəʊmɪəm/ *n.* Orig. Anglicized as †**encomy**. Pl. **-iums, -ia**. M16. [L f. Gk *egkōmion* eulogy, use as n. of neut. of adj. (sc. *epos* speech), f. as EN-[2] + *komos* revel.] A formal or high-flown expression of praise; a panegyric.

encompass /ɪnˈkʌmpəs, ɛn-/ *v.t.* Also †**in-**. ME. [f. EN-[1], IN-[2] + COMPASS *n.*] 1 Surround, encircle; envelop, contain; include comprehensively, embrace. ME. †b Outwit. *rare* (Shakes.). Only in L16. †2 Make a circuit round, go all round. M17–L18. 3 = COMPASS *v.* I. L19.

1 GIBBON His throne was encompassed with domestic enemies. A. MOOREHEAD Living in a little capsule, encompassed by a huge unknown wilderness. V. F. WEISSKOPF Human experience encompasses much more than any given system of thought can express. 3 H. L. CAMERON What earthly reason could Captain Thistleby have for encompassing my destruction?

encompassment *n.* the action of encompassing; the state of being encompassed: E17.

†**encomy** *n.* see ENCOMIUM.

encoop /ɪnˈkuːp, ɛn-/ *v.t. poet.* M19. [f. EN-[1] + COOP *n.*[1]] Coop up.

encoppicement /ɪnˈkɒpɪsm(ə)nt, ɛn-/ *n.* M20. [f. EN-[1] + COPPICE *n.* + -MENT.] The promotion and preservation of coppices.

encore /ˈɒŋkɔː/ *int.*, *n.*, & *v.* E18. [Fr. = still, again, of disputed origin; not used in the Eng. sense.] A *int.* Again, once more. E18. B *n.* A spectators' or audience's demand for an item to be performed again, or for a further item to be performed after the nominal end of a concert etc. Also, an item performed in response to such a demand. M18. C *v.t.* Call for the repetition of (an item) or a repetition by (a performer). M18.

encounter /ɪnˈkaʊntə, ɛn-/ *n.* Also †**in-**. ME. [(O)Fr. *encontre*, f. as next.] 1 a A meeting of adversaries in conflict; a duel, a battle. ME. b *gen.* A meeting, esp. by chance or unexpectedly. M17. c A session, or participation, in an encounter group. M20. †2 A lovers' meeting; an amatory approach. *rare* (Shakes.). Only in L16. †3 Manner, behaviour. *rare* (Shakes.) Only in L16.

1 SIR W. SCOTT The Saxons.. and the Gael.. had many a desperate and bloody encounter. *fig.*: SHAKES. *Rich. III* This keen encounter of our wits. b HENRY MILLER As a result of that chance encounter on the street we met frequently thereafter. B. LOVELL The first encounter of a spacecraft with Saturn.

Comb.: **encounter group**: of people seeking emotional adjustment through close physical and emotional contact with one another.

encounter /ɪnˈkaʊntə, ɛn-/ *v.* Also †**in-** ME. [OFr. *encontrer* (mod. *rencontrer*) f. Proto-Romance, f. L IN-[2] + *contra* against.] 1 *v.t.* Meet as an adversary; confront in battle. ME. 2a *v.t.* & (w. pl. subj.) *i.* Meet, come upon, (a person or thing), esp. by chance or unexpectedly. E16. b *v.t.* Meet with, experience, (difficulties, opposition, etc.). E19. †3 *v.t.* & *i.* Express opposition (to); thwart; dispute. M16–L18. †4 *v.i.* Meet *with*; contend *with* as an adversary. M16–L18. †5 *v.t.* Go to meet; approach. *rare* (Shakes.). Only in E17.

1 GIBBON The two kings encountered each other in single combat. 2a BYRON We never met before, and never.. may again encounter. T. HARDY The first person they encountered on entering the main street was the schoolmaster. b M. ESSLIN Ionesco encountered a rawer, more brutal world.

†**encounterer** *n.* E16. [f. prec. + -ER[1].] 1 An adversary; a contrary, an opposite. E16–M17. 2 A forward person; a flirt. *rare* (Shakes.). Only in E17.

encourage /ɪnˈkʌrɪdʒ, ɛn-/ *v.t.* Also †**in-**. LME. [(O)Fr. *encourager*, f. as EN-[1] + *corage* COURAGE *n.*] 1 Give courage, confidence, or hope to. LME. 2 Make sufficiently confident or bold *to do* a specified action. Also foll. by *to* a deed. LME. 3 Urge, incite; recommend, advise. Foll. by *to do*. L15. 4 Stimulate (a person, personal activity) by help, reward, etc.; patronize; abet. M17. 5 Allow, promote, or assist (an activity or situation); foster, cherish. L17.

1 J. RHYS You have.. encouraged me when I'd nearly given up. 2 D. M. FRAME The success of Montaigne's first two books encouraged him to write his third. 3 O. MANNING He had never encouraged Mrs. Trimmer to talk. 4 M. W. MONTAGU No woman dares.. encourage two lovers at a time. R. LARDNER Rita's aunt had encouraged the romance. 5 H. ACTON Reading was tolerated but not encouraged by her father.

encourager *n.* M16. **encouraging** *a.* that encourages or tends to encourage M17. **encouragingly** *adv.* M17.

encouragement /ɪnˈkʌrɪdʒm(ə)nt, ɛn-/ *n.* Also †**in-**. M16. [(O)Fr., f. as prec.: see -MENT.] The action or process of encouraging; the fact of being encouraged; a fact or circumstance that encourages.

encover /ɪnˈkʌvə, ɛn-/ *v.t. rare.* Also **in-** /ɪn-/. LME. [f. EN-[1], IN-[2] + COVER *v.*[2]] Cover completely.

Encratite /ˈɛnkrətʌɪt/ *n.* L16. [Late L *encratita*, f. patristic Gk *egkratitai* pl., f. *egkratēs* self-controlled, continent, f. as EN-[2] + *kratos* strength: see -ITE[1].] A member of any of several early Christian sects who carried ascetic practices to extremes.

†**encrease** *n.*, *v.*, †**encreasement** *n.* vars. of INCREASE *n.*,*v.*, INCREASEMENT.

encrimson /ɪnˈkrɪmz(ə)n, ɛn-/ *v.t.* Also **in-** /ɪn-/. L16. [f. EN-[1], IN-[2] + CRIMSON.] Make or dye crimson.

encrinal /ˈɛnkrɪn(ə)l, ɛnˈkrʌɪn(ə)l/ *a.* M19. [f. ENCRINUS + -AL[1].] = ENCRINITAL.

encrini *n.* pl. of ENCRINUS.

encrinite /ˈɛnkrɪnʌɪt/ *n.* E19. [f. next + -ITE[1].] *Palaeont.* 1 A crinoid, *esp.* a fossil crinoid. E19. 2 Limestone containing a large proportion of fossil crinoids. M20.

encriˈnital *a.* of, pertaining to, or of the nature of an encrinite; encrinitic: M19. **encrinitic** /-ˈnɪtɪk/ *a.* containing fossil crinoids M19.

encrinus /ˈɛnkrɪnəs, ɛnˈkrʌɪnəs/ *n.* Pl. **-ni** /-nʌɪ/. M18. [mod.L, f. Gk EN-[2] + *krinon* lily.] A fossil crinoid; *spec.* one belonging to the extinct genus *Encrinus* of stalked crinoids.

encroach /ɪnˈkrəʊtʃ, ɛn-/ *v.* & *n.* Also †**in-**. LME. [OFr. *encrochier* seize, fasten upon, f. as EN-¹ + *crochier* to crook, f. *croc* hook f. as CROOK *n.*] A *v.* †**1** *v.t.* Seize; obtain wrongfully. LME–M17. **2** *v.i.* Intrude usurpingly on another's territory, rights, etc.; make gradual inroads at the expense of something else. (Foll. by *on*, *upon*.) M16. **3** *v.i.* Advance gradually beyond due limits. M16.

2 STEELE I shall not encroach upon your Time. W. S. CHURCHILL The jungle had already encroached avidly upon the track. 3 G. GORDON The encroaching lines of spreading varicose veins at the back of her .. legs.

B *n.* Encroachment. E17.

encroacher *n.* L16. **encroachment** *n.* the action or an act of encroaching LME.

en croûte /ɑ̃ krut/ *adv. phr.* L20. [Fr.] In a pastry crust.

encrown /ɪnˈkraʊn, ɛn-/ *v.t.* Now *rare.* L15. [f. EN-¹ + CROWN *n.*] Put or form a crown on.

encrust /ɪnˈkrʌst, ɛn-/ *v.* Also (earlier) **in-** /ɪn-/. E17. [Fr. *incruster* f. L *incrustare*, f. as IN-² + *crusta* CRUST *n.*] **1** *v.t.* & *i.* (Cause to) form into a crust; (cause to) deposit a crust *on*. E17. **2** *v.t.* Ornament or decorate (a surface) with an overlay of precious material. M17. **3** *v.t.* Cover with a crust or solid coating; form a crust or coating on. L17. **4** *v.t.* Enclose as *in* a crust. *rare.* E18.

2 GIBBON The outside of the edifice was encrusted with marble. 3 P. LIVELY Rose pink rock encrusted with a greyish green lichen.

encrustate *v.*, **-ation** *n.* vars. of INCRUSTATE *v.* etc.

encrypt /ɛnˈkrɪpt/ *v.t.* M20. [f. EN-¹ + *crypt* in *cryptogram* etc.] Convert into code, esp. to prevent unauthorized access; conceal *in* something by this means.

encryption *n.* the process of encrypting M20.

enculturation /ɪnˌkʌltjʊˈreɪʃ(ə)n, ɛn-/ *n.* M20. [f. EN-¹ + CULTURE *n.* + -ATION.] The process by which the values and norms of a society are passed on to or acquired by its members.

en'culturate *v.t.* subject to enculturation; incorporate (a person) into a culture: M20. **en'culturative** *a.* of, pertaining to, or constituting enculturation M20.

†**encumber** *n.* Also **in-**. ME–M17. [(O)Fr. *encombre*, f. *encombrer*: see next.] The state of being encumbered; an encumbrance.

encumber /ɪnˈkʌmbə, ɛn-/ *v.t.* Also **in-** /ɪn-/. ME. [(O)Fr. *encombrer* block up, f. as EN-¹ + OFr. *combre* river barrage = med.L *combrus* barricade of felled trees.] †**1** Cause suffering or trouble to; harass; (of temptation, passions) overcome. ME–M17. †**2** Involve or entangle *in*. LME–E18. **3** Hamper, impede (a person, movement, etc.); act as a check or restraint on. LME. **4** Fill or load with something obstructive or useless; block up. LME. **5** Burden with duties, debts, etc.; burden (an estate) with a mortgage. L16. †**6** Fold (the arms). *rare* (Shakes.). Only in E17.

3 LD MACAULAY He could not be persuaded to encumber his feeble frame with a cuirass. 4 J. PRIESTLEY I have not .. encumbered my doctrine with .. difficulties. W. S. CHURCHILL The rest walked home across the corpses which encumbered the plain. 5 J. GALSWORTHY He had never committed the imprudence of .. encumbering himself .. with children.

encumberment /ɪnˈkʌmbəm(ə)nt, ɛn-/ *n.* Now *rare.* Also **in-** /ɪn-/. ME. [OFr. *encombrement*, f. as prec.: see -MENT.] **1** The action of encumbering; the state or fact of being encumbered. ME. †**2** Molestation, disturbance; Satanic temptation. ME–L16. †**3** An encumbrance. E–M17.

encumbrance /ɪnˈkʌmbr(ə)ns, ɛn-/ *n.* Also **in-** /ɪn-/. ME. [OFr. *encombrance*, f. *encombrer*: see ENCUMBER *v.*, -ANCE.] †**1** Encumbered state or condition; trouble, molestation. ME–M16. **2** A thing that encumbers; an impediment, a hindrance; a burden, a useless addition; an annoyance. LME. **3** *Law.* A right or interest in land possessed by someone other than the owner of the land, as a lease, mortgage, etc. E17. **4** A person dependent on another for support; a dependant. M18.

2 R. MACAULAY I decided to get rid of the tent, which was a heavy encumbrance. 3 T. LUNDBERG The assets are free of any lien or encumbrances. 4 **without encumbrance** having no children.

encumbrancer *n.* (*Law*) a person who has an encumbrance on a piece of land M19.

†**encursion** *n.* var. of INCURSION.

encurtain /ɪnˈkəːt(ə)n, ɛn-/ *v.t.* LME. [OFr. *enco(u)rtiner*, f. as EN-¹ + as CURTAIN *n.*] Surround with or as with a curtain; shroud, veil.

-ency /(ə)nsi/ *suff.* [f. or after L *-entia* -ENCE. Cf. -ANCY.] Forming ns. of quality, as *efficiency*, or state, as *presidency*, but not of action (cf. -ENCE).

encyclic /ɛnˈsʌɪklɪk, ɪn-, -ˈsɪk-/ *a.* & *n.* E19. [f. as next: see -IC.] = ENCYCLICAL.

encyclical /ɛnˈsɪklɪk(ə)l, ɪn-, -ˈsʌɪk-/ *a.* & *n.* M17. [Late L *encyclicus*, f. Gk *egkuklios* circular, general, f. as EN-² + *kuklos* circle: see -ICAL.] A *adj.* Of an ecclesiastical letter, now esp. one issued by the Pope: intended for extensive circulation. M17. B *n.* A papal letter sent to all bishops of the Roman Catholic Church. M19.

encyclopaedia *n.*, **-paedian** *n.* & *a.*, etc. vars. of ENCYCLOPEDIA etc.

encyclopedia /ɛnˌsʌɪkləˈpiːdɪə, ɪn-/ *n.* Also **-paed-**. M16. [mod.L f. pseudo-Gk *egkuklopaideia* for *egkuklios* (cf. ENCYCLICAL) *paideia* general education.] **1** The circle of learning; a general course of instruction. Now *rare* or *obs.* M16. **2** A book or set of books containing extensive information on all branches of knowledge, or on one particular subject, usu. arranged alphabetically. M17.

2 **the Encyclopedia** *Hist.* the French encyclopedia compiled in the 18th cent. by Diderot, d'Alembert, and others, and its successors. *walking encyclopedia*: see WALKING *ppl a.*

encyclopedian /ɛnˌsʌɪkləˈpiːdɪən, ɪn-/ *n.* & *a.* Also **-paed-**. E17. [f. prec. + -AN.] A *n.* †**1** = ENCYCLOPEDIA 1. Only in E17. **2** An encyclopedist. *rare.* M19. B *adj.* Encyclopedic. M19.

encyclopedic /ɛnˌsʌɪkləˈpiːdɪk, ɪn-/ *a.* Also **-paed-**. E19. [f. as prec. + -IC.] Of, pertaining to, or resembling an encyclopedia; embracing all branches of learning; full of information, comprehensive.

R. FRY His intellectual apprehension was .. heightened, and his knowledge .. became encyclopedic.

encyclopedical *a.* M17. **encyclopedically** *adv.* M19.

encyclopedise *v.* var. of ENCYCLOPEDIZE.

encyclopedism /ɛnˌsʌɪkləˈpiːdɪz(ə)m, ɪn-/ *n.* Also **-paed-**. M19. [f. as next + -ISM.] **1** Encyclopedic learning or knowledge. M19. **2** The doctrines advocated by the French Encyclopedists. M19.

encyclopedist /ɛnˌsʌɪkləˈpiːdɪst, ɪn-/ *n.* Also **-paed-**. M17. [f. as next + -IST.] **1** A compiler of or contributor to an encyclopedia; *esp.* (usu. **E-**) any of the compilers of the French Encyclopedia. M17. **2** A person who attempts to deal with every branch of knowledge. L19.

encyclopedize /ɛnˌsʌɪkləˈpiːdʌɪz, ɪn-/ *v.t.* Also **-paed-**, **-ise**. E19. [f. ENCYCLOPEDIA + -IZE.] Arrange as an encyclopedia; describe in an encyclopedia.

encypher *v.* var. of ENCIPHER.

encyst /ɪnˈsɪst, ɛn-/ *v.* Also **in-** /ɪn-/. E18. [f. EN-¹, IN-² + CYST.] *Biol.* **1** *v.t.* Enclose in a cyst. Chiefly as *encysted* ppl a. E18. **2** *v.i.* Become enclosed in a cyst; form a cyst. L19.

encys'tation *n.* = ENCYSTMENT M19. **encystment** *n.* the process of becoming encysted M19.

end /ɛnd/ *n.* [OE *ende* = OFris. *enda*, *-e*, OS *endi* (Du. *einde*), OHG *enti* (G *Ende*), ON *endir*, *endi*, Goth. *andeis*, f. Gmc, f. IE: cf. Skt *anta* end, boundary, death.] I With ref. to space. **1** An extreme limit or outermost part of a portion of space or of something extended in space. *obs.* exc. in *the end(s) of the earth* etc. below. OE. †**b** A boundary. LME–L16. **2** A limit of size or quantity. Now usu. in neg. contexts. OE. **3** A division or region of a country, city, etc.; *obs.* exc. in *east end* s.v. EAST *a.*, *west end* s.v. WEST *a.* OE. **b** An outlying part of a village or small town; an outlying property. Usu. preceded by a descriptive name. M19. **4** A proportion, a fraction. Only w. adjs. of quantity. *obs.* exc. *dial.* OE. **b** A piece that has been detached or left; a fragment, a remnant. L15. **c** A part, a portion; *esp.* (w. possess. adj.) the part of an enterprise, activity, etc., with which a person is involved. E20. **5** Either of the two extremities of a line, or of the greatest dimension of any object; a part of anything which includes either of its two extremities. ME. **b** *Bowls* & *Curling.* A portion of play in which all the bowls or stones are delivered from one particular end of the green or rink. L17. **c** *Archery.* The place at which a mark is set up; the number of arrows shot from one end of a range. E19. **d** One half or side of a sports ground, a court, etc.; the part occupied by either of two opposing teams or players. M19. **e** *Amer. Football.* A player at the end of the line; a winger; the position occupied by such a player. L19. **6** The surface which bounds an object at either extremity; the head of a cask. E16. **7a** A length of thread pointed with a bristle. Also more fully *shoemaker's end*. L16. **b** In full *cable's end*. A short length of cable. M17. **c** *N. Amer.* In full *end of steel*. The limit to which a railway extends; a terminus. E20.

2 J. S. MILL There was no end to the advantages. 3b E. M. FORSTER Howards End. 4b P. STUBBES Scraps or .. short ends of lace. CIGARETTE-*end*. c N. SHUTE Honey would have to come back to this country to tell us his end of it. *fig.*: S. BRILL Glich is the financial end, but policy comes from me. 5 J. WESLEY I was quickly wet to my toe's end. J. RATHBONE Mr. Curtis remained standing at the end of the bed. R. CAMPBELL We would corner him at the shallow end of the bath. L. GARFIELD There was a disturbance at the other end of the hall. d D. L. SAYERS The slogger smote a vigorous ball from the factory end.

II With ref. to time or serial order. **8** The limit of duration of a period of time; the termination or conclusion of an action, process, state, etc. OE. **b** The latter or final part. LME. **9** Termination of existence; destruction, downfall; a person's death. OE. **10** Ultimate state or condition. Chiefly in biblical quotations and allusions, often misinterpreted in sense 9. OE. †**11** A termination of doubt or debate; a resolution, a settlement. ME–M16. †**12** The completion of an action; the accomplishment of a purpose. ME–L17. **13** An intended result; an aim, a purpose. ME. **14** An outcome, a result. Now *rare.* LME. **15** A final cause or purpose; the object for which a thing exists. LME.

8 *Daily Telegraph* Mr Benn did not speak beyond thanking the Chancellor at the beginning and end of the meeting. *attrib.*: *Scotsman* New annual premiums received .. totalled £16.41 million in the three months to end-September. 9 S. LEACOCK If I should meet my end here. 13 V. WOOLF Everybody in the crowded street .. had some end in view. 15 H. J. LASKI His love of liberty, which is the true end of government.

Phrases: **all ends over** or **up** thoroughly. **and there's** (or **so**) **an end** *arch.* and this is, or shall be, an end. *at a loose end*: see LOOSE *a.* **at an end** finished, exhausted. *at loose ends*: see LOOSE *a.* *at one's wit's* or *wits' end*: see WIT *n.* **at the end** at last. *at the end of the day*: see DAY *n.* *be on* (or *at*) *the* RECEIVING *end*. *best end*: see BEST *a.* etc. **be the end of** be the death or downfall of. *big end*: see BIG *a.* *bitter end*: see BITTER *a.*, *n.*² BUSINESS *end*. *cable's end*: see sense 7b above. **change ends** switch from occupying one half of a ground, court, etc., to the other, and change the direction of play. **choose ends** select the direction in which one wishes to play. *come to a bad end*, *an end*: see COME *v.* *come to a sticky end*: see STICKY *a.*² 4b. *deep end*: see DEEP *a.* *defensive end*: see DEFENSIVE *a.* 1. *dirty end of the stick*: see DIRTY *a.* *east end*: see EAST *a.* *end of steel*: see sense 7c above. **end on** with the end facing one, or facing any object; with the end adjoining the end of the next object. **end to end** with the ends in contact, lengthways. †**for (an) end** in conclusion, finally. **for this end** = *to this end* below. **from end to end** from one extremity to the other, throughout the length of something. *get hold of the wrong end of the stick*: see STICK *n.*¹ **go end for end** *Naut.* (of a boat) be upset. **have at one's fingers'** or **tongue's end** know by heart. **have the better** or **worse end (of the staff)** get the best, or worst, of it. *hinder end*: see HINDER *a.*

in the end ultimately, in the long run. **keep one's end up** sustain one's part in an undertaking or performance; hold one's own. *little end*: see LITTLE *a.* *loose end*: see LOOSE *a.* **make an end of** put a stop to. **make (both) ends meet** live within one's income; maintain an adequate income. **no end** *colloq.* (*a*) a vast number or amount *of*, a remarkable example *of*; (*b*) *advb.* very much. *odds and ends*: see ODDS *n.* 2b. **on end** (*a*) in an upright position; (*b*) consecutively, continuously. **put an end to** stop, abolish, destroy. *rear end*: see REAR *a.*[1], *adv.* & *n.* **right** or **straight on end** consecutively, immediately. *shallow end*: see SHALLOW *a.*, *n.*, & *adv.* *sharp end*: see SHARP *a.* & *adv.* **shift end for end** *Naut.* reverse (a rope, spar, etc.) so that one end is where the other used to be; upset (a boat). *shoemaker's end*: see sense 7a above. *small end*: see SMALL *a.* **straight on end** = *right on end* above. *the beginning of the end*: see BEGINNING *n.* 4. **the end** (*a*) *colloq.* the last straw, the limit of endurability; (*b*) *US slang* the best, the ultimate. *the end of one's tether*: see TETHER *n.* *the end of the earth*: see *the ends of the earth* below. **the end of the line** or **road** *fig.* the point at which hope or endeavour has to be abandoned. **the end of the world** *fig.* a calamitous matter or situation (only in neg. contexts). **the end(s) of the earth** the most distant regions of the earth. *the right* or *wrong end of the stick*: see STICK *n.*[1] *the thin end of the wedge*: see WEDGE *n.* *the world's end*: see WORLD *n.* *tight end*: see TIGHT *a.* *to the end of the chapter*: see CHAPTER *n.* **†to the end that** in order that. **to this end** for this purpose. **turn end for end** put each end of (a thing) where the other end used to be. *west end*: see WEST *a.* **without end** endlessly, for ever. *world without end*: see WORLD *n.*

Comb.: **end-around** *n.* & *a.* (*a*) *n.* (*Amer. Football*) an offensive play in which an end runs with the ball behind his or her own team's line and round the opposite end; (*b*) *adj.* (*Computing*) involving the transfer of a digit from one end of a register to the other; **end-artery** *Anat.* an artery which supplies almost all the blood to a part of the body and does not anastomose with itself or other arteries; **end-game** the final stage of a game of chess, bridge, etc., when few men or cards remain; **end-gate** *US* a tailboard; **end grain** the grain of wood seen when it is cut across the growth rings; **end-leaf** a usu. blank leaf inserted at one or other end of a bound book; **end line** (*a*) a boundary line marking the end of a field or court in various games; (*b*) a line forming a conclusion; **end-man** *US* (chiefly *Hist.*) a man at the end of a line of blackface minstrels who engaged in comic repartee with the interlocutor; **end-member** the item at one end of a series; **end moraine**: formed or forming at the forward edge of a glacier; **endnote**: similar to a footnote but placed with others at the end of a book or chapter; **end organ** *Anat.* a specialized encapsulated ending of a sensory or motor nerve; **end-paper** a blank leaf placed at the beginning or end of a book (usu. in *pl.*); **end-piece** a piece at the end of a structure or composition; **end-plate** *Anat.* each of the discoidal expansions of a motor nerve where its branches terminate on a muscle fibre; **end-play** a method of play employed in the last few tricks of a game of bridge in order to force an opponent into making a disadvantageous discard or lead; **end-point** (*a*) the final stage of a process, period, etc.; *Chem.* the point in a titration (usu. marked by a colour change) at which a reaction is complete; (*b*) a point at the end of a line; **end-product** a final product, esp. of a radioactive decay series or a manufacturing process; **end result** the final outcome; **end run** *US* (*a*) *Football* an attempt to run with the ball round one flank of the team; (*b*) an evasive tactic, esp. in war or politics; **end-scraper** *Archaeol.* a flint scraper whose working edge is at one end of a blade or flake, transverse to the long axis; **end standard** a standard of length in the form of a metal bar or block, two of whose faces are the standard distance apart; **end-stopped** *a.* (of verse) having a pause at the end of each line; **end user** the ultimate user of a product; **end zone** *N. Amer.* (*a*) the rectangular area at each end of a football field between the end line and the goal-line; (*b*) in ice hockey, a section at each end of a rink extending from the neutral zone to the goal-line.

end /ɛnd/ *v.*[1] [OE *endian* = OFris. *endia*, OS *endiōn* (Du. *einden*), OHG *entōn* (G *enden*), ON *enda*.] **†1** *v.t.* Finish, complete. OE–M18. **2** *v.t.* Put an end to, cause to cease; destroy. OE. **†b** Kill. ME–E17. **3** *v.i.* Come to an end. OE. **b** Foll. by *in*: have as its result or conclusion; lead to. ME. **c** Die. Now *rare*. ME. **d** Come eventually to a specified state. Usu. foll. by *up*. L19. **4** *v.t.* Bring to an end, conclude, (an action, speech, one's life, etc.). ME. **5** *v.i.* Of a portion of space, an object, etc.: terminate, have its end or extremity. LME.

2 SOUTHEY That merciful deed For ever ends thy suffering. 3 J. BUCHAN Before the War ended I was travelling far and wide. b H. J. LASKI Political life, like human life, ends in death. d G. GREENE Englishmen who have started with the idea of attacking apartheid and ended trapped . . in a Bantu girl's bed. J. JOHNSTON Sometimes good people end up in prison. 4 G. BERKELEY We ended the day with music at St. Agnes. R. BROOKE Night ends all things. 5 SCOTT FITZGERALD There was a sharp line where my ragged lawn ended. J. FOWLES The beach ended in a fall of rocks.

Phrases, & with advs. in specialized senses: **end by doing** come eventually to do. **end it (all)** *colloq.* commit suicide. *end one's days*: see DAY *n.* *end or mend*, *mend or end*: see MEND *v.* **end up** put on end; (see also sense 3d above). *war to end war(s)*: see WAR *n.*[1]

ender *n.* LME.

end /ɛnd/ *v.*[2]*t.* *obs.* exc. *dial.* E17. [Origin uncertain: perh. dial. var. or corruption of IN *v.*, infl. by END *v.*[1]] Put (corn etc.) into a barn; make into a haystack; get in.

end- *comb. form* see ENDO-.

-end /ɛnd/ *suff.* Repr. L *-endus*, *-da*, *-dum*, of the gerundive of vbs in *-ere*, forming ns. usu. w. the sense 'person (or thing) to be treated in a specified way', as *addend*, *dividend*. The neut. gerundial ending is sometimes retained as in *addendum*, *agendum*, etc.

end-all /ˈɛndɔːl/ *a.* & *n.* LME. [f. END *v.*[1] + ALL *pron.*] **†A** *adj.* Ultimate, absolute. Only in LME. **B** *n.* A thing that ends everything or is final; *the* supreme purpose or thing of significance. Chiefly in *the* BE-ALL *and end-all*. E17.

endamage /ɪnˈdamɪdʒ, ɛn-/ *v.t.* LME. [f. EN-[1] + DAMAGE *n.*] **1** Affect adversely, harm. LME. **†2** Inflict material injury or damage on; damage, spoil. L15–E19.

endamagement *n.* the action of endamaging; the state of being endamaged: L16.

endanger /ɪnˈdeɪn(d)ʒə, ɛn-/ *v.t.* Also **†in-**. LME. [f. EN-[1], IN-[2] + DANGER *n.*] **†1** Expose (a person) to infringement of his or her rights; make liable to punishment by another person. Usu. in *pass.* (foll. by *to* the other person). LME–L16. **2** Put in danger. E16. **†b** Make (a person) liable *to do*; put in peril *of doing*. M16–M18. **†3** Subject (a person) to the will of another. M–L16. **†4** Incur the risk of, chance. L16–L18. **†5** Cause the danger of, make probable, (something untoward). E17–L18.

2 E. ROOSEVELT An epidemic that might endanger everybody in that area. F. HERBERT No woman wants her loved ones endangered. **endangered species**: in danger of becoming extinct. 4 ADDISON Unless they turned back quickly they would endanger being benighted. 5 SOUTHEY So as to endanger setting it on fire.

endangerer *n.* L17. **endangerment** *n.* the action of endangering; the state of being endangered: L16.

endarch /ˈɛndɑːk/ *a.* E20. [f. ENDO- + Gk *arkhē* beginning, origin.] *Bot.* Of xylem or its development: formed or occurring from the centre of a stem towards the periphery.

endarken /ɪnˈdɑːk(ə)n/ *v.t.* Now *rare*. L16. [f. EN-[1] + DARKEN.] Make dark, obscure (*lit.* & *fig.*).

†endart *v.* var. of INDART.

endarterectomy /ˌɛndɑːtəˈrɛktəmi/ *n.* M20. [f. ENDO- + ARTERY + -ECTOMY.] Surgical removal of part of the inner lining of an artery; an instance of this.

endarteritis /ˌɛndɑːtəˈrʌɪtɪs/ *n.* L19. [f. ENDO- + ARTERITIS.] *Med.* Inflammation of the inner lining of an artery.

endaspidean /ɛndəˈspɪdɪən/ *a.* L19. [f. mod.L *Endaspideae*, obs. taxonomic name, f. as ENDO- + Gk *aspid-*, *aspis* shield: see -AN.] Possessing or designating a bird's tarsal sheath with an anterior series of scutella on its outer side.

en daube /ɑ̃ doːb/ *adv. phr.* E20. [Fr.: cf. DAUBE.] Stewed, braised.

endear /ɪnˈdɪə, ɛn-/ *v.t.* Also **†in-**. L16. [f. EN-[1], IN-[2] + DEAR *a.*[1], after Fr. *enchérir* (f. *en* + *cher* dear).] **†1** Enhance the price or value of. L16–E19. **b** Represent as valuable or important; exaggerate. E–M17. **†2** Win the affection of; deepen (affection). L16–E18. **b** Bind by obligation of gratitude. E–M17. **3** Make dear *to* someone; create affection for (a person or thing). E17. **†4** Hold dear; treat affectionately. E17–E18.

3 H. KELLER The tenderness and sympathy which endeared Dr. Bell to so many hearts. P. USTINOV He immediately endeared himself to the liberal elements in his entourage.

endearance *n.* (*rare*) the action of endearing; the state of being endeared: M18. **endearing** *ppl a.* inspiring or manifesting affection M17. **endearingly** *adv.* E18.

endearment /ɪnˈdɪəm(ə)nt, ɛn-/ *n.* Also **†in-**. E17. [f. ENDEAR + -MENT.] **†1** An enhancement; an exaggeration. Only in E17. **†2** An obligation of gratitude. Only in 17. **3** The action of endearing; the fact of being endeared. Also, a thing that endears. M17. **4** An expression of love or fondness; a caress. E18. **†5** Affection, fondness. E18–E19.

4 D. LODGE Hero and heroine were exchanging husky endearments.

endeavour /ɪnˈdɛvə, ɛn-/ *v.* & *n.* Also ***-or**, **†in-**. LME. [f. *put oneself in devoir* s.v. DEVOIR 2: see -OUR.] **A** *v.* **†1** *v.refl.* & *i.* Exert oneself. LME–M17. **†2** *v.t.* Exert (one's power, thoughts, etc.). *rare*. L16–M17. **3** *v.i.* Try, make an effort for a specified object; attempt strenuously (*to do*). L16. **4** *v.t.* Use effort for; attempt (an action). Long *arch.* L16.

3 J. S. MILL If we are endeavouring after more riches. T. HARDY Charlotte vainly endeavoured to hide her confusion.

B *n.* The action of endeavouring; effort directed to attain an object; a strenuous attempt. LME.

COLERIDGE O Liberty! with profitless endeavour Have I pursued thee. T. E. LAWRENCE My determined endeavour is to scrape through with it. E. V. KNOX Fumbling with the screws of the windscreen, an endeavour which I have long proved to be vain. **do one's endeavour(s)** do one's best, do all one can.

endeavourer *n.* †(*a*) a person who endeavours; (*b*) in full *Christian Endeavourer*, a member of the Young People's Society of Christian Endeavour, a religious association begun in the US in 1881: L16.

†endebted *ppl a.* var. of INDEBTED.

endeca- *comb. form*, **endecasyllable** *n.*, etc., vars. of HENDECA- etc.

endeictic /ɛnˈdʌɪktɪk/ *a.* M17. [Gk *endeiktikos* probative, indicative, f. *endeiknunai* point out: see -IC. Cf. APODEICTIC, DEICTIC.] Serving to show or demonstrate.

endemial /ɛnˈdiːmɪəl, ɪn-/ *a.* Now *rare* or *obs.* L17. [f. Gk *endēmios* (see next) + -AL[1].] = ENDEMIC *a.*

endemic /ɛnˈdɛmɪk/ *n.* & *a.* M17. [Fr. *endémique* or mod.L *endemicus*, f. Gk *endēm(i)os*, pertaining to a people, native, f. as EN-[2] + *dēmos* people: see -IC.] **A** *n.* **1** An endemic disease. M17. **2** An endemic plant or animal. M20.

B *adj.* **1** (Of a disease, condition, etc.) habitually present in a certain area as a result of permanent local factors; of common occurrence; rife. E18. **2** Of a plant or animal: native to, and esp. restricted to, a certain country or area. M19.

1 J. G. COZZENS An occupational disease, endemic among social-service workers. L. NAMIER Hurricanes and slave troubles were endemic to the West Indies. G. STEINER Barbarism and political savagery are endemic in human affairs. D. ACHESON Curfews, 'roundups', and arrests became endemic.

endemical *a.* = ENDEMIC *a.* 1 M17. **endemically** *adv.* in an endemic manner; habitually: M17. **endemicity** /ɛndɪˈmɪsɪti/ *n.* the condition or fact of being endemic L19. **endemism** /ˈɛndɪmɪz(ə)m/ *n.* endemicity, esp. as regards the geographical distribution of plants and animals L19.

endenization /ɪnˌdɛnʌɪˈzeɪʃ(ə)n, ɛn-/ *n.* Now *rare*. L16. [f. ENDENIZE + -ATION.] The process of making someone a denizen; naturalization, enfranchisement; the fact of being endenizened.

†endenize *v.t.* L16. [Alt. of ENDENIZEN with assim. to vbs in -IZE.] **1** = ENDENIZEN. L16–M18. **2** Spirit away; change into superhuman form. E–M17.

endenizen /ɪnˈdɛnɪz(ə)n, ɛn-/ *v.t.* L16. [f. EN-[1] + DENIZEN *n.*] Make a denizen or citizen; naturalize (*lit.* & *fig.*), enfranchise.

For other words beginning with *en-* see the entry for **en-**[1]

endergonic /ɛndəː'gɒnɪk/ *a.* M20. [f. ENDO- + Gk *ergon* work + -IC.] *Sci.* Accompanied by the absorption of energy.

endermic /ɛn'dəːmɪk/ *a.* M19. [f. EN-[2] + Gk *derma* skin + -IC.] *Med.* Acting on or through the skin.

endermically *adv.* M19.

en déshabillé /õ deɪza'biːjeɪ, *foreign* ɑ̃ dezabije/ *a.* & *adv. phr.* Also Anglicized as **en déshabille** /õ deɪzə'biːl/, **en dishabille** /õ dɪsə'biːl/. L17. [Fr., f. *en* IN *prep.* + *déshabillé* DISHABILLE.] In a state of undress or of partial dress; casually dressed.

ending /'ɛndɪŋ/ *n.* OE. [f. END *v.*[1] + -ING[1].] **1** The action of END *v.*[1]; an instance of this; termination, conclusion, completion, etc. OE. **2** A concluding or terminating part, esp. of a literary work, metrical line, or piece of music. Also, an inflectional or formative suffix. ME.

1 W. MORRIS A fair ending crowned a troublous day. 2 *happy ending*: see HAPPY *a.* *weak ending*: see WEAK *a.*

endingless *a.* M20.

ending /'ɛndɪŋ/ *ppl a.* ME. [f. END *v.*[1] + -ING[2].] **1** That ends; final. ME. †**2** Dying. *rare* (Shakes.). Only in L16.

en dishabille *a.* & *adv. phr.* see EN DÉSHABILLÉ.

endite /'ɛndʌɪt/ *n.* L19. [f. ENDO- + -ITE[1].] *Zool.* An appendage on the inner side of a crustacean limb.

†**endite** *v.*[1] see INDICT *v.*[1]

†**endite** *v.*[2] see INDITE *v.*[1]

†**enditement** *n.* see INDICTMENT.

endive /'ɛndʌɪv, -dɪv/ *n.* LME. [(O)Fr. f. med.L *endivia* f. med.Gk *indibi* f. L *intibum* f. Gk *entubon*.] †**1** A sowthistle; some similar yellow-flowered plant. Only in LME. **2** (The blanched leaves of) a blue-flowered plant of the composite family, *Cichorium endivia*, grown as a salad (chiefly in a form with curled much-dissected leaves) or as a vegetable (in a form with wavy undivided leaves, more fully *Batavian* or *broad-leaved endive*). Also (in full *wild endive*), the wild form of the related plant, chicory, *Cichorium intybus*. LME. **3** Blanched chicory crowns. Also *French endive*. Chiefly *N. Amer.* M20.

endless /'ɛndlɪs/ *a.* & *adv.* OE. [f. END *n.* + -LESS.] **A** *adj.* **1** Having no end in (future) time, eternal. OE. **b** Interminable, incessant. OE. **2** Having no end in space; boundless; of infinite length. LME. **3** Of an immaterial thing, number, quality, etc.: boundless, infinite; *colloq.* innumerable, countless, unlimited. LME. **4** Of a belt, chain, etc.: made in the form of a loop, e.g. for continuous action round a set of wheels. E19.

1 STEELE Death . . is a short Night, followed by an endless Day. b G. VIDAL A wild mountain clan, given to endless drinking bouts. 2 W. BLACK The endless miles of moor. J. F. LEHMANN Airmen passed . . in endless streams. 3 D. H. LAWRENCE He had brought them endless presents. A. THWAITE Her endless curiosity.

†**B** *adv.* Infinitely, eternally. Only in ME.

endlessly *adv.* LME. **endlessness** *n.* (*a*) the quality of being endless; (*b*) a thing that has no end: ME.

endlong /'ɛndlɒŋ/ *prep., adv.,* & *adj.* Now chiefly *north.* [OE *andlang* prep. (see ALONG *a.*[2]), repl. in ME by forms partly f. END *n.* + LONG *a.*[1], partly f. ON *endlangr* adj. Cf. -LONG.] **A** *prep.* From end to end of; over the length of; along (as opp. to across). OE. **B** *adv.* **1** From end to end, lengthwise. OE. **2** At full length; horizontally. *obs.* exc. *north.* LME. **3** Straight on, straight through. *obs.* exc. *north.* LME. **4** On end, vertically. E17. **C** *adj.* **1** Extended lengthwise. *obs.* exc. *north.* L15. **2** Set on end, perpendicular. *rare.* E18.

endmost /'ɛndməʊst/ *a.* OE. [f. END *n.* + -MOST.] Nearest to the end, furthest, most distant.

endo- /'ɛndəʊ/ *comb. form.* Bef. a vowel also **end-**. [Repr. Gk *endon* within: see -O-.] Internal, inner; inside.

endoatmos'pheric *a.* occurring or operating within the atmosphere L20. **endo'cardial** *a.* †(*a*) situated within the heart; (*b*) of or pertaining to the endocardium: M19. **endocar'ditic** *a.* affected with or suffering from endocarditis M19. **endocar'ditis** *n.* inflammation of the lining membrane of the heart, esp. that of the valves M19. **endo'cardium** *n.* the smooth membrane lining the cavities and valves of the heart L19. **endocarp** *n.* (*Bot.*) the inner layer of the pericarp of a fruit, which lines the seed chamber E19. **endo'centric** *a.* (*Ling.*) designating a compound or construction whose distribution is the same as that of one of its constituents M20. **endocervical** /-'səːvɪk(ə)l, -sə'vʌɪk(ə)l/ *a.* situated or occurring within the cervix of the womb E20. **endo'cervix** *n.* (*Anat.*) the mucous membrane lining of the cervix of the womb M20. **endo'cranial** *a.* of or pertaining to the cavity or inside of the skull (*endocranial cast*, a cast of this cavity, taken as a guide to the size and shape of the brain) L19. **endocuticle**, **-'ticula** *n.* (*a*) the flexible laminated inner part of the arthropod procuticle; (*b*) the inner part of the cuticle surrounding animal hairs: E20. **endo'cyclic** *a.* (*Chem.*) situated inside a ring E20. **endocytose** /-'sʌɪtəʊz/ *v.t.* (*Biol.*) take in by endocytosis, engulf L20. **endocytosis** /-sʌɪ'təʊsɪs/ *n.* (*Biol.*) the taking in of matter by a living cell by invagination of its membrane M20. **endocytotic** /-sʌɪ'tɒtɪk/ *a.* of, pertaining to, or formed by endocytosis L20. **endo'dontal** *a.* = ENDODONTIC M20. **endo'dontia** *n.* = ENDODONTICS M20. **endo'dontic** *a.* of or pertaining to endodontics M20. **endo'dontically** *adv.* according to endodontic methods M20. **endo'dontics** *n.* the branch of dentistry that deals with the tooth pulp and its diseases M20. **endo'dontist** *n.* a practitioner or specialist in endodontics M20. **endoenzyme** *n.* (*a*) (now *rare*) an enzyme which acts within the cell producing it; (*b*) an enzyme which breaks bonds other than terminal ones in a long-chain molecule: E20. **endo'ergic** *a.* (*Sci.*) = ENDERGONIC M20. **endo'glossic** *a.* pertaining to or involving the use of a country's native language, esp. where this is not one of the world's major languages L20. **endo'lithic** *a.* (*a*) containing a design on stone that extends inwards; (*b*) *Biol.* living in or penetrating into stone: L19. **endolymph** *n.* the fluid in the membranous labyrinth of the ear M19. **endolym'phatic** *a.* of, pertaining to, or containing endolymph L19. **endometrial** /-'miːt-/ *a.* of or pertaining to the endometrium M19. **endometri'osis** /-miːt-/ *n.* (a condition marked by) the occurrence of endometrial tissue outside the womb E20. **endometriotic** /-miːtrɪ'ɒtɪk/ *a.* of or pertaining to endometriosis M20. **endometritis** /-mɪ'trʌɪtɪs/ *n.* inflammation of the endometrium L19. **endometrium** /-'miːt-/ *n.* [Gk *mētra* womb] the mucous membrane lining the womb L19. **endomi'tosis** *n.*, pl. **-toses** /-'təʊsiːz/, *Biol.* division of chromosomes in a cell nucleus without the subsequent division of the nucleus, giving rise to polyploidy M20. **endomitotic** /-'tɒt-/ *a.* (*Biol.*) pertaining to or involving endomitosis M20. **endo'mixis** *n.* (*Biol.*) nuclear disintegration and re-formation without conjugation in some lower ciliates E20. **endo'normative** *a.* (*Ling.*) drawing on usage within a language for models or standards M20. **endo'nuclease** *n.* (*Biochem.*) an enzyme which cleaves a polynucleotide chain by separating nucleotides other than the two end ones M20. **endonucleo'lytic** *a.* (*Biochem.*) pertaining to or involving the removal of a nucleotide from a polynucleotide molecule other than from the end M20. **endonucleo'lytically** *adv.* (*Biochem.*) in an endonucleolytic manner L20. **endo'parasite** *n.* a parasite that lives in the internal organs of its host L19. **endopara'sitic** *a.* of, pertaining to, or being an endoparasite L19. **endo'peptidase** *n.* (*Biochem.*) an enzyme which breaks peptide bonds other than terminal ones in a peptide chain M20. **endophyte** *n.* †(*a*) *rare* the part of a tree inside the bark; (*b*) a plant which lives inside another plant: M19. **endophytic** /-'fɪtɪk/ *a.* of, pertaining to, or being an endophyte L19. **endopod**, **en'dopodite** *ns.* (*Zool.*) the inner branch of a biramous limb or appendage in some crustaceans L19. **endo'polyploid** *a.* (*Genetics*) exhibiting endopolyploidy M20. **endo'polyploidy** *n.* (*Genetics*) polyploidy that is due to endomitosis M20. **endo'psychic** *a.* contained or occurring in the mind E20. **endopterygote** /ɛndɒp'tɛrɪgəʊt/ *a.* & *n.* (*Zool.*) (designating) an insect whose wings develop internally at first and which passes through a pupal stage E20. **endo'skeletal** *a.* of or pertaining to an endoskeleton; of the nature of or having an endoskeleton: L19. **endoskeleton** *n.* a skeleton inside the body, as in vertebrates M19. **endosome** *n.* (*a*) *rare* the central part of some sponges; (*b*) a body of chromatin in the nucleus of some cells; a nucleolus: L19 **endosperm** *n.* nutritive material surrounding the embryo in some plant seeds M19. **endo'spermic** *a.* of or pertaining to endosperm L19. **endospore** *n.* (*a*) the inner layer of the membrane or wall of some spores; (*b*) a spore formed in a case or theca; a naked spore before it develops a cell wall; (*c*) a resistant asexual spore that develops inside a vegetative bacterial cell: L19. **en'dosteal** *a.* (*a*) of or pertaining to the endosteum; (*b*) situated in or derived from the inside of a bone: M19. **en'dosteally** *adv.* inside a bone L19. **en'dosteum** *n.* a layer of vascular tissue lining the cavity that is present in some bones L19. **endostyle** *n.* (*Zool.*) a groove in the pharynx of some lower chordates that secretes mucus that aids the ingestion of food particles M19. **endo'sulfan** *n.* a sulphur-containing compound used as an insecticide on fruit, vegetables, and forage M20. **endo'symbiont** *n.* an endosymbiotic organism M20. **endosymbi'osis** *n.* symbiosis in which one of the symbiotic organisms lives inside the other M20. **endosymbi'otic** *a.* of or pertaining to endosymbiosis; (of an organism) living in such a relationship: M20. **endosymbi'otically** *adv.* in an endosymbiotic manner L20. **endo'toxic** *a.* of, pertaining to, or caused by an endotoxin E20. **endo'toxin** *n.* a toxin present in a bacterial cell, *esp.* one that is released only when the cell disintegrates E20. **endotracheal** /-'treɪkɪəl, -trə'kiːəl/ *a.* situated or occurring within the trachea; performed by way of the trachea: L19. **endotracheally** /-'treɪkɪəli, -trə'kiːəli/ *adv.* by way of the trachea M20. **endotrophic** /-'trəʊfɪk, -'trɒfɪk/ *a.* *Bot.* (of a mycorrhiza) penetrating into a root L19.

endocrine /'ɛndəkrʌɪn, -krɪn/ *a.* & *n.* E20. [f. ENDO- + Gk *krinein* to separate.] *Physiol.* **A** *adj.* Designating a gland that secretes directly into the blood or lymph; of or pertaining to such glands or their secretions (hormones). Cf. EXOCRINE. E20. **B** *n.* An endocrine gland. E20.

endocrino'logic (chiefly *US*), **-'logical** *adjs.* of or pertaining to endocrinology M20. **endocrino'logically** *adv.* as regards the endocrine glands or their activity M20. **endocri'nologist** *n.* an expert in or student of endocrinology M20. **endocri'nology** *n.* the branch of medicine that deals with the endocrine glands and hormones E20.

†**endoctrinate** *v.* see INDOCTRINATE.

†**endoctrine** *v.* see INDOCTRINE.

endoderm /'ɛndədəːm/ *n.* M19. [f. ENDO- + Gk *derma* skin.] **1** *Biol.* The inner germ layer of the embryo in early development; cells or tissue derived from this; such cells as forming the lining of the cavity of coelenterates. M19. **2** *Bot.* = ENDODERMIS. Formerly, a layer of cambium between phloem and xylem. M19.

endodermal /ɛndəʊ'dəːm(ə)l/ *a.* L19. [f. prec. and next + -AL[1].] Pertaining to or of the nature of endoderm or endodermis; derived from endoderm.

Also **endo'dermic** *a.* L19.

endodermis /ɛndəʊ'dəːmɪs/ *n.* L19. [f. ENDODERM after *epidermis*.] *Bot.* An inner layer of cells in the cortex of a root and of some stems, surrounding a vascular bundle.

endogamy /ɛn'dɒgəmi/ *n.* M19. [f. ENDO- + -GAMY, after POLYGAMY.] **1** *Anthropol.* The custom of marrying only within the limits of a local community, clan, or tribe. M19. **2** *Biol.* The fusion of reproductive cells from related individuals. E20.

endo'gamic *a.* of or pertaining to endogamy L19. **endogamous** *a.* practising endogamy; of or pertaining to endogamy: M19.

endogen /'ɛndədʒ(ə)n/ *n.* Now *rare* or *obs.* M19. [Fr. *endogène*, f. as ENDO-: see -GEN.] *Bot.* A plant whose stem grows by the development of new material inside it, with no differentiation into wood and bark.

endogenetic /ˌɛndəʊdʒɪ'nɛtɪk/ *a.* L19. [f. ENDO- + -GENETIC.] **1** *Sci.* Having an internal cause or origin. L19. **2** *Geol.* Formed or occurring inside the earth. E20.

endo'genesis *n.* = ENDOGENY L19.

endogenic /ɛndəʊ'dʒɛnɪk/ *a.* M20. [f. ENDO- + -GENIC.] *Geol.* = ENDOGENETIC 2.

endogenous /ɛn'dɒdʒɪnəs, ɪn-/ *a.* M19. [f. as ENDOGEN: see -GENOUS.] **1** *Bot.* Of, pertaining to, or designating a plant that grows by developing new material inside it. Now *rare* or *obs.* M19. **2** *Geol.* Formed or occurring within some structure or rock mass; *esp.* = ENDOGENETIC 2; *Bot.* developing from deep rather than superficial tissue. M19. **3** Having an internal cause or origin; *spec.* (*Med.* & *Psychiatry*) having a cause inside the body or self, not attributable to any external or environmental factor. L19.

3 M. C. GERALD Endogenous depression is said to exist when the precipitating factors are not known.

endogenously *adv.* M19. **endogeny** *n.* growth or development from within L19.

endomorph /ˈɛndə(ʊ)mɔːf/ *n.* L19. [f. ENDO- + -MORPH.] **1** A mineral or crystal surrounded by a different mineral. L19. **2** A person whose build is soft and round (with noticeable development of tissue derived from embryonic endoderm, as viscera). M20.

endoˈmorphic *a.* of, pertaining to, or characteristic of an endomorph; of the nature of an endomorph: L19. **endomorphy** *n.* the state or property of being an endomorph M20.

endomorphism /ɛndəʊˈmɔːfɪz(ə)m/ *n.* E20. [Fr. *endomorphisme*, f. as prec.: see -ISM.] **1** *Geol.* The alteration of cooling molten rock by reaction with the surrounding rock mass or assimilation of fragments of it. E20. **2** *Math.* A homomorphism of a set into itself. M20.

endophora /ɛnˈdɒfərə/ *n.* L20. [f. ENDO- after *anaphora*.] *Ling.* An endophoric reference or relation.

endophoric /ɛndəˈfɒrɪk/ *a.* L20. [f. prec. + -IC.] *Ling.* Referring to something within the text.

endoplasm /ˈɛndəplaz(ə)m/ *n.* L19. [f. ENDO- + -PLASM.] *Biol.* The inner, usu. granular, part of the cytoplasm of some cells, e.g. amoebae.

endoˈplasmic *a.* of, pertaining to, or occurring in endoplasm; chiefly in *endoplasmic reticulum*, a network of membranes in the cytoplasm of a cell, involved in protein and lipid synthesis M20.

endorphin /ɛnˈdɔːfɪn/ *n.* L20. [f. END(OGENOUS + M)ORPHIN(E.] Any of a group of peptides that occur in the brain and bind to the same receptors as morphine, thereby inhibiting pain.

endorsation *n.* see INDORSATION.

endorse /ɪnˈdɔːs, ɛn-/ *n.* L16. [App. f. the vb.] *Her.* A vertical stripe borne on either side of a pale and having a width one-quarter (sometimes one-eighth) that of the pale.

endorse /ɪnˈdɔːs, ɛn-/ *v.t.* Also **in-** /ɪn-/. L15. [med.L *indorsare* f. L IN-^{2} + *dorsum* back. Superseded earlier ENDOSS.] **I 1** Write a supplementary or official comment or instruction on (a document), esp. on the back, often to extend or limit its provisions; *spec.* sign (a bill of exchange) on the back to accept responsibility for paying it; sign (a cheque) on the back to make it payable to someone other than the stated payee. Also, write (a comment etc.) *on* a document; inscribe (a document) *with* (a comment etc.); make (a bill etc.) payable *to* another person by a signature on the back. L15. †**2** With double obj.: describe (a person) as; represent as being. L16–M17. **3** Confirm (a statement, opinion, etc.); declare one's approval of; vouch for. M17. **4** Make a record of an offence on (a licence, esp. a driving licence). M19. **b** In *pass.* Of a Black in South Africa: be moved out of an urban area because of not satisfying the conditions that would qualify him or her to continue living there. Usu. foll. by *out of.* M20.

1 SIR W. SCOTT Pointing out the royal warrant indorsed thereon. DICKENS We will indorse the parcel 'Pay the porter 2/6 extra for immediate delivery.' G. ORWELL For distances of less than a hundred kilometres it was not necessary to get your passport endorsed. 3 P. H. STANHOPE Such were the statements of Mr. Fox, but is there . . one man willing to endorse them? L. DEIGHTON Hanratty looked like a gardener . . , and this was endorsed by a shabby suit and unpolished . . shoes.

II 5 *Her.* As *endorsed* pa. pple. **a** = ADDORSED. E16. **b** Of wings: turned back to back. M18. **c** Of a pale: placed between two endorses. M19. **6** Load the back of (an animal) *with.* L17.

6 MILTON Elephants indorsed with towers.

endorsable *a.* able to be endorsed; transferable by endorsement; (of an offence) incurring the endorsement of the offender's driving licence: M18. **endorˈsee** *n.* a person to whom a bill etc. is assigned by endorsement M18. **endorser** *n.* L17. **endorsible** *a.* (now *rare*) = ENDORSABLE E18.

endorsement /ɪnˈdɔːsm(ə)nt, ɛn-/ *n.* Also **in-** /ɪn-/. M16. [f. prec. + -MENT.] **1** A comment, signature, etc., with which a document is endorsed; the action or an act of endorsing. M16. **b** A record of an offence entered on a licence, esp. a driving licence. E20. **2** Confirmation, ratification; approving testimony; an approving comment. M17.

2 R. L. STEVENSON I give the statement as Mackay's, without endorsement.

endoscope /ˈɛndəskəʊp/ *n.* M19. [f. ENDO- + -SCOPE.] *Med.* An instrument that can be introduced into the body to give a view of the inside of an organ.

endoˈscopic *a.* M19. **endoˈscopically** *adv.* M20. **enˈdoscopist** *n.* a person who uses an endoscope M20. **enˈdoscopy** *n.* the use of an endoscope M19.

endosmosis /ɛndɒzˈməʊsɪs/ *n.* Orig. (now *rare* or *obs.*) **endosmose** /ˈɛndɒzməʊz/. E19. [Fr. *endosmose*, f. as ENDO- + Gk *ōsmos* pushing: see -OSIS.] Osmotic diffusion of solvent or solute into a vessel or cell.

endosˈmotic *a.* M19. **endosˈmotically** *adv.* L19.

†**endoss** *v.t.* LME. [(O)Fr. *endosser*, f. as EN-^{1} + *dos* back. Repl. by ENDORSE *v.*] **1** Write on the back of (a document); write (words) *on* a document. LME–E17. **2** Inscribe or portray on any surface. LME–L16. **3** Put (clothing) on one's back. *rare.* LME–E19.

endothelium /ɛndə(ʊ)ˈθiːlɪəm/ *n.* Pl. **-ia** /-ɪə/. L19. [mod.L, f. ENDO- + Gk *thēlē* nipple + -IUM.] *Anat.* The layer of cells lining the blood-vessels, the heart, and the lymphatic vessels. Also, the layer of cells lining serous cavities (cf. MESOTHELIUM).

endothelial *a.* L19. **endotheliˈoma** *n.*, pl. **-mas**, **-mata** /-mətə/, a tumour developing from endothelial tissue L19. **endotheliˈomatous** *a.* of or resembling an endothelioma E20.

endotherm /ˈɛndə(ʊ)θəːm/ *n.* M20. [f. ENDO- after *homoiotherm*.] **1** *Zool.* An endothermic animal. M20. **2** *Physical Chem.* A curve corresponding to an endothermic reaction. M20.

endothermic /ɛndəʊˈθəːmɪk/ *a.* L19. [f. as ENDO- + THERMIC.] **1** *Chem.* Accompanied by, or (of a compound) formed with, the absorption of heat. L19. **2** *Zool.* Dependent on or capable of internal generation of heat. M20.

endothermy /ˈɛndəʊθəːmi/ *n.* E20. [f. ENDO- + Gk *thermos* heat + -Y^{3}.] **1** *Med.* = DIATHERMY. *rare.* E20. **2** *Zool.* The internal generation of heat by the body of an animal as a means of controlling its temperature. M20.

endow /ɪnˈdaʊ, ɛn-/ *v.t.* Also (earlier) †**in-**. LME. [Legal AN *endouer*, f. as EN-^{1} + (O)Fr. *douer*, f. L *dotare*, f. *dot-*, *dos* dowry, rel. to *dare* give.] **1** Provide a dower for (a widow). Formerly also, give a dowry to (a woman). LME. **2** Enrich with property; bequeath or give a permanent income to (a person, institution, etc.); establish (a lectureship, annual prize, etc.) by providing the funds needed to maintain it. LME. **3** Enrich or provide *with* an ability, talent, attribute, etc.; invest *with* a quality or (formerly) a privilege; in *pass.*, be possessed of or (*well* etc.) provided with talent or favourable qualities. Also foll. by †*in*, †*of*. LME. †**4** Of a personal attribute or quality: be inherent in (a person). *rare* (Shakes.). Only in E17.

2 B. PYM Wealth could not be more nobly used than in . . endowing a number of fellowships. 3 R. L. STEVENSON Mentally, he was endowed above the average. J. I. M. STEWART The trade of playwright . . does endow one at times with something of the actor's assurance. A. STORR The patient endows the therapist with attributes which are predominantly parental. Q. BELL He was genial and well-endowed.

endower *n.* L16.

endowment /ɪnˈdaʊm(ə)nt, ɛn-/ *n.* Also †**in-**. LME. [f. ENDOW + -MENT.] **1** The action of endowing. LME. **2** An ability, talent, attribute, etc., with which a person is endowed. M16. **3** The property or finance with which a person, institution, etc., is endowed. L16.

2 J. S. HUXLEY She was a person of great intellectual endowment. 3 LD BRAIN Voluntary hospitals . . were supported by endowments and voluntary contributions.

Comb.: **endowment assurance, insurance (policy)** a form of life insurance (policy) providing for the payment of a sum to the insured on a specified date or to his or her estate on earlier death; **endowment mortgage**: in which the borrower pays interest only until an endowment policy matures, its proceeds then being used to repay the capital.

†**endrench** *v.* see INDRENCH.

endrin /ˈɛndrɪn/ *n.* M20. [f. END(O- + DIELD)RIN.] A chlorinated hydrocarbon insecticide, $C_{12}H_8Cl_6O$, a stereoisomer of dieldrin.

†**endship** *n.* L16–E18. [f. END *n.* + -SHIP. Cf. *township*.] A small suburb; a hamlet.

endsville /ˈɛn(d)zvɪl/ *n. US slang.* Also **E-**. M20. [f. END *n.* + -S^{1} + -VILLE.] **1** The greatest, the best; the imaginary home of good things or people. M20. **2** = *the end of the road* s.v. END *n.* M20.

†**enduce** *v.* var. of INDUCE.

endue /ɪnˈdjuː, ɛn-/ *v.* Also **in-** /ɪn-/. LME. [(O)Fr. *enduire*, partly f. L *inducere* lead in (see INDUCE), partly f. as EN-^{1} + *duire* f. L *ducere* lead; assoc. in sense w. L *induere* put on (clothes).] †**1** *v.t.* Induct into an ecclesiastical living or a lordship. Only in LME. †**2** *v.t.* & *i.* Orig. (of a hawk), pass (the contents of the crop), or the contents of (the crop), into the stomach. Later, digest (*lit.* & *fig.*). LME–E18. **3** *v.t.* Orig., assume (a different form), take the form of. Later, put on (a garment). LME. **4** *v.t.* Clothe (a person). Usu. foll. by *with*. LME. †**b** Overlay, cover. *rare.* M17–L18. **5** *v.t.* †**a** = ENDOW 1, 2. LME–M17. **b** Endow *with* an ability, talent, attribute, etc. Freq. in *pass.* LME. †**c** Invest *with* an honour, dignity, etc. M–L16. †**d** Supply *with* something. *rare* (Shakes.). L16–E17. †**6** *v.t.* Bring up, educate, instruct. Only in 16. **b** Bring *to* a certain state or condition. *rare* (Shakes.). Only in E17.

3 G. SANDYS Next, Phantasus . . indues a tree, Earth, water, stone. LYTTON Who had not yet endued his heavy mail. 5b J. BUTLER We know. we are endued with capacities of action, of happiness and misery.

endungeon /ɪnˈdʌndʒ(ə)n/ *v.t. arch.* L16. [f. EN-^{1} + DUNGEON *n.*] Put into or confine in a dungeon.

Endura /ɛnˈdjʊərə/ *n.* L19. [mod.L, f. OProv. *endurar* endure, fast.] *Eccl. Hist.* The physical privations (freq. fatal) undergone by the Cathars after consolamentum to prevent recontamination of the soul.

endurable /ɪnˈdjʊərəb(ə)l/ *a.* E17. [f. ENDURE + -ABLE.] **1** Capable of enduring, likely to endure; durable. Now *rare.* E17. **2** Able to be endured. E18.

1 *Blackwood's Magazine* Rock-rooted castles, that seem endurable till the solid globe shall dissolve. 2 J. UPDIKE Life . . was scarcely endurable—a torture of headaches, sleeplessness, . . and anxiety.

enduraˈbility *n.* (*rare*) M19. **endurableness** *n.* (*rare*) L18. **endurably** *adv.* (*rare*) E19.

endurance /ɪnˈdjʊər(ə)ns, ɛn-/ *n.* Also †**in-**. L15. [(O)Fr., f. *endurer*: see ENDURE, -ANCE.] **1** Duration or continued existence in time; ability to last. L15. †**b** Protraction of an existing condition. *rare* (Shakes.). Only in E17. **2** Something which is endured; a hardship. M16. **3** The fact, habit, or power of enduring something unpleasant; long-suffering, patience. L16. **4** The ability of a thing to last or hold out; *esp.* the ability of a metal or other substance to withstand the repeated application of stress. L19.

1 L. M. HAWKINS Sermons of four hours' endurance. M. ARNOLD This is why Byron's poetry had so little endurance in it. 3 *American Humorist* Prolonging his visit beyond all endurance. F. KING He had a rare talent for endurance, bearing with insults and injuries . . with uncomplaining fortitude. 4 *Scientific American* The spectacular endurance test . . when a Bellanca plane stayed aloft for 51 hours 11 minutes.

endure /ɪnˈdjʊə, ɛn-/ *v.* Also †**in-**. ME. [(O)Fr. *endurer* f. L *indurare* harden, f. *in-* EN-^{1} + *durus* hard.] **1** *v.t.* & *i.* Undergo, bear, (pain, opposition, hardship, etc.), esp. without giving way. ME. **b** Of a thing: withstand (strain, pressure, etc.) without being damaged; be subjected to. LME. †**c** Withstand as an adversary; sustain. LME–E18. †**2** *v.t.* Harden (*lit.* & *fig.*); strengthen. LME–L16. **3** *v.i.* Remain in existence, last, persist. Formerly also, remain in a specified condition, place, etc. LME. †**b** Be continued through space; extend from one point to another. Only in 16. 4 *v.t.* Experience without resisting, submit to; bear, tolerate. Also foll. by *to do, that*. Freq. w. neg. L15. †5 *v.t.* Permit of, be compatible with. L16–E19.

1 G. GREENE So long as one is happy one can endure any discipline. M. L. KING A creature who could quietly endure, silently suffer and patiently wait. c DEFOE We were obliged to endure the whole weight of the imperial army. 3 H. LATIMER So this great king endured a leper all the days of his life. H. KISSINGER Only those agreements endure which both sides have an interest in maintaining. R. SCRUTON Even at the point of death the will to live endures. 4 M. W. MONTAGU Men endure everything while they are in love. G. GREENE He longs to be off. He cannot endure this place.

endurant *a.* (*rare*) ready to endure; that endures or is capable of enduring: M19. †**endurement** *n.* the action of enduring; hardship: E17–E18. **endurer** *n.* (*rare*) a person who endures something L16. **enduring** *ppl a.* that lasts, that continues in existence or in the memory LME. **enduring** *prep.* (*obs.* exc. *US dial.*) during LME. **enduringly** *adv.* M19. **enduringness** *n.* M19.

enduro /ɪnˈdjʊərəʊ, ɛn-/ *n.* Pl. **-os**. M20. [f. ENDUR(ANCE + -O.] A long-distance race for motor vehicles that is designed to test endurance rather than speed.

endways /ˈɛndweɪz/ *adv.* Also (*rare*) **-way** /-weɪ/. LME. [f. END *n.* + -WAY, -WAYS.] 1 In the direction of the ends; end to end; lengthwise. LME. 2 In a direct line, continuously. *obs.* exc. *dial.* L16. 3 With the end foremost, uppermost, or towards the viewer. Also *endways on*. L17.

1 J. SMEATON The stress upon the legs is always endways. 3 E. A. R. ENNION North Street, most of its . . houses endways on.

endwise /ˈɛndwʌɪz/ *adv.* & *a.* M17. [f. END *n.* + -WISE.] A *adv.* 1 = ENDWAYS 3. M17. 2 = ENDWAYS 1. E19. B *adj.* Acting or occurring endwise. L19.

ene /iːn/ *a.* M20. [f. -ENE.] *Chem.* Designating a pericyclic reaction in which, in its simplest form, two alkene molecules rearrange to form one.

-ene /iːn/ *suff.* [Alt. of -INE⁵.] 1 *Chem.* Forming the names of unsaturated hydrocarbons, as *ethylene, benzene, naphthalene*; *spec.* denoting the presence of one double bond between carbon atoms (cf. DIENE, TRIENE). 2 Forming the names of synthetic or proprietary products, as *corticene*.

1 J. S. CLARKE This third type of isomerism . . is apparent in but-2-ene.

en échelon /ɑ̃n eʃlɔ̃/ *a.* & *adv. phr.* Also *en e-*. E19. [Fr.] (Arranged) in an echelon. Cf. *in echelon* s.v. ECHELON *n.* 1.

enema /ˈɛnɪmə/ *n.* Pl. **-mas**, **-mata** /-ˈmɑːtə/. LME. [Late L f. Gk, f. *enienai* send or put in, inject, f. as EN-² + *hienai* send.] *Med.* A quantity of liquid or gas forced into the rectum or colon, esp. to expel the contents; an act of introducing fluid in this way; a syringe or other appliance used for the purpose.

high enema: see HIGH *a. low enema*: see LOW *a.*

enemy /ˈɛnəmi/ *n.* & *a.* ME. [OFr. *enemi* (mod. *ennemi*) f. L *inimicus*, f. as IN-³ + *amicus* friend, friendly.] A *n.* 1 A person who nurses hatred for or seeks to harm a person, group, or cause; an adversary, an antagonist. (Foll. by *of, to.*) ME. b A thing which is prejudicial to something or counteracts its effect or influence. LME. 2 A member of a hostile army or nation; an armed foe; a ship, aircraft, etc., of a hostile nation. ME. 3 *The* hostile force; *the* army etc. of a nation at war with one's own. L16. 4 *the enemy*, time. Chiefly in *how goes the enemy? colloq.* M19.

1 H. JAMES He had no enemies; he was an extremely amiable fellow, and universally liked. b W. PENN Vice, the Enemy of Religion. 2 G. BANCROFT All outside the family, tribe, or nation were usually held as enemies. 3 G. ORWELL Except at night, when a surprise attack was always conceivable, nobody bothered about the enemy.

Phrases: **(be) nobody's enemy but one's own** (be) responsible only for one's own misfortunes. **be one's own worst enemy** have the habit of bringing trouble upon oneself by one's own actions or behaviour. **enemy of the people**: a common form of indictment, esp. by Communist leaders, against a political opponent. **the enemy (of mankind)** the devil. **the great** or **last enemy** death. **the old enemy** the devil.

B *adj.* †1 Adverse, unfriendly, hostile. (Foll. by *to, with.*) ME–E18. 2 Of or pertaining to a hostile force or nation. Now only *attrib.* LME.

1 SWIFT Some evil genius, enemy to mankind. 2 *enemy action, hands, ship*, etc.

eneolithic /iːnɪəˈlɪθɪk/ *a.* Also **aen-**. E20. [f. L *aeneus* of copper or bronze + -O- + Gk *lithos* stone + -IC.] *Archaeol.* = CHALCOLITHIC *a.*

energetic /ɛnəˈdʒɛtɪk/ *a.* M17. [Gk *energētikos* active, f. *energein* operate, effect, f. as EN-² + *ergon* work: see -IC.] 1 Powerfully operative or effective. *arch.* M17. 2 Characterized by having much energy; strenuously active; forcible, vigorous. L18. 3 *Sci.* Of or pertaining to energy. E20.

1 P. G. TAIT The most energetic chemicals. 2 J. AUSTEN On the misery of what she had suffered . . she was energetic. G. B. SHAW Bursting into energetic action and shaking hands heartily. R. WEST An energetic woman, full of good sense and worldly wisdom.

energetical /ɛnəˈdʒɛtɪk(ə)l/ *a.* L16. [f. as prec. + -AL¹.] 1 *Philos.* Operative, effective; active as opp. to passive. *arch.* L16. †2 = ENERGETIC 1. Only in M17. 3 = ENERGETIC 2. Now *rare*. M17.

energetically /ɛnəˈdʒɛtɪk(ə)li/ *adv.* L18. [f. ENERGETIC or prec.: see -ICALLY.] 1 In an energetic manner. L18. 2 *Sci.* As regards energy; in terms of the energy released or required. M20.

2 *Nature* Membrane retrieval . . would be energetically a less costly process.

energetics /ɛnəˈdʒɛtɪks/ *n.* M19. [f. ENERGETIC: see -ICS.] 1 The branch of science that deals with energy. M19. 2 The properties of a system as they concern its energy and its energy flows and changes. L19.

2 *Nature* Marsupials . . have acquired mammalian-type energetics.

energic /ɪˈnəːdʒɪk, ɛ-/ *a.* M17. [f. ENERGY + -IC.] †1 = ENERGETIC 1. M17–M18. 2 = ENERGETIC 2. Now *rare*. E18.

†**energical** *a.* (*rare*) M16–E18.

energid /ˈɛnədʒɪd/ *n.* Now *rare* or *obs.* L19. [f. as ENERGY: see -ID².] *Biol.* The nucleus of a cell and the cytoplasm with which it interacts.

energize /ˈɛnədʒʌɪz/ *v.* Also **-ise**. M18. [f. ENERGY + -IZE.] 1 *v.t.* Infuse energy into (a person, activity, etc.). M18. b Supply energy, esp. by means of an electric current, for the operation of (a device). L19. 2 *v.i.* Expend energy, work; exercise one's powers. M18.

1 R. MAY You felt fear, and it energized you to rush for safety.

energiˈzation *n.* M20. **energizer** *n.* a person who or thing which energizes someone or something (*psychic energizer*: see PSYCHIC *a.* 3) M18.

energumen /ɛnəˈgjuːmən/ *n.* Also **-mene** /-miːn/. E18. [Late L *energumenus*, f. Gk *energoumenos* pa. pple of *energein* work in or upon, f. as EN-² + *ergon* work.] 1 A person believed to be possessed by the devil or an evil spirit. E18. 2 An enthusiast, a fanatic, a zealot. E18.

eˌnerguˈmenical *a.* (*rare*) L17.

energy /ˈɛnədʒi/ *n.* M16. [Fr. *énergie* or late L *energia* f. Gk *energeia*, f. as EN-² + *ergon* work: see -Y³.] 1 Force or vigour of expression. M16. 2 The exercise of power; active operation, working. E17. 3a *sing.* & in *pl.* Power actively and effectively used. M17. b In *pl.* Individual powers in use; activities, exertions. M18. 4 (Latent) ability or capacity to produce an effect. L17. 5 Vigour of action, utterance, etc.; a person's capacity for and tendency to strenuous exertion. E19. 6 *Sci.* The ability to do work, i.e. move a body. Orig., that possessed by a body by virtue of its motion. E19. b This ability provided in a readily utilized form, such as electric current or piped gas; resources that can be drawn on for this purpose. E20.

4 J. R. LOWELL Institutions which could bear and breed such men as Lincoln and Emerson had surely some energy for good. A. KOESTLER A sparse, dark wiry figure, charged with nervous energy. 5 L. HELLMAN The energy that had made us sprint into the zoo, running from monkey house to bird house. N. MITFORD They were eating up my time and energy in a perfectly shameless way. 6 E. RUTHERFORD The enormous emission of energy from a radioactive substance. R. DAWKINS Energy such as ultraviolet light from the sun. *atomic energy, chemical energy, electrical energy, mechanical energy, radiant energy, solar energy*, etc. *binding energy*: see BINDING *ppl a.* KINETIC *energy*. *latent energy*: see LATENT *a. potential energy*: see POTENTIAL *a.* b S. BELLOW The postwar prosperity of capitalism was based on cheap energy.

Comb.: **energy band** *Physics* a group of states of a quantized system characterized by a continuous range of energy values which the system is capable of having; **energy gap** (*a*) *Physics* a gap between adjacent energy bands, such that a particle cannot pass from the lower band to the higher without some minimum increase in its energy; (*b*) a national or global shortage of fuel and other sources of power. *energy level*: see LEVEL *n.* 4c.

enervate /ˈɛnəveɪt/ *a.* E17. [L *enervatus* pa. pple of *enervare*: see next, -ATE².] 1 Lacking moral, literary, or artistic vigour; spiritless; effeminate. E17. 2 Lacking physical strength. E18.

enervate /ˈɛnəveɪt/ *v.t.* E17. [L *enervat-* pa. ppl stem of *enervare* extract the sinews of, weaken, f. *e-* E- + *nervus* sinew: see -ATE³.] 1 Deprive of vigour or vitality; debilitate; weaken mentally, morally, or (formerly) physically. E17. †2 Destroy the force or authority of (an argument, doctrine, etc.); make ineffectual. E17–M19. b Disparage. E–M17. †3 Cut the tendons of; *spec.* hamstring (a horse). M17–M18.

1 Q. BELL She was enervated and chafed by the excitements and disappointments of the previous months. JAN MORRIS A heavy, dank, enervating environment.

enervatingly *adv.* in an enervating manner L20. **enervative** *a.* (*rare*) tending to enervate M19.

enervation /ɛnəˈveɪʃ(ə)n/ *n.* LME. [Late L *enervatio(n-)*, f. as prec.: see -ATION.] †1 Impairment of a right or privilege. Only in LME. 2 The action of enervating; the state of being enervated. M16.

enerve /ɪˈnəːv/ *v.t. obs.* exc. *poet.* LME. [(O)Fr. *énerver* f. L *enervare*: see ENERVATE *v.*] = ENERVATE *v.*

†**enervous** *a.* M17–M18. [f. L *enervis* (f. *e-* E- + *nervus* sinew) + -OUS.] Lacking nerve or strength; powerless, futile.

Enets /ˈɛnɛts/ *n.* & *a.* M20. [Russ.] A *n.* Pl. same. A member of a Samoyedic people inhabiting north central Siberia; the Uralic language of this people (also called *Yenisei Samoyed*). Cf. NENETS. M20. B *attrib.* or as *adj.* Of or pertaining to the Enets or their language. L20.

en évidence /ɑ̃n evidɑ̃ːs/ *adv. phr.* E19. [Fr.] In or at the forefront; conspicuously.

†**enew** *v.t.* LME–E17. [OFr. *enewer, eneauer*, f. as EN-¹ + *eau* water.] Of a hawk etc.: drive (a water-bird) into the water.

enface /ɪnˈfeɪs, ɛn-/ *v.t.* M19. [f. EN-¹ + FACE *n.*, after *endorse*.] Write, print, or stamp something on the face of (a document); write, print, or stamp (something) on the face of a document.

enfacement *n.* something that is written, overprinted, etc., on a document M19.

en face /ɑ̃ fas/ *adv. phr.* M18. [Fr.] With the face to the front, facing forwards; *Bibliogr.* on the facing page. Cf. EN REGARD.

en famille /ɑ̃ famiːj/ *adv. phr.* E18. [Fr.] At home, with one's family; as one of the family, informally.

enfant gâté /ɑ̃fɑ̃ gɑte/ *n. phr.* Pl. **-s -s** (pronounced same). E19. [Fr. = spoilt child.] A person given undue flattery or indulgence.

enfantillage /ɑ̃fɑ̃tijaːʒ/ *n.* E19. [(O)Fr., f. OFr. *enfantil* f. L *infantilis*: see INFANTILE, -AGE.] A childish action or prank.

enfants gâtés, terribles *n. phrs.* pls. of ENFANT GÂTÉ, TERRIBLE.

enfant terrible /ɑ̃fɑ̃ tɛribl/ *n. phr.* Pl. **-s -s** (pronounced same). M19. [Fr. = terrible child.] A person who causes embarrassment by ill-considered, or unorthodox behaviour or speech; an unconventional person.

enfeeble /ɪnˈfiːb(ə)l, ɛn-/ *v.t.* ME. [OFr. *enfeblir, -lier*, f. as EN-¹ + *feble* FEEBLE *a.*] Make feeble, weaken.

For other words beginning with *en-* see the entry for **en-**¹

enfeeblement *n.* the action of enfeebling; the state of being enfeebled: M17. **enfeebler** *n.* (*rare*) E17.

†**enfelon** *v.t.* L15–M19. [OFr. *enfelonner*, *-ir*, f. as EN-[1] + *felon* furious: see FELON *n.*[1] & *a.*] Make furious, enrage.

enfeoff /ɪnˈfiːf, -ˈfɛf, ɛn-/ *v.t.* Also †**in-**. See also INFEFT. LME. [AN *enfeoffer* (AL *enfeoffare*), OFr. *enfeffer*, f. as EN-[1] + *fief*: see FEE *n.*[2]] **1** *Law* (now *Hist.*). Put (a person) in possession of a fee or fief, under the feudal system; convey freehold property to by feoffment. (Foll. by *in*, *of*, *with*, †*on*.) LME. **2** *fig.* Hand over, give up possession of. L16.

enfeoffment /ɪnˈfiːfm(ə)nt -ˈfɛf-, ɛn-/ *n. obs.* exc. *Hist.* LME. [f. prec. + -MENT.] *Law.* The action of enfeoffing, feoffment; the state of being enfeoffed; a property conveyed or held by feoffment.

en fête /ɑ̃ fɛːt/ *pred. a. phr.* M19. [Fr.] Prepared for or engaged in holiday-making or celebration.

enfetter /ɪnˈfɛtə, ɛn-/ *v.t.* L16. [f. EN-[1] + FETTER *n.*] Put in fetters (*lit.* & *fig.*); enslave *to* another.

enfever /ɪnˈfiːvə, ɛn-/ *v.t.* M17. [f. EN-[1] + FEVER *n.*] Afflict with fever; *fig.* incense, enrage.

Enfield /ˈɛnfiːld/ *n.* M19. [An area of Greater London.] In full *Enfield rifle*. Any of various bolt-operated rifles made at the Royal Small Arms Factory, Enfield, or designed in imitation of them. Cf. LEE-ENFIELD.

enfilade /ɛnfɪˈleɪd/ *n.* & *v.* E18. [Fr., f. *enfiler* thread on a string, pierce or traverse from end to end, f. as EN-[1] + *fil* thread: see FILE *n.*[2], -ADE.] A *n.* **1** *Mil.* †**a** The situation of a post such that it commands the whole length of a line. Only in E18. **b** Gunfire directed along a line from end to end (also *enfilade fire*); an act of firing in this way. L18. **2** A suite of rooms with doorways in line with each other; a vista between rows of trees etc. E18.

B *v.t. Mil.* Subject to enfilade; cover the whole length of (a target) with a gun or guns. E18.

CLIVE JAMES The Germans installed concrete gun emplacements to enfilade the beaches.

enfile /ɪnˈfʌɪl, ɛn-/ *v.t.* LME. [Fr. *enfiler*: see ENFILADE.] †**1** Hang *up* or thread on a string. LME–L17. **2** *Her.* In *pass.* Of a charge: pierce or thread (another charge). (Foll. by *by*, *with*.) M19.

†**enfire** *v.t.* L15. [f. EN-[1] + FIRE *n.*] **1** Excite, arouse the passions of. L15–M19. **2** Set on fire. E16–E17.

enflame *v.* see INFLAME.

enflesh /ɪnˈflɛʃ, ɛn-/ *v.t.* M16. [f. EN-[1] + FLESH *n.*] Chiefly *Theol.* Give bodily form to.

enfleshment *n.* the action or an act of enfleshing; (an) incarnation: M20.

enfleurage /ɒ̃fləˈrɑːʒ/ *n.* M19. [Fr., f. *enfleurer* saturate with the perfume of flowers, f. as EN-[1] + *fleur* FLOWER *n.*: see -AGE.] The extraction of perfumes from flowers by means of oils and fats.

enflower /ɪnˈflaʊə, ɛn-/ *v.t.* E16. [f. EN-[1] + FLOWER *n.*] Adorn with flowers.

enflurane /ɛnˈflʊəreɪn/ *n.* L20. [f. *en-* of unkn. origin + FLU(O)R- + -ANE.] *Pharm.* A liquid, $CHF_2{\cdot}O{\cdot}CF_2{\cdot}CHFCl$, used as an inhalational general anaesthetic similar to halothane but less potent.

†**enfold** *n.* see INFOLD *n.*

enfold /ɪnˈfəʊld, ɛn-/ *v.*[1]*t.* Also (*arch.*) **in-** /ɪn-/. LME. [f. EN-[1], IN-[2] + FOLD *n.*[2], *v.*[1]] †**1** Involve; imply, entail; embroil *in*. LME–M17. **2** Wrap up *in* or *with* something; envelop, enclose. L16. **3** Encompass, encircle; clasp, embrace. L16. **4** Fold, shape into folds. Formerly also *fig.*, make involved or intricate. E17.

2 E. A. FREEMAN The royal robes in which the body had been enfolded. 3 E. M. FORSTER He simply enfolded her in his manly arms.

enfolder *n.* M16. **enfoldment** *n.* (*a*) *arch.* the action of enfolding; †(*b*) a thing that enfolds: L16.

enfold /ɪnˈfəʊld, ɛn-/ *v.*[2]*t. rare.* Also **in-** /ɪn-/. E17. [f. EN-[1], IN-[2] + FOLD *n.*[1]] Shut up (livestock) in a fold.

†**enforce** *n.* LME–L17. [f. the vb.] Effort, exertion.

enforce /ɪnˈfɔːs, ɛn-/ *v.* Also (*arch.*) **in-** /ɪn-/. ME. [OFr. *enforcier*, (also mod.) *enforcir*, f. Proto-Romance, f. L IN-[2] + *fortis* strong.] **I** Put force or strength in. †**1** *v.i.* & *refl.* Strive physically or mentally; exert oneself. (Foll. by *to do.*) ME–L16. †**2** *v.t.* Strengthen physically or morally; reinforce; encourage. (Foll. by *to do.*) LME–L17. †**3** *v.i.* Grow stronger; become violent. Only in LME. †**4** *v.t.* Intensify, make more vigorous; strengthen (a feeling). LME–L18. **5** *v.t.* Urge, press home, (an argument, demand, etc.). Formerly also, emphasize. LME.

4 S. JOHNSON The temptations to do ill are multiplied and enforced. 5 RUFUS ANDERSON Hoapile enforced his claim by an argument from a reciprocity of rights and duties.

II Use force on. †**6** *v.t.* Drive or impel by physical or moral force (*to*, *from* a place, belief, etc.). ME–M17. †**7** *v.t.* Overcome by violence; conquer; rape. LME–M17. †**8** *v.t.* Exert force on, press hard on; *fig.* press or urge with arguments, pleas, etc. LME–M17. **9** *v.t.* Compel, constrain, or oblige (*to do*). *arch.* LME.

III Produce or impose by force. †**10** *v.t.* Produce or obtain by physical or other force; extort *from* a person. M16–L17. **11** *v.t.* Compel the occurrence or performance of; impose (a course of action) *on* a person. E17. **12** *v.t.* Compel the observance of (a law, rule, practice, etc.); support (a demand, claim, etc.) by force. E17.

10 ROBERT BURTON By the striking of a flint fire is inforced. 11 B. JOWETT To enforce the education of their children upon unwilling parents. *Observer* A telephone call from Moscow or Washington would be enough to enforce their withdrawal. 12 R. OWEN He called on party officials to enforce strict Marxist orthodoxy in the arts.

enforcer *n.* a person, organization, etc., that enforces something; *slang* a person who imposes his will on others by violence and intimidation, esp. as a member of a criminal gang: L16. **enforcingly** *adv.* forcibly; earnestly, impressively: L16.

enforceable /ɪnˈfɔːsəb(ə)l, ɛn-/ *a.* M19. [f. prec. + -ABLE.] Able to be enforced.

enforceaˈbility *n.* E20. **enforceableness** *n.* M19.

enforcedly /ɪnˈfɔːsɪdli, ɛn-/ *adv.* LME. [f. ENFORCE *v.* + -ED[1] + -LY[2].] †**1** Forcibly, violently. LME–L16. **2** Under compulsion. L16.

enforcement /ɪnˈfɔːsm(ə)nt, ɛn-/ *n.* L15. [OFr., f. as ENFORCE *v.*: see -MENT.] **1** Constraint, compulsion; a constraining or compelling influence. Now *rare.* L15. †**2** The action or an act of assaulting or overcoming by violence. Only in L16. **3** The forceful pressing of an argument, demand, etc. L16. **4** The (forcible) extraction of payment; the process of compelling observance of a law, regulation, etc. L16. †**5** (A) reinforcement, esp. of an army etc. M17–M18.

3 S. SMILES It cost him many years of arguing, illustration, and enforcement. 4 SIR W. SCOTT The occasion seemed to require an enforcement of domestic discipline. attrib.: *enforcement agency, officer*, etc.

Comb.: **enforcement notice**: issued by a local authority in Britain and specifying a breach of planning legislation that the recipient is required to remedy.

enforcible /ɪnˈfɔːsɪb(ə)l, ɛn-/ *a.* Also †**in-**. L16. [f. ENFORCE *v.* + -IBLE.] = ENFORCEABLE. Formerly, forcible, compelling.

enforciˈbility *n.* M20.

†**enform** *v.* see INFORM *v.*

†**enfouldered** *a. rare* (Spenser). Only in L16. [Origin uncertain: perh. f. EN-[1] + OFr. *fouldre* (mod. *foudre*) thundercloud + -ED[1].] Full of thunderbolts; black as a thundercloud.

enframe /ɪnˈfreɪm, ɛn-/ *v.t.* Also **in-** /ɪn-/. M19. [f. EN-[1], IN-[2] + FRAME *n.*] **1** Frame, surround like a frame. M19. **2** Set in or as in a frame. L19.

†**enfranch** *v.* L16–M17. [AN *enfranchir*: see next.] = next.

enfranchise /ɪnˈfran(t)ʃʌɪz, ɛn-/ *v.t.* Also †**in-**. LME. [OFr. *enfranchiss-* lengthened stem of *enfranchir*, f. as EN-[1] + *franc*, *franche* free: see FRANK *a.*[1]] **1** Invest (a town) with municipal rights, esp. the right of representation in parliament. LME. **2** Grant (a person) the rights of a citizen, esp. the right to vote. LME. †**3** Admit to membership of a municipality, guild, corporation, etc. LME–M17. **4 a** Give (a slave, serf, etc.) liberty. M16. **b** Release from confinement. Chiefly *fig.* M16. †**c** Free from political domination. E–M17. **5** Release from obligatory payments or legal liabilities; convert (a leasehold or copyhold property) to freehold. L16.

4b A. S. BYATT David . . talked excitedly too, enfranchised from the solitude of his fat and silence.

enfranchisable *a.* L19. **enfranchisement** /-ɪz-/ *n.* the action of enfranchising; the state of being enfranchised: L16. **enfranchiser** *n.* M17.

enfrenzy /ɪnˈfrɛnzi, ɛn-/ *v.t.* Now *rare* or *obs.* M17. [f. EN-[1] + FRENZY *n.*] = FRENZY *v.* Chiefly as *enfrenzied* ppl a.

engage /ɪnˈgeɪdʒ, ɛn-/ *n.* Also †**in-**. L16. [f. the vb.] †**1** Promise, agreement. Only in L16. †**2** Entanglement, danger. Only in E17. **3** The engaging of swords. M19.

engage /ɪnˈgeɪdʒ, ɛn-/ *v.* Also †**in-**. LME. [(O)Fr. *engager* f. Proto-Romance, f. as EN-[1], IN-[2] + base of WAGE *n.*] **I** Pledge, secure. **1** *v.t.* †**a** Make over as a pledge; pawn; mortgage. LME–M17. **b** *fig.* Pledge (one's life, honour, etc.); put at risk, compromise. Now *rare.* M16. †**c** Make (a person) security for a commitment. L16–M17. **2** *v.i.* Pledge oneself (*to do*, *that*); guarantee; enter into a contract or undertaking (*to do*; also *with* an employee or worker). M16. **b** Foll. by *for*: answer for, guarantee; undertake to do, promise. M17. **c** Take service with or *with* an employer. M18. **3** *v.t.* Bind by a legal or moral obligation (*to* a party or deed; *to do*). E17. **b** *spec.* Bind by a promise of marriage, betroth. Usu. in *pass.* E18. **c** In *pass.* Have a social or business engagement arranged; be occupied in a meeting. L19. **4** *v.t.* Urge, persuade, induce. Now *rare.* M17. **5** *v.t.* Win over as an adherent or ally. *arch.* L17. **6** *v.t.* Fascinate, charm. Now *rare.* E18. **7** *v.t.* **a** Hire for work, take on as an employee; *refl.* take up employment (foll. by *to* the employer). M18. **b** Secure for one's own use; arrange beforehand to occupy or use; book, reserve. M18.

1b A. FRASER He would engage his soul for the reliability of all present. 2 O. WILDE: I . . engage to have it done by September. b A. HAMILTON He could not engage for their safety. 3 J. L. MOTLEY He declined engaging himself not to recall his foreign soldiery. P. G. WODEHOUSE Horace was engaged to marry . . Valerie. b M. PUZO Sonny was formally engaged to Sandra. c OED I am engaged for tomorrow, but could dine with you on Monday. 4 T. KEIGHTLEY He engaged them to declare in his favour. 7a C. CHAPLIN We were able to engage a maid to come twice a week. J. CONRAD An American ship where . . he had dared to engage himself. b W. S. MAUGHAM She had offered to engage a room . . in the house of the woman. E. WAUGH The tables are all engaged.

II Involve, entangle. †**8** *v.t.* Entangle physically; ensnare. L16–L17. †**9** *v.t.* & *i.* Involve, commit, (oneself) *in* an undertaking, quarrel, etc. Also foll. by other preps. L16–L18. †**10** *v.i.* & *t.* (Cause to) enter *into* or involve oneself *in* a place from which withdrawal is difficult. M17–M19. **11** *v.i.* Enter upon or occupy oneself *in* an activity, interest, etc. Formerly also foll. by *on*. M17. **12** *v.t.* Keep occupied or busy, provide occupation for, (a person, a person's thoughts, etc.). Usu. in *pass.*, foll. by *in* (*on*, *with*). M17. **13** *v.t.* Attract and hold fast (a person's attention, interest, etc.). M18. **b** Draw (a person) into a conversation. Usu. foll. by *in*. E20. **14** *Archit.* Fasten, attach; let part of (a column) into a wall. Usu. in *pass.* M18. **15** *v.i.* & *t.* Of part of a mechanism: come into contact with or fit into a corresponding part, so as to prevent or transmit movement; cause to do this; interlock (*with*). Also, put a motor vehicle into (gear, or a specified gear). M19.

11 J. BARZUN Nations where intellectuals engage . . in politics and state service. 12 E. WAUGH The local police were engaged in directing all traffic . . to the course. W. S. CHURCHILL Colonisation . . was the task that engaged the Western pioneers. 13 STEELE Her form . . engaged the eyes of the whole congregation in an instant. R. TRAVERS A mystery which engaged the attention of the press for some time. b A. POWELL Templar tried . . to engage the girl in conversation. 15 V. NABOKOV Press home until you hear or feel the

magazine catch engage. *Autosport* He could not engage third properly. W. BOYD Then the gears were engaged . . and the car slowly pulled away.

III With ref. to combat. 16a *v.i.* Enter into combat. Usu. foll. by *with*. M17. b *v.t.* Bring (forces) into battle (*with*). M19. 17 *v.t.* Enter into combat with, attack. L17. 18 *v.t.* & *i.* Of combatants: bring (weapons) together preparatory to fighting. L17.

16a SOUTHEY The mob . . did not venture to engage against musketry and cannon. 17 F. FITZGERALD American troops successfully engaged the enemy main forces and killed a great number. 18 H. ALLEN Since there are no seconds . . I shall simply count three and engage.

engager *n.* a person who engages someone or *in* something, or enters into an engagement; *spec.* (*Hist.*) a person who approved of the secret treaty made between Charles I and Scottish rulers in 1647: E17.

engagé /ɑ̃gaʒe, ɒŋgaˈʒeɪ/ *n.* & *a.* E19. [Fr., pa. pple of *engager* ENGAGE *v.*] A *n. Hist.* = ENGAGEE. *N. Amer.* E19. B *adj.* Of writers, artists, etc., or their works: showing social or political commitment. M20.

engageants /ɑ̃gaʒɑ̃, ɒŋgəˈʒɑːnts/ *n.pl. obs.* exc. *Hist.* L17. [Fr. †*engageantes* use as n. of fem. pl. of †*engageant* enticing, pretty, pres. pple of *engager* ENGAGE *v.*: see -ANT[1].] Double ruffles that fall over the wrists.

engaged /ɪnˈgeɪdʒd, ɛn-/ *a.* E17. [f. ENGAGE *v.* + -ED[1].] 1 That has been engaged; *spec.* under a promise to marry; *Archit.* (of a column) partly let into a wall. E17. 2 Of a telephone number or line, or a lavatory: unavailable because already in use. Of a tone: signifying that the telephone number called is engaged. L19. 3 = ENGAGÉ *a.* M20.

†**engagedness** *n.* L17–M18.

engagee /ɪŋgeɪˈdʒiː, ɛŋ-/ *n.* E19. [f. ENGAGE *v.* + -EE[1].] A person engaged for service or work; *spec.* (*N. Amer. Hist.*) a boatman hired by a fur-trader or explorer.

engagement /ɪnˈgeɪdʒm(ə)nt, ɛn-/ *n.* Also (earlier) †**in-**. E17. [(O)Fr., f. as ENGAGE *v.*: see -MENT.] †1 A legal or moral obligation; a tie; an attachment. E17–L18. 2 The fact or state of being or becoming engaged, *spec.* to marry. M17. b = COMMITMENT 5b. M20. 3 A formal promise, agreement or undertaking. *arch.* M17. b An appointment with another person; an agreement to meet. E19. c In *pl.* Promises to pay; financial commitments. M19. 4 An encounter between parties at war; a battle. M17. †5 The action of mortgaging property; a mortgage. Only in M17. †6 An inducement, a motive. M–L17. 7 A piece of business requiring a person's attention or presence; *esp.* a paid appointment, a job. L18.

2 W. J. M. RANKINE Another method of effecting engagement . . by wheels in rolling contact. S. SPENDER Within three weeks of our engagement . . we were married. A. STORR He broke off his engagement. 3 E. K. KANE An engagement was drawn up . . with the signatures of all the company. b B. TARKINGTON He . . apologized for having an engagement which made his departure necessary. c OED Mr. A. B. is unable to meet his engagements. 4 A. EDEN A big naval engagement with the German fleet. 7 W. COWPER From all his wearisome engagements freed. M. FONTEYN The season of 1910 was a limited summer engagement using dancers contracted to the Imperial Theatres.

Comb.: **engagement ring**: given by a man to a woman when they agree to marry each other.

engaging /ɪnˈgeɪdʒɪŋ, ɛn-/ *a.* L17. [f. ENGAGE *v.* + -ING[2].] That engages; *esp.* charming, winning, attractive.

J. SCOTT Several most engaging views. F. BUNSEN She . . has always the same engaging manner.

engagingly *adv.* M17. **engagingness** *n.* E18.

engaol *v.* var. of ENJAIL.

en garçon /ɑ̃ garsɔ̃/ *adv. phr.* E19. [Fr.] As or in the manner of a boy or a bachelor.

engarland /ɪnˈgɑːlənd, ɛn-/ *v.t.* Chiefly *poet.* L16. [f. EN-[1] + GARLAND *n.*] Encircle (as) with a garland.

engarrison /ɪnˈgarɪs(ə)n, ɛn-/ *v.t. obs.* exc. *Hist.* Also †**in-**. L16. [f. EN-[1], IN-[2] + GARRISON *n.*] Serve or station as a garrison in; protect by a garrison; *fig.* entrench or establish firmly (oneself).

†**engastrimyth** *n.* L16–E18. [Fr. *engastrimythe* f. Gk *eggastrimuthos*, f. as EN-[2] + *gastri* dat. of *gastēr* belly + *muthos* speech.] A ventriloquist.

†**engastrimythic** *a.*: only in M19.

Engelmann spruce /ˈɛŋg(ə)lmən ˈspruːs/ *n. phr.* Also **Engelmann's spruce** /-mənz/. M19. [f. George *Engelmann* (1809–84), US botanist + SPRUCE *n.*] A large alpine spruce, *Picea engelmannii*, of western N. America.

engem /ɪnˈdʒɛm, ɛn-/ *v.t. rare.* Also **in-** /ɪn-/. Infl. **-mm-**. E17. [f. EN-[1], IN-[2] + GEM *n.*] Set (as) with gems; bejewel.

†**engeminate** *v.* see INGEMINATE *v.*

engender /ɪnˈdʒɛndə, ɛn-/ *v.* Also †**in-**. ME. [(O)Fr., *engendrer* f. L *ingenerare*, f. as IN-[2] + *generare* GENERATE *v.*] 1 *v.t.* a Of a male: beget (offspring). *arch.* ME. †b Of a female: conceive; bear. ME–L17. c Of parents or ancestors, countries, situations, etc.: produce (living beings). LME. 2 *v.t.* Give rise to, bring about, (a state of affairs, a quality, feeling, etc.). ME. †3 Produce in the course of nature; generate, develop, (a natural product). LME–L18. †4 *v.i.* Have sexual intercourse, copulate, (*with*); breed, procreate. LME–E19. †5 *v.i.* Come into being, arise, originate. LME–M19. †6 *v.t.* Contract (a disease). E16–E17.

2 DRYDEN Immoderate Study engenders a grossness in the Mind. A. STORR A basic mistrust engendered by the circumstances of his early childhood. 5 DRYDEN Thick clouds are spread, and storms engender there.

engenderer *n.* LME. **engenderment** *n.* †(*a*) development, origin; (*b*) the action of engendering: L16.

engendrure /ɪnˈdʒɛndrʊə, ɪn-/ *n. arch.* Also **-dure** /-djʊə/, †**in-**. ME. [OFr. *engendr(e)ure*, f. as prec.: see -URE.] †1 The action of engendering. ME–M16. 2 A person's parentage or origin. LME.

engild /ɪnˈgɪld, ɛn-/ *v.t. poet.* Pa. pple **-gilt** /-ˈgɪlt/, **-gilded**. LME. [f. EN-[1] + GILD *v.*[1]] = GILD *v.*[1]

engine /ˈɛndʒɪn/ *n.* Also (*Sc.*, in senses 1 & 2) **ingine** /ɪnˈdʒʌɪn/. ME. [(O)Fr. *engin* f. L *ingenium* natural quality, talents, clever device, f. as IN-[2] + *gen-* base of *gignere* beget.] 1 Natural talent, wit; genius. *obs.* exc. *Sc.* ME. †b A person's disposition. Chiefly *Sc.* M16–E17. †2 Ingenuity; cunning. ME–M17. †3 An instance or product of ingenuity or cunning; an artifice, a plot; a snare. ME–L18. 4 An instrument; a tool. *arch.* ME. b Orig., any offensive weapon. Later, a large weapon with some form of mechanism. Now *arch.* & *Hist.* ME. †c An instrument of torture, *esp.* the rack. LME–L17. d A contrivance for catching game, fish, etc. L15. †5 The universe, or a particular division of the world, as a working entity. E–M16. 6†a A person regarded as another's instrument or agent, a tool. M16–M18. b A thing that is an agent or instrument (*of* an end or achievement). L16. 7 A contrivance consisting of a number of moving parts that work together to produce a desired physical effect. Now *rare* exc. as below & as the 2nd elem. of comb. M17. 8 A fire engine. *arch.* M17. 9 A stationary steam engine. E19. 10 A railway locomotive. M19. 11 A machine for producing energy of motion from some other form of energy, esp. heat that the machine itself generates. M19.

1 SIR W. SCOTT A man of quick ingine and deep wisdom. 4 H. POWER Our modern Engine the Microscope. b M. INNES A sling would . . be an engine to reckon with on bare ground. *fig.*: B. FRANKLIN The stage and the press . . became battering engines against religion. 6b *Times* We have been the engines of world growth. 7 ADAM SMITH Engines for knitting gloves or stockings. *Physics Bulletin* A small ruling engine capable of ruling plane or concave gratings . . with a pitch of 300 lines/mm. *beer-engine*: see BEER *n.*[1] 9 *atmospheric engine*: see ATMOSPHERIC *a.* 1. 11 *car engine, oil engine, petrol engine, rocket engine, Wankel engine*, etc.

Comb.: **engine-driver**: *spec.* a train driver; **engineman** a person who works on or operates an engine; **engine-room** a room containing engines, esp. a ship's engines; **engine-turning** the engraving of symmetrical patterns on metals by machine.

engine /ˈɛndʒɪn/ *v.* ME. [OFr. *enginier* f. med.L *ingeniare*, f. L *ingenium*: see prec. In sense 4 f. the n.] †1 *v.t.* Ensnare; deceive. Only in ME. †2 *v.t.* & *i.* Contrive, devise; plan *to do*. LME–E17. †3 Torture; assault (a place) with engines of war. LME–E17. 4 Fit (a ship etc.) with an engine. M19.

engined /ˈɛndʒɪnd/ *a.* Also (in sense 1) †**ingined**. E17. [f. ENGINE *n.* + -ED[2].] †1 Minded, disposed. *Sc. rare.* Only in E17. 2 Having an engine of a specified kind or position, or engines of a specified number. Only as 2nd elem. of comb., as *rear-engined, twin-engined*, etc. M20.

engineer /ɛndʒɪˈnɪə/ *n.* Also †**in-**. ME. [Orig. f. OFr. *engigneor* (mod. *ingénieur*) f. med.L *ingeniator*, f. *ingeniare*: see ENGINE *v.* Later f. mod.Fr. *ingénieur* or It. *ingegnere*, f. Proto-Romance, with suff. assim. to -EER.] 1 *Hist.* A designer and constructor of military works. Formerly also, a builder of engines of war. ME. b A soldier in a division of an army that specializes in engineering and (orig.) the design and construction of military works. L18. 2 A designer or maker of engines. L15. †b *fig.* An author or designer *of* something; a plotter. L16–E18. 3 More fully *civil engineer*. A person whose occupation is the design, construction, and maintenance of works of public utility, e.g. roads, bridges, and canals. E17. b A person who works in any branch of engineering, esp. as a qualified professional. M19. 4 A person in charge of an engine, now esp. a marine engine; *N. Amer.* an engine-driver. E17.

1b *Royal Engineers*: see ROYAL *a.* 3b *chemical engineer*: see CHEMICAL *a. electrical engineer*: see ELECTRICAL *a. mechanical engineer*: see MECHANICAL *a.* SANITARY *engineer*. STRUCTURAL *engineer*.

engineership *n.* the occupation or position of an engineer M17.

engineer /ɛndʒɪˈnɪə/ *v.* L17. [f. the n.] 1 *v.i.* Work as an engineer. L17. 2 *v.t.* Design, make, or build as a work of engineering. M19. 3 *v.t.* Arrange, contrive, or bring about, esp. artfully. M19. 4 *v.t.* Guide carefully, manoeuvre. *US.* M19.

1 R. W. EMERSON The grand tools with which we engineer. 2 M. HOWARD Margaret . . called in the electric company to engineer a heating system. *Scientific American* Gibson has . . engineered a bacterium capable of producing . . an enzyme that breaks down . . parathion. 3 G. GREENE I engineered a row on purpose and sacked him.

engineering /ɛndʒɪˈnɪərɪŋ/ *n.* E18. [f. ENGINEER *v.* + -ING[1].] 1 The work done by, or the occupation of, an engineer; the application of science for directly useful purposes, as construction, propulsion, communication, or manufacture. E18. 2 The action of working artfully to bring something about. L18. 3 A field of study or activity concerned with deliberate alteration or modification in some particular area. E20.

1 H. B. TRISTRAM An ancient roadway of which the engineering . . could be easily traced. **civil engineering** the branch of engineering that deals with the design, construction, and maintenance of works of public utility (see ENGINEER *n.* 3). *chemical engineering*: see CHEMICAL *a. electrical engineering*: see ELECTRICAL *a. mechanical engineering*: see MECHANICAL *a. military engineering*: see MILITARY *a.* STRUCTURAL *engineering*. 3 GENETIC *engineering*. *human engineering*: see HUMAN *a. planetary engineering*: see PLANETARY *a. social engineering*: see SOCIAL *a.*

Comb.: **engineering brick**: with high resistance to crushing, and low absorption of moisture; **engineering science** engineering as a field of study.

engineless /ˈɛndʒɪnlɪs/ *a.* L19. [f. ENGINE *n.* + -LESS.] That is without an engine.

enginery /ˈɛndʒɪn(ə)ri/ *n.* E17. [f. ENGINE *n.* + -ERY.] †1 The art of constructing engines; military engineering. Only in 17. 2 Engines; machinery; *esp.* (*poet.*) engines of war, artillery. M17.

engird /ɪnˈgəːd, ɛn-/ *v.t.* Chiefly *poet.* Pa. t. & pple **-girt** /-gəːt/, **-girded**. M16. [f. EN-[1] + GIRD *v.*[1]] = next.

For other words beginning with *en-* see the entry for **en-**[1]

engirdle /ɪnˈɡəːd(ə)l, ɛn-/ *v.t.* L16. [f. EN-[1] + GIRDLE *n.*[1]] Form a girdle or ring round; encircle, surround.

†**engirt** *v.*[1]*t.* L16. [f. EN-[1] + GIRT *v.*[1]] **1** Put a girdle or ring round; surround *with*. L16–M17. **2** = ENGIRDLE. E17–M18.

engirt *v.*[2] pa. t. & pple of ENGIRD.

†**engiscope** *n.* var. of ENGYSCOPE.

englacial /ɪnˈɡleɪʃ(ə)l, -sɪəl; ɛn-/ *a.* L19. [f. EN-[1] + GLACIAL.] Situated, occurring, or formed inside a glacier.

englacially *adv.* E20.

Englander /ˈɪŋɡləndə/ *n.* Earlier in NEW ENGLANDER. E19. [f. *England* + -ER[1], partly infl. by G *Engländer*.] A native or inhabitant of England; an English person.

Little Englander: see LITTLE *a.*

English /ˈɪŋɡlɪʃ/ *a.* & *n.* [OE *englisċ*, occas. *ænglisċ*, f. as ANGLE *n.*[2]: see -ISH[1].] **A** *adj.* **1** Of, pertaining to, or designating the group of Germanic peoples (Saxons and Jutes, as well as Angles) who invaded and settled in Britain in the 5th cent. AD, or (in post-Conquest times) the pre-Conquest Germanic inhabitants of England and their descendants. Long *obs.* exc. *Hist.* OE. **2** Designating the language of the English; written or spoken in English. OE. **3** Designating a person who is a native or inhabitant of England; of or pertaining to England or English people. ME. **4** Marked by the characteristics of an English person. M16.

2 R. W. EMERSON Our English Bible is a wonderful specimen of . . the English language. **3** H. HUNTER An English ship which had sailed round the world. J. D. SALINGER He drove over last Saturday with this English babe. **4** A. PHELPS A mind compact with sturdy and solid English elements.

B *n.* **1** Orig., the language spoken by the Germanic invaders of Britain in the 5th cent. AD. Now, the language descended from this, used in Britain, Ireland, Australia, New Zealand, the US, Canada, and many other countries. OE. **b** The English language as used in a particular area or period or by a particular writer; a particular kind of English. ME. **c** A person's facility in using English; the English language at a person's command. LME. **d** The English word or expression equivalent in meaning to a given word etc. Foll. by *for*. E20. **2** (*The*) English people; (*the*) English soldiers or forces. Treated as *pl.* L16. **3** A size of type (equal to about 14 points) between great primer and pica. Now *Hist.* L16. **4** In full *plain English*. The sense expressed plainly in English; the plain sense. Usu. foll. by *of*. M17. **5** (Also **e-**.) = SIDE *n.* 18. *US.* M19. **6** English language or literature as a subject to be studied. L19.

1 G. ORWELL The fight against bad English is not frivolous. **b** *Caribbean Studies* The various Creoles and creolized Englishes of the Caribbean. *American English*, *British English*, *pidgin English*, *Shakespeare's English*, etc. **c** T. HARDY His English, though not good, was quite intelligible to her. **d** R. KEARTON I cannot remember the English for it. **2** H. A. L. FISHER American divisions had fought with the French and English. **4** ADDISON An Oneirocritick, or, in plain English, an interpreter of dreams. H. FIELDING The English of all which is . . that I am in the wrong. **6** J. I. M. STEWART I had always come first in . . English.

Special collocations & phrases: *Basic English*: see BASIC *a.* 1. *Black English*: see BLACK *a.* *Early English*: see EARLY *a.* **English basement** *US* a basement with windows and its own entrance. *English bond*: see BOND *n.*[2] 9. **English breakfast** a substantial breakfast including cooked food. **English Canadian** an English-speaking Canadian (cf. *French Canadian* s.v. FRENCH *a.*). **English disease** †(*a*) melancholia; (*b*) rickets; (*c*) = *British disease* s.v. BRITISH *a.* *English elm*: see ELM 1. **English English** English as spoken by English people. *English flute*: see FLUTE *n.*[1] *English galingale*: see GALINGALE 2. *English maidenhair*: see MAIDENHAIR 2. *English horn*: see HORN *n.* **English Miss** a prim or prudish unmarried woman (cf. MISS *n.*[2]). *English muffin*: see MUFFIN 1a. *English mustard*: see MUSTARD *n.* 1. **English opening** *Chess*: in which the queen's bishop's pawn is advanced two squares on the first move. **English rose** a typically attractive light-complexioned English girl. **English setter** a long-haired usu. white or partly white sporting dog. **English sickness** = *English disease* (c) above. *English springer* (*spaniel*): see SPRINGER 6. †**English treacle** the plant water germander, *Teucrium scordium*. *English walnut*: see WALNUT 1. *Indian English*: see INDIAN *a.* **Middle English** English as it was between Old English and 1470 or 1500 and the advent of printing, characterized particularly by a reduced system of grammatical inflections, an increased lexical borrowing from other languages, esp. French and Latin, and a highly varied orthography. **modern English** English as it has been since 1470 or 1500. *Norman English*: see NORMAN *a.* 1. **Old English** (*a*) English as it was before about 1150 or the Norman Conquest, a West Germanic inflected language (comprising four main dialects, Kentish, Mercian, Northumbrian, and West Saxon); also called *Anglo-Saxon*; (*b*) *Typogr.* a form of black letter resembling that used by early English printers; (*c*) *Old English sheepdog*: see OLD *a.* & *adv.* *the English Channel*: see CHANNEL *n.*[1] 6. **the King's** or **Queen's English** the English language as correctly written or spoken.

Englishism *n.* (*a*) an English idiom or form of speech; (*b*) English character or practices; attachment to what is English: E19. **Englishness** *n.* E19.

English /ˈɪŋɡlɪʃ/ *v.t.* Also **e-**. LME. [f. the adj.] **1** Translate into English; give the English equivalent of. LME. †**2** Put into plain English, describe in simple terms. L16–L17. **3** = ENGLISHIZE 2. E19.

3 R. G. WHITE When a foreign word has been transplanted into our speech . . it should be thoroughly Englished.

Englisher /ˈɪŋɡlɪʃə/ *n.* In sense 2 also **e-**. M17. [f. ENGLISH *a.*, *v.* + -ER[1].] **1** An English subject; a native or inhabitant of England. Chiefly *Sc.* M17. **2** A person who translates a book etc. into English. E19.

Englishize /ˈɪŋɡlɪʃʌɪz/ *v.t.* Also **-ise**. L18. [f. ENGLISH *n.* & *a.* + -IZE.] †**1** Bring to England, cause to live in England. *rare*. Only in L18. **2** Make English; give an English form or character to; Anglicize. M19.

Englishiˈzation *n.* L20.

Englishly /ˈɪŋɡlɪʃli/ *adv.* LME. [f. ENGLISH *n.* & *a.* + -LY[2].] †**1** In English; by means of an English expression. LME–M16. **2** In the manner of English people or England. E17.

Englishman /ˈɪŋɡlɪʃmən/ *n.* Pl. **-men**. [OE *Englisċmon*, f. as ENGLISH *a.* & *n.*, MAN *n.*] A man who is English by birth, descent, or naturalization.

Englishry /ˈɪŋɡlɪʃri/ *n.* LME. [AN *englescherie*, AL *englescheria*, f. ENGLISH *n.* & *a.*: see -ERY.] **1** The fact of being English in character or (now *Hist.*) by birth or descent. LME. **2** *Hist.* The part of a population, esp. in Ireland, that is of English descent. L15. **3** English people. *rare*. M19.

1 E. E. EVANS His objections to the system . . reveal his Englishry. **3** M. TWAIN The Norman Conqueror came over to divert the Englishry.

Englishwoman /ˈɪŋɡlɪʃwʊmən/ *n.* Pl. **-women** /-wɪmɪn/. LME. [f. ENGLISH *a.* & *n.* + WOMAN *n.*] A woman who is English by birth, descent, or naturalization.

Englishy /ˈɪŋɡlɪʃi/ *a.* L19. [f. ENGLISH *n.* & *a.* + -Y[1].] Characteristically English.

Eng. Lit. /ɪŋ ˈlɪt/ *n. phr.* M19. [Abbrev. of *English literature*.] English literature, as a subject of academic study.

englobe /ɪnˈɡləʊb, ɛn-/ *v.t.* E17. [f. EN-[1] + GLOBE *n.*] **1** Shape into a globe. E17. **2** Enclose in or as in a globe. Chiefly *fig.* M19.

englut /ɪnˈɡlʌt, ɛn-/ *v.t. arch.* Also †**in-**. Infl. **-tt-**. L15. [OFr. *englotir* (mod. *engloutir*) f. late L *inglut(t)ire*, f. as IN-[2] + *gluttire* swallow. In sense 2 directly f. EN-[1], IN-[2] + GLUT *v.*[1]] **1** Swallow, gulp down. L15. **2** Glut, satiate. L15.

englyn /ˈɛŋlɪn/ *n.* Pl. **englyns**, **englynion** /ɪŋləˈnɪən, ɛn-/. L16. [Welsh.] In Welsh poetry, a stanza (usu. a quatrain) having any of various strictly prescribed metrical structures.

engobe /ɑ̃ɡɔb/ *n.* M19. [Fr.] A mixture of white clay and water applied as a coating to pottery to cover the natural colour or to provide a ground for decoration; = SLIP *n.*[1] 3.

engolden /ɪnˈɡəʊld(ə)n, ɛn-/ *v.t.* & *i.* E19. [f. EN-[1] + GOLDEN.] Make or become golden.

engore /ɪnˈɡɔː, ɛn-/ *v.*[1]*t.* Now *rare* or *obs.* L16. [f. EN-[1] + GORE *n.*[1]] Make gory, stain with blood.

†**engore** *v.*[2]*t. rare* (Spenser). Only in L16. [f. EN-[1] + GORE *v.*[1]] Gore, wound deeply; *fig.* enrage.

engorge /ɪnˈɡɔːdʒ, ɛn-/ *v.* Also (*rare*) **in-**. L15. [OFr. *engorgier* feed to excess (mod. *engorger* obstruct, congest), f. as EN-[1], GORGE *v.*] **1** *v.t.* & *i.* Gorge; feed greedily, fill to excess or to capacity. L15. **b** In *pass.* Be filled to excess; be crammed *with*; *Med.* be congested with fluid, esp. blood. Cf. GORGE *v.* 2a. L16. **2** *v.t.* Devour greedily; swallow up. M16.

1 *Nature* Ticks attach to the skin of their host . . , engorging on blood. **2** *Times Lit. Suppl.* Enlarging the appetite of the consuming public so as to enable it to engorge a growing volume and variety of goods.

engorgement *n.* the action of engorging; the state of being engorged, *esp.* (*Med.*) congestion of a tissue or organ with fluid, esp. blood: M16. **engorger** *n.* L16.

engouement /ɑ̃ɡumɑ̃/ *n.* E19. [Fr., lit. 'obstruction in the throat'.] Unreasoning fondness; (an) infatuation.

engouled /ɪnˈɡuːld, ɛn-/ *a.* M19. [f. (O)Fr. *engoulé* pa. pple of *engouler* gobble up, f. as EN-[1] + OFr. *goule* (mod. *gueule*) throat: see -ED[1]] *Her.* Of a bend, cross, etc.: entering the mouth of an animal.

engrace /ɪnˈɡreɪs, ɛn-/ *v.t.* Also †**in-**. L16. [f. EN-[1], IN-[2] + GRACE *n.*] †**1** Introduce into the favour of another. L16–M17. **2** *Theol.* Endow with grace. L19.

†**engraff** *v.t.* Also **in-**. LME–M19. [f. EN-[1], IN-[2] + GRAFF *v.*] = ENGRAFT 1, 2.

engraft /ɪnˈɡrɑːft, ɛn-/ *v.* Also †**in-**. See also earlier ENGRAFF. L16. [f. EN-[1], IN-[2] + GRAFT *v.*[1]] **1** *v.t.* & *i.* = GRAFT *v.*[1] 1,4. (Foll. by *into*, *upon*.) L16. **2** *v.t.* Implant, incorporate, (*in* or *into* an already existing system etc.); add *on* to an already existing base; = GRAFT *v.*[1] 2a. L16. †**3** *v.t.* Add to the stock of a trading company. L17–L18. †**4** *v.t.* Introduce smallpox virus into (a person's system); inoculate. Only in E18. **5** *v.t.* = GRAFT *v.*[1] 6. L19.

2 H. FIELDING Acquiring solid lasting habits of virtue, and ingrafting them into our character. JAS. GRANT It had been added to, or engrafted on, the tall, old, square baronial tower.

engraftment *n.* the action or an act of engrafting; a graft: M17.

engrail /ɪnˈɡreɪl, ɛn-/ *v.t.* LME. [OFr. *engresler* (mod. *engrêler*) make thin, f. as EN-[2] + *graisle*, *gresle* (mod. *grêle*) thin f. L *gracilis*.] **1** Chiefly *Her.* Make small semicircular indentations in the edge of. Chiefly as *engrailed* pa. pple. LME. **2** Decorate *with* a border, metalwork, colours, etc. *obs.* exc. *poet.* LME. †**3** Indent, incise; sculpture in intaglio. M16–L18. **4** Give a serrated appearance to; roughen. L16.

engrailed *a.* that has been engrailed; having the edge decorated with curvilinear indentations; (of a coin) having a series of such indentations or of raised dots around the margin: LME.

engrain *v.* see INGRAIN *v.*

engram /ˈɛnɡram/ *n.* E20. [G *Engramm*, f. as EN-[2] + Gk *gramma* letter.] A memory-trace; *spec.* a permanent and physical alteration of brain tissue postulated to account for the existence of memory.

engrammatic /ɛnɡrəˈmatɪk/ *a.* E20.

en grande tenue /ɑ̃ ɡrɑ̃ːd təny/ *adv. phr.* M19. [Fr.] In full dress.

†**engrandize** *v.t.* Also **-ise**, **in-**. M17–L19. [Fr. *engrandiss-* lengthened stem of *engrandir*, f. It. *ingrandire*; assim. to vbs in -IZE. Cf. AGGRANDIZE.] Make great; increase in importance, estimation, or rank.

en grand seigneur /ɑ̃ ɡrɑ̃ sɛɲœːr/ *adv. phr.* E19. [Fr.] In the manner of a nobleman.

engrasp /ɪnˈɡrɑːsp, ɛn-/ *v.t.* Now *rare* or *obs.* L16. [f. EN-[1] + GRASP *n.* or *v.*] Grasp (*lit.* & *fig.*); embrace, seize.

engrave /ɪnˈɡreɪv, ɛn-/ *v.*[1] Also †**in-**. Pa. pple **-ed**, (*arch.*) **-en**. L15. [f. EN-[1], IN-[2] + GRAVE *v.*[1], after Fr. †*engraver*.] **1** *v.t.* Inscribe or ornament (a hard surface or object) with incised marks. L15. **2** *v.t.* Carve (an inscription, figure, etc.) upon a surface or object; *fig.* fix indelibly *in* or *on* the memory, heart, etc. M16. †**3** *v.t.* Portray or represent by sculpture. M16–E17. 4 *v.t.* & *i.* Produce a representation of (a picture, lettering, etc.) for printing by removal of part of the surface of a plate or block. M17.

1 S. SMILES To engrave spoons and forks with crests and ciphers. 2 O. WISTER July third was to be engraved inside the wedding ring. W. S. MAUGHAM Isobel had a good memory and the various turns of the long discussion had engraved themselves upon it. 4 WILKIE COLLINS I get my bread by drawing and engraving on wood for the cheap periodicals.

†**engravement** *n.* = ENGRAVING I, 2 E17–E18.

†**engrave** *v.*[2]*t.* Also **in-**. M16–L17. [f. EN-[1], IN-[2] + GRAVE *n.*[1] or *v.*[1]] Put in a grave; entomb, bury.

†**engraven** *v.t.* Also **in-**. E17–L18. [Perh. alt. of ENGRAVE *v.*[1], due to anal. of vbs with pref. EN-[1] and suff. -EN[5].] = ENGRAVE *v.*[1]

engraver /ɪnˈɡreɪvə, ɛn-/ *n.* Also †**in-**. L16. [f. ENGRAVE *v.*[1] + -ER[1].] 1 A person who engraves something. L16. 2 An engraving tool. E19. 3 In full *engraver beetle*. A bark beetle of the genus *Ips*, which makes channels in the surface of the sapwood of trees. L19.

engraving /ɪnˈɡreɪvɪŋ, ɛn-/ *n.* E17. [f. ENGRAVE *v.*[1] + -ING[1].] 1 The action of ENGRAVE *v.*[1]; the art of the engraver. E17. 2 An engraved figure or inscription. *rare.* E17. 3 A print made from an engraved plate. E19.

engrenage /ɑ̃ɡrənaːʒ/ *n.* Pl. pronounced same. E20. [Fr., lit. 'gearing', f. *engrener* feed corn into (a threshing-machine), throw into gear, f. as EN-[1], GRAIN *n.*[1]: see -AGE.] 1 A set of circumstances that trap one; an organization or society regarded as full of snares. E20. 2 The process of preparing for effective joint action. M20.

engroove /ɪnˈɡruːv, ɛn-/ *v.t.* Also **in-** /ɪn-/. M19. [f. EN-[1], IN-[2] + GROOVE *n.* or *v.*] 1 Work (something) into a groove. M19. 2 Form a groove in. L19.

en gros /ɑ̃ ɡro/ *adv. phr.* E18. [Fr.] In general, in broad terms.

engross /ɪnˈɡrəʊs, ɛn-/ *v.t.* Also †**in-**. LME. [Ult. f. as EN-[1], GROSS *a.* In branch I f. AN *engrosser*, med.L *ingrossare*, f. OFr. *grosse*, med.L *grossa* large writing; in branch II f. OFr. *en gros*, med.L *in grosso* in bulk, wholesale f. late L *grossus* GROSS *a.*; in branch III f. (O)Fr. *engrosser*.] I Use large writing. 1 Write out in a large, clear hand; make a fair copy of. Now usu., express in legal form; produce (a legal document) in its final or definitive form. LME. †2 Settle or agree (a matter). LME–E16. †3 Make a written record of; enter in a formal document or list. LME–M17.

II Deal with on a large scale. 4 Orig. (now *Hist.*), buy up wholesale; *esp.* corner the market in (a commodity) in order to control the price. Later (now *arch.*), concentrate (property, privileges, functions, etc.) in one's own possession; monopolize. LME. †b Buy up large amounts of (land, tenements, etc.). M16–L18. †5 Amass, collect from all quarters. LME–E17. 6 Require the entire use of, utilize all of. E17. 7 Of an object of thought or feeling: fully occupy (the mind, affections, time, etc.). M17. 8 Absorb the whole attention of (a person). Usu. in *pass.* (foll. by *in*, *with*). E18.

4 H. T. BUCKLE Seeing a single person engross the conversation. 6 J. HARVEY The firm expanded... It came to engross every machine that had to do with building. 7 W. COWPER My morning is engrossed by the garden. 8 M. BARING Mademoiselle was engrossed in a French novel. A. HIGGINS He lost all interest in activities that had formerly engrossed him.

†III Make dense. 9 Thicken (a liquid); condense (a vapour). LME–L16. 10 Make (the body) gross or fat; coarsen (the mind). LME–E19. 11 Make thick or bulky; enlarge. L15–M17. b Add to the numbers of (an army); draw up (troops) in a compact body. E16–M17.

engrossedly /-sɪdli/ *adv.* in an engrossed manner, with absorbed attention M19. **engrosser** *n.* (now *Hist.*) LME. **engrossing** *ppl a.* that engrosses; *spec.* that fully absorbs one's attention or interest: L16. **engrossingly** *adv.* M19. **engrossingness** *n.* M19. **engrossment** *n.* (*a*) the action of engrossing; the state of being engrossed; (*b*) a thing that is engrossed, *spec.* the definitive copy of a legal document: E16.

engulf /ɪnˈɡʌlf, ɛn-/ *v.t.* Also †**-gulph**, (*arch.*) **in-** /ɪn-/. M16. [f. EN-[1], IN-[2] + GULF *n.*] 1 Swallow up (as) in a gulf or abyss; flow over and swamp. M16. 2 Affect powerfully, overwhelm; preoccupy, engross. L16. 3 *refl.* & in *pass.* Of a river: discharge itself into the sea; disappear underground. *arch.* M17.

1 J. KOSINSKI I was hurled into.. the brown filth, which parted under my body to engulf me. D. BAGLEY The waters of Santego Bay arose to engulf the town. *fig.*: E. WELTY The ancient deck chair.. engulfed her like a hammock. 2 D. ACHESON A bitter debate engulfed the United States. W. S. CHURCHILL The loneliness and apathy which engulfed her after Albert's death.

engulfment *n.* the action of engulfing; the process of being engulfed: E19.

†**engyscope** *n.* Also **engi-**. M17–M19. [f. Gk *eggus* near at hand + -SCOPE.] A microscope; *spec.* a reflecting microscope.

†**enhabit** *v.* var. of INHABIT.

enhalo /ɪnˈheɪləʊ, ɛn-/ *v.t.* M19. [f. EN-[1] + HALO *n.*] Surround (as) with a halo.

enhance /ɪnˈhɑːns, -hans, ɛn-/ *v.* Also †**in-**. ME. [AN *enhauncer* prob. alt. of OFr. *enhaucier* f. Proto-Romance, f. L IN-[2] + *altus* high.] †1 *v.t.* Lift, raise; raise the level of. ME–L16. †2 *v.t.* Exalt in rank, wealth, etc.; elevate spiritually or morally; lift up with pride; praise. ME–M17. 3 *v.t.* a Make appear greater; exaggerate. LME. b Raise in degree; heighten, intensify, (a quality, attribute, etc.). L16. 4a *v.t.* Raise (a price or value); increase (a charge or cost). LME. b *v.i.* Of property: rise in price. Formerly (of prices): rise. L15. 5 *v.t.* Increase *in* (or formerly, in) price, value, importance, attractiveness, etc. Also, improve in quality, utility, or (formerly) beauty. E16.

3a G. DOWNES The satirist wished to enhance the infirmity of Philip. b GIBBON These delights were enhanced by the memory of past hardships. 5 *Which Computer?* The ¼-inch tape streamer storage system.. has been enhanced to back-up the.. disc drives.

enhancer *n.* LME. **enhancive**, ***-sive** *a.* tending to enhance M19.

enhancement /ɪnˈhɑːnsm(ə)nt, -hans-, ɛn-/ *n.* M16. [f. prec. + -MENT.] 1 Something that enhances; *esp.* an extra facility; a supplementary payment. M16. 2 The action or process of enhancing; the fact of being enhanced. L16.

1 *Oxford Times* £2.48 per hour plus enhancements for evening and weekend work.

†**enhappy** *v.t.* E17–M18. [f. EN-[1] + HAPPY *a.*] Make happy or prosperous.

†**enharden** *v.t.* E16–L19. [f. EN-[1] + HARDEN *v.*] Make (a person) hard.

enharmonic /ɛnhɑːˈmɒnɪk/ *a.* & *n.* E17. [Late L *en(h)armonicus* f. Gk *enarmonikos*, f. as EN-[2] + *harmonia* HARMONY: see -IC.] *Mus.* A *adj.* 1 *Hist.* Designating (ancient Greek music based on) a tetrachord divided into two quarter-tones and a major third. E17. 2 Pertaining to, involving, or designating musical intervals smaller than a semitone, esp. the relationship between notes which are equal only in a scale of equal temperament (e.g. C sharp and D flat); (of an instrument or keyboard) sounding more than 12 notes to an octave. L18. B *n.* 1 In *pl.* Enharmonic music. E17. 2 A note belonging to an enharmonic interval. L19.

enharmonical *a.* = ENHARMONIC *a.* M18. **enharmonically** *adv.* L19.

enhearse *v.* var. of INHEARSE.

enhearten /ɪnˈhɑːt(ə)n, ɛn-/ *v.t.* Now *rare.* E17. [f. EN-[1] + HEARTEN *v.*] Encourage; embolden.

enheaven *v.* var. of INHEAVEN.

†**enherit** *v.* see INHERIT.

†**enheritable** *a.*, †**enheritance** *n.* vars. of INHERITABLE, -ANCE.

enhungered /ɛnˈhʌŋɡəd/ *a.* Now *rare.* L15. [Alt. of AHUNGERED, ANHUNGERED by substitution of EN-[1] for the pref.] Hungry.

enhypostasia /ˌɛnhʌɪpəˈsteɪzɪə/ *n.* L19. [f. EN-[2] + Gk *hupostasis* HYPOSTASIS + -IA[1].] *Theol.* The personhood of Christ as existing through (and only through) the hypostasis.

enhypostatic /-ˈstat-/ *a.* L19. **enhyˈpostatize** *v.t.* (*rare*) unite in one hypostasis or person L19.

For other words beginning with *en-* see the entry for **en-**[1]

enigma /ɪˈnɪɡmə/ *n.* Also †**aen-**. Pl. **enigmas**, **enigmata**. M16. [L *aenigma* f. Gk *ainigma*, f. base of *ainissesthai* speak allusively or obscurely, f. *ainos* fable.] 1 A riddle, usu. one involving metaphor. Formerly also, an obscure or allusive speech. M16. 2 A perplexing, mysterious, or unexplained thing. E17. 3 An enigmatic person. E20.

enigmatize *v.* (now *rare*) †(*a*) *v.t.* symbolize; (*b*) *v.t.* & *i.* make or become enigmatic: M17.

enigmatic /ɛnɪɡˈmatɪk/ *a.* E17. [Fr. *énigmatique* or late L *aenigmaticus*, f. as prec.: see -ATIC.] Of the nature of an enigma; perplexing, obscure; (of a person) baffling others' conjecture as to character, sentiments, identity, etc.; mysterious.

J. THURBER As enigmatic as the face of Mona Lisa.

enigˈmatical *a.* = ENIGMATIC M16. **enigˈmatically** *adv.* L16.

†**enigmatist** *n.* E17–E18. [L *aenigmatista* f. Gk *ainigmatistēs*, f. *ainigma* ENIGMA: see -IST.] A person who writes enigmas or who speaks enigmatically.

enisle /ɛnˈʌɪl, ɪn-/ *v.t.* Also **in-** /ɪn-/. E17. [f. EN-[1], IN-[2] + ISLE *n.*[1]] 1 Make into an island. E17. 2 Place or settle on an island; *fig.* isolate. M19.

2 M. ARNOLD In the sea of life enisled.. we mortal millions live alone.

enjail /ɪnˈdʒeɪl, ɛn-/ *v.t.* *arch.* Also **-gaol**, **in-** /ɪn-/. L16. [f. EN-[1], IN-[2] + JAIL *n.*] Shut up in, or as in, a jail.

enjamb /ɪnˈdʒam, ɛn-/ *v.* E17. [Fr. *enjamber* stride over, go beyond, f. as EN-[1] + (O)Fr. *jambe*: see JAMB.] †1 *v.i.* Encroach. Only in E17. 2 *v.t.* *Pros.* Continue (a sentence) without a pause beyond the end of a line, couplet, or stanza. Chiefly as *enjambed* ppl a. L19.

enjambment /ɪnˈdʒam(b)m(ə)nt, ɛn-/ *n.* Also **enjambement** /ɪnˈdʒam(b)m(ə)nt, ɛn-, *foreign* ɑ̃ʒɑ̃bmɑ̃/. M19. [Fr. *enjambement*, f. as prec.: see -MENT.] *Pros.* An instance of enjambing.

enjealous /ɪnˈdʒɛləs, ɛn-/ *v.t.* *arch.* Also (earlier) †**in-**. E17. [f. EN-[1], IN-[2] + JEALOUS.] Make jealous.

enjewel /ɪnˈdʒuːəl, ɛn-/ *v.t.* Also †**in-**. Infl. **-ll-**, ***-l-**. E17. [f. EN-[1], IN-[2] + JEWEL *n.*] Adorn with jewels or like a jewel.

enjoin /ɪnˈdʒɔɪn, ɛn-/ *v.t.* Also †**in-**. ME. [(O)Fr. *enjoi(g)n-* stem of *enjoindre* f. L *injungere* join, attach, impose, f. as IN-[2] + *jungere* JOIN *v.*] 1 Prescribe authoritatively (an action, conduct, etc.); *arch.* impose (a duty, penance, penalty, etc.). (Foll. by *on*, *upon*, †*to* a person.) ME. b Command or call upon (a person) *to do*; order *that*. ME. c Pledge *to* an observance. Formerly, sentence *to* a penalty. LME. †2 Join together. LME–L17. 3 Prohibit, forbid; *esp.* (*Law*) prohibit or restrain by an injunction. (Foll. by *from*.) L16.

1 A. J. AYER The sort of action that is enjoined or forbidden by some ecclesiastical authority. b SCOTT FITZGERALD 'Don't mention it,' he enjoined me. F. HERBERT I enjoin you to practice the meditation of peace.

enjoiner *n.* L16. **enjoinment** *n.* the action of enjoining; an injunction: M17.

enjoinder /ɪnˈdʒɔɪndə, ɛn-/ *n.* M19. [f. ENJOIN after *rejoinder*.] An imposition, a duty, an obligation.

enjoy /ɪnˈdʒɔɪ, ɛn-/ *v.* LME. [OFr. *enjoier* give joy to, (refl.) enjoy, f. as EN-[1] + *joie* JOY *n.*, or OFr. *enjoïr* enjoy, rejoice, f. as EN-[1] + *joïr* f. L *gaudere*.] 1 *v.i.* †a Be in a state of joy; rejoice. LME–M16. b Enjoy oneself. Only in imper. *N. Amer.* M20. 2 *v.t.* Take delight or pleasure in; have, use, or experience with delight. LME. b Have sexual intercourse with (usu. a woman). M16. 3 *v.t.* Have the use or benefit of (something pleasant or advantageous). LME. b Experience. L16. †4 *v.t.* Make happy, give pleasure to. L15–E17. 5 *refl.* Have a pleasant or delightful time. M17.

2 E. M. FORSTER Don't pretend you enjoyed lunch, for you loathed it. 3 I. MURDOCH A guest bedroom, which also enjoyed a view of the lawn. b H. VENN At best, she enjoys poor health. 5 OED He is enjoying himself at the seaside.

enjoyaˈbility *n.* the quality of being enjoyable; the degree to which something is enjoyable: L20. **enjoyable** *a.* able to be enjoyed; delightful: M17.

enjoyableness *n.* M19. **enjoyably** *adv.* L19. **enjoyer** *n.* L16. **enjoyingly** *adv.* (*rare*) with enjoyment. M19.

enjoyment /ɪnˈdʒɔɪm(ə)nt, ɛn-/ *n.* M16. [f. prec. + -MENT.] **1** The action or state of enjoying something. M16. **2** Pleasure; something that gives pleasure. M17.

1 LD MACAULAY He would protect the Established Church in the enjoyment of her legal rights.

†**enkennel** *v.t. rare.* L16. [f. EN-[1] + KENNEL *n.*[1]] **1** Lodge as in a kennel. L16–E17. **2** Contain like a kennel. Only in M19.

enkephalin /ɛnˈkɛf(ə)lɪn/ *n.* M20. [f. Gk *egkephalos* brain: see ENCEPHALO-, -IN[1].] *Biochem.* Either of two pentapeptide endorphins occurring in the brain.

enkindle /ɪnˈkɪnd(ə)l, ɛn-/ *v.* Also †**in-**. M16. [f. EN-[1], IN-[2] + KINDLE *v.*[1]] **1** *v.t.* **a** Excite or inflame (strong feeling). M16. **b** Cause (a flame, fire, etc.) to blaze up. L16. **2** *v.t.* **a** Arouse strong feeling in. Formerly also foll. by *to* a purpose or object, *to do* an action. M16. **b** Set on fire. Now *rare.* M16. **c** Light up, illuminate (*lit.* & *fig.*). L19. †**3** *v.i.* Catch fire; burst into flame. M16–M18.

2c D. H. LAWRENCE He saw her face strangely enkindled.

enkindler *n.* M19.

enknot *v.* var. of INKNOT.

enlace /ɪnˈleɪs, ɛn-/ *v.t.* LME. [OFr. *enlacier* (mod. *enlacer*) f. Proto-Romance, f. as IN-[2] + Proto-Romance alt. of L *laqueus* noose. Later taken as f. EN-[1] + LACE *n.*] **1** Encircle tightly; surround closely; embrace. LME. **2** Interlace, entwine, entangle. LME. **3** Pattern like lace. M19.

3 N. FREELING Woodcutters' paths . . enlace every hill.

enlacement *n.* M19.

en l'air /ɑ̃ lɛːr/ *adv. phr.* E18. [Fr.] In the air; *Ballet* while leaping vertically; *Mil.* while unsupported.

enlarge /ɪnˈlɑːdʒ, ɛn-/ *v.* Also †**in-**. ME. [OFr. *enlarger, -ir*, f. as EN-[1] + *large* LARGE *a.* In branch II after OFr. *eslargir* (mod. *élargir*) set free.] **I 1** *v.t.* Make larger or wider; increase the size or extent of. Also (now *rare*) intensify, increase. ME. **b** *v.t.* Increase (esp. a person's thoughts or feelings) in range or scope; make more comprehensive. M16. †**c** *v.t.* Make appear larger; exaggerate. L16–M18. **d** *v.t. Law.* Extend (the time allowed for an action). M17. **e** *v.t.* & *i. Photogr.* Reproduce on a larger scale. M19. **2** *v.i.* Become larger, wider, or more comprehensive; expand, increase. L15. †**b** Become stronger or more violent. E17–M18. **3a** *v.i.* & †*refl.* Speak or write in more detail; expatiate. Usu. foll. by *on*, *upon.* E17. †**b** *v.i.* Foll. by *on*: add to (a plan); amplify (a hint). E18–E19.

1 D. CECIL The party . . was enlarged by a steady stream of friends and neighbours. *refl.*: SHAKES. *1 Hen. VI* Glory is like a circle in the water, Which never ceaseth to enlarge itself. **b** C. LAMB His fine suite of rooms . . were enough to enlarge a man's notions of himself. **2** B. JOWETT As our knowledge increases, our perception of the mind enlarges. **3a** B. PYM She had not enlarged on this bald statement.

II 4 *v.t.* Set free, release. *arch.* LME.

†**III 5** *v.t.* & *i.* Give generously to or *to*; endow generously *with* gifts. L15–M17.

Phrases: **enlarge an estate** *Law* convert an estate from a tenancy or leasehold to a freehold. **enlarge the heart** make a person's heart swell with gratitude or pride; increase a person's sympathies.

enlarger *n.* a person who or thing which enlarges; *spec.* an apparatus for producing photographic enlargements M16.

enlargement /ɪnˈlɑːdʒm(ə)nt, ɛn-/ *n.* Also †**in-**. M16. [f. prec. + -MENT.] **I 1** (An) increase in size, extent, or scope; (an) increase in sympathies or understanding. M16. **b** A photographic print that is larger than the negative from which it is produced. M19. **2** Expatiation on a subject; verbal amplification. *arch.* M17.

1 GEO. ELIOT An enlargement of the chapel . . absorbed all extra funds.

II 3 Release from confinement. *arch.* M16. †**4** (The right to) freedom of action; a privilege. E–M17. **5** Absence of inhibition in praying or preaching. *arch.* M17.

enleague /ɪnˈliːɡ, ɛn-/ *v.t.* Now *rare.* Also (earlier) **in-** /ɪn-/. E17. [f. EN-[1], IN-[2] + LEAGUE *n.*[2] or *v.*] Unite in, or as in, a league.

enlèvement /ɑ̃lɛvmɑ̃; ɪnˈliːvm(ə)nt, ɛn-/ *n.* Pl. pronounced same. M18. [Fr., f. *enlever* carry off: see -MENT.] An abduction.

†**enlight** *v.t.* & *i.* Also **in-**. OE–E19. [OE *inlīhtan* shine, f. IN-[1] + *līhtan* (see LIGHT *v.*[2]). Later f. EN-[1] + LIGHT *v.*[2]] Shed light (on), *lit.* & *fig.*; light *up.*

enlighten /ɪnˈlʌɪt(ə)n, ɛn-/ *v.t.* Also †**in-**. ME. [Orig. f. prec. + -EN[5], later f. EN-[1], IN-[2] + LIGHTEN *v.*[2] or LIGHT *n.* + -EN[5].] †**1** Make luminous. ME–E19. **2** Give spiritual knowledge or insight to. LME. †**b** Remove blindness from (eyes). Freq. *fig.* LME–E18. **3** Shed light on, illuminate, (*lit.* & *fig.*). Now *arch.* & *poet.* L16. **4** Instruct; inform (*on* a matter); (chiefly as *enlightened* pa. pple) make free from prejudice or superstition. M17. †**5** Provide (a room, town, etc.) with light or lighting. M17–M19. †**6** Revive, exhilarate. Only in M17.

2 G. VIDAL Siddhartha became the enlightened one or Buddha. 4 ADDISON Before the World was enlightened by Learning and Philosophy. CONAN DOYLE I had no glimmer of what was in his mind, nor did he enlighten me.

enlightenedness *n.* the state or quality of being enlightened M19. **enlightener** *n.* a person who or thing which enlightens, esp. mentally or spiritually L16.

enlightenment /ɪnˈlʌɪt(ə)nm(ə)nt, ɛn-/ *n.* M17. [f. prec. + -MENT.] **1** The action of mentally or spiritually enlightening; the state of being so enlightened. M17. **2** *the Enlightenment*, the philosophical movement that occurred in Europe, esp. France, in the 18th cent., in which reason and individualism came to be emphasized at the expense of tradition. M19.

enlink /ɪnˈlɪŋk, ɛn-/ *v.t.* Also †**in-**. L15. [f. EN-[1], IN-[2] + LINK *n.*[2] or *v.*[1]] Fasten together with links; connect closely. Chiefly *fig.*

enlist /ɪnˈlɪst, ɛn-/ *v.* Also †**in-**. M16. [f. EN-[1], IN-[2] + LIST *n.*[3] or *v.*[4], perh. after Du. *inlijsten* inscribe on a list.] **1a** *v.t.* Enrol (another, (now *rare*) oneself) in one of the armed services. M16. **b** *v.i.* Volunteer for and be accepted by one of the armed services. L18. **2** *v.t.* Engage or secure (a person, his or her services, etc.) as help or support. L16.

1a **enlisted man** *US* a man in any of the armed services who ranks below a commissioned or warrant officer, *esp.* one ranking below a non-commissioned or petty officer. 2 H. KELLER I wrote to my friends about the work and enlisted their sympathy.

enlis'tee *n.* a person who is enlisted or who enlists for the armed services M20. **enlister** *n.* a person who enlists others for the armed services M19. **enlistment** *n.* the action or process of enlisting M18.

†**enlive** *v.t.* Also **in-**. L16–M17. [f. EN-[1], IN-[2] + LIFE *n.*, after LIVE *v.*] = next.

enliven /ɪnˈlʌɪv(ə)n, ɛn-/ *v.t.* Also †**in-**. M17. [f. prec. + -EN[5].] †**1** Give life to; restore to life. M17–M18. **2** Give fuller life to, animate, invigorate; stimulate. M17. **3** Make lively or cheerful; relieve the monotony or dreariness of. E18.

enlivener *n.* M17. **enlivening** *n.* (*a*) the action of the vb; (*b*) a thing that enlivens someone or something: L17. **enliveningly** *adv.* in an enlivening manner M19. **enlivenment** *n.* the action of enlivening; the state of being enlivened; a thing that enlivens someone or something: L19.

enlock /ɪnˈlɒk, ɛn-/ *v.t.* Also †**in-**. L16. [f. EN-[1], IN-[2] + LOCK *v.*[1]] Lock up, shut in, enclose.

†**enlumine** *v.t.* LME. [(O)Fr. *enluminer* f. med.L *inluminare* (L *illuminare*), f. as IN-[2] + *lumin-*, *lumen* light: cf. ILLUMINATE *v.*] **1** Light up, illuminate; *fig.* enlighten, make clear; shed lustre upon. LME–E17. **2** Illuminate (a manuscript). LME–E16.

enmarble /ɪnˈmɑːb(ə)l, ɛn-/ *v.t. rare.* Also (earlier) **emmarble** /ɪˈmɑːb(ə)l, ɛ-/. L16. [f. EN-[1], EM-[1] + MARBLE *n.*] Convert into marble; sculpture in or adorn with marble.

†**enmarvel** *v.* see EMMARVEL.

en masse /ɑ̃ mas, ɒ̃ ˈmas/ *adv. phr.* L18. [Fr.] In a mass; all together, as a group.

enmesh /ɪnˈmɛʃ, ɛn-/ *v.t.* E17. [f. EN-[1] + MESH *n.* Cf. IMMESH.] Catch or entangle in, or as in, a mesh or net.

enmeshment *n.* entanglement L19.

enmity /ˈɛnmɪti/ *n.* ME. [OFr. *enemi(s)tié* (mod. *inimitié*) f. Proto-Romance, f. L *inimicus*: see ENEMY, -ITY.] **1** The disposition or feelings of an enemy; ill will, hatred. ME. **2** The condition of being an enemy; a state of mutual hostility. LME. †**3** (Something with) a harmful or prejudicial influence. LME–E17.

1 M. MEYER To those who did not arouse his enmity, he could be charming. 2 P. H. GIBBS Old enmities and jealousies still smouldering across the frontiers. 3 SHAKES. *Lear* To wage against the enmity o' th' air.

enmuffle /ɪnˈmʌf(ə)l, ɛn-/ *v.t. rare.* E17. [f. EN-[1] + MUFFLE *v.*] Muffle up.

ennead /ˈɛnɪad/ *n.* M16. [Gk *ennead-*, *enneas*, f. as next: see -AD[1].] A set of nine; *spec.* each of the six divisions in Porphyry's collection of Plotinus' works, each of which contains nine books.

enneagon /ˈɛnɪəɡɒn/ *n.* M17. [f. Gk *ennea* nine + -GON.] A plane figure with nine straight sides and nine angles.

ennew /ɪˈnjuː, ɛn-/ *v.t.* Long *rare.* Also †**in-**. LME. [f. EN-[1], IN-[2] + NEW *a.*, after L *innovare* (see INNOVATE).] Make new; renew. Formerly also, repeat, do again.

ennit /ˈɛnɪt/ *int. dial.* M20. [Repr. a pronunc.] Isn't it. Cf. INNIT.

ennoble /ɪˈnəʊb(ə)l, ɛn-/ *v.t.* Also †**in-**. L15. [(O)Fr. *ennoblir*, f. as EN-[1], IN-[2], NOBLE.] **1** Make noble, impart nobility to; dignify; elevate or refine in character. L15. †**2** Make famous or illustrious. M16–L18. **3** Give the rank of a noble to (a person); make (a person) a peer or peeress. L16. †**4** Of light: make conspicuous. *rare.* Only in 17.

1 R. W. EMERSON He who does a good deed, is instantly ennobled. H. ALLEN It was set with seed pearls . . and ennobled with a gilt pattern.

ennoblement *n.* (*a*) the action of ennobling; the state or fact of being ennobled; †(*b*) a thing which ennobles: E17. **ennobler** *n.* L18.

en noir /ɑ̃ nwaːr/ *adv. phr.* M19. [Fr.] On the black side; in the worst light.

ennui /ɒnˈwiː, *foreign* ɑ̃nɥi/ *n.* & *v.* M18. [Fr. f. L *in odio*: see ANNOY *n.*] **A** *n.* Mental weariness and dissatisfaction arising from lack of occupation or interest; boredom. M18.

R. HUGHES The ship's monkey, . . with no pig now to tease, nearly died of ennui. S. O'FAOLÁIN The long ennui of those empty days.

B *v.t.* As *ennuied*, *ennuyed* pa. pple = ENNUYÉ. E19.

ennuyant /ɑ̃nɥijɑ̃/ *a.* L18. [Fr., pres. pple of *ennuyer*: see next, -ANT[1].] That gives rise to ennui; boring.

ennuyé /ɑ̃nɥije/ *a.* Fem. **-ée**. M18. [Fr., pa. ppl a. of *ennuyer* bore, f. *ennui*: see ENNUI.] Affected with ennui; bored.

Also **ennuyéd**, **ennuyé'd** *a.* M19.

Eno /ˈiːnəʊ/ *n.* L19. [f. J. C. *Eno* (*c* 1828–1915), Eng. pharmacist.] Proprietary name for a laxative and antacid preparation. Also *Eno's* (*Fruit Salt*).

eno- *comb. form* see OENO-.

Enochic /iːˈnɒkɪk/ *a.* L19. [f. *Enoch* (see below) + -IC.] Of, pertaining to, or characteristic of a person called Enoch, *spec.* the biblical son of Cain (*Gen.* 4:17), or the apocryphal Book of Enoch.

Also **Enochian** *a.* E20.

enol /ˈiːnɒl/ *n.* M20. [f. -ENE + -OL, or back-form. f. ENOLIC.] *Chem.* Any organic compound containing the unsaturated alcohol group ·CH:C(OH)· as a tautomeric form of a corresponding keto-compound.

KETO-ENOL.

enolase /ˈiːnəleɪz/ *n.* an enzyme involved in glycolysis and gluconeogenesis in the body M20. **enolate** /-nəl-/ *n.* (a compound containing) the carbanion of an enol M20. **e'nolic** *a.* L19. **enolization** /ˌiːnəlʌɪˈzeɪʃ(ə)n/ *n.* conversion into an enol or an enolic group M20.

enomotarch /ɪˈnɒmətɑːk/ *n. rare.* E17. [Gk *enōmotarkhēs*, f. *enōmotia* (see next) + *-arkhēs*

-ARCH.] *Gk Hist.* The commander of an enomoty.

enomoty /ɪˈnɒməti/ *n. rare.* E17. [Gk *enōmotia* band of sworn soldiers, f. as EN-[2] + *omnunai* swear: see -Y[3].] *Gk Hist.* A division in the Spartan army.

enophthalmos /ɛnɒfˈθalmɒs/ *n.* Also **-mus** /-məs/. L19. [(mod.L *enophthalmus*) f. as EN-[2] + Gk *ophthalmos* eye.] Abnormal retraction of the eyeball into the socket.

enorm /ɪˈnɔːm/ *n.* & *a.* LME. [Fr. *énorme* adj. or L *enormis*: see ENORMOUS.] †A *n.* A monstrous act. Also, wickedness. LME–M16. **B** *adj.* †**1** Of a sin, crime, etc.: monstrously wicked. L15–E18. †**2** Abnormal; extravagant. E16–M18. **3** Vast; enormous. *arch.* L16.

Phrases: **enorm lesion**, †**hurt** *Sc. Law* considerable damage in respect of property or rights.

†**enormious** *a.* LME–M17. [f. L *enormis* (see ENORMOUS) + -OUS.] = ENORMOUS.

enormity /ɪˈnɔːmɪti/ *n.* LME. [(O)Fr. *énormité* f. L *enormitas*, f. *enormis*: see next, -ITY.] **1** Orig., deviation from moral or legal rectitude. Now, the quality of being outrageous; monstrous wickedness. LME. **2** Orig., a crime, a transgression. Now, a monstrous offence; a gross irregularity, a serious error. LME. †**3** Abnormality, irregularity; an abnormal or irregular thing. L15–M19. **4** Enormous size, enormousness; daunting magnitude. Freq. considered *erron.* L18.

1 D. JACOBSON The enormity of the crime he wanted to commit. 2 M. RENAULT He was committing an enormity by being out of bed in the middle of the night. JO GRIMOND Lawyers . . stride on, turning a blind eye to the enormities of their profession. 4 *Times* A wide-angle lens captures the enormity of the Barbican Centre. *Listener* People were not really aware of the enormity of that problem.

enormous /ɪˈnɔːməs/ *a.* M16. [f. L *enormis* (f. *e-* E- + *norma* pattern) + -OUS.] **1** Excessive in size or intensity; very large, huge; very great. M16. †**b** That has grown too much in power or importance. M17–M18. †**2** Deviating from normality; abnormal, irregular; monstrous, shocking; outrageous, wicked. M16–E19.

1 G. S. FRASER *Cursor Mundi* is an enormous poem of 30,000 lines. A. THWAITE Kingsley went to enormous trouble for the son of his old companion.

enormously *adv.* E17. **enormousness** *n.* M17.

enosis /ɪˈnəʊsɪs, ˈɛnəsɪs/ *n.* M20. [mod.Gk *henōsis*, f. *hena* one: see -OSIS.] Political union, *esp.* that proposed between Greece and Cyprus.

enotic /-ˈnɒt-/ *a.* M20. **enotist** *n.* /ɪˈnəʊtɪst/ an advocate of enosis M20.

enough /ɪˈnʌf/ *a., n., & adv.* [OE *genōg, genōh* = OFris. *enōch*, OS *ginōg* (Du. *genoeg*), OHG *genuog* (G *genug*), ON *gnógr*, Goth. *ganōhs* f. Gmc, rel. to OE *ġenēah*, OHG *ginah*, Goth. *ganah* it suffices. Cf. 'NOUGH, NUFF.] **A** *adj.* Sufficient in quantity, number, etc.; not less than what is needed. (Used in concord with a preceding or following n., and predicatively.) OE.

J. CONRAD It has not soil enough . . to grow a single blade of grass. M. SINCLAIR Five weeks of it were enough to kill him. G. GREENE I've given her enough bromide to put her out of action till morning. J. IRVING If three or four people get stuffed into a car seat, nobody has enough room. *Country Life* There are enough hotels . . to suit any pocket.

B *n.* That which is sufficient; as much as is needed. OE.

A. P. HERBERT She could see enough of herself to be sure that she looked well. E. FROMM The greedy can never have enough, can never be 'satisfied'. *Proverb*: Enough is as good as a feast. **enough!** stop!, say no more! **enough and to spare** plenty, a great deal. **enough of —** no more of — is wanted. **enough said** no more need be said. **have had enough** (**of something**) be satiated with or tired of something. **have enough to do** (**to achieve something**) have no easy task. **more than enough** = *enough and to spare* above.

C *adv.* (In mod. Eng. *enough* normally follows the wd it qualifies.) **1** Sufficiently; in a quantity or degree that satisfies or is effectual. OE. **2** (In vaguer sense.) With intensive force: fully, quite. Implying disparagement of what is conceded: tolerably, fairly. E17.

1 J. M. COETZEE He felt strong enough to get up. B. GUEST He stayed long enough to drink eleven cups of tea. 2 O. MANNING The quarrel began mildly enough. *aptly enough, oddly enough, strangely enough*, etc. *fair enough!*: see FAIR *a. right enough*: see RIGHT *adv.* **sure enough** undeniably, as was or might have been expected. **b** D. H. LAWRENCE She was intelligent enough, but not interested in learning.

enounce /iːˈnaʊns, ɪ-/ *v.t.* E19. [Fr. *énoncer* f. L *enuntiare* ENUNCIATE after *announce, pronounce*.] **1** State in definite terms; enunciate. E19. **2** State publicly, proclaim. E19. **3** Utter, pronounce, (words etc.). E19.

enouncement *n.* M19.

enow /ɪˈnaʊ/ *a., n., & adv.*[1] Now *arch. & dial.* [OE *ġenōge*, nom. and accus. pl. of *ġenōġ* ENOUGH.] **A** *adj.* = ENOUGH *a.* (Orig. in concord w. a pl. n. only.) OE. **B** *n.* = ENOUGH *n.* ME. **C** *adv.* = ENOUGH *adv.* ME.

enow /ɪˈnaʊ/ *adv.*[2] L18. [Contr. of *e'en* (= *even*) *now* or for *the now*.] **1** Just now, a moment ago. *Sc. & dial.* L18. **2** By and by, presently. *dial.* L18.

en pantoufles /ɑ̃ pɑ̃tufl/ *adv. phr.* E20. [Fr., lit. 'in slippers'.] Relaxed, off guard; in a free and easy manner or atmosphere.

en passant /ɑ̃ pasɑ̃, ɒ̃ paˈsɑːnt/ *adv. phr.* E17. [Fr.] In passing, by the way.

J. JONES Then he writes *en passant* that his old landlady is dead. ***take a pawn en passant*** *Chess* take (with one's own pawn on the fifth rank) a pawn that has just made an initial move of two squares, as if that pawn had moved only one square.

en pension *adv. phr.* see PENSION *n.*

en permanence /ɑ̃ pɛrmanɑ̃ːs/ *adv. phr.* M19. [Fr.] Permanently.

en place /ɑ̃ plas/ *adv. phr.* E19. [Fr.] In place, in position.

enplane /ɪnˈpleɪn, ɛn-/ *v.t. & i.* M20. [f. EN-[1] + PLANE *n.*[4]] = EMPLANE.

en plein /ɑ̃ plɛ̃/ *adv. phr.* L19. [Fr. = in full.] *Gambling.* Entirely on one number or side; with the whole of one's bet.

en plein air /ɑ̃ plɛn ɛːr/ *adv. phr.* L19. [Fr.] In the open air.

en poste /ɑ̃ pɔst/ *adv. phr.* M20. [Fr.] In an official diplomatic position (at a specified place).

en prince /ɑ̃ prɛ̃ːs/ *adv. phr.* L17. [Fr.] Like a prince; in a princely or luxurious manner.

en principe /ɑ̃ prɛ̃sip/ *adv. phr.* E20. [Fr.] In principle.

enprint /ˈɛnprɪnt/ *n.* M20. [f. *enlarged print*.] A photographic print of the standard size produced by developing and printing companies, made by printing the whole of a negative to a moderate enlargement.

en prise /ɑ̃ priːz/ *adv. phr.* E19. [Fr.] *Chess.* In a position to be taken.

†**enquest** *n.* var. of INQUEST.

enquirable *a.*, **enquiration** *n.* vars. of INQUIRABLE, INQUIRATION.

enquire *v.*, **enquiry** *n.* see INQUIRE etc.

enrage /ɪnˈreɪdʒ, ɛn-/ *v.* Also †**in-**. L15. [OFr. *enrager* become enraged (mod. also = enrage), f. as EN-[1], RAGE *n.*] †**1** *v.t.* As *enraged* pa. pple. Maddened by anger, pain, etc.; frenzied. (Foll. by *by, with*.) L15–E18. †**2** *v.i.* **a** Be distracted or maddened by hunger, thirst, etc. Foll. by *for*. E–M16. **b** Become very angry. M16–L18. **c** Prevail with violent or destructive effect. M16–E17. **3** Make very angry. Chiefly as *enraged* pa. pple. E16. †**4** *v.t.* Make violent; exacerbate; inflame (a wound etc.). E16–M18.

enragedly *adv.* in an enraged manner L16. **enragedness** *n.* the state of being enraged E17. **enragement** *n.* the action of enraging; the state of being enraged; (formerly) rapture: L16.

†**enrail** *v.* see INRAIL.

†**enrange** *v.t. rare.* LME. [f. EN-[1] + RANGE *n.*[1], *v.*[1]] **1** Arrange; rank. LME–L16. **2** Range or ramble in (a forest). *rare* (Spenser). Only in L16.

enrank /ɪnˈraŋk, ɛn-/ *v.t.* Now *rare* or *obs.* L16. [f. EN-[1] + RANK *n.*] Set (esp. soldiers) in a line or lines.

en rapport *adv. phr.* see RAPPORT.

enrapt /ɪnˈrapt, ɛn-/ *a. poet.* E17. [f. EN-[1] + RAPT *a.*] Enraptured; deeply absorbed in something.

enrapture /ɪnˈraptʃə, ɛn-/ *v.t.* Also †**in-**. M18. [f. EN-[1] + RAPTURE.] Delight intensely, ravish, entrance; inspire with poetic fervour.

enravish /ɪnˈravɪʃ, ɛn-/ *v.t.* Now *rare.* L16. [f. EN-[1] + RAVISH.] Delight intensely, enrapture.

en regard /ɑ̃ rəgaːr/ *adv. phr.* E20. [Fr.] *Bibliogr.* On the facing page. Cf. EN FACE.

enregister /ɪnˈrɛdʒɪstə, ɛn-/ *v.t.* Also (earlier) †**in-**. LME. [(O)Fr. *enregistrer*, f. as EN-[1] + *registre* REGISTER *n.*[1]] Enter in a register or official record; put on record as law.

enregiˈstration *n.* registering, recording; *esp.* the mind's recording of actions that consequently become habitual or automatic E20.

en règle /ɑ̃ rɛgl/ *adv. phr.* E19. [Fr.] In order, according to form.

en retraite /ɑ̃ rətrɛt/ *adv. phr.* M19. [Fr.] In retirement.

en revanche /ɑ̃ rəvɑ̃ːʃ/ *adv. phr.* E19. [Fr.] In return, as compensation; in revenge.

enrheum /ɪnˈruːm, ɛn-/ *v.t. rare.* M17. [OFr. *enrheumer* (mod. *enrhumer*), f. as EN-[1], RHEUM *n.*[1]] Affect with catarrh; give a cold to. Chiefly as *enrheumed* pa. pple.

enrich /ɪnˈrɪtʃ, ɛn-/ *v.* Also †**in-**. LME. [(O)Fr. *enrichir*, f. as EN-[1] + *riche* RICH *a.*] **1** *v.t.* Make rich or wealthy; *fig.* endow with mental or spiritual wealth. LME. **b** Make splendid with (esp. costly) decoration. L15. **2** *v.i.* Increase one's wealth. *rare.* E16. **3** *v.t.* Add to the wealth of; add something valuable or worthwhile to. L16. **b** Make (soil, land) more productive; fertilize. E17. **4** *v.t.* Make richer in quality, colour, flavour, etc.; heighten, enhance. E17. **b** Improve the nutritive quality of (food) by adding vitamins or nutrients. M20. **5** *v.t.* Increase the proportion of a particular constituent in (a substance); *spec.* increase the proportion of uranium-235 in (uranium). E20.

3 R. W. EMERSON Owen has . . enriched science with contributions of his own. SAKI He had enriched her pantheon of personal possessions with a clever piece of work. 4 B. BAINBRIDGE Freda had hoped working in a factory would enrich Brenda's life. 5 *Nature* Calcium salts enriched in the non-radioactive nuclides ^{46}Ca and ^{48}Ca are now available.

enricher *n.* a person who or thing which enriches someone or something E17. **enrichingly** *adv.* in a way that enriches someone or something E19.

enrichment /ɪnˈrɪtʃm(ə)nt, ɛn-/ *n.* E17. [f. prec. + -MENT.] **1** The action or process of enrichment; the condition of being enriched. E17. **b** *Sci.* The proportion of a particular, usu. fissile, isotope in a quantity of an element (when greater than the natural proportion). Also, the increase in this proportion above the natural figure. M20. **2** Something that enriches; an ornament on a building, statue, etc. M17.

†**enridged** *a. rare* (Shakes.). Only in E17. [f. EN-[1] + RIDGE *n.*[1] + -ED[1].] Ridged.

enring /ɪnˈrɪŋ, ɛn-/ *v.t. poet.* L16. [f. EN-[1] + RING *n.*[1]] Form a ring round, encircle; put a ring on.

enripen /ɪnˈrʌɪpən, ɛn-/ *v.t. rare.* M17. [f. EN-[1] + RIPEN.] Make ripe, mature (*lit.* & *fig.*).

enrobe /ɪnˈrəʊb, ɛn-/ *v.t.* L16. [f. EN-[1] + ROBE *n.*[1]] Dress in a robe; cover with a robe or a coating.

enrober *n.* L16.

enrol /ɪnˈrəʊl, ɛn-/ *v.* Also ***-ll**, †**in-**. Infl. **-ll-**. LME. [OFr. *enroller* (mod. *enrôler*), f. as EN-[1] + *rolle* ROLL *n.*[1]] **I 1** *v.t.* **a** Write (a name) on a list, register, etc.; place (a person) on a list by adding a name. LME. **b** Incorporate as an acknowledged member (*in* a group). LME. **c** Place on the list of an army, make a member of an army; recruit (an army). L16. **2** *v.t. Hist.* Record in the documents of a court of justice; write (a deed etc.) on a roll or parchment; give legal form to. LME. **3** *v.t.* Set down in a record. Also, commemorate, celebrate. L15. **4** *v.i.* Enter one's name on a list, register, etc., esp. as a commitment to membership of a society, class, etc. (foll. by *in, for*); join *as* a member, student, etc. E20.

1a *State Enrolled Nurse*: see STATE *n.* **b** LYNDON B. JOHNSON Men and women were enrolled in classes of their choice. *fig.*: W. IRVING Determined . . to enrol myself in the fraternity of authorship. 3 G. HERBERT Small it is, in this poore sort To enroll thee. 4 P. ACKROYD He . . enrolled as a graduate student. M. FORSTER She enrolled for a six-month cookery course.

II 5 *v.t.* Form into a roll or rolls; wrap or enfold *in* or *with*. Now *rare*. LME.

enro'llee *n.* (*N. Amer.*) a person who has been enrolled M20. **enrolment** *n.* (*a*) the action of enrolling; the process of being enrolled; (*b*) the number of people who have been or may be enrolled, esp. in a school, university, etc.; (*c*) *Hist.* a documentary record, esp. of a deed: LME.

enroot /ɪn'ruːt, ɛn-/ *v.t.* Also **in-** /ɪn-/. LME. [f. EN-[1], IN-[2] + ROOT *n.*[1]] Chiefly as *enrooted* ppl. a. 1 Implant deeply in the mind; fix firmly as a custom. LME. 2 Fix by the root. L15. †3 Entangle like roots. *rare* (Shakes.). Only in L16.

enrough /ɪn'rʌf, ɛn-/ *v.t. poet.* E17. [f. EN-[1] + ROUGH *a.*] Make (the sea) rough.

enround /ɪn'raʊnd, ɛn-/ *v.t.* Long *rare*. LME. [f. EN-[1] + ROUND *n.*[1]] Surround.

en route *adv. phr.* see ROUTE *n.* & *v.*

ens /ɛnz/ *n.* Pl. **entia** /'ɛntɪə, 'ɛnʃɪə/. M16. [Late L *ens* use as n. of pres. pple formed from *esse* be, on the supposed anal. of *absens* ABSENT *a.* & *n.*, to translate Gk *on* use as n. of pres. pple of *einai* be.] 1 *Philos.* etc. Something which has existence; a being, an entity, as opp. to an attribute or quality. M16. †2 The essence; the essential part. L16–M18.

1 ***ens necessarium*** /nɛkɛ'sɑːrɪəm, nɛsɛ'sɛːrɪəm/ [mod.L = necessary being] a necessarily existent being; God. ***ens rationis*** /ratɪ'əʊnɪs, raʃɪ-/, pl. ***entia rationis***, [med.L = being of the mind] an entity of reason; a being with no existence outside the mind. ***ens reale*** /reɪ'ɑːli, rɪ'eɪli/, pl. ***entia realia*** /-lɪə/ [med.L = real being] a being existing independently of any finite mind. **ens realissimum** /reɪə'lɪsɪməm, rɪə-/ [mod.L] the most real being; God.

ensaint /ɪn'seɪnt, ɛn-/ *v.t.* L16. [f. EN-[1] + SAINT *n.*] Make a saint, canonize; regard as a saint.

ensample /ɛn'sɑːmp(ə)l/ *n. arch.* ME. [AN *ensa(u)mple* alt. of OFr. *essample* EXAMPLE *n.*] = EXAMPLE *n.*

¶The mod. arch. use is due chiefly to reminiscences of New Testament passages where the wd occurs in AV and RV.

†ensample *v.t.* LME–M17. [f. the n.] = EXEMPLIFY 2a, 3.

ensanguine /ɪn'saŋgwɪn, ɛn-/ *v.t.* Also (earlier) **†in-**. E17. [f. EN-[1], IN-[2] + L *sanguin-*, *sanguis* blood.] Stain with blood; make bloody or the colour of blood.

†enschedule *v.t. rare* (Shakes.). Only in L16. [f. EN-[1] + SCHEDULE *n.*] Put in a schedule.

ensconce /ɪn'skɒns, ɛn-/ *v.* Also **†in-**. L16. [f. EN-[1], IN-[2] + SCONCE *n.*[2]] †1 *v.t.* Provide with defensive earthworks; fortify. L16–M19. †2 *v.t.* & *i.* Shelter within or behind a fortification. L16–M18. 3 *v.t.* Establish or settle (esp. oneself) in a place for reasons of safety, security, or comfort. (*rare* bef. E19.) L16.

3 J. C. POWYS John and Mary had ensconced themselves on a small eighteenth-century sofa.

enscroll /ɪn'skrəʊl, ɛn-/ *v.t.* M19. [f. EN-[1] + SCROLL *n.*] 1 *Her.* Depict together with a scroll. *rare*. M19. 2 Write, record in writing. E20.

enseal /ɪn'siːl, ɛn-/ *v.t.* ME. [OFr. *enseeler*, f. as EN-[1] + *seel* SEAL *n.*[2]] 1 Fix a seal on; attest or confirm by sealing. Now *rare* or *obs.* ME. 2 Close with a seal, seal up. *arch.* ME.

†enseam *v.*[1]*t.* L15–L18. [Alt., through confusion with next, of OFr. *essaïmer* (mod. *essimer*), f. as ES- + *saïm* SEAM *n.*[3]] Cause (a hawk, a horse) to lose superfluous fat.

†enseam *v.*[2]*t. rare.* M16–E17. [OFr. *ensaïmer* (mod. *ensimer*, †*ensémer*), f. as EN-[1] + *saïm* SEAM *n.*[3]: cf. prec.] Soil or load with grease.

†enseam *v.*[3]*t. rare.* L16–E17. [Origin unkn.] Include; bring or contain together.

enseam /ɪn'siːm, ɛn-/ *v.*[4]*t.* E17. [f. EN-[1] + SEAM *n.*[1], *v.*] 1 Mark as with a seam. E17. †2 Sew or stitch up in. Only in E17.

†ensear *v.t. rare.* L15–E17. [f. EN-[1] + SERE *a.*] Dry up.

ensearch /ɪn'səːtʃ, ɛn-/ *v. arch.* Also **†in-**. ME. [OFr. *encerchier*, *-serchier*, f. as EN-[1] + *cerchier* (mod. *chercher*) SEARCH *v.*[1]] †1 *v.t.* Search into, investigate. ME–L16. 2 *v.t.* Search; scrutinize, examine. LME. †3 *v.t.* Search for, seek out. LME–M16. †4 *v.i.* Make a search; inquire. LME–L16.

†enseint *a.* var. of ENCEINTE *a.*

ensemble /ɒ̃'sɒ̃ːb(ə)l, ɒn'sɒmb(ə)l, *foreign* ɑ̃sɑːmbl (*pl. same*)/ *adv.* & *n.* LME. [(O)Fr. f. Proto-Romance, f. L *insimul*, f. as IN-[2] + *simul* at the same time.] A *adv.* Together; at the same time. Long *rare*. LME.

B *n.* 1 (The parts of) a thing viewed as a whole; the overall effect or appearance of something. Cf. earlier TOUT ENSEMBLE. M18. 2a The unity of performance achieved by two or more players, singers, or dancers performing together. E19. b A group of stage artistes who perform together in a production; *esp.* the supporting actors or dancers as opp. to the stars or principals. E20. c A scene on stage in which the ensemble or the whole cast appear; a piece of music performed by an ensemble. E20. d A group of singers or musicians, esp. a small group of soloists, who perform together. M20. 3 A set of (usu. women's) clothes that harmonize and are worn together; an outfit. E20. 4 *Sci.* A notional collection of systems of identical constitution but not necessarily in the same state; the family of possible outcomes or states of a given system; *spec.* a collection of particles large enough for its behaviour to be described statistically. E20.

1 J. BRODSKY They started to build, not separate buildings but whole architectural ensembles. 2a *Gramophone* There is just one spot of slightly poor ensemble where the castanets come in. b *attrib.*: *Flicks* The star . . is . . heading an ensemble cast of many familiar Allen regulars. c *Times* Lifar's opening *Noir et Blanc* . . put the company through its paces in a series of testing solos and ensembles. d *vocal ensemble*, *wind ensemble*, etc. 4 R. C. TOLMAN The properties of a thermodynamic system . . may be studied with the help of the average properties of an appropriately chosen representative ensemble of systems.

Comb.: **ensemble acting** or **playing**: in which all the roles are presented as contributing equally to a production.

†ensense *v.* see INSENSE.

ensepulchre /ɪn'sɛpəlkə, ɛn-/ *v.t.* Also ***-cher**. E19. [f. EN-[1] + SEPULCHRE.] Swallow up and destroy; engulf.

enserf /ɪn'səːf, ɛn-/ *v.t.* L19. [f. EN-[1] + SERF.] Make a serf; deprive of political rights.

enserfment *n.* the action of enserfing M20.

ensete /ɛn'siːti/ *n.* L18. [Amharic.] An Ethiopian tree of the banana family, *Ensete ventricosum*, with edible flower-heads and seeds. Also called *Abyssinian banana*.

enshadow /ɪn'ʃadəʊ, ɛn-/ *v.t.* L15. [f. EN-[1] + SHADOW *n.*] Put in shadow, shade; conceal *from*.

ensheath /ɪn'ʃiːθ, ɛn-/ *v.t.* Also **-sheathe** /-'ʃiːð/. L16. [f. EN-[1] + SHEATH *n.*[1], SHEATHE *v.*] Enclose or conceal like a sheath.

enshell *v.* var. of INSHELL.

†enshield *a. rare* (Shakes.). Only in E17. [Origin uncertain: perh. f. EN-[1] + SHIELD *n.*[1], but cf. next.] Shielded, concealed.

enshield /ɪn'ʃiːld, ɛn-/ *v.t. rare.* M19. [f. EN-[1] + SHIELD *v.* Cf. prec.] Guard or screen as with a shield.

enshrine /ɪn'ʃraɪn, ɛn-/ *v.t.* Also **†in-**. LME. [f. EN-[1], IN-[2] + SHRINE *n.*] 1 Enclose (as) in a shrine; place in a receptacle appropriate for a precious or revered object. LME. 2 Contain as a shrine does; contain or embody in a way that protects or preserves. E17.

1 *fig.*: W. SPALDING Papal orthodoxy sat enshrined in the Escurial. 2 SAKI Her drawing-room . . enshrined the memorials or tokens of past and present happiness. R. A. KNOX It was necessary to enshrine Christian truths in a more exact, a more elaborate setting than of old. ANTHONY SMITH The rights of the ordinary individual, acquired over centuries and enshrined in law.

enshrinement *n.* the action of enshrining; a thing that enshrines; an embodiment: M19.

enshroud /ɪn'ʃraʊd, ɛn-/ *v.t.* L16. [f. EN-[1] + SHROUD *n.*[1]] Cover as with a shroud; completely envelop; hide from view.

G. BROWN Moscow was enshrouded in fog and my aircraft had to be diverted. *fig.*: W. H. DIXON The crimes . . were enshrouded in the deepest mystery.

ensialic /ɛnsʌɪ'alɪk/ *a.* M20. [f. EN-[2] + SIALIC *a.*[1]] *Geol.* Originating or occurring in or on sialic material; of or pertaining to structures or phenomena of this kind.

ensient /ɛnsɪ'ɛnt/ *a.* E18. [Alt. of ENSEINT *a.*] *Law.* Of a woman: pregnant.

ensiform /'ɛnsɪfɔːm/ *a.* & *n.* M16. [f. L *ensis* sword + -FORM.] A *adj.* Shaped like a sword-blade; *spec.* (of a leaf) long and narrow with sharp edges and a pointed tip, like an iris leaf. M16.

ensiform cartilage = XIPHISTERNUM.

B *n.* An ensiform object; *spec.* = *ensiform cartilage* above. E20.

ensign /'ɛnsʌɪn, -sɪn, -s(ə)n/. *n.* LME. [(O)Fr. *enseigne* f. as INSIGNIA. Cf. ANCIENT *n.*[2]] 1 A signal, a rallying cry; a watchword, a slogan. Chiefly *Sc.* Long *rare*. LME. 2 A characteristic, a sign (*of* something). *arch.* LME. 3 A conventional symbol, an emblem; *esp.* a badge of office; in *pl.*, heraldic bearings, as much of a heraldic achievement as is depicted. LME. 4 A military or naval standard; a flag; *spec.* a flag flown at the stern of a vessel to show its nationality; in Britain, each of three such flags with the union flag in one corner (see below). LME. †5 A body of men serving under the same flag; a troop. M16–M17. 6 A standard-bearer (*Hist.*); an infantry officer of the lowest commissioned rank, a second lieutenant, (*Hist.* exc. in the Foot Guards); an officer in the Yeomen of the Guard. L16. 7 An officer of the lowest commissioned rank in the US navy. M19.

2 R. L. STEVENSON If the Indian Empire, the trade of London, and all the . . ensigns of our greatness should pass away. 3 M. R. MITFORD Those ensigns of authority, the keys. 4 **blue ensign** orig. the ensign of the rear admiral's squadron, now that of naval auxiliary vessels. **red ensign** orig. the ensign of the admiral's squadron, now that of the British merchant navy. **white ensign** orig. the ensign of the rear admiral's squadron, now that of the Royal Navy and Royal Yacht Squadron.

ensigncy *n.* (*Hist.*) the rank or position of an ensign M18.

ensign /'ɛnsʌɪn/ *v. obs.* exc. *Her.* L15. [OFr. *ensignier*, *enseigner* f. med.L *insignare* for L *insignire* mark, distinguish, f. as IN-[2] + *signum* SIGN *n.*] †1 *v.t.* & *i.* Indicate, point out. L15–L16. †2 *v.t.* Teach, instruct. L15–L16. 3 *v.t.* Mark with a sign or badge. Now only *Her.*, distinguish or ornament (a charge) by depicting some object placed above it. L16.

†ensignment *n.* LME. [(O)Fr. *enseignement*, f. as prec.: see -MENT.] 1 Instruction; a lesson; a means of instruction, an example. LME–E17. 2 A badge of office. M16–E17.

ensilage /'ɛnsɪlɪdʒ, ɛn'sʌɪlɪdʒ/ *n.* & *v.* L19. [Fr., f. *ensiler* f. Sp. *ensilar*, f. *en-* (f. as IN-[2]) + SILO: see -AGE.] A *n.* 1 The process of making silage. L19. 2 Silage. L19. B *v.t.* Treat (fodder) by ensilage; turn into silage. L19.

ensile /ɛn'sʌɪl/ *v.t.* L19. [Fr. *ensiler*: see prec.] = ENSILAGE *v.*

ensimatic /ɛnsʌɪ'matɪk/ *a.* M20. [f. EN-[2] + SIMATIC.] *Geol.* Originating or occurring in or on simatic material; of or pertaining to structures or phenomena of this kind.

†ensinew *v.* var. of INSINEW.

ensky /ɪn'skʌɪ, ɛn-/ *v.t. poet.* E17. [f. EN-[1] + SKY *n.*] Place in the sky or in heaven. Usu. in *pass.*

enslave /ɪn'sleɪv, ɛn-/ *v.t.* Also **†in-**. E17. [f. EN-[1], IN-[2] + SLAVE *n.*[1]] 1 Make (a person) completely subject to or dominated by habit, superstition, passion, or the like. E17. 2 Make a slave of, reduce to slavery; deprive of political freedom. M17.

1 J. GLASSCO I was . . enslaved by the beauty of Paris.

enslavement *n.* the action of enslaving; the state of being enslaved: L17. **enslaver** *n.* E18.

For other words beginning with *en-* see the entry for **en-**[1]

ensnare /ɪn'snɛː, ɛn-/ *v.t.* Also **†in-**. L16. [f. EN-[1], IN-[2] + SNARE *n.*] Catch in a snare. Chiefly *fig.*, beguile, lure; entangle in difficulties.
ensnarement *n.* (now *rare*) the action of ensnaring; the state or fact of being ensnared; a bait, a trap: E17. **ensnarer** *n.* (now *rare*) M17.

ensnarl /ɪnsnɑːl, ɛn-/ *v.t.* Also (earlier) **†in-**. LME. [f. EN-[1], IN-[2] + SNARL *n.*[1]] Entangle or catch as in a snarl or ravelled knot. Now only *fig.*

ensorcell /ɪn'sɔːs(ə)l, ɛn-/ *v.t.* Also **-el**. Infl. **-ll-**. M16. [(O)Fr. *ensorceler* alt. of OFr. *ensorcerer*, f. as EN-[1] + *sorcier* SORCERER.] Enchant, bewitch; fascinate.
ensorcellment *n.* magic, enchantment M20.

ensoul /ɪn'səʊl, ɛn-/ *v.t.* Also (earlier) **in-** /ɪn-/. E17. [f. EN-[1], IN-[2] + SOUL *n.*] **1** Put or take into the soul; unite with the soul. Now *rare*. E17. **2** Infuse a soul into; fill effectually. E17.
2 C. GORE An organism ensouled by the indwelling word. *New Scientist* God would be more likely to ensoul the fetus at birth.
ensoulment *n.* the introduction of a soul into something M20.

ensphere /ɪn'sfɪə, ɛn-/ *v.t.* Also **in-** /ɪn-/. E17. [f. EN-[1], IN-[2] + SPHERE *n.*] **1** Enclose (as) in a sphere; encircle. E17. **2** Shape into a sphere. M17.
enspherement *n.* (*rare*) M19.

†enspire *v.* see INSPIRE.

enstamp /ɪn'stamp, ɛn-/ *v.t.* Also (earlier) **†in-**. L16. [f. EN-[1], IN-[2] + STAMP *v.*] Stamp, imprint, (a mark etc.) *on* something; put a mark on, mark *with*.

†enstate *v.* var. of INSTATE.

enstatite /'ɛnstətʌɪt/ *n.* M19. [f. Gk *enstatēs* adversary (from its refractory nature) + -ITE[1].] *Min.* An orthorhombic magnesium silicate that is a member of the pyroxene group and occurs as translucent crystals of varying colours in igneous rocks and meteorites.

†ensteep *v.* var. of INSTEEP.

enstool /ɪn'stuːl, ɛn-/ *v.t.* L19. [f. EN-[1] + STOOL *n.*] Place on the stool of a W. African chief; enthrone (a chief).

enstyle *v.* var. of INSTYLE.

ensuant /ɪn'sjuːənt, ɛn-/ *a.* L16. [f. ENSUE + -ANT[1].] **†1** Appropriate *to* what has preceded. *rare*. Only in L16. **2** Ensuing, following; consequent (*on*). L19.

ensue /ɪn'sjuː, ɛn-/ *v.* Also **†in-**. LME. [OFr. *ensiw-*, *ensu-* stem of *ensivre* (mod. *ensuivre*) f. Proto-Romance, f. L *insequi*, f. as IN-[2] + *sequi* follow.] **†1** *v.t.* & *i.* Follow (a person); follow in (the steps of someone). LME–E17. **†2** *v.t.* Pursue, chase. LME–M16. **†3** *v.t.* Follow the guidance or example of; follow (one's inclination); take (advice). LME–L16. **4a** *v.i.* Be subsequent; occur or arise afterwards, esp. as a result or consequence; result *from* (also foll. by *on*, *upon*, *†by*, *†of*). LME. **†b** *v.t.* Succeed, come after, be subsequent to; result from. L15–M18. **†5** *v.t.* Correspond to. LME–E17. **6** *v.t.* Seek after, aim at. *arch.* L15. **†7** *v.t.* Carry out (a plan); follow (an occupation); follow up; spend (a period of one's life). E16–E17.
4a T. HARDY One quarter of the trees would die away during the ensuing August. R. LYND Thereupon a long argument ensued.
ensuer *n.* (*rare*) M16.

en suite /õ 'swiːt, *foreign* ɑ̃ sɥit/ *adv.*, *a.*, & *n. phr.* Also (esp. as adj. & n. phr.) **ensuite** /õ'swiːt/. L18. [Fr.] **A** *adv. phr.* **1** In agreement or harmony (*with*). Now *rare* or *obs.* L18. **2** In a row, with one room leading into another; as part of the same set of rooms. (Foll. by *with*.) E19. **b** As part of the same set of objects. (Foll. by *with*.) M20.
2 *Cornish Guardian* 4 bedrooms (2 with shower rooms en suite).
B *a. phr.* Of a room: that is en suite; forming part of the same set, immediately adjoining. M20.
C *n. phr.* An en suite room, *esp.* an en suite bathroom. L20.

†ensurance *n.* see INSURANCE.

ensure /ɪn'ʃʊə, ɛn-/ *v.t.* LME. [AN *enseürer* alt. of OFr. *asseürer* ASSURE. Cf. INSURE.] **1** Make sure, convince. Chiefly *refl.* & in *pass.* Long *rare*. LME. **†2** Promise to (a person). (Foll. by *to do*, *that*.) LME–M17. **†3** Engage, pledge, (a person); *esp.* become engaged to, espouse. LME–E17. **†4** Guarantee, warrant. LME–M18. **5** Secure, make safe, (*against*, *from*, a risk etc.). LME. **†b** Insure (a life, property, etc.) L17–M18. **6** Make certain the occurrence of (an event, situation, outcome, etc.). (Foll. by *that*.) M18. **7** Secure (a thing) *for* or *to* a person. Also foll. by double obj. L18.
5 J. REYNOLDS Ensure us from all error and mistake. 6 F. TUOHY Concessions had to be made, to ensure his silence. M. AMIS Everything has to be *just so*—and I.. ensure that it is. 7 LEIGH HUNT It ensures us an intercourse with a nation we esteem.
ensurer *n.* (*rare*) M17.

enswathe /ɪn'sweɪð, ɛn-/ *v.t.* Chiefly *poet.* L16. [f. EN-[1] + SWATHE *n.*[1] or *v.*] Wrap or bind (as) in a bandage; swathe.
enswathement *n.* a thing that enswathes or envelops; the state of being enswathed: L19.

ent- *comb. form* see ENTO-.

-ent /(ə)nt/ *suff.* [Fr. or its source L *-ent-* pres. ppl stem of vbs of 2nd, 3rd, and 4th conjugations, or *-ant-* (see -ANT[1]).] Forming adjs. denoting existence of action, as *effluent*, or state, as *convenient*, or ns. denoting an agent, as *president*, *referent*, *superintendent*, usu. f. vbs. Conflicting Eng., Fr., & L analogies have produced much inconsistency of use of *-ent* and *-ant*.

entablature /ɛn'tablətʃə, ɪn-/ *n.* Also **†in-**. E17. [f. It. *intavolatura* boarding (partly through Fr. ENTABLEMENT), f. *intavolare* board up, f. as IN-[2] + *tavola* table: see -URE.] **1** *Archit.* The part of a classical building that is above and supported by the columns, comprising architrave, frieze, and cornice. E17. **2** A structure analogous to a classical entablature. M19.
2 H. JAMES Fireplaces of white marble, the entablature of which was adorned with a delicate.. 'subject'.
entablatured *a.* M19.

entablement /ɛn'teɪb(ə)lm(ə)nt, ɪn-/ *n.* M17. [Fr., f. *entabler*, f. as EN-[1] + *table*: see TABLE *n.*, -MENT.] *Archit.* **1** = ENTABLATURE 1. Now *rare* or *obs.* M17. **2** The horizontal platform(s) supporting a statue, above the dado and the base. E19.

†entail *n.*[1] ME. [(O)Fr. *entaille*, f. as ENTAIL *v.*[1]] **1** Sculpture. ME–E16. **2** Shape, pattern; the cut of a garment; guise, semblance. ME–M16.

entail /ɪn'teɪl, ɛn-/ *n.*[2] Also **†in-**. LME. [f. ENTAIL *v.*[2]] **1** *Law.* The settlement of the succession of land or other property so that it cannot subsequently be bequeathed or sold but must pass to a designated class of descendants; the line of succession so prescribed. LME. **2** *fig.* Restriction to a prescribed succession of people; transmission as an inalienable inheritance; a secured inheritance. LME. **3** The fact of being necessarily consequent *upon*. M17.
2 J. MARTINEAU The natural entail of disease and character. J. BAYLEY Poets oppressed by the modern entail of the poet as self. 3 R. W. HAMILTON The entail of vice upon the circumstances of the present life.

†entail *v.*[1]*t.* LME. [OFr. *entaillier* (mod. *entailler*) f. med.L *intalliare*, f. as IN-[2] + *talliare* cut: see TAIL *v.*[1]] **1** *v.t.* Carve; cut into; decorate with carvings. LME–M17. **2** *v.i.* Cut (*into*). *rare* (Spenser). Only in L16.

entail /ɪn'teɪl, ɛn-/ *v.*[2]*t.* Also **†in-**. LME. [f. EN-[1], IN-[2] + AN *taile* TAIL *n.*[2] or *tailé* TAIL *a.*] **1** *Law.* Settle (land etc.) by entail; *fig.* confer as if by entail, bestow as an inalienable possession (*on*). LME. **†2** Attach inseparably *to*; attach, associate. Also foll. by *upon*. L16–E18. **3** Impose (inconvenience, expense, etc.) *on* or *upon* a person. M17. **4** Necessitate as a consequence; have as an inevitable accompaniment, involve. E19.
1 M. R. MITFORD The house and park.. were entailed on a distant cousin. 3 SIR W. SCOTT Which shall.. entail disgrace on all who have to do with it. 4 D. ATHILL He had no conception of what a real job.. entailed.
entailable *a.* L17. **entailer** *n.* a person who entails property L18. **entailment** *n.* the action or an act of entailing something; *Philos.* the strict or logically necessary implication of one proposition by another: M17.

†entame *v.*[1]*t.* ME. [(O)Fr. *entamer* alt. of *atamer*: see ATTAME.] **1** Cut into, wound. ME–L15. **2** Make the first cut in; *fig.* begin. Only in L15.

entame /ɪn'teɪm, ɛn-/ *v.*[2]*t.* L15. [f. EN-[1] + TAME *a.*] Tame; subdue.

entamoeba /ɛntə'miːbə/ *n.* Also ***-meba**. Pl. **-bae** /-biː/, **-bas**. E20. [mod.L, f. ENTO- + AMOEBA.] An amoeba of the parasitic genus *Entamoeba*, of which one species causes dysentery in man and another is a harmless commensal in the colon.

entangle /ɪn'taŋg(ə)l, ɛn-/ *v.t.* Also **†in-**. LME. [f. EN-[1], IN-[2] + TANGLE *n.*[2], *v.*] **1** Cause to be held in something that is tangled or that impedes movement or extrication. LME. **2** Involve (a person etc.) in difficulties, doubtful undertakings, etc. LME. **b** Involve (a person) in a compromising relationship *with* another. L19. **3** Make tangled; interlace so that separation is difficult. M16. **4** Make complicated or intricate; complicate *with*. L17.
1 ADDISON Lest she should entangle her Feet in her Petticoat. *fig.*: BURKE Nets that entangle the.. silken wings of a tender conscience. 2 J. A. FROUDE The Pope.. had endeavoured to entangle his nephew in the conspiracy. b F. HUME He became entangled with a lady whose looks were much better than her morals. 4 L. STERNE Two other circumstances which entangled this mystery.
entangler *n.* L16.

entanglement /ɪn'taŋg(ə)lm(ə)nt, ɛn-/ *n.* Also **†in-**. L16. [f. prec. + -MENT.] **1** The action of entangling; the condition or an instance of being entangled. L16. **2** A thing that entangles; a complication, an embarrassment. M17. **b** *Mil.* An extensive barrier designed to impede an enemy's movements, now often made of stakes and tangled barbed wire. M19. **3** A compromising, usu. amorous, relationship. M19.

entasis /'ɛntəsɪs/ *n.* Pl. **-ases** /-əsiːz/. M17. [mod.L f. Gk, f. *enteinein* to strain.] *Archit.* A slight bowing of the shaft of a column (introduced to correct the visual illusion of concavity).

entelechy /ɛn'tɛləki, ɪn-/ *n.* LME. [Late L *entelechia* f. Gk *entelekheia*, f. as EN-[2] + *telei*, dat. of *telos* end, perfection + *ekhein* be in a (certain) state: see -Y[3].] *Philos.* **1** In Aristotle's use: the condition in which a potentiality has become an actuality; *spec.* the essential nature or informing principle of a living thing; the soul. LME. **b** *Biol.* A supposed vital principle that guides the development and functioning of an organism. E20. **2** In Leibniz's use: a monad. L19.

entellus /ɪn'tɛləs, ɛn-/ *n.* M19. [*Entellus*, an old man in Virgil's *Aeneid*.] The hanuman monkey. Also *entellus langur*, *monkey*.

entemple /ɪn'tɛmp(ə)l, ɛn-/ *v.t.* E17. [f. EN-[1] + TEMPLE *n.*[1]] Enclose as in a temple; enshrine.

†entend *v.* see INTEND.

†entender *v.t.* Also **in-**. L16–M18. [f. EN-[1], IN-[2] + TENDER *a.*] Make tender; soften (the heart).

†entendment *n.* see INTENDMENT.

†entent *n.*, *v.* see INTENT *n.*, *v.*

entente /ɑːn'tɑːnt, *foreign* ɑ̃tɑ̃ːt/ *n.* M19. [Fr.] A friendly understanding, esp. between States; a group of States sharing such an understanding.

entente cordiale /ɑ̃tɑ̃ːt kɔrdjal, ɑːn,tɑːnt kɔːdɪ'ɑːl/ *n. phr.* Pl. ***-s -s*** (pronounced same). M19. [Fr.] An entente, *spec.* (*Hist.*) that arrived at by France and Britain in 1904.

†entention *n.* var. of INTENTION.

†ententive *a.* see INTENTIVE.

entepicondylar /,ɛntɛpɪ'kɒndɪlə/ *a.* L19. [f. ENTO- + EPICONDYLE + -AR[1].] *Anat.* *entepicondylar foramen*, a foramen in the humerus of many vertebrates just above the medial epicondyle.

†enter *n.* LME–L16. [f. the vb.] The action, power, or right of entering; an entrance, a passage.

enter /ˈɛntə/ *v.* ME. [(O)Fr. *entrer* f. L *intrare*, f. *intra* within.] **1 a** *v.i.* Go or come in or (*arch.*) *in*; (as a stage direction, in 3 pres. subjunct.) come on stage. Also foll. by *into* a specified place, region, etc. ME. **b** *v.t.* Go or come into (a place, medium, etc.); go within the bounds of (a country etc.). ME. **†c** *v.t.* Seize (a crown, a throne). M16–M17. **d** *v.t.* Force an entrance into; break into. L16. **†2 a** *v.i.* Come or fall *into* a state or condition. ME–E18. **b** *v.t.* Come or pass into (a certain condition). Formerly also, take upon oneself (a position), take up (an occupation). Now *rare.* M16. **3** *v.i. Law.* Take possession of land, esp. as an assertion of ownership. Also foll. by *†in, into, (up)on.* LME. **4 a** *v.i.* Penetrate deeply into or *into* something. LME. **b** *v.t.* Pierce, penetrate; *spec.* (of a male) have sexual intercourse with; insert the penis into the vagina of (a woman). E17. **5 a** *v.i.* Become a member of an organization. (Foll. by *at, in, into.*) LME. **b** *v.t.* Become a member of; take up one's vocation in; begin to live, study, etc., in. E17. **6** *v.i.* Begin; make a beginning; engage in an activity. Now only *Sc. dial.*, begin work, *esp.* begin harvest. LME. **7** *v.t.* Put *into*; insert, introduce. Now chiefly *techn.* LME. **8 a** *v.t.* Record in a register, diary, account-book, etc.; record particulars in (a journal), write up. Also foll. by *up.* LME. **b** *v.t.* Register (a vessel) entering or leaving a port; register with the authorities details of (goods being exported or imported). M17. **c** *v.i.* & *t.* Register as a competitor in a race, contest, etc.; submit (an animal, an inanimate object) for judging in a competition; become a competitor in (a race, contest, etc.). (Foll. by *for, in.*) L17. **d** *v.t. US Hist.* Get (public land) registered in one's name as the intending occupier or owner. L18. **e** *v.t.* Foll. by *up*: complete a series of entries in (an account-book etc.). L19. **9** *v.t.* **a** Give (an animal or bird) its first exercises or training; break in (a horse); (foll. by *at, to*) put (an untrained animal or bird) on the scent of a quarry. L15. **†b** Instruct (a person) initially; initiate. (Foll. by *in.*) M16–M19. **10** *v.t.* Formerly, take the first steps in, begin, (an activity). Now, begin (a period of time). E16. **11** *v.t.* Put or bring (a person) into something, esp. on to a ship. *arch.* E16. **12** *v.t.* **a** Procure admission into or *into* a society or an employment for (a person); admit as a member. Formerly also, bring (a person) *into* a specified state or relationship. L16. **b** Engage (an employee). M17. **13** *v.t.* Record in due form in a court of law, a deliberative body, etc. Also foll. by *up.* L16. **14** *v.t.* Look at or turn to a particular place in (a mathematical table). L16.

1a F. MARRYAT We.. entered into a noble forest. T. STOPPARD The door.. opens and two men enter. *transf.*: M. W. MONTAGU During these Excuses, enter Edgcombe. *break and enter*: see BREAK *v.* **b** D. H. LAWRENCE They had entered a wide river, from the narrow one. T. F. POWYS A flock of sheep all clamouring to enter a field. **enter one's head, mind** (of a thought, idea, etc.) occur to one, cross one's mind. *enter the lists*: see LIST *n.*[1] 7b. 4a *the iron entered into his soul*: see IRON *n.* **b** S. MARCUS He ejaculates without succeeding in entering her. 5a BOSWELL He could not.. enter where.. he could not have an able tutor. **b** T. HARDY Your scheme was to be a University man and enter the church. J. BUCHAN In 1914 he entered the Cabinet as President of the Board of Agriculture. 7 DAVID POTTER The die is hardened and entered into a soft steel roller. 8a J. STEINBECK The names were entered in the book. G. GREENE She hadn't entered the journal every day, and I had no wish to read every entry. *Personal Software* You must enter the coordinates of your shape as DATA in line 9000. **c** *Washington Post* Last year's winner.. did not enter this year. *Times* Davies.. has entered the French and Dutch open championships next month. 9a P. WAYRE After several weeks both birds would fly.., and it was time to enter them to a lure. 10 G. B. SHAW I have now entered my 93rd year. C. ISHERWOOD George has felt himself entering a new phase. J. SIMMS The discussions.. entered a period of intense upheaval. 12a I. WALTON Having entred Edward into Queens Colledge. E. PEACOCK He therefore entered himself as a clerk to a solicitor. 13 A. PULLING The defendant failed to appear, and judgment was entered. *transf.*: J. L. AUSTIN Now we must enter two caveats.

With preps. in specialized senses: **enter into, †in** (*a*) take upon oneself (a commitment, duty, relationship, etc.); bind oneself by, subscribe to, (an agreement); (*b*) engage in the consideration of (a matter); (*c*) form part of, be an element of; be relevant to; (*d*) take an interest in; sympathize with; **enter on, upon** (*a*) take the first steps on; begin to travel on; †(*b*) begin an attack on; (*c*) begin to deal with or consider.

enterable *a.* E18. **enterer** *n.* M16.

enter- /ˈɛntə/ *comb. form*[1]. Also **entre-** /ˈɛntrə/. [Repr. (O)Fr. *entre-* f. L *inter-*: see INTER-.] Forming compounds w. the senses 'between', 'among', 'mutually'. Now repl. by INTER-. The compounds of Eng. origin in which it occurs either are obs. or have been refashioned w. *inter-*.

enter- *comb. form*[2] see ENTERO-.

entera *n.* pl. of ENTERON.

enteral /ˈɛntər(ə)l/ *a.* E20. [Partly f. as ENTERIC + -AL[1], partly back-form. f. *parenteral.*] *Med.* Enteric; (of feeding, feeds, etc.) involving or passing through the intestine, either in the normal way (via the mouth etc.) or through an artificial opening (opp. PARENTERAL).

enterally *adv.* M20.

†enterchange *n.*, *v.* vars. of INTERCHANGE *n.*, *v.*

enterclose /ˈɛntəkləʊs/ *n. obs.* exc. *Archit.* Also **†inter-**. LME. [OFr. *entreclos* (in med.L *interclausum*), f. *entre-* ENTER-[1] + *clos* CLOSE *n.*[1]] A partition; a space partitioned off.

†entercommon *v.* & *n.* see INTERCOMMON.

†entercommune *v.* see INTERCOMMUNE.

†entercommunicate *v.*, **-ation** *n.* see INTERCOMMUNICATE etc.

†entercourse *n.* see INTERCOURSE.

†enterdiction *n.* see INTERDICTION.

†enterfere *v.* var. of INTERFERE.

†enterfold *v.* var. of INTERFOLD.

enteric /ɛnˈtɛrɪk/ *a.* & *n.* E19. [Gk *enterikos*, f. ENTERON: see -IC.] *Anat.* & *Med.* **A** *adj.* **1** Of, pertaining to, or occurring in the intestines. E19. **2** = *enteric-coated* below. E20.

1 **enteric fever** typhoid or paratyphoid fever.

Comb.: **enteric-coated** *a.* (of a capsule) coated so that the contents are released in the intestine after passage through the stomach unaltered.

B *n.* Enteric fever. E20.

entering /ˈɛnt(ə)rɪŋ/ *n.* ME. [f. ENTER *v.* + -ING[1].] **1** The action of ENTER *v.* ME. **†2** An entrance; a door, a gate, etc.; an opening. LME–M16.

enteritis /ɛntəˈraɪtɪs/ *n.* E19. [f. Gk ENTERON + -ITIS.] *Med.* Inflammation of the intestine, esp. acute inflammation of the small intestine, usu. accompanied by diarrhoea.

†enterlace *v.* see INTERLACE *v.*

†enterlard *v.* see INTERLARD.

†enterline *v.* see INTERLINE *v.*[1]

†enterlude *n.* see INTERLUDE.

†entermarriage *n.*, **-marry** *v.* vars. of INTERMARRIAGE, INTERMARRY.

†entermeddle *v.* var. of INTERMEDDLE.

†entermise *n.* Also **inter-**. L15. [OFr. *entremise*, f. *entremetre* (mod. *-mettre*), repr. L *intermittere* and *intromittere*: see INTERMIT, INTROMIT.] **1** Business. Only in L15. **2** Interposition, intervention. E17–E18.

entero- /ˈɛntərəʊ/ *comb. form* of Gk *enteron* intestine: see -O-. Bef. a vowel also **enter-**.

entero'biasis *n.*, pl. **-ases** /-əsiːz/, infestation with or disease caused by pinworms of the genus *Enterobius* M20. **enterocele** *n.* [Gk *kēlē* tumour] a hernia or cyst containing part of the intestine E17. **enterochro'maffin** *a.* (*Histol.*) designating chromaffin cells of the epithelium of the gastro-intestinal and respiratory tracts M20. **entero'coccus** *n.* any streptococcus that occurs in the intestine E20. **enterocoel(e)** *n.* (*Zool.*) (part of) a coelom that is or has been in communication with the archenteron L19. **entero'coelic, -'coelous** *adjs.* (*Zool.*) of or pertaining to an enterocoel L19. **enterocoely** *n.* (*Zool.*) development of a coelom by outpocketing of the archenteron M20. **enteroco'litis** *n.* inflammation of the small intestine and the colon M19. **enterocyte** *n.* a cell of the intestinal epithelium M20. **entero'cytic** *a.* of, pertaining to, or involving enterocytes M20. **entero'gastrone** *n.* a hormone secreted by the small intestine that inhibits gastric secretion and peristalsis M20. **enterohe'patic** *a.* of or pertaining to the intestine and the liver; *spec.* designating the circulation of bile salts etc. from their place of formation in the liver to the intestine, where they are reabsorbed into the blood and returned to the liver: M20. **enterohepa'titis** *n.* = *blackhead* (c) s.v. BLACK *a.* L19. **entero'kinase** *n.* an enzyme secreted by the duodenum that converts trypsinogen to trypsin E20. **enterolith** *n.* a stone or a hardened lump of faeces that forms in the intestine L19. **ente'ropathy** *n.* (a) disease of the intestine L19. **enteropneust** /ˈɛntərə(ʊ)pnjuːst/ *n.* (*Zool.*) a hemichordate of the class Enteropneusta, comprising animals with gill slits that open into the pharynx, e.g. the acorn worm E20. **ente'rostomy** *n.* (an instance of) the surgical formation of a permanent opening into the intestine through the abdominal wall, so as to bypass the stomach when feeding or the colon when eliminating waste L19. **enteroto'xaemia** *n.* (*Vet. Med.*) toxaemia due to an enterotoxin M20. **enterotoxi'genic** *a.* (of bacteria) producing an enterotoxin M20. **enterotoxige'nicity** *n.* the property of being enterotoxigenic; the degree to which something is enterotoxigenic: L20. **entero'toxin** *n.* a toxin produced in or affecting the intestine, such as those causing food poisoning and cholera E20. **Entero-'Vioform** *n.* (proprietary name for) a preparation of clioquinol used to prevent and treat travellers' diarrhoea M20. **entero'viral** *a.* of or pertaining to an enterovirus M20. **enterovirus** *n.* any of a group of picornaviruses which typically occur in the gastro-intestinal tract, but including the poliovirus, Coxsackie virus, echo-virus, and the virus of hepatitis A M20.

enteron /ˈɛntərɒn/ *n.* Pl. **-ra** /-rə/. M19. [Gk.] An alimentary canal or cavity, esp. of an embryo or coelenterate.

†enterplede *v.* var. of INTERPLEAD.

enterprise /ˈɛntəprʌɪz/ *n.* LME. [(O)Fr. *entreprise* use as n. of fem. pa. pple of *entreprendre*, later var. of *emprendre*: see EMPRISE.] **1** A piece of work taken in hand, an undertaking; *esp.* one that is bold, hazardous, or arduous. LME. **b** A business firm, a company. L19. **2** Disposition to engage in enterprises; initiative and imagination. L15. **†3** The action of overseeing or managing. M16–E19. **4** The action of engaging in enterprises; *esp.* activity undertaken with an economic or commercial end in view. M18.

1 G. F. KENNAN For a small country.. to launch an all-out military attack on Russia was a fantastic enterprise. J. W. KRUTCH The search for one kind of knowledge.. is the legitimate enterprise of science. 2 E. F. BENSON American enterprise had already largely repaired the destruction caused by the earthquakes. C. P. SNOW The present generation hasn't got a scrap of enterprise. 4 T. BENN All forms of enterprise, including nationalized industries.. the banks and insurance companies. *free enterprise*: see FREE *a.* *private enterprise*: see PRIVATE *a.*

Comb.: **enterprise culture** a capitalist society in which entrepreneurs are given specific encouragement; **enterprise zone** an area in which a government seeks to stimulate enterprise by granting financial concessions to businesses operating there.

enterprise /ˈɛntəprʌɪz/ *v.* Now *rare.* LME. [Partly f. prec.; partly f. Fr. *entrepris* pa. pple of *entreprendre* (see prec.).] **†1** *v.t.* Attack; make helpless or embarrassed. LME–E16. **2** *v.t.* Take on (a work, a condition); attempt, undertake, (a challenging or arduous task). (Formerly foll. by *to do.*) L15. **3** *v.i.* Make an attempt, undertake an arduous task. E16.

enterpriser *n.* a person who engages in an enterprise; now *esp.* an entrepreneur: E16.

enterprising /ˈɛntəprʌɪzɪŋ/ *a.* E17. [f. prec. + -ING[2].] Orig., that undertakes; foolhardy; scheming. Now, showing initiative and imagination; resourceful.

SCOTT FITZGERALD An enterprising office-boy can make his way to the top.

enterprisingly *adv.* E19.

†enterrogate *v.* var. of INTERROGATE.

†entersert *v.* var. of INTERSERT.

†entersole *n.* var. of ENTRESOL.

†entersparse *v.* var. of INTERSPERSE.

For other words beginning with *en-* see the entry for **en-**[1]

†entertain *n.* L16. [f. the vb.] 1 The action of entertaining a guest; treatment of a person as a guest. L16–M17. b = ENTERTAINMENT 4c. M–L17. 2 Mental acceptance. E–M17. 3 Conversation; social behaviour. E–M17. 4 Pleasure; an amusement. Only in 17.

entertain /ɛntəˈteɪn/ *v.* LME. [Repr. tonic stem of (O)Fr. *entretenir* f. Proto-Romance base, f. L *inter* among + *tenere* to hold.] 1 *v.t.* a Keep up, maintain, (a state of things, a process, action, etc.). Now *arch. rare.* LME. †b Keep in existence; keep in repair. L15–L17. †2 *v.t.* Keep in a certain state or condition. L15–E18. b Support, provide for, (a person). M17–L18. †3 *v.t.* Hold mutually. L15–L16. †4 *v.t.* Deal with; treat in a specified manner. L15–M17. 5 *v.t.* & *i.* Have (a person) as a guest; show hospitality (to). L15. †6 *v.t.* Receive; allow to enter; accept. M16–E18. b Receive and contain; accommodate. M17–E18. 7 *v.t.* Keep (a person) in one's service; hire (a servant), take *into* one's service. Now *rare.* M16. †8 *v.t.* Encounter, meet. *rare.* L16–M17. †9 *v.t.* Take upon oneself; engage in. L16–E18. 10 *v.t.* Keep or maintain in the mind; harbour, cherish; experience (a feeling). L16. b Admit to consideration; receive (an idea). E17. 11 *v.t.* Occupy the attention, time, etc., of; converse with. *arch.* L16. †b Occupy (time). L16–L17. †c Engage (enemy forces). L16–M17. 12 *v.t.* & *i.* Engage agreeably the attention (of); amuse. E17.

1a H. H. MILMAN Entertaining a friendly correspondence with the orthodox Queen Theodelinda. 5 J. BUCHAN He patronizes the drama and entertains lavishly. J. L. WATEN Mother was in the best room entertaining four ladies. 10 H. L. MENCKEN All the major religions . . entertain the concept of an infinite future. J. GLASSCO She entertained feelings of the purest and most venomous hatred. b G. F. KENNAN A new proposal was being entertained in the entourage of Colonel House. JOHN BROOKE It sounds fantastic that such beliefs could be seriously entertained. 11 CHESTERFIELD I have so often entertained you upon these important subjects. 12 C. LAMB My favourite occupations . . now cease to entertain. K. A. PORTER When they entertain themselves at their numerous . . feasts. D. BAGLEY He entertained them with a hilarious account of some of his experiences.

entertainable *a.* L17.

entertainer /ɛntəˈteɪnə/ *n.* M16. [f. prec. + -ER[1].] A person who entertains; *spec.* a professional provider of amusement or entertainment.

Washington Post He . . had performed with such entertainers as Bob Hope.

entertaining /ɛntəˈteɪnɪŋ/ *a.* M17. [f. as prec. + -ING[2].] †1 Hospitable. *rare.* Only in M17. †2 Supporting life. *rare.* Only in L17. 3 Agreeable, interesting; *esp.* diverting, amusing. L17.

3 G. BERKELEY A part of knowledge both useful and entertaining.

entertainingly *adv.* E17. **entertainingness** *n.* E19.

entertainment /ɛntəˈteɪnm(ə)nt/ *n.* LME. [f. as prec. + -MENT.] †1 Maintenance; support. LME–M18. b *sing.* & in *pl.* Pay, wages. M16–E18. †2 Treatment (of people); manner of behaviour. M16–M17. 3 Occupation, occupying *of* time. Long *rare.* M16. 4 Hospitable provision for the wants of a guest. Now *rare.* M16. b The action of receiving or providing for a guest. L16. c A meal; *esp.* a formal or elegant meal, a banquet. Now *rare.* E17. †5 The action of keeping a person in, or of taking a person into, one's service; employment. L16–M17. †6 The action of receiving or accepting something, as information, a present, a proposal, etc. L16–E18. †7 Reception (of a person); manner of reception. L16–L17. 8 The action of occupying a person's attention agreeably; amusement. L16. b A thing which entertains or amuses someone, *esp.* a public performance or exhibition designed to entertain people. M17. †9 Accommodation, esp. of a ship in a harbour. L17–E18. 10 The action of harbouring or cherishing in the mind a feeling, idea, etc. M19. b The consideration of an idea, proposal, etc. M19.

4 G. P. R. JAMES Take order that lodging and entertainment be prepared at York. b *Law Times* The proprietor . . undertakes to provide for the entertainment of all comers. 8 H. CECIL The general atmosphere of colour and light-heartedness provide a good afternoon's entertainment. b A. J. P. TAYLOR The cinema threatened humbler forms of entertainment. 10 E. MIALL The deliberate entertainment of this selfish design.

†entertake *v.t. rare* (Spenser). Only in L16. [f. ENTER-[1] + TAKE *v.*, as tr. Fr. *entreprendre* (see ENTERPRISE *n.*).] Entertain, receive.

†entertangle *v.* var. of INTERTANGLE.

†entertissued *a.* var. of INTERTISSUED.

†enterview *n.*, *v.* vars. of INTERVIEW *n.*, *v.*

†enterweave *v.* var. of INTERWEAVE.

enthalpy /ˈɛnθ(ə)lpi, ɛnˈθalpi/ *n.* E20. [f. Gk *enthalpein* warm in, f. as EN-[2] + *thalpein* to heat: see -Y[1].] *Physics.* The total heat content of a system, expressed as a thermodynamic quantity obtained by adding its free energy to the product of its pressure and volume.

enthral /ɪnˈθrɔːl, ɛn-/ *v.t.* Also **†in-**, ***-ll**. Infl. **-ll-**. LME. [f. EN-[1], IN-[2] + THRALL *n.*] 1 Reduce to the condition of a thrall; make a slave. Now *rare.* LME. 2 Enslave mentally or morally; *esp.* captivate, please greatly. Chiefly as *enthralled* pa. pple, *enthralling* ppl a. L16.

2 T. NEWTON A man should not . . enthrall his credit and honour to Harlots. E. JENKINS He was enthralled by the . . spell of the orator. E. WAUGH Most of the subject matter was entirely new to me and I found it enthralling.

enthraldom *n.* (*rare*) the state or condition of being enthralled M17. **enthralment** *n.* the action of enthralling; the state or condition of being enthralled: E17.

enthrone /ɪnˈθrəʊn, ɛn-/ *v.t.* Also **†in-**. E16. [f. EN-[1], IN-[2] + THRONE, repl. ENTHRONIZE.] 1 Set (a king, bishop, etc.) on a throne, esp. with ceremony; formally invest with the authority of a king, bishop, etc.; *fig.* give or ascribe supreme authority or honour to. E16. 2 Place in a high and prominent position. M19.

1 M. E. BRADDON If she seem an angel to you, enthrone her in your heart of hearts. 2 J. CONRAD The . . private office . . where old Heidig . . sat enthroned.

enthronement *n.* the action of enthroning; the fact of being enthroned: L17.

enthronize /ɪnˈθrəʊnʌɪz, ɛn-/ *v.t.* Now *rare.* Also **-ise**, **in-** /ɪn-/. LME. [OFr. *introniser* f. late L *intronizare* f. Gk *enthronizein*, f. as EN-[1] + *thronos* THRONE *n.*: see -IZE.] = ENTHRONE 1.

enthroniˈzation *n.* = ENTHRONEMENT E16.

enthuse /ɪnˈθjuːz, ɛn-/ *v.* Orig. *US.* E19. [Back-form. f. ENTHUSIASM.] 1 *v.t.* & *i.* Make enthusiastic; arouse enthusiasm. E19. 2 *v.i.* Show enthusiasm; gush. L19.

†enthusian *n.* M17–E18. [f. Gk *enthousia* = *enthousiasmos*: see next, -AN.] A person (seemingly) possessed by a god or in a prophetic frenzy.

enthusiasm /ɪnˈθjuːzɪaz(ə)m, ɛn-/ *n.* E17. [Fr. *enthousiasme* or late L *enthusiasmus* f. Gk *enthousiasmos*, f. *enthousiazein* be inspired or possessed by a god, f. *enthous*, *entheos* inspired, f. as EN-[2] + *theos* god.] †1 Possession by a god; supernatural inspiration; prophetic or poetic frenzy. Also, an occasion or manifestation of any of these. E17–L18. 2 Extravagant religious emotion; imagined inspiration. *arch.* M17. 3 Strong intensity of feeling in favour of something or someone arising from a strong conviction of correctness, worthiness, effectiveness, etc.; passionate eagerness or interest. (Foll. by *for*, *to do.*) E18. b An object of such feeling. E20.

1 H. HICKMAN Nothing made the Anabaptists so infamous as their pretended enthusiasms or revelations. 3 C. MACKENZIE The health and happiness of George and his future wife were drunk with enthusiasm. M. GIROUARD A combination of interest in everything . . with an especial enthusiasm for the Englishness of England. A. POWELL There was not much enthusiasm for this suggestion. b M. SADLEIR Godwin, whose . . achievements in fiction were among Bulwer's youthful enthusiasms.

enthusiast /ɪnˈθjuːzɪast, ɛn-/ *n.* & *a.* E17. [Fr. *enthousiaste* or eccl.L *enthusiastes* member of a heretical sect f. Gk *enthousiastēs* person inspired, f. *enthousiazein*: see prec.] A *n.* 1 A person who believes that he or she is the recipient of divine communications; a person of extravagant religious beliefs or emotions. *arch.* E17. †2 A person (seemingly) possessed by a god or in a prophetic frenzy. M17–E18. 3 A person full of enthusiasm about something or someone (foll. by *for*, *of*, †*to*). Also, a visionary, a self-deluded person. E18. B *adj.* Enthusiastic. Now *rare.* L17.

enthusiastic /ɪnˌθjuːzɪˈastɪk, ɛn-/ *a.* & *n.* E17. [Gk *enthousiastikos*, f. *enthousiazein*: see ENTHUSIASM, -IC.] A *adj.* †1 Pertaining to or of the nature of extravagant religious emotion or divine possession. E17–M19. †2 Irrational, quixotic. L17–L18. 3 Full of enthusiasm, characterized by enthusiasm; of the nature of enthusiasm, rapturous. M18.

3 J. R. GREEN Enthusiastic joy hailed the accession of Elizabeth. D. H. LAWRENCE Over supper he became enthusiastic about Canada. J. F. LEHMANN Party Going . . received an early batch of enthusiastic reviews.

†B *n.* = ENTHUSIAST *n.* 1, 2. E17–E18.

enthusiastical *a.* (*a*) *arch.* = ENTHUSIASTIC *a.*; †(*b*) visionary; fanatically devoted to an idea or belief: L16. **enthusiastically** *adv.* L17.

enthymeme /ˈɛnθɪmiːm/ *n.* Also **†-mem**, & in L form **enthymema** /ɛnθɪˈmiːmə/, pl. **-memas**, **-memata** /-ˈmiːmətə/. M16. [L *enthymema* f. Gk *enthumēma*, f. *enthumeisthai* consider, infer, f. as EN-[2] + *thumos* mind.] 1 *Logic.* A syllogism in which one premiss is not explicitly stated. M16. †2 *Rhet.* An argument based on merely probable grounds. E17–M19.

enthymematic /-mɪˈmatɪk/ *a.* of, pertaining to, or containing an enthymeme E19. **†enthymematical** *a.* = ENTHYMEMATIC L16–L17.

entia *n.* pl. of ENS.

entice /ɪnˈtʌɪs, ɛn-/ *v.t.* Also **†in-**. ME. [OFr. *enticier* prob. f. Proto-Romance 'set on fire', f. L IN-[2] + alt. of *titio* firebrand.] †1 Incite (*to* a course of action); provoke (*to* anger etc.). ME–E17. 2 Persuade or attract by the offer of pleasure or advantage. (Foll. by *from*, *to* a place, course of action, etc.) ME.

2 EVELYN Beer mingled with Honey, to entice the Wasps. W. BLACK My Lady strove to entice him into the general talk. H. JAMES The English . . want to entice us away from our native land.

enticer *n.* LME. **enticingly** *adv.* in an enticing manner E17.

enticement /ɪnˈtʌɪsm(ə)nt, ɛn-/ *n.* Also **†in-**. ME. [OFr., f. as prec.: see -MENT.] †1 Incitement; something that incites. ME–L16. 2 The action of enticing; a means or method of enticing, an allurement. M16.

†entierty *n.* see ENTIRETY.

entify /ˈɛntɪfʌɪ/ *v.t. rare.* E19. [f. late L *ent-* stem of ENS + -I- + -FY.] *Philos.* Make into an entity; attribute objective reality to.

entincture /ɪnˈtɪŋ(k)tʃə, ɛn-/ *v.t.* M18. [f. EN-[1] + TINCTURE *n.*] = TINCTURE *v.*

entire /ɪnˈtʌɪə, ɛn-/ *a.*, *adv.*, & *n.* Also **†in-**. LME. [AN *enter*, (O)Fr. *entier*, fem. *-ière*, f. Proto-Romance, f. L *integrum* neut. of INTEGER.] A *adj.* I 1 Whole; with no part excepted. LME. 2 Complete in itself, constituting a whole; containing all essential parts. LME. b Designating a kind of mixed beer. *arch.* M18. 3 Realized in its full extent; thorough, unqualified. LME. b Of a person: wholehearted in belief etc.; uncompromising, confirmed. M16. 4 Wholly of one piece; continuous, undivided. Now chiefly *Sci.* LME. b Having an unbroken outline; not indented. M18. 5 Intact, unbroken; undiminished, unimpaired; *arch.* not fatigued or wounded. L16. b Of a male animal: not castrated. L18. 6 Pure, unmixed, homogeneous. Now only in abstract sense, passing into sense 3. L16. 7 Wholly reserved (*to* a person), unshared, set apart. E17. 8 *Her.* Of a charge, esp. a cross: (having its extremities) attached to the sides of a shield. L17.

1 J. TYNDALL Sufficiently strong to bear the entire weight of the body. 2 J. A. SYMONDS In justice the whole of virtue exists entire. 3 E. BOWEN Naomi's own good faith was so entire that it would never occur to her. b OED: He is an entire believer in Christianity. **4 rank entire** *Mil.* (in) an unbroken formation.

II Ethical senses. †9 Irreproachable, blameless. LME–L18. †10 Characterized by integrity; incorruptible, honest. LME–E18. †11 Of a feeling etc.: genuine, earnest, sincere. LME–E18. †12 Inward, intimate. *rare.* L15–L16.

12 SPENSER Casting flakes of lustful fire .. into their hearts and parts entire.

†**B** *adv.* Completely; sincerely. Only in LME.

C *n.* **1** The whole; the full extent. Now *rare.* L16. **2** Entirety. *rare.* E17. **3** Entire beer (see ENTIRE *a.* 2b). *arch.* E19. **4** An uncastrated stallion. M19. **5** *Philately.* A whole stamped envelope, wrapper, etc. (used or unused). L19.

entirely *adv.* & †*a.* ME. **entireness** *n.* LME.

entirety /ɪnˈtʌɪərəti, -ˈtʌɪəti, ɛn-/ *n.* Also (earlier) †**-tierty**. ME. [(O)Fr. *entièreté* f. L *integritas*, f. INTEGER: see -TY[1].] **1** Completeness; integrity; perfection. Freq. in *in its entirety* below. ME. **b** *Law.* The entire or undivided possession of an estate. ME. **2** The whole, the sum total. Now *rare.* M19.

1 in its etc. **entirety** in its etc. complete form; as a whole. **b by entireties** with husband and wife each deemed seised of a whole estate (now replaced in the UK by joint tenancy).

Entisol /ˈɛntɪsɒl/ *n.* M20. [f. ENTI(RE + -SOL.] *Soil Sci.* A soil of an order comprising mineral soils that have not yet differentiated into distinct horizons.

entitative /ˈɛntɪtətɪv/ *a.* Now *rare.* E17. [med.L *entitativus* (in Scotist phr. *actus entitativus*), f. *entitat-*: see ENTITY, -IVE.] **1** Pertaining to the mere existence of something. E17. **2** Having real existence. M19.

entitatively *adv.* L17.

entitle /ɪnˈtʌɪt(ə)l, ɛn-/ *v.t.* Also †**in-**. LME. [AN *entitler*, OFr. *entiteler*, (also mod.) *intituler*, f. late L *intitulare*, f. as IN-[2] + *titulus* TITLE *n.*] **1** Give (a book, picture, composition, etc.) a title or (formerly) a heading or superscription. LME. †**b** Dedicate (a book) *to* a person. LME–E17. †**c** Ascribe (a book etc.) *to* an author. M16–E18. †**2** Write down under headings. LME–L16. **3** Give (a person) a title or designation indicating rank, office, etc. Now *rare.* LME. **4** Orig., give (a person) the title *to* an estate. Now (chiefly of circumstances, qualities, etc.), confer on (a person or thing) a rightful claim *to* something or a right *to do.* LME. †**b** Invest *with* an honour, office, etc. L16–M17. †**5** Regard or treat (a person) as having a title *to* something; represent as the agent, cause, or subject of a specified thing (foll. by *in, to*); *refl.* lay claim *to.* LME–E18. **b** Impute *to.* Only in M17.

1 B. COTTLE A clear .. way of entitling the tunes is to name them after their composers. 3 W. FULBECKE The kings .. of England entitling themselues kings .. of Fraunce. 4 W. HENRY The remaining salts .. have no properties sufficiently important to entitle them to a separate description. V. BRITTAIN A green card which entitled me to sit in the .. Press gallery. A. BRINK It's a free country and every man is entitled to his own views.

entitlement *n.* (*a*) *rare* a means of entitling, a name; (*b*) the fact of being entitled or qualified; (*c*) something to which a person is entitled, *esp.* a state benefit: M19.

†**entitule** *v.* var. of INTITULE.

entity /ˈɛntɪti/ *n.* L15. [Fr. *entité* or med.L *entitas, -tat-*, f. late L *ent-* stem of ENS: see -TY[1].] **1 a** Existence, being, as opp. to non-existence; the existence of a thing as opp. to its qualities or relations. L15. **b** Essence, essential nature. M17. **2** All that exists. E17. **3** A thing that has a real existence, as opp. to a relation, function, etc. E17.

1 V. SACKVILLE-WEST The one who had .. the strongest sense of his own entity. 3 M. MUGGERIDGE I became aware of the British Empire .. as a geographical and political entity. G. F. KENNAN How could the people .. act as a collective entity .. unless they were .. organized.

ento- /ˈɛntəʊ/ *comb. form.* Bef. a vowel also **ent-**. [Repr. Gk *entos* within: see -O-.] = ENDO-.

entoblast *n.* (*Biol.*) †(*a*) *rare* a cell nucleolus; (*b*) endoderm, *esp.* that of an embryo: M19. **entoderm** *n.* (*Biol.*) = ENDODERM I L19. **ento'dermal** *a.* (*Biol.*) = ENDODERMAL L19. **ento'parasite** *n.* = ENDOPARASITE L19. **entopara'sitic** *a.* = ENDOPARASITIC L19. **entophyte** *n.* = ENDOPHYTE (b) M19. **entophytic** /-ˈfɪtɪk/ *a.* = ENDOPHYTIC M19. **entotym'panic** *a.* (*Anat.*) situated within the tympanum L19. **ento'zoal** *a.* of, pertaining to, or designating an entozoon M19. **entozoon** /-ˈzəʊɒn/ *n.*, pl. **-zoa** /-ˈzəʊə/, an animal that lives inside another, esp. as a parasite M19.

entoil /ɪnˈtɔɪl, ɛn-/ *v.t. arch.* & *poet.* L16. [f. EN-[1] + TOIL *n.*[2]] Trap; ensnare. Chiefly *fig.*

entomb /ɪnˈtuːm, ɛn-/ *v.t.* Also †**in-**. LME. [OFr. *entomber*, f. as EN-[1] + *tombe* TOMB.] **1** Place in a tomb; bury; enclose as in a tomb. LME. **2** Serve as a tomb for; receive like a tomb. M17.

entombment *n.* M17.

entomo- /ˈɛntəməʊ/ *comb. form.* [Repr. Gk *entomon* insect, neut. of *entomos* adj., cut up, f. as EN-[2] + *temnein* to cut.] Insect(s).

ento'mogenous *a.* (esp. of a fungus) living as a parasite in or on an insect M19. **entomo'pathogen** *n.* an organism or other agent that causes disease in insects L20. **entomopatho'genic** *a.* causing disease in insects L20. **ento'mophagous** *a.* that eats insects M19. **ento'mophagy** *n.* the state of being entomophagous; the practice of eating insects: M20. **ento'mophilous** *a.* (of plants) fertilized by the agency of insects L19. **ento'mostracan** *a.* & *n.* (*Zool.*) (designating) any lower crustacean, i.e. one other than a malacostracan M19.

entomology /ɛntəˈmɒlədʒi/ *n.* M18. [Fr. *entomologie* or mod.L *entomologia*, f. as ENTOMO-, -LOGY.] The branch of zoology that deals with insects.

entomo'logic *a.* M20. **entomo'logical** *a.* E19. **entomo'logically** *adv.* M20. **entomologist** *n.* L18. **entomologize** *v.i.* practise entomology; collect or study insects: E19.

entone *v.* see INTONE *v.*

entoproctan /ɛntə(ʊ)ˈprɒkt(ə)n/ *n.* & *a.* E20. [f. mod.L *Entoprocta* (see below), f. as ENTO- + Gk *prōktos* anus (as having the anus within the lophophoral ring): see -AN.] *Zool.* **A** *n.* A member of the phylum Entoprocta of acoelomate invertebrates. Cf. BRYOZOAN, ECTOPROCTAN. E20. **B** *adj.* Of, belonging to, or characteristic of Entoprocta. E20.

'entoproct *a.* & *n.* = ENTOPROCTAN M20. **entoproctous** *a.* = ENTOPROCTAN *a.* L19.

entoptic /ɪnˈtɒptɪk, ɛn-/ *a.* L19. [f. ENTO- + OPTIC *a.*] Of a visual phenomenon: originating inside the eye.

entoptically *adv.* M20.

entourage /ˈɒntʊrɑːʒ, ɒntʊ(ə)ˈrɑːʒ/ *n.* M19. [Fr., f. *entourer* surround, f. *entour* surroundings, use as n. of adv. = 'round about': see -AGE.] A group of people in attendance on or accompanying someone important. Also, surroundings, environment.

en tout cas /ɑ̃ tu kɑ/ *n.* & *a. phr.* L19. [Fr. = in any case or emergency.] **A** *n. phr.* A parasol which also serves as an umbrella. L19. **B** *a.* & *n. phr.* (***En-Tout-Cas.***) (Proprietary name designating) a hard tennis-court. M20.

entr'acte /ˈɒntrakt, *foreign* ɑ̃trakt (*pl. same*)/ *n.* M19. [Obs. Fr. (now *entracte*), f. *entre* between + *acte* act.] The interval between two acts of a play; a performance or entertainment which takes place during an interval.

entrail /ˈɛntreɪl/ *n.*[1] Also †**in-**. Usu. in *pl.* ME. [(O)Fr. *entraille(s)* (now only pl.) f. med.L *intralia* alt. of L *interanea* use as n. of neut. pl. of *interaneus* internal, f. *inter:* see INTERIOR.] **I** *sing.* †**1** *collect.* The intestines; the body's internal parts. ME–M17. **2** An internal organ, *esp.* an intestine. Now *rare.* LME.

II In *pl.* **3** The internal organs of a man or other animal; *spec.* the bowels, the intestines. ME. †**4** The seat of the emotions; the heart, the soul. LME–L18. **5** *fig.* The innermost parts (*of* something). LME.

3 A. C. CLARKE She was covered in blood .. hacking away at the entrails of a ten foot tiger shark. 5 E. TEMPLETON He spent all his time probing into the entrails of their engines.

†**entrail** *v.* & *n.*[2] M16. [OFr. *entreillier*, f. as EN-[1] + *treille* trellis-work.] **A** *v.t.* Entwine; interlace. M16–M18. **B** *n.* A coil. *rare* (Spenser). Only in L16.

entrain /ɑ̃trɛ̃/ *n.* M19. [Fr.] Enthusiasm, animation.

entrain /ɪnˈtreɪn, ɛn-/ *v.*[1]*t.* M16. [(O)Fr. *entraîner*, f. as EN-[1] + *traîner* drag: see TRAIN *v.*] **1** Draw away with or after oneself; *fig.* bring on as a consequence. Now *rare.* M16. **2** (Of a current or fluid) incorporate and sweep along in its flow; incorporate (air) in concrete. L19. **3** *Biol.* **a** *v.t.* Of a rhythm or rhythmically varying thing: cause (another) gradually to fall into synchronism with it. L20. **b** *v.i.* Fall into synchronism in such circumstances. (Foll. by *to*.) L20.

1 HENRY MILLER I entrained only my own ruin, my own bankruptcy. 2 *Nature* As the melt water rises up the side of an iceberg, it entrains .. warmer, saltier water from the environment. 3b *Scientific American* All sighted birds will entrain to the light from a single electroluminescent panel.

entrainment *n.*[1] the action or process of entraining or becoming entrained L19.

entrain /ɪnˈtreɪn, ɛn-/ *v.*[2] L19. [f. EN-[1] + TRAIN *n.*[1]] **1** *v.t.* Put (esp. troops) on a train. L19. **2** *v.i.* Go on board a train. L19.

2 H. NICOLSON We then go to the station and entrain for Detroit.

entrainment *n.*[2] (*rare*) the action or fact of entraining L19.

en train /ɑ̃ trɛ̃/ *adv. phr.* L18. [Fr.] Afoot, under way; in or into the swing of something; occupied (*with*).

entrammel /ɪnˈtram(ə)l, ɛn-/ *v.t.* Infl. **-ll-**, ***-l-**. L16. [f. EN-[1] + TRAMMEL.] †**1** Bind or plait (the hair). L16–E17. **2** Fetter, hamper. E17.

entrance /ˈɛntr(ə)ns/ *n.* L15. [OFr., f. *entrer* ENTER *v.*: see -ANCE.] **1** Power, right, or opportunity of entering; admission. L15. **b** More fully *entrance fee.* A charge made for being allowed to enter or join. M17. **2** The action of coming or going in; *Mus.* = ENTRY 1C. E16. **b** The action of entering into an office, duty, etc. M16. **c** An act of coming on stage by an actor or actress. L16. †**3** The beginning (of a period of time etc.); the first part (of a book etc.). M16–M18. **4** A means by which something is entered; a door, a gate, a passage, etc.; the mouth of a river; a point of entering something. M16. †**5** The action of entering or writing up in a record; something so entered. L16–M19. **6** The forward part of a ship's hull below the waterline. L18.

1 J. GALSWORTHY One paid a shilling for entrance and another for the programme. C. S. FORESTER A door .. which gave entrance to a smaller room. 2 A. RADCLIFFE La Motte was interrupted by the entrance of the ruffian. S. SPENDER The entrance of the whole orchestra at the end of a fugal introduction. 4 G. M. TREVELYAN Gladstone .. made competitive examination the normal entrance to the Civil Service. J. WEIDMAN I walked in through the Broadway entrance .. then out the Thirty-Eighth Street side.

Phrases: **Great Entrance** in Orthodox Churches, the procession in which bread and wine are brought to the altar during the Liturgy. **Lesser** or **Little Entrance** in Orthodox Churches, the ceremony in which the book of the Gospels is laid on the altar during the Liturgy.

Comb.: *entrance fee*: see sense 1b above; **entrance form**: filled in by someone applying to be admitted to an organization, esp. a college or school; **entrance wound**: made by a bullet etc. where it enters the body.

entrance /ɪnˈtrɑːns, ɛn-/ *v.t.* Also †**in-**. L16. [f. EN-[1], IN-[2] + TRANCE *n.*] **1** Affect with delight or wonder and seemingly put into a trance; captivate, delight. Usu. in *pass.* L16. **b** Carry away in or as in a trance. L16. **2** Put into a trance. E17.

1 A. P. HERBERT Engrossed, entranced, he forgot about time, and about humanity. 2 ADDISON The Nine Days' Astonishment, in which the Angels lay entranced.

entrancement *n.* the action of entrancing; the state of being entranced: M17. **entrancing** *ppl a.* captivating, delightful M19. **entrancingly** *adv.* M19.

entrant /ˈɛntr(ə)nt/ *n.* & *a.* E17. [Fr., pres. pple of *entrer* ENTER *v.*: see -ANT[1]. Cf. earlier INTRANT.] **A** *n.* **1** A person who takes legal possession of land etc. Long *rare.* E17. **2** A person who enters a profession, becomes a member of an organization, etc. E19. **3** A person who comes or goes into a room, a place, etc. M19. **4** A competitor; a candidate in an examination. M19.

4 *Washington Post* Nearly two-thirds of the .. entrants will be competing in their first .. race.

B *adj.* That enters. Long *rare* or *obs.* M17.

entrap /ɪnˈtrap, ɛn-/ *v.t.* Also †**in-**. Infl. **-pp-**. M16. [OFr. *entrap(p)er*, f. as EN-[1] + *trappe* TRAP *n.*[1]] **1** Catch in or as in a trap; bring unawares into difficulty or danger. M16. **b** Beguile *into*; *spec.* induce to commit a crime in order to secure a prosecution. M19. **2** Involve in verbal contradiction. E17.

1 *Scientific American* The filter . . would selectively entrap any magnetic particles. b *Times* He has acted as an agent provocateur to entrap people and implicate them in crimes which otherwise would not have been committed.

entrapment *n.* (*a*) the action or fact of entrapping; the condition of being entrapped; (*b*) a means of entrapping, a trap: L16. **entrapper** *n.* a person who entraps someone or something L16.

en travesti *adv. phr.* see TRAVESTY *n.* 2.

entre- *comb. form* var. of ENTER-[1].

entreasure /ɪnˈtrɛʒə, ɛn-/ *v.t.* LME. [f. EN-[1] + TREASURE *v.*] Store up (as) in a treasury.

entreat /ɪnˈtriːt, ɛn-/ *v.* Also (now *rare*) **in-** /ɪn-/. LME. [OFr. *entraitier*, f. as EN-[1] + *traitier* TREAT *v.*] **1** *v.t.* Treat (a person etc.) in a specified way. *arch.* LME. †**2** *v.i.* Enter into negotiations (*with* a person; *of*, *for* a thing). LME–E17. †**3** *v.i.* Of a speaker, writer etc.: treat of or deal with a subject. (Foll. by *of*, *upon*.) LME–L17. **b** *v.t.* Deal with, handle, (a subject or question). E16–L17. **c** *v.t.* Occupy oneself with (a pastime etc.); pass (time). *rare*. Only in L16. †**4** *v.i.* Plead *for* (a person, a favour, etc.). LME–E19. †**5** *v.t.* Persuade by pleading or supplication; (of circumstances etc.) induce *to do*. LME–M17. **6** *v.t.* Request earnestly; beseech, implore, (a person). E16. **7** *v.t.* Ask earnestly for (a thing). (Foll. by *of* a person.) L16.

1 T. FULLER The pope ill entreated and imprisoned his messengers. 6 A. J. CRONIN I entreat you to give us shelter for the night. V. S. REID For the sake of your family, go away, I entreat you. 7 J. MILLER To entreat of the gods what they will not give.

†**entreatable** *a.* able to be handled; manageable; placable: LME–E18. †**entreatance** *n.* (*a*) treatment (of a person); (*b*) intercession: M16–E17. †**entreater** *n.* a negotiator, a mediator; a petitioner, a suitor: E16–L17. †**entreatful** *a.* (*rare*, Spenser) full of entreaty, supplicating: only in L16. **entreatingly** *adv.* in an entreating way, pleadingly M19. †**entreative** *a.* of the nature of or characterized by entreaty E17–M18.

entreatment /ɪnˈtriːtm(ə)nt, ɛn-/ *n. arch.* M16. [f. prec. + -MENT.] †**1** Discussion, negotiation; a conversation. M16–E17. **2** Treatment (of a person). E19.

entreaty /ɪnˈtriːti, ɛn-/ *n.* Also †**in-**. LME. [f. as prec. after TREATY.] †**1a** Treatment of a person; handling; management (of animals). LME–L17. **b** Treatment of a subject; discussion, investigation. LME–E17. †**2** Negotiation. LME–E17. **3** An earnest request, a supplication. L16.

3 E. B. BROWNING Refusing to give an ear to my husband's entreaties about seeing a physician.

entrechat /ɑ̃trəʃa (*pl. same*), ˈɑːntrəʃɑː/ *n.* L18. [Fr. f. It. (*capriola*) *intrecciata* complicated (caper).] A leap in which a ballet dancer strikes the heels together or crosses the feet a number of times while in the air.

entrecôte /ˈɒntrəkəʊt, *foreign* ɑ̃trəkoːt (*pl. same*)/ *n.* M19. [Fr., lit. = between rib.] More fully *entrecôte steak*. A boned steak cut off the sirloin.

entredeux /ɑ̃trədø/ *n.* Pl. pronounced same. M19. [Fr., lit. = between two.] An insertion of lace, linen, etc., in sewing.

†**entredit** *n.* see INTERDICT *n.*

†**entredite** *n.*, *v.* see INTERDICT *n.*, *v.*

entrée /ˈɒntreɪ, *foreign* ɑ̃tre (*pl. same*)/ *n.* E18. [Fr.: see ENTRY.] **1** *Mus.* **a** A piece of instrumental music, usu. resembling a march, forming the first part of a suite or divertissement, or introducing a character etc. on stage. E18. **b** A group of dances on one theme in 17th- and 18th-cent. French ballet; an act of a 17th- or 18th-cent. French opera-ballet. L18. **2** The action or manner of entering. M18. **b** The entrance of the performers in a play, circus, or other large show. E19. **3** The privilege or right of entrance; admission, esp. to a royal court. M18. **4** A dish served between the fish course and the main meat course; *N. Amer.* the main dish of a meal. M18.

2 M. EDGEWORTH Nothing could be more awkward than our entrée. 3 Q. BELL She certainly had the entrée to a feminine aristocratic circle. CLIVE JAMES For 50 cents I bought the entrée into the hard-core section of a big bookshop.

Phrases: ***entrée en matière*** /ɑ̃ matjɛːr/ [Fr., lit. = entry into the matter] an opening remark or statement; the beginning of a literary work.

†**entremess** *n.* Also **inter-**. ME–M18. [OFr. *entremes* (mod. *entremets*), f. *entre* between + *mes* (mod. *mets*) MESS *n.*] Something served between the courses of a banquet.

entremet /ɑ̃trəmɛ/ *n.* Pl. pronounced same, /-z/. L15. [Fr. *entremets*: see prec.] **1** In *pl.* Side dishes. L15. **2** *sing.* & in *pl.* (treated as *sing.* or *pl.*). A sweet dish; a dessert; *rare* a side dish. M18.

entrench /ɪnˈtrɛn(t)ʃ, ɛn-/ *v.* Also **in-** /ɪn-/. M16. [f. EN-[1], IN-[2] + TRENCH *n.*, *v.*] **1** *v.t.* Place within a trench; surround with a trench or trenches as fortification; establish firmly in a defensible position. M16. **2** *v.t. fig.* Fortify as if in a trench; *spec.* (*Polit.*) safeguard by constitutional provision; provide for the legal or political perpetuation of. L16. **3** *v.i.* & *refl.* Establish a well-defended position. L16. †**4** *v.t.* Make (a wound) by cutting. *rare*. L16–E17. **5** *v.i.* Encroach, trespass, (*upon*); trench. M17.

1 WELLINGTON A camp which they had strongly entrenched. 2 *Daily Telegraph* What was proposed amounted to entrenching the political supremacy of the native Melanesian people at the expense of the Indians. 3 W. S. CHURCHILL He held all the Channel ports, and had entrenched himself from Namur through Antwerp to the sea. 5 J. WESLEY Let not the gentlewoman entrench upon the Christian.

entrenched /ɪnˈtrɛn(t)ʃt, ɛn-/ *ppl a.* Also **in-** /ɪn-/. L16. [f. prec. + -ED[1].] **1** Surrounded with or as with a trench; fortified; firmly established. L16. **b** *Polit.* Of constitutional legislation, esp. a clause or provision: unable to be repealed except under more than usually stringent conditions. M20. **2** Dug out like a trench. L16.

1 BURKE Their . . stations . . were strong intrenched camps. L. HUDSON Some assaults on previously entrenched beliefs have been so violent.

entrenchment /ɪnˈtrɛn(t)ʃm(ə)nt, ɛn-/ *n.* Also **in-** /ɪn-/. L16. [f. as prec. + -MENT.] **1** A position fortified by trenches; a fortification. L16. **2** Now chiefly *Polit.* The action or an instance of entrenching. M17.

entre nous /ɑ̃trə nu/ *adv. phr.* L17. [Fr.] Between ourselves; in private.

entrepôt /ˈɒntrəpəʊ, *foreign* ɑ̃trəpo (*pl. same*)/ *n.* E18. [Fr. (earlier †*entrepost*, †*-pos*), f. *entreposer* store, f. *entre* among + *poser* to place: see INTER-, POSE *v.*[1]] **1** A storehouse for the temporary deposit of goods, provisions, etc.; *rare* temporary deposit. E18. **2** A commercial centre to which goods are brought for import and export, and for collection and distribution. M18.

2 *attrib.*: *Times* Bahrain island was destined to become the centre of entrepôt trade for the Persian Gulf.

entrepreneur /ˌɒntrəprəˈnəː/ *n.* E19. [Fr., f. *entreprendre* undertake + *-eur* -OR.] **1a** A director of a musical institution. E19. **b** A person who organizes entertainments, esp. musical performances. M19. **2** A person who undertakes or controls a business or enterprise and bears the risk of profit or loss; a contractor who acts as an intermediary. M19.

entrepreneurial /-ˈn(j)əː-/ *a.* of or pertaining to entrepreneurs or their activities; having the function or character of an entrepreneur: E20. **entrepreneurialism** /-ˈn(j)əː-/ *n.* = ENTREPRENEURSHIP M20. **entrepreneurially** /-ˈn(j)əː-/ *adv.* M20. **entrepreneurism** *n.* = ENTREPRENEURSHIP L20. **entrepreneurship** *n.* entrepreneurial activity or skills M20.

entresol /ˈɒntrəsɒl, *foreign* ɑ̃trəsɔl (*pl. same*)/ *n.* Also †**entersole**, **intersole**. E18. [Fr. f. Sp. *entresuelo*, f. *entre* between + *suelo* storey.] A low storey between the ground floor and the first floor of a building; a mezzanine storey.

entrism *n.* var. of ENTRYISM.

entropion /ɪnˈtrəʊpɪən, ɛn-/ *n.* L19. [f. Gk EN-[2] after *ectropion*.] Introversion of the eyelid.

entropy /ˈɛntrəpi/ *n.* M19. [f. Gk EN-[2] + *tropē* transformation: see -Y[3].] **1** *Physics.* A thermodynamic quantity that represents numerically the extent to which a system's thermal energy is unavailable for conversion into mechanical work (the change of entropy of a system when it undergoes a reversible process is equal to the amount of heat it absorbs or emits divided by the absolute temperature of the system). Also (equivalently), the degree of disorder of a system, measured in terms of the natural logarithm of the probability of occurrence of its particular arrangement of particles. M19. **2** A logarithmic measure of the average information rate of a message or language. M20.

1 *fig.*: *Observer* A busy mess-making inspector who spreads entropy wherever his inquiring hooter intrudes.

enˈtropic *a.* of or pertaining to entropy; characterized by or resulting from entropy: M20. **enˈtropically** *adv.* as regards entropy; in an entropic manner: L20.

†**entrude** *v.* see INTRUDE.

entrust /ɪnˈtrʌst, ɛn-/ *v.t.* Also **in-** /ɪn-/. E17. [f. EN-[1], IN-[2] + TRUST *n.*] **1** Invest with a trust; give (a person etc.) the responsibility for a task, a valuable object, etc. Foll. by *with*; (arch.) *in*, *to do*; †*for*, formerly also *absol.* E17. **2** Commit the safety of (a thing or person) or the execution of (a task) *to* a person, a thing, etc. E17.

1 L. BRUCE I was entrusted with the unromantic job of weeding. G. GREENE He was going to entrust him with what amounted to his life. 2 N. MOSLEY You should not entrust the administration of details to subordinates. A. BROOKNER Sofka had paid a . . visit to Mr Cariani before entrusting the girls to his . . tuition.

entrustment *n.* (*a*) the action of entrusting; the fact of being entrusted; †(*b*) a position of trust; a duty with which one is entrusted: M17.

entry /ˈɛntri/ *n.* ME. [(O)Fr. *entrée*, f. Proto-Romance use as n. of L *intrata* fem. pa. pple of *intrare* ENTER *v.*: see -Y[5].] **1** = ENTRANCE *n.* 2, 2c. ME. **b** A ceremonial entrance (by a person of rank). M16. **c** The start or resumption of a performer's part in a musical composition. L19. **d** *Bridge.* (A card providing) an opportunity to transfer the lead to one's partner or one's dummy. L19. **2** = ENTRANCE *n.* 1. ME. †**3** = ENTRANCE *n.* 3. ME–E20. **4** = ENTRANCE *n.* 4. ME. **b** A short passage between houses. Formerly also, an approach to a house. LME. **5** *Law.* The actual taking possession of land etc. by entering or setting foot on it. LME. **6** = ENTRANCE *n.* 2b. Also, the action of becoming a member of an organization. LME. †**7** A place used for lodgings or business. LME–M19. **8** Something entered in a register, diary, account-book, etc.; an item in an index; a word, phrase, etc., defined in a dictionary, (such a word etc. and) the accompanying portion of text. LME. **b** A record in a custom-house of goods imported and exported. LME. **c** A thing which has been entered for, or a person who has entered, a contest, race, etc.; the entrants for a contest, race, etc., collectively. L19. †**9** A dance between the parts of an entertainment; a musical entrée. M17–E18. **10** More fully *young entry*: the hounds that are receiving their initial training in any one season; a single such hound. Orig. (now *rare*), the initial training of hounds. M19.

1 **make entry** come or go in; come on stage. b L. P. HARTLEY The landlord . . held the door open, so that Irma seemed to make a little entry. 2 O. MANNING The manager warned him that, caught again, he would be forbidden entry . . to the hotel. 4 SHAKES. *Macb.* I hear a knocking At the south entry. *port of entry*: see PORT *n.*[1], PORT *n.*[3] 5b. 6 H. WILSON Rockingham's entry into office . . marked a turning-point. 8 V. WOOLF On a shelf were her diaries. . . And I made her read an entry. J. BARZUN A truly modern dictionary would add an entry under 'human': 'the opposite of admirable'. *Acorn User* To alter an entry, type in a new one. *double entry*: see DOUBLE *a.* & *adv.* *single entry*: see SINGLE *a.* c B. PYM I have recently been judging entries for the Southern Arts Association Prize. *new entry*: see NEW *a.*

For other words beginning with *en-* see the entry for **en-**[1]

Comb.: **entry form** an application form for a competition; **entryman** *US* a person who enters upon public land with the intention of settling; **entry permit**: giving authorization for a foreigner to enter a country; **Entryphone** (proprietary name for) a telephonic link with a remote unlocking facility by which a caller can summon attention, identify himself or herself to a person inside a building or room, and be admitted; **entryway** *US* a way in to somewhere or something, an entrance.

entryism /ˈɛntrɪɪz(ə)m/ *n.* Also **entrism** /ˈɛntrɪz(ə)m/. M20. [f. ENTRY + -ISM.] The policy or practice of joining an organization, esp. a political one, with the intention of subverting its aims and activities.

entryist *n.* & *a.* L20.

Entscheidungsproblem /ɛntˈʃaɪdʊŋsproˌbleːm, ɛntˈʃʌɪdʊŋs,prɒbləm/ *n.* M20. [G, f. *Entscheidung* decision.] *Math.* & *Logic.* = *decision problem* s.v. DECISION 3.

†**entune** *v.t.* LME. [Alt. of INTONE *v.*: cf. TUNE *n.*] 1 = TUNE *v.* 2a. LME–E17. 2 = TUNE *v.* 3a. L15–M16.

entwine /ɪnˈtwʌɪn, ɛn-/ *v.* Also †**in-**. L16. [f. EN-[1], IN-[2] + TWINE *v.*[1]] 1a *v.t.* & *i.* Twine or twist together; interweave. L16. b *v.t.* Make by twining. L17. 2 *v.t.* Clasp, enfold, embrace. M17. 3 *v.t.* Encircle (an object) *with* another; wind (an object) *around* or *about* another. L18.

1a SOUTHEY The Old Man Entwines the strong palm-fibres. b W. DE LA MARE The simplest bird entwines a nest. 2 TENNYSON True wife, Round my true heart thine arms entwine. 3 C. BOUTELL A vine-branch entwined about a rod.

entwinement *n.* the action of entwining; the state of being entwined: M17.

entwist /ɪnˈtwɪst, ɛn-/ *v.t. arch.* Also **in-** /ɪn-/. L16. [f. EN-[1], IN-[2] + TWIST *v.*] Clasp with or form into a twist; twist in *with*.

enubilate /ɪˈnjuːbɪleɪt/ *v.t. rare.* M18. [L *enubilat-* pa. ppl stem of *enubilare*, f. *e-* E- + *nubilus* cloudy, f. *nubes* a cloud: see -ATE[3].] Make clear.

enucleate /ɪˈnjuːklɪət/ *a.* L19. [L *enucleatus*, f. as next: see -ATE[2].] *Biol.* Deprived of its nucleus.

enucleate /ɪˈnjuːklɪeɪt/ *v.t.* M16. [L *enucleat-* pa. ppl stem of *enucleare* extract the kernel from, make clear, f. *e-* E-, NUCLEUS: see -ATE[3].] 1 Clarify, explain. *arch.* M16. 2 *Biol.* Deprive (esp. a cell) of its nucleus. L16. 3 *Surg.* Remove (a tumour) from its capsule or (an eye) from its socket without rupturing it. M19.

enucleation /ɪˌnjuːklɪˈeɪʃ(ə)n/ *n.* M17. [Fr. *énucléation* or med.L *enucleatio(n-)*, f. as prec.: see -ATION.] The action or an instance of enucleating.

enumerate /ɪˈnjuːməreɪt/ *v.t.* Pa. pple **-ated**, †**-ate.** E17. [L *enumerat-* pa. ppl stem of *enumerare*, f. *e-* E- + *numerus* number: see -ATE[3].] Specify as in a list, mention (a number of things) one by one; ascertain the number of.

enumeraˈbility *n.* the fact or quality of being enumerable M20. **enumerable** *a.* = DENUMERABLE L19. **enumerative** *a.* that enumerates; concerned with enumeration: M17. **enumeratively** *adv.* E20. **enumerator** *n.* a person who or thing which enumerates; *spec.* a person employed in taking a census: M19.

enumeration /ɪˌnjuːməˈreɪʃ(ə)n/ *n.* M16. [Fr. *énumeration* or L *enumeratio(n-)*, f. as prec.: see -ATION.] 1 The action of enumerating; *spec.* the process of recording names and addresses etc. for a census. M16. 2 A list, a catalogue. E18.

enunciate /ɪˈnʌnsɪeɪt/ *v.* E17. [L *enuntiat-* pa. ppl stem of *enuntiare*, f. *e-* E- + *nuntiare* ANNOUNCE.] 1 *v.t.* Express (an idea, theory, proposition, etc.) in definite terms. E17. 2 *v.t.* & *i.* Pronounce, articulate, (a spoken word etc.). M18. 3 State publicly, proclaim. M19.

1 F. L. WRIGHT Although Laotse . . first enunciated the philosophy, it probably preceded him. 2 W. DE LA MARE Meticulously enunciating each syllable of each word. 3 L. MACNEICE I listened to the voice of London enunciating facts for the masses.

enunciable *a.* M17. **enunciator** *n.* E19.

enunciation /ɪˌnʌnsɪˈeɪʃ(ə)n/ *n.* M16. [(O)Fr. *énonciation* or L *enuntiatio(n-)*, f. as prec.: see -ATION.] 1 The action or manner of enunciating. M16. †2 A proposition, a statement. L16–M18. 3 The form of words in which a proposition is stated. L18.

enunciative /ɪˈnʌnsɪətɪv/ *a.* M16. [L *enunciativus*, f. *enuntiare*: see ENUNCIATE, -IVE.] 1 That serves to enunciate; declaratory (*of*). M16. 2 Pertaining to vocal utterance. M19.

enure *v.* var. of INURE *v.*[1]

enuresis /ɛnjʊəˈriːsɪs/ *n.* E19. [mod.L, f. Gk *enourein* urinate in.] Involuntary urination, *esp.* bedwetting.

enuretic /-ˈrɛt-/ *a.* & *n.* (a person) affected with enuresis M20.

enurn *v.* var. of INURN.

enurny /ɪˈnəːni, ɛ-/ *a.* Now *rare.* M16. [AN *eno(u)rné* f. OFr. *ao(u)rné* pa. pple of *ao(u)rner*: see ADORN *v.*] *Her.* Of a bordure: charged or decorated with animals.

envassal /ɪnˈvas(ə)l, ɛn-/ *v.t.* Long *rare.* Infl. **-ll-**, ***-l-**. E17. [f. EN-[1] + VASSAL *n.*] Make a vassal of.

†**enveigh** *v.* var. of INVEIGH.

†**enveigle** *v.* var. of INVEIGLE.

enveil /ɪnˈveɪl, ɛn-/ *v.t.* Also †**in-**. M16. [f. EN-[1], IN-[2] + VEIL *n.*] Cover (as) with a veil; place a veil on.

envein *v.* see INVEIN.

envelop /ɪnˈvɛləp, ɛn-/ *v.t.* Also (now *rare*) **-ope**, †**in-**. LME. [OFr. *envoluper*, *-oper* (mod. *envelopper*), f. as EN-[1] + base repr. also by DEVELOP.] 1 Wrap up (as) in an outer covering or garment. LME. 2 Serve as a wrapping for; enclose, contain. L16. 3 Surround and touch on all sides, esp. so as to conceal; cause to be so surrounded; *fig.* shroud, make obscure; affect deeply or overwhelmingly. (Foll. by *in*.) L16. †4 Cover on the inside, line. *rare* (Spenser). Only in L16. 5 Of troops: (partly) surround. L17.

1 M. DE LA ROCHE Wright . . brought his great coon coat, in which he enveloped himself on the platform. 2 DAY LEWIS The waters which envelop an embryo in the womb. 3 A. J. CRONIN The sun . . enveloped them in a bath of light. E. WAUGH A fog came up quite suddenly . . , enveloping men and quarry. SLOAN WILSON She had seen . . her father stagger out carrying her mother, both their bodies enveloped in flames. J. HERRIOT A sudden misery enveloped me.

enveloping *n.* (*a*) the action of the vb; (*b*) a wrapping; wrapping material: L17. **envelopment** *n.* (*a*) the action of enveloping something; the state of being enveloped; (*b*) a thing that envelops something: M18.

envelope /ˈɛnvələʊp, ˈɒn-/ *n.* & *v.* Also (earlier) †**em-**. M16. [Fr. *enveloppe*, f. *envelopper*: see prec.] A *n.* 1 A wrapper, a covering; an enveloping layer or structure. M16. 2 *spec.* The covering of a letter, now a piece of paper folded to form a packet, usu. with a flap that can be sealed, for completely enclosing a document etc. E18. 3 *Fortif.* An earthwork in the form of a parapet or small rampart. E18. 4a *Math.* A curve or surface that is tangential to each of a family of curves or surfaces. L19. b A curve passing through the maxima or minima of a sound wave or other oscillatory signal. E20. 5 The flexible gas container that gives a balloon or airship buoyancy. E20. 6 The sealed rigid outer covering of a vacuum tube. M20.

1 H. WILLIAMSON Goodbye, brothers: your mortal envelopes lie here in Mother Earth. *Guns Review* A 225 grain round nosed bullet with a cupro nickel envelope. *floral envelope*: see FLORAL *a.* 2 *stamped addressed envelope*: see STAMP *v.* 4b *International Musician* Acoustic instruments change their sound quality according to the way they're played, . . in terms of brilliance, envelope, pitch, . . and so on.

B *v.t.* Put (a letter) in an envelope. *colloq.* M19.

envenom /ɪnˈvɛnəm, ɛn-/ *v.t.* Also †**in-**. ME. [(O)Fr. *envenimer*, f. as EN-[1] + *venim* VENOM.] †1 Poison (a person or animal) by contact, bite, etc. ME–E18. 2 Put venom on or into (a weapon etc.); taint (the air etc.) with poison; make poisonous. ME. 3 Infuse venom or bitterness into (actions, feelings, words, etc.), embitter; corrupt morally, taint. ME.

2 *Nature* Several surgeon fishes appear to have envenomed spines. 3 A. P. HERBERT An envenomed old lady . . muttered maledictions on the Conservative Government.

en ventre sa mère /ɑ̃ vɑ̃ːtr sa mɛːr/ *adv. phr.* Also ***mere***. L18. [Fr. = in its mother's womb.] *Law.* In the womb.

†**envermeil** *v.t. rare.* ME–E19. [OFr. *envermeilli(e)r*, f. as EN-[1], VERMEIL *a.* & *n.*] Tinge as with vermilion; make red.

enviable /ˈɛnvɪəb(ə)l/ *a.* E17. [f. ENVY *v.*[1] + -ABLE.] That is to be envied; such as to arouse envy.

I. MURDOCH To sleep with a clear conscience every night is indeed enviable.

enviaˈbility *n.* E20. **enviableness** *n.* (*rare*) M19. **enviably** *adv.* E19.

envier /ˈɛnvɪə/ *n.* LME. [f. ENVY *v.*[1] + -ER[1].] A person who envies.

†**envigour** *v.* see INVIGOUR.

envious /ˈɛnvɪəs/ *a.* ME. [AN = OFr. *envieus* (mod. *-eux*), f. *envie* ENVY *n.* after L *invidiosus* INVIDIOUS: see -OUS.] I 1 Full of envy; showing or feeling envy (*of*). ME. †2 Malicious, spiteful. ME–E18. †3 Grudging; parsimonious. L16–M17. †4 Enviable. L16–M17.

1 G. GISSING Cecily, whose powers of conversation and charms of manner made her bitterly envious. C. PETERS He was contemptuous of Bulwer's novels, but envious of their success.

II [Infl. by ENVY *v.*[2]] †5 Emulous; full of emulation. ME–E19.

enviously *adv.* LME. **enviousness** *n.* LME.

environ /ɪnˈvʌɪrən, ɛn-/ *v.t.* Also †**in-**. ME. [OFr. *environer* (mod. *-onner*), f. *environ* surroundings, around, f. as EN-[1] + *viron* circuit, f. *virer* VEER *v.*[2]] 1 Form a ring round, surround, encircle; beset, beleaguer, (*with*). ME. 2 Envelop, enclose. Formerly also, wrap up; conceal. LME. †3 Go round in a circle, make a circuit round. LME–M17.

1 T. TRAHERNE On every side we are environed with enemies. *Daedalus* The American lives in a society in which his successful manipulation of the environing conditions . . is crucial to his sense of himself. 2 J. TYNDALL We were environed with an atmosphere of perfect purity.

environing *n.* (*a*) the action of the vb; (*b*) a thing or things that environ; environment, surroundings; †(*c*) a circumference: LME.

environment /ɪnˈvʌɪrənm(ə)nt, ɛn-/ *n.* E17. [f. ENVIRON *v.* + -MENT.] 1 The action of environing; the state of being environed. *rare.* E17. 2 The set of circumstances or conditions, esp. physical conditions, in which a person or community lives, works, develops, etc., or a thing exists or operates; the external conditions affecting the life of a plant or animal. Also, physical conditions viewed in relation to the possibility of life. E19. 3 The region surrounding a place. M19. 4 Context, setting, *spec.* (*Phonet.*) that of a speech sound. M19. 5 A large artistic creation intended to be experienced with several senses while one is surrounded by it. M20. 6 *Computing.* The structure and conditions within which a computer can operate; the combination of hardware, software, interfaces, etc., which enables a user to operate a system. M20.

2 A. KOESTLER Processes by which heredity and environment shape a man's character. J. D. WATSON I wished to remain in the stimulating environment of Copenhagen. ANTHONY HUXLEY Such alien environments as that of Jupiter. *Times* We offer highly competitive salaries, . . an environment receptive to new ideas. **the environment** the totality of the physical conditions in which a human society lives. 3 J. S. BLACKIE The environment of this loch put me in mind of Grasmere.

environmental /ɪn,vʌɪrənˈmɛnt(ə)l, ɛn-/ *a.* L19. [f. prec. + -AL[1].] 1 Of or pertaining to the (physical) environment. L19. 2 Concerned with the conservation of the environment; not harmful to the environment. L20.

environmentally *adv.* by means of the, or an, environment; as regards (the conservation of) the environment (*environmentally sensitive area*, an area designated as containing landscapes or wildlife threatened by unrestricted development or industrial use): L19.

environmentalist /ɪn,vʌɪrənˈmɛnt(ə)lɪst, ɛn-/ *n.* & *a.* E20. [f. prec. + -IST.] A *n.* 1 A person who holds or advocates the view that environment, esp. as opp. to heredity, has a dominant influence on the development of an

For other words beginning with *en-* see the entry for **en-**[1]

individual or society. E20. 2 A person who is concerned about or seeks to protect the environment, esp. from pollution. L20. B *adj.* Of or pertaining to environmentalism or environmentalists. M20.

environmentalism *n.* E20. **en,vironmenta'listic** *a.* M20.

environs /ɪn'vʌɪrənz, ɛn-, 'ɛnvɪrənz/ *n.pl.* M17. [Fr., pl. of *environ*: see ENVIRON *v.*] The district surrounding a place, esp. an urban area. (Foll. by *of*.)

envisage /ɪn'vɪzɪdʒ, ɛn-/ *v.t.* E19. [Fr. *envisager*, f. as EN-[1], VISAGE.] 1 Look straight at. Chiefly *fig.*, face up to (danger etc.). *arch.* E19. 2 Contemplate, regard, esp. in a particular way; imagine, esp. as a possibility or a future event; expect *that*. E19.

1 KEATS To envisage circumstance, all calm, That is the top of sovereignty. R. MACAULAY Two pairs of . . eyes envisaged that remote wilderness. 2 E. BOWEN Sickness not having been envisaged, there was no sickroom. W. GOLDING I drew in my breath . . as I envisaged the appearance I must have presented.

envisagement *n.* L19.

envision /ɛn'vɪʒ(ə)n/ *v.t.* E20. [f. EN-[1] + VISION *n.*] Foresee, envisage, visualize.

envoi /'ɛnvɔɪ/ *n.* Also (earlier) **-voy**. LME. [(O)Fr., f. *envoyer* send, f. phr. *en voie* on the way.] The concluding part of a literary work, *esp.* a short stanza concluding a ballade; *arch.* an author's concluding words, dedication, etc.

†envolve *v.* var. of INVOLVE.

envoy /'ɛnvɔɪ/ *n.*[1] M17. [Fr. *envoyé* use as n. of pa. pple of *envoyer*: see ENVOI.] 1 A representative sent by one monarch or government to another on diplomatic business; a diplomat; now *spec.* an envoy extraordinary. M17. 2 An agent, a messenger, a representative. L17.

1 **envoy extraordinary** †(*a*) a minister charged with a special or temporary mission; (*b*) a minister plenipotentiary, ranking below an ambassador and above a chargé d'affaires.

envoyship *n.* the position or function of an envoy M18.

envoy *n.*[2] see ENVOI.

envy /'ɛnvi/ *n.* ME. [(O)Fr. *envie* f. L *invidia*, f. *invidere* look maliciously upon, grudge, f. as IN-[2] + *videre* see.] †1 Hostility; malice; enmity. ME-E18. b Unpopularity, odium. L16-L17. 2a A feeling of resentful or discontented longing aroused by another person's better fortune, situation, etc. (Foll. by *of*, †*at* the person, *at*, *of* a thing.) ME. b The object or ground of envy. M19. †3 [Infl. by Fr.] Longing, desire; enthusiasm. LME-E17.

2a E. O'BRIEN I noticed with envy that her legs were delicately tanned. b *Times* We had . . a musical education system that was the envy of the world.

envyful *a.* (long *obs.* exc. *Sc.*) full of envy or malice M16.

envy /'ɛnvi/ *v.*[1] LME. [(O)Fr. *envier*, f. as prec.] 1 *v.t.* Feel envy of (a person); wish to have the good fortune, possessions, etc., of (another person). Also, regard (the better fortune etc.) of another with resentment or discontent; wish to have (another person's good fortune etc.). Also w. double obj. LME. †2 *v.i.* & *t.* Feel envious, grudging, or hostile; feel envious or resentful *that*. LME-L17. †3 Give reluctantly or refuse to give (a thing) *to* a person; begrudge; treat (a person) grudgingly; regard with dislike or disapproval. M16-L18.

1 G. GREENE Daintry also envied him his wife; she was so rich, so decorative. C. JACKSON His many friends . . envied his popularity. B. PYM She wished she had a dog . . and envied two young men with a small mongrel.

†envy *v.*[2]*t.* & *i.* LME-E17. [OFr. *envier* f. L *invitare* challenge: cf. VIE *v.*] Vie (with).

enwall /ɪn'wɔːl, ɛn-/ *v.t.* Also **in-** /ɪn-/. Now *rare.* LME. [f. EN-[1], IN-[2] + WALL *n.*[1]] Enclose within a wall; act as a wall to.

enweave *v.* var. of INWEAVE.

enwheel /ɪn'wiːl, ɛn-/ *v.t. obs.* exc. *poet.* E17. [f. EN-[1] + WHEEL *n.*] Encircle, surround.

enwiden /ɛn'wʌɪd(ə)n, ɪn-/ *v.t. rare.* L16. [f. EN-[1] + WIDEN.] Widen, expand.

enwind /ɪn'wʌɪnd, ɛn-/ *v.t.* Chiefly *poet.* Also **in-**. Infl. as WIND *v.*[1] L16. [f. EN-[1], IN-[2] + WIND *v.*[1]] Wind itself around, surround with windings; make into a coil.

enwomb /ɪn'wuːm, ɛn-/ *v.t. arch.* & *poet.* Also **†in-**. L16. [f. EN-[1], IN-[2] + WOMB *n.*] 1 Contain like a womb; bury *in* or shut up as in a womb. L16. 2 Make pregnant. Long *rare* or *obs.* L16. 3 Hold or place in a womb. Now *rare* or *obs.* E17.

enwrap /ɪn'rap, ɛn-/ *v.t. arch.* Also **in-** /ɪn-/. Infl. **-pp-**. LME. [f. EN-[1], IN-[2] + WRAP *v.*] 1 Wrap, envelop, enfold, (*in*, *with*). LME. †2 Implicate, entangle, (*in*); involve in a common fate *with* another. LME-E19. 3 Involve, entail. LME. 4 Engross or absorb in thought, sleep, etc. L16.

enwrapment *n.* (*rare*) (*a*) the action of enwrapping; the state of being enwrapped; (*b*) a wrapping, a covering: M18. **enwrapping** *n.* (*a*) the action of the vb; (*b*) a fold: M16.

enwreathe /ɪn'riːð, ɛn-/ *v.t.* Now chiefly *literary.* Also **in-** /ɪn-/. L15. [f. EN-[1], IN-[2] + WREATHE *v.*] Surround as with a wreath; encircle like a wreath.

enwrought *a.* var. of INWROUGHT.

Enzed /ɛn'zɛd/ *n. Austral.* & *NZ colloq.* E20. [Repr. pronunc. of *NZ* as abbrev. of *New Zealand*.] New Zealand; a New Zealander.

Enzedder *n.* a New Zealander M20.

enzootic /ɛnzəʊ'ɒtɪk/ *a.* & *n.* L19. [f. EN-[2] + Gk *zōion* animal + -IC.] (Designating) a disease of animals that is prevalent in a particular locality.

enzyme /'ɛnzʌɪm; *in sense 1 also* ɛn'ziːmi/ *n.* M19. [In sense 1 f. EN-[2] + Gk *zumē* leaven; in sense 2 f. G *Enzym*, f. mod.Gk *enzumos* leavened.] 1 The leavened bread used for the Eucharist in the Greek Orthodox Church. M19. 2 A protein produced by living cells and functioning as a catalyst in a specific biochemical reaction. L19.

enzy'matic *a.* E20. **enzy'matically** *adv.* M20. **en'zymic** *a.* L19. **en'zymically** *adv.* M20.

enzymology /ɛnzʌɪ'mɒlədʒi/ *n.* E20. [f. prec. + -OLOGY.] The branch of biochemistry that deals with enzymes.

en,zymo'logical *a.* M20. **enzymologist** *n.* M20.

eo- /'iːəʊ/ *comb. form.* [f. Gk *ēos* dawn: see -O-.] Earliest, oldest; initial.

eoan /iː'əʊən/ *a. poet.* E17. [f. L *eous* f. Gk *ēōios*, f. *ēōs* dawn: see -AN.] Of or pertaining to the dawn; eastern.

Eocene /'iːə(ʊ)siːn/ *a.* & *n.* M19. [f. EO- + Gk *kainos* new, recent.] *Geol.* A *adj.* Designating or pertaining to the second epoch of the Tertiary period or sub-era, following the Palaeocene and preceding the Oligocene, or (formerly) this together with the Palaeocene and Oligocene. M19. B *n.* *The* Eocene epoch; the series of rocks dating from this time, bearing evidence of an abundance of mammals, including early forms of horses, bats, and whales. M19.

eo ipso /eɪəʊ 'ɪpsəʊ/ *adv. phr.* L17. [L, abl. of *idipsum* the thing itself.] By that very act (or quality); through that alone; thereby. Cf. IPSO FACTO.

Eolian, -ic *adjs.* see AEOLIAN, -IC.

éolienne /ˌəʊlɪ'ɛn/ *n.* Now *rare.* Also **aeol-, eol-**. E20. [Fr., fem. of *éolien* of the wind, f. *Éole* Aeolus, god of the winds, f. Gk *aiolos* changeful: see -IAN.] A fine dress fabric of silk and wool.

eolith /'iːə(ʊ)lɪθ/ *n.* L19. [f. EO- + -LITH.] *Archaeol.* Any of the roughly chipped stones found in Tertiary strata and orig. thought to be the earliest human artefacts, but now regarded as naturally formed; *loosely* any apparent artefact of natural origin.

eolithic /iːə(ʊ)'lɪθɪk/ *a.* & *n.* Also **E-**. L19. [Fr. *éolithique*, f. as EO- + -LITHIC.] *Archaeol.* (Designating or pertaining to) the earliest period represented by worked flints with eoliths interpreted as being of artificial origin.

eon *n.* see AEON.

Eonism /'iːənɪz(ə)m/ *n.* Also **e-**. E20. [f. Charles d'Éon (1728-1810), Fr. adventurer who wore women's clothes + -ISM.] Transvestism, esp. by a man.

Eonist *n.* a (usu. male) transvestite E20.

For other words beginning with *en-* see the entry for **en-**[1]

eo nomine /eɪəʊ 'nəʊmɪni, 'nɒmɪneɪ/ *adv. phr.* E17. [L, abl. of *id nomen* that name.] Under that name; that is so called; explicitly.

eosin /'iːə(ʊ)sɪn/ *n.* Also **†-ine**. L19. [f. Gk *ēos* dawn + -IN[1].] A bromine derivative of fluorescein, obtained as a fluorescent red powder, or one of its red salts or other derivatives, used as dyes, biological stains, constituents of red inks, etc.

eosinophil /iːə(ʊ)'sɪnəfɪl/ *a.* & *n.* Also **-phile** /-fʌɪl/. L19. [f. prec. + -PHIL.] A *adj.* Readily stained by eosin. L19. B *n.* A kind of phagocytic granulocyte with large eosinophil granules in its cytoplasm. E20.

,eosino'philia *n.* an increased number of eosinophils in the blood, as in some allergic disorders and parasitic infections E20. **,eosino'philic** *a.* (*a*) = EOSINOPHIL *a.*; (*b*) of, pertaining to, or exhibiting eosinophilia: E20. **,eosi'nophilous** *a.* = EOSINOPHIL *a.* L19.

eotechnic /iːə(ʊ)'tɛknɪk/ *a.* M20. [f. EO- + Gk *tekhnikos*: see TECHNIC.] Designating or pertaining to the first stage of industrial development.

-eous /ɪəs/ *suff.* [f. L *-eus* + -OUS. Cf. -ACEOUS, -ANEOUS.] Forming adjs. w. the sense 'of the nature of, resembling', as *erroneous*, *gaseous*.

ep- *pref.* see EPI-.

epacrid /ɛ'pakrɪd/ *n.* L19. [Partly f. next, partly f. mod.L *Epacrideae* = Epacridaceae (see below): see -ID[2].] Any shrub or small tree of the largely Australian family Epacridaceae, resembling the heaths but with usu. epipetalous stamens and anthers opening by slits; *spec.* any member of its type genus, *Epacris* (see next).

epacris /ɛ'pakrɪs/ *n.* E19. [mod.L, f. Gk *epi* on + *akron* summit, because chiefly alpine.] Any of various Australian heathlike shrubs of the genus *Epacris* (family Epacridaceae: see prec.), with pink or white tubular flowers in the axils of the leaves.

epact /'iːpakt/ *n.* M16. [(O)Fr. *épacte* f. late L *epactae* pl., f. Gk *epaktai* intercalated (sc. *hēmerai* days) fem. pl. of *epaktos* brought in f. *epagein* bring in, f. as EPI- + *agein* lead.] 1 The age of the moon in days at the beginning of a calendar year. M16. 2 The period of about 11 days by which the solar year is longer than the lunar year; any of these days. L16. 3 An intercalated day or period. *rare.* E17.

†epaenetic *a.* L17-M18. [Gk *epainetikos*, f. *epainein* to praise: see -IC.] Expressing or containing praise, laudatory.

epagomenic /ɛpəgə'mɛnɪk/ *a.* M19. [f. Gk *epagomenē* (sc. *hēmera* day) pa. pple of *epagein*: see EPACT, -IC.] Intercalary; (of a god) worshipped on intercalary days.

epa'gomenal, epa'gomenous *adjs.* E20.

epana- /'ɛpənə, ɛ'panə/ *comb. form.* Bef. a vowel **epan-**. [f. EPI- + Gk *ana* up, again.] *Rhet.* Used in ns. and derived adjs. w. the sense 'return, repetition'.

e'panodos *n.* (*a*) repetition of a sentence in an inverse order; (*b*) a return to the regular thread of discourse after a digression: L16.

epanalepsis /ˌɛpənə'lɛpsɪs/ *n.* M16. [Gk *epanalēpsis* repetition, f. *lēpsis* a taking: see EPANA-.] The repetition of a word or clause following intervening matter.

epanaleptic *a.* & *n.* (*a*) *adj.* characterized by epanalepsis; (*b*) *n.* an instance of epanalepsis: E20.

epanaphora /ɛpə'naf(ə)rə/ *n.* M16. [Gk = reference, f. *phora* a carrying: see EPANA-.] = ANAPHORA 1.

epanaphoral *a.* E20.

épanchement /epɑ̃ʃmɑ̃/ *n.* Pl. pronounced same. M19. [Fr., lit. 'discharge, effusion', f. *épancher* pour out (something) f. late L alt. of cl.L *expandere* EXPAND: see -MENT.] An outpouring or disclosure of one's thoughts or feelings. Also, a relationship marked by mutual trust and the exchange of confidences.

eparch /'ɛpɑːk/ *n.* M17. [Gk *eparkhos*, f. as EPI- + -ARCH.] 1 The governor of a civilian eparchy. M17. 2 The chief bishop of an ecclesiastical eparchy. L17.

eparchy /'ɛpɑːki/ *n.* L18. [Gk *eparkhia*, f. *eparkhos*: see prec., -Y[3].] 1 A province in the

Orthodox Church. L18. 2 *Hist.* A province of ancient Greece; a smaller division (corresponding to a part of a present-day nomarchy) of modern Greece. L18.

eparterial /ɛpɑːˈtɪərɪəl/ *a.* L19. [f. EPI- + ARTERIAL.] *Anat.* Of a branch of a bronchus: situated above the pulmonary artery.

épatant /epatɑ̃/ *a.* E20. [Fr., pres. ppl a. of *épater* flabbergast.] Shocking (to conventional persons); daring.

épater /epate/ *v.t.* Only in inf. E20. [Fr. = flabbergast.] Startle, shock. Esp. in phr. below.
épater les or ***le bourgeois*** /lɛ, lə burʒwa/ shock the conventionally-minded.

epaule /ɛˈpɔːl/ *n.* E18. [Fr. *épaule*: see EPAULETTE.] *Fortif.* The place where the face and flank of a bastion meet.

epaulement /ɛˈpɔːlm(ə)nt/ *n.* Also †**esp-**. L17. [Fr. *épaulement* (earlier *esp-*), f. *épauler* protect by an epaulement, f. *épaule*: see EPAULETTE, -MENT.] *Fortif.* A parapet or breastwork, esp. one protecting the flank.

épaulement /epolmɑ̃/ *n.* Pl. pronounced same. M19. [Fr.: see prec.] *Ballet.* A stance in which one shoulder is turned forward and the other drawn back, with the head facing over the forward shoulder; correct positioning of the shoulders.

epaulette /ˈɛpəlɛt, -pɔːl-, ɛpəˈlɛt/ *n.* Also **-let**. L18. [Fr. *épaulette* dim. of *épaule* shoulder f. L SPATULA, (in late L) shoulder-blade: see -ET[1], -ETTE.] 1 An ornamental shoulder-piece worn on a military or other uniform, usu. as a sign of rank. L18. b A military officer; a commission. E19. 2 A small shoulder-plate on a suit of armour. E19. 3 A loop or tab on the shoulder of a coat; a piece of trimming on the shoulder of a dress etc. M19.
1 W. STYRON A blue jacket whose shoulders glittered with the epaulets of an army colonel. 3 D. BOGARDE Singh carefully removed the folded cap from his epaulette.
epauletted *a.* having or wearing epaulettes E19.

epaxial /ɛˈpaksɪəl/ *a.* L19. [f. EPI- + AXIAL.] *Anat.* Situated on the dorsal side of an axis.

épée /ˈeɪpeɪ, *foreign* epe (*pl. same*)/ *n.* L19. [Fr. = sword f. OFr. *espee*: see SPAY.] A sharp-pointed duelling-sword used (blunted) for fencing; the art of fencing with this.
épéist /ˈeɪpeɪɪst/, ***épéiste*** /epeist/ *n.* a fencer who uses or is proficient with an épée E20.

epeiric /ɛˈpʌɪrɪk/ *a.* E20. [f. as next + -IC.] *Geol.* Of a sea: connected with the ocean but situated on a continent or continental shelf.

epeirogeny /ɛpʌɪˈrɒdʒəni/ *n.* Also **epir-**. L19. [f. Gk *ēpeiros* mainland, continent + -GENY.] The formation and alteration of continents by the (esp. vertical) movement of the earth's crust; an episode of this.
epeirogenesis /ɪˌpʌɪrə(ʊ)ˈdʒɛnɪsɪs/ *n.* = EPEIROGENY E20. **epeirogenetic** /ɪˌpʌɪrə(ʊ)dʒɪˈnɛtɪk/ *a.* E20. **epeirogenic** /ɪˌpʌɪrə(ʊ)ˈdʒɛnɪk/ *a.* L19. **epeiroˈgenically** *adv.* M20.

ependyma /ɛˈpɛndɪmə/ *n.* L19. [Gk *ependuma*, f. *ependuein* put on over, f. as EPI- + EN-[2] + *duein* put.] *Anat.* The epithelial layer lining the cerebral ventricles and the central canal of the spinal cord in vertebrates.
ependymal *a.* L19.

epenthesis /ɛˈpɛnθɪsɪs/ *n.* Pl. **-eses** /-ɪsiːz/. M16. [Late L f. Gk, f. *epenthe-* stem of *epentithenai* insert, f. as EPI- + EN-[2] + *tithenai* to place.] The development of a sound or an unetymological letter in a word, e.g. the *b* in *thimble*.
epenthesize *v.t.* introduce or modify by epenthesis L19.

epenthetic /ɛpɛnˈθɛtɪk/ *a.* M19. [Gk *epenthetikos*, f. *epenthesis*: see prec., -IC.] Of or pertaining to epenthesis; (of a sound or letter) that has come to be inserted in a word.

epeolatry /ɛpɪˈɒlətri/ *n.* M19. [f. Gk *epeos*, *epos* word + -O- + -LATRY.] The worship of words.

epergne /ɪˈpəːn/ *n.* E18. [Perh. f. Fr. *épargne* saving, economy.] An ornament (often with branches) for the centre of a dinner-table, for holding flowers, fruit, etc.

epexegesis /ɛˌpɛksɪˈdʒiːsɪs/ *n.* Pl. **-eses** /-iːsiːz/. L16. [Gk *epexēgēsis*, f. as EPI-, EXEGESIS.] The addition of a word or words to clarify the meaning; the word(s) so added.
epexegetic(al) /-ˈdʒɛt-/ *adjs.* M19. **epexegetically** /-ˈdʒɛt-/ *adv.* L19.

eph- *pref.* see EPI-.

ephah /ˈiːfə/ *n.* LME. [Heb. *ʼēpāh*, prob. f. Egyptian.] *Hist.* An ancient Hebrew dry measure equivalent to the bath (of about 40 litres or 9 gallons).

ephebe /ɛˈfiːb, ɪ-, ˈɛfiːb/ *n.* L19. [L *ephebus* f. Gk *ephēbos*, f. as EPI- + *hēbē* early manhood.] A young man; *spec.* in ancient Greece, one from 18 to 20 years old undergoing military training.
ephebic *a.* M19.

ephebeum /ɛfɪˈbiːəm/ *n.* Pl. **-bea** /-ˈbiːə/. L17. [L f. Gk *ephēbeion*, f. *ephēbos* EPHEBE.] *Gk Hist.* A palaestra court where young men could take exercise.

ephebiatrics /ɪˌfiːbɪˈatrɪks, ɛ-/ *n.* M20. [f. Gk *ephēbos* (see EPHEBE) after *geriatrics*, *paediatrics*.] The branch of medicine that deals with adolescents and their diseases.
ephebiaˈtrician *n.* an expert in or student of ephebiatrics M20.

ephectic /ɛˈfɛktɪk/ *n.* & *a.* M17. [Gk *ephektikos* adj., f. *epekhein* hold back, reserve (judgement).] A *n.* A member of the Sceptic school of philosophy in ancient Greece. M17. B *adj.* Characterized by suspension of judgement. L17.

ephedra /ɛˈfɛdrə/ *n.* E20. [mod.L (see below) f. L = equisetum, f. Gk.] Any of the trailing or scrambling evergreen gymnospermous shrubs of the genus *Ephedra* (family Ephedraceae), native to warm arid regions and with almost leafless stems like an equisetum.

ephedrine /ˈɛfədriːn/ *n.* Also **-in** /-ɪn/. L19. [f. prec. + -INE[5], -IN[1].] An alkaloid, $C_{10}H_{15}NO$, found in some ephedras and made as a sympathomimetic drug for use esp. as a bronchodilator for hay fever, asthma, etc.

ephelis /ɪˈfiːlɪs, ɛ-/ *n.* Pl. **-lides** /-lɪdiːz/. M18. [L f. Gk *ephēlis*, (in pl.) rough facial spots.] *Med.* A freckle; *collect.* any of various kinds of skin discoloration.

ephemera /ɪˈfɛm(ə)rə, -ˈfiːm-, ɛ-/ *n.*[1] & *a.* LME. [med.L, use as n. of fem. of late L *ephemerus* lasting only a day f. Gk *ephēmeros*, f. as EPI- + *hēmera* day.] A *n.* Pl. **-ras**, **-rae** /-riː/. †1 A fever lasting only one day. LME–E19. 2 Orig. = EPHEMERON 2. Now, a winged insect of the genus *Ephemera* or the order Ephemeroptera, a mayfly. Cf. EPHEMERID *n.* L17. 3 A person or thing of short-lived interest or use. M18.
3 S. JOHNSON These papers of a day, the Ephemerae of learning.
†B *adj.* Of a fever: lasting one day. LME–M16.

ephemera *n.*[2] *pl.* see EPHEMERON.

ephemerae *n.pl.* see EPHEMERA *n.*[1]

ephemeral /ɪˈfɛm(ə)r(ə)l, -ˈfiːm-/ *a.* & *n.* L16. [f. Gk *ephēmeros* (see EPHEMERA *n.*[1] & *a.*) + -AL[1].] A *adj.* 1 Chiefly *Zool.* & *Med.* Beginning and ending in the same day; existing for one day or a few days only. L16. 2 In existence, or of interest or use, for a short time only; transitory. M17.
2 A. THWAITE Much of Gosse's energy was going into ephemeral journalism.
B *n.* 1 An insect that lives only one day. L16. 2 A thing or person of transitory existence or of short-lived interest or use. E19.
ephemeralism *n.* = EPHEMERALITY E20. **ephemeˈrality** *n.* ephemeral quality; in *pl.*, ephemeral matters: E19. **ephemerally** *adv.* M19. **ephemeralness** *n.* E20.

†ephemeran *a.* & *n.* M17–E18. [f. EPHEMERA *n.*[1] + -AN.] = EPHEMERAL *a.*, *n.* 1.

ephemerid /ɪˈfɛm(ə)rɪd, -ˈfiːm-/ *n.* L19. [mod.L *Ephemeridae* (see below), f. *Ephemera* genus name: see EPHEMERA *n.*[1] & *a.*, -ID[3].] An insect of the order Ephemeroptera (cf. EPHEMERA *n.*[1] 2), *esp.* one of the family Ephemeridae.

†ephemerid *a.* E19–E20. [L *ephemerid-* stem of *ephemeris*: see next, -ID[2].] = EPHEMERAL *a.* 2.

ephemeris /ɪˈfɛm(ə)rɪs, -ˈfiːm-/ *n.* Also (f. the pl.) †**-rides**. Pl. **ephemerides** /ɛfɪˈmɛrɪdiːz/ E16. [L f. Gk, f. *ephēmeros*: see EPHEMERA *n.*[1]] 1 A table giving the position of a celestial object at daily or other regular intervals throughout a period; a book containing such tables and other astronomical information, an astronomical almanac. E16. 2 *gen.* An almanac, a calendar. Now *rare* or *obs.* L16. †3 A diary, a journal. L16–L17. 4 = EPHEMERA *n.*[1] 2, 3. E19.
Comb.: **ephemeris time** *Astron.* a time-scale defined in terms of the orbital motion of the planets.
†**ephemerist** *n.*[1] a person who makes or uses an ephemeris M17–M18.

ephemeron /ɪˈfɛm(ə)rɒn, -ˈfiːm-/ *n.* Pl. **-rons**, **-ra** /-rə/. L16. [Gk *ephēmeron* neut. of *ephēmeros*: see EPHEMERA *n.*[1] & *a.*] †1 A plant described by ancient writers as living only one day or causing death within one day. L16–M17. 2 An insect that lives only one day, or spends only one day in its winged form. Cf. EPHEMERA *n.*[1] 2. L16. 3 A short-lived person, institution, or production. L18. 4 As *ephemera* pl. Printed or written items produced for short-term use, as tickets, posters, and greetings cards. M20.
3 T. SHARPE Of all ephemera he found television commentators the least to his liking. 4 M. AMIS Faddy ephemeron covered its walls: posters of Jimi Hendrix, Auden and Isherwood, Rasputin.
ephemerist *n.*[2] a person who collects (printed or written) ephemera L20. **ephemerous** *a.* = EPHEMERAL *a.* M17.

Ephesian /ɪˈfiːʒ(ə)n/ *n.* & *a.* LME. [f. L *ephesius*, Gk *ephesios*, f. Gk *Ephesos* Ephesus: see -AN.] A *n.* 1 A native or inhabitant of Ephesus, an ancient Greek city on the west coast of Asia Minor. In *pl.* (treated as *sing.*), St Paul's Epistle to the Ephesians, a book of the New Testament. LME. †2 A close companion. *rare* (Shakes.). Only in L16. B *adj.* Of or pertaining to Ephesus or its inhabitants. L19.

Ephesine /ˈɛfɪsɪn/ *a.* M16. [Late L *Ephesinus*, f. *Ephesus*: see prec., -INE[1].] Of or pertaining to Ephesus; chiefly *Eccl.*, referring to the Council of Ephesus in 431 or to liturgical uses believed to have originated in Ephesus.

ephialtes /ɛfɪˈaltiːz/ *n.* Now *rare* or *obs.* LME. [Gk *ephialtēs*.] An evil spirit supposed to cause nightmares; nightmare.

ephod /ˈiːfɒd, ˈɛfɒd/ *n.* LME. [Heb. *ʼēpōd*.] 1 *Hist.* A sleeveless garment worn by priests in ancient Israel. LME. 2 A clerical garment. Formerly also, priestly office or influence. E17.

ephor /ˈɛfɔː/ *n.* Also **E-**. Pl. **ephors**, **ephori** /ˈɛfərʌɪ/. L16. [L *ephorus* or its source Gk *ephoros* overseer, f. as EPI- + base of *horan* see.] 1 *Gk Hist.* In Sparta and other Dorian states, any of the magistrates with executive, judicial, and disciplinary power who came to have power over the king's conduct. L16. 2 In modern Greece: an overseer, a superintendent. E19. 3 A prefect at the Edinburgh Academy. L19.
ephoral /-f(ə)r(ə)l/ *a.* M19. **ephorate** /-f(ə)rət/ *n.* the office of ephor; the body of ephors: M19.

Ephthalite /ˈɛfθəlʌɪt/ *n.* & *a.* L19. [Late Gk *Ephthalitos*: see -ITE[1].] *Hist.* (Of, pertaining to, or designating) a White Hun.

ephyra /ˈɛfɪrə/ *n.* Pl. **-rae** /-riː/. M19. [mod.L f. Gk *Ephura* a Nereid and an Oceanid.] *Zool.* A larval jellyfish, after separation from the scyphistoma.

epi- /ˈɛpi/ *pref.* Usu. **ep-** /ɛp, *unstressed* ɪp/ bef. an unaspirated vowel, **eph-** /ɛf, *unstressed* ɪf/ bef. an aspirated one. [Repr. Gk *epi* on, near to, above, in addition.] 1 Occurring, esp. in scientific wds, w. the senses 'on', as *epicycle*, *epigraph*, 'above, overlying', as *epicotyl*, *epidermis*, 'near to', as *epipubis*, 'in addition', as *epiphenomenon*. 2 *Chem.*, *Min.*, & *Geol.* In names of substances, denoting (*a*) analogy or similarity of composition, (*b*) a bridge in a molecule.
epiˈcalyx *n.*, pl. **-yces** /-ɪsiːz/, **-yxes**, *Bot.* a whorl of small bracts like sepals surrounding the true calyx in certain plants, esp. members of the mallow family L19. **epicarp** *n.* (*Bot.*) the outermost layer of the pericarp in a fleshy fruit; the peel, the skin: E19. **epichile** /-kʌɪl/ *n.* [Gk *kheilos* lip] *Bot.* the flat projecting outer part of the hinged labellum found in some orchids M19. **epichlorˈhydrin** *n.* *Chem.* a cyclic epoxide, C_3H_5OCl, that is a toxic flammable volatile liquid used esp. in the manufacture of epoxy resins M19.

epi'chordal *a.* (*Zool.*) situated or occurring on the dorsal side of the notochord L19. **epi'clastic** *a.* (*Geol.*) (of rock) formed on the earth's surface by the alteration of pre-existing rocks L19. **epi'cormic** *a.* (*Bot.*) [Gk *kormos* trunk (of a tree)] (of a shoot or branch) growing from a previously dormant bud on the trunk or a limb of a tree E20. **epicotyl** /-'kɒtɪl/ *n.* (*Bot.*) the part of an embryo or seedling stem above the cotyledon(s) L19. **epi'cranial** *a.* of or pertaining to the scalp M19. **epicuticle, -'ticula** *n.* (*a*) the thin waxy outer layer covering insects and other arthropods; (*b*) the thin membrane forming the outer part of the cuticle of animal hairs etc.: E20. **epicu'ticular** *a.* of or pertaining to the epicuticle M20. **epi'diorite** *n. Geol.* any rock formed from a basic igneous rock by metamorphism, with the original pyroxene transformed into amphibole L19. **epifluo'rescence** *n.* fluorescence of an object in an optical microscope when irradiated from the viewing side L20. **epi'focal** *a.* situated above the focus of an earthquake L19. **epi'lithic** *a.* (*Bot.*) growing on stone E20. **epi'otic** *a.* & *n.* (*Zool.*) (*a*) *adj.* situated above the ear; *spec.* designating one of the five otic bones that may be present in vertebrates; (*b*) *n.* an epiotic bone: L19. **epipe'lagic** *a.* of, pertaining to, or designating the upper layer of the ocean, down to 100 or 200 metres M20. **epi'petalous** *a.* (*Bot.*) (of stamens) attached to petals M19. **epi'pharynx** *n.* (*Zool.*) any of various structures developed from the roof of the mouth cavity in some insects and arachnids E19. **epi'plankton** *n.* plankton in the upper layer of the sea, down to about 100 metres L19. **epiplank'tonic** *a.* of, pertaining to, or designating epiplankton M20. **epiplasm** *n.* the cytoplasm remaining in the ascus of a fungus after the dispersal of its spores L19. **epip'teric** *a.* & *n.* (*Anat.*) (designating) a small Wormian bone sometimes found between the parietal and the greater wing of the sphenoid L19. **epip'terygoid** *a.* & *n.* (*Zool.*) (designating) a slender vertical bone situated above the pterygoid in the skull of some reptiles and primitive tetrapods L19. **epi'pubic** *a.* (*Zool.*) situated on the pubis; of the nature of an epipubis. L19. **epi'pubis** *n.* (*Zool.*) a cartilage or bone in front of the pubis in amphibians, reptiles, and marsupials: L19. **epi'scleral** *a.* (*Anat.*) of, pertaining to, or overlying the surface of the sclera of the eye M19. **epispore** *n.* (*Bot.*) the outer covering of a spore of a lichen or fern M19. **epi'stoma, epistome** *n.* (*Zool.*) a structure or region above or over the mouth in some invertebrates M19. **epi'theca** *n.* (*a*) a calcareous layer surrounding part of the theca of some corals; (*b*) the outer of the two overlapping halves of the cell wall of a diatom: M19. **epi'thecium** *n.*, pl. **-ia**, *Bot.* the surface layer of the fruiting body in certain lichens and fungi L19. **epitope** *n.* [Gk *topos* place] *Med.* the part of an antigen molecule to which an antibody molecule attaches itself M20. **epi'topic** *a.* (*Med.*) of or pertaining to an epitope M20. **epi'trochlear** *a.* (*Anat.*) situated above or near the trochlea of the elbow-joint M20. **epizone** *n.* (*Geol.*) a metamorphic zone characterized by moderate temperature, low pressure, and high stress M20.

epibiont /ɛpɪ'bʌɪɒnt/ *n.* M20. [f. EPI- + -BIONT.] An organism living upon the surface of another, esp. non-parasitically.

epibiotic /ˌɛpɪbʌɪ'ɒtɪk/ *a.* M20. [f. EPI- + Gk *biōtikos* pertaining to life: see BIOTIC.] Pertaining to or designating an epibiont.

epiblast /'ɛpɪblast/ *n.* E19. [f. EPI- + -BLAST.] **1** *Bot.* A projection resembling a flap opposite the scutellum on the embryo of some grasses. E19. **2** *Biol.* The outermost layer of a young embryo before it differentiates into ectoderm and mesoderm. Also called *ectoblast*. L19.

epi'blastic *a.* L19.

epiboly /ɛ'pɪbəli/ *n.* Also **-le**. L19. [Gk *epibolē* throwing or laying on, f. *epiballein* throw on, f. as EPI- + *ballein* throw; assim. to -Y[3].] *Biol.* The process by which one set of cells spreads over and surrounds another by dividing more rapidly, as in gastrulation. Cf. EMBOLY.

epi'bolic *a.* L19.

epic /'ɛpɪk/ *a.* & *n.* Also †**-ick**. L16. [L *epicus* f. Gk *epikos*, f. *epos*: see EPOS, -IC.] **A** *adj.* **1** Narrating at length the adventures or achievements of one or more heroic figures, in the manner of the *Iliad* and *Paradise Lost*; of or pertaining to compositions of this kind. L16. **2** Of the kind described in epic poetry; grand and heroic; impressive in scope, grandeur, etc. M18.

2 N. MONSARRAT A survivor of what must have been an epic sea battle. D. HALBERSTAM He was . . as much a hero and a personage of that epic era as Eisenhower.

B *n.* †**1** An epic poet. Only in M17. **2** An epic poem. E18. **3a** An imaginative work of any form seen as embodying a nation's conception of its past history. M19. **b** A film or novel based on an epic narrative or heroic in type or scale; *colloq.* an exceptionally long, expensive, or lavish entertainment. E20. **4** Something in real life regarded as a fit subject for an epic. M19. **5** The genre of epic literature. M20.

3b T. WOGAN On television I've endured the rigours of 'Miss World' . . and other epics. 4 D. H. LAWRENCE Her life was the epic that inspired their lives. 5 M. H. ABRAMS Epic and tragedy are the king and queen of poetic forms.

epical *a.* = EPIC *a.* E19. **epically** *adv.* M19.

epicanthus /ɛpɪ'kanθəs/ *n.* M19. [f. EPI- + CANTHUS.] A fold of skin from the upper eyelid that covers the inner angle of the eye, occurring in Mongolians and as a congenital anomaly in other people.

epicanthic *a.* having or pertaining to an epicanthus E20.

epicardium /ɛpɪ'kɑːdɪəm/ *n.* Pl. **-dia** /-dɪə/. M19. [f. EPI- + *-cardium*, after *pericardium*.] **1** *Anat.* The visceral part of the serous pericardium, covering the heart. M19. **2** *Zool.* Either of two hollow outgrowths from the pharynx in some ascidians. L19.

epicardiac *a.* L19. **epicardial** *a.* E20.

epicedium /ɛpɪ'siːdɪəm/ *n.* Pl. **-ia** /-ɪə/, **-iums**. Also (earlier, now *rare*) Anglicized as **epicede** /'ɛpɪsiːd/, (now *rare*) in Gk form as **epicedion** /ɛpɪ'siːdɪən/. M16. [L f. Gk *epikēdeion* use as n. of neut. of *epikēdeios* funeral (adj.), f. as EPI- + *kēdos* care, grief, mourning.] A funeral ode.

epicedial *a.* M17. **epicedian** *a.* & *n.* (*a*) *adj.* funereal, elegiac; †(*b*) *n.* = EPICEDIUM: E17.

epicene /'ɛpɪsiːn/ *a.* & *n.* LME. [Late L *epicœnus* f. Gk *epikoinos*, f. as EPI- + *koinos* common.] **A** *adj.* **1** *Gram.* Of a noun or pronoun: that may refer to either sex without changing its grammatical gender; denoting both males and females. LME. **2** Of indeterminate sex; characteristic of both sexes. Also, effeminate. E17. **3** For or used by both sexes. E17.

2 T. HARDY What had at first appeared as an epicene shape, the decreasing space resolved into a cloaked female. 3 A. DUGGAN The men . . wore long epicene gowns.

B *n.* **1** A person of indeterminate sex; an effeminate person. E17. **2** An epicene noun or pronoun. E17.

epicenter *n.* see EPICENTRE.

epicentral /ɛpɪ'sɛntr(ə)l/ *a.* & *n.* M19. [Sense A.1 f. Gk *epikentros* (see next); sense A.2 f. next: see -AL[1].] **A** *adj.* **1** *Zool.* Situated on a vertebral centrum. M19. **2** Of, pertaining to, or containing an epicentre. L19. **B** *n. Zool.* An epicentral spine. M19.

epicentre /'ɛpɪsɛntə/ *n.* Also ***-ter**, & in sense 1 in mod.L form (now *rare*) **epicentrum** /ɛpɪ'sɛntrəm/, pl. **-ra** /-rə/. L19. [Gk *epikentron* neut. of *epikentros* situated on a centre, f. as EPI- + *kentros* CENTRE *n.* & *a.*] **1** The point on the earth's surface directly above the focus of an earthquake. L19. **2** *fig.* The centre or heart of something, esp. something unpleasant. M20.

2 G. SWIFT At the very epicentre of the slaughter, on the infamous Western Front.

épicerie /episri/ *n.* Pl. pronounced same. E20. [Fr.: see SPICERY.] A grocer's shop in France.

epicheirema /ˌɛpɪkʌɪ'riːmə/ *n.* L17. [mod.L f. Gk *epikheirēma* attempt, f. *epikheirein* undertake, f. as EPI- + *kheir* hand.] *Logic.* In Aristotle's use, an attempted proof that is not conclusive; (by misunderstanding, now *rare*) a syllogism in which one or both of the premisses is supported by a reason.

epicism /'ɛpɪsɪz(ə)m/ *n. rare.* M19. [f. EPIC + -ISM.] The manner, style, etc., characteristic of epics.

epicist *n.* a writer of epic poetry M19.

†**epick** *a.* & *n.* var. of EPIC.

epiclesis /ɛpɪ'kliːsɪs/ *n.* Also **-kl-**. Pl. **-cleses** /-'kliːsiːz/. L19. [Gk *epiklēsis*, f. *epikalein* call on, f. as EPI- + *kalein* to call.] *Chr. Ch.* The part of the Eucharistic prayer in which the descent of the Holy Spirit is invoked on the elements or the communicants.

epicondyle /ɛpɪ'kɒndɪl, -dʌɪl/ *n.* M19. [Fr. *épicondyle*, mod.L *epicondylus*, f. (as) EPI- + CONDYLE.] *Anat.* A protuberance above or on the condyle of a long bone, *esp.* either of the two at the elbow end of the humerus.

epicondylar *a.* M20. ˌ**epicondy'litis** *n.* a painful condition of an epicondyle or epicondylar region of the humerus; tennis elbow: M20.

epicontinental /ˌɛpɪkɒntɪ'nɛnt(ə)l/ *a.* E20. [f. EPI- + CONTINENTAL.] *Geol.* Situated on a continent or continental shelf; *spec.* = EPEIRIC.

epicritic /ɛpɪ'krɪtɪk/ *a.* E20. [Gk *epikritikos* adjudicatory, f. *epikrinein* decide, f. as EPI- + *krinein* to judge: see -IC.] *Physiol.* Involving fine discrimination of sensory (esp. cutaneous) stimuli.

epicure /'ɛpɪkjʊə/ *n.* LME. [med.L *epicurus* appellative use of *Epicurus* f. Gk *Epikouros* Epicurus: see EPICUREAN *n.* 1.] †**1** (**E-**.) = EPICUREAN *n.* 1. LME–L18. **2** A person whose main concern is sensual pleasure, esp. eating; a glutton. *arch.* M16. **3** A person who cultivates a refined taste, esp. for food and drink. L16.

epicurish *a.* (*rare*) M16.

epicurean /ˌɛpɪkjʊ(ə)'riːən/ *n.* & *a.* Also †**-ian**. LME. [(O)Fr. *épicurien* or L *epicureus*, *-ius* f. Gk *epikoureios* f. *Epikouros* Epicurus: see below, -EAN.] **A** *n.* **1** Usu. **E-**. A disciple or student of Epicurus (341–270 BC), a Greek philosopher who held that the highest good is pleasure (identified with the practice of virtue), that the gods do not concern themselves with human affairs, and that the world results from the chance combination of atoms; a person who holds similar views. LME. **2** A person devoted to pleasure, now esp. refined sensuous enjoyment. L16.

B *adj.* **1** (Usu. **E-**.) Of or pertaining to Epicurus or his philosophy. L16. **2** Pertaining to or exhibiting a devotion to pleasure, esp. of a refined or sensuous kind; characteristic of or suited to such a person. E17.

Also †**epicureal**, **-ial** *a.* M16–E18.

epicureanism /ɛpɪ'kjʊərɪənɪz(ə)m/ *n.* M18. [f. prec. + -ISM.] **1** Usu. **E-**. The philosophical system of Epicurus. M18. **2** Adherence to the principles of Epicurus; devotion to a life of pleasure, esp. of a refined or sensuous kind. M19.

2 O. WELLES She knew how to eat, with the careful epicureanism of a woman who is used to having the best.

†**epicurian** *n.* & *a.* var. of EPICUREAN.

†**epicurise** *v.* var. of EPICURIZE.

epicurism /'ɛpɪkjʊ(ə)rɪz(ə)m/ *n.* L16. [Partly f. L *Epicurus* (see EPICUREAN *n.* 1) after Fr. *épicurisme*, partly f. EPICURE + -ISM.] **1** Usu. **E-**. = EPICUREANISM 1. Now *rare*. L16. †**2** The pursuit of pleasure; sensuality; gluttony. L16–L18. **3** The disposition and habits of an epicure; cultivated taste in food and drink. E17.

†**epicurize** *v.i.* Also **-ise**. L16–E18. [f. L *Epicurus* (see EPICUREAN *n.* 1) or EPICURE + -IZE.] Live or behave as an epicure; feast daintily or luxuriously.

epicycle /'ɛpɪsʌɪk(ə)l/ *n.* LME. [(O)Fr. *épicycle* or late L *epicyclus* f. Gk *epikuklos*, f. as EPI- + *kuklos* circle.] A circle whose centre moves round the circumference of a larger circle; *spec.* (*Hist. Sci.*) such a circle in the Ptolemaic system, in which the planets were regarded as moving in circles whose centres moved round larger circles (deferents) centred on the earth.

epicyclic /-'sʌɪk-, -'sɪk-/ *a.* & *n.* (*a*) *adj.* of, pertaining to, or involving epicycles; designating a gear in which one wheel travels round the outside or the inside of another wheel with which it meshes; (*b*) *n.* an epicyclic gear: M19. **epicyclical** /-'sʌɪk-, -'sɪk-/ *a.* = EPICYCLIC *a.* M19.

epicycloid /ɛpɪ'sʌɪklɔɪd/ *n.* L18. [f. prec. + -OID.] A curve traced by a point on the circumference of a circle as it rolls round the outside of a fixed circle (or, formerly, round the inside: cf. HYPOCYCLOID).

epicy'cloidal *a.* E19.

Epidaurian /ɛpɪˈdɔːrɪən/ *n.* & *a.* M16. [f. Gk *Epidauros*, L *Epidaurus* (see below) + -IAN.] *Gk Hist.* **A** *n.* A native or inhabitant of Epidaurus, a city in ancient Greece in the NE Peloponnese which was a centre for the cult of Asclepius. M16. **B** *adj.* Of or pertaining to Epidaurus or Epidaurians. E17.

epideictic /ɛpɪˈdʌɪktɪk/ *a.* L18. [Gk *epideiktikos*, f. as EPI- + *deiknunai* to show: see -IC.] Using oratorical skill to praise or censure; characterized by a display of such skill.

†epidemial *a.* M16–E19. [OFr., f. *épidémie*: see next, -AL^{1}.] = EPIDEMIC *a.* 1.

epidemic /ɛpɪˈdɛmɪk/ *a.* & *n.* E17. [Fr. *épidémique*, f. (O)Fr. *épidémie* f. late L *epidemia* f. Gk *epidēmia* prevalence of a disease, f. *epidēmios* prevalent, f. as EPI- + *dēmos* people: see -IC.] **A** *adj.* **1** Of a disease: normally absent or infrequent in a population but liable to outbreaks of greatly increased frequency and severity; temporarily widespread. E17. **2** Chiefly of something deprecated: widespread, prevalent, universal. M17.

1 *Scientific American* One rickettsial disease, epidemic typhus, has been for centuries a great scourge of mankind. 2 *Listener* It is .. a type of character more than a political party. But it is epidemic enough .. to produce .. much damage.

B *n.* A temporary but widespread outbreak of a particular disease; *fig.* a sudden marked increase in the extent or currency of something. M18.

V. BRITTAIN The ferocious influenza epidemic was already making us short of staff. *New Scientist* The epidemic of prejudice and discrimination towards HIV-infected people.

epidemical *a.* (now *rare*) = EPIDEMIC *a.* E17. **epidemically** *adv.* M17. **epidemicity** /-ˈmɪsɪti/ *n.* the quality of being epidemic L19.

epidemiology /ˌɛpɪdiːmɪˈɒlədʒi/ *n.* L19. [f. Gk *epidēmia* (see prec.) + -OLOGY.] The branch of medicine that deals with the incidence and transmission of disease in populations, esp. with the aim of controlling it; the aspects of a disease relating to its incidence and transmission.

Listener The aetiology and epidemiology of the disease are not yet well understood.

epidemioˈlogic *a.* (chiefly *US*) M20. **epidemioˈlogical** *a.* M19. **epidemioˈlogically** *adv.* L19. **epidemiologist** *n.* L19.

†epidemy *n.* L15–M19. [OFr. *ypidime*, *impidemie*, (also mod.) *épidémie*: see EPIDEMIC, -Y^{3}.] An epidemic; *spec.* the plague.

epidendrum /ɛpɪˈdɛndrəm/ *n.* Also **-dron** /-drən/. L18. [mod.L (see below), f. as EPI- + Gk *dendron* tree.] Any orchid of the genus *Epidendrum* (or formerly included in it), comprising chiefly epiphytic plants of tropical America.

epiderm /ˈɛpɪdəːm/ *n.* Now *rare* or *obs.* M19. [Fr. *épiderme* f. late L EPIDERMIS.] = EPIDERMIS.

epidermis /ɛpɪˈdəːmɪs/ *n.* E17. [Late L f. Gk, f. as EPI- + *derma* skin.] **1** The surface epithelium of the skin of an animal, overlying the dermis. E17. **2** The outer animal integument of a shell. M18. **3** The outer layer of tissue in a plant, except where it is replaced by periderm. E19.

epidermal *a.* E19. **epidermic** *a.* M19. **epidermical** *a.* (now *rare*) L17. **epidermically** *adv.* M19. **epidermoid**, ˌ**epiderˈmoidal** *adjs.* (composed of tissue) resembling epidermis; of the nature of epidermis: M19. ˌ**epiderˈmolysis** *n.* a condition in which the epidermis loosens and extensive blistering occurs, occurring esp. in babies L19.

epidiascope /ɛpɪˈdʌɪəskəʊp/ *n.* E20. [f. EPI- + DIA-^{1} + -SCOPE.] An optical projector giving images of both opaque and transparent objects.

epididymis /ɛpɪˈdɪdɪmɪs/ *n.* Pl. **epididymides** /ɛpɪdɪˈdɪmɪdiːz/. Cf. earlier DIDYMIS. E17. [Gk *epididumis*, f. as EPI- + *didumos* testicle, twin, f. *duo* two.] *Anat.* A convoluted duct on the posterior surface of the testis, where sperm are stored and along which they pass to the vas deferens.

epididymal *a.* L17. **epididyˈmectomy** *n.* (an instance of) surgical removal of an epididymis E20. **epididyˈmitis** *n.* inflammation of the epididymis M19.

epididymo- /ɛpɪˈdɪdɪməʊ/ *comb. form.* L19. [f. prec. + -O-.] *Med.* Of or pertaining to the epididymis and —, as *epididymo-orchitis* etc.

epidosite /ɪˈpɪdəsʌɪt/ *n.* M19. [Alt. of EPIDOTE: see -ITE^{1}. Cf. Gk *epidosis* an additional giving.] *Geol.* A metamorphic rock composed chiefly of epidote and quartz.

epidote /ˈɛpɪdəʊt/ *n.* E19. [Fr. *épidote*, f. Gk *epididonai* give in addition, f. as EPI- + *didonai* give (w. ref. to the great length of the crystals).] *Min.* A basic silicate of calcium, aluminium, and iron that occurs as monoclinic usu. green crystals in many metamorphic rocks. Also, any of several rock-forming silicates of analogous composition.

epidotic /-ˈdɒt-/ *a.* M19. **epidotiˈzation** *n.* the process of becoming epidotized L19. **epidotized** *a.* metamorphically altered into epidote M20.

epidural /ɛpɪˈdjʊər(ə)l/ *a.* & *n.* L19. [f. EPI- + DURA *n.*^{1} + -AL^{1}.] *Med.* **A** *adj.* Situated or administered in the spinal canal immediately outside the dura mater. L19.

Sun The painless-birth method is known as epidural anaesthesia.

B *n.* A local anaesthetic administered into the epidural space of the spinal canal, used esp. in childbirth to produce a loss of sensation below the waist without affecting consciousness. L20.

epifauna /ˈɛpɪfɔːnə/ *n.* E20. [f. EPI- + FAUNA.] The animal life which lives on (rather than in) the seabed or on a marine animal or plant.

epiˈfaunal *a.* M20.

epigamic /ɛpɪˈgamɪk/ *a.* L19. [f. EPI- + Gk *gamos* marriage + -IC.] *Zool.* Of the colours or behaviour of animals: having the property of attracting members of the opposite sex.

epigastrium /ɛpɪˈgastrɪəm/ *n.* L17. [Late L *epigastrion* f. Gk use as n. of neut. sing. of *epigastrios* over the belly, f. as EPI- + *gastr-*, *gastēr* belly.] *Anat.* The upper central region of the abdomen.

epigastric *a.* M17. **†epigastrical** *a.* E–M17.

epigeal /ɛpɪˈdʒiːəl/ *a.* M19. [f. as EPIGEOUS: see -AL^{1}.] *Bot.* = EPIGEAN; (of germination) marked by an elongation of the hypocotyl so that the cotyledons are pushed above the ground.

epigean /ɛpɪˈdʒiːən/ *a.* L19. [f. as EPIGEOUS: see -AN.] *Bot.* & *Zool.* Growing or living on or close to the ground.

epigene /ˈɛpɪdʒiːn/ *a.* E19. [Fr. *épigène* f. Gk *epigenēs*, f. as EPI- + -GENE.] **1** Of a crystal: chemically altered after its formation; pseudomorphic. Now *rare*. E19. **2** *Geol.* Occurring or formed at or near the earth's surface. L19.

epigenic /-ˈdʒɛn-/ *a.* = EPIGENE 2 L19.

epigenesis /ɛpɪˈdʒɛnɪsɪs/ *n.* M17. [f. EPI- + -GENESIS.] *Biol.* (now *Hist.*). (A theory of) the development of an organism by progressive differentiation of an initially undifferentiated whole (freq. opp. *preformation*). Also (earlier), formation by successive accretion of parts.

epigenetic /ˌɛpɪdʒɪˈnɛtɪk/ *a.* & *n.* L19. [f. prec. after *genetic*.] **1** *Biol.* Of, pertaining to, or of the nature of epigenesis. Also, resulting from external influences, not genetic. L19. **2** *Geol.* Of a deposit or feature: formed later than the rock etc. in which it is enclosed or situated. E20.

epigenetically *adv.* L19.

epigenetics /ˌɛpɪdʒɪˈnɛtɪks/ *n.* M20. [f. prec.: see -ICS.] The branch of biology that deals with the effect of external influences on development.

epigeous /ɛpɪˈdʒiːəs/ *a.* M19. [f. Gk *epigeios*, f. as EPI- + *gē* earth: see -OUS.] *Bot.* & *Zool.* = EPIGEAN.

epiglottis /ɛpɪˈglɒtɪs/ *n.* Also (earlier) Anglicized as **†epiglot**. LME. [Gk *epiglōttis*, f. as EPI- + *glōtta* tongue. Cf. GLOTTIS.] A thin leaf-shaped flap of cartilage, situated immediately behind the root of the tongue, which covers the entrance to the larynx during swallowing and prevents food from entering the windpipe.

epiglottal *a.* M20. **epiglottic** *a.* L19. ˌ**epiglottiˈditis** *n.* = EPIGLOTTITIS M19. ˌ**epigloˈttitis** *n.* inflammation of the epiglottis M19.

epigone /ˈɛpɪgəʊn/ *n.* Pl. **epigones**, **epigoni** /ɪˈpɪgənʌɪ, ɛ-/. Also **-gon** /-gən/. M18. [In pl. f. Fr. *épigones* f. L *epigoni* f. Gk *epigonoi*, pl. of *epigonos* offspring, f. as EPI- + *-gonos*, f. *gignesthai* be born.] A member of a succeeding (and less distinguished) generation.

A. BURGESS The generation of traitors—Alfred Adler, Carl Jung, and all their wretched epigones.

epigram /ˈɛpɪgram/ *n.* LME. [Fr. *épigramme* or L *epigramma* f. Gk, f. as EPI- + -GRAM.] **1** A short poem leading up to and ending in a witty or ingenious turn of thought. LME. **2** = EPIGRAPH 2. *obs.* exc. *Hist.* M16. **3a** A concise pointed saying. L18. **b** Epigrammatic expression. M19.

3a R. W. CHURCH He liked .. to generalize in shrewd and sometimes cynical epigrams.

epigrammist *n.* (*rare*) an epigrammatist M17.

epigrammatic /ˌɛpɪgrəˈmatɪk/ *a.* E17. [Late L *epigrammaticus*, f. L *epigrammat-* stem of *epigramma* EPIGRAM: see -IC, -ATIC.] Of or pertaining to epigrams; of the nature or in the style of an epigram; concise, pointed.

epigrammatical *a.* E17. **epigrammatically** *adv.* E19.

epigrammatise *v.* var. of EPIGRAMMATIZE.

epigrammatist /ɛpɪˈgramətɪst/ *n.* L16. [Late L *epigrammatista* f. Gk *epigrammatistēs*, f. *epigrammatizein*: see next, -IST.] A maker of epigrams.

epigrammatism *n.* epigrammatic style E19.

epigrammatize /ɛpɪˈgramətʌɪz/ *v.* Also **-ise**. L17. [Gk *epigrammatizein*, f. *epigramma* (see EPIGRAM), or f. L *epigrammat-* (see EPIGRAMMATIC) + -IZE.] **1** *v.t.* Express in an epigrammatic style. L17. **b** Make the subject of an epigram. M19. **2** *v.i.* Compose epigrams; write or speak in an epigrammatic style. E19.

epigrammatizer *n.* E19.

epigramme /ˈɛpɪgram/ *n.* M18. [Fr. *épigramme*, app. a fanciful use of *épigramme* = EPIGRAM.] *Cookery.* A small piece of meat, usu. lamb, served as an entrée.

epigraph /ˈɛpɪgrɑːf/ *n.* L16. [Gk *epigraphē*, f. *epigraphein* write on, f. as EPI- + *graphein* write.] **†1** The superscription of a letter, book, etc.; the imprint on a title-page. L16–E19. **2** An inscription, *esp.* one on a tombstone, building, statue, etc.; a legend on a coin. E17. **3** = MOTTO *n.* 2. M19.

2 C. THIRLWALL The epigraph of the thousand citizens who fell .. at Chaeronea. 3 *Economist* Towards the end of the book Mr Chevalier uses an epigraph from Daniel Halevy.

epiˈgraphic *a.* of or pertaining to epigraphs or epigraphy M19. **epiˈgraphical** *a.* = EPIGRAPHIC L19. **epiˈgraphically** *adv.* L19.

epigraphy /ɪˈpɪgrəfi, ɛ-/ *n.* M19. [f. prec. + -Y^{3}: see -GRAPHY.] **1** Inscriptions collectively. M19. **2** The branch of knowledge that deals with the interpretation, classification, etc., of inscriptions; the palaeography of inscriptions. M19.

epigrapher *n.* an expert in or student of inscriptions L19. **epigraphist** *n.* an epigrapher M19.

epigyne /ˈɛpɪdʒʌɪn/ *n.* Also in L form **epigynum** /ɛpɪˈdʒʌɪnəm/. L19. [mod.L *epigynum*, f. EPI- + Gk *gunē* woman, female.] *Zool.* The arachnid ovipositor; the external genital plate of spiders.

epigynous /ɪˈpɪdʒɪnəs, ɛ-/ *a.* M19. [f. mod.L *epigynus*, f. EPI- + Gk *gunē* woman (used for 'pistil'): see -OUS.] *Bot.* Of a flower: having the ovary completely enclosed in the receptacle and the stamens, sepals, etc., situated above it. Of stamens, sepals, etc.: so situated. Cf. HYPOGYNOUS, PERIGYNOUS.

epigyny *n.* epigynous condition L19.

epigynum *n.* see EPIGYNE.

epiklesis *n.* var. of EPICLESIS.

epiky /ˈɛpɪki/ *n.* Long *obs.* exc. *Hist.* E16. [med.L *epikeia*, *epieikeia* f. Gk *epieikeia*, f. as EPI- + *eikos* reasonable.] Reasonableness, equity, esp. as a legal principle.

epilate /ˈɛpɪleɪt/ *v.t.* L19. [f. Fr. *épiler* (f. as ES- + L *pilus* hair) after *depilate*.] Remove hair from.

epiˈlation *n.* L19.

epilepsy /ˈɛpɪlɛpsi/ *n.* M16. [Fr. *épilepsie* or late L *epilepsia* f. Gk *epilēpsia*, f. *epilab-* stem of *epilambanein* seize, attack, f. as EPI- + *lambanein* take hold of.] A condition in which a person has intermittent paroxysmal attacks of disordered

For other words beginning with *epi-* see the entry for **epi-**

brain function usu. causing a loss of awareness or consciousness and sometimes convulsions.

epileptic /ɛpɪˈlɛptɪk/ *a.* & *n.* E17. [Fr. *épileptique* f. late L *epilepticus* f. Gk *epilēptikos*, f. *epilēpsia*: see prec., -IC.] A *adj.* 1 Of, pertaining to, or of the nature of epilepsy. E17. 2 Affected with epilepsy. E17.

1 *Financial Times* An irate spasmodic fit bordering on the epileptic.

B *n.* A person with epilepsy. M17.

epileptical *a.* E17. **epileptically** *adv.* L19. **epileptiform** *a.* resembling (the symptoms of) epilepsy M19. **epilepto'genic**, **ˌepilep'togenous** *adjs.* producing epileptic attacks L19. **epileptoid** *a.* resembling or of the nature of epilepsy M19.

epilimnion /ɛpɪˈlɪmnɪən/ *n.* Pl. **-nia** /-nɪə/. E20. [f. EPI- + Gk *limnion* dim. of *limnē* lake.] The upper, warmer layer of water in a stratified lake.

epilobium /ɛpɪˈləʊbɪəm/ *n.* L18. [mod.L, f. EPI- + Gk *lobos* lobe, pod, with ref. to the insertion of the corolla at the end of the long ovary.] Any of various plants constituting the genus *Epilobium* (family Onagraceae), with terminal racemes of pink or purplish flowers; a willowherb.

epilog *n.*, **-ise** *v.* see EPILOGUE, EPILOGIZE.

epilogist /ɪˈpɪlədʒɪst/ *n.* E18. [f. EPILOG(UE + -IST.] The writer or speaker of an epilogue.

epilogistic /ɛˌpɪləˈdʒɪstɪk/ *a.* (*rare*) of the nature of an epilogue L18.

epilogize /ɪˈpɪlədʒʌɪz, ɛ-/ *v.* Also **-ise**. E17. [Gk *epilogizesthai*, f. *epilogos*: see next, -IZE.] 1 *v.i.* Deliver an epilogue. E17. 2 *v.i.* Serve as an epilogue or ending. M17. 3 *v.t.* = EPILOGUE *v.* M19.

epilogue /ˈɛpɪlɒg/ *n.* & *v.* LME. [(O)Fr. *épilogue* f. L *epilogus* f. Gk *epilogos*, f. as EPI- + *logos* saying, speech: see -LOGUE. Cf. PROLOGUE.] A *n.* Also ***-log**. 1 The concluding part of a literary work; a postscript. LME. 2 A speech or short poem addressed to the spectators by one of the actors at the end of a play. L16. †3 *Rhet.* The concluding part of a speech; a summary. Only in M17.

1 *Financial Times* The epilogue . . summarizes the lives of surviving children. *fig.*: *Economist* Oman's establishment of diplomatic relations with Russia is the epilogue to the Dhofar rebellion.

B *v.t.* Provide an epilogue to. E17.

epilogical /ɛpɪˈlɒdʒɪk(ə)l/ *a.* (*rare*) pertaining to or resembling an epilogue L19. †**epiloguize** *v.i.* & *t.* = EPILOGIZE M17-M18.

epiloia /ɛpɪˈlɔɪə/ *n.* E20. [f. EPIL(EPSY after *paranoia*.] *Med.* Tuberous sclerosis.

epimedium /ɛpɪˈmiːdɪəm/ *n.* L18. [mod.L (see below) f. Gk *epimēdion*.] Any of various low-growing creeping perennial herbs of the genus *Epimedium*, of the barberry family, which includes barrenwort, *E. alpinum*.

epimer /ˈɛpɪmə/ *n.* E20. [f. EPI- + -MER.] *Chem.* Either of two stereoisomers differing in configuration about one asymmetric carbon atom when others are present in the molecule.

epimerase /ɪˈpɪm-, ɛ-/ *n.* an enzyme which catalyses inversion at an asymmetric carbon atom in a molecule containing more than one such atom M20. **epi'meric** *a.* E20. **epimerism** /ɪˈpɪm-, ɛ-/ *n.* the fact or condition of having epimers E20. **epimerization** /ɪˌpɪmərʌɪˈzeɪ-, ɛ-/ *n.* the conversion of one epimer into another E20. **epimerize** /ɪˈpɪm-, ɛ-/ *v.t.* convert (one epimer) into another M20.

epimera *n.* see EPIMERON.

epimere /ˈɛpɪmɪə/ *n.* L19. [f. EPI- + -MERE.] 1 *Zool.* = EPIMERON. L19. 2 *Embryol.* The part of the mesoderm that divides to form the dermatome, myotomes, and sclerotomes. L19.

epimerite /ɪˈpɪmərʌɪt, ɛ-/ *n.* L19. [f. EPI- + Gk *meros* part + -ITE[1].] *Zool.* An anterior extension of the body in some protozoans that is used as an organ of attachment.

epimeron /ɛpɪˈmiːrən/ *n.* Also †**-ra**, †**-rum**. Pl. **-ra** /-rə/. M19. [f. EPI- + Gk *mēros* thigh.] *Zool.* 1 Part of the lateral wall of a somite of a crustacean. M19. 2 The posterior sclerite of the thoracic pleuron of some insects. L19.

epimeral *a.* M19.

epimorphic /ɛpɪˈmɔːfɪk/ *a.* M20. [f. EPI- + Gk *morphē* form + -IC.] Of, pertaining to, or designating epimorphosis or an epimorphism.

epimorphism /ɛpɪˈmɔːfɪz(ə)m/ *n.* M20. [f. EPI- + Gk *morphē* form + -ISM.] *Math.* A homomorphism of one set onto another.

epimorphosis /ˌɛpɪmɔːˈfəʊsɪs/ *n.* E20. [f. EPI- + MORPHOSIS.] *Zool.* Regeneration in which a new part is produced by the growth of new tissue. Opp. MORPHALLAXIS.

epimyth /ˈɛpɪmɪθ/ *n.* M19. [Gk *epimuthion* use as n. of neut. of *epimuthios* coming after the fable, f. as EPI- + *muthos* fable.] The moral of a fable.

epinasty /ˈɛpɪnasti/ *n.* L19. [f. EPI- + Gk *nastos* pressed together + -Y[3].] *Bot.* A tendency in part of a plant to grow more rapidly on the upper side, so that it curves downwards.

epi'nastic *a.* L19.

-epine /ɪˈpiːn/ *suff.* [f. EPI- + -INE[5].] *Chem.* Occurring in the names of compounds whose molecule includes an unsaturated seven-membered ring containing nitrogen.

epinephrine /ɛpɪˈnɛfrɪn, -riːn/ *n.* Chiefly *US.* Also **-rin** /-rɪn/. L19. [f. EPI- + Gk *nephros* kidney + -INE[5], -IN[1].] = ADRENALIN.

epineural /ɛpɪˈnjʊər(ə)l/ *a.* & *n.* M19. [f. EPI- + NEURAL.] *Zool.* A *adj.* 1 Situated on a neural arch. M19. 2 Lying over and parallel to a nerve. E20. B *n.* An epineural spine in a fish. M19.

epineurium /ɛpɪˈnjʊərɪəm/ *n.* L19. [f. EPI- + Gk *neuron* nerve.] *Anat.* The outer sheath of connective tissue round a nerve trunk.

epinician /ɛpɪˈnɪsɪən/ *a.* M17. [f. next + -AN.] Celebrating victory.

epinicion /ɛpɪˈnɪsɪən/ *n.* Now *rare*. Also **-cium** /-sɪəm/. E17. [Gk *epinikion* use as n. of neut. of *epinikios* of victory, f. as EPI- + *nikē* victory.] A song of triumph.

epipalaeolithic /ˌɛpɪpalɪə(ʊ)ˈlɪθɪk, -peɪl-/ *a.* & *n.* Also ***-paleo-**. E20. [f. EPI- + PALAEOLITHIC.] *Archaeol.* (Designating or pertaining to) a period or culture that seems to show features of both the palaeolithic and the mesolithic periods and may be transitional between them.

epiphanous /ɪˈpɪf(ə)nəs, ɛ-/ *a.* E19. [Sense 1 f. Gk *epiphanēs*, f. as next, sense 2 f. next: see -OUS.] 1 Resplendent. *rare*. E19. 2 = EPIPHANIC. L20.

epiphany /ɪˈpɪf(ə)ni, ɛ-/ *n.* ME. [Ult. f. Gk *epiphainein* to manifest, f. as EPI- + *phainein* show: see -Y[3]. In sense 1 f. (O)Fr. *épiphanie* f. eccl.L *epiphania* pl. & sing. f. eccl.Gk *epiphania* pl.; in sense 2 partly f. Gk *epiphaneia* manifestation.] 1 (Also **E-**.) A Christian festival observed on 6 January, in the Orthodox Church commemorating the baptism of Jesus and in the Western Church the manifestation of Jesus to the Gentiles in the persons of the Magi. ME. 2 A manifestation of some divine or superhuman being. E17. 3 Any sudden and important manifestation or realization. M19.

2 E. IRVING The second coming . . the glorious Epiphany of God our Saviour. M. AYRTON Dionysus, whose apotheosis, or epiphany, . . was as a bull. 3 T. EAGLETON *The Prelude* draws back from the tragic brink to which its isolated epiphanies allude. F. FERGUSSON The final perception or epiphany . . with which the play ends.

Comb.: **Epiphanytide** the period of the Church's year beginning with and immediately following Epiphany.

epi'phanic *a.* of the nature of an epiphany M20. **epiphanize** *v.t.* make manifest, reveal M20.

epiphenomenon /ˌɛpɪfɪˈnɒmɪnən/ *n.* Pl. **-mena** /-mɪnə/. E17. [f. EPI- + PHENOMENON.] 1 *Med.* A secondary symptom occurring with a disease but not necessarily regarded as its result or cause. E17. 2 *Philos.* & *Psychol.* A concomitant or by-product of something; *spec.* consciousness or mental phenomena regarded as by-products of the physical activity of the brain and nervous system that do not influence behaviour. L19.

epiphenomenal *a.* of the nature of or pertaining to epiphenomena L19. **epiphenomenalism** *n.* the doctrine that consciousness is an epiphenomenon L19. **epiphenomenalist** *a.* & *n.* (*a*) *adj.* of or pertaining to epiphenomenalism; (*b*) *n.* an advocate of epiphenomenalism: E20.

epiphonema /ˌɛpɪfəˈniːmə/ *n.* M16. [L f. Gk *epiphōnēma*, f. *epiphōnein* call to.] *Rhet.* An exclamatory sentence or striking reflection, which sums up or concludes a discourse or passage.

epiphora /ɪˈpɪf(ə)rə, ɛ-/ *n.* L16. [L f. Gk = a bringing to or upon, f. as EPI- + *pherein* carry.] 1 *Rhet.* A figure in which one word is repeated impressively at the end of several sentences. Now *rare* or *obs.* L16. 2 *Med.* Excessive watering of the eye. M17.

epiphragm /ˈɛpɪfram/ *n.* In sense 2 also in L form **epiphragma** /ɛpɪˈfragmə/. M19. [mod.L *epiphragma* f. Gk = lid, f. as EPI- + *phragma* fence.] 1 *Zool.* The layer of hardened secretion with which a snail closes its shell before hibernation. M19. 2 *Bot.* A membrane closing the mouth of the spore-case or fruiting body in some mosses and fungi. M19.

epiphyllous /ɛpɪˈfɪləs/ *a.* E19. [f. EPI- + Gk *phullon* leaf + -OUS.] *Bot.* Growing or inserted on a leaf.

epiphyllum /ɛpɪˈfɪləm/ *n.* M19. [mod.L (see below), f. as EPI- + Gk *phullon* leaf, the flowers being borne on flattened leaflike branches.] A cactus of the tropical American genus *Epiphyllum*, with flattened stems and large fragrant red or yellow flowers, *esp.* the night-flowering cactus *E. hookeri*.

epiphysis /ɪˈpɪfɪsɪs, ɛ-/ *n.* Pl. **-physes** /-fɪsiːz/. M17. [mod.L f. Gk *epiphusis*, f. as EPI- + *phusis* growth.] 1 A part of a bone, esp. an extremity of a long bone, which during growth is separated from the main part by cartilage that eventually ossifies. M17. 2 The pineal gland. More fully *epiphysis cerebri* /ˈsɛrɪbrʌɪ/ [L *cerebrum* brain]. L19.

epiphyseal, **-ial** /ɛpɪˈfɪzɪəl/ *adjs.* M19. **epiphysitis** /ɪˌpɪfɪˈsʌɪtɪs, ɛ-/ *n.* (*Med.*) inflammation of an epiphysis or of the cartilage separating it from the main part of the bone L19.

epiphyte /ˈɛpɪfʌɪt/ *n.* M19. [f. EPI- + -PHYTE.] A plant (esp. one that is not parasitic) which grows on another plant.

epi'phytal *a.* (now *rare*) = EPIPHYTIC M19. **epiphytic** /-ˈfɪtɪk/ *a.* of, pertaining to, or designating an epiphyte or epiphytes M19. **epiphytical** /-ˈfɪt-/ *a.* (now *rare*) = EPIPHYTIC M19. **epiphytically** /-ˈfɪt-/ *adv.* M19. **epi'phytous** *a.* (now *rare*) = EPIPHYTIC M19.

epiphytotic /ˌɛpɪfʌɪˈtɒtɪk/ *a.* & *n.* L19. [f. as prec. after *epizootic*.] (Designating) a plant disease that is temporarily prevalent over a large area.

epipleural /ɛpɪˈplʊər(ə)l/ *a.* M19. [f. Gk *epipleuros*, f. as EPI- + *pleura* rib: see -AL[1].] *Zool.* Situated on a rib.

epiplocele /ɪˈpɪpləsiːl, ɛ-/ *n.* E17. [Gk *epiplokēlē*, f. as EPIPLOON + -CELE.] *Med.* A hernia in which part of the omentum protrudes.

epiploic /ɛpɪˈpləʊɪk/ *a.* M17. [f. next + -IC.] *Anat.* Of or pertaining to the omentum.

epiploic foramen: connecting the two sacs of the peritoneum.

epiploon /ɪˈpɪpləʊɒn, ɛ-/ *n.* Now *rare*. LME. [Gk f. *epiplein* sail or float on.] 1 The omentum. LME. 2 The fat-body of an insect. E19.

epipodite /ɪˈpɪpədʌɪt, ɛ-/ *n.* M19. [f. next + -ITE[1].] *Zool.* A process on the outer side of the protopodite of a limb in some crustaceans.

Also **epipod** /ˈɛpɪpɒd/ *n.* L19.

epipodium /ɛpɪˈpəʊdɪəm/ *n.* Pl. **-ia** /-ɪə/. M19. [mod.L f. Gk *epipodion* use as n. of neut. of *epipodios* on the feet, f. as EPI- + *pod-*, *pous* foot.] *Zool.* A ridge running round the side of the foot in some molluscs.

epipodial *a.* L19.

epirogeny *n.* var. of EPEIROGENY.

Epirot /ɪˈpʌɪrət, ɛ-/ *n.* & *a.* Also **-rote** /-rəʊt/. L16. [Gk *ēpeirōtēs*, f. *ēpeiros* land, mainland: see -OT[2], -OTE.] A *n.* 1 A native or inhabitant of ancient or modern Epirus in NW Greece and southern Albania. L16. †2 (**e-**.) A person who lives inland. Only in M17. B *adj.* Of or pertaining to Epirus or its people. M19.

For other words beginning with *epi-* see the entry for **epi-**

episcopable /ɪˈpɪskəpəb(ə)l, ɛ-/ *a.* L17. [f. EPISCOPATE *v.* + -ABLE.] Eligible to be made a bishop.

episcopacy /ɪˈpɪskəpəsi, ɛ-/ *n.* M17. [f. eccl.L *episcopatus* EPISCOPATE *n.* after *prelacy*: see -ACY.] 1 Government of a Church by bishops; the system of church government in which there is an order of bishops. M17. 2 = EPISCOPATE *n.* 4. M17. 3 = EPISCOPATE *n.* 1. Now *rare.* L17. 4 = EPISCOPATE *n.* 3. Treated as *sing.* or *pl.* L18.

1 A. WOOD He was never a cordial friend to Episcopacy, but rather a patron of the Non-conformists. 2 P. H. BLAIR Remaining at first at Lindisfarne, but removing to Hexham during the episcopacy of Cuthbert.

episcopal /ɪˈpɪskəp(ə)l, ɛ-/ *a.* & *n.* LME. [(O)Fr. *épiscopal* or eccl.L *episcopalis*, f. *episcopus* BISHOP *n.*: see -AL[1].] A *adj.* 1 Of or pertaining to a bishop or bishops. LME. 2 Of or pertaining to episcopacy. Formerly also, advocating episcopacy. M17. 3 (Of a Church) constituted on the principle of government by bishops, possessing bishops; belonging to such a Church. M18.

1 W. JONES The episcopal ring . . was considered a symbol of sacerdotal authority. B. MOORE An Abbot with episcopal powers. *vicar episcopal*: see VICAR 3. 2 R. NELSON The Christian Church . . gives full Testimony in behalf of Episcopal Government. 3 I. SHAW She was . . sending her . . son to an exclusive, all-boys' Episcopal school. *Christian Socialist* An episcopal priest. **Episcopal Church**: *spec.* a Church of the Anglican Communion in the US, Scotland, and some other countries.

B *n.* = EPISCOPALIAN *n.* E18.

episcoˈpality *n.* (*rare*) episcopal manner or bearing; episcopacy; an episcopate: E17. **episcopally** *adv.* as a bishop; at the hands of a bishop; as an episcopal Church: M17.

episcopalia /ɪˌpɪskəˈpeɪlɪə, ɛ-/ *n.pl.* M19. [med.L, neut. pl. of *episcopalis* EPISCOPAL.] 1 *Hist.* Customary payments made by the clergy to the bishop of their diocese. M19. 2 Vestments, buildings, etc., belonging to a bishop. E20.

episcopalian /ɪˌpɪskəˈpeɪlɪən, ɛ-/ *a.* & *n.* L17. [f. EPISCOPAL + -IAN.] A *adj.* (Usu. **E-**.) Belonging to or designating an episcopal Church or the Episcopal Church. L17. B *n.* An adherent of episcopacy; (usu. **E-**) a member of an episcopal Church or the Episcopal Church. M18.

episcopalianism *n.* the principles of episcopal Churches or Episcopalians E19.

episcopate /ɪˈpɪskəpət, ɛ-/ *n.* M17. [eccl.L *episcopatus*, f. *episcopus* BISHOP *n.*: see -ATE[1].] 1 The position or office of a bishop. M17. 2 An episcopal see, a bishopric. E19. 3 Bishops collectively; *the* body of bishops in a Church. Treated as *sing.* or *pl.* M19. 4 The period during which a bishop holds office. L19.

1 G. PRIESTLAND We do not believe the Church of England . . should play with the episcopate as if it were a privately-owned treasure. 2 DISRAELI The Church Temporalities' Bill in 1833 . . suppressed ten Irish episcopates. 4 E. A. FREEMAN In the third year of his episcopate he was driven out.

†**episcopate** *v.i.* & *t.* M17–E18. [Late L *episcopat-* pa. ppl stem of *episcopare* be (in med.L also, make) a bishop, f. eccl.L *episcopus* BISHOP *n.*: see -ATE[3]. Cf. BISHOP *v.*[1]] Act as or make a bishop.

episcope /ˈɛpɪskəʊp/ *n.*[1] E20. [f. EPI- + -SCOPE.] An optical projector giving images of opaque objects.

epiˈscopic *a.* E20.

episcope /ɪˈpɪskəpi, ɛ-/ *n.*[2] Also **-é** /-eɪ/. M20. [Gk *episkopē* watching over, f. as EPI- + *skopē* watch.] The pastoral supervision exercised by a bishop.

episcopicide /ɪˈpɪskəpɪsʌɪd, ɛ-/ *n. rare.* L17. [f. eccl.L *episcopus* BISHOP *n.* + -I- + -CIDE.] †1 Murder of a bishop. L17–M18. 2 A person who or thing which causes the death of a bishop. *joc.* E20.

episcopize /ɪˈpɪskəpʌɪz, ɛ-/ *v.* Also **-ise**. M17. [f. eccl.L *episcopus* BISHOP *n.* + -IZE. Cf. EPISCOPATE *v.*] 1 *v.t.* Make (a person) a bishop. M17. 2 *v.i.*, & *t.* (w. *it*). Rule as a bishop; assume the role of a bishop. Now *rare* or *obs.* L17. 3 *v.t.* Bring under episcopal government; make episcopalian. M18.

episcotister /ɪˈpɪskətɪstə, ɛ-, ˌɛpɪskəˈtɪstə/ *n.* E20. [f. Gk *episkotizein* throw a shadow or darkness over, f. as EPI- + *skotos* darkness: see -IST, -ER[1].] A device used in experimental psychology for producing intermittent illumination of an object, consisting of a disc with a sector removed rotating in front of a light source.

episematic /ˌɛpɪsɪˈmatɪk/ *a.* L19. [f. EPI- + SEMATIC.] *Zool.* Of coloration, markings, etc.: serving to assist recognition by members of the same species.

episememe /ɛpɪˈsiːmiːm/ *n.* M20. [f. EPI- + SEMEME.] *Ling.* The meaning of a tagmeme or of a grammatical construction.

episiotomy /ɪˌpɪsɪˈɒtəmi, ɛ-/ *n.* L19. [f. Gk *epision* pubic region + -TOMY.] Enlargement of the vulval orifice by incision into the perineum, performed to facilitate childbirth; an operation of this kind.

episode /ˈɛpɪsəʊd/ *n.* L17. [Gk *epeisodion* use as n. of neut. of *epeisodios* coming in besides, f. as EPI- + *eisodos* entrance, f. *eis* into + *hodos* way, passage.] 1 *Hist.* In Greek tragedy, an interpolated passage of dialogue between two choric songs. L17. 2 A scene or digression complete in itself but forming part of a continuous narrative; each of a series of connected incidents or scenes. L17. b Each of the different successive broadcasts that go to make up a television or radio serial. E20. 3 An incident or finite period in a person's life or the history of something, considered in isolation. L18. 4 *Mus.* A passage between successive statements of a subject or theme. M19.

2 G. S. FRASER Full of exciting episodes as it is . . *Beowulf* moves nevertheless with sad deliberate dignity. b A. ROAD To produce a single 25 minute episode of the show costs £44,000. 3 N. CALDER Important episodes of mountain-building. I. MURDOCH A psychotic episode is sometimes of value in altering a pattern of consciousness. 4 *transf.*: N. FRYE The body of the poem is arranged in the form ABACA, a main theme repeated twice with two intervening episodes, as in the musical rondo.

episodic /ɛpɪˈsɒdɪk/ *a.* E18. [f. prec. + -IC.] 1 Of the nature of an episode; incidental. E18. 2 Occurring in or characterized by episodes; occasional, sporadic. E18.

1 G. MAXWELL My earlier sojourn in the Hebrides . . in retrospect seemed episodic. 2 GEO. ELIOT His episodic show of regard. *British Medical Journal* Episodic joint inflammation.

episodal /-ˈsəʊ-/ *a.* (*rare*) = EPISODIC L19. **episodical** *a.* = EPISODIC M17. **episodically** *adv.* M18. **episodicity** /ɛˌpɪsəˈdɪsɪti/ *n.* (*Geol.*) episodic quality or character M20.

episome /ˈɛpɪsəʊm/ *n.* M20. [f. as EPI- + -SOME[3].] *Genetics.* A genetic element inside some cells (as the DNA of some bacteriophages) able to replicate independently and also in association with a chromosome.

epiˈsomal *a.* M20. **epiˈsomally** *adv.* M20.

epispastic /ɛpɪˈspastɪk/ *a.* & *n.* Now *rare.* M17. [mod.L *epispasticus* f. Gk *epispastikos*, f. *epispan* attract, f. as EPI- + *span* to draw: see -IC.] *Med.* A *adj.* Producing a blister or a serous discharge. M17. B *n.* A blister; a substance for producing blisters. L17.

epistasis /ɪˈpɪstəsɪs, ɛ-/ *n.* Pl. **-ases** /-əsiːz/. E19. [Gk = a stoppage, f. *ephistanai* to check, stop, f. as EPI- + *histanai* put.] 1 *Med.* A film that forms on urine after it has stood. *rare.* E19. 2 *Med.* The checking of a bodily discharge. *rare.* E19. 3 *Genetics.* An interaction of genes that are not alleles; *esp.* the suppression of the effect of one such gene by another. E20.

Also **epistasy** /ɪˈpɪstəsi, ɛ-/ *n.* [Gk *epistasia* dominion] E20.

epistatic /ɛpɪˈstatɪk/ *a.* E20. [f. EPI- + STATIC, after *hypostasis*, *hypostatic*.] *Genetics.* Of, exhibiting, or caused by epistasis. (Foll. by *on*, *over*, *to*.)

epistaxis /ɛpɪˈstaksɪs/ *n.* Pl. **-staxes** /-ˈstaksiːz/. L18. [mod.L f. Gk, f. *epistazein* bleed at the nose, f. as EPI- + *stazein* drip.] Bleeding from the nose; a nosebleed.

epistemic /ɛpɪˈstiːmɪk, -ˈstɛm-/ *a.* E20. [f. Gk *epistēmē*: see EPISTEMOLOGY, -IC.] *Philos.* & *Ling.* Of or relating to (the extent of) knowledge or knowing, or its linguistic expression.

R. QUIRK We have epistemic modality expressing the degree of speaker's knowledge (e.g. *He may go* = 'I think it possible that he will').

epistemically *adv.* E20.

epistemics /ɛpɪˈstiːmɪks, -ˈstɛm-/ *n.* M20. [f. prec.: see -ICS.] The branch of science that deals with knowledge and understanding.

epistemology /ɪˌpɪstɪˈmɒlədʒi, ɛ-/ *n.* M19. [f. Gk *epistēmo-* comb. form of *epistēmē* knowledge, f. *epistasthai* know (how to do) + -OLOGY.] The branch of philosophy that deals with the varieties, grounds, and validity of knowledge.

eˌpistemoˈlogical *a.* L19. **eˌpistemoˈlogically** *adv.* in an epistemological manner; with reference to epistemology: L19. **epistemologist** *n.* L19.

episternum /ɛpɪˈstəːnəm/ *n.* M19. [f. EPI- + STERNUM.] *Zool.* 1 The upper part of the sternum in mammals; an interclavicle in some other vertebrates. M19. 2 The anterior sclerite of the thoracic pleuron of some insects. M19.

episternal *a.* situated on the sternum; of, pertaining to, or of the nature of an episternum: M19.

epistle /ɪˈpɪs(ə)l/ *n.* OE. [Orig. directly f. L *epistola* f. Gk *epistolē*, f. as EPI- + *stellein* send. In ME reintroduced f. OFr. (mod. *épître*).] 1 A letter, *esp.* one of a literary, formal, or public nature. Now freq. *joc.* or *rhet.* OE. b A literary work in the form of a letter, usu. in verse. LME. c A preface or letter of dedication at the beginning of a literary work. *obs.* exc. in *dedicatory epistle*, *epistle dedicatory*. E17. 2 *Chr. Ch.* a Any of various books in the New Testament which originated as apostolic letters to Christian communities and individuals. ME. b (**E-**.) *The* New Testament reading that precedes the Gospel in the Eucharist. LME.

2a CATHOLIC *Epistles. pastoral epistles*: see PASTORAL *a.* *Comb.*: **Epistle side** *Chr. Ch.* the south end of an altar, from which the Epistle is traditionally read.

epistle /ɪˈpɪs(ə)l/ *v.t.* & *i. rare.* L16. [f. the n.] = EPISTOLIZE. Also, write in a letter.

epistler /ɪˈpɪs(t)lə/ *n.* L16. [f. EPISTLE *n.*, *v.* + -ER[1].] 1 The writer of an epistle. L16. 2 *Chr. Ch.* = EPISTOLER 1. Now *rare* or *obs.* M17.

†**epistolar** *a.* LME–E18. [L *epistolaris*: see next, -AR[1].] = EPISTOLARY.

epistolary /ɪˈpɪst(ə)l(ə)ri/ *a.* M17. [Fr. *épistolaire* or L *epistolaris*, f. *epistola*: see EPISTLE *n.*, -ARY[2].] 1 Of or pertaining to (the writing of) epistles or letters. M17. 2 In the form of a letter or letters; contained in or conducted by letters. M17.

1 H. ACTON Some writers adapt themselves to their correspondents, even to the extent of changing their epistolary style. 2 T. JEFFERSON I recall . . the days of our former intercourse, personal and epistolary. *Notes & Queries* The year of the original epistolary form of the novel.

Also **epistolatory** *a.* E18.

epistoler /ɪˈpɪst(ə)lə/ *n.* M16. [Sense 1 f. OFr. *epistelier* or med.L *epistolaris*, *-arius* (see prec., -ER[2] 2); sense 2 f. Fr. †*épistolier* f. L *epistolaris*, f. *epistola* EPISTLE *n.*] 1 *Chr. Ch.* The reader of the Epistle at the Eucharist. M16. 2 A letter-writer. M17.

†**epistolic** *a.* M18. [Gk *epistolikos*, f. *epistolē*: see EPISTLE *n.*, -IC.] 1 = EPISTOLOGRAPHIC. Only in M18. 2 = EPISTOLARY. Only in L18.

†**epistolical** *a.* = EPISTOLARY M17–M18.

epistolise *v.* var. of EPISTOLIZE.

epistolist /ɪˈpɪst(ə)lɪst/ *n.* M18. [f. L *epistola* EPISTLE *n.* + -IST.] = EPISTLER 1.

epistolize /ɪˈpɪst(ə)lʌɪz/ *v. arch.* Also **-ise**. M17. [f. L *epistola* EPISTLE *n.* + -IZE.] 1 *v.i.* Write a letter or letters. M17. 2 *v.t.* Write a letter to (a person), correspond with. M18.

1 H. JAMES Be assured that the amount of thinking of you . . is out of all proportion to the amount of epistolizing. 2 BYRON St. Paul need not trouble himself to epistolize the present brood of Ephesians.

epistolizer *n.* M17.

epistolographic /ɪˌpɪst(ə)ləˈɡrafɪk/ *a. arch.* L17. [Gk *epistolographikos*, f. *epistolē*: see EPISTLE *n.*, -O-, -GRAPHIC.] (Of an alphabet or script) used in writing letters; *spec.* designating the demotic script of ancient Egypt.

e,pisto'lography *n.* letter-writing M19.

epistolophobia /ɪ,pɪst(ə)lə'fəʊbɪə/ *n.* E19. [f. (as) prec. + -PHOBIA.] A marked reluctance to write letters.

epistrophe /ɪ'pɪstrəfi, ɛ-/ *n.* L16. [Gk *epistrophē*, f. *epistrephein* turn about, f. as EPI- + *strephein* to turn.] *Rhet.* Repetition of a word at the end of successive clauses.

epistyle /'ɛpɪstʌɪl/ *n.* Orig. in L form †**-stylium**. M16. [Fr. *épistyle* or L *epistylium* f. Gk *epistulion*, f. as EPI- + *stulos* column.] *Archit.* = ARCHITRAVE I.

episyllogism /ɛpɪ'sɪlədʒɪz(ə)m/ *n.* M19. [f. EPI- + SYLLOGISM.] *Logic.* A syllogism the major premiss of which is proved by a preceding syllogism.

,**episyllo'gistic** *a.* L19.

epitaph /'ɛpɪtɑːf, -taf/ *n.* & *v.* LME. [(O)Fr. *épitaphe* f. L *epitaphium* funeral oration f. Gk *epitaphion* use as n. of neut. of *epitaphios* over or at a tomb or burial, f. as EPI- + *taphos* obsequies, tomb.] **A** *n.* An inscription upon a tomb; a brief composition characterizing a dead person. LME.

fig.: R. W. EMERSON The rolling rock leaves its scratches on the mountain . . the fern and leaf their modest epitaph in the coal.

B *v.t.* Describe in an epitaph; write an epitaph about. L16.

epitapher *n.* (*rare*) L16. **epi'taphic** *a.* L19. †**epitaphical** *a.*: only in L16. **epitaphize** *v.t.* = EPITAPH *v.* M19.

epitaphial /ɛpɪ'tafɪəl/ *a. rare.* M19. [f. Gk *epitaphios*: see prec., -AL[1].] Of, pertaining to, or contained in epitaphs.

epitaphian *a.* †(*a*) delivered at a funeral; (*b*) = EPITAPHIAL: M17.

epitasis /ɪ'pɪtəsɪs, ɛ-/ *n.* Pl. **-ases** /-əsiːz/. L16. [mod.L f. Gk, f. *epiteinein* intensify, f. as EPI- + *teinein* stretch.] The second part of a play, in which the action begins; the part of a play etc. where the plot thickens.

epitaxy /'ɛpɪtaksi/ *n.* M20. [Fr. *épitaxie*, f. as EPI-: see -TAXY.] The growth of crystals on a crystalline substrate which determines their orientation.

epi'taxial *a.* grown by or resulting from epitaxy M20. **epi'taxially** *adv.* so that epitaxy occurs; by an epitaxial process: M20. **epi'taxis** *n.* = EPITAXY M20.

epithalamium /,ɛpɪθə'leɪmɪəm/ *n.* Also (earlier) **-ion** /-ɪən/. Pl. **-iums, -ions, -ia** /-ɪə/. L16. [(L f.) Gk *epithalamion* use as n. of neut. of *epithalamios* nuptial, f. as EPI- + *thalamos* bridal chamber.] A song or poem in celebration of a wedding.

epithalamial *a.* L19. **epithalamic** /-'lamɪk/ *a.* M18. **epi'thalamy** *n.* (now *rare* or *obs.*) = EPITHALAMIUM L16.

epithalamus /ɛpɪ'θaləməs/ *n.* E20. [f. EPI- + THALAMUS.] *Anat.* The dorsal part of the diencephalon, which includes the pineal gland.

epithelia *n.* pl. of EPITHELIUM.

epitheliomuscular /ɛpɪ,θiːlɪə(ʊ)'mʌskjʊlə/ *a.* M20. [f. next + -O- + MUSCULAR.] Functioning as both epithelial and muscular tissue, as in some coelenterates; of or pertaining to such tissue.

epithelium /ɛpɪ'θiːlɪəm/ *n.* Pl. **-ia** /-ɪə/. M18. [mod.L, f. EPI- + Gk *thēlē* teat, nipple + -IUM.] **1** *Anat.* Tissue of the kind that covers the surface of the body and lines some hollow structures in humans and animals, consisting of sheets of cells bound closely together without intervening connective tissue; a particular kind or portion of such tissue. M18. **2** *Bot.* A layer of glandular cells such as those which line resin and gum canals. M19.

epithelial *a.* of, pertaining to, or of the nature of epithelium M19. **epitheliali'zation** *n.* = EPITHELIZATION M20. **epithelioid** *a.* resembling epithelium or epithelial cells L19. ,**epitheli'oma** *n.*, pl. **-mas, -mata** /-mətə/, a tumour of epithelial tissue, *esp.* a malignant tumour of squamous epithelium, a squamous-cell carcinoma L19. ,**epitheli'omatous** *a.* affected with or of the nature of an epithelioma L19. ,**epitheli'osis** *n.* a condition marked by a proliferation of epithelial cells M20. **epithelization** /,ɛpɪθiːlʌɪ'zeɪʃ(ə)n/ *n.* the process of becoming covered with or converted into epithelium M20.

epithem /'ɛpɪθɛm/ *n.* Also (earlier) †**-thima**. LME. [L *epithema* f. Gk *epithema, -thēma*, f. *epitithenai*: see next.] **1** A liquid applied to the body externally, esp. as a compress or poultice; the application of this. *arch.* LME. **2** *Bot.* A group of water-secreting cells below the epidermis of the leaves of many plants. E20.

†**epithemation** *n.* = EPITHEM I LME–E18.

epithet /'ɛpɪθɛt/ *n.* & *v.* L16. [Fr. *épithète* or L *epitheton* use as n. of neut. of Gk *epithetos* attributed, pa. ppl a. of *epitithenai* put on, add, f. as EPI- + *tithenai* to place.] **A** *n.* **1** A word or phrase expressing a quality or attribute regarded as characteristic of the person or thing mentioned. L16. **2** A significant appellation; a suitably descriptive term. L16. †**3** A term, an expression. *rare* (Shakes.). L16–E17. **4** An offensive or derogatory expression used of a person; a term of abuse, a profanity. L19. **5** Chiefly *Bot.* & *Microbiol.* In the binomial system of nomenclature: the element of a scientific name (typically in the form of an adj. in agreement with the generic name) indicating the species, variety, etc. E20.

1 GEO. ELIOT Hollow, empty—is the epithet justly bestowed on Fame. **2** B. C. BRODIE We . . employ the French term of ennui, for want of an equally appropriate epithet in English. *transferred epithet*: see TRANSFER *v.* 1b. **5** R. D. MEIKLE The willow was described by Smith as *Salix oleifolia* . . , an unfortunate choice of epithet since it was antedated by *S. oleifolia* of Villars. *specific epithet*: see SPECIFIC *a.*

B *v.t.* Describe using an epithet, apply an epithet to. E17.

G. MACDONALD Woeful Miss Witherspin, as Mark had epitheted her.

epitheted *a.* (*a*) containing many epithets; (*b*) designated by an epithet, esp. one too coarse to mention: E19. **epi'thetic** *a.* †(*a*) = EPITHETED (a); (*b*) pertaining to or of the nature of an epithet: M18. **epi'thetical** *a.* = EPITHETIC E18. **epi'thetically** *adv.* (*rare*) M19. **epithetize** *v.t.* (*rare*) = EPITHET *v.* E18.

†**epitheton** *n.* M16–E18. [L: see prec.] An attribute; an epithet.

†**epithima** *n.* see EPITHEM.

†**epithumetic** *a.* see EPITHYMETIC.

†**epithyme** *n.* LME–E18. [L *epithymon* f. Gk *epithumon*, f. as EPI- + *thumon* thyme.] A dodder, *Cuscuta epithymum*, parasitic on wild thyme.

epithymetic /,ɛpɪθɪ'mɛtɪk/ *a.* Also (earlier) †**-thum-**. M17. [Gk *epithumētikos*, f. *epithumein* to desire, f. as EPI- + *thumos* soul, appetite: see -IC.] Connected with desire or appetite.

epitomator /ɪ'pɪtəmeɪtə, ɛ-/ *n.* E17. [f. L *epitomat-* pa. ppl stem of *epitomare*, f. as next: see -ATOR.] A person who writes an epitome of a larger work.

epitome /ɪ'pɪtəmi, ɛ-/ *n.* Also (*non-standard*) **-my**. E16. [L f. Gk *epitomē*, f. *epitemnein* cut into, cut short, f. as EPI- + *temnein* to cut.] **1** A summary or abstract of a written work; a condensed account. E16. **2** A thing that represents another in miniature; a person who or thing which embodies a quality etc.; a typical example. E16.

1 L. HUTCHINSON To number his virtues is to give an epitome of his life. *Daily Telegraph* Apply . . with an epitome of past commercial and engineering experience. **2** W. HOLTBY Local government was an epitome of national government. J. FOWLES She was an epitome of all the most crassly arrogant traits of the . . British Empire.

Phrases: **in epitome** in miniature; in a summary.

epi'tomic *a.* of the nature of an epitome M17. **epi'tomical** *a.* = EPITOMIC E17. **epitomist** *n.* the writer of an epitome E17.

epitomize /ɪ'pɪtəmʌɪz, ɛ-/ *v.t.* Also **-ise**. L16. [f. EPITOME + -IZE.] **1** Make an epitome of, abridge; give a condensed account of, summarize. L16. †**b** Reduce to a smaller scale. M17–E18. **2** Contain in a small compass; contain or express in brief the whole of; be a perfect example of, typify. E17.

1 J. A. FROUDE I shall . . in a few pages briefly epitomize what passed. **2** I. MURDOCH She epitomised everything he didn't care for about women.

epitomi'zation *n.* the action of epitomizing; an epitome: E19. **epitomizer** *n.* E17.

epitomy *n.* see EPITOME.

epitrichium /ɛpɪ'trɪkɪəm/ *n.* L19. [f. EPI- + Gk *trikhion* dim. of *trikh-, thrix* hair.] *Anat.* A thin layer of cells covering the epidermis of an embryo, usu. disappearing before birth.

epitrichial *a.* L19.

epitrite /'ɛpɪtrʌɪt/ *n.* E17. [L *epitritos* f. Gk = in the ratio of 4 to 3, f. as EPI- + *tritos* third.] *Class. Pros.* A metrical foot consisting of one unstressed and three stressed syllables.

epitrochoid /ɛpɪ'trɒkɔɪd, -'trəʊ-/ *n.* M19. [f. EPI- + Gk *trokhos* wheel + -OID.] A curve traced by a point on a radius or extended radius of a circle that rolls outside another circle.

,**epitro'choidal** *a.* E19.

epitrope /ɪ'pɪtrəpi, ɛ-/ *n.* M16. [Late L f. Gk *epitropē*, f. *epitrepein* yield, f. as EPI- + *trepein* to turn.] *Rhet.* A figure of speech in which permission is given to an opponent, either seriously or ironically.

epizeuxis /ɛpɪ'zjuːksɪs/ *n.* L16. [Late L f. Gk, f. as EPI- + *zeuxis* yoking, f. *zeugnunai* to yoke.] *Rhet.* The vehement or emphatic repetition of a word.

epizoon /ɛpɪ'zəʊɒn/ *n.* Pl. **-zoa** /-'zəʊə/. M19. [f. EPI- + Gk *zōion* animal.] An animal that lives on the surface of another, esp. as a parasite.

epizoic *a.* living on the surface of an animal; of or pertaining to epizoa: M19.

epizootic /,ɛpɪzəʊ'ɒtɪk/ *a.* & *n.* L18. [Fr. *épizootique*, f. *épizootie*, f. as EPI- + Gk *zōion* animal: see -OTIC.] **A** *adj.* Of an animal disease: normally absent or infrequent in a population but liable to periods of greatly increased frequency; temporarily widespread. L18. **B** *n.* A temporary but widespread outbreak of a particular disease among animals; an epizootic disease. M19.

,**epizoot(i)o'logic(al)** *adjs.* of or pertaining to epizootiology M20. ,**epizooti'ology**, **-zoo'tology** *n.* the branch of science that deals with the incidence and transmission of disease in animal populations, esp. with a view to controlling them; the aspects *of* an animal disease to do with its incidence and transmission: M20. **epi'zooty** *n.* = EPIZOOTIC *n.* L18.

epoch /'iːpɒk/ *n.* Also (earlier) †**-cha**. E17. [mod.L *epocha* f. Gk *epokhē* stoppage, fixed point of time, f. *epekhein* stop, take up a position, f. as EPI- + *ekhein* hold, be in a certain state.] **I** A point in time. **1** The initial point in a system of chronology; a date from which succeeding years are numbered. Now *rare*. E17. †**2** The date of origin of a situation, institution, etc.; an event marking such a date. M17–E19. **3** The beginning of a distinctive period in the history of something or someone. Cf. ERA 3. M17. **4** The date or time of an event. Now *rare* exc. as below. M17. **b** A point in time defined by the occurrence of particular events or by the existence of a particular state of affairs. E18. **c** *Astron.* The point in time at which a particular phenomenon takes place; an arbitrarily fixed date relative to which planetary or stellar measurements are expressed. E18.

3 L. M. MONTGOMERY I've had a splendid time . . . It marks an epoch in my life. **4** T. JEFFERSON Inform him what . . you expect to deliver, with the epochs of delivery. **b** E. R. PITMAN It was an epoch never to be forgotten . . when she commenced labouring in Joppa.

II A period of time. **5** Orig., a chronological period characterized by the numbering of years from a particular noteworthy event (cf. ERA 1a). Now = ERA 1b. E17. **6** *Geol.* A division of geological time; *spec.* a subdivision of a period, corresponding to a stratigraphic series. E19. **7** *Physics.* The time interval between the zero of time measurement and the zero of a simple harmonic motion; (also *epoch angle*) the angular separation corresponding to this. L19.

5 H. J. LASKI No man was so emphatically representative of his epoch as Adam Smith. D. LESSING Poor people lived there as the rich have done in previous epochs. **6** *Scientific American* The basis for dividing geologic time into eras, periods and epochs.

W. C. PUTNAM The Pliocene Epoch, which merged with the Pleistocene, saw the rise of the living . . animals of the Earth.

Comb.: *epoch angle*: see sense 7 above; **epoch-making** *a.* such as marks the beginning of a new epoch; historic, of major importance; remarkable.

epochal /ˈɛpɒk(ə)l, iːˈpɒk-/ *a.* L17. [f. prec. + -AL[1].] 1 Of or pertaining to an epoch or epochs. L17. 2 Forming or characterizing an epoch; epoch-making. M19.

epochally *adv.* M20.

epoché /ˈɛpɒki/ *n.* E20. [f. Gk *epokhē* (see EPOCH) in sense 'suspension of judgement'.] *Philos.* (In Greek Scepticism) refusal to adopt a judgement or belief, when the necessary knowledge is not attainable; (in Phenomenology) the setting aside of assumptions and known facts in order to perceive the essence of a phenomenon.

epode /ˈɛpəʊd/ *n.* E17. [Fr. *épode* or L *epodos* f. Gk *epōidos*, f. as EPI- + *ōidē* ODE.] 1 A Greek lyric poem composed of couplets in which a long line is followed by a shorter; a serious poem. E17. 2 The part of a Greek lyric ode following the strophe and antistrophe. L17.

éponge /epɔ̃ːʒ/ *n.* E20. [Fr. f. L *spongia* SPONGE *n.*[1]] Sponge cloth.

eponychium /ɛpəˈnɪkɪəm/ *n.* L19. [mod.L, f. EPI- + Gk *onukh-*, *onux* nail.] *Anat.* The epidermis from which a nail develops in the foetus; the film of epidermis covering the root of a nail, the cuticle.

eponym /ˈɛpənɪm/ *n.* M19. [Gk *epōnumos* given as a name, giving one's name to a thing or person, f. as EPI- + -O- + -NYM.] 1 A person whose name has given rise (in fact or by repute) to the name of a people, place, institution, etc.; a personal name used as a common noun or used to form a common noun. M19. b A name or noun formed in this way. L19. 2 An Assyrian functionary who gave his name to his year of office. M19. 3 A person who is identified with something. L19.

1 G. GROTE Pelops is the eponym or name-giver of the Peloponnesus. A. BURGESS The eponym of H. G. Wells's *Christina Alberta's Father*, a retired laundry manager. b *Daily Telegraph* It would be absurd to compile a list of eponyms without mentioning . . 'malapropism' or 'stentorian'. 3 C. MERIVALE Saturn becomes the eponym of all useful and humane discovery.

epoˈnymic *a.* of, pertaining to, or using eponyms; eponymous: M19. **epoˈnymically** *adv.* M20. **eˈponymist** *n.* a person who is an eponym M19. **eˈponymous** *a.* (of a person) giving his or her name to something; (of a thing) named after a particular person: M19. **eˈponymously** *adv.* L20.

eponymus /ɪˈpɒnɪməs, ɛ-/ *n.* M19. [mod.L f. as prec.] A historical or mythical person who is an eponym.

eponymy /ɪˈpɒnɪmi, ɛ-/ *n.* M19. [Gk *epōnumia* derived or significant name, f. as EPONYM: see -Y[3].] 1 Eponymic nomenclature; the practice of explaining names of peoples, places, etc., by referring them to the name of a historical or mythical person. M19. 2 The year of office of an Assyrian eponym. L19.

epoophoron /ɛpəʊˈɒf(ə)rɒn/ *n.* L19. [f. EPI- + Gk *ōophoron* neut. of *ōophoros* bearing eggs, f. *ōion* egg + *-phoros* bearing.] *Anat.* In the female, a group of vestigial tubules derived from the upper mesonephros, between an ovary and a Fallopian tube, corresponding to the male epididymis. Cf. PAROOPHORON.

epopee /ˈɛpəpiː/ *n.* Now *rare.* L17. [Fr. *épopée* f. as next.] An epic poem, an epic; epic poetry.

epopoeia /ɛpəˈpiːə/ *n. arch.* L16. [Gk *epopoiia*, f. *epos* (see EPOS) + *poiein* make.] = EPOPEE.

epopt /ˈɛpɒpt/ *n.* L17. [Late L *epopta* f. Gk *epoptēs*, f. as EPI- + *op-* see.] *Gk Hist.* A person fully initiated into the Eleusinian mysteries.

epos /ˈɛpɒs/ *n.* M19. [L f. Gk = word, song, f. *ep-* stem of *eipein* say.] 1 Epic poetry; an epic poem; *esp.* narrative poetry embodying a nation's conception of its past history. M19. 2 = EPIC *n.* 4. M19.

epox- *comb. form* see EPOXY-.

epoxide /ɪˈpɒksʌɪd/ *n.* M20. [f. EPI- + OXIDE.] *Chem.* A compound whose molecule contains an oxygen atom linked to two carbon atoms as part of a ring; a cyclic ether.

Comb.: **epoxide resin** an epoxy resin.

epoxiˈdation *n.* the formation of an epoxide by addition of an oxygen atom to a carbon–carbon double bond M20. **epoxidize** *v.t.* convert into an epoxide by epoxidation M20.

epoxy /ɪˈpɒksi, ɛ-/ *n.* & *v.* M20. [f. next as adj.] A *n.* Epoxy resin; epoxy glue or cement. M20. B *v.t.* Infl. **epoxied, epoxyed.** Glue with epoxy glue or cement. L20.

epoxy- /ɪˈpɒksi, ɛ-/ *comb. form.* Bef. a vowel also **epox-**. Also as attrib. adj. **epoxy.** E20. [f. EPI- + OXY-.] 1 *Chem.* Designating or containing the group ·C·O·C· as it occurs in epoxides. E20. 2 (Only as adj.) Pertaining to or derived from an epoxide; *esp.* designating thermosetting synthetic resins containing epoxy groups, and substances made from them, used esp. as coatings and adhesives. M20.

1 *epoxy-compound, ring*, etc. 2 *epoxy glue, paint*, etc.

épris /epri/ *a.* Fem. ***éprise*** /epriz/. L18. [Fr., pa. ppl a. of *(s')éprendre* become attached or enamoured, f. as ES- + L *prehendere* seize.] Enamoured (*of*); taken *with*.

EPROM /ˈiːprɒm/ *n.* Also **eprom.** L20. [f. erasable programmable *ROM*.] *Computing.* A read-only memory whose contents can be erased by a special process (e.g. irradiation with ultraviolet light) and replaced.

eprouvette /ɛpruːˈvɛt/ *n.* Also **é-**. L18. [Fr. *éprouvette*, f. *éprouver* try, test: see -ETTE.] *Hist.* An apparatus for testing the strength of gunpowder.

epsilon /ˈɛpsɪlɒn, ɛpˈsʌɪlɒn/ *n.* E18. [Gk *e psilon* lit. 'bare e', short e written ε.] 1 The fifth letter (*E*, ε) of the Greek alphabet; *Astron.* (preceding the genitive of the L name of the constellation) the fifth brightest star in a constellation. E18. 2 An examiner's fifth-class mark; a person of low intelligence. E20.

Epsom /ˈɛpsəm/ *n.* Also **e-**. M17. [A town in Surrey, SE England.] 1 In full *Epsom water.* The water of a mineral spring at Epsom. M17. 2 In full *Epsom salt(s).* Orig., salts (chiefly magnesium sulphate) obtained from Epsom water. Now, hydrated magnesium sulphate as used medicinally, as a purgative etc. M18. 3 The racecourse on Epsom Downs, where the Derby and the Oaks are run; the principal race meeting held there. E19.

epsomite /ˈɛpsəmʌɪt/ *n.* E19. [f. prec. + -ITE[1].] Hydrated magnesium sulphate, occurring as a white efflorescence in caves and near springs and as orthorhombic crystals.

Epstein–Barr virus /ɛpstʌɪnˈbɑː vʌɪrəs/ *n. phr.* M20. [M. A. *Epstein* (b. 1921), Brit. virologist + Y. M. *Barr* (b. 1932), Irish-born virologist + VIRUS.] A DNA herpesvirus which causes infectious mononucleosis and is associated with Burkitt's lymphoma and nasopharyngeal carcinoma.

ept /ɛpt/ *a.* M20. [Back-form. f. INEPT.] Adroit, competent; appropriate, effective.

eptitude *n.* M20. **eptly** *adv.* L20.

epulary /ˈɛpjʊləri/ *a.* Now *rare.* L17. [L *epularis*, f. *epulum* banquet: see -ARY[2].] Of or pertaining to a feast.

epulation /ɛpjʊˈleɪʃ(ə)n/ *n.* Now *rare.* M16. [L *epulatio(n-)*, f. *epulat-* pa. ppl stem of *epulari* to feast, f. *epulum* banquet: see -ATION.] Feasting; a feast.

epulis /ɪˈpjuːlɪs, ɛ-/ *n.* Pl. **-lides** /-lɪdiːz/. M19. [mod.L f. Gk *epoulis*, f. as EPI- + *oulon* gum.] *Med.* A localized swelling of the gums.

epulotic /ɛpjʊˈlɒtɪk/ *n.* & *a.* Now *rare* or *obs.* M17. [Gk *epoulōtikos*, f. *epoulousthai* be covered with scars, f. as EPI- + *oulē* scar.] *Med.* (A medicine or ointment) that induces cicatrization.

†**epulotical** *a.* E–M17.

epurate /ˈɛpjʊreɪt/ *v.t.* Now *rare* or *obs.* L18. [f. (O)Fr. *épurer*, f. *pur* PURE *a.*: see -ATE[3].] Purify, purge. Freq. *fig.*

epuˈration *n.* E19.

epyllion /ɪˈpɪlɪən, ɛ-/ *n.* Pl. **-llia** /-lɪə/. L19. [Gk *epullion* dim. of *epos*: see EPOS.] A narrative poem resembling an epic in style or matter but of shorter extent.

equability /ɛkwəˈbɪlɪti/ *n.* M16. [L *aequabilitas*, f. as next: see -ITY.] 1 The quality of being equable; freedom from fluctuation or variation. M16. †2 Ability to be regarded as equal; comparability. L16–E19. †3 Well-balanced condition. L16–E17.

equable /ˈɛkwəb(ə)l/ *a.* M17. [L *aequabilis*, f. *aequare* make level or equal, f. *aequus* level, even, equal: see -ABLE.] †1 = EQUITABLE. Only in M17. 2 Of motion, temperature, the feelings, etc.: uniform, free from fluctuation or variation. L17. 3 Free from inequalities; uniform throughout; equally proportioned. L17.

2 A. T. THOMSON Mercury is . . adapted for thermometers; its expansion being most equable. M. F. MAURY The equable climates of Western Europe. P. H. JOHNSON He remained equable, sweet tempered and slow to anger. 3 C. THIRLWALL A new valuation . . with a view to a more equable system of taxation.

equableness *n.* M17. **equably** *adv.* E18.

equaeval /ɪˈkwiːv(ə)l, ɛ-/ *a.* Now *rare.* M19. [f. L *aequaevus*, f. *aequus* equal + *aevum* age: see -AL[1].] Of equal age; belonging to the same period.

Also †**equaevous** *a.*: only in M17.

equal /ˈiːkw(ə)l/ *a.*, *adv.*, & *n.* LME. [L *aequalis*, f. *aequus* level, even, equal: see -AL[1].] A *adj.* 1 Of a surface: even; level; on the same level. *arch.* LME. 2 Identical in amount, size, number, value, intensity, etc. LME. 3 Possessing a (specified or implied) quality or attribute to the same degree; on the same level as regards rank, power, excellence, etc.; *spec.* (of voices) belonging to the same register. Also foll. by *to*, *with*. E16. †4 Fair, just, impartial. E16–M18. 5 = EQUABLE 2. E17. †6 Uniform in appearance, size, or other property. M17–L18. 7 Evenly proportioned or balanced; uniform in effect or operation. M17. 8 Adequate in ability, resources, quantity, etc. Now only foll. by *to*. L17.

2 E. HUXLEY The company employs about equal numbers of each, but . . Pakistanis are coming into the lead. **all** or **other things being equal** circumstances being evenly balanced. 3 D. H. LAWRENCE No part should be subordinate to any other part: all should be equal. J. M. MURRY That was the excitement; but the dismay was equal. F. WELDON She had thought the Christian equal to the Jew; no more nor less. 5 GIBBON He proceeded, in a firm and equal tone. 7 GLADSTONE The Church contemplates with equal eye the whole of God's ordinances. **it is equal to me** it makes no difference to me, it's all the same to me. *separate but equal*: see SEPARATE *a.* 8 ARNOLD BENNETT He had . . proved equal to the enormously difficult situation. B. BAINBRIDGE I was not in very good health then, and not equal to duty at all.

Special collocations: **equal opportunity** the opportunity or right to be considered for employment or promotion without discrimination on certain grounds, as race, sex, or disability; the practice or policy of not discriminating in this way (freq. *attrib.* or in *pl.*). **equal pay** (the policy of giving) the same rate of pay for a particular job irrespective of the sex of the person doing it. **equal rights** (the policy of giving) the same rights for people of different races, both sexes, etc. *equal temperament*: see TEMPERAMENT *n.* 9.

†B *adv.* Equally. L16–M17.

C *n.* 1 A person who is equal to another in rank, ability, etc., or (formerly) age. L16. 2 *an equal*, a state of equality, a par. *obs.* exc. *dial.* L16.

1 D. H. LAWRENCE She knew herself to be the social equal, if not the superior, of anyone she was likely to meet.

equal /ˈiːkw(ə)l/ *v.* Infl. **-ll-**, ***-l-**. L16. [f. prec.] 1 *v.t.* Make equal; bring to the same level (*lit.* & *fig.*). *arch.* L16. †2 *v.t.* Consider or represent as equal; liken, compare. L16–E19. 3 *v.t.* Be or become equal to; match, rival. L16. 4†a *v.i.* Cope on equal terms *with. rare* (Shakes.). Only in L16. b *v.t.* Produce something equal to; reciprocate in equal measure. E17.

1 DRYDEN Rebellion equals all. 3 V. WOOLF Nothing on earth can equal this happiness. S. PLATH Let *a* equal acceleration and let *t* equal time. 4b DRYDEN Answer'd all her Cares, and equal'd all her Love.

Comb.: **equal(s) sign** the symbol =, used to indicate mathematical or other equality.

equalist *n.* (*rare*) a person who asserts the equality of certain (indicated) persons or things M17.

equalise *v.*, **equaliser** *n.* vars. of EQUALIZE etc.

equalitarian /ɪˌkwɒlɪˈtɛːrɪən, iː-/ *a.* & *n.* L18. [f. EQUALITY + -ARIAN.] = EGALITARIAN.

equalitarianism *n.* M19.

equality /ɪˈkwɒlɪti, iː-/ *n.* LME. [OFr. *equalité* (mod. *égalité*) f. L *aequalitas*, f. *aequalis*: see EQUAL *a.*, -ITY.] **1 a** The condition of being equal in quantity, magnitude, value, intensity, etc. LME. **b** *Math.* A symbolic expression of the fact that two quantities are equal; an equation. M20. **2** The condition of having equal rank, power, excellence, etc., with others. LME. †**3** Fairness, impartiality. LME–L17. **4** Evenness, uniformity. Now *rare*. LME. †**b** Evenness of mind or temper; equability. L15–M18.

1 C. V. WEDGWOOD Their votes . . would bring the supporters and the antagonists . . very nearly to an equality. 2 SOUTHEY Ye are all equal. . . Equality is your birth-right. S. UNWIN Her strong feelings about equality of the sexes.

Comb.: **Equality State** *US* (a popular name for) Wyoming, the first state to give women the vote.

equalize /ˈiːkwəlʌɪz/ *v.* Also **-ise**. L16. [f. EQUAL *a.* + -IZE, partly after Fr. *égaliser*.] †**1** *v.t.* = EQUAL *v.* 3. L16–E19. †**2** *v.t.* Consider to be equal, treat as equal; equate. Foll. by *to*, *with*. L16–M18. †**3** *v.t.* Bring to one level. L16–M17. **4 a** *v.t.* Make equal in magnitude, number, intensity, etc. E17. **b** *v.i. Sport.* Bring one's own side's score up to that of the other side. L19. **5** *v.t.* Make equal in rank, power, etc. M17. **6** *v.t.* Make uniform. E19. **7** *Electr.* **a** *v.t.* Correct or modify (a signal etc.) with an equalizer. E20. **b** *v.i.* Compensate *for* by means of an equalizer. M20. **8** *v.i.* Become equal. E20.

5 H. T. BUCKLE The invention of gunpowder equalised all men on the field of battle. 6 K. JOHNSTON The rich forest lands . . which equalise the temperature. 8 *Scientific American* The salty water . . poured through the hole until the pressure equalized.

equaliˈzation *n.* L18.

equalizer /ˈiːkwəlʌɪzə/ *n.* Also **-iser**. L18. [f. prec. + -ER[1].] **1** A person who aspires to be equal in rank, power, etc., to another. *rare*. L18. **2** A thing which makes equal. L18. **b** *Electr.* A passive network designed to modify a frequency response, esp. in such a way as to compensate for distortion. E20. **c** *Sport.* A goal, run, etc. that equalizes the score. E20. **d** A revolver, a firearm; a weapon. *slang* (orig. *US*). M20.

equally /ˈiːkw(ə)li/ *adv.* LME. [f. EQUAL *a.* + -LY[2].] **1** To an equal degree or extent. LME. **2** In equal shares or amounts. LME. **3** Uniformly; in uniform degree or quantity. LME. **4** According to the same rule or measure. Formerly also, impartially, equitably. E16. †**5** On a level; in a line *with*. L16–E18.

1 V. WOOLF She . . sat there . . equally poised between gloom and laughter. *Oxfam Review* Equally, the new relationship . . offers new opportunities. 2 R. RENDELL There was two hundred thousand and she left it equally between her four kids. 3 HUGH MILLER The population, formerly spread pretty equally over the country.

equalness /ˈiːkw(ə)lnɪs/ *n.* M16. [f. as prec. + -NESS.] **1** = EQUALITY 1a, 2. M16. †**2** Fairness, impartiality. Only in M16. †**3** Uniformity, evenness. M16–L18.

equanimity /ɛkwəˈnɪmɪti, iː-/ *n.* E17. [L *aequanimitas*, f. *aequus* even + *animus* mind: see -ITY.] †**1** Fairness, impartiality, equity. E17–M18. **2** Tranquillity of mind or temper; composure; resignation, acceptance of fate. E17.

2 V. BRITTAIN I refused to be . . impressed . . but such equanimity was difficult to achieve. S. SPENDER He faced adverse criticism with an equanimity which astonished me.

equanimous /ɪˈkwanɪməs, iː-/ *a.* M17. [f. L *aequanimus*, f. *aequus* even + *animus* mind: see -OUS.] Characterized by equanimity.

equanimously *adv.* M17. **equanimousness** *n.* (*rare*) M18.

equant /ˈiːkwənt/ *n.* & *a.* M16. [L *aequant-* pres. ppl stem of *aequare*: see next, -ANT[1].] **A** *n. Hist. Sci.* An imaginary circle introduced with the purpose of reconciling the planetary movements with the Ptolemaic hypothesis of uniform circular motion. M16. **B** *adj.* **1** *Hist. Sci.* Designating an equant. L16. **2** *Min.* Of a crystal: having its different diameters approximately equal in length. E20.

equate /ɪˈkweɪt, iː-/ *v.* LME. [L *aequat-* pa. ppl stem of *aequare* make equal, f. *aequus* EQUAL *a.*: see -ATE[3].] †**1** *v.t.* Make (bodies) equal; balance. *rare*. LME–M18. †**2** *v.t.* Take the average of. Only in LME. **3** *v.t. Astron.* Make a numerical adjustment to (an observation or calculation) in order to compensate for an irregularity or error. M17. **4** *v.t.* Chiefly *Math.* State the equality of (a thing) *to* or *with* another; put in the form of an equation. L17. **5** *v.t.* Treat or regard as equivalent. Foll. by *with* (also *to*). M19. **6** *v.i.* Be the equivalent of; be equal to; agree or correspond with. Foll. by *with* (also *to*). M20.

5 ANTHONY SMITH It is no longer possible to equate death with the lack of a heart beat. 6 M. STOTT Cleanliness does not equate with godliness.

equataˈbility *n.* the property of being equatable M20. **equatable** *a.* able to be equated L19. **equative** *a.* & *n.* (*Ling.*) (an expression, inflection, etc.) expressing equality, identity, or resemblance E20.

equation /ɪˈkweɪʒ(ə)n/, *in sense 1 also* -ʃ(ə)n/ *n.* LME. [(O)Fr. *équation* or L *aequatio(n-)*, f. as prec.: see -ATION.] **1** The action of making equal or equating; the state of being equal or in equilibrium; a balance. LME. †**b** *Astrol.* Equal partition, esp. of the heavens into twelve houses. Only in LME. †**2** *Math.* The action of stating the identity in value of two quantities or expressions. L16–L17. **3** A mathematical formula affirming the equivalence of two symbolic or numerical expressions (indicated by the sign =); *fig.* (the relationship between) the factors to be taken into account when considering a matter. L16. **b** *Chem.* A formula indicating a reaction by means of the symbols for the elements or compounds involved in it. E19. **4** *Astron.* A numerical quantity added to or subtracted from an observed or calculated one to compensate for an irregularity or error; the action or an act of making such an adjustment. M17.

1 J. W. KRUTCH Our characteristic equation of 'going to school' with 'getting an education'. A. F. DOUGLAS-HOME To establish an equation which would combine full employment with a steady level of prices. 3 S. THEMERSON There are some exceptions to the equation 1 + 1 = 2. *Which?* There have been some changes to that equation which may tip the balance in favour of diesel. *Laplace's equation*, *Planck('s) equation*, *Schrödinger('s) equation*, etc. **equation of state** *Sci.*: showing the relationship between the values of the pressure, volume, and temperature of a substance at any one time. **4 equation of time** the difference between mean solar time (as shown by clocks) and apparent solar time (indicated by sundials), which varies with the time of year. **human equation** = *personal equation* (b) below. **personal equation** (*a*) *Astron.* an individual's time of reaction or habitual inaccuracy in making observations; a correction or allowance made for this; (*b*) personal prejudice or bias.

equational /ɪˈkweɪʒ(ə)n(ə)l/ *a.* M19. [f. prec. + -AL[1].] **1** Pertaining to or involving the use of equations. M19. **2** *Biol.* Pertaining to or designating a chromosome division in which the two chromatids of each reduplicated chromosome separate longitudinally, prior to being incorporated into two daughter nuclei. E20. **3** *Gram.* Of a sentence, phrase, etc.: that has a copula, expressed or understood; copular. M20.

1 W. S. HATCHER An equational proof.

equationally *adv.* in terms of equations; by means of equations or an equational division: L19.

equator /ɪˈkweɪtə/ *n.* LME. [(O)Fr. *équateur* f.) med.L *aequator*, in full *circulus aequator diei et noctis* circle equalizing day and night, f. as EQUATE: see -OR.] **1** *Astron.* The great circle of the celestial sphere whose plane is perpendicular to the earth's axis and which is equidistant from the two celestial poles; when the sun is on it, the day is the same length as the night throughout the world. Also *celestial equator*. LME. **2** The great circle of the earth which is equidistant from the two poles and marks the division between the northern and southern hemispheres. E17. **b** A circle on any spherical body that divides it into two equal parts; *esp.* one equidistant from two poles of rotation. M18. **3 a** The part of a magnet midway between the poles, where its field is weakest. M17. **b** *magnetic equator*, the irregular line, passing round the earth in the neighbourhood of the geographical equator, on which the earth's magnetic field is horizontal. M19. **4** *Biol.* The plane of division of a cell or nucleus lying midway between the poles and at right angles to a line joining them. L19.

2b *New Yorker* Possible landing sites along the moon's equator.

equatorward *a.* & *adv.* (moving or facing) towards the equator E20. **equatorwards** *adv.* equatorward L19.

equatorial /ɛkwəˈtɔːrɪəl/ *a.* & *n.* Also †**-eal**. M17. [f. prec. + -IAL.] **A** *adj.* **1** *gen.* Of or pertaining to an equator. M17. **2** Of or pertaining to the earth's equator; situated, existing, or occurring on or near the equator. E18. **b** Of the orbit of a satellite: lying in the plane of the equator. M20. **3** Of an astronomical telescope or its mounting: such that the telescope can be rotated about one axis in the plane of the equator and another parallel to the earth's axis, so that the diurnal motion of a celestial object anywhere in the sky can be followed by rotation about the latter axis only. L18.

1 **equatorial plate** *Biol.* = METAPHASE *plate*. 2 E. WAUGH Shading their eyes from the brilliant equatorial sun. *Discovery* This pull of the sun sets up equatorial bulge.

B *n.* An equatorial telescope. L18.

equatorially *adv.* E19.

equerry /ɪˈkwɛri, ˈɛkwəri/ *n.* Also †**esquiry**, †**querry**. E16. [Fr. †*escu(i)rie* (now *écurie* stable) f. OFr. *escurie*, *esquierie* company of squires, prince's stables, f. *esquier* ESQUIRE *n.*; perh. assoc. w. L *equus* horse. Sense 1 seems to be based on OFr. *esquier d'esquierie* squire of stables.] **1** Orig., a groom, *spec.* an officer in the service of a royal or noble person charged with the care of the horses. Now, an officer in the British royal household whose duty is to attend on a particular member of the royal family. E16. †**2** The stables belonging to a royal or princely household; the body of officers in charge of them. M16–E19.

1 H. NICOLSON An . . equerry telephoned from the palace to warn them that H.M. was in a furious temper.

equerryship *n.* the position of an equerry E17.

equestrian /ɪˈkwɛstrɪən, ɛ-/ *a.* & *n.* M17. [f. L *equestr-*, *equester* belonging to a horseman, f. *eques* horseman, knight, f. *equus* horse: see -IAN.] **A** *adj.* **1** Of or pertaining to horse-riding; (of a person) skilled in horse-riding. M17. **b** On horseback; (of a portrait or statue) representing a person on horseback. E18. **2** *Hist.* Of or pertaining to an order of knights in the Roman and Holy Roman Empires. L17.

1 J. G. EDGAR Their mettled palfreys and their equestrian grace. J. CHEEVER A statue of a man on horseback that displayed a suit of equestrian armor.

B *n.* A rider or performer on horseback. L18.

equestrial *a.* (now *rare*) = EQUESTRIAN *a.* M16. **equestrianism** *n.* M19.

equestrienne /ɪˌkwɛstrɪˈɛn/ *n.* M19. [Alt. of prec. after fem. ns. in *-enne*, as *Parisienne*.] A female equestrian.

equi- /ˈiːkwi, ɛ-/ *comb. form.* Also †**aequi-**. [Repr. L *aequi-*, f. *aequus* equal: see -I-.] Used in wds adopted f. L, and in Eng. wds modelled on these, and as a freely productive pref., w. the sense 'equal(ly), in an equal degree'.

equianalˈgesic *a.* producing an equal analgesic effect M20. **equiaˈtomic** *a.* (of an alloy or intermetallic compound) containing equal numbers of atoms of two particular constituent elements M20. **equiaxe** *a.* [Fr. *équiaxe*] = EQUIAXED E19. **equiaxed** *a.* (of a crystal) having all its axes the same length M19. **equicaˈloric** *a.* (of food) equivalent as regards content of calories M20. **equiˈdifferent** *a.* (*Math.*, now *rare* or *obs.*) having equal differences, in arithmetic proportion L17. **equidiˈmensional** *a.* (of a particle) having approximately equal dimensions in each direction M20. **equiˈfinal** *a.* having the same result M20. **equifiˈnality** *n.* the condition of being equifinal E20. **equiform** *a.* having the same form L19. **equi'formity** *n.* uniformity M17. **equi'molar** *a.* (*Chem.*) (*a*) containing an equal number of moles; (*b*) = EQUIMOLECULAR (a): E20. **equimo'lecular** *a.* (*Chem.*) (*a*) containing an equal number of molecules; (*b*) = EQUIMOLAR (a): E20. **equi'multiple** *n.* any of a set of numbers each of which is the same multiple of a number in another set M17. **equi'numerous** *a.* (*Math.* & *Logic*) containing the same number of elements (foll. by *with*) M20. **equi'radial** *a.* (*rare*) having equal radii E19. **equi-'signal** *a.* designating the line or zone along which the signals from two radio beacons are equally strong, detection of this equality confirming position on the line; of or pertaining to a navigation system that works on this principle: M20. **equivalve** *a.* (of a bivalve mollusc or its shell) having valves that are of similar size and shape M19. **equivo'luminal** *a.* (of a wave) occurring without a change in the volume of each part of the medium through which it passes L19. **equivote** *n.* (*US*) a tied vote M17.

equiangular /i:kwɪ'aŋgjʊlə, ɛ-/ *a.* M17. [f. late L *equiangulus*, f. as EQUI- + *angulus* ANGLE *n.*[2]: see -AR[1].] (Of a figure) having all its angles equal; having angles equal to those of something else (foll. by *with*).

equiangular spiral a spiral such that the angle between the tangent and the radius vector is the same for all points of the spiral; also called *logarithmic spiral*. ˌ**equiangu'larity** *n.* the condition or fact of being equiangular M17.

equicrural /i:kwɪ'krʊər(ə)l/ *a.* E17. [f. late L *equicrurius* isosceles, f. as EQUI- + *crur-*, *crus* leg: see -AL[1].] Of a triangle: isosceles. Of a cross: having limbs of equal length.

equid /'ɛkwɪd/ *n.* L19. [mod.L *Equidae* (see below), f. L *equus* horse: see -ID[3].] A mammal of the family Equidae of odd-toed ungulates, which includes horses, asses, and zebras.

equidistance /i:kwɪ'dɪst(ə)ns, ɛ-/ *n.* E17. [Fr. *équidistance*, f. as next.] The fact of being equidistant.

at equidistance at equal distances.

equidistant /i:kwɪ'dɪst(ə)nt, ɛ-/ *a.* L16. [(O)Fr. *équidistant* or med.L *equidistant-*, f. as EQUI-, DISTANT.] **1** Separated by an equal distance or equal distances. L16. **2** Of lines, linear features, etc.: everywhere the same distance apart, parallel. L16. **3** Pertaining to or possessing the property that distances on a map are correctly proportioned along all lines radiating from a particular point or all lines parallel to either a line of latitude or a line of longitude. M19.

1 ANTHONY SMITH Both the quick-witted and the dim-witted are equally exceptional, being equidistant from the central norm. 2 H. REPTON The banks of a natural river are never equidistant.

equidistantly *adv.* L16.

†**equilater** *a.* L16–L18. [(O)Fr. *équilatère* or late L *aequilaterus*: see next.] = next.

equilateral /i:kwɪ'lat(ə)r(ə)l, ɛ-/ *a.* L16. [Fr. *équilateral* or late L *aequilateralis*, f. *aequilaterus*, f. as EQUI- + L *later-*, *latus* side: see -AL[1].] Having all its sides of equal length; (of a hyperbola) having axes of equal length and asymptotes at right angles.

†**equiliber** *n.* var. of EQUILIBRE.

equilibrant /ɪ'kwɪlɪbr(ə)nt, i:-/ *n.* L19. [Fr. *équilibrant*, f. *équilibrer* equilibrate, f. *équilibre* f. as EQUILIBRIUM.] *Mech.* A force or system of forces capable of balancing another and producing equilibrium with it.

equilibrate /i:kwɪ'lʌɪbreɪt, ɪ'kwɪlɪ-, i:-/ *v.* M17. [Late L *aequilibrat-* pa. ppl stem of *aequilibrare*, f. as EQUI- + *libra* balance: see -ATE[3].] **1** *v.t.* Bring into or keep in equilibrium; cause to balance (*with*). M17. **2** *v.i.* & *t.* Be in equilibrium (with); balance. E19. **3** *v.i.* Approach a state of equilibrium. M20.

1 DE QUINCEY To equilibrate the supply with the demand. 3 *Journal of Endocrinology* The Petri dishes were . . allowed to equilibrate for 24 h in an incubator.

e'quilibrator *n.* a device for maintaining or restoring equilibrium E20.

equilibration /ˌi:kwɪlʌɪ'breɪʃ(ə)n, ɪˌkwɪlɪ-, i:-/ *n.* E17. [Late L *aequilibratio(n-)*, f. as prec.: see -ATION.] The action of bringing into or keeping in equilibrium; the state of being in equilibrium. Foll. by *to*, *with*.

†**equilibre** *n.* Also **-ber**. E17–E19. [Fr. *équilibre* f. as EQUILIBRIUM.] = EQUILIBRIUM.

equilibria *n.pl.* see EQUILIBRIUM.

equilibrial /i:kwɪ'lɪbrɪəl, ɛ-/ *a.* L18. [f. EQUILIBRIUM + -AL[1].] Of or pertaining to equilibrium.

equilibriate /i:kwɪ'lɪbrɪeɪt, ɛ-/ *v.t.* & *i.* M17. [f. EQUILIBRIUM + -ATE[3].] = EQUILIBRATE 1, 2.

equilibrio /i:kwɪ'lɪbrɪəʊ, ɛ-/ *n.* Now *rare.* M17. [L *aequilibrio*, abl. of *aequilibrium* EQUILIBRIUM.] Equilibrium. Only in *in equilibrio*.

equilibrious /i:kwɪ'lɪbrɪəs, ɛ-/ *a.* Now *rare.* M17. [f. EQUILIBRIUM + -OUS.] In equilibrium; evenly balanced.

equilibrise *v.* var. of EQUILIBRIZE.

equilibrist /ɪ'kwɪlɪbrɪst, i:-; i:kwɪ'lɪb-, ɛ-/ *n.* M18. [f. EQUILIBRIUM + -IST.] A person who performs feats of balancing, *esp.* a tightrope-walker.

equili'bristic *a.* L19.

equilibrium /i:kwɪ'lɪbrɪəm, ɛ-/ *n.* Pl. **-iums**, **-ia**. E17. [L *aequilibrium*, f. as EQUI- + *libra* balance.] **1** A well-balanced state of mind or feeling; equanimity, poise. E17. **b** A state of indecision or neutrality produced by opposing influences of equal force. L17. **2** A condition of balance between opposing physical forces. M17. **3** A state in which the influences or processes to which a thing is subject cancel one another and produce no overall change or variation. L17. **b** *Econ.* A situation in which supply and demand are matched and prices stable. L19.

1 R. GITTINGS He was shaken by circumstances out of the philosophic and poetic equilibrium he had gained that winter. **b** W. PALEY That indifference and suspense, that waiting and equilibrium of the judgement. 3 *Scientific American* At equilibrium the number of granules drifting down . . must be matched by the number of granules drifting up. T. LUPTON Interferences with the equilibrium between the individual and the social reality around him.

Phrases: *dynamic equilibrium*: see DYNAMIC *a.* **neutral equilibrium**: in which a body remains in its new position after being disturbed. RADIATIVE *equilibrium*. RADIOACTIVE *equilibrium*. **stable equilibrium**: in which a body returns to its initial position after being disturbed. **unstable equilibrium**: in which a body continues to move in the direction given it by a disturbing force.

equilibrize /ɪ'kwɪlɪbrʌɪz/ *v.t.* Also **-ise**. M19. [f. prec. + -IZE.] Bring into equilibrium; balance.

†**equinal** *a.* E17–M19. [f. L *equinus* (see next) + -AL[1].] Equine.

equine /'i:kwʌɪn, 'ɛk-/ *a.* & *n.* L18. [L *equinus*, f. *equus* horse: see -INE[1].] **A** *adj.* Of or pertaining to a horse or horses; resembling (that of) a horse; affecting horses. L18. **B** *n.* A horse; an equid. L19.

equinely *adv.* in an equine manner; like a horse: L19.

equinoctial /i:kwɪ'nɒkʃ(ə)l, ɛ-/ *a.* & *n.* LME. [(O)Fr. *équinoctial* f. L *aequinoctalis*, f. *aequinoctium*: see EQUINOX, -AL[1].] **A** *adj.* **1** Pertaining to a state of equal day and night. LME. **2** Pertaining to the period or point of an equinox; happening near the time of an equinox, *esp.* designating gales that prevail near the autumnal equinox. L16. **3** Equatorial. L16.

1 equinoctial circle, line the celestial or terrestrial equator. **equinoctial point** = EQUINOX 2. **2** *equinoctial armilla*: see ARMILLA 1. **equinoctial day**: of 12 hours duration. **equinoctial month**: containing one or other of the equinoxes.

B *n.* **1a** The celestial equator. LME. **b** The terrestrial equator. Now *rare.* L16. †**2** = EQUINOX 1. LME–M17. **3** An equinoctial gale. M18.

equinox /'i:kwɪnɒks, ɛ-/ *n.* LME. [(O)Fr. *équinoxe* or L *aequinoctium* (med.L *equinoxium*), f. as EQUI- + *noct-*, *nox* night.] **1** Either of the two occasions in the year when the day is the same length as the night throughout the world, as the sun crosses the celestial equator. LME. **b** The condition of having the days and nights of equal length. Now *rare.* LME. **2** *Astron.* Either of the two points on the celestial sphere where the celestial equator intersects the ecliptic. LME. †**3** The terrestrial equator. L16–E18.

1 *autumnal equinox*: see AUTUMNAL *a.* 1. *vernal equinox*: see VERNAL *a.* 1.

equip /ɪ'kwɪp/ *v.t.* Infl. **-pp-**. E16. [Fr. *équiper* (cf. AN *eskipeson* equipment, med.L *eschipare* man (a vessel)), prob. f. ON *skipa* man (a vessel), fit up, arrange, f. *skip* SHIP *n.*] **1** Fit out or provide with what is necessary for action etc.; provide with arms or apparatus. (Foll. by *with*.) E16. **b** Provide *with* money; finance. L17. **2** Array, dress; dress up or fit out (esp. oneself) for a journey, enterprise, etc. L17. **3** Provide with the physical or mental abilities for a task etc. Usu. in *pass.* L18.

1 J. LONDON He had sought to equip himself with the tools of artistry. D. CARNEGIE The farm was equipped with a fine-looking dairy. 2 W. IRVING Chinook warriors . . equipped in warlike style. H. I. JENKINSON The tourist will do well to equip himself with good strong boots. 3 R. FRAME Her character didn't equip her for the task of being a diplomat's wife.

equipage /'ɛkwɪpɪdʒ/ *n.* M16. [Fr. *équipage*, f. *équiper*: see prec., -AGE.] **I** Equipment. †**1** The crew of a ship. *rare.* M16–M18. †**2** The action of fitting out a ship, arming a soldier, etc. L16–L17. †**3** The state or condition of being equipped. L16–M17. **4** Apparatus of war; all that an army requires for encampment, transport, etc.; the tackle of a ship. L16. †**b** Clothing, costume, attire; *esp.* military uniform or trappings. L16–E19. **c** Equipment for a journey, expedition, etc. E17. †**d** Apparatus in general. M17–M18. **5** Small articles of domestic furniture, as china, glassware, etc. L17. **6** Articles for personal ornament or use; a case of these. E18.

4 R. BEATSON With the guns, sails, rigging, and other equipage. **c** N. HAWTHORNE A few carpet-bags and shawls, our equipage for the night.

II The appurtenances of rank, social position, etc. †**7** Formal state or order; style of living etc. L16–M18. †**8** A retinue, a following. L16–E19. †**9** The money required to maintain an official establishment. Also more fully *equipage money*. M17–M18. **10** A carriage and horses with attendants; a carriage of this kind. E18.

7 G. BURNET She made an equipage far above what she could support. 10 J. FOWLES Horses being curried and groomed, equipages being drawn out.

†**III** [As if f. EQUI-.] **11** Equal step; equivalence. Chiefly in (*go*, *march*, etc.) *in equipage* (*with*). E–M17.

†**equipage** *v.t.* L16–L18. [f. the n.] Provide with an equipage, equip.

equiparate /ɪ'kwɪpəreɪt/ *v.t.* *rare.* M17. [L *aequiparat-* pa. ppl stem of *aequiparare* compare, liken, f. *aequipar*, f. as EQUI- + *par* equal: see -ATE[3].] †**1** Reduce to a level. Only in M17. **2** Regard as equivalent; equate. (Foll. by *to*, *with*.) L17.

equiparation /ɪˌkwɪpə'reɪʃ(ə)n/ *n.* Now *rare.* LME. [L *aequiparatio(n-)*, f. as prec.: see -ATION.] †**1** Impartial treatment. Only in LME. **2** The action of equating or (formerly) comparing. E17. †**b** A comparison. E–M17.

equipartition /ˌi:kwɪpɑ:'tɪʃ(ə)n, ˌɛ-/ *n.* E20. [f. EQUI- + PARTITION *n.*] *Physics.* The equal distribution of the kinetic energy of a system among its various degrees of freedom; the principle that this exists for a system in thermal equilibrium.

équipe /ekip/ *n.* Also **e-**. Pl. pronounced same. M20. [Fr. = group, team, f. as EQUIP.] A motor-racing stable; a team, esp. of sports players.

equipendency /ɛkwɪ'pɛnd(ə)nsi/ *n.* *rare.* M17. [f. EQUI- + PENDENCY.] The state or condition of hanging in equipoise.

Also †**equipendence** *n.*: only in E17.

equipment /ɪ'kwɪpm(ə)nt/ *n.* E18. [Fr. *équipement*, f. as EQUIP: see -MENT.] **1** Things used in equipping; articles used or required for a particular purpose; apparatus. E18. **b** An item of equipment. Orig. only in *pl.* L18. **2** The action of equipping; the state of being equipped; the manner in which a person or thing is equipped. M18. **3** Intellectual resources. M19.

1 R. HOLMES A mass of carefully prepared equipment, including camp-beds, cutlery, Arabic

guides. 2 R. W. EMERSON The admirable equipment of their Arctic ships carries London to the pole.

equipoise /ˈɛkwɪpɔɪz, iː-/ *n.* & *v.* M17. [f. EQUI- + POISE *n.*[1], repl. the phr. *equal poise.*] **A** *n.* **1** Equality or equal distribution of weight; equilibrium, esp. of intellectual, moral, or social forces or interests. M17. **2** A counterpoise; a balancing force. L18.

1 W. S. CHURCHILL We had scored one goal and our opponents two, and there the struggle hung in equipoise for some time. A. G. GARDINER The swift transitions by which the mind in times of stress seeks to keep its equipoise.

B *v.* **1** *v.t.* Serve as an equipoise to; counterbalance. M17. †**2** *v.i.* Balance *with*. *rare.* Only in M17. **3** *v.t.* Place or hold in equipoise; hold (the mind) in suspense. M18.

1 W. S. LANDOR No Praise Can equipoise his virtues. 3 I. D'ISRAELI He had to equipoise the opposite interests of the Catholics and the Evangelists.

equipollence /iːkwɪˈpɒl(ə)ns, ɛ-/ *n.* LME. [OFr. *equipolence* (mod. *équipollence*), f. *equipolent*: see next, -ENCE.] **1** Equality of power, authority, signification, etc. LME. **2** *Logic.* An equivalence between two or more propositions. LME.

Also **equi'pollency** *n.* E17.

equipollent /iːkwɪˈpɒl(ə)nt, ɛ-/ *a.* & *n.* LME. [OFr. *equipolent* (mod. *équipollent*) f. L *aequipollent-* of equal value, f. as EQUI- + *pollere* be strong.] **A** *adj.* **1** Possessing equal power, authority, effectiveness, validity, etc. LME. **2** Identical in meaning or result; equivalent. L16. **b** *Logic.* Of a proposition etc.: expressing the same thing as another, but in a different way. M17.

1 W. S. LANDOR A maritime power . . equipollent on the sea with France.

B *n.* Something that has equal power, effect, significance, etc.; an equivalent. E17.

equipollently *adv.* M17.

equiponderance /iːkwɪˈpɒnd(ə)r(ə)ns, ɛ-/ *n.* Now *rare.* E18. [f. next: see -ANCE.] Equality of weight; equilibrium.

Also **equi'ponderancy** *n.* E18.

equiponderant /iːkwɪˈpɒnd(ə)r(ə)nt, ɛ-/ *a.* M17. [med.L *aequiponderant-* pres. ppl stem of *aequiponderare*, f. as EQUI- + *ponderare* weigh: see PONDER *v.*, -ANT[1].] Of equal weight or (formerly) density; evenly balanced (now only *fig.*).

†**equiponderate** *a.* M16–E19. [med.L *aequiponderatus* pa. pple of *aequiponderare*: see prec., -ATE[2].] Equal in weight; in equilibrium. (Foll. by *to*, *with*.)

equiponderate /iːkwɪˈpɒnd(ə)reɪt, ɛ-/ *v.* M17. [med.L *aequiponderat-* pa. ppl stem of *aequiponderare* (see EQUIPONDERANT, -ATE[3]), or alt. of PREPONDERATE *v.*[1] by substitution of EQUI- for *pre-*.] **1** *v.t.* Counterpoise, counterbalance. M17. †**2** *v.i.* Be in a state of equipoise. M17–E19.

1 O. WALKER To equiponderate the prejudices of pleasure and interest.

ˌ**equiponde'ration** *n.* balancing; balance: M17.

†**equiponderous** *a.* M17–E18. [f. EQUI- + L *ponder-*, *pondus* weight + -OUS.] Of equal weight or density; of equal authority.

equipotent /iːkwɪˈpəʊt(ə)nt, ɛ-/ *a.* L19. [f. EQUI- + POTENT *a.*[2]] Chiefly *Pharm.* Equally powerful; having equal potencies.

equipotential /ˌiːkwɪpəˈtɛnʃ(ə)l, ˌɛ-/ *a.* & *n.* L17. [f. EQUI- + POTENTIAL.] **A** *adj.* †**1** Of equal authority. Only in L17. **2** *Physics.* (Of a line or surface) composed of points all at the same potential; having the same potential. M19. **3** *Biol.* Of embryonic tissue: having the same potentiality throughout for subsequent development. E20. **B** *n.* *Physics.* An equipotential line or surface. E20.

ˌ**equipotenti'ality** *n.* (*Biol.*) E20.

equipper /ɪˈkwɪpə/ *n.* M19. [f. EQUIP + -ER[1].] A person who or thing which equips.

equiprobability /ˌiːkwɪprɒbəˈbɪlɪti, ˌɛ-/ *n.* E20. [f. EQUI- + PROBABILITY.] The property of being equally probable.

equiprobable /iːkwɪˈprɒbəb(ə)l, ɛ-/ *a.* E20. [f. EQUI- + PROBABLE.] Equally probable.

equirotal /iːkwɪˈrəʊt(ə)l, ɛ-/ *a.* M19. [f. EQUI- + L *rota* wheel + -AL[1].] Having back and front wheels of equal diameter.

equisetum /ɛkwɪˈsiːtəm/ *n.* Pl. **-ta** /-tə/, **-s.** L17. [mod.L (see below) f. L *equisaetum*, f. *equus* horse + *saeta* bristle.] Any plant of the genus *Equisetum*, comprising rhizomatous herbaceous plants allied to the ferns and found worldwide except in Australasia, with hollow furrowed jointed stems freq. with whorled branches, and leaves reduced to nodal sheaths; a horsetail.

equitable /ˈɛkwɪtəb(ə)l/ *a.* M16. [Fr. *équitable*, f. *équité* EQUITY, with active meaning of the suff., as (e.g.) in *charitable*: see -ABLE.] **1** Characterized by equity or fairness; fair, just. Now chiefly of actions, arrangements, etc. M16. **2** *Law.* Pertaining to equity; (of a right, claim, etc.) valid or recognized in equity as opp. to common law. M17.

1 J. GATHORNE-HARDY How can it be equitable to exclude some of them from the benefits? 2 *Times* Equitable mortgagees of a house in . . Hackney.

equita'bility *n.* L20. **equitableness** *n.* M17. **equitably** *adv.* M17.

equitant /ˈɛkwɪt(ə)nt/ *a.* L18. [L *equitant-* pres. ppl stem of *equitare*: see next, -ANT[1].] *Bot.* Of a leaf: having its base folded and partly enclosing the leaf next above it, as in an iris.

equitation /ɛkwɪˈteɪʃ(ə)n/ *n.* M16. [Fr. *équitation* or L *equitatio(n-)*, f. *equitat-* pa. ppl stem of *equitare*, f. *equit-*, *eques* horseman, f. *equus* horse: see -ATION.] **1** The action or art of riding on horseback; horsemanship. M16. **2** A ride or outing on horseback. E18.

2 J. BARTH Our daily equitations changed. . . Now we generally rode silently.

equity /ˈɛkwɪti/ *n.* ME. [(O)Fr. *équité* f. L *aequitas*, f. *aequus* equal: see -ITY.] **1** Fairness, impartiality; even-handed dealing. ME. **2** That which is fair and right. Long *rare.* LME. **3** *Law.* The recourse to general principles of justice to correct or supplement common and statute law; the part of a legal system based on this; *spec.* the part of English law originally administered by the Lord Chancellor and later by the Court of Chancery (superseded by the Chancery Division of the High Court since 1875). L16. **4** A right which is recognizable in a court of equity; an equitable right. E17. **5** The value of a mortgaged property after deducting charges and claims against it. L19. **6** The issued share capital of a company (also *equity capital*); the shareholders' interest in a company; in *pl.*, ordinary shares. E20. **7** (**E-**.) (The name of) an actors' trade union in Britain and in the US and Canada. E20.

1 J. R. LOWELL There is a singular equity and absence of party passion. 4 **equity of redemption** the right of a mortgagor over the mortgaged property, *esp.* the right to redeem the property on payment of the principal, interest, and costs. 5 *negative equity.* 6 *Investors Chronicle* Bunzl now controls 24 per cent of the equity. *Times* The shift in portfolio preferences of . . investors from bonds to equities. 7 Q. CRISP I know I am an actor because I have an Equity card.

Comb.: *equity capital*: see sense 6 above; **equity draftsman** *arch.* a barrister who composes pleadings in a court of equity.

equivalence /ɪˈkwɪv(ə)l(ə)ns/ *n.* LME. [(O)Fr. *équivalence* f. med.L *aequivalentia*, f. *aequivalent-*: see EQUIVALENT, -ENCE.] **1** The condition of being equivalent. LME. **2** An instance of being equivalent. E20.

1 **principle of equivalence** *Physics* = *equivalence principle* below.

Comb.: **equivalence class** *Math.* the class of all members of a set that are in a given equivalence relation; **equivalence principle** *Physics* a basic postulate of general relativity, stating that at any point of space-time the effects of a gravitational field cannot be experimentally distinguished from those due to an accelerated frame of reference; **equivalence relation** *Math.* a reflexive, symmetric, and transitive relation between elements of a set.

equivalency /ɪˈkwɪv(ə)l(ə)nsi/ *n.* M16. [f. med.L *aequivalentia*: see prec., -ENCY.] **1** = EQUIVALENCE 1. M16. **2** = EQUIVALENCE 2. M20.

equivalent /ɪˈkwɪv(ə)l(ə)nt/ *a.* & *n.* LME. [(O)Fr. *équivalent* f. late L *aequivalent-* pres. ppl stem of *aequivalere*, f. as EQUI- + *valere* be strong: see -ENT.] **A** *adj.* †**1** Of persons or things: equal in power, rank, authority, or excellence. (Foll. by *to*, *with*, *for*.) LME–L17. **2** Equal in value, significance, or meaning. (Foll. by *to*, †*with*, †*for*.) E16. **3** That is virtually the same thing; having the same effect. (Foll. by *to*.) M17. **4** Having the same relative position or function; corresponding. (Foll. by *to*.) M17. **5** *Chem.* Of a quantity of a substance: just sufficient to combine with or displace a specified quantity of another substance. M17. **6** *Math.* Belonging to the same equivalence class. M20.

2 H. ADAMS The minstrel, or *menestrier*, became very early a word of abuse, equivalent to blackguard. R. OWEN Speedboats and crystal chandeliers at prices equivalent to a lifetime's wages. 3 **equivalent circuit** a notional electric circuit in which components such as resistors and capacitors are interconnected so as to reproduce the behaviour of a more complicated circuit or device and simplify its analysis. 4 N. CHOMSKY We have the right to maintain missiles on the Russian border . . , but . . they do not have the equivalent right. 5 **equivalent weight** the weight of a substance that is equivalent to 8 grams of oxygen or 1.0079 grams of hydrogen (formerly, to 1 gram of hydrogen).

B *n.* **1** Something equal in value or worth. Also, something tantamount or virtually identical. E16. **2** A word, expression, sign, etc., of equivalent significance. M17. **3** *Chem.* An amount of a substance whose weight is the equivalent weight of the substance. E19.

1 J. BRAINE Susan was a princess and I was the equivalent of a swine-herd. J. BARZUN The expert, the Ph.D. or his equivalent, is everywhere. I. MURDOCH She was used to doing things on the hunting field which seemed the equivalent of suicide. 2 A. LURIE He . . made a neutral noise, the auditory equivalent of a shrug.

Phrases: **mechanical equivalent of heat** the amount of mechanical energy that is equivalent to a standard amount of thermal energy, now 1 calorie (= 4.1868 joule).

equivalently *adv.* (*a*) to an equivalent extent or degree; (*b*) as an equivalent term; with equivalent significance; †(*c*) virtually, in effect: E16.

equivocacy /ɪˈkwɪvəkəsi/ *n.* *rare.* M17. [f. late L *aequivocus* (see next) + -ACY.] Equivocal character.

equivocal /ɪˈkwɪvək(ə)l/ *a.* & *n.* M16. [f. late L *aequivocus*, f. L *aequus* equal + *vocare* to call: see -AL[1].] **A** *adj.* **1a** Of evidence, signs, etc.: of uncertain or doubtful significance. M16. **b** Of sentiments, an attitude, etc.: undecided. L18. **2** Capable of more than one interpretation; ambiguous. L16. †**b** Of a person: expressing himself or herself in equivocal terms. *rare* (Shakes.). Only in E17. **3** Of uncertain nature. M17. †**4** Equal in name but not in reality. M17–M18. **5** Of a person, condition, tendency, etc.: questionable, suspicious; of doubtful merit or character. L18.

2 K. A. PORTER Messages disguised in equivocal phrases. 3 SIR W. SCOTT The equivocal spirits called fairies. 5 R. ELLMANN His male friendships included some that were equivocal.

†**B** *n.* An equivocal term; a homonym. M17–M18.

equivo'cality *n.* the quality or condition of being equivocal; something which is equivocal: M18. **equivocally** *adv.* †(*a*) nominally; (*b*) so as to admit of more than one application or interpretation; ambiguously: L16. **equivocalness** *n.* M17.

equivocate /ɪˈkwɪvəkət/ *n.* *rare.* L17. [f. the vb.] A word identical with another in form but not in meaning.

equivocate /ɪˈkwɪvəkeɪt/ *v.* LME. [Late L *aequivocat-* pa. ppl stem of *aequivocare*, f. *aequivocus*: see EQUIVOCAL, -ATE[3].] †**1** *v.t.* & *i.* Use (a word) in more than one sense; apply (a word) to more than one thing. LME–L17. **2** *v.i.* Use ambiguous words or expressions in order to mislead; prevaricate. L16. †**3** *v.t.* Insinuate or evade (a point, oath, etc.) by equivocation. E–M17.

2 D. HALBERSTAM Stevens ducked and faked and equivocated and finally, cornered, he admitted.

equivocatingly *adv.* in an equivocating manner M17. **equivocator** *n.* L16.

equivocation /ɪˌkwɪvəˈkeɪʃ(ə)n/ *n.* LME. [Late L *aequivocatio(n-)*, f. as prec.: see -ATION.] †**1** =

For other words beginning with *equi-* see the entry for **equi-**

EQUIVOQUE *n.* 4; the use of words that are ambiguous. LME–E19. 2 *Logic.* A fallacy arising from the use of the same term in different senses in a syllogism. L16. 3 The use of ambiguous words or expressions in order to mislead; the use of an expression that is literally false but is true with the user's mental addition; an equivocal word or expression. E17.

3 J. A. FROUDE The Bishop . . stooped to an equivocation too transparent to deceive any one. *fig.*: W. C. WILLIAMS Such resolves would lead . . to death, definitely and without equivocation.

equivoque /ˈiːkwɪvəʊk, ˈɛ-/ *a.* & *n.* Also **-voke**. LME. [(O)Fr. *équivoque* or late L *aequivocus*: see EQUIVOCAL.] †A *adj.* = EQUIVOCAL. LME–M17.

B *n.* †1 A thing which has the same name as something else. L16–M17. 2 An expression capable of more than one meaning; a pun; wordplay, punning. E17. 3 = EQUIVOCATION 3. *rare.* E17. 4 The fact of having more than one meaning or interpretation; ambiguity. E19.

2 T. F. DIBDIN Who mistook equivoque, abuse, and impudence, for wit. *Times Lit. Suppl.* Tony Augarde . . finds time for *bouts rimés*, echo poems and equivoques. 4 J. F. W. HERSCHEL Confusion, owing to the equivoque between the lunar and calendar month.

Equuleus /ɪˈkwʊlɪəs/ *n.* M18. [L = small horse, dim. of *equus* horse.] (The name of) a small inconspicuous constellation of the southern hemisphere, near the celestial equator between Aquarius and Delphinus; the Little Horse.

er /əː, ə/ *int.*, *v.*, & *n.* M19. [Imit.] A *int.* Expr. the inarticulate sound made by a speaker who hesitates or is uncertain what to say. M19. B *v.i.* Make this sound. M20. C *n.* An utterance of this sound. M20.

-er /ə/ *suff.*[1] [OE *-ere* f. Gmc.] Forming ns. 1 Forming ns. f. ns. and adjs. w. the senses (i) 'a person (orig. *spec.* a man) involved in or with, esp. as an occupation or profession', as *hatter, probationer, tiler*, etc., some in adaptations of L wds in *-graphus, -logus*, as *geographer, astrologer*, etc.; (ii) 'a person originating or resident in (a place)', as *cottager, foreigner, Londoner, New Yorker, northerner, villager*, etc.; (iii) 'a person or thing belonging to or connected with', as *airliner, old-timer, sixth-former, whaler*, etc.; (iv) 'a person who or thing which has or is', as *double-decker, fiver, porker, second-rater, three-wheeler*, etc.; (v) 'a thing or action, done by or involving', as *back-hander, header*, etc. 2 Forming ns. f. almost all vbs and some ns. w. the senses (i) 'a person (orig. *spec.* a man) who or animal which does, an instrument, machine, occurrence, action, etc., which does', as *blotter, computer, eye-opener, lifer, lover, maker, miler, pointer, poker, shaker, singer, wheeler-dealer*, etc.; (ii) 'a thing suitable for', as *broiler* etc.; (iii) in *fruiterer, sorcerer*, etc., a pleonastic extension of wds in -ER[2].

-er /ə/ *suff.*[2] (not productive). 1 Repr. OFr. *-er* f. L *-aris* -AR[1] (now usual) in ns., as *sampler* etc. 2 Repr. AN *-er* (OFr. *-ier*) f. L *-arius, -arium* (see -ARY[1]) in ns. w. the senses 'a person or thing connected with', as *butler, danger, mariner*, etc., 'a receptacle for', as *garner* etc. 3 Repr. OFr. *-eüre* f. L *-atura* in ns., as *bracer* etc., or OFr. *-eör* (mod. *-oir*) f. L *-atorium*, as *laver* etc. 4 Var. of -OR (repl. *-our*).

-er /ə/ *suff.*[3] [OE *-ra* (fem., neut. *-re*) adj., *-or* advb., both f. Gmc.] Forming the compar. of adjs. and advs., now esp. of wds of one syllable and occas. of two, as *colder, narrower*, etc.

¶Mod. spelling conventions are as follows: Wds in *-e* drop the *e*, as *brave*: *braver*; a final single consonant other than *h, w*, or *x* is doubled if preceded by a single-letter vowel, as *grim*: *grimmer*; in most adjs. and a few advs. in *-y* the *y* becomes *i*, as *early*: *earlier*, similarly in wds in *-ey*, as *gooey*: *gooier*.

-er /ə/ *suff.*[4] (not productive). [Repr. AN inf. ending of vbs.] Forming ns., freq. in *Law*, w. the sense '(a single instance of) the vbl action, a document effecting this', as *cesser, dinner, disclaimer, misnomer, supper*, etc.

-er /ə/ *suff.*[5] [OE *-(e)rian* = OS, OHG *-arōn*, ON *-ra*, f. Gmc.] Forming frequent. and iterative vbs f. (parts of) vbs or on sound-imitation, as *clamber, clatter, mutter, shudder, slumber, twitter*, etc.

-er /ə/ *suff.*[6] Also **-ers** /əz/. M19. Added to shortened forms of wds to form slang & colloq. equivalents, as *brekker, footer, rugger*, etc., among which *soccer* has passed into general use. As well as appearing in pls., as *Divvers* etc., the var. *-ers* is used esp. in proper names (e.g. *Twickers* = Twickenham) and to form adjectives, as *bonkers, crackers, preggers, starkers*, etc.

¶Orig. Rugby School slang, adopted at Oxford University, and then into wider use.

era /ˈɪərə/ *n.* Also (earlier) †**ae-**. M17. [Late L *aera* number used as basis of reckoning, item of account, epoch from which time is reckoned, f. pl. of L *aer-, aes* copper, money, counter.] 1 a A system of numbering years from a particular noteworthy event; a period of years so numbered. Cf. EPOCH 5. M17. b A period of history characterized by a particular state of affairs, series of events, etc.; a distinctive period in the history of something or someone. Cf. EPOCH 5. M18. 2 = EPOCH 1. Now *rare.* M17. 3 = EPOCH 3; a date or event marking the beginning of a distinctive period. E18. 4 A date or period to which an event is assigned. Now *rare.* E18. 5 *Geol.* A major division of geological time that is a subdivision of an eon and is itself divided into periods. L19.

1b M. HUNTER Stone tools . . used well into the era of bronze. J. BARZUN The cataclysm of revolution . . opened a new era of art and thought called Romanticism. 3 W. H. DIXON The landing of this English Governor was an era in their lives. 5 W. C. PUTNAM The Cenozoic, which is the contemporary Era, is a time of mammalian dominance.

Phrases: *Christian Era*: see CHRISTIAN *a.* *Common Era*: see COMMON *a.* **era of good feeling** (also w. initial caps.) *US Hist.* a period in the presidency of Monroe (1817–24) when there was virtually only one political party. *vulgar era*: see VULGAR *a.*

Comb.: **era-making** *a.* = EPOCH-*making*.

eradiation /ɪˌreɪdɪˈeɪʃ(ə)n/ *n.* M17. [f. *e-* E- + RADIATION.] 1 The action of radiating. M17. 2 Something that is radiated; an emanation. L17.

eˈradiate *v.i.* & *t.* (long *rare* or *obs.*) M17.

eradicable /ɪˈradɪkəb(ə)l/ *a.* M19. [f. next + -ABLE.] Able to be eradicated.

¶Earlier in INERADICABLE.

eradicate /ɪˈradɪkeɪt/ *v.t.* LME. [L *eradicat-* pa. ppl stem of *eradicare*, f. *e-* E- + *radic-, radix* root: see -ATE[3].] 1 Pull up or out by the roots, uproot. LME. 2 Remove or destroy completely; extirpate, get rid of. E17.

2 *New York Times* The Government has a fundamental . . interest in eradicating racial discrimination in education.

eradicant *a.* & *n.* (a substance) intended to eradicate a particular pest or disease from a particular area M20. **eradicated** *ppl a.* that has been eradicated; *Her.* (of a tree) depicted with its roots exposed: M17. **eradicator** *n.* M17.

eradication /ɪˌradɪˈkeɪʃ(ə)n/ *n.* LME. [L *eradicatio(n-)*, f. as prec.: see -ATION.] The action of eradicating; total destruction.

eradicative /ɪˈradɪkətɪv/ *a.* LME. [OFr. *eradicatif, -ive*, f. as ERADICATE after *palliatif* PALLIATIVE: see -IVE.] Tending or able to eradicate disease.

erasable /ɪˈreɪzəb(ə)l/ *a.* M19. [f. next + -ABLE.] Able to be erased; (of a medium or device) allowing what is on it or in it to be erased.

¶Earlier in INERASABLE.

erasaˈbility *n.* M20.

erase /ɪˈreɪz/ *v.* & *n.* L16. [L *eras-* pa. ppl stem of *eradere*, f. *e-* E- + *radere* to scrape.] A *v.t.* 1 *Her.* Represent (the head or a limb of an animal) with a jagged or torn edge. Only as *erased* ppl a., *erasing* vbl n. L16. 2 Rub out or obliterate (something written, typed, drawn, or engraved); remove *from* in this way; remove (a recorded signal) from magnetic tape etc. L17. b Remove all traces of (something) from or *from* one's memory or mind. L17. 3 Remove a recorded signal from (magnetic tape etc.). M20.

2b C. CHAPLIN I did my best to erase that night's horror from my mind. P. ROSE If it were possible to erase the past, to go back . . and try again.

B *n.* The action of erasing a magnetic tape etc. Usu. *attrib.* M20.

erase facility, head, etc.

erasement *n.* (now *rare*) E18. **eraser** *n.* a person who or thing which erases something; *spec.* a piece of (synthetic) rubber or plastic for erasing pencil or ink marks: L18. **erasion** *n.* (*rare*) the action or an act of erasing something L18. **erasive** *a.* (*rare*) that tends to erase something M17.

Erasmian /ɪˈrazmɪən/ *a.* & *n.* L19. [f. *Erasmus* (see below) + -IAN.] A *adj.* Pertaining to, characteristic of, or after the manner of Erasmus (*c* 1466–1536), Dutch humanist; designating the system of pronunciation he advocated for classical Greek. L19. B *n.* A follower of Erasmus; a person who holds the views of Erasmus. L19.

Erasmianism *n.* (*rare*) M18.

erastes /ɛˈrasteɪs, -z/ *n.* Pl. ***-tai*** /-tʌɪ/. L20. [Gk *erastēs* lover, f. *eran* be in love with.] *Gk Hist.* An older man who desires a younger man. Cf. EROMENOS.

Erastian /ɪˈrastɪən/ *n.* & *a.* M17. [f. *Erastus* (see below) + -IAN.] A *n.* A follower of the (supposed) doctrines of Erastus (1524–83), Swiss physician and theologian; a person who maintains the ascendancy of the State over the Church in ecclesiastical matters, or the State's right to legislate on ecclesiastical matters. M17. B *adj.* Characterized by, embodying, or designating the doctrine of Church and State held by Erastians. E19.

Erastianism *n.* L17.

erasure /ɪˈreɪʒə/ *n.* M18. [f. as ERASE + -URE.] 1 The action or an act of erasing something. M18. 2 The place where a letter etc. has been erased. L19.

2 J. BARNES We use infra-red light to pierce erasures in the correspondence.

†**erber** *n.*[1] var. of ARBER.

†**erber** *n.*[2] see ARBOUR.

erbium /ˈəːbɪəm/ *n.* M19. [f. *Ytterby*, Sweden (cf. YTTERBIUM) + -IUM.] A soft malleable metallic chemical element of the lanthanide series, atomic no. 68, used in special alloys. (Symbol Er.)

erbia *n.* erbium oxide, Er_2O_3, a pink powder M19.

erbswurst /ˈəːbzwəːst/ *n.* L19. [G, f. *Erbse* pea + *Wurst* sausage.] Seasoned pease-meal compressed into a sausage shape and used for making soup.

ere /ɛː/ *adv.*, *prep.*, & *conj.* Also (now *Sc.*) **ear**. [OE *ǣr* = OFris., OS, OHG *ēr* (Du. *eer*, G *eher*), Goth. *airis* f. compar. of Gmc base. Cf. AIR *adv.*, OR *adv.*, *prep.*, & *conj.*[1]] A *adv.* 1 Early; soon. Now only *Sc.* OE. †2 a Sooner, earlier. OE–M17. b Rather, in preference. ME–M16. †3 Formerly; on a former occasion; just now. OE–M17.

B *prep.* Before (in time). Freq. in *ere then, ere this*, etc. Now *arch.* & *poet.* OE.

SIR W. SCOTT I trust the King is ere this out of their reach. M. SKINNER Eerie the hush in England ere the storm.

C *conj.* 1 Of time: before. Also *ere ever, ere yet*, †*ere than*, †*ere that*. Now *arch.* & *poet.* OE. †2 Of preference: rather than. OE–LME.

1 TOLKIEN I would give you a gift ere we go. E. MUIR Time seemed finished ere the ship passed by.

¶See also ERELONG, ERENOW.

erect /ɪˈrɛkt/ *a.* LME. [L *erectus* pa. pple of *erigere* set up, f. *e-* E- + *regere* to direct.] 1 Upright; not bending or stooping; (of a line or surface) vertical; (of an optical image) having the same orientation as the object, not inverted. LME. †2 Of the mind or expression: uplifted; alert. M16–L18. 3 Of hair: standing up from the skin, bristling. Of a tail: standing out stiffly from the body. M18. 4 Of the penis or clitoris, or the nipples: enlarged and firm, esp. as a result of sexual arousal. L19.

1 J. STEINBECK As the sharp sun struck day after day, the leaves of the young corn became less stiff and erect. F. KING He walked briskly down the corridor . . , head erect and shoulders braced. *fig.*: C. THIRLWALL A spirit as erect as the King's tiara.

erectly *adv.* M17. **erectness** *n.* M17.

erect /ɪˈrɛkt/ *v.* LME. [L *erect-* pa. ppl stem of *erigere*: see prec.] **I** Elevate, raise. **1** *v.t.* Set in an upright position; make erect. LME. **†2** *v.t.* Direct upwards; lift up (one's eyes, hands, or head); raise; set in a high position. LME–E18. **†3** *v.t.* Raise in importance, dignity, etc.; elevate to an office, position, etc. LME–E18. **†4** *v.t.* Rouse, excite, embolden, (the mind, oneself). M16–M18.

1 A. GORDON The Charioteers . . bowed to the Ground, then erected themselves. 2 E. PAGITT The Bishop . . erecting his hands stood . . with his face to the Altar. 3 STEELE We have seen . . Monarchs erected and deposed.

II Construct; establish. **5a** *v.t.* Build, construct; set up (a statue, pole, etc.); *fig.* devise (a theory), form (a conclusion). LME. **b** *v.i.* Be built. Only in *be erecting*. L17. **6** *v.t.* **†a** Raise (an army). L15–L17. **b** Establish, found, (an office, corporation, institution, etc.); initiate (a project, scheme, etc.). Now *rare*. M16. **7** *v.t. Geom.* Draw (a line) perpendicular to a given line; draw (a figure) with a given line as base. M17. **8** *v.t. Astrol.* Construct (a horoscope, a chart of the sky). M17. **9** *v.t.* Foll. by *into*: set up or present as; give the character or status of; form into. L17.

5a QUILLER-COUCH A freshly-formed mound . . such as children erect over a thrush's grave. T. CAPOTE A barricade that state troopers had erected at the entrance. L. DEIGHTON Trestle tables . . had been erected in the garage. 6b D. HUME The Jesuits, a new order of regular priests erected in Europe. 9 G. SAINTSBURY The fallacy of erecting the practice of one . . style of literature into a code . . for all time.

erectable *a.* E19. **erective** *a.* †(*a*) tending to erect something; (*b*) pertaining to or involving erection of the penis: E17.

erectile /ɪˈrɛktʌɪl/ *a.* M19. [Fr. *érectile*, f. as prec.: see -ILE.] Able to be erected; (of tissue, an organ) able to become erect when suitably stimulated.

erecˈtility *n.* the quality of being erectile M19.

erection /ɪˈrɛkʃ(ə)n/ *n.* LME. [((O)Fr. *érection* f.) L *erectio(n-)*, f. as ERECT *v.*: see -ION.] **1** The action or an act of erecting; an erect position. LME. **2** An erect state of an organ, *spec.* the penis; an occurrence of this. L15. **3** A thing that is erected or built; a building. E17.

1 BURKE Any . . innovation which may amount to the erection of a dangerous nuisance. H. H. WILSON Their respect for his memory was evinced by the erection of a monumental column. 3 D. BREWSTER A wooden erection said to have been Newton's private observatory.

erector /ɪˈrɛktə/ *n.* M16. [f. ERECT *v.* + -OR.] **1** A person who erects something; a machine for assembling parts of buildings. M16. **2** A muscle which maintains an erect state of a part or an erect posture of the body. M19. **3** (**E-**.) (Proprietary name for) a construction toy consisting of components for making model buildings and vehicles. Chiefly in *Erector set*. *N. Amer.* E20.

erelong /ɛːˈlɒŋ/ *adv. arch.* Also **ere long**. L16. [f. ERE *prep.* + LONG *n.*] Before long; soon.

eremacausis /ˌɛrɪməˈkɔːsɪs/ *n.* M19. [f. Gk *ērema* quietly + *kausis* burning, f. *kaiein* to burn.] The gradual decomposition of organic material into elements and simple compounds in the presence of air and moisture.

eremejevite *n.* var. of JEREMEJEVITE.

†eremitage *n.* var. of HERMITAGE.

eremite *n.* see HERMIT.

eremitic, **eremitical** *adjs.* see HERMITIC, HERMITICAL.

eremurus /ɛrɪˈmjʊərəs/ *n.* Pl. **-ri** /-rʌɪ, -riː/, **-ruses**. E19. [mod.L (see below), f. Gk *erēmos* solitary + *oura* tail.] Any of various hardy perennial plants of the Asiatic genus *Eremurus*, of the lily family, cultivated for their dense racemes of white, yellow, or reddish flowers; the foxtail lily.

erenach *n.* var. of HERENACH.

erenow /ɛːˈnaʊ/ *adv. arch.* Also **ere now**. LME. [f. ERE *prep.* + NOW *n.*] Before this time.

erepsin /ɪˈrɛpsɪn/ *n.* E20. [f. L *eripere* (see next) + PEPSIN.] *Biochem.* A proteolytic fraction in the intestinal juice, consisting of a mixture of peptidases.

ereption /ɪˈrɛpʃ(ə)n/ *n.* E17. [L *ereptio(n-)*, f. *erept-* pa. ppl stem of *eripere*, f. *e-* E- + *rapere* seize: see -ION.] The action or an act of snatching or seizing.

erethism /ˈɛrɪθɪz(ə)m/ *n.* E19. [Fr. *éréthisme* f. Gk *erethismos*, f. *erethizein* irritate: see -ISM.] *Med.* Abnormally increased sensitivity or responsiveness in a part of the body; abnormal restlessness of mind and emotional sensitivity.

eˈrethic, **ereˈthistic** *adjs.* L19.

erewhile /ɛːˈwʌɪl/ *adv. arch.* ME. [f. ERE *prep.* + WHILE *n.*] A while before, some time ago.

Erewhonian /ɛrɪˈwəʊnɪən/ *a.* & *n.* L19. [f. *Erewhon* (see below), a partial reversal of *Nowhere* + -IAN.] **A** *adj.* Of, belonging to, or characteristic of the book *Erewhon* (1872) by Samuel Butler, or the utopia it describes. L19. **B** *n.* An inhabitant of Erewhon. E20.

erf /əːf/ *n.* Chiefly *S. Afr.* Also **†erve**. Pl. **erfs**, **erven** /ˈəːv(ə)n/. L17. [Du. = land, yard.] A piece of land; a building plot or site.

erg /əːg/ *n.*[1] L19. [Gk *ergon* work.] *Physics.* A unit of work or energy, equal to the amount of work done by a force of one dyne when its point of application moves one centimetre in the direction of the force; 10^{-7} joule.

erg /əːg/ *n.*[2] Pl. **areg** /ˈarɛg/. L19. [Fr. f. Arab. *ʿirḳ*, *ʿerg*.] An area of shifting desert sand-dunes, esp. in the Sahara.

ergastic /əːˈgastɪk/ *a.* L19. [f. Gk *ergastikos* capable of working, f. *ergon* work: see -IC.] *Cytol.* Pertaining to or designating the storage and waste products of metabolic activity in a cell.

ergastoplasm /əːˈgastə(ʊ)plaz(ə)m/ *n.* E20. [Fr. *ergastoplasme*, f. Gk *ergastikos*: see prec., -O-, PLASM.] The ribosome-carrying components in the cytoplasm of a cell, part of the endoplasmic reticulum.

ergastoˈplasmic *a.* E20.

ergastulum /əːˈgastjʊləm/ *n.* Pl. **-la** /-lə/. E19. [L f. Gk *ergastērion* workshop.] A building like a prison housing slaves on an estate (*Rom. Hist.*); any building for slaves or prisoners of war.

ergative /ˈəːgətɪv/ *a.* & *n.* M20. [f. Gk *ergatēs* worker + -IVE.] *Ling.* **A** *adj.* Designating a case which is used to mark the subject of a transitive verb, as in Eskimo and Basque; possessing or belonging to such a case; functioning as such a case although not distinctively inflected as one. M20. **B** *n.* (A word in) the ergative case. M20.

ergaˈtivity *n.* the state or condition of being ergative M20.

ergatocracy /əːgəˈtɒkrəsi/ *n.* E20. [f. Gk *ergatēs* worker: see -O-, -CRACY.] Government by workers; a government made up of workers.

-ergic /ˈəːdʒɪk/ *suff.* [f. Gk *ergon* work + -IC.] *Physiol.* Releasing, involving, or mimicking a specified substance as a neurotransmitter, as *adrenergic*, *cholinergic*, etc.

ergo /ˈəːgəʊ/ *adv.* & *n.* LME. [L.] **A** *adv.* Therefore. LME.

CLIVE JAMES The . . hotel is in the eastern, *ergo* Arab, part of the city.

B *n.* Pl. **-os**. A use of or occurrence of the word 'ergo'; a logical conclusion. Long *rare*. L16.

ergoism *n.* pedantic adherence to logically constructed rules E18.

ergo- /ˈəːgəʊ/ *comb. form.* [Gk *ergon* work: see -O-.] Work, energy.

ergosphere *n.* (*Astron.*) a postulated region round a black hole, from which energy could escape L20.

ergocalciferol /ˌəːgə(ʊ)kalˈsɪfərɒl/ *n.* M20. [f. ERGO(STEROL + CALCIFEROL.] *Biochem.* = CALCIFEROL.

ergodic /əːˈgɒdɪk/ *a.* E20. [f. G *ergoden*, f. Gk *ergon* work + *hodos* way: see -IC.] Of, pertaining to, or possessing the property that in the limit all points in a space are covered with equal frequency, or that each sufficiently large selection of points is equally representative of the whole.

ergoˈdicity *n.* the quality or property of being ergodic M20.

ergograph /ˈəːgə(ʊ)grɑːf/ *n.* L19. [f. ERGO- + -GRAPH.] An instrument for measuring and recording the work done by particular groups of muscles.

ergogram *n.* a record or tracing made by an ergograph E20. **ergoˈgraphic** *a.* L19.

ergometer /əːˈgɒmɪtə/ *n.* L19. [f. ERGO- + -METER.] An instrument or machine which measures work or energy, esp. the work done in a spell of exercise.

G. A. SHEEHAN Subjects working on a bicycle ergometer at fifty-six per cent of aerobic capacity.

ergometry *n.* the use of an ergometer M20.

ergometrine /əːgə(ʊ)ˈmɛtriːn, -ɪn/ *n.* M20. [f. ERGOT + Gk *mētra* womb + -INE[5].] *Pharm.* An oxytocic alkaloid in ergot that is an amide of lysergic acid and is given to control bleeding after childbirth. Cf. ERGONOVINE.

ergonomics /əːgəʊˈnɒmɪks/ *n.* M20. [f. ERGO- after *economics*.] The field of study that deals with the relationship between people and their working environment, as it affects efficiency, safety, and ease of action.

ergonomic *a.* of or pertaining to ergonomics; (of an object or design) devised in accordance with the findings of ergonomics; (designed to be) conducive to efficient use: M20. **ergonomically** *adv.* M20. **erˈgonomist** *n.* an expert in or student of ergonomics M20.

ergonovine /əːgə(ʊ)ˈnəʊviːn/ *n.* Chiefly *US*. M20. [f. ERGOT + L *novus* new + -INE[5].] = ERGOMETRINE.

ergophobia /əːgə(ʊ)ˈfəʊbɪə/ *n. joc.* E20. [f. ERGO- + -PHOBIA.] Fear or dislike of doing work.

ergosterol /əːˈgɒstərɒl/ *n.* E20. [f. ERGOT + -STEROL.] *Biochem.* A steroid alcohol, $C_{28}H_{44}O$, that is found in ergot and many other fungi and produces vitamin D_2 under ultraviolet irradiation.

Also **†ergosterin** *n.*: only in L19.

ergot /ˈəːgɒt/ *n.* L17. [Fr. = cock's spur f. OFr. *ar(i)got*, *argoz* of unkn. origin.] **1** A disease of rye and certain other grasses in which the seeds become replaced by hard black sclerotia of a fungus of the genus *Claviceps*, esp. *C. purpurea*, giving the appearance of a cock's spur; a sclerotium, or sclerotia, of this kind; a fungus causing such a disease. L17. **2** (A preparation or extract of) the dried sclerotia of this fungus used medicinally for the alkaloids they contain, esp. to induce contraction of the uterus. M19. **3** A small horny protrusion on the back of the fetlock of most horses. L19.

1 *Rolling Stone* Her explanation was ergot poisoning. F. T. BROOKS Some of the ergots fall to the ground.

ergoted *a.* affected with ergot M19. **ergotized** *a.* = ERGOTED E19.

ergotamine /əːˈgɒtəmiːn/ *n.* E20. [f. ERGOT + AMINE.] *Pharm.* The pharmacologically active isomer of an alkaloid present in some kinds of ergot, chiefly used to treat migraine.

ergotism /ˈəːgətɪz(ə)m/ *n.* M19. [f. as prec. + -ISM.] **1** Acute or chronic poisoning by ergot alkaloids, with symptoms that may include vomiting, diarrhoea, itching, coma, or dry gangrene of the extremities. M19. **2** The occurrence of ergot in grasses. M19.

ergotoxine /əːgə(ʊ)ˈtɒksiːn, -ɪn/ *n.* E20. [f. ERGOT + TOXIN + -INE[5].] *Med.* An oxytocic mixture of three ergot alkaloids, used in obstetrics and to treat migraine; an alkaloid in such a mixture.

erh hu /əː ˈhuː/ *n. phr.* Also ***erhu***. E20. [Chin. *èrhú*, f. *èr* two + *hú* bowed instrument.] A Chinese two-stringed musical instrument played with a bow.

eria /ˈɪərɪə/ *n.* Also **eri** /ˈɪəri/. M19. [Assamese *eriyā* adj., *eri* n., f. *erā* castor oil plant.] (The cocoon of) an Indian saturniid silk moth, *Attacus ricini*. Usu. *attrib.*

eria cocoon, *moth*, *silk*, etc.

eric /ˈɛrɪk/ *n.* L16. [Ir. *éiric.*] *Ir. Hist.* A blood-fine or financial compensation which had to be paid by a murderer to the family or dependants of the victim.

erica /ˈɛrɪkə/ *n.* E17. [mod.L f. Gk *ereikē*.] Any of various shrubs of the genus *Erica* (family Ericaceae), characterized by narrow rigid revolute leaves and bell-shaped waxy purple or pink flowers; a heath.

eri'caceous *a.* of or pertaining to the family Ericaceae, which comprises chiefly shrubs and small trees and includes the heaths, heather, rhododendron, and azalea M19.

ericetal /ɛrɪˈsiːt(ə)l/ *a.* & *n.* M19. [f. mod.L *ericetum* land dominated by erica, f. L *erica* + -ETUM: see -AL[1].] *Bot.* (A plant) that grows normally on heath or moorland.

ericoid /ˈɛrɪkɔɪd/ *a.* E20. [f. ERIC(A + -OID.] Belonging to plants of the genus *Erica* and allied genera; resembling such plants, esp. in respect of their narrow revolute leaves.

Eridanus /ɛˈrɪdənəs/ *n.* M16. [L, a river in Gk mythol. in which Phaethon drowned.] (The name of) a long winding constellation of the southern hemisphere that extends from near Orion to near Hydrus; the River.

eriff /ˈɛrɪf/ *n. rare.* L17. [Origin unkn.] †1 A two-year-old canary. L17–M18. 2 A newly initiated rogue or thief. *slang.* E18.

erigeron /ɪˈrɪdʒərɒn, ɛ-/ *n.* E17. [L = groundsel f. Gk, f. *ēri* early + *gerōn* old man (f. its early flowering and hoary appearance or white pappus). In sense 2 mod.L f. same source.] †1 Groundsel. E–M17. 2 Any of various plants of the genus *Erigeron*, of the composite family, resembling daisies, chiefly with white, pink, or mauve ray-florets. Also called *fleabane*. E19.

erineum /ɪˈrɪnɪəm, ɛ-/ *n.* Pl **-nea** /-nɪə/. L19. [mod.L, f. as ERINOSE.] †1 A fungus supposed to be the cause of erinose. Only in L19. 2 = ERINOSE. E20.

erinnic /ɪˈrɪnɪk, ɛ-/ *a. rare.* E19. [f. L *Erinnys*, Gk *Erinus* a Fury + -IC.] Characteristic of a Fury.

Also †**erinnical** *a.* E17.

erinose /ˈɛrɪnəʊz, -s/ *n.* E20. [f. Gk *erineos* woolly, f. *erion* wool + *-ose* alt. of -OSIS.] An area of a leaf densely covered with white hairs, caused by the presence of mites; the condition of having such an area. Freq. *attrib.*

eriometer /ɛrɪˈɒmɪtə/ *n.* E19. [f. Gk *erion* wool + -O- + -METER.] An instrument for measuring the diameter of fine fibres by optical means.

†**Erisch** *a.* & *n.* see ERSE.

eristic /ɛˈrɪstɪk/ *a.* & *n.* M17. [Gk *eristikos*, f. *erizein* wrangle, f. *eris* strife.] A *adj.* Of or pertaining to controversy or disputation; *spec.* (of an argument or arguer) aimed or aiming at victory rather than truth. M17. B *n.* 1 A person given to disputation. M17. 2 The art of disputation. M19.

†**eristical** *a.* E17–E18. **eristically** *adv.* M20.

Eritrean /ɛrɪˈtreɪən/ *a.* & *n.* E20. [f. *Eritrea* (see below) + -AN.] A *adj.* Of or pertaining to Eritrea, now a province of northern Ethiopia. E20. B *n.* A native or inhabitant of Eritrea. M20.

erk /əːk/ *n. slang.* Also **irk.** E20. [Origin unkn.] 1 A naval rating; an aircraftman. E20. 2 A disliked person. M20.

erlang /ˈəːlaŋ/ *n.* M20. [A. K. *Erlang* (1878–1929), Da. mathematician.] A unit used to express the intensity of traffic in telephone lines, corresponding to that in one line continuously occupied.

Erlebnis /ɛrˈleːpnɪs/ *n.* Pl. ***-nise*** /-nɪsə/. E20. [G, lit. 'experience', f. *leben* to live.] A conscious experience undergone, as opp. to the content or the memory of one.

Erlenmeyer flask /ˈəːlənmʌɪə flɑːsk/ *n. phr.* L19. [E. *Erlenmeyer* (1825–1909), Ger. chemist.] A conical flat-bottomed laboratory flask with a narrow neck.

erl-king /ˈəːlkɪŋ/ *n.* L18. [Partial tr. G *Erlkönig* lit. 'alder-king', mistr. Da. *ellerkonge* king of the elves.] *Gmc Mythol.* A bearded giant who lures little children to the land of death.

ermelin /ˈəːm(ə)lɪn/ *n.* Now *arch.* or *poet.* M16. [Origin uncertain: cf. Fr. *hermeline*, *armeline*, med.L *armelinus*, and next.] = ERMINE *n.* 1, 2.

ermine /ˈəːmɪn/ *n.* & *v.* ME. [OFr. *ermine*, (also mod.) *hermine*, prob. f. med.L (*mus*) *Armenius* Armenian (mouse), equiv. to L *mus Ponticus* mouse of Pontus.] A *n.* 1 A stoat; *esp.* one with white fur and black-tipped tail, the coat it has in winter in northern regions. ME. 2 The white fur of an ermine as used in clothing, often with the black tails displayed for the sake of effect. ME. b In *pl.* Trimmings or garments made from this fur. L15. 3 *Her.* One of the two chief furs, consisting of a white field covered with distinctive black markings. Cf. VAIR. LME. 4 A symbol of purity or honour, esp. with ref. to the use of ermine in the robes of judges and peers. L18.

2 *attrib.*: G. DOWNES The ermine mantle wherein the female is robed. 4 W. GODWIN Reluctant to fix an unnecessary stain upon the ermine of their profession.

B *v.t.* Cause to have the appearance of ermine. E19.

ermined /ˈəːmɪnd/ *a.* L15. [f. ERMINE *n.* + -ED[2].] 1 *Her.* Covered with the distinctive markings of ermine. L15. 2 Trimmed with ermine; resembling ermine. L15. 3 Robed in ermine; that has been made a judge or a peer. M18.

ermines /ˈəːmɪnz/ *n.* M16. [Origin uncertain: perh. f. OFr. *hermines* pl. of *herminet*, dim. of *hermine* ERMINE *n.*] *Her.* A fur that is the reverse of ermine, with white markings on a black field.

erminites /ˈəːmɪnʌɪts/ *n.* M16. [Fr. *herminite*.] *Her.* A fur resembling ermine but with markings that have a red hair on each side.

erminois /əːmɪˈnɔɪz/ *n.* M16. [OFr. (*h*)*erminois*, f. *hermine* ERMINE *n.*] *Her.* A fur resembling ermine but having black markings on a gold field.

erne /əːn/ *n.* Also ***ern.** [OE *earn* = MLG *arn*, *arnt* (Du. *arend*), OHG *arn*, ON *ǫrn* f. Gmc base.] An eagle; *esp.* a sea-eagle.

Ernestine /ˈəːnɪstʌɪn/ *a.* M19. [f. *Ernest* (see below) + -INE[1].] *Hist.* Designating or pertaining to the elder of the two lines of the house of Frederick the Gentle, Elector of Saxony, which originated with his son Ernest (1441–86) and lost the electoral title to the Albertine line in 1547. Cf. ALBERTINE.

erode /ɪˈrəʊd/ *v.* E17. [Fr. *éroder* or L *erodere*, f. *e-* E- + *rodere* gnaw.] 1 *v.t.* Destroy imperceptibly, little by little; corrode; *Geol.* (of rivers, wind, etc.) gradually wear away (soil, the land, etc.). E17. b *fig.* Make gradually to be of less and less value, strength, etc. M20. 2 *v.t. Geol.* Form by erosion. M19. 3 *v.i.* Cause erosion. M19. 4 *v.i.* Undergo erosion, wear away; *fig.* diminish gradually in value, strength, etc. E20.

1 D. ATTENBOROUGH Rain and rivers eroded the soft sandstones. b *What Mortgage* Inflation erodes the real cost of repayments as time goes on. 2 J. S. HUXLEY The fantastic shapes into which wind, water, and ice had eroded the Alpine ranges. 4 C. FREEMAN The earth . . had eroded so that the tree roots were exposed. *Daily Telegraph* The real value of the grant would erode through inflation.

erodable *a.* = ERODIBLE L20. **erodible** *a.* prone to erosion E20.

erogenic /ɛrəˈdʒɛnɪk/ *a.* L19. [Irreg. f. EROS + -GENIC.] = next.

erogenous /ɪˈrɒdʒɪnəs, ɛ-/ *a.* L19. [Irreg. f. EROS + -GENOUS.] Of a part of the body: sensitive to sexual stimulation; capable of giving sexual pleasure when touched or stroked. Esp. in *erogenous zone*.

eromenos /ɛˈrəʊmɛnɒs/ *n.* Pl. ***-noi*** /-nɔɪ/. L20. [Gk *erōmenos* pa. pple of *eran* be in love with.] *Gk Hist.* A young man desired by an older man. Cf. ERASTES.

-eroo /əˈruː/ *suff. colloq.* (chiefly *N. Amer.*, *Austral*, & *NZ*). [Fanciful.] Forming ns. f. vbs w. the senses 'large of the type or class', 'overwhelming', 'remarkable', 'unexpected', as *flopperoo*, *peacheroo*, *sockeroo*, etc.

Eros /ˈɪərɒs, ˈɛrəʊz/ *n.* Pl. **Erotes** /ɪˈrəʊtɛz/, **Eroses** /ˈɪərɒsɪz, ˈɛrəʊzɪz/. Also **e-.** L17. [L f. Gk.] 1 Love; the god of love, Cupid; earthly or sexual love. L17. 2 In Freudian psychology, the urge for self-preservation and sexual pleasure. Cf. THANATOS. E20.

erose /ɪˈrəʊs/ *a.* L18. [L *erosus* pa. pple of *erodere*: see ERODE.] *Bot.* & *Zool.* Having the margin irregularly denticulate, as if bitten by an animal.

erosion /ɪˈrəʊʒ(ə)n/ *n.* M16. [Fr. *érosion* f. L *erosio(n-)*, f. *eros-* pa. ppl stem of *erodere*: see -ION.] 1 The action or process of eroding something; the state of being eroded. M16. 2 An instance of erosion. E18.

erosional *a.* caused by or resulting from erosion E20. **erosionist** *n.* (*Geol.*) a person who believes the contours of the land are due to erosion of the surface M19.

erosive /ɪˈrəʊsɪv/ *a.* M19. [f. L *eros-* (see prec.) + -IVE.] Having the property of eroding.

erosiveness *n.* M20. **ero'sivity** *n.* E20.

erotema /ɛrəˈtiːmə/ *n.* Long *rare.* M16. [Late L f. Gk *erōtēma*, f. *erōtan* to question.] *Rhet.* = EROTESIS.

Erotes *n.pl.* see EROS.

erotesis /ɛrəˈtiːsɪs/ *n.* M16. [Late L f. Gk *erōtēsis*, f. *erōtan* to question.] *Rhet.* A figure of speech in which the speaker asks a question, with the confident expectation of a negative answer.

erotetic /-ˈtɛtɪk/ *a.* interrogatory M19.

erotic /ɪˈrɒtɪk/ *a.* & *n.* M17. [Fr. *érotique* f. Gk *erōtikos*, f. *erōt-*, *erōs* sexual love: see -IC.] A *adj.* Of or pertaining to sexual love; amatory, *esp.* tending to arouse sexual desire or excitement. M17. B *n.* 1 An erotic poem. M19. 2 A doctrine or science of love. M19.

erotical *a.* (*rare*) = EROTIC E17. **erotically** *adv.* L19. **eroticism** /-sɪz(ə)m/ *n.* erotic spirit or character; sexual excitement; the use of erotic material or practices: L19. **eroticist** /-sɪst/ *n.* a person given to the use of erotic material or practices M20.

erotica /ɪˈrɒtɪkə/ *n.pl.* M19. [f. Gk *erōtika* neut. pl. of *erōtikos*: see prec.] Orig., matters of love. Now, literature or art that is intentionally erotic.

I. MONTAGU My . . approach to literature included the pages in the bookseller's catalogue labelled 'Erotica'.

eroticize /ɪˈrɒtɪsʌɪz/ *v.t.* Also **-ise.** E20. [f. EROTIC + -IZE.] Make erotic, endow with an erotic quality; stimulate sexually.

erotici'zation *n.* M20.

erotise *v.* var. of EROTIZE.

erotism /ˈɛrətɪz(ə)m/ *n.* M19. [f. Gk *erōt-*, *erōs* sexual love + -ISM.] Sexual desire or excitement; eroticism.

erotize /ˈɛrətʌɪz/ *v.t.* Also **-ise.** M20. [f. as prec. + -IZE.] = EROTICIZE.

eroto- /ɪˈrɒtəʊ/ *comb. form* of Gk *erōt-*, *erōs* sexual love: see -O-.

eroto'genic *a.* = EROGENOUS E20. **erotology** /ɛrəˈtɒlədʒi/ *n.* the description of sexual love and lovemaking; the field of study that deals with sexual love: L19. **eroto'mania** *n.* excessive or morbid erotic desire; preoccupation with sexual passion: M19. **eroto'maniac** *n.* & *a.* (*a*) *n.* a person affected by erotomania; (*b*) affected by or symptomatic of erotomania: M19.

err /əː/ *v.* ME. [OFr. *errer* f. L *errare* f. base rel. to Goth. *airzei* error, *airzjan* lead astray, OS, OHG *irri* (G *irre*) astray.] †1 *v.i.* Roam, wander. ME–L17. 2 *v.i.* Go astray; stray *from* one's path or direction; deviate *from* a target or aim. *arch.* ME. 3 *v.i.* Go morally astray; sin. ME. 4 *v.i.* Make a wrong judgement, form a wrong opinion; make a mistake, blunder; (of a statement etc.) be incorrect. ME. †5 *v.t.* Do (something) wrongly or sinfully; make a mistake in. ME–M17.

3 G. B. SHAW To come to the bosom of her Church as an erring but beloved child. 4 I. MURDOCH The Goncourt jury . . might sometimes err, but they would never make a crass or fantastic mistake. **err on the right side** act so that the most likely error to occur is the least harmful one. **err on the side of** act with more rather than less of (a specified quality etc.).

erra'bility *n.* (now *rare* or *obs.*) liability to err, fallibility E18. **errable** *a.* (now *rare* or *obs.*) fallible LME. **erringly** *adv.* in an erring way E19.

errancy /ˈɛr(ə)nsi/ *n.* E17. [f. ERRANT *a.*: see -ANCY.] The condition of erring or being in error.

errand /ˈɛr(ə)nd/ *n.* [OE *ǣrende* = OFris. *ērende*, OS *ārundi*, OHG *ārunti*, f. Gmc base obscurely rel. to ON *eyrindi*, *ǫrindi*, *erindi*: ult. origin unkn.] 1†a A message, a verbal communication to be repeated to a third party.

OE–M18. **b** *spec.* in *Chr. Ch.* A petition or prayer presented through a saint. ME. **2a** A journey made for a special purpose; an expedition, a mission. *arch.* exc. *poet.* & *rhet.* OE. **b** A short journey on which a person is sent to take a message, collect goods, or perform some similar small task. M17. **3** The business on which a person goes or is sent; the object of a journey. ME.

1 R. STANYHURST Tel your King, from me, this errand. 2b V. GLENDINNING The oddest errand... To buy a dressing-gown for a nun. C. CHAPLIN I was made to.. run errands and do odd jobs. I. COMPTON-BURNETT Can I write letters, or go on errands? 3 W. PALEY The errand which brought him to Jerusalem.

Phrases: **errand of mercy** a journey to give help or relieve distress. **fool's errand** a pointless undertaking. †**make an errand** (*a*) make a short journey; (*b*) find a pretext for going.

Comb.: **errand-boy, -girl**: whose job is to run errands, esp. (formerly) for a shopkeeper.

errant /ˈɛr(ə)nt/ *a.* & *n.* See also ARRANT. ME. [Branch I f. (O)Fr. *errant* pres. pple of *errer* ERR and of OFr. *errer* travel (f. late L *iterare*, f. L *iter* journey). Branch II f. L *errant-* pres. ppl stem of *errare* ERR: see -ANT[1].] **A** *adj.* & (*arch.*) as *pres. pple.* **I 1** Travelling, itinerant; (esp. of a knight) wandering in search of adventure. Freq. *postpositive*. Now *literary* exc. in KNIGHT ERRANT. ME. †**2a** = ARRANT 2. LME–L18. **b** = ARRANT 3. M17–E18.

1 **errant polychaete** *Zool.* any of various active carnivorous marine polychaete worms not confined to tubes or burrows.

II 3 Astray, wandering; straying from the correct way; erratic. LME. **4** Erring in opinion, conduct, etc.; deviating from an accepted standard. E17.

3 P. ZWEIG The errant boy returns, a prodigal son, to embrace his family. DICKENS With an errant motion of his hands as if he could have torn himself. 4 G. F. WATTS Correcting errant taste in dress.

B *n.* A knight errant; a person who is errant. M17.

errantly *adv.* randomly; purposelessly: M19. **errantry** *n.* the condition of being errant; the condition, conduct, or ideas of a knight errant (cf. KNIGHT-ERRANTRY): M17.

errata /ɛˈrɑːtə, -ˈreɪt-/ *n.* L16. [L, pl. of ERRATUM.] **I 1** *pl.* of ERRATUM. L16. **II** *sing.* Pl. **-ta's, -taes** /-təz/. **2** A list of errors in a text. M17. †**3** = ERRATUM. M17–E18.

†**errate** *n.* see ERRATUM.

erratic /ɪˈratɪk/ *a.* & *n.* LME. [OFr. *erratique* f. L *erraticus*, f. *errat-* pa. ppl stem of *errare*: see ERR, -IC.] **A** *adj.* **1** Irregular or uncertain in movement; having no fixed course or direction. LME. †**b** Of a disease or pain: moving from one part of the body to another. M16–M18. **c** Itinerant; nomadic; vagrant. *arch.* M17. **2** Inconsistently variable in behaviour or habit; unpredictable; irregular or eccentric in opinion. M19.

1 A. C. CLARKE The animal was moving in a curiously erratic path, .. making little darts to right or left. 2 M. E. BRADDON He did not appear at luncheon, but.. he is always erratic.

Special collocations: **erratic block, boulder**: that differs from the surrounding rock and is thought to have been brought from a distance by glacial action. †**erratic star** a planet.

B *n.* **1** An erratic person. E17. **2** = *erratic block* above. M19.

erratical *a.* (now *rare* or *obs.*) = ERRATIC *a.* E17. **erratically** *adv.* E17. **erraticism** /-sɪz(ə)m/ *n.* erratic tendencies; an instance of erratic behaviour: L19. **erraticness** *n.* E20.

erratum /ɛˈrɑːtəm, -ˈreɪt-/ *n.* Pl. **-ta** /-tə/. Earlier Anglicized as †**-ate**. M16. [L = error, use as n. of neut. pa. pple of *errare* ERR.] An error in a printed or written text; *esp.* one noted in a list appended to a book or published in a subsequent issue of a journal.

errhine /ˈɛraɪn/ *n.* Now *rare* or *obs.* E17. [mod.L *errhinum* f. Gk *errinon*, f. *en* in + *rhin-*, *rhis* nostril.] **1** A medicinal preparation which induces sneezing when applied inside the nose. E17. †**2** A pointed plug of lint steeped in such a substance for insertion in a nostril. E17–M18.

erroneous /ɪˈrəʊnɪəs, ɛ-/ *a.* LME. [OFr. or L *erroneus*, f. L *erro(n-)* truant, vagabond, f. *errare*: see ERR, -EOUS.] **1** Of an opinion, statement, doctrine, etc.: containing errors; mistaken, incorrect; (formerly) heretical. LME. **b** Of a legal proceeding: faulty, irregular; rendered invalid by error. LME. †**2** Of a person, life, action, etc.: going astray morally or intellectually; criminal; misguided; heretical. LME–E19. †**3** Wandering, moving aimlessly; vagrant. M17–L18.

1 G. BUDD The erroneous impression that abscesses exist in the liver only. 2 S. JOHNSON That erroneous clemency. BYRON The book which treats of this erroneous pair.

erroneously *adv.* E16. **erroneousness** *n.* E17.

error /ˈɛrə/ *n.* Also (earlier) †**-our**. ME. [OFr. *err(o)ur* (mod. *erreur*) f. L *error*, f. *errare* ERR: see -OR.] **I 1** The condition of erring in opinion or belief; a mistaken opinion or belief. ME. **2** Something done incorrectly because ignorance or inadvertence; a mistake. ME. **b** *Law.* A mistake in matter of law appearing in the proceedings of a court of record. L15. **c** *Baseball.* A mistake by a fielder. L19. **3** A mistake in moral behaviour, a transgression; wrongdoing. ME. †**4** A flaw; a malformation. LME–L18. **5** The amount by which an observed or approximate numerical result differs from the true or exact one. E18. **6** *Philately.* A postage stamp that differs from the usual form by having wrong wording, colour, etc. M19.

1 C. LUCAS The general notion that springs are colder in summer and warmer in winter is but a vulgar error. V. KNOX This circumstance has led those into error. B. JOWETT Actions done in error. 2 J. GALSWORTHY It was not her fault; it was her error of judgment. O. MANNING He was expected to pick up her errors of grammar and pronunciation. *clerical error*: see CLERICAL *a.* 2. **b writ of error**: brought to procure the reversal of a judgement, on the ground of error. 5 *probable error*: see PROBABLE *a.* *random error*: see RANDOM *a.* *standard error*: see STANDARD *a.* *systematic error*: see SYSTEMATIC *a.*

II 7 The action of wandering; a devious or winding course. *obs.* exc. *poet.* E16.

Comb.: **error bar** a line through a point on a graph, parallel to one of the axes, which represents the uncertainty or error of the corresponding coordinate of the point; **error box** *Astron.* a quadrilateral area of sky whose dimensions correspond to the uncertainty of a measured position inside it; **error circle** *Astron.* a circular area of sky with the same significance as an error box.

errorist *n.* a person who tends to make errors or who encourages error M17. **errorless** *a.* M19.

-ers *suff.* var. of -ER[6].

ersatz /ˈɜːsats, ˈɛː-, *foreign* ɛrˈzats/ *a.* & *n.* L19. [G = compensation, replacement.] **A** *adj.* Made or used as a (usually inferior) substitute for something else. L19.

New Yorker I stole packets of sugar and containers of ersatz cream. T. LEARY The external social drama which is as dehydrated and ersatz as TV.

B *n.* An ersatz thing. L19.

Erse /ɜːs/ *a.* & *n.* Now *arch.* or *derog.* Orig. †**Erisch**, †**Ersch**. LME. [Early Sc. var. of IRISH.] **A** *adj.* Orig., of or pertaining to Ireland or the Scottish Highlands; *spec.* of or pertaining to Highland Gaelic; written or spoken in Highland Gaelic. Later, of or pertaining to the Gaelic spoken in Ireland, Irish. LME. **B** *n.* The Gaelic language; latterly *spec.* Irish Gaelic, Irish. L15.

erst /ɜːst/ *adv.* & *a.* [OE *ǣrest* superl. corresp. to *ǣr* ERE = OS *ērist* (Du. *eerst*), OHG *ērist* (G *erst*): see -EST[1].] **A** *adv.* †**1** Earliest, first in order of time. OE–LME. †**2** In the first place, in preference to doing something else. OE–E19. †**3** At first, initially. OE–E17. †**4** Sooner; before a specified time or event. ME–L16. **5a** Long ago, formerly, of old. *arch.* exc. *poet.* ME. †**b** Recently; not long ago. L15–L18. †**B** *adj.* Occurring first in time. OE–ME.

Phrases: †**at erst** (now, or then) and not before; at once.

erstwhile /ˈɜːstwaɪl/ *adv.* & *a.* L16. [f. ERST + WHILE *adv.*] **A** *adv.* Formerly; hitherto. *arch.* L16.

W. GOLDING His hair was frizzed and much lighter than erstwhile. R. SCRUTON The conservative will find the practice of politics as difficult as he has erstwhile found its theory.

B *adj.* Former. E20.

W. C. WILLIAMS The erstwhile chicken house has been a studio for years.

Ertebølle /ɜːtəˈbɜːlə/ *a.* Also **-bölle, -bolle**. E20. [Place in Jutland, Denmark.] *Archaeol.* Designating or pertaining to a late mesolithic culture in the western Baltic, the final phases of which show neolithic influence.

erubescence /ɛrʊˈbɛs(ə)ns/ *n. rare.* LME. [Late L *erubescentia*, f. as next: see -ESCENCE.] Erubescent quality; blushing. Formerly, shame.

erubescent /ɛrʊˈbɛs(ə)nt/ *a.* M18. [L *erubescent-* pres. ppl stem of *erubescere* blush, f. *e-* E- + *rubescere* redden, f. *rubere* be red: see -ESCENT.] Reddening; blushing.

eruca /ɪˈruːkə/ *n. rare.* Orig. Anglicized as †**eruke**. LME. [L: see next.] A caterpillar; a larva.

erucic /ɪˈruːsɪk/ *a.* M19. [f. L *eruca* rocket (the plant), caterpillar + -IC.] *erucic acid*, a solid unsaturated fatty acid, $C_{21}H_{41}COOH$, present in mustard seeds and rape seeds.

eruciform /ɪˈruːsɪfɔːm/ *a.* L19. [f. as prec. + -I- + -FORM.] Having the form of a caterpillar.

eruct /ɪˈrʌkt/ *v.i.* & *t.* Now *rare.* M17. [L *eructare*: see next.] = ERUCTATE. Also, rise in the course of eructation.

eruction *n.* (*rare*) E17.

eructate /ɪˈrʌkteɪt/ *v.* Now *rare.* M17. [L *eructat-* pa. ppl stem of *eructare*, f. *e-* E- + *ructare* to belch: see -ATE[3].] **1** *v.t.* Expel or emit violently. Chiefly *fig.* M17. **2** *v.i.* Of a person: belch. L18.

eructation /iːrʌkˈteɪʃ(ə)n, ɪ-/ *n.* LME. [L *eructatio(n-)*, f. as prec.: see -ATION.] **1a** Belching; a belch. LME. **b** (A) volcanic eruption; emission *of* something by a volcano. M17. **2** Material that is emitted. E17.

érudit /erydi, ɛrʊˈdiː/ *n.* Also **erudit** /ˈɛrʊdɪt/. E19. [Fr., f. as next.] A scholar.

erudite /ˈɛrʊdʌɪt/ *a.* & *n.* LME. [L *eruditus* pa. pple of *erudire* instruct, train, f. *e-* E- + *rudis* rude, untrained: see -ITE[2].] **A** *adj.* **1** Learned, scholarly. Formerly, trained, instructed. LME. **2** Of writing etc.: that shows great learning. M16. **B** *n.* An erudite person, a scholar. *rare.* M19.

eruditely *adv.* E16. **eruditeness** *n.* E19.

erudition /ɛrʊˈdɪʃ(ə)n/ *n.* LME. [OFr. *érudition* or L *eruditio(n-)*, f. *erudit-* pa. ppl stem of *erudire*: see prec., -ITION.] †**1** Instruction, education; what is taught; a maxim. LME–M18. **2** Orig., the state of being instructed or trained (foll. by *in*, *of*). Now, acquired knowledge, esp. in the humanities; learning, scholarship. M16.

1 H. FIELDING This gift Jenny had.. improved by erudition. 2 G. B. SHAW This simple faith in my accomplishment as a linguist and my erudition as a philosopher.

eruditional *a.* M17.

†**eruke** *n.* see ERUCA.

erump /ɪˈrʌmp/ *v.i. rare.* M17. [L *erumpere*: see ERUPT.] Break out; erupt; burst forth.

erumpent /ɪˈrʌmpənt/ *a.* M17. [L *erumpent-* pres. ppl stem of *erumpere*: see next, -ENT.] That bursts forth; *spec.* (*Bot.*) projecting from a surface or substratum.

erupt /ɪˈrʌpt/ *v.* M17. [L *erupt-* pa. ppl stem of *erumpere*, f. *e-* E- + *rumpere* burst forth.] **1** *v.i.* (Of volcanic material) be ejected in the course of an eruption; (of a rash, boil, etc.) appear on the skin; *gen.* (chiefly *fig.* exc. as below) come out of something (as if) with violence or rupture; burst forth. M17. **b** *v.i.* & *t.* (in *pass.*). Of a tooth: emerge through the skin of the gums in the course of development. M19. **2** *v.t.* Of a volcano, geyser, etc.: eject in an eruption. M18. **3** *v.i.* (Of a volcano, geyser, etc.) be in a state of eruption; suddenly become noisily active (foll. by *in*, *into*). L18.

1 W. OWEN Will toe-nails cease to grow; pimples to erupt? JO GRIMOND You could dangle a mussel.. over the water and suddenly a fish would erupt and seize it. 2 *Nature* On the lunar surface.. basalt magmas were erupted. 3 J. IRVING When no strong leader emerged,

the kingdom of Thak erupted in . . rebellion. S. BRETT The audience erupted into laughter and applause. R. FRAME After just a couple of hours . . my mother erupted, yelling at the guards.

eruption /ɪˈrʌpʃ(ə)n/ *n.* LME. [OFr. *éruption* or L *eruptio(n-)*, f. as prec.: see -ION.] **1** The appearance on the skin of a rash or a collection of boils or the like; a rash; a pathological alteration of the appearance of the skin. LME. **2** The action or an act of bursting or breaking out from natural or artificial limits. M16. **b** The emergence of a tooth through the skin of the gums in the course of development. M19. **3a** A sudden occurrence of something calamitous or noisy, as disease or laughter; an outbreak, an outburst. L16. **b** A spell of activity in which a volcano ejects lava, ash, etc., usu. violently; a spell of activity in which a geyser ejects hot water. M18. **4** A thing that bursts out; a sudden rush of flame, water, or the like. L17.

3a HUGH WALPOLE Before the eruption of the civil war.

eruptional *a.* M19.

eruptive /ɪˈrʌptɪv/ *a.* & *n.* M17. [f. ERUPT + -IVE.] **A** *adj.* Tending to erupt; of, pertaining to, or characterized by (an) eruption; (of rock) formed by the cooling and solidification of magma or (esp.) lava. M17.

BYRON The volcano's fierce eruptive crest. C. M. YONGE Illness of an eruptive kind.

B *n.* An eruptive rock. L19.

†**erve** *n.* var. of ERF.

erven *n.pl.* see ERF.

-ery /əri/ *suff.* [Fr. *-erie*, partly f. Proto-Romance, f. L *-ario-* + *-ia* -Y³; partly f. OFr. *-ere*, *-eor* (mod. *-eur*) f. L *-ator*, + *-ie* -Y³.] Forming ns. f. ns. and vbs in which it denotes (*a*) things of a certain kind, as *confectionery, greenery, machinery, scenery*; (*b*) a place of work, as *bakery, brewery*; *US* a place where things can be bought, as *bootery, eatery*; a place where plants or animals live or are reared, as *orangery, piggery, rockery, rookery, sealery*; (*c*) a state or condition, as *bravery, slavery*; an occupation, as *archery, midwifery*; (*d*) characteristic qualities, ideas, or actions (often *derog.*), as *knavery, popery, tomfoolery*.

eryngium /ɪˈrɪndʒɪəm/ *n.* L16. [mod.L f. L *eryngion* f. Gk *ērugion* dim. of *ērugos* sea holly.] Any of various umbelliferous plants of the genus *Eryngium*, with prickly leaves and blue or white flowers in thistle-like heads; *esp.* sea holly, *E. maritimum*.

eryngo /ɪˈrɪŋgəʊ/ *n.* Pl. **-o(e)s**. L16. [It. or Sp. *eringio* f. L *eryngion* ERYNGIUM.] †**1** The candied root of the sea holly, *Eryngium maritimum*, eaten as a sweet and considered an aphrodisiac. L16–E18. **2** Sea holly; any other plant of the genus *Eryngium*. M17.

erysipelas /ɛrɪˈsɪpɪləs/ *n.* LME. [L f. Gk *erusipelas*, perh. f. base of *eruthros* red + *pel-* in *pella* skin.] An acute, sometimes recurrent, disease caused by a streptococcal infection and characterized by large raised red patches on the skin, esp. of the face and legs, with fever and severe general illness.

SWINE *erysipelas*.

ˌ**erysiˈpelatose** *a.* = ERYSIPELATOUS E18.

erysipelatous /ˌɛrɪsɪˈpɛlətəs/ *a.* M17. [f. med.L *erysipelatus* (f. Gk *erusipelat-*, *erusipelas* ERYSIPELAS) + -OUS.] Pertaining to or of the nature of erysipelas; affected with erysipelas.

erysipeloid /ɛrɪˈsɪpɪlɔɪd/ *n.* L19. [f. ERYSIPELAS + -OID.] Dermatitis of the hands due to infection with swine erysipelas.

erythema /ɛrɪˈθiːmə/ *n.* L18. [Gk *eruthēma*, f. *eruthainein* be red, f. *eruthros* red.] Redness of the skin, usually in patches, as a result of injury or irritation.

erythemal *a.* erythematous; causing erythema: M20. ˌ**erytheˈmatic** *a.* erythematous L18. **erythematous** *a.* of, pertaining to, or symptomatic of erythema M19.

erythr- *comb. form* see ERYTHRO-.

erythraemia /ɛrɪˈθriːmɪə/ *n.* Also *__-thremia__. M19. [f. ERYTHRO- + -AEMIA.] †**1** The oxygenation of the blood in the lungs. *rare*. Only in M19. **2** An abnormally high concentration of red cells in the blood; a disease so characterized, *esp.* polycythaemia vera. E20.

erythraemic *a.* characteristic of or characterized by erythraemia E20.

erythrasma /ɛrɪˈθrazmə/ *n.* L19. [f. ERYTHRO- + Gk *-asma* (cf. CHLOASMA).] A chronic skin disease caused by a corynebacterium and characterized by scaling discoloured patches on areas of moist skin in contact with each other.

erythremia *n.* see ERYTHRAEMIA.

erythrina /ɛrɪˈθriːnə/ *n.* L18. [mod.L, f. Gk *eruthros* red.] Any of various leguminous tropical trees and shrubs of the genus *Erythrina*; = *coral tree* (b) s.v. CORAL *n.*

erythrine /ˈɛrɪθriːn, ɪˈrɪθriːn/ *n.* Now *rare*. M19. [f. as next + -INE⁵.] = ERYTHRITE 2.

erythrism /ˈɛrɪθrɪz(ə)m/ *n.* L19. [f. Gk *eruthros* red + -ISM.] *Zool.* Abnormal or excessive redness, as in the plumage or fur of a bird or animal; a red variety of a species.

eryˈthristic *a.* exhibiting erythrism E20.

erythrite /ˈɛrɪθrʌɪt, ɪˈrɪθrʌɪt/ *n.* M19. [f. as prec. + -ITE¹.] **1** A flesh-coloured variety of feldspar. Now *rare* or *obs.* M19. **2** *Min.* A hydrated arsenate of cobalt and nickel occurring as a secondary mineral in red or pink translucent monoclinic crystals. Also called *cobalt bloom, red cobalt (ore)*, (earlier) ERYTHRINE. M19. **3** *Chem.* = ERYTHRITOL. Now *rare*. M19.

erythritol /ɪˈrɪθrɪtɒl/ *n.* L19. [f. ERYTHRITE + -OL.] *Chem.* An optically active tetrahydric alcohol, $C_4H_{10}O_4$, occurring in certain lichens and algae, the nitrate of which is used as a vasodilator.

erythro- /ɪˈrɪθrəʊ/ *comb. form* of Gk *eruthros* red, and of ERYTHROCYTE: see -O-. Bef. a vowel **erythr-**.

erythroblast *n.* a nucleated cell which develops into an erythrocyte L19. **erythroˈblastic** *a.* containing or involving erythroblasts E20. **erythroblasˈtosis** *n.* the presence of erythroblasts in the blood; *spec.* (more fully *erythroblastosis foetalis*) haemolytic disease of the newborn, a severe anaemia that results when the mother develops antibodies against the blood of the foetus: M20. **erythroˈgenic** *a.* causing redness, esp. of the skin E20. **erythroleuˈkaemia** *n.* (*Med.*) a rare acute form of leukaemia with proliferation of erythroblasts and leucoblasts E20. **erythromeˈlalgia** *n.* [Gk *melos* limb] pain in the extremities, esp. the feet, with dilatation of the blood-vessels and reddening of the skin L19. **erythroˈmycin** *n.* an antibiotic isolated from *Streptomyces erythreus*, similar in its effects to penicillin M20. **erythrophagocyˈtosis** *n.* the phagocytosis of erythrocytes M20. **erythroˈphobia** *n.* (*a*) fear of blushing; (*b*) a visual hypersensitivity to the colour red: L19. **erythrophore** *n.* a red pigment cell in an animal E20. **erythropoiesis** /-pɔɪˈiːsɪs/ *n.* the formation of red blood cells E20. **erythropoietic** /-pɔɪˈɛtɪk/ *a.* pertaining to or characterized by erythropoiesis E20. **erythropoietin** /-pɔɪˈɛtɪn/ *n.* a hormone secreted by the kidneys that increases the rate of formation of red blood cells M20. **eryˈthropsia** *n.* [Gk *-opsia* seeing] a visual disorder in which everything appears red L19. **erythrosin** *n.* a brown powder, related to eosin, which gives a red colour in aqueous solution and is used as a biological stain and to colour food L19.

erythrocyte /ɪˈrɪθrəsʌɪt/ *n.* L19. [f. ERYTHRO- + -CYTE.] One of the principal cells in the blood of vertebrates, containing the pigment haemoglobin and transporting oxygen and carbon dioxide to and from the tissues. Also called *red (blood) cell, red corpuscle*.

erythrocytic /-ˈsɪtɪk/ *a.* of or pertaining to an erythrocyte; involving erythrocytes; (of malaria parasites etc.) occurring inside an erythrocyte: E20. **erythrocyˈtosis** *n.* an increased number of erythrocytes in the blood, esp. as a secondary symptom E20.

erythroid /ˈɛrɪθrɔɪd/ *a.* M19. [f. ERYTHRO- + -OID.] **1** Of a red colour. *rare*. M19. **2** Of or pertaining to erythrocytes or their precursors. E20.

erythrol /ˈɛrɪθrɒl/ *n.* L19. [f. ERYTHRITE + -OL.] *Chem.* = ERYTHRITOL.

erythronium /ɛrɪˈθrəʊnɪəm/ *n.* Pl. **-iums, -ia** /-ɪə/. E19. [mod.L, f. Gk *saturion eruthronion* red-flowered orchid.] Any of various ornamental spring-flowering bulbs of the genus *Erythronium* of the lily family; = *dog's tooth violet* s.v. DOG'S TOOTH 1.

erythrose /ɪˈrɪθrəʊz, -s, ˈɛrɪ-/ *n.* E20. [f. ERYTHRITE + -OSE².] A liquid tetrose sugar, $CHO{\cdot}(CHOH)_2{\cdot}CH_2OH$, existing as two optical isomers and differing from threose in having the hydroxyl groups on the second and third carbon atoms on the same side of the carbon chain.

es- /ɛs, *unstressed* ɪs/ *pref.* (not productive). Repr. OFr. *es-* (= It. *s-*) f. L *ex-* out, utterly (see EX-¹), as *escape, escheat*. Cf. A-⁷.

-es *suff.*¹ see -S¹.

-es *suff.*² see -S².

Esalen /ˈɛsələn/ *n.* & *a.* M20. [*Esselen*, an extinct N. American Indian people of the Californian coast.] (Designating) an alternative philosophy and technique aimed at increasing a person's self-awareness and potential by psychological and physiotherapeutic means.

Esau /ˈiːsɔː/ *n.* M17. [The biblical patriarch Isaac's elder twin son, who sold his birthright (*Gen.* 25:25 ff.).] A person who prefers present advantage to permanent rights or interests.

escalade /ɛskəˈleɪd/ *n.* L16. [Fr., or Sp. *escalada*, *-ado*, = It. *scalata*, f. med.L *scalare* SCALE *v.*²: see -ADE.] The action or an act of scaling the walls of a fortified place by means of ladders.

Also **escalado** /ɛskəˈlɑːdəʊ/ *n.* (*arch.*), pl. **-oes**, L16.

escalade /ɛskəˈleɪd/ *v.t.* E19. [f. the n.] Climb and get over (a wall) by means of ladders.

escalate /ˈɛskəleɪt/ *v.* E20. [Back-form. f. ESCALATOR.] **1** *v.i.* Travel on an escalator. E20. **2** *v.t.* & *i.* (Cause to) increase or develop, esp. by successive stages. M20.

2 M. L. KING The white liberal must escalate his support for the struggle for racial justice. M. EDWARDES A dispute arose, initially involving one man, . . and then escalated until some 14,000 employees . . went out on indefinite strike. N. MAILER It all escalated from car stealing up to armed robbery.

escalation /ɛskəˈleɪʃ(ə)n/ *n.* M20. [f. prec. + -ATION.] The process or an act of increasing in scale, scope, etc., by successive stages; (a) step-by-step development, esp. of a war or dispute.

escalator /ˈɛskəleɪtə/ *n.* Orig. *US*. E20. [f. ESCALADE *v.* + -ATOR, after *elevator*.] A staircase consisting of an endless chain of steps driven by a motor and continuously ascending or descending.

fig.: *Economist* Prices and wages are fellow-travellers on the same upward escalator.

Comb.: **escalator clause, contract**, etc.: providing for a change in prices etc. to meet specified contingencies.

escalatory /ɛskəˈleɪt(ə)ri/ *a.* M20. [f. ESCALATE + -ORY².] Tending to escalate; conducive of or constituting escalation.

escaline /ˈɛskəlɪn/ *n.* Also **-lin**. L17. [Fr., f. Du. *schelling*, G *Schilling*: see SHILLING.] Orig., a Flemish coin. Later, any of various coins used in South Africa and the southern States of the US.

escallonia /ɛskəˈləʊnɪə/ *n.* L19. [mod.L, f. *Escallon*, 18th-cent. Spanish traveller + -IA¹.] Any of various chiefly evergreen pink- or white-flowered shrubs of the S. American genus *Escallonia* (often included in the saxifrage family), used for hedging in mild coastal districts.

escallop /ɪˈskaləp, ɛ-, -ˈskɒl-/ *n.* L15. [OFr. *escalope* shell. Cf. SCALLOP.] **1** = SCALLOP *n.* 2b. L15. **2** = SCALLOP *n.* 1. E17. **3** *Her.* A figure of a single valve of a scallop, borne as a charge. Also *escallop-shell*. E17.

Comb.: **escallop-shell** (*a*) = SCALLOP *shell*; (*b*) an ornamental imitation of a scallop shell; (see also sense 3 above).

escalloped *a.* = SCALLOPED E17.

escalope /ɪˈskaləp, ɛ-, -ˈskɒl-, ˈɛskələʊp/ *n.* Also **escalop, escallope**. E19. [Fr. f. OFr. = shell. Cf. ESCALLOP.] A thin slice of boneless meat or (occas.) fish; *esp.* a special cut of veal from the leg.

escapable /ɪˈskeɪpəb(ə)l, ɛ-/ *a.* M19. [f. ESCAPE *v.* + -ABLE.] Able to be escaped or avoided.

¶Earlier in INESCAPABLE.

escapade /ˈɛskəpeɪd, ɛskəˈpeɪd/ *n.* M17. [Fr. f. Sp. or Prov., f. *escapar* to escape, f. Proto-

Romance: see ESCAPE *v.*, -ADE.] †1 An act of escaping from confinement or restraint; an escape. M17–M19. 2 An instance of irresponsible or unorthodox conduct. E19.

2 SIR W. SCOTT A youthful escapade, which might be easily atoned.

escape /ɪˈskeɪp, ɛ-/ *n.* ME. [Orig. f. OFr. *eschap*, f. *eschaper* (see ESCAPE *v.*); later f. the vb. Aphet. to SCAPE *n.*[1]] 1 The action or an act of escaping, or the fact of having escaped, from captivity, danger, etc. ME. **b** (A) leakage of liquid, gas, electricity, etc. L19. **c** The action of escaping from the gravitational force of a planet or other celestial object. M20. 2 The possibility or a means of escaping; a way out; a fire-escape. LME. **b** An outlet for liquid; *esp.* a sluice etc. to convey surplus water from a canal. L19. †3 A breaking of rules or conventions; a transgression, an (amorous) escapade. LME–L17. **b** A mistake; *esp.* a clerical or printer's error. L16–M19. **c** An involuntary outburst of feeling; a shaft of wit. E17–L18. 4 (A means of) mental or emotional distraction from the realities of life. M19. 5 A garden plant growing wild; an animal or bird which has escaped from captivity L19.

1 JONSON What, has he made an escape! which way? **b** OED There is an escape of gas in the kitchen. 2 N. COWARD Nothing's any use. There's no escape, ever. K. AMIS For many of them, .. to be a priest is an escape from the poverty. 4 D. W. HARDING Readers who .. would turn to her .. for relief and escape.

Comb.: **escape clause**: specifying the conditions under which a contracting party is freed from an obligation; **escape code** *Computing* = *shift code* s.v. SHIFT *n.* 15c; **escape committee** a group of prisoners that plans and coordinates escapes from a prison camp etc.; **escape hatch**: serving as an emergency exit in a submarine, ship, aircraft, etc.; **escape key** *Computing*: that either terminates the current operating mode or changes the functions of other keys; **escape road** a slip-road for the use of vehicles failing to negotiate a bend or hill; **escape shaft**: for the escape of miners if the ordinary shaft becomes blocked; **escape speed** = *escape velocity* below; **escape valve**: to allow the escape of steam etc. when the pressure gets too great; **escape velocity** the lowest velocity at which a body must be projected into space if it is not eventually to return by gravitational attraction; **escape wheel** a toothed wheel in the escapement of a watch or clock.

escape /ɪˈskeɪp, ɛ-/ *v.* ME. [AN, ONFr. *escaper* (OFr. *eschaper*, mod. *échapper*), f. Proto-Romance, f. as EX-[1] + med.L *cappa* cloak: see CAP *n.*[1] Aphet. to SCAPE *v.*[1]] 1 *v.i.* Break free *from* captivity; free oneself by fleeing or struggling. Also foll. by *out of*. ME. **b** Of a fluid, powder, etc.: leak or seep out; pass out. Of an object: come out (as if) from confinement. LME. †2 *v.t.* Escape from (prison, a person's control, etc.). ME–M17. 3 *v.t.* Succeed in avoiding (something unwelcome); elude (a person's grasp). ME. 4 *v.i.* Avoid capture, punishment, or something unwelcome; get off safely; go unpunished. ME. †**b** Recover from serious illness. LME–L15. 5 *v.t.* Elude (observation, search); fail to be noticed or recollected by (a person). ME. 6 *v.t.* Be uttered inadvertently by; issue involuntarily from (a person, a person's lips). LME.

1 C. HILL The King escaped from his captivity at Hampton Court. N. MONSARRAT Three hundred others escaped by means of ropes let down from these bastions. **b** J. L. WATEN From the darkness within a pungent odour escaped. W. GOLDING They had heaped up her .. hair out of the way on her head, though a curl or two had escaped. 3 W. MAXWELL Very few families escape disasters of one kind or another. A. S. NEILL You can't escape becoming smug and dignified if you are an inspector. 4 AV *Acts* 27:44 They escaped all safe to land. DONNE He may escape with his life. G. B. SHAW We court the danger; but the real delight is in escaping. S. LEWIS His wife, his clamoring friends, sought to follow him, but he escaped. 5 E. M. FORSTER The name escaped her. What was the name? J. HERSEY He tried to escape her glance by keeping his back turned. 6 T. HARDY The words had no sooner escaped her than an expression of unutterable regret crossed her face.

escaper *n.* E17.

escapee /ɛskeɪˈpiː, ɪˈskeɪpiː/ *n.* M19. [f. ESCAPE *v.* + -EE[1].] A person who has escaped, *esp.* an escaped prisoner.

escapeless /ɪˈskeɪplɪs, ɛ-/ *a.* M19. [f. ESCAPE *n.*, *v.* + -LESS.] Unavoidable; impossible to escape (from).

escapement /ɪˈskeɪpm(ə)nt, ɛ-/ *n.* See also SCAPEMENT (earlier). L18. [Fr. *échappement*, f. *échapper*: see ESCAPE *v.*, -MENT.] **1a** A mechanism in a clock or watch that alternately checks and releases the train by a fixed amount and transmits a periodic impulse from the spring or weight to the balance-wheel or pendulum; a mechanism in a typewriter that shifts the carriage a fixed amount when a key is pressed and released. L18. **b** The mechanism in a piano which allows a hammer to move away after striking a string. L19. **2a** The action of escaping. *rare*. E19. **b** A means of escape; an outlet. *arch.* M19.

1 *duplex escapement*: see DUPLEX *a.* 1.

escapism /ɪˈskeɪpɪz(ə)m, ɛ-/ *n.* M20. [f. ESCAPE *n.* + -ISM.] The tendency to seek, or practice of seeking, distraction or relief from reality.

L. D. WEATHERHEAD Religion that was mere escapism.

escapist /ɪˈskeɪpɪst, ɛ-/ *n.* & *a.* M20. [f. ESCAPE *n.* + -IST.] **A** *n.* 1 A person who escapes or tries to escape from captivity etc. M20. 2 A person who seeks distraction or relief from reality or who indulges in escapism. M20.

2 E. WAUGH Turning their backs on the world of effort and action. .. Happy, drab escapists.

B *adj.* Providing distraction or relief from reality; involving or characteristic of escapism. M20.

A. STORR Escapist phantasies. W. STYRON The escapist euphoria of a tax dodger seeking to lose his past in Rio de Janeiro.

escapologist /ɛskeɪˈpɒlədʒɪst, ɛskəˈpɒl-/ *n.* E20. [f. ESCAPE *n.* + -OLOGIST.] A person, esp. a performer, skilled in freeing himself or herself from the constraints of knots, handcuffs, confinement, etc.

esˌcapoˈlogical *a.* M20. **escapology** *n.* the methods and techniques of escaping, *esp.* those of an escapologist M20.

escarbuncle /ɪˈskɑːbʌŋk(ə)l, ɛ-/ *n.* L15. [OFr. (mod. *escarboucle*) f. as ES-, CARBUNCLE.] *Her.* A charge representing a carbuncle stone.

escargot /ɛˈskɑːgəʊ, ɪ-/ *n.* Pl. pronounced same. L19. [Fr. f. OFr. *escargol* f. Prov. *escaragol*.] A snail as an article of food.

†**escarmouche** *n.* LME–E19. [(O)Fr.: see SKIRMISH *n.*] A skirmish; *fig.* a fit of anger.

escarole /ˈɛskərəʊl/ *n.* *N. Amer.* E20. [Fr. f. It. *scar(i)ola* f. late L (*e*)*scariola*, f. L *escarius* used as food, f. *esca*: see ESCULENT.] A variety of endive with broad undivided leaves, used in salads.

escarp /ɪˈskɑːp, ɛ-/ *n.* L17. [Fr. *escarpe* f. It. *scarpa* slope. Cf. SCARP *n.*[2]] 1 *Fortif.* = SCARP *n.*[2] 1. L17. 2 *gen.* = SCARP *n.*[2] 2. M19.

escarp /ɪˈskɑːp, ɛ-/ *v.t.* E18. [Fr. *escarper*, f. as prec.] Make into or provide with an escarp.

escarpment /ɪˈskɑːpm(ə)nt, ɛ-/ *n.* E19. [Fr. *escarpement*, f. as prec.: see -MENT.] 1 *Fortif.* = ESCARP *n.* 1. E19. 2 A steep slope, *esp.* one at the edge of a plateau or separating areas of land at different heights; *Geogr.* the steep slope of a cuesta. E19.

escartelee /ɪˈskɑːtəliː, ɛ-/ *a.* Also **-ellé** /-əleɪ/. L17. [OFr. *escartelé* pa. pple of *escarteler* (mod. *écarteler*) divide into quarters, f. as ES- + *quartier* QUARTER *n.*] *Her.* Of a cross: quadrate. Of a line of partition: having a single square indentation. Usu. *postpositive*.

-esce /ɛs/ *suff.* [Repr. L *-escere*.] In or forming vbs, usu. inceptive, as *coalesce*, *effervesce*, *evanesce*, etc.

-escence /ˈɛs(ə)ns/ *suff.* [Repr. Fr. *-escence* or L *-escentia*, f. as next: see -ENCE.] In or forming ns. corresp. to adjs. in -ESCENT, as *deliquescence*, *effervescence*, *obsolescence*, etc.

Also **-escency** *suff.*

-escent /ˈɛs(ə)nt/ *suff.* [Repr. Fr. *-escent* or L *-escent-* pres. ppl stem of vbs in *-escere*: see -ESCE, -ENT.] In or forming adjs. w. the sense 'beginning to assume a particular state, variation of colour, etc.', as *effervescent*, *iridescent*, *obsolescent*, *phosphorescent*, *putrescent*, etc.

eschalot /ˈɛʃəlɒt/ *n.* E18. [Fr. *eschalotte* (now *échalotte*) alt. of OFr. *esc(h)alo(i)gne*: see SCALLION. Cf. SHALLOT.] A shallot onion.

eschar /ˈɛskɑː/ *n.* LME. [Fr. *eschare* (now *escarre*) or late L *eschara*: see SCAR *n.*[2]] A dry dark slough or scab, *esp.* one caused by burning.

escharotic /ɛskəˈrɒtɪk/ *a.* & *n.* E17. [Fr. *escharotique* (now *escar(r)otique*) or late L *escharoticus* f. Gk *eskharōtikos*, f. *eskhara*: see SCAR *n.*[2], -OTIC.] **A** *adj.* Tending to produce eschars, caustic. E17. **B** *n.* An escharotic substance. M17.

eschatocol /ˈɛskətəʊkɒl/ *n.* L19. [f. Gk *eskhatos* last + *kolla* glue, after PROTOCOL.] The concluding section of a charter, containing the attestation, date, etc.; a concluding clause or formula.

eschatology /ɛskəˈtɒlədʒi/ *n.* M19. [f. Gk *eskhatos* last + -OLOGY.] The branch of theology that deals with the four last things (death, judgement, heaven, and hell) and the final destiny of the soul and of humankind; a doctrine or belief about the second coming or the kingdom of God.

realized eschatology: see REALIZE 1.

ˌeschatoˈlogical *a.* M19. **ˌeschatoˈlogically** *adv.* in relation to eschatology E20. **eschatologist** *n.* L19. **eschatologize** *v.t.* give an eschatological character to E20.

eschaton /ˈɛskətɒn/ *n.* M20. [Gk *eskhaton* neut. of *eskhatos* last.] *Theol.* The final event in the divine plan.

C. H. DODD The *eschaton*, the divinely ordained climax of history.

†**eschaufe** *v.t.* LME–M16. [OFr. *eschaufer* (mod. *échauffer*) f. Proto-Romance var. of L *excalefacere*, f. as EX-[1] + *calefacere*: see CHAFE *v.*] Heat, make warm; *fig.* excite.

escheat /ɪsˈtʃiːt, ɛ-/ *n.* & *v.* ME. [OFr. *eschete* f. Proto-Romance, ult. f. L *excidere* fall away, escape, f. as EX-[1] + *cadere* fall.] **A** *n.* **I** *Law.* 1 Land that reverted to the feudal lord when the tenant died leaving no one eligible to succeed under the terms of the grant (*Hist.*); (now *US* exc. *Hist.*) property that reverts to the state or (formerly) the Crown when the owner dies intestate without heirs or (in Britain) was attainted; *Sc.* property that is forfeited or confiscated. ME. 2 The reversion of an escheat by intestacy or (in Scotland) forfeiture. Now *Sc.* & *US* exc. *Hist.* LME. 3 *Hist.* The right of appropriating property that is subject to escheat. LME. 4 *Hist.* A writ to obtain possession of such property. LME. †**II** 5 Forced contribution, plunder; in *pl.*, booty. L16–E17.

B *v.* *Law* (now *Sc.* & *US* exc. *Hist.*). 1 *v.t.* Make an escheat of; hand over as an escheat *to* or *into*. LME. **b** Forfeit. *Sc.* LME. 2 *v.i.* Revert by escheat *to* a lord, the Crown, or a state; become an escheat. LME.

2 H. KEMELMAN Without any other beneficiary the whole amount would escheat to the State.

escheatable *a.* subject to escheat L16. **escheatage** *n.* (now *rare*) the right of succeeding to an escheat E17. **escheatment** *n.* forfeiture or lapsing by escheat M19. **escheator** *n.* an officer formerly appointed to deal with escheats in a county LME. **escheatorship** *n.* the office of escheator L16.

eschew /ɪsˈtʃuː, ɛ-/ *v.* LME. [OFr. *eschiver* f. Proto-Romance, f. Gmc base of OHG *sciuhen*, G *scheuen* shun. Cf. SHY *a.*] †1 *v.t.* Avoid, escape, keep clear of (a danger, place, or person). LME–E18. 2 *v.t.* Carefully or deliberately abstain from, avoid, or shun (an action, indulgence, etc.). LME. †3 *v.i.* Get off, escape. LME–M16.

1 LD BERNERS To eschewe .. the displeasure of my lorde. ROBERT BURTON A woman a man may eschue, but not a wife. 2 W. BEVERIDGE They must not only eschew evil but do good. H. JAMES She looked for a bench that was empty, eschewing a still emptier chair. E. WAUGH Old-fashioned people .. who today eschew the telephone. A. FRASER He eschewed equally the Roman Catholic tenets .. and the Puritan practices.

eschewal *n.* the action or an act of eschewing L16. **eschewer** *n.* L16. **eschewment** *n.* the action of eschewing M19.

eschscholtzia /ɪˈʃɒltsɪə, ɪsˈkɒlʃə, ɛ-/ *n.* Also **-olzia**. L19. [mod.L, f. J. F. *Eschscholtz* (1793–1831), Russian-born naturalist and traveller + -IA[1].] Any of various poppies of the Californian genus *Eschscholtzia*, of the poppy family; esp. *E. californica* (Californian poppy), much grown for its brilliant yellow or orange flowers and glaucous, finely divided leaves.

esclandre /ɛsklɑ̃ːdr/ *n.* Pl. pronounced same. M19. [Fr. f. eccl.L *scandalum*: see SCANDAL *n.*] Unpleasant notoriety; a scandal, a scene.

esclavage /ɛsklavaːʒ/ *n.* Now *rare* or *obs.* Pl. pronounced same. M18. [Fr., lit. slavery, f. (O)Fr. *esclave* SLAVE *n.*[1]] A necklace composed of chains, rows of beads, etc., supposed to resemble a slave's fetters.

escopette /ɛskə(ʊ)ˈpɛt/ *n.* *US Hist.* E19. [Sp. *escopeta* (assim. to Fr. *escopette* f. It.) f. It. *schioppetto* dim. of *schioppo* carbine f. med.L *sclop(p)us* harquebus: see -ETTE.] A kind of carbine formerly used in Mexico and the southern US.

escort /ˈɛskɔːt/ *n.* L16. [Fr. *escorte* f. It. *scorta* use as n. of fem. pa. pple of *scorgere* guide, conduct f. late or med.L, ult. f. as EX-[1] + L *corrigere* set right, CORRECT *v.*] **1** A body of armed men accompanying a traveller or travellers for protection, for surveillance, or as a mark of honour, or acting as a guard for baggage, provisions, treasure, etc. L16. **b** A warship or warships accompanying merchant ships or other vessels for protection; a fighter aircraft accompanying bombers for protection. E20. **2** A person or group of persons accompanying someone on a journey for courtesy's sake or for protection or guidance. M18. **b** A person accompanying another socially; *esp.* a man accompanying a woman to a dance, party, etc. M20. **3** Attendance in the capacity of an escort; the protection or company of an escort. M19.

1 WELLINGTON Colonel Trant with his division attacked the escort of the military chest. **b** *attrib.*: W. S. CHURCHILL The First Cruiser Squadron . . had been . . employed on escort duties at sea. 2 G. VIDAL Because of our police escort, we did not have to go through the usual formalities. J. WAINWRIGHT I've organised a uniformed escort, for the coffin. **b** K. TENNANT Miss O'Shea was drinking ginger-beer and her escort had a shandy. *attrib.*: E. JONG He had taken some Japanese businessmen there with girls from an escort service. 3 J. MARTINEAU The elder deities were compelled to . . attend in escort to the Eastern idol. C. S. FORESTER He usually had to leave Lady Emily to hunt . . under the escort of . . his aides-de-camp.

escort /ɪˈskɔːt, ɛ-/ *v.t.* E18. [Fr. *escorter*, f. *escorte*: see prec.] Act as an escort to; accompany for protection, guidance, courtesy, etc.

LD MACAULAY He was escorted by a bodyguard under the command of Sarsfield. J. AGATE She . . insisted on escorting me to the door herself.

escortage *n.* (*US*) the company or protection of an escort L19.

†escot *v.t.* *rare* (Shakes.). Only in E17. [OFr. *escoter*, f. *escot* (mod. *écot*): see SCOT *n.*[2]] Pay a reckoning for, maintain.

escribe /ɪˈskrʌɪb, iː-, ɛ-/ *v.t.* M16. [f. *e-* E- + L *scribere* write. Cf. EXSCRIBE.] **†1** = EXSCRIBE I. *rare*. Only in M16. **2** *Geom.* = EXSCRIBE 2. L19.

†escript *n.* LME–E18. [OFr.: see SCRIPT *n.*[1]] A written document; *spec.* a writ.

escritoire /ɛskriːˈtwɑː/ *n.* L16. [OFr. = study, writing-box (mod. *écritoire* writing-desk) f. med.L SCRIPTORIUM.] A writing-desk with drawers etc., a bureau.

escrod /ɪˈskrɒd, ɛ-/ *n.* *US* (now *rare*). M19. [Origin unkn. Cf. SCROD.] = SCROD.

escroll /ɪˈskrəʊl, ɛ-/ *n.* Also (*Sc.*) **-ol.** E17. [OFr. *escroele* dim. of *escroe*: see next.] **†1** = ESCROW *n.* E17–M18. **2** *Her.* = SCROLL *n.* 4b. E17.

escrow /ɪˈskrəʊ, ɛ-/ *n.* & *v.* M17. [AN *escrowe*, OFr. *escroe* scrap, scroll f. med.L *scroda* f. Gmc base of SHRED *n.*] **A** *n.* **1** *Law.* A deed held by a third party and taking effect only when a stated condition is fulfilled. M17. **2** A deposit or fund held in trust or as a security. *N. Amer.* L19.

2 *attrib.*: *New Yorker* Banks began to advertise escrow services for drilling ventures. **in escrow** in trust as an escrow.

B *v.t.* Place in escrow. *US.* E20.

escuage /ˈɛskjʊɪdʒ/ *n.* *obs.* exc. *Hist.* E16. [AN, OFr., f. *escu* (mod. *écu*) shield (f. L *scutum*) + -AGE. Cf. SCUTAGE.] **1** Personal service in the field for a period of forty days each year, the chief form of feudal tenure. E16. **2** = SCUTAGE. L16.

escudero /ɛskʊˈdɪərəʊ/ *n.* *arch.* Pl. **-os.** E17. [Sp., f. as next.] A shield-bearer; an esquire; an attendant.

escudo /ɛˈskuːdəʊ/ *n.* Pl. **-os.** E19. [Sp. & Port., f. L *scutum* shield: cf. ÉCU, SCUDO.] The basic monetary unit of Portugal, and formerly of some other countries that were or had been Portuguese or Spanish territories.

esculent /ˈɛskjʊl(ə)nt/ *a.* & *n.* E17. [L *esculentus*, f. *esca* food, f. *esse* eat: see -ULENT.] **A** *adj.* Fit for food, eatable. E17. **B** *n.* Something that is fit for food or eatable, *esp.* a vegetable. E17.

escutcheon /ɪˈskʌtʃ(ə)n, ɛ-/ *n.* L15. [AN, ONFr. *escuchon* (OFr. *escusson*, mod. *écusson*) f. Proto-Romance f. L *scutum* shield.] **1** *Her.* The shield or shield-shaped surface on which a coat of arms is depicted; the shield together with its armorial bearings; a representation of this, a coat of arms; a shield-shaped charge, an inescutcheon. L15. **†b** A hatchment. Also *funeral escutcheon.* M17–E19. **2** A shield-shaped area or object; a protective plate, *spec.* one round a keyhole. M17. **b** The middle of a ship's stern where the name is placed. M19. **3** *fig.* Reputation. Only in wider metaphors, esp. *a blot on one's escutcheon.* L17.

1 *escutcheon of* PRETENCE. 2 *Practical Wireless* F. M. Tuner. . . Neat escutcheon and tuning dial. 3 P. G. WODEHOUSE It will undoubtedly tarnish the Ickenham escutcheon.

escutcheoned *a.* M18.

-ese /iːz/ *suff.* [Repr. OFr. *-eis* (mod. *-ois*, *-ais*) f. Proto-Romance f. L *-ensis*.] **1** Forming adjs. and ns. (pl. same) from names of foreign countries and towns, w. the sense '(a native or inhabitant) of', as *Cantonese*, *Japanese*, *Portuguese*, *Viennese*, etc. **2** Forming ns. f. personal names and other nouns w. the sense 'the language or style of', as *Carlylese*, *computerese*, *Johnsonese*, *officialese*, etc. Freq. *derog.*

esemplastic /ɛsɛmˈplastɪk/ *a.* E19. [f. Gk *hes* into + *hen* neut. of *heis* one + -PLASTIC, irreg. after G *Ineinsbildung* forming into one.] Moulding into one, unifying.

C. N. MANLOVE No esemplastic imagination is at work to weld the particulars into a whole.

eserine /ˈɛsəriːn/ *n.* M19. [Fr. *ésérine*, f. Efik *esere*: see -INE[5].] = PHYSOSTIGMINE.

esker /ˈɛskə/ *n.* Also **eskar.** M19. [Ir. *eiscir.*] A long narrow sinuous ridge, usu. of sand and gravel, deposited by a stream flowing under a former glacier or ice sheet.

Eskimo /ˈɛskɪməʊ/ *n.* & *a.* Pl. same, **-os.** Also **Esquimau**, pl. **-aux** /-əʊ(z)/. L16. [Da. f. Fr. *Esquimaux* pl. f. Algonquian: cf. Abnaki *askimo* raw-flesh eater.] **A** *n.* **1** A member of a people inhabiting the Arctic coasts of eastern Siberia, Alaska, Canada, and Greenland. Cf. INUIT, YUIT. L16. **2** Either or both of the two main languages (Inupiaq and Yupik) of this people. M18. **3** = *Eskimo dog* below. M19.

Comb.: **Eskimo-Aleut(ian)** *n.* & *a.* (of) the language family comprising Eskimo and Aleut.

B *attrib.* or as *adj.* Of or pertaining to the Eskimo or their languages. M18.

Eskimo curlew a curlew, *Numenius borealis*, that breeds in northern Canada. **Eskimo dog** a sturdy dog with webbed feet and slanting eyes, used by Eskimos for pulling sledges and hunting. **Eskimo pie** (chiefly *N. Amer.*) (US proprietary name for) a bar of chocolate-coated ice-cream. **Eskimo roll** a complete rollover in canoeing, from upright to capsized to upright.

¶For the Eskimo of Canada the term *Inuit* is now preferred by many Canadians.

Eskimoid *a.* resembling (that of) an Eskimo, similar in racial type to the Eskimo E20.

Esky /ˈɛski/ *n.* *Austral.* Also **e-.** M20. [Origin uncertain: perh. f. ESKIMO + -Y[6].] A portable insulated container for keeping food and drink cool.

¶Proprietary name in Australia.

esne /ˈɛzni/ *n.* Long *obs.* exc. *Hist.* [OE *esne* = OHG *asni*, Goth. *asneis* day-labourer.] A serf, a hireling.

esophagus *n.* etc.: see OESOPHAGUS etc.

esophoria /ɛsəˈfɔːrɪə/ *n.* L19. [f. Gk *esō* (see next) + -PHORIA.] *Med.* A tendency for the visual axes to converge; latent convergent strabismus.

esoteric /ɛsəˈtɛrɪk, iːs-/ *a.* & *n.* M17. [Gk *esōterikos*, f. *esōterō* inner, compar. of *esō* within, f. *es*, *eis* into: see -IC.] **A** *adj.* **1** (Of a philosophical doctrine, mode of speech, etc.) designed for or appropriate to an inner circle of advanced or privileged disciples; communicated or intelligible only to the initiated; (of a person) initiated into or belonging to an inner circle. Opp. EXOTERIC *a.* I. M17. **2** Not openly stated or admitted; confidential; secret. M19.

1 M. HUNTER The magician is an esoteric figure—part priest, part philosopher, part artist. G. MURRAY Unless we are to interpret the word 'poetry' in some esoteric sense of our own. P. LARKIN The esoteric areas of Neoplatonic symbolism . . and the history of inner literary conventions. H. ACTON This passion for reading set her apart from her sisters though she shared their esoteric jokes. **Esoteric Buddhism** a system of theosophical doctrines alleged to have been transmitted by an inner circle of Buddhists. 2 LD MACAULAY His esoteric project was the original project of Christopher Columbus. A. M. FAIRBAIRN Strauss had hardly the stuff in him to be an exoteric Conservative while an esoteric Radical.

B *n.* **1** A person initiated into esoteric doctrines. M17. **2** In *pl.* Esoteric doctrines or treatises. E18.

esoterical *a.* esoteric M19. **esoterically** *adv.* M18.

esoterica /ɛsəˈtɛrɪkə, iːs-/ *n.pl.* E20. [Gk *esōterika* neut. pl. of *esōterikos* ESOTERIC.] Esoteric items or publications; esoteric details.

esotericism /ɛsəˈtɛrɪsɪz(ə)m, iːs-/ *n.* M19. [f. ESOTERIC + -ISM.] **1** (Belief in) an esoteric doctrine. M19. **2** (A tendency towards) esoteric or obscure language or thought; an instance of this. L19.

1 R. ADAMS Something . . beside which all older religious notions would appear . . an esotericism as shallow as the whispered secrets of children.

esotericist *n.* an adherent of esoteric doctrines L19.

esoterism /ɪˈsɒtərɪz(ə)m/ *n.* M19. [f. Gk *esōterō*: see ESOTERIC, -ISM.] = prec.

esotery /ˈɛsət(ə)ri/ *n.* esoteric doctrine or knowledge M18.

esotropia /ɛsəˈtrəʊpɪə/ *n.* L19. [f. Gk *esō* (see ESOTERIC) + *tropē* turning (n.) + -IA[1].] *Med.* Convergent strabismus.

esox /ˈiːsɒks/ *n.* E16. [L f. Gaulish.] A large freshwater fish, *esp.* a pike. Now only as mod.L genus name.

espacement /ɪˈspeɪsm(ə)nt, ɛ-/ *n.* M19. [Fr., f. *espacer* SPACE *v.*: see -MENT.] **1** The action of spacing, or of placing at suitable intervals. M19. **2** The distance at which trees or crops are set apart when planted. M20.

espada /eˈspaða, ɛˈspɑːdə/ *n.* Pl. **-as** /-as, -əz/. E18. [Sp. f. L *spatha* sword, SPATHE.] **†1** A Spanish sword. *rare*. Only in E18. **2** A matador. L19.

espadon /ɛspəˈdɒn/ *n.* M19. [Fr. f. It. *spadone* augm. of *spada* sword f. L *spatha* sword, SPATHE.] *Hist.* A large two-handled sword of the 15th to 17th cents.

espadrille /ɛspəˈdrɪl, ˈɛspədrɪl/ *n.* L19. [Fr. f. Prov. *espardi(l)hos*, f. *espart* esparto.] A light canvas shoe with plaited fibre sole, orig. worn in the Pyrenees; an alpargata.

espagnole /ɛspaɲɔl/ *n.* M19. [Fr. (fem.), lit. 'Spanish', f. OFr. *espaignol*, *espaigneul*: see SPANIEL.] In full *espagnole sauce*. A simple brown sauce.

espagnolette /ˌɛspanjəˈlɛt, ɛ-/ *n.* E19. [Fr., f. *espagnol* Spanish: see prec., -ETTE.] A kind of bolt used for fastening French windows, in which a single handle operates fasteners at the top and bottom of the window.

espalier /ɪˈspaljə, ɛ-/ *n.* & *v.* M17. [Fr. f. It. *spalliera*, f. *spalla* shoulder f. L SPATULA, (in late L) shoulder-blade.] **A** *n.* **1** A fruit tree or ornamental shrub trained on a lattice or a framework of stakes. M17. **†2** A row of trees or shrubs trained in this way. Only in E18. 3 A lattice or framework, or one of the stakes, on which a tree or shrub is trained. M18. B *v.t.* Train as an espalier. E19.

esparcet /ɪˈspɑːsɪt, ɛ-/ *n.* Long *rare*. M17. [Fr. *esparcette*, †*-et*, f. OFr. *espars* (mod. *épars*) f. L *sparsus* SPARSE *a.*: see -ETTE.] A kind of sainfoin.

esparto /ɛˈspɑːtəʊ, ɪ-/ *n.* Pl. **-os**. M19. [Sp. f. L *spartum* f. Gk *sparton* rope.] A tough grass, *Stipa tenacissima*, growing in Spain and N. Africa and used in paper-making. Also *esparto grass*.

†**espaulement** *n.* var. of EPAULEMENT.

especial /ɪˈspɛʃ(ə)l, ɛ-/ *a.* LME. [OFr. (mod *spécial*) f. L *specialis*: see SPECIAL.] 1 Special as opp. to general. Formerly also, particular, individual, specific; provided for a particular purpose. *arch.* LME. 2 Pre-eminent, exceptional. *obs.* in *pred.* use. LME. 3 Pertaining chiefly to one particular person or thing. M19.

1 SHAKES. *Oth.* There is especial commission come from Venice. S. RICHARDSON I shall dispatch what I shall farther write . . by an especial messenger. **in especial** in particular, especially, particularly. 2 J. TYNDALL One fact of especial importance. I. MURDOCH He had always known and knew it now with an especial terror. 3 B. JOWETT I must repeat one thing . . for your especial benefit.

especialness *n.* (long *rare* or *obs.*) E17.

especially /ɪˈspɛʃ(ə)li, ɛ-/ *adv.* LME. [f. prec. + -LY[2].] In an especial manner, to an especial degree; chiefly, more than in other cases.

†**espeler** *n. rare*. L15-E18. [Origin unkn. Cf. SPELLER *n.*[2]] = SPILLER *n.*[2]

†**espelers** *n.pl.* see SPELLER *n.*[2]

esperance /ˈɛsp(ə)r(ə)ns/ *n.* LME. [(O)Fr. *espérance*, f. *espérer* to hope f. L *sperare*: see -ANCE.] Expectation, hope. *obs.* exc. *Hist.* as the motto of the Percy family, used as a battle-cry.

SHAKES. *1 Hen. IV* Now Esperance! Percy! And set on.

Esperanto /ɛspəˈrantəʊ/ *n.* L19. [f. Dr *Esperanto* (Esperanto for 'Hoping One'), pen-name of its inventor (see below).] An artificial language invented in 1887 for universal use by the Polish physician Dr L. L. Zamenhof (1859–1917), and based on roots common to the chief European languages with endings standardized.

Esperantist *n.* a person who knows Esperanto or advocates its use as a world language E20.

espial /ɪˈspʌɪ(ə)l, ɛ-/ *n.* LME. [OFr. *espiaille* action of spying, (in pl.) spies, f. *espier* ESPY: see -AL[1].] 1a The action or an act of spying or keeping watch. *arch.* LME. b The action of espying; the fact of being espied. L16. †2 A body of spies; a spy, a scout. LME-E19.

1a DICKENS The Captain . . cut a small hole of espial in the wall. b M. INNES She must slip to the other side and risk espial from the house.

espiegle /ɪˈspjeɪɡ(ə)l, *foreign* ɛspjɛɡl/ *a.* Now *rare*. E19. [Fr. (*Ul*)*espiegle* f. Du. *Uilenspiegel* (= G *Eulenspiegel*), f. *uil* OWL *n.* + *spiegel* mirror f. L *speculum*. Cf. *owlglass* s.v. OWL *n.*] Frolicsome, roguish.

espieglerie *n.* frolicsomeness, roguishness E19.

espionage /ˈɛspɪənɑːʒ, -ɪdʒ/ *n.* L18. [Fr. *espionnage*, f. *espionner* espy, f. *espion* SPY *n.*: see -AGE.] The practice of spying or using spies, esp. to obtain secret information.

INDUSTRIAL *espionage*.

esplanade /ɛspləˈneɪd, -ˈnɑːd/ *n.* L16. [Fr. f. It. *spianata* f. fem. of L *explanatus* flattened, levelled, pa. pple of *explanare*: see EXPLAIN, -ADE.] 1 *Fortif.* a The glacis of a counterscarp. Formerly, an area of flat ground on the top of a rampart. L16. b A level open space separating a citadel from the town that it commands. E18. 2 *gen.* Any level open space, *esp.* one where the public may walk; a road along the sea front of a resort. L17.

2 F. MUIR Virginia Water . . had in its esplanade of shops a . . coin-operated drycleaners.

esplees /ɪˈspliːz, ɛ-/ *n.pl.* M17. [AN *esple(t)z* pl. of OFr. *espleit*, *esploit* revenue: see EXPLOIT *n.*] The crops, rents, services, etc., obtained from land; the land yielding these.

†**espontoon** *n.* L18-M19. [Fr. *esponton*: see SPONTOON.] = SPONTOON.

espousal /ɪˈspaʊz(ə)l, ɛ-/ *n.* LME. [OFr. *espousaille* sing. of *espousailles* (mod. *épousailles*) f. L *sponsalia* betrothal, use as n. of neut. pl. of *sponsalis* adj., f. *spons-*: see next, -AL[1]. In sense 4 also infl. by ESPOUSE *v.*] 1 In *pl.* & †*sing.* (The celebration of) a marriage or betrothal. *arch.* LME. †2 *sing.* & in *pl.* The marriage vows; the married state. Chiefly in *break one's espousal*, *hold espousal*. LME-L16. †3 An espoused person; a husband, a wife. L15-E17. 4 The action or an act of espousing a cause etc. Foll. by *of*. L17.

4 HOR. WALPOLE Political reasons forbid the open espousal of his cause.

espouse /ɪˈspaʊz, ɛ-/ *v.t.* LME. [OFr. *espouser* (mod. *épouser*) f. L *sponsare*, f. *spons-* pa. ppl stem of *spondere* betroth. Cf. SPOUSE *v.*] 1 Take (a person, esp. a woman) as spouse; marry. LME. †2 Join in marriage (*lit.* & *fig.*). *rare*. Only in L16. †3 Betroth (a person, esp. a woman); pledge, commit. (Foll. by *to*.) E-M17. 4 Take to oneself or make one's own (a cause, quarrel, etc.); become a supporter of (a party); adopt, embrace (a doctrine, theory, profession, way of life). E17.

1 HOR. WALPOLE Before Edward had espoused the lady Grey, he had been contracted to the lady Eleanor Butler. 2 SHAKES. *2 Hen. VI* In presence of . . twenty reverend bishops, I . . was espous'd. 3 AV *Luke* 1:27 A virgine espoused to a man whose name was Ioseph. 4 M. MUGGERIDGE They . . espouse all the right causes— . . divorce reform, raising the school age, abolition of capital punishment. P. ACKROYD A man . . who espoused the principles of classical order and hierarchy.

espouser *n.* (*a*) a person who espouses a cause etc.; a supporter; †(*b*) a person who brings about an espousal or espouses a woman: M17.

espressivo /ɛsprɛˈsiːvəʊ/ *adv.* & *a.* L19. [It., f. L *expressus*: see EXPRESS *a.*, *adv.*, & *n.*[2]] *Mus.* (Performed) with expression of feeling.

espresso /ɛˈsprɛsəʊ/ *n.* Also **ex-** /ɛkˈsprɛs-/. Pl. **-os**. M20. [It. (*caffè*) *espresso*, f. *espresso* squeezed, pressed out, f. L *expressus*: see EXPRESS *a.*, *adv.*, & *n.*[2]] 1 Coffee made by forcing steam through ground coffee beans. M20. 2 A coffee bar etc. where such coffee is sold. Also *espresso bar*, *café*, etc. M20.

espringal /ɪˈsprɪŋɡ(ə)l, ɛ-/ *n. obs.* exc. *Hist.* E17. [(O)Fr. *espringale*, f. *espringuer* to spring, dance f. Frank. *springan* SPRING *v.*[1]] A medieval military machine for throwing stones, bolts, and other missiles.

esprit /ɛspri, ɛˈspriː, ˈɛspriː/ *n.* L16. [Fr. f. L *spiritus* SPIRIT *n.*] Vivacious wit.

esprit de corps /də ˈkɔː/ [see CORPS] regard for the honour and interests of the body to which one belongs; team spirit. ***esprit de l'escalier*** /də lɛskalje/ [lit. 'of the steps'] a clever remark that occurs to one after the opportunity to make it is lost. ***esprit fort*** /fɔːr/, pl. ***-s -s*** (pronounced same), [= strong] a strong-minded person, *esp.* one who claims independence of thought. *point d'esprit*: see POINT *n.*[2]

espy /ɪˈspʌɪ, ɛ-/ *v.* ME. [OFr. *espier* (mod. *épier*): see SPY *v.*] 1 *v.t.* Discover by looking out; catch sight of, esp. at a distance; descry, discern; detect (a flaw etc.). ME. b Perceive by chance or unexpectedly. L15. 2 *v.i.* & †*t.* Act as a spy (on); keep a look out (for); make a close examination (of). *arch.* LME.

1 AV *Gen.* 42:27 As one of them opened his sack . . , he espied his money. SWIFT The seamen espied a rock within half a cable's length of the ship. J. WESLEY These skilful wrestlers espy the smallest slip we make. 2 R. GREENE Espy her loves, and who she liketh best.

†**esquadron** *n.* L16-M18. [OFr. (mod. *escadron*), f. as SQUADRON.] A squadron of cavalry.

-esque /ɛsk/ *suff.* [Repr. Fr. *-esque* f. It. *-esco* f. med.L *-iscus*.] In and forming adjs. w. the sense 'resembling in style or characteristics', as *arabesque*, *burlesque*, *Daliesque*, *romanesque*, etc.

Esquimau *n.* & *a.* var. of ESKIMO.

esquire /ɪˈskwʌɪə, ɛ-/ *n.* Earlier as SQUIRE *n.*[1] LME. [OFr. *esquier* (mod. *écuyer*) f. L *scutarius* shield-bearer, f. *scutum* shield: see -ARY[1].] 1 Orig. (now *Hist.*), a young nobleman who, in training for knighthood, acted as shield-bearer and attendant to a knight. Later, a man belonging to the higher order of English gentry, ranking next below a knight. LME. b *Hist.* Any of various officers in the service of a king or nobleman. L15. c A landed proprietor, a country squire. *arch.* L16. 2 A title of courtesy (now only in formal use and in addresses of letters) placed after the name of a man (orig. one with the rank of esquire, sense 1a or b) when no other title is used. Abbrev. *Esq.* LME. 3 A man who escorts a woman in public. Now *rare*. E19.

1 T. H. WHITE The exaggerated courtesy which was expected of pages before they became esquires on their way to knighthood. b *Notes & Queries* In 1536 Heneage took over Norris' post of esquire of the King's body.

esquireship *n.* the rank of esquire; the service of an esquire: E17. **esquiress** *n.* a female armour-bearer or page L16.

esquire /ɪˈskwʌɪə, ɛ-/ *v.t. rare*. M17. [f. the n.] 1 Raise to the rank of esquire. M17. 2 Escort (a lady). L18. 3 Address as 'Esquire'. L19.

†**esquiry** *n.* var. of EQUERRY.

esquisse /ɛskis/ *n.* Pl. pronounced same. M18. [Fr. f. It. *schizzo*: see SKETCH *n.*[1]] A rough or preliminary sketch.

esraj /ɛˈsrɑːdʒ/ *n.* E20. [Bengali *esrāj*.] A three- or four-stringed Indian musical instrument with added sympathetic strings.

esrog *n.*, **esrogim** *n.pl.* see ETROG *n.*[1]

ess /ɛs/ *n.*[1] M16. [Repr. pronunc. of *S*, *s* as the letter's name.] The letter S, s; something S-shaped.

collar of esses: see COLLAR *n.*

Ess /ɛs/ *n.*[2] M19. [f. Fr. ESSENCE *n.*] In full *Ess Bouquet*. A kind of perfume.

-ess /ɛs, ɪs/ *suff.*[1] [Repr. Fr. *-esse* f. Proto-Romance f. late L *-issa* f. Gk.] In and forming ns. denoting females, as *actress*, *adulteress*, *countess*, *goddess*, *lioness*, etc., sometimes w. the sense 'wife of', as *ambassadress*, *mayoress*, etc.

¶Nouns in *-er*, *-or*, etc., which are not sex-specific, where such exist, are now often preferred.

-ess /ɛs/ *suff.*[2] (not productive). [Repr. OFr. *-esse*, *-ece* f. L *-itia*: cf. -ICE[1].] In ns. of quality formed f. adjs., as *duress*, *largess*, etc.

essart /ɪˈsɑːt, ɛ-/ *n.* M19. [OFr., = AN ASSART *n.*] *Hist.* = ASSART *n.* 1.

essart /ɪˈsɑːt, ɛ-/ *v.t.* & *i.* *obs.* exc. *Hist.* E18. [OFr. *essarter*: see ASSART *v.*] = ASSART *v.*

essay /ˈɛseɪ/ *n.* L16. [(O)Fr. *essai*, f. *essayer*: see next. Cf. ASSAY *n.*] I1 A trial, a test; an experiment. L16. 2 = ASSAY *n.* 5. *obs.* exc. *Hist.* L16. 3 A trial specimen, a sample; an example; a rehearsal. Now only *spec.* in *Philately*, a trial design of a stamp yet to be accepted. E17. †4 *Hunting*. The breast of a deer, the part in which its fatness was tested; the testing of a deer's fatness. Only in 17.

1 A. BEVAN At this point an essay in collective action was tried.

II5 An attempt, an endeavour. (Foll. by *at*, *in*; *to do*.) L16. 6 A short prose composition on any subject. L16. †7 A first tentative attempt at learning, composition, etc.; a first draft. M17-L18.

5 C. S. FORESTER The hand which he extended to the door missed its objective at the first essay. 6 D. LODGE They . . handed in . . essays written in the style of F. R. Leavis. 7 DRYDEN The first of Homer's Iliads (which I intended as an Essay to the whole work.)

essay'ette *n.* a short essay L19. **e'ssayical** *a.* essayistic M19. **essayism** *n.* the writing of essays; essayistic quality: E19. **essaylet** *n.* = ESSAYETTE L19.

essay /ɛˈseɪ/ *v.* L15. [Alt. of ASSAY *v.* by assim. to (O)Fr. *essayer* f. Proto-Romance, f. late L *exagium* weighing, a weight, f. L *exag-* base of *exigere*: see EXACT *a.*] 1 *v.t.* = ASSAY *v.* 1, 6. *arch.* L15. 2 *v.t.* & *i.* Attempt to accomplish or perform (a deed, task, etc.); make an attempt (at); undertake or try *to do*. M16. †3 = ASSAY *v.* 4. L17-E19.

1 POPE She . . No arts essay'd, but not to be admir'd. 2 P. G. WODEHOUSE Valerie Twisleton was about to essay the mad task of defying this woman. G. GREENE Only Mrs Smith had essayed violence. A. BURGESS These pieces . . which essayed serious art, got

nowhere. A. HAILEY They had even essayed some sex. E. BOWEN Several foreign firms, having essayed to set up factories in Dublin, decamped.

essayer *n.* (*a*) an assayer; †(*b*) a person who attempts to treat a certain subject or form of composition; an essayist: L16.

essayist /ˈɛseɪɪst/ *n.* E17. [f. ESSAY *n.*, *v.* + -IST.] 1 A writer of essays. E17. 2 A person who carries out tests or trials. (Foll. by *of*.) Now *rare* or *obs.* M18.

essay'istic(al) *adjs.* in the style of a literary essay; discursive, informal: M19.

esse /ˈɛsi/ *n.* M16. [L, use as n. of *esse* be.] Essential nature, essence, esp. as opp. to BENE ESSE.

Listener No Anglican could possibly dream of claiming that Establishment . . is of the *esse* of the Church. IN ESSE.

essence /ˈɛs(ə)ns/ *n.* LME. [(O)Fr. f. L *essentia*, irreg. f. *esse* be + after Gk *ousia* being, f. *ont-* pres. ppl stem of *einai* be: see -ENCE.] 1 *Theol.* The uniquely triune intrinsic nature of God, in respect of which the three persons of the Trinity are one. LME. 2 The substance of which something consists, *esp.* a celestial or elemental substance. LME. 3 The intrinsic nature or character of something; that which makes it what it is; the attributes, constituents, etc., that something must have for it not to be something else and that serve to characterize it. LME. b The most important or indispensable quality or element of anything. L16. †4 In ancient and medieval philosophy, an element additional to the four elements of the material world; = QUINTESSENCE 1. Chiefly in *fifth essence*. LME–M19. 5 A distillate or extract from a plant or medicinal substance, having its active constituents or characteristic properties in a concentrated form; perfume, scent, etc., esp. as an alcoholic solution of volatile substances. E16. 6 A spiritual or immaterial entity. Formerly, anything (immaterial or material) that exists. L16. 7 The foundation of a thing's existence; the reality underlying phenomena. L16. †8 Existence regarded as a fact or as a property possessed by something. L16–L17. †9 Importance. E–M17.

3 N. MITFORD The whole tradition is in its essence monastic. J. M. COETZEE He is neither cannibal nor laundryman, these are mere names, they do not touch his essence. **nominal essence**: of an abstract or conceptual entity. **real essence**: of something perceptible by the senses. b H. BELLOC He was carefully warned that surprise was the essence of this charming tradition. T. E. HULME The essence of poetry to most people is that it must lead them to a beyond of some kind. I. MURDOCH What goes on inwardly in the soul is the essence of each man, it's what makes us individual people. 5 J. GALSWORTHY The odour of flowers, . . of essences that women love, rose suffocatingly in the heat. *bath essence*, *coffee-essence*, *vanilla essence*, etc. 6 SHAKES. *Oth.* Her honour is an essence that's not seen. 7 M. H. ABRAMS Art imitates the world of appearance and not of Essence. E. M. FORSTER It is unmanageable because it is a romance, and its essence is romantic beauty.

Other phrases: **in essence** fundamentally, essentially. **(of) the essence (of)** indispensable or important (to).

Comb.: **essence-peddler** *US* (*a*) a pedlar of medicines; (*b*) a skunk.

essence /ˈɛs(ə)ns/ *v.t.* Now *rare*. M17. [f. the n.] Perfume with essence.

Essene /ˈɛsiːn/ *n.* LME. [L *Esseni* pl. f. Gk *Essēnoi*, perh. f. Aram.] A member of a Jewish ascetic sect of the 1st cent. BC and the 1st cent. AD who lived communally and are widely regarded as the authors of the Dead Sea Scrolls.

E'ssenian *n.* & *a.* †(*a*) *n.* = Essene; (*b*) *adj.* of, pertaining to, or resembling the Essenes: E18. **E'ssenic** *a.* of the nature of Essenism M19. **E'ssenical** *a.* (now *rare* or *obs.*) = ESSENIC M17. **Essenism** *n.* the doctrine and practice of the Essenes; an Essenic tendency: M19.

essenhout /ˈɛs(ə)n(h)əʊt/ *n.* *S. Afr.* E19. [Afk. f. MDu. *eschenhout*, f. *esch* ASH *n.*[1] + *hout* timber: see HOLT *n.*[1]] = ESSENWOOD.

essential /ɪˈsɛnʃ(ə)l/ *a.* & *n.* ME. [Late L *essentialis*, f. L *essentia*: see ESSENCE *n.*, -IAL.] A *adj.* 1 That is such in the absolute or highest sense. ME. †b Thorough, complete. E17–E18. 2 Of or pertaining to a thing's essence. LME. 3†a Dependent on the intrinsic character of something. E16–L19. b *Med.* Of hypertension or (formerly) any disease: of unknown cause. L19. 4 Absolutely indispensable or necessary. E16. 5 Constituting or forming part of a thing's essence; fundamental to its composition. M16. b Affecting the essence of anything; significant, important. L18. †6 Having existence; real, actual. M16–M17. 7 Of the nature of or resembling an essence, extract, or perfume. M17. 8 *Mus.* (Of a note) belonging to the chord, as opp. to a passing note, appoggiatura, etc.; (of a sharp or flat) in the key signature, not accidental. E18.

1 W. SPARROW The love of God is essentiall happiness. b T. DEKKER He's a most essentiall gentleman. 2 **essential difference** *Logic* = DIFFERENTIA. 4 T. THOMSON Silica . . is an essential ingredient in mortar. I. MURDOCH It was . . essential that he should leave her alone. H. READ A certain complexity of experience is essential to eloquence. *Observer* It is not essential for our people to know everything. **essential amino acid, fatty acid**: needed for growth but not synthesized by the body. 5 P. TILLICH It is a consequence of that which is not his essential being but is accidental in him. A. LURIE It's the essential part of my work, without which there wouldn't be . . any stories. M. HUNTER The mere fact of being human implies an essential loneliness in each of us. b N. PEVSNER The persistence over two hundred years of the Perpendicular style without any essential changes. 7 **essential oil** a volatile oil obtained by distillation and having the characteristic odour of the plant etc. from which it is extracted.

B *n.* 1 An indispensable or fundamental characteristic, element, or thing. Usu. in *pl.* Formerly also (in *pl.*), the three vows of chastity, poverty, and obedience indispensable to monastic life. LME. †2 Existence, being. *rare*. L15–M17.

1 G. MAXWELL I had brought with me on my back the essentials of living for a day or two while I prospected.

essentialize *v.t.* †(*a*) *rare* give essence or being to; (*b*) formulate in essential form, express the essential form of: M17. **essentialness** *n.* M17.

essentialism /ɪˈsɛnʃ(ə)lɪz(ə)m/ *n.* M20. [f. prec. + -ISM.] 1 *Philos.* A belief that things have a set of characteristics which make them what they are, and that the task of science and philosophy is their discovery and expression; the doctrine that essence is prior to existence (cf. EXISTENTIALISM). M20. 2 The view that all children should be taught on traditional lines the ideas and methods regarded as essential to the prevalent culture. M20.

essentialist /ɪˈsɛnʃ(ə)lɪst/ *n.* & *a.* E18. [f. as prec. + -IST.] A *n.* †1 A nonjuror who believed that the usages omitted from the 1552 Prayer Book were essential. *rare*. Only in E18. 2 A person who follows or advocates essentialism. M20. B *adj.* Of or pertaining to essentialism. M20.

essentiality /ɪˌsɛnʃɪˈalɪti/ *n.* LME. [Late L *essentialitas*, f. as ESSENTIAL: see -ITY.] 1 Essence, intrinsic nature. LME. 2 The quality or fact of being essential; necessity. M17. 3 An essential point or element. Formerly, an essential quality. Now only in *pl.* M17.

essentially /ɪˈsɛnʃ(ə)li/ *adv.* LME. [f. ESSENTIAL + -LY[2].] 1 In essence or character. LME. †2 On the grounds of the actual nature of something or someone. L16–E17. †3 In fact, really. *rare* (Shakes.). Only in L16. 4 With respect to the essential points; substantially, fundamentally; indispensably. M18.

1 BARONESS ORCZY A cool, balmy, late summer's night, essentially English in its suggestion of moisture. A. S. BYATT We try to see things as they *are*, *essentially*, not as they first appear to be. 4 G. B. SHAW Joan was persecuted essentially as she would be persecuted today.

essenwood /ˈɛs(ə)nwʊd/ *n.* L19. [Partial tr. Afk. ESSENHOUT.] Either of two large African evergreen trees of the mahogany family, *Ekebergia capensis* and *Trichilia emetica*, whose wood is used for furniture.

†**essera** *n.* M16–E19. [mod.L (whence Fr. *essère*) f. Arab. *aš-šarā* (the) dry scab, itch.] A rash similar to that caused by nettles; a variety of nettle-rash.

Essex /ˈɛsɪks/ *a.* & *n.* L16. [A county in SE England.] A *adj.* 1 *Essex calf*, a calf reared in Essex; *contempt.* (now *rare*), a person of that county. L16. 2 *Essex pig*, a black pig with a white stripe round the body and white feet, of a kind formerly bred for pork and bacon; *US* a black pig of a kind bred for pork and bacon. M19. 3 *Essex board*, a kind of fibreboard. M20. B *n.* Pl. same. An Essex pig. L19.

essexite /ˈɛsɪksʌɪt/ *n.* L19. [f. *Essex* County, Massachusetts, USA, where the first examples were found: see -ITE[1].] *Geol.* A granular igneous rock typically containing labradorite and nepheline.

essive /ˈɛsɪv/ *a.* & *n.* L19. [Finn. *essiivi*, f. L ESSE: see -IVE.] (Designating) a case in Finnish and certain other languages expressing a continuous state of being.

essoin /ɛˈsɔɪn/ *n.* Orig. †**assoin**. ME. [OFr. *essoi(g)ne* (AL *essonium*), f. *essoi(g)nier* ESSOIN *v.*] 1 *Law* (now *Hist.*). (The offering of) an excuse for non-appearance in court at the appointed time, on grounds of illness, pilgrimage, etc. ME. †2 *gen.* An excuse; making of conditions, parleying, delay. ME–L16.

essoin /ɛˈsɔɪn/ *v.* Orig. †**assoin**. ME. [OFr. *essoi(g)nier* f. med.L *exsoniare*, f. as EX-[1] + *sonia* lawful excuse, f. Frank.: cf. OHG *sunnia* hindrance = OS *sunnea* want, lack, ON *syn* refusal, denial, Goth. *sunjon* to excuse.] 1 *v.t.* *Law* (now *Hist.*). Excuse for non-appearance in court. Formerly also *gen.*, excuse. ME. †2 *v.t.* & *i.* Avoid (a person); shun contact (with). Only in ME. †3 *v.i.* Excuse oneself, decline, refuse. LME–L15.

essoinee /ɛsɔɪˈniː/ *n.* M17. [f. prec. + -EE[1].] *Law* (now *Hist.*). A person who had been essoined.

essoiner /ɛˈsɔɪnə/ *n.* ME. [AN *essoigniour*, f. *essoignier*: see ESSOIN *v.*, -ER[1].] A person who offered an excuse for someone else's non-appearance in court. Now *Hist.*

essonite /ˈɛsənʌɪt/ *n.* Also **he-** /ˈhɛ-/. E19. [f. Gk *hēssōn* less (as being less hard and heavy than other garnets) + -ITE[1].] *Min.* = CINNAMON *stone*.

est /ɛst/ *n.* L20. [Acronym, f. *E*rhard *S*eminars *T*raining, f. the name of W. *Erhard* (b. 1935), who devised est in the US.] A philosophy and technique aimed at developing self-awareness and a person's potential by means that include motivational methods from the world of business.

-est /ɪst/ *suff.*[1] [OE *-ost-*, *-ust-*, *-ast-*, and with umlaut *-est-*, *-st-*, both f. Gmc. Cf. Gk *-isto-*, Skt *iṣṭha-*.] Forming the superl. of adjs. and advs., now esp. of wds of one syllable and occas. of two, as *hardest*, *narrowest*, etc. The umlaut form survives in *best*, *eldest*.

¶ Mod. spelling conventions are as follows: Wds in *-e* drop the *e*, as *sore: sorest*; a final single consonant other than *h*, *w*, or *x* is doubled if preceded by a single-letter vowel, as *big: biggest*; in most adjs. and a few advs. in *-y* the *y* becomes *i*, as *early: earliest*, similarly in wds in *-ey*, as *gooey: gooiest*.

-est /ɪst/ *suff.*[2] *arch.* Also **-st**. [OE *-est*, *-ast*, *-st* = OHG *-ist* etc., Goth. *-is* etc.] Forming the 2nd person sing. of vbs, as *canst*, *doest*, *dost*, *findest*, *gavest*, etc.

establish /ɪˈstablɪʃ, ɛ-/ *v.* See also STABLISH. LME. [OFr. *establiss-* lengthened stem of *establir* (mod. *établir*) f. L *stabilire*, f. *stabilis* STABLE *a.*: see -ISH[2].] I *v.t.* 1 Institute or ordain permanently by enactment or agreement; *spec.* give legal form and recognition to (a Church) as the official Church of a country. LME. †b Secure or settle (property etc.) *on* or *upon* a person. LME–M17. 2 Set up on a permanent or secure basis; bring into being, found, (a government, institution, business, etc.). LME. †3 Make stable or firm; strengthen (*lit.* & *fig.*); ratify, confirm; restore (health). L15–E19. 4 Place (a person) in a secure position; put into residence or occupation; set up in business, appoint (esp. a civil servant) to a permanent post. L16. †b Provide for the maintenance of (a dependant etc.). M17–L19. 5 Initiate and secure acceptance of (a custom, belief, etc.); gain and keep (a position, a reputation). L16. **b** Introduce into a film or play and secure the identity or position of (a character, set, etc.). M20. **6** Place beyond dispute; ascertain, demonstrate, prove. E18.

1 J. STRUTT This edict was established, for the regulation of the Christian army . . during the Crusade. J. SMEATON Having first established that they should quit the work at nights. **the Established Church** *spec.* the Church of England or of Scotland. **b** SHAKES. *Macb.* We will establish our estate upon Our eldest, Malcolm. **2** W. S. CHURCHILL In 1851 the new colony of Victoria . . was established. ALDOUS HUXLEY Ask yourself what chance the loyalists ever had of establishing a liberal régime. **3** J. AUSTEN Harriet's cheerful look and manner established hers. **4** B. TARKINGTON He expected to get his family established at the seashore by the Fourth of July. D. CECIL Recently ordained and established as a curate . . at Overton. A. POWELL The Pimleys had established themselves in a . . block of flats . . not far from Battersea Bridge. **5** J. ROSENBERG Rembrandt's reputation as a portrait painter was very soon established. W. GOLDING Adults who tried to establish contact with him were never successful. **establish a suit** *Cards* play so that all one's remaining cards in a suit may take tricks. **6** E. BOWEN This has been suspected; now it's established, known. A. FRASER It was up to him to establish who, if anyone, could help him.

II *v.i.* **7** Take up residence, settle. L17.

establishable *a.* able to be established M17. **establisher** *n.* L15.

establishment /ɪˈstablɪʃm(ə)nt, ɛ-/ *n.* See also STABLISHMENT. L15. [f. prec. + -MENT.] **I** Something established. †**1 a** A settled arrangement, an established practice; a settled constitution or government. L15–L18. **b** *Fr. Hist.* A code of law. E19. **2** An organized body maintained for a State purpose; the (number of) personnel of a regiment, ship, etc. L17. **b** An institution or business; the premises or personnel of this. E19. **c** A household; its members collectively, *esp.* the servants. E19. **3 a** (**E-**.) The ecclesiastical system established by law; the Established Church. Also *Church Establishment.* M18. **b** (Usu. **E-**.) *The* group in society exercising authority or influence and seen as resisting change; any influential or controlling group. E20.

2 peace, war establishment reduced, increased, army etc. in time of peace, war. **b** I. MURDOCH Miss Quentin was at the hairdresser . . an expensive Mayfair establishment **c** N. MONSARRAT Two maids, a chef, and an ancient gardener . . were all that was left of an establishment which had formerly numbered sixteen. **3** J. H. NEWMAN Keble, Rose, and Palmer, represented distinct parties in the Establishment. D. L. SAYERS Having been brought up in the odour of the Establishment, he was familiar with this odd dissenting peculiarity. **b** D. LODGE Radicals looking for an issue on which to confront the Establishment.

II The action of establishing; the fact of being established. **4** A settled or stable condition, permanence; calmness of mind. M16. **b** Settlement in life; *spec.* (now *rare*) marriage. L17. **c** A settled income, a means of livelihood. E18. †**5** Something which strengthens, supports, or confirms. M16–M17. †**6 a** The action of settling the constitution and practices of an established Church. M17–E18. **b** The action of making a church an established Church; the fact or status of being an established Church. Formerly also, the legal recognition of a religious body. M17. **7** The length of time between the transit of a new or full moon across the meridian at a given place and the occurrence of the following high tide. M19.

4 C. MORGAN It gave her a sense of establishment to go continually to the same place. **b** J. AUSTEN He would willingly give up much wealth to obtain an early establishment. **c** W. COWPER It will afford me some sort of an establishment, at least for a time.

establishmentarian /ɪˌstablɪʃm(ə)nˈtɛːrɪən/ *n.* & *a.* M19. [f. prec. + -ARIAN.] **1** (A person) belonging to, or supporting the principle of, an established Church. M19. **2** (A person) belonging to or supporting the Establishment; (a person) having conservative views. M20.

establishmentarianism *n.* L19.

estacade /ɛstakad/ *n.* Pl. pronounced same. E17. [Fr. f. Sp. *estacada*: see STOCKADE.] A dyke made of piles or stakes in water or marshy ground in order to impede an enemy.

estafette /ɛstafɛt/ *n.* Pl. pronounced same. E17. [Fr. f. It. *staffetta* dim. of *staffa* stirrup, f. Langobardic: see -ETTE.] *Hist.* A mounted courier.

estalagem /istaˈlaʒim/ *n.* M19. [Port., f. *estala* stable f. Gmc base of STALL *n.*[1]] A Portuguese inn.

†**estall** *v.t.* Only in L16. [OFr. *estaler* place, fix, etc., in AL *estallare* assign terms for payment: see STALL *v.*[1], INSTALMENT *n.*[2]] Arrange the payment of (a debt) in instalments.

†**estalment** *n.* L16–M18. [f. AN *estalement* f. OFr. *estaler*: see prec., -MENT. Cf. INSTALMENT *n.*[2]] (An) arrangement to pay by instalments; an instalment.

estamin /ˈɛstəmɪn/ *n.* In sense 2 also **-mene, -mine** /-miːn/. E18. [OFr. *estamine* (mod. *étamine*) f. Proto-Romance f. L *staminea* use as n. of fem. of *stamineus* made of thread, f. *stamen* thread.] **1** = ETAMINE. E18. **2** A twilled woollen dress fabric. M19.

estaminet /ɛstaminɛ/ *n.* Pl. pronounced same, /-z/. E19. [Fr. f. Walloon *staminé* byre, f. *stamo* pole to which a cow is tethered in a stall, prob. f. G *Stamm* stem, trunk.] Orig., a café where smoking was allowed. Now, a small unpretentious café selling wine, beer, etc.

estampage /ɪˈstampɪdʒ, *foreign* ɛstɑ̃paːʒ (*pl. same*)/ *n.* Now *rare.* L19. [Fr., f. (O)Fr. *estamper* STAMP *v.*: see -AGE.] *Archaeol.* An impression on paper of an inscription; *spec.* a squeeze, a rubbing.

estancia /ɛˈstansɪə; *foreign* estanˈθia, -ˈsia (*pl.* -s)/ *n.* M17. [Sp., lit. 'station' = OFr. *estance* dwelling f. med.L *stantia* f. L *stant-* pres. ppl stem of *stare* to stand.] A cattle-ranch in Latin America or the southern US.

estanciero /ɛˌstansɪˈɛːrəʊ, *foreign* estanθiˈero/ *n.*, pl. **-os** /-əʊz, *foreign* -ɔs/, the keeper of an estancia, a cattle-rancher M19.

estate /ɪˈsteɪt, ɛ-/ *n.* ME. [OFr. *estat* (mod. *état*), f. L *status*: see STATE *n.*] **I** Condition. **1** State or condition (material, moral, physical, etc.). *arch.* ME. **b** A particular state, condition, or stage of life. *obs.* exc. in certain phrs. ME. **2** Condition as regards health, prosperity, etc. *arch.* LME. †**b** Natural or normal condition; good condition, health, well-being. LME–L16.

1 E. A. FREEMAN The wall, in its first estate, seems to have been merely a dyke of earth and rough stones. BROWNING In prime of life, perfection of estate. F. NORRIS This was his final estate, a criminal. **b** *Book of Common Prayer* To live together . . in the holy estate of matrimony. **man's** or **woman's estate** manhood or womanhood. **2** H. A. L. FISHER The best and most permanent contribution which that age was able to make to the relief of man's estate.

II Status, authority; a category of people with this. **3** Standing in the world, degree of rank or dignity; *esp.* high rank. *arch.* ME. †**b** A person of high rank. LME–M17. **4** Grandeur, pomp, state. *obs.* exc. *poet.* LME. **5** A particular class or category of people in a community or nation. Now *rare.* LME. **6** A class or order forming part of the body politic and sharing in government; *spec.* in Britain, each of the three Estates of the Realm (see below). LME. **b** In *pl.* An assembly of the governing classes or their representatives. E17. †**7** The authority of a monarch; governmental authority and administration. LME–L17. †**8** Form of government, constitution. Only in 17. †**9** A body politic, a state. E17–M18.

3 C. F. ALEXANDER The rich man in his castle, The poor man at his gate, God made them, high or lowly, And ordered their estate. **4 cup, chair,** etc., **of estate**: used on ceremonial or state occasions. **5** R. RECORDE This Rule is . . profitable for all estates of men. *Nature* The scientific estate is passing through a troubled period. **6** GLADSTONE The concessions of the spiritual estate of the realm. **b** C. V. WEDGWOOD The meeting of the Dutch Estates at The Hague.

III (A piece of) land; property. **10** Property, possessions, fortune, capital. *arch.* ME. **b** The collective assets and liabilities of a person, esp. one deceased or bankrupt. M19. **11** *Law.* The interest that a person has in land or other property. LME. **12** A landed property, *esp.* a large one. M18. **b** A property on which is grown a crop not native to Britain, as grapes, tea, coffee, or rubber. M19. **c** A residential or industrial district planned as a whole by one owner or local authority; the aggregate of tied public houses belonging to one brewery. L19.

IV 13 In full *estate car, estate wagon.* A car designed to carry both passengers and goods, usu. with folding rear seats and a rear door in place of a boot. M20.

10b J. WAINWRIGHT A legacy . . from the estate of some uncle. **11** *estate in fee, estate tail,* etc. **12** U. LE GUIN The family still owned an estate of seven thousand acres and fourteen villages. **b** P. V. PRICE The great wines are . . bottled at the estates where they are made. **c** C. PRIEST Now it was an estate, with thirty-six identical houses placed in a neat circular avenue. *council estate, industrial estate,* etc. *housing estate*: see HOUSING *n.*[1]

Other phrases: †**after one's estate** according to one's means. *cloth of estate*: see CLOTH *n.* 1. *enlarge an estate*: see ENLARGE *v.* †**make an estate of a thing** give an interest in or title to a thing *to* a person. **the** (**three**) **Estates of the Realm** (*a*) the three groups constituting Parliament, now the Lords Temporal (peers), the Lords Spiritual (bishops), and the Commons; (*b*) the Crown, the House of Lords, and the House of Commons. **Third Estate** (chiefly *Hist.*) the English commons; the French bourgeoisie and working class before the Revolution. **fourth estate** orig., any group regarded as having power in the land; now *spec.* the press.

Comb.: **estate agent** (*a*) a steward or manager of a landed estate; (*b*) a person who acts as agent and intermediary in the sale or lease of buildings and land; **estate-bottled** *a.* = DOMAINE-*bottled*; *estate car*: see sense 13 above; **estates bursar** a person in charge of the property that belongs to a college or university as endowment or investment; **estate duty** an estate tax levied in Britain between 1889 and 1975; **estate tax** a tax on the estate of a deceased person before it passes to the beneficiaries, such as inheritance tax in Britain; *estate wagon*: see sense 13 above.

estate /ɪˈsteɪt, ɛ-/ *v.t.* Now *rare* or *obs.* L16. [f. the n.] †**1** Bestow as an estate *on* or *upon*; let (land) *out*. L16–M17. **2** Establish (a person) in an estate; endow *with* possessions. E17. †**b** Provide with an estate or property. E–M17. †**3** Put into a particular state or condition; establish (*in*). E17–E18.

1 SHAKES. *Mids. N. D.* All my right of her I do estate unto Demetrius. **2** JASPER MAYNE I have estated her in all I have.

estated /ɪˈsteɪtɪd, ɛ-/ *a.* E17. [f. ESTATE *n.*, *v.* + -ED[2], -ED[1].] Having wealth or (esp. landed) property.

esteem /ɪˈstiːm, ɛ-/ *n.* ME. [(O)Fr. *estime*, f. *estimer*: see next.] †**1** Value, worth; reputation. ME–E19. †**2** Estimate, valuation; estimated value. E16–L17. **3** Estimation, opinion, judgement. *arch.* L16. **4** Favourable opinion, regard, respect. E17.

1 W. IRVING All these were of precious esteem, being family reliques. **2** J. BARGRAVE They put an esteem upon them, and I [was] made pay dear for them. **3** L. P. HARTLEY She sank in his esteem . . below the already lowly position occupied by women as a class. **4** M. MUGGERIDGE Something too banal to be taken seriously or held in esteem. *parity of esteem*: see PARITY *n.*[1] 1.

esteem /ɪˈstiːm, ɛ-/ *v.* LME. [(O)Fr. *estimer* f. L *aestimare* estimate, assess.] †**1** *v.t.* Estimate the number, quantity, or magnitude of. (Foll. by *at*, *to*, *to be*.) LME–E18. †**2 a** *v.t.* Assign a value to; assess, appraise; *fig.* assess the merit of. LME–L18. **b** *v.t.* Judge, form an opinion of. M16–E17. **c** *v.i.* Have a (specified) opinion *of*; be of the opinion *that*. M16–M18. **3** *v.t.* Regard as being; consider *as*, *to be*. E16. **4** *v.t.* Hold in (favourable or unfavourable) estimation; think (highly, little) of. M16. **b** Think highly of, respect. M16. †**c** Regard as important. L16–M17.

3 J. GALSWORTHY Black and mauve for evening wear was esteemed very chaste. SAKI The sort of secretary that any public man would esteem as a treasure. **4** G. GORER In a great many cases the presence or absence of a factor are quite differently esteemed. **b** D. CECIL A man she esteemed rather than loved. *Belfast*

Telegraph Fellow workers . . regret the death of the brother of their esteemed colleague . . and tender deepest sympathy.

†**esteemable** *a.* estimable, highly regarded E17–M18. **esteemer** *n.* M16.

ester /ˈɛstə/ *n.* M19. [G, prob. f. *Essig* vinegar (f. L *acetum*) + *Äther* ether.] Any organic compound in which a hydrogen atom in an acid is replaced by an alkyl, aryl, etc., group, as in fats and essential oils.

N. G. CLARK Lower, volatile esters are responsible for the fragrance and flavour of most fruits and flowers.

esterase /ˈɛstəreɪz/ *n.* an enzyme which hydrolyses an ester into an acid and an alcohol, phenol, etc. E20. **esterification** /ɪˌstɛrɪfɪˈkeɪʃ(ə)n, ɛ-/ *n.* the process of forming an ester; conversion of an acid into an ester: L19. **esterify** /ɪˈstɛrɪfʌɪ, ɛ-/ *v.t.* convert into an ester E20.

Esth /ɛsθ, ɛst/ *n.* & *a.* Now *rare.* M19. [G.] = ESTONIAN.

esthesis *n.*, **esthete** *n.*, **esthetic** *a.* & *n.*, etc. see AESTHESIS etc.

esthiomene /ɛsθɪˈɒmiːn/ *n.* LME. [med.L *esthiomenus* f. Gk *esthiomenos* pres. pple pass. or middle of *esthiein* eat.] Orig., gangrene; a gangrenous sore. Now, (the ulcerated genital lesions of) the disease lymphogranuloma venereum.

†**Esthonian** *a.* & *n.* var. of ESTONIAN.

estimable /ˈɛstɪməb(ə)l/ *a.* L15. [(O)Fr. f. L *aestimabilis*, f. *aestimare*: see ESTEEM *v.*, -ABLE. Earlier in INESTIMABLE.] †1 Able to be estimated, valued, or appraised. L15–E19. †2 Valuable; of great worth. L16–E19. †3 Important. L16–M18. 4 Worthy of esteem or regard. L17.

estimableness *n.* M18. **estimably** *adv.* M19.

estimate /ˈɛstɪmət/ *n.* LME. [f. the vb, or perh. f. L *aestimatus* vbl n., f. *aestimare*: see ESTEEM *v.*, -ATE[1].] †1 Intellectual ability or comprehension. Only in LME. †2 The action or an act of valuing or appraising; (a) valuation. M16–L17. †3 Repute, reputation. L16–M17. 4 A judgement of the character or qualities of a person or thing, or of a state of affairs etc.; estimation, opinion. L16. 5 An approximate judgement of the number, quantity, position, etc., of something; the number etc. so assigned. M17. b In *pl. The* statements of proposed public expenditure that the British Government presents to Parliament each year. M18. 6 A statement produced by a contractor or other tradesman of the price he or she expects to charge or will charge for doing a specified job; the price so stated. M18.

4 T. HARDY The journey was a fearfully heavy one . . at her own estimate. P. LARKIN He was mistaken if he expected her to be flattered by his estimate of her. 5 G. BERKELEY The estimates we make of the distance of objects. LYNDON B. JOHNSON The police estimate of the total crowd . . was more than a quarter of a million.

estimate /ˈɛstɪmeɪt/ *v.t.* Pa. pple **-ated**, †**-ate**. L15. [L *aestimat-* pa. ppl stem of *aestimare*: see ESTEEM *v.*, -ATE[3].] †1 = ESTEEM *v.* 4. L15–M18. †2 = ESTEEM *v.* 3. *rare.* M16–L18. †3 Assign a value to; assess, appraise. L16–M18. 4 Form an opinion of; gauge. M17. 5 Form a numerical estimate of or *that*; put *at* a specified number etc. by estimation; judge by estimation *to be* etc. M17.

4 S. JOHNSON While an author is yet living, we estimate his powers by his worst performance. 5 A. CARNEGIE The loss . . was estimated at fully a third of the total quantity. B. RUSSELL Remains . . estimated to belong to a period about one million years ago. J. HILTON He pondered, . . calculating distances, estimating times and speeds. P. D. JAMES He estimated that Lampart would arrive in about five minutes. N. CHOMSKY An estimated 70,000 people took part.

estimation /ɛstɪˈmeɪʃ(ə)n/ *n.* LME. [OFr., or L *aestimatio(n-)*, f. as prec.: see -ATION.] †1 Comprehension, intuition. Only in LME. †2 The action of valuing or assessing; a statement of price or value; (a) valuation. LME–L18. b Estimated value; a valuable. M16–L18. 3 The process of forming an approximate judgement of the number, quantity, position, etc., of something. LME. 4 Opinion, judgement, esp. as to the worth or character of a person or thing. LME. †b Conjecture, guessing. *rare* (Shakes.). Only in L16. 5 Appreciation, esteem; repute; the importance of a place. *arch.* M16.

4 J. LONDON Martin took a great slump in Maria's estimation. 5 G. CANNING Wishing to know in what estimation he was held by mankind.

estimative /ˈɛstɪmətɪv/ *a.* Now *rare.* LME. [OFr. *estimatif, -ive* or med.L *estimativus*, f. as ESTIMATE *v.*: see -IVE.] 1 Adapted for estimating; capable of estimating. LME. †2 Estimated. E–M17.

estimator /ˈɛstɪmeɪtə/ *n.* E17. [L *aestimator*, f. as ESTIMATE *v.*: see -OR.] 1 A person who estimates. E17. 2 *Statistics.* A method for arriving at an estimate of a value; a quantity used or evaluated as such an estimate. M20.

estimatory /ɛstɪˈmeɪt(ə)ri/ *a.* M18. [f. prec. or L *aestimatorius*, f. as prec.: see -ORY[2].] Involving or of the nature of an estimate.

estival *a.*, **-ate** *v.*, **-ation** *n.*, etc. see AESTIVAL etc.

estoc /ˈɛstɒk/ *n.* M19. [(O)Fr., prob. f. OFr. *estochier* lunge (mod. *estoquer* wound (a bull) mortally) f. MDu., MLG *stoken*: see STOKER.] *Hist.* A short sword used for thrusting.

estocada /estoˈkaθa, ɛstəˈkɑːdə/ *n.* E20. [Sp., f. *estoque* sword (f. (O)Fr. ESTOC) + *-ada* -ADE. Cf. next.] *Bullfighting.* The thrust that finally kills the bull.

†**estocado** *n.* M–L16. [f. Fr. *estocade* f. It. *stoccata*, f. *stocco* sword f. (O)Fr. ESTOC: see -ADO. Cf. prec.] An estoc; a blow or gesture with an estoc.

estoile /ɪˈstɔɪl, ɛ-/ *n.* L16. [OFr. (mod. *étoile*) f. L *stella* star.] *Her.* A charge in the form of a star with (usu. six) wavy points or rays.

Estonian /ɪˈstəʊnɪən, ɛ-/ *a.* & *n.* Also †**Esthonian**. E18. [f. mod.L *Est(h)onia*, f. ESTH after *Saxonia* etc.: see -AN.] **A** *adj.* Of or belonging to Estonia, a country situated on the south side of the Gulf of Finland. E18. **B** *n.* 1 A native or inhabitant of Estonia. E18. 2 The Finno-Ugric language of Estonia. M19.

estop /ɪˈstɒp/ *v.t.* Infl. **-pp-**. LME. [AN, OFr. *estop(p)er, estouper* (mod. *étouper*) stop up, impede (med.L *estoppare*) f. late L deriv. of L *stuppa* oakum.] 1 Stop (as) with a dam, plug, etc. *arch.* LME. 2 *Law.* Bar or preclude by estoppel. (Foll. by *from, to do.*) M16.

2 H. HALLAM The lord who had granted the charter of franchise was estopped from claiming him again.

estoppage *n.* stoppage; *Law* the condition of being estopped: E18.

estoppel /ɪˈstɒp(ə)l/ *n.* M16. [OFr. *estoup(p)ail* plug, stopper, f. as prec.: see -AL[1].] 1 *Law.* The principle which precludes a person from asserting something contrary to what is implied by his or her previous action or statement or by a previous judicial determination concerning that person. M16. †2 An obstruction (to a watercourse). E–M17.

estouffade /ɛstufad/ *n.* Pl. pronounced same. L19. [Fr. f. It. *stuf(f)ata* pa. pple of *stufare* to stew, f. *stufa* stove f. pop.L, ult. f. Gk *tuphos* smoke: cf. STEW *v.*] (A dish of) meat cooked very slowly in its own vapour.

estovers /ɪˈstəʊvəz, ɛ-/ *n.pl.* L15. [Pl. of AN *estover* (AL *estoverium*) use as n. of *estover*, OFr. *estoveir* be necessary, based on L *est opus* it is necessary: see -ER[4].] *Law.* 1 In full *common of estovers.* The right to take wood for fuel, repairs, or other necessary purpose from land one does not own, esp. land of which one is the tenant or lessee. L15. 2 Wood to which a person is entitled by common of estovers; necessaries allowed by law. L16.

estrade /ɛˈstrɑːd/ *n.* L17. [Fr. f. Sp. ESTRADO.] Orig., a slightly raised platform or dais for persons of rank to sit or recline on. Later, any dais.

estradiol *n.* see OESTRADIOL.

estrado /ɛˈstrɑːdəʊ/ *n.* Now *rare.* Pl. **-os**. L16. [Sp. f. L STRATUM.] 1 A room or part of a room richly furnished and used for reclining; a drawing-room. L16. 2 A platform. M19.

estral *a.*, **estrane** *n.* see OESTRAL, OESTRANE.

estrange /ɪˈstreɪn(d)ʒ, ɛ-/ *v.t.* L15. [AN *estraunger*, OFr. *estranger* (mod. *étranger*) f. L *extraneare* treat as a stranger, f. *extraneus*: see EXTRANEOUS. Cf. STRANGE *a.*] 1 Keep away or apart from or *from* an accustomed place, occupation, etc. *arch.* L15. †b Withhold *from* a person's perception or knowledge. Only in 17. †c Make (a person) a stranger *to.* E–M18. 2 Destroy or divert the affection, trust, loyalty, etc., of (a person); destroy or divert (such a feeling); cause to turn away in feelings or affection (*from*). L15. 3 Cut off from a community; remove (a possession or subject) from the ownership or dominion of someone. (Foll. by *from.*) *arch.* E16. †4 Make unlike one's normal self; make insane; madden. M16–E17. 5 Make unfamiliar in appearance; disguise. *arch.* E17.

1 I. D'ISRAELI Edward, long estranged from his native realm. 2 BURKE You are going to estrange his majestys confidence from me. W. S. CHURCHILL The Dutch rule of the conquered Belgian cities had estranged their inhabitants. *Morning Star* The murdered woman . . was identified . . as his estranged wife. 3 J. HOOKER Infidels estranged from the house of God.

estrangedness /-(d)ʒdnɪs, -dʒɪdnɪs/ *n.* the state of being estranged M17.

estrangelo /ɪˈstraŋɡələʊ, ɛ-/ *n.* M18. [Syriac *estrangelō*, thought to be f. Gk *stroggulos* rounded.] An archaic form of Syriac script.

estrangement /ɪˈstreɪn(d)ʒm(ə)nt, ɛ-/ *n.* M17. [f. ESTRANGE *v.* + -MENT.] The action of estranging or becoming estranged; the state of being estranged; alienation.

E. JONES There were quarrels that led to lasting estrangements.

†**estranger** *n.*[1] L15. [OFr.: see STRANGER *n.*] 1 A person belonging to another family, nation, or district; a stranger; a foreigner. L15–M17. 2 *Law.* = STRANGER *n.* 6b. L16–E18.

estranger /ɪˈstreɪn(d)ʒə, ɛ-/ *n.*[2] E17. [f. ESTRANGE *v.* + -ER[1].] A person who or thing which estranges.

estray /ɪˈstreɪ, ɛ-/ *n.* E16. [AN, f. AN & OFr. *estraier* STRAY *v.*[1]] 1 *Law.* A valuable or domesticated animal found wandering and unclaimed by its owner. E16. 2 *gen.* Anything that has strayed or wandered. L16.

estray /ɪˈstreɪ, ɛ-/ *v.i. arch.* M16. [AN & OFr. *estraier* STRAY *v.*[2]] Stray; go astray.

estreat /ɪˈstriːt, ɛ-/ *n.* & *v.* See also EXTREAT. ME. [AN *estrete*, OFr. *estraite*, use as n. of fem. pa. pple of *estraire* extract f. L *extrahere.*] **A** *n. Law.* 1 A copy of a legal record, *esp.* one of a fine or recognizance for use by an officer of the court. ME. †2 In *pl.* Fines or other payments enforced by a court. LME–M17. **B** *v.t.* Chiefly *Law.* Extract a copy of the court record of (a fine, recognizance, etc.) for use in prosecution; enforce (a fine); enforce forfeiture of (bail, a recognizance, etc.). E16.

estrepement /ɪˈstriːpm(ə)nt, ɛ-/ *n.* E16. [AN, OFr., f. *estreper* (whence AL *estrepare*) f. L *extirpare* EXTIRPATE: see -MENT.] *Law.* Damage to an estate caused by a tenant.

estrich /ˈɛstrɪtʃ/ *n.* Also **-idge** /-ɪdʒ/. LME. [OFr. *estruc(h)e* var. of *ostrusce* OSTRICH.] †1 Var. of OSTRICH. LME–E18. 2 *Comm.* The fine down of the ostrich. M19.

estriche /ˈɛstrɪtʃ/ *n.* [OE *ēast-rīć*, f. as EAST + *rīć* kingdom.] †1 Orig., the East Frankish kingdom. Later, any eastern kingdom. OE–ME. 2 In full *estriche board.* Timber from Norway or the Baltic. *obs.* exc. *Hist.* LME.

estridge *n.* var. of ESTRICH.

estrin, estriol *ns.* vars. of OESTRIN, OESTRIOL.

estro /ˈɛstro/ *n.* E17. [It. f. L OESTRUS frenzy.] Inspiration, impulse.

estrogen, estrone *ns.* see OESTROGEN, OESTRONE.

estropiated /ɪˈstrɒpɪeɪtɪd, ɛ-/ *a.* E20. [f. Fr. *estropier* cripple, disfigure f. It. *stroppiare* alt. of *storpiare*, f. L *turpis* ugly or *stuprare* defile, ravish: see -ATE[3], -ED[1].] Crippled; disfigured.

estrous *a.*, **estrum**, **-us** *ns.* see OESTROUS *a.* etc.

estuarial /ɛstjʊˈɛːrɪəl/ *a.* L19. [f. as next + -AL[1].] Of or pertaining to an estuary.
Also **estuarian** *a.* L19.

estuarine /ˈɛstjʊ(ə)rʌɪn/ *a.* M19. [f. ESTUARY + -INE[1].] Of or belonging to an estuary; *esp.* (of strata, organisms, etc.) formed, deposited, or occurring in an estuary.
P. LEVI How to drain a huge estuarine valley and make . . grazing land.

estuary /ˈɛstjʊ(ə)ri/ *n.* Also †**ae-**. M16. [L *aestuarium* tidal part of a shore, estuary, f. *aestus* heat, swell, surge, tide: see -ARY[1].] **1** A tidal opening or inlet. Now *rare* exc. as in sense 2. M16. **2** *spec.* The tidal mouth of a large river, where the tide meets the stream. L16. †**3** A vapour-bath. Only in M17. †**4** A place where liquid boils up; *fig.* mental turmoil. L17–E19.

†**estuation** *n.* var. of AESTUATION.

estufa /eˈstufa/ *n.* M19. [Sp., corresp. to OFr. *estuve* (mod. *étuve*): see STEW *n.*[1]] **1** An underground chamber in which a fire is kept permanently alight, used as a place of assembly by the Pueblo Indians. M19. **2** A heated chamber in which Madeira is stored and matured. L19.

†**estuosity** *n.* M17–M18. [f. L *aestuosus* full of heat, f. *aestus* heat: see -OSITY.] Heated condition.

esurience /ɪˈsjʊərɪəns, ɛ-/ *n.* E19. [f. next: see -ENCE.] The state of being esurient.
Also **esuriency** *n.* E19.

esurient /ɪˈsjʊərɪənt, ɛ-/ *a.* L17. [L *esurient-* pres. ppl stem of *esurire* be hungry, desiderative vb from *es-* pa. ppl stem of *esse* eat: see -ENT.] **1** Hungry; impecunious and greedy. *arch.* & *joc.* L17. **2** Gastronomic. E19.
esuriently *adv.* L19.

et /ɛt/ *conj.* ME. [L.] And. Only in med. & mod.L phrs.: see below.
et al. /al/ (*a*) [abbrev. of L *alii*, *aliae*, *alia* masc., fem., & neut. pl. of *alius* other] and others; (*b*) [abbrev. of L ALIBI] and elsewhere. **et sequens** /ˈsɛkwɛnz/ [L, pres. pple of *sequi* follow] and the following (usu. abbrev. to *et seq.*). **et sequentes** /sɛˈkwɛntiːz/ [L, masc. & fem. pl. of *sequens*], **et sequentia** /sɛˈkwɛntɪə/ [L, neut. pl. of *sequens*] and the following things (usu. abbrev. to *et seq.*, *et seqq.*). ET CETERA.

-et /ɪt/ *suff.*[1] [OFr. (fem. *-ete*, mod. *-ette*) = It. *-etto*, *-etta*, f. Proto-Romance *-itto*, *-itta*, perh. not of Latin origin.] In ns., orig. dims., mostly derived from Fr., as *bullet*, *fillet*, *hatchet*, *pullet*, *tablet*, etc., but also from It., as *nonet*.
¶Largely superseded in mod. wd-formation by the rel. -ETTE, -LET, exc. in wds modelled on *duet*, *quartet*.

-et /ɪt/ *suff.*[2] [OE *-et*, *-ett* = Goth. *-iti*, OHG *-izzi*.] Forming neut. vbl and denominative ns., as *thicket* etc.

eta /ˈiːtə/ *n.*[1] LME. [Gk *ēta*.] **1** The seventh letter (*H*, *η*) of the Greek alphabet. LME. **2** Freq. written *η*. **a** *attrib.* *Astron.* (Preceding the genitive of the L name of the constellation) denoting the seventh brightest star in a constellation. L18. **b** *Physics.* In full *eta meson*. A meson with zero isospin and spin and a mass of 549 MeV. M20.
2b eta prime a meson like the eta meson except for having a mass of 958 MeV.
Comb.: **eta patch** a large fan-shaped patch by which rigging can be attached to the envelope of an airship.

eta /ˈeɪtə/ *n.*[2] Pl. same. L19. [Jap.] A member of an outcast class in Japan. Cf. HININ.

eta *n.*[3] var. of ITA.

etaerio /ɛˈtɪərɪəʊ/ *n.* Pl. **-os**. M19. [Fr. *etairion*, *-ium* f. Gk *hetaireia* association.] *Bot.* An aggregate fruit, as a strawberry or raspberry.

etagere /ɛtəˈʒɛː/ *n.* Also **étagère** /etaʒɛr (*pl. same*), ɛtəˈʒɛː/. M19. [Fr. *étagère*, f. *étage* shelf, STAGE *n.*] A piece of furniture with a number of open shelves on which to display ornaments etc.

étalage /etalaːʒ/ *n.* Pl. pronounced same. E20. [Fr., f. *étaler* to display.] A display, a show.
B. CAMPBELL The étalage of leaves at the entrance to many robins' nests.

etalon /ˈɛtəlɒn/ *n.* Also **é-**. E20. [Fr. *étalon* lit. 'standard of measurement'.] *Physics.* A pair of half-reflecting flat plates of glass or quartz fixed parallel to one another a small distance apart, used to produce interference patterns.

etamine /ˈɛtəmiːn/ *n.* Also **é-**. E18. [Fr. *étamine*: see ESTAMIN.] A lightweight open-weave fabric of coarse yarn, now usu. cotton or worsted.

étang /etɑ̃/ *n.* Pl. pronounced same. M19. [Fr. f. OFr. *estanc*: see STANK *n.*] A shallow pool or small lake, *esp.* one resulting from the blocking of streams by sand-dunes along the French Mediterranean coast.

etaoin /ˈɛtəɔɪn/ *n.* M20. [See below.] More fully *etaoin shrdlu* /ˈʃəːdluː/. (A slug containing) the letters *e*, *t*, etc. produced by running the finger down the first one or two vertical lines of keys on a Linotype machine, used as a temporary marker and sometimes printed by mistake; any absurd or unintelligible sequence of type. Cf. SHRDLU.

etatism /ɛˈtɑːtɪz(ə)m/ *n.* Also ***étatisme*** /etatism/. E20. [Fr. *étatisme*, f. *état* state: see ESTATE *n.*, -ISM.] The extreme authority of the State over the individual citizen.
etatist, ***étatiste*** *a.* characterized by or exhibiting etatism M20.

†***état-major*** *n.* L18–L19. [Fr., f. *état* (see prec.) + *major* MAJOR *n.*[1]] The staff of an army, regiment, etc.; a managing or governing body.

et cetera /ɛtˈsɛt(ə)rə, ɪt-/ *adv.*, *n.*, & *v.* Also **etcetera**, **et caetera**. ME. [L, f. *et* and + *cetera* the rest, neut. pl. of *ceterus* remaining over.] **A** *adv.* And the rest; and similar things; and so on; and the customary continuation. Also redupl. ME.
J. GRENFELL A long line of intellectuals—father, grandfather, etcetera. F. W. CROFTS Yours, etc., *Leon Felix*. *Sunday Times* Squads of sexologists, whole studios full of raped girls, etc., etc.
B *n.* **1** (An instance of) the adverb *et cetera*. L16. **2** Something not mentioned explicitly, esp. for reasons of delicacy or propriety. Formerly *spec.*, (in *pl.*) trousers. L16. **3** A number of unspecified things or persons. M17. **4** In *pl.* (The usual) additions; extras, sundries. E18.
1 *New York Times* Etcetera etcetera was followed by blah-blah-blah. **2** J. CARY You don't know your etc. from an etc. **4** E. BOWEN She began to pack her compact, comb and other etceteras.
C *v.* Replacing a suppressed verb. M19.
H. KINGSLEY I am etcetera'd if I stand it.
¶Often abbrev. to *etc.* or *&c.*

etch /ɛtʃ/ *n.*[1] L16. [Contr.] = EDDISH 2.

etch /ɛtʃ/ *n.*[2] L19. [f. the vb.] **1** The action or process of etching; an act or method of etching. L19. **2** *Printing.* A liquid applied to a lithographic stone so as to form a crust that protects some areas from ink. M20.

etch /ɛtʃ/ *v.* M17. [Du. *etsen* f. G *ätzen* f. OHG *azzen*, *ezzen* f. Gmc causative f. as EAT *v.*] **1** *v.t.* Engrave (metal, glass, or stone) by coating it with a protective layer, drawing in this with a needle, and then covering with acid or other corrosive that attacks the parts the needle has exposed; *esp.* engrave (a plate) in this way in order to print from it; use this process to produce (a picture) or a picture of (a subject). M17. **b** Engrave by any method; *Sci.* selectively dissolve the surface of (a crystal or crystalline material) with a solvent. M18. **c** *fig.* Produce or affect as if by etching; cause to stand out clearly or vividly. M19. **2** *v.i.* Engage in the art of etching. M17. **3** *v.t.* Corrode; eat *out*, remove *from*, (with an acid or other solvent). M17.
1 A. B. JAMESON All the Illustrations . . have been newly etched on steel. **c** J. BUCHAN The far mountains were etched in violet against a saffron sky. A. CARTER The dry air etched his face full of fine lines.
Comb.: **etch figure**, **pit** a depression on the face of a crystal that is produced by the action of a solvent and is indicative of the crystal's microstructure.
etchable *a.* able to be etched or to be made visible by etching M20. **etchant** *n.* a corrosive or dissolving agent used for etching M20. **etcher** *n.* a person who etches M17.

etching /ˈɛtʃɪŋ/ *n.* M17. [f. prec. + -ING[1].] **1** The action of ETCH *v.*; the art of the etcher. M17. **2** A copy or representation produced by the process of etching; an impression from an etched plate. M18.
2 HOR. WALPOLE His etchings for Aesop's fables.
Comb.: **etching ground** the protective substance with which a surface is coated preparatory to etching.

Eteocretan /ˌiːtɪəˈkriːt(ə)n, ɛt-/ *n.* & *a.* E17. [f. Gk *Eteokrēt-*, *-krēs*, f. *eteos* true + *Krēs* Cretan: see -AN.] **A** *n.* **1** A member of a pre-Greek people of Crete. E17. **2** The language of this people. E20. **B** *adj.* Of or pertaining to the Eteocretans or their language. L19.

eteostichon /ɛtɪˈɒstɪkɒn/ *n.* *rare.* Also †**-stic.** M17. [f. Gk *eteos* genit. of *etos* year + *stikhos* row, rank.] = CHRONOGRAM.

eternal /ɪˈtəːn(ə)l, iː-/ *a.*, *n.*, & *adv.* LME. [OFr. *eternal*, *-nel* (mod. *éternel*) f. late L *aeternalis*, f. L *aeternus* contr. of *aeviternus* eternal, f. *aevum* age: see -AL[1].] **A** *adj.* **1** That will always exist; that has always existed; without a beginning or an end in time; everlasting. LME. **b** Pertaining to eternal things; having eternal consequences. E17. **c** Not conditioned by time; not subject to time relations. M17. **2** Permanent; enduring. L15. **b** Having a persistent resolve. *rare* (Shakes.). Only in E17. **c** Tediously persistent; recurring, incessant. L18. **3** Infernal; extremely abhorrent. Now *slang* or *dial.* L16. **4** Of a truth, principle, etc.: valid for all time; immutable, unalterable. L17.
1 *eternal life*: see LIFE *n.* **2** J. P. CURRAN The condition upon which God hath given liberty to man is eternal vigilance. A. ALISON Summits . . wrapped in eternal snow. O. MANNING He'd . . have wasted his life as a sort of eternal student. **the Eternal City** Rome. **c** C. MCCULLOUGH Their palates longed for a change from the eternal round of . . mutton chops, mutton stew. **eternal triangle** a relationship of three people involving sexual rivalry.
B *n.* **1** *the Eternal*, God, the Deity. L16. †**2** Eternity, endless time. Chiefly in *from eternal*. E17–M18. **3** In *pl.* Eternal things. M17.
C *adv.* Eternally, for ever. E17.
eternalism *n.* (*a*) eternalness; an eternal character or nature; (*b*) *Philos.* the belief that the universe has no beginning and no end: L19. **eterˈnality** *n.* = ETERNALNESS L15. **eternally** *adv.* (*a*) throughout eternity, for ever; (*b*) continually, incessantly; (*c*) immutably: LME. **eternalness** *n.* the state or quality of being eternal M18.

eternalize /ɪˈtəːn(ə)lʌɪz/ *v.t.* Also **-ise**. E17. [f. prec. + -IZE.] **1** = ETERNIZE 2. E17. **2** = ETERNIZE 1. E19. **3** = ETERNIZE 3. M19.
2 S. J. PERELMAN We eternalized baby shoes . . dipped them in bronze for ash trays. **3** A. J. DAVIS It contains truth eternalised.
eternaliˈzation *n.* E20.

eterne /ɪˈtəːn, iː-/ *a.*, *n.*, & *adv.* *arch.* & *poet.* LME. [OFr., f. L *aeternus* ETERNAL *a.*] **A** *adj.* Eternal. LME. **B** *n.* †**1** Eternity. Chiefly in *from eterne*. LME–L15. **2** *the eterne*, that which is eternal, *spec.* (*Eterne*) God. E17. †**C** *adv.* Eternally. Only in 16.

eternise *v.* var. of ETERNIZE.

eternity /ɪˈtəːnɪti, iː-/ *n.* LME. [OFr. *éternité* f. L *aeternitas*, f. *aeternus* ETERNAL *a.*: see -ITY.] **1** The quality, condition, or fact of being eternal; eternal existence. LME. **b** Perpetual or long-lasting continuance, esp. of fame. LME. **c** In *pl.* *The* eternal truths or realities. M19. **2** All of time past or time to come, or both jointly; infinite time, without a beginning or an end. LME. **b** A very great or apparently endless length of time; a tediously long time. E18. **3** In *pl.* Eternity of time viewed as consisting of successive ages. LME. **4** Timelessness; a state to which time has no application; the condition into which the soul enters at death; the afterlife. L16.
1 D. BREWSTER An argument . . to prove the eternity of the world. **2** HOBBES 'Natural' are those which have been Lawes from all Eternity. **b** J. MOXON Those Grey Kentish Bricks . . will last to Eternity. D. H. LAWRENCE At last, after an eternity, Cicio came along the platform. **3** E. B. BROWNING A clock Which strikes the hours of the eternities. **4** DAY LEWIS I had a vision of eternity in my sleep. **launch into eternity** (cause to) die.

Comb.: **eternity ring**: given as a symbol of lasting love and usu. set with an unbroken circle of stones.

eternize /ɪˈtəːnʌɪz, ˈiːtənʌɪz/ *v.t.* Also **-ise**. M16. [Fr. *éterniser* or med.L *eternizare*, f. L *aeternus* ETERNAL *a.*: see -IZE.] 1 Prolong indefinitely; make permanent; perpetuate (fame, memory, etc.). M16. 2 Make eternally famous, immortalize. L16. 3 Make eternal in duration or character. L16.

1 E. R. EDDISON Creatures . . eternized in amber.

eterniˈzation *n.* E17.

Etesian /ɪˈtiːʒɪən, ɪˈtiːz-, ɪˈtiːʒ(ə)n/ *a.* & *n.* Also **e-**. E17. [f. L *etesius* annual f. Gk *etēsios*, f. *etos* year: see -AN.] (Designating) a dry north wind blowing over the Aegean and eastern Mediterranean in the summer.

eth /ɛð/ *n.* Also **edh**. M19. [Da. *edh*, perh. repr. the sound of the letter.] The letter ð or đ, capital Ð, introduced in Old English to represent the voiced and voiceless dental fricatives /ð/ and /θ/; the letter in the form ð, ð, used in Old Norse and Icelandic to represent the voiced dental fricative /ð/. Also, the phonetic symbol ð, used *spec.* in the International Phonetic Alphabet to represent this voiced dental fricative.

¶Eth was used interchangeably with the letter thorn in Old and Middle English, and both were superseded by the digraph *th* with the advent of printing. In this dictionary eth is not used in early English forms, which are regularized with thorn.

eth- /ɛθ, iːθ/ *comb. form* of ETHYL, as *ethambutol*, *ethene*, etc.

-eth /ɪθ/ *suff.*[1] *arch.* Also **-th**. [OE *-eþ*, *-aþ*, *-þ* = OHG *-it* etc., Goth. *-iþ* etc.] Forming the 3rd person pres. sing. of vbs, as *doeth*, *doth*, *findeth*, *saith*.

-eth *suff.*[2] var. of -TH[2].

ethacrynic /ɛθəˈkrɪnɪk/ *a.* M20. [f. ETH- + ACRY(LIC + PHE)N(OXY- + ACET)IC.] *ethacrynic acid*, a powerful diuretic drug used to treat oedema.

ethambutol /ɛˈθambjʊtɒl/ *n.* M20. [f. ETH- + AMINE + BUT(AN)OL.] A derivative of ethylenediamine used as a bacteriostatic agent to treat tuberculosis.

ethanal /ˈɛθ(ə)nal/ *n.* M20. [f. next + -AL[2].] *Chem.* = ACETALDEHYDE.

ethane /ˈiːθeɪn, ˈɛθ-/ *n.* L19. [f. ETHER *n.*[1] + -ANE.] *Chem.* A colourless odourless flammable gas, C_2H_6, that is a simple alkane and a constituent of petroleum and natural gas.

Comb.: **ethanediol** = ETHYLENE *glycol*.

Ethanim /ˈɛθənɪm/ *n.* M16. [f. Heb. *yeraḥ hā-ʾēṯānīm* month of steady-flowing rivers, f. *ēṯān* ever-flowing.] In the Jewish calendar, = TISHRI.

ethanoic /ɛθəˈnəʊɪk/ *a.* L19. [f. ETHANE + -OIC.] *Chem.* = ACETIC I.

ethanoate *n.* = ACETATE I M20. **ethanoyl** *n.* = ACETYL E20.

ethanol /ˈɛθənɒl/ *n.* E20. [f. ETHANE + -OL.] *Chem.* A colourless volatile flammable liquid alcohol, C_2H_5OH, present in alcoholic drinks (cf. ALCOHOL 4), produced by the fermentation of hexose sugars, and used as a solvent, antifreeze, fuel, and intermediate; ethyl alcohol.

ethanolamine /-ˈnɒl-, -ˈnəʊl-/ *n.* each of three compounds which are derived from ammonia by successive replacement of hydrogen atoms with the group $\cdot C_2H_4OH$, melt near room temperature, and are used to form soaps by combination with fatty acids; *spec.* 2-aminoethanol, $H_2N{\cdot}C_2H_4OH$, used to purify gases: L19. **ethaˈnolic** *a.* M20.

ethchlorvynol /ɛθklɔːˈvʌɪnɒl/ *n.* M20. [f. ETH- + CHLOR-[1] + alt. of VIN(YL + -OL.] *Pharm.* A short-acting sedative and hypnotic used to treat insomnia.

¶A proprietary name for this drug in the US and Canada is PLACIDYL.

ethel /ˈɛθ(ə)l/ *n.*[1] Long *obs.* exc. *Hist.* [OE *æþel*, *ēþel*, *ōþel* = OS *ōþil*, OHG *uodal*, ON *óðal*, f. Gmc: see UDAL. Cf. ATHEL, ATHELING.] (An) ancestral land or estate; patrimony; (a) native land.

ethel *a.* & *n.*[2] var. of ATHEL.

ethene /ˈɛθiːn/ *n.* M19. [f. ETH- + -ENE.] *Chem.* = ETHYLENE.

ethenoid *a.* = ETHYLENIC E20.

ether /ˈiːθə/ *n.*[1] In senses 1–3 also (*arch.*) **aether**. LME. [OFr. *ether* or L *aether* f. Gk *aithēr* upper air, f. base of *aithein* kindle, burn, shine.] 1 *Hist.* A substance formerly believed to occupy space beyond the sphere of the moon and to compose the stars and planets. LME. 2 The clear sky; the region above the clouds; the substance formerly believed to occupy this, above the air of the lower region. Now *poet.* & *literary*. L16. b Air. E18. 3 A very rarefied and highly elastic substance formerly believed to permeate all space, including the interstices between the particles of matter, and to be the medium whose vibrations constituted light (and radio waves); the notional medium of radio transmission; *the ether* (colloq.), radio as a medium or art form. M17. †b Any hypothetical very rarefied fluid. L17–L18. 4 *Chem.* a A pleasant-smelling colourless volatile liquid, $(CH_3CH_2)_2O$, made by the action of sulphuric acid on ethanol and used as a solvent, intermediate, and anaesthetic. M18. †b A compound formed by the action of any other acid on ethanol. L18–M19. c Any organic compound of the type ROR′, where R, R′ are alkyl, aryl, etc., groups. Formerly also (more fully *compound ether*) = ESTER. M19.

2 A. UTTLEY Her voice floated . . through the silvery atoms of air and the mysterious ether to the great moon. 3 J. S. HUXLEY A . . request I made over the ether. 4c **diethyl ether** = sense 4a above.

etherate *n.* (*Chem.*) any compound whose molecule contains an ether molecule, esp. $(C_2H_5)_2O$ E20.

ether *v.* & *n.*[2] var. of EDDER.

ethereal /ɪˈθɪərɪəl/ *a.* & *n.* Also **-ial**, **aeth-**. E16. [f. L *aethereus*, *-ius* f. Gk *aitherios*, f. *aithēr*: see ETHER *n.*[1], -AL[1].] A *adj.* 1 Of or pertaining to the region above the clouds (ETHER *n.*[1] 2); (chiefly *poet.*) heavenly, celestial. E16. 2 Of the nature of or resembling the ether (ETHER *n.*[1] 1, 3); light, airy, attenuated; pertaining to or involving the ether. E16. 3 Resembling (a) spirit, impalpable; of unearthly delicacy and refinement. M17. 4 *Chem.* Of or pertaining to ether (ETHER *n.*[1] 4a); resembling (that of) ether. E19.

1 J. WILKINS The extreme Coldness of the Æthereal Air. MILTON Go, heavenly Guest, Ethereal Messenger. 2 H. POWER The aetherial Medium (wherein all the Stars and Planets do swim). *Scientific American* Loudspeakers are . . used instead of headphones, so that the entire family can enjoy the etherial entertainment. **ethereal oil** = *essential oil* s.v. ESSENTIAL *a.* 7. 3 R. LEHMANN People said how ethereal she'd grown to look, how spiritual. S. SPENDER Music . . at once so ethereal and yet so earthly. 4 N. G. CLARK Lower ketones have an ethereal or fruity odour.

B *n.* 1 The ethereal principle, the spirit or essence. Now *rare* or *obs.* M17. 2 An ethereal being, a spirit. M18.

ethereˈality *n.* the quality of being ethereal or beyond material analysis E19. **etherealiˈzation** *n.* the action or process of etherealizing M19. **etherealize** *v.t.* make ethereal in substance or appearance; spiritualize, refine: E19. **ethereally** *adv.* E17. **etherealness** *n.* M18.

etherean /ɪˈθɪərɪən/ *a.* *rare*. Also **-ian**. M17. [f. as ETHEREAL + -AN.] Heavenly, refined; (of a colour) soft, subdued.

ethereous /ɪˈθɪərɪəs/ *a.* Also **-ious**. M17. [f. as ETHEREAL + -OUS.] Composed of, or of the nature of, ether (ETHER *n.*[1] 1, 2, 3).

etherial *a.* & *n.*, **etherian**, **etherious** *adjs.* vars. of ETHEREAL, -EAN, -EOUS.

etheric /ˈiːθ(ə)rɪk/ *a.* L19. [f. ETHER *n.*[1] + -IC.] Of or pertaining to the ether (ETHER *n.*[1] 3).

Spiritualist What we carry over with us at death is our mind, and . . the etheric body.

Also **eˈtherical** *a.* M17.

etherify /ˈiːθ(ə)rɪfʌɪ/ *v.t.* M19. [f. ETHER *n.*[1] + -I- + -FY.] *Chem.* Convert into an ether.

etherifiˈcation *n.* E19.

etherise *v.* var. of ETHERIZE.

etherism /ˈiːθ(ə)rɪz(ə)m/ *n.* L19. [f. ETHER *n.*[1] + -ISM.] Addiction to ether; the symptoms or state produced by taking ether as a stimulant or intoxicant.

etherize /ˈiːθ(ə)rʌɪz/ *v.t.* Also **-ise**. M18. [f. ETHER *n.*[1] + -IZE.] †1 Electrify. *rare*. Only in M18. 2 Mix with ether, add ether to. Chiefly as *etherized* ppl a. E19. 3 *Chem.* = ETHERIFY. *rare*. E19. 4 Administer ether to; anaesthetize with ether. M19.

etheriˈzation *n.* M19.

Ethernet /ˈiːθənɛt/ *n.* L20. [f. ETHER *n.*[1] + NET(WORK *n.*] *Computing*. A system of communication for local area networks by coaxial cable that prevents simultaneous transmission by more than one station; a network using this.

etheromania /ˌiːθ(ə)rə(ʊ)ˈmeɪnɪə/ *n.* L19. [f. ETHER *n.*[1] + -O- + -MANIA.] Addiction to ether.

etheromaniac *n.* a person so addicted L19.

ethic /ˈɛθɪk/ *n.* LME. [In branch I f. (O)Fr. *éthique*, L *ethice*, Gk (*hē*) *ēthikē* (sc. *tekhnē* art, science); in branch II f. OFr. *éthiques*, med.L *ethica* pl. f. Gk (*ta*) *ēthika*; fem. sing. and neut. pl of Gk *ēthikos*, f. as ETHOS: see -IC, -ICS.] I *sing.* 1 = sense 4 below. Now *rare* or *obs.* LME. 2 A set of moral principles, *esp.* those of a specified religion, school of thought, etc. L19.

2 P. MEDAWAR It is part of the puritan ethic that any activity so pleasurable must be harmful. *Protestant ethic*: see PROTESTANT *a.* *social ethic*: see SOCIAL *a.*

II In *pl.* 3 A treatise on ethics (sense 4 below), *spec.* the one written by Aristotle. LME. 4 Usu. treated as *sing.* The science of morals; the branch of knowledge that deals with the principles of human duty or the logic of moral discourse; the whole field of moral science. L16. 5 The moral principles or system of a particular leader or school of thought; the moral principles by which any particular person is guided; the rules of conduct recognized in a particular profession or area of human life. M17.

4 SITUATION *ethics*. 5 R. W. DALE The ethics of dining. G. B. SHAW The ethics of vivisectionists.

ethic /ˈɛθɪk/ *a.* LME. [Fr. *éthique* or L *ethicus* f. Gk *ēthikos*, f. as ETHOS: see -IC.] 1 = ETHICAL *a.* I. LME. 2 = ETHICAL *a.* 2. L16.

ethical /ˈɛθɪk(ə)l/ *a.* & *n.* E17. [f. prec. + -AL[1].] A *adj.* 1 Of or pertaining to morality or the science of ethics; pertaining to morals. E17. 2 Dealing with the science of ethics or questions connected with it. M17. 3 In accordance with the principles of ethics; morally correct, honourable; conforming to the ethics of a profession etc. L19. 4 Of a medicine or drug: not advertised to the general public, and usu. available only on a doctor's prescription. M20. 5 *Finance*. Designating investment in enterprises whose activities do not offend against the investor's moral principles. L20.

1 J. MACKINTOSH The ethical principles of Hobbes, are completely interwoven with his political system. D. HALBERSTAM A woman with a strong ethical sense. *ethical* RELATIVISM. 2 J. RUSKIN Ethical and imaginative literature. 3 C. BEATON Many buyers . . are eminently ethical and have a respect for the couturier's work. C. POTOK How ethical it was . . to give Danny books to read behind his father's back.

B *n.* An ethical medicine or drug. M20.

ethicalism *n.* devotion to ethical ideals L19. **ethiˈcality** *n.* ethical principles or behaviour; an ethical principle: L19. **ethically** *adv.* M17. **ethicalness** *n.* L17.

ethician /ɛˈθɪʃ(ə)n/ *n.* *rare*. E17. [f. ETHIC *n.* + -IAN.] = ETHICIST.

ethicise *v.* var. of ETHICIZE.

ethicist /ˈɛθɪsɪst/ *n.* L19. [f. ETHIC *n.* + -IST.] An expert in ethics; a writer on ethics; a person who is guided by or adheres to principles of ethics or morality in opposition to religion.

ethicism *n.* devotion to ethics or ethical ideals L19.

ethicize /ˈɛθɪsʌɪz/ *v.* Also **-ise**. E19. [f. as prec. + -IZE.] 1 *v.i.* Discuss ethics; moralize. *rare*. E19. 2 *v.t.* Make ethical, impart an ethical element to. L19.

ethico- /ˈɛθɪkəʊ/ *comb. form*. E18. [Repr. Gk *ēthiko-* comb. form of *ēthikos*: see ETHIC *a.*, -O-.] Forming compound adjs. w. the sense 'ethical and —', as in *ethico-religious*, *ethico-social*, etc.

ethide /ˈɛθʌɪd, ˈiːθ-/ *n.* M19. [f. ETH- + -IDE.] *Chem.* Any binary compound of ethyl.

ethidium /ɛˈθɪdɪəm/ *n.* M20. [f. ETH- + -IDE + -IUM.] *Biochem.* (The cation of) ethidium bromide.

Comb.: **ethidium bromide** a purple derivative of phenanthridine used as a trypanocide, to stain DNA, and to destroy the superhelical structure of DNA.

ethine, **ethinyl** *ns.* vars. of ETHYNE, ETHYNYL.

ethionamide /εθɪˈɒnəmʌɪd/ *n.* M20. [f. ETH- + THIO- + AMIDE.] *Pharm.* An antibiotic, $C_8H_{10}N_2S$, which is active against mycobacteria and has been used to treat tuberculosis.

ethionic /εθʌɪˈɒnɪk/ *a.* M19. [f. ETHER *n.*[1] + THIONIC.] Chem. *ethionic acid*, an acid, $HO_3S{\cdot}C_2H_4{\cdot}O{\cdot}SO_3H$, known only in solution and obtained by the action of water on ethionic anhydride; *ethionic anhydride*, a crystalline cyclic compound, $C_2H_4S_2O_6$, formed by the action of sulphur trioxide on ethylene or ethanol.

ethionine /εˈθʌɪəniːn/ *n.* M20. [f. ETH- after METHIONINE.] *Chem.* An amino acid, $C_6H_{13}NO_2S$, that is the ethyl homologue of methionine and inhibits protein synthesis.

Ethiop /ˈiːθɪɒp/ *n.* & *a. arch.* Also †**Aeth-**. ME. [L *Aethiops*, *Aethiop-* f. Gk *Aithiops*, *Aithiop-* Ethiopian, f. *aithein* to burn + *ōps* face.] A *n.* = ETHIOPIAN *n.* 1. ME.

B *attrib.* or as *adj.* 1 Black. E17. †2 Of or pertaining to Ethiopia. *rare.* Only in M17.

1 KEATS Ivy . . Shading its Æthiop berries.

Ethiopian /iːθɪˈəʊpɪən/ *n.* & *a.* Also †**Aeth-**. ME. [f. *Ethiopia* (see below), *Aethiopia* (f. L *Aethiops*: see prec., -IA[1]) + -AN.] A *n.* 1 A native or inhabitant of Ethiopia, a region, now a country, in NE Africa bordering the Red Sea; *arch.* a Black, a dark-skinned person. ME. 2 An advocate or supporter of Ethiopianism. E20.

B *adj.* 1 Of or pertaining to Ethiopia; *arch.* Black, dark-skinned. L16. 2 Designating a zoogeographic region comprising Africa south of the Sahara. L19. 3 Of or pertaining to Ethiopianism. E20.

1 **Ethiopian serenader** *arch.* a blackface minstrel.

Ethiopianism *n.* a religious movement in sub-Saharan Africa which first appeared in the 1890s and was influenced by Black nationalism E20.

Ethiopic /iːθɪˈɒpɪk/ *a.* & *n.* Also †**Aeth-**. M17. [L *aethiopicus* f. Gk *aithiopikos*, f. *Aithiop-*: see ETHIOP, -IC.] A *adj.* Orig. = ETHIOPIAN *a.* 1. Now, designating the languages Ethiopic and Geez; written in or employing one of these languages. M17. B *n.* Any of several Semitic languages related to Arabic and spoken in Ethiopia and neighbouring areas. Also = GEEZ. E18.

†**Ethiopical** *a.*: only in L16.

†**Ethiops** *n.* Also **Aeth-**. E18–M19. [med.L *aethiops* f. L *Aethiops* ETHIOP *n.*] Any of various black or dark-coloured compounds of metals; *spec.* = *Ethiops mineral* below.

Ethiops martial black iron oxide. **Ethiops mineral** black mercury sulphide.

ethisterone /εˈθɪst(ə)rəʊn/ *n.* M20. [f. ETHYNYL + TESTOSTERONE.] A synthetic progestogen derived from testosterone which is used to treat menstrual disorders.

ethmoid /ˈεθmɔɪd/ *a.* & *n.* M18. [Gk *ēthmoeidēs*, f. *ēthmos* sieve: see -OID.] *Anat.* A *adj.* Of, pertaining to, or designating a bone at the root of the nose forming part of the cranium, with perforations through which pass the olfactory nerves. M18. B *n.* The ethmoid bone. M19.

Also **ethˈmoidal** *a.* M18.

ethnarch /ˈεθnɑːk/ *n.* M17. [Gk *ethnarkhēs*, f. *ethnos* nation + *-arkhēs* -ARCH.] A governor or leader of a nation or people; a ruler of a province.

ethnarchy *n.* (*a*) the province ruled by an ethnarch; (*b*) the position or post of an ethnarch: E17.

ethnic /ˈεθnɪk/ *n.* & *a.* LME. [eccl.L *ethnicus* heathen f. Gk *ethnikos*, f. *ethnos* nation: see -IC.] A *n.* †1 A person who is not a Christian or a Jew; a pagan, a heathen. LME–E18. 2 *Gk Hist.* An epithet that denotes nationality and is derived from or corresponds to the name of a people or city. E19. 3 A member of an ethnic group or minority. Chiefly *N. Amer.* M20.

2 J. A. CRAMER The Greek ethnic of each town or place has been subjoined.

B *adj.* 1 Pertaining to nations neither Christian nor Jewish; pagan, heathen. *arch.* L15. 2 Pertaining to race, ethnological; peculiar to a race or nation; indigenous. M19. 3 (Of a population group) sharing a distinctive cultural and historical tradition, often associated with race, nationality, or religion, by which the group identifies itself and others recognize it; belonging to or characteristic of such a group; *US colloq.* foreign, exotic. M20. b Of music: characteristic of a particular population group, or incorporating elements of this kind. M20.

2 C. THUBRON Within a few years the ethnic Russians . . will be a minority in their own empire. S. FREEDMAN An ethnic Chinese who escaped Vietnam by boat. 3 *Guardian* Ethnic minorities will hopefully be tempted into the force by the fact that a black and female PC is given a starring role. *Daily Telegraph* Problems facing ethnic businessmen. L. DEIGHTON It was a good meal, and not too damned ethnic. **ethnic minority** an ethnic group differing racially or culturally from the rest of the community.

ethnical *a.* †(*a*) pagan, heathenish; (*b*) of or pertaining to race; ethnological: LME. **ethnically** *adv.* L16. **ethnicism** /-sɪz(ə)m/ *n.* †(*a*) paganism, heathenism; a pagan superstition; (*b*) the pagan religions of antiquity; (*c*) consciousness of or emphasis on racial or national identity: E17. **ethnicist** /-sɪst/ *n.* (*a*) an ethnologist; (*b*) a supporter of one of more ethnic groups; (*c*) an enthusiast for the culture, food, dress, etc., of one or more ethnic groups: M19.

ethnicity /εθˈnɪsɪti/ *n.* L18. [f. prec. + -ITY.] †1 Paganism; pagan superstition. *rare.* Only in L18. 2 Ethnic character; the fact or sense of belonging to a particular ethnic group. M20.

2 *Toronto Sun* Kasparov . . is half-Jewish and half-American—an ethnicity more typical of the dominant Soviet players. *Times Educ. Suppl.* Those excluded on grounds of race, ethnicity, and social class.

ethno- /ˈεθnəʊ/ *comb. form.* [f. Gk *ethnos* nation: see -O-.] Nation, people, culture.

ethnoarchaeoˈlogical *a.* of or pertaining to ethnoarchaeology L20. **ethnoarchaeˈologist** *n.* an expert in or student of ethnoarchaeology L20. **ethnoarchaeˈology** *n.* the branch of knowledge that deals with the investigation of the social organization and other ethnological features of a present-day society on the basis of its material culture, in order to draw conclusions about past societies from their material remains M20. **ethnoboˈtanical** *a.* of or pertaining to ethnobotany L19. **ethnoboˈtanically** *adv.* from an ethnobotanical point of view E20. **ethnoˈbotanist** *n.* an expert in or student of ethnobotany M20. **ethnoˈbotany** *n.* the traditional knowledge and customs of a people relating to plants; the branch of knowledge that deals with these: L19. **ethnocentred** *a.* centred on one or more ethnic groups L20. **ethnoˈcentric** *a.* centred on one's own race or ethnic group; based on or characterized by a tendency to evaluate other races or groups by criteria specific to one's own; having assumptions or preconceptions originating in the standards, customs, etc., of one's own race or group: E20. **ethnoˈcentricism** *n.* = ETHNOCENTRICITY L20. **ethnocenˈtricity** *n.* the fact of being ethnocentric; ethnocentric character: M20. **ethnoˈcentrism** *n.* = ETHNOCENTRICITY E20. **ethnocide** *n.* the deliberate and systematic destruction of the culture of an ethnic group, esp. within a larger community L20. **ethnoˈcultural** *a.* pertaining to or having a particular ethnic group L20. **ethnoˈgenesis** *n.* the formation or emergence of an ethnic group within a larger community M20. **ethˈnogeny** *n.* the branch of anthropology that deals with the origin of races, peoples, and nations L19. **ethnohiˈstorian** *n.* an expert in or student of ethnohistory M20. **ethnohiˈstoric**, **-ical** *adjs.* of or pertaining to ethnohistory M20. **ethnoˈhistory** *n.* the branch of knowledge that deals with the history of races and cultures, esp. non-Western ones M20. **ethnoˈlinguist** *n.* an expert in or student of ethnolinguistics M20. **ethnolinˈguistic** *a.* pertaining to ethnolinguistics E20. **ethnolinˈguistics** *n.* the branch of linguistics that deals with the relations between linguistic and cultural behaviour E20. **ethnoˈmedicine** *n.* the branch of knowledge that deals with the traditional medical remedies and lore of a people L20. **ethnomethodoˈlogical** *a.* of or pertaining to ethnomethodology M20. **ethnomethoˈdologist** *n.* an expert in or student of ethnomethodology M20. **ethnomethoˈdology** *n.* a method of sociological analysis that examines how individuals in everyday situations construct and maintain the social order of those situations M20. **ethnomusicoˈlogical** *a.* of or pertaining to ethnomusicology M20. **ethnomusiˈcologist** *n.* an expert in or student of ethnomusicology M20. **ethnomusiˈcology** *n.* the branch of knowledge that deals with the music of cultures, esp. as an aspect of sociocultural behaviour M20. **ethnonym** *n.* a proper name by which a people or ethnic group is known; *spec.* a people's or group's own name for itself: M20. **ethnopharmaˈcology** *n.* the branch of knowledge that deals with the traditional drugs and medicinal substances of a people L20. **ethnophaulism** /-ˈfɔːlɪz(ə)m/ *n.* [Gk *phaulisma* disparagement] an expression that contains a disparaging reference to another people or ethnic group (e.g. *Dutch courage*) or is a contemptuous name for them (e.g. *Dago*) M20. **ethnoscience** *n.* the branch of knowledge that deals with the different ways the world is perceived and categorized in different cultures M20. **ethnoseˈmantic** *a.* of or pertaining to ethnosemantics M20. **ethnoseˈmantics** *n.* the branch of knowledge that deals with the way members of a speech community categorize their experience, as inferred from the semantic organization of vocabulary M20.

ethnography /εθˈnɒgrəfi/ *n.* E19. [f. ETHNO- + -GRAPHY.] The scientific description of races and peoples with their customs, habits, and mutual differences; an example of this.

ethnographer *n.* a person who writes such descriptions; an expert in or student of ethnography: M19. **ethnoˈgraphic**, **-ical** *adjs.* M19. **ethnoˈgraphically** *adv.* in an ethnographical manner; from an ethnographical point of view: M19.

ethnology /εθˈnɒlədʒi/ *n.* M19. [f. ETHNO- + -LOGY.] The branch of knowledge that deals with the characteristics of different peoples and the differences and relationships between them.

ethnoˈlogic, **-ical** *adjs.* M19. **ethnoˈlogically** *adv.* in an ethnological manner; from an ethnological point of view: M19. **ethnologist** *n.* M19.

ethogram /ˈiːθəgram/ *n.* M20. [f. Gk *ēthos* nature or disposition of animals, (in pl.) customs + -GRAM.] (A catalogue of) all the different kinds of behaviour or activity exhibited by an animal.

ethology /iːˈθɒlədʒi/ *n.* M17. [L *ethologia* f. Gk, f. *ēthos*: see ETHOS, -LOGY.] †1 The portrayal of character by mimic gestures, mimicry; an exposition of or treatise on manners. *rare.* M–L17. 2 The science of character formation. M19. 3 The branch of science that deals with animal behaviour, esp. in the wild. L19.

ethoˈlogical *a.* M18. **ethologist** *n.* M18.

ethos /ˈiːθɒs/ *n.* M19. [Gk *ēthos* nature, disposition.] The characteristic spirit of a culture, era, community, institution, etc., as manifested in its attitudes, aspirations, customs, etc.; the character of an individual as represented by his or her values and beliefs; the prevalent tone of a literary work in this respect.

M. SARTON The daring sense that anything could be said . . was surely one of the keys to the Bloomsbury ethos. R. FRY The general atmosphere—the ethos, which the works of art of a period exhale. D. L. EDWARDS Baptist congregations . . providing a . . popular alternative to an Anglicanism still aristocratic in its ethos.

ethosuximide /iːθəʊˈsʌksɪmʌɪd/ *n.* M20. [f. ETH- + -O- + phonet. alt. of SUCCINIMIDE.] 3,3-Ethylmethylsuccinimide, a drug given orally to suppress petit mal seizures.

ethoxide /ɪˈθɒksʌɪd/ *n.* L19. [f. ETHOXY- + -IDE.] *Chem.* A salt or simple compound containing the ethoxyl radical, as *sodium ethoxide*, $NaOC_2H_5$.

ethoxy- /ɪˈθɒksi/ *comb. form.* Also as attrib. adj. **ethoxy**. L19. [f. ETH- + OXY-.] *Chem.* Designating or containing an ethoxyl group.

ethoxyˈethane *n.* = ETHER *n.*[1] 4a L20.

ethoxyl /εˈθɒksʌɪl, -sɪl/ *n.* M19. [f. as prec. + -YL.] *Chem.* The radical $CH_3CH_2O{\cdot}$, derived from ethanol. Usu. in *comb.*

ethoxylated *a.* containing an introduced ethoxyl group M20.

†**ethroclite** *a.* & *n.* see HETEROCLITE.

ethrog *n.* see ETROG *n.*[1]

†**ethrogene** *a.* see HETEROGENE.

ethyl /ˈεθʌɪl, -θɪl, ˈiː-/ *n.* M19. [G, f. *Äther* ether + -YL.] *Chem.* The radical $CH_3CH_2{\cdot}$ derived from ethane, present in ethanol, ether, etc. Usu. in *comb.*

Comb.: **ethyl acetate** a colourless volatile liquid with a fruity smell, $CH_3COOC_2H_5$, used as a solvent; **ethyl alcohol** = ETHANOL; **ethylamine** a strongly basic liquid, $C_2H_5NH_2$; **ethylbenzene** *n.* a colourless liquid, $C_6H_5{\cdot}C_2H_5$, used in the manufacture of styrene; **ethyl chloride** a gas stored under pressure as a colourless flammable liquid and used as a solvent, anaesthetic, and intermediate; **ethyl ether** = ETHER *n.*[1] 4a.

ethylate *v.t.* introduce an ethyl substituent into (a compound) M19. **e'thylic** *a.* M19.

ethylene /'ɛθɪliːn, -θ(ə)l-/ *n.* M19. [f. prec. + -ENE.] A flammable gas, $CH_2{:}CH_2$, present in coal gas, natural gas, and crude oil, given off by ripening fruit, and used as an intermediate and to make polyethylene.

Comb.: **ethylenediamine** a viscous liquid, $(NH_2{\cdot}CH_2{\cdot})_2$, used in making detergents and emulsifying agents (*ethylenediamine tetra-acetic acid* = EDTA s.v. E, E); **ethylene glycol** a sweet-tasting liquid, $(HO{\cdot}CH_2)_2$, used esp. as an antifreeze; **ethylene oxide** a flammable toxic gas, $(CH_2)_2O$, used as an intermediate and fumigant.

ethy'lenic *a.* containing, derived from, or characteristic of ethylene; *spec.* designating a double bond between two carbon atoms: L19. **ethy'lenically** *adv.* in the manner of the ethylene molecule, by virtue of an ethylenic bond M20.

ethylidene /iː'θʌɪlɪdiːn, ɛ'θɪl-/ *n.* M19. [Fr. *éthylydène*, f. *éthylène* ETHYLENE + infixed *-yd-* f. *aldéhyde* ALDEHYDE.] *Chem.* The radical $CH_3C{=}$. Usu. in *comb.*

ethyne /'iːθʌɪn, 'ɛθ-/ *n.* Also **-ine**. L19. [f. ETH- + -INE[5], -YNE.] = ACETYLENE.

ethynyl /'ɛθɪnʌɪl, -nɪl/ *n.* Also **-inyl**. M20. [f. prec. + -YL.] The radical CH⋮C·. Usu. in *comb.*

Comb.: **ethynyloestradiol** a synthetic oestrogen with greater potency than oestradiol.

etic /'ɛtɪk/ *a.* M20. [f. PHONETIC *a.*] Designating a generalized non-structural approach to the description of a particular language or culture. Also (of language or behaviour), not serving to distinguish meaning but conveying information about the particular characteristics of a person. Cf. EMIC.

-etic /'ɛtɪk/ *suff.* [f. or after Gk *-etikos*, *-ētikos*: cf. -IC.] Forming adjs. (and ns.), as *paretic*, *pathetic*, *peripatetic*, *prothetic*, etc. (often corresp. to ns. in *-esis*).

†etik *a.* & *n.* see HECTIC *a.* & *n.*

etin /'iːtɪn/ *n.* Now *Sc.* (*arch.*) [OE *e(o)ten* = ON *jǫtunn* (Sw. *jätte*, Da. *jette*).] A giant.

-etin /'ɛtɪn/ *suff.* [After QUERCETIN.] Forming ns. denoting aglycones, usu. by replacing *-in* in the name of the glycoside from which the aglycone is obtained, as in *phloretin*, *quercetin*, etc.

etiolate /'iːtɪə(ʊ)leɪt/ *v.t.* L18. [Fr. *étioler* f. Normandy Fr. *(s')étieuler* grow into haulm, f. *ét(i)eule* (OFr. *esteule*, *estuble*, mod. *éteule*): see STUBBLE *n.*, -ATE[3].] Make (a plant) pale by excluding light; give a pale and sickly hue to (a person); *fig.* cause to lose vigour or substance. Chiefly as *etiolated* ppl a.

B. ANDERSON Marxist and liberal theory have become etiolated in a late Ptolemaic attempt to 'save the phenomena'.

etio'lation *n.* L18.

etiology *n.* var. of AETIOLOGY.

etiquette /'ɛtɪkɛt, ɛtɪ'kɛt/ *n.* M18. [Fr. *étiquette* TICKET *n.*, etiquette.] **1** The conventional rules of personal behaviour in polite society; the prescribed ceremonial of a court; the formalities required in diplomatic intercourse; the order of procedure established by custom in the armed services, Parliament, etc.; the unwritten code restricting professional persons in what concerns the interests of their colleagues or the dignity of their profession. M18. **†2** A rule of etiquette; an observance prescribed by etiquette. L18–E19. **3** A label. *rare.* M19.

1 JAS. MILL It was to him that, in etiquette, the command of the expedition belonged. R. L. STEVENSON I consulted him upon a point of etiquette: if one should offer to tip the American waiter? DAY LEWIS My father was very much the professional clergyman, having a strong sense of clerical etiquette. **2** M. B. KEATINGE Some of the etiquettes of his majesty's court are rather whimsical.

eti'quettical *a.* M19.

etna /'ɛtnə/ *n.* Also **†aetna**. M19. [An active volcano in Sicily.] A vessel (in the form of an inverted cone placed on a saucer) for heating a small quantity of liquid by burning spirit.

etoile /ɪ'tɔɪl, 'ɛtw(ə)l/ *n.* M18. [Fr.: see ESTOILE.] *Her.* = ESTOILE.

Eton /'iːt(ə)n/ *n.* L19. [*Eton* College, Eng. public school founded by Henry VI on the Thames opposite Windsor.] **1** *Eton blue*, a light blue used as the school colour at Eton. L19. **2** *Eton collar*, a broad and stiff collar worn outside a coat-collar. L19. **3** *Eton jacket*, a short black open-fronted jacket, pointed at the back and cut square at the hips, formerly worn by the younger boys at Eton. L19. **4** In full *Eton suit*, a suit of an Eton jacket with trousers or skirt. L19. **5** *Eton fives*, a form of fives played by pairs in a three-walled court, the design of which is based on an area outside the chapel at Eton. L19. **6** *Eton crop*, a close-cropped style of cutting women's hair. E20.

Etonian /-'təʊnɪən/ *n.* & *a.* (*a*) *n.* a person educated at Eton College; (*b*) *adj.* of, pertaining to, or characteristic of Eton College: M17.

etorphine /ɛ'tɔːfiːn/ *n.* M20. [f. ET(HENE + M)ORPHINE.] A synthetic derivative of morphine used esp. to immobilize large wild animals.

étourderie /eturdəri/ *n.* M18. [Fr., f. next.] Thoughtlessness, carelessness; a thoughtless act, a blunder.

étourdi /eturdi/ *a.* & *n.* Also (fem.) **-ie**. Pl. pronounced same. L17. [Fr., pa. ppl a. of *étourdir* stun, make dizzy.] (A person who is) thoughtless or irresponsible.

étrenne /etrɛn/ *n.* Pl. pronounced same. E19. [Fr. f. OFr. *estreine* ult. f. L *strena*.] A New Year's gift; a Christmas-box.

etrier /'eɪtrɪeɪ; *foreign* etrije (*pl. same*)/. *n.* Also **é-**. M20. [Fr. *étrier* stirrup, etrier.] *sing.* & in *pl.* A short rope ladder with a few solid rungs, used by climbers.

etrog /'ɛtrɒg/ *n.*[1] Also **eth-**, **es-** /'ɛs-/. Pl. **-s**, **-im** /-ɪm/. L19. [Heb. *'eṯrōg*.] A citron fruit as used ritually in the Jewish Feast of Tabernacles.

Etrog /'ɛtrɒg/ *n.*[2] M20. [See below.] Any of the statuettes by the Canadian sculptor S. Etrog (b. 1933), formerly awarded annually for achievement in Canadian film-making.

Etrurian /ɪ'trʊərɪən/ *n.* & *a.* E17. [f. L *Etruria*: see ETRUSCAN *a.*, -AN.] **A** *n.* = ETRUSCAN *n.* 1. E17. **B** *adj.* = ETRUSCAN *a.* 1. E17.

Etruscan /ɪ'trʌsk(ə)n/ *a.* & *n.* E18. [f. L *Etruscus* + -AN.] **A** *adj.* **1** Of or pertaining to (the people of) ancient Etruria, an area of Italy roughly corresponding to present-day Tuscany; of or in the language of ancient Etruria. E18. **2** Designating a kind of encaustic pottery made orig. in the 18th cent. by Josiah Wedgwood in imitation of ancient Etruscan pottery. M18. **3** Designating a style of decorative bookbinding with ornamentation based on the patterns on ancient Etruscan pottery. M19. **B** *n.* **1** A native or inhabitant of ancient Etruria. M18. **2** The language of the Etruscans, not yet deciphered and of unknown affinities. L18.

Etru'scologist *n.* an expert in or student of Etruscology L19. **Etru'scology** *n.* the branch of knowledge that deals with Etruscan history and antiquities L19.

-ette /ɛt/ *suff.* [Repr. OFr. fem. *-ette*: see -ET[1].] Forming ns. w. the senses 'small', as *cigarette*, *kitchenette*; 'imitation or substitute', as *flannelette*, *leatherette*; 'female', as *suffragette*, *usherette*.

ettle /'ɛt(ə)l/ *v.* & *n.* Chiefly & now only *Sc.* & *north.* ME. [ON *ætla* (also *etla*, *atla*) think, conjecture, purpose, destine, apportion, f. Gmc (whence OE *eaht*, OHG *ahta*, G *Acht* consideration) f. base also of Goth. *aha* mind, *ahma* spirit.] **A** *v.* **I 1** *v.t.* Intend, purpose, plan, attempt, (a thing, *to do*). ME. **†b** Arrange; prepare. ME–E16. **2** *v.t.* Destine, ordain, assign. ME. **3** *v.i.* Direct one's course; set out (*for*). ME. **b** Aim *at*, make an effort *at*; take aim (*at*, *for*). E18. **4** *v.t.* Aim (a blow, a missile) *at* a person or target (*lit.* & *fig.*); direct (speech, actions) to an object. LME. **II 5** *v.t.* Guess, conjecture; expect, anticipate. ME. **B** *n.* **1** Chance, opportunity. M18. **2** Aim, intent, purpose. L18.

étude /'eɪtjuːd, eɪ'tjuːd; *foreign* etyd (*pl. same*)/ *n.* M19. [Fr.: see STUDY *n.*] An instrumental piece, esp. for the piano, which concentrates on a particular aspect of technique or allows a display of virtuosity.

etui /ɛ'twiː/ *n.* Also **etwee**. E17. [Fr. *étui*, OFr. *estui* prison, f. OFr. *estuier* shut up, keep, save. Cf. STEW *n.*[2], TWEE *n.*[1], TWEEZE *n.*, TWEEZER.] A small usu. ornamental case for needles etc. Formerly also, a case for surgical instruments.

-etum /'iːtəm/ *suff.* Pl. **-etums**, **-eta** /'iːtə/. L17. [L *-etum* neut. of *-etus*.] Forming ns. denoting: (*a*) a collection or plantation of different plants of a group, as ARBORETUM, PINETUM; (*b*) *Ecol.* an association dominated by the species or genus from which it is named.

etwee *n.* var. of ETUI.

-ety *suff.* see -ITY.

etymologicon /ˌɛtɪmə'lɒdʒɪkɒn/ *n.* M17. [mod.L f. Gk *etumologikon*, neut. sing. (sc. *biblion* book) of *etumologikos* pertaining to etymology, f. *etumologos*: see ETYMOLOGY, -IC.] A book in which etymologies are traced and recorded; an etymological dictionary.

etymologize /ɛtɪ'mɒlədʒʌɪz/ *v.* Also **-ise**. M16. [med.L *etymologizare*, f. L *etymologia*: see next, -IZE.] **1** *v.t.* Give or suggest an etymology or derivation for. M16. **2** *v.i.* Study etymology; search into the origins of words; give or suggest etymologies for words. M17.

etymologi'zation *n.* (*rare*) L15.

etymology /ɛtɪ'mɒlədʒi/ *n.* LME. [OFr. *ethimologie* (mod. *étymologie*) f. L *etimologia* (med.L *ethymologia*, *ethim-*) f. Gk *etumologia*, f. *etumologos* student of etymology, f. *etumon*: see next, -OLOGY.] **1** An account of, or the facts relating to, the formation or development of a word and its meaning; the process of tracing the history of a word. LME. **†b** The original meaning of a word as shown by its etymology. L16–E18. **2** The branch of grammar that deals with the way individual words are inflected. *arch.* L16. **3** The branch of linguistics that deals with the etymologies of words. M17.

1 FOLK *etymology*.

etymologer *n.* = ETYMOLOGIST E17. **ˌetymo'logic** *a.* = ETYMOLOGICAL E19. **ˌetymo'logical** *a.* of or pertaining to etymology; in accordance with etymology: L16. **ˌetymo'logically** *adv.* in an etymological manner, according to the principles of etymology M18. **etymologist** *n.* M17.

etymon /'ɛtɪmɒn/ *n.* Pl. **-mons**, **-ma** /-mə/. L16. [L f. Gk *etumon* use as n. of neut. sing. of *etumos* true.] **†1** The original form of a word; the word or combination of words from which a given word has been corrupted. L16–L18. **†2** The original or primary meaning of a word. *rare.* E17–M19. **3** A word from which some given word is derived by borrowing, modification, etc. M17.

eu- /juː/ *pref.* [Repr. Gk *eu-*, f. *eu* well, f. *eus* good.] Used chiefly in wds derived f. Gk or formed on Gk analogies w. the senses 'good, well' or (*Med.*) 'normal' (opp. DYS-).

eubac'terial *a.* of, pertaining to, or involving eubacteria L20. **eubac'terium** *n.*, pl. **-ria**, (*a*) a bacterium of the genus *Eubacterium*, which includes anaerobic rods occurring in the intestines of vertebrates, animal and plant products, tissue infections, and soil; (*b*) a true bacterium as distinct from an archaebacterium: M20. **eucaine** *n.* [after *cocaine*] a synthetic derivative of piperidine formerly used as a local anaesthetic L19. **euca'tastrophe** *n.* a happy ending in a story, a sudden or unexpected coming right of events M20. **eu'centric** *a.* (of an electron microscope stage) having the field and focus unchanged when the specimen is tilted L20. **eu'chlorine** *n.* an explosive gas composed of chlorine and chlorine dioxide E19. **euchro'matic** *a.* (*Biol.*) staining like euchromatin M20. **eu'chromatin** *n.* (*Biol.*) chromosome material that stains normally, i.e. diffusely when the nucleus is not dividing, and is genetically active M20. **eucone** *a.* (of the eyes of certain insects) having a crystalline cone L19. **eugeo'clinal** *a.* (*Geol.*) = EUGEOSYNCLINAL L20. **eugeocline** *n.* (*Geol.*) = EUGEOSYNCLINE L20.

eugeosyn'clinal *a.* (*Geol.*) of or pertaining to a eugeosyncline M20. **eugeo'syncline** *n.* (*Geol.*) a geosyncline containing volcanic rocks and a greater depth of sediment than a miogeosyncline M20. **eu'globulin** *n.* (*Biochem.*) the fraction of serum globulin which is insoluble in pure water E20. **eu'hedral** *a.* (of a mineral crystal in a rock) bounded by its proper faces, unrestrained by the proximity of adjacent crystals E20. **eu'photic** *a.* pertaining to or designating the upper layers of a body of water, where enough light penetrates for photosynthesis E20. **eupnoea** /juːp'niːə/ *n.* [Gk *pnoē* breathing] natural or normal breathing E18. **eupnoeic** /juːp'niːɪk/ *a.* characterized by eupnoea; (of breathing) natural, normal: E20. **eu'social** *a.* (*Zool.*) showing an advanced level of social organization, in which a single female or caste produces the offspring and non-reproductive individuals cooperate in caring for the young M20. **eustele** *n.* (*Bot.*) a stele, characteristic of gymnosperms and dicotyledons, in which the vascular tissue is in separate strands in which the phloem occurs on one side or both sides of the xylem E20. **eu'stelic** *a.* (*Bot.*) having a eustele M20. **eu'thyroid** *a.* (*Med.*) having a normally functioning thyroid gland M20. **eu'thyroidism** *n.* (*Med.*) euthyroid state E20.

eubages *n.pl.* var. of EUHAGES.

Euboic /juː'bəʊɪk/ *a.* L16. [L *Euboicus* f. Gk *Euboikos*, f. *Euboia* Euboea: see below, -IC.] Of or belonging to Euboea, the largest of the Greek islands after Crete.

Euboic talent a weight in use at the time of the Persian war.

Also **Euboean** /juː'biːən/ *a.* L17.

eucalypt /'juːkəlɪpt/ *n.* L19. [Abbrev.] = EUCALYPTUS 1.

eucalyptus /juːkə'lɪptəs/ *n.* Pl. **-tuses, -ti** /-tʌɪ/. E19. [mod.L, f. Gk EU- + *kaluptos* covered, f. *kaluptein* cover, conceal; so called from the unopened flower and its protective covering.] 1 Any of the genus *Eucalyptus* of flowering evergreen trees and shrubs, of the myrtle family, including species important as forest trees in Australia and grown elsewhere for their hardwood, oils, gums, and resins, and as ornamentals. E19. 2 In full *eucalyptus oil*. Any essential oil from eucalyptus leaves, used esp. in pharmacy, flavourings, and perfumery. L19.

eucalyptian *a.* L19. **eucalyptic** *a.* M19. **eucalyptol** *n.* a volatile essential oil, 1,8-cineole, present in the oils of eucalyptus, cajuput, wormseed, and lavender L19.

eucaryotic *a.* var. of EUKARYOTIC.

eucharis /'juːkərɪs/ *n.* M19. [Gk *eukharis* gracious, f. as EU- + *kharis* grace.] Any of the Central and S. American genus *Eucharis* of evergreen bulbous plants, of the amaryllis family, grown in hothouses for their large white bell-shaped flowers.

Eucharist /'juːk(ə)rɪst/ *n.* Also **e-**. LME. [OFr. *eucariste* (mod. *eucharistie*) f. eccl.L *eucharistia* f. eccl.Gk *eukharistia* giving of thanks, (earlier) gratitude, f. Gk *eukharistos* grateful, f. as EU- + *kharizesthai* show favour, give freely, f. *kharis* grace.] I *Chr. Ch.* 1 One of the sacraments, the central act of Christian worship, in which bread and wine are consecrated and consumed as Christ's body and blood, to be a memorial of his sacrifice on the Cross; a service or rite in which this is done. LME. †2 A pyx. LME-M16. 3 The consecrated Eucharistic elements, *esp.* the bread. M16.

1 *Church Times* Members . . want to supplement the conventional Eucharists with a service which will attract newcomers. G. WAINWRIGHT The volume . . lists some thirty Lutheran Eucharists.

II *gen.* 4 Thanksgiving. E17.

eucha'ristize *v.t.* consecrate (bread or wine) in a Eucharist E18.

Eucharistic /juːkə'rɪstɪk/ *n.* & *a.* Also **e-**. E17. [f. prec. + -IC.] †A *n.* = EUCHARIST 4. E17-E18. B *adj.* 1 Of or pertaining to the Eucharist, or thanksgiving generally. M17. 2 Of the nature of or resembling the Eucharist. M19.

Eucharistical *a.* = EUCHARISTIC *a.* 1, 2 M16. **Eucharistically** *adv.* M17.

Euchite /'juːkʌɪt/ *n.* L16. [Late L *euchita*, *eucheta* f. Gk *eukhitēs*, *eukhētēs*, f *eukhē* prayer: see -ITE[1].] A member of a 4th-cent. Christian sect which believed that salvation could be gained only through incessant prayer.

Euchologion /juːkə'ləʊdʒɪən, -'lɒdʒ-/ *n.* Also **Euchology** /juː'kɒlədʒi/, **e-**. M17. [Gk *eukhologion*, f. *eukhē* prayer: see -OLOGY.] A book of prayers or religious rites; *spec.* a book of the Orthodox Church containing the Eucharistic rites and other liturgical matter.

euchre /'juːkə/ *n.* & *v.* E19. [G dial. *Jucker(spiel)*.] A *n.* 1 A card-game for 2 to 4 players in which the highest cards are the joker (if used), the jack of trumps, and the other jack of the same colour in a pack with the lower cards removed, the aim being win at least three of the five tricks played. E19. 2 An instance of euchring or being euchred. M19.

B *v.t.* 1 Prevent (a bidder) from winning three or more tricks at euchre, thereby scoring points oneself. E19. 2 Cheat, trick, (*into*, *out of*); deceive, outwit. M19. 3 Exhaust; ruin, finish, do for, (a person). Usu. in *pass. Austral.* M20.

2 T. PYNCHON They have euchred Mexico into some such Byzantine exercise. 3 K. S. PRICHARD I've got to get water for me horses . . or we're euchred.

euclase /'juːkleɪz/ *n.* E19. [Fr., f. Gk EU- + *klasis* breaking (so called from its brittleness).] *Min.* A hydrated basic silicate of beryllium and aluminium occurring as pale monoclinic crystals sometimes valued as gems.

Euclid /'juːklɪd/ *n.* L16. [Gk *Eukleidēs*, a mathematician of Alexandria, fl. 300 BC.] (A copy of) the works of Euclid, esp. *The Elements*, long the principal textbook of geometry.

Euclidean /juː'klɪdɪən/ *a.* Also **-ian**. E18. [f. L *Euclideus*, Gk *Eukleideios* (f. as prec.) + -EAN, -IAN.] Of or pertaining to Euclid; that is according to the principles of Euclid.

Euclidean geometry the geometry of ordinary experience, based on the axioms of Euclid, esp. the one stating that parallel lines do not meet. **Euclidean space**: that of ordinary experience, for which Euclidean geometry holds.

eucomis /'juːkəmɪs/ *n.* E19. [mod.L (see below), f. Gk *eukomēs* beautiful-haired, f. as EU- + *komē* hair.] Any of various bulbous African plants of the genus *Eucomis*, of the lily family, having the flower-spike crowned by large leaflike bracts. Also called *pineapple lily*.

eucrasia /juː'kreɪsɪə, -zɪə/ *n.* LME. [med.L f. Gk *eukrasia* good temperament, f. as EU- + *krasis* CRASIS: see -IA[1].] A good or normal state of health. Orig., a well-balanced mixture of bodily humours.

eucrasy /'juːkrəsi/ *n.* Long *rare* or *obs.* E17. [f. prec.: see -Y[3].] = prec.

†eucratic *a.* LME-L18. [f. Gk *eukratos*, f. *eukrasia*: see EUCRASIA, -IC.] Having good and bad points, with the good predominating.

eucrite /'juːkrʌɪt/ *n.* M19. [f. Gk *eukritos* easily discerned, f. as EU- + *kritos* separated, f. *krinein* to separate: see -ITE[1].] 1 *Geol.* A highly basic gabbro containing anorthite or bytownite, together with augite. M19. 2 An achondritic stony meteorite composed principally of anorthite and augite. L19.

†euctical *a.* M17-M18. [f. Gk *euktikos* f. *eukhesthai* pray f. *eukhē* prayer, + -AL[1].] Pertaining to prayer; supplicatory.

eudaemon *n.*, **-daemonic** *a.*, etc., vars. of EUDEMON etc.

eudaimonia /juːdʌɪ'mɒnɪə/ *n.* E20. [Gk, f. as EUDEMON: see -IA[1]. Cf. EUDEMONY.] *Philos.* Happiness or well-being consisting in the full realization of human potential, esp. (in Aristotle's ethics) in rational activity exhibiting excellence.

eudaimonism *n.* var. of EUDEMONISM.

eudemon /juː'diːmən/ *n.* Also **-daem-**. E17. [Gk *eudaimōn* fortunate, happy, f. as EU- + *daimōn* genius, DEMON *n.*[1]] 1 = AGATHODEMON. E17. 2 The eleventh of the twelve astrological houses. L17.

eudemonic /juːdiː'mɒnɪk/ *a.* Also **-daem-**. M19. [Gk *eudaimonikos*, f. EUDAIMONIA: see -IC.] Conducive to happiness.

eudemonics /juːdiː'mɒnɪks/ *n.pl.* (treated as *pl.* or *sing.*). Also **-daem-**. M19. [f. as prec.: see -ICS.] The art of pursuing life with happiness as the ultimate goal.

eudemonism /juː'diːmənɪz(ə)m/ *n.* Also **-daem-, -daim-**. E19. [f. as EUDEMON + -ISM.] An ethical system based on the view that the aim of moral action is personal fulfilment and well-being.

eudemonist *n.* & *a.* (*a*) *n.* a believer in eudemonism; (*b*) *adj.* = EUDEMONISTIC: E19. **eudemo'nistic** *a.* of or pertaining to eudemonism or eudemonists M19.

eudemony /juː'diːməni/ *n. rare.* Also **-daem-**. M18. [f. Gk EUDAIMONIA: see -Y[3].] Happiness; *spec.* = EUDAIMONIA.

eudiometer /juːdɪ'ɒmɪtə/ *n.* L18. [f. Gk *eudios* fine (of weather), f. as EU- + *dios* heavenly, genit. of *Zeus* god of the sky: see -OMETER. So called because an increase in the oxygen content of the air was formerly thought to accompany fine weather.] Orig., an instrument for measuring the oxygen content of the air. Now, any instrument for measuring and analysing gases by volume; *spec.* a graduated glass tube in which gases are chemically combined by a spark between two terminals.

,eudio'metric *a.* M19. **,eudio'metrical** *a.* L18. **,eudio'metrically** *adv.* E19. **eudiometry** *n.* E19.

Eudist /'juːdɪst/ *n.* & *a.* L19. [f. *Eudes* (see below) + -IST.] A *n.* A member of the Congregation of Jesus and Mary, founded for secular clergy by St Jean Eudes (1601-80), French missioner, and now concerned chiefly with secondary education in France, Canada, etc. L19. B *adj.* Of, pertaining to, or designating the Eudists. E20.

eufunctional /juː'fʌŋkʃ(ə)n(ə)l/ *a.* M20. [f. EU- + FUNCTIONAL *a.*] That performs a function well.

Euganean /juː'geɪnɪən/ *a.* & *n.* E17. [f. It. *Euganei* f. L, a people of northern Italy: see -EAN.] A *adj.* Designating a group of hills south-west of Padua. E17. B *n.* In *pl.* The Euganean Hills. L19.

euge /'juːdʒi/ *n.* Now *rare* or *obs.* M17. [L f. Gk = well done!] An expression of approval, a commendation.

eugenesis /juː'dʒɛnɪsɪs/ *n.* L19. [f. EU- + -GENESIS.] The production of fit and healthy offspring, esp. by deliberate outbreeding or selection of individuals.

euge'nesic, euge'netic *adjs.* L19.

eugenia /juː'dʒiːnɪə/ *n.* L18. [mod.L (see below), f. Prince *Eugene* of Savoy (1663-1736), Austrian general.] Any of various mostly tropical American trees of the genus *Eugenia*, of the myrtle family.

eugenic /juː'dʒɛnɪk/ *a.* L19. [f. as next + -IC.] Of or pertaining to eugenics.

eugenically *adv.* E20. **eugenicist** /-sɪst/ *n.* an expert in, or a student or advocate of, eugenics E20. **eugenist** *n.* & *a.* (*a*) *n.* = EUGENICIST; (*b*) *adj.* = EUGENIC: E20.

eugenics /juː'dʒɛnɪks/ *n.* L19. [f. EU- + -GEN + -ICS.] The science dealing with factors that influence the hereditary qualities of a race and with ways of improving these qualities, esp. by modifying the fertility of different categories of people.

negative eugenics: see NEGATIVE *a.* *positive eugenics*: see POSITIVE *a.*

eugenol /'juːdʒɪnɒl/ *n.* L19. [f. EUGENIA + -OL.] A liquid phenol, $C_{10}H_{12}O_2$, present in many essential oils, esp. clove oil; 4-allyl-2-methoxyphenol.

Euglena /juː'gliːnə/ *n.* M19. [mod.L (see below), f. EU- + Gk *glēnē* eyeball, socket of joint.] A single-celled freshwater flagellate of the genus *Euglena* (variously classed as a protozoan and an alga), which can form a green scum on stagnant water.

euglenoid *n.* & *a.* (*a*) *n.* a flagellate of the order containing *Euglena*, comprising mostly green or colourless organisms with one or two flagella and a gullet reservoir; (*b*) *adj.* resembling or characteristic of *Euglena* or a euglenoid (*euglenoid movement*, a rhythmical movement in which waves of expansion and contraction pass along the body): L19.

euhages /juːˈheɪɡiːz/ *n.pl.* Also **-bages** /-ˈbeɪɡiːz/. E17. [L, alt. of Gk *ouateis*: see OVATE *n.*[1] Cf. VATES.] Ancient Celtic priests or natural philosophers.

euhemerism /juːˈhiːmərɪz(ə)m/ *n.* M19. [f. L *Euhemerus* f. Gk *Euēmeros*, Sicilian writer (*c*316 BC) who maintained that the gods and goddesses of Gk mythol. were deified men and women: see -ISM.] The interpretation of myths as traditional accounts of real historical events and people.
euhemerist *n.* & *a.* (*a*) *n.* a euhemeristic person; (*b*) *adj.* = EUHEMERISTIC: M19. **euhemeˈristic** *a.* inclined to euhemerism; exhibiting or characterized by euhemerism: M19. **euhemerize** *v.* (*a*) *v.t.* subject to a euhemeristic interpretation; (*b*) *v.i.* follow the euhemeristic method of interpretation: M19.

eukaryotic /juːkarɪˈɒtɪk/ *a.* Also **-cary-**. M20. [f. EU- + Gk *karuon* nut, kernal + *ōtēs* -OT[2].] *Biol.* (Of a cell) characterized by a discrete nucleus with a membrane, and other organelles; (of an organism) composed of such cells, belonging to the group which includes most organisms other than bacteria; of or pertaining to a eukaryotic cell or organism.
ˈeukaryote *n.* a eukaryotic organism (opp. PROKARYOTE) M20.

eulachon /ˈjuːləkɒn/ *n.* Also **oolichan** /ˈuːlɪkən/ and other vars. M19. [Lower Chinook *ú̜ł̣xan*.] A small oily food fish, *Thaleichthys pacificus*, of the Pacific coast of N. America, belonging to the smelt family. Also called *candle-fish*.

Euler /ˈɔɪlə/ *n.* M19. [L. *Euler* (1707–83), Swiss mathematician.] Used *attrib.* and in *possess.* with ref. to Euler's discoveries in mathematics.
Euler's constant the limit as *n* tends to infinity of $1 + \frac{1}{2} + \frac{1}{3} + \ldots + \frac{1}{n} - \ln n$ (approximately 0.57715). **Euler's formula** or **theorem** any of various formulae and theorems arrived at by Euler, esp. $V + F - E = 2$, where *V*, *F*, and *E* are the numbers of vertices, faces, and edges of any simple convex polyhedron.
Eulerian /-ˈlɪərɪən/ *a.* L19.

eulogia /juːˈləʊdʒɪə, ɛvləˈɡiːə/ *n.* Pl. **-iae** /-iiː/. M18. [Late (eccl.) L = consecrated bread f. eccl.Gk = blessing, praise, f. Gk: see EULOGY.] *Eccl.* = ANTIDORON. Also, consecrated bread reserved for communicating those not present at the Eucharist.

eulogic /juːˈlɒdʒɪk/ *a. rare.* M18. [f. EULOGY + -IC.] = EULOGISTIC.
eulogically *adv.* M17.

eulogise *v.* var. of EULOGIZE.

eulogium /juːˈləʊdʒɪəm/ *n.* E17. [med.L = praise, app. blending of L *elogium* inscription on a tomb (see ELOGIUM) and med.L *eulogia* (see EULOGY).] = EULOGY 2.

eulogize /ˈjuːlədʒʌɪz/ *v.t.* Also **-ise.** E19. [f. next + -IZE.] Deliver or write a eulogy on; extol.
R. HAYMAN Lectures.. which tended to denigrate Czech achievements while eulogizing the primacy of German culture.
eulogizer *n.* a eulogist E19.

eulogy /ˈjuːlədʒi/ *n.* LME. [f. med.L *eulogium*, *eulogia* praise, f. Gk *eulogia*, f. as EU-, -LOGY.] 1 High praise. LME. 2 A speech or piece of writing in praise of a person or thing, esp. a person who has recently died. L16. †3 *Eccl.* = EULOGIA. Only in 18.
2 P. G. WODEHOUSE He embarked forthwith on an eulogy of his late playmate.
eulogism *n.* = EULOGY 2 M18. **eulogist** *n.* a person who delivers or writes a eulogy E19. **euloˈgistic** *a.* of the nature of a eulogy, laudatory (foll. by *of*) E19. **euloˈgistically** *adv.* M19.

Eumenides /juːˈmɛnɪdiːz/ *n.pl.* L17. [(L f.) Gk, f. *eumenēs* well-disposed, friendly, f. as EU- + *menos* spirit.] The Greek Furies.

eunomia /juːˈnəʊmɪə/. *n.* M19. [Gk, f. as EU- + *-nomia*: see -NOMY. Cf. EUNOMY.] A political condition of good law well administered.

Eunomian /juːˈnəʊmɪən/ *n.* & *a.* LME. [f. *Eunomius* (see below) + -AN.] *Eccl.* A *n.* A follower of Eunomius, 4th-cent. bishop of Cyzicus on the Sea of Marmara, who developed an extreme form of Arianism. LME. B *adj.* Of or pertaining to Eunomius or Eunomians. L18.

eunomic /juːˈnɒmɪk/ *a.* M20. [f. EUNOMIA + -IC.] Law-abiding; socially well ordered.

eunomy /ˈjuːnəmi/ *n. rare.* E18. [f. Gk EUNOMIA: see -Y[3].] = EUNOMIA.

eunuch /ˈjuːnək/ *n.* & *v.* OE. [L *eunuchus* f. Gk *eunoukhos* = bedroom guard, f. *eunē* bed + forms of *ekhein* keep.] A *n.* 1 A castrated man; such a man employed as a harem attendant or (*Hist.*) charged with important affairs of state in Mediterranean countries. OE. 2 *fig.* A person or thing with some kind of incapacity, specified or implied; an ineffectual person. L16. 3 = CASTRATO. M18.
1 GIBBON The private apartments of the palace were governed by a favourite eunuch. 2 BYRON The intellectual eunuch Castlereagh.
Comb.: **eunuch flute** *Hist.* a tubular musical instrument which produces notes from a membrane vibrated by the human voice.
B *v.t.* = EUNUCHIZE. Now *rare.* E17.
eunuchism *n.* the process or custom of making eunuchs; the condition of being a eunuch; emasculation: E17. **eunuchize** *v.t.* castrate; reduce to the condition of a eunuch; emasculate (*lit.* & *fig.*): M17. **eunuchry** *n.* (*rare*) the state of being a eunuch M19.

eunuchoid /ˈjuːnəkɔɪd/ *a.* & *n.* L19. [f. prec. + -OID.] A *adj.* Resembling or having the characteristics of a eunuch; having reduced sexual characteristics. L19. B *n.* A eunuchoid person. L19.
eunuˈchoidal *a.* M20. **eunuchoidism** *n.* E20.

euonymus /juːˈɒnɪməs/ *n.* M18. [mod.L (Linnaeus) f. L *euonymos* (Pliny) use as n. of Gk *euōnumos* having an honoured or auspicious name, f. as EU- + *onuma* name: see -NYM.] Any of various shrubs and small trees of the genus *Euonymus* (family Celastraceae), which includes the spindle tree, *E. europaeus*.

Eupad /ˈjuːpad/ *n.* E20. [f. *E*dinburgh *U*niversity *P*athological *D*epartment (where it was invented), w. joc. ref. to EU- and PAD *n.*[3], as = good pad.] *Pharm.* An antiseptic dry dressing of chlorinated lime mixed with boric acid.

eupathy /ˈjuːpəθi/ *n.* E17. [Gk *eupatheia* happy condition of the soul, f. as EU- + base of *pathos* feeling: see PATHOS, -Y[3].] In Stoic philosophy, each of three rational dispositions of the mind (joy, caution, and will).

eupatorium /juːpəˈtɔːrɪəm/ *n.* M16. [mod.L f. Gk *eupatorion* agrimony, *Agrimonia eupatoria*, f. Mithridates *Eupator* (120–63 BC), king of Pontus: see -IUM.] Any of various plants of the genus *Eupatorium*, of the composite family, largely of tropical America but including one British native, the hemp agrimony, *E. cannabinum*.

†eupatory *n.* LME–M17. [L *eupatoria* f. Gk *eupatorion*: see prec., -Y[3].] Hemp agrimony (see prec.). Formerly also, wood-sage, *Teucrium scorodonia*.

eupatrid /juːˈpatrɪd, ˈjuːpətrɪd/ *n.* & *a.* Pl. **eupatrids, eupatridai** /juːˈpatrɪdʌɪ/, **eupatridae** /juːˈpatrɪdiː/. M19. [Gk *eupatridēs* person of noble ancestry, f. as EU- + *patēr* father.] A *n.* In ancient Greece, a member of the hereditary aristocracy of Athens; *gen.* a person of noble descent. M19. B *adj.* Of, pertaining to, or belonging to the eupatrids. M19.

eupepsia /juːˈpɛpsɪə/ *n.* E18. [Gk *eupepsia* digestibility, f. *eupeptos*: see next, -IA[1].] Good digestion; absence of indigestion.

eupeptic /juːˈpɛptɪk/ *a.* L17. [f. Gk *eupeptos* easy to digest, having a good digestion, f. as EU- + *peptein* to digest: see -IC.] †1 Helping digestion. *rare.* Only in L17. 2 Having good digestion. M19. 3 Characteristic of or resulting from good digestion. M19. b Cheerful, well-disposed, optimistic. M20.
3 CARLYLE A massiveness of eupeptic vigour.
eupeptically *adv.* M20. **eupepˈticity** *n.* the condition resulting from good digestion M19.

euphausiid /juːˈfɔːzɪɪd/ *n.* & *a.* Also **-sid** /-zɪd/. L19. [f. mod.L *Euphausia* genus name, f. Gk EU- + *phainein* to show + *ousia* substance: see -ID[3].] (Of, pertaining to, or designating) any of a group of marine shrimplike, planktonic, mostly luminescent, malacostracan crustaceans that includes krill.
euphausiacean *n.* a member of the order or suborder Euphausiaceae of euphausiids M20.

euphemious /juːˈfiːmɪəs/ *a. rare.* M19. [f. Gk *euphēmos*: see EUPHEMISM, -IOUS.] 1 = EUPHEMISTIC. M19. 2 Considered respectable. M19.
euphemiously *adv.* M19.

euphemise *v.* var. of EUPHEMIZE.

euphemism /ˈjuːfɪmɪz(ə)m/ *n.* Also (now *rare*) in late L form **euphemismus** /juːfɪˈmɪzməs/. L16. [Gk *euphēmismos*, f. *euphēmizein* speak fair, f. *euphēmos* fair of speech, f. as EU- + *phēmē* speaking: see -ISM.] 1 A figure of speech in which an offensive, harsh, or blunt word or expression is avoided and one that is milder but less precise or accurate is used instead. L16. 2 The milder word or expression used in an instance of euphemism. L18.
2 T. PYNCHON 'Foreign workers', a euphemism for civilian prisoners brought in from countries under German occupation.
euphemist *n.* a person who uses euphemisms M19.

euphemistic /juːfɪˈmɪstɪk/ *a.* M19. [f. prec.: see -IST, -IC.] Pertaining to euphemism; of the nature of a euphemism; containing a euphemism.
euphemistical *a.* L19. **euphemistically** *adv.* by way of euphemism M19.

euphemize /ˈjuːfɪmʌɪz/ *v.t.* & *i.* Also **-ise.** M19. [Gk *euphēmizein*: see EUPHEMISM, -IZE.] Speak or write (of) euphemistically.
euphemizer *n.* L19.

euphenics /juːˈfɛnɪks/ *n.* M20. [f. EU- + PHEN(OTYPE + -ICS.] The improvement of the bodily functioning or development of a person by medical or other means.
euphenic *a.* M20.

euphonia /juːˈfəʊnɪə/ *n.* Now *rare.* L16. [Late L: see EUPHONY, -PHONIA.] = EUPHONY.

euphonic /juːˈfɒnɪk/ *a.* M18. [f. EUPHONY + -IC.] 1 Of or pertaining to euphony. M18. 2 = EUPHONIOUS. E19.
euphonical *a.* M17. **euphonically** *adv.* M19.

euphonious /juːˈfəʊnɪəs/ *a.* L18. [f. as prec. + -IOUS.] Full of or characterized by euphony; pleasing to the ear.
A. S. BYATT I want a name like Bowen, or Sackville ..; euphonious but plain.
euphoniously *adv.* M19.

euphonise *v.* var. of EUPHONIZE.

euphonism /ˈjuːf(ə)nɪz(ə)m/ *n.* Also in L form **†euphonismus.** L18. [f. as EUPHONY + -ISM.] The habit of using euphonious words; a euphonious expression.
euphoˈnistic *a.* chosen with regard to euphony; aiming to be euphonious: M19.

euphonium /juːˈfəʊnɪəm/ *n.* M19. [f. Gk *euphōnos*: see EUPHONY, -IUM.] A valved brass wind instrument of tenor-bass pitch, used especially in brass and military bands.

euphonize /ˈjuːf(ə)nʌɪz/ *v.t.* Also **-ise.** L18. [f. EUPHONY + -IZE.] Make euphonious; alter (a word) for the sake of euphony.
euphoniˈzation *n.* L19.

euphonon /juːˈfəʊnɒn/ *n.* E19. [Gk *euphōnon* neut. of *euphōnos*: see EUPHONY.] An obsolete musical instrument which resembled the upright piano in form and the organ in tone.

euphonous /ˈjuːf(ə)nəs/ *a.* E19. [f. next + -OUS.] = EUPHONIOUS.

euphony /ˈjuːf(ə)ni/ *n.* LME. [Fr. *euphonie* f. late L *euphonia* f. Gk *euphōnia*, f. *euphōnos* well-sounding, f. as EU-: see -PHONY. Cf. EUPHONIA.] 1 The quality, esp. of spoken words, of having a pleasant sound; the pleasing effect of sounds free from harshness. LME. 2 *Philol.* The tendency to phonetic change giving easier pronunciation. L19.
1 J. I. M. STEWART 'Albert Talbert' is lacking in euphony and even a shade ludicrous.

euphorbia /juːˈfɔːbɪə/ *n.* LME. [Alt. (by assim. to -IA[1]) of L *euphorbea*, f. *Euphorbus* (fl. 1st cent. BC), physician to Juba II, king of Mauretania.] Any herb or shrub of the genus *Euphorbia* (family Euphorbiaceae); = SPURGE *n.*
ˌeuphorbiˈaceous *a.* of or pertaining to the family Euphorbiaceae M19.

For other words beginning with *eu-* see the entry for **eu-**

euphorbium /juːˈfɔːbɪəm/ *n.* ME. [L *euphorbeum, -bium* f. Gk *euphorbion*, f. *Euphorbus*: see prec., -IUM.] 1 The resinous gum of certain succulent plants of the genus *Euphorbia*, formerly used as an emetic and purgative. ME. †2 = EUPHORBIA. E17–M18.

euphoria /juːˈfɔːrɪə/ *n.* Also (now *rare*) **euphory** /ˈjuːf(ə)ri/. L17. [mod.L f. Gk, f. *euphoros* borne well, healthy, f. as EU- + *pherein* to bear: see -IA[1], -Y[3].] Orig., a state of well-being, esp. as produced in a sick person by a medicine. Now, a strong feeling of well-being, cheerfulness, and optimism, *esp.* one based on overconfidence or overoptimism; a mood marked by this, as symptomatic of a mental illness or the influence of drugs.

W. STYRON Cans of beer . . helped perpetuate my euphoria.

euphoriant *n.* & *a.* (a drug) inducing euphoria M20. **euphoric** /-ˈfɒrɪk/ *a.* & *n.* (*a*) *adj.* accompanied or characterized by euphoria; elated, ecstatic; (*b*) a euphoriant: L19. **euphorically** *adv.* M20.

euphrasia /juːˈfreɪzɪə/ *n.* E18. [med.L f. Gk, lit. 'cheerfulness', f. *euphrainein* gladden, f. as EU- + *phrēn* mind.] Any plant of the genus *Euphrasia*, of the figwort family; *esp.* = *eyebright* s.v. EYE *n.*

euphrasy /ˈjuːfrəzi/ *n. arch.* LME. [Anglicized f. med.L EUPHRASIA.] = *eyebright* s.v. EYE *n.*

Euphratean /juːˈfreɪtɪən/ *a.* L19. [f. *Euphrates* (see below) + -AN.] Of, pertaining to, or bordering on the River Euphrates, a long river of SW Asia that flows into the Persian Gulf.

euphuism /ˈjuːfjuːɪz(ə)m/ *n.* L16. [f. *Euphues*, a fictional character (see below), f. Gk *euphuēs* well-endowed by nature, f. as EU- + *phu-* (= be) in *phuē* growth: see -ISM.] 1 A literary and conversational style imitative of that found in John Lyly's *Euphues* (1578–80), which was fashionable in the late 16th and early 17th cents. and is characterized by an abundance of antitheses, alliteration, and similes referring to natural history and mythology; any artificial and affected style; high-flown language. L16. 2 An instance of euphuism; a euphuistic expression. L19.

euphuist *n.* a person who uses euphuism L16. **euphuˈistic(al)** *adjs.* E19. **euphuˈistically** *adv.* M19.

eupione /ˈjuːpɪəʊn/ *n.* Now *rare.* M19. [Gk *eupiōn* very fat, f. as EU- + *piōn* fat; assim. to -ONE.] A volatile oily liquid obtained by the distillation of wood, tar, etc.

euploid /ˈjuːplɔɪd/ *a.* E20. [f. as EU- + -PLOID.] *Genetics.* Having an equal number of all the chromosomes of the haploid set.

euploidy *n.* euploid condition E20.

Eur- *comb. form* see EURO-.

Eurafrican /jʊ(ə)rˈafrɪk(ə)n/ *a.* & *n.* Also (exc. in sense A.1) **Euro-African** /jʊərəʊ-/. L19. [f. EURO- + AFRICAN.] A *adj.* 1 *Anthropol.* Designating a dark-skinned people supposed to have inhabited regions on both sides of the Mediterranean. L19. 2 Of or pertaining to both Europe and Africa, or countries or people of both continents. E20. 3 Of mixed European and (Black) African descent; *spec.* designating Coloured people in South Africa. E20. B *n.* A Eurafrican person (see sense A.3 above). E20.

euraquilo /jʊ(ə)rˈakwɪləʊ/ *n.* Also **euroaquilo** /jʊ(ə)rəʊˈakwɪləʊ/. L16. [L *euroaquilo* north-east wind, f. as EURUS + *aquilo* N wind.] A stormy north-east or NNE wind blowing in the eastern Mediterranean. Cf. EUROCLYDON.

Eurasian /jʊ(ə)ˈreɪʃ(ə)n, -ʒ(ə)n/ *a.* & *n.* M19. [Partly f. EURO- + ASIAN, partly f. *Eurasia* Europe and Asia together: see -AN.] A *adj.* 1 Of mixed European and Asian (formerly esp. Indian) descent. M19. 2 Of or pertaining to Europe and Asia considered as one continent. M19. B *n.* A person of mixed European and Asian (formerly esp. Indian) descent. M19.

Eurasiatic /jʊ(ə)r,eɪʃɪˈatɪk, -eɪʒ-/ *a.* & *n.* Also **Euro-Asiatic** /jʊərəʊeɪʃ-/. M19. [f. EURO- + ASIATIC.] A *adj.* = EURASIAN *a.* 2. M19. B *n.* A person of Eurasiatic origin. M20.

Euratom /jʊ(ə)rˈatəm/ *n.* M20. [f. *European Atomic Energy Community.*] An international organization (now administratively part of the European Community) established in 1958 to coordinate the development and use of nuclear energy in some European countries.

eureka /jʊ(ə)ˈriːkə/ *int.* & *n.* Also **E-**. E17. [Gk *heurēka*, 1st person sing. pf. of *heuriskein* find: uttered by Archimedes when he hit upon a method of determining the purity of gold.] A *int.* Expr. exultation at a sudden discovery. E17. B *n.* 1 A cry of *eureka!* M17. 2 A fortunate discovery. M19. 3 (**E-**.) (Proprietary name for) an alloy of copper and nickel used for electrical filament and resistance wire. E20.

eurhythmic /jʊ(ə)ˈrɪðmɪk/ *a.* In sense 2 also ***eury-**. M19. [Partly f. EURHYTHMY + -IC, partly back-form. f. next.] 1 Of, pertaining to, or having harmonious proportions or regularity. M19. 2 Involving eurhythmics. E20.

eurhythmical *a.* = EURHYTHMIC 2 E20. **eurhythmist** *n.* a person who practises or advocates eurhythmics E20.

eurhythmics /jʊ(ə)ˈrɪðmɪks/ *n.* Also ***eury-**. E20. [f. EU- + RHYTHM + -ICS.] A system of dance or rhythmical bodily movements, seeking to express the content of a piece of music or poetry, freq. used for educational and therapeutic purposes.

eurhythmy /jʊ(ə)ˈrɪðmi/ *n.* In sense 2 also ***eury-**. L16. [L *eur(h)ythmia* proportion f. Gk *euruthmia*, f. as EU- + *rhuthmos* proportion, RHYTHM: see -Y[3].] 1 Harmonious proportions, esp. in a building; symmetry; regularity. L16. 2 = EURHYTHMICS. M20.

euriballi *n.* var. of JURIBALLI.

Euripidean /jʊ(ə),rɪpɪˈdiːən/ *a.* E19. [f. L *Euripideus* f. Gk *Euripideios*, f. *Euripidēs* (see below): see -AN.] Of, pertaining to, or characteristic of the Athenian tragic poet Euripides (484–406 BC), or his works, style, etc.

euripus /jʊ(ə)ˈrʌɪpəs/ *n.* Pl. **-pi** /-ʌɪ/. L16. [L = strait (esp. that between Euboea and the mainland of Greece), canal f. Gk *euripos*, f. as EU- + *rhipē* a rushing.] †1 Rapid inhalation and exhalation during the use of tobacco. *rare.* Only in L16. 2 A strait or sea-channel with strong or irregular currents. E17. 3 An artificial channel; a canal. M18.

euro /ˈjʊərəʊ/ *n.*[1] *Austral.* Also **uroo, yuro.** Pl. **-os.** M19. [Aborig.] The wallaby *Macropus robustus.*

Euro /ˈjʊərəʊ/ *n.*[2] & *a. colloq.* L20. [Abbrev. of EUROPEAN.] A *n.* Pl. **-os.** 1 A European. Also, a Eurocommunist. L20. 2 = EUROBOND, EURODOLLAR. L20. B *adj.* Of, pertaining to, or characteristic of (esp. Western) Europe or its inhabitants. L20.

Euro- /ˈjʊərəʊ/ *comb. form.* Bef. a vowel also **Eur-** /jʊ(ə)r/. [f. *Europe*, EUROPEAN: see -O-.] Forming ns. and adjs. w. ref. to (*a*) Europe as a continent or a collection of countries; (*b*) the European Community (EC) or the European Parliament, as *Euro-candidate, Euro-election*, etc.; (*c*) money and securities held outside their country of origin, as *Euro-credit, Eurofinance.*

Euro-Aˈmerican *a.* & *n.* (*a*) *adj.* of or pertaining to both Europe and America; (*b*) *n.* a person with both European and American connections; a Westerner: E20. **Eurobabble** *n.* (*colloq.*) = EUROSPEAK L20. **Eurobond** *n.* an international bond issued outside the country in whose currency its value is stated M20. **Euroˈcentric** *a.* = EUROPOCENTRIC M20. **Eurocenˈtricity, Euroˈcentrism** *ns.* = EUROPOCENTRISM L20. **Eurocheque** *n.* a collaborative banking arrangement enabling account-holders from one European country to use their cheques in another; a cheque issued under this arrangement: M20. **Euroˈcommunism** *n.* a form of Communism in western European countries emphasizing acceptance of democratic institutions and independence of Soviet influence L20. **Euroˈcommunist** *n.* & *a.* (*a*) *n.* an adherent of Eurocommunism; (*b*) *adj.* of or pertaining to Eurocommunism or Eurocommunists: L20. **Euˈrocracy** *n.* (*colloq.*) government by Eurocrats L20. **Eurocrat** *n.* (*colloq.*) a bureaucrat of any of various European organizations, esp. the European Community M20. **Euro-currency** *n.* money held outside the country (usu. the US or Japan) in whose currency its value is stated M20. **Eurodollar** *n.* a US dollar deposited or held outside the US (not necessarily in Europe) L20. **Euromarket** *n.* (*a*) the Common Market of the European Community; (*b*) the European money market; the market of a particular Euro-currency: M20. **Euromissile** *n.* a medium-range nuclear weapon deployed in Europe L20. **Euro-MP** /jʊərəʊemˈpiː/ *n.* a Member of the European Parliament L20. **Euroˈparliament** *n.* the European Parliament L20. **Europarliamenˈtarian** *n.* = EURO-MP L20. **Europarliaˈmentary** *a.* of or pertaining to the European Parliament L20. **Eurosceptic** *n.* a person who is not enthusiastic about increasing the powers of the European Community L20. **Eurospeak** *n.* the allegedly unattractive language used by Eurocrats L20. **Eurostraˈtegic** *a.* relating to defence strategy in Europe; *spec.* (of nuclear weapons) designed for deployment and use within Europe, having a strike capability limited to Europe: L20. **Euroˈsummit** *n.* a summit meeting of European Community heads of government L20. **Eurovision** *n.* Europe-wide television provided by the collaboration of European broadcasting networks M20.

Euro-African *a.* & *n.* see EURAFRICAN.

euroaquilo *n.* var. of EURAQUILO.

Euro-Asiatic *a.* & *n.* var. of EURASIATIC.

euroclydon /jʊ(ə)rˈɒklɪd(ə)n/ *n.* E17. [New Testament Gk *eurokludōn*, f. Gk *Euros* (see EURUS) + *kludōn* wave, billow.] = EURAQUILO; any tempestuous wind.

Europaeo- /jʊərəˈpiːəʊ/ *comb. form.* Also **-peo-**. [f. L *Europaeus* European + -O-.] Of or pertaining to Europe and, as *Europaeo-Asiatic* etc.

European /jʊərəˈpiːən/ *n.* & *a.* L16. [Fr. *européen*, f. L *europaeus*, f. *Europa* Europe f. Gk *Eurōpē*: see -EAN.] A *n.* 1 A native or inhabitant of the continent of Europe. L16. 2 A person of European descent living outside Europe; a White person, esp. in a country with a non-White population. L17. 3 A person concerned with Europe as a whole; *spec.* an advocate of membership of the European Community. M20.

3 A. F. DOUGLAS-HOME Harold Macmillan had always been a keen European.

B *adj.* 1 Of, pertaining to, or characteristic of the continent of Europe or its inhabitants. E17. 2 Occurring in or extending over Europe. M17. 3 Concerned with Europe as a whole rather than its individual countries, *spec.* designating various economic and defence organizations or unions of western Europe. L19.

1 J. CONRAD He had the pose of a Buddha preaching in European clothes. **European plan** *N. Amer.* a method of charging for a hotel room exclusive of meals. 3 G. MEREDITH I am neither German nor French nor . . English. I am European and Cosmopolitan. **European Community** the association of countries formed in 1967 from the European Economic Community, the European Coal and Steel Community, and Euratom. **European Court** (*a*) the European Court of Human Rights, set up by the Council of Europe to enforce its European Convention on Human Rights; (*b*) the Court of Justice of the European Community, with jurisdiction created by the treaties of its predecessor Communities and compulsory in States which expressly accept it. **European Currency Unit** a notional unit of currency used within the European Monetary System and in trading Eurobonds. **European Economic Community** an economic and political association of certain European countries as a unit with internal free trade and common external tariffs; the Common Market. **European Monetary System** a system by which the exchange rates of some European Community countries are kept within certain limits in relation to each other and to the average of all European Community currencies. **European Parliament** the principal representative and consultative body of the European Community.

Europeanly *adv.* M19.

Europeanise *v.* var. of EUROPEANIZE.

Europeanism /jʊərəˈpiːənɪz(ə)m/ *n.* E19. [f. EUROPEAN + -ISM.] 1 Something peculiar to or characteristic of Europe or Europeans; European behaviour, culture, etc. E19. 2 (Advocacy of) the ideal of a unified Europe; *spec.* support for the European Community. M20.

Europeanist *n.* & *a.* (a person) advocating a unified Europe or supporting the European Community M20.

Europeanize /jʊərəˈpiːənʌɪz/ *v.t.* Also **-ise** L18. [f. as prec. + -IZE.] Make European in appearance, form, manner, or extent.
Listener These cards contain pictures of.. Europeanised biblical scenes.
Europeaniˈzation *n.* L19.

Europeo- *comb. form* var. of EUROPAEO-.

europium /jʊ(ə)rˈəʊpɪəm/ *n.* E20. [f. *Europe* + -IUM.] A metallic chemical element of the lanthanide series, atomic no. 63. (Symbol Eu.)

Europocentric /jʊ(ə),rəʊpə(ʊ)ˈsɛntrɪk/ *a.* M20. [f. *Europe* + -O- + -CENTRIC.] Having or regarding Europe as its centre; presupposing the supremacy of Europe and Europeans in world culture etc.
Europocenˈtricity, Europocentrism *ns.* the condition of being Europocentric; a Europocentric doctrine: M20.

eurus /ˈjʊərəs/ *n.* Long *rare.* LME. [L f. Gk *Euros.*] The east or south-east wind; (E-) the god of the east or south-east wind.

eury- /ˈjʊəri/ *comb. form* of Gk *eurus* wide. Opp. STENO-.
euryˈbathic *a.* [Gk *bathos* depth] (of aquatic life) capable of living at varying depths E20. **euryhaline** /-ˈheɪlʌɪn, -ˈheɪliːn/ *a.* [Gk *halinos* of salt] *Biol.* tolerating a wide range of salinity L19. **euryˈhydric** *a.* (*Biol.*) tolerating a wide range of humidity M20. **euˈryphagous** *a.* (*Zool.*) capable of feeding on a wide range of items E20. **eurytherm, euryˈthermal** *adjs.* (*Biol.*) able to tolerate a wide range of temperature L19. **euryˈthermic** *a.* = EURYTHERMAL E20. **euryˈthermous** *a.* = EURYTHERMAL M20. **eurytope** *n.* (*Ecol.*) a eurytopic organism L19. **euryˈtopic** *a.* (*Ecol.*) (of an organism) tolerating a wide range of types of habitat or ecological conditions M20.

eurypterid /jʊ(ə)ˈrɪptərɪd/ *n.* L19. [f. mod.L *Eurypterus* genus name, f. EURY- + Gk *pteron* wing: see -ID[3].] Any of the Eurypterida, extinct aquatic arthropods of Palaeozoic times, similar to scorpions but often larger and with a terminal pair of paddle-shaped appendages.

eurythmic *a.*, **eurythmics** *n.*, etc. see EURHYTHMIC etc.

Eusebian /juːˈsiːbɪən/ *a.* & *n.* L17. [f. *Eusebius* (see sense 2 below) + -AN.] **A** *adj.* †**1** Designating some kind of pear. Only in L17. **2** Of or pertaining to any of various early Christian saints and bishops called Eusebius; *spec.* designating the Arians of the 4th cent. AD, who included Eusebius of Nicodemia (d. *c*342) and Eusebius of Caesarea (*c*260–*c*340). M19.
2 **Eusebian canons** tables compiled by Eusebius of Caesarea to illustrate the parallelism between corresponding passages in the different Gospels.
B *n. Hist.* A member of the Eusebian Arians. M18.

Euskarian /juːˈskɛːrɪən/ *a.* & *n.* M19. [f. Basque *Euskara, Eskuara, Uskara* the Basque language + -IAN.] **A** *adj.* Basque; *esp.* in ethnology, designating pre-Aryan characteristics in Europeans supposedly typified by the Basques. M19. **B** *n.* A Basque person. L19.

Eusol /ˈjuːsɒl/ *n.* Also **e-**. E20. [f. *E*dinburgh *U*niversity *sol*ution, after EUPAD.] *Pharm.* An antiseptic solution of chlorinated lime and boric acid.

Eustachian /juːˈsteɪʃ(ə)n/ *a.* M18. [f. *Eustachius*, Latinized form of the name of Bartolomeo *Eustachio* (d. 1574) + -AN.] *Eustachian tube*, the passage running through the temporal bone and connecting the middle ear and the nasopharynx, by virtue of which the air pressure is the same on both sides of the tympanum.

eustasy /ˈjuːstəsi/ *n.* M20. [Back-form. f. next, after mod.L *-stasis* corresp. to *-static*: see -Y[3].] *Geogr.* A uniform worldwide change of sea level.

eustatic /juːˈstatɪk/ *a.* E20. [f. as EU- + STATIC.] *Geogr.* Accompanying or forming part of a worldwide change of sea level.
eustatically *adv.* M20.

Euston Road /juːstən ˈrəʊd/ *a. phr.* M20. [A road in London, site of a former School of Drawing and Painting (1938–9).] Designating a group of English post-impressionist realistic painters of the 1930s and their type of art.

eustyle /ˈjuːstʌɪl/ *a.* & *n.* L17. [L *eustylos* f. Gk *eustulos* with pillars well placed, f. as EU- + *stulos* pillar.] *Archit.* **A** *adj.* Of a building, colonnade, etc.: having the spaces between columns equal to 2¼ or 2½ times their diameters. L17. **B** *n.* The distance between columns in a eustyle structure. M19.

eusuchian /juːˈsjuːkɪən/ *n.* & *a.* L19. [f. mod.L *Eusuchia* (see below), f. as EU- + Gk *soukhos* crocodile: see -IAN.] **A** *n.* A crocodile of the suborder Eusuchia, which includes the only extant members of the order Crocodylia. L19. **B** *adj.* Of, pertaining to, or designating this suborder. L19.

eutaxitic /juːtakˈsɪtɪk/ *a.* L19. [f. EU- + Gk *taxis* arrangement + -ITE[1] + -IC.] *Petrogr.* Having or designating a banded rock structure.

eutaxy /ˈjuːtaksi/ *n.* Long *rare.* E17. [Fr. *eutaxie* f. Gk *eutaxia*, f. as EU- + -TAXY.] Good or established order or arrangement.

eutectic /juːˈtɛktɪk/ *n.* & *a.* L19. [f. Gk *eutēktos* easily melting, f. as EU- + *tēkein* melt: see -IC.] **A** *n.* **1** A mixture whose constituents are in such proportions that it melts and solidifies at a single temperature that is lower than the melting point of the constituents or any other mixture of them. L19. **2** A eutectic point. M20.
B *adj.* Of, pertaining to, or designating a eutectic, its melting point, or the point representing its melting point in a phase diagram. L19.
A. H. COTTRELL This is the ternary eutectic point at which the liquid is in equilibrium with all three solids.
eutecˈtiferous *a.* giving rise to or having a eutectic E20. **eutectoid** *n.* & *a.* (pertaining to or designating) a solid analogous to a eutectic, having a minimum transformation temperature between a solid solution and a mechanical mixture of solids E20.

euthanasia /juːθəˈneɪzɪə/ *n.* E17. [Gk, f. as EU- + *thanatos* death: see -IA[1].] **1** A gentle and easy death. E17. **2** A means of bringing about such a death (chiefly *fig.*, *of* something). M18. **3** The action of bringing about such a death, esp. of a person who requests it as a release from incurable disease. M19.
2 D. HUME Absolute monarchy.. is.. the true *Euthanasia* of the British constitution.
euthanasiac *a.* L20. **euthanasian** *a.* L19. **euˈthanatize** *v.t.* (*rare*) = EUTHANIZE L19. **ˈeuthanize** *v.t.* subject to euthanasia; put (an animal) to death humanely: L20.

euthanasy /juːθəˈneɪzi/ *n.* Now *rare.* M17. [Anglicized f. prec.: see -Y[3].] = EUTHANASIA 1.

euthenics /juːˈθɛnɪks/ *n.* E20. [f. Gk *euthēneein* thrive + -ICS.] The science or art that deals with improving the conditions of life and the environment as an aid to human well-being.

eutherian /juːˈθɪərɪən/ *a.* & *n.* L19. [f. mod.L *Eutheria* (see below), f. as EU- + Gk *thēria* pl. of *thērion* wild animal: see -AN.] (Pertaining to or designating) an animal of the infraclass Eutheria, comprising all mammals which develop a placenta (as opp. to marsupials and monotremes).

Eutopia /juːˈtəʊpɪə/ *n.* M16. [mod.L, f. Gk EU- + *topos* place: see -IA[1]. First used with a play on UTOPIA.] A place of ideal happiness or good order.
¶Often wrongly regarded as the correct form of UTOPIA, which has largely superseded it.

eutrapelia /juːtrəˈpiːlɪə/ *n.* M20. [Gk, f. *eutrapelos* pleasant in conversation, f. as EU- + *trepein* to turn: see -IA[1].] Wit, repartee; liveliness; urbanity.
†**eutrapely** *n.* (*rare*) eutrapelia; reprehensible levity: L16–L17.

eutrophic /juːˈtrəʊfɪk, -ˈtrɒf-/ *n.* & *a.* L19. [f. (as) next + -IC.] **A** *n.* A medicine that promotes good nutrition. *rare.* L19. **B** *adj.* Of a lake, swamp, etc.: rich in organic or mineral nutrients, *esp.* so rich that the resultant growth and decay of algae and other plants depletes the oxygen content significantly. M20.
eutrophicate *v.t.* make (more) eutrophic M20. **ˌeutrophiˈcation** *n.* the process of becoming eutrophic M20.

eutrophy /ˈjuːtrəfi/ *n.* E18. [Gk *eutrophia*, f. as EU- + -TROPHY.] **1** Good nutrition. *rare.* Only in E18. **2** The state of being eutrophic. M20.

Eutychian /juːˈtɪkɪən/ *n.* & *a.* LME. [eccl.L *Eutychianus*, f. *Eutyches*, Gk *Eutukhēs*: see -IAN.] *Eccl. Hist.* **A** *n.* A follower of the doctrine of Eutyches (*c*378–454), who held that the human nature of Christ was lost in the divine. LME. **B** *adj.* Of, pertaining to, or adhering to the doctrine of Eutyches. L16.
Eutychianism *n.* the Eutychian doctrine E17.

euxenite /ˈjuːksɪnʌɪt/ *n.* M19. [f. as EU- + Gk *xenos* stranger: see -ITE[1]. So named from its containing many rare constituents.] *Min.* A niobate and tantalate of yttrium and other rare earth elements and uranium, occurring as brownish-black orthorhombic crystals in granite pegmatites.

evacuable /ɪˈvakjʊəb(ə)l/ *a.* M20. [f. EVACUATE + -ABLE.] Able to be evacuated.

evacuant /ɪˈvakjʊənt/ *n.* & *a.* M18. [L *evacuant-* pres. ppl stem of *evacuare*: see next, -ANT[1].] **A** *n.* A medicine that induces some kind of bodily discharge, as defecation, vomiting, or sweating; *esp.* a purgative. M18. **B** *adj.* Having the property of an evacuant. E19.

evacuate /ɪˈvakjʊeɪt/ *v.* Pa. pple **-ated**, †**-ate**. LME. [L *evacuat-* pa. ppl stem of *evacuare* empty (bowels), (in late L) nullify, (in med.L) remove (contents), f. *e-* E- + *vacuus* empty: see -ATE[3].] **1** *v.t.* Empty, clear out the contents of (esp. the bowel or other bodily organ); produce a vacuum in (a vessel). Formerly, deplete (a person) of bodily humours or (the body) of blood, sweat, etc. LME. **b** Empty *of* contents; *fig.* deprive *of* value or force. L16. †**2** *v.t.* Esp. of a medicine or a medical regimen: eliminate from the body (harmful matter, a disease). LME–L18. †**3** *v.t.* Chiefly *Theol.* & *Law.* Make void, annul. E16–L18. **4** *v.t.* & *i.* Excrete (faeces); discharge (ingested material) through the bowel; *gen.* discharge, give off. Formerly, discharge (any matter) from the body or a part of it. E17. †**b** *v.i.* Of air, water, etc.: escape, empty out. M17–E19. **5** *v.t.* Clear (a building) of occupants. Formerly also, clear (a country or region) of or *of* inhabitants, troops, etc. E17. **6** *v.t.* Remove (inhabitants, inmates, troops), esp. to a place of safety from a place that has become dangerous. M17. **7** *v.t.* & *i.* a *Mil.* (Cause to) relinquish the occupation of (a country, town, position, etc.). E18. **b** *gen.* Withdraw from, leave, (premises etc.). E19. **8** *v.t.* Remove (fluid contents) so as to leave a void. *obs.* exc. *Surg.* E18.
1 E. LINKLATER They also chronicled.. a boil evacuated in October of the same year. b A. W. HADDAN To evacuate the sacraments of grace, and to regard them as merely acted prayers. 4 D. L. SAYERS Where arsenic was taken with.. a meal, nearly the whole of it would be evacuated within twenty-four hours. 5 *New York Times* The warning calls had enabled the police to evacuate the building before the explosion. 6 P. H. GIBBS I am in charge of a contingent of nurses and nuns just evacuated from the Belgian front. T. GUNN During the Blitz I was evacuated to a school in the country. 7 J. CONRAD He had had a lot to do with royalists.. after Toulon was evacuated. N. GORDIMER It had been forced to evacuate and was operating from some temporary hideout. b *Fortune* Flanders has evacuated her house to rent it to the Reagan staff for $5,500 a month. *Washington Post* 22 miles downstream,.. 1,200 of 3,600 residents have evacuated.
evacuator *n.* E17.

evacuation /ɪˌvakjʊˈeɪʃ(ə)n/ *n.* LME. [Late L *evacuatio(n-)*, f. as prec.: see -ATION.] **1** The action or an act of evacuating; *spec.* (*a*) defecation; (*b*) the removal of the contents, esp. air, from a vessel; (*c*) the withdrawal of troops; the removal of occupants or inhabitants. LME. †**2** The action of making invalid; cancelling, nullification; refutation. M16–M18. **3** A quantity of evacuated or excreted matter. E17.
1 attrib.: *Arizona Daily Star* Nuclear refugees at an evacuation center.

evacuative /ɪˈvakjʊətɪv/ *a.* E17. [Fr. *évacuatif*, *-ive*, f. *évacuer* f. L *evacuare* EVACUATE: see -IVE.] Tending to cause evacuation; of or pertaining to evacuation.

For other words beginning with *en* see the entry for **en-**

evacuee /ɪˌvakjuːˈiː/ *n.* Orig. in Fr. form ***évacué***, (fem.) **-ée**, /evakɥe/. E20. [Fr. *évacué* pa. ppl a. of *evacuer* f. L *evacuare* EVACUATE: see -EE[1].] A person who has been evacuated.

evade /ɪˈveɪd/ *v.* L15. [Fr. *évader* f. L *evadere*, f. *e-* E- + *vadere* go.] **1** *v.t.* Escape by contrivance from (attack, adverse designs, a pursuer, etc.); avoid, elude. L15. **2** *v.i.* Get away, escape. (Foll. by *from*, *out of*.) Now *rare*. E16. **3** *v.t.* Contrive to avoid (esp. a duty; *doing*); avoid giving a direct answer to (a question, a questioner); escape yielding to (an argument, obligation, etc.) by means of sophistry; defeat the intention of (a law, stipulation, etc.). E17. **4** *v.i.* Practice evasion. E18. **5** *v.t.* Of things: elude, baffle (efforts, power, etc.). E18.

3 C. IVES An opportunity for evading a question somewhat embarrassing to answer. G. GREENE Clues which point to James having evaded military service with insufficient excuse. A. BURGESS The novelist who lives abroad is trying to evade taxation or bad weather. C. P. SNOW Now he could evade talking about himself. 5 H. G. WELLS Emotion that evades definition.

evadable *a.* M19. **evader** *n.* M18. **evadingly** *adv.* in an evading manner, evasively M19.

evagation /iːvəˈɡeɪʃ(ə)n/ *n.* L15. [Fr. *évagation* or L *evagatio(n-)*, f. *evagat-* pa. ppl stem of *evagari*, f. *e-* E- + *vagari* wander: see -ATION.] †**1** Wandering of the thoughts, spirit, etc. L15–L17. **2** A digression in speech or writing. M17. **3** The action of wandering away or of departing from a locality, course, etc.; (an instance of) rambling, roving. E18.

evaginate /ɪˈvadʒɪneɪt/ *v.t.* M17. [L *evaginat-* pa. ppl stem of *evaginare* unsheath, f. *e-* E- + *vagina* sheath: see -ATE[3].] **1** Unsheath. *rare*. Only in M17. **2** *Med.* Turn (a tubular organ) inside out; evert. M17.

evagiˈnation *n.* (*a*) the action of evaginating; (*b*) an evaginated portion: M17.

evaluate /ɪˈvaljʊeɪt/ *v.t.* M19. [Back-form., after (O)Fr. *évaluer*, f. next: see -ATE[3].] **1** Work out the numerical value or equivalent of; find a numerical expression for. M19. **2** *gen.* Ascertain the amount or value of; appraise, assess. L19.

2 J. S. HUXLEY To read all previous work on the subject, in order to evaluate one's own results correctly.

evaluable *a.* L19. **evaluator** *n.* M20.

evaluation /ɪˌvaljʊˈeɪʃ(ə)n/ *n.* M18. [f. (O)Fr. *évaluation*, f. *évaluer*, f. *é-* (f. as ES-) + OFr. *value*: see VALUE *n.*, -ATION.] **1** The action of valuing in monetary terms; a calculation or statement of value; (a) valuation. Now *rare*. M18. **2** The action or an act of evaluating; (an) assessment of worth. L18.

2 E. BAKER My opinion of the manuscript can be accepted as a general evaluation of the writer's ability.

evaluative /ɪˈvaljʊətɪv/ *a.* E20. [f. EVALUATE + -IVE.] Expressing, constituting, or providing a judgement as to the value of something; designed or serving to evaluate.

New York Times Viewers have become increasingly evaluative, judgmental and critical of the programming. *English World-Wide* Pupils took part in an evaluative test.

evanesce /iːvəˈnɛs, ɛv-/ *v.i.* M19. [L *evanescere*, f. *e-* E- + *vanus* empty: see -ESCE.] Pass out of existence, disappear.

C. P. SNOW I felt the burden of worry evanesce.

evanescent /iːvəˈnɛs(ə)nt, ɛv-/ *a.* E18. [f. L *evanescent-* pres. ppl stem of *evanescere*: see prec., -ESCENT.] **1** On the point of vanishing or becoming imperceptible; too small to perceive. E18. **2** That quickly vanishes or passes away; having no permanence. M18. **b** *Bot.* Of a part of a plant: not permanent. L18.

2 L. EDEL Seeking to find words that would convey elusive and evanescent thought.

evanescence *n.* the process or fact of vanishing away; the quality of being evanescent: M18. **evanescently** *adv.* M19.

evangel /ɪˈvan(d)ʒɛl, -(d)ʒ(ə)l/ *n.*[1] *arch.* Also **-gile** /-(d)ʒɪl/. ME. [(O)Fr. *évangile* f. eccl.L *evangelium* f. Gk *euaggelion* (in eccl. use) good news, (in cl.Gk) reward for bringing good news, f. *euaggelos* bringing good news, f. as EU- + *aggelein* announce.] **1** The message of redemption of the world through Christ; the religious teaching contained in the New Testament; the Christian religion. ME. **2a** The record of Christ's life as contained in the four Gospels. LME. **b** Any of the Gospels. LME. **3** A copy of the Gospels, esp. as used in taking an oath. Usu. in *pl.* LME. †**4** Something confidently asserted or taken to be true. Only in 17. **5** A political or social creed regarded as in some way analogous to a doctrine of salvation. M19. **6** A message of good news. M19.

1 SIR W. SCOTT That worthy man . . teacheth the Evangel in truth and sincerity.

evangel /ɪˈvan(d)ʒɛl, -(d)ʒ(ə)l/ *n.*[2] L16. [Gk *euaggelos*: see prec.] An evangelist; *fig.* a person with a message to communicate.

New Yorker The people will take it as a 'message of solidarity' from the human-rights evangel.

Evangeliary /iːvanˈdʒɛlɪəri/ *n.* Also in L form **Evangeliarium** /iːvandʒɛlɪˈɛːrɪəm/, pl. **-ria** /-rɪə/. M19. [eccl.L *evangeliarium*, f. *evangelium*: see EVANGEL *n.*[1], -ARY[1].] = EVANGELISTARY.

evangelic /iːvanˈdʒɛlɪk, ɛv-/ *a.* & *n.* L15. [eccl.L *evangelicus* f. eccl.Gk *euaggelikos*, f. Gk *euaggelos*: see EVANGEL *n.*[1], -IC.] **A** *adj.* **1a** = EVANGELICAL *a.* 1b. L15. **b** Of or pertaining to the Gospel narrative or the four Gospels. L16. **2** (Usu. **E-**.) **a** = EVANGELICAL *a.* 2a. L16. **b** = EVANGELICAL *a.* 2b. E19. †**B** *n.* (Usu. **E-**.) = EVANGELICAL *n.* E17–E19.

evangelical /iːvanˈdʒɛlɪk(ə)l, ɛv-/ *a.* & *n.* M16. [f. prec. + -AL[1].] **A** *adj.* †**1a** = EVANGELIC *a.* 1b. M16–M18. **b** Of, pertaining to, or in accordance with the teaching of the gospel or the Christian religion. M16. **2** (Usu. **E-**.) a Protestant; *spec.* of or designating certain Churches in Europe (esp. that in Germany) which are, or were originally, Lutheran rather than Calvinistic. M16. **b** Of, pertaining to, characteristic of, or designating the school of Protestants which lays particular stress on salvation by faith in the atoning death of Christ, and denies that good works and the sacraments have any saving efficacy. L18. **3** Of or pertaining to an evangelist or a preacher of the gospel. *rare*. M17. **4a** Eager to share an enthusiasm or belief with others. E20. **b** = EVANGELISTIC 1b. M20.

1b G. BURNET Faith . . separated from the other Evangelical Graces. **evangelical prophet** Isaiah, viewed as prophesying the life of Christ and anticipating gospel doctrines in his writing. 2b G. PRIESTLAND Some evangelical papers . . profess to be speaking to the world, but do it in a language only intelligible to the converted. *Times* His . . piety was Evangelical rather than Modernist. *Christadelphian* Creationist writers from the Evangelical movement. 4a *Sunday Telegraph* Robin is evangelical about riding through France. b *Nature* An evangelical plea for the introduction of these difference equations into elementary mathematics courses.

B *n.* (Usu. **E-**.) **1** A Protestant; *spec.* a member of any Church called Evangelical. M16. **2** A member of the Evangelical school of Protestants, esp. within the Church of England. E19.

evangelicalism *n.* the doctrines or ethos of Evangelicals; adherence to the Evangelical school: M19. **evangelically** *adv.* M16.

evangelican /iːvanˈdʒɛlɪk(ə)n, ɛv-/ *a.* & *n.* Also **E-**. M19. [f. as prec. + -AN.] **A** *adj.* = EVANGELICAL *a.* 2b. M19. **B** *n.* = EVANGELICAL *n.* 2. L19.

evangelicanism *n.* M19.

evangelicity /ɪˌvan(d)ʒəˈlɪsɪti/ *n.* M19. [f. EVANGELIC, EVANGELICAL + -ICITY.] The quality of being evangelical.

evangelise *v.* var. of EVANGELIZE.

evangelism /ɪˈvan(d)ʒ(ə)lɪz(ə)m/ *n.* E17. [f. EVANGEL *n.*[2], EVANGELIC + -ISM.] **1** The preaching or promulgation of the gospel; activity as an evangelist. E17. **2** Adherence to or profession of Evangelical doctrines. E19. **3** Faith in the gospel. *rare*. M19. **4** Zealous advocacy of a cause or doctrine; proselytizing zeal. E20.

evangelist /ɪˈvan(d)ʒ(ə)lɪst/ *n.* ME. [(O)Fr. *évangéliste* f. eccl.L *evangelista* f. eccl.Gk *euaggelistēs*, f. *euaggelizesthai* EVANGELIZE: see -IST.] **1** Any of the writers of the four Gospels, Matthew, Mark, Luke, and John. ME. **2a** A person, esp. a layman, engaged in itinerant Christian missionary work. LME. **b** A person who preaches the gospel or brings it to a non-Christian people. M16. **c** A zealous advocate or promulgator of a cause or doctrine. L20. †**3** A book or copy of the Gospels. E16–E18.

2c CARLYLE The French Revolution found its Evangelist in Rousseau.

evangelistary /ɪˌvan(d)ʒəˈlɪstəri/ *n.* Also in L form **evangelistarium** /ɪˌvan(d)ʒ(ə)lɪˈstɛːrɪəm/, pl. **-ria** /-rɪə/. M17. [med.L *evangelistarium* f. eccl.L *evangelista*: see prec., -ARY[1].] **1** A book containing the portions of the Gospels that form part of the liturgy. M17. **2** A copy of the Gospels. M19.

evangelistic /ɪˌvan(d)ʒəˈlɪstɪk/ *a.* M19. [f. EVANGELIST + -IC.] **1** Of or pertaining to evangelists or evangelism; concerned with the spreading of the gospel. M19. **b** Concerned with or aimed at communicating a belief or enthusiasm; hortatory. L20. **2** Of or pertaining to the four evangelists. M19. **3** Of or pertaining to the Evangelical school. M19.

evangelistical *a.* (*rare*) M17. **evangelistically** *adv.* E20.

evangelium /iːvanˈdʒɛlɪəm/ *n.* Now *rare* or *obs.* M16. [eccl.L: see EVANGEL *n.*[1]] The gospel; a proclamation of the gospel.

evangelize /ɪˈvan(d)ʒ(ə)lʌɪz/ *v.* Also **-ise**. LME. [eccl.L *evangelizare* f. eccl.Gk *euaggelizesthai*, f. *euaggelos*: see EVANGEL *n.*[1], -IZE.] **1** *v.i.* Proclaim the gospel; act as an evangelist. LME. †**2** *v.t.* Proclaim as good news; preach about. LME–L17. **3** *v.t.* Preach the gospel to; (seek to) convert to Christianity. M17. **4** Imbue with the spirit of the gospel; interpret in an evangelical sense. L17.

2 J. MARBECK From that time the kingdome of God was evangelized. 3 *Presbyterian Herald* They are forbidden to evangelize the Malays, who are mostly Muslim.

evangeliˈzation *n.* M17. **evangelizer** *n.* LME.

evangile *n.* var. of EVANGEL *n.*[1]

evanid /ɪˈvanɪd/ *a. arch.* E17. [L *evanidus* rel. to *evanescere* EVANESCE: see -ID[1].] **1** Vanishing; of short duration; evanescent, fleeting. E17. **2** Faint, weak. M17. †**3** Of a colour: merely apparent. M17–M18.

evanish /ɪˈvanɪʃ/ *v.i.* Now *rare*. ME. [OFr. *evaniss-* lengthened stem of *evanir* f. Proto-Romance: see E-, VANISH *v.*] Vanish; die away or *away*.

evanishment *n.* L18.

Evans gambit /ˈɛv(ə)nz ˌɡambɪt/ *n. phr.* M19. [f. William Davies *Evans* (1790–1872), Welsh sea-captain and chess-player.] *Chess.* A gambit in which, following the Italian opening, White offers to sacrifice the queen's knight's pawn.

evaporable /ɪˈvap(ə)rəb(ə)l/ *a.* M16. [Fr. *évaporable* or med.L *evaporabilis*, f. *evaporare* EVAPORATE *v.*: see -ABLE.] Able to be evaporated.

evaporaˈbility *n.* M19.

evaporate /ɪˈvapərət/ *n. rare*. E20. [f. the vb.] *Geol.* = EVAPORITE.

evaporate /ɪˈvapəreɪt/ *v.* Pa. pple **-ated**, †**-ate**. LME. [L *evaporat-* pa. ppl stem of *evaporare*, f. *e-* E- + *vapor* steam: see -ATE[3].] **1** *v.t.* Convert into vapour or gas; drive off in the form of vapour. Orig., drive out (bodily humours) in the form of vapour. (Foll. by *into*, *off*.) LME. **2** *v.i.* Of a liquid or solid: give off or become vapour, pass off into the air etc. as vapour; decrease in bulk by evaporation. M16. †**3** *v.i.* Be emitted in the form of vapour; be exhaled. M16–L18. **4** *v.t.* Emit in the form of vapour; lose by evaporation. E17. **5** *v.t.* & *i.* Reduce (a solution etc.) *to* a residuum by evaporation; subject to evaporation. M17. **6** *v.i.* Of an emotion, a situation, wealth, etc.: pass away like vapour; be wasted or dissipated. (Foll. by *into*.) M17. **7** *v.i.* Of a person: disappear; leave; die. *joc.* E18.

1 R. W. EMERSON The sun evaporates the sea. 2 D. ATTENBOROUGH The more liquid part of it . . quickly evaporates. 4 ANTHONY HUXLEY The leaf would evaporate almost as much water as it would without its skin. 5 LD RUTHERFORD The filtrate was evaporated to dryness. **evaporated milk**: concentrated by partial

evaporation of its liquid content. 6 E. J. HOWARD Her impatience to see him had evaporated.

evaporator *n.* a person who or thing which evaporates, *esp.* an apparatus in which things can be evaporated E19.

evaporation /ɪ,vapəˈreɪʃ(ə)n/ *n.* LME. [f. L *evaporatio(n-)*, f. as prec.: see -ATION.] 1 The action or process of gradually turning from liquid or solid into vapour, or of passing away as vapour; an instance of this. LME. 2 The action or an act of evaporating a liquid or driving off the liquid part of something. LME. 3 Vapour given off by evaporation. Usu. in *pl.*, vapours, exhalations, fumes. LME. 4 Emission of vapour, esp. water vapour. Formerly also, emission of breath, fire, or sweat. M16.

1 D. ATTENBOROUGH Evaporation under the grilling sun has made the waters very salty. 4 ANTHONY HUXLEY Stomata control the evaporation from the leaf.

evaporative /ɪˈvap(ə)rətɪv/ *a.* & *n.* LME. [Late L *evaporativus*, f. as EVAPORATE *v.*: see -IVE.] A *adj.* Producing evaporation; employing or produced by evaporation. LME.

evaporative cooling: produced by the evaporation of a liquid.

†B *n.* A medicine that supposedly drew out bodily humours as vapour. Only in LME.

evaporatively *adv.* M20.

evaporimeter /ɪ,vapəˈrɪmɪtə/ *n.* E19. [f. EVAPOR(ATION + -IMETER.] An instrument for measuring the rate of evaporation.

evaporite /ɪˈvapərʌɪt/ *n.* E20. [Alt. of EVAPORATE *n.*: cf. -ITE[1].] *Geol.* A sedimentary salt deposit left after the evaporation of a body of water; a rock produced in this way.

evapoˈritic *a.* pertaining to or characteristic of an evaporite M20.

evapotranspiration /ɪ,vapəʊtranspɪˈreɪʃ(ə)n, -trans-/ *n.* M20. [f. EVAPO(RATION + TRANSPIRATION.] The loss of water from the land to the atmosphere by evaporation from the soil and transpiration from plants.

e,vapotranˈspirative *a.* L20. **e,vapotranˈspire** *v.t.* & *i.* lose (water) by evapotranspiration M20.

evasible /ɪˈveɪzɪb(ə)l/ *a.* M19. [f. L *evas-* (see next) + -IBLE.] Able to be evaded.

evasion /ɪˈveɪʒ(ə)n/ *n.* LME. [OFr. *évasion* f. L *evasio(n-)*, f. *evas-* pa. ppl stem of *evadere* EVADE: see -ION.] 1 A means of evading a duty, question, etc.; an evasive argument, a prevaricating excuse. LME. b The action or an act of evading; dodging, prevarication. E17. 2 Escape from confinement or danger. Now *rare*. LME. †b The possibility or a means of escape. L16–M18. 3 The action of avoiding or escaping a blow, pursuit, etc., by contrivance. M17. 4 The action of coming or going out. *rare*. M17.

1 E. BAKER Evasions often revealed more than direct statements. b H. T. BUCKLE I deem anonymous writing . . to be an evasion of responsibility. *tax evasion*: see TAX *n.*

evasive /ɪˈveɪsɪv/ *a.* E18. [f. L *evas-* (see prec.) + -IVE.] 1 Of a person: exhibiting or given to evasion; tending to avoid direct or unambiguous replies. E18. 2 Of an action or utterance: constituting or containing evasion; equivocal. M18.

1 O. MANNING Clarence squirmed under these questions, shrugged and was evasive. 2 B. PLAIN He had given her an evasive answer. **evasive action**: taken to avoid something unpleasant.

evasively *adv.* M18. **evasiveness** *n.* M18.

Eve /iːv/ *n.*[1] [OE *Ēfe* f. late L *Eva* f. Heb. *Ḥawwāh*, perh. rel. to *ḥay* alive or Aram. *ḥewyā* serpent.] The first woman in Hebrew tradition.

daughter of Eve a woman, *esp.* one regarded as showing a typically feminine trait. **not know from Eve** have no knowledge of the appearance of (a woman).

eve /iːv/ *n.*[2] ME. [Orig. a two-syll. var. of EVEN *n.*[1] For similar loss of *n* cf. CLEW *n.*, GAME *n.*, MAID *n.*] 1 = EVENING 2. *arch.* exc. *poet.* ME. 2 The evening or day before a saint's day or church festival; *gen.* the evening or day before any date or event. ME. 3 The time immediately preceding any event or action. L18.

2 *Christmas Eve*: see CHRISTMAS *n.* *Ember eve*: see EMBER *a.* 3 V. BRITTAIN The poet's death on the eve of the Dardanelles campaign.

Comb. **eve-churr** †(*a*) the mole-cricket; (*b*) the nightjar; **eve-jar** the nightjar; **eve-of-poll** *a.* of, pertaining to or occurring in the period immediately preceding the polling in an election.

evection /ɪˈvɛkʃ(ə)n/ *n.* M17. [L *evectio(n-)*, f. *evect-* pa. ppl stem of *evehere* carry out, elevate, f. *e-* E- + *vehere* carry.] †1 A lifting up; elevation, exaltation (*lit.* & *fig.*). Only in M17. 2 A periodic inequality in the moon's motion manifested as a displacement in longitude, caused by the perturbing effect of the sun. E18.

even /ˈiːv(ə)n/ *n.*[1] [OE *ǣfen* rel. to synon. OFris. *ēvend*, OS *āband*, MLG, MDu. *āvont* (Du. *avont*), OHG *āband* (G *Abend*).] 1 The latter part of the day, the evening. *obs.* exc. *poet.* & *dial.* OE. 2 = EVE *n.*[2] 2. *obs.* exc. *dial.* ME.

1 R. KIPLING Bring it to my house this even.

Comb.: **evenfall** the beginning of evening.

even /ˈiːv(ə)n/ *a.* & *n.*[2] [OE *efen* = OFris. *even*, *iven*, OS *eben* (Du. *even*, *effen*), OHG *eban* (G *eben*), ON *jafn*, Goth. *ibns*, f. Gmc.] A *adj.* 1 Of land, ground, etc.: level, flat, not hilly or sloping; of uniform height. OE. b Horizontal. *obs.* exc. in phrs. below. LME. 2 Of an action, movement, etc.: uniform, smooth; free from fluctuations; (of temper, the mind, etc.) equable, unruffled. OE. 3 Orig., (of a weight or balance) true, accurate. Later, (of conduct, laws, etc.) equal, just, impartial. OE. †4 (Of a path) straight, direct; (of speech or action) direct, straightforward; (of an object) straight ahead. ME–E17. 5 Equal in rank, power, etc.; on a par *with*, on equal terms *with*. ME. 6 Equal in size, number, quantity, etc. ME. b Of a chance, bet, etc.: as likely to succeed as not; fifty-fifty. L16. 7 Of a surface or line: without bumps or hollows or other irregularities; smooth. ME. 8 Medium, average; of proper magnitude. Now *rare* or *obs.* ME. 9 Level *with*; neither higher nor lower. *arch.* LME. b In the same plane or line (*with*); parallel. LME. †10 Exact, precise. LME–E17. 11 Of a whole number: exactly divisible by two, without leaving a remainder. Of a thing in a series: numbered with or known by such a number. Opp. *odd*. LME. 12 Accurately coincident or aligned. LME. 13 Uniform throughout in texture, colour, quality, etc. LME. 14 (Of a person) neither owing money nor owed; square, quits; (of accounts, affairs, etc.) having no balance or debt on either side. LME. 15 Equally balanced. L16. 16 Of a sum of money, a number, etc.: not involving fractions; expressible in a round number. M17.

1b *on* or *with an even keel*: see KEEL *n.*[1] 2 T. H. HUXLEY The even rhythm of the breathing. R. KIPLING Every tale was told in the even, passionless voice of the native-born. 5 BYRON I could not . . class My faults even with your own! W. S. CHURCHILL We worked together on even terms, more like brother and sister than mother and son. 6 **of even date** *Law* & *Comm.* of the same date. b BYRON Still their salvation was an even bet. *New York Times* Democrats believe they have a better-than-even chance at winning the seat. 7 J. M. NEALE When the snow lay round about, deep and crisp and even. A. PATON Kumalo would have stumbled, though the road was straight and even. 12 H. GARLAND His smile . . displayed fine, even teeth. 13 A. N. WILSON His face was scarlet . . so that flesh and acne blended into an even hue. 14 HARPER LEE Cecil had thirty cents, too, which made us even. **be** or **get even** (**with**) have one's revenge (on), retaliate (against). *break even*: see BREAK *v.* 16 E. DICKINSON I wondered . . if Father'd multiply the plates—To make an even Sum. *Offshore* Discovery of the Sundari field . . brings the number of oil fields in the Natomas SE Sumatra territory to an even dozen.

Other phrases: *honours are even*: see HONOUR *n.*

Special collocations: *even break*: see BREAK *n.*[1] 11b. **even hands** †(*a*) *at* or *of even hands*, on equal terms; with neither gain nor loss; (*b*) *be even hands* (Sc.), be even or quits *with*. **even money** (*a*) a sum expressible in a whole or a round number; (*b*) an even chance; betting odds of 1 to 1, offering a win equal to the stake. *even parity*: see PARITY *n.*[1] 3d. **even Stephen**(**s**), **Steven**(**s**) /ˈstiːv(ə)n(z)/ *colloq.* even, equal, level; *esp.* an even chance.

B *n.* †1 *on even* = ANENT *prep.* (of which it is an early form). OE–ME. †2 Nature, kind; *one's* like. Only in ME. †3 Ability, resources. Only in ME. †4 *the even*, the plain truth *of* something. Only in L16. 5 *Sport.* In *pl.* Something expressed in a whole or round number. L19.

5 **in evens** (run 100 yards or metres) in 10 seconds.

even /ˈiːv(ə)n/ *v.* [OE *efnan* and (*ġe*)*efnian*, f. as EVEN *a.*] 1 *v.t.* Liken, compare, (*to*). *obs.* exc. *dial.* OE. b Treat or represent as equal. (Foll. by *to*, *with*.) Now chiefly *Sc.* ME. †c Make equal in rank, dignity, etc. Only in ME. †2 *v.t.* Level (*to* or *with* the ground etc.); raze. OE–M17. 3 *v.t.* Make even, level, or straight; smooth. ME. †b Bring up to or restore to a level; bring into line. LME–M19. c Lower to a specified level (*lit.* & *fig.*); demean. *obs.* exc. *dial.* M17. †4 *v.i.* Be equal or comparable. (Foll. by *to*, *with*.) Only in ME. 5 *v.t.* Match, equal. *rare*. LME. †b Keep pace with. *rare* (Shakes.). Only in E17. 6 *v.t.* Make equal in magnitude; balance (an account), settle (a debt); come to agreement over (a point of difference). M16. †b Make (a person) even or quits *with* another. *rare* (Shakes.). Only in E17. †7 Cause to fit or match. M16. †8 *v.t.* Make (a balance) even. E17–E18.

1 C. READE Would ye even a beast to a man? b G. SAINTSBURY A touch of pathos, . . to be evened only to Shakespere's. 6 T. MAYNARD A wonderful chance to even old scores. *Billings (Montana) Gazette* Sheridan, Wyoming evened its record at 1-1.

With advs. in specialized senses: **even out** (*a*) make even or level; (*b*) become even or normal. **even up** compensate exactly; balance; make equal.

even /ˈiːv(ə)n/ *adv.* Also (*arch.*, *dial.*, & *poet.*) **e'en** /iːn/. [OE *efne* = OFris. *efne*, OS *efno* (Du. *even*), OHG *ebano* (G *eben*), f. WGmc.] I In senses closely related to the adj. †1 Evenly, regularly, uniformly. OE–E18. †2 Equally. OE–L16. †3 In exact agreement. ME–M17. 4 Directly, straight; due (east etc.). *obs.* exc. *dial.* ME.

II As an intensive or emphatic particle. 5 With ref. to manner or time, or (formerly) position, shape, or quality: exactly, just, (*so*, *thus*, *as*, etc.); in the same way *as*; at the same time *as* (also foll. by *while*, †*with*, etc.). Formerly also, just now, just then; close at hand. *arch.* & *rhet.* OE. 6 Quite, fully, (esp. w. following numeral). *obs.* exc. foll. by *to*: right up to, as far as. *arch.* OE. 7 Used to emphasize the identity or nature of a following person, thing, or circumstance. Also, namely, that is to say. *arch.* OE. b (Usu. **e'en**.) Bef. a vb: just, simply; nothing else but. *arch.* & *dial.* M16. 8 Implying an extremeness of the case mentioned in comparison with a weaker or more general one implied or expressed. Usu. preceding the wd, phr., or cl. emphasized. L16. b Emphasizing a compar.: still, yet. M18.

5 SHAKES. *Sonn.* Let your love even with my life decay. YEATS The souls even while you speak Have slipped out of our bond. R. KIPLING He made his prayer (Even as you and I!). I. MURDOCH I looked back at Flora . . and even as I looked I saw that she was starting to cry. 6 AV *Phil.* 2:8 He . . became obedient unto death, even the death of the cross. 7 AV *Zech.* 11:10 I tooke my staffe, euen Beautie, and cut it. b J. BENTHAM Since it is begun, e'en let it take its course. 8 M. EDGEWORTH Even this stupid gardener . . is as useful to society as I am. D. H. LAWRENCE He was roughly, even cruelly received. A. LURIE He couldn't get her to listen, or even stand still. E. WAUGH Ludovic was not successful in the . . competition. His sonnet was not even commended. A. GUINNESS Actors were always close to her heart, even when she disapproved of them. J. FOWLES There's no lock on the door, . . you can't shut it even. *New York Times* I'm not sure, even if we tried, if we could put it out. b M. AMIS My position will be even stronger.

Phrases: *even just*: see JUST *adv.* **even now** (*a*) at this very moment; (*b*) now, as well as previously; (*c*) *poet.* a very short time ago. †**go even** agree (*with*).

even- /ˈiːv(ə)n/ *comb. form* of EVEN *a.*, *adv.*, orig. repr. a Gmc stem.

even-ˈaged *a.* (of a forest) composed of trees that are of approximately the same age E20. †**even-Christian** *n.* a fellow Christian OE–E17. **even-ˈeven** *a.* (*Nuclear Physics*) (*a*) pertaining to nuclei of even mass number only; (*b*) designating nuclei containing even numbers of protons and neutrons: M20. **even-ˈhanded** *a.* fair, impartial, balanced, E17. **even-ˈhandedly** *adv.* fairly, impartially L19. **even-ˈhandedness** *n.* fairness, impartiality M19. **even-ˈodd**

a. (of an atomic nucleus) having an even number of protons and an odd number of neutrons M20.

evendown /ˈiːv(ə)ndaʊn/ *adv.* & *a. Sc.* & *north.* Also **even down**. ME. [f. EVEN- + DOWN *adv.*] A *adv.* †1 Straight down. Only in ME. 2 Downright; quite; completely. M19. B *adj.* 1 Downright, sheer, out and out; (of a person, also) straightforward, direct. E18. 2 Straight, perpendicular; *esp.* (of rain) coming straight down. M18.

†evene *v.i.* M17–E18. [Fr. †*évenir* (OFr. *esvenir*) f. L *evenire*: see EVENT *n.*] Happen, result.

evener /ˈiːv(ə)nə/ *n.* LME. [f. EVEN *v.* + -ER[1].] A person who or thing which makes even; *spec.* something which distributes the load equally between two or more horses used for draught.

evening /ˈiːv(ə)nɪŋ/ *n.* [OE *ǣfnung*, f. *ǣfnian* grow towards night, f. as EVEN *n.*[1]: see -ING[1].] †1 The process or fact of dusk falling; the time about sunset. OE–M16. 2 The close of day; *esp.* the time from about 6 p.m., or sunset if earlier, to bedtime. LME. b *fig.* The declining or closing period of life, or of anything compared to a day. Usu. foll. by *of*. E17. c Afternoon. *dial.* (*Eng.*, *US*, & *Austral.*) L18. 3 An evening spent in a particular way. L18. 4 *ellipt.* As *int.* Good evening. *colloq.* E20. 5 *ellipt.* = *evening paper* below. *colloq.* M20.

2 A. BLEASDALE It is early evening, going or just gone dark. A. YOUNG Long June evenings. b : T. COLLINS Intending . . to spend the evening of his life indulging his hobby of chemistry. 3 C. BEATON The wow of the evening was Carmen, the belly-dancer.

Phrases: **last evening** yesterday evening. **of an evening** *colloq.* habitually in the evening. *social evening*: see SOCIAL *a.* **this evening** (during) the evening of today. **tomorrow evening** (during) the evening of tomorrow.

Attrib. & *comb.*: In the senses 'of or pertaining to evening', 'existing, taking place, etc., during the evening', 'operating, acting, or on duty during the evening', as *evening breeze*, *flight*, *meal*, *train*, *walk*. Special combs., as **evening class**: held in an evening for adults who wish to learn about a particular subject or interest or to acquire a particular skill; **evening dress** the clothes prescribed by fashion to be worn in the evening on formal occasions; **evening grosbeak** a N. American grosbeak, *Coccothraustes vespertinus*, with yellow colouring; *evening* LYCHNIS; **evening paper** a newspaper published after about midday; **evening prayer** the Anglican service of evensong; **evening primrose** any plant of the genus *Oenothera* (see OENOTHERA) with flowers opening in the evening and wilting the next day (cf. *sundrops* s.v. SUN *n.*[1]); **evening school**: providing teaching in the evenings; **evening star** a planet, esp. Venus, when visible in the west after sunset; **evening suit** a formal suit prescribed by fashion to be worn in the evening.

evenings /ˈiːv(ə)nɪŋz/ *adv. colloq.* & *dial.* (chiefly *N. Amer.*). M17. [Pl. of prec.: cf. DAYS, NIGHTS *advs.* (earlier uses of -S[3] being identified w. -S[1]).] In the evening, every evening.

evenliness /ˈiːv(ə)nlɪnɪs/ *n.* Long *obs.* exc. *Sc.* [OE *efnlicnesse*, f. as next + -NESS.] The quality of being even; suitability; composure, equanimity.

evenly /ˈiːv(ə)nli/ *a.* Long *obs.* exc. *Sc.* OE. [f. EVEN *a.* + -LY[1].] †1 Equal; (of a date) the same. OE–E17. 2 (Of a person) fair, impartial; (of a surface) smooth, level. LME.

evenly /ˈiːv(ə)nli/ *adv.* OE. [f. EVEN *a.* + -LY[2].] †1a In an equal degree or proportion. OE–LME. b In equal shares, equally; as much on one side as on the other. LME. c To the same degree throughout. E17. 2 Without inclination or advantage to either side; impartially, equitably. ME. †3 Exactly; in exact agreement. ME. 4 So as to present an even or uniform surface, form, or line; without inequalities in level, colour, consistency, etc. LME. 5 With equanimity; serenely, tranquilly; (of a movement or action) without variation, uniformly. LME. 6†a In a straight line, directly. *rare* (Shakes.). Only in L16. b (On a) level *with*. L16.

1b E. FEINSTEIN We are evenly bad at the business of providing for one another's needs. 2 T. ARNOLD A single battle, evenly contested. 4 B. PYM It is drying lighter, and quite evenly too. J. M. COETZEE He counted thirty tents evenly spaced over the camp terrain. 5 J. STEINBECK He settled back and ate more slowly now, chewed evenly.

evenness /ˈiːv(ə)nnɪs/ *n.* [OE *efenniss*, f. EVEN *a.* + -NESS.] 1 Fairness in judicial matters. Formerly, equity, righteousness. OE. 2 The quality or state of being smooth or level, or exactly divisible by two. LME. †3 A balanced state or condition, equilibrium; equipoise. LME–M17. 4 Uniformity; regularity; calmness of mind, equanimity. L16.

4 A. J. ELLIS The evenness with which a Frenchman pronounces the syllables. P. G. WODEHOUSE The placid evenness of Kirk's existence began to be troubled. *Nature* This function . . compounds species richness . . and . . evenness (the apportionment of individuals among the species present).

evensong /ˈiːv(ə)nsɒŋ/ *n.* [OE *ǣfensang*, f. EVEN *n.*[1] + SONG *n.*[1]] 1 *Eccl.* (Also **E-**.) Orig. (now *Hist.*) the service of vespers in the pre-Reformation Western Church. Now, an Anglican service held in the afternoon or evening and having a set form, with prayers, psalms, canticles, Bible readings, and a recitation of the Creed. OE. 2 The time about sunset. *arch.* ME. 3 A song sung in the evening. LME.

event /ɪˈvɛnt/ *n.* & *v.* L16. [L *eventus*, f. *event-* pa. ppl stem of *evenire* come out, result, happen, f. *e-* E- + *venire* come.] A *n.* 1 Something that happens or is thought of as happening; an occurrence, an incident; now *esp.* one that is significant or noteworthy. L16. b *spec.* Each of a set of outcomes that are mutually exclusive and have a certain computable probability of occurrence. M19. c An item in a programme of sport; an occasion held out as offering attractions to the public. M19. d In *pl.* What is happening or has happened. M19. e *Sci.* A point of space-time. E20. f *Physics.* A single ionization, decay, or reaction of a subatomic particle. M20. 2 The outcome of a course of proceedings; a consequence, a result. Now only in certain phrs. (see below). L16. †3 That which befalls a person or thing; fate. L16–L17. 4 The (actual or contemplated) fact of a thing's happening; the occurrence *of*. Now chiefly in *in the event of* below. E17.

1 V. BRITTAIN The events reported in the newspapers seemed too incredible to be taken seriously. V. GLENDINNING The fountain playing was an event; it had been turned off all through the war. c P. ROTH His events were discus, shot, and javelin. *Western Morning News* Fund-raising events are being organised. *Observer* A three-day antique coin event starting on Tuesday. d E. MIALL Events have proved us right. G. B. SHAW I did not foresee this turn of events. f *Scientific American* The events yielding a positron and a neutral pion should be easier to identify. 2 SIR W. SCOTT He then took his aim . . and the multitude awaited the event in breathless silence. 4 P. G. WODEHOUSE Anonymous letters are too frequently traced to their writers, and the prospect of facing Kirk in such an event did not appeal to him.

Phrases: **after the event** afterwards rather than at the time or beforehand (*be wise after the event*, explain something after it occurs without having foreseen it; blame others for not having foreseen something). **at all events** in any case; whatever happens or happened. *double event*: see DOUBLE *a.* & *adv.* *happy event*: see HAPPY *a.* **in any** or **either event** = *at all events* above. **in the event** (*a*) as things turn(ed) out; (*b*) *US* = *in the event of* below. **in the event of** if (something specified) should happen; should (it) be the case.

Comb.: **event horizon** *Astron.* a notional surface from beyond which no matter or radiation can reach an observer; *spec.* the Schwarzschild sphere of a black hole.

B *v.i.* Take part in horse trials. Chiefly as *eventing* vbl n. M20.

eventer *n.* a horse or rider that takes part in horse trials L20. **eventless** *a.* without (noteworthy) events E19. **eventlessly** *adv.* L19. **eventlessness** *n.* L19.

eventful /ɪˈvɛntfʊl, -f(ə)l/ *a.* E17. [f. EVENT *n.* + -FUL.] 1 Full of striking events. E17. 2 Fraught with important issues; momentous. L18.

1 LD MACAULAY The changes which fourteen eventful years had produced. 2 SOUTHEY Thalaba . . waited calmly for the eventful day.

eventfully *adv.* E20. **eventfulness** *n.* M19.

eventide /ˈiːv(ə)ntʌɪd/ *n. arch.* exc. in *eventide home*. [OE *ǣfentīd*, f. as EVEN *n.*[1], TIDE *n.*] The time of evening; evening.

Comb.: **eventide home** a home for old people (orig. one maintained by the Salvation Army).

†eventilate *v.t.* E17. [L *eventilat-* pa. ppl stem of *eventilare*, f. *e-* E- + *ventilare* VENTILATE.] 1 Expose to the wind or air; fan; winnow (corn); aerate (blood). Only in 17. 2 *fig.* Discuss. Only in M17.

†eventilation *n.* M17–M18.

eventration /iːvɛnˈtreɪʃ(ə)n/ *n.* M19. [Fr. *éventration*, f. *éventrer* eviscerate, f. *é-* (f. as ES-) + *ventre* stomach: see VENTER *n.*[1], -ATION.] 1 *Med.* The extrusion outside the abdominal cavity of some of its contents. M19. 2 The action of opening an animal's belly. L19.

eventual /ɪˈvɛn(t)ʃʊəl/ *a.* E17. [f. L *eventus* EVENT *n.* + -UAL, after *actual*.] †1 Of or pertaining to events; of the nature of an event. Only in 17. 2 Of the nature of a result; consequential. L17. b Ultimately resulting. E19. †3 Of a stipulation: conditional. Of an army: to be raised if required. L17–L18. 4 That will arise or happen under certain circumstances. *arch.* M18. †5 That happens to exist. M–L18.

eventuality /ɪˌvɛn(t)ʃʊˈalɪti/ *n.* M18. [f. prec. + -ITY.] 1 A possible event; a contingency. M18. 2 *Phrenol.* The faculty of observing and remembering the order of succession in events; the supposed organ of this faculty. E19.

1 C. RYAN Although he had been ordered not to destroy it, Harmel was prepared for the eventuality.

eventually /ɪˈvɛn(t)ʃʊ(ə)li/ *adv.* M17. [f. as prec. + -LY[2].] †1 In result, as distinct from by intention. M17–E18. 2 In the event, in the end, ultimately. L17. †3 To provide against a contingency; in conditional terms. M–L18.

2 J. N. ISBISTER The cancer that eventually killed him. J. KOSINSKI Eventually, he forgot about it.

eventuate /ɪˈvɛn(t)ʃʊeɪt/ *v.i.* Orig. *US.* L18. [f. as EVENT *n.* + -ATE[3], after *actuate*.] 1 Have a (specified) result; turn out (well or badly); result *in*. L18. 2 Happen, result, come about. E19.

1 A. J. ROSS The crisis had eventuated favourably. M. L. KING The bravery of the Indian . . had ultimately to eventuate in defeat. 2 D. ACHESON Should this procedure eventuate it would be necessary for me to release . . a statement.

eventuˈation *n.* M19.

ever /ˈɛvə/ *adv.* Also (*poet.*) **e'er** /ɛː/. [OE *ǣfre*; ult. origin unkn.] I Always, at all times. 1 Throughout all time, or all past or future time; eternally, perpetually; throughout one's life. Now usu. w. sense limited by following adv., prep., or conj., as *after(ward)*, *before*, *since*. Also *ever and ever*. OE. 2 On all occasions; whenever possible or appropriate; = ALWAYS 1. *literary* & *north.* OE. 3 Constantly, incessantly; with continual recurrence. OE. b With compar. or (usu. in *comb.*) pres. pple to denote a continued increase or decrease. ME. †4 Imparting a distrib. sense to following indef. pron. or adv.; emphasizing the distrib. function of following distrib. wd. Cf. EVERY, EVERYWHERE. OE–ME.

1 *Book of Common Prayer* He liveth and reigneth ever one God. CARLYLE Ever must the Sovereign of Mankind be entitled King. LYTTON They would live happy ever after. A. BROOKNER Terrified of spiders ever since she was tiny. 2 GOLDSMITH He attacked the largest ships, and almost ever with success. SCOTT FITZGERALD The image of her mother, ever carried with her. P. G. WODEHOUSE It was ever her way to come swiftly to the matter in hand. 3 H. GUNTRIP A fearless thinker whose mind was ever on the move. b M. MCLUHAN The ever more specialist activities of literate society. *Nature* The ever increasing number of synthetic chemicals in the environment.

II At any time. Chiefly w. comparison, condition, negation, or question. 5 At any time. OE. b Immediately following a superl.: that there has been at any time. E20. 6 On any supposition, by any chance, at all. OE. b After interrog. pron., adv., etc., to emphasize a question or an assertion of ignorance. Cf. HOWEVER, WHATEVER. *colloq.* L16. 7 In any degree. Only in *ever the* followed by compar., & in *ever so*, *such* below. M17.

5 J. BUCHAN The worst man I have ever known. M. LAVIN He won't give in, now or ever. I. MURDOCH The stream, more choked than ever with its debris. J. M. COETZEE Have you ever seen a doctor about your mouth? b *Guardian* The biggest ever postbag of telegrams. 6 G. W. DASENT To get above ground as fast as ever she could. J. STEINBECK If they ever know themselves, the land will be theirs. b T. TROLLOPE Where ever am I to find a girl that can pull me out of my chair in the way you do? O. MANNING I don't know why you ever started.

Phrases: **as ever is** or **was** (*postpositive*) *colloq.* nothing less than. **did you ever?** *colloq.* have you seen or heard the like? **ever and again** or **anon** *arch.* occasionally. †**ever as** as long as; as often as; wherever. †**ever now and now** or **and then** every now and then. **ever so** (*a*) [f. earlier *never so*] to any possible degree; (*b*) *colloq.* very; (*c*) *slang* very much. **ever such a —** (w. following adj. & n.) *colloq.* a very —. **ever yours, yours ever**: in ending a letter to a close friend etc. *for ever*: see FOREVER. **if ever there was one** & vars. (asserting that the person or thing just mentioned is a perfect or undoubted instance of its kind). **is he** or **she ever** *N. Amer. slang* he or she is very. NEVER *ever*. *yours ever*: see *ever yours* above.

Comb.: **ever-being** *a.* that always is; **ever-blessed** *a.* always blessed, always (to be) adored; **ever-blooming** *a.* flowering throughout the growing season; **everdamp** a transfer paper with a hygroscopic coating to keep it moist; **ever-during** *a.* (*arch.*) always enduring, everlasting; **ever-living** *a.* that lives for ever, immortal (*lit.* & *fig.*); **ever-ready** *a.* & *n.* (*a*) *adj.* permanently accessible, available, or prepared; (*b*) *n.* an ever-ready person or thing.

Everest /ˈɛv(ə)rɪst/ *n.* E20. [Mount *Everest* in Nepal and Tibet, the world's highest mountain, f. Sir George *Everest* (1790–1866), Surveyor-General of India.] 1 The highest peak of attainment, difficulty, etc. E20. 2 A very large pile or heap. M20.

everglade /ˈɛvəgleɪd/ *n. US.* E19. [Prob. f. EVER + GLADE *n.*²] A marshy tract of land that is mostly under water and covered with tall grass. Usu. in *pl.* (w. cap. initial), *the* marshes of this kind in S. Florida.

evergreen /ˈɛvəgriːn/ *n.* & *a.* M17. [f. EVER + GREEN *a.*] A *n.* A tree or shrub that has green foliage all the year round. M17. B *adj.* 1 Of a tree or shrub: having green foliage all the year round. Of a leaf: lasting until the following season of growth. Opp. DECIDUOUS 2. L17. 2 Always green and fresh (*lit.* & *fig.*). L18.

1 *evergreen alkanet*: see ALKANET 2. *evergreen hazel*: see HAZEL *n.*¹ **evergreen oak** = *holm-oak* s.v. HOLM *n.*² 2.

everlasting /ɛvəˈlɑːstɪŋ/ *a.*, *n.*, & *adv.* ME. [f. EVER + LASTING *a.*] A *adj.* 1 Lasting for ever; infinite in future, or past and future, duration. ME. 2 Lasting so long as to seem or be treated as eternal. ME. b Lasting too long; repeated too often. M17. 3 Of a fabric, contrivance, etc.: almost infinitely durable, very slow to wear out. L16. 4a Of a plant: perennial. Chiefly in *everlasting pea* below. L16. b Of a flower: keeping its shape and colour when dried. L18.

1 AV *Isa.* 9:6 The mighty God, the everlasting Father. J. UPDIKE His soul has gone to everlasting fire! *everlasting* DEATH. *everlasting life*: see LIFE *n.* 2 POPE See Cromwell, damn'd to everlasting fame! DE QUINCEY Mighty gates of everlasting rock. b H. HALLAM The tedious descriptions of spring, and the everlasting nightingale. 4a **everlasting pea** a leguminous plant, *Lathyrus latifolius*, with large ornamental coloured flowers. b **everlasting flower** = sense B.4 below.

B *n.* 1 Eternity. Chiefly in *for*, *from* and *to everlasting*. LME. 2 *the Everlasting*, God, the Eternal. LME. 3 A stout fabric; *spec.* a strong twilled woollen cloth. L16. 4 Any of various plants, chiefly of the composite family, with papery flower-heads that keep their shape and colour when dried, *esp.* helichrysum; the flower of such a plant. Also called *immortelle*. L18.

1 I. WATTS From everlasting thou art God To endless years the same. 4 B. PYM Two wreaths of . . mauve everlastings and white chrysanthemums. **mountain everlasting** = *cat's-foot* (c) s.v. CAT *n.*¹ **pearl** or **pearly everlasting** an ornamental N. American plant, *Anaphalis margaritacea*, with shiny white flower-heads.

C *adv.* †1 For ever, throughout eternity. *rare.* Only in L15. 2 Very, exceedingly, excessively. *US slang.* L17.

2 K. D. WIGGIN She'd kick the ladder from out under her, everlastin' quick.

everlastingly *adv.* LME.

everlastingness /ɛvəˈlɑːstɪŋnɪs/ *n.* LME. [f. prec. + -NESS.] 1 The quality or fact of being everlasting; endless or eternal existence. LME. 2 Endless future duration. Formerly also = ETERNITY 2. LME. †3 = ETERNITY 4. LME–M19.

everly /ˈɛvəli/ *adv.* Long *obs.* exc. *Sc.* LME. [f. EVER + -LY².] Always, continually.

evermore /ɛvəˈmɔː/ *adv.* ME. [Orig. two wds, f. EVER + MORE *adv.*] 1 For all future time. *arch.* ME. 2 Always, constantly, continually. ME. 3 In expressed or implied neg. contexts: at any future time, ever again, any longer. Formerly also, in any degree. LME.

1 WORDSWORTH A life of peace . . that hath been, is, and shall be evermore. 2 SOUTHEY Yonder roar . . evermore increasing, Still louder, louder, grows. 3 SHAKES. *Sonn.* I may not evermore acknowledge thee. E. B. BROWNING Not in England evermore.

Phrases: *for evermore*: see FOREVERMORE.

eversible /ɪˈvəːsɪb(ə)l/ *a.* L19. [L *evers-* pa. ppl stem of *evertere* EVERT: see -IBLE.] Able to be everted.

eversion /ɪˈvəːʃ(ə)n/ *n.* LME. [Fr. *éversion* or L *eversio(n-)*, f. *evers-*: see prec., -ION.] †1 The action of overthrowing; the condition of being overthrown; an overthrow (*lit.* & *fig.*). LME–E19. 2 *Med.* The action of turning an organ or other structure outwards or inside out; the condition of being everted. M18.

eversive /ɪˈvəːsɪv/ *a.* E18. [f. as EVERSIBLE + -IVE.] Tending to the overthrow of or *of* something.

evert /ɪˈvəːt/ *v.t.* M16. [L *evertere*, f. *e-* E- + *vertere* turn.] 1 Cast from power, overthrow (a government or regime); frustrate (a purpose); upset (a judgement, doctrine, etc.). *arch.* M16. †2 Cast down (a building); defeat (an enemy). M–L16. †3 Draw or turn aside (*lit.* & *fig.*). L16–M17. †4 Turn upside down; upset (*lit.* & *fig.*); disturb. *rare.* Only in 17. 5 Chiefly *Med.* Turn (an organ or other structure) outwards or inside out. Chiefly as *everted* pa. pple. L18.

4 JONSON The very thought Everts my soul with passion. 5 R. F. BURTON The lips are tumid and everted. S. BECKETT Her eyes, rolling now and everted.

evertebrate /ɪˈvəːtɪbrət/ *n.* & *a.* L19. [f. *e-* E- + L VERTEBRA + -ATE². Cf. VERTEBRATE *a.* & *n.*] *Zool.* = INVERTEBRATE.

Everton toffee /ɛvət(ə)n ˈtɒfi/ *n. phr.* M19. [*Everton*, a district of Liverpool in NW England.] 1 A brittle toffee orig. made in Everton, similar to butterscotch but containing cream or evaporated milk. M19. 2 Coffee. *arch. rhyming slang.* M19.

evertor /ɪˈvəːtə/ *n.* E20. [f. EVERT + -OR.] *Anat.* A muscle that turns or rotates a part outwards.

every /ˈɛvri/ *a.* (in mod. usage also classed as a *determiner*) & *pron.* [OE *ǣfre ǣlc* 'ever each': see EVER, EACH.] A *adj.* 1 Used bef. a sing. n. to give the same sense in relation to individuals as does *all* bef. the pl. n. in relation to the aggregate of them (almost = EACH *a.*, but with a stronger connotation of generality or universality). Also, each of a merely notional aggregate. (Preceding the n. & all adjs. exc. possess. prons. Formerly also foll. by *a(n)* interposed bef. the n.; and preceding *the* + superl. adj. (now replaced by *even*).) OE. b Used bef. a number or numeral adj., or a period of time, to denote continued repetition or recurrence at the stated intervals. LME. c Each (of two). *obs.* exc. *dial.* L16. †2 With *n.pl.* All severally. (Usu. w. defining wd interposed.) M16–L17. †3 With *n.sing.* Any. M16–M18. 4 With *n.sing.* All possible —s; the utmost degree of. L19.

1 SOUTHEY To see every person in his class at least once a week. OED 'Each theory is open to objection' relates to an understood enumeration of theories, but 'Every theory is open to objection' refers to all theories that may exist. T. HARDY Every spare minute of the following days he hovered round the house. J. C. POWYS They hide every sign of water. J. STEINBECK Every bit of electric wire had been requisitioned. S. J. PERELMAN The inescapable conviction that my every move is somehow being observed. *at every turn*: see TURN *n. every bit as*: see BIT *n.*² **every inch** every bit (*of*); entirely, in every respect. **every last** *slang* absolutely every. *every man jack*: see JACK *n.*¹ **every now and again, every now and then** from time to time. *every* ONCE *in a while.* **every penny** all one's money; all the money. **every so often** = *every now and again* above. **every time** *colloq.* on all occasions, without fail or exception, certainly (freq. as an affirmative exclam.). **every way** in every way, in every respect. **every which way** (chiefly *N. Amer.*) in every direction; *from* every direction. See also EVERYBODY, EVERYDAY, EVERYONE, etc. b G. B. SHAW You shock me . . every second time you open your mouth. G. GREENE At each station on the Outer Circle a train stopped every two minutes. *every* FEW. **every other —** every second —, every alternate —. 2 SHAKES. *Temp.* I'll resolve you . . of every These happen'd accidents. 3 GOLDSMITH The weakness of the wall which every earthquake might overturn. 4 F. WELDON I . . showed her every kindness. *Guardian* Every effort should be made to sow the seed thinly.

B *pron.* †1 Everybody. ME–E16. †2 Distributed to each member of an aggregate; = EACH *pron.* 2. ME–L15. 3 Each, or every one, *of* several persons or things. (Formerly often treated as *pl.*). Now *obs.* exc. *dial.*, *poet.*, & in *all and every* s.v. ALL *pron.* & *n.* 4. LME.

3 DEFOE Every of the said chirurgeons is to have twelvepence a body. 3 C. K. STEAD These words / spaced out between wave- / break in every of its modes.

Phrases: †**every other** each other.

¶The form *ever each* (orig. *evereche, everych*) was corrupted into *every each* and has occas. been used *arch.* in this form.

everybody /ˈɛvrɪbɒdi/ *pron.* Orig. two wds. M16. [f. prec. + BODY *n.*] Every person. Also as antecedent of pl. pron.

BYRON Everybody does and says what they please. V. WOOLF Everybody in the house is sick of beef and mutton. J. STEINBECK Pilon knew everybody and everything about everybody. **everybody else** all other persons.

everyday /ˈɛvrɪdeɪ; *as pred. adj.* ɛvrɪˈdeɪ/ *n.* & *a.* LME. [f. EVERY + DAY *n.*] A *n.* †1 Each day in continued succession. *rare.* Only in LME. 2 A weekday, a day other than Sunday. *dial.* L19.

B *attrib.* or as *adj.* 1 Of or pertaining to every day, daily; pertaining to Sundays and weekdays alike. M17. 2 Worn or used on ordinary days. M17. 3 To be met with every day, unremarkable, ordinary; (of people and their attributes) commonplace, mediocre, inferior. M18.

1 F. NIGHTINGALE The everyday management of a sick-room. 2 DICKENS Mr. Quilp invested himself in his every-day garments. 3 COLERIDGE Persons of no every-day powers and acquirements. *Times* The everyday activity of shopping. G. SWIFT This sort of thing is not exactly everyday.

everydayness *n.* M19.

†**everydeal** *n.* & *a.* ME. [f. EVERY + DEAL *n.*¹] A *n.* Every part, the whole. Following a n. or pron.: every part (of it). ME–M16. B *adv.* In every part, in every respect; entirely, wholly. ME–E18.

everyhow /ˈɛvrɪhaʊ/ *adv. rare.* Also as two wds. M19. [f. EVERY + HOW *adv.*] In every way.

everylike /ˈɛvrɪlʌɪk/ *adv.* Long *obs.* exc. *dial.* LME. [f. EVER + obs. var. of ALIKE *adv.*; later prob. regarded as f. EVERY + LIKE *a.*] †1 Always in a similar fashion; continually. Only in LME. 2 From time to time, at intervals. *dial.* M19.

Everyman /ˈɛvrɪman/ *n.* Pl. **-men**. E20. [Name of the protagonist in a 15th-cent. morality play, f. EVERY + MAN *n.*] The ordinary or typical person, 'the man in the street'.

everyone /ˈɛvrɪwʌn/ *pron.* Also as two wds. ME. [f. EVERY + ONE *n.* & *pron.*] = EVERYBODY. Also as antecedent of pl. pron.

C. P. SNOW She was loyal about him with everyone. I. MURDOCH Everyone has had their adventures. **everyone else** = EVERYBODY *else*.

everyplace /ˈɛvrɪpleɪs/ *adv. N. Amer.* Orig. as two wds. E20. [f. EVERY + PLACE *n.*¹] In every place, everywhere.

everything /ˈɛvrɪθɪŋ/ *pron.* & *n.* Formerly as two wds. ME. [f. EVERY + THING *n.*¹] A *pron.* 1 All things, all; (with following adj.) all that is —;

colloq. a great deal. ME. 2 *pred.* The thing of supreme importance. *colloq.* L19.

1 T. HARDY Everything had been done that could be done. H. JAMES In spite of everything these points had helped him. M. KEANE Perhaps everything would still be all right. E. J. HOWARD Everything possible was flush with the walls. O. MANNING I have lost everything. R. P. JHABVALA Everything is covered with mildew. *everything coming* (or *going*) *one's way*: see WAY *n.* **have everything** *colloq.* possess every attraction, advantage, or requirement. *have everything one's own way*: see WAY *n.* 2 G. B. SHAW The idle pleasure of the moment is everything.

B *n.* Something of every kind. Usu. in *pl. joc.* L18.

everyway /ˈɛvrɪweɪ/ *adv.* Occas. as two wds. L16. [f. EVERY + WAY *n.*: cf. ALWAY, ANYWAY.] In every way, manner, or direction; in every respect.

everywhen /ˈɛvrɪwɛn/ *adv.* Occas. as two wds. M19. [f. EVERY + WHEN.] At all times, always.

everywhere /ˈɛvrɪwɛː/ *adv.* & *n.* Formerly also as two wds. ME. [Partly f. EVER + YWHERE, partly f. EVERY + WHERE.] A *adv.* 1 In every place or part. ME. 2 In many places; of common occurrence. *colloq.* E20.

1 K. GRAHAME The Otters have hunted everywhere . . without finding the slightest trace. E. BOWEN The mist's muffling silence could be everywhere felt. **everywhere else** in every other place. 2 *News Chronicle* Lamé is everywhere. F. SWINNERTON Nothing in the room had been changed; newly gathered Talisman roses . . were everywhere.

B *n.* All places or directions; *the* infinite. LME.

D. H. LAWRENCE Everywhere seemed silent. *here, there, and everywhere*: see HERE *adv.*

everywhereness *n.* (*arch.*) ubiquity, omnipresence L17.

everywheres /ˈɛvrɪwɛːz/ *adv. US colloq.* & *dial.* M19. [f. prec. + -S[3].] = EVERYWHERE *adv.*

everywhither /ˈɛvrɪwɪðə/ *adv. arch.* Orig. as two wds. LME. [f. EVERY + WHITHER *adv.*] In every direction.

eve-star /ˈiːvstɑː/ *n. obs.* exc. *poet.* LME. [f. EVE *n.*[2] + STAR *n.*[1]] = EVENING *star*.

Evian /ˈeɪvɪan, *foreign* evjɑ̃/ *n.* Also **É-**. M19. [See below.] In full *Evian water*. A non-effervescent mineral water obtained from Évian (in full Évian-les-Bains), a spa town in eastern France.

evict /ɪˈvɪkt/ *v.t.* LME. [L *evict-* pa ppl stem of *evincere*, f. *e-* E- + *vincere* conquer.] 1 *Law* (now *Hist.*). Recover (property or the title to property) *from* a person by legal process. Also foll. by *of*. LME. 2 Expel (a person, esp. a tenant) from land or a building, usu. by legal process; drive out (a population). (Foll. by *from, out of,* †*of*.) M16. †3 Conquer, overcome, (a country, adversary, etc.); obtain by conquest. M16–M17. †4 Defeat in argument or litigation; refute (an opinion); convince or convict (*of*). L16–M17. †5 Prove, settle by argument. L16–E18.

evic'tee *n.* an evicted tenant L19. **evictor** *n.* E19.

eviction /ɪˈvɪkʃ(ə)n/ *n.* LME. [Late L *evictio(n-)*, f. as prec.: see -ION.] 1 *Law* (now *Hist.*). The recovery of property by legal process. LME. 2 The action of evicting a person, esp. a tenant. L16. †3 The action of conquering a country or of obtaining something by conquest. Only in E17. †4 The action of defeating a person in argument or of refuting an opinion; conviction of an accused person. E17–E18. †5 (A) proof, (a) demonstration. E17–L18.

evidence /ˈɛvɪd(ə)ns/ *n.* ME. [(O)Fr. *évidence* f. L *evidentia*, f. *evident-*: see EVIDENT, -ENCE.] I *gen.* †1 An example. Only in ME. 2 An indication, a sign; indications, signs. ME. 3 Facts or testimony in support of a conclusion, statement, or belief. (Foll. by *for, (in favour) of, against* the conclusion etc.; *of, from* the facts etc.) ME. †b Something serving as a proof. LME–E18. †4 Manifestation, display. LME–E18. 5 The quality or condition of being evident; clearness, obviousness. M17.

2 M. E. HERBERT The country they were traversing gave evidence of careful cultivation. R. L. STEVENSON We were surrounded by so many evidences of expense and toil. 3 G. B. SHAW There is the same evidence for it as for anything else that happened millions of years before we were born. E. WAUGH I refuse to believe the evidence of my eyes. . . These creatures simply do not exist.

II *Law.* 6 Information (in the form of personal or documented testimony or the production of material objects) tending or used to establish facts in a legal investigation; a piece of information of this kind. LME. b Material admissible as testimony in a court of law. E19. 7 A document by means of which a fact is established; *esp.* (in *pl.*) title-deeds. *obs.* exc. *Hist.* LME. †8 A person who provides testimony or proof; a witness. L16–E19.

6 *Daily Telegraph* From the evidence given at the inquiry, certain breaches occurred of the Acts and regulations.

Phrases: **bear evidence** give evidence in a court of law. **call in evidence** call (a person) as a witness in a court of law. *circumstantial evidence*: see CIRCUMSTANTIAL *a.* I. *external evidence*: see EXTERNAL *a.* 4. HEARSAY *evidence*. **in evidence** present; visible; conspicuous; (see also *call in evidence* above). *internal evidence*: see INTERNAL *a. rules of evidence*: see RULE *n. secondary evidence*: see SECONDARY *a.* **turn King's, Queen's,** or (*US*) **State's evidence** (of an accomplice in a crime) testify for the prosecution.

evidence /ˈɛvɪd(ə)ns/ *v.* E17. [f. the n.] 1 *v.t.* = EVINCE 6. E17. 2 *v.t.* Serve as or give evidence for; attest. E17. †3 *v.t.* Establish by evidence; demonstrate, prove. M17–E19. 4 *Law.* †a *v.t.* Relate as a witness. M17–E19. b *v.i.* Testify, appear as a witness. Now *rare*. M17.

1 L. M. MONTGOMERY Gilbert . . had evidenced no recognition whatever of the existence of Anne Shirley. 2 R. V. JONES The Germans seemed to be taking it seriously as evidenced by their demands for heavy water.

†**evidencer** *n.* a witness L16–M18.

†**evidency** *n.* M16. [L *evidentia*: see EVIDENCE *n.*, -ENCY.] 1 = EVIDENCE *n.* 5. M16–E19. 2 = EVIDENCE *n.* 2. L16–E19.

evident /ˈɛvɪd(ə)nt/ *a.* & *n.* LME. [(O)Fr. *évident* or L *evident-*, *-dens*, f. *e-* E- + pres. pple of *videre* see: see -ENT.] A *adj.* 1 Obvious (to the eye or mind); plain or clear to see or understand; apparent. Formerly also (of objects), conspicuous. LME. †2 Of a sign, testimony, etc.: certain, indubitable. LME–M17.

1 E. F. BENSON The whole place, as could be seen at the most cursory glance, had been laid out with skill and care, but not less evident were the signs of subsequent neglect. N. MAILER It was evident to me that Yuriko was in love with him. I. MURDOCH Stagdon's evident assumption that most decisions . . were now taken by Miss Casement maddened Rainborough.

B *n.* Something that serves as evidence; *spec.* in *Sc. Law*, a document proving a person's title to something; usu. in *pl.*, title-deeds. LME.

evidentness *n.* M16.

evidential /ɛvɪˈdɛnʃ(ə)l/ *a.* E17. [med.L *evidentialis*, f. L *evidentia*: see EVIDENCE *n.*, -AL[1].] †1 Resting on documentary evidence. *rare*. Only in E17. 2 Of the nature of or providing evidence; serving to attest. M17. 3 Of, pertaining to, or based on evidence. M17.

2 F. W. FARRAR That Paul should have passed . . from one direction of life to the very opposite is evidential of the power and significance of Christianity. *Times* The court had their written answer which had evidential value. 3 E. B. TYLOR The basis of theological science must be historical as well as evidential.

evidentially *adv.* M17.

evidentiary /ɛvɪˈdɛnʃ(ə)ri/ *a.* E19. [f. L *evidentia* EVIDENCE *n.* + -ARY[1].] = EVIDENTIAL 2, 3.

evidently /ˈɛvɪd(ə)ntli/ *adv.* LME. [f. EVIDENT + -LY[2].] 1 So as to be distinctly visible or perceptible; without possibility of mistake or misunderstanding. Now *rare* or *obs.* LME. 2 Plainly, obviously. Now usu. parenthetically or modifying a sentence: it is plain (that); it would seem (that); seemingly, apparently; (as a comment on a statement or a reply to a question) so it appears. L16.

1 GIBBON An act which evidently disclosed his intention of transmitting the empire to his descendants. 2 D. HUME Reason was so evidently on their side. T. HARDY A frame of embroidered card-board—evidently the work of feminine hands. J. KOSINSKI The audience . . evidently approved his words. F. SWINNERTON Evidently they were brother and sister. *New York Times* Werblin does not speak to his former partners and, when asked why, will say curtly: 'Evidently, I don't like them.' R. RENDELL 'Were they old pals or something?' 'Evidently'

evil /ˈiːv(ə)l, -vɪl/ *n.*[1] OE. [f. the adj.] 1 Wickedness, moral depravity, sin; whatever is censurable, painful, malicious, or disastrous; the evil part or element of anything. OE. †2 A wrongdoing, a crime, a sin. OE–E17. 3 *the evil*, (*collect. pl.*) people. ME. †4 A disaster, a misfortune. ME–L18. 5 A disease, a sickness. *obs.* exc. *dial.* in *gen.* sense. ME. b Hist. *the* (*king's*) *evil*, scrofula. LME. 6 Any particular thing that is physically or morally harmful. ME.

1 G. B. SHAW Evil should not be countered by worse evil but by good. 6 H. WILSON Whatever is decided will be wrong—it is a choice of evils. P. CAREY Honey Barbara submitted to the evils of alcohol with a guilty flush.

Phrases & comb.: **evildoer** a person who does evil. **evildoing** wrongdoing. **lesser evil, lesser of two evils** the less harmful of two evil things; the alternative that has fewer drawbacks. *speak evil of*: see SPEAK *v. the social evil*: see *social evil* s.v. SOCIAL *a.*

evilness *n.* OE.

†**evil** *n.*[2] *rare* (Shakes.). Only in E17. [Origin unkn.] A privy, a lavatory.

evil /ˈiːv(ə)l, -vɪl/ *a.* [OE *yfel* = OS *ubil*, OFris., MDu. *evel* (Du *euvel*), OHG *ubil* (G *Übel*), Goth. *ubils*, f. Gmc.] 1 Morally depraved, bad, wicked. OE. 2 Causing pain or trouble; unpleasant, offensive, disagreeable. OE. †b Hard, difficult, (*to do*). ME–M16. †3 Unsound; unwholesome; poor, unsatisfactory; defective. OE–E17. b Of a workman, work, etc.: unskilful. E16–L18. 4 Harmful, prejudicial; malicious; (of an omen) boding ill; (of a reputation) unfavourable. ME. 5†a Of conditions, fortune, etc.: unfortunate, miserable. ME–E17. b Of a period of time: characterized by misfortune; unlucky, disastrous. LME.

1 AV *Gen.* 8:21 The imagination of mans heart is evil from his youth. *Christian Science Monitor* The villains are led by a freakishly evil woman. 2 P. MATTHIESSEN Not once have I seen him downhearted or tired, nor has he responded . . to my own evil temper. J. STEINBECK The evil music filled the night. 4 W. S. CHURCHILL Adams spread evil rumours of their conduct.

Special collocations: **evil day** = *evil hour* below. **evil days** a time when a person suffers misfortune. **evil eye** a malicious look; such a look superstitiously believed to do material harm; the ability to cast such looks. **evil hour** a time of ill luck, disaster, etc. **Evil One** the Devil. **evil spirit** a demon. **evil will** (now *rare*) malicious intention or purpose.

evil /ˈiːv(ə)l, -vɪl/ *adv. obs.* exc. in comb. [OE *yfele*, f. as prec.] = EVILLY.

Comb.: †**evil-favoured** *a.* having a repulsive appearance; **evil-liver** a person who lives a sinful life; **evil-looking, -smelling** *adjs.* having an evil look, smell.

evilly /ˈiːvəli, -vɪli/ *adv.* LME. [f. EVIL *a.* + -LY[2].] 1 Wickedly; with evil purpose or result; unfavourably. LME. †2 Faultily; insufficiently; incorrectly; improperly. M16–L17.

evince /ɪˈvɪns/ *v.t.* L16. [L *evincere*: see EVICT.] †1 Prove by argument or evidence; establish; *rare* vindicate. L16–E19. †2 Overcome, subdue. Only in 17. †3a Convince. E17–L18. b Confute. Only in 17. †4 Compel or extort by argument or persuasion. Only in M17. 5 Be an indication of; serve as evidence for; attest. M17. 6 Reveal the presence of (a feeling, quality, etc.); exhibit; give evidence of. E19.

1 J. AUSTEN The pleasantness of an employment does not always evince its propriety. 5 E. BOWEN The two were typical in their point of view, as evinced by the lectures they gave. 6 S. BELLOW Leventhal, evincing neither anger nor satisfaction, though he felt both, rose.

†**evinceable** *a.* = EVINCIBLE: only in L16. **evincible** *a.* demonstrable L16. **evincive** *a.* indicative E19.

Evipan /ˈɛvɪpan/ *n.* Also **e-**. M20. [Origin unkn.] *Pharm.* (Proprietary name for) the drug hexobarbitone.

evirate /ˈiːvɪreɪt, ˈɛ-/ *v.t.* E17. [L *evirat-* pa. ppl stem of *evirare* castrate, f. *e-* E- + *vir* man: see -ATE[3].] Castrate; emasculate.

eviration /iːvɪˈreɪʃ(ə)n, ɛv-/ *n.* E17. [L *eviratio(n-)*, f. as prec.: see -ATION.] Emasculation; the state of being emasculated.

evirato /ɛvɪˈrɑːtəʊ/ *n.* Pl. **-ti** /-ti/. L18. [It., use as n. of pa. pple of *evirare* f. L: see EVIRATE.] *Hist.* = CASTRATO.

†**evirtuate** *v.* M17. [f. (O)Fr. *(s')évertuer*, f. *é-* (f. as ES-) + *vertu* strength, VIRTUE: see -ATE[3].] 1 *v.t.* Deprive of virtue, strength, or authority. M17–L18. 2 *v.refl.* Exert oneself. Only in M17. 3 *v.i.* Exert an influence. Only in L17.

eviscerate /ɪˈvɪsəreɪt/ *v.* Pa. pple **-ated**, (now *poet.*) **-ate** /-ət/. L16. [L *eviscerat-* pa. ppl stem of *eviscerare*, f. *e-* E- + VISCERA: see -ATE[3].] 1 *v.t.* Disembowel; gut (*lit.* & *fig.*). L16. †2 *v.t.* Bring out the innermost secrets of. *rare.* E–M17. 3 *v.t.* Elicit the essence of. *rare.* M17. 4 *v.t.* Deprive *of* important or significant content; weaken, attenuate, emasculate. M19. 5 *v.t. Surg.* Remove the contents of (an eyeball). L19. 6 *v.i.* Of viscera: protrude through a surgical incision. M20.

1 W. FAULKNER The house had not been damaged: merely eviscerated. 4 T. S. ELIOT The parched eviscerate soil Gapes at the vanity of toil.

evisceˈration *n.* M17. **eviscerator** *n.* a person who eviscerates something, or a device for eviscerating something, esp. carcasses M20.

evitable /ˈɛvɪtəb(ə)l/ *a.* E16. [(O)Fr. *évitable* (f. *éviter* f. L *evitare*) or L *evitabilis*, f. *evitare*: see EVITE, -ABLE.] Avoidable. (Now usu. in neg. contexts.)

†**evitate** *v.t. rare.* L16–E17. [L *evitat-* pa. ppl stem of *evitare*: see EVITE, -ATE[3].] = EVITE.

evitation /ɛvɪˈteɪʃ(ə)n/ *n.* LME. [L *evitatio(n-)*, f. *evitare*: see next, -ATION.] Avoidance.

evite /ɪˈvʌɪt/ *v.t. arch.* exc. *Sc.* E16. [f. (O)Fr. *éviter* or L *evitare*, f. *e-* E- + *vitare* shun.] Avoid, shun.

eviternity *n.* var. of AEVITERNITY.

evocable /ˈɛvəkəb(ə)l/ *a.* L19. [Fr. *évocable*, f. *évoquer* f. L *evocare*: see EVOKE, -ABLE.] Able to be evoked.

evocate /ˈɛvə(ʊ)keɪt/ *v.t.* M17. [L *evocat-* pa. ppl stem of *evocare*: see EVOKE, -ATE[3].] †1 Call forth. Only in M17. 2 Call up (spirits) from the dead or (events) from the past. L17.

evocation /ɛvə(ʊ)ˈkeɪʃ(ə)n/ *n.* LME. [f. L *evocatio(n-)*, f. as prec.: see -ATION.] †1 *Gram.* A reduction of the third person to the first or second. LME–M17. †2 a The calling of a person from a specified place or association; the summoning of a person's spirit from its abode. L16–M17. b *Rom. Hist.* The practice of calling upon the gods of a besieged city to forsake it and come over to the besiegers. M17. 3 The transfer of a legal case or action to a higher court. Now *Hist.* M17. 4 The action or an act of evoking a spirit; a formula used for this purpose. M17. 5 In Platonic theory, the calling to mind or recollection of knowledge acquired in a previous state of existence. M17. †6 = AVOCATION 3, 4. M18–E19. 7 The action or an act of calling into existence or activity something non-existent or latent; something that brings to mind a specified memory, image, or feeling. (Foll. by *of*.) L18. 8 The action by which a chemical produced in one part of an embryo causes another part to develop in a particular way. M20.

7 W. FAULKNER The sum, the amount of the reward—the black, succinct evocation of that golden dream.

evocative /ɪˈvɒkətɪv/ *a.* M17. [L *evocativus*, f. as EVOCATE: see -ATIVE.] Having the property of evoking; *esp.* bringing to mind some memory, image, or feeling; having imaginative associations. (Foll. by *of*.)

R. SCRUTON Whether music can actually describe the world or whether it is merely evocative. P. NORMAN 'Mummy', to Louis, was a vaguely thrilling word, evocative of someone young you could cuddle up to in bed.

evocatively *adv.* M20. **evocativeness** *n.* M20.

evocator /ˈɛvə(ʊ)keɪtə/ *n.* L18. [L f. as EVOCATE: see -OR.] 1 A person who evocates or evokes something; *esp.* one who calls up a spirit. L18. 2 A chemical produced in one part of an embryo which causes another part to develop in a particular way; a morphogen. M20.

evocatory /ɪˈvɒkət(ə)ri, ɛvə(ʊ)ˈkeɪt(ə)ri/ *a.* E18. [Late L *evocatorius*, f. as EVOCATE: see -ORY[2].] Having the function or property of evoking spirits; evocative.

evoe /ɪˈvəʊi/ *int.* & *n.* Also **evohe**. L16. [L *eu(h)oe* f. Gk *euoi*.] (An utterance of) a Bacchanalian exclamation expr. elation or boisterousness.

evoke /ɪˈvəʊk/ *v.t.* E17. [L *evocare*, f. *e-* E- + *vocare* to call: perh. after Fr. *évoquer*.] 1 Call forth; *esp.* call up (a spirit etc.) by the use of magic charms. E17. 2 Transfer (a legal case or action) to a higher court. Now *Hist.* M18. 3 Call into being or activate (a memory, image, feeling, etc.); create in the imagination; produce (a response). M19.

1 T. WARTON To evoke the Queen of the Fairies. 3 H. J. LASKI The theory . . never produced in England the enthusiasm it evoked in France. C. MACKENZIE This statement evoked a murmur of agreement from the audience. V. S. PRITCHETT He had a loud, resonant voice and, being a fairish actor, could evoke the gallop of horses . . instantly.

evoker *n.* M19.

évolué /evolɥe/ *n.* & *a.* Pl. of n. pronounced same. M20. [Fr., pa. pple of *évoluer* evolve.] (Characteristic of or designating) an African who has had a European education or has adopted European ways or attitudes.

evolute /ˈiːvəluːt, ˈɛv-/ *n.* & *a.* M18. [L *evolutus* pa. pple of *evolvere* EVOLVE.] *Math.* (Designating) a curve that is the locus of the centres of curvature of a given curve (its involute) and is the envelope of the normals; so called because a point on a taut string unwound from the evolute traces the involute.

evolute /ˈiːvəluːt, -ljuːt, ˈɛv-/ *v.* L19. [Back-form. f. EVOLUTION.] 1 *v.i.* = EVOLVE 8. L19. 2 *v.t.* *Journalese.* = EVOLVE *v.* I. L19.

evolution /iːvəˈluːʃ(ə)n, ˈljuː-, ˈɛv-/ *n.* E17. [L *evolutio(n-)* (unrolling and) reading of a papyrus roll, f. *evolut-* pa. ppl stem of *evolvere* EVOLVE: see -ION.] 1 *Mil.* & *Naut.* A movement of a body of troops or ships carried out to change their disposition. E17. b *gen.* A wheeling about; each of a series of usu. ordered or deliberate movements, as of a dancer or a machine part. Usu. in *pl.* L17. 2 The action of opening out or unfolding; chiefly *fig.*, the orderly passage of a long train of events or of the time containing them. M17. 3 The process of developing in detail what is implicit in an idea or principle; the development of an argument; an outcome of such a process. L17. 4 The development of an animal or plant, or part of one, from a rudimentary to a mature state. L17. b Any process of gradual change occurring in something, esp. from a simpler to a more complicated or advanced state; the passage of something through a succession of stages. Also, origination by natural development as opp. to production by a specific act. E19. c A process by which different kinds of organism come into being by the differentiation and genetic mutation of earlier forms over successive generations, viewed as an explanation of their origins. M19. 5 *Math.* a The process of finding a root of some given quantity. *arch.* E18. b The process of obtaining an involute from an evolute. Now *rare.* E18. 6 Chiefly *Biol.* Emergence or protrusion from an envelope, seed, vesicle, etc. M18. 7 The process of giving off gas, heat, light, or sound. E19.

1b P. G. WODEHOUSE 'Do you do Swedish exercises?' 'I go through a series of evolutions every morning.' 4 J. T. NEEDHAM Nature . . ever exerting its Fecundity in a successive Evolution of organised Bodies. b *Times* The evolution of massive stars. J. PLAMENATZ They have quarrelled about the stage that capitalism has reached in the course of its evolution, how close it is to collapse. c G. M. TREVELYAN The whole idea of evolution and of 'man descended from a monkey' was totally incompatible with existing religious ideas. D. MORRIS At some point in the evolution of the squirrel family, the ancestors of this animal must have split off from the rest.

Phrases: **theory of evolution** (*a*) *Hist.* the hypothesis that an embryo or seed is a development of a pre-existing form which contains the rudiments of all the parts of the future organism; (*b*) the theory that present-day organisms have come into being through a process of evolution (sense 4c above).

evolutional *a.* of, pertaining to, or produced by evolution M19. **evolutionally** *adv.* in an evolutional way L19.

evolutionary /iːvəˈluːʃ(ə)n(ə)ri, ˈljuː-, ɛ-/ *a.* M19. [f. prec. + -ARY[1].] 1 Of or pertaining to evolution or development; dealing with or assuming the theory of evolution. M19. 2 Of, pertaining to, or performing the evolutions or manoeuvres of troops or ships. M19.

1 J. L. HARPER Species caught in different evolutionary pathways may face the same selective forces. E. C. MINKOFF Evolutionary biology. *London Review of Books* Taxonomists classify themselves as cladists or evolutionary systematists.

evolutionarily *adv.* in an evolutionary way; from an evolutionary standpoint: M20.

evolutionise *v.* var. of EVOLUTIONIZE.

evolutionism /iːvəˈluːʃ(ə)nɪz(ə)m, -ˈljuː-, ɛ-/ *n.* M19. [f. EVOLUTION + -ISM.] The theory of evolution; evolutionary assumptions or principles. Opp. *creationism*.

Times Lit. Suppl. The evolutionism inherent in Marx's general conception of history.

evolutionist /iːvəˈluːʃ(ə)nɪst, -ˈljuː-, ɛ-/ *n.* & *a.* M19. [f. as prec. + -IST.] A *n.* 1 *Mil.* A person skilled in evolutions. *rare.* M19. 2 A person who believes in or advocates the theory of evolution; an expert in or student of evolution. L19. B *adj.* Of or pertaining to evolutionism or an evolutionist. L19.

ˌ**evolutioˈnistic** *a.* L19.

evolutionize /iːvəˈl(j)uːʃ(ə)nʌɪz, ɛ-/ *v.t.* & *i.* Also **-ise**. L19. [f. EVOLUTION + -IZE.] Develop in the course of evolution; change gradually.

evolutive /iːvəˈl(j)uːtɪv, ɛ-/ *a.* L19. [f. EVOLUT(ION + -IVE.] Pertaining to, tending to, or promoting evolution.

evolvant /ɪˈvɒlv(ə)nt/ *n.* L20. [f. next + -ANT[1].] *Biol.* An evolved or deliberately modified form of an organism, esp. a bacterium, or of an enzyme.

evolve /ɪˈvɒlv/ *v.* E17. [L *evolvere* unroll, unfold, f. *e-* E- + *volvere* to roll.] I *v.t.* 1 Make more complicated or organized; bring to fuller development; develop. E17. 2 Disclose gradually to the mind; present in orderly sequence. M17. 3 Give off (gas, heat, etc.) as a result of internal processes. E19. 4 Bring out (something implicit or potential); deduce (a conclusion, law, etc.) from data; develop (a notion); work out (a theory). M19. 5 Produce or develop in the course of evolution. Usu. in *pass.* M19. 6 Produce (a condition, process, etc.) as a natural consequence. M19.

1 H. MOORE At some point you'd see something in the doodling, . . and from then on you could evolve the idea. 4 A. CARNEGIE Order was soon evolved out of chaos. W. GOLDING Roger Mason had evolved a method of dealing with Rachel. 5 H. T. LANE Teeth were first evolved not for purposes of mastication, but for attack and defence.

II *v.i.* 7 Gradually come into view or take shape; arise as a natural consequence; *spec.* (of an organism, part, or feature) come into being through evolutionary development. E18. 8 Undergo evolution (*into*). M19.

7 J. MCPHEE Gradually—as they added a room, razed a woodshed, . . —a new cabin evolved. J. GATHORNE-HARDY The British Nanny evolved out of . . a particular society. J. S. HUXLEY Leakey was convinced that early man had evolved in Africa. 8 L. MACNEICE They must . . have evolved late into sea-creatures. *Scientific American* The more massive a star is, the faster it evolves. F. SPALDING His [artistic] method evolved into a formula during the 1960s.

evolvable *a.* M19. **evolvement** *n.* a process of evolving M19. **evolver** *n.* E19.

evolvent /ɪˈvɒlv(ə)nt/ *a.* & *n.* E18. [L *evolvent-* pres. ppl stem of *evolvere* EVOLVE: see -ENT.] †A *adj.* Math. *evolvent line*, a tangent to an evolute. Only in E18. B *n.* 1 *Math.* The involute of a curve. Now *rare* or *obs.* E18. 2 Something that gives rise to or evolves something else. Also, something that is evolved. M19.

†evomit *v.t.* LME–E18. [L *evomit-* pa. ppl stem of *evomere* spew out, f. *e-* E- + *vomere* to vomit.] Vomit, throw up, (the contents of the stomach).
†evomition *n.* M17–E18.

evulgate /ɪˈvʌlgeɪt/ *v.t.* Now *rare* or *obs.* L16. [L *evulgat-* pa. ppl stem of *evulgare*, f. *e-* E- + *vulgare* spread among the multitude, f. *vulgus* multitude: see -ATE[3].] Make commonly known; divulge; publish.
evulˈgation *n.* M17.

evulse /ɪˈvʌls/ *v.t.* M18. [L *evuls-*: see next.] Pull out, tear away.

evulsion /ɪˈvʌlʃ(ə)n/ *n.* LME. [L *evulsio(n-)*, f. *evuls-* pa. ppl stem of *evellere* pluck out, f. *e-* E- + *vellere* pluck.] Forcible extraction.

evviva /ɛvˈviːva/ *n.* L19. [It., f. *e* 'and' (f. L *et*) used intensively + *viva*: see VIVA *n.*[1]] A shout of applause or acclamation.

Evzone /ˈɛvzəʊn/ *n.* & *a.* Also **e-**. L19. [mod.Gk *euzōnas*, *-os* n. f. Gk adj. = dressed for exercise, f. as EU- + *zōnē* girdle.] (Designating) a member of a select infantry regiment of the Greek army whose members wear a distinctive uniform that includes a fustanella.

ewe /juː/ *n.*[1] [OE *ēowu* = OFris. *ei*, OS *ewwi* (MDu. *oie*, Du. *ooi*), LG *ouw* (*lamm*, OHG *ouwi*, *ou* (G *Aue*), ON *ær*, f. Gmc f. IE wd repr. also by L *ovis*, Gk *o(w)is*. Cf. YOWE.] A female sheep, *esp.* a fully grown one; a female of various related animals.
Comb.: **ewe lamb** a female lamb; *fig.* one's most cherished possession (alluding to *2 Sam.* 12); **ewe-neck** a horse's neck whose upper outline curves inwards instead of outwards; **ewe-necked** *a.* (of a horse) having a ewe-neck.

Ewe /ˈeɪweɪ/ *a.* & *n.*[2] M19. [Ewe.] **A** *adj.* Of, pertaining to, or designating a Kwa language of Ghana, Togo, and Benin, or the people who speak this language. M19. **B** *n.* Pl. same. The Ewe language; a member of the Ewe people. L19.

ewer /ˈjuːə/ *n.*[1] LME. [AN *ewer*, *aiguer* f. ONFr. *eviere*, (O)Fr. *aiguière*, f. Proto-Romance f. fem. of L *aquarius* pertaining to water, f. *aqua* water: see -ER[2].] A jug with a wide mouth, *esp.* a water-jug of the kind formerly used in bedrooms.

†ewer *n.*[2] LME–E17. [OFr. f. L *aquarius*: see prec., -ER[2].] = next.

ewerer /ˈjuːərə/ *n.* LME. [f. prec. or next: see -ER[1].] *Hist.* A servant who supplied those at table with water to wash their hands.

ewery /ˈjuːəri/ *n.* Also **ewry** /ˈjuːri/. LME. [f. EWER *n.*[1] + -Y[3]: see -ERY.] **1** A place where ewers, towels, etc., were formerly kept; a department administratively responsible for this, esp. in the royal household. LME. **†2** The ewers, towels, etc., that a ewerer looked after. LME–L15.

ewest /ˈjuːɪst/ *adv. Sc.* E16. [Origin unkn.] Close at hand.

ewhow /ɛˈhwuː/ *int. Sc.* E19. [f. EH + *whow* var. of HOW *int.*[1]] Alas!

Ewigkeit /ˈeːvɪçkaɪt, ˈeɪvɪgkʌɪt/ *n.* Also **e-**. L19. [G = eternity.] Eternity; infinity.
into the Ewigkeit *joc.* into thin air.

Ewing /ˈjuːɪŋ/ *n.* E20. [J. *Ewing* (1866–1943), US pathologist.] *Ewing's tumour* or *sarcoma*, a rare malignant tumour of bone occurring in childhood and adolescence.

ewry *n.* var. of EWERY.

†ewt *n.* var. of EFT *n.*

ex /ɛks/ *n.* & *a.* E19. [EX-[1] 3.] **A** *n.* Pl. **exes, ex's** /ˈɛksɪz/. A person who formerly occupied a position etc. denoted by the context; *spec.* a former husband or wife. E19. **B** *adj.* Former, outdated. E19.

ex /ɛks/ *v.t.* M20. [Repr. pronunc. of *X, x.*] Cross *out* with an X, = X *v.* 2.

ex /ɛks/ *prep.* M19. [L = out of.] **1** *Comm.* Of stocks and shares: without, excluding. M19. **2** Of goods: out of, sold direct from, (a ship, warehouse, etc.). Of an animal: out of (a specified dam). L19.
1 *Daily Telegraph* The shares were traded ex the one-for-one scrip issue. **ex dividend** (with ref. to share prices) not including a dividend about to be paid. **2** *Lancet* The standard hospital model costs £115 ex factory. *Horse & Hound* Malicious, Ch. 1961 by Helioscope ex Blackball by Shut out.

ex- /ɛks, ɪks, ɪgz/ *pref.*[1] [L, f. as prec. Used bef. vowels, *c, f, h, p, q, s, t*: cf. E-, EF-.] **1** In vbs f. L (directly or through (O)Fr.) w. the senses 'out', as *exclude*, 'upward', as *extol*, 'thoroughly', as *excruciate*, 'bring into a state', as *exasperate*, 'remove, expel, relieve of', as *expatriate*, *exonerate*, *excoriate*. Also in wds (ult.) derived f. such vbs, as *exasperation*, *exclusive*, *excrescence*, *extension*. Occas. forming ns. directly f. Eng. ns., as *exclosure*, *exflagellation*, *exsolution*. **2** Occas. (E- preferred) forming adjs. w. the sense 'not having, deprived of', as *exalbuminous*. **3** As a freely productive pref. forming ns. f. titles of office, status, etc., w. the sense 'former(ly)', as *ex-convict*, *ex-husband*, *ex-president*, *ex-Prime-Minister*, *ex-serviceman*, *ex-servicewoman*.

ex- /ɛks/ *pref.*[2] Repr. Gk *ex-* out (of), as *exodus*, *exorcism*. Occas. intensive, as *exomologesis*.

exa- /ˈɛksə/ *comb. form.* [f. H)EXA-, 10^{18} being $(10^3)^6$, suggested by the supposed analogy of *tera-*, *tetra-*: cf. PETA-.] Used in names of units of measurement to denote a factor of 10^{18}, as *exametre* etc. Abbrev. *E.*

exacerbate /ɪgˈzasəbeɪt, ɛkˈsas-/ *v.t.* M17. [L *exacerbat-* pa. ppl stem of *exacerbare*, f. as EX-[1] 1 + *acerbare* make harsh or bitter, f. *acerbus* harsh, bitter, grievous: see -ATE[3].] Increase the sharpness of (a pain), the severity of (an illness), the bitterness of (a feeling), etc.; aggravate. Also, provoke the resentment of (a person).
J. BERGER The unfamiliar climate . . may have further exacerbated her nervous condition. J. MASTERS Such a step would merely exacerbate an already touchy situation. J. P. HENNESSY Trollope had been exacerbated by the noise of an itinerant German band.
exacerbatingly *adv.* in an exacerbating way M20.

exacerbation /ɪgˌzasəˈbeɪʃ(ə)n, ɛkˌsas-/ *n.* LME. [Late L *exacerbatio(n-)*, f. as prec.: see -ATION.] **1** The action of provoking to anger or bitterness; (an instance of) embittered feeling. LME. **2** (An) increase in the severity of a disease, punishment, etc.; *esp.* a paroxysm of a fever etc. E17.
2 *British Medical Journal* Several patients took 30–50 mg salbutamol a day during exacerbations.

exact /ɪgˈzakt, ɛg-/ *a.* & *adv.* M16. [L *exactus* pa. pple of *exigere* complete, bring to perfection, examine, ascertain, f. as EX-[1] 1 + *agere* perform.] **A** *adj.* **I** Precise, accurate. **1** Of a law or rule, discipline, etc.: permitting no deviation; strictly or punctiliously observed. M16. **2** Of an action or process, knowledge, research, etc.: complete in every detail; minutely thorough. M16. **3** Of a person: marked by accuracy of knowledge, observation, workmanship, etc. Of a judge: strict, rigorous. L16. **4** Of a result, numerical quantity, statement, etc.: not approximated in any way; completely accurate and precise. E17. **5** Of a likeness, representation, description, etc.: corresponding in every detail. M17. **6** Of a method, a scientific instrument, etc.: marked by precision, esp. of measurement; not allowing vagueness or uncertainty. M17.
1 JAS. MILL The troops were kept in . . exact discipline. W. BOYD He was excluded from the phenomenally exact social rankings which obtained in . . Nairobi society. **2** A. RADCLIFFE He gave an exact acquaintance with every part of elegant literature. **3** C. BRONTË She was an exact, clever manager. **4** OED A is an exact multiple of B. J. CONRAD Get the exact bearings of his swag. E. O'NEILL Blow me if them warn't her exact words! P. BROOK The dosage is so subtle that it is impossible to establish the exact formula. **5** W. S. MAUGHAM A word for which . . there is no exact equivalent in English. K. CLARK An exact replica. **6** F. MYERS No spoken language has yet been found exact enough to express the highest generalisations. **exact science** a science (e.g. mathematics, chemistry) capable of absolute or quantitative precision.
II Perfected, consummate. **†7** Of a person: highly skilled or accomplished; refined as regards taste. L16–E18. **†8** Of a quality, condition, etc.: consummate, refined, perfect. L16–E18. **†9** Of an object: highly wrought, elaborate. Of a building: well designed. E17–E18.
7 MILTON Eve, now I see thou art exact of taste. **8** R. LOVELL The hearing is most exact in the hare.
†B *adv.* Exactly, precisely. L16–L18.
POPE There's a Rehearsal, Sir, exact at one.
exactness *n.* M16.

exact /ɪgˈzakt, ɛg-/ *v.* LME. [L *exact-* pa. ppl stem of *exigere*: see prec.] **1** *v.t.* Demand and enforce the payment of (a debt, penalty, etc.), the performance of (a task), the concession of (something desired), etc.; force to give or pay. (Foll. by *from*, (arch.) *of*.) LME. **†b** Extort money from (a person). M–L16. **2** *v.t.* Of circumstances etc.: make desirable or necessary; call for. L16. **†3** *v.i.* Impose contributions *on* or *upon*. L16–E18. **4** *v.t. Law.* Call on (a defendant) to appear in court. Now *rare* or *obs.* E17. **5** *v.t.* Extract forcibly. *arch.* M17. **6** *v.t.* Inflict (vengeance) *against* or *from*. M19.
1 AV *2 Kings* 23:35 Iehoiakim . . exacted the siluer and the golde . . of euery one according to his taxation. E. JONES An indefatigable worker himself, he exacted the same standard from his assistants. H. J. LASKI William's advisers who exacted an oath of obedience from the clergy. **2** R. BOYLE I must withhold my Beleef . . till their Experiments exact it. **5** T. FULLER It passeth my Chymistrie to exact any agreement herein out of the contrariety of writers.
exactable *a.* M19.

exacta /ɪgˈzaktə, ɛg-/ *n. N. Amer.* M20. [Amer. Sp. *quiniela exacta* exact quinella.] *Betting.* = PERFECTA.

exacter /ɪgˈzaktə, ɛg-/ *n.* M16. [f. EXACT *v.* + -ER[1].] **1** = EXACTOR 4. M16. **2** = EXACTOR 1, 3. L16.

exacting /ɪgˈzaktɪŋ, ɛg-/ *a.* L16. [f. EXACT *v.* + -ING[2].] Making excessive demands, esp. on one's strength, skill, attention, etc.; hard to satisfy.
A. E. STEVENSON His ability . . to fulfill the demands of his exacting office. A. HALEY The state of repair failed to measure up to their exacting standards.
exactingly *adv.* M19. **exactingness** *n.* M19.

exaction /ɪgˈzakʃ(ə)n, ɛg-/ *n.* LME. [F f. L *exactio(n-)*, f. as EXACT *v.*: see -ION.] **1** The action or an act of exacting a payment, service, etc. LME. **b** In *pl.* Pressing demands made (*on* a person's time etc.). M20. **2** The action or an act of demanding more money etc. than is due; (an) extortion. LME. **3** A sum of money (arbitrarily) exacted. LME.
1b D. M. DAVIN I was . . wary of other people's drama and frugal of the exactions it makes on one's energy. **2** F. HALL We may, without being chargeable with exaction, ask of him to remit . . the rigour of his requirements. **3** BURKE The small balance . . remaining of the unjust exaction.

exactitude /ɪgˈzaktɪtjuːd, ɛg-/ *n.* M18. [F, f. *exact* f. as EXACT *a.*: see -TUDE.] Accuracy; attention to small details. Formerly also, perfect correctness (of a statement).
P. DE VRIES Dry martinis mixed with pharmaceutical exactitude.

exactly /ɪgˈzaktli, ɛg-/ *adv.* M16. [f. EXACT *a.* + -LY[2].] **†1** To a perfect degree; completely. M16–E18. **2** With careful attention to detail or conformity to rule; meticulously. Now *rare.* M16. **3** Accurately, precisely; without discrepancy, vagueness, or uncertainty. M17. **b** As a comment on a statement or a reply to a question: just so; I entirely agree. *colloq.* M19. **c** Used w. expressed or implied neg. when the statement denied is replaced by another of similar effect. L19.
2 H. MARTINEAU He paid for his lodging exactly and regularly. **3** H. JAMES It is exactly three months to a day since I left Northampton. M. SINCLAIR She didn't know what it was exactly. T. STOPPARD What exactly do you do in there? SCOTT FITZGERALD Exactly what it was she did not know. M. SINCLAIR He behaved exactly as if he had expected her. B. SPOCK At exactly 6 a.m., . . no earlier, no later. **c** OED Without exactly denying it, he led me to believe it was not true. **not exactly** (*a*) not quite, but close to (being); (*b*) *colloq. iron.* not at all, by no means.

exactor /ɪgˈzaktə, ɛg-/ *n.* LME. [L, f. as EXACT *v.* + -OR.] **1** A person who makes illegal or unreasonable demands; an extortioner. LME. **†2** An officer of justice who extorted confessions and carried out sentences. LME–L16. **3** A person who collects taxes, dues, or customs. *arch.* L16. **4** A person who insists on a task, service, etc., as a matter of right; a person who makes demands. L16.

exactress *n.* (*rare*) a female exactor E17.

†exaestuation *n.* Also **exest-**. M17–E18. [L *exaestuatio(n-)*, f. *exaestuat-* pa. ppl stem of *exaestuare* boil, foam, seethe, f. as EX-[1] I + *aestuare* boil etc., f. *aestus* heat (n.): see -ATION.] A boiling, an overheating, a fermentation.

exaggerate /ɪɡˈzadʒəreɪt, ɛɡ-/ *v.* M16. [L *exaggerat-* pa. ppl stem of *exaggerare*, f. as EX-[1] I + *aggerare* heap up, f. *agger* heap, mound: see -ATE[3].] †1 *v.t.* Pile up, accumulate, (*lit.* & *fig.*). M16–L17. †2 *v.t.* Dwell on the greatness of (a virtue, fault, etc.), emphasize. M16–M18. 3 *v.t.* & *i.* Represent (a thing) as greater than it really is; overstate, indulge in overstatement. (Earlier in EXAGGERATION I.) E17. 4 *v.t.* Increase immoderately (a condition); make (a physical feature) of abnormal size. (Earlier in EXAGGERATION 3.) M19.

2 MONMOUTH It was.. praiseworthy in Bishop Jovius to exaggerate the praises of.. his Benefactors. 3 G. GREENE One is inclined to exaggerate the value of another country's films. I. MCEWAN He exaggerates a lot, and turns his past into stories to tell at the bar. 4 LEIGH HUNT A nose exaggerated by intemperance. J. E. T. ROGERS The existing distress was exaggerated by this great social change.

exaggeratedly *adv.* to an excessive degree M19. **exaggeratingly** *adv.* in an exaggerating or hyperbolic manner E19. **exaggerative** *a.* marked by or given to exaggeration L18. **exaggeratively** *adv.* M19. **exaggerativeness** *n.* L19. **exaggerator** *n.* a person who or thing which exaggerates E17. **exaggeratory** *a.* = EXAGGERATIVE M18.

exaggeration /ɪɡˌzadʒəˈreɪʃ(ə)n, ɛɡ-/ *n.* M16. [L *exaggeratio(n-)*, f. as prec.: see -ATION.] 1 (A) representation of something as greater than it really is; (a) hyperbolic statement. M16. b *Fine Art.* (A) representation of a subject in which the features are emphasized or given excessive colouring. M18. †2 The action of dwelling on the greatness of a virtue, fault, etc.; emphasis. L16–M18. 3 (An) abnormal intensification of a condition. M17.

1 T. H. HUXLEY The exaggeration of the vertical height in the diagram. G. B. SHAW It is hardly an exaggeration to say that they discuss nothing else.

†exagitate *v.t.* M16. [L *exagitat-* pa. ppl stem of *exagitare*, f. as EX-[1] I + *agitare* AGITATE *v.*: see -ATE[3].] 1 Torment with pain; harass, persecute. M16–L17. 2 Debate, discuss. M16–M18. 3 Inveigh against. L16–L17. 4 Disturb, set in quicker motion, (the blood, breathing, etc.). E17–M18.

†exagitation *n.* E17. [L *exagitatio(n-)*, f. as prec.: see -ATION.] 1 Stirring up; (an) excitement. E17–M18. 2 Discussion. Only in E17.

exalbuminous /ɛksalˈbjuːmɪnəs/ *a.* M19. [f. EX-[1] 2 + L *albumin-*, ALBUMEN + -OUS.] *Bot.* Having no albumen in the seed.

exalt /ɪɡˈzɔːlt, ɛɡ-/ *a. poet.* E19. [f. next or its pa. pple.] Exalted.

exalt /ɪɡˈzɔːlt, ɛɡ-/ *v.t.* LME. [L *exaltare*, f. as EX-[1] I + *altus* high.] 1 Raise aloft; elevate. Now *arch.*, *rhet.*, & *humorously pedantic.* LME. b Raise (the voice) in speech or song; raise (a song); make (music). *arch.* M16. 2 Raise to a higher rank, station, etc.; *refl.* (*arch.*) assume a superior position. LME. b Make (more) excellent or sublime; give a lofty character to; dignify. Chiefly as *exalted* ppl a. E17. 3 Praise highly, extol. LME. 4 Make rapturously excited. Formerly, elate with pride, joy, etc. Chiefly as *exalted* pa. pple. LME. 5 Intensify, heighten. Formerly, increase (a price). LME. †6 Raise (a substance) to a higher degree of purity or potency; refine, concentrate. Also, make (a physical effect) more powerful. L15–E19. 7 *Astrol.* In *pass.* Of a planet: be in the sign of the zodiac where it exerts its greatest influence. M17. 8 Stimulate (a faculty) to greater activity. M18.

1 J. BARLOW Exalt your heads, ye oaks. 2 AV *1 Kings* 1:5 Then Adoniiah the sonne of Haggith exalted himselfe, saying, I wil be king. D. H. LAWRENCE Do away with the masters, exalt the will of the people. **exalted personage** a person of high (usu. princely or royal) rank. b DAY LEWIS Proud and poor, the Anglo-Irish exalted their snobbery into a tribal mystique. R. LEHMANN They parted in exalted peace of mind. W. CATHER That exalted serenity that sometimes came to her at moments of deep feeling. 3 J. BERGER Strong nations.. can only exalt and glorify their sons who.. sacrifice their life for.. an ideal. 4 CLARENDON The covenanters.. were very reasonably exalted with this success. G. B. SHAW Lunatics, exalted by.. visions of a dawning millennium. 5 M. SCHAPIRO His [Van Gogh's] first aim was intensity, a firm.. image exalted by daring colour. 6 J. RAY Other stones being exalted to that degree of hardness. *fig.*: BURKE This is Jacobinism sublimed and exalted into its most pure essence. 8 GEO. ELIOT Trivial causes had the effect of rousing and exalting the imagination.

exaltedly *adv.* in an exalted manner; with exaltation: L18. **exaltedness** *n.* exalted quality, rank, etc. M17. **exalter** *n.* L15.

exaltation /ɛɡzɔːlˈteɪʃ(ə)n, ɛks-/ *n.* LME. [(O)Fr., or late L *exaltatio(n-)*, f. L *exaltat-* pa. ppl stem of *exaltare*: see EXALT *v.*, -ATION.] 1 The action of raising aloft; the state of being raised or elevated. Orig. only in *Exaltation of the Cross* below. LME. b A group *of* larks in flight. (*rare* bef. E19.) LME. 2 Elevation in rank, power, etc.; *esp.* the elevation of a monarch to a throne. Formerly also, elevated rank, culmination of fortune. LME. b The raising of a thing to a high degree of excellence; exalted degree; an exalted manifestation. M17. 3 *Astrol.* The position of a planet in the zodiac in which it exerts especially great influence. LME. †4 The action or an act of raising a substance to a higher degree of purity or potency. L15–M18. 5 Rapturous excitement; elation. L15. 6 Intensification. M18.

1 **Exaltation of the Cross** a feast observed in the Roman and Orthodox Churches on 14 September in honour of the Cross of Christ, to commemorate either the exposition of the supposed True Cross in 629 after its recovery from the Persians, or the dedication by Constantine in 335 of the basilica built on the site of the Holy Sepulchre. 2 DEFOE Joseph.. told them the story of his exaltation in Pharaoh's court. b LD MACAULAY That chivalrous spirit.. was found in the highest exaltation among the Norman nobles. 5 G. ORWELL The exaltation, the lunatic enthusiasm, was still in his face.

exalté /egzalte/ *a.* & *n.* Fem. **-ée**. Pl. of n. pronounced same. M19. [Fr., pa. ppl a. of *exalter* f. as EXALT *v.*] (A person who is) elated or impassioned.

exam /ɪɡˈzam, ɛɡ-/ *n. colloq.* M19. [Abbrev.] = EXAMINATION 2.

examen /ɛɡˈzeɪmɛn/ *n.* E17. [L = tongue of a balance, (fig.) examination, f. *exigere* weigh accurately: see EXACT *a.*] †1 A critical dissertation or treatise, a disquisition. E17–M18. 2 (An) examination, (an) investigation. Now *rare.* E17. b *Eccl.* A formal examination of the soul or conscience. M17. †3 (An) investigation by experiment; a test. M17–M18. 4 The pointer of a balance. *rare.* M19.

examinable /ɪɡˈzamɪnəb(ə)l, ɛɡ-/ *a.* L16. [f. EXAMINE *v.* + -ABLE.] 1 *Law.* Subject to examination; cognizable. L16. 2 *gen.* Able to be examined (in). E17. b *Eccl. Hist.* Of a person: eligible to be examined for admission to Holy Communion. *Sc.* E18.

2 G. ADAMS The smallest examinable quantity of matter. *Times Lit. Suppl.* A subject which was both teachable (which.. partly meant examinable) and.. useful.

examinaˈbility *n.* L19.

examinant /ɪɡˈzamɪnənt, ɛɡ-/ *n.* L16. [L *examinant-* pres. ppl stem of *examinare*: see EXAMINE *v.*, -ANT[1].] †1 A person who is being examined as a witness; a person undergoing an examination as to fitness for church membership, ordination, etc. L16–E19. 2 A person who examines, an examiner. E17.

examinate /ɪɡˈzamɪnət, ɛɡ-/ *a.* & *n.* LME. [L *examinatus* pa. pple of *examinare*: see EXAMINE *v.*, -ATE[2].] †A *adj.* Examined; interrogated under torture. LME–E19. B *n.* 1 A person under examination, either as a witness or an as accused person. M16. 2 A person who is examined for suitability or proficiency; an examination candidate. L16.

examination /ɪɡˌzamɪˈneɪʃ(ə)n, ɛɡ-/ *n.* LME. [(O)Fr. f. L *examinatio(n-)*, f. *examinat-* pa. ppl stem of *examinare*: see EXAMINE *v.*, -ATION.] 1 a The action of judging or testing critically or by a standard, esp. one's conscience. LME. b The action of inspecting something or performing tests on it in order to investigate its nature, condition, or qualities; *spec.* a medical examination. M17. 2 (The action of conducting) a test of a person's knowledge or proficiency in which he or she is required to answer questions or perform tasks. LME. 3 Formal interrogation, esp. of a witness or an accused person; a trial. LME. b (A record of) the statements made by a witness or accused person when examined. M16. †4 A testing, a trial, an assay, (*lit.* & *fig.*). E–M16. 5 The action of searching, investigating, or inquiring into a subject, statements, etc. M16.

1b **medical examination** = MEDICAL *n.* 2. 3 **examination-in-chief**: made by the party calling the witness to give evidence.

Comb.: **examination paper** a paper of questions to be answered; a candidate's written answers.

examinational *a.* E19.

examinator /ɪɡˈzamɪneɪtə, ɛɡ-/ *n.* M16. [Late L, f. L *examinat-* pa. ppl stem of *examinare* EXAMINE *v.*: see -ATOR.] 1 = EXAMINER 3. Chiefly *Sc.* M16. †2 = EXAMINER 2. M17–M19. †3 = EXAMINER I. *Sc.* M18–M19.

examinatorial /ɪɡˌzamɪnəˈtɔːrɪəl, ɛɡ-/ *a.* M19. [f. late L *examinatorius* + -AL[1].] Of or pertaining to an examiner or an examination.

examine /ɪɡˈzamɪn, ɛɡ-/ *n. obs.* exc. *Sc.* & *Hist.* L15. [f. the vb.] (An) examination.

examine /ɪɡˈzamɪn, ɛɡ-/ *v.* ME. [(O)Fr. *examiner* f. L *examinare* weigh accurately, f. *examin-* EXAMEN.] †1 *v.t.* Assay, prove, (precious metal); *fig.* put (a person) to the test. Only in ME. 2 *v.t.* Investigate the nature, condition, or qualities of (something) by close inspection or tests; inspect closely or critically (*spec.* one's conscience); scrutinize; search (baggage); verify (calculations, account-books); give (a person) a medical examination. Formerly also, judge or try by a standard. ME. 3 *v.t.* Inquire into, investigate, (a subject); consider or discuss critically; try to ascertain (*whether*, *how*, etc.). ME. 4 *v.t.* & *i.* Test the knowledge or proficiency of (a person, esp. a pupil or candidate) by questioning (*in* or *on* a subject). LME. 5 *v.t.* Interrogate formally (esp. a witness or an accused person). Formerly also, investigate the guilt or innocence of (an accused person). LME. †b Interrogate under torture. L16–E18. 6 *v.i.* Look or inquire *into*. M19.

2 C. P. SNOW She examined the shelves, note-book in hand. L. HELLMAN The man in front was having his passport examined. L. JONES He.. walks nervously around the room examining books and paintings. 3 T. REID We shall examine this theory afterwards. G. B. SHAW We must examine why it occurred. *need one's head examined*: see HEAD *n.*

examiˈnee *n.* a person under examination; a person who is a candidate in an examination: L18. **examiningly** *adv.* in an examining manner; searchingly: L19.

examiner /ɪɡˈzamɪnə, ɛɡ-/ *n.* ME. [f. prec. + -ER[1].] †1 A person who examines or interrogates a witness or an accused person. ME–L17. 2 A person who inquires into facts or investigates the nature or condition of something; an investigator. LME. 3 A person appointed to examine a pupil, candidate, etc., or to set an examination. E18.

2 *medical examiner*: see MEDICAL *a.* 3 SATISFY *the examiners.*

examinership *n.* the office or post of examiner M19.

examplar /ɪɡˈzɑːmplə, ɛɡ-/ *n.* Now *rare.* LME. [OFr. *examplaire* var. of *exemplaire*: see EXEMPLAR *n.*] 1 A model; a perfect specimen (of some quality); a person or thing to be imitated. LME. 2 Orig., a copy, a transcript. Now, a copy of a book. LME. †3 A needlework sampler. M–L16.

example /ɪɡˈzɑːmp(ə)l, ɛɡ-/ *n.* LME. [OFr. (mod. *exemple*), alt. after L of *essample* (whence ENSAMPLE *n.*, aphet. SAMPLE *n.*) f. L *exemplum*, f. *eximere* take out (see EXEMPT *a.*).] 1 A typical instance; a fact or thing illustrating a general principle; a person or thing illustrating a certain quality etc. LME. b A specimen, an instance; a copy of a book, esp. a rare one. M16. 2 A person whose punishment is a warning or deterrent to others; an instance of such a punishment. LME. 3 A parallel case; a case with which comparison may be made. LME. 4 A precedent appealed to for justification. Now *rare* or *obs.* LME. 5 Action or conduct regarded as something that ought to or may be imitated; a person whose conduct ought to be imitated. LME. 6 *Logic.* An argument in which a premiss is assumed from a particular instance. M16. 7 A problem or exercise designed to illustrate a principle or technique in mathematics etc. L17.

1 J. B. PRIESTLEY This is an admirable example of the public spirit of the Norwich citizens. M. TIPPETT Socrates thinks there are four common examples of divine madness. b H. NEMEROV The bison, Except for a few examples kept in cages, Is now extinct. 2 D. CUSACK Should be expelled. Make an example of her. 3 *American Speech* The name *Istanbul* replaced *Constantinople.* There are many similar examples. 5 J. F. KENNEDY England's example in disarming unilaterally had not been followed by the other countries. A. C. BOULT Toscanini was an example to us all in his attitude of humble service to the composer and his music.

Phrases: **beyond example** surpassing or without comparison. **for example** by way of illustration. **give, set an example** (or **a good, bad,** etc., **example**) act in such a (good, bad) manner as to induce imitation. **without example** having no comparable instance.

example /ɪɡˈzɑːmp(ə)l, ɛɡ-/ *v.t.* LME. [f. the n.] †1 Set a precedent for; justify by precedent. LME–L16. 2 Exemplify; provide a model of; find or give an instance of. Now only in *pass.* LME. 3 Set an example to. Formerly also (of a thing), serve as an example or warning to. Now *rare.* L16. †4 Indicate (a person) as an example. E–M17.

2 J. MORLEY A fervid assiduity that has not often been exampled.

†**exanguine** *a.* var. of EXSANGUINE.

exanimate /ɪkˈsanɪmət, ɛk-/ *a.* M16. [L *exanimatus* pa. pple of *exanimare* deprive of life, f. as EX-[1] 1 + *anima* breath of life: see -ATE[2].] 1 Dead; lifeless (in appearance); inanimate. M16. 2 Deprived of or lacking animation or courage. M16.

exanimate /ɪkˈsanɪmeɪt, ɛk-/ *v.t.* Now *rare.* M16. [L *exanimat-* pa. ppl stem of *exanimare*: see prec., -ATE[3].] †1 Dishearten, dispirit. M16–M17. †2 Kill. L16–M17. 3 Make breathless or unconscious. L19.

ex animo /ɛks ˈanɪməʊ/ *adv. phr.* E17. [L = from the soul, f. as EX *prep.* + *animo* abl. of *animus* soul.] Heartily, sincerely.

exannulate /ɪkˈsanjʊlət, ɛk-/ *a.* M19. [f. EX-[1] 2 + ANNULUS + -ATE[2].] *Bot.* Having no annulus round the sporangium, as in certain ferns.

ex ante /ɛks ˈanti/ *a.* & *adv. phr.* M20. [mod.L, f. as EX *prep.* + L *ante* before.] Chiefly *Econ.* A *adj. phr.* Based on prior assumptions or expectations; predicted, prospective. M20. B *adv. phr.* Before the event, in advance, beforehand. M20.

exanthema /ɪkˈsanθɪmə, ɛksanˈθiːmə/ *n.* Pl. **exanthemata** /ɪksanˈθiːmətə, ɛk-/, **-themas.** Also **exanthem** /ɪkˈsanθɪm/. M17. [Late L f. Gk *exanthēma* eruption, f. as EX-[2] + *antheein* to blossom, f. *anthos* flower.] *Med.* The rash or skin signs of an acute, esp. febrile, disease; a disease characterized by this.

exantheˈmatic *a.* E19. **exanˈthematous** *a.* M18.

†**exantlate** *v.t.* M–L17. [L *exantlat-* pa. ppl stem of *exantlare* or *exanclare* draw out (a liquid): see -ATE[3].] Exhaust.

†**exantlation** *n.* (*a*) the action of drawing something out like water from a well; (*b*) exhaustion: M17–E18.

exarate /ˈɛksəreɪt/ *a.* L19. [L *exaratus* pa. pple of *exarare* plough up, write on a wax tablet, f. as EX-[1] 1 + *arare* to plough: see -ATE[2].] *Entomol.* Of a pupa: having the appendages free from the body.

exaration /ɛksəˈreɪʃ(ə)n/ *n.* Now *rare* or *obs.* M17. [Late L *exaratio(n-)*, f. *exarare*: see prec., -ATE[3].] The action of writing or of engraving on stone; a composition.

exarch /ˈɛksɑːk/ *n.* L16. [eccl.L *exarchus* f. Gk *exarkhos* leader, chief, f. as EX-[2]: see -ARCH.] 1 *Hist.* A governor or vicegerent of a distant province under the Byzantine emperors. L16. 2 In the Orthodox Church: any of certain bishops next in rank below a patriarch, with oversight of a province and (now or formerly) jurisdiction over a metropolitan; a primate of an autocephalous Church; a bishop appointed as a patriarch's representative in a distant part. L16.

Exarchist *n.* (*Hist.*) a supporter of the Exarch of Bulgaria against the Patriarch of Constantinople during the schism of 1872–1945 E20.

exarch /ˈɛksɑːk/ *a.* L19. [f. EX-[2] + Gk *arkhē* beginning, origin.] *Bot.* Of xylem or its development: formed or occurring from the periphery of a stem towards the centre.

exarchate /ˈɛksɑːkeɪt/ *n.* M16. [med.L *exarchatus*, f. as EXARCH *n.*: see -ATE[1].] 1 The office or position of an exarch. M16. 2 The province under the jurisdiction or rule of an exarch. L16.

exasperate /ɪɡˈzasp(ə)reɪt, ɛɡ-/ *v.* Pa. pple **-ated,** (*arch.*) **-ate** /-ət/. M16. [L *exasperat-* pa. ppl stem of *exasperare*, f as EX-[1] 1 + *asper* rough: see -ATE[3].] 1 *v.t.* & *i.* Irritate (a person) to annoyance or anger. (Formerly foll. by *to, to do.*) M16. 2 *v.t.* Intensify (ill feeling, wickedness); increase the fierceness of (disease, pain, appetite, etc.); exacerbate. M16. †3 *v.t.* Make more painful, aggravate; exaggerate (something unpleasant). M16–M18. †4 *v.t.* Irritate physically; chafe. M16–L17. †5 *v.t.* Make harsh or rugged; make (a law) more severe. L16–M18. †6 *v.i.* Become worse; (of a person) become enraged. M17–M18.

1 E. F. BENSON This tender assurance served only to exasperate Aunt Catherine. E. WAUGH It was an exasperating moment when we landed at Rome . . and were told we could not proceed.

exasperated *a.* that has been exasperated; (of a person) very irritable, mildly angry, esp. as a result of provocation or frustration: L16. **exasperatedly** *adv.* L19. **exasperatedness** *n.* M18. **exasperatingly** *adv.* in an exasperating manner M19. **exasperater** *n.* M17. **exasperator** *n.* M18.

exasperation /ɪɡˌzaspəˈreɪʃ(ə)n, ɛɡ-/ *n.* M16. [L *exasperatio(n-)*, f. *exasperat-*: see prec., -ATION.] 1 The condition of being exasperated; irritation; anger. Formerly also, an instance of this. M16. 2 The action or an act of exasperating; something that exasperates. E17. b Exacerbation of a disease. M17.

1 M. SPARK Mr. Lloyd looked round with offended exasperation. 2 GEO. ELIOT He had made ties for himself which . . were a constant exasperation.

exaspidean /ɛksaˈspɪdɪən/ *a.* L19. [f. mod.L *Exaspideae*, f. as EX-[1] 1 + Gk *aspid-*, *aspis* shield: see -EAN.] *Zool.* Possessing or designating a bird's tarsal sheath with an anterior series of scutella on its outer side.

†**exauctorate** *v.t.* Pa. pple **-ated, -ate.** L16. [L *exauctorat-* pa. ppl stem of *exauctorare* dismiss from service, f. as EX-[1] 1 + *auctor*: see AUTHOR *n.*, -ATE[3].] 1 Deprive (a law etc.) of authority. L16–L17. 2 Depose from office, deprive of rank. E17–E19.

†**exauctoration** *n.* E17–M19.

excalceate /ɪksˈkalsɪeɪt, ɛks-/ *v.t.* Now *rare* or *obs.* E17. [L *excalceat-* pa. ppl stem of *excalceare*, f. as EX-[1] 1 + *calceus* shoe: see -ATE[3].] Remove the shoes of, make barefoot, esp. as a symbolic gesture.

excalceˈation *n.* M18.

excamb /ɪkˈskamb, ɛk-/ *v.t.* & *i.* *Sc. Law.* L15. [med.L *excambiare*, f. as EX-[1] + late L *cambiare*: see CHANGE *v.*] Exchange (land).

excamber *n.* E17.

excambion /ɪkˈskambɪən, ɛk-/ *n.* *Sc. Law.* LME. [med.L *ex(s)cambio(n-)*, f. as prec.: see -ION.] An exchange of land.

excandescence /ɛkskanˈdɛs(ə)ns/ *n.* Now *rare.* L17. [L *excandescentia*, f. *excandescere* grow white-hot, f. as EX-[1] 1 + *candescere* become light, white, or hot, f. *candere* be white: see -ESCENCE.] The state of being glowing hot. Chiefly *fig.*, warmth of temper, spirits, etc.; passion; anger.

Also †**excandescency** *n.* E17–E19.

†**excantation** *n.* *rare.* L16–M19. [Alt. of *incantation* after L *excantare* bring out by enchantment, f. as EX-[1] 1 + *cantare* sing (see CHANT *v.*).] The action of removing something by enchantment.

excarnate /ɪkˈskɑːnət, ɛk-/ *a.* M19. [Late L *excarnatus*, f. *excarnare*: see next, -ATE[2].] Chiefly *Archaeol.* Stripped of flesh.

excarnate /ɪkˈskɑːneɪt, ɛk-/ *v.t.* Now *rare.* M17. [Late L *excarnat-* pa. ppl stem of *excarnare*, f. as EX-[1] 1 + *carn-*, *caro* flesh: see -ATE[3].] Remove the flesh from.

excarˈnation *n.* (*a*) the action of removing flesh; *spec.* the exposure of a corpse to let the flesh decay before it is buried; (*b*) loss of corporeal form, disembodiment: M19.

ex cathedra /ɛks kəˈθiːdrə, ˈkaθɪdrə/ *adv.* & *a.* E17. [L = from the (teacher's) chair, f. as EX *prep.* + CATHEDRA.] A *adv.* Authoritatively; as an official pronouncement; *esp.* (*RC Ch.*) with the full weight of the Pope's office as divinely appointed guardian of Christian faith and morals. E17.

Redemption Tidings The Pope . . claims to be infallible only when he speaks ex cathedra on faith and morals.

B *adj.* Authoritative, official; given *ex cathedra*; dogmatic. E19.

excavate /ˈɛkskəveɪt/ *ppl a.* *rare.* L16. [L *excavatus* pa. pple of *excavare*: see next, -ATE[2].] Hollowed out.

excavate /ˈɛkskəveɪt/ *v.* L16. [L *excavat-* pa. ppl stem of *excavare*, f. as EX-[1] 1 + *cavare* make or become hollow, f. *cavus* hollow: see -ATE[3].] 1 *v.t.* Make hollow by removing material from inside; make a hollow or hollows in; *esp.* remove material from (the ground) so as to make a hole. L16. 2 *v.t.* Make (a hole, channel, etc.) by removing material. M19. 3 *v.t.* Uncover or investigate by digging; unearth (*lit.* & *fig.*); *esp.* make a systematic exploration of (an archaeological site) by this means. M19. 4 *v.t.* Extract by digging. M19. 5 *v.i.* Make an excavation; take part in an archaeological excavation. M19.

1 DICKENS The foot of the cliff is excavated into a cavern. 2 C. LYELL One of them began to excavate a hole. 3 J. A. MICHENER He had dreamed of excavating one of the silent mounds in the Holy Land. *American Notes & Queries* It excavates thousands of titles not found in the usual bibliographies. 4 *Mining Magazine* About 60,000 t of gold ore had been excavated at the mine. 5 E. WILSON The deeper I have excavated, the more surely I have satisfied myself that the best was underneath.

excavation /ɛkskəˈveɪʃ(ə)n/ *n.* E17. [Fr., or L *excavatio(n-)*, f. as prec.: see -ATION.] 1 The action or an act of excavating, *spec.* as part of the archaeological investigation of a site. E17. 2 An excavated space; a cavity, a hollow. L18.

1 B. TARKINGTON Excavations for the cellars of five new houses were in process. C. G. SELIGMAN The skeletal remains recovered from excavations during Archaeological Surveys. 2 W. H. BARTLETT The wine-press was an oblong excavation in the rock.

excavational *a.* L20.

excavator /ˈɛkskəveɪtə/ *n.* E19. [f. EXCAVATE *v.* + -OR.] 1 A person who excavates; *esp.* one who excavates an archaeological site. E19. 2 A thing that excavates; *esp.* a machine (now usu. self-propelled) for removing soil from the ground. M19.

exˈcavatory *a.* of or pertaining to excavation or the work of an excavator M19.

excave /ɪkˈskeɪv, ɛk-/ *v.i.* & †*t.* *rare.* L16. [L *excavare*: see EXCAVATE *v.*] Excavate.

†**excecate** *v.t.* Pa. pple **excecated,** (earlier) **excecate.** E16–M17. [L *excaecat-* pa. ppl stem of *excaecare*, f. as EX-[1] 1 + *caecus* blind: see -ATE[3].] Make blind (*lit.* & *fig.*).

excecation /ɛksɪˈkeɪʃ(ə)n/ *n.* Now *rare* or *obs.* E16. [f. prec. + -ATION.] †1 Mental or spiritual blindness; the action of bringing into this condition. E16–M17. 2 The action or an act of blinding, esp. as a punishment. E17.

excedent /ɪkˈsiːd(ə)nt, ɛk-/ *n.* Now *rare* or *obs.* M17. [L *excedent-* pres. ppl stem of *excedere*: see next, -ENT.] An excess; something which exceeds.

exceed /ɪkˈsiːd, ɛk-/ *v.* LME. [(O)Fr. *excéder* f. L *excedere* go away or out, surpass, f. as EX-[1] 1 +

cedere go.] **1** *v.t.* Pass beyond or go over (a boundary, a specified point). *arch.* LME. †**b** Transgress (a law). LME–L18. **c** Go beyond the limit set by, do more than is warranted by, (a privilege, one's authority, etc.). M16. **2** *v.t.* Be greater or more numerous than; be heavier than; go faster than. (Foll. by *by*.) LME. †**b** Be too great or too much for. L16–M18. **3** *v.t.* Surpass, outdo; be superior to. (Foll. by *in*.) LME. †**4** *v.i.* Go beyond the bounds of propriety; go too far; be immoderate. LME–M18. **b** Exaggerate. E18–E19. **5** *v.i.* Be pre-eminent; be greater or better; preponderate. L15. **6** Chiefly at Cambridge University: have extra or special food at a meal; (of the food) be in extra quantity. L16.

2 E. ROOSEVELT My actual expenses always exceeded these figures. M. MEYER The membership .. should not exceed nine. R. BRADBURY His gift .. exceeded the weight limit by no more than a few ounces. E. F. BENSON It was binding on drivers not to exceed such a speed. 3 TENNYSON One whose rank exceeds her own. M. SCHORER In sheer clumsiness of style no living writer exceeds him. 5 SHAKES. *Lucr.* The guilt being great, the fear doth still exceed. B. JOWETT Men always choose the life which exceeds in pleasure.

exceedable *a.* (*rare*) E17.

exceeding /ɪk'siːdɪŋ, ɛk-/ *vbl n.* L15. [f. prec. + -ING[1].] **1** *gen.* The action of EXCEED *v.* Formerly also, an instance of this, an unusual or excessive action or performance; the quality of surpassing others, excellence. L15. **2a** In *pl.* Chiefly at Cambridge University: extra food allowed on festival days. E17. †**b** Usu. in *pl.* An amount in excess of calculation or what is usual; an excess, a surplus. E18–M19.

exceeding /ɪk'siːdɪŋ, ɛk-/ *a.* & *adv.* L15. [f. as prec. + -ING[2].] **A** *adj.* †**1** Going beyond the bounds of propriety; going to extremes. L15–M18. **2** Surpassing; extremely great; pre-eminent in amount or degree. Chiefly *attrib.* M16. †**3** Supremely good. M–L16.

1 E. SANDYS Why was Anna so exceeding in craving children at the hands of God? 2 LD MACAULAY The exceeding badness of the beer which he brewed. J. M. MURRY Recompensed for his exceeding suffering.

B *adv.* Exceedingly. *arch.* M16.

WORDSWORTH A virtuous household, though exceeding poor.

exceedingly *adv.* †(*a*) so as to outdo others; (*b*) extremely, very; very much: L15. **exceedingness** *n.* (long *rare*) L16.

excel /ɪk'sɛl, ɛk-/ *v.* Infl. **-ll-**. LME. [L *excellere*, f. as EX-[1] 1 + *celsus* lofty.] **1** *v.i.* Be pre-eminent in the possession of some quality or the performance of some action. (Foll. by *at*, *as*, *in*.) LME. **2** *v.t.* Be superior to (a person or thing) in the possession of some quality or the performance of some action; outdo, surpass. (Foll. by *in*.) LME. **b** Surpass (another's qualities or work). *rare.* E17. †**3** *v.t.* Be greater than, exceed; be too much for, overpower. M17–E18.

1 J. A. SYMONDS How could a Spartan .. excel in any fine art? E. M. FORSTER They were .. deficient where she excelled. J. HILTON He .. excelled at games. J. P. HENNESSY Trollope excelled at evoking the spirit as well as the appearance of any place. N. MITFORD She excelled as a hostess. 2 Z. GREY Sally wanted to look beautiful, to excell all the young ladies who were to attend. A. FRASER The coronation .. excelled in splendour anything he had conceivably expected. b S. JOHNSON He has excelled every composition of the same kind.

excellence /'ɛks(ə)l(ə)ns/ *n.* LME. [(O)Fr., or L *excellentia*, f. *excellent-*: see EXCELLENT, -ENCE.] **1** The state or fact of excelling; the possession of good qualities or abilities to an eminent or unusual degree; surpassing merit, skill, or worth. LME. **2** Something in which a person or thing excels; an excellent feature, quality, or ability. LME. †**3a** An excellent personality. LME–L18. **b** = EXCELLENCY 3b. L16–L18.

1 N. ARNOTT The brightest examples have arisen of intellectual and moral excellence. D. HALBERSTAM The drive in television news was no longer for pure excellence, a drive to be better .. than the other two networks. PAR EXCELLENCE. 2 A. P. STANLEY The great excellence of the eastern table-land was .. in pasture. J. H. NEWMAN Civilized nations allow that foreigners have their specific excellences.

excellency /'ɛks(ə)l(ə)nsi/ *n.* ME. [L *excellentia*: see prec., -ENCY.] **1** = EXCELLENCE 1. Now *rare* or *obs.* ME. †**b** Something that excels or takes the highest place; the best *of*. Only in 17. **2** (Usu. **E-**.) A designation of an important personage or dignitary; *spec.* the title of respect given to ambassadors, governors, and (*US*) Roman Catholic archbishops and bishops. Chiefly w. possess. adj. M16. **3** = EXCELLENCE 2. Now *rare.* E17. †**b** *The* thing that makes something excellent. M17–E19.

2 W. WHISTON His Excellency the Muscovite Ambassador.

excellent /'ɛks(ə)l(ə)nt/ *a.*, *adv.*, & *n.* LME. [(O)Fr. f. L *excellent-* pres. ppl stem of *excellere*: see EXCEL, -ENT.] **A** *adj.* **1** That excels in some respect (either good or bad); (of a quality) existing in a greater degree; outstanding, supreme. Now *rare* or *obs.* exc. as in sense 3. LME. †**2** Excelling in rank or dignity; exalted, highly honourable. LME–E18. **3** Pre-eminent; extremely good. E17.

1 HENRY MORE The excellent usefulness of the Horse. D. HUME Elizabeth .. was an excellent hypocrite. 2 AV *Ps.* 148:13 Let them praise the Name of the Lord, for his Name alone is excellent. 3 M. INNES Folk with intelligences ranging from moderate through good to excellent. G. GREENE The Opera Society had given an excellent rendering of Patience.

†**B** *adv.* Excellently. LME–M18.

C *n.* **1** In *pl.* Excellences. *rare.* L15. **2** *the excellent*, (*collect. pl.*) excellent people. E17.

excellently *adv.* in an excellent manner or degree, extremely well LME.

excelsior /ɛk'sɛlsɪɔː/ *int.* & *n.* L18. [L, compar. of *excelsus*, f. as EX-[1] 1 + *celsus* lofty: see -IOR.] **A** *int.* Go higher! L18.

LONGFELLOW A voice replied, far up the height, Excelsior!

B *n.* **1** Curled shavings of soft wood for stuffing, packing, etc. Orig. *US.* M19. **2** A person who or thing which reaches or aspires to reach higher. L19. **3** (Usu. **E-**.) A very small size (3 points) of type. Chiefly *US.* E20.

1 V. NABOKOV A boy with hair like excelsior. 2 D. H. LAWRENCE Up he goes! Up like a bloomin' little Excelsior In his Sunday clothes!

excentral /ɪk'sɛntr(ə)l, ɛk-/ *a. rare.* M19. [f. EX-[1] 1 + L *centrum* + -AL[1].] = ECCENTRIC *a.* 3.

excentric *n.* & *a.* see ECCENTRIC.

excentricity *n.* see ECCENTRICITY.

except /ɪk'sɛpt, ɛk-/ *ppl a.*, *prep.*, & *conj.* LME. [L *exceptus* pa. pple of *excipere*: see prec.] †**A** *ppl a.* Excepted, not included; exempted. LME–M17.

1 SHAKES. *Rich. III* Richard except, those whom we fight against Had rather have us win.

B *prep.* **1** Excepting, with the exception of, but. LME. †**2** Leaving out of account; in addition to, besides. *rare.* L15–M18.

1 N. COWARD Nobody knows we're here except Freda. G. HOUSEHOLD No sign of life except swooping bats. 2 T. AMORY Except the hours of sleep, we were rarely from each other.

C *conj.* **1** Used bef. a statement of fact that forms an exception to a statement just made. Usu. foll. by *that*: with the exception *that*. LME. **2** Unless. *arch.* exc. *poet.* L15. **3** Used bef. an adv., phr., or cl. expressing a respect in which a preceding statement is not applicable. L15.

1 DAY LEWIS Irish nursemaids of whom I remember nothing except that one .. was called Eva. A. PRICE I thought he was you, at the door. Except he doesn't knock. 2 W. OWEN Except you share With them in hell the sorrowful dark of hell. 3 L. BRUCE I wouldn't ever wear it, naturally—except maybe on Halloween. V. WOOLF There is no truth about life .. except what we feel. J. C. POWYS You can't break through life except by dying. E. WAUGH They .. left him in his room with no desire except to sleep. I. MURDOCH He never said this except jokingly to Harriet. **except for** exception being made for, were it not for; = sense B.1 above.

except /ɪk'sɛpt, ɛk-/ *v.* LME. [L *except-* pa. ppl stem of *excipere*, f. as EX-[1] 1 + *capere* take.] **I1** *v.t.* Specify as not included in a category or group; exclude (*from*). As *excepted* pa. pple freq. *postpositive.* LME. **2** *v.i.* Make objection (*against*), object or take exception (*to*). Now *rare.* LME. †**3** *v.t.* Offer or allege as an objection (*against*, *to*); object (*that*). L16–M18. †**4** *v.t.* Take exception to; protest against. *rare* (Shakes.). Only in L16.

1 J. BRYCE The Church excepted, no agent did so much. K. TYNAN From their collective guilt I except Miss Zinkeisen alone.

†**II5** Accept. LME–M17.

exceptable *a.* M20.

excepting /ɪk'sɛptɪŋ, ɛk-/ *prep.* & *conj.* L15. [f. EXCEPT *v.* + -ING[2].] **A** *prep.* **1** If one excepts. L15. **2** With the exception of, except. M16.

2 GOLDSMITH This was received with great approbation by all, excepting my wife.

B *conj.* **1** Unless. M17. **2** = EXCEPT *conj.* 3. Now *rare.* M17.

exception /ɪk'sɛpʃ(ə)n, ɛk-/ *n.* LME. [(O)Fr. f. L *exceptio(n-)*, f. as EXCEPT *v.*: see -ION.] **I1** The action of excepting someone or something from a group, the scope of a proposition, etc.; the state or fact of being so excepted. LME. **2** A person who or thing which is excepted; *esp.* a particular case or individual that does not follow some general rule or to which a generalization is not applicable. Foll. by *to*, †*from*. LME. **3** *Law* (now *Hist.*). A plea made by a defendant in bar of a plaintiff's action; *Sc.* a defence. Also, an objection made to the ruling of a court during the course of a trial; a plaintiff's objection to a defendant's affidavit or answer as insufficient. LME. †**4** A plea tending to evade the force of an opponent's argument; a formal objection to a proceeding, a person's fitness for office, etc. LME–L17. **5** Objection, demur, cavil; a complaint, a criticism. Now *rare* or *obs.* exc. in phrs. below. L15. †**b** Dislike, dissatisfaction. *rare* (Shakes.). Only in E17.

1 G. C. LEWIS This exception of women and children from the whole community. 2 B. RUSSELL 'Unsupported bodies in air fall' is a general rule to which balloons .. are exceptions. A. C. BOULT Sir Henry was most kind to younger musicians and I was no exception. 5 S. PEPYS Sir C. Sedley's exceptions against both words and pronouncing were very pretty.

†**II6** = ACCEPTION 1. LME–E17.

Phrases: **beyond exception** = *without exception* (b) below. **take exception (to)** object (to), take offence (at). **without exception** (*a*) with no one or nothing excepted (emphasizing the universality of a proposition etc.); (*b*) beyond reproach or suspicion. **with the exception of** except for.

exceptionable *a.* (*a*) to which exception may be taken; (*b*) exceptional: L17. **exceptionableness** *n.* (*rare*) M17. **exceptionably** *adv.* (*rare*) in an exceptionable manner; exceptionally: E19. **exceptionary** *a.* (*rare*) of, pertaining to, or indicative of an exception; exceptional: L18. **exceptionless** *a.* without an exception; not admitting of an exception: L16.

exceptional /ɪk'sɛpʃ(ə)n(ə)l, ɛk-/ *a.* M19. [f. prec. + -AL[1], after Fr. *exceptionnel*.] Of the nature of or forming an exception; unusual, out of the ordinary; special; (of a person) unusually good, able, etc.

I. MURDOCH The exceptional pallor of their skin .. put the onlooker .. in mind of Grecian marbles. J. BERGER The unusualness of both the things which were happening confirmed that the occasion was exceptional. R. JARRELL She herself was a very exceptional person.

exceptionalism *n.* the belief that a certain thing constitutes an exception in relation to others of its class, *spec.* (*Polit.*) that the peaceful capitalism of the US is an exception to the Marxist law of the inevitability of violent class struggle E20. **exceptio'nality** *n.* exceptional character or quality; an exceptional thing: M19. **exceptionally** *adv.* (*a*) unusually, outstandingly; (*b*) as an exception to rule or custom: M19. **exceptionalness** *n.* L19.

exceptious /ɪk'sɛpʃəs, ɛk-/ *a.* Now *rare.* E17. [f. EXCEPTION + -OUS, after *captious*.] Disposed to make objections; cavilling, captious.

exceptiousness *n.* L17.

exceptis excipiendis /ɛk,sɛptɪs ɛksɪpɪ'ɛndɪs/ *adv. phr.* L19. [Late L, f. abl. pl. of L *exceptus* pa. pple, and of *excipiendus* gerundive, of *excipere*: see EXCEPT *v.*] With appropriate exceptions.

exceptive /ɪk'sɛptɪv/ *a.* & *n.* L16. [Late L *exceptivus*, f. as EXCEPT *v.*: see -IVE.] **A** *adj.* **1** *Logic* & *Gram.* Introducing or making an exception; (of a proposition) having a subject that specifies an exception. L16. 2 Of people, their utterances, etc.: disposed or tending to take exception; captious. E17. B *n. Logic* & *Gram.* An exceptive proposition or word. L16.

†exceptless *a. rare* (Shakes.). Only in E17. [Irreg. f. EXCEPT *v.* + -LESS.] Making no exception.

exceptor /ɪk'sɛptə, ɛk-/ *n.* M17. [In sense 1 f. EXCEPT *v.* + -OR; in sense 2 f. late L, f. as EXCEPT *v.*] †1 A person who objects or takes exception; an objector. M–L17. 2 A reporter or clerk; *spec.* a clerk under the later Roman Empire. *obs.* exc. *Hist.* L17.

†excern *v.t.* & *i.* L16–M18. [L *excernere* EXCRETE.] Of a living organism or organ: separate (waste matter) preparatory to expelling it. Also, excrete.

excerpt /'ɛksəːpt, ɪk'səːpt, ɛk-/ *n.* Pl. **-s, †-a.** E17. [L *excerptum* use as n. of neut. pa. pple of *excerpere*: see next.] 1 An extract from a book, manuscript, musical work, etc. E17. 2 An offprint. *rare.* L19.

excerpt /'ɛksəːpt, ɪk'səːpt, ɛk-/ *v.* M16. [L *excerpt-* pa. ppl stem of *excerpere*, f. as EX-[1] 1 + *carpere* pluck.] 1a *v.t.* & *i.* Reproduce (a chosen passage) from a text; choose (a passage) for this purpose. M16. b *v.t.* Take quotations or choose passages from. L19. †2 *v.t.* Take out, remove. M16–E17.

1a O. SACKS 'The Man Who Fell out of Bed' is excerpted from *A Leg to Stand On.* b *American Speech* None of the volumes excerpted goes beyond 1967–68.

excerption /ɪk'səːpʃ(ə)n, ɛk-/ *n.* E17. [L *excerptio(n-)*, f. as prec.: see -ION.] 1 An excerpt. Formerly also, a collection of excerpts. E17. 2 The action of choosing or taking excerpts. M19.

excerptor *n.* (*rare*) L17.

excess /ɪk'sɛs, ɛk-, *attrib.* 'ɛksɛs/ *n.*, *a.*, & *v.* LME. [(O)Fr. *excès* f. L *excessus*, f. *excess-* pa. ppl stem of *excedere* EXCEED.] A *n.* I†1 The action of going out; adjournment. *rare.* LME–E17. 2 In full *excess of mind* or *soul.* An ecstasy; a trance. LME–E17. †3 (A display of) extravagant emotion. LME–M18. 4 In *pl.* & †*sing.* Extravagant violation of law, decency, or morality; outrageous acts or conduct. LME. 5 The action or an act of exceeding the limits of moderation, esp. in eating or drinking; (an) indulgence. LME. 6 The state of being in greater quantity or degree than is usual, necessary, appropriate, or beneficial; superabundance; an extreme or excessive amount or degree *of* something. LME. b *Chem.* An amount of a substance greater than that needed to effect a given reaction or change. E19. 7 The amount by which one number or quantity exceeds another; *spec.* a sum payable by an insured party in the event of a claim, the insurer paying the amount by which the claim exceeds this sum. LME. †b Usury, interest. *rare* (Shakes.). Only in L16. 8 The fact of exceeding something else in amount or degree; preponderance. Formerly also, the fact of surpassing or excelling others. E17. †9 Departure *from* custom, reason, etc. E–M18. 10 The action or an act of exceeding one's authority, rights, etc. E19.

4 P. WARNER He.. allowed his army to commit all the excesses that are particularly hateful. 5 O. W. HOLMES What had he been doing to get his head in such a state?—had he.. committed an excess? H. ACTON Reading was Nancy's sole excess: in everything else she was moderate. B. BAINBRIDGE Liverish from the previous night's excess. N. ANNAN Walking.. to dispel the excesses of Christmas Eve dinner. 6 ISAIAH BERLIN All the criticisms directed against this or that writer for an excess of bias or fancy. K. AMIS Excess of energy was really her trouble. A. BURGESS Tired eyes, as from an excess of recent deskwork. **to excess** to an inappropriate or overindulgent extent, excessively. b C. L. BLOXAM The carbonates of potash and soda are fused with an excess of arsenious acid. 8 **in excess of** more than.

†II 11 = ACCESS *n.* 1b. M16–M17.

B *adj.* Constituting an excess; *esp.* exceeding the appropriate or stipulated amount. Usu. *attrib.* (After M17 *obs.* until L19.) LME.

H. JAMES He was not absolutely simple, which would have been excess; he was only relatively simple, which was quite enough. B. SPOCK The body.. gets rid of excess water through the urine. B. TRAPIDO There is excess rubbish piling up.. beside the overflowing rubbish bin. **excess fare** payment due for travelling further or in a higher class than one's ticket allows. **excess luggage** luggage over the weight for which free carriage is permitted. **excess postage** payment due when the stamps on a letter etc. are insufficient.

C *v.t.* 1 Subject to an excess fare. L19. 2 Declare (an employee) redundant. *US.* L20.

excessive /ɪk'sɛsɪv, ɛk-/ *a.* & *adv.* LME. [(O)Fr. *excessif*, *-ive* f. med.L *excessivus*, f. L *excess-*: see prec., -IVE.] A *adj.* †1 Transgressing the bounds of law, decency, or morality. LME–M17. 2 Exceeding what is right, appropriate, or desirable; immoderate; given to excess. LME. †3 Exceeding what is usual; exceedingly great. L15–L17.

2 OED Avoid the company of excessive drinkers. ARNOLD BENNETT The doctor.. apparently saw nothing excessive in leaving two patients in charge of one unaided woman. J. M. MURRY An excessive and indiscriminating admiration of Wordsworth.

†B *adv.* Excessively. M16–L18.

excessively *adv.* (*a*) in an excessive amount, to an excessive degree; immoderately; †(*b*) wastefully, prodigally; greedily: LME. **excessiveness** *n.* L15.

exchange /ɪks'tʃeɪndʒ, ɛks-/ *n.* LME. [AN *eschaunge*, OFr. *eschange* (Fr. *échange*), f. *eschangier* (see next); *ex-* by assim. to L EX-[1].] 1 The action, or an act, of reciprocal giving and receiving (*of* goods, money, prisoners, blows, ideas, etc.). LME. b *Chess.* A capture first by one player and then by the other, as part of a single combination or manoeuvre. M18. c A reciprocal arrangement in which two people in different countries but usu. in similar roles change places for a period. E20. d A brief conversation, a discussion; an argument; a sequence of letters between correspondents. M20. 2 The giving and receiving of money for its equivalent in money of the same or another country; the trade of a money-changer. LME. †b The profit obtained by a money-changer or moneylender. M16–M18. 3a A building, office, institution, etc., used for the transaction of business or for monetary exchange. LME. b In full *telephone exchange.* A place where telephone calls are connected between different lines. L19. c A Labour Exchange. L19. 4a = *bill of exchange* s.v. BILL *n.*[3] 9. LME. b The financial system by which commercial transactions, esp. between parties in different countries, are effected without the transmission of money, e.g. by bills of exchange; interconversion of different currencies; (in full *rate of exchange*, *exchange rate*) the value assigned to a currency for the purpose of interconversion with another. L15. 5 Replacement *of* one thing by another. Formerly also, alteration, variation, change. LME. 6 A person or thing offered or given in exchange or substitution for another. L15. b A copy of a newspaper that is sent to another newspaper office in return for a copy of its newspaper; the newspaper received in return. Also more fully *exchange paper.* L18. 7 *Law* (now *Hist.*). A mutual grant of equal interests. L16. 8 A saloon, a drinking-place. *US colloq.* M19. 9 *Med.* An amount of a foodstuff regarded as replacing an equivalent quantity of another that is not allowed in a diet. M20.

1 N. MONSARRAT A straight exchange, the veal loaf for the barrel. *Proverb*: (Fair) exchange is no robbery. c *exchange professor*, *student*, etc. d J. JONES This exchange of letters between a middle-aged clerk and a girl. P. L. FERMOR Her husband had come in a little while before and overheard our exchange. C. PRIEST Polite exchanges and pleasantries.

Phrases: *bill of exchange*: see BILL *n.*[3] 9. *foreign exchange*: see FOREIGN *a.* **in exchange** as a thing exchanged (*for*). *labour exchange*: see LABOUR *n.* *local exchange*: see LOCAL *a.* *lose the exchange*: see *win the exchange* below. *medium of exchange*: see MEDIUM *n.* *par of exchange*: see PAR *n.*[1] 2a. *post exchange*: see POST *n.*[4] *private branch exchange*: see PRIVATE *a.* *rate of exchange*: see sense 4b above. *stock exchange*: see STOCK *n.*[1] & *a.* *telephone exchange*: see sense 3b above. **win** or **lose the exchange** *Chess* capture or lose a rook in exchange for a bishop or knight.

Comb.: **exchange control** governmental control of currency exchange between countries; **exchange force**: between atoms or subatomic particles and involving an exchange of charge, spin, or other coordinates; *exchange paper*: see sense 6b above; *exchange rate*: see sense 3b above; **Exchange Rate Mechanism** a method of stabilizing exchange rates in the European Monetary System by giving each currency a fixed exchange rate with the ecu; **exchange transfusion** *Med.* the simultaneous removal of some of a sick person's blood and replacement by normal blood; **exchange value** value when exchanged, exchangeable value.

exchange /ɪks'tʃeɪndʒ, ɛks-/ *v.* LME. [OFr. *eschangier* (mod. *échanger*), f. *é-* EX-[1] + *changer* CHANGE *v.*] 1 *v.t.* Dispose of by exchange or barter; relinquish (something) and receive something else in return; give up (a prisoner) to the enemy in return for one taken by them. (Foll. by *for*, *against*, †*with* the thing received.) LME. †b Obtain (something) in exchange *for.* L16–E17. †2 *v.t.* = CHANGE *v.* 4. LME–L16. 3 *v.t.* Give and receive reciprocally; make an exchange of. Foll. by sing. or pl. obj. *with* a person. E17. 4 *v.i.* Of money, articles of trade, etc.: be receivable as an equivalent *for.* L18. 5 *v.i.* Undergo or take part in an exchange; be replaced in an exchange; *spec.* (of an officer) pass *out of* a regiment or ship (*into* another) by exchange with another officer. L18.

1 C. DAY They had exchanged their regular jackets for black alpaca coats. 3 DAY LEWIS He was for ever buying, selling or exchanging books. W. CATHER Lou and Oscar exchanged outraged looks. J. WAIN They never passed each other without exchanging a word or two. 5 *Good Housekeeping* Daisy, a 14-year-old who exchanged with a 15-year-old French girl.

exchanger *n.* (*a*) a person who exchanges; *Hist.* a money-changer, a money-dealer; (*b*) a device in which something is exchanged, *spec.* = *heat-exchanger* s.v. HEAT *n.*: LME.

exchangeable /ɪks'tʃeɪndʒəb(ə)l, ɛks-/ *a.* L16. [f. prec. + -ABLE.] †1 = COMMUTATIVE 1. *rare.* Only in L16. 2 Able to be exchanged (*for*). M17. 3 Of value: estimated in terms of the value of the goods for which a thing may be exchanged. L18.

exchangea'bility *n.* L18.

exchequer /ɪks'tʃɛkə, ɛks-/ *n.* & *v.* ME. [AN *escheker*, OFr. *eschequier* (mod. *échiquier*) f. med.L *scaccarium* chessboard, f. *scaccus* CHECK *n.*[1] (see CHECK *int.*, -ER[2]); *ex-* by assoc. with EX-[1]. So called w. ref. to the chequered tablecloth on which accounts were orig. kept by means of counters. Aphet. to CHEQUER *n.*[1]] A *n.* In senses 2–4 usu. E-. †I 1 A chessboard; = CHEQUER *n.*[1] 1. ME–L15.

II 2 *Hist.* A department of state established under the Norman kings of England that dealt with the collection and administration of the royal revenues and with legal disputes about them. ME. 3 Orig. (now *Hist.*), the Government department responsible for the receipt and custody of the money collected by the departments of revenue. Now, the Government's account at the Bank of England whose balance forms the Consolidated Fund. LME. b *the Exchequer*, the contents of the Exchequer. M17. 4 *Hist.* More fully *Court of Exchequer*, *Exchequer of Pleas.* A former court of law (merged in the High Court of Justice in 1873) which historically represented the Anglo-Norman Exchequer in its judicial capacity. L15. b Either of the two analogous courts that formerly existed in Scotland and Ireland. E19. 5 A royal or national treasury. M16. 6 The monetary possessions of a private person, an institution, etc. E17.

Phrases: *Chancellor of the Exchequer*: see CHANCELLOR 2. *Court of Exchequer*, *Exchequer of Pleas*: see sense 4 above. *Marshal of the Exchequer*: see MARSHAL *n.*[1] 4. *stop of the exchequer*: see STOP *n.*[2]

Comb.: **exchequer bill** *Hist.* a bill of credit with varying interest issued by authority of Parliament; **exchequer-chamber** *Hist.* the room in the Exchequer where judges and officials met; (also *Court of Exchequer Chamber*) any of several former courts of appeal; a former forum of debate comprising all the judges.

B *v.t.* †1 Place in an exchequer or treasury. *rare.* Only in E18. 2 *Hist.* Proceed against (a person) in the Court of Exchequer. E19. b Seize as contraband. E19.

excide /ɛk'sʌɪd/ *v.t.* M18. [L *excidere* EXCISE *v.*[1]] Cut out.

excimer /ˈɛksɪmə/ *n.* M20. [f. EXCI(TED + DI)MER.] *Chem.* An exciplex, esp. formed from two identical atoms or molecules.

excipient /ɛkˈsɪpɪənt/ *a.* & *n.* E18. [L *excipient-* pres. ppl stem of *excipere* take out, receive, f. as EX-[1] 1 + *capere* take: see -ENT.] †A *adj.* That takes exception. Only in E18. B *n.* 1 An inactive substance that serves as the vehicle or medium for a drug. M18. 2 The material or surface that receives the pigments in painting. M19.

exciplex /ˈɛksɪplɛks/ *n.* M20. [f. EXCI(TED + COM)PLEX *n.*] *Chem.* A molecule formed by a metastable bond between two atoms or molecules and existing only in an excited state.

excipulum /ɛkˈsɪpjʊləm/ *n.* Also Anglicized as **exciple** /ˈɛksɪp(ə)l/, **excipule** /ˈɛksɪpjuːl/. M19. [L = receptacle, f. *excipere*: see EXCIPIENT, -ULE.] *Bot.* A layer of tissue underlying and containing the hymenium in the apothecium of a lichen.

excise /ˈɛksʌɪz/ *n.* L15. [MDu. *excijs* (also *accijs*), perh. f. Proto-Romance vbl n. f. L *accensare* to tax, f. as AC- + *census* tax, CENSUS.] 1 A tax, a toll. L15. 2 *spec.* A duty levied on goods produced or sold within a country and on licences granted for certain activities. L16. †3 Payment or imposition of excise duty. E–M18. 4 The government office responsible for the collection of excise duty, in Britain now called the *Board of Customs and Excise*. L18.

2 *attrib.*: *Cornish Guardian* Guilty to . . stealing an excise licence for a works truck. *excise duty*, *officer*, etc.

Comb.: **excise law**: *spec.* (*US*) a licensing law; **exciseman** an officer employed to collect excise duty and prevent infringement of the excise laws; **excisemanship** the post of exciseman.

excise /ɪkˈsʌɪz, ɛk-/ *v.*[1]*t.* L16. [L *excis-* pa. ppl stem of *excidere*, f. as EX-[1] 1 + *caedere* to cut.] 1 Chiefly *Bot.* & *Zool.* Notch or hollow out some of the substance of. Chiefly as *excised* pa. pple. L16. †2 Circumcise (esp. a woman or girl). E–M17. 3 Remove or expunge (a passage) from or *from* a book etc. M17. 4 Cut out physically (a growth, organ, etc.); remove or take out as if by cutting. M19.

3 H. R. Reynolds Marcion excised other portions of the Gospel which contradict his views. 4 J. R. S. Fincham F can not only be integrated into the chromosome but can also be excised from it. *fig.*: W. H. Auden Where abnormal / growths of self-love are excised / by the crude surgery of a / practical joke.

excisable *a.*[1] able or needing to be excised M19.

excise /ˈɛksʌɪz, ɪkˈsʌɪz, ɛk-/ *v.*[2]*t.* M17. [f. EXCISE *n.*] 1 Impose excise duty on (a thing). M17. 2 Force (a person) to pay excise duty; *arch.* overcharge. M17.

exˈcisable *a.*[2] (of a person or thing) liable to (the imposition of) excise duty L17.

excision /ɪkˈsɪʒ(ə)n, ɛk-/ *n.* L15. [(O)Fr. f. L *excisio(n-)*, f. as EXCISE *v.*[1]: see -ION.] 1 The action of cutting off from existence; the condition of being so cut off; destruction. L15. 2 The action of excising a growth or organ from the body, a passage from a book, etc.; something so removed. M16. 3 The action of expelling a person from a religious society; excommunication. M17.

2 A. Powell Considerable excisions had been made . . but it had returned . . with orders for further expurgation.

excisional *a.* M20.

excitability /ɪkˌsʌɪtəˈbɪlɪti, ɛk-/ *n.* L18. [f. next + -ITY.] 1 The property in plant and animal tissue of responding to a certain kind of stimulus. L18. 2 The quality in a person of being prone or susceptible to excitement. E19.

excitable /ɪkˈsʌɪtəb(ə)l, ɛk-/ *a.* E17. [f. EXCITE + -ABLE.] Able to be excited; responsive to stimuli; prone or susceptible to excitement, easily excited. (Foll. by *to*.)

N. Hawthorne He is . . wonderfully excitable to mirth. E. Bowen Keyed up by the sudden electric light, her manner was swaggering and excitable. *Scientific American* In excitable cells calcium channels open in response to the action potential.

excitableness *n.* M19.

excitant /ˈɛksɪt(ə)nt, ɪkˈsʌɪt(ə)nt, ɛk-/ *a.* & *n.* E17. [f. EXCITE + -ANT[1], perh. after Fr. *excitant*.] (An agent) that excites or stimulates.

A. John The sea air is known to be an excitant. *Nature* The central excitant action of *d*-amphetamine.

ˈ**excitancy** *n.* the property of being (an) excitant M19.

†**excitate** *v.t.* M16–M17. [L *excitat-* pa. ppl stem of *excitare*: see EXCITE, -ATE[3].] = EXCITE in senses current bef. M17.

excitation /ɛksɪˈteɪʃ(ə)n/ *n.* LME. [(O)Fr. f. late L *excitatio(n-)*, f. as prec.: see -ATION.] 1 The state of being excited; an instance of this. Now chiefly w. ref. to inanimate things: cf. EXCITEMENT 3b. LME. 2 The action or an act of exciting, esp. (in mod. use) tissue, electrical devices, atoms, etc. (see EXCITE 4, 5). LME. 3 Something that excites; a stimulus; an encouragement. *arch.* E17.

1 J. McPhee He told the story without modulation, without a hint of narrative excitation. H. M. Rosenberg The excitations associated with spin waves are also quantised. 2 T. H. Huxley The excitation of the retina proper. *Scientific American* The excitation of the electron from the valence band to the conduction band. *attrib.*: *Radio & Electronics World* The device reverts to its 'blank' state when the ac excitation voltage is removed.

excitative /ɪkˈsʌɪtətɪv, ɛk-/ *a.* L15. [Fr. *excitatif*, *-ive*, f. med.L *excitativus*, f. as EXCITATE: see -ATIVE.] Able or tending to excite. (Foll. by *of*.)

†**excitator** *n. rare.* L17–M19. [f. EXCITATE + -OR.] A person who or thing which excites; *spec.* in *Electr.*, an instrument for discharging a Leyden jar without giving the operator a shock.

excitatory /ɪkˈsʌɪtət(ə)ri, ɛk-/ *a.* E19. [f. as EXCITATE: see -ORY[2].] Producing or tending to produce excitation; produced by excitation.

excite /ɪkˈsʌɪt, ɛk-/ *v.* ME. [(O)Fr. *exciter* or L *excitare* frequent. of *exciere* call out or forth, f. as EX-[1] 1 + *ciere* move, call.] 1a *v.t.* & *i.* Instigate, incite, move, stir up, (a person, God, the soul, etc.). (Foll. by *to*, *to do*, *into doing*.) ME. †b *v.t.* Provoke, challenge. ME–L15. 2 *v.t.* Call into being (a faculty, feeling, etc.); rouse (what is dormant or latent). LME. †b Rouse from sleep, or unconsciousness; bring back to life. LME–L15. †c Call up (a spirit). LME–M17. 3 *v.t.* Induce or provoke (an action, a manifestation); bring about (an active condition). LME. 4 *v.t.* Stimulate (living matter) so as to produce or increase its activity. LME. 5 *v.t.* Magnetize or electrify (a substance or body); produce electrical activity in; produce (an electric current). Also, sensitize (a photographic film etc.). M17. b *Physics.* Cause to emit radiation; cause emission of (a spectrum); raise (an atom, electron, etc.) to a higher energy state. E20. 6 *v.t.* & *i.* Arouse strong emotion (in); *esp.* make very interested or eager. M19.

1a P. Kavanagh He looked like a spirited fellow who could be excited into doing two men's work. 2 T. Hardy The footman whose curiosity had been excited. W. S. Maugham Her prettiness was not the sort that excites carnal desires. 3 J. L. Motley Fire-ships, intended only to excite a conflagration of the bridge. S. Leacock The very name 'Spy' excites a shudder of apprehension. P. Ackroyd Her behaviour was exciting more comment. J. Heller He was distressed . . by how little attention his presence excited. 5 W. Garnett The idea . . was to use . . the current produced by the armature to excite its own electro-magnet. b H. M. Rosenberg The higher the temperature, the more electrons will be excited to the conduction band. 6 E. Waugh They let me up . . and said I wasn't to excite you. *Listener* Last week's legitimate television drama failed to excite.

excited /ɪkˈsʌɪtɪd, ɛk-/ *ppl a.* M17. [f. prec. + -ED[1].] 1 Of a substance, body, or device: that has been excited; magnetized; electrified; stimulated. M17. b *Physics.* Of an atom, electron, etc.: able to lose energy by emitting radiation. M17. 2 Stirred by strong emotion, agitated; characterized by excitement. M19.

1b **excited state** a state of a quantized system with more energy than the ground state. 2 E. Bowen Cecilia, strung-up, excited, not knowing where to begin. M. Frayn The excited screaming of the children playing.

excitedly *adv.* M19. **excitedness** *n.* E20.

excitement /ɪkˈsʌɪtm(ə)nt, ɛk-/ *n.* LME. [f. EXCITE + -MENT.] 1 The action of exciting; the fact of being excited. *rare.* LME. 2†a A motive, an incentive, (*to* action); an exhortation (*to do*); something that tends to produce a specified feeling. E17–M19. b An occasion of emotional excitement. L19. 3a *Med.* A state of overactivity in an organ. Now *rare* or *obs.* L18. b The state of being emotionally excited. Cf. EXCITATION 1. M19.

2b *Economist* No great excitements are expected from the last witnesses before the congressional committees. 3b S. Middleton Fisher stood hot with excitement. M. Tippett I can remember the excitement when *Back to Methuselah* was first published.

exciter /ɪkˈsʌɪtə, ɛk-/ *n.* LME. [f. EXCITE + -ER[1].] 1 A person who or thing which excites a person, feeling, event, etc. Formerly, an instigator. LME. 2 A device for producing excitation in another device; *spec.* (*a*) a small generator or battery that provides the energizing current for the field magnets of a main generator or motor; (*b*) *Electronics* part of a transmitter, radar, etc., that generates an internal constant-frequency signal. L19.

exciting /ɪkˈsʌɪtɪŋ, ɛk-/ *ppl a.* E17. [f. EXCITE + -ING[2].] 1 That excites a person; *esp.* arousing great interest or eagerness. E17. 2 Of a cause, esp. that of a disease: immediately preceding the result. E19. 3 That excites something inanimate, as an electric current, radiation (see EXCITE 5). L19.

1 J. T. Story Beautiful girl; exciting too, rowing the river in her nightie. Day Lewis Sunday was the most exciting day of my week. 3 *Nature* The gel was stained . . and photographed using exciting light at 254 nm.

excitingly *adv.* M19. **excitingness** *n.* E20.

excitive /ɪkˈsʌɪtɪv, ɛk-/ *a.* L18. [f. EXCITE + -IVE.] Tending to excite; productive *of*.

excitomotor /ɪkˈsʌɪtəʊməʊtə, ɛk-/ *a.* L19. [f. EXCITOR + MOTOR *n.* & *a.*] *Physiol.* Producing or increasing motor activity.

Also **excitoˈmotory** *a.* M19.

exciton /ˈɛksɪtɒn, ɪkˈsʌɪ-, ɛk-/ *n.* M20. [f. EXCIT(ATION + -ON.] *Physics.* A mobile concentration of energy in a crystalline material consisting of an excited electron and an associated hole.

exciˈtonic *a.* M20.

excitor /ɪkˈsʌɪtə, ɛk-/ *n.* E19. [f. EXCITE + -OR, after *motor*.] 1 = EXCITER 1. E19. 2 *Anat.* An efferent nerve whose stimulation increases the action of the part it supplies. M19.

excitory /ɪkˈsʌɪt(ə)ri/ *a.* E19. [f. EXCITE + -ORY[2].] Producing or tending to produce excitation.

excitron /ˈɛksɪtrɒn/ *n.* M20. [f. EXCIT(ATION + -TRON.] *Electronics.* A kind of mercury-arc rectifier with a pool of mercury as the cathode and a grid to control the conduction from a hot spot maintained throughout the conduction cycle.

exclaim /ɪkˈskleɪm, ɛk-/ *n. rare.* L15. [f. (as) EXCLAIM *v.*] An exclamation, an outcry.

exclaim /ɪkˈskleɪm, ɛk-/ *v.i.* & *t.* L16. [Fr. *exclamer* or L *exclamare*, f. as EX-[1] 1 + *clamare*: see CLAIM *v.*] Speak or say suddenly, excitedly, or forcefully, esp. in expression of anger, pain, delight, surprise, etc.; cry out. (Foll. by *that*.)

J. A. Froude The people exclaimed that they were betrayed by the gentlemen. D. H. Lawrence Men in the crowd exclaimed and groaned. L. M. Montgomery 'Oh, do you really think so?' exclaimed Anne.

With preps. in specialized senses: **exclaim against** *arch.* protest loudly against. **exclaim at** (*a*) *arch.* = *exclaim against* above; (*b*) cry out in admiration at. **exclaim on, upon** *arch.* (*a*) = *exclaim against* above; (*b*) apostrophize.

exclaimer *n.* L17.

exclamation /ɛkskləˈmeɪʃ(ə)n/ *n.* LME. [(O)Fr., or L *exclamatio(n-)*, f. *exclamat-* pa. ppl stem of *exclamare*: see prec., -ATION.] 1 The action of exclaiming; a sudden impassioned or emphatic utterance, a cry. LME. 2 A loud protest or complaint (*against*). *arch.* LME. 3 *Gram.* An interjection. M19.

1 E. F. Benson Lucia suddenly gave a little exclamation of annoyance. 2 J. Priestley What exclamation and abuse must he not expect?

Comb. & *phrases*: **exclamation mark**, (*US*) **exclamation point** a punctuation mark (!) used to show the exclamatory nature of the preceding phrase etc., and in *Math.* to indicate a factorial; **note of exclamation** = *exclamation mark* above.

exclamative /ɪk'sklamətɪv, ɛk-/ *a.* & *n. rare.* M18. [f. as next + -IVE.] A *adj.* = EXCLAMATORY 2. M18. B *n.* An exclamatory expression. M20.

exclamatory /ɪk'sklamət(ə)ri, ɛk-/ *a.* L16. [f. L *exclamat-*: see EXCLAMATION, -ORY[2].] 1 That exclaims; that gives rise to exclamation. L16. 2 Constituting or marking an exclamation. E18.

1 DONNE An intemperate . . and exclamatory Sorrow. 2 K. TYNAN Exclamatory titles like *Cheep!* and *Oh! Joy!*

exclamatorily *adv.* M19. **exclamatoriness** *n.* (*rare*) L20.

exclaustration /ɛksklɔː'streɪʃ(ə)n/ *n.* M20. [mod.L *exclaustratio(n-)*, f. as EX-[1] + L *claustrum* (see CLOISTER *n.*).] Permission for a religious to live outside a religious community, dispensed from community obligations and the jurisdiction of the superior.

ex'claustrate *v.t.* grant exclaustration to M20.

exclave /'ɛkskleɪv/ *n.* L19. [f. EX-[1] + EN)CLAVE *n.*] A region belonging to a country but surrounded by another country, as viewed by the former (cf. ENCLAVE *n.*).

exclosure /ɪk'skləʊʒə, ɛk-/ *n.* E20. [f. EX-[1] + CLOSURE, after *enclosure*.] An area from which unwanted animals are excluded.

exclude /ɪk'skluːd, ɛk-/ *v.t.* LME. [L *excludere*, f. as EX-[1] I + *claudere* to shut.] I Keep out (what is outside). 1 Deny entry or access to; shut out from a place. (Foll. by *from*, †*out of*, †2nd obj.) LME. 2 Deny membership or participation to; debar from a right or privilege, prohibit from an activity, etc. (Foll. by *from*, †2nd obj.) LME. 3 Give no place to; prevent the occurrence or use of; make impossible, preclude. LME. b Be incompatible with. LME. 4 Omit from a category, series, etc., or from the scope of a statement, enactment, etc. Cf. EXCLUDING. LME. b Of a term, statement, etc.: fail to include in its scope or meaning. M16. 5 Reject from consideration, dismiss, rule out. L16.

1 EVELYN When Branches are so thick . . that they . . exclude the sun. G. MAXWELL A wire gate [was] fitted to the gallery stairs, so that he could . . be excluded from the studio. 2 W. S. CHURCHILL He excluded him from all share in the wars. J. R. ACKERLEY My father's decision to exclude me from his confidence. 3 A. RADCLIFFE The thick foliage excluded all view of the country. J. BARZUN It was decreed that politics and religion should be excluded from general conversation. b H. SPENCER Absolute indifference excludes the conception of will. 4 J. B. PRIESTLEY These Lancashire towns—and this excludes industrial villages . . —have not the derelict look of some places elsewhere. b E. F. SCHUMACHER They [judgements] are based on a definition of cost which excludes all 'free goods'. 5 G. B. SHAW In spite of the virginity she had vowed . . she never excluded the possibility of marriage for herself. **law** or **principle of excluded middle** or **third** *Logic*: that either a proposition or its negative must be true.

II Thrust out (what is inside). 6 Banish, expel. LME. 7 Eject forcibly from a receptacle; *esp.* hatch from an egg. LME.

excludable, -ible *adjs.* M20.

excluder /ɪk'skluːdə, ɛk-/ *n.* M17. [f. prec. + -ER[1].] 1 A person who excludes someone; *spec.* one who attempts to exclude a candidate from an office by voting against him or her; *Hist.* a supporter of the Exclusion Bill. M17. 2 A device for keeping something out; *spec.* = *queen excluder* s.v. QUEEN *n.* M19.

2 *draught-excluder*: see DRAUGHT *n.*

excluding /ɪk'skluːdɪŋ, ɛk-/ *prep.* M17. [Use of pres. pple of EXCLUDE *v.* 4: see -ING[2].] If one does not take into account; apart from, except. Also, to the exclusion of.

C. DARWIN In all other respects, excluding fertility, there is a close general resemblance between hybrids and mongrels.

exclusion /ɪk'skluːʒ(ə)n, ɛk-/ *n.* LME. [L *exclusio(n-)*, f. *exclus-* pa. ppl stem of *excludere*: see EXCLUDE, -ION.] 1 The action or an act of excluding; (an instance of) shutting out from a place, debarring from an office or society, rejecting from consideration, etc. LME. 2 Something that excludes or is excluded, esp. from the terms of a contract. M17.

Phrases: **Bill of Exclusion** = *Exclusion Bill* below. **method, process of exclusion**(s) the process of discovering the cause of a phenomenon or the solution of a problem by eliminating alternative hypotheses in turn. **to the exclusion of** so as to exclude.

Comb.: **Exclusion Bill** *Hist.* a bill of 1680 seeking to bar James Duke of York (the future James II) from the succession, on the grounds of his being a Roman Catholic; **exclusion clause** a clause disclaiming liability for something under a contract; **exclusion order** *Law* (*a*) a statutory instrument preventing a suspected terrorist from entering Great Britain, or Northern Ireland, or the UK, (*b*) a court order barring the husband of a battered wife from the matrimonial home; **exclusion principle** *Physics* the principle that no two fermions of the same kind can be in the same quantum state; also called *Pauli('s) exclusion principle*; **exclusion zone** a zone into which entry is forbidden; *spec.* a delimited area which ships, aircraft, etc., of a given country (or foreign ships etc. in general) are warned not to enter.

exclusionary *a.* of or pertaining to exclusion; having the effect of excluding; *exclusionary rule*, a rule forbidding the use of certain types of evidence in court, esp. (*US*) that obtained in violation of a defendant's constitutional rights: E19. **exclusioner** *n.* (*obs.* exc. *Hist.*) a supporter of the Exclusion Bill L17.

exclusionist /ɪk'skluːʒ(ə)nɪst, ɛk-/ *n.* & *a.* M18. [f. prec. + -IST.] A *n.* A person who favours excluding someone from a privilege, right, situation, etc.; *spec.* in *Hist.*, (*a*) = EXCLUSIONER; (*b*) *Austral.* a free settler who opposed the granting of full civic rights to ex-convicts. M18. B *adj.* Of, pertaining to, or designating an exclusionist or exclusionists; characterized by exclusionism. E19.

exclusionism *n.* the principles of an exclusionist M19.

exclusive /ɪk'skluːsɪv, ɛk-/ *n.* & *a.* L15. [med.L *exclusivus*, f. L *exclus-*: see EXCLUSION, -IVE.] A *n.* †1 An excluding agent. Only in L15. 2 An exclusive proposition or word: see sense B.1 below. M16. 3 An exclusive person: see sense B.7 below. E19. 4 *Hist.* An Australian exclusionist. M19. 5 An exclusive news item, article, etc.: see sense B.5b below. E20.

B *adj.* 1 Of a proposition: in which the predicate is asserted to apply to the subject specified and no other. Of a word: effecting such a restriction. L16. 2 Of a statement, enumeration, etc.: excluding something, *spec.* one or both of the specified terminal points. M17. 3 = EXCLUSORY. *rare.* M17. 4 Not admitting of the simultaneous existence *of* something; incompatible. E18. 5 Of a right, privilege, quality, etc.: possessed or enjoyed by the individual(s) specified and no others; confined or restricted *to*. M18. b Of a news item, article, etc.: published solely in one specified newspaper or periodical. Of a design, product, etc.: (stated to be) available from only one establishment or firm. (Foll. by *to*.) M19. 6 Pursued, employed, etc., to the exclusion of all else; sole, only. L18. 7 Of a group, esp. a social circle, or a member of one: (excessively) reluctant to admit outsiders to membership. E19. 8 Of an establishment etc.: used or patronized by a restricted (esp. aristocratic) social group; high-class, fashionable. M20.

3 **exclusive voice** the right of veto. 4 G. B. SHAW A confusion of the mutually exclusive functions of judge and legislator. *exclusive OR*: see OR *n.*[2] 5 E. WAUGH There would be a sitting room for your exclusive use. b *Daily Telegraph* Furs from Grosvenor Canada . . are exclusive to Harrods. 6 C. DARWIN Natural Selection has been the main but not exclusive means of modification. H. SPENCER Exclusive devotion to work has the result that amusements cease to please. 7 T. BENN An exclusive priestly caste claiming a monopoly right to speak on behalf of the Almighty. (*the*) *Exclusive Brethren*: see BROTHER *n.* 8 J. CONRAD Her movements are commented on in the most exclusive drawing-rooms. *London Calling* Claridges, probably the most exclusive hotel in the world.

exclusively *adv.* (*a*) to the exclusion of all else; formerly (foll. by *of*, *to*), to the exclusion of specified persons or things; †(*b*) = EXCLUSIVE *adv.* 1: LME. **exclusiveness** *n.* M18. **exclusivism** *n.* a doctrine or policy of systematic exclusion, esp. of foreigners; the practice of excluding: M19. **exclusivist** *n.* & *a.* (*a*) *n.* an advocate of exclusivism; also, a person who maintains the exclusive validity of a theory; (*b*) *adj.* advocating or practising exclusivism: L19. **exclusi'vistic** *a.* exclusivist; exclusive: M20. **exclu'sivity** *n.* the quality of being exclusive; the right to exclusive use: E20.

exclusive /ɪk'skluːsɪv/ *adv.* LME. [med.L, f. *exclusivus* (see prec.) + advb. ending *-e*.] 1 So as not to include the limits or extremes in a series. Opp. *inclusive*. LME. 2 Foll. by *of*: †(*a*) to the exclusion of; †(*b*) apart from, not to mention; (*c*) excluding, not counting. L17.

1 E. CHAMBERS He sent him all the Gazettes, from No. 195 to No. 300 exclusive. 2 J. LOCKE To Inherit all . . exclusive . . of his brethren. F. SHERIDAN I . . should (exclusive of any other reasons) have thought myself bound. J. TYNDALL The châlet . . contained four men exclusive of myself and my guide.

exclusory /ɪk'skluːs(ə)ri, ɛk-/ *a.* L16. [Late L *exclusorius*, f. L *exclus-*: see EXCLUSION, -ORY[2].] Having the power or function of excluding. (Foll. by *of*.)

†excoct *v.t.* LME. [L *excoct-* pa. ppl stem of *excoquere*, f. as EX-[1] I + *coquere* cook, melt.] 1 Purge away by heat. LME–M17. 2 Remove the moisture from; ripen, mature. L16–E18. 3 Extract (esp. a metal) by heat. Only in 17.

†**excoction** *n.* (*rare*) the action of extracting by heat E17–E18.

excogitate /ɪks'kɒdʒɪteɪt, ɛks-/ *v.t.* E16. [L *excogitat-* pa. ppl stem of *excogitare* find out by thinking, f. as EX-[1] I, COGITATE.] Think out, devise, (something; *how*).

excogitative *a.* concerned with or having the power of excogitating M19. **excogitator** *n.* M19.

excogitation /ˌɛkskɒdʒɪ'teɪʃ(ə)n/ *n.* M16. [L *excogitatio(n-)*, f. as prec.: see -ATION.] 1 The action of devising in the mind. M16. 2 Something devised, a contrivance, a plan. M17.

excommunicable /ɛkskə'mjuːnɪkəb(ə)l/ *a.* L16. [f. EXCOMMUNICATE *v.* + -ABLE.] Liable to be excommunicated; (of an offence) punishable by excommunication.

excommunicant /ɛkskə'mjuːnɪk(ə)nt/ *n.* L16. [eccl.L *excommunicant-* pres. ppl stem of *excommunicare*: see EXCOMMUNICATE *v.*, -ANT[1].] 1 An excommunicated person. L16. 2 = EXCOMMUNICATOR. *rare.* M17.

excommunicate /ɛkskə'mjuːnɪkət/ *a.* & *n.* E16. [eccl.L *excommunicatus* pa. pple of *excommunicare*: see next, -ATE[2].] (A person who is) excommunicated.

excommunicate /ɛkskə'mjuːnɪkeɪt/ *v.t.* LME. [eccl.L *excommunicat-* pa. ppl stem of *excommunicare*, f. EX-[1] I + L *communis* COMMON *a.*, after *communicare* COMMUNICATE *v.*: see -ATE[3].] Sentence to exclusion from the Christian sacraments or from communication with the faithful; expel from a religious society or community.

excommunicative *a.* = EXCOMMUNICATORY E19. **excommunicator** *n.* a person who excommunicates M17. **excommunicatory** *a.* expressing excommunication; (of a person) disposed to excommunicate: E17.

excommunication /ˌɛkskəmjuːnɪ'keɪʃ(ə)n/ *n.* LME. [eccl.L *excommunicatio(n-)*, f. as prec.: see -ATION.] 1 The action of excommunicating. LME. 2 The sentence by which a person is excommunicated. M17.

excommunion /ɛkskə'mjuːnjən/ *n.* M17. [f. COMMUNION after *excommunication*.] = EXCOMMUNICATION.

ex-con /ɛks'kɒn/ *n. slang.* E20. [Abbrev.] = EX-CONVICT.

exconjugant /ɛks'kɒndʒʊg(ə)nt/ *n.* E20. [f. EX-[1] 3 + L *conjugant-* pres. ppl stem of *conjugare* CONJUGATE *v.*] Each of a pair of micro-organisms that have recently been in conjugation.

ex-convict /ɛks'kɒnvɪkt/ *n.* M19. [f. EX-[1] 3 + CONVICT *n.*] A person who has served a term in prison, esp. recently.

excoriate /ɪk'skɔːrɪeɪt, ɛks-/ *v.t.* Pa. pple **-ated**, (*arch.*) **-ate** /-ət/. LME. [L *excoriat-* pa. ppl stem of *excoriare*, f. as EX-[1] I + *corium* skin, hide: see -ATE[3].] 1 Remove portions of the skin (or analogous membrane) from, esp. by corrosive action or abrasion. LME. 2 Peel off (skin); remove (a lining membrane) by corrosion, abrasion, etc. M16. †3 Flay, skin, (a person or animal). M16–E19. 4 *fig.* Make a scathing attack on. M20.

1 M. BEERBOHM My wrists, my ankles, are excoriated.

excori'ation *n.* (*a*) the action or an act of excoriating; an excoriated place on the body, a sore; (*b*) scathing criticism, invective: LME.

excorticate /ɪk'skɔːtɪkeɪt, ɛks-/ *v.t.* Pa. pple **-ated**, †**-ate**. LME. [Late L *excorticat-* pa. ppl stem of *excorticare*, f. as EX-[1] I, CORTEX: see -ATE[3].] Remove the bark from (a tree) or the shell from (a nut).

ˌ**excorti'cation** *n.* E18.

excrement /'ɛkskrɪm(ə)nt/ *n.*[1] & *v.* M16. [Fr. *excrément* or L *excrementum*, f. *excre-* pa. ppl base of *excernere* EXCRETE: see -MENT.] A *n.* 1 *sing.* & in *pl.* Faeces. Formerly, any matter excreted or given out by the body or a plant. M16. †2 In *pl.* Something which remains after a process of sifting or refining; dregs, lees, refuse. M16–L17. B *v.i.* Defecate. *rare.* M17.

excre'mental *a.* pertaining to or consisting of excrement; of the nature of excrement: L16. **excremen'titial** *a.* (*rare*) = EXCREMENTAL E17. **excremen'titious** *a.*[1] = EXCREMENTAL L16. †**excrementitiously** *adv.* M17–L18. †**excrementitiousness** *n.*: only in M17.

†**excrement** *n.*[2] M16. [L *excrementum*, f. *excrescere*: see EXCRESCENCE, -MENT.] 1 Something which grows out or forth, *esp.* hair, nails, or feathers; an outgrowth (*lit.* & *fig.*). M16–E18. 2 Growth, increase. Only in E17.

†**excrementitious** *a.*[2] of the nature of or consisting of an outgrowth M17–M18.

†**excresce** *v.* & *n.* LME. [L *excrescere*: see next.] A *v.i.* & (*rare*) *t.* Increase, esp. inordinately; exceed what is usual; grow out. LME–L17. B *n.* An excess amount; an increase. Chiefly *Sc.* M16–E19.

excrescence /ɪk'skrɛs(ə)ns, ɛks-/ *n.* LME. [L *excrescentia*, f. *excrescent-* pres. ppl stem of *excrescere* grow out, f. as EX-[1] I + *crescere* grow: see -ENCE.] 1a An abnormal or diseased outgrowth on a person, animal, or plant; a disfiguring or unsightly addition (*lit.* & *fig.*). LME. b Something that grows out naturally; an appendage. Now *rare.* M17. †2 The action of growing out; immoderate growth, abnormal increase. M16–M18. 3 Exuberance; an exuberant outburst. Formerly, overblown pride, swagger. Now *rare.* E17.

1a J. A. MICHENER The awful modern excrescences that monopolized the town—the hot-dog stands.., the Moorish motels. b H. MOORE Sculpture had become overgrown with moss, weeds—all sorts of surface excrescences.

excrescency *n.* (now *rare*) (*a*) the state or condition of being excrescent; (an) abnormal development; †(*b*) = EXCRESCENCE 3: M16.

excrescent /ɪk'skrɛs(ə)nt, ɛks-/ *a.* L15. [L *excrescent-*: see prec., -ENT.] 1 Increased by addition, greater; constituting more than the normal quantity. Now *rare.* L15. 2 That grows out naturally. Now *rare* or *obs.* M17. 3 Growing abnormally; forming or constituting an excrescence; redundant, superfluous. M17. 4 *Philol.* Of a sound or letter in a word: due merely to euphony, not to derivation. L19.

excre'scential *a.* of the nature of an excrescence; redundant, superfluous: M19.

†**excression** *n.* E17–E18. [Irreg. f. L *excrescere* (see EXCRESCENCE) for EXCRETION *n.*[2]] = EXCRESCENCE I.

excreta /ɪk'skriːtə, ɛk-/ *n.pl.* M19. [L, use as n. of neut. pl. of *excretus* pa. pple of *excernere* EXCRETE.] Waste matter discharged from the body; *esp.* faeces, urine.

excretal *a.* M19.

excrete /ɪk'skriːt, ɛk-/ *v.* E17. [L *excret-* pa. ppl stem of *excernere*, f. as EX-[1] I + *cernere* sift.] †1 *v.t.* Of a drug, physician, etc.: cause the excretion of (matter). E–M17. 2 *v.t.* & *i.* Separate and expel (esp. waste products of metabolism) from the body, an organ, a cell, etc. M17.

2 C. DARWIN Certain plants excrete sweet juice. P. PARISH Some drugs are.. quickly and easily excreted. C. RYCROFT Squids.. excrete their ink in order to repel predators.

excreter *n.* M19. **excretive** *a.* able to excrete or promote excretion M17. **excretory** *a.* & *n.* (*a*) *adj.* having the function of excreting; pertaining to the process of excretion; also, of the nature of excreta; (*b*) *n.* (now *rare*) an excretory vessel or duct: L17.

excretion /ɪk'skriːʃ(ə)n, ɛk-/ *n.*[1] E17. [Fr. *excrétion* or L *excretio(n-)*, f. as EXCRETE: see -ION.] 1 The action or process of excreting; *spec.* emptying of the bowels. E17. 2 Material which is excreted. M17.

†**excretion** *n.*[2] E17–E18. [Late L *excretio(n-)*, f. *excret-* pa. ppl stem of *excrescere*: see EXCRESCENCE, -ION.] = EXCRESCENCE I, EXCREMENT *n.*[2] I.

†**excriminate** *v.t. rare.* M16–L18. [f. EX-[1] I + (as) CRIMINATE.] Clear of an imputation; shift an imputation from (one person) *upon* another.

excruciate /ɪk'skruːʃɪeɪt, ɛk-/ *v.t.* L16. [L *excruciat-* pa. ppl stem of *excruciare* torment, f. as EX-[1] I + *cruc-*, *crux* cross: see -ATE[3].] 1 Torment acutely (a person's senses). Formerly also, subject to physical torture; rack (one's brains). Now chiefly *hyperbol.* L16. 2 Torture mentally, inflict extreme mental anguish on. L16.

excruciating /ɪk'skruːʃɪeɪtɪŋ, ɛk-/ *a.* L16. [f. prec. + -ING[2].] That excruciates; agonizing; *joc.* or *hyperbol.* (of a song, joke, etc.) so bad as to cause pain to the hearer.

B. TARKINGTON He.. was stabbed by excruciating pains in his legs. E. F. BENSON She sings the melody of the first movement of the 'Unfinished'. It is quite excruciating, but recognizable.

excruciatingly *adv.* E19.

excruciation /ɪkˌskruːʃɪ'eɪʃ(ə)n, ɛk-/ *n.* E17. [L *excruciatio(n-)*, f. as EXCRUCIATE: see -ATION.] The action or an act of excruciating; the state of being excruciated.

excubitor /ɪk'skjuːbɪtə, ɛk-/ *n.* L18. [L, agent-n. f. *excubare* lie on guard, f. as EX-[1] I + *cubare* lie down: see -OR.] 1 A watchman, a sentinel. *rare.* L18. 2 *Rom. Hist.* A member of one of the four companies into which the imperial guard was divided. M19.

exculpate /'ɛkskʌlpeɪt/ *v.* M17. [med.L *exculpat-* pa. ppl stem of *exculpare*, f. as EX-[1] I + L *culpa* blame: see -ATE[3].] 1 *v.t.* & (*rare*) *i.* Of a person, court, etc.: free (a person) from blame, clear from an accusation. (Foll. by *from.*) M17. 2 *v.t.* Of a thing: provide grounds for exculpating; vindicate. Formerly also, justify. E18.

1 G. GROTE The latter stood exculpated on both charges. R. W. CLARK Freud's wish to exculpate himself from blame for the patient's treatment.

excul'pation *n.* (*a*) the action or an act of exculpating; (*b*) a ground for exculpating; an excuse: E18. **ex'culpatory** *a.* serving or intended to exculpate L17.

excur /ɪk'skɜː, ɛk-/ *v.i. rare.* Infl. **-rr-**. M17. [L *excurrere*: see next.] †1 Stray, digress, (*lit.* & *fig.*); go to an extreme. M–L17. 2 = EXCURSE 2. M19.

excurrent /ɪk'skʌr(ə)nt, ɛk-/ *a.* E17. [L *excurrent-* pres. ppl stem of *excurrere* run out, f. as EX-[1] I + *currere* run: see -ENT.] 1 Overflowing, superabundant. *rare.* Only in E17. 2a That runs or flows out. E19. b Serving as or providing an exit. M19. 3 *Bot.* Of a tree, trunk, etc.: having or designating an undivided main trunk. Of the midrib of a leaf: projecting beyond the tip or margin. M19.

excurse /ɪk'skɜːs, ɛk-/ *v.i.* M18. [L *excurs-*: see next.] 1 Run off, wander, digress. Chiefly *fig.* M18. 2 Make or go on an excursion. L18.

excursion /ɪk'skɜːʃ(ə)n, ɛk-/ *n.* & *v.* L16. [L *excursio(n-)*, f. *excurs-* pa. ppl stem of *excurrere*: see EXCURRENT, -ION.] A *n.* 1†a The action or an act of running out or of going beyond limits or to extremes. L16–M18. b Extension, projection. Formerly, an extending or projecting part. Now *rare* or *obs.* M17. 2 *Mil.* A sally, a sortie, a raid. *obs.* exc. in *alar(u)ms and excursions* s.v. ALARM *n.* L16. 3†a A digression in speech or writing. L16–E19. b *Astron.* A deviation from a regular path. E17. †4 An outburst of feeling; a sally of wit; an overstepping of the limits of propriety or custom; an escapade, a transgression; a vagary. E17–L18. 5 A journey or ramble made with the intention of returning to the starting-point (*lit.* & *fig.*); *spec.* a pleasure-trip taken esp. by a number of people to a particular place. L17. 6 (The extent of) a movement to and fro of an oscillatory body or fluctuating quantity; (the extent of) a variation from an average value. L18. b A sudden large increase in the output of a nuclear reactor. M20.

5 J. BRYCE The only excursion into the historical domain which I shall have to ask the reader to make. B. CHATWIN Their first excursion into the outside world was a visit to the Flower Show. J. A. MICHENER Evening excursions to historic sites like.. the poetic ruins of Caesarea. 6 C. FORD The excursion of the bass strings is greater. *Scientific American* At higher levels.. there should be large temperature excursions caused by alternating layers of atmospheric gas heated by compression and cooled by expansion. *Wireless World* To limit the maximum excursion of the reference voltage.

Comb.: **excursion fare**, **ticket**, **train**: for an excursion, usu. at a reduced rate.

B *v.i.* Make or go on an excursion. *arch.* L18.

excursional *a.* of or pertaining to an excursion M19. **excursionary** *a.* of the nature of an excursion; going on an excursion: M18. **excursionist** *n.* a person (esp. one of a party) making or going on an excursion M19. **excursionize** *v.* (*a*) *v.t.* (*rare*) explore (a district) by making excursions; (*b*) *v.i.* = EXCURSION *v.*: E19.

excursive /ɪk'skɜːsɪv, ɛk-/ *a.* L17. [f. as EXCURSE + -IVE, perh. after *discursive.*] 1 Of the nature of an excursion; consisting of excursions or digressions. L17. 2 Making or tending to make excursions; ranging widely; apt to stray, digressive; desultory. M18.

1 W. IRVING We are wandering.. into excursive speculations. 2 S. JOHNSON An intelligence perpetually on the wing, excursive, vigorous, and diligent. A. HELPS Do keep to the point, my excursive friends.

excursively *adv.* L18. **excursiveness** *n.* M18.

excursus /ɪk'skɜːsəs, ɛk-/ *n.* Pl. **excursuses**, **excursus** /-suːs/. E19. [L = excursion, f. as EXCURSE.] 1 A fuller treatment in an appendix of some point in the main text of a book, esp. an edition of the classics. E19. 2 A digression within a narrative in which some point is discussed at length. M19.

excurvation /ɛkskɜː'veɪʃ(ə)n/ *n.* E19. [f. EX-[1] I + CURVATION.] Outward curvature.

excusable /ɪk'skjuːzəb(ə)l, ɛk-/ *a.* LME. [OFr. f. L *excusabilis*, f. *excusare* EXCUSE *v.*: see -ABLE.] 1 Of a person: deserving or able to be excused or acquitted. (Foll. by †*of.*) Now *rare.* LME. 2 Of an action, conduct, etc.: admitting of excuse. LME.

2 *excusable homicide*: see HOMICIDE I.

excusa'bility *n.* (*rare*) = EXCUSABLENESS E18. **excusableness** *n.* the quality of being excusable M17. **excusably** *adv.* E17.

excusal /ɪk'skjuːz(ə)l, ɛk-/ *n.* L16. [f. EXCUSE *v.* + -AL[1]; cf. *refusal.*] The action or an act of excusing; the fact of excusing.

†**excusation** *n.* ME. [OFr. f. L *excusatio(n-)*, f. *excusat-* pa. ppl stem of *excusare*: see EXCUSE *v.*, -ATION.] 1 A real or alleged ground for being released from an obligation or excused an action; an excuse; a pretext; a plea for forgiveness or leniency. ME–M17. 2 The action of offering an excuse, defence, or apology. LME–M19. 3 Release or freedom from an obligation, duty, etc. LME–M16.

excusator /ɪk'skjuːzətə, ɛk-/ *n. obs.* exc. *Hist.* M17. [Late L *excusator*, f. L *excusat-* pa. ppl stem of *excusare*: see EXCUSE *v.*, -ATOR.] A person who makes an excuse, defence, or apology; *spec.* one officially authorized to do so.

excusatory /ɪk'skjuːzət(ə)ri, ɛk-/ *a.* LME. [med.L *excusatorius*, f. as prec.: see -ORY[2].] Tending or meant to excuse; making or containing an excuse; apologetic.

excuse /ɪk'skjuːs, ɛk-/ *n.* LME. [(O)Fr., f. *excuser*: see next.] 1 The action of excusing a person or an action; now *esp.* indulgence, pardon. LME. 2 Something offered as a reason for being excused. LME. 3 Something that serves to excuse or gives ground for excusing; a justification, a reason. LME. 4 = APOLOGY *n.*[1] 4. *colloq.* M19.

1 JOHN MORGAN I heartily pray the excuse and pardon of every Reader. LYTTON The old woman gave me a note of excuse. 2 A. LURIE I was so sure Kenneth wouldn't want to go that I . . gave an excuse for him. A. MOTION I make my excuses early, and lie on my unmade bed. 3 D. DU MAURIER His wife was a scold, but that was no excuse to kill her. T. S. ELIOT I was glad of the excuse for coming up to London.

excuseless *a.* (long *rare*) without excuse M16.

excuse /ɪk'skjuːz, ɛk-/ *v.* ME. [OFr. *escuser* (mod. *excuser*) f. L *excusare* free from blame, f. as EX-[1] 1 + *causa* accusation.] 1 *v.t.* & *i.* Seek to clear (a person) wholly or partially from blame without denying or justifying the action concerned; try to extenuate (an acknowledged fault). Formerly also, clear of blame by alleging *that.* ME. †2 *v.t.* Maintain the innocence of (a person); defend from an accusation (*of*); seek to justify (an action). ME–L17. 3 *v.t.* Obtain exemption for (a person); give reasons for the exemption of (a person) *from* a duty or obligation. ME. †b Decline (a deed, *to do*) with apologies. M16–M18. †4 *v.t.* Save (someone) from punishment or harm, esp. by taking someone's place; take the place of and so exempt from a duty. (Foll. by *of, from.*) ME–E18. 5a *v.t.* In *pass.* Have a sufficient excuse; be freed from blame. ME. b *v.t.* & *i.* Of a property, circumstance, etc.: serve as an excuse (for). M16. 6 *v.t.* Release from a task, duty, or obligation; dispense from payment, attendance, etc. (Foll. by *from,* 2nd obj.) ME. 7 *v.t.* Accept a plea in exculpation of (a person), forgive; judge leniently on the grounds of extenuating circumstances. LME. b Admit apology for, overlook, condone, (a fault, offence, impropriety, etc.); regard (an action) indulgently. LME. 8 *v.t.* Refrain from exacting; dispense with. M17.

1 I. WALTON I should rather excuse myself, then censure others. E. HAYWOOD She excused . . having made him wait. 2 R. HOLINSHED To excuse him of the death of the archbishop. 3 V. WOOLF He went off laughing, excusing himself on the score of business. b J. HILDROP He pressed me . . to dine with him, which I excused. 5b G. GREENE The man looked sick and tired enough to excuse any artifice. TOLKIEN You speak evil of that which is fair . . , and only little wit can excuse you. 6 OED The jury were excused from attendance for the rest of the week. D. ATHILL I had been excused games for all of one term. 7 B. JOWETT The people may be excused for following tradition only. E. M. FORSTER You must excuse me if I say stupid things, but my brain has gone to pieces. b F. W. ROBERTSON The boldest heart may be excused a shudder. H. E. BATES Are you married? . . Excuse my asking a personal question. 8 LYTTON From our royal court We do excuse your presence.

Phrases: **be excused** *colloq.* be allowed to leave the room (esp. to relieve oneself) or the table; urinate, defecate. **excuse me** an apology for interruption, lack of ceremony, etc.; an expression of polite or diffident dissent; (*excuse-me dance,* a dance in which one may take another person's partner). **excuse oneself** ask permission or apologize prior to leaving.

excuser *n.* †(*a*) *rare* a substitute, a deputy; (*b*) a person who offers or makes excuses: LME. **excusive** *a.* tending to excuse; that excuses: L16.

†**excuss** *v.t.* L16. [L *excuss-* pa. ppl stem of *excutere,* f. as EX-[1] 1 + *quatere* shake.] 1 Investigate thoroughly; discuss; get (the truth) *from* a person. L16–E18. 2 Shake off, cast off, get rid of, (*lit.* & *fig.*). E–M17. 3 *Law.* Seize (a debtor's goods) in execution of a warrant etc. Only in E18.

†**excussion** *n.* E17. [L *excussio(n-),* f. as prec.: see -ION.] 1 The action of shaking off or getting rid of something. Only in 17. 2 *Law.* Seizure of goods for debt. E17–E18.

excyst /ɛk'sɪst/ *v.i.* E20. [f. EX-[1] 1 + CYST, after *encyst.*] *Biol.* & *Med.* Emerge from a cyst.

excystation, excystment *ns.* (an instance of) emerging from a cyst. E20.

ex-directory /ɛksdɪ'rɛkt(ə)ri, -dʌɪ-/ *a.* M20. [f. EX *prep.* + DIRECTORY *n.*] Of a telephone number or subscriber: not listed in the directory through the subscriber's choice.

ex div /ɛks 'dɪv/ *adv. phr.* M19. [Abbrev.] *Comm.* = *ex dividend* s.v. EX *prep.* 1.

exeat /'ɛksɪat/ *n.* E18. [L = let him or her go out, 3rd person sing. pres. subjunct. of *exire* EXIT *v.*[1]] 1 A permission for temporary absence from a college or other institution. E18. 2 A permission granted by a bishop to a priest to move to another diocese. M18.

1 P. ACKROYD He had been given a day's exeat from the hospital where he was being treated.

exec /ɪg'zɛk, ɛg-/ *n. colloq.* L19. [Abbrev.] = EXECUTIVE *n.* 4.

execrable /'ɛksɪkrəb(ə)l/ *a.* LME. [(O)Fr. *exécrable* f. L *execrabilis* (in act. and pass. senses), f. *ex(s)ecrari*: see next, -ABLE.] †1 Expressing or involving a curse; awful, fearful. LME–M17. 2 Of a person or thing: deserving to be cursed; detestable. L15. †3 Piteous, horrifying. L15–E19. 4 Of wretched quality; abominable, bad beyond description. M18.

2 *New York Times* The others who were wounded in the execrable attack on the synagogue. 4 D. MURPHY Some past tenant with execrable taste had left the whole place superficially hideous.

execrably *adv.* L16.

execrate /'ɛksɪkreɪt/ *v.* M16. [L *execrat-* pa. ppl stem of *ex(s)ecrari* curse, f. as EX-[1] 1 + *sacrare* devote religiously, f. *sacr-, sacer* holy: see -ATE[3].] 1 *v.i.* Utter curses. M16. 2a *v.t.* Invoke evil upon; express loathing for; abhor. M16. †b *v.t.* & *i.* Pronounce a curse (upon); declare accursed. *rare.* Only in L17. †3 *v.t.* Make no longer holy; dedicate to evil. L16–M17.

2a B. RUSSELL The symbol of a new order, admired by some, execrated by many.

execrative *a.* of or pertaining to execration; characterized by or containing an execration: M19. **execrator** *n.* L16. **execratory** *a.* of the nature of an execration; execrative: E17.

execration /ɛksɪ'kreɪʃ(ə)n/ *n.* LME. [L *execratio(n-),* f. as prec.: see -ATION.] 1a The action or an act of pronouncing a curse upon a person. *obs.* exc. *Hist.* LME. b The uttering of curses; swearing. L17. 2 Loathing, abhorrence. L16. 3 An uttered curse, an imprecation. E17. 4 An object of cursing. *arch.* E17.

executant /ɪg'zɛkjʊt(ə)nt, ɛg-/ *n.* & *a.* M19. [Fr. *exécutant* pres. pple of *exécuter*: see next, -ANT[1].] A *n.* A person who executes, carries out, or performs something, esp. music. M19. B *adj.* That performs music. *rare.* M19.

executancy *n.* power and skill in performing music M19.

execute /'ɛksɪkjuːt/ *v.* Pa. pple **-ted,** †**-te.** LME. [(O)Fr. *exécuter* f. med.L *executare,* f. L *ex(s)ecut-* pa. ppl stem of *ex(s)equi* follow up, carry out, pursue judicially, punish, f. as EX-[1] 1 + *sequi* follow.] I Carry out, perform, etc. 1a *v.t.* & *i.* Carry out, put into effect, (a plan, purpose, command, sentence, law, will, etc.). LME. †b *v.t.* Display or manifest (a sentiment or principle) with practical effect. LME–L17. 2a *v.t.* Perform (a planned or skilled operation or movement). LME. †b *v.t.* & *i.* Perform or celebrate (a ceremony or religious service). LME–M18. c *v.t.* Perform acts of (justice, cruelty, etc.). *arch.* M16. 3 *v.t.* Fulfil (a function), discharge (an office). LME. 4 *v.t.* Go through the formalities required for (a legal act); make (a legal instrument) valid by signing, sealing, etc. M16. 5 *v.t.* Produce (a work of art or skill) from a design; perform (a piece of music). M18.

1 V. CRONIN To execute her plan Catherine needed the help of a friendly power. T. PYNCHON Oedipa had been named also to execute the will in a codicil dated a year ago. 2a G. BOYCOTT Richards . . executed his more aggressive strokes quite beautifully. 3 S. KINGSLEY I do solemnly swear that I will faithfully execute the office of President of the United States. 4 **execute an estate** convey or confer an estate in property etc., esp. by some particular operation of law. 5 K. CLARK It is in one of Neumann's great buildings . . that Tiepolo executed his masterpiece.

II Perform an execution on. 6 *v.t.* Put to death as a judicial punishment for a crime; kill as a political act. LME.

6 L. DURRELL The authorities arrested and executed the Archbishop.

executable *a.* L18. **executer** *n.* = EXECUTOR 2 M16.

execution /ɛksɪ'kjuːʃ(ə)n/ *n.* LME. [(O)Fr. *exécution* f. L *ex(s)ecutio(n-),* f. *ex(s)ecut-*: see prec., -ION.] 1 The action or an act of putting a person to death, esp. as a judicial punishment. Formerly also, any judicial, usu. corporal, punishment. LME. 2 The action or an act of executing a plan, purpose, command, law, etc. LME. b The enforcement by a public officer of the judgement of a court of law; *esp.* the seizure of the goods or person of a debtor in default of payment. E16. †c The practical display or manifestation of a sentiment or principle. L16–M17. 3 Destructive effect; infliction of damage or slaughter; destruction, esp. of a country refusing to pay a levy. Now chiefly in *do execution.* E16. †4 Action, operation. M16–E18. b Efficiency or excellence in action. M16–E17. 5 The carrying out of a planned or skilled operation or movement, the production of a work of art or skill; the (manner of) performance of a piece of music. Formerly, the performance of a ceremony or religious service. M16. †b An act of executing a movement, work of art, etc.; a deed; a musical performance. Usu. in *pl.* L16–E18. c Excellence in performance, esp. of music. L18. 6 The fulfilment or discharge of a function or office. L16. 7 The performance of the formalities required to validate a legal document. L18.

1 N. MOSLEY His method of execution was to inflict innumerable small wounds so that his victims did not know that they were dying. 2 H. JAMES There are a great many good ideas that are never put into execution. c SHAKES. *3 Hen. VI* Scarce I can refrain The execution of my big-swol'n heart Upon . . that cruel child-killer. 3 *fig.*: THACKERAY Black eyes, which might have done some execution had they been placed in a smoother face. 5 S. BECKETT I managed a few steps of creditable execution and then fell. H. READ The charm of a great master's drawing is partly the extraordinary skill and sureness of its execution. *Personal Software* It has a speed of execution close to that of machine code.

executionary *a.* E20.

executioner /ɛksɪ'kjuːʃ(ə)nə/ *n.* M16. [f. prec. + -ER[1].] 1 An official who carries out a death sentence. M16. 2 *gen.* A person who carries out a judgement or sentence. L16. 3 A person who executes a plan, purpose, command, law, etc. Now *rare.* L16.

1 *fig.* SHAKES. *Rich. III* Though I wish thy death, I will not be thy Executioner.

executioneress *n.* a female executioner M17.

executive /ɪg'zɛkjʊtɪv, ɛg-/ *a.* & *n.* LME. [med.L *executivus,* f. L *execut-*: see EXECUTE, -IVE.] A *adj.* 1 Pertaining to execution; having the function of putting something into effect; *spec.* designating the branch of government that deals with putting into effect laws and judicial sentences. LME. 2 Of or pertaining to the executive of a government. E19. 3 Apt or skilful in execution or performance. E19.

1 *Gramophone* Difficulties that appear to be as much executive as interpretational. *New York Times* This is the first time in the history of the Congress and the executive branch that we have worked out jointly an arms control proposal. *National Observer (US)* Executive editor of the Washington Post. *Times* Arrangements for the special constitutional assembly . . are to be made by the party's executive committee. 2 *Time* Executive clemency if they were convicted was discussed with the President. **Executive Council** *Austral.* a body presided over by the Governor-General or Governor and consisting of ministers of the Crown, which gives legal form to Cabinet decisions etc. **executive privilege** the privilege, claimed by the President for the executive branch of the US Government, of withholding information in the public interest. **executive session** *US* a private meeting (orig. of the Senate for executive business).

B *n.* 1 The executive branch of a government. L18. 2 The person or persons in whom is vested the supreme executive authority of a country or state, esp. the US President (also called *Chief Executive*) or the Governor of a State of the US. L18. 3 Any group or body concerned with administration or management; the executive committee of an organization. M19. 4 A person in an executive position in a business; a person skilled in executive or administrative work; a businessman, a businesswoman. E20.

1 *Daily Telegraph* Separation of powers between the legislature, the executive and the judiciary. 3 *Times* The executive of the Iron and Steel Trades Confederation . . voted 19 to 1 to back the . . pay-restraint package.

executively *adv.* in execution, in performance; by the action of an executive: LME.

executor /ɪɡˈzɛkjʊtə, ɛɡ-; *in sense 2* ˈɛksɪkjuːtə/ *n.* ME. [AN *execut(o)ur* f. L *executor*, f. *execut-*: see EXECUTE, -OR.] 1 A person appointed by a testator to execute his or her will. ME. 2 *gen.* A person who executes a plan, purpose, command, law, etc.; an agent, a performer; *Sc. Law* a person who executes a warrant. *arch.* LME. †3 = EXECUTIONER I. L15–E17.

1 literary executor a person entrusted with a dead writer's unpublished works etc.

executorship *n.* the office or duty of an executor E16.

executorial /ˌɛksɪkjʊˈtɔːrɪəl/ *a.* & *n.* L15. [med.L *executorialis*, f. as next: see -AL[1].] A *adj.* 1 *executorial letters*, a papal mandate for the appointment of a designated person to a benefice. L15. 2 Of or pertaining to an executor; *Sc. Law* pertaining to the execution of a warrant. M18. †B *n. Sc. Law.* A legal authority or instruction used to execute a decree or sentence. E16–E19.

executory /ɪɡˈzɛkjuːt(ə)ri, ɛɡ-/ *a.* LME. [Late L *executorius*, f. L *executor*: see EXECUTOR, -ORY[2].] 1 Of a law: in force, operative. Now *rare.* LME. 2 Of a law, contract, etc.: not yet put into effect or performed; due to come into effect at a future date. L16. 3 Of or pertaining to execution or putting into effect. M17. 4 = EXECUTIVE *a.* I. M17.

executrix /ɪɡˈzɛkjʊtrɪks, ɛɡ-/ *n.* Pl. **-trices** /-trɪsiːz/, **-trixes**. LME. [Late L *executrix*, f. L EXECUTOR: see -TRIX.] A female executor, esp. of a will.

executry /ɪɡˈzɛkjʊtri, ɛɡ-/ *n.* LME. [f. EXECUTOR + -Y[3].] †1 = EXECUTORSHIP. LME–L19. 2 *Sc.* The movable property of a deceased person. M17.

†**exede** *v.t.* M17–M18. [L *exedere*, f. as EX-[1] I + *ed-*, *esse* eat.] Corrode, eat away.

exedra /ˈɛksɪdrə, ɪkˈsiːdrə, ɛk-/ *n.* Also **exhedra** /ˈɛkshɪdrə, ɪksˈhiːdrə, ɛks-/. Pl. **-drae** /-driː/. E18. [L f. Gk, f. as EX-[2] + *hedra* seat.] 1 *Class. Hist.* A hall or arcade with seats, attached to a palaestra or a private house and used for conversation. E18. b *gen.* An apse, a recess, a large niche. M19. 2 = CATHEDRA. E18.

†**exeem** *v.* var. of EXEME.

exegesis /ɛksɪˈdʒiːsɪs/ *n.* Pl. **-geses** /-ˈdʒiːsiːz/. E17. [Gk *exēgēsis*, f. *exēgeisthai* interpret, f. as EX-[2] + *hēgeisthai* to guide.] (An) exposition, esp. of Scripture; a gloss, an explanatory note or discourse.

M. ARNOLD A very small experience of Jewish exegesis will convince us. L. VAN DER POST He was to give me a long exegesis on the origin and meaning of tennis.

exegesist *n.* = EXEGETE 2 M19.

exegete /ˈɛksɪdʒiːt/ *n.* M18. [Gk *exēgētēs*, f. *exēgeisthai*: see prec.] 1 *Gk Hist.* An interpreter or expounder of sacred lore. M18. 2 A person skilled in exegesis; an expositor (*of* a subject, doctrine, etc.). M19.

exegetic /ɛksɪˈdʒɛtɪk/ *a.* M17. [Gk *exēgētikos*, f. *exēgeisthai*: see EXEGESIS, -IC.] = EXEGETICAL. (Foll. by *of.*)

exegetical /ɛksɪˈdʒɛtɪk(ə)l/ *a.* E17. [f. as prec. + -AL[1].] †1 Of the nature of a gloss; explanatory. (Foll. by *of, to.*) E17–E18. 2 Of, pertaining to, or of the nature of exegesis; expository. M19.

2 exegetical theology exegetics.

exegetically *adv.* M17.

exegetics /ɛksɪˈdʒɛtɪks/ *n.* M19. [f. as EXEGETIC: see -ICS.] The branch of theology that deals with the interpretation of Scripture.

exegetist /ɛksɪˈdʒiːtɪst/ *n.* M19. [f. EXEGETE + -IST.] = EXEGETE 2.

†**exeme** *v.t.* Chiefly *Sc.* Also **exeem**. E16. [L *eximere*: see EXEMPT *a.* & *n.*] 1 Free from pain, care, etc.; exempt from a payment, penalty, or obligation. (Foll. by *from.*) E16–E20. 2 Take away, remove; select or except *from.* Only in 17.

exempla *n.* pl. of EXEMPLUM.

exemplar /ɪɡˈzɛmplə, ɛɡ-/ *n.* LME. [(O)Fr. *exemplaire* f. late L *exemplarium*, f. *exemplum* EXAMPLE *n.*: see -AR[2].] 1 A model for imitation; an example. LME. b The model, pattern, or original after which something is made; an archetype. E17. 2 A typical instance; a specimen; a typical embodiment (*of* a quality etc.). LME. 3 A copy of a book etc; a transcript. Formerly also, the original of a book from which copies are made. LME. 4 A parallel instance. L17.

1 R. FRY The exemplar which men put before themselves was the civilisation of Greece and Rome. 2 V. S. PRITCHETT He seems a promising exemplar of the human being exposed to everything without the support of a settled society.

exemplarism *n.* (*Theol.*) (*a*) the doctrine that divine ideas are the source of finite realities; (*b*) the doctrine that Christ became incarnate as an exemplar to humankind: L19. **exemplarist** *a.* & *n.* (*Theol.*) (*a*) *adj.* of or pertaining to exemplarism; (*b*) *n.* a person who believes in or advocates exemplarism: E20.

†**exemplar** *a.* LME–L18. [Late L *exemplaris*, perh. through (O)Fr. *exemplaire* (adj.): see prec., -AR[1].] = EXEMPLARY *a.*

†**exemplarly** *adv.*: only in 17.

exemplarity /ɛɡzɛmˈplarɪti/ *n.* E17. [med.L *exemplaritas*, f. late L *exemplaris*: see EXEMPLARY *a.* & *adv.*, -ITY.] The quality of being exemplary; exemplariness.

exemplary /ɪɡˈzɛmpləri, ɛɡ-/ *n.* Now *rare.* LME. [Late L *exemplarium*: see EXEMPLAR *n.*, -ARY[1].] 1 An example; a model, a pattern of conduct. LME. †2 A copy of a book; a transcript. M16–E18.

exemplary /ɪɡˈzɛmpləri, ɛɡ-/ *a.* & *adv.* L16. [Late L *exemplaris*, f. L *exemplum* EXAMPLE *n.*: see -ARY[2].] A *adj.* 1 Of a person, quality, etc.: fit for imitation. L16. 2 Of a thing: serving as a model or pattern; archetypal. L16. 3 Of a kind liable to become an example; remarkable, signal, extraordinary. *arch.* L16. 4 Of a penalty, punishment, etc.: serving as a warning or deterrent. E17. 5 Serving as a specimen or type; typical. E17. †6 Of or pertaining to an example; providing examples; illustrative. E17–E19.

1 A. KOESTLER Your behaviour remains exemplary and spotless. G. SWIFT I became a docile, dutiful, even an exemplary son. 4 **exemplary damages** *Law*: exceeding those necessary to compensate for actual loss and awarded to mark disapproval of the defendant's conduct.

†B *adv.* In an exemplary manner; to an exemplary degree. E17–L18.

exemplarily *adv.* E17. **exemplariness** *n.* the quality of being worthy of imitation M17.

exempli causa /ɪɡˌzɛmpli ˈkɔːzə; ɛɡ-; ˈkaʊzə/ *adv. phr.* Now *rare.* M16. [L, f. genit. of *exemplum* EXAMPLE *n.* + abl. of *causa*: see CAUSE *n.*] = EXEMPLI GRATIA.

exemplification /ɪɡˌzɛmplɪfɪˈkeɪʃ(ə)n, ɛɡ-/ *n.* LME. [AN, and med.L *exemplificatio(n-)*, f. *exemplificat-* pa. ppl stem of *exemplificare*: see EXEMPLIFY, -FICATION.] 1 The action or an act of exemplifying or showing by example. LME. 2 An attested copy or transcript of a record, deed, etc. LME. 3 A thing that exemplifies; an example, an illustration. L16.

exemplificational *a.* E19. **e'xemplifi,cative** *a.* illustrative E19.

exemplify /ɪɡˈzɛmplɪfʌɪ, ɛɡ-/ *v.* LME. [med.L *exemplificare*, f. L *exemplum* EXAMPLE *n.*: see -FY.] 1 *v.t.* Make an official or attested copy of (esp. a legal document). LME. †b Copy (a document); quote in writing. L16–E18. 2a *v.t.* Illustrate by examples; find or provide an example of. LME. b *v.i.* Quote examples by way of illustration. L16. c *v.t.* Be or serve as an example of. L18. †3 *v.t.* & *i.* Set a (good) example (to). LME–E16. †4 *v.t.* Adduce, quote, use as an example; compare *to* by way of example. E16–L18. †5 *v.t.* Make after an example or model. L16–L17. †6 *v.t.* Make an example of (a person). Only in M17. †7 *v.t.* Manifest or display an example of (a quality etc.). M–L17.

2a D. CECIL Her stories do exemplify her moral point of view. b C. BROOKE-ROSE The professor exemplified with a vivid comparison from the animal kingdom. c W. STYRON Talk about your lovesick fool, how I exemplified such a wretch!

exemplifiable *a.* (*rare*) E19. **exemplifier** *n.* M16.

exempli gratia /ɪɡˌzɛmpli ˈɡreɪʃə; ɛɡ-/ *adv. phr.* M17. [L, f. genit. of *exemplum* EXAMPLE *n.* + abl. of *gratia*: see GRACE *n.*] For example, for instance. Usu. abbrev. *e.g.*

exemplum /ɪɡˈzɛmpləm, ɛɡ-/ *n.* Pl. **-pla** /-plə/. L19. [L.] An example; an illustrative or moralizing story.

exempt /ɪɡˈzɛm(p)t, ɛɡ-/ *a.* & *n.* LME. [L *exemptus* pa. pple of *eximere* take out, deliver, free, f. as EX-[1] I + *emere* take.] A *adj.* 1 Not exposed or subject to something unpleasant or inconvenient; not liable to a charge, tax, etc. (Foll. by *from*, †*of.*) LME. b Free *from* a defect, weakness, etc. L16. 2 Independent of, not owing obedience to, a superior authority. Now *Hist.* (of religious foundations). (Foll. by *from.*) LME. b Not subject to influence or control. (Foll. by *from.*) M17.

1 R. C. TRENCH They whom Christ loves are no more exempt than others from their share of earthly trouble and anguish. J. BERGER He is exempt on medical grounds from military service. b SHELLEY From custom's evil taint exempt and pure. 2 A. P. STANLEY The Primate . . preferred to avoid the question of the exempt jurisdiction of Westminster. b GLADSTONE There is no European country in which ecclesiastical societies are exempt from civic control.

B *n.* 1 *Eccl.* A person or establishment not subject to episcopal jurisdiction. *obs.* exc. *Hist.* M16. †2 An inferior cavalry officer in the French army who commanded in the absence of the captain and lieutenant and was exempt from ordinary military duty. L17–E19. 3 A French police officer. *obs.* exc. *Hist.* L17. 4 = EXON *n.*[1] E18. 5 An exempted person; *esp.* one not liable to payment of tax or military service etc. M19.

exempt /ɪɡˈzɛm(p)t, ɛɡ-/ *v.t.* Pa. pple **-ed**, (*arch.*) **exempt**. LME. [f. as prec., orig. in pa. ppl form: see -ED[1].] 1 Grant immunity or freedom from or *from* a liability to which others are subject. LME. 2 Take or put away; remove, cut off; single out. (Foll. by *from, out of.*) Now *rare* or *obs.* LME. †3 Debar, exclude, *from.* LME–L17. †4 Omit from a category or enumeration; except. (Foll. by *from, out of.*) LME–M18.

1 J. A. FROUDE Clergy who committed felony were no longer exempted from the penalties of their crimes. R. D. LAING I was exempted from military service because of asthma. S. UNWIN My . . campaign to exempt books from Customs Clearance Charges.

exemptible *a.* E17.

exemptile /ɪɡˈzɛm(p)tɪl, ɛɡ-/ *a.* Now *rare.* E17. [Late L *exemptilis*, f. *eximere*: see EXEMPT *a.* & *n.*, -IL, -ILE.] Removable.

exemption /ɪɡˈzɛm(p)ʃ(ə)n, ɛɡ-/ *n.* LME. [(O)Fr., or L *exemptio(n-)*, f. *exempt-* pa. ppl stem of *eximere*: see EXEMPT *a.* & *n.*, -ION.] 1 The action of exempting or the state of being exempted from something unpleasant or inconvenient; (granting of) immunity. LME. b *Eccl.* Freedom from control by one's normal superior, usu. the bishop of the diocese, and immediate subjection to either the superior of one's religious house or order, or the Pope. LME. c Freedom from a defect or weakness. M17. †2 Removal; exception, exclusion. M16–L17.

exencephaly /ɛksɛnˈsɛf(ə)li, -ˈkɛf-/ *n.* Also in mod.L form **-cephalia** /-sɪˈfeɪlɪə, -kɛ-/. E20. [f. EX-[2] + Gk *egkephalos* brain + -Y[3], -IA[1].] A condition in which part of the brain protrudes through the skull.

exence'phalic *a.* E20.

exenterate /ɪkˈsɛntəreɪt, ɛk-/ *v.t.* E17. [L *exenterat-* pa. ppl stem of *exenterare*, after Gk *exenterizein*, f. as EX-[2] + *enteron* intestine: see -ATE[3].] Remove the contents of (part of the body, esp. the orbit); remove (an eyeball). Orig., disembowel.

exente'ration *n.* M17.

exequatur /ɛksɪˈkweɪtə/ *n.* E17. [L, 3rd pers. sing. pres. subjunct. of *exequi* (see EXECUTE) = let him or her perform.] 1 *RC Ch.* A government's authorization for a bishop to exercise his office in its territory, or for any papal enactment to take effect there; a claim by a government that such authorization is required or can be withheld. E17. 2 An official recognition of a consul by a foreign government, authorizing him or her to exercise office. L18.

exequial /ɪk'siːkwɪəl, ɛk-/ *a.* E17. [L *exsequialis*, f. *exsequiae*: see EXEQUY, -IAL.] Of or pertaining to a funeral.

exequy /'ɛksɪkwi/ *n.* Orig. †**exequies** (as *sing.*). LME. [OFr. *exequies*, f. L accus. *exsequias* (nom. *-iae*) funeral procession or ceremonies, f. *exsequi* follow after, accompany: see EXECUTE.] 1 In *pl.* & †*sing.* Funeral rites; a funeral ceremony. LME. 2 A funeral ode. *poet.* L19.

†**exerce** *v.* Chiefly *Sc.* LME. [(O)Fr. *exercer* f. L *exercere*: see EXERCISE *n.*] 1 *v.t.* Carry out or perform (a deed etc.); fulfil (a duty), exercise (a right or office); exert, wield, (justice, power, etc.). LME–L18. 2 *v.t.* & *i.* Keep (a person) busy, engage the attention (of); train, discipline. LME–L16. 3 *v.t.* Display, exhibit, (an emotion or quality). Only in 16.

†**exercent** *a.* M17–E18. [L *exercent-* pres. ppl stem of *exercere*: see EXERCISE *n.*] Exercising the duties of or practising one's profession or position, esp. that of an advocate.

exercise /'ɛksəsʌɪz/ *n.* ME. [(O)Fr. *exercice* f. L *exercitium*, f. *exercere* keep busy, practise, f. as EX-[1] I + *arcere* keep in, keep away.] 1 The employment or application of an organ, faculty, right, etc.; the exertion *of* influence or power; the practice *of* a virtue, function, profession, etc. ME. †b The (method of) use *of* a weapon. LME–L17. 2 Practice for the sake of physical, mental, or spiritual training or improvement. ME. b Disciplinary suffering; a trying experience; a state of distress or anxiety; a painful mental struggle. Now *rare.* LME. †c Acquired skill. *rare* (Shakes.). Only in E17. 3†a The action or an act of training or drilling troops, scholars, etc. LME–E19. b A military drill or parade; in *pl.*, military training, athletics, etc. M16. 4 Exertion of the muscles, limbs, etc., esp. for the sake of strength or health. LME. 5 A task set or performed for training the body or mind, or as a test of proficiency, esp. in some particular skill. M16. b A dissertation, composition, etc., submitted for a degree; a disputation, a viva voce. M16. c Something written by a pupil; something designed to afford practice to a learner. E17. d Any written composition; an essay, a sermon, a treatise. E18. e In *pl.* Formal acts or ceremonies on some special occasion, esp. the conferment of a degree. *N. Amer.* M19. †6 A habitual occupation; a customary practice. M16–M18. 7 A religious observance or act of worship; a sermon; an act of preaching or prophesying. M16. b The discussion of a passage of Scripture; a meeting of a Presbytery for such a discussion; a Presbytery. *Sc.* L16. c The practice and performance of religious ceremonies, worship, etc; the right to this. M17.

1 R. G. COLLINGWOOD Reconstructed historically, often not without the exercise of considerable historical skill. *New York Times* The exercise of the right of self-determination cannot be denied. 4 A. E. T. WATSON These horses have their own boys, who ride at exercise. JO GRIMOND She was much given to exercise, in her younger days chiefly golf, later long walks. 5 P. G. WODEHOUSE Kirk.. was engaged on his daily sparring exercise with Steve Dingle. S. LEWIS He stood on the sleeping-porch and did his day's exercises. M. GIROUARD His stone-faced stables are an elaborate and convincing exercise in neo-Palladianism. *Times Educ. Suppl.* The damage limitation exercise meant that plans.. were put on ice. *manual exercise*: see MANUAL *a.* c E. BLISHEN If I gave the class an exercise he rarely got beyond writing the date. FIVE-*finger exercise.*

Comb. & phrases: **exercise book** a notebook in which to do school exercises; a book containing set exercises; **exercise bicycle** or (*colloq.*) **bike** a stationary apparatus used for exercise, in which a person can sit and pedal against resistance, like a cyclist; **exercise yard** an enclosed area used for physical exercise; **the object of the exercise** the essential purpose of an action or procedure.

exercise /'ɛksəsʌɪz/ *v.* LME. [f. the n.] I *v.t.* 1 Employ, put to practical effect, (a faculty, skill, right, etc.); exert, wield, (force, influence, justice, etc.); practise acts of (cruelty, duplicity, etc.); have (an effect). LME. 2 Keep (a person) occupied or busy. Now only *refl.* & in *pass.* LME. †b Till (the ground). LME–L17. †c Use (an instrument or remedy); work (an animal). E16–M18. 3 Train (a person) by practice; drill (soldiers); exert (the body, muscles, etc.) for the sake of strength or health; cause (an animal) to do this. Also, subject to ascetic discipline. LME. †b Accustom, inure. M16–E17. c Practise the use or deployment of (a weapon). E18. †4 Perform, carry out, esp. habitually; take part in (an action, game, ceremony, religious service); play (a part); practise (a religion). LME–E19. b Pursue or ply (an occupation or trade); practise (an art, language, etc.); carry out the functions of (an office). LME–L18. 5 Tax the powers of; engage the attention of; *esp.* vex, worry. M16.

1 W. S. MAUGHAM He exercised great ingenuity in disguising old sets so that they looked new. G. F. KENNAN Kerensky's final defeat exercised a highly divisive effect on Western opinion. R. LYND Garrick and Kean exercise a spell on us. 2 J. P. MAHAFFY He and his fellows were all exercised as jurymen in deciding political and social disputes. 3 G. B. SHAW I, with a bigger body to exercise and quite as much energy, must loaf and loll. 5 C. RYCROFT Dreams are a continuation in sleep of thoughts which were exercising the sleeper while he was awake. ANTHONY SMITH Poe was much exercised by this thought.

II *v.i.* †6 Perform or practise one's occupation (*on*); discourse *on* a subject. E16–E18. 7 Conduct or engage in a religious exercise or service; interpret Scripture. *obs.* exc. *Sc.* M16. 8 Take exercise; go through exercises for practice; (of a soldier) drill. E17.

8 J. MILLER When you start to exercise, your heart automatically speeds up.

exercisable *a.* able to be exercised, employed, or enforced M18. **exerciser** *n.* a person who or thing which exercises; *esp.* an apparatus for use in exercising the limbs etc.: M16.

exercitant /ɪg'zəːsɪtənt, ɛg-/ *n.* M19. [Fr. f. L *exercitant-* pres. ppl stem of *exercitare*: see next, -ANT[1].] A person engaged in spiritual exercises.

exercitation /ɪg,zəːsɪ'teɪʃ(ə)n, ɛg-/ *n.* LME. [L *exercitatio(n-)*, f. *exercitat-* pa. ppl stem of *exercitare* frequent. of *exercere*: see EXERCISE *n.*, -ATION.] †1 (Any particular form of) physical exercise. LME–M17. 2 The action or an act of exercising a faculty, skill, power, etc. LME. b A display of (esp. literary or oratorical) skill; an essay, a composition. M17. 3 The action or an act of training by practice; a task undertaken for this purpose, an exercise. L15. †4 The practising of a trade; the habitual performance of actions. L16–M17. 5 (An act of) worship or religious observance. M17.

exercitor /ɪg'zəːsɪtə, ɛg-/ *n.* L17. [L, f. *exercit-* pa. ppl stem of *exercere*: see -OR.] *Rom.* & *Sc. Law* (now *Hist.*). A person to whom the daily profits of a ship belonged; a person who conducted a shipping business.

exerci'torian *a.* M19.

Exercycle /'ɛksəsʌɪk(ə)l/ *n.* Orig. *US.* Also **e-**. M20. [f. EXER(CISE *n.* + BI)CYCLE *n.*] (Proprietary name for) an exercise bicycle.

exergonic /ɛksəː'gɒnɪk/ *a.* M20. [f. EX-[2] + Gk *ergon* work + -IC.] *Sci.* Accompanied by the release of energy.

exergue /ɪk'səːg, ɛk'səːg, 'ɛksəːg/ *n.* L17. [Fr. f. med.L *exergum*, f. Gk EX-[2] + *ergon* work.] *Numism.* A small space on a coin or medal, usu. on the reverse below the principal device, for the date, the engraver's initials, etc.; the inscription placed there.

exergual /-g(ə)l/ *a.* M19.

exergy /'ɛksədʒi/ *n.* M20. [f. EX-[2] after *energy.*] *Physics* & *Chem.* The maximum amount of work that can be obtained from a process, or from a system by reversible processes.

exert /ɪg'zəːt, ɛg-/ *v.* M17. [L *ex(s)ert-* pa. ppl stem of *ex(s)erere* put forth, f. as EX-[1] I + *serere* bind, entwine, join. Cf. EXSERT.] †1 *v.t.* Perform, practise, (an action or operation). M17–M18. 2 *v.t.* Push out or up; discharge (a seed); emit (light). *obs.* exc. *Bot.* M17. †3 *v.t.* Bring to light, reveal. L17–M18. 4 *v.t.* Exercise, apply, bring to bear, (a quality, force, etc.), esp. with considerable effort or effect. L17. 5 *v.refl.* & †*i.* Use efforts or endeavours, strive, (*to do*; *for* a thing). M18.

4 R. HAYMAN The teacher who probably exerted the most direct personal influence on him. M. SARTON It was finally hunger that exerted enough pressure to get Laura up. 5 M. SPARK He had a sense of having exerted himself a great deal.

exertive *a.* tending to exert M19. †**exertment** *n.* (*rare*) the action or an act of exerting L17–M19.

exertion /ɪg'zəːʃ(ə)n, ɛg-/ *n.* M17. [f. prec. + -ION.] †1 The action or an act of displaying; (a) manifestation. M17–L18. 2 The action or an act of exerting something, esp. a faculty, power, etc. (Foll. by *of.*) L17. 3 The action or an act of exerting oneself (physically or mentally); (an) effort; vigorous action. L18.

1 J. AUSTEN An exertion of spirits which increased with her increase of emotion. 3 D. L. SAYERS She has, by her own exertions, made herself independent. N. MAILER The Filipinos jogged and panted from their exertion.

exes /'ɛksɪz/ *n.pl.* *colloq.* M19. [Abbrev.] Expenses.

†**exestuation** *n.* var. of EXAESTUATION.

Exeter /'ɛksɪtə/ *n.* L18. [A city in SW England.] 1 *Exeter carpet*, a type of rare hand-knotted carpet made in Exeter in the 18th cent. L18. 2 *Exeter Hall*, a type of evangelicalism represented by gatherings which took place in a former building of this name in the Strand, London. M19.

exeunt /'ɛksɪʌnt/ *v.i.* (*defective*). L15. [L, 3rd person pl. pres. indic. of *exire*: see EXIT *v.*[1]] A stage direction: (actors, or the characters whose names follow) leave the stage. Cf. EXIT *v.*[1]

exeunt omnes /'ɒmniːz/ all leave the stage.

ex facie /ɛks 'feɪʃi/ *adv. phr.* M19. [f. L *ex* out of + *facie* abl. of *facies* FACE *n.*] *Sc. Law.* On the face (of a document); so far as appears from a document.

exfiltrate /'ɛksfɪltreɪt/ *v.t.* & *i.* L20. [Back-form. f. next.] *Mil.* Remove (personnel or units) from behind enemy lines; covertly withdraw (an agent) from a dangerous position.

exfiltration /ɛksfɪl'treɪʃ(ə)n/ *n.* L19. [f. EX-[1] I + FILTRATION; in sense 2 perh. after *infiltration.*] 1 The action or process of filtering or seeping out. *rare.* L19. 2 *Mil.* The action of exfiltrating. M20.

exflagellation /,ɛksfladʒə'leɪʃ(ə)n/ *n.* E20. [f. EX-[1] I + FLAGELLATION.] *Zool.* The formation or shedding of flagella; the development of microgametes resembling flagella.

ex'flagellate *v.i.* undergo exflagellation E20.

exfoliate /ɪks'fəʊlɪeɪt, ɛks-/ *v.* M17. [Late L *exfoliat-* pa. ppl stem of *exfoliare* strip of leaves, f. L EX-[1] I + *folium* leaf: see -ATE[3].] 1 *v.t.* Cast off, shed, (the cuticle, the surface of a bone, etc.) in the form of thin layers or scales; *Surg.* remove the surface of (a bone etc.) in this form. M17. 2 *v.i.* Of bone, skin, a mineral, etc.: separate or come off in thin layers or scales. Of a tree: throw off layers of bark. L17. 3 *v.t.* & *i.* Unfold, develop. E19.

3 F. C. L. WRAXALL Questions exfoliated themselves. *New Yorker* Taking an active part in the exfoliating New York art scene.

exfoli'ation *n.* (*a*) the action or process of exfoliating; (*b*) a layer or scale produced by this: L17. **exfoliative** *n.* & *a.* (*a*) *n.* (*rare*) something which produces exfoliation; (*b*) *adj.* causing or promoting exfoliation; involving or marked by exfoliation: L17.

ex gratia /ɛks 'greɪʃə/ *adv.* & *a. phr.* M18. [L, f. *ex* from + *gratia* GRACE *n.*] (Done, given, etc.) as a favour or without (esp. legal) compulsion.

exhalation /ɛksə'leɪʃ(ə)n/ *n.* LME. [L *exhalatio(n-)*, f. *exhalat-* pa. ppl stem of *exhalare* EXHALE *v.*[1]: see -ATION.] 1 The action or an act of exhaling. LME. 2 *sing.* & in *pl.* Something which is exhaled; a mist, a vapour; an effluvium, a scent. LME. 3 A body of (usu. ignited) vapour; a meteor. *arch.* M16. 4 *Geol.* An emission of volcanic or magmatic gases into the atmosphere. E20.

2 S. O'FAOLÁIN The damp . . rose in curling exhalations from the pavements.

exhalative /ɛks'halətɪv, ɪks-/ *a.* pertaining to exhalation L16. **exhalatory** /ɛks'halət(ə)ri, ɪks-/ *a.* exhalative E19.

exhale /ɪks'heɪl, ɛks-/ *v.*[1] LME. [(O)Fr. *exhaler* f. L *exhalare*, f. as EX-[1] 1 + *halare* breathe.] **1** *v.i.* Be given off as vapour, evaporate. (Foll. by *from.*) LME. **2** *v.i.* & (in *pass.*) *v.t.* Of blood etc.: pass or be passed slowly and in minute quantities through tissue. Now *rare*. LME. **3** *v.t.* Draw up or drive off in the form of vapour; cause to evaporate. L16. **4** *v.t.* Expel from within by breathing; breathe out (life, words, a prayer, etc.). L16. **5** *v.t.* Give off or send up (vapour, fumes, etc.) from the surface; give off like a vapour. L16. **6** *v.t.* Give vent to (anger, enthusiasm, etc.); dissipate (strong emotion). *arch.* M18. **7** *v.i.* Make an expiration, breathe out. M19.

1 R. W. EMERSON When flowers reach their ripeness, incense exhales from them. 3 SIR W. SCOTT Bitumen and sulphur, which the burning sun exhaled from the waters of the lake. 4 H. JAMES She exhaled a moan of relief. A. GRAY Tilting her head back to exhale smoke from her nostrils. 5 J. CONRAD His whole person exhaled a charm. G. GREENE A white handkerchief . . exhaled as . . sweet an odour as a whole altar of lilies.

exhalable *a.* L17. **exhalant** *n.* & *a.* †(*a*) *n.* an exhalant vessel or organ; (*b*) *adj.* that exhales; conveying blood etc. in minute quantities: L18. **exhalement** *n.* (an) exhalation M17.

†exhale *v.*[2] L16. [f. EX-[1] 1 + HALE *v.*[1]] **1** *v.t.* & *i.* Draw (a thing) out of something, *spec.* (the sword) from the scabbard; drag (a person) away. L16–E17. **2** *v.t.* Cause (blood, tears, etc.) to flow (*from*). L16–E17. **3** *v.t.* Raise (a person) to a higher position; exalt. L16–M17.

exhaust /ɪg'zɔːst, ɛg-/ *n.* M19. [f. EXHAUST *v.*] **1** The exit or expulsion from an engine of steam, gas, or other motive fluid that has done its work of propulsion; the fluid so expelled; the pipework etc. through which this occurs, *esp.* the exhaust-pipe of a motor vehicle. M19. **2** (An apparatus for) the production of an outward current of air by creating a partial vacuum. M19.

1 N. CALDER Lead injected into the air by car exhausts. J. COLVILLE The exhaust of our fighters streaked the blue sky with white lines. attrib.: *exhaust gas, manifold, stroke*, etc.

Comb.: *exhaust manifold*: see MANIFOLD *n.* 5; **exhaust-pipe**: by which gaseous combustion products are expelled from an engine into the air.

†exhaust *a.* E16–E18. [L *exhaustus* pa. pple of *exhaurire*: see next.] Exhausted.

exhaust /ɪg'zɔːst/ *v.* Pa. pple **exhausted**, **†exhaust**. M16. [L *exhaust-* pa. ppl stem of *exhaurire*, f. as EX-[1] 1 + *haurire* draw (water), drain.] **1** *v.t.* Draw out (air or other gas). Formerly, draw (anything) off or out (*lit.* & *fig.*). M16. **†b** Take a draught of; drink or suck up. L16–L17. **2** *v.t.* Use up or consume completely; account for the whole of. M16. **3** *v.t.* Empty by drawing the contents off or out; drain; empty *of* (specified contents). E17. **4** *v.t.* Drain (a person, country, etc.) of strength or resources, or (a soil) of nutritive ingredients; tire out. Freq. as *exhausted, exhausting* ppl adjs. M17. **5** *v.t.* Draw out all that is essential or interesting in (an object of investigation or exposition); treat or study (a subject) so as to leave nothing further to be explained or discovered. E18. **6** *v.i.* Of steam: escape from an engine as exhaust. M19. **7** *v.i.* Of an engine or vehicle: discharge its exhaust (*into* etc.). E20.

1 G. BIRD Exhaust the air from beneath the bladder. M. EARBERY These things we have exhausted from the sacred Scriptures. 2 J. S. MILL A sufficient number of drawings to exhaust all the possible combinations. A. BEVAN As time went on the iron ore was exhausted. J. CHEEVER The father's replies were short-tempered. . . His patience was exhausted. 3 LD RUTHERFORD Sealed in an exhausted tube of hard glass. 4 W. STUBBS The Thirty Years' War exhausted Germany. O. MANNING Harriet, suddenly exhausted, wished she were in bed. 5 A. NEWMAN They had quickly exhausted the . . topic. 7 *Scientific American* The Lockheed L1011 tail engine exhausts through the end of the fuselage.

exhaustedly *adv.* in an exhausted manner M19. **exhaustedness** *n.* exhausted state or condition M19. **exhauster** *n.* a person who or thing which exhausts; *esp.* a device for removing air or gas: M18. **exhausti'bility** *n.* the quality of being exhaustible M19. **exhaustible** *a.* able to be exhausted M17. **exhaustingly** *adv.* in an exhausting manner L19. **exhaustless** *a.* (*literary*) incapable of being exhausted, inexhaustible E18. **†exhaustment** *n.* (*rare*) the action or an act of exhausting something, esp. resources; the state of being exhausted: E17–M19. **†exhausture** *n.* the action of exhausting something; state of being exhausted; an instance of this: L16–L18.

exhaustion /ɪg'zɔːstʃ(ə)n, ɛg-/ *n.* E17. [Late L *exhaustio(n-)*, f. L *exhaust-*: see prec., -ION.] **1** The action of draining something of a resource or emptying it of its contents; the state of being so depleted or emptied. E17. **2** Total loss of strength or vitality in a person. M17. **3** The removal or extraction *of* air from a vessel. M17. **4** The process or an act of establishing a conclusion by eliminating alternatives. (Earliest in *method of exhaustions* below.) L17. **5** The action or process of consuming something or using it up completely. M19.

1 H. DAVY When cattle are fed upon land not benefited by their manure, the effect is always an exhaustion of the soil. *Nature* In the next tube the exhaustion has been carried further. 2 A. KOESTLER Dance himself into a frenzy followed by exhaustion. 4 **method of exhaustions** *Math.* a way of proving the equality of two magnitudes by demonstrating the contradiction which occurs if one is greater or less than the other.

exhaustive /ɪg'zɔːstɪv, ɛg-/ *a.* L18. [f. EXHAUST *v.* + -IVE.] **1** Tending to exhaust a subject; leaving no part unexamined or unconsidered; thorough, complete, comprehensive. L18. **2** Tending to drain of strength, energy, or resources; exhausting. E19.

1 GLADSTONE I shall attempt in this limited work no exhaustive survey. L. GOULD She had made an exhaustive New York psychiatrist list. 2 M. KEANE Her day of exhaustive detective work.

exhaustively *adv.* E19. **exhaustiveness** *n.* E19.

exhedra *n.* var. of EXEDRA.

exheredate /ɪks'hɛrɪdeɪt, ɛks-/ *v.t.* Now *rare* exc. *Sc.* M16. [L *exheredat-* pa. ppl stem of *exheredare*, f. as EX-[1] 1 + *hered-*, *heres* heir: see -ATE[3].] Disinherit.

exheredation /ˌɛkshɛrɪ'deɪʃ(ə)n/ *n.* LME. [L *exheredatio(n-)*, f. as prec.: see -ATION.] Disinheritance.

exhereditation /ˌɛkshərɛdɪ'teɪʃ(ə)n/ *n.* *rare*. L16. [L *exhereditat-* pa. ppl stem of *exhereditare*, f. *exheredare*: see EXHEREDATE, -ATION.] = prec.

exhibit /ɪg'zɪbɪt, ɛg-/ *n.* E17. [L *exhibitum* neut. sing. of pa. pple of *exhibere*: see next.] **1a** *Law.* A document or object produced in a court and referred to and identified in written evidence. Formerly also, a document certified as having been attested by a witness. E17. **b** A detailed and formal statement of particulars, esp. of debts, liabilities, etc. E18. **2** In *pl.* The letters of orders and other documents which a beneficed or licensed Anglican priest may be required to produce at the first visitation after his admission; the fees payable on presenting these. E17. **3** A showing, a display; a production in evidence. M17. **b** = EXHIBITION 6. *N. Amer.* L19. **4** An item on display in an exhibition, museum, etc.; the collection of items sent by any one contributor. M19.

1 **exhibit A** the first exhibit in a case; *fig.* something regarded as evidence or the most important evidence. 3 *Times* The power to compel an exhibit of books of account. b S. BELLOW An exhibit of his pictures at a women's club. 4 J. BARNES Two exhibits in a side cabinet are easy to miss.

exhibit /ɪg'zɪbɪt, ɛg-/ *v.* Pa. pple **-ited**, **†-it**. LME. [L *exhibit-* pa. ppl stem of *exhibere*, f. as EX-[1] 1 + *habere* to hold.] **I** Show. **1** *v.t.* Hold out or submit (a document) for inspection, esp. as evidence in a court of law. LME. **2** *v.t.* Submit for consideration; present, prefer, (a petition, accusation, etc.). LME. **3a** *v.t.* Manifest to the senses, esp. sight; present to view. E16. **†b** *v.i.* Of a thing: reveal itself, be manifest. M17–M18. **4** *v.t.* Set out in words or figures, detail. Now *rare*. M16. **5** *v.t.* & *i.* Show (an item) publicly for entertainment, instruction, or in a competition; have (an item) on show in an exhibition. E18. **6** *v.t.* Represent by a figure, drawing, etc. L18. **b** Present a delineation or embodiment of in words or in actions. M19. **7** *v.t.* Indicate the presence of; give evidence of. L18.

3a J. TYNDALL The lake . . exhibits the colour of pure water. G. ORWELL Big Brother is the guise in which the Party chooses to exhibit itself to the world. B. BAINBRIDGE These remarks seemed perfectly genuine, as really exhibiting the state of his mind. 5 G. GISSING He exhibited one picture only. *Listener* There are twice as many nations exhibiting. 6 J. NICHOLSON One of these branches is exhibited in the figure. b LD MACAULAY In the power of exhibiting character by means of dialogue he was deficient. 7 O. HENRY He exhibited no signs of flinching. P. G. WODEHOUSE His employer had exhibited a disquieting disposition to blame him for everything.

II Offer, administer. **†8** *v.t.* Offer, present, (sacrifice, praise, etc.); administer (an oath). L15–M17. **†9** *v.t.* Provide, grant, (*to*); defray (expense). L15–M17. **†10** *v.i.* & (*rare*) *t.* Provide maintenance *to* a student; support, maintain. E17–M19. **11** *v.t.* Administer (medicine, a drug). Now *rare*. E17.

exhibitable *a.* M19. **exhibitant** *n.* †(*a*) a person who preferred or presented an accusation; (*b*) *gen.* a person who exhibits something: L17. **exhibiter** *n.* (now *rare*) = EXHIBITOR L16. **exhibitor** *n.* a person who exhibits something, esp. in a show or exhibition M17.

exhibition /ɛksɪ'bɪʃ(ə)n/ *n.* LME. [(O)Fr. f. late L *exhibitio(n-)*, f. as prec.: see -ION.] **I** Provision. **†1** Maintenance, support. LME–E18. **†2a** *sing.* & in *pl.* An allowance of money for a person's support; a pension; a salary. L15–M18. **b** A gift, a present. L16–E17. **3†a** Financial assistance given to a student. Only in 16. **b** A monetary award given to a student for a fixed period from the funds of a school, college, etc., usu. after a competitive examination. M17. **4** The administration of a medicine, drug, etc. Now *rare* or *obs.* L18.

1 J. STRYPE To bestow £8 . . towards the use and exhibition of three grammar scholars. 2a SWIFT He . . is driven to live in exile upon a small exhibition. b SHAKES. *Oth.* I would not do such a thing for . . petticoats, nor caps, nor any petty exhibition. 3b H. CARPENTER He also managed to win an Exhibition . . in Natural Science to Christ Church.

II Showing, a show. **5** The action or an act of exhibiting; manifestation; (a) visible show or display (of a feeling, quality, etc.). L17. **6** A public display of items to give pleasure or instruction, or as a competition. M18. **b** A public examination or display of the attainments of students. *US.* L18. **7** Something that is exhibited; a sight, a spectacle. Now *rare*. L18.

5 A. B. JAMESON Dunstan never would have dared such an exhibition of presumption. P. G. WODEHOUSE The exhibition of his virtues and the careful suppression of his defects. *attrib.*: A. CHRISTIE I do a couple of exhibition dances . . with Raymond . . he's the tennis and dancing pro. **make an exhibition of oneself** behave in so ostentatious or conspicuous a manner as to appear ridiculous or contemptible. 6 N. SHUTE An exhibition of Australian religious paintings at the National Gallery. *attrib.*: *New Yorker* Sumptuous exhibition catalogues proclaim their status as ideal gifts.

exhibitional *a.* M19. **exhibitioner** *n.* †(*a*) *rare* a person who paid for another's maintenance; (*b*) a student who has been awarded an exhibition; (*c*) an exhibitor: L16.

exhibitionism /ɛksɪ'bɪʃ(ə)nɪz(ə)m/ *n.* L19. [f. prec. + -ISM.] **1** (A psychosexual disorder characterized by) exposure of the genitals to strangers. L19. **2** A tendency towards display or extravagant behaviour. E20.

exhibitionist /ɛksɪ'bɪʃ(ə)nɪst/ *n.* & *a.* E19. [f. as prec. + -IST.] **A** *n.* **1** A person who takes part in an exhibition or public performance. *rare*. E19. **2** A person who indulges in exhibitionism. L19. **B** *attrib.* or as *adj.* Of, pertaining to, or displaying exhibitionism. E20.

exhibitio'nistic *a.* characterized by or given to exhibitionism M20. **exhibitio'nistically** *adv.* E20.

exhibitive /ɪg'zɪbɪtɪv, ɛg-/ *a.* L16. [mod.L *exhibitivus*, f. L *exhibit-*: see EXHIBIT *v.*, -IVE.] **1**

Having the property of exhibiting or showing; illustrative. (Foll. by *of*.) L16. †2 Having the function of imparting or communicating. (Foll. by *of*.) Only in 17.

exhibitively *adv.* E17.

exhibitory /ɪgˈzɪbɪt(ə)ri, ɛg-/ *n.* & *a.* E17. [Late L *exhibitorius*, f. as EXHIBIT *v.*: see -ORY[1], -ORY[2].] †A *n.* A procedure relating to the administration of a medicine, drug, etc. *rare*. Only in E17. B *adj.* Intended to exhibit or to cause to be exhibited; of or pertaining to exhibition. L18.

exhilarant /ɪgˈzɪlər(ə)nt, ɛg-/ *n.* & *a.* E19. [Fr. f. L *exhilarant-* pres. ppl stem of *exhilarare*: see next, -ANT[1].] A *n.* A medicine, drug, etc., that promotes exhilaration; a stimulant, a euphoriant. Now *rare*. E19. B *adj.* That exhilarates; exhilarating. M19.

exhilarate /ɪgˈzɪləreɪt, ɛg-/ *v.t.* M16. [L *exhilarat-* pa. ppl stem of *exhilarare*, f. as EX-[1] I + *hilaris* cheerful: see -ATE[3].] Make cheerful or merry; enliven, gladden; thrill, invigorate.

DICKENS It seemed greatly to delight and exhilarate him to say so. A. WILSON The exhilarating weather of April with its lively south-east breezes. A. MCCOWEN I was also exhilarated by the sense of power that I felt on the stage.

exhilaratingly *adv.* in an exhilarating manner M19. **exhilarative** *a.* tending to exhilarate E19. **exhilarator** *n.* (*rare*) a person or thing which exhilarates E19.

exhilaration /ɪg,zɪləˈreɪʃ(ə)n, ɛg-/ *n.* E17. [Late L *exhilaratio(n-)*, f. as prec.: see -ATION.] 1 The action or means of exhilarating; an exhilarating influence. E17. 2 The condition or feeling of being exhilarated. E17.

1 LONGFELLOW There was.. that wild exhilaration in the air. 2 K. M. E. MURRAY Periods of great depression.. were.. outnumbered by his times of exhilaration.

exhorbitant *a.* & *n.* var. of EXORBITANT.

exhort /ɪgˈzɔːt/ *v.* & *n.* LME. [(O)Fr. *exhorter* or L *exhortari*, f. as EX-[1] I + *hortari* encourage.] A *v.t.* 1 Admonish earnestly; urge (a person) to praiseworthy conduct (foll. by *to* do, *to* a course of action). LME. 2 Recommend (something) earnestly; insist upon. *arch.* E16.

1 LD MACAULAY The people would be exhorted to liberality. P. KAVANAGH The Faithful were exhorted to receive Holy Communion. L. A. G. STRONG The referee was exhorting the pair. 2 J. A. FROUDE He.. again exhorted a reform.

B *n.* = EXHORTATION. Now *rare* or *obs.* L15.

exhorter *n.* a person who exhorts someone or something; *spec.* in some Christian Churches, a person appointed to give religious exhortation under the direction of a minister: M16.

exhortation /ɛgzɔːˈteɪʃ(ə)n/ *n.* LME. [(O)Fr. or L *exhortatio(n-)*, f. *exhortat-* pa. ppl stem of *exhortari*: see prec., -ATION.] 1 The action or an act of exhorting. LME. 2 A set speech delivered for the purpose of exhorting; *esp.* a formal or liturgical address. LME.

1 M. SPARK Exhortations to Freddy.. to come home from heathen posts to Christian Harrogate. R. F. HOBSON Punishment and exhortation had no effect and psychiatric help was sought.

exhortational *a.* L20.

exhortative /ɪgˈzɔːtətɪv, ɛg-/ *a.* LME. [L *exhortativus*, f. *exhortat-*: see EXHORTATION, -IVE.] = next.

exhortatory /ɪgˈzɔːtət(ə)ri, ɛg-/ *a.* LME. [Late L *exhortatorius*, f. L *exhortat-*: see EXHORTATION, -ORY[2].] Of, pertaining to, or containing exhortation; intended to exhort.

exhumate /ɛksˈ(h)juːmeɪt, ɪgˈzjuː-/ *v.t.* Now *rare*. M16. [med.L *exhumat-*: see next, -ATE[3].] = EXHUME I.

exhumation /ɛks(h)juːˈmeɪʃ(ə)n, ɛgzjuː-/ *n.* LME. [med.L *exhumatio(n-)*, f. *exhumat-* pa. ppl stem of *exhumare*: see next, -ATION.] The action or an act of exhuming.

ˈ**exhumator** *n.* an exhumer E19.

exhume /ɛksˈ(h)juːm, ɪgˈzjuːm/ *v.t.* LME. [med.L *exhumare*, f. L EX-[1] I + *humus* ground.] 1 Dig out, unearth, (*lit.* & *fig.*); remove (something buried) from beneath the ground; *esp.* disinter a body with legal permission. LME. 2 *Geol.* Expose (a land surface) that was formerly buried. Chiefly as *exhumed* ppl a. L19.

exhumer *n.* a person who exhumes something M19.

ex hypothesi /ɛks hʌɪˈpɒθəsʌɪ/ *adv. phr.* E17. [mod.L, f. L *ex* by + abl. of late L HYPOTHESIS.] According to the hypothesis (made); supposedly.

exies *n.pl.* var. of AIXIES.

exigeant /egziʒɑ̃/ *a.* Fem. **-ante** /-ɑ̃ːt/. L18. [Fr., pres. ppl a. of *exiger* f. L *exigere*: see EXACT *a.* & *adv.*] Exacting, demanding.

M. EDGEWORTH Those *exigeante* mothers who expect always to have possession of a son's arm.

exigence /ˈɛksɪdʒ(ə)ns, ˈɛgzɪ-/ *n.* LME. [(O)Fr., or late L *exigentia*, f. *exigent-*: see EXIGENT *a.*, -ENCE.] †1 = EXIGENCY I. LME–E19. 2 Urgent need or necessity. L16. 3 A situation calling for urgent measures; a crisis, an emergency. M17.

2 S. SPENDER Political exigence was never a justification for lies. 3 M. C. CLARKE Falstaff is equal to any exigence.

exigency /ˈɛksɪdʒ(ə)nsi, ˈɛgzɪ-; ɪgˈzɪdʒ(ə)nsi, ɛg-/ *n.* L16. [Late L *exigentia*: see prec., -ENCY.] 1 What is demanded by a given situation; a requirement, a need. Now usu. in *pl.* L16. 2 (An instance of) urgent need or necessity. In *pl.*, desperate straits. M17. 3 Pressing or urgent quality; stringency (of requirements). M18.

1 A. POWELL His system of bookselling was designed to suit his own convenience, rather than the.. exigencies of the trade. 2 DRYDEN The Romans in great Exigency, sent for their Dictator from the Plow. ADDISON We.. complain of our want of bullion and must at last be reduced to the greatest exigencies. 3 W. ROBERTSON Such immediate.. assistance as the exigency of her affairs required. S. DONALDSON There had been a special timbre of exigency in Terrel's.. voice.

exigent /ˈɛksɪdʒ(ə)nt, ˈɛgzɪ-/ *n.*[1] *obs.* exc. *Hist.* Also †**-end**. ME. [AN *exigende* f. med.L *exigenda* neut. pl. of gerundive of L *exigere*: see EXACT *a.* & *adv.*] *Law.* A writ instructing a sheriff to summon a defendant to appear and answer the plaintiff, or else be declared an outlaw.

†**exigent** *n.*[2] LME. [OFr., f. as EXIGENT *a.*] 1 A time or state of pressing need; a critical situation. Also, an end, a climax. LME–E18. 2 In *pl.* Needs, requirements. Only in 17. 3 A required amount. *rare*. Only in M19.

exigent /ˈɛksɪdʒ(ə)nt, ˈɛgzɪ-/ *a.* E17. [L *exigent-* pres. ppl stem of *exigere*: see EXACT *a.* & *adv.*, -ENT.] 1 Urgent, pressing. E17. 2 Demanding more (*of* something) than is reasonable; exacting. E19.

exigently *adv.* L19.

exigenter /ˈɛksɪdʒ(ə)ntə, ˈɛgz-/ *n. obs.* exc. *Hist.* E16. [AN, f. *exigente*, *exigende*: see EXIGENT *n.*[1], -ER[2].] *Law.* An officer of the Court of Common Pleas (or, in the 18th and 19th cents., of the Court of King's or Queen's Bench) responsible for making out exigents.

exigible /ˈɛksɪdʒɪb(ə)l, ˈɛgz-/ *a.* E17. [Fr., f. *exiger* f. L *exigere*: see EXACT *a.* & *adv.*, -IBLE.] Of a duty, sum of money, etc.: able to be required; due; chargeable.

exiguity /ɛksɪˈgjuːɪti, ɛgzɪ-/ *n.* E17. [L *exiguitas*, f. *exiguus*: see next, -ITY.] Exiguous quality; scantiness.

exiguous /ɪgˈzɪgjʊəs, ɛg-/ *a.* M17. [L *exiguus*, f. *exigere* weigh exactly: see EXACT *a.* & *adv.*, -OUS.] Scanty in size, amount, etc.; extremely small.

S. SASSOON My exiguous diary has preserved a few details of that.. march. J. I. M. STEWART An art-student living.. on some exiguous bursary.

exiguously *adv.* M20. **exiguousness** *n.* M18.

exilarch /ˈɛksɪlɑːk/ *n.* L19. [f. EXILE *n.*[1] + -ARCH, tr. Aram. *rēš gālūṯā* chief of the exile.] Any of the hereditary leaders of the Jewish community in Babylon from the 2nd to about the 10th cent., to whom Jews in other eastern countries paid homage.

exile /ˈɛksʌɪl, ˈɛgz-/ *n.*[1] ME. [(O)Fr. *exil* Latinized alt. of earlier *essil* f. L *exilium*, f. *exul* banished person.] 1 Expulsion from one's own country to live abroad, imposed as a sentence or punishment; penal banishment; residence abroad enforced by law or political power. ME. b Prolonged residence in a foreign country, either voluntary or imposed by circumstances; expatriation. LME. †2 Devastation or wasteful destruction of property. LME–E17.

1 M. M. KAYE You.. will be deposed and sent away to spend the remainder of your life in exile. b W. S. CHURCHILL Huguenots.. driven into exile by religious persecution. *internal exile*: see INTERNAL *a. tax exile*: see TAX *n.* **the Exile** the captivity of the Jews in Babylon in the 6th cent. BC.

exile /ˈɛksʌɪl, ˈɛgz-/ *n.*[2] ME. [Prob. f. (O)Fr. *exilé* pa. pple of *exiler* EXILE *v.*, with muting of final syll., as in ASSIGN *n.*, infl. by L *exul*.] 1 A person obliged by law or compelled by circumstances to live abroad. Also, a person who does this from choice. ME. 2 More fully *exile-tree*, *exile-oil-plant*. In the Indian subcontinent: a tree, *Thevetia peruviana* (family Apocynaceae), introduced from the W. Indies or tropical America. M19.

1 D. ATHILL He was an Egyptian.. and had been living for some years as an exile in Germany. *tax exile*: see TAX *n.*

exile /ˈɛksʌɪl/ *a.* Now *rare* or *obs.* LME. [f. L *exilis*: see -ILE.] †1 Slender, shrunken, thin; diminutive. LME–L17. 2 Scantily endowed; poor; (of soil) meagre, barren. LME. †3 Thin in consistency; fine, tenuous, insubstantial. E17–L18.

exile /ˈɛksʌɪl, ˈɛgz-/ *v.t.* ME. [OFr. *exil(i)er* (mod. *exiler*) alt. of *essilier* f. late L *exiliare*, f. *exilium* EXILE *n.*[1]] 1 Banish (a person) from his or her native country or (*fig.*) a favourite place, environment, etc. (Foll. by *from*, *to*, †2nd obj.) ME. 2 Discard, get rid of. Now *rare*. LME. †3 Ravage, lay waste. LME–M16.

1 J. AUSTEN You are fitted for society and it is shameful you should be exiled from it. J. R. GREEN The exiled Greek scholars were welcomed in Italy. 2 E. BOWEN For these.. occasions, ladies went tailormade; coaching, indeed, created its own fashions, exiling fussy, draped skirts.

exilement *n.* (now *rare*) LME. †**exiler** *n.* LME–M17.

exilian /ɪgˈzɪlɪən, ɪkˈsɪ-; ɛg-, ɛk-/ *a.* L19. [f. L *exilium* (see EXILE *n.*[1]) + -AN.] = next.

exilic /ɪgˈzɪlɪk, ɪkˈsɪ-; ɛg-, ɛk-/ *a.* L19. [f. EXILE *n.*[1] + -IC.] Of or pertaining to a period of exile, esp. that of the Jews in Babylon; in exile.

P. ACKROYD The isolation of an exilic writer like Turgenev.

†**exilient** *a.* M17–E18. [L *ex(s)ilient-* pres. ppl stem of *ex(s)ilire*, f. as EX-[1] I + *salire* to jump, spring.] Leaping up (as) with joy; exultant, rapturous.

†**exilience** *n.* E17–E18.

†**exilition** *n.* M17–E18. [Irreg. f. L *ex(s)ilire* (see prec.) + -ITION.] A jumping up, a springing forth.

exility /ɪgˈzɪlɪti, ɪkˈsɪ-; ɛg-, ɛk-/ *n. arch.* LME. [L *exilitas*, f. *exilis*: see EXILE *a.*, -ITY.] 1 Slenderness, thinness; smallness of size, extent, etc. LME. †2 Impoverishment. M16–L18. 3 Thinness of texture or consistency; fineness, tenuity. E17.

eximious /ɪgˈzɪmɪəs, ɛg-/ *a.* Now *rare*. M16. [L *eximius* set apart, select, f. *eximere*: see EXEMPT *a.*, -OUS.] Distinguished, outstanding, pre-eminent.

exinanition /ɪk,sɪnəˈnɪʃ(ə)n, ɛk-/ *n.* Now *rare*. E17. [L *exinanitio(n-)*, f. *exinanire* make empty, f. as EX-[1] I + *inanis* empty.] 1 The action of emptying or draining (*lit.* & *fig.*); emptied or drained condition. E17. 2 The action or an act of emptying of pride, self-will, or dignity; abasement, humbling, *spec.* (*Theol.*) that taken upon himself by Christ. E17.

1 JER. TAYLOR Fastings to the exinanition of spirits.

exine /ˈɛksɪn, -ʌɪn/ *n.* L19. [perh. f. EX-[2] + Gk *in-*, *is* fibre.] *Bot.* The tough outer wall of a pollen grain. Opp. INTINE.

exist /ɪgˈzɪst, ɛg-/ *v.i.* E17. [Prob. back-form. f. EXISTENCE. Cf. L *ex(s)istere* emerge, present oneself, come into being, (in late L) be (aux.), f. as EX-[1] I + *sistere* take a stand.] 1 Have objective reality or being. E17. 2 Have being in a specified place or form or under specified conditions. Of a relation, circumstance, etc.: be found, subsist. (Foll. by advb. phr., *as*, †n. or adj. compl.) E17. 3 Continue alive or in being; maintain existence. Also, live, esp. under adverse conditions. L18.

1 J. S. MILL The man called father might still exist though there were no child. G. SAINTSBURY Plays . . formed a large . . part of such literary pastime as existed. 2 N. ARNOTT Which substances . . usually exist as airs. R. H. MOTTRAM There was a stronger link between them than existed with the others of the family. G. ORWELL Similar slits existed in thousands . . throughout the building. P. W. ATKINS Ice-VII . . exists only when the pressure exceeds 25000 atm. 3 V. BRITTAIN Love still existed . . in a world dominated by winter and death. N. SHUTE If the Geiger counter was correct, no life could exist there for more than a few days. R. P. GRAVES He would just be able to exist on his salary.

exister *n.* (*rare*) L19. **existing** *ppl a.* that exists; *esp.* that exists now or existed at the time in question, current: M18.

existence /ɪɡˈzɪst(ə)ns, ɛɡ-/ *n.* LME. [(O)Fr., or late L *existentia*, f. *ex(s)istent-* pres. ppl stem of *ex(s)istere*: see prec., -ENCE.] †1 Reality, as opp. to appearance. Only in LME. 2 The fact or state of existing; actual possession of being. LME. b Continued being; *spec.* continued being as a living creature, life, esp. under adverse conditions. M17. 3a Something that exists; an entity, a being. E17. b All that exists. M18. 4 A mode or kind of existing. M18.

2 JAS. MILL It created some evils . . which previously had no existence. C. HILL Some men were questioning the existence of witches. *bring, come*, etc., *into existence*. *call into existence*: see CALL *v.* **in existence** existing. b W. S. LANDOR I shall remember his [friendship] to the last hour of my existence. *the struggle for existence*: see STRUGGLE *n.* 3a H. FIELDING I have heard of a man who believed there was no real existence in the world but himself.

Comb.: **existence problem, theorem**, etc.: dealing with the existence of a mathematical or philosophical entity.

†**existency** *n.* = EXISTENCE 2, 3, 4 E17–E19.

existent /ɪɡˈzɪst(ə)nt, ɛɡ-/ *a.* & *n.* M16. [L *ex(s)istent-*: see prec., -ENT.] A *adj.* 1 That exists or has being. Opp. *non-existent*. M16. 2 Existing now or at the time in question; contemporary. L18. B *n.* A person who or thing which exists. M17.

existential /ɛɡzɪˈstɛnʃ(ə)l/ *a.* L17. [Late L *existentialis*, f. *existentia*: see EXISTENCE, -AL[1].] 1 Of or relating to existence. L17. 2 *Logic.* Of a proposition etc.: predicating existence. E19. 3 *Philos.* Of or pertaining to existence, esp. human existence, as opp. to the essence of things; existentialist. M20.

2 **existential import** the assumption made in a proposition that something denoted by it, esp. the subject-term, exists. **existential quantifier**: asserting that something exists of which a related proposition is true.

existentially *adv.* E19.

existentialism /ɛɡzɪˈstɛnʃ(ə)lɪz(ə)m/ *n.* M20. [tr. Da. *existents-forhold* (Kierkegaard) condition of existence, f. prec. + -ISM.] A modern philosophical trend, the leading tenet of which is that a person (unlike a thing) has no predetermined essence but forms his or her essence by acts of pure will. Cf. ESSENTIALISM.

existentialist *n.* & *a.* (*a*) *n.* an advocate or adherent of existentialism; (*b*) *adj.* of, pertaining to, or characteristic of existentialism: M20. ˌ**existentiaˈlistic** *a.* L20.

existible /ɪɡˈzɪstɪb(ə)l, ɛɡ-/ *a. rare.* E18. [f. EXIST *v.* + -IBLE.] Capable of existing.

existiˈbility *n.* L17.

†**existimation** *n.* M16–E18. [L *existimatio(n-)*, f. *existimat-* pa. ppl stem of *existimare*, f. as EX-[1] I + *aestimare* ESTEEM *v.*: see -ATION.] Valuation of a person in respect of his or her qualities; public standing or reputation.

exit /ˈɛksɪt, ˈɛɡzɪt/ *n.* L16. [L EXITUS.] 1 A departure of an actor etc. from the stage during a scene; *fig.* a person's death. L16. 2 *gen.* A departure from any place or situation. Also, freedom or opportunity to depart. M17. 3 A means of egress, esp. from a public building; an outlet, a way out. L17. b A place where traffic can leave a motorway etc.; a slip-road provided at such a place. M20. 4 *Cards* (esp. *Bridge*). The action of deliberately losing the lead; a card enabling one to do this. M20.

2 G. P. R. JAMES The man had just given admittance or exit to some one. J. LONDON Arthur was leaving the room, and Martin Eden followed his exit with longing eyes. *port of exit*: see PORT *n.*[3] 5b. 3 B. JOWETT An enclosure . . which was surrounded by a great ditch and had no exit. J. GASKELL We walked up the aisle . . and bunked out through the emergency exit.

Comb.: **exit line** a line spoken by an actor or actress immediately before leaving the stage; **exit permit** = *exit visa* below; **exit poll** an unofficial poll, esp. for the media, in which voters leaving a polling station are asked how they voted; **exit visa** a visa enabling one to leave a country; **exit wound**: made by a bullet passing out of the body.

exit /ˈɛksɪt, ˈɛɡzɪt/ *v.*[1]*i.* (*defective*). M16. [L, 3rd person sing. pres. indic. of *exire* go out, f. as EX-[1] I + *ire* to go.] A stage direction: (the last speaker, or the character whose name follows) leaves the stage. Cf. EXEUNT.

transf.: COLERIDGE So exit Clotilda, and enter Bertram.

exit /ˈɛksɪt, ˈɛɡzɪt/ *v.*[2] E17. [f. EXIT *n.*] 1 *v.i.* Make one's exit or departure, esp. from a stage; leave any place; *fig.* die. E17. 2 *v.i. Cards* (esp. *Bridge*). Lose the lead deliberately. M20. 3 *v.t.* Leave, get out of. L20.

1 C. HAMPTON He exits . . into the bedroom, leaving the stage empty. F. SMYTH The bullet had . . exited just behind his right ear.

exite /ˈɛksʌɪt/ *n.* L19. [f. Gk *exō* outside + -ITE[1].] *Zool.* Each of the lateral lobes on the outer side of some crustacean limbs.

exitial /ɪɡˈzɪʃ(ə)l, ɛɡ-/ *a.* Long *rare.* LME. [L *exitialis*, f. *exitium* destruction: see -AL[1].] Destructive to life, fatal.

exition /ɪkˈsɪʃ(ə)n, ɛk-/ *n.* Now *rare* or *obs.* L17. [L *exitio(n-)*, f. *exit-* pa. ppl stem of *exire*: see EXIT *v.*[1], -ION.] (A point of) exit or departure.

†**exitious** *a.* M16–E18. [L *exitiosus*, f. *exitium* destruction: see -OUS.] = EXITIAL.

exitus /ˈɛksɪtəs/ *n.* M17. [L, f. *exit-* pa. ppl stem of *exire*: see EXIT *v.*[1]] A departure; an exodus. Now only *Med.*, a fatal termination to an illness, a death.

ex-libris /ɛksˈlɪbrɪs, -ˈliːb-, -ˈlʌɪb-, -ˈliːbriːs/ *n.* Pl. same. L19. [L, lit. 'out of the books or library (of —)'.] An inscription, label, etc., indicating the owner of a book; *esp.* a bookplate.

ex-librism *n.* the collecting of bookplates L19. **ex-librist** *n.* L19.

ex-meridian /ɛksməˈrɪdɪən/ *a.* M19. [f. EX-[1] I + MERIDIAN *n.*] *Navigation.* (Of an observation of the sun or other celestial object) not taken on the meridian, but close enough to it to be reducible to a meridian altitude; involving or calculated from such an observation.

Exmoor /ˈɛksmʊə, -mɔː/ *a.* & *n.* E19. [*Exmoor*, SW England: see below.] A *adj.* Designating (breeds of) livestock found in or originating from Exmoor, a hilly region on the Devon-Somerset border, *esp.* (*a*) a breed of horned short-woolled sheep; (*b*) a breed of small heavy-maned pony. E19. B *n.* An Exmoor sheep or pony. E19.

ex nihilo /ɛks ˈniːhɪləʊ, ˈnʌɪ-/ *adv. phr.* L16. [L.] Out of nothing.

exo- /ˈɛksəʊ/ *comb. form.* [Gk *exō* outside: see -O-.] Outer, external.

exoatmosˈpheric *a.* occurring or operating outside the atmosphere M20. **exobioˈlogical** *a.* of or pertaining to exobiology or its subject-matter M20. **exobiˈologist** *n.* an expert in or student of exobiology M20. **exobiˈology** *n.* the branch of science that deals with the possibility of life on other planets or in space M20. **exocarp** *n.* (*Bot.*) the outer layer of the pericarp of a fruit M19. **exoˈcentric** *a.* (*Ling.*) designating a compound or construction whose distribution is not the same as that of any of its constituents; not endocentric: E20. **exocuticle, -ˈticula** *n.* (*a*) the hard, chitinous outer part of the arthropod procuticle; (*b*) the middle part of the cuticle surrounding animal hairs etc.: E20. **exoˈcyclic** *a.* (*a*) *Zool.* (of an irregular sea urchin) having the anus displaced from its usual apical position; (*b*) *Chem.* situated outside a ring: L19. **exocyˈtosis** *n.* (*Biol.*) the release of matter by a living cell M20. **exocyˈtotic** *a.* characterized by or subjected to exocytosis L20. **exoˈdontia** *n.* the extraction of teeth E20. **exoˈdontist** *n.* a specialist in exodontia E20. **exoelectron** *n.* an electron spontaneously emitted from a metal surface following abrasion or fracture M20. **exoenzyme** *n.* (*a*) an enzyme which acts outside the cell producing it; (*b*) an enzyme which breaks terminal bonds of long-chain molecules: E20. **exoˈergic** *a.* (*Sci.*) = EXERGONIC M20. **exoˈergically** *adv.* (*Sci.*) with the release of energy L20. **exoerythroˈcytic** *a.* (of malaria parasites etc.) occurring outside the red blood cells M20. **exoˈglossic** *a.* pertaining to or involving the use of a language that is not native to the country concerned L20. **exoˈnarthex** *n.* the outer vestibule of an Orthodox church M19. **exoˈnormative** *a.* (*Ling.*) drawing on foreign usage as a model for the native language M20. **exoˈnuclease** *n.* (*Biochem.*) an enzyme which removes successive nucleotides from the end of a polynucleotide molecule M20. **exonucleolytic** /-ˈlɪtɪk/ *a.* (*Biochem.*) involving the removal of successive nucleotides from the end of a polynucleotide molecule L20. **exonucleoˈlytically** *adv.* (*Biochem.*) in an exonucleolytic manner L20. **exonym** *n.* a place-name other than that used by the residents of the place concerned M20. **exoˈpeptidase** *n.* (*Biochem.*) an enzyme which breaks the terminal peptide bonds of peptide chains M20. **exopod, eˈxopodite** *ns.* (*Zool.*) the outer branch of a biramous limb or appendage in some arthropods L19. **exopterygote** /ɛksɒpˈtɛrɪɡəʊt/ *a.* & *n.* (*Zool.*) (designating) an insect whose wings develop externally and whose young usually resemble the adult, there being no real pupal stage E20. **exoˈskeletal** *a.* of or pertaining to an exoskeleton; of the nature of or having an exoskeleton: L19. **exoskeleton** *n.* a hard outer layer of an animal body M19. **exosphere** *n.* the outermost part of a planet's atmosphere M20. **exoˈspheric** *a.* of or pertaining to an exosphere; occurring in an exosphere: M20. **exospore** *n.* (*a*) the outer layer of the membrane or wall in some spores; (*b*) a spore formed by separation and release from a sporophore: M19. **exotoxin** *n.* a toxin released by a living micro-organism into its surroundings E20. **exotropia** /-ˈtrəʊpɪə/ *n.* [Gk *tropē* turning] *Med.* divergent strabismus L19.

Exocet /ˈɛksəsɛt/ *n.* L20. [Fr. = flying fish, f. L *exocetus* f. Gk *exōkoitos* sleeping out, fish that comes up on the beach, f. as EXO- + *koitos* bed.] (Proprietary name for) a kind of rocket-propelled short-range guided missile used esp. in tactical sea warfare. Also *Exocet missile*.

exocrine /ˈɛksə(ʊ)krʌɪn, -krɪn/ *a.* E20. [f. EXO- + Gk *krinein* to separate.] *Physiol.* Of, pertaining to, or designating a gland that secretes through a duct. Cf. ENDOCRINE.

exoculation /ɛkˌsɒkjʊˈleɪʃ(ə)n/ *n.* Now *rare* or *obs.* M17. [med.L *exoculatio(n-)*, f. L *exoculat-* pa. ppl stem of *exoculare* deprive of eyes, f. as EX-[1] + *oculus* eye: see -ATION.] The action of putting out a person's eyes; blinding.

exode /ˈɛksəʊd/ *n.*[1] Also †**exod**. ME. [Anglicized f. EXODUS; in sense 1 through (O)Fr. *Exode*.] †1 = EXODUS 1. ME–L16. 2 = EXODUS 2. *rare.* M18.

exode /ˈɛksəʊd/ *n.*[2] L17. [Fr. f. L EXODIUM.] *Class. Hist.* 1 In Roman drama, a comic interlude or farce following something more serious. L17. 2 In Greek drama, the end or catastrophe of a play. M18.

exoderm /ˈɛksə(ʊ)dəːm/ *n.* L19. [f. EXO- + Gk *derma* skin.] *Biol.* = ECTODERM.

exodermal /ɛksə(ʊ)ˈdəːm(ə)l/ *a.* E20. [f. prec. and next + -AL[1].] Pertaining to or of the nature of exoderm or exodermis.

exodermis /ɛksə(ʊ)ˈdəːmɪs/ *n.* E20. [f. EXO- after *endodermis*, *epidermis*.] *Bot.* A specialized layer of a root beneath the epidermis or velamen.

exodium /ɪkˈsəʊdɪʌm, ɛk-/ *n.* E17. [L f. Gk *exodion* use as n. of neut. sing. of *exodios* pertaining to an exit, f. *exodos*: see EXODUS.] = EXODE *n.*[2]

exodus /ˈɛksədəs/ *n.* Also (*rare*) **exody** /-di/. OE. [eccl.L *Exodus* f. Gk *exodos*, f. as EX-[2] + *hodos* way.] 1 (**E-**.) (The name of) the second book of the Bible, relating the release of the Israelites from their bondage in Egypt and their journey to Canaan. OE. 2 A departure, usu. of many people; an emigration; *spec.* the departure of the Israelites from Egypt. E17.

2 S. BRETT Charles and Frances joined the exodus to the bar.

ex officio /ɛks əˈfɪʃɪəʊ/ *adv.*, *a.*, & *n.* M16. [L, f. *officium* duty, OFFICE *n.*] A *adv.* & (usu. w. hyphen) *adj.* (That is such) by virtue of one's office. M16.

ex-officio oath *Hist.*: under which a person could be compelled to answer questions whose answers would expose him or her to censure or punishment.

B *n.* A person or officer serving ex officio. E19.

exogamy /ɪk'sɒɡəmi, ɛk-/ *n.* M19. [f. EXO- + -GAMY.] 1 *Anthropol.* The custom by which a man is obliged to marry outside his own community, clan, or tribe. M19. 2 *Biol.* The fusion of reproductive cells from unrelated individuals. E20.

exo'gamic *a.* of or pertaining to exogamy L19. **exogamous** *a.* practising exogamy; of or pertaining to exogamy: M19.

exogen /'ɛksədʒ(ə)n/ *n.* Now *rare* or *obs.* M19. [Fr. *exogène*, f. as EXO-: see -GEN.] *Bot.* A plant whose stem grows by the development of new material on the outside.

exogenetic /ˌɛksə(ʊ)dʒɪ'nɛtɪk/ *a.* L19. [f. EXO- + -GENETIC.] 1 *Sci.* Having an external cause or origin. L19. 2 *Geol.* Formed or occurring at the surface of the earth. E20.

exogenic /ɛksə(ʊ)'dʒɛnɪk/ *a.* E20. [f. EXO- + -GENIC.] = EXOGENETIC.

exogenous /ɪk'sɒdʒɪnəs, ɛk-/ *a.* M19. [f. mod.L *exogena* exogen (after cl.L *indigena* native (n. & adj.)) + -OUS.] 1 *Bot.* Of, pertaining to, or designating a plant that grows by developing new material on the outside. Now *rare* or *obs.* M19. 2 *Geol.* Formed or occurring outside some structure or rock mass; *esp.* = EXOGENETIC 2; *Bot.* developing from superficial rather than deep tissue. M19. 3 Having an external cause or origin; *spec.* (*Med.*) caused by an organism, event, agent, etc., operating outside the body; environmental. L19.

exogenously *adv.* L19.

exolete /'ɛksəliːt/ *a.* & *n.* E17. [L *exoletus* pa. pple of *exolescere*, become adult, fall out of use.] A *adj.* Disused, obsolete; insipid, effete. Long *rare* or *obs.* E17. B *n.* An effete person. *rare.* M20.

exolution /ɛksə'luːʃ(ə)n/ *n.* Now *rare.* E17. [L *ex(s)olutio(n-)*, f. *ex(s)olut-* pa. ppl stem of *ex(s)olvere* loosen, f. as EX-[1] + *solvere* loosen, let go: see -ION.] †1 The action of loosening or setting free; *esp.* (formerly) the emission of the principles called 'animal spirits', thought to be the cause of fainting. E17–M19. 2 Faintness, light-headedness; relaxation of the body's faculties. M17.

exomologesis /ˌɛksəmɒlə'ɡiːsɪs/ *n.* Pl. **-geses** /-'ɡiːsiːz/. L16. [Gk *exomologēsis*, f. *exomologein* confess, f. as EX-[2] + *omologein* agree, admit.] *Chr. Ch.* A full or public confession.

exomphalos /ɪk'sɒmfələs, ɛk-/ *n.* L16. [Gk = prominent navel, f. as EX-[2] + *omphalos* navel.] A protrusion of some of the contents of the abdomen through the umbilicus.

exon /'ɛksɒn/ *n.*[1] M18. [Repr. pronunc. /ɛgzɔ̃/ of Fr. EXEMPT *a.* & *n.*] Each of the four officers acting as commanders of the Yeomen of the Guard. Cf. EXEMPT *n.* 4.

exon /'ɛksɒn/ *n.*[2] L20. [f. *ex(pressed* pa. pple of EXPRESS *v.*[1] + -ON.] *Genetics.* A segment of a DNA or RNA molecule that contains coding information for a protein. Cf. INTRON.

exonic /ɪk'sɒnɪk, ɛk-/ *a.* L20.

exoner /ɪɡ'zəʊnə, ɛɡ-/ *v.t. obs.* exc. *Sc. Law.* E16. [Fr. *exonérer* f. L *exonerare* EXONERATE.] Relieve of a responsibility; free from or *from* blame or liability.

exonerate /ɪɡ'zɒnəreɪt, ɛɡ-/ *v.* Pa. pple **-ated**, (*arch.*) **-ate** /-ət/. LME. [L *exonerat-* pa. ppl stem of *exonerare*, f. as EX-[1] + *oner-*, *onus* burden: see -ATE[3].] 1 *v.t.* Free from or *from* blame or reproach; relieve from the blame or burden *of*. LME. 2 *v.t.* Take a burden from; relieve *of* a burden or possession; unload, make lighter, (a ship, one's conscience, etc.). Now *rare.* E16. 3 Relieve of a duty, obligation, payment, etc. Foll. by *from*, †*of*. M16. †4 *v.t.* & *i.* Discharge the contents of (the body, bowels, etc.). M16–L19. †5 *v.refl.* Of a river, sea, blood-vessel, etc.: empty or flow *into*. L16–E18. †6 *v.t.* Discharge, pour off, (a liquid, body of water, etc.) *into*; get rid of (people, a population). Only in 17.

1 H. JAMES An affectionate farewell might help to exonerate him from the charge of neglect. Q. BELL The evidence .. tends to exonerate her. 2 WELLINGTON Success would certainly exonerate our finances. 4 **exonerate nature, oneself** defecate.

exonerative *a.* tending to relieve of an obligation etc. E19.

exoneration /ɪɡˌzɒnə'reɪʃ(ə)n, ɛɡ-/ *n.* M16. [L *exoneratio(n-)*, f. *exonerare*: see prec., -ATION.] 1 The action or an act of freeing from blame or relieving of a duty or burden. M16. †2 Defecation. M17–L18.

†**exoneretur** *n.* M18–M19. [L = let him or her be discharged, 3rd person sing. pres. subjunct. pass. of *exonerare*: see EXONERATE.] *Law.* (The record of) the discharge of a bail when an action was withdrawn or settled or the prisoner taken to prison.

Exonian /ɪk'səʊnɪən, ɛk-/ *a.* & *n.* M19. [f. L *Exonia* Exeter + -IAN.] A *adj.* Of or pertaining to Exeter, a city in SW England. M19. B *n.* A native or inhabitant of Exeter. L19.

exonumia /ɛksə(ʊ)'njuːmɪə/ *n.pl.* (also treated as *sing.*) M20. [f. EXO- + NUM(ISMATIC + -IA[2].] Objects of historical interest that resemble coins or currency, such as medals and tokens.

exophora /ɪk'sɒf(ə)rə/ *n.* L20. [f. EXO- after *anaphora*.] *Ling.* An exophoric reference or relation.

exophoria /ɛksə'fɔːrɪə/ *n.* L19. [f. EXO- + -PHORIA.] *Med.* A tendency for the visual axes to diverge; latent divergent strabismus.

exophoric /ɛksə'fɒrɪk/ *a.* E20. [f. EXOPHORIA (& EXOPHORA) + -IC.] 1 *Med.* Having exophoria. E20. 2 *Ling.* Referring to something outside the text. L20.

exophthalmos /ɛksɒf'θalmɒs/ *n.* Also **-mus** /-məs/. E17. [(mod.L *exophthalmus* f.) Gk *exophthalmos*, f. as EX-[2] + *ophthalmos* eye.] Abnormal protrusion of the eyeball.

exophthalmia *n.* = EXOPHTHALMOS E18. **exophthalmic** *a.* characterized by exophthalmos L19.

exorable /'ɛks(ə)rəb(ə)l/ *a.* Now *rare.* M16. [L *exorabilis*, f. *exorare* implore, f. as EX-[1] 1 + *orare* pray: see -ABLE.] Able to be moved by entreaty.

exora'bility *n.* (*rare*) L19.

exorbitance /ɪɡ'zɔːbɪt(ə)ns, ɛɡ-/ *n.* LME. [f. as next: see -ANCE.] 1 (A) transgression of law or morality; an offence; misconduct, criminality. *arch.* LME. 2 The fact of being excessive or immoderate; extravagance; *esp.* gross excessiveness of a price, demand, etc. E17. 3 (An) eccentricity, (an) irregularity; (a) divergence from a prescribed track. Also, an attack of insanity. Now *rare* or *obs.* M17.

exorbitancy /ɪɡ'zɔːbɪt(ə)nsi, ɛɡ-/ *n.* E17. [f. next: see -ANCY.] †1 = EXORBITANCE 1. E17–E18. 2 = EXORBITANCE 3. Now *rare* or *obs.* E17. 3 = EXORBITANCE 2. Formerly also, (a) disposition to exceed one's rights; excessive greed. M17.

exorbitant /ɪɡ'zɔːbɪt(ə)nt/ *a.* & *n.* Also **exhor-**. LME. [Chr.L *exorbitant-* pres. ppl stem of *exorbitare* go out of the track, f. as EX-[1] + *orbita* ORBIT *n.*: see -ANT[1].] A *adj.* 1 a *Law.* Of a case, offence, etc.: anomalous, outside the intended scope of a law. Of a power, privilege, or enactment: abnormal, irregular. LME. †b *gen.* Abnormal, irregular; eccentric; frantic, wild. E17–E18. 2 Excessive, immoderate. Now chiefly of a price, demand, etc.: grossly excessive; far in excess of what is reasonable or appropriate. LME. b Of an object, etc.: disproportionately or excessively large. *arch.* M17. †3 Deviating *from* a specified rule or principle; (of a remark etc.) irrelevant. LME–L17. †4 Transgressing the bounds of law, decency, or morality; M16–E18.

2 G. GREENE One resents being moved by so exorbitant an agony. *Times* These so-called bureaux de change are charging exorbitant rates of commission.

†B *n.* A person who or thing which exceeds proper bounds. *rare.* E17–E18.

exorbitantly *adv.* M17.

exorbitate /ɪɡ'zɔːbɪteɪt, ɛɡ-/ *v.i.* Now *rare* or *obs.* E17. [Late L *exorbitat-* pa. ppl stem of *exorbitare*: see prec, -ATE[3].] Deviate or stray from the usual course (*lit.* & *fig.*).

exorbitation /ɪɡˌzɔːbɪ'teɪʃ(ə)n, ɛɡ-/ *n.* Now *rare* or *obs.* E17. [Late L *exorbitatio(n-)*, f. *exorbitare*: see prec., -ATION.] (A) deviation from the usual course.

exorcise *v.* var. of EXORCIZE.

exorcism /'ɛksɔːsɪz(ə)m, 'ɛksə-/ *n.* LME. [eccl.L *exorcismus* f. eccl.Gk *exorkismos*, f. *exorkizein* exorcize, f. as EX-[2] + *orkos* oath: see -ISM.] 1 The action or an act of exorcizing or expelling an evil spirit. LME. †2 The action of calling up spirits; the rites performed for this purpose. LME–M17. 3 A formula recited for the purpose of exorcizing. M16.

exorcist /'ɛksɔːsɪst, 'ɛksə-/ *n.* LME. [eccl.L *exorcista* f. Gk *exorkistēs*, f. *exorkizein*: see prec., -IST.] 1 A person who drives out evil spirits by invocation etc. LME. b *Eccl. Hist.* The third of the four minor orders in the RC Church, one of whose functions was the exorcizing of evil spirits. M16. †2 A person who seeks or purports to conjure up spirits. Only in E17.

1b C. MACKENZIE Cassandra Batt .. was officially sexton, but acted as .. exorcist, doorkeeper, and subdeacon as well. 2 SHAKES. *Jul. Caes.* Thou like an Exorcist, hast conjur'd up My mortified Spirit.

exor'cistic *a.* of or pertaining to an exorcist or exorcism M20. **exor'cistical** *a.* = EXORCISTIC M17.

exorcize /'ɛksɔːsʌɪz/ *v.t.* Also **-ise**. LME. [(O)Fr. *exorciser* or eccl.L *exorcizare* f. Gk *exorkizein*: see EXORCISM, -IZE.] 1 Conjure up (an evil spirit); solemnly call upon (an evil spirit) *to do*. Now *rare.* LME. 2 Drive away or expel (an evil spirit) by invocation or the use of some holy name. (Foll. by *from*, *out of*.) M16. 3 Free or clear (a person or place) *of* evil spirits, malignant influences, etc. M17.

2 *fig.*: L. P. HARTLEY Wealth had not exorcised her fear of money. 3 LYTTON Muttering hymns, monks huddled together .. as if to exorcize the land of a demon.

exorci'zation *n.* LME. **exorcizement** *n.* the action of exorcizing; exorcizing influence: L18. **exorcizer** *n.* E16.

exordium /ɪɡ'zɔːdɪəm, ɛɡ-/ *n.* Pl. **-iums, -ia** /-ɪə/. L16. [L, f. *exordiri* begin, f. as EX-[1] 1 + *ordiri* begin.] The beginning of anything; *esp.* the introductory part of a discourse or treatise.

exordial *a.* introductory; of or pertaining to an exordium: L17.

exosmosis /ɛksɒz'məʊsɪs/ *n.* Orig. (now *rare* or *obs.*) **exosmose** /'ɛksɒzməʊs/. E19. [Fr. *exosmose*, f. Gk EX-[2] + *ōsmos* pushing: see -OSIS.] Osmotic diffusion of solvent or solute out of a vessel or cell.

exossate /ɪk'sɒseɪt, ɛk-/ *v.t. rare.* E18. [L *exossat-* pa. ppl stem of *exossare* to bone, f. as EX-[1] 1 + *oss-*, *os* bone: see -ATE[3].] Deprive of bones; bone.

†**exossation** *n.* E17–E18. [f. as prec.: see -ATION.] The action or practice of causing fruit to grow without stones.

exostosis /ɛksɒs'təʊsɪs/ *n.* Pl. **-toses** /-'təʊsiːz/. L16. [Gk *exostōsis* outgrowth of bone, f. as EX-[2] + *osteon* bone: see -OSIS.] An outgrowth of bony tissue on a bone.

e'xostosed *a.* affected with exostosis M18. **exostotic** /-'tɒtɪk/ *a.* of, pertaining to, or of the nature of an exostosis M19.

exostracize /ɪk'sɒstrəsʌɪz, ɛk-/ *v.t.* Also **-ise**. M19. [Gk *exostrakizein*, f. as EX-[2] + *ostrakizein* OSTRACIZE.] Banish by ostracism.

exoteric /ɛksə(ʊ)'tɛrɪk/ *a.* & *n.* M17. [L *exotericus* f. Gk *exōterikos*, f. *exōterō* outer, compar. of *exō* outside: see -IC.] A *adj.* 1 (Of a philosophical doctrine, mode of speech, etc.) designed for or intelligible to outsiders; (of a disciple) not admitted to esoteric teaching; dealing with ordinary topics. Opp. ESOTERIC *a.* 1. M17. b Current among the general public; popular; ordinary. E19. 2 Pertaining to the outside; external. Now *rare.* M17.

1 *Times Lit. Suppl.* A market surely exists for an exoteric study of Wittgenstein's notoriously recondite ideas.

B *n.* 1 An uninitiated person; an outsider. L17. 2 In *pl.* Exoteric doctrines or treatises. M18.

exoterical *a.* M17. **exoterically** *adv.* M18. **exotericism** /-sɪz(ə)m/ *n.* (belief in) exoteric doctrines L19. **exotericist** /-sɪst/ *n.* a person who believes in exoteric doctrines M20.

exotherm /ˈɛksə(ʊ)θəːm/ *n.* E20. [f. EXO- + Gk *thermē* heat.] *Chem.* 1 A substance that liberates heat during its formation and absorbs heat on decomposing. E20. 2 A sudden liberation of heat in a process. M20.

exoˈthermal *a.* = EXOTHERMIC E20. **exoˈthermally** *adv.* = EXOTHERMICALLY L19.

exothermic /ɛksə(ʊ)ˈθəːmɪk/ *a.* L19. [Fr. *exothermique*, f. as EXO-, THERMIC.] *Chem.* Accompanied by, or (of a compound) formed with, the liberation of heat.

exothermically *adv.* in an exothermic manner M20. ˌ**exotherˈmicity** *n.* the property of being exothermic; the quantity of energy liberated in an exothermic reaction: M20.

exotic /ɪgˈzɒtɪk, ɛg-/ *a.* & *n.* L16. [L *exoticus* f. Gk *exōtikos*, f. *exō* outside.] **A** *adj.* 1 Of a word, fashion, plant, disease, etc.: introduced from abroad, not indigenous. Formerly also, belonging to another country, foreign, extrinsic, alien (*to*). L16. 2 Of behaviour, dress, a language, etc.: strikingly different, attractively unusual; glamorous. Formerly, outlandish, uncouth. E17. **b** Of, pertaining to, or characteristic of a foreigner or something foreign. Now *rare*. M17. 3 Of fuels, metals, etc.: of a kind not used for ordinary purposes or not ordinarily met with; specially produced or developed. M20.

1 G. W. TURNER Exotic pines now account for more than half of New Zealand's output of timber. *Times Lit. Suppl.* Minorities who have brought their exotic faiths from continents formerly under British domination. 2 H. INNES The cigarette was Turkish and the scent of it was an exotic intrusion in that solitude of snow and fir. W. CATHER Beside Alexandra lounged a strikingly exotic figure in a tall Mexican hat.

Special collocations: **exotic dancer** a striptease dancer.

B *n.* 1 A plant or animal that is not indigenous. M17. 2 A person of foreign origin. M17. 3 A striptease dancer. M20.

†**exotical** *a.* E17–E18. **exotically** *adv.* L17. **exoticism** /-sɪz(ə)m/ *n.* exotic character; something exotic: M19. **exoticness** *n.* M17.

exotica /ɪgˈzɒtɪkə, ɛg-/ *n.pl.* L19. [L, neut. pl. of *exoticus* EXOTIC.] Exotic things.

exotism /ˈɛksətɪz(ə)m, ˈɛgzə-/ *n.* Also ***exotisme*** /egzɔtism/. E19. [Fr. *exotisme*, f. *exotique*, f. as EXOTIC: see -ISM.] Resemblance to what is foreign; a foreign air.

expand /ɪkˈspand, ɛk-/ *v.* LME. [L *expandere*, f. as EX-[1] I + *pandere* to spread.] 1 *v.t.* Spread or stretch (a thing) out, esp. to its fullest extent; extend, open out. Formerly also, spread abroad, diffuse, (a report etc.). LME. 2 *v.i.* Become extended; spread out, unfold. M16. 3 *v.t.* †**a** Give full expression to (a feeling), pour out. M17–E19. **b** Express at greater length, develop, (an idea); write out (a contraction) in full; *Math.* rewrite (a product, power, or function) as a sum, give the expansion of. E19. 4 *v.t.* Widen the boundaries of, increase the area, scope, etc., of; enlarge, dilate. M17. 5 *v.i.* Become greater in area, bulk, capacity, etc.; become larger; *fig.* increase the scope of one's activity or the scale of operations of something; take in or go *into* a new area of activity. L18. 6 *v.i.* Throw off reserve; become expansive; expatiate *on*. E19.

1 LEIGH HUNT Sicily then lay expanded like a map beneath our eyes. O. MANNING He.. expanded his mouth in a significant smirk. 2 W. WITHERING Flowers.. expand at 6 or 7, and close at 2 in the afternoon. 3b H. J. LASKI Priestley.. was encouraged by friends to expand his argument into a general treatise. 4 I. WATT I.. believe that its use should be expanded rather than curtailed. 5 P. L. FERMOR Water is the one thing that expands when it freezes instead of contracting. S. NAIPAUL The sweat stains expanded across the back of his shirt. J. HARVEY The firm expanded and took in truck-mixers. *Marketing Week* Marks & Spencer is making a second attempt to expand into record sales. *fig.*: J. DICKEY My heart expanded with joy at the thought. 6 D. H. LAWRENCE Dr Mitchell was beginning to expand. With Alvina he quite unbent.

expandaˈbility *n.* the property of being expandable M20. **expandable** *a.* able to be expanded E20. **expander** *n.* a person who or thing which expands; *esp.* something used to increase bulk or versatility (*chest-expander*: see CHEST *n.*): M19. **expandible** *a.* = EXPANDABLE L20.

expanded /ɪkˈspandɪd, ɛk-/ *ppl a.* M17. [f. prec. + -ED[1].] 1 That has expanded or has been expanded. M17. 2 *Gram.* Designating a tense in which a form of the verb *to be* is used with a present participle. E20.

1 **expanded metal** sheet metal slit and stretched into a lattice. **expanded plastic** lightweight cellular plastic used esp. for packaging and insulation.

expanding /ɪkˈspandɪŋ, ɛk-/ *ppl a.* L18. [f. as prec. + -ING[2].] That expands.

expanding bullet = DUMDUM. **expanding universe** the universe regarded as continually expanding, with the galaxies receding from one another.

expanse /ɪkˈspans, ɛk-/ *n.* M17. [mod.L *expansum* firmament, use as n. of neut. of L *expansus* pa. pple of *expandere* EXPAND.] 1 An area of or *of* something presenting a wide unbroken surface; (*arch.*) *the* firmament. M17. 2 The distance to which something expands or is expanded. M19.

1 R. L. STEVENSON The bay was perfect—not a ripple.. upon its blue expanse. M. SPARK They were crossing the Meadows, a gusty expanse of common land.

expanse /ɪkˈspans, ɛk-/ *v.t. arch.* L15. [f. as next.] = EXPAND I, 4.

expansible /ɪkˈspansɪb(ə)l, ɛk-/ *a.* L17. [f. L *expans-* pa. ppl stem of *expandere* EXPAND: see -IBLE.] 1 Able to be enlarged or expanded, esp. by heat. L17. 2 Able to be opened or spread out. M18.

expansiˈbility *n.* E18.

expansile /ɪkˈspansʌɪl, ɛk-/ *a.* M18. [f. as prec. + -ILE.] Capable of causing or undergoing expansion; of or pertaining to expansion.

expansion /ɪkˈspanʃ(ə)n, ɛk-/ *n.* E17. [Late L *expansio(n-)*, f. as EXPANSIBLE: see -ION.] 1 The action of spreading out or extending; the condition of being spread out or extended. E17. 2 Something spread out, an expanse; (*arch.*) *the* firmament. E17. †**b** The immensity of space. L17–E18. 3 The action or process of making or becoming greater in area, bulk, capacity, etc.; enlargement, dilatation; the amount or degree of this. M17. **b** An increase in the scope of the activities or the scale of the operations of a company, country, etc. M19. **c** Increase in the amount of territory ruled or controlled by a country. L19. 4 The detailed expression of what is implicit in a statement; the writing out in full of something abbreviated; *Math.* the process of working out a product, power, or function and expressing it in simpler terms as a sum; the sum itself. E19. 5 An enlarged portion; something formed by the expansion of a thing. M19.

1 POPE The gilded clouds in fair expansion lie. D. H. LAWRENCE The lotus.. opens with an expansion such as no other flower knows. 3 S. H. VINES Alternate expansion and contraction of the tissue. **b** *Times* Encouraging the expansion of exports. J. W. KRUTCH What we call prosperity depends upon continual expansion. 5 J. TYNDALL This lake is simply an expansion of the river Rhone.

Comb.: **expansion bit** a drilling bit that can be adjusted to drill holes of different sizes; **expansion board** a circuit board that can be connected to or inserted in a computer to give extra facilities; **expansion bolt**: that expands when inserted, no thread being required; **expansion box** (*a*) a chamber to allow for expansion of a fluid or into which expansion occurs; (*b*) a unit that can be connected to a computer to give extra facilities; **expansion card** = *expansion board* above; **expansion engine** a steam engine in which expansion of the steam in the cylinder contributes to the force on the piston; **expansion joint**: made to allow for the thermal expansion of the parts that it joins; **expansion slot** a place in a computer where an expansion board can be added.

expansional *a.* E20. **expansionary** *a.* tending or directed towards (economic) expansion M20.

expansionist /ɪkˈspanʃ(ə)nɪst, ɛk-/ *n.* & *a.* M19. [f. prec. + -IST.] **A** *n.* A person who advocates a policy or theory of (now usu. territorial or economic) expansion. M19. **B** *adj.* Of, pertaining to, or advocating such a policy or theory. L19.

expansionism *n.* E20. **expansioˈnistic** *a.* = EXPANSIONIST *a.* M20.

expansive /ɪkˈspansɪv, ɛk-/ *a.* M17. [f. as EXPANSIBLE + -IVE.] 1 Tending or able to expand, spread out, or occupy a larger space. M17. **b** Of a force, movement, etc.: tending to cause expansion. M17. **c** Of an engine, process, etc.: working by the expansion of steam or hot gases. L18. 2 Free from reserve in feeling or speech; genially frank or communicative. M17. 3 Having wide bounds, broad, extensive; (of interests, sympathies, etc.) wide-ranging, comprehensive. E19.

1 *fig.*: C. SAGAN The human spirit is expansive; the urge to colonize new environments lies deep within many of us. 2 JO GRIMOND In expansive moods they have gone further, asserting that they descend from Huguenot weavers. 3 *Chicago Tribune* The expansive residential districts of suburban Kansas City. W. H. AUDEN The expansive dreams of constricted lives.

expansively *adv.* M19. **expansiveness** *n.* E19. **expanˈsivity** *n.* M19.

†**expansum** *n.* M17–L18. [mod.L (see EXPANSE *n.*): used to render Heb. *rāqīaʻ*, lit. 'beaten out'.] *The* firmament (cf. EXPANSE *n.* 1).

ex parte /ɛks ˈpɑːti/ *adv.* & *a. phr.* As adj. freq. ***ex-parte***. E17. [L = from a or the side.] **A** *adv. phr.* 1 Orig., on the part *of*. Now (*Law*), on behalf of. E17. 2 *Law.* On behalf of or with reference to only one of the parties concerned (and without notice to the adverse party). L17.

2 *Times* The owners.. applied to the Divisional Court ex parte for leave to issue the.. writs.

B *adj. phr.* 1 *Law.* Of an application, injunction, deposition, etc.: made, issued, etc., by or for only one party in a case. L18. 2 Of a statement etc.: one-sided, partial. E19.

expat /ɛksˈpat/ *n. colloq.* M20. [Abbrev.] = EXPATRIATE *n.*

expatiate /ɪkˈspeɪʃɪeɪt, ɛk-/ *v.* Pa. pple **-ated**, (*arch.*) **-ate** /-ət/. M16. [L *ex(s)patiat-* pa. ppl stem of *ex(s)patiari*, f. as EX-[1] I + *spatiari* to walk, f. *spatium* space.] 1 *v.i.* & †*refl.* Wander about at will; roam unrestrained. Now *rare*. M16. 2 *v.i.* Speak or write at great length on a topic; dilate. Usu. foll. by *on*. E17. 3**a** *v.t.* Extend or diffuse (a thing) so that it covers a wide area. Now *rare* or *obs.* E17. †**b** *v.i.* & *refl.* Widen its scope or area; expand, extend. M17–L18.

1 J. R. LOWELL Winter-flies.. crawl out.. to expatiate in the sun. 2 D. CARNEGIE For the next hour he expatiated on the peculiar.. virtues of the plumbing market. 3 T. ADAMS Princes expatiate their dominions.

expatiater *n.* a person who expatiates M19. **expatiative** *a.* (*a*) having a tendency to expand; (*b*) given to roaming freely: E19. **expatiator** *n.* = EXPATIATER M18. **expatiatory** *a.* marked by lengthy discourse; prone to talk at length: E19.

expatiation /ɪkˌspeɪʃɪˈeɪʃ(ə)n, ɛk-/ *n.* E17. [f. prec.: see -ATION.] †1 Expansion, development; an extended portion. E–M17. 2 The action or an act of roaming at will. Also (*rare*), liberty to roam. M17. 3 (A) lengthy treatment of a topic. E19.

expatriate /ɪksˈpatrɪət, -ˈpeɪt-, ˈɛks-/ *n.* & *a.* E19. [f. as next: see -ATE[2].] **A** *n.* Orig., an exile. Now, a person who lives from choice in a foreign country. E19.

C. P. SNOW An American expatriate, corrupted by Europe in the Jamesian style.

B *adj.* Orig., exiled. Now, living in a foreign country from choice. Also, of or relating to an expatriate or expatriates. E19.

C. THUBRON Many of his contemporaries never forgave Turgenev for his expatriate life.

expatriatism *n.* the condition or fact of being an expatriate L20.

expatriate /ɪksˈpatrɪeɪt, -ˈpeɪt-, ɛks-/ *v.* M18. [L *expatriat-* pa. ppl stem of *expatriare*, f. as EX-[1] I + *patria* native country: see -ATE[3].] 1 *refl.* & (*rare*) *v.i.* Leave one's country voluntarily; emigrate, settle abroad. Also, renounce one's citizenship. M18. 2 *v.t.* Expel (a person) from his or her native country; banish, exile. E19.

expatriˈation *n.* L18.

†**expect** *n. rare.* L16–E17. [f. the vb.] = EXPECTATION 3.

expect /ɪkˈspɛkt, ɛk-/ *v.* M16. [L *ex(s)pectare*, f. as EX-[1] I + *spectare* to look.] **I** *v.i.* †1 Defer action; wait. M16–M18. †2 Foll. by *for*: look forward to. L16–M17. 3 Of a female: be pregnant. Chiefly & now always in *be expecting. colloq.* Cf. sense 6b below. E19.

1 HENRY MORE A Dog expects till his Master has done picking of the bone. 3 A. DESAI I was married, Sarla was expecting.

II *v.t.* †4 Wait for, await. Of a destiny: be in store for. L16–E19. b Wait to see or know (*what, how, when,* etc.). L16–L18. 5 Regard as about or likely to happen; look forward to the occurrence of (an event). (Foll. by *that, to do*; someone or something *to do*.) L16. 6 Look forward to the arrival of (a person, esp. a guest) or the receipt of (something). L16. b Be pregnant with (a child). Cf. sense 3 above. E20. 7 Believe that it will prove to be the case that or *that*; suspect, suppose. L16. 8 Look for as due or requisite from another. (Foll. by someone or something *to do*.) E17.

4 GIBBON The . . king of the Goths, instead of expecting the attack of the Legions, boldly passed the Danube. W. COWPER Prisons expect the wicked. b W. GODWIN Mr. Tyrrel expected every moment when he would withdraw. 5 M. EDGEWORTH They expected a visit in a few hours. J. TYNDALL The Mur . . was by no means so bad as we had expected. J. CONRAD You can't expect to have it always your own way. E. O'NEILL It's just as well to expect the worst and you'll never be disappointed. C. P. SNOW I expect I shall be able to manage. E. J. HOWARD She was always expecting something wonderful to happen to her. 6 T. HARDY He expected a reply on the second morning . . but none came. G. B. SHAW Oh, Juggins, we're expecting Mr and Mrs Knox to tea. J. BUCHAN I . . may be absent for days. Expect me back when you see me. b J. HERRIOT Helen was expecting our baby this week-end. 7 S. O. JEWETT He's got too unwieldy to tackle a smart coon, I expect. B. PYM I expect your mother lies awake till you get in. 8 W. CATHER He seemed to expect his wife to do the talking. A. FRASER Much was traditionally expected of a royal prince in the way of benevolence.

expected *ppl a.* that is expected, that one would expect; *expected value* (Math.), a value of a variable, calculated by adding all the possible values, each multiplied by the probability of its occurrence: L16. **expectedly** *adv.* (*a*) in the manner expected; (*b*) (introducing a sentence) it is to be expected that: M18. **expecter** *n.* L16. **expecting** *ppl a.* †(*a*) expected; (*b*) expectant: E17. **expectingly** *adv.* L17.

expectable /ɪkˈspɛktəb(ə)l, ɛk-/ *a.* L16. [f. prec. + -ABLE. In sense 1 after Sp. *espectable* f. L *spectabilis*, f. *spectare* look at.] †1 Distinguished, illustrious. Only in L16. 2 That ought to be or is expected. M17.

2 I. BARROW In that measure which is expectable from the natural infirmity . . of man. *Chambers's Journal* The machine . . can handle all expectable types of envelope.

expectably *adv.* M20.

expectance /ɪkˈspɛkt(ə)ns, ɛk-/ *n.* E17. [f. as next: see -ANCE.] 1 The state of waiting for something; esp. in *after long expectance*. Formerly also, the state of waiting to know (*what, how, when,* etc.). *arch.* E17. 2 The action or state of expecting the occurrence of something; expectation. Now *rare.* E17. †3 Grounds for expecting something; prospect, esp. of inheriting. E17–L18.

1 SHAKES. *Tr. & Cr.* There is expectance here from both the sides What further you will do. 2 H. SLINGSBY Great expectance their is of a happy Parliament. 3 E. PARSONS An aunt . . from whom he has great expectances. **†in expectance** in prospect.

expectancy /ɪkˈspɛkt(ə)nsi, ɛk-/ *n.* E17. [L *ex(s)pectantia*, f. *ex(s)pectant-*: see EXPECTANT, -ANCY.] 1 (An) expectation of a coming event; (an) expectant attitude. E17. b An object of hope or expectation. *arch.* E17. 2 The extent to which an expectation may reasonably be entertained; the prospective chance of an event. E17. 3 Chiefly *Law.* The condition of being expected. Usu. in *in expectancy.* M17. 4 The position of being a prospective heir. E19. 5 What a person is entitled to expect; *spec.* a prospective inheritance. M19.

1 O. HENRY Sick with expectancy of the news he feared. D. PARKER There was an air of expectancy about them . . as of those who wait for a curtain to rise. b WORDSWORTH The Nation hailed Their great expectancy. 2 *life expectancy*: see LIFE *n.* 3 BURKE A practical reputation, to do any good, must be in possession, not in expectancy.

expectant /ɪkˈspɛkt(ə)nt, ɛk-/ *a.* & *n.* LME. [L *ex(s)pectant-* pres. ppl stem of *ex(s)pectare* EXPECT *v.*: see -ANT[1].] A *adj.* 1 In an attitude of expectation; waiting to see what will happen, etc. LME. 2 Of a person: having or foreseeing the prospect of coming into a certain position, succeeding to an inheritance, etc. LME. b Expecting the birth of a child. Chiefly in *expectant mother.* M19. 3 To be expected; *esp.* (*Law*) due to come to a person in reversion. E17. 4 Of a method (esp. a medical treatment), a policy, etc.: that leaves events to take their course. E19.

1 D. H. LAWRENCE A little group of expectant people, waiting to see the wedding. 2 LYTTON A pious Catholic, expectant of the cardinal's hat. 3 A. TUCKER We encourage ourselves to any . . disagreeable task by prospect of the profit expectant therefrom. **expectant heir** *Law* a person with a reversionary right or hope of succession to a property.

B *n.* 1 A person who is expecting an event, a benefit, etc.; *spec.* one who has the prospect of succeeding to property, a position, etc. E17. 2 A candidate for office. Formerly (*Sc.*), a candidate for the ministry who has not yet been licensed to preach. M17.

expectantly *adv.* M19.

expectation /ɛkspɛkˈteɪʃ(ə)n/ *n.* M16. [L *ex(s)pectatio(n-)*, f. *ex(s)pectat-* pa. ppl stem of *ex(s)pectare* EXPECT *v.*: see -ATION.] 1 The action of waiting for someone or something. Now passing into sense 3: expectant waiting. M16. b *Med.* The expectant method (see EXPECTANT *a.* 4). L17. 2 A preconceived idea of what will happen, what someone or something will turn out to be, etc.; the action of entertaining such an idea. M16. 3 The state or mental attitude of expecting something to happen; expectancy. M16. 4 A thing expected or looked forward to. L16. †5 Promise of future excellence; esp. in *of (great* etc.) *expectation.* L16–L18. 6 Grounds for expecting; *esp.* (in *pl.*) prospects of inheriting wealth. E17. 7 The condition of being expected. Only in *in expectation.* M17. 8 Degree of probability that something will occur, expressed numerically; *Math.* = *expected value* s.v. EXPECTED. E18. 9 Supposition with regard to the present or the past. L18.

1 R. SOUTH A daily Expectation at the gate, is the readiest Way to gain Admittance into the House. 2 J. BUTLER Our expectations that others will act so and so in such circumstances. B. PYM Emma had so far failed to come up to her mother's expectations. J. LE CARRÉ Was Mundt to make a dramatic return to his home country, against all expectation? 3 E. O'NEILL His face beams with the excited expectation of a boy going to a party. 6 AV *Ps.* 72:5 My soule waite thou onely vpon God; for my expectation is from him. J. R. ACKERLEY Mr. Burckhardt died . . intestate . . so that all my father's expectations came to nothing. 7 T. REID Belief of good or ill either present or in expectation. 8 *expectation of life, life expectation*: see LIFE *n.*

expectative /ɪkˈspɛktətɪv, ɛk-/ *a.* & *n.* L15. [med.L *expectativus*, f. L *ex(s)pectat-*: see prec., -IVE.] A *adj.* 1 *Eccl.* Relating to the reversion of benefices etc.; reversionary. L15. 2 = EXPECTANT *a.* 4. E17.

1 **grace expectative, expectative grace** *Hist.* a mandate given by a king or pope conferring the right of succession to a benefice.

B *n.* †1 A thing looked forward to; a prospective benefit. E16–M18. 2 = *grace expectative* (see sense A.1). L16.

expective /ɪkˈspɛktɪv, ɛk-/ *a. rare.* M17. [f. EXPECT *v.* + -IVE.] = EXPECTATIVE *a.*

expectorant /ɪkˈspɛkt(ə)r(ə)nt, ɛk-/ *n.* & *a.* M18. [L *expectorant-* pres. ppl stem of *expectorare*: see next, -ANT[1].] A *n.* An expectorant medicine. M18. B *adj.* Of a medicine: causing increased production of sputum, and so facilitating clearance of the bronchial passages. E19.

expectorate /ɪkˈspɛktəreɪt, ɛk-/ *v.* E17. [L *expectorat-* pa. ppl stem of *expectorare*, f. as EX-[1] 1 + *pector-*, *pectus* breast: see -ATE[3].] †1 *v.t.* Of a medicine: enable (sputum) to be expelled from the chest or lungs. E17–L18. 2 *v.t.* Eject from the throat or bronchial passages by coughing, hawking, etc. M17. 3 *refl.* & *v.i.* Relieve one's feelings. *arch.* M17. 4 *v.i.* Clear one's throat or bronchial passages of sputum; clear one's mouth of saliva, spit. E19.

2 E. B. BROWNING A woman expectorated blood violently as an effect of the experiment.

expecto'ration *n.* the action or an act of expectorating or spitting; expectorated matter: E17. **expectorative** *n.* & *a.* (*rare*) †(*a*) *n.* = EXPECTORANT *n.*; (*b*) *adj.* of or marked by expectoration: M17. **expectorator** *n.* †(*a*) = EXPECTORANT *n.*; (*b*) a person who expectorates or spits: L17.

expede /ɪkˈspiːd, ɛk-/ *v.t. Sc.* Now *rare.* M16. [L *expedire*: see EXPEDITE *v.*] †1 Deal with; accomplish, complete, settle. M16–L18. 2 Send out or issue (a document) officially. M16. †3 Send, esp. quickly; dispatch. L16–M17.

ex pede Herculem /ɛks ˌpɛdɪ ˈhəːkjʊlɛm/ *adv. phr.* M17. [L = Hercules from his foot.] Inferring the whole of something from an insignificant part, as Pythagoras supposedly calculated Hercules' height from the size of his foot.

expedience /ɪkˈspiːdɪəns, ɛk-/ *n.* LME. [f. as next: see -ENCE.] 1 = EXPEDIENCY 1. Now *rare* or *obs.* LME. †2 Haste, speed, dispatch. Also, something that requires this; an enterprise, an expedition. L15–E17. 3 = EXPEDIENCY 2. E17.

expediency /ɪkˈspiːdɪənsi, ɛk-/ *n.* E17. [Partly f. late L *expedientia*, partly f. next: see -ENCY.] 1 The quality or state of being expedient; suitability to the circumstances or conditions of the case; fitness, advantage. E17. 2 The consideration of what is expedient, as a motive or rule of action; the consideration of what is politic as opp. to what is just and right. E17. b In *pl.* Motives of expediency, the requirements of expediency. M19.

1 C. MIDDLETON In some perplexity . . about the expediency of the voyage. 2 I. D'ISRAELI Where political expediency seems to violate all moral right. B. BETTELHEIM His choice of work must not be due to mere convenience, chance or expediency. b J. S. MILL These reasons must arise from the special expediencies of the case.

expedient /ɪkˈspiːdɪənt, ɛk-/ *a.* & *n.* LME. [L *expedient-* pres. ppl stem of *expedire*: see EXPEDITE *v.*, -ENT.] A *adj.* I 1 Advantageous (in general or to a definite purpose); fit, proper; suitable to the circumstances of the case. Foll. by *for*, †*to*. Usu. *pred.* LME. 2 Useful or politic as opp. to right or just; advisable on practical rather than moral grounds. L18.

1 T. BEDDOES These, if not necessary to the existence of vegetables, may be expedient to their flourishing state. W. TAYLOR The most expedient settlements for a trading country. F. L. WRIGHT To use our new materials . . in ways that were not only expedient but beautiful. 2 J. MCPHEE Because everybody in Alaska hates Anchorage it is politically expedient to put the capital in a new place.

†II 3 Hasty, expeditious, speedy; (of a march) direct. L15–L16.

B *n.* A means of attaining an end; a shift; a resource. LME.

R. H. TAWNEY What is venial as an occasional expedient is reprehensible when carried on as a regular occupation. I. COLEGATE Her widely admired 'natural look' was achieved by the simple expedient of not taking much trouble over her clothes.

expediently *adv.* LME. **expedientness** *n.* (*rare*) M18.

expediential /ɪkˌspiːdɪˈɛnʃ(ə)l, ɛk-/ *a.* M19. [f. EXPEDIENCY + -AL[1].] Of, pertaining to, or having regard to what is expedient.

expedientially *adv.* (*rare*) L19.

expeditate /ɪkˈspɛdɪteɪt, ɛk-/ *v.t. obs.* exc. *Hist.* E16. [med.L *expeditat-* pa. ppl stem of *expeditare*, f. as EX-[1] 1 + *ped-*, *pes* foot, on the analogy of med.L *excapitare* decapitate.] Deprive (a dog) of claws or the ball of the foot to restrict free movement in hunting etc.

expedi'tation *n.* E16.

expedite /ˈɛkspɪdʌɪt/ *a.* Now *rare.* M16. [L *expeditus* pa. pple of *expedire*: see next, -ITE[2].] 1 Prompt, speedy, expeditious. M16. †2 Clear of obstacles or impediments (*lit.* & *fig.*); free from difficulties. L16–L17. †3 Unencumbered;

unrestricted in movement; active, nimble; (of a soldier) lightly equipped. L16–L18. 4 Of a thing: ready for immediate use; handy; serviceable. E17. †5 Of a person: prompt, alert, ready. Only in 17.

expedite /ˈɛkspɪdʌɪt/ *v.t.* L15. [L *expedit-* pa. ppl stem of *expedire* extricate (orig. free the feet), put in order, f. as EX-[1] I + *ped-*, *pes* foot: see -ITE[2].] **1** Deal with, accomplish; dispatch, perform quickly. L15. **2** Help forward, hasten the progress of. E17. **3** Send out or issue (a document etc.) officially; dispatch (a message, a courier); send out (troops, munitions). Now *rare.* E17. †**4** Clear of difficulties; clear up (confusion); facilitate (action or movement); disentangle, untie. Only in 17.

1 B. TAYLOR Such is my wish: dare thou to expedite it. 2 K. M. E. MURRAY The Press would not agree to the extra expense.. without a guarantee that production would thereby be.. expedited.

expediter *n.* = EXPEDITOR L19. **expeditor** *n.* a person who expedites something; *spec.* a progress chaser: M20.

expedition /ɛkspɪˈdɪʃ(ə)n/ *n.* LME. [(O)Fr. *expédition* f. L *expeditio(n-)*, f. as prec.: see -ITION.] †**1** The action of expediting something; prompt performance or supply of something; dispatch. LME–M17. **2a** A sending or setting forth with martial intentions; a warlike enterprise. LME. **b** A journey, voyage, or excursion made for a specific purpose. L16. †**3** The action of issuing official documents or other articles; a document so issued. L15–L18. **4** Quick movement; promptness, speed; dispatch. L16. **5** A body, esp. a military force, sent out for a specific purpose. L17.

1 †**in expedition** in the condition of being expedited. 2a R. HAKLUYT He conquered not in that expedition. b J. WYNDHAM There are notes of the places to which my expeditions took me. *fishing expedition*: see FISHING *n.* 4 MILTON With winged expedition, Swift as the lightning glance. W. PENN With all possible vigilance and expedition. 5 A. F. DOUGLAS-HOME The advance of a punitive expedition sent by King Henry.

expeditioner *n.* (*rare*) an expeditionist M18. **expeditionist** *n.* a person who makes, or takes part in, an expedition M19. **expeditionary** *a.* & *n.* (*a*) *adj.* of or pertaining to an expedition; sent on an (esp. military) expedition; (*b*) *n.* an expeditionist: E19.

expeditious /ɛkspɪˈdɪʃəs/ *a.* L15. [f. prec.: see -ITIOUS[1].] **1** Speedily performed or given; conducive to speedy performance. L15. **2** Of a person: acting or moving with expedition; speedy. L16.

1 J. G. MURPHY Equipped for expeditious travelling. 2 J. A. FROUDE The German commission was as expeditious as the Spanish had been dilatory.

¶Rare bef. 17.

expeditiously *adv.* E17. **expeditiousness** *n.* E18.

expel /ɪkˈspɛl, ɛk-/ *v.t.* Infl. **-ll-**. LME. [L *expellere*, f. as EX-[1] I + *pellere* to drive, thrust.] **1** Eject; cause to depart or emerge, esp. by the use of force; banish from a place; discharge (a bullet). (Foll. by *from.*) LME. **2** Compel the departure of (a person) from a society, community, etc.; *esp.* enforce the departure of (a student) from an educational establishment as a punitive measure. (Foll. by *from*, †2nd obj.) M16. †**3** Reject from attention or consideration. L16–M18. †**4** Keep off, exclude, keep out. *rare* (Shakes.). Only in E17.

1 E. HUXLEY In 1290 Edward I expelled the Jews. W. GOLDING She drew, puffed, expelled long coils of smoke. *Daily Telegraph* They were expelled on a flight leaving for Namibia later in the day. P. NORMAN He strove.. to expel even from his mind all that might be incriminating or unseemly. 2 SOUTHEY Whoever acted contrary.. should be expelled the Society. M. MITCHELL They had just been expelled from.. the fourth university that had thrown them out in two years.

expellable *a.* M17. **expeˈllee** *n.* a person who has been expelled L19. **expeller** *n.* M16.

expellent /ɪkˈspɛlənt/ *n.* & *a.* Also **-ant**. E19. [L *expellent-* pres. ppl stem of *expellere* EXPEL: see -ENT.] **A** *n.* A medicine believed to expel unwholesome matter. *rare.* E19. **B** *adj.* That expels or tends to expel. M19.

†**expence** *n.* var. of EXPENSE.

expend /ɪkˈspɛnd, ɛk-/ *v.t.* LME. [L *expendere*, f. as EX-[1] I + *pendere* weigh, pay. Cf. SPEND *v.*] **I 1** Spend (money); devote (care, time, effort); employ for a given purpose. Formerly also, spend completely, consume (resources) in outlay. (Foll. by *on* an object, *in* an action, *doing.*) LME. **2** Use up (material, strength, etc.) in any operation. Formerly also, consume (provisions). M18. **3** *Naut.* Lose (spars, masts, etc.) in fighting, by storm, etc. Also, use up (spare rope) by winding it round a spar etc. E19.

1 L. STEFFENS The promoter had expended nearly $300,000 in securing the legislation. P. G. WODEHOUSE He had expended much thought on the subject. C. RYCROFT Freud expended much ink and energy trying to prove that artists are neurotics. 2 JOHN PHILLIPS After the currents had expended themselves. G. ORWELL A convenient way of expending labour power without producing anything that can be consumed. 3 F. MARRYAT Have you expended any boat's masts?

†**II 4** Weigh mentally; consider, determine accurately. M16–L17.

expender *n.* LME.

expendable /ɪkˈspɛndəb(ə)l, ɛk-/ *a.* & *n.* E19. [f. prec. + -ABLE.] **A** *adj.* That may be expended; regarded as not worth preserving or saving; not normally reused; unimportant, able to be sacrificed to achieve an object. E19.

W. L. WHITE In a war anything can be expendable—money or gasoline or equipment or most usually men.

B *n.* An expendable person or object. M20.

expendaˈbility *n.* L20. **expendably** *adv.* L20.

expenditor /ɪkˈspɛndɪtə, ɛk-/ *n.* L15. [med.L, f. *expenditus* irreg. pa. pple (after *venditus* sold) of *expendere*: see EXPEND, -OR.] A person in charge of expenditure; *spec.* (now *Hist.*) an officer appointed to disburse the money collected by tax for the repair of sewers.

expenditure /ɪkˈspɛndɪtʃə, ɛk-/ *n.* M18. [f. EXPEND after prec.: see -URE.] **1a** The action or practice of expending money, care, time, effort, etc. M18. **b** The action or process of using up; consumption. E19. **2** An amount expended. L18.

1a ADAM SMITH The collection and expenditure of the public revenue. GEO. ELIOT He disliked all quarrelling as an unpleasant expenditure of energy. 2 R. P. GRAVES The move had.. reduced his income and increased his expenditure. J. BRAINE My salary didn't allow for casual expenditures of nearly ten bob.

expense /ɪkˈspɛns, ɛk-/ *n.* & *v.* Also †**-ence**. LME. [AN, alt. of OFr. *espense* f. late L *expensa* (sc. *pecunia* money) fem. of pa. pple of L *expendere* EXPEND.] **A** *n.* **1** The action or an act of expending something; the state of being expended; disbursement; consumption; loss; = EXPENDITURE I. Now *rare.* LME. †**2** Money expended; an amount expended. LME–M18. **3** Burden of expenditure; the charge or cost involved in or required for something; in *pl.*, the charges etc. incurred by a person in the course of working for another or undertaking any enterprise; the amount paid in reimbursement. LME. **b** A cause or occasion of expense. L19.

1 S. JOHNSON This exuberance of money displayed itself in wantonness of expence. U. LE GUIN The protein issue.. was now insufficient for full normal expense of energy. 2 W. PETTY Where a People thrive, there the income is greater than the expence. 3 A. PARSONS Those who can afford the expence, usually go to.. the sea coast. *Daily Telegraph* The home eleven had got 52 at an expense of two wickets. V. WOOLF Nancy, dressed at enormous expense by the greatest artists in Paris. F. TUOHY Vince's fat cheque to cover the expenses of a prolonged stay in Paris. b OED His sons have been a great expense to him.

Phrases: **at a person's expense** causing a person to spend money or suffer injury, ridicule, etc. **at the expense of** so as to cause loss, damage, or discredit to; to the detriment of. **put to (great** etc.**) expense** cause to spend (much etc.) money.

Comb.: **expense account** (*a*) an account in which are recorded other than capital payments made by a business; (*b*) a list of an employee's expenses payable by an employer.

B *v.t.* **1** Charge (a business) with expenses incurred. E20. **2** Offset (an expense) against taxable income. M20.

†**expenseful** *a.* costly, expensive; extravagant: E17–E18. †**expenseless** *a.* inexpensive; frugal: M17–L18.

expensive /ɪkˈspɛnsɪv, ɛk-/ *a.* E17. [f. L *expens-* pa. ppl stem of *expendere* EXPEND + -IVE. Assoc. early with EXPENSE.] **1** Given to profuse expenditure (of money, effort, etc.) or consumption (of time, health, etc.); lavish, extravagant. Now *rare.* E17. **2** Causing much expense, costly; making a high charge; highly-priced, dear. M17.

1 STEELE Young Men.. are.. so expensive both of their Health and Fortune. J. GILCHRIST A regular arrangement of extracts.. is.. more expensive of time. 2 J. A. FROUDE The father.. was unable to give the child as expensive an education as he had desired. W. MAXWELL The two upstairs rooms are.. expensive to heat in winter.

expensively *adv.* E17. **expensiveness** *n.* M17.

expergefaction /ɪkˌspəːdʒɪˈfakʃ(ə)n, ɛk-/ *n.* Now *rare* or *obs.* M17. [Late L *expergefactio(n-)*, f. L *expergefact-* pa. ppl stem of *expergefacere* awaken, arouse, f. *expergere* awaken, arouse: see -FACTION.] The action of awaking or rousing; the state, condition, or fact of being awakened or aroused.

experience /ɪkˈspɪərɪəns, ɛk-/ *n.* LME. [(O)Fr. *expérience* f. L *experientia*, f. *experiri* try: see -ENCE.] **1** †**a** The action of putting to the test, trial. LME–M17. **b** A procedure carried out to test or demonstrate something; an experiment. Now *rare* or *obs.* LME. **2** Proof by actual trial; practical demonstration. *obs.* exc. as passing into sense 3. LME. **3** Actual observation of or practical acquaintance with facts or events, considered as a source of knowledge. LME. **4** A state, condition, or event that consciously affects one; the fact or process of being so affected. LME. **b** A state of mind or feeling forming part of the inner religious life; a state or phase of religious emotion. L17. **5** The state of having been occupied in any branch of study or affairs; the extent or period of such an occupation; the aptitudes, skill, judgement, etc., thereby acquired. L15. **6** Knowledge resulting from actual observation or practical acquaintance, or from what one has undergone. M16. †**b** A fact, maxim, or rule based on experience; something expertly fashioned. L16–L17. **7** What has been experienced; the events that have taken place within the knowledge of an individual, a community, the human race, etc. E17.

1a J. SHIRLEY Make Experience of my loyalty, by some service. 3 T. REID Experience informs us only of what has been, but never of what must be. 4 LD MACAULAY Both.. had learned by experience how soon James forgot obligation. J. BARZUN Boredom is not the trivial, harmless experience that common speech assumes. S. BARSTOW I'd never been involved in a wedding before.. it's what you might call an experience. *peak experience*: see PEAK *n.*[1] & *a.* 5 SHAKES. *Two Gent.* His years but young, but his experience old. G. GORER The belief that experience is unnecessary, because 'nature teaches'. 6 J. TYNDALL I had had but little experience of alpine phenomena. G. GREENE My experience of diaries is they always give things away. 7 A. P. HERBERT In all her experience as a model. J. HELLER To write about the Jewish experience in America.

experience /ɪkˈspɪərɪəns, ɛk-/ *v.t.* M16. [f. the n.] †**1** Make trial or experiment of; test, try. M16–L18. †**2** Ascertain or prove by experiment or observation. (Foll. by obj. cl., *that.*) M16–M18. †**3** Give experience to; make experienced; train (soldiers); in *pass.*, be informed or taught by experience. M16–M17. **4** Have experience of; feel, suffer, undergo. L16. **5** Learn (a fact) by experience; find (*how*, *what*, *that*). Now *rare.* L16.

4 SIR W. SCOTT The hottest weather I ever experienced. W. GOLDING Free-will cannot be debated but only experienced, like a colour or the taste of potatoes. D. MURPHY I experienced an almost hysterical elation. I. MURDOCH The most.. peaceful sleep that I had experienced for a long time. *experience* RELIGION.

experienceable *a.* able to be experienced E20. **experiencer** *n.* †(*a*) *rare* an experimenter; (*b*) a person who experiences something: M17.

experienced /ɪk'spɪərɪənst, ɛk-/ *a.* M16. [f. EXPERIENCE *n.*, *v.*: see -ED², -ED¹.] 1 Having experience; wise or skilful through experience. (Foll. by *in.*) M16. †2 Tried, tested, approved; = EXPERT *a.* 3. M16–L18. 3 = EXPERIENT *a.* 2. Long *rare.* E17.

1 H. MARTINEAU The stray sheep may come back experienced in pasturage. R. L. FOX A famous shield-to-shield rally by a battalion of Philip's most experienced veterans. 2 S. JOHNSON To.. counteract by experienced remedies every new tendency. 3 A. ALISON Experienced grievances.

experient /ɪk'spɪərɪənt, ɛk-/ *a.* & *n.* LME. [L *experient-* pres. ppl stem of *experiri*: see EXPERIENCE *n.*, -ENT.] A *adj.* †1 = EXPERIENCED 1. LME–M17. 2 Met with in the course of experience. *rare.* E20. B *n.* †1 Something experienced, tested, or tried. *rare.* Only in E17. 2 A person who experiences something or undergoes an experience. L19.

experiential /ɪkˌspɪərɪ'ɛnʃ(ə)l, ɛk-/ *a.* E19. [f. EXPERIENCE *n.* + -IAL, after *inferential* etc.] Of, pertaining to, or derived from experience or observation.

experientialism *n.* the theory or doctrine that all knowledge is based on experience M19. **experientalist** *n.* a supporter of or adherent of experientialism L19. **experientially** *adv.* with regard to experience, in or by experience M17.

experiment /ɪk'spɛrɪmənt, ɛk-/ *n.* ME. [OFr., or L *experimentum*, f. *experiri*: see EXPERIENCE *n.*, -MENT.] I 1 The action of trying something or putting it to the test; a test, a trial. (Foll. by *of.*) *arch.* ME. †b An expedient or remedy to be tried. L16–E18. 2 An action or procedure undertaken to make a discovery, test a hypothesis, or demonstrate a known fact. LME. 3 A procedure or course of action tentatively adopted without being sure that it will achieve its purpose. L16. 4 The process or practice of conducting an experiment; experimentation. L17. 5 The equipment for a scientific experiment. M20.

2 J. D. WATSON He.. visited other labs to see which new experiments had been done. 3 B. JOWETT The experiment had never been tried of reasoning with mankind. 4 D. L. SAYERS She bought drugs in order to prove by experiment how easy it was.. to get hold of deadly poisons.

†II 6 A practical proof; a specimen, an example. ME–L17. 7 Practical acquaintance with a person or thing; (an) experience. (Foll. by *of.*) M16–M18.

†**experimentarian** *a.* & *n.* (a philosopher) relying on experiment M17–E19. †**experimently** *adv.* by experience LME–E19.

experiment /ɪk'spɛrɪmənt, ɛk-/ *v.* LME. [f. the n.] †1 *v.t.* = EXPERIENCE *v.* 4. LME–E18. †2 *v.t.* Ascertain or establish by trial. L15–E19. 3 *v.t.* Make trial or experiment of; test, try. Now *rare.* E16. 4 *v.i.* Perform an experiment or experiments (*on*, *with*). L18.

3 S. LESLIE He had.. experimented their theories in his laboratory. 4 B. SPOCK You can experiment to see which precautions.. work best. E. BOWEN She experimented with the four-speed gear.

experimen'tation *n.* the action or process of experimenting; a series of experiments: L17. **experi'mentative** *a.* of the nature of an experiment; inclined to make an experiment: E19. **experimenter** *n.* a person who experiments M16.

experimental /ɪkˌspɛrɪ'mɛnt(ə)l, ɛk-/ *a.* L15. [med.L *experimentalis*, f. L *experimentum* EXPERIMENT *n.*: see -AL¹.] †1 Of a person: having actual or personal experience of something. Of a thing: coming within the range of experience; observed. L15–M18. 2 Based on experience as opp. to authority or conjecture; founded on experience only, empirical. Formerly also, discovered by experience. E16. 3 Based on, derived from, or making use of experiment; *esp.* designating (a specialist in) a branch of knowledge based on experiment. L16. 4 Of or pertaining to experiments; used in or for experiments. L18. 5 Of the nature of an experiment; tentative; adopted or begun without assurance of success; *spec.* designating an educational establishment, artistic endeavour, etc., run or developed on non-traditional lines. E19.

2 E. M. GOULBURN To bring myself and others to an experimental knowledge of God. 3 B. LOVELL Astronomical investigations are almost completely observational and not experimental. *experimental chemist, physics, psychologist, psychology*, etc. 4 J. N. LOCKYER The spectrum of potassium.. varies very much under different experimental conditions. 5 JAS. MILL A first and experimental attempt. R. L. STEVENSON Wine in California is still in the experimental stage. M. GORDON Headmaster of an experimental school.

experimentalism *n.* (*a*) (adherence to) the principles of the empirical approach in philosophy or science; (*b*) *rare* experimental research, experimentation: M19. **experimentalist** *n.* (*a*) a scientist concerned with experimental research; a skilled experimenter; (*b*) a person given to experimenting with new methods of procedure etc.: M18. **experimentalize** *v.i.* perform or try experiments (*on*) E19. **experimentally** *adv.* (*a*) by or through experience; (*b*) by means of experiment: L16.

experimented /ɪk'spɛrɪmɛntɪd, ɛk-/ *ppl a.* Now *rare* or *obs.* L15. [f. EXPERIMENT *v.* + -ED¹.] 1 Experienced; versed or practised *in* a subject. L15. †2 Proved, tested, or known by experience or experiment; ascertained, authenticated. M16–E19. †3 = EXPERIENT *a.* 2. L17–E19.

experimentum crucis /ɪkˌspɛrɪmɛntəm 'kruːsɪs, 'kruːkɪs; ɛk-/ *n. phr.* M17. [mod.L = crucial experiment.] A decisive test showing which of several hypotheses is correct.

expert /'ɛkspəːt/ *n.* E19. [Fr., use as n. of (O)Fr. *expert* adj.: see next.] 1 A person with the status of an authority (*in* a subject) by reason of special skill, training, or knowledge; a specialist. Freq. *attrib.* E19. 2 A person who is expert or who has gained skill from experience. (Foll. by *at*, *in*, *with.*) M19. 3 A person who looks after or maintains machinery, esp. in a shearing shed; the manager of a team of shearers. *Austral. slang.* E20.

1 W. BESANT My writing was well known; experts swore that the forgery was by me. I. A. RICHARDS A human relation between the expert and his lay audience must be created. *Essentials* The fitter will rely on keen eyes.. and expert knowledge. *Times* The court decides in the end, there are expert witnesses. 2 E. K. KANE Hans Christian.. an expert with the kayak and javelin.

expert /'ɛkspəːt/ *a.* LME. [(O)Fr. alt. of *espert* after L *expertus* pa. pple of *experiri* try.] †1 Experienced (*in*); having experience (*of*). LME–L17. 2 Trained by practice or experience; skilled, skilful, (*at*, *in*, *with*). LME. †3 Tried, proved by experience; = EXPERIENCED 2. LME–E17.

1 W. PETTY A Protestant Militia of 25,000, the most whereof are expert in war. 2 E. E. HALE The Florentine was not expert in ecclesiastical matters. T. CAPOTE The expert execution of the crimes. R. WEST He was becoming an expert player of the administrative game. J. STEINBECK She was so expert with the rolling-pin that the dough seemed alive.

expert system a computer program into which has been incorporated the knowledge of experts on a particular subject so that non-experts can use it for making decisions, evaluations, or inferences.

expertly *adv.* LME. **expertness** *n.* M17.

expert /'ɛkspəːt/ *v.* L19. [f. EXPERT *n.*] 1 *v.t.* Examine as an expert. *N. Amer. colloq.* L19. 2 *v.i.* Look after or maintain the machinery and tools of a shearing shed. Chiefly as *experting* vbl n. *Austral. slang.* M20.

expertise /ɛkspəː'tiːz/ *n.* M19. [Fr.] Expert opinion or knowledge; know-how, skill, or expertness in something.

expertize /'ɛkspətʌɪz/ *v.i.* & *t.* Also **-ise**. L19. [f. EXPERT *n.* + -IZE.] Give an expert opinion (on); evaluate.

expiable /'ɛkspɪəb(ə)l/ *a.* Now *rare.* L16. [Fr., or eccl.L *expiabilis*, f. *expiare*: see EXPIATE *v.*, -ABLE.] Able to be expiated.

†**expiate** *a. rare* (Shakes.) Only in L16. [L *expiatus* pa. pple of *expiare*: see next, -ATE².] Of an appointed time: fully come; past.

expiate /'ɛkspɪeɪt/ *v.* L16. [L *expiat-* pa. ppl stem of *expiare*, f. as EX-¹ 1 + *piare* seek to appease (by sacrifice), f. *pius* PIOUS: see -ATE³.] †1 *v.t.* Put an end to (pain etc.) by death; extinguish (rage) by suffering to the full. L16–E17. †2 *v.t.* Cleanse (a person or place) of or *of* guilt or pollution by religious ceremonies. E–M17. 3 *v.t.* Avert (a predicted evil). *obs.* exc. *Hist.* E17. 4 *v.t.* & †*i.* w. *for.* Atone or make amends for. E17. 5 *v.t.* Extinguish the guilt arising from (a sin); constitute atonement for. E17. 6 *v.t.* Pay the penalty of (an offence). M17.

4 P. USTINOV His father's heresies.. would sooner or later have to be expiated. 5 H. JAMES His fault had been richly expiated by these days of impatience and bereavement. C. H. SISSON To be seen naked was a shame Which only death could expiate. 6 LD MACAULAY Some of the girls who had presented the standard to Monmouth at Taunton had cruelly expiated their offence.

expiation /ɛkspɪ'eɪʃ(ə)n/ *n.* LME. [L *expiatio(n-)*, f. as prec.: see -ATION.] 1 The action or an act of making atonement for a crime etc.; the condition of being expiated. LME. †b The action of ceremonially cleansing of guilt or pollution. M16–M17. 2 A means by which atonement is made. M16.

1 W. STYRON My crime was ultimately beyond expiation. 2 D. ATHILL The suffering was no expiation because it was of his own making.

Phrases: **day, feast**, etc., **of expiation** *arch.* the Day of Atonement. **in expiation (of)** for the purpose of expiating (for). **make expiation** atone.

expiator /'ɛkspɪeɪtə/ *n.* M19. [L, f. *expiare*: see EXPIATE *v.*, -OR.] A person who makes expiation for a sin, crime, etc.

expiatory /'ɛkspɪət(ə)ri/ *a.* L15. [eccl.L *expiatorius*, f. as prec.: see -ORY².] Serving to expiate. (Foll. by *of.*)

expilation /ɛkspɪ'leɪʃ(ə)n/ *n.* Now *rare.* M16. [L *expilatio(n-)*, f. *expilat-* pa. ppl stem of *expilare* plunder, f. as EX-¹ 1 + *pilare* fix firmly: see -ATION.] The action of plundering.

expiration /ɛkspɪ'reɪʃ(ə)n/ *n.* LME. [L *ex(s)piratio(n-)*, f. *ex(s)pirat-* pa. ppl stem of *ex(s)pirare*: see EXPIRE, -ATION.] †1a A vapour, an exhalation. LME–M17. b Change into vapour, evaporation. E16–M17. †2 The action of breathing one's last; death. M16–E19. 3 = EXPIRY 1. M16. 4 The action or an act of breathing out. L16. 5 (An) emission *of* air, vapour, etc. M17.

3 W. S. MAUGHAM It was at the expiration of their term [of hard labour] that their real punishment began. *Los Angeles Times* A customer.. had noticed that the expiration date on a cottage cheese carton had passed. 4 F. H. RAMADGE The impeded expiration.. caused.. the lower lobes of the lung to be exceedingly enlarged. 5 T. HARDY There came.. an utter expiration of air from the whole heaven in the form of a slow breeze.

expiratory /ɛks'pʌɪrət(ə)ri/ *a.* M19.

expire /ɪk'spʌɪə, ɛk-/ *v.* LME. [(O)Fr. *expirer* f. L *ex(s)pirare* breathe out, f. as EX-¹ 1 + *spirare* breathe.] I Die; come or bring to an end. †1 *v.t.* Breathe out (the soul, one's last breath, etc.) in the act of dying. LME–E18. 2 *v.i.* Of a person or animal: breathe for the last time, die. Of a fire etc.: die out. LME. 3 *v.i.* Of a period of time: come to an end; *rare* elapse, pass. Of an action, state, legal title, etc: cease, die out; become void or extinct through lapse of time. LME. †4 *v.t.* Bring to an end; conclude; make (a charter, gift, etc.) invalid or void. LME–E17.

2 S. KING A young man.. had remained in a coma for fourteen years before expiring. J. THURBER He tossed away his cigar and watched it expire in the damp night grass. 3 J. GALSWORTHY The agreement.. was for a period of five years, of which one only had expired. P. USTINOV At midnight.. a British ultimatum expired, and Britain was.. at war.

II Exhale, emit. 5 *v.t.* & *i.* Breathe out (air etc.). Opp. *inspire.* L16. 6 Pass out like a breath; be exhaled; (of a wind, flame, projectile, etc.) rush forth. Now *rare.* E17. †7 *v.t.* Give off or emit (a perfume, vapour, etc.), exhale; (of a volcano) emit (flames). E17–E19.

expi'ree *n.* (*Hist.*) a person sentenced to transportation to Australia whose term of punishment had expired E19. **expirer** *n.* L18.

expiry /ɪk'spʌɪri, ɛk-/ *n.* M18. [f. prec. + -Y³.] 1 The end or termination of a period of time, a contract, a truce, etc. M18. 2 Dying, death. *rare.* L18.

expiscate /ɪk'spɪskeɪt, ɛk-/ *v.t.* Chiefly *Sc.* Now *rare.* E17. [L *expiscat-* pa. ppl stem of *expiscare* fish out, f. as EX-[1] I + *piscare* to fish: see -ATE[3].] Fish out, find out, (a fact etc.); investigate; elucidate.

expis'cation *n.* E17.

explain /ɪk'spleɪn, ɛk-/ *v.* LME. [L *explanare*, f. as EX-[1] I + *planus* flat, PLAIN *a.*[1], to which the mod. spelling is assim.] 1 *v.t.* & *i.* Make clear or intelligible (a meaning, difficulty, etc.); clear of obscurity or difficulty; give details of (a matter, *how*, etc.) LME. †b Speak one's mind *against*, *upon*. E-M18. c *v.t.*, & *i.* w. subord. cl. Say in explanation. M19. †2 Make smooth (the forehead or face). M16-M17. †3 *v.t.* & *i.* Open out, unfold (an object). E17-E18. b *v.t.* Make plainly visible. E-M17. 4 *v.t.* State the meaning or significance of; interpret. E17. 5 *refl.* Make clear one's meaning; give an account of one's motives or conduct. E17. 6 *v.t.* Account for; make clear the cause or origin of. M18.

1 M. GRAY He took a card from his pocket... 'That will explain to Dr. Everard,' he said. J. A. MICHENER He was weary from trying to explain ideas to people who could not visualize them. C. P. SNOW Briers had been explaining to his superiors what he intended to do. *Daily Telegraph* The Blackfoot chief.. explained how the braves used to drive buffalo. c R. LANGBRIDGE Tears came into Susette's eyes... 'I have bitten my tongue,' Susette explained. R. H. MOTTRAM The nursing sister.. explaining that the occupants were more or less convalescent. 3 **explain (itself) into** develop into. 4 **explain away** modify or remove the force of (esp. offensive language, awkward facts, etc.) by explanation. 5 *Economist* Mr Kitson, who has refused to withdraw his reported remarks, will be asked to explain himself. 6 A. LURIE Knowing about Roz explains a lot.

explainable *a.* E17. **explainer** *n.* L16.

explanandum /ɛksplə'nandəm/ *n.* Pl. **-da** /-də/. L19. [L, neut. gerundive of *explanare* EXPLAIN.] *Philos.* = EXPLICANDUM. Cf. next.

explanans /ɛksplə'nanz/ *n.* Pl. **-nantia** /-'nantɪə/. M20. [L, pres. pple of *explanare* EXPLAIN.] *Philos.* = EXPLICANS. Cf. prec.

explanate /'ɛksplənert/ *a.* M19. [L *explanatus* pa. pple of *explanare* EXPLAIN: see -ATE[2].] *Zool.* Spread out flat.

explanation /ɛksplə'neɪʃ(ə)n/ *n.* LME. [L *explanatio(n-)*, f. *explanat-* pa. ppl stem of *explanare* EXPLAIN: see -ATION.] 1 The action or an act of explaining. LME. 2 A statement, circumstance, etc., which makes clear or accounts for something. E17. 3 A declaration made with a view to mutual understanding and reconciliation. M19.

1 G. B. SHAW An unfortunate child.. receiving an elaborate explanation of the figures on a clock dial. 2 A. RADCLIFFE La Motte now asked for an explanation of the scene. E. O'NEILL For there must be a cause and a rational explanation.

explanative /ɪk'splanətɪv, ɛk-/ *a.* E17. [Late L *explanativus*, f. L *explanat-*: see prec., -IVE.] Explanatory.

explanatory /ɪk'splanət(ə)ri, ɛk-/ *a.* E17. [Late L *explanatorius*, f. *explanat-*: see EXPLANATION, -ORY[2].] Serving, or intended to serve, as explanation; (of a person) disposed to explain.

DICKENS He rendered himself as explanatory as he could.

explanatorily *adv.* M19. **explanatoriness** *n.* M18.

explant /'ɛksplɑːnt/ *n.* E20. [f. the vb.] A piece of tissue, an organ, etc., that has been explanted.

explant /ɪk'splɑːnt/ *v.t.* L16. [mod.L *explantare*, f. L EX-[1] I + *plantare* to plant.] †1 Send out as an offshoot. Only in L16. 2 Remove (living tissue) from its original site, esp. to initiate a culture of it in a nutrient medium. E20.

explan'tation *n.* (*a*) the action of explanting; †(*b*) an offshoot: L16.

†**expletion** *n.* E17-E18. [L *expletio(n-)*, f. *explere*: see next, -ION.] The action of filling; repletion; fulfilment.

expletive /ɪk'spliːtɪv, ɛk-/ *a.* & *n.* LME. [Late L *expletivus*, f. *explere* fill out, f. as EX-[1] I + *plere* fill: see -IVE.] A *adj.* Introduced merely to make up a required quantity; *esp.* (of a word or phrase) serving to fill out a sentence or metrical line. Formerly also (of a conjunction), correlative. LME. B *n.* 1 A word or phrase used to fill out a sentence or metrical line. E17. b An oath; a meaningless exclamation. E19. 2 A person who or thing which serves merely to fill up space. L17.

1b A. GUINNESS Tony let fly a stream of expletives.

expletively *adv.* E17.

expletory /ɪk'spliːt(ə)ri, ɛk-/ *a.* L17. [f. L *explet-* pa. ppl stem of *explere*: see prec., -ORY[2].] = EXPLETIVE *a.*

explicable /ɪk'splɪkəb(ə)l, ɛk-, 'ɛksplɪkəb(ə)l/ *a.* M16. [Fr., or L *explicabilis*, f. *explicare*: see EXPLICATE, -ABLE.] Able to be explained or accounted for.

ISAIAH BERLIN Everything is in principle explicable, for everything has a purpose.

explicably *adv.* M20.

explicandum /ɛksplɪ'kandəm/ *n.* Pl. **-da** /-də/. M19. [L, neut. gerundive of *explicare*: see EXPLICATE.] *Philos.* The fact, thing, or expression to be explained or explicated. Cf. EXPLANANDUM, next.

explicans /ɛksplɪ'kans/ *n.* Pl. **-cantia** /-'kantɪə/. L19. [L, pres. pple of *explicare*: see EXPLICATE.] *Philos.* The explaining part of an explanation; in the analysis of a concept or expression, the part that gives the meaning. Cf. EXPLANANS, prec.

explicate /'ɛksplɪkeɪt/ *v.* M16. [L *explicat-* pa. ppl stem of *explicare* unfold, f. as EX-[1] I + *plicare* to fold: see -ATE[3].] †1 *v.t.* Unfold, unwrap; open out (a bud, leaf, etc.); spread out, display. M16-E18. b Make larger in area or volume. L16-M17. 2 *v.t.* & *i.* Give details (of). Now *rare*. M16. 3 *v.t.* Explain, make clear. M16. †b *refl.* Make clear one's meaning. M16-M17. 4 *v.t.* Develop the meaning or implication of (a principle, notion, etc.). E17. †5 *v.t.* = EXPLAIN 6. E17-E18. †6 *v.t.* Unravel, solve, (a difficulty etc.); disentangle, extricate *from* (a difficulty etc.). Also foll. by *out of*. E17-E18.

3 M. AMIS I explicated a Donne sonnet.

explicatory /ɛksplɪ'keɪt(ə)ri, ɛk'splɪkət(ə)ri/ *a.* E17.

explication /ɛksplɪ'keɪʃ(ə)n/ *n.* E16. [Fr., or L *explicatio(n-)*, f. as prec.: see -ATION.] 1 The action or an act of stating or describing in detail. E16. 2 The action or an act of making clear the meaning of something; (an) interpretation. M16. †b An exposition; a paraphrase. M17-L18. 3 (The result of) the process of developing the meaning or implication of a principle, notion, etc. E17. †4 The action of unfolding a flower, leaf, etc. Only in M17. †5 The action or an act of accounting for the cause or origin of a phenomenon etc. L17-M18. †6 = EXPLANATION 3. E-M18.

explication de texte /ɛksplikasjɔ̃ də tɛkst/ *n. phr.* Pl. ***explications de texte*** (pronounced same). M20. [Fr.] A detailed textual examination of a literary work; the making of such examinations.

explicative /ɪk'splɪkətɪv, ɛk-, 'ɛksplɪkətɪv/ *a.* & *n.* E17. [Fr. *explicatif*, f. *expliquer* explain, f. L *explicare*: see EXPLICATE, -IVE.] A *adj.* †1 Expansive. *rare*. Only in E17. 2 Explanatory, interpretative; *spec.* in *Logic* (of a judgement), that explains the predicate from analysis of the subject. M17. B *n.* An explicative term or phrase. L18.

explicatively *adv.* M18.

explicator /'ɛksplɪkeɪtə/ *n.* E17. [L, f. *explicare*: see EXPLICATE, -OR.] An explainer.

explicit /ɪk'splɪsɪt, ɛk-/ *a.* E17. [Fr. *explicite*, or L *explicitus* pa. pple of *explicare*: see EXPLICATE.] 1 Distinctly expressing all that is meant; leaving nothing merely implied or suggested; unambiguous; clear. E17. b Describing or portraying the naked body or intimate sexual activity. L20. 2 Of a person, personal qualities, a book, etc.: outspoken; unreserved in expression. E18. 3 *Math.* Of a function: having the dependent variable defined directly in terms of the independent variable(s). E19.

1 H. KISSINGER We had had communications from Chou En-Lai sufficiently explicit for our less supple minds to grasp. **explicit faith** *Theol.* the acceptance of a doctrine with a clear understanding of all it involves. b *Times* A national newspaper carried explicit photographs of himself and his wife. 2 G. GREENE Her biography.. is a useful and sometimes explicit corrective to Mrs Cecil Chesterton's vulgar and inaccurate study.

explicitly *adv.* M17. **explicitness** *n.* M17.

explicit /'ɛksplɪsɪt/ *v.* & *n.* ME. [Late L; either 3rd person sing. = here ends, pl. *expliciunt*, or abbrev. of *explicitus est liber* the book is unrolled.] †A *v.i.* (*defective*). A statement placed at the end of a book, chapter, etc.: (the book etc.) ends here. ME-M19. B *n.* The end; a conclusion. Cf. INCIPIT. M17.

explode /ɪk'spləʊd, ɛk-/ *v.* M16. [L *explodere* drive out by clapping, hiss off the stage, f. as EX-[1] I + *plaudere* clap the hands.] 1 *v.t.* Reject with scorn (an opinion, proposal, etc.); discard. Now (*rare*) only in *pass.* M16. b Discredit, bring into disrepute (a theory), show to be fallacious. M17. †2 *v.t.* Clap or hiss (a play etc.) off the stage; *gen.* drive away with disapproval; cry down. E17-E19. †3 *v.t.* Force out, expel, esp. with violence and sudden noise. M17-E19. 4 *v.i.* Expand, burst, or shatter with extreme violence and noise; *fig.* give vent suddenly to emotion; burst forth; appear suddenly, esp. as a success. L18. b Increase suddenly or rapidly, esp. in size, numbers, amount, etc. M20. 5 *v.t.* Cause to expand, burst, or shatter with extreme violence and noise. L18. 6 *v.t.* Separate into its constituent parts; *spec.* show in or as a diagram with each component displaced outwards and separated from its neighbours but retaining its relative position. M20.

1 C. G. B. DAUBENY As new views came into vogue, or old errors became exploded. b CONAN DOYLE One forms provisional theories and waits for time or fuller knowledge to explode them. 3 DISRAELI The exploded cork whizzed through the air. 4 E. PEACOCK 'Confound him!' or some stronger expletive exploded from the Earl's lips. J. UPDIKE The tires of planes touching down frequently explode from the heat. *Times* When it exploded six years ago alternative cabaret was unhampered by any precedent. **exploding wire** a wire subjected to a sudden and very high electric current so that it explodes violently. b *Countryman* The problems of feeding the exploding world population. *Weekend Australian* Business-finance news has exploded.. in Australia and the US. 5 P. G. WODEHOUSE It only needs a spark to explode a powder-magazine. E. L. RICE He inflates the bag and explodes it with a blow of his fist. 6 DAVID POTTER Booklets may be broken down or exploded into separate sheets. *exploded diagram*, *drawing*, etc.

explodable *a.* L19. **exploder** *n.* M17.

explodent /ɪk'spləʊd(ə)nt, ɛk-/ *n.* M19. [L *explodent-* pres. ppl stem of *explodere* EXPLODE.] *Phonet.* = PLOSIVE *n.*

exploit /'ɛksplɔɪt/ *n.* ME. [OFr. *espleit*, *esploit*, fem. *esploite*, (mod. *exploit* achievement), f. L *explicitum*, *-ta* neut. & fem. pa. pples of *explicare* EXPLICATE.] †1 Progress, speed; success; furtherance. ME-E16. †2 An attempt to gain advantage over or to subdue a person or place; a military enterprise. LME-M18. 3 An act, a feat, usu. of exceptional skill or bravery. M16.

3 G. SWIFT He wrote a book about his exploits,.. and for a few years he was one of the war-heroes.

exploit /ɪk'splɔɪt, ɛk-/ *v.* LME. [OFr. *espleiter* (mod. *exploiter*) accomplish, enjoy, f. L *explicare* EXPLICATE. In sense 4 f. mod.Fr.] †1 *v.t.* Accomplish, achieve, perform. LME-L18. †2 *v.i.* Act with effect; get on; prosper. LME-E17. †3 *refl.* Exert oneself. L15-M16. 4 *v.t.* Work (a mine); make use of (natural resources); utilize for one's own ends, take advantage of, (a person, esp. an employee, etc.). M19.

4 T. BENN To make sure that the resources of the North Sea were exploited for the benefit of the nation. H. MACMILLAN My close ties with America.. could be usefully exploited. DAY LEWIS Like all children, I mercilessly exploited this kindness.

exploita'bility *n.* the property of being exploitable M20. **exploitable** *a.* †(*a*) able to be accomplished; (*b*) able to be exploited: E17. **exploitage** *n.* exploitation M19. **exploitative** *a.* of, pertaining to, or involving exploitation, esp. of people L19. **exploi'tee** *n.* a person who is exploited M20. **exploiter** *n.* L19. **exploitive** *a.* = EXPLOITATIVE E20.

exploitation /ɛksplɔɪˈteɪʃ(ə)n/ *n.* E19. [Fr. f. OFr. *expletation*, f. as prec.: see -ATION.] The action or practice of exploiting something or someone.

exploration /ɛkspləˈreɪʃ(ə)n/ *n.* M16. [Fr., or L *exploratio(n-)*, f. *explorat-* pa. ppl stem of *explorare*: see EXPLORE, -ATION.] †1 a (An) examination, (an) investigation. *obs.* exc. as in sense b. M16–L17. b *Med.* A close examination of a wound, organ, etc., esp. for diagnostic purposes, with or without surgery. M19. 2 The action or an act of exploring a country, place, etc. E19.

explorational *a.* E20.

explorative /ɪkˈsplɒrətɪv, ɛk-/ *a.* M18. [f. L *explorat-* (see prec.) + -IVE.] = EXPLORATORY.

exploratively *adv.* M19.

explorator /ˈɛkspləreɪtə/ *n.* LME. [L, f. as prec.: see -OR.] †1 A person employed to collect information; *esp.* a military scout, a spy. LME–L17. †2 A person who searches diligently. L16–L17. 3 = EXPLORER. M19.

exploratorium /ɪkˌsplɒrəˈtɔːrɪəm, ɛk-/ *n.* L20. [f. EXPLORAT(ION + -ORIUM.] A museum or similar centre at which visitors have the opportunity of actively participating by handling exhibits, performing prearranged experiments, etc.

exploratory /ɪkˈsplɒrət(ə)ri, ɛk-/ *a.* & *n.* LME. [L *exploratorius*, f. *explorat-*: see EXPLORATION, -ORY[2].] A *adj.* 1 Of or pertaining to exploration. LME. 2 Undertaken for purposes of exploration; built or used for such purposes. E17. b Of a surgical operation or procedure: performed in order to ascertain the nature of a disorder or the scope for treatment; diagnostic. M19. 3 Carrying out exploration, exploring. M19.

2 SOUTHEY Exploratory travels. *Offshore* Shell Oil Co. hit oil in an exploratory well.

B *n.* = EXPLORATORIUM. L20.

explore /ɪkˈsplɔː, ɛk-/ *v.* M16. [Fr. *explorer* f. L *explorare* search out, f. as EX-[1] I + *plorare* utter a cry.] 1 *v.t.* Investigate (a fact, a cause, *why*, etc.). M16. †b Search for; search out. E17–E19. 2 *v.t.* Examine, scrutinize; *esp.* examine (a country, area, building, etc.) by going through it. L16. b Examine by touch; probe (a wound). M18. 3 *v.i.* Go on an excursion or exploration (*to*). E19. 4 *v.i.* Conduct a search *for*. L19.

1 S. WEINBERG In the late 1940's a 'big bang' cosmological theory was being explored by George Gamow. **explore every avenue** investigate every possibility. 2 R. MACAULAY I went on exploring Jerusalem and the country round it. E. BOWEN Meggatt haunted her dressing-table, explored her cosmetics. **exploring coil** a flat coil of insulated wire connected to a galvanometer, used for finding the strength of a magnetic field from the current induced in the coil when it is quickly turned over or withdrawn. b A. J. CRONIN She leaned forward and with the forefinger of one hand lightly explored the contours of his face.

explorement *n.* (*rare*) exploration M17. **explorer** *n.* a person who explores; an apparatus or device for exploring: L17. **exploringly** *adv.* in an exploring manner M19.

explosion /ɪkˈspləʊʒ(ə)n, ɛk-/ *n.* E17. [L *explosio(n-)*, f. *explos-* pa. ppl stem of *explodere* EXPLODE: see -ION.] 1 The action or an act of forcing out or emitting something suddenly, esp. with violence and noise. E17. b *Phonet.* = PLOSION. M19. †2 The action of scorning or rejecting an opinion, proposal, etc. M17–L18. 3 The action or an act of bursting or flying into pieces with extreme violence and noise; the loud noise accompanying this. M18. b *Golf.* More fully *explosion shot*. A shot in which the ball is made to jump out of a bunker by striking the sand just behind the ball. E20. 4 A sudden outbreak or show of emotion. E19. 5 A sudden or rapid increase, esp. in size, numbers, or amount. M20.

1 C. DARWIN The sudden explosion of viscid matter. 3 N. MONSARRAT There was a shattering explosion as a bomb hit the water. 4 SIR W. SCOTT Elspat was prepared for the first explosion of her son's passion. 5 *Time* Latin America is in the midst of a 'population explosion'. M. KLINE The explosion of mathematical activity.

explosiˈbility *n.* liability to explode L19. **explosible** *a.* liable to explode L18.

explosive /ɪkˈspləʊsɪv, ɛk-/ *a.* & *n.* M17. [f. EXPLOS(ION + -IVE.] A *adj.* 1 Tending to force out with violence and noise. M17. 2 Forced out or produced by an explosion. M18. 3 Tending to explode or to cause an explosion. L18. 4 Of, or pertaining to, or of the nature of, an explosion. M19. 5 *Phonet.* = PLOSIVE *a.* M19.

1 W. B. CARPENTER An expulsion of the offending particle by an explosive cough. C. G. WILLIAMS The explosive force will be less than it should be. 2 **explosive bolt**: released by being blown out of position by an explosive charge. **explosive rivet**: containing an explosive charge by means of which it is fixed in place. 3 M. BARING His relations with his two sisters were perpetually strained and often violently explosive. *Economist* Markings for detonators and other explosive material. 4 T. H. HUXLEY They combine with explosive violence, if exposed to sunshine. A. C. BENSON 'Art' .. is .. a snappish, explosive word.

B *n.* 1 A substance that can be made to explode. L19. 2 *Phonet.* = PLOSIVE *n.* L19.

1 **high explosive** an explosive which detonates and is significantly more powerful than gunpowder, which merely burns rapidly.

explosively *adv.* E19. **explosiveness** *n.* E19.

Expo /ˈɛkspəʊ/ *n.* Also **e-**. Pl. **-os**. M20. [Abbrev. of EXPOSITION.] A large international exhibition.

expolitio /ɛkspəˈlɪtɪəʊ, -ˈlɪʃ-/ *n.* L16. [L, f. *expolit-* pa. ppl stem of *expolire* polish, embellish, f. as EX-[1] I + *polire* polish.] *Rhet.* A figure of speech in which something is expressed in several different ways in order to give a fuller illustration.

expone /ɪkˈspəʊn, ɛk-/ *v.t.* Long chiefly *Sc.* LME. [L *exponere*: see EXPOUND.] 1 Set forth in words, declare. LME. 2 Expound, explain, interpret. LME. †3 Expend (effort, money). L15–L16. †4 Expose *to* danger etc. M16–M17.

exponence /ɪkˈspəʊn(ə)ns, ɛk-/ *n.* L19. [f. next: see -ENCE.] 1 The function of an exponent. *rare*. L19. 2 *Ling.* The realization of a linguistic category or feature in speech or writing; the relation between categories etc. and exponents of them. M20.

Also **exponency** *n.* L19.

exponent /ɪkˈspəʊnənt, ɛk-/ *a.* & *n.* L16. [L *exponent-* pres. ppl stem of *exponere*: see EXPOUND, -ENT.] A *adj.* That expounds or interprets. L16.

B *n.* 1 A number or symbol indicating a particular power of a quantity, usu. written above and to the right of the symbol representing that quantity; the power so indicated. L17. 2 A person who or thing which expounds, interprets, or illustrates; *esp.* a person who exemplifies something in his or her action. Also, an advocate or a supporter *of* something. E19. 3 A person who or thing which stands as a type, symbol, or index *of* something. E19. 4 *Ling.* An instance or realization in speech or writing of a linguistic category or feature. M20.

1 M. KLINE Newton used .. fractional exponents, as in $x^{2/3}$. 2 A. C. BOULT He was the last great exponent of the rule that the right hand beats time while the left adds the expression. V. BROME A leading exponent of psychoanalysis. A. F. DOUGLAS-HOME If the exponents of snatch and grab were allowed to get away with their spoils. H. MACMILLAN Masses of statistics poured out by the eager exponents of Communist success. 3 H. MARTINEAU Price is the exponent of exchangeable value.

expoˈnentiate *v.* (*a*) *v.t.* (*Math.*) make an exponent in an exponentiation; (*b*) *v.i.* increase exponentially: L20. ˌ**exponentiˈation** *n.* (*Math.*) the operation of raising one quantity to the power of another E20.

exponential /ɛkspə(ʊ)ˈnɛnʃ(ə)l/ *a.* & *n.* E18. [Fr. *exponentiel*, f. as prec: see -IAL.] *Math.* A *adj.* (Of an equation or quantity) involving an independent variable as (part of) an exponent; represented by or pertaining to such an equation or quantity; *esp.* (of a process or phenomenon) proceeding with something multiplied by a constant factor in successive equal periods of time; increasingly rapid or steep. E18.

C. P. SNOW The income from Tolstoy's books rose in a steady exponential curve. J. ZIMAN The exponential growth of science. **exponential time** *Computing* the time required for a computer to solve a problem, where this time is an exponential function of the size of the input.

B *n.* An exponential quantity. L18.

exponentially *adv.* E20.

exponible /ɪkˈspəʊnɪb(ə)l, ɛk-/ *n.* & *a.* M16. [med.L *exponibilis*, f. *exponere*: see EXPOUND, -IBLE.] (Designating) a proposition that admits of or requires explanation.

export /ˈɛkspɔːt/ *n.* & *a.* L17. [f. the vb.] *Comm.* A *n.* 1 An article that is exported; usu. in *pl.*, (the amount or value of) exported goods. L17. 2 The action of exporting. E19.

1 N. BARBER Exports from Egypt shot up. *invisible exports*: see INVISIBLE *a.* 2 J. R. GREEN The export of arms to Spain.

Comb.: **export reject** an imperfect article withdrawn from export and sold on the home market; **export surplus** the amount by which a country's exports exceed its imports.

B *adj.* Designating an article of a (usu. high) quality suitable for exporting. L19.

H. CARMICHAEL A bottle of your export special.

export /ɪkˈspɔːt, ɛk-, ˈɛkspɔːt/ *v.* L15. [L *exportare*, f. as EX-[1] I + *portare* carry.] †1 *v.t.* Take away. L15–E18. 2 *v.t.* & *i.* Send (esp. goods) to another country. M17. 3 *v.t. Computing.* Transmit (data) from a system for use elsewhere. L20.

2 *fig.*: W. COWPER Hast thou .. Exported slavery to the conquered East?

exportaˈbility *n.* the quality of being exportable L19. **exportable** *a.* able to be exported E18. **exporter** *n.* L17.

exportation /ɛkspɔːˈteɪʃ(ə)n/ *n.* E17. [L *exportatio(n-)*, f. *exportat-* pa. ppl stem of *exportare*: see EXPORT *v.*, -ATION.] 1 The action or practice of exporting. E17. †2 a = EXPORT *n.* 1. Usu. in *pl.* M17. b Something carried out. *rare.* E19. 3 *Logic.* The principle that if two propositions together imply a third, then the first of them on its own implies that the second implies the third. E20.

expose /ɪkˈspəʊz, ɛk-/ *v.* LME. [(O)Fr. *exposer*, based on L *exponere* (see EXPOUND) but re-formed on L pa. pple *expositus* and (O)Fr. *poser*: see POSE *v.*[1]] 1 *v.t.* Lay open *to* something undesirable, as danger, ridicule, censure, etc.; subject *to* risk. LME. 2 *v.t.* Place in an unsheltered position; leave without protection; uncover; put (a plant) out in the open air. Formerly also, risk, imperil. LME. 3 *v.t.* Cause or allow to be seen; exhibit openly, display; disclose, reveal, show. LME. b *Eccl.* Exhibit (the Host, a relic) for adoration. M17. 4 *v.t.* Disclose (a secret, intention, etc.). Formerly (now *dial.*), explain, describe in detail. L15. 5 a *v.t.* Foll. by *to*: lay open to the action or influence of. L16. b In *pass.* Of something outdoors: be open *to* a particular quarter, be situated in a certain aspect. E18. c *v.t.* & *i.* Subject (a photographic film or plate) to light or the radiation to which it is sensitive. M19. 6 *v.t.* Offer for or *for* sale. Also foll. by *to*. Now chiefly *Sc.* E17. 7 *v.t.* Compel to be out of doors; *esp.* (*Hist.*) leave an infant to perish for want of shelter. E17. †8 *v.t.* Publish (a discourse); put (coin) in circulation. M17–M18. 9 *v.t.* Unmask, show up, (an error, impostor, etc.); hold up to ridicule or reprobation (a misdeed, a wrongdoer). L17. †b Hold up to ridicule (what is not a fault). L17–L18.

1 JOHN BROOKE On her western frontiers Hanover was exposed to attack from France. 2 C. MILNE Up here we are now a little more exposed. 3 B. JOWETT The dead are only to be exposed for three days. J. CONRAD Blunt had unbuttoned his .. jacket, exposing a lot of starched shirt-front. J. HAWKES A dreary expanse of blackened tree stumps exposed at low tide. **expose oneself** display one's body indecently in public. 5a A. DAVIS Once they had been exposed to the realities of the prison and judicial systems. 9 R. MACAULAY When I'm exposed I shall own up and admit it was a hoax. M. AMIS I didn't worry about the lies being exposed.

exposable *a.* M20. **exposal** *n.* the fact of exposing or of being exposed E17. **exposedness** *n.* the state or condition of being exposed E17. **exposer** *n.* E17.

exposé /ɪkˈspəʊzeɪ, ɛk-; *foreign* ɛkspoze (*pl.* same)/ *n.* Also ***expose**. E19. [Fr., pa. pple of *exposer*: see prec.] 1 An orderly statement of facts. E19. 2 A showing up or revelation of something discreditable. E19.

1 A. S. BYATT A reasoned exposé of alternative courses of action. 2 *New York Review of Books* The headline-making exposé of a nation's indifference to the Holocaust.

exposit /ɪk'spɒzɪt, ɛk-/ *v.t.* L19. [L *exposit-*: see EXPOSITOR.] Reveal, show; expound.

exposita /ɪk'spɒzɪtə, ɛk-/ *n.* Now *rare.* E19. [L, fem. sing. (sc. *propositio*) of *expositus* pa. pple of *exponere*: see EXPOUND, PROPOSITION *n.*] *Logic.* = CONVERTEND.

exposition /ɛkspə'zɪʃ(ə)n/ *n.* ME. [(O)Fr., or L *expositio(n-)*, f. *exposit-*: see EXPOSITOR, -ION.] 1 (An) interpretation, (an) explanation; an expository article or treatise, a commentary. ME. 2 The action or process of stating or describing, in speech or writing; a detailed statement or description. LME. b *Logic.* Formerly, any of various forms of argument. Now, the adducing of an empirically evident case in support of a general truth. L16. c *Mus.* The first main section of a movement in sonata form; the opening section of a fugue. M19. †3 The action or practice of exposing infants. L16–L19. 4 The action or an act of exposing to view, esp. (*Eccl.*) the Host or a relic. Formerly also, (an) exposure of a misdeed. M17. b An exhibition, a show, *esp.* a large or international one. M19. †5 = EXPOSURE 1b. L17–M19.

1 W. SPARROW The exposition of the Bible. R. P. GRAVES The lectures were .. scholarly expositions of the classical text. 2 J. MORLEY Clear exposition was the only thing needed to convert him to the theory.

expositional *a.* of the nature of an exposition, explanatory M19. **expositionally** *adv.* M20. **expositionary** *a.* inclined to exposition; expositional: L19.

expositive /ɪk'spɒzɪtɪv, ɛk-/ *a.* & *n.* L15. [f. EXPOSITION + -IVE.] A *adj.* Descriptive; explanatory; expository. L15. †B *n.* An exposition; an argument. L15–L17.

expositor /ɪk'spɒzɪtə, ɛk-/ *n.* ME. [(O)Fr. *expositeur* or late L *expositor*, f. L *exposit-* pa. ppl stem of *exponere*: see EXPOUND, -OR.] 1 A person who or book which explains or interprets something. ME. 2 A person who describes something in detail; a narrator. LME.

expository /ɪk'spɒzɪt(ə)ri, ɛk-/ *n.* & *a.* LME. [Late L *expositorius*, f. L *exposit-*: see prec., -ORY[2].] A *n.* A book which explains or interprets, *esp.* a written commentary. LME. B *adj.* Of or pertaining to exposition; of the nature of or containing an exposition, explanatory. L16.

expositorily *adv.* M17.

ex post /ɛks 'pəʊst/ *a.* & *adv. phr.* M20. [mod.L, f. as EX *prep.* + L *post* after.] Chiefly *Econ.* A *adj. phr.* Based on past events or actual results; occurring afterwards; actual rather than predicted; retrospective. M20. B *adv. phr.* After the event; retrospectively. M20.

ex post facto /ɛks pəʊst 'faktəʊ/ *adv.* & *a. phr.* M17. [Erron. division of L *ex postfacto* in the light of subsequent events, f. *ex* from, out of + abl. of *postfactum* that which is done subsequently.] A *adv. phr.* After the event, after the fact; retrospectively. M17. B *adj. phr.* Done after another thing; *esp.* (of a law) applied retrospectively. L18.

expostulant /ɪk'spɒstjʊlənt, ɛk-/ *a.* L19. [L *expostulant-* pres. ppl stem of *expostulare*: see next, -ANT[1].] Expostulating.

expostulate /ɪk'spɒstjʊleɪt, ɛk-/ *v.* M16. [L *expostulat-* pa. ppl stem of *expostulare*, f. EX-[1] 1 + *postulare* demand.] †1 *v.t.* Ask for; demand; ask *how* or *why.* M16–L17. †2 *v.i.* State a complaint. Only in M16. †3 *v.i.* Discourse. L16–L18. 4 *v.i.* Talk earnestly in order to protest at a person's action or to dissuade him or her. (Foll. by *with* the person, *about*, *on*, etc., a subject.) L16. 5 *v.t.* †a Complain of (a grievance); remonstrate about (a matter) *with* someone. L16–E18. †b Debate (a matter), esp. as an aggrieved person. L16–L18. c Say in expostulation. Now only w. spoken wds as obj.: say as an expostulation. L16.

4 D. H. LAWRENCE Connie expostulated roundly, and was angry with both of them. W. GOLDING I began to expostulate at the wasted time. H. KISSINGER Semenov .. started expostulating on the dangers of accidental or unauthorized missile launches. 5c V. WOOLF 'Tut-tut-tut,' Mrs Lynn-Jones expostulated.

expostulative *a.* that expostulates M19. **expostulatively** *adv.* in an expostulating manner L19. **expostulator** *n.* E18. **expostulatory** *a.* characterized by or of the nature of expostulation L16.

expostulation /ɪkˌspɒstjʊ'leɪʃ(ə)n, ɛk-/ *n.* M16. [L *expostulatio(n-)*, f. as prec.: see -ATION.] 1 The action or an act of expostulating. M16. 2 A spoken remonstrance, protest, or reproof. L16.

†**exposture** *n. rare* (Shakes.). Only in E17. [f. EXPOSE after *posture* etc.] = EXPOSURE 1.

exposure /ɪk'spəʊʒə, ɛk-/ *n.* E17. [f. EXPOSE + -URE.] 1 The action of exposing; the fact or state of being exposed; *esp.* (*a*) the fact of being without shelter or protection from bad weather; (*b*) the unmasking of a wrongdoer. (Foll. by *to.*) E17. b The way in which something is situated in relation to compass direction, wind, sunshine, etc. M17. c A surface laid open to view, or to the operation of some agency. L19. 2 The action or an act of subjecting a photographic film or plate to light etc.; the length of time for which it is exposed; the combination of shutter speed and aperture; each of the sections of a film which can be or have been separately exposed. M19. 3 The extent to which an insurance company is at risk from any particular contingency; orig. *spec.* (the risk of) the spread of fire from one property to another. M19. b *Comm.* The financial commitment of a bank or other company in any particular country, activity, or asset; the risk associated with this. L20. 4 *Mountaineering.* The openness or insecurity of a climber's position; the climber's awareness of this. M20. 5 The condition of being brought to the attention of the public; publicity achieved through broadcasting or advertising. M20. 6 Experience, esp. of a specified kind of work. M20.

1 *Nature* Exposure to cigarette smoke during pregnancy. J. B. MORTON Hands that are .. red from exposure to sun and rain. B. BETTELHEIM Prisoners died .. as a result of exposure on the parade grounds. **indecent exposure** the intentional act of publicly displaying one's body in an indecent manner. b M. MCCARTHY The back windows .. had a southern exposure. c *Scientific American* Fossiliferous exposures of middle Devonian rocks. 2 *Photographer* It takes .. 36 exposure 35mm films. *double exposure*: see DOUBLE *a.* & *adv.* *multiple exposure*: see MULTIPLE *a.* 6 *City Limits* At Lewisham theatre children are getting exposure to the Thespian arts.

Comb.: **exposure meter** *Photogr.*: for measuring illumination and giving the exposure to use with a given film etc.

expound /ɪk'spaʊnd, ɛk-/ *v.* ME. [OFr. *espondre* f. L *exponere* expose, publish, exhibit, explain, f. as EX-[1] 1 + *ponere* to place.] 1 *v.t.* & *i.* Explain (what is difficult or obscure); comment on (a text or author); *esp.* comment on or interpret (a religious text). ME. b *v.t.* Give the significance or meaning of (a dream, symbol, riddle, etc.). *arch.* LME. †c *v.t.* Give the meaning of (a word or name), translate. LME–M17. †d *v.t.* Interpret the motives of (a person). Only in 17. †e *refl.* Explain one's meaning. E–M17. 2 *v.t.* Set out, declare, state in detail, (esp. a doctrine, opinion, idea, etc.). LME. b *Math.* Express in figures or symbols. Now *rare.* E18. 3 *v.t.* †a Foll. by *concerning*, *of*: explain (a statement) as referring to. LME–E18. b Now chiefly *Law.* Give a particular interpretation to, interpret in a particular way. M16. †c Translate (in a specified way). M16–E17.

1 E. ROOSEVELT He expounded at length the philosophy of Thomas Aquinas. 2 R. HAYMAN The doctor gave lectures expounding his theories.

expoundable *a.* L19. **expounder** *n.* LME.

†**express** *n.*[1] E16. [f. EXPRESS *v.*[1]] 1 A graphic representation, an image; *fig.* a type, a model. E16–M17. 2 The action or an act of expressing or representing by words, signs, or actions; expression. M17–E18. 3 A condition or product in which something is expressed; a manifestation. M17–M19. 4 A mode of speech, a phrase; an utterance. M–L17. b A specific mention, statement, or injunction. M–L17.

express /ɪk'sprɛs, ɛk-; *as attrib. adj. also* 'ɛksprɛs/ *a.*, *adv.*, & *n.*[2] LME. [(O)Fr. *exprès* f. L *expressus* distinctly or manifestly presented, pa. pple of *exprimere* (cf. EXPRESS *v.*[1]).] A *adj.* I†1 Stated, explicitly recorded. LME–L17. 2 Definitely stated and not merely implied; definitely formulated; explicit; unmistakable in import. LME. †b Outspoken; free from vacillation. L16–L18. 3 Specially designed for a particular object; done, made, or sent for a special purpose. LME. 4 Operating at high speed; designed for such operation; very fast. (Earliest in *express train* below; orig. so called as serving a particular destination.) M19.

2 H. MARTINEAU Mr. Stanley's answer was express and clear. E. CALDWELL Evelyn Summerall had planned the cocktail party for the express purpose of having them meet. b HENRY MORE I love to feel myself of an express and settled judgment. 3 J. MORLEY The social union is the express creation .. of the Deity. 4 DICKENS Going about the country at express pace. E. BOWEN Matchett is sending Anna's white velvet dress to the express cleaners.

II 5 Of an image, form, etc.: truly depicting the original, exact. *arch.* E16.

Special collocations: **express delivery** a system for the immediate postal delivery of an item. **express lift**: which does not stop at every floor. **express messenger** a messenger specially dispatched; *spec.* one employed to convey items sent by express delivery. **express rifle**: discharging the bullet at high speed. **express train** a train running to a particular destination and stopping at few intermediate stations; a fast train.

B *adv.* †1 Clearly, plainly, unmistakably; in distinct terms, positively. LME–E18. †2 Directly *against*; exactly; completely. LME–L16. 3 Specially, on purpose, for a particular end; at high speed; by express messenger or train. LME.

3 J. R. LOWELL A piece of news worth sending express.

C *n.* 1 a An express messenger. Freq. in titles of newspapers. E17. b A message sent by an express messenger, a dispatch. M17. 2 A company undertaking the transport of parcels, money, etc., more rapidly and securely than routine freight; items so sent. Chiefly *US.* M19. 3 a An express train. M19. b An express rifle. L19.

2 OED The books will be sent by express. attrib.: *express clerk, company, office, wagon*, etc. *pony express*: see PONY *n.* 3a *Orient Express*: see ORIENT *n.*

Comb.: **expressman** *US* a man employed in transmitting parcels etc., esp. as an employee of an express company.

expressage *n.* (*US*) (the charge for) the sending of a parcel etc. by express M19. **expressness** *n.* M17.

express /ɪk'sprɛs, ɛk-/ *v.*[1] LME. [OFr. *expresser* f. Proto-Romance, f. L EX-[1] 1 + *pressare* PRESS *v.*[1]: repr. in use L *exprimere.*] I Press out. 1 *v.t.* Get by pressing, squeezing, or wringing; *fig.* extort or elicit by pressure. Formerly also, expel or get rid of by force. (Foll. by *from*, *out of.*) LME. b *v.t.* & *i.* *spec.* Squeeze out (milk etc.) from the breast. M20. 2 *v.t.* Emit or exude as if by pressure. *arch.* E17. 3 *v.t.* Press or squeeze out the contents of. Now *rare.* M17.

II Portray, represent. 4 *v.t.* Orig., represent by sculpture, drawing, or painting; portray, depict. Now only, convey a notion of (a fact, characteristic, etc.) in a drawing etc. LME. †b Be an image or likeness of; resemble. L15–L17. 5 *v.t.* Represent in language; put into words; give utterance to (a feeling, an intention). LME. b Of a word, phrase, or statement: represent (a thought, sentiment, or state of affairs); denote, mean, signify. E16. †6 *v.t.* Mention, specify; give an account of, describe; describe as. LME–L18. b *v.i.* Make mention, give an account, *of.* LME–E16. 7 *v.t.* Represent by a symbol or symbols, symbolize; *Math.* represent (a number, relation, property, etc.) by a figure, symbol, or formula, esp. (a quantity) *in terms of* another. LME. 8 *v.t.* Manifest by external signs, betoken, (esp. a personal feeling or quality). LME. 9 *v.t.* State or mention explicitly. L16. 10 *v.t.* *Genetics.* Cause (an inherited characteristic or component, a gene) to appear in a phenotype. Usu. in *pass.* E20.

4 HOR. WALPOLE Loggan used long strokes in expressing flesh. b DRYDEN Kids and Whelps their Sires and Dams express. 5 *Law Reports* The lease correctly expressed the bargain between the parties. N. SHUTE He expressed his thanks for all that they had done. J. CONRAD What he seemed mostly concerned for was the 'stride forward', as he expressed it. **express oneself** say what one means or thinks (*on* a subject, *well*, *aptly*, etc.). b S. BUTLER No words can express too strongly the caution which should be used. J. L. AUSTIN Sentences expressing commands or wishes. 6 T. HEYWOOD Heardsman, thou hast exprest a monstrous beast. J. YORKE M. Milles in his Catalogue never expresseth him. W. COWPER I would express him simple, grave, sincere. 7 E. STILLINGFLEET A Child to express coming into the world, an old man for going out of it. 8 J. AUSTEN Never did tone express indifference plainer. M. GIROUARD The interior of each house expressed the artistic personality of its owners. 9 G. BERKELEY Hints and allusions, expressing little, insinuating much.

expressedly /-sɪdli/ *adv.* avowedly; explicitly, expressly: M16. **expresser** *n.* (*a*) a person who or thing which expresses; (*b*) a person with great powers of expression: L16. **expressible** *a.* E17. **expressor** *n.* = EXPRESSER E17.

express /ɪk'sprɛs, ɛk-/ *v.*²*t.* Orig. *US.* E18. [f. EXPRESS *n.*²] Send by express delivery or an express messenger.

expression /ɪk'sprɛʃ(ə)n, ɛk-/ *n.* LME. [(O)Fr. or L *expressio(n-)*, f. *express-* pa. ppl stem of *exprimere* (cf. EXPRESS *v.*¹): see -ION.] 1 The action or an act of pressing or squeezing out. LME. †b Something obtained in this way. Only in 17. 2 The action of expressing something in words or symbols; the utterance of feelings, intentions, etc.; manifestation of a feeling or quality by an external sign or token. Formerly also, explicit mention, description. LME. 3 A spoken utterance, a written declaration; an action, state, or fact whereby some feeling, quality, etc., is manifested or symbolized; a sign, a token. Now only foll. by *of*. E17. 4 Manner or means of expressing in language; wording, diction. E17. b A word, a phrase, a form of speech. M17. c *Math.* A collection of symbols that jointly express a quantity. L18. 5 In painting, sculpture, etc., the mode of expressing character, sentiment, action, etc. E18. b *Mus.* Manner of performance that expresses the feeling of a passage. L18. 6 Capacity of the face, voice, or attitude for expressing feeling or character; the appearance of the face, or the intonation of the voice, as indicating a person's feelings. L18. 7 *Genetics.* The appearance in a phenotype of a character or effect attributed to a particular gene; the manner or degree of this; the process by which possession of a gene leads to the appearance in the phenotype of the corresponding character. E20.

2 TENNYSON Adeline . . beyond expression fair. J. A. FROUDE To encourage the fullest expression of public feeling. M. TIPPETT He uses words as discourses and reserves the expression of artistic emotion for tone. *free expression*: see FREE *a.* 3 J. GILBERT The death of Christ was the expression of Divine love. B. JOWETT Your words . . are the very expression of my own feelings. 4 GEO. ELIOT He had not a great range of expression. b J. A. FROUDE Ambiguous expressions were explained away when challenged. B. PYM She was still 'under the doctor', as the expression was. D. LODGE She was brainwashed, if you'll pardon the expression. c A. S. EDDINGTON Simplifying the algebraic expressions. 5 J. RUSKIN Masterpieces of expression. b M. E. BRADDON She played with brilliancy, and . . with expression. 6 J. MOORE There is more expression in the countenances of French women. DICKENS 'Can't I!' said Abbey, with infinite expression. M. FRAYN A quiet level voice without expression of any sort. A. SILLITOE An expression of anger spread over his face. R. WARNER He looked at me with a doubtful and cunning expression in his . . eyes. 7 R. R. GATES Families can differ greatly in the degree of expression of polydactyly.

Comb.: **expression-mark** *Mus.* a sign or word indicating the expression required of a performer; **expression-stop** *Mus.* a stop in a harmonium allowing expression by means of varied air pressure.

expressional *a.* E19.

expressionism /ɪk'sprɛʃ(ə)nɪz(ə)m, ɛk-/ *n.* Also **E-**. E20. [f. prec. + -ISM.] A style of painting, drama, music, etc., expressing the inner experience of the artist rather than impressions of the physical world.

expressionist *a.* & *n.* (*a*) *adj.* practising expressionism; expressionistic; (*b*) *n.* an expressionist artist: M19. **expressio'nistic** *a.* of or produced by expressionists; characterized by expressionism: E20. **expressio'nistically** *adv.* E20.

expressionless /ɪk'sprɛʃ(ə)nlɪs, ɛk-/ *a.* E19. [f. as prec. + -LESS.] 1 That is not expressed. *rare.* E19. 2 Lacking expression. M19.

2 H. KINGSLEY A small man, with an impenetrable, expressionless face.

expressionlessly *adv.* L19. **expressionlessness** *n.* M19.

expressive /ɪk'sprɛsɪv, ɛk-/ *a.* LME. [Fr. *expressif*, *-ive* or med.L *expressivus*, f. L *express-*: see EXPRESSION, -IVE.] †1 Tending to press out or expel. *rare.* Only in LME. 2 Of, pertaining to, or concerned with expression; having the function of expressing. L15. 3 Full of expression, characterized by expression; (of a word, gesture, etc.) expressing its meaning with striking force, significant. Formerly also (of a statement), explicit. E17. 4 Of a person: open or emphatic in expressing opinions, feelings, etc. (Foll. by *of*.) *rare.* E17. †5 Expressing itself in action; tending to outward manifestation. E17–M18. 6 Serving to express, indicate, or represent. Foll. by *of*. L17.

2 J. JASTROW The receptive powers are in advance of the expressive ones. 3 R. W. CHURCH His Latin . . is singularly forcible and expressive. J. B. PRIESTLEY The instant look of horror on his expressive face. 4 C. LAMB We felt as we had been not enough expressive of our pleasure. 6 S. WILLIAMS Tables expressive of this diurnal variation. M. EDGEWORTH An air of dignity which seemed expressive of conscious innocence.

expressively *adv.* L15. **expressiveness** *n.* M17. **expre'ssivity** *n.* (*a*) *Genetics* the kind or degree of phenotypic expression of a gene; (*b*) the quality of being expressive: M20.

expressless /ɪk'sprɛslɪs, ɛk-/ *a. arch.* L16. [f. EXPRESS *a.* + -LESS.] That cannot be expressed; inexpressible.

expressly /ɪk'sprɛsli, ɛk-/ *adv.* LME. [f. EXPRESS *a.* + -LY².] 1 Distinctly, positively; in plain terms, explicitly. Formerly also, in full detail; with distinct enunciation. LME. †2 Avowedly, directly. LME–L17. 3 For the express purpose; on purpose. E17.

1 P. USTINOV Peasants were expressly forbidden to leave the estates. 3 J. BUCHAN Leithen . . has come here expressly to save the lady.

expresso *n.* var. of ESPRESSO.

†**expressure** *n.* LME. [f. L *express-* (see EXPRESSION) + -URE. Cf. L *pressura* pressure.] 1 Something which serves to press out or expel. *rare.* Only in LME. 2 An image, a picture. *rare* (Shakes.). Only in L16. 3 Expression by words or signs; manifestation, description. E17–M18. 4 The action of pressing or squeezing out; pressure. M17–M19.

expressway /ɪk'sprɛsweɪ, ɛk-/ *n. N. Amer.* & *Austral.* M20. [f. EXPRESS *a.* + WAY *n.*] A motorway through or bypassing a city.

†**exprobrate** *v.t.* Also **-bate**. M16. [L *exprobrat-* pa. ppl stem of *exprobrare*, f. as EX-¹ 1 + *probrum* shameful deed: see -ATE³.] 1 Make (something) a subject of reproach. M16–M17. 2 Reproach (a person). M–L17. 3 Reprobate, censure. Only in M19.

exprobration /ɛksprə'breɪʃ(ə)n/ *n.* Now *rare* or *obs.* LME. [L *exprobratio(n-)*, f. *exprobrat-*: see prec., -ATION.] †1 The action or an act of upbraiding or speaking reproachfully. LME–M19. 2 A reproachful utterance; reproachful language. M16. †3 Something which acts as a reproach. Only in L17.

ex professo /ɛks prə'fɛsəʊ/ *adv. phr.* L16. [L f. as EX *prep.* + abl. of *professus*: see PROFESS.] By profession; professedly.

expromission /ɛksprə'mɪʃ(ə)n/ *n.* Now *Hist.* E19. [mod.L *expromissio(n-)*, f. L *expromiss-*: see next, -ION.] A legal arrangement in which a creditor allowed a third party to assume responsibility for a debt in place of the original debtor.

expromissor /ɛksprə'mɪsə/ *n.* Now *Hist.* L17. [Late L, f. L *expromiss-* pa. ppl stem of *expromittere* promise or agree to pay, f. as EX-¹ + *promittere*: see PROMISE *n.*, -OR.] A person who agreed to pay; *esp.* one who took the place of a debtor in a case of expromission.

†**expropriate** *a. rare.* Only in LME. [med.L *expropriatus* pa. pple of *expropriare*: see next, -ATE².] Expropriated; *spec.* debarred from owning property.

expropriate /ɪks'prəʊprɪeɪt, ɛks-/ *v.t.* Pa. pple **-ated**, †**-ate**. L16. [med.L *expropriat-* pa. ppl stem of *expropriare*, f. as EX-¹ 1 + PROPRIUM property: see -ATE³.] 1 Take out of the owner's hands, esp. for one's own use: *spec.* (of a public authority) take away (land) for public use or benefit. L16. 2 Dispossess (a person) of ownership; deprive of property. (Foll. by *from*.) E17. †3 Renounce control of; give up *to*. M17–L18.

1 F. FITZGERALD The French had simply expropriated the village land to build their own farms. W. GOLDING A Royal Decree expropriated the land. 2 M. B. BROWN The need of industrial capitalism for expropriated labourers.

expropriator *n.* M19.

expropriation /ɪks,prəʊprɪ'eɪʃ(ə)n, ɛks-/ *n.* LME. [Orig. f. med.L *expropriatio(n-)*, f. *expropriat-* (see prec.); in mod. use directly f. prec.: see -ATION.] †1 Renunciation (*of*). LME–M17. 2 The action or an act of expropriating. M19.

ex proprio motu /ɛks ,prəʊprɪəʊ 'məʊtuː, ,prɒ-/ *adv. phr.* L17. [Late L = by own motion.] = MOTU PROPRIO; *spec.* in *Law*, by decision of a court without anyone's application.

†**expugn** *v.t.* LME. [OFr. *expugner* or L *expugnare* take by storm, f. as EX-¹ 1 + *pugnare* to fight.] 1 Capture by fighting; take by storm; assault, attack, storm. LME–M17. 2 Overcome or expel by force of arms; conquer, overpower. LME–E18.

†**expugnable** *a.* L16–L18. [OFr. f. L *expugnabilis*, f. *expugnare*: see prec., -ABLE.] Able to be captured or conquered.

†**expugnatory** *a.* E17–M18. [L *expugnatorius* conquering, f. *expugnat-* pa. ppl stem of *expugnare*: see EXPUGN, -ORY².] Adapted for attack, offensive.

expulsatory /ɪk'spʌlsət(ə)ri, ɛk-/ *a.* L16. [f. L *expulsat-* pa. ppl stem of *expulsare*: see next, -ORY².] = EXPULSIVE 1.

expulse /ɪk'spʌls, ɛk-/ *v.t.* LME. [L *expulsare* frequent. of *expellere* EXPEL.] Drive out, esp. with force, (*lit.* & *fig.*); eject, expel; evict.

expulser *n.* (now *rare*) M16.

expulsion /ɪk'spʌlʃ(ə)n, ɛk-/ *n.* LME. [L *expulsio(n-)*, f. *expuls-* pa. ppl stem of *expellere* EXPEL: see -ION.] The action or an act of expelling; the fact or condition of being expelled.

expulsionist *n.* a person who supports or advocates the expulsion of someone L19.

expulsive /ɪk'spʌlsɪv, ɛk-/ *a.* LME. [(O)Fr. *expulsif*, *-ive* f. late L *expulsivus*, f. *expuls-*: see prec., -IVE.] 1 Tending or having the power to expel, esp. from the body. LME. †2 Tending to repel. E–M17.

expulsory /ɪk'spʌls(ə)ri, ɛk-/ *a. rare.* LME. [med.L *expulsorius*, f. L *expulsor* expeller, f. *expuls-*: see EXPULSION, -OR, -ORY².] Of or pertaining to expulsion; expulsive.

expunct /ɪk'spʌŋkt, ɛk-/ *v.t.* L16. [L *expunct-* pa. ppl stem of *expungere* EXPUNGE.] Expunge, erase.

expunction /ɪk'spʌŋkʃ(ə)n, ɛk-/ *n.* E17. [L *expunctio(n-)*, f. as prec.: see -ION.] 1 The action of expunging; erasure. E17. b *Palaeogr.* The indication of an erasure or cancellation to be made in a manuscript by means of dots placed beneath the relevant letter or letters. M20. †2 A wiping out, a removal. E–M17.

expunctuation /ɛk,spʌŋktjʊ'eɪʃ(ə)n/ *n.* M20. [Blend of EXPUNCTION and PUNCTUATION.] = EXPUNCTION 1b.

expunge /ɪk'spʌndʒ, ɛk-/ *v.t.* E17. [L *expungere* mark for deletion by points set above or below, f. as EX-¹ 1 + *pungere* to prick.] 1 Strike out, erase, omit, (a name or word) from a list, (a phrase or passage) from a text. E17. 2 *fig.* Wipe out, efface; annihilate, destroy; annul; put an end to. E17. 3 Get rid of, remove. E17.

2 E. F. BENSON Certain moments she wanted to expunge completely from his mind. Y. MENUHIN A culture cannot be expunged from the face of the earth by political directive. 3 H. E. MANNING To expunge God from Science.

expunger *n.* E17.

expurgate /ˈɛkspəːgeɪt/ *v.* E17. [L *expurgat-* pa. ppl stem of *expurgare*, f. as EX-¹ 1 + *purgare*: see PURGE *v.*, -ATE³.] †1 *v.t.* Purge or cleanse (the body etc.) of excremental material. E-M17. 2 *v.t.* & *i.* Remove from (a book) passages regarded as objectionable. L17.

expurgator *n.* a person who expurgates M17. **ex,purga'torial** *a.* (*a*) of or pertaining to an expurgator; (*b*) tending to expurgate or purge: E19. **expurgatory** /ɪkˈspəːgət(ə)ri, ɛk-/ *a.* of or pertaining to expurgation; tending to expurgate or purge; *Expurgatory Index*: see INDEX *n.* 6b: M17.

expurgation /ɛkspəːˈgeɪʃ(ə)n/ *n.* LME. [Partly f. L *expurgatio(n-)* in med.L sense of 'cleansing, freeing from impurities', f. as prec.; partly f. prec.: see -ATION.] †1 The action or an act of cleansing from impurity (*lit.* & *fig.*). LME-M17. 2 The action or an act of removing impurities or objectionable elements. L16. 3 *spec.* The action or an act of removing from a book passages regarded as objectionable. E17. †4 *Astron.* The reappearance of the sun after an eclipse; emersion. M18-M19.

expurge /ɪkˈspəːdʒ, ɛk-/ *v.t.* Now *rare.* L15. [Fr. *expurger* alt. of OFr. *espurger* f. L *expurgare* EXPURGATE.] 1 Cleanse, purify, (*from*, *of*). L15. 2 Remove (something offensive, excremental material). M16. b Expunge from a book. M17. 3 = EXPURGATE 2. M17.

exquisite /ˈɛkskwɪzɪt, ɪkˈskwɪzɪt, ɛk-/ *a.*, *adv.*, & *n.* LME. [L *exquisitus* pa. pple of *exquirere* search out, f. as EX-¹ 1 + *quaerere* search, seek.] A *adj.* †1 Carefully ascertained or adjusted; accurate, exact; careful, precise. LME-M18. b Of a specified disease; accurately so named; typical, genuine. Only in 17. †2a Of language, expression, or terms: carefully or aptly chosen; uncommon; affected, overlaboured. L15-L17. †b Of an expedient, explanation, or reason: ingeniously devised, far-fetched. Of studies: abstruse. L15-M17. c Of food and drink: carefully chosen; choice; dainty, delicious. Now *rare* or *obs.* exc. as passing into sense 5. M16. 3 Elaborately devised or carried out, highly finished; carried to a high degree of perfection or completeness. *obs.* (merged in sense 5). M16. b Of a quality, disposition, or habit: cultivated to a high degree of intensity; consummate, extreme. M16. †4 Of a person: accomplished in a particular field; excellent, perfect. (Foll. by *at*, *in*, *to do*.) M16-E19. 5 Of such consummate excellence, beauty, or perfection as to excite intense delight or admiration; of great delicacy or beauty. L16. 6 Of pain, pleasure, etc.: intense, acute; keenly felt. M17. 7 Of the power of (mental or physical) feeling, the senses, etc.: keenly sensitive to impressions; acutely susceptible to pain, pleasure, etc.; delicate, finely-strung. M17.

1 MILTON Be not over exquisite To cast the fashion of uncertain evils. 2b SHAKES. *Twel. N.* I have no exquisite reason for't, but I have reason good enough. G. HAVERS The English . . well understand all the most exquisite points of Navigation. 3 W. CAVE Put to death with the most exquisite arts of torture. J. STRYPE Wherein he hath done such exquisite service to the Protestant cause. b JAS. MILL The exquisite ignorance and stupidity of the Mysoreans in the art of war. 4 B. FRANKLIN A most exquisite mechanic. 5 P. H. GIBBS The rose garden showed some exquisite blooms. *Times* Armed robbery, planned with exquisite skill by intelligent, determined men. 7 LD MACAULAY He had an exquisite ear, and performed skilfully on the flute.

B *adv.* Exquisitely. Now *rare.* E16.

C *n.* A person (esp. a man) who is overnice in dress etc.; a fop, a dandy. E19.

exquisitely *adv.* LME. **exquisiteness** *n.* M16. **exquisitism** *n.* (*a*) foppishness, dandyism; (*b*) *rare* overprecision: M19. **ex'quisitively** *adv.* (*rare*) exquisitely M17.

ex rel. /ɛks ˈrɛl/ *prep. phr.* M19. [Abbrev.] = next.

ex relatione /ɛks rɪˌleɪʃɪˈəʊni/ *prep. phr.* E17. [L.] *Law.* By relation of; according to the report of, as reported by.

exsangueous *a.* var. of EXSANGUIOUS.

exsanguinate /ɪkˈsaŋgwɪneɪt, ɛk-/ *v.t.* M19. [L *exsanguinatus* drained of blood, f. as EX-¹ 2 + *sanguin-*, *-guis* blood: see -ATE³.] Drain of blood.

exsangui'nation *n.* the action of exsanguinating; severe loss of blood: E20.

exsanguine /ɪkˈsaŋgwɪn, ɛk-/ *a.* Also †**exang-**. M17. [f. EX-¹ 2 + SANGUINE *a.*, after L *exsanguis* bloodless: see next, -INE¹.] Bloodless; without sufficient blood, anaemic; *fig.* lacking vigour or substance.

exsan'guineous *a.* (*obs.* exc. *Hist.*) bloodless M17.

exsanguious /ɪkˈsaŋgwɪəs, ɛk-/ *a.* Also **-eous.** M17. [f. L *exsanguis* bloodless, f. as EX-¹ 2 + *sanguis* blood: see -IOUS, -EOUS.] = EXSANGUINE.

exscind /ɪkˈsɪnd, ɛk-/ *v.t.* M17. [L *exscindere* cut out, f. as EX-¹ 1 + *scindere* to cut.] Cut out, excise, (*lit.* & *fig.*). Formerly also, destroy (a nation).

exscribe /ɪkˈskrʌɪb, ɛk-/ *v.t.* E17. [L *exscribere*, f. as EX-¹ 1 + *scribere* write.] †1 Copy or write out, transcribe. E17-E18. 2 *Geom.* Draw (a circle) outside a triangle so that it touches one side and the lines obtained by producing the other two sides. L19.

†**exsculp** *v.t. rare.* L16-M18. [L *exsculpere*, f. as EX-¹ 1 + *sculpere* cut, carve.] Cut out, hollow out by cutting.

exsect /ɪkˈsɛkt, ɛk-/ *v.t.* M17. [L *exsect-* pa. ppl stem of *exsecare* cut out, f. as EX-¹ 1 + *secare* to cut.] Cut out (*lit.* & *fig.*), remove (as) by cutting.

exsection /ɪkˈsɛkʃ(ə)n/ *n.* E17. [L *exsectio(n-)*, f. as prec.: see -ION.] Chiefly *Surg.* The action or an act of cutting out or away; (an) excision.

exsert /ɪkˈsəːt, ɛk-/ *v.t.* M17. [f. as EXERT.] †1 = EXERT 4. Only in M17. 2 *Biol.* Push out; cause to protrude. E19.

exsertion *n.* (*rare*) the action of exserting; the state or fact of being exserted: L19.

exsertile /ɪkˈsəːtɪl, ɛk-/ *a.* E19. [Fr., f. *exsert* exserted f. L *ex(s)ertus* pa. pple of *ex(s)erere*: see EXERT, -ILE.] *Biol.* Able to be exserted.

ex-service /ɛk(s)ˈsəːvɪs/ *a.* Also **-services** /-ˈsəːvɪsɪz/. E20. [f. EX-¹ 3 + SERVICE *n.*¹] Having belonged to one of the fighting services; pertaining to former servicemen or servicewomen.

Special collocations & comb.: **ex-serviceman** a former serviceman. **ex-servicewoman** a former servicewoman.

exsibilate /ɪkˈsɪbɪleɪt, ɛk-/ *v.t.* Long *rare* or *obs.* E17. [L *exsibilat-* pa. ppl stem of *exsibilare*, f. as EX-¹ 1 + *sibilare* hiss: see -ATE³.] Hiss off the stage; dismiss ignominiously.

,exsibi'lation *n.* M17.

exsiccate /ˈɛksɪkeɪt/ *v.t.* Pa. pple **-ated**, †**-ate**. LME. [L *exsiccat-* pa. ppl stem of *exsiccare*, f. as EX-¹ 1 + *siccare*, f. *siccus* dry: see -ATE³.] Make dry; remove moisture from; drain of all water.

exsiccation /ɛksɪˈkeɪʃ(ə)n/ *n.* LME. [L *exsiccatio(n-)*, f. as prec.: see -ATION.] The action of drying or draining; complete removal or absence of moisture.

exsiccative /ˈɛksɪkeɪtɪv, ɪkˈsɪkətɪv, ɛkˈsɪ-/ *a.* & *n.* Now *rare* or *obs.* LME. [med.L *exsiccativus*, f. as EXSICCATE: see -ATIVE.] (A medicine or other substance) having the power of making dry.

ex silentio /ɛks sɪˈlɛntɪəʊ, -ˈlɛnʃ-/ *adv. phr.* E20. [L = from silence.] By or from a lack of evidence to the contrary.

New York Review of Books Historians do not ordinarily go for the argument *ex silentio.*

exsolution /ɛksəˈluːʃ(ə)n/ *n.* E20. [f. EX-¹ 1 + SOLUTION.] *Geol.* The process by which a homogeneous solution, esp. a solid solution, separates into two or more distinct phases; the action or an act of passing out of solution.

ex'solve *v.t.* & *i.* (cause to) separate out from or be removed from a solution M20.

exspuition /ɛkspjʊˈɪʃ(ə)n/ *n.* M17. [L *exspuitio(n-)*, f. *exspuere*, f. as EX-¹ 1 + *spuere* to spit: see -ITION.] The action of spitting out; spittle.

†**exstacy, -sy** *n.* & *v.* vars. of ECSTASY.

†**exstatic** *a.* & *n.* var. of ECSTATIC.

†**exstillation** *n.* var. of EXTILLATION.

exstipulate /ɪkˈstɪpjʊlət, ɛk-/ *a.* E19. [f. EX-¹ 2 + STIPULA, STIPULE: see -ATE².] *Bot.* Lacking stipules.

exstrophy /ˈɛkstrəfi/ *n.* M19. [f. EX-² + Gk *stroph-* (see STROPHE) + -Y³.] *Med.* A congenital defect in which the wall of a hollow organ such as the bladder communicates with the exterior.

†**exstruct** *v.t.* Also **extruct**. M16-M18. [L *exstruct-* pa. ppl stem of *exstruere*, f. as EX-¹ 1 + *struere* build.] Build or pile up.

exsuccous /ɪkˈsʌkəs, ɛk-/ *a.* Now *rare.* M17. [L *exsuccus* without juice, f. as EX-¹ 2 + *succus* juice: see -OUS.] Lacking juice, sapless; dry (*lit.* & *fig.*).

exsuction /ɪkˈsʌkʃ(ə)n, ɛk-/ *n.* Long *rare* or *obs.* M17. [f. EX-¹ 1 + SUCTION.] The action of sucking or drawing out something, esp. air.

exsufflate /ˈɛksʌfleɪt/ *v.t.* M17. [Late (esp. eccl.) L *exsufflat-* pa. ppl stem of *exsufflare*, f. as EX-¹ 1 + L *sufflare*: see SUFFLATE.] Orig., blow out, blow away. Now only *Hist.*, do this as an exorcism or in token of renunciation of the devil.

exsu'fflation *n.* (*a*) (*obs.* exc. *Hist.*) the action or an act of exsufflating; (*b*) *Med.* the removal by blowing of material from a body cavity, esp. the respiratory tract: E16.

exsufflicate /ɪkˈsʌflɪkət, ɛk-/ *a. literary. rare.* E17. [App. arbitrary f. EXSUFFLATE.] Puffed up, inflated; blown (*lit.* & *fig.*).

†**exsuperate** *v.t.* L16-E18. [L *exsuperat-* pa. ppl stem of *exsuperare*, f. as EX-¹ 1 + *superare* rise above, f. *super* above: see -ATE³.] Overtop, surpass; overcome.

exsurge /ɪkˈsəːdʒ, ɛk-/ *v.i. rare.* L16. [L *exsurgere*, f. as EX-¹ 1 + *surgere* rise.] Rise up, start out.

exsurgent *a.* †(*a*) arising, emerging; (*b*) rising above the rest: E17.

exta /ˈɛkstə/ *n.pl. Hist.* M17. [L.] The viscera; *spec.* the entrails of a victim from which omens were interpreted by a soothsayer.

†**extacy, -sy** *n.* & *v.* vars. of ECSTASY.

extant /ɪkˈstant, ɛk-, ˈɛkstənt/ *a.* M16. [L *ex(s)tant-* pres. ppl stem of *ex(s)tare* be prominent or visible, exist, f. as EX-¹ 1 + *stare* stand: see -ANT¹.] †1 Able to be publicly seen, found, or reached; accessible. M16-M17. 2 Projecting or protruding from a surface. (Foll. by *above*, *from*, etc.) *arch.* M16. 3 Conspicuous, manifest. Now *rare.* M16. 4 In existence, *esp.* (of a document etc.) still existing, surviving. Formerly also, (of time) present; (of a fashion) current. M16.

4 G. L. HARDING There are scratched or hammered on some rocks outlines of various animals then extant. M. MEYER Gosse's reply is not extant.

†**extatic** *a.* & *n.* var. of ECSTATIC.

extemporal /ɪkˈstɛmp(ə)r(ə)l, ɛk-/ *a.* Now *rare* or *obs.* L16. [L *extemporalis* arising out of the moment, f. *ex tempore*: see EXTEMPORE, -AL¹.] 1 Done or said without premeditation; impromptu, extempore. L16. †2 (Of a person) able to speak, or given to speaking, extempore; (of a faculty) pertaining to extempore speech or action. L16-M17.

†**extemporally** *adv.* L16-L17. †**extemporalness** *n.*: only in M17.

extemporaneous /ɪkˌstɛmpəˈreɪnɪəs, ɛk-/ *a.* M17. [Late L *extemporaneus*, f. as prec.: see -ANEOUS.] 1 = EXTEMPORE *a.* 1. M17. 2 = EXTEMPORARY 3. Of a medicine: requiring preparation at the time of prescription (opp. *officinal*). E18.

extemporaneously *adv.* L18. **extemporaneousness** *n.* M18.

extemporary /ɪkˈstɛmp(ə)r(ə)ri, ɛk-/ *a.* L16. [f. EXTEMPORE + -ARY¹, after *temporary.*] †1 Sudden, unexpected; occasional, casual. L16-M18. 2 = EXTEMPORE *a.* 1. E17. 3 Hastily built or prepared; makeshift. M17.

extemporarily *adv.* M17. **extemporariness** *n.* L17.

extempore /ɪk'stɛmp(ə)ri, ɛk-/ *adv., n., & a.* M16. [L *ex tempore* on the spur of the moment, f. as EX *prep.* + *tempore* abl. of *tempus* time.] A *adv.* 1 Without premeditation or preparation; impromptu. (Now chiefly of speaking or of performing music.) M16. †2 At once, immediately. L16–M17.

1 †**live extempore**: for the present without regard for the future. **pray extempore**: without using a set form of prayer. **speak extempore**: without notes or other preparation.

†B *n.* An unprepared improvised speech, composition, or performance. L16–E19.

C *adj.* 1 Of a speech, musical performance, etc: spoken or done without preparation, esp. without written notes. Of a speaker or performer: performing without preparation. E17. 2 Occasional; sudden, unprepared for. (Now only of personal actions, w. some notion of sense 1.) M17. 3 Makeshift, contrived for the occasion. L17.

1 A. THWAITE His extempore lectures on Gray were particularly successful. 2 W. IRVING He was somewhat subject to extempore bursts of passion.

extemporize /ɪk'stɛmpərʌɪz, ɛk-/ *v.* Also **-ise**. M17. [f. prec. + -IZE.] 1 *v.i.* Speak extempore; compose or perform music extempore. M17. 2 *v.t.* Compose, perform, or produce extempore. E19.

1 E. HEATH I played the organ at which he had extemporized so often. 2 W. H. AUDEN He amused himself / extemporising moral, / highly moral, iambics.

extempori'zation *n.* M19. **extemporizer** *n.* E19.

†**extempory** *adv.* & *a.* E17–L18. [Anglicization.] = EXTEMPORE *adv.* & *a.*

extend /ɪk'stɛnd, ɛk-/ *v.* ME. [L *extendere* stretch out, f. as EX-[1] 1 + *tendere* stretch.] I Assess, value; take possession of. 1 *v.t. Law* (now *Hist.*). Value (land); *esp.* value (the land of a debtor) in order to find by when the creditor will be paid from its rental. ME. 2 *v.t.* a *Law* (now *Hist.*). Take possession of (land etc.) by a writ of extent or in payment of any other debt. L15. b *gen.* Take possession of by force. Now *rare* or *obs.* E17.

II Stretch, lengthen. 3 *v.t.* & †*i.* Straighten or spread out (esp. the body, limbs, etc.) at full length. LME. b Write out (notes, an abbreviation, etc.) in full; *esp.* transcribe (shorthand notes) in longhand. M17. 4†a *v.t.* Stretch or pull out (something) to its full size; distend (a vessel etc.); hold or maintain in a stretched condition; *rare* train (a vine). LME–L18. b *v.t.* Cause (a horse) to lengthen its stride. E18. c *v.refl.* (Of a horse) exert itself to the full, esp. in response to a challenge; (of an athlete etc.) use all one's efforts, exert oneself to the full. M19. d *v.t.* In *pass.* Of a horse, sportsman or sportswoman, etc.: be challenged into making maximum effort. E20. e *v.i.* Of a horse: lengthen the stride. L20. 5 *v.i.* & *t.* (Cause to) stretch or span over or *over* a period of time or a distance; (cause to) reach to or *to* a certain point. Also foll. by *into, through*, etc. LME. 6 *v.t.* Prolong in duration. LME. b Make longer, continue further in space. M16. c Develop further; bring nearer to completion. E18. 7a *v.t.* Spread out (*over*); cause to cover a space or area. LME. b *v.i.* Cover an area; stretch out in various directions; (of a law, obligation, quality, etc.) have a certain range or scope. LME. †8 *v.t.* Exaggerate. E16–E17. 9 *v.t.* a Increase the scope or range of application of. L16. b Increase the quantity or bulk of (a product) by the addition of another substance. M20.

3 H. JAMES Elizabeth, whose august person had extended itself upon a huge . . bed. 4c E. WAUGH An indolent, humorous clergyman, who we did not think was extending himself fully in coaching us. 5 STEELE His Troops are extended from Exilles to Mount Genevre. T. COLLINS On our right, the bare plain extended indefinitely. P. KAVANAGH Untrimmed hedges with briars extending well out into the fields. 6 SHAKES. *Macb.* You shall offend him, and extend his Passion. b W. BOYD The gleaming walnut dining table was fully extended to accommodate the family. A. BRIGGS During the fourth century . . some of the greatest Roman villas were built or extended. c ISAIAH BERLIN They consequently seek to extend historical knowledge to fill gaps in the past. 7b G. GREENE The land belonging to it extended in a semi-circle three miles deep from the last cottage. F. O'BRIEN His knowledge of physics . . extended to Boyle's Law and the Parallelogram of Forces. 9a H. SPENCER The invention . . enabled men to extend the principles of mechanics to the atmosphere. G. VIDAL He merely used Christianity to extend his dominion over the world.

III Stretch or hold out; offer. 10 *v.t.* Stretch or hold out (the hand or something held in it). LME. 11 *v.t.* Grant (kindness, mercy, patronage, etc.) *to*; offer (a welcome, invitation, etc.). Formerly also, vent (malice), inflict (vengeance), issue (a legal process), *against, upon*. L15.

10 J. BERGER The hostess . . extends her arm in beckoning invitation. 11 M. EDGEWORTH You should extend to me the same . . indulgence. D. CARNEGIE A man who has to refuse . . invitations extended by friends.

extenda'bility *n.* = EXTENSIBILITY L20. **extendable** *a.* = EXTENDIBLE M17. **extendi'bility** *n.* the property of being extendible L15. **extendible** *a.* able or (*Law*, now *Hist.*) liable to be extended L15.

extended /ɪk'stɛndɪd, ɛk-/ *a.* LME. [f. prec. + -ED[1].] 1 Lengthened, prolonged, (in space or time). LME. b Of an insurance policy: continuing to provide cover after the payment of premiums is discontinued. L19. c *Bibliogr.* Of the page of a book: having had the inner margin restored. M20. 2 Stretched out, spread out. M16. b Of a horse's gait: lengthened as far as possible without breaking. Cf. COLLECTED 2. L18. 3 *Law* (now *Hist.*). Of property: valued; taken possession of as payment of a debt. E17. 4 *Philos.* Having or possessing the quality of extension; occupying space. M17. 5 Increased in scope, area or range; widespread, extensive. E18.

Special collocations: **extended burial** *Archaeol.*: with the body laid at full length (cf. *crouched burial* s.v. CROUCH *v.* 1). **extended family** *Sociol.*: comprising not only one couple and their children but also consanguineous and conjugal relatives living in the same household or near by. **extended-play** *a.* (*a*) designating a record with more playing time than a single though of similar size; (*b*) designating a recording tape that is longer but thinner than the standard.

extendedly *adv.* M17. **extendedness** *n.* L17.

extender /ɪk'stɛndə, ɛk-/ *n.* ME. [f. as prec. + -ER[1].] 1 *gen.* A person who or thing which extends something. Formerly, *spec.* in *Law*, a surveyor or valuer of property, esp. under a writ of extent. ME. †2 = EXTENSOR. E17–L18. 3 A substance added to a product to dilute the colour, increase the bulk, or vary some other property. E20.

extense /ɪk'stɛns, ɛk-/ *n.* & *a.* Long *rare* or *obs.* E17. [OFr., or L *extensus* pa. pple of *extendere* EXTEND.] †A *n.* 1 An expanse. Only in E17. 2 Extension. Only in M17. B *adj.* Extensive; extended. M17.

extensible /ɪk'stɛnsɪb(ə)l, ɛk-/ *a.* E17. [Fr., or med.L *extensibilis*, f. L *extens-* pa. ppl stem of *extendere*: see EXTEND, -IBLE.] Able to be extended; extensile.

extensi'bility *n.* M17. **extensibleness** *n.* E18.

extensile /ɪk'stɛnsʌɪl, ɛk-/ *a.* M18. [f. L *extens-*: see EXTENSION, -ILE.] Able to be extended; (of a tongue, tentacle, etc.) able to be protruded.

extension /ɪk'stɛnʃ(ə)n, ɛk-/ *n.* LME. [Late L *extensio(n-)*, f. L *extens-*, *extent-* pa. ppl stem of *extendere*: see EXTEND, -ION.] 1 The action of extending the body or a limb; the holding out or up of the hand or arm. LME. b *Surg.* The application of axial traction to a fractured or dislocated limb or to an injured or diseased spinal column to restore it to its normal position. E17. †2 The action of stretching or straining something; a stretched or strained state; distension, swelling. E16–E19. 3 (An) increase in scope or range. L16. b In full *university extension*. Extramural teaching provided by a university or college. M19. 4 The scope or range of an immaterial thing. E17. b *Logic.* The range of a term or concept as measured by the number of kinds of object which it denotes or contains. L17. 5a Size, spatial extent. Now *rare*. E17. b *Physics* & *Philos.* The property of occupying space; spatial magnitude. E17. c Something that occupies space. M18. 6 An increase in duration or in the time allowed for something, *spec.* the sale of alcoholic drinks. M17. †7 The fact of being spread out; an expanse (of country). L17–L18. 8a (An) increase in length or area. L18. b A part of something that extends or enlarges it; *esp.* one added for this purpose, e.g. to a building or a motorway. M19. c (The number of) a subsidiary telephone distant from the main instrument or switchboard. E20. 9 The condition or fact of extending to a certain distance or in a certain direction. L18. 10 The action of adding up a horizontal line of figures or of computing a subtotal, as on an invoice; the figure thus obtained. M19. 11 *Ballet.* A position with the leg stretched at an angle from the body; the ability to hold such a position; the height above the waist that a dancer can raise one leg. M20. 12 The utmost lengthening of a horse's stride at a particular pace. M20.

3 S. SONTAG The metaphor of the psychic voyage is an extension of the romantic idea of travel. b attrib.: *extension course, lecture, student*, etc. 4 J. REYNOLDS The same extension of mind which gives the excellence of genius. 8b S. BECKETT His head is framed in headrest which is a narrower extension of backrest. B. PYM A cottage . . with that rather ugly 'extension' stuck on at the side. 9 E. K. KANE Showing . . the former extension of the Esquimaux race to the higher north.

Comb.: **extension bellows, tube**: added to a camera between the body and lens to shorten the distance of closest focus of an object so that close-up pictures can be taken.

extensionless *a.* (*Philos.*) lacking extension in space or duration in time E20.

extensional /ɪk'stɛnʃ(ə)n(ə)l, ɛk-/ *a.* M17. [f. prec. + -AL[1].] Of, pertaining to, or possessing extension; *spec.* (*Logic* & *Philos.*) concerned with the objects denoted rather than the predicates applied; having the truth value unaltered if a constituent is replaced by another with the same denotation or extension.

extensio'nality *n.* (*Philos.*) the state or fact of being extensional E20. **extensionally** *adv.* by way of or in terms of extension L19.

extensity /ɪk'stɛnsɪti, ɛk-/ *n.* M19. [f. L *extens-*: see EXTENSION, -ITY.] The quality of having (a certain) extension.

extensive /ɪk'stɛnsɪv, ɛk-/ *a.* LME. [Fr. *extensif*, *-ive* or late L *extensivus*, f. as prec.: see -IVE.] 1 Possessing, characterized by, or pertaining to spatial extension; occupying space. Formerly, characterized by swelling. LME. †2 Of metal: readily beaten into a thinner, more extensive form. Only in 17. 3 Of an immaterial thing (formerly also of a person or personal qualities): far-reaching, wide in scope, range, or application; comprehensive; lengthy. E17. 4 Tending to cause extension; having the effect of extending. M17. 5 *Logic.* Of or pertaining to extension; denoting or applying to a number of different objects or kinds of object. L17. 6 Of a material thing: having a wide extent, occupying a large surface or space. L18. 7 *Econ.* Of a method of farming etc.: in which a relatively small crop is obtained from a large area with a minimum of attention and expense. M19.

1 P. W. ATKINS The internal energy of a system depends on the amount of material it contains. . . This is an example of an extensive property. 3 B. BETTELHEIM Our society seems to be . . expecting more extensive technology to solve the problems it creates. 6 A. BROOKNER A largish house set in extensive gardens.

extensively *adv.* L16. **extensiveness** *n.* M17.

extensometer /ɛkstɛn'sɒmɪtə/ *n.* L19. [f. L *extens-*: see EXTENSION, -OMETER.] An instrument for measuring the extension or other deformation of a body under applied stress; an instrument using such deformations to record the elastic strain in metals, concrete, etc.

extensor /ɪk'stɛnsə, ɛk-/ *n.* E18. [Late L f. as prec.: see -OR.] *Anat.* A muscle which extends or straightens a limb etc. Also *extensor muscle*. Cf. FLEXOR.

extent /ɪk'stɛnt, ɛk-/ *n.* ME. [AN *extente* f. med.L *extenta* use as n. of fem. of L *extentus* pa. pple of *extendere* EXTEND.] **I** *Law* (now *Hist.*). **1** The action or an act of valuing property, esp. for the purpose of taxation; the value assigned in such a case. ME. †**b** A tax levied on such a valuation; income from property so valued. ME–M18. **2** Seizure of property in execution of a writ; (a) sequestration. L16. †**b** *fig.* An attack. L16–E17. **c** A writ to recover debts adjudged by a court of record as due to the Crown, under which the body, lands, and goods of the debtor could all be seized at once to compel payment of the debt. Also *writ of extent*. M17.

2b SHAKES. *Twel. N.* In this uncivil and unjust extent Against thy peace.

II *gen.* **3** The amount of space over which a thing extends; size, dimensions, amount. L15. **4** Width or limits of application; scope; the limit to which something extends. L16. †**b** Enlargement in scope or operation. M17–E18. †**5** The action of extending justice, kindness, etc. L16–M17. **6** A space or area of a specified kind; the whole *of* an area. E17. **7** *Logic.* = EXTENSION 4b. M17. **8** *Campanol.* The total possible number of distinct changes in a given method. E20.

3 A. J. TOYNBEE The western pampa's vast extent can no longer be seen with the eye. J. HERSEY It was then that he first realised the extent of the damage. **4** E. PAUL The drinks were watered to such an extent that temperance was automatically accomplished. L. DURRELL He was now alarmed at the extent to which it might become possible to hate her. J. GASKELL He can do what he likes with them to quite an extent. H. MACMILLAN I share to the fullest extent the responsibility of all the decisions. **6** R. GLOVER Th' imperial race That rul'd th' extent of Asia. C. WATERTON You may see a sloping extent of noble trees. G. P. MARSH They occupied only a small extent of England.

†**extent** *a.* LME–M17. [L *extentus*: see prec.] = EXTENDED 1, 2, 4, 5.

extenuate /ɪk'stɛnjʊeɪt, ɛk-/ *v.t.* Pa. pple **-ated**, (earlier) †**-ate**. LME [L *extenuat-* pa. ppl stem of *extenuare* thin, reduce, diminish, f. as EX-[1] 1 + *tenuis* thin: see -ATE[3].] **1** Make (a person, the body, etc.) thin; emaciate. *arch.* LME. **2** State at a low figure; disparage the magnitude or importance of; underrate. *arch.* E16. **b** Treat (a crime, a fault, guilt) as of trifling importance; *esp.* (try to) lessen the seeming seriousness of (a crime etc.) by partial excuse; (of a circumstance) lessen the guilt of (a crime etc.). L16. **c** Plead partial excuses for, try to justify. M18. †**3** Diminish in size, number, or amount; lessen (a quality etc.) in degree; mitigate (a law). M16–L18. **4** Thin out in consistency, make less dense. Now *rare* or *obs.* M16. †**5** Thin out (hair); make thin or narrow; beat (metal) into thin plates, draw into fine wire. M16–L17. †**6** Disparage (a person, action, attribute, etc.); diminish in honour. E17–E18.

2b B. BAINBRIDGE The prisoner's age and previous good character were extenuating circumstances. **c** A. RADCLIFFE She.. endeavoured to extenuate the conduct of Madame La Motte.

extenuatingly *adv.* in an extenuating manner L19. **extenuative** *a.* & *n.* (a thing) tending to extenuate L16. **extenuator** *n.* M18. **extenuatory** *a.* E19.

extenuation /ɪk,stɛnjʊ'eɪʃ(ə)n, ɛk-/ *n.* LME. [L *extenuatio(n-)*, f. as prec.: see -ATION.] **1a** The action or an act of making or becoming emaciated. *arch.* LME. †**b** The action or an act of diminishing in size or volume. E17–L18. †**2** The action or an act of lessening a quality etc. in degree; (a) weakening; (an) impoverishment; mitigation of blame or punishment. M16–E18. **3** The action or an act of lessening or trying to lessen the guilt of a crime etc. by partial excuse. L16. **4** The action or an act of belittling or underrating. E17.

3 P. G. WODEHOUSE Some excuse, some theory in extenuation of his behaviour, is.. urgently needed.

exterior /ɪk'stɪərɪə, ɛk-/ *a.* & *n.* E16. [L, compar. of *exter* external: see -IOR.] **A** *adj.* **1** Further from the centre, outer, (opp. *interior*). Of an action etc.: manifested on the surface, outward, visible. E16. **2** Situated or coming from outside; external (*to*). M16. †**3** Concerned with externals. M16–L18. **4** *Cinemat.* Outdoor. L20.

1 C. CLARKE Beatrice possesses a fund of hidden tenderness beneath her exterior gaiety. **exterior angle**: between a side of a triangle or polygon and the adjacent side produced. **exterior to** on the outer side or outside of. **2** F. L. WRIGHT It cannot be changed.. by the exterior pressures of any outward circumstances. *exterior* BALLISTICS.

B *n.* **1** An outward part, feature, etc. Usu. in *pl.* L16. **2** The outer surface of something. L17. **3** An outward or visible aspect or demeanour, esp. as concealing a different one. E19. **4** An outdoor scene in a play or film; a film or film sequence shot outdoors. L19.

1 SHAKES. *Merry W.* She did.. course o'er my exteriors with.. a greedy intention. **2** H. DOUGLAS Wooden frames, covered on the exterior with sheet copper. **3** J. CONRAD He was in reality of a timid disposition under his manly exterior.

exteriorly *adv.* (*a*) with outward act; in externals; (*b*) on the surface; in an exterior position: M16.

exteriorise *v.* var. of EXTERIORIZE.

exteriority /ɪk,stɪərɪ'ɒrɪti, ɛk-/ *n.* E17. [f. EXTERIOR + -ITY.] **1** The state of being outside or of having external existence; outwardness. E17. **2** Devotion to external instead of to inward and spiritual things. L19.

exteriorize /ɪk'stɪərɪərʌɪz, ɛk-/ *v.t.* Also **-ise**. L19. [f. as prec. + -IZE.] Make exterior; *Surg.* bring to the surface of the body or outside it. Also, give external form to, attribute external existence to.

R. HAYMAN He could exteriorize all his anxiety by writing.

exteriori'zation *n.* L19.

exterminable /ɪk'stəːmɪnəb(ə)l, ɛk-/ *a. rare.* M17. [f. as next + -ABLE.] Able to be exterminated or destroyed.

exterminate /ɪk'stəːmɪneɪt, ɛk-/ *v.t.* Pa. pple **-ated**, †**-ate**. LME. [L *exterminat-* pa. ppl stem of *exterminare* (in cl.L only in sense 1, in Vulgate in sense 2), f. as EX-[1] 1 + *terminus* boundary: see -ATE[3].] †**1** Drive beyond the boundaries of a state, community, etc.; banish. (Foll. by *from*, (*out*) *of*.) LME–L17. **2** Destroy utterly, kill, (a person or other living thing); kill all the members of (a race, sect, nation, etc.); make extinct; put a complete end to (an opinion). M16. †**3** Abolish, put an end to, (a thing). L16–L18. †**4** *Math.* Eliminate (an unknown quantity). M18–E19.

2 R. S. R. FITTER When the woods around Hampstead.. were grubbed up.. plants such as the tutsan.. were exterminated. A. BURGESS Jews had been.. tortured, sent to labour camps, exterminated.

exterminative *a.* = EXTERMINATORY L19. **exterminator** *n.* †(*a*) a person who banishes someone; (*b*) a person who exterminates or destroys someone or something; *spec.* (*N. Amer.*) a person employed to destroy vermin: LME. **exterminatory** *a.* tending to exterminate L18.

extermination /ɪk,stəːmɪ'neɪʃ(ə)n/ *n.* LME. [Late L *exterminatio(n-)*, f. as prec.: see -ATION.] †**1** Banishment, expulsion. LME–M17. **2** Total destruction, extinction. M16. †**3** *Math.* Elimination. M18–E19.

Comb.: **extermination camp** a concentration camp for the mass killing of people, *esp.* one of those set up in Nazi Germany.

†**extermine** *v.t.* LME–M17. [(O)Fr. *exterminer* f. L *exterminare*: see EXTERMINATE.] = EXTERMINATE 1, 2, 3.

extern /ɪk'stəːn, ɛk-/ *a.* & *n.* Also **-erne**. M16. [Fr. *externe* or L *externus*, f. *exter*: see EXTERIOR.] **A** *adj.* **1** = EXTERNAL *a.* 1. Now *rare* (*poet.*). M16. **2** = EXTERNAL *a.* 4. Now *rare.* M16. †**3** Situated in, belonging to, or designating a foreign country. M16–M17. **4** = EXTERNAL *a.* 3a, c. (Foll. by *to*.) Now chiefly *poet.* L16. **5** Connected with a community but not resident in it. Cf. sense B.2 below. M19. **B** *n.* †**1** Outward appearance. *rare* (Shakes.). Only in L16. **2** A person attached to a community or institution but not resident in it; *esp.*: (*a*) (in a strictly enclosed order of nuns) a sister who lives outside the enclosure and goes on outside errands; (*b*) (in a hospital) a non-resident doctor, worker, or patient; (in a school) a non-boarding pupil [Fr. *externe*]. E17.

external /ɪk'stəːn(ə)l, ɛk-/ *a.* & *n.* LME. [f. med.L, f. L *exter*: see prec., -AL[1].] **A** *adj.* **1** Outwardly visible or manifest; consisting of outward acts or observances. LME. **2** Of or situated on the outside or visible part of something; *Anat.* situated towards the outer surface of the body (opp. *internal*). L16. **b** Of a remedy or treatment: applied to the exterior of the body. E18. **3a** Situated outside or beyond the limits of a given object. (Foll. by *to*.) L16. †**b** = EXTERN *a.* 3. Only in L16. **c** Of a thing presented in sense-perception: (regarded as) existing independently of the mind perceiving it. M17. **4** Originating or acting from outside. M17. **5** Having an outside object or sphere of operation; *spec.* relating to foreign countries or foreign affairs. L18. **6** Of a student or an examiner: taking or marking examinations of a university of which he or she is not a resident member. Of an examination or a degree: taken or obtained by an external student. L19. **7** *Computing.* Not contained in the central processing unit. Also = PERIPHERAL *a.* 3. M20.

1 J. BUTLER The external worship of God. C. DARWIN Fertility in the hybrid is independent of its external resemblance to either pure parent. **2** T. HARDY The surgeon.. said that the external bruises were mere trifles. *external ear*: see EAR *n.*[1] **3a** C. RYCROFT Hallucinations.. are experienced as though they were external to the person constructing them. *external* RELATION. **b** J. STEINBECK External realities.. she obliterated by refusing to believe in them. **external world** the totality of external objects. **4** B. BETTELHEIM The need to ascribe inner conflict to some external force. **external evidence**: derived from a source independent of the thing discussed. **5** H. JAMES National questions.. of external as well as of domestic and of colonial policy.

B *n.* **1** In *pl.* Outward forms, observances, etc., as opp. to inner realities or substance. Also (*arch.*), outward features. M17. **2** External objects or circumstances; inessentials. M17. **3** The exterior; an outward surface or aspect. *arch.* L18.

1 R. SOUTH Adam was.. glorious in his externals; he had a beautiful body. M. M. FISKE Dwell in this artificial world [*sc.* the theatre], and you will know only the externals of acting. **2** M. L. KING What shall it profit a man, if he gain the whole world of externals.. and lose the internal—his own soul? **3** SOUTHEY Deformity and hollowness beneath The rich external.

externally *adv.* L16.

externalise *v.* var. of EXTERNALIZE.

externalism /ɪk'stəːn(ə)lɪz(ə)m, ɛk-/ *n.* M19. [f. EXTERNAL + -ISM.] **1** Excessive regard for outward form, esp. in religion. M19. **2** Devotion to the external world. L19.

externalist *n.* & *a.* (a person) that manifests externalism L19.

externality /ɛkstəː'nalɪti/ *n.* L17. [f. as prec. + -ITY.] **1** The quality of being external; *esp.* (*Philos.*) the fact of existing outside the perceiving subject. L17. **2** An external object or circumstance; an outward feature or characteristic. M19. **3** = EXTERNALISM. M19. **4** *Econ.* A side-effect or consequence (of an industrial or commercial activity) which affects other parties without this being reflected in the cost or the price of the goods or services involved. M20.

externalize /ɪk'stəːn(ə)lʌɪz, ɛk-/ *v.t.* Also **-ise**. M19. [f. EXTERNAL *a.* + -IZE.] Make external; embody, give external form to; treat as existing or occurring in the external world. Also, reduce to external observances.

externali'zation *n.* the action of externalizing; an embodiment: E19.

externat /ɛkstɛrna/ *n.* Pl. pronounced same. M19. [Fr., f. *externe*: see EXTERN *n.*] A day-school.

externate /'ɛkstəneɪt, ɪk'stəːneɪt, ɛk-/ *v.t. rare.* L19. [f. EXTERN *a.* + -ATE[3].] = EXTERNIZE.

exter'nation *n.* M19.

externe *a.* & *n.* var. of EXTERN.

externise *v.* var. of EXTERNIZE.

externity /ɪk'stəːnɪti, ɛk-/ *n.* E18. [f. EXTERN *a.*

+ -ITY.] The quality of being external or outward; external characteristics.

externize /ɪk'stəːnʌɪz, ɛk-/ *v.t.* Also **-ise**. M19. [f. as prec. + -IZE.] Embody in external form; externalize.

externi'zation *n.* M19.

exteroceptor /'ɛkstərəʊ,sɛptə/ *n.* E20. [Perh. f. EXTER(IOR or EXTER(NAL + -O- + RE)CEPTOR.] *Physiol.* A sensory receptor which receives external stimuli.

extero'ceptive *a.* E20.

exterritorial /,ɛkstɛrɪ'tɔːrɪəl/ *a.* L18. [f. EX-[1] I + TERRITORIAL, after next.] = EXTRATERRITORIAL.

exterritorially *adv.* M19.

exterritoriality /ɛkstɛrɪ,tɔːrɪ'alɪti/ *n.* L18. [Fr. *exterritorialité*, f. as EX-[1] I, TERRITORIAL, -ITY.] = EXTRATERRITORIALITY.

†**extill** *v.i.* & *t.* M17–E19. [L *exstillare*, f. as EX-[1] I + *stillare* to drop, f. *stilla* drop.] Come or send out in drops, exude.

†**extillation** *n.* Also **exstill-**. E17–E18. [f. L *exstillat-* pa. ppl stem of *exstillare*: see prec., -ATION.] An act of coming out in drops; in *pl.*, matter that has come out thus.

extinct /ɪk'stɪŋkt, ɛk-/ *a.* (orig. *pa. pple*). LME. [L *ex(s)tinctus* pa. pple of *ex(s)tinguere*, f. as EX-[1] I + *stinguere* quench.] 1 Of a fire, light, candle, etc.: extinguished; no longer burning. LME. b Of life, hope, disease, or anything compared to a light or fire: ended, no longer existing; devoid of any brilliance or light. L15. c Of a volcano: no longer erupting, having lost its capacity to erupt. M19. †2 Of a person: blotted out of existence; no longer living. L15–L17. 3 No longer used, recognized, etc.; discontinued, obsolete. Of a peerage or title: having no valid claimant. L15. 4 That has died out: (*a*) (of a family, race, etc.) having no living representative; (*b*) (of a species etc.) no longer surviving in the world at large or in a given locality. L17.

1 R. BYFIELD It tooke fire .. but was quickly extinct. J. GALSWORTHY He would sit .. brooding .., a cigar extinct between his lips. b R. LEHMANN His voice was flat .. and his eyes looked extinct. c **extinct volcano** *fig.* a person who has lost the energy, reputation, etc., he or she once possessed. 3 W. CRUISE Such a power, though extinct at law, would .. be enforced in equity. 4 C. DARWIN Megatherium, Toxodon, and other extinct monsters.

†**extinct** *v.* LME–M17. [L *ex(s)tinct-* pa. ppl stem of *ex(s)tinguere*: see prec.] = EXTINGUISH.

extincteur /ɛkstɛ̃ktœːr/ *n.* Pl. pronounced same. L19. [Fr. f. L *ex(s)tinctor*, f. as prec.: see -OR.] A fire extinguisher.

extinction /ɪk'stɪŋkʃ(ə)n, ɛk-/ *n.* LME. [L *ex(s)tinctio(n-)*, f. as EXTINCT *v.*: see -ION.] 1 The action or process of making or becoming extinct; the state or fact of being extinct; destruction, annihilation; abolition, suppression. LME. 2 *Physics.* Reduction in the intensity of light or other radiation as it passes through a medium or object. L18. b The appearance of darkness when a crystal is illuminated through a polarizer and viewed through another polarizer placed in a plane parallel to the first but oriented at right angles to it. L19.

1 R. S. R. FITTER Londoners .. have uprooted some of the more striking plants of the London area almost to the point of extinction. T. S. ELIOT The progress of an artist is .. a continual extinction of personality. J. A. MICHENER Many times .. the Jews would be threatened with extinction. 2 *attrib.*: G. E. HUTCHINSON The transmission is low and the extinction coefficient high in the infrared.

extinctive /ɪk'stɪŋktɪv, ɛk-/ *a.* LME. [Orig. f. med.L *extinctivus*, f. as EXTINCT *v.*; in mod. use f. prec.: see -IVE.] Tending or having the power to extinguish. Formerly, tending to reduce inflammation.

†**extincture** *n. rare* (Shakes.). Only in L16. [f. EXTINCT *v.* + -URE.] Extinction, quenching.

extine /'ɛkstɪn, -tʌɪn/ *n.* M19. [f. L *ext(imus* outermost + -INE[1].] *Bot.* = EXINE.

extinguish /ɪk'stɪŋgwɪʃ, ɛk-/ *v.* M16. [f. L *ex(s)tinguere*: see EXTINCT *a.*, -ISH[2]. Cf. DISTINGUISH.] I *v.t.* 1 Cause (a fire, light, etc.) to cease to burn or shine; quench, put out. M16. 2 Do away with completely, put an end to; stifle, quench, (a feeling, faculty, etc.); nullify, make void, (a right, claim, etc.); suppress (an institution, office, etc.). M16. b Wipe out (a debt) by full payment. M17. 3 Surpass by superior brilliance. *arch.* M16. 4 Exterminate, make extinct, (a family, race, etc.); *arch.* kill (a person). L16. 5 Reduce (an opponent) to silence. *colloq.* L19.

1 W. TREVOR He extinguished the light and mounted the stairs in darkness. *fig.*: D. CECIL Nothing could wholly extinguish the flame of genius. 2 J. YEOWELL Though the bishopric .. merged into the archbishopric .. it was not extinguished. C. S. FORESTER The rain .. extinguished the last chance of victory. E. F. SCHUMACHER Nationalisation extinguishes private proprietary rights. W. CATHER Something came up in him that extinguished his power of feeling and thinking. 3 M. O. W. OLIPHANT The men .. were quite transcended and extinguished by their wives.

II *v.i.* 6 Be extinguished, suppressed, etc.; become extinct. Now *rare.* L16.

extinguishable *a.* E16.

extinguishant /ɪk'stɪŋgwɪʃ(ə)nt, ɛk-/ *n.* M20. [f. prec. + -ANT[1]. Cf. *coolant, lubricant*, etc.] A material used to put out fires.

extinguisher /ɪk'stɪŋgwɪʃə, ɛk-/ *n.* M16. [f. EXTINGUISH + -ER[1].] 1 *gen.* A person who or thing which extinguishes something. M16. 2 A hollow conical cap for extinguishing a candle. M17. 3 = *fire extinguisher* s.v. FIRE *n.* E19.

extinguishment /ɪk'stɪŋgwɪʃm(ə)nt, ɛk-/ *n.* E16. [f. as prec. + -MENT.] 1 The action of extinguishing a light, feeling, right, institution, etc.; the state of being extinguished. E16. †2 Extermination *of* a family, race, etc.; extinct condition. M16–M17.

1 *Daily Telegraph* The end result is virtual extinguishment—for the footpath or bridleway .. has legally ceased to exist.

extirp /ɪk'stəːp, ɛk-/ *v.t.* Long *arch.* LME. [(O)Fr. *extirper* L *ex(s)tirpare*: see next.] †1 = EXTIRPATE 5. LME–M17. 2 = EXTIRPATE I. L15. †3 = EXTIRPATE 4. L15–M17. †4 = EXTIRPATE 2, 3. M16–L17.

extirpate /'ɛkstəpeɪt/ *v.t.* Pa. pple **-ated**, (*obs.* exc. *Sc.*) **-ate** /-ət/. M16. [L *ex(s)tirpat-* pa. ppl stem of *ex(s)tirpare*, f. as EX-[1] I + *stirps* stem or stock of a tree: see -ATE[3].] 1 Root out, eradicate, get rid of, (a heresy, vice, or other immaterial thing). M16. 2 Do away with as such (a specified category or grouping of people); break up (an organization). Formerly, expel (an individual). (Foll. by *from, out of.*) M16. 3 Kill all the members of (a race, sect, nation, etc.); make extinct. (Foll. by *out of.*) L16. 4 Pull up by the roots, destroy totally, (a tree or plant). E17. 5 Chiefly *Surg.* Remove or excise completely from the body (something regarded as having roots). M17.

1 D. MURPHY Our antagonisms had become too deeply rooted for either of us to extirpate them. 2 LD MACAULAY It is .. one of the first duties of every government to extirpate gangs of thieves. P. ACKROYD A small Anglican religious community .. which was extirpated by Parliamentary troops. 3 J. FERRIAR The Pygmies were extirpated by their wars. M. MCCARTHY Extinct and extirpated species, like the passenger pigeon. 5 G. B. SHAW Operations which consist of amputating limbs and extirpating organs.

extirpative *a.* (*Surg.*) acting or tending to extirpate LME. **extirpator** *n.* a person who or thing which extirpates E18.

extirpation /ɛkstə'peɪʃ(ə)n/ *n.* LME. [Fr., or L *ex(s)tirpatio(n-)*, f. as prec.: see -ATION.] 1 *Surg.* The complete removal or excision of an organ or diseased part. LME. 2 The action of expelling or destroying as undesirable; eradication of a vice or heresy; extermination of a race, species, etc. LME. 3 The action of pulling up by the roots. L17.

extispex /ɪk'stɪspɛks, ɛk-/ *n.* Pl. **-spices** /-spɪsiːz/. E18. [L, f. EXTA + *-spex*, f. *specere* look at.] *Rom. Hist.* = HARUSPEX.

extispicy /ɪk'stɪspɪsi, ɛk-/ *n.* L17. [L *extispicium*, f. as EXTISPEX: see -Y[4].] *Rom. Hist.* Inspection of the entrails of sacrificial victims in order to predict the future; haruspicy.

extol /ɪk'stəʊl, ɛk-/ *v.t.* Also ***-oll**. Infl. **-ll-**. LME. [L *extollere*, f. as EX-[1] I + *tollere* raise.] †1 Lift, raise. LME–M17. †2 Raise in rank or dignity; exalt. Also, uphold the authority of. LME–E18. 3 Praise enthusiastically. LME. †4 In a bad sense: make too much of, exaggerate. L15–M17. †5 Make swollen with pride, joy, etc. E16–M17.

3 C. CHAPLIN She extolled the virtues of Joe, stressing how hard he had worked.

extoller *n.* E17. **extolment** *n.* (*arch.*) the action or an act of praising; (a) eulogy: E17.

extorsion /ɪk'stɔːʃ(ə)n, ɛk-/ *n.* L19. [med.L *extorsio(n-)* var. of late L *extortio(n-)*: see EXTORTION.] Rotation of the eyeballs in which the tops move away from each other and the bottoms approach each other.

extorsive /ɪk'stɔːsɪv, ɛk-/ *a. rare.* M17. [med.L *extorsivus*, f. *extors-* var. of L *extort-*: see EXTORT *v.*, -IVE.] Tending to extort; obtained by extortion.

†**extort** *a.* LME–L16. [L *extortus* pa. pple of *extorquere*: see next.] Extorted, wrongfully obtained.

extort /ɪk'stɔːt, ɛk-/ *v.* E16. [L *extort-* pa. ppl stem of *extorquere*, f. as EX-[1] I + *torquere* to twist.] 1 *v.t.* Obtain (money, a promise, a concession, etc.) from a reluctant person by threat, force, importunity, etc. (Foll. by *from*, †*upon*.) E16. b Of a circumstance, influence, etc.: compel, constrain, (a given reaction). M17. 2 *v.t.* Subject (a person) to extortion. Long *rare.* M16–E17. 3 *v.i.* Indulge in extortion. *arch.* L16. 4 *v.t.* Extract (a meaning, an inference) *from* words, data, etc., in defiance of their natural interpretation. E17.

1 W. S. CHURCHILL Adolescent ruffians who extorted pennies and apples from tradesmen in return for not breaking their windows. E. M. DELAFIELD Mary .. only finally married him when consent had been extorted from Mr. Ponsonby on his deathbed. b JAS. MILL A situation which extorted the compassion of Englishmen. 4 SHAKES. *Twel. N.* Do not extort thy reasons from this clause.

extorter *n.* L16.

extortion /ɪk'stɔːʃ(ə)n, ɛk-/ *n.* & *v.* ME. [Late L *extortio(n-)*, f. as prec.: see -ION.] A *n.* 1 The action or an act of extorting money etc.; (an) exaction. ME. 2 *spec.* in *Law* (now *Hist.*). The unlawful taking of money by a public official under pretext of his or her office. L16. 3 *hyperbol.* An exorbitant demand. Also, an exorbitant sum. M18.

1 J. A. FROUDE By bribery and extortion he had obtained vast sums of money. J. S. BREWER The Dover boatmen, whose extortions may boast the prescription of three centuries.

B *v.* 1 *v.i.* Indulge in extortion. L15. 2 *v.t.* Charge exorbitantly. *obs.* exc. *dial.* M17.

extortionable *a.* (*rare*) = EXTORTIONARY M17. **extortionary** *a.* given to or characterized by extortion E19. **extortioner** *n.* a person who indulges in or is given to extortion LME. **extortionist** *n.* = EXTORTIONER L19.

extortionate /ɪk'stɔːʃ(ə)nət, ɛk-/ *a.* L18. [f. prec. + -ATE[2].] Characterized by extortion. Now chiefly in *hyperbol.* use: charging grossly excessive prices; (of a price or charge) grossly excessive, exorbitant.

extortionately *adv.* M20.

†**extortious** *a.* LME–L18. [f. EXTORTI(ON + -OUS, after *captious*.] Characterized by or acquired through extortion.

extortive /ɪk'stɔːtɪv, ɛk-/ *a.* M17. [f. EXTORT *v.* + -IVE. Cf. med.L *extortivus*.] Having a tendency to extort.

extra /'ɛkstrə/ *a.*, *n.*, & *adv.* M17. [Prob. f. EXTRAORDINARY, after similar forms in Fr. & G.] A *adj.* Beyond or more than the usual, stipulated, or specified amount or number; additional; more than is necessary. M17.

T. JEFFERSON Money .. for any extra wants of our own troops. W. E. H. LECKY Soldiers were employed on extra pay to make the roads. L. P. HARTLEY Isabel hired the extra chairs and tea-things.

Special collocations: **extra cover** *Cricket* (the position of) a fieldsman between cover-point and mid-off but further from the wicket. **extra time**: sometimes allowed for continued play after the normal finishing time of a football etc. match when the scores are then equal.

B *n.* **1** Something that is extra or additional; something given in addition or for which an extra charge is made; an extra charge or fee; an additional or special issue of a newspaper; in cricket, a run scored otherwise than by hitting the ball and running; *US* a coach specially hired or laid on. L18. **2** An additional person; *spec.* on the stage or in films, a person engaged temporarily for a minor part or to be present during a crowd scene. L18.

1 L. CARROLL 'With extras?' .. 'Yes .. we learned French and Music.' DICKENS 'What's the rent?' .. 'One pound per week... The boots and clothes are extras.' OED The builder took the contract very low, hoping to recoup himself by extras.

C *adv.* More than usually; additionally; in excess of the usual, specified, or expected amount. E19.

C. KINGSLEY He must be an extra good boy that day. M. DICKENS There will be two extra for dinner. N. BLAKE Packets of .. henbane and deadly nightshade, sixpence extra. **extra dry** or **sec** (of champagne) very slightly sweetened.

Comb.: **extra-special** *n.* & *a.* (*a*) *n.* the last edition of a London evening paper; an extra edition of a publication; (*b*) *adj.* designating such an edition; *fig.* (*colloq.*) very special; exceptionally good or fine.

extra /'ɛkstrə/ *prep. rare.* E17. [L *extra* f. *extera* abl. fem. of *exter* external.] Outside, externally to.

extra- /'ɛkstrə/ *pref.* [(chiefly med.) L *extra-* f. cl.L *extra* outside, beyond: see EXTRA *prep.* In cl.L and late L in a few adjs.: see EXTRAMUNDANE, EXTRAORDINARY.] Forming adjs. (usu. f adjs.) w. the senses 'situated outside', 'not coming within the scope of'. Opp. INTRA-.

extra'cellular *a.* (*Biol.*) situated or occurring outside a cell M19. **extra'cellularly** *adv.* (*Biol.*) outside a cell L19. **extracor'poreal** *a.* (involving something) situated or occurring outside the body M19. **extracor'poreally** *adv.* outside the body E20. **extra'cranial** *a.* situated or occurring outside the skull L19. **extracu'rricular** *a.* not coming within the scope of the normal curriculum; *fig.* outside the normal routine, *esp.* extramarital: E20. **extra'dural** *a.* (*Med.*) = EPIDURAL *a.* E20. **extra-e'ssential** *a.* not included in the essence of something M17. **extra-e'ssentially** *adv.* as something extra-essential M17. **extra-Euro'pean** *a.* situated or occurring outside Europe; pertaining to matters outside Europe; (of a plant or animal) not found in Europe: E19. **extraga'lactic** *a.* situated, occurring, or originating outside the Galaxy M19. **extrahe'patic** *a.* situated or occurring outside or beyond the liver M20. **extra-'illustrated** *a.* (of a book) having pictures stuck into it from another source M20. **extra-illu'stration** *n.* the action or practice of sticking pictures into a book from another source E20. **extra-'illustrator** *n.* a person who practises extra-illustration L19. **extra'legal** *a.* that is beyond the province of law, not regulated by law M17. **extra'legally** *adv.* as an extralegal matter or act M20. **extra'limital** *a.* situated, occurring, or derived from outside a particular area L19. **extralin'guistic** *a.* that is outside the field of linguistics or bounds of language E20. **extra'literary** *a.* that is outside the province of literature M20. **extra'logical** *a.* that lies outside the legitimate domain of logic M19. **extra'marital** *a.* involving or constituting a (usu. sexual) relationship between a married person and someone other than his or her spouse E20. **extra'maritally** *adv.* in an extramarital way M20. **extra-'metrical** *a.* that represents a syllable additional to what the metre requires or will accommodate M19. **extra-'musical** *a.* that is outside the field of music, or not an intrinsic part of music E20. **extra-parlia'mentary** *a.* occurring or existing outside or independently of Parliament L19. **extra-pa'rochial** *a.* that is outside the limits of a parish, or exempt from parish obligations (*lit.* & *fig.*) L17. **extra'punitive** *a.* (*Psychol.*) of, pertaining to, or designating a person who reacts aggressively to frustration, or unreasonably blames events or other people M20. **extra'punitively** *adv.* (*Psychol.*) in an extrapunitive manner M20. **extra'punitiveness** *n.* (*Psychol.*) extrapunitive quality M20. **extrapyra'midal** *a.* (*Anat.*) involving or designating nerves concerned with motor activity that descend from the cortex to the spine and are not part of the pyramidal system E20. **extra'sensory** *a.* (regarded as) derived by means other than the known senses, e.g. by telepathy, clairvoyance, etc. (*extrasensory perception*, a person's supposed faculty of perceiving by such means) M20. **extraso'matic** *a.* deriving from events external to an individual M20. **extra'systole** *n.* (*Med.*) a heartbeat outside the normal rhythm E20. **extrate'rrestrial** *a.* & *n.* (a being, esp. an intelligent one) existing or occurring beyond the earth's atmosphere M19. **extrate'rrestrially** *adv.* elsewhere than on or in the earth or its atmosphere M20. **extra'tropical** *a.* situated, existing, or occurring outside the tropics L18. **extra-'uterine** *a.* existing, formed, or occurring outside the uterus E18. **extra'vascular** *a.* situated or occurring outside the vascular system; not vascular in nature: E19. **extra'vascularly** *adv.* outside the vascular system E20. **extrave'hicular** *a.* occurring outside a spacecraft in space M20.

extract /'ɛkstrakt/ *n.* LME. [L *extractum* use as n. of neut. of *extractus* pa. pple to *extrahere*: see EXTRACT *v.*] †**1** A summary, an outline. LME–M17. **2** *Sc. Law.* A warrant empowering the performance of some judicial act; a properly authenticated copy of a legal or public record. M16. †**3** Something drawn or taken out of a thing; *fig.* the essential part of a matter. L16–M17. **4** A substance extracted from another substance or a thing, e.g. by treating with solvents which are then evaporated; a preparation containing the active principle of a substance in concentrated form. L16. **5** A passage from a book, manuscript, etc.; an excerpt, a quotation. M17. †**6** = EXTRACTION 2. M17–L18.

3 N. BACON The extract of all is, that he was chosen by the People and Parliament. 4 L. VAN DER POST The designs were .. dyed ink-black with some vegetable extract. *malt extract, pituitary extract*, etc. *fluid extract*: see FLUID *a.* 5 L. C. KNIGHTS Place beside the extract quoted from Halifax a passage .. from *Love for Love.* 6 J. MORSE The first child of European extract, born in New England.

extract /ɪk'strakt, ɛk-/ *a.* (orig. *pa. pple*). Long *obs.* exc. *Sc.* See also EXTRAUGHT. LME. [L *extractus* pa. pple of *extrahere*: see next.] **1** Extracted; derived, descended. LME. †**2** Distraught. M16–E17.

extract /ɪk'strakt, ɛk-/ *v.t.* LME. [L *extract-* pa. ppl stem of *extrahere*, f. as EX-¹ I + *trahere* draw.] **1** Draw out of a containing body or cavity, usu. with some degree of force, effort, dexterity, etc.; remove (something firmly fixed, esp. a tooth). LME. **b** Get (money, consent, a confession, etc.) from a person in the face of initial unwillingness. LME. **2** Obtain (constituent elements, juices, etc.) from a thing or substance by chemical or physical means. LME. **b** Subject (a substance or thing) to a chemical or physical procedure in order to obtain a constituent. L19. †**3** In *pass.* Be derived or descended (*from*). Also foll. by *of*. L15–L17. **4** Derive (happiness, amusement, understanding, etc.) from a specified source or situation; draw out (the sense of something); infer (a principle, right, etc.). L16. **5** *Math.* Calculate (a root of a number). L16. **6** *Sc. Law.* Make a copy of (a recorded judgement) with a view to executing it. L16. **7** Take (a part) from a whole; *esp.* copy out (a passage in a book etc.). (Foll. by *from, out of.*) L16.

1 SHAKES. *Meas. for M.* Putting the hand in the pocket and extracting it clutch'd. S. KINGSLEY Jacob .. extracts a horseshoe from the fire. E. J. HOWARD He extracted a battered packet of Gold Flake from the breast pocket of his shirt. b H. JAMES He extracted from Mrs Touchett a promise that she would bring her niece. 2 N. CALDER To extract vast quantities of metal from low-grade ores. 4 GEO. ELIOT [He] means to extract the utmost possible amount of pleasure .. out of this life. J. BRAINE My brain .. began to extract the hard inescapable facts from the scrawled figures and abbreviations. 7 MILTON Woman is her Name, of Man Extracted. G. SAINTSBURY A great many maxims .. might be extracted from his works.

extracta'bility *n.* the quality of being extractable M20. **extractable** *a.* able to be extracted L17. **extracted** *ppl a.* derived, drawn out; *spec.* (of an animal) obtained by controlled breeding; (of honey) separated from the uncrushed comb by centrifugal force or gravity: L17. **extracting** *ppl a.* †(*a*) *rare* (Shakes.) distracting; (*b*) that extracts: E17.

extractant /ɪk'straktənt, ɛk-/ *n.* M20. [f. EXTRACT *v.* + -ANT¹.] A substance used to extract another from a solution, tissue, etc.

extraction /ɪk'strakʃ(ə)n, ɛk-/ *n.* LME. [(O)Fr. f. late L *extractio(n-)*, f. as prec.: see -ION.] **1** The action or process of extracting; an act of extracting, esp. a tooth. LME. **2** Origin, lineage, descent. L15. †**3** An extract. L16–L17. †**4** An inference, a deduction. *rare.* E17–E19.

extractive /ɪk'straktɪv, ɛk-/ *n.* & *a.* LME. [Partly f. med.L *extractivus* (f. as EXTRACT *v.*), partly f. EXTRACT *v.*: see -IVE.] **A** *n.* †**1** A plaster or medicine for drawing out harmful matter. Only in LME. **2** A substance left after the removal of vegetable extracts. E19. **3** A substance that can be extracted, an extract. M19.

B *adj.* †**1** Esp. of a plaster or medicine: tending to extract; capable of extracting. L16–M18. **2** Able to be extracted; of the nature of an extract. L18. **3** Concerned with the extraction of natural resources or products, esp. non-renewable ones. M19.

3 *Arizona Daily Star* A degree in Mineral Dressing or Extractive Metallurgy.

extractor /ɪk'straktə, ɛk-/ *n.* E17. [f. EXTRACT *v.* + -OR.] A person or thing which extracts something; *spec.* (*a*) the part of a breech-loading gun which removes the cartridge; (*b*) an instrument for extracting honey from honeycombs.

Comb.: **extractor fan** a ventilating fan in a window or wall to remove stale air.

extractory *a.* E18.

extra dictionem /ˌɛkstrə dɪktɪ'əʊnɛm/ *a. phr.* E19. [L, tr. Gk *exō tēs lexeōs* outside the wording.] Of a logical fallacy: not arising from the wording used to express it.

extradite /'ɛkstrədʌɪt/ *v.t.* M19. [Back-form. f. next.] **1** Give up (a person) into the jurisdiction of another State in an action of extradition. M19. **2** Of a State: obtain the extradition of (a person) from another country. L19.

2 *Daily Telegraph* Grob .. had been extradited from France on charges alleging involvement with fraud.

extraditable *a.* liable or making liable to extradition L19.

extradition /ɛkstrə'dɪʃ(ə)n/ *n.* M19. [Fr., f. as EX-¹ I, TRADITION *n.*] The surrender or delivery of a person into the jurisdiction of another State in order that he or she may be tried by that State for a crime committed there.

Comb.: **extradition treaty**: by which two States mutually bind themselves to extradite people to each other's jurisdiction in specified circumstances.

extrados /ɪks'treɪdɒs, ɛk-/ *n.* L18. [Fr., f. L *extra* outside + Fr. *dos* back.] *Archit.* The upper or outer curve of an arch; *esp.* the upper curve of the voussoirs which form the arch. Cf. INTRADOS.

†**extraduce** *a. rare.* L16–E18. [L *ex traduce*, f. *ex* out of + *traduce* abl. of *tradux* vine-shoot trained for propagation.] Derived (as) from a parent stock; hereditary.

extra-foraneous /ɛkstrəfə'reɪnɪəs/ *a. arch.* L18. [f. EXTRA- + L *foris* door + -ANEOUS.] Outdoor.

extrajudicial /ɛkstrədʒuː'dɪʃ(ə)l/ *a.* M17. [med.L *extrajudicialis*, f. as EXTRA-, JUDICIAL.] **1** That is not part of the proceedings in court or of the case before a court; (of an opinion, confession, etc) not made in court, informal. M17. **2** That is outside the ordinary course of law or justice; not legally authorized; unwarranted. M17.

extrajudicially *adv.* L16.

extramission /ɛkstrə'mɪʃ(ə)n/ *n.* M17. [med.L *extramissio(n)-*, f. as EXTRA-, MISSION *n.*] (An) emission. Now only *Hist.*, the supposed emission of rays from the eyes as part of the visual process.

extramundane /ɛkstrə'mʌndeɪn/ *a.* M17. [Late L *extramundanus*, f. *extra mundum* outside the world or universe.] **1** (Pertaining to a region) situated beyond the earth. M17. **2** Situated outside or beyond the universe; pertaining to what is beyond the universe. E18. **3** *fig.* Remote, pertaining to things not of this world. E19.

extramural /ɛkstrə'mjʊər(ə)l/ *a.* M19. [f. L *extra muros* outside the walls + -AL¹.] **1** Situated or occurring outside the walls or boundaries of a town or city. M19. **2** Pertaining to or designating instruction given under the auspices of a university or college but intended for people other than its students. L19.

extramurally *adv.* E20.

extraneous /ɪkˈstreɪnɪəs, ɛk-/ *a.* M17. [f. L *extraneus* + -OUS.] 1 Of external origin; introduced or added from without; foreign *to* the object to which it is attached or which contains it. M17. 2 Not part of the matter in hand. (Foll. by *to*.) M17. 3 Of a person: not belonging to a specified group, family, etc. M17.

1 M. BAILLIE An extraneous body can be .. easily introduced into their bladder. G. P. MARSH The Low-German dialects were .. exposed to extraneous disturbing forces.

extraˈneity *n.* (*rare*) the state or quality of being extraneous M19. †**extraneize** *v.t.* (*rare*) make extraneous, remove M17–L18. **extraneously** *adv.* M18. **extraneousness** *n.* L19.

extraordinaire /ɪkˌstrɔːdɪˈnɛː, ɛk-, *foreign* ɛkstr(a)ɔrdinɛːr/ *postpositive a.* M20. [Fr., f. as next.] Remarkable, outstanding; (of a person) unusually active or successful in a specified respect.

extraordinary /ɪkˈstrɔːd(ə)n(ə)ri, ɛkˈstrɔː-, ɛkstrəˈɔːdɪn(ə)ri/ *a.*, *n.*, & *adv.* LME. [L *extraordinarius*, f. *extra ordinem* out of order, exceptionally, extraordinarily.] A *adj.* 1 Out of the usual or regular course or order; special. Formerly also, acting unusually, partial. LME. †b *Mus.* = ACCIDENTAL *a.* 2. L16–M18. †c Not according to rule, out of order. M17–E18. 2 Of an official etc.: outside or additional to the regular staff; specially employed. Freq. *postpositive* in titles, denoting secondary status. L16. 3 Of a kind not usually met with, exceptional; now *esp.* so exceptional as to provoke astonishment, admiration, or disapproval. L16. 4 Exceeding what is usual in amount, degree, extent, or size, esp. to the point of provoking astonishment, admiration, or disapproval. L16. †5 Additional to what is usual, extra. Freq. *postpositive*. M17–E19.

1 DEFOE Let him .. take some extraordinary measures to get in his debts. H. SECOMBE The extraordinary general meeting of Panteg Parish Council was under way. **extraordinary ray** *Optics* in double refraction, the ray that does not obey the ordinary laws of refraction. 2 W. BLACKSTONE Another species of extraordinary juries, is the jury to try an attaint. AMBASSADOR *extraordinary*. *envoy extraordinary*: see ENVOY *n.*[1] 3 P. H. JOHNSON I thought how extraordinary it was that so kind a man could be so cruel. A. N. WILSON Verdi's *Falstaff*... 'Extraordinary, isn't it, he was *eighty* when he wrote it.' 4 J. TYNDALL The sun met us here with extraordinary power. 5 M. M. SHERWOOD Spending a few extraordinary shillings.

B *n.* 1 Something extraordinary; an extraordinary quality or bearing; an extraordinary action, incident, etc. Now only in *pl.* (*rare*). L16. b In *pl.* Extraordinary receipts or payments. *arch.* L16. †2 An extraordinary envoy; a supernumerary official. Only in 17. 3 Orig., something extra; an additional or supplementary item. Now only, an extra allowance or expense. M17.

3 HOR. WALPOLE Munchausen .. presented an ample bill of extraordinaries for forage, etc.

†C *adv.* Extraordinarily. M17–L18.

extraordinarily *adv.* to an extraordinary degree, in an extraordinary manner M16. **extraordinariness** *n.* E17.

extrapolate /ɪkˈstrapəleɪt, ɛk-/ *v.* M19. [f. EXTRA- + INTER)POLATE *v.*] †1 *v.t.* Remove (a passage) from written material. *rare*. Only in M19. 2 *v.t.* & *i.* Extend (a range of values, a curve) on the assumption that the trend exhibited inside the given part is maintained outside it; assume the continuance of a known trend in inferring or estimating an unknown value; *gen.* predict on the basis of known facts or observed events. Also, obtain (an estimate, an extension of a given range etc.) by doing this; infer, or make an inference, *from*. L19. 3 *v.i.* Foll. by *to*: reach (a specified value) when extrapolated. E20.

2 S. WEINBERG Our calculations allow us to extrapolate the expansion of the universe backward in time. LD RUTHERFORD The effective straggling coefficient .. was calculated from this extrapolated curve. *Times Lit. Suppl.* His documents are .. comments on a particular colony at a particular time; .. it is hard work to extrapolate from them any general view about all the colonies. 3 *Nature* The line shown .. is a physical impossibility since it extrapolates to −666 at 4,599 Myr.

extrapolable, **extrapolatable** *adjs.* M20. **extrapoˈlation** *n.* the action or process, or an act, of extrapolating L19. **extrapolative** *a.* characterized by extrapolation; of the nature of extrapolation; employing or given to extrapolation: E20. **extrapolator** *n.* M20. **extrapolatory** *a.* M20.

extraposition /ɛkstrəpəˈzɪʃ(ə)n/ *n.* E20. [f. EXTRA- + POSITION *n.*] *Gram.* The placing of a word or group of words outside or at the end of a clause instead of within, while retaining the sense, as in *the rain, it raineth every day*.

extraˈpose *v.t.* subject to extraposition; move *from* or *to*: M20.

extraprovincial /ɛkstrəprəˈvɪnʃ(ə)l/ *a.* L17. [med.L *extraprovincialis*, f. *extra provinciam* outside the province.] Situated beyond the limits of a province; pertaining to travel outside a province.

extraterritoriality /ˌɛkstrətɛrɪtɔːrɪˈalɪti/ *n.* M19. [f. mod.L *extra territorium* outside the territory + -AL[1] + -ITY.] The freedom accorded to ambassadors etc. from the jurisdiction of the territory in which they reside. Also, the right of or claim to jurisdiction of a country over individuals living abroad or companies operating abroad; the status of people living in a country but not subject to its laws.

ˌextraterriˈtorial *a.* M19.

†**extraught** *a.* (orig. *pa. pple*). Only in 16. [Var. of EXTRACT *a.*; cf. *distraught*.] = EXTRACT *a.*

extravagance /ɪkˈstravəg(ə)ns, ɛk-/ *n.* M17. [Fr., f. as EXTRAVAGANT, -ANCE.] †1 A going out of the usual path (*lit.* & *fig.*); a digression; the position or fact of straying *from* a prescribed path. Only in M17. 2 An instance or kind of extravagant behaviour; an extravagant thing; *esp.* an absurd statement or action; a purchase or payment difficult to justify except as a whim or indulgence. M17. 3 The quality of being extravagant, esp. in writing, speech, or thought. L17. 4 Prodigality or wastefulness in expenditure, household management, etc. E18.

1 MILTON A doctrine of that extravagance from the sage principles of piety. 2 M. MEYER Another of his lifelong extravagances, clothes. R. DAWKINS Extravagances such as the tails of male birds of paradise. 4 M. EDGEWORTH Such extravagance, to give .. a silver penny, for what you may have for nothing.

extravagancy /ɪkˈstravəg(ə)nsi, ɛk-/ *n.* E16. [f. next: see -ANCY.] †1 The action or an act of wandering or departing from one's course. E16–M17. 2 = EXTRAVAGANCE 2. E16. 3 = EXTRAVAGANCE 3. Formerly also, eccentricity; impropriety, unbecomingness. Now *rare* or *obs.* M17. †4 = EXTRAVAGANCE 4. M17–E19.

extravagant /ɪkˈstravəg(ə)nt, ɛk-/ *a.* & *n.* LME. [med.L *extravagant-*, f. L EXTRA- + *vagant-* pres. ppl stem of *vagari* wander: see -ANT[1]. Also infl. in gen. sense by Fr. *extravagant*, It. *(e)stravagante*.] A *adj.* †1 Widely divergent or discrepant; irrelevant. (Foll. by *from*, *to*.) LME–M17. †2 Varying widely from what is usual or proper; unusual, abnormal, strange; unbecoming, unsuitable. LME–E18. 3 *RC Ch.* Designating certain medieval papal decrees, orig. not collected in the decretals. LME. 4 Exceeding the bounds of reason; showing a lack of restraint or moderation; absurdly or astonishingly excessive or elaborate. L16. 5 That wanders out of bounds; straying, vagrant. *obs.* exc. w. allus. to Shakes. E17. †b Of a soldier: not assigned to one place of duty; having a roving commission. Only in 17. †6 Spreading or projecting beyond bounds; straggling. E–M17. 7 Exceeding the bounds of economy or necessity in expenditure, way of life, etc.; profuse, prodigal, wasteful; (of a price) exorbitant. E18.

2 T. FULLER Persons .. treacherously slain, which occasioned their hasty .. and extravagant interment. 4 W. H. IRELAND The extravagant panegyrist of various living characters. G. SAINTSBURY It is .. not in the least extravagant to regard Sir Thomas Browne as the greatest prose-writer in the English language. F. KING Her writing, backward-sloping and all extravagant loops and swirls. 5 SHAKES. *Haml.* Th' extravagant and erring spirit hies To his confine. 6 EVELYN Cutting the too thick and extravagant Roots a little. 7 M. ROBERTS Madly extravagant and out of season, but I felt like having a treat.

B *n.* 1 *RC Ch.* An extravagant decree. E16. †2 A person who strays or wanders (*lit.* & *fig.*). L16–M17. †3a An exceptional or eccentric person; a fanatic. E17–E18. b A person who is extravagant in expenditure, way of life, etc. M18–E19. †4 An extravagant act, statement, etc. E17–E18.

extravagantly *adv.* E17.

extravaganza /ɪkˌstravəˈganzə, ɛk-/ *n.* M18. [Alt. (after EXTRA-) of It. *estravaganza* (usu. *strav-*), f. *(e)stravagante* f. as EXTRAVAGANT.] 1 Extravagance of language or behaviour. Now *rare*. M18. 2 A literary, musical, or dramatic composition of an extravagant or fanciful character. L18.

extravagate /ɪkˈstravəgeɪt, ɛk-/ *v.i.* E17. [f. EXTRAVAGANT + -ATE[3].] 1 Stray *from* a right course, a text, *into* error, etc. E17. 2 Wander at large; roam at will. M18. 3 Exceed what is proper or reasonable. E19.

extravaˈgation *n.* E17.

†**extravage** *v.i.* L17–M18. [f. prec. or EXTRAVAGANT.] Go beyond the sphere of duty; digress; ramble.

extravasate /ɪkˈstravəseɪt, ɛk-/ *a. obs.* exc. *poet.* M17. [f. next after adjs. in -ATE[2].] That has extravasated; that is not contained inside a vessel.

extravasate /ɪkˈstravəseɪt, ɛk-/ *v.* M17. [f. EXTRA- + L *vas* vessel + -ATE[3].] Chiefly *Med.* 1 *v.t.* Let or force out (a fluid, esp. blood) from the vessel that naturally contains it. M17. 2 *v.i.* Of blood, lava, etc.: flow out; undergo extravasation. L17.

extravaˈsation *n.* (chiefly *Med.*) an escape or effusion of blood or other fluid, esp. from many small vessels into surrounding tissue; a quantity of blood etc. that has escaped: L17.

†**extravase** *v.t.* & *i.* M17–M19. [Fr. *extravaser*, f. as EXTRA- + L *vas* vessel.] = EXTRAVASATE *v.*

extraversion /ɛkstrəˈvəːʃ(ə)n/ *n.* L17. [f. EXTRA- + VERSION.] †1 A turning outwards (*lit.* & *fig.*); a making manifest. *rare*. L17–E18. 2 = EXTROVERSION 3. E20.

extraversive *a.* = EXTROVERSIVE M20.

extravert /ˈɛkstrəvəːt/ *n.* E20. [f. prec. Cf. CONVERT *n.*] = EXTROVERT *n.*

extravert /ˈɛkstrəvəːt/ *v.t.* M17. [f. EXTRA- + L *vertere* to turn.] †1 Make manifest. M–L17. 2 = EXTROVERT *v.* M17.

†**extreat** *n.* L15. [Var. of ESTREAT, with *ex-* for *es-* after L.] 1 = ESTREAT *n.* L15–E18. 2 Extraction. Only in L16.

extrema *n.pl.* see EXTREMUM.

extremal /ɪkˈstriːm(ə)l, ɛk-/ *n.* E20. [f. EXTREMUM: see -AL[1].] *Math.* (A function represented by) a curve the integral along which has a maximum or minimum value; a surface the integral over which has such a value.

extremal /ɪkˈstriːm(ə)l, ɛk-/ *a.* LME. [f. EXTREME, (in sense 2) EXTREMUM + -AL[1].] †1 Outermost. Only in LME. 2 *Math.* Of or pertaining to extreme qualities or configurations, or highest or lowest values. M20.

extreme /ɪkˈstriːm, ɛk-/ *a.*, *n.*, & *adv.* LME. [(O)Fr. *extrême* f. L *extremus*, f. *exter* outer.] A *adj.* 1a (Of a quality, condition, or feeling) existing in a very high degree, very great or intense; (of an action, measure, etc.) very severe or violent; (of a case or circumstance) having some characteristic in the utmost degree. LME. †b Of a material agent: effective to a very high degree; very powerful. L15–M18. c Of a person: going to great lengths; advocating severe or drastic measures; immoderate in opinion. Formerly also, strict, severe. M16. d Of an opinion, fashion, etc.: immoderate, excessive. L19. 2 Outermost, furthest from the centre; endmost, situated at an end. LME. b Furthest; very far advanced in any direction; utmost, uttermost. L16. 3 Last, latest. Now *rare* or *obs.* Cf. *extreme unction* below. L15.

1a J. BUCHAN Mr Craw's face showed extreme irritation. H. G. WELLS This is only a very extreme instance of the general state of affairs. V. WOOLF Here at college, where the stir and presence of life are so extreme. 2 R. WARNER Flats . . built at the extreme edge of the aerodrome. **extreme and mean ratio** *Math.*: represented by a line divided according to the golden section, so that the ratio of its length to that of the longer part is the same as the ratio of the length of the longer part to that of the shorter (viz. 1.61803 . . .). †**extreme parts** the extremities of the body. **b** B. BAINBRIDGE The extreme end of the corrider. 3 **extreme unction** *RC Ch.* (former name for) the sacrament of anointing the sick, esp. those thought to be near death.

B *n.* †**1** The utmost or terminating point or verge; an end, an extremity (in time or space). M16–E19. **2** A very high degree; *the* utmost degree. M16. †**b** In *pl.* Straits, extremities, adversity. M16–M17. **3a** Something which is situated at one end of anything; either of two things as far as possible from each other in position, nature, or condition. M16. **b** *Math.* The first or last term of a series or proportion. Now *rare* or *obs.* L16. **c** *Logic.* The subject or predicate in a proposition; the major or minor term in a syllogism. E17. **4** An excessive degree, a very great length; an extreme measure. L16.

1 in (**the, his,** or **her**) **extremes** in the last moments of life. 3a G. GREENE It's strange how the human mind swings back and forth, from one extreme to another. *Proverb*: Extremes meet. **go to the other extreme** take a diametrically opposite course of action. 4 MRS H. WOOD I never thought the masters would go to the extreme of a lock-out. J. ROSENBERG An enthusiastic temperament such as his easily led to extremes.

Other phrases: **in (the) extreme** to an extreme degree, extremely.

†**C** *adv.* To an extreme degree, extremely. L16–E19.

extremely *adv.* †(*a*) to the uttermost degree; with a very great degree of some quality, esp. severity; (*b*) to or in an extreme degree; very much: L15. **extremeness** *n.* M16.

extremism /ɪkˈstriːmɪz(ə)m, ɛk-/ *n.* M19. [f. EXTREME + -ISM.] **1** Tendency to be extreme. M19. **2** The views or actions of extremists. E20.

extremist /ɪkˈstriːmɪst, ɛk-/ *n.* & *a.* M19. [f. as prec. + -IST.] **A** *n.* A person who holds extreme opinions or advocates extreme measures; a person who tends to go to extremes. M19. **B** *adj.* Of or pertaining to extremists or extremism. E20.

extremity /ɪkˈstrɛmɪti, ɛk-/ *n.* LME. [OFr. *extrémité* or L *extremitas*, f. *extremus*: see EXTREME, -ITY.] **1** The terminal point or portion of anything; the very end. LME. **b** In *pl.* The outermost parts of the body; the hands and feet. L15. †**2** = EXTREME *n.* 3a. Usu. in *pl.* LME–L16. **3** = EXTREME *n.* 2. LME. **4** A condition of extreme urgency or need; the utmost point of adversity. LME. **5** Great intensity of emotion or (formerly) action. Formerly also, a violent outburst. E16. †**6** Extreme severity or rigour (of a reprimand, punishment, etc.). M16–M17. **b** Extreme severity *of* weather. M16–E19. †**7** (An) extravagance in opinion, behaviour, or expenditure. M16–E18. **8** The last moments of a person's life. *arch.* E17. **9** An extreme measure. Usu. in *pl. arch.* M17. **10** Extremeness. M19.

1 W. BECKFORD Both extremities of the cross aisles are terminated by altar-tombs. 4 QUILLER-COUCH The man whom in his extremity I clothed and fed. 5 O. SACKS Those who are enduring extremities of suffering, sickness and anguish.

extremum /ɪkˈstriːməm, ɛk-/ *n.* Pl. **-mums, -ma** /-mə/. E20. [L, use as n. of neut. of *extremus* extreme.] *Math.* A value of a function that is a maximum or a minimum (either relative or absolute).

extricable /ˈɛkstrɪkəb(ə)l, ɪkˈstrɪk-/ *a.* E17. [f. next: see -ABLE. Cf. earlier INEXTRICABLE.] †**1** Able to be unravelled or solved. E17–E18. **2** Able to be set free or got out. L18.

extricate /ˈɛkstrɪkeɪt/ *v.t.* E17. [L *extricat-* pa. ppl stem of *extricare*, f. as EX-[1] 1 + *tricae* perplexities: see -ATE[3].] **1** Unravel; clear of tangles or (*fig.*) perplexities. Now *rare.* E17. **2** Get (a person) out of a difficulty, entanglement, etc.; remove, usu. with difficulty or dexterity, from what physically holds or contains someone or something. (Foll. by *from, out of.*) M17. **3** *Chem.* Release (gas) during a reaction. Now *rare* or *obs.* L18.

2 C. JACKSON After much embarrassed wriggling on her part he had extricated the offending garment. P. ACKROYD A foreigner who might extricate her from the world of Edwardian respectability. P. ROTH Suicide was the only way he might ever be able to extricate himself from his confusion and pain.

extriˈcation *n.* (*a*) the action of extricating; (*b*) hatching (from an egg): E17.

extrinsic /ɪkˈstrɪnsɪk, ɛk-/ *a.* M16. [Late L *extrinsecus* outer, f. L *extrinsecus* outwardly, f. *exter* external + *-im* as in *interim* + *secus* alongside of: see -IC.] †**1 a** Situated on the outside. *rare.* Only in M16. **b** Pertaining to the outside, external. M18. **2** Of a cause or influence: operating from outside, extraneous. E17. **3** Pertaining to an object in its external relations. Now *rare.* E17. **4** Due to external circumstances, not inherent. E17. **5** Not included, not forming part. Foll. by *to.* M17. **6** *Physics.* Characteristic of or designating a semiconductor in which the electrical conduction is due chiefly to electrons or holes provided by an added dopant. M20.

1b K. AMIS You are denied visitors . . And all extrinsic aids, like news. 4 HAZLITT Without any extrinsic advantages of birth.

Special collocations: **extrinsic factor** vitamin B_{12}. **extrinsic muscle**: originating beyond a part and acting on it as a whole.

extrinsical *a.* (now *rare*) = EXTRINSIC L16. **extrinsically** *adv.* L16. **extrinsicism** /-sɪsɪz(ə)m/ *n.* the view that the truth of religious dogma is received rather than demonstrated; an extrinsic thing: E20.

extrinsicate /ɪkˈstrɪnsɪkeɪt, ɛk-/ *v.t. rare.* M17. [f. EXTRINSIC + -ATE[3].] Exhibit outwardly, express.

extro- /ˈɛkstrəʊ/ *pref.*, alt. of EXTRA- after INTRO-, used by way of antithesis to this.

extrorse /ɪkˈstrɔːs, ɛk-/ *a.* M19. [Late L *extrorsus* adv., in an outward direction, f. L *extra* (see EXTRA *prep.*) + *versus* towards, pa. pple of *vertere* turn.] *Bot.* Of an anther: releasing its pollen on the outside of the flower.

extrospective /ɛkstrəˈspɛktɪv/ *a.* E20. [f. EXTRO- after INTROSPECTIVE.] Not introspective; regarding external objects rather than one's own thoughts and feelings.

extroversion /ɛkstrəˈvəːʃ(ə)n/ *n.* M17. [f. EXTRO- + VERSION.] **1** Chiefly *Med.* The action of turning, or the condition of being turned, outwards or inside out. M17. †**2** The diversion or wandering of a person's attention during a mystical experience. M17–L18. **3** *Psychol.* The fact or tendency of having one's thoughts and interests directed chiefly towards things outside the self. Opp. INTROVERSION. E20.

extroversive *a.* (*Psychol.*) characterized by or given to extroversion E20.

extrovert /ˈɛkstrəvəːt/ *n.* & *a.* E20. [Var. of EXTRAVERT *n.* after INTROVERT *n.*: see EXTRO-.] *Psychol.* (A person) given to or characterized by extroversion; (designating) a sociable or unreserved person.

extroverted *a.* = EXTROVERT *a.* E20. **extrovertish** *a.* somewhat extrovert; like that of an extrovert: M20.

extrovert /ɛkstrəˈvəːt/ *v.t. rare.* L17. [f. EXTRO- + L *vertere* to turn.] Give an outward direction to.

†**extruct** *v.* var. of EXSTRUCT.

extrude /ɪkˈstruːd, ɛk-/ *v.* M16. [L *extrudere*, f. as EX-[1] 1 + *trudere* to thrust.] **1** *v.t.* Thrust or force out; expel. (Foll. by *from.*) M16. **b** Shape (metal, plastic, etc.) by forcing through dies. E20. **2** *v.i.* Be extruded; protrude. M19.

1 G. VIDAL Ticker-tape machines extruded tapes in code. E. BOWEN Still more ornate pieces have been extruded to the outlying wings.

extrudable *a.* L20. **extruder** *n.* (*a*) a machine that shapes materials by forcing them through dies; (*b*) *Typogr.* an ascender, a descender: M20.

extrusion /ɪkˈstruːʒ(ə)n, ɛk-/ *n.* M16. [med.L *extrusio(n-)*, f. L *extrus-* pa. ppl stem of *extrudere*: see prec., -ION.] **1** Forceful expulsion from a place, position, privilege, etc. M16. **2** Expulsion by mechanical force, esp. of molten, fluid, or plastic material; *spec.* the shaping of metal or plastic by forcing through a die. M17. **3** An article made by extrusion. E20.

extrusive /ɪkˈstruːsɪv, ɛk-/ *a.* E19. [f. L *extrus-*: see prec., -IVE.] Tending to extrude; able to be extruded; *Geol.* (of rock) having been extruded to the earth's surface as lava or ash.

extry /ˈɛkstri/ *a., adv.,* & *n. colloq.* & *dial.* (chiefly *US*). M19. [Alt.] = EXTRA *a., adv.,* & *n.*

extubation /ɛkstjʊˈbeɪʃ(ə)n/ *n.* L19. [f. EX-[1] + IN)TUBATION.] *Med.* The removal of tubes from an intubated patient.

ˈextubate *v.t.* remove tubes from L20.

extuberant /ɪkˈstjuːb(ə)r(ə)nt, ɛk-/ *a.* Now *rare* or *obs.* L16. [L *extuberant-* pres. ppl stem of *extuberare*: see next, -ANT[1].] Swelling out, protuberant.

†**extuberance** *n.* (*a*) the quality or condition of being extuberant; (*b*) a swelling, a projection: E17–E19. †**extuberancy** *n.* = EXTUBERANCE M17–E18.

†**extuberate** *v.i.* & *t. rare.* E17–M18. [L *extuberat-* pa. ppl stem of *extuberare* swell out, f. as EX-[1] 1 + *tuber* swelling: see -ATE[3].] (Cause to) swell out or up.

extund /ɪkˈstʌnd, ɛk-/ *v.t.* E17. [L *extundere*, f. as EX-[1] 1 + *tundere* to beat.] Produce with effort, hammer out.

exuberance /ɪɡˈzjuːb(ə)r(ə)ns, ɛɡ-/ *n.* M17. [Fr. *exubérance* f. L *exuberantia*, f. *exuberant-*: see next, -ANCE.] **1** A superabundance, esp. of something abstract. M17. †**b** An abundance of good things. L17–M18. **2** An overflow; a profuse outgrowth; a protuberance. Now *rare.* M17. **3** The quality or condition of being exuberant; luxuriance of growth in a plant; abundance of high spirits and good health in a person. M17. **b** Copiousness or superfluity in expression. E18. **c** An extravagance, an excessive outburst. M19.

1 J. GALSWORTHY This resentment expressed itself in . . an exuberance of family cordiality. 3 *Listener* A man who had lost his youthful exuberance.

Also **exuberancy** *n.* E17.

exuberant /ɪɡˈzjuːb(ə)r(ə)nt, ɛɡ-/ *a.* LME. [Fr. *exubérant* f. L *exuberant-* pres. ppl stem of *exuberare*, f. as EX-[1] 1 + *uberare* be fruitful, f. *uber* fruitful: see -ANT[1].] **1 a** Of affection, joy, health, etc.: overflowing, abounding. LME. **b** Of people or their actions etc.: effusive in display of feeling; *esp.* full of high spirits and good health. E16. **2** Growing luxuriantly; produced in excess. E16. **b** Of speech or writing: copious, diffuse, lavishly ornamented. M17. **3** Luxuriantly fertile; abundantly productive. M17. **4** Of a fountain, stream, etc.: overflowing. L17. **5** Of wealth, stores, display, etc.: lavish, abundant, profuse. L17.

1a E. F. BENSON She should be in the highest and most exuberant spirits at their little dinner. **b** A. POWELL He gave an exuberant greeting. 2 A. N. WILSON The exuberant frizz of hair which blew from the hood of her . . duffle coat. 3 D. G. ROSSETTI Love's exuberant hotbed.

exuberantly *adv.* M17.

exuberate /ɪɡˈzjuːbəreɪt, ɛɡ-/ *v.* L15. [L *exuberat-* pa. ppl stem of *exuberare*: see prec., -ATE[3].] †**1** *v.t. Alch.* Make (mercury) act effectively. L15–L17. **2** *v.i.* Be exuberant; abound, overflow. E17. **3** *v.i.* Develop *into*; indulge *in* with exuberant feeling. Now *rare.* E18.

Exucontian /ɛksjʊˈkɒntɪən/ *n.* & *a.* M19. [f. eccl.Gk *exoukontios* (f. phr. *ex ouk ontōn* out of non-being) + -AN.] *Eccl.* (Designating) an Arian.

exudate /ˈɛɡzjʊdeɪt/ *n.* L19. [L *ex(s)udat-* pa. ppl stem of *ex(s)udare*: see EXUDE, -ATE[2].] An exuded substance; a quantity of exuded material; *spec.* (*Med.*) a mass of cells and fluid that has seeped out of blood-vessels or an organ, e.g. in inflammation or malignancy. Cf. TRANSUDATE.

†**exudate** *v.t.* & *i.* M17–L18. [f. as prec.: see EXUDE, -ATE[3].] = EXUDE.

exudation /ɛɡzjʊˈdeɪʃ(ə)n/ *n.* E17. [Late L *exsudatio(n-)*, f. as prec.: see -ATION.] **1** The process of exuding. E17. **2** Something which is exuded; *esp.* something given off like a vapour. E17.

2 B. MALAMUD The cold rose like an exudation from the marble floor.

eˈxudative *a.* (chiefly *Med.*) pertaining to or characterized by exudation M19.

exude /ɪɡˈzjuːd, ɛɡ-/ *v.* L16. [L *ex(s)udare*, f. as EX-[1] 1 + *sudare* to sweat.] **1** *v.i.* Ooze out; pass off slowly through pores, an incision, etc. L16. **2** *v.t.* Give off (moisture, a smell, etc.) in this way. M18. **3** *v.t.* (Of a person) show strongly (a personal characteristic or other immaterial quality); (of a place) have a strong atmosphere of. L19.

3 D. H. LAWRENCE He seemed to exude pride . . as he walked about.

exulcerate /ɪɡˈzʌlsəreɪt, ɛɡ-/ *v. arch.* M16. [L *exulcerat-* pa. ppl stem of *exulcerare*, f. as EX-[1] 1 + *ulcer-*, *ulcus*: see ULCER *n.*, -ATE[3].] †**1** *v.t.* & *i.* Cause ulcers (in). M16–M18. †**2** *v.i.* Break out in ulcers or sores. L16–E18. **3** *v.t.* Exasperate, irritate; wound (feelings); aggravate (a state). L16. **4** *v.i.* Act as an irritant or torment. L17.

exulceration /ɪɡˌzʌlsəˈreɪʃ(ə)n, ɛɡ-/ *n.* M16. [L *exulceratio(n-)*, f. as prec.: see -ATION.] **1** Ulceration; the early stages of ulceration. Now *rare* or *obs.* M16. **2** An ulcer, a sore. M16. **3** Exasperation; embitterment. L16.

exult /ɪɡˈzʌlt, ɛɡ-/ *v.* L16. [L *ex(s)ultare*, frequent. of *exsilire* leap up, f. as EX-[1] 1 + *salire* to leap.] †**1** *v.i.* Spring or leap up; leap for joy. L16–E18. **2** *v.i.* Rejoice greatly, be elated. (Foll. by *in*, *at*, *on*, *over*; *to do*.) L16. **3** *v.t.* Say exultingly. E20.

exultingly *adv.* in an exulting manner M17.

exultancy /ɪɡˈzʌlt(ə)nsi, ɛɡ-/ *n.* E17. [Late L *ex(s)ultantia*, f. L *ex(s)ultant-* pres. ppl stem of *ex(s)ultare*: see prec., -ANCY.] (An) exultant state; exultation; a joyous rapture.

Also **exultance** *n.* M17.

exultant /ɪɡˈzʌlt(ə)nt, ɛɡ-/ *a.* M17. [L *ex(s)ultant-* pres. ppl stem of *ex(s)ultare*: see EXULT, -ANT[1].] Triumphantly or rapturously joyful.

exultantly *adv.* L19.

exultation /ɛɡzʌlˈteɪʃ(ə)n/ *n.* LME. [L *ex(s)ultatio(n-)*, f. *ex(s)ultat-* pa. ppl stem of *ex(s)ultare*: see EXULT, -ATION.] **1** The action or a state of exulting; (the expression of) triumphant joy or rapture. LME. **2** An object exulted over, a cause of great joy. L15. **3** In *pl.* Shouts of joy. L16.

1 J. R. GREEN The exultation of the Court over the decision of the judges. J. BALDWIN There arose in him an exultation and a sense of power.

Exultet /ɪɡˈzʌltɛt, ɛɡ-/ *n.* M19. [L = let it rejoice, 3rd person sing. pres. subjunct. of *ex(s)ultare* EXULT.] *RC Ch.* The prose sung by the deacon at the blessing of the Paschal Candle on Easter Eve, of which *Exultet iam angelica turba* are the opening words.

exululate /ɛkˈsjuːljʊleɪt/ *v.i. rare.* E17. [L *exululat-* pa. ppl stem of *exululare*, f. as EX-[1] 1 + *ululare* howl: see ULULATE.] Howl, cry out.

exuluˈlation *n.* E18.

exumbrella /ɛksʌmˈbrɛlə/ *n.* L19. [f. EX-[1] + UMBRELLA.] *Zool.* The outer, convex, side of the umbrella of a jellyfish.

exumbrellar *a.* L19.

exundant /ɪkˈsʌnd(ə)nt, ɛk-/ *a.* M17. [L *exundant-* pres. ppl stem of *exundare* gush forth, overflow, f. as EX-[1] 1 + *undare* rise in waves, f. *unda* wave: see -ANT[1].] Overflowing, superabundant.

exundation /ɛksʌnˈdeɪʃ(ə)n/ *n.* Now *rare.* L16. [L *exundatio(n-)*, f. *exundare*: see prec., -ATION.] The action or an act of overflowing (by water).

exurb /ˈɛksəːb/ *n.* Orig. *US.* M20. [f. L *ex* out of + *urbs* city, or back-form. f. next.] A district outside a city or town, *esp.* a prosperous one beyond the suburbs.

exurban /ɛkˈsəːb(ə)n/ *a.* E20. [f. EX-[1] + URBAN, after SUBURBAN.] Of or belonging to a district outside a city or town, esp. an exurb.

exurbanite *n.* & *a.* (orig. *US*) (*a*) *n.* a person who lives in an exurb; (*b*) *adj.* = EXURBAN: M20.

exurbia /ɛkˈsəːbɪə/ *n.* Orig. *US.* M20. [f. EX-[1] + *-urbia*, after SUBURBIA.] Exurbs collectively; the region outside the suburbs of a city.

†**exust** *v.t. rare.* E17–E19. [L *exust-* pa. ppl stem of *exurere*, f. as EX-[1] 1 + *urere* burn.] Burn up.

†**exustion** *n.* L16–E18. [L *exustio(n-)*, f. as prec.: see -ION.] Destruction by burning; the action of burning something.

exute /ɪɡˈzjuːt, ɛɡ-/ *v.t. obs.* exc. *Hist.* M16. [L *exut-* pa. ppl stem of *exuere*: see next.] Strip (a person) *of*; divest or deprive *of*.

exuviae /ɪɡˈzjuːviiː, ɛɡ-/ *n.pl.* M17. [L = clothing stripped off, skins of animals, spoils, f. *exuere* divest oneself of.] Cast skins, shells, or other shed outer parts of animals, whether recent or fossil; *spec.* (*Zool.*) sloughed skins; *fig.* remnants, remains.

exuvial *n.* & *a.* †(*a*) *n.* (in *pl.*) spoils; (*b*) *adj.* pertaining to or of the nature of exuviae: M17. **exuviate** *v.t.* & *i.* shed (as) exuviae, moult M19. **exuviˈation** *n.* M19.

ex vi termini /ɛks viː ˈtəːmɪniː/ *adv. phr.* Now *rare* or *obs.* E18. [mod.L = from the force of the term.] By definition; by implication.

ex-voto /ɛksˈvəʊtəʊ/ *n.* & *a.* Pl. of n. **-os**. L18. [L *ex voto* f. *ex* out of, from + *voto* abl. sing. of *votum*: see VOTE *n.*] (Designating) something offered in fulfilment of a vow previously taken.

ex-votive *a.* M19.

†**ey** *n.* OE–M16. [OE *ǣġ* = OS, OHG (Du., G) *ei*, Crimean Goth. *ada*, f. Gmc., prob. ult. rel. to L *ovum*, Gk *ōion*.] = EGG *n.*

†**ey** *int.* var. of AY *int.*[2]

-ey *suff.*[1] see -Y[1].

-ey *suff.*[2] see -Y[6].

eyalet /ɛˈjɑːlɛt/ *n.* M19. [Turk., f. Arab. *iyāla(t)* management, administration, f. *ʼāla* govern.] = VILAYET.

eyas /ˈʌɪəs/ *n.* & *a.* Orig. †**nyas**. L15. [(O)Fr. *niais* (orig.) bird taken from the nest, (now) silly person, f. Proto-Romance f. L *nidus* nest. Initial *n* lost by misdivision as in ADDER *n.*[1]; sp. with *ey-* may be due to assoc. with EY *n.*] A *n.* **1** A young hawk in the nest, or taken from it for training; a hawk whose training is incomplete. L15. **2** A child, a youthful or immature person. L16. **B** *attrib.* or as *adj.* Unfledged, youthful. L16.

eye /ʌɪ/ *n.* [OE *ēaġe*, (Anglian) *ēġe* = OFris. *āgc*, OS *ōga* (Du. *oog*), OHG *ouga* (G *Auge*), ON *auga*, Goth. *augo*, f. Gmc. The OE pl. *ēaġan* survives in north. *een* and arch. *eyne* (Spenser); pl. *-s* dates from LME.] **I** **1** The organ of sight in humans and animals; the region of the face surrounding this. OE. **b** The imagined organ of sight as attributed to the heart, mind, or other quasi-personified things. OE. **c** The (usu. human) eye as characterized by the colour of its iris. ME. **2** *sing.* & in *pl.* **a** A look, a glance, a gaze. OE. **b** The aspect of a person's face as expressing his or her feelings. ME. **3** The eye as possessing the power or faculty of vision. ME. **b** A person or animal whose power of vision is used by another (usu. blind) person. LME. **c** A detective, a detective agency, *esp.* a private one. *slang.* E20. **d** A mechanical or electrical device resembling an eye in function. M20. **4a** *sing.* & in *pl.* The sense of seeing; ocular perception. ME. **b** An attentive look; attention, regard; observation, supervision. ME. **c** *sing.* & in *pl.* Point of view, way of looking at a thing; opinion, judgement. ME. **d** Range of vision, view, sight. Now *rare* or *obs.* exc. *fig.* in *one's mind's eye* below. L16. **5** The faculty of visual perception, appreciation, or judgement, either in general or with some specific reference. M17.

1 ALDOUS HUXLEY Behind their bifocal lenses his eyes were bright with excitement. J. STEINBECK Kino's eyes opened, and he looked first at the lightening square. G. B. SHAW Her eyes are red from weeping. b R. KIPLING Cities and Thrones and Powers Stand in Time's eye, Almost as long as flowers, Which daily die. c I. MURDOCH The light brown eyes gazed in her direction. 2a W. COWPER Modestly let fall your eyes. b POPE View him with scornful, yet with jealous eyes. 3 C. ISHERWOOD Her eyes no longer see him. *National Observer* (*US*) Right before your eyes on the wide screen. b WORDSWORTH Thou best Philosopher . . thou Eye among the blind. d W. H. AUDEN Let me pretend that I'm the impersonal eye of the camera Sent out . . to shoot on location. 4a J. LE CARRÉ It's for his eyes only. b T. MEDWIN I had . . fallen under the eye of the Government. G. F. KENNAN Lloyd George, with an eye to his political fortunes at home, chose to head the British delegation in person. c D. HUME Persons not lying under . . attainder were innocent in the eye of the law. R. DAHL Nanny . . in my eyes was filled with more wisdom than Solomon.

II An object resembling the eye in appearance, shape, function, or relative position. **6a** The small hole in a needle for taking the thread. OE. **b** A small hole in bread or (now usu.) cheese. LME. **c** A hole made in a tool for the insertion of a handle or some other object. M16. **d** An opening or passage in a millstone, kiln, etc., for the introduction or withdrawal of substances; the entrance or exit of a fox's earth, a mine shaft, etc. M16. **7** A mark or spot resembling an eye occurring on eggs, insect wings, etc.; *esp.* any of the marks near the end of the tail feathers of a peacock; each of the three spots on one end of a coconut. LME. **b** *Geol.* A lens-shaped inclusion with a different texture from the surrounding rock. L19. **8** An object resembling an eye on a plant; *esp.* (*a*) an axillary bud or leaf bud; (*b*) the centre of a flower; (*c*) the remains of the calyx on a fruit. LME. **9** In *pl.* Spectacles. Now *rare.* E16. **10** A loop, a ring; *esp.* a loop of thread in a hook and eye (see HOOK *n.* 1c); *Naut.* a loop at the end of a rope, *esp.* one at the top end of a shroud or stay. L16. **11** *fig.* A place regarded as a centre of learning, culture, or the like. L16. **12a** *Archit.* The centre of any part, esp. of a volute. E18. **b** The centre of a vortex or eddy; *esp.* the calm centre of a hurricane or storm. M19. **c** The dense centre of a shoal of fish. M19. **d** The brightest spot or centre of light; *esp.* the part of a furnace observed through the sight-hole. L19. **e** The main mass of lean meat in a rasher of bacon, cutlet, etc. M20. **13** A prominent natural object, such as a hill or island. Only in place-names. M19. **14** The opening through which the water of a fountain or spring wells up. M19. **15** A mass of ore left in a mine to be worked when other ore is becoming scarce or inaccessible; *fig.* (*Austral.* & *NZ*) *the* choicest portion, esp. of land. M19. **16** *Naut.* In *pl.* (in full *eyes of her*, *eyes of the ship*). The extreme forward part of a ship. M19.

6a AV *Matt.* 19:24 It is easier for a camel to goe thorow the eye of a needle. 8 B. TRAPIDO Withered potatoes sprouting at the eyes.

†**III** **17** A slight shade, tinge, or hint *of* something. Only in 17.

Phrases etc.: **a gleam**, **glint**, **in one's eye** a barely formed idea; a child who has not yet been conceived. (**all**) **my eye** (**and Betty Martin**) (all) nonsense. **an eye for an eye** [alluding to *Exod.* 21:24] revenge, retaliation in kind. APPLE *of one's* (or *the*) *eye*. *a smack in the eye*: see SMACK *n.*[2] **a twinkle in one's eye** = *a gleam in one's eye* above. *a wipe in the eye*: see WIPE *n.* **be all eyes** watch attentively. BELIEVE *one's eyes*. *blue eye*: see BLUE *a.* *cast an eye*: see CAST *v.* **cast sheep's eyes at** = *make sheep's eyes at* below. *catch the eye of*: see CATCH *v.* †**change eyes** exchange amorous glances. *clap eyes on*: see CLAP *v.*[1] 9. **close one's eyes to** or **against** ignore, refuse to recognize or consider. *cock one's eye*: see COCK *v.*[1] 6. *collect eyes*: see COLLECT *v.* 1. *compound eye*: see COMPOUND *a.* *cry one's eyes out*: see CRY *v.* 5d. *damn your* (or *my* etc.) *eyes!*: see DAMN *v.* *deadeye*: see DEAD *a.* **do a person in the eye** defraud, thwart, or humiliate a person. *easy on the eye(s)*: see EASY *a.* 1b. *electric eye*: see ELECTRIC *a.* *evil eye*: see EVIL *a.* **eye of day** *poet.* the sun. **eyes down** *colloq.* the start of play at bingo. **eyes front**, **left**, or **right** *Mil.* (a command to) turn the head in the direction stated. **eyes on stalks**: widened in amazement, inquisitiveness, etc. *eyes right*: see *eyes front* above. *find favour in the eyes of*: see FAVOUR *n.* *Flemish eye*: see FLEMISH *a.* & *n.* **get one's eye in** *Sport* accustom oneself to the prevailing conditions. *glass eye*: see GLASS *n.* & *a.* **go eyes out** *Austral. colloq.* make every effort. *green eye*: see GREEN *a.* *green in one's eye*: see GREEN *n.* *grey eye*: see GREY *a.* **half an eye** a very slight degree of ocular perception (*see with half an eye*: at a glance, without effort). *have a drop in one's eye*: see DROP *n.* 3b. **have an eye for** be quick to notice. **have an eye to** have as one's object; prudently consider. **have eyes bigger than one's belly** or **stomach** wish or expect to eat more than one can. **have eyes for** be interested in (*only have eyes for*, desire nothing or no one but). **have eyes to see** be observant or discerning. **have one's eye on** (*a*) = *keep an eye on* below; (*b*) desire or hope to obtain. *here's mud in your eye!*: see MUD *n.*[1] **hit one in the eye** (of a fact, object, etc.) be very obvious. *in a pig's eye*: see PIG *n.*[1] †**in eye** in sight or view. **in one's eye** in one's imagination; in mind. **in the eye(s) of —** as far as — is concerned, in the view of. **in the public eye** receiving much public attention. *in the* TWINKLING *of an eye*. **in the wind's eye** against the direction of the wind. †**into eye** into sight or view. *jump to the eyes*: see JUMP *v.* **keep an eye on** keep under observation. **keep an** or **one's eye(s) open, out, peeled,** or **skinned** be watchful; watch carefully *for*. *keep one's weather eye* (*open*): see WEATHER *n.* *keep one's eye on the ball*: see BALL *n.*[1] 2. *lay an eye on, lay eyes on*: see LAY *v.*[1] *leap to the eye*: see LEAP *v.* *lift* (*up*) *one's eyes*: see LIFT *v.* **look a person in the eye** look directly or unashamedly at a person. **lose an eye** become unable to see with one eye. *magic eye*: see MAGIC *a.* **make (sheep's) eyes at** look amorously at. *meet the eye*: see MEET *v.* *mind one's eye*: see MIND *v.* †**mingle eyes** = *change eyes* above. *my eye*: see *all my eye* above. *naked eye*: see NAKED *a.* *needle's eye*: see NEEDLE *n.* *not bat an eye*: see BAT *v.*[2] 2. **one in the eye** a disappointment or setback *for* someone regarded as deserving it. **one's mind's eye** one's mental view or imagination. **open a person's eyes** (*a*) cause a person to stare in astonishment; (*b*) enlighten or undeceive a person. *pass one's eye over*: see PASS *v.* *pipe the* or *one's eye(s)*: see PIPE *v.*[1] 4c. *private eye*: see PRIVATE *a.* *pull the wool over a person's eyes*: see WOOL *n.* **run an eye over** examine cursorily. **see eye to eye** be of one mind, think alike. *seeing eye*: see SEEING *ppl a.* **set eyes on** see, catch sight of. **shut one's eyes to** or **against** = *close one's eyes to* above. *spit in the eye of*: see SPIT *v.*[2] *straight eye*: see STRAIGHT *a.*[1] *strong eye*: see STRONG *a.* *tail of the eye*: see TAIL *n.*[1] *the glad eye*: see GLAD *a.* **the mind's eye** = *one's mind's eye* above. *third eye*: see THIRD *a.* & *n.* *throw dust in a person's eyes*: see DUST *n.* *turn a blind eye* (*to*): see BLIND *a.* **up to one's** or **the eyes** deeply or heavily (involved, engaged, etc.); to the limit. *wash one's eyes*: see WASH *v.* *wipe one's* or *a person's eye*: see WIPE *v.* **with one eye on** directing one's attention partly to. **with one's eyes open** in full awareness. **with one's eyes shut** (*a*) without full awareness; (*b*) with great ease. *would give one's eyes*: see GIVE *v.*

Comb.: **eye bank** a stock of corneas taken from people soon after death and used for replacing defective corneas in blind people; **eyebath** a small cup-shaped vessel for applying lotion etc. to the eye; **eye-beam** a beam or glance of the eye; **eye-black** mascara; **eye-bolt** a bolt or bar with an eye at one end for a hook, ring, etc.; **eyebright** any of various plants of the genus *Euphrasia*, of the figwort family, many of which were formerly valued as a remedy for weak eyes (*red eyebright*: see RED *a.*); **eye-catcher** a person who or thing which catches the eye; **eye-catching** *a.* striking; attractive; prominent; **eye contact** the state or practice of looking at another's eyes while he or she is looking at one's own; **eye-cup** = *eyebath* above; **eye dialect** a form of writing in which spellings are altered in order to represent a dialectal pronunciation; **eye-drop** a tear; in *pl.*, a solution for applying to the eye; **eyehole** (*a*) *arch.* the eye socket; (*b*) a hole to look through; **eye language** interpersonal communication by means of the expression of the eyes; **eye-legible** *a.* in a form that can be read by eye, without a magnifier or reader; **eye-level** the level seen by eyes looking straight ahead; the height of the eyes; **eye-liner** a cosmetic applied in a line around the eye; **eye mask** a covering for the eyes; *spec.* one of soft material soaked with a lotion for refreshing the eyes; **eye-opener** (*a*) *US* a dram, *esp.* one taken in the morning; (*b*) a thing that enlightens or surprises; (*c*) a person who or thing which is outstandingly attractive; **eye-opening** *a.* that enlightens or surprises; **eye-patch** = PATCH *n.*[1] 1c; **eye pencil** a pencil for applying lines of make-up around the eyes; **eyepiece** the lens or combination of lenses in a telescope or microscope by which the image is viewed or magnified; **eye-pit** (*a*) the eye socket; (*b*) the depression between the eye and the orbit; **eye-rhyme** a correspondence (of words in a poem) in spelling but not in pronunciation; **eye-service** *arch.* the doing of work only when watched by an employer or master; **eye-shade** a visor for protecting the eyes from strong sunlight; **eye-shadow** make-up applied to the eyelids or around the eyes; **eyeshot** (*a*) seeing-distance, range of sight; (*b*) a glance, a sudden look; **eye socket** the orbit of the eye; **eye splice** a splice made by turning back the strands at the end of a rope and interlacing them with the preceding part of the rope; **eye-stalk** *Zool.* a movable stalk supporting the eye in some animals; **eye strain** weariness of the eyes resulting from excessive or incorrect use; †**eyestrings** the muscles, nerves, or tendons of the eye which were formerly supposed to break or crack at death or loss of sight; **eyestripe** a stripe on a bird's head which encloses or appears to run through the eye; **eye-tooth** one of the canine teeth directly under or next to the eye, esp. in the upper jaw (*cut one's eye-teeth*: see CUT *v.*; *would give one's eye-teeth*: see GIVE *v.*); **eyewash** (*a*) a lotion for the eye; (*b*) *slang* something said or done merely for appearance or effect; humbug; **eyewater** (*a*) tears; (*b*) lotion for the eye; (*c*) the aqueous or vitreous humour of the eye; **eyewear** spectacles, contact lenses, and other things worn on the eyes; **eye-wink** (*a*) a look or glance; (*b*) the time it takes to wink, an instant; **eyewitness** *n.* & *v.* (*a*) *n.* a person who can testify from his or her own observation; a person who has seen a particular thing done or happen; (*b*) *v.t.* be an eye-witness of (an event); **eye-worm** a filarial worm that infects the eye and subcutaneous tissue of man and other primates in tropical Africa.

eyelike *a.* resembling an eye E17.

eye /ʌɪ/ *v.* Infl. **eyeing, eying.** M16. [f. the n.] **1** *v.t.* Fix the eyes upon, look at, observe. M16. †**b** Regard or look upon *as*. M–L17. **2** *v.t.* Keep an eye on; watch closely. L16. **b** Look at amorously or with sexual interest, ogle. L20. †**3** *v.t.* See, perceive. L16–L18. †**4** *v.t.* Have or keep in view; look to; aim at. L16–M17. †**5** *v.i.* Appear to the eye, look. *rare* (Shakes.). Only in E17. **6** *v.t.* Pierce a hole in (a needle etc.). M19. **7** *v.i.* Of an egg: form an eye (see EYE *n.* 7). E20.

1 W. GASS She sniffs the air and eyes a sailing cloud. 2 R. COBB The two groups eyed one another, listlessly but without hostility. b S. NAIPAUL He eyed a shapely mulatto girl. 3 POPE The paths of gods what mortal can survey? Who eyes their motion? 5 SHAKES. *Ant. & Cl.* My becomings kill me when they do not eye well to you.

eyeable *a.* (*a*) visible; (*b*) visually attractive: L18. **eyer** *n.* (*rare*) (*a*) an observer; (*b*) a maker of eyes in needles: LME.

eyeball /ˈʌɪbɔːl/ *n.* & *v.* L16. [f. EYE *n.* + BALL *n.*[1]] **A** *n.* **1** The globe of the eye, a firm white sphere within the eyelids that is formed by the sclera and the cornea. L16. **2** The pupil of the eye. Now *rare* or *obs.* L16.

1 **eyeball to eyeball** confronting closely; with neither party yielding.

B *v.t.* & *i.* Look (at), stare (at). *N. Amer. colloq.* E20.

eye-bree /ˈʌɪbriː/ *n. obs.* exc. *Sc.* & *dial.* OE. [f. EYE *n.* + BREE *n.*[1]] †**1** The eyelid. OE–L18. †**2** An eyelash. L16–E17. **3** = EYEBROW 1. L18.

eyebrow /ˈʌɪbraʊ/ *n.* LME. [f. EYE *n.* + BROW *n.*[1]; repl. EYE-BREE.] **1** The arch of short fine hair along the ridge above each eye; an artificial imitation of this. LME. **2** *Archit.* A fillet. E18.

Phrases & comb.: *cock an eyebrow* or *one's eyebrows*: see COCK *v.*[1] 6. **eyebrow pencil** a cosmetic pencil for drawing lines to accentuate the eyebrows. **eyebrow tweezers** tweezers for extracting unwanted hairs from the eyebrows. **raise one's eyebrow(s), an eyebrow** show surprise or disbelief (*at*). **up to the eyebrows** = *up to the eyes* s.v. EYE *n.*

eyebrowed *a.* having eyebrows M19. **eyebrowless** *a.* M19.

eyed /ʌɪd/ *a.* LME. [f. EYE *n.* + -ED[2].] **1** Having eyes. Usu. with preceding n. or adj. LME. †**b** Gifted with sight; clear-sighted. L16–M17. **2** Of cheese, an implement, etc.: having a hole or holes. LME. **3** Ornamented with marks like eyes; spotted. E19.

1 SCOTT FITZGERALD The owl-eyed man. *blue-eyed, green-eyed*, etc. 3 KEATS Eyed like a peacock.

eyedness *n.* the fact of having one eye or a specified eye dominant, or of preferring to use it. M20.

eyeful /ˈʌɪfʊl, -f(ə)l/ *n.* M19. [f. EYE *n.* + -FUL.] **1** As much as the eye can take in at once; a complete view, a good look at something. M19. **2** An exhilarating sight; *spec.* a strikingly attractive person. *colloq.* E20.

eyeglass /ˈʌɪɡlɑːs/ *n.* & *v.* E17. [f. EYE *n.* + GLASS *n.*] **A** *n.* †**1** The lens of the eye. *rare* (Shakes.). Only in E17. **2** The lens of an optical instrument to which the eye is applied. M17. **3** A lens for assisting defective eyesight, a monocle; in *pl.*, a pair of these held in position by hand or supported on the bridge of the nose; *sing.* & in *pl.* (*N. Amer.*), (a pair of) spectacles. Formerly, a magnifying glass, a microscope. M18. **B** *v.t.* & *i.* Look through an eyeglass (at). *rare.* E19.

eyeglassed *a.* provided with an eyeglass or eyeglasses M19. **eye-glassy** *a.* (*colloq.*) (supposedly) characteristic of one wearing an eyeglass; haughtily superior: L19.

eyelash /ˈʌɪlaʃ/ *n.* M18. [f. EYE *n.* + LASH *n.*[1]] **1** Any of the hairs on the edge of the eyelid. Formerly, the line of such hairs. M18. **2** A hair's breadth, a minute distance. M20.

eyeless /ˈʌɪlɪs/ *a.* LME. [f. EYE *n.* + -LESS.] **1** That is without an eye or eyes. LME. **2** Deprived of the eyes. L16. **3** Blind. E17.

eyelet /ˈʌɪlɪt/ *n.* & *a.* LME. [OFr. *oillet* (mod. *œillet*), dim. of *oil* (mod. *œil*) eye f. L *oculus*: see -ET[1].] **A** *n.* **1** A small round usu. reinforced hole in leather, cloth, sailcloth, etc., for a lace, ring, or rope to pass through. LME. **2** A hole or slit in a wall, usu. for observation. LME. **3** A small eye, *esp.* one in a butterfly's wing. L16.

Comb.: **eyelet hole** = EYELET *n.* 1, 2.

B *attrib.* or as *adj.* Of embroidery or fabric: composed of numerous small holes. E20.

eyelet /ˈʌɪlɪt/ *v.t.* M19. [f. EYELET *n.*] Make eyelets in. Chiefly as *eyeleted* ppl a., *eyeleting* vbl n.

eyelid /ˈʌɪlɪd/ *n.* ME. [f. EYE *n.* + LID *n.*] Either of the upper and lower folds of skin that meet when the eye is closed.

hang on by the eyelids *fig.* have only a slight hold. *not bat an eyelid*: see BAT *v.*[2] 2. *third eyelid*: see THIRD *a.* & *n.*

eyesight /ˈʌɪsʌɪt/ *n.* ME. [f. EYE *n.* + SIGHT *n.*] **1** The power or faculty of seeing. ME. **2** The action or an act of seeing; a look; observation. Now *rare* or *obs.* ME. †**3** The range of the eyes. ME–M17.

1 J. MCPHEE His eyesight was not much better than what was required to see a blueberry inches away. 2 CARLYLE Things . . known to us by the best evidence, by eyesight.

eyesome /ˈʌɪs(ə)m/ *a.* Now *poet.* L16. [f. EYE *n.* + -SOME[1].] Attractive.

eyesore /ˈʌɪsɔː/ *n.* ME. [f. EYE *n.* + SORE *n.*[1]] †**1** Soreness of the eyes. ME–M16. **2** An ugly object or mark; something that is offensive to the eyes. M16. **3** A cause of annoyance, offence, or vexation. M16. †**4** A scar, flaw, or defect on a horse. L17–E18.

3 S. RUSHDIE This slum is a public eyesore, can no longer be tolerated.

eyespot /ˈʌɪspɒt/ *n.* E19. [f. EYE *n.* + SPOT *n.*] **1** A kind of lily with a red spot in the middle of each leaf. E19. **2** A spot resembling an eye, esp. on a plant or animal. L19. **3** A small light-sensitive area of some invertebrates that serves in place of an eye. L19. **4** Any of several fungal diseases of sugar cane, cereals, and other grasses which causes yellowish oval spots on the leaves and stems. E20.

4 *sharp eyespot*: see SHARP *a.* & *adv.*

eyespotted *a.* having spots resembling eyes L16.

Eyetalian /ʌɪˈtalɪən/ *a.* & *n. slang.* M19. [Repr. non-standard or joc. pronunc. of ITALIAN.] (An) Italian.

Eyetie /ˈʌɪtʌɪ/ *n.* & *a. derog. slang.* E20. [f. prec. + -IE.] = prec.

eye view /ʌɪ ˈvjuː/ *n. phr.* Also **eye-view.** M18. [f. *bird's eye view* s.v. BIRD *n.*] Used after a possess. wd or phr. to denote what is seen from the viewpoint of the person or thing specified.

ALDOUS HUXLEY How should one look at other people? . . Should one take the Freud's-eye view or the Cézanne's-eye view? *Listener* From his own eye-view Sir Compton has no lack of items to add to the history of his time.

eyot /eɪt, ˈeɪət/ *n.* L17. [Var. of AIT *n.*[1], infl. by *islet* and Fr. *îlot*.] = AIT *n.*[1]

eyra /ˈeɪrə/ *n.* E17. [Sp. f. Tupi-Guarani (*e*)*irára*.] In full *eyra cat*. A wild cat, *Felis yagouaroundi*, in its red phase, found from Argentina and Paraguay to southern Texas.

eyre /ɛː/ *n.* Now *Hist.* ME. [OFr. *eire* f. L *iter* journey.] **1** Itineration, circuit. Chiefly in *justice in eyre* below. ME. **2** The circuit court held by a justice in eyre. LME.

1 **justice in eyre** an itinerant judge who rode from county to county to hold courts.

eyrie /ˈɪəri, ˈʌɪəri, ˈɛːri/ *n.* Also **aerie, aery, eyry.** L15. [med.L *area, aeria, eyria*, prob. f. (O)Fr. *aire* f. L *area* level piece of ground, (in late L) nest of a bird of prey.] **1** The nest of a bird of prey, esp. an eagle, or of any other bird which builds high up; *fig.* a human residence built at a great height. L15. †**2** A young bird of prey. L16–E17.

ezan /ɛˈzʌn/ *n.* M18. [Pers. & Turk. pronunc. of Arab. *ʼadān*.] = AZAN.

F

F, f /ɛf/, the sixth letter of the modern Eng. alphabet and of the ancient Roman one, corresp. to Gk digamma (ϝ) (repr. /w/), Semitic waw (repr. the sounds of *w* (approx.) and *u*). The sound now normally represented by the letter is a voiceless labiodental fricative consonant, except in *of* where it is voiced. Pl. **F's, Fs.** Cf. EFF.

I 1 The letter and its sound. **2** The shape of the letter.

2 f-hole either of a pair of sound-holes resembling an ʃ or reversed ʃ in shape, in the belly of a musical instrument of the violin family. **F-shaped** *a.* having a shape or cross-section like the capital letter F.

II Symbolical uses. **3** Used to denote serial order; applied e.g. to the sixth group or section, sheet of a book, etc. **4** *Mus.* (Cap. F.) The fourth note of the diatonic scale of C major. Also, the scale of a composition with F as its keynote. **5** The sixth hypothetical person or example. **6** (Usu. cap. F.) Designating the sixth-highest class (of academic marks etc.). **7** *F-layer*, the highest, most strongly ionized stratum of the ionosphere. Also called *Appleton layer.*

4 F clef the bass clef.

III 8 Abbrevs.: (A small selection only is given here. Those all in caps. or small caps. also occur with a full stop after each letter; some of those all in caps. also occur (i) with initial cap. only, (ii) in small caps.) **F.** = Fahrenheit; Father; Fellow of. **F** = (*Physics*) farad(s); (*Bacteriol.*) fertility; (*Biol.*) filial generation; fine (pencil-lead, or (*Physics*) denoting the hyperfine quantum number, expressing the resultant of nuclear spin I and electronic angular momentum J); fibre (in *F Plan*, (US proprietary name for) a type of high-fibre diet); (*Chem.*) fluorine. **f** = (*Photogr.*) focal length (prefixed to numbers indicating the ratio between the focal length of a camera lens and the diameter of the aperture, as *F*/2.8 or *F*2.8, *F*/4 or *F*4, etc.); *f-number*, *f/number*, any of these numbers; (*Physics* & *Chem.*) fundamental (orig. designating one of the four main series (S, P, D, F) of lines in atomic spectra, now more frequently applied to electronic orbitals, states, etc., possessing three units of angular momentum (as *f-electron*, *f-orbital*, etc.)). **f.** = female; filly; folio; following page etc.; foreign; (*slang*) fuck, fucking (sometimes printed *f*—). **f** = (as *pref.*) femto-; (*Mus.*) forte; frequency. **FA** = Fanny Adams, (freq. in *sweet FA*); Football Association; (*slang*) fuck all (freq. in *sweet FA*). **FAA** = (*US*) Federal Aviation Authority; Fleet Air Arm. **FAD** (*Biochem.*) = flavin adenine dinucleotide. **Fahr.** = Fahrenheit. **FANY** = First Aid Nursing Yeomanry. **FAO** = Food and Agriculture Organization (of the United Nations). **FAQ** = fair average quality. **f.a.s.** = free alongside ship. **fav.** = favourite (esp. in horse-racing). **FBA** = Fellow of the British Academy. **FBI** (*US*) = Federal Bureau of Investigation. **FC** = Football Club. **FCC** (*US*) = Federal Communications Commission. **FCL** = full container load. **FCO** = Foreign and Commonwealth Office. **fcp.** = foolscap. **FD** = [L] *Fidei Defensor* Defender of the Faith. **FDA** (*US*) = Food and Drugs Administration. **FDC** = first-day cover; [Fr.] *fleur-de-coin*. **Fe** (*Chem.*) = [L] *ferrum* iron. **Feb.** = February. **FET** (*Electronics*) = field-effect transistor. **ff.** = folios; following pages etc. **ff** = fortissimo. **fff** = fortissimo. **FFV** (*US*) = first family or families of Virginia. **FHB** = family hold back (when guests are sharing a meal). **Fid. Def.** = [L] *Defensor Fidei* Defender of the Faith. **FIFA** /ˈfiːfə/ = [Fr.] *Fédération Internationale de Football Association* International Football Federation. **fi. fa.** = fieri facias. **FIFO** /ˈfʌɪfəʊ/ (*Computing*) = first in, first out. **fig.** = figure. **FIMBRA** = Financial Intermediaries, Managers, and Brokers Regulatory Association. **FJI** = Fellow of the Institute of Journalists. **FL** = Florida. **fl.** = [L] *floruit* he or she flourished; fluid. **Fla.** = Florida. **flor.** = [L] *floruit* he or she flourished. **FLQ** = [Fr.] *Front de Libération de Quebec* Quebec Liberation Front. **Flt. Lt.** = Flight Lieutenant. **Flt. Off.** (*Hist.*) = Flight Officer. **Flt. Sgt.** = Flight Sergeant. **FM** = Field Marshal; frequency modulation. **Fm** (*Chem.*) = fermium. **fm.** = fathom(s). **FO** = Flying Officer; (*Hist.*) Foreign Office. **fo.** = folio. **f.o.b.** = free on board. **fol.** = folio. **f.o.r.** = free on rail. **FP** = former pupil; freezing point. **fp** = forte piano. **FPA** = Family Planning Association. **FPS** = Fellow of the Pharmaceutical Society. **fps, f p s** = feet per second; foot-pound-second. **Fr.** = Father; French. **Fr** (*Chem.*) = francium. **fr.** = franc(s). **FRCS** = Fellow of the Royal College of Surgeons. **FRG** = Federal Republic of Germany. **Fri.** = Friday. **Frl.** = [G] *Fräulein*. **FRS** = Fellow of the Royal Society. **FRSE** = Fellow of the Royal Society of Edinburgh. **FSA** = Fellow of the Society of Antiquaries. **FSH** (*Biochem.*) = follicle-stimulating hormone. **FSSU** = Federated Superannuation Scheme for Universities. **FT** = *Financial Times* (*FT index*, any of a number of stock indices published daily by the *Financial Times*). **Ft.** = Fort. **ft** = feet; foot. **FTC** (*US*) = Federal Trade Commission. **FT-SE** (*Stock Exch.*) = *Financial Times*-Stock Exchange index (of 100, 250, or 350 shares on the London Stock Exchange). **fur.** = furlong(s). **fwd** = forward. **f.w.d.** = four-wheel drive; front-wheel drive. **f.y.** (*US*) = fiscal year.

fa *n.* var. of FAH.

faamafu /faaˈmafʊ/ *n.* M20. [Samoan.] In Samoa, home-brewed liquor.

faa-Samoa /faa saːˈmɒʌ/ *n.* M20. [Samoan.] The Samoan way of life.

fab /fab/ *a. colloq.* M20. [Abbrev.] = FABULOUS *a.* 3c.

Also **fabby** *a.* L20.

Fabian /ˈfeɪbɪən/ *n.* & *a.* L16. [L *Fabianus* of the Fabian gens of ancient Rome.] **A** *n.* †**1** *Flaunting Fabian*, a roistering swashbuckler. Only in L16. **2** A member of the Fabian Society, or a sympathizer with its ideals. L19. **B** *adj.* **1** Of or pertaining to the Fabian gens of ancient Rome. M18. **2** After the manner of the cautious and delaying tactics employed by the Roman general Q. Fabius Maximus to wear out an enemy. L18. **b** Designating or pertaining to a socialist society founded in 1884, which advocates a policy of cautious and gradual political change. L19.

Fabianism *n.* the doctrines of the Fabian Society L19. **Fabianist** *n.* & *a.* E20.

fabism *n.* var. of FAVISM.

fable /ˈfeɪb(ə)l/ *n.* ME. [OFr. f. L *fabula* story, f. *fari* speak.] **1** A fictitious narrative or statement. ME. **2** A myth, legend; myths or legends in general. ME. **3** A short story, esp. one in which animals are the characters, which conveys a moral. ME. **4** A fiction invented to deceive. ME. **5** A ridiculous or untrustworthy story; idle talk. LME. †**6** Talk, discourse. *rare.* LME–L16. **7** A person who or thing which has become proverbial. *arch.* M16. **8** Something falsely claimed to exist, or having no existence outside popular legend etc. L16. **9** The plot of a play or poem. Formerly also, a play. *arch.* M17.

fable /ˈfeɪb(ə)l/ *v.* LME. [OFr. *fabler* f. L *fabulari* talk, discourse, f. as prec.] †**1** *v.i.* Speak, converse. *rare.* LME–L16. †**2** *v.i.* **a** Tell fictitious tales. LME–E19. **b** Talk idly. L16–L19. **3** *v.i.* Tell lies. (Foll. by *with*). *arch.* M16. **4** *v.t.* Talk about or relate fictitiously. M16.

fabled *ppl a.* (*a*) having no real existence; (*b*) described or celebrated in fable: E17. **fabler** *n.* LME.

fabliau /ˈfablɪəʊ, fabljo/ *n.* Pl. **-aux** /-əʊz, -o/ E19. [Fr. f. OFr. (Picard) *fablia(u)x* pl. of *fablel* dim. of *fable*: see FABLE *n.*] A verse tale, usu. burlesque in character, from the early period of French poetry.

fabric /ˈfabrɪk/ *n.* L15. [(O)Fr. *fabrique* f. L *fabrica* trade, manufactured object, workshop, forge, f. *faber* worker in metal, stone, etc. Cf. FORGE *n.*] **1** A building, an edifice. *arch.* L15. †**2** A machine, an appliance. L16–M17. **3** The construction or designing of a building, an animal's body, a vehicle, etc.; *spec.* the construction and maintenance of a church. E17. **4** A building in which work or manufacture is carried on; a factory. M17. **5** A structure; a frame; the basic structure (walls, floor, and roof) of a building. M17. **6** A type of construction or formation; texture. M17. **7** A manufactured textile, (a) woven, knitted, or felted material; a similar material made of chemically bonded fibres (also *non-woven fabric*). Formerly also, a manufactured material generally. M18. **8** The substance or structural material of something, *esp.* the woven tissue or fibre of a textile. E19.

5 H. G. WELLS The whole fabric of social life, conduct, law, property, confidence. 7 L. DEIGHTON I will buy new fabric for the front-room curtains.

fabric /ˈfabrɪk/ *v.t.* Infl. **-ck-**. E17. [f. the n.] Construct, fashion, frame, make (a material or immaterial object). (Foll. by *up, out.*)

fabricable /ˈfabrɪkəb(ə)l/ *a.* M20. [Late L *fabricabilis*, f. L *fabricare*: see FABRICATE, -ABLE.] Able to be shaped; *spec.* able to be formed into the shape required for a finished product.

fabricaˈbility *n.* M20.

fabricant /ˈfabrɪk(ə)nt/ *n.* Now *rare.* M18. [Fr., pres. pple of (O)Fr. *fabriquer* f. L *fabricare*: see next, -ANT[1].] A maker, a manufacturer.

fabricate /ˈfabrɪkeɪt/ *v.t.* LME. [L *fabricat-* pa. ppl stem of *fabricari*, *-are*, f. *fabrica*: see FABRIC *n.*, -ATE[3].] **1** Make with skill; manufacture; construct (something material or immaterial). LME. **b** Form into the shape required for a finished product. E20. **2** Invent (a lie, dishonest story, etc.); forge (a document). L18.

fabricative *a.* L18.

fabrication /fabrɪˈkeɪʃ(ə)n/ *n.* L15. [f. L *fabricatio(n-)*, f. as prec.: see -ATION.] **1** The action or process of manufacturing or constructing something; a structure. L15. **2** The action of inventing a lie, dishonest story, etc., or of forging a document; a false statement, an invention, a forgery. L18.

2 T. WRIGHT The common account of his death is a mere fabrication.

fabricator /ˈfabrɪkeɪtə/ *n.* E17. [L, f. *fabricare*: see FABRICATE, -OR.] **1** A person who or thing which fabricates. E17. **2** *Archaeol.* A rod-shaped flint implement, perh. used in the manufacture of other flint tools. L19.

Fabry-Pérot /fabrɪˈpɛrəʊ/ *n.* E20. [f. C. *Fabry* (1867–1945) and A. *Pérot* (1863–1925), Fr. physicists.] *Physics.* Used *attrib.* to designate devices invented by Fabry and Pérot.

Fabry-Pérot etalon = ETALON. **Fabry-Pérot interferometer** an interferometer incorporating an etalon.

fabular /ˈfabjʊlə/ *a.* L17. [L *fabularis*, f. *fabula* FABLE *n.*: see -AR[1].] Pertaining to or of the nature of a fable; fabulous.

fabulate /ˈfabjʊleɪt/ *v.* E17. [L *fabulat-* pa. ppl stem of *fabulari*: see FABLE *v.*, -ATE[3].] †**1** *v.i.* Narrate in fables. Only in E17. †**2** *v.t.* Relate as a fable or myth. Only in E17. **3** *v.t.* Invent, fabricate. M19.

fabuˈlation *n.* M18. **fabulator** *n.* L15.

fabulist /ˈfabjʊlɪst/ *n.* L16. [Fr. *fabuliste*, f. L *fabula* FABLE *n.*: see -IST.] **1** A person who relates or composes fables or legends. L16. †**b** A professional storyteller. Only in 17. **2** A person who invents dishonest stories; a liar. E17.

†**fabulize** *v.* E17. [f. L *fabula* FABLE *n.* + -IZE.] **1** *v.i.* Invent fables. E17–E19. **2** *v.t.* Concoct, invent; relate as legend *that*; make into a fable. M17–E19.

fabulosity /fabjʊˈlɒsɪti/ *n.* E17. [L *fabulositas*, f. *fabulosus*: see next, -ITY.] **1** The quality of being fabulous; fictitiousness, mythical character. E17. †**2** A fabulous thing, a fable. E17–E19.

fabulous /ˈfabjʊləs/ *a.* LME. [f. Fr. *fabuleux* or L *fabulosus*, f. *fabula* FABLE *n.*: see -ULOUS.] **1** Of the nature of a fable; full of fables; unhistorical; known only or chiefly through fable. LME. **2** Given to relating fables. Now *rare*. M16. †**b** Fond of listening to fables. L16–M17. **3a** Resembling a fable, absurd. *rare*. M16. **b** Like things found only in fable; astonishing. E17. **c** Excellent, marvellous, terrific. *colloq.* M20. **4** Of alleged existences or facts: belonging to fable, legendary. L16. †**b** Of a doctrine or notion: based on or arising in fable. E17–L18. **5** Celebrated in fable. E17.

3c A. ROSS Trueman puffed at a cigarette and said he felt fabulous. 4 H. ADAMS On all the old churches you can see 'bestiaries' . . of fabulous animals, symbolic or not.

fabulously *adv.* L16. **fabulousness** *n.* L16.

faburden /faˈbəːd(ə)n/ *n. obs.* exc. *Hist.* LME. [Perh. f. Fr. *faux-bourdon* lit. 'false hum', assim. to FAH, BURDEN *n.*] **1** A type of improvised polyphony, popular in England from the 15th cent. to the Reformation. LME. **2** The refrain or chorus of a song. L16.

façade /fəˈsɑːd/ *n.* M17. [Fr., f. as next, after It. *facciata*: see -ADE.] **1** The face or front of a building, *esp.* the principal front, looking on to a street or open space. M17. **2** An outward appearance or front, *esp.* one which is deceptive. L19.

1 R. MACAULAY The south façade has rounded arched windows and moulding and carving. JO GRIMOND One wing was a façade of gothic windows with nothing behind them. 2 R. COBB Behind the façade of giggles there existed a person who was rather unhappy.

façadism *n.* (*a*) a style or practice in architecture which lays emphasis on the design and elegance of the façades of buildings; (*b*) the practice of preserving the façade of a building whose interior has been destroyed: M19. **façadist** *n.* a person who practices façadism L20.

face /feɪs/ *n.* ME. [(O)Fr. f. Proto-Romance alt. of L *facies* form, appearance, visage, aspect, prob. rel. to *fax* torch.] **I** The front of the head. **1** The front part of the head, from the forehead to the chin; the visage, the countenance; the corresponding part of the head of an animal, insect, or other creature. ME. **b** A representation of a human countenance. L15. **c** (A form of address to) a person, esp. one admired or despised to some degree. *slang.* E20. **2** The countenance as a means of expressing feelings, character, etc.; what is shown by one's expression; a grimace. ME. **b** Command of facial expression; composure, coolness, effrontery. M16. **3** Sight, presence. Chiefly in phrs. below. ME. **4** The front part of the head, as the part presented in encounters and confrontations; confrontation, opposition. LME. **5** The countenance with regard to beauty. L16. **b** Make-up, cosmetics. *colloq.* E20.

1 E. BAKER Norma could see the criminal's face clearly, both full-front and in profile. 2 N. MOSLEY She made a face as if there was something bitter on her tongue. b LONGFELLOW I wonder that any man has the face To call such a hole the House of the Lord.

II The visible part or surface of a thing. **6** The surface or one of the surfaces of anything. ME. †**b** *Astrol.* One third of a sign of the zodiac, extending over 10 degrees in longitude. LME–E19. **c** An even or polished surface. L19. **7** Either side of a coin or medal, *esp.* the side bearing the effigy. Formerly also (*slang*), a coin. E16. **8** *gen.* The outer or upper side of a two-sided object; the front as opp. to the back. E17. **b** The inscribed side of a document etc. M17. **c** The marked or picture side of a playing-card. M17. **9a** *Archit.* The façade of a building; the exposed surface of a stone in a wall; the front of an arch. E17. **b** *gen.* The principal side, often vertical or steeply sloping, presented by an object; *spec.* the front of a cliff, a geological fault, etc. M17. **c** An open slope or hillside. *NZ.* M19. **10** Each of the surfaces of a solid. E17. **11** The dial-plate of a clock or a watch. L17. **12** The acting, striking, or working surface of an implement, tool, etc.; the striking surface of a golf club, cricket-bat, hockey-stick, lacrosse-stick, etc. E18.

7 *fig.*: R. HOGGART The other side of the coin which has 'sincerity' on its face. 8 G. R. PORTER Diagonal lines . . across the face of the cloth. E. BECKETT The face of a wheel which turns in a gear. 9b O. MANNING The snow was . . sliding wetly down from the rock faces above the houses. 10 F. HOYLE A uniform cube . . resting on one of its faces on the ground. 11 R. DAVIES The big clock's pallid face . . said it was a quarter to midnight.

III Outward appearance. **13** External appearance, look; semblance *of*. Now chiefly of immaterial objects. LME. **14** Outward show; disguise, pretence; a pretext. LME. **15** Visible state or condition; aspect. L16. **b** The physical conformation of a country. L17.

13 J. BRYCE The problems of the world . . are always putting on new faces.

IV *techn.* **16** *Fortif.* The outer surface of a wall, esp. of one of the curtain walls of a bastion. L15. **b** Either of two walls in a bastion which form a salient angle. L17. **17** *Typogr.* The printing surface of type or of a punch; a particular style of type. L17. **18** *Mining.* The end of a tunnel, stope, etc., at which work is progressing; the principal surface from which coal is being removed. E18. **19** *Mil.* Each of the sides of a battalion when it is formed into a square. M19.

17 *bold-face*, *fat-face*, *old-face*, etc. 18 B. T. WASHINGTON It was . . a mile from the opening of the coal-mine to the face of the coal.

V f. the vb. **20** *Ice Hockey* & *Lacrosse.* More fully *face-off*. The act of facing off (see FACE *v.* 8). L19.

Phrases: **before the face of** in the sight of. *black in the face*: see BLACK *a. blue in the face*: see BLUE *a.* 1b. **do one's face** *colloq.* apply make-up to one's face. *face down(wards)*: see *face up(wards)* below. **face to face** looking one another in the face; directly; clearly. **face to faceness** directness, clearness. **face to face with** confronting. **face up(wards)**, **down(wards)**: having the face or front in the direction indicated. *fling (something) in (a person's) face*: see FLING *v.* **fly in the face of** openly oppose or disobey. †**from face to foot** *rare* (Shakes.) from head to toe. *grind the faces of*: see GRIND *v. have a face as long as a fiddle*: see FIDDLE *n.* **have the face** be shameless enough. *hide one's face*: see HIDE *v.*[1] **in face of** = *in the face of* (a) below. **in one's face** directly at one, straight against one. **in the face of** (*a*) in front of; when confronted with; in spite of; (*b*) in the presence of. *laugh in a person's face*: see LAUGH *v. laugh on the other* (or *wrong*) *side of one's face*: see LAUGH *v. long face*: see LONG *a.*[1] **look a person in the face** confront a person with a steady gaze, implying courage, defiance, etc. **lose face** [tr. Chin. *diū liǎn*] be humiliated, lose one's good name or reputation. **loss of face** humiliation, loss of reputation. **make a face** = *pull a face* below. **on the face of** in the words of. **on the face of it** *fig.* obviously, plainly; superficially, apparently. **open one's face** *US slang* speak. *pull a face*: see PULL *v.* **put a good** (or **bold** etc.) **face on** (**something**) make (a matter) look well, face with courage. **put a new face on** alter the aspect of. **put one's face on** *colloq.* apply make-up to one's face. **save** (**one's**) **face** avoid public humiliation, save one's reputation. **set one's face against** steadfastly oppose. *set one's face like a flint*: see FLINT *n.* & *a.* **set one's face to**, **towards** look or aim towards. *show one's face*: see SHOW *v.* **shut one's face** *slang* be quiet, stop talking. SUNDAY *face*. **the acceptable face of** the tolerable or attractive manifestation or aspect of. **the face of the earth** the surface of the earth; anywhere. **the unacceptable face of** the intolerable or unattractive manifestation or aspect of. *three faces under* (or *in*) *a hood*: see THREE *a.* **to one's face** openly in one's sight or hearing; boldly, directly. *turn one's face to the wall*: see WALL *n.*[1] *wash its face*: see WASH *v. wipe an expression, a smile*, etc. *off a person's* or *one's face*: see WIPE *v.*

Comb.: **face-ache** (*a*) neuralgia; (*b*) *slang* a mournful-looking person; **face-bone** the cheek-bone; **face-brick** *US* a facing brick; **face-card** = *court-card* s.v. COURT *n.*[1]; **face-centred** *a.* (of a crystal structure) in which an atom or ion occurs at each vertex and at the centre of each face of the unit cell; **face-cloth** (*a*) a cloth for laying over and protecting the face; (*b*) a woollen fabric with a smooth surface; (*c*) a cloth for washing the face; **face-cream** cream applied to the face to improve the complexion; **face-flannel** = *face-cloth* (c) above; **face-fungus** *colloq.* a man's facial hair, a beard; **face-glass** the glass window of a diver's helmet; **face-guard** a mask for protecting the face; **face-lift** the operation of face-lifting; an improvement in appearance; **face-lifting** (*a*) an operation to remove wrinkles by tightening the skin of the face; (*b*) *fig.* the refacing or redecoration of a building; **face-mask** a mask covering the nose and mouth or the nose and eyes; *face-off*: see sense 20 above; **face-pack** a preparation designed to help the complexion, spread on the face and removed when dry; **face-painter** (*a*) a painter of portraits; (*b*) one who applies paint to the face; **face-painting** portrait painting; **face-piece** (*a*) a part of the rudder of a ship; (*b*) a diver's face-glass; (*c*) a face-mask; **face-plate** (*a*) an enlarged end or attachment on the mandrel of a lathe, on which work can be mounted; (*b*) a plate protecting a piece of machinery; (*c*) a diver's face-glass; **face-play** facial movement in acting etc.; **face-powder** a cosmetic powder for reducing the shine on the face; **face-saver** a thing or event that saves one's face or saves one from humiliation; **face-saving** *n.* & *a.* preserving one's reputation, credibility, etc. **face-symbol** *Cryst.* a symbol designating the face or plane of a crystal; **face value** the nominal value as stated on a coin, note, etc.; apparent value or nature, esp. as opp. to actual value; **face-worker** a miner who works at the coalface.

face /feɪs/ *v.* LME. [f. the n.] **I** Confront, look at or towards. **1** *v.i.* Show a bold face; brag, swagger. *obs.* exc. *dial.* LME. †**b** Be false. Only in L16. **2**†**a** *v.t.* Confront with assurance or impudence; bully. LME–M17. **b** *v.t.* Meet face to face; confront or oppose bravely or with confidence. M17. **c** *v.t.* & *i.* foll. by *up to*. Consider seriously (an idea, a fact, etc.); accept the inevitability, irrevocability of. L18. **3** *v.i.* **a** Look in a certain direction. (Foll. by *to*, *towards*.) L16. **b** Be situated with the face or front in a specified direction. (Foll. by *on*, *to*.) L18. **4** *v.t.* Look towards; be situated opposite to, front towards. M17. **b** Of an engraving, illustration, etc.: stand on the opposite page to. M18. **5** *v.i.* Chiefly *Mil.* Turn around so as to be looking in a specified direction. Also foll. by *about*, *round*. M17. **6** *v.t.* †**a** Direct the looks of. Only in M17. **b** *Mil.* Cause (soldiers) to turn and front in a certain direction. M19. **7** *v.t.* Turn (a playing-card etc.) face up. L17. **8** *v.i. Ice Hockey* & *Lacrosse.* Start or restart play by dropping the puck, or ball, between the sticks of two opposing players. Also foll. by *off*. M19. **b** *v.t.* Place (the puck or ball) in this way to start or restart play. Also foll. by *off*. M19.

2a **face out of** exclude shamelessly from; bully out of. b LYNDON B. JOHNSON India faced an important governmental crisis early in 1966. **face down** overcome (a person) by a show of determination or by browbeating. **face out** see (something) through with effrontery or impudence. **face the music** accept resolutely difficult or unpleasant consequences. c M. L. KING My fears began to go. . . I was ready to face anything. **face the facts** not shrink from or confront the truth, esp. when unwelcome. **let's face it** we must recognize an unwelcome fact. 3a J. DICKEY I faced ahead . . and watched the rest of the light come. 4 H. JAMES He was one of the men who fully face you when they talk of themselves. S. GIBBONS The cowsheds faced the house. 5 F. A. GRIFFITHS Right or left about three-quarters face.

II Put a face or facing on. **9** *v.t.* Provide (a garment) with facings. M16. †**b** Trim, deck, adorn. M16–L17. **10** *v.t.* Cover (a surface) with a layer of another material. L17. **11** *v.t.* Smooth the face or surface of. Also foll. by *down*, *up*. M19. **12** *v.t.* Coat (tea) with some colouring substance. Also foll. by *up*. M19.

9 R. GRAVES His uniform was now the green tunic

faced with red. 10 A. GRAY The tenements were faced with grey stone instead of red.

faced /feɪst/ *a.* E16. [f. FACE *n.* + -ED[2].] Having a face or expression of a specified kind; having a surface of a specified kind. Chiefly as 2nd elem. of comb., as *fresh-faced* etc.

faceless /ˈfeɪslɪs/ *a.* M16. [f. FACE *n.* + -LESS.] †1 Lacking face or courage; cowardly. M–L16. 2 Without a face; without identity; anonymous, characterless. M19.

2 C. THUBRON One of those faceless apartment blocks. S. MIDDLETON He had been faceless, a powerful name at the bottom of official orders.

facelessly *adv.* L20. **facelessness** *n.* M20.

facer /ˈfeɪsə/ *n.* E16. [f. FACE *n.*, *v.* + -ER[1].] †1 A person who shows a bold face; a braggart, a bully. E16–E17. 2 A large cup or tankard, *esp.* one filled to the brim. *slang.* Now *rare* or *obs.* E16. 3 A blow in the face; a head-on blow. E19. b *fig.* A great and sudden difficulty; a setback. E19.

facet /ˈfasɪt, -ɛt/ *n.* & *v.* E17. [Fr. *facette* dim. of *face* FACE *n.*: see -ET[1].] A *n.* 1 One side of a many-sided body, esp. when flat and smooth; *spec.* any of the cut and polished faces of a gem. E17. b *fig.* A particular side or aspect of something. E19. 2 *Zool.* Any of the segments of a compound eye. M19.

1 H. ADAMS The facets of the hexagon . . are more pleasing than the rounded surfaces of the cone. R. DAHL The different shades of green on the planes and facets of each clipped tree. b P. GALLICO An expert at every facet of the game. E. ROOSEVELT Certain sides of Franklin's character or particular facets of his personality.

B *v.t.* Cut or form facets upon. L19.

faceted *a.* having facets; of a form which has many faces or aspects: M19. **faceting** *vbl n.* the action or process of cutting or forming facets L19.

facete /fəˈsiːt/ *a.* *arch.* E17. [L *facetus* graceful, pleasant, witty.] 1 = FACETIOUS. E17. †2 Elegant, graceful, polished. Only in M17.

facetiae /fəˈsiːʃiiː/ *n.pl.* E16. [L *facetiae* pl. of *facetia* jest, f. *facetus*: see prec.] 1 Pleasantries, witticisms. E16. 2 *Bookselling.* Pornography. M19.

facetious /fəˈsiːʃəs/ *a.* L16. [Fr. *facétieux*, f. *facétie* f. L *facetia*: see prec., -OUS.] †1 Of manners etc.: polished, urbane. Only in L16. 2 Given to or characterized by pleasantry or joking, now esp. where inappropriate or trivializing; witty, humorous, amusing. L16.

2 J. CHEEVER The first was a facetious essay, attacking the modern toilet seat.

facetiously *adv.* E18. **facetiousness** *n.* M16.

Fach /fax/ *n.* Also *f-*. M19. [G = compartment, division, shelf.] A line of work or business; a department of activity; *métier.*

facia /ˈfeɪʃə/ *n.* M18. [Var. of FASCIA.] 1 = FASCIA I. *rare.* M18. 2 The plate over a shop front on which is written the occupier's name, trade, etc. L19. 3 The instrument panel or dashboard of a motor vehicle. E20.

facial /ˈfeɪʃ(ə)l/ *a.* & *n.* E17. [med.L *facialis*, f. L *facies*: see FACE *n.*, -AL[1].] A *adj.* †1 *Theol.* Of vision etc.: face to face; open. E17–E18. 2 Of or pertaining to the face. E19. 3 Of or belonging to the visible part or surface of something. M19.

2 A. N. WILSON Hugh was making a number of agonized facial gestures to Jen. **facial angle** the angle formed by two lines, one running from the nostril to the ear and the other from the nostril to the forehead. **facial nerve** either of the seventh pair of cranial nerves, supplying the facial muscles and the tongue. *facial sauna*: see SAUNA *n.*

B *n.* †1 The facial angle. *rare.* Only in E19. 2 A beauty treatment for the face. E20.

facially *adv.* M17.

faciation /feɪsɪˈeɪʃ(ə)n/ *n.* E20. [f. L *facies* (see FACE *n.*) + -ATION.] *Ecol.* A community containing more than one of the dominant species in an association.

faciendum /fakɪˈɛndəm, feɪʃɪ-/ *n.* Pl. ***-da*** /-də/. M19. [L = thing to be done, neut. gerundive of *facere* make, do.] *Philos.* A thing that should be done.

facient /ˈfeɪʃ(ə)nt/ *n.* *rare.* M17. [L *facient-*: see next.] A person who does something; a doer.

-facient /ˈfeɪʃ(ə)nt/ *suff.* [Repr. L *facient-* making, pres. ppl stem of *facere* do, make.] Forming adjs. and ns. w. the sense '(substance etc.) producing an action or state' as *abortefacient, calefacient, rubefacient.*

facies /ˈfeɪʃiiːz/ *n.* Pl. same. E17. [L: see FACE *n.*] 1 †a *joc.* The face. Only in E17. b *Med.* The appearance or expression of the face, esp. when characteristic of a particular disease. L19. 2 *Sci.* General aspect or appearance. E18. b *spec.* *Geol.* The character of a rock formation as displayed by its composition, texture, fossil content, etc.; a formation or body presenting a unified set of properties. M19. c *Ecol.* The characteristic set of dominant species in a habitat. E20.

facile /ˈfasʌɪl, -sɪl/ *a.* L15. [Fr., or L *facilis*, f. *facere* do, make: see -ILE.] 1 a Easily done or won (esp. in a contemptible way); presenting few difficulties. L15. †b Easy to use or understand. M16–L18. c Superficial, without depth. E20. 2 Easily led; flexible, compliant, yielding; weak-minded. *arch.* exc. *Sc. Law.* E16. 3 Not harsh or severe; affable, courteous, relaxed. L16. 4 Working easily or freely; fluent, ready. E17.

1a W. BEVERIDGE All other acts of piety will be facile and easy to him. c ALDOUS HUXLEY His models offered him facile consolations. J. UPDIKE The oracle spoke a great deal of facile, impudent, and traitorous nonsense. 4 D. HALBERSTAM The rewrite man turned reporter, very facile, very quick, a story banged out in ten minutes.

facilely *adv.* L15. **facileness** *n.* (now *rare*) M16.

facile princeps /ˌfasɪlɪ ˈprɪnsɛps/ *a.* & *n.* *phr.* M19. [L.] (A person who is) easily first; the acknowledged leader or chief.

facilitate /fəˈsɪlɪteɪt/ *v.t.* E17. [Fr. *faciliter* f. It. *facilitare* f. *facile* (f. L *facilis*: see FACILE), after L *debilitare* DEBILITATE, etc.] 1 Make easy or easier; promote, help forward (an action, result, etc.). E17. 2 Lessen the labour of, assist (a person). Now *rare.* M17. 3 *Physiol.* Increase the likelihood of, strengthen (a response); bring about the transmission of (an impulse). E20.

1 D. BAGLEY The revolving door had been taken away to facilitate passage in and out of the hotel. A. STORR They often used hypnosis to facilitate recall.

facilitative *a.* tending to facilitate something M19. **facilitator** *n.* a person who or thing which facilitates something E19.

facilitation /fəsɪlɪˈteɪʃ(ə)n/ *n.* E17. [f. as prec. + -ATION.] 1 The action or an act of facilitating something. E17. b A means of facilitating something, a help. Now *rare.* M17. 2 *Physiol.* The increased excitability of a neurone beyond a stimulated ganglion or synapse, resulting in an increased response to a stimulus. L19.

facilitatory /fəˈsɪlɪtət(ə)ri/ *a.* M20. [f. FACILITATE + -ORY[2].] Of, pertaining to, or involved in facilitation; intended to facilitate.

facility /fəˈsɪlɪti/ *n.* LME. [Fr. *facilité* or L *facilitas*, f. *facilis*: see FACILE, -ITY.] †1 Gentleness, lightness. Only in LME. 2 a Unimpeded opportunity. Now also, an amenity or service which enables something to be done. E16. b In *pl.* Favourable conditions for the easy or easier performance of something, *esp.* the physical means or equipment required in order to do something. E19. 3 The fact or condition of being easy or easily done; freedom from difficulty. M16. 4 Aptitude, dexterity; ease or readiness of speech, action, etc. M16. b Fluency of style. L16. †5 Courtesy, affability. M16–L18. 6 Pliancy, readiness to be led or persuaded. *arch.* exc. *Sc. Law.* M16. 7 Ease, indolence. Now *rare* or *obs.* E17.

2a *Guardian* The bank should . . consider extending this survival facility to students' parents. *Times Educ. Suppl.* An edit facility so that the pupils can . . correct their work if they wish. b C. FRANCIS Calcutta had few facilities . . no wharves, pontoons or landing stages. W. TREVOR There were full toilet and washing facilities. 3 BURKE The facility with which government has been overturned in France. 4 N. WEST The pleasures he received . . had decreased as his facility had increased.

facing /ˈfeɪsɪŋ/ *n.* LME. [f. FACE *v.* + -ING[1].] 1 The action of FACE *v.* Also foll. by *about, off,* etc. LME. 2 Material covering part of a garment for contrast or strength; in *pl.*, the contrasting cuffs, collar, etc., of a military or military-style jacket. M16. 3 A superficial coating; the material of such a coating; *spec.* the outer layer of stone or brick which forms the face of a building, wall, bank, etc. L16.

2 S. RICHARDSON I made robings and facings of a pretty bit of printed calico.

Comb.: **facing brick** a brick used in the outer wall of a building.

facinorous /fəˈsɪn(ə)rəs/ *a.* *arch.* M16. [L *facinorosus*, f. *facinus, facinor-* (bad) deed, f. *facere* do, make: see -OUS.] Extremely wicked.

†**facinorious** *a.* = FACINOROUS E–M17. **facinorousness** *n.* E18.

facio- /ˈfeɪʃɪəʊ/ *comb. form* of L FACIES face: see -O-.

facioˈplegic *a.* pertaining to paralysis of the face E20. **ˌfacioˌscapulo-ˈhumeral** *a.* pertaining to the face, scapula, and arm E20.

fack *n.* see FACT.

façon de parler /fasɔ̃ də parle/ *n.* *phr.* Pl. ***façons de parler*** (pronounced same). E19. [Fr.] A way or manner of speaking; a mere phrase or formula.

façonné /fasɔne/ *a.* & *n.* Pl. of n. pronounced same. L19. [Fr., pa. ppl a. of *façonner* fashion.] (Designating) a material into which a design has been woven.

façons de parler *n.* *phr.* pl. of FAÇON DE PARLER.

facsimile /fakˈsɪmɪli/ *n.*, *a.*, & *v.* Orig. †**fac simile**. L16. [mod.L, f. L *fac* imper. of *facere* do, make + *simile* neut. of *similis* SIMILAR.] A *n.* †1 The making of an exact copy, esp. of writing; imitation. L16–M17. 2 An exact copy, esp. of writing, printing, a picture, etc.; a reproduction. L17. 3 *spec.* A system for producing a copy by radio etc. transmission of signals from scanning an original. L19.

2 J. BRAINE My wife and I aren't exact facsimiles of that couple . . but we belong to the same world. B. MOORE A facsimile of an old chapter-house record book . . its original now destroyed. **in facsimile** so as to be an exact reproduction.

Comb.: **facsimile telegraphy** the transmission of copies of documents etc. by means of radio signals from which copies can be made using suitable receiving equipment.

B *attrib.* or as *adj.* That is a facsimile; exactly copied or like. M18.

F. H. A. SCRIVENER Elaborate facsimile editions of the chief codices.

C *v.t.* & *i.* Make or be a facsimile (of). M19.

facsimilize *v.t.* (*rare*) reproduce exactly, make a facsimile of E19.

fact /fakt/ *n.* Also (repr. dial. pronunc., now *US*) **fack** /fak/. L15. [L *factum* use as n. of neut. pa. pple of *facere* do, make.] 1 †a (An) action, a deed; *esp.* a noble or brave action, an exploit, a feat. L15–E19. b An evil or wrongful action; a crime. Now only in *before* or *after the fact, confess the fact.* M16. †2 The act of making, doing, or performing. Chiefly in *in the* (*very*) *fact.* M16–E19. 3 Truth; reality. L16. 4 A thing known for certain to have occurred or to be true; a datum of experience. M17. 5 A thing assumed or alleged as a basis for inference. E18. 6 *Law. collect. sing.* & in *pl.* Events or circumstances as distinct from their legal interpretation. E18.

1a MILTON He who most excels in fact of Arms. J. AUSTEN Gracious in fact if not in word. b W. HARRISON He is . . hanged . . neere the place where the fact was committed. I. BANKS Will I agree to be an accomplice after the fact? 2 W. IRVING She was detected . . in the very fact of laughing. 3 B. JOWETT Imagination is often at war with reason and fact. 4 E. M. FORSTER The facts are that she has been in England for three days and will not see us. C. ISHERWOOD You keep ignoring the fact that I *have* been back there. 5 OED The writer's facts are far from trustworthy. 6 J. M. LELY A jury . . decides all the issues of fact.

Phrases: *a matter of fact*: see MATTER *n.* **as a matter of fact** actually. *brute fact*: see BRUTE *a.* **fact of life** a thing (esp. unpleasant) the existence of which cannot be ignored. **facts and figures** precise information. **hard fact** inescapable truth. **in fact, in point of fact** in reality; (in summarizing) in short. *issue of fact*: see ISSUE *n.* *Theatre of Fact*: see THEATRE *n.* **the fact of the matter** the truth. **the facts of life** *colloq.*, *euphem.* details of the human sexual functions.

Comb.: **fact-finder** a person engaged in fact-finding; **fact-finding** *n.* & *a.* (*a*) *n.* the finding out of facts, the discovery and establishment of the facts of an issue; (*b*) *adj.* engaged in finding out facts; (esp. of a committee etc.) set up to discover and establish the facts of an issue; **fact-sheet** a paper on which facts relevant to an issue are set out briefly.

factful *a.* (*rare*) L19.

facta *n.pl.* see FACTUM.

factice /ˈfaktɪs/ *n.* Also †**-is**. L19. [G *Factis*, *Faktis*, f. L *facticius* artificial, f. *facere* make.] A substance resembling rubber made by vulcanizing unsaturated vegetable oils and used chiefly as a compounding ingredient in rubber.

facticity /fakˈtɪsɪti/ *n.* M20. [f. FACT + -ICITY.] The quality or condition of being a fact; factuality.

faction /ˈfakʃ(ə)n/ *n.*[1] L15. [(O)Fr. f. L *factio(n-)*, f. *fact-* pa. ppl stem of *facere* do, make: see -ION.] †**1 a** The action of doing or making something; an instance of this. L15–L17. **b** A way of behaving or acting. M16–E17. **2** A group or class of people; *spec.* a (self-interested or turbulent) party, esp. in politics. E16. **b** *Rom. Hist.* Any of the companies involved in chariot races in the circus. E17. **3** Self-interested or turbulent party strife or intrigue; dissension; the prevalence of a partisan spirit. M16. †**b** A quarrel. L16–M17.

2 D. LODGE The membership quickly split into two factions, one.. respectful and conciliatory, the other determined to be bold. 3 W. S. CHURCHILL The religious passions of former years now flowed into the channels of political faction.

factionary *n.* & *a.* (a) partisan M16. **factio'neer** *n.* & *v.* (now *rare*) (*a*) *n.* = FACTIONIST; (*b*) *v.i.* promote faction or a faction: E18. **factionist** *n.* a promoter or member of a faction; a partisan: E17.

faction /ˈfakʃ(ə)n/ *n.*[2] M20. [Blend of FACT and FICTION *n.*] Fiction based on real events or characters, documentary fiction; an example of this.

-faction /fakʃ(ə)n/ *suff.* [Repr. L *-factio(n-)*: see FACTION *n.*[1]] In and forming ns. of action related to vbs in -FY, as (*-fy* repr. L *facere*, Fr. *faire*) *satisfaction* etc., (*-fy* repr. L *-ficare*, Fr. *-fier*) *petrifaction* etc.

factional /ˈfakʃ(ə)n(ə)l/ *a.* M17. [f. FACTION *n.*[1] + -AL[1].] Of or pertaining to a faction or factions; characterized by faction.

factionalism *n.* a state characterized by faction; tendency to factional differences; the factional spirit: E20. **factionalist** *a.* of or pertaining to factionalism, factional M20. **factionalize** *v.t.* & *i.* divide into factions, (cause to) become factional L20. **factionally** *adv.* L19.

factious /ˈfakʃəs/ *a.* M16. [Fr. *factieux* or L *factiosus*, f. *factio(n-)*: see FACTION *n.*[1], -OUS.] Characterized by or pertaining to faction or a faction.

factiously *adv.* (now *rare*) L16. **factiousness** *n.* L16.

†**factis** *n.* var. of FACTICE.

factitious /fakˈtɪʃəs/ *a.* M17. [L *facticius*, f. *fact-*: see FACTION *n.*[1], -ITIOUS[1].] **1** Made by human skill or effort, not naturally occurring or produced. Now *rare*. M17. †**b** Of soil etc.: not original to an area. L17–E19. **2** Made for a special purpose; not genuine; not natural or spontaneous, artificial. L17.

1 J. BRYANT One was a natural eminence.. The other was a factitious mound. 2 R. WEST Stage plays .. arouse in the audience factitious emotion.

factitiously *adv.* L18. **factitiousness** *n.* M17.

factitive /ˈfaktɪtɪv/ *a.* & *n.* M19. [mod.L *factitivus*, irreg. f. L *factitare* frequent. of *facere* do, make: see -IVE.] *Gram.* **A** *adj.* Of a verb: expressing the notion of making a thing to be of a certain character (e.g. *paint* the door green). Also designating the object etc. of such a verb. M19. **B** *n.* A factitive verb. L19.

factive /ˈfaktɪv/ *a.* E17. [med.L *factivus* creative, practical, f. *fact-*: see FACTION *n.*[1], -IVE.] †**1** Tending or able to make; concerned with making. E–M17. **2** *Gram.* Orig., factitive. Now usu., designating or pertaining to a verb taking an assumed fact as object (e.g. English *know*, *regret*, *resent*). L19.

fac'tivity *n.* M17.

factoid /ˈfaktɔɪd/ *n.* & *a.* L20. [f. FACT + -OID.] **A** *n.* An assumption or speculation that is reported and repeated so often that it becomes accepted as a fact; a simulated or imagined fact. L20. **B** *adj.* That is a factoid; having the character of a factoid; containing factoids. L20.

factor /ˈfaktə/ *n.* LME. [Fr. *facteur* or L *factor*, f. *fact-*: see FACTION *n.*[1], -OR.] **I** †**1** A doer, a maker, a performer, a perpetrator. LME–M19. **2 a** An agent, a deputy, a representative. Now chiefly *Sc.* LME. **b** An estate manager, a land-agent; a bailiff. Also, a person appointed by a court to manage property. Now *Sc.* M16. **3** *Comm.* A person buying and selling on commission for another; esp. a mercantile agent entrusted with goods with a view to their sale. LME. **b** *Hist.* Any of the third class of employees of the East India Company. L17. **c** A person or agency that takes over and collects debts owed to other (esp. finance) companies. E20. †**4** A partisan, an adherent. E16–E18. **5** *US Law.* In certain States, a garnishee. *rare.* L19.

1 CLARENDON An avow'd Factor and Procurer of that odious Judgement. 3 W. IRVING Mahomet.. was employed by different persons as.. factor in caravan journeys to Syria.

II 6 *Math.* Each of the numbers or quantities that make up a given number or expression when multiplied together. L17. **7** A circumstance, fact, or influence which tends to produce a result; an element or component of something; a measured or quantifiable property. E19. **b** *Genetics.* A gene or other heritable agent that determines a hereditary character. E20. **c** *Biochem.* Any of a number of substances in the blood (identified by numerals) which are involved in coagulation. E20.

6 C. HUTTON For that *zy* may be positive, the signs of the two factors *z* and *y* must be alike. 7 E. F. BENSON The serene indulgence towards the doings of others which.. is.. a factor.. that makes for peace and pleasantness. M. M. KAYE Many factors.. prevented them from becoming friends: caste, upbringing and environment. *chill factor*, *X factor*, etc. *factor of safety*: see SAFETY *n.* **c factor VIII** or **eight** a beta globulin the congenital deficiency of which causes haemophilia.

Comb.: **factor analysis** (a) statistical calculation of the relative importance of a number of factors regarded as influencing a set of values; **factor group** *Math.* a group G/H the elements of which are the cosets in a given group G of a normal subgroup H of G; **factor theorem** *Math.*: that, given a polynomial $f(x)$, if $f(a) = 0$ then $(x - a)$ is a factor of $f(x)$, and vice versa.

factorage *n.* (*a*) the action or professional service of a factor; (*b*) commission or charges paid to a factor: E17. †**factoress** *n.* a female factor E17–E18. **factorship** *n.* the office or position of a factor or agent L16.

factor /ˈfaktə/ *v.* E17. [f. the n.] **1** *v.i.* Act as a factor or agent. E17. **b** Sell (debts) to a factor. M20. **2** *v.t.* Deal with (goods, money, etc) as a factor or agent. E17. **3** *v.t. Math.* = FACTORIZE 2. M19. **4** *v.t.* (Foll. by *in*, *into*) introduce as a factor; (foll. by *out*) exclude from an assessment. Chiefly *N. Amer.* L20.

factorable *a.* (*Math.*) able to be factorized; expressible as a product of factors: M20.

factorial /fakˈtɔːrɪəl/ *n.* & *a.* E19. [f. FACTOR *n.* + -IAL.] **A** *n. Math.* The product of a series of factors; *spec.* the product of an integer and all lower integers (expressed by !: $4! = 4 \times 3 \times 2 \times 1$). E19. **B** *adj.* Chiefly *Math.* Of or pertaining to a factor or factors. M19.

factorially *adv.* by reference to factors E20.

factorize /ˈfaktəraɪz/ *v.* Also **-ise**. M19. [f. FACTOR *n.* + -IZE.] **1** *v.t. US Law.* In certain States: make (a third party) a garnishee. *rare.* M19. **2** *v.t. Math.* Resolve into factors; express as a product of factors. M19. **b** *v.i.* Admit of being resolved into factors. E20.

factorizable *a.* (*Math.*) E20. **factori'zation** *n.* the operation of resolving a quantity into factors; a product of factors: L19.

factory /ˈfakt(ə)ri/ *n.* M16. [Ult. f. (as) FACTOR *n.* + -Y[3], (branch III) -Y[4]. In branch II repr. Port. *feitoria* (= It. *fattoria*, Sp. *factoria*, Fr. †*factorie*, later *factorerie*); in branch III after late L *factorium* (recorded in sense 'oil-press').] **I 1** The employment, office, or position of a factor. *Sc.* M16. **II 2** *Hist.* An establishment for traders doing business in a foreign country; a merchant company's foreign trading station. L16. **III 3** A building or buildings with equipment for manufacturing; a workshop; a works. E17. **4** A prison; a police station. *slang.* M19.

Comb.: **Factory Act(s)** an act or acts of Parliament regulating the operation of factories in the interest of the health and safety of employees; **factory farm** a farm using intensive methods of farming (esp. of livestock) usu. in an artificial environment, organized on industrial lines; **factory farming** running a factory farm, using the method of a factory farm; **factory floor** *fig.* the workers in an industry as opp. to the management etc.; **factory ship** a ship accompanying a fishing (orig. a whaling) fleet to process the catch; a fishing ship with facilities for immediate processing of the catch; **factory trawler** a trawler with facilities for processing its catch.

factotum /fakˈtəʊtəm/ *n.* Also †**fac totum**. M16. [med.L *factotum*, f. L *fac* imper. of *facere* do, make + *totum* the whole.] **1** Orig. †*dominus* or *magister factotum* [L = master], †*Johannes factotum* [= John]. A person who does all kinds of work; a jack of all trades; a person with delegated general powers; a servant who manages all his master's affairs. M16. **2** *Typogr.* A decorative woodblock with a space in the centre for the insertion of an initial capital letter. *obs.* exc. *Hist.* L17.

1 D. CECIL A general factotum, at one moment his personal attendant helping him to adjust his clothes, at another his confidential secretary.

factual /ˈfaktʃʊəl/ *a.* M19. [f. FACT after ACTUAL.] Concerned with or of the nature of fact(s); actual, real, true.

W. LIPPMANN Factual knowledge of the social order .. statistics, censuses, reports. C. MILNE Story books and factual books—or as they are more usually called, fiction and non-fiction.

factually *adv.* M19. **factualness** *n.* E20.

factualism /ˈfaktʃʊəlɪz(ə)m/ *n.* M20. [f. prec. + -ISM.] *Philos.* The theory maintaining that facts are pre-eminent and fundamental.

factualist *n.* & *a.* (*a*) *n.* an adherent of factualism; (*b*) *adj.* of or pertaining to factualism or factualists: M20.

factuality /faktʃʊˈalɪti/ *n.* L19. [f. as prec. + -ITY.] The state or quality of being factual; realism of representation; truth to fact.

factum /ˈfaktəm/ *n.* Pl. **facta** /ˈfaktə/, **factums**. M18. [L: see FACT. In sense 2 through Fr. legal usage.] †**1** *Math.* The product of two or more factors multiplied together. M18–E19. **2** *Law.* An act, a deed; a statement of fact(s). L18.

facture /ˈfaktʃə/ *n.* LME. [(O)Fr. f. L *factura*: see FEATURE *n.*] **1** The manner or style of making something; construction; workmanship. Now *rare.* LME. **2** The action or process of making something; manufacture. Now *rare.* L15. **3** *Art.* The quality of the execution of a painting, esp. of its surface. L19.

facty /ˈfakti/ *a. colloq.* L19. [f. FACT + -Y[1].] Full of facts; (of a person) concerned primarily with facts, deficient in emotion or imagination.

facula /ˈfakjʊlə/ *n.* Pl. **-lae** /-liː/. E18. [L, dim. of *fac-*, *fax* torch: see -ULE.] *Astron.* A bright spot or streak on the sun's disc.

facular *a.* of, pertaining to, or of the nature of a facula or faculae L19. **faculous** *a.* = FACULAR M19.

facultate /ˈfak(ə)lteɪt/ *v.t. rare.* M17. [med.L *facultare* make possible, f. L *facultas* FACULTY: see -ATE[3].] Authorize, empower.

facultative /ˈfak(ə)ltətɪv/ *a.* E19. [Fr. *facultatif*, *-ive*, f. *faculté*: see next, -ATIVE.] **1** Permissive; optional; contingent. E19. **b** *attrib.* in *Biol.* Capable of but not restricted to a particular (specified) function, mode of life, etc. Opp. OBLIGATE *a.* 2. L19. **2** Of or pertaining to a faculty. M19.

faculty /ˈfak(ə)lti/ *n.* LME. [(O)Fr. *faculté* f. L *facultas*, f. *facilis* FACILE: see -TY[1].] **I 1** An ability, aptitude, or competence for a particular kind of action (sometimes natural as opp. to acquired). Formerly also, ability in general. LME. †**b** A personal quality; disposition. L15–E17. **2** Means, resources; possessions, property. Now *rare* exc. in *faculty theory* below. LME. †**3** A power or capacity of a thing; an active property. L15–E18. 4 An inherent power or property of the body or an organ; a physical capability. Freq. in *pl.* L15. 5 An inherent power or property of the mind, as reason, memory, etc.; a mental capability. Freq. in *pl.* L16.

1 D. H. LAWRENCE He had the faculty of making order out of confusion. 2 A. YOUNG The prices . . are beyond their faculties. 4 S. SASSOON One man had lost that necessary faculty . . his eyesight. 5 H. JAMES His faculties—his imagination, his intelligence, his affections, his senses.

II †6 *gen.* A branch of knowledge. LME–M18. 7 A branch of learning (orig. esp. theology, law, medicine, or arts) taught and studied at a university or (now) polytechnic or college; a department of a university etc. teaching a specific branch of learning; the staff and students of such a department; (chiefly *N. Amer.*) the teaching staff of a university or college. LME. 8 An art, a trade, an occupation, a profession. *arch.* LME. 9 The members of a profession regarded as one body; *spec.* (*arch.*) *the* medical profession. E16.

7 M. ARNOLD At Bonn there is a Protestant faculty of theology. *Dean of Faculty*: see DEAN *n.*[1] 6. 8 R. NEVE A . . Soap-boyler . . and another Gentleman of the same Faculty. 9 T. HOOD Bacon . . was once in vogue amongst the Faculty for weak digestions. *Faculty of Advocates*: see ADVOCATE *n.* 1.

III 10 The power, freedom, or right of doing something, given by law or by a superior. E16. b An authorization, a licence; *esp.* (*Eccl.*) a dispensation to perform an action or hold a position otherwise illegal. M16.

10 M. ARNOLD Something . . anti-social which the State had the faculty to judge and the duty to suppress. b *Book of Common Prayer* None shall be . . a Deacon, except he be Twenty-three year of age, unless he have a Faculty.

Comb.: **faculty psychology**: in which certain mental faculties are seen as accountable for the phenomena of mind; **faculty theory**: that each person should contribute to public taxation according to his or her ability.

facultied *a.* accredited by a faculty; endowed with a faculty: M19.

facund /ˈfak(ə)nd, fəˈkʌnd/ *n.* & *a.* *arch.* ME. [As n. f. OFr. *faconde* f. L *facundia*, f. *facundus*, f. *fari* speak. As adj. f. OFr. *facond* f. L *facundus*.] †**A** *n.* Eloquence. ME–L15. **B** *adj.* Eloquent. LME.

faˈcundity *n.* eloquence M16.

facy /ˈfeɪsi/ *a.* *dial.* & *slang.* E17. [f. FACE *n.* + -Y[1].] Impudent, cheeky.

fad /fad/ *n.* *colloq.* (orig. *dial.*). M19. [Prob. 2nd elem. of earlier FIDFAD. Cf. earlier FADDY.] 1 An individual's peculiar notion, rule of action, or preference; a whim, a crotchet. M19. 2 Something briefly but enthusiastically taken up, esp. by a group; a craze. M19.

1 G. K. CHESTERTON A Socialist crank with some particular fad about public parks. D. WELCH It was one of Orvil's fads that he only liked bread in the form of toast. 2 M. STOTT Odd how furnishing fads change as decisively . . as styles in dress.

Comb.: **fadmonger** a faddist.

faddish /ˈfadɪʃ/ *a.* M19. [f. prec. + -ISH[1].] Given to fads; marked by fads.

faddishly *adv.* E20. **faddishness** *n.* L19.

faddism /ˈfadɪz(ə)m/ *n.* L19. [f. as prec. + -ISM.] Tendency to follow fads.

faddist *n.* L19.

faddle /ˈfad(ə)l/ *v.* & *n.* *dial.* & *colloq.* L17. [Cf. FAD, FONDLE, etc. See also FIDDLE-FADDLE.] **A** *v.* 1 *v.t.* Fondle (a child). L17. 2 *v.i.* Spend time idly or in play. M18. **B** *n.* Nonsense, trifling. M19.

faddy /ˈfadi/ *a.* *colloq.* (orig. *dial.*). E19. [Prob. f. as FAD *n.* + -Y[1].] Of a person: fussy about trifles, full of fads; *spec.* particular in matters of food. Of a thing: pursued as a fad.

faddiness *n.* M19.

fade /feɪd/ *n.* ME. [f. the vb.] 1 The action or an act of fading or losing freshness, vitality, or colour. Long *rare* in *gen.* use. ME. 2 A disappearance from the scene; a (quick or unobtrusive) departure. Chiefly in *do* or *take a fade*. *US slang.* E20. 3 *Cinemat.*, *Television*, & *Broadcasting.* (An instance of) fading a picture or sound. Also, a gradual decrease or increase in the brightness of a picture or the volume of a sound. See also FADE-IN, FADE-OUT. E20. 4 Reduction in the effectiveness of a motor vehicle's braking system. M20. 5 A ball's swerved course, deviation of a ball from a straight course, esp. in golf; a (slice) stroke or shot causing this. M20.

fadeproof *a.* resistant to fading; retaining colour or brightness: E20.

fade /feɪd; *in sense 3 foreign* fad/ *a.* ME. [(O)Fr.: see next.] 1 Lacking in brilliance of colour; dull, pale, wan. Long *arch.* ME. †2 Lacking in freshness or vitality; withered, languishing. ME–M18. 3 That has lost its taste; *fig.* insipid, uninspiring. Now only as a Gallicism. LME.

fade /feɪd/ *v.* ME. [OFr. *fader*, f. *fade* vapid, dull, faded, prob. f. Proto-Romance source blending L *fatuus* FATUOUS and *vapidus* VAPID.] **I** *v.i.* †1 Lose strength or vitality; grow weak, waste away. ME–L16. 2 Lose freshness; droop, wither. LME. 3 Lose brightness or brilliance of colour; grow dim or pale. LME. 4 Become indistinct, disappear gradually. Also foll. by *away*. L16. 5 Disappear from the scene mysteriously or unobtrusively; *slang* depart, go. Freq. foll. by *away*, *out*. M19. 6 Of (esp. broadcast) sound: decrease gradually in volume, die away (usu. foll. by *out*). Foll. by *in*, *up*: (of broadcast sound) increase gradually in volume from an inaudible level. L19. 7 Of a radio signal: fluctuate in strength as a result of varying atmospheric conditions. Chiefly as *fading* vbl n. E20. 8 *Cinemat.* & *Television.* Foll. by *out*, *in*: (of a picture etc.) gradually disappear from, become visible on, the screen. E20. 9 Of a motor vehicle's brake: become gradually less effective. M20. 10 Of a ball: deviate from a straight course, esp. in golf in a deliberate slice. M20.

2 A. UTTLEY Roses . . bloomed . . faded, and scattered their brown leaves on the grass. *fig.*: J. BRAINE One of those . . women whose good looks fade almost overnight. 3 A. J. CRONIN The light began to fade and they looked for a shelter for the night. L. DEIGHTON The once red . . flags . . had faded to a light pink in the sunlight. 4 W. IRVING I saw the last blue of my native land fade away. J. LE CARRÉ As the morning dragged on her hopes faded, and she knew he would never come. E. REVELEY Tango faded from his mind as though she had never been. 5 J. B. PRIESTLEY 'My wife,' Mr. Rathbury muttered, fading out. 6 E. WELTY The whole sound of the sea faded behind the windbreak.

II *v.t.* †11 Deprive of freshness, strength, or vigour; *spec.* taint, corrupt. LME–L18. 12 Cause to lose colour or brightness; make dull or pale. Formerly, lose the brilliance of (a colour). M16. 13 *Gambling.* Match the bet of (another player). *N. Amer. slang.* L19. 14 *Cinemat.* & *Television.* Cause (a picture etc.) to fade *out* or *in*: see sense 8 above. E20. 15 *Broadcasting.* Foll. by *out* (*down*), *in* (*up*): reduce, increase, (sound) gradually in volume. E20. 16 Cause (a ball) to fade or deviate from a straight course, esp. in golf. M20.

12 E. O'NEILL Dungaree trousers faded by many washings. W. BOYD The sun has faded all the bright colours to grey and blue.

fadable *a.* (*rare*) liable to fade (earlier in UNFADABLE) M17. **faded** *ppl a.* that has lost freshness, vitality, or colour; no longer fresh or bright: L15. **fadeless** *a.* not subject to fading; perpetually fresh or bright: M17.

fade-in /ˈfeɪdɪn/ *n.* E20. [f. FADE *v.* + IN *adv.*] 1 *Cinemat.*, *Television*, & *Broadcasting.* A gradual increase in the visibility of a picture or the volume of a sound. E20. 2 *Theatr.* A gradual brightening of the stage. M20.

Fade-Ometer /feɪdˈɒmɪtə/ *n.* Also **Fadeom-**, **Fadom-**. E20. [f. FADE *n.*, *v.* + -OMETER.] (Proprietary name for) a machine for testing the fastness of colours by subjecting them to an accelerated weathering process.

fade-out /ˈfeɪdaʊt/ *n.* E20. [f. FADE *v.* + OUT *adv.*] 1 A (gradual or unobtrusive) disappearance or departure; *spec.* death. Chiefly *US slang.* E20. 2 *Cinemat.*, *Television*, & *Broadcasting.* A gradual lessening in the visibility of a picture or the volume of a sound. E20. 3 *Theatr.* A gradual dimming of the stage. M20. 4 A temporary interruption of radio communication; fading (see FADE *v.* 7). M20.

fader /ˈfeɪdə/ *n.* E20. [f. FADE *v.* + -ER[1].] An apparatus for controlling the volume of sound in a cinema film or the signal in sound or television broadcasting.

fadge /fadʒ/ *n.*[1] *Sc.* & *north.* LME. [Origin unkn.] A flat thick loaf or bannock.

fadge /fadʒ/ *n.*[2] *dial.* & *techn.* L16. [Origin unkn.] A bundle, a load; *esp.* (*Austral.* & *NZ*) a small bale or part-filled sack of wool.

fadge *n.*[3] var. of FODGE.

fadge /fadʒ/ *v.* Now chiefly *dial.* L16. [Origin unkn.] **I** *v.i.* †1 Be consistent, be suitable, be suited, (foll. by *with*, *to*); suit, agree, (foll. by *with*). L16–M18. 2 Get on, thrive; (of an event) come off; (of a person) succeed in an enterprise. *obs.* exc. *dial.* L16. 3 Deal with a situation; manage, cope, (†*with*). *obs.* exc. *dial.*, *Newfoundland*, & *W. Indies.* L16. †4 Consent *to do.* L16–M17. 5 Get on well, hit it off, (*with* a person). Now *arch.* & *dial.* E17.

1 T. FULLER The Study of the Law did not fadge well with him. 2 SIR W. SCOTT I shall be impatient to hear how your matters fadge. 3 W. COWPER We . . have none but ourselves to depend on. . . Well, we can fadge. 5 MILTON They shall . . be made, spight of antipathy, to fadge together.

II *v.t.* 6 Put the parts of (an object) together somehow. Now only foll. by *up*. L17.

fading /ˈfeɪdɪŋ/ *ppl a.* LME. [f. FADE *v.* + -ING[2].] Subject to loss of colour or brightness; that fades.

fadingly *adv.* M17. **fadingness** *n.* M17.

fado /ˈfaːdu, ˈfɑːdəʊ/ *n.* Pl. **-os** /-uʃ, -əʊz/. E20. [Port., lit. 'fate'.] A type of popular (freq. plaintive) Portuguese song and dance, with a guitar accompaniment.

Fadometer *n.* var. of FADE-OMETER.

fady /ˈfeɪdi/ *a.* E18. [f. FADE *v.* + -Y[1].] Tending to fade or become less bright.

faecal /ˈfiːk(ə)l/ *a.* Also ***fecal**. M16. [f. as next + -AL[1].] Of the nature of or containing faeces.

faeces /ˈfiːsiːz/ *n.pl.* Also ***feces**. LME. [L, pl. of *faex* dregs.] 1 Sediment, dregs. LME. 2 Waste matter discharged from the bowels; excrement. LME.

faecula *n.*, †**faeculent** *a.* see FECULA, FECULENT.

faena /faˈena/ *n.* E20. [Sp., lit. 'task'.] *Bullfighting.* A series of passes with cape and sword by a matador, preparatory to the kill.

Faenza /fɑːˈɛntsə/ *n.* & *a.* M19. [A city in Emilia-Romagna province, N. Italy: cf. FAIENCE.] (Designating) faience made at Faenza in the 16th cent.

faerie *n.* & *a.* see FAERY.

Faeroese /fɛːrəʊˈiːz/ *a.* & *n.* Also **Faroese**, **Faröese**. M19. [f. *Faeroes* (see below) + -ESE.] **A** *n.* Of or pertaining to the Faeroes, a group of islands in the N. Atlantic between the Shetland Islands and Iceland, and a semi-autonomous province of Denmark. M19. **B** *n.* Pl. same. 1 A native or inhabitant of the Faeroes. M19. 2 The Norse language of the Faeroes. L19.

faery /ˈfeɪəri, ˈfɛːri/ *n.* & *a.* *arch.* Also (now chiefly in sense A.1) **faerie**. L16. [Archaizing var. of FAIRY, introduced by Spenser.] **A** *n.* 1 The enchanted world of fays, esp. as portrayed in Spenser's *Faerie Queene*; fairyland. Also, the inhabitants of this world. L16. 2 A supernatural being; a fay, a fairy. L16.

1 N. P. WILLIS A grass so verdant . . that it seemed the very floor of faëry. YEATS The Land of Faery, where nobody gets old and godly and grave. 2 KEATS Zephyr, blue-eyed Faery, turn.

B *adj.* Belonging to or suggestive of the world of fays; enchanted; beautiful but unreal. L16.

MILTON Faerie Elves. H. ALLEN Pines and crags faëry with September mists.

faff /faf/ *v.* & *n.* L18. [Cf. next.] **A** *v.* 1 *v.i.* & *t.* Of a wind: blow in puffs (on). *dial.* L18. 2 *v.i.* Bustle ineffectually, fuss. *dial.* & *colloq.* L19.

2 N. COWARD The Welfare Officers appeared, . . faffed about, . . and retired in due course.

B *n.* 1 A puff of wind. *dial.* L19. 2 *fig.* (An) ineffectual fussing, a dither. *colloq.* L19.

faffle /ˈfaf(ə)l/ *v.i.* L16. [Imit.] **1** Stutter, stammer. *dial.* L16. **2** Flap idly in the wind. Chiefly *dial.* L18. **3** Fuss, bustle ineffectually. *dial.* & *colloq.* L19.

fag /fag/ *n.*[1] LME. [Origin unkn.] **1** A knot in cloth. LME. **2** A sheep-tick. *dial.* & *Sc.* L18.

fag /fag/ *n.*[2] L15. [Origin unkn. In sense 4 abbrev. of FAG-END.] †**1** Something that hangs loose; a flap. Only in L15. **2** A last remnant, a fag-end (*lit.* & *fig.*); *spec.* the end of a cigarette. L16. **3** A leftover strip of land; also, tufts of last year's grass not grazed down. *dial.* L19. **4** A cigarette (orig. of a cheap sort). L19.

fag /fag/ *n.*[3] L18. [f. FAG *v.*[1]] **1** A fatiguing or unwelcome task; drudgery. Also, exhaustion. *colloq.* L18. **2** In a public school: a junior boy who performs menial tasks for a senior. Also *transf.*, a drudge. L18.

1 A. WHITE It saves a lot of fag to have someone to scrub my back. J. R. ACKERLEY He can quite well . . find the journey up too much of a fag.

fag /fag/ *n.*[4] *derog. slang* (chiefly *N. Amer.*). E20. [Abbrev.] = FAGGOT *n.* 8.

Comb.: **fag hag** a woman who consorts habitually with homosexual men.

fag /fag/ *v.*[1] Infl. **-gg-**. M16. [Origin unkn. Cf. FLAG *v.*[2]] **1** *v.i.* Grow weary or less eager, flag. Formerly also, swerve or turn aside *from*, *into*. *obs.* exc. *dial.* M16. **2** *v.i.* Work until one is exhausted; toil, exert oneself. L18. **3** *v.t.* Make thoroughly weary; tire out, exhaust. Freq. foll. by *out*. Usu. in *pass.* E19. **4** *v.t.* In a public school, of a senior boy: use the services of (a junior) for menial tasks. E19. **5** *v.i.* In a public school, of a junior boy: perform menial tasks for a senior. Formerly (*Cricket*), act as a fieldsman to a senior boy (usu. foll. by *out*). E19. **6** *v.t.* *Naut.* Unravel the ends of (a rope). M19.

2 F. BURNEY All day I am fagging at business. JOYCE Hot day coming. Too much trouble to fag up the stairs. 3 D. LODGE I feel quite fagged after all that effort.

fag /fag/ *v.*[2]*t.* *dial.* Infl. **-gg-**. M19. [Origin unkn. Cf. BAG *v.*[2]] = BAG *v.*[2]

fag-end /ˈfagɛnd/ *n.* E17. [f. FAG *n.*[2] + END *n.*] **1** The last part of a piece of cloth, freq. of a coarser texture than the rest. Chiefly *transf.*, the last part or tail-end of something, remaining after the best has been used up. E17. **2** An untwisted end of a rope. L18. **3** A cigarette-end. Cf. FAG *n.*[2] 4. *colloq.* E20.

1 W. GOLDING He was our lodger, hanging on to the fag-end of his life.

fagger /ˈfagə/ *n.* M19. [f. FAG *v.*[1] + -ER[1].] **1** A person who works hard. M19. **2** = FAGMASTER. M19.

faggot /ˈfagət/ *n.* & *v.* Also ***fagot**. ME. [(O)Fr. *fagot* f. It. *fagotto* dim. of Proto-Romance back-form. f. Gk *phakelos* bundle.] **A** *n.* **1** A bundle of sticks or twigs tied together as fuel; *Hist. spec.* one used in burning heretics alive. Hence, the punishment of being burnt alive for heresy. ME. †**b** *Mil.* A fascine. LME–E18. **2** A bunch (*of* herbs etc.); *fig.* a collection (*of* (esp. immaterial) things). L15. **3** A bundle of iron or steel rods bound together for reheating, welding, and hammering into bars. M16. **4** As a term of abuse: an objectionable (old) woman, child, animal, etc. Chiefly *dial.* L16. †**5** A person engaged temporarily to fill another's place at the muster of a regiment or to keep up its strength. L17–E19. **6** *Hist.* = *faggot vote* below. E19. **7** A kind of rissole or meatball made of minced pig's liver or other offal mixed with bread or suet, herbs, etc. Usu. in *pl.* Orig. *dial.* M19. **8** A male homosexual, esp. of an effeminate type. *slang* (orig. *US*). *derog.* E20.

1 H. LATIMER Running out of Germany for fear of the fagot. A. E. COPPARD They had begun to make three faggots of the wood they had collected. **bear** or **carry a faggot** *Hist.*: in token of having renounced heresy. 2 R. W. EMERSON The . . liturgies of churches are . . a fagot of selections. E. LINKLATER Carrying a great faggot of Easter lilies.

Comb.: **faggot-iron**: in the form of bars or masses, produced by welding together a faggot of iron bars; **faggot-stitch(ing)**: resembling the faggoting of drawn-thread work, used to join two pieces of material; **faggot vote** *Hist.* a vote manufactured by the nominal transfer to a person, not otherwise qualified, of sufficient property to enable him to vote.

B *v.* **1** *v.t.* Surround with or set on faggots (a person convicted of heresy). *rare.* M16. †**2** *v.i.* Of a former heretic: carry a faggot or wear an embroidered faggot in token of recantation. Only in M16. **3** *v.t.* Tie together (as) in a faggot. L16. **4** *v.t.* *Metall.* Fasten or pile together (bars or rods of iron) for reheating and welding. Freq. as *faggoted* ppl a. M19. **5** *v.i.* Make faggots or bundles of sticks or twigs. L19. **6** *v.t.* Ornament (needlework) with faggoting; join (pieces of material) by faggot-stitch. E20.

3 *fig.*: J. C. HARE Things essentially . . different, bundled and fagoted together for the occasion.

faggoter *n.* (*rare*) a person who makes faggots or faggoting L15. **faggoting** *n.* (*a*) the action of the vb; (*b*) embroidery in which a number of threads are drawn out and a few cross-threads tied together in the middle (suggestive of faggots); the joining of materials in a similar manner: M19.

faggoty /ˈfagəti/ *a.* Also ***fagoty**. M19. [f. FAGGOT *n.* + -Y[1].] **1** Obsessed with faggots or the burning of heretics. *rare.* M19. **2** Of, resembling, or suggestive of a male homosexual or homosexuals. *slang* (orig. *US*). E20.

faggy /ˈfagi/ *a.* *slang* (chiefly *N. Amer.*). M20. [f. FAG *n.*[4] + -Y[1].] = FAGGOTY 2.

Fagin /ˈfeɪgɪn/ *n.* M19. [A character in Dickens's *Oliver Twist*.] A trainer of thieves; a receiver of stolen goods; a thief.

fagmaster /ˈfagmɑːstə/ *n.* L19. [f. FAG *n.*[3] + MASTER *n.*[1]] In a public school: the senior boy for whom a junior fags.

fagot *n.* & *v.* see FAGGOT.

fagotto /faˈgɔtto, fəˈgɒtəʊ/ *n.* Pl. ***-tti*** /-t(t)i/, ***-ttos*** /-təʊz/. E18. [It.: see FAGGOT.] *Mus.* A bassoon. Also, a primitive form of this, a curtal.

fagoty *a.* see FAGGOTY.

fah /fɑː/ *n.* Also **fa**. ME. [f. L *fa(muli)*: see UT.] *Mus.* The fourth note of a scale in a movable-doh system; the note F in the fixed-doh system.

fahlerz /ˈfɑːlɛːts/ *n.* L18. [G, f. *fahl* ash-coloured, gray + *Erz* ore.] *Min.* Any grey copper ore of the system whose typical forms are tetrahedrite and tennantite.

fahlore /ˈfɑːlɔː/ *n.* E19. [Partial tr.] = prec.

Fahrenheit /ˈfar(ə)nhʌɪt, ˈfɑːr-/ *n.* & *a.* M18. [Gabriel Daniel *Fahrenheit* (1686–1736), Ger. physicist who invented the mercury thermometer.] **A** *n.* The thermometric scale introduced by G. D. Fahrenheit, in which water freezes at 32° and boils at 212° under standard conditions. M18. **B** *adj.* Designating or pertaining to this scale; *postpositive* (with a specified temperature) on this scale. E19.

faience /fʌɪˈɒs, feɪ-, -ˈɑːns/ *n.* & *a.* Also **faï-**, **fay-**. L17. [Fr. *faïence* f. *Faïence* FAENZA.] (Designating) tin-glazed or decorated earthenware or pottery (orig. that made at Faenza in N. Italy).

faik /feɪk/ *v.t.* *Sc.* LME. [Perh. aphet. f. Sc. var. of DEFALK.] **1** Reduce (a total); deduct (a sum). LME. **2** Spare, excuse, let off. L18.

fail /feɪl/ *n.*[1] ME. [OFr. *fai(l)le* (mod. *faille*), f. as FAIL *v.*] **1** = FAILURE 1, 2. Now only in *without fail*, definitely, for certain, irrespective of difficulties, (now only used to strengthen an injunction or promise, formerly also with statements of fact). ME. **2** = FAILURE 4. Long *rare* in *gen.* sense. L15. **b** *spec.* A failure to achieve the required standard in an examination. M20. †**3** Death. *rare* (Shakes.). Only in E17.

1 SHAKES. *Wint. T.* What dangers, by his Highness' fail of issue, May drop upon his kingdom. S. BECKETT He won't come this evening . . But he'll come tomorrow Without fail. 2 †**for fail** as a precaution against failure. 3 SHAKES. *Hen. VIII* How grounded he his title to the crown Upon our fail?

fail /feɪl/ *n.*[2] *Sc.* Also **feal**. LME. [Origin unkn.] A thick sod or piece of turf, esp. as used for building walls etc.; such sods collectively.

fail and divot *Law* (now *Hist.*) a servitude conferring the right to remove sods for building, roofing, etc.

Comb.: **fail-dyke** a wall built of sods.

fail /feɪl/ *v.* ME. [(O)Fr. *faillir* be wanting, f. Proto-Romance alt. of L *fallere* disappoint the expectations of, deceive.] **I** Be or become deficient. **1** *v.i.* & †*t.* Be lacking (to). Now only, of something needed: be unavailable. See also FAILING *prep.* ME. †**b** *v.i.* Of a number: be wanting to complete a sum. Only in ME. **c** *v.i.* & *t.* Chiefly of time: be inadequate (for the needs of). *arch.* ME. **2** *v.i.* & *t.* Of supplies, resources, etc.: run low, become inadequate (for the needs of). ME. **3** *v.i.* Cease to exist; become extinct. ME. †**b** Of a period of time: come to an end, expire. LME–E17. **4** *v.i.* Lose force or intensity; (of light etc.) grow dim or faint; (of a sound, a smell, etc.) die away, become indistinct; (of health, faculties, etc.) become weak or impaired, become too weak for one's needs. ME. **b** *v.t.* Of health, faculties, etc.: become too weak for the needs of. ME. **5** *v.i.* Of a person: decline in health or vigour, flag; *spec.* lose strength with the approach of death. ME. **b** Die. *obs.* exc. *dial.* E17. **6** *v.t.* & *i.* Not give due or expected service (to a person) at a time of need; prove unreliable as a resource or source of aid (to). ME. **7** *v.i.* Prove defective when tested; (of a structure or other material thing) give way under pressure. Of machinery etc.: break down, cease to function. Formerly also, of soldiers: not stand up to the enemy. ME.

1 H. MAUNDRELL Shaded over head with Trees, and with Matts when the boughs fail. c AV *Heb.* 11:32 The time would faile mee to tell of Gideon. 2 SPENSER The breath gan him to fayle. J. LOCKE Where the credit and money fail, barter alone must do. H. BELLOC The grass was brown, our wells had failed. 3 AV *Ps.* 12.1 The faithfull faile from among the children of men. W. BLACKSTONE The blood of the Kempes shall not inherit till the blood of the Stile's fail. 4 S. STURMY Let slip thine Anchor, the Wind fails. SHELLEY The Champak's odours fail Like sweet thoughts in a dream. G. ORWELL The light was failing, but there was no difficulty in recognizing her. b E. A. FREEMAN The heart of Eustace failed him. D. BLOODWORTH Rumours that Mao's health is failing have sent the Hong Kong stock exchange plummeting. B. UNSWORTH His eyes were failing, he could not see with any distinctness. 5 W. S. CHURCHILL We shall not flag or fail We shall go on to the end. J. CARY She had . . been obliged to stay in bed, and the village said that she was failing at last. b SHAKES. *Hen. VIII* Had the King in his last sickness fail'd. 6 G. GREENE Mr Opie had spoken rapidly . . and Dr Czinner found his knowledge of English failing him. E. CALDWELL To let a glance . . speak for them when words failed. 7 T. FORSTER Abundance of berries . . is said to presage a hard winter, but this [rule] often fails. D. SHANNON Brakes fail on a hill. I. HAMILTON First the telephone failed, then the electricity.

II Experience a deficiency. **8** *v.t.* Be destitute of, lack. Now *rare.* ME. **9** *v.i.* Be lacking *in* an essential quality or part; *arch.* be destitute *of*. ME.

8 R. JEFFERIES I fail words to express my utter contempt. 9 J. GAY A dancing-master . . seldom fails of the scarlet stocking. B. JOWETT The Dialogue fails in unity.

III Fall short in performance or attainment. **10** *v.i.* Be remiss in the performance of a duty (foll. by *in*); neglect or omit *to do*. ME. †**b** *v.t.* Omit to perform (a customary or expected action). LME–E18. **c** *v.t.* Not keep (a promise, appointment, etc.). Formerly also, disappoint (a person's expectations). *arch.* E16. **11** *v.i.* Foll. by *of*: come short of hitting (a target), attaining (one's purpose or goal), achieving (an effect) etc. Formerly also, escape (a fate). ME. **b** *v.t.* Fall short of (a target), miss (one's footing); not succeed in obtaining (something sought). Long *arch.* LME. †**12** *v.i.* Deviate from what is true or correct; err, be at fault. (Foll. by *from*, *of*.) ME–L16. **13** *v.i.* Be unsuccessful in an attempt or enterprise. (Foll. by *in*, *to do*.) ME. **b** Of an attempt, plan, etc.: meet with no success; miscarry. LME. **14** *v.i.* Of a crop etc.: give no return; prove unproductive. ME. **15** *v.i.* Of a firm etc.: become insolvent. L17. **16** *v.i.* & *t.* Of a candidate: fall short of the required standard in (an examination or test). L19. **b** *v.t.* Of an examiner: adjudge (a candidate) to have failed. L19.

10 S. HILL I cannot be said . . to have failed in carrying out my duty. J. LE CARRÉ Liz . . ignored her . . , failed to reply when she addressed her. b DEFOE My morning Walk with my Gun, which I seldom failed. c A. SEEGER I shall not fail that rendezvous. 11 GOLDSMITH A weak king . . seldom fails of having his authority despised. I. ASIMOV When our missing robot failed of location anywhere. b MILTON Though that seat of earthly bliss be fail'd, A fairer Paradise is founded now. J. CARROLL Several Celtic crosses . . failed the level of Colman's chin. 12 T. STARKEY The ordur of our law . . in the punnyschment of theft . . faylyth much from gud cyvylyte. 13 T. HARDY How could he succeed in an enterprise wherein . . Phillotson had failed? L. STEFFENS When tact and good humour failed, he applied force. L. VAN DER POST For once the charm of hot food . . failed to cheer me. b J. R. GREEN A revolt which failed . . through the desertion of their Head. 14 TENNYSON The year in which our olives fail'd. 15 G. GREENE Racketeers who make money out of receiverships as the big firms fail. 16 C. M. YONGE Almost all of them failed in arithmetic. ANTHONY SMITH He had failed a Cambridge exam owing to . . inadequacy in geometry.

IV †17 *v.t.* [After L *fallere*.] Deceive, cheat. *rare* (Spenser). Only in L16.

17 SPENSER So lively and so like that living sence it fayld.

Phrases & comb.: †**fail little** or **not much of, to do** come close to experiencing (a given fate). **fail safe** (of a mechanism) return to a danger-free position or state in the event of a breakdown. **fail-safe** *a.* (of a mechanical or electrical device, procedure, etc.) returning or involving return to a danger-free position or state in the event of breakdown; *gen.* totally reliable or safe. *words fail me*: see WORD *n.*

failed *ppl a.* (*a*) decayed; (of a person) infirm, decrepit; (*b*) that has been unsuccessful; (of a candidate for a degree) that has not passed: L15. **failer** *n.* LME.

failing /ˈfeɪlɪŋ/ *n.* LME. [f. FAIL *v.* + -ING[1].] **1** The action of FAIL *v.* LME. **2** A defect of character; a weakness. L16.

2 L. WOOLF Sharp ruined himself by drinking—a by no means uncommon journalistic failing.

failing /ˈfeɪlɪŋ/ *prep.* E19. [pres. pple of FAIL *v.*] In default of; in the absence of.

E. WAUGH We hoped Sebastian might give us luncheon. . . Failing him we can always try Boy Mulcaster.

faille /feɪl/ *n.* M16. [(O)Fr.] †**1** A kind of hood or veil worn by women. M16–L17. **2** A light ribbed silk fabric. M19.

failure /ˈfeɪljə/ *n.* M17. [AN (legal) *failer* for OFr. *faillir* FAIL *v.*, inf. used as n. (see -ER[4]); assim. to -OR, (later) -URE. Cf. *leisure, pleasure*.] **1** (A) cessation in the existence or availability of something. M17. **2** (An) omission to do or *to do* something due or requisite; default. M17. †**3** A slight fault; a failing, a shortcoming. M17–E18. **4** (An instance of) failing to effect one's purpose; (a) lack of success. M17. **b** A person who or thing which turns out unsuccessful. M19. **5** The process or fact of failing in health or strength, giving way under pressure, etc.; (a) cessation in the functioning of a mechanism, an organ of the body, etc. L17. **6** The process of becoming or the state of being insolvent. E18.

1 M. ELPHINSTONE On the failure of issue . . an adopted son succeeds. 2 T. LUNDBERG Failure to make returns . . could lead to prosecution. 4 J. R. SEELEY We see efforts ending in feebleness and failure. b E. F. BENSON Minorca . . had been a dismal failure as far as she was concerned. D. CUSACK I feel such a failure I don't seem to get anywhere. 5 *Happy Landings* 106 [accidents] were attributable to engine failures. E. H. GOMBRICH An increasing failure of nerve. *heart failure, renal failure*, etc.

fain /feɪn/ *pred. a.* & *adv.* Now *arch.* & *dial.* [OE *fæġ(e)n* corresp. to OS *fagan, -in*, ON *feginn*, f. Gmc, f. base repr. by OE *ġefēon* rejoice. Cf. next.] **A** *adj.* **1** Happy, well-pleased. Freq. in *full fain, glad and fain*. Foll. by *of, to do, that*. OE. **2** Glad or content under the circumstances *to do*. (Passing into sense 2b.) ME. **b** Obliged, left with no alternative but *to do*. E16. **3** Disposed, inclined, eager. Foll. by †*of, for, to do*. ME. †**b** Apt, wont, *to do*. L16–M17. **4** Fond. Formerly also, well-disposed, favourable. Long *obs.* exc. *Sc.* ME.

1 SHAKES. *1 Hen. VI* Are glad and fain by flight to save themselves. 2b I. D'ISRAELI Ascham, indeed, was fain to apologise for having written in English. E. BOWEN She was so blind to them down there that they were fain to stand pretending.

B *adv.* Gladly, willingly. Now chiefly in *would fain*. ME.

M. AMIS The boy . . had wrested from the girl some article . . which she would fain recover.

fainly *adv.* (*rare*) M16. **fainness** /-n-n-/ *n.* (chiefly *Sc.* & *north.*) eagerness, gladness ME.

fain /feɪn/ *v.*[1] Long *obs.* exc. *Sc.* [OE *fæġnian* (f. as prec.) = OS, OHG, Goth. *faginōn*, ON *fagna*. See also FAWN *v.*[1] Survival in Sc. prob. due to influence f. Norw. dial. *fegna* to welcome, f. ON *fagna*.] †**1** *v.t.* & *i.* (Cause to) be glad; rejoice. OE–LME. †**2** *v.t.* Welcome (a person). ME–L15. **3** *v.t.* = FAWN *v.*[1] I. LME. **4** *v.t.* Like (a person or thing, *to do*); be fond of. L16.

fain /feɪn/ *v.*[2]*t.* & *i.* *slang* (chiefly *children's*). Orig. *dial.* Also (earlier) **fen** /fɛn/. E19. [Origin uncertain: perh. f. as FEIGN *v.* 5 or alt. of FEND *v.*] Forbid (some move or action in a game, esp. marbles); claim exemption from (some unwelcome task or role in a game). Freq. in *fain(s) I, fain(s) it*.

fainaigue /fəˈneɪɡ, -iːɡ; fɪ-/ *v.* *dial.* Now *rare* or *obs.* M19. [Perh. f. OFr. *fornier* deny, ult. f. L *foris* outside, away + *negare* deny. Cf. FINAGLE.] **1** *v.t.* & *i.* Revoke (a suit etc.) at cards. M19. **2** *v.t.* & *i.* Fail in a promise (to). M19. **3** *v.t.* Cheat, deceive. L19.

fainéant /ˈfeɪneɪɒ̃; *foreign* fɛneɑ̃ (*pl.* of *n.* same)/ *n.* & *a.* E17. [Fr., f. *fait* 3rd person sing. of *faire* do + *néant* nothing.] **A** *n.* A person who does nothing, an idler, an inactive official. E17. **B** *adj.* Indolent, idle, inactive. E19.

faineancy /-ənsi/ *n.* = FAINÉANTISM M19. ***fainéantise*** /fɛneɑ̃tiːz, ˌfeɪneɪɒ̃ˈtiːz/ *n.* [Fr.] = FAINÉANTISM E17. **fainéantism, -isme** /ˈfeɪneɪɒ̃tɪz(ə)m/ *n.* the state or quality of being a fainéant; indifference, idleness, inactivity: L19.

faint /feɪnt/ *n.* See also FAINTS. ME. [f. FAINT *a.*, *v.*] †**1** Faintness. ME–M16. **2** An act or state of fainting. E19.

2 E. CRISPIN Bent forward . . as though putting his head down to ward off a faint. **in a dead faint** completely unconscious.

faintless *a.* (now *rare*) unflagging L16.

faint /feɪnt/ *a.* Also (now only *Comm.* in sense 6b, formerly also in sense 1) **feint**. ME. [OFr. *faint, feint* pa. pple of *faindre, feindre* FEIGN.] **1** Feigned, simulated. Now *rare*. ME. †**2** Shirking, lazy; sluggish. ME–L17. **3** Lacking in courage, cowardly. Now chiefly in *faint heart*. ME. **4** Weak or dizzy through fear, hunger, exhaustion, etc.; inclined to faint. Foll. by †*of, with*. ME. **b** Inducing faintness; (of a smell) sickly; (of an atmosphere) oppressive. *arch.* E16. **5**†**a** Esp. of a person or animal: weak, sickly, out of condition. LME–M18. **b** Of an action, purpose, etc.: feeble, half-hearted. L16. **6** Making a slight or feeble impression on the senses; hardly perceptible, dim, indistinct; (of a colour) pale. LME. **b** *spec.* Designating the pale blue or neutral-tinted lines ruled on paper as a guide for handwriting. M19.

1 THACKERAY We wear feint smiles over our tears and deceive our children. 4 A. J. CRONIN From surprise and shock she actually turned faint. b WOODES ROGERS The Weather was very wet, hot and faint. 5b J. F. LEHMANN The hopes still clung on, faint graspings at the idea that all might be well after all. *damn with faint praise*: see DAMN *v.* 2. 6 A. RANSOME A glimmer, faint at first, grew brighter. E. CALDWELL She whispered in a voice so faint that she could barely hear it herself. A. N. WILSON The very faint whiff of after-shave lotion he always exuded. R. C. HUTCHINSON I hadn't even the faintest idea what beauty was before I fell in love.

Special collocations & comb.: **faint heart** a cowardly spirit, cowardliness. **faint-heart** *a.* & *n.* (*a*) *adj.* timid, cowardly; (*b*) *n.* a coward. **faint-hearted** *a.* lacking courage, cowardly. **faint-heartedly** *adv.* in a faint-hearted manner. **faint-heartedness** the quality or state of being faint-hearted, cowardliness.

faintest *n.* (*colloq.*) *the* slightest idea or notion M20. **faintish** *a.* somewhat faint M17. **faintishness** *n.* M18. **faintness** *n.* LME.

faint /feɪnt/ *v.* ME. [f. the adj.] **1** *v.i.* Grow or become faint; lose heart or courage, give way; decline, fade, flag, wilt. ME. **2** *v.i.* Lose consciousness, esp. temporarily through a fall in blood pressure; fall in a swoon. Also foll. by *away*. LME. **3** *v.t.* Make faint, enfeeble. Now *rare*. LME.

1 E. BOWEN The sky shone . . fainting down to the fretted line, but was being steadily drained by the dark below. J. COLVILLE The P.M. went to France to bolster up the fainting French morale. D. HALL Water its foliage as well as the soil, or you may . . find your basil has 'fainted.' 2 J. STEINBECK That big stupid horse fainted from the heat. E. FERBER For the first time in her healthy twenty-odd years Leslie Lynnton had fainted dead away. **fainting fit** a faint, a swoon. 3 SHAKES. *Hen. VIII* It faints me To think what follows.

fainter *n.* E19. **faintingly** *adv.* (now *rare*) in a fainting manner, like a person who is fainting L16.

faintly /ˈfeɪntli/ *adv.* ME. [f. FAINT *a.* + -LY[2].] †**1** Feignedly, deceitfully. ME–M18. **2** In a faint manner; feebly, indistinctly; to an almost imperceptible degree, very slightly. ME. †**3** Hardly, scarcely. E16–M17.

2 STEELE To praise faintly the good Qualities of those below them. SCOTT FITZGERALD She . . heard them still singing faintly a song . . , very remote in time and far away. M. LAVIN The room . . was only faintly lit. G. GREENE His brother . . would be faintly surprised by this visit.

faints /feɪnts/ *n.pl.* Also **feints**. E18. [Pl. of FAINT *n.*] The impure spirit which comes over first and last in the process of distillation.

fainty /ˈfeɪnti/ *a.* *obs.* exc. *poet.* & *dial.* M16. [f. FAINT *a.* + -Y[1].] **1** Orig., faint, weak, languid. Later chiefly, inclined to faint. M16. **2** Causing faintness; sickly. L16.

fair /fɛː/ *n.*[1] Also (now esp. in sense 2, *pseudo-arch.*) **fayre**. ME. [OFr. *feire* (mod. *foire*) f. late L *feria* holiday, sing. of cl.L *feriae* religious festivals, holy days.] **1** A regular gathering of buyers and sellers at a time and place ordained by charter, statute, or custom. Now *esp.* (a part of) such a gathering devoted entirely to amusements (also *fun-fair*). ME. **b** An exhibition, esp. one designed to publicize a particular product or the products of one industry, country, etc. E19. **2** = FÊTE *n.* 1b. L19.

1 J. CARLYLE A mere cattle-fair; no booths with toys and sweeties. R. DAHL The fair came once a year with the swings and roundabouts and bumping cars. **a day after the fair** too late. *Bartholomew fair*: see BARTHOLOMEW 2. *mop fair*: see MOP *n.*[5] b A. CADE An annual pilgrimage to the Frankfurt Book Fair.

Comb.: **fairground** an outdoor area on which a fair is held.

fair /fɛː/ *a.*, *adv.*, & *n.*[2] [OE *fæġer* = OS, OHG *fagar*, ON *fagr*, Goth. *fagrs*, f. Gmc.] **A** *adj.* **1** Pleasing to the sight; (of a person, esp. a woman) beautiful. *arch.* OE. †**2** Pleasing to the smell or hearing. OE–LME. **3** Of words, a speech, a promise, etc.: initially attractive or pleasing; specious; flattering. OE. †**4** Of speech, diction: elegant, fluent. ME–L15. **5** Of an amount, a fortune, etc.: considerable, handsome. ME. †**6** *gen.* Desirable, pleasing; excellent. ME–L17. **7** (Of complexion, hair) light not dark, blond; having a light complexion or light hair. ME. **8** Of the weather: favourable; fine, bright, sunny. ME. **b** Of the wind: favourable to a ship's course. LME. **9** Physically clean or sound. Latterly chiefly of water: pure, clear, clean. ME. **10** Of character, reputation, conduct: free from moral stain, unsullied, spotless. *arch.* ME. **11** Of a person, action, argument, etc.: just, unbiased, equitable, impartial; legitimate, in accordance with the rules or standards. ME. **b** Of conditions, etc., esp. in sport: offering an equal chance of success. E18. **12** Of speech, behaviour, action, etc.: courteous, gracious, gentle. Formerly also, of a person's countenance: kindly. ME. **b** In courteous address: kind, dear. *arch.* LME. **13** Likely to succeed; promising; (of an omen) propitious. ME. **14** Unobstructed, clear, open; (now chiefly *dial.*) open to view, plainly to be seen. ME. **15** Now chiefly *Naut.* Of a line, surface, etc.: free from irregularities; smooth, even. L15. **16** Of handwriting: neat, legible. L17. **17** (Of degree or quality) moderate, adequate, reasonable; (of an amount etc.) not excessive but sufficient. L19. **b** Complete, utter, thorough. *slang* & *Austral.* & *NZ.* L19.

1 MILTON The fairest of her daughters Eve. J. RUSKIN A fair building is . . worth the ground it stands on. 3 B. JOWETT The Sophists have plenty of brave words and fair devices. 5 A. SILLITOE A shrewdness that gained him a fair living from the small acreage of garden he cultivated. 7 J. GALSWORTHY The girl with the fair hair . . , the fair arms emerging from a skin-tight bodice. 8 C. RYAN The weather for the next three days would be fair with little cloud and virtually no winds. b C. FRANCIS The wind was still fair—that is, it was coming from a direction other than ahead. 11 ISAIAH BERLIN We must seek to be fair, and not praise and blame arbitrarily. P. ANGADI Nanny . . can no longer deal with them all, it's not fair to ask it of her. b G. P. R. JAMES That would not matter if the ground were fair. 12 J. LOGAN I have used both fair and foul words. 13 A. BURGESS If I kill you now and give myself up to the police, there's a fair chance that I may hang. 14 R. FORD The fairest though farthest way about is the nearest way home. 16 A. THWAITE Kindly copy My words in your fair hand. 17 H. JAMES The storm had given fair warning of its approach. J. GARDNER A pretty fair job to judge by the car and the paint on the house. b N. COWARD They can ramp about among obscure English essayists and have a fair beano.

B *adv.* 1 Beautifully, handsomely. Now *rare.* OE. 2 Courteously, kindly. Now only in *speak (a person) fair*, address civilly. OE. †b In a proper or suitable manner; befittingly. ME–M17. †3 Gently, without haste or violence. Chiefly in *fair and easily, softly.* OE–E19. 4 Promisingly, auspiciously; favourably. *obs.* exc. in *bid fair*: see BID *v.* 6b. OE. 5 Honestly, impartially; according to the rules. ME. 6 Completely; fully; to a considerable degree. Now *dial.*, *N. Amer.*, *Austral.*, & *NZ.* ME. †b Clearly, plainly. LME–L17. c Directly, straight, due (north etc.) Now chiefly *Sc.* L15. 7 Evenly, on a level. Chiefly *dial.* E18.

1 SHAKES. *1 Hen. IV* The moon shines fair. 5 P. DEMING He had tried so many times . . and so fair, and every time a failure. 6 H. L. WILSON The thing fair staggered me.

Special collocations, comb., & *phrases* (of adj. & adv.): **a fair cop** a justifiable arrest. *a fair crack of the whip*: see WHIP *n. a fair deal*: see DEAL *n.*[3] 3. **a fair field and no favour** equal conditions in a contest. *a fair shake*: see SHAKE *n.* **a fair treat** *colloq.* a very enjoyable or attractive thing or person. *bid fair*: see BID *v.* 6b. **by fair means or foul** with or without violence or fraud. **fair and square** *a.* & *n. phr.* (*a*) *adj.* honest, above-board; (*b*) *adv.* honestly, justly, determinedly, straightforwardly, exactly. **fair copy** matter transcribed or reproduced after final correction; **fair-copy** *v.t.* write out or reproduce after final correction. *fair dinkum*: see DINKUM *a. fair do(s)*: see DO *n.*[1] 1c. **fair enough!** *colloq.* that's reasonable. **fair-face(d)** *adjs.* (*a*) having a fair complexion; (*b*) having a (usu. deceptively) attractive appearance; (*c*) (of brickwork etc.) not plastered. *fair fall*: see FALL *v. fair game*: see GAME *n.* **fair-haired** *a.* (*a*) blond; (*b*) (of a person) favourite, much loved. **fairlead(er)** *Naut.* a device, usu. on deck or on a spur, for guiding a rope and preventing it from cutting or chafing. **fair maid** = FUMADO. **fair-minded** *a.* just, unbiased. **fair-mindedly** *adv.* justly, without bias. **fair-mindedness** justness, absence of bias. **fair name** good reputation. **fair play** (*a*) honest, upright conduct; (*b*) equal conditions for all. **fair-spoken** *a.* (of a person) courteous, bland. **fair-to-middling** *a.* (*colloq.*) slightly above average. **fair-trade** (*a*) trade carried on legally; (*b*) smuggling. **fair-trader** a smuggler. **fairway** (*a*) a navigable channel in a river etc.; the regular course or track of a ship; (*b*) the closely-mown part of a golf course, excluding hazards, between the tee and the putting green. **fair-weather** *a.* fit or suitable only for fine weather (*fair-weather friend*: not good in a crisis). **in a fair way to** likely to (succeed etc.). **keep, part, fair** *arch.* remain, part, on good terms. *play fair*: see PLAY *v. the fair(er) sex*: see SEX *n.* **write out fair** = *fair-copy* above.

C *n.* †1 Beauty, good looks. In *pl.* points of beauty. OE–M17. 2 That which is fair; *the fair* aspect, etc.; fair play. LME. 3 A fair thing; *esp.* (*arch.* or *poet.*) a woman. LME.

Phrases etc.: **fair's fair** *colloq.* (reciprocal) fairness is called for. **for fair** *US slang* completely, altogether.

fair /fɛː/ *v.* OE. [f. FAIR *a.*] 1 *v.i.* †a Appear or become beautiful or clean. OE–LME. b Of the weather: clear. Also foll. by *away, off, up.* E19. †2 *v.t.* Make fair, beautify. ME–L16. 3 *v.t.* Make (the surface of a ship etc.) smooth and regular. M19.

Comb.: **fairwater** a structure on a ship etc. for assisting its passage through water.

fairing /ˈfɛːrɪŋ/ *n.*[1] L16. [f. FAIR *n.*[1] + -ING[1].] A present, *esp.* one bought at a fair; *fig.* one's deserts.

fairing /ˈfɛːrɪŋ/ *n.*[2] M19. [f. FAIR *v.* + -ING[1].] The action of making the surface of a ship, aircraft, motor vehicle, etc., smooth and streamlined; a structure added for this purpose.

fairish /fɛːrɪʃ/ *a.* & *adv.* E17. [f. FAIR *a., adv.* + -ISH[1].] A *adj.* 1 Moderately good, passable; *dial.* tolerably well (in health). E17. 2 Considerable in amount, quite large. L19. B *adv.* Quite, fairly. *colloq.* & *dial.* M19.

Fair Isle /ˈfɛːr ʌɪl/ *a.* chiefly (*attrib.*). M19. [One of the Shetland islands.] Designating any of various traditional multi-coloured geometric designs for knitting or a woollen article knitted in such a design.

Fairlight Clay /ˈfɛːlʌɪt ˈkleɪ/ *n. phr.* L19. [f. *Fairlight* a town in Sussex + CLAY *n.*] A band of shales and clays of the Wealden series extending through Kent and East Sussex.

fairly /ˈfɛːli/ *adv.* LME. [f. FAIR *a.* + -LY[2].] I 1 †a Beautifully, handsomely. LME–L19. b Legibly, neatly. *rare.* L16. 2 Gently, peaceably, softly. Long only *Sc.* LME. 3 Properly, suitably. L16. †b Courteously, respectfully. *rare* (Shakes.). L16–E17. 4 By proper means, legitimately; impartially, justly. M17.

1a BYRON To make The skin . . appear more fairly fair. 2 SHAKES. *Two Gent.* They parted very fairly in jest. 4 DEFOE We came honestly and fairly by the ship. J. MITCHELL Miss Culhampton . . deserves more praise than I can fairly give her.

II 5 Completely, fully; actually. L16. 6 Clearly, plainly. M17. 7 Moderately, tolerably; to a considerable degree; acceptably. E19.

5 M. SINCLAIR Left to himself, the Vicar fairly wallowed in his gloom. L. GARFIELD The thin child whose sharp face is fairly shining with pleasure. 6 SIR W. SCOTT [I] saw the bonny city lie stretched fairly before me. 7 E. BOWEN 'You see well from here . . or at any rate, fairly'. A. T. ELLIS She didn't look quite so odd . . but she still looked fairly odd. F. SWINNERTON They all left happy, and on the whole . . fairly sober.

Phrases: **fairly and squarely** = *fair and square* s.v. FAIR *adv.*

fairness /ˈfɛːnɪs/ *n.* OE. [f. FAIR *a.* + -NESS.] 1 The quality or condition of being fair to look at; beauty. OE. †b Of the weather: fineness. LME–M18. 2 Honesty, impartiality, justice. LME. †3 Fair or peaceable means. LME–M16. 4 Lightness of complexion or hair; blondness. L16.

fairy /ˈfɛːri/ *n.* & *a.* See also FAERY. ME. [OFr. *faerie, faierie* (mod. *féerie*), f. as FAY *n.*[2]: see -ERY.] A *n.* 1 The mythical land of fays, fairyland; the inhabitants of fairyland collectively; enchantment. Long *rare.* ME. 2 A mythical small being with human form, popularly believed to possess magical powers and to interfere in human affairs (with either good or evil intent); now *esp.* such a being with the form of a delicate beautiful female, usu. with wings. LME. 3 *transf.* †a An enchantress. *rare* (Shakes.). Only in E17. b A small graceful woman or child. M19. c A male homosexual. *slang, derog.* L19.

1 *good fairy*: see GOOD *a.*

B *adj.* 1 That is a fairy; of or pertaining to fairies; enchanted; fictitious. L16. 2 Fairy-like; delicate, finely formed. L18.

Special collocations & comb.: **fairy armadillo** either of two very small furry burrowing armadillos, *Chlamyphorus retusus* and *C. truncatus*, having a series of plates attached to the spine and heavily armoured at the rear. **fairy cake** a small individual sponge cake, usu. iced and decorated. **fairy cycle** a low small-wheeled bicycle for a child. *fairy flax*: see FLAX *n.* 2a **fairy-floss** *Austral.* candyfloss. **fairy godmother** a fairy who acts as a protector to a mortal child; *fig.* a benefactress. **Fairyland** the home of the fairies; an enchanted region. **fairy lights** small coloured lights used for decoration, esp. on Christmas trees. **fairy martin** an Australian martin, *Petrochelidon ariel*, predominantly black and white with a red-brown crown. **fairy moss** = AZOLLA. **fairy penguin** the little (blue) penguin, *Eudyptula minor*, found on the south coasts of Australia and New Zealand. **fairy prion** a prion, *Pachyptila turtur*, which breeds on the coasts of SE Australia, New Zealand, and the Falkland Islands, and has a bluish bill and bluish feet. **fairy-ring** a circular band of grass darker than that around it, caused by the growth of fungi, but popularly attributed to the dancing of fairies. **fairy rose** a miniature variety of China rose (*Rosa chinensis*). **fairy story** a fairy tale. **fairy tale** (*a*) a tale about fairies, or about a strange incident, coincidence, marvellous progress etc.; an unreal or incredible story, a fabrication; (*b*) the enchanted world of fairy tales, fairy tales as a genre. **fairy tern** (*a*) a small black-crowned Australasian tern, *Sterna nereis*; (*b*) the white tern, *Gygis alba*, of tropical oceans. *fairy thimble(s)*: see THIMBLE *n.* 8. **fairy wren** any of various small Australasian songbirds of the genus *Malurus* (family Maluridae), with a long cocked tail and freq. with bright blue coloration in the male.

fairyism *n.* (*a*) the magical power of fairies; (*b*) fairy-like conditions or characteristics: E18. **fairy-like** *a.* resembling (that of) a fairy L16.

faisandé /fɛzɑ̃de/ *a.* E20. [Fr., pa. pple of *faisander* hang (game) up until it is high.] Affected, artificial, theatrical; piquant, sensational, improper.

A. POWELL Orgies organised by *faisandé* party-givers in days by.

fait accompli /fɛt akɔ̃pli; fɛɪt əˈkɔ̃pli, əˈkɒmpli/ *n. phr.* M19. [Fr. = accomplished fact.] A thing done and irreversible before those affected learn of it.

faith /feɪθ/ *n.* & *v.* ME. [AN *fed*, OFr. *feid, feit* (/-θ/), f. L *fides*, f. var. of base also of *fidus* trustworthy, *fidere* to trust. Cf. FAY *n.*[1]] A *n.* I Confidence, belief. 1 Confidence, reliance, belief esp. without evidence or proof. (Foll. by *in.*) ME. b Belief based on testimony or authority. M16. 2 What is or should be believed; a system of firmly-held beliefs or principles; a religion. ME. 3 *Theol.* Belief in the doctrines of a religion, esp. such as affects character and conduct. LME. b The spiritual apprehension of divine truth or intangible realities. LME. †4 The power to convince; authority, credibility. LME–E19. b Attestation, confirmation, assurance. LME–M18.

1 J. H. NEWMAN To have faith in God is to surrender oneself to God. *Encounter* Citizens who have lost faith in government and almost in democratic institutions too. b T. H. HUXLEY The absolute rejection of authority . . the annihilation of the spirit of blind faith. 2 C. MCCULLOUGH Though she abandoned her faith for Paddy, she refused to adopt his in its stead. A. STORR Communism, . . although not a religion, is certainly a faith. 3 SWIFT Faith is an entire Dependence upon the Truth, the Power, the Justice, and the mercy of God. R. D. LAING We are not satisfied with faith, in the sense of an implausible hypothesis irrationally held. b E. M. GOULBURN Faith . . the faculty by which we realize unseen things.

II Fidelity. †5 A pledge, a solemn promise. ME–L17. 6 The duty of fulfilling a trust or promise; allegiance, obligation. ME. 7 The fulfilment of a trust or promise; fidelity, loyalty. ME.

5 R. WATSON Jane, here I geue to thee my faythe and truthe . . I wyll marrye thee. 6 WILLIAM PHILLIP The Lords . . took their oaths of faith and allegiance unto Don Philip. 7 EVELYN Persons of great faith to his Majesty's cause.

Phrases: **act of faith** †(*a*) = AUTO-DA-FÉ; (*b*) an action demonstrating (religious) faith. *article of faith*: see ARTICLE *n.* 9. **bad faith** treachery, intent to deceive. **breach of faith** (an act of) insincerity or treachery. **break (one's) faith** break one's word; be disloyal. **by my faith** *arch.* truly (in asseverations). *confession of faith*: see CONFESSION 7. *Defender of the Faith*: see DEFENDER. *explicit faith*: see EXPLICIT *a.* **give faith to** believe in, give credence to. **good faith** honesty of intention, sincerity. **i'faith** *arch.* = *in faith* below. *implicit faith*: see IMPLICIT 2. **in faith** *arch.* truly (in asseverations). **keep (one's) faith** keep one's word; be loyal. **on faith** on trust. **on the faith of** relying on the security of. **pin one's faith on** or to, **put one's faith in** believe implicitly, rely on completely. **the faith** the true religion.

Comb.: **faith cure, curer,** (*US*) **curist, -healer, -healing**: acting by faith and prayer, not drugs or other conventional medicine.

†B *v.i.* (foll. by *in, on*) & *t.* Believe, give credit to. LME–E17.

Faithist *n.* & *a.* (*a*) *n.* a member of a sect whose religion is based on the 'Kosmon Bible' or 'Oahspe' and on angelic communications; (*b*) *adj.* of or pertaining to this sect: L19. **faithworthy** *a.* (*arch.*) worthy of belief, trustworthy M16.

faithful /'feɪθfʊl, -f(ə)l/ *a.*, *n.*, & *adv.* ME. [f. FAITH *n.* + -FUL.] A *adj.* 1 Full of (esp. religious) faith; believing, pious. *arch.* ME. 2 Loyal, constant, steadfast; true *to* (a person (esp. a sexual partner), one's word or beliefs). ME. †b Of a promise etc.: containing a pledge of fidelity; binding. LME–E17. 3 Thorough in performing one's duty; conscientious. LME. 4 Trustworthy, veracious; reliable. LME. 5 True to the fact or original; accurate. E16.

2 DRYDEN Naturally good, and faithfull to his word. J. BARNES I may have discarded Christian sexual ethics, but I do believe in being faithful to one person at a time. 5 D. M. FRAME Handsome or ugly, he must paint a faithful likeness.

B *n.* 1 *The* true believers, *the* orthodox members of any religious community; esp. *the* Muslims; *the* loyal adherents of a (political) party. LME. 2 A true believer; one of the faithful; a loyal follower. LME.

1 J. PRIESTLEY The faithful received the eucharist every Lord's day. LD MACAULAY A communion service at which the faithful might sit. A. J. P. TAYLOR The I.L.P. had only contributions from the faithful. *Commander of the Faithful*: see COMMANDER 1. 2 J. ARCHER He addressed the party faithfuls in twenty-three new members' constituencies.

C *adv.* = FAITHFULLY. Long *non-standard.* M16.
faithfulness *n.* LME.

faithfully /'feɪθfʊli, -f(ə)li/ *adv.* LME. [f. FAITHFUL *a.* + -LY[2].] †1 With full faith, trust or confidence. LME–E17. 2 With fidelity; loyally, conscientiously, sincerely. LME. 3 In accordance with the facts; accurately, correctly. LME. 4 With binding assurances; solemnly, sincerely. LME.

2 J. CONRAD The duty had been faithfully and cleverly performed. **Yours faithfully**: a customary formula for closing a business or formal letter. 3 J. MITCHELL My duty was to report as faithfully as possible on the life of people as I found them. 4 E. O'NEILL Promise me faithfully never to forget your father!

faithless /'feɪθlɪs/ *a.* & *n.* ME. [f. FAITH *n.* + -LESS.] A *adj.* 1 Without confidence or trust; lacking (religious) faith, unbelieving. ME. 2 Unfaithful, insincere, false to one's promises, perfidious, disloyal. LME. 3 Unreliable, unstable, delusive. Now *rare* or *obs.* E17. B *n.* *The* non-believers, the people without faith. M16.
faithlessly *adv.* M17. **faithlessness** *n.* E17.

faitour /'feɪtə/ *n.* Long *arch. rare.* ME. [AN (= OFr. *faitor* doer, maker) f. L FACTOR *n.*: see -OUR.] An impostor, a cheat; *esp.* a vagrant shamming illness or pretending to tell fortunes.

faja /'faxa/ *n.* M19. [Sp.] In Spain and Spanish-speaking countries: a sash, a girdle.

fajita /fə'hiːtə, *foreign* fa'xita/ *n.* Pl. **-as** /-əz, *foreign* -as/. L20. [Mex. Sp., lit. 'little strip or belt'.] (A dish of) small strips of grilled spiced beef or chicken rolled in a tortilla with chopped vegetables, grated cheese, etc., and topped with sour cream. Usu. in *pl.*

fake /feɪk/ *n.*[1] E17. [Origin unkn.: rel. to FAKE *v.*[1]] *Naut.* A single turn of a coiled rope or hawser.

fake /feɪk/ *a.* & *n.*[2] Orig. *slang.* L18. [Rel. to FAKE *v.*[2]] A *adj.* Spurious, counterfeit, sham. L18.

Glasgow Herald Fake whisky ... the symptoms following consumption are similar to those of gastric poisoning. G. GREENE He gave her a bright fake smile.

B *n.* 1 A trick, a dodge: an act of pretence or deceit. E19. b *Sport.* A feint, a misleading movement to deceive an opponent. M20. 2 Something not genuine, a forgery, a sham. Orig. *spec.* (*slang*), a news story of questionable authenticity or that has been much embellished. M19. b A person who is not genuine; a charlatan, an impostor. L19. 3 Any of various substances used in manufacturing or furbishing; any substance used in a deception. M19.

2 N. FREELING The big bronze bowl .. was not as he had hoped fourth-century Gallo-Roman, but a pretty impudent Italian fake.

Comb.: **fake book** *Jazz* a book of music containing the basic chord-sequences of tunes.

fake /feɪk/ *v.*[1]*t.* LME. [Origin unkn.: rel. to FAKE *n.*[1]] *Naut.* Lay (a rope) in coils so that it runs clear; coil.

fake /feɪk/ *v.*[2] Orig. *slang.* E19. [Origin uncertain: perh. var. of FEAGUE.] 1 *v.t.* Do something to (a person or thing); *spec.* rob, steal, assault, kill. *slang.* Now *rare* or *obs.* E19. 2 *v.t.* Make presentable or plausible; alter so as to deceive; contrive out of poor or sham materials. Also foll. by *up.* M19. 3 *v.t.* & *i.* Improvise (music); ad lib. *colloq.* E20. 4 *v.t.* Imitate or counterfeit, esp. in order to deceive. E20. 5 *v.t.* & *i.* Feign, simulate; pretend. M20. 6 *v.i.* & *t.* *Sport.* Feint; deceive (an opponent) by a misleading movement. M20.

2 R. BOLDREWOOD The horse-brand .. had been 'faked' or cleverly altered. G. B. SHAW What else could the poor old chap do but fake up an answer fit for publication. 3 *Melody Maker* One had to 'fake' saxophone and banjo parts from those of such other instruments as were catered for in the score. 4 J. ARCHER David Stein .. had achieved notoriety in the art world by faking 300 paintings and drawings by well-known Impressionists. *poodle-fake*: see POODLE *n.* 5 E. O'NEILL I .. hid my face in my hands and faked some sobs. N. ALGREN The big boob lay pretending to sleep and anyone could see at a glance he was faking. 6 J. LEHANE The .. player may begin to fake his opponent to force a defensive mistake.

fakement /'feɪkm(ə)nt/ *n.* Orig. *slang.* E19. [f. prec. + -MENT.] A dodge, a trick; an act of faking.

faker /'feɪkə/ *n.* Orig. *slang.* E19. [f. as prec. + -ER[1]. See also FAKIR 2.] A person who fakes; a swindler.

fakery /'feɪk(ə)ri/ *n.* Orig. *slang.* L19. [f. as prec. + -ERY.] Deception, trickery; the practice of faking.

A. CLARE The history of ESP, astrology, poltergeist phenomena is the history of charlatanry and fakery.

faki /'feɪki, 'fa-/ *n.* L16. [Arab. *fakīh* one learned in Islamic law. Cf. ALFAQUI.] An expert in Islamic law; (in parts of Africa) a teacher in a Koran school.

fakir /'feɪkɪə; *in sense 1 also* 'fa-/ *n.* In sense 1 also (*arch.*) **faquir**. E17. [Arab. *fakīr* poor (man), partly through Fr. *faquir.* Sense 2 alt. of FAKER by pop. etym.] 1 A Muslim (or *loosely* Hindu) religious mendicant or ascetic. E17. 2 = FAKER. *US.* L19.

fa-la /fɑː'lɑː/ *n.* L16. [f. a meaningless refrain.] A kind of madrigal popular in the 16th and 17th cents.

Falabella /falə'bɛlə/ *n.* L20. [Julio *Falabella* (d. 1981), Argentinian breeder.] (An animal of) a breed of miniature horse, the adult of which does not usually exceed 75 cm in height.

falafel /fə'lɑːf(ə)l/ *n.* Also **felafel**. Pl. same. M20. [Egyptian colloq. Arab. *falāfil*, pl. of Arab. *fulful, filfil* pepper.] A ball or fritter of spiced minced pulses or other vegetables, eaten fried and usu. in bread.

Falange /fə'lan(d)ʒ, fə'lɑːn(d)ʒ/ *n.* & *a.* Also **Ph-**. M20. [Sp. = PHALANX.] (Designating or pertaining to) either of two political parties: (*a*) a Fascist and right-wing party in Spain; (*b*) a right-wing Christian (Maronite) party in Lebanon.

Falangism *n.* the principles of the (Spanish or Lebanese) Falange M20. **Falangist** *n.* & *a.* (*a*) *n.* an adherent of the (Spanish or Lebanese) Falange; (*b*) *adj.* of or pertaining to Falangism or Falangists: M20.

Falasha /fə'lɑːʃə/ *n.* Pl. same, **-s**. E18. [Amharic = exile, immigrant.] A member of an Ethiopian group holding the Jewish faith (many of whom are now resident in Israel). Also called *Black Jew*.

falbala /'falbələ/ *n.* E18. [Fr., of unkn. origin. See also FURBELOW *n.*] A trimming for women's petticoats, etc.; a flounce.

falcate /'falkeɪt/ *a.* E19. [L *falcatus*, f. *falx, falc-* sickle: see -ATE[2].] Chiefly *Bot.* & *Zool.* Bent or curved like a sickle; hooked.
†**falcation** *n.* a falcate condition or thing M17–E18.

falcated /'falkeɪtɪd/ *a.* E18. [f. as prec. + -ED[1].] 1 *Astron.* Appearing crescent-shaped. E18. 2 = prec. Chiefly in *falcated teal*, a duck, *Anas falcata*, native to China and NE Asia, named from the long sickle-shaped inner secondary feathers of the male. M18.

falces *n.* pl. of FALX.

falchion /'fɔːl(t)ʃ(ə)n/ *n.* Also †**fau(l)ch-** & other vars. ME. [OFr. *fauchon*, f. Proto-Romance, f. L *falx, falc-* sickle. Latinized sp. w. *-l-* f. 16.] 1 A broad curved sword with the edge on the convex side. Later, a sword of any kind. ME. †2 A billhook. L15–M17.

Falcidian /fal'sɪdɪən/ *a.* M17. [f. *Falcidius*, Roman proconsul *c* 40 BC + -AN.] *Rom. Hist.* Designating or prescribed by a law which ordained that a Roman citizen must leave at least a quarter of his estate to his legal heirs.

falciform /'falsɪfɔːm/ *a.* M18. [f. L *falx, falc-* sickle + -I- + -FORM.] Chiefly *Anat.* Sickle-shaped, curved, hooked.

falciform ligament a ligament separating the right and left lobes of the liver and joining the organ to the diaphragm and anterior abdominal wall.

falciparum /fal'sɪpərəm/ *n.* M20. [mod.L (see below), f. L *falc(i)-* *falx* sickle + *-parum*: see -PAROUS.] A protozoan, *Plasmodium falciparum*, which causes a severe form of malaria with tertian or subtertian fever. Chiefly in *falciparum malaria*.

falcon /'fɔː(l)k(ə)n, 'fɒlk(ə)n/ *n.* ME. [(O)Fr. *faucon* obl. case of *fauc* f. late L *falco, falcon-*, f. *falx, falc-* sickle, or Gmc base of OHG *falco*, whence Du. *valk*, G *Falke* falcon. Latinized sp. w. *-l-* f. 15.] 1 Orig., any of the diurnal birds of prey used in falconry (cf. HAWK *n.*[1]); *esp.* any of the smaller long-winged birds. In mod. use, any of numerous birds of prey, the majority belonging to the genus *Falco*, characterized by long, pointed wings. ME. b *Falconry. spec.* The female of this. Cf. TIERCEL. LME. 2 A representation of a falcon. LME. 3 *Hist.* A kind of light cannon used from the 15th to the 17th cent. L15.

1 *Eleonora's falcon, gyrfalcon, lanner falcon, peregrine falcon, saker falcon*, etc. †**falcon-gentle** (the female of) the peregrine falcon.

falconer /'fɔː(l)k(ə)nə, 'fɒlk(ə)nə/ *n.* LME. [AN *fauconer*, OFr. *-ier* (mod. *fauconnier*), f. *faucon*: see prec., -ER[2].] A person who breeds, keeps, and trains falcons or other birds of prey; one who hunts with such birds, a follower of the sport of falconry.

falconet /'fɔː(l)k(ə)nɪt/ *n.* M16. [In sense 1 f. It. *falconetto* dim. of *falcone* FALCON; in sense 2 f. FALCON: see -ET[1].] 1 *Hist.* A light cannon used in the 16th and 17th cent. M16. 2 A small falcon or bird resembling a falcon; *spec.* any of various small falcons belonging to the genus *Microhierax* or a related genus. M19.

falconry /'fɔː(l)k(ə)nri, 'fɒlk(ə)nri/ *n.* L16. [Fr. *fauconnerie*, f. as FALCON: see -RY.] The breeding, keeping, and training of falcons or other birds of prey; the sport or practice of hunting using such birds.

faldage /'faldɪdʒ/ *n.* Also †**fold-**. ME. [AL *faldagium*, f. as FOLD *n.*[1] + *agium*: see -AGE. Var. after FOLD *n.*[1]] *Hist.* †1 Rent paid for a fold or pen. Only in ME. 2 *Law.* The right of the lord of a manor to graze a tenant's sheep in folds on his land, in order to manure it. LME.

falderal /'faldəral/ *n.* Also **folderol** /'fɒldərɒl/ E19. [f. a meaningless refrain in songs.] A gew-gaw, a trifle; nonsense, trivial display.

E. GARRETT That his darling might never want for fal-de-rals. *Times* Erisichthon published with much puffing and falderal a recipe for Cold Duck soup.

faldetta /fal'dɛtta, fal'dɛtə/ *n.* M19. [It., dim. of *falda* fold of cloth, skirt.] A combined hood and cape worn by women in Malta.

†**faldistory** *n.* L17–M19. [med.L *faldistorium* var. of *faldistolium*: see next.] *Eccl.* The seat or throne of a bishop within the chancel of a cathedral.

faldstool /'fɔːldstuːl/ *n.* [Late OE *fældestōl*, *fyld(e)stōl* f. Gmc, f. base of FOLD *v.*[1], STOOL *n.* Partly f. med.L *faldistolium* f. WGmc.] *Eccl.* 1 A seat (freq. folding) used by a bishop or other prelate when not occupying the throne or when officiating in any church other than his own. LOE. 2 A movable folding stool or desk at which worshippers kneel; *esp.* one used by a monarch at his or her coronation. E17. 3 A small desk at which the Litany is said or sung. E17.

fale /ˈfɑːle/ *n.* E20. [Samoan.] A Samoan house with open sides and a thatched roof.

Falernian /fəˈləːnɪən/ *a.* & *n.* M17. [f. *Falernus* (see below) + -IAN.] Chiefly *Hist.* A *adj.* Of or pertaining to *Falernus ager*, an ancient district in Campania, Italy, famous for its wine. M17. B *n.* Falernian wine. E18.

Also †**Falerne** *a.* & *n.* E17–M18.

Faliscan /fəˈlɪsk(ə)n/ *n.* & *a.* L17. [f. L *Faliscus* + -AN.] (A native or inhabitant) of the ancient Etrurian city of Falerii.

Also **Faliscian** *n.* (*rare*) E17.

Falklands /ˈfɔː(l)kl(ə)ndz/ *a.* Also **Falkland**. L19. [The *Falklands*, informal name of the Falkland Islands in the S. Atlantic.] Of or pertaining to the Falkland Islands.

Falklander *n.* a native or inhabitant of the Falkland Islands L19.

fall /fɔːl/ *n.*[1] Now *dial.* [OE *-fealle* = OHG *falla* (G *Falle*), f. the vb. Cf. FALL *n.*[2] V.] A trapdoor, a trap.

¶Prob. the 2nd elem. of PITFALL, but there now usu. taken as FALL *n.*[2] or *v.*

fall /fɔːl/ *n.*[2] ME. [Partly f. ON (= fall, death in battle, sin, downfall); partly f. the vb. Cf. FELL *n.*[4]] I A falling from a height or to a lower level. 1 A dropping down from a height or relative height, esp. by the force of gravity. ME. b A descent of rain, snow, etc.; the amount that falls. L16. †c Shedding of blood. *rare* (Shakes.). Only in L16. †d The downward stroke of a sword etc. *rare* (Shakes.). L16–E17. e The descent or approach of night, twilight, winter, etc. *rare.* exc. in *nightfall*. M17. f Birth of lambs etc. by dropping from the parents; the number born. L18. 2 The time of year when leaves fall from trees; autumn. Now chiefly *N. Amer.* M16. 3 The manner in which something falls. M16. 4 Depreciation; a reduction in price, value, etc. M16. 5 Downward direction of a surface or outline; a slope, a declivity. M16. b *Naut.* The slope of a ship's deck; the difference in level between decks. M17. c The distance through which anything descends; the amount of the descent. L17. 6 A sinking down (of waves, the sun, etc.); subsidence; *fig.* decline, decay. L16. b The decline or closing part of a day, year, or life. E17. 7 The falling of a stream of water down a declivity; *sing.* & (freq.) in *pl.* a cascade, a waterfall. L16. 8 A lowering of the voice, a musical note, etc.; a cadence. E17. 9 A sinking of liquid in a measuring instrument; a lowering of pressure or temperature; a registering of this on an instrument. E19.

1 F. SMITH One of them, by a fall from the Parapet .., was killed. *rainfall, snowfall*, etc. 2 J. MCPHEE In early fall, towards the end of August, they gathered berries. 4 *Times* There have been some quite remarkable price falls in the year. 5 T. GRAY A natural terrass .. with a gradual fall on both sides. 6 W. MORRIS The wide sun reddened towards his fall. 7 R. RAYMOND The roar of the falls is heard in the distance. REVERSING *falls*. 8 SHAKES. *Twel. N.* That strain again. It had a dying fall.

II A falling over from an upright position. 10 A falling from an upright position to the ground; a controlled act of falling, esp. as a stunt or in judo. ME. b *Cricket.* The loss of a wicket. L19. 11 *fig.* A giving in to temptation; moral descent or ruin. ME. b *Theol. The* lapse into a sinful state resulting from Adam's transgression. Also *the Fall of Man.* ME. †c The cause of a moral fall. M16–E17. d An arrest; a period in prison. *Criminals' slang.* L19. 12 Death, destruction, overthrow. ME. 13 *Wrestling.* A bout; a throw which keeps an opponent on the ground for a specified time. M16. 14 The surrender or capture of a city, fortress, etc. L16. 15 A felling of trees; the timber felled in one season. L16.

10 B. PYM She might have had a fall and be unable to move or get to the phone. 12 B. HARRIS The fall of one of the greatest men in Europe .. Oliver Cromwell. 14 H. J. LASKI The .. vice which preceded the fall of Carthage and of Rome.

III 16 A linear measure consisting of the 40th part of a furlong; the corresponding square measure. *obs.* exc. *Sc.* & *north.* LME.

IV 17 One's fortune, lot, or fate; what befalls one. *obs.* exc. *Sc.* LME.

V (Cf. FALL *n.*[1]) 18 An article of dress, *esp.* one which hangs from or lies over something, as a veil, a flat collar, etc. E16. b Any item of material which hangs from something, *esp.* one which is decorative or ornamental. Also, a hairpiece or hairstyle in which the hair is long and falls down naturally. M17. c The long hair hanging over the faces of certain terriers. E20. 19a A rope in hoisting-tackle, to which the power is applied. M17. b *Naut.* In *pl.* The tackles by which lifeboats are hoisted or lowered from the davits. E19. 20 *gen.* Something which falls or has fallen. M18. 21 *Bot.* In *pl.* The parts or petals of a flower which bend downwards; *spec.* the outer perianth-segments of an iris (cf. STANDARD *n.* 4). L18.

18 S. E. FERRIER The Chantilly fall which embellished the front of her bonnet. b LADY BIRD JOHNSON Her hair simple but elegant with a fall. 20 *rainfall, rockfall, windfall*, etc.

Phrases: *break a fall*: see BREAK *v.* **fall of the leaf** *rare* autumn. *free fall*: see FREE *a. ride for a fall*: see RIDE *v. take a fall*: see TAKE *v. the Fall (of Man)*: see sense 11b above. **try a fall** contend *with* (an opponent).

Comb.: **fall-board** a shutter hinged at the bottom; **fall-breaker** a thing which breaks a fall; **fallfish** a N. American cyprinoid freshwater fish, *Semotilus corporalis*; **fall-front** *n.* & *a.* (having) a front part that drops or can be let down; **fall guy** *slang* an easy victim, a scapegoat; *fall* HERRING; **fall-leaf** *n.* & *a.* (*US*) = DROP-LEAF; **fall-line** (*a*) *Physical Geogr.* a narrow zone, distinguished by the occurrence of falls and rapids where rivers and streams cross it, marking the geological boundary between an upland region and a plain (*spec.* in *US*, between the Piedmont and the Atlantic coastal plain); (*b*) *Skiing* the natural route down a slope; **fall money** *Criminals' slang* money set aside by a criminal for use in the event of arrest; **fall-rope** a rope used for lifting; **fall-trap** = FALL *n.*[1]; **fall zone** = *fall-line* (a) above.

fall /fɔːl/ *v.* Pa. t. **fell** /fɛl/; pa. pple **fallen** /ˈfɔːl(ə)n/. [OE *feallan, fallan* = OFris., ON *falla*, OS, OHG *fallan* (Du. *vallen*, G *fallen*) f. Gmc. Cf. FELL *v.*[1]] I *v.i.* Descend from a height or to a lower level. 1 Drop or come down from a height or relative height, esp. by the force of gravity. OE. b Of rain, hail, darkness, etc.: descend, come down (as) from the upper atmosphere. OE. c *fig.* Of calamity, fear, sleep, etc.: come down *on, upon.* ME. d Of the young of animals: be dropped or born. LME. 2 Become detached and drop off. ME. 3 Descend, sink; *esp.* (of water, flames, a storm, etc.) subside, ebb, abate. ME. b Decline physically or morally. ME. †c Of the sun etc.: go down, set. LME–L19. 4 Of a river etc.: discharge itself, flow *into.* ME. 5 Of the face or facial expression: lose animation, assume a look of dismay or disappointment. LME. b Of the eyes or glance: be cast down. L19. 6 Of sound, esp. the voice, a musical note, etc.: become lower or quieter. LME. †7 Reduce in size; become thinner or leaner; (of swelling) go down. M16–E19. 8 Decrease, become reduced; go down in price or value. L16. 9 Of land: slope. L16. 10 Of feathers, leaves, etc.: droop, hang down. L16. 11 Of speech etc.: issue or proceed *from.* E17. 12 (Of liquid in a measuring instrument) sink to a lower point; (of a measuring instrument) register a lowering of pressure or temperature. M17. b Of temperature: become lower. L19.

1 M. KEANE I unhooked my gold dress and let it fall .. round my feet. S. BRETT The curtain fell for the interval. *free-fall*: see FREE *a.* b V. WOOLF Darkness fell as sharply as a knife in this climate. 2 E. BOWEN The .. last leaves still clung to the trees, as though they would not fall. 3 P. S. BUCK A still grey day when the wind fell and the air was quiet and warm. 6 J. C. POWYS The names .. kept rising and falling like a musical refrain. 8 H. WILSON Our majority .. had fallen to two when we lost Leyton. *Financial Times* Short sterling .. fell slightly to 87.79. 9 A. PATON The ground falls away from one's feet to the valley below. 12 A. CALDCLEUGH The thermometer in the winter seldom falls to freezing.

II *v.i.* Lose an upright position. 13 Prostrate oneself in reverence or supplication. OE. 14 Stumble or be drawn *into* (a trap, danger, error, etc.). OE. 15 Be brought or come suddenly to the ground. ME. b *Cricket.* Of a wicket: be knocked down by the ball to dismiss a batsman (also registering the dismissal of a batsman by any means). Of a batsman: be out *to* a catch, bowler, etc. L18. 16 Yield to temptation, sin; lose honour or moral standing. ME. b Be arrested; be sent to prison. *Criminals' slang.* L19. 17 *fig.* Of a fortification, empire, government, etc.: succumb to attack or opposition, be destroyed or overthrown. ME. b *Cards.* Be captured by a higher card. (Foll. by *to.*) E18. 18 Drop down wounded or dead; die by violence. ME. 19 Of a building etc.: come down in fragments, tumble in ruins. ME.

13 R. P. JHABVALA Realising who it was, they fell at the Nawab's feet. 15 *Dogworld* A dozen exhibitors slipped and fell in the mud. 16 D. LESSING It was because Adam ate the apple that he was lost, or fell. 17 L. NAMIER Lord North's government has fallen. 18 J. R. GREEN The greater part of the higher nobility had fallen in battle.

III *v.i.* Happen, occur, become. 20 (Of a lot, choice, etc.) chance *on*, light *on*; be allotted or apportioned *to*; come as a burden or duty *to*, devolve (*up*)*on.* ME. †21 Appertain, belong. Foll. by *to, for.* ME–M16. 22 Come into a specified state or position (by chance, naturally, in the course of events, or unawares); pass *into* (†*in*, †*to*) a specified state or position. ME. †b Come as a consequence or result. ME–L17. †c Change for the worse. (*in*)*to* LME–L16. d Of light, the sight, a movement, etc.: have or take a specified direction, have a specified position, settle *on.* L16. e Be (naturally) divisible *into.* M17. 23 Occur, come to pass, happen; come at a specified time, have as date. ME. 24 With compl.: become. (Foll. by adj., n. (now only *heir*), (now *dial.*) prep. phr., (*arch.*) *to be.*) LME. 25†a Of an office, living, etc.: become vacant. M16–L18. b Of a benefice or its revenues: lapse. L16.

20 C. THIRLWALL The suspicion of disaffection .. fell on a man of eminent talents. M. MEYER It fell to her to see to his personal needs. 22 AV *Luke* 10:30 A certaine man went downe from Hierusalem to Iericho, and fel among theeues. T. HARDY He fell into a heavy slumber and did not wake till dawn. A. HALEY Quiet fell when Tom made it clear he wished to speak. D. BARNES Before it fell into Nora's hands, the property had been in the .. family. *fall behind* etc. d G. MACDONALD The sound of a closing door .. fell on my ear. E. M. FORSTER To the left fell the shadow of the embankment. J. RATHBONE I .. moved the candle, and its light fell on the red hair of Rubén. e A. EDEN The pictures at Windlestone fell naturally into three categories. 23 W. HOLDER The Vernal Equinox, which .. fell upon the 21st of March. LONGFELLOW I am rather sorry that the Exhibition falls so late in the year. 24 J. A. FROUDE All the offices fell vacant together. G. GREENE He fell silent .. as though aware of an indiscretion.

IV *v.t.* 26†a Overthrow, bring down. ME–E17. b Fell (trees). Now *dial.* exc. *US, Austral.*, & *NZ.* LME. 27 Have as one's share; get, obtain. *obs.* exc. *dial.* LME. 28 Let fall, drop. Now only in *Campanol.* L15. †b Give birth to (a lamb etc.). L16–M17. †29 Lower. E17–L18.

Phrases: *bottom falls out of*: see BOTTOM *n.* **fair fall —** *arch.* may good befall —. *fall by the wayside*: see WAYSIDE *n. fall flat*: see FLAT *a. fall foul of*: see FOUL *adv. fall from grace*: see GRACE *n. fall in love*: see LOVE *n.* **fall into line** take one's place in a rank; collaborate with others, do as others. *fall into place*: see PLACE *n.*[1] *fall into the habit of*: see HABIT *n.* **fall in two** collapse, disintegrate. **fall on hard** or **evil times** suffer misfortune. **fall on one's face** (*a*) prostrate oneself in reverence; (*b*) fail ridiculously. **fall on one's feet** get out of difficulty or be successful, esp. unexpectedly or by good luck. **fall on one's sword** kill oneself with a sword. **fall over oneself** *colloq.* (*a*) be very clumsy; (*b*) be very hasty or eager (*to do*). **fall short** (*a*) be or become insufficient or inadequate; (*b*) (of a shot, missile, etc.) not go far enough; (foll. by *of*) fail to obtain or reach. *fall to one's share*: see SHARE *n.*[2] *fall to pieces*: see PIECE *n.* **fall to the ground** *fig.* (of a plan etc.) come to nothing, be abandoned, fail. *fall to the lot of*: see LOT *n.* **foul fall —** *arch.* may evil befall —.

With advs. in specialized senses: **fall aboard** (*a*) fall foul of (a ship, †a person); †(*b*) quarrel *with.* **fall about** *colloq.* be helpless, esp. with mirth; laugh uncontrollably. **fall apart** collapse, disintegrate. **fall astern** (of a ship) drop behind. **fall away** (*a*) withdraw one's support, desert, revolt, apostatize, (*from*); (*b*) become few or thin; decay, perish, vanish. **fall back** (*a*) give way, retreat; (*b*) *fall back on, upon*, have recourse to, rely on when in difficulty. **fall behind** be outstripped, stop keeping up. **fall down** (*a*) (of a ship) travel down towards the sea; †(*b*) sicken; (*c*) *fall down* (*on*) come to grief (over), fail (in). **fall in** (*a*) (of a building) collapse inwards; †(*b*) make one's way in, (of a ship) take a course for land; (*c*) (now *rare*) happen, occur; (*d*) *Mil.* (cause to) get into line; (*e*) agree; concur in an arrangement; †(*f*) make up a quarrel; (*g*) come to an end, terminate; (of a debt etc.) become due; (of land etc.) become available; (of a lease) run out; (*h*) *fall in for*, come in for, get, incur; (*i*) *fall in upon*, come upon or drop in upon by chance; (*j*) *fall in with*, come upon by chance, happen to meet; agree with; accede to, go along with (views, plans); humour (an opinion etc.); harmonize with, coincide with. **fall off** (*a*) step aside, withdraw; (*b*) *Naut.* (of a ship) fail to keep its head to the wind; deviate to leeward; (*c*) part company, become estranged; (*d*) decrease in size or number; deteriorate, decline. **fall on** (*a*) attack, join battle; (*b*) (now *rare*) begin, set to work. **fall out** (*a*) disagree, quarrel (*with*); (*b*) come to pass, occur; prove to be, turn out, *esp.* turn out well; (*c*) *fall out of* (*Mil.*), leave or be dismissed from (the ranks). **fall over** †(*a*) go over *to* (an enemy); (*b*) *Sc.* fall asleep; (*c*) not stay upright, topple over; (*fall over backwards*: see BACKWARD *adv.* 1). **fall through** break down, fail, miscarry. **fall to** (*a*) close automatically; (*b*) set to, begin working, eating, fighting, etc. **fall together** †(*a*) close, collapse; (*b*) *Phonet.* (of sounds) become identical.

With preps. in specialized senses: **fall a —** *arch.* begin *doing*, †an action. **fall aboard —** fall foul of (a ship). **fall behind —** be outstripped by, stop keeping up with. **fall down —** *arch.* descend or travel down (a river etc.). **fall for** (*colloq.*, orig *US*) be captivated or deceived by; yield to the attractions of; (see also sense 21 above). **fall from —** *arch.* forsake allegiance to; abandon; (see also Phrases above). **fall into —** †(*a*) come into or within; make a hostile approach to, make an inroad into; (*b*) engage in, begin, (esp. conversation, *with*); (*c*) comply with, accommodate oneself to; adopt (a habit etc.); (see also senses 4, 14, 22, & Phrases above). **fall on —** †(*a*) begin (an action or state, *doing*), set about; (*b*) attack, assault; (*c*) come across, light on; (*d*) have recourse to, make use of; (see also senses 1c, 20, 22d, & Phrases above). **fall to —** †(*a*) be drawn to, become a follower of; †(*b*) agree with, accede to; (*c*) *arch.* apply oneself to, begin, (an action, *doing*); (*d*) be killed or defeated by; (see also senses 15b, 17b, 20, 21, 22 above). **fall under —** (*a*) be classed among; (*b*) be subjected to. **fall upon —** = *fall on* above; (see also senses 1c, 20 above). **fall within —** be included in, come within the scope of.

†fallace *n.* ME–M17. [(O)Fr. f. as FALLACY.] = FALLACY 1, 2.

fallacion /fəˈleɪʃ(ə)n/ *n.* Now *rare*. Also **-ian**. M16. [Irreg. f. FALLACY, or f. FALLACIOUS after *suspicious, suspicion*.] = FALLACY 2.

fallacious /fəˈleɪʃəs/ *a.* E16. [(O)Fr. *fallacieux* f. L *fallaciosus*, f. as next: see -ACIOUS.] 1 Containing a fallacy. E16. 2†a Deceitful. M17–M18. b Deceptive, misleading. M17. 3 Causing disappointment, delusive. M17.

fallaciously *adv.* M17. **fallaciousness** *n.* L17.

fallacy /ˈfaləsi/ *n.* L15. [L *fallacia*, f. *fallax, -ac-*, f. *fallere* deceive: see -ACY. Cf. earlier FALLACE.] 1†a Deception, guile, trickery; a deception; a lie. L15–M18. b Deceptiveness, unreliability. L16. 2 A deceptive argument, a sophism; *spec.* in *Logic*, a flaw which vitiates a syllogism; one of the types of such flaws. Also, sophistry. M16. 3 An error, *esp.* one founded on false reasoning. Also, delusion, error. L16. †4 Fallibility. *rare*. M17–L18. 5 Unsoundness of opinion, an argument, etc.; delusiveness, disappointing character. L18.

2 J. GOODWIN I shall . . proceed to show the fallacies and other weaknesses of those pretences. **fallacy of accident** the fallacy of arguing from one point to another where the two points agree, or do not agree, purely by accident. **fallacy of misplaced concreteness** the fallacy of considering an abstract entity to be more concrete than it actually is. PATHETIC *fallacy*. 3 J. MARQUAND The fallacy that all Chinese look alike.

fal-lal /faˈlal, falˈlal/ *n.*, *a.*, & *v.* *arch.* E18. [Perh. suggested by FALBALA.] A *n.* A piece of finery or frippery. Usu. in *pl.* E18. †B *adj.* Affected, finicking, foppish. M18–M19. C *v.i.* Behave or dress in an affected or finicking manner; idle, dally, procrastinate. M19.

fallal(l)ery *n.* tawdry finery M19.

fall-away /ˈfɔːləweɪ/ *n.* L17. [f. FALL *v.* + AWAY *adv.*] †1 An apostate. Only in L17. 2 A falling off. L19.

fall-back /ˈfɔːlbak/ *a.* & *n.* M18. [f. FALL *v.* + BACK *n.*[1] (sense A.1), BACK *adv.*] A *adj.* 1 Of a chaise etc.: having a back which can be let down. *US*. M18. 2 That may be used in an emergency; *spec.* (of a wage) comprising a minimum amount, paid when work is not available. M20.

2 *Times* 5000 dockers were without work and receiving 'fall-back' pay.

B *n.* 1 A reserve; something which may be used in an emergency, *esp.* a fall-back wage. M19. 2 A falling back, depression. L19.

1 B. GUEST If that plan fell through, he had a fall-back in 'Lady E'.

fallen /ˈfɔːl(ə)n/ *ppl a.* & *n.* LME. [pa. pple of FALL *v.*] A *ppl a.* 1 That has fallen. Also *fallen-in, -off*, etc. LME. 2 Of flesh etc.: shrunken, emaciated. E18.

1 W. WITHERING The fallen branches of trees. J. JORTIN The Messiah was to restore fallen man. *New Republic* The miserable pensions that are being paid to the widows of fallen soldiers. D. H. LAWRENCE The grass plot was strewn with fallen leaves. G. GREENE This book . . should do much to raise Stevenson's . . fallen reputation. *fallen angel*: see ANGEL *n.* *fallen arch*: see ARCH *n.*[1] 3b. **fallen woman** a woman who has lost her chastity, honour, or standing; a prostitute.

B *n.pl.* *The* people who have fallen, esp. in battle. M18.

W. D. NEWTON The corpses of the fallen were trodden . . beneath . . heedless soles.

fallenness /-n-n-/ *n.* L19.

faller /ˈfɔːlə/ *n.* LME. [f. FALL *v.* + -ER[1].] 1 A person who or animal or thing which falls. Also *faller-away, -out*, etc. LME. 2 A person who fells trees. Chiefly *dial.*, *US*, *Austral.*, & *NZ*. M19.

fallibilism /ˈfalɪbɪlɪz(ə)m/ *n.* L19. [f. as next: see -ISM.] *Philos.* The principle that propositions concerning empirical knowledge cannot be proved.

fallibilist *a.* maintaining or accepting fallibilism L19.

fallible /ˈfalɪb(ə)l/ *a.* & *n.* LME. [med.L *fallibilis*, f. L *fallere* deceive: see -IBLE.] A *adj.* 1 Liable to err or to be deceived. LME. 2 Liable to be erroneous; unreliable. LME.

1 H. H. MILMAN The papal power . . the representative of fallible man. 2 W. HUBBARD Uncertain and fallible Reports.

B *n.* A person who is fallible. *rare*. E18.

falliˈbility *n.* the state or fact of being fallible; an instance of this; (cf. earlier INFALLIBILITY): M17. **fallibly** *adv.* M16.

falling /ˈfɔːlɪŋ/ *n.* ME. [f. FALL *v.* + -ING[1].] 1 The action of FALL *v.*; an instance of this. Also *falling-off, -out*, etc. ME. 2 A thing which falls or has fallen. Now *rare*. LME. †3 A hollow, a declivity. M16–E18.

1 SHAKES. *Haml.* O Hamlet, what a falling off was there. W. C. WELLS The falling of the mercury in the barometer. LONGFELLOW The silent falling of snow. F. D. DAVISON The business of falling, hauling and sawing pine logs. P. KURTH Their abrupt falling-out had done nothing to alter her conviction. **(as) easy as falling off a log** *colloq.* very easy.

Comb.: **falling sickness** *arch.* epilepsy.

falling /ˈfɔːlɪŋ/ *ppl a.* ME. [f. FALL *v.* + -ING[2].] 1 That falls. ME. 2 *Pros.* & *Phonet.* Of a foot, rhythm, etc.: having the stress at the beginning, decreasing in stress. M19.

Special collocations: **falling band** a collar which falls flat around the neck, fashionable during the 17th cent. *falling diphthong*: see DIPHTHONG *n.* 1. **falling leaf** *Aerobatics* a manoeuvre in which an aeroplane is stalled and side-slipped while losing height. **falling star** a meteor, a shooting star. **falling weather** *dial.* & *US* rain, snow, or hail.

fall-off /ˈfɔːlɒf/ *n.* L19. [f. FALL *v.* + OFF *adv.*] A reduction, a withdrawal; diminution.

Fallopian /fəˈləʊpɪən/ *a.* E18. [f. *Fallopius* Latinized form of the name of Gabriello *Fallopio* (1523–62), It. anatomist: see -AN.] Designating any of various anatomical structures reputedly discovered by Fallopius; esp. *Fallopian tube*, (in a female mammal) either of the tubes that lead from the ovaries to the cavity of the uterus.

Fallot /ˈfaləʊ, *foreign* falo/ *n.* E20. [Étienne Louis Arthur *Fallot* (1850–1911), Fr. physician.] Med. *Fallot's tetralogy, tetralogy of Fallot*, a condition in which four congenital cardiac abnormalities occur together, accompanied by cyanosis.

fallout /ˈfɔːlaʊt/ *n.* M20. [f. FALL *v.* + OUT *adv.*] (The deposition of) airborne radioactive debris from a nuclear explosion. Also *fig.*, a consequence, esp. side-effects, of an unexpected kind.

fallow /ˈfaləʊ/ *n.* ME. [Prob. f. FALLOW *v.* Cf. MLG *valge* (G *Felge*).] †1 (A piece of) ploughed land. ME–E18. 2 (A piece of) ground that is left uncultivated after being ploughed and harrowed, in order to restore its fertility. E16. 3 The state of lying fallow; an interval during which land is allowed to lie fallow. E16.

2 **green fallow**: planted with a green crop. *summer-fallow*: see SUMMER *n.*[1] 3 J. BILLINGSLEY Twelve successive crops of wheat, without an intervening fallow.

fallow /ˈfaləʊ/ *a.*[1] [OE *falu* (*fealu*), infl. *fealwe* etc. = OS *falu* (Du. *vaal*), OHG *falo* (G *fahl*, *falb*), ON *fǫlr*, f. Gmc.] Of a pale brownish- or reddish-yellow colour.

fallow deer a Mediterranean deer, *Cervus dama*, widely naturalized in European parks and forests, which is smaller than the red deer and has a dappled fawn summer coat.

fallow /ˈfaləʊ/ *a.*[2] LME. [f. FALLOW *n.*] 1 Of land: left uncultivated for the current year or longer (esp. in *lie* or *lay fallow*). Formerly also, ploughed in readiness for sowing. LME. 2 *fig.* Potentially useful but not put to use; inactive, uncreative. M17. 3 *transf.* Esp. of an animal: not pregnant. M18.

1 W. STYRON Great tracts of bramble-choked red earth gone fallow and worthless. 2 J. THURBER He had resumed work after a long fallow period. B. BETTELHEIM Decision-making is a function which . . tends to atrophy when it lies fallow.

fallowness *n.* E17.

fallow /ˈfaləʊ/ *v.t.* & (*rare*) *i.* [OE *fealgian*. Cf. LG *falgen*, MHG *valgen, velgen*.] 1 Plough and break up (land) for sowing. OE. 2 Break up and leave fallow (land) with a view to destroying weeds, mellowing the soil, etc. LME.

falsary /ˈfɔːls(ə)ri, ˈfɒls-/ *n.* *arch.* LME. [L *falsarius*, f. *falsus*: see next, -ARY[1].] 1 A person who forges or fraudulently alters a document. LME. †2 A deceitful person. L16–L17.

false /fɔːls, fɒls/ *n.*, *a.*, & *adv.* OE. [L *falsum* neut. of *falsus*, orig. pa. pple of *fallere* deceive; in ME reinforced by or newly formed f. OFr. *fals*, *faus*, fem. *false* (mod. *faux, fausse*) f. L *falsus*.] A *n.* †1 Fraud, deceit; *esp.* counterfeiting of money. OE–LME. †2 A deceitful person. Only in ME. 3 Something which is untrue or deceptive; (a) falsehood. *arch.* LME.

3 R. GREENE Such reports more false than truth contain. TENNYSON Earth's falses are heaven's truths.

B *adj.* I Deceptive, misleading. 1 Of a statement etc.: deliberately asserting what is known to be untrue: ME. b Of a person (esp. a witness), speech, etc.: deliberately untruthful; lying. ME. 2 Of a person, conduct, etc.: offering no firm basis for trust; disloyal, treacherous, (*to*). Also, insincere, affected. ME. †b Of ground, a foundation, etc.: not firm, treacherous. L16–L17. 3 Of an appearance, indication, etc.: deceptive, illusory; apparent, not real. Of a medium of vision: that distorts the object viewed through it. ME. 4 Of a weight, measure, etc.: dishonestly contrived to give an incorrect reading. Of dice: loaded. ME. 5 Not genuine; sham, spurious; (of a coin, jewel, etc.) made in fraudulent imitation from base materials; (of a document) forged. ME. b Of a person: that pretends or is falsely claimed to be (what is denoted by the n.). ME. c Of a quality, action, etc.: simulated, feigned. ME. d Esp. of hair or other features of the body: worn as a disguise, to conceal a defect, for cosmetic reasons, etc. L16. e Of a name or other personal attribute: adopted in place of the true one to disguise one's identity etc.; assumed. L19.

6 Of a manoeuvre, signal, etc.: intended to mislead an opponent, pursuer, etc. LME. 7 Of something naturally occurring: superficially resembling the thing properly so called but lacking its essential qualities or functions. Used esp. in names of plants, animals, and gems. LME. 8 Of a structure etc.: supplementing or substituted for the one properly so called. LME.

1 R. MAUGHAM If we find your claim to be James Steede is false, if you're an impostor. D. M. WALKER It is an offence . . to apply a false or misleading trade description to any goods. *Oxford Mail* Roy Jenkins . . dismisses Labour's plans . . as a 'false prospectus'. b SHAKES. *Rich. III* The envious slanders of her false accusers. 2 POPE They . . false to Phoebus, bow the knee to Baal. C. BRONTË Her promises are hollow—her offers false. O. WILDE The false friend coming close to him so as to betray him with a kiss. CONAN DOYLE He won her with his title . . and his false London ways. D. H. LAWRENCE They were all going about in a lugubrious false way, feeling they must not be natural or ordinary. b DRYDEN Graze not too near the Banks, my . . sheep, the Ground is false. 3 G. B. SHAW The ghastliness of a beautiful thing seen in a false light. L. DURRELL Her gratitude . . creates the illusion that she communicates with her fellow, but this is false. 5 JOSEPH HALL Criples that pretend false soares. G. ALLEN A swindler has two sets [of diamonds]—one real, one false. J. LE CARRÉ The agent was given . . a false passport. b R. SOUTH All pretended false Messiahs vanish'd upon the Appearance of Christ the true one. c I. MURDOCH I could . . imagine her face, pulled into that false sadness with glee looking through. *Sunday Times* I don't like people who have this false modesty. I know that I am beautiful. d G. B. SHAW He claps on the false nose, and is . . grotesquely transfigured. G. GREENE A flashy and false blonde. e R. A. FREEMAN Now, a common thief, he was sneaking in under a false name. A. SILLITOE He joined [the army] too young by giving a false age. 6 W. DAMPIER Had we enter'd the Port upon the false signal, we must have been taken. W. BLACKSTONE Putting out false lights in order to bring any vessel into danger. A. AINGER Lamb had a love of . . putting his readers on a false scent. 7 ST G. J. MIVART The superior or false vocal cords. G. H. WILLIAMS False planes, apparent crystal faces, whose position is not that of true crystal planes. *false acacia, false brome, false cypress, false hellebore, false killer, false oat(-grass), false scorpion, false topaz, false vampire*, etc. 8 E. WAUGH The dome was false . . Its dome was merely an additional storey full of segmental rooms.

II Mistaken, wrong. 9 Of an opinion, proposition, etc.: not in accordance with the truth or the facts; erroneous, untrue. ME. 10 Not conforming with orthodox practices or rules; incorrect, invalid. LME. b Of a musical note: wrong in pitch, out of tune. L15. 11 Of a movement or manoeuvre: made at the wrong moment or in the wrong direction; misjudged. Freq. in *false move, step*. E18. 12 Of pride, a scruple, etc.: arising from mistaken notions; misguided. Also, of hope, confidence, etc.: having no substantial basis; unjustified. E18.

9 *Book of Common Prayer* From all false doctrine, heresie, and schism . . Good Lord, deliver vs. S. JOHNSON The same proposition cannot be at once true and false. LD MACAULAY It may perhaps correct some false notions. A. J. P. TAYLOR The cabinet acknowledged that its expectation of a short war had proved false. 10 SHAKES. *L.L.L.* I smell false Latin; 'dunghill' for unguem. LD MACAULAY The heralds tell us . . that to put colours on colours, or metals on metals, is false blazonry. A. POWELL You . . look at life with a false perspective. b M. KEANE His voice was as wrong to me as a false note in music. 11 F. CLISSOLD A false step might have swept us below into an immense crevasse. *Today* One false move could cost Sally her life. T. STOPPARD He tries to leave, the first of several false exits by him. 12 S. HILL Doctor Sparrow . . may toss his head with all the false confidence of a mistaken diagnosis. *Truck & Driver* Mantova . . had been lulled into a false sense of security. *Times* The facts should be spelled out . . without false regard for the prickliness of . . minorities.

Special collocations & comb.: **false alarm**: given without reason, either to mislead or under misapprehension of danger. **false arrest** *US* wrongful arrest. **false bedding** *Geol.* = CROSS-BEDDING. *false bitter-sweet*: see BITTER-SWEET *n.* 4. **false bottom** a horizontal partition above the actual bottom of a vessel, box, etc., *esp.* one forming a secret compartment. *false* BROME. **false card**: played (esp. in bridge) so as to give a misleading impression of one's strength in the suit led. **false-card** *v.i.* play a false card. **false ceiling** a dummy ceiling fixed below the actual one, e.g. to accommodate wires, conduits, etc. **false colours** *Naut.* (freq. *fig.*) a flag to which one is not entitled, flown in order to deceive (esp. in *(sail) under false colours*). **false conception** *Med.* (*a*) = MOLE *n.*[4]; (*b*) pseudopregnancy. **false concord** *Gram.* a breach of the rules governing the agreement of words within a sentence. **false dawn** a transient light which precedes the true dawn by about an hour, esp. in eastern countries; *fig.* a promising sign which comes to nothing. **false economy** a superficial saving that indirectly causes increased expenditure. **false face** (*a*) a mask; (*b*) a treacherous or two-faced person. **false fire** †(*a*) a discharge of blank shot; (*b*) *Naut.* (*Hist.*) a kind of flare used as a night signal, or to mislead an enemy. **false front** (*a*) see FRONT *n.* 8b; (*b*) a façade used to conceal the height of a building. *false gallop*: see GALLOP *n.* **false god**: falsely claimed to exist. **false imprisonment** *Law* unlawful restriction placed on a person's liberty or movements. **false keel** an additional keel attached to the bottom of a ship's keel to strengthen it. **false key** a skeleton key. *false molar*: see MOLAR *n.* 1. **false point** a mistaken act of pointing by a game-dog. **false-point** *v.i.* (of a game-dog) point in error. **false position**: in which one is compelled to act in a manner inconsistent with one's true nature or principles. **false pretences** (orig. *Law*) misrepresentations designed to create an erroneous impression, esp. in order to obtain money (*Hist.*) or affection from someone. **false quantity** an incorrect use of a long for a short vowel or syllable, or vice versa (esp. in Latin verse). **false quarter** a horizontal crack in a horse's hoof, caused by injury to the coronet. **false relation** *Mus.* the simultaneous or adjacent appearance in different voices of two conflicting notes, freq. the major and minor third of the same triad. **false start** (in racing) a wrong start, necessitating return to the starting-point; *fig.* an unsuccessful attempt to begin something. **false teeth** removable artificial teeth made by or for a dentist to replace missing ones. *false vampire*: see VAMPIRE 3a. **false whorl** *Bot.* an arrangement simulating a whorl; *spec.* a verticillaster. **false witness** *arch.* perjury (esp. in *bear false witness*, commit perjury). **falsework** temporary supports enabling the construction of a building etc. to proceed until it is self-supporting.

C *adv.* 1 Untruthfully. *arch.* ME. 2 Treacherously, deceitfully. Chiefly in *play false* S.V. PLAY *v.* L16. 3 Improperly, wrongly. *arch.* L16.

1 SHELLEY If I speak false, then may my father perish. 2 W. F. HARVEY Your . . wife has played false to you and has . . read that letter, and betrayed its contents to your enemy. 3 T. MOORE False flew the shaft, though pointed well. See also *ring false* S.V. RING *v.*[1]

falsely *adv.* ME. **falseness** *n.* the quality of being false; an instance of this: ME.

false /fɔːls, fɒls/ *v.t.* ME. [OFr. *falser* (mod. *fausser*) f. late L *falsare*, f. *falsus*: see FALSE *a.*] †1 Counterfeit (money); forge (a document). ME–M16. †b Introduce falsehoods into; falsify. LME–L16. †c *false a blow*, make a feint. Only in L16. 2 Break, violate, (one's word). Long *arch. rare.* ME. †3 Claim to be false. Esp. in *false a doom* (*Sc.*), impugn a judgement by appealing to a higher court. ME–E18. 4 Flatter or wheedle deceptively. *dial.* L19.

2 T. HARDY Past regretting Loves who have falsed their vow.

falsehood /ˈfɔːlshʊd, ˈfɒls-/ *n.* Earlier (*obs.* exc. *dial.*) **-head** /-hɛd/. ME. [f. FALSE *a.* + -HEAD, -HOOD.] †1 Deceitfulness, treachery. ME–M16. 2 Lack of conformity with the truth; (intentional) falsity. ME. b (An) untrue belief or doctrine. ME. 3 Fraudulent practice, deception; an instance of this, a counterfeit. Now *rare* or *obs.* ME. 4 An untruthful statement; a lie. ME. 5 Untruthful speaking; lying. M17. 6 *Sc. Law.* = FALSET *n.*[1] 2. L17.

2 T. BEDDOES He has . . shewn the falsehood of the conclusion. S. NAIPAUL Truth and falsehood were inextricably intertwined in that statement. b A. HELPS Each age has to fight with its own falsehoods. 3 MILTON Hee . . Artificer of fraud . . was the first That practised falshood under saintly shew. 4 R. L. STEVENSON Another man who never told a formal falsehood in his life may yet be himself one lie. INJURIOUS *falsehood.* 5 E. STILLINGFLEET Herodotus was . . suspected of falshood.

falset /ˈfɔːlsɛt, ˈfɒls-/ *n.*[1] Chiefly *Sc.* LME. [OFr. f. late L *falsatum* neut. pa. pple of *falsare*: see FALSE *v.*] 1 Falsehood, deceit. LME. †2 *Sc. Law.* (A) fraudulent transaction; (a) forgery etc. LME–M17.

†**falset** *n.*[2] Only in 18. [Anglicization.] = FALSETTO *n.*

falsetto /fɔːlˈsɛtəʊ, fɒl-/ *n.* & *a.* L18. [It., dim. of *falso* FALSE *a.* Cf. Fr. *fausset.*] A *n.* Pl. **-os.** 1 A high-pitched voice (esp. of an adult male) forced to notes above its natural register. L18. 2 A person who sings in such a voice. L18. B *attrib.* or as *adj.* Above the natural register, high-pitched. E19.

falsettist *n.* = FALSETTO *n.* 2 L19.

falsies /ˈfɔːlsɪz, ˈfɒls-/ *n.pl.* M20. [f. FALSE *a.* + -IE + -S[1].] Shaped pads for increasing the apparent size of the female breasts.

falsification /ˌfɔːlsɪfɪˈkeɪʃ(ə)n, ˌfɒls-/ *n.* M17. [med.L *falsificatio(n-)*, f. *falsificat-* pa. ppl stem of *falsificare*: see next, -ATION.] 1 The action of making false; *esp.* (*a*) the fraudulent alteration of a document, of weights and measures, etc.; (*b*) the misrepresentation of a fact. M17. 2 The action of showing to be false or erroneous; the proving of an item in an account to be wrongly inserted. Also, disappointment of a person's expectations. M19.

falsificator *n.* a person who falsifies E17.

falsify /ˈfɔːlsɪfʌɪ, ˈfɒls-/ *v.* LME. [(OFr. *falsifier* f.) med.L *falsificare*, f. L *falsificus* making false, f. *falsus* FALSE *a.*: see -FY.] 1 *v.t.* Show to be false or erroneous. LME. b Fail to fulfil (a prediction, expectation, etc.). L16. 2 *v.t.* Alter (a document etc.) fraudulently. E16. †b Debase with impurities; adulterate. M16–M17. c Make incorrect or unsound; make (a balance or standard) untrue. L16. d Misrepresent, distort, (a fact etc.). M17. †3 *v.t.* Break, violate, (a promise etc.). M16–L17. †4 *v.t.* Make in fraudulent imitation; counterfeit, fake. M16–L17. †5 *v.t.* & *i. Fencing.* Pretend to aim (a blow); feint. L16–L17. †6 *v.i.* Make a false statement; deal in falsehoods (*with*). E17–L18.

1 T. JEFFERSON No man can falsify any material fact here stated. b WILKIE COLLINS The prognostications of our . . friends were pleasantly falsified. 2 D. BREWSTER He . . falsified the document by the substitution of a paragraph. c AV *Amos* 8:5 Making the Ephah small, and the shekel great, and falsifying the balances by deceit. I. D'ISRAELI He falsified accentuation, to adapt it to his metre. d R. SCRUTON I shall try to show how the Marxist's picture . . falsifies the realities of politics. 3 R. GREENE Aeneas . . falsified his faith to Dido. 4 M. LISTER They stampt and falsified the best ancient Medals so well. 6 SIR T. BROWNE His wisdome will hardly permit him to falsifie with the Almighty.

falsiˌfiaˈbility *n.* (*Philos.*) the quality of being falsifiable M20. **falsifiable** *a.* able to be falsified; *Philos.* (of a proposition) that can be shown to be false: E17. **falsifier** *n.* M17.

falsism /ˈfɔːlsɪz(ə)m, ˈfɒls-/ *n.* M19. [f. FALSE *a.* + -ISM.] A statement which is self-evidently false. Also, a platitude which is not even true. Opp. *truism*.

falsity /ˈfɔːlsɪti, ˈfɒls-/ *n.* ME. [L *falsitas*, f. *falsus*: see FALSE *a.*, -ITY.] 1 Untruthfulness, insincerity. Formerly also, deceitfulness, treachery. ME. 2 A false doctrine, proposition, or statement; a falsehood, an error. Also, false doctrines or statements collectively. LME. 3 Incompatibility with the facts; lack of truth. L16.

falsobordone /ˌfalsoborˈdoːne/ *n.* Also ***falso bordone***. Pl. **-ni** /-ni/. M18. [It., f. *falso* FALSE *a.* + *bordone* BOURDON. Cf. Fr. FAUX-BOURDON.] *Mus.* A technique of singing psalms in harmony, following simple chord progressions.

Falstaffian /fɔːlˈstɑːfɪən, fɒl-/ *a.* E19. [f. *Falstaff* (see below) + -IAN.] Characteristic of or resembling Sir John Falstaff, a fat, jolly, dissipated knight who features in Shakespeare's plays *Henry IV*, *Henry V*, and *The Merry Wives of Windsor*. Also, resembling the 'ragged regiment' recruited by Falstaff (*2 Hen. IV*).

faltboat /ˈfaltbəʊt/ *n.* Also **-boot.** E20. [(Partial tr.) G *Faltboot*, f. *falten* to fold + *Boot* boat.] A small collapsible boat.

falter /ˈfɔːltə, ˈfɒl-/ *v.*[1] & *n.* Also †**faulter.** LME. [Perh. f. FOLD *v.*[1] (occas. used of the faltering of the legs and tongue) + *-ter*, as in TOTTER *v.*] A *v.* **1** *v.i.* Walk unsteadily; stumble, stagger. Of the limbs: give way, totter. LME. **b** Of an inanimate thing: move spasmodically as if in hesitation; tremble, quiver. M19. **2** *v.i.* Speak in hesitant or broken tones; stammer. LME. **b** *v.t.* Utter in a hesitant voice. (Foll. by *forth, out.*) M18. **3** *v.i.* Show indecision; hesitate. Also, of courage, hope, etc.: give way, flag. E16. **4** *v.i.* Show loss of energy, momentum, or functioning. Of a breeze: die away. M18. **5** *v.i.* Of a person: fail in strength; collapse. *obs.* exc. *dial.* L18.

1 R. WISEMAN He felt his legs faulter. I. MCEWAN Like a newborn calf, the girl took a few aimless steps which faltered in embarrassment. b J. L. MOTLEY The .. Rhine as it falters languidly to the sea. 2 A. MOOREHEAD He faltered when he came to speak of .. Wills and fell back .. in tears. b H. H. MILMAN The Dean faltered out that he meant no harm. D. PAE 'Why would you have Ralph discharged?' she faltered. 3 G. VIDAL Only once did I falter in the course of the ritual. A. BROOKNER She was oddly nervous, her earlier resolution faltering. 4 N. MONSARRAT There was no more coal, so the power-stations faltered. C. FRANCIS Progress slowed down only when the wind faltered. A. WEST The conversation faltered for a moment.

B *n.* An instance of faltering; an unsteadiness of voice, progress, etc. M19.

falteringly *adv.* in a faltering or hesitant manner E17.

falter /ˈfɔːltə, ˈfɒl-/ *v.*[2] E17. [Perh. f. var. of OFr. *fautrer* to strike.] Thresh (barley etc.) a second time in order to break off the awns.

falutin /fəˈluːtɪn/ *n.* & *a.* E20. [Abbrev.] = HIGHFALUTIN.

falx /falks/ *n.* Pl. **falces** /ˈfalsiːz/. E18. [L = sickle.] **1** *Anat.* In full *falx cerebri* /ˈsɛrəbrʌɪ/ [of the brain]. The sickle-shaped fold of the dura mater on the midline of the brain between the cerebral hemispheres. E18. **2** *Zool.* = CHELICERA. Also = PATURON. Now *rare* or *obs.* M19.

fam /fam/ *n.* & *v. slang.* Now *rare* or *obs.* L17. [Abbrev. of FAMBLE *n.*] A *n.* = FAMBLE *n.* L17. **B** *v.t.* Feel, handle. E19.

famatinite /faməˈtiːnʌɪt/ *n.* L19. [f. Sierra de *Famatina*, mountain range in Argentina: see -ITE[1].] *Min.* A cubic sulphide of copper and antimony usu. occurring as grey metallic crusts or massive deposits.

famble /ˈfamb(ə)l/ *n. slang.* Now *rare* or *obs.* M16. [Perh. f. the vb.] **1** A hand. M16. **†2** A ring. Only in L17.

famble /ˈfamb(ə)l/ *v.i. obs.* exc. *dial.* LME. [Perh. rel. to FUMBLE *v.* Cf. Sw. *famla*, Da. *famle* grope.] Speak imperfectly; stammer, stutter.

fame /feɪm/ *n.* ME. [OFr. f. L *fama* report, fame.] **I 1** Personal reputation, *esp.* good personal reputation. ME. **2** The condition of being much talked about, (esp. favourably); renown; reputation derived from great achievements. ME. **†3** Infamy, bad repute. ME–L16.

1 *ill fame*: see ILL *a.* & *adv.* 2 M. ESSLIN Ionesco's flowering into a dramatist of world-wide fame. **fame and fortune** worldly success and riches as a goal or achievement. *Hall of Fame*: see HALL *n.* **of — fame** known or famous from —.

II 4 Public report, rumour, (freq. personified); a report, a rumour. Now *rare.* ME.

fameful *a.* (now *rare*) famous L16. **fameless** *a.* L16.

fame /feɪm/ *v.*[1]*t.* ME. [OFr. *famer*, f. as FAME *n.* Cf. med.L *famare.*] **1** Tell or spread as news, report. Now only in *pass.*, be currently reported *as, to be, to do. arch.* ME. **2** Make famous, speak much of. Now chiefly as *famed* ppl a., famous, celebrated, (*for*). LME.

1 KEATS The fancy cannot cheat so well As she is fam'd to do. 2 N. HAWTHORNE A corpulent, jolly fellow, famed for humour. *Country Quest* Edward I, the famed Hammer of the Scots.

†fame *v.*[2]*t.* Only in ME. [Aphet. f. OFr. *afamer* (mod. *aff-*), f. L *ad* AF- + *fames* hunger. Cf. FAMISH.] Starve, famish.

familia /fəˈmɪlɪə/ *n.* Pl. **-iae** /-ɪʌɪ/. E18. [f. as FAMILY.] *Rom. Law* & *Hist.* A household under one head regarded as a unit; the area of land regarded as sufficient to support one family.

familial /fəˈmɪljəl/ *a.* E20. [Fr., f. L *familia* FAMILY: see -AL[1].] Of, pertaining to, or characteristic of (the members of) a family; *Med.* occurring in several members of a family.

familiar /fəˈmɪlɪə/ *a.* & *n.* ME. [(O)Fr. *familier* f. L *familiaris*, f. *familia* FAMILY: see -AR[1].] A *adj.* **1** On a family footing, extremely friendly, intimate, (*with*); *spec.* sexually intimate (*with*). ME. **b** Unduly intimate (*with*). Long *rare.* LME. **2** Of or pertaining to one's family or household. Now *rare.* LME. **†3** Courteous, affable. LME–M18. **4** Informal, unceremonious; occas., excessively informal, impertinent, taking liberties *with.* LME. **5** Of an animal: domesticated, tame. Now *rare.* L15. **6** Well known, known from long or close association, recognized by the memory. (Foll. by *to.*). L15. **†b** Homely, plain; easily understood. E16–L19. **c** Common, current, habitual, usual. M16. **7** Well or habitually acquainted *with.* E16. **†8** Of food etc.: congenial, suitable. E–M17.

1 S. JOHNSON Time and intercourse have made us familiar. **familiar angel** a guardian angel. **familiar spirit** a demon attending and obeying a witch etc. 4 L. STRACHEY The young visitor, ignorant of etiquette, began to make free with the toys on the floor, in a way which was a little too familiar. T. H. WHITE You must never be familiar, rude or vulgar with them. 6 J. G. COZZENS The music was not familiar to Ernest. O. MANNING Relieved and delighted to see a familiar face. 7 W. MARCH She never saw him in person, and is familiar only with his photographs.

B *n.* **1** A member of a person's family or household. Now only *RC Ch.*, a person belonging to the household of the Pope or a bishop, who has domestic but not menial responsibilities. ME. **b** An officer of the Inquisition, chiefly employed in arresting and imprisoning the accused. M16. **2** A close friend or associate; a close acquaintance *of.* LME. **3** A familiar spirit. L16.

familiarism *n.* (now *rare*) a colloquialism M18. **familiarly** *adv.* LME. **familiarness** *n.* (now *rare*) familiarity E17.

familiarise *v.* var. of FAMILIARIZE.

familiarity /fəmɪlɪˈarɪti/ *n.* ME. [(O)Fr. *familiarité* f. L *familiaritas*, f. *familiaris*: see FAMILIAR, -ITY.] **1** The state of being extremely friendly; intimacy *with* (a person); *spec.* sexual intimacy (*with*). ME. **b** Undue intimacy. LME. **†c** A familiar person or friend; a circle of friends. Only in M17. **†2** The quality proper to a member of a family; behaviour due from a close friend etc.; devotion, fidelity. LME–L16. **3** Informality, unceremoniousness, impertinence; the treatment of inferiors or superiors as equals. LME. **b** An instance of familiar behaviour; something allowed only on the ground of intimacy; an act of sexual intimacy, a caress, kiss, etc. Usu. in *pl.* M17. **†4** Suitableness (of food etc.). M16–M17. **5** Close or habitual acquaintance (*with*); the quality of being known from long or close association, recognizability. E17.

3 *Proverb*: Familiarity breeds contempt. b L. STRACHEY The Duchess had grown too fond of her major-domo. There were familiarities. 5 H. ACTON She could claim familiarity with the painters .. of the avant-garde. M. KEANE I did not want to know it so well that familiarity could dissolve my assurance.

familiarize /fəˈmɪlɪərʌɪz/ *v.* Also **-ise.** E17. [Fr. *familiariser*, f. *familiaire* FAMILIAR *a.* + *-iser* -IZE.] **1** *v.t.* Make habitual or well known (*to*). E17. **†2** *v.t.* Domesticate, tame (an animal). M–L17. **3** *v.t.* Accustom, habituate, *to, to do.* Now *rare.* M17. **4** *v.t.* Make (oneself, another, a person's mind, etc.) well acquainted or at ease *with.* L17. **5** *v.refl.* & *i.* Adopt a familiar manner (*with*). Now *rare.* L17. **†6** *v.t.* Make (a person's manner) affable. E–M18. **7** *v.t.* Bring into familiar use; popularize. Now *rare.* M18.

4 J. A. FROUDE Wolsey .. familiarized Henry with the sense that a reformation was inevitable. A. GUINNESS Having arrived early in order to familiarise myself with my surroundings.

familiari'zation *n.* M18. **familiarizer** *n.* L19.

Familist /ˈfamɪlɪst/ *n.* Also **f-.** L16. [f. FAMILY + -IST.] **1** *Hist.* A member of the sect called the Family of Love (see FAMILY). L16. **†2** The head of a family, a family-man. E–M17.

Familism *n.* (*Hist.*) the doctrine and practice of the Familists M17.

familistère /familistɛːr/ *n.* Now *rare.* Pl. pronounced same. L19. [Fr., alt. of *phalanstère* PHALANSTERY after L *familia* FAMILY.] The home of a group of people living together as one family.

Also **familistery** /famɪˈlɪst(ə)ri/ *n.* (*rare*) M19.

familistic /famɪˈlɪstɪk/ *a.* In sense 1 also **F-.** M17. [f. FAMILIST + -IC.] **†1** Of or pertaining to the Familists or Familism. Only in M17. **2** Of or pertaining to a family. M17.

†familistical *a.* M17–E18.

famille /famiːj/ *n.* M19. [Fr. = family.] **1** *famille de robe* /də rɒb/ [lit. 'of the robe'], a French family founded by a lawyer or with a legal tradition. M19. **2** *famille jaune* /ʒoːn/, *noire* /nwaːr/, *rose* /roːz/, *verte* /vɛrt/, Chinese enamelled porcelain of particular periods in the 17th and 18th cents., of which the predominant colour is, respectively, yellow, black, red, and green. L19.

family /ˈfamɪli, -m(ə)l-/ *n.* & *a.* LME. [L *familia* household, f. *famulus* servant: see -Y[3].] A *n.* **I** Of people or animals. **1 a** The servants of a house or establishment; the retinue of a nobleman etc. Now *arch.* or *Hist.* LME. **b** The staff of a high-ranking military officer or State official. E19. **2** The descendants of a common ancestor; a house, a lineage. LME. **b** A race; a people assumed to be descended from a common stock. L16. **3** A group of people living as one household, including parents and their children, boarders, servants, etc.; such a group as an organizational unit of society. E16. **4** A group of individuals or nations bound together by political or religious ties or other ties of interest. L16. **b** (The members of) a local organizational unit of the Mafia. *colloq.* M20. **5** The group of people consisting of one set of parents and their children, whether living together or not; any group of people connected by blood or other relationship; a pair of animals and their young. M17. **6** A person's children regarded collectively; a set of offspring. M17.

2 DAY LEWIS I am of Anglo-Irish stock on both sides of my family. 3 A. POWELL The French family with whom I was to stay. *extended family, joint family, nuclear family, single-parent family*, etc. 5 A. HECHT Though they mean only good, Families can become a sort of burden. 6 L. STRACHEY By her he had a large family of sons and daughters.

II Of things. **7** *gen.* A group of things significantly connected by common features. E17. **8** *Biol.* A basic taxonomic grouping ranking above genus and below order. M18. **9** A group of languages consisting of all those ultimately derived from one early language. M18. **10** *Math.* A group of curves etc. obtained by varying one quantity. M18. **11** A group of musical instruments with the same fundamental method of sound-production. M19.

7 *Computing Equipment* A family of hard disk subsystems. 8 ANTHONY HUXLEY Orchids from one of the largest of plant families.

Phrases: **Family of Love** *Hist.* a sect which gained many adherents in England in the 16th and 17th cents., and which stressed the importance of love and held that absolute obedience was due to all governments. *happy families, family*, see HAPPY *a.* *Holy Family*: see HOLY *a.* **in a family way** in a domestic manner; informally. **in the family way** *colloq.* pregnant. **of (good) family** descended from noble or worthy ancestors. *start a family*: see START *v.* **†the family** *slang* the criminal community.

B *attrib.* or as *adj.* Of or pertaining to the family or a particular family; intended for families; suitable for families or all the family. E17.

J. B. PRIESTLEY Without the impudent indecencies, and so entirely suitable for family entertainment. M. B. BROWN A general lack of initiative in third- and fourth-generation family firms. *Rolling Stone* Because I was Jewish, I was also family. A. CLARE A family history of alcoholism. *TV Guide* (*Canada*) The family dog disappears.

Comb. & *special collocations*: **family allowance, benefit**: paid by the State or an employer to a parent or guardian of a child; **family bible** a bible used at family prayers and often having space for registering family births, deaths, etc., on its flyleaves; **family butcher**: concentrating on supplying meat to families rather than to institutions etc.; **family circle** (*a*) the company of people making up a family and its closest friends; (*b*) a gallery in a theatre etc. above the dress circle; **family credit** = *family income supplement* below; **Family Division** a division of the High Court dealing with adoption, divorce, and other family matters; **family doctor** a general practitioner, normally consulted by, and often regarded also as a friend of, a family; **family hotel** a hotel with special facilities or terms for families; **family income supplement** in Britain, a regular payment by the State to a family with an income below a certain level; **family likeness** a resemblance between members of the same family; **family living** *Eccl.* a benefice in the gift of the head of a family; **family man** a man with a family; a man who spends much time with his family; **family name** a surname; a name traditionally given to members of a family; **family planning** birth control, contraception; **family portrait** a portrait of a member of a family; **family room** *N. Amer.* a living- or recreation room commonly used by all members of a family; **family skeleton** a secret source of pain or shame to a family; **family-tree** a genealogical diagram tracing the generations of a family; a diagram tracing the relationships of languages of the same family.

famine /ˈfamɪn/ *n.* LME. [(O)Fr., f. *faim* hunger f. L *fames*.] 1 Severe scarcity of food throughout a region; an instance or period of such scarcity. LME. 2 Lack of food, hunger; starvation. *arch.* LME. 3 Violent appetite, as of a famished person. Now *rare*. LME. 4 Extreme dearth of something specified, material or immaterial. E17.

4 G. ORWELL This was one of the periods of tobacco famine and there was not a cigarette in the place.

Comb.: **famine prices**: raised by scarcity.

famish /ˈfamɪʃ/ *v.* LME. [f. FAME *v.*[2] + -ISH[2].] 1 *v.t.* Reduce to the extremes of hunger; starve. LME. 2 *v.t.* Kill with hunger, starve to death. LME. 3 *v.i.* a Suffer extreme hunger. M16. †b Die of starvation. M16–L18.

famished *a.* starved; *colloq.* very hungry: LME. **famishing** *a.* starving; *colloq.* very hungry: L16. **famishment** *n.* the state, condition, or process of being famished L15.

famose /faˈməʊz/ *a.* & *v.* Long *arch.* LME. [L *famosus*: see next, -OSE[1].] †A *adj.* = FAMOUS *a.* LME–E17. B *v.t.* = FAMOUS *v.* L16.

famous /ˈfeɪməs/ *a.* LME. [AN *famous*, OFr. *fameus* (mod. *-eux*) f. L *famosus*, f. *fama* FAME *n.*: see -OUS.] 1 Celebrated, renowned, well-known, (*for*). LME. 2 Notorious. *arch.* LME. 3 Of good repute; reliable, respectable. *Sc.* Now *rare*. LME. †4 Common, usual. E16–M18. 5 Excellent, splendid. *colloq.* L17.

1 R. JARRELL Is he really famous? .. I never heard of him before I got here. JAN MORRIS Oxford is chiefly famous for her University. *famous last words*: see *last words* s.v. LAST *a.*

famousness *n.* M16.

famous /ˈfeɪməs/ *v.t. arch.* LME. [f. the adj.] Make famous, celebrate.

famously /ˈfeɪməsli/ *adv.* LME. [f. FAMOUS *a.* + -LY[2].] †1 Commonly, openly, notoriously. LME–E18. 2 In a famous or celebrated manner; notably; as is celebrated or well known; according to fame. L16. 3 Excellently, splendidly. *colloq.* E17.

2 SHAKES. *Rich. III* This land was famously enrich'd With politic grave counsel. C. M. J. MACCABE The eighteenth century is, famously, the great century of linguistic regulation. 3 THACKERAY Will any gentleman have some sherry and soda-water ..? It clears the brains famously. C. BARRETT We got on famously .. Jim was as honest as they make them.

famulus /ˈfamjʊləs/ *n.* Pl. **-li** /-lʌɪ, -liː/. M19. [L = servant.] An attendant, esp. on a scholar or a magician.

fan /fan/ *n.*[1] OE. [L *vannus* winnowing-fan. See also VAN *n.*[1]] 1a A basket or shovel used for separating grain from chaff by tossing in the air. *obs.* exc. *Hist.* OE. b Any device or machine for winnowing grain. M17. 2 A device (usu. folding, and sector-shaped when spread out) for moving the air to cool one's face etc.; *esp.* one to be held in the hand. M16. 3 Something which, esp. when spread out, has the shape of a fan, as a bird's tail, a wing, a leaf, a tracery in a roof, etc. L16. b A fan-shaped alluvial deposit formed esp. where a stream begins to descend a gentler slope. M19. 4 *Naut.* (A blade of) a screw used in propelling vessels. L18. 5 A rotating apparatus usu. consisting of an axle or spindle with arms bearing flat or curved blades, esp. for producing a current of air as a means of ventilation etc. E19. b A small sail for keeping the head of a windmill towards the wind. E19. c An apparatus in a motor vehicle for sending a current of cold air over the radiator. E20.

1a AV *Matt.* 3:12 Hee .. whose fanne is in his hand .. will .. gather his wheat .. but .. burne vp the chaffe. B. JOWETT The grain shaken and winnowed by fans. 2 G. HUNTINGTON She opened her big feather fan .. and swept it slowly to and fro. 3 KEATS The fans Of careless butterflies. D. M. MULOCK The large brown fan of a horse-chestnut leaf. E. WAUGH The head-lamps .. spread a brilliant fan of light. C. CONRAN Slice the brains and spread them .. in a fan. *Rhenish fan*: see RHENISH *a.* 1. 5 J. MASTERS The fans in the ceiling whirred noisily, blowing hot air down on my head. (*when*) *the shit hits the fan*: see SHIT *n.*

Comb.: **fan belt**: transmitting torque from the engine of a motor vehicle to the fan that cools the radiator; **fan dance**: in which the dancer is nude but partially concealed by fans; **fanfoot**, pl. **-feet**, **-foots**, (*a*) any of various noctuid moths of the family Hypeninae; (*b*) a gecko of the genus *Ptyodactylus*, with fan-shaped toes; **fan heater**: in which an electric fan drives air over an electric heater into a room etc.; **fan-jet** a jet engine with additional thrust from cold air drawn in by a fan; **fanlight** a (fan-shaped) window over a door or other window; **fan mussel** (the shell of) any of various large marine bivalve molluscs of the genus *Pinna* and family Pinnidae, with fragile elongate triangular shells; **fan palm** a palm tree of a kind having palmate leaves; **fan-tracery**, **-vaulting** *Archit.*: composed of pendent semi cones covered with cusped panel work. See also FANTAIL.

fanlike *a.* resembling a fan E19. **fanwise** *adv.* in the manner of a fan L19.

†**fan** *n.*[2] *rare* (Shakes.). Only in E17. [f. FAN *v.*] The action or result of fanning.

fan /fan/ *n.*[3] L17. [Abbrev. of FANATIC.] †1 A fanatic. *rare*. Only in L17. 2 A keen and regular spectator of a (professional) sport or supporter of a (professional) sports team; a devotee of a specified amusement, performer, etc.; *gen.* an enthusiast for a particular person or thing. Orig. *US*. L19.

2 H. V. MORTON The fight fans howling like a pack of hungry wolves.

Comb.: **fan club** an organized group of devotees of a theatrical etc. celebrity; **fan mail** the letters sent to a celebrity by his or her fans.

fandom *n.* E20.

Fan /fan/ *n.*[4] & *a.* Also **Fang**. M19. [Fr., presumably f. Fan *Pangwe*.] (A member of, of or pertaining to,) an African people of the Ogowe basin in western equatorial Africa; (of) the Bantu language of this people.

fan /fan/ *v.* Infl. **-nn-**. OE. [f. FAN *n.*[1] See also VAN *v.*[1]] 1 *v.t.* Winnow (grain etc.). OE. b Winnow away (chaff); drive away or scatter like chaff. LME. 2 *v.i.* Make a movement as with a fan; flap; flutter; (of the wind) blow. Now *rare*. LME. b Be wafted gently along; move as by a gentle beating of the wings. *rare*. E17. 3 *v.t.* Move or drive (the air) with a fan. LME. b Move like a fan, wave. *arch.* M17. 4 *v.t.* Blow gently and refreshingly on; cool by blowing gently on. L16. 5 *v.t.* Drive a current of air (as) with a fan upon, so as to cool (a face etc.), to kindle (a flame etc.); *fig.* increase, foment, promote, (excitement etc.). E17. b Sweep away (as) by the wind from a fan. E19. 6 *v.t.* a Beat, rate soundly. Now chiefly *US*. L18. b Feel, search by feeling; *esp.* search (a person) for weapons etc. M19. 7 *v.t.* & *i.* Spread out or *out* in the shape of a fan. L19. 8 *v.i.* & *t. Baseball*. (Cause to) strike out. L19.

1 A. B. SOYER White oats .. are fanned, cleaned, and carried to a mill. b MILTON As chaff which, fanned, The wind drives. 2 SHAKES. *Hen. V* Turn the sun to ice with fanning in his face with a peacock's feather. M. TWAIN To feel the .. night breezes fan through the place. b E. K. KANE We managed to fan along at a rate of two knots an hour. 3 SOUTHEY The birds of heaven .. fann'd around him The motionless air of noon. b MILTON The willows .. Fanning their joyous leaves to thy soft lays. 4 COLERIDGE It fanned my cheek Like a meadow-gale of spring. C. MERIVALE Terraces, fanned by cool breezes from the sea. 5 H. WILLIAMSON To fan the embers in the hearth until the dry sticks burst into flame. J. S. HUXLEY The award fanned my poetic ambitions. A. T. ELLIS She .. plucked a large ivy leaf to fan herself. **fan the flame** *fig.* increase excitement etc. b SIR W. SCOTT To fan the flies from my ladie's face. 6b E. WALLACE No policeman has the right to 'fan' a prisoner until he gets into the police station. 7 A. MOOREHEAD The creek fans out into innumerable channels. K. CROSSLEY-HOLLAND That ash soared and its branches fanned over gods and men.

fana /fəˈnɑː/ *n.* M19. [Arab. *fanā'* annihilation.] In Sufism, the obliteration of human attributes and of consciousness of self and their replacement by a pure consciousness of God.

Fanagalo /ˈfanəɡaləʊ, ˈfanaɡalɔː/ *n.* Also **-ko-** /-kə-/. M20. [Nguni *fana ka lo*, f. *fana* be like + *ka* possess. suff. + *lo* this.] A pidgin of southern Africa, esp. among miners, made up of elements of Zulu, Xhosa, English, and Afrikaans. Formerly called *Kitchen Kaffir*.

¶The word *Kaffir* being regarded as derogatory by Africans, the new name *Fanagalo* came to be adopted by mining authorities and other employers.

fanal /ˈfeɪn(ə)l/ *n.* Long *arch. rare*. Also **ph-**. M17. [Fr. f. It. *fanale*.] A beacon, a lighthouse. Also, a (ship's) lantern.

fanam /fʌˈnɑːm/ *n.* M16. [Arab. f. Malayalam *paṇam*.] *Hist.* A small coin, formerly current in southern India.

Fanar *n.* var. of PHANAR.

fanatic /fəˈnatɪk/ *a.* & *n.* M16. [Fr. *fanatique* or L *fanaticus* pertaining to a temple, inspired by a god, frenzied, f. *fanum* temple: see FANE *n.*[2], -ATIC.] A *adj.* 1 Of an action, speech: such as might result from possession by a god or demon. Of a person: frenzied, mad. Long *rare*. M16. 2 = FANATICAL 2. E17.

1 R. BAKER A fanatick fellow .. gave forth, that himselfe was the true Edward. 2 T. PENNANT The cloisters .. fell victims to fanatic fury. W. IRVING The Fanatic legions of the desert. C. POTOK What annoyed him was their fanatic sense of righteousness, their absolute certainty that .. they alone had God's ear.

B *n.* †1 A mad person; a religious maniac. M17–E19. 2 A fanatical person, a person filled with excessive and mistaken enthusiasm, esp. in religion (orig. esp. Nonconformism). M17.

1 M. CASAUBON One Orpheus, a mere fanatick. 2 J. A. FROUDE The Jews .. were troublesome fanatics whom it was equally difficult to govern or destroy. R. MACAULAY They were both fanatics when they set their hearts on anything.

fanatical /fəˈnatɪk(ə)l/ *a.* M16. [f. prec. + -AL[1].] †1 = FANATIC *a.* 1 M16–M17. 2 Of a person, action, etc.: characterized by or filled with excessive and mistaken enthusiasm, esp. in religion. M16. †b Extravagant. *rare* (Shakes.). Only in L16. †c Nonconformist in religion. *derog.* L17–E18.

1 P. HOLLAND The men shaking & wagging their bodies .. after a fanaticall fashion. 2 GEO. ELIOT I call a man fanatical when .. he .. becomes unjust and unsympathetic to men who are out of his own track. c A. WOOD Mr. John Fairclough .. a non-conforming minister, was buried in the fanatical burial place.

fanatically *adv.* L17. **fanaticalness** *n.* M17.

fanaticise *v.* var. of FANATICIZE.

fanaticism /fəˈnatɪsɪz(ə)m/ *n.* M17. [f. FANATIC *a.* + -ISM.] The quality of being fanatical; excessive and mistaken enthusiasm, esp. in religion; an instance of this.

fanaticize /fəˈnatɪsʌɪz/ *v.* Also **-ise**. E18. [f. as prec. + -IZE.] 1 *v.i.* Act in a fanatical manner. E18. 2 *v.t.* Make fanatical; make a fanatic of. E19.

†**fanatism** *n.* L17–E19. [Fr. *fanatisme*.] Fanaticism.

fanchon /fɑ̃ʃɔ̃/ *n.* Pl. pronounced same. L19. [Fr., dim. of female name *Françoise*.] Chiefly *Hist.* (A side-piece or trimming of) a kerchief.

fanciable /ˈfansɪəb(ə)l/ *a.* M20. [f. FANCY *v.* + -ABLE.] That may be fancied; *spec.* (of a person) sexually attractive.

fancical /ˈfansɪk(ə)l/ *a.* Chiefly *dial.* L17. [f. FANCY *n.*: see -ICAL.] Fanciful.

fancier /ˈfansɪə/ *n.* M18. [f. FANCY *v.* + -ER[1].] A person who fancies something; *spec.* a connoisseur or follower of something; an amateur breeder of plants or animals. Freq. w. specifying wd.

LD MACAULAY People who, in their speculations in politics, are not reasoners, but fanciers. *Observer* Unlike most mouse fanciers, he keeps detailed written records of the genetic background of all his strains. *pigeon-fancier, rose-fancier,* etc.

fanciful /ˈfansɪfʊl, -f(ə)l/ *a.* E17. [f. FANCY *n.* + -FUL.] 1 Characterized by or displaying fancy in design; fantastically designed, ornamented, etc.; odd-looking. E17. 2 Suggested by fancy; imaginary, unreal. M17. 3 Disposed to indulge in fancies, whimsical, capricious. Also (now *rare*), characterized by the possession of fancy. M17.

1 SIR W. SCOTT She wears a petticoat . . I would it were . . of a less fanciful fashion. E. BOWEN She smiled at the memory . . as at any fanciful object, cameo or painted fan, . . valued once. 2 SAKI This chronicle of wonderful things, half fanciful, half very real. 3 COLERIDGE Milton had a highly imaginative, Cowley a very fanciful mind. E. WAUGH You may think me fanciful . . but . . I feel sometimes I can see the old house smiling to itself.

fancifully *adv.* M17. **fancifulness** *n.* M17.

fancy /ˈfansi/ *n.* & *a.* LME. [Contr. of FANTASY *n.*] A *n.* 1 Capricious or arbitrary preference; individual taste; an inclination (*to do*), a liking (*for*). LME. †b *spec.* Inclination in love. M16–E18. 2 A supposition with no solid basis; an arbitrary notion. L15. 3 Caprice, changeful mood; a caprice, a whim. L16. †4 = FANTASY *n.* 1. L16–E18. 5 Delusory imagination; unfounded belief; a delusion. L16. 6 Orig., imagination, *esp.* creative imagination. Later, the aptitude for the invention and development of illustrative or decorative imagery. L16. 7 Something pleasing or entertaining. Now usu., something fancied, as a horse to win a race. L16. 8 Inventive design; an invention, an original device, a contrivance. Formerly also *spec.*, a musical composition in an impromptu style. L16. †9 = FANTASY *n.* 2. E–M17. 10 Taste, critical judgement. Now *rare.* M17. 11 *the Fancy*, those with a certain common hobby or interest, fanciers, *esp.* patrons of boxing; the art of boxing. M18. 12 A fancy article; *esp.* a fancy cake. M19. 13 The art of breeding an animal etc. to develop particular points of conventional beauty or excellence; one of these points. L19.

1 G. MACDONALD What could have made Miss Crowther take such a fancy to the boy? R. DAVIES I've always had a fancy for the name Mungo. B. PYM I've always had a fancy to go there. **catch** or **take the fancy (of)** please, attract. 2 COLERIDGE As wild a fancy as any of which we have treated. 3 LD MACAULAY The antipathy of the nation to their religion was not a fancy that would yield to the mandate of a prince. 4 W. WOLLASTON We know matters of fact by the help of . . impressions made upon phansy. 5 A. P. STANLEY Which . . claims to be founded not on fancy . . but on Fact. J. WYNDHAM The . . childish fancies were on me again. I found myself waiting for . . horrible things. 6 M. PATTISON That ocean-horse in which the poetic fancy of the sea-roving Saxons saw an emblem of their . . vessels. G. HUNTINGTON Everyone in fancy . . went up those steps into the secret gardens. 8 T. HERBERT Adorned with . . fancies of Arabic characters. 9 P. HOLLAND Dreadfull spectres and fansies skreaking hideously round about him. 10 ADDISON Palaces . . built with an excellent Fancy. 11 R. L. STEVENSON A copy of *Boxiana*, on the fly-leaves of which a youthful member of the fancy kept a chronicle. 12 M. BRAGG A box of teacakes and fancies.

B *adj.* (usu. *attrib.*) 1 Involving or resulting from caprice; (of an action) capricious, whimsical; (of a price etc.) extravagant. M17. 2 Ornamental, not plain; (of foods etc.) of particularly fine quality; (of flowers etc.) particoloured. M18. b Dealing in or selling fancy goods. E19. 3 Added for ornament or extraordinary use. L18. 4 Based on fancy or imagination rather than fact. E19. 5 Of an animal etc.: bred to develop particular points of conventional beauty or excellence. E19. 6 Of a person: being an object of inclination or fancy. E19.

1 DICKENS As a display of fancy shooting, it was extremely varied and curious. J. T. MICKLETHWAITE They will give a fancy price for a work by a Leighton. 2b THACKERAY She buys a couple of begilt Bristol boards at the Fancy Stationers. 4 H. ROGERS We . . look at this wonderful character as a fancy portrait. 6 T. S. ELIOT One o' them fancy lads—a good soldier and fond o' the ladies.

Special collocations & comb.: **fancy bread** bread not of the ordinary texture, size, and weight. **fancy cake** a small iced cake. **fancy dress** (a) fanciful costume, esp. representing an animal, a character in history or fiction, etc. (*fancy-dress ball* a dance at which fancy dress is worn). **fancy-free** *a.* not in love (freq. in *footloose and fancy-free*). **fancy franchise** *Hist.*: based on complicated or arbitrary qualifications. **fancy man** (*a*) *slang, derog.* a man living on the earnings of a prostitute, a pimp; (*b*) *slang, derog.* a woman's lover; (*c*) in *pl.* = *the fancy* (see sense 11 above). **fancy-piece** *slang, derog.* = *fancy woman* below. **fancy-sick** *a.* (*arch.*) love-sick. **fancy woman** *slang, derog.* a kept mistress, a man's lover. **fancy-work** ornamental sewing etc.

fanciless *a.* (*arch.*) M18. **fancily** *adv.* M20. **fanciness** *n.* M20.

fancy /ˈfansi/ *v.t.* M16. [Partly f. FANCY *n.*, partly contr. of FANTASY *v.*] †1 Please, attach by liking *to*. M–L16. 2 Take a fancy to, like; be pleased with. Also, have an appetite for; be sexually attracted to. M16. b Select (a horse) as the likely winner of a race. M19. 3 Frame in fancy; conceive, imagine; suppose oneself to perceive. Freq. (*colloq.*) in imper. expr. surprise or incredulity. M16. †4 Arrange fancifully or artistically; contrive, design, plan. E17–M18. †5 Liken in fancy *to*, transform in fancy *into*. M17–M19. †6 Allot or ascribe in fancy. Only in M17. 7 Believe without being able to prove; be inclined to suppose; rather think *that*. L17. 8 Have an unduly high opinion of, pride oneself on, (oneself, one's own actions, abilities, or qualities). M19. 9 Breed (animals etc.) or grow (plants) to develop particular points of conventional beauty or excellence. M19.

1 R. GREENE Fast fancied to the Keepers bonny Lasse. 2 R. GRAVES Caligula sold him the sword-fighters whom nobody else seemed to fancy. C. P. SNOW I don't specially fancy having to deal with the old lady's kind of people. A. DRAPER I fancied a pie and chips. M. GEE She still looks quite a good lay. I think she fancies me a bit. b P. G. WODEHOUSE Ocean Breeze is fancied . . for a race . . at Goodwood. 3 M. PATTISON We read Bingley, and fancy we are studying ecclesiastical history. R. L. STEVENSON You can fancy the excitement into which that letter put me. I. MURDOCH Fancy Bruno being interested in sex at his age. 4 M. W. MONTAGU Furniture . . so well fancied and fitted up. 5 SOUTHEY Hast thou never . . fancied Familiar object into some strange shape? 6 N. BACON Fame hath fancied him that Title. 7 W. COBBETT The estate, I fancy, is theirs yet. A. S. NEILL I fancy that stern disciplinarians are men who hate to be irritated. D. MURPHY What I recollect, or fancy I recollect, is standing at the head of the stairs. 8 H. CONWAY I was conceited and fancied my game at whist. 9 H. MAYHEW Pigeons are 'fancied' to a large extent.

†**fand** *v.* var. of FOND *v.*[1]

fandangle /fanˈdaŋg(ə)l/ *n.* M19. [Perh. alt. of next after *newfangle*.] Fantastic ornament; nonsense, tomfoolery.

fandango /fanˈdaŋgəʊ/ *n.* Pl. **-o(e)s.** M18. [Sp.] 1 A lively Spanish dance for two in 3/4 or 6/8 time, usu. accompanied by guitars and castanets; a piece of music for this dance. M18. 2 A social assembly for dancing, a ball. Now *rare* or *obs.* M18. 3 = FANDANGLE. M19.

fane /feɪn/ *n.*[1] *obs.* exc. *dial.* [OE *fana* = OS, OHG *fano* (G *Fahne*), ON *fani*, Goth. *fana*, f. Gmc: rel. to L *pannus* (piece of) cloth. See also VANE.] †1 A flag, a banner, a pennant. OE–E19. 2 A weathercock. LME.

fane /feɪn/ *n.*[2] *poet.* LME. [L *fanum.*] A temple.

fanega /fəˈneɪgə/ *n.* E16. [Sp.] A former Spanish dry unit of capacity usu. equal to a bushel or a bushel and a half.

fanfare /ˈfanfɛː/ *n.* & *v.* M18. [Fr., ult. of imit. origin.] A *n.* 1 A short, showy, or ceremonious sounding of trumpets, bugles, etc.; a flourish; *fig.* an elaborate welcome. M18. 2 A style of decoration for the bindings of books, developed in France in the 16th cent., in which each cover is divided into symmetrical compartments of varying shapes and sizes by a continuous interlaced ribbon. Freq. *attrib.* L19.

1 *fig.*: A. COOKE With very little fanfare Parliament passed a Clean Air Act.

B *v.i.* Sound a fanfare. M19.

fanfaron /ˈfanfərɒn/ *n.* & *a.* Now *rare.* E17. [Fr., f. as prec.: see -OON.] A *n.* 1 A blusterer, a braggart; a person who makes a parade *of* something. E17. †2 = FANFARE *n.* 1. Only in M19. B *adj.* Braggart, boastful. L17.

fanfaronade /ˌfanfarəˈneɪd, -ˈnɑːd/ *n.* & *v.* M17. [Fr. *fanfaronnade*, f. as prec.: see -ADE.] A *n.* 1 Boisterous or arrogant talk, brag; ostentation; an instance of this. M17. 2 = FANFARE *n.* 1. E19. B *v.i.* Bluster, swagger. *rare.* M19.

fang /faŋ/ *n.*[1] LOE. [ON *fang* capture, grasp, embrace, OFris., OS, OHG *fang*, f. Gmc base repr. by FANG *v.*[1] See also VANG.] 1 Something caught or taken; booty, spoils; the proceeds of a robbery etc. Long *obs.* exc. *Sc.* LOE. 2†a A capture, a catch; a tight grasp or grip. LME–E17. b Power, ability (*lit.* & *fig.*); *esp.* the power of suction of a pump. *Sc.* & *north.* L18. 3 *Naut.* a = VANG. E16. b In *pl.* The valves of a pump-box. *rare.* M19. 4 A trap, a snare (*lit.* & *fig.*). *obs.* exc. *Sc.* M16. 5 A canine tooth, esp. of a dog or wolf. In *pl.* also *gen.* the teeth of a dog, wolf, or other animal noted for strength of jaw. M16. b The venom-tooth of a serpent. E19. c A human tooth. *colloq.* M19. 6 A claw, a talon. *obs.* exc. *dial.* M17. 7 An embedded pointed tapering part; *esp.* (the prong of) the root of a tooth. Also, a spike, the tang of a tool. M17. 8 A passage etc. constructed for the conveyance of air in a mine. *dial.* M17.

5 R. CAMPBELL A huge male baboon, with razor-sharp fangs. *transf.*: BROWNING Fangs of crystal set on edge in his demesne. b C. DARWIN Each horn is tubular, like an adder's fang. c C. CHAPLIN The boss . . had . . no upper teeth except one fang. **on the fang** *Austral. slang* eating. **put in the fangs** *Austral. slang* demand money etc. 7 R. WEST Mamma had forgotten to put a hole for the fang of the buckle in the belt.

fangless *a.* L16.

Fang *n.*[2] & *a.* see FAN *n.*[4] & *a.*

fang /faŋ/ *v.*[1] Long *obs.* exc. *dial.* or (occas.) *arch.* [OE *fōn*, superseded in ME by forms deriving from *fangen* pa. pple. Cf. OFris *fā*, OS, OHG *fahan*, ON *fá*, Goth. *fāhan* rel. to L *pangere* fix. Cf. FANG *n.*[1]] 1 *v.t.* Capture, seize; catch (fish etc.); lay hold of, grasp. OE. †b Get (at), obtain; get together, collect. LME–E17. 2 *v.t.* Receive, accept. OE. †3 *v.t.* Take (arms, counsel, leave, a name, one's way, etc.); undertake (battle). Also foll. by *to* (*be*): take (a person or thing) for (a purpose). OE–M16. 4 *v.i.* Seize, take hold *on*; take *to*, turn *to*; proceed *to* or *against*; set on, attack. OE. †5 *v.t.* Set about, begin *on*; start *to do*. OE–ME. 6 *v.t.* Promise, resolve, undertake. ME. †7 *v.i.* Take one's way, go; swerve *from*. LME–M16.

fang /faŋ/ *v.*[2]*t.* E19. [f. FANG *n.*] 1 Strike with a fang or fangs, bite. E19. 2 Prime (a pump) by pouring in sufficient water to start it. E19.

fanged /faŋd/ *a.* E17. [f. FANG *n.*[1] + -ED[2].] Furnished with a fang or fangs; having fangs (of a specified kind).

back-fanged: see BACK-. *front-fanged*: see FRONT *n.*, *a.*, & *adv.*

fangle /ˈfaŋg(ə)l/ *n.* & *v.* M16. [f. NEWFANGLED.] A *n.* 1 *new fangle*, a new fashion, whim, or invention; a novelty. *contempt.* Now *rare.* M16. †2 A fantastic, foppish, or silly contrivance; a piece of finery; foppery, fuss. L16–L17. B *v.t.* Fashion, fabricate; trick out. *contempt. obs.* exc. *dial.* M17.

fanglement *n.* (*a*) the action of fashioning something; (*b*) something fashioned, an invention, a contrivance: M17.

fanglomerate /fanˈglɒm(ə)rət/ *n.* E20. [f. FAN *n.*[1] + CONGLOMERATE *n.*] *Geol.* A rock consisting of consolidated fragments originally deposited in an alluvial fan.

fango /ˈfaŋgəʊ/ *n.* E20. [It. = mud, dirt.] Mud

of a kind obtained from thermal springs in Italy, used in curative treatment at spas etc.

fannell /ˈfan(ə)l/ *n. obs.* exc. *Hist.* M16. [med.L *fanula* or *fanonellus*, dim. rel. to FANON.] = FANON I.

fanner /ˈfanə/ *n.* E16. [f. FAN *n.*[1], *v.* + -ER[1].] †1 A person who winnows grain etc. E16–M17. 2 (An appliance forming part of) a device for winnowing grain etc. L18. 3 = FAN *n.*[1] 5. *rare.* M19. 4 More fully *wind-fanner.* The kestrel. (Cf. earlier *wind-vanner* s.v. VANNER *n.*[1] 2.) *dial.* M19. 5 A person who waves or operates a fan. L19.

Fannie Mae /fanɪ ˈmeɪ/ *n. phr. US slang.* M20. [Alt. of acronym *FNMA* (see below) after the forenames *Fanny, Mae.*] The Federal National Mortgage Association, a (now private) corporation which buys and sells mortgages.

fanny /ˈfani/ *n.*[1] L19. [Origin unkn.] 1 The female genitals. *coarse slang.* L19. 2 The buttocks. *N. Amer. slang.* E20.

2 fanny belt, fanny pack = *bumbag* s.v. BUM *n.*[1]

fanny /ˈfani/ *n.*[2] E20. [Perh. f. female name *Fanny.* Cf. FANNY ADAMS I.] *Naut.* A tin container for drink.

fanny /ˈfani/ *v.* & *n.*[3] *slang.* M20. [Origin unkn.] A *v.t.* Deceive or persuade by glib talk. M20. B *n.* Glib talk, a tall story. M20.

Fanny Adams /fanɪ ˈadəmz/ *n. slang.* L19. [A girl who was murdered in about 1867.] 1 *Naut.* Tinned meat; stew. L19. 2 More fully *sweet Fanny Adams.* Nothing at all. Cf. *FA.* E20.

¶In sense 2, sometimes interpreted as a euphemism for 'sweet fuck all'.

fanon /ˈfanən/ *n.* LME. [(O)Fr. f. Frank. = OS, OHG *fano*: see FANE *n.*[1] Cf. GONFANON.] 1 = MANIPLE I. LME. 2 A liturgical garment worn by the Pope when celebrating a solemn pontifical mass. M19.

fantabulous /fanˈtabjʊləs/ *a. slang.* M20. [Blend of FANTASTIC *a.* and FABULOUS *a.*] Of almost incredible excellence.

fantad *n.* var. of FANTOD.

fantail /ˈfanteɪl/ *n.* E18. [f. FAN *n.*[1] + TAIL *n.*[1]] 1 A fan-shaped tail or lower end. E18. 2 A broad-tailed variety of the domestic pigeon. Also *fantail pigeon, dove.* M18. 3 Any of numerous monarch flycatchers of the largely SE Asian and Australasian genus *Rhipidura* (also *fantail flycatcher*). M19. 4 The projecting part of the stern of a boat. L19. 5 The fan of a windmill. M20.

fantailed *a.* E19.

fan-tan /ˈfantan/ *n.* L19. [Chin. *fān tān,* (Cantonese) *fāan tāan.*] 1 A Chinese gambling game in which the players try to guess the remainder, after division by four, of a number of coins etc. hidden under a bowl. L19. 2 A card-game with a play of sevens and sequences on them. E20.

fantasia /fanˈteɪzɪə, fantəˈziːə/ *n.* E18. [It.: see FANTASY *n.*] 1 A musical or other composition in which the form is of minor importance, or which is based on a familiar tune or several familiar tunes. E18. 2 An Arab display involving horseback riding, dance, etc. M19.

fantasied /ˈfantəsɪd, -zɪd/ *a. arch.* Also **ph-**. M16. [f. FANTASY *n., v.*: see -ED[2], -ED[1].] Framed by the fancy; full of esp. strange or new fancies, imaginative; capricious, whimsical.

fantasise *v.* var. of FANTASIZE.

fantasist /ˈfantəsɪst/ *n.* Also (in sense 1) **ph-**. M19. [f. FANTASY *n.* + -IST.] 1 = FANTAST. M19. 2 A person who fantasizes; a writer of fantasies. E20.

fantasize /ˈfantəsʌɪz/ *v.* Also **ph-, -ise.** E20. [f. as prec.: see -IZE.] 1 *v.i.* Have a fantasy or fanciful vision; indulge in fantasy. E20. 2 *v.t.* Visualize in fantasy, represent in the fancy. M20.

fantasque /fanˈtask/ *n.* & *a.* Now *rare.* L17. [Fr., pop. form of *fantastique* FANTASTIC.] †A *n.* Fancy, whim. L17–E18. B *adj.* Fanciful, fantastic; curious. E18.

fantassin /ˈfantəsɪn/ *n.* Now *rare.* M18. [Fr. f. It. *fantaccino,* f. *fante* foot-soldier. Cf. INFANTRY.] A foot-soldier.

fantast /ˈfantast/ *n.* Also (*arch.*) **ph-**. L16. [Orig f. med.L f. Gk *phantastēs* boaster; later through G *Phantast.*] A visionary, a dreamer; a flighty impulsive person.

fantastic /fanˈtastɪk/ *a.* & *n.* Also (*arch.*) **ph-**. LME. [(O)Fr. *fantastique* f. med.L *fantasticus,* late L *phantasticus* f. Gk *phantastikos,* f. *phantazein* make visible, *phantazesthai* have visions, imagine, f. *phantos* visible, f. *phan-* base of *phainein* show: see -IC.] A *adj.* 1 Existing only in the imagination; fabulous, unreal. Now *spec.* perversely or irrationally imagined. LME. †2 = FANTASTICAL *a.* 2. LME–L18. †b Of poetry: concerned with fantasy or illusory appearance. *rare.* L16–M17. †3 Pertaining to or of the nature of a phantasm. L15–E18. 4 Fanciful; capricious, arbitrary; *esp.* extravagantly fanciful, odd and irrational in behaviour. Formerly also, having a lively imagination. L15. 5 Eccentric, quaint, or grotesque in design, conception, construction, or adornment. Cf. earlier FANTASTICAL *a.* 5. E17. b Making light elaborate dance steps. Chiefly in phrs. below (after Milton *L'Allegro* 33). M17. 6 Arbitrarily devised. Cf. earlier FANTASTICAL *a.* 6. Now *rare.* M17. 7 Unbelievable; incredibly great; extraordinary; excellent. *colloq.* M20.

1 D. L. SAYERS When people are very ill, they sometimes get fantastic ideas. 3 J. FLETCHER Is not this a fantastic house we are in, and all a dream we do? 4 G. WITHER Let no fantastique Reader now condemne Our homely Muse. R. W. EMERSON Great believers are always reckoned . . impracticable, fantastic, atheistic. 5 W. SPALDING Vaulted halls adorned with the usual fantastic arches. B. TAYLOR The witch with fantastic gestures draws a circle. W. BOYD The sort of mad impossible fantastic lie a desperate man would dream up. **b the light fantastic (toe)** *joc.* dancing. **trip the light fantastic** *joc.* dance. 6 H. N. HUMPHREYS Occasionally fantastic variations of well-known inscriptions occur. 7 P. H. GIBBS You here too? It's fantastic really. T. STOPPARD Fantastic woman I took there—titian hair, green eyes, dress cut down to here. *Newbury Weekly News* Their support . . raised a fantastic sum.

B *n.* 1 A person who has fanciful ideas or indulges in wild notions. Now *arch. rare.* M16. †2 A person given to fine or showy dress; a fop. L16–L17.

fantasticness *a.* (now *rare*) M16.

fantastical /fanˈtastɪk(ə)l/ *a.* & *n.* Also (*arch.*) **ph-**. LME. [f. prec. + -AL[1].] A *adj.* 1 = FANTASTIC *a.* I. LME. 2 Of or pertaining to fantasy as a product or faculty of the mind; imaginative. Now *rare.* E16. †3 = FANTASTIC *a.* 3. M16–E18. 4 = FANTASTIC *a.* 4. M16. †5 = FANTASTIC *a.* 5. M16–E17. 6 = FANTASTIC *a.* 6. M16.

1 R. G. COLLINGWOOD The way in which we distinguish real from fantastical ideas. 2 G. W. KNIGHT *Macbeth* is fantastical and imaginative beyond other tragedies. 4 D. L. SAYERS A man so slight and fantastical in manner.

B *n.* = FANTASTIC *n.* I. Now *arch. rare.* E17.

fantastiˈcality *n.* (*a*) fantastic character or quality, eccentricity, grotesqueness; (*b*) something that is fantastic, a whim: L16. **fantasticalness** *n.* †(*a*) *rare* the condition of being subject to phantasms; (*b*) fantasticality: M16.

fantastically /fanˈtastɪk(ə)li/ *adv.* E16. [f. FANTASTIC *a.* or FANTASTICAL *a.*: see -ICALLY.] †1 Through the exercise of fancy or imagination. E16–L17. 2 In a fantastic manner; capriciously; eccentrically. M16. 3 To a fantastic degree; unbelievably; extremely. *colloq.* E20.

fantasticate /fanˈtastɪkeɪt/ *v.* E17. [f. FANTASTIC *a.* + -ATE[3].] †1 *v.t.* Frame in fancy. Only in E17. 2 *v.i.* Frame fantastic notions, fantasize. Now *rare.* E17. 3 *v.t.* Make fantastic. M20.

fantastiˈcation *n.* the action of fantasticating; (a) fantastic speculation; (a) fantastic display or show; ostentation, affection: L19.

fantastico /fanˈtastɪkəʊ/ *n.* Pl. **-o(e)s.** L16. [It. = fantastic.] An absurd or irrational person; an eccentric; a fantastically-dressed person.

fantastry /ˈfantastri/ *n.* Long *rare.* Also **ph-**. M17. [f. as FANTAST + -RY.] Fantastic creation or display; delusory or illusory character; a fantasy.

fantasy /ˈfantəsi, zi/ *n.* Also **ph-**. LME. [OFr. *fantasie* (mod. *fantaisie*) = It. *fantasia* f. L *phantasia* f. Gk = appearance (later phantom), faculty of imagination, etc., f. *phantazein* make visible: see FANTASTIC, -Y[3]. See also FANCY *n.*] †1a Mental apprehension of an object of perception; the faculty by which such apprehension is made. LME–M17. b The image impressed on the mind by an object of sense. LME–L16. †2 A spectral apparition, a phantom; an illusory appearance. LME–L16. 3 Delusory imagination, hallucination; the fact or habit of deluding oneself by imaginary perceptions or reminiscences. Now *rare* or *obs.* LME. 4 (A product of) imagination; the process, faculty, or result of forming mental representations of things not actually present; (an) extravagant or visionary fancy. LME. b An ingenious, tasteful, or fantastic invention or design; *Mus.* a fantasia. LME. c A mental image. E19. d A daydream arising from conscious or unconscious wishes or attitudes. E20. e A literary genre concerned with imaginary worlds and peoples; a composition in this genre. M20. 5 A supposition resting on no solid grounds; whimsical or visionary speculation. LME. 6 Caprice, changeful mood; an instance of this; a caprice, a whim. LME. †7 Inclination, liking, desire. LME–E17.

3 SMOLLETT He will . . be sometimes misled by his own phantasy. 4 J. R. LOWELL Fantasy, the image-making power common to all who have the gift of dreams. A. S. NEILL In dreams we have nightmares; but in fantasy, we have a certain control. M. SARTON We made up endless fantasies about what we would do when we were rich. P. DAVIES Release from gravity represents an unusually compelling fantasy. b DICKENS A monstrous fantasy of rusty iron. d P. LAFITTE The Rorschach test invites him to enact his very vaguest fantasies, as when he sees pictures in the fire. e F. BROWN Fantasy deals with things that are not and cannot be. *Which Micro?* A fully-animated televised fantasy. 5 W. D. WHITNEY All that would be to them less than fancy—mere fantasy. 6 G. BURNET It was . . out of no light fantasy . . that he thus refused it. 7 R. HAKLUYT He fell into a fantasie and desire to . . know how farre that land stretched.

fantasy /ˈfantəsi, -zi/ *v.* Also **ph-**. LME. [OFr. *fantasier,* f. as prec.] 1 *v.t.* Imagine in a visionary manner. LME. 2 *v.i.* Indulge in fantasy; fantasize. M16. †3 *v.t.* Take a fancy to, be favourably inclined to. M16–M17.

Fante /ˈfanti/ *n.* & *a.* Also **-ti, -tee** /-tiː/. E19. [Fante.] A *n.* 1 One of two main varieties of Akan spoken in Ghana, the other being the mutually intelligible Twi. E19. 2 Pl. **-s**, same. A member of a people inhabiting southern Ghana. L19.

B *adj.* Of or pertaining to the Fantes or their language. M19.

go Fante *arch.* = *go native* s.v. NATIVE *a.*

fantigue /fanˈtiːg/ *n. dial.* E19. [Origin unkn.] A state of anxiety or excitement; an instance of this, *esp.* a fit of ill humour.

fantoccini /fantotˈtʃiːni, fantəˈtʃiːni/ *n.* L18. [It., pl. of *fantoccino* dim. of *fantoccio* puppet, f. *fante* boy.] 1 *pl.* Mechanically worked puppets. L18. 2 *sing.* A marionette show. L18.

fantod /ˈfantɒd/ *n. colloq.* Also **-tad** /-tad/. M19. [Origin unkn.] A state of fidgetiness, uneasiness, or unreasonableness; *the fantods,* nervous depression or apprehension, the fidgets, 'the creeps'.

fanzine /ˈfanziːn/ *n.* M20. [f. FAN *n.*[3] + MAGA)ZINE *n.*] A magazine for fans, esp. those of science fiction.

†**fap** *a. slang.* L16–E19. [Origin unkn.] Drunk, intoxicated.

Fapesmo /fəˈpɛzməʊ/ *n.* L16. [A mnemonic of scholastic philosophers, A indicating a universal affirmative proposition, and E a universal negative proposition.] *Logic.* The indirect mood of the first syllogistic figure, sometimes treated as the fourth-figure mood, = FESAPO.

faquir *n.* see FAKIR.

far /fɑː/ *a.* Compar. †**farrer,** FARTHER *a.,* FURTHER *a.* Superl. †**farrest,** FARTHEST *a.,* FURTHEST *a.*; also FARMOST. [OE *feorr* = OFris. *fēr, fīr,* OS *fer,* OHG *fer,* f. WGmc; prob. f. the adv.] 1 Situated at a great distance; situated a long way off. OE. b Remote in time, nature, or relationship. M16. 2 Extending to a great distance; long. ME. 3 More distant; being the further of two. LME.

1 H. JAMES That's another of the things I love, living in far countries. b J. CONRAD In the far future gleamed . . the big mansion. 3 G. GREENE It wasn't safe to cross the bridge . . for all the far side of the river was in the hands of the Vietminh.

Phrases, special collocations, & comb.: *a far cry*: see CRY *n.* **Far East** the extreme eastern countries of the Old World, *esp.* China and Japan. **Far Eastern** *a.* of or pertaining to the Far East. **Far West** orig., the region to the west of early N. American settlements; now, the region west of the Great Plains (taking in the Rocky Mountains and the Pacific coast). **Far Wester** = *Far-Westerner* below. **Far Western** *a.* of or pertaining to the Far West. **Far Westerner** a settler in or inhabitant of the Far West.

farness *n.* (*a*) remoteness; (*b*) *arch.* distant parts: LME.

far /fɑː/ *v.t.* Long *obs.* exc. *dial.* Infl. **-rr-**. [OE *feorran*, *fyrran* = OHG *firren*, ON *firra*, f. Gmc, f. base of FAR *adv.*] Put far off, remove.

E. GASKELL I wish the man were farred who plagues his brains wi' striking out new words.

far /fɑː/ *adv.* & *n.* Compar. FARTHER *adv.*, FURTHER *adv.*; superl. FARTHEST *adv.*, FURTHEST *adv.* [OE *feor(r)* = OFris. *fēr*, *fīr*, OS *fer*, *ferro* (Du. *ver*), OHG *fer*, *ferro*, ON *fjarri*, Goth. *fairra*, f. Gmc compar. formation on IE base repr. also by Skt *para*, Gk *pera* further.] **A** *adv.* 1 At a great distance, a long way off. OE. 2 To a great distance; to a remote place. OE. †b Over a large area, widely. ME–L17. 3 By a great deal. (With a compar. or superl., vb, etc., indicating inequality; modifying an adj., adv., etc., implying variation from a standard.) OE. b By a great interval or space. LME. 4 To or at an advanced point in space or time; to a great length or degree. ME. 5 Preceded by *as*, *how*, *so*, *thus*, etc.: at or to a specific distance, to a specific extent. ME.

1 K. GRAHAME A remote common far from habitation. 2 J. CONRAD They would have to go . . go far away. 3 B. JOWETT They were not far wrong. C. P. SNOW It was far too good to miss. b J. THOMSON Far distant from their native soil. 4 O. MANNING Her irritation did not carry her very far.

Phrases & comb.: **as far as** (*a*) right to, not short of, (a place); (*b*) to whatever extent; *as far as it etc. goes*, within its etc. limitations; (*c*) *N. Amer.* with regard to, as for; **by far** by a great amount. *far and away*: see AWAY *adv.* 2. **far and near** in every part, everywhere. **far and wide** over a wide area, everywhere. **far be it from me to** — I would on no account —. **far-back** *a.* remote, inaccessible, ancient. **far between** infrequent (FEW *and far between*). **far-come** *a.* (*arch.*) come from a great distance. **far-down** *a.* situated or existing far below. **far-famed** *a.* widely known, celebrated. **far-flung** *a.* (*rhet.*) widely extended, remote. **far forth** *arch.*, †**farforth** *adv.* †(*a*) to a great distance or extent; (*b*) to a definite degree or (formerly) distance (in *so*, †*as*, †*thus far forth*). **far from** *fig.* almost opposite to, anything but. **far gone** advanced in time; very ill, mad, tired, or drunk; much in debt; (foll. by *in*). **far-off** *a.* remote, distant. **far or near** anywhere. **far-out** *a.* distant; *fig.* unconventional, avant-garde; (as *int.*) excellent! **far-reaching** *a.* widely applicable; carrying many consequences. **far-seeing** *a.* prescient; prudent. **far-sighted** *a.* (*a*) far-seeing; (*b*) seeing distant things more clearly than those close to. **far-sightedly** *adv.* in a far-sighted manner. **far-sightedness** the capacity to be far-sighted, far-sighted quality. *go far*: see GO *v.* **go too far** *fig.* go beyond the limits of reason, courtesy, etc. **how far** to what extent or distance. *in so far (as)*: see IN *prep. not go far*: see GO *v.* **so far** to such an extent or distance; until now. **so far as** in so far as; as far as. **so far so good** progress has been satisfactory until now. **thus far** = *so far* above.

B *n.* Ellipt. after preps. (chiefly *from*): a distant place, a considerable distance. ME.

farad /ˈfarad/ *n.* M19. [f. FARADAY.] *Physics.* The SI unit of electrical capacitance, being the capacitance of a capacitor in which one coulomb of charge causes a potential difference of one volt between the plates. (Symbol F.)

¶Orig. proposed with different specifications, and as a unit of electrical charge.

faradaic /farəˈdeɪɪk/ *a.* L19. [f. as next + -IC.] *Physics.* Produced by or associated with electrical induction; inductive, induced.

faradaism /ˈfarədeɪɪz(ə)m/ *n.* L19. [f. next + -ISM.] = FARADISM.

Faraday /ˈfarədeɪ/ *n.* In sense 2 **f-**. M19. [Michael *Faraday* (1791–1867), Eng. scientist.] *Physics* & *chem.* **I** 1 Used *attrib.* and in *possess.* to designate things discovered, invented, or explained by Faraday. M19.

Faraday cage an earthed metal screen surrounding a piece of equipment to protect it from external electrostatic interference. **Faraday constant** = sense 2 below. **Faraday effect** the rotation of the plane of polarization of electro-magnetic waves when transmitted through certain substances in a magnetic field that has a component parallel to the direction of transmission. **Faraday's constant** = sense 2 below. **Faraday('s) dark space**: between the negative glow and the positive column in a low-pressure discharge tube. **Faraday's law** (*a*) a law stating that when the magnetic flux linking a circuit changes, an electromotive force is induced in the circuit proportional to the rate of change of the flux linkage; (*b*) a law stating that the amount of any substance deposited or liberated during electrolysis is proportional to the quantity of charge passed and to the equivalent weight of the substance.

II 2 That quantity of electric charge which is required to flow in order to deposit or liberate one gram-equivalent of any element during electrolysis (approx. equal to 96.490 coulomb). E20.

faradic /fəˈradɪk/ *a.* L19. [f. prec. + -IC.] = FARADAIC.

faradism /ˈfarədɪz(ə)m/ *n.* L19. [f. as prec. + -ISM.] Electrotherapy (using induced alternating currents).

faradiˈzation *n.* (now *rare*) treatment by faradism M19. **faradize** *v.t.* (now *rare*) treat by faradism M19.

farandole /far(ə)nˈdəʊl, ˈfar(ə)ndəʊl/ *n.* M19. [Fr., f. mod.Prov. *farandoulo*.] A Provençal communal dance usu. in 6/8 time; a piece of music for this dance or in this time.

farang /faˈraŋ/ *n.* M19. [Thai f. FRANK *n.*[1]: cf. FERINGHEE.] Among Thais: a foreigner, *esp.* a European.

far-away /ˈfɑːrəweɪ, fɑːrəˈweɪ/ *a.* & *n.* E19. [f. FAR *adv.* + AWAY *adv.*] **A** *adj.* 1 Remote in time, space, or relationship. E19. 2 Of a look or expression: absent, dreamy. Of a voice: sounding faint, distant, or abstracted. L19. **B** *n.* A remote place; the distance. *arch.* & *poet.* E19.

far-awayness *n.* L19.

farce /fɑːs/ *n.*[1] LME. [OFr. = stuffing, f. as FARCE *v.*] Forcemeat, stuffing.

farce /fɑːs/ *n.*[2] E16. [Fr. = prec., used metaphorically of interludes etc.] 1 A dramatic work intended only to excite laughter, often by presenting ludicrously improbable events. E16. b The branch of drama consisting of such works. L17. 2 Anything fit only to be laughed at; a hollow pretence, a mockery. L17.

1b A. S. NEILL Our school dramas tend toward comedy and farce rather than tragedy. 2 S. RAVEN He knows nothing and has taught nothing. The end of term exams were a mere farce.

farcer *n.* a person who writes or acts in a farce. E19. **farcify** *v.t.* turn into a farce M19.

farce /fɑːs/ *v.t.* ME. [OFr. *farsir* (mod. *farcir*), f. L *farcire* stuff.] 1 Cram or stuff (*with*). Also foll. by *up*. Now *rare*. ME. †b *Cookery.* Stuff with forcemeat, herbs, etc. LME–M18. †2 Stuff or force *into*, *through*. LME–E17. 3 Lard, embellish, garnish. Also foll. by *up*. LME. 4 *Eccl.* Amplify (a liturgical formula) by the insertion of certain words; interpolate a (vernacular) comment in (an epistle etc.). M19.

1 W. DE LA MARE A mind Farced up with all I have learned and read.

farceur /farsœːr (*pl. same*), fɑːˈsəː/ *n.* L17. [Fr., f. †*farcer* act farces + *-eur* -OR.] 1 A joker, a wag. L17. 2 An actor or writer of farces. L19.

farcical /ˈfɑːsɪk(ə)l/ *a.*[1] E18. [f. FARCE *n.*[2] + -ICAL.] Of, pertaining to, or resembling farce; extremely ludicrous or futile.

G. MURRAY The wild and farcical nature of the old comedy. A. FRASER The action would have been farcical if men's lives had not been at stake.

farciˈcality *n.* (an instance of) farcical quality M19. **farcically** *adv.* L18.

farcical /ˈfɑːsɪk(ə)l/ *a.*[2] Now *rare* or *obs.* M18. [f. FARCY + -ICAL.] Of or pertaining to farcy.

farcy /ˈfɑːsi/ *n.* Also (earlier) †**farcin**. LME. [(O)Fr. *farcin* f. late L *farciminum*, *farcimen*, f. *farcire* to stuff.] 1 Glanders, esp. in chronic form. Also (*US*), a bacterial disease of cattle, marked by swelling and inflammation of lymph nodes. LME. 2 More fully *farcy bud*, *button*. A small lymphatic growth characteristic of glanders. LME.

farcied *a.* affected with farcy M19.

fard /fɑːd/ *n.* Now *arch.* or *Hist.* M16. [(O)Fr., f. as next.] Paint, esp. white paint, for the face.

fard /fɑːd/ *v.t.* *arch.* LME. [(O)Fr. *farder*.] 1 Paint (the face) with cosmetics, orig. with fard. Freq. as *farded* ppl a. LME. 2 *transf.* & *fig.* Embellish, gloss over. M16.

fardel /ˈfɑːd(ə)l/ *n.*[1] ME. [OFr. (mod. *fardeau*) bundle, load, f. Proto-Romance: see -EL[2].] 1 A small pack, a parcel, a bundle. *arch.* ME. 2 A burden, esp. *fig.* of sin, sorrow, etc. LME. †3 A wrapping, *esp.* an item of clothing. LME–M17. 4 The omasum or third stomach of a ruminant. Also *fardel-bag*. M19.

1 *fig.*: H. ROGERS A fardel of myths. 2 BYRON These fardels of the heart.

fardel /ˈfɑːd(ə)l/ *n.*[2] *obs.* exc. *Hist.* LME. [Contr., f. as FOURTH *a.* + DEAL *n.*[1] See also FARL.] A fragment, a piece; *spec.* a quarter.

†**fardel** *v.t.* L15. [f. FARDEL *n.*[1] In sense 2 perh. assoc. with FURL *v.*] 1 Make into a bundle; bundle *up*. L15–E18. 2 *Naut.* = FURL *v.* L16–E18.

fare /fɛː/ *n.*[1] [OE *fær* neut., *faru* fem., both f. base of FARE *v.*] **I** †1 A coming or going; a course, a passage; a journey, a voyage. OE–M18. b An expedition; *spec.* a fishing voyage. OE–M16. †2 A travelling company, a troop. ME–M17. 3†a A road, a way, a path. LME–M18. b A spoor or track, esp. of a rabbit or hare. *obs.* exc. *dial.* L15. 4 Orig., a journey for which a price is paid. Later, the cost of conveyance of a passenger (formerly also of goods). LME. 5 A passenger (*rarely* passengers) paying to travel in a public vehicle, esp. a taxi. M16. b A load, a cargo; *spec.* (*US*) a catch of fish. E17.

4 O. MANNING He had not even the bus fare to and from his lodging. 5 R. RENDELL I was driving the mini-cab, I'd just dropped a fare.

II 6 Mode of behaviour; bearing, demeanour, appearance. *obs.* exc. *dial.* ME. †b Display, pomp. Only in ME. †7 A course of action or events; proceedings, business. ME–M16. b Noisy activity; fuss, commotion, uproar. ME–L15. 8 State of affairs; (good or bad) fortune. *obs.* exc. *poet.* ME. †b Good fortune, prosperity, success. ME–M18. 9 Food with regard to quality or quantity; food and drink provided. ME.

9 T. C. WOLFE The magic of strange foods and fruits was added to familiar fare. *bill of fare*: see BILL *n.*[3]

Comb.: **farebox** a locked receptacle on a bus or other public vehicle into which passengers drop their fares; **fare indicator** a device for registering the fares paid or due in a public vehicle; **fare-stage** a part of the route of a public vehicle (esp. a bus) considered for the purpose of calculating the fare; the stop marking the limit of a stage.

†**fare** *n.*[2] ME–M18. [It. *faro* f. L *pharus*, Gk PHAROS.] = PHARE *n.* 3.

fare /fɛː/ *n.*[3] *obs.* exc. *dial.* M16. [Var. of FARROW *n.*] A young pig; a litter of pigs.

fare /fɛː/ *v.* [OE *faran* = OFris., ON *fara*, OS, OHG, Goth. *faran* (Du. *varen*, G *fahren*), f. Gmc f. IE.] **I** 1 *v.i.* Journey, travel, make one's way. Foll. by *forth*: depart, set out. Now *arch.* & *literary.* OE. †2 *v.i.* Go, move, advance, proceed; flow, run. OE–M19. 3 *v.t.* Bear, carry, convey. *rare.* ME.

1 M. ARNOLD Through the deep noontide heats we fare. J. W. JOHNSON One puts on one's best clothes and fares forth. 2 SPENSER One knocked at the dore, and in would fare.

II 4 *v.i.* Get on in a specified manner (*well*, *ill*, etc.); have luck or treatment of a specified (*good*, *bad*, etc.) kind. OE. b Be entertained, be fed or feed oneself in a specified manner (*well* etc.). *arch.* LME. 5 *v.i. impers.* in *it fares, it fared*, etc.: it happens, it happened, etc.; it turns out, it turned out, etc. ME. †6 *v.i.* Act, behave, conduct oneself; deal *with*, do *by*. ME–L17. 7 *v.i.* †a Seem or act *as though, as if*. LME–M17. b Seem likely or incline *to do, to be*. *arch.* M19.

4 P. KAVANAGH He did not care for his sisters, and was not worried how they fared in life. **fare thee** or **you well** *imper.* = FAREWELL *int.* b E. K. KANE Our breakfast, for all fare alike, is hard tack. 5 SWIFT Beware . . that it fare not with you as with your predecessor.

farer *n.* a traveller (chiefly as 2nd elem. of comb., as *seafarer, wayfarer*, etc.) LME.

farewell /fɛːˈwɛl; *as adj. usu.* ˈfɛːwɛl/ *int., n., v., & adj.* LME. [f. imper. of FARE *v.* + WELL *adv.*] A *int.* 1 As an expression of goodwill or a polite salutation on parting: goodbye. *arch.* LME. 2 *fig.*: As an expression of regret or an exclamation: goodbye to or *to*; no more of. *arch.* or *poet.* LME.

2 J. FORDYCE Farewel to real friendship, farewel to convivial delight.

B *n.* 1 An utterance of the word farewell; leave-taking, departure, parting good wishes. LME. †2 An aftertaste. M17–M18.

1 M. SPARK We had already said our farewells on the day before my departure. *sailor's farewell*: see SAILOR *n.* *soldier's farewell*: see SOLDIER *n.* *take farewell*: see TAKE *v.*

C *v.t.* 1 Bid or say goodbye to; take leave of. L16. 2 Mark the departure or retirement of (a person) with a ceremonial occasion. E20.

1 R. F. BURTON She farewelled me with her dying eyes.

D *adj.* Pertaining to, accompanying, or signifying a leave-taking. M17.

K. MOORE Are you going to give a farewell party?

fare-you-well /fɛːjʊwɛl/ *n. US colloq.* Also **-thee-** /-ðɪ-/. L19. [f. *fare you well* s.v. FARE *v.* 4.] *to a fare-you-well*, to the utmost degree, completely.

farfel /ˈfɑːf(ə)l/ *n.* Also ***farfal, ferfel*** /ˈfɑː-/. Pl. same, ***-s***. L19. [Yiddish *farfal, farfil, ferfel* (pl.), f. MHG *varveln* noodles, noodle soup.] Ground or granulated noodle dough; in *pl.*, granules or pellets of this.

†far-fet *ppl a.* ME–L17. [f. FAR *adv.* + pa. pple of FET.] 1 = FAR-FETCHED 1. ME–L17. 2 = FAR-FETCHED 2. M16.

far-fetched /fɑːˈfɛtʃt, ˈfɑːfɛtʃt/ *ppl a.* M16. [f. FAR *adv.* + pa. pple of FETCH *v.* Cf. prec.] 1 Brought from far. *arch.* M16. 2 Of an idea, argument, simile, etc.: strained, unnatural, improbable. L16.

far-fetchedness *n.* M19.

farina /fəˈrʌɪnə, -iːnə/ *n.* LME. [L *farina*, f. *far* corn.] 1 Flour, meal. LME. 2 Any powdery substance or substance in powdered form. E18.

farinaceous /farɪˈneɪʃəs/ *a.* M17. [Late L *farinaceus*, f. as prec.: see -ACEOUS.] 1 Consisting of, made of, or characterized by flour or meal. M17. 2 Yielding flour or starch; starchy. M17. 3 Having a mealy nature or appearance. M17. †4 Covered with fine powder. M17–E19.

faring /ˈfɛːrɪŋ/ *n.* M16. [f. FARE *v.* + -ING[1].] 1 The action of FARE *v.* M16. 2 In *pl.* Made dishes. Now *rare.* M17.

farinha /fəˈriɲə, fəˈriːnjə/ *n.* E18. [Port., f. as FARINA.] = CASSAVA 2.

farinose /ˈfarɪnəʊs/ *a.* E18. [Late L *farinosus*, f. L FARINA: see -OSE[1].] Covered with or yielding farina; of the nature of farina, finely powdered.

farkleberry /ˈfɑːk(ə)lb(ə)ri/ *n.* M18. [Prob. alt. of WHORTLEBERRY.] A shrub or small tree, *Vaccinium arboreum*, bearing black berries, native to the south-eastern US.

farl /fɑːl/ *n.* Chiefly *Sc.* L17. [Contr. of FARDEL *n.*[2]] Orig., a quarter of a thin cake of flour or oatmeal. Later, any such thin cake, whether quadrant-shaped or not.

farm /fɑːm/ *n.* ME. [(O)Fr. *ferme* f. med.L *firma* fixed payment, f. L *firmare* fix, settle, confirm, (in med.L) contract for, f. L *firmus* FIRM *a.*] 1 *Hist.* a A fixed annual amount, in money or kind, payable as rent, tax, etc. ME. b A fixed annual sum accepted as composition for taxes or other moneys collected. Also, a fixed charge imposed on a town, county, etc., to be collected within its limits. LME. c The allowing of a person to collect and keep the revenues from taxes etc. in return for a fixed sum; the privilege of so collecting taxes etc. M17. 2 The condition or arrangement of being let at a fixed rent (in *have, let, set*, etc. *in, to*, etc. *farm*). ME. †3 A lease. L15–M17. 4 A tract of land held (orig. on lease) under one management for the purposes of cultivation or the rearing of certain animals (for food or fur etc.). See also *funny farm* s.v. FUNNY *a.*, HEALTH *farm*. E16. b A tract or tracts of water used for the breeding or rearing of fish or other animals (usu. of a specified kind). M19. 5 A farmhouse. M16. 6 A place where children are farmed (see FARM *v.*[2] 4). *derog.* M19. 7 A prison hospital. *arch. slang.* L19. 8 A storage installation for oil etc. M20.

4 J. R. GREEN The farms of Lothian have become models of agricultural skill. *dairy farm, mink farm, poultry farm*, etc. *collective farm*: see COLLECTIVE *a.* 4. *home farm*: see HOME *a.* SEWAGE *farm*. b *fish farm, oyster farm, trout farm*, etc. 6 *baby-farm* etc.

Comb.: **farm-hand** a person who works on a farm; **farmhold** *arch.* a quantity of land held and cultivated as a farm; **farm land**: used or suitable for farming; **farmstead, -steading** a farm with the buildings on it; **farm-wife** a farmer's wife.

farm /fɑːm/ *v.*[1]*t.* Long *obs.* exc. *dial.* [OE *feormian*, of unkn. origin.] Cleanse, empty.

farm /fɑːm/ *v.*[2] LME. [f. FARM *n.*] †1 *v.t.* Rent (land etc.). LME–E18. 2 *v.t.* Collect the fees or proceeds of (a tax, office, etc.) on payment of a fixed sum. M16. 3 *v.t.* a Let (land) to a tenant. Also foll. by *out*. Now *rare.* L16. b Allow a person to collect and keep the revenues from (a tax) or the proceeds of (an undertaking etc.) in return for a fixed sum. Also foll. by *out*. E17. c Hire out the labour of (a person etc.). Also foll. by *out*. E17. 4 *v.t.* Take over, for a fee, the care of (a person, esp. (*derog.*) a child), maintenance of (an institution etc.), or performance of (a task etc.); (freq. foll. by *out*) arrange for another or others so to take over the care etc. of, delegate (work) to a subcontractor. M17. 5 *v.i.* Be a farmer, till the soil. E18. 6 *v.t.* Cultivate, till. E19. 7 *v.t.* & *i. Cricket.* Of a batsman: contrive to receive most of (the bowling). M20.

2 M. PATTISON The Tidemann farmed . . the tin-mines belonging to the Duchy of Cornwall. 4 DICKENS The parish authorities . . resolved, that Oliver should be 'farmed'. *New Statesman* One term 'farmed out' with a man tutor. *Globe & Mail* (*Toronto*) How could you get a strike going when the work can be so easily farmed out somewhere else?

farmable *a.* that may be farmed or leased; suitable for farming: E17.

farman *n.* var. of FIRMAN.

farmer /ˈfɑːmə/ *n.* LME. [AN *fermer*, (O)Fr. *fermier*, combining uses of med.L *firmarius*, *firmator*, f. *firma*: see FARM *n.* In more mod. uses prob. f. FARM *v.*[2] + -ER[1].] 1 A person who is allowed to collect and keep the revenues from taxes etc. in return for a fixed sum. LME. †2 A person who cultivates land for the owner; a bailiff, a steward. LME–L16. 3 Orig., a person who rents land for the purpose of cultivation. Now *gen.*, a person who cultivates a farm, as tenant or owner; one who farms land or rears certain animals (usu. of a specified kind). LME. †b A person who leases a weir or mill. LME–E16. 4 A person who farms children (*derog.*), a task, etc. M19.

1 H. AINSWORTH Speculators, farmers of revenues, and others. 3 *dairy farmer, fish-farmer, mink-farmer, poultry-farmer, trout-farmer*, etc. 4 *baby-farmer*.

Comb.: **farmer-general**, pl. **farmers-general**, [tr. Fr. *fermier général*] a person who collected taxes etc. in a district of France before the Revolution; **farmer's lung** a pulmonary disease caused by allergy to fungal spores from mouldy hay etc.

farmeress *n.* (now *rare*) (*a*) a woman who farms land; (*b*) a farmer's wife: L16. **farmeˈrette** *n.* (chiefly *US*) a woman or girl who farms land E20. **†farmerly** *a.* like a farmer M17–L18.

farmery /ˈfɑːməri/ *n.*[1] M17. [f. FARM *n.* + -ERY.] The buildings, yards, etc., belonging to a farm.

farmery *n.*[2] var. of FERMERY.

farmhouse /ˈfɑːmhaʊs/ *n.* M16. [f. FARM *n.* + HOUSE *n.*[1]] 1 A dwelling-house attached to a farm; *spec.* the chief such dwelling-house. M16. 2 More fully *farmhouse loaf*. A loaf of bread of an oval or rectangular shape with a curving top. M20.

farming /ˈfɑːmɪŋ/ *vbl n.* L16. [f. FARM *v.*[2] + -ING[1].] 1 *gen.* The action of FARM *v.*[2] L16. 2 *spec.* The business of cultivating land, raising stock, etc. M18.

2 *dairy-farming, high farming, organic farming, sheep-farming*, etc.

farmost /ˈfɑːməʊst/ *a.* E17. [f. FAR *a.* + -MOST.] Furthest, most remote.

farmyard /ˈfɑːmjɑːd/ *n.* & *a.* M18. [f. FARM *n.* + YARD *n.*[1]] A *n.* The yard or enclosure attached to a farmhouse. M18. B *attrib.* or as *adj.* Coarse, disgusting, uncouth. E20.

farnesol /ˈfɑːnɪsɒl/ *n.* E20. [G, f. mod.L (*Acacia*) *farnesiana* a plant that is a source of the alcohol, f. Odoardo *Farnese* (1573–1626), It. cardinal: see -OL.] *Chem.* A terpenoid alcohol, $C_{15}H_{25}OH$, that occurs in various essential oils and is used in the preparation of scents.

far niente /far nɪˈɛnte/ *n. phr.* E19. [It. = doing nothing.] Idleness; *dolce far niente*.

faro /ˈfɛːrəʊ/ *n.*[1] Also (earlier) **†pharaoh, †pharo.** E18. [Fr. PHARAON, perh. as a name of the king of hearts. Cf. PHARAON 2.] A gambling card-game, in which the players bet on the order in which certain cards will appear when taken singly from the top of the pack.

Comb.: **faro bank** (*a*) a gaming house where faro is played; (*b*) the banker's stake, against which the other players put their stakes;

faro /faro/ *n.*[2] M19. [Fr.] A type of beer made in Belgium around Brussels.

Faroese, -öese *a.* & *n.* var. of FAEROESE.

farol /faˈrol, fəˈrəʊl/ *n.* Pl. ***faroles*** /faˈroles/, ***farols*** /fəˈrəʊlz/. M20. [Sp., lit. 'lantern'.] *Bullfighting.* A movement in which the bullfighter draws the bull by passing the cloak back rapidly over his own head.

farouche /fəˈruːʃ/ *a.* M18. [Fr., alt. of OFr. *faroche, forache* f. med.L *forasticus*, f. L *foras* out-of-doors.] Sullen, shy.

F. PARTRIDGE Her face has . . become less farouche, and her manner more confident. G. CHARLES He was not . . very articulate in discussion. Rather farouche.

farouchely *adv.* M20.

farraginous /fəˈreɪdʒɪnəs/ *a.* E17. [f. L *farrago*, *-gin-* (see next) + -OUS.] Hotchpotch, miscellaneous.

farrago /fəˈrɑːgəʊ, fəˈreɪgəʊ/ *n.* Pl. **-os, *-oes.** M17. [L = mixed fodder for cattle, (fig.) a medley, f. *far* spelt, corn.] A confused group; a medley, a mixture, a hotchpotch.

A. BURGESS Such a repetitive farrago of platitudes. M. GEE A farrago of madness and morals and murder of the language.

farrant /ˈfar(ə)nt/ *a. Sc.* & *north.* Also (earlier) **-and** /-(ə)nd/. LME. [Perh. application of *farande* north. pres. pple of FARE *v.*] 1 †a Comely, handsome. Only in LME. b Proper, becoming, dignified. LME. 2 Having a specified appearance, disposition, or temperament, as *evil-farrant, well-farrant*, etc. LME.

farrantly *adv.* LME.

farrash *n.* var. of FERASH.

farrier /ˈfarɪə/ *n.* & *v.* M16. [OFr. *ferrier* f. L *ferrarius*, f. *ferrum* horseshoe, iron: see -IER.] A *n.* 1 A smith who shoes horses; a person who treats the diseases and injuries of horses. M16. 2 An official with care of the horses in a cavalry regiment. M19. B *v.* 1 *v.i.* Practise farriery. E18. 2 *v.t.* Treat (a horse) as a farrier does. E19.

farriery *n.* the art of the farrier; *spec.* veterinary surgery with regard to horses: M18.

farrow /ˈfarəʊ/ *n.* [OE *færh* (*fearh*) = OHG *farah*, f. WGmc f. IE base also of L *porcus*, Gk *porkos*: see PORK. In sense 3 f. the vb. See also FARE *n.*[3]] 1 A young pig. OE. 2 A litter of pigs. L16. 3 An act of farrowing. E17.

2 R. D. BLACKMORE Two farrows of pigs ready for the chapman. 3 P. HOLLAND One sow may bring at one farrow twenty pigges.

farrow /ˈfarəʊ/ *a.* Chiefly *Sc.* L15. [Flem. *verwe*, *varwe*, in *verwekoe*, *varwekoe*, †*verrekoe* cow that has become barren.] Of a cow: not in calf, not having produced a calf.

farrow /ˈfarəʊ/ *v.t.* & *i.* ME. [f. the n.] Of a sow: give birth to (young).
GOLDSMITH A sow .. farrowed fifteen pigs at a litter. M. WEBB When our sow farrowed, we were to keep all the piglets.

farruca /fəˈruːkə/ *n.* E20. [Sp., fem. of *farruco* Galician or Asturian, f. *Farruco* pet-form of male forename *Francisco*.] A type of flamenco dance.

†**farry** *v.t.* & *i.* L17–E19. [Back-form. f. FARRIER *n.*] = FARRIER *v.*

farsakh /ˈfɑːsak/ *n.* L19. [Pers. & Arab., rel. to FARSANG.] = FARSANG.

farsang /ˈfɑːsaŋ/ *n.* E17. [Pers., rel. to PARASANG.] An Iranian (Persian) unit of distance now equal to 6km (3.7 miles).

Farsi /ˈfɑːsiː/ *n.* & *a.* L19. [f. Arab. *fārsī*, f. *Fārs* f. Pers. *Pārs* Persia, PARSEE.] (Of or pertaining to) the (modern) Persian language.

fart /fɑːt/ *n.* Now *coarse slang.* LME. [f. the vb.] 1 An emission of wind from the anus. (Used as a type of something worthless.) LME. 2 A contemptible person. *slang.* M20.
1 SNOO WILSON This process isn't working... It's not worth a fart. 2 M. GORDON Some old fart who should've been dead years ago.

fart /fɑːt/ *v.* Now *coarse slang.* [OE (in *feorting* vbl n.) corresp. to MLG *verten*, OHG *ferzan*, MHG *verzen*, *vurzen* (G *farzen*, *furzen*), ON (with metathesis) *freta*, f. Gmc.] 1 *v.i.* Emit wind from the anus. OE. 2 *v.t.* Emit as wind from the anus. M17. 3 *v.i.* Fool *about* or *around*. E20.
1 J. P. DONLEAVY When someone farted in my house you could smell it in every room. 3 J. WAINWRIGHT Look! It's important. Stop farting around.
farter *n.* L16.

farther /ˈfɑːðə/ *v.t.* Now *rare.* LME. [Var. of FURTHER *v.*] †1 = FURTHER *v.* 3. *rare.* Only in LME. 2 = FURTHER *v.* 1. L16.
fartherance *n.* (*rare*) = FURTHERANCE L18.

farther /ˈfɑːðə/ *adv.* & *a.* ME. [Var. of FURTHER *adv.*, *a.*] A *adv.* 1 More forward; to or at a more advanced point in space or time. ME. 2 To a greater extent; = FURTHER *adv.* 2. LME. 3 In addition, moreover; = FURTHER *adv.* 3. LME. 4 At a greater distance; = FURTHER *adv.* 4. LME.
1 V. WOOLF The gulls rose in front of him and .. settled again a little farther on.
B *adj.* †1 = FURTHER *a.* 1. ME–M16. 2 More extended, additional; = FURTHER *a.* 2. LME. 3 More distant or advanced, remoter; = FURTHER *a.* 3. M16.
3 R. L. STEVENSON Where we have .. crossed a chain of mountains, it is only to find another .. upon the farther side. I. MURDOCH In the farther future, when you have made yourself right with the authorities. *Farther India* = *Further India* s.v. FURTHER *a.* 3.
¶The forms *farther*/*further* displaced the regular compar. of FAR *adv.*, *a.* as being largely coincident in meaning. Until recently, *farther* was preferred of physical distance, *further* in figurative contexts, but *further* is now usual in all contexts.
†**farthermore** *adv.* & *a.* (*a*) *adv.* = FURTHERMORE; (*b*) *adj.* remoter: ME–E17.

farthermost /ˈfɑːðəməʊst/ *a.* L15. [Var. of FURTHERMOST.] Most distant or remote, furthest.

farthest /ˈfɑːðɪst/ *a.* & *adv.* LME. [Var. of FURTHEST.] A *adj.* 1 Most distant or remote. LME. 2 Longest. M17.
1 W. JONES The farthest limits of the kingdom. **at (the) farthest** = *at (the) furthest* s.v. FURTHEST *a.*
B *adv.* To or at the greatest distance. L16.

farthing /ˈfɑːðɪŋ/ *n.* [OE *fēorþing*, -*ung*, f. *fēorþa* FOURTH, perh. after ON *fjórðungr* quarter: see -ING³.] 1 *Hist.* A quarter of an old penny; a British coin of this value (no longer legal tender). OE. 2 More fully *farthing-land.* A measure of land varying in extent from a quarter of an acre to thirty acres (approx. 0.1 to 12 hectares). Now *dial. rare.* OE. †3 In full *farthing noble*, *farthing of gold.* A quarter noble. LME–E17. 4 *fig.* A very little, the least possible amount. Usu. in neg. contexts. LME.
1 F. W. ROBERTSON A miser .. hoards farthings. 4 STEELE The gentleman .. has told her he does not care a farthing for her. *brass farthing*: see BRASS *n.*
farthingsworth *n.* as much as can be bought or sold for a farthing; a very small amount: ME.

farthingale /ˈfɑːðɪŋgeɪl/ *n.* Also †**vardingale.** E16. [OFr. *verdugale*, *vertugalle*, alt. of Sp. *verdugado*, f. *verdugo* rod, stick, f. *verde* green.] *Hist.* A framework of hoops, or a hooped petticoat, formerly used to extend the skirts of women's dresses.
Comb.: **farthingale chair** a 17th-cent. chair with a wide seat, a low straight back, and no arms.

†**farthingdeal** *n.* LME–M19. [Repr. OE *fēorþan dǣl*, accus. of *fēorþa* FOURTH *a.* + *dǣl* DEAL *n.*¹] A fourth part; *spec.* the fourth part of an acre.

fartlek /ˈfɑːtlɛk/ *n.* M20. [Sw., f. *fart* speed + *lek* play.] A method of training for middle- and long-distance running, in which the athlete runs over country, mixing fast with slow work.

fasces /ˈfasiːz/ *n.pl.* L16. [L, pl. of *fascis* bundle.] 1 *Rom. Antiq.* Rods in a bundle with an axe, carried by lictors before the superior magistrates as an emblem of power. L16. 2 (Symbols of) authority or power. E17.

fascet /ˈfasɪt/ *n.* M17. [Origin unkn.] In glass-manufacturing, a tool used to introduce glass bottles into the annealing oven.

Fasching /ˈfaʃɪŋ/ *n.* E20. [G.] In southern Germany and Austria: carnival, the carnival season, which lasts from Epiphany to Shrove Tuesday.

Fasci /ˈfaʃi/ *n.pl.* E20. [It., pl. of *fascio*: see FASCISM.] In Italy: groups of men organized politically, such as those in Sicily *c*1895 or those of the Fascists.

fascia /ˈfaʃɪə, ˈfeɪ-, -ʃə/ *n.* Pl. **-iae** /-ɪiː/, **-ias.** See also FACIA. M16. [L = band, fillet, casing of a door etc., rel. to FASCES.] 1 *Archit.* A horizontal band of wood, stone, brick, or marble, esp. as used in an architrave. M16. †b A ceiling coved on two opposite sides only. M17–E18. †2 A band (for the hair or head), a fillet. L16–E17. 3 Any object, or collection of objects, that gives the appearance of a band or stripe. E18. 4 *Anat.* A thin sheet of connective tissue enclosing a muscle or other organ; the connective tissue forming this. L18. 5 = FACIA 2. E20. 6 = FACIA 3. E20.

fasciate /ˈfaʃɪeɪt, -ʃɪət/ *a.* L19. [f. as next: see -ATE².] *Bot.* = FASCIATED *a.* 3.

fasciate /ˈfaʃɪeɪt/ *v.t.* Long *rare.* M17. [L *fasciat-* pa. ppl stem of *fasciare* swathe, f. FASCIA: see -ATE³.] Bind with or as with a fascia.

fasciated /ˈfaʃɪeɪtɪd/ *a.* E18. [f. FASCIA + -ATE² + -ED¹. Cf. Fr. *fascié*.] †1 *Archit.* Of a ceiling: coved on two opposite sides only. Only in E18. 2 Marked with bands or stripes. M18. 3 *Bot.* Exhibiting abnormal fusion of parts or organs normally separate, resulting in a flattened ribbon-like structure. Cf. FASCIATION 1. M19.

fasciation /faʃɪˈeɪʃ(ə)n/ *n.* M17. [f. as FASCIATE *v.*: see -ATION.] 1 The binding up of a limb etc. with bandages; a bandage. Long *rare* or *obs.* M17. 2 The growing together of contiguous parts; *esp.* (*Bot.*) fasciated condition (FASCIATED 3). L17.

fascicle /ˈfasɪk(ə)l/ *n.* L15. [L *fasciculus* dim. of *fascis*: see FASCES, -CULE. Cf. FASCICULE, FASCICULUS.] 1 Chiefly *Sci.* A small bundle, a bunch; *Bot.* a cluster of short stalks, roots, etc.; *Anat.* a bundle of (muscle, nerve, etc.) fibres. L15. 2 Each part of a book published in instalments. M17.
fascicled *a.* = FASCICULATE L18.

fascicular /faˈsɪkjʊlə/ *a.* M17. [f. as FASCICULE + -AR¹.] Chiefly *Sci.* Of, pertaining to, or of the nature of a fascicle (FASCICLE 1).

fasciculate /faˈsɪkjʊleɪt, -lət/ *a.* L18. [f. as prec. + -ATE².] Chiefly *Sci.* Arranged, growing, or occurring in a fascicle or fascicles (FASCICLE 1).
fasciculated *a.* = FASCICULATE L18. **fascicuˈlation** *n.* the state of being fasciculate; *spec.* (*Med.*) irregular spontaneous contraction of small groups of muscle fibres: L19.

fascicule /ˈfasɪkjuːl/ *n.* L17. [L *fasciculus* (see FASCICLE), after Fr. *fascicule*. Cf. FASCICULUS.] †1 A handful. Only in L17. 2 = FASCICLE 1. *rare.* M18. 3 = FASCICLE 2. L19.

fasciculus /faˈsɪkjʊləs/ *n.* Pl. **-li** /-lʌɪ, -liː/. E18. [L: see FASCICLE. Cf. FASCICULE.] 1 Chiefly *Sci.* = FASCICLE 1. E18. 2 = FASCICLE 2. M19.

fasciitis /fasɪˈʌɪtɪs, faʃɪ-/ *n.* Also **fascitis** /fəˈsʌɪtɪs, -ʃʌɪ-/. L19. [f. FASCIA + -ITIS.] *Med.* Inflammation of the fascia of a muscle etc.

fascinate /ˈfasɪneɪt/ *v.* L16. [L *fascinat-* pa. ppl stem of *fascinare*, f. *fascinum* spell, witchcraft: see -ATE³.] I *v.t.* †1 Bewitch, put under a spell. L16–M17. 2 Of a serpent etc.: deprive (a victim) of the power of escape or resistance by a look or by being in sight (formerly associated with witchcraft). M17. 3 Formerly, enslave (the faculties), paralyse (the judgement). Now, attract irresistibly, charm, enchant. M17.
3 P. SCOTT The range of Tusker's knowledge of the world had astonished him, fascinated him.
II *v.i.* 4 Be irresistibly attractive, charming, or enchanting. L19.
fascinated *a.* that has been fascinated; irresistibly attracted (*by*), charmed (*by*, *with*): E18. **fascinatedly** *adv.* L19. **fascinating** *a.* that fascinates; irresistibly attractive, charming: M17. **fascinatingly** *adv.* M19. **fascinative** *a.* having power to fascinate, tending to fascinate M19.

fascination /fasɪˈneɪʃ(ə)n/ *n.* E17. [L *fascinatio(n-)*, f. as prec.: see -ATION.] 1 The casting of a spell; sorcery; a spell. *obs.* exc. *Hist.* E17. †b The state of being under a spell. M17–M18. 2 Fascinating quality; the power to fascinate; an irresistible attractiveness. L17. b A serpent's power to fascinate a victim. L18. 3 The state of being fascinated; an instance of this, an irresistible feeling of attraction. (Foll. by *by*, *for*, *with*.) M19.
2 M. TIPPETT He exercised a tyrannical fascination over them. R. F. HOBSON The luring fascination of the unknown. 3 *Christian Science Monitor* Qaddafi doesn't reject Western technology, he has a fascination for it.

fascinator /ˈfasɪneɪtə/ *n.* M18. [L, f. as FASCINATE: see -OR.] 1 A magician. *arch.* M18. 2 An irresistibly attractive or charming person. M19. 3 A headscarf worn by women, either crocheted or made of a soft material. L19.

fascine /faˈsiːn/ *n.* & *v.t.* L17. [Fr. f L *fascina*, f. *fascis* bundle.] A *n.* A long faggot used for engineering purposes and (esp. in war) for lining trenches, filling ditches, etc. L17. B *v.t.* Fill up, protect, or strengthen with fascines. E19.

fasciola /fasɪˈəʊlə/ *n.* Pl. **-lae** /-liː/. M19. [L = small bandage.] *Anat.* In full *fasciola cinerea* /sɪˈnɪərɪə/, pl. *fasciolae cinereae* /-rɪiː/ [L *cinereus* = ash-coloured]. A thin layer of grey matter in the hippocampal formation of the brain.
faˈsciolar *a.* of or pertaining to the fasciola; *fasciolar gyrus* = FASCIOLA: L19.

fascioliasis /fasɪəˈlʌɪəsɪs/ *n.* Pl. **-ases** /-əsiːz/. L19. [f. mod.L *Fasciola* (see below), f. as prec.: see -IASIS.] *Med.* Infestation (of man or animals) with the liver fluke, *Fasciola hepatica*; the disease resulting from this.

Fascism /ˈfaʃɪz(ə)m, -sɪz(ə)m/ *n.* Also **f-.** E20. [It. *fascismo*, f. *fascio* bundle, group f. pop.L *fascium* for L *fascis* bundle: see -ISM.] The principles and organization of the Italian Fascists, the Italian Fascist movement; a similar nationalist and authoritarian movement in another country; *loosely* right-wing authoritarianism.
Also ***Fascismo*** /faˈʃizmo/ *n.* [It.] E20.

Fascist /ˈfaʃɪst, -sɪst/ *n.* & *a.* Also **f-.** E20. [It. *Fascista*, f. as prec.: see -IST.] A *n.* A member of a body of Italian nationalists, which was organized in 1919 to oppose Communism in Italy and controlled the country from 1922 to 1943; a member of any similar nationalist and authoritarian organization in another country; *loosely* any person with right-wing authoritarian political views. E20. B *adj.* Of, pertaining to, or characteristic of Fascism or Fascists. E20.
Fascisti /faˈʃisti/ *n.pl.* [It.] the Italian Fascists E20. **Faˈscistic** *a.* of or pertaining to Fascism or Fascists; having Fascist ideals: M20. **Faˈscistically** *adv.* E20.

fa'scistoid *a.* resembling (that of) a Fascist; tending towards Fascism: M20.

fascitis *n.* var. of FASCIITIS.

fash /faʃ/ *n.*[1] *Sc.* & *north.* E18. [f. the vb.] Trouble, vexation; bother; something that gives trouble.

fash /faʃ/ *n.*[2] *slang.* L19. [Abbrev.] Fashion.

fash /faʃ/ *a. slang.* L20. [Abbrev.] Fashionable.

fash /faʃ/ *v.* Chiefly *Sc.* & *north.* M16. [Early mod.Fr. *fascher* (now *fâcher*) f. Proto-Romance, f. L *fastus* disdain.] **1** *v.t.* Annoy, trouble, bother, weary, (oneself, another). M16. **2** *v.i.* Weary, be annoyed; trouble oneself; take trouble. (Foll. by *of, to do.*) L16.

1 SIR W. SCOTT Never fash yoursel' wi' me . . but look to yoursel'.

fashery *n.* annoyance, worry; something that causes worry: M16.

fashion /ˈfaʃ(ə)n/ *n.* ME. [AN *fasun*, (O)Fr. *façon* f. L *factio(n-)*, f. *fact-* pa. ppl stem of *facere* make, do: see -ION.] **1** Make, build, shape; appearance; characteristic form. In early use also, face, features. *arch.* ME. **2** A particular make, shape, style, or pattern; *spec.* a particular style of clothing. ME. **3** *gen.* (A) manner, (a) mode, (a) method, (a) way. LME. **4** Mode of action, demeanour; in *pl.*, behaviour, manners, gestures. Now *rare.* LME. †**5** The action or process of making; workmanship as contributing to value. LME–L18. **6** Prevailing custom, a current or conventional usage, esp. of a particular period or place or among a particular class of society; *spec.* (a) current style in clothing, hairstyle. L15. **b** *The* mode of dress, etiquette, furniture, speech, etc., prevalent at a particular time; *the* person who or thing which it is fashionable to admire or discuss. M16. †**c** In *pl.* Manners and customs. Chiefly in *know, learn, see, (the) fashions.* M16–E18. **d** Fashionable people; *the* fashionable world. E19. **7** Social status; *spec.* high social status, esp. as shown by dress and behaviour. Chiefly in *man, woman,* etc., *of fashion. arch.* L15. **8** Kind, sort. Now *rare.* M16. **9** A mere form, pretence. *obs.* exc. *Sc.* in *make fashion*, pretend. L16.

3 H. JAMES He had never yet heard a young girl express herself in just this fashion. D. H. LAWRENCE He tried to talk to Alvina in a fatherly fashion. J. B. PRIESTLEY Nottingham seems gayer, in its own robust Midland fashion, than other provincial towns. N. SHUTE They bathed in leisurely fashion. **after a fashion** not satisfactorily, but somehow or other. **after the fashion of** in the manner of, like. **in a fashion** = *after a fashion* above. 6 B. PYM Dresses of the thirties and earlier, now coming back into fashion. W. BRONK Fashions in ornamental planting change. P. F. BOLLER At that time fashion dictated that women's skirts should be short. A. LURIE Fashions by and large imitated the clothes that little girls had worn. b B. TRAPIDO I wore it, as was then the fashion, well over half way up my thighs.

Comb.: Forming advs. f. ns. and adjs. w. the sense 'in the manner or fashion of, -wise', as *crab-fashion, Roman-fashion*, etc. W. the sense 'fashionable, stylish', as *fashion jewellery* etc. Special combs., as **fashion-conscious** *a.* aware of and concerned about fashion; **fashion house** a business establishment displaying and selling high-quality clothes; **fashion-monger** a person who studies and follows fashion; **fashion-paper** a journal dealing with fashionable life, esp. current fashions in dress; **fashion piece** *Naut.* either of the two timbers in the underbody of a ship which form the shape of the stern; **fashion plate** a picture showing a fashion, esp. in dress; *fig.* a person who dresses in the current fashion.

fashionist *n.* a follower of fashion E17. **fashionless** *a.* L16.

fashion /ˈfaʃ(ə)n/ *v.t.* LME. [f. the n., after (O)Fr. *façonner.*] **1** Make, create, form, mould. LME. **b** Contrive, manage. Long *obs.* exc. *dial.* M16. †**c** Represent. *rare* (Spenser). Only in L16. **2** Make into a specified shape; model *according to, after, like*; shape *into, to.* E16. **3** Give a form suitable *to, to do*; accommodate, adapt *to.* Now *rare.* E16. †**4** Change the fashion of; modify, transform. Foll. by *to.* E16–M18. †**b** Counterfeit, pervert. *rare* (Shakes.). Only in L16.

1 J. CLAVELL A cross . . that he fashioned out of two pieces of driftwood. H. KISSINGER The team the new President brought together to fashion a global strategy. J. M. COETZEE Whether he knew no way of fashioning a lamp or a candle. 2 J. KOSINSKI The boys would . . fashion them into pistols.

fashioner *n.* M16.

fashionable /ˈfaʃ(ə)nəb(ə)l/ *a.* & *n.* L16. [f. FASHION *v., n.* + -ABLE.] **A** *adj.* †**1** Able to be fashioned or shaped (*to*). L16–M17. **2** Dressing or behaving according to the current or best fashion. E17. **3** Conformable to fashion; in vogue, generally accepted; of, pertaining to, characteristic of, or frequented by fashionable people. E17. †**b** Of a good fashion or appearance; stylish. M17–E18. †**4** Merely formal. E–M17.

3 N. COWARD Funny how the South of France has become so fashionable in the summer, isn't it? L. HELLMAN My hair, . . straight in a time when it was fashionable to have curls.

B *n.* A fashionable person. Usu. in *pl.* L18.

fashiona'bility *n.* M19. **fashionableness** *n.* E17. **fashionably** *adv.* E17.

fashioned /ˈfaʃ(ə)nd/ *a.* LME. [f. FASHION *v., n.*: see -ED[1], -ED[2].] **1** That has been fashioned, esp. in a specified way; (of a stocking) shaped to fit the contour of the leg. LME. **2** As 2nd elem. of comb.: of the specified description of fashion. Esp. in OLD-FASHIONED. L16.

1 *fully-fashioned*: see FULLY *adv.*

fashious /ˈfaʃəs/ *a. Sc.* & *north.* M16. [Fr. †*fascheux* (now *fâcheux*), f. *fascher* (*fâcher*): see FASH *v.*, -IOUS.] Causing anxiety or trouble; tiresome.

fasola /ˈfɑːsɒlɑː, -səʊl-/ *n.* M20. [f. FA *n.* + SOL *n.*[1] + LA *n.*] *Mus.* A system of solmization in which the progression of syllables used is fa, sol, la, fa, sol, la, mi.

fast /fɑːst/ *n.*[1] ME. [ON *fasta* = OS, OHG *fasta*, f. Gmc base of FAST *v.*] **1** An act or instance of fasting. ME. †**b** The action of fasting; abstinence from food. *rare.* E17–L18. **2** A day or season appointed for fasting. ME.

1 **break one's fast** stop fasting, take breakfast. 2 H. SEGAL She kept the yearly fast and went to the synagogue.

Comb.: **fast-day** a day appointed for fasting.

fast /fɑːst/ *n.*[2] LME. [ON *festr*, f. *festa* fasten, f. *fastr* FAST *a.*] *Naut.* A rope or chain for mooring.

†**fast** *n.*[3] L17–M18. [Fr. *faste* f. L *fastus.*] Arrogance, pompousness.

fast /fɑːst/ *n.*[4] M19. [f. the adj.] Something that is fast or fixed; *esp.* a body of rock or ice.

fast /fɑːst/ *a.* [OE *fæst* = OFris. *fest*, OS *fast* (Du. *vast*), OHG *festi* (G *fest*), ON *fastr*, f. Gmc.] **I 1** Firmly fixed in place; not easily moved; physically stable. *arch.* OE. **b** Constant, steadfast. Now *rare.* OE. **c** (Of sleep) deep, unbroken, sound; experiencing deep sleep. Now *dial.* L16. **d** Of a colour: that will not quickly fade or wash out. M17. **e** Of an organism: resistant to the stain-removing or toxic action of a (specified) agent. Usu. as 2nd elem. of comb. E20. †**2** Of a fortress or district: secure against attack. OE–M17. **3** Compact, solid, hard. *obs.* exc. *dial.* OE. **b** Frozen. *N. Amer.* Now *rare* or *obs.* E18. **4** Constipated. Long *obs.* exc. *dial.* OE. **5** Firmly attached or tied; that cannot easily escape or be extricated. ME. **6**†**a** Mean, niggardly. Only in ME. **b** Tenacious. Foll. by *of.* Now *rare.* E16. **7** Closed firmly, bolted, locked. ME.

1 *bedfast*: see BED *n.* c R. MACAULAY A remarkably fast sleeper. 5 G. MAXWELL I had to make the rope fast to a stump. 7 D. L. SAYERS He tried the handle, but the door was fast.

II 8 Rapid, swift, quick-moving; imparting quick motion. ME. **b** Of a clock or watch: indicating a time more advanced than the true time. M19. **c** *Photogr.* (Of film etc.) needing only brief exposure; (of a lens) shortening the necessary exposure time, having a large aperture; (of a shutter) providing a brief exposure time. E20. **9** Of a person: dissipated, extravagant, pleasure-loving, studiedly unconventional, immoral. M18. **10** Suitable for or productive of quick movement; (of a cricket pitch, tennis-court, putting-green, etc.) on which a ball bounces or runs freely. M19.

8 I. MURDOCH He did not run, he just walked at a fast steady pace. 9 J. S. HUXLEY He got into a fast set . . and took to gambling.

Phrases: *fast and* FURIOUS. **fast and** (or †**or**) **loose** an old cheating game; *fig.* inconstancy; *play (at) fast and loose*, ignore one's obligations, be unreliable, trifle. *hard and fast*: see HARD *a.* **make fast** bind, connect, fix firmly. **take fast hold of** hold or grasp tightly.

Special collocations & comb.: **fastback** (*a*) *Bookbinding* (a book with) a binding in which the backs of the sections adhere to the sheets; (*b*) (a motor car with) a back that slopes in a continuous line down to the bumper. **fastball** *N. Amer.* (*a*) a rapidly pitched ball in baseball; *fig.* a deception, an unfair action to gain an advantage; (*b*) a form of the game of softball. **fast-boat** a whaling boat which has attached itself to a whale by harpooning it. **fast bowler** *Cricket*: employing fast bowling. **fast bowling** *Cricket*: in which the ball travels at high speed. **fast break** in basketball, handball, etc., a swift attack from a defensive position. **fast-break** *v.i.* make a fast break. **fast breeder (reactor)** a breeder reactor in which fission is caused mainly by fast neutrons. *fast buck*: see BUCK *n.*[8] **fast foe** *arch.* a person who is unwaveringly hostile to one. **fast food** wholly or partially pre-prepared for quick sale or serving. **fast-food** *a.* (*US*) produced without special effort or expense. **fast friend** a staunch or firm friend. **fast friendship** staunch or firm friendship. **fasthold** (now *rare*) a stronghold. **fast ice**: covering seawater but (usu.) attached to land. **fast land** *US* land lying above the high-water mark. **fast lane** a traffic lane on a motorway etc. intended for overtaking; *fig.* a means or route of rapid progress, a highly pressured lifestyle. **fast neutron** a neutron of high kinetic energy; *esp.* one released in nuclear fission and not slowed by any moderator. **fast one** *slang* an unfair action to gain an advantage (esp. in *pull* (or *put over*) *a fast one*). **fast reactor** a nuclear reactor in which fission is caused mainly by fast neutrons. **fast-talk** *v.t.* (*N. Amer. colloq.*) persuade by rapid or deceitful talk. **fast track** a track for fast trains; *fig.* a means or route of rapid progress. **fast-track** *v.t.* (*colloq.*) give priority to, treat as urgent. **fast train** an express train which stops at few intermediate stations. **fast-twitch** *a.* (of a muscle fibre) that contracts rapidly, providing strength rather than endurance. **fast worker** *colloq.* a person who makes rapid progress, esp. in winning another's affections.

fastish *a.* M19.

fast /fɑːst/ *v.* [OE *fæstan* = OFris. *festia*, (M)Du. *vasten*, OHG *fastēn*, (G *fasten*), ON *fasta*, Goth. *fastan*, f. Gmc.] **1** *v.i.* Abstain from all or some kinds of food, as a religious observance or as a ceremonial expression of grief. (Foll. by *on* the food taken.). OE. **2** *v.i. gen.* Go without food. Formerly also, go without drink. Foll. by *from.* OE. †**3** *v.t.* Pass (time) fasting; observe (a day etc.) as a time of abstinence. ME–L17. **4** *v.t.* Deprive of all or some kinds of food. M19.

faster *n.* ME.

fast /fɑːst/ *adv.* [OE *fæste* = OS *fasto* (Du. *vast*), OHG *fasto*, (G *fast* almost), ON *fast*, f. Gmc base of FAST *a.*] **1** With firm grasp or attachment; securely. OE. †**b** With strict observance. ME–M16. **c** So as to be unable to move. E16. **2** So as not to be moved or shaken; so as to close firmly; fixedly. OE. †**b** Earnestly, steadily. ME–M17. †**c** Stoutly, strongly. ME–L16. **3** In a close-fitting manner; tightly. ME. **4** Close; very near. *arch.* ME. †**5** Soon, immediately. ME–L18. **6** Quickly, rapidly. ME. **b** Readily, with alacrity. *obs.* exc. in *fast enough.* LME. **c** In quick succession. L16. **7** In a dissipated manner, extravagantly, unconventionally, immorally. Chiefly in *live fast.* L17.

1 D. H. LAWRENCE The girl sat very insecurely, clinging fast. 2 C. MEW We caught her, fetched her home at last And turned the key upon her, fast. 6 A. P. HERBERT In truth the hare was travelling only half as fast as an express train. c SHELLEY My thoughts come fast.

Phrases: †**as fast as** as soon as. *fast and* FURIOUS. **fast asleep** sound asleep. **sleep fast** sleep soundly. **stick fast** be unable to move or make progress (*lit.* & *fig.*). *thick and fast*: see THICK *adv.*

Comb.: **fast-forward** *n., a.,* & *v.* (*a*) *n.* & *a.* (designating) a control on a machine using sound or videotape which enables the tape to be wound forward quickly; (*b*) *v.t.* & *i.* (cause to) be wound forward quickly.

fasten /ˈfɑːs(ə)n/ *n.* Long *obs.* exc. *Sc.* & *north.* in comb. [OE *fæsten* f. Gmc, f. base of FAST *v.* Rel. to OS *fastunnia*, Goth. *fastubni.*] = FAST *n.*[1]

Comb.: **Fasten(s) -een, -eve, -even, Tuesday** *Sc.* & *north.* the day before the beginning of the fast of Lent; Shrove Tuesday.

fasten /ˈfɑːs(ə)n/ *v.* [OE *fæstnian* = OFris. *festna*, OS *fastnon*, OHG *fastinōn*, *fest-*, f. WGmc, f. base of FAST *a.*: see -EN[5].] **I** *v.t.* †**1** Make sure or stable; establish, confirm; ratify (an agreement). OE–M17. †**2** Make unable to move, immobilize. OE–M17. **3** Attach to something else; fix or hold securely in position; secure with a clasp, button, latch, bolt, seal, etc.; (now *Naut.*) attach together the parts of. ME. **b** *fig.* Direct (a look, thoughts, etc.) keenly (*up*)*on*; fix (a nickname, imputation, etc.) (*up*)*on*. ME. †**c** Deliver effectively (a blow); imprint (a kiss). (Foll. by (*up*)*on*.) E16–L17. **4** Secure as a means of connection (a clasp, button, tie, etc.); (foll. by *off*) secure (a thread etc.) with a knot, extra stitches, etc. ME. †**5** Make solid, strengthen, harden. ME–L16. **6** Join or bind in a contract (*with*), latterly *spec.* as an apprentice. Long *obs.* exc. *dial.* LME. **7** Close with a grip (the hands, teeth). Long *obs.* exc. *dial.* M16.

3 J. AUSTEN The chaise arrived, the trunks were fastened on. E. M. FORSTER The rope that fastened Leonard to the earth. F. L. WRIGHT Three thicknesses of boards . . , the boards fastened together with screws. E. J. HOWARD He leaned out of the window to fasten back the shutter. b SAKI The character she had fastened on to him. A. J. CRONIN He felt Blodwen Page's eye fastened on him with a certain inquiry. 4 P. D. JAMES He fastened his seat belt without speaking.

II *v.i.* **8a** Foll. by *on*, *upon*: lay hold of, seize on, single out for attack or attention, avail oneself eagerly of (a pretext etc.). ME. **b** Foll. by *on to*, *to*: affix oneself to, take a grip of, seize; *spec.* harpoon (a whale). E19. †**9** Without following prep.: take hold, attach oneself; take up a position. LME–M18. †**10** Become solid, harden, set. M17–M18. **11** Become unable to move, be immobilized. M18. **12** Admit of being fixed or secured. E19.

8a M. DUFFY No delicious titbit of local information to fasten on. b J. A. MICHENER His hind quarters where two wolves had fastened onto him.

fastener /ˈfɑːs(ə)nə/ *n.* L16. [f. prec. + -ER[1].] A person who or thing which fastens something; a device for fastening.

zip-fastener: see ZIP *n.*[1] 4.

fastening /ˈfɑːs(ə)nɪŋ/ *n.* ME. [f. as prec. + -ING[1].] †**1** (Something which provides) strengthening, support. Only in ME. **2** The action of FASTEN *v.* ME. **3** A device which fastens something. LME.

Fasti /ˈfastʌɪ, -tiː/ *n.* Also **f-**. E17. [L, pl. of *fastus* (*dies*), a lawful day, a day on which the courts sat.] **1** *Rom. Hist.* A calendar or calendars showing the permitted days for legal and public business, festivals, games, anniversaries, etc. E17. **2** *transf.* A chronological register of events, lists of office-holders, etc. L17.

fastidious /faˈstɪdɪəs/ *a.* LME. [L *fastidiosus*, f. *fastidium* loathing: see -IOUS.] †**1** Disagreeable, distasteful. LME–M18. †**2a** Disgusted. M16–L17. **b** Proud, disdainful, scornful. E17–L18. **3** Scrupulous or overscrupulous in matters of taste, cleanliness, propriety, etc.; squeamish. E17.

3 M. MEYER So fastidious in his tastes and so shy of human contact.

fastidiously *adv.* E17. **fastidiousness** *n.* M16.

fastidium /faˈstɪdɪəm/ *n. rare.* M18. [L, f. *fastus* FAST *n.*[3]] Disgust; ennui.

fastigiate /faˈstɪdʒɪət, -eɪt/ *a.* M17. [f. L *fastigium* tapering point, gable + -ATE[2].] **1** Sloping upwards or tapering to a point. *rare.* M17. †**2** Having a flat surface at the top; *esp.* corymbose. L18–M19. **3** *Bot.* Of a tree etc.: having the branches more or less parallel to the main stem. M19.

fastigium /faˈstɪdʒɪəm/ *n.* L17. [L: see prec.] The apex, the summit; *Archit.* the ridge or gable end of a roof, a pediment.

fasting /ˈfɑːstɪŋ/ *n.* ME. [f. FAST *v.* + -ING[1].] **1** The action of FAST *v.*; an instance of this. ME. †**2** = FAST *n.*[1] 2. LME–M17.

Comb.: **fasting blood sugar** the concentration of sugar in the blood after a period of fasting; **fasting-day** a fast-day.

fastly /ˈfɑːstli/ *adv.* Now *arch. rare* OE. [f. FAST *a.* + -LY[2].] = FAST *adv.*

fastness /ˈfɑːs(t)nɪs/ *n.* OE. [f. FAST *a.* + -NESS.] **I1** The quality or state of being firmly fixed; stability. Formerly also, firm attachment. OE. †**b** Fidelity, loyalty, (*to*). L16–M17. †**2** Compactness, density, solidity; (of style) conciseness. M16–L17. †**3** Security, difficulty of access; safety, strength. L16–L17. **4** Rapidity, swiftness, quickness. M17. **5** Dissipation, extravagance, unconventionality, immorality. M19.

II6 A stronghold, a fortress. OE. †**7a** Support, help. Only in LME. **b** A fastening. L17–L19.

6 C. HILL He lured the Scottish Army away from its fastness at Stirling. *fig.*: A. S. BYATT It never does the academic fastnesses real harm to be shaken.

fastuous /ˈfastjʊəs/ *a.* Now *rare.* M17. [Late L *fastuosus*, in cl.L *fastosus*, f. *fastus* FAST *n.*[3]: see -OUS, -UOUS.] Haughty, arrogant, pretentious, ostentatious.

fastuously *adv.* L17. **fastuousness** *n.* M17.

fat /fat/ *n.*[1] See also VAT *n.*[1] [OE *fæt* = MLG, Du. *vat*, OHG *faz* (G *Fass*), ON *fat*, f. Gmc.] **1** A vessel; *esp.* a large vessel for liquids, a tub, a cask. Long only *Sc.* OE. **2** A unit of capacity equal to eight bushels. *obs.* exc. *Hist.* LME. †**3** A cask for dry goods. M16–E19.

fat /fat/ *n.*[2] LME. [f. the adj.] **1** The fat part of something. LME. **b** The richest or choicest part. *obs.* exc. in *the fat of the land* below. LME. **c** Fatness, corpulence. E18. **d** *Theatr.* A part which gives the player the opportunity of appearing to advantage. E19. **2** The oily or greasy substance of which the fat parts of animal bodies are largely composed; any variety of this, distinguished by its provenance. Also (more fully *vegetable fat*), a similar substance made from plant products. M16. **b** *Chem.* Any of a class of compounds which are glyceryl esters of carboxylic acids and which include the compounds forming the typical constituents of animal fat. L19. **3** In *pl.* Fat cattle or sheep. *Austral.* & *NZ.* L19.

2 *bacon fat*, *pork fat*, etc.

Phrases etc.: **a bit of fat** *colloq.* a piece of good luck. *chew the fat*: see CHEW *v.* *green fat*: see GREEN *a.* **the fat is in the fire** an explosion of anger is sure to follow. **the fat of the land** the best of everything (chiefly in *live off* or *on the fat of the land*).

Comb.: **fat-body** *Zool.* an organ in the haemocoel of an insect which acts as a store of nutrients, esp. lipids and glycogen; **fat-soluble** *a.* soluble in fats or oils.

fatless *a.* E19. **fatlike** *a.* resembling fat E18.

fat /fat, fa/ *n.*[3] Now *rare.* M19. [Fr., f. Prov. *fat* stupid, ignorant, f. L *fatuus* FATUOUS *a.*] A presumptuous, conceited dandy; a fop.

fat /fat/ *a.* Compar. & superl. **-tt-**. [OE *fǣt(t)* = OFris. *fatt*, *fett*, MDu., MLG *vett* (Du. *vet*), OHG *feizzet* (G *feist*), f. WGmc pa. pple formation on Gmc vb, f. adj.] **I1** Well-fed, plump. Now chiefly, too plump, corpulent. OE. **b** Of larger size than is usual; large in comparison with others of the same species. L19. **2** Of an animal: made plump for slaughter, fattened up. OE. **b** Of grain or fruit: well-developed; ripe, juicy. Now *rare.* LME. **3** Thick, full; *Typogr.* characterized by thick strokes of abnormal width. ME.

1 J. STEINBECK Ma was heavy, but not fat; thick with child-bearing and work. *fig.*: SHAKES. *Merch. V.* I will feed fat the ancient grudge I bear him. 2 DEFOE Whether he or she was fattest and fittest to kill first. b R. WEST If you roll the little withered ones between your fingers they taste sweet and rich like big fat ones. 3 J. RABAN Their briefcases were fat with glossy promotional literature.

II4 Containing much fat or oil; greasy, oily, unctuous. OE. **5** Containing a high proportion of some particular component; (of wood) resinous; (of coal) bituminous; (of clay) sticky; (of limestone) nearly pure, slaking easily; *rare* (of air) thick, dense. Formerly also, (of water) thick, turbid; (of wine etc.) fruity, full-bodied. LME. **6** Of an actor's part etc: offering abundant opportunity for skill and display; impressive. M18.

4 J. DAVIES The Milk . . is so fat, that it makes a Cream two fingers thick. 6 P. G. WODEHOUSE True acting part, the biggest in the piece, full of fat lines.

III7 Rich, fertile; (of a benefice, job, lawsuit, etc.) yielding good returns, plentiful. Formerly also, (of a person) affluent, wealthy. ME.

7 J. FOWLES Incumbents of not notably fat livings do not argue with rich parishioners. P. S. BUCK They planted seed upon the earth that was fat with the richness of the dried water.

IV8 Slow-witted, stupid; indolent, complacent. L16.

8 SHAKES. *Haml.* Duller shouldst thou be than the fat weed That roots itself in ease.

Special collocations, phrases, & comb.: **a fat chance** *slang* no or hardly any possibility. **a fat lot** *slang* a small amount (*of*), hardly any. **fat cat** *slang* a wealthy person, *esp.* a wealthy politician, civil servant, or businessman. **fat dormouse** = *edible dormouse* s.v. EDIBLE *a.* **fat-face** *a.* (*Typogr.*) designating a type characterized by thick strokes of abnormal width. **fat-faced** *a.* having a fat face; *Typogr.* = *fat-face* above. **fat-head** a stupid person. **fat-headed** *a.* stupid. **fat-headedness** stupidity. **fatmouth** *n.* & *v.* (*US slang*) (*a*) *n.* a loudmouth; (*b*) *v.i.* talk too much. **fatstock** livestock made fat for slaughter. **fat-witted** *a.* dull, stupid. *grease the fat pig*: see GREASE *v.*

fatly *adv.* †(*a*) plentifully; (*b*) to a great extent; (*c*) clumsily: L15.

fat /fat/ *v. arch.* Infl. **-tt-**. OE. [f. the adj.] †**1** *v.t.* [tr. Heb. *diššēn.*] Anoint (the head); load (an altar) with fat. OE–L17. †**b** Cover with fat or grease; *gen.* cover thickly. LME–M17. **2** *v.t.* & *i.* (Cause to) grow fat. ME. **3** *v.t.* Fertilize (soil etc.). LME.

2 **kill the fatted calf** [*Luke* 15] celebrate; *esp.* receive a returned prodigal with joy.

fatter *n.* (*a*) a person who (formerly also, a food which) fattens; †(*b*) an animal which grows fat (quickly etc.): E16.

fatal /ˈfeɪt(ə)l/ *a.* LME. [(O)Fr., or L *fatalis*, f. *fatum* FATE *n.*: see -AL[1].] †**1** Allotted or decreed by fate. (Foll. by *to*.) LME–E18. **b** Condemned by fate; doomed *to*. E16–M17. **2** Of or concerned with destiny. Formerly also, prophetic, ominous. LME. **3** Fateful, decisive, important. LME. **4** Destructive; ruinous; resulting in death (*to*); (of a weapon, bait, etc.) deadly, sure to kill. E16. **b** Causing serious harm, disastrous. L17. **5** Of the nature of fate; inevitable, necessary. E17.

1 R. BENTLEY It is fatal to our author ever to blunder when he talks of Egypt. 2 **the Fatal Sisters** the Fates. **the fatal thread**: supposedly spun by the Fates, determining the length of a person's life. 3 M. GEE That fatal night when all her dreams came to a premature and bloody end. 4 V. WOOLF There is some flaw in me—some fatal hesitancy. J. A. MICHENER If the venom entered the bison anywhere near the head or face, it was invariably fatal. b T. HARDY It was a fatal omission of Boldwood's that he had never once told her she was beautiful. G. VIDAL The hairdresser had made the fatal error of using the wrong dyes. 5 N. HAWTHORNE What a hardy plant was Shakespeare's genius, how fatal its development.

fatally *adv.* (*a*) as predetermined by fate; (*b*) with fatal result: LME. **fatalness** *n.* M17.

fatalism /ˈfeɪt(ə)lɪz(ə)m/ *n.* L17. [f. prec. + -ISM, perh. after Fr. *fatalisme.*] **1** Belief in fatality; the doctrine that all events are predetermined by fate. L17. **2** Submission to or compliance with this doctrine. M18.

fatalist /ˈfeɪt(ə)lɪst/ *n.* & *a.* M17. [f. as prec. + -IST, perh. after Fr. *fataliste.*] **A** *n.* A person who believes or accepts that all events are predetermined by fate. M17. **B** *adj.* Of or pertaining to fatalism or fatalists. M19.

fata'listic *a.* of, pertaining to, or of the nature of fatalism M19. **fata'listically** *adv.* M19.

fatality /fəˈtalɪti, feɪ-/ *n.* L15. [Fr. *fatalité* or late L *fatalitas*, f. L *fatalis*: see FATAL, -ITY.] **1** The quality of causing death or disaster; a fatal influence. L15. **b** A disastrous event, a calamity; *esp.* a death caused by an accident, in war, etc. M19. **2** = FATE *n.* 2. Now *rare.* L16. **3** The quality or condition of being predetermined, esp. doomed, by fate; the agency or supremacy of fate; subjection to fate. M17.

1 B. ANDERSON He undermined all the racist fatalities that underlay Dutch colonial ideology. 3 J. BUTLER A Fatality supposed consistent with what we certainly experience does not destroy the proof of an intelligent author and Governor of nature. J. A. SYMONDS The fatality attending an accursed house.

fata morgana /ˌfɑːtə mɔːˈɡɑːnə/ *n.* E19. [It. = fairy Morgan, sister of King Arthur, whose legend was carried to Sicily by Norman settlers.] A kind of mirage most frequently seen in the Strait of Messina between Italy and Sicily, attributed in early times to fairy agency; an illusion.

fate /feɪt/ *n.* LME. [Orig. f. It. *fato*, later f. its source L *fatum* lit. 'that which has been spoken', neut. pa. pple of *fari* speak.] 1 The power or agency which, according to popular belief, predetermines all events from eternity. LME. b *Mythol.* A goddess of destiny, *esp.* each of the three Greek, Roman, or Scandinavian goddesses of destiny. E16. 2 That which is destined to happen, esp. to a person; a person's or thing's appointed lot. LME. b The ultimate condition of a person or thing. M18. 3 Death, destruction, ruin, downfall. LME.

1 A. LOOS Our paths seemed to cross each other and I told him . . a thing like that was nearly always the result of fate. P. BAILEY We did hope . . that everything would be for the best . . but Fate thought otherwise, didn't she? b H. ALLEN That Fate who sits at the gates of first beginnings and tangles the threads of life. 2 D. H. LAWRENCE He was expressionless, neutralized, possessed by her as if it were his fate. L. STRACHEY A curious fate awaited this young man. b N. MAILER The fate of the campaign was being determined elsewhere. S. HAZZARD A couple whose fates could not be predicted with confidence.

Phrases: *a fate worse than* DEATH. **as sure as fate** quite certain(ly). *book of fate*: see BOOK *n.* **decide, fix, seal, a person's fate** determine what will become of a person. *tempt fate*: see TEMPT *v.*

fate /feɪt/ *v.t.* L16. [f. the n.] Preordain, predestine. Now only in *pass.* (foll. by *to be* or *do*); also *impers.* in *it is fated, it was fated*, etc. (foll. by *that*).

I. D'ISRAELI It was fated that England should be the theatre of the first of a series of Revolutions. J. CONRAD We knew we were fated . . to hear about one of Marlow's inconclusive experiences.

fated /ˈfeɪtɪd/ *a.* L16. [f. FATE *n.*, *v.* + -ED[2], -ED[1].] 1 Preceded by an adv. or adj.: having a particular fate. *rare* exc. in *ill-fated* L16. †2 Fateful. *rare* (Shakes.). Only in E17. 3 Decreed, determined or controlled by fate. E18. 4 Doomed to destruction. E19.

3 I. MURDOCH This was the moment, and Edward believed in fated moments. 4 LD MACAULAY Cavalry . . were fast approaching the fated city.

fateful /ˈfeɪtfʊl, -f(ə)l/ *a.* E18. [f. FATE *n.* + -FUL.] 1 Of an utterance etc: prophetic. E18. 2 = FATAL 4. M18. 3 Fraught with destiny, important, momentous, decisive. E19. 4 Controlled by or showing the influence of fate. L19.

3 J. GALSWORTHY The confusion of patriotism and personalities left behind by the fateful gathering. 4 E. PEACOCK As fateful as a Greek tragedy.

fatefully *adv.* M19. **fatefulness** *n.* L19.

Fatha *n.* var. of FATIHAH.

fat hen /fatˈhɛn/ *n. phr.* L18. [f. FAT *v.* + HEN *n.*] Any of various weeds with succulent leaves, esp. the goosefoot *Chenopodium album* and (*dial.*) the oraches *Atriplex patula* and *A. prostrata*. Also (*Austral.* & *NZ*) any of various plants of these genera, sometimes eaten as vegetables.

father /ˈfɑːðə/ *n.* & *a.* [OE *fæder* = OFris. *feder*, OS *fadar* (Du. *vader*), OHG *fater* (G *Vater*), ON *faðir*, Goth. *fadar*, f. Gmc. f. IE, whence also L *pater*, Gk *patēr*, Skt *pitṛ*.] A *n.* 1 A male parent of a human being (used as a form of address by a son or daughter, and sometimes a son- or daughter-in-law, and sometimes also familiarly by the mother of a man's child or children); a man who undertakes the responsibilities of a father towards a child; (now *rare*), any man who gives away a bride. Also, a male parent of an animal. OE. 2 A male ancestor, a forefather, a progenitor; *esp.* the founder of a race or family. OE. b An originator, a founder, a designer; a man who gives the first influential example of something immaterial. LME. 3 A man who shows paternal care or kindness; a man to whom filial obedience and reverence are due; a patron (of literature etc.). OE. b *Eccl.* A man responsible for the spiritual care, guidance or instruction of a person (also *spiritual father*); a confessor (in full (arch.) *ghostly father*). ME. c A priest belonging to a religious order; the superior of a monastic house. Later also used as a title preceding the name of any priest (abbrev. *F.*, *Fr.*). ME. 4 *Chr. Ch.* (Usu. **F-**.) God; the first person of the Trinity. Formerly also, Christ. OE. 5 Used as a title of respect for an old and venerable man (or for something personified as such). ME. 6 Each of the leading men or elders of a city or an assembly; *esp.* a senator of ancient Rome. Usu. in *pl.* LME. b The oldest member, the doyen of a society etc.; the presiding member or president. E17. 7 *Computing.* A tape of data from which the current version has been generated, retained for security reasons. M20.

1 I. MCEWAN Robert was desperate to be a father, desperate to have sons. *fig.*: B. F. TAYLOR Fox river, Rock river, Mississippi, the old Father of them all. *adoptive father, biological father, birth father, foster-father, natural father*, etc. 2 R. KIPLING Excellent herbs had our fathers of old. b R. V. JONES Hugo Meynell, known the world over as the father of English foxhunting. 3 E. A. FREEMAN Scots . . owed no duty to Rome . . but only to their Father and Lord at Winchester. 5 T. GRAY Say, Father Thames . . Who foremost now delight to cleave With pliant arm thy glassy wave? 6 A. DUGGAN He attended the Senate, and occasionally delivered a short speech to the assembled Fathers. b SMOLLETT I will take your place . . and think myself happy to be hailed 'Father of the Feast'.

Phrases: *Apostolic Fathers*: see APOSTOLIC *a.* 1. *be gathered to one's fathers*: see GATHER *v.* 2. **Church Fathers** = *Fathers of the Church* below. CITY *fathers*. *conscript fathers*: see CONSCRIPT *a.* 1. **Father of English poetry**: Chaucer. **Father of History**: Herodotus. **Father of lies**: the Devil. *father of the chapel*: see CHAPEL *n.* **Father of the House of Commons**: the member with the longest continuous service. **Fathers of the Church** early Christian writers, esp. of the first five centuries. *Father Superior*: see SUPERIOR *a.* *founding father*: see FOUNDING *a.* *ghostly father*: see sense 3b above. *God the Father, God the Son, and God the Holy Spirit* (or *Ghost*): see GOD *n.* *Greek Fathers*: see GREEK *a.* **Holy Father**: the Pope. *Our Father*: see OUR *a.* 1b. *Pilgrim Father*: see PILGRIM *n.* 4. **Right, Most Reverend Father in God** the titles of a Church of England bishop and archbishop respectively. *Roman father*: see ROMAN *a.* *spiritual father*: see sense 3b above. **the child is father to the man** tendencies in childhood foreshadow adult development. **the father (and mother) of** a *colloq.* a very severe (beating etc.); a very big (overdraft, row, etc.). *the Seraphic Father*: see SERAPHIC *a.* *the wish if father to the thought*: see WISH *n.* *White Father*: see WHITE *a.*

B *attrib.* or as *adj.* (Freq. w. hyphen.) That is a father. M17.

Special collocations & comb.: *Father Christmas*: see CHRISTMAS *n.* & *int.* **father-figure** an older man (esp. of influence) who is revered for paternal characteristics, and who may serve as an emotional substitute for a father. **father-in-law**, pl. **fathers-in-law**, (*a*) the father of one's wife or husband; (*b*) (now *rare*) a stepfather. **fatherland** a person's native country, now esp. Germany. **father-lasher** the short-spined sea scorpion, *Myoxocephalus scorpius*, found in N. Atlantic coastal waters. **father-long-legs** = DADDY-*long-legs*. **father right** the custom by which dynastic succession passes only in the male line. **Father's Day** a day on which fathers are conventionally honoured, usu. the third Sunday in June. *Father Time*: see TIME *n.*

father /ˈfɑːðə/ *v.t.* LME. [f. the n.] 1 Procreate as a father; be or become the (biological) father of, beget. LME. b Originate, found (a doctrine etc.) M16. 2 Appear as, or acknowledge oneself as, the father of (a child) or (later) the author of (a book); take responsibility for. LME. 3 Act as a father to, look after. *arch.* LME. 4 Name the father of (a child); fix the paternity of (a child) or origin or source of (a thing); attribute (a piece of work etc.). Foll. by †*of*, *on*, *upon*. M16. b *refl.* Indicate one's paternity. *obs.* exc. *dial.* L16. c Foist, impose *on*, *upon*. E19.

1 *fig.*: A. PRICE Arrogance that was fathered on pride by boredom. 2 LD MACAULAY By these two distinguished men Paterson's scheme was fathered. 4 D. LIVINGSTONE And coolly fathered the traffic on the Missionaries.

fatherhood /ˈfɑːðəhʊd/ *n.* Also †**-head**. LME. [f. FATHER *n.* + -HOOD, -HEAD.] 1 The quality or state of being a (real or spiritual) father. LME. †2 Paternal authority. LME–L17. †3 With possess. adj. (as *your* etc. *fatherhood*): a title of respect esp. to a high-ranking clergyman, (rarely) to God, and to any man with a claim to respect. LME–L17.

fatherless /ˈfɑːðəlɪs/ *a.* & *n.* LOE. [f. as prec. + -LESS.] A *adj.* 1 Without a father; having a dead, absent, or unknown father. LOE. 2 Of a book etc.: anonymous. *obs.* exc. as *fig.* use of sense 1. E17. B *absol.* as *n. pl. The* fatherless people as a class, *the* fatherless children as a class. LOE.

fatherlessness *n.* E18.

fatherlike /ˈfɑːðəlʌɪk/ *a.* & *adv.* LME. [f. as prec. + -LIKE.] A *adj.* †1 Resembling one's father. LME–E17. 2 Such as is proper to a father, fatherly. L16. B *adv.* In a fatherly manner, as a father. E16.

fatherly /ˈfɑːðəli/ *a.* LOE. [f. as prec. + -LY[1].] †1 Ancestral. LOE–M17. 2 Of or pertaining to a (real or spiritual) father; paternal. Now only of feelings, conduct, or character. LME.

fatherliness *n.* M16.

fatherly /ˈfɑːðəli/ *adv.* LME. [f. as prec. + -LY[2].] In a fatherly manner.

fathership /ˈfɑːðəʃɪp/ *n.* LME. [f. as prec. + -SHIP.] Fatherhood, paternity.

fathogram /ˈfaðəɡram/ *n.* M20. [f. FATHO(M *n.* + -GRAM.] A tracing, made by an echo-sounder, representing the varying depth of water beneath a moving vessel.

fathom /ˈfað(ə)m/ *n.* Pl. **-s**, (with a number also) same. [OE *fæþm* corresp. to OFris. *fethem*, OS *faþmos* pl. two arms outstretched (Du. *vadem*, *vaam* 6 feet), OHG *fadum* cubit (G *Faden* 6 feet), ON *faðmr* embrace, bosom, f. Gmc.] †1 In *pl.*, the embracing arms; *sing.* that which embraces or contains, a lap, a bosom. Only in OE. b *fig.* Grasp, power. OE–E17. 2 A measure of the length covered by the outstretched arms; this measure standardized to 6 feet (1.8288 m.), now chiefly used in soundings. Formerly also, a cubit. OE. †b The stretching of the arms to their fullest extent. E17–L18. c *fig.* (Breadth of) comprehension. *arch.* E17. d In *pl.* Depths. E17. 3 A quantity of esp. wood, coal, peat, etc., now usu. 6 ft square in cross-section, whatever the length. M16.

2 J. MASEFIELD The swaying weeds ten fathom beneath the keel. R. BOLT Take anchor rope . . it's a penny a fathom. C. S. LEWIS His pictures . . plunged me a few fathoms deeper into my delight. c SHAKES. *Oth.* Another of his fathom they have none. d T. MIDDLETON Swallow up his father . . Within the fathoms of his conscience.

fathom /ˈfað(ə)m/ *v.* [OE *fæþmian*, f. as FATHOM *n.*] 1 *v.t.* Encircle with extended arms as in measuring. Formerly also, embrace, clasp, envelop. *arch.* OE. 2 *v.t.* Measure the depth of (water) with a sounding line; sound; *fig.* get to the bottom of, penetrate, comprehend fully; investigate (†*into*). L16. 3 *v.i.* Take soundings (*lit.* & *fig.*). Formerly also, enquire *into*. E17.

1 SIR W. SCOTT Trees . . so thick that a man could not fathom them. 2 E. LONGFORD Her insatiable desire to fathom people's characters. R. OWEN I spent a long time trying to fathom this puzzling line of thought.

fathomable *a.* (earlier in UNFATHOMABLE) M17. **fathomer** *n.* a person who or an instrument which fathoms L16.

fathomless /ˈfað(ə)mlɪs/ *a.* E17. [f. prec. + -LESS.] †1 That cannot be encircled with the arms. *rare* (Shakes.). Only in E17. 2 Of measureless depth; incomprehensible. M17.

fathomlessly *adv.* E19.

fatidic /feɪˈtɪdɪk, fə-/ *a.* M17. [L *fatidicus*, f. *fatum* FATE *n.* + *-dicus*, f. weak var. of base *dicere* say: see -IC.] = next.

fatidical /feɪˈtɪdɪk(ə)l, fə-/ *a.* E17. [f. as prec. + -AL[1].] Prophetic; gifted with prophetic power.

fatigable /ˈfatɪɡəb(ə)l/ *a.* Also **fatiguable** /fəˈtiːɡ-/. E17. [OFr. f. late L *fatigabilis*, f. L *fatigare*: see FATIGUE *v.*, -ABLE. Cf. earlier INFATIGABLE.] Able to be fatigued; easily tired.

fatigaˈbility, **fatiguaˈbility** *n.* susceptibility to fatigue E20.

fatigate /ˈfatɪɡeɪt/ *v.t. obs.* exc. *dial.* M16. [L *fatigat-* pa. ppl stem of *fatigare* FATIGUE *v.*: see -ATE³.] = FATIGUE *v.* 1.

†**fatigation** *n.* LME–E18. [OFr. f. L *fatigatio(n-)*, f. as prec.: see -ATION.] Weariness; (an) action causing weariness.

fatiguable *a.* var. of FATIGABLE.

fatigue /fəˈtiːɡ/ *n.* M17. [Fr., f. as next.] 1 (An) action, task, or duty which causes weariness. M17. 2 Weariness caused by bodily or mental exertion. E18. b The condition of weakness in metals or other solid substances caused by cyclic variations in stress. Now esp. in *metal fatigue*. M19. c A condition of muscles, organs, cells, or (esp. luminescent) materials characterized by a (temporary) reduction in power, efficiency, or sensitivity following prolonged use or activity. L19. d A lessening of the response to charitable appeals and situations of need as a result of overexposure to them. Usu. as a 2nd elem. of comb. L20. 3 The non-military duty or duties of a soldier, sometimes allotted as punishment. L18. b In *pl.* Garments worn by a soldier on fatigue. M19. c = *fatigue-party* below. L19.

1 D. M. FRAME The aim of Montaigne's retirement . . was to rest from the fatigues of court. 2 D. LESSING Anna was now so tired . . that fatigue was like heavy hands dragging down her legs and her arms. c J. BRONOWSKI This is what causes fatigue, and blocks the muscle action until the blood can be cleaned with fresh oxygen. d *aid fatigue, compassion fatigue, donor fatigue*, etc. 3 H. WILLIAMSON One of the fatigues was the digging of ditches for the burying of water pipes. b E. JONG The kids buy . . war toys and child-sized fatigues.

Comb.: **fatigue-dress** the dress of a soldier on fatigue; **fatigue-party** a party of soldiers on fatigue.

fatigueless *a.* E19. **fatiguesome** *a.* (now *rare*) M18.

fatigue /fəˈtiːɡ/ *v.t.* L17. [(O)Fr. *fatiguer* f. L *fatigare* exhaust as with riding or working, weary, harass, f. *ad fatim, affatim* to satiety, to bursting, enough (cf. *fatiscare, -ari* burst open, gape open).] 1 Tire, weary, exhaust. L17. 2 Weaken (a material etc.) esp. by the application of stress; induce fatigue in (a muscle, organ etc.). L18.

fatiguingly *adv.* in a fatiguing manner, so as to cause fatigue E19.

Fatihah /ˈfɑːtɪhə, ˈfat-/ *n.* Also **-ha**; **Fatha** /ˈfɑːtə/. E19. [Arab. *al-Fātiḥa* the opening (Sura), use as n. of fem. pple *fātiḥa* opening, f. *fataḥa* to open.] The short first sura of the Koran, used by Muslims as an essential element of the ritual prayer.

fatiloquent /feɪˈtɪləkwənt/ *a. rare.* M17. [f. L *fatiloquus*, f. *fati-* comb. form of *fatum* FATE *n.* + *-loquus*, f. *loqui* speak, after *eloquent*, etc.] Prophetic; declaring fate.

Fatimid /ˈfatɪmɪd/ *n.* & *a.* Also **-ide** /-ʌɪd/. M19. [f. Arab. *Fāṭima* Fatima (see below) + -ID³.] (Designating or pertaining to) a descendant of Fatima, the daughter of Muhammad, and her husband Ali, cousin of Muhammad, esp. a member of the dynasty which ruled in parts of N. Africa, Egypt, and Syria from 909 to 1171.

Also **Fatimite** /-ʌɪt/ *n.* & *a.* E18.

fatiscent /fəˈtɪs(ə)nt/ *a.* E19. [L *fatiscent-* pres. ppl stem of *fatiscere* yawn: see -ENT.] Having chinks or clefts; cracked.

fatism *n.* var. of FATTISM.

fatling /ˈfatlɪŋ/ *n. arch.* E16. [f. FAT *v.* + -LING¹.] A calf, lamb, or other young animal fattened for slaughter.

fatness /ˈfatnɪs/ *n.* OE. [f. FAT *a.* + -NESS.] 1 The quality or state of being fat; plumpness, obesity. OE. †b Oiliness. Only in LME. †2 A greasy or oily substance; an unctuous layer or deposit in soil. OE–E18. 3 Richness, abundance (of food); fertility (of land). Formerly also, (a) fertilizing property or substance; the richest part of land etc. *arch.* exc. *US.* OE.

3 T. HARDY The oozing fatness and warm ferments of the Var Vale.

Fatso /ˈfatsəʊ/ *n. slang* (*joc.* & *derog.*). Pl. **-oes**. M20. [presumably f. pl. of FAT *n.*² fat person + -O.] (A nickname for) a fat person.

fatten /ˈfat(ə)n/ *v.* M16. [f. FAT *a.* + -EN⁵.] 1 *v.t.* Make fat (esp. animals for slaughter). M16. b *v.i.* Cause fatness. M17. 2 *v.t.* Fertilize, enrich, (soil etc.). M16. 3 *v.i.* Grow or become fat. (Foll. by †*in, on, with*). L17.

1 GIBBON The forest of Lucania, whose acorns fattened large droves of wild hogs. *fig.*: A. COOKE He tolerated, even fattened the newspaper myth of a locker-room tough guy. b T. COLLINS His cookery doesn't fatten, but it fills up. 3 V. S. PRITCHETT Bertie's pink face fattened with delight.

fattener *n.* a person who or thing which fattens; *esp.* an animal which fattens (early, slowly, etc.): E17. **fattening** *ppl a.* (*a*) causing fatness or increase in weight; (*b*) that grows fat: L17.

fattish /ˈfatɪʃ/ *a.* LME. [f. FAT *a.* + -ISH¹.] Somewhat fat; plump.

fattism /ˈfatɪz(ə)m/ *n.* Also **fatism**. L20. [f. FAT *a.* + -ISM.] Prejudice or discrimination against fat people.

fattist *n.* & *a.* (*a*) *n.* a person who practises fattism; (*b*) characterized by fattism: L20.

†**fattrels** *n.pl. Sc.* L18–E20. [Fr. †*fatraille* trumpery, things of no value.] Ribbon-ends; a loose, trailing piece of cloth etc.

fatty /ˈfati/ *a.* & *n.* LME. [f. FAT *a.*, *n.*² + -Y¹.] A *adj.* 1 Resembling or of the nature of fat; oily, greasy. LME. †2 (Of a plant) full of sap, juicy; (of an animal) plump. LME–E17. 3 Of soil: fertile, rich. LME. 4 Consisting of or containing fat; adipose. L15. 5 Marked by abnormal deposition of fat. M19.

Special collocations: **fatty acid** *Chem.* any of the series of open-chain carboxylic acids including those found as esters in fats and oils. **fatty degeneration** tissue degeneration, e.g. of the liver or heart, marked by the deposition of fat in the cells of the tissue.

B *n.* (A nickname for) a fat person. L18.

fattiness *n.* L16.

fatuitous /fəˈtjuːɪtəs/ *a.* M18. [f. next + -OUS.] Characterized by fatuity.

fatuity /fəˈtjuːɪti/ *n.* M16. [Fr. *fatuité* or L *fatuitas*, f. *fatuus* foolish: see -ITY.] The state or condition of being fatuous; folly (crass) stupidity; (now *rare* exc. *Sc. Law*) imbecility, dementia.

E. WAUGH The endless succession of Hollywood films, the slick second-rateness of the best of them, the blank fatuity of the worst.

fatuoid /ˈfatjʊɔɪd/ *n.* E20. [f. mod.L *fatua* (see below) fem. of L *fatuus* (see next) + -OID.] A mutant form of the cultivated oat, prob. representing a partial reversion to the wild oat, *Avena fatua*.

fatuous /ˈfatjʊəs/ *a.* E17. [f. L *fatuus* foolish, silly, insipid + -OUS.] †1 Tasteless, vapid. Only in E17. 2 Of a person, personal action, feeling, etc.: vacantly silly, purposeless, idiotic. M17. 3 In a state of dementia or imbecility. Now *rare* exc. *Sc. Law.* M18.

fatuously *adv.* L19. **fatuousness** *n.* L19.

fatwa /ˈfatwɑː/ *n.* Also **fetwa**. E17. [Arab. *fatwā*, f. *ʼaftā* decide a point of law: see MUFTI *n.*¹] A (usu. written) decision on a point of Islamic law given by a mufti.

faubourg /fobuːr (*pl. same*), ˈfəʊbʊəɡ/ *n.* L15. [Fr.: cf. med.L *falsus burgus* not the city proper.] A part of a town or city lying outside the gates, a suburb, *esp.* a suburb of Paris.

faucal /ˈfɔːk(ə)l/ *a.* M19. [f. next. + -AL¹.] = FAUCIAL; *spec.* in *Phonet.* (now *rare*), guttural.

fauces /ˈfɔːsiːz/ *n.pl.* LME. [L *fauces* throat.] *Anat.* The cavity at the back of the mouth from which the larynx and the pharynx open out.

faucet /ˈfɔːsɪt/ *n.*¹ LME. [(O)Fr. *fausset* f. Prov. *falset*, f. *falsar* bore (= (O)Fr. *fausser* damage, break into).] †1 A peg or spigot to stop the vent-hole in a cask etc. LME–M18. 2 A tap for drawing liquor from a barrel etc. Now *dial.* & *US.* LME. 3 A tap for drawing any liquid or gas from a pipe or vessel; *spec.* one providing access to a supply of piped water for household etc. *US.* M19. 4 The enlarged section of a pipe made to receive the spigot end of the next section. *US.* L19.

†**faucet** *n.*² L17–E18. [Alt. of FACET.] A facet; a faceted stone.

†**fauchion** *n.* var. of FALCHION.

faucial /ˈfɔːʃ(ə)l/ *a.* E19. [f. L *fauci-*, *fauces* FAUCES + -AL¹. Cf. FAUCAL.] Of, pertaining to, or proceeding from the fauces.

faugh /fɔː/ *int.* Also **foh**. M16. [Natural exclam.] Expr. disgust.

†**faulchion** *n.* var. of FALCHION.

Faulknerian /fɔːkˈnɪərɪən/ *a.* M20. [f. William *Faulkner* (see below) + -IAN.] Of or pertaining to the American novelist William Faulkner (1897–1962) or his writings.

fault /fɔːlt, fɒlt/ *n.* ME. [OFr. *faut(e)* (mod. *faute*) f. Proto-Romance use as n. of fem. and neut. of pa. pple of L *fallere* FAIL *v.*] 1 Deficiency, lack, or want *of*. Formerly also *absol.*, lack of food or necessities of life. Now *arch.* or *poet.* ME. †2 Default, failing, neglect. ME–L16. 3 A defect, imperfection, or blemish of character, constitution, structure, workmanship, appearance, etc. ME. 4 Something wrongly done; (a) transgression; (an) offence. LME. b A failure in an attempt; a slip, an error, a mistake. E16. c *Tennis* etc. A violation of the rules; a stroke or move which incurs a penalty; *esp.* a service in which the ball falls outside prescribed limits. L16. d *Showjumping*. A penalty point incurred for an error in performance. E20. 5 Responsibility for something wrong, culpability. Also, a defect causing something wrong or undesirable. LME. †6 An unsound or damaged place; *Mil.* a gap in the ranks. E16–L17. 7 *Hunting*. A break in the line of scent; loss of scent; a check caused by this. L16. 8 *Geol.* A fracture in a rock formation, marked by the relative displacement and discontinuity of strata on either side of the plane of the fracture. L18. 9 A break or other defect in an electric circuit. M19.

1 R. W. EMERSON And, fault of novel germs, Mature the unfallen fruit. 3 HOBBES Do not see . . any fault, in the administration of their common businesse. D. LIVINGSTONE His independence and love of the English were his only faults. c *foot-fault*: see FOOT *n.* 4 F. W. ROBERTSON A restless, undefinable sense of fault. B. JOWETT A fault which is most serious . . ; the fault of telling a lie. b I. WATTS There must be some fault in the deduction. 5 TENNYSON Creatures voiceless through the fault of birth. G. ORWELL It won't be my fault if old Victory Mansions doesn't have the biggest outfit of flags in the whole street. 6 SHAKES. *John* Patches set upon a little breach Discredit more in hiding of the fault. 8 *normal fault, overthrust fault, reverse fault, strike-slip fault, thrust fault, transform fault, wrench fault*, etc.

Phrases: **at fault** (*a*) *Hunting* having lost the scent; (*b*) puzzled, unsure what to do; (*c*) culpable, to blame. *double fault*: see DOUBLE *a.* & *adv.* **find fault (with)** make an adverse criticism (of), complain (of). **in fault** *arch.* culpable, at fault. **to a fault** (usu. of a commendable quality etc.) excessively. **with all faults** at the buyer's risk.

Comb.: **fault-block** a mass of displaced rock bounded by or between faults; **fault breccia**: consisting of compacted rock fragments produced by the mechanical stress of faulting and usu. lying along the line of the fault; **fault-finder** a person who (esp. habitually) finds fault; **fault-finding** *n.* & *a.* (*a*) *n.* the action or habit of finding fault, captious criticism; (*b*) *adj.* that finds fault, esp. habitually; **fault-line** *Geol.* the line of intersection of a fault with the earth's surface or with a horizontal plane (*fault-line scarp, valley*: produced secondarily along a fault-line by erosion).

faultful *a.* (*arch.*) faulty, culpable L16.

fault /fɔːlt, fɒlt/ *v.* LME. [f. the n. Perh. also infl. by OFr. *fauter.*] †1 *v.i.* Be wanting or absent. LME–E16. 2 *v.i.* Come short of an accepted standard, fail. Long *rare.* LME. 3 *v.i.* Commit a fault; go or do wrong; offend. (Foll. by *against, to, toward.*) *arch.* LME. 4 *v.t.* Find fault with, blame, censure. LME. b Declare to be or mark as faulty. L16. †5 *v.t.* Stand in need of, lack. LME–L15. †6 *v.i.* Be deficient or lacking *in*. E16–E17. †7 *v.i.* Make a mistake, blunder. M16–M18. 8 *v.t. Geol.* Cause a fault or faults in; break the continuity of (a stratum etc.). Chiefly as *faulted* ppl a., *faulting* vbl n. M19.

3 T. CARTWRIGHT He that marrieth another, faulteth against the former wife. BROWNING Had I died for thee I had faulted more. 4 *American Speech* Of all the productions of the publishing world, dictionaries are . . the most likely to be faulted by reviewers. b *Spectator* His final conclusion at least cannot be faulted. 7 CHESTERFIELD His tongue stammering and faulting.

faulting *n.* (*a*) the action of the vb; (*b*) *Geol.* an instance of causing a fault or faults, a break in the continuity of a stratum etc.: LME. **faulture** *n.* (*rare*) something blemished or imperfect, a failing, (the commission of) an error E19.

faulter /ˈfɔːltə, ˈfɒlt-/ *n. Sc.* & *north.* LME. [f. prec. + -ER[1].] A person who commits a fault; a culprit, an offender.

†faulter *v.* var. of FALTER *v.*[1]

faultless /ˈfɔːltlɪs, ˈfɒlt-/ *a.* LME. [f. FAULT *n.* + -LESS.] **1** Without defect, imperfection, or blemish; irreproachable. LME. **2** Guiltless, innocent. Long *obs.* exc. as passing into sense 1. E16.

1 E. A. FREEMAN The faultless model of a ruler. M. BARING Her French accent was perfect, her diction faultless.

faultlessly *adv.* E17. **faultlessness** *n.* L16.

faulty /ˈfɔːlti, ˈfɒlti/ *a.* LME. [Partly f. FAULT *n.* + -Y[1], partly after Fr. *fautif.*] **1** Defective, imperfect, blemished. LME. **2** Guilty; to blame. Long *rare* or *obs.* LME. **3** Of the nature of a fault; censurable, wrong. M16. **4** Having imperfections or failings. L16.

1 W. DAMPIER They made a new Boltsprit . . our old one being very faulty. I. MURDOCH Homer is imperfect. Science is imperfect. Any high thinking of which we are capable is faulty. 3 E. M. GOULBURN A faulty habit of mind. 4 J. BUTLER To forgive injuries . . so peculiarly becomes an imperfect, faulty creature. S. RICHARDSON His reputed faulty morals.

faultily *adv.* M16. **faultiness** *n.* M16.

faun /fɔːn/ *n.* LME. [(O)Fr. *faune* or L *Faunus* an ancient Italian god worshipped by shepherds and farmers and identified with Gk Pan.] *Class. Mythol.* A member of a class of ancient Italian rural deities in human form with goat's ears and tail (and later with goat's legs), characterized by lustfulness.

faunal *a.*[1] (*rare*) L16.

fauna /ˈfɔːnə/ *n.* Pl. **-nae** /-niː/, **-nas**. L18. [mod.L application of *Fauna*, an ancient Italian rural goddess, sister of *Faunus* (see prec.). Cf. FLORA.] **1** *collect. sing.* & in *pl.* The animals or animal life of a given area, habitat, or epoch. Cf. FLORA. L18. **2** A treatise or list of these. L19.

faunal *a.*[2] L19. **faunally** *adv.* M18. **faunist** *n.* an expert in or student of fauna M18. **fauˈnistic** *a.* of or pertaining to a faunist or fauna: L19. **fauˈnistical** *a.* faunistic L19. **fauˈnistically** *adv.* in a faunistic manner L19.

Fauntleroy /ˈfɔːntlərɔɪ/ *n.* L19. [f. the novel *Little Lord Fauntleroy* (1885) by Frances Hodgson Burnett.] More fully *Little Lord Fauntleroy* **1** *Fauntleroy suit, costume*, a boy's velvet suit with a lace collar. L19. **2** A boy resembling 'Little Lord Fauntleroy'; a gentle-mannered or elaborately dressed boy (freq. *iron.*). E20.

faunule /ˈfɔːnjuːl/ *n.* E20. [f. FAUNA + -ULE.] *Ecol.* The fauna of a specified small habitat, *esp.* a group of fossils from one small area.

fausen /ˈfɔːz(ə)n/ *n.* Long *obs.* exc. *dial.* M16. [Origin unkn.] An eel. Also *fausen-eel*.

faussebraie /ˈfɔːsbreɪ/ *n.* Also **-braye**. L15. [Fr., f. *fausse* fem. of *faux* false + *braie* = med.L *braca* dyke, embankment.] *Fortif.* An artificial mound or wall thrown up in front of the main rampart. Formerly also, a covered way.

faust /fɔːst/ *a. rare.* L17. [L *faustus*, f. base of *favere* favour.] Happy.

†faustity *n.* E17–E18.

Faustian /ˈfaʊstɪən/ *a.* L19. [f. Johann *Faust* (see below) + -IAN.] Of, pertaining to, or characteristic of Johann Faust (Johannes Faustus) a wandering astrologer and necromancer who lived in Germany *c* 1488–1541, who was reputed to have sold his soul to the Devil.

faute de mieux /fot də mjø/ *adv.* & *a. phr.* M18. [Fr.] (Used) for want of a better alternative.

†fauter *n.* var. of FAUTOR.

fauterer /ˈfɔːt(ə)rə/ *n.* Now *rare* or *obs.* M17. [Extended f. prec.: see -ER[1]. Cf. *caterer.*] = FAUTOR 1.

fauteuil /fotœːj/ *n.* Pl. pronounced same. M18. [Fr. f. OFr. *faudestuel, faldestoel*: see FALDSTOOL.] **1** An armchair. *arch.* M18. **2** A theatre stall, seat in a bus, etc., resembling an armchair. M19.

fautor /ˈfɔːtə/ *n.* Now *rare.* Also **†-er**. ME. [(O)Fr. *fauteur* f. L *fautor*, f. *favere* favour: see -OR.] **1** An adherent, a partisan, a supporter. ME. **†2** A protector, a patron. LME–L17.

fautorship *n.* the fact or condition of being a fautor M19. **†fautress** *n.* a female fautor L16–E18.

fauve /fəʊv/ *n.* & *a.* E20. [Fr., lit. 'wild animal'.] **A** *n.* = FAUVIST *n.* E20. **B** *adj.* = FAUVIST *a.* Also, vividly coloured. M20.

fauvism /ˈfəʊvɪz(ə)m/ *n.* E20. [Fr. *fauvisme*, f. as FAUVE + -ISM.] A style of painting with vivid use of colour, orig. that of the school of Henri Matisse (1869–1954).

fauvist /ˈfəʊvɪst/ *n.* & *a.* Also ***fauviste*** /fovist (*pl. of n. same*)/. E20. [Fr. *fauviste*, f. as FAUVE + -IST.] **A** *n.* An adherent of fauvism. E20. **B** *adj.* Of or pertaining to fauvism or fauvists. E20.

faux /fəʊ/ *a.* L20. [Fr.] Orig. & chiefly *Fashion.* Imitation, false, fake.

Time Not the real thing, of course, but thick faux furs.

faux bonhomme /fo bɔnɔm/ *n. phr.* Pl. ***faux bonshommes*** /fo bɔ̃zɔm/. E20. [Fr. = false good-natured man.] A sly and shifty person who assumes an open and good-natured manner.

faux-bourdon /foburdɔ̃/ *n.* Pl. pronounced same. L19. [Fr.] = FABURDEN.

faux-naïf /fonaif, fəʊnʌɪˈiːf/ *n.* & *a.* Pl. pronounced same. M20. [Fr., f. as *faux* false + NAÏF.] **A** *n.* A person who pretends to be ingenuous or naive. M20. **B** *adj.* **1** Of a work of art: self-consciously or meretriciously simple and artless. M20. **2** Of a person: pretendedly ingenuous or naive. M20.

faux pas /fo pɑ, fəʊ ˈpɑː/ *n. phr.* Pl. same /pɑ, ˈpɑːz/. L17. [Fr., f. *faux* false + *pas* step.] A false step; an act that compromises one's (esp. a woman's) reputation; an offence against social convention; an indiscreet remark or action.

fave /feɪv/ *n.* & *a. slang.* M20. [Abbrev.] **A** *n.* = FAVOURITE *n.* 1. M20. **B** *adj.* = FAVOURITE *a.* M20.

†favel *n.* ME. [OFr. *fauvel*, f. *fauve* fallow-coloured: see -EL[2].] **1** (The name of) a fallow-coloured or chestnut horse, *esp.* one proverbial as the type of fraud, cunning, or duplicity. Chiefly in *curry favel* (see CURRY *v.*[1] 1). ME–E17. **2** (The personification of) cunning or duplicity. LME–L16.

favela /faˈvela/ *n.* M20. [Port.] A Brazilian shack, shanty, or slum. Usu. in *pl.*

Faverolle /ˈfavərɒl, -ˈrəʊl/ *n.* E20. [Prob. f. *Faverolles* in the department of Seine-et-Oise, France.] (A bird of) a breed of domestic fowl originated in France by crossing light Brahmas or Dorkings with Houdans.

favic /ˈfeɪvɪk/ *a.* L19. [f. FAVUS + -IC.] *Med.* Of or pertaining to favus.

favism /ˈfeɪvɪz(ə)m/ *n.* Also **-bism** /-bɪz(ə)m/. E20. [f. It. *favismo*, f. *fava* broad bean f. L *faba* bean: see -ISM.] *Med.* An allergic syndrome involving haemolytic anaemia, manifested after eating or exposure to broad beans and associated with an inherited enzyme deficiency.

favonian /fəˈvəʊnɪən/ *a.* M17. [L *favonianus*, f. *Favonius* the west wind: see -IAN.] Of or pertaining to the west wind; gentle, propitious.

favor *n., v.*, **favorable** *a.*, etc., see FAVOUR *n.* etc.

favour /ˈfeɪvə/ *n.* Also ***favor**. ME. [OFr. *favour, -or* (mod. *faveur*) f. L *favor, -oris*, f. *favere* regard with good will, rel. to *fovere* cherish.] **1** Propitious or friendly regard; esteem, liking. Formerly also, a liking, a preference. ME. **b** Approving disposition towards a thing; inclination to commend, sanction, or adopt. E19. **2** Kindness beyond what is due or usual; gracious or friendly action arising from special goodwill. LME. **b** An instance of this; an act of exceptional kindness as opp. to one of duty or justice; *euphem.* in *pl.*, a woman's allowing of sexual intercourse with her. L16. **c** *Comm.* A letter. *arch.* M17. **3 †a** Lenity, mitigation of punishment; a lenient act. Also, an indulgence, a privilege. LME–L18. **b** Leave, permission, pardon. *arch.* L16. **4** Partiality towards a litigant etc., too lenient or too generous treatment. LME. **5** Aid, support, furtherance. LME. **6** Something which draws affection or goodwill; attraction, beauty; an attraction, a charm. *arch.* LME. **7** Appearance, aspect, look. *arch.* L15. **b** The countenance, the face. *arch.* E16. **†c** A feature. L16–M17. **8** Something given or worn as a mark of favour, celebration, or allegiance, as a knot of ribbons, a rosette, a cockade, etc. L16.

1 SIR W. SCOTT His young Life-guardsman, for whom he seemed to have taken a special favour. LD MACAULAY Rochester . . stood high in the favour of the King. *curry favour*: see CURRY *v.*[1] 5. **find favour (in the eyes of)** be liked (by), prove acceptable (to). 2 SIR W. SCOTT I have a friend . . who will . . do me so much favour. b TENNYSON I came to ask a favour of you. N. MARSH Do me a favour and get the hell out of this, will you? 3a SHAKES. *Merch. V.* That, for this favour, He presently become a Christian. b **under favour** if one may venture to say so. 4 P. MASSINGER Not swayed or by favour or affection. *a fair field and no favour*: see FIELD *n. without fear or favour*: see FEAR *n.*[1] 5 J. S. C. ABBOTT He begged permission, under favor of the night, to surprise the Bellerophon. **in favour of** on behalf of, in support of, on the side of, to the advantage of. **in one's favour** to a person's advantage. 6 AV *Ecclus* 40:21 Thine eye desireth fauour and beautie. A. HELPS It takes away much of the favour of life. 7 T. FULLER Palestine . . tricked and trimmed with many new Cities, had the favour thereof quite altered. W. RAND To learn the favour of his Countenance from his Picture. b J. RAY By their virtuous behaviour compensate the hardness of their Favour. 8 W. HOLTBY Paper caps bearing the favours of the Kingsport team. T. H. WHITE The great champion would fight under a favour of her own.

favourless *a.* (long *rare*) E16.

favour /ˈfeɪvə/ *v.* Also ***favor**. LME. [OFr. *favorer* f. med.L *favorare*, f. L *favor*: see prec.] **1** *v.t.* Regard with favour; have a liking or preference for; approve. LME. **2** *v.t.* Show favour to, treat kindly; countenance, encourage. LME. **b** Indulge or oblige (a person) *with*. LME. **†3** *v.i.* Show favour (*un*)*to*. LME–M16. **4** *v.t.* Treat with partiality; side with, take the part of. LME. **5** *v.t.* Aid, support; show oneself propitious to. LME. **b** Of a circumstance, fact, etc.: lend confirmation or support to (esp. a belief, doctrine, etc.); point in the direction of. M16. **6** *v.t.* Deal gently with; avoid putting too much strain on (a limb etc.); ease, save, spare. *colloq.* E16. **7** *v.t.* Resemble in face or features; occas., have a look of. *colloq.* E17. **8** *v.t.* Of circumstances, weather, etc.: prove advantageous to (a person); be the means of promoting (an operation or process); facilitate. M17.

1 E. STILLINGFLEET Josephus seems to favour the division of the City into three parts. 2 S. BUTLER A strong bias within . . to favour the deceit. Q. BELL To be, if not spoiled, outrageously favoured. b LYTTON Fielding twice favoured me with visits. 4 OED The examiner was accused of having favoured his own pupils. 5 BURKE If Providence should . . favour the allied arms. *absol.*: BROWNING Had but fortune favored. b C. C. ABBOTT Every indication favored rain. 6 DICKENS This habit . . favours my infirmity. 7 E. WELTY Becky's the one she takes after. . . You don't favor him. 8 W. THOMSON The darkness of the night favoured the enterprise.

favourer *n.* LME.

favourable /ˈfeɪv(ə)rəb(ə)l/ *a.* Also ***favorable**. ME. [(O)Fr. *favorable* f. L *favorabilis*, f. *favor*: see FAVOUR *n.*, -ABLE.] **1** That regards with favour; inclined to countenance or help; well-disposed, propitious. ME. **b** Gracious; kindly, obliging. Now *arch. rare.* E16. **†2** Winning favour; pleasing; comely. LME–L16. **b** Admissible, allowable. *rare.* Only in M17. **†3** Showing undue favour, partial, (*to*). Only in LME. **4** Advantageous, convenient; facilitating one's purpose or wishes; helpful, suitable. LME.

5 That is in favour of, approving, commendatory. M17. †b Tending to palliate or extenuate. L17–L18. 6 That concedes what is required or requested; auspicious, promising; giving consent. M18. b Of a patient's condition, progress, etc.: satisfactory, favouring recovery. E20.

1 SHAKES. *Tam. Shr.* Happier the man whom favourable stars Allots thee for his lovely bedfellow. E. A. FREEMAN King Swegen was lending a favourable ear to their prayers. b SHAKES. *2 Hen. IV* Unless some dull and favourable hand will whisper music to my weary spirit. 4 CLARENDON A place very favourable for the making Levies of Men. T. PENNANT Sail with a favourable breeze. 5 DEFOE Giving a favourable account of the place. 6 GIBBON The eunuch . . soon returned with a favourable oracle.

favourableness *n.* M16. **favourably** *adv.* LME.

favoured /ˈfeɪvəd/ *a.*[1] Also ***favored**. LME. [f. FAVOUR *n.* + -ED[2].] Having a favour or favours of a specified kind; *esp.* having a specified sort of appearance or features. Chiefly as 2nd elem. of comb., as *well-favoured* etc.

favouredly *adv.* M16. **favouredness** *n.* M16.

favoured /ˈfeɪvəd/ *a.*[2] Also ***favored**. M17. [f. FAVOUR *v.* + -ED[1].] Having been favoured.

G. GREENE The favoured few who visited him at Rye. **most favoured nation**: to which a State has granted by treaty etc. the greatest political or commercial privileges, *esp.* to which a State accords the lowest scale of import duties.

favourite /ˈfeɪv(ə)rɪt/ *n.* & *a.* Also ***favorite**. L16. [Fr. †*favorit* (now *favori*, *-ite*) f. It. *favorito* pa. pple of *favorire*, f. *favore* FAVOUR *n.*] A *n.* 1 A person or thing regarded with particular favour and preferred above others. L16. b A competitor generally expected to win; *esp.* a race-horse etc. at the shortest odds. E19. 2 A chosen intimate companion of a monarch or other person in power, esp. when unduly favoured. L16. †3 A supporter, a well-wisher, a friend, a follower. Only in L16. 4 A curl or lock of hair hanging loose on the temple (as fashionable during the 17th and 18th cents.). *obs.* exc. *Hist.* L17.

1 DAY LEWIS She sang . . 'Kathleen Mavourneen' and other popular favourites of the time. S. BELLOW An older brother was the favourite; she was neglected. b H. CECIL The favourite for the Oaks is My Conscience and the betting on it is 2 to 1 against. 2 S. SPENDER D— . . behaved to me like a spoiled favourite towards a mad prince. 3 SHAKES. *1 Hen. VI* This factious bandying of their favourites. 4 J. GAY Sooner I would . . with immodest fav'rites shade my face.

B *adj.* Regarded with especial favour or liking, preferred above others. E18.

S. KAUFFMANN A bottle of their favourite wine, sparkling Burgundy. A. THWAITE They treated him like a favourite nephew—sharing his interests, listening to his poems. **favourite son** *US* a person who has endeared himself particularly to his country or State; *esp.* a candidate for presidential or other high office who has the support of the constituency or the political leaders of his own State.

favouritism /ˈfeɪv(ə)rɪtɪz(ə)m/ *n.* Also ***favoritism**. M18. [f. prec. + -ISM.] 1 Undue partiality; the unfair favouring of one person or group at the expense of another. M18. 2 The state or condition of being a favourite. E19.

1 I. D'ISRAELI Truth will always prevail over literary favouritism. 2 *Times* Grattan continued to enjoy its favouritism with the analysts, rising another 6p.

favus /ˈfeɪvəs/ *n.* M16. [L = honeycomb.] *Med.* A contagious skin disease affecting the face and scalp, characterized by yellow crusts made up of the threads of the fungus *Trichophyton schoenleini* and skin debris; a similar disease affecting fowls. Also called *honeycomb ringworm*.

fawn /fɔːn/ *n.*[1] & *a.* LME. [(O)Fr. *faon* (†*foun*, †*feon*) f. Proto-Romance, f. L *fetus* offspring, FOETUS.] A *n.* 1 A young deer, esp. a fallow deer; a buck or doe of the first year. LME. †2 *gen.* A young animal, a cub. L15–E17. 3 A light yellowish brown. L19.

1 **in fawn** (of a deer) pregnant.

Comb.: **fawn-colour(ed)** (of) the colour fawn.

B *adj.* Of a light yellowish brown. M20.

†**fawn** *n.*[2] L16–M18. [f. FAWN *v.*[1]] An act of fawning; a servile cringe.

fawn /fɔːn/ *v.*[1] ME. [Var. (repr. OE *fagnian*) of FAIN *v.*[1]] 1 *v.i.* Of an animal, esp. a dog: show affection or pleasure esp. by tail-wagging, grovelling, or whining. ME. †2 *v.t.* Fawn on; caress. ME–L15. 3 *v.i.* Behave servilely or abjectly; affect a cringing pleasure or fondness. ME.

With preps. in specialized senses: **fawn on, upon** (*a*) show delight at the presence of; lavish caresses on; (*b*) affect a servile fondness for, behave cringingly to.

fawner *n.* a person who fawns, cringes, or flatters, a toady LME.

fawn /fɔːn/ *v.*[2] LME. [f. FAWN *n.*[1]] 1 *v.t.* Of a deer: give birth to (a fawn). Long *rare* or *obs.* LME. 2 *v.i.* Give birth to a fawn. L15.

fawning /ˈfɔːnɪŋ/ *a.* LME. [f. FAWN *v.*[1] + -ING[2].] 1 Showing affection or pleasure by tail-wagging etc.; fondling. LME. 2 Showing servile deference, flattering. L16.

fawningly *adv.* L16. **fawningness** *n.* a fawning disposition or demeanour, cringing behaviour, servility L17.

fax /faks/ *n.*[1] Long *obs.* exc. *dial.* [OE *feax* = OFris. *fax*, OS, OHG *fahs*, ON *fax* (Norw. *faks*).] The hair of the head.

¶The final element in the names *Fairfax*, *Halifax*.

faxed *a.* having hair, hairy; *faxed star*, a comet: OE.

fax /faks/ *n.*[2] *pl. informal.* M19. [Repr. pronunc.] Facts.

fax /faks/ *n.*[3] & *v.* M20. [Repr. abbrev. of FACSIMILE.] A *n.* 1 Facsimile; facsimile telegraphy; *esp.* a message etc. sent or a copy obtained by such a method. M20. 2 A fax machine. L20.

Comb.: **fax machine**: for sending and receiving faxes.

B *v.t.* Transmit by facsimile telegraphy. L20.

faxable *a.* L20. **faxer** *n.* L20.

fay /feɪ/ *n.*[1] Long *arch. rare.* ME. [OFr. *fei* (mod. *foi*), earlier *feit*, *feid*: see FAITH.] Faith.

G. P. R. JAMES By my fay, the place seems a fortress instead of an abbey.

fay /feɪ/ *n.*[2] *literary.* LME. [OFr. *fa(i)e* (mod. *fée*) f. L *fata* the Fates (pl. of *fatum* FATE *n.*) taken as fem. sing. in Proto-Romance.] A fairy.

fay /feɪ/ *n.*[3] M18. [f. FAY *v.*[2]] Surface soil, esp. containing loose stones etc. and needing to be cleared; dross.

fay /feɪ/ *n.*[4] E20. [Abbrev.] = OFAY.

fay /feɪ/ *v.*[1] [OE *fēgan* = OS *fogian* (Du. *voegen*), OHG *fuogen* (G *fügen*) f. WGmc.] †1 *v.t.* Fit, adapt, or join (*lit.* & *fig.*); put together; fix in position. OE–ME. 2 *v.i.* Suit, do, go on favourably, succeed. *obs.* exc. *dial.* ME. 3a *v.t.* Fit (a piece of timber) closely and accurately *to* (another). M18. b *v.i.* Of a piece of timber: fit closely to another, so as to leave no intervening space. M18. 4 *v.i.* Fit *in*, fit. *US.* M19.

fay /feɪ/ *v.*[2]*t.* Now *dial.* ME. [ON *fægja*.] Cleanse; cleanse and polish; clean out; clear away.

fayalite /ˈfeɪəlʌɪt/ *n.* M19. [f. *Fayal*, an island in the Azores: see -ITE[1].] *Min.* An orthorhombic iron silicate which is an end-member of the olivine family of minerals.

fayence *n.* & *a.* var. of FAIENCE.

fayre *n.* see FAIR *n.*[1]

faze /feɪz/ *v.*[1]*t.* Orig. *US.* Also **phase**. M19. [Var. of FEEZE *v.*] Disconcert, perturb. (Usu. in neg. contexts.)

F. ROBB Although Cope might be only a fishing skipper no gilded plutocrat was going to faze him.

†**faze** *v.*[2] see FEAZE *v.*

fazenda /fəˈzɛndə/ *n.* E19. [Port. = Sp. HACIENDA.] In Portugal, Brazil, and other Portuguese-speaking countries: an estate, a large farm; the homestead belonging to such an estate etc.

fazendeiro /fazɛnˈdɛːrəʊ/ *n.* a person who owns or occupies a fazenda E19.

†**fazle** *v.i.* LME–M17. [Rel. to G *faselen*, Du. *vezelen*.] Ravel (*out*).

†**feague** *v.t.* Also **feak**. See also FIG *v.*[3] L16. [Perh. f. as next. Cf. FAKE *v.*[2]] 1 Beat, whip; punish; bring down. Foll. by *away*: set going briskly, work hard at. L16–E19. 2 = FIG *v.*[3] 2. Only in L18.

feak /fiːk/ *v.*[1] Also (earlier) **feat** /fiːt/. E16. [G *fegen* cleanse, sweep.] *Falconry.* 1 *v.t.* Wipe (the beak); wipe the beak of. E16. 2 *v.i.* Of a hawk: wipe the beak after feeding. L16.

feak *v.*[2] var. of FEAGUE.

feal *n.* var. of FAIL *n.*[2]

feal /fiːl/ *a. arch.* M16. [OFr., alt. of *feil* f. L *fidelis*: see next.] Faithful, constant, loyal.

fealty /ˈfiːəlti/ *n.* ME. [OFr. *feau(l)te*, *fealte* (mod. *féauté*) f. L *fidelitas*, f. *fidelis* faithful, f. *fides* FAITH: see -TY[1].] 1 A feudal tenant or vassal's (acknowledgement of the obligation of) fidelity to his lord. ME. 2 *gen.* Allegiance, fidelity. M16.

1 G. BURNET The Bishops were also obliged to swear fealty to the Prince. SIR W. SCOTT Each bent the knee To Bruce in sign of fealty.

fear /fɪə/ *n.*[1] [OE *fǣr* corresp. to OS *vār* ambush, MDu. *vare* fear (Du. *gevaar* danger), OHG *fāra* ambush, stratagem, danger, deceit (G *Gefahr* danger), f. Gmc.] †1 A sudden calamity; danger. Only in OE. 2 The painful emotion caused by the sense of impending danger or evil; an instance of this. ME. b A state of alarm or dread. ME. 3 Apprehension or dread *of*, *to do*, *that*, *lest*. Esp. in *for fear* (*of* etc.) in order to avoid the risk (of). ME. b A feeling of mingled dread and reverence towards God or (formerly) any rightful authority. ME. 4 Reason for alarm. Also formerly, something that is to be dreaded. Now *rare*. LME. †b Ability to inspire fear. E–M17. 5 Solicitude, anxiety for the safety of a person or thing. Now chiefly in (*in*, *for*) *fear of one's life*. L15.

2 A. N. WILSON Fear gripped him, a quite physical sensation, a tightening of the lungs, a weak fluttering in the stomach. F. WELDON 'Cows kill four people a year . . ' said Bella, who always had a statistic to back up a fear. *personified*: COLERIDGE Pale Fear Haunted by ghastlier shapings. b E. GRIFFITH I set out . . in fear and trembling. 3 H. KELLER I could not suppress an inward fear . . lest I should fail. J. GARDNER The fear that every minute detail might not go perfectly. L. DEIGHTON Extension phones that a servant could use to eavesdrop without fear of discovery. b AV *Ps.* III:10 The feare of the Lord is the beginning of wisedome. 4 COVERDALE *Ps.* 53:5 They are afrayed, where no feare is.

Phrases: *for fear* (*of* etc.): see sense 3 above. **put the fear of God into** terrify. **without fear or favour** impartially. **no fear** *colloq.* no chance, not likely, certainly not.

fear *n.*[2] var. of FIAR *n.*

fear /fɪə/ *v.* [OE *fǣran* = OS *fāron* lie in wait (MDu. *vaeren* fear), OHG *fārēn* plot against, lie in wait, ON *færa* taunt, slight: cf. Goth. *ferjans* pl., liers-in-wait.] I1 *v.t.* Inspire with fear, frighten. Now *arch.* & *dial.* OE. †2 *v.t.* Drive (*away*, *to*, *into*) by fear. LME–M17. b Deter *from* (a course of conduct etc.) LME–M17.

2 SHAKES. *Meas. for M.* A scarecrow . . to fear the birds.

II3 *v.t.* Revere (esp. God). OE. 4 *v.i.* & (*arch.*) *refl.* Be afraid (*lest*, †*of*). LME. 5 *v.t.* Be afraid of (a person, thing, or anticipated event); hesitate *to do*; shrink from *doing*. LME. 6 *v.i.* Be apprehensive *for*. LME. †b *v.t.* Be apprehensive about. M16–M17. 7 *v.t.* Have an uneasy sense of the probability of, be afraid *that*; apprehend or anticipate (something unpleasant). L15. †8 Regard with distrust; doubt. L16–M18.

3 DEFOE If you fear God . . as your father. 4 C. MARLOWE I fear me he is slain. **never fear** *colloq.* there is no danger of that. 5 DRYDEN He would have spoke, but . . fear'd Offence. E. CLODD What man cannot understand he fears. 6 DRYDEN Let the greedy merchant fear for his ill-gotten gain. 7 A. TROLLOPE I fear we are all in your black books. M. PATTISON London had ceased to fear a foreign foe.

feared *ppl a.* (*a*) (now *dial.*) frightened, afraid; timid (*of*, *for*, *to do*); (*b*) regarded with fear: ME. **fearer** *n.* M16. **fearingly** *adv.* †(*a*) in a terrifying manner; (*b*) timidly: M16.

fearful /ˈfɪəfʊl, -f(ə)l/ *a.* & *adv.* ME. [f. FEAR *v.* + -FUL.] A *adj.* I1 Causing fear or terror; dreadful, terrible; inspiring reverence. ME. 2 Notable of its kind, esp. in badness; annoying; exceedingly bad, long, boring, etc. *colloq.* M17.

1 W. FULKE A flying Dragon . . very fearefull to looke upon. 2 DAY LEWIS As a result of . . arriving a whole day late . . I got into a fearful fluster.

II 3 Frightened; timid, apprehensive, nervous. (Foll. by *of*, *that*, *lest*, *to do*.) LME. †b Anxious *about*, *of* (something). M–L16. †4 Cautious, wary. E16–L18. 5 Of a look, word, etc.: showing signs of fear. M16. 6 Full of reverence. L16.

3 ADDISON Th' impatient Greyhound . . Bounds . . to catch the fearful Hare. 5 SOUTHEY Hasty, yet faltering in his fearful speech.

B *adv.* Exceedingly, excessively. Now *dial.* M17.

fearfully *adv.* (*a*) dreadfully, terribly; to a fearful extent; *colloq.* exceedingly, excessively; (*b*) timidly, nervously, anxiously, cautiously: LME. **fearfulness** *n.* the quality or state of being affected by fear; the capacity of inspiring fear: LME.

fearless /ˈfɪəlɪs/ *a.* L16. [f. FEAR *n.*[1] + -LESS.] 1 Unaffected by fear, bold; showing no sign of fear. L16. †2 Not regarded with fear; giving no cause for fear. L16–M18.

fearlessly *adv.* L16. **fearlessness** *n.* E17.

fearnought /ˈfɪənɔːt/ *n.* & *a.* M18. [f. FEAR *v.* (in imper.) + NOUGHT.] (Of) a strong thick kind of woollen cloth used for weather-resistant clothes, porthole covers, etc. Cf. DREADNOUGHT *n.* 1.

Also **fearnothing** *n.* & *a.* E18.

fearsome /ˈfɪəs(ə)m/ *a.* M18. [f. FEAR *v.*, *n.*[1] + -SOME[1].] Fear inspiring; frightful, dreadful; appalling, esp. in appearance.

fearsomely *adv.* L19. **fearsomeness** *n.* L19.

†**feasance** *n.* M16–M18. [AN *fesa(u)nce*, (O)Fr. *faisance*, f. *fais-* pres. stem of *faire* do: see -ANCE.] The execution of a condition, obligation, feudal service, etc.

feasibility /fiːzɪˈbɪlɪti/ *n.* E17. [f. next: see -ITY.] 1 The quality or state of being feasible. E17. 2 A feasible thing. *rare.* M17.

Comb.: **feasibility report**, **study**: on or into the practicability of a proposed plan.

feasible /ˈfiːzɪb(ə)l/ *a.* LME. [(O)Fr. *faisable*, †*faisible*, f. *fais-* pres. stem of *faire* do: see -IBLE.] Practical, possible; manageable, convenient, serviceable; *colloq.* plausible.

D. LIVINGSTONE It seems feasible that a legitimate . . trade might take the place of the present unlawful traffic. D. LODGE Christian unity is now a feasible objective for the first time since the Reformation.

feasibleness *n.* M17. **feasibly** *adv.* M17.

feast /fiːst/ *n.* ME. [OFr. *feste* (mod. *fête*), f. L *festa* neut. pl. (taken as fem. sing. in Proto-Romance) of *festus* festal, joyous. Cf. FÊTE *n.*] 1 A religious anniversary observed with rejoicing. ME. b An annual village festival (orig. held on the feast-day of the saint to whom the parish church is dedicated). M16. 2 A sumptuous meal or entertainment; a banquet, esp. public, for many guests. Also formerly, a series of such entertainments. ME. †3 Rejoicing, festivity. ME–M17. 4 An ample and delicious meal; *fig.* delight or gratification to the mind or senses. LME.

2 BUNYAN Mr. Carnal Security did again make a feast for the town of Mansoul. 4 T. GRAY Voices, that were a perfect feast to ears that had heard nothing but French operas. TOLKIEN The evening meal seemed a feast . . wine . . bread and butter, and salted meats, and dried fruits, and good red cheese.

Phrases: *double feast*: see DOUBLE *a.* & *adv.* *feast of* EXPIATION. **feast of reason** intellectual talk. *feast of weeks*: see WEEK *n.* **immovable feast** a religious feast celebrated on the same date every year. **make feast** (*a*) *arch.* make merry; feast; †(*b*) show honour or respect to, make much of (a person); fête. **movable feast** a religious feast of which the date varies from year to year; *joc.* a meal etc. taken at no regular time.

Comb.: **feast-day**: on which a feast is held.

feast /fiːst/ *v.* ME. [OFr. *fester* (mod. *fêter*), f. as prec. Cf. FÊTE *v.*] 1 *v.i.* & (*arch.*) *t.* w. *it.* Partake of a feast; feed sumptuously *on*, *upon*; *fig.* regale or gratify oneself *on*, *upon*. ME. †b *v.i.* Enjoy oneself. *rare* (Shakes.). Only in E17. 2 *v.t.* Provide a feast for; entertain sumptuously; pass (time etc.) *away* in feasting; *fig.* regale, gratify. ME.

1 LYTTON I have . . feasted upon the passions. V. CRONIN Feasting late at night on oysters, champagne and spiced dishes. 2 DEFOE Our men . . feast themselves here with fresh provisions. E. L. DOCTOROW She . . feasted her eyes on the little girl.

feaster *n.* †(*a*) a provider of a feast; (*b*) a partaker of a feast; a person who lives luxuriously: LME.

feastful /ˈfiːstfʊl, -f(ə)l/ *a. arch.* LME. [f. prec. + -FUL. Perh. suggested by FESTIVAL.] Of or pertaining to feasting; given to feasting; festive.

feat /fiːt/ *n.* LME. [OFr. *fet*, (also mod.) *fait* f. L *factum* FACT.] †1 An action, a deed, a course of conduct; overt action. LME–M18. b = FACT 1b. L15–M16. 2 A noteworthy act or achievement; an action showing dexterity or strength; a surprising trick. Formerly esp. a noble or brave deed. LME. †3 A kind of action; a pursuit, an employment, an art, a profession. LME–M17. †4 The art or knack of doing something. LME–L17. †5 Fact; actuality. LME–E16.

1 SIR W. SCOTT He changed his mortal frame By feat of magic mystery. 2 J. B. MORTON The feat of remaining under water for half an hour in a steel casket has been performed by an Egyptian. M. HUNTER A leader, who outdid them all in feats of daring. D. FRASER He speared a wolf . . a rare feat.

feat of arms an achievement in battle or tournament, esp. in single combat.

feat /fiːt/ *a.* & *adv.* Now *arch.* & *dial.* ME. [OFr. *fet* (mod. *fait*) f. L *factus* lit. 'made (for something)': see FACT.] A *adj.* 1 Fitting, suitable, *for*, *to*; becoming; elegant; neat. ME. 2 Apt; smart, adroit; deft; dexterous, nimble. LME. †3 Affected. M16–E18.

1 SHAKES. *Temp.* Look how well my garments sit upon me, Much feater than before. 2 J. GAY The featest maid That e'er . . delightsome gambol play'd.

B *adv.* Featly. Now *rare* or *obs.* LME.

featness *n.* L16.

†**feat** *v.*[1]*t.* LME. [f. FEAT *a.*] 1 Equip, make fit. LME–L17. 2 Show as elegant. *rare* (Shakes.). Only in E17.

feat *v.*[2] see FEAK *v.*[1]

feather /ˈfɛðə/ *n.* [OE *feþer* = OFris. *fethere*, OS *feþara* (Du. *veer*), OHG *fedara* (G *Feder*), ON *fjǫðr* f. Gmc, f. IE base repr. also by Skt *patra* wing, Gk *pteron*, *pterux* wing, L *penna* PEN *n.*[2]] I As an appendage. 1 Any of the appendages growing from a bird's skin, consisting of a partly hollow horny shaft or midrib, fringed with vanes of barbs; in *pl.*, plumage. OE. †2 In *pl.* Wings. OE–E17. 3 Plumage; *fig.* attire. ME. b (A) type of plumage; (a) species (of bird). L16. 4 A bird; *collect.* gamebirds. E17.

1 N. TINBERGEN Fighting Cranes preen their feathers in between fights. 2 W. RALEIGH Josephus gave all Noah's children feathers, to carry them far away. 3 THACKERAY I saw him in full clerical feather. b S. RUTHERFORD Fowls of a feather flock together.

II As a detached object. 5 A feather as a detached object; in *pl.* or *collect.*, feathers as a material. OE. †6 A pen. OE–L18. 7 A piece or pieces of feather attached to the base of an arrow, to direct its flight; a flight. LME. 8 A plume worn as a decoration or crest. LME. 9 A very light object; a trivial thing. M16. b = FEATHERWEIGHT 1. M18.

7 R. BOYLE The Feathers that wing our Arrows. 9 SHAKES. *All's Well* You boggle shrewdly; every feather starts you.

III Something resembling a feather. 10 a A tuft of hair, *esp.* one standing upright on a person's head or growing in a different direction to the rest of a horse's coat. M16. b A fringe of long hair on the legs etc. of a dog, horse, etc. L16. c The foamy crest of a wave; the wake left by a submarine periscope. M19. 11 A projecting rib or tongue on an implement, piece of machinery, etc.; *esp.* one intended to fit into a groove. Also, a longitudinal strengthening rib on a shaft. M18. 12 *Confectionery.* One of the degrees in boiling sugar. Now *rare.* E19. 13 A blemish or flaw resembling a feather (in an eye, a precious stone, etc.). M19.

IV [f. the vb.] 14 *Rowing.* The action of feathering. M19.

Phrases: **a feather in one's cap, hat**, etc. (*fig.*) an achievement to be proud of. *birds of a feather*: see BIRD *n.* CONTOUR *feather*. *fine feathers*: see FINE *a.* & *adv.* **in fine, full, high**, etc. **feather** in good spirits, health, or condition. *fur and feather*: see FUR *n.*[1] 2c. **of the same, that, every, feather** of the same etc. kind or character. *Prince of Wales' feathers*: see PRINCE *n.* **(show) the white feather** (display) cowardice (a white feather in a game-bird's tail being a mark of bad breeding). **smooth a person's ruffled** etc. **feathers** restore a person's equanimity, appease a person. **you could have knocked me** etc. **down with a feather** I etc. was astonished.

Comb.: **feather-brain** a foolish, dim-witted person or intelligence; **feather-brained** *a.* foolish, dim-witted; **feather-cut** a hairstyle in which hair is cut to be thin and wispy like a feather; **feather duster** a brush made of feathers for dusting; **feather-foil** water violet, *Hottonia palustris*; **feather-grass** a Eurasian perennial grass, *Stipa pennata*, grown as an ornamental for its feathery inflorescences; **feather-footed** *a.* having feet covered with feathers; *fig.* moving silently and quickly; **feather-head** = *feather-brain* above; **feather-headed** *a.* = *feather-brained* above; *feather* HYACINTH; **featherman** (*obs.* exc. *Hist.*) a dealer in feathers; **feather ore** jamesonite or a similar native sulphide of lead and antimony occurring in fibrous or capillary form; **feather palm** a palm tree of a kind having pinnate leaves; **feather-pate** = *feather-brain* above; **feather-pated** *a.* = *feather-brained* above; **feather-stitch** *n.* & *v.* (*a*) *n.* an ornamental zigzag stitch; (*b*) *v.t.* & *i.* sew (with) this stitch; **feathertail** *a.* = *feather-tailed* below; *feathertail glider* = *flying mouse* s.v. FLYING *ppl a.*; **feather-tailed** *a.* (of a small marsupial) having a tail with a row of long stiff hairs along each side; *feather-tailed possum*, a small arboreal possum, *Distoechurus pennatus*, found in New Guinea; **feather-tongue** *v.t.* (*Carpentry*) provide with a tongue or projection for fitting into a groove; **feather-top grass** a grass with a feathery inflorescence, *esp.* one of the genus *Calamagrostis* or *Pennisetum*; **feather-topped** *a.* (*Hist.*) (of a wig) frizzed at the top; **featherwife** (*obs.* exc. *Hist.*) a woman who prepares and deals in feathers; **feather-work** the art of working in feathers.

feather-like *a.* resembling (that of) a feather L16.

feather /ˈfɛðə/ *v.* [OE *gefiþrian*; re-formed (in pa. pple) in ME f. the n.] I Cover or provide with feathers. †1 *v.t.* Give wings to (*lit.* & *fig.*). OE–E19. 2 *v.t.* Provide, clothe, or adorn, (as) with feathers; *spec.* fit (an arrow) with a feather. ME. †b Wound with an arrow. LME–L16. †3 *v.i.* & *refl.* Grow or get feathers; become fledged. LME–L18. †4 *v.t.* Of a cock: cover with outspread feathers; mate with (a hen). *rare.* LME–E18. 5 *v.t.* a Line with feathers. M16. b Coat with feathers. Chiefly in *tar and feather*. M18.

1 T. L. BEDDOES Blessings of mine Feather your speed! 3 D. PELL The Vulture . . beholds her young to thrive and feather. 5a **feather one's (own) nest** appropriate things for oneself, enrich oneself when opportunity occurs.

II Give the appearance of feathers. 6 *v.t.* = FEATHER-EDGE *v.* E17. 7 *v.t.* & *i.* *Rowing.* Turn (an oar) so as to pass through the air edgeways. M18. b Rotate (propeller blades) about their axes so that they offer minimal resistance to forward motion through air or water; vary the angle of incidence of (helicopter rotors etc.). M19. 8 *v.i.* Move or float like a feather or feathers; grow in a feathery shape or form. L18. b Of cream: rise on the surface of coffee etc. like small feathers. Orig. *US.* M19. 9 *v.i.* *Hunting.* Of a dog: make a quivering movement with the tail and hindquarters while searching for a scent. E19.

8 R. D. BLACKMORE The wave and dip of barley feathering to a gentle July breeze.

feather bed /ˈfɛðəbɛd, fɛðəˈbɛd/ *n. phr.* & *v.* As vb usu. **feather-bed.** OE. [f. FEATHER *n.* + BED *n.*] A *n.* 1 A bed or mattress stuffed with feathers. OE. 2 *fig.* Something (esp. a job, situation, etc.) comfortable or easy. Freq. *attrib.* L17. 3 In *pl.*, treated as *sing.* A stonewort of the genus *Chara*; a bed of stoneworts. E19. B *v.t.* Infl. **-dd-**. Provide with, esp. economic, advantages or comforts; pamper, make things easy for. M20.

feather-bedding *n.* making or being made comfortable by favourable (esp. economic) treatment; *spec.* the employment of superfluous staff: E20.

feathered /ˈfɛðəd/ *a.* OE. [f. FEATHER *n.*, *v.*: see -ED[2], -ED[1].] 1 Having feathers; provided or fitted with a feather or feathers. OE. b Pertaining to or consisting of animals with feathers. E17. 2 (Apparently) having wings; winged, fleet. Chiefly *poet.* L16. 3 Formed or arranged like feathers; like a feather or feathers; having markings resembling a feather or feathers. L16.

1 **feathered friend** (*colloq.* or *iron.*) a bird.

feather-edge /ˈfɛðərɛdʒ/ *n.* & *v.* E17. [f. FEATHER *n.* + EDGE *n.*] A *n.* The fine edge of a wedge-shaped board or plank. Freq. *attrib.* E17. B *v.t.* Cut to a feather-edge; produce a feather-edge on. M17.

featherfew /ˈfɛðəfjuː/ *n.* ME. [Alt.] = FEVERFEW.

feathering /ˈfɛð(ə)rɪŋ/ *n.* M16. [f. FEATHER *v.* + -ING[1].] 1 The action of FEATHER *v.* M16. 2 Plumage; the feathers of an arrow; structure or markings like a feather or feathers. M16. 3 *Archit.* Cusping in tracery. E19.

featherless /ˈfɛðəlɪs/ *a.* LME. [f. FEATHER *n.* + -LESS.] Without feathers.
featherlessness *n.* E18.

featherlet /ˈfɛðəlɪt/ *n.* M19. [f. FEATHER *n.* + -LET.] A small feather.

featherweight /ˈfɛðəweɪt/ *n.* & *a.* E19. [f. FEATHER *n.* + WEIGHT *n.*] A *n.* 1 A weight at which boxing etc. matches are made, intermediate between bantamweight and lightweight, in the amateur boxing scale now being between 54 and 57 kg, though differing for professionals, wrestlers, and weightlifters, and according to time and place; a boxer etc. of this weight. Also formerly, the lightest weight allowed to be carried by a horse in a handicap race. E19. 2 A very light person or thing. M19. B *adj.* Very light in weight; (of a boxer etc.) that is a featherweight, of or pertaining to featherweights. L19.

feathery /ˈfɛð(ə)ri/ *a.* & *n.* M16. [f. FEATHER *n.* + -Y[1].] A *adj.* Having or covered with feathers; resembling feathers in appearance or lightness; tipped or fringed (as) with feathers; stuffed with feathers. M16. B *n.* Pl. **-ies**. A golf ball stuffed with feathers. L19.
featheriness *n.* L17.

featly /ˈfiːtli/ *a. arch.* E19. [f. FEAT *a.* + -LY[1].] Graceful, neat.

featly /ˈfiːtli/ *adv. arch.* LME. [f. FEAT *a.* + -LY[2].] In a feat manner; gracefully, neatly, nimbly, deftly.

featural /ˈfiːtʃ(ə)r(ə)l/ *a.* L19. [f. FEATURE *n.* + -AL[1].] Of or pertaining to a feature or the features.
featurally *adv.* E19.

feature /ˈfiːtʃə/ *n.* LME. [OFr. *feture, faiture* form f. L *factura* formation, creature, f. *fact-* pa. ppl stem of *facere* do: see -URE.] 1 Form, shape; proportions, esp. of the body. Long *arch.* LME. †b A form, a shape, a creation; a creature. LME–M17. †c Good shape or looks. Only in L16. †2 A part of the body; an element of bodily form. LME–M18. 3 A part of the face; in *pl.* freq. (the proportions or lineaments of) the face. LME. 4 A distinctive or characteristic part of a thing; a part that arrests attention by its prominence etc.; *Ling.* a distinct quality of a linguistic element which may have contrastive value. L17. b A distinctive or prominent article or item in a newspaper, magazine, etc. M19. c A feature film or programme. E20.

1 T. FULLER The king fell much enamoured of her feature. 2 SWIFT I agreed in every Feature of my Body with other Yahoos. 3 A. C. CLARKE His features relaxed into a slight smile. D. M. THOMAS Her face, in which the eyes were the best feature. 4 R. L. STEVENSON A world almost without a feature; an empty sky, an empty earth. H. PEARSON His after-dinner snooze was still a regular feature of his day. R. P. GRAVES A feature of the house was the impressive hallway. *distinctive feature*: see DISTINCTIVE *a.* 1. c C. JACKSON The movie over.. to be replaced with the next feature, Charlie Chaplin in *The Gold Rush*. *double feature*: see DOUBLE *a.* & *adv.*

Comb.: **feature film** a film of some length intended to form the main item in a cinema programme; **feature-length** *a.* of the length of a typical feature film or programme; **feature programme** a broadcast based on one specific subject; **feature writer**: who writes a feature or features in a magazine etc.

feature /ˈfiːtʃə/ *v.* M18. [f. the n.] 1 *v.t.* Resemble in features, favour. Now chiefly *dial.* M18. 2 *v.t.* Affect the features of; be a feature of. Now *rare.* E19. 3 *v.t.* Outline or portray the features of; picture. E19. 4 *v.t.* Make a special display, attraction, or feature of; give prominence to, esp. in play, film, etc. L19. 5 *v.i.* Be a feature or special attraction; participate or play an important part *in.* M20.

1 J. HAWTHORNE She featured her mother's family more than her father's. 2 A. W. KINGLAKE Knolls and ridges which featured the landscape. 3 J. GALSWORTHY He lay awake, featuring Fleur.. recalling her words. 4 C. CHAPLIN I was to have my name featured.. at the top of the bill. B. BAINBRIDGE Bernard's first appearance on television, in a programme featuring his work. 5 *Times* Libraries.. feature prominently in many of the local authority cuts.

featured /ˈfiːtʃəd/ *a.* L15. [f. FEATURE *n.*, *v.*: see -ED[2], -ED[1].] 1 Fashioned, formed, shaped; furnished with or having features (of a specified kind). L15. †b Well-formed; comely. M16–L18. 2 Shaped into or expressed by features or form. Now *rare.* M18. 3 Made a feature or special attraction. L19.

1 JOSEPH HALL Thy nose.. is.. featured like some curious Turret. 3 *Globe & Mail (Toronto)* The featured artists were Paula Robinson, flute; James Campbell, clarinet.

featureless /ˈfiːtʃəlɪs/ *a.* L16. [f. FEATURE *n.* + -LESS.] 1 Without good features, ugly. *rare.* L16. 2 Without features; having no prominent features; uninteresting, uneventful. E19.

2 *Punch* The month will be so featureless. I. COLEGATE The house is square and more or less featureless.
featurelessness *n.* L19.

featurely /ˈfiːtʃəli/ *a.* Now *rare.* E19. [f. FEATURE *n.* + -LY[1].] Having strongly marked features; characteristic, typical.
featureliness *n.* E19.

featurette /fiːtʃəˈrɛt/ *n.* M20. [f. FEATURE *n.* + -ETTE.] A short feature film or programme.

†featy *a.* E17–L19. [f. FEAT *a.* + -Y[1]. Cf. FITTY *a.*] Neat, pretty; clever.

feaze /fiːz/ *v. obs.* exc. *Naut.* Also (earlier) **†faze**. M16. [Prob. f. LDu. naut. term: cf. MLG, MDu. *vēse* fringe, frayed edge, rel. to OE *fæs, fas*, OHG *faso, fasa* fringe (G *Faser* fibre, filament, *fasern* fray out).] 1 *v.i.* Of a rope etc.: unravel or fray at the end. M16. 2 *v.t.* Unravel or fray (a rope etc.). L16.

febricitant /fɪˈbrɪsɪt(ə)nt/ *n.* & *a.* Long *rare.* M16. [L *febricitant-* pres. ppl stem of *febricitare* have a fever, f. *febris* fever: see -ANT[1].] (A person) affected with fever.

febricula /fɪˈbrɪkjʊlə/ *n.* Now *rare* or *obs.* M18. [L *febricula* dim. of *febris* fever: see -CULE.] *Med.* A slight fever of short duration.

febrifacient /fɛbrɪˈfeɪʃ(ə)nt/ *a.* & *n. rare.* E19. [f. L *febris* fever + -FACIENT.] *Med.* A *adj.* Producing fever. E19. B *n.* A substance that causes fever. E19.

febrific /fɪˈbrɪfɪk/ *a.* Earlier in ANTIFEBRIFIC. E18. [Fr. †*fébrifique*, f. L *febris* fever: see -FIC.] Producing fever; feverish.

febrifugal /fɛˈbrɪfjʊg(ə)l, fɛbrɪˈfjuːg(ə)l/ *a.* M17. [f. (as) next + -AL[1].] Serving or intended to reduce fever, anti-febrile.

febrifuge /ˈfɛbrɪfjuːdʒ/ *n.* & *a.* L17. [Fr. *fébrifuge*, f. L *febris* fever: see -FUGE.] A *n.* A medicine to reduce fever; a cooling drink. L17. B *adj.* = FEBRIFUGAL. E18.

febrile /ˈfiːbrʌɪl/ *a.* M17. [Fr. *fébrile* or med.L *febrilis*, f. L *febris* fever: see -ILE.] Of or pertaining to fever; produced by or indicative of fever; feverish.

fig.: M. LASKI Her continued febrile chatter about the evening obscurely troubled Roy.
febrility /fɪˈbrɪlɪti/ *n.* feverishness L19.

Febronian /fɛˈbrəʊnɪən/ *a.* & *n.* L19. [f. *Febronius* (see below) + -IAN.] *Eccl. Hist.* A *adj.* Of or pertaining to 'Justinus Febronius' (J. N. von Hontheim of Trier, Germany) or his doctrine (published in 1763) that national Roman Catholic Churches should be as far as possible independent of Rome. L19. B *n.* An adherent of Febronius or his views. L19.
Febronianism *n.* the doctrine of Febronius M19.

February /ˈfɛbrʊəri, ˈfɛbjʊəri/ *n.* ME. [OFr. *feverier* (mod. *février*), f. late L (Proto-Romance) *febrarius* for L *februarius*, f. *februa* (neut. pl.) a Roman festival of purification held on 15 February. Later refash. after L.] The second month of the year in the Gregorian calendar, containing twenty-eight days, except in a leap year when it has twenty-nine. Also *fig.*, w. allusion to the rain and melting snows considered characteristic of the month in Britain and elsewhere in the northern hemisphere. Also (*pop.*) called *February fill-dyke* (referring to its rain and snows).

attrib.: SHAKES. *Much Ado* What's the matter, That you have such a February face, So full of frost, of storm and cloudiness?

februation /fɛbrʊˈeɪʃ(ə)n/ *n.* Now *rare.* M17. [L *februatio(n-)*, f. *februare* purify (cf. prec.): see -ATION.] A ceremonial purification.

fecal *a.* see FAECAL.

feces *n.pl.* see FAECES.

Fechner's law /ˈfɛxnəz lɔː/ *n. phr.* L19. [Gustav Theodor *Fechner* (1801–87), Ger. psychologist.] *Psychol.* A law stating that the strength of a sensation is a logarithmic function of the strength of the stimulus. Also called *Weber–Fechner law.*

fecial *a.* & *n.* var. of FETIAL.

feck /fɛk/ *n. Sc.* & *north.* L15. [Aphet. f. var. of EFFECT *n.*] 1 The greater or better part; a great quantity. L15. †2 The purpose, the intended result; the point (of a statement etc.). L15–E17. 3 Efficacy, efficiency, value. M16.

1 R. BURNS I hae been a devil the feck o' my life. 3 J. GALT Your laddie there's owre young to be o' ony feck in the way o' war.
feckful *a.* efficient M16. **feckfully** *adv.* E17. **feckly** *adv.* †(*a*) indeed; (*b*) mostly; almost: L17.

feck /fɛk/ *v.t. slang* (chiefly *Anglo-Ir.*). E19. [Perh. var. of FAKE *v.*[2]] Steal.

J. O'FAOLAIN Clan na Gael.. is making ructions over sums they say were fecked in New York.

fecket /ˈfɛkɪt/ *n. Sc.* L18. [Origin unkn.] An under waistcoat or vest.

feckless /ˈfɛklɪs/ *a.* Orig. *Sc.* & *north.* L16. [f. FECK *n.* + -LESS.] Feeble, futile, ineffective, aimless; irresponsible.

A. SILLITOE We'd left our topcoats at home, but kids are ever feckless.
fecklessly *adv.* M19. **fecklessness** *n.* M17.

fecula /ˈfɛkjʊlə/ *n.* Also **faec-**. Pl. **-lae** /-liː/ L17. [L *faecula* crust of wine, dim. of *faex* dregs, sediment: see -CULE.] 1 Sediment resulting from infusion of crushed vegetable matter; *esp.* starch obtained in this way. Also *gen.*, sediment, dregs. L17. 2 Faecal matter of insects or other invertebrates. E20.

feculence /ˈfɛkjʊl(ə)ns/ *n.* M17. [(O)Fr. *féculence* or late L *faeculentia*, f. *faeculentus*: see next, -ENCE.] 1 Feculent matter; filth; scum. M17. 2 The quality or state of being feculent; foulness. M19.
Also †**feculency** *n.* E17–E19.

feculent /ˈfɛkjʊl(ə)nt/ *a.* Also †**faec-**. L15. [Fr. *féculent* or L *faeculentus*, f. as FAECES: see -ULENT.] 1 Containing or of the nature of faeces or dregs; filthy; turbid; foul, fetid. L15. †2 Covered with faeces. *rare* (Spenser). Only in L16.

fecund /ˈfɛk(ə)nd, ˈfiːk-/ *a.* LME. [Fr. *fécond* or L *fecundus.*] 1 Highly productive, esp. of offspring; prolific, fertile. LME. 2 Producing fertility, fertilizing. L17. 3 *Demography.* Capable of bearing children. Cf. FECUNDITY 3, FERTILE 1b. E20.

1 A. BROOKNER Fecund and beaming, Evie found motherhood the easiest thing in the world.

fecundability /fɪˌkʌndəˈbɪlɪti/ *n.* E20. [f. prec. + -ABILITY, after It. *fecondabilità.*] The probability of becoming pregnant within a given period of time, esp. a month or a menstrual cycle.

fecundate /ˈfɛk(ə)ndeɪt, ˈfiːk-/ *v.t.* M17. [L *fecundat-* pa. ppl stem of *fecundare*, f. *fecundus* fecund: see -ATE[3].] 1 Make productive. M17. 2 = FERTILIZE 2. E18.

1 J. R. LOWELL Even the Trouvères.. could fecundate a great poet like Chaucer. 2 U. LE GUIN There were no insects to fecundate flowering plants.

fecundation /fɛk(ə)nˈdeɪʃ(ə)n, fiːk-/ *n.* M16. [f. as prec.: see -ATION.] Fertilization; impregnation.

fecundify /fɪˈkʌndɪfʌɪ/ *v.t.* Long *rare* or *obs.* E18. [f. FECUND + -I- + -FY.] = FECUNDATE.

fecundity /fɪˈkʌndɪti/ *n.* LME. [Fr. *fécondité* or L *fecunditas*, f. *fecundus* fecund: see -ITY.] **1** The capacity to reproduce, fertility, productiveness, esp. in abundance. LME. **2** The capacity for making productive or fertile. M17. **3** *Demography.* Reproductive capacity; the maximum number of live births calculated to be possible in a given population. Cf. FERTILITY 3. M19.

1 A. BURGESS Why . . complain of fecundity when god commanded us to be fruitful?

fed /fɛd/ *n. US.* Also (esp. in sense 3) **F-**. L18. [Abbrev. of FEDERAL, FEDERALIST.] **1** = FEDERALIST *n.* L18. **2** An official of the US federal government; *esp.* a member of the US Federal Bureau of Investigation. *slang.* E20. **3** = *Federal Reserve Bank* or *Federal Reserve Board* s.v. FEDERAL *a.* M20.

2 T. LEARY He starts out like a fed, and now he's offering me acid.

fed /fɛd/ *a.* LME. [pa. pple of FEED *v.*] **1** Supplied with food; nourished. LME. **†2** Fattened. M16–E17. **3** *fed up*, surfeited, disgusted, extremely bored or tired, (*with*). E20.

Phrases: **fed to death**, **fed to the (back) teeth** = sense 3 above.

fed *v.* pa. t. & pple of FEED *v.*

fedai /fəˈdɑːiː/ *n.* Pl. (in sense 1) same, **-s**, (in sense 2) **fedayeen** /fɛdʌɪˈjiːn/. L19. [Arab. & Pers. *fidāʾī* one who gives his life for another, f. *fadā* ransom (someone with something).] **1** *Hist.* An Ismaili Muslim assassin. L19. **2** In *pl.* (*fedayeen*). Guerrillas in Muslim countries; *esp.* (*a*) Arab guerrillas operating against the Israelis; (*b*) Marxist paramilitary groups operating in Iran. M20.

fedan *n.* var. of FEDDAN.

fedayeen *n.pl.* see FEDAI.

feddan /fɛˈdɑːn/ *n.* Also ***fedan***. E19. [Arab. *faddān* a yoke of oxen, an acre.] A measure of land used in Egypt and some other Arab countries, equivalent to 0.405 hectare (about one acre) or more in certain areas.

federacy /ˈfɛd(ə)rəsi/ *n.* Now *rare.* M17. [f. FEDERATE *a.* (see -ACY) or abbrev. of CONFEDERACY.] **1** The state of being joined by a treaty; an alliance. M17. **2** = CONFEDERACY 3. E19.

federal /ˈfɛd(ə)r(ə)l/ *a.* & *n.* Also (esp. in senses A.3, B.) **F-**. M17. [f. L *foedus*, *foeder-* covenant: see -AL¹. Cf. Fr. *fédéral.*] **A** *adj.* **1** Of or pertaining to a covenant or treaty. Now only *spec.* in *Theol.*, pertaining to or based on the doctrine of God's Covenant with Adam as representing humankind and with Christ as representing the Church. M17. **2** Of, pertaining to, or of the nature of a system of government in which several States form a central political unity but remain independent in internal affairs. Cf. UNITARY *a.* 2. M17. **b** Of or pertaining to the central government as distinguished from the separate units constituting it. L18. **3** *US Hist.* (Usu. **F-**.) Favouring a central or federal government; *esp.* of or pertaining to the Federalist party or the Northern States and their supporters or troops in the Civil War. L18. **4** Comprising an association of largely independent units. E20.

2 A. F. DOUGLAS-HOME Ways . . which would give to the three territories a Federal structure. b A. E. STEVENSON Some of the federal aid might take the form of . . grants to the states. 4 *Times Lit. Suppl.* The geography and diverse character of Wales made a federal university of scattered colleges a necessity.

Special collocations: **federal district** the district used as the seat of federal government. *federal land-bank*: see LAND-BANK 2. **Federal Reserve Bank** *US* each of twelve regional banks which regulate and serve the member banks of the Federal Reserve System. **Federal Reserve Board** *US* the board regulating the Federal Reserve System and consisting of governors appointed by the US President with Senate approval. **Federal Reserve System** the US national banking system of reserve cash available to banks. **federal territory** the territory used as the seat of federal government.

B *n. US Hist.* (Usu. **F-**.) A supporter of the Union government or (esp.) a soldier in Union armies in the American Civil War. M19.

federally *adv.* (*a*) *Theol.* on the basis of a covenant; (*b*) in the manner of a federation: M17.

federalise *v.* var. of FEDERALIZE.

federalism /ˈfɛd(ə)rəlɪz(ə)m/ *n.* L18. [Fr. *fédéralisme*, f. *fédéral* FEDERAL *a.*: see -ISM.] (The principle of) a federal system of government; advocacy of this; *spec.* in *US Hist.* (usu. **F-**) the principles of the Federalists.

federalist /ˈfɛd(ə)rəlɪst/ *n.* & *a.* L18. [Fr. *fédéraliste*, f. *fédéral*: cf. FEDERAL & see -IST.] **A** *n.* A person who supports federalism; *spec.* in *US Hist.* (usu. **F-**) a member or supporter of the Federalist party. L18. **B** *adj.* Of, pertaining to, or favouring federalism or federalists; *spec.* in *US Hist.* (usu. **F-**) designating or pertaining to the party advocating a federal union of American colonies after the War of Independence. E19.

federaˈlistic *a.* inclined to federalism, somewhat federalist M19.

federalize /ˈfɛd(ə)rəlʌɪz/ *v.t.* Also **-ise**. E19. [Fr. *fédéraliser*, f. *fédéral* FEDERAL *a.*: see -IZE.] Unite in a federal union or government; place under federal jurisdiction.

federate /ˈfɛd(ə)rət/ *n.* & *a.* L17. [L *foederatus* pa. ppl formation on *foedus*, *foeder-* covenant + *-atus* -ATE². Cf. Fr. *fédéré.*] **A** *n.* **1** A party to a covenant. *rare.* L17. **2** *Fr. Hist.* [tr. Fr. *fédéré.*] A deputy to the Fête of the Federation, July 14, 1790; a member of one of the armed associations formed during the first French Revolution, or during the Hundred Days; a member of the Commune in 1871. L18. **B** *adj.* Federated, confederate. E18.

federate /ˈfɛdəreɪt/ *v.t.* & *i.* E19. [Late L *foederat-* pa. ppl stem of *foederare*, f. *foedus*, *foeder-*: see prec., -ATE³.] Unite in or form into a league or federation.

A. J. AYER All the factories in a given industry should be federated into a Guild. P. SCOTT There had been an attempt to get the rulers of the Tradura agency states to federate.

federation /fɛdəˈreɪʃ(ə)n/ *n.* E18. [Fr. *fédération* f. late L *foederatio(n-)*, f. as prec.: see -ATION.] **1** The action of federating; *esp.* the union of several States etc. under a federal government, each remaining independent in internal affairs. E18. **2** A federated society; a federal group of States etc. L18.

federationist *n.* a supporter of federation M19.

federative /ˈfɛd(ə)rətɪv/ *a.* L17. [f. L *foederat-* (see FEDERATE *v.*) + -IVE; perh. partly f. Fr. *fédératif.*] **1** Of or pertaining to the formation of a covenant or alliance. Now *rare.* L17. **2** Of, pertaining to, or of the nature of a federation; forming part of a federation; inclined to federation. L18.

†fedity *n.* M16–M18. [L *foeditas*, f. *foedus* foul: see -ITY.] Foulness, loathsomeness; in *pl.*, foul or loathsome practices.

fedora /fɪˈdɔːrə/ *n.* Orig. *US.* L19. [f. *Fédora*, title of a drama (1882) by Victorien Sardou (1831–1908).] A low soft felt hat with a curled brim and the crown creased lengthways.

†fee *n.*¹ [OE *feoh*, *fioh*, *fēo* = OFris. *fia*, OS *fehu* cattle, property (Du. *vee* cattle), OHG *fihu*, *fehu* cattle, property, money (G *Vieh* cattle), Goth. *faihu* f. Gmc var. of IE base, repr. by Skt *paśu*, L *pecu* cattle (cf. L *pecunia* money).] **1** Livestock, cattle. OE–M16. **2** Movable property. OE–L16. **3** Money. OE–L17.

fee /fiː/ *n.*² ME. [AN = OFr. *feu*, *fiu*, *fieu*, (also mod.) *fief*, pl. *fiez* f. Proto-Romance var. of med.L *feodum*, *feudum*, derived f. Frank. base, rel. to OHG *fehu*, OE *fēo*, etc.: see prec.] **1 a** *Feudal Law.* (Tenure of) an estate in land (in England always a heritable estate) in return for homage and service to a superior lord by whom it is granted; an estate so held, a fief, a feudal benefice. ME. **b** *Common Law.* (Tenure of) a heritable estate in land. See also earlier FEE SIMPLE, FEE TAIL. M16. **†2** Homage paid by a vassal to a superior; service, employment. ME–L16. **3** A territory held in fee; a lordship. Now *arch.* or *Hist.* LME. **†4** The heritable right to an office of profit, held feudally, or to a pension or revenue. LME–E19. **†5** A tribute to a superior. LME–E17. **†6** A perquisite, an incidental benefit attaching to employment etc. LME–M18. **b** Any allotted portion. L16–M17. **7 †a** A prize, a reward. LME–M17. **†b** A bribe. M16–M17. **c** A gratuity, a tip. L16. **8** A fixed salary or wage. Also in *pl.*, wages. *obs.* exc. *Hist.* LME. **9** The sum payable to a public officer in return for the execution of relevant duties. LME. **10** The sum paid for admission to an examination, a society, a public building, etc. LME. **11** The remuneration due to a lawyer, physician, or other professional person, for consultation etc. L16. **12** In *pl.* Regular payment for tuition at school, university, etc. E17. **13** More fully *transfer fee.* The money paid to an employer for the transfer of an employee, esp. for the transfer of a footballer. L19.

1a **in fee** by a heritable right subject to feudal obligations. *in one's* DEMESNE *as of fee.* **b at a pin's fee** *arch.* at the value of a pin, at very little value. **hold in fee** *fig.* (*arch.*) hold as one's absolute and rightful possession. 8 R. SIMPSON The post of King's standard-bearer, with the fee of six shillings . . a day. 9 R. L. FOX Aristotle did receive a handsome fee for his services, and . . died a rich man. 10 J. K. JEROME There is a grotto in the park which you can see for a fee. 11 V. PACKARD His standard fee for offering advice is $500 a day. *retaining fee*: see RETAIN *v.* 2b.

fee /fiː/ *v.* Pa. t. & pple **feed**, **fee'd**. LME. [f. prec.] **†1** *v.t.* Grant (a person) a fief or feudal estate. LME–L15. **2** *v.t.* Engage for a fee; *Sc.* hire (a servant etc.). LME. **†b** Bribe. LME–E19. **3** *v.t.* Give a fee or payment to. E16. **4** *v.i.* Take service *with*, hire oneself *to*. M17.

3 W. CATHER It wasn't necessary to fee porters or waiters. E. JONG They are Whores fer hire to anyone that fees 'em.

Comb.: **feeing market** *Hist.* a twice-yearly hiring-market at which farm hands hired themselves out for the next six months.

feeb /fiːb/ *n. US slang.* E20. [Abbrev. of FEEBLE *a.* & *n.*] A feeble-minded or stupid person.

feeble /ˈfiːb(ə)l/ *a.* & *n.* ME. [AN, OFr. *feble*, var. of *fieble* (mod. *faible*), later forms of *fleible*, f. L *flebilis* that is to be wept over, f. *flere* weep: see -BLE.] **A** *adj.* **1** Lacking physical strength, frail, weak, (now only of living things). ME. **2** Lacking intellectual or moral strength. ME. **†3** Poor, mean, scanty. Foll. by *of*: poorly supplied. ME–L16. **4** Lacking energy, force, or effect. ME. **5** Faintly perceived; indistinct, dim. M19.

1 G. M. FRASER He was still in shocking pain and entirely feeble. 4 C. WILSON The feeble argument fails to do justice to Jung's basic conception. 5 J. RHYS Amélie brought out candles . . but the night swallowed up the feeble light.

Comb.: **feeble-minded** *a.* of very low intelligence; *spec.* having a mental age of 8 or 9 or an IQ of between 50 and 70. **feeble-mindedness** the state of being feeble-minded.

B *n.* **1** A weak, frail, or ineffectual person. ME. **2** *Fencing.* The blade of a sword from the middle to the point. Cf. FOIBLE *n.* 1, FORTE *n.*¹ 1. M17. **3** A weakness, a foible. *rare.* L17.

feebleness *n.* ME. **feebling** *n.* a feeble person, a weakling L19. **feeblish** *a.* L17. **feebly** *adv.* ME.

feeble /ˈfiːb(ə)l/ *v.* ME. [f. the adj.] **1** *v.i.* Become feeble. Now *rare* or *obs.* ME. **2** *v.t.* Make feeble; weaken. *arch.* ME.

2 A. E. COPPARD The illness feebled him.

feebless /ˈfiːblɪs/ *n.* Long *arch. rare.* ME. [OFr. *feblesse* (mod. *faiblesse*), f. *feble* FEEBLE *a.*: see -ESS².] Weakness, infirmity; poor health.

feed /fiːd/ *n.* L16. [f. the vb.] **1** The action or an act of eating or feeding; the taking or giving of food. L16. **2** Grazing; pasturage, pasture. L16. **3** Food for animals, fodder. L16. **b** Food for humans. *US colloq.* E19. **4** A meal of corn, oats, etc. given to a horse or other animal. M18. **5** A (large or sumptuous) meal; a feast. *colloq.* E19. **6** The action or process of supplying something, as fuel or material to a machine etc.; the mechanism or means of supply. M19. **b** The (amount of) material supplied. M19. **7** *Theatr.* An actor etc. who provides lines or cues for another to react to; a comedian's straight man. Cf. earlier FEEDER 11. E20.

3 M. SHADBOLT Turnips for next year's winter feed. 5 B. BEHAN They're all bloody big fellows . . from eating bloody great feeds and drinking cider. 6 P. BENJAMIN Graduating the feed of the paper to the exact speed of the machine. D. L. SAYERS A commercial vehicle with a leaking feed. 7 S. BRETT Wilkie was a grand feed, but that's all he was. I was the funny one.

Phrases: **on the feed** (of fish) feeding or seeking food. **off one's feed** having no appetite. **out at feed** turned out to graze.

Comb.: **feed-bag** a nosebag; **feed check (valve)** a valve between a feed-pipe and a boiler to prevent return of feed-water; **feed cock**: which regulates the flow of water to a boiler etc.; **feed crop** barley, beans, wheat, etc., grown for animal food; **feed crusher, cutter** a machine for processing feed; **feed dog** the mechanism in a sewing-machine which feeds the material under the needle; **feed-floor** *US* a floor off which cattle etc. can eat food; **feedlot** an area or building where livestock are fed or fattened up; **feed-pipe**: which takes water etc. from a feed-tank to a boiler or other machine; **feed pump**: which supplies water, fuel, etc., to a machine; **feed-room** *US* & *NZ* a room in which animal feed is stored; **feedstock** raw material to supply a machine or industrial process; **feed-stuff** fodder; **feed-tank** a tank containing a supply of water for a steam locomotive, a boiler, etc., or for drinking; a tank containing liquid for a machine or industrial process; **feed-trough** (*a*) a trough between railway lines from which a steam locomotive scoops up water; (*b*) *US* a trough in which food for animals is placed; **feed-water** a supply of water for a boiler etc.

feed /fiːd/ *v.*[1] Pa. t. & pple **fed** /fɛd/. [OE *fēdan* = OFris. *fēda*, OS *fōdean* (Du. *voeden*), OHG *fuoten*, ON *fœða*, Goth. *fōdjan*, f. Gmc.] I *v.t.* 1 Give food to, supply with food; suckle. OE. b Put food into the mouth of. LME. †c Graze, pasture, (cattle etc.). LME–M18. 2 Provide with nourishment or sustenance; support. OE. 3 Serve as food or sustenance for. ME. 4 Fill with food, pamper; fatten *up* (cattle etc.). ME. 5 Keep continuously supplied (with water, fuel, working material, etc.); insert further coins etc. into (a meter) for continued functioning. ME. b Relay or supply electrical signals or power to, esp. as part of a larger network or system. L19. c *Football* etc. Give a pass or passes to. L19. d *Theatr.* Supply (an actor etc.) with lines or cues to react to; act as straight man to (a comedian). Cf. earlier FEEDER 11. E20. e *Jazz*. Play an accompaniment for (a soloist); provide as an accompaniment. Orig. *US*. M20. 6 Gratify, seek to satisfy (an appetite, passion, etc.); sustain (a person) *with* hope etc. ME. 7 Cause to be eaten or grazed by cattle etc.; use (land) as pasture; give as food (*to*). M17. 8 Of cattle etc.: eat, feed on, graze. Also foll. by *down*, *off*. E18. 9 Foll. by *back*: return by feedback. E20.

1 E. M. FORSTER Tom shall feed us on eggs and milk. b *refl.*: H. D. TRAILL His meal might be served up to him on costly dishes, but he fed himself with his fingers. 2 I. WATTS God . . feeds the strength of every Saint. 5 J. BARLOW She . . fed The turning spindle with the twisting thread. P. THEROUX There was a swimming pool nearby, fed by a waterfall. 6 J. MARSTON This morne my vengeance shall be amply fed. R. KNOLLES Craftily feeding him with the hope of libertie. 7 A. SILLITOE He wanted fish to . . feed to the cat. 8 R. JEFFERIES The sheep have fed it too close for a grip of the hand.

II *v.i.* 10 Take food, eat; (of a baby etc.) suckle. Foll. by *off*, *on*: consume, be nourished by. ME. 11 Of material: pass continuously *to*, *into* a machine, reservoir, etc. M17. 12 Foll. by *back*: return as feedback. M20.

10 POPE Devouring dogs . . fed on his trembling limbs. A. UPFIELD Cows feeding off the same grass as myxomatized rabbits. *Lancet* The baby fed well and gained weight.

Phrases: *bite the hand that feeds one*: see BITE *v.* **feed a part** *Theatr.* fill out a part with trivial details etc. **feed (full and) high** supply with rich and abundant food. *feed the fishes*: see FISH *n.*[1]

Comb.: **feed-forward** the modification or control of a process by its anticipated or predicted results or effects (cf. FEEDBACK).

feedable *a.* M17.

feed, fee'd *v.*[2] pa. t. & pple of FEE *v.*

feedback /ˈfiːdbak/ *n.* E20. [f. FEED *v.* + BACK *adv.*] 1 The return of a fraction of the output signal from one stage of an electric circuit, amplifier, etc., to the input of the same or a preceding stage; the signal so returned. E20. 2 *Biol.*, *Psychol.*, etc. Modification or control of a process or system by its results or effects, esp. by the difference between a desired and actual result. M20. 3 Information about the result of an experiment, performance, etc.; response. M20.

Phrases: **negative feedback** feedback which tends to cause a decrease in the output signal, or, more widely, which tends to attenuate the effect of which it is part. **positive feedback** feedback which tends to cause an increase in the output signal, or, more widely, which tends to amplify the effect of which it is part.

feeder /ˈfiːdə/ *n.* LME. [f. FEED *v.* + -ER[1].] 1 A person who supports, sustains, or supplies food for another, an animal, etc. LME. †b The host of a parasite; *derog.* a person who keeps another as a sycophant or spy. L16–E19. 2 A person who fattens up livestock for market. LME. b A person who attends to the feeding of a flock, a shepherd, (*lit.* & *fig.*). LME. c A person who supervises the feeding or training of horses, hounds, fighting cocks, etc. L18. 3 A consumer of food (esp. in a specified manner). M16. †b A person dependent on another for sustenance; a servant. Only in E17. c An animal (being) fattened for market. Now chiefly *US*. L18. 4 A person who or thing which supplies material to a machine in regulated quantities. M17. 5 *Mining*. A smaller lode falling into the main lode or vein. E18. b An underground spring; an escape of water or gas. E18. 6 A natural or artificial water course which flows into another body of water; a tributary (*lit.* & *fig.*). L18. b A branch road, railway line, air service, etc., linking outlying districts with the main lines of communication. M19. 7 A device used in feeding; *slang* a spoon; a baby's bottle or bib; a receptacle from which animals etc. may feed. E19. 8 The bowler in certain ball games. Also, a game resembling rounders. E19. 9 A reservoir of liquid metal to be supplied to a casting; a channel or means of supply of liquid metal. M19. 10 *Electr. Engin.* A heavy untapped main for carrying electrical energy to a distribution point or system. L19. b An electrical connection between an aerial and a transmitter or receiver of electromagnetic waves. E20. 11 *Theatr.* = FEED *n.* 7. L19.

feeding /ˈfiːdɪŋ/ *n.* OE. [f. FEED *v.* + -ING[1].] 1 The action of FEED *v.* OE. 2 Food, diet. Now *rare*. LME. 3 Grazing-land, pasturage. *obs.* exc. *dial.* LME.

Comb.: **feeding-bottle** a bottle fitted with a teat from which a baby can suck milk etc.; **feeding-cup** a small vessel with a spout for feeding liquid to an invalid lying down; **feeding-time** the time at which captive animals etc. are fed.

fee-farm /ˈfiːfɑːm/ *n.* LME. [AN *fee-ferme*, OFr. *feuferme*, *fiofferme*: see FEE *n.*[2], FARM *n.* Cf. FEU-FARM.] *Law*. 1 Tenure by which land is held in fee simple subject to a perpetual fixed rent, without other services; the estate or the land so held. LME. 2 More fully *fee-farm rent*. The rent paid for an estate so held. LME.

fee-farmer *n.* a person who holds a fee-farm E16.

fee-faw-fum /ˌfiːˌfɔːˈfʌm/ *n.* Now *rare*. L17. [The first line of doggerel spoken by the giant in the fairy tale 'Jack the Giant Killer' ('Jack and the Beanstalk') on seeing Jack.] 1 A bloodthirsty person. L17. 2 Nonsense, such as might terrify children. E19.

feel /fiːl/ *n.* ME. [f. the vb.] †1 Perception, consciousness, understanding, knowledge. *Sc.* & *north.* ME–E18. 2 Sensory awareness; the sense of touch. Now only in *to the feel*. ME. 3 The action or an act of feeling or testing by touch. LME. b An instance of 'feeling up' (see FEEL *v.* 1c). *slang*. M20. 4 A (mental or physical) feeling or sensation. LME. 5 The sensation characteristically produced by an object, situation, etc. M18.

Phrases: **have a feel for** have a natural talent for or understanding of (a subject etc.). *raw feel*: see RAW *a.*

feel *a.* var. of FIEL.

feel /fiːl/ *v.* Pa. t. & pple **felt** /fɛlt/. [OE *fēlan* = OFris. *fēla*, OS *gifōlian* (Du. *voelen*), OHG *fuolen* (G *fühlen*), f. WGmc.] I 1 *v.t.* Touch, esp. with the hand or finger(s); examine or explore by touching. OE. b *v.i.* Use the hand, finger, or other part of the body to touch. L16. c *v.t.* Touch or caress the genitals of (a person). Freq. foll. by *up*. *slang*. M20. 2 *v.t.* Test, discover, or ascertain by handling or touching; try to ascertain by touch *whether*, *if*, *how*. ME. b *fig.* Test or discover by cautious trial; sound out a person, the strength of an enemy, etc. Also foll. by *out*. ME. 3 *v.i.* Grope about; search *in*, *for*, etc., by touch. LME. b *v.t.* Ascertain the presence or nature of anything by or as by touch. Freq. foll. by *out*. M19.

1 W. TREVOR He felt the leaves of the rubber plant, taking them in turn between thumb and forefinger. b M. LEITCH He began to feel with his hands along the edges of the door. c J. KEROUAC We used to get next to pretty young daughters and feel them up in the kitchen. 2 OED The surgeon felt if any bones were broken. b D. ACHESON Relations with him became easier . . as we felt one another out. 3 E. J. HOWARD He . . felt hopefully in his pockets for pennies, but there were none. b H. R. MILL The form of the floor of the ocean has thus been gradually felt out point by point.

II 4 *v.t.* Perceive through physical sensation, esp. the sense of touch. OE. b Perceive by taste or smell. *obs.* exc. *dial.* ME. c *v.i.* Have or be capable of having sensations of touch. ME. †5 *v.t.* Perceive mentally, become aware of. OE–E17. 6 *v.t.* Be conscious of (a sensation, emotion, etc.); experience, undergo. Foll. by simple obj., obj. w. inf. or (esp. adj.) compl., *that*. ME. b *v.t.* Be physically affected or injured by; be emotionally affected by; behave as if conscious of. LME. c *v.i.* w. compl. Be conscious of being, regard oneself as. E19. d *v.i.* Be inclined *to do*. *US*. M19. 7 *v.i.* w. compl. Have a particular notion; be in a particular frame of mind; have a sensation or experience *as if*, *as though*. ME. 8 *v.t.* †a Think, hold as an opinion. LME–M16. b Have an impression or conviction of; believe *that*; consider *to be*. E17. 9 *v.i.* w. compl. Be consciously perceived (esp. through the sense of touch) as; produce the sensation of being, give the impression of being; seem *as if*, *as though*. L16. 10 *v.i.* Have one's sensibilities aroused; experience emotion; have sympathy *with*, have compassion *for*. E17.

4 J. STEINBECK She could feel his warm breath against her skin. b E. B. RAMSAY I feel a smell of tea. 6 C. MARLOWE I feel Thy words to comfort my distressed soul! POPE You . . Shall feel your ruling passion strong in death. T. HARDY Not having exerted myself . . I felt no sleepiness whatever. A. CARNEGIE I had never . . felt the power and majesty of music to such a high degree. b HARPER LEE Our mother died when I was two, so I never felt her absence. S. BELLOW On my way home, feeling the vodka I've drunk. c J. HERRIOT I felt rather a lout in my working clothes among the elegant gathering. 7 G. B. SHAW I feel as if I were sitting on a volcano. C. P. SNOW Sometimes I felt anxious about what was being said in there. 8b H. JAMES I was certain you would come—I have felt it all day. D. H. LAWRENCE I feel you don't love him, dear. I'm almost sure you don't. 9 A. CALDCLEUGH The air felt chilly. M. ROBERTS It feels as though they've only been together for a little while. 10 LD MACAULAY A moderate party . . had always felt very kindly towards the Protestant Dissenters. Y. WINTERS The insane, who sometimes perceive and feel with great intensity.

Phrases: *feel a person's collar*: see COLLAR *n.* *feel good*: see GOOD *a.* *feel in one's bones*: see BONE *n.* **feel like** (*a*) feel as though, feel similar to; (*b*) desire (a thing), have an inclination towards *doing*. **feel no pain** *slang* be insensibly drunk. **feel oneself** be fit, confident, etc. **feel oneself into** enter imaginatively into, bring oneself to identify or empathize with. **feel one's feet** = *find one's feet* s.v. FIND *v.* **feel one's legs** be conscious of one's powers, be at one's ease. *feel one's oats*: see OAT *n.* **feel one's way** find one's way by groping; proceed cautiously. **feel one's wings** = *feel one's legs* above. *feel small*: see SMALL *a.* **feel the draught, the pinch** *colloq.* feel the adverse effects of changed (esp. financial) conditions. **feel the pulse of** feel an artery to ascertain the heartbeat rate (and so the state of health) of; *fig.* ascertain the intentions or sentiments of. *feel the weight of*: see WEIGHT *n.* **feel up to** feel capable of or ready to face. *feel wretched*: see WRETCHED *a.* 1 a. **make one's presence felt** have an effect on others, influence proceedings.

feelable *a.* that can or may be felt LME.

feeler /ˈfiːlə/ *n.* LME. [f. FEEL *v.* + -ER¹.] **1** A person who feels an emotion; a person who understands or experiences something. LME. **2** A person who perceives by the senses, esp. by touch. E16. **3** *Zool.* An organ in certain animals for testing things or searching for food by touch, as an antenna or a palpus. M17. **4** A tentative hint or proposal put out to test opinion. M19. **5** More fully *feeler gauge*. A thin (usu. metal) strip of a known thickness, used to measure narrow gaps or clearances; a device with such strips. M20.

1 P. THOMPSON We are to be the main feelers of the consequences. J. R. LOWELL He was not a strong thinker, but a sensitive feeler. 2 N. FAIRFAX All hearers deaf, all feelers numb. 3 R. F. CHAPMAN Elongation, such as occurs in the cockroach, is possibly associated with the use of antennae as feelers. 4 *Sun (Baltimore)* The Germans also were making peace feelers both to Britain and the United States and to Russia with the object of splitting the Allies.

feeling /ˈfiːlɪŋ/ *n.* ME. [f. FEEL *v.* + -ING¹.] **1** The action of FEEL *v.* ME. **2** Physical sensibility other than sight, hearing, taste, or smell; the sense of touch. ME. **b** (A) physical sensation; a perception due to this. ME. **3** The condition of being emotionally affected or committed; an emotion (*of* fear, hope, etc.). ME. **b** In *pl.* Emotions, susceptibilities, sympathies. L18. **4** Consciousness; an emotional appreciation or sense (*of* a condition etc.). LME. **5** A belief not based solely on reason; an attitude, a sentiment. LME. **6** Capacity or readiness to feel (esp. sympathy or empathy); sensibility. LME. †**7** Knowledge of something through experience of its effects. E16–M17. **8** The quality felt to belong to a thing; the general emotional effect produced (esp. by a work of art) on a spectator or hearer. L16.

2 ADDISON The Sense of Feeling can indeed give us a Notion of . . Shape. **b** R. G. COLLINGWOOD A hundred people . . may all feel cold, but each person's feeling is private to himself. 4 J. T. MICKLETHWAITE The feeling of perfect equality inside the church. 5 B. JOWETT They have the feelings of old men about youth. 6 D. HUME The delicacy of his feeling makes him sensibly touched. 8 R. WARNER There was a feeling of space about the room.

Phrases: **bad feeling** animosity. *better feelings*: see BETTER *a.* etc. **good feeling** benevolence, amity, the avoidance of unkindness. **hurt the feelings of** upset, offend. **ill feeling** bad feeling, malice, animosity. MIXED *feelings*.

feelingless *a.* E19. **feelingful** *a.* E20.

feeling /ˈfiːlɪŋ/ *a.* LME. [f. FEEL *v.* + -ING².] **1** Capable of sensation; sentient. LME. **2** Fully realized; vivid, acute, heartfelt. M16. **3** Of language etc.: expressing or indicating emotion. L16. **4** Affected by emotion; sensitive, sympathetic, compassionate. E17.

feelingly /ˈfiːlɪŋli/ *adv.* LME. [f. prec. + -LY².] †**1** With accurate perception, sensibly; appropriately. LME–M17. **2** So as to be felt or leave an impression behind. LME. **3** By or from personal feeling or knowledge; in a heartfelt manner; with emotion. M16. †**4** Sensitively. L18–E19.

feelthy /ˈfiːlθi/ *a. slang.* M20. [Joc. imitation of foreign pronunc. of FILTHY *a.*] Obscene.

G. GORER Little bronze figures of an obscenity which resembles feelthy postcards.

feely /ˈfiːli/ *n.* M20. [f. FEEL *v.* + -Y¹. Cf. MOVIE.] A (hypothetical) film augmented by tactual effects. Freq. in *the feelies*.

feer /fɪə/ *v.t.* Also **pheer, veer**. LME. [Perh. f. OE *fyrian* make a furrow, f. *furh* FURROW *n.*] Mark off (land) for ploughing.

feering *n.* (*a*) the action of the vb; (*b*) = LAND *n.*¹ 6a: M18.

feerie *a.* var. of FEIRIE.

fee simple /fiː ˈsɪmp(ə)l/ *n. phr.* LME. [AN: see FEE *n.*², SIMPLE *a.*] *Law.* Tenure of a heritable estate in land etc. for ever and without restriction to any particular class of heirs; an estate so held.

feet *n.* pl. of FOOT *n.*

fee tail /fiː ˈteɪl/ *n. phr.* LME. [AN *fee tailé* = AL *feudum talliatum*: see FEE *n.*², TAIL *a.*] *Law.* (Tenure of) a heritable estate entailed or restricted to some particular class of heirs of the person to whom it is granted.

feetless /ˈfiːtlɪs/ *a.* Now *rare.* E17. [f. FEET + -LESS.] Without feet, footless.

feeze /fiːz/ *n.* LME. [f. next. See also VEASE.] **1** A rush; a violent impact. Also, a rub. Now *dial.* & *US.* LME. **2** A state of alarm. *US dial.* M19.

feeze /fiːz/ *v.t. obs.* exc. *dial.* Also †**pheeze**. [OE *fēsian*, of unkn. origin. Cf. FAZE *v.*¹] †**1** Drive; drive off or away; put to flight. OE–L17. **2** Frighten. LME. **3a** Do for (a person). Esp. in threat *I'll feeze you.* L16. **b** Beat, flog. E17.

fegary /fɪˈgɛːri/ *n. dial.* & *colloq.* Now *rare.* E17. [Alt. of VAGARY.] Usu. in *pl.* **1** A vagary, a prank; a whim, an eccentricity. E17. **2** A gewgaw, a trifle; finery in dress. E18.

fegs /fɛgz/ *n.* & *int. obs.* exc. *Sc.* & *dial.* Also **fecks**. L16. [Perh. f. FAY *n.*¹ or FAITH + -KIN(S.)] (A meaningless noun) expr. solemn conviction or astonishment.

i'fegs = *i'faith* s.v. FAITH *n.*

fehi *n.* var. of FEI.

Fehling /ˈfeɪlɪŋ/ *n.* L19. [Hermann von *Fehling* (1812–85), Ger. chemist.] *Fehling('s) reaction, test*, the reaction of Fehling's solution with aldehydes, used as an analytical test esp. for aldose sugars. *Fehling('s) solution*, an alkaline solution of copper(II) sulphate and a tartrate.

Fehm *n.*, **Fehmgericht** *n.* vars. of VEHME, VEHMGERICHT.

fei /ˈfeɪi/ *n.* Also **fehi, fe'i**. E19. [Tahitian.] (The fruit of) a type of banana widely grown in Polynesia and Melanesia, which is characterized by violet sap and erect inflorescences.

feign /feɪn/ *v.* ME. [(O)Fr. *feign-* pres. stem of *feindre* f. L *fingere* form, conceive, contrive.] **1** *v.t.* Fashion materially. *rare.* ME. **2** *v.t.* Invent (a story, excuse, etc.); forge (a document); counterfeit. *arch.* ME. **3** *v.t.* Allege, maintain fictitiously. ME. †**4a** *v.refl.* & *i.* Disguise one's sentiments; dissemble. ME–M16. **b** *v.t.* Disguise, conceal. ME–L16. †**5** *v.i.* & *refl.* Avoid duty by false pretences, shirk; be reluctant *to do.* ME–M16. **6** *v.t.* Make a show of, simulate, pretend to. ME. **b** *v.i.* Practise simulation. E17. **7** *v.refl.* & (now usu.) *i.* w. compl. Pretend to be; pretend *to be, to do.* ME. **8** *v.t.* Represent in fiction. Now *rare.* LME. †**b** *v.i.* Make fictitious statements. LME–M17. **9** *v.t.* Imagine (what is unreal). Now *rare.* LME. †**b** Believe erroneously and arbitrarily. M16–E18. **c** Assume fictitiously for purposes of calculation. *arch.* L17. †**10** *v.t.* Adulterate. *rare.* LME–E17. †**11** *v.t.* & *i.* Pretend to deal (a blow etc.). LME–M17. †**12** *v.i.* & *t. Mus.* Sing softly, hum; sing with due regard to the accidentals not indicated by old notation. LME–E17.

6 P. PEARCE Tom could not feign interest in what seemed so far away in time. A. SCHLEE Charlotte . . feigned a weakness she did not entirely feel. 7 DEFOE Satan made David feign himself mad. Q. CRISP The only method . . by which one can survive one's emotions is to feign not to have them.

feignedly /ˈfeɪnɪdli/ *adv.* in a feigned manner. LME. **feignedness** /ˈfeɪnɪdnɪs/ *n.* the quality of being feigned LME. **feigner** *n.* LME. **feigning** *n.* (*a*) the action of the vb; †(*b*) an assumption, a fiction: LME. **feigningly** *adv.* in a feigning manner LME.

feijão /feɪˈ(d)ʒãuː/ *n.* M19. [Port. f. L *phaseolus* bean.] Any of various edible beans, *esp.* a form of haricot bean, *Phaseolus vulgaris*, used as a staple item of diet in Brazil. Cf. FEIJOADA.

feijoa /feɪˈ(d)ʒəʊə; fɛ-, fiː-, -ˈjəʊə/ *n.* L19. [mod.L (see below), f. J. da Silva *Feijó* (1760–1824), Brazilian naturalist.] An evergreen shrub or small tree of the tropical S. American genus *Feijoa*, of the myrtle family; the edible green fruit of this, which resembles the guava.

feijoada /feɪˈ(d)ʒwaðə, -də/ *n.* M20. [Port., f. FEIJÃO.] A Brazilian stew made with black beans and pork, sausage, etc., served with rice.

Feinne /ˈfeɪnjə/ *n.pl.* Also **Fein**. L18. [Ir. *féinne* genit. sing. (taken as pl.) of FIAN.] The Fenian warriors of Irish history and legend.

feint /feɪnt/ *n.* L17. [(O)Fr. *feinte* use as n. of fem. of pa. pple of *feindre* FEIGN.] **1a** *Fencing, Boxing*, etc. A blow, cut, or thrust intended to deceive and distract the opponent. L17. **b** *Mil.* A movement made in order to deceive an enemy. L17. **2** An assumed appearance; a pretence. L17.

feint *a.* see FAINT *a.*

feint /feɪnt/ *v.i.* ME. [Sense 1 f. Fr. *feint* (see FAINT *a.*); sense 2 f. FEINT *n.*] †**1** Deceive. ME–L17. **2** *Mil., Boxing, Fencing*, etc. Make a sham attack. Foll. by *at, on, upon.* M19.

feints *n.pl.* var. of FAINTS.

feirie /ˈfɪəri/ *a. Sc.* Also **feerie**. LME. [Perh. rel. to FERE *a.*] Fit to travel; nimble, vigorous.

feirily *adv.* M16.

feis /fɛʃ, feɪʃ/ *n.* In sense 1 also **fes(s)**. Pl. **feiseanna** /-ʃənə/. L18. [Ir. = wedding feast, feast, festival.] **1** An assembly of kings, chiefs, etc., formerly believed to be a kind of early Celtic parliament. L18. **2** An Irish or Scottish festival of the arts, resembling the Welsh Eisteddfod. L19.

feist *n.* see FIST *n.*²

feisty /ˈfʌɪsti/ *a. N. Amer. colloq.* L19. [f. FEIST + -Y¹.] Aggressive, excitable, touchy; plucky, spirited.

feistily *adv.* L20. **feistiness** *n.* L20.

felafel *n.* var. of FALAFEL.

Felapton /fəˈlaptɒn/ *n.* M18. [A mnemonic of scholastic philosophers first used in med.L, E indicating a universal negative proposition, A a universal affirmative proposition, and O a particular negative proposition.] *Logic.* The fourth mood in the third syllogistic figure, in which the major premiss is a universal negative, the minor premiss a universal affirmative, and the conclusion a particular negative.

feldgrau /ˈfɛltgraʊ/ *n.* & *a.* M20. [G = field-grey.] (Of) a dark grey, = *field-grey* s.v. FIELD *n.*

feldsher /ˈfɛldʃə/ *n.* Also ***-scher***. L19. [Russ. *fel'dsher* f. G *Feldscher* field surgeon.] In Russia and the former USSR: a person with practical training in medicine and surgery, but without professional medical qualifications; a physician's or surgeon's assistant; a local medical auxiliary.

feldspar /ˈfɛl(d)spɑː/ *n.* Also **felspar** /ˈfɛlspɑː/. M18. [Alt. of G *Feldspat(h)*, f. *Feld* FIELD *n.* + *Spat(h)* SPATH w. substitution of synonym. SPAR *n.*³; *fels-* by false etym. f. G *Fels* rock.] *Min.* Any of a large class of monoclinic or triclinic aluminosilicate minerals which are mostly colourless or pink and include many common rock-forming minerals.

aventurine feldspar: see AVENTURINE 2.

feldspathic /fɛl(d)ˈspaθɪk/ *a.* Also **felspathic** /fɛlˈspaθɪk/. M19. [f. as prec. + -IC.] *Min.* Of the nature of feldspar; containing (much) feldspar.

feldspathoid /ˈfɛl(d)spəθɔɪd/ *n.* Also **felspath-** /ˈfɛlspəθ-/. L19. [f. as prec. + -OID.] *Min.* Any of a group of minerals chemically similar to the feldspars, but containing less silica.

feldspa'thoidal *a.* M20.

Félibre /felibr/ *n.* Pl. pronounced same. L19. [Fr. f. Prov. *felibre* any one of the teachers in the temple whom the child Jesus questioned, f. late L *fellibris* var. of *fellebris* nursling f. L *fellare* to suck.] A member of a society founded in 1854 by Provençal writers to maintain and purify Provençal as a literary language and to promote the artistic interests of the South of France.

Félibrism /ˈfeɪlɪbrɪz(ə)m/ *n.* E20. [f. prec. + -ISM.] (The principles of) the movement instituted by the Félibres.

felicide /ˈfiːlɪsʌɪd/ *n.* M19. [f. L *feles* cat + -CIDE.] The killing of a cat or cats.

felicific /fiːlɪˈsɪfɪk/ *a.* M19. [L *felicificus*, f. *felix* happy: see -FIC.] Making or tending to make happy.

felicitate /fɪˈlɪsɪteɪt/ *v.* E17. [Late L *felicitat-* pa. ppl stem of *felicitare* make happy, f. *felix* happy: see -ATE³.] **1a** *v.i.* Cause happiness. *rare.* E17. **b** *v.t.* Make happy. Now *rare.* M17. **2** *v.t.* Regard as or pronounce to be happy or fortunate. Now *spec.* congratulate (a person, *on*). M17.

felicitation /fɪˌlɪsɪˈteɪʃ(ə)n/ *n.* E18. [f. prec.: see -ATION.] **1** Congratulation. E18. **2** A congratulatory speech or message, a congratulation. Usu. in *pl.* L18.

felicitous /fɪˈlɪsɪtəs/ *a.* M18. [f. FELICITY + -OUS.] 1 Happy; showing or marked by great happiness. Formerly also, fortunate, prosperous, successful. (Earlier in FELICITOUSLY 1.) M18. 2a Of an action, manner, etc.: very apt, well suited to the occasion. L18. b Of a person: happy or pleasantly apt in expression, manner, or style. E19. 3 Pleasing, delightful. L19.

1 J. RUSKIN In the refinement of their highly educated..benevolent and felicitous lives. 2a O. WILDE Your poems are most charming, and your choice of epithets exquisite and felicitous. 3 J. ROSENBERG There is something particularly felicitous about this painting, which has aroused the highest enthusiasm.

felicitously /fɪˈlɪsɪtəsli/ *adv.* M16. [f. prec. + -LY².] 1 Happily, prosperously, successfully. *rare.* M16. 2 Aptly; with striking appropriateness or grace. E19.

felicity /fɪˈlɪsɪti/ *n.* LME. [(O)Fr. *félicité* f. L *felicitas*, f. *felix*, *felic-* happy: see -ITY.] 1 The state or an instance of being happy; happiness, bliss. LME. 2 A cause or source of happiness. LME. 3 Prosperity, good fortune, success. Now *rare.* LME. †b In *pl.* Prosperous circumstances; successful enterprises; successes. LME–M18. c A stroke of fortune; singular fortunateness (of an occurrence); a fortunate trait. M18. 4 An appropriateness in invention or expression. E17. b A happy inspiration; a well-chosen expression. M17.

felid /ˈfiːlɪd/ *n.* L19. [mod.L *Felidae* (see below), f. L *feles* cat: see -ID³.] *Zool.* An animal of the family Felidae, which includes the cats, lion, tiger, leopard, etc.

feline /ˈfiːlʌɪn/ *a.* & *n.* L17. [L *felinus*, f. *feles* cat: see -INE¹.] A *adj.* Of or pertaining to cats; characteristic of a cat; resembling a cat in any respect. L17.

LYTTON The feline care with which he stepped aside from any patches of mire.

B *n.* A cat (chiefly *joc.*); *gen.* any felid. M19.

felinely *adv.* M19. **felinity** /fɪˈlɪnɪti/ *n.* M19.

felix culpa /ˌfiːlɪks ˈkʌlpə, ˌfeɪlɪks, ˈkʊlpɑː/ *n. phr.* M20. [L, lit. 'happy fault', from the Exultet in the liturgy for Holy Saturday.] *Theol.* The Fall of Man or the sin of Adam as resulting in the blessedness of the Redemption; *transf.* an apparent error or tragedy with happy consequences.

fell /fɛl/ *n.*¹ [OE *fel(l)* = OFris., OS *fel* (Du. *vel*), OHG *fel* (G *Fell*), ON *ber-fjall* bear-skin, Goth. *þruts-fill* 'swelling skin', f. Gmc f. IE base repr. also by L *pellis*, Gk *pella* skin.] 1 The skin or hide of an animal, usu. with the hair, wool, etc. OE. b Human skin. OE. 2 A covering of hair, wool, etc., esp. when thick or matted; a fleece. L16.

1 R. GRAVES A lion of tawny fell. *flesh and fell*: see FLESH *n.* b P. HOLLAND That kind of dropsy wherein water runneth between the fell and the flesh. 2 J. R. LOWELL The surly fell of Ocean's bristled neck.

Comb.: **fellmonger** a person who prepares skins for leather-making; *arch.* a dealer in hides and skins; **fell-wool** wool pulled from sheepskins as opp. to that shorn from the living animal.

fell /fɛl/ *n.*² Now chiefly *north.* & *Sc.* ME. [ON *fjall* and *fell* hill, mountain, prob. rel. to OS *felis*, OHG *felis*, *felisa* (G *Fels*) rock.] 1 A hill, a mountain. *obs.* exc. in proper names as *Bowfell*, *Scafell*, etc. ME. 2 A stretch of high moorland, a ridge, a down. ME.

Comb.: **fell-field** *Ecol.* (an area of) a habitat characteristic of tundra, with scattered low-lying vegetation and stony soil; **fell hound** (an animal of) a variety of foxhound orig. bred for hunting in hill country.

†**fell** *n.*³ *rare* (Spenser). Only in L16. [L *fel* (*fell-*) gall.] Gall; rancour.

fell /fɛl/ *n.*⁴ E17. [f. FELL *v.*¹ Cf. FALL *n.*²] 1 A fall of lambs (see FALL *n.*² 1f). E17. 2 A cutting down of timber; the amount of timber cut down in one season. M17. 3 The sowing down of the edge of a seam to form a smooth surface. L19.

fell /fɛl/ *a.* & *adv.* ME. [OFr. *fel* f. Proto-Romance, whence also (f. obl. case) FELON *n.*¹ & *a.*] A *adj.* 1 Fierce, cruel, ruthless; terrible, destructive. Now only *poet.* or *rhet.* ME. 2 Keen, piercing; intensely painful or destructive. Now *dial.*, *poet.*, or *rhet.* ME. †3 Hot, angry, enraged. ME–L16. 4 Full of spirit, doughty. *obs.* exc. *dial.* ME. b Eager *for*, *on*, †*to*. *obs.* exc. *dial.* M17. 5 Shrewd, clever, cunning. *obs.* exc. *Sc.* & *dial.* ME. 6 Exceedingly great, mighty. *obs.* exc. *Sc.* E16.

1 F. O'BRIEN Fell adders hiss and poisonous serpents roll. 2 G. TURBERVILLE Small arrowis, cruel heads, that fel and forked be.

Phrases: *at* or *in one fell swoop*: see SWOOP *n.* 2b.

B *adv.* In a fell manner; cruelly, fiercely; eagerly; greatly. ME.

L. G. GIBBON Mistress Melon was a fell good worker.

fellness *n.* (*obs.* exc. *dial.* or *poet.*) the quality of being fell; cruelty; fierceness; keenness: LME.

fell /fɛl/ *v.*¹*t.* [OE *fellan*, *fyllan* = OFris. *falla*, *fella*, OS *fellian* (Du. *vellen*), OHG *fellen* (G *fällen*), ON *fella* f. Gmc base, causative of FALL *v.*] 1 Cause to fall; knock or strike down (a person or animal, formerly a building etc.); cut down (a tree). OE. b Lay low, kill. OE. †2 Bring or let down, lower. ME–E17. 3 Stitch down (the edge of a seam) so that it lies flat over the other edge and leaves a smooth surface. M18.

1 R. GRAVES The Tiger then felled him with a.. blow on the side of his head. L. K. JOHNSON Let no more trees be felled or else the forest will be bare. b J. HELLER Gold was positive he would be..felled by a heart attack.

fellable *a.* (of a tree etc.) that may be felled L16.

fell *v.*² pa. t. of FALL *v.*

fella /ˈfɛlə/ *n.* Also **fellah**. M19. [Repr. an affected or non-standard pronunc. of FELLOW *n.* Cf. FELLER *n.*²] = FELLOW *n.* 8.

fellah /ˈfɛlə/ *n.*¹ Pl. **-aheen, -ahin**, /-əhiːn/, **-ahs**. M18. [Arab. *fallāḥ*, colloq. pl. *fallāḥīn*, tiller of the soil, f. *falaḥa* split, till the soil.] A peasant in an Arabic-speaking country, esp. in Egypt.

fellah *n.*² var. of FELLA.

fellaheen, -ahin *n.* pl. of FELLAH *n.*¹

fellate /fɛˈleɪt/ *v.t.* & *i.* L19. [L *fellat-* pa. ppl stem of *fellare* suck.] Perform fellatio (on).

fellator *n.* a person who performs fellatio L19. **fellatrix** *n.* a female who performs fellatio L19.

fellatio /fɛˈleɪʃɪəʊ, -ˈlɑːt-/ *n.* L19. [mod.L, f. L *fellatus* pa. pple, f. as prec.] Sucking or licking of a sexual partner's penis.

fellation /fɛˈleɪʃ(ə)n/ *n.* L19. [f. (as) prec.: see -ION.] = prec.

feller /ˈfɛlə/ *n.*¹ LME. [f. FELL *v.*¹ + -ER¹.] 1 A person who fells a person, animal, or (esp.) timber. LME. 2 An attachment on a sewing-machine for felling seams etc.; a person who fells seams etc. L19.

feller /ˈfɛlə/ *n.*² E19. [Repr. an affected or non-standard pronunc. of FELLOW *n.* Cf. FELLA.] = FELLOW *n.* 8.

(young) feller-me-(or my-)lad a frivolous or irresponsible young man, esp. used as a disapproving form of address.

felloe /ˈfɛləʊ/ *n.* Also **felly** /ˈfɛli/. [OE *felg*, pl. *felga*, corresp. to MLG, MDu. *velge* (Du. *velg*), OHG *felga* (G *Felge*), of unkn. origin.] The outer rim or a part of the rim of a wheel, supported by the spokes; each of the curved pieces which join together to form a wheel rim.

fellow /ˈfɛləʊ/ *n.* & *a.* LOE. [ON *félagi*, f. *fé* (= OE *feoh* FEE *n.*¹) + Gmc base of LAY *v.*¹] A *n.* 1 A person who shares with another in anything; a partner, a colleague, an ally. Now *rare.* LOE. †b In a bad sense: an accomplice. LME–M19. †c A partaker or sharer *of*. LME–M17. 2 A companion, an associate, a comrade. Now usu. in *pl.* ME. †b *spec.* A female companion. ME–E17. 3 Either of a pair; a partner, a counterpart, a match. ME. 4 An equal in rank, ability, or kind. ME. b A contemporary. Usu. in *pl.* L19. 5 A member of a company or party with common interests. ME. 6a Any of the incorporated senior members of a college or collegiate foundation. LME. b A member of the governing body in certain universities. M19. c An elected graduate holding a stipendiary position in a college for a period of research. L19. 7 A member, or sometimes a privileged member, of certain learned societies. LME. 8 A man, a boy. *colloq.* LME. 9†a (Used as form of address to) a servant or other person of low station. LME–L16. b A despised person. LME. †c A Black. *US.* M18–M19.

2 H. COGAN Brave men, their fellows in arms. 3 JOYCE One boot stood upright..the fellow of it lay upon its side. 4 E. FAIRFAX His fellowes late shall be his subjects now. BYRON Danger levels man and brute, And all are fellows in their need. 7 *Fellow of the British Academy*, *Fellow of the Royal Society*, etc. 8 J. CARLYLE He looked dreadfully weak still, poor fellow! G. STEIN Rose had lately married Sam Johnson a decent honest kindly fellow. P. H. GIBBS All very innocent, he thought...A fellow must amuse himself now and then.

Phrases etc.: *fellow-me-* (or *my-*)*lad*: see *young fellow-me-* (or *my-*)*lad* below. **good fellow** an agreeable or convivial companion. *hail-fellow(-well-met)*: see HAIL *int.* **jolly fellow** = *good fellow* above. **my dear fellow, my good fellow**: used as forms of address, now sometimes implying censure. *stout fellow*: see STOUT *a.* *teaching fellow*: see TEACHING *ppl a.* **(young) fellow-me-(or my-)lad** = (*young*) *feller-me-lad* s.v. FELLER *n.*²

B *attrib.* or as *adj.* 1 (Sometimes hyphenated.) Belonging to the same class; associated in joint action; in the same relation to the same object. M16. 2 Equivalent *to*. Now *rare.* E17.

1 *fellow Christian*, *fellow guest*, *fellow man*, *fellow member*, *fellow prisoner*, *fellow student*, *fellow sufferer*, etc. 2 H. BUSHNELL They..have nothing fellow to God in their substance.

Comb. & special collocations: **fellow-citizen** a citizen of the same city as another; **fellow-citizenship** the state of being fellow-citizens; **fellow-commoner** †(*a*) a joint-partaker with others, *esp.* a person who eats at the same table; (*b*) *Hist.* any of a privileged class of undergraduates at Oxford, Cambridge, or Dublin, entitled to dine at the fellows' table; (*c*) a person who has a right of common with others; **fellow-countryman** a person who belongs to the same country as another; a compatriot; **fellow creature** a person or animal made by the same creator, *spec.* by God; **fellow-heir** a joint heir; **fellow soldier** a soldier who fights under the same standard or on the same side as another; **fellow subject** a subject of the same monarch; **fellow-travel** *v.i.* sympathize with the aims and general policy of the Communist Party or other party or movement; **fellow-traveller** (*a*) a person who travels with another; (*b*) a non-Communist who sympathizes with the aims and general policy of the Communist Party; *transf.* a person who sympathizes with but is not a member of another party or movement.

fellowess *n.* (now *rare*) a female fellow, a woman L15.

fellow /ˈfɛləʊ/ *v.t.* Now *rare.* ME. [f. the n.] 1†a Join in partnership or companionship *with*, *to*. ME–L16. b Make an equal *with*, *to*. LME. †2 Accompany, be associated with; be a partner in. LME–M17. 3 Equal, match. M17.

3 P. HEYLIN It will be a palace..not fellowed in Europe.

†**fellow-feel** *v.i.* E17–E18. [Back-form. f. next.] Share the feelings of others; sympathize *with*.

fellow-feeling /fɛləʊˈfiːlɪŋ/ *n.* E17. [f. FELLOW *n.* + FEELING *n.*, tr. L *compassio*, Gk *sympatheia* SYMPATHY.] 1 Sympathy. E17. 2 A sense of common interest. Now *rare.* E18.

fellowless /ˈfɛləʊlɪs/ *a.* LME. [f. FELLOW *n.* + -LESS.] 1 Without a partner or companion. *rare.* LME. 2 Without an equal, matchless. L16.

fellowlike /ˈfɛləʊlʌɪk/ *a.* & *adv. obs.* exc. *poet.* L15. [f. FELLOW *n.* + -LIKE.] A *adj.* †1 Companionable, sympathetic. L15–M17. 2 Like a partner or companion. E16. †B *adv.* 1 Like one's fellows, similarly. Only in M16. 2 Sociably. L16–L17.

fellowly /ˈfɛləʊli/ *a.* & *adv. obs.* exc. *poet.* & *rhet.* ME. [f. as prec. + -LY¹.] A *adj.* †1 Pertaining to or befitting friends or companions. ME–L16. 2 Companionable, sociable. LME. B *adv.* On equal terms; sociably; familiarly. ME.

fellowship /ˈfɛlə(ʊ)ʃɪp/ *n.* & *v.* ME. [f. FELLOW *n.* + -SHIP.] A *n.* 1 Participation, sharing; community of interest, sentiment, or nature.

ME. †b Partnership, (a) membership in a society. LME–E17. 2 Companionship, company, society. ME. 3 Intimate personal communion; intercourse. ME. †b Communication. M16–E17. 4 Friendliness; the spirit of comradeship; an instance of this. ME. 5 A body of fellows or equals; a company. Now *rare*. ME. 6 = COMMUNION 4. LME. 7 A guild, a corporation, a company. LME. †b The members of a guild or corporation. LME–M17. c An association of any kind; a society, a club, a fraternity. M16. 8†a The body of fellows in a college or university; the society constituted by the fellows. L15–L18. b The status or emoluments of a fellow in a college, learned society, etc.; a post as a fellow in a college etc. E16. 9 *Math.* The process of calculation by which gain or loss is divided among partners. M16.

1 SWIFT Joining with us here in the fellowship of slavery. 2 J. LOCKE To have fellowship with those of his own kind. 4 R. L. STEVENSON Life forces men apart and breaks up the goodly fellowships for ever. R. H. TAWNEY A band of comrades, where fellowship should be known for life. 6 **the right hand of fellowship** admission or entitlement to communion. 7c J. P. DONLEAVY The Student Christian Movement is a fellowship of students who desire to understand the Christian faith. 8b S. SPENDER If they . . obtained fellowships, generally they became absorbed into the Oxford hierarchy.

B *v.* †1 *v.t.* Unite in fellowship; associate *with*, *to*. LME–M16. †2 *v.t.* Accompany. LME–L15. 3 *v.t.* Admit to fellowship; enter into participation or comradeship with. Now only in religious use. LME. 4 *v.i.* Join in fellowship; associate *with*. Now only in religious use & chiefly *US*. LME.

felly *n.* var. of FELLOE.

felly /ˈfɛli/ *adv.* ME. [f. FELL *a.* + -LY².] 1 Fiercely, cruelly; destructively. ME. †b Bitterly, keenly; terribly. LME–L16. c Exceedingly. *dial.* E19. †2 Craftily, cunningly. Only in LME.

felo de se /ˌfiːləʊ dɪ ˈsiː, ˌfɛ-, ˈseɪ/ *n. phr.* Pl. ***felones de se*** /fɪˌləʊniːz/, ***felos de se*** /ˌfiːləʊz/. E17. [AL *felo* FELON *n.*¹ & *a.*, *de se* of himself.] 1 A person who commits suicide (formerly a criminal act in the UK) or any malicious act which leads to his or her own death; *fig.* a self-destructive person or thing. E17. 2 Suicide. L18.

felon /ˈfɛlən/ *n.*¹ & *a.* ME. [(O)Fr. (n. & adj.), obl. case of *fel* (see FELL *a.*) = Prov. *fel(on)* f. med.L *fel(l)o*, *fel(l)on-*, of unkn. origin.] A *n.* 1 A person who has committed felony. ME. †2 A wicked person, a villain; the Devil; an evil spirit. ME–E19.

Comb.: **felon-setting** *Anglo-Ir.* informing on or otherwise helping to catch a criminal.

B *adj.* 1 Cruel, fierce, terrible, wild; wicked; murderous. *arch.* ME. †b Angry, sullen. LME–M16. †2 Brave, sturdy. LME–L16. †3 Impressively large. *Sc.* LME–E17.

felon /ˈfɛlən/ *n.*² ME. [App. a specific application of prec.: cf. med.L *fel(l)o* in same sense.] A whitlow; an abscess, boil, or inflamed sore; inflammation (of a part of an animal).

Comb.: **felon-grass** *north.* & *Sc.* any of several plants reputed to cure felon in cattle; esp. masterwort, *Peucedanum ostruthium*.

felones de se *n. phr. pl.* see FELO DE SE.

felonious /fɛˈləʊnɪəs, fɪ-/ *a.* LME. [f. FELONY + -OUS.] 1 Of or pertaining to felony; of the nature of felony. Earliest in FELONIOUSLY. LME. b Of a person: that has committed felony. M19. 2 Wicked, atrociously criminal. Now chiefly *poet.* L16.

feloniously *adv.* LME. **feloniousness** *n.* E18.

†**felonous** *a.* LME. [f. FELON *n.*¹ + -OUS.] 1 Wicked. LME–L16. 2 Fierce, cruel, violent; bold, sturdy. LME–L16.

felonry /ˈfɛlənri/ *n.* M19. [f. FELON *n.*¹ + -RY.] The class of felons; *Hist.* the convict population in Australia.

felony /ˈfɛləni/ *n.* ME. [(O)Fr. *félonie*, f. as FELON *n.*¹ & *a.*: see -Y³.] †1 Wickedness; anger; deceit, treachery. ME–M16. †2 A crime, a misdeed, a sin. ME–E16. 3 *Feudal Law.* An act committed by a vassal which involved the forfeiture of his fee. ME. 4 Crime regarded by the law as grave, and usu. involving violence; an instance of this. (Formerly distinguished from *misdemeanour*.) ME.

4 **felony de se** /dɪ ˈseɪ/ [L = of himself] = FELO DE SE 2.

felos de se *n. phr. pl.* see FELO DE SE.

felsenmeer /ˈfɛlzənmiːr/ *n.* Pl. **-e** /-ə/. E20. [G, lit. 'rock-sea'.] *Physical Geogr.* An expanse of angular frost-riven rocks which may develop on a flat terrain in arctic and alpine climates; a boulder field.

felsic /ˈfɛlsɪk/ *a.* E20. [Contr. of FELDSPAR and SILICA: see -IC.] *Geol.* Of, pertaining to, or designating a group of light-coloured minerals including feldspars, feldspathoids, quartz, and muscovite; (of rock) containing a high proportion of such minerals. Cf. MAFIC.

felsite /ˈfɛlsʌɪt/ *n.* L18. [f. *fels-* in FEL(D)SPAR + -ITE¹.] *Geol.* Any fine-grained igneous rock consisting mainly of feldspar and quartz.

felsitic /fɛlˈsɪtɪk/ *a.* L20.

felspar *n.* var. of FELDSPAR.

felspathic *a.*, **-oid** *n.* vars. of FELDSPATHIC, -OID.

felstone /ˈfɛlstəʊn/ *n.* M19. [Partial tr. G *Felsstein*, f. *Fels* rock + *Stein* stone.] *Geol.* = FELSITE.

felt /fɛlt/ *n.* & *a.*¹ [OE *felt* = OS *filt* (Du. *vilt*), (O)HG *filz*, f. WGmc base rel. to that of FILTER *n.*] A *n.* 1 A fabric made of wool or other fibrous materials consolidated by heat and mechanical action so that the fibres are matted together. OE. 2 A piece of felt; something made of felt, *esp.* a felt hat. Formerly also, a filter made of felt or other material. LME. b A piece of woven cloth with a felted nap used in paper-making. M18. 3 A thickly matted mass of hair or other fibrous substance; *dial.* couch grass. LME. B *attrib.* or as *adj.* Made of felt. LME.

felt pen, **felt tip**, **felt-tip(ped) pen** a pen with a felt point.

feltlike *a.* resembling felt E17. **felty** *a.* feltlike M19.

felt /fɛlt/ *ppl a.*² L16. [pa. pple of FEEL *v.*] That is or has been felt; of which one is aware.

feltness *n.* L19.

felt /fɛlt/ *v.*¹ ME. [f. the n.] 1 *v.t.* Make of felt. Chiefly as *felted* ppl a. ME. 2 *v.t.* Make into felt; bring to a feltlike consistency; press together. E16. 3 *v.i.* Form into feltlike masses, become matted together. L18. 4 *v.t.* Cover with felt. L19.

felt *v.*² pa. t. & pple of FEEL *v.*

felter /ˈfɛltə/ *n.*¹ ME. [f. FELT *v.*¹ + -ER¹.] A person who makes or works with felt.

felter /ˈfɛltə/ *n.*² Long *obs.* exc. *dial.* E17. [f. FELTER *v.*] A tangle, a matted mass.

felter /ˈfɛltə/ *v.t. obs.* exc. *dial.* LME. [OFr. *feltrer* (mod. *feutrer*), f. *feltre* (mod. *feutre*) f. med.L *feltrum*, *filtrum*: see FILTER *n.*] 1 Tangle (hair etc.); mat together. LME. 2 Entangle; encumber. M16. †3 Filter. M16–E17.

felting /ˈfɛltɪŋ/ *n.* L17. [f. FELT *v.*¹ + -ING¹.] 1 The action of FELT *v.*¹ L17. 2 Felted cloth. E19.

felucca /fɛˈlʌkə/ *n.* E17. [It. *feluc(c)a* prob. f. Sp. †*faluca* perh. f. Arab. word of uncertain origin; cf. Moroccan Arab. *flūka*.] A small vessel propelled by lateen sails or oars, or both, formerly used in the Mediterranean area for coastal transport or trading, and still in use on rivers, esp. the Nile.

felwort /ˈfɛlwəːt/ *n.* [OE *feldwyrt*, f. as FIELD *n.* + WORT *n.*¹] The autumn gentian, *Gentianella amarella*, a plant with dull purple flowers found esp. in chalk and limestone grassland. Formerly also, any of several gentians grown in gardens, esp. *Gentiana lutea*.

fem /fɛm/ *n.*¹ *slang. derog.* L20. [Abbrev.] An effeminate man.

fem *n.*² see FEMME.

female /ˈfiːmeɪl/ *a.* & *n.* ME. [(O)Fr. *femelle* f. L *femella* dim. of *femina* woman. The present form is due to assoc. w. *male*.] A *adj.* 1 Of, pertaining to, or designating the sex which can bear offspring or produce eggs; in organisms which undergo sexual reproduction, designating, pertaining to, or producing gametes (ova) that can be fertilized by male gametes. ME. b Of a plant, flower, etc.: bearing pistils but lacking stamens; fruit-bearing. L18. 2 Of a plant, mineral, or other object: having a colour or other property associated with femaleness, esp. as being inferior to a corresponding male property etc. Now *rare* exc. in certain collocations (see below). LME. 3 Composed or consisting of women or girls or of female animals or plants. M16. 4 Of, pertaining to, or characteristic of, women or girls or female animals. Formerly also, effeminate; weak. L16. 5 Of a mechanical instrument etc.: hollowed or moulded in order to receive a corresponding or male part. M17.

1 *female child, female dog, female ostrich, female salmon*, etc. 3 MILTON That fair femal Troop . . that seemd of Goddesses. 4 G. GREENE It lacks the female touch. A man's den. A. S. BYATT She began to feel very female, an attendant servant-cum-girl-friend, his woman.

B *n.* 1 A female person, animal, or plant; (the member(s) of) the female sex. ME. 2 A woman or girl as distinguished from a man or boy; *gen.* (now only *derog.* or *joc.*) a woman, a girl. ME.

1 F. MARRYAT The stag . . was . . acting as a sentinel for the females. H. G. WELLS The female of the species . . by the age of fifteen has a clearer sense of reality in these things than most men have to the doddering end of their days.

Special collocations & *comb.*: **female circumcision** incision or removal of some of the genitals of a girl or woman (sometimes including infibulation). **female condom** a contraceptive and prophylactic sheath that a woman can insert into her vagina before sexual intercourse. **female fern** = *lady-fern* s.v. LADY *n.* **female hemp** (*obs.* exc. *Hist.*) = *fimble hemp* s.v. FIMBLE *n.* **female impersonator** a male performer dressed and acting as a woman. **female rhyme** a feminine rhyme (see FEMININE *a.* 3b). *female screw*: see SCREW *n.*¹ 1.

femalely *adv.* (*rare*) M19. **femaleness** *n.* the quality of being female L19. **femality** /fɪˈmalɪti/ *n.* female nature or characteristics M17. **femalize** *v.* †(*a*) *v.i.* become effeminate; (*b*) *v.t.* give a feminine ending to (a word): L17.

feme /fiːm, fɛm/ *n.* M16. [AN, OFr. (mod. FEMME), f. L *femina* woman.] 1 A woman. *obs.* (–M17) exc. in phrs. below. M16. 2 *Law.* A wife. L16.

Phrases: **feme covert** /ˈkʌvət/ [see COVERT *a.* 5] *Law* a married woman. **feme sole** /səʊl/ *Law* (*a*) an unmarried woman, *esp.* a divorcee; (*b*) *Hist.* a married woman who trades etc. alone or independently of her husband.

femerell /ˈfɛm(ə)rɪl/ *n.* LME. [OFr. *fumeril* louvre (in med.L *fumerillum*, *-ellum*).] Chiefly *Hist.* A louvre or covered aperture on the roof of a kitchen, hall, etc., for ventilation or escape of smoke.

femic /ˈfɛmɪk/ *a.* E20. [Contr. of FERROMAGNESIAN: see -IC.] *Petrogr.* Designating, belonging to, or characteristic of a large category of igneous rocks whose chemical composition (broadly non-aluminous and ferromagnesian) can be expressed as a combination of certain normative minerals (notably pyroxene and olivine). Cf. SALIC *a.*²

femicide /ˈfɛmɪsʌɪd/ *n.* E19. [Irreg. f. L *femina* woman + -CIDE, after *homicide*.] The killing of a woman.

feminal /ˈfɛmɪn(ə)l/ *a.* LME. [med.L *feminalis*, f. L *femina* woman: see -AL¹. Cf. OFr. *feminal*.] Of or pertaining to women; womanly, feminine.

feminality /fɛmɪˈnalɪti/ *n.* (*a*) female nature; (*b*) a female trait or peculiarity (usu. in *pl.*): M17.

femineity /fɛmɪˈniːɪti/ *n.* E19. [f. L *femineus* womanish (f. *femina* woman) + -ITY.] Womanliness; womanishness.

feminie /ˈfɛmɪni/ *n. arch.* LME. [OFr. *femenie*, f. L *femina* woman.] Womankind. In early use *spec.* the Amazons; also, their land.

feminine /ˈfɛmɪnɪn/ *a.* & *n.* LME. [(O)Fr. *féminin*, *-ine* or L *femininus*, *-ina*, f. *femina* woman: see -INE¹.] A *adj.* 1 Of a person or animal: female. Now *rare*. LME. †b Of an object to which sex is attributed, esp. a celestial body: female. L16–M19. 2 Of or pertaining to women; characteristic or regarded as characteristic of women; womanly. LME. b Womanish; effeminate. *derog.* Long *rare* or *obs.* LME. 3 *Gram.* Designating the gender to which belong words classified as female on the basis of sex or some arbitrary distinction, such as form; (of a word) belonging to this gender; (of a suffix, inflection, etc.) used with or to form words of this gender. LME. b *Pros.* & *Mus.* [Orig. in Fr. verse, of feminine wds ending in mute *-e* (used as a feminine suff.).] Of a rhyme or the ending of a verse or phrase: having the final syllable or note unaccented. E17.

1 SHAKES. *L.L.L.* A soul feminine saluteth us. 2 A. WILSON Women scholars were primarily women and should not disregard the demands of feminine fashion. M. AMIS Men are often urged, by women, to recognize the feminine side of their nature. 3 J. STODDART Every noun denoting a female animal is feminine. b J. A. WESTRUP The feminine endings in the melody are similar to those found in early eighteenth-century instrumental music. **feminine caesura**: not immediately following a stress.

B *n.* 1 A woman. Formerly also, woman, women. Now *rare.* L15. 2 *Gram.* A word classified as feminine; the feminine gender. M16.

femininely *adv.* M17. **feminineness** *n.* M19.

femininist /ˈfɛmɪnɪnɪst/ *n. rare.* L19. [f. prec. + -IST.] = FEMINIST *n.*

femini'nistic *a.* E20.

femininity /fɛmɪˈnɪnɪti/ *n.* LME. [f. as prec. + -ITY. Cf. FEMINITY.] 1 The characteristic quality or qualities of woman; womanliness; the state or fact of being female. LME. b Effeminacy. M19. 2 Womankind. *rare.* LME.

1 M. FONTEYN Tamara Karsavina .. is seductive, enchanting, coquettish, demure, innocent, or haughty .. She captures every aspect of femininity. b T. P. O'CONNOR Features delicate almost to femininity.

feminise *v.* var. of FEMINIZE.

feminism /ˈfɛmɪnɪz(ə)m/ *n.* M19. [f. L *femina* woman + -ISM; in sense 2 f. Fr. *féminisme.*] 1 The qualities of a female; *spec.* in *Med.*, the development of female secondary sexual characteristics in a male. M19. 2 Advocacy of equality of the sexes and the establishment of the political, social, and economic rights of women; the movement associated with this. L19.

2 L. WOOLF The kind of fact which made—and makes—feminism the belief or policy of all sensible men.

feminist /ˈfɛmɪnɪst/ *a.* & *n.* L19. [Fr. *féministe*, f. L *femina* woman: see -IST.] A *adj.* Of or pertaining to feminism or the advocacy of women's equality and rights. L19. B *n.* An advocate of feminism or women's equality or rights. Cf. earlier FEMININIST. E20.

femi'nistic *a.* E20.

feminity /fɪˈmɪnɪti/ *n.* LME. [(O)Fr. *féminité* f. med.L *feminitas*, f. L *femina* woman: see -ITY.] 1 = FEMININITY 1. LME. b = FEMININITY 1b. M17. 2 = FEMININITY 2. LME.

feminize /ˈfɛmɪnʌɪz/ *v.* Also **-ise.** M17. [f. L *femina* + -IZE. Cf. Fr. *féminiser.*] 1 *v.t.* Make feminine or female; make characteristic of or associated with women. M17. b Induce female physiological characteristics in. E20. 2 *v.i.* Become or grow feminine. *rare.* M19.

femini'zation *n.* the action of feminizing; the process of becoming feminized; the state of being feminized (*testicular feminization*: see TESTICULAR 1): M19.

feminoid /ˈfɛmɪnɔɪd/ *a.* E20. [f. L *femina* woman + -OID.] Feminine (but not female); of female form or appearance.

femme /fam; *in senses 8, 9 also* fɛm/ *n.* In sense 9 also ***fem*** /fɛm/. Pl. ***femmes*** /fam, famz; fɛmz/. L17. [Fr.: see FEME.] I In phrases. 1 *femme couverte* /kuvɛrt, kʊˈvəːt/, pl. *couvertes* /-vɛrt, -ˈvəːts/ [see COVERT *a.* 5], = FEME *covert.* L17. 2 *femme de chambre* /də ʃɑ̃ːbr, ˈʃɑːmbrə/ [lit. 'of the (bed)room'], a lady's maid. M18. 3 *femme incomprise* /ɛ̃kɔ̃priːz/, pl. *incomprises* /-priːz/, a woman who is misunderstood or unappreciated. M19. 4 *femme de ménage* /də menaːʒ, meɪˈnɑːʒ/ [lit. 'of the household'], a charwoman, a domestic help. L19. 5 *femme du monde* /dy mɔ̃ːd, duː mɔːnd/, a woman of the world. L19. 6 *femme fatale* /fatal, faˈtɑːl/, pl. *fatales* /-tal, -ˈtɑːl/, a dangerously attractive woman. E20. II Simply. 7 *gen.* A woman, a wife. *rare.* E19. 8 A girl. *US slang.* E20. 9 A lesbian taking a traditionally feminine role. *slang.* M20.

femora *n.pl.* see FEMUR.

femoral /ˈfɛm(ə)r(ə)l/ *a.* & *n.* L18. [f. L FEMUR, *femor-* + -AL¹.] Chiefly *Anat.* A *adj.* Of or pertaining to the femur or thigh. L18.

femoral artery: running down the front of the upper thigh and the rear of the lower thigh, continuing into the popliteal artery.

B *n.* The femoral artery. M19.

femoro- /ˈfɛmərəʊ/ *comb. form.* [f. as prec. + -O-.] Used in *Anat.* & *Med.* to form words in senses 'of the femur', 'femoral and —', as *femoro-fibular, femoro-popliteal.*

femto- /ˈfɛmtəʊ/ *comb. form.* [f. Da. or Norw. *femten* fifteen: see -O-.] Used in names of units of measurement to denote a factor of 10^{-15}, as *femtosecond* etc. Abbrev. *f.*

femur /ˈfiːmə/ *n.* Pl. **femurs, femora** /ˈfɛm(ə)rə/. L15. [L = thigh.] 1 The thigh-bone in vertebrates. Formerly also, the thigh. L15. 2 The third articulated segment of the leg in insects and some other arthropods. M19.

fen /fɛn/ *n.*¹ [OE *fen(n)* = OFris. *fen(n)e*, OS *fen(n)i* (Du. *veen*), OHG *fenna, fenni* (G *Fenn*), ON *fen*, Goth. *fani* clay, f. Gmc.] 1 (A tract of) low land covered wholly or partly with shallow water or subject to frequent flooding; *Ecol.* wet land with alkaline, neutral, or only slightly acid peaty soil (cf. BOG *n.*¹). OE. 2 Mud, filth, excrement. Long *obs.* exc. *dial.* OE.

1 **the Fens** low-lying districts of Cambridgeshire, Lincolnshire, and neighbouring counties in eastern England, which were formerly marshland but have been drained for agriculture since the 17th cent.

Comb.: **fen-berry** the cranberry; **fen-fire** a will-o'-the-wisp; **fenman** a native or inhabitant of the Fens; **fen-runners** long skates for skating on fens; *fen sedge*: see SEDGE 1; *fen tiger*: see TIGER *n.* 4a.

fenner *n.* a native or inhabitant of the Fens M19.

fen /fɛn/ *n.*² Long *obs.* exc. *dial.* [OE *fyne.* The mod. form (with *e* for OE *y*) is Kentish. Cf. FENNY *a.*², FINEW *v.*] †1 Mould, mildew, moisture. Only in OE. 2 A mould that attacks the hop plant. M18.

fen /fʌn/ *n.*³ Pl. same. M19. [Chin. *fēn* a hundredth part.] A monetary unit of China, equal to one-tenth of a jiao.

fen *v.* see FAIN *v.*²

fence /fɛns/ *n.* ME. [Aphet. f. DEFENCE *n.*] †1 The action of defending. ME–E16. †2 Means or method of defence. LME–M18. 3 A railing or barrier constructed of posts of any of various materials connected by wire, planks, etc., used to enclose and prevent entry to and exit from a field, yard, etc.; *arch.* a bulwark, a defence. LME. b A structure for a horse to jump over in a competition, race, etc. M19. 4 The action or art of fencing. M16. 5 A person who or an establishment which deals in stolen goods. L17. 6 A guard, guide, or gauge designed to regulate the movements of a tool, machine, etc. E18.

3 R. CAMPBELL The corrugated iron fence which separated our two gardens. 4 A. DUGGAN Our enemies would use the same tricks of fence.

Phrases: *electric fence*: see ELECTRIC *a. live fence*: see LIVE *a.* **mend one's fences** (*a*) *US* (of a member of Congress) renew contact with the electors, improve political relationships; (*b*) *gen.* renew contact or make peace with a person. **over the fence** *Austral. colloq.* unreasonable, unjust. *rush one's fences*: see RUSH *v.*² 8. **sit on the fence** remain neutral in a contest, not take sides, not commit oneself. **sunk fence**: placed along the bottom of a ditch, or formed by a ditch. *zigzag fence*: see ZIGZAG *a.*

Comb.: **fence lizard** a N. American spiny lizard, *Sceloporus undulatus*; **fence-mending** the action of mending one's fences, renewal of contact, improving of (political) relationships; **fence-month** (*a*) the period (about 30 days) of fawning for deer, during which hunting was forbidden; (*b*) the close season for fishing; **fence-row** *US* an uncultivated strip of land on each side of and below a fence; **fence-shop**: selling stolen goods; **fence-sitter** a person who sits on the fence, a person who will not commit himself or herself; **fence-sitting** the action of sitting on the fence, refusal to commit oneself.

fenceful *a.* (now *rare* or *obs.*) protecting, shielding E17.

fence /fɛns/ *v.* LME. [f. the n.] 1 a *v.t.* Protect, shield, screen, (*from, against*); fortify, surround (as) with a fence (foll. by *about, in, round, up*); keep *off* with a fence. LME. b *v.t.* Repel, keep *out* or *off. arch.* L16. †c *v.i.* Provide defence or protection *against.* L17–M18. 2 *v.t. Sc. Law.* Open the proceedings of (a court of law, *Hist.* the Parliament) by the use of a form of words forbidding the unnecessary interruption or obstruction of the proceedings. LME. 3 *v.i.* Practise the art or sport of fencing. L16. b Engage in skilful argument; parry, evade answering (a question). (Foll. by *with.*) M17. 4 *v.t.* & *i.* Deal in (stolen goods). E17. 5 *v.i.* Of a horse etc.: jump fences. L19.

1a E. BIRNEY Lieutenant Smith began to write rapidly, his arm fencing the paper from Turvey's gaze. R. C. HUTCHINSON The houses were formidably fenced off with barbed wire. b SIR W. SCOTT A cup of sack shall fence the cold. 3a J. D. WATSON Afternoons were spent at a gymnasium learning how to fence. b B. UNSWORTH In all our conversations I was fencing with him, scoring off him all the time.

fencer /ˈfɛnsə/ *n.* L16. [f. FENCE *v.* + -ER¹.] 1 A person who practises the art or sport of fencing. Formerly also, a professional sword-fighter; a gladiator. L16. 2 A receiver of stolen goods. L17. 3 A horse which jumps fences (*well, badly*, etc.). E19. 4 A person who puts up or mends fences. E19.

fenchone /ˈfɛntʃəʊn/ *n.* L19. [G *Fenchon*, f. *Fenchel* fennel: see -ONE.] *Chem.* A fragrant liquid terpenoid ketone, $C_{10}H_{16}O$, found esp. in fennel and thuja oils.

fenchane *n.* a liquid saturated bicyclic hydrocarbon, $C_{10}H_{18}$, from which fenchone and the fenchenes are formally derived E20. **fenchene** *n.* any of a series of isomeric liquid terpenes of formula $C_{10}H_{16}$, obtained by reducing fenchone L19.

fencible /ˈfɛnsɪb(ə)l/ *a.* & *n.* ME. [Aphet. f. DEFENSIBLE.] A *adj.* 1 Of a person: fit and liable for defensive military service. Formerly also, of arms or armour: able to be used for defence. Chiefly *Sc. obs.* exc. *Hist.* ME. b *Hist.* Of a military force: composed of soldiers liable only for home service. L18. †2 Of a fortress, town, etc.: able to be defended; well-fortified. L16–E19. †3 Able to serve as a fence or enclosure. E18–E19.

2 SPENSER No fort so fencible .. But that continuall battery will rive. 3 SIR W. SCOTT The thorn hedges are nearly fencible.

B *n. Hist.* A soldier liable only for home service. L18.

fencing /ˈfɛnsɪŋ/ *n.* LME. [f. FENCE *v.* + -ING¹.] 1 The action of protecting or setting up a defence *against* something. Long *rare* or *obs.* LME. 2 *Sc. Law.* The formal opening of a court of law or (*Hist.*) the Parliament. M16. 3 The practice, art, or sport of engaging in combat with swords, esp. according to a set of rules using foils, épées, or sabres to score points. L16. b The action of engaging in skilful argument or evading questions. E17. 4 A fence, an enclosure, a railing; fences collectively; material for fences. L16. 5 The action of putting up a fence. E17. 6 The action (by a horse) of jumping a fence. E19. 7 The action or practice of dealing in stolen goods. M19.

fend /fɛnd/ *n. Sc.* & *dial.* M17. [f. the vb.] 1 Defence, protection. M17. 2 An effort; an attempt; the action or activity of making an effort or efforts. E18.

fend /fɛnd/ *v.* ME. [Aphet. f. DEFEND.] 1 *v.t.* & *i.* = DEFEND. Now *poet.* or *arch.* ME. 2 *v.t.* Keep from or away, ward off. Now usu. foll. by *off.* LME. 3 *v.t.* Forbid; prevent (*from*). Cf. FAIN *v.*² *obs.* exc. *dial.* LME. 4 *v.i.* Make an effort, strive, struggle. M16. b Foll. by *for*: look after, provide for (usu. oneself). E17. c Fare, manage. *Sc.* & *dial.* E18. 5 *v.t.* Support, maintain. Chiefly *Sc.* & *dial.* M17.

1 **fend and prove** (now *dial.*) argue, wrangle. 2 C. RYCROFT Go to bed with hot Horlick's malted milk to fend off night starvation. 4 D. H. LAWRENCE A man has to fend and fettle for the best. b G. SWIFT We don't need him any more .. we can fend for ourselves. 5 SIR W. SCOTT They are puirly armed, and warse fended wi' victual.

fendy *a.* (*dial.*) resourceful, managing; active: E18.

Fendant /fɑ̃dɑ̃/ *n.* E20. [Swiss Fr.] (The grape producing) a dry white wine of SW Switzerland.

fender /ˈfɛndə/ *n.* ME. [f. FEND *v.* + -ER¹.] **I 1 a** *Naut.* A piece of old cable, matting, rubber, etc., hung over a vessel's side to protect it against chafing or impact. ME. **b** A large piece of timber fixed as a guard to protect a pier or dockwall. L16. **c** A low metal frame fitted to a fireplace to prevent coals from rolling outside the hearth. M17. **d** A sluice(-gate). M19. **e** A mudguard; a wing or bumper of a motor vehicle. *N. Amer.* E20. **2** *gen.* Anything used to keep something off or prevent collision. E17.

1a V. SACKVILLE-WEST Those little fenders which prevent a ship from bumping too roughly against the quay. c G. ORWELL To sit in a room like this, in an armchair beside an open fire with your feet in the fender.

II 3 = DEFENDER. *obs.* exc. *dial.* LME.

Comb.: **fender-bender** *slang* (chiefly *N. Amer.*) a (usu. minor) collision between vehicles; **fender-stool** a long footstool placed close to the fender of a fireplace.

†**feneration** *n.* L16–L18. [L *faeneratio(n-)*, f. *faenerare*, *-ari* lend on interest, f. *faenus*, *faenor-* interest: see -ATION.] Usury.

fenestella /fɛnɪˈstɛlə/ *n.* LME. [L, dim. of *fenestra* window: see -EL².] **1** *Archit.* A small window or opening in a wall, esp. in the side of an altar or confessio, enabling the relics inside to be seen. LME. **b** A small niche in the wall on the south side of the altar in a church, containing the piscina and often the credence. L18. **2** *Palaeont.* A fossil bryozoan of Palaeozoic age. Chiefly as mod.L genus name. M19.

†**fenester** *n.* ME–E19. [OFr. *fenestre* (mod. *fenêtre*) f. as next.] A window.

fenestra /fɪˈnɛstrə/ *n.* Pl. **-trae** /-triː/. E19. [L = window.] **1** *Bot.* A small mark or scar left by the separation of the seed from the ovary. *rare.* E19. **2** *Anat.* A small hole or opening in a bone; *esp.* either of two openings, covered by membranes, in the inner ear (see below). M19. **3** *Med.* **a** A perforation in a surgical instrument other than in the handle. Also, an opening in a dressing. L19. **b** A hole cut surgically in any structure of the body; *esp.* one made by fenestration. M20.

2 **fenestra ovalis** /əʊˈvɑːlɪs, -ˈveɪl-/ [L = oval window] the opening between the middle ear and the vestibule. **fenestra rotunda** /rəˈtʌndə/ [L = round window] the opening between the cochlea and the middle ear.

fenestral /fɪˈnɛstr(ə)l/ *a.* Now *rare.* L17. [f. as prec. + -AL¹.] Of or pertaining to a window.

fenestrate /fɪˈnɛstrət, ˈfɛnəstrət/ *a.* M19. [L *fenestratus* pa. pple of *fenestrare* provide with openings or windows, f. as FENESTRA; see -ATE².] Having an opening. Now *spec.* in *Bot.* & *Zool.*, having small perforations or transparent areas.

fenestrate /fɪˈnɛstreɪt, ˈfɛnəstreɪt/ *v.t.* L19. [L *fenestrat-* pa. ppl stem of *fenestrare*: see prec., -ATE³.] Provide with small holes or openings; perforate.

fenestrated /fɪˈnɛstreɪtɪd, ˈfɛnəstreɪtɪd/ *a.* E19. [f. as FENESTRATE *a.* + -ED¹.] = FENESTRATE *a.* Also, (of a surgical instrument) having one or more fenestrae.

fenestration /fɛnɪˈstreɪʃ(ə)n/ *n.* M19. [f. as FENESTRATE *v.* + -ION.] **1** *Archit.* The arrangement of windows in a building. M19. **2** *Bot.* & *Zool.* The condition of being fenestrate. L19. **3** *Surg.* (The operation of cutting) an artificial opening into the labyrinth of the ear, used to restore hearing in cases of otosclerosis. L19.

feng-shui /ˈfɛŋʃuːi, ˈfʌŋ-/ *n.* L18. [Chin., f. *fēng* wind + *shuǐ* water.] In Chinese mythology, a system of spirit influences, good and evil, which inhabit the natural features of landscapes; a kind of geomancy for dealing with these in choosing sites for houses or graves.

Fenian /ˈfiːnɪən/ *n.* & *a.* E19. [f. OIr. *féne* one of the names of the ancient population of Ireland, confused with *fiann* FIAN the guard of legendary kings: see -IAN.] **A** *n.* **1** Any of the band of mercenary warriors of Irish history and legend who acted as permanent guard of the high king of Ireland. E19. **2** A member of a 19th-cent. league among the Irish in the US and Ireland for promoting revolution and the overthrow of the British Government in Ireland. M19. **B** *adj.* Of or pertaining to the Fenians or Fenianism. M19.

Fenianism *n.* the principles, purposes, or methods of the 19th-cent. Fenians M19.

fenks /fɛŋks/ *n.pl.* E19. [Origin unkn.] The fibrous parts of a whale's blubber, which contain the oil; the refuse of blubber when melted.

fennec /ˈfɛnɛk/ *n.* L18. [Arab. *fanak* f. Pers. *fanak*, *fanaj*.] More fully *fennec fox*. A small fox, *Vulpes zerda*, which inhabits deserts from Morocco to Arabia and is notable for its very large ears.

fennel /ˈfɛn(ə)l/ *n.* [OE *finugl*, *finule* fem., *fenol*, *finul* masc., and OFr. *fenoil*, f. L *faeniculum* dim. of *faenum* hay.] An aromatic yellow-flowered umbelliferous herb, *Foeniculum vulgare*, with feathery leaves used to flavour fish sauces, salad dressings, etc. Also, any of various similar or related plants (see below).

Phrases & comb.: *dog-fennel*: see DOG *n.* **fennel-flower** any of various plants of the genus *Nigella*, of the buttercup family; esp. *N. sativa* (black cumin), the seeds of which are used as a flavouring. **fennel-giant** *arch.* = *giant fennel* below. **Florence fennel** = FINOCCHIO. **giant fennel** any of various large Mediterranean umbellifers of the genus *Ferula*, related to fennel. *hog's fennel*: see HOG *n.* **sweet fennel** = *Florence fennel* above.

fennish /ˈfɛnɪʃ/ *a.* L16. [f. FEN *n.*¹ + -ISH¹.] **1** = FENNY *a.*¹ 1. L16. **2** Belonging to or produced from a fen. L16.

Fennoscandian /fɛnəʊˈskandɪən/ *a.* E20. [f. G *fennoskandisch* adj., f. L *Fenni* the Finns + -O-: see SCANDIAN *a.*] *Geol.* Designating or pertaining to the ancient land mass in NW Europe comprising most of Scandinavia, Finland, and adjacent parts of Russia.

fenny /ˈfɛni/ *a.*¹ OE. [f. FEN *n.*¹ + -Y¹.] **1** Of the nature of a fen; boggy, swampy. OE. †**b** Muddy, dirty. OE–M17. **2** Inhabiting, growing, or produced in a fen. Now only of plants. M16.

1 *Watsonia* Crowinstown Lake .. has a fenny margin .. but is becoming acid on the west side. 2 SHAKES. *Macb.* Fillet of a fenny snake, In the cauldron boil and bake.

fenny *a.*² see VINNY *a.*

fenoterol /fɛnəˈtɛrɒl/ *n.* L20. [f. *feno-* repr. PHENO- + *-ter-* arbitrary elem. + -OL.] *Pharm.* A sympathomimetic agent used esp. as a bronchodilator in the treatment of asthma.

fenster /ˈfɛnstə/ *n.* E20. [G = window.] *Geol.* An opening eroded through a stratum in a region of overfolding or overthrusting, exposing a younger stratum beneath.

fent /fɛnt/ *n.* & *v.* LME. [(O)Fr. *fente* slit, f. use as n. of fem. pa. pple of L *findere* cleave, split. See VENT *n.*¹] **A** *n.* **1** A short slit or opening in a robe, *esp.* the opening at the throat; a placket. Now chiefly *dial.* LME. **2** A remnant of cloth. M19.

1 *fig.* L. DURRELL Rumours .. had begun to scuttle about the fents and warrens of the old town. 2 *attrib.*: H. MITCHELL I hunted the fent shops for remnants of gay prints.

B *v.t.* Make slits in. *rare.* L16.

fenugreek /ˈfɛnjʊɡriːk/ *n.* [OE *fenogrecum*, superseded in ME by forms f. (O)Fr. *fenugrec*, f. L *faenugraecum*, for *faenum Graecum* 'Greek hay': the Romans used the dried plant for fodder.] A leguminous plant, *Trigonella foenum-graecum*, with aromatic seeds used to flavour curries etc. Also *gen.*, any plant of the genus *Trigonella*.

bird's-foot fenugreek: see BIRD *n.* **sweet fenugreek** = *Darling clover* s.v. DARLING *n.*²

feod *n.* see FEUD *n.*²

†**feodal** *a.* var. of FEUDAL *a.*¹

feodary *n.* var. of FEUDARY.

feoff /fiːf, fɛf/ *v.t.* Now *rare* or *obs.* ME. [AN *feoffer*, OFr. *fieuffer*, *fieffer*, f. as FIEF *n.*] **1** *Law.* Put in legal possession; = ENFEOFF *v.* 1. ME. †**2** Confer (a heritable possession) *on*, *upon*. L16–M17.

feoffee /fɛˈfiː/ *n. obs.* exc. *Hist.* LME. [AN *feoffé* pa. pple of *feoffer*: see prec., -EE¹.] *Law.* **1** More fully *feoffee in* or *of trust*. A trustee invested with a freehold estate in land, latterly esp. for charitable or other public purposes. LME. **2** The person to whom a feoffment is made. M16.

feoffer *n.* var. of FEOFFOR.

feoffment /ˈfiːfm(ə)nt, ˈfɛf-/ *n. obs.* exc. *Hist.* ME. [AN, f. as FEOFF *v.*: see -MENT.] *Law.* **1** The action of putting a person in possession of property, rents, etc., under the feudal system; the mode of conveying freehold property by livery of seisin. ME. **b** More fully *feoffment of* or *upon trust*, *feoffment to uses*. A conveyance of land to one person in trust for another, or for certain uses. L15. †**2** Possession of property as a result of feoffment; the property itself. Only in ME. †**3** A deed of feoffment. LME–L17.

1 **charter** or **deed of feoffment**: recording or (later) effecting a feoffment.

feoffor /ˈfiːfə, ˈfɛfə/ *n. obs.* exc. *Hist.* Also **-er**. LME. [AN *feoffour*, f. as FEOFF *v.*: see -OUR, -OR.] *Law.* **1** A person who makes a feoffment to another. LME. †**2** = FEOFFEE. LME–E17.

-fer /fə/ *suff.* Also (see below) **-ifer**. [L = carrying, bearing, f. *ferre* carry, bear.] Forming (usu. w. intermediate -I-) ns. w. the sense 'a person or thing having, containing, or carrying', as *aquifer*, *crucifer*, *rotifer*, etc.

féra /fera/ *n.* Pl. pronounced same. Also ***ferra***. E19. [Swiss Fr.] A whitefish from any of certain Alpine lakes.

feracious /fəˈreɪʃəs/ *a.* Now *rare.* M17. [f. L *ferac-*, *ferax* f. *ferre* to bear: see -ACIOUS.] Bearing abundantly; fruitful, prolific.

CARLYLE A world so feracious, teeming with endless results.

feracity /fəˈrasɪti/ *n.* Now *rare.* LME. [L *feracitas*, f. as prec.: see -ACITY.] The quality of being feracious.

ferae naturae /ˌfɪəriː nəˈtʃʊəriː, ˌfɛraɪ nəˈtjʊəraɪ/ *pred.* & *postpositive a.* & *n. phr.* M17. [L = of wild nature.] Chiefly *Law.* Undomesticated or wild (animals).

Feraghan /ˈfɛrəɡɑːn/ *n.* E20. [Pers., f. *Ferghana*, a region in central Asia.] A costly handmade Persian rug, usu. of cotton.

feral /ˈfɪər(ə)l/ *a.*¹ E17. [L *feralis* pertaining to funeral rites or to the dead.] **1** Deadly, fatal. Now *rare* or *obs.* E17. **2** Funereal, gloomy. Now *arch.* or *poet.* M17.

feral /ˈfɪər(ə)l, ˈfɛr(ə)l/ *a.*² & *n.* E17. [f. L *fera* wild animal, use as n. (sc. *bestia*) of *ferus* wild + -AL¹.] **A** *adj.* **1** Of, pertaining to, or resembling, a wild animal; savage, fierce, brutal. E17. **2** Wild, untamed, uncultivated. M17. **b** Chiefly of animals: belonging to or forming a wild population ultimately descended from individuals which escaped from captivity or domestication; born of such an animal in the wild. M19.

1 I. MURDOCH Her intense animal face was blazing with health and vitality and feral curiosity. 2b *Watsonia* The fact that a plant can maintain itself .. where it was planted, without further care .. is not sufficient to justify calling it feral. **feral pigeon** the common pigeon of town and city centres and elsewhere, that is descended from domesticated forms of the rock dove, *Columba livia*.

B *n.* A wild beast; a domesticated animal living wild. M17.

Ferangi *n.* var. of FERINGHEE.

ferash /fɛˈraʃ/ *n.* Also **farrash**. E17. [Pers. & Urdu *farrāš* f. Arab. = a person who spreads out bedding, carpets, etc.] A servant in some Muslim countries; *spec.* a menial performing heavy domestic tasks.

ferberite /ˈfɔːbərʌɪt/ *n.* E19. [f. surname *Ferber* (see below) + -ITE¹.] †**1** [J. J. *Ferber* (1743–90), Swed. mineralogist.] *Geol.* A variety of gneiss. Only in E19. **2** [Rudolph *Ferber*, 19th-cent. Ger. mineralogist.] *Min.* A monoclinic ferrous tungstate (isostructural with wolframite) usu. occurring as black elongated prisms. M19.

fer-de-lance /fɛː də ˈlɑːns/ *n.* Pl. **fers-de-lance** (pronounced same), **fer-de-lances**. L19.

[Fr. = iron (head) of lance.] A highly venomous tropical American pit viper, *Bothrops atrox*.

fer-de-moline /fɛːdəmə'lʌɪn/ *n.* Pl. ***fers-*** (pronounced same). LME. [Fr. *fer de moulin* lit. 'iron of mill'.] *Her.* A charge resembling the iron support of a millstone.

fere /fɪə/ *n. arch.* Also †**yfere**. [OE *ġefēra*, f. Gmc base of Y- + (ult.) ablaut var. of base of FARE *v.* (Northumb. *fœra*.] **1** A comrade, a partner; a friend or companion of either sex. OE. **2** A husband or wife; the mate of an animal etc. ME. †**3** An equal, a peer. ME–E19.

1 TENNYSON The lamb . . raceth freely with his fere. **2** B. TAYLOR Paris . . Took thee, the widow, as his fere.

fere /fɪə/ *a.* Long only *Sc.* ME. [ON *fœrr* ult. f. Gmc ablaut var. of base of FARE *v.* Cf. FEIRIE.] Sound, strong; in good health.

feretory /'fɛrət(ə)ri/ *n.* ME. [OFr. *fiertre* f. L *feretrum* f. Gk *pheretron* bier, f. *pherein* bear, assim. to wds in *-tory*.] **1** A (portable) shrine containing the relics of a saint. ME. **2** A small room or chapel in which shrines were deposited. LME. **3** A bier. LME.

feretrum /'fɛrətrəm/ *n. rare.* Pl. ***-tra*** /-trə/. L15. [L: see FERETORY.] = FERETORY 1.

feretto /fə'rɛtəʊ/ *n.* Now *rare* or *obs.* M17. [It. *ferretto* (*di spagna* 'of Spain'), dim. of *ferro* iron f. L *ferrum*.] Copper calcined with sulphur or zinc sulphate, used to colour glass.

ferfel *n.* var. of FARFEL.

fergusonite /'fəːgəs(ə)nʌɪt/ *n.* E19. [f. Robert *Ferguson* (1799–1865), Sc. physician + -ITE[1].] *Min.* A tetragonal niobate and tantalate of iron, cerium, yttrium, and other elements, usu. occurring as grey, yellow, or brown prisms.

feria /'fɪərɪə, 'fɛ-/ *n.* LME. [L = holiday: see FAIR *n.*[1] In sense 2 through Sp.] **1** *Eccl.* A weekday, *esp.* one on which no festival falls. LME. **2** In Spain and Spanish-speaking America: a fair. M19.

†**ferie** *n.* [OFr.] = FERIA 1 LME–E17.

ferial /'fɪərɪəl, 'fɛr-/ *a.* LME. [(O)Fr. *férial* or its source med.L *ferialis*, f. as prec.: see -AL[1].] **1** *Eccl.* Designating or pertaining to an ordinary weekday as opp. to a day appointed for a festival or fast. LME. †**2** *Sc. Law.* Designating a day or time when courts of law were closed and legal process was invalid. LME–E18. **3** Of or pertaining to a holiday. L15.

†**feriation** *n.* E17–E19. [med.L *feriatio(n-)*, f. L *feriat-* pa. ppl stem of *feriari* make holiday, f. as FERIA: see -ATION.] The keeping of a holiday; cessation of work.

ferine /'fɪərʌɪn/ *a.* M17. [L *ferinus*, f. *fera*: see FERAL *a.*[2], -INE[1].] **1** Bestial. M17. **b** Of, pertaining to, or resembling, a wild animal; untamed, savage. L17. **2** Of a disease: malignant. *rare.* M17.

1 J. NORRIS To . . suffer the ferine and brutish part to get the Ascendant over that which is Rational and Divine. **b** J. S. BLACKIE Dogs and cocks . . and other ferine combatants.

Feringhee /fə'rɪŋgi/ *n. Anglo-Ind.* Also **Ferangi** /fə'raŋgi/. E17. [Urdu f. Pers. *firangī* f. base of FRANK *n.*[1]] **1** In India and parts of the Middle East, a European. Freq. *derog.* E17. **2** A Eurasian of Portuguese-Indian descent. *obs.* exc. *Hist.* M18.

Ferio /'fɛrɪəʊ/ *n.* M16. [L = to strike dead, taken as a mnemonic of scholastic philosophers, E a universal negative proposition, I a particular affirmative proposition, and O a particular negative proposition.] *Logic.* The fourth mood of the first syllogistic figure, in which a universal negative major premiss and a particular affirmative minor yield a particular negative conclusion.

Ferison /fɛ'rʌɪs(ə)n/ *n.* E16. [A mnemonic of scholastic philosophers: see prec.] *Logic.* The sixth mood of the third syllogistic figure, in which a universal negative major premiss and a particular affirmative minor yield a particular negative conclusion.

ferity /'fɛrɪti/ *n.* M16. [OFr. *ferite* or L *feritas*, f. *ferus* wild: see -ITY.] **1** The quality or state of being wild or savage; wildness, ferocity. M16. **2** Barbarity; savage cruelty or inhumanity. Now *rare* or *obs.* E17. **3** Primitive or barbarous condition. M17.

ferk *v.* var. of FIRK.

ferlie *a.*, *n.*, & *v.* var. of FERLY.

ferling /'fəːlɪŋ/ *n. obs.* exc. *Hist.* [OE *fēorþling*, f. *fēorþa* FOURTH + -LING[1].] †**1** A quarter of a penny; a farthing. OE–E18. **2** The fourth part of a piece of land; each of four wards of a borough etc. E17.

ferly /'fəːli/ *a.*, *n.*, & *v.* Now chiefly *Sc.* & *dial.* Also **ferlie**. [OE *fǣrlić*, f. as FEAR *n.*[1] + -LY[1].] **A** *adj.* †**1** Sudden, unexpected. OE–LME. †**2** Dreadful, frightful, terrible. ME–L16. **3** Strange, wondrous; remarkable, surprising. ME.

B *n.* †**1** Wonder, astonishment. ME–L15. **2** Something strange or wonderful, a marvel; a curiosity, a novelty. ME. **b** A strange, unpleasant, or monstrous person or animal. L18.

2 DAY LEWIS Those ferlies you'll not behold Till the guardians of that valley have crossed Your hand with fairy gold.

C *v.i.* Wonder, marvel *at*. LME.

R. BURNS They'll . . ferlie at the folk in Lon'on.

fermail /'fəːmeɪl/ *n.* L15. [(O)Fr., (OFr. also *-aille*), f. med.L *firmaculum*, *ferm-* clasp, brooch, buckle, f. *firmare* fix: see FIRM *v.*, -AL[1].] Chiefly *Her.* A buckle, a clasp.

Fermat /'fəːmɑː/ *n.* E19. [Pierre de *Fermat* (1601–65), Fr. mathematician.] *Math.* Used in *possess.* and *attrib.* to designate concepts introduced by Fermat.

Fermat number any number of the form $2^{2^n}+1$, where n is a positive integer. **Fermat's last theorem** a conjecture (of which Fermat noted that he had 'a truly wonderful proof'), that if n is an integer greater than 2, $x^n + y^n = z^n$ has no positive integral solutions. **Fermat's theorem** (*a*) a theorem that if p is a prime and a an integer not divisible by p, then $a^{p-1} - 1$ is divisible by p; (*b*) = *Fermat's last theorem* above.

fermata /fəː'mɑːtə/ *n.* Pl. **-tas**, **-te** /-teɪ/. L19. [It.] *Mus.* (A sign indicating) an unspecified prolongation of a note or rest.

ferment /'fəːmɛnt/ *n.* LME. [(O)Fr., or L *fermentum* f. *fervere* boil: see -MENT.] **1** Leaven, yeast; a fermenting agent; *arch.* an enzyme. LME. **2** = FERMENTATION 1. E17. **b** *fig.* Agitation, excitement, tumult. L17.

1 J. GRIGSON To make the ferment, cream the yeast and sugar . . and whisk in the water. **2** G. BERKELEY The first ferment of new wine. **b** E. MANNIN He had thought to sleep but the ferment of his thoughts did not permit of it.

ferment /fə'mɛnt, fəː-/ *v.* LME. [(O)Fr. *fermenter* f. L *fermentare*, f. *fermentum*: see prec.] **1** *v.i.* Undergo fermentation. LME. **b** *transf.* & *fig.* Become excited or agitated; be exacerbated. L17. **2** *v.t.* Subject to fermentation; cause fermentation in. L15. **b** *transf.* & *fig.* Excite, stir up; exacerbate, foment. M17.

1b I. COMPTON-BURNETT It is a good thing to speak of things openly. . . Then nothing can ferment and fester underneath. **2b** R. W. EMERSON The Christianity which fermented Europe.

fermenta'bility *n.* the quality of being fermentable L18. **fermentable** *a.* able to be fermented M18. **fermenter**, **-or** *n.* (*a*) a vessel in which fermentation takes place; (*b*) an organism which causes fermentation: E20.

fermental /fə'mɛnt(ə)l/ *a.* M17. [f. FERMENT *n.* + -AL[1].] Pertaining to or of the nature of a ferment or fermentation.

fermentate /'fəːmənteɪt/ *v.t.* Now *rare* or *obs.* L16. [L *fermentat-* pa. ppl stem of *fermentare* FERMENT *v.*: see -ATE[3].] Cause to ferment; leaven.

fermentation /fəːmɛn'teɪʃ(ə)n/ *n.* LME. [Late L *fermentatio(n-)* f. as prec.: see -ATION.] **1** A biochemical process of the nature of that involved in the action of yeast on sugars or dough, involving effervescence, evolution of heat, and chemical breakdown of the substance acted on. LME. **2** *fig.* (A state of) excitement or agitation. M17.

Comb.: **fermentation lock** a valve placed on top of a vessel of fermenting wine etc. to enable gas to escape.

fermentative /fə'mɛntətɪv/ *a.* M17. [f. as FERMENTATE + -IVE.] **1** Pertaining to or of the nature of fermentation; developed by fermentation. M17. **2** Tending to cause or undergo fermentation. M17.

fermentescible /fəːmɛn'tɛsɪb(ə)l/ *a.* L17. [f. FERMENT *v.*: see -ESCE, -IBLE.] Capable of causing or undergoing fermentation.

fermentive /fə'mɛntɪv/ *a.* M17. [f. FERMENT *n.*, *v.* + -IVE.] Tending to produce fermentation.

fermentum /fə'mɛntəm, fəː-/ *n.* E18. [med.L use of L = yeast: see FERMENT *n.*] *RC Ch.* (now *Hist.*). A portion of the Eucharistic oblation sent from the papal mass to a neighbouring presbyter.

fermery /'fəːm(ə)ri/ *n.* Also **farm-** /'fɑːm-/. LME. [Aphet. f. OFr. *enfermerie* f. med.L *infirmaria* INFIRMARY.] *Hist.* An infirmary, esp. of a monastery.

Fermi /'fəːmi/ *n.* E20. [Enrico *Fermi* (1901–54), Italian-born physicist.] **I 1** Used *attrib.* to denote principles and concepts arising from Fermi's work. E20.

Fermi energy, **level** the energy of the Fermi surface. **Fermi statistics** = FERMI-DIRAC STATISTICS. **Fermi surface** a surface in momentum space representing the maximum energy, at absolute zero, of the electrons in a crystal lattice with respect to their direction of motion.

II 2 (**f-**.) A unit of length used in nuclear physics, equal to 10^{-15} m. M20.

Fermi-Dirac statistics /ˌfəːmɪdɪ'rak stəˌtɪstɪks/ *n. phr.* E20. [FERMI + P. A. M. *Dirac* (1902–84), Eng. physicist.] *Physics.* A type of quantum statistics, introduced by Fermi and Dirac, used to describe systems of identical particles which obey the exclusion principle.

fermion /'fəːmɪɒn/ *n.* M20. [f. FERMI + -ON.] *Physics.* A particle that has an antisymmetric wave function, and hence half-integral spin, and can be described by Fermi-Dirac statistics. Cf. BOSON.

fermium /'fəːmɪəm/ *n.* M20. [f. FERMI + -IUM.] A radioactive metallic chemical element of the actinide series, atomic no. 100, which is produced artificially. (Symbol Fm.)

fern /fəːn/ *n.* [OE *fearn* = MDu. *væren* (Du. *varen*), OHG *farn* (G *Farn*), f. WGmc.] Any of the numerous vascular cryptogams of the order Filicopsida, which reproduce by means of spores borne usu. on the underside of the fronds, which are typically pinnately divided (freq. repeatedly); *collect.* a quantity of ferns.

beech-fern, *buckler-fern*, *flowering fern*, *lady-fern*, *male fern*, *royal fern*, *tree-fern*, *walking fern*, etc.

Comb.: **fern ally** a member of various orders of vascular cryptogams related to the ferns, e.g. the clubmosses, horsetails, and quillworts; **fern-bird** a warbler, *Bowdleria punctata*, with spiny tail feathers, native to New Zealand; *fernbrake*: see BRAKE *n.*[1] 1; **fern crushing** *NZ* the inhibition of fern growth, chiefly by grazing with cattle etc.; **fern-house** a conservatory in which ferns are grown; **fern-owl** the nightjar; **fernland** (*a*) *NZ* land covered with fern; (*b*) (**F-**) (chiefly *Austral.*) New Zealand; **Fernleaf** *slang* New Zealander; **fern-seed** the supposed seed of the fern, believed before the reproduction of ferns was understood to be invisible and to render the possessor invisible.

fernery *n.* a place where ferns are grown; a glass case, planter, or conservatory for growing ferns: M19. **fernless** *a.* L19. **fernlike** *a.* resembling (that of) a fern or fern frond M17. **ferny** *a.* of, pertaining to, or resembling, fern; having abundant ferns: E16.

fern /fəːn/ *a.* & *adv.* Long *obs.* exc. *dial.* in FERNYEAR. [OE *fyrn* cogn. w. OS *furn*, *forn* formerly, ON *forn* (adj.) ancient.] **A** *adj.* Former, ancient, past, of old. OE. †**B** *adv.* Formerly, long ago, a long time. OE–LME.

fern /fəːn/ *v.* LME. [f. the n.] **1** *v.t.* Cover with fern. *rare.* LME. †**2** *v.i.* Feed on fern. L16–L17.

†**fernambuck** *n.* L16–E18. [Alt. of *Pernambuco*, a seaport in Brazil, now Recife.] = BRAZIL *n.*[1] 1.

ferntickle /'fəːntɪk(ə)l/ *n.* Long *obs.* exc. *dial.* LME. [Origin unkn.] A freckle; a small mark or blemish on the skin.

fernyear /'fəːnjɪə/ *n.* & *adv.* Long *obs.* exc. *dial.* As n. also **fern year**. OE. [f. FERN *a.* + YEAR *n.*[1]] **A** *n.* †**1** A past year; olden times. OE–L18. **2**

Last year. LME. †**B** *adv.* In past years; in the course of last year. OE–E19.

ferocious /fəˈrəʊʃəs/ *a.* M17. [f. L *feroc-*, *ferox* fierce: see -IOUS.] **1** Savage, bloodthirsty; fierce, destructive. M17. **2** Indicative of or characterized by ferocity. E18. **3** Very great, extreme; very unpleasant. *colloq.* L19.

1 S. LEWIS The ferocious Colonel bellowed 'What the hell would I do that for?' **2** C. MACKENZIE His scowl became absolutely ferocious. **3** M. ALLINGHAM I say, there's a ferocious draught somewhere.

ferociously *adv.* L18. **ferociousness** *n.* M18.

ferocity /fəˈrɒsɪti/ *n.* M16. [(O)Fr. *férocité* or its source L *ferocitas*, f. as prec.: see -ITY.] The quality or state of being ferocious; habitual fierceness or savageness; a ferocious act.

E. WAUGH The charity of religion tempered her ferocity as an antagonist.

-ferous /f(ə)rəs/ *suff.* Also (see below) **-iferous.** [Repr. Fr. *-fère* or L *-fer* carrying, bearing (see -FER) + -OUS.] Forming (usu. w. intermediate -I-) adjs. w. the sense 'having, containing, or carrying', as *auriferous*, *fructiferous*, *pestiferous*, etc.

ferra *n.* var. of FÉRA.

ferrament /ˈfɛrəm(ə)nt/ *n.* Also in L form **ferramentum** /fɛrəˈmɛntəm/, pl. **-ta** /-tə/. LME. [OFr. *ferrement* f. L *ferramentum* implement of iron, f. *ferrum* iron: see -MENT.] An iron instrument or tool (usu. in *pl.*); in *pl. esp.* ironwork on windows etc.

Ferrarese /fɛrəˈriːz/ *n.* & *a.* L16. [It., f. *Ferrara* (see below) + -ESE.] **A** *n.* Pl. same, †**-s.** A native or inhabitant of Ferrara, a city in Emilia-Romagna in N. Italy. L16. **B** *adj.* Of or pertaining to Ferrara. L19.

ferrate /ˈfɛreɪt/ *n.* M19. [f. L *ferrum* iron + -ATE[1].] *Chem.* A salt formed (as) from ferric oxide, Fe_2O_3, and a base; a salt containing oxyanions of trivalent iron.

ferredoxin /fɛrɪˈdɒksɪn/ *n.* M20. [f. L *fer(rum* iron + REDOX + -IN[1].] *Biochem.* Any of certain iron-containing proteins which participate in intracellular electron-transfer processes.

Ferrel /ˈfɛr(ə)l/ *n.*[1] E20. [W. *Ferrel* (1817–91), US meteorologist.] *Meteorol.* **1** *Ferrel's law*: that winds are deflected by Coriolis forces, to the right and left in the northern and southern hemispheres respectively. E20. **2** *Ferrel cell*, an atmospheric convection cell in which air rises at latitude 60° N. or S. and sinks at latitude 30°. E20.

ferrel *n.*[2] & *v.* var. of FERRULE *n.* & *v.*

ferreous /ˈfɛrɪəs/ *a. rare.* M17. [f. L *ferreus*, f. *ferrum* iron: see -EOUS.] **1** Of or pertaining to iron; consisting of or containing iron. M17. **2** Like iron in hardness or colour. E19.

†**ferrer** *n.* Also **-our.** LME–L18. [OFr. *fereor*, *ferour* (mod. *ferreur*), f. med.L *ferrator*, f. *ferrare* shoe horses, f. L *ferrum* iron, (in med.L) horseshoe: see -ER[2].] A blacksmith; *esp.* a farrier.

ferret /ˈfɛrɪt/ *n.*[1] LME. [OFr. *fuiret*, (also mod.) *furet*, by suff. substitution from OFr. *fu(i)ron*, f. Proto-Romance, f. late L *furo*, *furon-* thief, ferret, f. L *fur* thief: see -ET[1].] **1** A half-tamed variety of polecat, freq. with white or pale fur, kept for driving rabbits from burrows, killing rats, etc. LME. **2** *fig.* A detective; a person who searches assiduously. E17.

1 black-footed ferret a rare mammal, *Mustela nigripes*, resembling the polecat and native to N. American prairies.

ferrety *a.* resembling (that of) a ferret E19.

ferret /ˈfɛrɪt/ *n.*[2] L16. [Prob. f. It. *fioretti* floss-silk, pl. of *fioretto* dim. of *fiore* FLOWER *n.*] †**1** *ferret-silk*, floss-silk. L16–E17. **2** A stout cotton or silk tape. *arch.* M17.

ferret /ˈfɛrɪt/ *v.* LME. [f. FERRET *n.*[1] Cf. Fr. *fureter.*] **1 a** *v.i.* Hunt with ferrets. Chiefly as *ferreting* vbl n. LME. **b** *v.t.* Clear (a burrow etc.) by means of a ferret. L15. **2** *v.t.* Drive out (as) with a ferret. (Foll. by *about*, *away*, *forth*, *off*, *out.*) L16. **3 a** *v.t.* Bother, worry, (a person); hunt or search *out* (also foll. by *up*). L16. **b** *v.i.* Worry, be concerned (*about*); search or rummage about. L16.

1b R. JEFFERIES Even if the burrows be ferreted, in a few weeks this great hole shows signs of fresh inhabitants. **2** D. H. LAWRENCE Ferretted the rats from under the barn. **3a** L. DEIGHTON Does he sniff round to see what he can ferret out? **b** A. SILLITOE I'll just nip round to see your dad, and tell him you're here, in case he should ferret about you. E. BOWEN Eva . . ferreted under a gauntlet, laid bare her wristwatch.

ferreter *n.* ME.

ferreting /ˈfɛrɪtɪŋ/ *n. arch.* L17. [f. FERRET *n.*[2] + -ING[1].] = FERRET *n.*[2]

ferri- /ˈfɛri/ *comb. form.* [f. L *ferrum* iron: see -I-.] Of or containing iron, esp. in the ferric (trivalent) state. Cf. FERRO-.

ferricrete *n.* (*Geol.*) a breccia or conglomerate cemented by iron compounds E20. **ferricy'anic** *a.* (*Chem.*): *ferricyanic acid*, an unstable brown solid acid, $H_3Fe(CN)_6$ M19. **ferri'cyanide** *n.* (*Chem.*) a salt containing the anion $Fe(CN)_6^{3-}$ M19.

ferriage /ˈfɛrɪɪdʒ/ *n.* Also **ferryage.** ME. [f. FERRY *n.*, *v.* + -AGE.] **1** The fare paid for the use of a ferry. ME. **2** The action or means of ferrying a person or thing across water. LME.

ferrian /ˈfɛrɪən/ *a.* M20. [f. prec. + -AN.] *Min.* Having a constituent element partly replaced by ferric iron. Cf. FERROAN.

ferric /ˈfɛrɪk/ *a.* L18. [f. L *ferrum* iron + -IC.] **1** *gen.* Of, pertaining to, or containing iron. L18. **2** *Chem.* Of or containing iron in the trivalent state. Cf. FERROUS. M19.

2 ferric acid a hypothetical parent acid of the ferrates.

ferrier /ˈfɛrɪə/ *n.* Now *rare.* Also **ferryer.** ME. [f. FERRY *v.* + -ER[1].] A person who operates a ferry, a ferryman.

ferriferous /fɛˈrɪf(ə)rəs/ *a.* E19. [f. L *ferrum* iron + -FEROUS.] Producing or yielding iron.

ferrimagnetism /fɛrɪˈmagnɪtɪz(ə)m/ *n.* M20. [f. FERRI- + MAGNETISM.] A form of magnetism resembling but weaker than ferromagnetism, that is associated with antiparallel alignment of neighbouring atoms or ions having unequal magnetic moments.

ferrimagnet *n.* a ferrimagnetic solid M20. **ferrimag'netic** *a.* & *n.* (*a*) *adj.* pertaining to or exhibiting ferrimagnetism; (*b*) *n.* = FERRIMAGNET: M20.

Ferris wheel /ˈfɛrɪs wiːl/ *n. phr.* L19. [G. W. G. *Ferris* (1859–96), Amer. engineer + WHEEL *n.*] A giant, vertical revolving wheel with passenger cars on its periphery, used at amusement parks etc.

ferrite /ˈfɛraɪt/ *n.* M19. [f. L *ferrum* iron + -ITE[1].] **1** A mixed oxide of ferric iron and another metal or metals; *spec.* a compound of formula MFe_2O_4 (where M is a divalent metal), many examples of which have magnetic and electrical properties which make them suitable for use in high-frequency electrical components. M19. **2** *Metall.* An allotrope of pure iron which has a body-centred cubic crystal structure and is present as a solid solvent in low-carbon steels. L19. **3** *Petrogr.* A microscopic particle of amorphous iron oxide present in a rock. L19.

ferritic /fəˈrɪtɪk/ *a.* (*Metall.*) containing, composed of, or characteristic of ferrite E20.

ferritin /ˈfɛrɪtɪn/ *n.* M20. [f. FERRI- + -*t*- + -IN[1].] *Biochem.* A water-soluble protein containing ferric iron, involved in storing iron in mammalian metabolism.

ferro- /ˈfɛrəʊ/ *comb. form.* [f. L *ferrum* iron: see -O-.] Of, connected with, or containing iron; (in alloy names) containing iron and (another metal), as *ferrochromium*, *-manganese*, *-vanadium*, etc.; *Chem.* of iron in the ferrous (divalent) state (cf. FERRI-).

ferro-'alloy *n.* an alloy of iron and one or more other metals, esp. as used in metallurgical processing E20. **ferro'concrete** *n.* & *a.* (of) reinforced concrete E20. **ferrocy'anic** *a.* (*Chem.*): *ferrocyanic acid*, a white solid acid, $H_4Fe(CN)_6$ E19. **ferro'cyanide** *n.* (*Chem.*) a salt containing the anion $Fe(CN)_6^{4-}$ E19. **ferro'prussiate** *n.* (chiefly *Photogr.*) = FERRICYANIDE; *attrib.* designating a blueprint process involving potassium ferricyanide and ferric ammonium citrate: L19.

ferroan /ˈfɛrəʊən, fəˈrəʊən/ *a.* M20. [f. prec. + -AN.] *Min.* Having a constituent element partly replaced by ferrous iron. Cf. FERRIAN.

ferrocene /ˈfɛrəsiːn/ *n.* M20. [f. FERRO- + *-cene* from *cyclopentadiene.*] *Chem.* An orange crystalline compound, $Fe(C_5H_5)_2$, having a molecule in which two parallel planar aromatic cyclopentadiene ligands enclose an iron atom in a sandwich structure.

ferroelectric /ˌfɛrəʊɪˈlɛktrɪk/ *a.* & *n.* M20. [f. FERRO- + ELECTRIC.] *Physics.* **A** *adj.* Of, relating to, or having the property of exhibiting a permanent electric polarization and hysteresis when subjected to an electric field. M20. **B** *n.* A ferroelectric body or substance. M20.

ferroelectrically *adv.* M20. **ferroelec'tricity** *n.* the quality of being ferroelectric; the phenomena exhibited by ferroelectric substances M20.

ferromagnesian /ˌfɛrə(ʊ)magˈniːʒ(ə)n, -zjən/ *a.* E20. [f. FERRO- + MAGNESIAN.] Of a rock or mineral: containing iron and magnesium as major components.

ferromagnetic /ˌfɛrə(ʊ)magˈnɛtɪk/ *a.* & *n.* M19. [f. FERRO- + MAGNETIC.] **A** *adj.* †**1** = PARAMAGNETIC *a.* 2. M–L19. **2** Of, pertaining to, or exhibiting ferromagnetism. L19. **B** *n.* A ferromagnetic (orig. = paramagnetic) body or substance. M19.

ferro'magnet *n.* a ferromagnetic body or substance M20. **ferromagnetically** *adv.* M20.

ferromagnetism /fɛrə(ʊ)ˈmagnɪtɪz(ə)m/ *n.* M19. [f. FERRO- + MAGNETISM.] Orig., paramagnetism. Now, the form of magnetism shown by metallic iron, cobalt, and nickel, which is characterized by a large magnetic permeability and the phenomenon of hysteresis, and is associated with parallel alignment of the magnetic moments of neighbouring atoms.

ferronnerie /fɛrɔnri, fɛˈrɒnəriː/ *n.* & *a.* Also ***ferronerie.*** E20. [Fr. = iron work, wrought iron.] (Designating) decoration with a motif of arabesques and scrolls, used on pottery etc.

ferronnière /fɛrɔnjɛːr (*pl. same*); fɛˌrɒnɪˈɛː/. *n.* Also ***ferronière.*** M19. [Fr. = a frontlet, a coronet worn on the forehead: after Leonardo da Vinci's portrait *La Belle Ferronnière.*] An ornamental chain with a central jewel, worn around the head.

ferrosoferric /fərəʊsə(ʊ)ˈfɛrɪk/ *a.* M19. [f. mod.L *ferrosus* ferrous + -O- + FERRIC.] *Chem.* Of both ferrous and ferric iron. Only in *ferrosoferric oxide*, magnetite, magnetic iron oxide, Fe_3O_4.

†**ferrour** *n.* var. of FERRER *n.*

ferrous /ˈfɛrəs/ *a.* M19. [f. L *ferrum* iron + -OUS.] **1** *Chem.* Of or containing iron in the divalent state. Cf. FERRIC 2. M19. **2** Of iron; (chiefly of an alloy) containing iron in significant quantities. Orig. & freq. in *non-ferrous.* L19.

ferrugineous /fɛrʊˈdʒɪnɪəs/ *a.* M17. [f. L *ferrugineus* (see next) + -OUS: see -EOUS.] = next.

ferruginous /fɛˈruːdʒɪnəs/ *a.* M17. [f. L *ferrugo*, *-gin-* iron rust, dark red (f. *ferrum* iron) + -OUS. Cf. Fr. *ferrugineux.*] **1** Of the nature of or containing iron or its compounds (orig. iron rust). M17. **2** Of the colour of rust; reddish-brown. M17.

2 ferruginous duck a diving duck, *Aythya nyroca*, with predominantly dark rust-brown plumage; also called *white-eyed pochard.*

ferrule /ˈfɛruːl, ˈfɛr(ə)l/ *n.* & *v.* Also **ferrel** /ˈfɛr(ə)l/. E17. [Alt. (prob. by assim. to L *ferrum* iron, and -ULE) of earlier VERREL. Cf. VIRL.] **A** *n.* A (usu.) metal ring or cap for strengthening, *esp.* one for preventing the end of a stick, tube, etc., from splitting or wearing. E17.

H. ALLEN The ferrule of a cane was heard clicking on the mosaics in the vestibule.

B *v.t.* Provide or fit with a ferrule. L17.

ferruled *a.* provided with a ferrule M19.

ferruminate /fɛˈruːmɪneɪt/ *v.t.* Long *rare* or *obs.* E17. [L *ferruminat-* pa. ppl stem of *ferruminare* to cement, f. *ferrumen*, *-min-* cement, f. *ferrum* iron: see -ATE[3].] Cement, solder, unite.

ferrumi'nation *n.* E17.

ferry /ˈfɛri/ *n.* ME. [ON *ferja* ferryboat, or *ferju* as in *ferjukarl*, *-maðr* ferryman, *ferjuskip* ferryboat = Du. *veer*, MHG *vër(e)* (G *Fähre*), f. Gmc, f.

base of FARE v.] 1 A passage or place where a boat etc. regularly transports passengers, vehicles, or goods across a stretch of water. ME. 2 A boat etc. for transporting passengers, vehicles, or goods across a stretch of water. ME. b A module for transporting an astronaut from the surface of a planet etc. to the spacecraft. M20. 3 A service for transporting passengers, vehicles, or goods, across a stretch of water by boat etc.; *Law* the right to operate and to levy a toll for such a service. E18. b A service for delivering aircraft to the user by flying, esp. across a sea or a continent. E20. c A service carrying passengers and goods usu. short distances by air. M20.

Comb.: **ferryboat** = sense 2 above; **ferry-bridge** a type of ferryboat in which a train is transported across a river or bay; **ferryman** a person who keeps or looks after a ferry.

ferry /ˈfɛri/ *v.* [OE *ferian* reinforced by forms f. cognate ON *ferja* = OS *ferian*, OHG *ferren* (MHG *vern*), Goth *farjan*, f. Gmc, f. base of FARE *v.*] 1 *v.t.* Carry, transport, take from one place to another, esp. across a stretch of water (formerly also, the sea) by boat. (Foll. by *over*, *across*.) OE. b Work (a boat) across a stretch of water. L18. c Fly (an aircraft) to a delivery-point. E20. 2 *v.i.* Go across water by boat. Formerly also, go, depart. (Foll. by *over*.) OE.

1 R. CAMPBELL He ferried the stone across on rafts. M. MUGGERIDGE They would ferry my father about from meeting to meeting. 2 R. BURNS When death's dark stream I ferry o'er.

ferryable *a.* (*rare*) (of a river etc.) that may be crossed in a boat etc. L19.

ferryage *n.* var. of FERRIAGE.

ferryer *n.* var. of FERRIER.

fers-de-lance *n.pl.* see FER-DE-LANCE.

fers-de-moline *n.* pl. of FER-DE-MOLINE.

fertile /ˈfəːtʌɪl/ *a.* LME. [Fr. f. L *fertilis*, f. *ferre* to bear: see -ILE.] 1 (Of soil) rich in the materials needed to support vegetation; fruitful; (of an animal or plant) able to produce offspring; (of a seed or egg) able to develop into a new individual; *fig.* (of the mind) inventive, productive of ideas. LME. b *Demography.* Productive of (live-born) children. Cf. FECUND 3. E20. c *Nuclear Physics.* Able to be transformed into a fissile isotope by the capture of a neutron. M20. 2 Tending to assist productiveness. L16. †3 Abundant. E–M17.

1 A. J. TOYNBEE The soil . . was fertile and needed only water to make it productive. A. BEVAN The sense of injustice arising from gross inequalities . . is a fertile source of discontent. *Lancet* The number of children that a fertile couple have depends on . . the efficiency of the contraceptive methods they use. **Fertile Crescent** a semicircular region stretching from the eastern Mediterranean to the Persian Gulf.

fertilely *adv.* L16. **fertileness** *n.* L16.

fertilisation *n.*, **-ise** *v.*, **-iser** *n.* vars. of FERTILIZATION etc.

fertility /fəˈtɪlɪti/ *n.* LME. [Fr. *fertilité* f. L *fertilitas*, f. *fertilis* FERTILE: see -ITY.] 1 The quality of being fertile; fruitfulness; productiveness. LME. 2 In *pl.* Productive powers. Now *rare.* E17. 3 *Demography.* Productiveness; the actual number of (live) births. Cf. FECUNDITY 3. M19.

fertilization /ˌfəːtɪlʌɪˈzeɪʃ(ə)n/ *n.* Also **-isation**. M19. [f. next + -ATION.] The action or process of fertilizing.

double fertilization: see DOUBLE *a.* & *adv.*

fertilize /ˈfəːtɪlʌɪz/ *v.t.* Also **-ise**. M17. [f. FERTILE + -IZE. Cf. Fr. *fertiliser*.] 1 Make (esp. soil) fertile or productive. M17. 2 *Biol.* Cause (a female individual, plant, egg, etc.) to develop a new individual by the introduction of male reproductive material. M19.

1 H. ACTON The fortunes of England depended on the use of natural manure in fertilizing the soil. 2 S. SPENDER Fertilized another master's wife and left the school under a pregnant cloud.

fertilizable *a.* M19.

fertilizer /ˈfəːtɪlʌɪzə/ *n.* Also **-iser**. M17. [f. prec. + -ER[1].] 1 A substance which fertilizes soil etc.; manure, *esp.* an artificially prepared substance containing nitrogen, phosphorus, or potassium added to soil in order to fertilize it. M17. 2 An agent of fertilization in plants. M19.

ferula /ˈfɛrjʊlə/ *n.* LME. [L = giant fennel, rod.] 1 An umbelliferous plant of the genus *Ferula*; giant fennel. LME. 2 A long splint. Now *rare* or *obs.* LME. 3 = FERULE 2. L16.

feruˈlaceous *a.* (now *rare*) resembling the giant fennel M17.

ferule /ˈfɛruːl/ *n.* & *v.t.* LME. [L FERULA.] A *n.* 1 = FERULA 1. Now *rare* or *obs.* LME. 2 A rod, cane, or other instrument of punishment; *esp.* a flat ruler with a widened end. L16. B *v.t.* Beat or strike with a ferule. L16.

fervency /ˈfəːv(ə)nsi/ *n.* L15. [f. OFr. *fervence* or its source late L *ferventia*, f. *fervent-* pres. ppl stem of *fervere*: see FERVENT, -ENCY.] 1 Intensity of heat. Now *rare.* L15. 2 Intensity of feeling; ardour; zeal. M16.

Earlier †**fervence** *n.* LME–L16.

fervent /ˈfəːv(ə)nt/ *a.* ME. [OFr., f. L *fervent-* pres. ppl stem of *fervere* boil, glow: see -ENT.] 1 Of a person, personal feeling, etc.: ardent, intense; earnest. ME. b (Of a sea, storm, uproar, etc.) violent; (of a pestilence) raging. Now *rare* or *obs.* LME. 2 Hot, burning, boiling. Formerly also in *Med.* (of a bodily humour or a disease) hot, violent; (of a medicine) of violent effect. LME. †b Of cold: severe, intense. LME–M17.

1 C. P. SNOW His interest was as fervent, as vivid and factual, as it must have been when he was a young man. D. M. THOMAS Madame Serebryakova even claimed to be a fervent admirer of Frau Erdman's voice.

fervently *adv.* †(*a*) burningly, severely; (*b*) ardently, intensely: LME. **ferventness** *n.* (now *rare*) LME.

fervid /ˈfəːvɪd/ *a.* L16. [L *fervidus*, f. *fervere*: see prec., -ID[1].] 1 Burning, glowing, hot. Now *poet.* L16. 2 Intense; impassioned. M17.

1 QUILLER-COUCH It was so pleasing to find a breeze up there allaying the fervid afternoon. 2 P. G. WODEHOUSE In a situation which might have stimulated another to fervid speech, George Pennicut contented himself with saying 'Goo!'

fervidly *adv.* M19. **fervidness** *n.* L17.

fervor *n.* see FERVOUR.

fervorous /ˈfəːv(ə)rəs/ *a.* Now *rare.* E17. [f. prec. + -OUS.] Full of fervour.

fervour /ˈfəːvə/ *n.* Also ***-or**. ME. [OFr. *fervo(u)r* (mod. *ferveur*) f. L *fervor*, f. *fervere*: see FERVENT, -OR.] 1 (An instance of) intense feeling, ardour, passion, zeal. ME. 2 (A condition of) intense heat. Formerly also, seething or turbulence in water. LME.

1 E. F. BENSON Her heart had remained, indeed, most inconveniently young, its sympathies were all with youth and its fervours. B. PLAIN A sudden brightness came into the little face, a fervor so glowing. 2 SHELLEY Those deserts . . whose . . fervors scarce allowed A bird to live.

fes *n.* see FEIS.

Fesapo /ˈfɛsəpəʊ/ *n.* E19. [A mnemonic of scholastic philosophers, E indicating a universal negative proposition, A a universal affirmative proposition, and O a particular negative proposition.] *Logic.* The fourth mood of the fourth syllogistic figure, in which a particular negative conclusion is drawn from a universal negative major premiss and a universal affirmative minor premiss. Cf. FAPESMO.

Fescennine /ˈfɛsɪnʌɪn/ *a.* E17. [L *Fescenninus* pertaining to Fescennia: see below, -INE[1].] Of or pertaining to Fescennia in Etruria, known for scurrilous dialogues in verse; licentious, obscene, scurrilous.

fescue /ˈfɛskjuː/ *n.* & *v.* Also (earlier) †**festu**. LME. [OFr. *festu* (mod. *fétu*) f. Proto-Romance, f. L *festuca* stalk, stem, straw.] A *n.* †1 A straw, a twig; something small or trivial. LME–E17. 2 A small stick etc. for pointing out the letters to children learning to read; a pointer. Now *rare.* E16. 3 Any of various perennial freq. wiry and tufted grasses constituting the genus *Festuca*; any of several slender annual grasses constituting the genus *Vulpia*. Also *fescue-grass*. M18.

3 *Chewings fescue*, *rat's-tail fescue*, *red fescue*, *sheep's fescue*, etc.

†B *v.t.* Direct or assist in reading, using a fescue. M17–M18.

fess /fɛs/ *n.*[1] Also **fesse**. L15. [OFr. *fesse* alt. of *faisse* f. L FASCIA.] *Her.* An ordinary consisting of a broad horizontal stripe across the middle of the field, usu. occupying one-third of the shield.

in fess (of more than one charge) in the position of a fess, arranged horizontally.

Comb.: **fess point** a point at the exact centre of a shield.

fess *n.*[2] see FEIS.

fess /fɛs/ *v.i. colloq.* Also **'fess**. E19. [Aphet. f. CONFESS.] Confess, own *up*.

L. M. ALCOTT I shall tell them myself . . and "fess" to mother how silly I've been.

fesse *n.* var. of FESS *n.*[1]

fest /fɛst/ *n.* Orig. *US.* M19. [G = festival.] A festival, a special occasion. Chiefly as 2nd elem. of comb., as *filmfest*, *songfest*. Cf. GABFEST.

festa /ˈfɛstə/ *n.* E19. [It. f. L: see FEAST *n.*] In Italy, a feast, a festival, a holy day.

festal /ˈfɛst(ə)l/ *a.* & *n.* L15. [OFr. f. late L *festalis*, f. *festum*, (pl.) *festa*: see FEAST *n.*, -AL[1].] A *adj.* Of, pertaining to, or given up to, a feast or festivity; in holiday mood, joyous. L15.

DE QUINCEY The ball-room wore an elegant and festal air.

B *n.* A feast, a festivity. *poet.* E19.

¶Rare bef. M18.

festally *adv.* M19.

fester /ˈfɛstə/ *n.* Now *rare.* LME. [OFr. *festre* f. L FISTULA.] 1 Orig. = FISTULA. Later, a sore, an ulcer; a suppurating place. LME. †2 A cicatrice or scar (over a festering wound). L15–M16.

fester /ˈfɛstə/ *v.* LME. [f. the n., or OFr. *festrir*, f. as prec.] 1 *v.i.* Of a wound or sore: (orig.) gather or produce pus, ulcerate; (now usu.) suppurate. LME. b Of poison etc.: infect surrounding parts, rankle. Foll. by *into*: become by festering. Now chiefly *fig.* of grief etc. LME. 2 *v.i.* Putrefy, rot. LME. 3 *v.t.* Cause to ulcerate or suppurate; *fig.* allow (malice etc.) to rankle. LME. †b Cicatrize. LME–M16.

1 C. ISHERWOOD I had cut it on a piece of tin . . and now it had suddenly festered and was full of poison. b H. WOTTON Ancient quarrels . . festering in his breast. BURKE Smitten pride smarting from its wounds, festers into new rancour. 2 SHAKES. *Sonn.* Lilies that fester smell far worse than weeds. 3 J. MARSTON I . . festred rankling malice in my breast. R. ESTCOURT Take heed, lest your ungentle Hand shou'd fester what you mean to heal.

festerment *n.* (*rare*) the process or state of festering; *dial.* something that festers: M19.

†**festial** *n.* L15–E18. [med.L *festialis* perh. error for *festivalis*: see FESTIVAL.] = FESTIVAL *n.* 1.

festilogy /fɛˈstɪlədʒi/ *n.* Also **-ology** /-ɒlədʒi/. M19. [med.L *festilogium*, f. L *festum* feast: see -LOGY.] A treatise on ecclesiastical festivals.

†**festin** *n.* Also **-ine**. E16–M19. [Fr., Sp. *festin*, It. FESTINO *n.*[2]] = FESTINO *n.*[2]

festinate /ˈfɛstɪnət, -eɪt/ *a.* Now *rare.* E17. [L *festinatus* pa. pple, f. as next: see -ATE[2].] Hasty, hurried.

festinately *adv.* L16.

festinate /ˈfɛstɪneɪt/ *v.t.* & †*i. rare.* L16. [L *festinat-* pa. ppl stem of *festinare* hurry: see -ATE[3].] Hasten, speed.

festination /fɛstɪˈneɪʃ(ə)n/ *n.* M16. [L *festinatio(n-)*, f. as prec.: see -ATION.] 1 Haste, speed. Now *rare.* M16. 2 *Med.* A gait with short fast tottering steps that occurs in some cases of Parkinson's disease. L19.

†**festine** *n.* var. of FESTIN.

Festino /fɛˈstʌɪnəʊ/ *n.*[1] M16. [A mnemonic of scholastic philosophers, E indicating a universal negative proposition, I a particular affirmative proposition, and O a particular negative proposition.] *Logic.* The third mood of the second syllogistic figure, in which a particular negative conclusion is drawn from a universal negative major premiss and a particular affirmative minor premiss.

†**festino** *n.*[2] Pl. **-o(e)s**. M18–M19. [It., dim. of FESTA.] An entertainment, a feast.

festival /ˈfɛstɪv(ə)l/ *a.* & *n.* LME. [OFr. f. med.L *festivalis*, f. as next: see -AL[1].] A *adj.* 1 Of or befitting a feast or feast day. Now only *attrib.*

& usu. taken as n. LME. †2 Joyful, merry. L16–L17.

B *n.* †1 A book containing an exhortation for each feast day. L15–E17. 2 A (time of) festive celebration or merrymaking; a feast day. L16. b A (usu. periodic) series of theatrical or musical performances, films, etc., of special importance. E19. 3 = FÊTE *n.* 1b. *US.* M19.

2 B. TARKINGTON People were gayest on New Year's Day; they made it a true festival. b *Publishers Weekly* The annual Shakespeare festival at Stratford-on-Avon.

Comb.: **festival-day**: on which a festival is held.

festive /ˈfɛstɪv/ *a.* M17. [L *festivus*, f. *festum*, (pl.) *festa*: see FEAST *n.*, -IVE.] 1 Of or befitting a feast or festival; joyous, cheerful. M17. 2 Of a person: fond of feasting, jovial; (of a place, season, etc.) devoted to a feast or feasting. M18.

1 G. HUNTINGTON Order something festive, perhaps champagne. **the festive season** *spec.* the period around Christmas.

festively *adv.* E19.

festivity /fɛˈstɪvɪti/ *n.* LME. [(O)Fr. *festivité* or L *festivitas*, f. as prec.: see -ITY.] 1 A festive celebration, a feast; (an occasion of) rejoicing or gaiety. In *pl.*, festive proceedings. LME. †2 Festive quality or condition; suitability for a festival; cheerfulness. M16–L17.

1 E. SUMMERSKILL Weddings, golden weddings, funerals, and other festivities.

festiveness *n.* M20. **festivous** *a.* (now *rare* or *obs.*) = FESTIVE M17.

festology *n.* var. of FESTILOGY.

festoon /fɛˈstuːn/ *n.* M17. [Fr. *feston* f. It. *festone* festal ornament, f. L *festa*: see FEAST *n.*, -OON.] 1 A chain or garland of flowers, leaves, ribbons, drapery, etc. (suspended in a curve between two points). M17. b *transf.* Something hanging like a festoon. M19. 2 *Archit.* A carved or moulded ornament representing a festoon. M17. 3 A small brown moth of oakwoods, *Apoda limacodes*. L19.

1 J. RUSKIN The curved rock from which the waterfall leaps into its calm festoons.

festoonery *n.* something arranged in festoons, arrangement in festoons M19.

festoon /fɛˈstuːn/ *v.t.* L18. [f. the n.] Adorn (as) with or form into festoons; hang up in festoons; cover, drape.

G. SANTAYANA A gold watch-chain heavily festooning a big paunch. T. GUNN Ivy-festooned statues of Greek gods.

Festschrift /ˈfɛs(t)ʃrɪft/ *n.* Also **f-**. Pl. **-schriften** /-ʃrɪftən/, **-s**. E20. [G, lit. 'celebration-writing'.] A volume of writings collected in honour of a scholar, freq. presented to mark an occasion in his or her life.

†festu *n.* see FESCUE.

†festual *a.* E16–M19. [f. L *festum*, (pl.) *festa* FEAST *n.* after *spiritual* etc.] Festal, festival.

festucine /ˈfɛstjʊsʌɪn/ *a. rare.* M17. [f. L *festuca* stalk, straw + -INE^1.] Straw-coloured.

fet /fɛt/ *v.t. obs.* exc. *dial.* Infl. **-tt-**. Pa. t. & pple **fet**. [OE *fetian*: see FETCH *v.*] 1 = FETCH *v.* 1. OE. 2 = FETCH *v.* 3. OE. 3 = FETCH *v.* 2. ME. 4 = FETCH *v.* 5. ME. 5 = FETCH *v.* 7. ME. 6 = FETCH *v.* 6. M16. 7 = FETCH *v.* 8a. M16.

feta /ˈfɛtə/ *n.* Also **fetta**. M20. [mod.Gk *pheta*.] A white salty Greek ewe's-milk cheese.

fetal *a.* var. of FOETAL.

fetalisation, **-ization** *ns.* vars. of FOETALIZATION.

fetation *n.* var. of FOETATION.

fetch /fɛtʃ/ *n.*^{1} M16. [f. the vb.] 1 An act of fetching, a reach, a sweep, (*arch.*); *spec.* a sheepdog's bringing of sheep back to the handler by the most direct route (the third stage of sheepdog trials). M16. 2 A contrivance, a stratagem, a trick. Now *arch. rare.* M16. 3 *Naut.* a An act of tacking. Now *rare.* M16. b The line of a continuous stretch of water from point to point, e.g. of a bay or of open sea, or traversed by wind or waves. M19. 4 An indrawn or caught breath; a sigh. *dial.* M19.

1 J. C. SHAIRP A great fetch of imaginative power. 2 H. BUSHNELL No ingenious fetches of argument.

fetch /fɛtʃ/ *n.*^{2} L17. [Origin unkn.] The apparition or double of a (usu. living) person.

M. LEADBEATER She believed she had seen his fetch as a forerunner of his death.

†fetch *n.*^{3} see VETCH.

fetch /fɛtʃ/ *v.* [OE *feċċ(e)an* alt. of *fetian* FET *v.*, prob. rel. to OE *fatian*, OFris. *fatia*, OHG *fazzōn* (G *fassen*) grasp, perh. orig. 'put in a vessel', f. base of FAT *n.*^{1}, VAT *n.*] 1 *v.t.* & *i.* Go in search of and bring back (a person or thing); collect (a person or thing). OE. †2 *v.t.* Obtain, get, come by. ME–M17. b *Cricket.* Score (a specified number of runs). M18–E20. 3 *v.t.* Cause to come; succeed in bringing; elicit. LME. 4 *v.t.* Deal (a blow); make (a stroke). Usu. w. indirect obj. Now *colloq.* LME. b Strike (a person). Now chiefly *US.* M16. 5 *v.t.* Derive, deduce, infer, borrow. Now *rare* or *obs.* M16. 6 *v.t.* Draw (breath); heave (a sigh); utter (a groan etc.). Now *arch. rare.* M16. 7 *v.t.* Make, perform, (a movement); take (a walk etc.). *arch.* exc. *US.* M16. 8 Orig. *Naut.* a *v.t.* Arrive at, reach; come up with (a boat etc.). M16. b *v.i.* Take a course; bring a boat etc. up. L16. †c *v.t.* Get into (the wake of a boat etc., the course of the wind). E17–M18. 9 *v.t.* Of a commodity: realize, sell for (a price). Formerly also (of money) purchase (a commodity). E17. 10 *v.t.* Move to interest, admiration, or delight; attract. *colloq.* E17.

1 R. L. STEVENSON 'Rum,' he repeated, 'Rum! rum!' I ran to fetch it. M. DRABBLE Do let me come and fetch you, because look, it's raining outside. E. ALBEE Fetch, . . puppy, go fetch. *deep-fetched*: see DEEP *adv.* FAR-FETCHED. 2 H. LATIMER Christ sent this man unto the priest to fetch there his absolution. 3 Y. MENUHIN They could fetch such extraordinary sounds from primitive instruments. 4 P. BARKER She fetched me such a swipe across the face. 5 E. STILLINGFLEET Many great Families . . fetched their pedegree from the Gods. 6 T. BEDDOES The child . . was still fetching deep sobs. 7 THACKERAY Mr. Warrington . . was gone to fetch a walk in the moonlight. 8a B. STOKER With the wind blowing from its present quarter . . she should fetch the entrance of the harbour. 9 D. J. ENRIGHT Artichokes fetch a good price in France. 10 J. K. JEROME To say that the child has got its father's nose . . fetches the parents.

Phrases, & with advs. & preps. in specialized senses: **fetch about** (*a*) (esp. *Naut.*) make a movement, a turn, etc.; (*b*) swing round (the arm, a weapon) to gather impetus; †(*c*) contrive, devise, plan. *fetch a gutser*: see GUTSER *n.* **fetch and carry** (orig. of a dog) run backwards and forwards with things, be a mere servant. **fetch around** = *fetch round* below. **fetch away** = *fetch way* below. **fetch down** bring or force down. **†fetch in** surround, enclose; take in (*lit.* & *fig.*). **†fetch off** get the better of, make an end of. **fetch out** draw out, develop, display. **fetch round** revive, recover; (cause to) regain consciousness. **fetch up** (*a*) (orig. *Naut.*) reach, come in sight of, get to (a place etc.); come to a stop, end up (*at*, *in*, etc.); (*b*) vomit; †(*c*) raise, elevate; (*d*) overtake, come up (*with*); (*e*) make up (lost ground etc.); (*f*) *US* bring up, rear (children). **fetch way** *Naut.* move or shift from its proper place; break loose.

Comb.: **fetch-and-carry** the action of fetching and carrying; a person who fetches and carries; **fetch-up** a coming to a standstill; stopping.

fetcher *n.* LME.

fetching /ˈfɛtʃɪŋ/ *a.* L16. [f. prec. + -ING^2.] †1 Contriving, scheming, crafty. Only in L16. 2 Alluring, fascinating, delightful, attractive. *colloq.* L19.

fetchingly *adv.* L19.

fetch-light /ˈfɛtʃlʌɪt/ *n.* L17. [f. FETCH *v.*, *n.*^{2} + LIGHT *n.*] A corpse-candle, *esp.* one supposedly seen before a death moving from the person's house to his or her grave.

fête /feɪt, fɛt/ *n.* Also **fete** LME. [Fr., f. OFr. *feste* FEAST *n.*] 1 A festival, an entertainment, a fair. LME. b A sale or bazaar, esp. out of doors, designed to raise money for charity. L19. 2 A religious festival, a saint's day. E19.

fête /feɪt, fɛt/ *v.t.* Also **fete**. E17. [f. the n., after Fr. *fêter*.] Entertain (a person) with a fête or feast, make much of (a person); give a fête in honour of, commemorate or celebrate by a fête.

V. CRONIN Alexis Orlov, then being feted . . as the victor of Chesme Bay.

fête champêtre /fɛt ʃɑ̃pɛːtr/ *n. phr.* Pl. ***-s -s*** (pronounced same). L18. [Fr., f. as FÊTE *n.* + *champêtre* rural.] An outdoor or pastoral entertainment, a rural festival.

fête galante /fɛt galɑ̃t/ *n. phr.* Pl. ***-s -s*** (pronounced same). E20. [Fr., f. as FÊTE *n.* + *galante* fem. of *galant* GALLANT *a.*] A *fête champêtre*, esp. as depicted in an 18th-cent. French genre of painting; a painting in this genre.

fêtes champêtres, ***galantes*** *n. phrs.* pls. of FÊTE CHAMPÊTRE, GALANTE.

fetial /ˈfiːʃ(ə)l/ *a.* & *n. obs.* exc. *Hist.* Also **fecial**. M16. [L *fetialis* (erron. *fec-*), of unkn. origin.] **A** *n.* In ancient Rome: a member of a group of priests who acted as heralds and performed the rites connected with the declaration of war and conclusion of peace. M16. **B** *adj.* Of or pertaining to a fetial; heraldic, ambassadorial. M16.

fetich(e) *n.* var. of FETISH.

fetichism *n.* var. of FETISHISM.

feticide *n.* var. of FOETICIDE.

fetid /ˈfɛtɪd, ˈfiːt-/ *a.* Also **foetid**. LME. [L *fetidus* (erron. *foet-*) f. *fetere* to stink: see -ID^1.] Foul-smelling, stinking.

M. MITCHELL The smell of sweat, of blood, of unwashed bodies, of excrement rose up in waves . . until the fetid stench almost nauseated her.

fetidly *adv.* M19. **fetidness** *n.* E18.

fetiferous *a.* var. of FOETIFEROUS.

fetish /ˈfɛtɪʃ/ *n.* Also **-ich(e)**. E17. [Fr. *fétiche* f. Port. *feitiço* charm, sorcery, use as n. of adj. 'made by art', f. L *facticius* FACTITIOUS.] 1 Orig., an object used by peoples of W. Africa as an amulet or means of enchantment. Later more widely, an inanimate object reverenced as having magical powers or as being animated by a spirit. E17. b An object, principle, etc., irrationally reverenced, esp. in an obsessive manner. M19. c *Psychol.* A non-sexual part of the body, object, action, etc. acting as a focus for sexual desire. L19. †2 In representations of Black speech: incantation, worship; an oath. E18–E19.

1 H. ALLEN The witch-doctor's horrible little manikin, a fetish with . . a blind, silly face. G. GORER The lucky mascot, the fetish which will preserve its owner from misfortune. b E. FIGES I made a fetish of being always punctual, always punctilious and conscientious.

fetisheer /fɛtɪˈʃɪə/ *n.* Now *rare.* Also **fetisher** /ˈfɛtɪʃə/. E17. [Port. *feiticeiro*, f. *feitiço* (see FETISH), later infl. by Fr. *fétiche* or Eng. FETISH.] 1 A person believed to have power over fetishes; a witch-doctor, a priest. E17. 2 = FETISH 1. *rare.* M17.

fetishise *v.* var. of FETISHIZE.

fetishism /ˈfɛtɪʃɪz(ə)m/ *n.* Also **fetich-**. E19. [f. FETISH + -ISM.] (A religion, lifestyle, psychological condition, etc., involving) devotion to or reverence for a fetish or fetishes.

fetishist *n.* & *a.* (*a*) *n.* a person who has a fetish or who worships a fetish or fetishes; (*b*) *adj.* fetishistic M19. **feti'shistic** *a.* of, pertaining to, or characteristic of, fetishism; of the nature of a fetish M19.

fetishize /ˈfɛtɪʃʌɪz/ *v.t.* Also **-ise**. M20. [f. FETISH + -IZE.] Make a fetish of; pay undue respect to, overvalue.

fetishi'zation *n.* M20.

fetlock /ˈfɛtlɒk/ *n.* ME. [Corresp. to Du. *vetlok*, Flem. *vitlok*, MHG *vizzeloch*, *-lach* (G *Fissloch*) rel. to G *Fessel* fetlock, deriv. of Gmc var. of base of FOOT *n.*] 1 The part of a horse's leg where the tuft of hair grows behind the pastern-joint. ME. 2 = FETTERLOCK 1. Now *rare.* L17.

fetlocked *a.* (*rare*) hobbled or fastened by the fetlock; shackled: E18.

fetor /ˈfiːtə/ *n.* Also **foetor**. L15. [L *fetor* (erron. *foet-*), f. *fetere*: see FETID; -OR.] A foul or offensive smell; a stench.

fetta *n.* var. of FETA.

fetter /ˈfɛtə/ *n.* [OE *feter* corresp. to OS pl. *feteros* (Du. *veter* lace), OHG *fezzera* (early mod.G *Fesser*), ON *fjǫturr*, f. Gmc, f. IE base of FOOT *n.*] 1 A chain or shackle (orig. for the feet); a bond; a handcuff. Usu. in *pl.* OE. b In *pl.* Captivity. E18. 2 Anything that confines or impedes; a restraint. OE.

2 J. LONDON His neck chafed against the starched fetter of a collar. O. NASH A dinner engagement . . is no longer a fetter, Because liars can just . . lie their way out of it.

fetterless *a.* E17.

fetter /ˈfɛtə/ *v.t.* [OE *ġefeterian, -fetran* f. as FETTER *n.* or f. ON *fjǫtra*.] 1 Bind (as) with fetters; chain, shackle. OE. 2 Impose restraint on; confine, impede. E16.

1 W. IRVING I now fettered my horse to prevent his straying. 2 J. PRIESTLEY The best faculties . . may be sunk and fettered by superstition.

fetterer *n.* (*rare*) E17.

fetterlock /ˈfɛtəlɒk/ *n. arch.* LME. [f. FETTER *n.* + LOCK *n.*[2]] 1 A portable lock for a shackle or hobble; a padlock. LME. b The padlock as a heraldic or symbolic badge or device. LME. †2 = FETLOCK 1. L16–M19.

fettle /ˈfɛt(ə)l/ *n.*[1] *obs.* exc. *Sc.* & *north.* [OE *fetel* = OHG *fezzil* (G *Fessel*) chain, band, ON *fetill* bandage, strap, f. Gmc base meaning 'grasp, hold'.] A strip or band of material; a belt, a bandage, a handle on a pannier etc.

fettle /ˈfɛt(ə)l/ *n.*[2] Orig. *dial.* M18. [f. the vb.] Condition, state, trim. Now chiefly in *in good, fine,* etc., *fettle*

J. AGATE The old lady was in tremendous fettle and looking as imposing as ever.

fettle /ˈfɛt(ə)l/ *v.* Now *dial.* & *techn.* LME. [f. FETTLE *n.*[1]] 1 *v.t.* Make ready, arrange, put to rights, tidy; groom (a horse etc.). LME. b Hit (a person). *dial.* M19. c *techn.* Prepare, clean, trim, (the rough edge of a metal casting, pottery before firing, a furnace, etc.). L19. 2 *v.refl.* & *i.* Get oneself ready, prepare, (for battle etc.). Long *obs.* exc. *dial.* LME. b *v.i.* Busy oneself, fuss. M18.

fettler *n.* a person who fettles; *esp.* a repairer of railway lines: L19.

fettuccine /fɛtʊˈtʃiːni/ *n.pl.* Also **fettucine**. E20. [It., pl. of *fettuccina*, dim. of *fetta* slice, ribbon.] Ribbons of pasta; an Italian dish consisting largely of this and usu. a sauce.

fetus *n.* var. of FOETUS.

fetwa *n.* var. of FATWA.

feu /fjuː/ *n.* & *v.* L15. [OFr.: see FEE *n.*[2]] *Sc. Law.* A *n.* 1 Orig., a feudal tenure in which land is granted by one person to another in return for an annual payment in place of military service. Now, a perpetual lease for a fixed sum. L15. b A piece of land held in feu. L18. 2 *Feudal Law.* = FEE *n.*[2] 1a. E17.

1 **in** or **upon feu** (of tenured land) subject to certain payments or services.

Comb.: **feu duty** the annual sum payable on a feudal tenure.

B *v.t.* Grant (land) on feu. L16.

feu /fø/ *a.* E19. [Fr.] Of a person: deceased, late.

†feuage *n.* E17–E18. [OFr., f. *feu* FIRE *n.*: see -AGE.] = FUMAGE.

feuar /ˈfjuːə/ *n.* L16. [f. FEU *n.* + -AR[2].] *Sc. Law.* = FIAR.

feud /fjuːd/ *n.*[1] & *v.* ME. [OFr. *fede, feide* f. MLG, MDu. *vēde*, MLG *veide*, corresp. to OHG *fēhida* (G *Fehde*) = OE *fǣhþu* enmity, OFris. *fāithe, fēithe*, f. Gmc base of FOE.] A *n.* 1 Active hatred, hostility, ill will. *obs.* exc. *dial.* ME. 2 A state of bitter and lasting mutual hostility, esp. between two families, tribes, or individuals, marked by murderous assaults in revenge for previous injury. LME. 3 A quarrel, contention. M16.

2 E. A. FREEMAN Carrying out an ancestral deadly feud. F. FITZGERALD The Catholics . . and old-fashioned political parties continued their fierce blood feuds. 3 C. S. FORESTER Jimmy and Doris quarrelled ceaselessly . . continuing a feud that . . originated some time back.

B *v.i.* Conduct a feud. L17.

K. CROSSLEY-HOLLAND If . . feuding families could not settle a dispute . . it was brought before a court.

feud /fjuːd/ *n.*[2] Also (now *rare*) **feod**. ME. [med.L *feudum, feodum*: see FEE *n.*[2]] *Hist.* = FEE *n.*[2] 1a, 3.

feudal /ˈfjuːd(ə)l/ *a.*[1] Also **†feodal**. E17. [med.L *feudalis, feodalis*, f. as prec.: see -AL[1].] 1 Of or pertaining to a feud or fief. E17. 2 Of or pertaining to the holding of land in feud; designating or pertaining to a medieval European system of administration, jurisdiction, land tenure, etc. (or similar system elsewhere), based on the relationship between a vassal and his superiors, the highest lord of which was often the king, and by which land was granted (ultimately to a vassal who worked the land) in return for homage, military service, and other duties. M17.

1 M. HALE Wales, that was not always the feudal Territory of . . England. 2 GIBBON The first rudiments of the feudal tenures. T. BENN The feudal nonsense of a hereditary title.

feudally *adv.* in a feudal manner; under feudal conditions: M19. **feudalism** *n.* the feudal system or its principles M19. **feudalist** *n.* a representative or a supporter of the feudal system E19. **feudalistic** *a.* of the nature of or inclined to feudalism L19.

feudal /ˈfjuːd(ə)l/ *a.*[2] *rare.* E19. [f. FEUD *n.*[1] + -AL[1].] Of or pertaining to a feud or state of bitter hostility.

feudalise *v.* var. of FEUDALIZE.

feudality /fjuːˈdalɪti/ *n.* E18. [Fr. *feudalité, féod-*, f. *feudal, féodal*, f. as FEUDAL *a.*[1]: see -ITY.] †1 *Law.* Fealty. Only in Dicts. E18–M19. 2 Feudal quality or state; the principles and practice of the feudal system. L18. 3 A feudal regime; a power like that of feudalism; a feudal holding or fief. E19.

2 J. S. MILL The very essence of feudality was . . the fusion of property and sovereignty.

feudalize /ˈfjuːd(ə)lʌɪz/ *v.t.* Also **-ise**. E19. [f. FEUDAL *a.*[1] + -IZE.] Make feudal, bring under the feudal system; convert (lands) into feudal holdings; reduce (persons) to the position of feudal vassals.

feudaliˈzation *n.* M19.

feu d'artifice /fø dartifis/ *n. phr.* Pl. ***feux d'artifice*** (pronounced same). L17. [Fr., lit. 'fire of artifice'.] A firework show; a firework.

feudary /ˈfjuːdəri/ *n.* & *a.* Now *arch.* or *Hist.* Also **feod-**. LME. [med.L *feodarius*, f. as FEUD *n.*[2]: see -ARY[1].] A *n.* 1 A person who holds lands of an overlord on condition of homage and service; a feudal tenant, a vassal. LME. b A subject, a dependant, a servant. E17. †2 An officer responsible for receiving the revenues of wards of court. L15–M18.

1 T. FULLER Accepted of the Jewish King to be honourary feodaries unto him.

B *adj.* Feudally subject (*to*). L16.

†feudatary *n.* & *a.* L16. [med.L *feudatarius*, f. *feudat-*: see next, -ARY[1].] A *n.* = FEUDATORY *n.* 2. L16–E19. B *adj.* = FEUDATORY *a.* Only in 17.

feudatory /ˈfjuːdət(ə)ri/ *a.* & *n.* L16. [med.L *feudatorius*, f. *feudat-* pa. ppl stem of *feudare* enfeoff, f. as FEUD *n.*[2]: see -ATE[3], -ORY[2].] A *adj.* Owing feudal allegiance *to*, subject *to*; under overlordship. L16.

P. F. TYTLER The petty chiefs . . had for a long period been feudatory to the Norwegian crown.

B *n.* 1 A feud, a fief, a fee; a dependent lordship. M17. 2 A person who holds lands by feudal tenure; a feudal vassal. M18.

feu de joie /fø də ʒwa/ *n. phr.* Pl. ***feux de joie*** (pronounced same). E17. [Fr., lit. 'fire of joy'.] I †1 A bonfire. E17–L18. 2 A salute fired by rifles etc. on occasions of ceremony or public rejoicing. E18. II 3 *fig.* A joyful thing or occasion; a celebration. M17.

feudist /ˈfjuːdɪst/ *n.*[1] Now *US.* L16. [f. FEUD *n.*[1] + -IST.] A person who has a feud with another.

¶Rare bef. E20.

feudist /ˈfjuːdɪst/ *n.*[2] E17. [Fr. *feudiste* or mod.L *feudista*, f. as FEUD *n.*[2]: see -IST.] 1 A writer on feuds or fiefs; an authority on feudal law. E17. †2 A person living under the feudal system. E17–M18.

feu-farm /ˈfjuːfɑːm/ *n.* LME. [OFr. *feuferme*: see FEE-FARM.] *Sc. Law.* Tenure by which land is held of a superior on payment of an annual sum.

feu follet /fø fɔlɛ/ *n. phr.* Pl. ***feux follets*** (pronounced same). M19. [Fr., lit. 'frolicsome fire'.] A will-o'-the-wisp, an ignis fatuus, (*lit.* & *fig.*).

feuillemorte /fœjmɔrt/ *a.* L16. [Fr. = dead leaf. Cf. FILEMOT.] Of the colour of a dead leaf, brown or yellowish brown.

†feuillet *n.* Only in 18. [Fr. *feuillette* f. med.L *folietta* a measure of wine.] A half hogshead.

feuilleton /ˈfəːɪtɒ̃, *foreign* fœjtɔ̃ (*pl. same*)/ *n.* M19. [Fr., f. *feuillet* dim. of *feuille* leaf: see -ET[1], -OON.] (A part of a newspaper etc. devoted to) fiction, criticism, light literature, etc.; an article or work suitable for or printed in that part.

E. JONES He earned part of his living by writing regular feuilletons for the local press.

feuilletonist /ˈfəːɪtɒnɪst/ *n.* Also ***feuilletoniste*** /fœjtɔnist (*pl. same*)/. M19. [Fr. *feuilletoniste*, f. as prec. + *-iste* -IST.] A writer of feuilletons.

feuilletoˈnistic *a.* characteristic of feuilletonists L19.

Feulgen /ˈfɔɪlg(ə)n/ *n.* E20. [R. J. *Feulgen* (1884–1955), Ger. biochemist.] Used *attrib.* to denote a technique devised by Feulgen for preferentially staining chromosomes or other bodies containing DNA.

feux d'artifice, de joie, follets *n. phrs.* pls. of FEU D'ARTIFICE etc.

fever /ˈfiːvə/ *n.* & *v.* OE. [L *febris*; reinforced in ME by AN *fevre*, (O)Fr. *fièvre* f. L.] A *n.* 1 An abnormally high temperature of the body as a whole; any of various diseases characterized by this. OE. 2 A state of intense nervous excitement or agitation. ME.

1 I. MURDOCH Jealousy inhabited her like a fever making her shake and sweat. *blackwater fever, Lassa fever, relapsing fever, scarlet fever, yellow fever*, etc. **fever and ague** (now *US*) malaria. *hay fever*: see HAY *n.*[1] 2 W. EMPSON The fever and multiplicity of life . . are contrasted with the calm of the external space.

Comb.: **fever heat** the high temperature of the body in fever; *fig.* fever pitch; **fever pitch** a state of abnormal excitement; **fever therapy** the treatment of disease by induced fever.

B *v.* 1 *v.t.* Affect (as) with a fever. E17. 2 *v.i.* Be seized with a fever. M18.

1 R. L. STEVENSON The stir and speed of the journey . . fever him, and stimulate his dull nerves.

feveret *n.* (now *rare*) a slight fever E18.

feverfew /ˈfiːvəfjuː/ *n.* OE. [L *febrifuga, -fugia*, f. as prec. + *fugare* drive away; forms f. L superseded in ME by those f. AN *feiverfue*.] An aromatic white-flowered herb of the composite family, *Tanacetum parthenium*, used to treat migraine and formerly as a febrifuge.

feverish /ˈfiːv(ə)rɪʃ/ *a.* LME. [f. FEVER *n.* + -ISH[1].] 1 (Of food, climate, etc.) causing or tending to cause fever; (of a country etc.) infested with fever. LME. 2 Having symptoms (resembling those) of a fever. Formerly also, ill of a fever. M17. b Of the nature or indicative of a fever. L17. 3 Excited; restless; hectic. M17.

1 G. CAMPBELL Tracts which are exceedingly feverish in summer. 2 J. AUSTEN Though heavy and feverish . . a good night's rest was to cure her. b J. STEINBECK His face was puffed and feverish. 3 B. RUBENS Rabbi Zweck frantically opened every drawer, rummaging through their contents with feverish fingers.

feverishly *adv.* †(*a*) with the symptoms of fever; (*b*) excitedly, restlessly: M17. **feverishness** *n.* M17.

feverous /ˈfiːv(ə)rəs/ *a.* LME. [f. FEVER *n.* + -OUS.] 1 = FEVERISH 2. LME. 2 = FEVERISH 1. E17. 3 = FEVERISH 3. E17.

feverously *adv.* M17.

few /fjuː/ *a.* (in mod. usage also classed as a *determiner*), *pron.*, & *n.* [OE *fēawe, fēawa* contr. *fēa* = OFris. *fē*, OS *fa(o)* OHG *fao, fō*, ON *fár*, Goth. pl. *fawai* f. Gmc f. IE base also of L *paucus*, Gk *pauros* small.] A *adj.* 1 With *n.pl.* Not many, hardly any; a small number (with *compar.* & *superl.*). (Preceding the n. and other adjs. but following any determiners (the def. article, demonstratives, possessives, etc.) or ordinal numerals (also *last, next*); also pred. after *be* etc.) OE. 2 With *n.pl.* *A* small number of. (Preceding the n. and other adjs.) ME. b *A* small quantity of. Long *obs.* exc. *dial.* LME. 3 Of a company or number: small. Now *rare.* LME.

1 J. CONRAD Packing his few belongings. P. G. WODEHOUSE George Pennicut contented himself with saying 'Goo!' He was a man of few words. R. S. THOMAS After the few people have gone. P. SCOTT Marriages and christenings, of which there seemed . . to be fewer than there were funerals. *Times* They have few, if any, close friends. W. BOYD Temple spent the next few days in an . . attempt to find someone who would admit he was a 'problem'. *Economist* There are very few openings in universities at the moment. 2 J. CONRAD In a very few hours I arrived. A. UTTLEY The leaves had gone, all but a few odd ones. 3 *New York*

Times The fewest number of firemen in the history of the city.

B *pron.* & *n.* **1** *absol.* Few people or things understood contextually; not many *of*, hardly any *of*. (Also modified by adv. as *very, many.*) OE. **2** *A* small number (*of*). ME. **b** *A* good bit, *a* considerable extent. *arch. slang.* M18. **3** *The* small company (specified or understood). Now usu. *the* minority, *the* elect; *spec.* (**F-**) *the* Royal Air Force pilots who took part in the Battle of Britain. M16.

1 SHAKES. *Hen. V* We few, we happy few, we band of brothers. A. HELPS How few of your fellow-creatures can have the opportunity. G. B. SHAW Very few of them are fortunate enough to enjoy this advantage. G. GREENE Few . . drank anywhere else. 2 C. ISHERWOOD Most of the boys looked up and grinned . . , only a few were sullen. J. C. POWYS Courtly travellers, a few of whom were bound for Oxford. **b** W. IRVING Determined to astonish the natives a few!

Phrases: **a good few** *colloq.* a considerable number (of). *catch, get,* etc. *a few z's*: see Z, z 1b. **every few** once in every small group of (days, miles, etc.), at intervals of a few (days, miles, etc.). **few and far between** neither numerous nor frequent. **have a few** *spec.* (*colloq.*) have a few alcoholic drinks. **in few** *arch.* in few words, in short, briefly. **no fewer than** as many as (a specified number). **not a few, quite a few** *colloq.* a considerable number (of or *of*). *of few words*: see WORD *n.* **some few** some but not at all many (*of*).

fewness *n.* small number or quantity OE.

fewmet /ˈfjuːmɪt/ *n.* Also **fumet**. LME. [(f. AN var. of) OFr. *fumees* (pl.), f. *fumer* (repr. L *fimare*) to dung.] *sing.* & (usu.) in *pl.* The excrement of a deer.

fewter /ˈfjuːtə/ *n.* & *v.* Long *obs.* exc. *Hist.* LME. [OFr. *feutre, fautre* f. med.L *filtrum*: see FILTER *n.*] A *n.* A support or rest for a spear attached to a saddle or side of a breastplate and lined with felt to absorb the shock of impact. LME.

B *v.t.* Put (a spear) in a fewter. LME.

T. H. WHITE They fewtered their spears again, and thundered into the charge.

†fewterer *n.* ME–E19. [AN *veutrier* (= AL *veltrarius*) f. OFr. *veutre, v(e)autre, veltre* (mod. *vautre*) boar-hound, f. Proto-Romance contracted and dissimilated form of L *vertragus* greyhound, of Gaulish origin.] A keeper of greyhounds. More *widely*, an attendant.

fewtrils /ˈfjuːtrɪlz/ *n.pl. dial.* M18. [Cf. FATTRELS.] Little things, trifles.

DICKENS I ha' gotten decent fewtrils about me agen.

fey /feɪ/ *a.* Long chiefly *Sc.* [OE *fǣġe* = OS *fēgi* (Du. *veeg*), OHG *feigi* (G *feige* cowardly), ON *feigr* f. Gmc.] **1** Fated to die, at the point of death (as manifested by strange exultant behaviour supposedly portending death). Formerly also, accursed, unlucky; weak, feeble. OE. **b** Disordered in mind, behaving strangely like a person about to die; possessing or displaying magical or supernatural powers. Now freq. *iron.*, affected. L18. **†2** Leading to or portending death; fatal. ME–L18.

1 R. BURNS Thro' they dash'd, and hew'd, and smash'd, Till fey men died awa. **b** J. LE CARRÉ His interlocuter was whimsical if not downright fey.

feyly *adv.* M20. **feyness** *n.* L19.

fez /fɛz/ *n.* Pl. **fezzes**. E19. [Turk. *fes*, perh. through Fr. *fez*, named after *Fez* (now *Fès*) in Morocco, once the chief place of manufacture.] A flat-topped conical red hat with a tassel worn by men in some Muslim countries, and formerly the national head-dress of the Turks.

fezzed *a.* wearing a fez M19.

fiacre /fɪˈɑːkrə; *foreign* fjakr (*pl. same*)/ *n.* L17. [Fr., f. the Hôtel de St *Fiacre*, rue St Antoine, Paris, where such vehicles were first hired out.] A small four-wheeled horse-drawn carriage.

†fial *n.* var. of PHIAL.

Fian /fiːn/ *n.* Also **Fiann**. Pl. **Fianna** /ˈfiːənə/, **Fians**. L18. [Ir. *fian* (pl. *fianna*), orig. 'band of warriors and hunters'. Cf. FEINNE.] = FENIAN *n.* 1.

fiancé /fɪˈɒnseɪ, -ˈɑːns-, -ˈɒ̃s-/ *n.* Fem. **-ée**. M19. [Fr., f. (O)Fr. *fiancer* betroth, f. OFr. *fiance* a promise.] A man or woman engaged to be married to another; the person to whom one is engaged.

fianchetto /fɪənˈtʃɛtəʊ, -ˈkɛtəʊ/ *n.* & *v.* M19. [It., dim. of *fianco* FLANK *n.*] *Chess.* A *n.* Pl. **-oes**. The development of a bishop by moving it one square to a long diagonal of the board. M19.

B *v.t.* Develop (a bishop) in this way. E20.

Fiann *n.* var. of FIAN.

Fianna Fáil /fɪˌanə ˈfɔɪl/ *n. phr.* E20. [Ir. f. *fianna* (see FIAN) + *Fáil* genit. of *Fál* an ancient name for Ireland.] An Irish Republican Party founded in 1926 by De Valera, in opposition to the Anglo-Irish treaty of 1921.

fiant /ˈfʌɪənt/ *n.* M16. [L, first wd in formula *fiant literae patentes* 'let letters patent be made out'.] *Hist.* A warrant addressed to the Irish Chancery for a grant under the Great Seal.

fiants /ˈfɪənts/ *n.pl.* Long *arch.* Also **†fuants**. L16. [OFr. *fient*, (also mod.) *fiente* dung, repr. pop.L development of L *fimus*. The specialization of sense seems to be English.] *Hunting.* The excrement of certain animals, e.g. the fox and the badger.

fiar /ˈfiːə/ *n. Sc.* Also **fear**. L15. [f. FEE *n.*[2] + -AR[2]. Cf. FEUAR.] *Law.* A person who has the reversion of a property and is its ultimate owner.

fiasco /fɪˈaskəʊ, *in sense 1 foreign* ˈfjasko/ *n.* Pl. **-scos**, (sense 1) **-schi** /-ski/. M19. [It.; in sense 2 f. phr. *far fiasco* lit. 'make a bottle', with unexpl. allus.] **1** A bottle, a flask. (Not Anglicized.) M19. **2** A complete and ignominious failure, orig. of a dramatic or musical performance; an ignominious result. M19.

2 H. JAMES One of the biggest failures that history commemorates, an immense national *fiasco*.

fiat /ˈfʌɪat/ *n.* & *v.* LME. [L, 3rd person sing. pres. subjunct. of *fieri* = let it be done, let there be made. In sense A.2 short for *fiat lux* (Vulgate *Gen.* 1:3) = let there be light.] A *n.* **1** A formal authorization (orig. expressed by the L word *fiat* or a formula containing it) for a proposed arrangement, a request, etc.; *gen.* an authoritative pronouncement, a decree, an order. LME. **2** A command by which something is brought into being. L16.

1 F. FITZGERALD Japan took over French Indochina by diplomatic fiat. R. C. A. WHITE The unsatisfactory procedure of the writ of error on the fiat of the Attorney-General. 2 J. TYNDALL Was space furnished at once, by the fiat of Omnipotence, with these burning orbs?

Comb.: **fiat-money** *US* inconvertible paper money made legal tender by Government decree.

B *v.t.* Sanction by (official) pronouncement. M19.

J. S. LE FANU My uncle fiated the sexton's presentment, and the work commenced forthwith.

fib /fɪb/ *n. colloq.* M16. [Perh. short for FIBLE-FABLE.] **1** A person who tells (trivial or venial) lies. M16. **2** A (trivial or venial) lie. E17.

2 H. JAMES They are very sincere; they don't tell fibs.

fib /fɪb/ *v.*[1]*i. colloq.* Infl. **-bb-**. E17. [f. the n.] Tell a (trivial or venial) lie.

fibber *n.* E17. **fibbery** *n.* falsehood, lying M19.

fib /fɪb/ *v.*[2]*t.* & *i. slang.* Infl. **-bb-**. M17. [Origin unkn.] Administer a pommelling (to), esp. in boxing.

fiber, fiberglass *ns.* see FIBRE, FIBREGLASS.

fible-fable /ˈfɪb(ə)lfeɪb(ə)l/ *n.* Long *obs.* exc. *dial. rare.* L16. [Redupl. of FABLE *n.*] Nonsense.

Fibonacci /fiːbəˈnɑːtʃi/ *n.* L19. [Leonardo *Fibonacci* (fl. 1200), Tuscan mathematician.] Math. *Fibonacci('s) numbers, series*, etc., the series of numbers, 1, 1, 2, 3, 5, 8, . . , in which each number is the sum of the two preceding ones.

fibre /ˈfʌɪbə/ *n.* Also ***fiber**. LME. [(O)Fr. f. L *fibra*.] **†1** A lobe of the liver; in *pl.*, the entrails. LME–E17. **2** *Anat.* & *Zool.* Any threadlike structure forming part of the muscular, nervous, connective, or other tissue in an animal body. M16. **3** *Bot.* A threadlike element in plant tissue; *spec.* an elongated thick-walled cell lacking protoplasm. M17. **4** A slender subdivision of a root. M17. **5** A thread or filament forming part of a textile. Also, a thread formed from glass, metal, etc. E19. **6** *collect.* Any material consisting of animal, vegetable, or man-made fibres; *esp.* one that can be spun, woven, or felted. Also, fibrous structure. E19. **7** *fig.* Essential character or make-up. M19. **8** *Metall.* A structure characteristic of wrought metal in which there is a directional alignment or elongation of crystals or inclusions. M19. **9** The part of a foodstuff that cannot be digested or absorbed; roughage. Also *dietary fibre*. E20.

2 T. HOLCROFT In cold countries the fibres of the tongue must be less flexible. B. BAINBRIDGE Straining in every fibre I crouched there, panting. *yellow fibre*: see YELLOW *a.* 3 W. HAMILTON The vascular fibres of the bark. 5 F. SMYTH Smith set to work on the rest of the fluff, and found . . fibres of wool, cotton, . . and jute. *carbon fibre, glass fibre*, etc. 6 HUGH MILLER Pieces of coal which exhibit the ligneous fibre. *Wall Street Journal* The company entered the man made fiber field with rayon. 7 N. MONSARRAT We are not all made of the same stern fibre. *moral fibre*: see MORAL *a.*

Comb.: **fibreboard** (a sheet of) compressed wood or other plant fibre, used as a building material; **fibrefill** material made of synthetic fibres, used for padding garments, cushions, etc.; **fibre-optic** *a.* relating to or used in fibre optics; **fibre optics** the transmission of light by total internal reflection through fibres of glass or other transparent solids; **fibre-tip** *a.* & *n.* (*a*) *adj.* fibre-tipped; (*b*) *n.* a fibre-tipped pen; **fibre-tipped** *a.* (of a pen) having a tip made of tightly packed capillary fibres which hold the ink.

fibred *a.* furnished with fibres (chiefly as 2nd elem. of comb.) M17. **fibreless** *a.* having no fibres or strength M19. **fibrescope** *n.* a fibre-optic device for viewing inaccessible internal structures, esp. in the human body M20.

fibreglass /ˈfʌɪbəglɑːs/ *n.* Also ***fiberglass**, (US proprietary name) **Fiberglas**. M20. [f. FIBRE + GLASS *n.*] Any material consisting of glass filaments woven into a textile or paper, or embedded in plastic etc., for use as a construction or insulation material.

fibriform /ˈfʌɪbrɪfɔːm/ *a.* M19. [f. FIBRE + -I- + -FORM.] Having the form of a fibre or fibres.

fibril /ˈfʌɪbrɪl/ *n.* M17. [mod.L *fibrilla*: see next.] **1** *Bot.* The ultimate subdivision of a root. M17. **2** A small or delicate fibre; *spec.* a constituent strand of an animal, vegetable, or man-made fibre. Also, a threadlike molecular formation such as occurs in some colloidal systems and proteins. L17.

fibrilla /fʌɪˈbrɪlə, fɪ-/ *n.* Pl. **-llae** /-liː/. M17. [mod.L, dim. of *fibra* FIBRE.] = FIBRIL 2.

fibrillar *a.* of, relating to, or of the nature of a fibrilla M19. **fibrillary** *a.* = FIBRILLAR L18. **fibrilliform** *a.* having the form of a fibril M19. **fibrillose** *a.* (marked with fine lines as if) composed of or covered with fibrils E19.

fibrillate /ˈfʌɪbrɪleɪt, ˈfɪ-/ *v.* M19. [f. FIBRILLA + -ATE[3].] **1** *v.i.* Of blood: turn into fibrillae (in clotting). M19. **2** *v.i.* Of the muscles of the heart: contract irregularly fibril by fibril. E20. **3** *v.t.* *Paper-making.* Beat (vegetable fibre) down into its constituent fibrils. E20. **b** *v.i.* Of fibre: split up into fibrils. M20.

fibrillated *ppl a.* having a fibrillar structure M19.

fibrillation /fʌɪbrɪˈleɪʃ(ə)n, fɪ-/ *n.* M19. [f. as prec.: see -ATION.] **1** Arrangement into fibrils; formation of fibrillae; a fibrillated mass. M19. **2** *Med.* Irregular spontaneous contraction in the individual fibres of a muscle, esp. of the auricles or ventricles of the heart. L19. **3** *Paper-making.* The beating of vegetable fibre into its component fibrils. E20.

fibrin /ˈfʌɪbrɪn, ˈfɪ-/ *n.* E19. [f. FIBRE + -IN[2].] A protein forming fibres. Now only *spec.* an insoluble protein formed by enzyme action from fibrinogen when blood coagulates, which forms a fibrous network round the clot.

fibrinogen /fɪˈbrɪnədʒ(ə)n/ *n.* L19. [f. prec. + -GEN.] A soluble protein present in blood plasma, from which fibrin is formed during coagulation.

fibrinoid /ˈfʌɪbrɪnɔɪd/ *a.* & *n.* E20. [G, f. as FIBRIN + -OID.] *Med.* (Of the nature of or involving) a granular material, resembling fibrin in its staining properties, which is found in the placenta during pregnancy, as well as in various diseased tissues.

fibrinolysis /fʌɪbrɪˈnɒlɪsɪs/ *n.* E20. [f. FIBRIN + -LYSIS.] The breakdown of fibrin in blood clots.

fibrinolysin *n.* any of various enzymes which dissolve blood clots by breaking down the fibrin; *spec.* plasmin: E20. **ˌfibrinoˈlytic** *a.* pertaining to or causing fibrinolysis E20.

fibrinous /ˈfʌɪbrɪnəs/ *a.* M19. [f. FIBRIN + -OUS.] Composed of, containing, or of the nature of fibrin.

fibriˈnosity *n.* fibrinous quality L19.

fibro /ˈfʌɪbrəʊ/ *n. Austral.* & *NZ colloq.* Pl. **-os.** M20. [Abbrev.] = FIBRO-CEMENT. Also, a house composed mainly of this.

fibro- /ˈfʌɪbrəʊ/ *comb. form.* [L, f. *fibra* FIBRE: see -O-.] *Anat.* & *Med.* Forming ns. and adjs. w. the sense 'fibrous, of fibre,' chiefly in terms referring to fibrous tissue.

fibroadeˈnoma *n.*, pl. **-mas, -mata** /-mətə/, a tumour (esp. a benign tumour of the breast) formed of mixed fibrous and glandular tissue L19. **fibroadeˈnomatous** *a.* of the nature of a fibroadenoma L19. **fibroblast** *n.* any of the fibre-secreting cells in connective tissue L19. **fibroˈblastic** *a.* of, involving, or relating to fibroblasts L19. **fibrocartilage** *n.* fibrous cartilage, containing bundles or networks of fibres M19. **fibrocartiˈlaginous** *a.* of the nature of fibrocartilage M19. **fibro-ceˈment** *n.* a mixture of asbestos and cement, used in sheets for building E20. **fibroˈcystic** *a.* characterized by the development of fibrous tissue and cystic spaces M19. **fibrocyte** *n.* an inactive form of fibroblast found in mature fibrous tissue E20. **fibroˈgenesis** *n.* formation of (fibrous) connective tissue M20. **fibroˈgenic** *a.* causing fibrogenesis M20. **fibroˈplasia** *n.* proliferation of fibrous tissue, esp. in the process of healing E20. **fibrosarˈcoma** *n.*, pl. **-mas, -mata** /-mətə/, a sarcoma in which the predominant cell is a malignant fibroblast L19. **fibroˈvascular** *a.* (*Bot.*) consisting of a mixture of fibrous and vascular tissue M19.

fibroid /ˈfʌɪbrɔɪd/ *a.* & *n.* M19. [f. FIBRE + -OID.] **A** *adj.* Resembling, composed of, or characterized by fibrous tissue. M19. **B** *n. Med.* A tumour containing much fibrous tissue; *esp.* a fibrous myoma of the uterus. L19.

fibroin /ˈfʌɪbrəʊɪn/ *n.* M19. [f. FIBRO- + -IN[1].] A protein forming the main component of raw silk filaments, spiders' webs, etc.

fibrolite /ˈfʌɪbrəlʌɪt/ *n.* E19. [f. FIBRO- + -LITE.] *Min.* = SILLIMANITE.

fibroma /fʌɪˈbrəʊmə/ *n.* Pl. **-mas, -mata** /-mətə/. M19. [f. L *fibra* FIBRE + -OMA.] *Med.* A benign tumour of fibrous tissue.

fibrose /ˈfʌɪbrəʊs/ *a.* Now *rare.* L17. [mod.L *fibrosus*: see FIBRE, -OSE[1].] = FIBROUS.

fibrose /fʌɪˈbrəʊs/ *v.i.* L19. [Back-form. f. next.] Form fibrous tissue. Chiefly as *fibrosed*, *fibrosing* ppl adjs.

fibrosis /fʌɪˈbrəʊsɪs/ *n.* Pl. **-broses** /-ˈbrəʊsiːz/. L19. [f. L *fibra* FIBRE + -OSIS.] *Med.* (An) abnormal increase of fibrous tissue within an organ.

cystic fibrosis a hereditary disorder of the exocrine glands, in which the production of thick mucus leads to the blocking of the pancreatic ducts, intestines, bronchi, etc.

fibrositis /fʌɪbrəˈsʌɪtɪs/ *n.* E20. [f. FIBROSE *a.* + -ITIS.] *Med.* Any rheumatic disorder of uncertain origin believed to involve the fibrous tissue; *esp.* painful inflammation of the back and shoulder muscles.

fibrositic /fʌɪbrəˈsɪtɪk/ *a.* relating to or affected with fibrositis E20.

fibrotic /fʌɪˈbrɒtɪk/ *a.* L19. [f. as FIBROSIS: see -OTIC.] Affected with or characterized by fibrosis.

fibrous /ˈfʌɪbrəs/ *a.* E17. [f. FIBRE + -OUS. Cf. Fr. *fibreux.*] **1** Formed from or full of fibres. E17. **2** Resembling fibre or fibres. E18.

1 fibrous protein any of a class of proteins having an elongated freq. helical molecular structure with little folding. **fibrous tissue** the common connective tissue of mammals, consisting of fibrous collagen with fibroblasts or fibrocytes, forming ligaments, fasciae, etc.

fibrously *adv.* L19. **fibrousness** *n.* E18.

fibry /ˈfʌɪbri/ *a.* E19. [f. FIBRE + -Y[1].] Resembling a fibre; having many fibres.

fibster /ˈfɪbstə/ *n.* E19. [f. FIB *v.*[1] + -STER.] A person who tells fibs; a petty liar.

fibula /ˈfɪbjʊlə/ *n.* Pl. **-lae** /-liː/, **-las.** L16. [L *fibula* brooch, perh. f. base of *figere* to fix.] **1** *Anat.* The outer of the two bones between the knee and the ankle, articulating at its upper end with the tibia. L16. **2** *Antiq.* A clasp, a buckle, a brooch. L17.

fibular *a.* of, pertaining to, or (formerly) resembling the fibula of the leg E18.

-fic /fɪk/ *suff.* Also (see below) **-ific.** [Repr. (Fr. *-fique* f.) L *-ficus* making, doing, f. weakened base of *facere* make, do.] Forming (usu. w. intermediate -I-) adjs. corresp. to L adjs. in *-ficus* or modelled on them, (1) from ns., w. the sense 'making, producing', as *calorific, pacific, prolific*; (2) from adjs., w. the sense 'performing actions of a specified kind', as *magnific*, or, later, 'bringing into a specified state', as *beatific*; (3) from vbs, w. the sense 'causing to', as *horrific*; (4) from advs., w. the sense 'acting in a specified way', as *malefic*.

-fication /fɪˈkeɪʃ(ə)n/ *suff.* Also (see below) **-ific-.** [Repr. (Fr. *-fication* f.) L *-ficatio(n-)* corresp. to vb stems in *-fica(t-)-*.] Forming (usu. w. intermediate -I-) the regular ns. of action corresp. to vbs in -FY which represent or are modelled on L vbs in *-ficare*, as *glorification, purification, transmogrification.*

fice *n.* see FIST *n.*[2]

ficelle /fisɛl (*pl. same*), fɪˈsɛl/ *n.* L19. [Fr. = string.] **1** The off-white colour of much string. Only *attrib.* or in *comb.*, as *ficelle-colour(ed).* L19. **2** A (stage) device, an artifice. L19.

2 G. MURRAY Raids on women were a real cause of war, but they were also a . . favourite *ficelle* of fiction.

fiche /fiʃ (*pl. same*), fiːʃ/ *n.*[1] M20. [Fr., short for *fiche de voyageur.*] The registration form filled in by foreign guests in French hotels.

fiche /fiːʃ/ *n.*[2] Pl. same, **-s.** M20. [Abbrev.] = MICROFICHE.

Fichtean /ˈfɪxtɪən/ *a.* E19. [f. *Fichte* (see below) + -AN.] Of or connected with the German idealist philosopher Johann Gottlieb Fichte (1762–1814) or his views.

fichu /ˈfiːʃuː/ *n.* M18. [Fr., of unkn. origin.] A triangular piece of muslin, lace, or the like, worn by women round the neck and shoulders, and formerly also over the head.

fickle /ˈfɪk(ə)l/ *a.* [OE *ficol* rel. to *ġefic* deceit, *befician* deceive, and further to *fǣcne* deceitful, *fācen* deceit(ful), corresp. to OS *fēkan*, OHG *feihhan*, ON *feikn* portent.] **1** Deceitful, false. Now only (*Sc.*) of a place: treacherous, unsafe. OE. **2** Of a person, feelings, etc.: changeable in disposition, loyalty, affections, etc.; inconstant. ME. **3** Of a thing, esp. the weather: changeable, inconstant. LME.

1 M. O. W. OLIPHANT It's a fickle corner in the dark. **2** S. NAIPAUL A . . lover fighting to keep to himself the affections of a fickle mistress. M. IGNATIEFF They were dependent on the fickle mercy of their sons. **3** F. CHICHESTER The wind was unusually fickle, changing speed and direction every few minutes.

fickleness *n.* LME. **fickly** *adv.* ME.

fickle /ˈfɪk(ə)l/ *v.t. Sc.* & *dial.* M16. [f. the adj.] Baffle, perplex.

S. SMILES Other questions were put to 'fickle' him.

fico /ˈfiːkəʊ/ *n. arch.* Pl. **-os.** L16. [It. f. L *ficus* FIG *n.*[1] Cf. FIGO.] †**1** = FIG *n.*[1] 1c. L16–M17. **2** = FIG *n.*[1] 3. L16.

2 SHAKES. *Merry W.* 'Steal' foh! A fico for the phrase!

fictile /ˈfɪktʌɪl, -tɪl/ *a.* & *n.* E17. [L *fictilis*, f. *fict-*: see next, -ILE.] **A** *adj.* **1** Made of earth, clay, etc., by a potter. E17. **2** Of or pertaining to pottery or pottery manufacture. M19. **B** *n.* A piece of pottery. Now *rare.* M19.

fiction /ˈfɪkʃ(ə)n/ *n.* LME. [(O)Fr. f. L *fictio(n-)*, f. *fict-* pa. ppl stem of *fingere* fashion: see -ION. Cf. FEIGN.] **1** *gen.* A thing feigned or imaginatively invented; an invented statement or narrative; an untruth. LME. **2** *gen.* The action of feigning or of inventing imaginary events etc. (orig. *spec.* for the purpose of deception); imaginative invention as opp. to truth or fact. L15. **3** *spec.* Literature consisting of the narration of imaginary events and the portrayal of imaginary characters; (the genre comprising) novels and stories collectively. L16. **b** A work of fiction, a novel or story. L19. **4** *spec.* A conventionally accepted falsehood or pretence. L16. †**5** Fashioning, imitating; arbitrary creation; a device, a thing created. L16–L18.

1 GIBBON Such an anecdote may be rejected as an improbable fiction. **2** C. THIRLWALL The scene may . . have afforded temptation for fiction. F. WELDON How much is fiction and how much is true? **3** LYTTON Old people like history better than fiction. **b** G. ORWELL He's supposed to publish my next three fictions. **4** DICKENS By a . . pleasant fiction his single chamber was always mentioned in the plural. *legal fiction*: see LEGAL *a.*

fictionary *a.* (*rare*) = FICTIONAL L19. **fictioˈneer** *n.* a writer or inventor of fiction E20. **fictionist** *n.* a narrator or writer of fiction E19. **fictionize** *v.* (*a*) *v.t.* = FICTIONALIZE; (*b*) *v.i.* invent a fictional version of events etc.: M19.

fiction /ˈfɪkʃ(ə)n/ *v. rare.* E19. [f. the n.] **1** *v.t.* Feign; fictionalize. E19. **2** *v.i.* Admit of being fictionalized. M20.

fictional /ˈfɪkʃ(ə)n(ə)l/ *a.* M19. [f. FICTION *n.* + -AL[1].] Of, pertaining to, or of the nature of fiction; imaginatively invented.

fictioˈnality *n.* the quality or state of being fictional M20. **fictionaliˈzation** *n.* the action or process of fictionalizing M20. **fictionalize** *v.t.* make into fiction, give a fictional form to; give a fictional version of (an actual event etc.): E20. **fictionally** *adv.* L19.

†**fictious** *a.* E17–L19. [f. L *fict-* (see FICTION *n.*) + -IOUS.] Fictitious; characterized by fiction.

fictitious /fɪkˈtɪʃəs/ *a.* E17. [L *ficticius* f. *fict-*: see FICTION *n.*, -ITIOUS[1].] **1** Artificial, arbitrarily devised; counterfeit, imitation, sham. E17. **2** Imaginary, invented; unreal, false; (of a name or character) assumed. E17. **3** Of, pertaining to, or characteristic of literary fiction. L18. **4** Regarded as or called such by a legal or conventional fiction. M19.

1 H. CROOKE Distinguish betweene natural and fictitious precious Stones. **2** N. ROWE The fictitious Justice of the Gods. POPE Make use of Real Names and not of Fictitious Ones. **3** E. WAUGH How to invent names for fictitious characters without fear of prosecution. **4** H. J. S. MAINE Adoption, as a method of obtaining a fictitious son.

fictitiously *adv.* M17. **fictitiousness** *n.* M17.

fictive /ˈfɪktɪv/ *a.* L15. [Fr. *fictif*, *-ive* or med.L *fictivus*, f. L *fict-*: see FICTION *n.*, -IVE.] †**1** Given to feigning or in order to deceive. Only in L15. **2** Originating in fiction, created by the imagination; fictitious; unreal, sham. E17. **3** Concerned with the creation of fiction; imaginatively creative. M19.

2 W. H. AUDEN Into what fictive realms can imagination/translate you.

¶ Rare bef. 19.

fictively *adv.* L19. **fictiveness** *n.* L20.

ficus /ˈfiːkəs, ˈfʌɪkəs/ *n.* LME. [L *ficus* fig tree, fig.] **1** *Med.* A type of condyloma resembling a fig. Long *rare* or *obs.* LME. **2** A tree or shrub of the large genus *Ficus*, of the mulberry family, which includes the fig, *F. carica*, and the rubber plant, *F. elastica.* M19.

fid /fɪd/ *n.* & *v.* E17. [Origin unkn.] Chiefly *Naut.* **A** *n.* **1** A conical pin used to open the strands of rope in splicing. E17. **2** A plug of oakum for the vent of a gun. E17. **3** A square wooden or metal bar to support a topmast or topgallant; a bar used to support or steady anything. M17. **4** A small thick piece of anything; a bundle, a heap, a pile. In *pl.*, lots. *dial.* & *colloq.* M19. **B** *v.t.* Infl. **-dd-.** Fix (a topmast etc.) with a fid. E18.

-fid /fɪd/ *suff.* [L *-fidus* split: see TRIFID.] Forming adjs. with the sense 'divided into a specified number of parts', as *quadrifid*, or (in *Bot.*) 'divided in a specified way', as *palmatifid.*

fidalgo /fɪˈdalgəʊ/ *n. obs.* exc. *Hist.* Pl. **-os.** M17. [Port., contr. of *filho de algo* son of something. Cf. HIDALGO.] A Portuguese noble.

fiddle /ˈfɪd(ə)l/ *n.* [OE *fiþele* = (M)Du. *vedel* (*veel*), OHG *fidula* (G *Fiedel*), ON *fiðla* f. Gmc f. Proto-Romance, f. L *vitulari* celebrate a festival, be joyful (cf. *Vitula* goddess of victory and jubilation).] **I 1** A stringed musical instrument of the violin family; *spec.* a violin. Now chiefly *colloq.* or *derog.* OE. **2** A person who plays a fiddle; *transf.* (now *rare*) a person to whose music others dance, a jester, an entertainer. L16. **3** Something resembling a fiddle in shape; *esp.* (*Naut.*) a contrivance to stop things sliding off a flat surface in rough weather. M19. 4 Fiddling, fussing; a fuss, an inconvenience. L19. 5 A swindle, a fraud; a piece of cheating. *colloq.* L19.

2 F. MARRYAT He was.. the fiddle of the ship's company. 4 J. S. BLACKIE The eternal whirl and fiddle of life. 5 J. T. STORY This little harmless horse-racing racket and fiddle.

II 6 As *int.* Nonsense! Fiddlesticks! M19.

Phrases: *as fit as a fiddle*: see FIT *a.* **hang up one's fiddle** (chiefly *US*) retire from business, give up an undertaking. **hang up one's fiddle when one comes home** (chiefly *US*) cease to be cheerful or entertaining when in the company of one's family. **have a face as long as a fiddle** look miserable. **on the fiddle** engaged in a swindle or piece of cheating. **play first** (**second, third**) **fiddle** take a leading (or subordinate) role.

Comb.: **fiddle-back** (a chair with) a back shaped like the body of a fiddle; a chasuble similarly shaped; **fiddle-bow** the stringed bow with which a fiddle is played, a fiddlestick; **fiddle-case**: in which a fiddle is kept; **fiddle dock** a dock, *Rumex pulcher*, with fiddle-shaped leaves; **fiddle-fish** the monkfish, *Squatina squatina*; **fiddle-head** (*a*) = *scroll-head* s.v. SCROLL *n.* 2(b); (*b*) (in full *fiddle-head greens*) the new leaf of certain ferns, considered a delicacy; **fiddle-headed** *a.* having a fiddle-head or a fiddle-patterned handle; **fiddle-pattern**: in the shape of the body of a fiddle; **fiddle-patterned** *a.* (of cutlery) having the handle shaped like the body of a fiddle; **fiddle-string** any of the strings on a fiddle; **fiddlewood** (the timber of) any of various neotropical trees of the genus *Citharexylum*, of the verbena family, esp. the W. Indian *C. fruticosum* and *C. spinosum*.

fiddle /ˈfɪd(ə)l/ *v.* LME. [f. the n.] 1 *v.i.* Play the fiddle. LME. 2 *v.t.* Play (a tune etc.) on the fiddle. LME. 3 *v.i.* Be idle or frivolous; make aimless movements, toy or play *with*, *about*, *at*, etc.; fritter *away*. M16. 4a *v.t.* Cheat, swindle, falsify; get by cheating. *slang.* E17. b *v.i.* Cheat; intrigue. M19.

1 V. WOOLF An old Spaniard who fiddled.. so as to make a tortoise waltz. 3 SWIFT He took a pipe in his hand, and fiddled with it till he broke it. H. SMART They've had him fiddling about so long in the school, he's most likely forgot how to gallop. 4 G. CLARE He.. found out that the books had been fiddled, and how the fiddling had been done.

fiddlededee /fɪd(ə)ldɪˈdiː/ *int.* & *n.* L18. [f. FIDDLE *n.*, *v.* with a meaningless redupl. addition.] A *int.* Nonsense! L18. B *n.* Nonsense, absurdity. M19.

fiddle-faddle /ˈfɪd(ə)lfad(ə)l/ *n.*, *a.*, *v.*, & *int.* L16. [Redupl. of FIDDLE *n.*, *v.* Cf. GIBBLE-GABBLE.] A *n.* 1 Trifling talk or action; a trifling or trivial matter (usu. in *pl.*). L16. 2 A trifler, a gossip. Now *dial.* E17. B *adj.* Trifling, petty, fussy. E17. C *v.i.* Fuss, trifle, mess about. M17. D *int.* Nonsense! L17.

fiddler /ˈfɪdlə/ *n.* [OE *fiþlere* (= ON *fiðlari*), f. as FIDDLE *n.*: see -ER[1].] 1 A person who plays the fiddle. OE. 2 A trifler. Now *spec.* a person who makes aimless movements or who toys or plays with something. L16. 3a In full *fiddler crab.* Any of various small crabs of the genus *Uca*, the males of which have one claw larger than the other and held in position like a violinist's arm. E18. b = *fiddle-fish* s.v. FIDDLE *n.* Also, the shovel-nosed ray, *Trygonorhina fasciata*, of Australian waters (more fully *fiddler ray*). L19. 4 A cheat, a swindler, a falsifier. *slang.* M19. 5 A sixpence. *arch. slang.* M19.

1 *drunk as a fiddler*: see DRUNK *a.*

Comb.: **fiddler-back, fiddler beetle**, an Australian black scarab beetle, *Eupoecila australasiae*, with green fiddle-shaped markings; *fiddler crab*: see sense 3a above; *fiddler ray*: see sense 3b above; **Fiddler's Green** *Naut.* the sailor's Elysium, a place of wine, women, and song.

fiddlestick /ˈfɪd(ə)lstɪk/ *n.* LME. [f. FIDDLE *n.* + STICK *n.*[1]] 1 A bow with which a fiddle is played. LME. 2 An insignificant thing, a triviality. *colloq.* Now *rare.* E17. 3 *sing.* & (usu.) in *pl.* As *int.* Nonsense! E17.

2 W. IRVING We do not care a fiddlestick.. for.. public opinion. 3 THACKERAY Do you suppose men so easily change their natures? Fiddlestick! THOMAS HUGHES Fiddlesticks! it's nothing but the skin broken.

fiddley /ˈfɪdli/ *n.* L19. [Origin unkn.] *Naut.* An iron framework (usu. covered by a grating) round the deck opening leading to the engine-room and stokehold of a steamer; the space it encloses.

fiddling /ˈfɪdlɪŋ/ *a.* L16. [f. FIDDLE *v.* + -ING[2].] 1 That fiddles. L16. 2 Petty; futile, contemptible, inconsiderable; *colloq.* fiddly. M17.

fiddly /ˈfɪdli/ *a. colloq.* E20. [f. FIDDLE *v.* + -Y[1].] Requiring time or dexterity; pernickety.

fidei-commissum /ˌfʌɪdɪʌɪkɒˈmɪsəm/ *n.* E18. [L, neut. pa. pple of *fidei-committere* entrust a thing to a person's good faith, f. *fidei* dat. of *fides* FAITH + *committere* entrust, commit.] *Rom. Law.* A bequest in which an heir or legatee is instructed to transfer the legacy in whole or part to a third party.

fideicommissary *a.* [L *fidei commissarius*: see -ARY[1]] of, pertaining to, or of the nature of a fidei-commissum L19.

fideism /ˈfʌɪdiːɪz(ə)m/ *n.* L19. [f. L *fides* FAITH + -ISM.] The doctrine that knowledge depends on faith or revelation.

fideˈistic *a.* E20.

fidejussor /fʌɪdɪˈdʒʌsə/ *n.* E16. [L, f. *fide-jubere*, f. *fide* abl. of *fides* FAITH + *jubere* to order: see -OR 2.] *Rom. Law.* A person who authorizes the bail of or goes bail for another; a surety.

fidejussory *a.* [L *fidejussorius*] of or pertaining to surety or bail M18.

Fidelism /fɪˈdɛlɪz(ə)m/ *n.* Also in Sp. form **Fidelismo** /fɪdɛˈlɪzməʊ/ M20. [f. Sp. *Fidelismo*, f. *Fidel* Castro Ruz: see CASTROISM, -ISM.] = CASTROISM.

Fidelist *a.* of or pertaining to Fidel Castro or Fidelism M20.

fidelity /fɪˈdɛlɪti/ *n.* LME. [Fr. *fidélité* or L *fidelitas*, f. *fidelis* faithful, f. *fides* FAITH: see -ITY.] 1 Loyalty, faithfulness, unswerving allegiance (*to* a person, spouse, cause, etc.). LME. †b One's word of honour, one's pledge. M–L16. c *Ecol.* The degree of association of a species with a plant community. M20. 2 Trustworthiness, veracity, accuracy (of a thing, †a person); correspondence with an original, *spec.* the degree to which a reproduced or transmitted sound, picture, etc., resembles the original. M16.

1 G. BURNET They serve those that hire them.. with.. great Fidelity. R. DAWKINS Kittiwakes form monogamous pair-bonds of exemplary fidelity. 2 R. HOOKER The principall thing required in a witnesse is fidelitie. POPE Be very free of your Remarks.. in regard.. to the Fidelity of the Translation. G. STEINER Ancient literature.. was handed down with great fidelity. *high fidelity* see HIGH *a.*

Comb.: **fidelity bond, insurance**, etc.: taken out by an employer to indemnify him or her against losses incurred through an employee's dishonesty etc.

fidepromissor /ˌfʌɪdɪprɒˈmɪsə/ *n.* L19. [L, f. *fidepromittere*, f. *fides* FAITH + *promittere* to promise: see -OR.] *Rom. Law.* A person who pledges himself as security for another; a bail, a surety.

fidfad /ˈfɪdfad/ *n.* & *a.* Now *rare.* M18. [Contr. of FIDDLE-FADDLE.] A *n.* A person who gives attention to trifles, a fusspot; a trifle, a petty matter of detail. M18. B *adj.* = FIDDLE-FADDLE *a.* M19.

fidge /fɪdʒ/ *v.* & *n. dial.* & *colloq.* L16. [Perh. rel. to FIG *v.*[2], FYKE *v.*] A *v.i.* Move about restlessly or uneasily; be eager and restless; (of a limb) twitch. L16. B *n.* The action of fidgeting; the state of being fidgety; a fidgety person. M18.

fidget /ˈfɪdʒɪt/ *n.* L17. [Sense 1 prob. f. FIDGE *v.*; senses 2 & 3 f. FIDGET *v.*] 1 *sing.* & (usu.) in *pl.* Vague physical uneasiness, seeking relief in continual spasmodic movements; uneasiness, restlessness. Freq. *the fidgets.* L17. 2 A person who fidgets or causes others to fidget. E19. 3 The action or habit of fidgeting. M19.

fidget /ˈfɪdʒɪt/ *v.* L17. [f. the n.] 1 *v.t.* Cause to fidget; make uncomfortable, trouble, worry. L17. 2 *v.i.* Make spasmodic movements indicative of restlessness, uneasiness, or impatience; move restlessly. M18. b Be uneasy, worry. M19.

1 J. AUSTEN She says I fidget her to death. ALBERT SMITH The heat fidgetted them all by day. 2 J. HATTON The chairman fidgetted uneasily in his seat. S. HILL His hands, which usually fidgeted with papers or cigar tin, were folded. b J. H. EWING Mother fidgetted because I looked ill.

fidgeter *n.* E20. **fidgetingly** *adv.* in a fidgeting manner L19.

fidget pie /fɪdʒɪt ˈpʌɪ/ *n. phr.* Also (earlier) **fitchet pie** /fɪtʃɪt/. L18. [Origin unkn.] A savoury pie containing onions, apples, and bacon.

fidgety /ˈfɪdʒɪti/ *a.* M18. [f. prec. + -Y[1].] Inclined to fidget; uneasy, restless, impatient.

fidgetily *adv.* L19. **fidgetiness** *n.* L18.

fidibus /ˈfɪdɪbəs/ *n.* E19. [G, ult. origin unkn.] A paper spill for lighting a pipe etc.

Fido /ˈfʌɪdəʊ/ *n.* Also **FIDO**. M20. [Acronym, f. *Fog Investigation Dispersal Operation.*] A device enabling aircraft to land by dispersing fog by means of petrol-burners on the ground.

fiducial /fɪˈdjuːʃ(ə)l/ *a.* L16. [Late L *fiducialis*, f. L *fiducia* trust, f. *fidere* to trust: see -AL[1], -IAL.] 1 *Surveying, Astron.*, etc. Designating a line, point, etc., assumed as a fixed basis of comparison. L16. 2 *Theol.* Of, pertaining to, or of the nature of trust or reliance. E17.

fiducially *adv.* M17.

fiduciary /fɪˈdjuːʃ(ə)ri/ *n.* & *a.* L16. [L *fiduciarius*, f. *fiducia*: see prec., -ARY[1].] A *n.* †1 Something that secures trust. Only in L16. 2 A person who holds a position of trust with respect to someone else, a trustee. M17. B *adj.* 1a Holding something in trust, acting as trustee. *obs.* exc. *Rom. Law.* M17. b Held or given in trust. M17. c Of or pertaining to a trust, trustee, or trusteeship. M18. †2 Resembling or proceeding from trust. M–L17. 3 Of a paper currency: depending for its value on public confidence or securities. L19.

fiduciarily *adv.* †(*a*) trustfully; (*b*) under the conditions of a trust: M17.

fidus Achates /fʌɪdəs əˈkeɪtiːz/ *n. phr. literary.* E17. [L = faithful Achates: see ACHATES.] = ACHATES.

fie /fʌɪ/ *int.* & *n.* ME. [(O)Fr. *fi* f. L *fi* exclam. of disgust at a stench. Cf. ON *fý*.] A *int.* Expr. disgust, reproach, or (a pretence or assumption of) outraged propriety. *arch.* ME.

C. M. YONGE 'For shame, Viola! Oh fie! Oh Vi!' I said, in accordance with an ancient formula.

B *n.* An utterance of the word 'fie', a reproach, a protest. Now *rare.* M16.

fief /fiːf/ *n.* & *v.* E17. [(O)Fr.: see FEE *n.*[2] Cf. FEOFF *v.*] A *n.* = FEE *n.*[2] 1a. Also, one's sphere of operation or control. E17.

J. CLAVELL I served Lord Yoshi Chikitada.. when the clan's fief was no bigger than this village. H. WILSON It is his fief, an appointive bureaucracy.

†B *v.t.* Grant as a fief. Only in L18.

fiefdom *n.* a fief E19.

fie-fie /ˈfʌɪfʌɪ/ *a.* & *v. arch.* or *joc.* E19. [Redupl. of FIE.] A *adj.* Improper, of an improper or shocking character, causing (pretended) outrage. E19. B *v.i.* & *t.* Say 'fie' (to). M19.

fiel /fiːl/ *a.* Long *obs.* exc. *Sc.* Also **feel**. [OE *fǣle* = OHG *feili* (G *feil*). Sense 2 may be a different wd.] †1 Excellent, proper, good. OE–LME. 2 Comfortable, pleasant, cosy; soft, smooth. *Sc.* L18.

field /fiːld/ *n.* & *a.* [OE *feld*, corresp. to OFris., OS *feld* (Du. *veld*), OHG, G *Feld*, f. WGmc.] A *n.* I (A piece of) ground. †1 (A stretch of) open land. OE–L17. 2 (A piece of) land appropriated to pasture or tillage or some particular use, and usu. bounded by hedges, fences, etc. (Freq. w. specifying wd.) OE. 3 The ground on which a battle is fought; a battlefield. Freq. *the field.* ME. 4 A battle. *arch.* LME. †b Order of battle. E16–L17. 5 The country as opp. to a town or village. Now *arch.* & *dial.* LME. 6 A piece of ground put to a (usu. specified) use other than pasture or tillage. L16. 7 Country which is, or is to become, the scene of a campaign; the scene of military operations. Chiefly *the field.* E17. 8a An enclosed piece of ground for playing a game, as cricket, football, etc., or for athletic events; part of this as an area of attack or defence. M18. b *collect.* Field events (in athletics). *US.* E20. 9 *collect.* The players or partakers in an outdoor contest or sport; all competitors except a specified one or specified ones. M18. **b** *Cricket.* The side not batting. M19. **10** In *Cricket* etc., (the position of) a player stationed in a particular area of the field. E19. **11** A tract of ground abounding with some (usu. specified) natural product. M19.

1 C. MARLOWE Hilles and vallies, dales and fields. AV *Gen.* 2:5 Euery plant of the field. 2 J. RUSKIN The fields! . . All spring and summer is in them. R. BRAUTIGAN The older children . . had to work in the fields . . picking beans. *cornfield, turnip-field*, etc. 3 LD MACAULAY These three chiefs . . fled together from the field of Sedgemoor. *fig.*: B. L. FARJEON I bade her good-day, and left Captain Bellwood in possession of the field. 4 MILTON What though the field be lost? 5 SHAKES. *Mids. N. D.* In the town, the field, You do me mischief. 6 *airfield, bleachfield, playing-field*, etc. 7 J. A. MICHENER Days when a force of four hundred well-armed men could be put into the field. 8 *infield, outfield*, etc. 9 J. ARCHER They're into the straight mile—Minnow leads the field around the bend. *Horse & Hound* We had a large field out . . and hounds . . put on a spectacular performance. 10 M. R. MITFORD That exceedingly bad field . . caught him out. 11 C. CORNWALLIS Bowls filled with the precious metal, and . . labelled with the name of the field from which it was taken. *coalfield, diamond-field, gold-field, oilfield*, etc.

II An area of operation. **12** An area or sphere of action, operation, or investigation; a (wider or narrower) range of opportunities. ME. **b** Scope, opportunity, extent of material for action or operation. Now *rare* or *obs.* M17. **c** *Math.* An algebraic system with two operations that satisfy certain axioms analogous to those for the multiplication and addition of real numbers; a commutative ring that contains a unit element for multiplication and an inverse for each non-zero element. L19. **d** *Computing.* A set of one or more characters in a record which together represent a single item of information; an item that is or can be represented in this way. M20. **13** The space or range within which objects are visible from a particular viewpoint, or through an optical instrument, the eye, etc., in a given position. Freq. *field of observation, view, vision*, etc. M18. **14** *Physics.* A region in which some condition prevails, *esp.* a region of electric, gravitational, magnetic, etc., influence; the presence of such influence; the force exerted by such influence on a standard object. M19. **b** *Embryol.* A region of an embryo capable of developing into a particular organ or part of one. E20. **c** *Psychol.* An environment or situation regarded as a system of psychological forces with which an individual interacts. M20.

12 T. THOMSON A very interesting field of investigation. **b** SWIFT The matter . . will afford field enough for a divine to enlarge on. 13 A. BAIN The eye can take in a wide field at once. J. TYNDALL Organisms . . shooting rapidly across the microscopic field. R. HILLARY I noticed how small was my field of vision. H. READ As the mind perceives, it automatically selects and organizes the field of perception.

III An extended surface. **15** The surface on which something is portrayed; *esp.* (*Her.*) the surface of an escutcheon or of one of its divisions. Also, the groundwork of a picture, coin, flag, etc. LME. **16** A large stretch, an expanse, of sea, sky, ice, snow, etc., or *fig.* L16.

15 TENNYSON Sir Lancelot's azure lions . . Ramp in the field. 16 SHAKES. *Per.* Without covering, save yon field of stars. J. RUSKIN The snows round . . are the least trodden of all the Mont Blanc fields. A. BARRY The whole field of English history.

Phrases: *a fair field and no favour*: see FAIR *a.* **a good field** a large number of good competitors, a group of strong candidates. *back the field*: see BACK *v.* 5. *common field*: see COMMON *a.* *deep field*: see DEEP *a.* **depth of field** the distance between the nearest and the furthest objects that give an image judged to be in focus in a camera etc. *electric field*: see ELECTRIC *a.* **field of honour** the ground where a duel or battle is fought. *flood and field*: see FLOOD *n.* **hold the field** avoid being superseded. **in the field** on campaign; in the natural environment as opp. to headquarters, a laboratory, etc. **keep the field** continue a campaign. *long field*: see LONG *a.*[1] *magnetic field*: see MAGNETIC *a.* *open field*: see OPEN *a.* **play the field** *colloq.* avoid exclusive commitment to one person etc. *potter's field*: see POTTER *n.*[1] *short field*: see SHORT *a.* **take the field** begin a campaign. *track and field*: see TRACK *n.*

B *attrib.* or as *adj.* **1** Of an animal, plant, etc.: having the open country as a natural habitat. LME. **2** Of military equipment: light and mobile for use with armies in the field. L16. **3** Of a test, piece of research, work, etc.: carried out or achieved in the natural environment. L18.

1 C. CONRAN It might be easier to substitute ordinary field mushrooms. 3 A. PRICE Aske needs more field experience, at the sharp end.

Comb. & *special collocations*: **field-artillery** light ordnance fitted for travel and use in active operations; **field battery** a battery of light guns for use on a battlefield; **field-bed** (*a*) a camp-bed, *esp.* one for use on active service; (*b*) a bed made in the open; *field bindweed*: see BINDWEED I; **field-book**: used in the field by a surveyor for technical notes; **field boot** a military boot that is knee-length and close-fitting; **field character** a visible character that can be used in identifying a bird etc. in the field; **field-conventicle** an open-air conventicle; **field-cornet** *Hist.* a minor magistrate in charge of a district of the Cape Colony; **field-day** (*a*) *Mil.* (a day on which troops are drawn up for) a manoeuvring exercise, a review; (*b*) a day spent in the field for the purpose of hunting, exploration, etc.; (*c*) *fig.* a great occasion, a day noted for brilliant or important events, a triumph; **field-dressing** bandage, ointment, etc., for dressing a wound on the battlefield; **field-effect transistor** a semiconductor device in which the majority carriers flow along a channel whose effective resistance is controlled by a transverse electric field produced by a reverse bias applied to a gate region surrounding the channel; **field emission** the emission of electrons from the surface of a conductor under the influence of a strong electrostatic field as a result of the tunnel effect; *field emission microscope*, a device which utilizes this effect to produce an enlarged image of the emitting surface on a fluorescent screen; **field equation** any equation describing a field; *spec.* any of a series of equations relating to electromagnetic and gravitational fields established by J. C. Maxwell and Einstein respectively. **field event** an athletic event other than a race, such as weight-putting, jumping, discus-throwing, etc. (cf. *track event* s.v. TRACK *n.*); *field fleawort*: see FLEA *n.* **field general** *N. Amer. Football* = QUARTERBACK *n.* I; **field-glass(es)** a (usu. binocular) telescope for outdoor use; **field goal** in American football and basketball, a goal scored when the ball is in normal play; in American football also, a goal scored from a drop-kick or place-kick direct from a scrimmage; in rugby football, a goal scored from a drop-kick; **field-grey** *n.* & *a.* [tr. G *Feldgrau*] (of) a shade of grey, the regulation colour of the uniform of a German infantryman; **field guide** a book for the identification of birds, flowers, etc., in the field; **field hand** (orig. *US*, now chiefly *Hist.*) a person, esp. a slave, employed as a farm labourer; *field hockey*: see HOCKEY *n.*[1] I; **field hospital** a temporary military hospital esp. near a battlefield; **field madder** a Eurasian cornfield weed, *Sherardia arvensis*, of the madder family, with small pink flowers and whorled leaves; **field mark** a visible mark that can be used in identifying a bird etc. in the field; **field magnet**: providing magnetic flux in an electric generator or motor; **Field Marshal** an army officer of the highest rank; **field-meeting** †(*a*) a duel; (*b*) *Hist.* a religious meeting held in the open air; (*c*) an outdoor meeting of naturalists, archaeologists, etc.; **field mouse** = *wood mouse* s.v. WOOD *n.*[1] (also *long-tailed field mouse*); **field mushroom** a common edible mushroom, *Agaricus campestris*; **field mustard** charlock; **field notes** notes made by a surveyor, scientist, sociologist, etc., while engaged in fieldwork; **field officer** an army officer ranked above a captain and below a general; *field pea*: see PEA *n.*[1] 2; **field-preacher** a person who preaches in the open air; **field-preaching** the action or an act of preaching in the open air; **field rank** the rank of a field officer; **field scabious** a scabious of dry grassy places, *Knautia arvensis*; **field spaniel** a spaniel trained to retrieve; a spaniel closely allied to but larger than the cocker; **field sports** outdoor sports, *esp.* hunting, shooting, and fishing; **fieldstone** stone used in its natural form, esp. for building; **field strength** the intensity of an electric, magnetic, or other field (*field-strength meter* a device for measuring this); **field system** the system by which cultivated ground is subdivided into areas of arable, meadow, and pasture land; **field telegraph** a movable kind of telegraph for use on campaign; **field-test** *v.t.* test (a device) in the environment in which it is to be used; **field theory** a theory about a field of operation, investigation, or influence, or in which the idea of such a field is the dominant concept; *field vole*: see VOLE *n.*[2]; **fieldwork** (*a*) work carried out in the natural environment by a surveyor, collector of scientific data, sociologist, etc.; (*b*) *Mil.* a temporary fortification; (*c*) (now *Hist.*) the work of a field hand; **fieldworker** a person engaged in fieldwork.

fieldful *n.* as much or as many as a field will hold L19. **fieldward(s)** *adv.* towards the fields, in the direction of the fields E19.

field /fiːld/ *v.* E16. [f. the n.] †**1** *v.i.* Take the field, fight. Only in 16. **2** *v.i.* Act as a fielder or fieldsman in cricket, baseball, etc. E19. **3** *v.t.* Stop and return (the ball) in cricket, baseball, etc. M19. **b** *fig.* Deal competently with (a succession of questions etc.). E20. **4** *v.i.* Bet on the field against the favourite. L19. **5** *v.t.* Put (a football team etc.) into the field; select (a team or individual) to play. E20.

fielded /ˈfiːldɪd/ *a.* E17. [f. FIELD *n.*, *v.*: see -ED[2], -ED[1].] **1** Engaged on a battlefield, fighting in the open field. Long *arch. rare.* E17. **2** Of a ball in cricket, baseball, etc.: stopped (and returned). Of a succession of questions etc.: dealt (competently) with. L19. **3** Designed to form a field or fields; *Cabinet-making* designating a panel of wood etc. made to project slightly beyond the surface of its frame. E20.

fielden /ˈfiːld(ə)n/ *a.* & *n.* Long *dial. rare.* M16. [f. FIELD *n.* + -EN[4].] **A** *adj.* Level and open; consisting of fields. Formerly also, rural, rustic. M16. †**B** *n.* Open land, cultivated land. E17–E18.

fielder /ˈfiːldə/ *n.* ME. [f. FIELD *n.*, *v.* + -ER[1].] **1** A person who or animal which works in the fields. Long *rare* or *obs.* ME. **2** A person who backs the field against the favourite. M19. **3** In cricket, baseball, rounders, etc.: a member of the side that is not batting, a player on the side trying to get the other out, esp. one other than the bowler. M19.

fieldfare /ˈfiːldfɛː/ *n.* [Late OE *feldefare*, perh. f. as FIELD *n.* + the stem of FARE *v.*] A thrush, *Turdus pilaris*, with a grey head and rump, known in Britain chiefly as a winter visitor.

fieldsman /ˈfiːldzmən/ *n.* Pl. **-men.** E19. [f. FIELD *n.* + -'S[1] + MAN *n.*] In cricket, baseball, etc.: a member of the side that is not batting, a fielder.

fiend /fiːnd/ *n.* [OE *fēond* = OFris. *fiand*, OS *fiond* (Du. *vijand*), OHG *fiant* (G *Feind*), ON *fjándi*, Goth. *fijands*, f. pres. pple of Gmc vb whence OE *fēogan*, ON *fía*, Goth *fijan* hate. Cf. formation of FRIEND *n.*] †**1** An enemy, a foe. OE–ME. **2** = DEVIL *n.* I. OE. **3** An evil spirit; a demon, devil, or diabolical being. OE. **4** A person of superhuman wickedness, esp. cruelty or malignity. ME. †**b** A monster; the personification of a baleful or destructive influence. LME–L18. **c** A mischievous or annoying person; *esp.* (usu. w. specifying wd) a devotee, an addict. Freq. *joc.* E17.

2 MILTON The Gates . . belching outrageous flame . . since the Fiend pass'd through. SIR W. SCOTT What the foul fiend can detain the Master so long? *fiend* (*a*) HAET. *fiend's limb*: see LIMB *n.*[1] 3 F. BRAGGE Revenge . . makes a man a fiend incarnate. J. WESLEY Inflam'd with Rage like Fiends in Hell. 4 SPENSER That cursed man, that cruel feend of hell. **b** W. COWPER He calls for famine, and the meagre fiend Blows mildew from between his shrivel'd lips. **c** R. KNOX If religion, as Lenin said, is the opium of the people, he . . has done his best to make drug-fiends of us all. J. D. SALINGER Old Brossard was a bridge fiend, and he started looking around the dorm for a game.

fiendlike *a.* resembling a fiend, characteristic of a fiend L16. **fiendly** *a.* (*arch.*) †(*a*) hostile, unfriendly; (*b*) fiendish: OE.

fiendish /ˈfiːndɪʃ/ *a.* & *adv.* E16. [f. prec. + -ISH[1].] **A** *adj.* Resembling or characteristic of a fiend; superhumanly cruel and malignant; *colloq.* notably unpleasant, intractable, exasperating, etc. E16. **B** *adv.* Excessively, horribly. *rare.* M19.

fiendishly *adv.* in a fiendish manner; excessively, horribly L19. **fiendishness** *n.* E17.

fierasfer /fʌɪəˈrasfə/ *n.* M19. [mod.L *Fierasfer* former genus name f. Prov. *fieras-fèr*, *fielat-fèr*, f. OProv. *filat* thread, net (f. L *filum* FILE *n.*[2]) + *fèr* fierce, wild (f. L *ferus* wild).] = *pearlfish* (b) s.v. PEARL *n.*[1] & *a.*

fierce /fɪəs/ *a.* & *adv.* ME. [AN *fers*, OFr. *fiers* nom. of *fer*, *fier* (mod. *fier* proud) f. L *ferus* untamed.] A *adj.* 1 Of a violent and intractable temper; vehement in anger or hostility. ME. b Of a mechanism: violent, not smooth or easy in action, forceful in effect. E20. †2 High-spirited, brave, valiant. ME–L17. †3 Proud, haughty. ME–L16. 4 Angry, violent; vehemently raging; unpleasantly strong or intense. ME. 5 Ardent, eager; full of violent desire; furiously zealous or active. LME.

1 MILTON Moloc .. The fiercest Spirit That fought in Heav'n; now fiercer by despair. P. F. BOLLER A blooded brood stallion with a fierce and ungovernable nature. b D. HALLIDAY The brake was fiercer than I expected, but the thing was stable enough. 3 SHAKES. *2 Hen. VI* He is fierce and cannot brook hard language. 4 POPE Music the fiercest grief can charm. W. S. CHURCHILL A vessel which .. could ride out the fiercest storms of the Atlantic ocean. J. STEINBECK The fierce light of the burning house. 5 E. NICHOLAS He is .. fierce for the Duke of Gloucesters returne. POPE Vengeful slaughter, fierce for human blood.

B *adv.* In a fierce manner. Now *rare.* ME.

SHAKES. *1 Hen. VI* Mid-day sun fierce bent against their faces.

fiercely *adv.* ME. **fierceness** *n.* LME.

fieri facias /ˌfʌɪərʌɪ ˈfeɪʃɪas/ *n. phr.* LME. [L = cause to be made, f. *fieri* be made, come into being + *facias* 2nd person sing. pres. subjunct. of *facere* do, make.] *Law.* A writ to a sheriff for executing judgement.

fierté /fjɛrte/ *n.* Now *rare.* L17. [Fr., after *fier*: see FIERCE, -TY[1].] Haughtiness; high spirit.

fiery /ˈfʌɪəri/ *a.* ME. [f. FIRE *n.* + -Y[1].] 1 Consisting of fire; flaming with fire; fire-bearing. ME. 2 Looking like fire; brightly glowing or flaming; blazing red. ME. b Of eyes: flashing, ardent. M16. 3 Hot as fire; burning, red hot. ME. b Acting like fire; producing a burning sensation; inflaming. M16. c *Cricket.* Making the ball rise dangerously. L19. 4 Made, tested, or performed by the agency of fire. LME. 5 Ardent, eager, fierce, spirited; pugnacious, irritable. LME. b Of a horse: mettlesome. L16. 6 Of gas: liable to take fire, highly flammable. Of a mine etc.: containing such gas, liable to explosions. M18.

1 AV *Dan.* 3:23 These three men .. fell downe bound into the midst of the burning fierie furnace. DRYDEN He deals his fiery Bolts about. **fiery cross** (*a*) *Hist.* a wooden cross, charred and dipped in blood, used as a battle rallying-signal among Scottish clans; (*b*) a burning cross used as a symbol of intimidation by the Ku Klux Klan. 2 A. RADCLIFFE The sun threw a fiery gleam athwart the woods. 3 R. HOOKER The sword which is made fierie doth not only cut .. but also burne. b A. BAIN The fiery taste of alcoholic liquors. 4 AV *1 Pet.* 4:12 The fiery triall which is to trie you. 5 LD MACAULAY Adventures irresistibly attractive to his fiery nature. C. M. YONGE Charles, in his fiery petulance, declared that he would go. E. A. FREEMAN Such fiery zeal implies the firmest belief. b SHAKES. *Rich. II* The Duke .. Mounted upon a hot and fiery steed.

fierily *adv.* E17. **fieriness** *n.* LME.

fiesta /fɪˈɛstə/ *n.* M19. [Sp. = feast.] In Spain or Spanish America: a religious festival; *gen.* any festivity or holiday.

fife /fʌɪf/ *n.* & *v.* M16. [G *Pfeife* PIPE *n.*[1] or Fr. *fifre* f. Swiss G *Pfifre* (G *Pfeifer* PIPER).] A *n.* 1 A kind of small shrill flute, used chiefly along with drums in military music. M16. 2 A player of this instrument. M16. 3 The sound of this instrument. E17. B *v.* 1 *v.i.* Play the fife. L16. 2 *v.t.* Play (an air etc.) on the fife. L19.

fifer /ˈfʌɪfə/ *n.*[1] M16. [f. FIFE *v.* + -ER[1].] A player of the fife.

Fifer /ˈfʌɪfə/ *n.*[2] L19. [f. *Fife* (see below) + -ER[1].] A native or inhabitant of Fife, a local government region of east central Scotland (formerly a county and also known as 'the kingdom of Fife').

fife-rail /ˈfʌɪfreɪl/ *n.* E18. [Origin unkn.] *Naut.* A rail round the mainmast of a sailing ship, with belaying pins for running rigging. Formerly also a rail forming the upper fence of the bulwarks on each side of the quarterdeck and poop in a man-of-war.

fifteen /fɪfˈtiːn, ˈfɪftiːn/ *a.* & *n.* (*cardinal numeral*). [OE *fīftēne* (*-tīene*) = OFris. *fīftīne*, OS *fīftein* (Du. *vijftien*), OHG *fimfzehan* (G *fünfzehn*), ON *fimtán*, Goth. *fimftaihun*, f. Gmc base of FIVE, -TEEN.] A *adj.* 1 One more than fourteen (a cardinal numeral represented by 15 in arabic numerals, xv, XV in roman). OE. †2 = FIFTEENTH *a.* LME–E17.

1 R. L. STEVENSON Fifteen men on the dead man's chest. E. M. KNOWLES In his fifteen-page 'Introduction'. 2 LD BERNERS The fyftene day of May.

B *n.* 1 Fifteen persons or things identified contextually, as years of age, chances (in giving odds), minutes, shillings (now *Hist.*), pence, etc. OE. 2 One more than fourteen as an abstract number; the symbols or figures representing this (15 in arabic numerals, xv, XV in roman). LME. †3 Each of fifteen parts into which something was or might have been divided; *esp.* a tax of one-fifteenth formerly imposed on personal property. L15–M17. 4 The fifteenth of a set or series with numbered members, the one designated fifteen, (usu. *number fifteen*, or with specification, as *book fifteen*, *chapter fifteen*, etc.); a size etc. denoted by fifteen, a garment etc. of such a size, (also *size fifteen*). E16. 5 A set of fifteen; a thing having a set of fifteen as an essential or distinguishing feature; *spec.* (*a*) *Cribbage* the exact sum of fifteen made by the face value of two or more cards (a court-card being reckoned as ten), by which a player scores two points; (*b*) a team of fifteen in rugby football. M17.

1 **The Fifteen** the Jacobite rebellion of 1715. 5 R. KIPLING You're as good as in the First Fifteen already.

Comb.: Forming compound numerals with multiples of a hundred, as *915* (read *nine hundred and fifteen*, US also *nine hundred fifteen*), etc. In dates used for one thousand five hundred, as *1512* (read *fifteen twelve*), *fifteen-nineties*, etc. With ns. + -ER[1] forming ns. w. the sense 'something (identified contextually) being of or having fifteen —s', as *fifteen-tonner* etc. Special combs., as **fifteen-pounder** a gun throwing a shot that weighs fifteen pounds.

fifteenth /fɪfˈtiːnθ, ˈfɪftiːnθ/ *a.* & *n.* (*ordinal numeral*). [OE *fīftēoþa*, repl. in ME by forms f. FIFTEEN + -TH[2].] A *adj.* Next in order after the fourteenth, that is number fifteen in a series, (represented by 15th). OE.

H. FIELDING And here we put an end to the fifteenth book. J. RUSKIN Dull inventions of the fifteenth century. **fifteenth part** *arch.* = sense B.2 below.

B *n.* 1 The fifteenth person or thing of a category, series, etc., identified contextually, as day of the month, (following a proper name) person, esp. monarch or pope, of the specified name, etc. OE. 2 Each of fifteen equal parts into which something is or may be divided (*Hist.* a tax equal to one such part formerly imposed on personal property), a fraction which when multiplied by fifteen gives one, (= *fifteenth part* above). LME. 3 *Mus.* An interval embracing fifteen notes on the diatonic scale; a note a fifteenth above another given note; a chord of two notes a fifteenth apart. Also, an organ-stop sounding fifteen notes above the open diapason. LME.

1 N. TORRIANO She having had a very bad Night from the Fourteenth to the Fifteenth. 2 W. BLACKSTONE Tenths and fifteenths were temporary aids .. granted to the king by Parliament.

Comb.: forming compound numerals with multiples of a hundred, as *five-hundred-and-fifteenth* (*515th*) etc.

fifteenthly *adv.* in the fifteenth place M17.

fifth /fɪfθ/ *a.*, *n.*, & *adv.* (*ordinal numeral*). [OE *fīfta* = OFris. *fīfta*, OS *fīfto* (Du. *vijfde*), OHG *fimfto* (G *fünfte*), ON *fimti*, f. Gmc f. IE, whence also L *quintus*, Gk *pemptos*: see -TH[2].] A *adj.* Next in order after the fourth, that is number five in a series, (represented by 5th). OE.

W. COWPER Just made fifth chaplain of his patron lord. **fifth column** [tr. Sp. *quinta columna*] *Hist.* an extra body of supporters claimed by General Mola as being within Madrid when he besieged the city with four columns of Nationalist forces in 1936; *gen.* an organized body sympathizing with and working for the enemy within a country at war etc. **fifth columnist** a member of a fifth column, a traitor, a spy. **fifth gear** the fifth in a sequence of forward gears in a motor vehicle, bicycle, etc. **fifth-generation** *a.* (of a computer) belonging to a proposed new class of computer employing artificial intelligence. **Fifth Monarchy** the last of the five great empires referred to in the prophecy of Daniel (*Dan.* 2:44); *Fifth-Monarchy-man*, a member of a 17th-cent. sect who expected the immediate coming of Christ and advocated the repudiation of all other government and the establishment of his reign by force. **fifth part** *arch.* = sense B.2 below. **fifth position** *Ballet* the position, esp. when starting or finishing a step, in which the feet are placed turned outwards one immediately in front of but touching the other, so that the toe of the back foot just protrudes beyond the heel of the front foot; the corresponding position of the arms. **fifth wheel** (*a*) the extra wheel of a coach; (*b*) the horizontal turntable over the front axle of a carriage etc. as an extra support to prevent its tipping; (*c*) *colloq.* a superfluous person or thing. **smite under the fifth rib** *arch.* strike to the heart, kill. **take the Fifth (Amendment)** *US* appeal to Article V of the ten original amendments (1791) to the Constitution of the US, which states that 'no person .. shall be compelled in any criminal case to be a witness against himself'; (in extended use) decline to incriminate oneself.

B *n.* 1 The fifth person or thing of a category, series, etc., identified contextually, as day of the month, (following a proper name) person, esp. monarch or pope, of the specified name, forward gear, etc. OE. 2 *Mus.* An interval embracing five consecutive notes in the diatonic scale; a note a fifth above another given note; a chord of two notes a fifth apart. LME. 3 Each of five equal parts into which something is or may be divided, a fraction which when multiplied by five gives one, (= *fifth part* above). M16. 4 In *pl.* Articles of the fifth degree in quality; fifth-rate material. L19. 5 (A bottle containing) a fifth of a gallon of liquor. *US colloq.* M20.

1 SHELLEY Each fifth shall give The expiation for his brethren here. W. ROBERTSON The spoil .. after setting apart the king's fifth, was divided.

Comb.: Forming compound ordinal numerals with multiples of ten, as *forty-fifth* (*45th*), *five-thousand-and-fifth* (*5005th*), etc.

C *adv.* Fifthly. E16.

fifthly *adv.* in the fifth place E16.

fiftieth /ˈfɪftɪɪθ/ *a.* & *n.* (*ordinal numeral*). [OE *fīftigeoþa*, corresp. to ON *fimmtugandi*, f. FIFTY on the analogy of TENTH *a.* & *n.*: see -TH[2].] A *adj.* Next in order after the forty-ninth, that is number fifty in a series, (represented by 50th). OE.

AV *Lev.* 25:11 A Iubile shall that fiftieth yeere be vnto you. **fiftieth part** *arch.* = sense B.2 below.

B *n.* 1 The fiftieth person or thing of a category, series, etc., identified contextually. OE. 2 Each of fifty equal parts into which something is or may be divided, a fraction which when multiplied by fifty gives one, (= *fiftieth part* above). E19.

Comb.: Forming compound numerals with multiples of a hundred, as *one-hundred-and-fiftieth* (*150th*) etc., and (*arch.*) with numerals below ten, as *three-and-fiftieth* etc.

fifty /ˈfɪfti/ *a.* & *n.* (*cardinal numeral*). [OE *fīftiġ* = OFris., OS *fīftich* (Du. *vijftig*), OHG *fimfzug* (G *fünfzig*), ON ON *fimmtigr*, Goth. *fimftigjus*: see FIVE, -TY[2].] A *adj.* 1 Five times ten (a cardinal numeral represented by 50 in arabic numerals, l, L in roman). OE. 2 A large indefinite number of. E19.

1 BROWNING The new edition fifty volumes long. TENNYSON Better fifty years of Europe than a cycle of Cathay. 2 H. S. BLACKWOOD I'll not forget old Ireland, Were it fifty times as fair.

B *n.* 1 Fifty persons or things identified contextually, as years of age, points, runs, etc., in a game, chances (in giving odds), etc. OE. 2 A set of fifty; a thing having a set of fifty as an essential or distinguishing feature; *spec.* a fifty-pound note or fifty-dollar bill. OE. 3 Five times ten as an abstract number; the symbols or figures representing this (50 in arabic numerals, l, L in roman). LME. 4 The fiftieth of a set or series with numbered members, the one designated fifty, (usu. *number fifty*, or with specification, as *chapter fifty*, *verse fifty*, etc.); a size etc. denoted by fifty (also *size fifty*). E16. 5 In *pl.* *The* numbers from 50 to 59 inclusive, esp. denoting years of a century or units of a scale of temperature; *one's* years of life between the ages of 50 and 59. L19.

1 LEIGH HUNT A corpulent man of fifty. 2 AV *2 Kings* 1:13 Hee sent againe a captaine of the third

fiftie, with his fiftie. 5 R. B. ANDERSON A series of works published in the fifties and sixties.

Comb.: Forming compound numerals (cardinal or ordinal) with numerals below ten, as *fifty-nine* (59), *fifty-ninth* (59th), etc. , and (cardinals) with multiples of a hundred, as 350 (read *three hundred and fifty*, US also *three hundred fifty*), etc. Special combs., as **fifty-fifty** *adv.* & *a.* (*colloq.*, orig. *US*) (on a basis of) fifty per cent, with equal shares, half-and-half; **fifty-year rule** a rule that public records should normally become open to inspection fifty years after their compilation.

fiftyfold *a.* & *adv.* (*a*) *adj.* fifty times as great or as numerous; having fifty parts, divisions, elements, or units; (*b*) *adv.* to fifty times the number or quantity: OE. **fiftyish** *a.* about fifty (in age, measurements, etc.) E20.

fig /fɪg/ *n.*[1] ME. [(O)Fr. *figue* f. Prov. *fig(u)a* f. Proto-Romance alt. of L *ficus* fig tree, fig.] **1** A soft pear-shaped many-seeded fruit, eaten fresh or dried, which is borne by the widely cultivated Mediterranean tree *Ficus carica*; (more fully *fig-tree*) the tree which bears this fruit, a member of the mulberry family. Also, w. specifying wd, any of several other plants of the genus *Ficus* or unrelated plants having similar fleshy fruits; the fruit of such a plant. ME. **b** A banana, *esp.* a small one. Chiefly *W. Indies.* L16. **†c** More fully *fig of Spain*, *Italian fig*. A poisoned fig, used to kill a person secretly. L16–L17. **d** A raisin. *dial.* L18. **†2a** *sing.* & in *pl.* Haemorrhoids, piles. LME–M16. **b** An excrescence on the frog of a horse's hoof resembling a fig. L16. **3** A small, valueless, or contemptible thing. LME. **b** A small piece of tobacco. *US.* M19.

1 *Hottentot fig*, *Indian fig*, *Moreton Bay fig*.

Phrases: **not care, give, a fig for** regard as worthless or of no importance. **not worth a fig** of no value.

Comb.: **figbird** (*a*) = BECCAFICO; (*b*) any of various Australasian orioles of the genus *Sphecotheres*, feeding on fruit; **fig-marigold** = MESEMBRYANTHEMUM; **fig-parrot** = LORILET; **fig-pecker** = BECCAFICO; *fig-tree*: see sense 1 above; **figwort** any of various plants of the genus *Scrophularia* (family Scrophulariaceae), which bear dull, usu. purplish-brown flowers and were formerly thought useful against tuberculosis of the lymph nodes of the neck (scrofula).

figged *a.* = FIGGY E18. **figgy** *a.* (*a*) resembling figs; (*b*) (of a pudding) made with raisins: M16.

fig /fɪg/ *n.*[2] Now *rare* or *obs.* L16. [Fr. *figue* (in phr. *faire la figue*) f. It. *fica*.] An insulting gesture in which the thumb is thrust between two of the closed fingers or into the mouth.

fig /fɪg/ *n.*[3] M19. [f. FIG *v.*[3]] **1** Dress, equipment. Only in *in full fig* M19. **2** Condition, form. Esp. in *in fine, great, fig.* L19.

fig /fɪg/ *v.*[1]*t.* Now *rare* or *obs.* Infl. **-gg-**. L16. [f. FIG *n.*[2]] Insult by giving the fig to.

fig /fɪg/ *v.*[2]*i. obs.* exc. *dial.* Infl. **-gg-**. L16. [Var. of FYKE *v.* Cf. FIDGE *v.*] Move briskly and restlessly; jog to and fro.

fig /fɪg/ *v.*[3]*t.* Infl. **-gg-**. L17. [Var. of FEAGUE.] **†1** Fill (the head) with nonsense etc. Only in L17. **2** Cause (a horse) to be lively and carry its tail well by applying ginger to its anus. Also foll. by *out*, *up*. E19. **3** Foll. by *out*, *up*: dress, get up; make smart. E19.

Figaro /ˈfɪgərəʊ/ *n. arch. slang.* Pl. **-os**. M19. [The hero of *Le Barbier de Séville* and *Le Mariage de Figaro* by Beaumarchais (1732–99), and later in operas by various composers.] A barber.

fight /fʌɪt/ *n.* [OE *feohte*, *feoht*, *gefeoht*, f. base of the vb. Cf. OFris. *fiuht*, OS, OHG *fehta* (Du. *gevecht*), OHG *gifeht* (G *Gefecht*).] **1** The action of fighting. *arch.* OE. **2a** A hostile encounter between (esp. large organized) opposing forces, = BATTLE *n.* 1. Now *arch.* or *rhet.* OE. **b** A combat, esp. unpremeditated, between two or more people, animals, or other parties. Now also *spec.*, a boxing-match. ME. **3** *fig.* Strife, struggle for victory; a conflict against an opposing force. OE. **†4** A kind of screen used during naval encounters to conceal and protect the combatants. L16–L17. **5** Appetite or ability for fighting; pugnacity. E19.

2a P. HOLLAND The conflicts and fights at sea, in the first Punick warre. 3 SHELLEY What secret fight Evil and good . . Waged thro' that silent throng. P. SCOTT His old man's dream of a fight to the bitter end. 5 D. WELCH Great walls of fight and resistance.

Phrases: **make a fight of it, put up a fight** offer resistance. *running fight*: see RUNNING *ppl a.* **sham fight** an imitation battle held as a training exercise or for display. **show fight** not give in tamely.

fighty *a.* warlike, pugnacious ME.

fight /fʌɪt/ *v.* Pa. t. **fought** /fɔːt/, pa. pple **fought,** (*arch.*) **foughten** /ˈfɔːt(ə)n/. [OE *feohtan* = OFris. *fiuhta*, OS *fehtan* (Du *vechten*), OHG *fehtan* (G *fechten*) f. WGmc.] **1** *v.i.* Contend in war or battle or single combat. (Foll. by *against*, *with*, an opponent, *for* a person or thing supported or desired.) OE. **b** *v.refl.* Bring (oneself) *into*, *out of*, *to* a certain condition etc. by fighting. M17. **2** *v.i. transf.* & *fig.* Contend, struggle, strive for victory; campaign or strive determinedly to achieve something. (With constructions as sense 1.) OE. **3** *v.t.* Engage in or conduct (a battle, duel, etc.). ME. **b** Maintain (a cause, suit at law, quarrel, etc.) against opposition; contend over, contest (a question or election). E17. **c** Contend with (a horse etc.) for mastery. *US.* M19. **d** Win or make (one's way) by fighting. M19. **4** *v.t.* Engage or oppose in war, battle, or a duel, or with fists; war against. L17. **b** Strive to overcome, contend against (disease, fire, fear, etc.). L18. **5** *v.t.* Cause (cocks, dogs, etc.) to fight. L17. **6** *v.t.* Handle (troops, a ship, gun, etc.) in battle. L18. **7** *v.t.* Contend in single combat for (a prize). *rare.* E19.

1 J. WOLCOT He . . is ready to fight up to his knees in blood for her Majesty. I. MURDOCH She fought like a maniac. C. ISHERWOOD When they fought . . it was with fists and bottles and furniture. 2 E. CALAMY Men that fight against a Reformation. S. SPENDER He fought in the General Election . . in the Liberal cause. A. PRICE The trailing blackberry shoots . . were fighting with the vigorous crop of stinging nettles. 3 T. HARDY A midnight battle had been fought on the moors. b ADDISON He fights the cause Of honor, virtue, liberty, and Rome. d J. DIDION Maria tried to . . fight her way out of sleep. 4 DAY LEWIS The scene of a battle . . when the boys of Wexford had fought the oppressors. b TENNYSON She cannot fight the fear of death. J. DICKEY The whole search party have to fight rapids after rapids for hour after hour. 6 R. L. STEVENSON He told Captain Hotham to . . fight his vessel till she sank.

Phrases, & with advs. in specialized senses: *fight a person with his* or *her own weapons*: see WEAPON. **fight back** (*a*) *v.phr.t.* & *i.* resist; (*b*) *v.phr.t.* suppress (one's feelings). **fight down** overcome, suppress (one's feelings). *fight fair*: see FAIR *a.* **fight off** (*a*) *v.phr.t.* strive to defend oneself against, repel with effort; (*b*) *v.phr.i.* try to back out of something. **fight out** pursue (a fight etc.) to the end, settle by fighting (freq. in *fight it out*). **fight shy of** avoid, be unwilling to approach (a person, task, etc.). *fight tooth and nail*: see TOOTH *n.* **fight up against** (now *rare* or *obs.*) struggle against being overwhelmed by. *fight windmills*: see WINDMILL *n.* 1.

Comb.: **fight-back** a retaliation, a rally, a recovery; **fight-off** a contest to decide a tie, *spec.* in a fencing-match.

fightable *a.* E19.

fighter /ˈfʌɪtə/ *n.* [OE *feohtere* = OHG *fehtāri*. Later f. FIGHT *v.* + -ER[1].] **1** A person, animal, etc., who fights. OE. **2** A high-speed military aircraft designed mainly for aerial combat. E20.

Attrib. & *comb.*: In the sense 'designating or pertaining to a fighter (aircraft) or fighters', as *fighter cover*, *machine*, *pilot*, *plane*, *squadron*, etc. Special combs., as **fighter bomber** an aircraft serving as both a fighter and a bomber.

fighting /ˈfʌɪtɪŋ/ *vbl n.* ME. [f. FIGHT *v.* + -ING[1].] The action of FIGHT *v.*

Comb.: **fighting chair** *US* a fixed chair on a boat used by a person trying to catch large fish; **fighting chance** an opportunity of succeeding by great effort; *fighting cock*: see COCK *n.*[1] 1; **fighting drunk** *a.* (*colloq.*) drunk and quarrelsome; **fighting fit** *a.* fit enough to fight; at the peak of fitness; **fighting fund** a sum of money raised to finance a cause or campaign; **fighting mad** *a.* (*colloq.*) furiously angry; **fighting-sails** (chiefly *Hist.*) the sails retained by a ship going into action, formerly the courses and topsails only; **fighting talk** *colloq.* talk indicating a willingness to fight, talk likely to provoke a fight; **fighting-top** *Naut.* a circular gun platform placed high on the mast of a warship; **fighting trim** the state of readiness of a ship for battle; *fig.* excellent health or condition, readiness for action, (chiefly in *in fighting trim*); **fighting-weight** the specified weight or weight-range within which a boxer etc. must come to be eligible to fight in a certain class; an individual's ideal weight for fitness; **fighting words** *colloq.* words indicating a willingness to fight, words likely to provoke a fight.

fighting /ˈfʌɪtɪŋ/ *ppl a.* ME. [f. as prec. + -ING[2].] That fights, able and ready to fight; militant, warlike.

Siamese fighting fish: see SIAMESE *a.*

fightingly *adv.* M17.

fig-leaf /ˈfɪgliːf/ *n.* Pl. **-leaves** /-liːvz/. M16. [f. FIG *n.*[1] + LEAF *n.*[1]] **1** The leaf of a fig tree, *spec.* (with ref. to *Gen.* 3:7) when used as a covering to conceal the genitals. M16. **2** *fig.* A means of concealing something shameful or indecorous. Usu. in *pl.* M16.

2 C. KINGSLEY They tore off . . even the fig-leaves of decent reticence.

fig-leafed, -leaved *a.* (*a*) made of fig-leaves; (*b*) (of the genitals etc.) covered by fig-leaves: E18.

figment /ˈfɪgm(ə)nt/ *n.* LME. [L *figmentum*, f. base of *fingere* to fashion: see -MENT.] **1a** An invented statement, story, doctrine, etc. LME. **b** A thing which has no existence other than in the imagination. E17. **†2** Something moulded or fashioned; an image, model, etc. L16–M17.

1b P. PEARCE Neither a silly figment of her imagination nor a flesh-and-blood man.

figmental /fɪgˈmɛnt(ə)l/ *a.* of the nature of a figment, fictitious, imaginary M17.

†figo *n.* Pl. **-os**. L16–M17. [OSp. & Port.] = FICO.

SHAKES. *Hen. V* The Figo for thee then.

figuline /ˈfɪgjʊlɪn, -ʌɪn/ *a.* & *n.* Now *rare.* M17. [L *figulinus*, f. *figulus* potter: see -INE[1].] **A** *adj.* **1** Made of earthenware. M17. **2** Of earth: suitable for pottery. L17. **B** *n.* **1** Potter's clay. M19. **2** An earthen vessel. L19.

figura /fɪˈgjʊərə/ *n.* Pl. ***-rae*** /-riː/, ***-ras***. M20. [L: see FIGURE *n.*] **1** *Theol.* A type of a person. Cf. FIGURE *n.* 8. M20. **2** A person who represents a higher or supervening reality. *literary.* M20. **b** An act or deed that is representative or symbolic. M20.

figurable /ˈfɪgjʊrəb(ə)l/ *a.* E17. [(O)Fr., f. as FIGURE *v.*: see -ABLE.] Able to receive a definite figure or form; able to be represented figuratively.

figura'bility *n.* M18.

figurae *n.pl.* see FIGURA.

figural /ˈfɪgjʊr(ə)l/ *a.* LME. [OFr., or late L *figuralis*, f. *figura* FIGURE *n.*: see -AL[1].] **1** = FIGURATIVE 1, 2. LME. **†2** *Math.* = FIGURATE *a.* 3. M16–E18. **3a** *gen.* Pertaining to figures or shapes. Now *rare* or *obs.* M17. **b** *spec.* Of sculpture: consisting of human or animal figures, usu. in relief. M20. **4** *Mus.* Florid, embellished with a rapid repetitive accompaniment. L19.

3b *Times Lit. Suppl.* The figural sculpture on the Ruthwell Cross.

figurally *adv.* LME.

figurant /figyrɑ̃ (*pl. same*), ˈfɪgjʊr(ə)nt/ *n.* Fem. ***-ante*** /-ɑ̃ːt (*pl. same*), -(ə)nt/. L18. [Fr., pres. ppl a. of *figurer* FIGURE *v.*: see -ANT[1].] **1** A ballet-dancer. Now *rare* or *obs.* L18. **2** A supernumerary actor in a play; a (freq. non-dancing) performer with a supporting role in a ballet. L18.

figurante /figuˈrante, fɪgjʊˈranti/ *n.*[1] Pl. ***-ti*** /-ti/, ***-tes*** /-tɪz/. L18. [It., vbl adj. of *figurare* FIGURE *v.*] = FIGURANT 1. Now *rare* or *obs.*

figurante *n.*[2] see FIGURANT.

figuranti *n.pl.* see FIGURANTE *n.*[1]

figurate /ˈfɪgjʊreɪt/ *ppl a.* & *n.* L15. [L *figuratus* pa. pple, f. as next: see -ATE[2].] **A** *ppl a.* **1** Formed into or represented by a figure; having definite form or shape. L15. **†2** Based on figures or metaphors; figurative. M16–E18. **3** *Math.* Capable of representation by geometrical figures. Now only in *figurate numbers*, (series of) numbers, such as polygonal numbers, that can be represented as occupying a simple geometrical figure. E17. **4** *Mus.* = FIGURAL 4. E18. **B** *n.* A figurate thing, *esp.* a figurate number. Now *rare* or *obs.* E17.

figurate /ˈfɪgjʊreɪt/ *v.t.* L15. [L *figurat-* pa. ppl stem of *figurare* form, fashion, f. *figura* FIGURE *n.*: see -ATE[3].] †1 Liken *to*, compare *to*. Only in L15. †2 Represent by a figure or emblem. M16–M17. †3 Give figure or shape to; present in visible shape. E17–E18. 4 Speak of or treat figuratively; represent by a figure or metaphor. M17.

figuration /fɪgəˈreɪʃ(ə)n, -gjʊ-/ *n.* LME. [(O)Fr., or L *figuratio(n-)*, f. as prec.: see -ATION.] 1 The form, shape, outline, or contour of a thing. LME. b The action or process of giving shape to; assignment to a certain form. M16. †2 *Math.* The making of arithmetical figures; the multiplying of a number into itself. LME–L17. 3 Allegorical representation. M16. 4 *Mus.* Use of florid counterpoint; alteration by the introduction of passing notes, rapid figures, etc. L16. 5 Ornamentation by means of figures or designs. M17.

1 T. SMITH The different shapes and figurations of letters in several ages of the world. 3 W. FULKE The sacrament is not a bare figuration of the flesh of Christ. 4 *Listener* Short skirling woodwind figurations and languid dying falls on the solo cello.

figurative /ˈfɪgərətɪv, -gjʊ-/ *a.* LME. [Late L *figurativus*, f. as prec.: see -ATIVE.] 1 Emblematic, typical. LME. 2 Based on or using figures or metaphors; metaphorical, not literal. LME. 3 Containing or using many figures of speech. L16. †4 Pertaining to the use of graphic symbols or numbers. L16–E19. 5 Pertaining to or of the nature of pictorial or sculptural representation. E17. b *spec.* Of an artist, a style of painting, etc.: creating forms which are recognizably derived from objective sources without necessarily being clearly representational. M20. 6 *Mus.* = FIGURAL 4. E18.

2 COVERDALE By a figurative . . speech he declareth the horror . . of the damned. 3 W. BELSHAM Shakespeare . . is the most figurative writer in our language. 5b *Listener* Figurative painters today undoubtedly owe much to abstract expressionism.

figuratively *adv.* LME. **figurativeness** *n.* E18.

figure /ˈfɪgə/ *n.* ME. [(O)Fr. f. L *figura*, f. base of *fingere* to fashion: see -URE.] I Form, shape. †1 a The proper or distinctive form of a person or thing. ME–E17. b *gen.* The external form or shape of something. LME. 2 *Geom.* A definite form consisting of a two-dimensional space enclosed by a line or lines or a three-dimensional space enclosed by a surface or surfaces; any of the classes of these, as the triangle, circle, cube, etc. ME. 3 A person considered as a visible form. ME. b A person as an object of mental contemplation. M18. 4 The bodily shape or bodily frame of a person etc. LME. 5 a Style of living, *esp.* ostentatious living. *arch.* E17. b Importance, distinction; personal rank or standing. Now chiefly in *man* or *woman of figure*. *arch.* L17.

2 A. KOESTLER A geometrical figure on the blackboard. 3 L. HELLMAN A figure in the distance running up and down the beach. R. ELLISON A figure in a nightmare which the sleeper tries . . to destroy. b ISAIAH BERLIN Its most venerated figure, a cultivated, fastidious, and morally sensitive scholar. K. ISHIGURO All groups of pupils tend to have a leader figure. 4 T. DREISER Her rather slim and as yet undeveloped figure. DAY LEWIS Nor can I recall his face or figure.

II Represented form, likeness. 6 The image or representation of something material or immaterial. ME. †b An imaginary form. LME–L16. 7 A representation of the human form in sculpture, painting, etc.; a statue, a portrait. ME. 8 An emblem, a type. ME. †9 a A person acting a part. Only in LME. b A part enacted, a represented character. Also, a position, capacity. E17–E18.

6 BURKE He is their standard figure of perfection. 7 K. CLARK Round the merchants' church . . are life-size figures of the saints. J. BERGER The porcelain figure of the shepherdess. 8 C. CARTWRIGHT The Rock . . was a Type and a Figure of Christ.

III A written character. 10 A numerical symbol, esp. each of the ten used in arabic notation. ME. b A number, amount of money, or value, expressed in figures. M19. c In *pl.* Arithmetical calculations. E20. d *Cricket.* In *pl.* A bowler's average. M20. †11 *gen.* A letter of the alphabet, a symbol for a musical note, a mathematical symbol, or other written character. L16–M17.

10 L. P. HARTLEY He felt disinclined to go on totting up figures. S. WEINBERG Wavelengths given . . to eight significant figures. b J. F. KENNEDY The tremendous figures that the Germans were spending.

IV Devised form; design. 12 A diagram, an illustrative drawing. (Freq. abbrev. *fig.*) LME. 13 *Astrol.* A diagram of the aspects of the astrological houses; a horoscope. LME. 14 An ornamental arrangement of lines or other markings; a decorative pattern. L16. b *spec.* The pattern formed by the grain and knots in wood. L19. 15 An evolution or set of evolutions in dancing. Also, one of the divisions of a set dance. M19. 16 *Skating.* A movement or series of movements following a prescribed pattern and often beginning and ending at the same point. M19. b A movement in formation flying or swimming following a prescribed pattern. M20.

15 F. NORRIS A square dance was under way, the leader of the city band calling the figures.

V Repr. Gk *skhēma* form. 17 *Logic.* The form of a syllogism as determined by the position of the middle term. LME. 18 *Mus.* A short succession of notes which produce a single impression; a brief melodic or rhythmic motif out of which longer passages are developed. LME. 19 More fully *figure of speech*. A form of rhetorical expression which gives beauty, variety, force, etc., to a composition, as metaphor or hyperbole. LME. b A metaphor, a metaphorical expression. LME. 20 (Usu. F-.) In *pl.* (The name of) a class in a Roman Catholic school, college, or seminary, now only *spec.* the second class, immediately above Elements and below Rudiments, in certain Jesuit Schools. E17. 21 *Gram.* Any of the standard deviations from the normal forms of words, as elision, or from the rules of construction, as ellipsis. E17.

19 S. SONTAG My subject is not physical illness itself but the uses of illness as a figure or metaphor.

Phrases etc.: **cut a figure** = *make a figure* below. *double figures*: see DOUBLE *a.* & *adv. facts and figures*: see FACT. *father-figure*: see FATHER *n.* **figure four (trap)** an animal trap with a trigger set in the shape of a figure 4. *figure of* EIGHT. **figure of four (trap)** = *figure four trap* above. **figure of fun** a grotesque or ridiculous person. **figure of merit** a numerical expression taken as representing the performance or efficiency of a given device or material. *four-figure*: see *two-figure* below. *four figures*: see *two figures* below. **go the whole figure** *US* do something thoroughly, go the whole hog. **keep one's figure** not grow stout. **make a figure** (*a*) (with qualifying adj.) present a specified appearance, create a particular impression; (*b*) play a prominent or important part. *mother-figure*: see MOTHER *n.*[1] *parent-figure*: see PARENT *n. public figure*: see PUBLIC *a.* & *n. significant figure*: see SIGNIFICANT *a.* 1C. *three-figure*: see *two-figure* below. *three figures*: see *two figures* below. **two-figure, three-figure, four-figure**, etc. *adjs.* designating or involving (*a*) numbers respectively between 10 and 99, 100 and 999, 1000 and 9999, etc.; (*b*) numbers expressed to two, three, four, etc., significant figures. **two, three, four**, etc. **figures** a total between 10 and 99, 100 and 999, 1000 and 9999, etc.

Comb.: **figure-caster** (*a*) (now *rare*) a person who casts horoscopes; (*b*) a person who performs numerical calculations; **figure-casting** the action or practice of casting horoscopes; **figure-dance** a dance consisting of several distinct figures or divisions; **figure-dancer** a performer in a figure-dance; **figure-flinger** (long *rare*) = *figure-caster* (a) above; **figure-floating** the formation of set patterns by a group of swimmers floating in the water; **figure-skater** a person who practises figure-skating; **figure-skating** the art or practice of skating in figures or set patterns; **figure weaving** weaving of cloth with individual patterns or figures in it.

figureless *a.* without figure or a figure E17.

figure /ˈfɪgə/ *v.* LME. [(O)Fr. *figurer* f. L *figurare*, f. *figura* FIGURE *n.*] †1 *v.t.* Give figure to; form, shape. LME–L18. 2 *v.t.* Represent in a diagram or picture. LME. b Trace (a design, letter, etc.). E16. 3 *v.t.* Be an image or type of; represent typically. Now *rare*. LME. †4 *v.t.* Liken *to*. LME–E16. b Resemble. *rare*. M16–L18. 5 *v.t.* Express in a metaphorical sense; express by means of a metaphor or other image. LME. †b Adorn with figures of speech. M17–E18. 6 *v.t.* Ornament or adorn with a design or pattern; *Mus.* embellish with an accompaniment in quicker time. LME. †7 *v.t.* Prefigure, foretell. LME–L16. 8 *v.t.* Represent by speech or action. L15. 9 *v.t.* Picture in the mind; imagine. E17. 10 *v.i.* †a Stand for, lay claim to. Foll. by *for*. E–M17. b Appear, feature, make an appearance. Also, be conspicuous. M17. c Show off. (Foll. by *away*, *off*.) L18. d Foll. by *as*: appear in the character of, resemble. E19. 11 a *v.t.* Mark with numerical figures; express in figures. L17. b *v.t.* *Mus.* Mark (esp. the bass) with numbers in order to indicate the proper harmony. L17. c *v.i.* Use figures in arithmetic. M19. 12 *v.i.* & *t.* *Dancing*, *Skating*, etc. Perform (a figure or set of evolutions). Also foll. by *down*, *away*, *out*. M18. 13 *v.t.* Reckon, calculate; understand, ascertain. *colloq.* (orig. & chiefly *N. Amer.*). M19. 14 *v.i.* Foll. by *on*, *upon*: think over, consider; count on, expect. *colloq.* (chiefly *US*). M19. b (Of information received, an event, etc.) be understandable, make sense. Freq. w. impers. *it* (foll. by *that*). M20.

2 R. L. STEVENSON The Greeks figured Pan . . stamping his foot. H. ADAMS There are two series of windows, one figuring the . . followers of Louis VIII. 3 H. COGAN This boy leaned on his elbow upon the . . chair and figured mercy. 6 F. NORRIS A white paper figured with knots of pale green leaves. 9 E. L. LINTON All the pains and grief his imagination had ever figured. 10b E. M. FORSTER She was expected to figure at this function, and to figure largely. J. P. DONLEAVY There's the garden that's figured so prominently in my dreams. J. DIDION Maria tried to remember in which of the woman's stories Lee had figured. 13 J. D. SALINGER Even though I was pretty loaded, I figured I could . . use a few extra bucks. L. BRUCE It didn't work out the way I had figured it.

With advs. in specialized senses: **figure out** (*a*) work out, esp. by arithmetic or logic; (*b*) (chiefly *US*) understand, estimate; (see also sense 13 above). **figure up** reckon up with figures.

figurer *n.* M16.

figured /ˈfɪgəd/ *a.* LME. [f. FIGURE *v.*, *n.*: see -ED[1], -ED[2].] 1 Having a particular figure or shape. LME. †b Having a definite shape, structured. E17–L18. 2 Shaped into or represented by a figure or figures; *Math.* = FIGURATE *a.* 3. L15. 3 Adorned with patterns or designs. L15. 4 Adorned with rhetorical figures; figurative. E16. 5 Of a dance: consisting of figures. E18. 6 *Her.* Of the sun, moon, or other charge: drawn with a human face. M19. 7 *Mus.* = FIGURAL 4. L19.

1 T. DWIGHT Its summits are finely figured, and richly diversified. 3 T. SHERIDAN A pretty figured linen gown.

Special collocations: *figured bass*: see BASS *n.*[2]

figurehead /ˈfɪgəhɛd/ *n.* M18. [f. FIGURE *n.* + HEAD *n.*] 1 An ornamental carving, usually a bust or full-length figure, placed over the cutwater of a ship. M18. 2 A nominal leader, president, etc., who has little or no authority or influence. L19.

figurette /fɪgjʊˈrɛt/ *n. rare.* M19. [f. FIGURE *n.* + -ETTE.] = next.

figurine /ˈfɪgəriːn, -gjʊ-/ *n.* M19. [Fr. f. It. *figurina* dim. of *figura* FIGURE *n.*: see -INE[4].] A small modelled or sculpted figure; a statuette.

figurist /ˈfɪgjʊrɪst/ *n. obs.* exc. *Hist.* L16. [f. FIGURE *v.* + -IST.] A believer in the figurative nature of something, e.g. of the presence of Christ in the Eucharist.

Fijian /fiːˈdʒiːən/ *n.* & *a.* E19. [f. *Fiji* (see below) + -AN.] A *n.* 1 A native or inhabitant of the Fiji archipelago or the State of Fiji in the S. Pacific. E19. 2 The Austronesian language of the Fijians. M19. B *adj.* Of, pertaining to, or designating the Fiji archipelago, the Fijians, or their language. M19.

fike *v.* var. of FYKE *v.*

†**filace** *n.* Also **-aze**. LME–M16. [AN *filaz* file of documents f. med.L *filacium*, either f. L *filum* thread, FILE *n.*[2], or abbrev. of late L *chartophylacium* chest for papers, f. Gk *khartophulakion*, f. *khartēs* paper, CHART *n.* + *phulak-* (*phulassein*) to keep, guard.] *Law.* = FILE *n.*[2] 1.

filacer /ˈfɪləsə/ *n. obs.* exc. *Hist.* Also **-zer** /-zə/. E16. [Law Fr., f. as prec.: see -ER[2].] *Law.* An officer of the superior courts at Westminster who filed original writs and issued processes.

filagree *n.* var. of FILIGREE.

filament /ˈfɪləm(ə)nt/ *n.* L16. [Fr., or mod.L *filamentum*, f. late L *filare* spin, f. L *filum* thread: see -MENT.] **1** A fine flexible length of some material, esp. in a plant or animal, or produced artificially from glass, metal, etc.; *spec.* (*a*) a thin stream of light or wisp of smoke etc.; (*b*) a thread of man-made fibre. L16. **b** *Astron.* A narrow threadlike streamer from the sun's chromosphere or in its corona. M19. **c** A refractory conducting wire, now usu. made of tungsten, in an electric bulb or thermionic valve which is heated or made incandescent by the electric current. L19. **2a** *Bot.* The slender stalk which supports the anther. M18. **b** *Zool.* The barb of a down feather. M19.

1 J. GASKELL These aren't spiderwebs: . . they're mycelium filaments, the start of my mushrooms. F. KING Filaments of mist were beginning to curl over the sides of the island.

filamentary /fɪləˈmɛnt(ə)ri/ *a.* of, pertaining to, or of the nature of a filament or filaments M19. **filamented** *a.* having filaments L19. **filamentose** /fɪləˈmɛntəʊs/ *a.* = FILAMENTOUS M19. **filamentous** /fɪləˈmɛntəs/ *a.* (*a*) composed of or containing filaments; (*b*) resembling a filament; threadlike: L17.

filander /fɪˈlandə/ *n.*[1] Now *rare.* L15. [(O)Fr. *filandre* rel. to OFr. *filandrier*, *-iere* (mod. *filandière* fem.) spinner, ult. f. *filer* spin, f. late L *filare*: see prec.] A threadlike intestinal worm afflicting hawks; *sing.* & (usu.) in *pl.*, a disease caused by such worms.

filander *n.*[2] see PHILANDER *n.*

filar /ˈfʌɪlə/ *a.* L19. [f. L *filum* thread + -AR[1].] Of or pertaining to (a) thread; *esp.* (of an optical instrument) having threads or wires across its field of view.

filaree /fɪləˈriː/ *n. US.* L19. [Alt. of ALFILARIA.] = ALFILARIA.

filaria /fɪˈlɛːrɪə/ *n.* Pl. **-iae** /-iiː/, **-ias**. M19. [mod.L *Filaria* former genus name, f. L *filum* thread + *-aria* -ARY[1].] A parasitic nematode worm of the superfamily Filarioidea, which includes a number of organisms responsible for diseases in man.

filarial *a.* pertaining to, caused by, or of the nature of filariae L19.

filariasis /fɪˌlɛːrɪˈeɪsɪs, fɪləˈrʌɪəsɪs/ *n.* Pl. **filariases** /fɪˌlɛːrɪˈeɪsiːz, fɪləˈrʌɪəsiːz/. L19. [f. prec. + -IASIS.] *Med.* Any of a group of tropical diseases resulting from infection with filariae; *spec.* a disease, transmitted by mosquitoes, in which worms of the genera *Wuchereria* or *Brugia* are present in the lymph vessels, leading to elephantiasis.

Also **filariˈosis** *n.*, pl. **-oses** /-ˈəʊsiːz/, L19.

filature /ˈfɪlətʃə, -tjə/ *n.* M18. [Fr. f. It. *filatura*, f. *filare* spin f. late L *filare*: see -URE.] (An establishment for) the reeling of silk from cocoons.

filaze, **filazer** *ns.* vars. of FILACE, FILACER.

filbert /ˈfɪlbət/ *n.* LME. [AN *philbert*, dial. Fr. *noix de filbert* a nut ripe about St Philibert's day (20 or (old style) 22 August).] **1** A cultivated hazelnut, *esp.* one of a relatively elongated kind. Also, a tree producing these, esp. *Corylus maxima*. LME. **b** The head. *slang.* L19. **2** *Art.* In full *filbert brush*. A flat oval bristle brush used in oil-painting. M20.

filch /fɪltʃ/ *v.* & *n.* ME. [Origin unkn.] **A** *v.* **1** *v.t.* Steal, pilfer, snatch, (esp. things of small value); carry off furtively. (Foll. by *away*, *off*.) ME. **2** *v.i.* Engage in stealing or pilfering. M16. **3** *v.t.* Rob (*of* something). *rare.* M16.

1 HENRY MILLER If Curley didn't have the money he would filch it from his mother's purse. 2 GEO. ELIOT If I don't lie and filch somebody else will.

B *n.* **†1** A staff with a hook at one end, used to steal articles from hedges, open windows, etc. E17–E18. **2** A thing which has been filched. Now *rare.* E17.

filcher *n.* L16. **filching** *n.* (*a*) the action of the vb; (*b*) = FILCH *n.* 2: M16.

file /fʌɪl/ *n.*[1] [OE (Anglian) *fīl* = OS *fīla* (Du. *vijl*), OHG *fīhala*, *fīla* (G *Feile*), f. WGmc.] **1** An instrument (now usu. of steel) with small raised cutting edges or teeth on its surface(s), used for smoothing or shaping objects. OE. **b** *fig.* Discipline or hardship imposed for the benefit or cleansing of the soul etc.; a person who or thing (personified) which imposes this. ME. **2** A person, *esp.* an artful person; a fellow, a cove. *slang.* E19.

Comb.: **file-fish** any of numerous, chiefly tropical, fishes of the family Balistidae with rough skin suggesting the surface of a file; **file-shell** any of various bivalve molluscs belonging to the genus *Lima* and related genera, with rough shells; **file snake** any of various snakes that resemble a file in shape or texture; *spec.* (*a*) a wart snake; (*b*) *S. Afr.* a non-venomous colubrid snake of the genus *Mehelya*.

file /fʌɪl/ *n.*[2] E16. [f. FILE *v.*[3] reinforced by Fr. *fil* thread (f. L *filum*) & *file* (f. *filer* FILE *v.*[3]).] **I** Repr. Fr. *fil.* **1** A string, wire etc., on which documents etc. are run for keeping; a folder etc. for preserving papers, documents, etc., esp. arranged in a particular order for easy reference; a collection of papers so kept, esp. in an office, or in a court of law referring to a cause. Formerly also, a list, a catalogue. E16. **b** *Computing.* A collection of related records stored for use by a computer. M20. **2** *Her.* Each of the dependent points of a label. Formerly also, a label. M16. **†3** The thread, drift, or course of a story etc. M16–M17. **4** (More fully *file in the foot*) a disease in cattle and sheep characterized by lines or cracks in the hoofs. Formerly also, a disease in trees. Now *dial.* E17.

1 D. LODGE He nodded at a manilla file reposing on his otherwise immaculate desk.

II Repr. Fr. *file.* **5** A line of people (esp. soldiers) or things one behind the other. L16. **b** *Mil.* A small detachment of soldiers etc. (now usu. only two). E17. **6** *Chess.* Each of the eight lines of squares extending across the board from player to player. E17.

Phrases: **in file** one behind the other. *Indian file*: see INDIAN *a.* **on file** in a file or filing-system. **open file** *Chess*: on which there is no pawn of either colour (*seize the open file*, place a rook or the queen on an open file in a position such that that piece cannot immediately be driven from the file). *single file*: see SINGLE *a.* & *adv.*

Comb.: **file server** a device which manages access to one or more separately stored files of data.

file /fʌɪl/ *n.*[3] *slang* (long only *US*). Now *rare.* L17. [Origin unkn.] Earlier †*file-cloy*. A pickpocket.

file *n.*[4] var. of FILI.

file /fʌɪl/ *v.*[1] [OE *fȳlan* = MLG *vülen*, MHG *viulen*, f. WGmc, f. Gmc base also of FOUL *a.*] **1** *v.t.* = DEFILE *v.*[1] 2. *arch.* OE. **2a** *v.t.* = DEFILE *v.*[1] 1. *obs.* exc. *dial.* ME. **†b** *v.i.* = DEFILE *v.*[1] 6. ME–E17. **†3** *v.t.* **a** Defame, dishonour. ME–M17. **b** Accuse, blame; condemn, find guilty. ME–M18. **†4** *v.t.* = DEFILE *v.*[1] 3. Only in ME.

file /fʌɪl/ *v.*[2] ME. [f. FILE *n.*[1]] **1** *v.t.* & *i.* Smooth or shape (an object) with a file. ME. **2** *v.t.* Remove (roughness etc.) with a file. Now only w. *away*, *off*, *out*. ME. **3** *v.t.* Polish or elaborate (esp. a literary work) to perfection. LME.

1 C. MCCULLERS His . . wife sat filing her fingernails. 2 *fig.*: TENNYSON So grated down and filed away with thought. 3 SHAKES. *Sonn.* Precious phrase by all the Muses fil'd.

filer *n.*[1] ME.

file /fʌɪl/ *v.*[3] LME. [Fr. *filer* string on a thread, f. late L *filare* spin, f. L *filum* thread.] **I** Corresp. to FILE *n.*[2] I. **1a** *v.t.* Arrange (now only documents etc.) in a particular order for preservation and easy reference; place (a document etc.) on file; put *away* in a file. Formerly also, string on a thread. LME. **b** *v.t.* & *i.* Place (a document) on file among official records by formal procedures of registration; submit (an application for a patent, a petition for divorce, etc.) to the appropriate authority. E16. **c** *v.t.* & *i.* Assert a title to (a piece of land or a mining claim). *N. Amer.* L19. **2** *v.t.* Of a newspaper reporter: transmit (a story, information, etc.) to a newspaper. M20.

1a A. BURGESS I sent the silly thing to headquarters, but they will have filed it among the other missives of madmen. **filing cabinet**: with drawers for storing documents. **b** J. BARTH I petitioned for permission to file an amended complaint. T. LUNDBERG The company must file with Companies House . . a copy of the company's audited accounts. *Guardian* She filed successfully for divorce. 2 A. CARTER He filed copy to a New York newspaper for a living.

II Corresp. to FILE *n.*[2] II. **†3** *v.t.* Arrange (soldiers) in a file or files. L16–M17. **4** *v.i.* March or walk (*away*, *off*, etc.) in file. E17. **†b** *fig.* Keep pace with. *rare.* Only in E17.

4 J. GALSWORTHY The coffin was borne into the chapel, and, two by two, the mourners filed in behind it. G. W. TARGET If the bell does not ring for Assembly, I want you to file out and go into the hall quietly. b SHAKES. *Hen. VIII* My endeavours, Have ever come too short of my desires, Yet fil'd with my abilities.

filer *n.*[2] L19.

†file *v.*[4]*i.* *slang.* L17–M18. [f. FILE *n.*[3]] Pick pockets.

†filer *n.*[3] L17–E18.

filé /ˈfiːleɪ/ *n. US.* M19. [Fr., pa. pple of *filer* twist.] Pounded or powdered sassafras leaves used to flavour and thicken soup, esp. gumbo. Earliest in GUMBO *filé*.

filemot /ˈfɪlɪmɒt/ *a.* & *n. arch.* M17. [Alt. of FEUILLEMORTE.] (Of) a yellowish-brown or dead-leaf colour.

filet /ˈfiːleɪ, ˈfɪlɪt; *foreign* filɛ (*pl. same*)/ *n.*[1] M19. [Fr.: see FILLET *n.*] **1** = FILLET *n.* 9. Chiefly in phrs. below. M19. **2** A kind of net or lace with a square mesh. L19.

1 **filet de boeuf** /ˌfiːleɪ də ˈbəːf, *foreign* filɛ də bœf/ a fillet of beef. **filet mignon** /ˌfiːleɪ ˈmiːnjɔ̃, *foreign* filɛ miɲɔ̃/, pl. **mignons** (pronounced same) [see MIGNON] a slice cut from the small end of the tenderloin of beef. 2 *filet design*, *lace*, *net*, etc.

fili /ˈfɪli/ *n.* Also ***file***. Pl. ***-d(h)***. L19. [Ir. *fileadha*, *filidh*, pl. forms of *file* poet.] In medieval Irish legal tradition, a poet-seer, ranking above a bard.

filial /ˈfɪlɪəl/ *a.* & *n.* LME. [(O)Fr., or eccl.L *filialis*, f. L *filius* son, *filia* daughter: see -AL[1].] **A** *adj.* **1** Of a child; (esp. of sentiment, duty, etc.) due from a child. LME. **b** That is due to a child. M16. **2** Having the character or relationship of a child or offspring; *spec.* in *Biol.*, designating the offspring of a cross. LME.

1 A. BURGESS She fell in love with an older man . . filial deprivation had something to do with it. 2 **first filial generation** *Biol.* the immediate offspring of individuals selected for crossing. **second filial generation** *Biol.*: produced by interbreeding of individuals of a first filial generation.

†B *n.* An offshoot. M16–M18.

filiˈality *n.* filial quality or relation E17. **filially** *adv.* E17. **filialness** *n.* (*rare*) E18.

filiate /ˈfɪlɪeɪt/ *v.t.* L18. [med.L *filiat-* pa. ppl stem of *filiare* acknowledge as one's child, f. L *filius* son, *filia* daughter: see -ATE[3].] = AFFILIATE *v.* 3.

filiation /fɪlɪˈeɪʃ(ə)n/ *n.* LME. [(O)Fr. f. eccl. & med.L *filiatio(n-)* relationship as a child, (esp.) sonship, f. L *filius* son, *filia* daughter: see -ATION.] **1** The relationship (as) of a child (esp. a son) to his or her father; *spec.* in *Theol.*, the relationship (as) of a son to God; adoption (as a son) by God. LME. **2** = AFFILIATION 3. M16. **3** Descent or derivation *from*; the genealogical relation of one language, area of study, etc., to another. L18. **4** Formation of branches or offshoots; a branch or offshoot of a society or language. L18.

3 H. KURATH The relationships between the Indo-European dialects and their filiation in prehistoric times.

filibeg /ˈfɪlɪbɛg/ *n. Sc.* Also **fillebeg**, **philabeg**, & other vars. M18. [Gael. *feileadh-beag* little kilt, f. *feileadh* plaid + *beag* little.] The gathered and belted lower part of a plaid; a kilt.

filibuster /ˈfɪlɪbʌstə/ *n.* & *v.* Earlier **†flibutor**, **†flibustier**. L16. [Orig. f. Du. *vrijbuiter* FREEBOOTER; then (L18) f. Fr. *flibustier*; finally (M19) f. Sp. *filibustero*, f. Fr.] **A** *n.* **†1** *gen.* A freebooter. *rare.* Only in L16. **2** Any of a class of pirates who pillaged the Spanish colonies in the W. Indies in the 17th cent. L18. **3** A member of an American band of adventurers who incited revolution in various Latin American States in the mid 19th cent.; *gen.* a person who engages in unauthorized warfare against a foreign State.

M19. 4 An act of obstruction in a legislative assembly, esp by prolonged speaking; a person who engages in such an act. Chiefly *N. Amer.* L19.

4 D. HALBERSTAM It was not a short spiel, but a genuine filibuster, and it went on and on, reactionary and embarrassing.

B *v.* 1 *v.i.* Act as a filibuster or adventurer. M19. b *v.t.* Subject to the methods of a filibuster or adventurer. M19. 2 *v.i.* & *t.* Practise obstruction (against) in a legislative assembly. Chiefly *N. Amer.* L19.

2 H. WILSON Even if ministers were not filibustering to ensure that the Prime Minister's Questions were not reached. *New Scientist* Marcus Kimble MP . . was prepared to filibuster any attempts to give the offer statutory protection.

filibusterer *n.* M19. **filibusterism** *n.* the practice of, or inclination to, filibustering M19.

filices *n.* pl. of FILIX *n.*

filicic /fɪˈlɪsɪk/ *a.* M19. [f. G *Filixsäure* filicic acid, f. L *filic-* *filix* fern: see -IC.] Chem. *filicic acid*, a mixture of phenolic compounds, with anthelmintic properties, obtained from the rhizome of the male fern, *Dryopteris filix-mas*, and other ferns.

filicin *n.* filicic acid, or a crude extract containing it L19.

filicide /ˈfɪlɪsʌɪd/ *n.* M17. [f. L *filius* son, *filia* daughter + -CIDE.] 1 The action of killing a son or daughter. M17. 2 A person who kills a son or daughter. E19.

filid(h) *ns.* pls. of FILI.

filiform /ˈfʌɪlɪfɔːm/ *a.* M18. [f. L *filum* thread + -I- + -FORM. Cf. Fr. *filiforme.*] Having the form of a thread; threadlike.

J. MCPHEE The filiform leaves of the sundews were spread out like the spines of umbrellas.

filigrane /ˈfɪlɪgreɪn/ *n.* Also †**filigreen**. M17. [Fr. f. It. *filigrana*, f. L *filum* thread + *granum* seed. Cf. next.] = FILIGREE *n.*

filigree /ˈfɪlɪgriː/ *n.* & *v.* Also **fila-** /ˈfɪlə-/. L17. [Alt. of FILIGREEN.] A *n.* Ornamental work, orig. with beads or precious stones, of fine (usu. gold or silver) wire, twisted, plaited, and soldered into a delicate openwork design; anything delicate resembling this. L17.

Scientific American A filigree of gold inlaid inscriptions details each bell's musical properties. *attrib.*: A. RADCLIFFE Enclosed within a filigree screen of gold, lay the image of the saint.

B *v.t.* Work in or ornament with filigree. Chiefly as *filigreed* ppl a. L18.

J. A. MICHENER He had Texas-style boots, filigreed with silver.

†**filigreen** *n.* var. of FILIGRANE.

filing /ˈfʌɪlɪŋ/ *n.* LME. [f. FILE *v.*[2] + -ING[1].] 1 The action of FILE *v.*[2] LME. 2 A particle rubbed off by a file. Usu. in *pl.* LME.

filio-pietistic /ˌfɪlɪəʊpʌɪəˈtɪstɪk/ *a.* L19. [f. L *filius* son, *filia* daughter + -O- + PIETISTIC.] Marked by excess of filial piety.

Filipino /fɪlɪˈpiːnəʊ/ *n.* & *a.* Also (fem.) **-na** /-nə/. L19. [Sp., f. (*las Islas*) *Filipinas* the Philippines.] A *n.* Pl. **-os**, fem. **-as**. 1 A native or inhabitant of the Philippines in SE Asia, *esp.* one of Spanish or mixed descent. L19. 2 The national language of the Philippines, based on Tagalog. (Orig. called *Pilipino.*) M20. B *adj.* Of or pertaining to Filipinos or the Philippines, or their language. E20.

filix /ˈfʌɪlɪks, ˈfɪ-/ *n.* Pl. ***-lices*** /-lɪsiːz/. M18. [L.] *Bot.* A fern. Usu. in pl. *Filices*, the group of ferns as a whole.

filix mas /mɑːs/ [= male] an anthelmintic preparation obtained from the rhizome of the male fern, *Dryopteris filix-mas*.

fill /fɪl/ *n.*[1] [OE *fyllu* = OHG *fullī* (G *Fülle*), ON *fyllr*, Goth. *ufarfullei*, f. Gmc, f. base of FULL *a.* In senses 2–5 f. the vb.] 1 Enough to satisfy or sate; as much as one wants (*of* food etc.). OE. 2 A quantity sufficient to fill a space or container; a single charge. M16. 3 The action or an act of filling. *rare.* M18. b *Poker.* The act of filling one's hand. M19. 4 An embankment to fill or traverse a gully or hollow. M19. 5 Material used to fill a space or cavity. L19. b Auxiliary or secondary material inserted to ensure continuity in music, literature, etc. M20. c *Archaeol.* The body of material found in a pit etc. during excavation, of a later period than the feature itself. M20.

1 DRYDEN Away, my goats, away: for you have browz'd your fill. *fig.*: A. SETON She had had her fill of the cloisters and the hovering nuns, kindly as most of them were. 2 R. L. STEVENSON If there is a fill of tobacco among the crew . . pass it round. 5 J. S. FOSTER The fill is poorly compacted. b C. WATSON He knew . . what would tickle a sub-editor's fancy and help meet the insatiable demand for short 'fills'. c *World Archaeology* This layer . . accounted for most of the fill in the excavated portions of the site.

fill *n.*[2] see THILL *n.*[1]

fill /fɪl/ *v.* [OE *fyllan* = OFris. *fullia*, OS *fullian* (Du. *vullen*), OHG *fullen* (G *füllen*), ON *fylla*, Goth. *fulljan*, f. Gmc, f. base of FULL *a.*] I Make or become full. 1 *v.t.* Make full; put as much into (a receptacle etc.) as can be held; stock abundantly; populate densely. (Foll. by *with.*) OE. †b Impregnate. E–M17. 2 *v.i.* Become full (*with*). E17. b Of the eyes: brim with tears. L19. 3 *Naut.* a *v.t.* (Of the wind) cause (sails) to swell; cause (sails) to be swelled by the wind. E17. b *v.i.* Have sails distended by the wind; (of a sail) become distended by the wind. L17.

1 J. L. WATEN She filled the kettle and placed it on the stove. J. CONRAD The . . brutality . . filled him with a despairing desire to escape. 2 TENNYSON Twice a day the Severn fills. W. GASS Big Hans began pouring whiskey in the kid's mouth but the mouth filled without any getting down his throat.

II Occupy completely. 4 *v.t.* Occupy the whole capacity or extent of; spread over, pervade. OE. 5 *v.t.* Hold (a position); discharge the duties of (an office or post). LME. 6 *v.t.* Replace the emptiness of (space or time), occupy (a vacant space or time). M16. 7 *v.t.* Appoint a person to occupy (a vacant place or position). L16. 8 *v.t.* Plug (a hole or gap) with material; *spec.* in *Dentistry*, stop (a hollow tooth) with cement, amalgam, gold, etc. M19.

4 G. VIDAL Smoke filled the room. J. THURBER A detailed recital . . would fill a large volume. 5 G. GREENE He filled with perfect tact a part which combined assistant, secretary and male nurse. 6 B. JOWETT Amusements which fill a vacant hour. 7 E. A. FREEMAN The people at large claimed a voice in filling the episcopal chair.

III Satisfy, fulfil, complete. 9 *v.t.* Satisfy, satiate, glut. OE. †b *v.i.* Become sated. ME–L16. 10 *v.t.* Execute (a command), perform (a duty), fulfil (a promise, a prophecy). Now *rare* or *obs.* OE. †11 Make perfect, accomplish, complete (a task, a period of time, one's days). OE–E17. 12 *v.t.* Make up as an order or prescription. Chiefly *N. Amer.* M19. 13 *Poker* etc. a *v.i.* Complete a flush etc. by drawing the necessary cards. Of a flush etc.: be completed. M19. b *v.t.* Improve (one's hand) or complete (a flush etc.) by drawing the necessary cards. M19.

9 S. PEPYS I sat before Mrs. Palmer . . and filled my eyes with her. b SHAKES. *Ven. & Ad.* Glutton-like she feeds, yet never filleth.

IV With the introduced contents as obj. 14 *v.t.* Put into or *into* a receptacle with the intention of filling it; pour out or (now usu.) *out* (a drink etc.); load (corn etc.) on to a ship. ME.

14 W. DAMPIER Having fill'd our Water, cut our Wood, and got our Ship in a sailing posture. R. L. STEVENSON The other immediately filled some of the spirit into a tumbler.

Phrases: *back and fill*: see BACK *v.* 9. *fill a gap*: see GAP *n. fill the bill*: see BILL *n.*[3]

With advs. in specialized senses: **fill in** (*a*) add material to occupy the space within (a cavity, outline, etc.); (*b*) add what is wanted to complete (an unfinished document, blank cheque, etc.); (*c*) *slang* thrash, beat up; (*d*) find occupation during (a period of inactivity); (*e*) *colloq.* inform (a person) more fully (foll. by *on* a subject); (*f*) act as a substitute, stand in, (*for*). **fill out** (*a*) enlarge, become enlarged or plumper, to a desired or proper limit; (*b*) (chiefly *US*) = *fill in* (a) above; (see also sense 13 above). **fill up** (*a*) make or become full to capacity, fill completely; (*b*) provide what is needed to occupy the vacant parts or places in or deal with the deficiencies of; fill in (a document etc.); do away with (a pond etc.) by filling; stop up; (*c*) fill the tank of a motor vehicle with petrol etc.; †(*d*) complete or come up to the measure of, equal, satisfy.

Comb.: **fill-in** (*a*) a person or thing put in as a substitute or to fill a vacancy; (*b*) a briefing; **fill-up** a thing that fills something up; an act of filling up a petrol tank etc.

fillable *a.* L15.

filled /fɪld/ *ppl a.* L16. [f. FILL *v.* + -ED[1].] 1 That has been filled (freq. as 2nd elem. of comb.); made full; containing filling. Also *filled-in, -up*, etc. L16. 2 *spec.* Made up or extended by the use of foreign material; adulterated. L19.

fille de chambre /fij də ʃɑ̃ːbr/ *n. phr. arch.* Pl. ***filles de chambre*** (pronounced same). L17. [Fr.] A chambermaid; a lady's personal maid.

fille de joie /fij də ʒwa/ *n. phr.* Pl. ***filles de joie*** (pronounced same). E18. [Fr., lit. 'girl of pleasure'.] A prostitute.

filler /ˈfɪlə/ *n.*[1] L15. [f. FILL *v.* + -ER[1].] 1 A person who or thing which fills something or brings about fullness; a machine or device for filling. Also *filler-in, -up*, etc. L15. 2 Something used to fill a cavity, stop a gap, complete a load, make bulk, etc.; *spec.* (*a*) a substance used to fill cracks etc. in a surface before painting; (*b*) extraneous material inserted to avoid a gap in an utterance, a newspaper column, a broadcast, etc.; (*c*) an inert substance added to chemical compounds to give the desired bulk, texture, strength, etc. L16.

1 BYRON The fifteen hundred fillers of hot rooms, called the fashionable world. 2 M. A. K. HALLIDAY Exclamations and 'fillers' such as *oh, ah, quoi*! *Which?* Many outdoor fillers . . lack the flexibility to cope with the movement of timber as it gets wet and dries out again.

Comb.: **filler cap** a cap closing the pipe leading to the petrol tank of a motor vehicle; **filler hose** the hose of a petrol pump at a garage etc.

filler /ˈfɪlɛː/ *n.*[2] Also **fillér**. Pl. same. E20. [Hungarian *fillér*.] A monetary unit of Hungary, equal to one-hundredth of a forint.

filles de chambre, de joie *n. phrs.* pls. of FILLE DE CHAMBRE, DE JOIE.

fillet /ˈfɪlɪt/ *n.* ME. [(O)Fr. *filet* f. Proto-Romance dim. of L *filum* thread: see FILE *n.*[2], -ET[1].] I 1 A ribbon, string, or narrow band worn around the head to keep the hair in place or for ornament. ME. †2 An ornamental border or edging on a cloth, garment, furniture, etc. LME–E17. 3 A thin narrow band of anything; *Archit.* a narrow flat band separating two mouldings, a band between the flutes of a column. L15. b A strip of wood; *esp.* one fastened to a surface to serve as a support, to strengthen a joint, etc. M16. c *Her.* A horizontal division of a shield, a quarter of the depth of a chief. *rare.* L16. d A narrow band of painted, gilded, etc., decoration. In *Bookbinding*, a line impressed into a book cover; a wheeled tool for producing such lines. M17. e A ribbon of metal from which coin blanks are punched. M18. †4 A thread, a string; a thing resembling a thread or string, as a root fibre, the stamen of a plant, etc. M16–M18. 5 A strip of material for binding; a band, a bandage. M17. 6 A raised rim or ridge on any surface. E18. 7 A curve inside an angle serving to prevent concentration of stress. E20. b *Aeronaut.* A fairing at the junction of two surfaces to smooth the flow of air. M20. II 8 A band of nerve or muscle fibre, a tendon, the fraenum of the tongue. In *pl.*, the loins. LME. 9 A fleshy boneless piece of meat from near the loins or ribs of an animal; the undercut of a sirloin of beef. LME. b A boneless cut from a fish or fowl. E18. c The middle part of a leg of veal boned, rolled, and tied with string; a piece of beef, fish, etc., prepared in this way. E18.

Comb.: **fillet steak** the undercut of a sirloin of beef; **fillet weld** a weld of roughly triangular section joining two surfaces at right angles to each other.

fillet /ˈfɪlɪt/ *v.t.* E17. [f. the n.] 1 Bind with or as with a fillet; encircle with an ornamental band. E17. 2 Now chiefly *Bookbinding.* Mark or ornament with a fillet. E17. 3 Divide (meat, fish) into fillets; remove the bones from. M19.

1 D. M. MOIR Her golden tresses . . Were filleted up with roses. 2 B. FRANKLIN A book whose covering is filleted with gold. 3 *fig.*: *Times* Officers reporting to the general were sometimes called into the Colonel's office first and . . could have their information filleted.

filleter *n.* L19.

filleting /ˈfɪlɪtɪŋ/ *n.* L16. [f. FILLET *v.* + -ING[1].] 1 The action of FILLET *v.*; an instance of this. L16. 2 Binding tape, a piece of this; a band, a bandage. M17.

fillette /fijɛt/ *n.* Pl. pronounced same. M19. [Fr.] A young girl.

filling /ˈfɪlɪŋ/ *n.* ME. [f. FILL *v.* + -ING[1].] 1 The action of FILL *v.* Also *filling-in, -up*, etc. ME. 2 Something which fills or is used to fill a space or hole, stop up a gap, etc.; *spec.* (*a*) stones and rubble used to make up a bank or wall; (*b*) (chiefly *US*) weft; (*c*) (a quantity of) material used to fill a sandwich etc.; (*d*) cement, gold, etc., used to fill a cavity in a tooth; (a tooth filled with) a quantity of such material. LME. **b** Extraneous or inferior material used to add bulk or fill space. M17.

1 T. CHALMERS Such a filling up of the time as will keep you away from the evil communications. 2 D. JACOBSON She will make pancakes, with a filling of hot, spiced quince. F. SMYTH The teeth . . were in perfect condition apart from a single amalgam filling. b SWIFT The prefaces of Dryden . . meerly writ at first for filling To raise the volume's price a shilling.

Comb.: **filling station** an establishment selling petrol etc. to motorists.

filling /ˈfɪlɪŋ/ *a.* L16. [f. FILL *v.* + -ING[2].] That fills; *spec.* that makes the stomach feel full.

fillip /ˈfɪlɪp/ *n.* E16. [Imit.] 1 A smart blow (with the fist etc.). Now *rare.* E16. 2 A movement made by bending the last joint of the finger against the thumb and suddenly releasing it; a smart stroke or tap given in this way. M16. 3 A trifle; a moment. E17. 4 A stimulus, an incentive. E18.

1 J. STILL There was a knave not far, Who caught one good fillip on the brow with a door-bar. 2 BOSWELL The Prince . . by a fillip, made some of it [wine] fly in Oglethorpe's face. 3 BYRON Eat, drink, and love; the rest's not worth a fillip. 4 J. N. ISBISTER The interest from abroad . . was a great fillip to Freud.

fillip /ˈfɪlɪp/ *v.* LME. [Imit.] 1 *v.i.* Make a fillip with the fingers. LME. **b** *v.t.* Flip or flick (the fingers). E18. 2 *v.t.* Propel (a small missile, a coin, etc.) with or as with a fillip. M16. **b** Strike smartly; tap or flick with the finger. L16. 3 *v.t.* Urge, stimulate. M16.

2 A. FONBLANQUE Our aforesaid merchant filliped a nut sharply against his bullying giant. 3 SHELLEY Pour: that the draught may fillip my remembrance.

fillis /ˈfɪlɪs/ *n.* Also **ph-**. E20. [Fr. *filasse* tow.] *Hort.* A loosely twisted hemp or jute string, used for tying up plants etc.

fillister /ˈfɪlɪstə/ *n.* E19. [Perh. f. Fr. *feuilleret* in same sense.] A rabbet plane used in making window sashes (also *fillister plane*); a rabbet on the outer edge of a window-sash bar.

filly /ˈfɪli/ *n.* LME. [ON *fylja* (corresp. to OHG *fulī(n)*, *fulīhha*, MHG *fülhe*), f. Gmc base of FOAL *n.*] 1 A young female horse or other equid, *spec.* from the time of weaning to the age of 4 or 5. Cf. COLT *n.*[1], FOAL *n.* LME. 2 *transf.* A lively girl or young woman. *colloq.* E17.

Comb.: **filly-foal** a female foal.

film /fɪlm/ *n.* [OE *filmen* = OFris. *filmene* skin, f. WGmc, ult. f. base of FELL *n.*[1]] †1 A membrane. OE–M18. 2 A thin skin, sheet, coating, or layer, of some material. L16. 3 A fine thread or filament, as of gossamer, silk, etc. L16. 4 Dimness or an abnormal opacity affecting the eye. E17. 5 A thin mist; a haze. M19. 6 A coating of light-sensitive emulsion on a photographic plate etc. M19. **b** Plastic material coated with one or more layers of light-sensitive emulsion used in photography, cinematography, etc.; a roll of this. L19. 7 A drama, episode, event, etc., recorded on cinematographic film, magnetic tape, etc., for subsequent viewing. E20. **b** (The making of) films (esp. cinematographic) considered as an art form. E20. **c** In *pl.* The cinema industry. E20.

1 EVELYN A Wallnut . . the Shell lin'd with Films. 2 D. WELCH The light film of dust on the laurels. M. ATWOOD Sandwiches wrapped in plastic film. 3 C. DARWIN Like films of silk blown by the wind. 4 L. MORRIS O'er his glaring eyes the films of death Crept. 5 E. L. DOCTOROW She saw everything through a film of salt tears. 6 C. WALLACE Loading by touch is quite simple. . . The photographer should try it with an old film. 7 A. GRAY He watched a cowboy film in the staff club cinema. b T. BARR Film presents . . elements . . which are peculiar to itself and are not part of the theater. c I. MURDOCH Anna never tried to get into films.

Comb.: **film badge** a device containing photographic film which registers the wearer's exposure to radiation; **film buff** a person enthusiastic or knowledgeable about the cinema; *film clip* see CLIP *n.*[1] 2b; **film colour** *Psychol.* colour perceived as an opaque mist, unattached to a distinct surface; **filmcraft** the art or technique of making cinematographic films; **filmfest** a festival of films; **film-goer** a frequenter of the cinema; **film pack** a pack of sheets of photographic film for use in a plate camera; **filmset** *v.t.* set (matter for printing) by filmsetting; **filmsetter** an organization or person who does filmsetting; **filmsetting** *Printing* the setting of matter to be printed by projecting it on to a photographic film from which the printing surface is prepared; **film speed** (*a*) the degree of sensitivity to light of a photographic film; (*b*) the speed at which a cinematographic film passes through a camera or projector; **film star** a celebrated cinema actor or actress; **film stock** unexposed film; **film strip** a series of transparencies for projection, esp. as a teaching aid; **film unit** the actors, technicians, and equipment involved in recording (a part of) a film for the cinema, television, etc.

filmdom *n.* the world of cinema; (those involved in) the cinema industry: E20. **filmic** *a.* of, pertaining to, or resembling cinematography or the cinema; suitable for reproduction on film: M20. **filmically** *adv.* E20. **fil'mography** *n.* a list of cinematographic films by a particular director, actor, etc., or on a particular subject M20.

film /fɪlm/ *v.* E17. [f. the n.] 1 *v.t.* Cover with or as with a film. Also foll. by *over.* E17. **b** *v.i.* Become covered with a film; grow dim or hazy. Also foll. by *over.* M19. 2 *v.t.* Record (a scene, person, etc.) on cinematographic film or magnetic tape; make a film of (a book, play, etc.). L19. **b** *v.t.* & *i.* Make (a film etc.) for the cinema, television, etc.; take part in the making of (a film etc.). M20. 3 *v.i.* Be (well or ill) suited for reproduction on film. E20.

1 A. DESAI The dust filming the window pane. b D. LESSING The bird's eyes are filming, and blood wells from its open beak. 2 *Daily Telegraph* Cameras were allowed for the first time to film their Lordships inside their red-carpeted sanctum. A. S. NEILL I have seen *Hamlet* filmed. b *Daily Telegraph* The bear . . was filming a commercial in the Western Isles when he swam off. 3 W. SAROYAN The sort of face that would film well and look good on the screen.

filmable *a.* able to be filmed; suitable for reproduction on film: E20.

film noir /film nwaːr, fɪlm ˈnwɑː/ *n. phr.* Pl. **-s -s** (pronounced same). M20. [Fr., lit. 'black film'.] A cinematographic film of a gloomy or fatalistic nature; the branch of film consisting of such works.

filmy /ˈfɪlmi/ *a.* E17. [f. FILM *n.* + -Y[1].] 1 Forming a thin sheet or coating. E17. 2 Resembling a film; gauzy, resembling gossamer. E17. †3 Of a membranous structure. Only in M17. 4 Covered (as) with a film; dim, hazy. E19.

2 S. KAUFFMANN Her filmy negligee heightening the illusion that she floated. **filmy fern** any of various small ferns of the genera *Hymenophyllum, Trichomanes*, and related genera, with thin translucent fronds, forming sheets on moist rocks etc.; (*Tunbridge filmy fern*: see TUNBRIDGE 3). 4 G. SWIFT All I ever see in his eyes is a filmy gaze, fixed on the distance.

filmily *adv.* L19. **filminess** *n.* E18.

filo /ˈfiːləʊ/ *n.* Also **phyllo**. M20. [mod.Gk *phullo* leaf.] Dough that can be stretched into very thin leaves and layered so as to make sweet and savoury pastries; pastry made from this dough.

Filofax /ˈfʌɪlə(ʊ)faks/ *n.* M20. [Alt. after FILE *n.*[2], pl. of FACT *n.* (cf. FAX *n.*[2])] (Proprietary name for) a personal organizer.

filoplume /ˈfʌɪlə(ʊ)pluːm/ *n.* L19. [mod.L *filopluma*, f. L *filum* thread + *pluma* feather: see -O-.] *Ornith.* A thin hairlike feather.

filopodium /fʌɪlə(ʊ)ˈpəʊdɪəm/ *n.* Pl. **-ia** /-ɪə/. E20. [f. L *filum* thread + PODIUM.] *Zool.* A threadlike pseudopodium.

filopodial *a.* L20.

filoselle /ˈfɪləsɛl/ *n.* Also **†-sella**. M16. [Fr. f. It. *filosello*.] 1 (Silk thread similar to) floss silk. Also *filoselle silk.* M16. †2 A kind of material, prob. of silk and wool. Only in 17.

fils /fis/ *n.*[1] L19. [Fr. = son.] The son, junior: appended to a name to distinguish between a father and son of the same name. Cf. PÈRE 2.

House & Garden Russell *père* had been in banking. . . Russell *fils* . . thought this a bit-too-cramping project.

fils /fɪls/ *n.*[2] Pl. same. L19. [Colloq. pronunc. of Arab. *fals* a small copper coin: see FLOOSE.] 1 *Hist.* Any of various small copper coins in the Middle East. L19. 2 A monetary unit of Iraq, Bahrain, Jordan, Kuwait, and formerly various other Arab countries, equal to one-thousandth of a dinar. Also, a monetary unit of Yemen equal to one-hundredth of a riyal. M20.

filter /ˈfɪltə/ *n.* LME. [OFr. *filtre* var. of *feltre* (mod. *feutre* felt) f. med.L *filtrum*, f. WGmc base rel. to that of FELT *n.*] †1 (A piece of) felt. Only in LME. 2 A piece of felt, woollen cloth, or (now esp.) unsized paper, freq. in the shape of a conical funnel, etc., through which liquid may be passed to free it of suspended matter; any device with this function, as one with a stratum of sand, charcoal, or other porous material. M16. 3 A material used for filtering. *rare.* E19. 4 Any device or arrangement which removes or separates out constituents, as (*a*) a device for removing impurities from the air (also *air-filter*); (*b*) a screen for absorbing light of some or all colours (also *colour-filter, light-filter*); (*c*) a pad of absorbent material fitted at the mouth end of a cigarette to reduce harmful ingredients in the smoke; also, a cigarette with such a filter; (*d*) a sheet or block of material placed in the path of a beam of X-rays etc. in order to absorb radiation of certain wavelengths; (*e*) *Electronics* a circuit that attenuates all signals except those within one or more frequency bands; (*f*) an arrangement for the filtering of traffic: M19.

2 S. W. BAKER The natives had scraped small holes in the sand, as filters. *fig.*: A. ALISON The whole information . . was strained through the imperial filters. 4 I. ASIMOV Filters on his nose to keep out germs. P. SCOTT The box . . that had a filter on the lid to keep the contents dry. *Master Photographer* A set of glass filters . . for use at the light source to provide exact corrections or create effects.

Comb.: **filter aid** any substance added to a liquid or to a filtering medium to prevent the formation of an impervious filter cake; **filter-bed** a pond or tank with a false bottom covered with sand or gravel, acting as a filter; **filter cake** a deposit of insoluble material on a filter; **filter-feeder** an animal that obtains its nourishment by filter-feeding; **filter-feeding** the filtering and ingestion by an organism of nutrient matter suspended in water; **filter-paper** porous paper used for filtering; **filter-passing** *a.* (of a virus) filterable; **filter tip** a filter fitted at the mouth end of a cigarette; a cigarette with such a filter; **filter-tipped** *a.* having a filter tip.

filter /ˈfɪltə/ *v.* L16. [f. the n.] 1 *v.t.* Pass (a liquid, air, electrical signal, light, etc.) through a filter; pass as through a filter; remove constituents from. L16. **b** *v.i.* Engage in filtering liquid etc. L16. 2 *v.i.* Flow through a filter; pass as through a filter; percolate; move slowly, trickle; (of news etc.) leak *out*, come *through.* L18. **b** *spec.* Of road traffic: join traffic coming from another direction at a junction, esp. when other traffic from the same direction has to stop. E20. 3 *v.t.* Obtain (as) by passing through a filter. L18. **b** Foll. by *out*: separate or prevent the passage of (as) by a filter. E20. 4 *v.t.* Act as a filter to. M19.

1 LD RUTHERFORD The precipitate of lead sulphide was filtered off. D. ATTENBOROUGH Cilia around their mouths created a current of water and from it they filtered their food. B. A. FARRELL The patient had already been filtered through psychiatric and psychological interviews. 2 E. BOWEN Restrictions were being relaxed and Catholics were now filtering back again. P. GOODMAN The prosperous well-paying jobs do not filter down evenly to the poorest groups. A. GUINNESS A pale greenish light filtered through the window-panes. 4 K. WATERHOUSE The roller blind filtering a green, dead light over the empty desks.

filterer *n.* E19.

filterable /ˈfɪlt(ə)rəb(ə)l/ *a.* Also **filtrable**. E20. [f. prec. + -ABLE.] Able to be filtered; *spec.* (of a virus) able to pass through a filter that retains bacteria.

filtera'bility *n.* E20.

filth /fɪlθ/ *n.* & *v.* [OE *fȳlþ* = OS *fūliþa* (Du. *vuilte*), OHG *fūlida*, f. Gmc base of FOUL *a.*: see -TH[1].] A *n.* 1 †a Rotting or purulent matter; rottenness. OE–L17. b Dirt, esp. of a disgusting kind. ME. 2 *fig.* Moral defilement, vileness; corruption; obscenity. OE. b Foul or obscene language; obscene literature. M18. c *The* police. *derog. slang.* M20. †3 The quality or state of being foul; filthiness. ME–L16. 4 In *pl.* Types of dirt. Formerly also, foul acts (done or suffered), moral transgressions. Now *rare*. ME. 5 A vile person; a scoundrel; a slut, a whore. *obs.* exc. *dial.* ME. B *v.t.* Make foul, defile. *rare*. LME.

filthy /ˈfɪlθi/ *a.* & *adv.* ME. [f. FILTH *n.* + -Y[1].] A *adj.* 1 Corrupt; morally foul; obscene. ME. 2 Full of filth; covered with filth; dirty, foul. LME. †b Of air or clouds: murky, thick. L16–E17. 3 Disgraceful, contemptible, low, disgusting. LME. 4 Delighting in filth. Now *rare*. E16. 5 Of weather, a mood, etc.: extremely unpleasant. L19.

1 JILLY COOPER Telling such filthy stories at dinner that the great industrialist.. left the table in high dudgeon. 2 M. MOORCOCK I must have been utterly filthy I had not.. properly washed for at least six weeks. G. M. FRASER The whole place was filthy with refuse. b SHAKES. *Macb.* Hover through the fog and filthy air. 3 N. COWARD If he told you that, he's a filthy liar. **filthy lucre** [f. *Tit.* 1:11] dishonourable gain; *loosely* money. 5 P. BOOTH Don't take any notice of him. He's been in a filthy mood all day.

B *adv.* Filthily; to a disgusting extent. Now chiefly in *filthy rich*. E17.

filthify *v.t.* make filthy L18. **filthily** *adv.* M16. **filthiness** *n.* L15.

filthy /ˈfɪlθi/ *v.t.* E20. [f. the adj.] Make filthy.

filtrable *a.* var. of FILTERABLE.

filtrate /ˈfɪltreɪt/ *n.* M19. [f. as next: see -ATE[1].] The liquid that has passed through a filter.

filtrate /ˈfɪltreɪt/ *v.* E17. [mod.L *filtrat-* pa. ppl stem of mod.L *filtrare* filter: see -ATE[3].] 1 *v.t.* = FILTER *v.* 1. E17. 2 *v.i.* = FILTER *v.* 2. E18.

filtration /fɪlˈtreɪʃ(ə)n/ *n.* E17. [Fr., f. *filtrer* to filter: see -ATION.] 1 The action or process of filtering. E17. 2 Movement (as) through a filter; percolation. E17.

filtre /filtr/ *n.* Pl. pronounced same. M20. [Fr.] A filtering appliance for making coffee, which allows boiling water to pass through ground coffee into a cup or pot; coffee made with such an appliance.

fimble /ˈfɪmb(ə)l/ *n.* L15. [Du. *femel*, LG *fimel* f. Fr. (*chanvre*) *femelle* female (hemp).] More fully *fimble hemp*. The male plant of the hemp. Cf. *carl hemp* s.v. CARL *n.* 3.

fimble /ˈfɪmb(ə)l/ *v.i.* & *t.* Long *obs.* exc. *dial.* L16. [App. var. of FUMBLE *v.*, w. vowel suggesting lighter movement.] Move the fingers lightly and frequently over (something).

fimbria /ˈfɪmbrɪə/ *n.* Pl. **-iae** /-ɪiː/. M18. [Late L = border, fringe.] *Anat.*, *Bot.*, etc. A fringe; any of the threads or other projections forming a fringe; *spec.* any of a number of finger-like projections surrounding the ovarian end of a Fallopian tube.

fimbriate /ˈfɪmbrɪeɪt/ *a.* E19. [L *fimbriatus* fringed, f. as prec.: see -ATE[2].] 1 Chiefly *Bot.* & *Zool.* = FIMBRIATED 2. E19. 2 *Her.* = FIMBRIATED 1. L19.

fimbriated /ˈfɪmbrɪeɪtɪd/ *a.* L15. [f. as prec. + -ED[1].] 1 *Her.* Of a charge: bordered with a narrow band or edge. L15. 2 Chiefly *Bot.* & *Zool.* Fringed, bordered with hairs or hairlike processes. L17.

fimbriation /fɪmbrɪˈeɪʃ(ə)n/ *n.* M19. [f. as FIMBRIATE: see -ATION.] *Her.* The condition of being fimbriated; a border, a narrow edge.

fin /fɪn/ *n.*[1] [OE *fin(n)* = MLG *finne*, MDu. *vinne* (Du. *vin*), prob. ult. rel. to L *pinna* feather, wing.] I 1 An organ attached to various parts of the body in fishes and cetaceans, which serves for propulsion and steering in the water; a similar organ in some other animals. OE. 2 A finned animal; a fish. Now *rare*. M16.

1 J. WAIN Wicked sharks.. were swimming just below the surface, their fins poking out. *adipose fin, anal fin, dorsal fin, pectoral fin, ventral fin*, etc.

II A thing resembling a fin. †3 The lid (of the eye). Only in E17. 4 The baleen of a whale; a blade or thin strip of whalebone. Now *rare* or *obs.* M17. 5 A sharp lateral projection on the share or the coulter of a plough. M17. 6 A person's arm and hand; a hand. *slang*. Now *rare*. L18. 7 A small projecting surface on an aircraft or rocket, esp. for ensuring stability; a similar projection on other devices to improve heat transfer etc. M19. 8 A finlike appendage to a ship's bottom; a keel shaped like a dorsal fin inverted; a centreboard. L19. 9 A projecting attachment on a motor vehicle, esp. on the tail. M20. 10 An underwater swimmer's flipper. M20.

Comb.: **fin-back** = *fin whale* below; **finfoot**, pl. **-s**, any of a number of tropical aquatic birds of the family Heliornithidae, superficially resembling grebes but belonging to the same order as the cranes and rails; **fin-footed** *a.* having feet adapted for swimming by being webbed or lobate; **fin-ray** *Zool.* each of the long slender bony processes supporting the fins of a fish; **fin-toed** *a.* having lobate toes; **fin-weed** *dial.* rest-harrow; **fin whale** a large baleen whale, *Balaenoptera physalus*, which has a prominent dorsal fin (also called *common rorqual*).

finlike *a.* resembling a fin M17.

fin /fɪn/ *n.*[2] *slang*. M19. [f. FINNIP.] A five-pound or (*N. Amer.*) five-dollar note.

Fin *n.*[3] see FINN.

fin /fɪn/ *v.* Infl. **-nn-**. E16. [f. FIN *n.*[1]] 1 *v.t.* Cut off the fins from (a fish); cut up (a chub). E16. 2 a *v.t.* Swim in or along, as a fish; make (one's way etc.) by swimming under water. M19. b *v.i.* Swim under water. M20. 3 *v.t.* Provide (an aircraft, motor vehicle, etc.) with fins. M20.

finable /ˈfʌɪnəb(ə)l/ *a.* Also **fineable**. L15. [f. FINE *v.*[2] + -ABLE.] Liable for or subject to a fine; for which a fine may be imposed.

finagle /fɪˈneɪg(ə)l/ *v.* *colloq.* (orig. *US*). Also **phe-**. E20. [f. FAINAIGUE: see -LE[3].] 1 *v.i.* Use dishonest or devious means to bring something about; fiddle. E20. 2 *v.t.* Secure by dishonest or devious means. M20.

finagling *vbl n.* the action of the vb; an instance of this: E20.

final /ˈfʌɪn(ə)l/ *a.* & *n.* ME. [(O)Fr. *final* or L *finalis*, f. *finis* end: see -AL[1].] A *adj.* 1 Putting an end to something, *spec.* to uncertainty or conflict; not to be altered; conclusive. ME. 2 Marking the last stage of a process; ultimate. LME. 3 Having regard to end or purpose. LME. 4 Coming at the end (of a series, a word, etc.). M16.

1 CONAN DOYLE Some.. were complete failures, and as such will hardly bear narrating, since no final explanation is forthcoming. 4 J. BETJEMAN I put my final shilling in the meter. G. GREENE That final 'e' which so neatly distinguishes the artiste from the artist.

Special collocations & phrases: *final cause*: see CAUSE *n.* **final clause** *Gram.* a clause expressing purpose or intention (e.g. in English one introduced by *in order that* or *lest*). **final demand** an account which is a creditor's last attempt to procure money owed, before taking punitive measures. **final drive** the last part of the transmission in a motor vehicle. **final process** *Law* (now *Hist.*) process of execution. **final proof** *US Law* the process observed in paying for pre-empted land after six months' occupancy. **final solution** [tr. G *Endlösung*]: the German policy, from 1941, of exterminating Jewish people in Europe; the process of massacring these victims. *in the final analysis*: see ANALYSIS 1.

B *n.* 1 †a *for final*, finally, conclusively; *in final*, in conclusion. Only in LME. b Completion, an end. Now *rare*. L16. 2 A final thing; *spec.* (*a*) the final letter or sound of a word; (*b*) *Mus.* the principal note in any mode; (*c*) the last or deciding heat or game in a sports or other competition; (*d*) the last series of examinations; in *pl.*, the examinations of the last series, esp. at university etc.; (*e*) the edition of a newspaper published latest in the day. E17.

finale /fɪˈnɑːli/ *n.* M18. [It., as n. of adj. f. L *finalis*: see prec.] 1 The last movement or section or (formerly) note of a musical composition; the closing section of an act in an opera; the closing part of a drama or other public entertainment. M18. 2 The conclusion. L18.

finalise *v.* var. of FINALIZE.

finalism /ˈfʌɪn(ə)lɪz(ə)m/ *n.* L19. [f. FINAL + -ISM.] 1 The belief that an end or limit has been reached. *rare*. L19. 2 The doctrine that natural processes such as evolutionary changes are directed towards some end or goal. E20.

finalist /ˈfʌɪn(ə)lɪst/ *n.* L19. [f. FINAL + -IST.] 1 A person who believes that an end or limit has been reached. *rare*. L19. 2 A competitor who has qualified for a final; a candidate in the last of a series of examinations. L19.

finalistic /fʌɪnəˈlɪstɪk/ *a.* E20. [f. FINALISM: see -ISTIC.] Of or pertaining to the doctrine that natural processes such as evolutionary changes are directed towards some end or goal.

finality /fʌɪˈnalɪti/ *n.* M16. [Fr. *finalité* f. late L *finalitas*, f. L *finalis*: see FINAL, -ITY.] †1 An end in view; a guiding object. Only in M16. 2 The quality, condition, or fact of being final; the condition of being at the limit; the belief that something is final. M19. b A thing that is final; a final act, state, or utterance. M19. 3 The relation of being an end or final cause; the principle of final cause viewed as operative in the universe. M19.

finalize /ˈfʌɪn(ə)lʌɪz/ *v.* Also **-ise**. E20. [f. FINAL *a.* + -IZE.] 1 *v.t.* Complete, bring to an end, put in final form; approve the final form of. E20. 2 *v.i.* Bring something to completion, conclude. M20.

finaliˈzation *n.* M20.

finally /ˈfʌɪn(ə)li/ *adv.* LME. [f. FINAL *a.* + -LY[2], after OFr. *final(e)ment*, late L *finaliter*.] 1 In the end; lastly; at last. LME. b As a final point or conclusion (of a speech or piece of writing etc.). LME. 2 Once for all, irreversibly, decisively, conclusively. LME.

1 V. WOOLF Finally, .. he retired to Hampstead. J. M. COETZEE Sitting upright with his back to the wall, he finally fell asleep. b AV *2 Cor.* 13:11 Finally, brethren, farewell. 2 O. MANNING I suggest you see it before finally making up your mind to finance this venture.

finance /fʌɪˈnans, fɪ-; ˈfʌɪnans/ *n.* LME. [(O)Fr. = †end, †payment, money, f. *finer* make an end, settle, etc., f. *fin* end. The senses now current are from mod.Fr.] †1 Ending, an end. *rare*. LME–E17. †2 Payment of a debt; compensation; a ransom. LME–L16. †3 Supply (of goods); stock of money. L15–E16. †4 A tax; taxation; revenue. L15–L17. †5 Borrowing of money at interest. M16–E18. 6 In *pl.* The monetary resources of a monarch, State, company, or individual. M18. 7 The management of (esp. public) money; the science of levying and applying revenue. L18.

7 *high finance*: see HIGH *a.*

Comb.: **finance company, house** a company mainly concerned with providing money for hire-purchase transactions.

financist *n.* = FINANCIER *n.* 1 L19.

finance /fʌɪˈnans, fɪ-; ˈfʌɪnans/ *v.* L15. [f. the n.] †1 *v.i.* & *t.* Pay or put to ransom. Only in L15. 2 *v.i.* Engage in or manage financial operations; provide oneself with capital. E19. 3 *v.t.* Provide with money, esp. capital; provide money for. M19.

3 L. NAMIER The factor had to finance his West Indian correspondents—lend them money for the sake of consignments. M. GIROUARD School boards financed by a local school rate were to be set up in the towns.

fiˈnanceable *a.* L20. †**financer** *n.* = FINANCIER *n.* 2 M17–M18.

financeer *v.* var. of FINANCIER *v.*

financial /fʌɪˈnanʃ(ə)l, fɪ-/ *a.* & *n.* M18. [f. FINANCE *n.* + -IAL.] A *adj.* 1 Of or pertaining to revenue or money matters. M18. 2 In possession of money. *Austral.* & *NZ slang*. E20.

1 G. GORER By financial difficulties I do not mean absolute poverty. **financial modeller** a person engaged in financial modelling; a computer program for financial modelling. **financial modelling** computer-assisted construction of abstract models for financial calculations, projections, etc. **financial year** a year as reckoned for taxing or accounting (e.g. the British tax year, reckoned from 6 April). *financial wizard*: see WIZARD *n.* 2b.

B *n.* In *pl.* Shares in companies dealing in money. L20.

financialist *n.* = FINANCIER *n.* I M19. **financially** *adv.* L18.

financier /fʌɪˈnansɪə, fɪ-/ *n.* E17. [Fr., as FINANCE *n.*: see -IER.] 1 A person who is concerned with or skilled in finance, esp. establishing and managing public funds; a capitalist. E17. †2 *Fr. Hist.* An administrator, collector, or farmer of taxes before the Revolution. L17–M18.

financier /fʌɪnanˈsɪə, fɪn-/ *v.i.* Usu. *derog.* Also **financeer.** E19. [f. the n.] Conduct financial operations; swindle.

finca /ˈfɪŋka, ˈfɪŋkə/ *n.* E20. [Sp., f. *fincar* cultivate, perh. f. L *figere* fix, fasten, plant.] In Spain and Spanish America: landed property; a country estate; a ranch.

finch /fɪn(t)ʃ/ *n.* [OE *finć* = MDu. *vinke* (Du. *vink*), OHG *finc(h)o* (G *Fink*), f. WGmc.] Any of numerous small passerine birds, typically having short, stout beaks adapted for seed eating, belonging to the family Fringillidae and certain related families.

bullfinch, chaffinch, goldfinch, greenfinch, hawfinch, etc.

finchlike *a.* resembling (that of) a finch L19.

find /fʌɪnd/ *n.* E19. [f. the vb.] 1 An act or instance of finding; a discovery (of a fox, treasure, minerals, etc.). E19. 2 A thing which is found. M19. b A person who comes usefully to notice (public or one's own). L19.

2 J. LUBBOCK Bronze weapons are entirely absent from the great finds of the Iron Age. b R. DAVIES I'm sure this boy is a lucky find Do let's have him.

Phrases: **sure find** (*a*) *Hunting* a place where a fox etc. is sure to be found; (*b*) a person who or thing which is sure to be found.

Comb.: **find-place, -spot** *Archaeol.* the place where an object was found.

find /fʌɪnd/ *v.* Pa. t. & pple **found** /faʊnd/. [OE *findan* = OFris. *finda*, OS *findan*, *fiþan* (Du. *vinden*), OHG *findan* (G *finden*), ON *finna*, Goth. *finþan*, f. Gmc.] I Meet with or come upon by chance or in the course of events. 1 *v.t.* Become aware of or get possession of by chance; come across, meet with. OE. b *euphem.* Steal. *slang.* M19. 2 *v.t.* Come to have, obtain, receive, experience. OE. 3 *v.t.* Discover or perceive on inspection or consideration. ME. b *refl.* Come to be, or perceive oneself to be, in a specified state or position. LME. 4 *v.t.* Learn through experience or trial; regard as, prove (something) to be. ME. †5 *v.t.* Detect; discover the identity or true character of. ME–L18. 6 *v.t.* Feel, suffer from; perceive (a taste, smell, etc.). *obs.* exc. *dial.* LME. 7 *v.t.* Gain or recover the use of (one's limbs, powers, etc.). M16.

1 M. PATTISON In 1276, we find the Emperor and the King of England in constant communication. OED I found a shilling on the floor. W. STAFFORD Travelling through the dark I found a deer/dead on the edge of the Wilson River road. H. ROTH I found her sitting very quietly, as usual, in her large arm-chair. 2 J. M. NEALE Ye who now do bless the poor Shall yourselves find blessing. F. W. NEWMAN I . . despair of finding readers among those who seek solely for amusement. 3 E. HEMINGWAY I found I was quite drunk. H. L. MENCKEN I have found nothing in it save nonsense. b SCOTT FITZGERALD He found himself increasingly in a position to do as he wished. G. GREENE Myatt found himself alone. 4 T. HARDY I've tried to keep it from you, but have found I cannot. M. KEANE Joan did not find him amusing.

II Discover or attain (as if) by search or effort. 8 *v.t.* Discover or obtain by searching; rediscover (something lost). OE. b *v.t.* & *i.* Discover (game, a scent) in hunting. ME. c *v.refl.* Discover one's niche or vocation. M17. d *v.t.* Of an address: be adequate to enable a letter etc. to reach (a person). E20. 9 *v.t.* Ascertain by mental effort or calculation; discover by study or inquiry. OE. 10 *v.t.* Contrive, devise, invent; be the discoverer of (a scientific fact etc.). OE. 11 *Law.* †a *v.i.* Determine. Only in OE. b *v.t.* Authoritatively determine and declare (a person) to be *guilty*, *innocent*, etc., (an issue, offence, etc.) to be that specified, *that*; determine and deliver (a verdict). LME. c *v.t.* Ascertain the validity of (an indictment etc.). L15. d *v.i.* Determine and deliver a verdict (*against*, *for*, etc., the accused or a party in a dispute). E17. 12 *v.t.* Arrive at, reach; reach by a natural or normal process; *arch.* reach the conscience or understanding of. ME. 13 *v.t.* Succeed in obtaining; procure (money, sureties, bail, etc.); make or arrange to have (time, opportunity, etc.). ME. b Summon up (courage, resolution, strength, etc.). LME.

8 AV *Luke* 15:6 Reioyce with me, for I have found my sheepe which was lost. E. WAUGH Find another glass . . if you can. b *Field* Archen Hills was blank . . but hounds found at once in Woodend. c A. MILLER Not finding yourself at the age of thirty-four is a disgrace! 11b J. BUCHAN The jury found it a case of suicide while of unsound mind. d M. RICHLER The jury found in favour of the insurance company. 12 SOUTHEY Yet may a dagger find him. COLERIDGE Whatever *finds* me, bears witness for itself that it has proceeded from a Holy Spirit. I. MURDOCH A letter to the theatre finds me. 13 HOR. WALPOLE I just found a moment to write you a line. b OED At last he has found courage to speak.

III Provide. 14 *v.t.* Supply, provide, furnish. ME. 15 *v.t.* Provide for (a person, oneself); support, maintain. Foll. by *in*: supply with. ME. †b Serve to maintain. L15–L16.

14 E. A. FREEMAN The government required each county to find its quota of ships.

Phrases: **all found** (of servants' wages) with board and lodging provided. *find fault* (*with*): see FAULT *n.* *find favour* (*in the eyes of*): see FAVOUR *n.* **find God** experience religious conversion. **find (it) in one's heart to** (*a*) *arch.* desire to; (*b*) bring oneself to, be hard-hearted enough to, (usu. in neg. contexts). **find its way** be brought or get *into* etc. **find Jesus** experience conversion to Christianity. **find one's feet** learn to stand or walk, get the use of one's feet; *fig.* grow in ability or confidence, develop one's powers, acquire knowledge or capability in a new job etc. **find one's way** to contrive to reach, arrive at. *find* RELIGION. **find the lady** = THREE-*card trick*. **how do you find yourself?** how are you? **know where to find** understand (a person), know the views of. **take us as you find us** accept us as we are.

With advs. in specialized senses: **find out** (*a*) seek out, detect, discover; detect in an offence, discover the identity or true character of; (*b*) make a discovery, discover a fact, the truth, etc. **find up** (now *dial.*) discover by searching, seek out.

Comb.: **find-fault** a person who finds fault, a fault-finder.

findable *a.* able to be found LME.

finder /ˈfʌɪndə/ *n.* ME. [f. FIND *v.* + -ER¹.] 1 A person who finds something or someone. Also *finder-out* etc. ME. b A person whose occupation it is to find something, a prospector; *slang* a thief. M18. †2 A dog trained to seek out or retrieve game. LME–M19. 3 A thing which finds something; a contrivance or instrument for finding something. L16. b *spec.* A small telescope attached to a large one to help locate the object to be viewed. L18. c A part of a camera showing the extent of the picture, = *viewfinder* s.v. VIEW *n.* L19.

1 **finders keepers** *colloq.* whoever finds something is entitled to keep it.

fin de siècle /fɛ̃ də sjɛkl/ *n.* & *a. phr.* L19. [Fr. = end of century.] (Designating or characteristic of) the end of a century, *spec.* the nineteenth century; decadent.

†**findhorn** *n.* see FINNAN.

finding /ˈfʌɪndɪŋ/ *n.* ME. [f. FIND *v.* + -ING¹.] 1 The action or an instance of finding or discovering. ME. †2 The action of inventing or devising; a device. ME–M17. 3 The action of maintaining or supporting (a person etc.). ME. †b Keep, maintenance, support. LME–M16. †4 The action of providing or supplying. LME–L16. 5 A thing found; a discovery, a find. LME. 6 The result of a judicial or other formal inquiry; a verdict. Freq. in *pl.* M19. 7 In *pl.* A craftsman's tools and sundries. *US.* M19.

5 R. CARSON The full scope of the dangerous interaction of chemicals is . . little known, but disturbing findings now come regularly. 6 J. LANG The court-martial still adheres to its finding of murder.

Comb.: **finding-list** a list of books in a particular location or category in a library; **finding-store** *US* a shop selling craftsmen's findings.

†**findon** *n.* see FINNAN.

findrinny /ˈfɪndrɪni/ *n.* L19. [OIr. *findruine* f. early OIr. *findbruine*, f. *find* (mod. *fionn*) white + elem. prob. f. base of *bruth* heat.] White bronze.

fine /fʌɪn/ *n.*¹ ME. [(O)Fr. *fin* f. L *finis* end, (in med.L) a sum to be paid on concluding a lawsuit.] I End. 1 Cessation, termination, conclusion. Now only in *in fine* below. ME. †2 The end of life, death. ME–M16. †3 The limit; extremity, an extreme case. LME–M19. †4 The end in view; an aim, a purpose. LME–E17. †5 A consequence, a result. E16–E17.

1 **in fine** †(*a*) in the end, at last; (*b*) finally, to sum up, in short.

II 6 *Law.* The final agreement or settlement of a suit; *spec.* the compromise of a fictitious or collusive suit for the possession of land, formerly used as a form of conveyance. *obs.* exc. *Hist.* ME.

III A fee, a penalty. 7a A penalty of any kind. *arch.* ME. b A sum of money imposed as the penalty for breaking the law or a regulation. LME. †8 A sum of money offered or paid for exemption from punishment or as compensation for injury. ME–E17. †9 A fee paid for any privilege. LME–M18. 10 *Hist.* A fee paid to a feudal landlord by the tenant or vassal on the transfer or alienation of the tenancy. LME. b A sum of money paid by an incoming tenant in consideration of a low rent. E16.

7a J. S. BLACKIE We stood for our faith, when our life was the fine. b H. HALLAM Fines to the amount of £85,000 . . were imposed on the Covenanters.

Comb. **fine rolls** *Hist.* rolls recording payments made to the Crown for the granting of privileges, land, etc.

fine /fʌɪn/ *n.*² E17. [f. FINE *a.*] †1 A fine woman. E–M17. 2 Fine weather. M19. 3 A fine thing; *spec.* (in *pl.*), very small particles. L19.

2 C. LAMB You go about, in rain or fine, at all hours. 3 *New Yorker* There's no shale upstream . . No fines to contaminate it.

fine /ˈfiːnə/ *n.*³ L19. [Ir.] An ancient Irish family or sept.

fine /fin/ *n.*⁴ Pl. pronounced same. E20. [Fr., abbrev. of FINE CHAMPAGNE.] (A) French brandy; *spec.* = FINE CHAMPAGNE.

fine (de la) maison /(də la) mɛzɔ̃/ a house brandy.

fine /fʌɪn/ *a.* & *adv.* ME. [(O)Fr. *fin* f. Proto-Romance f. L *finire* FINISH *v.*] A *adj.* I 1 Of superior quality; very good of its kind. ME. 2 Free from dross or impurity; clear, pure, refined. ME. b Of gold or silver: containing a specified (high) proportion of pure metal. LME. c Of a liquid: pure, clear, transparent. Now chiefly *dial.* L15. †3 Sheer, absolute, perfect; *iron.* & *derog.* consummate, egregious. ME–E18. 4 Virtuous, morally upright; honourable, noble. ME. 5 Very skilful, highly accomplished. ME. 6 Excellent, of striking merit, admirable; (amongst collectors of coins, books, etc.) in a good but not excellent state of preservation. ME. b Good, enjoyable; (in weakened sense) satisfactory, acceptable, all right. M19. 7 Remarkably good-looking, handsome, beautiful; imposing, dignified. LME. b Of good size; large, well-grown. L16. 8 Of dress etc.: ornate, showy, smart. E16. 9 Characterized by or affecting refinement or elegance. M16. 10 Of a thought, saying, etc.: admirably conceived or expressed. L17. b Of speech, writing, etc.: ornate, elegant, affected. L18. c Flattering, complimentary; euphemistic. M19. 11 Of the weather, a day, etc.: bright, clear; free from rain or fog, and with some sunshine. E18. 12 In good health or spirits; well. L18.

1 S. RAVEN He drank half a bottle of very fine claret. 5 N. MITFORD He was said to be the finest billiards player in the British Isles. 6 G. SAINTSBURY The greatest artist could have done nothing finer. *iron.*: BROWNING A fine way to paint soul, by painting body So ill. b C. KINGSLEY He thought of the fine times coming when he would be a man. K. AMIS 'You don't mind, do you?' . . 'Fine with me.' 7 D. H. LAWRENCE He was a fine fellow, big, straight and fearless-looking. E. MANNIN A fine big house with a pillared porch, like a Greek temple. b MRS H. WOOD He is not a fine child, for he is remarkably small; but he is a very pretty one. 8 *Proverb*: Fine feathers make fine birds. 9 W. BESANT He's only a working man, you see. He hasn't got your fine ways. 10 HOBBES Two or three

fine sayings are not enough to make a wit. b H. CHAPONE Idle gallantry and unmeaning fine speeches. c J. MORLEY Hardly . . more than a fine name for self-indulgence. 11 A. AYCKBOURN It is a fine evening, the sun streams through the french windows. 12 H. HOOD There's nothing wrong with my heart. . . I'm fine, just fine.

II Delicate, subtle. 13 Delicately beautiful; exquisitely fashioned. LME. b Of emotion etc.: elevated, refined. E17. 14 Delicate in structure; thin, filmy. LME. b Very small; in small particles. M16. 15 Extremely thin or slender. LME. b *Cricket*. Behind the wicket and near the line of flight of the ball. M19. 16 Of a weapon, tool, etc.: having a sharp point or edge. LME. †17 Clever, subtle, ingenious; cunning, artful. LME–M18. 18 Capable of delicate perception or discrimination. M16. 19 Not easily perceptible; subtle, minute, precise. M16.

14 I. MCEWAN His hair was unnaturally fine, like a baby's. b J. STEINBECK A fine sandy dust arose from the land. 15 SPENSER Like a crane his neck was long and fyne. 18 A. BAIN The part endowed with the finer tactile power feels the other. 19 T. STOPPARD I was just explaining one or two of the finer points.

B *adv.* Now chiefly *colloq.* & *dial.* 1 Well, very well; completely, thoroughly. ME. 2 In a fine manner; elegantly. E16. 3 Delicately, subtly; precisely. L16.

1 D. MACDONALD Most of the tricks were good tricks and they worked fine. 2 SWIFT The neighbours who come here to dine Admire to hear me speak so fine.

Special collocations, comb., & phrases (of adj. & adv.): *as fine as fivepence*: see FIVE *a.* & *n.* **cut it fine** allow very little margin, time, space, etc. **fine and dandy** *colloq.* first-rate; (of a person) well. **fine-axe** *v.t.* face (stone) to a smooth surface by tapping with a mason's axe. *fine chemicals*: see CHEMICAL *n.* **fine cut** a kind of finely-shredded tobacco. **fine-cut** *a.* finely cut or shredded. **fine-draw** *v.t.* (*a*) sew together (two pieces of cloth, the edges of a rent, etc.) so that the join is barely perceptible; (*b*) draw out to extreme thinness or subtlety. **fine-drawn** *a.* (*a*) subtle, extremely thin; (*b*) *Sport* (now *rare*) reduced in weight by training. **fine feathers** gaudy plumage (*lit.* & *fig.*). **fine gentleman** a man characterized by refined manners and tastes; *derog.* a man of fashion, a dandy, a man who thinks himself above working. **fine-grain** *a.* fine-grained; *Photogr.* of or capable of producing an image which may be considerably enlarged without appearing grainy. **fine-grained** *a.* having a fine grain; consisting of small particles. **fine-hair** *v.t.* remove fine hairs or down from (a pelt). **fine-hand** *a.* written in a fine or delicate hand. **fine lady** a woman of quality or refinement; *derog.* a woman of fashion, a woman who thinks herself above working. **fine print** = *small print* s.v. SMALL *a.* **fine-spun** *a.* spun or drawn out to a fine thread, delicate, flimsy; *fig.* excessively subtle or refined, unpractical. **fine structure** small-scale or detailed variation in structure, texture, appearance, etc., *esp.* (*Physics*) the presence of closely-spaced lines in spectra (cf. HYPERFINE); *fine-structure constant*, a fundamental (and dimensionless) physical constant, equal to approximately 1/137, which occurs in expressions describing the fine structure of the atomic spectra of hydrogen, helium, etc. **fine-tooth comb** a comb with narrow close-set teeth; *go over* or *through with a fine-tooth comb* search or examine thoroughly. **fine-tooth-comb** *v.t.* comb (a person's hair) with a fine-tooth comb; *fig.* search or examine thoroughly. **fine-tune** *v.t.* make delicate adjustments to. **fine tuner** a device for fine tuning. **fine tuning** the process of making delicate adjustments (to an instrument etc., *fig.* the economy etc.). **fine-weather** *a.* fit or suitable only for fine weather. *fine weather for ducks*: see DUCK *n.*[1] **not put too fine a point** or **an edge (up)on it** speak bluntly. **one fine day** once upon a time. **one of these fine days** some day in the future. **one's finest hour** the time of one's greatest success. **run it fine** = *cut it fine* above.

†fine *v.*[1]*i.* & *t.* ME–L16. [OFr. *finer* f. Proto-Romance f. L *finis* end.] Bring or come to an end; finish.

fine /fʌɪn/ *v.*[2] ME. [f. FINE *n.*[1]] I†1 a *v.t.* Pay as a penalty, ransom, or composition. ME–L16. b *v.i.* Pay a penalty, ransom, or composition, *spec.* to avoid the duties of an office. (Foll. by *for*, *off*.) M16–M18. 2 *v.i.* Pay for a privilege or appointment. *obs.* exc. *Hist.* M16. 3†a *v.i.* Pay a sum on renewal of tenure. Only in L17. b *v.t.* Foll. by *down*, *off*: secure the reduction of (rent) by paying a lump sum. *obs.* exc. *Hist.* E18. II 4 *v.t.* Impose a fine on, punish by a fine. Formerly also *gen.*, punish. M16.

fine /fʌɪn/ *v.*[3] ME. [f. FINE *a.* Cf. Fr. *finer*, med.L *finare* refine.] 1 *v.t.* Make clear or pure, refine, (now only beer and wine). Also foll. by *down*. ME. †2 *v.t.* Make beautiful, embellish; smarten *up*. LME–M17. 3 *v.t.* Break into small particles; make less coarse. M16. 4 *v.i.* Of liquid: become clear, clarify. Also foll. by *down*. M16. 5 *v.t.* & *i.* Make or become more slender or attenuated; slim *down*, dwindle or whittle *away*. E19. 6 *v.i.* Of the weather: become clear, brighten *up*. Now chiefly *Austral.* L19.

1 *fig.*: BROWNING Fined and thrice refined I' the crucible of life. 5 E. THOMAS Twilight has fined to naught. N. FREELING Hard work and fresh air had fined her down so much that she suddenly found herself far too thin.

fineable *a.* var. of FINABLE.

fine art /fʌɪn 'ɑːt/ *n. phr.* M18. [f. FINE *a.* + ART *n.*[1], tr. Fr. *beaux-arts* (pl.).] 1 In *pl.* Those arts which appeal to the intellect or the sense of beauty, as literature, music, and esp. painting, sculpture, and architecture. M18. b *sing.* Any one of these arts; *transf.* a thing requiring a high degree of skill, a high accomplishment. L19. 2 These arts collectively, esp. as constituting a branch of practice or study. M19.

fine champagne /fin ʃɑ̃paɲ/ *n. phr.* M19. [Fr. = fine (brandy from) Champagne.] Old liqueur brandy from the Grande Champagne and Petite Champagne vineyards in the Charente, France; an example, glass, or drink of this. Cf. FINE *n.*[4]

†fineer *v.* var. of VENEER *v.*

Fine Gael /fiːnə 'geɪl/ *n. phr.* M20. [Ir., lit. 'tribe of Gaels'.] An Irish political organization and party which entered the Dáil in 1937 in succession to the United Ireland Party.

fineish /'fʌɪnɪʃ/ *a.* L16. [f. FINE *a.* + -ISH[1].] †1 Affecting refinement, fastidious. L16–M17. 2 Rather fine. M17.

fineless /'fʌɪnlɪs/ *a. rare.* E17. [f. FINE *n.*[1] + -LESS.] Boundless, infinite, unlimited.

finely /'fʌɪnli/ *adv.* ME. [f. FINE *a.* + -LY[2].] 1 Perfectly, completely, thoroughly. Long *obs.* exc. *Sc.* ME. 2 Superbly, excellently, beautifully; with great skill, to great effect. LME. †3 Cleverly, shrewdly, with cunning. M16–M17. 4 With delicacy or sensitivity. M16. 5 To a fine point or edge; minutely, precisely. M16. 6 Ornately, showily, smartly. M17.

fineness /'fʌɪnnɪs/ *n.* LME. [f. FINE *a.* + -NESS.] 1 *gen.* The quality or state of being fine. LME. 2 Purity of a metal, degree of freedom from alloy. Now *spec.* the number of parts per thousand of gold or silver in an alloy. L15. 3 Astuteness, cunning; an artifice, a stratagem. Now *rare.* E16.

1 LEIGH HUNT He wrote to the Prince of Orange upon the fineness of his troops. W. S. LANDOR As little as a silkworm knows about the fineness of her thread.

Comb.: **fineness ratio** the ratio of length to width in a ship's hull, aircraft fuselage, etc.

finer /'fʌɪnə/ *n.* Now *rare* or *obs.* LME. [f. FINE *v.*[3] + -ER[1].] A person who or thing which refines; a refiner.

finery /'fʌɪnəri/ *n.*[1] L16. [Fr. *finerie*, f. OFr. *finer* refine: see -ERY.] Chiefly *Hist.* A hearth where cast iron is made malleable or in which wrought iron or steel is made from pig-iron.

finery /'fʌɪn(ə)ri/ *n.*[2] L17. [f. FINE *a.* + -ERY, after BRAVERY.] 1 Showy dress or decoration. L17. 2 Looks, beauty; affected or ostentatious elegance or splendour. Now *rare.* E18.

fines herbes /finz ɛrb, fiːnz 'ɜːb/ *n. phr. pl.* M19. [Fr. = fine herbs.] Chopped mixed herbs used in cooking.

aux fines herbes /o, əʊ/ flavoured with chopped mixed herbs.

finesse /fɪ'nɛs/ *n.* & *v.* LME. [Fr., f. Proto-Romance, f. base of *fin* FINE *a.*: see -ESS[2].] A *n.* 1 Clarity, purity (esp. of metals); slenderness, delicacy. Now *rare.* LME. 2 Delicacy of manipulation or discrimination; refinement. M16. 3 Artfulness, cunning; subtle strategy. M16. 4 An artful stratagem; a ruse, a trick. M16. b *Cards.* An attempt to take a trick with a card lower than but not in sequence with a card of the same suit also held. M19.

1 P. GALLICO The finesse and delicacy of her wristbones. 2 J. CHEEVER She could wave a hornet away from her wineglass with great finesse. 3 J. AUSTEN She was not experienced in the finesse of love.

B *v.* 1 *Cards.* a *v.i.* Attempt to take a trick by a finesse. M18. b *v.t.* Play (a card) in a finesse. M18. 2 *v.i.* Use artifice or stratagem. L18. b *v.t.* Achieve by artifice; bring about or manage by delicate handling. E19.

2 M. E. BRADDON She diplomatized and finessed with them as if she had been canvassing the county. b D. EDGAR The wheeling and dealing, the brinkmanship and finessing of opponents, the whole elaborate political game.

finew *a.*, *v.* & *n.* see VINNY *a.*, *v.* & *n.*

finewed *a.* see VINNIED.

fingan *n.* var. of FINJAN.

finger /'fɪŋgə/ *n.* [OE *finger* = OFris. *finger*, OS, OHG *fingar* (Du. *vinger*, G *Finger*), ON *fingr*, Goth. *figgrs*, f. Gmc.] I 1 Each of the five terminal members of the hand, or each of the four, excluding the thumb. OE. 2 Formerly *gen.*, the breadth of a finger as a measure, ¾ inch. Now *spec.* (*slang*) an amount of liquor one finger-breadth deep in a glass, a small measure of liquor. LME. 3 A digit of an animal. Now *rare.* LME. 4 A part of a glove etc. which is made to receive a finger. M16. 5 Skill in fingering a musical instrument etc.; touch. Now *rare.* M18.

2 J. D. SALINGER I brought my glass over and poured myself out . . at least four fingers of Scotch.

II Something which resembles a finger. 6 A finger-like projection, esp. on a plant. LME. b A banana. L19. c A long narrow pier or other structure. M20. 7 Any small projecting rod etc. with a mechanical function; the pointer of a clock or watch (now *dial.*). L15. 8 A short and narrow object or piece of material, e.g. an item of food. M19. 9 *slang.* a A police officer, a detective. L19. b An informer. E20. c A pickpocket. E20. d A person who indicates victims to criminals. M20.

6 BROWNING Our fig tree . . has furled Her five fingers. c *Times* Aircraft can taxi to the . . 900 ft. long glazed pier, or 'finger', which stretches out from the terminal to provide completely enclosed passenger access. 7 T. HARDY On the clock's dull dial a foggy finger, Moving to set the minutes right. 8 J. JOHNSTON A plate of thin fingers of hot buttered toast. *fish finger* etc.

Phrases etc.: **all fingers and thumbs** clumsy, awkward. *auricular finger*: see AURICULAR *a.* 4. *burn one's fingers*: see BURN *v.* 10. *clean fingers*: see CLEAN *a.* *cross one's fingers*: see CROSS *v.* FIRST *finger*. *five-finger (exercise, grass)*: see FIVE *a.* & *n.* FOREFINGER. *fourth finger*: see FOURTH *a.* **get one's** (or **the**) **finger out** *slang* hurry up, begin work in earnest, take action, (freq. in *imper.*). **give the finger to** *slang* make an obscene gesture to (a person etc.) with the middle finger raised. *green fingers*: see GREEN *a.* **have a finger in the pie** be (esp. officiously) concerned in the matter. *index finger*: see INDEX *n.* *keep one's fingers crossed*: see CROSS *v.* *lady's finger*: see LADY *n.* & *a.* **lay a finger on** touch, however slightly (usu. in neg. & hypothetical contexts). **lay one's finger on** = *put one's finger on* below. **let slip through one's fingers** lose by letting go one's hold of, *fig.* miss the opportunity of. **lift a finger** make the slightest effort (usu. in neg. contexts). *little finger*: see LITTLE *a.* *long finger*: see LONG *a.*[1] *middle finger*: see MIDDLE *a.* **move a finger** = *lift a finger* above. **one's fingers itch** one is longing or impatient (*to do*). **point a** (or **the**) **finger at** (*a*) throw scorn on; (*b*) identify as responsible, accuse. **pull one's finger out** *slang* = *get one's finger out* above. **put a finger on** = *lay a finger on* above. **put one's finger on** point to or identify with precision (a cause of trouble etc.). **put the finger on** *slang* inform against; identify as a victim. **raise a finger** = *lift a finger* above. *ring finger*: see RING *n.*[1] *second finger*: see SECOND *a.* **shake one's finger at** *fig.* = *wag one's finger at* below. *snap one's fingers at*: see SNAP *v.* 7. **stir a finger** = *lift a finger* above. **take one's finger out** *slang* = *get one's finger out* above. *third finger*: see THIRD *a.* & *n.* **turn, twist, wind,** or **wrap round one's (little) finger** easily exert one's will over (a person), persuade without difficulty. *two fingers*: see TWO *a.* 1. **wag one's finger at** *fig.* reprove, rebuke. *white finger, fingers*: see WHITE *a.* *wind round one's (little) finger*: see *turn round one's (little) finger* above. *with a wet finger*: see WET *a.* *work one's fingers to* *the bone*: see BONE *n.* *wrap round one's* (*little*) *finger*: see *turn round one's* (*little*) *finger* above.

Comb.: **finger alphabet** a system of manual signs for communicating with the deaf; **finger-board** a flat strip of wood etc. at the top end of a stringed musical instrument, against which the strings are pressed to determine notes; **finger-bowl** a bowl for water etc. for rinsing the fingers at table, esp. after dessert; **finger-breadth** the width of the finger used as a measure; **finger-dry** *v.t.* & *i.* dry and style (hair) with the fingers; **finger food** food so served that it can conveniently be eaten without cutlery; **finger-glass** a glass for water etc. for rinsing the fingers at table, esp. after dessert; **finger-hole** one of a series of holes in a wind instrument which are opened and closed by the fingers in playing; **finger lake** a long narrow lake in a glaciated valley; **finger language** = *finger spelling* below; **finger-lickin', -licking** *adv.* & *a.* (*colloq.* (orig. *US*)) [f. proprietary slogan 'it's finger lickin' good'] (*a*) *adv.* to the extent that one licks one's fingers; (*b*) *adj.* tasty, appetizing; **finger-mark** a mark left on a surface by the touch of a (dirty) finger; **finger millet** a tropical cereal grass, *Eleusine coracana*, with digitate spikes; **fingernail** each of the nails of the fingers (*to one's fingernails*, completely, thoroughly); **finger-paint** *n.* & *v.i.* (use) a paint that can be applied with the fingers; **finger-pick** *n.* & *v.* (*a*) *n.* a plectrum worn on a finger; (*b*) *v.i.* & *t.* play (a guitar etc., music, esp. country and western) using a finger-pick; **finger-plate** a plate fastened on a door to protect it from finger-marks; **finger-pointing** *vbl n.* & *a.* (of or pertaining to) accusation; **finger-post** *n.* & *v.* (*a*) *n.* a signpost at a crossroads or junction; (*b*) *v.t.* indicate the direction of by means of a finger-post; **fingerprint** *n.* & *v.* (*a*) *n.* an impression made on a surface by a person's finger, esp. as used for identifying a criminal etc.; *fig.* any sign identifying a person, a distinctive characteristic; (*b*) *v.t.* record the fingerprint(s) of (a person); **finger puppet** a small puppet made to fit on a finger; **finger-ring** a ring worn on the finger; **finger's-breadth** = *finger-breadth* above; **finger-snap** a snap of the fingers; **finger spelling** manual signs for communicating with the deaf; **finger-stall** a sheath to protect a finger when injured or in a handicraft etc.; **finger-stone** †(*a*) a stone sufficiently small to be thrown by the hand; (*b*) a convexly tapering cylindrical stone; a belemnite; **finger-tight** *adv.* as tight as can be made by the hand; **finger-wave** a wave set in wet hair with the fingers.

fingered *a.* (*a*) having fingers (esp. of a specified kind); (*b*) resembling a finger: E16. **fingerful** *n.* as much as can be held on one finger or between two fingers; a small quantity: L19. **fingerless** *a.* without fingers E16. **finger-like** *a.* resembling (that of) a finger or fingers L18. **fingery** *a.* branching into fingers or finger-like divisions E19.

finger /ˈfɪŋgə/ *v.* LME. [f. the n.] †**1** *v.t.* Point at with a finger; point *out* (as) with a finger. LME–M18. **2** *v.t.* Play on (a musical instrument) with the fingers; play (a passage of music) with the fingers used in a particular way. LME. **b** Mark (written music) with signs or figures indicating the fingers with which the notes are to be played. E19. **3** *v.t.* Lay the fingers on with the intention to steal, pilfer, (*from*). M16. **4** *v.t.* Hold or turn about in one's fingers; put one's fingers on, touch with the fingers; do this repeatedly or restlessly. L16. **b** *v.t.* & *i.* Handle (money) with unworthy motives. L16. **5** *v.i.* Make restless or repeated movements (*at*) with the fingers; toy *with*. Formerly also *fig.*, long or grope *for*. M17. **6** *v.t.* Manipulate with the fingers; *fig.* elaborate, work up with minute labour. *rare*. E19. **7** *v.t.* Indicate (a victim) or supply (information) to criminals; inform on or identify (a criminal) to the police. *N. Amer. criminals' slang*. M20.

fingerer *n.* a person who fingers something; *esp.* a thief: M16.

finger-end /fɪŋgərˈɛnd/ *n.* Pl. **finger-ends**. Also **finger's end**, pl. **fingers' ends**. ME. [f. FINGER *n.* (+ -'S[1]) + END *n.*] The end or tip of a finger. Cf. FINGERTIP *n.*

at one's finger-ends = *at one's fingertips* s.v. FINGERTIP *n.* **have at one's finger-ends** = *have at one's fingertips* s.v. FINGERTIP *n.* **to the** (or **one's**) **finger-ends** = *to the fingertips* s.v. FINGERTIP *n.*

fingering /ˈfɪŋg(ə)rɪŋ/ *n.*[1] LME. [f. FINGER *v.* + -ING[1].] The action of FINGER *v.*; *Mus.* (the marking of written music to indicate) the method of using the fingers to play an instrument or a particular passage.

¶See also CROSS-FINGERING.

fingering /ˈfɪŋg(ə)rɪŋ/ *n.*[2] Orig. †**fingram**. E17. [Perh. alt. of OFr. *fin grain* fine grain: cf. GROGRAM.] †**1** (An example of) a kind of woollen cloth. *Sc.* E17–M18. **2** A kind of fine wool or yarn used for knitting. L17.

fingerling /ˈfɪŋgəlɪŋ/ *n.* & *a.* LME. [f. FINGER *n.* + -LING[1].] **A** *n.* †**1** Each of the fingers of a glove; a finger-stall. LME–L16. **2** A parr; any very young fish. E18. **3** A very small being. M19. **B** *attrib.* or as *adj.* Of a fish or other animal: small because still very young. L19.

fingertip /ˈfɪŋgətɪp/ *n.* & *a.* M19. [f. FINGER *n.* + TIP *n.*[1]] **A** *n.* The tip of a finger. (Cf. earlier FINGER-END.) M19.

at one's fingertips ready at hand. **have at one's fingertips** be thoroughly conversant with, have ready knowledge of. **to the** (or **one's**) **fingertips** through and through, in every way, completely.

B *attrib.* or as *adj.* **1** *Archaeol.* Of ornament: made with the fingertips. E20. **2** Of a garment: reaching to the fingertips. M20. **3** That can be controlled by a light movement of the fingers. M20.

fingle-fangle /ˈfɪŋg(ə)lfaŋg(ə)l/ *n.* *arch.* M17. [Redupl. of FANGLE *n.* Cf. FIDDLE-FADDLE.] A trifle; something whimsical or fantastic.

Fingo /ˈfɪŋgəʊ/ *n.* Pl. **-os**. E19. [Xhosa *mfengu* destitute wanderer.] (A member of) a people of South Africa made up of various groups driven from Natal in the early 19th cent. and now largely living in the eastern Cape Province.

†**fingram** *n.* see FINGERING *n.*[2]

fingrigo /ˈfɪŋgrɪgəʊ/ *n.* Pl. **-os**. L17. [Jamaican creole, perh. f. FINGERY *a.* + GO *n.*[1], *v.*] A W. Indian climbing shrub with large prickles, *Pisonia aculeata*, of the bougainvillea family.

finial /ˈfɪnɪəl, ˈfʌɪn-/ *a.* & *n.* LME. [f. unrecorded AN or AL, f. (O)Fr. *fin*, L *finis* end: see -AL[1].] †**A** *adj.* Final. LME–L15. **B** *n.* **1** *Archit.* An ornament which surmounts the apex of a roof, pediment, gable, tower-corner, canopy, etc.; the topmost part of a pinnacle. LME. **2** An ornamental knob or extremity on a piece of silverware, cutlery, etc. M20.

finialled *a.* having finials M19.

finical /ˈfɪnɪk(ə)l/ *a.* L16. [Prob. f. FINE *a.* + -ICAL, & orig. university slang; perh. suggested by MDu. *fijnkens* accurately, neatly, prettily.] Overparticular, precise, fastidious; *arch.* excessively delicate in workmanship or elaborate in detail.

finically *adv.* M17. **finicalness** *n.* L17. **finicality** /fɪnɪˈkalɪti/ *n.* (a) finical quality L16.

finicism /ˈfɪnɪsɪz(ə)m/ *n.* M19. [f. next + -ISM.] Finical affectation.

finick /ˈfɪnɪk/ *n.* E18. [Prob. back-form. f. FINICAL.] A finical person.

finick /ˈfɪnɪk/ *v.i.* Chiefly *dial.* M19. [Prob. back-form. f. next.] Perform work or act finically.

finicking /ˈfɪnɪkɪŋ/ *a.* & *n.* Also **finikin** /ˈfɪnɪkɪn/. M17. [f. FINICAL, w. suffix-substitution of -ING[2].] **A** *adj.* = FINICAL. Also, trifling. M17. †**B** *n.* (Usu. **finikin.**) **1** A variety of the domestic pigeon. E18–M19. **2** A finicking person. Only in M18.

finickingly *adv.* L19.

finicky /ˈfɪnɪki/ *a.* E19. [f. FINICAL, w. suffix-substitution of -Y[1], or f. FINICK *v.* + -Y[1].] = FINICAL. Also, needing much attention to detail.

D. HEWETT All sorts of .. delicacies to tempt Gwennie's finicky appetite. A. GUINNESS His rehearsals .. never became stodgy or finicky.

finickiness *n.* M19.

finif *n.* var. of FINNIP.

finify /ˈfʌɪnɪfʌɪ/ *v.t.* *obs.* exc. *US* & *dial.* L16. [f. FINE *a.* + -I- + -FY.] Make fine; adorn, decorate.

finikin *a.* & *n.* see FINICKING.

fining /ˈfʌɪnɪŋ/ *n.* LME. [f. FINE *v.*[3] + -ING[1].] **1** The action of FINE *v.*[3] LME. **2** *sing.* & (usu.) in *pl.* A substance used for clarifying liquid, now *spec.* beer or wine. L18.

finis /ˈfiːnɪs, ˈfɪnɪs, ˈfʌɪnɪs/ *n.* LME. [L *finis* end.] **1** At the end of a book: the end. LME. **2** The conclusion, the end, the finish; the end of life, death. L17.

finish /ˈfɪnɪʃ/ *n.* L18. [f. the vb.] **1** The last stage, the termination, the conclusion, the end; *spec.* (*a*) the end of a hunt, race, or other contest or event; the death of a fox; the point at which a race etc. ends; (*b*) the final taste impression of a wine etc. L18. **2** A thing which finishes, or gives completeness or perfection to something; *spec.* the last coat of paint or plaster laid on a surface; a veneer or other material added to something, usu. to enhance its appearance; a mode of finishing furniture etc. L18. **3** A place of entertainment open late (a possible last call on a night out). *arch. slang*. L18. **4** The condition or quality of being finished or perfected. E19. **5** Methylated spirit. *colloq.* Now *rare*. L19.

1 A. M. JOHNSON To look upon death .. as the finish of your sorrows! L. W. MEYNELL They were pieces in a game that still had to be played to a grim finish. **fight to the finish** a contest which lasts until one party is defeated. **from start to finish** throughout. **2** R. V. JONES The standard of finish was terrible, and .. no one who was doing a decent job would leave his work in that state.

Comb.: **finish line** = *finishing-line* s.v. FINISHING *n.*

finish /ˈfɪnɪʃ/ *v.* ME. [OFr. *feniss-* (mod. *finiss-*) lengthened stem of *fenir* (mod. *finir*) f. L *finire*, f. *finis* end: see -ISH[2].] **I** *v.t.* **1** Bring to an end, come to the end of, go through the last stage of, (a thing, *doing*). ME. **b** Foll. by *off*: provide with an ending. M19. **2** Bring to completion; make or do completely; complete. Also foll. by *off*. LME. **3** Perfect finally or in detail, put the final and completing touches to, (also foll. by *off*, *up*); complete or perfect the education of (a person, esp. a girl), the fattening of (cattle etc.), the manufacture of (woodwork, cloth, etc.) by surface treatment. LME. †**b** Make (*into*) by a final operation. E18–E19. **4** Deal with or dispose of the whole or the remainder of (an object); complete the consumption of (food, one's stock of something), the reading of (a book etc.). E16. **b** Kill, destroy; reduce to utter exhaustion or helplessness. Also foll. by *off*. Now chiefly *colloq.* E17.

1 SCOTT FITZGERALD When Jordan Baker had finished telling all this. E. WAUGH The colonel finished the last war as a brigadier. **2** S. BELLOW He was still finishing his work well within the deadlines. **4b** V. BRITTAIN Why couldn't a torpedo have finished me? R. INGALLS That just about finished the place for us.

II *v.i.* **5** Come to an end, reach the end, (also foll. by *up*); cease, leave *off*; end *in* (a thing), *by* (*doing*), *up* (in a particular state or place, (*by*) *doing*. LME. †**b** Die. LME–E17. **c** *Sport.* Come to the end of a course or race (in a particular condition or place). L19. **6** Foll. by *with*: complete one's use of or association with. L18.

5 B. FRANKLIN Partnerships often finish in quarrels. D. DU MAURIER Yawning a little as they waited for the sermon to finish. E. BOWEN The girl finished up with a rush. *Heritage Outlook* This was unfortunately denied to us at the last moment so we finished up in the Public Library. **c** D. FRANCIS Treetops broke down and finished last, limping.

finishable *a.* (earlier in UNFINISHABLE) M19.

finished /ˈfɪnɪʃt/ *ppl a.* L16. [f. prec. + -ED[1].] **1** That has been finished; ended, completed. L16. **2** Consummate, perfect, accomplished. E18.

¶Earlier in UNFINISHED.

finisher /ˈfɪnɪʃə/ *n.* E16. [f. as prec. + -ER[1].] **1** A person who or thing which finishes (something). E16. **2** *spec.* **a** A worker or machine performing the final operation in a manufacturing process. L17. **b** A discomfiting thing, a decisive or crushing blow (*lit.* & *fig.*). *colloq.* L18.

1 finisher of the law *joc.* (*arch.*) a hangman, an executioner.

finishing /ˈfɪnɪʃɪŋ/ *n.* LME. [f. as prec. + -ING[1].] **1** The action of FINISH *v.* Also *finishing-off*. LME. **2** A thing which gives a finished appearance; decoration, ornamental work. M17.

Comb.: **finishing-line, -post** a (real or imaginary) line, post, which marks the end of a race etc.; **finishing-school** a school for completing the education, esp. of girls, with an emphasis on the social graces.

finishing /ˈfɪnɪʃɪŋ/ *ppl a.* E18. [f. as prec. + -ING².] That finishes (something).

finishing stroke, touch a last action or added effect in the preparation or production of something (usu. in *pl.*).

finishment /ˈfɪnɪʃm(ə)nt/ *n.* Now *US.* LME. [f. as prec. + -MENT.] End, finishing; death.

finitary /ˈfʌɪnɪt(ə)ri/ *a.* M20. [f. next after UNITARY.] *Math.* Of a proof, relation, etc.: involving a finite number of steps or other entities.

finite /ˈfʌɪnʌɪt/ *a.* & *n.* LME. [f. L *finitus* pa. pple of *finire* FINISH *v.*] A *adj.* 1 Having bounds, ends, or limits; not infinite or infinitesimal. LME. b Having an existence subject to limitations and conditions. M17. †2 Fixed, determined, definite. L15–L17. 3 *Math.* (Of a line) having two ends; (of a numerical quantity) neither infinitely large nor infinitesimally small; corresponding to or represented by a finite number or a finite number of items. L16. 4 *Gram.* (Of a verb part) limited by number and person, not in the infinitive; (of a clause) containing a finite verb part. L18. 5 *Mus.* Of a canon: with a separately composed ending. M19.

1 C. P. SNOW Not in the vague future, but in finite time. E. L. DOCTOROW You will be left with a finite amount of money. 3 : *finite difference, finite group*, etc.

B *n.* A finite being or thing; *Gram.* a finite verb part or form. Also, that which is finite. E17.

finitely *adv.* M17. **finiteness** *n.* E17.

finite /ˈfʌɪnʌɪt/ *v.t.* E17. [f. the adj.] Make finite.

finitise *v.* var. of FINITIZE.

finitism /ˈfʌɪnʌɪtɪz(ə)m/ *n.* E20. [f. FINITE *a.* + -ISM.] 1 *Philos.* & *Theol.* The belief that the world, or some realm, or God, is finite. E20. 2 A view of mathematics that rejects the validity of actual infinities; *spec.* the doctrine that every proof should involve only a finite number of steps. M20.

finitist *n.* & *a.* (*a*) *n.* an adherent of finitism; (*b*) *adj.* characterized by or relating to finitism: L19. **finiˈtistic** *a.* M20.

finitize /ˈfʌɪnʌɪtʌɪz/ *v.t.* Also **-ise**. E20. [f. as prec. + -IZE.] Make finite.

finitude /ˈfɪnɪtjuːd/ *n.* M17. [f. as prec. + -TUDE.] The condition or state of being finite; finiteness.

finity /ˈfɪnɪti/ *n.* L17. [OFr. *finité*, f. *fini* pa. pple of *finir* to bound, f. L *finire* FINISH *v.*] Finiteness, finitude; an instance of this.

finjan /fɪnˈdʒɑːn/ *n.* Also **-gan** /-ˈgɑːn/. E17. [Arab. *finjān* f. Pers. *pingān* cup.] A small porcelain coffee-cup, used in the eastern Mediterranean region.

fink /fɪŋk/ *n.*¹ *N. Amer. slang. derog.* L19. [Origin unkn.] An unpleasant contemptible person; *spec.* (*a*) an informer; (*b*) a detective; (*c*) a strikebreaker. Cf. *ratfink* s.v. RAT *n.*¹

fink *n.*² var. of VINK.

fink /fɪŋk/ *v.*¹*i. non-standard.* L19. [Repr. a pronunc.] Think.

fink /fɪŋk/ *v.*²*i. N. Amer. slang.* E20. [f. FINK *n.*¹] 1 Inform (*on*). E20. 2 Back *out* (*on*). M20.

finkle /ˈfɪŋk(ə)l/ *n. obs.* exc. *dial.* ME. [L *faeniculum*: see FENNEL.] Fennel.

Finlander /ˈfɪnləndə/ *n.* Now *rare.* E18. [f. *Finland* (see FINN) + -ER¹.] = FINN.

Finlandization /fɪnləndʌɪˈzeɪʃ(ə)n/ *n.* Also **-isation**. M20. [f. *Finland* (see FINN) + -IZATION, tr. G *Finnlandisierung.*] *Hist.* A policy of benevolent neutrality towards the Soviet Union, such as was allegedly pursued by Finland from 1944; the adoption of such a policy.

ˈFinlandize *v.t.* induce (a country) to adopt a policy of benevolent neutrality towards the Soviet Union L20.

finless /ˈfɪnlɪs/ *a.* L16. [f. FIN *n.*¹ + -LESS.] Without fins.

finlet /ˈfɪnlɪt/ *n.* L19. [f. FIN *n.*¹ + -LET.] A small fin.

Finn /fɪn/ *n.* Also (now *rare*) **Fin**. [OE *Finnas* pl., corresp. to G *Finne*, ON *Finnr*; recorded as L *Fenni* (Tacitus), Gk *phinnoi* (Ptolemy).] A member of a people of Scandinavia and NE Europe speaking a Finno-Ugric language; a native or inhabitant of Finland.

¶ *Finn* and *Finland* do not correspond to terms used by the Finns themselves (who use *Suomi* & derivs.).

finnack *n.* var. of FINNOC.

finnan /ˈfɪnən/ *n.* Also †**findhorn**, †**findon**. E18. [f. *Findon*, a fishing village near Aberdeen (confused w. *Findhorn*, place and river).] More fully *finnan haddock*, (Sc.) *haddie.* A haddock cured with the smoke of green wood, turf, or peat.

finned /fɪnd/ *a.* ME. [f. FIN *n.*¹ + -ED².] Having a fin or fins (of a specified kind).

finner /ˈfɪnə/ *n.* L18. [f. FIN *n.*¹ + -ER¹.] = *fin whale* s.v. FIN *n.*¹

finnesko /ˈfɪnəskəʊ/ *n.* Also **fin(n)sko**. Pl. same. L19. [Norw. *finnsko*, f. *Finn* FINN + *sko* shoe.] A boot made of tanned reindeer skin with the hair left on the outside.

Finnic /ˈfɪnɪk/ *a.* M17. [f. FINN + -IC.] Of or pertaining to the Finns, the group of peoples ethnically allied to the Finns, or the group of languages allied to Finnish.

Finnicize /ˈfɪnɪsʌɪz/ *v.t.* (*rare*) give a Finnish form to E19.

finnied *a.* see VINNIED.

finnip /ˈfɪnɪp/ *n. slang.* Also **fin(n)if** /ˈfɪnɪf/. M19. [Origin uncertain: perh. repr. Yiddish *finef* five.] A five-pound or five-dollar note.

Finnish /ˈfɪnɪʃ/ *a.* & *n.* L17. [f. FINN + -ISH¹.] A *adj.* Of or pertaining to the Finns or (occas.) the group of peoples ethnically allied to the Finns. L17.

Finnish spitz a small stocky kind of spitz with a coarse reddish-brown coat.

B *n.* The Finno-Ugric language of the Finns. L18.

Finno- /ˈfɪnəʊ/ *comb. form.* [f. FINN + -O-.] Finnish or Finnic and —.

Finno-Ugrian /-ˈuːgrɪən, -ˈjuː-/ *a.* & *n.* = FINNO-UGRIC L19. **Finno-Ugric** /-ˈuːgrɪk, -ˈjuː-/ *a.* & *n.* (belonging to) the group of Uralic languages including Finnish, Estonian, Lappish, and Hungarian L19.

finnoc /ˈfɪnək/ *n. Sc.* (now *dial.*). Also **-ack**, **ph-**. E17. [Gael. *fionnag*, f. *fionn* white.] An immature sea trout or salmon.

finnow *n.*, *a.*, & *v.* see VINNY *a.*, *n.*, & *v.*

finnowed *a.* see VINNIED.

finnsko *n.* var. of FINNESKO.

finny /ˈfɪni/ *a.*¹ L16. [f. FIN *n.*¹ + -Y¹.] 1 Having a fin or fins. L16. 2 Of the nature of or like a fin. E17. 3 Teeming with fish; of or pertaining to fish. *literary.* M18.

finny *a.*², *v.* & *n.* see VINNY *a.*, *v.* & *n.*

fino /ˈfiːnəʊ/ *n.* Pl. **-os**. M19. [Sp. = FINE *a.*] A type of light-coloured dry sherry; a glass or drink of such sherry.

finocchio /fɪˈnɒkɪəʊ/ *n.* Also **-ochio**. E18. [It. f. pop.L var. of L *faeniculum*: see FENNEL.] A form of fennel with swollen leaf-bases, *Foeniculum vulgare* var. *azoricum*, eaten as a vegetable.

Finsen /ˈfɪns(ə)n/ *a.* E20. [N. R. *Finsen* (1860–1904), Da. physician.] Designating (apparatus used for) the treatment of skin diseases by ultraviolet light.

finsko *n.* var. of FINNESKO.

fiord /fjɔːd/ *n.* Also **fjord**. L17. [Norw. f. ON *fjǫrðr*. Cf. FIRTH *n.*², FORD *n.*] A long, narrow, and deep inlet of the sea between steep cliffs, as on the Norwegian coast (now ascribed to erosion by glaciers).

fiorin /ˈfʌɪərɪn/ *n.* E19. [App. f. Ir. *fiorthann* long coarse grass.] More fully *fiorin grass.* A tufted perennial grass, *Agrostis stolonifera*, that sends up stalks from a rooting decumbent base. Also called *creeping bent.*

fiorite /fɪˈɔːrʌɪt/ *n.* E19. [f. Santa *Fiora* in Tuscany, western Italy, where first described: see -ITE¹.] *Min.* A siliceous sinter that occurs as a pearly incrustation near hot springs and fumaroles.

fioritura /fɪˌɔːrɪˈtʊərə/ *n.* Pl. **-re** /-ri, -reɪ/. M19. [It., f. *fiorire* to flower.] *Mus.* A decoration or embellishment of a melody.

fip /fɪp/ *n. US arch. colloq.* E19. [Abbrev.] = *fippenny bit* s.v. FIPPENNY *a.*

fipenny *a.* & *n.* var. of FIPPENNY.

fippence /ˈfɪp(ə)ns/ *n. colloq.* Now *rare* or *obs.* E17. [Repr. a pronunc.] Fivepence.

fippenny /ˈfɪp(ə)ni/ *a.* & *n. arch.* Also **fipenny**. E19. [Repr. a pronunc. of *fivepenny*: see FIVE.] A *adj.* = *fivepenny* s.v. FIVE. E19.

fippenny bit *US* a Spanish half-real piece; a silver coin used in the Eastern US before 1857 and worth about six cents.

B *n.* A clasp-knife. *slang.* E19.

fipple /ˈfɪp(ə)l/ *n.* E17. [Cf. Icel. *flipi* lip of a horse.] A complete or partial plug at the head of a wind instrument, *esp.* a partial plug at the head of a recorder, whistle, etc., leaving a narrow channel for air; the narrow channel itself.

Comb.: **fipple flute** a flute which is played by blowing endwise.

fir /fəː/ *n.* LME. [Prob. f. ON *fyri-* (in *fyriskógr* fir-wood etc.) f. Gmc, f. base also of OE *furhwudu* fir-wood, OHG *forha* (G *Föhre*), ON *fura.* See also VAR *n.*] 1 An evergreen coniferous tree; now *esp.* one belonging to the genus *Abies* of the pine family, characterized by upright cones and flat needles usu. arranged in two rows. Also, a Douglas fir; a Scotch fir. Also *fir tree.* LME. 2 The wood of a fir. LME.

1 *balsam fir*: see BALSAM *n. Douglas fir*: see DOUGLAS *n.*¹ *red fir*: see RED *a. Scotch fir*: see SCOTCH *a.* **silver fir** a fir whose needles are white or silvery underneath, spec. *Abies alba*, a timber tree of central and southern Europe. *white fir*: see WHITE *a.*

Comb.: **fir balsam** = *balsam fir* above; **fir clubmoss** a European clubmoss, *Huperzia selago* (family Lycopodiaceae), with a branching form resembling a miniature tree; **fir cone** a cone of a fir or pine.

Firbolg /fɪəˈbɒlg, *foreign* fɪrˈbɔləg/ *n.* M18. [Ir., ult. origin unkn.] A member of a legendary early colonizing people of Ireland.

fire /ˈfʌɪə/ *n.* [OE *fȳr* = OFris., OS *fiur* (Du. *vuur*), OHG *fiur*, *fūir* (G *Feuer*) f. WGmc base, corresp. to Gk *pur.*] 1 The active principle operative in combustion, manifested as a hot bright shifting body of gas or as incandescence; such gas or incandescence. (One of the four elements of the ancients.) OE. b *spec.* The burning flame(s) of hell or purgatory. OE. c Volcanic heat; a flow of lava. Formerly also, a volcanic eruption. L16. 2 Fuel in a state of combustion; a mass of burning material in a grate, furnace, etc.; a heater with a flame or incandescent element. OE. b Fuel as a means of making a fire or setting something alight, *esp.* fuel that is already burning. *obs.* exc. *dial.* OE. c In full *Greek fire.* A flammable composition for setting light to enemy ships, works, etc., first used by the Greeks of Constantinople. *obs.* exc. *Hist.* ME. 3 Destructive burning, esp. of a large mass or area; a conflagration. As *int.*, warning of a fire. ME. 4 Lightning; a flash of lightning; a thunderbolt. ME. 5 Fever, inflammation; disease as a consuming agency. *arch.* ME. 6a A burning passion or emotion. ME. b Ardour of temperament; zeal, fervour, enthusiasm. E17. c Liveliness of imagination; vivacity; poetic inspiration. M17. 7 State of combustion. Chiefly in *on fire* below. LME. 8 Luminosity; a glowing or flashing appearance resembling that of fire. M16. 9 The action of firing guns etc. L16. 10 A flare, a firework; the flammable composition used in a firework or other combustible device. Orig. & now only in *false fire* s.v. FALSE *a.* E17. 11 Torture or death by burning. Now *rare.* M17. 12 The heating quality in liquors etc.; *joc.* a warming drink of liquor etc. M18. 13 *Cricket.* The tendency of a ball to fly up erratically, or of a wicket etc. to cause the ball to fly up. L19.

1 J. MABBE A face as red as fire. 2 F. M. FORD The fire . . was burning brightly; she must have just put coals on. *fig.*: POPE Some spark of your celestial fire. *electric fire, gas fire, open fire*, etc. 3 S. JOHNSON Now a rabble rages, now a fire. 6a SHAKES. *Merry W.* The wicked fire of lust. b M. AYRTON She's got no fire, Estelle, no go, no zing. 8 W. BLACK A great fire of sunset spread over the west. 9 J. G. FARRELL Rifle and revolver fire was almost continuous during . . the night.

Phrases etc.: *ball of fire*: see BALL *n.*[1] 3. **between two fires** shot at or attacked from two directions. BONFIRE. *catch fire*: see CATCH *v. cease fire, cease-fire*: see CEASE *v. coal(s) of fire*: see COAL *n.* **fire and brimstone** torment in hell. **fire and sword** burning and slaughter, esp. by an invading army. **fire in one's** (or **the**) **belly** ambition, driving force, initiative. **fires of heaven** *poet.* the stars. **give fire** (**to**) set alight, kindle. **go on fire** (chiefly *Sc.* & *Anglo-Ir.*) begin to burn. **go through fire** (**and water**) encounter or face all dangers, submit to the severest ordeal. *Great Fire*: see GREAT *a. Greek fire*: see sense 2c above. *hang fire*: see HANG *v.* **heavenly fires** *poet.* the stars. *holy fire*: see HOLY *a. indirect fire*: see INDIRECT *a. Kentish fire*: see KENTISH *a. line of fire*: see LINE *n.*[2] *miss fire*: see MISS *v.*[1] **no smoke without fire** no rumour without some basis in fact. **on fire** ignited, burning, (*like a house on fire*: see HOUSE *n.*[1]); *fig.* inflamed with passion, anger, zeal, etc. *open fire*: see OPEN *a. out of the (frying-)pan into the fire*: see PAN *n.*[1] **play with fire** trifle with dangerous matters. **pull out of the fire** = *snatch out of the fire* below. *pull the chestnuts out of the fire*: see CHESTNUT *n. Ring of Fire*: see RING *n.*[1] *running fire*: see RUNNING *a.* **save out of the fire** preserve as a remnant from a disaster. **set fire to** (**†in, †on**) apply fire to, cause to start burning, kindle, ignite. **set on fire** ignite, kindle; *fig.* inflame. **set the Thames on fire, set the world on fire** do something remarkable, make an impact, (usu. in neg. contexts). **snatch out of the fire** rescue from disaster or ruin. *St Anthony's fire*: see SAINT *n.* & *a. St Elmo's fire*: see SAINT *n.* & *a.* **strike fire** elicit sparks by friction or by a blow. **take fire** begin to burn. *the fat is in the fire*: see FAT *n.*[2] **under fire** being shot at; *fig.* being adversely criticized etc. *wandering fire*: see WANDERING *ppl a.* **where's the fire?** *joc.* what's the hurry? WILDFIRE.

Comb.: **fire-alarm** a device for or means of giving warning of fire; **fireback** (*a*) (a metal plate for) the back wall of an open hearth; (*b*) (also *fireback pheasant*) either of two pheasants of SE Asia, *Lophura ignita* and *L. erythrophthalma*; **fire-balloon** a hot-air balloon whose buoyancy is derived from a fire burning at its mouth; **fire-bird** any of various small birds with bright orange or red plumage, *esp.* (*US*) the Baltimore oriole; **fire-blanket** a sheet of usu. fireproof material with which to smother a fire in an emergency; **fire-blight**: see *pear-blight* s.v. PEAR *n.*; **fireboard** a board used to close up a fireplace; *US* a mantelpiece; **fire-bomb** *n.* & *v.* (*a*) *n.* an incendiary bomb; (*b*) *v.t.* attack or destroy with a fire-bomb or fire-bombs; **firebrat** a bristletail, *Thermobia domestica*, which frequents warm places in houses; **fire-break** an obstacle preventing the spread of (esp. grass or forest) fires, as an area of cleared or ploughed land; **fire-brick** a brick capable of standing intense heat without burning, used in grates etc.; **fire brigade** an organized body of people trained and employed to extinguish fires; **fire-bug** *colloq.* an incendiary, an arsonist; **fire certificate**: confirming that current statutory fire regulations have been complied with at a particular premises; **fireclay** clay of a kind used for making fire-bricks; **fire company** (*a*) a section of a fire brigade; (*b*) a fire-insurance company; **fire-control** a system of regulating the firing of guns from a ship or fort; the station from which such control is exercised; **fire coral** a branched stinging coral of the genus *Millepora* and suborder Milleporina; **fire-crack** a crack caused by heat, *esp.* one which occurs in metal being reheated or annealed; **firecracker** (chiefly *N. Amer.*) an explosive firework; **firecrest** a kinglet, *Regulus ignicapillus*, with a golden crest, found in woods and forests in central and southern Europe and Asia Minor; **fire cross** = *fiery cross* s.v. FIERY *a.*; **fire-cure** *v.t.* cure (esp. tobacco or leather) over a fire; **fire-curtain** (*a*) a fireproof curtain in a theatre etc.; (*b*) *Mil.* = CURTAIN *n.* 7; **firedamp** (a miner's name for) methane, which is explosive when mixed in a certain proportion with air; **fire department** *N. Amer.* a fire brigade; **fire-discipline** *Mil.* the training of soldiers to fire exactly as commanded, so that their actions are coordinated; *firedog*: see DOG *n.* 7; **fire door** a fireproof door to inhibit or prevent the spread of fire; **fire-drill** (*a*) a simple device for kindling fire consisting of a pointed stick and a piece of wood; (*b*) a rehearsal of the procedure to be used in case of fire; **fire engine** (*a*) a vehicle carrying equipment to fight and extinguish fires; (*b*) (*obs.* exc. *local*) a steam engine; **fire-escape** an emergency staircase, esp. on the outside of a building, enabling people to escape should fire break out; an apparatus serving the same purpose; **fire exit** a passage or door to go through to escape from fire; **fire extinguisher** an apparatus with a jet for discharging liquid chemicals, foam, etc., in order to extinguish fire; **fire-eyed** *a.* (*poet.*) having eyes glowing as with fire; **fire-fight** *Mil.* a struggle to establish superiority of fire-power over an enemy; a fight involving fire or firearms; **fire-fighter** a person whose task is to extinguish fires; a member of a fire brigade; **fire-fighting** the extinguishing of fires; **firefish** any of several scorpion fishes with venomous spines, esp. of the genera *Pterois* and *Dendrochirus*; **firefly** a winged nocturnal beetle that emits light, usu. in flashes, found esp. in the tropics; *spec.* one of the family Lampyridae; **fire-fork** (*obs.* exc. *dial.* or *Hist.*) a fork-shaped instrument for stirring up a fire, putting on fuel, etc.; **fire-guard** (*a*) a protective (usu. meshed) framework or grating, placed in front of an open fire in a room; (*b*) *N. Amer.* = *fire-watcher* below; (*c*) *N. Amer.* = *fire-break* above; **fire hall** *N. Amer.* a fire station; **fire-hearth** (*a*) a brick or stone area on which a fire is made; the hearth in front of a fireplace; (*b*) a cooking range or stove on a ship; **fire-hose** a hose-pipe for extinguishing fires; **firehouse** (*a*) (*obs.* exc. *dial.* or *Hist.*) a house with a fireplace in it; the room in a house where the family fire was; (*b*) *US* a fire station; **fire-hunting** *US* (*a*) the firing of timber to drive out game; (*b*) hunting at night with lights; *fire hydrant*: see HYDRANT; **fire insurance** insurance against losses by fire; **firelight** †(*a*) lightning; (*b*) the light given by a fire or fires; **fire-lighter** (*a*) a person who kindles a fire; (*b*) material for lighting fires, *esp.* a piece of flammable material used to help start a fire in a grate; **fire-line** (*a*) a fire-break; (*b*) a fire station telephone line for operation (not administrative) use; **fire-master** †(*a*) an officer of artillery who superintended the manufacture of explosives or fireworks; (*b*) (chiefly *Sc.*) the chief officer of a fire brigade; **fire-new** *a.* (*arch.*) brand-new; **fire-office** an office or company dealing in fire insurance; **fire-opal** a girasol; **fire-pan** a receptacle for holding or carrying fire; a brazier, a portable grate; **fire pink** a N. American campion, *Silene virginica*, with narrow scarlet petals; **fire-plough** a simple device for making fire, similar to a fire-drill; *fire-plug*: see PLUG *n.* 2; **fire-policy** a certificate from a fire-office guaranteeing compensation in case of fire; **fire-position** *Mil.* the position from which an attacking force opens fire during an advance; **fire-power** (*a*) *Mil.* the ability of the guns and missiles of a military force to inflict destruction; (*b*) *fig.* financial, emotional, or intellectual strength; **fire-practice** = *fire-drill* (b) above; **fireproof** *a.* & *v.t.* (make) able to resist fire or great heat; **fireproofing** (*a*) making proof against fire; (*b*) material used to make something fireproof; **fire-raid** an air raid with incendiary bombs; **fire-raiser** an arsonist; **fire-raising** arson, incendiarism; **fire-ranger** *N. Amer.* an official who keeps watch against the occurrence of forest fires; **fire-red** *a.* & *n.* (*a*) *adj.* red like fire; reddened by fire; (*b*) *n.* (*Comm.*) a brilliant red pigment with a strong resistance to oil and light; **fire-risk** (*a*) the risk of loss by fire; (*b*) the obligation of a fire-insurance company to make good loss by fire; (*c*) a property insured against fire, *esp.* one which is likely to go on fire; an object, state of affairs, etc., conducive to the outbreak of a fire; **fire-room** (*a*) a room containing a fireplace; (*b*) the furnace-room of a building or stokehold of a ship; **fire sale** a sale of goods (freq. at low prices) remaining after the destruction of commercial premises by fire; **fire-screen** (*a*) a movable screen to keep off the direct heat of a fire; (*b*) = *fire-guard* (a) above; (*c*) an ornamental screen placed in front of a fireplace when the fire is unlit; **fire-ship** (*a*) *Hist.* a ship loaded with combustibles etc. and set adrift among enemy ships etc. to ignite and destroy them; (*b*) *arch. slang* a person with venereal disease; a prostitute; **fire-shovel**: for putting coal etc. on a fire or for removing coal or ashes; **fire station** a building where a fire brigade is based, housing fire engines etc.; **fire-step** = FIRING-*step*; **fire-stick** (*a*) a burning brand; (*b*) = *fire-drill* (a) above; (*c*) an implement for stirring up a fire; **fire-storm** (*a*) *poet.* a storm of fire; (*b*) an intense conflagration into which surrounding air is drawn with great force, esp. resulting from incendiary or nuclear bombing; **fire-swallower** = FIRE-EATER 1; **fire-tongs**: for grasping coal etc.; **fire-trap** a building etc. without proper fire exits and in which a fire, once started, would spread easily; **fire-tree** *NZ* = POHUTUKAWA; **fire-vessel** (*a*) a receptacle for fire; (*b*) *Hist.* = *fire-ship* (a) above; **fire-walk** the ceremony of fire-walking; **fire-walker** a person who takes part in a fire-walk; **fire-walking** walking barefoot over hot stones, ashes, etc., a religious rite in Fiji and elsewhere, and formerly an ordeal in European countries; **fire wall** a fireproof wall to inhibit or prevent the spread of fire; **fire warden** *N. Amer.* an official employed to prevent or extinguish fires; **fire-watcher** a person engaged in fire-watching; **fire-watching** (*a*) tending a fire; (*b*) keeping watch for fires, esp. those caused by bombs; **fire-water** *colloq.* strong alcoholic liquor; **fireweed** any of several plants that spring up on burnt land; *spec.* rosebay willowherb; **firewoman** a female fire-fighter; **firewood** wood prepared for burning, fuel; **fire-worship** the treatment of fire as a god; *pop.* Zoroastrianism; **fire-worshipper** a person who treats fire as a god; *pop.* a Zoroastrian.

fire /ˈfʌɪə/ *v.* [OE *fȳrian*, f. FIRE *n.*] †**1** *v.t.* Supply with material for a fire. Only in OE. **2** *v.t.* Inspire, inflame; stimulate (the imagination); fill (a person) with enthusiasm. ME. **3** *v.t.* Set fire to with the intention of damaging or destroying. LME. **b** Light, kindle, burn, (a beacon, an explosive, waste vegetation, etc.). LME. **4** *v.t.* Light (gunpowder); discharge or let off (a gun, firework, etc.); explode (a mine). E16. **b** Eject or propel (a shot, bullet, or other missile) from or as from a gun etc. L16. **c** Produce or deliver (a broadside, salute, etc.) by discharge of guns. M19. **d** *fig.* Deliver (a speech, question, look, etc.) in a sharp explosive manner. M19. **5** *v.i.* **a** Of a gun etc.: go off. M16. **b** Discharge a gun or other firearm; shoot. M17. **6** *v.t.* Drive away or out by or as if by fire. (Foll. by *out.*) Now *rare* or *obs.* M16. **7 a** *v.i.* Become excited or inflamed. M16. **b** *v.t.* & *i.* Make or become hot or inflamed. *rare.* L17. **8** *v.t.* & *i.* (Cause to) glow or redden as if on fire. L16. **9** *v.i.* Of an explosive etc.: catch fire, be ignited. E17. **b** Of (a cylinder in) an internal-combustion engine: undergo ignition of its fuel. L19. **10** *v.t. Farriery.* Burn, cauterize. E17. **11** *v.t.* Subject to the action or effect of fire; bake (pottery etc.); dry or cure (tea or tobacco) by artificial heat. M17. **12 a** *v.t.* Supply (a furnace, engine, boiler, power station) with fuel. M18. **b** *v.i.* Make up a fire; light the fire of a furnace. Also foll. by *up.* M19. **c** *v.i.* Light a pipe, cigar, etc. Also foll. by *up. colloq.* M19. **13** *v.t.* & *i.* Of flax: be or become covered with black spots as if burnt. L18. **14** *Photogr.* **a** *v.t.* Release (the shutter of a camera). L19. **b** *v.i.* Take a photograph. Also foll. by *away, off.* L19. **15** *v.t.* Expel (a person) forcibly; dismiss, discharge. Also (*US*) foll. by *out.* L19.

2 R. K. NARAYAN Dead and decaying things seemed to .. fire his imagination. M. MOORCOCK To fire me with a sense of wonder at the marvels of science and technology. **3** F. O'BRIEN They made an attempt to fire the complete building by igniting a number of armchairs. **b** A. UTTLEY Hedges were trimmed and the cuttings fired in numerous little bonfires. **4** F. MARRYAT Edward fired his gun into the body of the man. **b** D. CARNEGIE Crowley .. grabbed the .. revolver, and fired another bullet into the prostrate body. P. CAMPBELL The shots had .. been fired near Portobello Bridge. **d** F. TUOHY Nor were the questions he now fired at the girl evidence of any real curiosity. **5b** E. HEMINGWAY The pistol did not fire. F. FITZGERALD Nhu's own troops were refusing to fire on the crowds. *fire into the brown* (*of them*): see BROWN *n.* 1. **7a** W. IRVING She fired up at the arrogance of the squire. **8** A. LANG Watching .. the dawn as it fired. **9b** *fire on all cylinders*: see CYLINDER 3. **12a** H. FAST She's built to be fired by coal. **14a** *Diver* All you have to do is load the film .. frame your subject, and fire the shutter. **15** A. MILLER When a man gets old you fire him, you have to, he can't do the work. P. MORTIMER He resigned before Reuters fired him. *hire and fire*: see HIRE *v.* 1.

With advs. in specialized senses: **fire away** begin or go ahead (esp. speaking), in a rapid and energetic manner; (see also sense 14b above). **fire up** (*a*) show sudden anger; (*b*) *N. Amer. colloq.* stimulate, fill with enthusiasm; (see also senses 12b, c above).

fireable *a.* able to be fired or set on fire M17.

firearm /ˈfʌɪərɑːm/ *n.* M17. [f. FIRE *n.* + ARM *n.*[2]] A portable weapon from which a missile is propelled by means of an explosive charge; a rifle, gun, pistol, etc. Usu. in *pl.*

fire-ball /ˈfʌɪəbɔːl/ *n.* LME. [f. FIRE *n.* + BALL *n.*[1]] **1** *Mil. Hist.* A ball filled with combustibles or explosives used as a projectile to damage an enemy or enemy fortifications. LME. **2** A ball of flame or fire; *spec.* (*a*) a large meteor; (*b*) a ball of lightning; (*c*) a ball of flame resulting from a nuclear explosion. M16. **3** *Her.* A bomb or grenade with fire issuing from the top, bottom, and both sides. M19. **4** *fig.* A very energetic person; a person with a fiery temper. M20.

fire-boot /ˈfʌɪəbuːt/ *n. obs.* exc. *Hist.* Also †**-bote**. L15. [f. FIRE *n.* + BOOT *n.*[1]] *Law.* The supplying of fuel to a fire; wood used for this purpose; the right of a tenant to take firewood from the landlord's estate.

firebox /ˈfʌɪəbɒks/ *n.* M16. [f. FIRE *n.* + BOX *n.*[2]] †1 A tinder-box. M16–M19. †2 A kind of firework. Only in M17. 3 The fuel-chamber of a steam boiler. L18.

firebrand /ˈfʌɪəbrand/ *n.* ME. [f. FIRE *n.* + BRAND *n.*] 1 A piece of burning wood. ME. 2 *fig.* A person who or thing which kindles strife, inflames passion, etc. LME. †3 = *brand-mark* (a) s.v. BRAND *n.* L17–E18.

2 W. HOLTBY Astell . . was a firebrand, a troubler of the peace.

fire-drake /ˈfʌɪədreɪk/ *n.* OE. [f. FIRE *n.* + DRAKE *n.*[1]] 1 *Gmc Mythol.* A fiery dragon. OE. †2 A fiery meteor. M16–M19. †3 A person with a fiery red nose. *rare* (Shakes.). Only in E17.

fire-eater /ˈfʌɪəriːtə/ *n.* L17. [f. FIRE *n.* + EATER.] 1 An entertainer who eats or pretends to eat fire. L17. 2 A person who is fond of fighting or quarrelling; (now *rare*) a duellist. E19.

fire-eating *ppl a.* that eats fire E19.

fire-fang /ˈfʌɪəfaŋ/ *v.* & *n.* *obs.* exc. *dial.* & *US.* E16. [f. FIRE *n.* + FANG *v.*[1]] A *v.t.* Scorch; damage (esp. barley, oats) by overheating; burn. Chiefly as *fire-fanged* ppl a. E16. B *n.* The state of being fire-fanged; damage from overheating. M18.

fire-flaught /ˈfʌɪəflɔːt, -flaxt/ *n.* Orig. *Sc.* Now *rare.* LME. [f. FIRE *n.* + FLAUGHT *n.*[1]] 1 Lightning, a flash of lightning. LME. 2 *transf.* A sudden burst or rush; a fiery glance. M17.

fire-iron /ˈfʌɪərʌɪən/ *n.* ME. [f. FIRE *n.* + IRON *n.*] †1 An implement of iron etc. for striking a light. ME–M16. 2 In *pl.* Implements for tending a domestic fire, usu. tongs, poker, and shovel. M17.

fireless /ˈfʌɪəlɪs/ *a.* L16. [f. FIRE *n.* + -LESS.] 1 Without energy, life, or imagination. L16. 2 Without a fire; devoid of fire. M17.

Comb.: **fireless cooker** an insulated chamber able to be brought to and maintained at a temperature high enough for cooking in; a haybox.

firelock /ˈfʌɪəlɒk/ *n.* M16. [f. FIRE *n.* + LOCK *n.*[2]] *Hist.* 1 A gunlock in which sparks were produced by friction or percussion to ignite the priming. M16. 2 A musket having this type of lock. L16. 3 A soldier armed with such a weapon. M17.

fireman /ˈfʌɪəmən/ *n.* Pl. **-men.** E17. [f. FIRE *n.* + MAN *n.*] 1 A person who uses firearms. E17. 2 A person who attends to a furnace or to the fire of a steam engine, steamship, etc.; a stoker. M17. 3 A person whose task is to extinguish fires, a fire-fighter. E18. 4 *Mining.* A person whose duty is to check mines for firedamp, supervise blasting, etc. M19.

2 R. P. WARREN The fireman . . bent to heave a shovelful of coal into the firebox door. 3 S. SPENDER A few scores of firemen . . relieved of fire-fighting duties. *visiting fireman*: see VISITING *ppl a.*

fireplace /ˈfʌɪəpleɪs/ *n.* L17. [f. FIRE *n.* + PLACE *n.*[1]] A place for a fire, *esp.* a partially enclosed place at the base of a chimney where a domestic fire is situated; the structure surrounding or area in front of this.

firer /ˈfʌɪərə/ *n.* E17. [f. FIRE *v.* + -ER[1].] 1 An incendiary, an arsonist. Now *rare* or *obs.* E17. 2 A person who sets anything on fire; a person who fires clay etc. E19. 3 A person who discharges a firearm; a gun etc. that fires in a specified way. M19.

fireside /ˈfʌɪəsʌɪd/ *n.* & *a.* M16. [f. FIRE *n.* + SIDE *n.*] A *n.* 1 Orig., the space under a chimney to the right and left of a domestic fire, occupied by two seats. Now, the space around a fireplace. M16. 2 *collect.* Those who sit around one's fire; one's household. *arch.* E18. 3 One's home, home life. M19.

B *adj.* 1 Situated beside or pertaining to a domestic fire. M18. 2 Intimate, relaxed; *esp.* designating an informal political talk broadcast to the nation. Orig. *US.* E19.

2 *Observer* Fireside chats from Number 10 Downing Street. *New Yorker* He talked of his private meetings with Gorbachev . . the 'fireside summit'.

fire-stone /ˈfʌɪəstəʊn/ *n.* OE. [f. FIRE *n.* + STONE *n.*] 1 A stone used in striking fire, *esp.* iron pyrites. Also, the flint of a firelock. *arch.* OE. 2 A stone that resists the action of fire, used for lining furnaces, ovens, etc. L15. b Any of certain soft calcareous sandstones. *local.* E18. 3 A hearth-stone. Now *rare.* E17.

firework /ˈfʌɪəwəːk/ *n.* M16. [f. FIRE *n.* + WORK *n.*] I 1 A combustible or explosive composition for use in war; a machine charged with such a composition. Now *rare* or *obs.* M16. 2 A device producing spectacular effects by the use of combustibles; a rocket, squib, etc. L16. †3 A set arrangement of such devices, forming a pictorial or ornamental design. L16–L18. 4 In *pl.* & †*sing.* A colourful and spectacular display of such devices. L16. b *fig.* In *pl.* A display of wit, passion, anger, etc. L17. †II 5 Work done by, in, or with fire. Only in 17. 6 A place where fuel is obtained; an apparatus for working with fire. Only in 17.

fireworker *n.* †(*a*) an artillery officer or other person who is concerned with explosives in war; (*b*) a person who makes fireworks: E17.

firing /ˈfʌɪərɪŋ/ *n.* LME. [f. FIRE *v.* + -ING[1].] 1 The action of setting something on fire. LME. b The action of catching fire. *rare.* L16. c The ignition of the fuel in a cylinder of an internal-combustion engine. L19. 2 Material for a fire, fuel. L15. 3 The discharging of a firearm etc. E16. b *Campanol.* The ringing of all the bells in a peal at once. L18. 4 *Farriery.* Cauterizing. M17. 5 The sudden drying and death of the leaves of a plant. L17. 6 The action of subjecting something to heat or fire; baking, curing. L18. 7 The action of supplying a furnace, boiler, etc. with fire or fuel. L19.

1 W. COBBETT Those meetings led . . to the firing and pulling down of houses. 3 R. BEATSON Night coming on, the firing on both sides ceased.

Comb.: **firing-line** the front line of troops in a battle; *fig.* the forefront in any conflict; **firing-party** a firing-squad; **firing-point** (*a*) the temperature at which a flammable oil is liable to spontaneous combustion; (*b*) in target shooting, the position from which the shots are fired; **firing-squad** a group of soldiers detailed to fire a salute at a military funeral or to shoot a condemned person; **firing-step** a board or ledge in a trench on which a soldier stands to fire.

firk /fəːk/ *v.* Also **ferk.** [OE *fercian, færcian,* prob. f. *fær*: see FARE *n.*[1]] †1 *v.t.* Bring, carry, conduct. OE–LME. 2 †a *v.refl.* & *i.* Urge oneself forward; move quickly, hasten. ME–L16. b *v.i.* Move about briskly; dance, frisk about, fidget. *obs.* exc. *Sc.* & *dial.* L16. 3 *v.t.* Urge, press hard; drive, drive away. Now only foll. by *off, out, up.* LME. 4 *v.t.* Beat, whip, trounce. *arch.* M16. †5 *v.t.* Cheat, rob; get (money, a living) by cheating. E17–E18.

4 G. A. SALA A poor rogue soundly firked at the post. 5 T. DEKKER As from poor clients lawyers firk money.

firker *n.* M17.

firkin /ˈfəːkɪn/ *n.* LME. [Prob. f. MDu. dim. of *vierde* fourth: see -KIN.] 1 A small cask for liquids, fish, butter, etc., originally containing a quarter of a barrel. LME. 2 A unit of capacity equal to half a kilderkin. LME.

firlot /ˈfəːlɒt/ *n.* *Sc.* Now *rare* or *obs.* L15. [AL *firlota, ferlota, ferthelota* (13) prob. f. ON *fjórði hlotr* fourth part: see FOURTH, LOT *n.*] (A container used as) a measure of capacity for corn etc. equal to a quarter of a boll.

firm /fəːm/ *n.* L16. [Sp. & (in senses 2, 3) It. *firma,* f. med.L (cf. FARM *n.*), f. L *firmare* strengthen, (in late L) confirm by one's signature, f. *firmus* FIRM *a.*] †1 One's autograph signature. L16–M18. †2 The name under which the business of a commercial enterprise is transacted. M18–M19. 3 A partnership or company for carrying on a business; a group of people working together, orig. (*derog.*) to further their own interests; a (criminal) organization or gang; a group of hospital doctors and their assistants. L18.

2 C. E. RIDDELL Trading under the firm of 'Grant & Co.' 3 R. KIPLING Wressley was the working-member of the Foreign Office firm. M. GIROUARD The house was . . decorated by the newly founded firm of Watts and Company. **long firm** a group of swindlers obtaining goods without paying. **(the) old firm** *colloq.* (the) established and reliable partnership.

firm /fəːm/ *a.* & *adv.* ME. [(O)Fr. *ferme* f. L *firmus.*] A *adj.* 1 Securely fixed; not easily moved; steady, stable. ME. 2 Not shaking or wavering; steady or controlled (esp. in motion). LME. 3 Fixed, settled, established; (of a decree, law, etc.) immutable; (of an offer) not liable to cancellation after acceptance. LME. †b Assured, secure (as a possession etc.). LME–M18. †c Certain, sure; valid. LME–L17. 4 Of a person, personal attribute, or action: not easily moved or swayed; steadfast; unwavering; resolute, determined. LME. 5 Of solid or compact structure or texture; resistant to pressure or impact; hard, sound, undecayed. LME. †6 Healthy, robust. Cf. INFIRM *a.* L16–L18. 7 Of a price, commodity, etc.: maintaining a level or value. M19.

1 OED Try whether the post is firm in the ground. C. S. LEWIS All the knots which you wished to be firm would come untied. †**firm land** dry land, solid earth; the mainland; *terra firma. on firm ground*: see GROUND *n.* 2 W. C. BRYANT O aged man, would that thy knees were firm As is thy purpose. R. L. STEVENSON He took my hand in his large firm grasp. 3 H. MACMILLAN In spite of some misunderstandings, the old alliance remained firm. 4 M. EDGEWORTH 'I am the count', replied he, in a firm tone. T. S. ELIOT Be firm with her . . Assert your right to a little privacy. J. RATHBONE They remained firm in the Catholic faith suffering persecution . . and like misfortunes. 5 L. DEIGHTON Its subsoil is firm enough to take the weight of a bombing plane. U. BENTLEY He had a firm, well-disciplined body. 6 POPE Lamented youth! in life's firm bloom he fell. 7 J. ARCHER Gold was still climbing and the Deutschmark . . remained firm, while the dollar was on the retreat.

Comb.: **firmware** *Computing* a permanent form of software built into certain kinds of computers.

B *adv.* Firmly; so as to be or remain firm. Now chiefly in *hold firm, stand firm.* ME.

firmish *a.* somewhat firm M19. **firmly** *adv.* LME. **firmness** *n.* M16.

firm /fəːm/ *v.* ME. [Partly (either through Fr. *fermer* or directly) f. L *firmare* (see FIRM *n.*); partly a new formation on FIRM *a.*] I *v.t.* 1 †a Establish, confirm, encourage (a person etc.); ratify, settle, strengthen (an agreement, title, etc.). ME–E19. †b Make (a document) valid by seal, signature, etc.; sign (one's name). E16–L17. c Foll. by *up*: make immutable or not liable to cancellation, confirm. *colloq.* L20. 2 Make firm or fast; fix securely (esp. plants *in* soil); hold firmly. LME. 3 Make compact or resistant to pressure; solidify. Also foll. by *up.* L16.

1 DRYDEN Jove has firm'd it with an Awfull Nod. b DRYDEN Your Father's hand, Firm'd with his Signet. c SNOO WILSON We'll firm up the deal later. 2 *Practical Gardening* Firm the plant well in but don't over compact the soil. 3 W. FOLKINGHAM Boggie and spungie grounds are . . firmed by frequent ouerflowing them with Fords.

II *v.i.* 4 Become firm; (of prices etc.) stabilize, improve after a decline. Also foll. by *up.* L19.

4 *Timber Trades Journal* The Scandinavian market, . . weak over recent months, is now showing signs of firming. R. WILLIAMS The whole picture was beginning to firm up in my mind.

firmament /ˈfəːməm(ə)nt/ *n.* Now *literary.* ME. [(O)Fr. f. L *firmamentum,* f. *firmare*: see FIRM *a.*, -MENT.] 1 The arch or vault of heaven with its clouds and stars; the sky, the heavens. Also formerly, heaven as God's dwelling place. ME. †2 A celestial sphere in Ptolemaic astronomy, *spec.* that of the fixed stars. ME–M17. †3 Anything which strengthens or supports; a substratum, a foundation. LME–E18.

1 J. G. FARRELL A low bank of cloud . . was slowly mounting over the entire firmament, concealing the stars. *fig.*: J. CHEEVER High in her firmament of gin, she looked critically at her brother.

firmamental /fəːməˈmɛnt(ə)l/ *a.* M16. [f. prec. + -AL[1].] 1 Of or pertaining to the firmament. M16. 2 Of the nature of a supporting framework or substratum. Now *rare* or *obs.* L17.

firman /ˈfəːmən, fəːˈmɑːn/ *n.* Also **farman** /ˈfɑːmən, fəˈmɑːn/. E17. [Pers. *firmān* = Skt *pramāṇa* (right) measure, standard, authority.] An edict or order issued by a Near Eastern ruler or official, esp. a grant, licence, passport, or permit.

†firmitude *n.* M16–E18. [L *firmitudo*, f. *firmus* FIRM *a.*: see -TUDE.] Firmness, solidity, strength, resolution.

†firmity *n.* LME–E18. [(O)Fr. *fermeté*, f. as FIRM *a.* Later refash. after L *firmitas*: see -ITY.] Firmness, solidity, stability; allegiance.

†firmless *a. poet.* L16–M18. [f. FIRM *a.* + -LESS.] Unsteady, shifting.

firn /fɪən/ *n.* M19. [G f. OHG *firni* old, rel. to OS *fern* past, *forn* formerly, ON *forn* ancient (Sw. *forn* former).] = NÉVÉ.

firry /ˈfəːri/ *a.* E19. [f. FIR + -Y[1].] Having many firs; of or pertaining to the fir.

first /fəːst/ *a.*, *adv.*, & *n.* (*ordinal numeral*). [OE *fyr(e)st* = OFris. *ferost*, *-est*, *ferst*, OHG *furist* (*furisto* prince, whence G *Fürst*), ON *fyrstr*, f. Gmc superl., f. IE base also of L *primus*, Gk *prōtos*, Skt *prathama*.] A *adj.* 1 Preceding all others in time, order, series, succession, etc.; earliest in occurrence, existence, etc.; basic; that is number one in a series; (represented by 1st). OE. b Occurring or presenting itself next after a given point of time (expressed or implied). E17. 2 Foremost or most advanced in position. OE. 3 Foremost in rank, importance, or excellence. ME. b In official titles: having precedence over all others. M18.

1 S. JOHNSON Each of the six first lines of the *Iliad* might lose two syllables. T. HARDY Mr Clare . . whose first wife had died . . married a second late in life. SCOTT FITZGERALD I thought of the first sheep I ever remember seeing. I. MURDOCH An April evening . . the big trees in first leaf. DAY LEWIS Memories from my first two years. G. GORDON For the first few years of his working life . . he had had to work every second Saturday. *first conjugation*, *first declension*, etc. b MORTIMER COLLINS I shall get back to London by the first train. 2 OED The first horse in the race. 3 J. OZELL Courage, a General's first Quality. H. MARTINEAU I was told a great deal about 'the first people in Boston'. b *first cellist*, *first lieutenant*, *First Lord of the Treasury*, *First Sea Lord*, *first violin*, etc.

B *adv.* 1 Before anyone or anything else, in time, rank, serial order, etc. OE. †b Originally. OE–E18. 2 Before another specified or implied thing, time, event, etc.; as the first point in a topic, argument, etc., in the first place. ME. b In preference to something else; rather; more likely. LME. 3 For the first time, then and not earlier. ME. 4 *ellipt.* Travelling first class. L19.

1 SCOTT FITZGERALD After greeting Rosemary and her mother he waited for them to speak first. *Proverb*: First come, first served. 2 A. R. PENNINGTON It is impossible for the priest to remit the sins of any unless they are first remitted by Christ. J. BUCHAN She could scarcely refuse to give him breakfast first. J. STEINBECK He . . slipped off first one shoe and then the other. b BROWNING Die? He'll bribe a gaoler or break prison first. 3 T. HARDY He . . surveyed people up and down when first making their acquaintance. G. GREENE In this story of . . Hunca-Munca . . the unmistakable Potter style first appears.

C *n.* I 1 The first person or thing of a category, series, etc., identified contextually, as day of the month, (following a proper name) person, esp. monarch or pope, of the specified name, base in baseball, etc. ME. 2 *The* first part, *the* beginning. LME. 3 *Her.* *The* tincture first mentioned in a blazon. M16.

1 OED He is always the first to find fault. S. BECKETT I was stopped by a second policeman, similar in all respects to the first. 2 F. MARRYAT We shall be able to stem the first of the flood. D. H. LAWRENCE It was wrong from the first It was wrong to begin with.

II 4 *gen.* A person who or thing which is first. L16. 5 *Mus.* The highest part of a duet, trio, etc. L18. 6 In *pl.* Goods of the best quality. E19. 7 (A person having) a place in the first class of an examination; (the winner of) first place in a race etc. M19. 8 A first-class compartment, carriage, or section, on a train etc. E20. 9 A first edition (of a book). E20. 10 = *first gear* below. E20. 11 The first known or discovered example of a thing; a first instance or occurrence, esp. of something notable. M20.

7 S. SPENDER To gain a First, a Scholarship, . . seemed as difficult as scaling some great height. J. DIDION She took all the jumping firsts at the . . horse show. 11 J. F. STRAKER 'I'm sorry about that, Paul'. That made another first: they had not used Christian names before.

Phrases etc.: **at first** at the beginning. **come in first** win a race. *double first*: see DOUBLE *a.* & *adv.* **feet first** with the feet in front. **first and foremost** first(ly) and most important(ly). **first and last** taking one thing with another, all in all, from start to finish. **first in, first out** (*a*) (of a system of accounting) in which the goods first acquired by a company are valued as though they are the first to be sold; (*b*) *Computing* (designating or pertaining to) a procedure in which the item removed from a buffer, queue, etc., is always the one that has been in the longest. **first of all** before anyone or anything else, firstly. **first off** *colloq.* (orig. *US*) at first, to begin with. **first or last** sooner or later. **first past the post** (designating) the winner of an election by virtue of receiving the most votes though perhaps not having an absolute majority. **first up** *Austral.* first of all, at the first attempt. *first-wicket partnership*: see WICKET 3b. **from first to last** throughout. **from the first** from the beginning. *for the first time*: see FOR *prep.* **head first** with the head in front. *in the first flight*: see FLIGHT *n.*[1] *in the first instance*: see INSTANCE *n.* **in the first place** first, firstly; to begin with. *of the first head*: see HEAD *n.* **of the first order** [Fr. *du premier ordre*] outstanding, excellent. *of the first water*: see WATER *n.* 10b. **the first** the beginning; even one elementary thing (*about*).

Special collocations & comb.: (As ordinal.) Forming compound ordinal numerals with multiples of ten, as *forty-first* (*41st*), *five-thousand-and-first* (*5001st*), etc. (As adj.) **first aid** help given to an injured person (until medical treatment is available); *first-aid post*, a place where first aid is available. **first-aider** a person trained or skilled in first aid. *first base*: see BASE *n.*[1] *first blood*: see BLOOD *n.* *first blush*: see BLUSH *n.* 1. **first-born** *a.* & *n.* (*a*) *adj.* that is born first, eldest; (*b*) *n.* one's first or eldest child. *first brush*: see BRUSH *n.*[2] 1. *First Cause*: see CAUSE *n.* *first chop*: see CHOP *n.*[3] **first coat** a first layer of paint etc. **first comer** a first or earliest arrival. *First Consul*: see CONSUL 2. **first cost** = *prime cost* s.v. PRIME *a.* *first cousin*: see COUSIN *n.* 1. **first cross** the crossing of two pure breeds; an offspring of such a cross. **first day** (*a*) Sunday, esp. among the Society of Friends; (*b*) the first day of issue of stamps etc.; (*first-day cover*: see COVER *n.*[1]). **first degree** *spec.* (*a*) the least serious category of burn; (*b*) the most serious category of crime (*principal in the first degree*: see PRINCIPAL *n.* 2a). **first-degree** *a.* (*a*) (of a burn) affecting only the epidermis; (*b*) *US* (of murder) premeditated and without mitigating circumstances. *first derivative*: see DERIVATIVE *n.* 3. **first edition** the first printed form in which a book etc. is published; the whole number of copies in this form; one copy in this form. **first finger** the finger next to the thumb. **first floor** the floor immediately above the ground floor; *N. Amer.* the ground floor. *First Folio*: see FOLIO *n.* **first-foot** *n.* & *v.* (chiefly *Sc.*) (*a*) *n.* the first person to cross the threshold in the New Year; (*b*) *v.i.* be such a person; go on a round of visits as a New Year begins (chiefly as *first-footing* vbl n.). **first-footer** a person who first-foots or goes first-footing. **first-fruits** (*a*) the first products of agriculture for the season, esp. as offered to God, *fig.* the first results of work etc.; (*b*) *Hist.* a payment to a superior by the new holder of an office, esp. an ecclesiastical office. **first gear** the lowest or bottom forward gear in a motor vehicle, bicycle, etc. **first-generation** *a.* (of a computer) distinguished by the use of vacuum tubes and belonging essentially to the period 1945–55. **first good** = SUMMUM BONUM. *first intention*. **first lady** the most important lady; *US spec.* the wife of the President, or another appointed woman acting as hostess for him. **first language** one's native language. *first lesson*: see LESSON *n.* 2. *first* LIEUTENANT. **first light** the time when light first appears in the morning. **first line** (orig. *Mil.*) the line of fighting forces or *fig.* the group of people who are most advanced or of the highest quality. *First Lord of the Treasury*: see TREASURY. **first love** (the emotion felt) the first time one falls in love; the person with whom one falls in love for the first time; one's favourite occupation, possession, etc. *first* MOVER. **first name** a person's personal given or Christian name, as opp. to his or her surname (*on first-name terms*, sufficiently friendly to address each other by first names). **first-name** *v.t.* address by first name, be on first-name terms with. **first night** the first public performance of a play etc. **first-nighter** a person who attends a first night or first nights. **first offender** an offender against the law against whom no previous conviction is recorded. **first officer** (*a*) the mate on a merchant ship; (*b*) the second in command to the captain on an aircraft. *first person*: see PERSON *n.* 6, 7. **first position** (*a*) *Mus.* the lowest possible position of the hand on the finger-board of a stringed instrument; (*b*) *Ballet* a disposition of the body in which the legs are together with heels touching, and the toes are turned out at a right angle. *first post*: see POST *n.*[6] *first quarter*: see QUARTER *n.* 7b. **first reading** the first of three successive occasions on which a bill must have been presented to a legislature before it becomes law, permitting its introduction. *first refusal*: see REFUSAL 2. **first school** a primary school intended for children between the ages of 5 and 8 or 9. *First Sea Lord*: see SEA. *First Secretary*: see SECRETARY *n.* **first sergeant** *US* the highest ranking non-commissioned officer in a company. *first sound*: see SOUND *n.*[2] *first storey*: see STOREY *n.* **first strike** an aggressive attack with nuclear weapons before their use by the enemy. *first string*: see STRING *n.* **first thing** (*a*) *the* most elementary or rudimentary thing (freq. in *not know the first thing about*); (*b*) *adv.* (*colloq.*) before anything else; (*c*) *first things first*, the most important things before any others. **first-time buyer** a person seeking to buy a home who has not previously owned one and so has none to sell. **first-timer** a person who does or is something for the first time. **First War** = *First World War* s.v. WORLD. *first water*: see WATER *n.* 10. **First World** (*a*) the US and USSR; (*b*) the developed countries apart from the (former) Communist bloc. *First World War*: see WORLD *n.*

firstness *n.* LME.

first class /fəːs(t) ˈklɑːs; *as adj. also* ˈfəːs(t)klɑːs/ *n. phr.*, *a.*, & *adv.* As adj. & adv. usu. **first-class**. L18. [f. FIRST *a.* + CLASS *n.*] A *n. phr.* The first (usu. the highest) of a series of classes into which people or things are grouped; a set of people or things grouped together as better than others; the best accommodation in a train, boat, aircraft, etc.; mail given preferential treatment; a compartment of a train etc. offering the best accommodation; (a person with) a place in the highest division of an examination list. L18.

B *adj.* Belonging to, achieving, travelling by, etc., the first class; of the best quality, very good; of the highest order. M19.

R. K. NARAYAN This threatened to develop into a first-class crisis. F. FORSYTH Harcourt-Smith was of the university intake, with a first-class degree. *Times* The price of the first class stamp has remained at 17p since September 1984.

Comb.: **first-classman** a person with a first-class degree.

C *adv.* By first-class accommodation in a train, boat, aircraft, etc.; by first-class mail; *colloq.* excellently. L19.

first hand /fəːstˈhand; *as adj. also* ˈfəːsthand/ *n. phr.*, *a.*, & *adv.* As adj. & adv. (now usu.) **firsthand**. M18. [f. FIRST *a.* + HAND *n.*] A *n. phr. at first hand*, directly from the first source, without intermediate agency. M18.

B *adj.* Of or pertaining to the first source, original; coming direct from the first source, derived from personal experience. M18.

H. GUNTRIP Those who criticize psychoanalysis rarely show firsthand knowledge of events in the field later than . . about 1908.

C *adv.* Directly from the first source, at first hand. M19.

S. KNIGHT The prostitutes had learned first-hand of a secret.

firstling /ˈfəːs(t)lɪŋ/ *n.* & *a.* M16. [f. FIRST *a.* + -LING[1].] A *n.* The first product or result of something; the first offspring of a season. Usu. in *pl.* M16. B *attrib.* or as *adj.* That is the first product or result; first-born. E17.

firstly /ˈfəːs(t)li/ *adv.* & *n.* M16. [f. FIRST *a.* + -LY[2].] A *adv.* As the first point in a topic, argument, etc.; in the first place. M16. B *n.* A use of the word *firstly*. *rare.* L17.

first-rate /fəːs(t)ˈreɪt; *as adj. also* ˈfəːs(t)reɪt/ *n.*, *a.*, & *adv.* Also (usual form in sense A.1) **first rate**. M17. [f. FIRST *a.* + RATE *n.*[1]] A *n.* 1 *Hist.* The highest of the rates or classes by which warships were distinguished according to the number of guns they carried. M17. 2 A warship of the first rate (*Hist.*); a person or thing of the highest class or rank (now *rare*). L17.

B *adj.* 1 *Hist.* Of a warship: of the first rate. L17. 2 Of the highest class or excellence; extremely good, excellent. *colloq.* M18.

2 M. E. G. DUFF As long as France remained a first-rate power. M. GORDON Her misfortune was to be a merely first-rate painter in an age of geniuses.

C *adv.* Excellently, very well. *colloq.* M19.

B. W. ALDISS 'You're looking first-rate' 'And you, Sicily evidently agrees with you'.

first-rater *n.* a first-rate person or thing E19.

firth /fəːθ/ *n.*[1] Chiefly *north. poet.* Now *rare* or *obs.* LME. [Metath. var. of FRITH *n.*[2]] A (hunting) forest; a coppice, a small wood.

firth /fəːθ/ *n.*[2] Orig. *Sc.* LME. [ON *fjǫrðr* FIORD: cf. FRITH *n.*[3]] An arm of the sea; a river estuary.

fisc /fɪsk/ *n.* Also (*Sc. Law*) **fisk**. L16. [Fr., or L FISCUS rush-basket, purse, treasury.] 1 *Hist.* Orig. the private treasury of the Roman emperors, later developing into a public treasury but retaining considerable imperial control. L16. b An exchequer. Now *rare*. L16. 2 *Sc. Law*. The public treasury or Crown to which estates lapse by escheat; the revenue to the Crown by escheat. Formerly also, the right of the Crown to the estate of a rebel. *obs.* exc. *Hist.* L17.

fiscal /ˈfɪsk(ə)l/ *a.* & *n.* M16. [Fr., or L *fiscalis*, f. *fiscus* treasury: see prec.] A *adj.* 1 Of or pertaining to a treasury. Now chiefly, of or pertaining to governmental financial matters. M16. 2 Of or pertaining to financial matters in general. Chiefly *US*. M19.

Special collocations: **fiscal agent** a bank or trust company appointed by a corporation etc. to act as its financial representative. **fiscal drag** *Econ.* (a deflationary effect on economic growth caused by) the tendency of tax yields to increase at a higher rate than inflation when tax allowances remain fixed. **fiscal engineer** *US* a specialist in fiscal engineering. **fiscal engineering** *US* management of the finances of a firm so as to take maximum advantage of tax exemptions etc. **fiscal year** (chiefly *N. Amer.*) a financial year (for the US Government, beginning 1 October (before 1976, 1 July)).

B *n.* 1 A legal official in any of various countries, having the function of public prosecutor and (in the Netherlands and formerly in Dutch Colonies) esp. concerned with revenue. Formerly also, an official of the treasury. M16. b *Sc.* = *procurator fiscal* s.v. PROCURATOR 3. L16. 2 [Afk. *fiskaal* = public official (cf. sense 1), hangman, from the birds' habit of impaling prey on thorns.] Any of a number of largely black and white African shrikes of the genus *Lanius*, spec. *L. collaris*. Freq. *fiscal shrike, bird*. Orig. *S. Afr.* L18. 3 A stamp given as a receipt for a payment of tax etc. M19. 4 A fiscal year (specified by a following date). Chiefly *US*. M20.

4 *National Observer* (*US*) Both houses . . approved a preliminary budget resolution setting forth targets . . for fiscal 1977, which begins Oct. 1.

fiscality /fɪˈskalɪti/ *n.* (*a*) exclusive or excessive regard to fiscal matters; (*b*) in *pl.*, fiscal matters: E19. **fiscally** *adv.* from a fiscal point of view M19.

Fischer-Tropsch /fɪʃəˈtrɒpʃ/ *n.* M20. [f. F. J. E. *Fischer* (1877–1948), and H. *Tropsch* (1889–1935), Ger. chemists.] *Chem.* Used *attrib.* to designate a process which produces hydrocarbons etc. through the catalytic hydrogenation of carbon monoxide.

fiscus /ˈfɪskəs/ *n.* Pl. **fisci** /ˈfɪskʌɪ/. M17. [L: see FISC.] = FISC 1, 1b.

H. ALLEN Coined silver dollars were lying idle in the Mexican fiscus.

fisgig *n.* & *a.* var. of FIZGIG *n.*[1] & *a.*

fish /fɪʃ/ *n.*[1] Pl. **-es** /-ɪz/, (usu.) same. [OE *fisċ* = OFris. *fisk*, OS, OHG *fisc* (Du. *visch*, G *Fisch*), ON *fiskr*, Goth. *fisks*, cogn. w. L *piscis*, f. IE.] 1 Orig., any animal living exclusively in water (now only as 2nd elem. of comb., as *crayfish*, *cuttlefish*, *jellyfish*, *shellfish*, and in *Cookery*). Now, any of a large and varied group of cold-blooded aquatic vertebrates possessing gills and fins. OE. b In full *tin fish*. A torpedo. *Naut. slang.* E20. c A dollar. *US slang*. E20. 2 (Usu. **F-**.) In *pl. The* constellation and zodiacal sign Pisces. OE. 3 The flesh of fish, esp. as food (opp. *flesh*, *fowl*). ME. 4 Usu. w. preceding (derog.) adj. A person. *colloq.* M18.

1 *angel-fish*, *angler-fish*, *bluefish*, *catfish*, *codfish*, *dogfish*, *hagfish*, *monkfish*, etc. c R. JESSUP Would a hundred fish do you? . . Would it be enough for the bus? 2 L. MACNEICE We all know you were born under the Fish. 4 P. SCOTT Her family . . were cold fish to a man.

Phrases: **a fish out of water** a person not in accustomed or preferred surroundings. *a nice, pretty, kettle of fish*: see KETTLE *n.* *be* FOOD *for fishes*. *blind fish*: see BLIND *a.* *bony fish*: see BONY *a.* *cartilaginous fish*: see CARTILAGINOUS 1. *cry stinking fish*: see STINKING *a.* **drink like a fish** drink (esp. alcohol) excessively. **feed the fishes** (*a*) be drowned; (*b*) be seasick. **fish and chips** fried fish with fried chipped potatoes. *Flying Fish*: see FLYING *ppl a.* **have other fish to fry** have more important business to attend to. *kettle of fish*: see KETTLE 1. **neither fish, nor flesh, nor good red herring** of indefinite character. *queer fish*: see QUEER *a.* & *n.* **royal fish** whales, porpoises, and sturgeon, if caught near the coast or cast ashore belonging to the Crown, or in the Duchy of Cornwall to the Prince of Wales. *soup and fish*: see SOUP *n.* *Southern Fish*: see SOUTHERN. *stinking fish*: see STINKING *a.* *walking fish*: see WALKING *ppl a.* *wet fish*: see WET *a.* *ye gods and little fishes*: see GOD *n.*

Comb.: **fish-basket** (*a*) a basket for carrying fish; (*b*) *US* a creel for catching fish; **fish-bowl** a (usu. glass) bowl in which to keep live (esp. ornamental) fish; **fish cake** a small cake of flaked or minced fish and mashed potato, often coated in batter or breadcrumbs and fried; **fish-carver** a knife for serving fish; **fish-day** (now *arch.* or *Hist.*) a day on which fish is eaten; a fast-day. **fish eagle** any eagle or other large bird of prey that feeds on fish; *spec.* any of certain eagles of the genus *Haliaeetus*; **fish-eaters** a knife and fork for eating fish; **fish-eye** *n.* & *a.* (*a*) *n.* a variety of moonstone; a diamond, an imitation diamond; (*b*) *adj.* (of a lens) wide-angled with a curved front; **fish farm** a place where fish are bred for food; **fish-farmer** a person engaged in fish-farming; **fish-farming** the breeding of fish for food; **fish finger** an oblong piece of flaked or minced fish coated in batter or breadcrumbs; **fish-fork** a small four-tined fork for eating fish; a large broad four-tined fork for serving fish; **fish-fry** (*a*) *US* a picnic where fish is fried and eaten; (*b*) = FRY *n.*[1] 3; **fishgarth** (now *arch.* & *dial.*) an enclosure on a river or the seashore for keeping or catching fish. **fish-glue** isinglass; **fish-hawk** the osprey; **fish-hook** (*a*) a bent piece of wire, usu. barbed, used for catching fish; (*b*) *Naut.* a hook forming part of the tackle used to raise an anchor; *fish-kettle*: see KETTLE 1; **fish-knife** a small broad blunt-edge knife for eating fish; a similar large knife for serving fish; **fish-ladder** a series of pools built like steps to enable fish to ascend a fall or dam; **fish louse** any of numerous small crustaceans of the class Branchiura, esp. of the genus *Argulus*, temporary parasites of fish; **fish-meal** ground dried fish used as fertilizer etc.; **fishmonger** a dealer in fish; **fishnet** *a.* & *n.* (*a*) *adj.* (of a garment or fabric, esp. of tights or stockings) open-meshed; (*b*) *n.* in *pl.*, fishnet tights or stockings; **fish-plate** *n.*[1] the perforated draining plate of a fish-kettle; **fish poison** (*a*) a substance toxic to fish; (*b*) any of certain plants, extracts of which have an intoxicating effect on fish; *esp.* Jamaican dogwood, *Piscidia piscipula*, and (*US*) buckeye; **fish-pond** a pond in which live fish are kept; *joc.* the sea, the ocean. **fish-pool** a pool in which live fish are kept; **fishpot** a wicker trap for eels, lobsters, etc.; **fish-sauce** a sauce made to be eaten with fish; **fish-slice** (*a*) a carving-knife for fish; (*b*) a cook's implement for turning or taking out fish or other (fried) food; **fish-sound** the swimming bladder of a fish; **fish supper** a dish of fried fish and chips to be eaten for supper; **fish-tank** a tank in which live (esp. ornamental) fish are kept; **fishwife** a woman who sells fish; a foul-mouthed abusive woman; **fishworm** *US* an earthworm; a worm used as bait for fish.

fishful *a.* containing many fish M16. **fishless** *a.* devoid of fish L16. **fishlike** *a.* resembling (that of) a fish E17. **fishling** *n.* (*rare*) a young or small fish M19.

fish /fɪʃ/ *n.*[2] Pl. **-es** /-ɪz/, same. E16. [Senses 1 & 2 prob., sense 3 certainly f. Fr. *fiche*, f. *ficher* fix, f. Proto-Romance intensive of L *figere* fix.] 1 A flat plate of iron, wood, etc. laid on a beam, rail, etc., or across a joint, to protect or strengthen it. E16. 2 *Naut.* A long piece of wood, concave on one side and convex on the other, lashed to a spar that has fractured or been weakened in order to strengthen it. M17. 3 A small flat piece of bone, ivory, etc., sometimes fish-shaped, used instead of money in card-games. E18.

Comb.: **fish-beam**: comprising an iron plate sandwiched between two beams; **fish-bolt** a bolt for fastening fish-plates and rails together; **fish-plate** *n.*[2] either of two plates holding rails together.

fish /fɪʃ/ *n.*[3] Pl. **-es** /-ɪz/, same. M17. [f. FISH *v.*[1]] 1 *Naut.* The purchase used in fishing an anchor. Earliest in *comb.* M17. 2 An act of fishing. *colloq.* L19. 3 An object accidentally left or dropped down the borehole of an oil well, hindering further drilling. M20.

fish /fɪʃ/ *v.*[1] [OE *fisċian* = OFris. *fiskia*, OS *fiskon* (Du. *vissen*), OHG *fiskōn* (G *fischen*), ON *fiska*, Goth. *fiskōn*, f. Gmc, f. base of FISH *n.*[1]] I *v.i.* 1 Catch or try to catch fish, esp. by using a net or hook and line etc. (Foll. by *for*.) OE. b *fig.* Try to convert other individuals to Christianity. LME. 2 Try to obtain or elicit a compliment, secret, etc., by indirect means or artifice. (Foll. by *for*.) M16. 3 Search for something in or under water; grope or feel in search for or *for* something concealed. M17. b (Try to) clear the borehole of a well of extraneous obstacles. E20. 4 Of water: provide (good or bad) sport for anglers. L19.

1 C. STEAD This waterside, where he had fished for gudgeon as a child. 2 J. AUSTEN I am not fishing; don't compliment me. 3 M. SHADBOLT Reg tossed the gun in the harbour. The police are still fishing for it. S. KING The pitchman sighed and fished inside his shirt. 4 J. BUCHAN Sim had always declared that it [a tarn] only fished well after rain.

II *v.t.* 5 Catch or try to catch (fish); collect (coral etc.) from the seabed. LME. 6 Try to catch fish in (a stretch of water); search (something) *for* (information, papers, etc.). LME. 7 Draw or pull (as) from water (foll. by *from*, *out*, *out of*, *up*); elicit, get *out* esp. by artifice, (a fact, opinion or secret). LME. b *Naut.* Draw the flukes of (an anchor) up close to the gunwale. L15. c Pull (a wire) through a conduit or between floors or walls by means of a stiff looped wire or other device pushed in from the nearer end. L19. 8 Use as a bait in fishing; use (a boat etc.) for fishing. L19. 9 Compete as a fisherman in (a fishing-competition). L19.

6 J. BUCHAN Remote glens where I could fish unfrequented streams. 7 J. G. COZZENS The sodden body fished out of dirty water. R. CHANDLER He fished a match out of his pants.

Phrases: **fish for oneself** rely on one's own efforts. **fish in troubled waters** make one's profit out of disturbances. **fish out** exhaust the fish from (a pool etc.).

fishaˈbility *n.* the property or condition of being fishable M20. **fishable** *a.* (of water) able to be fished in, suitable for fishing in E17.

fish /fɪʃ/ *v.*[2]*t.* E17. [f. FISH *n.*[2]] 1 Mend or strengthen (a spar etc.) with a fish or fishes. E17. 2 Join (rails) with a fish or fishes. M19.

fisher /ˈfɪʃə/ *n.* [OE *fisċere* = OFris. *fisker*, OS *fiskari* (Du. *visser*), OHG *fiscāri* (G *Fischer*), ON *fiskari*, f. Gmc, f. base of FISH *n.*[1]: see -ER[1].] 1 A person employed in catching fish, a fisherman. *arch.* OE. b *fig.* More fully *fisher of men* [*Matt.* 4:19]. An evangelist. OE. 2 An animal that catches fish for food. M16. b *spec.* A large N. American arboreal carnivore of the weasel family, *Martes pennanti*; the fur of this animal. L17. 3 A fishing boat. M19.

fisherman /ˈfɪʃəmən/ *n.* Pl. **-men**. LME. [f. prec. + MAN *n.*] 1 A person who catches fish for a living or for sport; an angler. LME. 2 A fishing boat. E17. 3 An animal that catches fish. *rare*. M17. 4 A person who retrieves objects left or dropped down the borehole of an oil well. E20.

1 **fisherman's bend** *Naut.* a knot tied by making a full turn round usu. the ring of an anchor and making one half hitch through the turn and a second round the standing part of the rope. **fisherman's knit** a type of thick ribbed knitting. **fisherman's knot**: used to join two small lines by tying an overhand knot in the end of each and around the opposite standing part. **fisherman's rib** = *fisherman's knit* above. **fisherman's story** or **tale** = *fishing story* s.v. FISHING *n.*

fishery /ˈfɪʃ(ə)ri/ *n.* E16. [f. FISH *v.*[1] + -ERY, or f. FISHER + -Y[3].] 1 The business, occupation, or industry of catching fish or other products from the sea, rivers, etc. E16. 2 (An establishment in) a place or district where fish are caught. L17. 3 *Law*. The right of fishing in certain waters. M18.

fishgig /ˈfɪʃgɪg/ *n.* Now *rare*. M17. [Alt., after FISH *n.*[1]] = FIZGIG *n.*[2]

fishify /ˈfɪʃɪfʌɪ/ *v.t.* L16. [f. FISH *n.*[1] + -I- + -FY.] Cause (flesh) to become like fish or insubstantial or wasted.

SHAKES. *Rom. & Jul.* O flesh, flesh, how art thou fishified!

fishing /ˈfɪʃɪŋ/ *n.* ME. [f. FISH *v.*[1] + -ING[1].] 1 The action of FISH *v.*[1] ME. 2 = FISHERY 3. *obs.* exc. *Hist.* LME. 3 = FISHERY 2. LME.

1 *coarse fishing, fly-fishing, line-fishing, pearl-fishing,* etc. *Attrib. & comb.*: Esp. w. sense 'used for or concerned with fishing', as *fishing boat, fishing net, fishing-port, fishing-smack, fishing-tackle, fishing-village.* Special combs., as **fishing expedition** *fig.* (*a*) a legal investigation with the purpose of discovering information on which to base a later proceeding; (*b*) a search undertaken not with the stated purpose but in the hope of discovering incriminating evidence; **fishing-line** a thin thread of silk, nylon, cord, etc. to which a baited hook, sinker, float, etc. are attached, used for catching fish; **fishing-rod** a long thin tapering rod, usu. jointed, to which a line is attached for angling; **fishing story** an exaggerated account of an incident.

fishing /ˈfɪʃɪŋ/ *ppl a.* M17. [f. FISH *v.*[1] + -ING[2].] 1 Of an animal: that catches fish. M17. 2 Of a question: asked in order to elicit information indirectly. E19.

1 **fishing frog** an angler-fish.

fishtail /ˈfɪʃteɪl/ *n.* & *v.* M19. [f. FISH *n.*[1] + TAIL *n.*[1]] A *n.* The tail of a fish; anything resembling this in shape or lateral movement; *esp.* an arrow unsteady in flight. M19.

Comb.: **fishtail burner** a gas burner producing a spreading flame.

B *v.i.* Swing the tail of an aircraft or the back of a vehicle from side to side (in aircraft to reduce the landing speed); move with the tail so swinging. E20.

fig.: R. CHANDLER A large black and gold butterfly fishtailed in and landed on a hydrangea bush.

fishy /ˈfɪʃi/ *a.* L15. [f. FISH *n.*[1] + -Y[1].] 1 Resembling a fish or some characteristic of a fish; *esp.* (of the eye) dull, vacant-looking. L15. 2 Smelling or tasting like fish. M16. 3 Containing many fish. Now only *poet.* or *joc.* M16. 4 Consisting of fish. L17. 5 Of dubious character, questionable. *colloq.* M19.

1 E. M. FORSTER Adams was whiskiefied and fishy-faced, and obviously a bully. 4 POPE Watery fowl, that seek their fishy food. 5 O. MANNING Poor old Yaki, innocently involved in this fishy business.

fishily *adv.* M19. **fishiness** *n.* M18.

fisk *n.* see FISC.

fisk /fɪsk/ *v.i.* Long *arch. rare.* LME. [Perh. frequent. (with *-k* suff. as in *walk, talk*) of OE *fȳsan* hurry, or of *fēsian, fȳsian* FEEZE *v.* Cf. synon. Sw. *fjäska* frequent. of *fjäsa* bustle, make a fuss.] Move briskly, frisk or whisk (*about*).

R. KIPLING Take *me* from Pevensey to fisk and flyte through fern and forest.

fissibility /fɪsɪˈbɪlɪti/ *n. rare.* L18. [f. L *fiss-* (see next) + -IBILITY.] The quality of being easily split.

fissile /ˈfɪsʌɪl/ *a.* M17. [L *fissilis*, f. *fiss-* pa. ppl stem of *findere* split: see -ILE.] 1 Inclined or tending to split; able to be split. M17. 2 *spec.* Able to undergo nuclear fission. M20.

1 GODFREY SMITH The plain fact is that the Labour Party is historically, fundamentally and . . irrevocably fissile.

fissility /fɪˈsɪlɪti/ *n.* the quality of being fissile L17.

fission /ˈfɪʃ(ə)n/ *n.* & *v.* E17. [L *fissio(n-)*, f. *fiss-*: see prec., -ION.] A *n.* 1 The action of splitting or dividing into pieces. E17. 2 *Biol.* The division of a cell or organism into new cells or organisms, as a mode of reproduction. M19. 3 *Physics.* The splitting of a heavy atomic nucleus into (usu.) two nuclei spontaneously or under the impact of another particle, with resulting release of energy. M20.

1 C. RYCROFT The absence of a native genius for compromise has led to complete fission. 2 BINARY *fission. multiple fission*: see MULTIPLE *a.*

Comb.: **fission bomb** an atomic bomb.

B *v.i.* & *t.* (Cause to) undergo fission. E20.

G. R. KEEPIN Those heavy nuclides which can be fissioned by thermal neutrons. G. SAMPSON When Latin lost its role and cultures began to fission along national lines in the Renascence.

¶ Rare before M19.

fissionaˈbility *n.* the quality of being fissionable M20. **fissionable** *a.* able to undergo fission; tending to undergo fission: M20.

fissiparous /fɪˈsɪp(ə)rəs/ *a.* M19. [Irreg. f. L *fissus* pa. pple of *findere* to split, after *viviparous* etc.] 1 *Biol.* Reproducing by fission; of or pertaining to reproduction by fission. M19. 2 Tending to split or divide; pertaining to splitting or division. L19.

2 R. QUIRK The fissiparous tendencies that local needs and nationalist susceptibilities are fostering.

fissiparity /fɪsɪˈparɪti/ *n.* (*a*) the quality of being fissiparous; (*b*) the process of fissiparous reproduction: L19. **fissiparously** *adv.* L19. **fissiparousness** *n.* M20.

fissiped /ˈfɪsɪpɛd/ *a.* & *n.* Also **-pede** /-piːd/. M17. [Late L *fissipes, -ped-*, f. L *fissus* (see prec.) + *pes, ped-* foot.] *Zool.* A *adj.* Having the toes separated. Now *spec.* designating those mammals of the order Carnivora other than the pinnipeds. M17. B *n.* A fissiped animal. Cf. PINNIPED. M17.

fissive /ˈfɪsɪv/ *a.* L19. [f. L *fiss-*: (see FISSILE) + -IVE.] Pertaining to or of the nature of fission.

fissle /ˈfɪs(ə)l/ *n.* & *v. Sc.* & *dial.* Also **fistle.** E18. [Imit.: cf. FIZZLE.] A *n.* 1 A rustling noise. Formerly also, a fuss. E18.

B *v.* 1 *v.t.* & *i.* Rustle. E18. †2 *v.i.* Move about restlessly; fidget. L18–L19.

1 W. MCILVANNEY Straw fissled, inventing shapes in the darkness.

fissural /ˈfɪʃ(ə)r(ə)l/ *a.* LME. [f. FISSURE *n.* + -AL[1].] Of or pertaining to a fissure or fissures; like a fissure; having fissures.

¶ In isolated use bef. L 19.

fissuration /fɪʃərˈeɪʃ(ə)n/ *n.* M19. [Fr., f. *fissurer*, f. as next: see -ATION.] The action or process of fissuring; the state of being fissured.

fissure /ˈfɪʃə/ *n.* & *v.* LME. [(O)Fr., or L *fissura*, f. *fiss-*: see FISSILE, -URE.] A *n.* 1 An opening, usu. long and narrow, made by cracking, splitting, or separation of parts. Orig. esp. in *Med.*, a linear wound or ulceration; now chiefly, a long cleft in rock or ice. LME. 2 *Her.* A diminutive of the bend sinister. L15. 3 The action of fissuring; the state of being fissured; sharp division. M17.

1 E. HEATH The Rift Valley, that great fissure in the earth which extends for a thousand miles. *fig.*: E. GELLNER Not *any* genetically transmitted trait will have the effect of producing a fissure in society. 3 R. D. LAING The fissure into self and ego, inner and outer, good and bad occurs.

Comb.: **fissure eruption** *Geol.* a steady emission of lava along a fissure in the earth's crust; **fissure vein** *Min.* a fissure in the earth's crust filled with valuable mineral.

B *v.* 1 *v.t.* Make a fissure or fissures in; split. M17. 2 *v.i.* Develop a fissure or fissures; crack. M19.

fissured *a.* having a fissure or fissures; broken up by fissures: L18.

fist /fɪst/ *n.*[1] [OE *fȳst* = OFris. *fest*, MLG *fūst* (Du. *vuist*), OHG *fūst* (G *Faust*), f. WGmc.] 1 The hand clenched with the fingers bent into the palm (so esp. in striking a blow and in holding something); grasp, grip. OE. 2 The hand. Now only *joc.* ME. b *Typogr.* A hand-shaped symbol with a pointing finger used to draw attention to a note etc. Also called *index*. Cf. HAND *n.* 8b. L19. 3 One's handwriting (now only *joc.*); *transf.* the style of transmitting by telegraph peculiar to an individual operator. L15.

1 R. L. STEVENSON The blind man clung close to me, holding me in one iron fist. E. BAKER He was sure Shillitoe would swing his right fist and tensed, ready to block the blow. 2 T. PYNCHON She was near the door with an unidentifiable drink in her fist.

Phrases: **give us your fist** shake hands. *hand over fist*: see HAND *n.* **make a fist at, of** *colloq.* bungle, be unsuccessful at. **make a good, poor,** etc. **fist at, of** *colloq.* make a good etc. attempt at, succeed in doing well etc.

Comb.: **fist-fight** a fight with bare fists, *esp.* a spontaneous one.

fistful *n.* the quantity held by a fist, a handful E17. **fistiˈana** *n.pl.* [-ANA] publications or other items concerning or associated with boxing M19.

fist /fʌɪst/ *n.*[2] Also (*Sc.* & *US*) **feist** /fʌɪst/, (*US*, esp. in sense 3) **fice** /fʌɪs/, **fiste** /fʌɪst/, (*obs.* exc. *dial.*) **foist** /fɔɪst/. ME. [Rel. to FIST *v.*[2], f. WGmc base. In branch II abbrev. of *fisting cur, dog,* etc.] I 1 An act of breaking wind. Formerly also, a foul smell. Now *rare* or *obs.* ME. 2 A puffball fungus. Long *obs.* exc. *dial.* L16. II *US* (forms other than *fist* usual). 3 A small dog, a cur. L18. 4 A person of little worth; a bad-tempered person. M20.

fist /fɪst/ *v.*[1]*t.* L16. [f. FIST *n.*[1]] 1 Strike with the fist, punch. L16. 2 Grasp with the fist. Now chiefly *Naut.*, handle (a sail, oar, etc.). E17. 3 Clench (the hand, the fingers) into a fist. M20.

1 *Daily Chronicle* The latter unobserved by the referee fisted the ball into the net. W. GOLDING He danced, fisted the air a bit, then gave an ejaculatory laugh. 2 SHAKES. *Coriol.* We have been down together in my sleep, Unbuckling helms, fisting each other's throat. 3 S. PLATH Then I fisted my fingers together and smashed them at his nose.

†**fist** *v.*[2]*i.* Also **foist.** OE–L17. [Rel. to FIST *n.*[2], f. WGmc base.] Break wind.

fisting cur, dog, hound a small pet dog.

fiste *n.* see FIST *n.*[2]

fisted /ˈfɪstɪd/ *a.* L16. [f. FIST *n.*[1] + -ED[2].] 1 As 2nd elem. of comb.: having a fist or hand of the specified kind. L16. 2 Having or using fists. *rare.* E19.

1 *close-fisted, ham-fisted,* etc.

†**fistic** *n.* M16–E18. [med.L *fisticum* f. Arab. *fustuk, -ak, fistik* ult. f. Gk *pistakion* PISTACHIO.] A pistachio. Also *fistic nut, tree.*

fistic /ˈfɪstɪk/ *a. colloq.* E19. [f. FIST *n.*[1] + -IC.] Pugilistic.

fistical *a.* M18.

fisticuff /ˈfɪstɪkʌf/ *v.* Also (now *rare*) **fisty-.** M17. [f. next.] 1 *v.t.* Strike with the fists. M17. 2 *v.i.* Fight with the fists. M19.

fisticuffs /ˈfɪstɪkʌfs/ *n.pl.* Also (now *rare*) **fisty-.** E17. [Prob. f. FISTY + CUFF *n.*[2] + -S[1].] Fighting with the fists.

B. CHATWIN Fifty years of fisticuffs had flattened his nose.

fistle *n.* & *v.* var. of FISSLE.

fistmele /ˈfɪstmiːl/ *n.* E17. [f. FIST *n.*[1] + MELE measure.] The distance from the end of the extended thumb to the opposite side of the hand, about 15 cm or 6 inches, used *spec.* in *Archery* to gauge the correct height of the string from the braced bow. Cf. SHAFTMENT *n.*[1]

fistula /ˈfɪstjʊlə/ *n.* Pl. **-lae** /-liː/, **-las.** LME. [L = pipe, flute; partly through OFr. *fist(u)le, festre* FESTER *n.*] 1 A reed instrument or pipe of the ancient Romans. LME. 2 A long pipelike ulcer; an abnormal passage between two internal structures of the body or between one such and the surface of the body. L15. b A passage in the body made for surgical purposes. L19. 3 A whale's spout; a slender tube in certain invertebrates. M17. 4 *Eccl.* (now *Hist.*). A tube through which communicants, esp. the Pope, received the consecrated wine. L17.

fistular /ˈfɪstjʊlə/ *a.* LME. [OFr. *fistulaire* or L *fistularis*, f. as prec.: see -AR[1].] 1 = FISTULOUS I. LME. 2 = FISTULOUS 2. E18.

fistulate /ˈfɪstjʊleɪt/ *v.* E17. [L *fistulat-* pa. ppl stem of *fistulare*, f. FISTULA: see -ATE[3].] †1 *v.i.* Form or grow into a fistula. Only in 17. †2 *v.t.* Make tubular. *rare.* Only in M18. 3 *v.t. Vet. Med.* Provide with an artificial fistula. M20.

fistulose /ˈfɪstjʊləʊs/ *a.* LME. [f. as next: see -OSE[1].] = FISTULOUS.

fistulous /ˈfɪstjʊləs/ *a.* LME. [f. L *fistulosus*, f. as FISTULA: see -ULOUS.] 1 *Med.* Pertaining to or of the nature of a fistula; having a fistula. LME. 2 Esp. *Bot.* Naturally tubular or pipelike in form; having or containing a tube or tubes. L16.

fisty /ˈfɪsti/ *a.* Now *rare.* L17. [f. FIST *n.*[1] + -Y[1].] Of or pertaining to fists or their use in fighting.

¶ Prob. repr. earlier in FISTICUFFS.

fistycuff *v.* see FISTICUFF.

fistycuffs *n.pl.* see FISTICUFFS.

fit /fɪt/ *n.*[1] Also **fytte.** [OE *fitt*, perh. identical with OHG *fizza* border of cloth (G *Fitze* skein of yarn, †thread with which weavers mark off a day's work) and ON *fit* hem: but cf. next.] 1 A section of a poem or song; a canto. *obs.* exc. *Hist.* OE. 2 A piece of music; a strain. *arch.* LME.

fit /fɪt/ *n.*[2] [OE *fitt*. Orig. meaning perh. 'juncture', 'meeting', 'match', which might relate this word to, or identify it with, prec.: cf. FIT *a.*, *v.*[1]] †I 1 Conflict, struggle. Only in OE. 2 A position of danger or excitement; a (painful, pleasant, etc.) experience or fate. LME–E17. b A mortal crisis. Only in L16.

2 CHAUCER This noble king . . The firste night had many a mery fitte With eche of hem. b SPENSER The life did flit away . . And all his senses were with deadly fit opprest.

II 3 A short period. Now only (*dial.*), a spell of weather of a specified kind. ME. 4 Orig., one of the paroxysms of a recurrent disease. Later, a short sudden attack of illness, now usu. one marked by convulsions or loss of consciousness. Also, a sudden uncontrollable outbreak of a symptom. M16. †b *spec.* An outbreak of madness (formerly viewed as a recurrent disease). L16–E18. c *spec.* An epileptic fit. Formerly, a fainting fit; an attack of hysteria. E18. d *hyperbol. sing.* & in *pl.* A violent emotional reaction, as of shock or displeasure; esp. in *have fits* or *a fit*, (orig. *US*) *throw a fit. colloq.* M19. 5 A sudden brief spell of (a given) activity, of inaction, of a specified feeling, etc. Also, a sudden impulse to action; a mood. L16. 6 A sudden violent outburst of laughter, tears, anger, etc. Usu. foll. by *of*. M17. 7 *Hist. Sci.* Either of two alternating states of a light wave at any given point in its path, characterized respectively by a tendency to be reflected by a transparent body and a tendency to be transmitted by it; the coming into being of either state, as a property of the wave. E18.

3 D. DYKE Which is not . . rooted, but onely for a fitte. SWIFT A fit of good weather would tempt me a week longer. 4 SHAKES. *Jul. Caes.* He had a fever . . And when the fit was on him, I did mark How he did shake. SMOLLETT I expect to be laid up with another fit of the gout. M. SPARK Sandy affected to have a fit of spluttering coughs. *apoplectic fit, epileptic fit, fainting fit*, etc. b SHAKES. *Tit. A.* Unless some fit or frenzy do possess her. c B. MACDONALD He . . begun to foam . . and I seen he was in a fit. d DAY LEWIS You'd better not tell your Auntie or she'd have a fit. 5 H. B. STOWE When the fit was on him, he would shoe a horse better than any man. CONAN DOYLE Now he has got an energetic fit and intends to do it. P. G. WODEHOUSE He had developed fits of absent-mindedness. N. MITFORD Her attitude of . . vagueness alternating with sudden fits of severity. 6 D. LESSING Maryrose and I . . burst into fits of helpless laughter. R. TRAVERS Ashe . . in a fit of temper flung it overboard.

Phrases: **beat to** or **into fits** *colloq.* defeat or excel thoroughly. **by fits, by** (or **in**) **fits and starts** with irregular bursts of activity, spasmodically. **give a person a fit** surprise or outrage a person. **give (a person) fits** *colloq.* defeat (a person) crushingly; *US* rebuke (a person) soundly. **in** (or **into**) **fits** in (or into) a state of hysterical amusement. *lick into fits*: see LICK *v. throw a fit*: see THROW *v.*

fit /fɪt/ *n.*[3] L17. [f. FIT *v.*[1]] 1 The process of making a person fit for something. Now only *spec.* (*US*), the training of a person for college. L17. 2 The fitting or adjustment of one thing to another, esp. a garment to the body; the way in which a garment, machine part, etc., fits. E19. b A garment etc. in respect of its fit. M19.

2 J. KOSINSKI The . . words meshed with each other like oiled millstones ground to a fine fit. A. LURIE Black men . . are noticeable for the . . superb fit of their clothes. b CONAN DOYLE The dress . . could not have been a better fit if I had been measured for it.

¶ See also FIT-OUT, FIT-UP.

fit /fɪt/ *a.* & *adv.* Compar. & superl. **-tt-**. LME. [Origin unkn.] A *adj.* †1 Of an object: possessing the right measurements or size; fitting exactly. (Foll. by *to*.) LME–E18. 2 Adapted to the requirements of the case; appropriate, suitable. (Foll. by *for, to do, to be done.*) LME. b *Biol.* Possessing or conferring the ability to survive and reproduce in a particular environment. LME. 3 Befitting the person or circumstances; right, proper. Now only *pred.* foll. by *to do, to be done.* LME. †b Needful *to be done.* E17–M18. 4 In a suitable condition; prepared, ready. Exc. *dial.* now only foll. by *for, to do, to be done.* M16. 5 Inclined, disposed. Now usu. (*colloq.* & *dial.*), angry, desperate, exhausted, etc., enough *to do.* L16. b Of a thing: likely or calculated *to do. colloq.* L18. 6 Of an adequate standard, sufficiently good; (of a person) qualified, competent, or worthy. (Foll. by *for, to do, to be done.*) L16. 7 In a suitable state for strenuous physical activity; *gen.* in good health. *colloq.* E18.

1 J. HARINGTON You must have a hollow key with a worm fit to that screw. 2 H. PRIDEAUX What is the fittest portion of our Substance to be set apart. E. O'NEILL Is that banshee schreeching fit music for a sick man? D. CUSACK A . . divergence of opinion regarding the fit penalty to be meted out. b *survival of the fittest.* 3 W. CONGREVE 'Tis fit Men should be coy, when Women woo. **see** or **think fit** decide or choose (*to do*, esp. an arbitrary or foolish thing). 4 H. GLASSE They will be fit to eat in two or three days. J. CONRAD We felt . . fit for nothing but placid staring. 5 DEFOE I am fit to hang myself because I can't find it out. J. H. NEWMAN He . . keeps you standing till you are fit to sink. **fit to be tied** in a very angry mood. b J. CONRAD Beastly beer . . rotten stuff fit to make an old he-goat yell if you poured it down its throat. 6 SHAKES. *Jul. Caes.* Let's carve him as a dish fit for the gods. B. FRANKLIN This is a business I am not fit for. SCOTT FITZGERALD He wasn't fit to lick my shoe. F. L. WRIGHT The dwelling became more fit for human habitation. M. EDWARDES He came to the conclusion that my activities . . were beyond reproach and that I was a fit person to join the NEB. 7 S. HILL Your digestive and nervous systems are perfect, you are fit and well. A. HAILEY He . . kept himself fit with a rigid daily exercise schedule. *fighting fit*: see FIGHTING *vbl n.* **fit as a fiddle, flea** extremely fit.

B *adv.* 1 With a close correspondence or fit. Now *rare* or *obs.* LME. 2 In a manner calculated or likely *to do. colloq.* & *dial.* E19.

1 W. RAND One cup would go fit into the other. 2 J. C. HARRIS Clarence Bullard was there, dressed up fit to kill. W. GASS Pa laughed fit to shake the house.

fit /fɪt/ *v.*[1] Infl. **-tt-**. Pa. t. & pple **fitted**, (*dial.* & *US*) **fit**. LME. [f. FIT *a.* exc. in sense 1, of unkn. origin.] I *v.t.* †1 Marshal, deploy, (troops). Only in LME. 2 Be suited to or appropriate for; befit. Usu. *impers.* in (*it*) *fits* etc. LME. 3 Meet the requirements of; suit. *obs.* exc. *dial.* L16. b In *pass.*, be suited (*dial.*). Formerly also (*refl.*), suit oneself. M17. 4 Esp. of a garment: be of the right measurements or proper shape and size for. Also (*fig.*), correspond to or accord with exactly. L16. 5 Bring into a suitable condition; make ready, fit, or competent. Exc. *dial.* now only foll. by *for, to, to do.* L16. 6 Provide (now esp. a thing) *with* what is suitable or necessary; equip. L16. 7 Make (a thing) correspond or conform to something else, adapt, adjust, (usu. foll. by *to*); find room for. L16. 8 Adjust (an object) to the contours of its receptacle or counterpart; fix, apply, etc., (an object) so that it exactly occupies a given position; try the fit of (a garment etc.). E17. 9a Give (a person) a deserved punishment; avenge oneself on, requite. Now *dial.* & *Austral.* E17. b Secure enough (genuine or false) evidence to convict, frame. Also foll. by *up*. Orig. *Austral.* L19. 10 Provide or adapt a garment etc. to suit the measurements of (a person). L17.

2 N. ROWE This Boldness does not fit a Stranger. H. SIDDONS What the contents of Middleton's letter were it fitted me not to inquire. 3 A. HORNECK A temptation which will fit one, will not fit another. 4 W. S. GILBERT To let the punishment fit the crime. QUILLER-COUCH The bullets in the . . body do not fit your pistols, but came from a larger pair. D. HAMMETT He wore . . a black overcoat that fitted him very snugly. *fit the bill*: see BILL *n.*[3] 5 AV *Rom.* 9:22 Vessels of wrath fitted to destruction. J. BRYCE It . . does not completely fit him to weigh the real merits of statesmen. R. MACAULAY Nature had not fitted her for learning. 6 I. WALTON I wil fit him to morrow with a Trout for his breakfast. DICKENS Apartments . . which were richly fitted with a polished wood. G. B. SHAW A small kitchen table . . fitted as a writing table with an old canister full of pens. 7 R. W. EMERSON Nature has a magic by which she fits the man to his fortunes. 8 H. HUNTER The tyrant . . who fitted the unhappy traveller to his bed of iron. J. CONRAD Shades . . fitted low over all the lights imparted to the room something of a forest's deep gloom. A. J. CRONIN He took the key . . and fitted it in the lock. M. FRAYN To fit all the pieces of the jig-saw together. 9 F. BURNEY With a look that implied—I'll fit you for this! 10 L. DURRELL At the dressmaker's, being fitted for a shark-skin costume.

II *v.i.* 11a Be proper or suitable. Usu. *impers.* in *it fits, it is fitting*, etc. Now *rare* or *obs.* L16. b Be in accord or harmonize *with*. Now *arch. rare.* L16. 12 Be of the right shape and size to occupy a given position; *fig.* be in harmony or accord with facts, circumstances, one's companions, etc. Usu. foll. by *in* (adv. & prep.), *into*, (*fig.*) *in with*. L17. 13 Esp. of a garment in relation to its wearer: be of the correct measurements. L18.

11a SPENSER Sometimes I joy when glad occasion fits. MILTON To appear as fits before th' illustrious lords. b SHAKES. *Tit. A.* Why dost thou laugh? It fits not with this hour. 12 OED This peg fits into this hole. K. AMIS My ideas work. Because they fit in with the way life's lived. *Woman's Illustrated* How would they fit in, in this new land? 13 G. GREENE The doors no longer quite fitted and had to be propped at night. T. CAPOTE His suits fitted as though he had borrowed them from a stout friend. *fit like a glove*: see GLOVE *n. the cap fits*: see CAP *n.*[1]

With advs. & preps. in specialized senses: **fit in** (adv. & prep.), **into** accommodate within a given space or (*fig.*) a schedule etc.; (see also sense 12 above). **fit on** adjust (a garment) to the body so that it fits exactly. **fit out** (chiefly *Naut.*) equip with all that is necessary in the way of stores, clothing, etc. **fit up** (*a*) equip, esp. with suitable furniture or appliances; (*b*) *slang* conceal or place incriminating evidence on; (see also sense 10b above).

fit /fɪt/ *v.*[2]*t.* & *i. Sc.* Infl. **-tt-**. L16. [Var. of FOOT *v.*] = FOOT *v.*

fit fair, fit the tee *Curling* position oneself to deliver a shot at the proper distance from the far tee.

fit /fɪt/ *v.*[3] Infl. **-tt-**. L16. [f. FIT *n.*[2]] †1 *v.t.* Force (a thing) by paroxysms *out of* its usual position. *rare* (Shakes.). Only in L16. 2 *v.i.* Have an epileptic fit, be seized by a fit. M20.

1 SHAKES. *Sonn.* How have mine eyes out of their spheres been fitted In the distraction of this madding fever!

fitch /fɪtʃ/ *n.*[1] *obs.* exc. *dial.* LME. [Var. of VETCH.] A vetch, any of various plants of the genus *Vicia* and allied genera; spec. *V. sativa*, grown for fodder (usu. in *pl.*).

¶ In AV *fitches* is used to render the Hebrew name of two non-leguminous cultivated plants: black cumin, *Nigella sativa* (*Isa.* 28:25), and spelt, *Triticum spelta* (*Ezek.* 4:9).

fitch /fɪtʃ/ *n.*[2] LME. [Early Du. *fisse, visse, vitsche*: cf. FITCHEW.] 1 The fur or hair of the polecat. LME. 2 A polecat. Now *dial.* L15. 3 In full *fitch-brush*. A brush made of polecat hair or hog's or other similar hair. M19.

fitch /fɪtʃ/ *n.*[3] E20. [Origin unkn.] *Basket-making*. A kind of plait in which two canes are twisted together in the same direction so as to enclose a crossing weft at each half-turn.

fitch /fɪtʃ/ *v. Sc.* & *north.* L15. [App. intermediate between FYKE *v.* and FIDGE *v.*] 1 *v.t.* Change the place of; shift. L15. 2 *v.i.* Move in small spurts from place to place. E17.

fitché /ˈfɪtʃeɪ/ *a.* Also **-ée, -y.** L16. [Fr. *fiché, -ée* pa. ppl a. of *ficher* to fix.] *Her.* Of a cross: having its lower limb tapered to a point.

fitched /fɪtʃt/ *a.* M16. [f. prec. + -ED[1].] *Her.* = prec.

fitchée *a.* var. of FITCHÉ.

fitchet /ˈfɪtʃɪt/ *n.* M16. [Dim. of FITCH *n.*[2]: see -ET[1].] 1 = FITCHEW. Also, a dark-coloured ferret resulting from a cross between a polecat and a ferret; a polecat-ferret. M16. 2 A weasel. *dial.* L17.

fitchet pie *n. phr.* see FIDGET PIE.

fitchew /ˈfɪtʃuː/ *n.* LME. [OFr. *ficheau* dial. var. of *fissel* (pl. *fissiaulx*), later *fissau*, dim. of a wd appearing in early Du. as *fisse, visse, vitsche*, whence ult. also FITCH *n.*[2]] 1 A polecat. LME. 2 The fur of the polecat. LME.

fitchy *a.* var. of FITCHÉ.

fitful /ˈfɪtfʊl, -f(ə)l/ *a.* L16. [f. FIT *n.*[2] + -FUL.] †1 Of a fever etc.: marked by fits or paroxysms. *rare.* L16–M18. 2 Marked by irregular bursts of activity or strength; spasmodic; capricious. E19.

1 SHAKES. *Macb.* After life's fitful fever he sleeps well. 2 E. MIALL The fitful and convulsive energy they have at times displayed. A. HALEY He dozed off into a fitful sleep.

fitfully *adv.* L18. **fitfulness** *n.* E19.

fitly /ˈfɪtli/ *a. rare.* L16. [f. FIT *a.* + -LY[1].] = FIT *a.*

fitly /ˈfɪtli/ *adv.* M16. [f. FIT *a.* + -LY[2].] 1 Suitably, appropriately. M16. †2 At an opportune moment. Only in E17.

2 AV *Prov.* 25:11 A word fitly spoken is like apples of gold.

fitment /ˈfɪtm(ə)nt/ *n.* E17. [f. FIT *v.*[1] + -MENT.] †1 The action of making fit or ready for something. *rare* (Shakes.). Only in E17. †2 That which is fitting; duty. *rare* (Shakes.). Only in E17. 3 A piece of fitted or fixed furniture; a part fitted to a machine etc. Usu. in *pl.* M19. 4 The process of fitting or attaching in a given position. L19.

3 N. BLAKE The cottage was snug enough, if somewhat austere in its fitments.

fitness /ˈfɪtnɪs/ *n.* L16. [f. FIT *a.* + -NESS.] 1 The quality of being suitable, qualified, or morally fit for something. L16. b *Biol.* (A numerical measure of) ability to survive and reproduce in a particular environment. L16. 2 Conformity with what circumstances require; propriety. L16. †3 Readiness, inclination. *rare* (Shakes.). Only in E17. †4 The quality of having exactly the right measurements. M17–L18. 5 The quality or state of being physically fit. M20.

1 *warrant of fitness*: see WARRANT *n.*[1] 2 **the (eternal) fitness of things** [orig. w. ref. to the ethical theories of Samuel Clarke (1675–1729)] the natural appropriateness of the existing order of things; what is fitting or appropriate.

fit-out /ˈfɪtaʊt/ *n.* E19. [f. FIT *v.*[1] + OUT *adv.*] The action of equipping with all that is necessary, esp. in dress; an outfit.

fitted /ˈfɪtɪd/ *ppl a.* E17. [f. FIT *v.*[1] + -ED[1].] 1 Suitable or qualified *for, to do*; calculated or likely *to do*. E17. 2 That has been fitted; (of a covering etc.) shaped so as to fit exactly; (of a cupboard) designed to fit a given space; (of a room, esp. a kitchen) equipped with (matching) units specially designed to fit their positions. E19.

1 R. WATSON How much.. Philip's power and character were fitted to excite jealousy. J. CAREY Being fifteen stone.. he was not well fitted for a career in ballet. 2 **fitted carpet**: cut to cover the whole floor of a room. **fitted sheet** a bed-sheet with box ends fitting closely round the mattress.

fittedness *n.* M17.

fitten /ˈfɪt(ə)n/ *n.* Long *obs.* exc. *dial.* Also **fitton**. LME. [Origin unkn.] A lie, an invention.

fitten /ˈfɪt(ə)n/ *a.* Now *dial.* (chiefly *US*). M17. [f. FIT *v.*[1] + -EN[6].] Suitable, fit.

W. FAULKNER He would see fitten to reveal it.

fitter /ˈfɪtə/ *n.* M17. [f. FIT *v.*[1] + -ER[1].] 1 *gen.* A person or thing which fits or adapts something. M17. 2 *spec.* A person who supervises the fitting, alteration, etc., of garments. M19. 3 A mechanic who assembles or repairs machine or engine parts. M19. 4 A person employed to fix installations or appliances of any kind. M19.

4 *gas-fitter, pipe-fitter*, etc.

†**fitter** *v.i.* & *t.* LME–E17. [Perh. rel. to MHG *vetze* (G *Fetzen*) rag, scrap: see -ER[5]. Cf. FRITTER *v.*] Break into very small pieces; shred.

fitters /ˈfɪtəz/ *n.pl. obs.* exc. *dial.* M16. [f. prec. See also FLITTERS, FRITTER *n.*[2]] Very small pieces; fragments, smithereens.

fitting /ˈfɪtɪŋ/ *n.* E17. [f. FIT *v.*[1] + -ING[1].] 1 The action of FIT *v.*[1]; *spec.* (*a*) the action or an act of fitting a garment to the wearer by a tailor or dressmaker; (*b*) the assembling and adjusting of machine parts. E17. 2 Something fitted; a piece of apparatus or furniture, a fixture. Usu. in *pl.* E19.

2 S. DELANEY The landlady pointed it out to me as part of the furniture and fittings.

Comb.: **fitting-room**: in which a garment etc. is fitted to the wearer; **fitting-shop** a place where machine parts are put together.

fitting /ˈfɪtɪŋ/ *ppl a.* LME. [f. FIT *v.*[1] + -ING[2].] 1 Becoming, proper, appropriate. LME. 2 Adjusted exactly to the contours of something. Now only with prefixed adv., as *close-fitting*. M16.

1 B. T. WASHINGTON In order that the distinguished visitor might have a fitting reception.

fittingly *adv.* M17. **fittingness** *n.* M17.

fitton *n.* var. of FITTEN *n.*

fitty /ˈfɪti/ *a. obs.* exc. *dial.* L16. [Prob. f. FIT *a.*, *v.*[1] or + -Y[1], but perh. partly alt. of FEATY.] Fitting, becoming; neat, trim.

fit-up /ˈfɪtʌp/ *n. slang.* M19. [f. FIT *v.*[1] + UP *adv.*[1]] 1 A stage or other theatrical accessory that can be fitted up for the occasion. M19. b In full *fit-up company*. A touring company which carries such properties with it. L19. 2 An act of concealing or placing incriminating evidence on a person. L20.

fitz /fɪts/ *n. obs.* exc. *Hist.* ME. [AN spelling of OFr. *fiz*, earlier *filz* (mod. *fils*), f. L *filius* son.] A son. Chiefly in patronymic designations, surviving as an elem. in surnames, e.g. *Fitzherbert, Fitzwilliam*, latterly sometimes bestowed on the illegitimate sons of princes.

J. WEST The contentions of Henry Fitz-empress with Eleanora of Guienne.

FitzGerald /fɪtsˈdʒɛr(ə)ld/ *a.* E20. [G. F. *FitzGerald* (1851–1901), Ir. physicist.] Sci. *FitzGerald(-Lorentz) contraction, effect* [LORENTZ], the relativistic foreshortening, in the direction of motion, of a body moving relative to the observer.

fiumara /fjuːˈmɑːrə/ *n.* E19. [It.] (The dried bed of) a mountain torrent, esp. in Italy.

five /fʌɪv/ *a.* & *n.* (*cardinal numeral*). [OE *fīf* = OFris., OS *fīf* (Du. *vijf*), OHG *fimf, finf* (G *fünf*), ON *fimm*, Goth. *fimf*, f. Gmc f. IE, whence also L *quinque*, Gk *pente*, Skt *pañca*.] A *adj.* One more than four (a cardinal numeral represented by 5 in arabic numerals, v, V in roman). OE.

G. GREENE A hand.. with five pennies in the palm. *five orders*: see ORDER *n.* **five positions** *Ballet* the five basic positions of the feet, with one of which most steps begin and end; the five corresponding positions of the arms. *the Five Nations*: see NATION *n.*[1] *the five senses*: see SENSE *n.* 8. *the five wits*: see WIT *n.* *the Five Wounds*: see WOUND *n.*

B *n.* 1 Five persons or things identified contextually, as parts or divisions, years of age, points, runs, etc., in a game, chances (in giving odds), minutes, inches, shillings (now *Hist.*), pence, etc. OE. 2 One more than four as an abstract number; the symbol or figure representing this (5 in arabic numerals, v, V in roman). OE. 3 A set of five; a thing having a set of five as an essential or distinguishing feature; *spec.* (*a*) a playing-card, domino, or face of a die marked with five pips or spots; (*b*) a five-pound note, a five-dollar bill. LME. 4 The fifth of a set or series with numbered members, the one designated five, (usu. *number five*, or with specification, as *book five, chapter five*, etc.); a size etc. denoted by five, a shoe, glove, garment, etc., of such a size, (also *size five*). E16. 5 The time of day five hours after midnight or midday (on a clock, watch, etc., indicated by the numeral five displayed or pointed to). Also *five o'clock*. M16.

1 E. BLYTON The five in the little cart all talked at once. *know how many beans make five*: see BEAN *n.* **take five** *colloq.* take a five-minute break; take a short break, relax. 2 L. EGAN What else looks like an S except a five? 3 A. TYLER 'How would you like that, sir?'.. 'Fives and ones.' **bunch of fives** *slang* a hand, a fist. 4 R. KIPLING Number Five was unpacking. *Radio Five*: see RADIO *n.* 3. 5 R. L. STEVENSON Where all the children dine at five.

Comb.: Forming compound cardinal numerals with multiples of ten from twenty to ninety, as *thirty-five*, (arch.) *five-and-thirty*, etc., and (*arch.*) their corresponding ordinals, as *five-and-thirtieth*, etc., and with multiples of a hundred, as *205* (read *two hundred and five*, US also *two hundred five*), etc. With ns. + -ER[1] forming ns. w. the sense 'something (identified contextually) being of or having five —s', as *five-seater* etc. Special combs., as **five-and-ten(-cent store)** *N. Amer.* a store where all the articles were originally priced at five or ten cents; *gen.* a cheap store; **five-corner** *sing.* & (usu.) in *pl.*, (the fruit of) any of several shrubs of the Australian coast of the genus *Styphelia*; **five-eighth** in Austral. & NZ rugby football, a player between the half-back and the three-quarter; **five-finger** (*a*) *sing.* & in *pl.*, any of various plants, *esp.* cinquefoil (also *five-finger grass*); (*b*) a starfish with the usual five arms; (*c*) *five-finger exercise*, an exercise on the piano for all the fingers; *fig.* an easy task; (*d*) *five-finger discount* (US slang), (the proceeds of) stealing or shoplifting; **five hundred** a form of euchre in which 500 points make a game; **five-leaf** (long *rare*) cinquefoil; **five-lined** *a.* consisting of or marked with five lines; **five o'clock shadow** beard growth which is visible on a man's face after about 5 p.m.; *five o'clock tea*: see TEA *n.* 5(a); **fivepence** (*a*) five pence, esp. of the old British currency before decimalization; *as fine as fivepence* (arch. colloq.), very smart; (cf. FIPPENCE); (*b*) (usu. two wds) since 1968, a coin worth five (new) pence; **fivepenny** *a.* worth or costing fivepence; (cf. FIPPENNY); **fivepin bowling, fivepins** a game in which five pins or skittles are set up and bowled at to be knocked down; **five-star** *a.* (*a*) given five stars in a grading, esp. where this indicates the highest quality; (*b*) having or being a military rank that is distinguished by five stars on the shoulder-piece of the uniform; **fivestones** jacks played with five stones; **five-year plan** a plan for the economic development of a country spread over five years, *esp.* the plan for the economic development of the former USSR, inaugurated in 1928.

fivefold *a.* & *adv.* (*a*) *adj.* five times as great or as numerous; having five parts, divisions, elements, or units; (*b*) *adv.* to five times the number or quantity: OE. **fiver** *n.* (*colloq.*) a five-pound note, a five-dollar bill: M19. **fivesome** *n.* a set of five persons or things; a game (esp. of golf) for five players: LME.

fives /fʌɪvz/ *n.*[1] M17. [Pl. of FIVE treated as sing.: ult. significance unkn.] A game in which a ball is struck by a gloved hand or a bat against one wall of a court.

Eton fives: see ETON 5. *Rugby fives*: see RUGBY 2. *Winchester fives*: see WINCHESTER *n.* 1.

Comb.: **fives-court** a prepared court where fives is played.

†**fives** *n.*[2]*pl.* var. of VIVES.

fix /fɪks/ *n.* E19. [f. the vb.] 1 A position from which it is difficult to escape, a predicament. *colloq.* E19. 2 Condition, state; (working) order. *US colloq.* E19. 3 The material used for lining a puddling-furnace. L19. 4 (A reliable indication of) the position of an aircraft, a ship, etc., found by bearings or astronomical observation; the action of obtaining such an indication; *transf.* an assessment or identification (of location, size, price, etc.). E20. 5 A bribe, bribery; an illicit arrangement. *slang.* E20. 6 A dose of a narcotic drug, *esp.* one (to be) taken by an addict. *slang.* M20. 7 The action of fixing or determining something, *spec.* the price of gold; the time at which such fixing takes place. L20.

1 TOLKIEN To find ourselves in the same fix or a worse one. G. M. FRASER Our little party was in an appalling fix. 2 H. WOODRUFF In getting a whole stable of horses into fix to trot races. 4 F. CHICHESTER I got a sun fix with the sextant. M. AMIS Five days of London time and still no fix on Selina. **radio fix** the position of a ship, aircraft, etc., found by radio. *running fix*: see RUNNING *ppl a.* 5 E. D. SULLIVAN It's impossible to scare tough hombres who can get $55 a barrel for beer that costs them $7. There's plenty leeway for the 'fix'. M. KINGTON The Peruvians have always claimed that the result was a fix and demanded a replay. 6 J. KEROUAC Bull was.. taking his fix.. jabbing with the needle into his.. arm. I. MURDOCH He needed her as a drug addict needs his fix.

†**fix** *a.* LME–L17. [OFr. (mod. *fixe*) or its source L *fixus*: see next.] Fixed.

fix /fɪks/ *v.* LME. [Partly f. prec., partly f. med.L *fixare*, f. L *fixus* pa. pple of *figere* fix, fasten.] I 1 *v.t.* Fasten, make firm or stable in position; place; attach (a bayonet) to the muzzle of a rifle etc.; secure against displacement; implant (principles, memory, etc.). Freq. foll. by *in, on, to.* LME. b *v.i.* Become firmly attached or implanted; adhere *to*. Now *rare* or *obs.* L17. c *v.t. Genetics.* Establish (a character, or the gene responsible for it) as a permanent property of subsequent generations. E20. 2 *v.t.* Direct steadily and unwaveringly; set (the eyes, gaze, affections, attention) *on, upon*. Also attract and hold (the eyes, gaze, attention, etc.). LME. b Make motionless with astonishment etc., hold spellbound. Now *rare*. M16. c Make (the eyes, features, etc.) rigid, as in death. E19. 3 *v.t.* Deprive of volatility or fluidity. Orig. *spec.* in *Alch.*, cause (a volatile spirit or essence) to combine with a tangible solid or liquid. L15. b (Of a plant or bacterium) assimilate (nitrogen or carbon dioxide) by converting it into a non-gaseous compound; *gen.* cause (an element) to form a compound. M19. c Preserve and harden (tissue etc.), esp. for microscopic examination. L19. 4 *v.i.* Lose volatility or fluidity; congeal. Now *rare* or *obs.* E17. 5 *v.t.* Secure from change, vacillation, or wandering; give stability or constancy to (the mind, thoughts, affections, purposes). E17. **b** Settle immovably the purposes or convictions of. Foll. by *against*, *for*, *on*, *to do*. Now only in *pass.* L17. **c** Make constant in devotion. (Foll. by *in*, *to*.) Now *rare* or *obs.* E18. **6** *v.t.* Make (a colour, a drawing, a photographic image, etc.) fast and permanent. M17. **7** *v.t.* Hold engaged or occupied, corner (*lit.* & *fig.*). Also, single out *with* one's eyes etc. M17.

1 E. HALL His head to be fixed on a pole. E. BUDGELL I resolved . . to fix his face in my memory. b S. RICHARDSON Prejudices in disfavour . . fix deeper . . than prejudices in favour. 2 T. HERBERT Could but these Idolaters fix their mind upon Heaven. BYRON A shrine would fix The eye upon its seeming crucifix. c SHELLEY Fix those tortured orbs in peace and death. 5 BACON Images are said by the Roman church to fix the cogitations . . of them that pray before them. c J. AUSTEN If a woman conceals her affection . . from the object of it, she may lose the opportunity of fixing him. 7 S. RICHARDSON As I entered one Room he went into another . . At last I fixed him speaking to Rachel.

II 8 *v.t.* Place definitely or more or less permanently; station, establish; locate; set *up*. *colloq.* M16. **b** Foll. by *up*: arrange the accommodation of (a person); attend to the wants of; provide *with*. L19. **9** *v.i.* **a** Take up one's position mentally. Now *rare* or *obs.* E17. **b** Foll. by *on*, *upon*: settle one's choice on, choose, select. M17. **c** Decide, determine, *to do*, arrange *for doing*. L18. **10** *v.i.* Settle, esp. permanently, take up one's position or abode. *arch.* E17. **11** *v.t.* Appoint or assign the precise position or time of; refer (a thing) to a definite place, time, etc. Formerly also, attribute exclusively *to*. M17. **b** Allocate or determine the incidence of (a responsibility, liability, etc.). Also, burden (a person) *with* costs, liability, etc. M19. **12** *v.t.* Settle definitely; specify, determine, (a thing, *that*); settle or determine the form of, give a permanent form to, arrest changes or development in (language, literature, etc.). M17. **13** *v.t.* Adjust, make ready for use, arrange in proper order, organize. Also get ready, put in order, tidy; prepare (food or drink); apply cosmetics to. Also foll. by *up*. M17. **b** Mend, repair; redecorate; alter with the purpose of improvement. Also foll. by *up*. M18. **c** Obtain the support of (a person) by illegal or dubious means, esp. bribery; arrange (the result of a match etc.) fraudulently. L18. **d** Arrange favourably for oneself; deal with, silence, kill (a person). *slang.* M19. **e** Castrate or spay (an animal). M20. **14** *v.i.* **a** Intend, arrange, make preparations *to do*. Also foll. by *up*. E18. **b** Put oneself in proper trim; dress up, smarten up. Also foll. by *up*. L18. **15** *v.t.* Fettle, line (a puddling-furnace) with a fix. L19. **16** *v.i.* & *refl.* Inject oneself with a narcotic drug. *slang.* M20.

8 T. TWINING The dining-table was fixed in the middle of the room. SOUTHEY We are fixed here for some time. b R. C. PRAED He'd . . fix up Mr. Sabine comfortably for the night. 9b H. J. BROOKE Our choice would probably fix on that which was most predominant. c J. KEBLE I have fixed to go to London. 10 GOLDSMITH Where luxury once fixes, no art can either lessen or remove it. 11 S. JOHNSON Here will I fix the limits of transgression. J. H. NEWMAN The full moon is not fixed to any certain day in either month. 12 SWIFT Some Method . . for ascertaining and fixing our Language for ever. SOUTHEY It was . . fixed that the brigadier should go.E. A. PARKES The War Office authorities have fixed the daily supply . . at 8 gallons. *fix a person's fate*: see FATE *n.* 13 B. HARTE Mother'll fix you suthin' hot. G. VIDAL She . . fixed her face in a compact mirror. b G. STEIN The smell of paint when they were fixing up the kitchen. c J. BETJEMAN I fix the Planning Officer . . and the Mayor. *Guardian* The mere suspicion that matches were being 'fixed' would be disastrous for the game. d O. W. HOLMES If you can't fix it so as to be born here [Boston], you can come and live here. P. G. WODEHOUSE 'Don't you worry. I'll fix him.' . . 'You wouldn't croak him?' e D. H. LAWRENCE Is he a gentleman or a lady?—Neither, . . I had him fixed. 14a J. B. PRIESTLEY I may be able to fix up for you both to go out to supper afterwards. E. WELTY I think she was fixing to pull him out of that bed. b W. FAULKNER You better go to the bathroom and fix up.

fixable, **-ible** *a.* L15.

fixate /fɪkˈseɪt/ *v.* L19. [f. L *fixus* (see FIX *a.*) + -ATE[3].] **1** *v.t.* Fix, make stable. Now *rare.* L19. **2** *v.i.* Be or become fixed. L19. **3** *v.t.* Direct one's eyes on, concentrate one's gaze directly on. L19. **4** *Psychol.* Arrest (part of one's libido) at an immature stage, causing an abnormal attachment to persons or things and abnormal emotional responses; cause (a person) to undergo this. Also *loosely*, in *pass.*, be or become obsessed with. Freq. foll. by *on*. E20.

2 O. SACKS Their eyes roll for a moment, and then fixate. 3 D. MORRIS The baby's eyes can now fixate objects. 4 W. MCDOUGALL The *libido* . . of every child normally becomes fixated upon the parent of the opposite sex. R. QUIRK We mustn't get fixated on the reception of contemporary fiction.

fixation /fɪkˈseɪʃ(ə)n/ *n.* LME. [med.L *fixatio(n-)*, f. *fixat-* pa. ppl stem of *fixare*: see FIX *v.*, -ATION.] **1** *Sci.* & *Med.* The action or process of fixing; *spec.* conversion, now esp. of nitrogen, to a non-gaseous form; immobilization of a limb, a fractured bone, a joint, or a displaced or floating organ. LME. **†2** The quality or condition of being non-volatile or able to resist the action of fire. E17–E18. **3** A fixed proportion or standard. Formerly also, a fixed habitation or location. Now *rare.* E17. **4** *gen.* The action or an act of fixing; the fact or condition of being fixed. M17. **5** The action or an act of concentrating the gaze directly on an object. L19. **6** *Psychol.* The arresting of part of the libido at an immature stage, causing an abnormal attachment to persons or things and abnormal emotional responses; *loosely* an obsession, concentration on one idea. (Foll. by *on*.) E20.

3 T. FULLER Far . . from Ipswich his first fixation. B. FRANKLIN No . . invariable fixation for coining can be made. 4 J. BENTHAM The fixation of the punishment not lying within the province of the jury. CARLYLE Yet it had attained no fixation or consistency. 5 G. F. STOUT The fixation of images is not accompanied by overt movement. 6 M. HUNTER Publishers with fixations on stories of English boarding-school life.

fixative /ˈfɪksətɪv/ *a.* & *n.* M17. [f. FIX *v.* + -ATIVE.] **A** *adj.* Tending to set or fix something, used for fixing. M17. **B** *n.* A substance used to set or fix something, as colours or drawings, hair, biological material before microscopic examination, volatile components of perfumes, etc. L19.

fixature /ˈfɪksətʃə/ *n.* Now *rare.* M19. [f. FIX *v.* after *curvature* etc.] A preparation used to hold hair in position.

fixed /fɪkst/ *ppl a.* Also (*arch.*) **fixt**. LME. [f. FIX *v.* + -ED[1].] **1** Definitely and permanently placed or assigned; stationary or unchanging in relative position; definite, permanent, lasting. LME. **2a** Directed steadily or intently towards an object. M16. **b** Made rigid or immobile (as in strong emotion or by death). M17. **3** Placed or attached firmly (*lit.* & *fig.*); made firm or stable in position. Also (now *rare*), resolved, intent, or set on something. L16. **b** *Her.* Of a cross: having the limbs attached to the edges of the escutcheon. *rare.* L17. **4a** Not easily volatilized; deprived of volatility. M17. **b** Unable to be distilled or evaporated without decomposition. E19. **5** Prepared, put in order. Now *rare.* M17. **6** *pred.* Situated (*well*, *badly*, etc.) in material or financial terms; (foll. by *for*) situated with regard to. *colloq.* M19. **7** Corrupted, bribed; having the result fraudulently prearranged. *slang.* L19.

1 MILTON In which of all these Orbes hath Man His fixed seat. C. THIRLWALL A fixt and uniform rent. M. PATTISON Every Hanse town was in its turn represented, according to a fixed cycle. B. JOWETT Colours which are dyed in this way become fixed. P. CAREY To . . disappear like the image on an improperly fixed photograph. 2a A. RADCLIFFE He regarded her with a fixed attention. R. WEST Under Kitty's fixed gaze I had to open a letter. b H. MARTINEAU The papers in his hand shook; but his countenance was fixed. 3 LD MACAULAY For all persecution he felt a fixed aversion. 6 M. LAURENCE Not wealthy, perhaps, but certainly nicely fixed. 7 L. STEFFENS Being in with the stables, I soon began to hear about 'fixed races'.

Special collocations & comb.: *fixed capital*: see CAPITAL *n.*[2] 2. **fixed focus** a camera focus at a distance from the lens that is not adjustable. **fixed idea** = IDÉE FIXE. **fixed income** income from a pension, investment, etc., that is set at a particular figure and does not rise with the rate of inflation. **fixed odds** odds in betting that are predetermined. **fixed oil** a non-volatile oil. **fixed point** (*a*) *Physics* a well-defined reproducible temperature, usu. that of a change of phase, used for calibration or for defining a temperature scale; (*b*) *Math.* a point that is unchanged by a given transformation or by each of a given set of transformations; (*c*) a time of day at which a particular item is always broadcast, the rest of the programme schedule being devised so as to accommodate it; (*d*) *Computing*, used *attrib.* to designate a mode of representing a number by a single sequence of digits whose values depend on their location relative to a radix point in a predetermined position in the sequence; **fixed star** a star as now commonly understood, with a seemingly unchanging position relative to the other stars (in contrast to planets, comets, and meteors); **fixed-wing** *a.* designating aircraft of the conventional type as opp. to rotating-wing aircraft such as helicopters.

fixedly /ˈfɪksɪdli/ *adv.* L16. **fixedness** /ˈfɪksɪdnɪs/ *n.* E17.

†fixen *n.* var. of VIXEN.

fixer /ˈfɪksə/ *n.* E17. [f. FIX *v.* + -ER[1].] **1** A person who fixes something; *spec.* a person who makes (esp. illicit) arrangements or bargains. E17. **2** A thing which fixes something; *spec.* a substance for fixing photographic images etc. M19.

fixidity /fɪkˈsɪdɪti/ *n.* Now *rare.* M18. [f. FIX *a.* or FIXED after *fluidity*: see -ITY.] Fixity.

fixing /ˈfɪksɪŋ/ *n.* E17. [f. FIX *v.* + -ING[1].] **1** *gen.* The action of FIX *v.*; a thing which fixes something. E17. **b** A method or means of fixing. *rare.* M17. **2** In *pl.* Apparatus, equipment; the trimmings of a dress or dish; adjuncts. E19.

fixit /ˈfɪksɪt/ *n.* E20. [f. FIX *v.* + IT *pron.*] **1** = FIXER 1. Esp. as a pseudo-surname in *Miss Fixit*, *Mr Fixit*, etc. E20. **2** The action or an act of fixing something. M20.

fixity /ˈfɪksɪti/ *n.* M17. [Partly f. FIX *a.* + -ITY, partly through Fr. *fixité*.] **1** The property of a substance of not evaporating or losing weight when heated. Now *rare* or *obs.* M17. **2** *gen.* The condition of not being liable to displacement or change; the quality of being fixed; stability, permanence. L18.

fixt *ppl a.* see FIXED.

fixture /ˈfɪkstʃə, -tjə/ *n.* L16. [Alt. of FIXURE after *mixture*.] **1** The action of fixing; the process of becoming fixed. Now *rare* or *obs.* L16. **b** The condition of being fixed; fixedness, fixity. E19. **2** *Law.* In *pl.* Accessory articles annexed to a house or piece of land and regarded as legally part of it. M18. **3** In *pl.* Appendages, adjuncts; apparatus. *N. Amer.* M18. **4** Anything fixed or securely fastened in position; anything made firm, stable, or immobile. L18. **5** A person or thing confined to or established in one place. Chiefly *pred.* L18. **6** A (date agreed for a) meeting, appointment, etc.; *esp.* (the date appointed for) a sporting event, as a match, race, etc. E19.

1 SHAKES. *Merry W.* The firm fixture of thy foot would give an excellent motion to thy gait. 3 J. C. OATES It had . . swivel-type reading lamps and mahogany fixtures. 5 L. AUCHINCLOSS For twenty-five years I've been a fixture in her home. 6 CLIVE JAMES My afternoon fixture in Hiroshima, the Toyo Kogyo plant. *Football Monthly* West Ham still have a third of their home fixtures remaining.

fixure /ˈfɪkʃə, -sjʊə/ *n.* Long *arch. rare.* E17. [Late L *fixura*, f. L *figere* FIX *v.*: see -URE.] Fixed condition, position, or attitude; fixedness, stability.

fiz *n.*, *v.* see FIZZ *n.*, *v.*

fizgig /ˈfɪzɡɪɡ/ *n.*[1] & *a.* Also **fis-**, (in sense 5) **phiz-**. E16. [Prob. f. FIZZ *v.* + GIG *n.*[1]] **A** *n.* **1** A giddy flirtatious young woman. *arch.* E16. **2** A kind of whirligig or spinning-top. *rare.* M17. **3** A kind of small firework, a cracker. *arch.* M17. **4** A piece of tawdry finery. Also, a silly notion, an absurd crotchet. *arch.* E19. **5** An informer. *Austral. slang.* E20. **B** *adj.* Flighty. *arch.* E20.

fizgig /ˈfɪzɡɪɡ/ *n.*[2] Long *rare.* See also FISHGIG. M16. [Prob. ult. f. Sp. *fisga* harpoon.] A kind of harpoon.

fizz /fɪz/ *n.* Also (now *rare*) **fiz.** M18. [f. the vb.] 1 A disturbance, a fuss. Long *rare* or *obs.* M18. 2 A hissing or spluttering sound. E19. 3 High spirits, dash, animation. *arch.* M19. 4 An effervescent drink, *esp.* champagne. *colloq.* M19.
Comb.: **fizz-boat** *NZ* a motor boat, a speedboat.

fizz /fɪz/ *v.* Also (now *rare*) **fiz,** infl. **-zz-.** M17. [Imit.] †1 *v.t.* Cause to make a fizz. Only in M17. 2 *v.i.* Make a hissing or spluttering sound; move with a fizzing sound. L17. 3 *v.i.* Foll. by *out*: fade or die away. M19.

fizzer /ˈfɪzə/ *n.* M19. [f. FIZZ *v.*, *n.* + -ER[1].] 1 An excellent or first-rate thing. M19. 2 = FIZZ *n.* 4. *rare.* L19. 3 *Cricket.* A very fast ball; a ball that deviates with unexpected speed after pitching. *colloq.* E20. 4 A charge-sheet. *Mil. slang.* M20. 5 A disappointing failure, a fiasco. *Austral. slang.* M20.

fizzle /ˈfɪz(ə)l/ *v.* & *n.* LME. [Imit.: see FIZZ *v.*, -LE[3]. Cf. FISSLE.] A *v.i.* †1 Break wind quietly. LME–M18. 2 Make a feeble hissing or spluttering sound. M19. 3 Fail, end in a fiasco; reach a lame conclusion. Freq. foll. by *out.* M19. B *n.* †1 The action of breaking wind quietly. L16–M18. 2 (The action of making) a feeble hissing or spluttering sound. M19. 3 A failure, a fiasco, a lame conclusion. Also foll. by *out.* M19.

fizzy /ˈfɪzi/ *a.* M19. [f. FIZZ *v.* + -Y[1].] (Given to) fizzing; effervescent.
fizzily *adv.* L20. **fizziness** *n.* L20.

fjeld /fjɛld/ *n.* M19. [Norw. (Bokmål) *fjeld* f. ON *fjall*: see FELL *n.*[2]] A high barren rocky plateau, esp. in Scandinavia.

fjord *n.* var. of FIORD.

flab /flab/ *n.* E19. [Sense 1 alt. of FLAP *n.*; sense 2 back-form. f. FLABBY.] 1 = FLAP *n.* 6b. *dial.* E19. 2 Flabbiness, overweightness; bodily fat. *colloq.* M20.
2 K. GILES She looks pretty good..no flab round the thighs yet.

flabbergast /ˈflabəgɑːst/ *v.t.* *colloq.* L18. [Origin unkn.] Dumbfound, confound, astonish. Freq. in *pass.*
R. PARK She gave a screech of astonishment and flopped into a chair, completely flabbergasted.

flabby /ˈflabi/ *a.* L17. [Expressive alt. of FLAPPY.] 1 Chiefly of flesh: hanging down, through its own weight; flaccid, limp. Of a person etc.: overweight. L17. 2 Of language, character, etc.: weak, lacking vigour. L18. 3 Damp, clammy. Now *rare.* L18.
1 J. GALSWORTHY Thanks to abstemious habits, he had not grown fat and flabby.
flabbily *adv.* M19. **flabbiness** *n.* E18.

flabellate /fləˈbɛleɪt/ *a.* E19. [f. L *flabellum* fan + -ATE[2].] *Bot.* & *Zool.* Fan-shaped.

flabelliform /fləˈbɛlɪfɔːm/ *a.* L18. [f. as prec. + -I- + -FORM.] = prec.

flabellum /fləˈbɛləm/ *n.* Pl. **-lla** /-lə/. M19. [L, f. *flabrum* gust, f. *flare* to blow: see -ELLUM.] A fan; *esp.* one carried in religious ceremonies.

flaccid /ˈflaksɪd, ˈflasɪd/ *a.* E17. [Fr. *flaccide* or L *flaccidus*, f. *flaccus* flabby: see -ID[1].] 1 Of flesh etc.: lacking stiffness, hanging or lying loose or in wrinkles, flabby, limp. E17. b *Bot.* Bending without elasticity; relaxed from lack of moisture, drooping. E17. 2 Of an immaterial thing: lacking vigour, feeble. M17.
1 H. WILLIAMSON Further exercises brought the aching flaccid muscles back into tension. 2 F. W. FARRAR His resolutions have been feeble, and his purposes flaccid. R. C. HUTCHINSON The flaccid voice of one whose reserves are long overdrawn.
flaccidity /flәkˈsɪdɪti, fləˈsɪ-/ *n.* L17. **flaccidly** *adv.* M19. **flaccidness** *n.* E18.

flacherie /ˈflaʃ(ə)riː/ *n.* L19. [Fr. = flaccidity.] An infectious disease of silkworms marked by digestive disorders and bodily flaccidity.

Flacian /ˈfleɪʃɪən/ *n.* & *a.* M16. [f. *Flacius* (see below) + -AN.] A *n.* A follower of Matthias Flacius (1520–75), a Lutheran theologian, who opposed the adiaphorist views advocated by Melanchthon; an anti-adiaphorist. M16. B *adj.* Of or pertaining to Matthias Flacius or his followers. L19.
Flacianist *n.* L19.

flack /flak/ *n.*[1] *slang* (chiefly *US*). M20. [Origin unkn.] A press agent; a publicity man. Also *flackman.*
flackery *n.* public relations, promotion, hype M20.

flack *n.*[2] var. of FLAK.

flack /flak/ *v.*[1] *obs.* exc. *dial.* LME. [Imit.; = MDu. *vlacken*, ON *flaka* (of a wound) gape, Icel. *flaka* to flap, hang loose.] 1 *v.i.* Flap, flutter; flap the wings; palpitate. LME. 2 *v.t.* Move or shake intermittently; flap, flick. M18. 3 *v.t.* Beat with a flail; rake (hay). M18. 4 *v.i.* Hang loosely. *dial.* E19.

flack /flak/ *v.*[2] *N. Amer. colloq.* M20. [f. FLACK *n.*[1]] 1 *v.i.* Act as a flack, disseminate favourable publicity. M20. 2 *v.t.* Speak in favour of, promote (a person or thing); disseminate (information etc.). L20.

flacker /ˈflakə/ *v.i.* & (*rare*) *t.* Now chiefly *dial.* LME. [Prob. rel. to OE *flacor* adj. (of arrows) flying, f. imit. base repr. also by MHG *vlackern* flicker (G *flackern*), ON *flǫkra*, *flǫkta* flutter. Cf. FLICKER *v.*] Flap (the wings), flutter.

flacket /ˈflakɪt/ *n.* *obs.* exc. *dial.* ME. [ONFr. *flasquet*, dim. of *flasque*: see FLASK *n.*, -ET[1].] A flask, bottle, or vessel; *esp.* a barrel-shaped liquor vessel.

flacon /flakɔ̃/ *n.* Pl. pronounced same. E19. [Fr.: see FLAGON.] A small stoppered bottle; *esp.* one for scent or smelling-salts.

fladge /fladʒ/ *n.* *slang.* M20. [Abbrev.] = FLAGELLATION 2b.

flag /flag/ *n.*[1] LME. [Rel. to Du. *flag*, Da. *flæg*: ult. origin unkn.] 1 Any of various plants, *esp.* irises, with sword-shaped leaves; *esp.* (more fully *water* or *yellow flag*) a yellow-flowered Eurasian iris, *Iris pseudacorus*, common in streams and pools. LME. b In *pl.* or *collect.* A kind of coarse grass. L16. 2 The blade or long slender leaf of a cereal or other plant. L16.
1 AV *Job* 8:11 Can the rush growe vp without myre? can the flag growe without water? *sweet flag*: see SWEET *a.* & *adv.* 2 R. JEFFERIES The wheat was then showing a beautiful flag.
Comb.: **flag-root** *N. Amer.* (the root of) sweet flag, *Acorus calamus.*

flag /flag/ *n.*[2] Cf. FLAGSTONE. LME. [Prob. of Scand. origin: cf. Icel. *flag* spot where a turf has been cut out, ON *flaga* slab of stone.] 1 A piece of turf; a sod; a slice of earth turned over by the plough. Also *collect.*, turf; ploughed earth. Long *dial.* (*East Anglia*). LME. 2 A flat slab of any fine-grained rock which may be split into flagstones; a flagstone; (in *pl.*) a pavement or floor of flagstones. LME.
2 G. JONES The sound of his boots on the kitchen flags. *Comb.*: W. J. LOCKE A narrow flag-paved street.

flag /flag/ *n.*[3] L15. [Origin unkn.] A quill-feather of a bird's wing. Usu. in *pl.* or as *flag-feather.*

flag /flag/ *n.*[4] M16. [Perh. orig. an application of the adj.] 1 A piece of bunting or other material, usu. oblong or square, attachable by one edge to a staff or halyard, and used as a standard, ensign, or signal, or for decoration or display. M16. 2 *spec.* *Naut.* A flag carried by a vessel to show that an admiral is in command. Hence, the emblem of an admiral's rank afloat; the admiral himself; a flagship. M17. 3 *spec.* A flag raised, dropped, waved, etc., to indicate the start or finish of a race. Hence, the moment so indicated. Also, a device on a chess-clock which falls when the time-limit is reached. M19. 4 The tail of an animal, *esp.* of a setter. M19. 5 An apron. *slang.* M19. 6 A small object or device resembling a flag; *esp.* a visible part of the mechanism in a taxi's meter etc., used to indicate availability. E20. 7 A statement of the name (and sometimes other details) of a newspaper or other publication, as printed on the page. M20. 8 *Computing.* A symbol or symbols used to indicate some property of the data in a record, *spec.* the truth of a statement. M20.
Phrases: **black flag** (*a*) a pirate's ensign; (*b*) a flag formerly hoisted outside a prison to announce the execution of a criminal. *chequered flag*: see CHEQUERED *a.* 1. **flag of convenience** a foreign flag under which a ship is registered in order to avoid financial charges etc. **flag of truce** a white flag used to signal the wish for a truce. **give** etc. **the honour of the flag** make etc. an acknowledgement of supremacy by lowering the flag to another. **hoist one's flag** (of an admiral) take up command. **hoist the flag** make a claim to discovered territory by raising one's national flag. **keep the flag flying** refuse to haul down one's flag and surrender; continue the fight (chiefly *fig.*). **lower** or **strike one's flag** take it down, *esp.* as a token of respect, submission, or surrender; (of an admiral) relinquish command. **put the flag(s) out** celebrate a victory or other event. *rally round the flag*: see RALLY *v.*[1] *red flag*: see RED *a.* **show the flag** (esp. of a naval vessel) make an official visit to a foreign port or elsewhere; *fig.* ensure that notice is taken of oneself, one's country, etc. *strike one's flag*: see *lower one's flag* above. **white flag** a flag of truce, a flag disclaiming hostile intention. *yellow flag*: see YELLOW *a.*
Comb.: **flag-boat** a boat serving as a mark in sailing-matches; **flag-captain** the captain of a flagship; **flag-day** a day on which a charity holds a street collection, and donors are given small paper badges as tokens; **Flag Day** *US* the anniversary (14 June) of the adoption of the Stars and Stripes in 1777; **flag-fall** the dropping of a flag to indicate the start of a race; **flag-flying** the flying of flags; *fig.* (*colloq.*) (*a*) (deliberate) overbidding at bridge; (*b*) = *kite-flying* (c) s.v. KITE *n.*; **flag-lieutenant** an admiral's aide-de-camp; **flag-list** the roll of flag-officers; **flagman** †(*a*) an admiral, a flag-officer; (*b*) a person who has charge of, carries, or signals with a flag; **flag-officer** an admiral, vice admiral, or rear admiral; a yacht-club commodore; **flag-pole** a flagstaff; **flag-rank** the rank of flag-officer; **flagstaff**, pl. **-staffs**, **-staves**, a pole or staff on which a flag is hoisted; **flag-station**: where trains stop only if signalled; **flag-wagging** *slang* (*a*) signalling with hand-held flags; (*b*) = *flag-waving* below; **flag-waver** a chauvinist, a political agitator; **flag-waving** trying to arouse popular enthusiasm, jingoism.
flagless *a.* not bearing a flag or flags M19. **flaglet** *n.* a small flag L19.

†**flag** *a.* L16–M18. [Origin unkn.] Hanging down, drooping (esp. of hair, an animal's tail).

flag /flag/ *v.*[1]*t.* Infl. **-gg-.** E16. [f. FLAG *n.*[2]] Pave with flagstones. Also, (of a stone) form the paving of.
flagging *vbl n.* (*a*) the action of the verb; (*b*) the material used in paving; the pavement: E17.

flag /flag/ *v.*[2] Infl. **-gg-.** M16. [Rel. to FLAG *a.*] 1 *v.i.* Hang down; flap about loosely. M16. †b *v.t.* Allow to droop; drop (the head, ears, tail, etc.). M17–M18. †2 *v.i.* (Of wings) move feebly; (of a bird) move its wings feebly; fly unsteadily or near the ground. L16–M18. 3 *v.i.* Become limp or flaccid; (of a plant) droop, fade. E17. 4 *v.t.* †a (Of a bird etc.) relax the efforts of (its wings) from fatigue; (of conditions etc.) impede (the wings). E17–E18. b Allow or cause to become languid; enfeeble. E17. 5 (The predominant sense.) *v.i.* Become feeble or unsteady in flight or motion; be unable to maintain one's speed, strength, or interest; lag through fatigue; become languid. M17. b Of an author, book, pleasure, conversation, etc.: wane in vigour or interest, grow dull. L17.
1 SHELLEY Its sails were flagging in the breathless noon. 2 SPENSER My Muse, whose fethers..Doe yet but flagg and slowly learn to fly. 4b J. M. FAULKNER Famine and fever flagged their forces. 5 E. BOWEN He never flagged in his wish that they should continue to learn. J. M. COETZEE The work was hard; by mid-morning K was flagging. b THOMAS HUGHES By degrees the cricket flagged, and most of the men went off.

flag /flag/ *v.*[3]*t.* Infl. **-gg-.** L17. [f. FLAG *n.*[1]] †1 Plant *about* with flags or reeds. Only in L17. 2 Tighten (the seams of a barrel) by means of flags or rushes. M18. 3 Cut off the flag or blade of (wheat). M19.

flag /flag/ *v.*[4]*t.* Infl. **-gg-.** L18. [f. FLAG *n.*[4]] 1 Provide with, decorate, or mark out (as) with flags; place a flag on or over. L18. b Mark with a small flag or tag so that relevant items may be readily found. M20. c *Computing.* Assign a flag (FLAG *n.*[4] 8) or flags to (information). M20. 2 Inform or communicate (as) by means of a flag or flags; *esp.* (also foll. by *down*) stop (a driver, vehicle, etc.) by waving or signalling; obtain (a lift) by such means. M19.
1 *Times* In honour of the day all the official buildings ..were flagged. *Scientific American* The presence of a transposon simultaneously generates a mutation..,

identifies itself . . and flags its location. 2 S. BELLOW He went into the middle of the street and flagged a cab. C. THUBRON I was flagged down for breaking one of the . . traffic laws. *absol.*: J. DIDION Mr McClellan met them . . , flagging wildly when he caught sight of the truck.

flagella *n.* pl. of FLAGELLUM.

flagellant /ˈfladʒ(ə)l(ə)nt, fləˈdʒɛl(ə)nt/ *n.* & *a.* L16. [L *flagellant-* pres. ppl stem of *flagellare* to whip, f. FLAGELLUM: see -ANT[1].] A *n.* 1 A person who scourges himself or herself as a religious discipline or penance; *esp.* a member of one of the bands of such people common in Europe in the 13th cent. and later. Usu. in *pl.* L16. 2 *gen.* A person who flagellates (himself or herself, or others) from cruelty, for sexual gratification, etc. L18. B *adj.* Given to flagellation, flagellating. L19.

flagellantism *n.* M19.

flagellar /fləˈdʒɛlə/ *a.* L19. [f. FLAGELLUM + -AR[1].] *Biol.* Of or pertaining to a flagellum or flagella.

flagellate /ˈfladʒ(ə)lət, -eɪt/ *a.* & *n.* M19. [f. FLAGELLUM + -ATE[2].] A *adj.* Having flagella; *esp.* of the nature of a flagellate, pertaining to flagellates. Also, flagelliform. M19. B *n.* Any member of the subphylum Mastigophora (formerly the class Flagellata) of microscopic protozoans, characterized by the possession of flagella (used for locomotion). L19.

flagellated *a.* provided with flagella L19.

flagellate /ˈfladʒəleɪt/ *v.t.* Pa. pple **-ated**, (*rare*) **-ate** /-ət/. E17. [L *flagellat-* pa. ppl stem of *flagellare*: see FLAGELLANT, -ATE[3].] Scourge, whip.

flagellator *n.* a person who flagellates M16. **flagellatory** *a.* pertaining to flagellation M19.

flagellation /fladʒəˈleɪʃ(ə)n/ *n.* LME. [eccl.L *flagellatio(n-)*, f. as FLAGELLATE *v.*: see -ATION. Sense 3 f. FLAGELLATE *a.* & *n.*] 1 (**F-**.) The scourging of Jesus; a picture representing this. LME. 2 *gen.* The action of scourging or flogging; a flogging. L15. b Beating as a means of sexual gratification. L19. 3 *Zool.* = EXFLAGELLATION. Also, the arrangement of flagella on an organism. L19.

ˈflagellative *a.* pertaining to flagellation M19.

flagelliform /fləˈdʒɛlɪfɔːm/ *a.* E19. [f. FLAGELLUM + -I- + -FORM.] *Biol.* Having the form of a flagellum.

flagellist /ˈfladʒ(ə)lɪst/ *n.* M19. [f. FLAGELLUM + -IST.] A flagellator.

flagellomania /ˌfladʒ(ə)lə(ʊ)ˈmeɪnɪə/ *n.* L19. [f. FLAGELLUM + -O- + -MANIA.] Enthusiasm for flogging (as a punishment); abnormal desire for flagellation of oneself or others.

flagellomaniac *n.* & *a.* L19.

flagellum /fləˈdʒɛləm/ *n.* Pl. **-lla** /-lə/. E19. [L, dim. of *flagrum* scourge.] 1 A whip, a scourge. Chiefly *joc.* E19. 2 *Biol.* A motile whiplike projection from a cell. Also, (*Bot.*) a runner, a creeping shoot. M19.

flageolet /fladʒəˈlɛt, ˈfladʒəlɪt/ *n.*[1] M17. [Fr., dim. of OFr. *flag(e)ol*, *flajol* f. Prov. *flaujol*, of unkn. origin: see -ET[1].] 1 A small wind instrument resembling the recorder, having six principal holes, including two for the thumb, and sometimes keys. M17. 2 An organ-stop having a tone similar to that of this instrument. M19.

flageolet /fladʒəˈlɛt, *foreign* flaʒɔlɛ (*pl. same*)/ *n.*[2] L19. [Fr., ult. f. L *phaseolus* bean: see -ET[1].] A small kind of (esp. French) kidney-bean. Also *flageolet bean*.

flagger /ˈflagə/ *n.*[1] M19. [f. FLAG *v.*[1], *n.*[2] + -ER[1].] 1 A person who lays down flagstones. M19. 2 A streetwalker. *slang.* Now *rare* or *obs.* M19.

flagger /ˈflagə/ *n.*[2] *obs.* exc. *Hist.* L19. [f. FLAG *n.*[4] + -ER[1].] A person who carries a flag before a traction-engine to warn of its approach.

flaggy /ˈflagi/ *a.*[1] LME. [f. FLAG *n.*[1] + -Y[1].] 1 Having many flags or reeds. LME. 2 Resembling a flag or reed. L16. 3 Consisting or made of flags or reeds. E17. 4 Of corn, straw, etc.: having a large blade (cf. FLAG *n.*[1] 2.). M19.

flaggy /ˈflagi/ *a.*[2] *obs.* exc. *dial.* M16. [f. FLAG *v.*[2] + -Y[1].] 1 Soft and flabby, flaccid. M16. 2 Hanging down limply or lankly, drooping, pendulous. L16.

flagginess *n.* M17.

flaggy /ˈflagi/ *a.*[3] M19. [f. FLAG *n.*[2] + -Y[1].] Of stone: readily split into flags, laminate.

flagitate /ˈfladʒɪteɪt/ *v.t. rare.* E17. [L *flagitat-* pa. ppl stem of *flagitare* demand earnestly: see -ATE[3].] Entreat, importune.

flagiˈtation *n.* M17.

flagitious /fləˈdʒɪʃəs/ *a.* LME. [f. L *flagitiosus*, f. *flagitium* importunity, shameful crime, f. *flagitare*: see prec., -IOUS.] Extremely wicked, criminal, villainous.

flagitiously *adv.* E17. **flagitiousness** *n.* L17.

flagon /ˈflag(ə)n/ *n.* LME. [(O)Fr. *flacon* f. late L *flasco*, *-on-* FLASK *n.*] 1 A large bottle for holding liquor; *spec.* (*a*) In early use, a metal bottle with a screw top, such as was carried by pilgrims; (*b*) A flattened globular glass bottle for wine or cider, holding nearly twice as much as an ordinary bottle (now usu. 1.13 litres). LME. 2a A vessel used to hold the wine at the Eucharist. L15. b A large vessel containing drink for use at table, usu. with a handle, spout, and lid. E16. 3 The amount of liquid held by a full flagon; a flagon and its contents. E17.

flagrance /ˈfleɪgr(ə)ns/ *n. rare.* E17. [(OFr.) f. as next; in mod. use f. FLAGRANT: see -ANCE.] 1 = FLAGRANCY 1. E17. 2 = FLAGRANCY 2. M19.

flagrancy /ˈfleɪgr(ə)nsi/ *n.* L16. [L *flagrantia*, f. *flagrant-*: see next, -ANCY.] 1 Glaring shamefulness; outrageousness, scandalousness, notoriety. L16. 2 *lit.* Blazing or glowing condition. *rare.* E17.

flagrant /ˈfleɪgr(ə)nt/ *a.* L15. [Fr., or L *flagrant-* pres. ppl stem of *flagrare* burn, blaze, be inflamed: see -ANT[1].] 1 †a Resplendent, glorious. Only in L15. b Blazing, burning, glowing; gaudy. *arch.* L15. †c Of a fluid: fiery, hot. Only in 17. †d Burning red from a flogging. E18–M19. †2 Of a feeling, passion, etc.: ardent, burning. E16–L18. 3 Of an offence, an offender: glaring, notorious, scandalous, blatant. E18. 4 Actually in progress; (of war etc.) raging. E19.

1b SOUTHEY The crackling hearth, Where heath and cistus gave their flagrant flame. CARLYLE A . . Dowager (who dresses . . in flagrant colours). *fig.*: DE QUINCEY Flagrant health, health boiling over in fiery rapture. 3 T. F. DIBDIN An indifferent General, and a flagrant traitor. ALDOUS HUXLEY Surprised in flagrant inattention, Jeremy started guiltily. W. C. WILLIAMS A flagrant miscarriage of justice in our local courts. 4 **in flagrant delict** = IN FLAGRANTE DELICTO.

flagrantly *adv.* M18. **flagrantness** *n.* (*rare*) E18.

flagrante delicto /fləˌgrantɪ dɪˈlɪktəʊ/ *adv. phr.* E19. [L = in the heat of the crime.] = IN FLAGRANTE DELICTO.

flagship /ˈflagʃɪp/ *n.* L17. [f. FLAG *n.*[4] + SHIP *n.*] 1 A ship bearing an admiral's flag, *esp.* one in a fleet or squadron. L17. 2 Something considered a leader or superior example of its kind; *spec.* the major product, model, etc., in a company's range. M20.

flagstone /ˈflagstəʊn/ *n.* M16. [f. FLAG *n.*[2] + STONE *n.*] 1 A flat stone suitable for paving etc.; (in *pl.*) a pavement or paved floor. M16. 2 Sandstone that can be split up into flags. E19.

flagstoned *a.* paved with flagstones L19.

flail /fleɪl/ *n.* & *a.* [OE, = OS *flegil*, (M)Du. *vlegel*, (O)HG *flegel*, f. WGmc, prob. f. L *flagellum* scourge, flail. In ME prob. f. OFr. *flaiel* or MDu. *vlegel.*] A *n.* 1 A threshing implement consisting of a wooden handle attached to a heavy free-swinging pole or club. OE. 2 Something resembling this; a whip, a scourge. LME. †3 Something which swings on a pivot, as the swing-bar of a gate, the clapper of a bell, the lever of a press. LME–L17. 4 A medieval weapon consisting of a (usu. iron) handle with a spiked club or lengths of chain attached. L15.

protestant flail a short staff weighted with lead carried by protestants at the time of the 'Popish plot' (1678–81).

B *attrib.* or as *adj. Med.* Of a part of the body: abnormally movable, hanging loosely. L19.

Comb. & *special collocations*: **flail chest** a condition in which multiple rib fractures cause excessive flexibility of the chest wall, sufficient to interfere with breathing; **flail-harvester**, **mower**, etc., a harvesting, mowing, etc., machine having free-swinging cutters mounted on a horizontal rotor; **flail-joint** *Med.* a joint showing grossly excessive mobility; *flail-mower*: see *flail-harvester* above; **flail-tank** a tank with flails attached, used to detonate mines.

flail /fleɪl/ *v.* L15. [f. the n.] 1 *v.t.* Scourge, beat; strike with or as with a flail. L15. b Thresh (corn etc.) with a flail. E19. 2 *v.i.* & *t.* Thrash about (with); wave or swing (an object) wildly or erratically. L19.

1 P. BAILEY She flailed the ancient carpet as if it contained demons instead of dust. 2 I. MCEWAN Clawing at their throats, retching, flailing their arms and falling to the grass. J. MONTAGUE Windshield wipers flail helpless against the rain.

flair /flɛː/ *n.*[1] Also **flare**. M17. [OFr. = a kind of flatfish.] A ray or skate.

flair /flɛː/ *n.*[2] L19. [Fr., f. *flairer* to smell f. Proto-Romance f. L *fragrare*: see FRAGRANT.] 1 An instinct for selecting or performing what is excellent or useful; instinctive discernment. Also, originality, stylishness. L19. 2 Special aptitude, ability, or enthusiasm *for*. E20.

1 U. LE GUIN He seemed to have lost the flair . . , the sense for where the really important problem lay. C. FREEMAN To wear an inexpensive dress with such flair that her friends were under the impression that she dressed extravagantly. 2 D. CARNEGIE With his Irish geniality, he had a flair for making people like him.

flair /flɛː/ *v.t.* E20. [f. FLAIR *n.*[2]] Sniff, smell out, scent; *fig.* detect.

Glasgow Herald We flair survivals of phrase and intonation lurking in the speech . . of very aged persons. *absol.*: J. MASEFIELD The fox . . flaired with his muzzle.

flaith /flɑː/ *n.* M19. [Irish.] *Ir. Hist.* The chief of an ancient family or *fine*.

flak /flak/ *n.* In sense 2 also **flack**. M20. [G, abbrev. of *fliegerabwehrkanone* lit. 'aviator-defence-gun'.] 1 Anti-aircraft fire (*spec.* German, in the war of 1939–45). M20. 2 *fig.* Strong adverse criticism; hostile reactions. M20.

1 J. BRAINE The bomb-aimer got a faceful of flak. 2 *Times* When someone left the office lights on during a power crisis, they . . got a good deal of flak in the morning.

Comb.: **flak-catcher** a person or organization whose job it is to deal with criticism on behalf of another. **flak-jacket** a protective jacket of heavy fabric reinforced with metal.

flake /fleɪk/ *n.*[1] ME. [Perh. f. ON *flaki*, *fleki* wicker shield (Da. *flage* hurdle).] 1 A (wattled) hurdle, sometimes used as a temporary gate. Now *dial.* ME. 2 A frame or rack for storing provisions, esp. oatcakes, or drying produce, esp. fish. LME. 3 *Mining.* A framework of boards used as a shelter from the weather. *obs.* exc. *dial.* M17. 4 *Naut.* A small stage or workmen's cradle hung over the side of a ship. M19.

flake /fleɪk/ *n.*[2] ME. [Immediate source unkn.: perh. senses of different origins. Cf. Norw. *flak* patch, flake, *flake* form into flakes, Sw. *isflak* ice floe, ON *flakna* flake off, split, Du. *vlak* spot, fleck, prob. f. Gmc. Cf. FLAW *n.*[1], FLAUGHT *n.*[1]] 1 = SNOWFLAKE 1. ME. b A small piece of down or fluff; something resembling this. M17. †2 A spot, a fleck, a blemish. LME–M16. 3 An ignited fragment thrown off by a fire; an isolated tongue of flame. LME. 4 A stratum or lamina; a thin sheet; *spec.* a (loose) sheet of ice, a floe. LME. 5 A small flattish fragment. E16. 6 A thin piece peeled or split off from a surface. L16. b *Archaeol.* A piece of stone detached from a larger block, esp. by human action in the course of the manufacture of implements. M19. 7 A bundle of parallel threads; a loose lock of hair. Cf. FLAKE *n.*[3] *arch.* L16. 8 One of the natural divisions of the flesh, *esp.* of certain fishes. E17. b Dogfish or other shark, as food. E20. 9 (A plant of) a variety of carnation with striped petals. Cf. BIZARRE *n.* 1, PICOTEE *n.* E18. 10 In *pl.* Any of various kinds of breakfast cereal; *esp.* cornflakes. E20.

Comb.: **flake culture** a primitive culture characterized by the use of stone implements made from flakes struck for the making of implements; **flake-stand** a cooling-tub for the worm of a still; **flake-white** a pigment made from flakes of white lead; **flake tool** *Archaeol.* a tool made from a flake struck for the making of a tool (*flake-tool culture* = *flake culture* above).

flake /fleɪk/ *n.*[3] E17. [Cf. FAKE *n.*[1] and G *Flechte* of same meaning.] = FAKE *n.*[1] Cf. FLAKE *n.*[2] 7.

flake /fleɪk/ *v.*[1] LME. [f. FLAKE *n.*[2]] 1 *v.i.* Fall as flakes. Orig., now *rarely*, of snow. LME. 2 *v.t.* Cover with or as with flakes (of snow etc.). E17. 3 *v.t.* Mark with flecks or streaks. E17. 4 *v.t.* Break flakes from; break or rub off in flakes. M17. b *v.i.* Come away or off in flakes; separate as flakes. M18. 5 *v.i.* & *t.* Break into small pieces; separate into flakes. M17.

1 D. M. MOIR Butterflies . . Down flaking in an endless stream. 2 LONGFELLOW His russet beard was already Flaked with patches of snow, as hedges sometimes in November. 4 E. B. TYLOR Most stone knives of the kind seem to have been used, as they were flaked off. W. RYE Watermen . . are believed to flake off their dirt . . by rubbing themselves against the sharp angles of square flint church towers. b B. BAINBRIDGE The plaster was flaking off the ceiling.

flaked *ppl a.*[1] (*a*) arranged in flakes or layers; (*b*) marked with flecks or streaks: L16. **flaker** *n.* a person who or thing which flakes; *spec.* an implement for flaking flint: L19. **flaking** *vbl n.* the action of the vb; the condition of being flaked or flecked; a flecked appearance: E19.

flake /fleɪk/ *v.*[2] L15. [Var. of FLACK *v.*[1], FLAG *v.*[2]] †1 *v.i.* Become languid or flabby; flag; (of a garment) fall in folds. L15–L16. 2 *v.i.* Lie about, laze, bask. *dial.* M17. 3 *v.i.* Faint or fall asleep (from exhaustion, drunkenness, etc.) Usu. foll. by *out. colloq.* M20.

3 K. HULME When you flaked, I didn't know whether to get a doctor or not.

flaked *ppl a.*[2] tired *out*, exhausted, unconscious, asleep M20.

flake /fleɪk/ *v.*[3]*t.* L19. [f. FLAKE *n.*[3] Cf. FAKE *v.*[1]] *Naut.* Lay (a rope) on the deck in coils so that it will run out freely when required; lay out (a chain cable) on the forecastle deck for examination; lay (a sail) down in folds on either side of the boom. Also foll. by *down*. Cf. FAKE *v.*[1]

flaky /ˈfleɪki/ *a.* L16. [f. FLAKE *n.*[2] + -Y[1].] 1 Consisting of or resembling flakes. L16. 2 Separating easily into flakes; (of pastry) consisting of thin flakes when baked. L17. 3 Full of locks or tufts of hair. Now *rare*. E19. 4 Crazy, eccentric. *N. Amer. slang.* M20.

flakily *adv.* M19. **flakiness** *n.* M18.

flam /flam/ *n.*[1], *v.*, & *a.* E17. [Origin uncertain: perh. abbrev. of FLIMFLAM or FLAMFEW.] A *n.* †1 A fanciful notion, a whim. Only in 17. †2 A fanciful composition of verse. M17–M18. 3 A fabrication or falsehood; (a piece of) deception; flattery, blarney. M17. B *v.t.* Deceive by a fabrication or trick, or by flattery. *obs.* exc. *dial.* & *US.* M17. †C *adj.* Counterfeit, fabricated, fictitious. Only in L17.

flam /flam/ *n.*[2] L18. [Prob. imit.] A type of stroke in side-drum playing, made by striking both sticks against the parchment leaving a slight interval between them.

R. GRAVES Could I call a double-flam From the drums.

flamant *a.* var. of FLAMMANT.

†**flamb** *v.t. Sc.* LME–M19. [AN *flaum(b)er*, Fr. *flamber* singe; orig. a var. of *flam(m)er* FLAME *v.*] Baste.

†**flambant** *a.* L16–L19. [Fr., f. *flamber* FLAME *v.*] Flaming.

flambé /flɑ̃be, ˈflɒmbeɪ/ *a.* & *v.* L19. [Fr., pa. pple of *flamber* singe, pass through flame.] A *adj.* 1 (Of a copper-based glaze) iridescent from the effects of a special firing process; (of a type of Chinese porcelain) characterized by such a glaze. L19. 2 Of food: covered with spirit and served alight. E20. B *v.t.* Pa. t. & pple ***-béed***. Cover (food) with spirit and set alight. M20.

flambeau /ˈflambəʊ/ *n.* Pl. **-s**, **-x** /-z/. M17. [(O)Fr., dim. of *flambe*, †*flamble*, f. L *flammula*, dim. of *flamma* FLAME *n.*] 1 A flaming torch, *esp.* one made of several thick waxed wicks. M17. 2 A large (branched) candlestick. L19.

1 *fig.*: A. E. HOUSMAN The chestnut casts his flambeaux.

flamboyant /flamˈbɔɪənt/ *n.* Also **-boyan** /-ˈbɔɪən/, **-boyante**. L19. [Prob. Fr., use as n. of FLAMBOYANT *a.*] The royal poinciana, *Delonix regia*. Also more fully *flamboyant tree*.

flamboyant /flamˈbɔɪənt/ *a.* M19. [Fr., pres. pple of *flamboyer* to blaze, flame, f. *flambe*: see prec.] 1 a *Archit.* Of a style: characterized by wavy flamelike lines. M19. b Resembling a flame in form; wavy. L19. 2 Gorgeously (flame-)coloured; (of a person, behaviour, etc.) florid, ostentatious, showy. M19.

1a *absol.*: N. PEVSNER French Flamboyant . . is compared unfavourably with English Perpendicular. b F. WILKINSON A so-called flamboyant blade, on which the edge was scalloped. 2 CONAN DOYLE His brilliant necktie, shining pin, and glittering rings were flamboyant in their effect. S. J. PERELMAN A young lady in flamboyant theatrical make-up appeared.

flamboyance, **-cy** *ns.* the quality of being flamboyant L19. **flamboyantly** *adv.* L19.

flamdoodle *n.* see FLAPDOODLE.

flame /fleɪm/ *n.* ME. [AN *flaum(b)e*, (O)Fr. *flam(m)e*, f. L *flamma*.] 1 (A portion of) ignited gas, typically incandescent and often tongue- or spire-shaped. ME. b The state of visible combustion; in *pl.* (w. *the*), fire, esp. w. ref. to death or destruction by burning. LME. 2 A burning intense emotion; passion; *esp.* love. Formerly also, genius, talent, esp. in writing. ME. b A lover; now usu. (*joc.*) in *old flame* a former lover. M17. 3 A bright beam of light; *fig.* brilliance, brilliant colouring. LME. 4 Something resembling a flame in shape or esp. in colour. E17. b The red-orange colour of flame. E18. 5 A pale noctuid moth, *Axylia putris*. E19.

1 DRYDEN Thrice to the vaulted Roof the Flames aspire. M. AMIS The flabby blue flame from the gas-ring. *fig.*: A. S. BYATT An atmosphere of smothered conflagration . . —not visible flame, but the uneasy smouldering . . of a bonfire. b E. O'NEILL Their cities shall vanish in flame, their fields shall be wasted. 2 MABEL COLLINS This flame of ardent ambition kept her alive. J. FOWLES Her eyes were all flame as she threw a passionate look back at Charles. 3 W. C. BRYANT The northern lights . . cold, wandering flames. 4 M. E. BRADDON The yellow stonecrop made a flame of colour on the top. b *attrib.*: *Vogue* His [a designer's] back-baring flame dress.

Phrases: **burst into flame**(s) ignite. *fan the flame*: see FAN *v.* **in flames** on fire (*shoot down in flames*: see SHOOT *v.*). *oil to* or *on the flames*: see OIL *n.* *old flame*: see sense 2b above.

Comb.: **flame-cell** *Zool.* a ciliated cell at the end of a protonephridium which creates a water current in the tubule; **flame gun** a flame-throwing gun used to destroy weeds, etc.; **flame nettle** any of various labiate plants of the genus *Solenostemon*, with variegated leaves, grown as house-plants; = COLEUS; **flame-projector** = *flame-thrower* below; **flame-proof** *a.* & *v.t.* (make) able to resist flames; **flame-retardant**, **-resistant** *adjs.* (of fabric etc.) not readily flammable; **flame test**: for detecting certain chemical elements by the characteristic colour they give to a flame; **flame-thrower** a weapon for throwing a spray of ignited fuel; **flame-trap** a device fitted to prevent the passage of flame through a system esp. in an internal-combustion engine; **flame tree** any of various trees with brilliant red or yellow flowers; *esp.* a bottle tree, *Brachychiton australis*, native to Australia; **flame-ware** cooking equipment, esp. of glass, that can withstand the heat of an open flame.

flameless *a.* burning without flame; devoid of flame: E17. **flamelet** *n.* a small flame M19. **flamelike** *a.* resembling (that of) a flame M16.

flame /fleɪm/ *v.* ME. [AN *flaum(b)er*, OFr. *flam(m)er*, (also mod.) *flamber*, f. *flam(m)e* FLAME *n.*] 1 *v.i.* Burn with a flame or flames; emit flames. ME. b *v.t.* Burn, set on fire, consume or destroy with flames. Long *rare*. L16. c *v.t.* Subject to the action of flame. L19. 2 *v.i.* Shine or glow (red) like flame. ME. 3†a *v.t.* Kindle, excite (emotion etc.). LME–M17. b *v.i.* (Of a person) be consumed *with* fury, passion, etc.; burst out into anger etc.; (of passion etc.) burst out. Also foll. by *out*, *up*. M16. 4a *v.t.* Send forth or convey by means of a flame. LME. b *v.i.* Move like flame. *poet.* M17.

1b *fig.*: T. S. ELIOT The brief sun flames the ice, on pond and ditches. c *American Speech* Allowing my loop wire to cool sufficiently after flaming it. 2 C. MACKENZIE A crimson spot flaming now on both of his cheekbones. 3b LD MACAULAY He flamed with indignation. E. WAUGH Love, patriotism, zeal for justice, and personal spite flamed within him. A. LURIE It is years since she flamed out like that at anyone. 4a T. A. COOK Beacon fires . . which flamed messages along the valley. b TENNYSON Once again thou flamest heavenward.

Comb. & *with advs. in specialized senses*: **flame out** (of a jet engine) lose power through extinction of the flame in the combustion chamber; **flame-out** (an instance of) loss of power through this cause.

flamer *n.* a person who or thing which flames; *arch. slang* something or someone glaringly conspicuous: L16.

flamen /ˈfleɪmɛn, ˈflɑː-/ *n.* Pl. **flamens**, **flamines** /ˈflamɪniːz/. ME. [L.] Chiefly *Rom. Hist.* A priest serving a particular god.

flamen dialis /dɪˈeɪlɪs, dɪˈɑːlɪs/ the flamen of Jupiter.

flamenco /fləˈmɛŋkəʊ/ *n.* & *a.* Pl. **-os**. L19. [Sp. = Fleming.] (Designating or pertaining to) a style of music played (esp. on the guitar) and sung by Spanish gypsies; (a song or dance) to music in this style.

flamfew /ˈflamfjuː/ *n.* Long *rare*. L16. [Fr. †*fanfelue* (now *fanfreluche*) f. med.L *famfaluca* bubble, lie, app. f. Gk *pompholux* bubble.] A bauble, a showy trifle.

flamines *n.pl.* see FLAMEN.

flaming /ˈfleɪmɪŋ/ *ppl a.* & *adv.* LME. [f. FLAME *v.* + -ING[2].] A *adj.* 1 That flames; in flames, on fire. LME. b Burning hot, fiery. M17. 2 Glowing, brilliant; (w. ref. to colour) bright, vivid. LME. b *fig.* Highly coloured; exaggerated; overlaudatory; (of an argument etc.) passionate. E17. 3 Blasted, damned, bloody. *colloq.* L19.

1 DAY LEWIS Like flaming swords they barred my way. b D. FRANCIS Flaming June had come and gone: it was raining again. 2 M. E. BRADDON The flaming poppies among the ripening corn. b SHAKES. *Tr. & Cr.* He having colour enough, and the other higher, is too flaming a praise for a good complexion. 3 ALAN BENNETT That flaming dog has messed on our steps again.

B *adv.* Damn, bloody. *colloq.* M20.

M. KINGTON Then flaming well think of something better.

flamingly *adv.* E17.

flamingo /fləˈmɪŋgəʊ/ *n.* Pl. **-o(e)s**. M16. [Sp. †*flamengo*, FLAMENCO flamingo, Fleming, fr. MDu. *Vlaminc* Fleming.] 1 Any of a number of wading birds of the family Phoenicopteridae, with pink or scarlet plumage, long slender legs and neck, and a heavy bent bill which is held upside down in the water when feeding. M16. 2 A deep pink colour. L19.

2 *attrib.*: V. WOOLF Lovely evenings, with . . flamingo clouds.

flammability /flaməˈbɪlɪti/ *n.* M17. [f. (as) next: see -ABILITY.] = INFLAMMABILITY.

¶Formerly obs. (M17 only) but revived (M20-): cf. next.

flammable /ˈflaməb(ə)l/ *a.* E19. [f. L *flammare*, f. *flamma* flame: see -ABLE.] = INFLAMMABLE.

¶Often preferred in official use to avoid the possible ambiguity of *inflammable*.

flammant /ˈflam(ə)nt/ *a. obs.* exc. *Her.* Also **flamant**. L15. [OFr. *flam(m)ant*, f. *flam(m)er* to FLAME *v.*] Flaming.

flammeous /ˈflamɪəs/ *a.* Now *rare*. M17. [f. L *flammeus* (f. *flamma* flame) + -OUS: see -EOUS.] Of the nature of, or resembling, flame, esp. in colour; shining, resplendent.

flammiferous /flaˈmɪf(ə)rəs/ *a. rare.* M17. [f. L *flammifer* + -OUS: see -FEROUS.] Bearing flame.

flammivomous /fləˈmɪvəməs/ *a. rare.* M17. [f. late L *flammivomus* (f. *flamma* flame + *-vomus* vomiting) + -OUS.] Vomiting out flame.

flammulated /ˈflamjʊleɪtɪd/ *a.* L19. [f. mod.L *flammulatus*, f. L *flammula* dim. of *flamma* flame: see -ED[1].] Of a reddish colour, ruddy. Chiefly in *flammulated owl*, a small owl, *Otus flammeolus*, native to western N. and Central America.

flammuˈlation *n.* (*rare*) a small flamelike marking M19.

flamy /ˈfleɪmi/ *a.* LME. [f. FLAME *n.* + -Y[1].] 1 Consisting of flames; flaming. LME. 2 Resembling flame, esp. in colour. LME.

flan /flan/ *n.* M19. [Fr., orig. = a round cake, f. OFr. *flaon*: see FLAWN.] 1 An open pastry or sponge case containing a (sweet or savoury) filling. Cf. earlier FLAWN. M19. 2 A disc of metal from which a coin is made. M19.

flancard /ˈflaŋkɑːd/ *n.* Also **flanchard** /ˈflantʃɑːd/. L15. [OFr., f. *flanc* FLANK *n.*] *Hist.* A piece of armour for the thigh, or for the flank of a horse.

flanch /flɑːn(t)ʃ/ *n.*[1] & *v.* Also **flaunch** /flɔːn(t)ʃ/. E18. [Origin uncertain: perh. f. FLAUNCH *n.*[1]] A *n.* = FLANGE *n.* 2. E18. B *v.* [Cf. OFr. *flanchir* bend.] 1 *v.i.* Spread *out*; slope outwards towards the top. L18. 2 *v.t.* Foll. by *up*: slope (esp. the outside of a chimney-shaft) inwards towards the top. M19.

flanching *n.* (*a*) the action or state of spreading outwards; (*b*) the sloping fillet of cement or mortar embedding the base of a chimney pot: M19.

flanch *n.*[2] var. of FLAUNCH *n.*[1]

flanchard *n.* var. of FLANCARD.

flanconade /ˈflaŋkəneɪd/ *n.* M17. [Fr., f. *flanc* FLANK *n.*: see -ADE.] *Fencing.* A thrust in the side.

Flanders /ˈflɑːndəz/ *n.* LME. [Du. *Vlaanderen* pl.: a region and former principality in the south-west of the Low Countries, now divided between Belgium, the Netherlands, and France.] Used *attrib.* to designate things originating in or associated with Flanders.

Flanders brick = *Bath brick* s.v. BATH *n.*[1] **Flanders poppy** a red corn poppy used as the emblem of the Allied soldiers who fell in the war of 1914–18; an artificial red poppy sold on behalf of the ex-service community and worn in Britain on Remembrance Day and the period directly preceding it (cf. POPPY *n.* 1c).

Flanderkin *n.* (*arch.*) a native or inhabitant of Flanders E16. **Flandrian** *a.* (*a*) (now *rare*) of or pertaining to Flanders or its inhabitants; (*b*) *Geol.* of, pertaining to, or designating the period following the end of the last glaciation in NW Europe: M17. **Flandrish** *a.* (*arch.*) Flemish ME.

flane /fleɪn/ *n.* Long only *Sc. arch.* [OE *flān* masc. and fem. = ON *fleinn* masc., cogn. w. OE *flā* FLO.] An arrow.

flane /flɑːn/ *v.i.* L19. [Back-form. f. FLÂNEUR.] Laze, saunter.

flânerie /flɑnri/ *n.* L19. [Fr., f. *flâner* lounge, saunter idly.] Idling.

flâneur /flɑnœːr/ *n.* Pl. pronounced same. M19. [Fr., f. *flâner* (see prec.) + *-eur* -OR.] An idler.

R. HOLMES Paris . . celebrated the idea of the *flâneur*, the man who drifts round the streets, gazing at everything.

flange /flan(d)ʒ/ *n.* & *v.* L17. [Origin uncertain: rel. to FLANCH *n.*[1] & *v.*] A *n.* 1 A part that widens out (now only in a vein of ore). L17. 2 A projecting flat rim, collar, or rib, serving esp. for strengthening, attachment, or (on a wheel) maintaining position on a rail. Also, a rim or fan standing out from the main part of a natural object. M18.

2 M. KINGSLEY The brown water . . striking a ridge of higher rock . . flew up in a lovely flange. J. MASTERS The wheels' flanges ground against the inside of the rail. *blank flange*: see BLANK *a.*

B *v.* [Cf. OFr. *flangir* bend.] 1 *v.t.* Provide with a flange. Chiefly as *flanged* ppl a. L18. 2 *v.i.* Widen out or *out*. E19. 3 *v.i.* Alter a sound recording by removing sound of a particular but varying frequency (orig. by pressing alternately on the flanges of the tape reels playing two copies of the recording simultaneously, now by means of a flanger). Usu. in *flanging* vbl n. L20.

flangeless *a.* E20. **flanger** *n.* (*a*) *US* a vertical scraper for clearing snow from railway tracks to allow room for the wheel-flanges; (*b*) a device that alters a sound signal by introducing a cyclically varying phase shift into one of two identical copies of the signal and recombining them: L19.

flank /flaŋk/ *n.* LOE. [(O)Fr. *flanc*, f. Frank. base meaning 'a side'.] 1 The fleshy or muscular part of the side of a person or animal, strictly that between the ribs and the hip. Formerly also, the belly; the womb. LOE. b A cut of meat, or a piece of hide, from the flank of an animal. M18. 2 The side part of anything, esp. a building, mountain, etc. E17. 3 The extreme right or left side of (esp.) an army or other body of people in military formation; a wing. M17. b *Fortif.* A part of a work so disposed as to defend another by flanking fire. L17. 4 The side of the tooth of a gear-wheel, or of a screw-thread, which makes effective contact with another surface. M19.

1 T. A. COWARD The Redwing . . can be distinguished by its long pale eye-stripe and reddish flanks. G. ORWELL From the hip to the knee her flank was against his. 2 A. MILLER They drive . . up a steep gorge whose flanks almost blot out the sky. 3 C. S. FORESTER A company commander then had to get his men forward again, watching his flanks. *fig.*: R. MAY To fight on both flanks—to oppose totalitarianism . . and to recover our . . belief in the worth and dignity of the person. **in flank** at the side.

Comb.: **flank forward** *Rugby Union* a wing forward.

flank /flaŋk/ *v.*[1] M16. [f. the n. Cf. Fr. *flanquer.*] †1 *v.i.* Deliver a raking fire. Only in M16. 2 *v.t.* Guard, strengthen, or defend, on the flank; attack or threaten the flank of; (of artillery) fire sideways on, rake. L16. 3 *v.t.* Be situated at the side of; *esp.* be situated on either side of. M17. 4 *v.t.* Dodge, evade. *US arch. slang.* M19.

2 SIR W. SCOTT An advanced angle . . with shot-holes for flanking the door-way. 3 E. GLASGOW A red brick house flanked by a stony hill. F. HERBERT She saw Paul approaching flanked by two small boys.

flank /flaŋk/ *v.*[2]*t.* M19. [Imit.: cf. *flick*, *spank.*] Flick; crack (a whip).

flanker /ˈflaŋkə/ *n.* & *v.* M16. [f. FLANK *v.*[1] + -ER[1].] A *n.* 1 A fortification for protecting or threatening a flank. M16. 2 One of a detachment of soldiers sent to guard the flanks of a military formation. L16. b A trick or swindle. Chiefly as *pull, work*, etc., *a flanker. slang* (orig. *Mil.*). E20. c *Rugby Union* etc. a flank forward, a wing forward. In *Amer. Football*, a player who lines up in a position to the outside of an end. M20. 3 A thing which flanks anything. E17. B *v.* [Cf. Du. *flankeren* f. Fr. *flanquer* FLANK *v.*[1]] 1 *v.t.* Protect on the flanks; protect or threaten from a flanker. *arch.* L16. 2 *v.i.* Make an attack on the flank. Now *rare* or *obs.* E17.

flannel /ˈflan(ə)l/ *n.* & *a.* Also (*obs.* exc. *dial.*) **-en** /-ən/. ME. [Prob. f. Welsh *gwlanen* woollen article, f. *gwlân* wool.] A *n.* 1 Any of various loose-textured soft woollen or man-made fabrics of plain or twilled weave and slightly napped on one side. ME. †b A Welshman. *rare* (Shakes.). Only in L16. 2 In *pl.* Underwear or other garments, *esp.* trousers, made of flannel. E17. 3 A small piece of (usu. cotton towelling) fabric for washing the face, hands, etc. E19. 4 Nonsense; flattery; bragging. *slang.* E20.

2 H. FAST He was . . dressed in gray flannels and a blue blazer.

Comb.: **flannelboard** = FLANNELGRAPH; **flannel-cake** a kind of thin wheat griddle-cake; **flannel flower** an Australian umbelliferous plant, *Actinotus helianthi*, the involucre of which resembles a snipped piece of white flannel; **flannel-mouth** *US slang* a flatterer, a braggart.

B *attrib.* or as *adj.* Made of flannel. L16.

J. D. SALINGER There was this very Joe Yale-looking guy, in a grey flannel suit.

flanneˈlette *n.* a napped cotton fabric imitating the texture of flannel L19. **flannelgraph** *n.* a sheet of flannel to which paper or cloth cut-outs will adhere, used esp. as a teaching aid M20. **flannelled** *a.* wrapped in flannel; wearing flannel trousers: L18. **flannelly** *a.* resembling flannel M19.

flannel /ˈflan(ə)l/ *v.* Infl. **-ll-**, ***-l-**. M19. [f. the n.] 1 *v.t.* Rub with a flannel; *rare* wrap in flannel. M19. 2 *v.t.* & *i.* Use flattery (on); bluff, mislead. *slang.* M20.

1 I. MCEWAN Steered him to the washbasin, was filling it with warm water and flanneling his face. 2 J. BRAINE I managed to flannel him into the belief that I approved of his particular brand of efficiency.

flannen *n.* & *a.* see FLANNEL *n.* & *a.*

flanque *n.* var. of FLAUNCH *n.*[1]

flap /flap/ *n.* ME. [f. the vb.] I The action of FLAP *v.* 1 A light blow or slap (with something broad and flexible). ME. 2 (The noise produced by) the motion of something broad and loose, *esp.* the up-and-down movement of a wing. L18. b *Phonet.* A consonantal sound produced by a single fast flapping motion of the tongue or other organ. M19. c A state of anxiety, agitation, or excitement; a fuss; *Mil.* an alert. *colloq.* E20.

1 SWIFT Give him a soft Flap on his Eyes. 2 C. KINGSLEY I can hear the flap and snort of the dogs' nostrils. J. TYNDALL A gnat can execute many thousand flaps of its little wings in a second. c *Punch* There is a flap because the price of bread is going up. **be in** or **get in(to) a flap** be or become anxious, agitated, or excited.

II Something that flaps. †3 Something broad and flat to strike with; *esp.* a fly swatter. LME–E18. 4 Something broad and flat hinged or attached on one side only, as a trapdoor, a table-leaf, the cover of a pocket, the seal of an envelope, etc. E16. b A hanging or pendent portion of a garment, hat, etc. M16. c A valve which opens and shuts on one hinged side. Also *flap-valve*. E19. d The gill-cover of a fish. E19. e The pendent portion(s) of a saddle. M19. f A hinged or sliding section of a wing or tailplane used to control lift etc.; an aileron. E20. 5 In *pl.* (A disease marked by) swollen glands in the mouth of a horse. L16. 6 Something broad and loose, irrespective of connection with anything else. E17. b A large, broad mushroom; an open mushroom-top. Cf. FLAB *n.* 1. M18. c A loose covering for the lower part of the abdomen. *US.* E19. 7 A girl or woman of light or loose character. *slang* (now *dial.*). M17. 8 *Surg.* A portion of skin or flesh separated from the underlying tissue, but remaining attached at the base while being transplanted to another site. Also, a piece of skin used as a graft. E19.

4 J. STEINBECK Casy spread the tent flaps with his hands and stepped out. *cat-flap*: see CAT *n.*[1] b C. T. DENT Tying the flaps of his hat over his ears. 6 THACKERAY The flap of a shoulder of mutton. 7 J. MABBE Fall to your flap, my Masters, kisse and clip.

Comb.: **flapmouth(ed)** (*slang, derog.*) (having) a mouth with broad, hanging lips; **flap-sight** a hinged sight on a rifle; **flap-table** a table with one or more hinged leaves; *flap-valve*: see sense 4c above.

flapped *a.* formed like a flap, pendulous; having a flap or flaps: M17. **flapless** *a.* E20.

flap /flap/ *v.* Infl. **-pp-**. ME. [Prob. imit.: cf. CLAP *v.*[1]] 1 *v.t.* & *i.* Strike with a sudden blow. Long *obs.* exc. *dial.* ME. 2a *v.t.* Cause to swing or sway about, flutter, or flop, esp. with accompanying noise. ME. b *v.i.* Of something attached at one point or side or loosely fastened: swing or sway about, flutter, flop (freq. making a noise); *fig.* (of ears) open wide, strain to hear something. E16. c Toss (esp. a pancake) smartly. M19. 3 *v.t.* Strike with something flexible and broad; (of a bird) strike with the flat of the wing; drive *away* or *off* in such a way. LME. b *v.i.* Make a flap or stroke. L16. 4a *v.t.* Move up and down, beat (the wings). LME. b *v.i.* (Of wings, flippers, arms, etc.) beat, move up and down; beat the wings etc. L17. 5 *v.i.* Of a bird, ship, etc.: travel with wings, sails, etc., flapping. L18. 6 *v.i.* Be upset, become agitated; fuss; panic. *colloq.* E20.

1 J. SKELTON I shall flappe hym as a fole to fall at my fete. 2a SOUTHEY I hear the wind, that flaps The curtain of the tent. J. STEINBECK Lennie flapped his big hands helplessly. b DICKENS The . . curtains flapped . . idly in the wind. P. PEARCE He unbuttoned his pyjama jacket and let it flap open. M. ERSKINE You get on and explain them . . Harris . . has his ears positively flapping. 3 J. H. WIFFEN Night's shrieking bird Flaps the friezed window with her wing. G. W. LE FEVRE Two men would run before me to flap away the flies. 4a J. G. WOOD The Swift does not flap its wings so often as the Swallow. b R. L'ESTRANGE 'Tis common for a duck to run flapping and fluttering away. 5 C. KINGSLEY A slate-blue heron . . flapped fifty yards up the creek.

flapdoodle /ˈflapduːd(ə)l/ *n.* *colloq.* Also ***flam-** /ˈflam-/. M19. [Arbitrary.] Nonsense, rubbish.

F. MARRYAT The gentleman has eaten no small quantity of flapdoodle . . it's the stuff they feed fools on.

flap-dragon /ˈflapdrag(ə)n/ *n.* & *v.* Long *rare* or *obs.* L16. [f. FLAP *v.* + DRAGON.] A *n.* (A raisin etc. as caught and eaten in) the game of snapdragon. L16. B *v.t.* Swallow as one would a snapdragon. *rare* (Shakes.). Only in E17.

flapjack /ˈflapdʒak/ *n.* E17. [f. FLAP *v.* + JACK *n.*[1]] 1 A flat cake or pancake; an apple turnover. E17. 2 A sweet biscuit made with rolled oats. M20. 3 A powder compact. M20.

flapper /ˈflapə/ *n.* L16. [f. FLAP *v.* + -ER[1].] 1 Something flat to strike with, esp. to make a noise; a fly-swatter. L16. 2 A person who flaps or strikes another, esp. to get his or her attention. Hence, a reminder. Now *rare* or *obs.* E18. 3 A newly fledged wild duck or partridge. Chiefly *dial.* M18. 4 Something hanging by one side or working on a hinge; *esp.* the striking part of a flail, a swingle. L18. b A fin or flipper; a crustacean's tail; (*slang*) the hand. Now *rare*. M19. c An irregular race meeting (cf. FLAPPING 2). *slang.* E20. 5 [Perh. f. FLAP *n.* 7, or a fig. use of sense 3.] †a A young prostitute; an immoral young girl. *slang.* L19–E20. b Orig., a young girl nearing maturity. Later, a young woman (esp. an unconventional or flighty one). *colloq.* L19. c *spec.* A (fashionable) young woman of the nineteen-twenties and -thirties. *colloq.* E20.

Comb.: **flapper vote** (*derog.*, now *Hist.*) the parliamentary vote granted to women of 21 and over in 1928.

flapperdom, **flapperhood** *ns.* the condition of being a flapper (sense 5b, c) E20. **flapperish** *a.* characteristic of or like a flapper E20.

†flappet *n.* L16–E18. [f. FLAP *n.* + -ET[1].] A little flap.

flapping /ˈflapɪŋ/ *vbl n.* LME. [f. FLAP *v.* + -ING[1].] 1 The action of FLAP *v.* LME. b *spec. Aeronaut.* The angular up-and-down oscillation of the blade of a helicopter about its hinge. M20. 2 A form of racing not subject to the rules of an official body. *slang.* E20.

flappy /ˈflapi/ *a.* L16. [f. FLAP *v.* + -Y[1].] †1 Flabby. *rare.* Only in L16. 2 That flaps, or has a tendency to flap. M19.

flare /flɛː/ *n.*[1] E19. [f. the vb.] 1 The action or quality of flaring; a dazzling irregular light; a sudden outburst of light or flame. E19. b *fig.* A dazzling display; a sudden outburst of emotion etc.; a sudden or loud noise. M19. c *Astron.* A sudden outburst of radiation from the sun (freq. *solar flare*) or a star. M20. 2 *Photogr.* Extraneous illumination of the film, due to internal reflections etc. M19. 3 A gradual swell or bulging outward (orig. in *Shipbuilding*); a gradual widening or spreading outward (esp. of a skirt etc.); that part which widens or spreads; (in *pl.*) flared trousers. M19. b *Aeronaut.* A lessening of the steepness of the glide path of an aircraft about to land. Also *flare-out.* M20. 4 (A device giving off) a bright flame, used as a signal or as illumination of a target etc.; a flame of burning waste gas from an oil-well etc. L19.

1 TOLKIEN Many of them carried torches, and in the flare I could see their faces. b H. E. BATES She got up with a flare of energy . . almost running. *Daily Telegraph* Amid a flare of trumpets, the procession returned. 3 J. AGEE A woman . . her face narrow beneath her flare of sunbonnet. 4 S. GIBBONS The wickering hissing of the gas flares which lit the hall and cast sharp shadows. *Lifeboat* His yacht . . was now in distress and firing flares.

Comb.: **flare-path** an area illuminated to guide aircraft in landing or taking off; **flare star** *Astron.* a star in which flares occur from time to time.

flareless *a.* M20.

flare /flɛː/ *n.*[2] *dial.* M19. [Origin unkn.] The fat about a pig's kidney.

flare *n.*[3] var. of FLAIR *n.*[1]

flare /flɛː/ *v.* M16. [Origin uncertain (perh. Scand.).] 1†a *v.t.* Spread out, display (one's hair). Only in M16. b *v.i.* Of hair etc.: spread out, stream (as if) in the wind. Now *rare.* L16. 2 *v.t.* & *i.* Spread out or display (oneself) conspicuously. Now *rare.* E17. 3 *v.i.* Of a ship's sides, a wineglass, a skirt, trousers, etc.: widen gradually in an upward or downward direction. E17. b *v.t.* Cause to spread or widen gradually outwards. Freq. as *flared* ppl a. M19. c *v.t.* & *i. Aeronaut.* Reduce the steepness of the glide path of (an aircraft) about to land. M20. 4 *v.i.* Burn with a spreading, unsteady flame; blaze or glow (as) with flame; *fig.* burst into sudden (usu. temporary) activity, emotion, etc. Freq. foll. by *out*, *up.* M17. b *v.t.* Light up with a flare; cause a candle to burn with an unsteady light; send by means of a flare. Also, burn off (waste gas) at an oil-well etc. M18.

2 GOLDSMITH A flaming torch, if flared round in a circle . . appears as a ring of fire. 3b T. MORRISON Jadine flared her nostrils. W. GOLDING His white trousers were flared at the bottom. 4 K. MANSFIELD Blue flowers and red flowers . . flared in the roadside hedges. E. WELTY The log shifted . . and light flared all over in the room. U. LE GUIN She was . . easily upset, and her temper flared at a word. *Times* Jeers and insults which flared into scattered stone-throwing. b J. R. GREEN The English beacons flared out their alarm along the coast.

Comb.: **flare-out** (*a*) = *flare-up* (a) below; (*b*) *Aeronaut.* = FLARE *n.*[1] 3b; **flare-up** (*a*) a sudden bursting out into flame, anger, excitement, etc.; (*b*) *Naut.* a signal flare.

flary /ˈflɛːri/ *a.* Now *rare.* M19. [f. FLARE *n.*[1] + -Y[1].] Having or resembling a flare or flares; *esp.* gaudy, showy.

flaser /ˈflɑːzə/ *n.* L19. [G, dial. form of *Flader* streak, vein.] *Geol.* Used *attrib.* and in *comb.* to denote (the presence of) a streaky structure characterized by lenses of little-altered parent rock in a rock metamorphosed by shearing, as *flaser-gabbro*, *flaser structure*, etc.

flash /flaʃ/ *n.*[1] Now *local.* In sense 1 also **flosh** /flɒʃ/. See also FLUSH *n.*[1] ME. [(O)Fr. *flache*, Central Fr. form of Picard and Norman dial. *flaque* f. MDu. *vlacke.*] 1 A pool, a marshy place. ME. 2 A water-filled hollow formed by subsidence due to rock salt extraction (esp. in Cheshire). L19.

flash /flaʃ/ *n.*[2] M16. [f. FLASH *v.*] I A burst of light. Cf. FLASH *v.* II. 1 A sudden, transitory burst or blaze of flame or light. M16. b A flashlight, an electric torch. E20. c A photographic flashlight; a photograph taken using this. M20. 2 A brief period of time (during which a flash is visible); an instant. Usu. in *in a flash* immediately, instantaneously. E17. 3 A brief outburst or transient display of something (seen as resembling a flash of light); *esp.* a sudden access of feeling or knowledge. E17. b A brief news dispatch or bulletin (orig. by telegraph, now on radio or television). M19. c A brief scene on film or television. E20. 4†a A piece of showy talk; an empty phrase. E17–M18. b Superficial brilliancy; ostentation. L17. c [f. FLASH *a.*] Thieves' slang, cant. Now chiefly *Hist.* M18. †5 A superficially brilliant or showy person. E17–E19. 6a A coloured patch of cloth on a uniform or other clothing, esp. on the upper arm or shoulder and with the distinguishing device of a regiment, country, etc. M19. b A patch of or *of* bright colour on a darker background. L20. 7 Excess metal, plastic, etc., forced between facing surfaces as two halves of a mould close up, forming a thin projection on the final object. E20. 8 A thin layer (of glass, chrome, etc.). E20.

1 K. CLARK The dark landscape is lit only by terrific flashes of lightning. *flash in the pan*: see PAN *n.*[1] c *electronic flash*: see ELECTRONIC *a.* 3 SHAKES. *Haml.* Your flashes of merriment that were wont to set the table on a roar. J. CONRAD He gave us a flash of his white teeth. ALDOUS HUXLEY To some people . . there come little flashes of illumination—momentary glimpses into the nature of the world. *hot flash*: see HOT *a.* 4b CLIVE JAMES The man was all artist, humble under the flash. c *patter flash*: see PATTER *v.*[1] 3. 6b C. PHILLIPS Leila's mother had large flashes of grey in her hair.

II A sudden movement of water. Cf. FLASH *v.* I. 9†a A splash of water; a large wave. E17–E18. b A sudden rush of water let down from a weir to increase the depth of the river temporarily. Also, a contrivance for producing this. L17. †10 A sudden burst of rain, wind, etc. M17–E19.

Comb.: **flash bulb**: producing a flash of light used for photography under conditions of low light; **flash burn**: caused by sudden intense heat, esp. from a nuclear explosion; **flash card**: with words etc., shown briefly to a child by a teacher as an aid to learning; **flash-cube** a set of (four) flash bulbs arranged as a cube and operated in turn; **flash-dry** *v.t.* dry in a very short time; **flash-flood** a sudden, destructive flood; **flash-freeze** *v.t.* freeze (food etc.) very rapidly so as to prevent the formation of ice crystals; **flash-gun** a device to hold and operate a camera flashlight; **flash-lamp** (*a*) a portable flashing electric lamp, *esp.* an electric torch; (*b*) = *flashlight* (b) below; **flashlight** (*a*) a flashing light used in signalling, lighthouses, etc.; (*b*) a device which provides a burst of intense illumination for photography in dark conditions; (*c*) = *flash-lamp* (a) above; **flash photolysis** *Chem.* the use of a very brief intense flash of light to bring about gas-phase decomposition or dissociation, usu. as a means of studying short-lived molecules etc.; **flashpoint** (*a*) the lowest temperature at which the vapour from an oil etc. will ignite in air; (*b*) *fig.* a point of climax at which violent action (as loss of temper, active hostility, etc.) begins; **flash powder** a powder which burns rapidly with a bright flash, esp. as formerly used in photography; **flash tube** a gas-discharge tube used to provide an electronic flash when a current is suddenly passed through it.

flashless *a.* without a flash, emitting no flash; (of gunpowder etc.) emitting no flash when ignited: E20.

flash /flaʃ/ *n.*[3] *rare.* L16. [Origin unkn.] = FLASHING *n.*[2]

flash /flaʃ/ *a.* Chiefly *colloq.* L17. [f. FLASH *n.*[2]] 1a Of or pertaining to thieves or prostitutes; *spec.* of thieves' slang, cant. *arch.* L17. b Of, pertaining to, or resembling sporting and betting men as a class, esp. patrons of boxing and racing. E19. 2 Gaudy, showy, superficially attractive; too smart. L18. 3 Counterfeit, sham. Now *rare* or *obs.* E19. 4 Knowing, fly, cheeky. *slang.* E19.

2 W. PLOMER A flash flat in Chelsea of a bogus elegance. 4 D. STUART Some flash young coot, to tell him how to shoe a horse!

Special collocations: *Flash Harry*: see HARRY *n.*[2] **flash-house** *arch.* a brothel.

flashly *adv.* E19. **flashness** *n.* M19.

flash /flaʃ/ *v.* ME. [App. imit.: cf. PLASH *v.*[2], DASH *v.*[1], SPLASH *v.*[1], SLASH *v.*] I Expr. movement of water. 1 *v.t.* Splash (water) *about*, (*up*)*on*. *obs.* exc. as passing into sense 6. ME. 2 *v.i.* Of the sea, a wave, a river, etc.: dash, break, flow swiftly. (Passing into sense 5.) LME. 3 *v.t.* Send a flash or rush of water down (a river, millstream, etc.). L18.

1 T. HERBERT The wave flashing upon our decks . . much salt water. 2 M. SCOTT The roaring surf was flashing up over the clumps of green bushes.

II With ref. to light or fire. Freq. w. advs. 4 *v.i.* Burst suddenly into flame or light; give out flame or sparks. LME. 5 *v.i.* Move swiftly, like a flash of light; burst suddenly into view or perception. LME. 6 *v.t.* (Cause to) emit or reflect (light, fire, etc.) like a flash or in flashes; cause to gleam or shine; send out swiftly. L16. b *v.t.* & *i. spec.* Signal to (other traffic) by causing one's vehicle's (head)lights to shine briefly or intermittently. M20. 7 *v.i.* Break out *into* sudden action, words, etc. E17. b Burst into sudden anger or excitement. Foll. by *out*, *up.* E19. 8 Chiefly *slang.* a *v.i.* Make a flash or display, show off. Now *rare.* E17. b *v.t.* Make a great display of, exhibit ostentatiously, show off. L18. c *v.t.* & *i.* Exhibit or expose (part of one's body, esp. the genitals) briefly and indecently. *slang.* M19. 9 *v.i.* Emit or reflect light suddenly or intermittently; gleam. L18. 10 *v.t.* Express or communicate by a flash or flashes; *esp.* send (a message, news, etc.) by radio, telegraph, etc. L18. b *v.t.* & *i. Cinemat.* Show or be shown briefly on the screen. E20. 11 *v.t.* Cover (glass etc.) with a thin layer or film of some material. M19.

4 J. TYNDALL Lightning flashed about the summits of the Jungfrau. J. BARNES Every third street-lamp flickered and flashed into life. 5 R. L. STEVENSON It flashed into my mind . . that . . the powder for the gun had been left behind. E. GLASGOW A bird and its shadow flashed over the winter fields. G. HEYER Often the answer to a problem will flash upon one in the night. 6 C. KINGSLEY Turning round I had a lantern flashed in my face. W. S. MAUGHAM A light was flashed and in that heavy darkness the sudden glare was terrifying. 7 A. H. GREEN The imprisoned steam flashes forth in repeated explosions. 8a SHAKES. *Timon* A naked gull, which flashes now a phoenix. b A. CARTER The blonde . . flashed a pair of vast, blue, indecorous eyes at the young reporter. 9 SHELLEY Like wingèd stars the fireflies flash and glance. R. MACAULAY Fierce black eyes that flashed while he spoke. 10 J. A. FROUDE The cannon . . flashed their

welcome through the darkness. *Listener* Electronic indicators which flash train times and platform numbers momentarily.

Comb. & with advs. in specialized senses: **flashback** *(a)* a flame moving rapidly back through a combustible vapour; *(b)* a scene in a film, novel, etc., which returns or changes to an earlier time. **flash-board** a board set up on a mill-dam to increase the flow of water through the mill; **flash over** make an (accidental) electric circuit by sparking across a gap; **flash-over** an accidental electrical discharge across a gap, esp. where the voltage is too great for the insulation on a conductor;

flasher /ˈflaʃə/ *n.* E17. [f. prec. + -ER[1].] †1 A person who splashes water. *rare.* E17–M18. 2 Something emitting flashes of light. Now *esp.* (a sign or signal using) an automatic device which switches a light or lights rapidly on and off. L17. †3 A flash person; *spec.* an attendant at a gaming-table. M–L18. 4 *Cricket.* A batsman inclined to play forcefully at balls wide of the off-stump. *colloq.* M20. 5 A person who exposes himself indecently. *colloq.* L20.

flashing /ˈflaʃɪŋ/ *n.*[1] L16. [f. FLASH *v.* + -ING[1].] The action of FLASH *v.*; an act or instance of this.

Comb.: **flashing-point** = *flashpoint* (a) s.v. FLASH *n.*[2]

flashing /ˈflaʃɪŋ/ *n.*[2] L18. [f. FLASH *n.*[3] + -ING[1].] A strip of non-porous material (esp. flexible metal) that excludes water from the junction of a roof covering with another surface; material used for this.

flashy /ˈflaʃi/ *a.* L16. [f. FLASH *n.*[2], *v.* + -Y[1].] †1 Splashing. L16–E17. †2 Watery; insipid; trifling, insubstantial. L16–M19. 3 Flashing, sparkling, brilliant. Hence, showy, of fine appearance, gaudy, cheaply attractive. Also, momentary. E17. †4 Excited, eager. M17–L18. 5 Of a person, an attribute, etc.: superficially brilliant; given to showing off; vain, conceited. L17.

3 H. BUSK One ruby glitter'd like the flashy Mars. C. J. LEVER The splendour of a very flashy silk waistcoat. C. LASSALLE The storm, flashy and loud, began as they ran downstairs. 5 G. COLMAN A young flashy Englishman will sometimes carry a whole fortune on his back. DE QUINCEY The secondhand report of a flashy rhetorician. A. TYLER Those black-haired, flashy, beauty-queen types.

flashily *adv.* M18. **flashiness** *n.* E17.

flask /flɑːsk/ *n.* [OE *flasce*, *flaxe* (in sense 2 f. Fr. *flasque* f. OFr. *flasche*, *flaske*) f. med.L *flasca*. In sense 3 prob. f. It. *fiasco* f. med.L *flasco*, *flascon*. Ult. origin unkn. Cf. FLAGON.] †1 A (wooden, skin, etc.) container for liquor. OE–LME. 2a *Founding.* A frame used to hold a mould for casting. M17. b *Dentistry.* A sectional metal container for holding a denture during vulcanization. M19. 3 A bottle, usu. of bulbous or conical shape, with a narrow neck; *esp.* a glass vessel used in chemistry, or (in a covering of wickerwork or plaited grass) for wine or oil. Now freq. *ellipt.*, a vacuum or thermos flask. L17.

3 *hip flask*, *powder flask*, *Thermos flask*, *vacuum flask*, etc.

flask /flɑːsk/ *v.t.* E18. [f. the n.] †1 Protect with wickerwork etc., as a flask is protected. Only in E18. 2 Put in a flask; *spec.* in *Dentistry*, place (a denture) in a flask and enclose with plaster prior to vulcanizing. M19.

flasket /ˈflɑːskɪt/ *n. arch.* ME. [f. ONFr. *flasquet* FLACKET.] 1 A container; *esp.* a (small) flask. ME. 2 A long shallow basket. LME.

flasque /flɑːsk/ *n.* M16. [Fr. *flasque* FLASK *n.* or alt. of *flanque* var. of FLAUNCH *n.*[1]] *Her.* A bearing resembling a flanch, but smaller, esp. in width.

flat /flat/ *n.*[1] ME. [f. the adj.] 1 A piece of level ground; a plain; the low ground through which a river flows. Freq. in *pl.* ME. b A tract of low-lying marshy ground; a swamp. E17. 2 (Without *pl.*) a That which is flat, the flat part of something; *spec.* *(a)* the broad surface of a sword etc. as opp. to the edge; *(b)* the inside *of* the open hand. LME. b Level country; *esp.* level ground without hedges or ditches for horse-racing; *the* season or occupation of flat-racing. M19. 3 A nearly level tract over which the tide flows or which is covered by shallow water; a shallow, a shoal. Usu. in *pl.* L15. 4 A tract of arable land, a ploughed section of a field; *esp.* each of the larger portions into which the common field was divided, a square furlong. *obs.* exc. *dial.* or *Hist.* E16. 5†a A die loaded by being shaved on one or more surfaces. M16–E18. b *gen.* Something of a broad thin shape, as a disc, a coin, a strip of wood, a piece of metal, etc. M16. 6 *Mus.* A note lowered a semitone below natural pitch; a sign (♭) indicating this lowering. L16. 7 A horizontal plane; a level. Formerly also, a plane figure. L16. b A flat space or flattened surface; *esp.* a worn patch on a tyre. L19. c In full *optical flat.* A block or lamina (usu. made of glass) with one or more surfaces made accurately plane and smooth, any unevenness etc. being small compared with the wavelength of light. L19. 8a A broad flat-bottomed receptacle; a flat-bottomed boat. M17. b A relatively long or broad and low article of dress, as a low-heeled shoe, (*US*) a low-crowned hat. E19. 9 A horizontal upper surface; *esp.* the horizontal part of a roof. Formerly also, a landing on a staircase, the tread of a stair. E18. 10 *Mining.* A horizontal (part of) a bed, stratum, or vein. M18. 11 A simpleton; someone who is (easily) taken in, a dupe. Freq. contrasted w. *sharp. arch. slang.* M18. 12 *Theatr.* A section of scenery mounted on a frame. L18. 13 *Naut.* a In *pl.* Timbers in the midships of a vessel. E19. b The partial deck or floor of a particular compartment. M19. 14 (The paint used for) a surface painted with a uniform matt finish. E19. 15 A flat tyre; a puncture. E20.

1 SHAKES. *Haml.* Till of this flat a mountain you have made. A. B. EDWARDS The river widens away before us; the flats are green on either side. b SHAKES. *Temp.* All the infections that the sun sucks up From bogs, fens, flats. 2a W. SNELGRAVE He gave me a slight blow .. with the flat of his Cutlace. DICKENS Here's old Bill Barley on the flat of his back. b J. WILSON Sic a .. body .. could never have been bred or born on the flat. 3 G. C. DAVIES At low water, the muds or flats are dry. *mudflat*, *sandflat*, etc. 6 *Mus. double flat*: see DOUBLE *a.* & *adv.* **sharps and flats** (*loosely*) the black keys of a piano. 7 J. BENTHAM A declivity is .. preferable by far to a dead flat. 11 THACKERAY 'You wouldn't be such a flat as to let three thousand a year go out of the family.' 12 **join the flats** *fig.* make a thing into a coherent whole; preserve the appearance of a consistent attitude. 15 J. M. CAIN I was in the filling station, fixing flats.

flat /flat/ *n.*[2] E19. [Alt. of FLET *n.*[1] by assoc. with FLAT *a.*] 1 A floor or storey in a house. Now *rare.* E19. 2 A dwelling comprising a room or rooms forming a unit (esp. self-contained) within a house or larger building, and freq. wholly or chiefly on one floor. E19.

Comb.: **flatmate** a person who shares a flat with another.

flatlet *n.* a small flat E20. **flatted** *a.* divided into, constructed as, or consisting (partly) of flats E20.

flat /flat/ *a.* & *adv.* Compar. & superl. **-tt-**. ME. [ON *flatr* = OHG *flaz* f. Gmc: ult. relationship uncertain.] A *adj.* I 1 Horizontally level; without inclination. ME. 2 Spread out, stretched, lying at full length. ME. b Of a building etc.: levelled with the ground; overthrown, razed. M16. c Lying in close apposition; with the whole length and breadth evenly in contact with a surface. M16. 3 Even, smooth, unbroken, without projection; (of the face, features, etc.) without prominence, not projecting; (of land) not undulating; (of a surface) smooth, level. ME. b Deflated, punctured. E20. c *Electronics.* Uniform in behaviour over a given range of frequencies; responding equally to signals of all frequencies. E20. 4 Having a broad level surface and little depth; *esp.* (of a foot) touching the ground with most or all of the lower surface in walking or standing, having little or no arch. LME. b Of a vessel: wide and shallow. L15. 5 (Of a tint etc.) of uniform depth and shade; *Photogr.* lacking contrast; (of paint etc.) not glossy. M18.

1 J. GWILT In India .. all buildings of any importance have flat roofs. 2 E. K. KANE The hunter is flat and motionless. R. KIPLING A big wind blew .. the tents flat. b SHAKES. *Coriol.* To lay the city flat, To bring the roof to the foundation. c H. J. STONOR The ladder was standing flat against the wall. 3 I. MURDOCH Flat cornlands where .. miles away against the sky one could perhaps see a silo. M. SPARK Miss Brodie's chest was flat, no bulges at all. b E. BOWEN My tyre .. went really flat. 4 W. DAMPIER The Booby is a Water-fowl .. her Feet are flat like a Ducks Feet. D. LARDNER This ruler consists of a flat piece of wood with a straight edge. (*as*) *flat as a pancake*: see PANCAKE *n.* 1. 5 W. M. CRAIG Throwing every mass of shadow into a flat tint. P. CAREY She uses a flat plastic paint.

II 6 Unrelieved by condition or qualification; absolute, downright, unqualified, plain. M16. b Impecunious, penniless, broke. Cf. *flat broke. US slang.* M19. 7 Completely lacking in attraction or interest; dull, lifeless; monotonous, insipid. L16. 8 Deficient in sense or mental vigour; stupid, dull, slow-witted. *arch.* L16. 9a *Mus.* Relatively low in pitch; *esp.* (of a note or singer) below true pitch; (of a key) having a flat or flats in the signature. L16. b Of a sound, voice, etc.: not clear and sharp, dead, dull. E17. 10†a Of an accent, syllable, etc.: unstressed. L16–E17. b *Gram.* Of a word, esp. an adverb: not distinguished by an ending characteristic of its part of speech. Now *rare.* L19. c *Phonet.* Of a sound: characterized by the downward shift of higher frequencies. M20. 11 Lacking energy or spirits, lifeless, dejected; depressed. E17. b Of trade etc.: depressed, inactive, sluggish. M19. c Of an electric battery: run down, discharged. M20. 12 Of drink etc.: lacking in flavour, stale; *esp.* having lost effervescence. E17. 13a Of a loan etc.: without interest. *US.* M19. b *Comm.* Unvarying, fixed, uniform; not varying with changed conditions or in particular cases. L19.

6 T. JEFFERSON In flat contradiction to their Arret of December last. T. KEIGHTLEY He claimed to be put in possession .. but met with a flat refusal. G. SAINTSBURY Such hints at rebellion .. were .. regarded as flat heresy. **leave flat** go away from (a person) without warning, drop suddenly and completely. **that's flat** let there be no doubt about it. 7 M. PATTISON A rather flat treatment of trite themes. E. GASKELL It seems so flat to be left behind. **fall flat** prove a failure, fail to win applause, response, etc. 8 J. R. SEELEY I look for nothing from empty, slow, flat people. 9a **B, E**, etc., **flat** a semitone lower than B, E, etc. b F. WELDON Annie had a flat, nasal telephone voice. 11 C. LAMB I am now calm, but sadly taken down and flat.

Special collocations & comb.: **flat arch** an arch with a flat intrados. **flat boat** *(a)* a broad flat-bottomed boat; *(b)* *US* a large roughly made boat formerly used for floating goods etc. down western rivers. **flat bottom** *(a)* = *flat-boat* above. **flat-bottom(ed)** *adjs.* (esp. of a boat) having a flat bottom. **flat-cap** (the wearer of) a cap with a low crown, *esp.* (now *Hist.*) a round cap worn in the 16th and 17th cents. by citizens of London. **flatcar** *N. Amer.* a railway wagon without raised sides or ends. **flatfish** any of numerous flat-bodied, bottom-dwelling bony fishes forming the order Heterosomata and including sole, plaice, turbot, etc. **flatfoot** *slang* a police officer. **flat-footed** *a.* *(a)* having flat feet; *(b)* (*colloq.*) downright, resolute; unready, unprepared; clumsy, uninspired. **flat-four** *a.* (of an engine) having four cylinders all horizontal, two on each side of the crankshaft. **flat-headed** *a.* *(a)* having or appearing to have a flat head; *(b)* *flat-headed borer* (US), the wood-boring larva of any of various beetles of the family Buprestidae. **flat-iron** *(a)* a domestic iron for pressing linen etc., heated by external means and usu. triangular in shape; *(b)* *colloq.* a boat, building, etc., like a flat iron in shape. **flatland** *(a)* a hypothetical land in space of two dimensions; *(b)* (orig. *US*) a region of flat land. **flat-nose** a flat-nosed person or animal. **flat-nosed** *a.* having a flat nose. **flat-pea** *Austral.* a leguminous shrub of the genus *Platylobium*, with flat pods. **flat race**: run over level ground, as opp. to a hurdle race or a steeplechase. **flat racing** the racing of horses in flat races. **flat rate** a rate of payment etc. that is the same in all cases, not proportional or otherwise variable. **flat spin** *(a)* *Aeronaut.* a nearly horizontal spin; *(b)* *colloq.* a state of agitation, panic. **flat-tail mullet** an Australian mullet, *Liza argentea*. **flat-top** *slang* *(a)* an aircraft carrier; *(b)* a man's short flat haircut. **flat tyre** *(a)* a deflated or punctured tyre; *(b)* (*N. Amer. colloq.*) a dull and spiritless person. **flatware** *(a)* crockery such as plates, saucers, etc. (opp. *hollow ware*); *(b)* *N. Amer.* cutlery. **flatwoods** *US* low-lying wooded country, esp. in Ohio, Alabama and Florida.

B *adv.* †1 Directly, exactly; due (*east* etc.). M16–M17. 2 Downright, absolutely, positively, plainly; completely, quite. L16. b Exactly, precisely. Orig. *US.* E20. 3 *Mus.* In a flat manner; a semitone below natural pitch. L17.

2 C. JENNER Sir Harry contradicted him flat. W. S. MAUGHAM You haven't turned it down flat? **flat out** at top speed, using all one's strength and resources. **b** J. CLARKE It took her about two minutes flat to step into jeans and sweater. 3 OED She has a tendency to sing flat.

flattish *a.* E17.

flat /flat/ *v.*[1] Infl. **-tt-**. L16. [f. the adj.] **1** *v.t.* = FLATTEN 1. Now *rare.* L16. †**2** *v.t.* Lay flat or level, raze, throw down. E–M17. **3** *Naut.* †**a** *v.i.* Of a ship: turn its head from the wind. Only in E17. **b** *v.t.* Force (the sail) flat or close against the mast. M17. **c** *v.i.* = FLATTEN 3b. M18. †**4** *v.t.* = FLATTEN 2. E17–E18. **b** *v.i.* = FLATTEN 2b. M17–E18. **5** *v.i.* = FLATTEN 3. Now *rare* or *obs.* exc. in *flat off*, *flat out* below. L17. **6** *v.t. Mus.* = FLATTEN 4. Now chiefly *US.* L17. **7** *v.t.* = FLATTEN 5. M19. **8** *v.t.* & *i.* Saw lengthwise through the thickness of (a plank etc.), so reducing the width. L19.

2 O. FELTHAM She hath.. flatted their strongest Forts. 3b W. MONSON He hears the Seamen cry.. flat a Sheet. 4 BACON An Orenge, Limon and Apple.. fresh in their Colour, But their Iuyce somewhat flatted. G. BURNET So great a length does.. flat the Hearers, and tempt them to sleep. **b** T. FULLER Their loyalty flatteth and deadeth by degrees. 5 **flat off** *US* (*rare*) slope gradually to a level. **flat out** *US* become gradually thinner; *fig.* fail (esp. in business), collapse. 6 W. APEL Variants in which some of the original tones are flatted.

Comb.: **flat-out** *US* a failure, a fiasco.

flatter *n.* (*a*) a worker who makes something flat; (*b*) a tool used in making things flat, esp. a blacksmith's broad-faced hammer: E18. **flatting** *vbl n.* (*a*) = FLATTENING; *esp.* the process of rolling out sheet metal; (*b*) (paint used for) a uniform matt coat: E17.

flat /flat/ *v.*[2]*i.* *Austral.* Infl. **-tt-**. L20. [f. FLAT *n.*[2]] Live in or share a flat (*with*).

flat-head /ˈflathɛd/ *n.* Also **flathead**. E18. [f. FLAT *a.* + HEAD *n.*] **1** (A member of) any of various peoples, esp. (**Flathead**) certain N. American Indian peoples such as Chinook, Choctaw, and Salish, who customarily practised head-flattening or (in the case of the Salish) were erroneously credited with so doing. E18. **2** A fish with a flattened head; *spec.* any of numerous marine fishes of the family Platycephalidae. L18. **3** A fool, a simpleton. *dial.* & *slang.* M19. **4** A hognose snake. *US.* L19.

Comb.: **flathead catfish** a large N. American catfish, *Pylodictis olivaris*, with long slender body and flattened head.

flatling /ˈflatlɪŋ/ *adv. arch.* & *dial.* Also **-lings** /-z/. LME. [f. FLAT *a.* + -LING[2].] **1** In a prostrate position, at full length, flat. LME. **2** With the flat side (esp. of a sword). LME.

†**flatlong** *adv.* L16–M17. [f. FLAT *a.* + -LONG.] **1** In or into a prostrate position. L16–M17. **2** With the flat side; with flat sides in contact. L16–M17.

flatly /ˈflatli/ *adv.* LME. [f. FLAT *a.* + -LY[2].] **1** In a flat or prostrate position. Long *rare* or *obs.* LME. **2** In a plain, blunt, or decisive manner; without hesitation, ambiguity, or qualification; absolutely, completely. M16. **3** In a dull or spiritless manner; without zest, insipidly; prosaically. M17. **4** With a small degree of curvature. Also, as on a flat surface; without relief. L18.

flatness /ˈflatnɪs/ *n.* LME. [f. FLAT *a.* + -NESS.] **1** The quality or condition of being flat or level. LME. **2** Absoluteness, unqualified condition. Also, outspokenness, plainness (of speech). L16. **3** Lack of sharpness and clarity in a sound; deadness of tone, voice, etc. E17. **4** Lack of spirit or energy; apathy, dejectedness; lack of mental acuteness or alertness. M17. **5** The quality in speech or writing of lacking animation, brilliance, or pointedness; prosaic dullness. M17. **6** The quality of having a small degree of curvature; reduced convexity. L17. **7** Lack of relief or prominence; the quality or state of having an even and unbroken surface. E18. **8** Deficiency in flavour; insipidity, vapidity. E18. **9** Lack of incident or interest, monotony; sluggishness of commercial activity. E19. **10** The condition of having great breadth or length in proportion to height or depth. L19.

flatten /ˈflat(ə)n/ *v.* Cf. FLAT *v.*[1] M17. [f. FLAT *a.* + -EN[5].] **1** *v.t.* Make flat in shape; reduce to a plane surface; make broad and thin; reduce the thickness or height of, esp. by pressure; squeeze or beat flat. M17. **2** *v.t.* Make flat, vapid, or insipid; make dull or spiritless; deprive of interest; deaden, depress. M17. **b** *v.i.* Become insipid or dull; lose spirit, droop. L17. **3** *v.i.* Be or become flat or flatter; lose convexity or protuberance; grow broad at the expense of thickness. Also foll. by *out.* E18. **b** *Naut.* Of the wind etc.: decrease in force. M18. **4** *v.t. Mus.* Lower in pitch by a semitone. E19. **5** *v.t.* Paint (a surface) with a matt finish; deprive (paint) of lustre. E19. **6** *v.t.* Knock down. Also, defeat crushingly, humiliate. *colloq.* L19.

1 D. L. SAYERS Bunter, like a steam-roller, had passed over everything, flattening out all traces of upheaval. F. O'CONNOR Flattening themselves against the side to let.. people through. W. GOLDING The water was smoother today as though the dead air were flattening it. 2 G. BURNET The odiousness of the crime grew at last to be so much flatten'd by the frequent executions. BURKE So far from endeavouring to excite this spirit, nothing has been omitted to flatten and lower it. **b** R. L'ESTRANGE Satisfactions that.. flatten in the very tasting. 3b G. ANSON The storm at length flattening to a calm. 6 M. GEE We would have flattened them, me and my mates in the army.

Phrases: **flatten in** *Naut.* extend a sail more nearly fore-and-aft of the vessel. **flatten out** *Aeronaut.* bring an aircraft into a position parallel with the ground; (of an aircraft) assume such a position.

flattener *n.* M18. **flattening** *vbl n.* the action or process of making or becoming flat; the condition of being flattened. E18.

flatter /ˈflatə/ *v.*[1] ME. [Origin unkn., perh. back-form. f. FLATTERY.] **1** *v.t.* Try to please or win the favour of by obsequious speech or conduct; pay obsequious attention to. ME. **2** *v.t.* Compliment unduly or insincerely, overpraise. ME. †**3** *v.i.* Of an animal, esp. a dog: display (apparent) pleasure or affection by tail-wagging, making a pleased sound, etc. LME–E17. **b** *v.t.* Touch or stroke lightly and caressingly. *rare.* L16–E18. **4** *v.t.* Gratify the vanity or self-esteem of; make (a person) feel honoured; gratify (a person's vanity). LME. **5** *v.t.* Encourage or cheer (a person) with hopeful or pleasing manifestations; inspire with (esp. unfounded) hope. LME. **b** Please or delude with the belief, idea, or suggestion *that.* Chiefly *refl.* L16. **6** *v.t.* Play upon the vanity or susceptibilities of (a person); beguile or persuade by blandishments; coax, wheedle. E16. **7** *v.t.* Beguile, charm away (sorrow etc.); charm *to* (tears etc.). *arch.* L16. **8** *v.t.* Of a painter, portrait, etc.: represent too favourably, exaggerate the good looks of. L16. **b** Show to the best advantage, make effective, emphasize the good points of. E20. **9** *v.t.* Gratify (the eye, ear, etc.). L17.

1 SHAKES. *Rich. II* I mock my name, great king, to flatter thee. 2 OED 'Your beautiful voice—' 'Ah! you are flattering me.' L. STEFFENS I did not flatter anybody: I told the truth as near as I could get it. 3 E. TOPSELL Dogges.. who would fawn & gently flatter vpon all those which came.. there. 4 W. H. PRESCOTT Others he flattered by asking their advice. P. ACKROYD A very clever young man who flattered her self-regard by becoming infatuated with her. 5 W. H. PRESCOTT Men had flattered themselves.. with the expectation of some change for the better. *absol.*: *Field* Two furlongs from home Maiden Erlegh looked dangerous, but he flattered only to deceive. **b** H. JAMES She flattered herself that she was a very just woman. 6 T. FULLER Or did he hope.. to flatter Heaven into a consent? 7 SHAKES. *Rich. III* Flatter my sorrows with report of it. 8 HOR. WALPOLE Oliver.. said to him '.. I desire you.. to paint my picture truly like me, and not flatter me.' *absol.*: CONAN DOYLE A good-looking woman, too, if the photograph does not flatter. **b** J. CHEEVER A grey silk dress—a cloth and a color that flattered her. 9 R. L. STEVENSON The beauty of the stone flattered the young clergyman's eyes.

flatterer *n.* ME. **flattering** *ppl a.* that flatters; *flattering unction* [Shakes. *Haml.*], a salve that one administers to one's own conscience or self-esteem: LME. **flatteringly** *adv.* LME.

†**flatter** *v.*[2]*i.* LME–E19. [Imit.: cf. *flacker*, *flutter*, *flitter*.] Float, flutter.

flattery /ˈflat(ə)ri/ *n.* ME. [OFr. *flaterie* (mod. *flatterie*), f. *flater* v. = flatter, prob. ult. f. Gmc base of FLAT *a.* w. meaning 'pat, smooth, caress'.] **1** The action or practice of flattering; undue or insincere praise; adulation; cajolery, blandishment. ME. **2** Gratifying deception, delusion. (Chiefly Shakes.). Long *rare* or *obs.* L16. **3** An act or instance of flattering. Now *rare.* L16.

1 GOLDSMITH Tyranny over his inferiors, and flattery to the queen. C. P. SNOW It sounded like flattery, like the kind of extravagant compliment he used to give her. 2 SHAKES. *Oth.* She is persuaded I will marry her, out of her own love and flattery. 3 R. BOYLE Your Custome to look ev'n upon Smal Praises as Flatteries.

flattie /ˈflati/ *n. colloq.* Also **-y**. L19. [f. FLAT *a.* + -IE, -Y[6].] **1** A flatfish. L19. **2** A flat-bottomed boat. L19. **3** A police officer. Cf. *flatfoot* s.v. FLAT *a.* L19. **4** A flat-heeled shoe. Orig. *US.* M20.

flatulence /ˈflatjʊl(ə)ns/ *n.* E18. [f. as next + -ENCE. Cf. next.] **1** Inflated or puffed-up condition, windiness, vanity; pomposity, pretentiousness. E18. **2a** The condition of being charged with gas. *rare* exc. as below. E19. **b** *spec.* The state or condition of having the stomach or other part of the alimentary canal charged with gas. M19. **c** The tendency of a food to produce flatus. M19.

flatulency /ˈflatjʊl(ə)nsi/ *n.* L16. [f. next + -ENCY.] **1a** = FLATULENCE 2c. L16. **b** = FLATULENCE 2b. M17. **2** *fig.* = FLATULENCE 1. M17.

flatulent /ˈflatjʊl(ə)nt/ *a.* L16. [Fr. f. mod.L *flatulentus*, f. L *flatus* blowing, blast, f. *flare* to blow: see -ULENT.] **I 1** Causing or apt to cause the formation of gas in the alimentary canal. L16. **2** Caused by, accompanied by, or troubled with an accumulation of gas in the alimentary canal. M17. **3** *fig.* Inflated, puffed up, windy, pretentious. M17.

1 M. DONOVAN Eaten in quantity it [beet-root] often proves flatulent. 2 G. BIRD Occasional attacks of indigestion, with flatulent eructations. 3 DRYDEN How many of those flatulent Writers have I known. K. AMIS Some flatulent work on textile trades in the time of the Tudors.

II 4†**a** Of a windy nature, full of air or wind. E17–M18. **b** Liable to, or prolific in, windy blasts. Long *rare* or *obs.* L17.

4b R. BOHUN The Spring and Autumn.. are the most Flatulent Seasons of the yeere.

flatulently *adv.* M19. **flatulentness** *n.* (*rare*) flatulence M16.

flatuosity /flatjʊˈɒsɪti/ *n.* Long *rare* or *obs.* L16. [f. next + -ITY.] †**1** A quantity of wind, air, or gas. L16–E17. **2** = FLATULENCE 2b. E17. **b** A tendency to cause flatulence. *rare.* E18.

†**flatuous** *a.* L16. [med.L *flatuosus*, f. L *flatus*: see next, -OUS.] **1** = FLATULENT 4. L16–E18. **2** = FLATULENT 1. Only in 17. **3** = FLATULENT 2. E17–E18. **4** = FLATULENT 3. M17–E18.

flatus /ˈfleɪtəs/ *n.* Pl. **-uses**. M17. [L *flatus*, f. *flare* to blow.] **1** Gas accumulated in the alimentary canal, or expelled from the anus; wind. M17. **2** A blowing, a blast; a breath, a puff of wind. Now *rare.* L17. †**3** A morbid inflation or swelling (*lit.* & *fig.*). E–M18.

flatwise /ˈflatwʌɪz/ *adv.* Also **-ways** /weɪz/, (*rare*) **-way** /-weɪ/. E17. [f. FLAT *a.* + -WISE, -WAYS.] With the flat side (esp. as opp. to the edge) uppermost, foremost, or applied to another surface.

flatworm /ˈflatwəːm/ *n.* M18. [f. FLAT *a.* + WORM *n.*] Any worm of the phylum Platyhelminthes, characterized by a flattened body with three cell layers, a blind gut, and no other body cavity, and including trematodes (flukes), cestodes (tapeworms), and turbellarians.

Flaubertian /fləʊˈbɛːtɪən, -ˈbəːt-/ *a.* E20. [f. *Flaubert* (see below) + -IAN.] Of, pertaining to, or characteristic of the French novelist Gustave Flaubert (1821–1880), or his writings.

flaucht *n.* var. of FLAUGHT *n.*[2]

flaught /flɔːt/ *n.*[1] Chiefly *Sc.* Cf. FLAKE *n.*[2], FLIGHT *n.*[3], FLAW *n.*[1] ME. [Prob. OE or ON f. Gmc, f. parallel bases of FLAKE *n.*[2], FLAW *n.*[1]] **1** A flash of light, lightning, or fire; a tongue of flame. See also FIRE-FLAUGHT. ME. 2 A flake of snow. LME. 3 Turf, greensward; a turf. Cf. also FLAG *n.*[2] I. LME. 4 A lock of hair. L18. 5 A sudden blast of wind (and rain). E19.

flaught /flɔːt/ *n.*[2] Chiefly *Sc.* Also **-cht**. Cf. FLOCHT. L16. [Var. of FLOCHT.] 1 = FLOCHT I. L16. 2 A spreading out, as of wings for flight. E19. 3 A flock of birds, a flight. E19. 4 The action of fleeing, flight. L19.

flaughter /ˈflaxtə/ *v. Sc. & north.* M18. [f. FLAUGHT *n.*[2] Cf. FLICHTER *v.*] 1 *v.t.* Flutter. Of a light: flicker. M18. 2 *v.t. & i.* Make or become angry, excited, or afraid. L18. 3 *v.t. & i.* Spread open, sprawl; knock down. M19.

flaunch /flɔːn(t)ʃ/ *n.*[1] Also **flanque** /flɑːŋk/, **flanch** /flɑːn(t)ʃ/. LME. [Perh. f. OFr. *flanche* (fem.) = *flanc* (masc.) FLANK *n.*] *Her.* A subordinary formed on each side of the shield by a line convex towards the centre, always borne double.

flaunched *a.* having flaunches L17.

flaunch *n.*[2] & *v.* var. of FLANCH *n.*[1] & *v.*

flaunt /flɔːnt/ *n.* Now *rare.* L16. [f. the vb.] †1 Showy dress, finery. L16–E17. 2 The action or habit of making a display. E17.

flaunt /flɔːnt/ *v.* M16. [Origin unkn.] 1 *v.i. & t.* (w. *it*). Display oneself ostentatiously or impudently; show off. M16. b *v.t.* (Now the usual sense.) Parade or flourish (oneself, one's possessions, abilities, etc.) provocatively or defiantly. E19. 2 *v.i.* Flutter or wave proudly. L16. 3 *v.t.* Flout. (Often considered to be *erron.*) E20.

1 W. IRVING The Miss Lambs might now be seen flaunting along the streets in French bonnets. b O. WILDE They flaunt their conjugal felicity in one's face, as if it were the most fascinating of sins. G. GREENE The little man . . flaunting his cane and battered bowler along the endless road out of the screen. 2 T. HOOD No pennons brave Flaunted upon the mast. 3 *Times* The Prime Minister . . referred to 'flaunting' the regulations.

flaunter *n.* L16. **flaunting** *ppl a.* (*a*) showy, gaudy, ostentatious; (*b*) waving gaily or proudly: M16. **flauntingly** *adv.* L16. **flaunty** *a.* given to ostentation or show; impudent, vain: L18.

flautando /flaʊˈtandəʊ/ *n. & adv.* E19. [It., pres. pple of *flautare* play the flute, f. *flauto* flute.] *Mus.* (A direction: with) a flutelike violin tone, produced either by playing harmonics or by bowing lightly over the finger-board.

Also ***flautato*** /flaʊˈtaːtəʊ/ *n. & adv.* M19.

flautino /flaʊˈtiːnəʊ/ *n.* Pl. **-os**. In sense 2 also **-na** /-nə/. E18. [It., dim. of *flauto* flute.] 1 A small flute or flageolet. E18. 2 A gemshorn organ-stop of 2-ft length and pitch. M19.

flautist /ˈflɔːtɪst/ *n.* M19. [It. *flautista*, f. *flauto* flute. Cf. earlier FLUTIST.] A person who plays the flute.

flauto /ˈflauto, ˈflaʊtəʊ/ *n.* Pl. **-ti** /-ti/, **-tos** /-təʊz/. E18. [It. = FLUTE *n.*[1]] 1 Orig., a recorder. Later, a flute. Also, the part played by such an instrument. E18. 2 An organ-stop of flute scale. L19.

1 ***flauto piccolo*** /ˈpikkolo, ˈpɪkələʊ/, pl. **-li** /-li/, **-los** /-ləʊz/, [= small] †(*a*) a small recorder; (*b*) a piccolo. ***flauto traverso*** /traˈverso, trəˈvəːsəʊ/, pl. **-si** /-si/, **-sos** /-səʊz/, a side-blown flute.

flavanthrone /fleɪˈvanθrəʊn, flə-/ *n.* Also **-ene** /-iːn/. E20. [G *Flavanthren*, f. as FLAVO- + ANTHRA(QUINONE: see -ONE, -ENE.] *Chem.* A yellow synthetic dye, $C_{28}H_{12}N_2O_2$, derived from anthraquinone. Also *flavanthrone yellow*.

flavescent /fləˈvɛs(ə)nt/ *a.* M19. [L *flavescent-* pres. ppl stem of *flavescere*, f. *flavus* yellow: see -ESCENT.] Turning a pale yellow; yellowish.

Flavian /ˈfleɪvɪən/ *a. & n.* L16. [L *Flavianus*, f. *Flavius* (see below): see -AN.] *Rom. Hist.* A *adj.* Of or pertaining to any of several distinguished Romans of the name of Flavius or the gens to which they belonged (among whose members were the emperors Vespasian, Titus, and Domitian). L16. B *n.* A member of the Flavian gens. M20.

flavin /ˈfleɪvɪn/ *n.* Also **-ine** /-iːn, -ɪn/. See also next. M19. [f. L *flavus* yellow + -IN[1], -INE[5].] 1 *Chem.* = QUERCETIN. M19. 2 *Biochem.* Any of a group of naturally occurring pigments which have a tricyclic molecular structure based on fused benzene, pyrazine, and pyrimidine rings, and include a number of biologically important substances such as riboflavin. M19.

Comb.: **flavin adenine dinucleotide, flavin mononucleotide** coenzymes derived from riboflavin (cf. FLAVOPROTEIN).

flavine /ˈfleɪviːn, -ɪn/. *n.* See also prec. M19. [f. as prec.: see -INE[5].] 1 See prec. M19. 2 Any of a group of yellow derivatives of acridine having antiseptic properties, e.g. acriflavine. E20.

flavo- /ˈfleɪvəʊ/ *comb. form* of L *flavus* yellow: see -O-. Used esp. in *Chem.*, sometimes w. the sense 'containing flavin'.

flavoˈprotein *n.* (*Biochem.*) any of a group of conjugated proteins having flavin mononucleotide or flavin adenine dinucleotide as cofactor, involved in oxidation-reduction reactions in the cell M20.

flavone /ˈfleɪvəʊn/ *n.* L19. [f. FLAVO- + -ONE.] A colourless crystalline tricyclic compound, 2-phenylbenzo-1,4-pyrone, $C_{15}H_{10}O_2$. Also, any derivative of this, many examples of which are yellow plant pigments.

flavonoid *n.* any of a large class of plant pigments having a structure based on or similar to that of flavone, including anthocyanins, anthoxanthins, etc., besides flavones M20. **flavonol** *n.* a hydroxy derivative of flavone, 3-hydroxyflavone, $C_{15}H_{10}O_3$; any derivative of this, many examples of which are yellow plant pigments: L19.

flavor *n.*, *v.* see FLAVOUR *n.*, *v.*

flavorous /ˈfleɪv(ə)rəs/ *a.* L17. [f. FLAVOUR *n.* + -OUS.] Full of flavour; pleasing to the taste and smell.

flavour /ˈfleɪvə/ *n.* Also ***-or**. LME. [OFr. *flaor* (infl. by *savour*) perh. f. Proto-Romance blending of L *flatus* blowing, breath and *foetor* stench.] 1 Fragrance, smell; an aroma; a trace of a particular odour. *arch.* LME. 2 The quality perceived by the sense of taste (aided by smell); a distinctive taste. L17. b A substance added to food etc. to impart a specific taste. L18. 3 *fig.* An undefinable characteristic quality; a slight admixture *of* a (usu. undesirable) quality. L17. 4 *Particle Physics.* A quantized property of quarks which differentiates them into at least six varieties (up, down, charmed, strange, top, bottom). Also, an analogous property of leptons. L20.

1 J. MASEFIELD The strong ammonia flavour Of horses' stables. 2 J. STEINBECK Doc was frying sausages, sprinkling a little chocolate over them. It gave them an odd and oriental flavour, he thought. **flavour of the month** a short-lived fashion; a person who or thing which is very popular for a short time. b M. PYKE Should a really convincing raspberry flavour be developed, will its use be wrong in the absence of raspberries? 3 H. L. MENCKEN There is always a flavour of doubt . . a feeling . . that, after all, the scoundrel *may* have something up his sleeve. *Company* Amsterdam . . is compared with Venice, but the flavour is totally different.

flavourful *a.* E20. **flavourist** *n.* a person who creates flavourings for drinks, perfumes, etc. L20. **flavourless** *a.* M18. **flavourlessness** *n.* M19. **flavoursome** *a.* M19. **flavoury** *a.* E18.

flavour /ˈfleɪvə/ *v.* Also ***-or**. LME. [f. the n.] 1 *v.i.* †a Be odorous, savour, smell. Only in LME. b Have the flavour *of*. L19. 2 *v.t.* Give flavour, taste, or scent to; season. M16.

1b M. CORELLI A strange sickening sense of unrest that flavoured of despair. 2 S. RUSHDIE Water flavoured with freshly squeezed limes.

flavoured *a.* (*a*) mixed with a flavouring agent; (*b*) having a (usu. specified) flavour: M18. **flavouring** *n.* (*a*) the action of the vb; (*b*) a perfume or flavour; *spec.* something used to give flavour to food or drink: LME.

flaw /flɔː/ *n.*[1] ME. [Perh. f. ON *flaga* slab of stone, prob. f. Gmc base parallel to that of FLAKE *n.*[2]] I A detached piece (cf. FLAKE *n.*[2], FLAUGHT *n.*[1]). Now chiefly *dial.* 1 A flake of snow; a spark or tongue of fire. ME. 2 A fragment, a splinter: *obs.* exc. *Sc.*, the point of a horseshoe nail which is snapped off after passing through the hoof; hence, something worthless. LME. 3 Turf; a single turf. Cf. also FLAG *n.*[2] I. E18. b The quantity of peats cut in a season. E19.

II A broken or faulty place. (Perh. earliest in WHITLOW.) 4 A defect, imperfection, or blemish. L15. b In a legal document, title, etc.: an invalidating defect or fault. E17. c A failure or shortcoming; a fault. M18. 5 A crack, fissure, or breach. E17. 6 A lie, a falsehood. *Sc.* E18.

4 E. WHARTON Two little lines near her mouth, faint flaws in the smooth curve of the cheek. b G. BURNET A Prince who knew there was a flaw in his title would always govern well. c J. G. COZZENS Now he could see it well enough as the flaw that it was, a defect in self-control. 5 SWIFT He that would keep his house in repair, must attend every little breach or flaw.

flawless *a.* without crack, defect, or imperfection M17. **flawlessly** *adv.* L19. **flawlessness** *n.* L19.

flaw /flɔː/ *n.*[2] E16. [Prob. f. MLG *vlāge*, MDu. *vlāghe* (Du. *vlaag*), the primary sense perh. being 'stroke'.] 1 A sudden blast or gust of wind. E16. b A short spell of rough weather. L18. †2 A sudden onset; a burst of feeling or passion; a sudden uproar. L16–L17.

flaw /flɔː/ *v.*[1]*i. & t.* E17. [f. FLAW *n.*[1]] Make or become faulty; break, crack.

P. COLQUHOUN Elm is very apt to flaw and splinter. *Times Lit. Suppl.* A fallacy that flaws the entire book.

flawed *ppl a.* imperfect, blemished; faulty, damaged. LME.

flaw /flɔː/ *v.*[2] *rare.* E19. [f. FLAW *n.*[2]] 1 *v.i.* Blow in gusts. E19. 2 *v.t.* Ruffle as a gust of wind does. L19.

flaw *v.*[3] see FLAY *v.*[1]

flawn /flɔːn/ *n. arch.* ME. [OFr. *flaon* (mod. FLAN) f. med.L *flado*, *fladon-*, f. Frank. (Du. *vlade*, *vla* custard), f. WGmc.] A custard or cheesecake. Also, a pancake. Cf. FLAN.

flax /flaks/ *n.* [OE *flæx* (*fleax*) = OFris. *flax*, (M)Du. *vlas*, OHG *flahs* (G *Flachs*), f. WGmc, prob. f. IE base repr. also by Gk *plekein*, L *plectere*, G *flechten* to plait.] I 1 A blue-flowered plant, *Linum usitatissimum* (family Linaceae) cultivated for its seed (linseed), and for textile fibre made from its stalks. OE. 2a With specifying wd: any of various related or similar plants. LME. b More fully *New Zealand flax*. A New Zealand plant, *Phormium tenax*, of the agave family, the leaves of which yield a fibre used for baskets etc. M19.

2a **fairy flax** *Linum catharticum*, bearing small white flowers and formerly used in laxative preparations. **pale flax** *L. bienne*, bearing pale blue flowers. **purging flax** = *fairy flax* above. TOADFLAX.

II 3 The fibre of the plant *Linum usitatissimum*, whether dressed or not; cloth made from this fibre, linen. OE. †b *spec.* The fibre as a material for making candle or lamp wicks; a wick. OE–M17. 4 A material resembling the fibres of the flax plant or similarly used. M16.

Comb.: **flax-blue** (of) the blue of the flax flower; **flax-brake, -break, -breaker** a device or machine to thresh out the fibres of flax; **flax-bush, -lily** *NZ* = sense 2b above; **flax-comb** an instrument for cleaning and straightening flax fibres; **flax-flower blue** = *flax-blue* above; **flax-hackle** = *flax-comb* above; *flax-lily*: see *flax-bush* above; **flax-seed** (*a*) linseed; (*b*) *US* a pupa of the hessian fly, which resembles a seed of flax.

flaxy *a.* made of flax; like flax: M17.

flax /flaks/ *v. US colloq.* M19. [f. the n.] 1 *v.t.* Beat severely. Usu. foll. by *out*. M19. 2 *v.i.* Foll. by *out*: tire, become exhausted. L19. 3 *v.i.* Foll. by (*a*)*round*: bestir oneself, bustle about. L19.

flaxen /ˈflaks(ə)n/ *a.* LME. [f. FLAX *n.* + -EN[4].] 1 Made of flax, linen. LME. 2 Of hair etc.: coloured like dressed flax, pale yellow. E16. 3 Of or pertaining to flax as a commercial product. E18.

flay /fleɪ/ *v.*[1]*t.* Also (*dial.*) **flaw** /flɔː/, †**flea**. [OE *flēan* = MDu. *vlae(gh)en* (Du. *vlaen*), ON *flá*, f. Gmc.] 1 Strip or pull off the skin or hide of; skin. OE. 2 Strip, peel *off* (the skin). ME. †b Tear off (a man's beard) together with the skin. ME–L15. 3 Strip off or severely damage portions of the skin from; excoriate. ME. 4 Remove or strip *off* (an outer covering, as peel, bark, etc.) Now chiefly *dial.* ME. b Pare (*off*) thin slices of (turf). L16. 5 Strip an outer covering from; peel. L16. †b Strip (a person) of clothing; undress. *rare* (Shakes.). Only in E17. c Strip (a building etc.) of its exterior covering or ornament. M17. 6 Rob or cheat (a person); pillage, plunder. *arch.*

L16. 7 Subject to acute pain or torture; *fig.* criticize severely, abuse. L18.

1 U. LE GUIN The tanned skins of rebels flayed alive. 2 F. M. FORD Those two women pursued that poor devil and flayed the skin off him. 3 LD MACAULAY The prospect of dying in Newgate, with a back flayed and an eye knocked out. 4 F. FORSYTH She was rusty, her paint blistered by the sun in many places, flayed off by salt spray in others. 6 J. A. FROUDE Plundering cities and temples and flaying the people with requisitions. 7 W. SAFIRE The antisloppiness brigade . . has flayed the cliché users.

Comb.: **flay-flint** a skinflint.

flayer *n.* LME.

flay *v.*[2] & *n.* var. of FLEY.

flea /fliː/ *n.* & *v.*[1] [OE *flēa(h)*, corresp. to MLG, MDu. *vlō* (Du. *vloo*), OHG *flōh* (G *Floh*), ON *fló*, f. Gmc.] A *n.* Any of various small wingless parasitic insects of the order Siphonaptera, which live on the skin of mammals and birds, feeding on blood, and are noted for their agility in jumping. Also (w. specifying wd), any of various invertebrates which jump or move jerkily like a flea. OE.

bat flea, *cat flea*, *dog flea*, *human flea*, etc. *fit as a flea*: see FIT *a.* 7. **go** or **send away with a flea in one's, his**, etc. **ear** go or send (a person) away discomfited by a reproof or rebuff.

Comb.: **fleabag** *slang* (*a*) a sleeping bag; (*b*) a shabby place, esp. lodgings; a shabby, unkempt person; **fleabane** any of various plants, esp. of the genera *Pulicaria* and *Erigeron* (family Compositae), reputed to drive away fleas; *spec.* (more fully *common fleabane*) *P. dysenterica*, a marsh plant bearing yellow flowers; **flea-beetle** any of numerous small jumping beetles of the family Chrysomelidae, many of which are serious plant pests; **flea-bite** (*a*) (the red spot caused by) the bite of a flea; *Med.* a petechial haemorrhage into the skin resembling this; (*b*) *fig.* a trifling inconvenience or discomfort; (*c*) a small reddish, brown, or black spot in the coloration of a horse, dog, or other animal; **flea-bitten** (*a*) bitten by or infested with fleas; (*b*) (of the coloration of an animal) sprinkled with flea-bites on a lighter ground; **flea-bug** *US.* = *flea-beetle* above; **flea-circus** a show of performing fleas; **flea-collar** a collar (for a dog or cat) impregnated with a substance that kills fleas; **flea-dock** butterbur; **flea-hopper** *US* a small jumping hemipteran insect of the family Miridae, injurious to plants; esp. *Halticus bracteatus* (garden flea-hopper) and *Psallus seriatus* (cotton flea-hopper); **flea-louse** a jumping plant-louse of the hemipteran family Psyllidae; **flea market** a street market; **flea-pit** *slang* an allegedly verminous place of public assembly; *esp.* a cinema; **fleawort** any of several plants of the genus *Tephroseris*, related to the ragworts; *esp.* (more fully *field fleawort*) *T. integrifolia*, a Eurasian plant of calcareous grassland.

B *v.t.* Rid of fleas. E17.

W. H. AUDEN The dog fleaing itself in the hot dust.

fleasome *a.* (*joc.*) full of fleas (usu. assoc. w. GLEESOME) M19. **fleay** /ˈfliːi/ *a.* E17.

†flea *v.*[2] var. of FLAY *v.*[1]

flead *n.* var. of FLEED.

fleam /fliːm/ *n.*[1] & *v.* Now *dial.* ME. [Alt. of FLUME *n.*] A *n.* Orig., a stream or river. Now, a mill stream, an artificial channel. ME. B *v.i.* Flow, stream (*away*). LME.

fleam /fliːm/ *n.*[2] LME. [OFr. *flieme* (mod. *flamme*) f. Proto-Romance alt. of late L *phlebotomus* (med.L *fledomum*, *fletoma*), f. Gk *phlebotomon* use as n. of neut. adj. (see PHLEBOTOMY).] *Med.* (now chiefly *Hist.*). A lancet used for blood-letting; latterly *esp.* one for the bleeding of horses.

flebile /ˈfleɪbɪleɪ/ *a.* E17. [It. f. L *flebilis* that is to be wept for; plaintive: see FEEBLE *a.*] *Mus.* Mournful, plaintive.

flèche /flɛʃ, fleɪʃ/ *n.* Pl. pronounced same. ME. [(O)Fr. = arrow.] †1 An arrow. Only in ME. 2 *Fortif.* A work in communication with the covered way, placed at the salient angle of the glacis. E18. 3 *Archit.* A slender spire, usu. of wood and rising from a roof. M19. 4 Any of the twenty-four points on a backgammon board. M19. 5 *Fencing.* In full *flèche attack.* A running attack. E20.

fléchette /fleɪˈʃɛt/ *n.* E20. [Fr., dim. of *flèche* arrow: see -ETTE.] *Mil.* A missile resembling a dart, dropped from an aircraft.

fleck /flɛk/ *n.*[1] L16. [Rel. to FLECK *v.*[1]] 1 A blemish, freckle, or spot in the skin. L16. b A patch of colour, light, etc. E19. 2 A small particle; a flake, a speck. M18.

1 E. FIGES Everything is different about old people. . . Those little brown flecks on the skin. b P. H. JOHNSON She smiled at the flecks of sunlight fluttering like moths about the ceiling. 2 C. LASSALLE There were little flecks of cork in her glass.

fleckless *a.* M19. **flecklessly** *adv.* L19.

fleck *n.*[2] var. of FLICK *n.*[2]

fleck *n.*[3] var. of FLICK *n.*[3]

fleck /flɛk/ *v.*[1]*t.* LME. [Origin uncertain; cf. ON *flekkr* n., *flekka* vb, or MLG, MDu. *vlecke* (Du. *vlek*) = OHG *flec*, *fleccho* (G *Fleck*, *flecken*), of unkn. origin.] Spot, streak; mark with flecks; dapple, variegate. Freq. as *flecked* ppl a.

G. SWIFT Little orange spots of mud flecked her stockings. S. KING Deep green eyes flecked with hazel.

fleck /flɛk/ *v.*[2] Long *obs.* exc. *dial.* M16. [Perh. var. of FLAG *v.*[2] Cf. FLEG *v.*[2]] Fly low; flit, flutter about.

fleck *v.*[3] see FLICK *v.*[2]

fleckered /ˈflɛkəd/ *a.* L15. [f. FLECK *v.*[1] + -ER[5] + -ED[1].] Marked with flecks; dappled; scattered in flecks.

GEO. ELIOT Seated . . in the fleckered shade of the ash tree.

fleckled /ˈflɛk(ə)ld/ *a.* L16. [f. FLECK *n.*[1] + -LE[1] + -ED[2].] Dappled; freckled.

flection *n.* var. of FLEXION.

fled *v.* pa. t. & pple of FLEE *v.*

fledge /flɛdʒ/ *a.* *obs.* exc. *dial.* LME. [Prob. repr. base of OE *unfligge*, glossing L *implumes* unfledged; corresp. to MDu. *vlugghe* (Du. *vlug*), OHG *flucchi* (G *flügge* is from LG), f. WGmc, f. base of FLY *v.*] 1 Of a young bird: fit to fly, fledged. LME. †b *fig.* High-spirited. LME–M17. 2 Provided *with* feathers for flight. M17.

2 *fig.* MILTON All the fond hopes, which forward Youth and Vanitie are fledge with.

fledgeless *a.* unfledged M18.

fledge /flɛdʒ/ *v.* & *n.* M16. [f. the adj.] A *v.* 1 *v.i.* Of a young bird: develop feathers large enough for flight; become fully plumed. M16. 2 *v.t.* Bring up (a young bird) until its feathers are developed enough for flight. L16. 3 *v.t.* Provide (a bird, an arrow) with feathers; adorn with feathers; cover (as) with feathers or down. L16.

1 *Bird Watching* Young ravens take about six weeks to fledge. 3 L. P. HARTLEY Low hills rose behind the town, green hills already fledged with autumn yellow.

B *n.* A feather or downlike covering. *rare.* E20.

D. H. LAWRENCE He had now a black fledge on his upper lip, a black finely-shaped line.

fledged *ppl a.* able to fly; *fig.* mature, independent: L16.

fledgling /ˈflɛdʒlɪŋ/ *n.* & *a.* Also **fledgeling**. M19. [f. FLEDGE *a.* + -LING[1], after *nestling*.] A *n.* A young bird just fledged; *fig.* an inexperienced person. M19.

B *attrib.* or as *adj.* Inexperienced; raw. M19.

E. JOHNSON He gave fledgling authors a chance to appear in print.

fledgy /ˈflɛdʒi/ *a.* *rare.* L16. [f. as prec. + -Y[1].] †1 Fledged; ready to fly. Only in L16. 2 Covered with feathers, feathery. E19.

flee /fliː/ *v.* Pa. t. & pple **fled** /flɛd/. [OE *flēon* = OFris. *flia*, OS *fliohan* (MDu. *vlīen*, Du. *vlieden*), OHG *fliohan* (G *fliehen*), ON *flý(j)a*, Goth. *þliuhan* f. Gmc. Already in OE confused with FLY *v.*] I *v.i.* 1 Run away from or as from danger; take flight; hasten or run for safety or protection. (Foll. by *from*, *out of*; *to*, *into*.) OE. b Get safely away, make one's escape. ME. 2 Withdraw hastily, go away, leave. Foll. by *from*, *out of*. OE. 3 = FLY *v.* I. Now only *poet.* OE. 4 Vanish, cease, pass away. ME.

1 E. BOWEN She fled to the back of the house and hid in a box-room. W. S. CHURCHILL The Marquis, brokenhearted, fled into exile. E. BLISHEN They fled, to be caught round the next corner. b G. ORWELL Goldstein had fled and was hiding no one knew where. 2 A. B. JAMESON Two years later he fled from society. 3 SHELLEY The dark arrow fled In the noon. 4 GIBBON The animating health and vigour were fled.

II *v.t.* 5 Run or hasten away from (a person, place, etc.); forsake. OE. 6 Avoid with dread or distaste; shun. OE. b Contrive to avoid; evade. Now *rare.* ME.

5 B. MALAMUD Hundreds of Jews are leaving the city as if fleeing the plague. *Bird Watching* Continental birds . . fleeing food failures.

fleece /fliːs/ *n.* [OE *flēos*, *flēs*, (WS) *flīes* = Du. *vlies*, MHG *vlies* (G *Vlies*), f. WGmc base; prob. ult. rel. to the base of L *pluma* feather.] 1 The woolly covering or pelt of a sheep or similar animal. OE. b *Her.* A charge representing a sheepskin with its wool suspended by a ring. E16. c A sheep; *collect.* sheep. L18. 2 The body or quantity of wool shorn from a sheep at one time. LME. b An act of robbery or cheating. Formerly also, a share of booty. E17. 3 A thing resembling a sheep's fleece in appearance or in consistency; *esp.* a rough abundant head of hair. E16. b Fabric with a fleecy consistency; a soft silky nap, esp. as a lining. M19.

1 **Golden Fleece** (*a*) *Gk Mythol.* a fleece of gold sought and won by Jason; (*b*) (in full *Order of the Golden Fleece*) an order of knighthood instituted in 1430 by Philip the Good, Duke of Burgundy. *double fleece*: see DOUBLE *a.* & *adv.* 2 SIR W. SCOTT Thou shalt have a necklace of jet at next shearing-feast, if our fleeces bear any price in the market. 3 POPE Soft as the fleeces of descending snow.

Comb.: **fleece-picker** (*NZ* & *Austral.*) a person who picks up fleeces in a shearing shed; **fleece-wool** wool from the main part of a fleece obtained at the annual shearings.

fleecelike *a.* resembling (that of) a fleece E18.

fleece /fliːs/ *v.* M16. [f. the n.] 1 *v.t.* & *i.* Obtain (money etc.) *from* a person by unfair means. Now *rare.* M16. 2 *v.t.* Strip (a person, city, etc.) of or *of* money, property, etc.; rob; charge an excessive amount. L16 3 *v.t.* Clip or shear the fleece from (a sheep). Now *rare.* E17. 4 *v.t.* Dapple or fleck with fleecy masses; cover (as) with a fleece. M18.

1 CARLYLE To divide what they fleeced from these poor drudges. 2 A. SILLITOE They aren't going to fleece an old salt like me and get away with it. 4 J. FOWLES The sky half blue, half fleeced with white clouds.

fleeceable *a.* M19. **fleeced** *a.* (*a*) provided with a fleece (of a specified kind); (*b*) that has been fleeced: L16. **fleecer** *n.* E17.

fleech /fliːtʃ/ *v.* *Sc.* & *north.* LME. [Origin uncertain: cf. OHG *flēhon* , *flēhen* flatter, beseech, MHG *vlēhen*, G *flehen* beseech, Du. *vleien* flatter.] 1 *v.t.* Coax, cajole, wheedle; beseech, entreat. LME. 2 *v.i.* Speak coaxingly or beseechingly; fawn. LME.

fleecy /ˈfliːsi/ *a.* & *n.* As n. also **-ie**. M16. [f. FLEECE *n.* + -Y[1].] A *adj.* 1 Consisting of fleeces; woollen. M16. 2 Covered with a fleece; fleeced. L16. 3 Resembling a fleece in colour or consistency; woolly; (of the sky) flecked with white clouds. M17. B *n.* A fleece-picker. *NZ* & *Austral. slang.* L19.

fleecily *adv.* L19. **fleeciness** *n.* M20.

fleed /fliːd/ *n.* Also **flead**. Chiefly *dial.* M19. [Origin unkn.] = FLICK *n.*[3]

fleer /ˈfliːə/ *n.*[1] Now *rare.* ME. [f. FLEE *v.* + -ER[1].] A person who flees.

fleer /flɪə/ *v.* & *n.*[2] LME. [Prob. of Scand. origin; cf. Norw. and Sw. dial. *flira*, Da. dial. *flire* grin, laugh derisively.] A *v.* †1 *v.i.* Grin, grimace; make a wry face as if about to cry. LME–L18. 2 *v.t.* & *i.* (w. *at*, †*upon*). Gibe, jeer, sneer at; laugh at mockingly or scornfully. LME. 3 *v.i.* Laugh in a coarse, impudent or fawning manner. Formerly foll. by *on*, *upon*. M16.

2 I. GURNEY Three jeering, fleering spectres, That walked abreast and talked of me. 3 *Daily Telegraph* Impudent-looking wenches . . leering and fleering and chuckling *con amore*.

B *n.* A mocking look or speech; a sneer. E17.

SHAKES. *Oth.* And mark the fleers, the gibes, and notable scorns, That dwell in every region of his face.

fleerer *n.* E17. **fleeringly** *adv.* in a fleering manner E17.

fleet /fliːt/ *n.*[1] [OE *flēot* (once) ship or ships collect., f. *flēotan* float, swim: see FLEET *v.*[1]] 1 A naval force; a number of warships under one commander-in-chief. More widely, a number of ships or boats sailing in company. OE. b *The* navy. E18. 2 A number of persons, birds, or other objects moving in company. Now *esp.* a group of vehicles or aircraft having the same proprietor or otherwise forming a unit. LME. 3 A set or row of drift-nets fastened together end to end. L18.

2 R. HOGGART Buses . . from a big town fleet. K. WATERHOUSE A fleet of electric trollies piled high with newspaper parcels.

Phrases & comb.: *Admiral of the Fleet, Fleet Admiral*: see ADMIRAL 3. **First, Second, Third, Fleet** (*Austral. Hist.*) groups of convict ships arriving in 1788, 1790, 1791 respectively. **Fleet Air Arm** (*Hist.*) the aviation service of the Royal Navy. **fleet in being** (chiefly *Hist.*) a fleet of warships considered as exerting a strategic influence by their mere existence. **flogging round the fleet** *Hist.* the punishment of being flogged alongside each vessel in the fleet.

fleet /fliːt/ *n.*[2] [OE *flēot* (also *flēote* or *-a*), corresp. to OFris. *flēt*, (M)Du. *vliet*, MHG *vliez*, ON *fljót*, f. Gmc base of FLEET *v.*[1]] 1 A place where water flows; a creek, an inlet. Now *dial.* or in proper names. OE. 2 *the Fleet*, (the name of) a stream (now covered) flowing into the Thames between Ludgate Hill and Fleet Street; *Hist.* the prison that stood near it. LME.

Comb.: **Fleet marriage** *Hist.* a wedding performed clandestinely by a Fleet parson (see below) in the Fleet; **Fleet parson** *Hist.* any of a number of disreputable clergymen to be found in or around the Fleet ready to perform clandestine marriages; **Fleet Street** [name of a street in London formerly devoted largely to the production and publication of daily newspapers] the British press; British journalism or journalists collectively.

fleet /fliːt/ *a.*[1] Now *dial.* Also **flet** /flɛt/. LME. [pa. pple of FLEET *v.*[2]] Of milk: skimmed.

fleet /fliːt/ *a.*[2] & *adv.*[1] *poet.* or *literary.* E16. [Prob. f. ON *fljótr*, f. Gmc base of FLEET *v.*[1]] **A** *adj.* 1 Swift in movement; nimble. Cf. FLEET *v.*[1] 7. E16. 2 Evanescent; transient. Cf. FLEET *v.*[1] 6. E19.

1 SHAKES. *L.L.L.* Their conceits have wings, Fleeter than arrows. K. CROSSLEY-HOLLAND Even Thialfi, as fleet of foot as any man in Midgard, was hard put to keep up with him. 2 BARONESS ORCZY A bright smile, fleet and sweet, illumined her dainty face.

B *adv.* Quickly, swiftly. L16.

L. G. GIBBON Tired though he was he came to her side right fleet enough.

fleetly *adv.* = FLEET *adv.*[1] L16. **fleetness** *n.* E17.

fleet /fliːt/ *a.*[3] & *adv.*[2] Now chiefly *dial.* E17. [Perh. f. OE cognate of Du. *vloot* shallow, f. Gmc base of FLEET *v.*[1]] **A** *adj.* Of water: shallow. E17. **B** *adv.* At or to a small depth; esp. in *plough* or *sow fleet.* M17.

fleet /fliːt/ *v.*[1] [OE *flēotan* float, swim = OFris. *fliāta*, OS *fliotan* (Du. *vlieten*), OHG *fliozan* (G *fliessen*), ON *fljóta* float, flow, f. Gmc.] **I** Float. 1 *v.i.* Rest on the surface of the water; be buoyed up; (of a vessel) be or get afloat. *obs.* exc. *dial.* OE. †2 *v.i.* Drift or float in water or air. OE–M18. **b** Move unsteadily, as if floating; sway; fluctuate, waver. LME–M17. 3 *v.i.* Swim. Long *obs.* exc. *Hist.* OE. †4 *v.i.* Travel by water, sail. ME–E18. **II** Flow, slip away, etc. 5 *v.i.* Of water, a river, etc.: flow. Long only *Sc.* ME. 6a *v.i.* Glide away or *away* vanish, fade (*away*). Now only of immaterial things: *esp.* (of time) pass rapidly, slip *away*. Formerly also, waste *away*, disintegrate. Cf. FLEET *a.*[2] 2. *arch.* ME. **b** *v.t.* Pass, while away (time). *rare.* E17. 7 *v.i.* Move swiftly; flit, fly (*away*). Cf. FLEET *a.*[2] 1. *arch.* LME. **III** 8 *v.t. Naut.* Change the position of, shift (a block, rope, etc.). L17.

fleet /fliːt/ *v.*[2]*t.* Now *dial.* Pa. pple **-ed**, †**fleet**. Cf. FLEET *a.*[1] LME. [Prob. f. OE *flēt* cream, f. base of *flēotan* FLEET *v.*[1]; but cf. also Du. *vlieten* (= FLEET *v.*[1]) used in this sense.] Remove the scum from the surface of (a liquid); *esp.* skim (milk, the cream from milk).

fleeting *n.* (*a*) the action of the vb; (*b*) in *pl.*, skimmings, curds: LME.

fleeting /ˈfliːtɪŋ/ *ppl a.* OE. [f. FLEET *v.*[1] + -ING[2].] †1 Floating; swimming. OE–L16. †2 Shifting, unstable; (of a person, an attribute) fickle, inconstant. ME–M17. †3 Flowing; fluid. ME–L17. 4 Passing or gliding swiftly away; (esp. of time, life) passing by rapidly; brief; transient; not permanent or enduring. M16.

2 MILTON Of such a variable and fleeting conscience what hold can be tak'n? 4 E. H. GOMBRICH The Impressionist preoccupation with the fleeting moment. A. N. WILSON All those girls had been fleeting presences in his life.

fleetingly *adv.* L19. **fleetingness** *n.* E18.

fleg /flɛg/ *n.*[1] *Sc.* E18. [f. FLEG *v.*[1]] A fright, a scare.

fleg /flɛg/ *n.*[2] *Sc.* Now *rare* or *obs.* E18. [Origin unkn.] A random blow or kick, a stroke.

fleg /flɛg/ *v.*[1]*t.* *Sc.* Infl. **-gg-**. E17. [Origin unkn. Cf. FLEY.] Frighten, scare.

fleg /flɛg/ *v.*[2]*i.* *Sc.* Infl. **-gg-**. L18. [Origin uncertain: perh. var. of FLAG *v.*[2], FLECK *v.*[2]] Flee, run off; fly away. (Foll. by *off.*)

†**flegm** *n.* var. of PHLEGM.

Flem /flɛm/ *n. colloq.* E20. [Abbrev.] = FLEMING *n.*[1] 1.

†**fleme** *v.t.* OE–E19. [OE *flīeman*, f. *flēam* flight f. Gmc f. ablaut var. of base of FLEE *v.*] Cause to flee; banish, exile.

¶ Only in isolated Sc. use after 16.

Fleming /ˈflɛmɪŋ/ *n.*[1] [Late OE *Flæmingi*, partly f. ON and partly f. MDu. *Vlaminc* (whence ON), f. *Vlām-* base of *Vlaanderen* Flanders: see -ING[3].] 1 A native or inhabitant of Flanders. LOE. †2 A Flemish ship. *rare.* Only in L16.

Fleming /ˈflɛmɪŋ/ *n.*[2] M20. [Sir John Ambrose *Fleming* (1849–1945), Eng. electrical engineer.] Physics. *Fleming's left-hand rule*, a mnemonic which represents the direction of the force exerted on a current-carrying conductor in a magnetic field by the second finger of the left hand, the directions of the current and the field being indicated by the first finger and thumb held perpendicularly to it and to each other. Also called *left-hand rule*.

Flemish /ˈflɛmɪʃ/ *a.* & *n.* ME. [MDu. *Vlāmisch* (Du. *Vlaamsch*) = OFris. *Flamsk*, assim. to FLEMING *n.*[1]: see -ISH[1].] **A** *adj.* 1 Of or pertaining to Flanders in the Low Countries, its people, or its language. ME. 2 Resembling a Fleming in habits and behaviour. *rare.* L16. **B** *n.* The West Germanic language of Flanders, comprising a group of Dutch dialects, now one of the two official languages of Belgium. E18.

Special collocations & comb.: *Flemish bond*: see BOND *n.*[2] **Flemish coil** *Naut.* a rope coiled down flat with the end coming to the centre and each coil closely packed within the preceding coil. **flemish-coil** *v.t.* (*Naut.*) = FLEMISH *v.* **Flemish eye** *Naut.* a kind of eye-splice in which the ends are scraped down, tapered, passed oppositely, marled, and served over with spun yarn. **Flemish horse** *Naut.* a short foot-rope at the yard-arms of a square-rigged ship.

flemish /ˈflɛmɪʃ/ *v.t.* M19. [f. the adj.] *Naut.* Coil or lay up (a rope) in a Flemish coil. Freq. foll. by *down*.

flense /flɛns/ *v.t.* Also **flench** /flɛn(t)ʃ/, **flinch** /flɪn(t)ʃ/. E19. [Da. *flensa* = Norw. *flinsa*, *flunsa* flay.] 1 Cut up and slice the fat from (a whale or seal). E19. 2 Flay or skin (a seal); strip off (the skin of a seal). L19.

flesh /flɛʃ/ *n.* [OE *flǣsć* = OFris. *flask*, OS *flēsk* (Du. *vlees*), OHG *fleisc* (G *Fleisch*), ON *flesk* pork, bacon, f. Gmc.] **I** 1 The soft substance of animal bodies, esp. the muscular part; the tissue which covers the bones and is enclosed by the skin. OE. 2 The tissue of animal bodies regarded as food (esp. as excluding fish and sometimes fowl); meat. Now chiefly in phrs. below or preceded by specifying wd. OE. 3 Quantity or excess of flesh in proportion to bone; plumpness, fat. Formerly also, good condition. M16. 4 The soft pulpy substance of a fruit or plant; the part which is enclosed by the rind and which encloses the core or kernel, esp. as regarded as an article of food. L16. 5 The visible surface of the human body, with reference to its colour and appearance. E17. **b** = FLESH-COLOUR. M19. 6 More fully *flesh side*. The side of a hide that adjoined the flesh. M17.

1 BUNYAN His . . sins, that stick as close to him as the flesh sticks to the bones. 2 T. NASHE The puffin that is halfe fish, halfe flesh. S. BARING-GOULD When a wolf has once tasted human flesh, he desires to taste it again. 3 E. GARRETT Its [a face's] once noble outlines were blurred by too much flesh. 4 ANTHONY HUXLEY A large pumpkin with bright orange flesh. 5b *attrib.*: F. H. BURNETT The . . foot and ankle wore a flesh silk stocking.

II 7 People of the same kindred or descent collectively; (one of) one's family. Now *rare* exc. in *one flesh, flesh and blood* below. OE. 8 That which has corporeal life; the animal kingdom; humankind. Now chiefly in *all flesh* below. OE. 9 The physical or material frame of man; the body. Now chiefly in biblical allusion or in *in the flesh* below. OE. **b** = BODY *n.* 3. OE. 10 The animal or physical nature of man; human nature as subject to material needs and limitations. OE. 11 The sensual appetites and inclinations as opp. to those of mind and soul; the carnal nature of man. ME.

7 SHELLEY What, if we . . were his own flesh, His children and his wife? 8 SHAKES. *Much Ado* As pretty a piece of flesh as any is in Messina. R. W. EMERSON He . . visits worlds which flesh cannot enter. 9 AV *Job* 19:26 Though . . wormes destroy this body, yet in my flesh shall I see God. W. HABINGTON My frighted flesh trembles to dust. 10 J. A. FROUDE The archbishop retired to his see to afflict his flesh with public austerities. 11 F. W. FARRAR Things which tend to the gratification of the flesh.

Phrases: **all flesh** whatever has bodily life. *a thorn in the* (or *one's*) *flesh*: see THORN *n.* 1b. **flesh and blood** *n.* (*a*) humankind; the body or its material; human nature with its emotions and infirmities; (*b*) *one's* (*own*) near relatives, descendants, or ancestors. **flesh-and-blood** *a.* actually living, not supernatural or imaginary. **flesh and fell** *n.* & *adv.* (*arch.*) (*a*) *n.* the whole substance of the body; (*b*) *adv.* entirely. *go the way of all flesh*: see GO *v.* **in flesh** *arch.* corpulent, well-fed, in good condition. **in the flesh** in bodily form, in life. **lose flesh** grow thinner. **make a person's flesh creep** or **crawl** frighten, horrify, or disgust, esp. with dread of the supernatural. *neither fish, nor flesh* (*nor good red herring*): see FISH *n.*[1] **one flesh** [*Gen.* 2:24] intimately united, esp. by virtue of marriage. *piece of flesh*: see PIECE *n.* *pound of flesh*: see POUND *n.*[1] *proud flesh*: see PROUD *a.* 8. **put on flesh** grow fatter. **sins of the flesh** sins related to sensual temptation, esp. unchastity. *the world, the flesh, and the devil*: see WORLD *n.*

Comb.: **flesh-brush** a brush used to stimulate the circulation by rubbing the skin; **flesh-fly** a fly which deposits its eggs or larvae in dead flesh, a meat-fly; *esp.* the black and grey fly *Sarcophaga carnaria*; **flesh-hook** (long *rare* or *obs.*) (*a*) a hook for removing meat from a pot; (*b*) a hook on which meat is hung; **flesh-meat** (*obs.* exc. *dial.*) flesh (occas. excluding pork or bacon) as an article of food; **fleshmonger** †(*a*) a butcher; †(*b*) a pander, a fornicator; (*c*) *arch. rare* a slave-dealer; **fleshpot** (*a*) *arch.* a pot in which flesh is cooked; (*b*) in *pl.* (with ref. to *Exod.* 16:3), luxurious living; **flesh-quake** *arch.* a trembling of the body; *flesh side*: see sense 6 above; **flesh tint** (*a*) = FLESH-COLOUR; (*b*) in *pl.*, a painter's rendering of flesh-colours; **flesh-worm** a worm that feeds on flesh; **flesh-wound** a wound which does not penetrate the bone or any vital organ.

fleshen *a.* (long *rare* or *obs.*) made of flesh (*lit.* & *fig.*); covered with flesh: LME. **flesher** *n.* (*a*) (chiefly *Sc.*) a butcher; (*b*) *US* a fleshing-knife: ME. **fleshhood** *n.* (*arch.*) the state or condition of being in the flesh, incarnation: LME. **fleshless** *a.* L16.

flesh /flɛʃ/ *v.* LME. [f. the n.] 1 †**a** *v.t.* & *i.* *Med.* Grow new tissue in (a wound); heal over. Only in LME. **b** *v.t.* Make fleshy, fatten (*lit.* & *fig.*). Long *rare.* E17. **c** *v.t.* Cover (bones etc.) with flesh; embody in flesh. M17. **d** *v.t.* & *i.* Foll. by *out*. Make or become (more) substantial. L19. 2 *v.t.* Give (a hound etc.) a piece of the flesh of the game killed in order to incite it; make (an animal) eager for prey by the taste of blood. M16. 3 *v.t.* **a** Initiate in or inure to bloodshed or warfare. M16. †**b** Initiate *in* or inure or habituate *to* any practice; harden (in wrongdoing). L16–E18. **c** Arouse or excite (a person) by a foretaste of success or gratification. Now *rare* or *obs.* L16. 4 *v.t.* Plunge (a weapon) into flesh; use (a sword etc.) for the first time on flesh, 'blood'. L16. **b** Gratify (lust, rage, etc.). Long *rare* or *obs.* E17. 5 *v.t.* Remove the flesh adhering to (a skin or hide). L18. 6 *v.t.* Paint flesh-colour. *rare.* M19.

1b H. G. WELLS We've fleshed ourselves a bit, eh? c T. FULLER This bare Sceleton of Time, Place, and Person must be fleshed with some pleasant passages. d J. LE CARRÉ The extra work that fleshed out his pension. 3a A. W. KINGLAKE He fleshed his troops . . with enterprises against the enemy's posts. c DRYDEN Him, flesh'd with slaughter, and with conquest crown'd. 4 SHAKES. *2 Hen. IV* The wild dog shall flesh his tooth on every innocent. *fig.*: J. R. LOWELL The poor youth, just fleshing his maiden pen in criticism. b SHAKES. *All's Well* This night he fleshes his will in the spoil of her honour.

fleshment *n.* (*rare*, Shakes.): only in E17.

flesh-colour /ˈflɛʃkʌlə/ *n.* & *a.* Also *-**color**. L16. [f. FLESH *n.* + COLOUR *n.*] A *n.* A light brownish pink, supposedly the colour of the flesh of a Caucasian seen through the skin. L16. B *attrib.* or as *adj.* Of this colour. E18.

flesh-coloured *a.* = FLESH-COLOUR *a.* M18.

fleshed /flɛʃt/ *a.* LME. [f. FLESH *n.*, *v.*: see -ED[2], -ED[1].] 1 Covered or furnished with flesh. (Freq. preceded by specifying wd.) LME. 2 Inured to or eager for battle or bloodshed. L16. †b Bent *upon* the destruction or injury of (a person). E–M17.

1 C. DARWIN A yellow or purple fleshed fruit. 2 SHAKES. *Rich. III* They were flesh'd villains, bloody dogs.

fleshing /ˈflɛʃɪŋ/ *n.* LME. [f. FLESH *v.*, *n.*: see -ING[1].] 1 a In *pl.* The pieces of flesh etc. scraped from a hide. LME. b The action of scraping pieces of flesh etc. from a hide. L18. †2 *Med.* The growth of new tissue in a wound. Only in LME. 3 The action of FLESH *v.* 2. L16. 4 In *pl.* Flesh-coloured tights, esp. as part of a stage costume. M19.

Comb.: **fleshing-knife** a large two-handled implement with a blunt edge used in fleshing hides.

fleshly /ˈflɛʃli/ *a.* & *adv.* OE. [f. FLESH *n.* + -LY[1].] A *adj.* I 1 Of or pertaining to desire or bodily appetites; lascivious, sensual. OE. †b Sexual. ME–L15. †2 Connected by or based on ties of flesh and blood, natural. OE–L16. 3 Unredeemed, unregenerate. Long *rare*. OE. 4 Of or pertaining to the material body; mortal; material as opp. to divine or spiritual. ME. 5 Pertaining to, concerned with, or influenced by (considerations concerning) life in this world; worldly. ME. II †6 Fat, plump; fleshy. LME–L17. 7 Consisting of flesh (*lit.* & *fig.*); *esp.* (of the heart) soft and tender as opp. to hard. Now *rare* or *obs.* LME. †B *adv.* 1 Bodily; materially. ME–M17. 2 Carnally, sensually, sexually. ME–L16.

fleshliness *n.* †(*a*) *rare* incarnate condition; (*b*) carnality; †(*c*) fleshiness, plumpness: OE.

fleshy /ˈflɛʃi/ *a.* LME. [f. FLESH *n.* + -Y[1].] 1 Well furnished with flesh, fat, plump. LME. 2 Of or pertaining to flesh; *esp.* consisting of flesh, without bone. Also *fig.* (now *rare*), of a heart etc.: soft, tender. LME. b Of plant or fruit tissue: pulpy, not fibrous. L16. c Corporeal, bodily. E17. †3 = FLESHLY 4. LME–M16. 4 Resembling flesh, like flesh. LME.

1 G. GREENE The fleshy and porky figure of the actor. 2 TINDALE The pistle of Christ.. written.. not in tables of stone, but in fleshy tables of the herte. c MILTON He, sovran priest.. Poor fleshy tabernacle entered. 3 COVERDALE *Job* 10:4 Hast thou fleszshy eyes then, or doest thou loke as man loketh? 4 J. ABERNETHY An increase of bulk, and a fleshy feel.

fleshiness *n.* LME.

flet /flɛt/ *n.*[1] [OE *flet(t)* = ON *flet*, ult. f. Gmc base of FLAT *a.*] †1 The floor or ground beneath one's feet. OE–LME. 2†a A dwelling, house, or hall. OE–LME. b The inner part of a house. *Sc.* LME.

Phrases: **fire and flet** *arch.* fire and houseroom.

flet /flɛt/ *n.*[2] *Sc.* L18. [App. repr. ON *flétta* plait, f. *flétta* = G *flechten* to plait.] A mat of plaited straw; *esp.* one placed on the back of a packhorse.

flet *a.* var. of FLEET *a.*[1]

fletch /flɛtʃ/ *v.t.* M17. [Alt. of FLEDGE *v.*, prob. infl. by next.] Provide (an arrow) with feathers for flight (*lit.* & *fig.*).

fletching *n.* (*a*) the action of the vb; (*b*) the feathers of an arrow: M20.

fletcher /ˈflɛtʃə/ *n.* ME. [OFr. *flech(i)er*, f. *fleche* arrow, ult. origin unkn.: see -ER[2].] A person who makes or trades in arrows (and occas. bows).

Fletcherian /flɛˈtʃɪərɪən/ *a.* M19. [f. *Fletcher* (see below) + -IAN.] Of, pertaining to, or characteristic of (the work of) the English dramatist John Fletcher (1579–1625).

Fletcherism /ˈflɛtʃərɪz(ə)m/ *n. obs.* exc. *Hist.* E20. [f. Horace *Fletcher* (1849–1919), US author + -ISM.] The practice of thorough mastication as advocated by Fletcher.

Fletcherite *n.* a follower of Fletcher E20. **fletcherize** *v.t.* masticate thoroughly E20.

fletton /ˈflɛt(ə)n/ *n.* Also **F-**. E20. [*Fletton*, a village in Cambridgeshire, southern England.] A type of brick made by a semi-dry process, orig. from the Oxford clay near Fletton. Also *fletton brick*.

fleur-de-coin /flœːrdəkwɛ̃/ *n.* L19. [Fr. = bloom of the minting-die.] *Numism.* Mint or perfect condition of a coin.

fleur-de-lis /flɔːdəˈliː/ *n. phr.* Pl. **fleurs-** (pronounced same). Also **-lys**; (*arch.* or *poet.*) **flower-de-luce** /flaʊədɪˈluːs/, pl. **-luces** /-ˈluːsɪz/. ME. [OFr. *flour de lys*, f. as *flour* FLOWER *n.* + *de* of + *lys* LILY, also assoc. with a fanciful L *flos deliciae* flower of delight.] 1 (The flower of) any of various plants of the genus *Iris*, of the iris family. ME. 2 The heraldic lily, composed of three petals bound together near their bases and traditionally supposed to have represented an iris, the head of a sceptre, or the top of a battleaxe or other weapon; *esp.* (*sing.* or in *pl.*) the former royal arms of France (characterized by this device). Also, the former royal family of France or (before 1789) the French standard, nation, or government. ME. 3 The representation or figure of the heraldic fleur-de-lis. Also (*Hist.*), a brand of such a form with which convicted criminals were branded under the French penal code. LME.

fleuret /ˈflɔːrɛt/ *n.*[1] Now *rare* or *obs.* M17. [Fr. (f. *fleur* flower) = It. *fioretto* dim. of *fiore* flower: see -ET[1].] A fencing-foil.

fleuret /ˈflʊəˈrɛt, flɔː-/ *n.*[2] E19. [Fr. *fleurette* dim. of *fleur* FLOWER *n.*: see -ET[1].] An ornament resembling a small flower.

fleurettée /ˈflɔːrəteɪ/ *a.* M16. [Fr. *fleuretté(e)*, f. *fleurette*: see prec.] *Her.* = FLORY.

fleuron /ˈflʊərɒn, ˈflɔː-, *foreign* flœrɔ̃ (*pl. same*)/ *n.* LME. [OFr. *floron* (mod. *fleuron*), f. *flour* FLOWER *n.*] 1 A flower-shaped ornament, used esp. in architecture or printing, as a device on coins, etc. LME. 2 A small pastry puff used for garnishing. Long *rare* or *obs.* M17. †3 = FLORET *n.* 1. *rare*. Only in E18.

fleury *a.* var. of FLORY *a.*

flew /fluː/ *n.*[1] L16. [Origin unkn.] In *pl.* The thick hanging lips of a bloodhound or similar dog.

flewed *a.* (long *rare*) having flews (of a specified kind) L16.

flew *n.*[2] var. of FLUE *n.*[1]

flew *a.*[1], *a.*[2] vars. of FLUE *a.*[1], *a.*[2]

flew *v.* pa. t. of FLY *v.*

flewet /ˈfluːɪt/ *n. obs.* exc. *Sc.* & *north.* L16. [Origin unkn.] A hard blow or stroke, a buffet.

flex /flɛks/ *n.*[1] M19. [L *flexus*, f. *flex-*: see FLEX *v.*] *Math.* A point of inflection.

flex /flɛks/ *n.*[2] E20. [Abbrev. of FLEXIBLE.] (A length of) flexible insulated wire for carrying low-current electricity, esp. to portable domestic appliances.

flex /flɛks/ *v.* E16. [L *flex-* pa. ppl stem of *flectere* bend.] 1 *v.t.* Cause to bend; *esp.* in *Anat.*, bend (a joint or limb), move or contract (a muscle) to bend a joint. E16. b *Geol.* Distort (strata). L19. c *Archaeol.* Place (a corpse) with the legs drawn up under the chin. Chiefly as *flexed* ppl a. E20. 2 *v.i.* Be or become bent; be capable of bending; (of a muscle etc.) contract. E20.

1 J. STEINBECK He flexed his muscles against his back. B. CHATWIN Young rooks were learning to flex their wings. **flex one's muscles** *fig.* give a show of aggression or strength. 2 *Scientific American* The arrow.. must flex slightly as it is launched. J. BERGER He saw the muscles.. down its haunches flex as it zigzagged.

flexed *ppl a.* that has been flexed, bent; (Her.) *flexed and reflexed*, having two extremities curved in opposite directions, as the letter S: L16. **flexing** *n.* the action of the vb; an instance of this, a bending: E20.

flexibility /flɛksɪˈbɪlɪti/ *n.* E17. [Fr. *flexibilité* or late L *flexibilitas*, f. L *flexibilis*: see next, -ITY.] 1 Ability to be bent, pliancy. E17. 2 Readiness to yield to influence or persuasion; pliancy of mind or disposition. M17. 3 Susceptibility of modification or alteration; capacity for ready adaptation. L18. b Chiefly *Mus.* Capacity of the voice or fingers for free, rapid, or varied execution or delivery. L18.

flexible /ˈflɛksɪb(ə)l/ *a.* & *n.* LME. [(O)Fr., or L *flexibilis*, f. as FLEX *v.* + -IBLE.] A *adj.* 1 Orig., able to be inclined or made favourable *to*. Now, willing or disposed to yield to influence or persuasion; able to be guided or easily led; manageable. LME. 2 Able to be bent; admitting of change in figure without breaking; yielding to pressure, pliable, pliant. LME. †3 Of a fluid: not rigid, yielding. Of a wind: variable in direction, shifting. Only in 17. 4 Able to be modified or adapted to various purposes or uses; supple; versatile. M17.

1 SHAKES. *3 Hen. VI* Women are soft, mild,.. and flexible. 2 ALDOUS HUXLEY Mitsima rolled out another piece of clay into a long flexible cylinder. ANTHONY HUXLEY Flexible garage doors composed of metal strips. 4 SYD. SMITH Some have been selected for flexible politics. LYTTON His voice was so deep and flexible. M. HUNTER So variable are the uses of language, so infinitely flexible their application. **flexible response** a strategy based on a spectrum of possible military responses to any threat.

B *n.* = FLEX *n.*[2] L19.

flexibleness *n.* (now *rare*) = FLEXIBILITY E17. **flexibly** *adv.* E17.

flexile /ˈflɛksʌɪl/ *a. arch.* M17. [L *flexilis*, f. *flex-*: see FLEX *v.*, -ILE.] 1 Easily bending or bent; supple, pliant; (of the features) mobile. M17. 2 a Easily directed or influenced; yielding. M17. b Capable of varied adaptation, versatile. M18.

fle'xility *n.* M17.

flexion /ˈflɛkʃ(ə)n/ *n.* Also (*rare*) **flection**. E17. [L *flexio(n-)*, f. *flex-*: see FLEX *v.*, -ION.] 1 The action or an act of bending, curvature; *esp.* the bending of a limb or joint by action of the flexor muscles. E17. 2†a *gen.* Alteration, change, modification. E–M17. b A modification of the sound or tone of the voice; inflection. M18. 3 The bent part of anything, a bend, a curve. E17. 4 *Gram.* Modification of the form of a word; *esp.* the change of ending in conjugation, declension, etc.; inflection. E17. 5 *Math.* = FLEXURE 6. E18.

flexional *a.* (*a*) of, pertaining to, or of the nature of flexion; (*b*) (of a language) based on flexions: M19. **flexionless** *a.* M19.

flexitime /ˈflɛksɪtʌɪm/ *n.* Also **flextime** /ˈflɛkstʌɪm/. L20. [f. FLEXIBLE + TIME *n.*] An arrangement whereby employees are free to vary their starting and finishing times (within prescribed limits), while working a contracted number of hours; working time so arranged.

†**flexive** *a.* E17–L18. [f. L *flex-*: see FLEX *v.*, -IVE.] Tending to bend, flexible.

flexography /flɛkˈsɒɡrəfi/ *n.* M20. [f. L *flexus*, f. *flex-*: see FLEX *v.*, -OGRAPHY.] A rotary printing method using rubber or plastic plates moulded in relief and special inks for printing esp. on packaging materials.

flexo'graphic *a.* M20.

flexor /ˈflɛksə/ *n.* E17. [mod.L, f. L *flex-*: see FLEX *v.*, -OR.] *Anat.* More fully *flexor muscle*. A muscle whose function is to bend a joint or limb. Cf. EXTENSOR.

flextime *n.* var. of FLEXITIME.

flexuous /ˈflɛksjʊəs/ *a.* E17. [f. L *flexuosus*, f. *flexus* a bending, f. *flex-*: see FLEX *v.*, -OSE[1], -OUS.] 1 Full of bends and curves; winding, sinuous. E17. 2 Moving in bends or waves, undulating. *rare*. E17.

flexuose *a.* (chiefly *Bot.*) = FLEXUOUS 1 E18. **flexu'osity** *n.* (*a*) the state or quality of being flexuous; (*b*) an instance of this, a winding: E17. **flexuously** *adv.* M17.

flexure /ˈflɛkʃə/ *n.* L16. [L *flexura*, f. *flex-*: see FLEX *v.*, -URE.] 1 The action or an act of flexing or bending; curvature. L16. 2 Flexed or bent condition; bent figure or posture; bending or winding form. E17. 3 Something that is bent; a bend, a curve; *spec.* the inner surface of a flexed joint. E17. †4 A tendency to bend or be bent; a strain. Only in M17. †5 Ability to bend or be bent. M17–E19. 6 *Sci.* The curving of a line or surface or solid, esp. from or towards a straight line, plane, etc. L17. 7 *Geol.* The bending of strata under pressure. M19.

flexural *a.* of or relating to flexure L19.

fley /fleɪ/ *v.* & *n. obs.* exc. *Sc.* & *north.* Also **flay**. ME. [ON *fleygja* ult. f. WGmc causative of FLY *v.*] A *v.* 1 *v.t.* Put to flight, frighten *away*. ME. 2 *v.t.* Frighten, scare, terrify. ME. 3 *v.i.* Be afraid; take fright. Long *rare* or *obs.* M18. B *n.* A fright, a scare. L18.

fleysome *a.* frightful, dreadful L18.

flibbertigibbet /flɪbətɪˈdʒɪbɪt/ *n.* LME. [Prob. imit. of meaningless chatter.] 1 Orig., a gossip or chatterer. Now usu. a flighty, irresponsible, or frivolous person. LME. 2a (A name for) a devil or fiend. *rare.* E17. b [After a character in Sir Walter Scott's novel *Kenilworth*.] An impish, mischievous child; a restless person, usu. grotesque in appearance. E19.

1 E. BOWEN I'd always been the bright one, Victor the quiet one; I'd been the flibbertigibbet, he'd been the steady. 2b O. HENRY Some venomous kobold or flibbertigibbet, whining, complaining, cursing.

flibbertygibbety *a.* (*rare*) irresponsible, frivolous L19.

†flibutor *n.* see FILIBUSTER.

flic /flɪk, *foreign* flik (*pl. same*)/ *n.* L19. [Fr.] A French police officer.

flicflac /ˈflɪkflak/ *n.* M19. [Fr.; imit. of a succession of sharp sounds.] *Ballet.* A lashing movement of the leg related to the fouetté.

flichter /ˈflɪxtə/ *v. Sc.* (now *local*). Also **flighter**. LME. [Prob. imit.; see -ER[5]. Var. form prob. infl. by FLIGHT *v.*] 1 *v.i.* Flutter, move irregularly or feebly; (of a light) flicker. LME. 2 *v.i.* Struggle; tremble, quiver. E16. 3 *v.t.* Alarm, startle. E18.

1 SIR W. SCOTT A branch of ivy flightering awa frae the wa'. 2 A. RAMSAY My flighteren heart gangs pittie-pattie.

flick /flɪk/ *n.*[1] LME. [Imit.] 1 A light, sharp, blow, esp. one given with something pliant, a whip, the fingernails, etc. LME. b A sudden movement, a jerk; *esp.* a snap or click of the fingers. M19. c (A stroke played with) a quick turn of the wrist, esp. in throwing or playing a ball; a turn of the ball. L19. 2 A slight, sharp, sound (produced by a light blow or sudden movement). M19. 3 Something that is flicked; a fleck (of light etc.). M19. 4 (A showing of) a motion picture; (in *pl.*) the cinema. Cf. FLICKER *n.*[2] 3. *slang.* E20.

1b P. H. GIBBS Waiters scurried about at the flick of Robin's fingers. 2 ALBERT SMITH The only . . sound . . being . . the flick of the driver's whip. 3 THACKERAY Flicks of yellow that the rushlight threw on the . . ceiling. 4 F. SWINNERTON Take her to the theatre, the ballet, the flicks. J. BRAINE Tea at the Raynton, then a flick.

Comb.: **flick-knife**: with a blade springing out when a button is pressed.

flick /flɪk/ *n.*[2] Chiefly *dial.* Also **fleck** /flɛk/. LME. [Alt. of FLIX *n.*[1]] The fur of a hare or rabbit; hence *collect.*, hares and rabbits.

flick /flɪk/ *n.*[3] *obs.* exc. *dial.* Also **fleck** /flɛk/. L16. [Origin uncertain: perh. same wd as FLICK *n.*[5], FLITCH *n.*] The fat around a pig's kidney.

flick /flɪk/ *n.*[4] *colloq.* (now *rare*). L19. [Origin unkn.] A fellow, a chap.

flick *n.*[5] see FLITCH *n.*

†flick *v.*[1]*t. Criminals' slang.* L17–M19. [Prob. f. FLICK *n.*[5] Cf. FLITCH *v.*] Cut.

flick /flɪk/ *v.*[2] & *adv.* Also ***fleck** /flɛk/. E19. [f. FLICK *n.*[1]] A *v.* 1 *v.t.* Strike or propel lightly and smartly with something flexible; jerk or flip *away*, *off*, etc. E19. b *spec.* Play or deliver (a ball) with a flick of the wrist etc. L19. 2 *v.i.* Move or go with quick, smart movements or vibrations; esp. riffle or look rapidly *through*, *over*, etc., (pages, a book, etc.) M19. 3 *v.t.* Make a light stroke or movement with (a whip etc.); move or shake with a flick. M19.

1 A. R. HOPE Flicking each other with our towels. S. GIBBONS She . . flicked the reminders of dinner off the table with Adam's drying-up towel. 2 J. GARDNER The porch lights flicked on and off. P. NORMAN The white label of the gramophone record flicks round and round. J. SIMMS He flicked through the notebook he always carried. 3 F. HERBERT A smile flicked the corners of the wrinkled old mouth. B. HINES She still swiped at him, and . . he still flicked his head back.

B *adv.* With a flick. *rare.* M19.

flicker /ˈflɪkə/ *n.*[1] E19. [Imit. of the bird's call.] Any of various American woodpeckers of the genus *Colaptes*; esp. *C. auratus* (more fully *common* or *northern flicker*).

flicker /ˈflɪkə/ *v.* & *n.*[2] [OE *flicorian*, *flycerian* (cf. LG *flickern*, Du. *flikkeren*), orig. synon. with FLACKER.] A *v.* 1 *v.i.* Of a bird: flutter. Now *rare.* OE. †2 *v.i.* Make caressing or fondling movements; act or look in a coaxing or affectionate manner; dally (*after*). ME–E19. †3 Waver, vacillate, act unreliably. ME–M18. 4 *v.i.* & (*rare*) *t.* (Cause to) flutter rapidly, quiver, undulate; wave to and fro. LME. 5 *v.i.* Flash up and die away rapidly (and repeatedly); (of flame) burn fitfully; (of light) vary rapidly in brightness. E17. 6 *v.t.* Cause to move rapidly or fitfully like a flicker of light; indicate by a flicker. M19.

2 DRYDEN Lavinia . . looks a little flickering after Turnus. 3 W. SHENSTONE A race of flickering knaves. 4 TENNYSON Nor cared the serpent . . to flicker with his double tongue. R. WARNER The beginnings of a smile flickered at the corners of her mouth. 5 C. MERIVALE A gleam of hope still flickered in their bosoms. M. DE LA ROCHE A gust came down the chimney and the night-light flickered. **flicker out** die away after a final flicker. 6 R. LANGBRIDGE He watched her eye-lashes flicker dismissal. D. H. LAWRENCE He . . flickered his two-forked tongue from his lips.

B *n.* 1 An act of flickering, a flickering movement. M19. 2 A wavering, unsteady light or flame. M19. b A rapid, rhythmic variation in illumination or sound; the visual or aural sensation caused by this. L19. c *spec.* A succession of abrupt changes in the image on a television etc. screen (esp. with an overlap between them), causing visual confusion. L19. 3 = FLICK *n.*[1] 4. *slang.* Now *rare.* E20.

1 D. BAGLEY The flame which burned without a flicker in the still air. *fig.*: A. S. BYATT She looked at him with a flicker of interest. 2 P. G. WODEHOUSE A flicker of lightning came and went in the darkness.

Comb.: **flicker fusion frequency** *Optics* the frequency of flicker above which the eye perceives a light source as constant; **flicker photometer**, **photometry** a photometer, a photometric technique, used for comparing the intensities of two light sources (esp. of different colours), which works by measuring the flicker produced when the same visual field is illuminated alternately by the two sources; **flickertail** *N. Amer.* = *Richardson's ground squirrel* s.v. RICHARDSON *n.*[1]

flickering *vbl n.* the action of the vb; an instance of this: LME. **flickeringly** *adv.* in a flickering manner M19. **flickery** *a.* that flickers, flickering L19.

flickermouse /ˈflɪkəmaʊs/ *n.* Now *dial.* Pl. **-mice** /-mʌɪs/. M17. [Alt. of FLITTER-MOUSE.] = BAT *n.*[3]

flier *n.* var. of FLYER.

flight /flʌɪt/ *n.*[1] [OE *flyht* corresp. to OS *fluht*, (M)Du. *vlucht* f. WGmc, f. Gmc base of FLY *v.*] 1 The action or manner of flying or moving through the air with or as with wings. OE. †b The power of flying. Only in ME. 2 Swift movement, esp. of a projectile through the air; *spec.* the passage of a projectile from a gun to a target. ME. b Swift passage *of* time. M17. c In games, the trajectory and pace of a ball through the air; the control or variation of this in order to deceive an opponent. L19. 3†a The wing of a bird. Only in ME. b *collect.* The flight-feathers. M18. 4 A flock of things passing through the air, *esp.* a flock of birds or insects. ME. b A volley of missiles, esp. arrows. Chiefly *Hist.* M16. c The young birds that take wing at one time. L16. d A company *of* angels. E17. e A migration or migrating body of birds or insects. E19. 5 A flight-arrow. Also, flight-shooting. LME. b The tail of a dart, by which it is balanced when in flight. M20. †6 A state of agitation or trembling. E–M16. 7 *Falconry.* The pursuit of game etc. by a hawk; the quarry being pursued. M16. 8 The distance which a bird, aircraft, missile, etc., can or does fly. E17. 9 A mounting, soaring, or excursion of the imagination, fancy, ambition, etc. M17. 10 A series of stairs running between two landings. E18. b A series of locks on a canal in graduated steps. M19. c A series of hurdles or rails usu. for racing over. M19. 11 The action or technique of travelling through the air or through space in an aircraft, spacecraft, etc. L18. b An instance of air or space travel; a timed journey by an airline from one place to another; a journey or voyage through the air or through space. L18. c A Royal Air Force unit consisting of about six aircraft; the members of such a unit. E20. 12 The husk or glume of oats. M19. 13 The lower part of the clapper of a bell. L19.

1 DAY LEWIS The butterflies whose dithering flight was no more erratic than my aunts' talk. D. ATTENBOROUGH Their wings were so small . . that they had lost the power of flight. 2 SHELLEY Ships, whose flight is swift along the wave. b MILTON The never-ending flight Of future days. c *Squash World* I tried . . to slow the ball down and put a bit of flight on it. 4 HARPER LEE Watching flights of martins sweep low over the . . rooftops. b W. OWEN Sudden successive flights of bullets streak the silence. e P. MATTHIESSEN The numerous dead redstarts . . —a whole migratory flight—that must have perished. 9 C. JOHNSTON A silence more expressive . . than all the flights of eloquence. 10 R. MACAULAY They climbed a steep, winding flight of stone stairs. J. S. FOSTER A landing serves as a rest between flights. 11b R. BRADBURY It was the boy's first flight into space, his very first time in a rocket. E. WELTY She had come on a night flight from Chicago.

Phrases: **in flight** flying, travelling through the air (see also INFLIGHT). **in the first** or **top flight** taking a leading place. **†of the same flight** *rare* (arrows) having the same power of flight; of equal size and weight. **take a** or **one's flight** fly, move swiftly through the air.

Comb.: **flight-arrow** a light, well-feathered arrow for long-distance shooting; **flight attendant** a passenger attendant in an aircraft; **flight bag** a small zipped bag with a shoulder-strap, as carried by air travellers; **flight call** (*a*) the cry made by a bird in flight; (*b*) an announcement at an airport, informing passengers that they may board their aircraft; **flight control** a system for directing the movement of aircraft, located either on the ground or in the aircraft itself; **flight crew** a team of people who ensure the effective operation and safety of an aircraft during its flight; **flight-deck** (*a*) the deck of an aircraft carrier on which aircraft take off and land; (*b*) the part of an aeroplane accommodating the pilot, navigator, etc.; **flight envelope** *Aeronaut.* the possible combinations of speed and altitude, speed and range, etc., of a particular kind of aircraft or aero-engine; **flight-feather** any of the feathers which support a bird in flight, comprising the primary and secondary feathers; **flight lieutenant** a rank in the Royal Air Force, immediately below squadron leader; **flight-line** (*a*) the course taken by (esp. migrating) birds; (*b*) a general area in an airfield including hangars, ramps, etc., where aircraft are parked and serviced; **flight net** a net used for catching birds; **flight-number** the identifying number of a scheduled aircraft flight; **flight officer** a rank in the Women's Royal Air Force, equivalent to flight lieutenant; an officer in the US air forces; **flight path** the planned or actual course of an aircraft or spacecraft; **flight plan** *Aeronaut.* the prearranged scheme for a particular flight; **flight-recorder** a device in an aircraft which records the technical details of each flight, for use in the event of an accident; **flight refuelling** the refuelling of an aircraft while in flight; **flight sergeant** a rank in the Royal Air Force, next above sergeant; **flight-shaft** = *flight-arrow* above; **flight-shooting** (*a*) *Archery* distance-shooting with flight-arrows; (*b*) shooting wildfowl in flight; **flight-shot** (*a*) the distance to which a flight-arrow is shot; a bowshot; (*b*) a shot taken at wildfowl in flight; **flight-test** *v.t.* test (an aircraft, rocket, etc.) during flight.

flightless *a.* (of birds, insects, etc.) lacking the power of flight L19.

flight /flʌɪt/ *n.*[2] ME. [Corresp. to OFris. *flecht*, OS, OHG *fluht* (Du. *vlucht*, G *Flucht*), ON *flótti* f. Gmc, f. base of FLEE *v.* Prob. already in OE.] 1 The action or manner of fleeing or running away from or as from danger etc.; hasty retreat. ME. 2 *Econ.* The selling of currency or withdrawal of investments etc. in anticipation of a fall in value. Foll. by *from.* E20.

1 H. DOOLITTLE My trip to Greece . . might have been interpreted as a flight from reality. C. CONNOLLY As escapes from the problem, as flights from guilt, they may be welcome. **put to flight** cause to flee, rout. **take (to) flight** run away, flee.

flight /flʌɪt/ *n.*[3] *obs.* exc. *dial.* L15. [Var. of FLAUGHT *n.*[1]] A flake of snow; a snowstorm.

flight /flʌɪt/ *v.* E16. [f. FLIGHT *n.*[1], *n.*[2]] †**1** *v.i.* Flutter; fluctuate. Cf. FLICHTER. *Sc. rare.* Only in E16. **2** *v.t.* Put to flight, rout; frighten. *obs.* exc. *dial.* L16. **b** Set flying, start in flight. E19. **3** *v.i.* †**a** Migrate. E17–M18. **b** Fly in flights. L19. **4** *v.t.* Feather (an arrow). M19. **5** *v.t.* Shoot (wildfowl) in flight. L19. **6** *v.t.* Vary the trajectory and pace of (a cricket ball etc.). E20.

flighted /ˈflʌɪtɪd/ *ppl a.* L16. [f. FLIGHT *n.*[1] + -ED[2].] **1** Having a certain flight or speed. *rare.* L16. **2** Feathered. M18. **3** Of steps: arranged in flights. E20.

flighter *v.* var. of FLICHTER.

flighty /ˈflʌɪti/ *a.* M16. [f. FLIGHT *n.*[1] + -Y[1].] **1** Swift, fleet. *rare.* M16. **2** Guided by whim or fancy rather than by judgement or common sense; fickle, frivolous. M18. **3** Insane, crazy. Now *rare.* E19.
1 P. MATTHIESSEN The animals are flighty now, and so I stalk them with more care. 2 H. G. WELLS Your wits might be flighty, but . . your character was sound. A. THWAITE Edmund, though young, was certainly not flighty.
flightily *adv.* L18. **flightiness** *n.* M18.

flim /flɪm/ *n. slang.* L19. [Abbrev. of FLIMSY *n.*] A £5 note.

flimflam /ˈflɪmflam/ *n.*, *a.*, & *v.* Also **flim-flam**. M16. [Symbolic redupl. formation with vowel variation: cf. WHIM-WHAM.] **A** *n.* **1** A trifle, a conceit. Now usu. *collect.*, nonsense. M16. **2** A contemptible trick. Now usu. *collect.*, humbug, deception. M16. **3** A confidence trick; confidence trickery. *slang.* L19.
1 W. A. WALLACE The wanderings of his dotage, and flim-flam after all. 2 *Times* No amount of public relations flim-flam can disguise the fact that extremists win.
B *adj.* Frivolous, nonsensical; fictitious, sham. L16.
R. HOLINSHED His slanderous reports are vnderpropt with flim-flam surmises.
C *v.t.* Infl. **-mm-**. Humbug, beguile (*into* something); *spec.* (*slang*) cheat (by a confidence trick). M17.
Punch Marketing practices that smacked of flimflamming the public.
flimflammer, **-flammery** *ns.* L19.

flimmer /ˈflɪmə/ *n.* Pl. same. M20. [G = tinsel.] *Biol.* A mastigoneme, esp. a slender one.

flimmer /ˈflɪmə/ *v.i.* L19. [Imit.: cf. G *flimmern.*] Flicker, move unsteadily.

flimsy /ˈflɪmzi/ *a.* & *n.* E18. [Prob. based on FLIMFLAM: see -SY.] **A** *adj.* **1** Frail, slight, insubstantial; easily destroyed, poorly put together. E18. **2** Trivial, paltry; frivolous, superficial. M18.
1 J. CHEEVER The walls were flimsy—part frosted glass and part plywood. 2 T. T. LYNCH The flimsy individual who has read fifty novels in a year, but nothing else. ISAIAH BERLIN A historical and emotional atmosphere for which the evidence is flimsy, but which is artistically indispensable.
B *n.* **1** A banknote. *slang.* Now *rare* or *obs.* E19. **2** A flimsy thing or material; *esp.* (a document on) thin paper (as used for taking copies on a typewriter etc.). M19.
2 D. L. SAYERS She . . shook the top sheet, carbons, and flimsies together.
flimsily *adv.* L18. **flimsiness** *n.* E18.

flinch /flɪn(t)ʃ/ *v.*[1] & *n.* M16. [OFr. *flenchir*, *flainchir* turn aside f. WGmc, whence also (M)HG *lenken* to bend, turn.] **A** *v.* †**1** *v.i.* Slink, sneak *off*, *away.* M16–E17. **2** *v.i.* Give way, draw back, turn aside, now esp. through a failure in courage or endurance; shrink *from* anything. L16. †**b** *v.t.* Withdraw (from), lose. L17–M19. **3** *v.i.* Shrink under pain, trouble, etc.; wince; blench. L17.
2 G. SANTAYANA Oliver never flinched in his determination to pursue higher things. C. MCCULLOUGH Too much of a land person . . to flinch from doing what had to be done. 3 E. BOWEN Rupert's wife . . stood . . breathing hard and flinching away from the lightning. J. HERRIOT The skin isn't broken, but he flinches if you press here.
B *n.* An act or instance of flinching. E19.

flincher *n.* L16. **flinchingly** *adv.* (*rare*) with flinching L19.

flinch *v.*[2] var. of FLENSE.

flinder /ˈflɪndə/ *n.* Long *obs.* exc. *dial.* ME. [Corresp. to Du. *vlinder* butterfly.] A moth or butterfly.

flindermouse /ˈflɪndəmaʊs/ *n.* Now *dial.* Pl. **-mice** /-mʌɪs/. L15. [f. prec. + MOUSE *n.*: cf. FLICKERMOUSE, FLITTER-MOUSE.] = BAT *n.*[3]

flinders /ˈflɪndəz/ *n.*[1] *pl.* LME. [Prob. of Scand. origin: cf. Norw. *flindra* thin chip or splinter.] Fragments, small pieces, splinters. Cf. FLITTERS, FITTERS.

Flinders /ˈflɪndəz/ *n.*[2] L19. [Capt. Matthew *Flinders* (1774–1814), Eng. navigator.] **1** *Flinders bar*, a soft iron bar placed vertically near a ship's compass to correct deviation due to magnetic induction. L19. **2** *Flinders grass*, any of various grasses esp. of the genus *Iseilema*, giving valuable forage. *Austral.* L19.

flindosa /flɪnˈdəʊzə/ *n. Austral.* Also **-sy** /-zi/. M19. [Alt. of mod.L *Flindersia* (see below), f. prec.] (The timber of) an Australian hardwood rainforest tree, *Flindersia australis* (family Rutaceae). Also called *Australian teak.*

fling /flɪŋ/ *n.* ME. [f. the vb.] **1** An attempt at or attack upon something; now *spec.* a sarcastic remark, a gibe. ME. **2** A hasty or reckless movement; a violent movement, a flinging about of the body. M16. **b** A dance involving vigorous movement; chiefly in *Highland fling* below. E19. **3** An act of flinging; a throw. L16. **4** A period of self-indulgence or pleasure; a good time; *spec.* a brief (usu. extramarital) affair. E19.
1 C. JOHNSTON A fling at the clergy never fails to raise a laugh. **have a fling at** (*a*) make an attempt at; (*b*) make a (verbal) attack on. 2 H. N. COLERIDGE The furious jerks and flings which . . [the shark] made. **Highland fling** a type of vigorous Scottish reel. **take the fling**(s) *Sc.* become bad tempered or unmanageable. 3 W. DE LA MARE After a few lasso-like flings of it, he had run the rope . . over one of a few large hooks. 4 Y. MENUHIN It was our fling, our time of freedom, of unconcern, of letting duty slide. A. LURIE Rosemary isn't looking for a fling She's looking for an undying passion.

fling /flɪŋ/ *v.* Pa. t. & pple **flung** /flʌŋ/. ME. [Perh. rel. to ON *flengja* (Sw. *flänga*, Da. *flænge*) flog.] **I** *v.i.* **1** Rush; go angrily or violently. ME. †**2** Come *together* in fighting; aim a blow (*at*). ME–L15. **3** (Of a horse etc.) kick and plunge violently; be unruly; (of a person) be restive or violent, struggle; freq. *fig.*, burst into invective or complaint. LME. **4** Dance, caper. *Sc.* E16.
1 LD MACAULAY The Chancellor . . flung away in a rage. S. MIDDLETON He flung back the way he had come. V. WOOLF Are we to fling off in a new direction? 3 SHAKES. *Macb.* Duncan's horses . . Turn'd wild in nature, broke their stalls, flung out. J. PAYN I had rather she had flung out at me.
II *v.t.* **5** Throw (*lit.* & *fig.*), hurl, cast, toss, propel, esp. with violence, malice, or recklessness. Freq. w. advs. LME. **b** Put suddenly or violently *into* prison etc. LME. **6** Spread out or extend (the arms etc.) suddenly; kick *up* (the heels). M17. **7** Send out, emit (light, sound, etc.). *arch.* M17. **8** Throw (oneself) *at*, *down*, *into*, *on*, etc.; *fig.* throw (oneself, one's efforts) *into* an activity etc. E18. †**9** Get the better of; cheat, swindle. *slang.* M18–M19. **10** Throw down to the ground; *esp.* (of a horse) throw (a rider). L18.
5 EDWARD WARD Fling dirt enough, and some will stick. T. HARDY She flung a cloak round her. QUILLER-COUCH I flung a short glance downward at the birches and black water. S. LEWIS The February city, where lorries flung up a spattering of slush. J. BUCHAN They would fling me a question or two about South Africa. b LD MACAULAY Laud was flung into the Tower. 6 E. FEINSTEIN She flung her arms round me, and sobbed. 7 MILTON The sun begins to fling His flaring beams. 8 LYTTON I flung myself into his arms and wept. J. RATHBONE He flung himself back in his chair. J. MCCARTHY She had flung all her energies into the rebellion. 9 C. JOHNSTON He cannot fling his worthy associate out of the whole spoil. 10 HOR. WALPOLE His horse started, flung him, and fell upon him. TENNYSON Never a man could fling him; for Willy stood like a rock.

Phrases, & with advs. in specialized senses: **fling aside** disregard; reject. **fling down** throw to the ground; overthrow; demolish. **fling off** abandon, disown; throw off the scent. **fling open** open suddenly or violently. **fling in a person's face** refer reproachfully to (a previous action, statement, etc., of that person). *fling in a person's teeth*: see TOOTH *n.* **fling to** shut suddenly or violently. **fling up** (*a*) throw up (a defensive mound etc.); (*b*) relinquish. **fling wide** = *fling open* above.
flinger *n.* E16.

flint /flɪnt/ *n.* & *a.* [OE = MDu. *vlint* rel. to OHG (G dial.) *flins* and perh. to Gk *plinthos* tile (see PLINTH).] **A** *n.* **1** A hard stone which consists of nearly pure silica and occurs as nodules which are steel-grey within and have a white crust. OE. **b** Anything hard and unyielding. ME. **2** (A piece of) this stone or, in modern devices, a metal (usu. a hard alloy containing misch metal), struck against iron or steel in order to produce sparks for ignition, e.g. in a flintlock gun, a cigarette lighter, etc. OE. **3** Any piece of flint; freq. a piece flaked or ground into a tool or weapon by prehistoric man. ME. **4 a** In full *flint glass.* A pure lustrous glass made from lead oxide, sand (orig., ground flint), and alkali. L17. **b** In full *flint corn.* Any of various varieties of maize having very hard kernels. Chiefly *US.* E18. **5** A journeyman tailor who refuses to submit to an employer's terms. Cf. DUNG *n.* 3. *slang. obs.* exc. *Hist.* M18.
1 b SIR W. SCOTT Callum, flint to other considerations, was penetrable to superstition. 3 J. DYER Ancient roads, o'er whose broad flints Such crowds have roll'd. J. A. MICHENER Flints . . sharpened to a glistening sheen on one serrated edge. **set one's face like a flint** be steadfast. *skin a flint*: see SKIN *v.*
B *attrib.* or as *adj.* Of flint. ME.
Comb.: *flint corn*: see sense A.4b above; *flint glass*: see sense A.4a above; **flint-hearted** *a.* hard-hearted; **flintlock** [LOCK *n.*[2] 3] (*Hist.*) (the lock of) a gun discharged by a spark from the flint igniting the primer; **flint paper** (*a*) a paper burnished or glazed to a high gloss; (*b*) an abrasive paper; **flintstone** = senses A.1, 2, 3 above; **flintwood** = *blackbutt* s.v. BLACK *a.*
flintless *a.* E19.

flinty /ˈflɪnti/ *a.* M16. [f. prec. + -Y[1].] Of or full of flint; resembling flint in colour, texture, hardness, or impenetrability.
J. L. WATEN The sun glared at us through flinty clouds. S. KING Her eyes were flinty, proud, and unbelieving.
Comb.: **flinty-hearted** *a.* having a hard heart or centre, hard-hearted.
flintily *adv.* L19. **flintiness** *n.* E17.

flip /flɪp/ *n.*[1] L17. [Perh. f. FLIP *v.* with the sense of 'whip up' into froth.] Orig., a mixed drink of beer and spirits heated with a hot iron. Now, a drink of spirits or wine beaten with egg and sugar, served either warm or iced.
egg-flip: see EGG *n.*
Comb.: **flip-dog**, (*US*) **-iron** a poker used to heat flip.

flip /flɪp/ *n.*[2] L17. [f. the vb.] **1** A sharp blow. L17. **2** A sudden jerk or movement, a flick; a turning over, a somersault. E19. **b** The springing of the barrel of a gun at the moment of discharge. L19. **3** A (short) flight in an aircraft; a quick trip or tour in any conveyance. *colloq.* E20.
1 W. BESANT The . . flips which we poor women have to endure from harsh masters. 2 G. C. DAVIES A derisive flip of their white tails. H. JAMES He gave a flip with a finger-nail to his cigarette. F. ASTAIRE They tossed Zenzo . . across the full length of the stage with a few double flips thrown in. 3 P. FIDDICK His pre-Easter flip to the Berlin Wall.
Comb.: **flip jump** a toe jump in figure-skating. **flip side** the reverse or less important side of a gramophone record.

flip /flɪp/ *a. colloq.* (orig. *dial.* & *US*). M19. [f. the vb.] Nimble, now usu. of tongue; glib, flippant.
Times The word 'schizophrenia' is flung about today with flip facility. J. LE CARRÉ He's too damn flip with his alibi.

flip /flɪp/ *v.* Infl. **-pp-**. M16. [Prob. contr. FILLIP *v.* but cf. FLIP-FLAP.] **1** *v.i.* Make a flip (*at*) with the fingers etc. M16. **2** *v.t.* Strike smartly with the fingers, a whip, etc.; flick. L16. **3** *v.t.* & *i.* Put (something) into motion with a flip or jerk;

move (something) with a flip or jerk; toss (a coin etc.). E17. 4 *v.i.* Fly in a (small) aircraft; make a short trip. *colloq.* E20. 5 *v.i.* Be or become wildly excited or enthusiastic; lose one's self-control; go mad. Also *flip one's lid* or (chiefly *US*) *wig*. *colloq.* M20.

1 S. GRAND Viciously flipping at the flowers . . with the stick he carried. 2 J. PYCROFT Minnie laughed and flipped her old friend with her glove. 3 M. BARING The boys . . began making pellets and flipping them at each other. J. STEINBECK They had to flip for who would go to the party first. B. BAINBRIDGE Freda kept flipping ash on the carpet. *Listener* The Ambassador flipped the switch: the lights went on. 5 *Boston Globe* Our food and service are great . . Your club treasurer will flip over our rates. G. SWIFT He'd flipped, he'd gone bananas.

Comb.: **flip chart** (orig. *US*) (a page of) a large pad erected on a stand and bound so that one page can be turned over at the top to reveal the next. **flip-top** *a.* (of a table) having additional sections at either end that can be drawn or folded outwards to increase the surface area; (of a package) that can be flipped open, usu. by pulling the top upwards and back.

Phrases, & with preps. in specialized senses: *flip one's lid* or *wig*: see sense 5 above. **flip through** look rapidly through (a book, index, etc.), flick through.

flipping *ppl a.* & *adv.* (*slang*) damned(ly), bloody E20.

flipe *n.*, *v.* vars. of FLYPE *n.*, *v.*

flip-flap /ˈflɪpflap/ *n.*, *adv.*, *v.*, & *a.* E16. [Redupl. of FLAP *n.* with vowel variation: cf. next.] **A** *n.* **1** Something that flaps. Now *rare* or *obs.* E16. **2** A kind of somersault. L17. **B** *adv.* With a repeated flapping movement. L16. **C** *v.t.* & *i.* Infl. **-pp-**. Flap. L16. **D** *adj.* That flaps. *rare.* M19.

flip-flop /ˈflɪpflɒp/ *n.*, *v.*, & *adv.* M17. [Redupl. of FLOP *n.* with vowel variation: cf. prec.] **A** *n.* **1** Something that flaps or flops. Now *esp.* a sandal consisting of a flat sole and straps. M17. **2** A (backward) somersault. Cf. FLIP-FLAP *n.* 2. *N. Amer.* E20. **3** *Electronics.* A switching circuit that changes from one stable state to another, or via an unstable state back to its stable state, in response to a triggering pulse. M20. **B** *v.t.* & *i.* Infl. **-pp-**. Flip or flap. L19. **C** *adv.* In a flapping manner. E20.

flippancy /ˈflɪp(ə)nsi/ *n.* M18. [f. next: see -ANCY.] The quality or an instance of being flippant.

flippant /ˈflɪp(ə)nt/ *a.* & *n.* E17. [f. FLIP *v.* + -ANT[1], perh. in imitation of heraldic adjs., as *couchant*, *trippant*.] **A** *adj.* **1** Nimble; pliant. *obs.* exc. *dial.* E17. **†2** Talkative, voluble, fluent. E17–L18. **†3** Sportive, playful. Only in 18. **4** Lacking in seriousness; treating serious matters lightly; disrespectful. E18.

4 E. M. FORSTER I should never have talked in this flippant, superficial way. G. A. BIRMINGHAM He resents the flippant mirth of those whom he regards as his inferiors.

B *absol.* as *n.* A flippant person. Now *rare.* L18. W. COWPER The flippant and the scold.

flippantly *adv.* M18. **flippantness** *n.* E18.

flipper /ˈflɪpə/ *n.* & *v.* E19. [f. FLIP *v.* + -ER[1].] **A** *n.* **1** A limb adapted for swimming, as the limb of a turtle, the (fore)limb of a seal, the wing of a penguin, etc. E19. **b** A flexible attachment to the foot used for underwater swimming, esp. by frogmen. M20. **2** The hand. *slang.* M19. **3** *Cricket.* A top-spinner given an extra flip of the fingers. M20. **B** *v.i.* Move by means of flippers. M20.

flirt /fləːt/ *n.* M16. [App. imit.: cf. FLICK *n.*[1], SPURT *n.*] **I 1 †a** A smart stroke of wit, a joke; a gibe. M16–E18. **b** A smart tap or blow. *obs.* exc. *dial.* L16. **2** A sudden jerk or movement; a quick throw or flick; a darting movement. L16. **3** *Horology.* A lever etc. for causing sudden movement. L18.

2 G. WHITE Hedge-sparrows have a remarkable flirt with their wings.

II 4 A person who behaves in a flirtatious manner; someone to flirt with. Formerly *esp.* a flighty young woman. M16. **†b** A promiscuous woman. E17–E18.

4 OUIDA Sabretasche had an universal reputation as a most unscrupulous flirt. E. J. HOWARD She wasn't a flirt; she never edged up to sex and backed off giggling.

flirtish *a.* resembling or characteristic of a flirt M17. **flirty** *a.* of, pertaining to, or characterized by, flirtation M19.

flirt /fləːt/ *v.* M16. [f. as the n.] **†1 a** *v.i.* & *t.* Sneer, gibe, scoff, *at* or at; turn up one's nose *at* or at. Formerly also, flare (the nostrils). M16–M18. **b** *v.t.* Give (a person) a sharp sudden blow. M16–M17. **2** *v.t.* Propel or throw with a jerk or sudden movement; give sudden motion to; flip, flick; spread (a bird's wing, tail, etc.) quickly; open and close (a fan) smartly. L16. **b** Blurt *out*. Now *rare* or *obs.* M17. **3** *v.i.* Move with a jerk, spring, dart. Now *rare.* L16. **4** *v.i.* Behave in a superficially amorous manner, dally. E17. **b** Toy *with* (an idea etc.); deal lightly or frivolously *with* (a serious matter). M19.

2 T. DEKKER Tis thy fashion to flirt inke in everie mans face. 3 R. L. STEVENSON The tails of his night-shirt flirting as he turned. 4 N. MITFORD He had danced and flirted . . with other people. b N. PODHORETZ The notion I had been flirting with of staying in England forever was out.

flirter *n.* E19.

flirtation /fləːˈteɪʃ(ə)n/ *n.* E18. [f. as FLIRT *n.* + -ATION.] The action or an instance of flirting (sense 4).

attrib.: SAKI If he got as far as the flirtation stage . . sheer perversity . . might carry him on to more definite courtship.

flirtational *a.* (*rare*) M19.

flirtatious /fləːˈteɪʃəs/ *a.* M19. [Irreg. f. prec. + -OUS on the analogy of *ambition*, *ambitious*: see -TIOUS.] Given to or of the nature of flirtation.

flirtatiously *adv.* M19. **flirtatiousness** *n.* L19.

†flirt-gill *n.* L16–E17. [f. FLIRT *n.*, *v.* + GILL *n.*[4]] A promiscuous woman. Cf. GILL-FLIRT.

flisk /flɪsk/ *v.* *obs.* exc. *dial.* L16. [Imit.: cf. WHISK *v.*] **1** *v.i.* Frisk about; be restless. L16. **2** *v.t.* Make restless or angry. L18. **3** *v.t.* Flick. L18.

flisky *a.* (*Sc.*) frisky E19.

flit /flɪt/ *n.* M19. [f. the vb.] **1** A removal, a (secret) change of abode, esp. in order to avoid a creditor. M19. **2** A light movement or touch; a flutter. L19. **3** (**F-**.) (Proprietary name for) an insecticide used esp. in the form of a spray. E20. **4** A homosexual. *US slang.* M20.

1 **do a flit** decamp. *moonlight flit*: see MOONLIGHT *n.* & *a.*

†flit *a.* *poet.* L16–M17. [Var. of FLEET *a.*[2], infl. by FLIT *v.*] Swift, nimble; fleeting, unsubstantial.

SPENSER Now, like a stag; now, like a faulcon flit.

flit /flɪt/ *v.* Infl. **-tt-**. ME. [ON *flytja* f. weak grade of base of *fljóta*: see FLEET *v.*[1]] **1** *v.t.* Remove to another place. Now chiefly *Sc.* & *north.* ME. **†b** Get rid of, drive *away*. LME–L16. **c** Shift (a tethered animal) to fresh grazing. E16. **†2** *v.t.* Change the condition or direction of. Only in ME. **3** *v.i.* Depart, migrate; move or pass away. Also foll. by *away*, *from*, *to*. ME. **b** Of time: pass away. L16. **4** *v.i.* **†a** Change in state, condition, or direction; alter, shift about. LME–E19. **b** Of a flame: flicker, die down. M19. **5** *v.i.* Pass lightly, softly, or rapidly. Freq. with *about*, *by*, *off*, *to and fro*, etc. LME. **b** Of a bird, bat, or other flying thing or creature: fly lightly and swiftly, make short flights. M16. **6** *v.i.* Move house; change one's abode, esp. secretly (cf. FLIT *n.* 1). Chiefly *north.* & *Sc.* E16.

1 G. W. DASENT They flitted home their goods and laid up the ship. 3 R. BURNS Like the Borealis race, That flit ere you can point their place. N. HAWTHORNE Our spirits must have flitted away unconsciously. 5 TENNYSON Unawares they flitted off, Busying themselves about the flowerage. W. H. AUDEN A shadow-train flitted foreshortened through fields. A. AYCKBOURN Flitting from woman to woman as the mood takes you. b T. CAMPBELL The bat flits to and fro. L. M. MONTGOMERY Fireflies were flitting over in Lovers' Lane. B. ENGLAND The helicopter flitted about with such dainty ease. 6 A. GUINNESS My mother and I flitted, leaving behind . . a wake of unpaid bills.

flitch /flɪtʃ/ *n.* Also (now *dial.*) **flick** /flɪk/. [OE *flicce*, corresp. to MLG *vli(c)ke*, ON *flikki* (whence dial. *flick*) f. Gmc, as in ON *flik* rag.] **1** The side of an animal, salted and cured. Now only, a side of bacon. OE. **2** A lengthwise slice of timber from a tree-trunk, esp. an outside slice. M18. **b** Any of several planks fastened together to form a compound beam. Also (in full *flitch-plate*), a strengthening plate added to a beam, girder, or any woodwork. L19. **3 a** A square piece of blubber from a whale. L18. **b** A steak cut from a halibut. L19.

1 B. CHATWIN A flitch of bacon was rammed into a rack in the rafters. **Dunmow flitch** a side of bacon presented periodically at Dunmow in Essex to any couple proving conjugal harmony for a year and a day.

Comb.: **flitch-beam** a compound beam, esp. one consisting of a metal plate between two slabs of wood; *flitch-plate*: see sense 2b above.

Also **flitchen** *n.* (*obs.* exc. *dial.*) LME.

flitch /flɪtʃ/ *v.t.* M19. [f. the n. Cf. earlier FLICK *v.*[1]] Cut into flitches; cut as a flitch is cut.

flite *n.*, *v.* vars. of FLYTE *n.*, *v.*

fliting *vbl n.* var. of FLYTING.

flitter /ˈflɪtə/ *n.*[1] M16. [f. FLIT *v.* + -ER[1].] A person who or thing which flits.

flitter /ˈflɪtə/ *n.*[2] *rare.* M17. [G.] A small thin metal square used in decoration.

flitter /ˈflɪtə/ *n.*[3] E19. [f. the vb.] A flittering or fluttering motion.

Comb.: **flitter-winged** *a.* having wings that flutter.

flitter /ˈflɪtə/ *v.* LME. [f. FLIT *v.* + -ER[5]. Cf. FLITTERS.] **1** *v.i.* Flit about; fly quickly, flutter. LME. **†2** *v.i.* Fly all about, fly *into* dust or pieces. M16–L17. **†3** *v.i.* Wither, droop. *rare.* L16–M19. **4** *v.t.* Cause to flit; shuffle (cards). *rare.* M19.

flittery *a.* (*rare*) (of ideas, feelings, etc.) uncertain, flitting about, wavering M19.

flitter-mouse /ˈflɪtəmaʊs/ *n.* Pl. **-mice** /-mʌɪs/. M16. [f. FLITTER *v.* + MOUSE *n.*, after Du. *vledermuis* or G *Fledermaus*. Cf. FLICKERMOUSE, FLINDERMOUSE.] = BAT *n.*[3]

flittern /ˈflɪt(ə)n/ *n.* Chiefly *dial.* L17. [Perh. rel. to next.] (A strip of wood from) an oak sapling.

flitters /ˈflɪtəz/ *n.pl.* Chiefly *dial.* & *US.* E17. [Alt. of FITTERS, assoc. w. FLITTER *v.* Cf. FLINDERS.] Fragments; splinters, tatters.

flitting /ˈflɪtɪŋ/ *vbl n.* ME. [f. FLIT *v.* + -ING[1].] **1** The action of FLIT *v.*: an instance of this. ME. **2** *spec.* The action of moving house, a removal. Now chiefly *north.* & *Sc.* ME. **b** The goods, furniture, etc., which are moved in a flitting; baggage. ME.

2 *moonlight flitting*: see MOONLIGHT *n.* & *a.*

flivver /ˈflɪvə/ *n.* *US slang.* E20. [Origin unkn.] A cheap motor car or aeroplane; a 'banger'.

flix /flɪks/ *n.*[1] M17. [Origin unkn.] Fur (of an animal). Cf. FLICK *n.*[2]

†flix *n.*[2] see FLUX *n.*

flixweed /ˈflɪkswiːd/ *n.* L16. [f. †*flix* var. of FLUX *n.* + WEED *n.*[1]: the plant was a supposed remedy for dysentery.] A Eurasian cruciferous plant, *Descurainia sophia*, with small yellow flowers and finely-divided leaves.

†flo *n.* Pl. **flon**. OE–E17. [OE *flā* weak fem., rel. to *flān* FLANE *n.*] An arrow.

float /fləʊt/ *n.* Also **†flote** (see also FLOTE-GRASS). OE. [Partly f. OE, ON *flot* floating state, OE *flota*, ON *floti* ship, fleet; partly f. the vb.] **I 1 a** The action or an act of floating. Formerly also, the condition of floating or being on the water; esp. in **†***on float* afloat. Now *rare.* OE. **b** An operation of floating a currency. L20. **†2** A stream, a river; the sea; a wave. ME–M17. **†3** The flood of the tide; an overflow from a river, a flood; esp. in *on float* in flood, at high water. E16–L18.

1 A. THACKERAY A romantic float in a gondola. 2 SHAKES. *Temp.* Upon the Mediterranean flote Bound sadly home for Naples. 3 *fig.*: A. M. BENNETT With all her animal spirits in the fullest float of exhilaration.

II A floating object. **4** A cork or other buoyant object used on a fishing-line to indicate by movement when a fish bites, or on a fishing net to support the edge. ME. **b** A hollow or inflated part or organ supporting an organism in the water. M19. **c** A buoyant device used to help an inexperienced swimmer remain afloat. L19. **d** A structure fitted to the alighting gear of an aircraft to enable it to float on water. L19. **5** A mass of weeds, ice, etc., floating on the surface of water. Now *rare.* M16. **6** Any of the boards or paddles of a water-wheel or paddle-wheel. E17. **7** A hollow ball or other similar device for regulating the water-level in a boiler, cistern, etc., or the petrol-level in the carburettor of a petrol engine. M18. **8** *Theatr. sing.* & in *pl.* The footlights. E19. **9** A soft drink with a scoop of ice-cream floating in it. Also *ice-cream float.* E20.

4 L. MACNEICE The handsome glass balls which are used as floats for nets. 9 J. DIDION She was also attracted to happy endings . . the Coke float that followed the skinned knee.

III A broad, level, shallow means of transportation. **10** A raft, a flat-bottomed boat. LME. **11** A low-bodied cart or vehicle; *esp.* a low-bodied battery-powered vehicle for delivering milk or other goods (also *milk float*). M19. **12** A platform on wheels with a display on it, used in processions. L19.

10 P. V. WHITE The saplings were soon bound together, and upon floats of hollow logs, by means of thongs. 12 A. BURGESS Behind him came floats with young people's tableaux—The Jazz Age, . . Prison Reform.

IV Misc. uses corresp. to senses of the vb. **13** A tool used in the making of archers' bows. *obs.* exc. *Her.* LME. **14** Any of various tools used for smoothing or levelling; *esp.* (*a*) a single cut file; (*b*) a plasterer's trowel; (*c*) a marble-worker's polishing block. M17. **15** Chiefly *Mining.* Loose rock or ore brought by water from its original formation. Also, particles of ore which do not settle readily in water. Also *float-ore* etc. L17. **16** A trench used for floating or irrigating land. L18. **17** *Weaving.* The passing of weft threads over a section of the warp without being interwoven; a thread or group of threads so passed. M19. **18** A government warrant confirming a prospective settler's claim to a part of a tract of public land put up for sale. *US.* M19. **19a** A sum of money in a shop etc. made available for change-giving or minor expenditures. E20. **b** The amount of money represented by cheques etc. in transit. Chiefly *US.* E20. **20** In critical path analysis, the period of time by which the duration of an activity may be extended. M20.

Comb.: **float-board** = sense 6 above; **float-chamber** a small chamber in a carburettor from which petrol, maintained at a constant level by the action of a float, is supplied to the jets; **float-cut** *a.* (of a file) single cut; **float glass**: manufactured by the float process (see below); **float-light** a lightship; *float-ore*: see sense 15 above; **floatplane** a seaplane equipped with floats; **float process**: for making plate glass by drawing it in a continuous sheet from the melting tank and on to the surface of molten metal for hardening.

float /fləʊt/ *v.* Also †**flote**. [Late OE *flotian* = OS *floton* (MDu. *vlōten*), ON *flota*, f. Gmc weak grade of base of FLEET *v.*[1] Reinforced in ME by OFr. *floter* (mod. *flotter*) f. Proto-Romance, prob. also f. Gmc.] **I** *v.i.* **1** Rest or move on the surface of a liquid without sinking; be or become buoyant; (of a stranded ship) get afloat. LOE. **2** Move gently, drift, on or as on the surface of a moving liquid; move or be suspended freely (*in* a liquid or gas etc.). Formerly also, (of a fish) swim. ME. **b** Move or depart in a casual or leisurely way; wander from place to place. *slang.* E20. **c** Of a currency: fluctuate in international exchange value according to market forces. M20. **d** *Electronics.* Of a part of an electric circuit: be unconnected to a source of fixed potential. M20. **3**†**a** Undulate, oscillate, be unsteady; spread in an undulating form; *fig.* waver. L16–E19. **b** Move or hover dimly before the eye or in the mind. L17. **4** *Comm.* Of an acceptance: be in circulation. L18. **5** *Weaving.* Of a thread: pass over or under several threads either of the warp or weft, instead of being interwoven with them. L19.

1 W. COWPER Her timbers yet are sound, And she may float again. T. H. HUXLEY Ice floats readily on water. 2 J. STEINBECK Any dead fish or sea bird that might have floated in on a rising tide. M. INNES A murmur of voices floated briefly down. A. POWELL Dark fumes floated above the houses. 3b B. PLAIN Her face floats over the pages . . and no matter what else I'm thinking, part of me is always thinking of her.

II *v.t.* **6** Cover with a liquid; irrigate (land); flood, drench, saturate. L16. **7a** Of water, the tide, etc.: support, set afloat, or bear along by the force of the current, (a buoyant object). E17. **b** Cause to be borne along on the surface of water, or to move gently in or through the air; transport by water. M18. **c** Bring into favour, launch (a company, scheme, etc.); put (shares in a company) up for sale on the stock market; air (an idea, theory, etc.); circulate (a rumour). M19. **d** Allow (a currency) to have a fluctuating exchange rate. L20. **8** Make smooth or level; *esp.* (*a*) in *Plastering*, level (the surface of plaster) with a trowel; (*b*) in *Farriery* (now *rare*), file the teeth (of a horse). E18.

6 J. AUSTEN He thought . . I should find the near way floated by this rain. 7b E. WAUGH Exquisite private jokes which they wrote on leaves and floated downstream. C. RYAN Makeshift ferries composed of rubber rafts were slowly floating trucks across the river. *Daily Telegraph* Barnes . . floated over a high cross and Lineker was there to nod it into the net. c F. FORSYTH Bormac was . . floated with an issue of half a million ordinary shares. H. KISSINGER Brezhnev . . floated the concept of 'a system of collective security in Asia.'

Comb.: **float-boat** † (*a*) a ship's longboat; (*b*) a raft; **float-stone** (*a*) a bricklayer's stone for smoothing bricks used in curved work; (*b*) a light porous stone that floats.

floatative *a.* tending to or producing flotation M19. **floating** *vbl n.* (*a*) the action of the verb; an instance of this; (*b*) (in *Plastering*) the second of three coats of plaster: M16.

floatable /ˈfləʊtəb(ə)l/ *a.* E19. [f. prec. + -ABLE.] **1** Of a river: capable of supporting floating objects, that can be floated on. Chiefly *US.* E19. **2** Capable of floating; buoyant. M19.

floata'bility *n.* L19.

floatage /ˈfləʊtɪdʒ/ *n.* Also **flot-**. E17. [f. FLOAT *n.*, *v.* + -AGE.] **1** The action or state of floating. E17. **2** (The right of appropriating) flotsam; floating masses. E17. **3a** *collect.* Ships etc. afloat on a river. M19. **b** The part of a ship above the water-line; freeboard. M19. **4** Floating power, buoyancy. L19.

floatation *n.* var. of FLOTATION.

floatel /fləʊˈtɛl/ *n.* Also **flotel**. M20. [Blend of FLOAT *v.* and HOTEL.] A hotel that floats (*esp.* a boat used as a hotel) or that is built over water; a floating accommodation block.

floater /ˈfləʊtə/ *n.* L16. [f. FLOAT *v.* + -ER[1].] **1** A person or thing which floats; *spec.* (*a*) (*US slang*) a dead body found floating in water; (*b*) *Austral.* a meat pie floating in pea-soup; (*c*) a piece of float-ore (see FLOAT *n.* 15). L16. **2** A voter who is not committed to any political party; (*US*, *derog.*) one whose vote may be bought. M19. **3** A person who frequently changes jobs or place of residence. *US.* M19. **b** An official order to leave a town, district or state; a sentence suspended on condition that the offender leaves the area. *US slang.* E20. **4** *Stock Exch.* A government stock certificate etc. recognized as security. L19. **5** A mistake, a gaffe. *slang.* E20.

float-grass *n.* var. of FLOTE-GRASS.

floating /ˈfləʊtɪŋ/ *ppl a.* L16. [f. FLOAT *v.* + -ING[2].] **1** That floats. L16. **2** Variable, unstable; (now esp. of a population) not fixed in a definite place. L16. **3** (Of financial capital) not fixed or permanently invested; (of a debt) short-term and unfunded; (of a currency or its exchange rate) fluctuating. E19. **b** *Comm.* (Of a cargo) at sea; *esp.* (of a marine insurance policy) providing cover for any ship and its cargo used by a shipping company on specified journeys. M19. **4** Having little or no attachment; disconnected. E19.

Special collocations: **floating anchor** a sea anchor. **floating bridge** (*a*) a bridge made of two small bridges with the uppermost able to be extended beyond the lower by means of pulleys, formerly used for crossing moats; (*b*) a bridge supported by a caisson or pontoon; (*c*) a ferry working on chains. *floating dock*: see DOCK *n.*[3] **floating island** (*a*) a detached floating mass of vegetation; (*b*) *Cookery* a dessert of custard with meringues etc. floating in it. **floating kidney** an abnormal condition in which the kidneys are movable; such a kidney. **floating light** (*a*) a lightship; (*b*) a lifebuoy with a light. **floating mill** *US* a mill constructed so as to float in a river and be worked by the current. **floating point** *Computing* a decimal point that does not occupy a fixed position in the numbers processed, part of the representation of a given number specifying the position of the point for that number; usu. *attrib.* as *floating-point*; **floating rib** each of the last two pairs of ribs, which have no anterior connection to each other or to the sternum. **floating voter**: not committed to any political party.

floatingly *adv.* M17.

floatsome *n.* see FLOTSAM.

floaty /ˈfləʊti/ *a.* LME. [f. FLOAT *n.*, *v.* + -Y[1].] †**1** Well-watered. Only in LME. **2** Capable of floating, buoyant. E17. **3** Of a garment or fabric: light and airy. L20.

floc /flɒk/ *n.* In *pl.* & *collect. sing.* E20. [f. FLOCCULUS.] A flocculent mass of fine particles and colloidal material.

flocci *n.* pl. of FLOCCUS.

floccillation /flɒksɪˈleɪʃ(ə)n/ *n. rare.* M19. [mod.L *floccillus* dim. of L FLOCCUS: see -ATION.] = CARPHOLOGY.

floccinaucinihilipilification /ˌflɒksɪˌnɔːsɪˌnɪhɪlɪˌpɪlɪfɪˈkeɪʃ(ə)n/ *n.* M18. [f. L *flocci*, *nauci*, *nihili*, *pili*, wds denoting 'at little value' + -FICATION.] The action or habit of estimating as worthless.

floccipend /ˈflɒksɪpɛnd/ *v.t.* Long *rare* or *obs.* M16. [f. L *flocci pendere* hold at little value.] Regard as insignificant; make no account of.

floccose /ˈflɒkəʊs/ *a.* M18. [Late L *floccosus*, f. L FLOCCUS: see -OSE[1].] **1** Furnished with a tuft or tufts of woolly hair. Now *rare* or *obs.* M18. **2** Covered with or composed of flocci. M19.

flocculate /ˈflɒkjʊleɪt/ *v.t.* & *i.* L19. [f. as FLOCCULUS: see -ATE[3].] Form into flocculent masses.

floccu'lation *n.* L19.

floccule /ˈflɒkjuːl/ *n.* M19. [f. as FLOCCULUS: see -ULE.] A small portion of matter like a flock or tuft of wool.

flocculent /ˈflɒkjʊl(ə)nt/ *a.* E19. [f. L FLOCCUS + -ULENT.] **1** Resembling tufts or flocks of wool; consisting of loose woolly masses. E19. **2** Covered with a short woolly substance; downy. L19.

flocculence *n.* the state or condition of being flocculent; the condition of containing flocci: M19.

flocculus /ˈflɒkjʊləs/ *n.* Pl. **-li** /-lʌɪ, -liː/. L18. [mod.L, dim. of L FLOCCUS: see -ULE.] **1** A floccule; *esp.* one held in suspension in or precipitated from a fluid. L18. **2** *Anat.* A small lobe on the undersurface of the cerebellum. M19. **3** *Astron.* A small cloudy wisp on the surface of the sun, revealed by the spectroheliograph. E20.

floccus /ˈflɒkəs/ *n.* Pl. **flocci** /ˈflɒksʌɪ/. M19. [L = FLOCK *n.*[2]] Something resembling a flock of wool; a tuft of woolly hairs or filaments.

flocht /flɒxt/ *n. Sc.* Cf. FLAUGHT *n.*[2] L15. [App. repr. OE parallel w. FLIGHT *n.*[1]] **1** A state of agitation or excitement; a flutter. L15. †**2** The action of fleeing, flight. *rare.* Only in E16.

flock /flɒk/ *n.*[1] [OE *flocc* = MLG *vlocke*, ON *flokkr*: ult. origin unkn.] **1** A band, body, or company of people. Now *obs.* exc. as in *transf.* from senses 2 and 3. OE. **b** In *pl.* Great numbers, 'swarms'. M16. **2** A number of animals of one kind, esp. birds, feeding or travelling together. ME. **3** A number of domestic animals of one kind, now usu. sheep, goats, or geese, kept together. ME. **4a** The Christian body, esp. in relation to Christ as the Good Shepherd; a congregation, esp. in relation to its pastor. ME. **b** A group of people, as children, pupils, etc., under the charge or guidance of one or more persons as parents, teachers, etc. L19.

1 LD BERNERS They parceyued a flocke of men of armes commynge togyder. b COVERDALE *2 Macc.* 14:14 The Heithen which fled out of Iewry . . came to Nicanor by flockes. 2 J. RATHBONE Flocks of larks and fieldfares rose ahead of me. 3 POPE He . . sitting down, to milk his flocks prepares. **flocks and herds** sheep and cattle. 4a AV *1 Pet.* 5:2 Feede the flocke of God which is among you. R. HOGGART Like the relationship laid down as proper between the minister and his flock.

Comb.: **flock-book** a list of pedigrees of sheep; **flock-master** a sheep-farmer; **flock pigeon** an

Australian bronzewing pigeon, *Phaps histrionica*, forming large flocks.

flockless *a.* L16.

flock /flɒk/ *n.*[2] ME. [(O)Fr. *floc* f. L FLOCCUS.] **1** A lock or tuft of wool, cotton, etc. Formerly also, the type of something worthless. ME. **2** In *pl.* & *collect. sing.* A material for quilting or stuffing made of wool-refuse or torn-up cloth. ME. **3** In *pl.* & *collect. sing.* Powdered wool or cloth, formerly used in thickening cloth and now in making flock-paper. L15. **4** *Chem.* In *pl.* Light loose masses precipitated. L16.

1 W. FULKE They look white, like flocks of wooll. J. LYLY I will never care three flocks for his ambition. 2 W. CONGREVE Put more flocks in her bed.

Comb.: **flock-bed, -mattress**: stuffed with flock; **flock-paper** wallpaper that has been sized and then sprinkled with powdered wool.

flocky *a.* (*a*) resembling flock; (*b*) floccose: LME.

flock /flɒk/ *v.*[1] ME. [f. FLOCK *n.*[1]] †**1** *v.t.* Gather (individuals) into a company; muster (troops); bring (crowds) *in*. ME–L16. **2** *v.i.* Congregate, go in great numbers, troop. Freq. w. advs. ME. †**3** *v.t.* Lead *away* to another flock. L16–L17. **4** *v.t.* Crowd or throng round (a person). Long *obs.* exc. *dial.* E17.

1 J. HOOKER So had he flocked in Englishmen to ouerrun his countrie. 2 G. GREENE Hundreds of women were flocking into the capital for market. J. M. COETZEE Who would not flock to see the entertainment? 4 JOHN TAYLOR Good fellowes trooping, flock'd me so.

flock /flɒk/ *v.*[2]*t.* M16. [f. FLOCK *n.*[2]] **1** Stuff with flock. Also, cover (a prepared surface of cloth, paper, etc.) with flock. M16. †**2** *fig.* Treat with contempt, regard as worthless. M–L16.

flockmeal /ˈflɒkmiːl/ *adv.* Long *arch. rare.* [OE *floccmǣlum*: see FLOCK *n.*[1], -MEAL.] By or in flocks, flock by flock.

floe /fləʊ/ *n.* E19. [Prob. f. Norw. *flo* f. ON *fló* layer, stratum. Cf. FLAW *n.*[1]] A sheet of floating ice; a detached portion of an ice-field. Also *ice floe*

floe ice ice floating in sheets.

flog /flɒg/ *v.* Orig. *slang.* Infl. **-gg-**. L17. [Prob. imit. or f. L *flagellare* FLAGELLATE *v.*] **1** *v.t.* Beat, whip; punish with repeated blows of a birch, cane, whip, etc.; drive (laziness etc.) out of or (learning etc.) into a person by beating. L17. **b** Urge (a horse etc.) on with a whip. L18. **2** *v.t.* Beat, lash, strike (an object etc.), esp. for a particular purpose; *Angling* cast a fly-line over (a stretch of water) repeatedly; *Cricket* punish (a bowler, the bowling). E19. **b** *v.i.* Of a sail: beat or flap heavily. M19. **3** *v.t.* **a** Defeat; excel. *slang.* M19. **b** Tire (*out*). Usu. in *pass. dial.* L19. **4** *v.t.* Sell, offer for sale (esp. worthless or shoddy goods or those illicitly obtained). Also, steal. *slang.* E20. **5** *v.i.* Proceed by violent, painful, or exhausting effort. E20.

1 F. E. SMEDLEY I have not forgotten the Greek and Latin flogged into us at Westminster. G. GORER Six women were publicly flogged.. till the blood ran down their backs. **flog to death** *colloq.* talk about, promote, etc., *ad nauseam.* b G. P. R. JAMES Take off the bridles.. and flog them down the valley. *flog a dead horse*: see DEAD *a.* etc. 2 J. F. W. HERSCHEL Trees were seen to flog the ground with their branches. b F. MARRYAT The storm-staysail.. flogged and cracked with a noise louder than the gale. 3a E. A. FREEMAN I think for position it flogs every place I know. b R. KIPLING I went to bed; for I was fair flogged out. 4 M. DRABBLE Let's go and look at the ghastly thing that Martin flogged us. *Listener* He was.. flogging quack remedies to innocents who needed protecting from him. 5 M. BINCHY It would be nicer than flogging all the way to Clarence Gardens.

flogger *n.* (*a*) a person who flogs; *colloq.* an advocate of corporal punishment; (*b*) *slang* a riding-whip; (*c*) a tool for removing the stoppers of casks, bottles, etc.: E18. **flogging** *vbl n.* the action of the vb, esp. the practice of corporal punishment; an instance of this; *flogging round the fleet*: see FLEET *n.*[1]: L17.

†**flon** *n.* pl. of FLO.

flong /flɒŋ/ *n.* L19. [Fr. *flan* FLAN.] Prepared paper for making stereotype moulds.

flood /flʌd/ *n.* [OE *flōd* corresp. to OFris., OS *flōd* (Du. *vloed*), OHG *fluot* (G *Flut*), ON *flóð*, Goth. *flōdus*, f. Gmc f. IE (as in Gk *plōein* swim, *plōtos* navigable).] **1** The flowing in of the tide. Also *flood-tide*. OE. **2** A body of flowing water; a river, a stream. *obs.* exc. *poet.* OE. **3** Water as opp. to land; the sea. *obs.* exc. *poet.* OE. **4** An overflowing or irruption of (a great body of) water over land not usually submerged, an inundation, a deluge. OE. **5** A profuse and violent outpouring (as) of water or other liquid; a swollen stream; a torrent, a downpour. ME. **6** In *pl.* Uterine haemorrhage. Long *rare* or *obs.* M17. **7** A floodlight. Freq. in *pl. colloq.* M20.

1 R. DONNELLY The young flood making close in shore. *fig.*: SHAKES. *Jul. Caes.* There is a tide in the affairs of men Which, taken at the flood, leads on to fortune. 2 W. SOMERVILLE Ev'ry.. hollow Rock, that o'er the dimpling Flood Nods pendant. 3 W. COWPER Swiftly dividing the flood, To a slave-cultured island we came. **flood and field** sea and land. 4 LD MACAULAY When the floods were out, he exposed his life to imminent risk. P. THEROUX The river.. was in full flood. *fig.*: TENNYSON His passions all in flood And masters of his motion. *Noah's Flood*: see NOAH I. **the Flood** = *Noah's Flood* s.v. NOAH I. 5 *Times* Karen Barber's flood of tears.. was all too understandable. J. ARCHER Andrew was surprised and touched by the flood of letters. 7 M. AYRTON Estelle switches on the big floods and the strips.

Comb.: **flood-hatch** a framework of boards sliding in grooves, to be raised in time of flood; a sluice, a floodgate; **flood-lamp** a floodlight; **floodlight** *n.* & *v.* (*a*) *n.* (a lamp providing) intense artificial light which eliminates all shadows on the surface illuminated; (*b*) *v.t.* illuminate with a floodlight or floodlights, esp. with the light projected from several directions; **floodlit** *ppl a.* illuminated by a floodlight or floodlights; **flood-mark** the high-water mark; **flood plain** a tract of low-lying ground which is often flooded by a river etc.; *flood-tide*: see sense I above.

floody *a.* (long *rare*) of, pertaining to, or of the nature of a flood LME.

flood /flʌd/ *v.* E17. [f. the n.] **1** *v.t.* Cover with a flood, inundate (*lit.* & *fig.*). E17. **2** *v.i.* Come (*in*) in great quantities; overflow; be or become flooded. M18. **3** *v.i.* Have a uterine haemorrhage. L18. **4** *v.t.* Pour (*out, away, back*) in a flood. Chiefly *fig. rare.* E19. **b** Drive *out* (of one's home etc.) by a flood or floods. Usu. in *pass.* E20. **5** *v.t.* Cover or fill with water, irrigate; deluge (a burning house, a mine, etc.) with water; (of rain) fill (a river) to overflowing; overfill (a carburettor) with petrol. M19.

1 E. WAUGH The domestic hot water machine has burst and flooded the kitchen quarters. E. PAUL When rationing ends and beef begins flooding the market. B. MALAMUD The river overflowed its banks, flooding the lower reaches of the city. **flooded box** *Austral.* coolabah. **flooded gum** *Austral.* any of several eucalypts growing in damp soil. 2 L. EVANS If it floods early, it scarce retires within its Banks in a Month. K. MOORE Thoughts of Rollo came flooding back. 4 C. MERIVALE The lifeblood of the provinces is flooded back upon Paris. 5 A. BAIN A violent storm has flooded the rivers. R. DAVIES He'll be drowned same as when the Cambrian pit was flooded!

floodable *a.* liable to flood, subject to inundation E19. **flooding** *n.* (*a*) in *pl.*, floods, *fig.* fullness, superabundance; (*b*) *gen.* the action of the vb; an instance of this; (*c*) a uterine haemorrhage: L17.

floodgate /ˈflʌdgeɪt/ *n.* ME. [f. FLOOD *n.* + GATE *n.*[1]] **1** A gate that may be opened or closed to admit or exclude (esp. flood) water; *spec.* the lower gate of a lock. ME. **b** *fig.* A restraint, barrier, or check, esp. on the emotions. ME. †**2** A stream that was closed by or passed through a floodgate; a strong stream, a torrent (*lit.* & *fig.*). LME–M17. **3** A sluice. Also (*dial.*), a gate suspended over a stream so as to rise with the water in flood time but prevent the passage of cattle etc. at low water. M16.

1b SHAKES. *Ven. & Ad.* Through the floodgates breaks the silver rain. THACKERAY The floodgates were opened, and mother and daughter wept. 3 *fig.*: C. CARTWRIGHT My Lord, you let a flood-gate of Arguments out. *attrib.*: SHAKES. *Oth.* My particular grief Is of so flood-gate and o'erbearing nature.

flookan /ˈfluːk(ə)n/ *n.* Also (earlier) **flooking** /ˈfluːkɪŋ/. E18. [Origin unkn.] *Mining.* A transverse vein of clayey material; the material forming this.

floor /flɔː/ *n.* [OE *flōr*, corresp. to (M)Du *vloer*, MHG *vluor* (G *Flur*), ON *flór*, f. Gmc.] **I** A level structure in a house or other building. **1** The layer of boards, bricks, tiles, stones, etc., covering the base of a room or other compartment; the lower surface of a room. Also in extended usage, the base of a cavity, etc. OE. **b** *fig.* A minimum, esp. of prices or wages. M20. **2** The lower surface of a set of rooms etc. extending on one level through a building; the set of rooms etc. on such a level; a storey. LME. **3a** The framework or underside of the ceiling of a room etc., considered in relation to the compartment above. L16. **b** The framework or structure of joists etc. supporting the flooring of a room. E18. **4** *Naut.* †**a** The deck. Only in 17. **b** The bottom of a vessel on either side of the keelson. Also, a floor-timber. E19. **5** *spec.* (passing into branch II). **a** The part of a legislative assembly which members sit in and speak from; the right to speak next in a debate. M18. **b** (The floor of) the part of a hall etc. used for dancing. M19. **c** (The floor of) a film or television studio where a programme etc. is shot. M20.

1 J. TYNDALL The stone floor was dark with moisture. G. STEIN The parlour had a thick and flowered carpet on the floor. PELVIC *floor*. **b** *Economist* A floor of only £12 a week on the wages of British artists. 2 M. GIROUARD The second and third floors overhung the lower half of the house. 3a *fig.*: C. BOWEN Then Caesar.. Bounding his throne by Ocean, his fame by the firmament floor. **b** P. NICHOLSON Floors in which bridging joists are used. 5a J. T. STORY I remember my maiden speech on the floor of the House. **c** M. KENNEDY I'll make a shooting script... It'll be something you can go on the floor with.

II A level space. **6** An artificial platform or levelled space designed for a particular activity (and freq. w. specifying wd). OE. **b** *transf.* The corn etc. laid on such a space for threshing; in the malting process, a batch of grain etc. laid at one time for steeping. LME. **7** A naturally level space or extended surface. Also (*colloq.* or *dial.*), the ground. LME. †**8** An area or region. *rare.* LME–E17.

6 *fig.*: W. COWPER Where flails of oratory thresh the floor. *threshing-floor*: see THRESHING *n.* 7 L. STEPHEN Forests of pine rise steeply from the meadow floor. *Times* With the field drawn tight around the bat and catches being snapped up off the floor. N. CALDER They lowered a camera to the ocean floor. 8 BACON Both of them.. fill a whole Floare or Orbe vnto certaine Limits.

III A surface as a foundation. **9** A surface on which something rests, a foundation. OE. **10** The stratum immediately beneath a seam of coal etc. M19.

9 J. SMEATON The arches are.. 6 feet from the floor to the springer. 10 T. H. HUXLEY Vegetable remains are also met with in rocks beneath the coal, forming what is called the floor.

IV A layer. **11** A layer, a stratum; a horizontal course. E18. **12** A unit of measurement used in embankment work, usu. equal to a volume 18 or 20 feet square by one foot deep. Now *rare* or *obs.* E18.

11 J. RAY Many Beds or Floors of all kinds of Sea-Shells.

Phrases: **cross the floor** join the opposing side of an assembly. *first floor*: see FIRST. **from the floor** (of a question, statement, etc.) given by an individual member at a meeting etc., as opp. to a representative of the platform etc. *ground floor*: see GROUND *n.* **mop the floor with** = *wipe the floor with* below. *second floor*: see SECOND *a.* **take the floor** (*a*) begin to dance on a dance-floor etc.; (*b*) *N. Amer.* speak in a debate. *third floor*: see THIRD *a.* & *n.* **wipe the floor with** *slang* inflict a humiliating defeat on, crush.

Comb.: **floorboard** *n.* & *v.* (*a*) *n.* a board forming a section of the floor of a room etc.; (*b*) *v.t.* (*US slang*) press (the accelerator pedal) down as far as possible, drive fast. **floorcloth** a cloth used for washing floors; **floor-lamp** *N. Amer.* a standard lamp; **floor-leader** *US* the leader of a party in a legislative assembly; **floor-length** *a.* reaching to the floor; **floor manager** (*a*) a person in charge of a floor; *esp.* a shop-walker; (*b*) the stage-manager of a television production; *floor-mop*: see MOP *n.*[2] I; **floor plan** the diagram of a floor, *esp.* one showing the rooms etc. on one storey of a building; **floor-polish** a manufactured substance for making floors glossy; **floor show** an entertainment presented on the floor of a restaurant, nightclub, etc., as opp. to on a stage; **floor-timber** *Naut.* each of the parts of the ship's timbers which are placed immediately across the keel; **floor-walker** *US* a shopwalker.

floorage *n.* (*rare*) a number of floors, an amount of flooring M18. **floorless** *a.* M19.

floor /flɔː/ *v.* LME. [f. the n.] **1** *v.t.* Cover or provide with a floor or floors; form or serve as the floor of. LME. **2** *v.t.* Bring to the floor or ground; knock down; cause to fall. M17. **3** *v.t.* Overcome, get the better of; defeat; confound, nonplus, baffle. Also (*arch. colloq.*), get through (a piece of work) successfully. E19. **b** *v.i.* Commit a fatal blunder, fail. Long *rare* or *obs.* M19. **4** *v.t.* Place *upon* (something) as a floor. *rare.* L19. **5** *v.t.* Hang (a picture) low on the wall. *rare.* L19.

1 S. PEPYS Looking over the joiners, flooring my dining-room. C. VANCOUVER The..sleeping place floored with flat stones. J. BUCHAN A cup in the hills, floored..with short, crisp pasture. **2** BYRON The usual excuse of floored equestrians. B. MALAMUD The Deputy Warden floored the Fixer with a blow. **3** DISRAELI I was the only man who could floor O'Connell. R. CHURCH Any word of more than one syllable floored me. N. ANNAN A..first-class man..could be expected to *floor* the bookwork in the early papers. **4** E. B. TYLOR The doctrine of a Heaven, floored upon a firmament.

floorer *n.* a person who or thing which floors; esp. (*a*) a knock-down blow; (*b*) a confounding or baffling thing: L18. **flooring** *n.* (*a*) the action of the vb; (*b*) a floor of a room etc.; the materials of which it is made; (*c*) in the malting process, the operation of spreading the grain on the malt-floor and treating it there: LME.

floose /fluːs/ *n.* Also **flus**, **†fluce**, & other vars. L16. [Arab. *fulūs* money, pl. of *fals* a small copper or bronze coin f. Gk. *phollis* FOLLIS. Cf. FILS *n.*[2]] A small coin of N. Africa, Arabia, India, and neighbouring countries; *collect.* money.

floozie /ˈfluːzi/ *n. colloq.* Also **-sie**, **-zy**. E20. [Origin uncertain: perh. rel. to FLOSSY *a.*] A girl or woman, *esp.* one of disreputable character.

flop /flɒp/ *n.* E17. [f. the vb.] **1** *gen.* The action of FLOP *v.*; an instance of this; a flopping motion; the heavy dull sound produced by this. E17. **b** Something loose and pendulous, a flap. E20. **2** A mass of thin mud or other viscous fluid. *dial.* M19. **3a** A successful act of trickery; an act of cheating. *US slang.* Now *rare* or *obs.* M19. **b** A reversal of attitude or behaviour; a sudden change of party or policy. *US colloq.* L19. **4** A dismal failure, a collapse; a person who or thing (esp. an enterprise) which fails; something unable to fulfil a role adequately. *colloq.* L19. **5** A flabby or soft person. *slang.* E20. **6** A bed; somewhere to spend the night. Also, a safe house for criminals. *slang.* E20.

1b P. ARROWSMITH David..pushed a flop of hair back off his forehead. **4** ROBERT ANDERSON That's a terrible thing..to make a flop of the first job you've got. I. HAMILTON As a social event the party was a flop. **5** F. O'CONNOR She was a great flop of a woman. **6** S. BELLOW The flop I found was in a tall clapboard hotel.

Comb.: **flop-eared** *a.* having pendulous ears; **flop-house** *slang* (orig. *US*) a doss-house.

¶Rare bef. 19.

flop /flɒp/ *v.* Infl. **-pp-**. E17. [Var. of FLAP *v.*] **1** *v.i.* Swing or sway about heavily and loosely. E17. **2** *v.i.* Move heavily, clumsily, or in an ungainly way; sit, kneel, lie, fall, etc., *down* awkwardly or suddenly. Also, make the dull sound of a soft body falling or a flat thing slapping the water. L17. **b** *v.i.* & *t.* (Cause to) change one's attitude or behaviour; (cause to) change sides; bring or come over. *US colloq.* L19. **3** *v.t.* Throw (*down*) suddenly, cause to fall heavily and noisily. E19. **4** *v.t.* Move (a wing, limb, etc.) heavily and loosely up and down. M19. **5** *v.t.* Strike with a sudden blow; close *up* with a blow. *dial.* (now *rare*). M19. **6** *v.t.* Achieve (success in an examination, good marks, etc.) by cheating. *US colloq.* Now *rare.* M19. **7** *v.i.* Fail dismally, collapse, disappoint expectations, prove inadequate. *colloq.* E20. **8** *v.i.* Sleep; spend the night. *slang.* E20.

1 R. JARRELL His fair hair kept flopping in his face. *fig.*: T. E. LAWRENCE A miserable squad flops like a wet dishcloth. **2** P. H. JOHNSON She flopped over like a rag doll. **b** C. R. COOPER Hurriedly lawmakers who had been opposed to it 'flopped' to the other side. **3** T. HOOD In bolts our bacon-hog..And flops him down in all the muck. **4** J. E. TENNENT Cawing and flopping his wings in the sky. **7** *Observer* If the play 'flops' after a run of..three or four nights. M. REYNOLDS Lenin supposedly tried to apply the teachings of Marx to Russia—and flopped. **8** M. SHADBOLT It's only tucker I need..and a place to flop at nights.

flopper *n.* (*US slang*) (*a*) a fraudster; (*b*) a person who deserts to the opposing political side or party: L19.

flop /flɒp/ *adv.* E18. [f. the vb.] With a flop, or flopping noise.

flopperoo /flɒpəˈruː/ *n. N. Amer. slang.* Also **floperoo**. M20. [f. FLOP *v.* + -EROO.] A flop, a failure.

floppy /ˈflɒpi/ *a.* & *n.* M19. [f. FLOP *v.* + -Y[1].] A *adj.* **1** Having a tendency to flop (*lit.* & *fig.*); limply flexible, flaccid. M19. **2** *floppy disc*, a flexible disc with a magnetic coating, used to store machine-readable data; this together with its protective envelope. L20. **B** *n.* A floppy disc. L20.

floppily *adv.* L19. **floppiness** *n.* L19.

flor /flɒr, flɔː/ *n.* L19. [Sp., lit. 'flower'.] A film of yeast allowed to develop on the surface during the making of fino sherry.

flora /ˈflɔːrə/ *n.* Pl. **-ras**, **-rae** /-riː/. E16. [L f. *flor-*, *flos* flower.] **1** (**F-**.) An ancient Italian goddess of fertility and flowers. Hence, the personification of nature's power to produce flowers. E16. **2** A catalogue of the plants of a defined area, with descriptions of them and/or stations for the more unusual species. L18. **3** The plants or plant life of a given area, habitat, or epoch. Cf. FAUNA. L18.

3 INTESTINAL *flora.*

Comb.: **Flora dance** *dial.* [see *floral dance* s.v. FLORAL *a.*] = *furry dance* s.v. FURRY *n.*; **Flora('s) day** *dial.* = FURRY *n.*

floral /ˈflɔːr(ə)l/ *a.* & *n.* M17. [L *Floralis* or directly f. L *flor-* (see prec.): see -AL[1].] A *adj.* **1** (**F-**.) Pertaining to or in honour of the goddess Flora. M17. **2** Of or pertaining to a flower or flowers. M18. **3** Pertaining to a flora or floras. L19.

Special collocations: **floral dance** [alt. of FURRY *n.*] = *furry dance* s.v. FURRY *n.* **floral diagram**: showing a cross-section of a flower, with the relative positions of petals, sepals, stamens, ovary, etc. **floral envelope** the perianth of a flower; the corolla and/or calyx. **floral formula**: expressing concisely the structure of a flower (the number and arrangement of parts), by means of letters, numerals, and symbols. **floral leaf** any of the modified leaves occurring in an inflorescence (bracts) or forming part of a flower (petals, sepals). **floral tribute** an offering of flowers at a funeral. *floral whorl*: see WHORL *n.* 3.

B *n.* **†1** (**F-**.) A dancer at a Roman festival in honour of Flora. Only in M17. **2** A fabric with a floral design. L19.

florally *adv.* E19.

Floreal /ˈflɔːrɪəl/ *n.* Also ***Floréal*** /flɔreal/. E19. [Fr. *Floréal*, f. L *floreus* flowery, f. *flor-*, *flos* flower: see -AL[1].] *Hist.* The eighth month of the French Republican calendar (introduced 1793), extending from 20 April to 19 May.

floreated *ppl a.* var. of FLORIATED.

Florence /ˈflɒr(ə)ns/ *n.* & *a.* ME. [(O)Fr., name of the chief city of Tuscany, western Italy, = early It. *Fiorenze* (now *Firenze*), f. L *Florentia.*] A *n.* **†1** A gold florin. ME–L16. **2** Any of several fabrics, *esp.* (*a*) *Hist.* a woollen cloth; (*b*) a lightweight silk dress fabric. L15. **†3** = *Florence wine* below. E–M18.

B *attrib.* or as *adj.* Made in or obtained from Florence. M16.

Florence fennel: see FENNEL *n.* **Florence flask** a long-necked glass flask, used to hold Florence oil. **Florence oil** a superior kind of olive oil. **Florence wine** *arch.* a red wine from Tuscany.

†florent *a.* L15–E18. [L *florent-* pres. ppl stem of *florere* FLOURISH *v.*: see -ENT.] Putting out flowers or leaves and shoots; *fig.* flourishing.

Florentine /ˈflɒr(ə)ntʌɪn/; *in senses A.5, B.2 also* -tiːn/ *n.* & *a.* ME. [(O)Fr. *Florentin*, *-ine* or L *Florentinus*, f. *Florentia*: see FLORENCE, -INE[1].] A *n.* **1** A native or inhabitant of Florence in Tuscany, western Italy. ME. **2** A fabric of silk or (formerly) cotton or worsted, used for garments. Cf. FLORENCE *n.* 2. M16. **3** A kind of pie; *esp.* meat etc. baked in a plate with a cover of pastry (and not in a pie-dish). Now *rare* or *obs.* L16. **4** The Italian dialect spoken in Florence. L16. **5** A kind of biscuit packed with nuts, glacé cherries, and other preserved fruit, coated on one side with chocolate. M20.

B *adj.* **1** Of, obtained from, or associated with the city of Florence. L16. **2** *Cookery.* Of eggs, fish, etc.: served on a bed of spinach or with spinach sauce. Usu. *postpositive.* M18. **3** *Embroidery.* Using Florentine stitch. E20.

1 Florentine iris a bearded iris with almost white flowers, *Iris* × *germanica* var. *florentina*, the chief source of orrisroot. **Florentine mosaic**: composed of pieces of semiprecious stone embedded in marble etc. to form patterns or pictures. **Florentine pie** *rare* = sense A.3 above. **Florentine stitch** *Embroidery*: worked in zigzag patterns on canvas.

flore pleno /ˌflɔːrɪ ˈpleməʊ, ˈpliːn-/ *a. phr.* L19. [L, lit. 'with a full flower'.] Double-flowered.

florescence /flɔːˈrɛs(ə)ns/ *n.* L18. [mod.L *florescentia*, f. L *florescent-* pres. ppl stem of *florescere* inceptive of *florere* to flower: see -ENCE.] The process of flowering or bursting into flower; the period of flowering. Now chiefly *fig.* Also (now *rare* or *obs.*), an inflorescence.

Scientific American The imported culture did not reach full florescence until the sixth century.

¶Earlier in REFLORESCENCE.

florescent *a.* (*rare*) bursting into flower, flowering (*lit.* & *fig.*) E19.

floret /ˈflɒrɪt, ˈflɔː-/ *n.* L17. [f. L *flor-*, *flos* flower + -ET[1].] **1** A small flower forming part of an inflorescence; *spec.* (*Bot.*) (*a*) any of the individual small flowers making up the ray or disc of a composite flower; (*b*) (in a grass) an individual lemma and palea, together with the flower they enclose. L17. **2** A tiny blossom or flowering plant; a floweret. L18. **3** Any of the segments into which a cauliflower or broccoli head may be divided. M20.

2 P. MATTHIESSEN A rock garden..set about with strap fern, edelweiss, and unknown alpine florets.

floreted *a.* covered or adorned with tiny flowers M19.

floriated /ˈflɔːrɪeɪtɪd/ *a.* Also **-eated**. M19. [Irreg. f. L *flor-*, *flos* flower + -I- + -ATE[2] + -ED[1].] Decorated with floral ornaments; *fig.* highly exaggerated.

floriate *a.* = FLORIATED L19. **flori'ation** *n.* a floral decoration; a musical flourish: M19.

floribunda /flɒrɪˈbʌndə, flɔː-/ *n.* L19. [mod.L, use as n. of fem. of *floribundus* flowering profusely, f. L *flor-*, *flos* flower + *-bundus* (as in *moribundus*), infl. by *abundus* copious.] A plant, esp. a type of garden rose (also *floribunda rose*), bearing its flowers in dense clusters.

florican /ˈflɔːrɪkan/ *n.* Also **-ikan**. L18. [Origin unkn.] Either of two small bustards native to the Indian subcontinent, (more fully *Bengal florican*) *Houbaropsis bengalensis*, and (more fully *lesser florican*) *Sypheotides indica.*

floriculture /ˈflɒrɪkʌltʃə, ˈflɔː-/ *n.* E19. [f. L *flor-*, *flos* flower + CULTURE *n.*, after *horticulture.*] The growing of (ornamental) flowers.

floricultural *a.* E19. **floriculturist** *n.* a person who practises or is skilled in floriculture M19.

florid /ˈflɒrɪd/ *a.* M17. [(Fr. *floride* f.) L *floridus*, f. *flor-*, *flos* flower or *florere* to flower: see -ID[1].] **1** Having many or (formerly) consisting of flowers; flowery. *arch.* M17. **2** *fig.* Profusely decorated as with flowers; highly (usu. excessively) ornate. Chiefly of speech or writing, or a speaker or writer: having or using many rhetorical ornaments or flowery words and phrases. M17. **b** *Archit.* Esp. of 15th- and 16th-cent. buildings: enriched with elaborate decoration. E18. **c** Of music: in which a simple theme is varied and embellished with melodic figures; figurate. Of counterpoint: consisting of a combination of different kinds. E18. **†3** Glowing with beauty; highly attractive. Of a colour: bright, glaring. M17–L18. **4** Having a ruddy or highly coloured complexion. Also, flushed *with* an emotion. M17. **†b** Of blood: bright red, i.e. from the arteries. M17–L18. **5** In the bloom of health; flourishing, vigorous. *arch.* M17. 6 Of a disease or its manifestations: occurring in a fully developed form. L20.

1 GOLDSMITH In florid beauty groves and fields appear. 2 R. FRY A lover of all that was rich, exuberant and even florid. P. ACKROYD My French is . . somewhat florid and literary. 3 J. BUTLER Florid and gaudy Prospects and Expectations. 4 N. MAILER The sort of heavy florid man who seems boyish at forty. E. L. DOCTOROW Morgan was now florid with excitement. 5 STEELE I . . attribute the florid old age I now enjoy, to my . . walks up Hedington-Hill. 6 *Lancet* Patients . . whose florid symptoms had not remitted with major tranquillisers.

flo'ridity *n.* florid quality E18. **floridly** *adv.* M17. **floridness** *n.* M17.

Florida /ˈflɒrɪdə/ *n.* M18. [A region (since 1845 a State) in the extreme south-east of the US.] Used *attrib.* to designate things found in, obtained from, or associated with Florida.

Florida moss an epiphytic bromeliad, *Tillandsia usneoides*, resembling lichen, distributed from the southern US to S. America. **Florida room** *N. Amer.* a kind of sun lounge or sheltered porch. *Florida snapping turtle*: see SNAPPING *ppl a.* 3. **Florida water** a toilet-water resembling eau-de-cologne, frequently containing orange-water.

Floridan /ˈflɒrɪd(ə)n/ *n.* & *a.* M18. [f. prec. + -AN.] = FLORIDIAN.

floridean /fləˈrɪdɪən/ *a.* Also **F-**. E20. [f. mod.L *Florideae* (see below) + -AN.] Belonging to the Florideae, a subclass of the Rhodophyceae (red algae); *floridean starch*, a reserve polysaccharide found in many red algae.

Also **florideous** *a.* (now *rare* or *obs.*) L19.

Floridian /fləˈrɪdɪən/ *n.* & *a.* Cf. FLORIDAN. L16. [f. FLORIDA + -IAN.] A *n.* An inhabitant (formerly, a N. American Indian) of Florida. L16. B *adj.* Of, pertaining to, or associated with Florida. E19.

floriferous /flɒˈrɪf(ə)rəs, flɔː-/ *a.* M17. [f. L *florifer* (f. *flori-* comb. form of *flos* flower) + -OUS: see -FEROUS.] Bearing (numerous) flowers.

floriferousness *n.* E18.

florigen /ˈflɔːrɪdʒ(ə)n, ˈflɒ-/ *n.* M20. [f. L *flori-* comb. form of *flos* flower + -GEN.] A hypothetical hormone in plants, not yet isolated but thought to induce flowering.

florikan *n.* var. of FLORICAN.

florilegium /flɒrɪˈliːdʒɪəm, flɔː-/ *n.* Also †**-legy**. Pl. **-ia** /-ɪə/, **-iums**. E17. [mod.L, lit. 'bouquet', f. L *flori-* comb. form of *flos* flower + *legere* to gather, tr. Gk *anthologion* ANTHOLOGY.] A collection of choice extracts from literature; an anthology. Also (*rare*), w. ref. to etymological sense: a book describing choice flowers.

florin /ˈflɒrɪn/ *n.* ME. [(O)Fr. f. It. *fiorino*, f. *fiore* flower: the coin orig. so named bore a lily (fleur-de-lis) on the reverse: see FLORENCE.] 1 A gold coin first issued at Florence in 1252. *obs.* exc. *Hist.* ME. 2 An English gold coin issued by Edward III, equivalent to six shillings or six shillings and eightpence in the currency of the day. *obs.* exc. *Hist.* L15. 3 Any of various (orig. gold or silver) coins current at various times on the Continent. Now only, the monetary unit of the Netherlands; a guilder. E17. 4 In modern British pre-decimal coinage: the silver, later cupro-nickel, two-shilling piece, first minted in 1849. M19.

4 GODLESS *florin*.

floripondio /flɔːrɪˈpɒndɪəʊ/ *n.* E17. [Sp. f. mod.L *floripondium*, app. f. L *flori-* comb. form of *flos* flower + *pondus* weight.] Either of two S. American plants of the nightshade family, *Brugmansia arborea* and *B. sanguinea*, allied to the thorn-apple.

florist /ˈflɒrɪst/ *n.* E17. [f. L *flor-*, *flos* flower + -IST, after Fr. *fleuriste* or It. *florista*.] A person who cultivates or breeds (ornamental) flowers, now esp. for sale. Also (now usu.), a dealer in (cut) flowers.

floristic /fləˈrɪstɪk/ *a.* & *n.* L19. [f. FLORA + -ISTIC.] A *adj.* Of or pertaining to floristics. L19. B *n.* In *pl.* (treated as *sing.*). The branch of phytogeography that deals with the distribution of plants. L19.

floristically *adv.* E20.

floristry /ˈflɒrɪstri/ *n.* E19. [f. FLORIST + -RY.] The art, study or business of a florist. Formerly, garden flowers collectively.

floruit /ˈflɒrʊɪt, ˈflɔːr-/ *n.* M19. [L, 3rd person sing. perf. indic. of *florere* to flourish.] The period during which a person etc. flourished.

H. W. WATKINS Professor de Groot puts his life at A.D. 65–135, and his *floruit* in the reign of Trajan.

florula /ˈflɔːrʊlə/ *n.* Pl. **-lae** /-liː/, **-las**. M19. [mod.L, dim. of L *Flora*: see FLORA, -ULE.] A small or circumscribed flora (FLORA 2, 3). Also, a small collection of plants from an area.

florulent /ˈflɔːrʊl(ə)nt, ˈflɒ-/ *a. rare.* L16. [L *florulentus*, f. *flor-*, *flos* flower: see -ULENT.] Covered with flowers or representations of flowers.

flory /ˈflɔːri/ *a.* Also **fleury** /ˈflʊəri/. LME. [OFr. *flo(u)ré* (mod. *fleuré*), f. *fleur* FLOWER *n.*: see -Y[5].] *Her.* Decorated with a fleur-de-lis or fleurs-de-lis; *esp.* (of a cross) having limbs tipped with fleurs-de-lis.

floscular /ˈflɒskjʊlə/ *a.* L18. [f. L *flosculus* (see next) + -AR[1].] *Bot.* = FLOSCULOUS 2.

floscule /ˈflɒskjuːl/ *n.* M17. [Fr., or L *flosculus* dim. of *flos* flower.] †1 Something resembling a small flower. Only in M17. 2 *Bot.* Any of the florets in a composite flower. Now *rare.* L18.

flosculous /ˈflɒskjʊləs/ *a.* M17. [f. as prec. + -OUS.] †1 Having the nature or flavour of a flower or flowers. M–L17. 2 *Bot.* Composed of florets (FLORET *n.* 1(a)); *spec.* consisting entirely of disc florets. Of a floret: belonging to the disc, tubular. M18.

flos ferri /flɒs ˈfɛraɪ/ *n. phr.* M18. [L, lit. 'flower of iron'.] *Min.* A branching coral-like variety of aragonite, often occurring with haematite.

flosh *n.* see FLASH *n.*[1]

floss /flɒs/ *n.*[1] Chiefly *Orkney* & *Shetland*. E17. [Cf. Norw. dial. *flos*, *flus* a strip peeled off, *flysja* to peel.] The stems of the soft rush, *Juncus effusus*, esp. as used for thatch or woven into ropes.

floss /flɒs/ *n.*[2] M18. [OFr. *flosche* down, pile on velvet, mod. *floche*, as in *soie floche* floss-silk; ult. origin unkn.] 1 The rough silk surrounding a silkworm's cocoon; *transf.* the silky down in maize and certain other plants. Also = *floss-silk* below. M18. 2 A downy or fluffy surface. Also, an accumulation of flossy particles; fluff. L18. 3 In full *dental floss*. Floss-silk or similar thread used to clean between the teeth. E20. 4 Usu. *candyfloss*. A (usu. pink or white) mass of fluffy spun sugar. M20.

2 F. NORRIS Overlaying the flush of rose in her cheeks . . was a faint sheen of down, a lustrous floss. 4 *fig.* (*attrib.*): R. HOGGART Invitations to a candy-floss world: the newer mass art.

Comb.: **floss-silk** (*a*) the rough silk broken off in winding a cocoon, esp. as carded and used in the manufacture of common silk; (*b*) untwisted silk fibres used in embroidery and crewel work.

floss /flɒs/ *n.*[3] M19. [G *Floss*, cogn. w. FLOAT *n.*] *Metall.* The molten slag floating on the iron in a puddling furnace.

floss /flɒs/ *v.t.* & *i.* L20. [f. FLOSS *n.*[2]] Clean between (the teeth) with dental floss.

flossy /ˈflɒsi/ *a.* M19. [f. FLOSS *n.*[2] + -Y[1].] 1 Resembling or consisting of floss (FLOSS *n.*[2]). M19. 2 Excessively grand or stylish; fancy, showy. Also, saucy, 'fresh'. *N. Amer. colloq.* L19.

flossied *ppl a.* (*colloq.*) dressed *up* in a showy style M20.

flot /flɒt, *foreign* flo (*pl. same*)/ *n.* L19. [Fr., lit. 'wave'.] A trimming of lace or loops of ribbon, arranged in overlapping rows.

flota /ˈfləʊtə/ *n.* L17. [Sp. = fleet.] *Hist.* The Spanish fleet which used to cross the Atlantic and bring back the products of America and the W. Indies. Formerly also *gen.*, a fleet.

flotage *n.* var. of FLOATAGE.

flotant /ˈfləʊt(ə)nt/ *a.* E17. [Fr. *flottant* pres. pple of *flotter* to float.] *Her.* Of a banner, ship, etc.: floating (in the wind, water, etc.).

flotation /fləʊˈteɪʃ(ə)n/ *n.* Also **float-**. E19. [f. FLOAT *v.* + -ATION, after Fr. *flottaison*. The spelling *flot-* adopted to conform with *flotilla*.] 1 The action or process of floating in a liquid etc.; the condition of keeping afloat. E19. 2 The action of floating a company or enterprise. L19. 3 The separation of the components of crushed ore etc. by their different capacities to float on a given liquid. E20.

1 *centre of flotation*: see CENTRE *n.* **line** or **plane of flotation**: in which the horizontal surface of a fluid intersects a body floating in it. 3 **froth flotation**: in which a frothing agent is added to the liquid used, causing the valuable particles to collect in the surface bubbles.

†**flote** *n.*, *v.* vars. of FLOAT *n.*, *v.*

flote-grass /ˈfləʊtgrɑːs/ *n.* Also **float-grass**. LME. [f. *flote* obs. var. of FLOAT *n.*, *v.* + GRASS *n.*] Any of various grasses or (formerly) sedges of marshy or watery places; now usu. floating sweet-grass, *Glyceria fluitans*.

flotel *n.* var. of FLOATEL.

flotilla /fləˈtɪlə/ *n.* E18. [Sp., dim. of *flota* = Prov. *flota*, OFr. *flote* (mod. *flotte*) fleet: see FLOTA.] A small fleet; a fleet of boats or small vessels.

flotsam /ˈflɒts(ə)m/ *n.* Also (*dial.*) **floatsome** /ˈfləʊt-/, (*arch.*) **flotson** /ˈflɒts(ə)n/. E17. [AN *floteson*, f. *floter* FLOAT *v.* For the form cf. JETSAM; cf. also LAGAN, WAVESON.] 1 *Law.* Wreckage of a ship or its cargo found floating on the surface of the sea. Usu. assoc. w. JETSAM. E17. 2 Timber etc. washed down by a stream. Orig. *dial.* E19. 3 *transf.* & *fig.* Things (or persons) discarded as worthless. M19. 4 Newly ejected oyster-spawn. L19.

3 R. BUCHANAN A mania for buying all sorts of flotsam and jetsam. P. GALLICO The flotsam of bums, drifters and down-and-outers.

flounce /flaʊns/ *n.*[1] L16. [f. FLOUNCE *v.*[1]] A sudden fling or jerk of the body or of a limb or limbs; a plunging or flopping movement; usu. such a movement as an expression of annoyance, impatience, or disdain.

flounce /flaʊns/ *n.*[2] E18. [Alt. of earlier FROUNCE *n.*[1], prob. by assim. to FLOUNCE *v.*[1]] A wide ornamental strip of material gathered and sewn by its upper edge, esp. round a woman's skirt, so that its lower edge hangs full and free.

H. JAMES She was dressed in white muslin, with a hundred frills and flounces.

flounce /flaʊns/ *v.*[1] & *adv.* M16. [Origin uncertain: perh. conn. w. Norw. *flunsa* hurry, Sw. dial. *flunsa* fall with a splash, or perh. of imit. origin, as *bounce*, *pounce*.] A *v.* 1 *v.i.* Dash, flop, plunge; go with agitated or violent motion, esp. as an expression of anger or annoyance. (Foll. by *in*, *off*, *out*, etc.) M16. †2 *v.t.* Dash, drive, or fling violently. L16. 3 *v.i.* Of a person or animal: make abrupt or jerky movements with the body or limbs; throw the body about. E17.

1 T. FULLER He commanded them all at once to flounce into the river. A. BROOKNER She flounces into the bathroom and does not speak to him. R. COBB Adopting his high-and-mighty manner and flouncing out in a fury. 3 J. SHUTE When one hath struck a great fish, he plungeth and flounceth.

B *adv.* With a flounce. Now *rare.* L16.

flounce /flaʊns/ *v.*[2]*t.* L17. [Alt. of earlier FROUNCE *v.*: cf. FLOUNCE *n.*[2]] 1 Curl, frizz, trim. *rare.* L17. 2 Adorn or trim with a flounce or flounces. E18.

2 M. R. MITFORD Striped muslin to flounce my gowns.

flouncing *n.* (*a*) the action of putting a flounce on a garment; (*b*) a flounce, the material of which a flounce is made: M18.

flouncy /ˈflaʊnsi/ *a.* Also **-ey**. E19. [f. FLOUNCE *n.*[2] + -Y[1].] Having flounces, flounced.

flounder /ˈflaʊndə/ *n.*[1] ME. [AN *floundre* (AL *flundra*), OFr. (and mod. Norman dial.) *flondre*, prob. of Scand. origin (cf. OSw. *flundra*, Da. *flynder*, ON *flyðra*).] 1 A small flatfish, *Platichthys flesus*, found in European coastal waters and rivers. Also (w. specifying wd), any of numerous small flatfishes of the families Pleuronectidae and Bothidae. ME. 2 A thing resembling a flounder in appearance: (*a*) *dial.* a liver fluke; (*b*) a tool formerly used to shape the front of a boot. M19.

1 *witch flounder*: see WITCH *n.*^{3} *yellowtail flounder*: see YELLOWTAIL.

flounder /ˈflaʊndə/ *v.* & *n.*^{2} L16. [Imit. (perh. a blending of FOUNDER *v.* and BLUNDER *n.*, *v.*) on the basis of the frequency of *fl-* in wds expressing impetuous, clumsy, or rough movement, as *fling*, *flounce*.] A *v.* 1 *v.i.* Orig., stumble. Later, plunge or tumble about, move clumsily, struggle along, as or as if in mud or deep water. L16. †2 *v.t.* Cause to stumble or struggle; confound. M–L17. 3 *v.i. transf.* Make mistakes; struggle or show confusion in thoughts or words; manage something badly or with difficulty. L17.

1 V. WOOLF She would jump straight into a stream and flounder across. A. UTTLEY She floundered along, bumping into outstretched boughs, tripping over stones. 3 L. P. HARTLEY To flounder for ever in these cruel uncertainties. P. BARKER Knowing how to cope with situations that left other people floundering.

B *n.* The action of the vb; an instance of this. M19.

flounderer *n.* M19. **flounderingly** *adv.* in a floundering manner M20.

flour /ˈflaʊə/ *n.* Also †**flower**. See also FLOWER *n.* ME. [Orig. form of FLOWER *n.*, becoming differentiated in the sense 'the finest part of meal'; the spelling *flower* was also used in this sense until early 19.] I 1 Orig., the finest quality of meal. Hence, the finer part of the meal of wheat or other grain, obtained by bolting. Now *esp.* wheatmeal. ME. 2 Any fine soft powder, *esp.* that obtained by the grinding of seeds, farinaceous roots, etc. LME.

1 E. RAFFALD Rub a little of the butter into the flour. *plain flour*, *self-raising flour*, *wholemeal flour*, etc. *cornflour*: see CORN *n.*^{1} 2 SOUTHEY A vessel laden with manioc flour. *Science* Turbid water . . charged with comminuted rock debris or 'glacial flour'.

†II See FLOWER *n.*

Comb.: **flour beetle** a small beetle of the genus *Tribolium*, the larvae of which feed on flour; **flour-bolt, -bolter** a flour sieve.

flour /ˈflaʊə/ *v.* LME. [f. the n.] 1 *v.t.* Sprinkle or cover with flour. LME. 2 *v.t.* Grind into flour. *US.* E19. 3 *v.t.* & *i. Mining.* Break up (a metal, esp. mercury), be broken up, into small sulphide-coated particles. M19.

1 A. CARTER The morning sky . . was as white as if it had been floured. P. BARKER Her arms were floured half-way to the elbow. 2 **flouring mill** a mill for making flour, as distinct from a grist-mill.

flourish /ˈflʌrɪʃ/ *n.* LME. [f. the vb.] 1 The blossom on a fruit tree. *Sc.* & *north.* LME. †b The condition of being in blossom. L16–E19. c *fig.* Prosperity, vigour; perfection, prime. L16. †2 A prolusion; a piece of ornamental preamble, preliminary to serious discussion or business. M16–E17. 3 Ostentatious embellishment; gloss. Now *rare.* L16. 4 *Mus.* a A fanfare of horns, trumpets, etc. L16. b A florid passage or style of composition; a short extemporized prelude or ornamental addition. M17. 5 An ostentatious gesture made with a weapon or other instrument; *spec.* a graceful sweeping movement made with a weapon at the start of a fencing-match. E17. b *gen.* A showy or extravagant gesture. M18. 6 A literary or rhetorical embellishment; a florid expression. E17. 7 An ornament of flowing curves about a letter or word in handwriting. M17. b A florid decoration; scrollwork, tracery. L17.

1c SIR W. SCOTT The flourish of his powerful relative's fortunes had burst forth in the finery of his dress. *Times* Shares retreat after early flourish. 4a A. SETON There was a great flurry and a flourish of trumpets. *fig.* (*collect.*): J. ARCHER An oil rig which, with much flourish and advance publicity, he had towed out to the Prospecta Oil site. b A. RAMSAY The fine flourishes of new musick imported from Italy. 5 STEELE Before he applied his weapon to my chin, he gave me a flourish with it. b W. VAN T. CLARK She . . got back into the coach with a flourish of her skirts. C. HAMPTON With a flourish, he produces a cauliflower from the paper bag. 7 A. DESAI She wrote in long, spidery flourishes. b A. ALVAREZ An ornamental iron gateway, painted black, its flourishes picked out in gold.

flourishy *a.* L19.

flourish /ˈflʌrɪʃ/ *v.* ME. [(O)Fr. *floriss-* lengthened stem of *florir* (now *fleurir*) f. Proto-Romance alt. of L *florere*, f. *flos*, *flor-* FLOWER *n.*: see -ISH^{2}.] I Blossom, thrive. 1 *v.i.* Of a plant or tree: grow vigorously, thrive. ME. b Flower, blossom. *obs.* exc. *Sc.* ME. 2 *v.i.* Thrive, prosper, be successful. ME. †3 *v.i.* Display vigour *in*, *with*; abound *in*, overflow *with*. ME–E18. 4 *v.i.* a Spend one's life or be active during a specified period. Foll. by *in*, *at*, *about*, etc. LME. b Be at the height of fame or excellence, be in one's prime. Also (*colloq.*), be in good health. M16.

1 N. MOSLEY It was a marvel so many flowers could flourish near a desert. B. PLAIN Like weeds in . . rain it had flourished, spreading roots and . . tentacles. 2 G. GREENE I doubt . . whether a lion would flourish on green things. M. HOLROYD Old pagan festivals, long-forgotten elsewhere, still flourished. D. M. THOMAS As her playing improved . . her career began to flourish. 4a W. IRVING James flourished nearly about the time of Chaucer and Gower. b N. BALCHIN He said, 'How's Marcia?' . . I just said, 'Oh, flourishing.'

II Adorn. †5 *v.t.* Adorn with flowers or verdure; cause to bloom. ME–E17. †6 *v.t. gen.* Adorn, embellish, decorate. ME–E18. b Embellish (a book or writing); decorate, illuminate. LME–M17. 7†a *v.t.* Embellish (words, a speech) with rhetorical phrases or flowery expressions. ME–L17. b *v.i.* Speak floridly and copiously *on* or *upon*; use florid language. Now *rare.* E18.

III Display ostentatiously. 8a *v.t.* Wave (something) about ostentatiously; brandish (a weapon etc.). Also, move (the limbs) about vigorously. LME. b *v.i.* Of a weapon: be brandished. Long *rare.* LME. 9a *v.t.* Make a display or parade of; show ostentatiously. LME. b *v.i.* Make a flourish or parade; show off, brag, swagger. Now *rare.* M16. †10 *v.i. Mus.* Play a short extemporized prelude before the real performance. M16–E19. b Of trumpets: sound a fanfare. L16–E18. †11 *v.i.* Move with a flourish; make sweeping movements. *rare.* E–M18.

8 DICKENS Looking at the dwarf . . as he flourished his arms and legs about. C. MORGAN When he recognized her, he would clutch at the handkerchief . . and flourish it in the air. J. MONTAGUE He flourished a sabre to rally troops and plunge across the Somme. 9a W. GOLDING A huge hoarding which was flourishing beans . . ten feet in the air. D. M. THOMAS She stormed in . . She flourished before me two photographs.

flourisher *n.* LME. **flourishing** *n.* the action of the vb; an instance of this; a decoration, ornamental detail: ME. **flourishingly** *adv.* L15. **flourishment** *n.* (*rare*) prosperity, thriving E18.

floury /ˈflaʊəri/ *a.* LME. [f. FLOUR *n.* + -Y^{1}.] Covered with flour or powder; of or resembling flour.

floury miller an Australian cicada, *Abricta curvicosta*, whose body is covered with white down.

flout /flaʊt/ *v.* & *n.* M16. [Perh. f. Du. *fluiten* whistle, play the flute, hiss (*uitfluiten*); cf. synon. G colloq. *pfeifen auf* 'pipe at'.] A *v.t.* & *i.* Treat or behave with disdain; mock, jeer; express contempt (for) by action or speech. Now usu. denoting indirect expression: openly disregard (a law, an opinion, etc.). M16.

BROWNING Ah, you may flout and turn up your faces. G. SAINTSBURY Locke . . had expressly flouted (or rather . . denounced) poetry as idle and pernicious. R. MACAULAY Those who live loosely and flout the laws. M. FRAYN If one is flouting the generally accepted rules of behaviour one must exercise discretion. †**flouting-stock** (*a*) an object of mockery; (*b*) = FLOUT *n.*

B *n.* A mocking speech or action. L16.

flouter *n.* L16. **floutingly** *adv.* L16.

flow /fləʊ/ *n.*^{1} LME. [f. the vb.] 1 The action or fact of flowing. LME. b The quantity that flows; rate of flowing. E19. c That which flows; flowing liquid. E19. 2†a A deluge, a flood. LME–L16. b An overflowing; *spec.* a periodical overflow of the Nile or other river. E17. 3 The incoming or rise of the tide. (Opp. *ebb.*) L16. 4 Any continuous movement resembling the flow of a river and connoting a copious supply; an outpouring, a stream. M17. b The loose or undulating way in which a garment, outline, etc., flows or hangs. M19. 5 More fully *plastic flow*. A gradual permanent deformation of a solid under stress, without fracture or loss of cohesion. L19.

1 SHELLEY The flow Of sudden tears. H. READ The natural flow of water towards the lower level of the sea. R. L. BRUCKBERGER All networks of radio and television and the flow of their waves. b L. DEIGHTON At first the flow was no faster than a kitchen tap. c J. WILSON The still flow of this majestic river. 3 J. RUSKIN The Thames tide, with its tossing wherries at the flow. 4 N. MITFORD There were no more big house parties, but a continual flow of people. D. LODGE I tried to stem her flow of intimate reminiscence. C. PRIEST My creative energy was undiminished . . there was nothing that could . . obstruct the flow. b J. RUSKIN In the folds of the drapery . . is a flow like that of waves.

Phrases: **flow of soul** genial conversation (as complement to *feast of reason*). **flow of spirits** sudden or (now usu.) habitual cheerfulness. †**set one's eyes at flow** *rare* (Shakes.) (cause to) weep.

Comb.: **flow-blue** a blue colour applied to pottery or porcelain which diffuses readily through the glaze; **flow chart**, **diagram** a diagram showing the movement or action of persons or things in any complex system, as an industrial plant or a computer program; **flow-line** (*a*) *Physics* an imaginary curve drawn in a fluid such that at each point the direction of motion of the fluid is along the tangent to the curve at that point; (*b*) (in *pl.*) the lines that appear on the surface of wrought metal when polished or etched, indicating the direction of flow of the metal during working; (*c*) any of the related routes followed by goods, materials, etc., in the various stages of manufacture or treatment; a path depicted on a flow chart; **flow(-line) production** the continual passage of goods from one piece of equipment to another in the successive stages of production; **flow-meter** an instrument for measuring the rate of flow of gas, liquid fuel, etc.; **flow pipe** the pipe by which hot water leaves the boiler in a heating or hot water system; *flow production*: see *flow-line production* above; **flow sheet** = *flow chart* above; **flowstone** *Geol.* rock deposited by water flowing in a thin sheet; a rock formation so formed. **flow structure** *Geol.* the structure in igneous rock produced by the flow of the molten mass before solidification.

flow /fləʊ/ *n.*^{2} Chiefly *Sc.* L17. [Perh. f. Icel. (ON) *flói* of the same meaning, rel. to *flóa* FLOW *v.*] 1 In full *flow moss*. A watery swamp, a morass. L17. 2 A quicksand. E19.

1 *attrib.*: *Daily Telegraph* The 'flow' country of Caithness and Sutherland, an open peat bog.

flow /fləʊ/ *v.* Pa. t. **flowed** /fləʊd/; pa. pple **flowed** /fləʊd/, †**flown**. [OE *flōwan*, cogn. w. ON *flóa* flood, MLG *vlōien*, Du. *vloeien* flow, f. Gmc base of FLOOD *n.*] I Glide along as a stream. 1 *v.i.* Of fluids, a stream, etc.: glide or run along, move along in a current. (Foll. by *along*, *down*, *out*, etc.) OE. b Of blood or other bodily fluid: circulate within the vessels of the body. ME. c Foll. by *over*: overflow. Long *rare.* E16. †2 *v.i.* Become liquid, melt. OE–M18. 3 *v.i.* a Of people: come or go as a stream, move smoothly or in a crowd. LME. b Of things: move as a stream, run smoothly and easily. Of electricity: move as a current, circulate. Of money: circulate within the economy, be transferred. LME. 4 Of hair, a garment, etc.: hang easily and gracefully, lie in undulating curves, stream. LME. †5 *v.t.* Cause to flow or run; make fluid. LME–M17. 6 *v.i.* Of talk, literary style, etc.: proceed smoothly. L16. 7 *v.i. Math.* Increase or diminish continuously by infinitesimal quantities. *arch.* E18. 8 *v.i.* Of a solid: undergo plastic flow (see FLOW *n.*^{1} 5). L19.

1 H. ALLEN The water . . was soon seen and heard to be flowing away at a rapid rate. I. MCEWAN Usually the canal flows north, but today it was completely still. O. HENRY A little iron bridge . . under which the small tortuous river flows. *fig.*: G. GREENE The stream of the unconscious continues to flow undisturbed. c SHAKES. *Ant. & Cl.* My lord Who is so full of grace that it flows over On all that need. 3a T. S. ELIOT A crowd flowed over London Bridge, so many. b A. BEVAN Investment flowed freely from Europe to America. A. MILLER The emotion flowing between them prevents anyone from speaking. G. GREENE Along the route to Tanyin flowed a fast stream of . . cars. *Acorn User* Data can flow between computers . . in two directions simultaneously. 4 G. MILLAR Wavy, brown hair flowing glossily over his round head. 6 A. S. BYATT

The conversation . . flowed easily enough. S. BRETT I think my version flows better . . sounds more poetic.

II Stream forth. 9 *v.i.* Gush out, well forth, spring; (of blood) be shed. OE. **b** Issue *from, out of*; result *from.* ME. **c** Of a person: pour out one's feelings. L17. 10 *v.i.* Of the sea or a tidal river: rise and advance, be in flood. Freq. in *ebb and flow.* Cf. EBB *v.* 1. OE. †**b** Of a river, esp. the Nile: overflow. Cf. FLOWN *ppl a.*[1] 1. ME–E17. †**c** Of the eyes: become overfull, run (with tears). ME–E18. 11 *v.i.* †**a** Of wealth etc.: abound. Only in OE. **b** Of wine etc.: run abundantly, be poured out unstintingly. L15. 12 *v.i.* Foll. by *with*: abound in, be plentifully supplied with. Now *rare* exc. in allusion to biblical phr. below. ME. 13 *v.t.* Cover or fill with water, flood. Now *rare.* LME. **b** Cover with any liquid, as varnish or glaze. Now *rare.* M19. 14 *v.t.* Produce (a liquid or stream of liquid). *rare.* M16.

9 D. CARNEGIE The blood flowing from his wounds left a crimson trail. *transf.*: B. PLAIN Ferns flowed out of hanging baskets at the windows. **b** H. G. WELLS The broad principles of action that flow from this wide conception of socialism. **c** TENNYSON The mother flow'd in shallower acrimonies. 10 *fig.*: E. M. FORSTER Waves of emotion broke, as if a tide of passion was flowing through the . . air. 12 AV *Exod.* 3:8 A lande flowing with milke and hony.

Comb.: **flow-on** *n.* & *a.* (*Austral.*) (*a*) consequences; (*b*) (designating or pertaining to) a wage or salary adjustment made for certain workers as a consequence of adjustments already made for other related workers.

flowage *n.* (*a*) the act of flowing; flooded state; (*b*) plastic flow: M19.

flower /ˈflaʊə/ *n.* Also (earlier) †**flour**. See also FLOUR *n.* ME. [AN *flur*, OFr. *flor, flour* (mod. *fleur*), f. L *flos flor-*. The orig. sp. *flour* was disused by L17 exc. in its specialized sense (see FLOUR *n.*).] **I** 1 The seed-bearing part of a plant, consisting botanically of reproductive organs (stamens and/or carpels) typically surrounded by a (usu. coloured) corolla and a (usu. green) calyx (or sometimes by a calyx alone). In popular use, such an organ when brightly coloured and conspicuous; a blossom, a bloom. ME. 2 A blossom (and usu. its stalk) considered independently of the growing plant, esp. as used in groups for decoration or as a mark of honour or respect. ME. 3 A representation of a flower in painting, embroidery, architecture, etc.; *esp.* = FLEUR-DE-LIS 3. ME. **b** *Typogr.* A stylized ornament, often based on the shape of a flower, printed in rows to form a decorative border, heading, etc. L18. 4 *fig.* Formerly, virginity. Now, a precious possession, an adornment. ME. 5 *fig. The* finest individual(s) out of a number of persons or things; the pick. ME. **b** *The* finest embodiment *of* a quality. ME. **c** *The* choicest part *of* something; *the* essential part *of* a matter. Cf. FLOUR *n.* LME. 6 In *pl.* Rhetorical embellishments; fine phrases. LME. 7 A flowering plant; *esp.* one grown for its flowers. LME. 8 *fig.* The most active or vigorous period of a person's life; one's prime. Formerly also, the period of a person's greatest prosperity. LME. 9 *Chem.* The powdery form *of* a substance, esp. one obtained by sublimation. In later use only in *pl. arch.* LME. **b** Of a plant: the state of being in bloom. Chiefly as *in flower, into flower.* E17. 10 [After Fr. *fleurs*, perh. alt. of *flueurs*: see FLUOR.] In *pl.* The menstrual discharge. Now *rare* or *obs.* LME. 11 Any of various fungoid growths. M16.

1 N. E. HICKIN Damp hedges . . golden with the yellow daisy-like flowers of fleabane. 2 E. O'NEILL And me still goin' every day to put flowers on Maw's grave. S. HILL Dorothea . . went out into the garden to cut some flowers for Eleanor. **flower of the hour** *US* a plant of the mallow family, *Hibiscus trionum*, which has short-lived pale yellow flowers with a purple eye and is native in warmer parts of the Old World (and naturalized in N. America). *language of flowers*: see LANGUAGE *n.*[1] **no flowers (by request)** an intimation that no wreaths etc. are desired at a funeral. *the Hundred Flowers*: see HUNDRED *a.* 4 LD MACAULAY A precious prerogative which . . even the Whigs allowed to be a flower properly belonging to the Crown. 5 L. VAN DER POST The generation which lost its finest flower in the First World War. R. H. MORRIESON Yuh were the flower of the district, Natalie. **b** TENNYSON Lancelot, the flower of bravery. **c** J. GAY I sip the tea's delicious flower. CARLYLE The flower of the matter is . . that they sit in secret. 6 R. BOYLE Discourses not tricked up with Flowers of Rhetorick. 7 **flower of Jove** a woolly campion, *Lychnis flos-Jovis*, cultivated for its bright pink flowers. *bellflower, cuckoo-flower, flannel flower, monkey-flower, passion-flower, sunflower, wallflower*, etc. 8 J. WEBB Jeffery Monmouth was in his Flower Anno 1156. SIR W. SCOTT He is a man in the flower of life, about thirty. J. B. PRIESTLEY We looked like the affluent society in full flower. 9 *flowers of sulphur, zinc*: see SULPHUR *n.*, ZINC *n.* 11 **flower of wine** a scum formed by certain yeasts on fermenting wine. **flowers of tan** a mould, *Fuligo varians*, found on tanbark, dead wood, etc.

†**II** See FLOUR *n.*

Comb.: **flower arrangement** the art of arranging flowers in vases etc. for artistic effect; **flower-bed** a garden bed in which flowers are grown; **flower-bug** (orig. *US*) any of various predatory hemipteran insects of the family Anthocoridae, occurring in flowers, on foliage, etc.; **flower children** = *flower people* below; **flower-fence** a W. Indian leguminous shrub, *Caesalpinia pulcherrima*, used for hedging in the tropics; **flower-fly** a dipteran insect which frequents flowers, *esp.* one of the family Syrphidae (hoverflies); **flower-girl** (*a*) a woman selling flowers, *esp.* in the street; (*b*) a small girl carrying or scattering flowers in front of the bride at a wedding; **flower-head** *Bot.* a dense compact inflorescence; *spec.* = CAPITULUM (b); **flower-pecker** any of various oriental and Australasian passerine birds of the family Dicaeidae; **flower people** a class of hippies, prominent in the late 1960s, who carried flowers as emblems of peace and love; **flower-piece** a picture or arrangement of flowers; **flowerpot** a small vessel, typically of red earthenware or plastic and tapering downwards, for holding soil in which a plant or plants may be grown; **flower power** the ideas of flower people, regarded as an instrument for changing the world; **flower-spike** = SPIKE *n.*[1] 2.

flowerful *a.* having many flowers M19. **flowerless** *a.* not flowering or adorned with flowers; *flowerless plant* (Bot.), a cryptogam: L15. **flowerlessness** *n.* M19. **flower-like** *a.* & *adv.* (*a*) *adj.* resembling (that of) a flower; (*b*) *adv.* in the manner of a flower: E17.

flower /ˈflaʊə/ *v.* ME. [f. the n., prob. after OFr. *florir, flourir* FLOURISH *v.*] **I** *v.i.* 1 Come into or be in flower; blossom, bloom. ME. **b** *fig.* Foll. by *into, to*: develop into. M19. 2 *fig.* Be in or attain one's fullest perfection, the highest stage in one's development, etc. Formerly, foll. by *in, of*: thrive in respect of, abound in. ME. †3 Of beer or wine: froth, mantle. LME–M18.

1b E. J. HOWARD A contentment that flowered . . almost to ecstasy. *Philadelphia Inquirer* She has flowered into young womanhood. 2 DAY LEWIS We who 'flowered' in the Thirties/were an odd lot.

II *v.t.* 4 Cover (as) with flowers. Also foll. by *over.* Now *rare.* LME. 5 Decorate with (esp. embroidered) representations of flowers or with floral patterns. E16. 6 *Hort.* Induce (a plant) to flower. M19.

4 W. BARTRAM Its thick foliage . . is flowered over with large milk-white . . blossoms. 5 *transf.*: M. ARNOLD The frost flowers the whiten'd window-panes.

flowering *n.* (*a*) in *pl.* figures of flowers; †(*b*) *sing.* blossoms collectively; (*c*) the action of the vb, the process of coming into flower: ME.

flowerage /ˈflaʊərɪdʒ/ *n.* L17. [f. FLOWER *n.*, *v.* + -AGE.] †1 The hanging up of bunches of flowers. Only in L17. 2 The process or result of flowering; flowers collectively. M19.

flower-de-luce *n.* see FLEUR-DE-LIS.

flowered /ˈflaʊəd/ *a.* LME. [f. FLOWER *n.*, *v.*: see -ED[2], -ED[1].] 1 Covered with flowers; decorated with (esp. embroidered) representations of flowers. LME. 2 Bearing flowers of a specified kind or number. L16. †3 In flower. M17–L18.

flowerer /ˈflaʊərə/ *n.* L18. [f. FLOWER *v.* + -ER[1].] 1 A person who decorates china etc. with floral patterns. L18. 2 A plant that flowers in a specified manner or at a specified time. M19.

floweret /ˈflaʊərɪt/ *n.* LME. [f. FLOWER *n.* + -ET[1].] 1 A small flower. Chiefly *literary.* LME. 2 = FLORET *n.* 3. E20.

flowering /ˈflaʊərɪŋ/ *ppl a.* LME. [f. FLOWER *v.* + -ING[2].] †1 At the height of one's vigour, beauty, prosperity, etc.; flourishing. LME–E17. 2 Of a plant: that is in bloom. E16. 3 = FLOWERY *a.* 1. L16. 4 That bears (conspicuous) flowers. Chiefly in names of plants contrasted with similar or allied species in which the flowers are inconspicuous or absent. L17.

1 **flowering age, youth** the prime of life or youth. 4 **flowering cherry** any of several species of *Prunus* grown for their ornamental flowers (and not their fruit). *flowering* CURRANT. *flowering* DOGWOOD. **flowering fern** = *royal fern* s.v. ROYAL *a.* **flowering raspberry** an American bramble, *Rubus odoratus*, with large rose-purple flowers and leaves resembling those of the maple. **flowering rush** a tall monocotyledonous aquatic plant, *Butomus umbellatus* (family Butomaceae), with umbels of pinkish flowers and rushlike triquetrous leaves. *flowering* WILLOW.

flowery /ˈflaʊəri/ *a.* & *n.* LME. [f. FLOWER *n.* + -Y[1].] **A** *adj.* 1 Having many flowers, covered with flowers. LME. **b** Composed of flowers, of the nature of flowers. M17. 2 Ornamented with figures of flowers or floral designs. LME. **b** *Her.* = FLEURY *a.* Now *rare* or *obs.* L17. 3 Characterized by flowers of speech; full of fine words and phrases. E17.

1 **flowery dell** *rhyming slang* a cell. **Flowery Empire, Land**, etc. China. 3 B. TAYLOR Smyrna is . . called, in the flowery tongue of the East, the 'Ornament of Asia'.

B *n.* [Abbrev. of *flowery dell* above.] A (prison or police) cell. E20.

flowerily *adv.* L19. **floweriness** *n.* M18.

flowing /ˈfləʊɪŋ/ *n.* OE. [f. FLOW *v.* + -ING[1].] 1 The action of FLOW *v.* OE. 2 †**a** An overflowing, a flood. ME–M17. **b** That which flows or streams out; a stream, a wave. Now *rare.* LME.

flowing /ˈfləʊɪŋ/ *ppl a.* OE. [f. FLOW *v.* + -ING[2].] 1 That flows; gliding or running along. OE. 2 Rising like the tide; brimming, abundant, copious. E16. 3 Of language or style: gliding easily or smoothly, fluent. M16. **b** Of manner or demeanour: easy, graceful, smooth. E17. 4 Of hair, a garment, etc.: hanging easily and gracefully, streaming, unconfined. E17. 5 Of lines or contours: smoothly continuous, not rigid or abrupt. E18.

2 R. BURNS All-cheering Plenty, with her flowing horn. 3 G. HAKEWILL A great wit, and flowing eloquence. 5 JAMES SMITH Tracery is . . flowing, where the lines branch out into leaves, arches, &c.

Special collocations: **flowing sail** *Naut.* a full unconfined sail; *flowing sheet*: see SHEET *n.*[2]

flowingly *adv.* E17. **flowingness** *n.* E18.

flown /fləʊn/ *ppl a.*[1] *arch.* E16. [Obs. pa. pple of FLOW *v.*] 1 In flood; *fig.* swollen (*with*), puffed up. Now only in allusion to Milton (see below). E16. †2 *Naut.* Of a sheet: slackened to allow free movement in the wind. E17–M18.

1 MILTON Then wander forth the Sons of Belial, flown with insolence and wine.

flown /fləʊn/ *ppl a.*[2] E16. [pa. pple of FLY *v.*] That has flown or been flown. Also foll. by *out* and preceding adj. as *far-flown, new-flown*

flown cover *Philately* an envelope or cover dispatched by airmail.

flown *v.*[1] pa. pple of FLY *v.*

†**flown** *v.*[2] pa. pple of FLOW *v.*

flu /fluː/ *n.* Also **'flu**, †**flue**. M19. [Abbrev.] = INFLUENZA.

G. BARKER She's in bed, she's got the 'flu. *Asian flu*: see ASIAN *a.* *French flu*: see FRENCH *a.* GASTRIC *flu.*

†**fluate** *n.* & *v.* L18. [Fr., f. *fluor* FLUORINE + -ATE[1].] **A** *n.* 1 = FLUORIDE. L18–M19. 2 A fluosilicate applied as a solution to building stone to make it harder and more durable. Only in L19. **B** *v.t.* Treat (stone) with fluate. Only in L19.

flub /flʌb/ *v.* & *n.* *N. Amer. colloq.* E20. [Origin unkn.] **A** *v.t.* & *i.* Infl. **-bb-**. Botch, bungle, mess *up*; perform badly. E20. **B** *n.* Something badly or clumsily done; a slip-up. M20.

flubdub /ˈflʌbdʌb/ *n.* Chiefly *US.* L19. [Origin unkn.] Nonsense, undue fuss; bombastic or inept language.

R. KIPLING Any God's quantity of fuss and flubdub to bury a man.

†**fluce** *n.* var. of FLOOSE.

fluctuant /ˈflʌktjʊənt/ *a.* M16. [(O)Fr., pres. pple of OFr. *fluctuer* f. L *fluctuare*: see next, -ANT[1].] 1 Moving like waves. Chiefly *fig.*, unstable, wavering. M16. 2 Floating (as) on waves; buoyant. *rare.* E17.

1 R. L'ESTRANGE How is it possible for any man to be at rest in this fluctuant wandering humour and opinion? 2 BACON Fluctuant as the ark of Noah.

fluctuate /ˈflʌktʃʊeɪt, -tjʊ-/ *v.* M17. [L *fluctuat-* pa. ppl stem of *fluctuare* undulate, f. *fluctus* current, flow, wave, f. stem of *fluere* flow: see -ATE^3.] 1 *v.i.* Undulate; move like or (as) on waves. Now *rare* or *obs.* M17. b *v.t.* Unsettle; cause to undulate. *rare.* L18. 2 *v.i.* Vary irregularly, be unstable or unsettled; vacillate, waver. M17.

2 J. JAY The Committee .. fluctuates, new members constantly coming in, and old ones going out. V. WOOLF She fluctuated between irritation and interest.

fluctuation /flʌktʃʊˈeɪʃ(ə)n, -tjʊ-/ *n.* LME. [(O)Fr., or L *fluctuatio(n-)*, f. as prec.: see -ATION.] 1 Vacillation, wavering; an instance of this. LME. 2 The action or condition of passing irregularly between one state and another; repeated variation. E17. b An alternate rise and fall in amount or degree. E19. 3 *Med.* Of a swelling: a consistency indicating the presence of fluid. E17. 4 *lit.* A wavelike motion. Now *rare.* M17.

1 L. MURRAY We should be plunged into a state of uncertainty and fluctuation. 2 I. D'ISRAELI Every modern language has always existed in fluctuation and change. b R. OWEN Fluctuations in the electricity supply .. render digital clocks inaccurate.

fluctuational *a.* of, pertaining to, or of the nature of fluctuation E20.

fluctuous /ˈflʌktjʊəs/ *a.* Now *rare* or *obs.* L16. [L *fluctuosus* full of waves f. *fluctus* wave: see -OUS.] Full of, or resembling, waves.

flue /fluː/ *n.*^{1} Also **flew**. LME. [MDu. *vluwe* fishing net (Du. *flouw* snipe net).] A kind of fishing net, either fixed or towed. Also *flue net.*

flue /fluː/ *n.*^{2} LME. [Origin unkn.] †1 The mouthpiece of a hunting horn. Only in LME. 2 Orig., a chimney. Now, a smoke-duct in a chimney, a duct allowing the exit of hot gases from a furnace etc.; a channel for conveying heat, esp. a hot-air passage in a wall; a tube for heating water in some kinds of boiler. L16. 3 The spout in a pawn shop. *slang.* E19. 4 The airway of a flue-pipe in an organ. L19.

2 N. GORDIMER Like torn paper drawn up a flue by the draught of flames. 3 **in flue** in pawn. **up the flue** (*a*) in pawn; (*b*) in a bad way, lost, dead.

Comb.: **flue-boiler** a boiler whose water-space is traversed by flues; **flue-brush** a round or cylindrical brush of stiff bristle or wire for cleaning the inside of a chimney or flue; **flue-cure** *v.t.* cure (tobacco) by artificial heat from flues; **flue-dust** dust which collects in the flue of a furnace; *spec.* metalliferous dust collected in the flue of a metallurgical furnace; **flue-gas** any mixture of gases from the flues of chemical or smelting factories; **flue-pipe** an organ-pipe into which air enters directly, i.e. without striking a reed; **flue-stop** an organ-stop controlling a flue-register; **flue-work** the flue-stops of an organ collectively.

flued *ppl a.* having a flue or duct E19. **flueless** *a.* without a flue E20.

flue /fluː/ *n.*^{3} L16. [App. f. Flem. *vluwe* of same meaning: cf. FLUFF *n.*^{1}] 1 A woolly or downy substance; down, nap. L16. 2 Soft light particles, fluff. L18.

1 *Observer* Nabokov .. wrote about the flue of a nymphet's arm. 2 DICKENS Its old-established flue under its old-established four-post bedsteads.

fluey *a.* covered in flue E19.

†**flue** *n.*^{4} var. of FLU.

flue /fluː/ *a.*^{1} *obs.* exc. *dial.* Also **flew**. LME. [Origin unkn.] 1 Shallow. LME. 2 Having a wide opening, splayed. L17.

flue /fluː/ *a.*^{2} *obs.* exc. *dial.* Also **flew**. E17. [Origin unkn.] Weak, sickly, delicate.

flue /fluː/ *v.t.* & *i.* L18. [App. f. FLUE *a.*^{1}] Make or become wider or divergent; splay.

fluellen /flʊˈɛlɪn/ *n.* Also **fluellin**. M16. [Alt. of Welsh *llysiau Llywelyn* Llewelyn's herbs: cf. the pers. name *Fluellen* (= Llewellyn) in Shakes.] †1 Any of several kinds of speedwell; *esp.* heath speedwell, *Veronica officinalis.* Also *male fluellen.* M16–M18. 2 Either of two creeping yellow-flowered cornfield weeds allied to the snapdragon, *Kickxia spuria* (more fully *round-leaved fluellen*), and *K. elatine* (more fully *sharp-leaved fluellen*). Also †*female fluellen.* L16.

†**fluence** *n.*^{1} E17. [f. as FLUENCY: see -ENCE.] 1 A stream. Only in E17. 2 A smooth and easy flow (of words etc.); readiness of utterance. Only in 17.

fluence /ˈfluːəns/ *n.*^{2} *colloq.* Also **'f-**. E20. [Aphaeretic form of INFLUENCE *n.*] A mysterious, magical, or hypnotic power. Chiefly in *put the fluence on* (a person or thing).

M. PROCTER If ever I saw a girl trying to put the 'fluence on a fellow it was Tess.

fluency /ˈfluːənsi/ *n.* E17. [f. next + -ENCY.] †1 Copiousness, abundance. E17–E18. 2 A smooth and easy flow (of words, wit, etc.); ready utterance; ease and readiness in speech etc. M17.

2 J. W. EBSWORTH The genuine sweetness and musical fluency of his best lyrics. J. BARZUN Thanks to his fluency in French and German he was able .. to make his ideas known.

fluent /ˈfluːənt/ *a.* & *n.* L16. [L *fluent-* pres. ppl stem of *fluere* flow: see -ENT.] A *adj.* 1 †a Flowing freely or abundantly; abounding *in.* L16–L17. b Giving freely; generous. Long *obs.* exc. *dial.* E17. c Of hair: abundant, flowing. *arch.* & *poet.* E17. 2 Articulate, expressing oneself quickly and easily; *esp.* able to speak a (specified) foreign language easily and without hesitation. L16. b Of speech, style, etc.: flowing easily and readily. Of language: used with skill; *esp.* (of a foreign language) spoken with facility. E17. c Of movement etc.: easy, graceful; not rigid or stiff. M19. 3 Of a liquid, stream, etc.: that flows; flowing. Now chiefly *transf.* & *fig.* E17. 4 (Of a substance) ready to flow, fluid; *fig.* not settled, liable to change. *arch.* E17. 5 *Math.* Continuously increasing or decreasing infinitesimally. *arch.* M18.

2 A. G. GARDINER Fluent talkers are not necessarily good conversationalists. b GEO. ELIOT A soft voice with a clear fluent utterance. R. GRAVES Criccieth's mayor addressed them First in good Welsh and then in fluent English. c E. HEMINGWAY He .. played a smoothly fluent game of billiards that contrasted with his own ninety-four-year-old brittleness. 3 J. S. C. ABBOTT Masses of cavalry, in fluent and refluent surges. 4 WORDSWORTH His quick hand bestowed On fluent operations a fixed shape. E. B. BROWNING The broad, fluent strata of pure air.

B *n.* †1 A current of water, a stream. L16–E18. 2 *Math.* A fluent quantity (see sense A. 5 above). *arch.* M18.

†**fluential** *a.* (*Math.*) = FLUENT *a.* 5 L18–E19. **fluently** *adv.* E17.

fluff /flʌf/ *n.*^{1} L18. [Prob. dial. var. of FLUE *n.*^{3} Cf. Flem. *vluwe* fluff, Du. *fluweel* velvet.] 1 Any light, loosely adhering, or flocculent material, such as that which separates from blankets etc. L18. b Soft fur or down. L19. 2 A piece of downy or feathery material; a soft or downy mass or bunch. M19. 3 A mistake made in speaking, playing music, a game, etc.; orig. & freq. *Theatr.*, a mistake in delivering one's lines. *colloq.* L19. 4 Something unimportant, a trifle; *collect.* trivia. E20.

1 E. O'BRIEN I saw fluff and dust .. under the bed. 2 J. R. LOWELL Tiny fluffs of feathered life. T. HARDY All this fluff of muslin about you. 3 *Daily Telegraph* In spite of a surprising number of fluffs, there was some excellent playing. 4 *American Notes & Queries* The more immediate monetary rewards to be gained by starring in a piece of unchallenging romantic fluff.

Phrases: *bit of fluff*: see BIT *n.*^{2} 6.

fluff /flʌf/ *v.*^{1} & *n.*^{2} *Sc.* & *north.* L18. [Imit.] A *v.* 1 *v.i.* & *t.* (in *pass.*) (Cause to) puff, pant. L18. b *v.t.* Blow *out* (a candle etc.). E20. 2 *v.i.* Flutter; move in the wind. E19. 3 *v.i.* Make a fuss. M19. B *n.* A puff, a whiff; a short blast, a small explosion. E19.

fluff /flʌf/ *v.*^{2} E19. [f. FLUFF *n.*^{1}] 1 *slang.* a *v.t.* Falsify, disguise the defects of, obscure. E19. b *v.i.* Bluff, lie. E20. 2 *v.i.* Obtain money by devious means; give short change, solicit tips. *Railway slang.* L19. 3 *v.i.* & *t.* Make or become fluffy; shake or be shaken *up* or *out* into a soft fluffy mass. L19. 4 *v.t.* Make into fluff. L19. 5 *v.t.* Put a soft surface on (the flesh side of leather). L19. 6 *v.i.* Move or float softly; settle *down* like a ball of fluff. L19. 7 *v.t.* & *i.* Make a mistake esp. in a game or performance; blunder, bungle, fail. *colloq.* L19.

1 H. WILSON To reach a clear decision, with nothing fluffed or obscure. b M. GILBERT Watch him .. he's fluffing... He's acting. Dangerous man. 3 N. BLAKE Birds huddled in the snow-laden hedges, their plumage fluffed out. K. HOM There is no need to 'fluff' the rice before serving it. 6 W. C. RUSSELL A fog .. fluffing thick and soft as feathers about the ship. 7 *Daily Telegraph* The very best the Minister can hope for is that he will not fluff lines given to him by his officials. DAY LEWIS I kept fluffing when I practised them [songs].

fluffy /ˈflʌfi/ *a.* E19. [f. FLUFF *n.*^{1} + -Y^1.] 1 Consisting of or resembling fluff; soft, downy. E19. 2 Covered with fluff, down, fur, or the like. M19. 3 Vague, indecisive, uncertain; feather-brained; *spec.* (*Theatr.*) unsure of one's lines. *colloq.* L19.

fluffily *adv.* E20. **fluffiness** *n.* M19.

flugelhorn /ˈfluːg(ə)lhɔːn/ *n.* M19. [G *Flügelhorn*, f. *Flügel* wing + *Horn* HORN *n.*] A brass wind instrument with a cup-shaped mouthpiece and a wide conical bore.

fluid /ˈfluːɪd/ *a.* & *n.* LME. [(O)Fr. *fluide* or L *fluidus* f. *fluere* flow: see -ID^1.] A *adj.* 1 Flowing or moving readily, not solid or rigid; *Physics* (of a substance) that consists of particles moving freely among themselves, has no fixed shape, and yields easily to external pressure; *fig.* changing readily, not settled or stable. LME. †2 Of speech etc.: fluent. L17–L18. 3 Operating by means of a liquid; that uses a liquid to transmit power. M19.

1 C. LUCAS The salt fuses readily, and runs very fluid. H. ARENDT Shifting and fluid cliques of society. W. S. CHURCHILL A moment of great hesitancy .., when everything was fluid and uncertain. 3 *fluid clutch, fluid coupling, fluid drive, fluid flywheel*, etc.

B *n.* 1 A fluid substance; a liquid, a gas; *esp.* a liquid preparation having a specified purpose. M17. 2 *spec.* A liquid constituent or secretion of a living organism. E18. 3 Any of various all-pervading substances postulated to account for physical phenomena. Chiefly *Hist.* M18.

1 *brake fluid, cleaning fluid*, etc. *ideal fluid*: see IDEAL *a.* 2 *cerebrospinal fluid, seminal fluid, synovial fluid*, etc.

Special collocations & comb.: **fluid amplifier** a fluidic device in which small changes in a low-energy flow of fluid produce corresponding changes in a much larger flow. **fluid dra(ch)m** a unit of liquid capacity: in Britain, equal to ⅛ fluid ounce (0.217 cu. in., 3.56 cc); in the US equal to 0.225 cu. in., 3.69 cc (see also FLUIDRAM). **fluid extract** (also ***fluidextract**) a concentrated solution (usu. in alcohol) of the active principle of a vegetable drug prepared to a standard strength. **fluid gram** a unit of liquid capacity equal to 1 cm^3: see also FLUIGRAM. **fluid mechanics** the branch of mechanics that deals with the flow of fluids and the way they respond to and exert forces. **fluid ounce** (also ***fluidounce**) a unit of liquid capacity: in Britain equal to 1/20 imperial pint (1.734 cu. in., 28.42 cc), in the US equal to 1/16 US pint (1.804 cu. in., 29.56 cc).

fluidly *adv.* L17. **fluidness** *n.* (*rare*) M17.

fluidal /ˈfluːɪd(ə)l/ *a.* L19. [f. FLUID + -AL^1.] Of or pertaining to fluids or flowing; *spec.* (of rocks) showing evidence of a former fluid state.

fluidextract *n.* see *fluid extract* s.v. FLUID.

fluidible /ˈfluːɪdɪb(ə)l/ *a.* E20. [f. FLUID + -IBLE.] Capable of changing shape like a fluid under pressure.

fluidic /fluːˈɪdɪk/ *a.* L19. [f. FLUID + -IC.] 1 Of the nature of a fluid. L19. 2 *Spiritualism.* Of or pertaining to the astral body. L19. 3 Of or pertaining to fluidics. M20.

fluidics /fluːˈɪdɪks/ *n.pl.* (usu. treated as *sing.*). M20. [f. FLUID + -ICS: see -IC.] The technique of using small interacting flows and fluid jets to perform functions or operate systems; the branch of technology that deals with this.

fluidify /fluːˈɪdɪfʌɪ/ *v.t.* M19. [f. FLUID + -I- + -FY.] Make (a substance) fluid.

fluidifi'cation *n.* M20.

fluidise *v.* var. of FLUIDIZE.

fluidism /ˈfluːɪdɪz(ə)m/ *n.* M19. [f. FLUID + -ISM.] 1 The theory which refers all diseases to the state of the bodily fluids. *obs.* exc. *Hist.* M19. 2 *Spiritualism.* The hypothesis of the existence of supersensible fluidic bodies. L19.

fluidist *n.* a believer in fluidism (either sense) L19.

fluidity /fluːˈɪdɪti/ *n.* E17. [f. FLUID + -ITY.] 1 The quality, condition, or degree of being fluid. E17. 2 The quality (of speech, movement, etc.) of flowing smoothly, fluency. E17. 3 *transf.* & *fig.*: The ability or tendency to change; flexibility, instability. E19.

fluidize /ˈfluːɪdʌɪz/ *v.* Also **-ise**. E19. [f. FLUID + -IZE.] 1 *v.i.* & *t.* Make or become fluid. E19. 2 Cause (a mass of finely divided solid) to acquire the characteristics of a fluid by the upward passage of gas etc. through it. M20.
fluidiˈzation *n.* the process of fluidizing; the state of being fluidized: M20. **fluidizer** *n.* an apparatus in which fluidization is carried out M20.

fluidounce *n.* see *fluid ounce* s.v. FLUID *a.*

fluidram /ˈfluːɪdram/ *n. US.* Also **-drachm**. M19. [Contr.] = *fluid dra(ch)m* s.v. FLUID.

fluigram /ˈfluːɪgram/ *n. US.* Also **-gramme**. L19. [Contr.] = *fluid gram* s.v. FLUID.

fluke /fluːk/ *n.*[1] [OE *flōc*, corresp. to ON *flóki*, rel. by ablaut to MLG, MDu. *flac*, OHG *flah* (G *flach*) flat.] 1 A flatfish; *esp.* a flounder. Now chiefly *dial.* OE. 2 Any of various parasitic flatworms (trematodes); *esp.* (also *liver fluke*) *Fasciola hepatica*, which occurs in the livers of affected sheep and has an intermediate stage in snails of the genus *Limnaea*. M17. 3 A variety of kidney potato. M19.
fluked *a.* = FLUKY *a.*[1] M19.

fluke /fluːk/ *n.*[2] M16. [Perh. f. FLUKE *n.*[1], from the shape.] 1 Either of the broad triangular plates on the arms of an anchor. M16. b A barb or the barbed head of an arrow, lance, harpoon, etc. E17. 2 Either of the two lobes of a whale's tail. E18.

fluke /fluːk/ *n.*[3] M19. [Origin uncertain: perh. of dial. origin.] 1 Orig. in *Billiards* and other games: a chance lucky stroke. Now more widely: a piece of luck, an unexpected success, an unlikely chance occurrence. M19. 2 A puff *of* wind, a chance breeze. L19.
1 CLIVE JAMES A swimming pool which by some fluke did not contain a floating body. *attrib.*: *Daily Chronicle* It was no fluke victory. 2 QUILLER-COUCH Swaying this way and that . . as corn is swayed by flukes of summer wind.

fluke /fluːk/ *v.*[1] M19. [f. FLUKE *n.*[2]] 1 *v.i.* Of a whale: use the flukes in swimming, dive showing the flukes. M19. 2 *v.t.* Secure (a whale carcass) by a rope or chain around the tail. L19.

fluke /fluːk/ *v.*[2]*t.* & *i.* M19. [f. FLUKE *n.*[3]] Orig. in *Billiards* and other games: achieve by or make a lucky stroke. Now more widely: do, get, etc., (something) by luck rather than skill.
Times Bennett . . tried for a cannon, but fluked the white. N. GOULD Even if he managed to fluke home in this trial. J. I. M. STEWART If I did fluke a place at Oxford.

fluky /ˈfluːki/ *a.*[1] Also **-ey**. M19. [f. FLUKE *n.*[1] + -Y[1].] Infested with parasitic flukes.

fluky /ˈfluːki/ *a.*[2] Also **-ey**. M19. [f. FLUKE *n.*[3] + -Y[1].] Lucky, obtained by chance rather than skill. Of wind etc.: erratic, uncertain.
flukily *adv.* L19. **flukiness** *n.* L19.

flume /fluːm/ *n.* ME. [OFr. *flum*, *flun* f. L *flumen* river, f. *fluere* to flow.] †1 A river, a stream; water. ME–M17. 2 An artificial channel conveying water etc. for industrial use, esp. for the transport of logs or timber. M18. b A water-chute used as a fairground ride etc.; a water-slide. L20. 3 A deep narrow channel or ravine with a stream running through it. Orig. *US.* L18.
2 B. TAYLOR Wooden flumes, raised on tall tressels, brought water . . to the diggings.
Phrases: **be, go up the flume** (*US slang*) come to grief, die.

flume /fluːm/ *v.* M19. [f. the n.] 1 *v.i.* Build flumes for a watercourse. M19. 2 *v.t.* Convey in a flume. L19. 3 Take water from (a river etc.) by means of a flume. L19.

flummadiddle /ˈflʌmədɪd(ə)l/ *n. US.* Also **flummer-, fum(m)a-** /ˈfʌmə-/, & other vars. M19. [Prob. f. FLUMMERY *n.*] 1 A dish made with stale bread, pork-fat, molasses, and spices, baked in the oven. M19. 2 Nonsense, humbug; something trivial or ridiculous. M19.

flummer /ˈflʌmə/ *v.t.* Now *rare* or *obs.* In sense 2 also **flummery** /flʌm(ə)ri/. M16. [Sense 1 prob. imit.; in sense 2 perh. back-form. f. FLUMMERY *n.*] †1 Repeat indistinctly, mumble. Only in M16. 2 Flatter; deceive by flattery. M18.

flummerdiddle *n.* var. of FLUMMADIDDLE.

flummery /ˈflʌm(ə)ri/ *n.* E17. [Welsh *llymru*, perh. related to *llymrig* bare, soft, slippery.] 1 A dish made with boiled, jellied oat- or wheatmeal. E17. b Any of various sweet dishes made with milk, flour, eggs, gelatin, etc. L17. 2 Flattery, empty compliment; nonsense, humbug. M18. b *collect.* Trifles, useless trappings or ornaments. L19.
2 THACKERAY These petitioners . . begin with a fine flummery about the . . eminent genius of the person whom they are addressing. b A. FRASER Even the celebration of Christmas was denounced as being a piece of Popish flummery.

flummery *v.* see FLUMMER.

flummox /ˈflʌməks/ *v. colloq.* Also **-mux**. M19. [Prob. dial., imit.] 1 *v.t.* Bewilder, confuse, confound, perplex, disconcert. M19. 2 *v.i.* Give in, give up, collapse. *US.* M19.
1 M. AMIS I sat flummoxed and muttering like a superannuated ghost. *absol.*: L. MACNEICE Voices that flummox and fool. 2 D. P. THOMPSON If he should flummox at such a chance, I know of a chap . . who'll agree to take his place.

flump /flʌmp/ *n.* M18. [f. the vb.] The action or sound of flumping; a heavy dull thud.

flump /flʌmp/ *v.* E17. [Imit.] 1 *v.i.* Fall or move heavily, flop *down*, with a dull noise. E17. 2 *v.t.* Set or throw *down* with a soft thud. E19.

flung *v.* pa. t. & pple of FLING *v.*

flunk /flʌŋk/ *v.* & *n.* Orig. *US.* E19. [Origin uncertain: cf. FUNK *n.*[3] & *v.*[2]] A *v.* 1 *v.i.* Give up, back down, fail utterly (also foll. by *out*). E19. b *spec.* Fail in an examination; (foll. by *out*) leave or be dismissed from school etc. because of academic failure. M19. 2 *v.t.* Fail (an examination); reject (an examination candidate). M19.
1b M. J. BRUCCOLI Fitzgerald came close to flunking out . . when he failed three of his six courses. 2 *Times* I was utterly . . depressed and flunked my A levels. A. MILLER If you don't start studyin' math he's gonna flunk you, and you won't graduate.
B *n.* A complete failure, esp. in an examination. M19.
flunker *n.* a person who fails an examination L19.

flunkey /ˈflʌŋki/ *n.*[1] Orig. *Sc.* Also **-ky**. M18. [Perh. rel. to FLANKER 'a person who stands at one's flank': see -Y[6].] 1 A liveried manservant, a footman; a menial attendant. Usu. *derog.* M18. 2 An obsequious or fawning person; a toady, a snob. M19. 3 A cook, kitchen-hand, or waiter. *US.* E20.
1 A. CARTER A braided, bewigged flunkey brought us a silver bucket of iced champagne. H. ROBBINS Now he wants me to buy him some flowers for a dame. . . I'm nothing but a flunkey around here.
flunkeydom *n.* the domain of flunkeys; flunkeys collectively; the spirit of a flunkey: M19. **flunkeyiˈana** *n. collect.* the sayings or characteristics of flunkeys M19. **flunkeyism** *n.* the manner, speech, etc., of a flunkey M19.

flunkey /ˈflʌŋki/ *n.*[2] *US.* M19. [f. FLUNK + -Y[6].] A person who fails, esp. in an examination; one who comes to grief through ignorance, a mug.

fluo- /ˈfluːəʊ/ *comb. form* of FLUORINE: see -O-. Cf. FLUORO-.
fluoˈborate *n.* a salt of fluoboric acid, containing the anion BF_4^- E19. **fluoˈboric** *a.* containing fluorine and boron; esp. in *fluoboric acid*, a strong acid, HBF_4, known only in aqueous solution: E19. **fluoˈcerite** *n.* (*Min.*) a hexagonal fluoride of cerium, lanthanum, and related elements, usu. occurring as colourless to pink prisms or tabular crystals M19. **fluoˈphosphate** *n.* a mineral or other substance that is both a fluoride and a phosphate L19. **fluoˈsilicate** *n.* a salt of fluosilicic acid, containing the anion SiF_6^{2-} M19. **fluosiˈlicic** *a.*: *fluosilicic acid*, a strong acid, H_2SiF_6, known in aqueous solution or as hydrates E19.

fluor /ˈfluːə/ *n.* E17. [L = flow, f. *fluere* to flow: see -OR. Cf. Fr. †*flueur*.] †1 In *pl.* The menstrual discharge. Cf. FLOWER *n.* 10. E–M17. †2 A flow, a flowing; a stream; an effluvium. M–L17. †3 A fluid state; a fluid mass; (in *pl.*) 'the humours' of the body. M17–E18. 4 *Min.* a [tr. G *Fluss*.] Any mineral of a kind less hard and more fusible than gems. Long *obs.* exc. *Hist.* M17. b A fluorine-containing mineral of this kind. Now *spec.* = FLUORSPAR. *arch.* L18.

fluor- *comb. form* see FLUORO-.

fluoranthene /flʊəˈranθiːn/ *n.* L19. [f. FLUORO- (the compound fluoresces) + PHEN)ANTH(R)ENE.] *Chem.* A crystalline tetracyclic aromatic hydrocarbon, $C_{16}H_{10}$, obtained from coal tar; any derivative of this.

fluorated /ˈflʊəreɪtɪd/ *a.* L18. [f. FLUOR- + -ATE[2] + -ED[1].] *Chem.* Combined with fluorine or hydrofluoric acid.

fluorene /ˈflʊəriːn/ *n.* L19. [f. FLUORO- (the compound fluoresces) + -ENE.] *Chem.* A crystalline tricyclic aromatic hydrocarbon, $C_{13}H_{10}$, obtained from coal tar; any derivative of this.

fluoresce /flʊəˈrɛs/ *v.i.* L19. [Back-form. f. FLUORESCENCE.] Exhibit fluorescence, be fluorescent.
fluorescer *n.* a fluorescent substance E20.

fluorescein /ˈflʊərəsiːn, -sɪn/ *n.* L19. [f. FLUORESCENCE + -EIN.] *Chem.* An orange-red crystalline solid, $C_{20}H_{12}O_5$, obtained by reaction of resorcinol and phthalic anhydride, which exhibits greenish-yellow fluorescence in visible light, is often used in solution as a marker or indicator, and has antiseptic properties.

fluorescence /flʊəˈrɛs(ə)ns, flɔː-/ *n.* M19. [f. FLUORSPAR (which exhibits this property) + -ESCENCE.] Electromagnetic radiation emitted by certain substances when they are subject to incident radiation (esp. violet or ultraviolet light or X-rays), electrons, or other particles; the property of absorbing light of short (freq. invisible) wavelength and emitting light of longer (visible) wavelength. Cf. PHOSPHORESCENCE.

fluorescent /flʊəˈrɛs(ə)nt, flɔː-/ *a.* M19. [f. as prec. + -ESCENT.] Having the property of or emitting fluorescence; pertaining to, resulting from, or of the nature of fluorescence.
fluorescent lamp, light, etc.: in which light is produced by fluorescence; *esp.* a discharge tube in which a phosphor on the inside of the tube is made to fluoresce by ultraviolet light from mercury vapour. **fluorescent screen** a screen coated with fluorescent material for displaying images produced by incident X-rays, electrons, or other radiation.
fluorescently *adv.* M20.

fluorian /ˈflʊərɪən/ *a.* M20. [f. FLUORINE + -IAN.] *Min.* Having a constituent element partly replaced by fluorine.

fluoric /ˈflʊərɪk/ *a.* L18. [Fr. †*fluorique*, f. *fluor* FLUOR: see -IC.] Of fluorine or fluorspar; †*fluoric acid*, hydrofluoric acid.

fluoridate /ˈflʊərɪdeɪt, ˈflɔː-/ *v.* M20. [Back-form. f. next.] 1 *v.t.* & *i.* Add traces of a fluoride or other source of fluoride ions to (water, toothpaste, food, etc.) in order to reduce or prevent tooth-decay. M20. 2 *v.t.* Treat (teeth) with a preparation containing fluoride. M20.

fluoridation /flʊərɪˈdeɪʃ(ə)n, flɔː-/ *n.* E20. [f. FLUORIDE + -ATION.] 1 The process by which a mineral absorbs fluorine. E20. 2 The addition of traces of a fluoride to drinking-water to prevent or reduce tooth-decay. M20. 3 = FLUORIDIZATION 2. M20.
fluoridationist *n.* a person who advocates the fluoridation of public water supplies M20.

fluoride /ˈflʊərʌɪd, flɔː-/ *n.* E19. [f. FLUORINE + -IDE.] *Chem.* A compound of fluorine with a less electronegative element or radical; a salt or ester of hydrofluoric acid.

fluoridization /ˌflʊərɪdʌɪˈzeɪʃ(ə)n, ˌflɔː-/ *n.* Also **-isation**. M20. [f. prec. + -IZATION.] 1 = FLUORIDATION 2. M20. 2 The application of a fluoride to the teeth to prevent or reduce decay. M20.
fluoridize *v.t.* M20.

fluorimeter /flʊəˈrɪmɪtə/ *n.* E20. [f. FLUOR(ESCENCE + -IMETER.] = FLUOROMETER 2.
fluoriˈmetric *a.* L20. **fluoriˈmetrically** *adv.* M20. **fluoˈrimetry** *n.* E20.

fluorinate /ˈflʊərɪneɪt, ˈflɔː-/ *v.t.* M20. [f. FLUORINE + -ATE³.] Treat with fluorine; *Chem.* introduce one or more fluorine atoms into (a compound or molecule), usu. in place of hydrogen. Also, fluoridate. Freq. as *fluorinated* ppl a.

fluoriˈnation *n.* M20.

fluorine /ˈflʊəriːn, ˈflɔː-/ *n.* E19. [f. FLUOR + -INE⁵.] An extremely reactive pale yellow gaseous chemical element, atomic no. 9, belonging to the halogen group. (Symbol F.)

fluorite /ˈflʊərʌɪt, ˈflɔː-/ *n.* M19. [f. FLUOR + -ITE¹.] *Min.* = FLUORSPAR.

fluoro- /ˈflʊərəʊ, ˈflɔː-/ *comb. form* of FLUORINE (less commonly FLUORIDE) or FLUORESCENCE: see -O-. Bef. a vowel also **fluor-**. Cf. FLUO-.

fluoˈrapatite *n.* (*Min.*) a variety of apatite containing a substantially higher proportion of fluorine than of chlorine M19. **fluoroˈcarbon** *n.* any of a large class of synthetic, chemically stable compounds of carbon and fluorine M20. **ˈfluoroform** *n.* an unreactive gas, CHF_3, that is the fluorine analogue of chloroform L19. **fluorophoˈtometer** *n.* a fluorometer (sense 2) incorporating a photometer E20. **fluorophotoˈmetric** *a.* of or pertaining to fluorophotometry M20. **fluorophoˈtometry** *n.* the use of the fluorophotometer M20. **fluoˈrosis** *n.* (a diseased state due to) poisoning by a fluorine compound E20.

fluorometer /flʊəˈrɒmɪtə, flɔː-/ *n.* L19. [f. prec. + -METER.] **1** A device used to measure the intensity of a fluoroscopic image. L19. **2** An instrument for measuring the intensity or other property of fluorescence. E20.

fluoroˈmetric *a.* of or pertaining to the fluorometer (sense 2) or fluorometry E20. **fluoroˈmetrically** *adv.* M20. **fluorometry** *n.* the use of a fluorometer (sense 2) E20.

fluoroscope /ˈflʊərəskəʊp, ˈflɔː-/ *n.* L19. [f. FLUORO- + -SCOPE.] An instrument with a fluorescent screen which is used with an X-ray source to give a visible X-ray image of an object.

fluoroˈscopic *a.* of or pertaining to a fluoroscope or fluoroscopy L19. **fluoroˈscopically** *adv.* M20. **fluoˈroscopy** *n.* the use of a fluoroscope L19.

fluorspar /ˈflʊəspɑː/ *n.* L18. [f. FLUOR + SPAR *n.*³] Calcium fluoride, CaF_2, occurring as a transparent or translucent mineral (colourless when pure but often variously coloured by impurities) which crystallizes in the cubic system and is used ornamentally and as a metallurgical flux. Cf. FLUOR *n.* 4b.

fluphenazine /fluːˈfɛnəziːn/ *n.* M20. [f. FLU(ORO- + PHEN(OTHI)AZINE.] *Pharm.* A phenothiazine derivative, $C_{22}H_{26}F_3N_3OS$, used as a tranquillizer.

¶A proprietary name for this drug in the US is PROLIXIN.

flurazepam /flʊəˈreɪzɪpam, -ˈraz-/ *n.* M20. [f. FLU(O)R(O- after DIAZEPAM.] *Pharm.* A benzodiazepine widely used as a hypnotic.

flurr /fləː/ *v.* Now *rare* or *obs.* M17. [Imit.] **1** *v.t.* Scatter, throw about. M17. **2** *v.i.* Fly up; whirr, flutter. L17.

flurry /ˈflʌri/ *n.* & *v.* L17. [f. prec., prob. after HURRY *n.*, *v.*] **A** *n.* **1** A sudden agitation of the air; a gust or squall. L17. **b** A sudden shower (*of* snow, rain, etc.); a rush (*of* birds etc.). Orig. *US.* L17. **2** A sudden commotion or excitement; nervous agitation or hurry; a sudden burst of activity. E18.

1 SWIFT The boat was overset by a sudden flurry from the north. b P. G. WODEHOUSE A scrambling flurry of blows at close quarters, and then . . they fell together. V. BRITTAIN An icy wind drove flurries of snow into my face. 2 W. IRVING How happy I was to . . leave behind me the hurry and worry and flurry of the city.

B *v.* **1** *v.t.* Confuse or agitate (as) by haste, noise, etc. M18. **2** *v.i.* Agitate the air; come down in flurries. L19.

1 F. BURNEY This flurried me violently, insomuch that my memory failed me. 2 E. P. ROE The petals of the cherry were flurrying down like snow in every passing breeze.

flurriedly *adv.* in a flurried manner M19.

flus *n.* var. of FLOOSE.

flush /flʌʃ/ *n.*¹ LME. [Var. of FLASH *n.*¹] A pool, a marshy place; = FLASH *n.*¹ 1. Now chiefly *Ecol.*, a piece of wet ground over which water flows but not in a definite channel.

flush /flʌʃ/ *n.*² E16. [Rel. to FLUSH *v.*¹] **I 1** A sudden rush of water, esp. as caused for a specific purpose. E16. **b** The stream from a mill-wheel. E19. **2** A (sudden) abundance or rush (*of* anything); *esp.* (*a*) a rush of emotion, elation produced by success, victory, etc., (*b*) a fresh growth (of grass etc.), freshness, vigour. Freq. *in the first flush, in full flush.* E16. **b** A flight of birds suddenly started up. L16. **3** The action of or a device for cleansing a drain, water-closet, etc., by flushing. L19.

2 J. T. STORY You do things in the early flush of marriage that you prefer to forget later on. P. V. WHITE Let me bring you the roses . . There's such a flush. D. ATTENBOROUGH The frogs feast on the great flush of insects that have . . come with the rain. 3 C. BEATON Her lavatory . . equipped with a gold handle which one pulled . . to bring about a discreetly gurgling flush of water. attrib.: *flush lavatory, toilet,* etc.

II 4 A glow of light or colour; *esp.* (a rush of blood causing) a reddening of the face, neck, etc. M17.

4 A. GUINNESS I felt an angry flush beginning to rise to my face. **hectic flush**: occurring in some wasting diseases. *hot flush*: see HOT *a.*

flush /flʌʃ/ *n.*³ E16. [Fr. †*flus, flux* (whence Flem. *fluys* and Sp. *flux*, It. †*flusso*) f. L *fluxus* FLUX *n.*] *Cards.* A hand of cards all of one suit, or including a prescribed number of one suit.

royal (straight) flush *Poker* a straight flush headed by an ace. **straight flush** a flush that is also a sequence.

flush /flʌʃ/ *a.*¹ M16. [Prob. rel. to FLUSH *v.*¹] **1** †**a** Lacking nothing, perfect. Only in M16. **b** Full to overflowing; *esp.* (of a stream etc.) in flood. E17. **c** Full of life or enthusiasm; vigorous. Now *rare* or *obs.* E17. **2** Plentifully supplied, esp. with money (foll. by *with, of*); prosperous; (of money) plentiful. L16. **b** Lavish, generous. *dial.* E18. **3** Blushing; flushed. *arch.* L16. **4** Even, level, in the same plane (*with* the adjacent surface); *spec.* (of a ship's deck) on one level. E17. **b** *Typogr.* Not indented or protruding. E20.

1c H. BROOKE Both appeared quite flush and confident of victory. 2 P. KAVANAGH Money was flush in those days and flowed . . freely. N. MAILER If . . you are flush and have a few dollars to spare, I'm sure my mother could use it. 3 M. DRAYTON Thy Cheeke, now flush with Roses. 4 JAS. GRANT The original castle starts flush from the edge of the rock. B. COTTLE The one high-walled mansion not flush with the line of the town street.

Comb.: **flush-decker** a ship with a flush deck.

flushness *n.* M17. **flushy** *a.* (now *rare*) E18.

flush /flʌʃ/ *a.*² L16. [f. FLUSH *n.*³] *Cards.* Orig., (of a player) holding a flush. Now usu. (of a hand or sequence) forming or including a flush.

flush /flʌʃ/ *v.*¹ ME. [Prob. imit. Perh. infl. by FLASH *v.*] **1** *v.i.* Move rapidly, dart, spring; *esp.* (of a bird) fly up suddenly, start up. ME. †**b** Of people: rush, swarm. LME–M17. **2** *v.t.* Cause (esp. a gamebird) to fly or start up; put up. L15. **b** Reveal; bring into the open; drive *out.* M20. **3** *v.i.* & *t.* (Cause to) spurt, rush out or flow with sudden violence. Now *rare.* M16. **4** *v.i.* Of blood: rush into and redden the face etc.; (of the face etc.) become red or hot, blush. L16. **b** *v.t.* Make red or ruddy; cause to blush or colour. Chiefly as *flushed* pa. pple. L17. **5** *v.i.* & *t.* (Cause to) glow *with* colour, light, etc. M17. **6** *v.t.* Inflame with pride or passion; encourage. Chiefly as *flushed* pa. pple. M17. **7** *v.t.* Fatten *up* (sheep); stimulate (ewes) with a good diet in the breeding season. M18. **8** *v.t.* Cleanse (a drain, lavatory, etc.) by a flow of water; dispose of anything thus (foll. by *away, down*). L18. **b** Flood (a meadow etc). M19. **9** *v.i.* Of a plant: send out shoots. E19. **b** *v.t.* Cause (a plant) to send out shoots. L19.

1 F. NORRIS With a startling rush of wings, a covey of quail flushed from the brush. 2 P. SCOTT A plan for flushing the tiger and driving it . . on to the guns. b R. H. MORRIESON The enthralled hush . . flushed a still sulking Herbert out of the bedroom. 3 J. RAY Milk . . heated to such a degree doth suddenly . . flush up and run over. 4 DRYDEN What means . . That blood, which flushes guilty in your face? H. JAMES She thrilled, she consciously flushed, and all to turn pale again. b W. COWPER Flushed with drunkenness. 5 J. R. LOWELL A meadow flushed with primroses. 6 BURKE Flushed with the insolence of their first inglorious victories.

flusher *n.* (also *flusherman*) a person employed to flush sewers M19. **flushing** *n.* the action of the vb; an instance of this: LME.

flush /flʌʃ/ *v.*²*t.* M19. [f. FLUSH *a.*¹ 4.] Make flush or level; fill in (a joint etc.) level with a surface; point.

flush /flʌʃ/ *adv.* E18. [f. FLUSH *a.*¹] With direct force or full effect; squarely. Also, level; (formerly) directly, straight.

Flushing /ˈflʌʃɪŋ/ *n.* M19. [A port in the Netherlands (Du. *Vlissingen*).] A type of rough, thick woollen cloth. Freq. *attrib.*

Flushinger /ˈflʌʃɪŋə/ *n.* L17. [f. as prec. + -ER¹.] *Hist.* A ship or sailor from Flushing.

flusker /ˈflʌskə/ *v. obs.* exc. *dial.* M17. [Prob. imit.: cf. FLUSH *v.*¹] **1** *v.i.* Flutter, fly erratically. M17. **2** *v.t.* In *pass.* Be flustered, confused. M19.

fluster /ˈflʌstə/ *v.* & *n.* E17. [Origin uncertain; perh. rel. to Icel. *flaustur* hurry, *flaustra* to bustle.] **A** *v.* **1** *v.t.* Confuse with drink, render slightly intoxicated. Passing into sense 3. E17. **2** *v.i.* Be excited, eager, or agitated; bustle. Now *rare.* E17. **3** *v.t.* Flurry, confuse, make nervous. Cf. sense 1 above. E18.

1 THACKERAY His head is flustered with burgundy. 2 P. KAVANAGH The mother flustered around the returned son, helping him off with his coat. 3 I. WALLACE The degree to which the news had flustered him was a surprise.

B *n.* Flurry, flutter, agitation; a confused or agitated state. Formerly also, an impressive bustle or show of activity. L17.

DAY LEWIS As a result of . . arriving a whole day late . . I got into a fearful fluster.

flustered *ppl a.* fuddled; confused, agitated, flurried: E17.

flustrate /ˈflʌstreɪt/ *v.t. arch. colloq.* E18. [f. FLUSTER *v.* + -ATE³.] = FLUSTER *v.* 1, 3.

fluˈstration *n.* M18.

flute /fluːt/ *n.*¹ ME. [OFr. *flahute, fleüte, flaüte* (mod. *flûte*) prob f. Prov. *flaüt*, perh. a blend of *flaujol* (see FLAGEOLET *n.*¹) and *laüt* LUTE *n.*¹] **1** A reedless woodwind instrument of cylindrical shape having holes along it stopped by fingers or keys, orig. with the mouthpiece at one end, now in the side near one end. ME. **b** A player of this instrument. M16. **2** An organ-stop similar in tone to this instrument. Also *flute-stop.* E17. **3** A tall slender wineglass used esp. for sparkling wine. M17. **4** A semicylindrical (longitudinal) groove: *spec.* (*Archit.*) in a column. M17.

1 **English flute** a recorder. *nose-flute*: see NOSE *n.* *transverse flute*: see TRANSVERSE *a.* *whistle and flute*: see WHISTLE *n.* 1c.

flutelike *a.* resembling (that of) a flute E18. †**flutenist** *n.* = FLUTIST M17–E18. **flutist** *n.* a flute player (cf. FLAUTIST) E17.

flute /fluːt/ *n.*² M16. [Sense 1 f. Du. *fluit* lit. = FLUTE *n.*¹; sense 2 f. Fr. *flûte*, of unkn. origin.] *Naut.* (now *Hist.*). **1** A Dutch sailing vessel with a rounded stern. M16. **2** A warship serving as a transport, with part of her armament removed. M17.

flute /fluːt/ *v.* LME. [f. FLUTE *n.*¹] **I 1** *v.i.* Play a flute or pipe. LME. **b** *v.t.* Play (a tune etc.) on a flute or pipe. M19. **2** *v.i.* & *t.* Whistle, sing, or speak, in flutelike tones. E19.

2 TENNYSON Some . . swan . . fluting a wild carol ere her death. S. O'FAOLÁIN The doves fluting long and slow in the deep woods. S. J. PERELMAN 'Too too divine having you,' she fluted.

II 3 *v.t.* Make flutes or grooves in; provide with or arrange in flutes. L16. **b** *v.i.* Hang or jut *out* in flutes. L19.

fluted *ppl a.* (*a*) having grooves or flutes; arranged in flutes; (*b*) having the tonal quality of a flute: E17. **fluter** *n.* (now *rare*) a flute player ME.

flutey *a.* var. of FLUTY.

fluting /ˈfluːtɪŋ/ *n.* L15. [f. FLUTE *v.* + -ING¹.] **1** The action of playing on the flute or making flutelike sounds; an instance of this. L15. **2** = FLUTE *n.*¹ 4. E17. **3** The action of making flutes in columns etc.; ornamentation with flutes; fluted work. E18.

flutter /ˈflʌtə/ *n.* M17. [f. the vb.] **1** The action or state of fluttering; vibration; an instance of this. M17. **b** *Med.* Abnormal rapid rhythmic contractions, esp. of the atrium of the heart. E20. **c** An (undesirable) oscillation of a wing or other part of an aircraft under stress. E20. **d** A rapid variation in the pitch or loudness of a sound, not audible as such but heard as distortion; a property in a reproducer that gives rise to this. Cf. WOW *n.*[1] 2. E20. †**2** Ostentatious display or fuss. M17–E19. **3** (A state of) tremulous excitement or agitation; esp. in *in a flutter*, (*colloq.*) *all of a flutter*. M18. **4** A small bet or speculation. *slang.* L19.

1 ADDISON An infinite Variety of Motions to be made use of in the flutter of a Fan. G. K. CHESTERTON The fine French kings came over in a flutter of flags and dames. *cause a flutter among the dovecots*: see DOVECOT. 2 R. BENTLEY They . . make a mighty flutter and triumph. 3 J. W. CROKER The flutter of her nerves . . makes her very miserable. DICKENS He immediately . . fell into a great flutter. 4 P. G. WODEHOUSE Here we all are—you with the money, me with the book— . . let's have a little flutter.

Comb.: **flutter-mill** *US* a mill worked by a flutter-wheel; **flutter-tongue** *n.* & *v.* (*a*) *n.* rapid tonguing used in playing wind instruments (freq. *attrib.*); (*b*) *v.t.* & *i.* perform or play (with) rapid tonguing; **flutter-wheel** a small water-wheel worked by the impact of a rapid stream of water from a chute.

flutter /ˈflʌtə/ *v.* [OE *floterian*, *-orian* frequent. of Gmc base of FLEET *v.*[1]: see -ER[5]. Cf. synon. G *flattern*, †*flotteren*, †*flutteren*.] †**1** *v.i.* Float about on water. OE–L18. **2** *v.i.* Of a bird, insect, etc.: flap the wings in a quivering manner in short flights or while stationary; fly in quick irregular movements. OE. **b** *v.t.* Move (something) *away* etc. by a quivering action (of the wings). E17. **3** *v.i.* Move (downwards, to and fro, etc.) with quick light vibrations; quiver; (of the heart or pulse) beat rapidly (and weakly). M16. **4** *v.t.* Flap (wings etc.) in a quivering manner; move or wave (a flag etc.) lightly; agitate, ruffle. E17. **b** *v.t.* Throw into confusion or excitement. M17. **5** *v.i.* Quiver with excitement; be agitated. M17. **6** *v.i.* Move about aimlessly or restlessly; hover. L17.

2 J. MCCOSH The moth fluttering about the light which is to consume it. **b** ALBERT SMITH Seeds, which the bird had fluttered from his cage. 3 GEO. ELIOT Here and there a leaf fluttered down. D. WELCH Her silk scarves fluttered in the wind. J. L. WATEN He saw a little smile flutter on Mother's lips and then disappear. 4 J. HERVEY The gay butterfly flutters her painted wings. W. STYRON She . . fluttered her eyelids and turned her gaze demurely down. B. BAINBRIDGE Nina fluttered her fingers at him. **b** E. WHARTON Young Mr Gryce's arrival had fluttered the maternal breasts of New York. *flutter the dovecots*: see DOVECOT. 5 THACKERAY Fluttering with her own audacity. 6 W. BLACK She . . kept fluttering about the hall, bothering the patient clerks with inquiries.

flutte'ration *n.* (now chiefly *US*) the action or state of fluttering; an instance of this; *esp.* confusion, bustle: M18. **flutterer** *n.* LME. **fluttering** *vbl n.* the action of the vb; an instance of this: LME. **flutteringly** *adv.* in a fluttering manner E19. **fluttery** *a.* liable to flutter, fluttering LME.

fluty /ˈfluːti/ *a.* Also **-ey**. E19. [f. FLUTE *n.*[1] + -Y[1].] Flutelike in tone; piping.

fluvial /ˈfluːvɪəl/ *a.* LME. [L *fluvialis*, f. *fluvius* river, f. *fluere* to flow: see -AL[1].] Of or pertaining to a river or rivers; found or living in rivers.

fluvialist *n.* a person who explains geological features as being due to the action of existing rivers E19.

fluviatile /ˈfluːvɪətʌɪl/ *a.* L16. [Fr. f. L *fluviatilis*, f. *fluviatus* moistened, wet, f. *fluvius*: see prec, -ILE.] Of or pertaining to a river or rivers; found or living in rivers; formed or produced by the action of rivers.

fluvio- /ˈfluːvɪəʊ/ *comb. form* of L *fluvius* river: see -O-.

fluvio'glacial *a.* (*a*) pertaining to or produced by the action of streams originating in glacial ice; (*b*) of, pertaining to, or produced by the combined action of, both rivers and glaciers: L19. **fluviola'custrine** *a.* of, pertaining to, or produced by the combined agency of, both rivers and lakes M19.

fluviology /fluːvɪˈɒlədʒi/ *n.* E20. [f. prec. + -LOGY.] The branch of science that deals with rivers; a body of knowledge concerning a river or rivers.

fluviometer /fluːvɪˈɒmɪtə/ *n.* M19. [f. as prec. + -METER.] An instrument for measuring the rise and fall of rivers.

flux /flʌks/ *n.* In sense 1 also †**flix**. LME. [(O)Fr., or L *fluxus*, f. *flux-* pa. ppl stem of *fluere* to flow.] **1** A flowing out (from the bowels, an organ, etc.) of fluid material; *esp.* an abnormal or excessive discharge of blood or excrement; (*arch.*) diarrhoea, dysentery. LME. **2** The action of flowing; the flowing in of the tide (esp. in *flux and reflux*). LME. **b** A stream, a flood: esp. *fig.*, of people, talk, etc. E17. **3** A continuous succession of changes of condition, composition, or substance. LME. **b** The passing away of life, time, etc. E17. **4** *Math.* Continued motion of a point etc. Later also = FLUXION 3. Now *rare* or *obs.* M17. †**5** A liquid or molten state. L17–L18. **6** Any substance which is mixed with a metal etc. in order to facilitate melting; a substance used to make colours fusible in enamelling, pottery, etc. E18. **7** *Physics.* **a** The rate of flow of any fluid, or of radiant energy, particles, etc., across a given area; the amount of this crossing a given area in a given time. M19. **b** (The number of) lines of magnetic induction or electric displacement passing through an area; the integral over the area of the component of the field strength normal to the area. Also *magnetic, electric, flux.* L19.

1 *bloody flux*: see BLOODY *a.* & *adv. white flux*: see WHITE *a.* 2 *fig.*: C. THIRLWALL The flux and reflux of the nations which fought and wandered in the countries. **b** J. CHEEVER I heard thunder, and a second later a flux of summer rain inundated the county. P. L. FERMOR The vehicle threaded its way through a flux of traffic. 3 L. EDEL The flux of the mind, its continuity and yet its continuous change. **in a state of flux** in an unstable condition. **b** J. THOMSON Thus to remain, Amid the flux of many thousand years. 7 *New Scientist* The thermal neutron flux . . will be . . 2×10^{13} neutrons per square centimetre per second. *Nature* The flux of hydrogen atoms in the solar wind. **b** J. A. FLEMING If . . a disc of iron is placed in a uniform field of magnetic force, the flux concentrates itself in the iron.

Comb.: **flux density** the quantity of (magnetic, electric, etc.) flux passing through unit area; **flux-gate (magnetometer)** a kind of magnetometer (used esp. in aerial surveys) consisting of one or more soft iron cores each surrounded by primary and secondary windings, the characteristics of the external magnetic field being determined from the signals produced in the secondary windings; **flux-line** any of a set of lines representing by their direction and density the direction and rate of flow of a fluid etc. or the direction and strength of a magnetic or electric field; **fluxmeter**: for measuring (changes in) magnetic etc. flux.

¶The var. *flix* survives in FLIXWEED.

†**flux** *a.* LME–L18. [L *fluxus* ppl a., f. *fluere* to flow.] In a state of flux, flowing, fluctuating.

flux /flʌks/ *v.* LME. [f. the n.] **1** *v.t.* Purge; cause a flux in (a person). Now *rare* or *obs.* LME. †**b** *v.i.* Undergo a flux. LME–M18. **2** *v.t.* & *i.* Make or become fluid; fuse, melt. L15. **3** *v.t.* Treat or heat with a flux (FLUX *n.* 6). L18. **4** *v.i.* Flow copiously. Now *rare.* E19.

†**fluxible** *a.* L15. [OFr, or late L *fluxibilis* liquid, f. *flux-* pa. ppl stem of *fluere* to flow: see -IBLE.] **1** Able to be melted, fusible. L15–M18. **2** Fluid. Also, pliable. M16–E18. **3** Liable to flux or change, variable. M16–L17.

†**fluxibility** *n.* L16–M18.

†**fluxile** *a.* E17–M19. [Late L *fluxilis* f. *flux-*: see prec., -ILE.] = FLUXIBLE 2, 3.

†**fluxility** *n.* M17–E18.

fluxion /ˈflʌkʃ(ə)n/ *n.* M16. [(O)Fr., or f. L *flux-*: see FLUXIBLE, -ION.] **1** = FLUX *n.* 1. Now *rare* or *obs.* M16. **2** The action of flowing (out); continuous motion; continual change. L16. †**b** = EFFLUVIUM 2. E17–M18. **3** *Math.* Increase or decrease of a continuously varying quantity; the rate of this. Now chiefly *Hist.*, in *method* etc. *of fluxions*, the Newtonian calculus. L17.

fluxional *a.* (*a*) *Math.* of or pertaining to fluxions; (*b*) resulting from or subject to flux; flowing, variable: M18. **fluxionary** *a.* (now *rare*) = FLUXIONAL M18. **fluxionist** *n.* (*Math.*, *Hist.*) a person who uses (the method of) fluxions M18.

†**fluxive** *a.* L16–E18. [med.L *fluxivus* fleeting, transitory, f. *flux-*: see FLUXIBLE, -IVE.] Liable to flow; fluid; fluctuating, variable.

fly /flʌɪ/ *n.*[1] Pl. **flies**. [OE *flȳġe*, *flēoge* = OS, OHG *flioga* (Du. *vlieg*, G *Fliege*), f. WGmc, f. Gmc base of FLY *v.*] **1** Any winged insect, as a bee, locust, moth, etc. Now usu. restricted to small winged insects of any group not popularly identifiable, or falling under sense 2 as below or as the 2nd elem. of comb. OE. **b** Any of various winged insects harmful to crops or animals; a disease caused by such an insect. E18. **2** A dipteran or two-winged insect; an insect of the order Diptera (comprising the true flies). OE. **b** *ellipt.* The tsetse-fly. *S. Afr.* M19. **3** *fig.* (A type of) something insignificant. ME. **4** *Angling.* A natural fly or an imitation of this consisting of a hook dressed with silk and feathers, etc., used as fishing-bait. L16. †**5** A familiar demon; *transf.* a spy, a flatterer. L16–M17. **6** *Printing.* **a** A printer's devil. *rare.* L17. **b** The person who or machine which takes the printed sheets from the press. M18. **7** (Usu. **F-**.) *The* constellation Musca. L17.

1 *alder-fly, caddis-fly, damselfly, firefly, greenfly, ichneumon fly, mayfly, sawfly, stonefly*, etc. **b** *hop-fly, potato-fly, sheep-fly*, etc. 2 *blowfly, crane-fly, horsefly, housefly, hoverfly, sandfly, warble fly*, etc. 3 HAZLITT He would not hurt a fly. 4 R. BRAUTIGAN I cast . . and let my fly drift. *dry fly, watchet fly, wet fly*, etc.

Phrases: **drink with the flies** (*Austral.* & *NZ slang*) drink alone. **fly in amber** *fig.* a curious relic. **fly in the ointment** [after *Eccles.* 10:1] a trifling circumstance that spoils the enjoyment or agreeableness of a thing. **fly on the wall** (*a*) an unperceived observer; (*b*) *Cinemat.* a film-making technique whereby events are observed realistically with minimum interference rather than acted out under direction. **fly on the wheel** a person who overestimates his or her own influence. **like flies** in large numbers or quantities. *Lord of the Flies*: see LORD *n.* **no flies on** *slang* no lack of astuteness in (a person); nothing shady or underhand about (a deal etc.). *squashed fly (biscuit)*: see SQUASH *v.* 1.

Comb.: **fly agaric** a poisonous mushroom, *Amanita muscaria*, with a white-spotted scarlet cap; **flybane** (*a*) any of various supposedly insecticidal plants, *esp.* catchfly; (*b*) *rare* poison for flies; **fly-bird** a hummingbird; **fly-bitten** *a.* †(*a*) fly-specked; †(*b*) = FLY-BLOWN (a); (*c*) stung by flies; **fly-book** a book-shaped case in which anglers keep fishing-flies; †**fly-cap** a kind of head-dress, shaped like a butterfly; **fly-dope** *N. Amer.* insect repellent; **fly-eater** an eater of flies; *spec.* any of several small Australasian warblers constituting the genus *Gerygone* (family Muscicapidae); **fly-fan** an instrument or motor-driven fan for driving away flies; **fly-fish** *v.i.* fish with a fly as bait; **fly-fishing** fishing with a fly; **fly-flap** *n.* & *v.* (*a*) *n.* an instrument for driving away flies; (*b*) *v.t.* strike with a fly-flap, beat, whip; **fly-flapper** (*a*) a person who drives away flies with a fly-flap; (*b*) a fly-flap; **fly-fungus** (*a*) = *fly agaric* above; (*b*) a parasitic fungus, *Entomophthora muscae*, which infests and kills houseflies and other insects; *fly honeysuckle*: see HONEYSUCKLE 2; **fly-hook** a hook baited with a fly; **fly-line** *n.*[1]: for fly-fishing; **fly-mould** = *fly fungus* (b) above; **fly-net** a net for keeping flies away; **fly orchid** an orchid, *Ophrys insectifera*, with small dark-purple flowers resembling flies; **fly-paper** paper treated with a sticky substance for catching and poisoning flies; **fly-rod**: for fly-fishing; **fly screen** a screen for keeping flies away; **fly-speck** (*a*) a small stain produced by the excrement of an insect; (*b*) a disease of apples etc., with small black surface specks, caused by the fungus *Leptothyrium pomi*; **fly-specked**, **-speckled** *adjs.* marked with fly-specks; **fly-spray** a spray, usu. an aerosol, containing a liquid for killing flies; **fly-strike** infestation of the skin of sheep with the maggots of blowflies; **fly-strip** an impregnated plastic strip for poisoning flies; **fly-swatter** a device for killing flies by hitting them; **fly-swish** = *fly-whisk* below; **flyweight** a weight in boxing and other sports below bantamweight, in the amateur boxing scale now being below 52 kg, though differing for professionals and in other sports, and according to time and place; (designating) a boxer etc. of this weight; *light flyweight*, (of) a weight in amateur boxing of below 49 kg, (designating) a boxer of this weight; **fly-whisk** an instrument for driving away flies; **fly-wire** screening designed to keep out flies.

fly /flʌɪ/ *n.*[2] Pl. **flies**, (in sense 3 also) **flys**. OE. [f. the vb.] **1** The action or an act of flying. OE. **b** The course of a ball, or the ball itself, as it travels through the air. M19. **2 a** The 32 points of a mariner's compass; a compass card. L16. **b** A speed-regulating device in a clockwork mechanism. L16. **c** A flywheel or other similar speed-regulating device in machinery. M17. **3** *Hist.* **a** A stagecoach. E18. **b** A lightweight covered carriage drawn by one horse. E19. **4** *Theatr.* In *pl.* The space above the front part of the stage. E19. **5** Orig., the sloping walls or roof of a tent. Now, the flap at the entrance of a tent. Also = *fly-sheet* (b) below. E19. **6** Waste cotton. E19. **7** A strip on a garment which contains or covers the fastening; *sing.* & (freq.) in *pl.*, the flap that hides the fastening at the front of a pair of trousers; the fastening itself. M19. **8** The breadth of a flag from the staff to the end. M19. **b** The part of a flag which is furthest from the staff. M19.

1b J. T. FARRELL A long high fly which was easily caught. **3b** P. V. WHITE The Bonners drove, in the family carriage and a hired fly. **4** H. ROSENTHAL The three rooms . . high up in the opera house on the level with the 'flies.' **5** P. MATTHIESSEN The others have rigged a fly over the fire and are making tea . . in this downpour. **7** G. GREENE The flies of his grey flannel trousers gaped from a lost button.

Phrases: **give it a fly** *Austral. slang* make an attempt, have a go. **have a fly at** *Austral. slang* make an attempt at, have a go at. **on the fly** (*a*) while in motion through the air; (*b*) *transf.* while active, busy, or on the move.

Comb.: **fly ash** ash resulting from the burning of powdered coal; **fly ball** *Baseball* a ball hit so as to be catchable; **fly boy** *US slang* a member of the Air Force, esp. a pilot; **fly bridge** an open deck with duplicate controls situated above the main bridge of a ship; a flying bridge; **fly camp** a temporary camp; **fly-cruise** a holiday starting with an air journey to the place where a sea-cruise begins; **fly drive** a holiday or a journey involving both flying and driving; **fly frame** *Spinning* a flyer frame; **fly-half** *Rugby Football* a stand-off half; **fly-kick** a kick, esp. in rugby, made while the ball is in the air; **flyleaf** a blank leaf at the beginning or end of a book; the blank leaf of a circular etc.; **fly-line** *n.*[2] the regular line of flight followed by a migrating bird; **flyman** (*a*) *Hist.* a person who drives a fly (sense 3b above); (*b*) *Theatr.* a person positioned in the flies to work the ropes etc.; **fly-nut** a screw nut with wings or projections enabling it to be tightened by hand; **fly page** either side of a flyleaf; **fly-post, -poster** *vs.t.* & *i.* display (handbills etc.) rapidly in unauthorized places; **flysheet** (*a*) a two- or four-page leaflet or circular; (*b*) a protective cover pitched outside and over a tent; **fly stitch** an embroidery stitch similar to chain stitch but open-ended; **fly-tip** *v.t.* carry out the fly-tipping of (rubbish etc.); **fly-tipping** the unauthorized dumping of building rubble or other waste; **flyway** (*a*) = *fly-line* above; (*b*) a vast area occupied by bird populations containing both winter and breeding grounds linked by migratory routes; **flywheel** a heavy-rimmed wheel attached to a revolving shaft to store momentum, usu. so as to regulate machinery.

fly /flʌɪ/ *a. slang.* E19. [Origin uncertain: perh. rel. to the vb.] **1** Knowing, sharp, wide awake. E19. **2** Of the fingers: nimble, skilful. Now *rare.* M19.

1 A. PRICE He was too fly to let anyone pin so much as a charity flag on him. P. ACKROYD Are you fly to what's going on? **put (someone) fly** inform, tell, (someone).

Special collocations: **fly cop** *US slang* a detective, a plain-clothes police officer. **fly-flat** *slang* a person who is or thinks he or she is wise, but is or gives the impression of being a fool. **fly-pitch** *slang* a street pitch. **fly-pitcher** *slang* a person who operates a fly-pitch; a street-trader.

flyness *n.* L19.

fly /flʌɪ/ *v.* Pa. t. **flew** /fluː/; pa. pple **flown** /fləʊn/. [OE *flēogan* = OFris. *fliāga*, OS (Du. *vliegen*), OHG *fliogan* (G *fliegen*), ON *fljúga*, f. Gmc.] **I 1** *v.i.* Move through the air with wings. (Foll. by *about*, *away*, *off*, *out*, etc.) OE. **b** *v.i. fig.* Of fame, a report, etc.: spread, become known. Also, (of words, thoughts, emotions, etc.) shift, change, or be exchanged swiftly and animatedly. ME. **c** *v.i.* Of a fish: spring from the water, rise into the air. Cf. *flying fish* s.v. FLYING *ppl a.* L16. **d** *v.t.* Cover by flying (a course or distance). E17. **2** *v.i.* Pass or rise quickly through the air. (Foll. by *away*, *off*, *up*, etc.) OE. **b** Of stairs: go straight up or down without change of direction. Now *rare.* L17. **c** Spring lightly, jump *over.* E18. **3** *v.i.* Move or travel swiftly, pass rapidly, rush along. (Foll. by *along*, *away*, *back*, etc.) ME. **b** *spec.* Of time: pass quickly, rush by. M16. **4** *v.i.* Move with a start or rush; spring, hasten; depart hurriedly. ME. **5** *v.i.* Be forced or driven off or away suddenly and quickly. (Foll. by *from*, *out of.*) ME. **b** In full *fly in pieces.* Break up suddenly, split up. L15. **c** Of a door or window: be thrown suddenly *open*, *up*, etc. E17. **d** Of money: be rapidly spent. M17. **e** *Baseball.* Hit a fly ball. (Foll. by *out.*) L19. **6** *Falconry.* **a** *v.i.* & *t.* Of a hawk: fly (*at*) and attack. LME. **b** *v.t.* & *i.* Send (a hawk) to fly and attack. E16. **c** *v.t.* Chase or attack with a hawk. L16. **7** *v.t.* Release (a bird) to fly; keep (birds) for racing, hunting, etc. E17. **b** Make (a kite) rise and stay aloft in the air. See also *fly a kite* below. M17. **8** *v.i.* Of a flag, garment, or other partially attached object: flutter, wave. M17. **b** *v.t.* Set or keep (a flag) flying. M17. **9** *v.i. Naut.* Of the wind: shift or veer suddenly. L17. **10** *v.i.* Of an aircraft or spacecraft: travel through the air or space at speed. M19. **b** Of a person: travel by aircraft, pilot an aircraft. E20. **11** *v.t.* Of an aircraft or its occupant(s): cover, traverse, or perform, by flying. L19. **b** Conduct or pilot (an aircraft). E20. **c** Convey or transport by aircraft. E20.

1 J. STEINBECK A pigeon flew in through the open hay door. **b** T. HARDY That young man's feelings had flown hither and thither between minister and lady. S. MIDDLETON Conversation and laughter were flying. **d** SHAKES. *Macb.* Ere the Bat hath flowne His Cloyster'd flight. **2** DRYDEN Golden stars flew up to light the skies. **3** J. TYNDALL The velocity with which the earth flies through space. D. H. LAWRENCE She flew along the terrace and up the steps to the roof. **b** S. MIDDLETON The first three days had passed slowly, but by Thursday time flew. **4** J. I. M. STEWART Mabel has to fly . . But she did so very much want to meet you. **5** LD BERNERS His hede flewe fro hys sholders. DAY LEWIS The squawking hens bouncing up and down . . straw and feathers flying. **c** G. GREENE Suddenly the door which I had pushed against so often before flew open. **7** J. CLAVELL It's one of my few rules: only to fly the falcons that I've trained. **b** *fig.*: TENNYSON O Madam, You fly your thoughts like kites. **8** R. BROOKE And the moon came down and danced to me, And her robe was white and flying. V. BRITTAIN The flags flying in the streets . . for Queen Victoria's Diamond Jubilee. **10** B. MOORE That's a helicopter, it could not fly all the way from Rome. **b** W. S. MAUGHAM When I said I wanted to learn to fly he said he'd fix it for me. DAY LEWIS The womb-like sensation of flying in an air-liner. **11** *Captain* The machine which flew the channel. N. SHUTE He was flying a courier service. **b** C. POTOK He flies big planes that drop bombs.

II 12 *v.i.* & *t.* = FLEE (exc. sense 3). OE.

Phrases: *as the crow flies*: see CROW *n.*[1] **fly a kite** *fig.* (*a*) raise money by an accommodation bill; (*b*) try something out; make an announcement or take a step in order to test public opinion; (*c*) *go fly a kite* (colloq., chiefly N. Amer.), go away. **fly at higher game** *fig.* have nobler ambitions. *fly-by-wire*: see WIRE *n.* **fly high** *fig.* (*a*) be ambitious, aim high; (*b*) prosper, flourish. *fly in pieces*: see sense 5b above. *fly off the handle*: see HANDLE *n.*[1] **fly past** make a ceremonial aircraft flight past some person or place. *fly the coop*: see COOP *n.*[1] **fly the track** (*US colloq.*) turn from the usual or expected course. **fly to arms** take up arms eagerly or suddenly. *go fly a kite*: see *fly a kite* (c) above. **let fly** (*a*) *v.phr.t.* discharge (a missile), utter (an oath, strong words, etc.); (*b*) *v.phr.i.* make a physical or verbal attack; fire, shoot, (*at*); (*c*) *v.phr.t. Naut.* allow (a sail or sheet) to fly loose; hoist (colours). **make the money fly** spend money quickly. *pigs might fly*: see PIG *n.*[1]

With advs. & preps. in specialized senses: **fly at, on, upon** spring upon violently, attack with fury. **fly in** (*a*) arrive by aircraft; (*b*) *fly in, into* fall or pass suddenly into (a passion, raptures, etc.). **fly off** (*a*) start away, leave suddenly; (*b*) *fig.* take another course, break away *from. fly on*: see *fly at* above. **fly out** (*a*) spring out, rush out suddenly; (*b*) burst out or explode in conduct, temper, etc.; (*c*) depart by aircraft. *fly upon*: see *fly at* above.

Comb.: **fly-back** (*a*) the return of the hands of a stopwatch or chronograph to zero; (*b*) the return of the scanning spot in a cathode-ray tube to the starting point; (*c*) the portion of each cycle of a sawtooth waveform in which the signal diminishes; **fly-by** (*a*) = *fly-past* (a) below; (*b*) a close approach of a spacecraft to a planet etc.; **fly-by-night** *n.* & *a.* (*a*) *n.* a person who makes night excursions or decamps by night in order to avoid debts; (*b*) *adj.* unreliable, dishonest; superficial, short-lived; **fly-in** (*a*) the action or an act of delivering troops, goods, etc., by air to a specified place; (*b*) a service or entertainment provided for people who have arrived by air; **fly-off** *n.* & *a.* (*a*) *n.* the action of flying off; (*b*) *adj.* (of a motor-vehicle brake) requiring a manual operation to put it on or off but not to keep it on; **flyover** (*a*) a road or rail bridge which crosses over a road or railway; (*b*) = *fly-past* (a) below; **fly-past** (*a*) the action of flying past, or of forming part of a procession of aircraft; (*b*) = *fly-by* (b) above; **fly-the-garter** a game in which players leap from one side of a 'garter' or line of stones over the back of another player; **flyunder** a road or railway which runs under another; **fly-up-the-creek** *US* (*a*) the green heron, *Butorides virescens*; (*b*) a flighty person; (*c*) a native or inhabitant of Florida.

flyable /ˈflʌɪəb(ə)l/ *a.* L16. [f. FLY *v.* + -ABLE.] †**1** Flying; that flies. Only in L16. **2** Able to be leapt over (on horseback). *colloq.* L19. **3** (Of weather) suitable for flying; (of goods) transportable by air; (of an aircraft) capable of flying, able to be flown. M20.

fly-away /ˈflʌɪəweɪ/ *a.* & *n.* Also **flyaway**. L18. [f. FLY *v.* + AWAY.] **A** *adj.* **1** Apt to fly away; *spec.* (of a person, action, etc.) sudden, impulsive, volatile, flighty. L18. **2** Of a garment: loose, streaming. M19.

1 *Daily Mirror* Spurned by her fly-away husband, Mick, Bianca Jagger dances alone. A. TYLER She developed a breathless, fly-away air.

B *n.* A person who or thing which flies away. E19.

fly-blow /ˈflʌɪbləʊ/ *n.* & *v.* M16. [f. FLY *n.*[1] + BLOW *n.*[2], *v.*[1]] **A** *n.* A fly's egg deposited in meat, carrion, etc.; a maggot hatched from this. M16. **B** *v.t.* Infl. as BLOW *v.*[1] **1** Of a fly etc.: deposit eggs on or in (meat etc.). Cf. earlier BLOW *v.*[1] 18. E17. **2** *fig.* Corrupt secretly, taint. E17.

fly-blown *a.* (*a*) full of fly-blows; tainted, impure, corrupt; (*b*) *Austral.* & *NZ slang* without any money, broke: E16.

fly-boat /ˈflʌɪbəʊt/ *n.* L16. [Du. *vlieboot* a boat used orig. on the *Vlie*, a channel off the north coast of the Netherlands; later assoc. with FLY *n.*[1]: see BOAT *n.*] **1** *Hist.* A fast sailing vessel, *esp.* a Dutch flat-bottomed boat, used for coastal trade or for warfare, exploration, etc. L16. †**2** A small boat; *esp.* a ship's boat. L16–E19. †**3** A fishing boat used in Shetland, a buss. E17–L18. **4** A swift passage-boat used on canals. M19.

flycatcher /ˈflʌɪkatʃə/ *n.* L16. [f. FLY *n.*[1] + CATCHER.] **1** Any of numerous birds that feed on insects, typically catching their prey by short flights from a perch, *esp.* (*a*) a member of the Old World family Muscicapidae; (*b*) = *monarch flycatcher* s.v. MONARCH *n.*; (*c*) = *tyrant-flycatcher* s.v. TYRANT *n.* 5. L16. **2** A person who or thing which catches flies. E17. **b** An insectivorous plant. M19.

1 *fantail flycatcher*, *least flycatcher*, *paradise flycatcher*, *pied flycatcher*, *spotted flycatcher*, etc.

flyer /ˈflʌɪə/ *n.* Also **flier**. LME. [f. FLY *v.* + -ER[1].] **1** Something which flies; a creature or thing that flies or is carried through the air. LME. **2** A person who runs away, a fugitive; a fleer. LME. **3** Each of a series of rectangular steps forming a straight flight. M17. **4** A mechanism which has a regular and fast-moving revolution, as: an appliance for regulating the motion of a roasting-jack; a sail of a windmill; the part of a spinning wheel which twists the thread as it leads it to and winds it on the bobbin. L17. **5** A person, animal, vehicle, train, etc., which moves with exceptional speed. L18. **b** A flying jump or leap. L19. **c** *Cricket.* A ball pitched short that flies up sharply. E20. **6** A speculative venture, *esp.* a speculative financial investment. *US.* M19. **7** A small handbill or flysheet, *esp.* one issued by the police or used for advertising purposes. *N. Amer.* L19. **8** An aircraft. L19. **b** An aviator. M20. **9** An ambitious or outstanding person; an excellent or outstanding thing. *colloq.* E20.

1 C. DARWIN Birds breeding on precipices, and good fliers, are unlikely to be exterminated. 5 E. WALLACE Fifty-Five is a flyer . . He did the five furlongs in fifty-eight and a fifth seconds. 7 *New Yorker* The police . . put out flyers asking witnesses . . to come forward. 8 H. G. WELLS The most efficient heavier-than-air fliers that had ever appeared. 9 T. PARKER People of higher rank . . say he's something of what's called a 'flyer'.

Phrases: **take a flyer** take a chance.

flying /ˈflʌɪɪŋ/ *vbl n.* ME. [f. FLY *v.* + -ING[1].] The action of FLY *v.*; *spec.* the action of guiding, piloting, or travelling in an aircraft or spacecraft.

Comb. (not all clearly separable from collocations of the ppl a.): **flying boat** (*a*) a boat-shaped car on a funfair roundabout; (*b*) a form of seaplane with a fuselage that resembles a boat; **flying corps** an aircraft unit for military or naval purposes; **flying field** an airfield; **flying machine** (now *arch.* or *Hist.*) a machine that can be flown in the air, *esp.* one that is heavier than air and depends on its motors for propulsion and lift; **Flying Officer** a rank in the Royal Air Force, immediately below Flight Lieutenant; **flying school** a place where people are taught to fly aircraft; **flying speed** the speed of an aircraft at take-off or in normal level flight; **flying squadron** a Royal Air Force unit or formation made up of several flights; (see also s.v. FLYING *ppl a.*); **flying suit** (*a*) a suit worn by someone piloting an aircraft; (*b*) a kind of one-piece trouser suit worn as a casual fashion garment.

flying /ˈflʌɪɪŋ/ *ppl a.* OE. [f. FLY *v.* + -ING[2].] 1 That flies. OE. 2 That flies about; *fig.* circulating, shifting about, itinerant, volatile. LME. 3 That passes through the air esp. quickly. M16. 4 That passes or travels swiftly, that passes by rapidly; (of a vehicle etc.) designed for rapid movement. M16. b Esp. of a trip or visit: passing, hasty, transient. Also, temporary. M16. 5 That flees, fleeing. L16. 6 Hanging loose; fluttering, waving. E17.

1 A. WINCHELL A menagerie of curious beasts, and crawling and creeping and flying things. 2 BUNYAN I hope they are but flying stories. W. SAUNDERS Flying pains and weaknesses of the limbs. 4 POPE Earth rolls back beneath the flying steed. b H. WILSON He paid me a flying visit.

Phrases: *come off, through, with flying colours*: see COLOUR *n.* †**under, with, a flying seal** (of a letter) having a seal but not closed, so that it can be read while in transit.

Special collocations (not all clearly separable from combs. of the vbl n.): **flying bomb** an unmanned aircraft with an explosive warhead. **flying bridge** †(*a*) a drawbridge; (*b*) a temporary bridge constructed for military purposes; (*c*) an auxiliary bridge situated higher than the main bridge of a yacht or other ship. **flying buttress** a buttress, usu. on an arch, which slants upwards to a wall from a pier or other support. **flying change** an equestrian movement in which the leading leg in the canter position is changed without loss of speed while the horse is in the air. *flying circus*: see CIRCUS *n.* 8. †**flying coach** a swift stagecoach. **flying coffin** *colloq.* a hazardous or vulnerable aeroplane. **flying column** a military force capable of rapid movement and independent operation. **flying doctor** a doctor who habitually visits patients in remote areas by aircraft. **flying dragon** = *flying lizard* below. *Flying* DUTCHMAN. **flying façade** a façade that rises above the level of the roof of a building. **flying fish** (*a*) any of various tropical fishes of the family Exocoetidae, capable of gliding considerable distances above the water by means of winglike pectoral fins; (*b*) *the Flying Fish*, (the name of) the constellation Volans. **Flying Fortress** the Boeing B-17, a US long-range heavy bomber developed in the late 1930s. **flying fox** (*a*) any of numerous fruit-eating bats, mainly of the genus *Pteropus*, found in India, Madagascar, SE Asia, and Australia; (*b*) (*Austral.* & *NZ*) a carrier operated by cables across a gorge etc. **flying gurnard** any of various tropical benthic marine fishes of the family Dactylopteridae, with greatly enlarged pectoral fins, able to leap out of the water. **flying horse** (*a*) a throw in wrestling, similar to the flying mare; (*b*) *the Flying Horse* (now *rare* or *obs.*), (the name of) the constellation Pegasus. **flying jenny** (chiefly *US*) a merry-go-round. **flying jib** (*a*) *Naut.* a light sail set on an extension of a jib-boom; (*b*) *slang* a loud-mouthed talker. **flying jump, leap**: made with a running start. *flying-kites*: see KITE *n.* 5a. *flying leap*: see *flying jump* above. **flying lemur** either of two SE Asian nocturnal arboreal mammals of the genus *Cynocephalus*, order Dermoptera, which resemble lemurs and can glide hundreds of feet by means of a membrane between the fore and hind limbs and the tail; also called *colugo*. **flying lizard** any arboreal agamid lizard of the SE Asian genus *Draco* able to glide short distances by means of skin membranes supported by elongated ribs. **flying mare** a throw in wrestling, in which one wrestler throws the other over his or her back using the other's arm as a lever. **flying mouse** the smallest gliding marsupial, *Acrobates pygmaeus* (family Burramyidae), of eastern Australia; also called *feathertail glider, pygmy glider*. **flying phalanger** any of various small Australasian marsupials of the genera *Petaura* and *Petauroides* (family Petauridae), that are able to make gliding leaps by means of furred skin membranes between fore and hind limbs; also called *glider*. **flying picket** (a member of) a group of striking workers who move from place to place picketing premises and companies other than those at which they are employed. †**flying post** a post travelling by relays of horses. **flying ring** each of a number of rings suspended in pairs or rows by swinging ropes, used in acrobatics and gymnastics. **flying saucer** a disc- or saucer-shaped unidentified flying object. *Flying Scotsman*: see SCOTSMAN 2. **flying shear** a device for shearing a long continuous length of metal into short pieces. **flying shore** a horizontal shore used to provide temporary support between two buildings. **flying spot** a small spot of light that moves rapidly over an object, the reflected or transmitted light from the spot being used to reproduce an image of the object. **flying squad** a division of a police force or other body organized for rapid movement. **flying squadron** a military detachment or other body organized for rapid movement; (see also s.v. FLYING *vbl n.*). **flying squid** any of various squid that are able to leap out of the water, esp. of the family Ommastrephidae. **flying squirrel** (*a*) any of various mainly Asian nocturnal squirrels able to make gliding leaps between trees by means of furred skin membranes between fore and hind limbs; (*b*) = *flying phalanger* above. **flying start** (*a*) a start in which the competitors pass the starting-point at full speed; (*b*) *fig.* an initial advantage, an excellent start. **flying tackle** a tackle in football etc. made while running or jumping. **flying trapeze** a trapeze on or from which acrobats swing to and fro. **flying wing** a type of aircraft designed without a fuselage or a tailplane.

flype /flʌɪp/ *n.* Chiefly *north.* Also **flipe**. M16. [Cf. Du. *fleb, flep* a woman's forehead cloth, Da. *flip* flap, FLYPE *v.*] A fold, a flap; *esp.* a hat-brim.

flype /flʌɪp/ *v.t.* Chiefly *Sc.* Also **flipe**. ME. [Cf. MDa. *flippe* to skin, FLYPE *n.*] 1 Strip off (the skin etc.), peel, flay. ME. 2 Turn up or down, fold back; turn inside out. M16.

flysch /flɪʃ/ *n.* M19. [Swiss G dial.] *Geol.* A thinly-bedded sedimentary deposit consisting of shales and marls alternating with coarser strata such as sandstones and conglomerates. Orig. *spec.* (**F-**), such a deposit of late Cretaceous to Oligocene age in the Alps.

flyte /flʌɪt/ *n. obs.* exc. *dial.* & *Sc.* Also **flite**. [OE *flīt*, f. *flītan*: see next.] †1 Contention, strife; abuse. OE–E17. 2 A scolding-match. M18.

flyte /flʌɪt/ *v. obs.* exc. *dial.* & *Sc.* Also **flite**. [OE *flītan* = OS *andflītan* contend, OHG *flīz(z)an* strive (G *sich befleissen* busy oneself).] †1 *v.i.* Contend, strive; argue noisily; chide. (Foll. by *against, on, with.*) OE–E18. 2a *v.t.* Chide, scold, (a person). LME. b *v.i.* Scold. (Foll. by *at.*) E16.

flyter *n.* a person who disputes or scolds OE. **flyting** *n.* (*a*) the action of the vb; contention, scolding, rebuking; (*b*) a contest of poetical invective, esp. as practised by 16th-cent. Scottish poets: ME.

fly-trap /ˈflʌɪtrap/ *n.* L18. [f. FLY *n.*[1] + TRAP *n.*[1]] 1 A plant which catches flies; *esp.* (in full *Venus('s) fly-trap*), a N. American marsh plant, *Dionaea muscipula* (family Droseraceae), which has hinged leaves able to spring shut and trap insects which touch sensitive trigger hairs. L18. 2 The mouth. *slang*. L18. 3 A trap for catching flies. E19.

foal /fəʊl/ *n.* & *v.* [OE *fola* = OFris. *fola*, OS *folo*, MDu. *volen*, (also mod.) *veulen*, OHG *folo* (G *Fohlen*), ON *foli*, Goth. *fula*, f. Gmc, rel. to synon. L *pullus*, Gk *pōlos*; cf. FILLY.] **A** *n.* 1 A horse or other equid before or soon after birth; a colt or filly, *esp.* one under one year of age. OE. b An elephant or camel of similar age. *rare*. LME. †2 A horse. ME–E16. 3 *Coalmining*. A young boy employed in the transporting of coal from the working face to the tramway. *obs.* exc. *Hist.* L18.

1 **in foal, with foal** (of a mare, she-ass, etc.) pregnant.

Comb.: **foalfoot** (now *dial.*) the plant coltsfoot, *Tussilago farfara*; **foal-tooth** each of the first teeth of a horse etc.;

B *v.t.* & *i.* Of a mare, she-ass, etc.: give birth to (a foal). LME.

foam /fəʊm/ *n.* [OE *fām* = (O)HG *feim*, f. WGmc f. IE, rel. to L *pumex* PUMICE *n.* and *spuma* SPUME *n.*] 1 A mass of small bubbles formed on the surface of water or another liquid by agitation, fermentation, etc. OE. b Foaming saliva issuing from the mouth; froth of perspiration on the coat of an animal. OE. c Foam for smothering fire, produced by adding a chemical agent to water or by other means; a chemical agent used in producing such foam. E20. 2 Foaming water, the sea. *arch.* OE. 3 Rubber or plastic solidified in a lightweight cellular mass with many small gas bubbles. Also *foam rubber, plastic*, etc. M20.

1 L. DURRELL The sighing of the waves as they thickened into roundels of foam. I. MCEWAN The white foam burst from the bottle's neck.

Comb.: **foamback** *a.* & *n.* (a fabric etc.) backed by a thin layer of synthetic foam; **foam extinguisher** a fire extinguisher generating a mass of foam; **foam flower** any of various N. American plants of the genus *Tiarella*, of the saxifrage family; esp. *T. cordifolia*, grown for its feathery racemes of small white or reddish flowers.

foamless *a.* E19.

foam /fəʊm/ *v.* [OE *fǣman* = OHG *feimen*, f. WGmc; superseded in ME by a new formation f. the n.] 1 *v.i.* Emit foam; froth at the mouth; be covered in foamy perspiration; *colloq.* be very angry. OE. †2 *v.t.* Cover (as) with foam. *rare*. ME–M16. †3 *v.i.* Emerge as foam. Only in LME. 4 *v.i.* Of a liquid: froth, gather foam; run foaming *along, down*, etc.; pass off or away in foam. LME. 5 *v.t.* Emit in or like foam; pour *out* with rage and violence. LME. 6a *v.t.* Fill with foaming liquor. *poet.* E18. b *v.i.* Of a cup etc.: be filled with foaming liquor. E19.

1 W. IRVING Fall down in convulsions [and] foam at the mouth. E. A. FREEMAN Still urging on his foaming horse. 4 T. C. WOLFE Below him a mountain stream foamed down its rocky bed. 5 W. COWPER They roam the earth . . foaming out their own disgrace.

foamingly *adv.* while foaming E17.

foamed /ˈfəʊmd/ *a.* E20. [f. FOAM *v.*, *n.*: see -ED[1], -ED[2].] 1 Covered with foam. E20. 2 Having or made to a cellular structure like that of foam. M20.

2 **foamed slag** a lightweight cellular building material made by solidifying a foam of molten blast-furnace slag.

foamy /ˈfəʊmi/ *a.* [OE *fāmiğ, fǣmiğ*, f. as FOAM *n.* + -Y[1].] 1 Covered with foam, full of foam, frothy. OE. 2 Consisting or of the nature of foam; of, pertaining to, or resembling foam. LME.

foaminess *n.* L19.

fob /fɒb/ *n.*[1] LME. [f. FOB *v.*[1]] †1 A cheat, an impostor. *rare*. Only in LME. 2 A trick, an artifice. Now *arch. slang*. E17.

fob /fɒb/ *n.*[2] L15. [Origin unkn.] 1 *gen.* Froth, foam. *dial.* L15. 2 The scum or froth produced during the manufacture of soap. M19.

fob /fɒb/ *n.*[3] M17. [Prob. of G origin (cf. G dial. *Fuppe* pocket): orig. a cant term.] 1 A small pocket in the waistband of trousers, for carrying a watch, money, or other valuables. M17. 2 The contents of the fob, cash. *rare*. L17. 3 (In full *fob-chain*) a chain attached to a watch carried in the fob; an ornamental attachment to a fob-chain; a tab on a key-ring. L19.

Comb.: *fob-chain*: see sense 3 above; **fob watch** a pocket-watch suitable for carrying in the fob.

fob /fɒb/ *v.*[1]*t.* Infl. **-bb-**. LME. [Cf. G *foppen* cheat, deceive, quiz, banter.] 1 Cheat, deceive. (Foll. by *of, out of.*) LME. 2 Foll. by *off*: a Put off deceitfully, put off *with* (something inferior); attempt to satisfy with an excuse or pretence; palm (something inferior) off *on*, pass off (something fraudulent) *as*. L16. †b Remove by deceit. E–M17. †3 Bring *into* or bestow *on* by trickery; pass off *on*; get up, procure, or promote, by trickery. M17–E19.

1 H. FIELDING While everyone else he is fobbing, He still may be honest to me. 2a H. JAMES She was the girl his mother would have fobbed off on him. G. HEYER How could I hope to fob myself off as Evelyn at such a gathering. E. TAYLOR You wouldn't be fobbed off or coaxed away from a subject. G. PRIESTLAND Let nobody try to fob them off with fairy tales about appropriate technology.

fob /fɒb/ *v.*[2]*t.* Infl. **-bb-**. E19. [f. FOB *n.*[3]] Put into one's fob; pocket.

fob /fɒb/ *v.*[3]*i. dial.* & *techn.* Infl. **-bb-**. M19. [f. FOB *n.*[2]] Froth, foam.

focaccia /fə'katʃə/ *n.* M20. [It.] A kind of flat savoury Italian bread made with oil and usually seasoned with herbs etc.

focal /'fəʊk(ə)l/ *a.* L17. [(mod.L *focalis*) f. FOCUS *n.*: see -AL[1].] 1 Of or pertaining to a focus; collected or situated at a focus. L17. 2 *Med.* Of a disease etc.: occurring at discrete foci; localized. L19.

Special collocations: **focal distance, length** the distance between the centre of a lens or mirror and the focus. **focal plane** the plane perpendicular to the axis of a lens or mirror and containing the focus. **focal point** a focus (of a lens etc. or *fig.*).

focally *adv.* at a focus M19.

focalize /'fəʊk(ə)lʌɪz/ *v.* Also **-ise**. M19. [f. prec. + -IZE.] 1 *v.t.* Bring (rays of light, heat, etc.) to a focus; focus. M19. 2 *v.t.* & *i.* Adjust or arrange the focus of (the eye). L19. 3 *v.t. Med.* Confine (a disease etc.) to a focus or foci. Chiefly as *focalized* ppl a. E20.

focali'zation *n.* L19.

foci *n.pl.* see FOCUS *n.*

†focile *n.* LME–E18. [med.L *focile* lit. 'steel for striking fire', FUSIL *n.*[2]] Either of the bones of the forearm or of the lower leg: the ulna or tibia (*greater focile*), the radius or fibula (*lesser focile*).

fo'c's'le *n.* see FORECASTLE.

focus /'fəʊkəs/ *n.* Pl. **foci** /'fəʊsʌɪ/, **focuses**. M17. [L = fireplace, domestic hearth.] 1 *Geom.* Any of a number of points from which the distances to any point of a given curve or solid obey a simple arithmetic relation, as (*a*) (of an ellipse) either of two points from which the distances to any point on the curve have a constant sum; (*b*) (of a parabola) a point whose distance from any point on the curve equals the distance from the directrix to the same point on the curve; (*c*) (of a hyperbola) either of two points from which the distances to any point on the curve have a constant difference. M17. 2a *Physics.* A point at which rays or waves (of light, heat, sound, etc.) meet after reflection or refraction, or (more fully *virtual focus*) from which divergent rays appear to proceed. M17. b The distance from a lens etc. to this point (= *focal length*); the position at which an object must be situated for the image of it given by a lens or mirror to be sharply defined; the adjustment (of a lens, the eye, etc.) necessary to produce a well-defined image; the state of producing a clear image thus. L17. c *fig.* A state of (unity and) clear definition. L18. 3 *Med.* The primary or principal site in the body of an infection, malignant growth, or other disease. L17. 4 The centre of attention, activity, or greatest energy; the place of origin of an earthquake, a storm, a volcanic eruption, etc. M18.

1 J. BRONOWSKI The orbit of a planet . . is a broad ellipse in which the sun is . . at one focus. 2a J. F. W. HERSCHEL A far greater heat than can be produced in the focus of any burning-glass. H. D. THOREAU We were exactly in the focus of many echoes. *principal focus*: see PRINCIPAL *a.* b F. T. PALGRAVE Rapid alteration of the eye's focus in looking at the landscape. R. MACAULAY The distant prospect . . neared and acquired focus and clarity. W. BOYD His headache wouldn't allow him to bring the small print into focus. *short focus*: see SHORT *a.* c W. S. JEVONS The transactions of many different individuals . . are brought to a focus. 4 W. FAULKNER The courthouse the center, the focus, the hub. M. H. ABRAMS To shift the focus of critical interest from audience to artist. A. HAILEY Nim remained in the witness chair, the focus of attention. R. P. GRAVES He became the focus for romantic stories.

Phrases: *conjugate focus*: see CONJUGATE *a.* **depth of focus** (*a*) = *depth of field* s.v. FIELD *n.*; (*b*) the distance between the two extreme axial points behind a lens at which an image is judged to be in focus. FIXED *focus*. **in, out of, focus** giving, not giving, a sharply defined image as seen through a lens, the eye, etc. *virtual focus*: see sense 2 above.

focusless *a.* without focus L19.

focus /'fəʊkəs/ *v.* Infl. **-s-, -ss-**. L18. [f. the n.] 1 *v.t.* Make converge to or as to a focus; bring into focus; adjust the focus of (the eye, a lens, etc.); concentrate *on*. L18. b *v.i.* Focus the eye, a lens, etc. M19. 2 *v.i.* Converge to or as to a focus; come into focus; come to a focus; concentrate or be concentrated *on*. M19.

1 R. BRADBURY I raised the beam of my flashlight . ., I focused it . . on the hole in the yellow ceiling. O. MANNING Guy tilted forward his glasses and tried to focus the spectacle before him. C. ACHEBE He took a little time to focus his eyes properly and decide who I was. H. M. ROSENBERG Electrons can be focussed into narrow beams by electrostatic or magnetic lenses. C. PRIEST I focused much of my distemper on London: I noticed only its bad qualities. 2 I. MURDOCH My eyes were dazed by the change of light and could not focus. H. KISSINGER Our concerns were still focusing on Iraq. A. BLEASDALE Miss Sutcliffe looks around the room, focuses finally on a big . . wardrobe. *Times* The DTI would not say whether the inspectors . . would focus on specific cases.

focusable *a.* L19. **focuser** *n.* a device for focusing; *spec.* an electrostatic or magnetic device for focusing particles: L19.

fodder /'fɒdə/ *n.* & *v.* [OE *fōdor* = MLG *vōder*, (M)Du. *voeder*, OHG *fuotar* (G *Futter*), ON *fóðr*, f. Gmc, f. base rel. to that of FOOD.] A *n.* †1 Food in general. OE–M17. 2 Food for cattle, horses, etc. Now *spec.* dried food, as hay, straw, etc., for stall-feeding. See also *cannon-fodder* s.v. CANNON *n.* OE.

Comb.: **fodder-cheese** cheese made from the milk of cows being foddered on hay.

B *v.t.* Give fodder to; feed *with* as fodder. In early use also *gen.*, feed. LME.

fodderer *n.* E17. **fodderless** *a.* M19.

fodge /fɒdʒ/ *n. Sc.* & *north.* Also **fadge** /fadʒ/. M18. [Origin unkn. Cf. next (earlier).] A short fat person.

fodgel /'fɒdʒ(ə)l/ *a. Sc.* E18. [Prob. f. prec.: see -EL[2].] Plump, buxom.

fodient /'fəʊdɪənt/ *a.* & *n. rare.* L17. [L *fodient-* pres. ppl stem of *fodere* dig: see -ENT.] A *adj.* Digging, burrowing. L17. B *n.* A burrowing animal. L19.

foe /fəʊ/ *a.* & *n.* Now *poet.* or *rhet.* OE. [Repr. two distinct OE wds: (i) *fāh* adj. = OFris. *fāch*, (ii) *ġefā* n., orig. use as n. of adj. = at feud (with), both = OHG *gifēh* at feud, odious, f. WGmc. After the pref. *ġe-* Y- was lost in early ME, the simple adj. and the orig. compound n. became coincident.] A *adj.* At feud *with*; hostile, inimical (*to*). Long *obs.* exc. in FOEMAN. OE.

B *n.* 1 Orig., an adversary in a feud or in mortal combat. Now more widely, a personal enemy or opponent, an ill wisher, *fig.* a thing inimical to one's well-being. OE. 2 A member of a hostile army or nation, an enemy in battle or war. ME. 3 *collect.* A hostile force, the enemy. L16.

1 POPE Embrace, embrace, my sons! be foes no more! 2 C. BOWEN Trojans eye me in wrath, and demand my life as a foe! C. DAY Aside from colds, . . his only foes were sick headaches. 3 C. RYAN A foe most of them remember as the fiercest soldiers they had ever encountered.

foehn *n.* see FÖHN.

foeman /'fəʊmən/ *n. arch.* & *literary.* Pl. **-men**. OE. [f. FOE *a.* + MAN *n.*] An enemy in war, an adversary.

foetal /'fiːt(ə)l/ *a.* Also **fet-**. E19. [f. FOETUS + -AL[1].] Of, pertaining to, or of the nature of a foetus; in the condition of a foetus.

foetal distress evidence of deteriorating condition of a foetus during labour.

foetalization /fiːt(ə)lʌɪ'zeɪʃ(ə)n/ *n.* Also **fet-, -isation**. M20. [f. prec. + -IZATION.] The retention into adult life of bodily characteristics which earlier in evolutionary history were only infantile.

'foetalized *a.* characterized by or manifesting foetalization M20.

foetation /fiː'teɪʃ(ə)n/ *n.* Also **fet-**. M17. [f. L *fetat-* pa. ppl stem of *fetare* (*foet-*) bring forth, breed, f. *fetus*: see FOETUS, -ATION.] The formation of a foetus or embryo.

foeticide /'fiːtɪsʌɪd/ *n.* Also **fet-**. M19. [f. FOETUS: see -CIDE.] The action of destroying a foetus or causing abortion.

foeti'cidal *a.* of or pertaining to foeticide L19.

foetid *a.* var. of FETID.

foetiferous /fiː'tɪf(ə)rəs/ *a.* Also **fet-**. M17. [f. L *fetifer*, f. *fetus*: see FOETUS, -FEROUS.] Producing offspring.

foetor *n.* var. of FETOR.

foetus /'fiːtəs/ *n.* Also **fet-**. LME. [f. L *fetus*, *foetus* pregnancy, giving birth, young offspring, abstract n. parallel to adj. *fetus* pregnant, productive.] An unborn viviparous animal in the womb, an unhatched oviparous animal in the egg; *esp.* an unborn human more than eight weeks after conception.

fog /fɒg/ *n.*[1] LME. [Origin uncertain: cf. Norw. *fogg*.] 1 The grass which springs up after hay has been cut; the aftermath. Also, long grass left standing in a pasture or among stubble and used as winter grazing. LME. 2 Moss. *Sc.* & *north.* LME.

1 **under fog** with the long grass left standing. YORKSHIRE *fog*.

fog /fɒg/ *n.*[2] M16. [Perh. back-form. f. FOGGY *a.*] 1 A thick cloud of minute water-droplets suspended in the atmosphere at or near the earth's surface, esp. when combined with dust or smoke; the obscurity produced by this. M16. b *transf.* Any abnormal darkened state of the atmosphere; an opaque mass *of* smoke. E17. 2 *fig.* A state of perplexity. Esp. in *in a fog*. E17. 3 *Photogr.* A deposit of silver on a negative or print etc., obscuring the image; an unwanted clouding. M19.

1 J. MASEFIELD Then fog came down . . and hid the seas. 2 J. GARDNER He wandered . . in a mental fog, unable to recognize his car when he saw it.

Comb.: **fog-bank** a dense haze at sea; **fog-bound** unable to proceed because of fog; **fog-bow** a phenomenon like a rainbow, produced by the action of light on fog; **fog-dog** = DOG *n.* 10; **foghorn** *n.* & *v.* (*a*) *n.* a sounding instrument (on a ship or on shore) warning ships in a fog; *fig.* (*colloq.*) a loud penetrating voice; (*b*) *v.t.* & *i.* (*colloq.*) utter or talk in a loud penetrating voice; **fog-lamp**: for improving visibility in fog; **fogman** a railwayman who places fog-signals; **fog-signal** (*a*) a detonator placed on a railway line in foggy weather to warn drivers; (*b*) (the signal given by) a foghorn .

fogless *a.* free from fog M19.

fog /fɒg/ *v.*[1] Infl. **-gg-**. L16. [f. FOG *n.*[2]] I *v.t.* 1 Surround or choke with fog; cover with fog or condensed vapour, steam or mist *up*. L16. 2 Put in a mental fog; bemuse, perplex. Also, make (an idea) confused. E19. 3 *Photogr.* Affect with an obscuring deposit of silver, make cloudy. M19. 4 *v.t.* Treat with something in the form of a spray, esp. an insecticide. Chiefly as *fogging* vbl n. M20.

1 W. BARLOW Somtimes by clouds it [the sun] is enueloped, and by mists fogged. A. HIGGINS Hot steam drifted about her, fogging up the window. 2 R. MACAULAY This reply had . . so fogged the poor reporter's mind that he had written no more.

II *v.i.* 5 *Hort.* Of a plant: damp *off*. M19. 6 Become covered or filled with fog; become covered with condensed vapour, steam or mist *up*. L19. 7 Place fog-signals on a railway line. Chiefly as *fogging* vbl n. L19.

6 T. O'BRIEN When his glasses fogged he did not bother to wipe them.

fog /fɒg/ *v.*[2] Infl. **-gg-**. E18. [f. FOG *n.*[1]] 1 *v.i.* Become overgrown with moss. *Sc.* E18. 2 *v.t. Agric.* Leave (land) under fog. Also, feed (animals) on fog or foggage. E19.

fogey *n.* var. of FOGY.

foggage /'fɒgɪdʒ/ *n. Sc.* L15. [med.L *fogagium*, f. FOG *n.*[1]: see -AGE.] 1 = FOG *n.*[1] L15. 2 (The right of) pasturing cattle on fog. *obs.* exc. *Hist.* L15.

fogger /'fɒgə/ *n.* L16. [Perh. f. *Fugger*, surname of a family of merchants and financiers of Augsburg in the 15th and 16th cents.] 1 A person given to underhand practices for the sake of gain; *esp.* a low-class lawyer. Long *obs.* exc. in PETTIFOGGER. L16. 2 A petty chapman; a pedlar. *dial.* E19. 3 A middleman between a nail-maker and a wholesale nail-merchant. *obs.* exc. *Hist.* M19.

foggy /ˈfɒgi/ *a.* L15. [In branch II certainly, and perh. in branch I also, f. FOG *n.*[1]] I 1 Of air, mist, etc.: thick and murky. Also, having the consistency of or filled with fog or thick mist. L15. b *fig.* Esp. of the understanding: confused, muddled. Of an idea or perception: indistinct. E17. 2 Of flesh etc.: spongy in consistency, flabby. Of a person or animal: unwholesomely fat or bloated. *obs.* exc. *dial.* M16. †3 Marshy, boggy. M16–M17. †4 Of beer: thick with floating particles. E17–M18. 5 *Photogr.* Obscured by a deposit of silver, cloudy. M19.

1b K. ISHIGURO My memory's so foggy these days. **not have the foggiest (idea** or **notion)** *colloq.* not have the slightest idea.

II 6 Resembling, consisting of, or covered with fog or rank grass; *Sc.* mossy. M17.

foggily *adv.* L16. **fogginess** *n.* M16.

fogle /ˈfəʊg(ə)l/ *n. arch. slang.* E19. [Origin unkn.] A (silk) handkerchief.

fogou /ˈfəʊguː/ *n.* L19. [Corn. *fogo, fougo.*] *Archaeol.* A Cornish form of souterrain.

fogram /ˈfəʊgrəm/ *n.* & *a. arch. slang.* M18. [Origin unkn.] A *n.* An old-fashioned person; a fogy. M18. B *adj.* Old-fashioned or antiquated in outlook. L18.

fogy /ˈfəʊgi/ *n.* & *a.* Also **fogey**, (*Sc.*) **foggie** /ˈfɒgi/. L18. [Rel. to prec.] A *n.* 1 An elderly or decrepit person, *esp.* one with old-fashioned or conservative ideas. Chiefly *old fogy. derog.* (orig. *Sc.*). L18. 2 An invalid or garrison soldier. *Sc.* (*obs.* exc. *Hist.*). L18.

1 J. RAE Some old fogey they have dragged out of retirement. **young fogy** a young person with markedly conservative tastes or ideas.

B *adj.* Antiquated in ideas or outlook; fogyish. *derog.* M19.

Sunday Telegraph The reactionary and Fogey elements at the Vatican.

fogydom *n.* the condition of a fogy M19. **fogyish** *a.* resembling or characteristic of a fogy L19. **fogyism** *n.* the ideas or condition of a fogy M19.

foh *int.* var. of FAUGH.

föhn /fəːn/ *n.* In sense 2 freq. **foehn.** M19. [G, in OHG *phōnno*, MHG *foenne*, ult. f. L (*ventus*) *Favonius* mild west wind.] 1 A warm dry south wind which blows down the valleys on the north side of the Alps. M19. 2 *Meteorol.* A warm dry katabatic wind developing on the lee side of a mountain range in response to air moving across the range. Also *föhn wind.* L19.

foible /ˈfɔɪb(ə)l/ *a.* & *n.* L16. [Fr., obs. var. of *faible*: see FEEBLE *a.*] †A *adj.* Weak, feeble. L16–E18.

B *n.* 1 *Fencing.* = FEEBLE *n.* 2. Cf. FORTE *n.*[1] 1. M17. 2 A special defect or peculiarity in a person's character etc., *esp.* one forming a source of misguided pride. L17.

2 THACKERAY A foible of Mr. Holt's.. was omniscience. A. FRATER He had flown with the emir.. and was familiar with his foibles at the controls.

foiblesse /fɛblɛs/ *n.* Now *rare* or *obs.* L17. [Fr., obs. var. of *faiblesse*, f. *faible* FEEBLE *a.*] A weakness of character; a failing; a liking or weakness *for*.

foie gras /fwɑː ˈgrɑː/ *n. phr. colloq.* Also **foie-gras.** E19. [Abbrev.] = PÂTÉ *de foie gras*.

foil /fɔɪl/ *n.*[1] ME. [Partly f. OFr. *foil* masc. f. L *folium* leaf, partly f. OFr. *foille* fem. (mod. *feuille*) f. L *folia* neut. pl. of *folium* treated as fem. sing. Cf. CINQUEFOIL, MILFOIL, TREFOIL.] 1 Metal (or †other substance) hammered or rolled into a thin sheet. Now also, metallized plastic film. ME. †2 A leaf; a heraldic representation of a leaf. LME–M16. 3†a *gen.* A thin layer of any material; a paring. LME–E17. b A counterfoil. Now *rare* or *obs.* L15. 4 A thin leaf of metal placed under a precious stone to increase its brilliance or under a transparent substance to give it the appearance of a precious stone. Formerly also, the setting of a precious stone. LME. 5 A sheet of metal foil (now usu. of a tin amalgam) placed behind the glass of a mirror as a reflector; *gen.* a background, a backing. L16. 6 A thing which or person who sets off another by contrast. L16. 7 *Archit.* Each of the small arcs between the cusps of a Gothic window or arch. M19.

1 K. AMIS To take the foil off the roasting capon and put it higher in the gas-oven. *aluminium foil, tinfoil*, etc. 4 H. FIELDING The finest brilliant requires a foil. 6 HAZLITT Real excellence does not seek for a foil in inferiority.

foil /fɔɪl/ *n.*[2] *arch.* L15. [f. FOIL *v.*[1] III.] 1 A setback or check in an enterprise; a repulse, a defeat. L15. †2 *Wrestling.* A throw not resulting in a complete fall. M16–L17.

1 C. MARLOWE Never had the.. Emperor So great a foil by any foreign foe. R. SOUTH It may give a man many a.. foil and many a disheartening blow.

foil /fɔɪl/ *n.*[3] L16. [f. FOIL *v.*[1] I. Cf. OFr. *foulis*, (O)Fr. *foulée* in same sense.] *Hunting.* 1 The track or scent of a hunted animal. L16. 2 A scent obliterating that of a hunted animal. M20.

1 **run (upon) the foil** (of a hunted animal) run over the same track a second time (and so baffle hounds).

foil /fɔɪl/ *n.*[4] L16. [Origin unkn.] A light blunt-edged fencing sword with a button on the point; in *pl.* & *sing.*, the exercise of fencing with such weapons.

foil /fɔɪl/ *n.*[5] M20. [Abbrev.] = HYDROFOIL.

Comb.: **foil-borne** (of a boat) lifted out of the water by means of hydrofoils; (of the motion etc. of a boat) taking place while the boat is so supported.

foil /fɔɪl/ *v.*[1] ME. [Perh. f. AN var. of (O)Fr. *fouler* full cloth, trample, ult. f. L *fullo* FULLER *n.*[1] The development in branch II is paralleled in DEFOIL, DEFOUL.] I In sense of Fr. *fouler*: cf. FULL *v.*[1] 1 *v.t.* Trample, tread down. *obs.* exc. *dial.* ME. 2 *v.t.* & *i. Hunting.* Cross (ground, a scent or track), or, formerly, travel *down* a stream, in such a way as to obliterate the scent. LME.

1 R. KNOLLES King Richard.. caused the ensignes of Leopold.. to be puld downe, and foiled under foot.

II Infl. by FOUL *a., v.* 3 *v.t.* Foul, pollute. *obs.* exc. *dial.* LME. †4 *v.t.* Violate the chastity of (a woman). LME–L16.

3 N. UDALL A man hath no honour to foile his handes on a woman.

III (Cf. earlier FOIL *n.*[2]) 5 *v.t.* Defeat or repulse (an opponent); beat off (an attack). Formerly also (in wrestling), inflict a foil or incomplete fall on. M16. †b *v.i.* Suffer defeat or discomfiture. L16–M17. c *v.t.* Outdo, surpass. L17. 6 *v.t.* Render ineffectual, frustrate, (a plan, attempt, etc.); frustrate the efforts or designs of (a person etc.). M16.

5 POPE Not fiercer woes thy fortitude could foil. 6 A. HOPKINS With enchanting waywardness he.. foils expectations. P. L. FERMOR Nets over the.. currant bushes foiled starlings but not us.

foil /fɔɪl/ *v.*[2]*t.* L16. [f. FOIL *n.*[1]] Chiefly as *foiled* ppl a. 1 Place foil under (a crystal etc.) to accentuate its brilliancy; *fig.* set off by contrast. L16. †2 Coat (glass, a mirror) with metal foil on one side as a reflector. Also, cover *over* (as) with foil. E17–E19. 3 *Archit.* Ornament with foils. M19.

foiling /ˈfɔɪlɪŋ/ *n.*[1] M16. [f. FOIL *v.*[1] + -ING[1].] The action of FOIL *v.*[1]; *esp.* the treading of a deer or other animal. Also, an animal's trail.

foiling /ˈfɔɪlɪŋ/ *n.*[2] L16. [f. FOIL *v.*[2] + -ING[1].] The action or process of FOIL *v.*[2]; *Archit.* ornamentation in the form of foils.

foilist /ˈfɔɪlɪst/ *n.* E20. [f. FOIL *n.*[4] + -IST.] A person who fences with a foil.

†**foillage** *n.* see FOLIAGE *n.*

†**foin** *n.*[1] ME–E18. [OFr. *foine* (mod. *fouine*), *faïne*, Walloon *fawine*, f. Proto-Romance deriv. of L *fagus* beech.] (The fur of) the beech-marten, *Martes foina*; in *pl.*, garments or trimmings of this fur.

foin /fɔɪn/ *n.*[2] *arch.* ME. [OFr. *foine, foisne* (mod. *fouine*) three-pronged fish-spear, f. L *fuscina* trident; partly f. FOIN *v.*] †1 A kind of spear. Only in ME. 2 A thrust made with a pointed weapon. LME. †3 = FOIL *n.*[4] M17–E18.

2 M. TWAIN Arthur smote.. Mordred with a foin of his spear.

foin /fɔɪn/ *v. arch.* LME. [f. FOIN *n.*[2]] 1 *v.i.* Make a thrust with or *with* a pointed weapon; lunge. Freq. foll. by *at* a person. LME. †2 *v.t.* Thrust at, stab. LME–M16.

1 *transf.*: G. CAVENDISH The boare continually foining at him with his great tuskes.

foison /ˈfɔɪz(ə)n/ *n.* ME. [(O)Fr. f. Proto-Romance f. L *fusio(n-)* outpouring: see FUSION, PROFUSION.] A *n.* 1 A plentiful supply, an abundance, (*of*); *esp.* a plentiful harvest. Formerly also (in *pl.*), abundant resources. *arch.* ME. 2 Inherent vigour, strength, or vitality. Now chiefly *Sc.* ME. 3 Sustaining power; nutriment. Now *dial.* & *Sc.* LME.

1 R. W. HAMILTON We anticipate the foison of an unknown husbandry. J. R. LOWELL He has a perennial foison of sappiness. 2 HENRY SMITH Such a foison hath your alms that.. it increases, like the widow's meal. 3 J. GEE The Liturgie.. is but dry meat, and hath no foison in it.

B *v.t.* Supply generously (*with*). Long *arch.* LME.

Maclean's Magazine Mr. Boyczuk won ribbons for his tray foisoned with grapes and apples.

foisonless *a.* (chiefly *Sc.*) (*a*) lacking strength, weak, exhausted; (*b*) not nutritious: E18.

foist /fɔɪst/ *n.*[1] LME. [f. as FUST *n.*[1]] †1 A wooden cask for wine etc. LME–M16. 2 A fusty smell. E19.

†**foist** *n.*[2] L15. [(O)Fr. *fuste* f. It. *fusta*, f. *fusto* stem, trunk or f. L *fustis* a cudgel.] 1 A vessel propelled both by sails and oars; a light galley. L15–L18. 2 A river barge. M16–E17.

†**foist** *n.*[3] L16. [f. FOIST *v.*[1]] 1 A rogue, a cheat; *spec.* a pickpocket. L16–L17. 2 A piece of roguery, a trick. E–M17. 3 A fraudulent insertion. M18–E19.

foist *n.*[4] see FIST *n.*[2]

foist /fɔɪst/ *v.*[1] M16. [Du. dial. *vuisten*, f. *vuist* FIST *n.*[1]] †1 *v.t.* & *i.* Palm (a false die) so as to be able to produce it at the right moment. Only in M16. b *v.i.* Practise roguery or deception; *spec.* pick a pocket. L16–L18. 2 *v.t.* Introduce *in*, *into* surreptitiously or unwarrantably. L16. 3 *v.t.* Impose (an unwelcome person or thing) *on*, *upon*; palm off or *off* (something worthless). Also, falsely fix the authorship of (a composition) *on*, *upon*. L16.

2 LYTTON The.. interpolations.. supposed to be foisted into the Odyssey. 3 MILTON The unskilfull fraud of him that foisted this Epistle upon Ignatius. G. A. SALA You have inferior articles foisted on you while being charged for the best. W. VAN T. CLARK Men.. only too willing to foist the burden.. on to others. G. GREENE God knows what Foreign Office type they might foist on us.

foist /fɔɪst/ *v.*[2] *obs.* exc. *dial.* L16. [f. FOIST *n.*[1] Cf. FUST *v.*] Become fusty.

†**foist** *v.*[3] var. of FIST *v.*[2]

foisty /ˈfɔɪsti/ *a.* E16. [f. FOIST *n.*[1] + -Y[1]. Cf. FUSTY.] Having a stale musty smell; fusty.

folacin /ˈfəʊləsɪn/ *n.* M20. [f. FOL(IC + AC(ID *n.* + -IN[1].] = FOLIC *acid.*

folate /ˈfəʊleɪt, ˈfɒl-/ *n.* M20. [f. FOLIC + -ATE[1].] *Biochem.* A salt or ester of folic acid.

fold /fəʊld/ *n.*[1] [OE *fald* contr. of *falæd, falod, -ud*, corresp. to OS *faled*, MLG *valt*, Du. *vaalt.*] 1 A pen or enclosure for livestock, esp. sheep. OE. b An enclosed piece of ground forming part of a farm. Now *rare.* LME. c The animals enclosed in a fold (now *rare*); *spec.* in *Sc.*, a herd of Highland cows used for breeding. M17. 2 *fig.* The Church, the body of Christian believers; *the* group of people who share a particular set of values etc. ME.

2 W. S. MAUGHAM He met an abbé who was celebrated for his success in bringing infidels and heretics back to the fold.

Comb.: **fold-course** *Hist.* the right of faldage; the land subject to this right.

foldless *a.*[1] having no fold or pen E19.

fold /fəʊld/ *n.*[2] ME. [f. FOLD *v.*[1]] 1 (Either of) the two parts of an object which are brought together in folding; the hollow between two such parts. ME. b A leaf of a book; each side of a double door. Now chiefly, a layer or thickness of cloth etc. E16. c A coil of a serpent's body or of string etc. L16. d An undulation or gentle curve of the ground; a slight hill or hollow. M19. e *Geol.* A bending or curvature in rock strata. M19.

2 The action of folding. Formerly also, an embrace. E17. b A manner or way of folding paper etc. L19. 3 A line or crease made by folding. M19.

1 A. GRAY The thick woollen stockings . . would not stay up but hung in folds round her ankles. G. HEYER Her crooked fingers worked amongst the folds of her silken skirt. d H. BELLOC That kind of landscape in which hills seem to lie in a regular manner, fold on fold, one range behind the other. 2 SHAKES. *Tr. & Cr.* And the weak wanton Cupid Shall from your neck unloose his amorous fold.

foldless *a.*[2] having no fold or crease M19.

fold /fəʊld/ *n.*[3] ME. [f. -FOLD in *manifold*, *threefold*, etc.] †1 A time, a repetition. Chiefly in *many a fold*. ME–L17. 2 (A specified number of) times. L17. 3 Each portion of a manifold thing. *rare*. E19.

2 N. ARNOTT The effect was found to be several fold greater than of steam from the same quantity of fuel.

fold /fəʊld/ *v.*[1] [OE *faldan*, *fealdan* = MDu. *vouden* (*vouwen*), OHG *faltan* (G *falten*), ON *falda*, Goth. *falþan*, f. Gmc. redupl. str. vb.] 1 *v.t.* Double or bend (a flexible thing) over on itself (also foll. by *in*, *over*, *together*); bend (a portion of a thing) *back*, *down*. OE. b *v.t. Geol.* Cause (rock strata etc.) to undergo bending or curvature. L19. 2 *v.t.* Lay (the arms etc.) together so as to overlap or intertwine; clasp (the hands) together or (now usu.) *together*. OE. †b Plait; mat (hair). LME–L16. 3 *v.t.* & *i.* Coil, wind. Now only w. *about*, *round*. ME. 4 *v.t.* Enclose (as) in a fold or folds, swathe, envelop (foll. by *in*, †*with*); embrace, clasp *in* one's arms or *to* one's breast. ME. 5 *v.i.* Yield to pressure so as to become folded, admit of being folded. Formerly also *fig.*, falter, lose courage; yield, succumb. Now chiefly as *folding* ppl a. ME. b *Geol.* Of rock strata etc.: undergo bending or curvature. M19. c Collapse; cease to function, go bankrupt. Also foll. by *up*. E20. †6 *v.t.* & *i.* Bend (oneself, a limb, etc.), bow. ME–E17.

1 W. H. AUDEN He envies those who have learned, / when reading newspapers, / how to fold them. 2 R. COBB Even if they had had wings, they would have kept them prudently folded. C. P. SNOW His hands, folded on his blotting-paper, stood out heavy-knuckled. 4 TENNYSON Shadows of the silver birk Sweep the green that folds thy grave. E. WHARTON Mrs Fisher . . had folded her in a demonstrative embrace. 5c A. BURGESS His trick cycle folded under him. S. BELLOW Competitors are trying to steal my chemist from me. Without him I'll have to fold.

With advs. in specialized senses: **fold away** make more compact by folding. **fold in** *Cookery* add (an ingredient) gently with a spoon, fork, etc., so as to mix it in without stirring or beating. **fold out** admit of being unfolded. **fold up** = *fold away* above; (see also sense 5c above).

Comb.: **foldaway** *a.* adapted to be folded away; **foldboat** [tr. G *Faltboot*] = FALTBOAT; **fold-out** *n.* & *a.* (an oversize page in a magazine etc.) which has to be unfolded by the reader; **fold-up** *a.* adapted to be folded up.

foldable *a.* L19.

fold /fəʊld/ *v.*[2]*t.* OE. [f. FOLD *n.*[1]] 1 Enclose (sheep etc.) in a fold; *fig.* bring into the body of Christian believers. Also foll. by *up*. OE. 2 Place sheep in a fold or folds on (a piece of land) to manure it. L17.

1 I. MURDOCH There was the distant sound of folded sheep.

-fold /fəʊld/ *suff.* [OE *-fald*, *-feald* = OFris., OS *-fald* (Du. *-voud*), (O)HG *-falt*, ON *-faldr*, Goth *-falþs*, cogn. w. FOLD *v.*[1] and w. Gk *-paltos*, *-plasios*, also w. *plo-* in *haplos*, and prob. w. L (*sim*)*plex*.] Forming adjs. and advs. from cardinal numerals and adjs. meaning 'many' w. the senses 'multiplied by', 'in an amount multiplied by', 'having so many parts', as in *threefold*, *manifold*, etc., and parallel ns. used with *a* w. the sense 'a specified number or amount of times' (cf. FOLD *n.*[3]).

†foldage *n.* var. of FALDAGE.

folder /ˈfəʊldə/ *n.*[1] Now *rare*. L16. [f. FOLD *v.*[2] + -ER[1].] A person who folds sheep, a shepherd.

folder /ˈfəʊldə/ *n.*[2] M17. [f. FOLD *v.*[1] + -ER[1].] 1 *gen.* A person who folds or doubles over something. Also foll. by *up*. M17. 2 A machine which folds paper etc. M19. 3 A folded pamphlet, circular, etc. *US*. L19. 4 A folding cover or holder for loose papers. E20.

¶ Earlier in UNFOLDER.

folding /ˈfəʊldɪŋ/ *n.* LME. [f. FOLD *v.*[1] + -ING[1].] 1 The action of FOLD *v.*[1]; an instance of this. LME. 2 A point or place of folding; a hill, a hollow; a group of hills or hollows; a fold of a garment. LME.

2 SIR W. SCOTT The foldings of his mantle green.

Comb.: **folding strength** the capacity of paper to withstand continuous alternate folding without tearing.

folding /ˈfəʊldɪŋ/ *ppl a.* E17. [f. FOLD *v.*[1] + -ING[2].] That folds; that is or can be folded.

folding door(s): consisting of two or more sections which can be folded against each other. **folding money** *colloq.* paper money.

folia /foˈlia/ *n.*[1] L18. [Port., lit. 'madness', f. Prov. Cf. FOLLY *n.*] A wild dance of Portuguese origin. Also, a special tune associated with this dance, esp. as a theme for instrumental variations.

folia *n.*[2] pl. of FOLIUM.

foliaceous /fəʊlɪˈeɪʃəs/ *a.* M17. [L *foliaceus*, f. *folium* leaf: see -ACEOUS.] 1 a *Bot.* Having the form or appearance of a leaf; (of a lichen) = FOLIOSE. Formerly, of a flower: having petals. M17. b Of or pertaining to a leaf or leaves; consisting of leaves. E19. 2 *Geol.* Consisting of, or of the nature of, thin leaflike plates. E18. 3 *Zool.* & *Entomol.* Shaped or arranged like leaves. E19.

foliage /ˈfəʊlɪɪdʒ/ *n.* & *v.* Also (earlier) **†foillage**. LME. [Alt. (after L *folium*) of (O)Fr. *feuillage*, †*foillage*, f. *feuille* leaf: see FOIL *n.*[1], -AGE.] A *n.* 1 Ornamental representation of leaves. Also (now *rare* or *obs.*), an instance of this. LME. 2 The leaves of a tree, plant, etc., collectively. E17.

2 J. HAWKES Every leaf gleams dully in the . . sun, and yet all are merged in the mass of heavy foliage.

Comb.: **foliage leaf** a normal green leaf (opp. petals and other modified leaves). **foliage plant**: grown for its decorative leaves rather than for its flowers.

B *v.t.* Decorate with foliage (real or representational). Chiefly as *foliaged* ppl a. M18.

foliar /ˈfəʊlɪə/ *a.* L19. [mod.L *foliaris*, f. L *folium* leaf: see -AR[1].] Of, pertaining to, or of the nature of a leaf.

foliar feed nutrients supplied to the leaves of a plant.

foliate /ˈfəʊlɪət, -eɪt/ *a.* E17. [L *foliatus* leaved, f. *folium* leaf: see -ATE[2].] †1 Of metal: beaten into foil. E17–E19. 2 Resembling a leaf; leaflike. M17. 3 Furnished with leaves. Also, decorated with representations of foliage. L17. 4 *Bot.* = FOLIOLATE. Cf. TRIFOLIATE. M19.

foliate /ˈfəʊlɪeɪt/ *v.* M17. [f. L *folium* leaf + -ATE[3]. With second part of sense 1 cf. med.L *foliare*.] 1 *v.t.* Apply foil or tin amalgam to (glass). Formerly also, beat (metal) into foil. M17. 2 *v.i.* Send out leaves. L18. 3 *v.i.* Split into thin leaflike sheets or laminae. L18. 4 *v.t. Archit.* Decorate (an arch etc.) with foils or leaf shapes. E19. 5 *v.t.* Mark the leaves of (a book or manuscript) with consecutive numbers. Cf. PAGINATE. M19.

2 *fig.*: A. BURGESS These [euphemisms] are foliating like triffids.

foliated /ˈfəʊlɪeɪtɪd/ *a.* M17. [f. FOLIATE *a.*, *v.* + -ED[1].] 1 Chiefly *Geol.* & *Min.* Composed of thin leaflike sheets or laminae. M17. 2 Having or consisting of leaves. E18. 3 Chiefly *Zool.* & *Conchol.* Shaped like a leaf or leaves; having leaflike processes. E19. 4 Decorated with carved foliage or with architectural foils. M19.

foliation /fəʊlɪˈeɪʃ(ə)n/ *n.* E17. [f. FOLIATE *a.*, *v.*: see -ATION.] 1 The process of bursting into leaf; the state of being in leaf. Also, a leaflike process or (formerly) scale. E17. †b The petals of a flower. L17–M18. c *Bot.* Arrangement of leaves in bud; vernation. L18. 2 Decoration of an arch etc. with foils; tracery made up of foils. E19. b An arrangement of carved foliage. L19. 3 *Geol.* The process or property of splitting into leaflike sheets or laminae; the laminae into which a crystalline rock divides. M19. 4 The consecutive numbering of the leaves in a book or manuscript. M19.

foliator /ˈfəʊlɪeɪtə/ *n.* M19. [f. FOLIATE *v.* + -OR.] A person who numbers the leaves of a book etc.

foliature /ˈfəʊlɪətʃə/ *n.* L17. [L *foliatura*, f. *foliatus* FOLIATE *a.*: see -URE.] (A cluster of) foliage. Also, carved foliage.

folic /ˈfəʊlɪk, ˈfɒl-/ *a.* M20. [f. L *folium* leaf + -IC.] *folic acid*, a vitamin of the B complex found in leafy green vegetables, liver, and kidney, whose deficiency causes pernicious anaemia and which is chemically a pteroylglutamic acid with one glutamic acid residue. Also called *folacin*, (chiefly *US*) *vitamin M*.

folie /ˈfɒli; *foreign* fɔli (*pl. same*)/ *n.* E19. [Fr.: see FOLLY *n.*] Mental illness, mania, madness. Chiefly in names of pathological conditions: see below.

folie à deux /ɑː ˈdəː, *foreign* a dø/ an identical delusion or mental disorder affecting two people living in close association. **folie de grandeur** /də grɒ̃ˈdəː, *foreign* grɑ̃dœːr/ delusions of grandeur. **folie du doute** /duː ˈduːt, *foreign* dy dut/ obsessive self-doubt.

foliferous *a.* var. of FOLIIFEROUS.

foliicolous /fəʊlɪˈɪkələs/ *a.* L19. [f. L *folii-* comb. form of *folium* leaf + -COLOUS.] Of a liverwort or fungus: growing or parasitic on leaves.

foliiferous /fəʊlɪˈɪf(ə)rəs/ *a.* Also **foliferous** /fə(ʊ)ˈlɪf-/. E19. [f. as prec. + -FEROUS.] Bearing leaves or leaflike appendages.

folio /ˈfəʊlɪəʊ/ *n.*, *a.*, & *v.* LME. [In sense A.I, a generalization of med.L use of abl. of L *folium* leaf, in references 'at leaf so-and-so', or a Latinization of It. *foglio*. In sense A.II, developed f. phr. *in folio*, f. It. *in foglio*.] A *n.* Pl. **-os**. I With ref. to numbering. 1 An individual leaf of paper, parchment, etc. (either loose as one of a series, or forming part of a bound volume) which is numbered on the recto or front side only. LME. 2 *Bookkeeping.* The two opposite sides of a ledger or account-book when they are used concurrently. Also, a single page of a ledger etc. showing both sides of an account. L16. 3 The page number in a printed book. L17. 4 A fixed number of words (in British legal documents etc. 72 or, in parliamentary proceedings, 90, in the US 100) used as a unit in reckoning the length of a document. M19.

II With ref. to size. 5 A size of book in which each leaf is half a standard printing-sheet. Usu. *in folio*. L16. 6 A sheet of paper folded once to form two leaves (four pages). E17. 7 A book or manuscript made up of sheets of paper folded once; a volume of the largest size. E17.

7 **First Folio** the first collected edition of Shakespeare's works, published in folio format in 1623.

B *adj.* Formed of sheets (or a sheet) folded once; (of a book) of the largest standard size. E17.

C *v.t.* Number the pages of. Chiefly as *folioing* vbl n. M19.

foliolate /ˈfəʊlɪələt, -eɪt/ *a.* M19. [f. next + -ATE[2].] *Bot.* Consisting of leaflets; (with numerical prefix) having the specified number of leaflets, as *3-foliolate*.

foliole /ˈfəʊlɪəʊl/ *n.* M18. [Fr. f. L *foliolum* dim. of *folium* leaf: see -OLE[1].] 1 *Bot.* Each of the divisions of a compound leaf; a leaflet. M18. 2 *Zool.* A small leaflike appendage. M19.

foliose /ˈfəʊlɪəʊz/ *a.* E18. [L *foliosus*, f. *folium* leaf: see -OSE[1].] Leafy; *spec.* (*a*) (of a liverwort) having the plant body differentiated into a stem and leaves (opp. *thalloid*); (*b*) (of a lichen) in which the thallus is lobed and leaflike and attached to the substrate by rhizoids (opp. *crustose*, *fruticose*).

foliot /ˈfɒlɪət/ *n.* ME. [OFr. = fowler's snare, (also mod.) foliot of a clock, prob. f. *folier* play the fool, f. *fol* foolish. In sense 2 cf. It. *folletto* = Fr. (*esprit*) *follet*, dim. of *fol*.] †1 Foolish or deluding talk. Only in ME. †2 A kind of goblin. Only in E17. 3 *Antiq.* The earliest form of escapement in clocks, consisting of a bar with adjustable weights on the ends. L19.

folium /ˈfəʊlɪəm/ *n.* Pl. **-ia** /-ɪə/. M18. [L.] **1** A leaf. Also, a leaflike process. Usu. in *pl.* M18. **2** *Geol.* A thin leaflike sheet, as of a schistose rock. Usu. in *pl.* L18. **3** Math. *folium of Descartes*, a cubic curve with a single node at which a single loop begins and ends. M19. **4** = FOLIO *n.* 6. *rare.* L19.

folivore /ˈfəʊlɪvɔː/ *n.* L20. [f. L *foli(i)-* comb. form of *folium* leaf: see -VORE.] *Zool.* An animal that feeds primarily on leaves.

folivorous /fə(ʊ)ˈlɪv(ə)rəs/ *a.* (of an animal) feeding primarily on leaves; (of diet) consisting of leaves: L20.

folk /fəʊk/ *n.* Pl. same, **-s**. [OE *folc* = OFris. *folk*, OS, OHG *folc* (Du. *volk*, G *Volk*), ON *folk* people, army, detachment, f. Gmc. Cf. VOLK.] **1** A people, a nation, a race; (of animals) a species, a kind. *arch.* OE. **2** In *pl.* (*folk*, †*folks*) & †*sing.* (A group of) people in relation to a superior, as the subjects of a king, the retainers or workpeople of a lord etc. *arch.* OE. **3** In *pl.* (*folk(s)*) & (now *arch.* & *dial.*) *sing.* People in general. Freq. w. qualifying adj. designating people of a certain group or class. Now chiefly *colloq.* OE. **4** In *pl.* (*folk(s)*). Relatives, members of one's family; *dial.* & *US* friends, neighbours. M17. **5** *ellipt.* = *folk music* below. M20.

2 G. PETTIE The maister of the house . . ought . . to shewe himself more seuere towards his owne folke, then towards others. 3 S. JOHNSON Folks want me to go to Italy. J. B. PRIESTLEY The working folk of Lancashire have much in common, of course, with their Yorkshire neighbours. I. SHAW I don't have a rich father, like some folks I know. *the wee folk*: see WEE *a.* 4 C. BROWN My folks didn't come up too much. Dad would never come any place to see me.

Attrib. & *comb.*: Esp. w. the sense 'of the (common) mass of people, traditional, popular', as *folk art, belief, culture, hero, legend, literature, myth, remedy, wisdom*, etc. Special combs., as **folk-blues** the original blues of the Blacks of the southern US, as opp. to composed imitations; **folk-club** a club where folk music is performed; **folk-dance** a dance of popular or traditional origin; a piece of music for such a dance; *folk epic*: see EPIC *n.*; **folk-etymologize** *v.t.* & *i.* alter by folk etymology; **folk etymology** the popular modifying of the form of a word to make it seem to be derived from familiar words, as *sparrowgrass* for *asparagus*; **folkfest** (chiefly *N. Amer.*) a festival of folk music or other elements of folk culture; *folk guitar*: see GUITAR *n.*; **folkland** *Hist.* land which was the property of the common people; **folk medicine** medicine of a traditional kind employing herbal remedies etc.; **folk memory** (a) recollection of the past persisting among a (group of) people; **folkmoot, folkmote** *Hist.* a general assembly of the people of a town, city, etc.; **folk music** music of popular or traditional origin; modern music composed in the style of this; **folk psychology** the psychology of races or peoples; **folk rock** folk music incorporating the stronger beat of rock music and usu. also electric stringed instruments etc.; **folksay** *US* traditional speech, the speech, proverbs, etc., of an oral tradition; **folk-singer** a singer of folk-songs; **folk-song** a song of popular or traditional origin; a modern composition in this style; **folk-tale** a tale of popular or traditional origin; **folk-way(s)** the traditional behaviour of a (group or class of) people; **folkweave** a rough loosely woven fabric.

folkie *n.* (*colloq.*) a folk-singer; a devotee of folk music: M20. **folkish** *a.* characteristic of the (common) people or traditional culture etc.; unsophisticated: M20. **folknik** *n.* [-NIK] a devotee of folk music M20.

folklore /ˈfəʊklɔː/ *n.* M19. [f. FOLK + LORE *n.*[1]] **1** The traditional beliefs, customs, songs, tales, etc., preserved in oral tradition among a (group of) people; the branch of knowledge that deals with these. M19. **2** Popular fantasy or belief. M20.

folkloric *a.* of or pertaining to folklore L19. **folklorish** *a.* resembling folklore E20. **folklorist** *n.* a person who studies folklore M19. **folkloˈristic** *a.* of or pertaining to folklore, of the character of folklore L19. **folkloˈristics** *n.* folklore as a branch of knowledge or a subject of research M20.

folksy /ˈfəʊksi/ *a.* M19. [f. FOLK + -SY.] **1** Friendly, sociable, informal. M19. **2** Having the characteristics of folk art or culture; *esp.* ostensibly or artificially folkish. M20.

folksiness *n.* M20.

folky /ˈfəʊki/ *a.* E20. [f. FOLK + -Y[1].] = FOLKSY 2.

folkiness *n.* M20.

folles *n.* pl. of FOLLIS.

follicle /ˈfɒlɪk(ə)l/ *n.* Also (*rare*) **-cule** /-kjuːl/. LME. [L *folliculus* little bag, dim. of *follis* bellows: see -CULE.] **1** *Anat.* Any of various small rounded saclike or vesicular structures, often having a secretory function; *esp.* (*a*) (also *hair follicle*) a secretory gland or cavity containing a hair-root; (*b*) any of the cavities in the ovary in which ova form. LME. **2** *Bot.* **a** A capsular fruit. Now *spec.* a single-carpelled fruit opening on one side only. E18. **b** An air-filled vesicle. L18.

1 GRAAFIAN *follicle*.

Comb.: **follicle-stimulating hormone** a pituitary hormone which promotes ripening of the follicles in the ovary and sperm formation in the testes; abbrev. *FSH*.

follicular /fɒˈlɪkjʊlə/ *a.* L17. [L *follicularis*, f. as prec.: see -AR[1].] **1** Of the nature of or resembling a follicle; consisting of follicles. L17. **2** Of or pertaining to a follicle or follicles; affecting follicles of a particular kind. M19.

folliculated /fɒˈlɪkjʊleɪtɪd/ *a.* L18. [f. as FOLLICLE + -ATE[2] + -ED[1].] Provided with a follicle or follicles.

follicule *n.* var. of FOLLICLE.

folliculitis /fəlɪkjʊˈlʌɪtɪs/ *n.* M19. [f. as FOLLICLE + -ITIS.] Inflammation of (esp. hair) follicles.

folliculose /fɒˈlɪkjʊləʊs/ *a.* E19. [L *folliculosus*, f. as FOLLICLE: see -OSE[1].] = FOLLICULAR 1.

folliful /ˈfɒlɪfʊl, -f(ə)l/. *a.* Long *obs.* exc. *dial.* M16. [f. FOLLY *n.* + -FUL.] Foolish.

follis /ˈfɒlɪs/ *n.* Pl. **folles** /ˈfɒliːz/. L19. [L.] *Hist.* A bronze or copper coin introduced by Diocletian in AD 296 and again used in Byzantine currency *c*800.

follow /ˈfɒləʊ/ *n.* L19. [f. the vb. See also FOLLOW-ON, FOLLOW-THROUGH, FOLLOW-UP.] **1** The action of FOLLOW *v.* L19. **2** *Billiards, Snooker*, etc. A stroke in which the cue-ball is struck above the centre in order to cause it to roll forward after the object-ball which it has set in motion; the impulse or spin given to the ball by such a stroke. L19.

follow /ˈfɒləʊ/ *v.* [OE *folgian* corresp. to OFris. *fol(g)ia, fulgia*, OS *folgon* (Du. *volgen*), OHG *folgēn* (G *folgen*), beside OE *fylġan*, ON *fylgja* accompany, help, lead, follow, pursue, f. Gmc.] I Go or come after; accompany; succeed. **1** *v.t.* & *i.* (foll. by *after*). Go or come after (a person or object in motion). OE. **2a** *v.t.* & (now *rare*) *i.* w. *after*, †*on*, †*upon*. Go after with intent to keep up, overtake, or catch; go in pursuit, chase, (a person or object in motion). OE. **b** *v.t.* & (now *rare*) *i.* w. *after*. Pursue (an object of desire); strive after, aim at. ME. †**c** *v.t.* Pursue (an affair) to its conclusion or accomplishment; prosecute; enforce (a law). Also foll. by *on, upon, against*. M16–L17. **3** *v.t.* Go after or along with (a person) as an attendant or companion; accompany; *fig.* be a (necessary) accompaniment to, be consequent upon. OE. **b** *v.t.* Go after as an admirer, suitor, etc. E17. **c** *v.t.* & *i.* Attend (the body of a deceased person) to the grave; *colloq.* attend (a person's funeral). E19. **4a** *v.t.* & *i.* Come after (something else) in sequence, order of time, etc. ME. **b** *v.i.* Happen or occur after something else; ensue. Formerly also, proceed, continue. (Foll. by *on*). LME. **c** *v.t.* Provide (a thing) *with* a sequel or a successor. L17. **5a** *v.i.* Result, be deducible, occur as a consequence. (Foll. by *from*, †*of*). ME. **b** *v.t.* Come after or succeed (something) as a consequence. L16.

1 J. R. GREEN One of the Norman strangers who followed in the wake of the Conqueror. E. BOWEN One by one they had followed each other out. J. CHEEVER The smell of fresh earth that follows a plow. 2a G. GREENE The chap who was following him had to queue up at the ordinary entrance and lost him. b T. GUNN The blue jay scuffling in the bushes follows some hidden purpose. c SHAKES. *2 Hen. IV* O, such a day, so fought, so followed, and so fairly won. 3 S. C. HALL The rheumatic . . creature who had 'followed' the family for more than forty years. b SHAKES. *Haml.* Do they hold the same estimation they did when I was in the city? Are they so followed? 4a E. BOWEN He went off to order the supper—just supper, they said, fish or something, with coffee to follow. W. TREVOR The Whitsun visitors would follow the Easter ones. b I. MURDOCH He had, since his retirement . . had no opportunities for self-indulgence, since Fanny's death had followed so soon after. 5a M. HOLROYD If friends were God's apology for families, it followed they should be as unlike one's own family as possible. b ANTHONY SMITH Fits can follow many of the ordinary vicissitudes of life, such as fright.

II Keep to or trace the course of. **6** *v.t.* Treat or take (a person) as a guide, leader, etc.; accept the authority or example of; espouse the opinions or cause of. OE. **7** *v.t.* Conform to, comply with, obey, or act upon or in accordance with, (advice, command, fashion, etc.). OE. †**b** Conform to in likeness, resemble, take after; imitate. OE–L17. **8** *v.t.* Pursue or practise (a way of life, a hobby, etc.); engage in or apply oneself to (work etc.); *esp.* earn a living at (a profession). OE. **9** *v.t.* Go forward along, keep to the track or course of, (a path etc.). ME. **10** *v.t.* & *i.* Keep track of mentally, understand, grasp the meaning of, (an argument, a speaker, etc.). L17. **b** *v.t.* Watch the progress or course of (a person or object in motion); take a close interest in the present state or progress of (events, a football team, etc.). L17.

6 ISAIAH BERLIN Kant insisted, following Rousseau, that a capacity for rational self-direction belonged to all men. 7 I. MURDOCH I . . followed my rule of never speaking frankly to women in moments of emotion. R. S. THOMAS And he writes there/in invisible handwriting the instructions/the genes follow. 8 G. GREENE The career of an *hôtelier* was not . . the one which the Jesuits had expected me to follow. 9 E. M. FORSTER Her track through the dew followed the path that he had turfed over. R. BRAUTIGAN I walked down . . from Steelhead, following the Klamath River. 10 J. GASKELL It is a bit difficult . . to follow technicalities in a foreign tongue. R. MACDONALD I don't quite follow I'm very stupid today. b R. DAVIES I don't suppose he made a move without you following him with your eyes. F. JOHNSON We are following with concern events in Germany.

Phrases: *follow in a person's footsteps*: see FOOTSTEP *n.* 1. *follow one's nose*: see NOSE *n.* *follow suit*: see SUIT *n.* *follow the crowd*: see CROWD *n.*[2] **follow the drum** *arch.* be a soldier. **follow the hounds** go hunting. *follow the plough*: see PLOUGH *n.* 3. **follow the sea** be a sailor. **follow the string** *Archery* (of a bow) take on a permanent curve from use.

With advs. in specialized senses: **follow on** (*a*) continue moving in the same direction as an object moving in front; provide continuation; (*b*) *Cricket* (of a team) go in to bat for a second innings immediately after failing in their first innings to reach a score a prescribed number of runs fewer than that of their opponent's first innings. **follow out** pursue to a conclusion; carry out (instructions) precisely. **follow through** continue to completion; *spec.* (*Golf, Cricket*, etc.) continue a stroke or action (esp. to the full extent of the swing), after the ball has been struck or (in bowling) released. **follow up** pursue steadily or closely; make further investigation of; reinforce by further action or support.

Comb.: **follow-me-lads** *arch.* [cf. Fr. *suivez-moi-jeune-homme*] curls or ribbons hanging loosely over the shoulder; **follow-my-leader,** (*N. Amer.*) **follow-the-leader** a game in which each player must do as the leader does, or pay a forfeit; **follow-spot** a spotlight that follows a performer on the stage.

followable *a.* LME.

follower /ˈfɒləʊə/ *n.* OE. [f. prec. + -ER[1].] **1a** An attendant, a servant, a companion. OE. **b** An adherent, a disciple; a person who follows an example, rule of conduct, etc. ME. **c** An admirer; *esp.* a man courting a maidservant who calls at the house to see her. *arch.* M19. **2a** A thing that comes after or succeeds something else. *rare.* LME. **b** A person who goes or comes after a person or object in motion; a pursuer. L16. **3** A young cow, horse, or hen. Chiefly *Sc.* & *north.* LME. **4** A mechanical part whose motion or action is derived from that of another part to which force is applied; *spec.* (*a*) a block or plate through which the pressure of a press, pile-driver, etc., is applied; (*b*) a wheel etc. deriving its motion from a driving-wheel, cam, etc. L17.

1a F. FERGUSSON He meets an old man with his servants . . and kills him and all his followers. 2b

SHAKES. *3 Hen. VI* Ah hark! The fatal followers do pursue.

following /'fɒləʊɪŋ/ *n.*[1] ME. [f. FOLLOW *v.* + -ING[1].] 1 The action of FOLLOW *v.* Also foll. by adv. ME. 2 A body of followers, attendants, or adherents. LME.

1 J. STRUTT Queen Elizabeth . . frequently indulged herself in following of the hounds. W. D. WHITNEY The following-up of a series of acts. 2 B. T. BRADFORD The bartender . . was something of a character and had a large following.

following /'fɒləʊɪŋ/ *a.*, *n.*[2], & *prep.* ME. [f. as prec. + -ING[2].] A *adj.* 1 That follows. ME. b *esp.* In introducing a statement etc.: now to be mentioned. ME. 2 *Naut.* Of a wind or sea: blowing or moving in the direction of the ship's course. E16.

1 SHAKES. *Lucr.* What following sorrow may on this arise. POPE His following shield the fallen chief o'erspread. *New Yorker* The following year, a grand jury . . questioned him. b A. THWAITE The son sent his father the following account of a visit.

B *absol.* as *n. The* fact(s), person(s), thing(s), etc., now to be mentioned. L18.

C *prep.* As a sequel to or consequence of; coming after in time. M20.

H. GARDNER He had . . become the idol of the West End stage, following the sensational success of a rather sentimental historical play.

follow-on /'fɒləʊɒn, fɒləʊ'ɒn/ *n.* & *a.* L19. [f. *follow on* s.v. FOLLOW *v.*] A *n.* The action or an act of following on. L19.

Cricket World In the first three hours of the follow-on came just 77 runs.

B *attrib.* or as *adj.* That follows on. L19.

Financial Times A large follow-on order . . for engines.

follow-through /fɒləʊ'θruː/ *n.* & *a.* L19. [f. *follow through* s.v. FOLLOW *v.*] A *n.* The action or an act of following through. L19.

P. METZLER He rolled his drives with long contact between ball and strings, and finished them with a full follow-through. *Times* Dealers reported that best levels could not be maintained because of a lack of follow-through.

B *attrib.* or as *adj.* That follows through. E20.

follow-up /'fɒləʊʌp/ *n.* & *a.* E20. [f. *follow up* s.v. FOLLOW *v.*] A *n.* The action or an act of following up; a continuation or repetition of an initial action; *esp.* (*a*) a second advertisement, letter, etc., referring to an earlier one; (*b*) *Med.* a renewal or continuation of contact with, or a re-examination of, a patient at an interval or intervals after treatment. E20.

Listener There was no evidence . . that the whole operation was planned . . as a follow-up to the occupation of Southern Thule. O. SACKS His wife became virtually exempt from migraine and in a six-month follow-up had suffered only two attacks.

B *attrib.* or as *adj.* That follows up; of or pertaining to (a) renewed or repeated action. E20.

folly /'fɒli/ *n.* & *v.* ME. [(O)Fr. *folie* madness, f. *fol* mad, foolish: see FOOL *n.*[1] & *a.*, -Y[3]. In sense 2b cf. also Fr. *folie* delight, favourite abode.] A *n.* 1 The quality or state of being foolish or deficient in understanding; lack of good sense; unwise conduct. ME. 2 An instance of foolishness; a foolish act, idea, practice, etc.; a ridiculous thing. ME. b A costly ornamental building (considered as) serving no practical purpose. L16. †3 Evil, wickedness; harm; (a) crime, (a) sin; *esp.* (an act of) lechery or fornication. ME–M17. †4 Madness; rage. ME–L17. 5 *Theatr.* In *pl.* (A revue with) glamorous female performers. E20.

1 T. GRAY Where ignorance is bliss, 'Tis folly to be wise. H. CARPENTER *The Tale of Tom Kitten* deals with the folly of forcing children into tidy clothes. 2 JOHN BROOKE To avoid the follies and weaknesses of his grandfather. b P. LEVI The Monument was a Gothic folly, a carved stone tower standing alone in a field. 5 *Ziegfeld Follies* etc.

B *v.i.* Act foolishly. *arch.* M18.

Folsom /'fəʊls(ə)m/ *a.* E20. [See below.] Designating or pertaining to a prehistoric culture first found near Folsom in NE New Mexico, USA, or its remains, esp. a type of fluted lanceolate projectile point.

foment /'fə(ʊ)mɛnt/ *n.* LME. [L *fomentum*: see next. In sense 3 prob. infl. by FERMENT *n.*] 1 = FOMENTATION 1b. Now *rare.* LME. 2 A thing that foments something; a stimulus, an encouragement. *obs.* exc. as passing into sense 3. E17. 3 = FERMENT *n.* 2b. L18.

2 HENRY MORE The foments of strife and palliations of hypocrisy. 3 T. JEFFERSON Should the present foment in Europe not produce republics everywhere.

foment /fə(ʊ)'mɛnt/ *v.t.* LME. [(O)Fr *fomenter* f. late L *fomentare*, f. L *fomentum* lotion, poultice, f. *fovere* heat, cherish.] 1 Bathe or poultice with fomentations; apply a fomentation to. LME. 2a Foster, stimulate, or instigate (a sentiment, a course of conduct, sedition, etc.). E17. b Promote the growth, development, effect, or spread of (something physical). *arch.* M17. †3 Excite, irritate. M17–E18. †4 Warm. Only in M17.

2a E. LONGFORD Strong hostility to Wellington was being fomented in the House of Lords. V. GLENDINNING She . . orchestrated and fomented the quarrels and alliances of her . . young men.

fomenter *n.* E16.

fomentation /fəʊmɛn'teɪʃ(ə)n/ *n.* LME. [(O)Fr., or late L *fomentatio(n-)*, f. *fomentat-* pa. ppl stem of *fomentare*: see prec., -ATION.] 1a The action or an act of applying a fomentation (sense 1b). LME. b A preparation of hot moist material or a warm or medicated lotion for application to the body. LME. 2 The action of fostering, stimulating, or instigating; an influence, a stimulus. E17. †3 The action of warming. Only in M17.

fomes /'fəʊmiːz/ *n.* Now only in pl. **fomites** /'fəʊmɪtiːz/. M17. [L = tinder.] †1 The cause or source of a disease or *fig.* of sin etc. M17–L18. 2 In *pl.* Inanimate carriers of infection; *spec.* the clothes, bedding, etc., of a person with a communicable disease. E19.

Fomorian /fə'mɔːrɪən/ *a.* & *n.* L19. [f. OIr. *fomoir*, later *fomhóir*, w. 2nd elem. possibly rel. to either Ir. *muir* sea or OE *mære* nightmare (see MARE *n.*[2]), + -IAN.] *Ir. Mythol.* (A member) of a race of pirates or giants.

†**fon** *n.*[1], *a.*, & *v.* ME. [Origin & exact interrelation unkn. See also FOND *a.*, FUN *v.*] A *n.* A fool. ME–L16. B *adj.* Foolish. LME–L16. C *v.* 1 *v.i.* Be foolish or infatuated; act the fool. LME–M16. 2 *v.t.* Make a fool of. Only in LME.

Fon /fɒn/ *n.*[2] & *a.* M19. [Fon.] A *n.* Pl. same, **-s**. 1 A member of a W. African people inhabiting the southern part of Benin. M19. 2 The Kwa language of this people, a close relative of Ewe. M19. B *attrib.* or as *adj.* Of or pertaining to the Fon or their language. M19.

fond /*in sense 3* fɒnd; *in senses 1 & 2 foreign* fɔ̃ (*pl. same*)/ *n.* Also †**fonds**. M17. [Fr. *fond*, *fonds* (now differentiated in sense) f. OFr. *fonz*, *fons* ult. f. L *fundus* bottom: cf. FUND *n.*] 1 Foundation, ground, groundwork. Now *rare.* M17. 2 = FUND *n.* 3. Now *rare.* L17. 3 = FUND *n.* 4 *obs.* exc. *Sc. dial.* L17.

¶Orig. Anglicized in all senses.

fond /fɒnd/ *a.* LME. [f. FON *n.*, *v.*: see -ED[2], -ED[1].] †1 Insipid, flavourless; sickly. LME–E19. 2 Infatuated, foolish. Now *esp.* foolishly credulous or confident. LME. 3 Imbecile; mad. *obs.* exc. *dial.* LME. 4 Eager, glad, inclined. Foll. by *to do*, †*of*. *obs.* exc. *Sc.* M16. 5 Foll. by *of*, †*on*: having a strong affection or liking for; (formerly) proud of. L16. 6a Of a person, an action, or attribute: overaffectionate, foolishly doting; tender, loving. L16. b Of an opinion, a sentiment, etc.: held with strong or unthinking affection, foolishly optimistic. M17. †7 Trifling, trivial. E–M17.

2 T. FULLER Never more to fright Children with fond tales of Bug-bears. 4 I. WATTS We are so fond to appear always in the right. 5 C. CONNOLLY He was fond of wine and very partial to grapes and figs. E. TEMPLETON She worries about Father . . I didn't know she was so fond of him. P. ROSE The melodramas in which he was fond of acting. 6a J. BUCHAN Every letter he wrote was treasured by a fond mother. D. WELCH She shook her head and smiled with fond reproach. b W. H. AUDEN Our fondest hopes were granted. E. P. THOMPSON It was the fond belief of the English people that the employment of spies . . was un-British.

fondish *a.* M19.

†**fond** *v.*[1] Also **fand**. [OE *fandian* corresp. in form to OFris. *fandia*, OS *fandon*, OHG *fantōn*.] 1 *v.t.* Put to the proof, try, test; tempt. OE–LME. 2 *v.t.* Attempt, undertake (*to do*, a deed). OE–L16. 3 *v.t.* Seek, look for. Only in ME. 4 *v.i.* & *refl.* Go, travel. ME–M17.

†**fond** *v.*[2] M16. [f. FOND *a.*] 1 *v.i.* Dote *on*, *upon*, *over*. M16–E17. 2 *v.t.* Make a fool of; beguile. M16–L17. 3 *v.t.* Caress, fondle; be fond of. L17–E18.

fonda /'fɒnda, 'fɒndə/ *n.* E19. [Sp., f. as FONDUK.] In Spain and Spanish-speaking countries: an inn, a hotel.

fondaco /'fɒndəkəʊ, *foreign* 'fondako/ *n.* Now *rare.* Pl. **-chi** /-ki/. L16. [It., f. as FONDUK.] In Italy etc.: a warehouse; formerly also, an inn, a hotel.

fondant /'fɒnd(ə)nt/ *n.* L19. [Fr., use as n. of pres. pple of *fondre* melt: see FOUND *v.*[2], -ANT[1].] A sweet made of a soft paste of flavoured (and usu. coloured) sugar; (more fully *fondant paste*) such a paste.

Comb.: **fondant icing**: made of fondant paste; *fondant paste*: see above.

fondle /'fɒnd(ə)l/ *v.* & *n.* L17. [Back-form. f. next.] A *v.* †1 *v.t.* Treat indulgently; pamper. L17–L18. 2 *v.t.* Handle or treat with fondness; caress, stroke lovingly or amorously. L18. 3 *v.i.* Behave or speak fondly or amorously (*with*, *together*, etc.). E19.

2 A. PATON Kumalo lifted him up, and wiped his nose clean, and kissed and fondled him. J. OSBORNE She puts out her hand, and runs it over his head, fondling his ear and neck. *Daily Express* Optician Geoffrey Wilson who fondled a young woman patient in his darkened consulting room was yesterday struck off. 3 DICKENS 'Foolish Nell', said the old man fondling with her hair.

B *n.* An act of fondling. E19.

fondler *n.* M18.

fondling /'fɒndlɪŋ/ *n.* Now *rare.* LME. [f. FOND *a.* + -LING[1].] †1 A foolish person. LME–L18. 2 A much loved person; a person much caressed or fondled; a pet. L16.

fondly /'fɒndli/ *a. rare.* L16. [f. FOND *a.* + -LY[1].] = FOND *a.* 2, 6.

fondly /'fɒndli/ *adv.* LME. [f. FOND *a.* + -LY[2].] †1 Foolishly, ignorantly. LME–M17. 2 Affectionately, tenderly, lovingly. L16. 3 With self-deceiving, affectionate, or foolish credulity. M18.

2 COLERIDGE Fondly in his arms he took Fair Geraldine. E. WAUGH She . . asked fondly about his injuries. 3 W. IRVING I will henceforth . . endeavour to be all that she fondly imagined me.

fondness /'fɒndnɪs/ *n.* LME. [f. FOND *a.* + -NESS.] 1 (An instance of) foolishness or folly. *obs.* exc. *dial.* LME. 2 Foolish or unreasoning affection or tenderness. L16. 3 Affection, tenderness; a strong (and unreasoning) inclination, partiality, propensity, or desire *for*. E17.

2 J. GAY By partial fondness shown . . we doat upon our own. 3 HANNAH MORE A mother's fondness reigns Without a rival. B. BAINBRIDGE Some people thought of foxgloves as weeds, but she had a fondness for them.

†**fonds** *n.* see FOND *n.*

fondue /'fɒnd(j)uː/ *n.* M19. [Fr., fem. pa. pple of *fondre* melt: see FOUND *v.*[2]] A dish of flavoured melted cheese. Also, any dish in which small pieces of food are dipped into a hot or boiling liquid.

fonduk /'fɒndʊk/ *n.* E18. [Arab. *funduq* f. Gk *pandokeion*, *pandokheion* inn.] In N. Africa: an inn, a hotel; a warehouse.

fons et origo /fɒnz ɛt 'ɒrɪgəʊ, ɒ'rʌɪgəʊ/ *n. phr.* E19. [L.] The source and origin (*of*). Earliest in *fons et origo mali* /'mɑːli/, the source and origin of evil.

A. N. WILSON The *fons et origo* of his devotion to Catholicism was that it was the ancient faith of Europe.

font /fɒnt/ *n.*[1] LOE. [L *fons*, *font-* spring, fountain, in specialized eccl. use *fons* or *fontes* *baptismi* water(s) of baptism.] 1 A receptacle, usu. of stone and free-standing, for the water used in baptism. Also *baptismal font*. LOE. b A receptacle for holy water. M16. c The reservoir for oil in a lamp. L19. 2 A spring, a fountain; the fount or source (of something). LOE.

Comb.: **font-name** (one's) baptismal name; †**font-stone** = sense 1 above; **fontware** *Computing* typesetting software designed to enable special printing fonts to be used.

fontful *n.* (*rare*) as much as a font will hold LME.

font /fɒnt/ *n.*[2] L16. [Fr. *fonte*, f. *fondre* melt: see FOUND *v.*[2] See also FOUNT *n.*[2]] 1 The action or process of casting or founding. Also, cast iron. *rare*. L16. 2 *Printing*. A complete set of type of a particular face and size; a set of characters of a consistent design (esp. as bought from a particular supplier) for the composition of text; a typeface. Also *font of type*. L17.

fontal /ˈfɒnt(ə)l/ *a.* & *n.* L15. [OFr., or med.L *fontalis*, f. L *fons*, *font-*: see FONT *n.*[1], -AL[1].] A *adj.* 1 a Of or pertaining to a fountain or spring. *rare*. L15. b Of or pertaining to the source or fountain-head of something; original, primary. L17. 2 Of or pertaining to a baptismal font; baptismal. L15.

1b COLERIDGE The fontal truths of natural religion.

B *n. Her.* A shell or urn (usu. supported by a mythological figure) from which a stream of water flows, symbolizing a river. L17.

fontanelle /fɒntəˈnɛl/ *n.* Also *-**el**. M16. [Fr. f. mod.L *fontanella* Latinization of OFr. *fontenelle* dim. of *fontaine* FOUNTAIN *n.*: see -EL[2].] †1 A hollow of the skin between muscles. Only in M16. †2 A natural or artificial outlet for bodily secretions, morbid fluids, or the like; *fig.* a source, an outlet. E17–M19. 3 Any of a number of soft areas of incomplete ossification in the skull of an infant, lying at junctions of more than two sutures. M18.

fontange /fɔ̃tɑ̃ːʒ/ *n.* Pl. pronounced same. L17. [Fr., f. the Duchesse de *Fontanges*, a mistress of Louis XIV.] *Hist.* (A hairstyle requiring the front hair to be curled into a high dressing on a wire frame, topped by) a topknot of ribbon or lace.

food /fuːd/ *n.* [Late OE *fōda*, f. Gmc: no exact counterparts in other Gmc langs. Cf. FEED *v.*, FODDER *n.*] 1 Substance(s) (to be) taken into the body to maintain life and growth, nourishment; provisions, victuals. LOE. †b One's livelihood. LOE–E17. c An article of food; a type of food. LME. d Solid nourishment, as opp. to drink. E17. 2 *fig.* Something providing spiritual, emotional, or mental sustenance. Now *spec.* matter or material to discuss or dwell on. LOE. †3 The act of eating. ME–L16. †4 That which is fed or nurtured; a child, a creature, a person. ME–L15. 5 Nutriment absorbed by a plant from the earth or air. M18.

1 T. R. MALTHUS Want of food . . the most efficient cause of the three immediate checks to population. SCOTT FITZGERALD After a day without food he began to grow hungry. 2 STEELE Praise is the Food of a great Soul. SOUTHEY A lively tale, and fraught With . . food for thought. L. RITCHIE There the reflective will find food for their meditations.

Phrases: **be food for fishes** be drowned. **be food for powder** be fit only to die in battle; be a soldier or soldiers. **be food for worms** be dead. *fast food*: see FAST *a.* *junk food*: see JUNK *n.*[2] *skin food*: see SKIN *n.*

Comb.: **food additive** a substance added to food as a colouring, flavouring, or preservative, or for some other non-nutritional purpose; **food call** the cry of a bird for food; **food-chain** *Ecol.* a series of organisms each dependent upon the next for food, esp. by direct predation; **food chemistry** the branch of science that deals with the chemical constitution of foods; **food cycle** *Ecol.* the system of interdependent food chains in a community; **food-fish** a fish used as food by humans; *food-pass*: see PASS *n.*[2] 14; **food poisoning** illness due to bacteria or toxins in food consumed; **food processor** a kitchen appliance or other machine for processing food by chopping, mixing, shredding, etc.; **food stamp** *US* a stamp exchangeable for food, issued cheaply to the needy; **foodstuff** an item of food, a substance used as food; **food value** the relative nourishing power of a food, nutritional value; **food web** *Ecol.* = *food cycle* above.

foodful *a.* (chiefly *poet.*) rich in food; nutritious M17. **foodless** *a.* LME.

foodaholic /fuːdəˈhɒlɪk/ *n. colloq.* Also **-oholic**. M20. [f. FOOD + -AHOLIC.] A person with an inordinate craving for or obsession with food; a compulsive eater.

foodie /ˈfuːdi/ *n. colloq.* Also **foody**. L20. [f. FOOD + -IE, -Y[6].] A person with a particular interest in food; a gourmet.

foodoholic *n.* var. of FOODAHOLIC.

foody *n.* var. of FOODIE.

foody /ˈfuːdi/ *a.* E17. [f. FOOD + -Y[1].] Full of food (*rare*); of or pertaining to food.

foo-foo /ˈfuːfuː/ *n.* Also **fufu**. M18. [Twi *fufuu*.] Dough made from boiled plantain.

fool /fuːl/ *n.*[1] & *a.* ME. [OFr. *fol* n. & a. (mod. *fol*, *fou* mad, madman) f. L *follis* bellows, inflated ball, (later, fig.) windbag, empty-headed person. See also TOMFOOL.] A *n.* 1 A person who behaves or thinks imprudently or unwisely; a silly person. ME. 2 A jester or clown, esp. as formerly retained in a great household. ME. 3 A person who is fooled or imposed on, a dupe. *arch.* exc. in *make a fool of*. LME. 4 A person with a mental handicap or mental illness. *obs.* exc. in *born fool*, *natural fool* (now only as gen. terms of abuse). LME.

1 T. DEKKER Fooles by lucky Throwing, oft win the Game. QUILLER-COUCH When first I met you . . I thought you a fool To-day you have grown into an unmitigated ass. *Proverbs*: A fool and his money are soon parted. A fool at forty is a fool indeed. A fool may give a wise man counsel. There's no fool like an old fool Fools rush in where angels fear to tread. 4 R. LASSELS The Pazzorella, where they keep madmen and fools.

Phrases & comb.: **act the fool** act foolishly; indulge in buffoonery or ridiculous behaviour. *All Fools' Day*: see ALL *a.* 2. APRIL *fool*. **be a fool for** be unable to resist the appeal or attractions of. **be a fool for one's pains** have one's trouble for nothing. **be a fool to** *arch.* be nothing in comparison with. **Feast of Fools** *Hist.* a burlesque festival sometimes celebrated in churches in the Middle Ages on New Year's Day. **fool's coat** the motley or particoloured coat of a fool or jester. **fool's cress** = *fool's watercress* below. **fool's** ERRAND. **fool's gold** any yellow mineral, *esp.* pyrite or chalcopyrite; *fig.* something deceptively attractive, profitable, etc., in appearance. **fool's mate** *Chess*: in which the first player is checkmated by the opponent's second move. **fool's paradise** a state of illusory happiness. **fool's parsley** an umbelliferous garden weed, *Aethusa cynapium*, with finely divided leaves, superficially resembling parsley. **fool's watercress** an aquatic umbelliferous plant, *Apium nodiflorum*, with pinnate leaves resembling those of watercress. **nobody's fool**, **no fool** a sensible person, not easily deceived. **play the fool** = *act the fool* above. *ship of fools*: see SHIP *n.* 1.

B *adj.* Foolish, silly, stupid. Now *colloq.* (chiefly *N. Amer.*). ME.

S. COLVIL Fighting is a fool thing. W. N. HARBEN He's goin' to ruin us with his fool notions. **fool hen** *US colloq.* a spruce grouse or similar bird, esp. when young or tame.

foolship *n.* (now *rare*) (*a*) the quality or state of being a fool; foolishness; (*b*) (with possess. pron., as *your* etc. *foolship*) a mock title of respect for a fool: L15.

fool /fuːl/ *n.*[2] L16. [Perh. transf. use of FOOL *n.*[1]] Orig. a confection of clotted cream, a custard trifle. Now, a purée of fruit (esp. gooseberries) mixed or served with cream or custard.

fool /fuːl/ *v.* LME. [f. FOOL *n.*[1] & *a.*] †1 *v.i.* Be or become foolish or insane. LME–L15. 2 *v.i.* Behave like a fool; play the fool, idle, trifle. L16. b Act as a clown or jester. E17. 3 *v.t.* Make a fool of; impose upon; dupe or trick (*out of*, *into*); deprive *of* or put *off* by trickery. L16. 4 *v.t.* Make foolish, infatuate. Now *rare* or *obs.* E17.

2 W. WYCHERLEY My heart is too much in earnest to be fooled with. THOMAS HUGHES You and I . . go fooling about with him, and get rusticated. b C. STEAD His weakness for playground leadership led him to cavort and fool. 3 ANTHONY SMITH As every sense can be fooled, every sensation can, therefore, be wrong. **you could have fooled me** *colloq.*: expr. scepticism or contradiction.

With advs. in specialized senses: **fool about** play the fool. **fool along** *US* go slowly or aimlessly. **fool around** play the fool; *US* hang about aimlessly; *colloq.* flirt, have an affair. **fool away** fritter or squander foolishly. **fool round** = *fool around* above.

foolery /ˈfuːləri/ *n.* M16. [f. FOOL *n.*[1] + -ERY. See also TOMFOOLERY.] The practice of fooling or acting foolishly; a foolish action or thing.

W. WARNER With . . Fooleries more than few I courted her.

foolhardy /ˈfuːlhɑːdi/ *a.* ME. [OFr. *folhardi* f. *fol* foolish (see FOOL *n.*[1] & *a.*) + *hardi* HARDY *a.*] Foolishly adventurous or bold; reckless; delighting in needless risks.

F. CHICHESTER It was a crazy, dangerous flight . . the most foolhardy I had ever attempted.

foolhardily *adv.* LME. **foolhardiness** *n.* ME.

foolish /ˈfuːlɪʃ/ *a.* ME. [f. FOOL *n.*[1] + -ISH[1].] 1 Lacking good sense or judgement; like or befitting a fool; indicative of or proceeding from folly; ridiculous. ME. 2 Humble, insignificant, trifling. Now *arch.* & *dial.* L16.

1 G. GREENE It was foolish, . . but one cannot always be logical. S. RAVEN You'd have a very good chance of a first if you tried. But . . you settle for what's just good enough to keep you from looking foolish. 2 R. BOLDREWOOD A hundred miles is . . no foolish ride.

foolishly *adv.* L15. **foolishment** *n.* foolishness E20. **foolishness** *n.* the quality or state of being foolish; a foolish act or thing: L15.

foolometer /fuːˈlɒmɪtə/ *n. joc.* M19. [f. FOOL *n.*[1] + -OMETER.] A standard for the measurement of fools or folly.

foolproof /ˈfuːlpruːf/ *a.* E20. [f. FOOL *n.*[1] + PROOF *a.*] Safeguarded against any kind of accident; so straightforward as to be incapable of misuse or mistake.

Times The cost of making nuclear reactors absolutely foolproof would outweigh their economic advantages.

foolscap /ˈfuːlzkap/, *in sense 2 also* -lsk-/ *n.* Also (earlier) **fool's cap**. E17. [f. FOOL *n.*[1] + -'S[1] + CAP *n.*[1]] 1 A fool's or jester's cap, usually hung with bells. Also, a dunce's cap. E17. 2 A former size of paper for printing, 13½ × 17 inches (about 340 × 430 mm). Also, a former size of writing paper, 13 × 8 inches (about 330 × 200 mm). L17. 3 An illustration of a fool's cap used as a watermark. L18.

foot /fʊt/ *n.* Pl. **feet** /fiːt/, (sense 7 also) **foot**, (sense 18) **foots**. [OE *fōt*, pl. *fēt* = OFris. *fōt*, OS *fōt*, *fuot* (Du *voet*), OHG *fuoz* (G *Fuss*), ON *fótr*, Goth *fōtus*, f. Gmc f. IE base repr. also by Skt *pad*, *pāda*, Gk *pous*, *pod-*, L *pes*, *ped-* foot.] I 1 The terminal part of the leg below the ankle-joint. OE. †b The leg and foot. LME–M17. c A diseased condition of the foot. Only w. specifying wd. M19. 2 Step, pace, tread. Freq. w. specifying wd. OE. †3 Power of walking or running. ME–M18. 4 a The end of a bed, couch, grave, etc., towards which the feet of an occupant are placed; the lower end of a table etc. LME. b The portion of a sock, stocking, etc., which covers the foot of the wearer. L16. 5 *Hist.* Infantry. Also † *men of foot*. M16.

1 J. STEINBECK His feet did not stamp the clods or feel the warmth . . of the earth. I. MURDOCH He lightly stroked the feet, probing between the long separated toes. c *Madura foot*, *trench foot*, etc. 2 F. MARRYAT I was not aware of your presence. Your foot is so light. B. JOWETT Dogs . . swift of foot. 3 H. BRACKEN Horses may alter as to their Speed or Foot. 4a D. DUNNETT At the foot of the bed stood Thorfinn. b W. HARRISON He will carrie his hosen . . to save their feet from wearing. 5 STEELE Their Foot repulsed the same Body of Horse in three successive Charges.

II 6 *Pros.* A unit of length with a varying number of syllables, one of which bears a main stress; a similar unit of speech. OE.

III 7 (Pl. also *foot*.) A unit of length; *esp.* one of one-third of a yard, equal to 30.48 centimetres. Also (w. specifying wd), an area or volume equal to that of a square or cube whose edges are one foot long. OE. b A distance or space of the least size. ME. 8 Any of various measures relating to specified commodities, *esp.* a measure used in tin-mining. Now chiefly *dial.* E17.

7 P. MASSINGER A room of eight feet square. R. HODGSON Spiders big as bladders lie Under hemlocks ten foot high. *cubic foot*, *square foot*. b SHAKES. *1 Hen. IV* I'll starve ere I'll rob a foot further.

IV 9 An adjustable piece of wood or iron fastened to the front of the beam of a wheelless plough and used to regulate the depth of ploughing. Also *plough-foot. obs.* exc. *Hist.* ME. **10** The lower (usu. projecting) part of an object which serves as a support; the base. LME. **11** The terminal point of the leg of a chair, table, pair of compasses, etc. LME. **12a** *Bot.* The part by which a petal is attached; the root of a hair. L17. **b** *Zool.* A locomotive or adhering organ of an invertebrate. M19. **13** *Printing.* Either of the two plane surfaces, divided by a groove, at the base of a type. L17. **14** *Mus.* The terminal portion of an organ-pipe. M19. **15** The plate in a sewing-machine which holds the material steady. L19.

10 D. L. SAYERS Three cut-glass goblets (one with a chipped foot). 11 D. BREWSTER Place one foot of the compasses in the quadrant *NF.*

V 16 The lowest part or bottom of a hill etc., or of any structure in an erect or sloping position, as a wall, ladder, staircase, etc. ME. **b** The beginning or end of the slope of a bridge. LME. **c** *Naut.* The lower edge of a sail. L17. **†17** Something written at the end of a document etc.; *spec.* (*a*) the sum or total of an account; (*b*) the refrain or chorus of a song. LME–E18. **18** *sing.* & (usu.) in *pl.* (*foots*). Dregs; refuse of oil etc.; coarse sugar. M16. **19** The lower end or bottom of (a page of) a document, list, etc. M17.

16 G. BERKELEY A town situate at the foot of Vesuvius. H. JAMES The lower hall stretched away at the foot of the stairs. 17 DRYDEN A trifling sum of Misery, New added to the foot of thy Account. 18 B. RANDOLPH They raise the foot of the oyl, so that thick and thin goes together. 19 W. WOLLASTON At the foot of the page.

†VI 20 = FOOTING 7. M16–E19. **b** Ground, reason. L17–L18. **21** Foothold, standing-ground. L16–M17. **22** Standard rate of calculation or valuation. L16–M18.

20 B. FRANKLIN I wish all correspondence was on the foot of writing and answering when one can. b HOR. WALPOLE The Prince excused his own inapplication on the foot of idleness. 21 F. KIRKMAN Hinder new love from getting foot in her heart. 22 J. LOCKE He must pay twenty per Cent. more for all the commodities he buys with the Money of the new Foot.

Phrases: *a foot in both camps*: see CAMP *n.*[2] 5. **at foot** (of a foal etc.) accompanying its mother. *athlete's foot*: see ATHLETE 1. **at the feet of** in the position of a disciple or subject of, or a suppliant to. *bind hand and foot*: see HAND *n. change one's feet*: see CHANGE *v. cold feet*: see COLD *a. cover one's feet*: see COVER *v.*[2] 1. *cut the grass from under a person's feet*: see GRASS *n. cut the ground from under a person's feet*: see GROUND *n.* **drag one's feet** be deliberately uncooperative or slow to act. *fall on one's feet*: see FALL *v. feel one's feet*: see FEEL *v. feet first*: see FIRST. *feet foremost*: see FOREMOST. **feet of clay** (cf. *Dan.* 2:33) fundamental weakness in a person who has appeared to be of great merit. *find one's feet*: see FIND *v.* FIRST-*foot.* **†foot and hand** stepping forward and striking simultaneously (*come in foot and hand*, attack an opponent by so doing). **foot in the door** a chance of ultimate success, an opportunity to progress, esp. in *have a* or *one's foot in the door*; cf. *toe in the door* s.v. TOE *n.* **foot to foot** *arch.* with one foot against an opponent's; in close combat. *from head to foot*: see HEAD *n.* **get one's feet wet** *fig.* begin to take an active part. **have one foot in the grave** be or appear to be near death. **have one's feet on the ground** be practical and sensible. *have the ball at one's feet*: see BALL *n.*[1] 2. **keep one's feet** avoid falling, remain upright. *land on one's feet*: see LAND *v.* 3. **my foot!** *colloq.*: contradicting contemptuously. *not let the grass grow under one's feet*: see GRASS *n.* **not put a foot wrong** not make a single mistake in behaviour or speech. *off one's feet*: see OFF *prep.* & *a.* **on foot** (*a*) walking or running as opp. to riding, driving, etc.; (*b*) (of an action etc.) afoot, in motion; *set on foot*, start (an action etc.). **on one's feet** standing or walking, *esp.* standing to make a speech; well enough to walk about. **on the right foot** at an advantage, in a favourable position, (esp. in *get off on the right foot*, make a good start). **on the wrong foot** at a disadvantage, in an awkward position, (esp. in *get off on the wrong foot*, make a bad start). *put one's best foot forward*: see BEST *a.* **put one's feet up** take a rest, esp. sitting or lying with one's feet propped up. **put one's foot down** (*a*) be firmly insistent or repressive; (*b*) accelerate a motor vehicle. **put one's foot in it** *colloq.* blunder, *esp.* inadvertently say or do something to cause offence or embarrassment. **set foot in** or **on** enter, go to, (a place etc.). *shake the dust off one's feet*: see DUST *n. sit at the feet of*: see SIT *v.* **stand on one's own (two) feet** be independent or self-reliant. *take the weight off one's feet*: see WEIGHT *n.* **to one's feet** to a standing position (in *get, jump,* etc. *to one's feet*). **tread under foot** *fig.* oppress. **under foot** on the ground, with regard to conditions for walking etc. **under one's feet** in one's way, obstructing one's actions or progress. *vote with one's feet*: see VOTE *v. walk a person off his* or *her feet*: see WALK *v.*[1] **with one's foot on the neck of** *arch.* completely dominating.

Comb.: **foot-and-mouth (disease)** a contagious virus disease of cattle etc. with ulceration of hoofs, around the mouth, etc.; **foot-bank** = BANQUETTE; **foot-bath** (*a*) an act of washing the feet; (*b*) a small shallow bath used for this; **footboard** a board, esp. in or on a vehicle, to support the foot or feet or to stand on; **foot-bone** the tarsus; **foot boy** †(*a*) a boy attendant; (*b*) *arch.* a page-boy; **footbrake** a brake in a vehicle operated by pressure of the foot; **foot breadth** *arch.* the breadth of a foot (as a measure); **footbridge** a bridge for pedestrians; **foot-candle** a disused unit of illumination equal to the illumination given by a source of one candela at a distance of one foot (equivalent to one lumen per square foot, 10.764 lux); **foot-cloth** †(*a*) a large richly ornamented cloth laid over the back of a horse; (*b*) *arch.* a carpet; **foot-drop** *Med.* a permanently downward position of the foot, due to paralysis of the dorsiflexor muscles; **footfall** *arch.* the sound of a footstep; **foot-fault** *n.* & *v.* (*Tennis*) (*a*) *n.* a fault consisting in overstepping the baseline or running etc. while serving; (*b*) *v.i.* make a foot-fault; **foot-folk** *arch.* foot-soldiers, infantry; **foot-gear** footwear; **foot guards** infantrymen with a special guarding function; now *spec.* (w. cap. initials) in the British army, the Grenadier, Coldstream, Scots, Irish, and Welsh Guards; **foothill** a hill lying at the base of a mountain or mountain range; **foothold** a place giving support for the feet, a surface for standing on, (*lit.* & *fig.*); an established place; a basis from which advantage may be gained or influence or support increased; cf. *toe-hold* s.v. TOE *n.*; **foot-lambert** a (disused) unit of surface brightness corresponding to the emission or reflection of one lumen per square foot; **†foot-land-raker** a footpad; **foot-licker** *arch.* a slave, a humble or fawning suppliant; **footlights** screened lights in front of a stage at the level of the actors' feet; (*fig.*) *the* acting profession; **foot-locker** *N. Amer.* a small trunk or chest; **foot-log** *US* a log used as a footbridge; **footloose** *a.* free to act or acting as one pleases, having no ties; **footmark** (*a*) *rare* a mark on the foot; (*b*) a footprint; **foot-muff** a covering of fur or similar material in which the feet are placed for warmth; **foot pace** (*a*) a walking pace; (*b*) a raised portion of a floor, a dais; (*c*) a hearthstone; (*d*) a half-landing; **footpad** [PAD *n.*[2]] *Hist.* a highway robber operating on foot; **foot page** *arch.* a boy servant or attendant; **foot-passenger** a person who walks as opp. to riding or driving, a pedestrian; **footpath** a path for walkers; a pavement for pedestrians at the side of a road; **footplate** a driver's and fireman's platform in a locomotive; **foot plough** a swing plough; **foot-pound** the quantity of energy expended when a force of one pound moves through a distance of one foot; *foot-*POUNDAL; **foot-pound-second** *a.* designating or pertaining to a system of measurement in which these form the basic units of length, mass, and time respectively; **foot-race** a race between competitors on foot; **footrest** a bench, stool, rail, etc., used to support the feet of a seated person; **foot-rope** *Naut.* (*a*) a bolt-rope to which the lower edge of a sail is sewn; (*b*) a rope below a yard, for sailors to stand on while furling or reefing; **foot-rot** (*a*) a bacterial disease of the foot in animals, esp. sheep; (*b*) a fungal disease of plants, affecting the base of the stem; **foot-rule** a rigid measure one foot long; **foot-soldier** an infantryman; **footsore** *a.* having sore feet, esp. from walking; **footstalk** *Bot.* & *Zool.* a small supporting stalk; a petiole, peduncle, or the like; **foot's pace** = *foot pace* (a) above; **footstall** the base or pedestal of a pillar or statue; **footstone** †(*a*) a base, a pedestal; (*b*) the foundation-stone of a building; (*c*) a (commemorative) stone at the foot of a grave; **footstool** (*a*) a stool for resting the foot or feet on while sitting (*lit.* & *fig.*); †(*b*) a stool on which to stand to reach a higher position; **footsure** *a.* sure-footed; **footwall** *Geol.* the fault block which lies below an inclined fault; **footwarmer** a contrivance or covering for keeping the feet warm; **foot-washing** the action or an act of washing the feet, esp. as a religious rite; **footway** a way or path for walkers or pedestrians; **footwear** what is worn on the feet; boots, shoes, socks, etc., collectively; **footwork** use of the feet in sports (esp. football), dancing, etc.; agility, adroitness; **footworn** *a.* (*arch.*) (*a*) worn by the feet; (*b*) footsore.

footless *a.* LME. **footlike** *a.* resembling a foot E20.

foot /fʊt/ *v.* LME. [f. the n.] **I 1** *v.i.* & (esp.) *t.* w. *it.* **a** Step, or tread to music or in time; dance. LME. **b** Walk, go on foot. L16. **2** *v.t.* Set foot on; walk, dance, etc., on or over. M16. **3** *v.t.* Settle or establish (a person, esp. oneself) in or *in* a specified place. Now *rare.* L16. **4** *v.t.* **a** Strike or push with the foot or feet; kick; spurn (*lit.* & *fig.*). Now *rare.* L16. **b** Of a bird, esp. a hawk: seize with the talons. L16. **5** *v.t.* Follow the tracks of; trace. L18.

1a DRYDEN A Quire of Ladies . . That featly footing seem'd to skim the Ground. b S. E. FERRIER He footed away as fast as his short legs . . permitted. G. GREENE The taxi drew up at the corner of a city street. 'We foot it from here.' 2 J. HENRY The ground we footed within the last three days is a very rugged isthmus. R. L. STEVENSON It was good to foot the grass. 4a SHAKES. *Merch. V.* You that did . . foot me as you spurn a stranger cur Over your threshold.

II 6 *v.t.* Make a foot for, add or attach a foot to. LME. **7a** *v.t.* Write the total at the foot of, add up (an account, bill, etc.). Freq. foll. by *up.* L15. **b** *v.t.* Pay or settle (a bill). *colloq.* E19. **c** *v.i.* Mount or total *up* to or *to* a particular sum. M19.

6 SMOLLETT The stockings which his wife footed for me. 7a H. B. STOWE The wall-paper was . . garnished with chalk memorandums, and long sums footed up. b T. C. WOLFE Tell him . . to spare no expense. I'll foot the bills.

footage /ˈfʊtɪdʒ/ *n.* L19. [f. FOOT *n.* + -AGE.] **1** Payment of miners by the linear foot of work; the amount paid or mined. L19. **2** A length in linear feet, esp. of cinematographic or television film used; material recorded on a length of such film. E20.

2 *New York Times* Some of the footage looked as though it had been filmed in Paris. *Broadcast* Close-up footage of the beetles, ants and worms.

football /ˈfʊtbɔːl/ *n.* & *v.* LME. [f. FOOT *n.* + BALL *n.*[1]] **A** *n.* **1** A large round or elliptical inflated ball, usu. of leather or (now) plastic. LME. **2** A primarily open-air game played with such a ball by two sides each seeking to move it across the opponents' goal-line by kicking or other permitted means; (manner or style of) the playing of this game. LME. **3** *fig.* A person or thing continually kicked or tossed or bandied about. M16.

2 *Listener* Most of the impressive football came from Real Madrid. *American football, Association football, Australian (Rules) football, five-a-side football, Gaelic football, rugby football,* etc. *football boot, club, ground, helmet, match, pitch, player,* etc. 3 L. ADAMIC The Yugoslav peoples were once again a football in international power politics.

Comb.: **football coupon** a coupon used in an entry for a football pool; **football hooligan** a person who engages in hooliganism while attending or travelling to or from a football match; *football pool(s)*: see POOL *n.*[2] 5b.

B *v.* **1** *v.t.* Kick or treat like a football. L16. **2** *v.i.* Play football. L19.

¶Without specification usu. understood as Association football in Britain, American football in the US, Canadian football in Canada, Australian Rules football in Australia, rugby football in NZ, or whatever form of the game is most commonly played in the particular country or area.

footballer *n.* a football player L19.

footed /ˈfʊtɪd/ *a.* LME. [f. FOOT *n.*, *v.*: see -ED[2], -ED[1].] **1** Having a foot or feet; having footlike appendages; (as 2nd elem. of comb.) having feet of a specified kind or number. LME. **2** Composed in metrical feet. Long *rare.* M16.

1 A. C. SWINBURNE Fair as the snow and footed as the wind. *bare-footed, cat-footed, flat-footed, four-footed, sure-footed,* etc.

footer /ˈfʊtə/ *n.*[1] E17. [f. FOOT *n.*, *v.* + -ER[1].] **1** A person who goes on foot, a pedestrian. Now *rare* exc. in FIRST-*footer.* E17. **2** *Bowls.* A small mat on which a player stands when delivering the ball. M19. **3** With numeral prefixed: a person or thing having a height or length of the specified number of feet. M19. **4** A bird, esp. a hawk, which is skilful in seizing prey in the talons. L19. **5** A line of information appearing at the foot of each page of a document, containing the date, the chapter-heading, etc. L20.

footer /ˈfuːtə/ *n.*[2] & *v. dial.* & *slang.* Now *rare.* M18. [Var. of FOUTRE.] **A** *n.* A worthless or idle person. M18. **B** *v.i.* Trifle, potter about, dawdle. M19.

footer /ˈfʊtə/ *n.*[3] *slang.* M19. [f. FOOTBALL *n.*: see -ER[6].] Football.

footie *n.* var. of FOOTY *n.*

footing /ˈfʊtɪŋ/ *n.* LME. [f. FOOT *v.* + -ING[1].] **I 1** The action of placing the feet, esp. so as not to slip or stumble; stable position of the feet, foothold. LME. **2** The action of walking, pacing, stepping, or dancing; a step, a tread. Formerly also, a dance. Now *rare.* M16. †**b** The action of setting foot on land. *rare* (Shakes.). Only in E17. **3** A mark or impression left by the foot or feet. Now *rare.* L16.

1 SIR W. SCOTT Unless he climb, with footing nice, A far projecting precipice. TOLKIEN He missed his footing on a round stone and fell into the cold water. 2 GOLDSMITH A squire from the country . . desirous of learning the new manner of footing. KEATS To him they bent their footing through the dews. b SHAKES. *Oth.* Whose footing here anticipates our thoughts A se'nnight's speed.

II 4 †**a** The foundation, ground, or basis on which something rests or from which it rises. LME–L17. **b** A projecting course or number of courses at the base of a wall etc. for support. E17. **5** Support for the foot; surface (of a specified kind) for walking or standing on. L16. **6** *gen.* A firm or secure position, an established place, a foothold. L16. **7** The basis on which or conditions under which an enterprise is established or operates; the position or status of a person in relation to others; a degree of intimacy etc. M17. **8** One's entrance on a new position, one's admittance to a trade, society, etc.; a fee required for this. E18.

5 SIR W. SCOTT Where scarce was footing for the goat. J. STEINBECK The bottom of the gulch levelled off, and the footing was sand. 6 A. TROLLOPE She had made good her footing in her aunt's house. 7 H. JAMES Ask them to take you in on the footing of a lodger. V. SACKVILLE-WEST Once we have finished all our business we may meet upon an equal footing. *Times* The stimulation of enterprise is best organized on a regional footing. 8 **pay (for) one's footing** pay the customary fee for admittance to a trade, society, etc.

III 9 The action of adding up a column of figures; a sum total. L15. **10** The action of making a foot for or attaching a foot to a stocking etc.; (a) material used for this. E16. **11** The attached edge of a lace trim. L17. **12** A piece of hard wood dovetailed to the end of an arrow nearest the pile. M19.

footle /ˈfuːt(ə)l/ *v.* & *n. slang.* L19. [Perh. f. FOOTER *v.* w. suff. substitution of -LE[3].] **A** *v.i.* Trifle (*about*), play the fool. L19. **B** *n.* Nonsense, twaddle; something trifling and silly. L19.

footler *n.* E20.

footling /ˈfuːtlɪŋ/ *a.* L19. [f. FOOTLE *v.* + -ING[2].] Trivial, silly.

G. B. SHAW Paraphrases of great works, made by footling people. J. CAREY Making up plots and complications, which he always found a bit footling.

footling /ˈfʊtlɪŋ/ *adv.* M18. [f. FOOT *n.* + -LING[2].] *Med.* Of a birth, presentation, delivery, etc.: with the feet foremost.

footman /ˈfʊtmən/ *n.* Pl. **-men.** ME. [f. FOOT *n.* + MAN *n.*] **1** An infantryman. ME. **2** A pedestrian; a (good, fast, etc.) walker or runner. *obs.* exc. *dial.* LME. **3** A servant or attendant accompanying a rider or carriage on foot. Also *running footman. obs.* exc. *Hist.* LME. **4** A liveried servant whose chief duties include attending to the employer's carriage and door and waiting at table. E18. **5** A trivet to hang on grate bars. M18. **6** Any of a number of moths belonging to the tiger moth family Arctiidae. E19.

footmanship *n.* (now *rare* or *obs.*) (*a*) the action of, or skill in, running or walking; (*b*) the occupation or office of a footman: M16.

footnote /ˈfʊtnəʊt/ *n.* & *v.* E19. [f. FOOT *n.* + NOTE *n.*[2]] **A** *n.* A note printed or written at the foot of a page etc.; *fig.* a piece of additional or incidental information. E19. **B** *v.t.* Supply with a footnote or footnotes; comment on in a footnote. M19.

footprint /ˈfʊtprɪnt/ *n.* M16. [f. FOOT *n.* + PRINT *n.*] **I** *lit.* **1** An impression left by the sole of the foot in walking, standing, etc. M16. **II 2** The ground area beneath a vehicle or aircraft that is affected by forces such as noise, pressure, or blast; the area of contact between a tyre and the ground. M20. **3** The area within which a broadcast signal from a particular source can be received. L20. **4** The area of desk space etc. occupied by a microcomputer or other piece of hardware. L20.

footsie /ˈfʊtsi/ *n.*[1] *colloq.* M20. [Joc. dim. of FOOT *n.*: see -IE. Cf. FOOTY *n.*] Amorous play with the feet.

G. FOWLER I played footsie with her during Don José's first seduction by Carmen. *fig.*: *Economist* Pakistan is . . despite recent games of footsie with Peking, a staunchly anti-communist ally.

Footsie /ˈfʊtsi/ *n.*[2] *colloq.* L20. [Alt. of *FT-SE* s.v. F, F, after prec.] The Financial Times-Stock Exchange 100 share index.

footslog /ˈfʊtslɒg/ *v.* & *n. colloq.* L19. [f. FOOT *n.* + SLOG *v.*] **A** *v.i.* Infl. **-gg-**. March or tramp laboriously. L19. **B** *n.* A laborious march or tramp. E20.

footslogger *n.* a person who footslogs; an infantryman: L19.

footstep /ˈfʊtstɛp/ *n.* ME. [f. FOOT *n.* + STEP *n.*[1]] **1** An impression made by a foot, a footprint. Now chiefly *fig.* in *follow* or *walk in a person's footsteps*, follow a person's example, take the same course of action as a person. ME. **2** A step or tread of the foot. M16. **b** A distance covered in a step. Now *rare.* L18. **3** A step on which to place the foot to ascend or descend. L16. **b** Chiefly *Hist.* A footboard for a printing-press operator. L17. **c** A bearing to sustain the foot of a vertical shaft or spindle. Also *footstep bearing.* M19. †**4** A vestige, a trace. L16–L18.

footy /ˈfʊti/ *n. colloq.* Also **-ie**. M20. [Joc. dim. of FOOT *n.*: see -Y[6], -IE. Cf. FOOTSIE *n.*[1]] **1** Also redupl. **footy-footy**. = FOOTSIE *n.*[1] M20. **2** Football. Chiefly *Austral.* & *NZ.* M20.

footy /ˈfuːti/ *a. dial.* & *colloq.* Also (earlier, *obs.* exc. *Sc.*) **fouty**. E18. [Var. of FOUGHTY.] Paltry, worthless, little and insignificant.

footy-footy *n.* see FOOTY *n.* 1.

foo yong *n. phr.* var. of FU YUNG.

foozle /ˈfuːz(ə)l/ *n. slang.* M19. [Rel. to next.] **1** A fogy; a stupid person, a bungler. Now *rare.* M19. **2** A clumsy failure, a botched attempt; *esp.* a bungled golf-stroke. L19.

foozle /ˈfuːz(ə)l/ *v.t. slang.* M19. [G dial. *fuseln* work badly: cf. FUSEL OIL.] Do clumsily, botch, bungle, (esp. a golf-stroke).

foozler *n.* L19.

fop /fɒp/ *n.* LME. [Origin unkn.] †**1** A foolish person. LME–E18. **2** A dandy, an exquisite. L17. †**3** A conceited person. M18–E19.

fopling *n.* a petty fop L17.

†**fop** *v.* Infl. **-pp-**. E16. [App. f. G *foppen* cheat, deceive: prob. orig. thieves' cant.] **1** *v.i.* Act foolishly, play the fool. Only in E16. **2** *v.t.* Make a fool of, cheat, dupe. Also, fob *off.* Only in 17.

foppery /ˈfɒp(ə)ri/ *n.* M16. [f. FOP *n.* + -ERY.] †**1 a** A foolish action, practice, idea, or statement; a thing foolishly esteemed. M16–M18. **b** Foolishness, stupidity. L16–E18. **2** The behaviour or manner characteristic of a fop; dandyism; an instance of this. L17. **b** (An example of) foppish finery. E18.

foppish /ˈfɒpɪʃ/ *a.* E17. [f. FOP *n.* + -ISH[1].] †**1** Resembling or befitting a fool. E17–E18. **2** Resembling or befitting a fop or dandy. L17.

foppishly *adv.* M17. **foppishness** *n.* E17.

for /fɔː, *unstressed* fə/ *prep.*, *conj.*, & *n.* [OE *for* = OFris., OS *for*, Goth. *faur*, prob. reduced form of Gmc prep. meaning 'before (of place and time)', repr. by OE FORE *prep.* = OFris., OS, OHG *fora*, beside OS, OHG forms with *-i*, viz. *furi* (G *für*) and ON *fyrir*.] **A** *prep.* **I** Before. Cf. FORE *prep.* †**1** In front of, in or into the presence of; (in oaths) before. OE–LME. †**2** Before in time. OE–ME. †**3** In preference to. OE–E16.

II Of representation, substitution, or exchange. **4** Representing, as a representative of. OE. **5** In place of, instead of; on behalf of. OE. **6** Introducing that with which something is (to be) exchanged: in exchange for; as the price or penalty of; in requital of. OE. **b** At the cost of, to the amount of. L18.

4 I. MURDOCH A fear not exactly of James but of something that James stood for. 5 H. JAMES You can see for yourself—she has got half the place down. G. GREENE He kept in the dusky background . . and let the ladies fight for him. V. S. PRITCHETT She had no one left to pray for. B. BAINBRIDGE She wasn't afraid of him; she was afraid for him. 6 T. HARDY There was to be one execution—only one—for arson. I. MURDOCH I bought up the entire stock for less than a pound. W. GOLDING I offer them the idea for free. b THOMAS HUGHES The Lord's men were out, by half-past twelve o'clock for ninety-eight runs. A. ALPERS He sent them a cheque for £5.

III 7 In defence or support of; on the side of; in favour of. Also *ellipt.*, in favour. Opp. *against.* OE. **b** In honour of; after. Chiefly in *name* (a child etc.) *for* (a person) (now chiefly *Austral.*, *N. Amer.*, & *Sc.*). E18.

7 T. HARDY Tupcome was for sleeping in Bristol that night, but Dornell . . insisted upon mounting and getting back. E. TEMPLETON In the Bible, one can find quotations for and against any human activity. J. GRENFELL She's always been one for sailors ever since she can remember. H. WILSON A tally of those for and against. b C. MCCULLOUGH There are streets named for him all over New Zealand.

IV Of purpose, result, or destination. **8** With the object or purpose of; with a view to; as preparatory to, in anticipation of; conducive to; leading to, giving rise to, with the result or effect of. OE. **b** With the purpose or result of benefiting; as a service to. Also, (chiefly following adjs., ns., or advs. of quality) as affecting beneficially or the reverse. OE. **c** With the purpose of being, becoming, or serving as. L15. **9** Used pleonastically before *to* and an infinitive w. the sense 'in order to do' or simply 'to do' (now *arch.* & *dial.*). Also (*US*) introducing a n. or pron. followed by an infinitive after vbs of wanting, liking, etc. ME. **10** In order to obtain, win (money etc.), save (one's life), etc. ME. **b** Indicating the object of a feeling or a faculty. L16. **11** In order to arrive at or reach; with the purpose of going to or towards, in the direction of. LME. **12** To be received by, to belong to; to be used by, with, or in connection with. LME. **13** Following a vb, adj., or n. of quality denoting suitability, appropriateness, appointment, purpose, or design; following a n. or as a predicate indicating the possession of such a quality. LME. **b** Following an adj. or adv. qualified by *too*, *enough*, etc. w. the sense 'to require', 'to allow', 'to constitute', etc. E19. **14** Introducing a n. or pron. followed by an infinitive w. the sense 'that he, she, etc. may, might, should, etc.' E16.

8 T. HARDY Seeing . . that somebody was there cleaning for Sunday he entered. M. KEANE I supposed you had been out for a healthy brisk walk. I. MURDOCH Now I must find Miranda and tell her to change for church. J. WAINWRIGHT The sexual assault in each case is motive enough for the murder. W. GOLDING Thackeray keeps us in suspense and ignorance for our own good. M. ROBERTS What are you doing that for? asks Beth, puzzled. b T. HARDY A bad job for thee, Christian, that you should have showed your nose then. V. WOOLF Nobody lives for himself alone. I. MURDOCH After all, it is for Clement that I am here. J. SIMMS Kiyoko was there; I would play for her. c DICKENS [He] went for a soldier, and never came back. G. EWART Had an egg for breakfast every morning. P. ACKROYD He . . slices two pieces of bread for toast. 9 G. WASHINGTON You must ride round ye back of ye Mountain for to get below them. A. TYLER His mother hated for Cody to mix with outsiders. A. F. LOEWENSTEIN You used to like for me to touch you, Billy. 10 LD MACAULAY Charles fled for his life. V. WOOLF Then she went to him for assurance. J. CHEEVER He was rude to his friends when they stopped in for a drink. A. WHITE I have worked for my living since I was 16. M. PROCTER They had phoned for their wheel man like calling for a taxi. b E. BOWEN He did not care for her looks or her clothes. M. KEANE He had a long briar in his hand and examined its point carefully for hairs. I. MURDOCH Why wantonly destroy one's palate for cheap wine? V. S. PRITCHETT One discovers a gift for saying things with two meanings. F. TUOHY I had developed a grudging admiration for him. 11 T. HARDY He made straight for the point whence proceeded the low roar. I. MURDOCH He wondered where Miranda was going,

and concluded that she was bound for the village shop. J. WAINWRIGHT I was starting for home the next day. **12** T. HARDY He is . . a perfect match for her. E. WAUGH Details of the costumes for a charity ballet. G. GREENE I've some bad news for all of you. I. MURDOCH I wear small oval rimless spectacles for reading. **13** T. HARDY Tell him flatly that you are not for him? R. MACAULAY It wasn't for me to question her. R. HARDY They were hunters and they were built for nothing else. G. GREENE I had the impression that the party was for tonight? G. HOUSEHOLD There was nothing for it but to go. A. CARTER You'll find a full account of the operation in *The Lancet* for June 1898. **b** A. CARTER His teeth were chattering too much for him to speak coherently. H. CARPENTER She has grown too big for the White Rabbit's house. **14** E. BOWEN And it would be a shame for you all to go, added Doreen. D. ABSE It took a long time for the dust to settle. V. S. PRITCHETT It was exciting for her to drive the old man dangerously fast.

V Of attributed or assumed character. **15** As being, as equivalent to, as; in the character of; (now *dial.*) as a type of. OE.

15 R. MACAULAY Anyhow, Hobart I knew for an ignorant person. S. O'FAOLÁIN Norah cursed him and all of us for a pack of cowards. T. E. LAWRENCE They'd have taken for granted I was too soft for man's work. W. STAFFORD We stood with wet towels over our heads for shade.

VI Of cause or reason. **16** By reason of, under the influence of (a feeling). OE. **17** Because of, on account of (a person or thing); on account of one's regard for. Also (*arch.*) in adjurations or exclamations: for the sake of. OE. **b** In consequence of, due to the effect of. Now chiefly after comparatives (otherwise usu. replaced by *from, of, through*). ME. **18** Indicating the presence or operation of something usu. as an obstacle or hindrance. OE. **b** In spite of, notwithstanding (*rare* exc. in *for all, any*, with n. or *that*). Also in conj. phr. *for all* (*that*), notwithstanding that, although (now *rare* in literary use). OE. †**c** As a precaution against, so as to prevent; against, from, of. ME–E18.

17 R. MACAULAY The artist's spirit, which loved beauty for what it was. V. WOOLF He had been arrested three times for attending seditious meetings. L. BRUCE I sort of felt sorry for the damned flies. I. MURDOCH Emily told him that he had married Harriet for snobbish reasons. **b** T. COOPER He lacketh teeth for age. G. GREENE Two young officers, who were obviously the worse for drink. **18** T. HARDY If it had not been for our Betty I should have gone long ago! M. SINCLAIR You can't see the text for the footnotes. D. WELCH I could not sleep for the squeaking of the crickets. A. CARTER There was hardly room to move for large chairs and cupboards. I. MURDOCH A clever face if it were not for a kind of childish timidity. **b** LEIGH HUNT I am not a very bad play-fellow . . for all I am so much bigger. W. GOLDING Somehow for all his apparent amiability a note that can only be called patronizing creeps in. W. H. AUDEN The flirtatious male . . never doubting That for all his faults he is loved. **c** J. MOXON That may hinder the Corner of the edge of the Chissel for coming at the Work.

VII Of correspondence or correlation. **19** Preceded and followed by the same n. indicating equality in number or quantity between objects compared or contrasted. ME. **20** Preceding a designation of number or quantity to which another is stated to correspond proportionally. LME.

19 W. OWEN Faces that used to curse me, scowl for scowl. *Listener* The difference, programme for programme, is fully three million. **20** J. BERESFORD It contains . . for one inch of lean four or five of stringy fat. *Times* In Britain and West Germany there are 1.3 murders a year for every 100,000 people.

VIII Of reference. **21** So far as concerns, with regard or respect to, concerning. ME. **22** Considering, or making the allowance required by, the usual nature of. L17.

21 G. GREENE For all he knew he was surrounded by friends. D. ABSE For my part I felt a righteous pride. G. HOUSEHOLD For the rest of the route there were enough old footprints. E. FEINSTEIN I could be a pile of clothes or papers for all the attention she gives me. **22** W. S. MAUGHAM He was talkative, forward for his age, a great reader, and clever.

IX Of duration and extension. **23** Marking actual or intended duration: during, throughout. LME. **24** Marking distance: over, to the extent of. M16.

23 M. KEANE It was really in her power to endure Nurse for a few days. F. TUOHY He shouted continuously for about four minutes. **24** M. G. LEWIS After travelling for five and twenty miles. R. HARDY At night you can see a fire on the plain for twenty miles.

Phrases & comb.: (A selection of cross-refs. only is included: see esp. other ns.) *all for*: see ALL *adv.* 1. *as for*: see AS *adv.* etc. **be for it** *slang* (orig. *Mil.*) be in or due for trouble or punishment. *for all* (*that*): see ALL *pron.* & *n.* 3. *for* BECAUSE. *for ever*: see EVER *adv. for free*: see FREE *a. for one thing*: see THING *n.*[1] **for-profit** *a.* profit-making. *for sale*: see SALE *n.* **for the first, second**, etc. **time** as a first, second, etc., instance. **I** etc. **for one** I etc. as one, I etc. as a unit in an aggregate. **now for —**: indicating desire for or anticipation or expectation of.

B *conj.* **1** Introducing a cl. containing the cause of a fact, the statement of which precedes or follows; because. *arch.* ME. **2** Introducing a new cl. or series of clauses containing the proof(s) of or reason(s) for believing what has previously been stated: seeing that, since. ME. †**3** In order that. ME–L16. †**4** *for and*, and moreover. E16–E17.

1 DRYDEN Why comes not he? . . for he's a puling sprite. **2** M. KEANE He did not know—how could he, for nobody told him? J. STEINBECK Do not touch it, for if you do . . , it will blind you. **3** SHAKES. *3 Hen. VI* And, for the time shall not seem tedious, I'll tell thee what befell me. **4** SHAKES. *Haml.* A pick-axe and a spade, a spade, for and a shrouding sheet.

C *n.* An argument or reason in favour of something. Chiefly in *the fors and againsts*. Cf. PRO *n.*[2] E19.

for- /fɔː, *unstressed* fə/ *pref.*[1] (no longer productive). [OE *for-, fær-* = OFris. *for-, fir-*, OS *for-*, OHG *fir-, far-* (Du., G *ver-*), Goth. *fair-, faur-*, corresp. to Gk *peri-, para-*, L *per-, por-*, Skt *pari, parā*, f. IE pref. with variation of form and meaning esp. (i) rejection, exclusion, prohibition, (ii) destruction, (iii) exhaustion.] **I** Forming vbs. **1** Forming vbs f. vbs, w. intensive privative sense 'away, off', as †*forthrow*. **2** Forming vbs f. vbs, w. the sense 'prohibit or exclude by —,' as *forbid*. **3** Forming vbs f. vbs, w. the sense 'abstain, neglect, renounce', as *forbear, forgo, forgive, forget, forsake, forswear*. **4** Forming vbs f. vbs, w. the sense '— wrongly or pervertedly', as †*forworship*. **5** Forming vbs f. vbs, w. the sense 'with destructive or painful effect', as *fordo, forhunger*, or 'asunder, in pieces', as †*forburst*. **b** Forming vbs f. ns., used only in pa. pple, w. the sense 'overpowered or troubled by', as †*forstormed*. **6** Forming vbs f. vbs, w. the sense 'excessively, so as to overwhelm', chiefly in pa. pple as †*forfrighted*, †*forpampered*, or 'so as to exhaust (oneself) by —', as *forwander*. **7** Forming trans. vbs f. intrans. or trans. vbs, w. the sense 'all over, extensively, thoroughly', as †*forbruise*. **8** Forming vbs f. vbs, w. intensive force, as †*fordread*. **9** Forming trans. vbs f. adjs. or ns, w. the sense 'make or give —', as †*forfeeble*, †*forlength*. **II** Forming adjs. **10** Forming adjs. f. adjs. w. intensive force, as †*forblack*, *forlorn*, †*forweary*.

for- /fɔː, *unstressed* fə/ *pref.*[2] (not productive). [Repr. OFr. *for-, fors-*, identical w. *fors* adv. (mod. *hors*) f. L *foris, foras* outside.] In wds adopted f. Fr., as *forfeit* etc.

for- *pref.*[3] see FORE-.

forage /ˈfɒrɪdʒ/ *n.* ME. [(O)Fr. *fourrage*, f. OFr. *fuerre* (mod. *feurre* straw) f. Frank. f. Gmc base of FODDER: see -AGE.] **1** Fodder for horses or cattle, now esp. for army horses. ME. **b** Food which animals etc. find for themselves. L17. **2** The action of foraging or providing forage; a raid or search for food or supplies. L15. †**b** The action of raging or ravening. L16–M17. †**3** In *pl.* Foragers. E16–E17.

1b T. HOOPER Flowers producing forage for the honeybee.

Comb.: **forage cap** an undress cap worn by the infantry; a peaked dress cap worn by the army and air force. **forage crop**: grown for animal feed; **forage-fish**: of interest to humans chiefly as food for more valuable fish; **forage-harvester** a machine for harvesting forage crops.

forage /ˈfɒrɪdʒ/ *v.* LME. [(O)Fr. *forrag(i)er*, f. as prec.] **I** *v.t.* **1** Obtain forage or supplies from; plunder, pillage. LME. **2** Supply with forage or food. M16. **3** Obtain by foraging or rummaging; search *out*. M17.

1 CARLYLE Noble and Peasant had been pillaged, ransomed, foraged, eaten-out by so many different Armies. **2** DISRAELI He foraged their pony . . and supplied them from his dairy. **3** THACKERAY His valet . . went out and foraged knowledge for him.

II *v.i.* **4** Seek out food or provisions; go out in search of food. M16. †**5** Gorge oneself; revel *in*. L16–L17. **6** Make inroads *on, upon*; raid. M17. **7** Make a search (*for*); rummage. M18.

4 J. K. JEROME Bread and butter, and jam, and bacon and eggs, and other things we foraged around the town for. R. MACDONALD Blackbirds were foraging under the trees and around a feeder. **5** SHAKES. *Hen. V* His most mighty father . . smiling to behold his lion's whelp Forage in blood of French nobility. **6** CHARLES I He permitteth his Souldiers to . . forrage upon the Countrey. **7** W. IRVING He passed many an hour foraging among the old manuscripts.

forager /ˈfɒrɪdʒə/ *n.* LME. [OFr. *forragier*, f. *forrage* FORAGE *n.*; also OFr. *forrageour* (mod. *fourrageur*) f. *forragier* FORAGE *v.*: see -ER[2].] †**1** A harbinger, a messenger. LME–E17. **2** A person (*spec.* a soldier) who forages; a member of a foraging party. L15. **3** An animal etc. which seeks its own food. E17. **b** An ant or other insect searching for food; an army ant. M19.

foralite /ˈfɔːrəlʌɪt/ *n.* M19. [f. L *forare* to bore + -LITE.] *Geol.* A tubelike marking in sandstones etc. resembling a worm burrow.

foram /ˈfɔːrəm/ *n.* E20. [Abbrev.] A foraminifer.

foramen /fəˈreɪmɛn/. *n.* Pl. **foramina** /fəˈramɪnə/. L17. [L *foramen, foramin-* f. *forare* to bore.] Esp. *Anat.* An opening, an orifice, a hole; a short passage.

EPIPLOIC *foramen.* **foramen magnum** /ˈmagnəm/ [L = large] a large hole in the occipital bone by which the spinal cord enters the skull. STENSEN'S *foramen.*

foraminate /fəˈramɪneɪt/ *v.t.* L16. [f. as next + -ATE[3].] Bore, pierce, perforate.

foraminifer /fɒrəˈmɪnɪfə/ *n.* Pl. **foraminifera** /fɒrəmɪˈnɪf(ə)rə/, **foraminifers**. M19. [f. L *foramin-* (see FORAMEN) + -I- + -FER.] *Zool.* A rhizopod of the chiefly marine order Foraminiferida, typically having a calcareous shell with perforations (foramina) through which pseudopodia extend, the fossils forming a major constituent of chalk and many marine oozes.

foramiˈniferal *a.* of or pertaining to foraminifera; containing or consisting of foraminifera: M19. **foramiˈniferan** *n.* & *a.* (*a*) *n.* = FORAMINIFER; (*b*) *adj.* of or pertaining to foraminifera: L20. **foramiˈniferous** *a.* having foramina; foraminiferal: M19.

†**foraminous** *a.* E17–E19. [f. as prec. + -OUS.] Full of holes, perforated, porous.

forasmuch /fərəzˈmʌtʃ/ *adv. arch.* ME. [Orig. 3 wds *for as much*, tr. OFr. *por tant que* for so much as.] *forasmuch as*, seeing that, since.

forastero /fɒrəˈstɛːrəʊ/ *n.* Pl. **-os**. M19. [Sp. = foreign.] Any of various medium-quality varieties of the cacao tree, orig. ones imported to Venezuela from the W. Indies. Cf. CRIOLLO.

foray /ˈfɒreɪ/ *n.* LME. [Prob. f. the vb.] **1** A hostile or predatory incursion; a raid; *gen.* an (adventurous) expedition. LME. †**2** Plunder, prey. LME–L16. †**3** The advance guard of an army. LME–L16.

1 D. LESSING They make frequent forays southwards to raid and plunder crops and livestock. A. POWELL Occasional forays into upper-crust life, spending a weekend at some country house.

foray /ˈfɒreɪ/ *v.* LME. [Back-form. f. FORAYER.] **1** *v.t.* Raid in search of forage or booty; plunder. Now *rare* or *obs.* LME. **2** *v.i.* Go on or make a foray. LME.

forayer /ˈfɒreɪə/ *n.* ME. [OFr. *forrier* (AN *forreiour*) forager (mod. *fourrier* quartermaster) f. Proto-Romance.] **1** A person who forays; a forager, a raider. ME. †**2** A person who goes on ahead; a messenger. ME–M16.

forb /fɔːb/ *n.* E20. [Gk *phorbē* fodder, forage, f. *pherbein* to feed.] Any herbaceous plant other than a grass.

forbad(e) *v.* pa. t.: see FORBID *v.*

forbear *n.* var. of FOREBEAR *n.*

forbear /fɔːˈbɛː/ *v.* Pa. t. **-bore** /-ˈbɔː/; pa. pple **-borne** /-ˈbɔːn/. [OE *forberan* = OHG *farberan* restrain, abstain, Goth. *frabairan* endure, f. base of FOR-[1], BEAR *v.*[1]] †**1** *v.t.* Bear, endure, submit to. OE–L16. **2** *v.t.* Bear with, have patience with, tolerate. Now chiefly *Sc.* OE. †**3** *v.t.* & *i.* Bear up against, control (oneself, one's emotions). OE–LME. **4** *v.t.* †**a** Dispense with, do without. OE–E17. †**b** Give up, part with, lose. ME–L16. **c** Keep away from, leave alone. Now chiefly *Sc.* ME. **5** *v.t.* & *i.* Abstain or refrain from or *from* (an action etc.); cease or decline *to do*. ME. **6** *v.t.* Refrain from using or uttering; hold back. ME. **b** *refl.* Restrain oneself. *rare.* M16. **7** *v.t.* Show mercy or indulgence to; spare. Now *rare.* ME. **b** *v.i.* Be patient; show forbearance. L16. **8** *v.t.* Give up (a claim, a lawsuit); refrain from enforcing or demanding, esp. the payment of (a debt). Now *rare.* LME.

1 CHAUCER I may not . . Forbere to ben out of your compagnie. 2 CAPT. J. SMITH I have forborne your insolencies. 4a W. BULLEN He is the best bonde slave . . and least can be forborne. b LYDGATE She hath forbore Her maydenhead. c SIR W. SCOTT I know all his haunts, and he cannot forbear them long. 5 E. B. BROWNING I forbore involving you in such a responsibility. J. K. JEROME His aspect was too wretched to invite conversation, and we forbore, therefore, to ask him questions. R. GRAVES Forbearing from the jealousy that . . he was convinced that she must feel. 6 POPE Forbear that dear, disastrous name. b AV *2 Chron.* 35:21 Forebeare thee from medling with God. 7 C. BOWEN May the splinters icy thy delicate feet forbear! b W. COWPER The kindest and the happiest pair Will find occasion to forbear.

forbearant *a.* tolerant, indulgent, patient M17. **forbearer** *n.* LME. **forbearing** *ppl a.* †(*a*) abstinent; (*b*) patient, long-suffering: LME.

forbearance /fɔːˈbɛːr(ə)ns/ *n.* L16. [f. prec. + -ANCE.] **1** Abstinence from enforcing what is due, esp. the payment of a debt. L16. **2** The action or habit of forbearing; an instance of this. L16. **3** Forbearing conduct or spirit; patient endurance, lenity. L16.

1 *Proverb*: Forbearance is no quittance. 2 T. JEFFERSON Laws which rendered criminal . . the forbearance of repairing to church. G. GROTE The various acts and forbearances which a man supposes to constitute the sum of his duty. 3 D. BREWSTER The man of the world treats the institutions of religion with more respect and forbearance. A. POWELL He behaved with great forbearance when I let his fire out.

Comb.: †**forbearance money** money paid to a creditor, in addition to interest, for allowing late payment of a debt.

†**forbid** *n.* *rare.* E17–M18. [f. the vb.] A forbidding, a prohibition.

forbid /fəˈbɪd/ *v.* Pa. t. **-bade** /-ˈbad, -ˈbeɪd/, **-bad** /-ˈbad/; pa. pple **-bidden** /-ˈbɪd(ə)n/, (*arch.*) **-bid**. [OE *forbēodan* = OFris. *forbiāda*, Du. *verbieden*, OHG *farbiotan* (G *verbieten*), Goth. *faurbiudan*, f. base of FOR-[1], BID *v.*] **I** *v.t.* **1** Command not to do, have, or use; not allow to exist or happen. Foll. by double obj. of the person commanded (orig. dat.) and the thing prohibited; a person, a thing, *that*, †*to do*; a person *from* (now *rare*), *to do*; a thing *to* a person; a thing *being done*, *to be done*. OE. **2** Exclude, keep back, hinder, restrain; make impossible or undesirable. With constructions as sense 1. OE. †**3** Ban, exile, debar. E17–E19.

1 LYTTON When strength and courage are forbid me. E. W. LANE He forbade both men and women from entering them. DICKENS Will you forbid him the house where I know he is safe? J. STEINBECK A law that requires you to pull your blinds down after sundown, and forbids you to pull them down before. G. GREENE The law that forbade the evidence in divorce cases being published. C. HILL Cromwell's first action on reaching Ireland was to forbid any plunder or pillage. 2 R. B. SHERIDAN The state I left her in forbids all hope. I. MURDOCH Hugo suggested that I should come and live with him, but some instinct of independence forbade this.

II *v.i.* **4** Not allow it, prevent it. Chiefly in exclams. LME.

4 SHAKES. *1 Hen. VI* I may not open; The Cardinal of Winchester forbids.

Phrases: *forbid the* BANNS. **God forbid (that)** may it not happen (that).

forbiddal *n.* (*rare*) = FORBIDDANCE M19. **forbiddance** *n.* the action or an act of forbidding; (a) prohibition: E17.

forbidden /fəˈbɪd(ə)n/ *a.* ME. [f. prec. + -EN[6].] **1** That has been forbidden; prohibited, banned; out of bounds. ME. **2** *Physics.* Designating or involving a transition between two quantum-mechanical states that does not conform to some selection rule, esp. for electric dipole radiation. E20.

1 J. CONRAD It is deadly because of its forbidden treasures. O. MANNING Harriet was doubtful about this essay into forbidden territory. *forbidden degrees*: see DEGREE *n.* **forbidden fruit** (*a*) the fruit forbidden to Adam (*Gen.* 2:17); *fig.* illicit pleasure; (*b*) any of several varieties of citrus fruit, *esp.* the shaddock, *Citrus maxima*. *forbidden ground*: see GROUND *n.*

forbiddenly *adv.* (*rare*) E17. **forbiddenness** /-n-n-/ *n.* M17.

forbidding /fəˈbɪdɪŋ/ *a.* L16. [f. as prec. + -ING[2].] **1** That forbids. L16. **2** Repellent, or uninviting appearance; formidable, stern. E18.

2 E. K. KANE We saw the same forbidding wall of belt-ice. L. DEIGHTON A forbidding figure: distant and cold and expert.

forbiddingly *adv.* M19. **forbiddingness** *n.* M18.

forbore *v.* pa. t., **forborne** pa. pple: see FORBEAR *v.*

forby /fəˈbʌɪ, fɔːˈbʌɪ/ *prep.* & *adv.* Also **-bye**. Now chiefly *Sc.* & *dial.* ME. [f. FOR-[3] + BY *prep.*, *adv.* Cf. G *vorbei*.] **A** *prep.* **1** Of motion: past, close by. ME. **b** Of position: hard by, near. L16. †**2** In preference to, before, beyond. Only in ME. **3** Beside, in comparison with. ME. **4** Besides, not to mention. M16. †**5** Through the means of, by. *rare* (Spenser). Only in L16.

1 SPENSER A goodly Lady did foreby them rush. 4 S. R. CROCKETT No doubt he had many a sin on his soul, forbye murder.

B *adv.* **1** Aside; nearby. ME. **b** Of motion or time: along, past. ME. **2** Besides, in addition. L16.

1 P. BUCHAN The blacksmith stood a little forby, wi' hammer in his hand. b W. STORY That time has been long forby. 2 SIR W. SCOTT But . . there was another reason forby.

force /fɔːs/ *n.*[1] ME. [(O)Fr. f. Proto-Romance, f. L *fortis* strong. In branch II f. FORCE *v.*[1]] **I 1** Physical strength as an attribute of living beings. Now *rare.* ME. **2** Strength, energy, violence, intense effect, as an attribute of physical action or movement; effort; *spec.* the strength or speed of a wind, as represented by numbers in the Beaufort Scale. ME. **3** Strength or power of a ruler, nation, etc.; *esp.* military strength or power. Formerly also, the strength of a fortress etc.; the fighting strength of a ship. ME. **4** A body of armed men, ships, etc., an army; in *pl.*, troops, the fighting strength of a nation or commander. ME. **b** *A* large part, number, or quantity (formerly also without preceding article); *the* majority. *obs.* exc. *Sc.* & *dial.* LME. **c** An organized body of workers etc. Also (*US Hist.*), the number of slaves in the service of a plantation owner etc. E19. **d** *The* police; a body of police. M19. **5** Physical strength exerted on an object or person, esp. in order to compel or constrain action; violence; (moral or physical) coercion, esp. in *by force*, by violent means, by compulsion. Formerly also, (a) constraint, (a) compulsion. ME. **b** *spec.* in *Law*. Unlawful violence against a person or thing. Formerly also, an act of this. M16. **6** Mental or moral strength. Now only, power of effective action in overcoming resistance etc. ME. **7** Value, importance. Now only, the real import, significance, or effect in context, of a word, statement, etc. ME. **8** Power (of a non-material thing) to control, influence, or produce an effect; efficacy; *esp.* power to convince or sway judgement. LME. **b** Legal validity, binding power of a law. LME. **c** Power of an artistic medium, as writing, painting, etc., to convey an impression or idea with vividness or effect. M19. **d** The ability of a dog to move sheep. *NZ* & *Austral.* M20. **9a** *Physics.* (The intensity of) an agency or influence that produces or tends to produce a change in the motion of a moving body, or produces motion or stress in a stationary body. M17. **b** Orig., the cause of motion, heat, electricity, etc., conceived as a principle or power. Now only *transf.* & *fig.*, an agency, influence, or source of power likened to a physical force; often in *pl.*, as *forces of nature*, *economic forces*. L18.

1 *Daily News* As soon as his recovered forces will justify the voyage and journey he will make the passage. 2 J. BRAINE She gave me a blow on my chest with more force than playfulness behind it. M. LEITCH His palms burned—they had taken the force of his tumble on the gritty road. B. MOORE The wind force increased, sending a great slap of water over the edge of the pier. 3 SHAKES. *3 Hen. VI* And lo where George of Clarence sweeps along, of force enough to bid his brother battle. 4 B. PLAIN A large force of Japanese planes attacked the United States naval facilities at Pearl Harbor. *fig.*: B. BETTELHEIM The story of Faust is that of a battle for his soul between the forces of light and darkness. b DEFOE Her maid, with a force of crying, said her master was dead. d G. GORER The Metropolitan Police is on a different footing to the numerous other forces in Britain. *Belfast Telegraph* If the Government expects members of the force and the Army to risk injuries . . it has got to pay up. 5 K. WHITE I have very little society and that is quite a force on my friends. *New York Times* The problem in Central America is not the show of force, it is the use of force. 8 L. P. HARTLEY It had the overwhelming force of any new obsession. D. JACOBSON He had no more to say, perhaps because he felt the force of my argument. c C. CLARKE Slender comes out in this play with extraordinary force.

II †**10** The plunger of a force-pump. L16–M18. **11** *Tennis* etc. A powerful stroke played with the purpose of forcing an error from the opponent; *spec.* in *Real Tennis*, such a shot aimed at the dedans. M17. **12** *Bridge* etc. A bid to which one's partner must reply, an act of forcing. M19. **13** *Billiards*. A stroke in which the cue-ball is struck off-centre causing it to stop or recoil at a particular angle. M19.

Phrases: **armed forces** (the people constituting) the fighting strength of a nation etc. *brute force*: see BRUTE *a.* *by force*: see sense 5 above. **by force of** by virtue of, by means of. **come into force** come into operation, take effect. *electromotive force*: see ELECTROMOTIVE *a.* *from force of habit*: see HABIT *n.* **in force** (*a*) in large numbers; (*b*) *Law* operative, binding, valid. **join forces** combine efforts. *life force*: see LIFE *n.* **put in force** enforce. *task force*: see TASK *n.* **with force and arms** *Law* (now *Hist.*) = VI ET ARMIS.

Comb.: **force cup** a rubber cup attached to a handle which clears a blocked drain by creating a vacuum in it; a plunger; **force-feed** *n.* & *v.* (*a*) *n.* a supply, esp. of lubricant, maintained under applied force or pressure; (*b*) *v.t.* feed (a prisoner, animal, etc.) by force; **force field** (chiefly *Sci. Fiction*) a region or barrier of (usu. invisible) force; **force-land** *v.i.* & *t.* [after FORCED *landing*] (cause to) make a forced landing; **force-out** *Baseball* a putting out of a base runner by necessitating an advance to the next base when it is not possible to do so safely; **force-pump** (*a*) a pump that forces water beyond the range of atmospheric pressure; (*b*) a kind of stomach-pump used for force-feeding; **force stroke** = sense 11 above.

force /fɔːs/ *n.*[2] Also **foss** /fɒs/. *north.* LME. [ON *fors* (Sw. *fors*, Da. *fos*).] A waterfall.

force /fɔːs/ *v.*[1] ME. [(O)Fr. *forcer*, f. as FORCE *n.*[1]] **I** Apply force. **1a** *v.t.* Compel or oblige (a person, oneself, etc.) *to do*, *into doing*, or *to* or *into* a course of action; rape (esp. a woman). ME. **b** *v.t.* & (now only *dial.*) *i.* Urge or push to the limits; strain or strive (*to do*). ME. **c** *v.t.* & *i.* *Cards*. Compel (a player) to trump or reveal the strength of a hand; compel a player to play (a certain card). M18. **d** *v.t.* *Baseball*. Put out (a base runner) by necessitating an advance to the next base when it is not possible to do so safely. Usu. foll. by *out*. M19. **e** *v.i.* *Tennis* etc. Use a force stroke. L19. **2a** *v.t.* Compel or constrain by physical, mental, moral, or circumstantial means; *Physics* modify by external action. LME. **b** *v.t.* & *i.* Of a sheepdog: move (sheep) in a certain direction. *Austral.* & *NZ*. E20. **3** *v.t.* Cause, bring about, or produce, by effort. M16. **4a** *v.t.* Overpower, capture, take by force, (a stronghold, defence, †troops); obtain by force, extort. L16. **b** *v.t.* Make a way by force through, break through, (a pass, enemy lines, etc.); break open (a lock, door, etc.). E17. **c** *v.i.* Make one's way *in*, *out*, *through*, or *up*, by force. Now *rare.* M17. **5** *v.t.* Drive, push, or propel violently or against resistance. Chiefly w. preps. or advs. L16. **6** *v.t.* Foll. by *on*, *upon*: impose or press (a thing) forcibly on (a person); oblige (a person) to turn or resort to (a thing). E17. †**b** Enforce (a law). *rare* (Shakes.). Only in E17. **c** Impose an unnatural or unusual sense or context on (a word, analogy, etc.). M17. **7** *v.t.* Hasten artificially the growth, development, or maturity of (a plant, farm animal, child, etc.). E17.

1a D. H. LAWRENCE She tried to force her mind to the contemplation of the new state of things. R. H. MOTTRAM He lay in bed until hunger forced him to rise. W. C. WILLIAMS He was insistent and forced her against her will to get into his car. **2a** W. S. CHURCHILL The President's . . use of the patronage at his disposal to force the repeal of the Silver Purchase Act. J. CHEEVER Her wicked sisters had got pregnant in order to force their marriages. **3** L. VAN DER POST I thought it useless to waste the energies of the whole party forcing a way through. A. MACLEAN He looked at me, forced a pale smile that was half apology, half recognition. **4a** T. JEFFERSON The people . . forced the prison of Saint Lazare. G. STEIN Sometimes it hurt so in him, . . it would force some slow tears from him. A. WILSON If he had forced from the public and the critics respect and hearing. **b** J. T. STORY I watched her open a locker, using a hatpin to force the lock. R. RENDELL It appears she was shot by someone who forced an entry to this house. **c** DRYDEN For Love they force thro' Thickets. **5** C. S. FORESTER The lower the brig would settle, . . the greater would be the pressure forcing water through the hole. E. BOWEN Had she been left alone . . life might yet have forced her on to her own feet. N. MOSLEY I thought I should force her mouth open by pressing my fingers between her teeth. **6** R. LANGBRIDGE Her lack of money had forced her back upon the most respectable costume which she had. N. MITFORD She gets a hold over people . . with her charm and her prestige and then forces her own values on them. **c** E. WHITE This is manifestly to force the Scripture. **7** ANTHONY HUXLEY Hyacinths and other bulbs we force in winter. K. M. E. MURRAY Regular schooling should not be begun too young, early 'forcing' being . . the cause of many boys of promise proving disappointments.

II Give, have force. †**8** *v.t.* Strengthen, reinforce; fortify. LME–E19. **b** Season, spice. LME–L15. **c** *v.t.* Clarify (wine) by a short process. M18–M19. †**9** *v.t.* & *i.* Be concerned, attach importance to, care (*for, of, to do*). Usu. in neg. contexts. LME–E17. †**10** *v.i.* Be of importance; matter, signify. LME–E17.

9 SHAKES. *Lucr.* I force not argument a straw.

Phrases: **force a card** *Conjuring* make a person choose a particular card unconsciously. **force a person's hand** compel a person to act prematurely or to adopt a policy unwillingly. **force a smile** make oneself smile, smile in spite of one's feelings. **force down** compel (an aircraft) to land. **force one's voice** strain to get notes beyond one's usual range or a degree of loudness beyond what is easy or natural. **force the bidding** raise the price rapidly at an auction. **force the game** (*Cricket* etc.) run risks to increase the rate of scoring. **force the issue** compel a decision. **force the pace** adopt a fast pace in a race in order to tire out one's adversary or adversaries quickly.

force /fɔːs/ *v.*[2]*t. obs.* exc. *Sc. dial.* LME. [AN *forcer*, f. OFr. *forces*, f. L *forfices*, FORFEX pair of scissors, clipping-shears.] Clip or shear (a fleece, a beard); *esp.* clip off the coarser upper part of (a fleece).

†**force** *v.*[3]*t.* LME–L18. [Alt. of FARCE *v.* by confusion with FORCE *v.*[1]] = FARCE *v.* I, Ib.

fig.: SHAKES. *Tr. & Cr.* Wit . . larded with malice and malice forced with wit.

¶ Surviving in FORCEMEAT.

forceable /ˈfɔːsəb(ə)l/ *a.* LME. [OFr. *forçable*, f. as FORCE *v.*[1]: see -ABLE. Cf. FORCIBLE.] **1** = FORCIBLE. Now *rare*. LME. **2** Able to be forced. L16.

forceably *adv.* LME.

forced /fɔːst/ *ppl a.* L15. [f. FORCE *v.*[1] + -ED[1].] **1** Compelled, imposed, or obtained by force; compulsory. L15. **2** Produced or maintained with effort; strained; (of a gesture etc.) affected, unnatural. L16. **3** Artificially made or prepared; *esp.* (of soil) disturbed by digging, having the topsoil raised. Long *obs.* exc. *dial.* E17. **4** Of a plant, crop, etc.: made to bear, or produced, out of the proper season. L17. **5** Of (a draught of) air: produced or supplied by artificial means, as a blower etc. M19.

1 I. MURDOCH A forced marriage which her free nature would resent and soon detest. **2** G. GORDON The forced, indeed intense, jollity he found himself . . assuming when conversing with certain members of the company. **4** E. BOWEN She thought they looked like forced roses, magnetized into being.

Special collocations & comb.: **forced-choice** *a.* (of a question, technique, etc.) requiring a choice to be made by the participant between a number of prearranged answers or alternatives. **forced labour** compulsory labour, usu. under rigorous conditions. **forced landing** an unavoidable landing by an aircraft in an emergency. **forced march**: requiring a special effort by troops etc. **forced move** a move in chess etc. to which there is no reasonable alternative.

forcedly /ˈfɔːsɪdli/ *adv.* M16. **forcedness** /ˈfɔːsɪdnɪs/ *n.* M17.

force de frappe /fɔrs də frap/ *n. phr.* Pl. ***forces de frappe*** (pronounced same). M20. [Fr. = striking force.] *Mil.* A striking force; *spec.* the French independent nuclear striking force.

forceful /ˈfɔːsfʊl, -f(ə)l/ *a.* & *adv.* M16. [f. FORCE *n.*[1] + -FUL.] **A** *adj.* **1** Full of force, powerful, strong; (of a speech etc.) impressive, effective. M16. **2** Acting with force, violent; (now *rare*) driven or propelled with force. L16. **B** *adv.* Forcefully. *rare.* E18.

1 P. G. WODEHOUSE One of those forceful characters which monopolize any stage on which they appear. **2** N. CHOMSKY An end to any forceful interference in the internal affairs of Vietnam or any other nation.

forcefully *adv.* L18. **forcefulness** *n.* E19.

forceless /ˈfɔːslɪs/ *a.* M16. [f. FORCE *n.*[1] + -LESS.] Without force; feeble.

force majeure /fɔrs maʒœːr/ *n. phr.* L19. [Fr. = superior strength.] Irresistible force, overwhelming power; *spec.* in *Law, Comm.*, etc., an unforeseeable course of events excusing fulfilment of a contract.

forcemeat /ˈfɔːsmiːt/ *n.* L17. [f. FORCE *v.*[3] + MEAT *n.*] A mixture of finely chopped meat or vegetables etc., seasoned and spiced, and chiefly used for stuffing or garnish.

forcené /forsəne/ *a.* E18. [Fr., pa. pple of *forcener, forsener*, be or become mad or enraged, f. OFr. *fors* (mod. *hors*) + *sen* sense.] *Her.* Of a horse: rearing or standing on its hind legs.

forceps /ˈfɔːsɛps, -sɪps/ *n.sing.* & *pl.* L16. [L.] **1** Also *pair of forceps*. A pair of pincers, usually held in one hand to obtain a firm grip on a small object, esp. in surgery or anatomical dissection, or in entomology. Also, in obstetrics, a large two-bladed instrument designed to encircle and pull upon the baby's head to assist delivery. L16. **2** *Zool.* An organ or part of the body that has the shape of, or may be used as, a forceps, e.g. the cerci of earwigs. Formerly also, either of the two branches of this. M17.

forcer /ˈfɔːsə/ *n.*[1] Long *obs.* exc. *Hist.* ME. [OFr. *forc(i)er*.] A chest, a coffer.

forcer /ˈfɔːsə/ *n.*[2] M16. [f. FORCE *v.*[1] + -ER[1].] **1** A person who or thing which forces. Now *esp.* a person who produces forced crops. M16. **2** An instrument or means of forcing; *esp.* (the plunger of) a force-pump. M17.

forces de frappe *n. phr.* pl. of FORCE DE FRAPPE.

forcible /ˈfɔːsɪb(ə)l/ *a.* & *adv.* LME. [Legal AN, OFr., f. as FORCE *v.*[1]: see -IBLE. Cf. FORCEABLE.] **A** *adj.* **1** Done by or involving the use of force or violence. Esp. in *Law* in *forcible detainer*: see DETAINER *n.*[2] I. LME. **2** Having force; now chiefly (of a person, action, speech, etc.) producing a powerful effect, convincing; formerly also, (of a person, material thing, or natural agency) strong, powerful. M16.

1 P. SCOTT They ate it in different ways, a few eagerly, most reluctantly, some by forcible feeding. **2** L. STEPHEN One man sees everything in the forcible light and shade of Rembrandt.

B *adv.* Forcibly. L16.

Comb.: **forcible-feeble** *n.* & *a.* [after Shakes. *2 Hen. IV*] (a person) disguising feebleness under a show of force.

forci'bility *n.* L18. **forcibleness** *n.* M16. **forcibly** *adv.* L15.

forcing /ˈfɔːsɪŋ/ *vbl n.* LME. [f. FORCE *v.*[1] + -ING[1].] The action of FORCE *v.*[1]

Comb.: **forcing frame, house** a frame, a building, where the growth or maturity of a plant, fruit, etc. is artificially hastened; **forcing pen** *Austral.* & *NZ* a pen into which sheep are forced or driven in order to guide them to a certain point.

forcipate /ˈfɔːsɪpeɪt/ *a.* M17. [f. L *forcip-* FORCEPS + -ATE[2].] Chiefly *Bot.* & *Zool.* Shaped like forceps; deeply forked.

Also **forcipated** *a.* M17.

forcy /ˈfɔːsi/ *a.* Chiefly *Sc.* & *north.* LME. [f. FORCE *n.*[1] + -Y[1].] Full of force, strong, active; (of weather) propitious for speedy growth or ripening of crops.

ford /fɔːd/ *n.* [OE *ford* = OFris. *forda*, OS *-ford* in place-names (Du. *voorde*), (O)HG *furt*, f. WGmc, Gmc base of FARE *v.*] **1** A shallow place where a river or other stretch of water may be crossed by wading or with a vehicle. OE. **2** A tract of water; a stream; the sea. *obs.* exc. *dial.* M16.

ford /fɔːd/ *v.* E17. [f. the n.] **1** *v.t.* Cross (water) by means of a ford. E17. **2** *v.i.* Cross (*over*) water by means of a ford. L17.

fordable *a.* E17. **fording** *n.* (*a*) the action of the vb; (*b*) a ford: M18.

fordeal /ˈfɔːdiːl/ *n.* & *a.* Long *obs.* exc. *Sc.* L15. [f. FOR-[2] + DEAL *n.*[1] (part).] **A** *n.* **1** Precedence; *arch.* advantage. L15. **2** A store, a reserve. E19. **B** *adj.* In reserve, in hand. E19.

fordo /fɔːˈduː/ *v.t. arch.* Also **fore-**. Pa. t. **-did** /-ˈdɪd/; pa. pple **-done** /-ˈdʌn/. [OE *fordōn* = OS *fardōn* (Du. *verdoen*), OHG *fartuon* (G *vertun*), f. base of FOR-[1], DO *v.*] **1** Kill; put an end to (life). OE. **2** Destroy, ruin, spoil, (a place, thing, †person); lay waste to (land). OE. **3** †**a** Abolish (an institution); annul (a law). OE–M19. **b** Do away with, remove, (an immaterial object, esp. sin). ME. †**4** Undo; make powerless, counteract, (poison, temptation, etc.). ME–E17. **5** As *fordone* pa. pple. Exhausted, tired out. M16.

1 SHAKES. *Haml.* This doth betoken The corse they follow did with desperate hand fordo it own life. **5** M. ARNOLD With Indian heats at last fordone.

fordrunken /fɔːˈdrʌŋk(ə)n/ *ppl a.* Long *arch.* [OE *fordruncen*, f. FOR-[1] + DRUNKEN *a.* (= MLG *verdrunken*).] Drunk, overcome with drink.

fore /fɔː/ *a.* & *n.* L15. [Independent use of FORE-.] **A** *adj.* †**1** Anterior in time, previous, former. L15–E18. **2** Situated in front. Freq. opp. *back, hind, aft.* E16.

2 J. SPOTTISWOOD The Cannon having made great breaches in the fore and back walls.

B *n.* The forepart of something, the front; the bow of a ship. (Earliest in *to the fore* below.) M17.

to the fore (*a*) (of a person) present, on the spot, alive, surviving; (*b*) (of money etc.) ready, available; (*c*) in full view, conspicuous; (*d*) *come to the fore*, come to the front, come into prominence, take a leading part.

fore /fɔː/ *adv., prep.* & *conj.* Also **'fore**. [OE *fore* = OFris. *for(e)*, *fara*, OS, OHG *fora* (Du. *voor*, G *vor*), Goth. *faura*, f. Gmc, rel. to Skt *pra, purā*, Gk *pro, para*, L *pro, prae, per*. From 16th cent. often regarded as abbrev. of *before*.] **A** *adv.* **1** Before in time, previously. Long *obs.* exc. *dial.* OE. †**2** Forward, forth. ME–M17. **3** See FORE AND AFT.

B *prep.* **1** Before in place, in the presence of. OE. **2** Before in time, previous to. *obs.* exc. *dial.* & *US.* OE. †**3** In support of; on account of. OE–LME. †**4** Before in order, in preference to. ME–M17.

1 SHAKES. *Wint. T.* Contract us fore these witnesses.

C *conj.* Before. *US.* E19.

American Speech My two boys died 'fore they was ten.

fore /fɔː/ *int.* M19. [Prob. aphet. f. BEFORE, AFORE.] *Golf.* As a warning to anyone in the probable line of flight of a ball: look out!

fore- /fɔː/ *pref.* Also (not productive) **for-**. OE. [Repr. FORE *adv.* & *prep.*, *a.*] **1** Forming vbs and their derivs. in senses 'before, in front', as *foreshorten*, 'beforehand, in advance', as *forecast, foreordain*. **2** Forming ns. in senses 'in front (of), front-', as *forecourt, forelimb*, 'that is the front part of', as *forearm*, 'of, near, or towards the bow of a ship or connected with the foremast, forward', as *forecastle, forehold*, 'that is in advance (of), anticipatory, precedent', as *forefather*, *forenoon.* 3 Formerly occas. forming preps., as *fore-again(st).*

fore'act *v.t.* & *i.* (now *rare*) act beforehand E17. **fore-a'gain(st)** *prep.* (long *obs.* exc. *Sc.*) over against, directly opposite L15. †**fore-alleged** *ppl a.* previously alleged L16–E18. **forebay** *n.* a reservoir or channel from which water is discharged to run a mill-wheel LME. †**forebell** *n.* the first of a peal of bells L15–E19. **forebitter** *n.* (*Naut.*) a sea-song, esp. sung for recreation E20. **forebody** *n.* †(*a*) the front part of a dress; (*b*) *Naut.* the forward part of the hull of a ship: E17. **forebow** *n.*[1] (*obs.* exc. *dial.*) [f. BOW *n.*[1]] (*a*) in *pl.*, the shoulders of an animal; (*b*) the prow of a ship: E16. †**forebow** *n.*[2] [f. BOW *n.*[3]] an arched frame on the front of a saddle E18–M19. **forebrain** *n.* (*Anat.*) the anterior part of the brain, including the cerebrum and diencephalon L19. **forebreast** *n.* (*a*) (now only *Sc.*) the forepart of something; orig. *spec.* the vanguard of an army; (*b*) *Mining* = FOREFIELD: LME. **forecabin** *n.* a cabin in the forward part of a vessel E19. **forecaddie** *n.* a caddie who goes ahead of golfers to see where the balls fall L18. **fore'call** *v.t.* call or ordain beforehand M17. **forecar** *n.* (now *rare*) an early kind of motorcycle having a passenger's seat in front E20. **forecarriage** *n.* the front part of the framework of a carriage M16. **fore-'cited** *ppl a.* previously cited L16. **forecon'ceive** *v.t.* (long *rare*) preconceive M16. **foredawn** *n.* the time preceding the dawn L19. **foreday** *n.* †(*a*) in *pl.*, preceding days, past life; (*b*) (chiefly *Sc.* & *US*) the early part of the day, before or around dawn: ME. **foredeck** *n.* the deck at the forward part of a ship; the forward part of the deck: E16. **fore'destine** *v.t.* (*rare*) predestine ME. **fore'destiny** *n.* (*rare*) destiny, fate M16. **foredoor** *n.* (now *rare*) a front door M16. **foredune** *n.* the part of a dune system nearest to the sea E20. **fore-elders** *n.pl.* (chiefly *north.*) ancestors, progenitors ME. **foreface** *n.* the front part of something, *esp.* the face of an animal; an iron framework forming the front part of a fireplace: M16. **forefield** *n.* (*Mining*) a coalface, *esp.* the most advanced part of a coalface currently being worked L17. **forefighter** *n.* (*rare*) a fighter in the front ranks LME. **fore'gain(st)** *prep.* (long *obs.* exc. *Sc.*) over against, directly opposite LME. **foregame** *n.* (now *rare*) a preliminary game L16. **foreganger** *n.* †(*a*) a forerunner, a predecessor; (*b*) *Naut.* a short piece of rope connecting a line to a harpoon in whale-fishing etc.; (*c*) *Naut.* a 15-fathom length of strong anchor chain which ran between an anchor and the rest of the cable, and could withstand extra wear and tear: ME. **foregate** *n.* a front gate LME. **foregift** *n.* (*Law*) a premium for a lease E18. **foreglance** *n.* (*a*) the action of glancing forward; (*b*) a glance beforehand: M19. **fore'guess** *v.t.* guess beforehand; anticipate, conjecture: LME. **foregut** *n.* (*Anat.* & *Zool.*) the anterior part of the gut L19. **forehammer** *n.* (*Sc.* & *north.*) a large hammer used by a blacksmith; a sledgehammer: LME. **fore'hear** *v.t.* & *i.* (now *rare*) hear beforehand L16. †**forehent** *v.t.* (*rare*) overtake, take in advance: only in L16. **forehock** *n.* a foreleg cut of pork or bacon E20. **forehold** *n.* (*Naut.*) (a section of) a hold in the forward part of a ship M17. **forehorse** *n.* the foremost horse in a team L15. **forein'tend** *v.t.* intend beforehand L16. **forelady** *n.* (chiefly *US*) = FOREWOMAN 2 L19. †**forelend** *v.t.* (*rare*, Spenser) grant previously: only in L16. †**forelie** *v.i.* (*rare*, Spenser) lie across the front of: only in L16. †**forelift** *v.t.* lift up in front L16–M18. **fore'live** *v.t.* & *i.* live before (another); exist previously: LME. **foreloader** *n.* a loader mounted on the front of a tractor etc. M20. **fore'mean** *v.t.* intend beforehand E17. †**foremention** *v.t.* mention beforehand L16–M18. **forenamed** *ppl a.* (*arch.*) named or mentioned before, aforesaid ME. **foreoath** *n.* (*Law*, now *Hist.*) in Anglo-Saxon England, an oath required of the party bringing a suit unless the fact complained of was manifest OE. **fore'order** *v.t.* order beforehand; preordain: L19. **fore'plan** *v.t.* plan beforehand L18. **foreplane** *n.* a carpenter's plane used for preliminary smoothing E18. **forepleasure** *n.* pleasure induced by sexual stimulation E20. **forepurpose** *n.* (now *rare* or *obs.*) a previous intent or design L16. **fore'purpose** *v.t.* (now *rare* or *obs.*) intend or resolve beforehand: M16. **forerank** *n.* the front rank, the most prominent place L16. †**fore-recited** *ppl a.* previously recited; aforesaid: E–M17. **forerib** *n.* a rib of beef for roasting, cut from just in front of the sirloin (freq. in *pl.*) M19. **forerider** *n.* a person who rides ahead; a scout, a messenger: L15. **foreseat** *n.* (now *Sc.* & *US*) a seat or position in front, esp. in church; the front part of a box-pew: L16. **fore'seize** *v.t.* (*rare*) take (something one is destined to receive) prematurely L17. **fore'shine** *v.i.* (*arch.*) shine forth; throw light forward: L16. **foreshock** *n.* a lesser shock preceding the main shock of an earthquake E20. †**foreshop** *n.* (chiefly *Sc.*) a shop fronting a street M17–E19. **foreside** *n.* the forepart; the front or upper side: LME. **fore'signify** *v.t.* prefigure, typify; foretell: M16. †**foreskirt** *n.* the front or a front part of a coat or robe below the waist M16–M17. **foresleeve** *n.* the part of a sleeve which covers the forearm; a loose ornamental sleeve formerly worn over an ordinary sleeve: LME. **fore'spent** *ppl a.* (now *rare*) spent previously L16. †**fore-spurrer** *n.* (*rare*, Shakes.) a person who spurs or presses on ahead: only in L16. **forestick** *n.* (*US*) the front stick lying on the andirons in a wood fire L18. **forestone** *n.* (*a*) a mass of rock which interrupts a vein of ore; (*b*) the front crosspiece of a blast-furnace: M17. **forestroke** *n.* a forward stroke in bell-ringing, sword-fighting, etc. L17. **fore'suffer** *v.t.* & *i.* suffer beforehand M19. **foretack** *n.* (*Naut.*) a rope by which the weather corner of a foresail is kept in place L15. **fore'teach** *v.t.* (*rare*) teach (a person, something) beforehand M16. **foretime** *n.* (*arch.*) the past, early days, old times L15. **foretooth** *n.* a front tooth (usu. in *pl.*) OE. **fore-understanding** *n.* (*rare*) instinctive knowledge or understanding; intuition: M16. **fore'utter** *v.t.* (*rare*) foretell L16. **forewheel** *n.* either of the front wheels of a four-wheeled carriage E18. **forewing** *n.* either of the anterior wings of an insect M19. **foreworld** *n.* the prehistoric or primeval world L18. **fore'write** *v.t.* write beforehand (chiefly as *forewritten* ppl a.) LME.

fore and aft /fɔːr (ə)nd 'ɑːft/ *adv.* & *a. phr.* As adj. usu. **fore-and-aft**. E17. [Perh. tr. phr. of LG origin: cf. Du. *van voren en van achteren.*] Chiefly *Naut.* A *adv.* 1 From stem to stern, lengthwise. E17. 2 Of position: in or at both bow and stern, all over the ship. E17. 3 Of motion or direction: backwards and forwards. E18. B *adj.* Placed or directed lengthwise. E19.

Comb. & *special collocations*: **fore-and-aft cap** a cap with a peak at each end; **fore-and-aft rigged** *a. phr.* (of a vessel) having sails set lengthwise as opp. to on yards; opp. *square-rigged* s.v. SQUARE *a.*

fore-and-after *n.* (*a*) a vessel, esp. a schooner, which is fore-and-aft rigged; (*b*) a fore-and-aft cap: E19.

fore-appoint /fɔːrə'pɔɪnt/ *v.t. arch.* M16. [f. FORE- + APPOINT.] Appoint beforehand.

fore-appointment *n.* previous appointment, preordination L16.

forearm /'fɔːrɑːm/ *n.* E18. [f. FORE- + ARM *n.*[1]] The part of the arm from the elbow to the wrist or fingertips; the corresponding part in the foreleg of an animal or the wing of a bird.

A. GRAY His sleeves were rolled well above his elbows exposing robust hairy forearms.

forearm /fɔːr'ɑːm/ *v.t.* L16. [f. FORE- + ARM *v.*[1]] Arm beforehand (freq. *fig.*).

E. M. GOULBURN We are forearmed against surprises. *Bird Watching* Forwarned is forearmed, for such knowledge alerts you to the .. likely species in the .. habitat you are visiting.

forebear /'fɔːbɛː/ *n.* Orig. *Sc.* Also **forbear**. L15. [f. FORE- + var. of BEER *n.*[2]] An ancestor, a forefather, (freq. in *pl.*).

W. MAXWELL Their forebears had perhaps come on a later wave of European migration.

forebode /fɔː'bəʊd/ *v.* E17. [f. FORE- + BODE *v.*[1]] 1 a *v.t.* Have a presentiment of (a thing, esp. something evil), *that*; anticipate. E17. b *v.i.* Conjecture, forecast. E18. 2 *v.t.* Betoken, portend. M17. 3 *v.t.* Announce beforehand, predict. M17.

1 POPE My soul foreboded I should find the bower Of some fell monster. 3 W. H. DIXON Old men foreboded evil days to come.

forebodement *n.* (*rare*) (a) foreboding M18. **foreboder** *n.* a person who or thing which forbodes L17. **forebodingly** *adv.* in a foreboding manner, predictively E19.

foreboding /fɔː'bəʊdɪŋ/ *n.* LME. [f. prec. + -ING[1].] 1 A prediction, a presage. LME. b A portent, an omen. LME. 2 A presentiment of coming evil. E17.

1 J. TYNDALL Heedless of the forebodings of many prophets of evil weather. 2 R. SUTCLIFF There was a queer superstitious feeling in him .. a queer foreboding of trouble to come. D. ACHESON The army, against the deepest forebodings of General Walker, moved forward.

forecame *v.* pa. t. of FORECOME.

forecast /'fɔːkɑːst/ *n.* LME. [f. the vb.] †1 a A plan, a plot. LME–M18. b A design, a purpose, an aim. M16–L17. 2 The action or faculty of forecasting; forethought, prudence. Now *rare.* M16. 3 A conjectural estimate, based on present indications, of something in the future, esp. of coming weather; a prediction. L17.

2 CARLYLE The doctrine, which Swift, with the keen forecast of genius, dimly anticipated. 3 C. LAMB A forecast of the wearisome day that lies before me. *Observer* The previous forecast of no serious gale.

forecast /'fɔːkɑːst/ *v.* Pa. t. & pple **-cast**, **-casted**. LME. [f. FORE- + CAST *v.*] 1 a *v.t.* & *i.* Contrive or plan beforehand; foreordain, predestine. *obs.* exc. *dial.* LME. b *v.t.* Consider beforehand. M16. 2 *v.t.* & *i.* Estimate or conjecture beforehand (future events or conditions, esp. the weather); predict. L15.

1a A. GOLDING At the first sight the thing which was forecast by good order, seemeth to happen by adventure. 2 MILTON If it happen as I did forecast. M. E. G. DUFF I am quite unable to forecast the future. E. O'BRIEN The weather bureau forecast sun.

forecastable *a.* L19. **forecaster** *n.* a person who forecasts M17. **forecastingly** *adv.* (now *rare* or *obs.*) with prior planning or consideration M16.

forecastle /'fəʊks(ə)l/ *n.* Also **fo'c's'le**. LME. [f. FORE- + CASTLE *n.*[1]] *Naut.* 1 *Hist.* A short raised deck at the front of a ship, orig. raised like a castle to command the enemy's decks. LME. 2 *Hist.* The forward part of the upper deck of a ship. L15. 3 The forward part of a ship, below the deck, where the sailors live. M19.

foreclose /fɔː'kləʊz/ *v.* ME. [(O)Fr. *forclos* pa. pple of *forclore*, f. as FOR-[2] + *clore* CLOSE *v.*: assoc. w. FOR-[1], FORE-.] I *v.t.* †1 Bar from escaping, prevent the passage or leaving of. Only in ME. 2 Exclude, bar, shut out completely. LME. 3 Hinder or prohibit (a person) *from, to do*; hinder the action or activity of. LME. b Prevent the performance or occurrence of (an action or event). M16. c Debar (a person) from enjoyment (*of*). M19. †4 Close fast, stop up, block up (an opening, way, etc.). L15–M18. 5 Establish an exclusive claim to. L16. 6 Settle (an arguable point) by anticipation. E18. 7 *Law.* Bar (a person entitled to redeem a mortgage) upon non-payment of the money due; deprive of the equity of redemption. E18. b Bar (a right of redemption); take away the power of redeeming (a mortgage). E18.

2 D. NEAL The Puritans being thus foreclosed and shut out of the Church. 3 G. BERKELEY A mind not hardened by impenitency, nor foreclosed by pride. b W. LIPPMANN One career excluding others, one course foreclosing its alternatives. 5 R. W. EMERSON And finding .. even virtue and truth foreclosed and monopolized. 7b G. SANTAYANA Tenants must occasionally be evicted and mortgages foreclosed.

II *v.i.* 8 Revoke the power of redeeming a mortgage. Freq. foll. by *on.* E18.

8 A. TROLLOPE A .. notice .. from the duke's lawyer, saying that he meant to foreclose.

foreclosure /fɔː'kləʊʒə/ *n.* E18. [f. FORE- + CLOSURE.] *Law.* The action of foreclosing a mortgage or depriving a mortgagor of the right of redemption; a proceeding to bar the right of redeeming mortgaged property.

forecome /fɔː'kʌm/ *v. rare.* Pa. t. **-came** /-'keɪm/; pa. pple **-come**. OE. [f. FORE- + COME *v.*] 1 *v.t.* Come before, anticipate. OE. 2 *v.t.* Gain the advantage of, overcome. OE. †3 *v.i.* Come before the usual time. Only in ME.

foreconscious /fɔː'kɒnʃəs/ *a.* & *n.* E20. [f. FORE- + CONSCIOUS *a.*, tr. G *vorbewusst.*] *Psychol.* (Of or pertaining to) that part of the mind below the threshold of immediate conscious attention, whose memories can be brought into the conscious field. Cf. PRECONSCIOUS.

forecourt /'fɔːkɔːt/ *n.* M16. [f. FORE- + COURT *n.*[1]] 1 An enclosed space in front of a building, an outer court. M16. b *spec.* The part of a filling-station where petrol is supplied. M20. 2 The front part of a court used for sports or games, *esp.* the part of a tennis-court between the service line and the net. E20.

1 E. METEYARD The ivy-clad cottage, with its forecourt or garden standing to the front. K. ISHIGURO We sat on a bench in the forecourt of the .. station.

foredge *n.* var. of FORE-EDGE.

foredo *v.* var. of FORDO.

foredoom /'fɔːduːm/ *n.* M16. [f. FORE- + DOOM *n.*[1]] A doom or judgement pronounced beforehand; destiny.

foredoom /fɔːˈduːm/ *v.t.* L16. [f. FORE- + DOOM *v.*] **1 a** Forecast, foreshadow. *rare.* L16. **b** Foreordain, predestine. L17. **2** Doom or condemn beforehand (*to*). E17.
2 Bosw. SMITH His efforts were . . foredoomed to failure.

fore-edge /ˈfɔːrɛdʒ/ *n.* Also **foredge.** M17. [f. FORE- + EDGE *n.*] The front or outer edge, esp. the outer vertical edge of a page or a book.
Comb.: **fore-edge painting** a picture or decoration on the fore-edge of a book.

fore-end /ˈfɔːrɛnd/ *n.* LME. [f. FORE- + END *n.*] **1** Now chiefly *Naut.* The front or front part of a place. LME. **b** In *pl.* The forward space in a submarine used for storing torpedoes and as living quarters for the crew. Also, the submarine ratings quartered there. M20. **2** The beginning or early part of a period of time. Now *Sc.* & *dial.* E17. **3** The front part of the stock of a gun, supporting the barrel. L19. **4** The hock of a foreleg of pork or bacon. E20.
Comb.: **fore-end loader** *Agric.* a loader attached to the front of a tractor or other vehicle.

forefather /ˈfɔːfɑːðə/ *n.* ME. [f. FORE- + FATHER *n.*: cf. ON *forfaðir.*] A person from whom one's father or mother is descended, an ancestor; a member of the past generations of a family or race. Usu. in *pl.*
J. W. KRUTCH Modern man has far more knowledge . . than his forefathers had. **Forefathers' Day** *US* 21 December, the anniversary of the landing of the first settlers at Plymouth, Massachusetts.
forefatherly *a.* of or pertaining to one's forefathers, ancestral M19.

forefeel /fɔːˈfiːl/ *v.t.* Pa. t. & pple **-felt** /-ˈfɛlt/. L16. [f. FORE- + FEEL *v.*] Feel beforehand, have a presentiment of.
forefeeling *n.* (*a*) the action of the vb; (*b*) a presentiment: M16.

forefend *v.* var. of FORFEND.

forefinger /ˈfɔːfɪŋgə/ *n.* LME. [f. FORE- + FINGER *n.*] The finger next to the thumb, the index finger.

forefoot /ˈfɔːfʊt/ *n.* Pl. **-feet** /-fiːt/. LME. [f. FORE- + FOOT *n.*, perh. after Du. *voorvoet* (cf. G *Vorderfuss*).] **1** Either of the front feet of a quadruped. LME. †**b** The hand. *joc. rare* (Shakes.). Only in L16. **2** *Naut.* The foremost piece of the keel of a ship. L18.
1 H. MCMURTRIE The long claws of their fore-feet enable them to dig with great effect. 2 B. GREENHILL The . . 'long' ship . . had a projecting forefoot, which came to be developed . . as a ram.

forefront /ˈfɔːfrʌnt/ *n.* LME. [f. FORE- + FRONT *n.*] **1** The principal face or foremost part, esp. of a building. Now *rare.* LME. **b** The front rank or vanguard of an army. L15. **2** *fig.* The very front; the leading or most important part or place. L16. **3** The beginning of a book, document, or literary work. Long *arch.* L16.
2 J. R. GREEN The great statutes which stand in the forefront of our laws. G. M. TREVELYAN They were in the forefront of progress and invention.

foregather *v.* var. of FORGATHER.

forego /fɔːˈgəʊ/ *v.*[1] *t.* & *i.* Pa. t. **-went** /-ˈwɛnt/; pa. pple **-gone** /-ˈgɒn/. OE. [f. FORE- + GO *v.*] Go before, precede in place or time.
A. D. T. WHITNEY Sublimely unaffected by all that had foregone. J. PAYNE His head forewent his feet and he fell to the ground.

forego *v.*[2] var. of FORGO.

foregoer /fɔːˈgəʊə, ˈfɔː-/ *n.*[1] LME. [f. FORE- + GOER.] †**1** A messenger sent before, a forerunner; *spec.* a purveyor. LME–M18. **2** A person who or thing which goes in front; a leader. Also, an example, a pattern. LME. **3** A predecessor. M16. **4** *Naut.* = FOREGANGER (b). L17.
2 R. BAXTER The promised Glory, and the future blessings that are its necessary Foregoers.

foregoer *n.*[2] var. of FORGOER.

foregoing /ˈfɔːgəʊɪŋ/ *a.* LME. [f. FOREGO *v.*[1] + -ING[2].] That goes or has gone before; preceding; previously mentioned.
T. HARDY Instead of new articles . . those that had been rejected in the foregoing summer were brought out again. *absol.*: HOR. WALPOLE Besides the foregoing, Lord Breadalbane has . . eleven portraits.

foregone /ˈfɔːgɒn, fɔːˈgɒn/ *ppl a.*[1] L16. [pa. pple of FOREGO *v.*[1]] That has gone before or gone by; (of time) past.
foregone conclusion (*a*) a decision or opinion come to in advance of the evidence or necessary facts; (*b*) a result that can be or could have been foreseen.

foregone *ppl a.*[2] var. of FORGONE *ppl a.*

foreground /ˈfɔːgraʊnd/ *n.* & *v.* L17. [f. FORE- + GROUND *n.* after Du. *voorgrond*: cf. G *Vordergrund.*] **A** *n.* **1** The part of a view which is in front and nearest the observer, esp. as represented in a picture. L17. **2** *fig.* The most conspicuous or prominent position. E19.
1 K. CLARK The composition is divided into a foreground with figures, and a very distinct landscape. 2 J. A. SYMONDS The Aeolians occupied the very foreground of Greek literature.
Comb.: **foreground music** music played in the foreground, which dominates over any other sound.
B *v.t.* Place in the foreground, make prominent; *spec.* (*Ling.*) draw attention to (a particular feature or message in a piece of writing) by means of esp. striking or unexpected linguistic devices. L19.
M. EATON This description tends to foreground narrative and script at the expense of other factors. *Fremdsprachen* In any informative text, the purpose should be foregrounded.
foregrounding *vbl n.* the action of the vb; *spec.* (*Ling.*) the action of emphasizing something by means of linguistic devices: M20.

forehand /ˈfɔːhand/ *n.* & *a.* M16. [f. FORE- + HAND *n.*] **A** *n.* †**1** An arrow for shooting straight in front of one. Only in M16. **2** The position in front or above; the upper hand, the advantage. *obs.* exc. *Sc.* M16. †**b** That which holds the front position; the vanguard. *rare* (Shakes.). Only in E17. **3** The part of a horse which would be in front of a rider. E17. **4** *Tennis, Badminton*, etc. A forehand stroke. E20.
4 *Tennis World* Her killer forehand is now supported by a . . top spin backhand. **on the forehand** (on the side on which one must strike) forehanded.
B *adj.* †**1** Designating an arrow for shooting straight before one. Only in L16. **2** Done or given at some earlier time; (of a payment) made in advance. *obs.* exc. *Sc.* L16. **3** Foremost, leading. *obs.* exc. *Sc.* M17. **4** *Tennis, Badminton*, etc. Designating a stroke played with the arm extended away from the body and the palm of the hand facing one's opponent. Also, designating an area of a court in which such a stroke is usually played. L19.
4 J. BARRINGTON The most efficient forehand volley is built up on a relatively short back-swing.
forehander *n.* (*Tennis, Badminton*, etc.) a forehand stroke E20.

forehanded /ˈfɔːhandɪd/ *a.* & *adv.* L16. [f. prec. + -ED[2].] **A** *adj.* †**1** (Of a horse) *well* etc. built in the forehand; (of a person) *well* etc. built. L16–L18. **2** Looking to the future; prudent, thrifty. Now *Sc.* & *US.* M17. **b** That has made provision for the future; comfortable, well-to-do. Now *US.* M17. **3** *Tennis, Badminton*, etc. Of a stroke: forehand. Now *rare.* L19.
2 J. R. LOWELL They were . . a thrifty forehanded race.
B *adv. Tennis, Badminton*, etc. With a forehand stroke. L19.
foreˈhandedness *n.* (*US*) the action of looking to the future; prudence, foresight: M19.

forehead /ˈfɒrɪd, ˈfɔːhɛd/ *n.* [OE *forhēafod*, f. FOR-[3], FORE- + *hēafod* HEAD *n.* Cf. OFris. *forhāfd*, MLG *vorhōved*, Du. *voorhoofd*, G *Vor(der)haupt.*] **1** That part of the face which extends from the level of the eyebrows up to the natural line of the hair. Also, the corresponding part of the face of an animal. OE. †**2** A feeling or attitude able to be expressed in a person's countenance; *spec.* innocence, modesty, assurance. LME–L18. **3** The front part, the forefront. L15.
1 E. HEMINGWAY Their helmets came low down over their foreheads and the side of their faces. 2 T. SHERIDAN No body . . could have the forehead or folly to turn it into ridicule.
foreheaded *a.* (now *rare*) having a forehead L16. **foreheadless** *a.* (now *rare* or *obs.*) having no forehead, lacking in shame or assurance E17.

foreign /ˈfɒr(ə)n/ *a.*, *n.*, & *adv.* ME. [OFr. *forein*, *forain* f. Proto-Romance, f. L *foras*, f. *fores* door. For the spelling with *-eign* cf. *sovereign.*] **A** *adj.* **I** Of another place. †**1** Out of doors, outside; *chamber foreign*, a privy, a lavatory. Only in ME. **b** Concerned with matters outside one's home, manor, etc. E17–E18. **2** Belonging to, coming from, or characteristic of, another country or nation. ME. **b** Belonging to or coming from another district, county, society, etc. LME. **3** Situated outside the country; not in one's own land. LME. **b** Situated outside an estate, district, county, etc. LME. **4** Carried on or taking place abroad, into or with another country. M16. **5** Dealing with matters concerned with other countries. L16.
2 H. BELLOC He fell, crying and howling in a foreign tongue to gods of his own in the northland. 3 C. ISHERWOOD I am in a foreign city, alone, far from home.
II Alien, not one's own. **6** Alien in character; extraneous, dissimilar, inappropriate, irrelevant. (Foll. by *to.*) LME. **b** Unfamiliar, strange. L19. **7** Belonging to or coming from other persons or things; not one's own. LME. †**b** Of a possession: other than personal. L16–E18. †**c** Not of one's household or family. *rare* (Shakes.). Only in E17. **8** Esp. of matter in tissue etc.: introduced from outside. E17.
6 H. MOORE Culture remains a foreign element, something outside the desires and necessities of everyday life. 7 R. BLACKMORE Machines . . Move by a foreign impulse, not their own.
Phrases: *chamber foreign*: see sense 1 above. *of foreign growth*: see GROWTH *n.*
B *n.* †**1** [Short for *chamber foreign*] A privy. ME–L16. †**2** A person or thing from another place; a foreigner, an outsider. ME–M17. **3** *ellipt.* Foreign language, foreign parts, etc. E17. **4** That part of a town which lies outside the borough or parish proper; in *pl.*, the outer court of, or the land immediately outside the precincts of, a monastery. *obs.* exc. in local place-names. M17.
3 P. O'DONNELL He was a foreigner and he babbled in foreign.
C *adv. Naut.* To or for foreign parts, abroad. Chiefly in *go foreign*, *sail foreign*, etc. E19.
Special collocations & *comb.*: **foreign affairs** matters abroad; *spec.* those concerning the interests of the home country. **foreign aid** money or goods given by one State to another. **Foreign and Commonwealth Office** (the building used for) the British government department dealing with foreign affairs. **foreign body** a piece of extraneous matter, esp. in tissue. **foreign devil** *derog.* [see KWAI-LO] in China, a foreigner, *esp.* a European. **foreign exchange** (dealings in) the currency of other countries. **foreign-going** *a.* (of a ship) going to foreign countries. *foreign legion*: see LEGION *n.* **Foreign Minister** a government minister responsible for foreign affairs (an equivalent of the British Foreign Secretary in many other countries). **Foreign Office** (the building used for) a government department dealing with foreign affairs; *spec.* (*Hist.* & *colloq.*) = *Foreign and Commonwealth Office* above. **Foreign Secretary** the head of the British Foreign and Commonwealth Office. *foreign trade*: see TRADE *n.*
foreignism *n.* (*a*) the imitation of what is foreign; (*b*) a phrase, idiom, etc., of foreign origin: M19. **foreignize** *v.t.* & *i.* make or become (as if) foreign M17. **foreignly** *adv.* L19. **foreignness** /-n-n-/ *n.* E17.

foreigner /ˈfɒr(ə)nə/ *n.* LME. [f. FOREIGN *a.* + -ER[1].] **1** A person born in or belonging to another country, esp. one whose language and culture differ from one's own. LME. **2** A person not belonging to a particular place or society; a stranger, an outsider. Now chiefly *dial.* LME. **3** Something originating abroad, *spec.* a foreign vessel; an imported animal or article. L17. **b** In *pl.* Foreign stocks and shares. L19. **4** Something done or made at work by an employee for his or her own benefit; a piece of paid work not declared to the relevant authorities. *slang.* M20.
1 A. LURIE Some foreigner who knows only a few words of your language. 2 F. WELDON She was reckoned a foreigner: she came from Crossley, five miles away. C. RAINE Children . . are foreigners in our world until they become naturalised. 3 ADDISON The lemons, the brandy, the sugar, and the nutmeg, were all foreigners. 4 A. BLEASDALE We're both goin' t' get prosecuted f' doin' a foreigner while we're on the dole.

forejudge /fɔːˈdʒʌdʒ/ *v.*[1] M16. [f. FORE- + JUDGE *v.*, after Fr. *préjuger*, L *praejudicare* PREJUDGE.] 1 *v.t.* Judge or determine beforehand or without a fair trial; prejudge. M16. †2 *v.t.* & *i.* w. *of*. Form an opinion of beforehand. E17–L18.

forejudgement *n.* a judgement made in advance M16.

forejudge *v.*[2] var. of FORJUDGE.

fore-kamer *n.* see VOORKAMER.

foreknow /fɔːˈnəʊ/ *v.* Pa. t. **-knew** /-ˈnjuː/; pa. pple **-known** /-ˈnəʊn/. LME. [f. FORE- + KNOW *v.*] 1 *v.t.* Know (of) in advance, foresee. LME. 2 *v.i.* Have previous knowledge *of*. E18.

foreknowledge /fɔːˈnɒlɪdʒ/ *n.* M16. [f. FORE- + KNOWLEDGE *n.*] Prior knowledge of an event etc., prescience.

G. GROTE Money lent with the foreknowledge that the borrower will be unable to pay it. SAKI Elaine felt a sudden foreknowledge of something disagreeable about to happen.

foreknown *v.* pa. pple of FOREKNOW.

forel /ˈfɒr(ə)l/ *n.* & *v.* Also **-rr-**. ME. [OFr. (mod. *fourreau*) sheath, f. *fuerre*, f. Frank. = OHG *fōtar*, *fuotar* case, cover (G *Futter* lining), Goth. *fōdr* sheath, f. Gmc, rel. to Skt *pātra* receptacle, f. *pāti* protects.] A *n.* †1 A scabbard. Only in ME. 2 A case or covering for a book or manuscript. Now *dial.* LME. 3 A kind of parchment resembling vellum, used to cover (account-) books. M16. 4 A selvedge, a border of cloth. Now *dial.* L17. B *v.t.* Cover (a book) with forel. *obs.* exc. *dial.* M17.

forelaid *v.* pa. t. & pple of FORELAY.

foreland /ˈfɔːlənd/ *n.* ME. [f. FORE- + LAND *n.*[1] Cf. ON *forlendi* land between hills and sea, Du. *voorland*.] †1 Land other than that customarily granted to tenants of a manor; such land granted temporarily on special terms. Only in ME. 2 A cape, a headland, a promontory. LME. b Land deposited by the action of the sea in front of a coast. L19. †3 A piece of land adjoining a street; a house or tenement facing a street. *Sc.* L15–L18. 4 A strip of land in front of something; a strip of land left between the foot of a wall or embankment and an adjacent moat or ditch. L16. 5 A stretch of borderland. M19. 6 *Geol.* A stable unyielding block of the earth's crust, against which compression produces a folded mountain range. E20.

2 R. RECORDE The great forlonde of Affrike, commonly called the cape of Good hope. 5 J. KITTO I looked towards the west, and beheld the forelands of Carmel.

forelay /fɔːˈleɪ/ *v.t.* Pa. t. & pple **-laid** /-ˈleɪd/. M16. [f. FORE- + LAY *v.*[1]] 1 Lie in wait for, waylay. *obs.* exc. *dial.* M16. †b Lie in ambush around or near (a place). M16–L17. 2 Plot or take action against; frustrate, hinder. Long *rare*. L16. 3 Lay down or plan beforehand; prearrange. *obs.* exc. *dial.* E17.

foreleg /ˈfɔːlɛg/ *n.* LME. [f. FORE- + LEG *n.*] Either of the front legs of a quadruped.

forelimb /ˈfɔːlɪm/ *n.* L18. [f. FORE- + LIMB *n.*[1]] Either of the anterior limbs of a vertebrate animal; a foreleg, wing, flipper, etc.

forelock /ˈfɔːlɒk/ *n.*[1] OE. [f. FORE- + LOCK *n.*[1]] 1 A lock of hair growing just above the forehead. OE. 2 The part of the mane of a horse etc. growing from the poll and hanging over the forehead. E18.

1 **take time, occasion, opportunity**, etc. **by the forelock** [cf. *Father Time* s.v. TIME *n.*] not let a chance slip away.

Comb.: **forelock-touching, -tugging** the action or an act of touching or plucking at one's hair as at the peak of a cap; *fig.* obsequiousness, servility.

forelock /ˈfɔːlɒk/ *n.*[2] & *v.* ME. [f. FORE- + LOCK *n.*[2]] Chiefly *Naut.* A *n.* A wedge or pin passed through a hole in a bolt etc. to keep it in place; a cotter. ME.

Comb.: **forelock bolt** a bolt with a hole for a forelock; **forelock hook** a hook by which a bunch of three yarns is twisted into a strand.

B *v.t.* Fasten with a forelock or cotter. LME.

forelook /ˈfɔːlʊk/ *n.* Now *US.* ME. [f. FORE- + LOOK *n.*] †1 Foresight, foreknowledge; providence. Only in ME. 2 A look ahead. L16.

forelook /fɔːˈlʊk/ *v.* ME. [f. FORE- + LOOK *v.*] †1 *v.t.* Have foreknowledge of, foresee; provide for. Only in ME. 2 *v.i.* Look ahead or to the future. L15. †3 *v.t.* Bewitch by a look. L16–E17.

foreman /ˈfɔːmən/ *n.* Pl. **-men**. ME. [f. FORE- + MAN *n.*, perh. after ON *formaðr* leader, or immed. f. Du. *voorman* (cf. G *Vormann*).] 1 a A chief servant; an overseer, a steward, a bailiff. ME. b A principal workman supervising other workers. L16. †2 A man who goes in front, a leader; a soldier in the front rank. LME–L17. 3 The appointed leader and spokesperson of a jury. E17. 4 The most prominent and influential person in an organization or society. *obs.* exc. *local* as a title of a municipal officer. E17.

1a J. Q. ADAMS I sometimes think I must come to this—to be the foreman upon my own farm. b J. SMEATON One of the masons . . offered himself as foreman over the stone-cutters.

foremanship *n.* the office or position of a foreman; supervision (as) by a foreman: M19.

foremast /ˈfɔːmɑːst/ *n.* L15. [f. FORE- + MAST *n.*[1]] 1 The mast of a ship (with two or more masts) nearest the bow. L15. 2 The station of being before the mast. Only *attrib.*, as *foremast man*, *seaman*, a sailor below the rank of petty officer. E17.

foremen *n.* pl. of FOREMAN.

foremilk /ˈfɔːmɪlk/ *n.* E20. [f. FORE- + MILK *n.*] 1 Colostrum. E20. 2 The first milk drawn from a cow etc. at each milking; the first part of the milk from a breast at a feed. E20.

foremost /ˈfɔːməʊst/ *a.* & *adv.* [OE *formest*, *fyrmest*, f. *forma* first with additional superl. suff. (see -EST[1]): later assim. to FORE- + -MOST.] A *adj.* 1†a First in a series. OE–M16. b First in time. Long *obs.* exc. *Sc.* ME. 2 Most notable or prominent; best, chief. OE. 3 Most advanced in position; (in) front. ME.

2 W. S. CHURCHILL Marlborough stood forth, even above his comrade, the great Eugene, as the foremost soldier of the age. A. FRASER The situation was naturally inimical to many of the Scots, foremost among them the Highlanders. 3 GOLDSMITH The giant . . was foremost now; but the Dwarf was not far behind. DICKENS The boat drove stern foremost before it [the tide].

B *adv.* Before anything else; in the first place. Now chiefly in FIRST *and foremost*. OE.

Phrases: **feet, head**, etc. **foremost** with the feet etc. in front, feet etc. first.

foremostly *adv.* (*rare*) E17.

foremother /ˈfɔːmʌðə/ *n.* L15. [f. FORE- + MOTHER *n.*[1], after *forefather*.] A female ancestor or predecessor. Usu. in *pl.*

M. STOTT A modern mother is spared much of the toil of her foremothers.

forename /ˈfɔːneɪm/ *n.* M16. [f. FORE- + NAME *n.*, after Fr. *prénom*, L *praenomen*, Du. *voornam*, etc.] A personal name which precedes the surname, a first name; in *Rom. Hist.* = PRAENOMEN.

forenight /ˈfɔːnʌɪt/ *n.* Long *obs.* exc. *Sc.* ME. [f. FORE- + NIGHT *n.*] The early part of the night; the evening.

forenoon /ˈfɔːnuːn/ *n.* Chiefly *arch.* exc. *Naut.* LME. [f. FORE- + NOON *n.*] The day until noon; the morning.

L. G. GIBBON As though it were nine o'clock in the forenoon and the sun shining bravely.

forensic /fəˈrɛnsɪk/ *a.* & *n.* M17. [f. L *forensis*, f. as FORUM: see -IC.] A *adj.* 1 Of, pertaining to, or used in a court of law, now *spec.* in relation to the detection of crime. M17. 2 Of, pertaining to, or employing forensic medicine. M20.

1 DICKENS In an imposing and forensic manner. F. FORSYTH Scotland Yard, among the copious facilities of its forensic science department, has a section devoted to voice analysis. **forensic medicine** the application of medical knowledge to legal problems. 2 P. D. JAMES We can be sure of nothing until we have . . the forensic reports.

B *n.* 1 A speech or written thesis setting out one side of a question. *US.* E19. 2 Forensic science (esp. as the designation of a department, laboratory, etc.). *colloq.* M20.

Independent I wonder what forensic would find under your fingernails.

forensically *adv.* M19.

foreordain /fɔːrɔːˈdeɪn/ *v.t.* LME. [f. FORE- + ORDAIN *v.*] Ordain or appoint beforehand, predestinate.

foreordination /ˌfɔːrɔːdɪˈneɪʃ(ə)n/ *n.* E17. [f. FORE- + ORDINATION.] Ordination or appointment beforehand, predestination; an instance of this.

Also **foreˈordinance** *n.* (*rare*) M16.

forepart /ˈfɔːpɑːt/ *n.* LME. [f. FORE- + PART *n.*] 1 The foremost part, the front; *spec.* the bow of a ship. LME. 2 *Hist.* A stomacher. E17. 3 The earlier part. E17.

1 W. DAMPIER The head or fore-part is not altogether so high as the Stern. 3 A. HAMILTON In the Forepart of the seventeenth Century.

forepassed /fɔːˈpɑːst/ *ppl a.* Now *rare.* Also **-past**. M16. [f. FORE- + *passed*, *past* pa. ppl a. of PASS *v.*] Already past; bygone, erstwhile.

forepaw /ˈfɔːpɔː/ *n.* E19. [f. FORE- + PAW *n.*[1]] Either of the front paws of an animal.

forepeak /ˈfɔːpiːk/ *n.* L17. [f. FORE- + PEAK *n.*[1] Cf. Du. *voorpiek*.] *Naut.* The front end of a hold or cabin in the angle of the bows of a ship.

foreperson /ˈfɔːpəːs(ə)n/ *n.* L20. [f. FORE- + PERSON *n.*] A foreman, a forewoman. (Used to avoid sexual distinction.)

forepiece /ˈfɔːpiːs/ *n.* M16. [f. FORE- + PIECE *n.*] The foremost or front piece of something; *Theatr.* a curtain-raiser.

foreplay /ˈfɔːpleɪ/ *n.* E20. [f. FORE- + PLAY *n.*] Sexual stimulation preceding intercourse.

foreprise, -prize *vs.* vars. of FORPRISE.

forequarter /ˈfɔːkwɔːtə/ *n.* LME. [f. FORE- + QUARTER *n.*] A front quarter of something, *spec.* of a carcass (of beef, lamb, etc.). In *pl.*, the front part of the body of a quadruped.

foreran *v.* pa. t. of FORERUN.

forereach /fɔːˈriːtʃ/ *v.* M17. [f. FORE- + REACH *v.*[1]] Chiefly *Naut.* 1 *v.i.* Make way into wind whilst tacking; shoot ahead, gain ground *on*. M17. 2 *v.t.* Gain ground on, overtake: *fig.* get the better of. E19.

foreright /fɔːˈrʌɪt/ *adv.*, *a.*, *prep.*, & *n.* *obs.* exc. *dial.* Also (*rare*) **-rights** /-ˈrʌɪts/. LME. [f. FORE- + RIGHT *a.*, *adv.*] A *adv.* Directly forward, in or towards the front, straight ahead. LME. B *adj.* 1 Of a path, current, etc.: direct; straight in front. E17. †b Of a wind: in one's favour. E–M17. 2 Of a branch: growing straight out. M18. 3a Rash, reckless, headstrong, stubborn. M18. b Honest, straightforward; blunt, plain-spoken. E19. C *prep.* †1 Straight along. Only in M17. 2 Opposite, over against, right in front of. M19. D *n.* 1 Something straightforward; direct or blunt speech. M18. b A branch growing straight out. L19. 2 Coarse wholemeal bread. L18.

foreroom /ˈfɔːruːm/ *n.* L15. [f. FORE- + ROOM *n.*[1]] 1 A compartment in the bow of an open boat. *obs.* exc. *Sc.* L15. 2 A front room, a parlour. Now *US.* E18.

forerun /fɔːˈrʌn/ *v.* Infl. **-nn-**. Pa. t. **-ran** /-ˈran/; pa. pple **-run**. OE. [f. FORE- + RUN *v.*] †1 *v.i.* Run on in front. OE–M17. 2 *v.t.* †a Run in front of, precede; act as herald of. ME–M18. b Be the precursor of (a future event etc.), indicate the coming of, foreshadow. L16. 3 *v.t.* Outrun, outstrip, (now only *fig.*). E16. 4 *v.t.* Anticipate, forestall. L16.

3 R. W. CHURCH Even genius . . cannot forerun the limitations of its day. 4 *Times Lit. Suppl.* Akenside who foreran e. e. cummings by using lower case 'i' for the first person pronoun.

forerunner /ˈfɔːrʌnə/ *n.* ME. [f. prec. + -ER[1].] 1 A person who runs ahead, *esp.* one who prepares or shows the way; a precursor, a herald, a guide. Now chiefly *fig.* ME. b *spec.* A skier who runs over the course as a preliminary to a skiing race in order to check for possible hazards and clear spectators from the course. M20. 2 In *pl.* The members of the advance guard of an army. M16. 3 A predecessor, an ancestor. L16. 4 A thing which precedes, prepares for, or foreshadows another. L16. 5 *Naut.* a = FOREGANGER (b). L17. b A piece of cloth attached to a log line to mark the end of the stray line. E19.

For other words beginning with *fore-* see the entry for **fore-**

1 M. MEYER The forerunners of Impressionism—Delacroix, Courbet, Corot and, especially, Turner and Constable. 3 L. STERNE My . . observations will be altogether of a different cast from any of my forerunners. 4 M. DE LA ROCHE Bright red-gold wavelets of cloud . . forerunners of the strong tide of day. V. BROME The highly successful London visit was the forerunner of many such visits.

foresaid /'fɔːsɛd/ *a.* & *n. obs.* exc. *Sc.* OE. [f. FORE- + SAID *ppl a.*] A *adj.* Previously mentioned, aforesaid. OE. B *n.* Chiefly *Law.* A person or matter previously mentioned. Usu. in *pl.* M16.

foresaid *v.* pa. t. & pple of FORESAY.

foresail /'fɔːseɪl/ *n.* L15. [f. FORE- + SAIL *n.*[1]] In a square-rigged vessel, the lowest sail on the foremast. In a fore-and-aft rigged vessel, a sail on the after side of the foremast. In a single-masted vessel, any triangular sail before the mast.

foresaw *v.* pa. t. of FORESEE.

foresay /fɔː'seɪ/ *v.t.* Now *rare* or *obs.* Pa. t. & pple **-said** /-'sɛd/. OE. [f. FORE- + SAY *v.*[1]] Say beforehand, predict.

foresee /fɔː'siː/ *v.* Pa. t. **-saw** /-'sɔː/; pa. pple **-seen** /-'siːn/. [OE *foresēon*, f. FORE- + *sēon* SEE *v.* In 16 perh. partly a new formation.] 1 *v.t.* Be aware of beforehand; predict (a thing, *that*). OE. †2 *v.t.* Prepare; provide for or against in advance. OE–M17. †3 *v.i.* Exercise foresight; make provision. LME–E17. 4 *v.i.* Foresee events. *rare.* M17.

1 V. BRITTAIN Few prophets foresaw . . an even more profound clash nearly ten years later.

foreseer *n.* M16.

foreseeable /fɔː'siːəb(ə)l/ *a.* E19. [f. prec. + -ABLE.] Able to be foreseen.

foreseeable future the period during which the general course of events can reasonably be predicted.

¶Earlier (L17) in UNFORESEEABLE.

foreseea'bility *n.* the quality of being forseeable; predictability: E20. **foreseeably** *adv.* so as to be foreseeable, in a foreseeable manner M20.

foreset /'fɔːsɛt/ *a.* E20. [f. FORE- + SET *ppl a.*] *Geol.* Of layers of sediment: deposited on the inclined, advancing, forward slope of a delta.

foreset /fɔː'sɛt/ *v.t.* Now *rare.* Infl. **-tt-**. Pa. t. & pple **-set**. OE. [f. FORE- + SET *v.*[1]] †1 Place in front, put first. OE–LME. 2 Arrange or settle beforehand; predetermine. M16.

foreshadow /'fɔːʃadəʊ/ *n.* M19. [f. FORE- + SHADOW *n.*, after next.] An indication or imperfect representation of something to come.

J. M. LUDLOW A truce is often the foreshadow of a peace.

foreshadow /fɔː'ʃadəʊ/ *v.t.* L16. [f. FORE- + SHADOW *v.*] Serve as a type or presage of, prefigure; suggest or indicate (something to come).

J. L. MOTLEY The surrender of Ghent foreshadowed the fate of Flanders.

foresheet /'fɔːʃiːt/ *n.* M17. [f. FORE- + SHEET *n.*[2]] *Naut.* 1 A rope by which the lee corner of a foresail is kept in place. M17. 2 In *pl.* The inner part of the bows of a boat having gratings on which the bowman stands. E18.

foreshew *v.* var. of FORESHOW.

foreship /'fɔːʃɪp/ *n.* OE. [f. FORE- + SHIP *n.*] The foremost part of a ship; the prow.

foreshore /'fɔːʃɔː/ *n.* M18. [f. FORE- + SHORE *n.*[1]] The part of a shore between high- and low-water marks, or between the water and land cultivated or built on.

P. NORMAN Miles of sand, the foreshore . . like some dark, wet ocean, with the real sea . . in the distance.

foreshorten /fɔː'ʃɔːt(ə)n/ *v.t.* L16. [f. FORE- + SHORTEN, prob. after Du. *verkorten.*] Show or portray (an object) with the apparent shortening due to visual perspective; *fig.* shorten, curtail, abridge.

J. REYNOLDS The best of the painters could not even foreshorten the foot. V. WOOLF Little men and women, foreshortened from this height, hurried along by the railings.

foreshot /'fɔːʃɒt/ *n.* Chiefly *Sc.* L17. [f. FORE- + SHOT *n.*[1]] 1 A projecting part of a building. L17. 2 *Distilling.* The first spirits obtained. L18.

foreshow /fɔː'ʃəʊ/ *v.t. arch.* Also **-shew**. Pa. pple **-showed, -shown** /-'ʃəʊn/. OE. [f. FORE- + SHOW *v.*] †1 Look out for; provide. OE–ME. 2 Foretell, give promise or warning of, prefigure. LME. †3 Show, display, betoken. L16–E17.

2 POPE Astrologers, that future fates foreshow. J. IMISON The falling of the mercury forshews thunder. 3 SHAKES. *Per.* Your looks foreshow You have a gentle heart.

†**foreshower** *n.* a person who foretells; a thing which prefigures or portends: M16–M18. **forshowing** *n.* (*a*) the action of the vb; (*b*) a prognostication, a sign or token of a future event: OE.

foresight /'fɔːsʌɪt/ *n.* ME. [f. FORE- + SIGHT *n.*, prob. after ON *forsjá, -sjó.*] 1 The action or faculty of foreseeing; prescience. ME. 2 Care or provision for the future; providence, prudence. ME. 3 A view forward; a prospect. LME. b The action or an act of looking forward (*lit.* & *fig.*). L16. 4 The front sight of a gun. E19. 5 *Surveying.* A sight taken looking forwards. M19.

1 JOSEPH HALL Want of foresight makes thee more merry. J. GALSWORTHY She had no foresight, and never went to meet trouble. 2 H. T. BUCKLE In hot climates, nature being bountiful, man is not obliged to use foresight. 3 J. B. MOZLEY The perpetual foresight of death.

foresighted *a.* having or using foresight; prescient, prudent: M17. **foresightedly** *adv.* M20. **foresightedness** *n.* E20. **foresightful** *a.* full of foresight L16.

foreskin /'fɔːskɪn/ *n.* M16. [f. FORE- + SKIN *n.*, after G *Vorhaut.*] The loose skin covering the end of the penis, the prepuce.

foreslack *v.* var. of FORSLACK.

foreslow *v.* var. of FORSLOW.

forespeak /fɔː'spiːk/ *v.*[1] Pa. t. **-spoke** /-'spəʊk/, (*arch.*) **-spake** /-'speɪk/; pa. pple **-spoken** /-'spəʊkən/, (*arch.*) **-spake**. ME. [f. FORE- + SPEAK *v.*] 1 †a *v.i.* Speak beforehand; make predictions, prophesy. ME–M17. b *v.t.* Say or speak of beforehand; foretell. Now *rare.* LME. 2 *v.t.* Order or reserve beforehand; bespeak. *obs.* exc. *Sc.* M17.

forespeaker *n.* (*obs.* exc. *Sc.*) a person who speaks for another; an advocate, a spokesman: ME.

forespeak *v.*[2] var. of FORSPEAK.

forespend *v.* var. of FORSPEND.

forespoke *v.*[1], *v.*[2] pa. t., **forespoken** *v.*[1], *v.*[2] pa. pple: see FORESPEAK *v.*[1], FORSPEAK.

forest /'fɒrɪst/ *n.* & *v.* ME. [OFr. (mod. *forêt*) f. late L *forestis* (*silva*) 'outside wood', a royal forest reserved for hunting, f. *foris* out of doors, outside; in AL *foresta, forestum.*] A *n.* 1 A large tract of land covered with trees and undergrowth sometimes mixed with pasture (in proper names also a district formerly forest but now cultivated); the trees growing in such a tract. ME. b *transf.* & *fig.* A large number, a dense mass. E17. 2a *Hist.* A (woodland) area, esp. owned by the monarch, kept for hunting and having its own laws and officers. ME. b A tract of wild land reserved for the stalking of deer. Also *deer-forest.* E18. †3 A wild uncultivated place; a wilderness. ME–M17.

1 U. LE GUIN The trees went on and on, . . endless, a forest all over the world. *Hercynian Forest, New Forest, Sherwood Forest,* etc. *rainforest*: see RAIN *n.*[1] b ARNOLD BENNETT A forest of pillars stood planted on the ground floor. 2a F. POLLOCK The presence of trees . . is not required to make a forest in this sense. The great mark of it is the absence of enclosures. 3 D. PELL Away she betakes her self into the great and wide Forrest of the Sea.

Comb.: **forest-bed** *Geol.* a stratum originating from a primeval forest; **forest devil** *Austral.* a device for removing tree stumps; **forest falcon** an American hawk of the genus *Micrastur*; **forest fire** an uncontrolled fire in woodland; **forest floor** the ground in a forest; *spec.* the layer of more or less decayed organic debris forming the upper soil of a forest; **forest fly** a parasitic fly of the genus *Hippobosca*; esp. *H. equina*, which is troublesome to horses, cattle, etc., and in Britain is found chiefly in the New Forest; **forest-green** *a.* & *n.* (of) any of various shades of green associated with forests, *esp.* Lincoln green; **forest kangaroo** = FORESTER 3a(b); **forest laws** *Hist.* laws enacted by Norman kings relating to the royal forests; **forest mahogany** *Austral.* (the timber of) any of several eucalypts, esp. *Eucalyptus resinifera*; **forest marble** an argillaceous oolitic limestone found in SW England, having conspicuous dendritic markings; also called *landscape marble*; **forest oak** *Austral.* casuarina; **forest park** an area of forest land open to the public and having recreational facilities; **forest ranger** an official who patrols, manages, and protects a (public) forest; **forest red gum** (the timber of) an Australasian tree, *Eucalyptus tereticornis*; **forest tree** a tree of any large species suitable for or growing in a forest; **forest wallaby** any of several wallabies of the genus *Dorcopsis*, that inhabit the forests of New Guinea.

B *v.t.* 1 Place in a forest. *rare.* E19. 2 Make into a forest; plant with trees. M19.

forested *a.* covered with forest; thickly planted with trees: E17. **forestful** *n.* as much or as many as a forest will hold M19. **forestless** *a.* L19.

forestage /'fɔːsteɪdʒ/ *n.* LME. [f. FORE- + STAGE *n.*] †1 The forecastle of a ship; a ship having a forecastle. LME–L15. 2 *Theatr.* The front part of a stage, esp. an apron stage. E20.

forestal /'fɒrɪst(ə)l/ *a.* E19. [f. FOREST *n.* + -AL[1].] Of or pertaining to a forest.

forestall /'fɔːstɔːl/ *n.* [OE *for(e)steall*, f. FORE- + *steall* (app.) a position taken up. In sense 2 f. FORE- + STALL *n.*[1], in AL *forstallum* a piece of land in front of a building.] †1 An ambush. In *Law*, the offence of waylaying a traveller on the highway; the jurisdiction of this. OE–E17. 2 *Hist.* A piece of armour attached to a horse's bridle to protect the face. E16. 3 Something at or facing the front; *spec.* the space in front of a farmhouse or the approach to it from a road. Long *obs.* exc. *dial.* M16.

forestall /fɔː'stɔːl/ *v.t.* ME. [f. the n.] 1 *Hist.* Intercept or buy up (goods etc.) before they come to market, esp. to force up the price (formerly an indictable offence). ME. b Spoil the trade of (a fair or market) by buying up goods beforehand or by dissuading sellers from bringing them. LME. †2 Lie in wait for, intercept, cut off. LME–M18. †3 Obstruct (a road, the entrance to a house, etc.) by armed force. LME–E17. 4 Hinder, obstruct, or prevent by anticipation. L16. †b Bar or deprive (a person) *from, of, out of* by prior action. L16–M17. †5 Preoccupy, secure beforehand; influence, prejudice. L16–L17. 6 Act before; anticipate (and make ineffective). L16. 7 Think of or deal with before the appropriate time. M17.

1 *fig.*: SWIFT To confine, forestall, and monopolize the beams of the sun. 4 R. MACAULAY She must get down to her . . book quickly, or she would be forestalled by all these tiresome people. 6 A. STORR Carefully and neatly dressed, in order to forestall any possible criticism of their appearance. 7 MILTON What need a man forestall his date of grief.

¶Earliest in AL *for(e)stallare* forestall the market, waylay, AN *forstallour* forestaller of markets.

forestaller *n.* ME.

forestalment /fɔː'stɔːlm(ə)nt/ *n.* Also *-**ll**-. E17. [f. prec. + -MENT.] The action or result of forestalling; an instance of forestalling.

forestation /fɒrɪ'steɪʃ(ə)n/ *n.* E20. [f. FOREST *n.* + -ATION.] The planting or establishing of a forest, afforestation.

forestay /'fɔːsteɪ/ *n.* ME. [f. FORE- + STAY *n.*[1]] 1 *Naut.* A stay from the head of the foremast to a ship's deck to support the foremast. ME. 2 *Printing.* A leg supporting the frame or ribs of a hand-press. M19.

forester /'fɒrɪstə/ *n.* ME. [(O)Fr. *forestier*, f. as FOREST *n.*: see -ER[2]. Cf. AL *forestarius.*] 1 An officer in charge of a forest or of growing timber. ME. 2 A person who lives in a forest. E16. 3a A bird or animal of the forest; *spec.* (*a*) a New Forest pony; (*b*) *Austral.* the Eastern grey kangaroo, *Macropus giganteus.* M17. b Any of various Palaearctic zygaenid moths of the genus *Ino*, having bright metallic green wings. Also (*N. Amer.*), any of various moths of the family Agaristidae. E19. 4 A forest tree. M17. 5 (**F-**.) A member of any of various friendly societies known as the (Ancient, Independent, etc.) Order of Foresters. M19.

forestial /fə'rɛstɪəl/ *a.* L17. [f. FOREST *n.* + -IAL.] Of or pertaining to a forest, forestal.

forestry /'fɒrɪstri/ *n.* L17. [f. as prec. + -RY.] 1 *Sc. Law* (now *Hist.*). The privileges of a royal forest; the estate to which these privileges are attached. L17. 2 Wooded country; a vast extent of trees. E19. 3 The art or science of planting and managing forests. M19.

foresty /ˈfɒrɪsti/ *a.* E17. [f. as prec. + -Y[1].] Like a forest; covered in forest.

foretaste /ˈfɔːteɪst/ *n.* LME. [f. FORE- + TASTE *n.*[1]] A taste beforehand, a partial enjoyment or suffering (*of*) in advance; an anticipation.

Review of English Studies This volume . . can offer only a foretaste of the riches that are promised when the whole project is complete.

foretaste /fɔːˈteɪst/ *v.t.* LME. [f. FORE- + TASTE *v.*] 1 Have a foretaste of, anticipate. LME. 2 Taste before another. *rare.* M17.

1 T. KEN Saints thus Celestial Joys fore-taste. 2 MILTON Foretasted Fruit Profan'd first by the Serpent.

foretell /fɔːˈtɛl/ *v.* Pa. t. & pple **-told** /-ˈtəʊld/. ME. [f. FORE- + TELL *v.*] 1 *v.t.* Tell of (an event etc.) before it takes place; predict, prophesy. ME. b Foreshadow, presage, be the precursor of. L16. †2 *v.i.* Speak *of* beforehand, prophesy *of.* ME–M17. †3 *v.t.* Inform or enjoin (a person) beforehand; state in advance. ME–L17.

1 E. M. FORSTER It is impossible to foretell the future with any degree of accuracy. b C. MCCULLERS The clouds . . grew steadily denser, and foretold a heavy summer rain. 2 MILTON To introduce One greater, of whose day he shall foretell. 3 HOBBES A Man is free to fore-tell, or not, what points he will insist upon.

foretellable *a.* E20. **foreteller** *n.* L16.

forethink /fɔːˈθɪŋk/ *v.*[1] Pa. t. & pple **-thought** /-ˈθɔːt/. OE. [f. FORE- + THINK *v.*[2]] 1 *v.t.* Think out beforehand, premeditate; contrive, plan. *obs.* exc. *dial.* OE. 2 *v.t.* Think of or contemplate beforehand; anticipate. ME. †3 *v.i.* Think beforehand *of.* L16–E18.

1 N. ROWE My brain forethought And fashion'd every action of my life. 2 W. BALDWIN Rather of a friend hope the best, then forethinke the worst. 3 J. NORRIS He could not make it without forethinking of it.

forethinker *n.* M19.

forethink *v.*[2] var. of FORTHINK *v.*[1]

forethought /ˈfɔːθɔːt/ *n.* ME. [f. FORE- + THOUGHT *n.*[1]] 1 Previous consideration; anticipation, premeditation. ME. †2 An idea or design previously thought out; an anticipation. ME–E18. 3 Care or thought for the future. LME.

1 GEO. ELIOT The title which she had never given him before came to her lips without forethought. 3 B. JOWETT Just so much forethought as is necessary to provide for the morrow.

foreˈthoughtful *a.* full of forethought; provident: E19. **foreˈthoughtfully** *adv.* L19. **foreˈthoughtfulness** *n.* M17.

forethought *v.* pa. t. & pple of FORETHINK *v.*[1]

foretoken /ˈfɔːtəʊk(ə)n/ *n.* OE. [f. FORE- + TOKEN *n.*] A sign of something to come.

foretoken /fɔːˈtəʊk(ə)n/ *v.t.* OE. [f. FORE- + TOKEN *v.*; later f. the n.] Indicate beforehand; portend.

B. MALAMUD Inspired by the change in her, hoping it might foretoken better luck for him.

foretold *v.* pa. t. & pple of FORETELL.

foretop /ˈfɔːtɒp, *Naut.* -təp/ *n.* ME. [f. FORE- + TOP *n.*[1]] 1a A lock of hair growing above or arranged on a person's forehead, a forelock; a similar part of a wig. Now *rare* or *obs.* ME. b A tuft of hair growing on or hanging over the forehead of an animal. Now chiefly *US.* E17. †2 (The front part of) the top of the head. LME–L18. 3 *Naut.* The top of a foremast, the platform around the head of the lower foremast. L15. 4 The front seat on top of a horse-drawn vehicle. *US.* M19.

fore-topgallant /fɔːtɒpˈgal(ə)nt, -təˈgal-/ *a.* E16. [f. FORE- + TOPGALLANT.] *Naut.* Designating or pertaining to a part of a mast above the foretopmast.

fore-topgallant mast, sail, yard, etc.

fore-topmast /fɔːˈtɒpmɑːst, -məst/ *n.* L15. [f. FORE- + TOPMAST.] *Naut.* The mast above the lower foremast.

fore-topsail /fɔːˈtɒps(ə)l, -seɪl/ *n.* L15. [f. FORE- + TOPSAIL.] *Naut.* The sail above the foresail.

pay with the fore-topsail: see PAY *v.*[1]

forever /fəˈrɛvə/ *adv.* & *n.* Also (now esp. in sense A.1) **for ever**. ME. [Orig. two wds, f. FOR *prep.* + EVER.] A *adv.* 1 For all future time, in perpetuity, (also *for ever and ever, for ever and a day,* (arch.) *for ever and ay*); *colloq.* for a very long time. ME. 2 Continually, incessantly, repeatedly. *colloq.* L18.

1 J. MORLEY Hitherto certainly, and probably it will be so for ever. E. FEINSTEIN Do people recover from such pain, or are they damaged forever? *Look Now* We felt that we'd known each other forever. — **for ever!** may — flourish! 2 *Daedalus* He is forever telling us what he will do and why.

B *n.* 1 (An) eternity, perpetuity. M19. 2 After vbs: a very long time. *colloq.* M20.

1 M. ANDERSON This is forever, here where we stand . . how does one spend a forever? 2 J. AIKEN They always take for ever to change. A. CARTER It seemed forever before he got to the centre of the stage.

foreverness *n.* the state or condition of lasting for ever, permanence E19.

forevermore /fərɛvəˈmɔː/ *adv.* Also **for evermore**. ME. [Orig. two wds, f. FOR *prep.* + EVERMORE.] For all future time, in perpetuity.

forewarn /fɔːˈwɔːn/ *v.*[1]*t.* ME. [f. FORE- + WARN *v.*[1]] 1 Warn, caution, or admonish beforehand. ME. 2 Announce beforehand, prophesy. *rare.* L16.

1 SHAKES. *3 Hen. VI* We were forewarned of your coming And shut the gates. *Proverb*: Forewarned is forearmed. 2 *Daily Telegraph* Nuns . . are worried that a holy relic is forewarning a world catastrophe.

forewarner *n.* LME. **forewarning** *n.* (*a*) the action of the vb; (*b*) a warning beforehand; prior notice or admonition: LME.

forewarn *v.*[2] var. of FORWARN.

forewent *v.*[1], *v.*[2] pa. t.: see FOREGO *v.*[1], FORGO.

forewoman /ˈfɔːwʊmən/ *n.* Pl. **-women** /-wɪmɪn/. E18. [f. FORE- + WOMAN *n.*] 1 A woman appointed as leader and spokesperson of a jury. E18. 2 A female worker supervising other workers. M19.

foreword /ˈfɔːwəːd/ *n.* M19. [f. FORE- + WORD *n.*, after G *Vorwort.*] A preface; a section of introductory remarks, esp. by a person other than the author of the main work.

forex /ˈfɒrɛks/ *n.* L20. [Abbrev.] *Comm.* The foreign exchange market; foreign exchange.

foreyard /ˈfɔːjɑːd/ *n.*[1] LME. [f. FORE- + YARD *n.*[1]] A yard or court in front of a building.

foreyard /ˈfɔːjɑːd/ *n.*[2] L15. [f. FORE- + YARD *n.*[2]] *Naut.* The lowest yard on a foremast.

forfare /fɔːˈfɛː/ *v.* Long *obs.* exc. *Sc.* OE. [f. FOR-[1] + FARE *v.*] 1 *v.i.* †a Pass away, perish, decay. OE–L16. b As *forfared* pa. pple. Worn out with travel, age, etc. LME. 2 *v.t.* Cause to perish, destroy. OE.

forfeit /ˈfɔːfɪt/ *n.* ME. [OFr. *forfet,* (also mod.) *forfait* crime, f. pa. pple of *for(s)faire* transgress (med.L *forisfacere*), f. as FOR-[2] + *faire* do: in sense 3 also infl. by the vb.] †1 A transgression, a crime, an offence; wilful injury. Also, breach or violation *of.* ME–E19. 2 Something to which the right is lost by the commission of a crime or fault; a penal fine; a penalty for breach of contract or neglect of duty. LME. 3 The losing of something by way of penalty; = FORFEITURE. LME. 4 A penalty for a breach of contract, neglect, etc., a fine, *esp.* a trivial fine for a breach of the rules of a club, game, etc.; an article surrendered as a penalty in a game. E17.

forfeit /ˈfɔːfɪt/ *a.* LME. [OFr. *forfet, -fait* pa. pple of *forfaire*: see prec.] (To be) given up as a penalty for an offence, a breach of agreement, etc. (Foll. by *to.*)

J. G. FARRELL The saying of prayers and sewing-up in bedding of those whose lives had been forfeit.

forfeit /ˈfɔːfɪt/ *v.* ME. [f. FORFEIT *n.*] 1†a *v.i.* Do wrong, sin, transgress. ME–M16. b *v.t.* Transgress against, violate (one's faith or oath). *rare.* LME. 2a *v.t.* Lose the right to, be deprived of, have to pay, as a penalty for crime, neglect, etc. LME. b *v.t.* Lose or give up, as a necessary consequence. LME. c *v.i.* Incur the penalty of forfeiture. Long *rare.* E18. 3 *v.t.* Of a governing power: subject (land, goods) to forfeiture; (chiefly *Sc.*) subject (a person) to forfeiture, deprive *of* estates. *obs.* exc. *Hist.* LME. †4 *v.t.* Exact a forfeit or fine from. L16–M18. †5 *v.t.* Cause the forfeiture, loss, or ruin of. E17–E18.

2 DEFOE My life and effects were all forfeited to the English government. B. CHATWIN He ran away three times and three times forfeited his wages. *forfeit (one's) bail*: see BAIL *n.*[1] b E. WAUGH In their austere trade they had forfeited the arts of leisure.

forfeitable *a.* liable to be forfeited, subject to forfeiture LME. **forfeiter** *n.* LME.

forfeiture /ˈfɔːfɪtʃə, -tjʊə/ *n.* LME. [OFr. *forfaiture,* f. as FORFEIT *n.* + -URE.] †1 Transgression of a law; crime; sin. LME–E17. 2 The fact of losing or becoming liable to deprivation of or *of* an estate, life, an office, right, etc., in consequence of an offence or breach of agreement. LME. †3 The penalty for an offence. LME–M17. 4 That which is forfeited; a fine. Now *rare* or *obs.* LME.

2 A. FRASER The penalty for high treason was death, as well as the forfeiture of titles and offices.

forfend /fɔːˈfɛnd/ *v.* Also **fore-**. LME. [f. FOR-[1] + FEND *v.*] †1 *v.t.* Forbid, prohibit. (Foll. by *to do.*) LME–L19. 2 *v.t.* & *i.* Avert, keep away, prevent, (esp. evil). Freq. in *Heaven* etc. *forfend! arch.* LME. 3 *v.t.* Secure or protect by precautionary measures. Now chiefly *US.* L16.

1 E. PAGITT Anselme . . forfended Priests to have Wives. J. BADCOCK This ingenious veterinarian forefends the practice of mixing clay in the stuffing. 2 C. S. LEWIS Heaven forfend I should be taken to mean that Wyvern is the same to-day.

forfex /ˈfɔːfɛks/ *n.* E18. [L.] 1 A pair of scissors. *joc.* E18. 2 *Entomol.* A pair of anal organs shaped like scissors, which cross when closed. E19.

forficate /ˈfɔːfɪkeɪt/ *a.* E19. [f. L *forfex, forfic-* pair of scissors + -ATE[2].] Shaped or functioning like a pair of scissors; deeply forked.

Also **forficated** *a.* M18.

forficulate /fɔːˈfɪkjʊlət/ *a.* L19. [f. L *forficula* dim. of *forfex* pair of scissors + -ATE[2].] Chiefly *Bot.* & *Zool.* Shaped like a (small) pair of scissors.

forfoughten /fɔːˈfɔːt(ə)n/ *ppl a. obs.* exc. *Sc.* & *north.* ME. [f. FOR-[1] + FOUGHTEN.] Wearied, worn-out, esp. with fighting.

forgather /fɔːˈgaðə/ *v.i.* Also **fore-**. L15. [Du. *vergaderen* meet, assemble (= G *vergattern*) assim. to FOR-[1], GATHER *v.*] 1 Gather together, assemble. L15. 2 Meet (*with*). E16. b Associate *with,* take *up* with. L18.

1 E. JONES They used to forgather regularly once a week in the Café. 2 R. FERGUSSON When I again Auld Reikie see, And can forgether, lad, with thee. S. R. CROCKETT The outsailed *Seahorse* and the deceived *Ariel* had forgathered off the Isle of Man.

forgave *v.* pa. t.: see FORGIVE.

forge /fɔːdʒ/ *n.* ME. [(O)Fr. f. Proto-Romance f. L *fabrica* trade, workshop, fabric.] 1 A smithy. ME. †2 Manufacture, construction; style of construction, make, workmanship. LME–L17. 3 A blacksmith's hearth or fireplace with attached bellows, used for heating iron to make it malleable. L15. 4 A hearth or furnace for melting or refining metals; a workshop etc. where this is done. L15.

1 JO GRIMOND A blacksmith's forge in which the smith in leather apron hammered out red-hot horse-shoes. 3 *fig.*: W. M. PRAED In laboured phrase and polished lie Wrought by the forge of flattery.

Comb.: **forge-man** a worker in a forge, a blacksmith; **forge-master** the manager or owner of a forge.

forge /fɔːdʒ/ *v.*[1] ME. [(O)Fr. *forger* f. L *fabricare* FABRICATE.] 1 *v.t.* Make, fashion, construct, (a material thing). *obs.* exc. as passing into sense 4. ME. 2 *v.t.* Make (something) in fraudulent imitation of something else; imitate fraudulently, counterfeit, (esp. a document, a signature, a banknote, etc.) in order to pass the fraudulent imitation off as genuine. ME. 3 *v.t.* Fabricate, invent, (a tale, a lie). Formerly also, coin (a word etc.). LME. 4 *v.t.* Shape by heating in a forge and hammering; beat into shape. LME. 5 *v.i.* Work at a forge; do a blacksmith's work. LME. 6 *v.i.* Commit forgery. Now *rare.* L16.

2 R. BUCHANAN As if I had . . forged the laird's name. R. GRAVES He had forged a document purporting to be a testimonial. 3 W. CAMDEN Some thinke it to be no ancient name, but forged by the writer of King Arthurs historie. C. KINGSLEY A charge

. . forged by that villain. 4 H. ALLEN The smith spent the afternoon forging two heavy chains. *fig.*: B. PYM A link might have been forged between two solitary people.

forgea'bility *n.* ability to be forged L19. **forgeable** *a.* able to be forged LME. †**forgeful** *a.* apt to forge, creative M18–E19. **forger** *n.* a person who forges something, esp. fraudulently LME. †**forgerer** *n.* a forger L16–E19.

forge /fɔːdʒ/ *v.*[2] *i.* & *t.* M18. [Perh. alt. of FORCE *v.*[1]] **1** *v.i.* Of a ship: make way esp. by momentum or pressure of wind or tide. M18. **2** *v.t.* Make *one's way* by momentum, esp. gradually and steadily. L19.

forge ahead take the lead esp. in a race, move forward rapidly.

forge /fɔːdʒ/ *v.*[3] *i.* M19. [Perh. f. FORGE *v.*[1] 4, with ref. to the sound.] = CLICK *v.*[1] 1b.

forgery /'fɔːdʒ(ə)ri/ *n.* L16. [f. FORGE *v.*[1] + -ERY.] **1** The making of a thing in fraudulent imitation of something else; *esp.* the forging of a document. L16. **b** Something that has been forged or counterfeited; *esp.* a forged document. L16. **c** The fact of being forged. *rare.* M17. **2** Orig., deception, a deceit. Later, fictitious invention. Now only *poet.* L16. †**3** The action or craft of forging metal. Only in 17.

1 SHAKES. *Lucr.* Guilty of treason, forgery, and shift. **b** B. JOWETT That . . one of the most excellent writings bearing the name of Plato should be a forgery.

forget /fə'gɛt/ *n.*[1] Chiefly *colloq.* M19. [f. FORGET *v.*] An instance of forgetting; a lapse of memory.

forget *n.*[2] var. of FORGETT.

forget /fə'gɛt/ *v.* Infl. **-tt-**. Pa. t. **-got** /-'gɒt/; pa. pple **-gotten** /-'gɒt(ə)n/, (*US*, *arch.*, & *poet.*) **-got.** [OE *forgietan* = OFris. *forjeta*, OS *fargetan* (Du. *vergeten*), OHG *firgezzan* (G *vergessen*), f. WGmc, f. base of FOR-[1] + GET *v.*] **1** *v.t.* Lose remembrance of; cease to retain in one's memory. (Foll. by simple obj., obj. cl.) OE. **b** *v.i.* Lose or cease to retain remembrance of something. LME. **c** *v.t.* Fail to recall to mind; not recollect. L18. **2** *v.t.* Omit or neglect through inadvertence. Usu. foll. by *to do.* OE. **b** *v.t.* Omit to take, leave behind inadvertently. ME. **c** *v.t.* Omit to mention, leave unnoticed, pass over inadvertently. M16. **3** *v.t.* Cease or omit to think of, let slip out of the mind, leave out of sight, take no note of. OE. †**b** *v.t.* Drop the practice of (a duty, virtue, etc.); lose the use of (one's senses). LME–L17. **c** *v.i.* Foll. by *about*: not recall the facts concerning; not remember to take action in the matter of. *colloq.* L19. **4** *v.t.* Neglect wilfully, disregard, slight. ME.

1 E. M. FORSTER I had forgotten we were dining out. S. SASSOON Why should I remember that and forget so much else? **c** TOLKIEN There is another danger . . which he does not see. . . He has forgotten Treebeard. 2 T. F. POWYS This order—that Mr. Pix never forgot to give. **b** SHAKES. *1 Hen. IV* A plague upon it! I have forgot the map. . . No, here it is. 3 J. CONRAD He was nearly forgotten. *absol.*: R. C. TRENCH God may forgive, man is not therefore to forget. **c** N. GOULD He had forgotten about that, it was such a long time ago. I. MURDOCH He had completely forgotten about his son and was not pleased to be reminded. 4 A. RADCLIFFE Why should I be in danger of forgetting what is due to my father?

Phrases etc.: **don't you forget it** *emphatic colloq.* remember it, keep it in mind. **forget (about) it** *imper.* (*colloq.*) take no more notice of it, there is no need for apology or thanks. **forget oneself** (*a*) neglect one's own welfare; (*b*) *arch.* lose consciousness; (*c*) act unbecomingly or unworthily.

forgetness *n.* (*rare*) forgetfulness LME. **forgettable** *a.* (earlier in UNFORGETTABLE) M19. **forgetter** *n.* LME. **forgetting** *vbl n.* (*a*) the action of the vb; †(*b*) the state of being unconscious, oblivion: ME.

forgetful /fə'gɛtfʊl, -f(ə)l/ *a.* LME. [f. prec. + -FUL.] **1** Apt, inclined, or liable to forget. (Foll. by *of.*) LME. **2** Heedless, neglectful. Foll. by *of*, *to do.* E16. **3** Inducing forgetfulness or oblivion. Chiefly *poet.* M16.

forgetfully *adv.* E18. **forgetfulness** *n.* LME.

forgetive /'fɔːdʒɪtɪv/ *a.* L16. [Perh. f. FORGE *v.*[1]] Skilled at making; inventive, creative.

forget-me-not /fə'gɛtmɪnɒt/ *n.* M16. [tr. OFr. *ne m'oubliez mie*: cf. MHG *vergiz min nicht* (G *Vergissmeinnicht*). In the 15th cent. worn as a lover's token.] **1** Any of various low-growing plants of the genus *Myosotis*, of the borage family; esp. *M. scorpioides*, which has bright blue flowers with a yellow centre; a flowering stem of such a plant. Also (locally or w. specifying wd), any of various (cultivated ornamental) plants resembling these, usu. with small, bright blue flowers. M16. †**2** The ground pine, *Ajuga chamaepitys.* Only in L16.

1 **Alpine forget-me-not** (*a*) any of various mountain plants of the genus *Myosotis*, esp. *M. alpestris*; (*b*) *N. Amer.* any of several plants of the Rocky Mountains of the *Eritrichium*, of the borage family. **Cape forget-me-not** a plant of the borage family native to southern Africa, *Anchusa capensis.* **Chinese forget-me-not** a hound's tongue, *Cynoglossum amabile*, native to eastern Asia.

Comb.: **forget-me-not blue** (of) a clear bright blue.

¶ Rare bef. E19.

forgett /'fɔːdʒɪt/ *n.* Also **forget.** L17. [Fr. FOURCHETTE.] A side-piece for a finger or thumb of a glove.

forgettory /fə'gɛt(ə)ri/ *n. joc. colloq.* Also **-ery.** E20. [Blend of FORGET *v.* and MEMORY.] The faculty of forgetting; faultiness of memory.

forgivable /fə'gɪvəb(ə)l/ *a.* Also **-giveable.** M16. [f. next + -ABLE.] Able to be forgiven.

forgivableness *n.* the quality of being forgivable L19. **forgivably** *adv.* in a manner that is excusable or deserves forgiveness (earlier in UNFORGIVABLY) E20.

forgive /fə'gɪv/ *v.* Pa. t. **-gave** /-'geɪv/; pa. pple **-given** /-'gɪv(ə)n/. [OE *forgiefan* corresp. to OS, OHG *fargeban* (Du. *vergeven*, G *vergeben*), ON *fyrirgefa* forgive, Goth. *fragiban* grant, f. Gmc, f. base of FOR-[1] + GIVE *v.*] †**1** *v.t.* Give, grant. OE–L15. **2** *v.t.* Pardon (an offence); cease to resent or claim requital for; remit (a debt). (Foll. by indirect obj. or *to* a person.) OE. **3** *v.i.* Pardon an offence or an offender; give up resentment against a person etc. OE. **4** *v.t.* Give up resentment against, pardon, (an offender) (foll. by *for*); (now *rare*) give up one's claim against (a debtor). ME. †**5** *v.t.* Give up (resentment, anger); give up one's resolve *to do.* ME–M16. **6** *v.t.* Make excuse or apology for, regard indulgently. M17.

2 T. MOORE Clonmell never forgave this to Grattan. *Time* A scheme that would forgive all debt. 3 POPE To err is human, to forgive, divine. 4 ARNOLD BENNETT He had forgiven his father for having thwarted his supreme ambition. 6 J. HIGGINS Forgive me for asking, Father, but are you American or Irish?

forgiver *n.* ME. **forgiving** *ppl a.* that forgives; inclined to forgive; indicating forgiveness: L17. **forgivingly** *adv.* M17. **forgivingness** *n.* M18.

forgiveness /fə'gɪvnɪs/ *n.* OE. [f. *forgiven* pa. pple of prec. + -NESS.] **1** The action of forgiving; the state of being forgiven. Formerly also, indulgent permission. OE. **2** Readiness to forgive. ME.

1 M. MILNER The trespasses that the prayer book says we also need forgiveness for. *Time* He advocates complete forgiveness of interest payments. 2 E. F. BENSON That higher power of forgiveness which is to forget.

forgo /fɔː'gəʊ, fə-/ *v.* Also **forego.** Pa. t. **-went** /-'wɛnt/; pa. pple **-gone** /-'gɒn/. OE. [f. FOR-[1] + GO *v.*] †**1** *v.i.* Go away, go past, pass away. OE–M16. **2** *v.t.* Go by, pass over; leave alone or undone, overlook, slight. Long *arch. rare.* OE. **3** *v.t.* Abstain or refrain from (an action, a procedure). OE. †**4** *v.t.* Let go (involuntarily); lose, forfeit. OE–L16. **5** *v.t.* Go from, forsake, leave. *arch.* ME. **6** *v.t.* Go without, deny to oneself; let pass, omit to take or use; give up, renounce. ME. †**7** *v.t.* Only as *forgone* pa. pple. Exhausted, esp. from travelling; faint with emotion. ME–L16.

3 E. A. FREEMAN We forego any comparison between the two men. 6 B. PYM They did not consider that it was necessary for them to forgo any of the pleasures.

forgoer /fɔː'gəʊə/ *n.* Also **fore-.** E17. [f. FORGO *v.* + -ER[1].] A person who forgoes something.

forgone /fɔː'gɒn/ *ppl a.* Also **fore-.** L19. [pa. pple of FORGO *v.*] That has been forgone.

forgot *v.* pa. t. & pple: see FORGET *v.*

forgotten *v.* pa. pple: see FORGET *v.*

forinsec /fə'rɪnsɪk/ *a. obs.* exc. *Hist.* M18. [med.L (*servitium*) *forinsecum*, f. L *forinsecus* (adv.) out of doors.] *forinsec service*, service due to the superior from whom one's lord held land.

†**forinsecal** *a.* M16–M18. [f. L *forinsecus* (see prec.) + -AL[1].] Foreign; alien, extrinsic.

forint /'fɒrɪnt/ *n.* M20. [Hungarian f. It. *fiorino*: see FLORIN.] The basic monetary unit of Hungary, equal to 100 filler.

forisfamiliate /ˌfɔːrɪsfə'mɪlieɪt/ *v.t.* L16. [med.L *forisfamiliat-* pa. ppl stem of *forisfamiliare*, f. *foris* outside + *familia* family: see -ATE[3].] *Civil & Sc. Law.* Liberate (a child) from family tutelage by giving him or her possession of part of his or her inheritance.

forisfamili'ation *n.* E17.

forjeskit /fə'dʒɛskɪt/ *a. Sc.* L18. [Origin uncertain: cf. FOR-[1], DISJASKIT.] Jaded, tired out.

forjudge /fɔː'dʒʌdʒ, fə-/ *v.t.* Also **fore-.** LME. [OFr. *forjugier*, f. as FOR-[2] + JUDGE *v.*: in med.L *for(is)judicare* dispossess.] **1** *Law.* Dispossess, oust, or exclude by a judgement. Foll. by *from*, *of*, or with *double obj.* Now *rare.* LME. †**2** Condemn judicially (*to* a penalty). LME–M18.

forjudger *n.* [-ER[4]] a judgement of sentence of deprivation, expulsion, or banishment L15.

fork /fɔːk/ *n.* [OE *forca*, *force* corresp. to OFris. *forke*, OS *furka*, OHG *furcha* (Du. *vork*, G (dial.) *Furke*), ON *forkr*, f. Gmc f. L *furca* pitchfork, forked stake, whence (O)Fr. *fourche*, ONFr. *fourque* (which reinforced the wd in ME).] **I** A pronged implement. **1** A pronged agricultural implement, usu. with a long straight handle, used for digging, lifting, carrying, or throwing, and formerly as a weapon. Cf. PITCHFORK *n.*[1] OE. †**b** The forked tongue of a snake. *rare* (Shakes.). Only in E17. **2** A (usu. metal) implement with two, three, or four prongs, used for holding food while it is cut, conveying food to the mouth or plate, and as a cooking utensil. (Freq. w. specifying wd.) LME. **3** A prong, *esp.* the prong of a fork. Usu. in *pl.* L17. **b** A pickpocket; in *pl.*, the fingers, esp. as used in picking a pocket. *arch. slang.* L17. **4** In full *tuning-fork.* A two-pronged steel instrument designed to give a particular note (esp. middle C) when struck. L18.

2 J. JOHNSTON People were eating cream cakes with tiny silver forks. *carving-fork*, *fish-fork*, *toasting-fork*, etc. *silver-fork*: see SILVER *a.*

II An object with two or more branches. †**5** In *pl.* (usu. treated as *sing.*) or *sing.* A gallows. ME–E19. †**b** *Rom. Antiq.* The yoke under which defeated enemies had to pass as a token of submission; a whipping-post. Only in 17. **6** A stake, stick, etc., with a forked end (used as a support for vines etc.). LME. **7** *Archit.* A pair of timbers supporting a roof-tree. LME. **8** A bifurcation or division into branches; the point at which something forks; each of the branches, prongs, etc., into which something forks. LME. **b** A person's leg (usu. in *pl.*). Also, the part of the human body at which the legs join the trunk. E17. **c** *Chess.* A simultaneous attack by one piece, esp. a knight, on two opposing pieces. M17. **d** The point at which one river divides or two rivers join; a branch, a tributary. Chiefly *N. Amer.* M18. **e** A flash (of forked lightning); a tongue (of flame). M19. †**9** A barbed arrowhead. *rare* (Shakes.). Only in E17. **10** A part of any machine or device having two or more prongs; *esp.* the part of a bicycle frame in which the (front or back) wheel revolves. M19.

8 G. MEREDITH Torches were struck in . . the trees, or in the fork of the branches. A. AYCKBOURN Turn left . . through the village, then take the right fork past the pub. **d** W. IRVING The fork of the Nebraska, where it divides itself into two . . beautiful streams.

Phrases: MORTON'S FORK.

Comb.: **forkball** *Baseball* a pitch in which the ball is held with the thumb, index finger, and middle finger spread; **fork-lift** (**truck** etc.) a vehicle with a pronged device for lifting and carrying heavy items; **fork lunch**(**eon**), **supper**, etc.: consisting of food suitable for eating with a fork alone, so that it can be eaten standing; **forktail** any of various animals with forked tails; *spec.* (*a*) a salmon in the fourth year of its growth; (*b*) any of several chiefly black and white thrushlike birds constituting the genus *Enicurus*, native to SE Asia; **fork-tailed** *a.* (esp. in names of birds etc.) having a forked tail.

forkful *n.* as much as may be lifted on a fork M17. **forklike** *a.* resembling (that of) a fork E17.

fork /fɔːk/ *v.* ME. [f. the n.] 1 *v.i.* Form a fork; have or divide into branches, bifurcate; diverge, esp. in a specified direction. ME. b *v.t. Chess.* Attack (two pieces) simultaneously with one piece. E18. 2 *v.t.* Make or form into the shape of a fork. M17. 3 *v.t.* Pick a pocket. *arch. slang.* L17. 4 *v.t. Mining.* Pump (a mine) dry; remove (water) by pumping. E18. 5 *v.t.* Move (as) with a fork; dig, throw, scoop *in*, *out*, *over*, etc., with a fork. E19. 6 *v.t.* & *i.* Foll. by *out*, *over*, *up*: hand over (esp. money), pay, give up. *colloq.* M19.

1 J. SYLVESTER The Tree, In two faire branches forking fruitfully. M. REID The lightning forked and flashed. C. MACKENZIE They came to where the track forked to their respective crofts. 5 T. BERGER He forked up a plump piece of meat and put it between his lips. *Amateur Gardening*: Fork a little peat into the soil. *absol.*: W. HOLTBY On the stacks beyond the chestnut trees, labourers were forking. 6 J. BARNES They had to . . fork out at Christmas, and fork out money.

forker *n.* L16.

forked /fɔːkt/ *a.* ME. [f. FORK *n.*, *v.*: see -ED[2], -ED[1].] 1 Having a fork or forks or a forklike end; shaped like a fork, bifurcate, divergent, cleft. ME. b Of a road: making or having a fork or forks; branching. E16. c Having (a specified number of) prongs or forks. M16. d *Hist.* Of an arrow: having a fork-shaped arrowhead; (of an arrowhead) fork-shaped. M16. e Of a mountain: cleft at the summit. *poet.* E17. †2 Of an argument: ambiguous, equivocal. M16–L17. 3 Horned; *fig.* cuckolded. Now *rare* or *obs.* L16. 4 Having the lower part of the trunk divided; two-legged. *rare.* E17.

Special collocations: **forked head** a forked arrow(head). **forked lightning**: in the form of a zigzag or a branching line. **forked tongue** a lying or deceitful tongue (freq. in *with (a) forked tongue*).

forkedly *adv.* E17. **forkedness** *n.* E17.

forky /ˈfɔːki/ *a.* L17. [f. FORK *n.* + -Y[1].] Forked, fork-shaped.

forkiness *n.* E17.

†**forlese** *v.t.* Pa. t. **-lore**; pa. pple **-lorn**. See also FORLORN *a.* [OE *forlēosan* = OFris *forliāsa*, OS *far-*, *forliosan* (Du. *verliezen*), OHG *firliosan* (G *verlieren*), Goth. *fraliusan*, f. Gmc, f. bases of FOR-[1], LOSE *v.*] 1 Lose. OE–M17. 2 Destroy; kill. OE–M17. b Ruin; put to shame; lead astray. Usu. in *pass.* ME–L16. 3 Leave, abandon, forsake. ME–E17.

†**forloff** *n.* see FURLOUGH.

forlorn /fəˈlɔːn/ *a.* & *n.* OE. [pa. pple of FORLESE.] A *adj.* †1 Morally lost; abandoned, depraved. OE–L17. 2a Foll. by *of*, *from*: forsaken by (a person); bereft or destitute of (a thing). Chiefly *poet.* ME. b Abandoned, forsaken, deserted; left alone, desolate. M16. 3†a Ruined, doomed to destruction. LME–E18. b Desperate, hopeless. E17. 4 In pitiful condition; of a wretched appearance. L16.

2a TENNYSON Mournful Œnone wandering forlorn Of Paris once her playmate. b E. BOWEN The stretch of forlorn marsh and sad sea-line. 4 E. F. BENSON Lucia had looked so tired, so forlorn, so young to be visited with such hopeless trouble.

†B *n.* 1 A forlorn person. E16–E19. 2 = FORLORN HOPE. M17–L18.

forlornity *n.* (*US*) forlornness M19. **forlornly** *adv.* M17. **forlornness** /-n-n-/ *n.* the state or quality of being forlorn OE.

forlorn hope /fəˌlɔːn ˈhəʊp/ *n. phr.* M16. [Du. *verloren hoop* lost troop, f. *verloren* pa. pple of *verliezen* (see FORLESE) and *hoop* company (see HEAP *n.*).] 1 *Mil.* A picked troop sent to the front to begin an attack; a storming party, a body of skirmishers. In *pl.* also, the people composing such a troop; adventurers. M16. b A dangerous or desperate enterprise. M18. †2 The losers at a gaming-table collectively. Also, a gambler's last stake. *slang.* E17–L18. 3 A faint hope; an enterprise unlikely to succeed. M17.

form /fɔːm/ *n.* Also (now only in sense 18) **forme**. ME. [(O)Fr. *forme* f. L *forma* mould, shape, beauty.] I Shape, arrangement of parts. 1 The visual aspect, esp. the shape or configuration, of a thing; the shape of a body. ME. †b Beauty, comeliness. LME–M17. c Shape and structure considered abstractly as an element in the arts. M19. d *Cryst.* More fully *crystal form*. A set of crystal faces all of which have the same relation to the symmetry elements. L19. †2 An image, a likeness, a representation. ME–E17. 3 A person or animal as visible or tangible. ME. 4 The particular mode in which a thing exists or manifests itself. ME. b A species, a kind, a variety; an artistic or literary genre. LME. c *Ling.* Any of the ways in which a word may be pronounced, inflected, or spelt; the external characteristics of a word or other unit as distinct from its meaning. M18. d *Bot.* A taxonomic grouping ranking below a variety, which contains organisms differing from a given variety, subspecies, etc., in some trivial, freq. impermanent, character, e.g. a colour variant. L19. †5 The way in which something is done or made; method, fashion. ME–M17. 6 A set, customary, or prescribed way of doing something; correct or usual procedure. ME. b The present state of affairs; what is happening or going on, what is to be done. *colloq.* M20. †7 A model, a type, a pattern, an example. LME–L17. 8 *Philos.* a In Platonic philosophy, the transcendent idea or archetype which serves as the pattern for a created thing. LME. b In Aristotelian and scholastic philosophy, the essential determinant principle of a thing; that which makes something (*matter*) a determinate species or kind of being. LME. c In Kantian philosophy, that element of knowledge which is supplied by the mind and gives reality and objectivity to the thing known, as distinct from the element (*matter*) supplied by feeling. E19. 9 Arrangement and expression of ideas esp. in the arts; style in musical or literary composition. LME. 10 A set or fixed order of words; the customary or legal method of drawing up a document etc. Also, a regularly drawn document. LME. †b A recipe, a prescription. LME–E17. c A document with blanks to be filled up. M19. 11a Behaviour according to prescribed or customary rules; observance of etiquette, decorum, etc. Also *derog.*, outward observance or conformity without intrinsic sincerity. LME. b Orig., a way of behaving oneself; an instance of a specified kind of behaviour; in *pl.*, manners. Later, a mode of behaviour or procedure in accordance with prescribed usage, etiquette, etc., a ceremony. Freq. *derog.*, a ritual without intrinsic meaning. L16. 12†a A grade or degree of rank, eminence, or quality. LME–E18. b Any of the classes in which schoolchildren may be placed according to age or ability. M16. 13 Orderly arrangement of parts; regularity, good order. L16. 14 Of a racehorse, an athlete, etc.: condition of health and training, fitness. Also, record of previous performances by a racehorse, an athlete, etc. M18. b Liveliness, good spirits. *colloq.* L19. c Criminal activity on public record. *slang.* M20.

1 A. MACLEAN The Schloss Adler was built in the form of a hollow square. J. S. FOSTER The fabric . . gives character and form to the spaces within it. c O. N. ROOD In painting . . colour is subordinate to form. *Dance Theatre Journal* Everything she had to say . . was right there in the dancing . . . She expressed everything through form. 3 D. WELCH I did not notice the dark form on the bench. I. MURDOCH Felix stood . . his tall form blotting out the evening star. 4 D. L. SAYERS The arsenic was taken in liquid form. B. MOORE God was there . . in the form of a wafer of bread and a chalice of wine. b A. S. BYATT A form is as good as the writer who chooses it. JO GRIMOND Traces of a primitive form of barley . . have been found. c MAX-MÜLLER The Chinese sound *ta* means, without any change of form, great, greatness, and to be great. 6b B. BAINBRIDGE What's the form tonight? You are coming, I take it. 9 J. R. LOWELL Form . . is the artistic sense of decorum controlling the coordination of parts. 10 D. L. SAYERS They were married in the old . . Prayer Book form, and the bride said 'Obey'. c L. VAN DER POST There was no filling in of forms in triplicate. 11a J. GRAHAME Giving thanks to God—not thanks of form, A word and a grimace, but reverently. b M. MITCHELL The old usages went on, must go on, for the forms were all that were left to them. 12a S. PEPYS Thinking is working, though many forms beneath what my Lady and you are doing. b MORTIMER COLLINS He was in the fifth form at Eton. 13 P. SCOTT My passion for form and order . . everything used but with care and kept clean. 14 S. L. ELLIOTT A bloke might try and get some form up and get in the football team next winter. *Observer* On 1984 form, there are eight drivers who stand a good chance of winning today. b P. BOOTH 'Dad's sure in good form today,' she yelled. c P. LAURIE The boy's elder brother had form for doping greyhounds.

II A material object. 15 A mould, frame, or block in or on which something is shaped. ME. b *spec.* A temporary structure for holding fresh concrete in shape while it sets. E20. 16 The lair of a hare. ME. 17 A long seat without a back, a bench. LME. 18 *Printing.* (Usu. **forme.**) Type set and locked in a chase ready for printing; a quantity of film arranged for making a plate etc. L15.

15 *Daily Telegraph* You warm a small amount of metal, put it in the scroll form and gradually pull it round to the shape. 16 M. BURTON A slight depression in the long grass known as a 'form', where the hare habitually crouches during the day. 17 A. UTTLEY They sat outside . . on long low forms. 18 F. NORRIS We begin to set Saturday's paper at about four Friday afternoon, and the forms are locked about two in the morning.

Phrases: **a matter of form** a point of correct procedure; *colloq.* mere routine. *bad form*: see *good form* below. *common form*: see COMMON *a.* *crystal form*: see sense 1d above. **good, bad,** etc., **form** complying with or offending against current social conventions. **in (due, proper) form** according to the conventions, (merely) formally. **in (good** etc.) **form** playing or performing well, in good spirits. *in proper form*: see *in due form* above. **off form** not performing well, not at one's best. **on form** = *in good form* above. *true to form*: see TRUE *a.*, *n.*, & *adv.*

Comb.: **form-board** a board with spaces to take blocks of various shapes and sizes, used in intelligence tests; **form book** a record of the performances of a racehorse etc.; **form catalogue** a library catalogue in which books of a certain kind or literary genre are listed together; **form class** (*a*) *Forestry* a group of trees having a similar form factor (see below); (*b*) *Ling.* a class of linguistic forms with grammatical features in common; **form-critic** a person who engages in form-criticism; **form-criticism** textual analysis of the Bible etc. by tracing the history of its content of proverbs, myths, and other forms; **form drag** the drag on a moving body resulting from its shape; **form factor** *Forestry* the ratio of the volume of a tree to that of a regularly-shaped body of the same height and base; **form-genus** (chiefly *Mycol.* & *Palaeont.*) a collective group of (parts of) organisms showing morphological similarities but not necessarily a genetic relationship; a group of similar trace fossils; **form-historian** = *form-critic* above; **form-history** = *form-criticism* above; **form-letter** a standardized letter to deal with frequently occurring matters; **form-line** *Cartography* a line drawn on a map to show the estimated configuration or elevation between the contour lines (usu. in *pl.*); **form-master, -mistress,** a teacher who has particular responsibility for a class of schoolchildren; **form quality** a quality of the whole of something rather than of its constituent parts; **form-room** the room where a class of schoolchildren is based; **form-species** a subdivision of a form-genus; **form sheet** (orig. *US*) = *form book* above; **form word** a word with a formal or grammatical function; **formwork** = sense 15b above.

formful *a.* (now *rare* or *obs.*) full of form or forms; shapely; imaginative: M18. **formless** *a.* shapeless, having no determinate or regular form L16. **formlessly** *adv.* L19. **formlessness** *n.* E18.

form /fɔːm/ *v.*[1] ME. [OFr. *fourmer*, (also mod.) *former* f. L *formare*, f. *forma* FORM *n.*] 1 *v.t.* Give form or shape to; fashion, mould. ME. †b *v.t.* Formulate; state formally. ME–L17. c *v.t.* Give a specified form to; fashion *into* a certain shape, *after*, *by*, *from*, *on*, a pattern. ME. †d *v.t.* Express by form, embody. *rare* (Spenser). Only in L16. e *v.i.* Orig., agree in form, fit *with*. Later, take a (specified) shape, be shaped *into*. E18. f *v.t. Electr.* Convert (a semiconductor device, the plates of a lead-acid accumulator, etc.) into a particular state by the application of a current or voltage. L19. 2 *v.t.* Mould (a person, the mind, a faculty, etc.) by discipline, experience, or education. ME. 3 *v.t.* Construct, frame, make, produce, (something); articulate (a word). ME. b *v.t.* Frame in the mind, conceive, (an idea, a judgement, etc.). Also (*obs.* exc. *dial.*), imagine.

L16. c *v.i.* Come into being. E19. 4 *v.t.* Go to make up; compose. LME. b Serve as, constitute; be one or a part *of*. E19. 5 *v.t. Ling.* Construct (a word) by derivation etc.; have (a case etc.) expressed by an inflection etc. LME. 6 *v.t.* Place in order, arrange; organize (persons or things) *into* a society, system, etc. LME. 7 *v.t.* & *i. Mil.* Arrange or draw up or *up* in order; assume or take up an arrangement in a (specified) formation. E18. 8 *v.t.* Develop or acquire (a habit); enter into or contract (a friendship, an alliance, etc.). M18.

1 MILTON The Rib he formd and fashond with his hands. c C. MCCULLOUGH A little silver brooch formed into the rising sun emblem. e L. STEPHEN A ridge of rocky peaks, forming into two ridges about its centre. 2 A. JESSOPP Rudely scrawled by some one whose hand is not yet formed. J. BAYLEY The inescapable burden of being formed by parents and by early traumas. 3 M. CONNELLY A large rustic table formed by driving four stakes into the ground and placing planks on top. A. CARNEGIE We had before this formed a small debating club. b G. GREENE She was forming a plan. Q. CRISP I formed no positive opinion of him whatsoever. c W. BRONK The stars .. form and evolve, .. explode in novae. 4 H. JAMES The two houses together formed a single dwelling. DAY LEWIS The simple fishermen who formed the greater part of his congregation. b E. A. FREEMAN A realm of which Northumberland constitutionally formed a part. G. VIDAL His statistics would form the basis of a report. 5 RICHARD MORRIS The verbs of the strong conjugation form the past tense by a change of the root-vowel. 6 J. R. GREEN The Clerks of the Royal Chapel were formed into a body of secretaries. 7 C. C. TRENCH They formed in squadron column. I. HAY On the command 'form fours', odd numbers will stand fast. 8 J. BUTLER Active habits are to be formed by exercise. T. HARDY I have never loved anybody .. I have not even formed a strong friendship.

form /fɔːm/ *v.*[2]*i.* Now *rare.* LME. [f. FORM *n.*] Of a hare: have its form (*in* a particular place), be placed.

-form /fɔːm/ *suff.* Also (see below) **-iform.** [Repr. Fr. *-forme*, L *-formis*, f. *forma* FORM *n.*] Forming (usu. w. intermediate -I-) adjs. w. the sense 'having the form of', as *cruciform* etc., and referring to the number of forms, as *uniform*, *multiform*, etc.

forma /ˈfɔːmə/ *n.* Pl. **-mae** /-miː/, **-mas.** E20. [L: see FORM *n.*] *Bot.* = FORM *n.* 4d.

formable /ˈfɔːməb(ə)l/ *a.* LME. [f. FORM *v.*[1] + -ABLE.] 1 Able to be created or formed; workable, plastic. LME. 2 Properly formed; formal, shapely. Long *obs.* exc. *dial.* LME.

forma'bility *n.* E19.

formal /ˈfɔːm(ə)l/ *n.* E17. [f. the adj.] 1 In *pl.* Things which are formal. *rare.* E17. 2 (An) evening dress; an occasion on which evening dress is worn. Chiefly *N. Amer.* M20.

2 M. BEADLE Young ladies .. wear short formals, and old ladies wear floor-length evening dresses. A. YORK She looked sufficiently virginal to be attending her first formal.

formal /ˈfɔːm(ə)l/ *a.* LME. [L *formalis*, f. *forma*: see FORM *n.*, -AL[1].] 1 a *Philos.* Of or pertaining to the form or constitutive essence of a thing; essential. LME. †b Pertaining to the specific form of an animal or plant. LME–L17. c Of or pertaining to the outward form, shape, appearance, arrangement, or external qualities of a thing. Formerly also (of knowledge), theoretical. M17. d *Logic.* Concerned with the form, not the matter, of reasoning. M19. 2 Of, pertaining to, or in accordance with recognized rules or conventions, esp. of art. LME. †b Of a story: elaborately constructed; circumstantial. L16–E18. †c Made in proper form, complete; veritable, unmistakable. M17–E18. †3 Having a definite principle; regular, methodical. LME–E18. b Well-formed, regular, shapely. LME–L16. c Sound in mind; sane. *rare* (Shakes.). Only in L16. 4 Of a person, action, etc.: rigorously observant of etiquette, convention, etc.; prim; (unduly) precise or ceremonious. E16. 5 Valid or correctly so called in virtue of its form; explicit and definite, not merely tacit or accepted as equivalent. M16. 6 Connected with or accompanied by form or ceremony; (of dress) suitable for a polite or ceremonial occasion. L16. †7 That is so merely in outward form or appearance. L16–M18. 8 (Excessively) regular or symmetrical; stiff, methodical. L16. 9 Merely a matter of convention; routine, perfunctory; having the form without the spirit. M17.

1a R. SOUTH Deceit is the formal, constituent reason of hypocrisy. c F. W. ROBERTSON All living unity is spiritual, not formal. 2 U. BENTLEY We've done away with formal grammar and parsing and all that rubbish. W. S. CHURCHILL The Treaty .. bound Louis, not only in formal terms, but by a gentleman's agreement, to recognise .. William III as King. 4 S. HILL Her voice was cool, formal. A. BROOKNER Her manners were charming and formal. 6 E. ROOSEVELT The President .. gave a formal reception for me: all were seated according to protocol. 8 M. GIROUARD The formal Italianate garden, with .. parterres patterned with bedded-out flowers. 9 G. GREENE The papers which might just get him past a formal cursory examination.

Special collocations: *formal cause*: see CAUSE *n.* **formal concept** [tr. G *formaler Begriff*] a concept of logic free from the descriptive content that would restrict it to any particular subject-matter. **formal education** education in an academic institution. *formal operations*: see OPERATION 6b. **formal sin** a forbidden or sinful action done with evil intent.

formalness *n.* L17.

formaldehyde /fɔːˈmaldɪhʌɪd/ *n.* L19. [f. FORMIC + ALDEHYDE.] A colourless, pungent, toxic gaseous aldehyde, HCHO, usu. prepared by oxidation of methanol and used as formalin or in the manufacture of plastics etc.; methanal. Cf. FORMALIN.

formalin /ˈfɔːm(ə)lɪn/ *n.* L19. [f. FORMALDEHYDE + -IN[1].] An aqueous solution of formaldehyde (37 per cent by weight), used as a disinfectant, preservative for biological specimens, etc.

formalini'zation *n.* treatment with formalin M20. **formalinize** *v.t.* treat with formalin E20.

formalise *v.* var. of FORMALIZE.

formalism /ˈfɔːm(ə)lɪz(ə)m/ *n.* E19. [f. FORMAL *a.* + -ISM.] 1 Strict or excessive adherence to prescribed forms; an instance of this. E19. 2 The use or observance of prescribed forms (esp. of worship) without regard to their inner significance. M19. b *Theol.* The basing of ethics on the form of the moral law without regard to intention or consequences. M20. 3 *Math.* a (The conception of pure mathematics as) the manipulation according to certain rules of intrinsically meaningless symbols. E20. b A particular mathematical theory or mode of description of a physical situation or effect. M20. 4 *Theatr.* A movement away from naturalism, originating in Russia *c* 1890; a symbolic and stylized manner of production. E20. 5 The theory held by an early 20th-cent. Russian literary group that form and technique are the means to and the goal of artistic creation; (excessive) concern with form and technique rather than content. M20.

1 C. MERIVALE Completely enchained by their dogmatic formalisms. 2 J. MORLEY The cant and formalism of any other degenerate form of active faith. 4 A. NICOLL We are here [in the Nō plays] confronted with a theatre in which formalism is dominant.

formalist /ˈfɔːm(ə)lɪst/ *n.* & *a.* E17. [Fr. *formaliste* or med.L *formalista*: see FORMAL *a.*, -IST.] A *n.* †1 A person supporting the religious group currently holding power; a time-server. E–M17. 2 A person excessively attached to forms; a stickler for etiquette, ceremony, or rules. M17. 3 An adherent or student of formalism. E20. B *adj.* Of or pertaining to formalism; formalistic. E20.

formalistic /fɔːməˈlɪstɪk/ *a.* M19. [f. FORMALIST + -IC.] Characterized by formalism.

formality /fɔːˈmalɪti/ *n.* M16. [Fr. *formalité* or med.L *formalitas*, f. *formalis*: see FORMAL *a.*, -ITY.] †1 Literary or artistic form or style. M16–L17. 2 Accordance with legal form. *rare.* M16. 3 Conformity to rules, propriety; rigid or merely conventional observance of forms. L16. †4 The formal or essential nature of something; the defining characteristic, a formal category. L16–M18. 5 The quality of being formal; precision of manners; stiffness of design. L16. 6 In *pl.* & *collect. sing.* Robes or insignia of office or dignity. *obs.* exc. *Hist.* L16. †b Ceremonial or distinctive dress. L17–E18. †7 Outward form; the appearance or semblance (*of* something). E–M17. †8 Method, regularity; uniform procedure. E–M17. 9†a Ceremonious attention (paid to a person). E17–M18. b A requirement of etiquette, regulation, or custom, (esp. with an implied lack of real significance). M17. 10 Ceremony, elaborate procedure. M17. 11 A formal or ceremonial act; a legal, authorized or customary procedure. L17.

3 F. ATTERBURY Nor was his Attendance on Divine Offices a matter of Formality and Custom, but of Conscience. 4 J. GOAD Motion is the Formality of Wind. JER. TAYLOR If it be propounded as evil, the will that chooses it under that formality is criminal. 5 R. FRAME He bows. I'm rather taken aback by his courtly formality. 7 MILTON Sacred things not perform'd sincerely .. are no way acceptable to God in their outward formality. 9a R. KNOLLES Entertaining him with all the formalities that feigned friendship could deuise. b G. ORWELL The confession was a formality, though the torture was real. 10 S. PEPYS A great deal of do and formality in choosing of the Council and officers. 11 E. HEMINGWAY We would have to be married under Italian law and the formalities were terrific.

formalize /ˈfɔːm(ə)lʌɪz/ *v.* Also **-ise.** L16. [f. FORMAL *a.* + -IZE, partly through Fr. *formaliser.*] †1 *v.t.* Impart or constitute the form or essence of. L16–L17. †2 *v.t.* & *i.* (foll. by *upon*). Raise scrupulous objections (to); cavil (at). L16–L18. †3 *v.t.* Cause to take sides, declare *oneself* for or against. L16–M17. 4 *v.t.* Give a formal or definite shape to; state or establish formally. M17. 5 *v.i.* Act with formality; be formal or ceremonious. Now *rare.* M17. 6 *v.t.* Make formal; make ceremonious, precise, or rigid; give legal formality to (a document etc.); imbue with formalism. L18.

4 M. O. W. OLIPHANT The gates .. shut against him, did no more than formalize that sentence of banishment. 5 J. HALES They turned .. their true Fasting into Formalizing and partial abstinence. 6 *New York Times* We have reached an agreement on the disability bill and we hope to have it formalized by Monday.

formalizable *a.* able to be formalized M20.

formally /ˈfɔːm(ə)li/ *adv.* LME. [f. FORMAL *a.* + -LY[2].] 1 In formal respects; as regards form. LME. †2 According to logical form; according to the principles of art or science. LME–L16. 3 Explicitly, expressly. E16. 4 In prescribed or customary form; with the formalities required to make an action valid or definite; in set form. M16. †5 Regularly; in the normal or usual manner; with exact correspondence. Only in 17. 6 With formality of manner, ceremoniously. E17. 7 As a matter of form; as a formality. L19.

1 F. BOWEN What is formally correct may be materially false. 3 W. BLACKSTONE Perhaps in no instance it has ever been formally expressed at the first institution of a state. 4 W. RAEPER MacDonald accepted the invitation formally after being presented with the official documents. 6 A. MASSIE Willy addressed Colette formally as '*vous*' while she called him '*tu*'.

formamide /ˈfɔːməmʌɪd/ *n.* M19. [f. FORMIC + AMIDE.] *Chem.* A colourless liquid amide, $HCONH_2$, derived from formic acid.

formant /ˈfɔːm(ə)nt/ *n.* E20. [G, f. L *formant-* pres. ppl stem of *formare* FORM *v.*[1]: see -ANT[1].] 1 Orig., the characteristic tone of a vowel sound; now, any of several characteristic bands of resonance which together determine the sound quality of a vowel. E20. 2 A morpheme occurring only in combination in a word or word-stem. M20.

forma pauperis /fɔːmə ˈpɔːpərɪs/ *n. phr.* L16. [L, lit. 'the form of a poor person'.] *Law.* (The condition of) a poor person, in respect of being able to bring a legal action without payment. Freq. in *in* or *sub forma pauperis*, as a poor person; *transf.* & *fig.* humbly, in supplication.

format /ˈfɔːmat/ *n.* M19. [Fr. f. G, f. L *formatus* (*liber*) shaped (book) pa. pple of *formare* FORM *v.*[1]] 1 The physical characteristics of a book or other object, esp. the shape and size. M19. 2 A style or manner of arrangement or procedure. M20. 3 An arrangement of data etc. for storage or processing by computer. M20.

1 H. WILLIAMSON Format is often taken to mean the style and general appearance of a book, as well as its shape and size. DAVID POTTER The first vertical format double-size stamp was issued. 2 V. PACKARD The overall format . . was: 'Basic pattern of 'good guys' versus 'bad men'.' *Which Computer?* Entering the date in the . . American format (month, day, year). 3 *attrib.*: B. F. GREEN An associated format statement . . specifies the precise manner in which the quantities appear in the input or output medium.

format /ˈfɔːmat/ *v.t.* Infl. **-tt-**. M20. [f. the n.] Chiefly *Computing.* Arrange or put into a format; impose a format on.

Times There are dot matrix printers . . which format each character as required. *QL User* The program formats a disk in such a fashion that equal amounts of storage are used for each record.

formate /ˈfɔːmeɪt/ *n.* Also †**formiate**. E19. [f. FORMIC + -ATE[1].] *Chem.* A salt or ester of formic acid.

formate /fɔːˈmeɪt/ *v.i.* E20. [Back-form. f. FORMATION.] Of an aircraft or pilot: take up formation *with*, fly in formation.

formation /fɔːˈmeɪʃ(ə)n/ *n.* LME. [(O)Fr., or L *formatio(n-)*, f. *format-* pa. ppl stem of *formare* FORM *v.*[1]: see -ATION.] 1 The action of forming, the process of being formed; creation, production. LME. b The action or process of forming an accumulator plate, semiconductor device, etc. Cf. FORM *v.*[1] 1f. L19. 2 A thing formed. M17. 3 The arrangement of the parts of something; structure, conformation. L18. b The disposition of fibres in a sheet of paper. E20. 4 Orig. *Mil.* A formal arrangement of persons or things (ships, aircraft, etc.) acting together as a unit. L18. 5 *Geol.* An assemblage of rocks or series of strata having some common characteristic. E19. 6 *Ecol.* A mature community of plant species adapted to particular conditions. L19.

1 J. ROSENBERG The atmosphere at home played an even greater role in the formation of his character. 4 J. A. FROUDE The usual Roman formation in battle was in triple line. **in formation** (of aircraft etc.) together, in a set pattern or configuration.

Comb.: **formation dancing** a variety of (competitive) ballroom dancing in which a team of couples dances a prepared routine; **formation flying** flying in formation; **formation-rule** *Logic* each of a set of rules together specifying permissible combinations of signs in a given system.

formational *a.* of or pertaining to a formation or formations L19. **formationally** *adv.* L19.

formative /ˈfɔːmətɪv/ *a.* & *n.* L15. [OFr. *formatif*, *-ive* or med.L *formativus*, f. *format-*: see prec., -ATIVE.] A *adj.* 1 Capable of forming or creating; serving to fashion. L15. b Of or pertaining to formation; *spec.* (*Archaeol.*, usu. F-) = PRECLASSIC. M19. 2 *Ling.* Of an inflectional or derivative affix: used in forming words. E18. 3 Of tissue: capable of growth and development. L19.

1 C. DARWIN The formative organs themselves are perfect in structure. b D. ARKELL The formative years of his life, between the ages of five and twelve.

B *n.* A formative element or agent. M18.

L. BLOOMFIELD Any unanalyzable word or formative is a morpheme. J. GALSWORTHY That essential formative of character, east wind.

formatively *adv.* M17. **formativeness** *n.* M19.

formatore /formaˈtoːre/ *n.* Pl. ***-ri*** /-ri/. M19. [It., agent-n. f. *formare* to form.] A modeller in wax or plaster; a technical assistant who repairs or restores pottery, metalwork, etc.

forme *n.* see FORM *n.*

†**forme** *a.* [OE *forma* = OFris. *forma*, OS *formo*, Goth. *fruma*, superl. f. base of FORE *adv.*] 1 Earlier or earliest in time or serial order; the first of two, former. OE–LME. 2 Foremost, first, in position, rank, etc. ME–E16.

formé, formée *adjs.* see FORMY.

formedon /ˈfɔːmɪdən/ *n. obs.* exc. *Hist.* L15. [AN f. AL *forma doni*, *forma donationis* form of gift.] *Law.* A writ of right formerly used to claim entailed property.

formée, formé *adjs.* see FORMY.

former /ˈfɔːmə/ *n.*[1] LME. [f. FORM *v.*[1] + -ER[1].] 1 A person who forms something; a maker, a creator, a shaper. LME. 2 A tool, mould, or other device used to form articles or shape material. M17. b *Electr.* A frame or core about which a coil is wound. L19. c *Aeronaut.* A transverse member that strengthens and gives shape to a wing or fuselage. E20.

1 R. CUDWORTH The Framer and Former of the Vniverse. 2 T. HOOPER The wax cups are prepared by dipping a wooden or glass former into molten beeswax.

†**former** *n.*[2] M16–E18. [OFr. *formoir* chisel (mod. *fermoir*): see -ER[2].] A kind of chisel or gouge.

former /ˈfɔːmə/ *a.* & *n.*[3] ME. [f. FORME *a.* + -ER[3]: cf. FOREMOST.] A *adj.* 1 Orig., earlier in time. Now chiefly, of the past, belonging to or occurring in an earlier period. ME. †b First, foremost. LME–E16. c Previously owned, occupied, frequented, etc. LME. d Designating a previous holder of an office etc.; sometime, ex-. Orig. *US.* E20. †2 At or towards the front. LME–L17. 3 The first or first mentioned of two (opp. *latter*). E17.

1 B. MOORE The last thing . . I want is to reopen our disagreements of former days. *Former Prophets*: see PROPHET. d S. LEWIS From the Babbitts' former house had come two much-carved rocking chairs. e *Daily Telegraph* Former Army Major, Brian Hart, had sued for wrongful dismissal. 3 A. WINCHELL The former locality . . has for many years been a favourite collecting-ground of geologists.

B *n.* *The* first or first mentioned of two people or things (opp. *latter*). L16.

C. FORD The former may be made by several methods.

-former /ˈfɔːmə/ *suff.* M19. [f. FORM *n.* + -ER[1].] A member of a specified class or form in a school.

DENNIS POTTER The choice of grammar school sixth-formers would be Oxford or Cambridge first.

formeret /ˈfɔːm(ə)rɛt/ *n.* L19. [Fr., f. *forme* FORM *n.*] *Archit.* A rib-moulding at the junction of a vault with the vertical wall; a wall rib.

formerly /ˈfɔːməli/ *adv.* L16. [f. FORMER *a.* + -LY[2].] †1 Before another or something else; first. L16–M17. 2 At some past time, in former days. L16. †3 A short time ago, just now. L16–M18.

2 E. WAUGH Now . . he found a naughty relish in what he had formerly shunned.

Formgeschichte /ˈfɔːmgəʃɪxtə/ *n.* E20. [G, f. *Form* form + *Geschichte* history.] = *form-criticism* s.v. FORM *n.*

†**formiate** *n.* var. of FORMATE *n.*

formic /ˈfɔːmɪk/ *a.* L18. [f. as next: see -IC.] 1 Chem. *formic acid*, a colourless irritant volatile liquid carboxylic acid, HCOOH, produced by various insects (esp. ants) and plants, and used in tanning and dyeing; methanoic acid. L18. 2 Of or pertaining to ants. *rare.* E19.

formica /fɔːˈmʌɪkə/ *n.*[1] LME. [L = ant.] †1 A disease characterized by small pustules and a burning and itching of the skin. LME–M16. 2 An ulcer, abscess, or excrescence, occurring esp. in a hawk's bill or a dog's ears. E17. 3 An ant. Now only as mod.L genus name. M19.

Formica /fɔːˈmʌɪkə/ *n.*[2] Also **f-**. E20. [Origin unkn.] (Proprietary name for) a hard, durable plastic laminate used esp. as a decorative heat-resistant surfacing material.

formicarioid /fɔːmɪˈkɛːrɪɔɪd/ *a.* & *n.* Also **-caroid** /-ˈkɛːrɔɪd/, **-cariid** /-ˈkɛːrɪɪd/. L19. [f. mod.L *Formicarius* genus name f. med.L *formicarium*: see next, -OID.] *Ornith.* Of or pertaining to, a bird of, the large neotropical passerine family Formicariidae, comprising the insectivorous antbirds.

formicary /ˈfɔːmɪk(ə)ri/ *n.* E19. [med.L *formicarium*, f. as FORMICA *n.*[1]: see -ARY[1].] An ants' nest; an anthill.

formicate /ˈfɔːmɪkeɪt/ *v.i. rare.* L17. [L *formicat-* pa. ppl stem of *formicare* crawl like an ant (said of the pulse or skin), f. *formica* ant: see -ATE[3].] Crawl like an ant; crawl (as if) *with* ants.

J. R. LOWELL An open space, which formicated with peasantry.

formication /fɔːmɪˈkeɪʃ(ə)n/ *n.* E18. [L *formicatio(n-)*, f. as prec.: see -ATION.] Chiefly *Med.* A sensation as of insects crawling over or under the skin.

formicid /ˈfɔːmɪsɪd/ *a.* & *n.* L19. [mod.L *Formicidae* (see below), f. *formica* ant: see -ID[3].] *Entomol.* (Of, pertaining to, or designating) an insect of the hymenopteran family Formicidae, which comprises the ants.

formicine /ˈfɔːmɪsʌɪn/ *a.* L19. [L *formicinus*, f. *formica* ant: see -INE[1].] Of or pertaining to ants; *spec.* designating ants (related to and resembling those) of the genus *Formica*.

formidable /ˈfɔːmɪdəb(ə)l, fɔːˈmɪd-/ *a.* LME. [Fr., or L *formidabilis*, f. *formidare* fear: see -ABLE.] To be dreaded or viewed with respect; likely to be hard to overcome, resist, or deal with.

J. S. HUXLEY Giant nettles with a formidable sting. A. STORR A formidable lady, rich, beautiful, energetic and self-willed.

formidaˈbility *n.* M18. **formidableness** *n.* M17. **formidably** *adv.* L17.

†**formidolous** *a. rare.* M17–L18. [L *formidolosus* causing or feeling dread, f. *formido* dread: see -OUS.] Causing fear, terrible; feeling fear, timorous.

forming /ˈfɔːmɪŋ/ *vbl n.* LME. [f. FORM *v.*[1] + -ING[1].] 1 The action of FORM *v.*[1]; the fact or process of being formed. LME. 2 *Electr.* = FORMATION 1b. Cf. FORM *v.*[1] 1f. E20.

formol /ˈfɔːmɒl/ *n.* L19. [f. FORMALDEHYDE + -OL.] = FORMALIN.

formolize *v.t.* = FORMALINIZE M20.

Formosan /fɔːˈməʊs(ə)n/ *a.* & *n.* M17. [f. *Formosa* the former (orig. Portuguese) name of Taiwan, f. L *formosa* (*insula* island) fem. of *formosus* beautiful: see -AN.] *Hist.* A *adj.* Of or pertaining to Formosa (now Taiwan) an island off the south-east coast of China. M17. B *n.* A native or inhabitant of Formosa; the language of Formosa. E18.

formose /ˈfɔːməʊs, -z/ *n.* L19. [f. FORMALDEHYDE + -OSE[2].] *Chem.* A mixture of hexose sugars formed from formaldehyde by a condensation reaction in the presence of weak alkali.

formosity /fɔːˈmɒsɪti/ *n.* Now *rare* or *obs.* LME. [OFr. *formosité* f. L *formositat-*, f. *formosus* beautiful, f. *forma* FORM *n.*: see -ITY.] Beauty; a beautiful thing.

formula /ˈfɔːmjʊlə/ *n.* Pl. **-lae** /-liː/, **-las**. E17. [L, dim. of *forma* FORM *n.*: see -ULE.] 1 A set form of words prescribed by authority or custom for use on ceremonial or social occasions; also (freq. *derog.*), a rule unintelligently or slavishly followed, a traditional or conventional belief or established method. E17. b A set form of words as a definition or an enunciation of a principle or (religious) doctrine; *esp.* a statement or method intended to reconcile different aims or opinions. E18. c *Literary Criticism.* A stock epithet, phrase, or line, repeated for various effects in literary composition, esp. epic poetry. L19. 2 A prescription; a list of ingredients, a recipe; *N. Amer.* baby food made up from a recipe. E18. 3a *Math., Physics*, etc. A general rule, principle, or relationship expressed in symbols, often as an equation. L18. b *Chem.* An expression of the atomic constituents of a compound by means of symbols and figures. M19. c In general scientific use, a group of symbols or figures condensing a set of facts. M19. 4 *Motor Racing.* The class or specification of a racing car, usu. expressed in terms of engine capacity. E20.

1 K. CLARK All art is to some degree symbolic and recognition depends on certain long accepted formulae. D. MACDONALD The formula for a best seller now includes a minimum of 'outspoken' descriptions of sexual activities. C. V. WEDGWOOD The executioner did not go through the usual formula of asking for, and receiving the forgiveness of his victim. b H. H. WILSON Forcing the Brahmins . . to repeat the Mohammedan formula of faith. P. G. WODEHOUSE It was plain that this girl and he were poles apart and could never hope to find a formula. c *transf.*: E. M. FORSTER He enters crying 'Revenge!' or 'My heart bleeds for humanity!' or whatever his

formula is. 2 T. MORRISON She was a wet-nurse . . and made her living from white babies. Then formula came and she almost starve to death. 3b *empirical formula*: see EMPIRICAL. c *dental formula*: see DENTAL *a. floral formula*: see FLORAL *a.* 4 *formula one, formula two, formula three, formula 5000*, etc.

formulable /ˈfɔːmjʊləb(ə)l/ *a.* L19. [f. FORMUL(ATE + -ABLE.] Able to be formulated.

formulae *n.pl.* see FORMULA.

formulaic /fɔːmjʊˈleɪɪk/ *a.* L19. [f. FORMULA + -IC.] Of the nature of a formula.
formuˈlaically *adv.* M20.

formular /ˈfɔːmjʊlə/ *n.* Long *rare.* LME. [f. as FORMULARY *n.*: see -AR[2].] = FORMULARY *n.*

formular /ˈfɔːmjʊlə/ *a. rare.* L18. [f. FORMULA + -AR[1].] 1 Formal, correct in form. L18. 2 = FORMULARY *a.* L19.
formularize *v.t.* = FORMULATE M19. **formulariˈzation** *n.* the action or an act of formularizing L19.

formularism /ˈfɔːmjʊlərɪz(ə)m/ *n.* E20. [f. next + -ISM.] Rigid adherence to or dependence on formularies.
Also **formularist** *n.* L19.

formulary /ˈfɔːmjʊləri/ *n.* M16. [Fr. *formulaire* or med.L *formularius* (*liber* book), f. as FORMULA: see -ARY[1].] 1 A collection or system of formulae; a document or book containing the set or prescribed form or forms, esp. of religious belief or ritual; *gen.* a formula. M16. 2 *Pharm.* A listing of medicinal drugs with their uses, methods of administration, etc. E19.

formulary /ˈfɔːmjʊləri/ *a.* E18. [f. FORMULA + -ARY[1].] Of the nature of a formula; of or pertaining to a formula or formulae; using formulae.

formulate /ˈfɔːmjʊleɪt/ *v.t.* M19. [f. FORMULA + -ATE[3], after (O)Fr. *formuler* f. med.L *formulare*, f. as FORMULA.] Reduce to or express (as) in a formula; put into a systematic form or statement.
H. ARENDT Romantic intellectuals who had formulated the main tenets of a conservative ideology.
formuˈlation *n.* (*a*) the action of formulating; (*b*) a material or mixture prepared according to a particular formula: L19. **formulator** *n.* E20.

formule /ˈfɔːm(j)uːl/ *n. rare.* L17. [(O)Fr. f. L FORMULA.] = FORMULA.

formulise *v.* var. of FORMULIZE.

formulism /ˈfɔːmjʊlɪz(ə)m/ *n.* M19. [f. FORMULA + -ISM.] Adherence to or dependence on conventional formulas.
formulist *n.* M19.

formulize /ˈfɔːmjʊlʌɪz/ *v.t.* Also **-ise**. M19. [f. FORMULA + -IZE.] Formulate; construct a formula for.
formuliˈzation *n.* M19.

formy /ˈfɔːmi/ *a.* Also (earlier) **-é**, **-ée**. LME. [Fr. *formé* pa. ppl a. of *former* FORM *v.*[1]] *Her.* Of a cross: = PATTÉE.

formyl /ˈfɔːmʌɪl, -mɪl/ *n.* M19. [f. FORMIC + -YL.] *Chem.* The radical ·CHO. Usu. in *comb.*
formylate *v.t.* introduce one or more formyl groups into (a compound or molecule) by chemical reaction M20. **formyˈlation** *n.* M20.

fornent /fɔːˈnɛnt, fə-/ *prep. Sc., Anglo-Ir.,* & *north.* Also **-nst** /-nst/. LME. [f. FORE *adv.* + ANENT.] 1 Opposite to, facing; alongside. LME. 2 With regard to, concerning. LME.
1 SIR W. SCOTT King Ahasuerus . . sate upon his royal throne fornent the gate of his house.

fornicate /ˈfɔːnɪkət/ *a.* E19. [L *fornicatus* vaulted, arched, f. as FORNIX: see prec., -ATE[2].] Arched, bending over.

fornicate /ˈfɔːnɪkeɪt/ *v.i.* M16. [eccl.L *fornicat-* pa. ppl stem of *fornicari*, f. L FORNIX, *fornic-* brothel, (orig.) arch, vaulted chamber: see -ATE[3].] Commit or indulge in fornication.

fornication /fɔːnɪˈkeɪʃ(ə)n/ *n.*[1] ME. [(O)Fr. f. eccl.L *fornicatio(n-)*, f. as FORNICATE *v.*: see -ATION.] 1 Voluntary sexual intercourse between esp. unmarried persons; (esp. in biblical use) adultery. ME. 2 *fig.* Idolatry. ME.
1 R. GRAVES Unjust that our mistress, . . a married woman, should commit adultery and yet unmercifully whip her for mere fornication.

fornication /fɔːnɪˈkeɪʃ(ə)n/ *n.*[2] *rare.* E18. [L *fornicatio(n-)*, f. as FORNICATE *a.*: see -ATION.] *Archit.* An arching, a vaulting.

fornicator /ˈfɔːnɪkeɪtə/ *n.* LME. [Late L, f. *fornicatio(n-)*: see FORNICATION *n.*[1], -OR.] A person who commits or indulges in fornication.
fornicatress *n.* = FORNICATRIX L16.

fornicatrix /ˈfɔːnɪkeɪtrɪks/ *n.* Pl. **-trices** /-trɪsiːz/, **-trixes**. L16. [Late L, fem. of FORNICATOR: see prec., -TRIX.] A woman who commits or indulges in fornication.
J. UPDIKE The hero throws Jo, the third of his willing fornicatrices, onto the bed full of guests' wraps.

fornix /ˈfɔːnɪks/ *n.* Pl. **-nices** /-nɪsiːz/. L17. [L = arch, vaulted chamber.] A thing resembling an arch. Chiefly *Anat.*, an arched organ or structure; *spec.* (*a*) (more fully *fornix cerebri* /ˈsɛrɪbrʌɪ/) a band of white fibres at the base of the brain; (*b*) any of the uppermost recesses of the vagina.

forold /fɔːrˈəʊld, fə-/ *v.i.* Long *dial.* [OE *forealdian*, f. FOR-[1] + *ealdian* grow old, f. *eald* OLD *a.* Cf. OHG *faralten* (G *veralten*).] Grow old, wear out with age. Now only as *forolded* ppl a.

†**forpass** *v.* LME. [OFr. *fo(u)rpasser*, f. *fors* FOR-[2] + *passer* PASS *v.*] 1 *v.t.* Surpass, excel; *rare* exceed (a time-limit). LME–E17. 2 *v.i.* Pass beyond; *rare* go past, pass. L15–L16.
2 SPENSER One day as hee forpassed by the plaine With weary pace.

forpet /ˈfɔːpɪt, -pɛt/ *n. Sc.* & *north.* Also **-pit** /-pɪt/. M17. [Alt. of *fourth part.*] A quarter of a peck.

forpine /fɔːˈpʌɪn, fə-/ *v.t.* & (*rare*) *i. arch.* ME. [f. FOR-[1] + PINE *v.*] (Cause to) pine or waste away; torture.

forpit *n.* var. of FORPET.

forprise /fɔːˈprʌɪz, fə-/ *v.t.* Now *rare.* Also **fore-**, **-prize**. LME. [AN *forpris(e)* pa. pple of *for(s)prendre* to except, f. *for(s-* FOR-[3] + *prendre* take.] Chiefly *Law.* Take out, except, exempt.

forrader *a.* & *adv.* see FORWARDER *a.* & *adv.*

forrel *n.* & *v.* var. of FOREL.

†**forridden** *a.* E16–E19. [f. FOR-[1] + *ridden* pa. pple of RIDE *v.*] Exhausted by (excessive) riding.

forrit /ˈfɒrɪt/ *adv. Sc.* & *north.* E18. [Alt. of FORWARD *adv.*] Forward(s), ahead.

†**forsado** *n.* Pl. **-os**. E17–M18. [Sp. *forçado* (now *forzado*). Cf. FORSARY.] A galley-slave.

forsake /fəˈseɪk/ *v.t.* Pa. t. **-sook** /-ˈsʊk/; pa. pple **-saken** /-ˈseɪk(ə)n/. [OE *forsacan* = OS *forsakan* (Du. *verzaken*), OHG *firsahhan*, f. WGmc, f. base of FOR-[1] + OE *sacan* quarrel, accuse: see SAKE *n.*[1]] †1 Decline or refuse (something offered, *to do*). OE–E17. b Avoid, shun, refuse to undertake or have to do with. ME–L16. c Deny (an accusation, oneself, etc.); deny or renounce allegiance to (God, a lord, etc.). ME–L16. 2 Give up, surrender, (esp. something valued). Passing into sense 3. OE. b Break off from or renounce (a task, plan, doctrine, or belief, or (esp.) a sin). Formerly also w. inf. as obj. ME. 3 Abandon, withdraw from; *esp.* withdraw one's help, friendship, or companionship from, desert. ME.
2 SHAKES. *Lucr.* And for himself himself he must forsake. b J. T. FOWLER The southern Picts . . had forsaken idolatry. 3 G. ORWELL His nerve so forsook him that he began shouting for mercy even before the beating began. B. PYM It was as if a monk should forsake his cloister to embrace the riches of the world.
forsaken *ppl a.* deserted, left solitary or desolate LME. **forsakenly** *adv.* L16. **forsakenness** /-n-n-/ *n.* E17. **forsaker** *n.* LME.

†**forsary** *n.* M16–E18. [Fr. †*forsaire*, -*çaire* (now *forçat*). Cf. FORSADO.] A galley-slave.

forset /fəˈsɛt/ *v.t.* Now *dial.* Infl. **-tt-**. Pa. t. & pple **-set**. [OE *forsettan*, f. as FOR-[1] + SET *v.*[1]: = MHG *versetzen.*] Beset; bar (a way); waylay, entrap, (a person).

forshape /fəˈʃeɪp/ *v.t.* Long *rare* or *obs.* OE. [f. FOR-[1] + SHAPE *v.*] Transform; *rare* disfigure.

†**forslack** *v.* Also **fore-**. ME. [f. FOR-[1] + SLACK *v.*] 1 *v.i.* Slacken. *rare.* ME–L16. 2 *v.t.* Be slack in, neglect; lose or spoil by slackness or delay. L16–M17.

forslow /fəˈsləʊ/ *v. arch.* Also **fore-**. OE. [f. as FOR-[1] + *slāwian* be slow, f. *slāw* SLOW *a.*] 1 *v.t.* Be slow about; lose or spoil by sloth; delay, neglect. OE. 2 *v.t.* Hinder, obstruct. L16. †3 *v.i.* Be slow or dilatory. Only in L16.
1 W. HUBBARD They were resolved to foreslow no opportunity. 2 R. C. SINGLETON What delay foreslows the laggard nights. 3 SHAKES. *3 Hen. VI* Forslow no longer; make we hence amain.

forsooth /fəˈsuːθ/ *adv. arch., iron.,* or *derog.* [OE *forsōþ*: see FOR *prep.*, SOOTH *n.*] In truth, indeed; truly.

forspeak /fɔːˈspiːk, fə-/ *v.t.* Also **fore-**. Pa. t. **-spoke** /-ˈspəʊk/; pa. pple **-spoken** /-ˈspəʊkən/. OE. [f. FOR-[1] + SPEAK *v.*] †1 Deny. Only in OE. †2 Renounce; *rare* forbid. OE–L16. †3 Speak against, speak ill of. LME–E17. 4 Bewitch or charm, esp. by excessive praising. Now only *Sc.* LME.
3 SHAKES. *Ant. & Cl.* Thou hast forspoke my being in these wars, And say'st it is not fit. 4 SIR W. SCOTT To obviate the risque of forspeaking . . add some little ejaculation expressive of deference to heaven or fortune.
forspeaker *n.* (now only *Sc.*) a witch, an enchanter LME.

forspend /fəˈspɛnd/ *v.t.* Also **fore-**. OE. [f. FOR-[1] + SPEND *v.*] †1 Spend, squander. OE–ME. 2 Exhaust, tire out. Chiefly as *forspent* ppl a. L16.

†**forstand** *v.t.* OE. [f. FOR-[1] + STAND *v.*] 1 Oppose, withstand. OE–E18. 2 [Cf. G *verstehen.*] Understand. OE–L19.

forsterite /ˈfɔːstərʌɪt/ *n.* E19. [f. J. R. *Forster* (1729–98), Ger. naturalist + -ITE[1].] *Min.* An orthorhombic magnesium silicate mineral of the olivine group forming white, yellow, or green crystals.

Forstner bit /ˈfɔːstnə bɪt/ *n. phr.* E20. [Benjamin *Forstner*, inventor.] A type of wood-drilling bit.

forswear /fɔːˈswɛː, fə-/ *v.* Pa. t. **-swore** /-ˈswɔː/; pa. pple **-sworn** /-ˈswɔːn/. OE. [f. FOR-[1] + SWEAR *v.*] 1 *v.t.* Renounce or abandon on oath, abjure, (a cause, one's country, *to do*, etc.). OE. 2 *v.i.* & *t.* (*refl.* & in *pass.*) Swear falsely, commit perjury. OE. 3 *v.t.* †a Swear by (a thing) falsely or profanely. Only in ME. b *v.t.* Swear (something) falsely; break, forsake, or go back on (an oath, sworn allegiance, etc.). *arch.* L16. 4 *v.t.* Deny or repudiate on oath or with strong protestation. LME.
1 ANTHONY SMITH The kind of self-denial which forswears virtually every sort of proven aid. 2 J. S. BLACKIE I have sworn to obey the laws, and I cannot forswear myself.
forswearer *n.* a perjurer LME. **forsworn** *ppl a.* perjured OE. **forswornness** /-n-n-/ *n.* (*rare*) OE.

forsythia /fɔːˈsʌɪθɪə, fə-/ *n.* M19. [mod.L (see below), f. William *Forsyth* (1737–1804), Eng. botanist: see -IA[1].] Any of various chiefly Chinese shrubs of the genus *Forsythia*, of the olive family, grown for their yellow bell-shaped flowers which appear in spring before the leaves.

fort /fɔːt/ *n.* See also FORTE *n.*[1] LME. [(O)Fr., or It. *forte*, use as n. of *fort*, *forte* strong: see next.] I 1 *Mil.* A building or place fortified for defensive or protective purposes, usu. surrounded with a ditch, rampart, and parapet, and garrisoned with soldiers; *fig.* a strong position, a stronghold. LME. 2 *Hist.* A trading-station (orig. fortified). *N. Amer.* L18.
1 **hold the fort** act as temporary substitute, cope with an emergency.
II See FORTE *n.*[1]

†**fort** *a.* LME–L18. [(O)Fr., f. L *fortis* strong.] Strong, powerful.

fort /fɔːt/ *v.* Chiefly *US.* M16. [f. the n.] 1 *v.t.* Defend or protect (a place) with a fortification; enclose or station (people) in or *in* a fort. M16. 2 *v.i.* Build a fort or a fortification. E18.

fortalice /ˈfɔːtəlɪs/ *n.* Also †**fortilage**. LME. [med.L *fortalitia*, -*itium*, f. L *fortis* strong.] Orig., a fortress. Now chiefly, a small fort or outwork of fortification.

forte /ˈfɔːteɪ, ˈfɔːti, fɔːt/ *n.*[1] Orig. †**fort**. M17. [Fr. *fort*, use as n. of *fort* (see FORT *n.*); the Fr. fem. form was substituted for the masc. in Eng., as in *locale*, *morale*. Pronunc. latterly infl. by next.] 1 *Fencing*. The stronger part of a sword-blade, from the hilt to the middle. Cf. FEEBLE *n.* 2, FOIBLE *n.* 1. M17. 2 The strong point of a person; the thing in which one excels. L17.

2 W. TREVOR He, as though repetition were his forte, repeated the words.

forte /ˈfɔːti/ *adv.*, *a*, & *n.*[2] E18. [It. = strong, loud, f. L *fortis* strong.] *Mus.* A *adv.* & *adj.* (A direction:) loud(ly). (Abbrev. *f.*) E18.

forte forte very loudly; abbrev. *ff.* *mezzo forte*: see MEZZO *adv.*

B *n.* A loud tone or passage. M18.

forte-piano /ˌfɔːtɪpɪˈanəʊ/ *n.*, *adv.*, & *a.* M18. [It.: see prec. and PIANO *adv.* & *a.*] *Mus.* A *n.* An early form of the pianoforte. M18. B *adv.* & *adj.* (A direction:) loud(ly) and then immediately soft(ly). (Abbrev. *fp.*) L19.

fortes *n.pl.* see FORTIS.

Fortescue /ˈfɔːtɪskjuː/ *n.* *Austral.* Also **f-**. L19. [Perh. f. FORTY + SKEWER (w. ref. to the abundant spines of the fish), alt. after the surname *Fortescue*.] A small scorpion fish, *Centropogon australis*, having poisonous spines.

forth /fɔːθ/ *adv.*, *prep.*, & *n.* [OE *forþ* = OS *forþ*, OFris. *forth* (Du. *voort*), MHG *vort* (G *fort*), f. Gmc (repr. by Goth. *faurþis* further), f. IE base repr. by FORE-.] A *adv.* 1 Of movement or direction: forwards, onwards. Formerly also used ellipt.: go forwards. *obs.* exc. in *back and forth*: see BACK *adv.* OE. 2 Forward, into view. Only w. such vbs as *bring*, *come*, *show*, etc., *forth*. Formerly also w. certain vbs where *out* is now used, as *lay forth*, *single forth*. OE. †b Used ellipt.: go or come forward, into view; come out *with*, utter. LME–M16. 3 Of movement: away or out from a place of origin, (temporary) residence, or confinement. Formerly also w. certain vbs where *out* is now used, as *lend forth*, *lock forth*. OE. b Used ellipt.: go away or out from. *arch.* ME. †c Of position: away; abroad; not at home. ME–E17. 4 Of extent in time: onwards, following immediately and continuously on from a specified point in time. *arch.* OE. †b Of action: continuously, persistently. OE–E19. †5 Of extent in space: onwards from a specified point or place, continuously in one direction without deviation. OE–M16. †6 At or to an advanced point in time, position, or progress. ME–L15.

2 E. BOWEN Forth into the midst stepped Hermione. A. CARTER Blackened statues stretched their arms forth, as if attempting to flee the fire. 3 I. MURDOCH The hilarious excitement which Christian had been holding in check throughout our interview burst wildly forth. R. GRAVES The seven years' curse is ended now That drove me forth from this kind land. c SHAKES. *Com. Err.* Say he dines forth, and let no creature enter. 4 AV *Ps.* 113:2 Blessed be the name of the Lord: from this time forth. b SIR W. SCOTT Now, men of death, work forth your will. 5 COVERDALE *Ezek.* 6:14 From the wildernesse off Deblat forth.

Phrases: *and so forth*: see SO *adv.*, *conj.*, & *a.* **forth of** (now only *poet.*) out of. †**forth with** along with, at the same time as. *hold forth*: see HOLD *v.*

B *prep.* †1 Forward, up to, to the extent of (chiefly w. *even*). Also in conj. phr. *forth that*: until. OE–LME. 2 Out or away from; (from) out of. Now *rare*. M16.

2 H. F. CARY Never fire, With so swift motion, forth a stormy cloud, Leap'd downward.

†C *n.* Free course. *rare* exc. in *have one's forth*, have outlet, have free course. LME–E17.

forth- /fɔːθ/ *comb. form*. OE. [f. FORTH *adv.*] Forming ppl adjs. (rarely vbs) and ns. of action and (*rare*) agent, as *forthgoing*, *forthspeaker*, *forthtell*, etc.

†**forthbring** *v.t.* (*a*) bear (offspring, fruit); (*b*) bring forward; utter. **forth'bringing** *vbl n.* (*a*) the action of FORTHBRING *v.*; (*b*) *esp.* the carrying forth of a body for burial. **forth'fare** *v.i.* †(*a*) die; (*b*) go away, depart. †**forthgo** *v.i.* (*a*) go forth, depart; (*b*) come forth, proceed. **forth'going** *n.* a going forth, a departure. **forth'going** *a.* that goes forth; *esp.* enthusiastic. **forth'putting** *n.* (*a*) the action of putting forth; (*b*) *US* obtrusive behaviour. **forth'putting** *a.* (now chiefly *US*) forward, obtrusive. †**forthset** *v.t.* set forth, display. **forth'setting** *n.* a display, an exhibition.

for that /fɔː ˈðat/ *conj.* *arch.* LOE. [See FOR *prep.* 17, THAT *conj.*] 1 For the reason that, because. LOE. †2 For the purpose that; in order that. LOE–L16.

1 SHAKES. *Merry W.* For that I love your daughter . . I must advance the colours of my love.

forthcome /fɔːθˈkʌm/ *v.* & *ppl a.* Now *rare*. OE. [Orig. f. FORTH- + COME *v.* In mod. use back-form. f. FORTHCOME *ppl a.*] A *v.i.* Come forth. OE. B *ppl a.* That has come forth or been issued. E19.

forthcomer *n.* E19.

forthcoming /fɔːθˈkʌmɪŋ/ *vbl n.* In sense 2 also **furthcoming**. M16. [f. FORTH- + COMING *n.*] 1 A coming forward or out. Formerly *esp.* an appearance in court. M16. 2 *Sc. Law.* An action brought by the arrester of property in order to make the proceeds of arrestment available. M17.

forthcoming /fɔːθˈkʌmɪŋ, *esp. attrib.* ˈfɔːθ kʌmɪŋ/ *ppl a.* L15. [f. FORTH- + COMING *a.*] 1 About or likely to come forth or appear; approaching (in time); (ready to be) produced when wanted, at one's disposal. L15. 2 Of a person: ready to make or meet advances; responsive, informative. M19.

1 H. KISSINGER I informed his Cabinet members that a final decision would be forthcoming within twenty-four hours. P. FULLER My reflections on these two great thinkers will be expanded . . in a forthcoming book. 2 *Punch* The War Minister . . was not very forthcoming on the question of dive bombers.

forthcomingness *n.* E19.

forthink /fɔːˈθɪŋk, fə-/ *v.*[1] Also **fore-**. [OE *forþenċan* (f. FOR-[1] + *þenċan* THINK *v.*[2]) = OHG *fordenchen* (G *verdenken*).] †1 *v.t.* Despise, distrust. Only in OE. †2 *v.refl.* & *i.* Repent (*of*), be sorry (*for*, *that*, *to do*). ME–M17. 3 *v.t.* Think of with pain or regret; repent of, be sorry for. Long chiefly *Sc.* ME.

2 G. WHETSTONE Forthinke of thy forepassed faultes. W. WARNER Wel may I fore think mee so to haue done. 3 R. BOLT If you will even now forthink and repent of your obstinate opinions, you may still taste his gracious pardon.

†**forthink** *v.*[2] ME. [f. FOR-[1] + THINK *v.*[1]] 1 *v.t.* Displease, cause regret to. ME–M16. 2 *v.t.* Cause regret or repentance in (a person). Foll. by *of*, *for*, *that*. ME–L16.

1 CHAUCER I nas, ne nevere to be I thenke, Ayens a thing that myght the forthenke. 2 A. KING It forthinkes me sore that I haue sinned.

†**forth on** *adv.* Also **forthon** OE. [f. FORTH *adv.* + ON *adv.*] 1 Straight away, forthwith. OE–ME. 2 Of time or space: onwards, forwards. L15–E17.

2 A. GOLDING From the beginning foorthon, Moyses and the Prophets gaue it you. SHAKES. *Timon* My free drift . . . flies an eagle flight . . forth on.

forthright /ˈfɔːθraɪt, fɔːθˈraɪt/ *adv.*, *a.*, & *n.* OE. [f. FORTH *adv.* + -RIGHT.] A *adv.* 1 Straight forward, in a direct manner. OE. 2 Straight away, immediately. ME.

1 KEATS Until impatient in embarrassment he forthright pass'd. 2 SPENSER Whose dore forthright To him did open as it had beene taught.

B *adj.* 1 Proceeding in a straight course. *arch.* OE. 2 Straightforward, outspoken; decisive, unhesitating; unswerving. M19.

1 R. L. STEVENSON A headlong, forth-right tide. 2 J. A. MICHENER He was an attractive man, forthright and generous in his impulses. M. FORSTER She was forthright and daring and could not stand artifice of any kind.

C *n.* A straight course. E17.

SHAKES. *Temp.* Here's a maze trod, indeed, through forth-rights and meanders!

forthrightly *adv.* M20. **forthrightness** *n.* straightforwardness L19.

forthward /ˈfɔːθwəd/ *adv.* & *a.* *arch.* [OE *forþweard*, f. FORTH *adv.* + -WARD. Cf. FORWARD *adv.*, *a.*, & *n.*] A *adv.* †1 Continually. Only in OE. 2 From a specified time onwards, hereafter. ME. 3 Forward, onward, ahead; out, away (from a place). ME. B *adj.* = FORWARD *a.* *rare*. L15.

forthwith /fɔːθˈwɪθ, -ð/ *adv.* ME. [Partly abbrev. of next, but partly f. *forth with* s.v. FORTH *adv.*, used absol.] †1 Along with, at the same time. Only in ME. 2 Immediately, at once, without delay. LME.

2 R. COBB She would write forthwith to my parents and let them know how I had behaved.

†**forthwithal** *adv.* ME–M16. [f. FORTH *adv.* + WITH *prep.* + ALL *pron.* Cf. WITHAL.] = FORTHWITH 2.

†**for-thy** *conj.* OE–M19. [OE *forþī*, *forþȳ*, f. FOR *prep.* + *þȳ*, instr. of THE: see THE *adv.*] For this reason, therefore.

fortieth /ˈfɔːtɪɪθ/ *a.* & *n.* (*ordinal numeral*). [OE *fēowertigoþa*, f. as FORTY + -TH[2].] A *adj.* Next in order after the thirty-ninth; that is number forty in a series, (represented by 40th). OE.

fortieth part *arch.* = sense B.2 below.

B *n.* 1 The fortieth person or thing of a category, series, etc., identified contextually. M18. 2 Each of forty equal parts into which something is or may be divided, a fraction which when multiplied by forty gives one, (= *fortieth part* above). E19.

Comb.: Forming compound numerals with multiples of a hundred, as *two-hundred-and-fortieth* (*240th*) etc., and (*arch.*) with numerals below ten, as *five-and-fortieth* etc.

fortification /ˌfɔːtɪfɪˈkeɪʃ(ə)n/ *n.* LME. [Fr. f. late L *fortificatio(n-)*, f. *fortificat-* pa. ppl stem of *fortificare*: see FORTIFY, -ATION.] I The action of fortifying. 1 *Mil.* The action of fortifying or providing with defensive works. LME. b The art or science of fortifying or providing with defensive works. M17. †2 Strengthening, corroboration, ratification. L15–E17. 3 The strengthening of wine with alcohol, esp. a spirit. L19. b The addition of nutrients, such as vitamins, to food. M20.

1 W. RALEIGH Much common good . . likely to arise with mutual fortification of both those kingdoms.

II 4 *Mil.* A defensive work; a wall, tower, earthwork, etc. Usu. in *pl.*, such works collectively. LME. b *transf.* & *fig.* A means of defence. L16. 5†a *Gunnery.* The additional thickness of metal serving to strengthen parts of a cannon. E–M17. †b *gen.* A means of strengthening. M–L17. c *spec.* The strengthening timbers etc. of a ship, esp. a whaling vessel. *rare*. E19.

4 C. LYELL Extensive fortifications to protect them from their enemies. **fortification spectra** = TEICHOPSIA.

fortified /ˈfɔːtɪfʌɪd/ *ppl a.* L15. [f. FORTIFY *v.* + -ED[1].] 1 Strengthened; provided with means of defence; protected with fortifications. L15. 2a Of wine: strengthened with alcohol, esp. a spirit. E20. b Of food: given an increased nutritive value, esp. by the addition of vitamins. E20.

fortify /ˈfɔːtɪfʌɪ/ *v.* LME. [(O)Fr. *fortifier* f. late L *fortificare*, f. L *fortis* strong: see -FY.] I Make strong. 1 *v.t.* Strengthen the structure of. LME. b *spec.* Strengthen (a gun) by additional thickness of metal; strengthen (a ship) by additional timbers etc. E17. c Cover or bind with some protective material or appliance. Now passing into senses 7 and 8. E17. 2 *v.t.* Impart strength or vigour to; give (a person, oneself) strength or endurance for some effort. LME. 3 *v.t.* a Strengthen mentally or morally; cheer, encourage. LME. b Confirm, add support to (a statement etc.). *arch.* LME. †4 *v.t.* Make more powerful or effective; reinforce with additional resources; garrison (a fortress). LME–E18. †5 *v.i.* Gain strength, grow strong. E–M17. 6 *v.t.* a Strengthen (wine) with alcohol, esp. a spirit. Freq. as *fortified* ppl a. L19. b Increase the nutritive value of (food), esp. with vitamins. M20.

1 DRYDEN The . . Bee . . Employ'd at home . . to fortify the Combs. c WELLINGTON Kegs . . well fortified with iron hoops. 2 B. BAINBRIDGE To fortify herself for the task ahead she allowed herself a little more brandy. 3a S. LEWIS The assurance of Tanis Judique's friendship fortified Babbitt's self-approval. b H. MARTINEAU A distinct charge is brought against you, fortified by particulars. 4 E. HALL He fortified Burdeaux with Englishmen. 6b *Which?* Instant potato contains no vitamin C, unless it has been fortified.

II Strengthen against attack. 7 *v.t.* Provide (a town etc.) with defensive works; protect with fortifications. LME. 8 *v.t.* Surround (an army etc.) with defences; put in a state of defence. L15. 9 *v.i.* Erect fortifications; establish a defensive position. L16.

7 W. ROBERTSON These were . . commanded to fortify Leith. 8 F. FITZGERALD The Vietnamese would have to fortify Vietnamese hamlets against other Vietnamese. 9 U. S. GRANT The enemy was fortifying at Corinth.

fortifiable *a.* E17. **fortifier** *n.* M16.

†**fortilage** *n.* var. of FORTALICE.

Fortin /ˈfɔːtɪn/ *n.* L19. [J. N. *Fortin* (1750–1831), Fr. instrument-maker.] *Fortin('s) barometer*, a barometer with an adjustable reservoir of mercury.

fortis /ˈfɔːtɪs/ *n.* & *a.* L19. [L = strong.] **A** *n.* Pl. (in sense 2) **-tes** /-tiːz/. 1 A variety of dynamite. L19. 2 *Phonet.* A fortis consonant. M20. **B** *adj. Phonet.* Of a consonant: strongly articulated; *spec.* designating the more or most strongly articulated of two or more homorganic consonants. E20.

¶ In *Phonet.* opp. *lenis.*

fortissimo /fɔːˈtɪsɪməʊ/ *adv.*, *a.*, & *n.* E18. [It., superl. of FORTE *adv.*, *a.*, & *n.*[2]] *Mus.* **A** *adv.* & *adj.* (A direction:) very loud(ly). (Abbrev. *ff.*) E18. **B** *n.* Pl. **-mos, -mi** /-mi/. A very loud tone or passage. M19.

fortitude /ˈfɔːtɪtjuːd/ *n.* ME. [(O)Fr. f. L *fortitudo, -din-*, f. *fortis* strong: see -TUDE.] 1 Moral strength or courage, esp. in the endurance of pain or adversity. (One of the four cardinal virtues.) ME. †2 Physical or structural strength. LME–E18. 3 *Astrol.* A dignity. Long *rare* or *obs.* M16.

1 C. C. TRENCH She bore with fortitude her husband's absence. J. BUCHAN To go tandem-driving with him at Oxford required fortitude, for he was very blind. 2 R. EDEN A beast . . excellinge all other beastes in fortitude and strength.

fortiˈtudinous *a.* endowed with or characterized by fortitude M18.

fortlet /ˈfɔːtlɪt/ *n.* ME. [f. FORT *n.* + -LET.] A small fort.

fortnight /ˈfɔːtnʌɪt/ *n.* [OE *fēowertīene niht*: see FOURTEEN, NIGHT *n.*] A period of two weeks.

Financial Times The Islamic year . . has less than a fortnight to run. **a fortnight (from) today, Monday, last Tuesday**, etc., a fortnight after today, Monday, last Tuesday, etc. **a fortnight on Monday** etc. a fortnight after Monday etc. **Monday, this day, today**, etc., **fortnight** a fortnight from Monday, this day, today, etc.

fortnightly /ˈfɔːtnʌɪtli/ *a.* & *n.* E19. [f. prec. + -LY[1].] **A** *adj.* Produced or occurring fortnightly; paid etc. fortnightly. E19. **B** *n.* A newspaper or magazine published fortnightly. (In earliest use spec. *The Fortnightly Review.*) E20.

fortnightly /ˈfɔːtnʌɪtli/ *adv.* E19. [f. as prec. + -LY[2].] Every fortnight, by the fortnight.

Fortran /ˈfɔːtran/ *n.* Also **f-**, **FORTRAN**. M20. [f. *for(mula tran(slation.*] (The name of) a programming language used esp. for scientific calculations.

fortravail /fɔːˈtraveɪl, fə-/ *v.t. obs.* exc. *Sc.* Also **-travel** /-ˈtrav(ə)l/. ME. [f. FOR-[1] + TRAVAIL *v.*] Exhaust with labour. Usu. in *pass.*

fortress /ˈfɔːtrɪs/ *n.* ME. [(O)Fr. *forteresse* strong place f. Proto-Romance, f. L *fortis* strong. Cf. FORT *n.*] A military stronghold, *esp.* a strongly fortified town fit for a large garrison.

K. CLARK His palace began as a fortress built on an almost impregnable rock. *fig.*: *Guardian* I have never seen a European policy as a policy of withdrawal into a fortress Europe.

fortress /ˈfɔːtrɪs/ *v.t. arch.* L15. [f. the n.] Fortify; protect (with or as with a fortress); serve as a fortress to.

fortuitism /fɔːˈtjuːɪtɪz(ə)m/ *n.* L19. [f. FORTUIT(OUS + -ISM.] The belief that adaptation in nature is due to mere chance.

fortuitist *n.* a person who believes in fortuitism L19.

fortuitous /fɔːˈtjuːɪtəs/ *a.* M17. [L *fortuitus*, f. *forte* by chance, f. *fors* chance, luck + -OUS.] That is due to or produced by chance; accidental, casual.

A. BRINK His presence is not fortuitous He has a role to play.

fortuitously *adv.* M17. **fortuitousness** *n.* the quality of being fortuitous, accident, chance M17.

fortuity /fɔːˈtjuːɪti/ *n.* M18. [Irreg. f. as prec.: see -ITY.] Fortuitousness; accident; a chance occurrence.

fortunate /ˈfɔːtʃ(ə)nət/ *a.* & *n.* LME. [L *fortunatus*, f. *fortuna*: see FORTUNE *n.*, -ATE[2].] **A** *adj.* 1 Favoured by fortune; lucky, prosperous. (Foll. by *to*, *to do.*) LME. 2 Bringing or presaging good fortune, auspicious, favourable. LME.

1 DAY LEWIS I was singularly fortunate to spend these summers of childhood among such people. *absol.*: *Scientific American* An armchair reader, envious of the fortunate who will visit the sites. 2 LD MACAULAY It ought to be considered as a most fortunate circumstance.

B *n.* A fortunate person or thing. Long *rare*. E17.

fortunateness *n.* M16.

†**fortunate** *v.t.* LME–L18. [L *fortunat-* pa. ppl stem of *fortunare*, f. *fortuna*: see FORTUNE *n.*, -ATE[3].] Make fortunate, give good fortune to, prosper.

fortunately /ˈfɔːtʃ(ə)nətli/ *adv.* M16. [f. FORTUNATE *a.* + -LY[2].] In a fortunate manner, luckily, successfully; (modifying a sentence) it is fortunate that.

W. S. MAUGHAM Bertha fortunately detested such festivities as did Miss Ley herself. G. VIDAL Fortunately, there were no ruins in sight.

fortune /ˈfɔːtʃuːn, -tʃ(ə)n/ *n.* ME. [(O)Fr. f. L *fortuna* chance as a divinity, (esp. good) luck.] 1 (Also **F-**.) Chance or luck as a power in human affairs; this power personified as a goddess. ME. †2 A chance, an accident; an adventure. ME–E18. b A mishap, a disaster. L15–E17. 3 *sing.* & in *pl.* The good or bad luck that befalls a person or an enterprise. LME. b A person's destiny. Chiefly in *tell a person's fortune* below. LME. 4 Good luck; success, prosperity. LME. 5 Position as determined by wealth; wealth; a substantial amount of money etc. M16. 6 *sing.* & in *pl.* A person's condition or standing in life; a prosperous condition. E17. 7 A wealthy woman, an heiress. *obs.* exc. in *marry a fortune* below. M17. 8 *Astrol.* A planet, esp. in a favourable aspect; *spec.* the planet Saturn, the planet Jupiter. L17.

1 LD MACAULAY When fortune changed . . his real propensities began to show themselves. 2 T. STANLEY Many other good Fortunes happening to the Athenians . . are recorded. 3 J. R. GREEN On the fortunes of Philip hung the fortunes of English freedom. A. C. BOULT It has not been my good fortune to see inside many of the great London homes. 4 J. HARINGTON A herald by great fortune found out his pedigree. 5 D. CARNEGIE George Eastman . . amassed a fortune of a $100 million. D. CAUTE A leather shoulder bag that had cost a fortune. 6 JANET MORGAN The Millers . . looked equally prosperous . . but their fortunes, too, were imperceptibly growing shakier.

Phrases: **a small fortune** a large amount of money. †**by fortune** by chance. *Fortune's wheel*: see WHEEL *n.* 8. *hostage to fortune*: see HOSTAGE *n.*[1] **make a, one's fortune** become rich. **man** etc. **of fortune** a person possessing great (usu. inherited) wealth. **marry a fortune** *arch.* marry a rich heiress. *push one's fortune*: see PUSH *v.* **seek, try, one's fortune** pursue, make trial of, one's luck, esp. in the hope of achieving wealth and position. **soldier of fortune** an adventurous person ready to take service under any person or State in return for money; a mercenary. **tell a person's fortune** supposedly foretell a person's future by palmistry etc. *tempt fortune*: see TEMPT *v. try one's fortune*: see *seek one's fortune* above. *wheel of fortune*: see WHEEL *n.*

Comb.: **fortune cookie** *N. Amer.* a baked dough cake containing a prediction etc. on a slip of paper; **Fortune 500, Fortune 1000**, *US* (an annual list of) the five hundred (from 1970 the one thousand) most profitable US industrial corporations. **fortune-hunter** a person who indulges in fortune-hunting; **fortune-hunting** attempting to secure a fortune for oneself, esp. by marrying a wealthy woman; **fortune-teller** a person who practises fortune-telling; **fortune-telling** supposedly foretelling a person's future by palmistry etc.

fortuneless *a.* L16.

fortune /ˈfɔːtʃuːn, -tʃ(ə)n/ *v.* LME. [OFr. *fortuner* f. L *fortunare* make fortunate, f. *fortuna*: see prec.] †1 *v.t.* Assign a (specified) fortune to (a person etc.); control the fortunes of. LME–E17. b Destine (a person) *to* (*to do* something); ordain (something) *to* happen. LME–E17. 2 *v.i.* Happen, chance, occur. Usu. *impers.* in *it fortuned that*. Now *arch.* or *poet.* LME. 3 *v.i.* †a Happen, chance, *to be*, *to do*. LME–L18. b Come by chance *on*. *rare.* M17. 4 *v.t.* Orig. (foll. by *off*, *out*), find a husband for (a girl) by providing a dowry. Later, endow with wealth or fortune, dower. Now *rare*. Cf. earlier FORTUNED 2. M18.

fortuned /ˈfɔːtʃ(ə)nd/ *a.* Now *rare*. LME. [f. FORTUNE *n.*, *v.*: see -ED[2], -ED[1].] 1 Having or characterized by a (specified) fortune. Formerly also, fortunate. LME. 2 Possessed of a fortune or portion, wealthy. M17.

†**fortunize** *v.t. rare*. Also **-ise**. L16–M17. [f. FORTUNE *n.* + -IZE.] Regulate the fortunes of; make fortunate.

forty /ˈfɔːti/ *a.* & *n.* (*cardinal numeral*). [OE *fēowertiġ* = OFris. *fiuwertich*, OS *fiwartich* (Du. *veertig*), OHG *fiorzug* (G *vierzig*), ON *fjórir tigir*, Goth. *fidwor tigjus*: see FOUR, -TY[2].] **A** *adj.* 1 Four times ten (a cardinal numeral represented by 40 in arabic numerals, xl, XL in roman). OE. b A large indefinite number. E17.

1 C. READE Dietrich's forty years weighed him down like forty bullets. **forty hours** in the Roman Catholic Church the continuous exposition of the Host for forty hours, used as an occasion of special devotion or intercession. **forty winks** *colloq.* a short sleep, *esp.* one taken after a meal; a nap. b G. HERBERT I have forty businesses in my hands.

B *n.* 1 Forty persons or things identified contextually, as years of age, points, runs, etc., in a game, chances (in giving odds), minutes, etc. OE. 2 A set of forty; a thing having a set of forty as an essential or distinguishing feature. ME. b One fourth of a quarter section of land, comprising forty acres (approx. 16.2 hectares). *US.* M19. 3 Four times ten as an abstract number; the symbols or figures representing this (40 in arabic numerals, xl, XL in roman). ME. 4 The fortieth of a set or series with numbered members; the one designated forty, (usu. *number forty*, or with specification, as *chapter forty*, *verse forty*, etc.); a size etc. denoted by forty, a garment etc. of such a size, (also *size forty*). E16. 5 In *pl.* The numbers from 40 to 49 inclusive, esp. denoting years of a century or units of a scale of temperature; *one's* years of life between the ages of 40 and 49. L19. 6 A crook, a thief, a sharper. *Austral. slang.* L19.

1 G. BERKELEY Alciphron is above forty. 5 GEORGIANA HILL What were called half-caps were worn in the early forties. HUNGRY *forties*. **roaring forties** stormy ocean tracts between latitude 40° and 50° south. **the Forties** the sea area between the north-east coast of Scotland and the south-west coast of Norway (from its depth of over 40 fathoms) (also *the long Forties*).

Comb.: Forming compound numerals (cardinal or ordinal) with numerals below ten, as *forty-nine* (*49*), *forty-first* (*41st*), etc. , and (cardinals) with multiples of a hundred, as *340* (read *three hundred and forty*, US also *three hundred forty*), etc. With ns. + -ER[1] forming ns. w. the sense 'something (identified contextually) being of or having forty —s', as *forty-seater* etc. Special combs., as **forty acre** *US* & *NZ* a section of land comprising forty acres; **forty-eight** (*a*) a plant-pot of which forty-eight are formed from one cast of clay; (*b*) in *pl.*, forty-eight leaves to the sheet in a printed book; (*c*) the forty-eight preludes and fugues of J. S. Bach; **forty-five** (*a*) *the Forty-five*, the Jacobite rebellion of 1745; (*b*) a card-game in which each trick counts five and the game is forty-five; (*c*) *N. Amer.* a revolver of .45 calibre; (*d*) a 45-rpm 7-inch microgroove gramophone record; **forty-footer** a forty-foot yacht; **forty-niner** a gold-digger who settled in California during the gold fever of 1849.

fortyfold *a.* & *adv.* (*a*) *adj.* forty times as great or as numerous; having forty parts, divisions, elements, or units; (*b*) *adv.* to forty times the number or quantity: OE. **fortyish** *a.* about forty (in age, measurements, etc.) E19.

forum /ˈfɔːrəm/ *n.* Pl. **-rums, -ra** /-rə/. LME. [L, rel. to *fores* (outside) door, orig. an enclosure surrounding a house.] 1 *Rom. Antiq.* The public place or market-place of a city; the place of assembly for judicial and other business, esp. at Rome. LME. b A place of or meeting for public discussion; a periodical etc. which provides an opportunity for conducting a debate. M18. **2** A court, a tribunal (*lit.* & *fig.*). L17.

1 GIBBON The principal Forum; which appears to have been of a circular, or rather elliptical form. b L. NKOSI During its .. run to town the bus becomes a great forum for the airing of political views. 2 *fig.*: J. MORLEY It is truth that in the forum of conscience claims an undivided allegiance.

Comb.: **forum shopping** (orig. *US*) the practice by a plaintiff of seeking out the court felt most likely to give a sympathetic hearing to his or her case.

forwander /fɔːˈwɒndə, fə-/. *v.i.* Now *arch.* exc. *Sc.* ME. [f. FOR-¹ + WANDER *v.*] Weary oneself with wandering; wander far and wide. Usu. in *pass.*

forward /ˈfɔːwəd/ *v.t.* L16. [f. FORWARD *adv.*] **1** Orig., put forward, set on foot. Later, help forward, promote. L16. **2** Accelerate the growth of (a plant etc.). E17. **3** †**a** Pass on, make known widely. Only in E18. **b** Send forward; send (a letter etc.) on to a further destination; *Comm.* dispatch (goods etc.). M18. **4** *Bookbinding.* Prepare (a book) for finishing by putting a plain cover on. L19.

1 E. A. FREEMAN To protect its rights and to forward its interests. M. DE LA ROCHE George Fennel .. came to see him, and still further forwarded his recovery. 2 SWIFT I forward the grass, and I ripen the vine. 3b W. GOLDING Forwarding address: Rinderpest, Bloemfontein, SA. J. N. ISBISTER His name was forwarded, and he was duly elected. **forwarding agent, merchant**, a person whose business is the receiving and shipment or transmission of goods.

forward /ˈfɔːwəd/ *adv.*, *a.*, & *n.* As adv. also **-wards** /-wədz/. [OE *forweard* var. of *forþweard*: see FORTHWARD.] **A** *adv.* **1** Towards the future, continuously onwards. Now chiefly in *from this day* etc. *forward, look forward to*, below. OE. **b** *Comm.* For future delivery or payment. L19. †**2** Further on in a series; onwards from a specified point. LME–M17. **3** Towards what is in front, onwards. LME. **4** Towards the front, in the direction in which one is facing. E16. **5** At an advanced point; in advance; ahead; at a point beyond another. E16. **6** *fig.* Onward, so as to make progress. E16. **7** To the front (from being behind); to the foreground (from being in the background); into view. E17. **8** *Naut.* & *Aeronaut.* In, near, to, or towards, the bow or nose. M17.

1 S. SMILES The elder student from that time forward acted as the Mentor of the younger one. **from this day** etc. **forward** from this day etc. onwards. *look forward to*: see LOOK *v.* b *Farmers Weekly* He sold 300t of feed barley forward in August for January collection. 2 MARVELL I am this day beginning my long journey to Archangel, and so forward. 3 M. SINCLAIR She hurled herself forward and he caught her. E. WAUGH The crowds .. shuffled forward towards the Abbey. *backward(s) and forward(s)*: see BACKWARD *adv.* 4. *fast-forward*: see FAST *adv.* *Great Leap Forward*: see GREAT *a.* *leap forward*: see LEAP *n.*¹ *put one's best foot forward*: see BEST *a.* etc. 4 E. BOWEN Lilian wore her hair forward over her shoulders in two .. braids. J. M. COETZEE His mother sat with .. her head drooping forward. *play forward*: see PLAY *v.* 5 AV *Num.* 32:19 Wee will not inherite with them on yonder side Iordane, or forward. 6 F. SWINNERTON Determination spurred her forward. **go forward** be going on, progress. 7 A. RADCLIFFE Dorothee, who had lingered far behind, was called forward. *bring forward*: see BRING *v.* *carry forward*: see CARRY *v.* **come forward** offer oneself for a task, post, etc. *put forward*: see PUT *v.*¹ *set forward*: see SET *v.*¹ 8 F. ASTAIRE To lie down in his bunk up forward just outside the cockpit.

Comb.: **forward-looking** *a.* (of a person etc.) progressive; **forward-scatter** *v.t.* scatter (radiation etc.) through an angle of less than 90° with respect to the original direction; **forward scatter(ing)** scattering of radiation etc. involving a change of direction of less than 90°; radiation etc. so scattered; *esp.* propagation of high-frequency radio waves beyond the horizon by scattering or reflection from the ionosphere.

B *adj.* †**1** Belonging to a front part or to the earliest part. Only in OE. **2** Situated in the forepart. Long *rare* or *obs.* in *gen.* sense. ME. **b** Orig., that lies in front. Later, that lies in the direction towards which one is moving. M17. **c** *Naut.* & *Aeronaut.* Belonging to the forepart of a ship etc.; that is in or near or to or towards the bow or nose. L19. **3** That is in an advanced state or condition; progressing towards maturity or completion. Chiefly *pred.* E16. **b** Of a plant, a crop, the season: well advanced, early. L16. **c** Of a pregnant animal: *in* or *with* foal etc. L17. **4** Ready, prompt, eager, (*to do*). Formerly also, inclined *to* or *for*. *arch.* E16. **b** Ardent, spirited, zealous. Now *rare* or *obs.* E17. **5** Presumptuous, pert. M16. **6** Well advanced for one's years, precocious. L16. **7** Directed towards a point in advance, onward, towards the front. E17. **b** *Cricket.* Designating or pertaining to a stroke made in playing forward (see *play forward* s.v. PLAY *v.*). L19. **c** *Football* etc. Of a pass: towards one's opponents' goal-line. L19. **8** Of opinions etc.: advanced, extreme; *esp.* favouring or advocating vigorous aggressive action. E17. **9a** *Comm.* Of a business transaction, contract, etc.: relating to future produce, delivery, etc. L19. **b** Prospective; advanced; with a view to the future. M20.

2 SHAKES. *All's Well* Let's take the instant by the forward top. b A. W. KINGLAKE Out of the forward horizon. c F. CHICHESTER The forward half of *Gipsy Moth* was in smooth water. D. LODGE Taking one's place in the forward passenger cabin of a wide-bodied jet. 3 MRS H. WOOD A sturdy little fellow .. sufficiently forward in walking to get about the room. *Landscape* The two wines at their best .. are fruity and forward, with a charm that develops early. 4 M. PATTISON Authors were always forward to send him copies of their learned publications. b WELLINGTON He is a gallant, forward officer. 5 W. S. MAUGHAM There was nothing saucy in her manner, forward or pert. 6 PRINCESS ALICE My children .. are so forward, clever, and spirited. 7 H. H. WILSON General Wood was compelled .. to undertake a forward movement. 8 *Pall Mall Gazette* Denouncing outrage and dynamite, and what are generally known as 'forward' measures. 9a *Daily News* Consumers will not pay this price for forward contracts. b *Financial Times* Elridge's forward planning was aggressive and ambitious.

C *n.* †**1** The fore or front part; the first part. OE–ME. **2** (The position of) an attacking player in football, hockey, etc. L19.

forwardly *adv.* in a forward manner; *US* in a forward direction: M16. **forwardness** *n.* E16.

forwarder /ˈfɔːwədə/ *n.* M16. [f. FORWARD *v.* + -ER¹.] A person who or thing which forwards something.

forwarder /ˈfɔːwədə/ *a.* & *adv.* Also (*joc. colloq.*) **forrader** /ˈfɒrədə/. L18. [Compar. of FORWARD *a.* & *adv.*: see -ER³.] Further forward.

can't get any or **no forwarder** can make no progress.

forwards *adv.* see FORWARD *adv.*, *a.*, & *n.*

†**forwarn** *v.t.* Also **fore-**. OE–E19. [f. FOR-¹ + WARN *v.*²] Prohibit, forbid.

†**forwaste** *v.t.* M16–M17. [f. FOR-¹ + WASTE *v.*] Waste; use up, exhaust; lay waste; make feeble.

†**forwear** *v.t.* Infl. as WEAR *v.*¹ See also FORWORN *a.* ME–E17. [f. FOR-¹ + WEAR *v.*¹] Wear out, wear away, exhaust.

forwearied /fɔːˈwɪərɪd/ *a. arch.* M16. [pa. pple of FORWEARY: see -ED¹.] Tired out.

forweary /fɔːˈwɪəri/ *v.t. arch.* ME. [f. FOR-¹ + WEARY *v.*] Weary, tire out.

forwent *v.* pa. t.: see FORGO.

forwhy /fəˈwʌɪ/ *adv.* & *conj.* Also as two wds. OE. [f. FOR *prep.* + WHY.] **A** *adv.* **1** *interrog.* For what reason, why? OE. †**2** *rel.* On account of which, wherefore. ME–E17.

1 W. KETHE For why? The Lord our God is good. K. HULME She is surprised by that, although she can't say for why.

B *conj.* **1** Because. ME. †**2** = FOR *conj.* 2. ME–E17.

forworn /fɔːˈwɔːn/ *a. arch.* E16. [pa. pple of FORWEAR.] Tired out.

foryield /fɔːˈjiːld, fə-/ *v.t. obs.* exc. *Sc.* [OE *forgieldan* = OHG *fargeltan* (G *vergelten*), f. as FOR-¹ + YIELD *v.*] Pay, recompense, requite.

forzando /fɔːtˈsandəʊ/ *adv.* & *a.* E19. [It., f. *forzare* to force.] *Mus.* (A direction:) with force or emphasis; = SFORZANDO.

Fosbury flop /fɒzb(ə)ri ˈflɒp/ *n. phr.* M20. [f. Richard (Dick) *Fosbury* (b. 1947), US athlete and 1968 Olympic gold-medallist + FLOP *n.*] A method of high jumping in which the athlete leaps head first and arches the back in attempting to clear the bar.

foss *n.*¹ var. of FOSSE.

foss *n.*² var. of FORCE *n.*²

fossa /ˈfɒsə/ *n.*¹ Pl. **fossae** /ˈfɒsiː/. M17. [L = ditch, f. fem. pa. pple of *fodere* dig.] *Anat.* A shallow depression or cavity.

fossa /ˈfɒsə/ *n.*² M19. [Malagasy *fosa*. Cf. next.] A red-brown catlike viverrid mammal, *Cryptoprocta ferox*, the largest carnivore of Madagascar.

fossane /ˈfɒseɪn/ *n.* L18. [Fr., f. as prec.] The Malagasy civet, *Fossa fossa*, a foxlike brown spotted nocturnal viverrid mammal of Madagascar.

fosse /fɒs/ *n.* Also **foss**. LOE. [(O)Fr., f. L *fossa*: see FOSSA *n.*¹] **1** A canal, a ditch, a trench; *esp.* one serving as a barrier or defence, a moat. Earliest as a name (now *the Fosse*, the *Fosse Way*) of one of the four great Roman roads in Britain, so called from the ditch on each side, and probably running from Axminster to Lincoln. LOE. †**2** A deep hole or pit; a grave or place for sacrifice. L15–M19. **3** *Anat.* = FOSSA *n.*¹ M18.

1 R. GRAVES Strengthening the ancient City ramparts, clearing and deepening the choked fosse. 2 F. FAWKES A deep round foss he made, And on the kindling wood the victim laid.

fossed *a.* (*rare*) surrounded (as) by a fosse L17.

fossé /ˈfɒseɪ/ *n.* Also (earlier, *Sc.*) **foussie** /ˈfuːsi/. E16. [Fr., f. late L *fossatum* neut. pa. pple of L *fossare* frequent. of *fodere* dig.] = FOSSE 1.

fossette /fɒˈsɛt/ *n.* M19. [Fr., dim. of *fosse*: see -ETTE.] Chiefly *Zool.* A small hollow or depression, as in a bone or shell.

fossick /ˈfɒsɪk/ *v.* Chiefly *Austral.* & *NZ.* M19. [Origin unkn.: sense 3 is almost certainly the earliest.] **1** *v.i.* In *Mining*, search for gold in abandoned workings, or by digging out crevices etc.; *gen.* search, rummage about or *about.* M19. **2** *v.t.* Search (a place etc.); dig *out* or *up.* M19. **3** *v.t.* Obtain by asking, ferret out. *dial.* L19.

1 C. BARRETT An Arab fossicking among potsherds on a low mound, held up a verdigrised copper coin. H. P. TRITTON Most were fossicking in the creeks and gullies and the old workings. P. CAREY The Joys were seen .. fossicking out at the tip for their neighbours' rejected furniture. 2 B. CRONIN No one will get to fossicking those tents while Pup's there. F. CHICHESTER I felt hungry and fossicked out the remains of the excellent jam and egg sandwiches.

fossicker *n.* M19.

fossil /ˈfɒs(ə)l, -sɪl/ *n.* & *a.* M16. [Fr. *fossile*, f. L *fossilis* dug up, f. *foss-* pa. ppl stem of *fodere* dig: see -ILE.] **A** *n.* †**1** A fossilized fish found, and believed to have lived, underground. Only in M16. **2** Orig., any rock or mineral dug out of the earth. Later, anything preserved in the strata of the earth and recognizable as the remains or vestiges of a plant or animal of a former (usu. prehistoric) geological period. E17. **3** A person, thing, or idea belonging to the past or incapable of development or change; a fossilized person or thing. M19. **4** A word or linguistic form preserved only in isolated regions or in set phrases or forms, as *hue* in *hue and cry*. M20.

2 JAN MORRIS The Dawn Redwood nearby was rediscovered .. in 1945, after centuries in which it was known only as a fossil. *attrib.*: D. ATTENBOROUGH Anyone can date many rocks .. and by doing so put into order the major events of fossil history. ZONAL (*guide*) *fossil*.

B *adj.* **1** Found buried in the earth, dug up. Now chiefly, of the nature of a fossil (sense A.2 above). M17. **2** Belonging to the past, antiquated; fixed; incapable of change or development. M19.

1 P. MATTHIESSEN Close by one print an imprint of lost ages, a fernlike fossil brachiopod in a broken stone. **fossil fuel** any fuel, as coal or petroleum, formed below ground from the remains of plants and animals during the geological past. 2 ALDOUS HUXLEY But in practice and emotionally he was a child, a fossil mid-Victorian child.

fossilate *v.t.* & *i.* (cause to) become a fossil E19. **fossiˈlation** *n.* L19. **fossildom** *n.* the condition or character of being a fossil L19. **fossiled** *a.* fossilized M19. **fossiˈliferous** *a.* containing fossils or organic remains L19. **fossilist** *n.* (now *rare*) a palaeontologist M18. †**fossilogy** *n.* palaeontology L18–M19.

fossilize /ˈfɒs(ə)lʌɪz, -sɪl-/ *v.t.* & *i.* Also **-ise**. L18. [f. FOSSIL *n.* + -IZE.] 1 (Cause to) become a fossil. L18. 2 (Cause to) become antiquated, fixed, or incapable of change or development. M19.

1 T. O'BRIEN He could.. imagine himself finally stopping and freezing and fossilizing. D. ATTENBOROUGH It is difficult to believe that.. a jellyfish could retain its shape long enough to be fossilized. 2 A. CARNEGIE Long years of peace had fossilized the service. B. M. H. STRANG Fossilised survivals of the old pattern of prenegation (*nill* = *won't*).

fossilizable *a.* E20. **fossiliˈzation** *n.* E19.

fossor /ˈfɒsə/ *n.* M19. [L = digger, miner, (in late L) gravedigger, f. *foss-*: see FOSSIL, -OR.] 1 *Eccl. Hist.* An officer of the early Christian Church charged with the burial of the dead. M19. 2 [mod.L *Fossores* former taxonomic division.] Any of various sphecoid or other hymenopteran insects with legs adapted for digging or nest-building; a digger-wasp. L19.

fossorial /fɒˈsɔːrɪəl/ *a.* M19. [f. med.L *fossorius* (f. as prec.) + -IAL.] 1 Of an animal: that habitually burrows or digs. M19. 2 Of or pertaining to burrowing animals; *esp.* (of a limb etc.) adapted for burrowing. M19.

fossula /ˈfɒsjʊlə/ *n.* Pl. **-lae** /-liː/. M19. [L, dim. of *fossa*: see FOSSA *n.*[1], -ULE.] Chiefly *Zool.* A small fossa or depression.

foster /ˈfɒstə/ *n.*[1] & *a.* [OE *fōster* f. Gmc base of FOOD + instr. suff. In branch A.II f. the adj.] **A** *n.* †**I1** Food, nourishment. OE–L17. 2 Care, keeping, fostering. *rare.* ME–M19. **II3** A foster-parent; a nurse. *arch.* OE. 4 A foster-child. Formerly also, offspring. Long only *Sc.* ME.

B *attrib.* or as *adj.* (Freq. w. hyphen.) 1 Having a specified familial relationship not by blood or adoption, but by virtue of nursing, bringing up, or care, as *foster-brother, foster-daughter, foster-sister, foster-son.* OE. 2 Concerned with the care of orphans, or children in need of a temporary but stable home. L19.

1 M. FORSTER My idea of happiness was to have a family... Even an adoptive or foster family would have sufficed. 2 T. KENEALLY When I was twelve I went to a foster-home, a childless couple in Connecticut.

Comb. & *special collocations*: **foster-child** a child nursed or brought up as their own by people other than his or her biological or adoptive parents; **foster-father** a man who brings up a child as his own; the husband of a wet-nurse; **foster-mother** (*a*) a woman who nurses and brings up a child as her own, or on behalf of the child's natural mother; (*b*) an apparatus for rearing chickens hatched in an incubator; **foster-nurse** a nurse who brings up a child as her own.

†**foster** *n.*[2] LME–L17. [Contr.] = FORESTER.

foster /ˈfɒstə/ *v.* [OE *fōstrian* (= ON *fóstra*), f. as FOSTER *n.*[1] & *a.*] 1 *v.t.* Nourish, feed. Now chiefly *fig.* OE. 2**a** *v.t.* & *i.* Raise (a child). Now only, nurse or bring up (a child) as a foster-child, be a foster-parent (to). ME. †**b** *v.t.* Teach or train *in* (beliefs, habits, etc.). LME–L16. **c** *v.t.* Of an authority etc.: assign (a child) to be fostered. Also foll. by *out.* L20. 3 *v.t.* Encourage, harbour, or nurse (a feeling); (of circumstances) be conducive to; promote the development of; (now only with mixture of sense 4) encourage or help the growth of (a plant etc.). (Foll. by *up.*) ME. †**b** *v.t.* Encourage *in* a habit etc. M16–M17. 4 *v.t.* Tend with affectionate care, cherish; keep warm. *arch.* LME.

1 SHAKES. *Cymb.* One bred of alms and foster'd with cold dishes. 2 S. JOHNSON A Laird, a man of wealth and eminence, sends his child.. to a tacksman or tenant to be fostered. *Sunday Telegraph* A West Indian friend who fosters and I had a party together with all our children. 3 A. STORR Teachers hope to detect and foster creativity in their pupils. K. CROSSLEY-HOLLAND If you want a friend whom you can wholly trust, foster his friendship. 4 GOLDSMITH What a viper have I been fostering in my bosom!

fosterable *a.* M19.

fosterage /ˈfɒst(ə)rɪdʒ/ *n.* E17. [f. prec. + -AGE.] 1 The action of fostering a child; responsibility for fostering a child. E17. 2 *Hist.* The custom among the Scottish and Irish nobility of employing a tenant as a foster-mother. L18. 3 The action of encouraging or promoting something. E19.

fosterer /ˈfɒst(ə)rə/ *n.* LME. [f. as prec. + -ER[1].] 1 A person who fosters a child, a foster-parent. LME. 2 A person who or thing which encourages or promotes something or someone; a patron. L16. 3 A foster-brother; a foster-child. *Anglo-Ir.* M18.

fosterling /ˈfɒstəlɪŋ/ *n.* OE. [f. FOSTER *n.*[1] & *a.* + -LING[1].] A foster-child, a nursling; a protégé.

fostress /ˈfɒstrɪs/ *n.* E17. [f. as prec. + -ESS[1].] A female fosterer.

fother /ˈfɒðə/ *n.* [OE *fōþer* = OS *fōþar* (Du. *voer*), OHG *fuodar* (G *Fuder*), f. WGmc base, prob. f. ablaut var. of base meaning 'stretch out', as in FATHOM *n.*] 1 A cart-load; *fig.* an enormous quantity (of gold or money). *obs.* exc. *dial.* OE. **b** A mass; a quantity (of people etc.). ME. 2 A specific weight (latterly usu. 19½ hundredweight, approx. 990 kg) used for lead or (rarely) coal. ME.

fother /ˈfɒðə/ *v.* L18. [Prob. f. Du. *voederen* (now *voeren*), or LG *fodern* = G *füttern* to line.] *Naut.* 1 *v.t.* Cover (a sail) with oakum and draw it over a leak with the intention of stopping it. L18. 2 *v.i.* Stop a leak by this method. E19.

fou /fuː/ *a. Sc.* M16. [Var. of FULL *a.*] Inebriated, drunk.

Foucault /ˈfuːkəʊ, *foreign* fuko/ *n.* M19. [J. B. L. *Foucault* (1819–68), Fr. physicist.] Used *attrib.* and in *possess.* to designate things discovered, devised, or worked on by Foucault.

Foucault current an eddy current. **Foucault('s) pendulum** a pendulum designed to demonstrate the earth's rotation by the rotation of its plane of oscillation.

foudroyant /fuːˈdrɔɪənt, *foreign* fudrwajɑ̃/ *a.* M19. [Fr., pres. pple of *foudroyer* strike (as) with lightning, f. *foudre* f. L *fulgur* lightning: see -ANT[1].] 1 Thunderous, noisy. Also, dazzling. M19. 2 Of a disease: beginning suddenly and in a very severe form. L19.

fouetté /fwete (*pl. same*), ˈfwɛteɪ/ *n.* M19. [Fr., pa. pple of *fouetter* to whip.] *Ballet.* A step in which a dancer stands on one *pointe* and executes a rapid sideways movement with the free leg.

fougade /fuːˈgɑːd/ *n.* Now *rare.* M17. [Fr. f. It. *fogata*, f. †*fogare* flee, fly: see -ADE.] = FOUGASSE.

fougasse /fuːˈgɑːs/ *n.* E19. [Fr., alt. of *fougade*: see prec.] *Mil.* A land-mine filled with pieces of rock, metal, etc., designed to fly in a given direction when the explosive is lit.

fought /fɔːt/ *ppl a.* M16. [pa. pple of FIGHT *v.*] That has been fought. Chiefly w. specifying adv., as *well fought.*

fought *v.* pa. t. & pple of FIGHT *v.*

foughten /ˈfɔːt(ə)n/ *ppl a. arch.* M16. [pa. pple of FIGHT *v.*] Designating a field on which a battle has been fought.

foughty /ˈfaʊti/ *a. dial.* See also FOOTY *a.* E17. [Corresp. to Du. *vochtig*, Sw. *fuktig*, Da. *fugtig* damp: prob. already in OE.] Musty.

foujdar /ˈfaʊdʒdɑː/ *n. Anglo-Ind.* L17. [Pers. *fawjdār* military commander, f. Arab. *fawj* troop + Pers. *dār* holder.] A police officer. Formerly also, a criminal judge in Bengal.

foul /faʊl/ *n.* OE. [f. FOUL *a.* In sense 3 partly f. FOUL *v.*] 1 That which is foul. Opp. FAIR *n.*[2] OE. 2 *sing.* & (occas.) in *pl.* A disease in the feet of cattle. Now usu. *foul-in-the-foot, foul of the foot.* E16. 3 A collision or entanglement, esp. in rowing or running. M18. 4 A violation of the rules of a game, *esp.* one involving interference with play by an opponent; *Boxing* an illegal punch (one below the belt, etc.). L19.

1 **foul befall** *arch.* may evil befall. 4 **claim a foul** demand points in one's favour in a game or match because of foul play on the part of an opponent.

foul /faʊl/ *a.* [OE *fūl* = OFris., OS, OHG *fūl* (Du. *vuil* dirty, G *faul* rotten, lazy), ON *fúll*, Goth. *fūls* stinking, f. Gmc, f. IE base also of L PUS, *putere* to stink, Gk *puon, puos, puar* pus.] **I** Not wholesome, clean, or attractive. 1 Highly offensive to the senses; *esp.* smelling of decay. OE. **b** Of a disease, sore, etc.: marked by festering or gangrene. OE. 2 Not clean; dirty, soiled. Now *arch.* & *dial.*, exc. with mixture of sense 1: disgustingly dirty, filthy. OE. **b** Of a road etc.: muddy. LME. 3 *fig.* Of a person, action, etc.: repugnant to the moral sense; revoltingly or detestably wicked, vile. Chiefly *rhet.* OE. †**b** Guilty of a charge; implicated in a crime. ME–E17. 4 Of speech etc.: indecent, obscene. Also, disgustingly abusive. OE. 5 Shameful, discreditable. ME. 6 Not attractive in appearance; ugly, unsightly. Now *arch.* & *dial.* ME. **b** Of a sound: not pleasing to the ear. Now *dial.* LME. 7 Of weather: wet and windy. ME. **b** *Naut.* Of wind or tide: unfavourable to sailing. E18. 8 Of a misfortune etc.: wretchedly bad, grievous. LME. 9 Of manner, conduct, etc.: marked by violence, rough, harsh. Also, of a method: unscrupulous, dishonest; (esp. in *by fair means or foul*). LME. **b** *Sports* & *Games.* Not (acting) according to the rules. L16. 10 Of air, water, etc.: filled with impurities or (now chiefly) noxious matter. M16. **b** Dull, discoloured. *arch.* L16. 11 Of a diet or eater: consisting of or eating coarse food or (now chiefly) carrion. E18. 12 *hyperbol.* Extremely unpleasant or disagreeable. *dial.* & *colloq.* L18.

1 N. SHUTE The whole city was becoming foul and beginning to smell. J. LE CARRÉ The foul stench of decaying fish oil. **b** SHAKES. *A.Y.L.* I will.. Cleanse the foul body of th' infected world. 2 C. S. LEWIS A hamper full of his foul linen for your wife to wash. D. DAVIE Pavements foul with miners' spittle. 3 AV *Mark* 9:25 Iesus.. rebuked the foule spirit. C. THIRLWALL Aristophanes must stand convicted.. of the foulest motives. LD MACAULAY A court foul with all the vices of the Restoration. E. O'NEILL It is a foul sin in the sight of Jehovah. 4 P. H. GIBBS 'I believe you've got a German mistress.' 'You have a foul mind.' G. B. SHAW I called her the foulest names until she gave in. A. SILLITOE He cursed them in foul, well-polished language. 5 MILTON The dire event, That with sad overthrow and foul defeat Hath lost us Heav'n. 6 AV *Job* 16:16 My face is fowle with weeping. R. W. EMERSON There is no object so foul that.. light will not make beautiful. 7 J. BUCHAN It's a foul day, so you'd better stop indoors. 8 MILTON Eadbald, vext with an evil Spirit, fell.. into foul fits of distraction. 9 R. W. EMERSON War is a foul game. **b** *Times* A foul shot on the pink cost him six points. 10 JOYCE The very air.. becomes foul and unbreathable when it has been long enclosed. 12 C. CONNOLLY I had a foul journey. CLIVE JAMES He was foul to his children because by growing up they reminded him that he would.. die. *Balance* I was in a foul temper and in no mood for the delights ahead.

II Not clear, obstructed. 13 Clogged or impeded with foreign matter. (Now chiefly of a gun barrel or (*dial.*) of land overgrown with weeds.) L15. 14 *Naut.* Of a coast or sea bottom: rocky. Of a ship: having its keel overgrown with seaweed, barnacles, etc. E17. 15 *Naut.* Entangled with or impeded by something, and thus not having free movement. (Foll. by *of.*) E17.

13 F. NIGHTINGALE If your chimney is foul, sweep it. 15 G. W. MANBY A small axe to cut away the line, in case of its getting foul when running out.

Special collocations & *comb.*: **foul anchor** (*a*) an anchor which has become caught in some impediment; (*b*) *spec.* an anchor which has got its cable twisted round the stock or flukes; a representation of this, used as the seal of the Lord High Admiral of Britain. **foul ball** *Baseball* a ball struck so that it falls outside the lines drawn from the home base through the first and third bases. **foul brood** any of several bacterial diseases of larval bees, marked by a sickly unpleasant smell in the hive. **foul copy** (now *rare*) a first copy, defaced by corrections (opp. *fair copy*). †**foul disease** or **evil** (*a*) epilepsy; (*b*) syphilis. **foul Fiend** the Devil. **foul line**: marking the boundary of a playing area etc. **foul mouth** a person who uses foul language. **foul-mouthed** *a.* using foul language. **foul-mouthedness** foul-mouthed quality. **foul papers** pages of a first copy, defaced by corrections. **foul play** (*a*) unfair play in a game; (*b*) *transf.* dishonest or unscrupulous dealings; *spec.* violent crime resulting in another's death. **foul proof** a proofreader's marked proof (opp. to the clean or corrected copy which succeeds it). *foul strike*: see STRIKE *n.*[1] 11a. *foul tip*: see TIP *n.*[2]

foully *adv.* ME. **foulness** *n.* foul quality or state; a foul substance or deposit: OE.

foul /faʊl/ *v.* [OE *fūlian* = OHG *fūlōn* (G *faulen*). In ME prob. a new formation f. the adj.] **1** *v.i.* Be or become foul, dirty, or clogged. Now freq. foll. by *up*. OE. **2** *v.t.* Make foul or dirty, esp. with excrement. ME. **b** *v.i.* Of an animal: defecate. L15. **3** *v.t. fig.* Pollute with guilt; dishonour, disgrace. ME. **4** *v.t.* Make ugly, deface. Long *arch.* ME. **5** *v.t.* Chiefly *Naut.* Cause to become entangled. Also, make immovable; block, obstruct (a sea bottom etc.). E18. **b** *v.i.* Become entangled. M19. **c** *v.t.* Run foul of, collide with. M19. **6** *v.t.* & *i. Sport.* Be guilty of foul play against (an opponent or member of an opposing team). L19. **7** *v.i. Baseball.* Hit a foul ball. L19.

1 G. DURRELL The water fouled very quickly, so that it had to be changed three times a day. 2 N. MONSARRAT Grand Harbour . . was fouled by scum . . and dead fish. Q. BELL A stray dog . . having fouled the carpets beyond bearing. **foul one's (own) nest** *fig.* (*a*) bring discredit on one's family etc. by one's actions; (*b*) speak disparagingly of one's family etc. 3 CHESTERFIELD Your *Commensaux*, who . . foul themselves with . . scoundrel gamesters. 4 *Daily News* Passing . . to the main line the engine fouled the points. **5 fouled anchor** = *foul anchor* s.v. FOUL *a.* **b** F. FRANCIS He will be perpetually fouling in the branches. **c** THOMAS HUGHES He managed . . to get into Iffley lock . . without fouling the gates.

With advs. in specialized senses: **foul off** *v.phr.t.* (in *pass.*) = *foul out* (b) below; **foul out** (*a*) *v.phr.i.* (of a baseball batter) be made out by hitting a foul ball which is caught on the fly by one of the opposing team; (*b*) *v.phr.t.* (in *pass.*) & *i.* (in basketball) be put out of the game for exceeding the permitted number of fouls; **foul up** *v.phr.t.* & *i.* (*fig.*) throw or be thrown into confusion, mess or be messed up.

fouling *n.* (*a*) the action of the vb; (*b*) a foul deposit: LME.

foul /faʊl/ *adv.* OE. [f. the adj.] †**1** In a loathsome or stinking manner. OE–M16. †**2** Shamefully, disgracefully. ME–L16. †**3** Grievously, sorely. ME–L16. †**4** In an ugly manner. Only in LME. **5** Not in the correct or regular manner. L17. **6** *Naut.* Into a state of entanglement, into collision. L17. **7** In a manner contrary to the rules of a game or of fair play. E18.

2 SHAKES. *Rich. III* I'll have this crown of mine cut from my shoulders Before I'll see the crown so foul misplaced. 3 SPENSER Two of . . her nephews are so fowle forlorne. **6 fall foul of** (*a*) come into collision with; (*b*) quarrel with; (*c*) make an attack on. **run foul of** = *fall foul of* (a) above. **7 play a person foul** *fig.* behave treacherously to a person.

Comb.: **foul-hook** *v.t.* hook (a fish) elsewhere than in the mouth.

Foulah *n.* & *a.* var. of FULAH.

foulard /ˈfuːlɑː, -ɑːd/ *n.* M19. [Fr., of unkn. origin.] **1** A thin printed or checked material of silk or of silk and cotton. M19. **2** A handkerchief of this material. L19.

foulé /fule/ *n.* L19. [Fr. = pressed (cloth), pa. pple of *fouler* FULL *v.*[1]] A light woollen dress material with a fibrous appearance.

foulmart *n.* var. of FOUMART.

foul-up /ˈfaʊlʌp/ *n. colloq.* (orig. *US*). M20. [f. FOUL *v.* + UP *adv.*[1]] A confused situation; a muddle, a mess.

foumart /ˈfuːmət, -mɑːt/ *n.* Now chiefly *dial.* Also **foul-** /ˈfaʊl-/. ME. [f. FOUL *a.* + unstressed form of OE *mearþ*: see MARTEN. Cf. MART *n.*[4]] The polecat, *Mustela putorius*. Also as a term of contempt.

found /faʊnd/ *n.*[1] M16. [f. FOUND *v.*[2]] The process of founding metal or material for glass.

†**of found** *Sc.* made of cast metal.

found /faʊnd/ *n.*[2] *Sc.* E17. [f. FOUND *v.*[1]] *sing.* & in *pl.* The foundations of a building.

found /faʊnd/ *ppl a.* LME. [pa. pple of FIND *v.*] **1** That has been found or discovered. Chiefly with preceding adv., as *new-found* LME. **2** Chiefly *Naut.* That is equipped or supplied. Only with preceding adv. etc., as *well found*. L18. **3** Obtained without effort or searching; *spec.* (*a*) (of a stone) taken from the surface of the ground, not quarried; (*b*) (of an artist's materials) taken from the natural environment and used unaltered to form artistic works [cf. Fr. *objet trouvé*]; (of art) based on such materials; (*c*) (of poetry) formed by taking an existing piece of prose and breaking it up into rhythmical units: L19.

found /faʊnd/ *v.*[1] ME. [(O)Fr. *fonder* f. L *fundare*, f. *fundus* bottom, foundation.] **I** *v.t.* **1** Lay the base or foundation of (a building). Sometimes simply, build, construct. Usu. in *pass.* Now *rare*. ME. **2** Be the original builder of (an edifice, town, etc.); establish (an institution) for the first time, esp. with provision for its future maintenance. ME. **3** Establish (something immaterial) on a firm basis, support, principle, etc.; base, ground. Of a thing: serve as a basis for. ME. **b** Ground (a person) *in* a subject of instruction. Long *arch.* LME.

1 AV *Matt.* 7:25 The windes . . beat vpon that house: and it fell not, for it was founded vpon a rocke. 2 C. THIRLWALL His son Lycaon founds the first city, Lycosura. L. STEPHEN De Foe founded the modern school of English novelists. H. FAST Thomas Seldon presided over the bank his father founded. 3 J. LUBBOCK A classification of insects founded on larvae. OED This novel is believed to be founded on fact. G. F. KENNAN His success at home had been founded . . on his appeal to common people. **b** H. ALLEN That you will undertake the instruction of the young clerk . . with the end in view of founding him in . . *Penmanship*.

II *v.i.* **4** Base one's opinion, (of an opinion etc.) be based, *on*, *upon*. Chiefly *Sc.* M19.

4 T. M. COOPER The rather inconclusive fact on which Innes founds.

founded *a.* (*a*) (with qualifying adv.) having a (good, bad, etc.) basis; (*b*) (without adv., *arch.*) having a firm foundation, well-justified: L15.

found /faʊnd/ *v.*[2]*t.* LME. [(O)Fr. *fondre* f. L *fundere* pour, melt.] †**1** Dissolve (ingredients) together. Only in LME. **2** Melt and mould (metal); cast or form (an article) by this process. E16. **3** Fuse to make glass; make (glass, a glass article) by fusing. L18.

found *v.*[3] pa. pple of FIND *v.*

foundation /faʊnˈdeɪʃ(ə)n/ *n.* LME. [(O)Fr. *fondation* f. L *fundatio(n-)*, f. *fundat-* pa. ppl stem of *fundare*: see FOUND *v.*[1], -ATION.] **1** The action of building on a firm substructure; the state of being so built. Now *rare*. LME. **2** *fig.* The action of establishing or constituting on a permanent footing; *esp.* the establishing of an institution with provision for its future maintenance. LME. †**b** The charter establishing a society, institution, etc., with rules for its maintenance. LME–M16. **3** A fund devoted to the permanent maintenance of an institution; an endowment. LME. **b** An institution (e.g. a college, hospital, monastery, etc.) maintained by an endowment. E16. **c** An organization with a permanent fund devoted to financing research, the arts, and other charitable causes. E20. **4** The solid ground or base (natural or artificial) on which a building rests. Also *sing.* & (usu.) in *pl.*, the lowest part of a building, constructed below ground level and supporting the weight of the whole. LME. **5** *fig.* That on which an immaterial thing is based or depends; an underlying principle or source, the basis of a report or belief, etc. LME. †**b** A basis of agreement. M17–L18. **c** In *pl.* The fundamental principles *of* a subject, esp. as a separate object of study. E19. **6** *transf.* Something on which other parts are overlaid; *esp.* (*a*) a basic underpart or backing of a hat, skirt, etc.; (*b*) (in knitting etc.) the first set of stitches, to which the rest are secured. M19. **b** A base for cosmetics. Usu. *attrib.*, as *foundation cream*. E20. **c** = *foundation garment* below. M20. **7** *Bee-keeping.* Sheets of beeswax placed in a frame for the bees to build their combs on. M19.

2 of the New (Old) Foundation (of a cathedral) in which the chapter was reconstituted (left intact) by Henry VIII at the Reformation. **3 on** (or †**of**) **the foundation** entitled to enjoy the funds of an endowed institution, i.e. by being a member of it. **b** M. MEYER Sweden then boasted two universities, both ancient foundations. **c** *Gulbenkian Foundation*, *Rockefeller Foundation*, etc. **4** *fig.*: P. G. WODEHOUSE A hearty laugh that rocked me to my foundations. **5** B. RUSSELL In all social animals . . cooperation . . has some foundation in instinct. R. HOGGART Girls who were . . the foundation of Leeds' predominance as a centre for ready-made clothing. M. MUGGERIDGE My mother's suspicions . . were quite without foundation.

Comb.: **foundation garment** a woman's corset or other supporting undergarment; **foundation member** = *founder member* s.v. FOUNDER *n.*[1] **foundation-school** an endowed school; **foundation-stone** a stone forming part of the foundations of a building, *esp.* one laid at a public ceremony to mark the beginning of the building; *fig.* a basis; **foundation stop** an organ-stop sounding only a note and its octaves.

foundational *a.* forming a foundation; basic, fundamental: L17. **foundationary** *a.* of or relating to a foundation M18. **foundationer** *n.* a person who is on the foundation of an endowed school or college M19. **foundationless** *a.* having no foundation or basis M17. **foundationlessness** *n.* L19.

founder /ˈfaʊndə/ *n.*[1] ME. [f. FOUND *v.*[1] + -ER[1].] **1** The original builder of a city or edifice. ME. **2** A person who sets up or establishes something for the first time; *esp.* a person who establishes an institution with an endowment for its future maintenance. ME. †**3** A person who supports or maintains another. M16–E17.

Comb.: **founder member** a member of an organization from the time when it was founded; **founder's kin** relatives of the founder of a school etc. who are thereby entitled to preferential treatment; **founder's shares** special shares issued to the founders or original subscribers of a public company, who receive a dividend only after the ordinary and preference share dividends have been paid.

foundership *n.* M16.

founder /ˈfaʊndə/ *n.*[2] ME. [f. FOUND *v.*[2] + -ER[1], perh. after (O)Fr. *fondeur*.] **1** A person who casts metals or makes articles of cast metal. ME. **2** A person who founds glass. M19.

1 *bell-founder*, *iron-founder*, etc.

founder /ˈfaʊndə/ *n.*[3] LME. [f. FOUNDER *v.* In sense 1 cf. Fr. *fondrilles*.] †**1** In *pl.* Sediment, dregs. Only in LME. **2** Inflammation of a horse's foot from overwork. Also, a similar disease in dogs. M16. **3** In full *body-founder*, *chest-founder*. Rheumatism of the chest muscles in a horse. M18. **4** A landslip. L19.

founder /ˈfaʊndə/ *v.* ME. [OFr. *fondrer*, *esfondrer* send to the bottom, submerge, collapse, f. Proto-Romance vbs f. alt. of L *fundus* bottom: cf. med.L *fundora* bottom, *funderare* founder.] **I** *v.t.* **1** Knock to the ground; fell. Long *obs.* exc. *Sc.* ME. **2** Cause to fall with lameness, fatigue, or (*fig.*) shock, dismay, etc.; *esp.* affect (a horse) with the founder. L16. **3** Cause (a ship) to fill with water and sink. M17.

2 S. BECKETT Like an old hack foundered in the street, struggling no more. E. BOWEN Shock foundered Eric, sent him silly all over.

II *v.i.* **4** Chiefly of a horse or its rider: fall to the ground, esp. from lameness. Also, stick fast in a bog. LME. **5** Of a structure: collapse, give way. L15. **6** Of a ship: fill with water and sink to the bottom. E17. **b** *fig.* Of a plan, hope, relationship, etc.: come to grief, fail. E17.

4 B. ENGLAND Ansell staggered, foundered dully. 5 C. LYELL The cliffs of Bawdsey . . are foundering slowly. 6 W. C. WILLIAMS Their ship . . had foundered in a storm at sea. **b** T. SHARPE Sir Godber's ideals had . . foundered on the rocks of financial necessity. GODFREY SMITH The development plans nearly foundered . . for lack of capital.

founderous /ˈfaʊnd(ə)rəs/ *a.* Chiefly *dial.* & *Law.* Also **foundrous**. L17. [f. FOUNDER *v.* + -OUS.] Causing a person or horse to founder; miry, full of potholes.

S. WEYMAN The road was deep and foundrous, and . . I was obliged to leave it . . to pass the worst places.

†**foundery** *n.* var. of FOUNDRY.

founding /ˈfaʊndɪŋ/ *n.* M17. [f. FOUND *v.*[2] + -ING[1].] **1** (The casting of metal in) the manufacture of articles of cast metal. M17. **2** (The fusing of materials in) the manufacture of glass. L18.

1 *bell-founding*, *iron-founding*, etc.

founding /ˈfaʊndɪŋ/ *ppl a.* E20. [f. FOUND *v.*[1] + -ING[2].] Associated in the foundation of an institution.

founding father *spec.* an American statesman at the time of the Revolution, esp. a member of the Federal Constitutional Convention of 1787. **founding member** = *founder member* s.v. FOUNDER *n.*[1]

foundling /ˈfaʊndlɪŋ/ *n.* ME. [f. pa. pple of FIND *v.* + -LING[1], perh. after (M)Du. *vondeling*.] An abandoned child of unknown parentage.

Comb.: **foundling hospital**, †**house** *Hist.* an institution caring for foundlings.

foundress /ˈfaʊndrɪs/ *n.* LME. [f. FOUNDER *n.*[1] + -ESS[1].] 1 A female founder; *esp.* a woman who founds an institute. LME. 2 *Zool.* A female which founds a colony. L19.

foundrous *a.* var. of FOUNDEROUS.

foundry /ˈfaʊndri/ *n.* Also †**foundery**. E17. [f. FOUND *v.*[2] + -RY, perh. after (O)Fr. *fonderie*.] 1 The art or business of founding or casting metal; metal castings. E17. 2 A building where metal or glass is founded. M17.

Comb.: **foundryman** a worker in a foundry.

fount /faʊnt/ *n.*[1] L16. [Prob. back-form. f. FOUNTAIN *n.* after *mount, mountain*.] A source of water; a spring. Now chiefly *fig.*

R. P. GRAVES Housman . . seems to have been a fount of amusing anecdotes.

fountful *a.* (chiefly *poet.*) full of springs E17.

fount /faʊnt/ *n.*[2] L17. [Alt.] *Printing.* = FONT *n.*[2] 2.

¶ Until the advent of computer typesetting the usual form in Britain, and still frequent there.

fountain /ˈfaʊntɪn/ *n.* ME. [(O)Fr. *fontaine* f. late L *fontana* use as n. (sc. *aqua* water) of *fontanus* adj. of *fons, font-* a spring.] 1 A natural spring; the source of a river, stream, etc. Now chiefly *poet.* & *arch.* exc. *S. Afr.* ME. b *fig.* A principal origin or source. LME. 2 A jet or number of jets of water made to spout artificially; a structure built for such a jet or jets to rise and fall in. Also = *drinking fountain* s.v. DRINKING *vbl n.* E16. b = SODA *fountain*. M19. 3 *Her.* A roundel barry wavy argent and azure, representing water. E17. 4 A small reservoir for holding liquid, esp. oil in a lamp or ink in a pen or printing-press. E18.

1 H. M. BRACKENRIDGE The greatest objection to this country is the want of fountains and running streams. b W. BLACKSTONE The French law, which is derived from the same feodal fountain.

Comb.: **fountain-head** the headwaters or source of a stream etc.; *fig.* an original source, esp. of information; **fountain-pen**: in which the nib is constantly replenished with ink from a reservoir inside the pen.

fountained *a.* supplied with fountains or springs E19. **fountaineer** *n.* (now *rare*) a person who operates or has charge of a fountain E17. **fountainless** *a.* devoid of springs or fountains L17. **fountainous** *a.* of the nature of a source; full of springs: M17.

fountain /ˈfaʊntɪn/ *v.i.* & *t.* L19. [f. the n.]. (Cause to) rise like the waters of a fountain.

four /fɔː/ *a.* & *n.* (*cardinal numeral*). [OE *fēower* = OFris. *fiūwer, fiōr*, OS *fiwar, fiuwar, fiori*, OHG *fior, fier* (Du., G *vier*), ON *fjórir*, Goth. *fidwōr*, f. Gmc f. IE, whence Skt *catvārah, catur-*, Gk *tessares*, L *quattuor*.] A *adj.* One more than three (a cardinal numeral represented by 4 in arabic numerals, iv, IV, rarely iiii, IIII, in roman). OE.

P. THOMAS They fired four Guns as Signals of Distress. E. L. LINTON He . . was the safest confidant to be found within the four seas. M. WEBB The meeting lasted four hours. DAY LEWIS Four tall windows on the ground floor. *cast, fling,* or *throw to the four winds*: see WIND *n.*[1] *four figures*: see FIGURE *n. four freedoms*: see FREEDOM *n.* **four walls** the walls of a room or a house, in extended usage the symbol of confinement within a restricted space. *within the four corners*: see CORNER *n.* 3.

B *n.* 1 Four people or things identified contextually, as parts or divisions, years of age, points, runs, etc., in a game, chances (in giving odds), minutes, inches, shillings (now *Hist.*), pence, horses in hand, etc. ME. 2 One more than three as an abstract number; the symbol(s) or figure(s) representing this (4 in arabic numerals, iv, IV, rarely (exc. on clock-faces) iiii, IIII, in roman). ME. 3 The time of day four hours after midnight or midday (on a clock, watch, etc., indicated by the numeral four displayed or pointed to). Also *four o'clock*. LME. 4 A set of four; a thing having a set of four as an essential or distinguishing feature; *spec.* (*a*) a playing-card, domino, or side of a die marked with four pips or spots; (*b*) a crew of four in a rowing boat; in *pl.*, boat races between such crews; (*c*) in *pl.*, four leaves to the sheet in a printed book; (*d*) an engine or motor vehicle with four cylinders; (*e*) *Cricket* a hit to the boundary for which four runs are scored (cf. SIX *n.* 4(e)); (*f*) four playing-cards of the same rank as a scoring combination (also in *pl.*). L15. 5 The fourth of a set or series with numbered members, the one designated four (usu. *number four*, or with specification, as *book four, chapter four*, etc.); a size etc. denoted by four, a shoe, glove, garment, etc., of such a size, (also *size four*). E16. 6 Each of a set of four; *spec.* (*a*) a large plant-pot of which four are formed from a cast of clay; (*b*) a candle of which four constitute a pound in weight. E19.

1 AV *2 Sam.* 21:22 These foure . . fell by the hand of Dauid. L. SIMOND An elegant post-chaise and four stopped at the door. 2 W. WHEWELL Four . . was held to be the most perfect number. 3 SWIFT If you'll be sure to come at four. 4 C. MACKENZIE Cosway was called away to make up a four at Bridge. J. ARCHER A four for Harvey . . and a six for the dealer. 5 E. WALLACE He had . . rowed 'four' in his boat. *Radio Four*: see RADIO *n.* 3.

Comb.: Forming compound cardinal numerals with multiples of ten from twenty to ninety, as *thirty-four*, (arch.) *four-and-thirty*, etc., and (*arch.*) their corresponding ordinals, as *four-and-thirtieth* etc., and with multiples of a hundred, as *204* (read *two hundred and four*, US also *two hundred four*), *5004* (read *five thousand and four*, US also *five thousand four*), etc. With ns. + -ER[1] forming ns. w. the sense 'something (identified contextually) being of or having four —s', as *four-seater, -wheeler*, etc. Special combs., as **four-ale** *Hist.* ale sold at fourpence a quart; a bar selling such ale; **four-ball** a golf match between two pairs with each player using a separate ball, the best ball on each side counting at each hole; **four-by-four** (*a*) *slang* a vehicle having four-speed transmission and four-speed auxiliary transmission; (*b*) *N. Amer.* a post or batten measuring four inches by four in cross-section; **four-by-two** (*a*) *Mil. colloq.* the cloth attached to a pull-through; (*b*) *derog. slang* a Jew; (*c*) *N. Amer.* & *Austral.* a post or batten measuring four inches by two in cross-section; also called *two-by-four*; **four-channel** *a.* & *n.* (designating) any of various systems for recording and playing back sound signals whereby, through the placing of four loudspeakers, the original front-to-back sound distribution may be reproduced as well as the side-to-side one of stereophony; **four-colour** *a.* having or pertaining to four colours; *four-colour problem*, a problem to prove that any plane map can be coloured with only four colours so that no two same-coloured regions have a common boundary; **four-cycle** *a.* = *four-stroke* below; **four-dimensional** *a.* having a fourth dimension in addition to length, breadth, and depth; **four-eyes** *slang* a bespectacled person; *four-figure*: see FIGURE *n.*; **four-flush** *n.* & *v.* (*a*) *n.* an almost worthless poker hand having four (not five) cards of the same suit; (*b*) *v.i.* (*US*) bluff, brag; **four-flusher** *US* a bluffer, a humbug; **four-foot** *a.* (*obs.* exc. *poet.*) four-footed; **four-footed** *a.* having or using four feet (*esp.* opp. to biped); quadruped; **four-four** *a.* & *n.* (*Mus.*) (designating) time or rhythm consisting of four crotchets in a bar; **Four-H club** *N. Amer.* a club for the instruction of young people in citizenry and agriculture (from supposedly improving head, heart, hands, and health); **four-handed** *a.* (*a*) (of a mammal) quadrumanous; (*b*) having or using four hands; (of a card-game etc.) for four players; (of a piece of keyboard music) for two players; **four hundred** *US* the highest social group in a locality; **four-in-hand** (*a*) a vehicle with four horses driven by one person on the box; (*b*) *US* a necktie (to be) worn tied in a loose knot with two hanging ends; *four last things*: see LAST *a.*; *four-leaf clover*: see CLOVER *n.*; **four-letter** *a.* consisting of four letters; *esp.* designating any of several coarse English monosyllabic words referring to sexual or excretory functions; *four-letter man*, an obnoxious person; **four o'clock** (*a*) (more fully *four o'clock flower*) = *marvel of Peru* s.v. MARVEL *n.*[1]; (*b*) the Australian friar-bird; (*c*) a light meal taken at about four o'clock; **four-on-the-floor** *N. Amer. slang* a manual gear lever; **four-part** *a.* (*Mus.*) composed for four parts or voices; **fourpence** four pence, esp. of the old British currency before decimalization; **fourpenny** *a.* (*a*) worth or costing fourpence; *fourpenny nail*, a nail 1½ inches long of which a thousand add up to four pounds in weight; (*b*) *fourpenny one* (*colloq.*), a hard blow, esp. to the face; **four-post** *a.* (of a bed) having four posts to support a canopy overhead; **four-poster** (**bed**) a four-post bed; **four pounder** a gun that throws a shot that weighs four pounds; **four-rowed** *a.* having four rows; *four-rowed barley*, a form of six-rowed barley, *Hordeum vulgare*, having four longitudinal rows of fertile spikelets; **fourscore** *arch.* eighty; **four-square** *a.*, *adv.*, & *n.* (*a*) *adj.* square-shaped, solidly based; resolute; (*b*) in a square form or position, resolutely; (*c*) *n.* (*arch.*) a figure having four equal sides; **four-star** *a.* & *n.* (*a*) *adj.* given four stars in a grading in which this denotes the highest standard or the next standard to the highest, excellent; having or designating a military rank distinguished by four stars on the shoulder-piece of the uniform; (*b*) *n.* something given a four-star grading, esp. petrol; **four-stroke** *a.* (of an internal-combustion engine) having a cycle of four strokes (intake, compression, combustion, and exhaust); **four-vector** [G *Vierervektor*] *Math.* a vector defined by four scalar components; *esp.* a space–time vector in relativity theory; **four-went(-ways)** (*obs.* exc. *dial.*) a point where four ways meet, a crossroads; **four wheel** *n.* & *a.* (*a*) *n.* a four-wheeled vehicle; (*b*) *adj.* having four wheels; acting on all four wheels of a vehicle; **four wheeler** a four-wheeled vehicle, *spec.* (*Hist.*) a four-wheeled hackney carriage.

fourfold *a.*, *adv.*, & *n.* (*a*) *adj.* four times as great or as numerous; having four parts, divisions, elements, or units; (*b*) *adv.* to four times the number or quantity; (*c*) *n.* (*rare*) a fourfold amount: OE. †**fourscorth** *a.* eightieth L16–E18.

†**fourbe** *n.* M17. [Fr., lit. (masc.) 'cheat, impostor', (fem.) 'imposture' in thieves' cant, (f. (fem.) *fourber* cheat,) f. *fourbe* adj., f. It *furbo* (adj.) astute, (n.) a cunning person.] 1 A cheat, an impostor. M17–M18. 2 A trick, an imposture. M–L17.

†**fourbery** *n.* Also **fur-**. M17–M19. [Fr. *fourberie*, f. *fourber*: see prec., -ERY.] A piece of deception; a fraud, a trick, an imposture. Also (*rare*), deceit, trickery.

Fourcault /ˈfʊəkəʊ/ *n.* E20. [Émile *Fourcault* (1862–1919), Belgian inventor.] Used *attrib.* to designate (apparatus used in) a continuous process for making sheet glass in which glass is drawn vertically upwards through a slot in a floating trough.

fourché /ˈfɔːʃeɪ/ *a.* Also **-ée**. L16. [Fr. *fourchée* forked, f. *fourche* (pitch)fork.] *Her.* Forked.

fourchette /fʊəˈʃɛt/ *n.* M18. [Fr., dim. of *fourche*: see FORK *n.*, -ETTE.] 1 *Anat.* Something forked or resembling a fork; *spec.* the fold of skin at the posterior edge of the vulva. M18. 2 A forked object, instrument, or device; *spec.* the forked piece between two adjacent fingers of a glove. M19. 3 In any of several card-games, a combination of cards immediately above and below the card led. L19.

Fourdrinier /fʊəˈdrɪnɪə, -ɪeɪ/ *n.* M19. [Henry (d. 1854) and Sealy (d. 1847) *Fourdrinier*, Brit. papermakers and patentees of such a machine.] In full *Fourdrinier* (†*Fourdrinier's*) *machine*. A machine for making paper as a continuous sheet by drainage on a wire mesh belt.

fourgon /furgɔ̃/ *n.* Pl. pronounced same. M19. [Fr.] A baggage-wagon, a luggage-van.

Fourier /ˈfʊrɪə, -rɪeɪ/ *n.* M19. [J. B. J. *Fourier* (1768–1830), Fr. mathematician.] *Math.* & *Physics.* Used *attrib.* and (less usu.) in *possess.* to designate various expressions etc. arising from the work of Fourier.

Fourier analysis the analysis of a complex waveform into a set of sinusoidal functions the frequencies of which form a harmonic series. **Fourier series** an infinite series of the form $\frac{1}{2}a_0 + (a_1 \cos x + b_1 \sin x) + (a_2 \cos 2x + b_2 \sin 2x) + \ldots$, (where the *a*s and *b*s are constants), used to represent or approximate a periodic function in Fourier analysis. **Fourier transform**, a function derived from another function and representing it by a spectrum of sinusoidal functions.

Fourierism /ˈfʊrɪərɪz(ə)m/ *n.* M19. [Fr. *Fouriérisme*, f. *Fourier* (see below) + -ISM.] A system for the reorganization of society in accordance with the phalansterian principles of the French socialist Charles Fourier (d. 1837).

Fourierist *n.* & *a.* (*a*) *n.* an adherent or student of Fourierism; (*b*) *adj.* of or pertaining to Fourierism: M19. **Fourieˈristic** *a.* = FOURIERIST *a.* L19.

fou rire /fu riːr/ *n. phr.* E20. [Fr., lit. 'mad laughter'.] (A fit of) wild or uncontrollable laughter.

Fournier /ˈfʊənɪə/ *n.* E20. [P. S. *Fournier* (see below).] A typeface modelled on types made by the French punch-cutter P. S. Fournier (d. 1768).

fourniture /furnity:r/ *n.* L19. [Fr., lit. 'furniture'.] = FURNITURE *n.* 7.

fourreau /'fʊərəʊ/ *n.* L19. [Fr., lit. 'sheath, scabbard'.] A close-fitting dress; an underskirt forming part of a dress.

fourrier /'fʊərɪə/ *n.* Long *obs.* exc. *Hist.* Also †**furrier**. LME. [Fr., f. OFr. *forrier*: see FORAYER.] A person going in advance of an army etc. to secure accommodation or other requirements; a purveyor, a quartermaster. Also, a harbinger, a courier.

foursome /'fɔ:s(ə)m/ *pron.*, *n.*, & *a.* ME. [f. FOUR + -SOME[2].] A *pron.* & *n.* 1 Formerly, four in all. Now, a group of four. ME. 2 *Golf.* A match for four people, with two playing on each side. M19. B *attrib.* or as *adj.* For four; *esp.* (of a dance) performed by four people together. E19.

fourteen /fɔ:'ti:n, 'fɔ:ti:n/ *a.* & *n.* (*cardinal numeral*). [OE *fēowertīene* = OFris. *fiuwertīne*, OS *fiertein* (Du. *veertien*), OHG *fiorzehan* (G *vierzehn*), ON *fjórtán*, Goth. *fidwōrtaihun*: see FOUR, -TEEN.] A *adj.* One more than thirteen (a cardinal numeral represented by 14 in arabic numerals, xiv, XIV in roman). OE. B *n.* 1 One more than thirteen, as an abstract number; the symbols or figures representing this (14 in arabic numerals, xiv, XIV in roman). OE. 2 Fourteen people or things identified contextually, as years of age, chances (in giving odds), minutes, shillings (now *Hist.*), pence, etc. LME. 3 The fourteenth of a set or series with numbered members, the one designated fourteen, (usu. *number fourteen*, or with specification, as *book fourteen*, *chapter fourteen*, etc.); a size etc. denoted by fourteen, a garment etc. of such a size, (also *size fourteen*). LME. 4 A set of fourteen; a thing having a set of fourteen as an essential or distinguishing feature. M20. 5 Any of a set of fourteen; *spec.* (*a*) a plant-pot of which fourteen are formed from one cast of clay; (*b*) a candle of which fourteen add up to a pound in weight. L20.

Comb.: Forming compound numerals with multiples of a hundred, as *514* (read *five hundred and fourteen*, US also *five hundred fourteen*), etc. In dates used for one thousand four hundred, as *1485* (read *fourteen eighty-five*), *fourteen-twenties*, etc. With ns. + -ER[1] forming ns. w. the sense 'something (identified contextually) being of or having fourteen —s', as *fourteen-tonner* etc.

four'teener *n.* something comprising fourteen parts; *esp.* (*a*) *rare* a poem of fourteen lines; (*b*) a line of fourteen syllables: E19.

fourteenth /fɔ:'ti:nθ, 'fɔ:ti:nθ/ *a.* & *n.* (*ordinal numeral*). [OE *fēowertēoþa*, repl. in ME by forms f. FOURTEEN + -TH[2]. Cf. ON *fjórtándi*.] A *adj.* Next in order after the thirteenth, that is number fourteen in a series, (represented by 14th). OE.

fourteenth part *arch.* = sense B.3 below.

B *n.* 1 The fourteenth person or thing of a category, series, etc., identified contextually, as day of the month, (following a proper name) person, esp. monarch or pope, of the specified name, etc. OE. 2 *Mus.* An interval embracing fourteen consecutive notes in the diatonic scale; a note a fourteenth above another given note; a chord of two notes a fourteenth apart, or based around the fourteenth of a note. L16. 3 Each of fourteen equal parts into which something is or may be divided, a fraction which when multiplied by fourteen gives one, (= *fourteenth part* above). E19.

Comb.: Forming compound numerals with multiples of a hundred, as *three-hundred-and-fourteenth* (*314th*) etc.

fourteenthly *adv.* in the fourteenth place M17.

fourth /fɔ:θ/ *a.*, *n.*, & *adv.* (*ordinal numeral*). [OE *fēo(we)rþa* = OS *fiortho* (Du. *vierde*), OHG *fiordo* (G *vierte*), ON *fjórði*, f. Gmc f. IE, whence also L *quartus*, G *tetartos*, Skt *caturtha*.] A *adj.* Next in order after the third, that is number four in a series, (represented by 4th). OE.

fourth day Wednesday. **fourth dimension** a property of bodies that would make them be to solids as solids are to surfaces; *Physics* time viewed as a quality resembling a length. *fourth estate*: see ESTATE *n.* **fourth finger** the finger fourth from the thumb, the little finger. **fourth gear** the fourth in a sequence of forward gears in a motor vehicle, bicycle, etc. **fourth-generation** *a.* (of a computer) distinguished by large-scale integrated-circuit technology and very large rapid-access memory and belonging essentially to the post-1970 period. **fourth part** *arch.* = sense B.3 below. **fourth position** *Ballet* the position, esp. when starting or finishing a step, in which the feet are placed turned outwards one in front of the other, separated by the distance of one step; the corresponding position of the arms. **fourth wall** *Theatr.* a proscenium opening through which a stage is seen. **Fourth World** those countries considered to be the poorest and most underdeveloped of the Third World.

B *n.* 1 The fourth person or thing of a category, series, etc., identified contextually, as day of the month, (following a proper name) person, esp. monarch or pope, of the specified name, etc. ME. b A person making up a foursome for a game, social event, etc. E19. c (A person having) a place in the fourth class in an examination list. E20. d = *fourth gear* above. E20. 2 *Mus.* An interval embracing four consecutive notes in the diatonic scale; a note a fourth above another given note; a chord of two notes a fourth apart, or based around the fourth of a note. L16. 3 Each of four equal parts into which something is or may be divided, a fraction which when multiplied by four gives one, a quarter, (= *fourth part* above). L16.

1 S. STURMY Three Right Lines being given, To find a fourth in proportion to them. J. O'HARA He . . had three quick drinks and was on his fourth. **Fourth of July**, **Glorious Fourth**: the anniversary of the Declaration of Independence of the United States (1776). J. GARDNER Selecting the Mahler Fourth. b T. S. ELIOT Wanting a fourth at bridge. c C. L. WRENN The consciousness in the minds of the Oxford authorities that Sweet had obtained a 'fourth' in greats. 3 *Scientific American* Mortality during pregnancy and delivery may account for a fourth of the deaths. *third(s)-and-fourth(s)*: see THIRD *n.* 2.

Comb.: Forming compound ordinal numerals with multiples of ten, as *fifty-fourth* (*54th*), *five-thousand-and-fourth* (*5004th*), etc.

C *adv.* Fourthly. L15.

fourthly *adv.* in the fourth place E16.

foussie *n.* see FOSSÉ.

fouter *n.* var. of FOUTRE.

fouth /fu:θ/ *n.* *Sc.* LME. [Var. of FULTH.] Fullness, plenty.

foutre /'fu:tə/ *n.* Now *rare* or *obs.* Also **fouter**, FOOTER *n.*[2] L16. [OFr., use as n. of inf. f. L *futuere* have sexual intercourse with (a woman).] 1 A valueless thing; the slightest amount. Esp. in *a foutre for —*, *not a foutre* (Cf. FUCK *n.* 3.) *slang.* L16. 2 A worthless or contemptible person. E18.

fouty *a.* see FOOTY *a.*

fovea /'fəʊvɪə/ *n.* Pl. **-eae** /-ɪi:/. L17. [L = small pit.] *Anat.* A small depression or pit; *esp.* the shallow pit in the retina at the back of the eye, which consists of cones and is the site of highest visual acuity (cf. *macula lutea* s.v. MACULA 2).

fovea centralis /sɛn'trɑ:lɪs/ [L = central] the fovea of the retina.

foveal *a.* of, pertaining to, or situated in a fovea L19. **foveate**, **-ated** *adjs.* having or distinguished by a fovea or foveae; pitted: M19.

foveola /fəʊ'vi:ələ/ *n.* Pl. **-lae** /-li:/. M19. [L, dim. of prec.] *Anat.* A small fovea.

foveolate *a.* having or distinguished by a foveola or foveolae; pitted: M19. **foveolated** *a.* = FOVEOLATE *a.* E19.

fovilla /fə'vɪlə/ *n.* Now *rare* or *obs.* L18. [mod.L, perh. alt. of *favilla*.] *Bot.* The substance contained in pollen cells.

fowl /faʊl/ *n.* Pl. same, **-s**. [OE *fugol* = OFris. *fugel*, OS *fugal*, OHG *fogal* (Du. *vogel*, G *Vogel*), ON *fugl*, Goth. *fugls*, f. Gmc, f. base of FLY *v.*] 1 A bird. *arch.* exc. as 2nd elem. of comb. (see below). OE. †b *spec.* A game-bird. M17–M18. 2 A domestic cock or hen; any of various gallinaceous birds chiefly kept for eggs and flesh. Also *US*, a domestic duck or turkey. ME. †3 In *pl.* Winged creatures. LME–M17. 4a *gen.* The flesh of fowl, esp. as food. Now only in *fish, flesh, and fowl*. L16. b *spec.* The flesh of a domestic cock or hen considered as food. M19.

1 E. TOPSELL To defend them from Eagles, and other ravening Fowls. MILTON Beasts of chase, or fowl of game In pastry built. *domestic fowl*: see DOMESTIC *a.* 2. *game-fowl*: see GAME *n.* *guinea-fowl*: see GUINEA 1. WATERFOWL. WILDFOWL. b EVELYN Sometimes we shot at fowls and other birds. 2 D. L. SAYERS I had half a dozen fowls to kill and pluck. 3 T. GAGE Battes, or Rear-mice and other fowle. 4b I. M. BEETON The remains of cold roast fowl.

Comb.: *fowl* CHOLERA; *fowl leucosis*: see LEUCOSIS 2; **fowl-paralysis** = MAREK'S DISEASE; **fowl pest** (*a*) = *fowl plague* below; (*b*) = NEWCASTLE *disease*; **fowl plague** an acute, highly contagious, and usually fatal virus disease affecting poultry; **fowl pox** a virus disease of poultry in which lesions appear on the feather-free parts of the body, or on the mucous membranes of the mouth, nose, or throat; **fowl-run** an enclosure for fowls; a breeding establishment for fowls.

fowl /faʊl/ *v.i.* OE. [f. the n.] Catch, hunt, shoot, or snare wild birds, esp. wildfowl.

fowler /'faʊlə/ *n.* OE. [f. prec. + -ER[1].] 1 A person who hunts birds, esp. wildfowl, for sport or food; a bird-catcher. OE. †2 A kind of light cannon, esp. for use on board ship. LME–M17.

fowling /'faʊlɪŋ/ *n.* LME. [f. as prec. + -ING[1].] The action of FOWL *v.*; the practice of catching, hunting, shooting, or snaring wild birds, esp. wildfowl.

Comb.: **fowling piece** a light gun for shooting wildfowl.

fox /fɒks/ *n.* [OE *fox* = OS *vuhs* (Du. *vos*), OHG *fuhs* (G *Fuchs*), f. Gmc.] I 1 Any of various sharp-snouted bushy-tailed carnivorous canids distinguished by a flattened skull and erect triangular ears; *esp.* the red-furred *Vulpes vulpes* (also *red fox*), an important beast of the chase in England and proverbial for its cunning. OE. 2 *fig.* a A cunning, sly, or crafty person. OE. b A freshman at a college etc. *US arch. slang.* M19. c An attractive woman. *N. Amer. slang.* M20. 3 The fur of the fox, esp. as dressed and used for clothing. LME. 4 Any of various animals related to the fox or considered to resemble it in appearance or habits. Usu. w. specifying wd. L16. 5 (Usu. **F-**.) Orig. *the Fox and Goose*. *The* constellation Vulpecula. L18.

1 R. BURNS Foxes and statesmen, subtile wiles ensure. W. HOLTBY Hounds . . lost their fox in Lipton Sticks. N. TINBERGEN Repeated raids by a fox in the egg-season. *Arctic fox*: see ARCTIC *a.* 1b. *crazy like* (or *as*) *a fox*: see CRAZY *a.* 3. **fox and geese** a game played on a board with pegs, draughtsmen, etc. **fox and hounds** a game in which one player is pursued by the other players. **play the fox** (*a*) act cunningly; (*b*) sham (illness etc.). *white fox*: see WHITE *a.* 2 J. ARBUTHNOT Don't you see how that old fox steals away your customers? 3 POINTED *fox*. 4 *flying-fox*, *sea-fox*, etc.

II Senses of obscure development. †6 A kind of sword. L16–E18. 7 A sourness in fermented beer caused during the brewing process. Long *rare* or *obs.* M18. 8 *Naut.* A strand formed by twisted rope-yarn and used as seizing. M18.

Comb.: **fox bane** a yellow-flowered aconite, *Aconitum vulparia*, native to central and southern Europe; **foxberry** the cowberry; **fox-chase** (*a*) *arch.* a fox-hunt; (*b*) a game in imitation of this; **fox-coloured** *a.* of a reddish-brown or -yellow colour; **fox-fire** *US* the phosphorescent light emitted by certain fungi on decaying timber; **fox-fur** (*a*) the dressed coat of a fox; (*b*) a garment lined or trimmed with such fur; **foxglove** (*a*) a tall woodland plant of the figwort family, *Digitalis purpurea*, which has tall spikes of purple or white bell-shaped flowers and is the source of digitalis; (*b*) any of various similar plants; *esp.* (formerly) mullein; **fox-grape** any of various N. American wild grapes, esp. *Vitis labrusca*, from which originate many cultivated varieties; **foxhole** (*a*) *Mil.* a hole in the ground used as a shelter against missiles or as a firing-point; (*b*) *fig.* a place of refuge or concealment; **foxhound** a kind of hound bred and trained to hunt foxes; **fox-hunt** *n.* & *v.* (*a*) *n.* a hunt for a fox or foxes with hounds; a meeting or association for this; (*b*) *v.i.* go fox-hunting; **fox-hunter** a person who takes part in a fox-hunt; **fox-hunting** *n.* the sport or action of hunting a fox or foxes with hounds; **fox-hunting** *ppl a.* that goes fox-hunting; fond of fox-hunting; **fox-mark** a brown spot or stain in the leaves of a book, a print, etc., caused by damp affecting impurities in the paper; **fox moth** a reddish-brown European eggar moth, *Macrothylacia rubi*, with black-and-yellow woolly larvae; **fox-red** *a.*

& *n.* (of) a bright reddish brown; **fox shark** the thresher shark; **fox skin** the skin of a fox; **fox snake** a large harmless colubrid snake of N. America, *Elaphe vulpina*; **fox sparrow** a red-tailed N. American sparrow, *Zonotrichia iliaca*; **fox squirrel** a squirrel, *Sciurus niger*, of the eastern US; **fox-terrier** a short-haired terrier bred for the unearthing of foxes, but kept chiefly as a pet.

foxery *n.* the characteristics or behaviour of a fox; craftiness, cunning: LME. **foxlike** *a.* resembling (that of) a fox; *esp.* crafty, cunning: L16. **foxship** *n.* (*a*) *rare* the character or qualities of a fox, foxiness; (*b*) (with possess. adj., as *your* etc. *foxship*) *joc.* a title or form of address given to a fox: E17.

fox /fɒks/ *v.* M16. [f. the n.] †1 *v.t.* Pierce with a sword, stab. M–L16. 2†a *v.t.* Achieve by crafty means. *rare.* Only in E17. b *v.i.* Act craftily, dissemble; sham illness etc. M17. 3 *v.t.* Intoxicate, make drunk, befuddle. Chiefly as *foxed* ppl a. *arch.* E17. †b Daze or stupefy (fish); make (fish) easy to catch by this means. M17–E19. 4 Deceive, puzzle, trick. M17. 5 *v.i.* Of beer: turn sour in the fermenting process. M18. 6 *v.t.* Repair (a boot or shoe) by renewing the upper leather; ornament (the upper of a shoe) with a strip of leather. L18. 7 *v.t.* Discolour (the leaves of a book, an engraving, etc.) with fox-marks; *transf.* discolour with spots or blotches. Chiefly as *foxed* ppl a. M19.

4 A. B. LONGSTREET Has he foxed you? U. BENTLEY I was foxed as how to cross the gulf that separated our two chairs. 7 ALAN BENNETT That foxed and fly-spotted fridge.

foxie /ˈfɒksi/ *n. Austral.* & *NZ.* E20. [Abbrev. of *fox-terrier*: see FOX *n.*, -IE.] A fox-terrier.

foxing /ˈfɒksɪŋ/ *n.* ME. [f. FOX *v.*, *n.* + -ING[1].] †1 A fox's trick, a clever ruse or deceit. Only in ME. 2 The action of FOX *v.* M18. 3 A strip of leather or other material used to ornament the upper of a boot or shoe. M18. 4 Discoloration, esp. of the leaves of a book etc. by fox-marks. L19.

Foxite /ˈfɒksʌɪt/ *n.* & *a.* L18. [f. C. J. *Fox* (see below) + -ITE[1].] *Hist.* A *n.* A political supporter or adherent of the Whig politician Charles James Fox (1749–1806), opponent of the younger Pitt. L18. B *adj.* Of or pertaining to Fox or the Foxites. L18.

foxtail /ˈfɒksteɪl/ *n.* LME. [f. FOX *n.* + TAIL *n.*[1]] 1 A fox's brush (formerly a badge of a fool or jester). LME. 2 Any of several grasses of the genus *Alopecurus*, with a soft spikelike panicle; esp. *A. pratensis*, a common grass of meadows. Also *foxtail-grass*. M16.

Comb.: *foxtail-grass*: see sense 2 above; **foxtail lily** = EREMURUS; **foxtail millet** the grass *Setaria italica*, with a dense spikelike panicle, grown as a cereal in warm countries and as fodder in the US.

foxtrot /ˈfɒkstrɒt/ *n.* & *v.* L19. [f. FOX *n.* + TROT *n.*[1]] A *n.* 1 A pace with short steps, as in changing from trotting to walking. L19. 2 A ballroom dance with slow and quick steps; a piece of music for this dance. E20. B *v.i.* Infl. **-tt-**. Dance a foxtrot. E20.

foxtrotter *n.* E20.

foxy /ˈfɒksi/ *a.* E16. [f. FOX *n.* + -Y[1].] 1 Foxlike; of the nature or appearance of a fox; *esp.* crafty, cunning. E16. b Of a woman: sexually attractive. *N. Amer. slang.* E20. 2a Of a painting: marked by an excessive predominance of reddish tints. L18. b *gen.* Fox-coloured; reddish-brown or -yellow. M19. 3 Discoloured or defective through atmospheric conditions, improper treatment, etc.; *spec.* (of the leaves of a book etc.) discoloured by fox-marks. E19.

1 TENNYSON Modred's narrow foxy face. M. GEE He's .. foxy in his dealings with his elders. b *Easyriders* Green eyes, 21 years old and foxy, would like to hear from a gorgeous man.

foxily *adv.* M20. **foxiness** *n.* L19.

foy /fɔɪ/ *n. obs.* exc. *dial.* L15. [Du. *fooi* tip, gratuity, MDu. *foye*, *voye* f. Fr. *voie* way, journey.] A parting entertainment, present, or drink, given by or to a person setting out on a journey.

foyaite /ˈfɔɪəʌɪt, ˈfəʊjəʌɪt/ *n.* L19. [f. *Foya* locality in Portugal + -ITE[1].] *Geol.* A type of nepheline-syenite rock, typically of trachytoid texture and containing orthoclase.

foyer /ˈfɔɪeɪ; *foreign* fwaje (*pl. same*)/ *n.* L18. [Fr. = hearth, home f. Proto-Gallo-Romance, f. L *focus* fire: see -ER[2].] 1 = FOCUS *n.* 4. L18. 2 A large room in a theatre or concert hall for the use of the audience during intervals. Also, the entrance-hall of a hotel, theatre, or other public building. M19.

†**fra** *prep.*, *adv.*, & *conj.* see FRO.

frab /frab/ *v.t. dial.* Infl. **-bb-**. M19. [Origin unkn.: cf. CRAB *v.*[1]] Harass, worry.

frabjous /ˈfrabdʒəs/ *a. joc. colloq.* L19. [Nonsense wd invented by Lewis Carroll.] Delightful, joyous.

frabjously *adv.* L19.

fracas /ˈfrakɑː/ *n.* Pl. same /-kɑːz/. E18. [Fr., f. *fracasser* f. It. *fracassare* make an uproar.] A disturbance, a row, an uproar.

R. MACAULAY An unseemly fracas with the police.

†**frache** *n.* M17–M19. [Origin unkn.] A metal tray for holding glassware in the annealing process.

†**fracid** *a.* M17–M19. [L *fracidus* soft, mellow (of olives), f. *frax*, pl. *fraces* lees of oil: see -ID[1].] Rotten from overripeness.

frack *a.* var. of FRECK *a.*

fractal /ˈfrakt(ə)l/ *n.* & *a.* L20. [Fr., f. L *fract-*: see FRACTION, -AL[1].] *Math.* A *n.* A curve having the property that any small part of it, enlarged, has the same statistical character as the whole. L20. B *adj.* Of the nature of a fractal; of or relating to fractals. L20.

fracted /ˈfraktɪd/ *a.* M16. [f. L *fract-* (see FRACTION) + -ED[1].] †1 Broken; *Math.* fractional. M16–E18. 2 *Her.* Having a part displaced as if broken. E19.

fractile /ˈfraktʌɪl/ *n.* M20. [f. FRACTION *n.* + -ILE.] *Statistics.* = QUANTILE.

fractile /ˈfraktʌɪl, -tɪl/ *a. rare.* E18. [f. L *fract-* (see FRACTION) + -ILE.] Fragile; of or relating to breakage.

fraction /ˈfrakʃ(ə)n/ *n.* LME. [(O)Fr. f. Chr.L *fractio(n-)* breaking (as of bread), f. L *fract-* pa. ppl stem of *frangere* break: see -ION.] 1 *Math.* A numerical quantity that is not a whole number; one or more aliquot parts of a unit or whole number; any quantity expressed as a numerator (written above a horizontal line) divided by a denominator (written below the line); a small proportion or (*loosely*) amount. LME. 2a The dividing of bread in the Eucharist. LME. b *gen.* The action of breaking or disrupting; (formerly) refraction. Now *rare* or *obs.* M16. †3 The result of breaking; the state of being broken; a fracture, a breach, a fissure. LME–L18. †4 An interruption of harmony; discord; a breach of the peace; a rupture. E16–L18. 5 A thing broken off; a disconnected portion; a small piece. Now *rare.* E17. 6 A portion of a one-square-mile section of undeveloped land. *US.* L18. 7 Each of the portions, differing in physical or chemical properties, into which a mixture may be separated by distillation or another process. M19. 8 An organized group of Communists within a non-Communist body such as a trade union; any deviant or schismatic group. E20.

1 L. A. G. STRONG Walter tried a massé shot, and missed by the fraction of an inch. B. BAINBRIDGE It skimmed the air a fraction above Adolf's head. *continued fraction*, *decimal fraction*, *improper fraction*, *proper fraction*, *vulgar fraction*, etc. 2b O. FELTHAM When the Affections are glewed to the world, Death makes not a Dissolution, but a Fraction.

fractional /ˈfrakʃ(ə)n(ə)l/ *a.* L17. [f. prec. + -AL[1].] 1 Of, pertaining to, or dealing with a fraction or fractions; comprising or being a fraction; of the nature of a fraction; incomplete, partial, insignificant. L17. 2 Pertaining to or involving separation of a mixture into fractions. M19. 3 Of or pertaining to a (Communist) fraction. E20.

1 *Financial Times* Fractional early gains were eventually replaced by equally minor falls.

Special collocations: **fractional crystallization** the separation of fractions of different chemical composition from a solution or liquid mixture by crystallization under varying physical conditions. **fractional currency**, **note** *N. Amer.*: of less value than the basic monetary unit. **fractional distillation** separation, by means of distillation usu. with a fractionating column, of a liquid mixture into fractions differing in boiling point (and hence chemical composition). *fractional note*: see *fractional currency* above.

fractionalism *n.* the doctrine or policy of a (Communist) fraction; factionalism, schism: M20. **fractionalist** *n.* & *a.* (*a*) *n.* an adherent of fractionalism; (*b*) *adj.* of or pertaining to fractionalists or fractionalism: M20. **fractionally** *adv.* L19.

fractionalize /ˈfrakʃ(ə)n(ə)lʌɪz/ *v.t.* Also **-ise.** M20. [f. prec. + -IZE.] Break up or separate into distinct parts or fractions.

fractionaliˈzation *n.* M20.

fractionary /ˈfrakʃ(ə)n(ə)ri/ *a.* L17. [f. FRACTION + -ARY[1].] 1 = FRACTIONAL 1. L17. 2 Dealing with or carried on by fractions or fragments; tending to divide into fractions. M19.

fractionate /ˈfrakʃəneɪt/ *v.* M19. [f. FRACTION + -ATE[3].] 1 *v.t. Chem.* etc. Separate into fractions by distillation or another method. M19. b *gen.* = FRACTIONALIZE. M20. 2 *v.i.* Break up into fractions. M20.

1 **fractionating column** a tall vessel with horizontal subdivisions and inert packing, in which vapour from a still passes upwards through descending condensate, the vapour becoming progressively enriched in more volatile components as it ascends, and the less volatile components becoming concentrated in the descending liquid.

fractioˈnation *n.* L19.

fractionize /ˈfrakʃənʌɪz/ *v.t.* Also **-ise.** L17. [f. FRACTION + -IZE.] Break up into fractions.

fractioniˈzation *n.* M20.

fractious /ˈfrakʃəs/ *a.* M17. [f. FRACTION + -OUS, prob. after *faction*, *factious*. Sense 1 perh. f. L *fract-* (see FRACTION) + -IOUS.] †1 Accompanied by breakage or rupture of parts. Only in M17. 2 Refractory, unruly; quarrelsome; cross, peevish. L17.

fractiously *adv.* M18. **fractiousness** *n.* E18.

fracto- /ˈfraktəʊ/ *comb. form.* L19. [f. L *fractus* broken + -O-.] *Meteorol.* Prefixed to names of cloud-types, w. the sense 'broken, fragmentary' (*fracto-cumulus*, *fracto-nimbus*).

fracture /ˈfraktʃə/ *n.* LME. [(O)Fr., or L *fractura*, f. *fract-*: see FRACTION, -URE.] 1 The action of breaking, the fact of being broken; breakage; *esp.* the breaking of a bone. LME. 2 The result of breaking, esp. of a bone, or (*Geol.*) of a stratum or strata under deformational stress; a crack, a division, a split. Formerly also, a broken part, a splinter. LME. 3 The way in which a rock or mineral breaks when subjected to a blow (as opp. to *cleavage*); the characteristic appearance of the freshly broken surface of a rock or mineral. L18. 4 *Phonol.* = BREAKING 1b. L19.

2 *comminuted fracture*, *compound fracture*, *greenstick fracture*, *open fracture*, *simple fracture*.

fracture /ˈfraktʃə/ *v.* L16. [f. the n.] 1 *v.t.* Cause a fracture in (esp. a bone). L16. b Impress, excite, amuse greatly. *US slang.* M20. 2 *v.i.* Break, suffer fracture. L19. 3 *v.t. Phonol.* = BREAK *v.* 1f. L19.

1 M. CUTLER I fell upon a large round timber and fractured two ribs. 2 H. M. ROSENBERG What determines the point at which the specimen will fracture?

fracturable *a.* L19.

frae *prep.*, *adv.*, & *conj.* see FRO.

fraena *n.* pl. of FRAENUM.

fraenulum /ˈfriːnjʊləm/ *n.* Also **fren-**. Pl. **-la** /-lə/. E18. [mod.L dim. of next.] 1 *Anat.* A small fraenum. E18. 2 *Entomol.* A bristle or group of bristles attached to the base of the hindwing in some butterflies and moths, serving to interlock with the forewing in flight. L19.

fraenum /ˈfriːnəm/ *n.* Also **frenum**. Pl. **-na** /-nə/. M18. [L = bridle.] *Anat.* A ligament or membranous fold serving to check the motion of the part to which it is attached, *esp.* any of those underneath the tongue.

ovigerous fraenum in some cirripedes, a fold of the mantle to which the fertilized egg-masses are attached.

fragile /ˈfradʒʌɪl/ *a.* L15. [(O)Fr., or L *fragilis*, f. base of *frangere* break: see -ILE.] †1 Morally weak or vulnerable; liable to sin. L15–M16. 2

Liable to break or be broken; weak, perishable, easily destroyed. M16. **b** Of a person: delicate in frame, constitution, or physique. M19.

2 BACON Of Bodies, some are Fragile; and some are Tough. *fig.*: G. VIDAL My own position here is fragile. **b** A. NEWMAN She looked . . young and fragile.

fragilely *adv.* M19. **fragileness** *n.* E18.

fragility /frə'dʒɪlɪti/ *n.* LME. [(O)Fr. *fragilité* or L *fragilitas*, f. *fragilis*: see prec., -ITY.] †**1** Moral weakness. LME–E17. **2** The quality of being fragile. L15.

2 *fig.*: S. JOHNSON The fragility of beauty.

fragment /'fragm(ə)nt/ *n.* LME. [Fr., or L *fragmentum*, f. base of *frangere* break; see -MENT.] **1** A broken off, detached, or incomplete part (*lit.* & *fig.*); a (comparatively) small (detached) portion; a broken piece; a part remaining when the rest is lost or destroyed. LME. **b** An extant portion of a written work which as a whole is lost; a portion of work left uncompleted by its author; a part of anything uncompleted. L16. †**2** As a term of contempt. *rare* (Shakes.). Only in E17.

1 CONAN DOYLE He held our cards in his hand, and he tore them up and stamped on the fragments. B. TARKINGTON It seemed to him that the last fragment of his familiar world had disappeared.

fragment /frag'mɛnt, 'fragm(ə)nt/ *v.t.* & *i.* E19. [f. the n.] Break or separate into fragments (*lit.* & *fig.*).

H. FAST The population of the car was fragmented by language and origin. V. GLENDINNING The family began to fragment; sisters died or married and moved away.

fragmented *a.* broken or separated into fragments; disjointed, fragmentary: E19.

fragmental /frag'mɛnt(ə)l, 'fragm(ə)nt(ə)l/ *a.* E19. [f. FRAGMENT *n.* + -AL[1].] = next.

fragmentally *adv.* E19.

fragmentary /'fragm(ə)nt(ə)ri/ *a.* E17. [f. FRAGMENT *n.* + -ARY[1].] **1** Of the nature of, or composed of, fragments; not complete or entire; disconnected or disjointed. E17. **2** *Geol.* Composed of fragments of previously-existing rock or other substances. M19.

1 E. K. KANE Becoming embarrassed in fragmentary ice. B. JOWETT His knowledge is fragmentary and unconnected.

fragmentarily *adv.* M19. **fragmentariness** *n.* M19.

fragmentation /fragmɛn'teɪʃ(ə)n/ *n.* L19. [f. FRAGMENT *n.* + -ATION.] The action of breaking or separating into fragments; the state of being fragmented; *spec.* in *Biol.*, separation into parts which form new individuals or units.

Comb.: **fragmentation bomb, grenade**: designed to disintegrate into small fragments on explosion.

fragmentize /'fragm(ə)ntʌɪz/ *v.t.* Also **-ise**. E19. [f. FRAGMENT *n.* + -IZE.] Break into fragments.

fragmenti'zation *n.* M20. **fragmentizer** *n.* a machine for breaking up scrap metal L20.

†**fragor** *n.* E17–E18. [L, f. base of *frangere* break: see -OR.] A loud harsh noise, a crash, din.

fragrance /'freɪgr(ə)ns/ *n.* & *v.* M17. [(O)Fr., or L *fragrantia*, f. *fragrant-*: see FRAGRANT, -ANCE.] **A** *n.* Sweetness of smell; sweet or pleasing scent; (in *Cosmetics*) a scent; *fig.* a pleasing emotional association. M17.

KEATS To . . share The inward fragrance of each other's heart. J. C. POWYS There was a faint fragrance of sap-filled grass in the air.

B *v.t.* Supply or fill with fragrance. *rare.* M19.

fragrancy /'freɪgr(ə)nsi/ *n.* L16. [L *fragrantia*: see prec., -ANCY.] The quality of being fragrant; sweetness of smell.

fragrant /'freɪgr(ə)nt/ *a.* LME. [Fr., or L *fragrant-* pres. ppl stem of *fragrare* smell sweet: see -ANT[1].] Emitting a pleasant odour; sweet-smelling.

R. BROOKE From the inland meadows, Fragrant of June and clover, floats the dark. E. WAUGH Dust hung in the cool air, fragrant as crushed herbs. **fragrant orchid** an orchid, *Gymnadenia conopsea*, with fragrant lilac flowers, frequent in calcareous grassland.

fragrantly *adv.* E16.

'fraid /freɪd/ *a. colloq.* L19. [Aphet. f. AFRAID.] Expr. regret: (I'm) afraid.

R. KIPLING Wish I could, Lizzie. 'Fraid I can't. D. GRAY 'So you won't go on working here?' 'No. 'Fraid not.'

frail /freɪl/ *n.*[1] LME. [OFr. *fraiel*, of unkn. origin.] A kind of basket made of rushes, used for packing figs, raisins, etc.; the quantity of fruit contained in this. Also *frail-basket*.

frail /freɪl/ *n.*[2] *dial.* E19. [Dissimilated form of FLAIL *n.*] A flail.

frail /freɪl/ *n.*[3] *slang* (chiefly *US*). E20. [f. the adj.] A woman.

frail /freɪl/ *a.* ME. [OFr. *fraile*, *frele* (mod. *frêle*) f. L *fragilis* FRAGILE.] **1** Morally weak; unable to resist temptation; (of a woman, *arch.*) unchaste. Now *literary.* ME. **2** Liable to break or be broken; easily crushed or destroyed; fragile, transient. ME. **3** Weak in constitution or health; susceptible to illness; weakened by illness. ME. †**4** Tender. *rare* (Spenser). Only in L16.

1 W. IRVING The leniency of one who felt himself to be but frail. E. A. FREEMAN A child of the frail Abbess of Leominster. 2 J. MARTINEAU A profounder but a frailer bliss. J. F. LEHMANN The sun burnt more fiercely through the frail shield of the willow leaves. 3 P. H. GIBBS She looked thin, frail, and over-worked. W. BOYD The shock was too much for his frail body and he died in . . the morning.

frailly *adv.* ME. **frailness** *n.* (now *rare*) ME.

frail /freɪl/ *v.t. US dial.* M19. [Prob. f. FRAIL *n.*[2]] Beat, thrash.

frailty /'freɪlti/ *n.* ME. [OFr. *fraileté* f. L *fragilitas*, f. *fragilis* FRAGILE: see -ITY.] **1** Moral weakness; instability of mind; liability to yield to temptation. ME. **b** A fault arising from moral weakness, a foible. E17. **2** Physical weakness, perishableness, infirmity, susceptibility to damage or destruction; an instance of this. Formerly also, a frail feature, a flaw. LME.

1 SHAKES. *Oth.* Is't frailty that thus errs? **b** J. CHEEVER They quarreled like adults, with a cunning knowledge of each other's frailties. 2 J. UPDIKE A man whose increasing physical frailty compelled retreat from social excitements.

fraise /freɪz/ *n.*[1] E17. [Fr., = mesentery of a calf, in transf. use.] **1** A ruff such as was worn in the 16th cent. and was again fashionable in the 19th cent. E17. **2** A defensive palisade round a fortification, placed near the berm. L18.

fraise /freɪz/ *n.*[2] L19. [Fr., f. *fraiser* enlarge a circular hole.] A tool used for enlarging a circular hole; *Horology*, a tool with several cutting edges.

fraise *n.*[3] var. of FROISE.

fraise /freɪz/ *v.t.* E18. [Fr. *fraiser*, f. as FRAISE *n.*[1]] *Fortif.* Fence or defend with or as with a fraise.

Fraktur /'fraktʊə/ *n.* L19. [G.] *Typogr.* A German style of black letter, the normal type used for printing German from the 16th to the mid 20th cent.

framable /'freɪməb(ə)l/ *a.* Also **frameable**. L16. [f. FRAME *v.* + -ABLE.] Able to be framed. Formerly also, conformable.

framboesia /fram'biːzɪə/ *n.* Also ***-bes-**. E19. [mod.L, f. as next: see -IA[1].] The disease yaws.

framboise /frɑːm'bwɑːz/ *n.* & *a.* L16. [(O)Fr. f. Proto-Gallo-Romance, conflation of L *fraga ambrosia* ambrosian strawberry.] **A** *n.* †**1** The raspberry. L16–M17. **2** A shade of pink: raspberry colour. M20. **B** *adj.* Of raspberry colour. E20.

frame /freɪm/ *n.* ME. [f. the vb.] †**I 1** Advantage, benefit, profit. Only in ME.

II Action or manner of framing. **2**†**a** A large body of people, an array. Only in LME. **b** An established order or system, esp. of government. L16. †**c** An arrangement of words; a formula in logic. E17–M18. †**3** Adapted or adjusted condition; definite form, regular procedure; order. L15–E19. **4** The action of framing or constructing; a contrivance, a plan. *obs.* exc. *N. Amer. slang*, a frame-up. M16. **5** Mental or emotional disposition or state. More fully *frame of mind.* M16. **6** The manner of framing; structure; constitution, nature. L16.

2b SHAKES. *Macb.* But let the frame of things disjoint, both the worlds suffer. **frame of reference** (*a*) a system of coordinate axes in relation to which position may be defined and motion conceived of as taking place; (*b*) a set of standards governing perceptual or logical evaluation or social behaviour. 3 SHAKES. *Haml.* Good my lord, put your discourse into some frame. 5 DEFOE In this thankful frame I continued. T. DREISER Short . . was in an exceedingly jovial frame of mind. 6 SPENSER The goodly frame . . of Castle Joyeous.

III A framed work, a structure. **7a** The universe, the heavens, the earth, or any part of it, regarded as a structure. ME. †**b** Any structure, device, or machine constructed of parts fitted together. LME–E18. **c** The animal, esp. the human body, with reference to its build or constitution. L16. **d** *Newfoundland.* A string of nets for catching seals. E19. **e** An emaciated animal (*Austral.* & *US*); in *pl.* (*Austral.*), draught cattle. L19. **8** A supporting structure; a structure of which the outline or skeleton is not filled in; a framework. LME. **b** *spec.* A structure of wood, steel, or concrete, which supports and forms an integral part of a building. LME. **c** A building, *esp.* a wooden one. Now only *US*, a frame house etc. (see below). LME. **d** A supporting structure used in embroidery. Formerly also, a loom. E16. **e** *Printing.* A piece of furniture carrying cases of type and other equipment, at which a compositor works. L17. **f** That part of a pair of spectacles which encloses the lenses and holds them in position. M19. **g** The rigid part of a bicycle. L19. **h** In *Snooker* etc., the triangular form used in setting up the red balls; these balls as set up, or the round of play required to pocket all the balls in order. Similarly in *Skittles* & *Tenpin Bowling*, each of the several innings forming a game. L19. **i** The supporting skeleton of a motor vehicle, aircraft (cf. *airframe* s.v. AIR *n.*[1]), etc. E20. **9** A surrounding structure, such as a case or border, in which something such as a picture or a pane of glass is set or let in. L16. **b** *Hort.* A portable or fixed structure covered with transparent material, used to protect seeds and young plants. L17. **c** An open box of slats in which bees build and which can be removed from the hive. L17. **d** Any of various utensils of which the outer case or border is an important part. E18. **e** *Cinemat.* Any of the series of separate pictures on a film. E20. **f** *Television.* A single complete image or picture built up from a series of lines. M20. **10** *Computing.* A complete or self-identifying message in a data communication system; a section of a recording on magnetic tape that comprises a single bit in each track. L20.

7c A. FRASER For all her slight frame, she was not unathletic. 8 P. S. BUCK The door was hung loosely upon a warped wood frame. *climbing frame*: see CLIMB *v.* I. *mainframe*: see MAIN *a.* *walking frame*: see WALKING *n.* *X-frame*: see X, X. ZIMMER *frame.* 9 T. S. ELIOT A photograph in a silver frame. *fig.*: H. CARPENTER Its opening and closing passages provide a frame to the narrative. **in the frame** under consideration, in the spotlight. **b** *cold frame*: see COLD *a.*

Comb.: **frame aerial** a radio aerial composed of a rectangle or loop of wire, adapted for directional reception; **frame-breaker** *Hist.* a Luddite; **frame drum**: with its head(s) stretched over a frame or hoop; **frame dwelling, house**, etc.: built of wood, supported by a framework of timbers; **frame-saw** a thin saw stretched in a frame, which gives it rigidity; **frame story**: that serves as a framework within which a number of other stories are told; **frame work** work done on or with a frame (cf. FRAMEWORK).

frameless *a.* having no frame M19.

frame /freɪm/ *v.* [OE *framian*, f. base of FROM. Cf. ON *frama* to further, advance, & related ON *fremja* to further, advance, perform, which prob. infl. the sense-development.] †**1** *v.i.* Profit, be of service. OE–ME. **2** *v.i.* Make progress; prosper, succeed; fare. *obs.* exc. *dial.* OE. †**3** *v.t.* Make ready for use; equip or adorn *with*. Only in ME. †**4** *v.t.* Prepare (timber) for use in building; hew out; perform the carpenter's work for (a building). ME–E18. **5** *v.t.* **a** Contrive, devise, invent (a plot, rule, story, etc.); compose; express. LME. **b** Conceive, imagine. *arch.* L16. †**c** Cause, produce. Only in L16. **d** Form, articulate, utter (words, sounds). E17. **6** *v.t.* Make, construct. LME. †**7a** *v.t.* Give shape to, form (with material object); compose, give expression to (the face). L15–E18. **b** *v.t.* Shape, direct (one's thoughts, actions, etc.) to a certain purpose; *arch.* dispose, lead, (a person). Foll. by *for*, *to*, *to do*. M16. **c** *v.t.* & *i.* Direct (one's steps); set out upon (a journey); shape one's course, go. *obs.* exc. *dial.* L16. **d** *v.i.* & *t.* Prepare, attempt, or pretend to do something; contrive *to* do something. Also, show promise in an activity. Now chiefly *dial.* E17. **8** *v.t.* Adapt, adjust, fit (chiefly an immaterial object) *to* or *into* (something). M16. †**b** *v.i.* Adapt oneself, conform. Of things: suit, fit. M16–M17. **9** *v.t.* Set or enclose in a frame; serve as a frame for. E18. **10** *v.t.* Concoct a false charge or accusation against; devise a scheme or plot with regard to; make the victim of a frame-up. *slang* (orig. *US*). E20.

5a M. MCCARTHY She . . stood looking out into the garden, endeavouring to frame an apology. R. P. GRAVES The motion was framed in anti-conservative terms. **frame up** *N. Amer. slang* prearrange (an event) surreptitiously and with sinister intent; plan in secret; fake the result of. **b** GEO. ELIOT He could frame to himself no probable image of love-scenes between them. **c** SHAKES. *2 Hen. VI* Fear frames disorder. **6** B. JOWETT The things in heaven are framed by the Creator in the most perfect manner. **7a** SHAKES. *3 Hen. VI* I can . . frame my face to all occasions. **b** S. PEPYS We were as merry as I could frame myself to be. J. KEBLE Thy silent grace, framing aright our lowly orisons. **c** E. BRONTË Frame upstairs, and make little din. **d** MRS H. WARD He frames well in speaking. **8** WORDSWORTH Unto this he frames his song. **9** J. CARLYLE I have your . . Villa framed and hung up. D. M. THOMAS Her long straight black hair framed a somewhat heavy face. **10** C. E. MULFORD Honest men framed, and guilty men let off for political reasons.

Comb.: **frame-up** (*colloq.*, orig. *US*) something that has been prearranged or concocted, esp. with a sinister intent; a conspiracy or plot, e.g. to incriminate a person on false evidence.

framed *a.* that has been framed; provided with a frame: LME. **framer** *n.* a person who frames something LME. **framing** *vbl n.* (*a*) the action of the verb; (*b*) a framework; a frame or set or system of frames: LME.

frameable *a.* var. of FRAMABLE.

framework /ˈfreɪmwəːk/ *n.* See also *frame work* s.v. FRAME *n.* L16. [f. FRAME *n.* + WORK *n.*] A structure made of parts joined to form a frame; *esp.* one designed to enclose or support; a frame, a skeleton.

F. C. BURNAND The old arm-chair, whose framework had been made any number of years ago. *fig.*: H. I. ANSOFF A large majority of decisions must be made within the framework of a limited total resource. *Tribune* A legal framework for individual workers' rights. **framework of reference** = *frame of reference* s.v. FRAME *n.* 2b.

frampold /ˈframp(ə)ld/ *a. obs.* exc. *dial.* L16. [Origin unkn.] **1** Peevish, cross. L16. **2** Of a horse: fiery, spirited. E17.

franc /fraŋk/ *n.* LME. [(O)Fr., derived from the legend *Francorum rex* king of the Franks, on gold coins first struck in the reign (1350–64) of Jean le Bon.] Orig., a gold coin used in medieval France; later, a silver coin used in France. Now, the basic monetary unit of France, Belgium, Switzerland, and other (formerly) French-speaking countries. Cf. CENTIME, RAPPEN.

franc-archer /frɑ̃karʃe/ *n.* Pl. ***franc-archers*** (pronounced same), ***francs-archers*** /frɑ̃zarʃe/. L17. [Fr., lit. 'free archer'.] *Fr. Hist.* A member of a body of archers established by Charles VII, and exempted from taxes in consideration of their services.

franchise /ˈfran(t)ʃʌɪz/ *n.* ME. [(O)Fr., f. *franc*, fem. *franche* free, FRANK *a.*[1] + *-ise*, repr. L *-itia*, -ESS[2].] †**1** Nobility of mind; liberality, magnanimity. ME–M17. †**2** Freedom; exemption from servitude or subjection. ME–M17. **3** A legal immunity or exemption from a particular burden or jurisdiction, granted to an individual, a corporation, etc. Now chiefly *Hist.* ME. **b** A percentage specified in a marine insurance policy below which the underwriter incurs no responsibility. M19. **4** A right or privilege granted by the power of the monarch to any individual or group of people. LME. **b** The powers granted by a governing body to any company set up for the public interest. *US.* E19. **c** The authorization granted to a sports club, certifying its existence and ownership. *N. Amer.* E20. **d** The authorization granted by a company to sell its products or services in a particular area. M20. **e** An outstanding player in a team sport. *US colloq.* M20. †**5** Freedom from arrest, granted to fugitives in certain privileged places; right of asylum or sanctuary. Also, an asylum, a sanctuary. LME–E17. **6** The freedom or full membership of a corporation or state; citizenship. LME. †**7** The area over which a privilege extends; a territory, domain. LME–L19. **8** The right of voting at public elections. L18. **b** Any one of the principles of qualification for the right to vote. L19.

3 P. HOLLAND A most famous towne . . with the franchises and right of a Colonie. **4** J. E. T. ROGERS The right of having a watermill was a franchise. **c** S. BELLOW The politics surrounding cable-TV franchises in Chicago. *Times* Liverpool is probably the only major city in England without a McDonald's franchise. **6** C. THIRLWALL Those citizens who had been deprived of their franchise for lighter offences. **8** V. S. NAIPAUL First election with universal adult franchise. **b** *fancy franchise*: see FANCY *n.* & *a.*

franchisal *a.* of or belonging to franchises L19. **franchiˈsee** *n.* a holder of a franchise (FRANCHISE *n.* 4d) M20. **franchiser** *n.* (*a*) *rare* a person who is entitled to vote; (*b*) a company which or person who grants franchises: M19. **franchisor** *n.* = FRANCHISER (b) M20.

franchise /ˈfran(t)ʃʌɪz/ *v.t.* LME. [(O)Fr. *franchiss-* lengthened stem of *franchir*, f. *franc*, fem. *franche* free: see FRANK *a.*[1] Cf. AFFRANCHISE, ENFRANCHISE.] Now chiefly as *franchised* ppl a., *franchising* vbl n. **1** Make or set free; invest with a franchise or privilege; = ENFRANCHISE. Now *rare.* LME. **2a** Confer certain powers on (a company set up for the public interest). *US.* E20. **b** Grant a franchise to; authorize (an individual) to sell certain products or services in a particular area. M20.

†**franchisement** *n.* [OFr.] = ENFRANCHISEMENT M16–E19.

†**Francic** *a.* L17–M19. [med.L *Francicus*, f. *Francus* FRANK *n.*[1]: see -IC.] Of or pertaining to the ancient Franks or their language.

francisc /franˈsɪsk/ *n.* Also in L form **-cisca** /-ˈsɪskə/. E19. [(Fr. *francisque* f.) med.L *francisca.*] *Hist.* A kind of battleaxe used by the ancient Franks.

Franciscan /franˈsɪsk(ə)n/ *n.* & *a.* L16. [Fr. *franciscain* f. mod.L *Franciscanus*, f. *Franciscus* Francis: see below, -AN.] **A** *n.* A friar or nun of the order founded by St Francis of Assisi in 1209. L16. **B** *adj.* Of or belonging to the order of St Francis; pertaining to the Franciscans. L16.

Franciscanism *n.* (*rare*) the system and practice of the Franciscans M19.

francise *v.* var. of FRANCIZE.

francium /ˈfransɪəm/ *n.* M20. [f. *France* country of the element's discoverer + -IUM.] A radioactive chemical element, atomic no. 87, which is the heaviest member of the alkali metal group and occurs as a decay product in uranium ores. (Symbol Fr.) Cf. VIRGINIUM

francize /ˈfransʌɪz/ *v.t.* Also **-ise**. M17. [Fr. *franciser*, f. *français* French.] Make French; *spec.* (in Quebec) cause to adopt French as an official or working language.

franciˈzation *n.* the action of making something French; the status thus conferred; *spec.* (in Quebec) the adoption of French as an official or working language: M17.

Franck-Condon /fraŋkˈkɒnd(ə)n/ *a.* E20. [J. *Franck* (1882–1964) and E. U. *Condon* (1902–74), US physicists.] *Physics.* Designating or associated with the principle that an electronic transition leaves the nuclear configuration of a molecule unchanged.

franco /ˈfraŋko/ *a.* & *adv.* L19. [It. (*porto*) *franco* free (carriage).] Of a foreign business transaction: free of any postal or delivery charge.

Franco- /ˈfraŋkəʊ/ *comb. form.* [f. med.L *Francus* FRANK *n.*[1] + -O-.] Forming adj. and n. combs. with the meaning 'French, Frankish or French and —', as *Franco-Canadian*, *Franco-German*, *Franco-Prussian*, *Franco-Roman*. Cf. GALLO-[1].

Francoˈmania *n.* a craze or excessive liking for France and French things L19. **Francophil(e)** *a.* & *n.* (a person who is) friendly towards France or fond of France and French things L19. **Francoˈphilia** *n.* friendliness towards France; excessive fondness for France and French things: M20. **Francophobe** *a.* & *n.* (a person who is) affected with Francophobia L19. **Francoˈphobia** *n.* dread or dislike of France and French things L19.

François Premier /frɑ̃swa prəmje/ *a. phr.* M19. [Fr. = Francis I (see below).] Designating the styles of architecture, furniture, etc., characteristic of the reign of Francis I, King of France 1515–47.

Francoist /ˈfraŋkəʊɪst/ *n.* & *a.* M20. [f. *Franco* (see below) + -IST.] **A** *n.* A supporter of (the policies of) General Francisco *Franco* y Bahamonde (1892–1975), Spanish Nationalist leader and later dictator of Spain. M20. **B** *adj.* Of, pertaining to, or supporting the regime, policies, or principles of Franco. M20.

francolin /ˈfraŋkəlɪn/ *n.* M17. [Fr. f. It. *francolino*, of unkn. origin.] Any of numerous African or Asian partridges belonging to the genus *Francolinus.*

Franconian /franˈkəʊnɪən/ *a.* & *n.* E19. [f. *Franconia* (see below) + -AN.] **A** *adj.* Of or pertaining to (the inhabitants of) Franconia, a region of Germany, formerly a duchy, bordering the River Main. E19. **B** *n.* **1** A native or inhabitant of Franconia. M19. **2** *collect.* A group of medieval West Germanic dialects, combining features of Low and High German. M20.

francophone /ˈfraŋkə(ʊ)fəʊn/ *n.* & *a.* Also **F-**. E20. [f. FRANCO- + Gk *phōnē* voice.] (A person who is) French-speaking.

francs-archers *n.pl.* see FRANC-ARCHER.

franc tireur /frɑ̃ tirœːr/ *n. phr.* Pl. **-s -s** (pronounced same). E19. [Fr. = free shooter.] An irregular soldier, a guerrilla fighter; *Hist.* a member of an irregular French light-infantry corps, originating in the Revolutionary wars.

frangible /ˈfrandʒɪb(ə)l/ *a.* LME. [OFr. or med.L *frangibilis*, f. *frangere* break: see -IBLE.] Able to be broken, breakable, fragile.

frangiˈbility *n.* L18.

frangipane /ˈfrandʒɪpeɪn/ *n.* L17. [Fr., f. as next.] **1** = FRANGIPANI 1. L17. **2** = FRANGIPANI 2. M19. **3** An almond-flavoured cream or paste. M19.

frangipani /frandʒɪˈpani, -ˈpɑːni/ *n.* Also (now *rare*) **-panni**. M19. [*Frangipani*, 16th-cent. It. marquis, inventor of a perfume for scenting gloves.] **1** A perfume resembling jasmine. Now *spec.* the scent of the blossom of the frangipani plant, or an imitation of it. M19. **2** A fragrant ornamental shrub or tree of the neotropical genus *Plumeria*, of the dogbane family, *esp.* red jasmine, *P. rubra.* L19.

franglais /frɑ̃glɛ/ *n.* M20. [Fr., blend of *français* French and *anglais* English.] A corrupt version of the French language marked by the indiscriminate use of words and phrases of British and American origin.

franion /ˈfranɪən/ *n.* Long *arch.* *rare.* M16. [Origin unkn.] A gallant, a lover. Also (Spenser), a promiscuous woman.

Frank /fraŋk/ *n.*[1] [OE *Franca* = OHG *Franko*, perh. named after a weapon: cf. OE *franca* javelin. Reinforced in ME by med.L *Francus*, (O)Fr. *Franc*, f. Gmc. Cf. SAXON.] **1** A member of the Germanic nation or nations that conquered Gaul in the 6th cent., and from which the country received the name France. OE. **2** In the eastern Mediterranean region: a person of Western nationality. Cf. FERINGHEE. L17.

†**frank** *n.*[2] LME–E19. [OFr. *franc* sty, f. Gmc.] An enclosure, *esp.* one for feeding hogs or other animals in, a sty.

frank /fraŋk/ *n.*[3] E18. [f. FRANK *v.*[2]] **1** *Hist.* The superscribed signature of a person entitled to send letters free of charge. E18. **b** A letter bearing such a signature. M18. 2 The mark or impression made on an envelope etc. by franking it; a franked cover. M20.

frank /fraŋk/ *n.*[4] *dial.* E19. [Imit. of the bird's cry.] The heron.

frank /fraŋk/ *n.*[5] *colloq.* (chiefly *N. Amer.*). M20. [Abbrev.] A frankfurter.

frank /fraŋk/ *a.*[1] ME. [(O)Fr. *franc*, *franche* f. med.L *francus* free. Orig. identical with the ethnic name *Francus* (see FRANK *n.*[1]).] 1 †a Free; not in slavery or captivity. ME–M17. b Free from restriction, obligation, or anxiety. Long *obs.* exc. *Hist.*, in (chiefly legal) collocations as FRANK-FEE, FRANK-PLEDGE, etc. ME. 2 Liberal, bounteous, generous. Now *rare.* ME. †3 Of a plant, tree, etc.: of superior quality, producing good or abundant fruit, flowers, etc. Also of a drug or remedy: of high quality, valuable. Cf. FRANKINCENSE. L15–M17. †4 Luxuriant in growth, vigorous. M16–E17. 5 Ingenuous, open, sincere; candid, outspoken. M16. b Undisguised, avowed. M18. c *Med.* Unmistakable, obvious. L19.

2 CARLYLE He..set about improvements..on a frank scale. 5 E. LINKLATER His scowl had vanished, and he smiled in a large, frank, and genial way. L. DURRELL Though she was evasive with the doctors she was perfectly frank with her friends. A. THWAITE Before they had even met, they were frank critics of each other's poetry. b A. WILSON He leaned his head back against the chair and gave way to frank laughter. c R. D. LAING Schizoid manifestations..perilously close to frank psychosis. *Lancet* Foul-smelling infected urine often containing frank blood.

†**Frank** *a.*[2] M16–L17. [f. FRANK *n.*[1]] Native to or characteristic of the Western nations of Europe.

frank /fraŋk/ *v.*[1]*t.* LME. [f. FRANK *n.*[2]] 1 Enclose and feed (*up*) in an enclosure. Long *rare.* LME. †2 Feed *up*, cram. M16–M17.

frank /fraŋk/ *v.*[2]*t.* E18. [f. FRANK *a.*[1]] 1 a *Hist.* Sign (a letter etc.) to ensure transmission free of charge. E18. b Put an official sign or mark on (a letter etc.), by mechanical means, to record payment of postage. Also *gen.*, put any official sign on (an envelope etc.). E20. c Put a postmark on (a letter etc.) or on top of (a postage stamp). M20. 2 *fig.* Facilitate the coming and going of (a person); provide with a social entrée to. *arch.* E19. 3 Pay the passage of (a person); convey gratuitously. *arch.* E19. 4 Exempt, make immune; *esp.* (*Hist.*) exempt from future payment of tax etc. L19.

1b F. RAPHAEL The envelopes ...were franked 'STUDENT'S EXERCISE'. DAVID POTTER Letters and packets are franked with a handstamp or machine impression. **franking machine**: for officially marking letters with a sign in lieu of a postage stamp and recording the cost of postage incurred. 2 T. COLLINS I have enough money to frank myself in a frugal way for some weeks. 3 J. H. BURTON An opportunity of being franked to Poland.

franker *n.* (*a*) a person who franks a letter; (*b*) a machine or device for franking letters: L18.

frankalmoign /'fraŋk(ə)lmɔɪn/ *n.* E16. [AN *fraunke almoigne*. Cf. FRANK *a.*[1], ALMOIGN.] *Law* (now *Hist.*). A feudal tenure in England by which a religious body could hold land perpetually, usu. in return for praying for the soul of the donor and his descendants.

Frankenstein /'fraŋk(ə)nstʌɪn/ *n.* M19. [The title of a novel (1818) by Mary Shelley whose eponymous main character constructed and gave life to a human monster. Often wrongly used as the name of the monster itself.] A terrible creation; a thing that becomes terrifying to its creator. Also *Frankenstein('s) monster.*

Franken'steinian *a.* M20.

Frankenthal /'fraŋk(ə)ntɑːl/ *n.* M19. [A town in the Palatinate, Germany.] In full *Frankenthal porcelain, ware*, etc. A porcelain made at Frankenthal from the middle to the end of the 19th cent.

frank-fee /'fraŋkfiː/ *n.* LME. [f. FRANK *a.*[1] + FEE *n.*[2]] *Law.* A tenure of land in fee simple; land so held.

frankfold /'fraŋkfəʊld/ *n. obs.* exc. *Hist.* E17. [f. FRANK *a.*[1] + FOLD *v.*[2]] *Law.* = FALDAGE 2.

frankfurter /'fraŋkfəːtə/ *n.* Also ***frankfurt.** L19. [G *Frankfurter Wurst* Frankfurt sausage.] A seasoned smoked beef and pork sausage, originally made at Frankfurt am Main in Germany.

frankincense /'fraŋkɪnsɛns/ *n.* LME. [OFr. *franc encens* lit. 'high-quality (see FRANK *a.*[1]) incense'.] An aromatic gum resin used esp. for burning as incense, obtained from trees of the genus *Boswellia* (family Burseraceae), native to Somalia. Also, a similar resin obtained from fir or pine trees. Also, a tree yielding such a resin.

Frankish /'fraŋkɪʃ/ *a.* & *n.* ME. [f. FRANK *n.*[1] + -ISH[1].] A *adj.* †1 Of or pertaining to France or the French. Only in ME. 2 Of or pertaining to the ancient Franks. LME. 3 Of or pertaining to the Western nations of Europe. (Cf. FRANK *n.*[1] 2.) *rare.* L16. B *n.* †1 The language or people of France. Only in ME. 2†a *collect. pl. The* ancient Franks. Only in ME. b The language of the ancient Franks. M19.

franklin /'fraŋklɪn/ *n.*[1] ME. [AL *francalanus*, f. *francalis* held without fees, f. *francus* free: see FRANK *a.*[1], -AL[1], -AN.] †1 A freeman. Only in ME. 2 A freeholder; *spec.* in the 14th and 15th cents., a member of a class of landowners of free but not noble birth, ranking below the gentry. Now only *Hist.* ME. †3 A liberal host. L16–E18.

2 LYTTON His dress was that of a substantial franklin.

Franklin /'fraŋklɪn/ *n.*[2] L18. [Benjamin *Franklin* (1706–1790), US statesman, inventor, and scientist.] 1 In full *Franklin stove.* A free-standing stove for heating a room. Also, a kind of iron fireplace. *N. Amer.* L18. 2 More fully *Franklin's rod.* A lightning conductor. *US. arch.* E19.

Fran'klinian *a.* & *n.* (*a*) *adj.* of, pertaining to, or characteristic of Benjamin Franklin; (*b*) *n.* a follower of Franklin: M18. **franklini'zation** *n.* (*Med.*, *arch.*) the therapeutic use of static electricity L19.

franklinite /'fraŋklɪnʌɪt/ *n.* E19. [f. *Franklin*, borough in New Jersey (ult. f. as prec.) + -ITE[1].] *Min.* An oxide of zinc and iron, often with some manganese, which is a mineral of the magnetite group and usu. occurs as black octahedral crystals.

frankly /'fraŋkli/ *adv.* M16. [f. FRANK *a.*[1] + -LY[2].] †1 Freely; without restriction or restraint. M16–E17. 2 Generously, bountifully; unconditionally, unreservedly. Now *rare.* M16. 3 Without concealment or reserve; avowedly, openly, plainly. M16. 4 With freedom of artistic expression. M19.

2 C. BRONTË The power of meriting the kindness.. so frankly offered. 3 E. BOWEN Quite frankly, the country gives me the creeps. J. BARTH Wingate told me frankly I was a damn fool. A. T. ELLIS The tourist haunts were..frankly bent on commerce and communication.

frankmarriage /'fraŋkmarɪdʒ/ *n.* ME. [AN *franc mariage*: see FRANK *a.*[1], MARRIAGE.] *Law* (now *Hist.*). A tenure by which a man and his wife held lands granted to them by the father or other blood relative of the wife, which were heritable for four generations, in return for no other service than fealty.

frankness /'fraŋknɪs/ *n.* M16. [f. FRANK *a.*[1] + -NESS.] 1 Freedom of manner or approach; candour, ingenuousness, openness; *spec.* outspokenness. M16. †2 Bounteousness, generosity. L16–M18. 3 Freedom of artistic expression. L18.

1 J. TYNDALL I shall offend them..by my frankness in stating this.

frank-pledge /'fraŋkplɛdʒ/ *n.* ME. [Law L *franciplegium*, Latinization of AN *fraunc plege*, f. AN *fraunc*, (O)Fr. *franc* FRANK *a.*[1] + *plege* PLEDGE *n.*, mistr. *frithborh* s.v. FRITH *n.*[1], through the altered forms *freoborg*, *friborg*, in which the 1st elem. was identified w. *free.*] *Law* (now *Hist.*). 1 Each of the mutually responsible members of a tithing etc. Also (occas.) the tithing itself. ME. 2 The system by which each member of a tithing was responsible for the good conduct of, or damage done by, every other member. LME.

2 **view of frank-pledge** a court held periodically for the production of the members of a tithing or later of a hundred or a manor.

frantic /'frantɪk/ *a.*, *n.*, & *adv.* Also †**fren-**, †**phren-**. LME. [(O)Fr. *frénétique* f. L *phreneticus* FRENETIC. The early change from *-e-* to *-a-* is unaccounted for.] A *adj.* 1 Of a person. a Mentally deranged, insane; violently or ragingly mad. Now *rare* or *obs.* LME. b Wildly excited; distraught with rage, pain, grief, or other emotion. E17. 2 Of an action, quality, etc.: pertaining to or displaying frenzy, uncontrolled, violent. E16. †b Of a disease: accompanied by delirium or frenzy. L16–E18. 3 Extreme, very great. *colloq.* E20.

1a A. B. JAMESON His father, believing him frantic, shut him up..in his chamber. b J. K. JEROME Little mishaps, that..drive you nearly frantic with rage, when they occur on the water. 2 H. KELLER I felt as if invisible hands were holding me, and I made frantic efforts to free myself. 3 I. MURDOCH He felt a.. frantic desire for a drink.

†B *n.* A person who is frantic; a lunatic, a delirious patient. LME–M18.

†C *adv.* In a frantic manner. *rare.* L16–M17.

frantically *adv.* M18. **franticly** *adv.* M16. **franticness** *n.* E16.

frap /frap/ *n. rare.* L16. [Imit.: cf. RAP *n.*[1]] A noise made by knocking.

frap /frap/ *v.* Infl. **-pp-**. ME. [OFr. *fraper* (mod. *frapper*).] 1 *v.t.* & †*i.* (w. *at*, *on*). Strike, beat. *obs.* exc. *dial.* ME. 2 *v.t. Naut.* Tie or bind together (esp. halyards) to increase tension or to prevent from blowing loose. M16.

frapping *vbl n.* (*a*) the action of the verb; (*b*) *Naut.* a rope for binding or lashing: E19.

†**frape** *n.*[1] ME–E18. [App. f. OFr. *frap* multitude, of unkn. origin.] A crowd; a mob, a rabble.

frape /freɪp/ *n.*[2] E18. [Prob. f. FRAP *v.*] 1 In full *frape-boat.* A type of boat with much frapping. *rare.* E18. 2 A rope used for mooring a boat. E20.

†**fraple** *v.i.* L16–E17. [Perh. f. OFr. *frapillier* grow angry or indignant.] Dispute, wrangle, bluster.

frapler /'fraplə/ *n. arch.* L16. [f. prec. + -ER[1].] A blusterer, a bully.

frappant /frapɑ̃/ *a.* L18. [Fr., pres. pple of *frapper* strike.] Striking, impressive.

frappé /frape, 'frapeɪ/ *a.* & *n.* M19. [Fr., pa. pple of *frapper* in sense of 'to ice (drinks)'.] A *adj.* (Chiefly of wine) iced, cooled; (of a drink) served with crushed ice. M19. B *n.* A drink served with crushed ice or frozen to a slushy consistency. E20.

Frascati /fra'skɑːti/ *n.* M20. [A district in Latium, Italy, SE of Rome.] A wine, usu. white, produced in the Frascati region.

frass /fras/ *n.* M19. [G, f. *fressen* devour (see FRET *v.*[1]).] The excrement of larvae; the refuse left behind by boring insects.

frat /frat/ *n.*[1] *N. Amer. slang.* L19. [Abbrev.] (A member of) a students' fraternity.

frat /frat/ *n.*[2] & *v. slang.* M20. [Abbrev.] A *n.* 1 Fraternization by troops. M20. 2 A woman with whom a soldier fraternizes. M20. B *v.i.* Infl. **-tt-**. Fraternize (*with*). M20.

fratter *n.* M20.

fratch /fratʃ/ *v.* & *n.* Also **thratch** /θratʃ/. LME. [Prob. imit.] A *v.i.* †1 Make a harsh or strident noise; creak. LME–L15. 2 Disagree, quarrel; scold. Now chiefly *dial.* E18. B *n.* A disagreement, a quarrel. E19.

fratchety, fratchy *adjs.* scolding, quarrelsome L19.

frate /'frɑːti, *foreign* 'fraːte/ *n.* Pl. **-ti** /-ti/. E18. [It., lit. 'brother'.] An Italian friar.

frater /'freɪtə/ *n.*[1] ME. [OFr. *fraitur* aphet. f. *refreitor*, f. late L *refectorium* REFECTORY.] *Hist.* The dining-room of a monastery; a refectory.

frater /'freɪtə/ *n.*[2] M16. [L = brother.] †1 An Abraham-man. M16–L17. †2 A friar. L16–M17. 3 A brother: a comrade. L18.

fraternal /frə'təːn(ə)l/ *a.* & *n.* LME. [med.L *fraternalis*, f. L *fraternus*, f. *frater* brother: see -AL[1].] A *adj.* Of, pertaining to, or characteristic of, a brother or brothers; brotherly. LME.

fraternal order *US* a brotherhood or friendly society. **fraternal polyandry**: in which a woman married to one man is also wife to that man's brother(s). **fraternal twin**: developed from a separate ovum and not necessarily closely similar to its sibling.

B *n. Med.* A fraternal twin. E20.

fraternally *adv.* E17.

fraternise *v.* var. of FRATERNIZE.

fraternity /frəˈtəːnɪti/ *n.* ME. [(O)Fr. *fraternité* f. L *fraternitas*, f. *fraternus*: see FRATERNAL, -ITY.] 1 A group or order of men organized for religious or devout purposes. ME. 2 A group of men associated by some common interest, or of the same class, occupation, etc.; a guild or company. LME. b A male students' society at a college or university, usu. with a name consisting of three letters of the Greek alphabet; a student association for academic and extracurricular activities. *N. Amer.* L18. 3 The relationship between brothers; brotherhood. LME. 4 The state or quality of being fraternal; brotherliness. LME.

2 A. J. CRONIN Emmy . . preferred always to stop at those cafés likely to be frequented by the sporting fraternity. 4 *Observer* Too much fratricide, too little fraternity.

fraternize /ˈfratənʌɪz/ *v.* Also **-ise**. E17. [Fr. *fraterniser* f. med.L *fraternizare*, f. *fraternus*: see FRATERNAL, -IZE.] 1 *v.i.* Form a friendship or associate (*with*), as a brother or brothers. E17. b *spec.* Enter into friendly relations or associate socially with or *with* troops of an occupying power or civilians of an occupied country, usu. in contravention of military orders; *esp.* (of a soldier) have sexual relations with a woman of an occupied country. L19. 2 *v.t.* Bring into fraternal association; unite as brothers. Now *rare.* M17.

1 SIR W. SCOTT Too little of a democrat to fraternize with an affiliated society of the *soi-disant* Friends of the People. b *transf.*: F. TRUEMAN It was made clear by Len Hutton that we should not fraternize with the West Indian cricketers. 2 COLERIDGE To know ourselves Parts and proportions of one wondrous whole! This fraternizes man.

fraterniˈzation *n.* [Fr. *fraternisation*] the action of fraternizing; fraternal association: L18. **fraternizer** *n.* L18.

fratery *n.* var. of FRATRY *n.*^{1}

frati *n.* pl. of FRATE.

fratricide /ˈfratrɪsʌɪd/ *n.* L15. [(O)Fr. or (in sense 1) L *fratricida*, (in sense 2) late L *fratricidium*, f. L *fratr-* *frater* brother: see -CIDE.] 1 A person who kills his or her brother or sister. L15. 2 The action of killing one's brother or sister. M16.

fratriˈcidal *a.* E19.

fratry /ˈfreɪtri/ *n.*^{1} Now *rare.* Also **-tery** /-t(ə)ri/. LME. [App. f. FRATER *n.*^{1} + -Y^{3}.] = FRATER *n.*^{1}

fratry /ˈfreɪtri/ *n.*^{2} *obs.* exc. *Hist.* M16. [med.L *fratria*, *fratreia* fraternity, app. infl. by Gk *phratria*.] A fraternity or brotherhood; a friary.

Frau /fraʊ/ *n.* Pl. **-en** /-ən/, **-s**. E19. [G. Cf. FROW *n.*^{1}] A German or Austrian woman. Freq. as a title, corresponding to *Mrs.*

fraud /frɔːd/ *n.* ME. [(O)Fr. *fraude* f. L *fraud-*, *fraus* deceit, injury.] 1 The use of false representations to gain unjust advantage; criminal deception. ME. b The quality of being deceitful; insincerity. Now *rare.* LME. †c A state of delusion. *rare* (Milton). M–L17. 2 An act or instance of deception; a dishonest artifice or trick. LME. 3 A method or means of deceiving; now *esp.* a person or thing not fulfilling expectation or description, an impostor. M17.

1 SWIFT They look upon fraud as a greater crime than theft. b LD MACAULAY Vices . . which are the natural defence of weakness, fraud and hypocrisy. c MILTON So glister'd the dire Snake, and into fraud Led Eve. 2 M. TWAIN It was a base fraud—a snare to trap the unwary. 3 W. COWPER Not all . . Can . . Discern the fraud beneath the specious lure. R. COBB He's a bit of a fraud . . well, let us say, he exaggerates.

Phrases: **in fraud of** so as to defraud. *pious fraud*: see PIOUS *a.*

Comb.: **fraudsman** a cheat, an impostor, a fraud. **fraud squad** a division of a police force appointed to investigate fraud.

fraudful *a.* fraudulent, treacherous LME. **fraudfully** *adv.* LME. **fraudless** *a.* (now *rare*) free from fraud L16. **fraudster** *n.* a person who commits fraud, *esp.* in business dealings L20.

fraudulence /ˈfrɔːdjʊl(ə)ns/ *n.* L15. [OFr., or eccl.L *fraudulentia*, f. L *fraudulentus*: see next, -ENCE.] The quality or fact of being fraudulent; deceit.

Also **fraudulency** *n.* (now *rare*) M17.

fraudulent /ˈfrɔːdjʊl(ə)nt/ *a.* LME. [OFr., or L *fraudulentus*, f. *fraud-*: see FRAUD, -ULENT.] 1 Guilty of or given to fraud; deceitful, dishonest. LME. 2 Characterized by, of the nature of, or accomplished by, fraud. LME. †3 *Med.* Putrefying, gangrenous. LME–E17.

2 *fraudulent preference*: see PREFERENCE 4.

fraudulently *adv.* with intent to deceive, dishonestly LME.

Frauen *n.pl.* see FRAU.

fraughan /frɔːn/ *n.* *Anglo-Ir.* E18. [Ir. *fraochán*.] = BILBERRY.

fraught /frɔːt/ *n.* *obs.* exc. *Sc.* ME. [MDu., MLG *vracht* (whence G *Fracht*) beside *vrecht* FREIGHT *n.*] †1 = FREIGHT *n.* 2. ME–L17. 2 = FREIGHT *n.* 1. LME. 3 = FREIGHT *n.* 2b. LME.

3 J. M. BARRIE To carry a fraught of water to the manse.

fraught /frɔːt/ *ppl a.* LME. [pa. pple of FRAUGHT *v.*] 1 Of a ship: laden. *arch.* LME. 2 Supplied, provided, equipped, *with*. Now *poet.* LME. 3 Foll. by *with*. Involving, attended *with*, full of, (meaning etc.); destined to produce, threatening or promising, (danger, difficulty, etc.). L16. 4 Causing or suffering anxiety or distress. M20.

2 SHAKES. *Lear* I would you would make use of your good wisdom, Whereof I know you are fraught. 3 P. G. WODEHOUSE A meeting with Oofy Prosser at this moment might be fraught with pain and embarrassment. K. CLARK An imaginary world, vaster, more dramatic and more fraught with associations. 4 D. FRANCIS Don't look so fraught . . . They said it was clear there now. V. GLENDINNING Poor Georgina died after only four years of fraught marriage.

fraught /frɔːt/ *v.t. arch.* Pa. t. & pple **fraught**, **fraughted**. See also FRAUGHT *ppl a.* LME. [MDu. *vrachten* load (a ship), f. as FRAUGHT *n.*] 1 = FREIGHT *v.* 1. *obs.* exc. as FRAUGHT *ppl a.* LME. †2 = FREIGHT *v.* 2. *Sc.* LME–L16. 3 Supply, provide, equip *with*. LME.

fraughtage *n.* †(*a*) = FREIGHTAGE 1; (*b*) = FREIGHT *n.* 2: LME. †**fraughter** *n.* (*Sc.*) = FREIGHTER 1 E16–L17.

fraughted *v.* pa. t. & pple see FRAUGHT *v.*

Fräulein /ˈfrɔɪlʌɪn, *foreign* ˈfrɔylaɪn/ *n.* L17. [G, dim. of FRAU.] An unmarried German woman; a German governess. Freq. as a title, corresponding to *Miss*.

Fraunhofer /ˈfraʊnhəʊfə/ *n.* M19. [Joseph von *Fraunhofer* (1787–1826), Bavarian optician and physicist.] 1 *Fraunhofer('s) lines*, dark (absorption) lines in solar and stellar spectra. M19. 2 *Fraunhofer('s) diffraction*, diffraction in which the pattern is a linear function of the phase variation across the diffracting aperture or object. Cf. FRESNEL *diffraction*. L19.

fraxetin /ˈfraksɪtɪn/ *n.* M19. [f. as next + -ETIN.] *Chem.* A hydroxy derivative, $C_{10}H_8O_5$, of coumarin, the aglycone of fraxin.

fraxin /ˈfraksɪn/ *n.* M19. [f. L *fraxinus* ash (tree) + -IN^{1}.] *Chem.* A coumarin glycoside found in the bark of ash, horse chestnut, and other trees. Cf. prec.

fraxinella /fraksɪˈnɛlə/ *n.* M17. [mod.L, dim. of L *fraxinus* ash tree, w. allus. to the pinnate leaves.] A Eurasian plant of the rue family, *Dictamnus albus*, with showy white flowers and fragrant leaves which secrete a volatile flammable oil. Also called *burning bush*, *gas plant*.

fray /freɪ/ *n.*^{1} LME. [f. FRAY *v.*^{1}] †1 An assault, an attack. LME–L16. 2 A disturbance, a stir; a noisy quarrel, a brawl; a fight, conflict (*lit.* & *fig.*). LME. 3 A feeling of fear; alarm, fright. *obs.* exc. *Sc.* LME.

2 W. S. CHURCHILL The South African Armoured division . . was very forward in the fray. A. UTTLEY Susan was drawn in the fray to dust and polish. P. USTINOV It was time for the clergy to enter the fray against the Catholics in the Kremlin.

fray /freɪ/ *n.*^{2} M17. [f. FRAY *v.*^{2}] The result of fraying; a frayed place.

fray /freɪ/ *v.*^{1} ME. [Aphet. f. AFFRAY *v.*, EFFRAY.] 1a *v.t.* Affect with fear, frighten. *obs.* exc. *poet.* & *dial.* ME. †b *v.i.* Be afraid, fear; tremble, shudder with fear. LME–M17. 2a *v.i.* Quarrel; make a disturbance, fight. *arch.* LME. †b *v.t.* Assault, attack; attack and drive *off*. LME–L16. 3 *v.t.* Frighten or scare away. (Foll. by *away*, *off*, *out*.) *arch.* E16.

1a *absol.*: SPENSER Instead of fraying they themselves did feare. 3 SIR W. SCOTT It is enough to fray every hawk from the perch.

fray /freɪ/ *v.*^{2} LME. [Fr. *frayer*, earlier *freiier*, *froiier*, f. L *fricare* rub.] 1 *v.t.* & *i.* Of a deer: rub (its head) against something to remove the velvet from its newly formed horns. LME. 2a *v.t.* Wear through by rubbing; ravel out the edge or end of (something woven or twisted); *fig.* strain (the nerves or temper). Formerly also, bruise. LME. b *v.i.* (Of material) become ragged at the edge, unravel; *fig.* (of nerves or temper) become strained. E18. 3 *v.t.* Clear, force, (a path, way, etc.). L18.

2a E. BOWEN The . ., situation more and more frayed the young men's already battle-strained nerves. D. LODGE O'Shea's suit was baggy and threadbare, his shirts were frayed. b G. GREENE The cuffs had frayed and been repaired. 3 J. G. FARRELL Think of . . the camel! Adapted . . for the desert regions through which it frays its diurnal passage.

fraying *vbl n.* (*a*) the action of the vb; (*b*) an abrasion on a tree, or the discarded velvet, resulting from a deer's fraying: LME.

frayn /freɪn/ *v.* [OE *fregnan*, *frīnan* = OS *fregnan*, ON *fregna*.] 1 *v.t.* & *i.* Ask. *obs.* exc. *dial.* OE. †2 *v.t.* Ask for, request. Only in ME.

frazil /ˈfreɪz(ə)l, frəˈzɪl/ *n.* *N. Amer.* L19. [Canad. Fr. *frasil* snow floating on water. Cf. Fr. *fraisil* cinders.] Slush consisting of small ice crystals formed in water too turbulent to freeze solid. Also *frazil ice*.

frazzle /ˈfraz(ə)l/ *v.* & *n.* *colloq.* (orig. *dial.* & *US*). E19. [Origin uncertain: perh. a blend of FRAY *v.*^{2} and FAZLE.] A *v.t.* & *i.* Fray, wear out, exhaust; *fig.* burn, char, shrivel up with burning. Freq. as *frazzled* ppl a. E19. B *n.* The state of being frazzled; a frazzled thing. Chiefly in (*burnt*, *worn*, *beaten*, etc.) *to a frazzle*. E19.

freak /friːk/ *n.* & *a.* M16. [Prob. of dial. origin.] A *n.* 1 A caprice, a whim, a vagary. M16. 2 Capriciousness. L17. 3 A capricious prank or trick. *arch.* E18. 4 A product of irregular or sportive fancy; (more fully *freak of nature*) an abnormal or irregular occurrence, an abnormally developed person or thing, a monstrosity. L18. 5 An unconventional person, a hippy; a homosexual; a person who undergoes narcotic hallucinations or a powerful emotional experience; a drug addict, *esp.* an addict of a specified drug; a person obsessed with a specified activity, thing, etc., an enthusiast. *colloq.* L19.

1 R. L. STEVENSON You should be able to stop and go on, and follow this way or that, as the freak takes you. 2 C. BRONTË A decent quiescence under the freak of manner, gave me the advantage. 3 A. TROLLOPE Expelled from Harrow for some boyish freak. 4 A. BURGESS Freaks—dwarfs, giants, Siamese twins, pinheads—are undeniably Other, but they are also ourselves. 5 B. W. ALDISS I was up early. I am a yoga freak.

B *attrib.* or as *adj.* Abnormal or capriciously irregular, freakish. Also, of or pertaining to freaks, unconventional. L19.

C. MCCULLERS A freak plant, a zinnia with six bronze petals and two red. K. M. E. MURRAY Unfortunately freak weather for August occurred and he arrived . . in snow. J. O'FAOLAIN He might have been ready to . . join some freak sect. **freak show** (at a fair) a sideshow featuring abnormally developed individuals.

freakdom *n.* freakishness L19.

freak /friːk/ *v.* M17. [f. FREAK *n.*; sense 1 perh. alt. of FRECK *v.* by assoc. with STREAK *v.*^{2}] 1 *v.t.* Fleck or streak randomly; variegate. Chiefly as *freaked* pa. pple. M17. 2 *v.i.* Gambol, frolic. *rare.* M17. 3 *v.t.* & *i.* (Cause to) undergo narcotic hallucinations or a powerful emotional experience; (cause to) become angry. Chiefly foll. by *out*. *slang.* M20.

1 R. GRAVES A wan winter landscape, Hedges freaked with snow. 3 D. ADAMS 'It's the wild colour scheme that freaks me,' said Zaphod. L. ALTHER When she was first doing therapy, it freaked her out.

Comb.: **freak-out** an intense emotional experience, *esp.* one resulting from the use of hallucinatory drugs.

freakish /ˈfriːkɪʃ/ *a.* L17. [f. FREAK *n.* + -ISH[1].] Capricious, whimsical; irregular, unpredictable; curious, grotesque.

freakishly *adv.* L19. **freakishness** *n.* L17.

freaky /ˈfriːki/ *a.* E19. [f. FREAK *n.* + -Y[1].] Freakish; *esp.* unconventional, weird.

freakily *adv.* M20. **freakiness** *n.* L19.

freath /friːð/ *v.t.* & *i. Sc.* E18. [Origin unkn.; cf. FROTH *n.*] (Cause to) froth or foam.

freck /frɛk/ *a. obs.* exc. *Sc.* & *north.* Also **frack** /frak/. [OE *frec, fric, fræc* = OHG *freh* covetous, greedy (G *frech* bold, insolent), ON *frekr* greedy, Goth. *faihufriks* avaricious.] 1 Eager, prompt, ready. OE. 2 Strong, vigorous. E16.

freckly *adv.* ME.

freck /frɛk/ *v.t.* E17. [Orig. pa. pple *freckt*, abbrev. of *freckled*: see next and cf. FREAK *v.*] Mark with spots or freckles; dapple.

freckle /ˈfrɛk(ə)l/ *n.* & *v.* Orig. (long *obs.* exc. *dial.*) **frecken** /ˈfrɛk(ə)n/. LME. [ON *freknur* pl. (Sw. *fräkne*, Da. *fregne*).] A *n.* 1 A light brown patch on the skin, usu. produced by exposure to the sun. LME. 2 *gen.* A small spot or discoloration. L15. B *v.* 1 *v.i.* Become marked with freckles. M16. 2 *v.t.* Mark with freckles. E17.

freckled *a.* (*a*) marked with freckles; spotted, dappled; †(*b*) (*rare*) resembling a freckle: LME. **freckly** *a.* covered with freckles E18.

free /friː/ *a.*, *n.*, & *adv.* [OE *frēo* = OFris., OS, OHG *frī* (Du. *vrij*, G *frei*), Goth. *freis*, f. Gmc f. IE, repr. by Skt *priya* dear, f. base meaning 'to love'.] A *adj.* I 1 Of a person: not or no longer in bondage, servitude, or subjection to another, having personal rights and social and political liberty as a member of a society or State. OE. †2 Noble, honourable, of gentle birth and breeding. Also, (of character and conduct) noble, honourable, generous, magnanimous. OE–M17. 3 Of a State, its citizens, and institutions: enjoying national and civil liberty, not subject to foreign domination or despotic or tyrannous government. ME. b *spec.* Designating (freq. w. cap. initial) a political or racial group actively opposed to an invading, occupying, or hostile power; *esp.* denoting those who continued resistance to Germany in the war of 1939–45 after the capitulation of their respective countries. M20.

1 B. RUSSELL Sympathy not only for free Greeks, but for barbarians and slaves. *Country Life* She wanted to be an artist and a free woman, refusing to be called 'Mrs'. *fig.*: J. DENHAM Who . . free from Conscience, is a slave to Fame. 2 SHAKES. *Oth.* I would not have your free and noble nature Out of self-bounty be abus'd. MILTON Thou Goddess fair and free. 3 SHAKES. *Cymb.* Till the injurious Romans did extort This tribute from us, we were free. S. SMILES Holland . . became the chief European centre of free thought, free religion, and free industry. b C. GRAVES The scattered remnants of the Free French, Free Dutch, Free Polish, and Free Norwegian fleets.

II 4 Acting from one's own will or choice and not compelled or constrained; determining one's own action or choice without outside motivation. OE. 5 Ready to do or grant something; acting willingly or spontaneously; (of an act) done of one's own accord; (of an offer or agreement) readily given or made, made with good will. ME. b Of a horse: ready to go, willing. L15. c Ready *to do* something; eager, willing, prompt. *obs.* exc. in *free to confess* below, where the adj. is now understood as sense 16b. M17. 6 Ready to give, liberal, lavish. Foll. by *of.* ME. b (Of a gift) given out of liberality or generosity, not in return or requital for something; unrequested, unsolicited. LME. 7 (Of speech) characterized by liberty in the expression of sentiments or opinions; uttered or expressed without reserve; plain-spoken. ME. b Not observing due bounds, licentious, loose. M19. 8 Acting without restriction or limitation; allowing oneself ample scope *in* doing something. L16. b Unstinted as to supply or quantity; coming forth in profusion; administered without stint; abundant, copious. M17. 9 Frank and open in conversation or dealings; ingenuous, unreserved. Also, forward, familiar, impudent. M17.

4 E. A. FREEMAN The choice of the electors would be perfectly free. 5c J. CLARE Mark . . his generous mind; How free he is to push about his beer. 6 S. BUTLER For Saints themselves will sometimes be Of Gifts that cost them nothing, free. 7 H. NELSON Gave Lord Hood my free opinion that 800 troops . . would take Bastia. L. J. JENNINGS Men used rather free expressions to each other . . in the days of the Regency. b TENNYSON Earl Limours Drank till he jested with all ease, and told Free tales. 8 POPE How free the present age is in laying taxes on the next. H. BRACKEN He gives us a Caution not to be too free with such Preparations. G. BERKELEY The free use of strong fermented liquors. b S. BARING-GOULD A monthly rose that was a free bloomer. 9 DEFOE I pressed him to be free and plain with me. R. B. SHERIDAN Not so free, fellow!

III 10 a Usu. foll. by *from*, *of*: released or exempt from, not liable to (a rule, penalty, or payment). OE. b Exempt from, having immunity from, not subject to (something regarded as hurtful or undesirable). ME. 11 Exempt from, or not subject to, some particular jurisdiction or lordship. Also, possessed of particular rights and privileges. ME. 12 Of real property: held without obligation on rent or service, freehold. *arch.* ME. 13 Given or provided without charge or payment, gratuitous. Also, admitted, carried, or placed without charge or payment. ME. 14 Invested with the rights or immunities of or *of*, admitted to the privileges of or *of* (a chartered company, corporation, city, or the like). LME. b Allowed the use or enjoyment *of* (a place etc.). L17. 15 Exempt from restrictions with regard to trade; not subject to tax, toll, or duty; allowed to trade in any market. M17.

10a LD MACAULAY Free from all the ordinary rules of morality. b J. FERRIAR Our own writers are not free from this error. N. LINDLEY The point . . appears to me . . free from any real difficulty. 13 DRYDEN Lazy Drones, without their Share of Pain, In winter Quarters free, devour the Gain. 14 J. LOCKE Is a Man under the Law of England? What made him Free of that Law? J. ENTICK The shop-keepers are obliged to be free of the city. b KEATS And I was free of haunts umbrageous.

IV 16 Not impeded, restrained, or restricted in actions, activity, or movement; unhampered, unfettered. ME. b At liberty, allowed, or permitted *to do* something. LME. c Unbiased, open-minded. Long *rare* or *obs.* M17. 17 Clear of obstruction; not blocked; open, unobstructed. ME. 18 Clear of something regarded as objectionable or an encumbrance. Foll. by *of*, *from.* ME. 19 Guiltless, innocent, acquitted. Now *rare* or *obs.* ME. 20 At liberty; able to move about or range at will; *esp.* not kept in confinement or custody, released from confinement or imprisonment; liberated. LME. 21 Of a material: yielding easily to operation; easily worked; loose and soft in structure. E16. b Of wood: without knots. L17. 22 Not fixed, fastened, or held in one particular place. L16. 23 Released from ties, obligations, and restraints. L16. b Released or exempt from work or duty; clear of engagements; (of a room, table, etc.) not occupied or in use. E17. 24 Allowable or allowed (*to* or *for* a person *to do* something); open or permitted *to. arch.* L16. b *Ling.* Designating a form that can occur in isolation. E20. c *Phonet.* Of a vowel: occurring in a syllable not ended by a consonant. M20. 25 Disengaged from contact or connection with some other body or surface; relieved from the pressure of an adjacent or superincumbent body. E18. 26 Of a literary or artistic style: not observing strict laws of form. Of a translation: not adhering strictly to the original, not literal. E19. 27 *Chem.* Not combined. E19. 28 *Physics.* Of a source of power: disengaged, available to do work. E19. 29 *Naut.* Of the wind: not adverse. M19.

16 A. RADCLIFFE Her dress . . was loosened for the purpose of freer respiration. B. JOWETT The various passions are allowed to have free play. b DICKENS She was free to come and go. 17 J. NARBOROUGH They did meet with no Ice, but a free and open Sea. SIR W. SCOTT And quickly make the entrance free. 18 R. HOLME A Woman all Hairy, no part of her Face free. C. LUCAS There is hardly any mine . . free from pyrite. 20 LD MACAULAY Deer, as free as in an American forest. J. MORLEY Calvin . . set free all those souls. *Times* He wanted the accused to be allowed to go free. 21 J. SMEATON This stone was capable of being thus wrought, and was so free to the tool. 22 MILTON The tawny lion, pawing to get free His hinder parts. 23 SHAKES. *Ant. & Cl.* Free, madam! no . . He's bound unto Octavia. b G. BURNET Coleman had a whole day free to make his escape. E. WAUGH There is no table free. K. AMIS What about lunch today? Are you free? 24 J. JACKSON It was free to everyone to bastinado a Christian where he met him. 25 R. KNOX At the free surface of the mucous membrane. 29 R. H. DANA We had the wind free . . sail after sail the captain piled on her.

Phrases: *be free with*: see *make free with* below. **for free** (*colloq.*, orig. *US*), provided without payment. **free and easy** *a.*, *adv.*, & *n. phr.* (*a*) *adj. phr.* unconstrained, natural, unaffected; unceremonious; careless, slipshod; morally lax, permissive; *free and easiness* a state or manner of being free and easy; (*b*) *adv. phr.* (*rare*) in a free and easy manner; (*c*) *n. phr.* (*arch. slang*) a convivial gathering. **free on board, rail**, etc. without charge for delivery to a ship, a railway wagon, etc. **free to confess** ready and willing to make a confession. *free warren*: see WARREN *n.*[1] 1b. **free, white, and over twenty-one** *colloq.* not subject to another person's control or authority, independent. **give** or **have a free hand** give or have complete liberty of action in an undertaking. **it's a free country** *colloq.* the (course of) action proposed is not illegal or forbidden. *Land of the Free*: see LAND *n.*[1] **make** or **be free with** take liberties with. *set free*: see SET *v.*[1] *the Wee Free Kirk*: see WEE *a.*

B *absol.* as *n.* †1 A person of noble birth or breeding; a knight or lady. OE–M16. 2 A free person. Long only as *collect. pl.*, *the* class of free people. See also *Wee Frees* s.v. WEE *a.* ME. 3 *Football.* A free kick. M19. 4 A free thing; *esp.* something for which no charge is made. E20.

C *adv.* 1 In a free manner; freely; *esp.* without cost or payment. ME. 2 *Naut.* Not close-hauled. E19.

1 DRYDEN Achitophel . . Disdain'd the golden Fruit to gather free. G. SEMPLE The Middle of the Current of the River, runs the freest. **free, gratis, and for nothing** *colloq.* absolutely without charge. 2 F. MARRYAT We were going about four knots and a half free.

Special collocations & comb.: *free agent*: see AGENT *n.* 4. **free alms** = FRANKALMOIGN. **free association** *Psychol.* the statement, by a person under test, of ideas evoked by those specified by the tester, without further suggestion or control by the tester; an idea or feeling so evoked. **free ball** *Snooker* the right to nominate any ball as the object ball, as a result of being snookered by a foul stroke; a ball so nominated. **freebase** *n.* & *v.* (*a*) *n.* cocaine purified by heating with ether, and taken by inhaling the fumes or smoking the residue; (*b*) *v.t.* purify (cocaine) thus. *free bench*: see BENCH *n.* 6. **free-born** *a.* (*a*) born to the rights and liberty of a citizen, not born to slavery; (*b*) of, pertaining to, or befitting a free-born person. **Free Church** (*a*) *gen.* a Church free from State control, *esp.* the Nonconformist as opp. to the Established Church; (*b*) *spec.* (also *Free Church of Scotland*) the Church formed by ministers seceding from the Scottish Presbyterian establishment (1843–1929). **free city** (*a*) *Hist.* a medieval sovereign city-state in Germany; (*b*) a semi-autonomous city under the authority of an international body. **free electron** an electron not bound in an atom or molecule. **free energy** *spec.* a thermodynamic property of a system that represents ability to do work. **free enterprise** the freedom of private business from State control. **free expression** the uninhibited expression of one's thoughts, feelings, and creative capacities. **free fall** motion under the force of gravity only, ballistic flight; unpowered motion in space; *esp.* the part of a parachute descent occurring before the parachute opens. **free-fall** *v.i.* move in a free fall. **free fight**: in which all present may join. **free float** (in critical path analysis) a float that can be utilized with no adverse effect on the timing of subsequent processes. **free-for-all** *a.* & *n.* (designating or pertaining to) a fight that is open to all, an unrestricted contest or discussion. **free gift**: made not in return for anything; *esp.* an object given away by a firm in order to promote sales of a product. **free grace** the unmerited favour of God. **free hand** the right of acting completely at one's own discretion, *esp.* in relation to a particular undertaking. **free-hand** *a.* (of a drawing) made without artificial aid to the hand. **free-handed** *a.* generous, *esp.* with money. **free-handedly** *adv.* generously. **free-handedness** open-handedness, generosity. **free-hearted** *a.* having a free heart; frank, open, unreserved; not burdened by anxiety, guilt, or suspicion; impulsive; generous, liberal. **free house** a public house or inn that does not belong to a brewery and may thus sell any brewer's liquor. **free kick** *Football* a kick which the opposing team are not allowed to hinder or block (under different rules for different forms of the game), as one allowed against a team committing an infringement or in other defined circumstances. *Free Kirk*: see KIRK *n.* **free labour** (*a*) labour of people who are free, not slaves; (*b*) labour of people who are not members of a trade union. **free library**: available for use without payment. **free list**: of persons or things to be admitted free of payment, duty, etc. **free-liver** a person who gives free indulgence to the appetites, esp. eating. **free-living** *a.* (*a*) (of a person) that is a free-liver; (*b*) *Biol.* living freely and independently, not attached to a substrate; *esp.* not parasitic or symbiotic. **freeload** *v.i.* (*slang*) behave as a freeloader. **freeloader** *slang* a person who eats or drinks or is accommodated free of charge, a sponger. **free love** (the doctrine permitting) sexual relations irrespective of marriage. **free lunch** (orig. *US*) a lunch given gratis, *esp.* by barkeepers to attract custom; *fig.* (w. allusion to the proverb *there's no such thing as a free lunch*) something for nothing. **free market**: in which prices are determined by unrestricted competition. *free pardon*: see PARDON *n.* 4b. **free pass** (a document giving the holder) the right to travel on a railway etc. or to enter a place of entertainment without paying. **free path** *Physics* (*a*) the distance which a molecule or other particle traverses without encountering another particle or colliding with a containing wall; (*b*) the distance a sound wave travels between successive reflections from the walls of an enclosure; (in both senses chiefly in *mean free path* s.v. MEAN *a.*[2]). **free period** a period in the regular timetable of an educational establishment during which a particular teacher or student has no definitely assigned duties. **free place** a place in a secondary fee-paying school awarded without charge to a particular student. **free port** (*a*) a port open to all traders; (*b*) a port area where goods are exempt from customs duty during loading and unloading. *Free Presbyterian Church*: see PRESBYTERIAN *a.* 1. **free-quarter** *Hist.* (*a*) the obligation or impost of having to provide free board and lodging for troops; (*b*) the right of troops to be billeted in free quarters; the necessity for troops of having to find free quarters. **free radical** *Chem.* an uncharged atom or group of atoms having one or more unpaired electrons available for bonding. **free range** *US* open pasture-land. **free-range** *a.* designating (eggs or meat from) hens or other domestic fowl given freedom of movement in seeking food. *free rein*: see REIN *n.*[1] **free school** (*a*) (chiefly *Hist.*) a school at which no fees are charged; (*b*) an independent school run on the basis of freedom from restriction for the pupils. **free selection** *Austral. Hist.* = SELECTION 4. **free skating** a competitive programme of variable skating figures performed to music. **free soil** *US Hist.* territory in which slaveholding was prohibited; *attrib.* pertaining to or designating a 19th-cent. political party opposing the extension of slavery beyond the original slave States. **free space** *Physics*: unoccupied by matter. **free speech** the right to express opinions of any kind without incurring a penalty. **free-spoken** *a.* not concealing one's opinions, frank, blunt. **free-standing** *a.* not attached or connected to another structure, not supported by a structural framework. **free State** (*a*) a State not subject to another; (*rare*) a republic; (*b*) *US Hist.* a State of the US in which slavery did not exist. **Free Stater** a native, inhabitant, or supporter of a particular free State, *esp.* (*Hist.*) of the Orange Free State or of the Irish Free State. **free stock** plants grown from seed to be used as rootstocks in grafting. **free-style** *a.* (*a*) *gen.* (of movement) unrestricted; (*b*) *spec.* (of a swimming-race) in which any style of stroke may be used; (of wrestling) with few restrictions on the holds permitted. **free-tailed bat** a molossid, *spec.* one of the genus *Tadarida*. **freethinker** a person who refuses to submit the reasoning process to the control of authority in religious belief; a rationalist. **freethinking** *n.* & *a.* (*a*) *n.* free thought; (*b*) *adj.* holding the principles of freethinkers. **free thought** the free exercise of reason in matters of religious belief, rationalism. **free trade** (*a*) an open and unrestricted trade; (*b*) trade or commerce left to follow its natural course without restriction on imports etc.; (*c*) *arch.* trade which evades the lawful customs duties, smuggling. **free-trader** a person who takes part in free trade; an adherent of free trade. **free vector** *Math.* a vector of which only the magnitude and direction are specified, not the position or line of action. **free verse** = VERS LIBRE. **free vote** a parliamentary vote not made subject to party discipline. *free warren*: see WARREN *n.*[1] 1b. **freeware** *Computing* software that is available without charge. **freeway** (orig. *US*) an express highway, esp. with restricted access; a toll-free highway. **free wheel** the driving-wheel of a bicycle able to revolve with the pedals at rest; a wheel or propeller that can run free of a clutch or other connection with motive power. **free-wheel** *v.i.* ride a bicycle without pedalling, coast; *fig.* move or act without effort or constraint. **free world** the non-Communist countries collectively (as referred to by them).

free /friː/ *v.t.* Pa. t. & pple **freed**. [OE *frēon*, *frēog(e)an* = ON *fría*, *friá*, f. Gmc, f. base of FREE *a.*] **1** Make free (*from*, †*of*); set at liberty; release or deliver from bondage or constraint. OE. **2** Relieve or deliver *from*, rid or ease *of* (a burden, obligation, inconvenience); exempt *from* (payment, tribute), confer immunity on. Formerly also, exempt (a church or similar foundation) from feudal services or exactions. OE. **b** Clear from blame or stain; show or declare to be guiltless; absolve, acquit. Long *obs.* exc. *Sc.* L16. **c** Relieve or rid of the presence of a person. Foll. by *from*, *of*. L16. †**d** Grant immunity *from* the operation of a thing; make safe and secure *from*. E–M17. †**3** Remove so as to leave the place clear, banish, get rid of. L16–M17. †**4** Leap or get clear over (a ditch or other obstacle). L16–L18. **5** Clear, disengage, or disentangle (a thing) from some obstruction or encumbrance; get (oneself) loose, extricate. Formerly also, open so as to allow free passage. E17. **b** *Naut.* Bail out water from (a ship). E17. **6** *Mining.* Register (a new mine, vein, etc.) by making the customary payment. E17. †**7** Frank (a letter). L18–E19.

1 C. KINGSLEY Then he freed one of these four men. B. JOWETT A philosophy which could free the mind from the power of abstractions. 2 D. HUME He freed their subjects from all oaths of allegiance. J. R. GREEN The towns had long since freed themselves from all payment of the dues.. exacted by the King. b AV *Rom.* 6:7 He that is dead, is freed from sinne. c H. MARTINEAU The gentleman soon chose to free the family of his presence. d D. PELL There are but few Trees.. that are free'd from the Thunder, save the Lawrel. 3 S. DANIEL Free thine owne torment, and my griefe release. 5 DRYDEN Nor cou'd their tainted Flesh with Ocean Tides Be freed from Filth. *fig.*: C. M. YONGE Having freed himself from his difficulties. 7 S. JOHNSON Please to free this letter to Miss L. Porter.

freer *n.* a person or agent who frees or sets free someone or something E17.

-free /friː/ *suff.* [FREE *a.*, *n.*, & *adv.*] Forming adjs. and advs. w. the sense 'free of or from (the first element)', as *carefree*, *dust-free*, *lead-free*, *rent-free*.

freebie /ˈfriːbi/ *a.* & *n.* *colloq.* (orig. *US*). M20. [Arbitrary expansion of FREE *a.*] **A** *adj.* Free, provided without charge. M20. **B** *n.* Something free, provided without charge; *esp.* a free gift, free hospitality, or the like. M20.

freeboard /ˈfriːbɔːd/ *n.* L17. [f. as FREE *a.* + BOARD *n.*; in sense 1 tr. AN *franc bord*, in AL *francum bordum*: see FRANK *a.*[1], BOARD *n.*] **1** *Law* (now *Hist.*). The right of claiming a certain portion of land outside the fence of a park or forest; the land thus claimed. L17. **2** *Naut.* The height of a ship's side between the water-line and the lowest part of the deck. E18.

freeboot /ˈfriːbuːt/ *v.i.* L16. [Back-form. f. next.] Act as a freebooter, plunder.

freebooter /ˈfriːbuːtə/ *n.* L16. [Du. *vrijbuiter*, f. as FREE *a.* + BOOTY + -ER[1]. See also FILIBUSTER.] A person who goes in search of plunder; a pirate; a piratical adventurer (*lit.* & *fig.*).

†**free-booty** *n.* E17. [f. as FREE *a.* + BOOTY after prec.] **1** Plunder or spoil (to be) taken by force. E17–M18. **2** Taking of booty, plundering. *rare.* Only in M17.

freedman /ˈfriːdmən/ *n.* Pl. **-men**. E17. [f. *freed* pa. pple of FREE *v.* + MAN *n.*] An emancipated (male) slave.

freedom /ˈfriːdəm/ *n.* [OE *frēodōm*: see FREE *a.*, -DOM.] **1** Exemption or release from slavery or imprisonment (*lit.* & *fig.*); personal liberty. OE. **2** The quality of being free from the control of fate or necessity; the power of self-determination attributed to the will. OE. †**3** The quality of being free or noble; nobility, generosity, liberality. ME–L16. **4** The state of being able to act without hindrance or restraint; liberty of action; the right *of*, *to do*. ME. **5** Exemption *from* a specific burden, charge, or service; an immunity. ME. **b** An immunity, privilege, or right possessed by a city, corporation, university, or other institution. Formerly also, a body possessing such an immunity etc.; the district over which a particular immunity etc. extended. L16. **6** Exemption from arbitrary, despotic, or autocratic control; independence; civil liberty. LME. †**7** Readiness or willingness to act. LME–E19. **8** The right of participating in the privileges attached to citizenship *of* a town or city (often given as an honour to distinguished people), or to membership *of* a company or trade. Also, the document or diploma conferring such freedom. LME. **b** Foll. by *of*: unrestricted access to or use of. M17. **c** The liberty or right to practise a trade; the fee paid for this. *obs.* exc. *Hist.* E18. **9** Foll. by *from*. The state of not being affected by (a defect, disadvantage, etc.); exemption. E17. **10** Orig., the overstepping of due customary bounds in speech or behaviour, undue familiarity. Now also, frankness, openness, familiarity; outspokenness. E17. **11** Facility or ease in action or activity; absence of encumbrance. E17. **12** Boldness or vigour of conception or execution. M17. **13** A piece of common land allotted to a freeman. *Sc.* M18.

1 R. GRAVES I became your slave.. and it was you who gave me my freedom. 2 J. LOCKE In this then consists Freedom, (*viz.*) in our being able to act.. according as we shall choose, or will. 4 O. SITWELL The septs of Ireland.. fighting for their personal ideal of freedom—the freedom to fight. 5 T. KEIGHTLEY Freedom from arrest, a privilege at that time necessary for the cause of liberty. 6 SWIFT Freedom consists in a people's being governed by laws made with their own consent. 7 BACON We found.. such a freedome and desire to take strangers.. into their bosom. 8 J. WESLEY They presented me with the freedom of the city. b J. H. BURTON Having conferred on you the freedom of the library, he will not concern himself by observing how you use it. 9 M. R. MITFORD There is a freedom from cant about the authoress. 10 R. BOYLE This Love, I have taken the freedom to style 'Seraphic Love'. BURKE I talked.. with the freedom I have long used to him on this and other subjects. 11 J. TYNDALL The sun's rays penetrate our atmosphere with freedom. 12 J. HOWELL I alwaies lov'd you for the freedom of your genius.

Phrases: *Bird of Freedom*: see BIRD *n.* **degree of freedom** (*a*) *Physics* each of the independent modes in which motion or displacement of a body can occur; (*b*) *Chem.* (in *pl.*) properties which can vary independently in a system of given composition; (*c*) *Statistics* (in *pl.*) independent quantities contributing to a distribution. *freedom of* CONSCIENCE. *freedom of* RELIGION. **freedom of speech** = *free speech* s.v. FREE *a.*, *n.*, & *adv. freedom of the press*: see PRESS *n.*[1] **Freedom of the Rule** *Sc.* liberty granted to a Scottish advocate to plead at the English bar. **the four freedoms** freedom of speech, freedom of religion, freedom from want or fear, and freedom of the will.

Comb.: **freedom fighter** a person who takes part in a resistance movement to an established political system; **freedom ride** *US* an organized ride in buses etc. as a demonstration against racial segregation.

Freefone /ˈfriːfəʊn/ *n.* Also **-phone**, **f-**. M20. [f. FREE *a.* + alt. of PHONE *n.*[2]] A telephone service whereby an organization pays the cost of certain incoming calls.

¶Proprietary name in the US.

freehold /ˈfriːhəʊld/ *n.* & *a.* LME. [tr. AN *fraunc tenement* 'free holding'.] **A** *n.* **1** A tenure by which an estate is held in fee simple, fee tail, or for term of life; a similar tenure of a dignity or office. LME. **2** An estate or office held by such a tenure. LME. **B** *attrib.* or as *adj.* Held by freehold; of the nature of or pertaining to freehold. E16.

freeholder /ˈfriːhəʊldə/ *n.* LME. [tr. AN *fraunc tenaunt* 'free tenant', in AL *francus tenans*.] A person who possesses a freehold estate; *Sc. Law* (now *Hist.*) a person who held land directly from the monarch, and who acquired by this the right to vote and to be elected to Parliament.

freelage /ˈfriːlɪdʒ/ *n. obs.* exc. *dial.* ME. [f. FREE *a.* + alt. of -LOCK.] 1 Freedom; a franchise, a privilege. Long *rare.* ME. 2 A heritable property. *Sc.* E19.

freelance /ˈfriːlɑːns/ *n., v., a.,* & *adv.* Orig. two wds. E19. [f. FREE *a.* + LANCE *n.*] A *n.* 1 *Hist.* A (medieval) mercenary, a *condottiere.* E19. 2 A person operating without permanent commitments in a particular sphere of activity; *spec.* a person who works, usu. in a specialist area, for no fixed employer. M19. B *v.i.* Act or work as a freelance. Freq. as *freelancing* vbl n. E20. C *attrib.* or as *adj.* Working as or done by a freelance or freelances. E20. D *adv.* As or by a freelance or freelances. M20.

freelancer *n.* a freelance M20.

freely /ˈfriːli/ *adv.* OE. [f. FREE *a.* + -LY².] 1 Of one's own accord, spontaneously; without constraint or reluctance; unreservedly, without stipulation; readily, willingly. OE. b With freedom of will or choice. ME. 2 Without restraint or reserve with regard to speech; unreservedly, frankly, openly, plainly. ME. 3 Without restraint or restriction on action or activity; without hindrance or interference. ME. b Without observance of or conformity to strict rule; loosely. M19. 4 Without stint; plentifully, abundantly; generously, liberally. ME. †5 In freedom; with the rights of free birth; without servitude; with absolute possession. ME–M17. †6 Nobly; excellently, beautifully. ME–L15. †7 Without payment or cost, gratis. Also, without punishment. ME–M18. 8 Entirely, completely; very. *Sc.* E16.

1 R. W. DALE He freely forgives the penitent. H. JAMES She told fibs as freely as she applied trimmings. b MILTON Because we freely love, as in our will To love or not. 2 LD MACAULAY She well knew that she was not handsome, and jested freely on her own homeliness. C. P. SNOW He began to talk more freely among strangers. 3 J. MORLEY The right of thinking freely and acting independently. J. CONRAD He moved freely. I. MURDOCH Caverns or grottos through which, bending double, one could freely pass. BREATHE *freely.* b MAX-MÜLLER Translate it somewhat freely. 4 DEFOE We ate very freely. 5 SHAKES. *Twel. N.* Thou shalt live as freely as thy lord To call his fortunes thine.

freeman /ˈfriːmən/ *n.* Pl. **-men**. OE. [f. FREE *a.* + MAN *n.*] 1 A man who is personally free, with the rights and liberty of a citizen, not a slave or serf or subject to a tyrannical or occupying power. OE. 2 A person who possesses the freedom of a city, borough, or company. ME.

freemartin /ˈfriːmɑːtɪn/ *n.* L17. [Origin unkn.: cf. Ir., Gael. *mart* cow (fattened for the market).] A hermaphrodite or imperfect female twin calf.

Freemason /ˈfriːmeɪs(ə)n/ *n.* Also **f-**. LME. [f. FREE *a.* + MASON *n.*] 1 A skilled worker in stone, a mason; *esp.* a member of a class of such workers who customarily moved from place to place to work on any great building project and who possessed a system of secret signs and passwords for recognition among themselves. Now only *Hist.* exc. as passing into sense 2. LME. 2 A member of a society for mutual help, called the *Free and Accepted Masons* and having elaborate secret rituals. Formerly & orig. also, an honorary member accepted into a society of Freemasons (sense 1). M17.

1 E. TOPSELL The master work-men, free masons, and carpenters. 2 *Times* He managed to keep his cool . . giving another officer a freemason's handshake.

Freemaˈsonic *a.* M19.

Freemasonry /ˈfriːmeɪs(ə)nri/ *n.* LME. [f. prec. + -RY.] †1 The craft or occupation of a skilled mason. Only in LME. 2 The system and institution of Freemasons. L18. 3 *fig.* Secret or tacit brotherhood; instinctive sympathy and understanding. E19.

3 E. TEMPLETON There existed a secret league, a kind of freemasonry. V. GLENDINNING There was a sort of freemasonry among those who . . stayed on in London during the worst of the war.

freeness /ˈfriːnɪs/ *n.* Now *rare.* LME. [f. FREE *a.* + -NESS.] 1 The quality or state of being free; freedom. LME. 2 Readiness; generosity. LME. 3 Unreservedness, frankness. M16. 4 Something free, provided without charge, esp. free hospitality. *W. Indies.* M20.

Freephone *n.* var. of FREEFONE.

Freepost /ˈfriːpəʊst/ *n.* Also **f-**. L20. [f. FREE *a.* + POST *n.*²] A postal service whereby an organization pays the postage costs for certain incoming letters.

freesia /ˈfriːzɪə/ *n.* L19. [mod.L (see below), f. Friedrich H. T. *Freese* (d. 1876), Ger. physician: see -IA¹.] Any of various plants (freq. hybrids) of the southern African genus *Freesia*, of the iris family, much grown for their fragrant tubular flowers of varied colours; a flowering stem of such a plant.

freestone /ˈfriːstəʊn/ *n.* ME. [f. as FREE *a.* + STONE *n.*; in sense 1 tr. OFr. *franche pere*, AL *lapis liber* lit. 'stone of superior quality': see FRANK *a.*¹] 1 Any of various fine-grained sandstones or limestones that can be cut or sawn easily. Also, a slab or piece of such stone. ME. 2 In full *freestone peach, nectarine.* A kind of peach or nectarine in which the stone becomes loose when the fruit is ripe. E19.

free will /friː ˈwɪl/ *n.* & *a. phr.* Also **free-will**. ME. [f. FREE *a.* + WILL *n.*¹, tr. late (eccl.)L *liberum arbitrium*, whence Fr. *libre arbitre.*] A *n.* 1 Spontaneous will, inclination to act without suggestion from others. ME. 2 The power of directing one's own actions unconstrained by necessity or fate. ME.

1 AV *Ezra* 7:13 All they . . which are minded of their owne free-will to goe vp to Ierusalem. 2 HOBBES The third way of bringing things to pass, distinct from necessity and chance, namely freewill.

B *attrib.* or as *adj.* (Usu. **free-will**.) Given readily or spontaneously, voluntary. M16.

BOSW. SMITH The free-will offerings of their golden ornaments by the Libyan women.

Comb.: **Free Will Baptist** a member of a N. American sect, of Welsh origin, of Arminian Baptists.

freewiller *n.* (*arch.*, *derog.*) a believer in the doctrine of free will, *esp.* an Arminian L17.

freeze /friːz/ *n.*¹ LME. [f. the vb.] 1 The action of FREEZE *v.*; *esp.* a state, coming, or period, of severe frost. LME. b *spec.* The fixing or stabilization of prices, wages, etc., at a certain level or figure; the prevention of assets, credits, etc., from being realized. M20. 2 A film-shot in which movement is arrested by the repetition of a frame; a facility for stopping a film or videotape at a particular frame. M20.

1 K. FIELD During a freeze there is no comfort in a southern house. *fig.*: J. D. SALINGER She gave me the big freeze when I said hello. b *New Statesman* A Socialist government should actively support a new nuclear freeze in Europe. *wage freeze*: see WAGE *n.* 2 M. EATON The credits come up . . on a freeze of Fletch's face.

Comb.: **freeze-frame, -shot** = sense 2 above.

†**freeze** *n.*² M17–E18. [Origin unkn.] Water used for diluting wine.

freeze /friːz/ *v.* Pa. t. **froze** /frəʊz/; pa. pple **frozen** /ˈfrəʊz(ə)n/, (*colloq.*) **froze**. See also FRORE. [OE *frēosan* = MLG, MDu. *vrēsen* (Du. *vriezen*), OHG *friosan* (G *frieren*), ON *frjósa*, f. Gmc f. IE base repr. by L *pruina* hoarfrost, Skt *pruṣvā*.] I *v.i.* 1 impers. in *it freezes, it is freezing*, etc.: the local temperature is such that water becomes solid through loss of heat; there is frost; *colloq.* it is bitterly cold. OE. 2 Of (a body of) water: be converted into or become covered with ice through loss of heat. Of any liquid: solidify through loss of heat. Also, (esp. of an object containing moisture) become hard and rigid in this way. ME. 3 Be or become fastened *to* or *together* by frost. LME. 4 Be affected by or have the sensation of extreme cold; be or feel very cold. Also, suffer the loss of vital heat; be brought *to death* in this way (freq. *hyperbol.*); die by frost. LME. b Have the feelings quenched or powers paralysed, esp. through experiencing an intensity of fright, shock, horror, or the like; be appalled, be terrified. M16. c Become rigid or motionless; stop abruptly and hold one's position. Also, (of a movement in a film) be arrested by the repetition of a frame. M19.

1 F. SMITH It snowed all night, and froze very hard. 2 J. MCPHEE With the arrival of cold, they [fruit] freeze on the vine, and when they thaw . . they are . . sweeter. R. V. JONES His transport was immobilized because the engine oil had frozen solid. 3 C. FRY He should stand in the winter sea Till his clothes freeze to his flesh. 4 COLERIDGE Her limbs did creep and freeze. C. LAMB His kitchen chimney was never suffered to freeze. J. D. SALINGER I wished I knew who'd swiped my gloves . . because my hands were freezing. b POPE Pale, trembling, tired, the sailors freeze with fears. J. P. MAHAFFY If I behold the tiny fish on which they put such a price I freeze with horror. c C. BRONTË The smile on his lips froze. *Listener* Whenever a sentry appeared, they froze.

II *v.t.* 5 Affect with frost; make hard or rigid, injure or kill, by extreme loss of heat; bring *to death* in this way (usu. in *pass.*; freq. *hyperbol.*). ME. 6a Congeal or inhibit the flow of (blood) as if by loss of heat; now chiefly *fig.* in *freeze someone's blood* below. Also, cause to experience an intensity of fright, shock, horror, or the like, appal, terrify; chill (the feelings); paralyse (powers). LME. b Cause (a liquid) to solidify by removal of heat; form ice on the surface of (a river, lake, etc.). Also = DEEP-FREEZE *v.* L15. 7 Make (assets, credits, etc.) temporarily or permanently unrealizable; fix or stabilize (prices, wages, etc.) at a stated level. E20. 8 Arrest at a certain stage of development or progress; make immobile; fix in a particular position. Also, arrest (a movement in a film) by repeating a frame. M20.

5 J. KOSINSKI The frost came, freezing everything solid under the snow. *transf.*: C. KINGSLEY Will she not freeze me too into stone? 6a S. RICHARDSON I should have melted her by love, instead of freezing her by fear. b JOHN ROSS We froze oil of almonds in a shot-mould. 7 J. D. MACDONALD The Feds . . froze the accounts balances. Money can come in. Nothing goes out. 8 G. ORWELL To arrest progress and freeze history at a chosen moment. A. COOKE Chaplin . . froze his stance and very slowly raised his elbows. *New Yorker* When the Japanese attacked Pearl Harbor he was frozen in his job.

Phrases, & with advs. in specialized senses: **freeze someone's blood** terrify someone. **freeze on to** *slang* take or keep tight hold of (*lit.* & *fig.*). **freeze out** *US slang* exclude from business, society, or other activity, by competition, boycotting, etc. **freeze over** *v.phr.i.* & *t.* (usu. in *pass.*) become covered, cover, with a coating of ice. **freeze up** (*a*) set fast in ice; (*b*) obstruct by the formation of ice. *till* or *until hell freezes* (*over*): see HELL *n.*

Comb.: **freeze-dried** *a.* preserved by freeze-drying; **freeze-dry** *v.t.* preserve (foodstuffs, blood plasma, pharmaceuticals, etc.) by freezing followed by subjecting to a high vacuum which removes ice by sublimation; **freeze-out** (*a*) *freeze-out poker*, a variety of poker in which the players, as fast as they lose their staked capital, drop out, all the money going to the player last remaining; (*b*) an act of freezing or forcing out; the exclusion of someone from business, society, or the like, by competition, boycotting, etc.; **freeze-thaw** *attrib. a.* (*Geol.*) designating the alternate freezing and thawing of water around rocks etc. as a mechanism for erosion; **freeze-up** the condition of being obstructed by the formation of ice; a period during which land or water is frozen, esp. so as to prevent travel; an area so affected; a frozen condition.

freezable *a.* L19. **freezy** *a.* (*rare*) chilled almost to freezing, bitterly cold LME.

freezer /ˈfriːzə/ *n.* M19. [f. prec. + -ER¹.] 1 A thing that freezes; *spec.* a refrigerated room or compartment designed to keep food frozen, a deep-freeze. M19. 2 An animal bred for export as a frozen carcass. *NZ.* L19. 3 A punch used in chasing metal to produce a frosted groundwork. L19.

freezing /ˈfriːzɪŋ/ *vbl n.* LME. [f. FREEZE *v.* + -ING¹.] The action of FREEZE *v.* Also, freezing point (see below).

V. CRONIN It was so cold—well below freezing—that Sophie's feet swelled.

Comb.: **freezing-mixture** a mixture of substances, such as salt and ice, which is used to produce temperatures below the freezing point of water; **freezing point** the temperature at which a liquid freezes; *spec.* that of water, 0°C, 32°F; **freezing tool** = FREEZER 3; **freezing works** *Austral.* & *NZ* a place where animals are slaughtered and the carcasses frozen for export.

freezing /ˈfriːzɪŋ/ *a.* & *adv.* M16. [f. as prec.: see -ING[2].] A *adj.* That freezes (*lit.* & *fig.*); *esp.* (of a person's manner, speech, etc.) coldly repressive, chilling; (of weather) bitterly cold. M16.

LD MACAULAY Many . . had been repelled by his freezing looks. G. VIDAL In freezing weather we went up to Susa. **freezing rain** rain composed of drops which freeze on impact with the ground or other solid surface.

B *adv.* *freezing cold*, bitterly cold. *colloq.* E20.

freezingly *adv.* LME.

freibergite /ˈfrʌɪbəːɡʌɪt/ *n.* M19. [f. *Freiberg*, a city in Saxony + -ITE[1].] *Min.* An argentiferous variety of tetrahedrite.

freieslebenite /frʌɪəzˈleɪbənʌɪt/ *n.* M19. [f. Johann K. *Freiesleben* (1774–1846), Ger. mining official + -ITE[1].] *Min.* A monoclinic sulphide of lead, silver, and antimony, usu. occurring as grey prisms with a metallic lustre.

freight /freɪt/ *n.* LME. [MLG, MDu. *vrecht*, var. of *vracht*: see FRAUGHT *n.*] 1 Hire of a ship or aircraft for transporting goods; the service of transporting goods in containers or by water, air, or (chiefly *US*) land, *esp.* as distinguished from express by being slower and cheaper; the charge for this. LME. 2 The cargo of a ship; a ship load; goods carried by freight (see sense 1). LME. b A load, a burden. E17. 3 More fully *freight train*. A goods train; (chiefly *US*) a container train. M19.

1 G. MAXWELL The box would have to travel freight and not in the passenger portion of the aircraft. S. BELLOW It'll cost two hundred bucks in freight. 2 E. LINKLATER One boat had already arrived and discharged its freight. *pull one's freight*: see PULL *v.* 3 M. B. HOUSTON There were four trains a day . . not counting the freights.

Comb.: **Freightliner** (proprietary name for) a container train; *freight ton*: see TON *n.*[1] 2; *freight train*: see sense 3 above.

†**freight** *ppl a.* LME. [Contr. of *freighted* pa. pple of prec.: cf. FRAUGHT *ppl a.*] 1 = FRAUGHT *ppl a.* 1. LME–E18. 2 = FRAUGHT *ppl a.* 2. M16–E17.

freight /freɪt/ *v.* LME. [f. the n. Cf. FRAUGHT *v.*] 1 *v.t.* Load (a ship) with cargo; hire or let out (a ship) for the transport of goods and passengers. LME. b *fig.* Load, burden. E19. 2 *v.t.* & *i.* Carry or transport (goods) as freight. M16.

1 E. BOWEN Having freighted a small vessel with their household effects, [they] themselves set sail for London. b G. VIDAL Dr. Ashok's voice was freighted with emotion. L. HUDSON People and places, apparently trivial, are heavily freighted . . with unspoken significance. 2 *Listener* Mown down on a turnpike by a container-lorry freighting lavatory-pans to the Midwest.

freightage /ˈfreɪtɪdʒ/ *n.* L17. [f. FREIGHT *v.* + -AGE.] 1 The freighting or hiring of a ship; the charge made for this; *gen.* the cost of transporting goods. L17. 2 = FREIGHT *n.* 2. E19. 3 Transport of goods. L19.

freighter /ˈfreɪtə/ *n.* L16. [f. FREIGHT *v.* + -ER[1]. Cf. earlier FRAUGHTER.] 1 A person who loads a ship, or who charters and loads a ship. L16. 2 A person who receives and forwards freight as a business; *US Hist.* a person who transported freight by wagon across the plains. E18. 3 A ship or aircraft for transporting freight; *US* a freight wagon. M19.

†**freightment** *n.* M16–M18. [f. FREIGHT *v.* + -MENT, after Fr. *frètement*.] (The document recording) the hiring of a ship.

Frelimo /frɛˈliːməʊ/ *n.* M20. [Port. acronym, f. *Fre*nte de *Li*bertação de *Mo*çambique Mozambique Liberation Front.] The nationalist liberation party of Mozambique, founded in 1962.

fremd /frɛmd/ *a.* *obs.* exc. *Sc.* & *north.* Also (*Sc.*) **fremmit** /ˈfrɛmɪt/. [OE *frem(e)de* = OFris. *fremethe*, OS *fremiþi* (Du. *vreemd*), OHG *fremidi* (G *fremd*), Goth. *framaþeis* strange, f. Gmc base of FROM.] 1 Foreign, not native. OE. 2 Strange, unknown. OE. 3 Estranged, hostile, unfriendly. OE. 4 Not related, not one's kin, of another family. ME.

fremdly *adv.* LME. **fremdness** *n.* strangeness, coldness L15.

fremescent /frɪˈmɛs(ə)nt/ *a.* *rare.* M19. [f. L *fremere* to roar + -ESCENT.] Growing noisy.

fremitus /ˈfrɛmɪtəs/ *n.* E19. [L, f. *fremere* to roar.] A dull roaring noise; *spec.* (*Med.*) a palpable vibration.

fremmit *a.* see FREMD.

French /frɛn(t)ʃ/ *a.* & *n.* [OE *frenċisċ* f. Gmc, f. base of FRANK *n.*[1]: see -ISH[1].] A *adj.* 1 Of or pertaining to the country of France in western Europe, its Romance language, or its people. OE. b French Canadian. L17. 2 Having a quality or qualities attributed to French things or people, esp. (*a*) refinement, (*b*) impropriety. LME.

2 A. RADCLIFFE Their sprightly melodies, debonnaire steps . . gave a character to the scene entirely French. J. GALSWORTHY I don't advise you to read it; it's very French.

Special collocations & comb.: *French artichoke*: see ARTICHOKE 1. **French bean** a kidney or haricot bean used as a vegetable, both as unripe sliced pods, and as ripe seeds; the plant (*Phaseolus vulgaris*) bearing such beans. **French bed, bedstead** a bedstead with no bedposts and with the headboard and footboard turned outwards. **French blue** *colloq.* a combination of amphetamine and barbiturate. **French brace** (*a*) a type of breast-drill; (*b*) *Theatr.* a hinged brace. **French bread** orig., a kind of fancy bread; now also = *French loaf* below. **French Canadian** *n.* & *a.* (*a*) *n.* a Canadian of French ancestry, a mainly French-speaking Canadian; the language spoken by such a person; (*b*) *adj.* of or pertaining to French Canada, French Canadians, or their language. **French chalk** a kind of steatite, used for marking cloth, removing grease and, in powder form, as a dry lubricant. **French clock** a clock made in France, *esp.* an elaborately decorated 18th-cent. clock. *French cotton*: see COTTON *n.*[1] **French cricket** an informal type of cricket without stumps in which the batsman is out if the ball hits his or her legs. †**French crown** an écu. **French cuff** a double cuff formed by turning back a long cuff and securing it with buttons or links. *French curve*: see CURVE *n.* 3. **French defence** *Chess* a defence beginning with the black king's pawn moving one square in reply to a two-square move of the white king's pawn. **French disease** (now *rare*) syphilis. **French door** = *French window* below. **French drain** a drain consisting of rubble through which water soaks away. **French dressing** a salad-dressing consisting of vinegar and oil, usu. seasoned. *French endive*: see ENDIVE 3. **French flu** = FRANCOPHILIA. **French fried potato** a (fried) potato chip. *French fry*: see FRY *n.*[2] 1c. **French grey** a shade of grey with a lavender tint. *French* HONEYSUCKLE. *French horn*: see HORN *n.* **French kiss** = *deep kiss* s.v. DEEP *a.* **French kissing** the practice of giving French kisses. **French knickers** wide-legged knickers. **French knot** *Embroidery* a stitch in which the thread is wound around the needle, which is then passed back through the fabric at almost the same point to form a small dot. **French lavender** a kind of lavender, *Lavandula stoechas*, with large purple bracts at the tops of the flower-spikes. **French leave** unannounced or unauthorized departure (or other action): chiefly in *take French leave*. *French letter*: see LETTER *n.*[1] 7. **French loaf** a long crisp loaf of bread. *French lungwort*: see LUNGWORT 1. **French maid** a lady's maid of French origin, to employ whom was freq. regarded as a status symbol in Victorian and Edwardian Britain. *French marigold*: see MARIGOLD *n.* 1. **French morocco** an inferior quality of Levant morocco. *French mustard*: see MUSTARD *n.* **French oak** †(*a*) the ilex; (*b*) *W. Indies* a W. Indian tree, *Catalpa longissima*, of the bignonia family. **French partridge** the red-legged partridge, *Alectoris rufa*. **French pink** *US* (*a*) a cornflower, *Centaurea cyanus*, naturalized in the US; (*b*) a sea pink. **French pleat** (*a*) a pleat at the top of a curtain consisting of three smaller pleats; (*b*) = *French roll* below. **French polish** a shellac solution used to produce a high gloss on wood; the smooth finish so produced. **French-polish** *v.t.* make smooth and glossy with French polish. **French-polisher** a person whose business is the French-polishing of woodwork. **French pox** (now *rare*) syphilis. **French Revolution** the revolution of 1789–99, in which the Bourbon monarchy in France was overthrown. **French roll** a hairstyle in which the hair is tucked into a vertical roll down the back of the head. **French roof** a mansard roof. **French seam**: in which the raw edges are enclosed. **French sixth** *Mus.* a chord consisting of a major third, augmented fourth, and augmented sixth. *French sorrel*: see SORREL *n.*[1] 2. **French stick** = *French loaf* above. **French tickler** *colloq.* a condom with stimulant protrusions. **French toast** (*a*) bread buttered on one side and toasted on the other; (*b*) bread coated in beaten egg and milk and fried. **French turnip** (the spindle-shaped root of) a navew, *Brassica napus* subsp. *rapifera*. **French twist** = *French roll* above. *French ultramarine*: see ULTRAMARINE *n.* 1. **French vermouth** dry vermouth. *French whisk*: see WHISK *n.*[1] 2c. **French window** a glazed door in an outside wall, serving both as a window and as a door.

B *n.* 1 The Romance language of France, spoken as a native language also in neighbouring countries (e.g. Belgium where it is one of the two official languages) and in parts of Canada, and the official language of a number of African countries. ME. b *euphem.* Bad language. Esp. in *excuse* (or *pardon*) *my French*. L19. 2 *collect. pl.* *The* people of France. Also (*rare*) without article, French people. M16. 3 Dry vermouth. M20. 4 Fellatio, cunnilingus. *slang.* M20.

1 *Norman French*: see NORMAN *a.* 1. *Old French*: see OLD *a.* *pedlar's French*: see PEDLAR. 3 M. GILBERT He was drinking double gins with single Frenches in them. 4 B. TURNER You can be whipped or caned . . or you can have French for another pound.

Frencher *n.* (*derog.*, *rare*) a Frenchman E19. **Frenchery** *n.* (*collect.*, *rare*) French goods, characteristics, etc. L16. **Frenchism** *n.* (*rare*) a French custom, idiom, or characteristic M18. **French-like** *adv.* & *a.* like or after the manner of the French, in French fashion M16. **Frenchly** *adv.* (now *rare*) in a (supposedly) French manner E16. **Frenchness** *n.* E16.

French /frɛn(t)ʃ/ *v.* Also **f-**. M17. [f. the adj.] †1 *French it*: speak French. *rare.* Only in M17. 2 *v.t.* Give a French form or style to; make French, translate into French. M18. 3 *v.t.* Teach (a person) French. *rare.* M19. 4 *v.i.* Of tobacco, cotton, or another plant: become diseased and distorted. *US.* M19. 5 *v.t.* & *i.* Practise fellatio or cunnilingus (with). *slang.* M20.

Frenchie *a.* & *n.* var. of FRENCHY.

Frenchify /ˈfrɛn(t)ʃɪfʌɪ/ *v.* Also **f-**. L16. [f. FRENCH *a.* + -I- + -FY.] 1 *v.t.* Make French in form, character, or manners. L16. †b As *Frenchified* ppl a.: afflicted with the French disease, i.e. syphilis. *slang.* M17–E18. 2 *v.i.* Become French in ideas, manners, etc. *rare.* L18.

1 A. BURGESS The hotel cuisine was good, though a bit Frenchified. J. JONES His Socialism was sadly frenchified and utopian, but his heart was sound.

Frenchifiˈcation *n.* M19.

Frenchman /ˈfrɛn(t)ʃmən/ *n.* Orig. two wds. Pl. **-men**. OE. [f. FRENCH *a.* + MAN *n.*] 1 A man of French birth or nationality. OE. †b An ancient Gaul. LME–E17. 2 A French ship. L15. 3 A scholar of the French language. *rare. colloq.* L17. 4 A tobacco plant affected by a deformity which causes the leaves to thicken and become narrow and distorted. *US.* L17. 5 A knife or straight-sided trowel used in pointing brickwork. L19. 6 The French or red-legged partridge, *Alectoris rufa*. L19.

Frenchwoman *n.*, pl. **-women**, (*a*) a woman of French birth or nationality; †(*b*) a woman of ancient Gaul: L16.

Frenchy /ˈfrɛn(t)ʃi/ *a.* & *n.* Also **Frenchie**. E19. [f. FRENCH *a.* + -Y[6], -IE.] A *adj.* Characteristic of what is French; French-like. E19.

H. N. COLERIDGE St. Pierre is a pretty . . town . . it is neat and Frenchy. C. O. SKINNER Word had gotten about that the plays in her repertoire were 'Frenchy', meaning naughty.

B *n.* A Frenchman, a Frenchwoman. Also, a French Canadian. *derog.* L19.

Frenchily *adv.* L19. **Frenchiness** *n.* L19.

frenetic /frəˈnɛtɪk/ *a.* & *n.* Also (now *rare*) **phrenetic**. LME. [(O)Fr. *frénétique* f. L *phreneticus* f. late Gk *phrenētikos*, for *phrenitikos*, f. *phrenitis* delirium, f. *phren-*, *phrēn* heart, mind: see -ITIS, -IC. Cf. FRANTIC.] A *adj.* 1 Of a person. †a Mentally deranged, insane. LME–L18. b Wildly excited, (over-)enthusiastic, fanatical. M16. †2 Of a disease: accompanied by delirium or temporary madness. LME–M18. 3 Of an action, quality, etc.: frenzied, erratic, uncontrolled. E16.

1b N. INGELO He esteems Prophetick Visions only as Dreams of phrenetick men. 3 D. M. DAVIN The demands she made on herself . . grew greater, more frenetic . . every year.

†B *n.* An insane or delirious person. E16–L19.

¶Formerly stressed on 1st syll.

†**frenetical** *a.* LME–L17. **frenetically** *adv.* M19.

†frentic *a.* & *n.* var. of FRANTIC.

frenulum *n.* var. of FRAENULUM.

frenum *n.* var. of FRAENUM.

†frenzical *a.* Also **ph-**. L16–M18. [f. next + -IC + -AL[1].] Crazy, insane; wildly enthusiastic.

Also **†frenzic** *a.* M–L16.

frenzy /ˈfrɛnzi/ *n.* & *a.* Also (now *rare*) **phrenzy**. ME. [(O)Fr. *frénésie* f. med.L *phrenesia* for L *phrenesis*, f. Gk *phren-*, *phrēn* mind: see FRENETIC, -Y[3].] A *n.* 1 Mental derangement, temporary insanity; the uncontrollable excitement of a paroxysm of mania. ME. 2 Mental agitation likened to insanity; a state of delirious fury, rage, enthusiasm, etc. Also, wild folly, craziness. LME. b A crazy notion or idea; a craze, a mania. M17.

1 C. THIRLWALL Subject to temporary fits of frenzy. K. LINES In a frenzy they disarranged their hair, tore their garments and rushed screaming out of the city. 2 H. INNES Smoking cigarette after cigarette in a frenzy of frustration. CONAN DOYLE Not.. the reasoned courting of an elderly man, but.. the passionate frenzy of youth. *fig.*: R. HUGHES An impudent leather cap; a frenzy of curls.

Comb.: **frenzy-fever** *arch.* a delirious fever.

B *adj.* †1 Mad, insane, crazy. L16–M17. 2 Angry. *dial.* M19.

frenzy /ˈfrɛnzi/ *v.* L18. [f. the n.] 1 *v.t.* Drive (a person, an animal, etc.) mad; infuriate, put into a frenzy. Chiefly as *frenzied* ppl a. L18. 2 *v.i.* Be in or go into a frenzy. *rare.* M20.

1 D. ACHESON The Department seemed like a pack of beagles in frenzied pursuit. J. G. FARRELL The frenzied crowd of maddened natives. *New Yorker* For all the hour.. that one of his pieces sometimes lasts.. he frenzies the keyboard.

frenziedly *adv.* M19.

Freon /ˈfriːɒn/ *n.* Also **f-**. M20. [Origin unkn.] Proprietary name for any of a series of halogenated hydrocarbons (containing fluorine and usu. chlorine or bromine) used esp. as refrigerants and aerosol propellants.

frequence /ˈfriːkw(ə)ns/ *n.* Now *rare.* LME. [(O)Fr. *fréquence* f. L *frequentia*: see next, -ENCE.] 1 A gathering of people in large numbers; a crowded condition; a crowd, a multitude. *arch.* LME. †2 Constant use of something; familiarity. Only in E17. 3 Frequent occurrence or repetition, frequency. E17.

frequency /ˈfriːkw(ə)nsi/ *n.* M16. [L *frequentia*, f. *frequent-*: see next, -ENCY.] †1 = FREQUENCE 1. M16–E18. †2 Constant use or repetition *of*. E17–L18. b Familiarity *with*, constant attendance *at*. M–L17. 3 *gen.* The fact of occurring often or of being repeated at short intervals; commonness of occurrence; rate of recurrence. M17. 4 *spec.*: a *Med.* The rate of recurrence *of* the pulse, respiration, or other periodic bodily function. M18. b *Physics* etc. The number of times in a second or other specified time interval that any regular oscillation or vibration is repeated, such as that associated with mechanical vibration, sound, electromagnetic radiation, alternating current, etc.; *esp.* the number of cycles per second of a carrier wave used for radio transmission, (*loosely*) a waveband, a channel. Also, a sound etc. having a definite frequency. M19. c *Statistics.* The (relative) number of times something occurs in a given sample. M19. d *Ecol.* A measurement of the way in which the members of a species are distributed in a community. E20.

3 HOR. SMITH The diminished frequency of wars. C. MCCULLOUGH He wasn't calling her *herzchen* any more; of late she had noticed its frequency declining. 4b L. DEIGHTON Jimmy.. was tuning his radio to the frequencies between 7050 and 7100 kilocycles. H. M. ROSENBERG A wave is usually characterized by its frequency and wavelength. A. BURGESS Bartlett had taken a stick microphone.. and intoned a frequency. *audio frequency*, *high frequency*, *intermediate frequency*, *low frequency*, *medium frequency*, *natural frequency*, *video frequency*, etc. d K. A. KERSHAW If a species has a frequency of 10 per cent then it should occur once in every ten quadrats examined.

Comb.: **frequency changer**, **converter** a device for changing the frequency of an alternating current; *spec.* in a superheterodyne receiver, for combining the incoming signal with that from the local oscillator to produce the intermediate frequency; **frequency curve** a frequency diagram in the form of a continuous curve; **frequency diagram**: in which frequency of occurrence is plotted against the value of the variable; **frequency distortion** distortion of a signal due to unequal amplification or attenuation of components of different frequency; **frequency distribution** (a mathematical expression giving) a classification of the members of a population according to the value assumed for each member by some variable; a measurement of how often a variable takes each of its possible values; **frequency modulation** variation of the frequency of a radio or other wave as a means of carrying information such as an audio signal; **frequency polygon** a frequency diagram containing a (small) finite number of data points, each point being joined to the next by a straight line; **frequency response** the way in which the output-input ratio of an amplifier or other device depends on the signal frequency.

frequent /ˈfriːkw(ə)nt/ *a.* & *adv.* LME. [(O)Fr. *fréquent* or L *frequent-*, *-ens*, crowded, frequent, of unkn. origin: see -ENT.] A *adj.* 1 †a Profuse, ample. Only in LME. b Numerous, abundant; found at short distances apart. M16. †2 Crowded, full. M16–E19. 3 Commonly used or practised; well or widely known. Now *rare.* M16. 4 (The prevailing sense.) Happening or occurring often or at short intervals; rapidly recurring. M16. 5 Addicted *to*; accustomed *to do*; inclined to indulge *in* or be repetitive *in*. Now *rare.* M16. 6 †a Often in company *with* (a person); conversant *in* (a subject). L16–M17. b Constant, habitual, regular. E17.

1b M. B. KEATINGE Walls.. flanked and crowned by frequent square towers. 2 DRYDEN 'Tis fit in frequent senate we confer. SHELLEY Halls, Frequent with crystal column. 3 A. STAFFORD I have not.. used any one word not frequent and familiar. 4 J. B. PRIESTLEY Jobs at which you have to be sustained by frequent cups of tea. J. D. SALINGER They gave me frequent warning to start applying myself. 5 SHAKES. *Wint. T.* He.. is less frequent to his princely exercises than formerly. JOSEPH HALL How frequent the Scripture is in the prohibition of this practice. 6b DAY LEWIS A farmer.. is the only frequent visitor.

B *adv.* Frequently, often. *colloq.* & *poet.* E17.

frequentist *n.* a person who believes that the probability of an event is the limit of its relative frequency in a large number of trials M20. **frequently** *adv.* (*a*) at frequent intervals, often, repeatedly; †(*b*) numerously: M16. **frequentness** *n.* (long *rare*) M17.

frequent /frɪˈkwɛnt/ *v.* L15. [(O)Fr. *fréquenter* or L *frequentare*, f. *frequent-*: see prec.] I *v.t.* 1 Visit or make use of (a place) often; go often or habitually to (a place, a house, meetings, etc.). L15. 2 Visit or associate with (a person); be with (a person) often. Now *rare.* L15. †3 Use habitually or repeatedly; practise. L15–M17. 4 Familiarize *with*. Long *obs.* exc. *Sc.* L16. †5 Crowd, fill; pack together; supply abundantly. L16–L17.

1 A. J. TOYNBEE This University City, which is frequented.. by thousands of students. G. GREENE Castle.. entered a bookshop he had frequented for several years now. 2 R. NORTH His Lordship had one friend that used to frequent him much.

II 6 *v.i.* Resort (*to* a place); associate *with* (a person); be often *in*, *about* (a place). *obs.* exc. *Sc.* L16.

6 POPE Far from all the ways Where men frequent.

frequentable *a.* (*rare*) that may be frequented, easily accessible L16. **frequenter** *n.* a person who frequents (a place, meetings, etc.) E17.

frequentation /friːkwənˈteɪʃ(ə)n/ *n.* LME. [Fr. *fréquentation* f. L *frequentatio(n-)*, f. *frequent-*: see FREQUENT *a.*, -ATION.] 1 The action or habit of visiting or frequenting; habitual attendance or association. LME. 2 †a The act of making use *of* regularly or often. Also, a custom, practice. E16–L17. b Frequent celebration of the sacraments. *rare.* E17.

frequentative /frɪˈkwɛntətɪv/ *a.* & *n.* M16. [Fr. *fréquentatif*, *-ive* or L *frequentativus*, f. *frequent-*: see FREQUENT *a.*, -ATIVE.] *Gram.* A *adj.* Of a verb, verbal form, or conjugation: expressing frequent repetition or intensity of action, as English *chatter*, *dribble*, *twinkle*, etc. M16. B *n.* A frequentative verb, verbal form, or conjugation. M16.

frere *n.* see FRIAR.

frescade /frɛsˈkɑːd/ *n.* M17. [Fr. f. It. *frescata*, f. *fresco* cool, fresh: see -ADE.] A cool, shady alley or walk.

fresco /ˈfrɛskəʊ/ *n.* & *v.* L16. [It. = cool, fresh. Earliest in *in fresco* repr. It. *affresco*, *al fresco* on the fresh (plaster). Cf. ALFRESCO.] A *n.* Pl. **-o(e)s**. 1 A method of painting in which water-colour is applied to wet, freshly laid plaster, so that the colours penetrate and become fixed as it dries. L16. b A painting produced by this method. L17. †2 Cool fresh air. E17–E19.

1 R. W. EMERSON The grand sibyls.. painted in fresco by Michel Angelo. b E. M. FORSTER On the ceiling was a fresco of the battle of Solferino.

Phrases: ***fresco buono*** /ˌfrɛsko ˈbwɔːno/ [= good] = sense A.1 above. ***fresco secco*** /ˌfrɛsko ˈsɛkko/ = SECCO *n.* 1. **in fresco** in the fresh air.

B *v.t.* Paint in fresco. E19.

L. M. MONTGOMERY Anne gazed at the ceiling as if it were frescoed with angels.

fresh /frɛʃ/ *a.*, *adv.*, & *n.* [OE *fersc* = OFris., MDu. *fersc* (Du. *vers*), OHG *frisc* (G *frisch*), ON *ferskr*, f. Gmc; replaced in ME by forms f. OFr. *freis* f. Proto-Romance f. same Gmc base.] A *adj.* I 1 (Of water) not salt; fit for drinking. Also, (now *rare*) of butter: unsalted. OE. b Of or pertaining to such water. Formerly also, of fish: freshwater. ME. 2 Of food: new as distinct from being preserved (by salting, pickling, smoking, drying, tinning, freezing, etc.). OE. 3 Retaining its original qualities, not deteriorated or changed by lapse of time; (of food) not stale or musty; (of a flower, memory, etc.) not faded; bright (in colour); clear; (of the complexion etc.) unsullied, looking young or healthy; (of clothing) clean. ME. †b Colourfully or finely dressed. LME–L16. 4 Not tired; full of energy; active, vigorous; refreshed. ME. †b Ready, eager, having an inclination (*to*, *to do*). ME–L17. c Of a cow: yielding a renewed or increased supply of milk, coming into milk. *US.* L19. 5 Esp. of air or water: pure, untainted, cool, refreshing, invigorating. LME. b Of the wind: having considerable force, quite strong; formerly also, springing up again. M16. c Of the weather: not frosty; rainy. *Sc.* & *north.* L18. 6 a Sober; *esp.* sobered up. *obs.* exc. *Sc.* LME. b Slightly intoxicated, tipsy. *arch.* E19. 7 [Perh. infl. by G *frech* impudent.] Forward, impertinent, free in behaviour. Orig. *US.* M19.

1 R. BOYLE He always found the ice fresh that floated upon the sea-water. b SHAKES. *Tit. A.* Till the fresh taste be taken from that clearness, And made a brine-pit with our bitter tears. 2 W. MARCH He liked them made from fresh coconut, not from that tasteless, shrivelled-up stuff that came in boxes. 3 I. M. BEETON It is particularly necessary that they should be quite fresh, as nothing is worse than stale eggs. R. P. WARREN Her clothes had looked perfectly fresh and unwrinkled. D. CUSACK Girls' voices, very fresh and young, sing the hymn. HARPER LEE See if you can tell us what happened, while it's still fresh in your mind. 4 J. HIGGINS Now.. I would like to sleep. I must be fresh for tonight's concert. 5 MILTON They among fresh dews and flowers Flie to and fro. W. BOYD Inhaling the.. fresher air on the first floor. 7 BETTY SMITH How fresh she must look—running after a feller like that. *Philadelphia Inquirer* That young, single dentist got fresh with me.

II 8 New, novel; not previously known, used, met with, etc. ME. b Additional, other, different. LME. 9 Recent, newly made; recently arrived, received, etc. ME. b Newly come *from* or *out of*. L17. 10 Raw, inexperienced; unsophisticated. L16.

8 CONAN DOYLE If the lady will not accept what is already known, why should any fresh discovery.. turn her from her purpose? I. MURDOCH Dorina was to have been a fresh start, a stepping-stone into some sort of elegant life. b G. ORWELL It appeared that they had engaged in fresh conspiracies from the very moment of their release. R. WEST Her face was contorted by a fresh spasm of weeping. 9 SWIFT The Author was then young.. and his reading fresh in his head. P. V. WHITE A Tannenbaum, smelling as such trees will when they bleed from fresh wounds. b E. BLISHEN A first-year form, thirty boys fresh from their junior schools. *City Limits* Fresh from winning the best director prize at Cannes. 10 DISRAELI Did you ever fight a duel? No!.. Well! you are fresh indeed!

Phrases & special collocations: BREATH *of fresh air*. **fresh as a daisy, as paint** bright, cheerful, active. *fresh blood*: see BLOOD *n.* **fresh breeze** a strong breeze, *spec.* a wind of force 5 (19–24 m.p.h.) on the Beaufort scale. *fresh off the irons*: see IRON *n.*

B *adv.* In a fresh manner; *esp.* newly. ME.

D. LESSING Picked fresh this morning, morning-picked country strawberries. **fresh out of** just sold or run out of (goods, supplies, etc.).

Comb.: *fresh-baked*, *fresh-caught*, etc.; **fresh-find** *v.t.* find (a deer) after the scent has been lost; **fresh-run** *a.* (of a fish, esp. a salmon) recently come up from the sea.

C *n.* 1 A rush of water in a stream; a flash flood; an ebb tide increased by heavy rain. M16. b A gust or squall (of wind). L17. 2 A pool, spring, or stream of fresh water. L16. 3 A freshwater stream running out into a tideway of salt water; (the land adjoining) the part of a tidal river above the salt water. Freq. in *pl. N. Amer.* M17. 4 The fresh or early part *of* a day, year, etc. E18.

freshish *a.* somewhat fresh M18. **freshness** *n.* the quality or condition of being fresh LME.

fresh /frɛʃ/ *v.* ME. [f. the adj.] 1 *v.t.* Refresh; cheer; renew. (Foll. by *up*.) *arch.* ME. 2 *v.i.* Of the sea: roughen. Formerly also, of the wind: increase in strength. L16.

freshen /ˈfrɛʃ(ə)n/ *v.* L17. [f. FRESH *a.* + -EN[5].] 1 *v.i.* Of the wind: increase in strength, begin to blow fresh. Also foll. by *up*. L17. 2a *v.t.* Renew, revive, give freshness to. Also foll. by *up*. M18. b *v.i.* Become (more) fresh; become bright or vivid. E19. c *v.i.* Wash one's hands and face, tidy one's hair and clothes, etc. Foll. by *up*. Chiefly *N. Amer.* M20. d *v.t.* Add fresh wine, spirits, etc., to (a drink which has been standing for some time); top up. M20. 3 *v.t.* & *i.* (Cause to) lose salt or saltness. L18. 4 *v.i.* Of a cow: give birth; come into milk. *US.* E20.

1 D. PAE The wind was again freshening into a gale. J. MASEFIELD It freshened up till it blew like thunder. 2a H. E. BATES A magical sweetness of dusty earth freshened by rain. J. GLASSCO The hundred yards in the cold night air freshened me up. **freshen the nip** *Naut.* alter the position of a rope etc. under strain, so as to expose a different part to friction. b C. BRONTË A greenness grew over those brown beds, .. freshening daily. S. NAIPAUL The air freshened as I approached the sea. c D. ADAMS Assuming you had landed by now and freshened up with a quick dip and shower. 3 *New Yorker* The Great Salt Lake .. has been freshening in recent years.

freshener *n.* a thing which freshens something M19.

fresher /ˈfrɛʃə/ *n. colloq.* L19. [f. FRESH *a.* + -ER[1].] A first-year student at university or polytechnic. Cf. FRESHMAN.

freshet /ˈfrɛʃɪt/ *n.* & *v.* L16. [Prob. f. OFr. *freschete* dim. of *freis* FRESH *a.*: see -ET[1].] A *n.* 1 A stream or rush of fresh water flowing into the sea; (now only *poet.*) a small freshwater stream. L16. 2 A flood of a river caused by heavy rain or melted snow. M17.

1 W. MCILVANNEY The river .. broke into a thousand freshets on the rocks. 2 S. N. CLEGHORN Wide and shallow in the cowslip marshes Floods the freshet of the April snow.

B *v.t.* & *i.* Flood (as) with a freshet. *rare.* M19.

freshly /ˈfrɛʃli/ *adv.* ME. [f. FRESH *a.* + -LY[2].] 1 Newly, recently. Now only w. ppl adjs. ME. b Anew, afresh. Now *rare.* LME. 2 With renewed vigour; (of the wind) briskly. Formerly also, fiercely, eagerly. ME. 3 Clearly, brightly; distinctly; sharply. Formerly also, gaily, magnificently. LME.

1 S. BEDFORD Outside the potting shed stood a large box of freshly dug garden earth. b J. STEINBECK The tears started freshly in Rose of Sharon's eyes. 2 TENNYSON [A breeze] gathering freshlier overhead. 3 SHAKES. *A.Y.L.* Looks he as freshly as he did the day he wrestled? J. W. BURGON The man lives freshly in the memory of his fellows.

freshman /ˈfrɛʃmən/ *n.* Pl. **-men**. M16. [f. FRESH *a.* + MAN *n.*] 1 A newcomer, a novice. Formerly also, a proselyte. M16. 2 A student during his or her first year (and esp. first term) at a university, college, polytechnic, or (*N. Amer.*) high school. L16.

1 *attrib.*: D. ACHESON The attitude of the leader of the Senate to a freshman senator. 2 R. JARRELL The first thing I do with a freshman .. is to shake her out of her ignorant complacency.

freshmanship *n.* the condition or state of being a freshman E17. **freshwoman** *n.* (*rare*), pl. **-women**, a female freshman E17.

freshwater /ˈfrɛʃwɔːtə/ *a.* LME. [f. FRESH *a.* + WATER *n.*] 1 Of, pertaining to, or living in water that is not salt. LME. 2 Unskilled, untrained, raw; now only, unaccustomed or new to the sea. L16. 3 Of an institution, college, etc.: insignificant; rustic, provincial. *US.* M19.

1 †*freshwater soldier*: see SOLDIER *n.* 4.

Fresison /frɪˈsʌɪs(ə)n/ *n.* E19. [A mnemonic of scholastic philosophers, E indicating a universal negative major, I a particular affirmative minor, and O a particular negative conclusion.] *Logic.* The fifth mood of the fourth syllogistic figure, in which a particular negative conclusion is drawn from a universal negative major premiss and a particular affirmative minor.

Fresnel /freɪˈnɛl/ *n.* M19. [A. J. *Fresnel* (1788–1827), Fr. physicist.] *Physics.* I 1 Used *attrib.* and in *possess.* to designate devices, phenomena, or concepts related to Fresnel's work in optics. M19.

Fresnel biprism = BIPRISM. **Fresnel diffraction** diffraction in which the pattern is a nonlinear function of the phase variation across the diffracting aperture or object (cf. *Fraunhofer('s) diffraction* s.v. FRAUNHOFER 2). **Fresnel lens** a lens consisting of a number of concentric annular sections, designed to produce a parallel beam free from spherical aberration. **Fresnel('s) rhomb** a glass parallelepiped in which, by total internal reflection, a beam of plane polarized light can be converted into a beam of circularly or elliptically polarized light travelling in the same direction.

II 2 (**f-**.) A unit of frequency equal to 10^{12} Hz. Also *fresnel unit*. M20.

fret /frɛt/ *n.*[1] LME. [f. FRET *v.*[1]] 1 The action or an act (as) of gnawing or wearing away; an eroded or decayed spot. Now *rare.* LME. b *sing.* & in *pl.* Colic. Now *dial.* E17. 2 (An) agitation or torment of the mind; (a state of) irritation, vexation, or peevishness; a cause of worry or irritation; a peevish utterance. LME. †3 A sudden disturbance of weather; a gust or squall (of wind). M16–M18. 4 Secondary fermentation of liquor. M17.

1 TENNYSON Before .. the busy fret Of that sharpheaded worm begins. 2 C. LAMB The fret and fever of speculation. E. GASKELL He heard his wife's plaintive fret. J. HILTON Repose from which all the fret of existence had ebbed away. **on the fret** [perh. infl. by other senses] in a state of irritation or impatience.

fret /frɛt/ *n.*[2] LME. [Prob. f. OFr. *frete* trellis, interlaced work (mod. *frette*), of unkn. origin: see FRET *v.*[2]] 1 Ornamental interlaced work; *esp.* a decorative network of jewels or flowers for the hair. LME. 2 *Her.* Orig., a figure formed by alternate interlacing bendlets and bendlets sinister. Later, a device consisting of two narrow bands in saltire interlaced with a mascle. LME. 3 An ornamental pattern composed of continuous combinations of straight lines, usu. joined at right angles. Also *Greek fret*. E17.

†**fretwise** *adv.* in the form of a fret, interlaced LME–E18.

fret /frɛt/ *n.*[3] E16. [Origin unkn.] Any of various bars or ridges on the finger-board of some stringed instruments (usu. those played by plucking) used for fixing the position of the fingers to produce the required notes.

Comb.: **fretboard** a finger-board provided with frets.

fret /frɛt/ *n.*[4] *obs.* exc. *dial.* L17. [OFr. *frete* (mod. *frette*) ferrule, ring.] An iron hoop circling the nave of a cartwheel.

fret /frɛt/ *n.*[5] *north.* M19. [Origin unkn.] More fully *sea fret*. Mist or drizzle coming in off the sea; a sea fog.

fret /frɛt/ *v.*[1] Infl. **-tt-**. [OE *fretan* = MLG, MDu. *vrēten* (Du. *vreten*), OHG *frezzan* (G *fressen*), Goth. *fraïtan*, f. Gmc bases of FOR-[1], EAT *v.* In sense 4 perh. orig. a separate wd: cf. Prov. *fretar*, It. *frettare*, mod.Fr. dial. *fretter*, ult. f. L *fricare* rub.] †1 *v.t.* Chiefly of animals: eat, devour, consume. OE–L16. 2a *v.t.* & *i.* Gnaw; consume, torment, or wear away by gnawing; destroy gradually or insidiously by corrosion, erosion, disease, etc. ME. b Of emotion: consume, torment. *obs.* exc. as passing into sense 3 in *fret the heart*. ME. †c *v.i.* Become eaten or corroded; wear away, decay. (Foll. by *off*, *out*.) L15–E19. 3a *v.t.* Chafe, irritate; annoy, distress, worry (a person, oneself); bring (*in*)*to* or into a specified condition by worrying. ME. b *v.i.* Worry, distress oneself with regret, discontent, or anxiety; express worry or peevish discontent. (Foll. by *about*, *at*, *over*, *that*, etc.) M16. c *v.t.* Spend or pass (time, one's life, etc.) in fretting. (Foll. by *away*, *out*.) E17. 4a *v.t.* Rub (*away*), chafe; cause to move against something with friction. ME. b *v.i.* Rub (*on*, *against*); fray *out*. M17. 5 *v.t.* & †*i.* (w. *into*, *through*, *to*.) Make (a way, hole, etc.) by gnawing or corrosion. LME. 6a *v.i.* Of a stream, the sea, etc.: flow or rise in little waves, move in agitation. M16. b *v.t.* Ruffle (water). L18. 7 *v.t.* & *i.* (Cause to) undergo secondary fermentation. Now chiefly *dial.* M17.

2 C. LAMB We cannot bear to have our thin wardrobe eaten and fretted into by moths. B. MASON The surface of these rock shelves is jagged, .. fretted away by the corrosive sea. b L. EDEL The nagging guilt, fretting at his heart. 3a R. LARDNER Mother had nearly fretted herself sick for fear I would be left. A. WAUGH The innumerable small annoyances that fret and harass us. b M. E. BRADDON Knows his own interest too well to fret and fume about trifles. R. C. HUTCHINSON Men do fret over trifles when there are larger things to crowd the mind. J. BARTH Jeannine .. began to fret in her crib. P. ACKROYD I fretted that I had no books to read in my cell. c SHAKES. *Macb.* Life's but a walking shadow, a poor player, That struts and frets his hour upon the stage. 4a F. RAPHAEL Fretting the carving knife between the roundels of the sharpener. **fretting corrosion** abrasion accompanied by chemical corrosion occurring where metal surfaces are held in contact, with some freedom of relative movement. b P. V. WHITE The old woman's head was barely fretting against the pillow. 5 J. WAIN What .. shape the sea has fretted into the land.

fretter *n.* (*a*) a thing which gnaws or eats away something, *esp.* a caterpillar which eats vines; (*b*) a person who or thing which irritates, chafes, or rubs something; (*c*) a person inclined to fret: E16. **frettingly** *adv.* in a fretting manner M17.

fret /frɛt/ *v.*[2]*t.* Infl. **-tt-**. Pa. pple **fretted**, †**fret**. LME. [Prob. f. OFr. *freté* (= AL *frectatus*, *frictatus*) pa. pple of *freter* rel. to *frete* trellis: see FRET *n.*[2]] 1 Chiefly as *fretted* ppl a. Decorate, *esp.* embroider, with interlaced work; ornament with gold, silver, or jewels. Long only *fig.* LME. 2 *Her.* Interlace; decorate with an interlaced pattern. LME. 3 Decorate (esp. a ceiling) with fretwork; carve into frets. M16.

1 LONGFELLOW White clouds sail aloft; and vapours fret the blue sky with silver threads. 3 H. READ He stood against the fretted hedge, which was like white lace.

fretting *n.* (*a*) the action of the vb; (*b*) a pattern or ornamentation so produced: LME.

fret /frɛt/ *v.*[3]*t.* Infl. **-tt-**. E17. [f. FRET *n.*[3]] Provide (a guitar etc.) with frets. Chiefly as *fretted* ppl a.

fretful /ˈfrɛtfʊl, -f(ə)l/ *a.* L16. [f. FRET *v.*[1] + -FUL.] †1 Corrosive, irritating. Only in L16. 2 Inclined to fret; worried, irritable, peevish; impatient, restless. E17. b Characterized by or apt to cause irritation. M18. 3 Of water etc.: agitated, troubled, broken into waves. E17.

fretfully *adv.* L18. **fretfulness** *n.* E17.

fretish /ˈfrɛtɪʃ/ *v.t.* Long *obs.* exc. *dial.* Also **-tt-**. E16. [OFr. *frediss-* lengthened stem of *fredir*, *freidir* (mod. *froidir*), f. *freid* (mod. *froid*) f. Proto-Romance alt. of L *frigidus* FRIGID: see -ISH[2].] Benumb, freeze. Now only as *fretished* ppl a., numb with cold.

†**fretize** *v.t.* L16–E18. [Rel. to OFr. *fraitis* decorated with fretwork.] = FRET *v.*[2] 3.

fretless /ˈfrɛtlɪs/ *a.*[1] *rare.* L19. [f. FRET *n.*[1], *v.*[1] + -LESS.] 1 Free from irritation or worry. L19. 2 Of water: calm, unruffled. L19.

fretless /ˈfrɛtlɪs/ *a.*[2] M20. [f. FRET *n.*[3] + -LESS.] Of a musical instrument: having no frets on the finger-board.

fretsaw /ˈfrɛtsɔː/ *n.* M19. [f. FRET *n.*[2] + SAW *n.*[1]] A saw with a narrow vertical blade stretched on a frame, used for cutting thin wood to form ornamental designs.

frettish *v.* var. of FRETISH.

fretty /ˈfrɛti/ *a.*[1] M16. [OFr. *freté*, f. *frete*: see FRET *n.*[2], -Y[5].] *Her.* Covered with alternate interlacing bendlets and bendlets sinister.

fretty /ˈfrɛti/ *a.*[2] M19. [f. FRET *v.*[1] + -Y[1].] Inclined to fret; irritable.

fretwork /ˈfrɛtwəːk/ *n.* E17. [f. FRET *n.*[2] + WORK *n.*] 1 *Archit.* Carved work in decorative patterns esp. of intersecting straight lines. E17. 2 The cutting of wood with a fretsaw to form ornamental designs; wood so cut. L19.

fretworked *a.* ornamented with or by fretwork L19.

Freudian /ˈfrɔɪdɪən/ *a.* & *n.* E20. [f. Sigmund *Freud* (1856–1939), Austrian neurologist and founder of psychoanalysis: see -IAN.] A *adj.* Of or pertaining to Freud or his methods or theories of psychoanalysis; *loosely* relating to (supposed) unconscious feelings. E20.

S. SPENDER A Freudian argument which told me that I only troubled about these things out of a sense of guilt. J. I. M. STEWART There was something Freudian about my forgetfulness. **Freudian slip** an unintentional (esp. spoken) error that seems to reveal subconscious feelings.

B *n.* A follower of Freud or his methods. E20.

Freudianism *n.* the theory, system, or methods of Freudian psychoanalysis E20. **Freudianly** *adv.* M20.

friable /ˈfrʌɪəb(ə)l/ *a.* M16. [Fr., or L *friabilis*, f. *friare* crumble into small pieces: see -ABLE.] Able to be easily crumbled or reduced to powder; crumbly.

friaˈbility *n.* the quality of being friable E17. **friableness** *n.* M17.

†**friand** *a.* L16–E19. [(O)Fr., = dainty, in OFr. vivacious, for *friant* pres. pple of *frire* FRY *v.*] Delicious to the palate; fond of delicate food, epicurean.

friandise /fri(j)ɑ̃diːz/ *n. rare.* Pl. pronounced same. L15. [Fr., f. *friand*: see prec., -ISE[1].] 1 A delicacy; dainty fare. L15. †2 Fondness for delicate fare. Only in E17.

friar /ˈfrʌɪə/ *n.* Also (earlier, long *arch.*) **frere** /frɛː/. ME. [(O)Fr. *frère* f. L *frater*, *fratr-* brother.] 1 Brother (chiefly *fig.*); comrade. Long *arch. rare.* ME. 2 A member of any of certain religious orders of men, *esp.* the four mendicant orders: the Franciscans (*Grey Friars*, *Friars Minor*), Augustinians (*Austin Friars*), Dominicans (*Black Friars*, *Friars Major*), and Carmelites (*White Friars*). ME. b In *pl.* The quarters of an order of friars; a name for the part of a town where such a friary once stood. ME. 3 Any of various fishes. *local.* E17. 4 *Printing.* A light patch amongst printed matter on a page, due to insufficient inking. (Cf. MONK *n.*[1] 2.) L17. 5 In full *friar-bird.* Any of various honeyeaters of the largely Australasian genus *Philemon*, members of which have black, partly naked heads. L18.

2 *Pied Friars*, *preaching friars*, etc.

Comb.: *friar-bird*: see sense 5 above; **friar's balsam** tincture of benzoin used as an application for ulcers and wounds, or as an expectorant.

friarly *a.* & *adv.* (*a*) *adj.* of or pertaining to friars, resembling or characteristic of a friar; (*b*) *adv.* after the manner of the friars: M16.

friary /ˈfrʌɪəri/ *n.* ME. [f. prec. + -Y[3].] 1 A fraternity or brotherhood of friars. ME. 2 A convent of friars. LME.

†**friation** *n.* M17–M18. [f. L *friat-* pa. ppl stem of *friare*: see FRIABLE, -ATION.] The action of rubbing or crumbling into small pieces.

frib /frɪb/ *n. Austral.* & *NZ.* E20. [Origin unkn.] A small short lock of wool from a sheep. Usu. in *pl.*

fribby *a.* & *n.* (*a*) *adj.* of the nature of a frib, consisting of fribs; (*b*) *n.* a frib: E20.

fribble /ˈfrɪb(ə)l/ *n.* & *a.* M17. [f. the vb.] A *n.* 1 A frivolous person, a trifler, a person not engaged in serious work. M17. 2 A trifling thing; a frivolous notion or characteristic. M19. 3 Frivolity, nonsense. Also *fribble-frabble.* M19. B *adj.* Trifling, frivolous, ridiculous. L18.

fribblish *a.* characteristic of or suited to a fribble; frivolous, trifling: M18.

fribble /ˈfrɪb(ə)l/ *v.* E17. [Symbolic.] †1 a *v.t.* & *i.* Stammer, mumble. Only in 17. b *v.i.* Falter; totter in walking. E18–M19. 2 *v.i.* Act aimlessly, behave frivolously, mess about. M17. b *v.t.* Foll. by *away*: part with lightly and wastefully, fritter. M17. 3 *v.t.* Frizzle (a wig). *Sc.* M18.

fribbler *n.* a trifler E18.

fricandeau /ˈfrɪkandəʊ/ *n.* & *v.* Also (earlier) †**-do.** E18. [Fr.] A *n.* Pl. **-eaux** /-əʊz/, †**-oes.** (A slice of) veal or other meat fried or stewed and served with sauce; an escalope; a fricassee of veal. E18. B *v.t.* Make into fricandeaux. M18.

fricassee /ˈfrɪkəsiː, frɪkəˈsiː/ *n.* & *v.* M16. [Fr. *fricassée* fem. pa. pple of *fricasser* cut up and stew in sauce.] A *n.* Meat sliced and fried or stewed and served with sauce; *esp.* a ragout of birds or small animals. M16. B *v.t.* Pa. t. & pple **-sseed.** Make a fricassee of; dress as a fricassee. M17.

†**frication** *n.* LME. [L *fricatio(n-)*, f. *fricat-* pa. ppl stem of *fricare* rub: see -ATION.] 1 The action or process of chafing or rubbing the body with the hands. LME–L17. 2 The action of rubbing the surface of one body against that of another; friction. M17–E18.

fricative /ˈfrɪkətɪv/ *a.* & *n.* M19. [mod.L *fricativus*, f. L *fricare* rub: see -ATIVE.] A *adj.* Of a consonant-sound: produced by the friction of the air-stream through a narrow opening in the mouth (as *v*, *s*). M19. B *n.* A fricative consonant. M19.

fricatrice /ˈfrɪkətrɪs/ *n.* Now *rare.* E17. [f. L *fricare* rub + -TRICE.] An unchaste woman.

friction /ˈfrɪkʃ(ə)n/ *n.* & *v.* M16. [Fr. f. L *frictio(n-)*, f. *frict-* pa. ppl stem of *fricare* rub: see -ION.] A *n.* 1 The action of chafing or rubbing the body or limbs, formerly much used in medical treatment. M16. b *Hairdressing.* A massage of the scalp. M20. 2 The rubbing of one body against another; attrition. E18. b *Med.* More fully *friction-murmur*, *-sound*, etc. A scratching sound heard in auscultation when the pleura or pericardium is roughened by inflammation. L19. 3 *Physics.* The resistance which a body encounters in moving over another body. E18. 4 *fig.* The jarring or conflict of wills, opinions, temperaments, etc. M18.

2 J. MORSE The rocks below . . are worn many feet deep by the constant friction of the water. 3 A. S. EDDINGTON Friction which has to be overcome when a train . . is kept moving uniformly. F. HOYLE There is very little friction indeed between one icy surface and another. **angle of friction** the maximum angle of slope at which one body will remain on another without sliding down. **coefficient of friction** the ratio between the force necessary to move one surface horizontally over another and the pressure between the two surfaces. STATIC *friction.* 4 T. C. WOLFE The friction between Helen and Eliza was often acute. A. KOESTLER Constant friction, flaring into heated quarrels.

Attrib. & *comb.*: Esp. in the sense 'working, esp. transmitting motion, by frictional contact', as *friction-brake*, *-clutch*, *-cone*, *-coupling*, *-disc*, *-gear(ing)*, etc. Special combs., as **friction-ball**: used in bearings to lessen friction; **friction match**: that ignites by friction; *friction-murmur*, *-sound*: see sense 2b above; **friction welding**: in which the heat is produced by rotating one component against the other under compression.

B *v.* 1 *v.i.* Move with friction; sustain friction. *rare.* M19. 2 *v.t.* Subject to friction; rub. *rare.* M19. 3 *v.t.* Impregnate (fabric) with rubber by rolling in a calender. M19.

frictionize *v.t.* = FRICTION *v.* 2 M19. **frictionless** *a.* free from or without friction M19. **frictionlessly** *adv.* L19.

frictional /ˈfrɪkʃ(ə)n(ə)l/ *a.* M19. [f. prec. + -AL[1].] Of or pertaining to friction; moved, produced, or operating by friction.

frictional electricity = STATIC *electricity.*
frictionally *adv.* L19.

Friday /ˈfrʌɪdeɪ, -di/ *n.*, *adv.*, & *a.* [OE *Frīgedæg*, corresp. to OFris. *frī(g)endei*, MLG, MDu. *vrīdach* (Du. *vrijdag*), OHG *frīatag* (G *Freitag*), = day of *Frīg* = ON *Frigg*, the wife of Odin, prop. use as n. of fem. of Gmc base of FREE *a.*: WGmc tr. late L *Veneris dies* day of the planet Venus (whence Fr. *vendredi*), based on Gk *Aphroditēs hēmera* day of Aphrodite.] A *n.* 1 The sixth day of the week, following Thursday. OE. 2 A reception or entertainment given on a Friday. M19.

1 **girl, Man, Friday** [f. *Man Friday* in Defoe's novel *Robinson Crusoe*] a helper, *esp.* an assistant who performs general duties in an office. **Golden Friday** the Friday in each of the Ember weeks. *Good Friday*: see GOOD *a. Man Friday*: see *girl Friday* above.

B *adv.* On Friday. Now *colloq.* ME.

H. KEMELMAN Friday the Rabbi slept late.

C *attrib.* or as *adj.* Of Friday; characteristic of Friday, esp. (formerly) as a day of fasting; taking place on Friday(s). L16.

Fridays *adv.* (*colloq.*) on Fridays, each Friday ME.

fridge /frɪdʒ/ *n. colloq.* Also **frig.** E20. [Abbrev.] = REFRIGERATOR.

Comb.: **fridge-freezer** an upright unit combining a refrigerator and a freezer, each self-contained.

fridge /frɪdʒ/ *v.* M16. [App. imit.: cf. FRIG *v.*, FIG *v.*[2], FIDGE *v.*] †1 *v.i.* Move restlessly, fidget. M16–L17. 2 *v.t.* & †*i.* Rub, fray, chafe; wear away by rubbing. Now chiefly *dial.* E17.

fried /frʌɪd/ *ppl a.* LME. [pa. pple of FRY *v.*: see -ED[1].] 1 Cooked by frying. LME. 2 Drunk. *slang.* E20.

fried *v.* pa. t. & pple of FRY *v.*

Friedel-Crafts reaction /friːd(ə)lˈkrɑːfts rɪˌakʃ(ə)n/ *n. phr.* L19. [f. Charles *Friedel* (1832–99), Fr. chemist + James M. *Crafts* (1839–1917), US chemist.] *Chem.* The catalytic alkylation or acylation of an aromatic compound in the presence of a Lewis acid such as aluminium chloride.

Friedreich /ˈfriːdrʌɪk, -x/ *n.* L19. [Nikolaus *Friedreich* (1825–82), Ger. neurologist.] *Med.* 1 *Friedreich('s) ataxia, disease*, a hereditary progressive ataxia with onset usu. in adolescence. L19. 2 *Friedreich's paramyoclonus*, = *paramyoclonus multiplex* s.v. PARA-[1]. L19.

friend /frɛnd/ *n.* & *a.* [OE *frēond* = OFris., OS *friund* (Du. *vriend*), OHG *friunt* (G *Freund*), ON *frændi*, Goth. *frijonds*, f. Gmc pres. pple of vb = 'to love', f. base of FREE *a.*] A *n.* 1 A person joined by affection and intimacy to another, independently of sexual or family love. OE. 2 A near relation. Usu. in *pl.*, those responsible for one. OE. 3 A person who is not hostile or an enemy to another; one who is on the same side. OE. 4 A person who wishes another, a cause, etc., well; a sympathizer, helper, patron, (*of*, *to*); (usu. in *pl.*) a supporter *of* an institution etc., who regularly contributes money or other help. ME. b A helpful thing. LME. c A person who acts for another, *esp.* (*Hist.*) as a second in a duel. E19. 5 An acquaintance, an associate; a stranger whom one comes across or has occasion to mention again. Freq. as *voc.* as a polite form or in irony, and (*Hist.*) used by members of the Society of Friends as the ordinary form of address. ME. 6 A romantic or sexual partner, a lover. Now a euphemism exc. where qualified as *boyfriend*, *girlfriend*, *lady-friend*, *man-friend*, etc. LME. 7 (**F-.**) A member of the Society of Friends. M17.

1 R. G. COLLINGWOOD An intimate and beloved friend of my own. *Proverb*: A friend in need is a friend indeed. 2 OED Handed over to the care of his friends. 3 J. MASTERS They'd said 'Friend', instead of giving the countersign. 4 J. PRIESTLEY The Gnostics . . were no friends to marriage. *Guardian* The twenty . . Friends of the Tate Gallery. b SHAKES. *Wint. T.* Good expedition be my friend. 5 R. KIPLING You musn't bang about as though Delhi station belonged to you, my friend. JONATHAN ROSS The local inspector's calling out friend Twite [a pathologist]. 6 *Guardian* The boy's mother . . was joined . . by a man described as her 'friend'.

Phrases: **be** or **keep friends** (**with**) be on good or intimate terms (with). *best friend(s)*: see BEST *a.* etc. *curate's friend*: see CURATE *n. feathered friend*: see FEATHERED 1. **friend at court** a person in a position to use his or her influence on one's behalf. **friends in high places** highly-placed people able or ready to use their influence on one's behalf. *keep friends* (*with*): see *be friends* (*with*) above. **make friends** (**with**) get on good or intimate terms (with). *man's best friend*: see MAN *n.* **my** etc. **learned friend** (a form of address used of) a fellow lawyer in court. **my** etc. **noble friend** (a form of address used of) a fellow member of the House of Lords. **my** etc. (**right**) **honourable friend** (a form of address used of) a fellow member of the House of Commons. NEXT *friend*. PLUMBER'*s friend*. PRISONER'*s friend*. *Society of Friends*: see SOCIETY 6a.

†**B** *adj.* Well-disposed, friendly, not hostile. (Cf. ENEMY *a.*) LME–L17.

friend /frɛnd/ *v.t.* ME. [f. the n.] †**1** Gain friends for. *rare.* Only in ME. **2** Make (a person) a friend or friendly; join in friendship. Usu. in *pass. obs.* exc. *dial.* LME. **3** Act as a friend to, befriend (a person or cause); help. *arch.* or *poet.* M16.

friended *a.* having a friend or friends (of a specified kind); (*rare*) befriended: LME. †**friending** *vbl n.* friendliness; the action of befriending someone or favouring one's friends: E–M17.

friendless /ˈfrɛndlɪs/ *a.* OE. [f. FRIEND *n.* + -LESS.] Destitute of friends.

friendlessness *n.* E19.

friendlike /ˈfrɛndlʌɪk/ *a.* M16. [f. FRIEND *n.* + -LIKE.] Like a friend or friends, friendly.

friendly /ˈfrɛn(d)li/ *a.* & *n.* OE. [f. FRIEND *n.* + -LY[1].] **A** *adj.* **1** Having the qualities or disposition of a friend, disposed to act as a friend, kind. OE. **2** Characteristic of or befitting a friend or friends; showing friendship. LME. **3** Of a thing: disposed or likely to be helpful; kindly, propitious, favourable, salutary. Foll. by *to*. LME. **b** Suitable to one's comfort, convenient. L17. **4** Favourably disposed; inclined to approve or help. LME. **5** Not hostile or in opposition; on amicable terms. (Foll. by *to*, *with*.) L16. **b** Not proceeding from or carried out with hostility; (of a football match or other game) outside any official competition. L19. †**6** Of things: not jarring or conflicting. Only in 18. **7** (**F-**.) Of or pertaining to the Society of Friends. L19. **8** *Computing* etc. Easy and convenient to use; designed with the needs of users in mind. L20. **9** Not harmful to the environment. L20. **10** Appended to nouns to form adjs. w. the senses 'adapted to', 'suitable for', 'not harmful to'. L20.

1 J. M. COETZEE This morning when I tried to be friendly he shook me off. **2** M. E. BRADDON Jernam acknowledged their courtesy with a friendly nod. **3** J. BUCHAN This time they had not the friendly night to shield them. **b** ADDISON On the first friendly Bank he throws him down. **4** J. C. MORISON The side of his history from which a friendly biographer would most readily turn away. **5** J. WEDGE Friendly aircraft in the distance. I. MCEWAN Our families must become friendly for reasons of diplomacy and business. **10** *USA Today* The most overtly yuppie-friendly show on air.

Special collocations: **friendly fire** *Mil.* gunfire from one's own side, *spec.* when causing accidental injury or damage to that side. **Friendly Society** any of various associations providing mutual insurance schemes.

B *n.* **1** A member of an indigenous people or tribe which is not hostile to invaders. Usu. in *pl.* M19. **2** A friendly football match or other game (see sense A.5b above). L19.

friendlily *adv.* in a friendly manner or spirit, like a friend L17. **friendliness** *n.* L15.

friendly /ˈfrɛn(d)li/ *adv.* OE. [f. FRIEND *n.* + -LY[2]. Later sometimes f. the adj.] In a friendly manner or spirit, friendlily.

friendship /ˈfrɛn(d)ʃɪp/ *n.* OE. [f. FRIEND *n.* + -SHIP.] **1** The state or relation of being a friend; association as friends. OE. **b** A relationship of friendliness or intimacy. OE. **2** Friendly feeling or disposition; friendliness. ME. †**3** A friendly act; a favour; friendly aid. ME–E17.

1 BACON Without friendship, society is but meeting. **b** J. MORLEY His friendship with two of the chief actors may have biassed his judgment. **2** A. J. P. TAYLOR Germany and Soviet Russia . . made a pact of mutual friendship at Rapallo.

frier *n.* var. of FRYER.

Friesian /ˈfriːzjən, -ʒ(ə)n/ *a.* & *n.* E20. [Alt. of FRISIAN.] (An animal of, of or pertaining to) a breed of usu. black and white large dairy cattle orig. bred in Friesland.

Friesic /ˈfriːzɪk/ *a.* M19. [f. G *Friese* (see FRISIAN) + -IC. Cf. FRISIC.] = FRISIAN *a.*

frieze /friːz/ *n.*[1] LME. [Fr. *frise*, f. med.L = Frisian (wool). Cf. FRIEZE *v.*[1]] **1** A kind of coarse woollen cloth with a nap, usually on one side only, orig. of Welsh, now esp. of Irish manufacture. LME. **2** Bruising or abrasion of the grain in leather. Orig. in †*frieze-leather*, frizzed leather. L16. †**3** Down on a plant; a tuft of this. M–L17.

1 J. DYER Frize of Cambria. F. O'BRIEN Your heavy great-coat of Galway frieze.

friezy *a.* (*a*) dressed in frieze; (*b*) resembling frieze: M19.

frieze /friːz/ *n.*[2] M16. [Fr. *frise* f. med.L *frisium*, var. of *frigium*, for L *Phrygium* (sc. *opus*) Phrygian work.] **1** *Archit.* In the entablature of an order, the member between the architrave and the cornice; a band of sculpture filling this. M16. **b** = HYPOTRACHELIUM. L16. **2** Any broad horizontal band of sculptured, painted, or other decoration, esp. on a wall near the ceiling; a horizontal paper strip bearing pictures or decoration, for mounting on a wall. M17.

2 R. MACAULAY A long frieze running right across under the windows, with carved flowers and trees. *fig.*: R. COBB The ever-rising frieze of evergreens composed of holly, yew and cypress.

friezeless *a.* having no frieze M19.

frieze /friːz/ *v.*[1]*t.* *obs.* exc. *Hist.* LME. [Fr. *friser* or Sp. *frisar*: see FRIZZ *v.*[1] Cf. FRIEZE *n.*[1]] Cover with a nap. Freq. as *friezed* ppl a.

friezer *n.* a person who friezes cloth LME.

frieze /friːz/ *v.*[2]*t.* M16. [Fr. *friser* rel. to *frise* FRIEZE *n.*[2]] Chiefly as *friezed* ppl a. **1** Embroider with gold; work (gold) into decorative patterns. Now *rare*. M16. **2** Cover (silver) with chased patterns. L17. **3** *Naut.* Decorate by painting (the bows, stern, and quarters of sailing ships). M18.

frig *n.*[1] var. of FRIDGE *n.*

frig /frɪɡ/ *v.* & *n.*[2] Now *coarse slang*. LME. [Perh. imit.: cf. FIDGE *v.*, FRIDGE *v.*, FYKE *v.*] **A** *v.* Infl. **-gg-**. **1** *v.i.* Move about restlessly; wriggle. *obs.* exc. *dial.* or passing into sense 3c. LME. †**2** *v.t.* Rub, chafe. E16–L17. **3** *v.t.* & *i.* Masturbate. Also = FUCK *v.* 1, 2. L17. **b** *v.t.* = FUCK *v.* 3. E20. **c** *v.i.* Muck or mess *about*, fool *around* (*with*); make *off*. Cf. FUCK *v.* 2b, etc. M20.

1 I. MURDOCH Sit down, Sarah, stop frigging about. **3** *fig.*: BYRON Such writing is sort of mental masturbation—he is always f—gg—g his *Imagination*. **b** R. FRAME It was the last straw . . 'Frig this tree. Just *frig* it!' **c** X. HERBERT Don't frig about. Give's my money or there'll be trouble.

B *n.* An act of frigging (sense 3). Also = FUCK *n.* 3. L19.

M. MCCARTHY I don't give a frig about Sinnott's heredity.

frigging *ppl a.* & *adv.* = FUCKING *ppl a.* & *adv.* E20.

frigate /ˈfrɪɡət/ *n.* L16. [Fr. *frégate* f. It. *fregata*, †*fragata* (whence Sp. *fragata*), ult. origin unkn.] **1** A light, swift vessel, powered by oar or sail. Now only *poet.* L16. **2** A fast-sailing merchantman. *obs.* exc. *Hist.* E17. **3a** *Hist.* A sailing warship; *spec.* one next in size to a ship of the line and carrying 28–60 guns. M17. **b** A general-purpose warship with mixed armament, usu. lighter than, or, in the US and some other navies, heavier than a destroyer; orig., any of a kind designed for convoy escort work. M20. **4** In full *frigate-bird*. Any of several large swift predatory sea birds constituting the genus *Fregata* and family Fregatidae, which have long wings, a long deeply forked tail, and a long hooked bill, and inhabit tropical oceans. M18.

Comb.: *frigate-bird*: see sense 4 above; **frigate-built** *a.* (*Hist.*) (of a sailing ship) having a descent of some steps from the forecastle or quarterdeck to the waist; **frigate mackerel** a small tropical tuna of the genus *Auxis*, esp. *A. thazard*.

frigger /ˈfrɪɡə/ *n.*[1] Now *coarse slang*. L16. [f. FRIG *v.* + -ER[1].] A person who masturbates or copulates.

frigger /ˈfrɪɡə/ *n.*[2] E20. [Origin unkn.] A small glass ornament or glass-maker's test sample.

friggle /ˈfrɪɡ(ə)l/ *v.i. obs.* exc. *Sc.* & *dial.* E17. [Frequent. of FRIG *v.*] Wriggle. Also, fuss.

fright /frʌɪt/ *n.* [OE *fryhto* metath. (Northumb.) alt. of *fyrhto*, -*u* = Goth. *faurhtei*, f. Gmc, f. base = afraid, repr. also by OE *forht*, OS *foroht*, -*aht*, OHG *foraht*, Goth. *faurhts*.] **1** (Sudden) fear, violent terror; alarm; an instance of this. OE. **2** Anything that inspires terror; *esp.* (*colloq.*) a person or thing of a grotesque or ridiculous appearance. M17.

1 E. O'NEILL He . . sinks back, too numbed by fright to move. R. MAUGHAM Oh, what a fright you gave me! . . I thought it was burglars. **in a fright** in a state of terror. *stage fright*: see STAGE *n.* **take fright** become frightened. **2** J. M. SYNGE The fright of seven townlands for my biting tongue. B. BAINBRIDGE Brenda looked such a fright—she had toothache . . and her jaw was swollen.

Comb.: **fright wig**: with the hair standing on end.

frighty *a.* (*rare*) †(*a*) causing fright; (*b*) suffering from fright, fearful: ME.

fright /frʌɪt/ *v.* Now only *poet.* & *dial.* See also FRIT *ppl a.* [OE (Northumb.) *fryhta* var. of *fyrhtan* = OFris. *fruchtia*, OS *forahtian*, OHG *furihten*, *for(a)htan* (G *fürchten*), Goth. *faurhtjan* f. Gmc base of FRIGHT *n.* Cf. next.] **1** *v.i.* Take fright; be afraid. Long *obs.* exc. *dial.* OE. **2** Frighten (*away*, *off*, etc.). OE.

frighted *ppl a.* frightened, scared; (*poet.*) pervaded with fear: L16.

frighten /ˈfrʌɪt(ə)n/ *v.t.* M17. [f. FRIGHT *n.* + -EN[5], superseding FRIGHT *v.*] Throw into a fright; terrify; alarm; scare *away*, *off*; drive *out of* a place etc., *into* submission etc., by fear or menace.

GEO. ELIOT If you can't . . frighten her off touching things, you must . . keep 'em out of her way. F. M. FORD In Ashburnham's face . . there was absolute panic. I was horribly frightened. W. S. CHURCHILL The activities of the early trade unions frightened the Government into oppressive measures. *frighten the horses*: see HORSE *n.* *frighten the life out of*: see LIFE *n.*

frightenable *a.* E19. **frightenedly** *adv.* L19. **frighteningly** *adv.* in a manner or to an extent that frightens M19.

frightener /ˈfrʌɪt(ə)nə/ *n.* M19. [f. FRIGHTEN *v.* + -ER[1].] A person who or thing which frightens; *spec.* (*slang*) a member of a criminal gang who intimidates its victims.

put the frighteners on *slang* intimidate, threaten.

frightful /ˈfrʌɪtfʊl, -f(ə)l/ *a.* ME. [f. FRIGHT *n.* + -FUL.] **1** Frightened, alarmed; timid. *obs.* exc. *dial.* ME. **2** Frightening, alarming; shocking, dreadful; appalling, hideous. Freq. *hyperbol.* (*slang*), notable of its kind, esp. in badness; very unpleasant, ugly, boring, etc. E17.

2 M. KEANE A hideous and wicked little hat, frightful to wear and frightful to behold. C. S. FORESTER Every man had turned tail and fled from that frightful musketry. W. S. CHURCHILL The casualties in this battle were frightful. I. MURDOCH Shut the window, there's a frightful draught.

frightfully *adv.* in a frightful manner; to a frightful extent or degree; (*slang*) extremely, excessively: E17. **frightfulness** *n.* the quality or state of being frightful; *spec.* [after G *Schrecklichkeit*] a deliberate military policy of terrorizing the enemy (esp. civilians): E17.

frightment /ˈfrʌɪtm(ə)nt/ *n. rare.* E17. [f. FRIGHT *v.* + -MENT.] The state of being in fear; something that causes fear.

frigid /ˈfrɪdʒɪd/ *a.* LME. [L *frigidus*, f. *frigere* be cold, f. *frigus* cold: see -ID[1].] **1** Intensely cold, devoid of warmth. LME. **2** Usu. of a woman: unable to achieve orgasm, sexually unresponsive. Formerly also, lacking in sexual vigour, impotent. M17. **3** Lacking ardour, apathetic; cold, indifferent, formal; (of a thing) chilling, depressing. M17. **b** Dull, insipid, flat. Now *rare*. M17.

1 C. P. SNOW The contrast between the warmth in bed and the frigid air one breathed. **frigid zone** each of two areas of the earth's surface, lying north of the Arctic Circle and south of the Antarctic Circle. **3** C. MERIVALE The nobles . . let matters take their course with frigid indifference. T. HARDY Anne went home . . bidding Loveday a frigid adieu. E. M. FORSTER 'Pardon me', said a frigid voice. '. . We will incommode you no longer.' **b** LD MACAULAY A hundred and sixty lines of frigid bombast.

frigidly *adv.* M17. **frigidness** *n.* (*rare*) E18.

Frigidaire /frɪdʒɪˈdɛː/ *n.* E20. [Fr., f. as next.] (Proprietary name for) a refrigerator.

frigidarium /frɪdʒɪˈdɛːrɪəm/ *n.* Pl. **-iums**, **-ia** /-ɪə/. E18. [L *frigidarium*, f. as FRIGID: see -ARIUM.] *Hist.* The room in Roman baths containing the final, cold, bath.

frigidity /frɪˈdʒɪdɪti/ *n.* LME. [Fr. *frigidité* f. late L *frigiditas*, f. as FRIGID: see -ITY.] **1** Intense coldness. LME. †**b** The quality of producing coldness. L16–M18. 2 Inability (usu. in a woman) to achieve orgasm; lack of sexual response. Formerly also, impotence. L16. 3 Lack of ardour or enthusiasm; apathy, coldness, indifference; formality. M17. b Lack of imagination; dullness, insipidity. Now *rare*. M17.

frigorific /frɪɡəˈrɪfɪk/ *a.* M17. [L *frigorificus*, f. *frigor-*, *frigus* cold: see -FIC.] Producing cold, cooling, freezing.

frijoles /friˈxoles, frɪˈhəʊlɛs/ *n.pl.* L16. [Sp., pl. of *frijol* bean, ult. f. L *phaseolus*.] Esp. in Mexican cookery: (a dish of) beans.

frikkadel /frɪkəˈdɛl/ *n. S. Afr.* L19. [Afrikaans f. Fr. *fricadelle*.] A fried or baked meatball; a rissole.

frill /frɪl/ *n.* & *v.* L16. [f. or rel. to Flem. *frul*.] A *n.* 1 An ornamental edging of woven material, of which one edge is gathered or pleated and the other left loose so as to have a wavy or fluted appearance. L16. b A decorative strip of paper etc. for garnishing a ham-bone, cake, etc. M19. 2 A fringe of hair, feathers, etc., resembling this; *esp.* a fringe of feathers round the neck of a pigeon. Hence, a frilled pigeon. M18. 3a An affectation of dress or manner, an air. Usu. in *pl. colloq.* M19. b Something merely ornamental; a useless embellishment; an optional extra; a showy accomplishment. Usu. in *pl. colloq.* (freq. *derog.*). L19. 4 The mesentery of an animal. L19.

1 *fig.*: A. CARTER The sea remained calm, there was scarcely the frill of a wave to be seen. 3a M. TWAIN He cussed me for putting on frills, and trying to be better than him. b M. MCCARTHY She had gone to a sound boarding-school.. with a well-rounded curriculum but no frills. J. C. OATES Jasper drove a smart, practical Ford, with few frills.

Comb.: **frill-lizard** an Australian agamid lizard, *Chlamydosaurus kingii*, with an erectile membrane around its neck.

B *v.* 1 *v.t.* Equip or decorate with a frill; be or become a frill for. Also, form into a frill. L16. 2 *v.t.* & *i. Photogr.* Cause (the film on a photographic plate) to rise in flutes at the edge; (of the film) rise thus. L19.

frilled *a.* provided or decorated with a frill or frills; naturally possessing a frill or frills; *frilled lizard* = *frill-lizard* s.v. FRILL *n.*: E19. **frillery** *n.* (a mass of) frills L19. **frilling** *n.* (*a*) the action of the vb; (*b*) frills collectively: E19.

frilly /ˈfrɪli/ *a.* & *n.* M19. [f. FRILL + -Y[1].] A *adj.* Having or resembling a frill or frills; full of frills; *colloq.* showy, decorative rather than functional. M19.

H. S. HARRISON I am a clerk.. My official title, of course, is a little more frilly. *Financial Times* A red cassock with a large frilly white collar.

B *n.* 1 In *pl.* (Frilled) underwear. *colloq.* E20. 2 = *frill-lizard* s.v. FRILL *n. Austral. colloq.* M20.

frilliness *n.* E20.

frim /frɪm/ *a. obs.* exc. *dial.* Compar. & superl. **-mm-**. [OE *freme* f. Gmc.] Vigorous, flourishing, luxuriant, rich; succulent, juicy; soluble, fusible.

Frimaire /frɪˈmɛː, *foreign* frimɛːr/ *n.* E19. [Fr., f. *frimas* hoar-frost.] *Hist.* The third month of the French Republican Calendar (introduced 1793), extending from 21 November to 20 December.

fringe /frɪn(d)ʒ/ *n.* & *a.* ME. [OFr. *frenge*, *fringe* (mod. *frange*) f. Proto-Romance metath. alt. of late L FIMBRIA, earlier only pl., fibres, shreds, fringe.] A *n.* 1 An ornamental bordering of threads left loose or made into tassels or twists, sometimes attached to a narrow band of fabric; *collect.* a piece of material forming this. ME. 2 Anything resembling this; a border or edging, *esp.* one that is broken or serrated; an edging of hair or fibres in an animal or plant. E17. b A portion of front hair cut short and arranged so as to hang over the forehead. L19. 3 An outer edge or margin; an outer limit of an area, population, sphere of activity, etc. Formerly also, an appendage, a sequel. M17. b A peripheral or secondary group, *esp.* an unofficial or unconventional one. E20. 4 *Optics.* A band or strip of contrasting brightness or darkness (usu. one of a series), produced by diffraction or interference of light. Also, a strip of false colour in an optical image. E18. 5 *ellipt.* = *fringe benefit* below. M20.

2 W. B. CARPENTER In Fishes the gills are composed of fringes. K. MANSFIELD On the edge of the sea a white silky fringe just stirred. W. CATHER A fringe of cedars grew along the edge of the cavern. 3 H. BELLOC An Inn.. that stood on the fringe of a larch wood. *Cornishman* Frank Gibson was left.. stuck out on the fringe of things. P. D. JAMES They were mostly theatrical people, on the fringe anyway. b *Sight & Sound* There is a fringe who bomb places.

Phrases: *Celtic fringe*: see CELTIC *a.* **lunatic fringe** a fanatical, eccentric, or visionary minority of a political party etc.

B *attrib.* or as *adj.* Existing on the edge or margin of anything; of secondary or minor importance; unofficial, unconventional. Formerly also, fringed. L16.

G. CHARLES Fringe characters, not big enough for the central roles. S. BRETT An actor friend.. was setting up a new fringe theatre company.

Special collocations & *comb.*: **fringe benefit** a perquisite or benefit provided by an employer to supplement a money wage or salary. **fringe medicine** the systems of health care that are not regarded as orthodox by the medical profession. **fringe net**: intended to confine a fringe of hair. **fringe-tree** a deciduous N. American shrub or small tree, *Chionanthus virginicus*, of the olive family, bearing white flowers in panicles.

fringer *n.* a person who occupies or belongs to a fringe (FRINGE *n.* 3) M20. **fringy** *a.* of the nature of or resembling a fringe; provided, decorated, or covered with fringes: M18.

fringe /frɪn(d)ʒ/ *v.* ME. [f. the n.] 1 *v.t.* Provide, decorate, or encircle with or as with a fringe. Chiefly as *fringed* ppl a. ME. 2 *v.t.* Act as a fringe to; appear as a fringe on. L18. 3 *v.i.* Spread like a fringe *away*, *off*, *out*, *over*, etc. Now *rare*. M19.

1 I. MURDOCH The open fields.. were fringed with ragged lines of elm and hawthorn. W. GOLDING The velvet cloth on the table was fringed with bobbles. **fringing reef** a coral reef forming a ring around an island. 2 E. B. TYLOR The Esquimaux who fringe the northern coast. G. L. HARDING The pink oleander fringes the banks of every stream.

fringing *vbl n.* (*a*) the action of the vb; (*b*) the formation or appearance of optical fringes; (*c*) the spreading of electric or magnetic lines of force at the edges of a region, so as to depart from the regular pattern within the region: LME.

fringilline /frɪnˈdʒɪlʌɪn/ *a.* L19. [f. L *fringilla* finch + -INE[1].] *Ornith.* Finchlike, of or pertaining to the finches; *spec.* designating or pertaining to members of the subfamily Fringillinae or the genus *Fringilla*, which includes the chaffinch and the brambling.

†friponnerie *n.* E18–E19. [Fr., f. *fripon* rogue. Cf. -ERY.] Roguery.

†fripper *n.* L16–L17. [Fr. *fripier*, alt. of OFr. *frepier*, f. *frepe* rag, old clothes, ult. origin unkn.: see -ER[2] 2.] = next.

fripperer /ˈfrɪp(ə)rə/ *n.* L16. [Extended form of prec.: see -ER[1] 2.] A dealer in second-hand clothing.

frippery /ˈfrɪp(ə)ri/ *n.* & *a.* M16. [Fr. *friperie*, OFr. *freperie*, f. *frepe*: see FRIPPER, -ERY.] A *n.* †1 Old or second-hand clothes; cast-offs. M16–E19. †2 A second-hand clothing shop. Also, trade in cast-offs. L16–M19. 3 Finery; *esp.* unnecessary or tawdry adornment in dress; an item of this. M17. b A knick-knack, a trifle. Also *collect.* E19. 4 Empty display; showy talk or writing; ostentation. E18.

3 ARNOLD BENNETT Mrs Hamps followed, the fripperies of her elegant bonnet trembling. S. T. WARNER All the state and frippery of a court. b *Sunday Times* When France did win the championship.. they didn't bother with such fripperies as backs. 4 E. A. FREEMAN All the fopperies and fripperies of chivalry. M. O. W. OLIPHANT A noble young gentleman amid all his frippery of courtier and virtuoso.

B *adj.* Trifling, frivolous; contemptible. E17.

frippet /ˈfrɪpɪt/ *n. slang.* E20. [Origin unkn.] A frivolous or showy young woman; such women collectively.

frisado *n.* var. of FRIZADO.

Frisbee /ˈfrɪzbi/ *n.* Also **f-**. M20. [Perh. f. the *Frisbie* bakery in Bridgeport, Connecticut, USA, whose pie-tins could be used similarly.] (US proprietary name for) a concave plastic disc which spins when thrown in the air and is used in a throwing and catching game; the game itself.

Punch I.. watched the hippies playing frisbee with our hub-caps. *ultimate Frisbee*: see ULTIMATE *a.*

frisé /ˈfriːzeɪ/ *a.* L19. [Fr., pa. pple of *friser*: see FRIEZE *v.*[1], FRIZZ *v.*[1]] Of, pertaining to, or designating a pile fabric with cut and uncut loops forming a pattern, chiefly used in upholstery.

Frisesomorum /ˌfrʌɪsɛsəˈmɔːrəm/ *n.* Also **Frisesmo** /frʌɪˈsɛsməʊ/. L16. [A mnemonic of scholastic philosophers, I indicating a particular affirmative major proposition, E a universal negative minor proposition, and O a particular negative conclusion.] The supposed indirect mood of the first syllogistic figure, in which a particular negative conclusion is drawn from a particular affirmative major premiss and a universal negative minor premiss. (Later sometimes taken to be the fourth-figure mood, FRESISON.)

frisette /frɪˈzɛt/ *n.* E19. [Fr., f. *friser* to curl, frizz: see -ETTE.] A cluster of usu. artificial curls attached to a band and worn on the forehead.

friseur /frizœːr/ *n.* Now *rare*. Pl. pronounced same. M18. [Fr., f. *friser* (see prec.) + *-eur* -OR.] A hairdresser.

Frisian /ˈfrɪzɪən/ *a.* & *n.* L16. [f. L *Frisii* Frisians, f. OFris. *Frīsa*, *Frēsa*, whence OE *Frīsa*, *Frēsa*, MDu. *Vriese* (Du. *Vries*), OHG *Friaso* (G *Friese*), ON *Frisir*: see -IAN.] A *adj.* Of, pertaining to, or characteristic of Friesland, a region including a northern province of the Netherlands and part of NW Germany, its language, or its inhabitants. L16. B *n.* 1 A native or inhabitant of Friesland. L16. 2 The West Germanic language of Friesland (now restricted in use to a small area of the NW Netherlands), the closest relative of English. M19.

Frisic *a.* (now *rare* or *obs.*) = FRISIAN *a.* L17.

frisk /frɪsk/ *a.*, *v.*, & *n.* LME. [OFr. *frisque* vigorous, alert, lively, merry, var. of *fri(s)che*, earlier *frique*, perh. ult. rel. to OHG *frisc* fresh, lively.] †A *adj.* Full of life; spirited, lively, frisky. LME–M19.

B *v.* 1 *v.i.* Skip, leap, dance, in a lively playful manner; gambol, frolic. E16. 2 *v.t.* Move or wave in a lively playful manner. M17. 3 *v.t.* Search (a person or place); *esp.* feel quickly over (a person) in search of a concealed weapon etc. Orig. *slang.* L18.

1 V. WOOLF She came frisking into the room; but her mind is a sedate, literal mind. F. TUOHY Ponies.. were frisking in the sunshine. 2 R. H. PATTERSON The tail is frisked up into the air in the liveliest manner possible. 3 F. FORSYTH The guards checked him at the gate, frisking him from ankles to armpits.

C *n.* 1 Orig. in *Equestrianism*, a caracole, a caper. Now *gen.*, a playful leap or skip, (*rare*) a whim. Also, friskiness. E16. 2 An act of frisking, a search (see sense B.3 above). Orig. *slang.* L18.

frisker *n.* a person who or thing which frisks M16.

frisket /ˈfrɪskɪt/ *n.* L17. [Fr. *frisquette* f. mod.Prov. *frisqueto*, f. Sp. *frasqueta*.] *Printing.* A thin iron frame hinged to the tympan of a hand-press, having tapes or paper stretched across it, for keeping the sheet in position and clean.

frisky /ˈfrɪski/ *a.* E16. [f. FRISK + -Y[1].] Given to frisking; lively, playful.

friskily *adv.* M19. **friskiness** *n.* E18.

frisson /frisɔ̃ (*pl. same*), ˈfrɪsɒn/ *n.* L18. [Fr. = shiver, thrill.] An emotional thrill; a shiver of excitement.

D. L. SAYERS It absolutely thrilled me. I got shudders all the way down my spine. A genuine frisson. W. BOYD The car.. seemed to trail a frisson of sexuality, like smoke.

frist /frɪst/ *n.* & *v. arch.* [OE *first*, *frist* = OFris. *ferst*, *first*, OS, OHG *frist* (G *Frist*), ON *frest*.] A *n.* †1 A period of time; a certain time. OE–ME. 2 A delay, a respite. Formerly also, a truce. ME. †B *v.* 1 *v.t.* & *i.* Grant respite to (a person); delay or postpone (a thing). ME–M17. 2 *v.t.* Lend (money etc.) on credit; give (a debtor) time for payment. LME–E19.

frisure /frɪˈzjʊə/ *n.* M18. [Fr., f. *friser*: see FRIZZ *v.*[1]] A style of curling or frizzing the hair.

frit /frɪt/ *n.* & *v.* Also **-tt.** M17. [It. *fritta* (perh. through Fr. *fritte*) use as n. of fem. pa. pple of *friggere* FRY *v.*] **A** *n.* **1** A calcined mixture of silica and fluxes, which can be melted to make glass. M17. **2** A vitreous composition from which soft porcelain, enamel, etc., are made. L18. **B** *v.t.* Infl. **-tt-**. Make into frit; fuse partially, calcine. E19.

frit /frɪt/ *ppl a. dial.* & *colloq.* E19. [pa. pple of FRIGHT *v.*] Frightened.

B. BEHAN I wasn't frit of the farmer's boy, a big lump of a lad.

frit-fly /ˈfrɪtflʌɪ/ *n.* L19. [f. L *frit* tiny particle on ear of corn + FLY *n.*[1]] A small black fly, *Oscinella frit*, which is a destructive pest of cereals.

frith /frɪθ/ *n.*[1] Long *obs.* exc. *Hist.* [OE *friþu* (also str. neut. *friþ*) = OFris. *frethu*, OS *friþu* (Du. *vrede*), OHG *fridu* (G *Friede*), ON *friðr*, f. Gmc.] **1** Peace; protection; safety, security. OE. †**2** A place where game or fish are preserved for hunting. ME–L16.

Comb.: **frithborh** [OE *friþborh*: see BORROW *n.*] = FRANK-PLEDGE; **frith-stool** †(*a*) a refuge, a sanctuary; (*b*) a seat (usu. of stone) formerly placed near the altar of some churches, providing sanctuary.

frith /frɪθ/ *n.*[2] [OE (*ġe*)*fyrhþe*, *fyrhþ*, f. Gmc, perh. ult. f. base of FIR.] **1** A wood; (sparsely) wooded country. Now chiefly *poet.* OE. **2** Land grown sparsely with trees or scrub; unused pasture-land; a clearing in a wood. Now *dial.* LME. **3** A hedge, esp. made of wattled brushwood; a hurdle for fencing. Now *dial.* LME. **4** Brushwood, undergrowth. Now *dial.* L16.

frith /frɪθ/ *n.*[3] ME. [f. as FIRTH *n.*[2]: perh. infl. by L *fretum* arm of the sea.] = FIRTH *n.*[2]

frith /frɪθ/ *v. obs.* exc. *dial.* LME. [f. FRITH *n.*[2]] **1** *v.t.* Fence in or surround with a hedge. LME. **2** *v.i.* Form a hedge of wattled brushwood; cut underwood. E19.

frithing *vbl n.* (*a*) the action of the vb; (*b*) material cut for hedging, brushwood: LME.

fritillaria /frɪtɪˈlɛːrɪə/ *n.* L16. [mod.L (see below), f. L *fritillus* dice-box (prob. w. ref. to the chequered corolla of *Fritillaria meleagris*) + *-aria* -ARY[1].] A plant of the genus *Fritillaria*, a fritillary, *esp.* any of the cultivated kinds.

fritillary /frɪˈtɪl(ə)ri/ *n.* M17. [f. as prec.: see -ARY[1].] **1** Any plant of the large genus *Fritillaria* of the lily family; *esp.* (*a*) wild snake's head, *F. meleagris*, which bears drooping purple or white bell-like flowers and grows in damp meadows; (*b*) crown imperial, *F. imperialis*. M17. **2** Any of numerous butterflies, chiefly nymphalids of the genera *Argynnis*, *Boloria*, *Speyeria*, etc., which are characteristically brown with dark brown or black spots. M19.

fritiniency /frɪˈtɪnɪənsi/ *n. rare.* M17. [f. L *fritinnire* twitter: see -ENCY.] Twittering.

fritt *n.* & *v.* var. of FRIT *n.* & *v.*

fritter /ˈfrɪtə/ *n.*[1] LME. [(O)Fr. *friture* f. Proto-Romance, f. L *frict-* pa. ppl stem of *frigere* FRY *v.*: see -ER[2].] **1** A piece of (usu. specified) meat, fruit, etc., coated in batter and deep-fried. LME. **2** *Whaling.* In *pl.* = FENKS. M17.

fritter /ˈfrɪtə/ *n.*[2] L17. [Alt. of FLITTERS: perh. rel. to MHG *vetze* (G *Fetzen*) rag, scrap.] **1** In *pl.* & (rarely) *sing.* Minute pieces, fragments, shreds; small or unimportant items. L17. **2** Frittering; excessive subdivision or complexity. E19.

2 T. RICKMAN This window is a series of small panels . . and these . . throw the building into fritter. V. WOOLF People have been staying here . . . such a fritter & agitation.

fritter /ˈfrɪtə/ *v.* E18. [f. prec.] **1** *v.t.* Usu. w. *away*: do away with piecemeal, wear down, attenuate; *esp.* waste (time, money, energy, etc.) on trifling matters. E18. **2** *v.t.* & *i.* Break or separate into minute pieces. Now *rare.* L18.

1 *Sunday Post* (*Glasgow*) You won't fritter the company profits on taxi fares. J. BARNES She had watched her mother's intelligence being frittered away on calculations about the price of tinned food.

fritterer *n.* M19.

fritto misto /fritto ˈmisto/ *n. phr.* E20. [It. = mixed fry.] A dish of various foods, usu. types of seafood, deep-fried in batter.

Fritz /frɪts/ *n.*[1] E20. [G, abbrev. of *Friedrich*, male forename.] A German; *esp.* a German soldier fighting in the war of 1914–18. Also, Germans, esp. German soldiers, collectively. Cf. JERRY *n.*[3]

fritz /frɪts/ *n.*[2] *slang* (orig. & chiefly *N. Amer.*). E20. [Origin unkn.] Only in *on the fritz*: out of order, broken, defective.

Friulian /friˈuːlɪən/ *a.* & *n.* L19. [f. *Friuli*, a district in NE Italy + -AN.] **A** *adj.* Of or pertaining to Friuli, its inhabitants, or the dialect spoken there. L19. **B** *n.* **1** A native or inhabitant of Friuli. M20. **2** The Rhaeto-Romance dialect spoken in Friuli. M20.

frivel *v.* var. of FRIVOL *v.*

frivol /ˈfrɪv(ə)l/ *a.* & *n.* Chiefly *Sc.* L15. [(O)Fr. *frivole*, f. as FRIVOLOUS. As n., reintroduced 19 f. the vb or f. mod.Fr.] †**A** *adj.* Frivolous; paltry; absurd. Also, fickle. L15–E17. **B** *n.* A frivolous thing or person; *esp.* a frivolous act. L15.

frivol /ˈfrɪv(ə)l/ *v.* Also **-el.** Infl. **-ll-**, ***-l-**. M19. [Back-form. f. FRIVOLOUS.] **1** *v.i.* Behave frivolously. M19. **2** *v.t.* Fritter (*away*). L19.

frivoller *n.* L19.

frivolity /frɪˈvɒlɪti/ *n.* L18. [Fr. *frivolité*, f. *frivole*, f. as next: see -ITY.] **1** The quality of being frivolous; frivolous behaviour. L18. **2** A piece of frivolous behaviour; a frivolous thing. M19.

frivolous /ˈfrɪv(ə)ləs/ *a.* LME. [f. L *frivolus* silly, trifling + -OUS.] **1** Of little or no value or importance, paltry; (of a claim, charge, etc.) having no reasonable grounds. LME. **2** Lacking seriousness or sense; silly. L15.

1 B. PYM I always try to switch my thoughts to something frivolous like clothes. R. C. A. WHITE Unless the application is clearly frivolous, it will usually be granted. 2 A. ALVAREZ He thought it frivolous and unbecoming to the serious figure he cut in the world.

frivolously *adv.* L16. **frivolousness** *n.* L16.

friz *n.*, *v.* vars. of FRIZZ *n.*, *v.*[1]

frizado /frɪˈzɑːdəʊ/ *n. obs.* exc. *Hist.* Also **-s-** /-s-/. M16. [Sp. *frisado* napped (cloth), f. *frisar* = Fr. *friser* raise a nap on (cloth), curl (hair): see FRIZZ *v.*[1], FRIEZE *v.*[1]] A fine worsted cloth with a nap, similar to baize.

†**frize** *v.* see FRIZZ *v.*[1]

frizz /frɪz/ *n.* Also **friz.** M17. [f. next.] The state of being frizzed or curled. Also, frizzed hair, a row of curls.

frizz /frɪz/ *v.*[1] Also **friz** (infl. **-zz-**); orig. †**frize.** LME. [(O)Fr. *friser*, perh. f. *fris-* stem of *frire* FRY *v.*; the vowel appears to have been shortened under the infl. of FRIZZLE *v.*[1]] **1** *v.t.* Rub (wash-leather etc.) with a pumice stone or blunt knife so as to remove the grain, soften the surface, and give a uniform thickness. LME. **2** *v.t.* Form (the hair, the nap of a cloth, etc.) into a mass of small crisp curls or tufts. L16. **3** *v.i.* Of the hair: form small crisp curls. L17.

2 A. CARTER A huge man . . with black hair frizzed out in a cloud down to his shoulders.

frizz /frɪz/ *v.*[2]*i.* Chiefly *dial.* M19. [f. as FRIZZLE *v.*[2]] Of food: make a sputtering or sizzling noise when frying; burn or dry up in cooking.

frizzle /ˈfrɪz(ə)l/ *v.*[1] & *n.*[1] M16. [f. FRIZZ *v.*[1]: see -LE[3].] **A** *v.* **1** *v.t.* Form (hair) into small crisp curls. M16. **2** *v.i.* Of hair: frizz, curl (*up*). E17.

1 A. TYLER The damp weather had frizzled her hair into little corkscrews.

B *n.* A small crisp curl; frizzled hair. E17.

frizzly *a.* consisting of frizzles or curls E18.

frizzle /ˈfrɪz(ə)l/ *v.*[2] & *n.*[2] M18. [f. FRY *v.* with imit. ending: see -LE[3]. Cf. FIZZLE, SIZZLE.] **A** *v.* **1** *v.t.* Burn or dry up (food) in cooking. M18. **2** *v.t.* & *i.* Fry, grill, or burn with a sputtering or sizzling noise. M19.

2 W. S. MAUGHAM He had four little fish cheerfully frizzling in a pan.

B *n.* The action, an act, or the noise of frizzling. L19.

frizzy /ˈfrɪzi/ *a.* L19. [f. FRIZZ *n.* + -Y[1].] Consisting of frizzles or small crisp curls; resembling a frizz.

frizziness *n.* E19.

fro /frəʊ/ *prep.*, *adv.*, & *conj.* Also (*Sc.* & *north.*) **frae** /freɪ/, †**fra.** ME. [ON *frá*, corresp. to OE *fram* FROM.] **A** *prep.* **1** *gen.* = FROM *prep.* Now only *Sc.* & *dial.* ME. †**2** Of, concerning. *rare.* Only in ME.

1 DONNE Cal vow'd men fro cloysters, dead from tombs. SIR W. SCOTT Well could he hit a fallow-deer Five hundred feet him fro. JAS. HOGG Up there rase ane wee wee man Franethe the moss-gray stane.

B *adv.* In a direction or position that is remote or apart, away. Formerly also, contrary, against. Now only in TO AND FRO. ME.

R. HOLLAND Sum said to and sum fra. A. FLEMING Passage to, fro, and through without danger.

†**C** *conj.* **1** From the time that, from the moment when, as soon as, when. LME–E16. **2** Since, seeing that. M16–E17.

Fröbel *n.* var. of FROEBEL.

frock /frɒk/ *n.* & *v.* LME. [(O)Fr. *froc* f. Frank., corresp. to OHG *hroc.*] **A** *n.* **1** A priest's or monk's long gown with loose sleeves; occas., a cassock. Also, priestly status or character. LME. **2** A man's upper garment; a long coat, tunic, or mantle. Now *rare* or *obs.* LME. **3** A woman's or girl's garment, consisting of a skirt and bodice; a dress. Formerly also, a skirted garment worn by young children of either sex. M16. **4** *Hist.* = SMOCK-FROCK 1. Formerly also = SMOCK-FROCK 2. E17. **b** A sailor's woollen jersey. E19. **5** †**a** A man's informal coat. E18–E19. **b** In full *frock-coat.* A man's double-breasted long-skirted coat not cut away in front and now worn chiefly on formal occasions. E19. **c** A person wearing such a coat; *esp.* (*derog.*) a politician, as opp. to a military man, concerned with the administration of the war of 1914–18. E20.

1 SIR W. SCOTT The Hermit by it stood, Barefooted, in his frock and hood. W. GLADDEN Such words as these . . cost the great Carmelite preacher . . his frock. 2 W. K. KELLY Kings at arms covered with long frocks of cloth of gold. **frock of mail** a mailcoat, armour. 3 A. TROLLOPE I don't think I've ever been in London since I wore short frocks. J. ARCHER She was dressed in a bright yellow frock. 4 C. WALFORD Dealers in haubergs, or waggoners' frocks. **b** L. DEIGHTON I know it's a roll-neck pullover but you sign for a Frock I'm not responsible for Naval Nomenclature. 5 J. HANWAY His regimentals . . are a blue cloth frock with silver brandenburgs. **b** *Observer* Contemptible as a soldier, Lord George was impossible as a 'frock'.

Comb.: *frock-coat*: see sense 5b above; **frock-coated** *a.* attired in a frock-coat;

B *v.t.* Provide with or dress in a frock; *fig.* invest with priestly office. Chiefly as *frocked* pa. pple. L16.

froe /frəʊ/ *n.* Now chiefly *US.* Also **frow,** (orig.) †**frower.** L16. [Use as n. of FROWARD *a.* in sense 'turned away'.] A wedge-shaped cleaving-tool having a handle set at right angles to the blade.

Froebel /ˈfrəʊb(ə)l, ˈfrəːb(ə)l/ *n.* Also **Fröbel.** L19. [F. W. A. *Fröbel* (see below).] Used *attrib.* to designate (a school organized according to) the system of child education by the use of kindergartens introduced by Friedrich W. A. Fröbel (1782–1852), German teacher and educationalist.

Froe'belian *a.* & *n.* (*a*) *adj.* of or pertaining to the Froebel system; (*b*) *n.* an adherent of the Froebel system: L19.

frog /frɒg/ *n.*[1] [OE *frogga*, a pet-form rel. to OE *forsć*, *frosć*, *frox*, = MLG, Du. *vorsch*, OHG *frosc* (G *Frosch*), ON *froskr*, f. Gmc. Cf. FROSK.] **1** Any of numerous amphibians of the order Anura (formerly Salientia), which develop from tadpoles and are tailless as adults; *esp.* (as distinct from *toad*) any of those which have a smooth skin and leap rather than walk. Freq. *spec.* (more fully *common frog*) one of the widespread Eurasian species *Rana temporaria*. OE. **b** With specifying wd: any of various animals held to resemble the frog in appearance or habits. L18. **2** A contemptible or repulsive person. *slang. derog.* Long *rare* or *obs.* exc. as below. ME. **b** A native or inhabitant of the Netherlands, a Dutchman. *derog.* Long *obs.* exc. *Hist.* M17. **c** (Also **F-**.) A Frenchman, a Frenchwoman (cf. *frog-eater* below). Also, the

French language. *slang. derog.* L18. **3** Any of various diseases of the throat or mouth; a swelling beneath the tongue. Now *rare* or *obs.* exc. in *frog in the throat* below. LME. **4** More fully *frog-stool.* A toadstool. Long *obs.* exc. *dial.* LME. **5** A hollow in the face of a brick. L19. **6** *Mus.* = NUT *n.* 9c. Orig. & chiefly *US.* E20.

1 *bullfrog, edible frog, tree frog, wood-frog,* etc. LEAP-FROG *n.* & *a., v.* b *fishing frog*: see FISHING *ppl a.* 1. HORNED *frog.* 2 L. OWEN These infernall frogs [Jesuits] are crept into the West and East Indyes. c W. FAULKNER Ask him... You can speak Frog. *attrib.*: S. TOWNSEND Another sex book.. by a Frog writer. 3 **frog in the throat** an irritation or apparent impediment in the throat, hoarseness.

Comb.: **frogbit** a floating monocotyledonous plant of stagnant water, *Hydrocharis morsus-ranae* (family Hydrocharitaceae), with white flowers and cordate leaves; also, an allied N. American plant, *Limnobium spongia*; **frog-eater** *slang, derog.* a Frenchman, a Frenchwoman, (cf. sense 2c above); **frog-eye** a fungal disease of plants (esp. tobacco and apple) marked by ring-shaped spots on leaves; **frog-face** (a person or animal having) a face thought to resemble that of a frog, with broad brow and nostrils and bulging eyes; *Med.* a type of facial deformity usu. caused by a tumour in the region of the nose; **frog-faced** *a.* having a frog-face; **frog-fish** (*a*) an angler-fish (cf. *fishing frog* s.v. FISHING *ppl a.* 1); (*b*) any of numerous fishes of the families Antennariidae and Brachionichthyidae, resembling angler-fishes esp. in attracting prey by means of a lure; (*c*) *S. Afr.* = TOADFISH 3; **froghopper** any of numerous jumping homopteran insects of the family Cercopidae, the larvae of which surround themselves with protective froth ('cuckoo-spit'); **frogland** (*a*) marshy land abounding with frogs; †(*b*) (**F-**) *derog.* the Netherlands; (*c*) (**F-**) *joc. derog.* France; **frog-lily** *US* a yellow water lily, *Nuphar advena*; **frogman** a person wearing a close-fitting suit of rubber or the like, with goggles and flippers, and equipped with self-contained breathing apparatus, for underwater operations (orig. attacking enemy ships); **frogmarch** *n.* & *v.* (*a*) *n.* (also **frog's march**) the action or an act of carrying a prisoner face downwards with each of four people holding a limb; (*b*) *v.t.* carry in this way; hustle forward (a refractory or reluctant person) after seizing from behind and pinioning the arms; **frogmouth** any of various Asian and Australasian birds resembling nightjars, of the families Podargidae and (more fully *owlet-frogmouth*) Aegothelidae (genus *Aegotheles*); **frog orchid** a small green-flowered orchid of short turf, *Coeloglossum viride*; *frog's march*: see *frogmarch* (a) above; **frog-spawn** (*a*) the spawn of a frog or frogs; (*b*) *colloq.* pond-slime; (*c*) *colloq.* tapioca or sago pudding; **frog-spit, -spittle** = *cuckoo-spit* s.v. CUCKOO *n.*; *frog-stool*: see sense 4 above.

froggery *n.* (*a*) a place where frogs are kept or where they are found in great numbers; (*b*) a colony of frogs: M18. **froggish** *a.* froglike M19. **froglet** *n.* a young or small frog E20. **froglike** *a.* resembling a frog M16. **frogling** *n.* a little frog; a tadpole: E17.

frog /frɒg/ *n.*[2] E17. [Origin uncertain: perh. f. prec., and also infl. by synon. It. *forchetta* dim. of *forca* and Fr. *fourchette* dim. of *fourche*: see FORK *n.* Cf. also FRUSH *n.*[2]] A piece of elastic horny substance growing in the middle of the sole of a horse's hoof.

frog /frɒg/ *n.*[3] E18. [Origin unkn.] **1** An attachment to a waist-belt to support a sword, bayonet, or similar weapon. E18. **2** An ornamental coat-fastening, originally forming part of military dress, consisting of a spindle-shaped button covered with silk or similar material and a loop through which it is passed. M18.

frogged *a.* (of a coat or other garment) fastened or ornamented with frogs L18.

frog /frɒg/ *n.*[4] M19. [Origin unkn.] A grooved piece of metal placed at the junction of the rails where one railway track crosses another.

frogging /ˈfrɒgɪŋ/ *n.*[1] M17. [f. FROG *n.*[1] + -ING[1].] Catching frogs, fishing for frogs.

frogging /ˈfrɒgɪŋ/ *n.*[2] L19. [f. FROG *n.*[3] + -ING[1].] The attachments or ornamental fastenings on a frogged garment.

froggy /ˈfrɒgi/ *n.* M19. [f. FROG *n.*[1] + -Y[6].] **1** A frog. *joc.* M19. **2** (Also **F-**.) A Frenchman, a Frenchwoman. *slang. derog.* L19.

froggy /ˈfrɒgi/ *a.* E17. [f. FROG *n.*[1] + -Y[1].] **1** Having (many) frogs. E17. **2** Of or like a frog or frogs. M19. **3** (Also **F-**.) French. *slang. derog.* M20.

Fröhlich's syndrome /ˈfrəːlɪks ˌsɪndrəʊm/ *n. phr.* E20. [f. Alfred *Fröhlich* (1871–1953), Austrian neurologist.] *Med.* A syndrome including obesity and lack of sexual development, which affects young males and is caused by a hypothalamic tumour.

froise /frɔɪz/ *n.* Also **fraise** /freɪz/. ME. [Origin uncertain: perh. f. OFr. f. pop.L var. of L *frixum, frixa* neut. and fem. pa. pple of *frigere* FRY *v.*] A kind of pancake or omelette, often containing slices of bacon.

†**frokin** *n.* E17–M18. [f. obs. Du. dim. of *vrouw*: see FROW *n.*[1], -KIN.] A Dutch girl or woman.

frolic /ˈfrɒlɪk/ *a., v.,* & *n.* E16. [Du. *vrolijk* adj., f. (M)Du. *vro* glad, joyous + *-lijk* -LY[1].] **A** *adj.* **1** Joyous, merry, mirthful; sportive, full of pranks. *arch.* E16. †**2** Free, liberal. Foll. by *of.* Only in L16.

1 G. ETHEREGE Then sparkling champagne.. Makes us frolic and gay. E. DARWIN Galantha.. prints with frolic step the melting snows.

B *v.* Infl. **-ck-**. **1** *v.i.* Play pranks, gambol, caper about (*with*). Formerly also, make merry. L16. **2** *v.t.* Make joyous or merry. Also, entertain by giving parties to. Now *rare* or *obs.* L16.

1 BYRON Its bounding crystal frolick'd in the ray. J. RUSKIN Horses.. frolicking with each other. 2 O. FELTHAM Virtue.. gives such Cordials, as frolick the heart. W. IRVING By dint of dinners, of feeding and frolicking the town.

C *n.* †**1** In *pl.* Humorous verses circulated at a feast. E–M17. **2** An outburst of fun, gaiety, or merriment; a prank. M17. **b** Fun, merriment, gaiety. L17. **c** A whim. *rare.* E18. **3** A scene or occasion of gaiety or mirth; a merrymaking, a merry party. M17.

2 B. FRANKLIN I spent no time in taverns, games, or frolics of any kind. J. R. LOWELL He.. often filled whole pages.. with the gay frolics of his pencil. b B. JOWETT All young creatures are full of motion and frolic. 3 H. MARTINEAU They meant to have a reaping frolic when the corn should be ripe.

frolicker *n.* E19. **frolicky** *a.* = FROLICSOME M18. †**frolicly** *adv.* mirthfully, gaily L16–L17. †**frolicness** *n.*: only in 17.

frolicsome /ˈfrɒlɪks(ə)m/ *a.* L17. [f. prec. + -SOME[1].] Full of playful mirth; inclined to frolic.

frolicsomely *adv.* L19. **frolicsomeness** *n.* E18.

from /frɒm, *unstressed* frəm/ *prep., adv.,* & *conj.* [OE *fram, from* = OS, OHG, Goth. *fram*, ON *frá* FRO, f. Gmc base = forward (= PRO-[1]) + *-m* suff.] **A** *prep.* Often used in association with *to* (a finishing-point). **1** Denoting departure or moving away: expr. relation with a person who or thing which is the starting-point or site of motion. OE. **2** Indicating the starting-point or the first of two boundaries of an extent in space. OE. **b** Indicating the starting-point in a series, esp. the lower limit in a series or range. OE. **3** Indicating the starting-point of an extent in time. Freq. foll. by *to*, denoting the passage of time or regular recurrence. OE. **4** Indicating someone or something left behind or at a distance by a person who or thing which withdraws or goes away. OE. **b** Indicating a place or object left on one side by a person who or thing which deflects or turns away. L16. **5** Indicating the (degree of) distance, remoteness, absence, etc., of a person or thing in a fixed position. OE. **b** Indicating absence: not with (a person), not at (a place). *arch.* ME. **6** Denoting removal, separation, exclusion, freedom, deliverance, privation, abstention, or similar negation of contact with a concrete or abstract object. OE. **7** Orig., denoting a qualitative remoteness, unlikeness, or incongruity. Now, indicating the unlikeness, distinction, or difference of the person or thing distinguished. OE. **8** Indicating a person as a source of action at some degree of distance, esp. as a giver or sender. OE. **9** Denoting the ground of a judgement or belief. Also, denoting a reason, cause, or motive. OE. **10** With another prep. following: indicating initial position or state. OE. **11** Indicating a state or condition which is or may be abandoned or changed for another. ME. **12** Denoting derivation, source, descent, or the like (*lit.* & *fig.*). ME. **13** Denoting the fixed place or position of origin of an action or motion the range of which extends beyond that point. L16. **14** Indicating a model, rule, or copy, or (now *rare*) a person or thing after whom or which another is named. L16. **15** Indicating the place etc. of origin of a person or thing. Also, indicating the range, field, etc., out of which a selection is or may be made. E17.

1 AV *Gen.* 4:16 And Cain went out from the presence of the Lord. H. JAMES She passed from room to room. E. BOWEN The funeral could not.. be expected to take place 'from' Wisteria Lodge. 2 M. PATTISON Neustria.. extended from the Meuse almost to the present southern limits of France. b G. WHITE The swallow lays from four to six white eggs. 3 SHAKES. *A.Y.L.* And so, from hour to hour, we ripe and ripe. C. BRONTË I knew him from a boy. P. KAVANAGH From half-past five that morning they had been up. 4 SHAKES. *3 Hen. VI* We will not from the helm to sit and weep. V. S. PRITCHETT When he came home from his London office. b W. S. MAUGHAM To divert him from his chosen path. 5 T. ARNOLD Veii lay about ten miles from Rome. b J. MOSER He was continually from home, running from one house to another. E. PARSONS Georgina she could not bear a moment from her sight. 6 M. ELPHINSTONE The narrow tract.. separated from Mékrán.. by the range of hills. J. BUCHAN The smug suburban life from which he had revolted. G. GREENE Shaded from the sun. 7 P. MASSINGER But this is from the purpose. L. CARROLL You can't tell one flower from another. W. GOLDING The novelists who stand out from the rest. 8 LD MACAULAY Independence, veracity, self-respect, were things not required by the world from him. R. KIPLING I got one really exciting letter from you. 9 DISRAELI Remarkable from the neatness.. of its architecture. T. RALEIGH A person suffering from senile dementia. V. WOOLF No one kills from hatred. G. GREENE 'It's good of you,' she said, and I could tell from her voice that she meant it. 10 MILTON The sacred well That from beneath the seat of Jove doth spring. H. MACKENZIE My grandmother.. looking at me from under her spectacles. 11 GOLDSMITH From being attacked, the French.. became the aggressors. BROWNING Temples.. which tremblingly grew blank From bright. 12 R. HENRY The greatest rivers sometimes flow from the smallest fountains. LD MACAULAY His chief pleasures were commonly derived from field sports. I. MURDOCH Harriet had acquired Ajax.. from the Battersea Dogs Home. 13 DRYDEN They mined it near, they battered from afar. L. CARROLL From their point of view they are perfectly right. R. HARDY Ceilings from the beams of which hung leaves of palm and sisal. I. MCEWAN Mary admired.. the view from the balcony. 14 SHAKES. *Tam. Shr.* For, sure, Æacides Was Ajax, call'd so from his grandfather. L. M. HAWKINS She sketched objects; she colored from nature. 15 F. HALL This list I could amplify from my own verbal stores. R. HARDY Pus from the infected wound ran against his fingers. D. ABSE The man on his right was from Manchester.

Phrases: (A selection of cross-refs. only is included: see esp. other ns.) *as from*: see AS *adv.* etc. *far from*: see FAR *adv. from a child*: see CHILD *n. from hand to mouth*: see HAND *n.* **from now on** now and in the future. †**from oneself** beside oneself, out of one's wits. **from out of** *arch.* out of, from within, from among. *from* PILLAR *to post. from the way*: see WAY *n.* **from time to time** occasionally, intermittently.

†**B** *adv.* Away. Cf. FRO *adv.* LME–E17.

E. TOPSELL A sliding snake.. Gliding along the altar, from and back.

†**C** *conj.* From the time when. LME–E17.

G. BABINGTON From wee rise till we goe to bed.

fromage frais /frɔmaʒ frɛ, frɒmɑːʒ ˈfreɪ/ *n. phr.* L20. [Fr. = fresh cheese.] Soft fresh cheese used esp. as a dessert, with or without added flavouring.

fromward /ˈfrɒmwəd/ *adj., adv.,* & *prep. obs.* exc. *dial.* [OE *fromweard*, f. FROM + -WARD.] †**A** *adj.* **1** Departing, about to depart. Only in OE. **2** Froward. ME–L16. **B** *adv.* **1** In a direction which leads from or is turned from a given place or object; *fig.* in a different or diverse way, contrarily. OE. †**2** Of time: onward from a given date. Only in LME. **C** *prep.* In a direction which leads or is turned from (an object etc.); away from. ME.

Also **fromwards** *adv.* & *prep.* (*obs.* exc. *dial.*) OE.

frond /frɒnd/ *n.* L18. [L *frond-*, *frons* leaf.] 1 *Bot.* A leaflike organ formed by the union of stem and foliage in certain flowerless plants, esp. ferns, and differing from the leaf in usu. bearing a fructification. Also *loosely*, any large compound leaf, e.g. of the palm, banana, etc. L18. 2 *Zool.* A leaflike structure. M19.

frondage *n.* fronds collectively; *loosely* foliage: M19. **frondlet** *n.* a little frond M19.

fronde /frɔ̃d/ *n.* Pl. pronounced same. L18. [Fr., lit. 'sling'.] 1 *Fr. Hist.* (Usu. ***F-***.) A political party in mid-17th-cent. France which rose in rebellion against Mazarin and the Court during the minority of Louis XIV. L18. 2 *transf.* A malcontent or disaffected party; violent political opposition. E19.

fronded /ˈfrɒndɪd/ *a.* M17. [f. (as) FROND + -ED[2].] †1 Having leaves or foliage (*lit.* & *fig.*). Only in M17. 2 Having fronds. L19.

frondent /ˈfrɒnd(ə)nt/ *a.* L17. [L *frondent-* pres. ppl stem of *frondere* send out leaves, f. as FROND: see -ENT.] Having leaves or fronds, leafy.

frondesce /frɒnˈdɛs/ *v.i.* E19. [L *frondescere* frequent. of *frondere*: see prec., -ESCE.] Send out leaves.

frondescent *a.* breaking into leaf E19. **frondescently** *adv.* in a frondescent manner M19.

frondescence /frɒnˈdɛs(ə)ns/ *n.* M19. [mod.L *frondescentia*, f. as prec.: see -ENCE.] 1 The process or period of sending out leaves. M19. 2 Fronds or leaves collectively. L19.

frondeur /frɔ̃dœːr/ *n.* Pl. pronounced same. L18. [Fr., f. FRONDE + *-eur* -OR.] 1 In *Fr. Hist.* (usu. ***F-***), a member of the *Fronde*. L18. 2 *transf.* A malcontent, a political rebel. M19.

frondiferous /frɒnˈdɪf(ə)rəs/ *a.* L16. [f. L *frondifer*, f. as FROND: see -OUS, -FEROUS.] Bearing leaves or fronds.

frondose /frɒnˈdəʊs/ *a.* E18. [L *frondosus*, f. as FROND: see -OSE[1].] Orig., leafy, leaflike. Now, covered with fronds; having the appearance of a frond.

frondosely *adv.* L19. **frondoseness** *n.* leafiness E18. †**frondosity** *n.* (*a*) leafiness; (*b*) a representation of leaves: M17–L18.

frondous /ˈfrɒndəs/ *a.* E19. [f. L *frondosus*: see prec., -OUS.] Leafy; *Bot.* bearing leaves and flowers on the same stem.

frons /frɒnz/ *n.* M19. [L: see FRONT *n.*] *Entomol.* The middle part of the face of an insect, between the eyes.

front /frʌnt/ *n.*, *a.*, & *adv.* ME. [(O)Fr. f. L *front-*, *frons* forehead, front.] **A** *n.* **I** 1 The forehead. Now only *poet.* & *rhet.* ME. **b** = FRONS. *rare.* E19. 2 The face. Now *rare* or *obs.* exc. in *front to front* below. LME. 3 Orig., the face as expressing emotion or character. Now, bearing, demeanour; degree of composure or confidence while under threat or in danger. LME. **b** *fig.* Outward appearance or aspect; a bluff; a pretext. Cf. sense 6d below. E20. 4 Effrontery, impudence. M17.

2 W. JONES Till thrice the sun his rising front has shown. **front to front** = *face to face* s.v. FACE *n.* 3 SIR W. SCOTT The .. unclouded front of an accomplished courtier. W. S. MAUGHAM She was putting on a bold front to conceal her wounded feelings. **b** A. BARON It was only a front He was scared stiff. P. BARKER The need to bluster, to keep up a front at all costs. 4 LD MACAULAY None of the commissioners had the front to pronounce that such a man could properly be made the head of a great college.

II Foremost part. 5 **a** The foremost line or part of an army, battalion, etc.; line of battle; the foremost part of the ground occupied or of the whole field of operations, the part next to the enemy. Also, the foremost part of a position, as opp. to the *rear*, the scene of actual fighting. LME. **b** The direction towards which a line of troops faces when formed. M19. **c** *transf.* & *fig.* A sector of activity regarded as resembling a military front (freq. w. specifying wd). E20. **d** A political group organized to pursue a particular objective or set of objectives. E20. 6 The side or part of an object which appears to look out or to present itself to the view; the forepart of something, as a vehicle or a building. Also, the side or part of an object (esp. opp. to the *back*) which is less remote from a spectator or which is naturally reached first, as the face in a mine or the like. LME. †**b** A frontier. Only in L16. **c** Land facing a road, a river, the sea, etc.; frontage; spec. *the* promenade of a seaside resort, often with adjoining gardens. M18. **d** A person or organization serving as a cover for subversive or illegal activities. Cf. sense 3b above. E20. 7 *Archit.* Any of the sides or faces of a building; *esp.* the one in which the main entrance is sited. LME. 8 †**a** = FRONTAL *n.* 2. LME–M16. **b** More fully *false front*. A half-wig covering the front of the head, worn with a cap or bonnet by women. Now only *Hist.* L17. **c** The part of a garment, esp. of a dress or shirt, which covers (the upper part) of the front of the body. Also, a false shirt-front. E19. †9 The first part or line of something written or printed. Also, a frontispiece. L16–E18. 10 A position or place situated before something or towards an observer; a forward position, a leading position in a race or contest. Only in phrs. with preceding prep., as *to*, *at*, *the front* (*of*), *come to the front*, *in front of*, etc. E17. 11 **a** *gen.* An advancing boundary at which physical properties alter markedly. M19. **b** *Meteorol.* A narrow transition zone at the boundary of an advancing mass of air of distinct properties; the line of intersection of such a boundary with the earth's surface; *esp.* the leading edge (*warm front*) or trailing edge (*cold front*) of the warm sector of a cyclonic weather system. E20.

5a MILTON Front to Front Presented stood in terrible array. E. HEATH The forces of the Republican government had been pushed back .. and the main front was along the River Ebro. *action front!*: see ACTION *n.* **go to the front** join troops on campaign. *Western Front*: see WESTERN *a.* **b change of front** a radical alteration of one's attitude or position on a particular subject. **change front** (of a line) face in another direction; *fig.* radically alter one's attitude or position on a particular subject. *second front*: see SECOND *a.* **c** *Times* The industry is fighting back on the marketing as well as the political front. H. KISSINGER Progress in superpower relations .. has to be made on a broad front. J. DIDION He .. is still Top Pineapple on the hospitality front. **d** *National Front*, *patriotic front*, *popular front*, etc. 6 F. W. MAITLAND The skin being thin, the writing on the front could be seen upon the back. N. SHAVE For curved blades, the hollow side is the front. *transf.*: SHAKES. *Sonn.* Philomel in summer's front doth sing. **front of (the) house** *Theatr.* the parts of the theatre in front of the proscenium arch; the staff of the theatre or their activities. **c** *sea front*, *waterfront*. G. GREENE A blow along the front'll do you good. **d** M. MILLER It's a front; the Commies control it. M. ERSKINE He was .. respectable-looking and meek, .. just the type to make an excellent front for Madame Rosario. 7 W. P. COURTNEY The fronts of the mansion were decorated with statues. P. PEARCE Along the fronts of the tall, narrow terrace houses she goes. 8b A. TROLLOPE The graces of her own hair had given way to a front. **c** *shirt-front*: see SHIRT *n.* *Y-fronts*: see Y, Y 2. 10 W. K. KELLY In the very front of danger. **come to the front** take up or move to a forward position; become conspicuous. **in front** advanced or facing an observer; in the lead. **in front of** (*a*) ahead of, in advance of; (*b*) confronting, in the presence of. 11a *Scientific American* A flame front burns back through the vapour. *wavefront*: see WAVE *n.* **b** *occluded front*: see OCCLUDE 5.

B *adj.* (*attrib.*). 1 Of or pertaining to the front, situated in front. E17. 2 *Phonet.* Of a sound: formed by raising the front part of the tongue, excluding the blade and tip, towards the hard palate. M19.

C *adv.* At the front; in front. M17.

E. HICKERINGILL The Enemy .. had beset them Front and Rear. *eyes front*: see EYE *n.* **front of** *US* in front of. **out front** (chiefly *N. Amer.*) (*a*) at or to the front, in front, in the forefront, to the fore; (*b*) *Theatr.* in the front of the stage; in the auditorium.

Comb. & *special collocations*: **front bench** a bench at the front of an assembly; *spec.* any of such in the House of Commons, occupied by members of the Cabinet or Shadow Cabinet; **front-bencher** an occupant of a front bench; *front burner*, *on the*: see BURNER 3; **front door** the principal entrance-door of a house or other building (*lit.* & *fig.*); **front end** (*a*) *colloq.* the forward part of a motor vehicle, train, etc.; (*b*) *Electronics* the tuner, local oscillator, and mixer of a superheterodyne receiver; (*c*) that part of a computer system that a user deals with directly, esp. a device providing input or access to a central computer or other parts of a network; freq. *attrib.* (w. hyphen); (*d*) *attrib.* (w. hyphen) designating money paid or charged at the beginning of a transaction; *front-end loading*, the recovering of fees and service charges at the beginning of a loan repayment period; **front-fanged** *a.* (*Zool.*) having venomous fangs at the front of the upper jaw; proteroglyphous, solenoglyphous; **front line** (*a*) = sense A.5a above (*front-line States*, a group of countries adjacent to South Africa and hostile to its policy of apartheid); (*b*) the players in a jazz band other than the rhythm section; **front-loader** a machine, esp. a washing machine, which is loaded from the front (rather than from the top); **front man** (*a*) (orig. *US*) a man acting as a front (see sense A.6d above); (*b*) the leader or most prominent member of a group of musicians; **front matter** (in a book or similar publication) the title page, preface, introduction, and any other matter preceding the text; **front money** (orig. *US*) money paid in advance or at the beginning of a business transaction; **front office** (orig. & chiefly *US*) a main or head office, *esp.* police headquarters; **front page** the first page of a newspaper, esp. as containing important or remarkable news; **front-pager** a famous or notorious person likely to figure as the subject of a story or article on a front page; **front room** a room, esp. a sitting-room, situated at the front of a house; **front runner** (orig. *US*) (*a*) an athlete, horse, or other contestant who runs best when in the lead or who can set a fast pace; (*b*) a leading contestant (*lit.* & *fig.*), the contestant most likely to succeed; **frontsman** *Hist.* a salesman who stands on the pavement in front of a shop; **frontstead** (now *dial.*) a piece of ground between the front of a house and the road or street; a forecourt, a front garden; **front yard** *N. Amer.* a piece of ground in front of a house, a front garden.

frontways *adv.* = FRONTWISE M19. **frontwise** *adv.* in a position or direction facing to the front L18.

front /frʌnt/ *v.* E16. [Partly f. OFr. *fronter*, f. *front* FRONT *n.*, partly directly f. FRONT *n.*] 1 *v.i.* Have one's or its front facing in a specified direction. E16. †**b** *v.t.* Set the front of (a building) in a specified direction. M17–E19. 2 *v.t.* Stand or be face to face with; meet, face boldly; confront; oppose. *arch.* L16. 3 *v.t.* Be or stand in front of; serve as a front to. L16. **b** *v.i.* Act as a front (FRONT *n.* 6d) *for* a person or organization. Orig. *US.* M20. **c** *v.t.* & *i.* Lead or be the most prominent member of (a group of musicians). Orig. *US.* M20. **d** *v.t.* Present (a television show etc.); appear as the major promoter of (a product). L20. †4 *v.t.* Introduce (a story) *with* a reference or topic; preface. L16–M18. 5 *v.t.* **a** Have the front towards; stand opposite to, face. E17. **b** Of a building: have its front on the side of (a street etc.). L17. 6 *v.t.* Set face to face *with*, confront *with*. E17. 7 Chiefly *Mil.* †**a** *v.i.* March in the front or first rank. *rare.* Only in E17. **b** *v.i.* Turn the front or face in a specified direction. M17. **c** *v.t.* & *i.* (Cause to) form a front or line. L18. 8 *v.t.* Adorn in front; provide with a front; face (*with* a specified material). M17. 9 *v.i.* Become or feel distended or swollen, esp. through the absorption of fluid. *Sc.* & *dial.* E19. 10 *v.t.* *Phonet.* Articulate (a sound) with the tongue further forward. L19. **b** *v.i.* Of a sound: be or become formed with the tongue further forward. M20.

1 H. MAUNDRELL Having a few small Rooms fronting outward. W. GOLDING The balcony fronted on the swollen river. 2 SHAKES. *Ant. & Cl.* Those wars which fronted mine own peace. F. NORRIS Singlehanded, Annixter fronted the monster. V. WOOLF Here she was fronting her audience. 3 W. GOLDING The iron railings that fronted Bounce's house. **d** *Listener* Drug firms are able to employ well-known media people to front their promotions. M. KINGTON A .. TV series. .. I think I'll get Frank Muir to front it. 4 T. BOSTON Solomon .. fronts his writings .. with most express gospel. 5a F. CLISSOLD Fronting us, rose the summit of Mont Blanc. **b** A. M. GILLIAM The church .. was to have fronted the Plaza. 6 F. W. ROBERTSON Fronting his patron .. with the stern unpalatable truth of God. 7b J. HAYWARD The third fronting to their flanckward spurr'd towards him. 8 T. DWIGHT The Presbyterian church .. is fronted with two towers.

fronted *ppl a.* having or formed with a front (of a specified kind) E17.

frontage /ˈfrʌntɪdʒ/ *n.* E17. [f. FRONT *n.* + -AGE.] 1 Land which abuts on a river or other stretch of water, or on a road. Also, the land between the front of a building and a road or the like. E17. 2 Extent of front. M19. 3 The front face or part of a building. M19. 4 The action of fronting in a certain direction; the fact of facing a certain way; exposure, outlook. M19.

1 A. C. BOULT Devonshire House.. enjoyed a frontage on the Green Park. 2 T. W. HINCHLIFF Shopkeepers.. get very little frontage to display their goods. 3 C. ISHERWOOD Dirty plaster frontages embossed with scroll-work. 4 D. G. MITCHELL It has no wide and open frontage to the sun.

Comb.: **frontage-road** *N. Amer.* a service road.

frontager *n.* the owner of land or property adjoining the seashore or a roadway: E17.

frontage /ˈfrʌntɪdʒ/ *v.t. rare.* E20. [f. the n.] Face; have the front towards.

frontal /ˈfrʌnt(ə)l/ *n.* ME. [OFr. *frontel* (mod. *frontal*) f. L *frontale* (pl. *frontalia*), f. *frons* FRONT *n.*: see -AL[1].] †1 a A band or ornament worn on the forehead. ME–M17. b = FRONTLET 1C. E17–M18. 2 A movable covering for the front of an altar, an altar-cloth. LME. b A decorated front for a tomb. L19. 3 The façade of a building. LME. †4 *Archit.* A pediment placed over a small door or window. L16–M18. 5 The frontal bone. M19.

frontal /ˈfrʌnt(ə)l/ *a.* M17. [mod.L *frontalis*, f. *frons*: see FRONT *n.*, -AL[1].] 1 Of or pertaining to the forehead. M17. 2 Of or pertaining to the forepart or foremost edge; of or on the front. M19. 3 Of, pertaining to, or depicting the front of a person, object, etc., or the façade of a building; (of sculpture) displaying frontality. L19.

1 **frontal bone** the cranial bone forming the forehead and the upper parts of the orbits. **frontal lobe** the lobe of the cerebrum lying behind the frontal bone. 2 **frontal assault, attack**: delivered directly on the front, not on the flank or rear. 3 H. WILLIAMSON Something.. apprehended in the retina of the eye, and not by a frontal stare. **full-frontal** *a.* (*a*) displaying the human body completely naked, seen from the front; (*b*) *fig.* holding nothing back, revealing all.

fron'tality *n.* [tr. Da. *frontalitet*] a principle in sculpture etc. according to which the figure is represented as seen from the full front E20. **frontally** *adv.* in a frontal manner; *esp.* by a frontal attack (*lit.* & *fig.*): E20.

frontier /ˈfrʌntɪə, frʌnˈtɪə/ *n.*, *a.*, & *v.* LME. [AN *frounter*, (O)Fr. *frontière*, f. Proto-Romance deriv. of L *frons*, *front-* FRONT *n.*] A *n.* †1 The front side, the forepart. Also (*rare*), the side that faces in a specified direction. LME–E17. †2 = FRONTLET 2. Only in LME. †3 The front line or foremost part of an army. LME–E16. 4 *sing.* or in *pl.* The part of a country that borders on another country; the marches; the border or extremity coterminous with that of another. LME. b The part of a country held to form the border or furthest limit of its settled or inhabited regions; *esp.* the western edge of settlement of the US before the Pacific settlement. L17. †5 A border fortress, a frontier town. LME–L18. b A barrier against attack. L16–E18. †6 A settler on the frontier; a frontiersman. L17–E18.

4 G. F. KENNAN Establishing an agreed frontier between Poland and Russia. *fig.*: A. PRICE The frontiers of treason are rarely so clearly defined.

Comb.: **frontiersman** a man living on a frontier, or on or beyond the borders of civilization.

B *adj.* 1 Of or belonging to the frontier of a country; situated on the frontier; bordering. E16. b Characteristic of life on a frontier; remote from the comforts of civilization; pioneering. M19. †2 Fronting; opposite. *rare.* Only in E17.

1 C. M. YONGE A few of the frontier castles had fallen into his hands. b H. D. THOREAU To live a primitive and frontier life. LADY BIRD JOHNSON An area that's called the American Alps and is still very much frontier.

C *v.* †1 *v.i.* Act as a frontier; border *on* or *upon*. L16–M17. 2 *v.t.* Stand on or form the boundary of; face; delimit. Formerly also, bar, oppose. Long *rare.* L16.

frontierism *n.* a mode of expression characteristic of the (US) frontier L19. **frontierless** *a.* E20.

frontignac /frɒntɪˈnjak/ *n.* Also **frontignan** /frɒntɪˈnjɒ̃/. E17. [Spurious form of *Frontignan* (see below), after many southern Fr. names in *-ignac*.] 1 A muscat wine originally made at Frontignan in the department of Hérault, France. E17. 2 The grape from which this wine is made. M17.

frontispiece /ˈfrʌntɪspiːs/ *n.* & *v.* L16. [Fr. *frontispice* or late L *frontispicium* façade of a building, f. L *frons*, *front-* FRONT *n.* + *-spicium* as in *auspicium* AUSPICE, assim. in spelling to PIECE *n.*] A *n.* 1 The principal face or front of a building; *esp.* the decorated entrance of a building. L16. 2 The pediment over a door or gate. Also, a sculptured or engraved panel. E17. 3 *gen.* The front part of something; *spec.* (chiefly *joc.*) the face or forehead. E17. †4 The first page of a book or pamphlet or what was printed on it; the title-page including illustrations and table of contents; an introduction or preface. E17–E18. 5 (Now the usual sense.) An illustration facing the title-page of a book. L17. B *v.t.* Provide with a frontispiece; represent on a frontispiece; put as a frontispiece. Now *rare.* E18.

frontless /ˈfrʌntlɪs/ *a.* E17. [f. FRONT *n.* + -LESS.] 1 Shameless, audacious, daring, brazen. Now *rare.* E17. 2 Not having a front. L19.

1 JONSON The.. most frontlesse piece Of solid impudence. 2 *Daily Express* She wore this startling backless—and nearly frontless—dress.

frontlessly *adv.* E17. **frontlessness** *n.* L17.

frontlet /ˈfrʌntlɪt/ *n.* L15. [OFr. *frontelet* dim. of *frontel*: see FRONTAL *n.*, -LET.] 1 An ornament or band worn on the forehead. L15. b = PHYLACTERY 1b. L16. †c (A cloth or bandage containing) a medicament applied to the forehead. E17–E18. d A piece of armour or harness for the forehead of an animal. E19. 2 A cloth hanging over the upper part of an altar frontal. Also, an ornamental border to an altar-cloth. M16. 3 The forehead: now only of an animal. M17. 4 The front or face of a building, mountain, etc. *rare.* E19.

1b AV *Exod.* 13:16 It shall be for a token vpon thine hand, and for frontlets betweene thine eyes.

fronto- /ˈfrɒntəʊ/ *comb. form.* M19. [Irreg. f. L *frons*, *frontis* FRONT *n.*: see -O-.] Used (chiefly *Anat.*) to form adjs. w. the sense 'of or pertaining to the forehead and —', as *fronto-nasal*, *-occipital*, *-parietal* etc.

frontogenesis /frʌntə(ʊ)ˈdʒɛnɪsɪs/ *n.* M20. [f. as FRONT *n.* + -O- + -GENESIS.] *Meteorol.* The formation or development of a front or fronts.

frontoge'netic *a.* M20.

frontolysis /frʌnˈtɒlɪsɪs/ *n.* M20. [f. as prec. + -LYSIS.] *Meteorol.* The decay or disappearance of a front or fronts.

fronto'lytic *a.* M20.

fronton /ˈfrʌnt(ə)n/ *n.* L17. [Fr. f. It *frontone*, augm. of *fronte* forehead: see FRONT *n.*, -OON. In sense 3 tr. Sp. *frontón*.] 1 A pediment. L17. 2 An altar frontal. *rare.* M18. 3 A building in which pelota is played. L19.

frontward /ˈfrʌntwəd/ *n.*, *adv.*, & *a.* Also **-wards** /-wədz/. M16. [f. FRONT *n.* + -WARD.] †A *n.* The direction towards the front. Only in M16. B *adv.* 1 Towards or in the direction of the front; to the front *of*. M19. 2 With the front or face in a specified direction. Foll. by *to*. *rare.* M19. C *adj.* Of or pertaining to the front. M19.

froom *a.* var. of FRUM.

†**froppish** *a.* M17–L18. [Perh. f. var. of FRAP *v.* + -ISH[1].] Froward, fretful, peevish.

†**froppishness** *n.* L17–M18.

frore /frɔː/ *pa. pple* & *a.* Also **frorn** /frɔːn/, †**froren**. ME. [Orig. pa. pple of FREEZE *v.*] 1 *pa. pple* & *ppl a.* Frozen. *obs.* exc. *dial.* ME. 2 *adj.* Intensely cold, frosty, frostlike. Now only *poet.* L15.

frory *a.* (now *rare* or *obs.*) frozen, frosty, intensely cold M16.

frosh /frɒʃ/ *n.*[1] *N. Amer. slang.* Pl. same. E20. [Alt. of FRESHMAN, perh. infl. by G *Frosch* frog, (dial.) grammar-school pupil.] A college freshman; *collect.* freshmen.

†**frosh** *n.*[2]: see FROSK *n.*

frosk /ˈfrɒsk/ *n.* Long *obs.* exc. *dial.* Also †**frosh.** [OE *forsc*, *frosc*, *frox*: see FROG *n.*[1]] A frog.

frost /frɒst/ *n.* [OE *frost*, usu. *forst* = OFris. *frost*, *forst*, OS, (O)HG *frost* (Du. *vorst*), ON *frost*, f. Gmc, f. weak grade of base of FREEZE *v.*: see -T[1].] 1 The action, state, or effect of freezing; the prevalence of a temperature below the freezing point of water; extreme cold; a frozen consistency. OE. 2 Frozen dew or vapour forming a white deposit. Also *hoar-frost*. OE. †b Ice. LME–L16. 3 *fig.* An influence that chills or depresses; *esp.* coldness of behaviour or temperament, frigidity; (*slang*) a coolness. ME. 4 A failure. *slang* (orig. *Theatr.*). L19.

1 SHAKES. *Rom. & Jul.* Death lies on her like an untimely frost Upon the sweetest flower. J. UPDIKE By night the frost cracks rocks with a typewriter staccato. **black frost** frost not accompanied by hoar-frost. **degrees of frost** degrees below freezing point. **Jack Frost** frost personified. **white frost** frost accompanied by hoar-frost. 2 POPE Groves that shine with silver frost. 3 W. H. MALLOCK He could not.. keep a slight frost from his manner. 4 R. LINDNER Look, Doc. This analysis is a frost, isn't it?

Comb.: **frostbound** *a.* affected by severe frost; **frost crack** a vertical split in a tree-trunk caused by freezing; **frost-fish** (*a*) (chiefly *NZ*) the scabbard-fish, *Lepidopus caudatus*; (*b*) *N. Amer.* a tomcod, *Microgadus tomcod*; **frost-flower** an ice-crystal resembling a flower; **frost grape** (the fruit of) any of several N. American wild vines, esp. *Vitis vulpina*, whose fruit turns sweet with the first frosts; **frost heave, heaving** the uplift of soil or other surface deposits due to expansion of groundwater on freezing; **frost-nail** *Hist.* a nail driven into a horse's shoe to prevent slipping in icy weather; **frost-nip** *n.* & *v.t.* (affect with) frostbite, usu. slight; **frost pocket** a small low-lying area affected by frost; **frost shattering** the disintegration or fracture of rock due to expansion of water freezing in cracks or pores; **frost-work** (decoration in imitation of) the tracery formed on the surface of glass etc. by frost (freq. *attrib.*).

frostless *a.* E18. **frostlike** *a.* resembling (that of) frost E19.

frost /frɒst/ *v.* E16. [f. the n.] 1 *v.t.* Make (a horse's shoe) rough by inserting frost-nails, to prevent slipping; shoe (a horse) in this way. *obs.* exc. *Hist.* E16. 2 *v.t.* Cover (as) with hoar-frost or rime; *spec.* give a frostlike surface or appearance to (glass etc.), make (glass) opaque. Chiefly as *frosted* ppl a. M17. b Turn (hair) white. M17. c Ice (a cake). Chiefly as *frosted* ppl a. Now *US.* M18. 3 *v.t.* Freeze; *esp.* injure (a plant etc.) by frost. E19. 4 *v.i.* Become covered (*over*, *up*) with frost. (*lit.* & *fig.*) L20.

2 D. WELCH Home-made lemonade stood in already frosted glasses. I. MURDOCH The door has an oval panel of opaque frosted glass. A. LURIE Eighteen wigs, one frosted with diamonds. 3 C. SAGAN High mountainous regions that remain frosted after the snows of the valleys have melted. 4 T. HOOPER The honey will 'frost',.. showing a white cloudy area.. often mistakenly thought to be deterioration.

frosting *n.* (*a*) the action of the vb; (*b*) a frosted surface; icing on a cake etc.: E16.

frostbite /ˈfrɒs(t)bʌɪt/ *n.* E19. [f. FROST *n.* + BITE *n.*] Necrosis produced by exposure to severe cold, usually affecting the superficial tissues of fingers and toes.

frostbite /ˈfrɒs(t)bʌɪt/ *v.t.* Pa. pple **-bitten** /-bɪt(ə)n/, (*rare*) **-bit** /-bɪt/. L16. [f. FROST *n.* + BITE *v.*] Injure with intense cold, expose to frost; affect with frostbite; sustain frostbite in (oneself, one's limbs).

frosty /ˈfrɒsti/ *a.* LME. [f. FROST *n.* + -Y[1]. Cf. OE *fyrstig*.] 1 Affected or characterized by frost, ice-cold. LME. 2 *transf.* & *fig.* Cold as frost, chilling; lacking ardour or warmth, frigid. LME. 3 (Appearing to be) covered with hoar-frost; (of the hair) white. LME.

1 J. TYNDALL The winter set in with clear frosty weather. 2 *Sunday Sun* (*Brisbane*) An interview.. was preceded by a gruelling examination from Mr Swan. The atmosphere was decidedly frosty. 3 *transf.*: SHAKES. *Tit. A.* My frosty signs and chaps of age.

frostily *adv.* E17. **frostiness** *n.* E18.

frot /frɒt/ *v.t.* Long chiefly *dial.* Infl. **-tt-**. ME. [OFr. *froter* (mod. *frotter*), ult. origin unkn.] Rub; polish; stroke, caress.

fig.: B. LEVIN Grudges and vendettas, regularly frotted into life. *absol.*: J. SCOTT The dog.. seemed a very friendly creature, standing tall.. to frot against the sergeant's leg.

froth /frɒθ/ *n.* LME. [ON *froða* or *frauð*, f. a Gmc base repr. also by OE *āfrēoþan* to froth.] 1

The aggregation of tiny bubbles in a liquid, caused by agitation, fermentation, effervescence, etc.; foam, spume. Also, a state of frothing. LME. **b** Foaming saliva. Now *rare*. LME. **c** Matter rising to the surface of a liquid during boiling etc.; scum. M16. **2** Something insubstantial or of little value. Formerly also, something immature or tender. LME. **3** A worthless person or persons; 'scum'. *derog.* Now *rare* or *obs.* L16.

1 O. WILDE Collecting contemporaneous things is like trying to hold froth in a sieve. D. L. SAYERS They walked .. slowly, so as not to set the beer all of a froth. *transf.*: D. HEWETT The pink nylon dress in a froth over her arm. 2 A. HORNECK Thou hast delighted in froth, and idle talk. 3 SHAKES. *Merry W.*: Froth and scum, thou liest!

Comb.: **froth-blower** (*joc.*) a beer-drinker; formerly esp. (*Froth-Blower*) as a member of a charitable organization; *froth flotation*: see FLOTATION 3.

froth /frɒθ/ *v.* LME. [f. the n. Cf. ON mutated form *freyða*.] **1** *v.i.* Emit froth; foam at the mouth; (of a liquid) gather froth, run foaming (*away*, *over*). LME. **2** *v.t.* Emit as or like froth. *rare.* LME. **3** *v.t.* Cause to foam, make frothy. E17. **4** *v.t.* Cover (as) with froth. E17.

1 T. HARDY His lips frothing like a mug of hot ale. K. MANSFIELD The water frothed up in the big soapy bowl with pink and blue bubbles. 2 TENNYSON Is your spleen froth'd out, or have ye more? 3 S. JOHNSON She .. made his coffee, and frothed his chocolate. 4 SMOLLETT His face frothed up to the eyes with soap lather.

frothy /ˈfrɒθi/ *a.* L15. [f. FROTH *n.* + -Y[1].] **1** Full of, covered with, or accompanied by froth; foamy. L15. **2** Consisting of or resembling froth. Also *fig.*, insubstantial, trifling, vain; (of a person) shallow. L16.

1 W. SOMERVILLE Wanton Joy .. had spilt the Cyder's frothy Flood. 2 E. LYALL A mere ranter, a frothy mob orator. A. BURGESS A frothy evening frock.

frothily *adv.* E18. **frothiness** *n.* E17.

frottage /ˈfrɒtɑːʒ, *foreign* frɔtaːʒ/ *n.* M20. [Fr. = rubbing, friction, f. *frotter*: see FROT.] **1** The practice of touching or rubbing against the (clothed) body of another person (usu. in a crowd), as a means of obtaining sexual gratification. M20. **2** *Art.* The technique or process of taking a rubbing from an uneven surface, such as grained wood, as a basis for an artistic work. M20.

frotteur /frɒˈtəː, *foreign* frɔtœːr (*pl. same*)/ *n.* [Fr.] a person who indulges in frottage (sense 1) L19. **frotteurism** /frɒˈtəːrɪz(ə)m/ *n.* = FROTTAGE 1 M20.

frottola /ˈfrɒtələ, *foreign* ˈfrottola/ *n.* Pl. **-le** /-leɪ, *foreign* -le/. M19. [It., lit. 'fib, tall story'.] *Mus.* A form of Italian comic or amorous song, esp. from the 15th and 16th cents.

frou-frou /ˈfruːfruː/ *n.* & *v.* L19. [Fr., imit.] **A** *n.* A rustling, esp. of skirts. Hence, frills, frippery. L19. **B** *v.i.* Move with a rustle (of skirts etc.). E20.

frough /fraʊ/ *a.* Long *dial.* Also **frow**. ME. [Origin unkn. Cf. FRUSH *a.*] Frail, brittle; not to be depended on.

froughy /ˈfraʊi/ *a.* Long *dial.* Also **frowy**. L16. [Perh. f. prec. + -Y[1].] **1** Musty, sour, stale. L16. **2** Of wood: spongy, brittle. M17.

frounce /fraʊns/ *n.*[1] LME. [(O)Fr. *fronce*, f. Frank., rel. to ON *hrukka* wrinkle. Cf. FLOUNCE *n.*[2]] †**1** A wrinkle. Also, a crease or pleat; *fig.* deceit. LME–E18. †**2** A flounce. Only in 17. **3** [Infl. by FROUNCE *v.*] (A piece of) vain display; elaboration. *rare.* L19.

frounce /fraʊns/ *n.*[2] LME. [Origin unkn.] *Falconry.* A sore in the mouth of a hawk.

frounce /fraʊns/ *v.* ME. [(O)Fr. *froncer*, also OFr. *froncir* wrinkle, fold, f. as FROUNCE *n.*[1]] **1** †**a** *v.t.* Fold or wrinkle; knit, purse (the brow, lips). ME–M17. **b** Knit the brow; (of the face) become wrinkled. Now *rare* or *obs.* LME. †**2** *v.t.* & *i.* Make or become creased or pleated. LME–E19. **3** *v.t.* Frizz, curl (hair, a wig). E16.

froust *n.* & *v.* var. of FROWST.

frousty *a.* var. of FROWSTY.

frow /fraʊ/ *n.*[1] LME. [Du. *vrouw* woman.] **1** A Dutchwoman. LME. †**2** A maenad or Bacchante. M16–E17. **3** A woman or lady, *esp.* a buxom one; a housewife. L16. **4** A slut; an immoral woman. *dial.* L18.

frow *n.*[2] var. of FROE.

frow *a.* var. of FROUGH.

froward /ˈfrəʊəd/ *adv.*, *a.*, *prep.*, & *n. arch.* As prep. also **-wards** /-wədz/. [Late OE *frāward*, f. as FRO + -WARD. Cf. FROMWARD.] †**A** *adv.* **1** In a direction leading away from a given person, place, or thing. LOE–L16. **2** Perversely; untowardly. ME–L16. **B** *adj.* Perverse, hard to please; refractory, ungovernable; untoward, unfavourable. ME. **C** *prep.* Long *rare.* (In a direction) away from. ME. †**D** *n.* A froward person or thing. LME–L16.

frowardly *adv.* LME. **frowardness** *n.* ME.

†**frower** *n.* see FROE.

frown /fraʊn/ *n.* L16. [f. the vb.] **1** A manifestation or sign of displeasure or disapproval. Now only as passing into sense 2. L16. **2** A furrowed or wrinkled state of the brow; a look expressing severity, disapproval, perplexity, or thought. Formerly also, the habit of frowning. E17.

1 DEFOE The father's frowns are a part of correction. 2 A. J. CRONIN His open and agreeable expression marred by the frown of a man harassed and overworked. A. LURIE A sharp W-shaped frown between his neat dark eyebrows.

frown /fraʊn/ *v.* LME. [OFr. *frognier*, *froignier* (surviving in *re(n)frogner*), f. *froigne* surly look, of Celt. origin (cf. Welsh *ffroen* nostril).] **1** *v.i.* Knit or furrow the brow in displeasure or thought; express disapproval or anger by a stern look (*at*, *on*, *upon*). LME. **b** Of a thing: present a gloomy or threatening aspect. E17. **2** *v.t.* **a** Drive or force *into*, (now *rare*) *away*, *down*, *off*, by a frown or frowns. L17. **b** Enforce, express, or produce by a frown or frowns. L18.

1 E. BLISHEN I would frown impatiently at the dispute. O. SACKS He thought again deeply, frowning in concentration. A. BLOND Others have been frowned upon for indulging in an unmanly .. occupation. b H. MARRYAT A deep ravine of frowning rocks. 2a N. WEBSTER I will be neither frowned nor ridiculed into error. b L. STEPHEN In 1861 the Schreckhorn .. still frowned defiance upon all comers.

frowner *n.* a person who frowns M17. **frowningly** *adv.* with a frown; in a frowning manner: M16.

frowst /fraʊst/ *n.* & *v.* Also **froust**. L19. [Back-form. from next.] **A** *n.* **1** Extra time in bed in the morning. Also, an armchair. *Public School slang.* L19. **2** (A laze or idle in) the stuffy or fusty warmth of a crowded or unventilated room. *colloq.* E20.

2 J. BETJEMAN Tea and a frowst with crumpets. J. R. ACKERLEY Ask for the window to be opened? Better not .. They preferred their frowst.

B *v.i.* Stay in a stuffy, warm, or fusty atmosphere, esp. lazily or idly; take pleasure in doing this. L19.

K. AMIS No use sitting about .. or frowsting by the fire with a book.

frowster *n.* E20.

frowsty /ˈfraʊsti/ *a.* Orig. *dial.* Also **frousty**. M19. [Origin uncertain: cf. OFr. *frouste* ruinous, decayed, FROUGHY, FROWZY.] Fusty, stuffy; warm and ill-ventilated; frowzy.

C. LASSALLE Their rooms had a frowsty, subterranean atmosphere.

frowstiness *n.* E20.

frowsy *a.* var. of FROWZY.

frowy *a.* var. of FROUGHY.

†**frowze** *n.* M16–E18. [Origin uncertain; perh. alt. of FROUNCE *n.*[1] with assim. to FRIZZ *n.*, FUZZ *n.*[1]] A woman's wig of frizzed hair.

frowzy /ˈfraʊzi/ *a.* Also (perh. infl. by FROWSTY) **frowsy**. L17. [Prob. rel. to earlier FROUGHY and later FROWSTY; ult. origin unkn.] **1** Smelling fusty, stuffy, or stale from being dirty, unwashed, or unventilated. L17. **2** Dirty, untidy, or neglected in appearance; slatternly, sluttish. E18.

1 N. COWARD Some frowsy little hotel. 2 K. A. PORTER Badly buttoned and frowsy-haired.

frowzily *adv.* L17. **frowziness** *n.* E18.

froze *v.* pa. t. & pple: see FREEZE *v.*

frozen /ˈfrəʊz(ə)n/ *ppl a.* ME. [pa. pple of FREEZE *v.*] **1** Solidified by exposure to cold; exposed to extreme cold; *spec.* (of food) preserved by refrigeration to below freezing point. ME. **b** *fig.* Frigid, unfriendly, unresponsive. L16. **2** Hard, rigid; fixed, immobile. L19. **b** *Billiards* etc. Of a ball: at rest in close contact with another ball or a cushion. *rare.* E20. **c** Of a credit or asset: impossible to liquidate or realize at maturity or some other given time. Cf. LIQUID *a.* 6. E20.

1 R. C. HUTCHINSON The road was still narrowed by a ridge of frozen snow. A. HIGGINS My hands were frozen . ., my feet chilled to the bone. M. PYKE Frozen chickens .. have become industrial products manufactured for a world market. b *the frozen* MITT. 2 **the frozen limit** *colloq.* the absolute limit; the ultimate of what is objectionable or unendurable.

frozenly *adv.* E18. **frozenness** /-n-n-/ *n.* M17.

frozen *v.* pa. pple of FREEZE *v.*

fructan /ˈfrʌktan/ *n.* M20. [f. FRUCTOSE + -AN.] *Biochem.* A polysaccharide whose constituent monosaccharides are fructoses; = FRUCTOSAN.

fructed /ˈfrʌktɪd/ *a.* E17. [f. L *fructus* fruit + -ED[2].] *Her.* Of a tree or plant: bearing fruit (usu. when of a different colour from the rest).

Fructidor /ˈfrʊktɪdɔː, *foreign* fryktidɔːr/ *n.* L18. [Fr., f. L *fructus* fruit + Gk *dōron* gift.] *Hist.* The twelfth month of the French Republican calendar (introduced 1793), extending from 18 August to 16 September. Also, the purge of conservative deputies that took place on the eighteenth day of that month (4 September) in 1797.

fructiferous /frʌkˈtɪf(ə)rəs/ *a.* M17. [f. L *fructifer* (f. *fructus* fruit) + -OUS: see -FEROUS.] Bearing or producing fruit.

fructiferously *adv.* M17.

fructification /ˌfrʌktɪfɪˈkeɪʃ(ə)n/ *n.* L15. [Late L *fructificatio(n-)*, f. L *fructificat-* pa. ppl stem of *fructificare*: see next, -ATION.] **1** The process of bearing fruit (now chiefly *Bot.*). Formerly also, fertilization. L15. **2** The fruit(s) of a flowering plant; the spore-bearing structures in a fern or other cryptogam. M18.

fructify /ˈfrʌktɪfʌɪ/ *v.* ME. [(O)Fr. *fructifier* f. L *fructificare*, f. *fructus* fruit: see -FY.] **1** *v.i.* Bear fruit, become fruitful. ME. **2** *v.t.* Cause to bear fruit; make fertile or productive. L15.

1 *fig.*: S. SMILES The good deed .. will live, even though we may not see it fructify. 2 J. A. MICHENER Without the aid of some god to fructify the earth the farmer was powerless. *fig.*: F. L. WRIGHT Cultural sterility .. might be saved and fructified by this ideal of an organic architecture.

fructivorous /frʌkˈtɪv(ə)rəs/ *a.* L17. [f. L *fructus* fruit + -VOROUS.] = FRUGIVOROUS.

fructosan /ˈfrʌktəsan/ *n.* E20. [f. FRUCTOSE + -AN.] *Biochem.* = FRUCTAN.

fructose /ˈfrʌktəʊz, -s/ *n.* M19. [f. L *fructus* fruit + -OSE[2].] *Chem.* A hexose sugar which occurs widely (esp. combined in sucrose) in fruit juices, syrups, and honey.

fructuous /ˈfrʌktjʊəs/ *a.* LME. [(OFr. f.) L *fructuosus*, f. *fructus* fruit: see -OUS.] **1** (Of a plant) bearing much fruit, prolific; (of soil) fertile. LME. **2** *fig.* Beneficial, advantageous. LME.

fructuously *adv.* LME. **fructuousness** *n.* M19.

frug /frʌg/ *n.* & *v.* M20. [Origin unkn.] **A** *n.* A vigorous dance performed to pop music, popularized in the 1960s. M20. **B** *v.i.* Infl. **-gg-**. Dance the frug. M20.

frugal /ˈfruːg(ə)l/ *a.* M16. [L *frugalis*, f. *frugi* indecl. adj. (orig. dat. of *frux* fruit) = economical, useful: see -AL[1].] **1** Careful or sparing in the use or supply of food, goods, etc.; economical. (Formerly foll. by *of*.) M16. **2** Of things, esp. food: provided in small quantity and with avoidance of excess; plain, simple. E17.

1 SHAKES. *Merry W.* I was then frugal of my mirth. R. LEHMANN A frugal wage-earner, managing on a few hundreds. 2 GOLDSMITH A frugal meal, which consisted of roots and tea.

fruˈgality *n.* frugal character E16. **frugally** *adv.* L16. **frugalness** *n.* E18.

†**frugiferous** *a.* M17–M18. [f. L *frugifer* (f. *frux frug-* fruit) + -OUS: see -FEROUS.] Bearing fruit; fruitful.

frugivore /ˈfruːdʒɪvɔː/ *n.* M20. [f. as next + -VORE.] An animal that feeds on fruit.

frugivorous /frʊˈdʒɪv(ə)rəs/ *a.* E18. [f. L *frug-*, *frux* fruit + -VOROUS.] Esp. of an animal: living on fruit; = FRUCTIVOROUS.

fruit /fruːt/ *n.* ME. [(O)Fr. f. L *fructus* (enjoyment of) the produce of the soil, harvest, fruit, revenue, f. *frui* enjoy f. base of *fruges* fruits of the earth.] **I 1** *sing.* & (now chiefly) in *pl.* Vegetable produce in general. Also *fruits of the earth* or *ground*. ME. **2** *sing.* & *collect. pl.* The edible product of a tree, shrub, or other plant, consisting of the seed and its envelope, esp. when sweet, juicy, and pulpy. Also *loosely*, another sweet juicy part of a plant, as the stalks of rhubarb, eaten similarly. Cf. VEGETABLE *n.* 2. ME. †**b** A fruit course of a meal; dessert. L16–E17. †**3** A fruit tree. Also, a food-plant. ME–M18. **4** *Bot.* The seed-bearing structure (the matured ovary) of a plant, as a means of reproduction etc. M18.

1 AV *Exod.* 23:10 Sixe yeres thou shalt sow thy land, and shalt gather in the fruites thereof. *first-fruit*: see FIRST. 2 M. HENRY The choicest fruits ripen slowly. E. O'NEILL Pompeia . . takes a peach from the bowl of fruit. *Proverb*: He that would eat the fruit must climb the tree. *breadfruit, kiwi fruit, miracle fruit, passion-fruit*, etc. *bear fruit*: see BEAR *v.*[1] DEAD SEA *fruit*. FORBIDDEN *fruit*. **in fruit** bearing fully formed fruit. *soft fruit*: see SOFT *a.* *stone fruit*: see STONE *n.*, *a.*, & *adv.* b SHAKES. *Haml.* My news shall be the fruit to that great feast. 4 C. DARWIN Winged seeds are never found in fruits which do not open.

II *transf.* & *fig.* **5** Offspring, progeny. More fully *fruit of the body, loins, womb*. (Orig. a Hebraism.) *arch.* ME. **6** *sing.* & in *pl.* Anything (concrete or abstract) produced by an activity, process, etc.; product, outcome. ME. **7** Advantage, profit. *arch.* ME. **8 a** A person easily imposed on; a dupe. *slang* (orig. *US*). L19. **b** In familiar greetings: fellow, chap. Only in *old fruit*. E20. **c** A (passive) male homosexual. *slang* (orig. *US*). E20.

5 SHAKES. *3 Hen. VI* King Edward's fruit, true heir to th' English crown. 6 G. GISSING Kindly, intimate talk, the fruit of a lifetime of domestic happiness. *Scouting* Get out that . . type-writer, unleash that tape-recorder . . and send us the fruits. 7 J. HOWE I read thy lines with fruit and delight.

Comb.: **fruit bar** a piece of dried and pressed fruit; **fruit-bat** any of numerous fruit-eating bats of the suborder Megachiroptera, which includes the flying foxes; **fruit-body** = *fruiting body* s.v. FRUIT *v.* 1; **fruit cake** (*a*) a cake made with dried fruit, nuts, spice, etc.; (*b*) *slang* (from phr. *nutty as a fruit cake*) an eccentric or crazy person; **fruit cocktail** finely-chopped fruit salad; **fruit-dove** any of numerous Australasian and Indonesian fruit-eating doves of the genera *Ptilinopus* and *Phapitreron*, many of which have brightly coloured plumage; WOMPOO *fruit-dove*; **fruit-farm**: on which fruit trees are grown; **fruit fly** (*a*) any of various dipteran flies of the families Tephritidae, whose larvae infest cultivated fruit (also *large fruit fly*); (*b*) any of various dipteran flies of the family Drosophilidae, which feed on rotting or fermenting fruit (also *small fruit fly*); **fruit gum** a fruit-flavoured piece of gelatin sucked as a sweet; **fruit-juice** the juice of (esp. citrus) fruit, served as a drink or appetizer; **fruit-knife**: for cutting fruit, with a silver etc. blade to withstand the acid; **fruit loaf** a kind of sweet bread or cake containing dried fruit and usu. baked in a rectangular tin; **fruit machine** a coin- or token-operated gaming-machine, in which a player is successful when certain combinations of symbols, usu. representing various kinds of fruit, appear; **fruit salad** an assortment of fruits cut up and served in syrup etc.; *slang* an array of campaign ribbons etc. worn on the chest; **fruit salts** effervescent health salts; *fruit set*: see SET *n.*[1] 8c; **fruit sugar** sugar obtained from fruit, *esp.* fructose; **fruit tree**: grown for its fruit; **fruit-wood** the wood of a fruit tree, esp. as used to make furniture.

fruit /fruːt/ *v.* LME. [f. the n.] **1** *v.i.* Bear fruit. LME. **2** *v.t.* Induce (a plant) to bear fruit. M17.

1 **fruiting body** the spore-producing organ in a fungus.

fruited *a.* bearing (much) fruit E17.

fruitage /ˈfruːtɪdʒ/ *n.* LME. [OFr., f. *fruit* FRUIT *n.*] **1** Fruit collectively. LME. **2** The process, season, or state of bearing fruit. L16. †**3** A decorative arrangement of fruits; a picture, carving, embroidery, etc., representing this. E17–E18.

fruitarian /fruːˈtɛːrɪən/ *n.* & *a.* L19. [f. FRUIT *n.* + -ARIAN, after *vegetarian*.] **A** *n.* A person who lives exclusively on fruit. L19. **B** *adj.* Of or pertaining to fruitarians or their diet. E20.

fruitarianism *n.* E20.

fruiter /ˈfruːtə/ *n.* ME. [(O)Fr. *fruitier*, f. *fruit* FRUIT *n.*: see -ER[2]. Later prob. f. FRUIT *n.*, *v.* + -ER[1].] **1** A fruit-grower. Formerly, a dealer in fruit; a household official in charge of fruit. ME. **2** A vessel engaged in the fruit-trade. M19. **3** A tree that fruits in a specified way. L19.

fruiterer /ˈfruːt(ə)rə/ *n.* LME. [Extension of prec. with -ER[1].] A dealer in, or (formerly) grower of, fruit.

†**fruiteress** *n.* a female fruiterer E18–E19.

fruitery /ˈfruːtəri/ *n.* Now *rare*. E17. [(O)Fr. *fruiterie*, f. *fruit* FRUIT *n.*: see -ERY.] †**1** A place where fruit is grown or stored. E17–E19. **2** Fruit collectively. E17.

fruitful /ˈfruːtfʊl, -f(ə)l/ *a.* LME. [f. FRUIT *n.* + -FUL.] **1** Of a tree etc.: bearing abundant fruit. Of soil, weather, etc.: inducing fertility in plants. LME. **2** Bearing many offspring; prolific. LME. **3** *gen.* Abundantly productive of ideas or some other immaterial thing. (Foll. by *of*, *in*.) LME. **4** Productive of good results; beneficial, rewarding. LME. †**5** Of a crop, reward, etc.: abundant, copious. Only in 17.

2 AV *Gen.* 1:22 God blessed them, saying, Be fruitfull, and multiply. 3 W. H. PRESCOTT His fruitful genius suggested an expedient. J. BUCHAN He was fruitful of notions . . he could suggest magnificent schemes. 4 H. J. LASKI Problems . . required the absence of passionate debate if they were in any fruitful fashion to be solved. 5 DRYDEN Harvests heavy with their fruitful weight, Adorn our fields.

fruitfully *adv.* LME. **fruitfulness** *n.* LME.

fruition /frʊˈɪʃ(ə)n/ *n.* LME. [(O)Fr. f. late L *fruitio(n-)*, f. L *fruit-* pa. ppl stem of *frui* enjoy: see FRUIT *n.*, -ION.] **1** Enjoyment; the pleasure arising from possession. Now *rare* or *obs.* LME. **2** [By association with FRUIT *n.*] **a** The state of being in fruit; fructification. L19. **b** *fig.* Successful outcome of a hope, plan, etc.; fulfilment, realization. L19.

1 *Book of Common Prayer* That we . . may after this lyfe have the fruicion of thy glorious Godhead. C. MARLOWE That perfect bliss . . , The sweet fruition of an earthly crown. 2a H. JAMES The apples in the . . orchards . . gave a suggestion of sour fruition here and there. b E. R. PIKE Trade unions . . were fed . . and brought to fruition by . . toilers in the British industrial scene. C. HILL Cromwell's design . . came to fruition only in 1657.

fruitist /ˈfruːtɪst/ *n.* E19. [f. FRUIT *n.* + -IST.] A person who cultivates fruit.

fruitive /ˈfruːɪtɪv/ *a.* M17. [med.L *fruitivus*, f. L *frui*: see FRUIT *n.*, -IVE.] Consisting of or based on enjoyment; having the faculty of enjoyment.

fruitless /ˈfruːtlɪs/ *a.* & *adv.* LME. [f. FRUIT *n.* + -LESS.] **A** *adj.* **1** Producing no fruit; barren, sterile. Formerly, producing no offspring. LME. **2** Producing no results; vain, unsuccessful, futile, unprofitable. LME.

2 C. BAX I have no money, and so it is fruitless to talk about a fine. I. MURDOCH What a lot of his . . strength he had wasted on fruitless controversies.

B *adv.* Fruitlessly, without avail. *poet.* M18.

T. GRAY I fruitless mourn to him that cannot hear.

fruitlessly *adv.* L16. **fruitlessness** *n.* E17.

fruitlet /ˈfruːtlɪt/ *n.* L19. [f. FRUIT *n.* + -LET.] A small fruit; (*Bot.*) a single member of an aggregate fruit.

fruity /ˈfruːti/ *a.* M17. [f. FRUIT *n.* + -Y[1].] **1** Of, relating to, or resembling fruit. M17. **2** Of wine: tasting of the fresh grape. M19. **3** *fig.* Full of rich quality; *esp.*: (of language) unduly strong; (of a story etc.) full of (usu. scandalous) interest or suggestion; (of the voice) mellow and deep, plummy. *colloq.* E20.

fruitily *adv.* E20. **fruitiness** *n.* M19.

frum /frʊm/ *a.* Also **froom**. L19. [Yiddish f. MHG *vrum* zealous (G *fromm* pious).] Esp. of a Jew: pious, religious, orthodox.

frumentaceous /fruːm(ə)nˈteɪʃəs/ *a.* *rare*. M17. [f. late L *frumentaceus*, f. L *frumentum*: see next, -ACEOUS.] Of the nature of or resembling wheat or other cereal plants.

frumentarious /fruːm(ə)nˈtɛːrɪəs/ *a.* *rare*. L17. [f. L *frumentarius*, f. L *frumentum* corn: see -ARIOUS.] Of or pertaining to corn.

frumentation /fruːm(ə)nˈteɪʃ(ə)n/ *n.* E17. [L *frumentatio(n-)*, f. *frumentat-* pa. ppl stem of *frumentari* provide with corn, f. *frumentum*: see next, -ATION.] *Rom. Hist.* A general charitable distribution of corn.

frumenty /ˈfruːm(ə)nti/ *n.* Also **furmety** /ˈfəːmɪti/. LME. [OFr. *frumentee*, *four-*, f. *frument*, *fourment* (mod. *froment* wheat) f. L *frumentum* corn: see -Y[5].] A dish made of hulled wheat boiled in milk and seasoned with cinnamon, sugar, etc.

frumious /ˈfruːmɪəs/ *a.* *joc.* *colloq.* L19. [Nonsense wd invented by Lewis Carroll.] Angrily ferocious. Cf. BANDERSNATCH.

†**frummagemed** *pa. pple* & *ppl a.* *slang*. L17–M19. [Origin unkn.] Choked, strangled, hanged.

frump /frʌmp/ *n.* M16. [Prob. shortening of FRUMPLE.] **1** A mocking speech or action; a snort, a sneer. *obs.* exc. *dial.* M16. **2** A derisive deception, a hoax. *obs.* exc. *dial.* L16. **3** In *pl.* Sulks, ill humour. *obs.* exc. *dial.* M17. **4** An old-fashioned dowdily-dressed, (orig.) ill-tempered woman or (rarely) man. E19.

4 M. FORSTER She looked like a middle-aged frump, even when she was young.

frump /frʌmp/ *v.* M16. [f. as prec.] †**1** *v.i.* Scoff, mock (*at*). M16–M19. **2** *v.t.* Mock, taunt, insult, snub. *obs.* exc. *dial.* L16. **3** *v.t.* Annoy, irritate. M19.

frumper *n.* L16.

frumpish /ˈfrʌmpɪʃ/ *a.* M17. [f. FRUMP *n.* + -ISH[1].] **1** Disposed to sneer, mocking; bad-tempered, cross. Now *rare*. M17. **2** Like a frump; characteristic of a frump; dowdy and old-fashioned. M19.

frumpishly *adv.* E20. **frumpishness** *n.* L19.

frumple /ˈfrʌmp(ə)l/ *v.* & *n.* LME. [f. MDu. *verrompelen*, f. *ver-* FOR-[1] + *rompelen* RUMPLE *v.*] **A** *v.t.* Wrinkle, crumple. Long *obs.* exc. *dial.* LME. †**B** *n.* A wrinkle. LME–L15.

frumpy /ˈfrʌmpi/ *a.* M18. [f. FRUMP *n.* + -Y[1].] **1** Bad-tempered, irritable. Now *rare*. M18. **2** Dowdy and old-fashioned. M19.

frumpily *adv.* M20. **frumpiness** *n.* E20.

frusemide /ˈfruːsəmʌɪd/ *n.* Also (chiefly *US*) **furosemide** /fjʊəˈrɒsəmʌɪd/. M20. [f. *fru-* alt. of FUR(YL + *sem-* of unkn. origin + -IDE.] *Pharm.* A strong diuretic, $C_{12}H_{11}ClN_2O_5S$, used esp. in the treatment of oedema.

frush /frʌʃ/ *n.*[1] Now only *Sc.* (*rare*). LME. [OFr. *fruis*, *frois*, f. *fruissier*, *froissier*: see FRUSH *v.*] †**1** A charge, a collision. LME–M16. **2** The noise of a crash, crashing. LME. **3** *collect.* Fragments, splinters. LME.

frushy *a.* brittle, fragile E17.

frush /frʌʃ/ *n.*[2] *obs.* exc. *dial.* M16. [Perh. f. Fr. *fourchette* (see FROG *n.*[2]), but cf. Norw., WFris. *frosk* in same sense.] The frog of a horse's foot. Also (*running frush*), the disease thrush which affects this.

frush /frʌʃ/ *a.* *Sc.* & *north.* E18. [Perh. f. the vb, but cf. FROUGH.] **1** Not firm in substance; soft; crumbly. E18. **2** Brittle, fragile. L18.

frush /frʌʃ/ *v.* ME. [OFr. *fruissier*, *froissier* (mod. *froisser*) f. pop.L, f. L FRUSTUM.] **1** *v.t.* Strike violently so as to injure or damage. *obs.* exc. *dial.* ME. **2** *v.i.* Rush violently (*in*, *out*, *together*). *obs.* exc. *dial.* LME. **3** *v.t.* Rub vigorously, scratch. *obs.* exc. *dial.* LME. †**4** *v.t.* Carve (a chicken); dress (a chub). LME–L18. †**5** *v.i.* Break, snap; become crushed. L15–M17. **6** *v.t.* Straighten, set upright (the feathers of an arrow). *obs.* exc. *Hist.* M16.

†**frust** *n.* M18–E19. [L FRUSTUM.] A fragment.

frusta *n.pl.* see FRUSTUM.

frustrable /ˈfrʌstrəb(ə)l/ *a.* *rare*. L16. [Late L *frustrabilis*, f. L *frustrari*: see FRUSTRATE *v.*, -ABLE.] Able to be frustrated or foiled.

†frustraneous *a.* M17–L18. [f. mod.L *frustraneus* (f. *frustra* in vain, after L *extraneus*) + -OUS.] Vain, ineffectual, unprofitable.

frustrate /ˈfrʌstreɪt/ *ppl a.* & *n.* L15. [L *frustratus* pa. pple of *frustrari*: see next, -ATE².] A *ppl a. arch.* 1 †a *Law.* Null, invalid. L15–M17. b *gen.* Ineffectual, fruitless, unavailing. E16. †2 Idle, pointless. E–M16. 3 †a Balked (*of*). M16–E18. b Deprived or destitute *of.* L16. 4 Of a hope, purpose, etc.: disappointed, defeated, futile. L16. B *n.* A frustrated, disappointed, or ineffective person. M20.

frustrate /frʌˈstreɪt, ˈfrʌ-/ *v.t.* Pa. pple **frustrated, †frustrate**. LME. [L *frustrat-* pa. ppl stem of *frustrari*, f. *frustra* in vain: see -ATE³.] 1 Balk, disappoint (a person). Now also, make discontented through inability to achieve one's desires (material, spiritual, or sexual) (esp. as *frustrated* pa. pple & ppl a.). Now *rarely* foll. by *of* (a desired object). LME. 2 Make ineffectual; counteract; disappoint (a hope, an expectation); foil (a plan). LME. b *Law.* Annul, invalidate. Now *esp.*, cause (a contract) to be terminated prematurely (see FRUSTRATION). E16.

1 W. DAMPIER Being frustrated of getting over the River. D. ATHILL On the threshold of anything promising he is always frustrated by disaster apparently beyond his control. R. F. HOBSON Feeling frustrated by this apparently insoluble problem. 2 L. STRACHEY The French intrigue must be frustrated at all hazards. W. S. CHURCHILL His hopes of invading England . . with French assistance were frustrated. E. MUIR These things we know and . . Either frustrate or . . endure. H. CARPENTER Her hopes of frustrating Meg's romance.

frustratedly *adv.* in a frustrated manner, through frustration L20. **frustrater** *n.* L17. **frustratingly** *adv.* in a frustrating manner, so as to cause frustration M20. **ˈfrustrative** *a.* tending to frustrate L15. **†frustratory** *a.* tending to frustrate L15–E18.

frustration /frʌˈstreɪʃ(ə)n/ *n.* M16. [L *frustratio(n-)*, f. as prec.: see -ATION.] The action or an instance of frustrating; the state of being frustrated; discontent arising from inability to achieve one's aims; *spec.* in *Law*, the premature termination of a contract by circumstances that make performance as envisaged by the terms of the contract impossible.

G. GROTE Aristeides ascribes the frustration of this attack to the valour of two . . generals. R. LINDNER The total frustration of his deepest affectional needs produced an emotionally starved individual. L. VAN DER POST When once more . . we found our way blocked . . , the sense of frustration was more than some of us could bear. S. HILL Almost in tears at the frustration of finding nothing he desired to buy.

frustrum *n.* var. of FRUSTUM.

†frustula *n.* pl. of FRUSTULUM.

frustule /ˈfrʌstjuːl/ *n.* M19. [L *frustulum* dim. of FRUSTUM: see -ULE.] *Bot.* The silicified cell wall of a diatom (with or without its contents), which consists of two valves or overlapping halves.

†frustulum *n.* Pl. **-la**. Only in 18. [L: see prec.] A small frustum.

frustum /ˈfrʌstəm/ *n.* Pl. **-tums, -ta** /-tə/. Also **frustrum** /ˈfrʌstrəm/. M17. [L = piece cut off.] 1 *Math.* The portion of a solid figure which remains after the upper part has been cut off by a plane parallel to the base, or which is intercepted between two planes. M17. 2 *gen.* A fragment or portion. *rare.* E18.

frutescent /frʊˈtɛs(ə)nt/ *a.* E18. [Irreg. f. as next + -ESCENT. Cf. med.L *frutescere* become shrubby.] *Bot.* Becoming shrubby; having the appearance or habit of a shrub.

frutescence *n.* shrubbiness L19.

frutex /ˈfruːtɛks/ *n.* Pl. **frutices** /ˈfruːtɪsiːz/. M17. [L.] *Bot.* A woody plant smaller than a tree; a shrub.

fruticetum /fruːtɪˈsiːtəm/ *n.* M19. [L = a place full of shrubs or bushes, f. as prec.] A collection of shrubs. Cf. ARBORETUM.

fruticose /ˈfruːtɪkəʊs/ *a.* M17. [L *fruticosus*, f. *frutic-* FRUTEX: see -OSE¹.] 1 *Bot.* Of the nature of a shrub; woody-stemmed. M17. 2 Resembling a shrub in appearance or manner of growth; *spec.* (of a lichen) having upright or pendulous branching thalli. E19.

fruz /frʌz/ *v.t. obs.* exc. *dial.* Infl. **-zz-**. E18. [Symbolic.] Spread out (hair) in a frizzy mass; ruffle.

fry /fraɪ/ *n.*¹ ME. [ON *frjó* = Goth. *fraiw*, of unkn. origin.] 1 *collect.* Young fish just produced from the spawn; *spec.* (more fully *salmon fry*) the young of salmon in their first year. ME. b The young of other creatures produced in very large numbers. L16. 2 Offspring, seed, young (of human beings); a man's children or family. (Cf. sense 4 below.) *obs.* exc. *dial.* LME. 3 The roe of a fish. LME. 4 Chiefly as *small fry*. The smaller kinds of fish or other animals; young or insignificant people (collectively or in a body); small or insignificant objects. L16.

1 *Coarse Fishing* Nearly all fry perish before growing beyond about . . 5 in. 4 N. COX We bring out not onely Pike and Carp, but lesser Fry. HOR. WALPOLE We have burned two frigates, and a hundred and twenty small fry. M. HUNTER My sister was still the oldest child there—which made the rest of us pretty small fry.

fry /fraɪ/ *n.*² M17. [f. the vb.] 1 (A dish of) food cooked by frying. M17. b Any of various internal parts of animals usu. eaten fried, esp. *lamb's fry* (see LAMB *n.*). L18. c More fully *French fry*. A (fried) potato chip. Usu. in *pl.* Chiefly *N. Amer.* E20. 2 †a Excessive heat. Only in M17. b The frying of a meal, a fry-up; *esp.* (*US*) a social gathering at which fried food is eaten. E19.

fry /fraɪ/ *v.* Pa. t. & pple **fried** /fraɪd/. ME. [(O)Fr. *frire* f. L *frigere*, cogn. w. Gk *phrugein*, Skt *bhṛjjati* grill.] 1 *v.t.* & *i.* Cook or undergo cooking in hot fat, usu. in a shallow pan. ME. 2 *v.t.* & *i. transf.* & *fig.* Burn or overheat, esp. with effects analogous to those of frying food; frizzle, scorch (freq. *hyperbol.*, of the sun). Also, torture or be tortured by fire. LME. b Execute or be executed in the electric chair. *US slang.* E20. †3 *v.i.* Boil, seethe, ferment, simmer. L16–L17.

1 V. S. PRITCHETT He . . cracked eggs, got breadcrumbs and soon fried one of his wonderful fish suppers. *deep-fried, -frying*: see DEEP *adv.* **†fry in one's own grease** be burnt alive; be tormented by one's own passions; suffer the consequences of one's own folly. **fry up** heat or reheat in a frying-pan. *have other fish to fry*: see FISH *n.*¹ 2 JONSON Earth and seas in fire and flame shall fry. SMOLLETT My uncle, frying with vexation. 3 SPENSER Ye might have seene the frothy billowes fry Vnder the ship.

Comb.: **frying-pan** a shallow pan in which food is fried (*out of the frying-pan into the fire*: see PAN *n.*¹); **fry-pan** = *frying-pan* above; **fry-up** a dish of fried food, *esp.* of cold food heated up in a frying-pan; the preparation of such a dish.

fryer /ˈfraɪə/ *n.* Also **frier**. M19. [f. prec. + -ER¹.] 1 A person who fries food, esp. fish, a vessel used in frying. M19. 2 A fish, chicken, etc., for frying. M19.

†fuants *n.pl.* var. of FIANTS.

fub /fʌb/ *n. obs.* exc. *dial.* Also **fubb, fubs** /-z/. E17. [Perh. a blending of *fat* and *chub*: cf. FUBSY.] 1 A small chubby person. E17. 2 Refuse wool. Also, long withered grass. E19.

fubby *a.* (*rare*) = FUBSY L18.

fubar /ˈfuːbɑː/ *a. US slang* (orig. *Mil.*). M20. [Acronym, f. *f*ouled (or *f*ucked) *u*p *b*eyond *a*ll *r*ecognition.] Ruined, spoiled, disastrously bungled.

fubsy /ˈfʌbzi/ *a. colloq.* L18. [f. prec.: see -SY.] Fat and squat. Also *fig.*, stuffy, old-fashioned.

Times Lit. Suppl. A fubsy disinclination to contemplate any kind of change.

fucate /ˈfjuːkeɪt/ *a.* Long *rare.* M16. [L *fucatus* pa. pple of *fucare* to colour, paint, dye, f. FUCUS: see -ATE².] Artificially coloured or painted; *fig.* falsified, disguised.

fuˈcated *a.* = FUCATE M16. **†fucation** *n.* (*rare*) (*a*) the action of painting the face; (*b*) counterfeiting: E17–E18.

fuchsia /ˈfjuːʃə/ *n.* L18. [mod.L, f. Leonhard *Fuchs* (1501–66), Ger. botanist: see -IA¹.] 1 Any of various ornamental shrubs of the chiefly S. American genus *Fuchsia*, of the willowherb family, having drooping flowers freq. with purple-red sepals and perigynous tube. L18. 2 A shade of red like that of the fuchsia flower. E20.

native fuchsia *Austral.* any of various shrubs, esp. of the genus *Correa* (of the rue family), with flowers resembling the fuchsia.

fuchsine /ˈfuːksiːn/ *n.* Also **-in** /-ɪn/. M19. [f. G *Fuchs* fox tr. Fr. *Renard*, name of the chemical company by which this product was first produced commercially + -INE⁵.] An aniline dye, a hydrochloride of rosaniline or pararosaniline, which forms green crystals but dissolves in water to form a deep-red solution and is used esp. as a biological stain; = MAGENTA *n.*

fuchsinophil /fʊkˈsɪnəfɪl/ *a.* Also **-phile** /-faɪl/. E20. [f. prec. + -O- + -PHIL.] *Biol.* Readily stained with fuchsine; produced by staining with fuchsine.

fuchsinoˈphilia *n.* affinity for fuchsine M20. **fuchsinoˈphilic** *a.* = FUCHSINOPHIL M20.

fuchsite /ˈfʊksaɪt/ *n.* M19. [f. J. N. von *Fuchs* (1774–1856), Ger. mineralogist + -ITE¹.] *Min.* A green chromium-containing variety of muscovite.

fuci *n.* pl. of FUCUS.

fuck /fʌk/ *n. coarse slang.* L17. [f. the vb.] 1 An act of copulation. L17. 2 A person, esp. a woman, considered in sexual terms or as a sexual partner. Also = FUCKER (b). L19. 3 The slightest amount (esp. in *not care* (or *give*) *a fuck*). Also in other phrs. as a meaningless intensifier. E20.

1 E. J. HOWARD Eat well, don't smoke, and a fuck was equal to a five-mile walk. 2 D. MAMET Don't get smart with me, you young fuck. 3 D. HOLBROOK Driver speed up. Come on, for fuck's sake. J. DIDION What in fuck am I supposed to do? P. CAREY How in the fuck is it that you don't know how to make a decent omelette?

fuck /fʌk/ *v. coarse slang.* E16. [Origin unkn.] 1 *v.i.* Copulate. E16. 2 *v.t.* Copulate with. L17. b Ruin, spoil; exhaust, wear out. M20. 3 *v.t.* & *i.* In imprecations and exclamations, freq. in imperative or optative form, expr. anger, hatred, irritation, etc.; damn, curse. Cf. DAMN *v.* 3, 3b. E20.

1 S. CONRAN Serge . . moved . . into the next-door room where he lived, ate and fucked. 2b A. BEATTIE 'Everything's fucked. . . What does it matter the way things *should* be?' 3 J. DIDION 'Oh fuck it,' she says then, and tears run down her cheeks. A. FUGARD Fuck legends. Me? . . I live my life here!

Phrases, & with advs. in specialized senses: **fuck about, around** fool about, mess about. **fuck off** go away, make off, (usu. in *imper.*). **fuck up** (*a*) ruin, spoil, mess up; disturb emotionally; (*b*) blunder, fail, make a serious error.

Comb.: **fuck-up** a mess, a disastrously bungled matter.

fucker *n.* (*a*) a person who copulates; (*b*) used as a general term of abuse: L16. **fucking** *ppl a.* & *adv.* (*a*) *ppl a.* (*lit.*) that copulates; (*b*) *ppl a.* & *adv.* (*fig.*) used as an intensifier: M16.

fucoid /ˈfjuːkɔɪd/ *a.* & *n.* M19. [f. FUCUS + -OID.] A *adj.* Of the nature of or resembling a seaweed, *spec.* any of the brown seaweeds of the order Fucales, exemplified by bladderwrack (genus *Fucus*); of or relating to such seaweeds. M19. B *n.* A seaweed of the order Fucales; a similar fossil marine plant. M19.

fuˈcoidal *a.* M19.

fucoxanthin /fjuːkəˈzanθɪn/ *n.* L19. [f. FUCUS + -O- + XANTHIN.] *Chem.* A brown carotenoid pigment occurring in and generally characteristic of the brown algae.

fucus /ˈfjuːkəs/ *n.* Pl. **fuci** /ˈfjuːsaɪ/. E17. [L *fucus* rock-lichen, red dye or cosmetic f. Gk *phukos* seaweed.] †1 Paint or make-up for beautifying the skin; a wash or colouring for the face. E17–M18. 2 A seaweed with leathery fronds: now *spec.* a member of the genus *Fucus*, e.g. bladderwrack, *F. vesiculosus*. E18.

fucused *a.* (long *rare*) beautified with paint, made-up L17.

fud /fʌd/ *n.*¹ *Sc.* & *north.* E18. [Origin unkn.] 1 The buttocks. E18. 2 The tail or scut of a rabbit, hare, or other animal. E18.

fud /fʌd/ *n.*² *slang* (chiefly *US*). M20. [Abbrev.] = FUDDY-DUDDY *n.*

fuddle /ˈfʌd(ə)l/ *n. slang.* L17. [f. the vb.] †1 Drink, liquor, booze. L17–E18. 2 Intoxication, drunkenness. M18. 3 Confusion, muddled state. E19. 4 A drinking-bout. E19.

3 T. E. WEBB He rushed about—Vain was his frenzied fuddle. 4 **on the fuddle** out on a prolonged spell of drinking.

fuddle /ˈfʌd(ə)l/ *v.* L16. [Origin unkn.] 1 *v.i.* Have a drinking-bout; tipple, booze. L16. 2 *v.t.* Intoxicate; confuse with drink or a drug. E17. 3 *v.t.* Stupefy, muddle, confuse. E17.

2 E. WAUGH I went to luncheon ... and drank enough wine to fuddle me slightly. P. LIVELY She had lain fuddled still from the sleeping pills. **fuddle one's cap** or **nose** get drunk. 3 S. COWPER He was quite fuddled with joy.

fuddler *n.* (now *rare*) a person who fuddles, a tippler L17.

fuddy-duddy /ˈfʌdɪdʌdi/ *n.* & *a. slang.* Also **fuddydud**. E20. [Origin unkn.] A *n.* An old-fashioned person; an ineffectual old fogy. E20.

Woman's Realm I work with fashionable young women, .. so I don't want to appear an old fuddy-duddy.

B *adj.* Old-fashioned, ineffectual, stuffy. E20.

Q. CRISP We must chart a course between the fuddy-duddy strictures of yesterday and the hapless chaos of today.

fudge /fʌdʒ/ *n.* L18. [f. the vb or int.] 1 Nonsense. L18. 2 A made-up story, a deception. Now *esp.* a putting together or patching up (esp. of facts or information) in a clumsy or underhand manner. L18. 3 An item inserted in a newspaper page, *esp.* a piece of late news. L19. 4 A soft crumbly or chewy kind of confectionery, made from milk, sugar, butter, etc. L19.

2 *Listener* A new way of settling disputes .. with the arbitrator resisting the usual fudge. 4 *attrib.*: V. NABOKOV Gooey fudge sundaes, musicals, movie magazines .. were .. on her list of beloved things.

fudge /fʌdʒ/ *v.* E17. [Perh. alt. of earlier FADGE *v.*] 1 *v.i.* Fit in with what is anticipated; turn out, result. Also, merge together. E17. 2 *v.t.* Put together, make up, or patch in a clumsy, makeshift, or underhand way; deal with incompetently. Often foll. by *up*. L17. b Thrust or force *in* awkwardly or irrelevantly; put or get *in* underhandedly. L18. 3 *v.i.* Talk nonsense. *rare.* M19. 4 *v.i.* Gloss over discrepancies or difficulties; prevaricate, temporize. L20.

1 SIR W. SCOTT We will see how the matter fudges. P. D. JAMES She saw the drab blacks and grays of the marching army fudge, dissolve. 2 J. I. M. STEWART A stupid question, fudged up by a tired examiner. H. WILSON Without fudging an issue on which a clear decision has to be reached. L. KENNEDY He had been caught fudging the books. b T. HEALD The public schools can fudge their pupils into Oxford and Cambridge.

fudgy *a.* (*a*) irritable, uneasy; (*b*) *US* botched, bungling: E19.

fudge /fʌdʒ/ *int.* M18. [f. the vb.] Nonsense! Rubbish!

Fuegian /fʊˈɪdʒɪən, ˈfweɪdʒɪən, -g-/ *a.* & *n.* E19. [f. (Sp.) Tierra del *Fuego* (see below), lit. 'land of fire' + -IAN.] A *adj.* Of or pertaining to Tierra del Fuego, (the largest island in) an archipelago at the southernmost tip of S. America, or its inhabitants. E19. B *n.* A member of an American Indian people inhabiting Tierra del Fuego. E19.

fuehrer *n.* var. of FÜHRER.

fuel /fjʊəl, ˈfjuːəl/ *n.* ME. [AN *fuaille*, *fewaile*, OFr. *fouaille* f. Proto-Romance, f. L *focus* hearth, (in late L) fire.] 1 Material for burning; combustible matter as used for fire, or as a source of heat or power. ME. b With *a* and *pl.*: a kind of fuel, as wood, coal, oil, etc. E17. 2 *fig.* Anything that sustains or inflames passion, excitement, etc. L16. 3 Food, or the constituents of food, as a source of energy. L19. 4 *spec.* a A liquid or other material which provides the power in an internal-combustion engine. L19. b A material which reacts with an oxidizer to produce thrust in a rocket engine. E20. c A material which reacts with an oxidizer to produce electricity in a fuel cell. E20. d A radioactive material used as a source of nuclear energy. M20.

1 SWIFT Dry grass and sea-weed, which I intended for feuel. b *white fuel*: see WHITE *a.* 2 A. BAIN Difficulty adds fuel to the flame. 3 L. J. BOGERT Calorie values are especially useful in thinking .. of food as body fuel.

Comb.: **fuel cell** a primary cell producing electric current direct from a chemical reaction between continuously-supplied materials; **fuel element** an assemblage of nuclear fuel and other materials for use in a reactor; *esp.* = *fuel rod* below; **fuel food**: that is rich in fats or carbohydrates and provides the body with energy; **fuel gauge** a meter indicating the quantity of fuel in a tank; *fuel injected, injection, injector*: see INJECTED, INJECTION, INJECTOR; *fuel rod*: see ROD *n.* 8b; **fuel-value** (*a*) the value of a combustible article as fuel; (*b*) the amount of energy available from (a quantity of) food.

fuelless /-l-l-/ *a.* L19.

fuel /fjʊəl, ˈfjuːəl/ *v.* Infl. **-ll-**, ***-l-**. L16. [f. the n.] 1 *v.t.* Provide or supply with fuel. L16. 2 *v.i.* Get or take in fuel. L19.

1 *City Limits* Fuelled by a rather transparent cynicism, the story speeds on to a finale. P. D. JAMES The craft would be fuelled and ready for sea. 2 *Successful Slimming* They have fuelled up with a couple of Mars Bars.

fueller *n.* (*a*) a person who or thing which supplies fuel; †(*b*) a domestic responsible for making the fires: LME.

fuff /fʌf/ *v.*, *n.*, & *int.* Chiefly *Sc.* & *dial.* E16. [Imit. Cf. FAFFLE *v.*] A *v.* 1 *v.i.* Puff. E16. 2 *v.i.* Of an animal, esp. a cat: spit. L17. 3 *v.t.* Puff (a tobacco-pipe). L18. B *n.* 1 A puff of wind; the spit of a cat; a whiff. M16. 2 A burst of ill temper. E19. C *int.* An exclamation in imitation of a sound, or expr. contempt. L18.

fuffle /ˈfʌf(ə)l/ *v.t.* *Sc.* *rare.* M16. [Imit.] Throw into disorder; jerk about; hustle.

fufu *n.* var. of FOO-FOO.

fug /fʌg/ *n.* & *v.* *colloq.* Orig. *dial.* & *School slang.* L19. [Origin unkn.] A *n.* A thick, stuffy, smelly atmosphere, *esp.* that of a crowded poorly-ventilated room. L19.

K. HULME In this fug of smoke and turpentine, who could sleep? *New Yorker* The warm, beery fug of the restaurant.

B *v.i.* Infl. **-gg-**. Stay in a stuffy atmosphere. Also foll. by *up*. L19.

fugged *ppl a.* (of a room or atmosphere) stuffy, thick L20. **fuggy** *a.* (of a room or atmosphere) warm, stuffy, and smelly, through lack of ventilation; (of a person) that lives in or enjoys such an atmosphere: L19.

fugacious /fjʊˈgeɪʃəs/ *a.* M17. [f. L *fugax*, *fugac-*, f. *fugere* flee: see -ACIOUS.] 1 Apt to flee away or flit; fleeting, transient, evanescent. M17. b Of a substance: volatile. L17. 2 *Bot.* & *Zool.* Falling or fading early; soon cast off. M18.

1 H. MARTINEAU The fugacious nature of life and time. 2 G. WHITE A single rose-like fugacious flower.

fugaciously *adv.* E19. **fugaciousness** *n.* M17.

fugacity /fjʊˈgasɪti/ *n.* E17. [f. as prec. + -ITY.] 1 The quality of being fugacious; instability; transitoriness; volatility. E17. 2 *Physics.* A thermodynamic property of a (real) gas which if substituted for the pressure or partial pressure in the equations for an ideal gas gives equations applicable to the real gas; an analogous property of a solid or liquid derived using equations of the same form. E20.

fugal /ˈfjuːg(ə)l/ *a.* M19. [f. FUGUE + -AL¹.] 1 *Mus.* Of the nature of or characteristic of a fugue or fugues. M19. 2 *Psychiatry.* Of the nature of a fugue; marked by fugues. M20.

1 A. HOPKINS A skilful alternation of fugal sections with more openly dramatic chordal writing. 2 O. SACKS An element of hysterical or fugal amnesia.

fugally *adv.* L19.

fugato /fjuːˈgɑːtəʊ, fuː-/ *adv.*, *a.*, & *n.* M19. [It. = fugued, f. *fuga* FUGUE.] *Mus.* A *adv.* & *adj.* In the fugue style, but not in strict or complete fugue form. M19. B *n.* Pl. **-os**. A passage in this style. L19.

-fuge /fjuːdʒ/ *suff.* [f. or after mod.L *-fugus*, f. L *fugare* put to flight.] Forming ns. and adjs. w. the sense '(an agent) that dispels or expels', as *febrifuge*, *vermifuge*.

fuggle /ˈfʌg(ə)l/ *n.* Also **fuggles** /-z/. L19. [Origin unkn.] A variety of hops used in beer making.

fughetta /fjuːˈgɛtə/ *n.* L19. [It., dim. of *fuga* FUGUE.] *Mus.* A short condensed fugue.

fugie /ˈf(j)uːdʒi/ *n.* *Sc. obs.* exc. *Hist.* L18. [Perh. f. L *fugae* in the law L phr. *in meditatione fugae* contemplating flight.] A cock that refuses to fight; a runaway; a coward.

Comb.: **fugie-warrant**: granted against a debtor, on sworn information that he or she intends to flee.

fugitate /ˈfjuːdʒɪteɪt/ *v.* M17. [Sense 1 f. next; sense 2 f. L *fugitat-* stem of *fugitare*, f. *fugere* flee: see -ATE³.] 1 *v.t.* *Sc. Law.* Declare fugitive, outlaw. M17. 2 *v.i.* Run away. *rare.* M19.

fugiˈtation *n.* (*a*) *Sc. Law* a judicial declaration of outlawry and its associated penalties; (*b*) the action of fleeing: M18.

fugitive /ˈfjuːdʒɪtɪv/ *a.* & *n.* LME. [(O)Fr. *fugitif*, *-ive* f. L *fugitivus*, f. *fugit-* pa. ppl stem of *fugere* flee: see -IVE.] A *adj.* 1 That has taken flight, esp. from duty, justice, an enemy, or a master. LME. b Apt or tending to flee; running away. E17. †2 Driven out, banished, exiled. LME–L16. 3 Moving from place to place; flitting, vagrant. Also *fig.*, fickle. LME. 4 Evanescent, fleeting, of short duration; (of an impression, colour, etc.) quickly fading. LME. b Of a substance: volatile. *rare.* M17. c = FUGACIOUS 2. *rare.* M19. 5 Of literature: of passing interest, ephemeral, occasional. M18.

1 E. KIRKE A Union officer refused to return a fugitive slave. W. DE LA MARE Betrayed and fugitive, I still must roam. 4 L. DURRELL Their appearances were fugitive and had the air of being illusory. 5 J. I. M. STEWART A pile of .. fugitive magazines concerned with theatrical affairs.

B *n.* 1 A person who flees or tries to escape from danger, an enemy, justice, a master, etc. LME. †b A deserter. M16–M17. c An exile, an outlaw. L16. 2 A person who or animal which shifts about or moves from place to place; a vagrant. L16. 3 Something transient, fleeting, or elusive. L17.

1 N. MONSARRAT These people were craven fugitives from war. c W. IRVING Fugitives from the Spanish and American frontiers. 2 J. CONRAD My other self, now gone from the ship .. to be a fugitive and a vagabond on the earth.

fugitively *adv.* (*rare*) M19. **fugitiveness** *n.* M17.

fugle /ˈfjuːg(ə)l/ *v.t.*¹ *arch.*, *dial.*, & *slang.* E18. [Origin unkn. See also HONEY-FUGGLE.] Cheat, trick.

fugle /ˈfjuːg(ə)l/ *v.*² M19. [Back-form. f. next.] 1 *v.i.* Do the duty of a fugleman (*lit.* & *fig.*); act as guide or director, signal. M19. 2 *v.t.* Exemplify, demonstrate. *rare.* M19.

fugleman /ˈfjuːg(ə)lmən/ *n.* Pl. **-men**. E19. [G *Flügelmann* flank-man, f. *Flügel* wing + *Mann* man.] 1 *Hist.* A well-drilled soldier placed in front of a regiment or company to demonstrate expert drilling etc. to the others. E19. 2 *transf.* & *fig.* A leader, organizer, or spokesman. E19.

fugu /ˈfuːguː/ *n.* M20. [Jap.] A puffer fish of the family Tetraodontidae, esp. as a Japanese delicacy.

fugue /fjuːg/ *n.* & *v.* L16. [Fr., or its source, It. *fuga* f. L *fuga* flight, rel. to *fugere* flee.] A *n.* 1 *Mus.* A polyphonic composition in which a short melodic theme, the subject, is introduced by one part or voice, and successively taken up by the others and developed by their interweaving. L16. 2 *Psychiatry.* A flight from or loss of the awareness of one's own identity, sometimes involving wandering away from home, and often occurring as a reaction to shock or emotional stress. E20.

1 **double fugue**: having two subjects each similarly treated. MIRROR *fugue.* 2 C. P. SNOW He was having fugues .. in which the bad news hadn't happened. *attrib.*: C. PRIEST The fugue state, .. like being in a continuous dream.

B *v.i.* *Mus.* Infl. **fuguing**, **fuging**. Compose or perform a fugue. L17.

fugued, **fuguing** *ppl adjs.* (*Mus.*) in the form of a fugue M19. **fuguist** *n.* (*Mus.*) a composer of fugues L18.

führer /ˈfjʊərə/ *n.* Also **fuehrer**. M20. [G *Führer* leader. Hitler's full title was *Führer und Reichskanzler.*] A (ruthless or tyrannical) leader; spec. *the Führer*, a title assumed by Hitler as leader of the German Reich.

Comb.: **führer principle** the principle that a führer

has the right to command and the people the duty to obey.

-ful /fʊl, f(ə)l/ *suff.* [f. FULL *a.*] 1 Forming adjs. Orig. used in composition with a preceding n. to form adjs. w. the sense 'full of or having,' as *beautiful*, *graceful*, or, in the 14th cent., w. the sense 'having the qualities of' as *masterful*, *powerful*. Later, in the 16th and 17th cents., forming adjs. from adjs. or L adj. stems with little change of meaning, as *direful*, *grateful* (perh. by analogy with older synonyms in *-ful*). In mod. Eng. forming adjs. from vb-stems w. the sense 'apt to, able to, accustomed to,' as *forgetful*, *mournful*, or occas. with passive force, as *bashful*. 2 Forming ns. (pl. **-fuls**, occas. **-sful**) w. the sense 'the amount that fills or would fill (a receptacle),' as *handful*, *mouthful*, *spoonful*.

Fulah /ˈfuːlə/ *n.* & *a.* Also **Foulah**, **Fula**. L18. [Cf. Fulfulde *pulo* Fulah person. Cf. FULBE, PEULH.] A *n.* Pl. **-s**, same. 1 A member of an African people who have tended to migrate eastwards over the centuries and who currently inhabit numerous African countries from Senegal to Sudan. L18. 2 The language of this people, Fulfulde. M19. B *attrib.* or as *adj.* Of or pertaining to the Fulahs or their language. M19.

Fulani /fʊˈlɑːni/ *n.* & *a.* Pl. **-s**, same. M19. [Hausa.] = FULAH *n.* & *a.*; *spec.* of or pertaining to, a member of, the Fulahs of northern Nigeria and adjacent territories.

Fulbe /ˈfʊlbeɪ/ *n.* Pl. **-s**, same. E20. [Fulfulde = Fulah people.] = FULAH *n.* 1.

Fulbright /ˈfʊlbrʌɪt/ *n.* M20. [J. William *Fulbright* (1905–95), US Senator.] 1 In full *Fulbright award*. An award, scholarship, etc., granted under the terms of the Fulbright Act of 1946, by which it was agreed with foreign countries that the money gained from the sale by the US government of surplus war properties should be used to finance higher learning. M20. 2 In full *Fulbright professor*, *scholar*, etc. A person in receipt of such an award. M20.

†fulciment *n.* M17–L18. [L *fulcimentum*, f. *fulcire*: see FULCRUM, -MENT.] A prop or support; *spec.* a fulcrum.

fulcrate /ˈfʌlkreɪt/ *a.* Now *rare* or *obs.* M18. [f. next + -ATE[2].] *Bot.* Supported by or having fulcra.

fulcrum /ˈfʊlkrəm, ˈfʌl-/ *n.* Pl. **-cra** /-krə/, **-crums**. L17. [L = post or foot of a couch, f. base of *fulcire* prop up, support.] 1 A prop or support; now *spec.* the point against which a lever is placed to get purchase or on which it turns or is supported. L17. 2 *fig.* The means by which or central source from which influence etc. is brought to bear. L17. 3a *Bot.* In *pl.* The accessory organs or appendages of a plant. Now *rare* or *obs.* L18. b *Zool.* Any of certain anatomical structures having a central position or supporting function, *spec.*: (*a*) a chitinous framework enclosing the pharynx in dipteran flies; (*b*) in rotifers, the stem of the incus of the mastax. M19.

1 J. S. FOSTER If the projecting arm were . . extended over a support or fulcrum . . counter movement could be obtained. 2 C. MERIVALE The consulship was the fulcrum from which the whole Roman world was to be moved. O. SACKS The fulcrum of her family, giving it balance and power.

fulcral *a.* (*rare*) relating to or of the nature of a fulcrum or fulcra L19.

fulfil /fʊlˈfɪl/ *v.t.* Also ***fulfill**. Infl. **-ll-**. [Late OE *fullfyllan*, f. FULL *a.* + *fyllan* FILL *v.*] 1 Fill up, make full. *arch.* LOE. †b Spread through the whole extent of, pervade. LME–L16. †2 Provide fully with what is wished for; satisfy the appetite or desire of. ME–E17. 3 Make complete, supply with what is lacking; replace (something); compensate for (a defect). *arch.* ME. †4 Hold or occupy (a vacant position); take (the place of something). ME–M16. 5 Bring to consummation, carry out (a prophecy, promise, etc.); satisfy (a desire, prayer). ME. b *refl.* Work out one's destiny; develop one's gifts or character to the full. M19. 6 Carry out, perform, do (something prescribed); obey or follow (a command, the law, etc.). ME. †b Perform, accomplish (a deed). ME–L16. c Meet the requirements of, answer (a purpose); comply with (conditions). L18. 7 Bring to an end, finish, complete (a period of time, piece of work, etc.). ME.

1 SIR W. SCOTT I have never known knight more fulfilled of nobleness. 5 T. HARDY He had promised silence and absence, and had fulfilled his promise literally. E. BOWEN The weather . . was once more fulfilling the expectations of visitors. b F. WELDON Liffey . . did temporary work in offices . . but felt that such work could hardly . . fulfil her. 6 J. H. NEWMAN In what sense do we fulfil the words of Christ? G. VIDAL He fulfilled his historic function with wit and dignity. c M. GORDON People who fulfil minimum standards of home care. ANTHONY SMITH Two patients . . had survived after fulfilling the British criteria for brain death. 7 AV *2 Sam.* 7:12 And when thy dayes be fulfilled, and thou shalt sleepe with thy fathers.

fulfiller *n.* a person who fulfils LME. **fulfilling** *n.* the action of the vb; an instance of this; (*rare*) something that fulfils: ME. **fulfilment** *n.* the action or an act or process of fulfilling; accomplishment, performance, completion: L18.

Fulfulde /fʊlˈfʊldeɪ/ *n.* & *a.* M20. [Fulfulde.] (Of) the Niger-Congo language of the Fulahs.

fulgent /ˈfʌldʒ(ə)nt/ *a.* Now *poet.* & *rhet.* LME. [L *fulgent-* pres. ppl stem of *fulgere* shine: see -ENT.] Shining, brilliant, glittering, resplendent.

†fulgence *n.* = FULGENCY: LME–M17. **†fulgency** *n.* brightness, splendour M17–L18. **fulgently** *adv.* (*rare*) L19. **fulgentness** *n.* (*rare*) E18.

fulgid /ˈfʌldʒɪd/ *a.* M17. [L *fulgidus*, f. *fulgere* shine: see -ID[1].] Flashing, glittering, shining.

fulgor /ˈfʌlgɔː, -gə/ *n. arch.* Also **fulgour**. M16. [L, f. *fulgere*: see prec., -OR.] A brilliant or flashing light; dazzling brightness, splendour.

fulgorous *a.* (*rare*) flashing, brilliant L18.

fulgorid /ˈfʌlgərɪd/ *n.* & *a.* L19. [mod.L *Fulgoridae* (see below), f. *Fulgora* genus name f. L = the goddess of lightning, f. *fulgur* lightning: see -ID[3].] *Entomol.* A *n.* A homopteran insect of the family Fulgoridae, which includes the lantern-flies. L19. B *adj.* Of, pertaining to, or designating this family. E20.

fulgural /ˈfʌlgjʊr(ə)l/ *a. rare.* M17. [Fr. f. L *fulguralis*, f. *fulgur* lightning: see -AL[1].] Of or pertaining to lightning.

fulgurant /ˈfʌlgjʊr(ə)nt/ *a.* M17. [L *fulgurant-* pres. ppl stem of *fulgurare* lighten, flash, f. *fulgur* lightning: see -ANT[1].] Flashing like lightning.

fulgurantly *adv.* (*rare*) L19.

fulgurate /ˈfʌlgjʊreɪt/ *v.i.* L17. [L *fulgurat-* pa. ppl stem of *fulgurare*: see prec., -ATE[3].] Emit flashes like lightning.

fulgurating *ppl a.* flashing like lightning; (of pain) darting through the body: L17.

fulguration /fʌlgjʊˈreɪʃ(ə)n/ *n.* M17. [L *fulguratio(n-)* lightning, esp. sheet-lightning, f. *fulgurat-*: see prec., -ATION.] 1 The action of lightening or flashing like lightning; usu. in *pl.*, flashes of lightning. Now *rare.* M17. 2 In assaying, a brightening in the appearance of a molten metal when only a thin film of lead remains on its surface. *obs.* exc. *Hist.* L17. 3 *Med.* The destruction of tissue by means of diathermy. E20.

1 *fig.*: E. CAIRD The continual fulgurations of deity.

fulgurite /ˈfʌlgjʊrʌɪt/ *n.* M19. [f. L *fulgur* lightning + -ITE[1].] *Geol.* (A piece of) sand or other substance fused or vitrified by lightning.

fulgurous /ˈfʌlgjʊrəs/ *a.* E17. [f. L *fulgur* lightning + -OUS.] Resembling, full of, or charged with lightning.

Fulham /ˈfʊləm/ *n. arch. slang.* Also **f-**. E16. [Perh. f. *Fulham* in London, once a haunt of gamesters.] A die loaded to ensure either a high throw (*high Fulham*) or a low throw (*low Fulham*).

†fuliginated *a. rare.* M17–L18. [f. L *fuliginatus*, f. *fuligo* soot: see -ATE[2], -ED[1].] Of a sooty colour or appearance.

fuliginous /fjuːˈlɪdʒɪnəs/ *a.* L16. [Late L *fuliginosus*, f. *fuligo*, *fuligin-* soot: see -OUS.] †1 Of a vapour or exhalation: thick and noxious, and said to be formed by organic combustion. L16–E18. 2 Of, containing, or resembling soot; sooty. E17. b Covered or blackened with soot. Chiefly *joc.* M18. 3 Sooty-coloured, dusky. E19.

2 R. C. HUTCHINSON The fuliginous interior of a one-roomed timber house. *fig.*: CARLYLE A very fuliginous set of doctrines.

fuligiˈnosity *n.* the condition or quality of being fuliginous or sooty; (in *pl.*) sooty matter: M18. **fuliginously** *adv.* M18. **fuliginousness** *n.* (long *rare*) L16.

fuligo /fjuːˈlʌɪgəʊ/ *n.* Now *rare.* M17. [L.] Soot.

full /fʊl/ *a.*, *adv.*, & *n.* [OE *full* = OFris. *foll*, *full*, OS *ful* (Du. *vol*), OHG *foll* (G *voll*), ON *fullr*, Goth. *fulls*, f. Gmc, f. IE: cogn. w. Gk *polus*, L *plenus*.] A *adj.* 1 Containing all (*of* a substance) that its limits will allow; having no space empty, replete. OE. b *postpositive.* = -FUL 2. Now *rare.* OE. c Of the heart etc.: overcharged with emotion, ready to overflow. ME. †d Of an office: occupied, not vacant. Foll. by *of*. L16–M18. †e Having the outline filled in; solid. L16–E18. f Of an animal: pregnant. Of a fish: containing roe. E17. 2 Foll. by *of*: holding or having plenty of; crowded with; containing many or much, characterized by. OE. b Having sufficient or ample for one's needs; wealthy. Long *obs.* exc. *dial.* L16. 3 Having eaten or drunk to repletion. *arch.* or *colloq.* OE. b Having had plenty *of*. Now only in biblical phrs. *full of years*, *honours*, *children*, etc. ME. c Sated, weary *of*. Freq. foll. by *up*. Now *Austral.* & *NZ slang.* ME. d Drunk. *slang* (chiefly *Sc.*, *Austral.*, *US*). M16. 4 Abundant, sufficient, copious, satisfying. OE. b Of a report etc.: complete, detailed. M17. 5 Complete, entire, perfect. OE. b Answering in every respect to a description; having all the qualifications or privileges of a designation. OE. †c Of a friend or enemy: avowed, wholehearted. OE–LME. 6 Reaching the specified or usual limit; whole. OE. b At or to the greatest degree or extent. LME. c Of an assembly: having all or most of its members present. M16. 7 Having a rounded outline; large, swelling, plump. OE. b Of a garment: amply cut; containing much material arranged in gathers or folds. L18. 8 Having or exerting great force; strong, vigorous. ME. b Of light: intense. Of colour: deep, rich, intense. Of sound: strong, resonant. Of flavour: rich, mellow. M17. 9 *Naut.* Of a sail: filled with wind. Of a ship: having the sails filled with wind. LME. 10 Engrossed with, absorbed in; unable to stop thinking or talking *of*. E17.

1 I. MURDOCH The sink had been blocked for several days and was full of . . water. S. BECKETT The hotels were full or would not let me in. b W. FULKE An egges shell full of dew. c DEFOE His heart was so full, he could say no more. 2 J. CONRAD It . . seemed a living thing full of fury. A. MCCOWEN His . . house which was always full of interesting people. 3 G. W. DASENT They ate and drank . . and when they were all full, they made a raft. c M. FRANKLIN He averred he was 'full up of life under the old man's rule'. 4 R. W. CHURCH He turned his studies to full account. Z. N. HURSTON Those full, hot meals he had left back in Alabama. b E. E. KAY The audience are quite at liberty to take the fullest notes they like. 5 G. GREENE I've got a full set now of these Irish coins. W. TREVOR He was offering a full removal service. b T. PARKER I'd like to stay in and perhaps get as high as full corporal. 6 S. HEANEY Given heavy rain and sun For a full week, the blackberries would ripen. b M. MCCARTHY The trees were in full leaf. c W. WALLACE He . . kept the academic senate waiting for him in full conclave. 7 F. WELDON Her breasts were full and round beneath the old sweater. b J. BRAINE However full her skirt, Elspeth always gave the impression that it was inadequate. 8 F. MANN The pulse feels full and forceful. 10 H. BRACKEN So full of themselves, that they reject all wise Counsel. J. CONRAD The biggest thing in the town, and everybody I met was full of it.

Special collocations, phrases, & comb.: **at full length** (*a*) lying stretched out; (*b*) without abridgement. *come full circle*: see CIRCLE *n.* **full age** an age at which a person is considered to have the status of an adult. *full and by*: see BY *adv.* **full as a bull** or **goog** *Austral.* & *NZ slang* extremely drunk. *full as a tick*: see TICK *n.*[1] **full-back** (the position of) a defending player placed near the goal in various ball games. **full blood** (a person or animal of) pure breeding. **full-blooded** *a.* (*a*) purebred, not hybrid; (*b*) vigorous, forceful, hearty, sensual. **full-bloodedly** *adv.* in a full-blooded manner, forcefully. **full-bloodedness** the fact or quality of being full-blooded. **full board** (*a*) the provision of a bed and all meals at a hotel etc.; (*b*) *Austral.* & *NZ* a full complement of shearers on the board. **full-bodied** *a.* rich in quality, tone, etc. **full-bottom** a full-bottomed wig. **full-bottomed** *a.* (of a wig) long at the back. **full brother, sister**: born of the same father and mother. *full chisel*: see CHISEL *n.*[1] 1. **full-colour** *a.* all in colour; having the full range of colours. **full-cream** *a.* unskimmed, made from unskimmed milk. **full dress**: worn on ceremonial or formal occasions (*full-dress debate*, a formal debate in which important speeches are made; *full-dress uniform*, military uniform worn for ceremonial parades etc.). *full* EMPLOYMENT. *full growth*: see GROWTH *n.* **full hand** *Poker* a hand containing three of a kind plus a pair. **full-hearted** *a.* (*a*) zealous, confident, courageous; (*b*) full of feeling, emotional. **full-heartedly** *adv.* in a full-hearted manner. **full-heartedness** the quality of being full-hearted. **full house** (*a*) = *full hand* above; (*b*) the maximum or a large attendance in a theatre, in Parliament, etc. **full-length** *a.* not shortened or abbreviated; (of a mirror, portrait, etc.) showing the whole height of the human figure. *full lock*: see LOCK *n.*[2] 13. **full marks** the maximum award in an examination or assessment. **full measure** not less than the amount stated. **full moon** the moon with the whole disc illuminated; the time when this occurs. **full-mouthed** *a.* (*a*) (of cattle etc.) having a full set of adult teeth; (*b*) (of a dog) baying loudly; (*c*) (of oratory etc.) sonorous, vigorous; †(*d*) having the mouth full of food. *full nelson*: see NELSON *n.*[2] *full of beans*: see BEAN *n.* **full-page** *a.* taking up the entire page of a newspaper etc. **full pay** the amount allowed while on active service or actively employed. *full pelt*: see PELT *n.*[2] 3. **full pitch** *Cricket* (*a*) a ball pitched right up to the batsman; (*b*) *advb.* without the ball having touched the ground. **full point** = *full stop* (a) below. **full professor** (orig. *US*) a professor of the highest grade in a university etc. **full-scale** *a.* not reduced in size; complete. **full score** (*Mus.*) a score giving the parts for all performers on separate staves. *full sister*: see *full brother* above. **full speed** (or **steam**) **ahead** an order to proceed at maximum speed or to pursue a course of action energetically. **full stop** (*a*) a punctuation mark (.) to show the end of a sentence or abbreviation; (*b*) a complete cessation; (as *int.*) that's all, without qualification (cf. *period*). *full term*: see TERM *n.* *full tilt*: see TILT *n.*[2] **full time** (*a*) the total normal working hours; (*b*) the end of a football or other match. **full-time** *a.* occupying or using all one's working time. **full-timer** a worker or student attending for the whole working day. **full toss** = *full pitch* (a) above. **full up** filled to capacity; replete. *full vent*: see VENT *n.*[2] **full word** *Ling.* having a meaning in itself. *give full weight to*: see WEIGHT *n.* *have one's hands full*: see HAND *n.* *in full cry*: see CRY *n.* *in full feather*: see FEATHER *n.* *in full swing*: see SWING *n.*[1] **in full view** entirely visible. *on a full stomach*: see STOMACH *n.* *the full treatment*: see TREATMENT *n.* 6.

B *adv.* **1** Very, exceedingly. *arch.* or *poet.* exc. in *know full well*, be very well aware (of). OE. **2** Completely, entirely, fully; quite (*as*). Now usu. in *comb.* OE. **3a** With ref. to points of the compass: due. Now *rare* or *obs.* LME. **b** Of position and direction: exactly, directly, straight. L16.

1 MILTON The imperial ensign . . full high advanced, Shone like a meteor. T. GRAY Full many a gem of purest ray serene. 2 C. KINGSLEY He weighed full fifteen stone. G. M. TREVELYAN Small children were sometimes set to work . . at an age full as early as the factory children of later times. **full out** thoroughly, completely; *esp.* at full power or speed. 3b M. ROBERTS She turns right round and looks him full in the face.

Comb.: **full-blown** *a.* (*a*) of a flower: in full bloom; (*b*) full of wind, puffed out; *fig.* fully developed, complete; **full-fashioned** *a.* = *fully-fashioned* s.v. FULLY *adv.*; **full-fledged** *a.* = *fully-fledged* s.v. FULLY *adv.*; *full-frontal*: see FRONTAL *a.* 3; **full-grown** *a.* having attained full size or maturity, fully grown; **full-rigged** *a.* (of a ship having three or more masts) carrying square sails on all masts; **full-rigger** a full-rigged ship; *full-summed*: see SUMMED *a.* 1.

C *n.* **1** With *of*: the whole; the complete scope, entire range, sum total. *arch.* ME. **2** A sufficient amount; enough to fill a receptacle; one's fill. Now chiefly *dial.* ME. **3** The period, point, or state of the greatest fullness or strength; the height or middle of a month, season, etc. ME. **b** *The* period or state of complete illumination of the moon's disc. LME. †**4** A set (of pans or kettles). LME–M17. **5** In Kent: a ridge of shingle or sand pushed or cast up by the tide. M19. **6** A herring full of milt or roe; *crown full*, one of the best quality. L19.

1 J. H. NEWMAN With my opinions, to the full of which I dare not confess. 2 G. W. DASENT They had all stared their full. 3 BROWNING June was not over Though past the full.

Phrases: **at (the) full** †(*a*) completely, at full length, to the full extent; (*b*) at the position or in the state of fullness. *crown full*: see sense 6 above. **in (†the) full** at full length, unabridged; to the full amount or sum due. **to the full** completely, fully, quite.

full /fʊl/ *v.*[1]*t.* ME. [Prob. back-form. f. FULLER *n.*[1] infl. by (O)Fr. *fouler* or med.L *fullare*. Cf. FOIL *v.*[1]] †**1** Beat, trample down; destroy. ME–M17. **2** Orig., clean or thicken (cloth) by treading or beating. Now, clean, shrink, and felt (woollen) cloth by heat, pressure, and moisture. LME.

2 : **fulling-mill** a mill in which cloth is fulled; a machine for fulling cloth.

full /fʊl/ *v.*[2] LME. [f. FULL *a.*] **1** *v.t.* Make full. Long *obs.* exc. *dial.* & *US Black English*. LME. **b** *v.i.* Be or become full. Now chiefly *dial.* & *US*, of the moon or tide. LME. †**2** *v.t.* Fulfil, complete. LME–M17. **3** *Dressmaking*. Gather up fullness, fold, pleat. M18.

†**fullage** *n.* L17–L18. [Perh. f. FULYIE.] Refuse, street-sweepings, filth.

fuller /ˈfʊlə/ *n.*[1] OE. [f. L *fullo* (of unkn. origin) + -ER[1].] A person whose occupation is to full cloth.

fuller's earth (or **clay**) a fine-grained clay used in fulling cloth and as an adsorbent. *fuller's teasel*: see TEASEL *n.* 1.

fullery *n.* (*rare*) = *fulling-mill* s.v. FULL *v.*[1] M18.

fuller /ˈfʊlə/ *v.* & *n.*[2] E19. [Origin unkn.] **A** *v.t.* Stamp (iron etc.) with a fuller (see sense B. below); form a groove or channel in. E19. **B** *n.* A grooved or rounded tool on which iron etc. is shaped; a groove made by this. M19.

fullerene /ˈfʊləriːn/ *n.* L20. [Abbrev. of BUCKMINSTERFULLERENE.] *Chem.* Any of several forms of carbon consisting of atoms joined together as a hollow structure.

full face /fʊl ˈfeɪs/ *n.*, *a.*, & *adv. phr.* Also **full-face.** E18. [f. FULL *a.* + FACE *n.* Cf. next.] **A** *n. phr.* **1** The face seen from the front and entirely visible to the observer; a full-face view. E18. **2** *Typogr.* A full-faced character; a font of such characters. L19. **B** *adj.* & *adv. phr.* As seen from the front; with the front or face entirely visible to the observer. L19.

full-faced /fʊlˈfeɪst/ *a.* E17. [f. FULL *a.* + FACE *n.* + -ED[2]. Cf. prec.] **1** Having a full or plump face. E17. **2** Having the face turned fully towards the observer or in some specified direction. E17. **3** *Typogr.* Of a character: having a face occupying the whole depth of type. E19.

fullness /ˈfʊlnɪs/ *n.* Also **fulness.** ME. [f. FULL *a.* + -NESS.] **1** The condition of containing something in abundance. ME. **b** In biblical language, all that is contained in the world. ME. †**c** Abundance, plenty. LME–E18. **2** Completeness, perfection. ME. **b** Copiousness or exhaustiveness (of knowledge, statement, etc.). M19. **3** The condition of being filled to capacity. LME. **4** Satiety; (the effects of) overindulgence. Now only, a feeling of having eaten (more than) enough. LME. **5** The quality (of sound, colour, etc.) of being full; richness. LME. **6** Roundness (of the body), plumpness. E17. **7** The condition (of a garment) of being full; the material gathered or folded to produce this. E19.

1b J. WESLEY The Earth and all her Fullness owns Jehovah for her sovereign Lord! c DEFOE Before I revelled in fullness, and here I struggled with hard fare. 2 G. PRIESTLAND Christianity . . hasn't yet been tried . . What right have we to expect its fullness in *our* time? b J. BARZUN He is replying . . with his customary fullness of illustration. 6 J. FERRIAR A certain degree of fullness improves the figure. 7 J. AUSTEN No fullness appears . . the back is quite plain.

Phrases: **fullness of the (or one's) heart** strong feelings or emotions. **in the fullness of time** at the destined time; eventually.

fully /ˈfʊli/ *v.t. slang.* M19. [f. the adv., in phr. 'fully committed for trial'.] Commit (a person) for trial.

fully /ˈfʊli/ *adv.* OE. [f. FULL *a.* + -LY[2].] In a full manner or degree; completely, entirely, thoroughly, exactly, quite.

Comb.: **fully-fashioned** *a.* (of a garment, esp. a stocking) shaped to fit closely; **fully-fledged** *a.* (of a young bird) having a full set of true feathers; *transf.* & *fig.* mature, of full rank or status.

fulmar /ˈfʊlmə/ *n.* L17. [Hebridean Norn dial. (Gael. *fulmair*), f. ON *fúll* FOUL *a.* (with ref. to the bird's habit of regurgitating oily stomach contents when disturbed) + *már* gull (cf. MEW *n.*[1]).] A gull-sized grey-and-white northern petrel, *Fulmarus glacialis*.

fulmen /ˈfʌlmən, ˈfʊl-/ *n.* Pl. ***-mina*** /-mɪnə/. L17. [L.] A thunderbolt; thunder and lightning, *esp.* as an attribute of Jupiter.

fulminant /ˈfʌlmɪnənt, ˈfʊl-/ *a.* & *n.* E17. [Fr., or L *fulminant-* pres. ppl stem of *fulminare*: see FULMINATE *v.*, -ANT[1].] **A** *adj.* **1** = FULMINATING. E17. **2** *Med.* Developing suddenly and rapidly. L19.

2 *Lancet* A fulminant disease which ends in death within 24 h.

B *n.* Something that fulminates; a thunderbolt; an explosive. *rare.* E19.

fulminate /ˈfʌlmɪneɪt, ˈfʊl-/ *n.* E19. [f. FULMINIC + -ATE[1].] *Chem.* A salt or ester of fulminic acid; *esp.* any of a number of unstable explosive salts of metals (e.g. that of mercury, used in detonators).

fulminate /ˈfʌlmɪneɪt, ˈfʊl-/ *v.* LME. [L *fulminat-* pa. ppl stem of *fulminare* lighten, strike with lightning (in sense 1 f. med.L *fulminare* issue ecclesiastical censures), f. *fulmen*, *fulmin-* lightning: see -ATE[3].] **1** *v.t.* Utter or publish (a formal denunciation). LME. **b** *v.i.* (Orig. of the pope) issue formal censures (*against*); rail or speak violently (*against*). M17. **c** *v.t.* Censure, condemn; denounce vehemently or in scathing terms. L17. **2** *v.i.* Emit thunder and lightning. *rare.* E17. **b** *v.t.* Cause to flash out like lightning. *rare.* M17. **c** *v.i.* Issue as a thunderbolt. M19. **3** *v.t.* & *i.* (Cause to) explode violently, detonate. M17. †**4** *v.i. Metall.* Of gold: suddenly become bright and uniform in colour. Cf. FULMINATION 3. Only in E18. **5** *v.i. Med.* Of a disease: come on or develop suddenly and severely. E20.

1 G. H. NAPHEYS Kings have fulminated their decrees against it. b BOSWELL The holy father used . . to fulminate with serious effect against the greatest powers in Europe. J. ADDAMS Tore his hair, and loudly fulminated in weird Italian oaths. c BURKE I would have the Laws rise . . to fulminate such vain and impious wretches. 3 W. GREGORY A dark powder is formed, which fulminates violently when heated.

fulminator *n.* a person who or thing which fulminates L19.

fulminating /ˈfʌlmɪneɪtɪŋ, ˈfʊl-/ *ppl a.* E17. [f. prec. + -ING[2].] **1** Sending out violent denunciations etc.; railing. E17. **2** Exploding with a loud noise or bright flash; highly explosive. M17. **3** *Med.* Of disease: coming on suddenly and progressing rapidly. E20.

2 **fulminating gold, mercury, silver**, etc. the explosive fulminate of gold, mercury, silver, etc. (see FULMINATE *n.*).

fulmination /fʌlmɪˈneɪʃ(ə)n, fʊl-/ *n.* E16. [L *fulminatio(n-)*, f. *fulminat-*: see FULMINATE *v.*, -ATION.] **1** The formal issuing of an ecclesiastical condemnation or censure; *gen.* violent denunciation or threatening; an outburst of indignation. E16. **2** The bursting out of thunder and lightning; a thunderbolt. Chiefly *fig.* E17. **3** *Metall.* A sudden uniform brightening of the appearance of gold. Cf. FULMINATE *v.* 4. Only in E17. **4** The action of detonating; violent explosion. M17.

fulminatory /ˈfʌlmɪnət(ə)ri, ˈfʊl-/ *a.* E17. [Fr. *fulminatoire*, f. as FULMINATE *v.*: see -ORY[2].] Sending out fulminations, thundering.

fulmine /ˈfʌlmɪn, ˈfʊl-/ *v.* L16. [(O)Fr. *fulminer* or L *fulminare*: see FULMINATE *v.*] **1** *v.t.* Emit (thunder or lightning); *fig.* flash out. *arch.* or *poet.* L16. **2** *v.i.* Speak out fiercely or energetically. (Now chiefly after Milton.) E17.

1 SPENSER As it had beene a flake Of lightning through bright heven fulmined. 2 MILTON Whose resistless eloquence . . Shook the Arsenal and fulmined over Greece.

fulmineous /fʌlˈmɪnɪəs, fʊl-/ *a. arch.* or *poet.* E18. [f. L *fulmineus*, f. *fulmen*, *fulmin-* lightning + -OUS: see -EOUS.] Of or pertaining to thunder or lightning.

fulminic /fʌlˈmɪnɪk, fʊl-/ *a.* E19. [f. L *fulmin-*, FULMEN + -IC. Cf. FULMINATE *v.* 3.] *Chem. fulminic acid*, a very unstable acid, CNOH, known only in ethereal solutions in which it polymerizes rapidly. Cf. FULMINATE *n.*

fulminous /ˈfʌlmɪnəs, ˈfʊl-/ *a.* M17. [f. L *fulmen*, *fulmin-* lightning + -OUS.] Of or pertaining to thunder or lightning; fulminating.

fulminuric /fʌlmɪˈnjʊərɪk, fʊl-/ *a.* M19. [f. FULMINIC + URIC.] *Chem. fulminuric acid*, any of a number of isomeric acidic compounds of formula $C_3H_3N_3O_3$; *esp.* nitrocyanoacetamide, $NO_2 \cdot CH(CN) \cdot CONH_2$.

fulminurate *n.* a salt or ester of fulminuric acid M19.

fulness *n.* var. of FULLNESS.

fulsome /ˈfʊls(ə)m/ *a.* ME. [f. FULL *a.* + -SOME[1].] **1** Abundant, plentiful; full, copious, rich. Now *rare.* ME. **2** Full and plump, well-grown; *derog.* overgrown. LME. †**b** Overfed, surfeited. M17–E19. **3** (Of food) coarse, heavy, filling, cloying; *gen.* satiating, wearisome, tedious. LME. **b** Having a sickly or nauseating taste. *obs.* exc. *Sc.* E17. **4** Physically disgusting; dirty, foul, loathsome. *obs.* exc. *Sc.* LME. †**b** Foul- or strong-smelling; rank. L16–E18. †**5** Offending against accepted standards of morals or taste; repulsive, odious, obscene. LME–E19. **b** Lustful, wanton. *rare* (Shakes.). Only in E17. **6** (Esp. excessively) complimentary or flattering; (too) effusive, (too) lavish, overdone. E17.

2 *fig.*: U. BENTLEY Fulsome white clouds, their bellies fleeced with grey, billowed over the moors. **3** JOSEPH HALL A little honie is sweet; much, fulsome. **4** ROBERT BURTON She vomited some 24 pounds of fulsome stuffe of all colours. **5** N. AMHURST What followed was too fulsome for the eyes of my chaste readers. **6** M. EDGEWORTH The fulsome strains of courtly adulation. B. PYM Thanks can never be too fulsome.

fulsomely *adv.* LME. **fulsomeness** *n.* LME.

fulth /fʊlθ/ *n.* Long *obs.* exc. *dial.* See also FOUTH. ME. [f. FULL *a.* + -TH[1].] Fullness, one's fill.

fulvid /ˈfʌlvɪd, ˈfʊl-/ *a.* Long *rare.* L16. [Late L *fulvidus*, f. L *fulvus* FULVOUS: see -ID[1].] = FULVOUS.

fulvous /ˈfʌlvəs, ˈfʊl-/ *a.* M17. [f. L *fulvus* reddish-yellow + -OUS.] Reddish-yellow; dull yellowish brown, tawny.

fulvous whistling duck, fulvous tree duck, a long-legged tawny-plumaged duck, *Dendrocygna bicolor*, native to E. Africa, the Indian subcontinent, and the New World tropics and subtropics.

fulyie /ˈfʊli, ˈfʊlji/ *v.* & *n. Sc.* Also **-zie**. LME. [Perh. f. (O)Fr. *fouler* trample underfoot: cf. FULL *v.*[1], FOIL *v.*[1]] **A** *v.t.* †**1** Trample, overcome, destroy. LME–E18. **2** Defile, pollute. E16. **B** *n.* Street-sweepings, refuse; filth; dung, manure. L15.

fum /fʌm/ *v.* Infl. **-mm-**. E17. [Imit.] †**1** *v.i.* Strum (on a guitar). Only in 17. **2** *v.t.* Thump, beat. *W. Indies.* L18.

fumadiddle *n.* var. of FLUMMADIDDLE.

fumado /fjuːˈmɑːdəʊ/ *n.* Now *dial.* Pl. **-o(e)s**. L16. [Sp., pa. pple of *fumar* to smoke f. L *fumare*: see FUME *v.*, -ADO. See also *fair maid* s.v. FAIR *a.* & *adv.*] A pilchard, orig. smoked, later salted and pressed.

fumage /ˈfjuːmɪdʒ/ *n.* Cf. FEUAGE. M18. [med.L *fumagium*, f. L *fumus* smoke: see -AGE.] *Hist.* A tax on hearths or chimneys.

fumaric /fjuːˈmarɪk/ *a.* M19. [f. mod.L *Fumaria* fumitory + -IC.] *Chem. fumaric acid*, a crystalline unsaturated dibasic acid, *trans*-HOOC·CH=CH·COOH, which is isomeric with maleic acid and occurs in fumitory and many other plants; *trans*-butenedioic acid.

ˈ**fumarate** *n.* a salt or ester of fumaric acid M19.

fumarole /ˈfjuːmərəʊl/ *n.* Also **-mer-**. E19. [It. †*fumaruolo* f. late L *fumariolum* vent, hole for smoke, dim. ult. of L *fumus* smoke + *-arium* -ARY[1]: see -OLE[1].] A vent in or near a volcano, from which hot vapour is emitted.

fumarolic /-ˈrɒlɪk/ *a.* of, pertaining to, or formed by a fumarole E20.

fumaroyl /ˈfjuːmərəʊʌɪl, -rəʊɪl/ *n.* M20. [f. FUMARIC + -OYL.] A divalent radical, *trans*-·OC·CH=CH·CO·, derived from fumaric acid. Usu. in *comb.*

Also **fumaryl** *n.* M19.

fumble /ˈfʌmb(ə)l/ *v.* & *n.* LME. [LG *fummeln*, *fommeln*, Du. *fommelen*, whence Sw. *fumla*: cf. FAMBLE *v.*] **A** *v.* **1** *v.i.* Use one's hands or fingers clumsily or ineffectually; grope (*about*, *at*, *for*, *with*); act hesitantly. LME. **b** *v.t.* Handle awkwardly or clumsily; *esp.* mishandle (a ball). E17. **2** *v.i.* & *t.* Copulate impotently or ineffectually (with). *slang.* E16. **3** *v.i.* & *t.* Speak (words) hesitantly or indistinctly; mumble, mutter. M16. **4** *v.t.* Wrap up clumsily, huddle together. Long *rare* or *obs.* L16.

1 I. MURDOCH I fumbled with the catch of the front door, my hands trembling with nervousness. E. FIGES I fumbled in my shopping bag . . for our supper. L. AUCHINCLOSS Mark would not fumble . . he would move with absolute assurance. *fig.*: V. WOOLF Fumbling in his mind for something to say. **b** P. V. WHITE Fumbling the letter out of its envelope. **fumble one's way** find one's way by groping. **2** *fig.*: GOLDSMITH Impotent posterity would in vain fumble to produce his fellow. H. REED The early bees are assaulting and fumbling the flowers. **3** SIR W. SCOTT Never lose time fumbling and prating about it. *Company* Bill fumbled through his final goodbyes.

B *n.* An act of fumbling; *esp.* a clumsy attempt; a mishandling of a ball. M17.

fumbler *n.* a person who fumbles E16. **fumblingly** *adv.* in a fumbling manner L16.

fume /fjuːm/ *n.* LME. [OFr. *fum* f. L *fumus* smoke, and OFr. *fume*, f. *fumer* f. L *fumare*: see next.] **I** Now usu. in *pl.* **1** The volatile matter produced by combustion; smoke. Now usu., odorous or fragrant smoke from burning tobacco, incense, diesel fuel, etc. LME. †**b** Something producing aromatic vapour. M16–E18. **2** An odour emitted from or by a substance or object. LME. **3** A vapour or gas (esp. a harmful or irritant one) given off by an acid or volatile substance. Formerly also, vapour given off by a substance when heated. LME. **b** A watery vapour, steam, or mist rising from the earth or sea. Now *rare.* M16. **4** A vapour or exhalation produced by the body; *esp.* (now only) a noxious vapour imagined to rise from the stomach to the brain as a result of (excess) food or alcohol. LME.

1 DICKENS The fumes of choice tobacco scent the air. L. T. C. ROLT Reeking with the fumes of spent gunpowder. **2** A. C. SWINBURNE The fume of the flowers of the night. **3** J. MILLER A patient who developed a spectacular tremor . . as the result of breathing in mercury fumes. **4** C. THIRLWALL The fumes of the wine . . thawed their reserve.

II *fig.* **5** (A fit of) anger, an irritable mood. Freq. as *in a fume* LME. **6** Something unsubstantial, transient, or imaginary. Now *rare.* M16. **7** Something which clouds or confuses the faculties or reason. L16.

5 N. COWARD You're all fuss and fume. **7** M. ARNOLD His head gets a little hot with the fumes of patriotism.

Comb.: **fume chamber, cupboard** (in a laboratory) a glazed enclosure in which to perform experiments involving harmful gases and vapours, which are removed by means of a ventilator; **fume hood**: for extracting harmful vapours in a laboratory etc.

fume /fjuːm/ *v.* LME. [(O)Fr. *fumer* or L *fumare* to smoke.] **1** *v.t.* Apply fumes to; expose to fumes; fumigate. LME. **b** Perfume (now only with incense); offer incense to. L15. †**c** Preserve by smoking. E–M17. †**2** *v.t.* Emit as vapour; disperse in vapour. L15–M19. **3** *v.i.* Be angry or irritated. E16. **b** *v.t.* Say or think angrily or irritably. Also, spend (time) in an angry state. L19. **4** *v.i.* Emit fumes, smoke, or vapour. M16. **5** *v.i.* (Of fumes etc.) issue, rise, be emitted; pass *away* or *off* as fumes. L16. †**b** Of alcohol or food: rise as fumes (*to* or *into* the brain). L16–E18. †**6** *v.i.* Become clouded or confused by alcohol, sleep, etc. *rare* (Shakes.). Only in E17.

1 **fumed oak**: darkened by exposure to ammonia fumes. **3** P. G. WODEHOUSE These formalities irked Judson. . . He wrote his name on the form . . fuming. **b** P. LIVELY I haven't time to be ill, she fumed. **4** C. D. WARNER The fire sputters and fumes. **fuming nitric acid** concentrated nitric acid containing excess dissolved nitrogen dioxide. *fuming sulphuric acid*: see SULPHURIC *a.* 1. **5** S. PLATH A faint chickeny aroma fumed up to my nostrils.

fumer *n.* (*rare*) E17. **fumingly** *adv.* in a fuming manner; angrily: L16.

fumerole *n.* var. of FUMAROLE.

fumet /fjuːˈmɛt/ *n.*[1] Also **-ette**. E18. [Fr., f. *fumer* FUME *v.*] **1** The smell of game when high; game flavour. E18. **2** A concentrated stock, usu. of game or fish, used as flavouring. E20.

fumet *n.*[2] var. of FEWMET.

fumette *n.* var. of FUMET *n.*[1]

†**fumid** *a.* M17–L18. [L *fumidus*, f. *fumus* smoke: see -ID[1].] Fuming, vaporous.

†**fumiferous** *a. rare.* M17–M19. [f. L *fumifer*, f. *fumus* smoke + -OUS: see -FEROUS.] Bearing or producing smoke.

fumigant /ˈfjuːmɪg(ə)nt/ *n.* L19. [L *fumigant-* pres. ppl stem of *fumigare*: see next, -ANT[1].] Something that fumigates; a substance used in fumigation.

fumigate /ˈfjuːmɪgeɪt/ *v.t.* M16. [L *fumigat-* pa. ppl stem of *fumigare*, f. *fumus* FUME *n.*: see -ATE[3].] **1** Scent with fumes; perfume. Now *rare* or *obs.* M16. **2** Apply fumes to; *esp.* disinfect or disinfest by the application of (chemical) smoke or fumes. L18.

fumigator *n.* (*a*) a person who fumigates; (*b*) an apparatus used for fumigating: L17. **fumigatory** *a.* (*rare*) of or pertaining to fumigation L18.

fumigation /fjuːmɪˈgeɪʃ(ə)n/ *n.* LME. [(O)Fr., or late L *fumigatio(n-)*, f. as prec.: see -ATION.] **1** The production of aromatic fumes; the action of perfuming with a preparation of herbs, perfumes, etc. Also, the preparation so used or the fumes produced. LME. **2** The action or process of applying (chemical) fumes or smoke, *esp.* as a disinfectant or disinfesting agent. LME. **3** (Exposure of a part of the body to) therapeutic fumes. Now *rare* or *obs.* LME.

fumish /ˈfjuːmɪʃ/ *a.* Long *arch. rare.* E16. [f. FUME *n.* + -ISH[1].] †**1** Of the nature of fumes, esp. as rising in the body (cf. FUME *n.* 4); emitting fumes. E16–L17. **2** *fig.* Irascible, bad-tempered; exhibiting anger. E16.

fumishly *adv.* L16. **fumishness** *n.* E16.

fumitory /ˈfjuːmɪt(ə)ri/ *n.*[1] Also †**fumiter**. LME. [(O)Fr. *fumeterre* f. med.L *fumus terrae* 'smoke of the earth'.] Any of various weeds of the genus *Fumaria* (family Fumariaceae), with spikes of pink or white tubular flowers and finely divided greyish leaves; esp. *F. officinalis*. Also, any plant of the related genus *Corydalis*.

fumitory /ˈfjuːmɪt(ə)ri/ *n.*[2] *rare.* M16. [Erron. f. med.L *fumatorium* chimney, louvre, f. L *fumat-* pa. ppl stem of *fumare* FUME *v.*: see -ORY[1].] †**1** A censer. Only in M16. **2** A place set apart for smoking or fumigation. E18.

fummadiddle *n.* var. of FLUMMADIDDLE.

fumose /fjuːˈməʊs/ *a.* Now *rare.* LME. [L *fumosus*, f. *fumus* smoke: see -OSE[1].] **1** Full of or giving off fumes. Formerly also = FUMOUS 1. LME. **2** Consisting of fumes or smoke, vaporous, smoky. LME.

†**fumosity** *n.* LME. [OFr. *fumosité* or med.L *fumositas*, f. as prec.: see -ITY.] **1** The state of fuming or being full of fumes; a fume or fumes. LME–M18. **2** The flatulent quality of some foods; the heady quality of alcohol; a fume supposed to rise to the brain from the stomach. LME–L17.

fumous /ˈfjuːməs/ *a.* Now *rare.* LME. [f. as FUMOSE: see -OUS.] †**1** Causing flatulence or (supposedly) a fume to rise to the brain from the stomach. LME–E18. †**2** Consisting of fumes, vaporous; fumy. LME–L18. †**3** Angry, furious. LME–L17. **4** Pertaining to smoke or (*joc.*) smoking. M17.

fumy /ˈfjuːmi/ *a.* E16. [f. FUME *n.* + -Y[1].] Composed of or full of fumes; of the nature of fumes; giving off or smelling of fumes; vaporous, smoky.

fun /fʌn/ *n.* & *a.* L17. [f. the vb.] **A** *n.* **1** A trick, a cheat, a hoax. *obs.* exc. *dial.* L17. **2** Amusement, light-hearted pleasure; jocularity, drollery. Also, something which provides this, a source of amusement. E18.

2 M. SHEARMAN Most footballers play for the fun and the fun alone. W. FEATHER Setting a good example for your children takes all the fun out of middle-age. J. WAIN You've had your fun, and now I'm going to have a baby. *Listener* The clothes were . . fun to wear.

Phrases: *figure of fun*: see FIGURE *n.* **for fun, for the fun of it** for amusement or excitement. **fun and games** (*colloq.*) exciting or amusing goings-on; *esp.* flirtation, carrying-on. **in fun** as a joke; not seriously. **like fun** (now *rare*) vigorously, quickly, much; *iron.* not at all. **make fun of, poke fun at** tease, ridicule. *Comb.*: **funfair** (a part of) a fair devoted to amusements and sideshows. **funfest** (*N. Amer.*) a gathering for the purposes of amusement. **fun run** an organized, largely uncompetitive, long-distance run involving mass participation of occasional (often sponsored) runners.

B *attrib.* or as *adj.* Amusing, entertaining, enjoyable, exciting; not serious. M19.

Sunday Express You can't rustle up enough fun people for a small party. G. PRIESTLAND Why don't you go to a fun place? Covent Garden! The Barbican! Limehouse!

fun /fʌn/ *v.* Infl. **-nn-**. L17. [Prob. orig. dial. var. of FON *v.*; later f. the n.] **1** *v.t.* Cheat, hoax, cajole *of*, *out of*. *obs.* exc. *dial.* L17. **2** *v.i.* Have fun; fool, joke. M19.

funambulator /fjuːˈnambjʊleɪtə/ *n. rare.* L17. [f. as next + -ATOR.] = next.

funambuˈlation *n.* tightrope walking, rope-dancing E18. **funambulatory** *a.* of or pertaining to rope-dancing; that walks on a tightrope: L17.

funambulist /fjuːˈnambjʊlɪst/ *n.* L18. [f. Fr. *funambule* or its source L *funambulus* (f. *funis* rope + *ambulare* walk) + -IST.] A rope-walker, a rope-dancer.

funambulism *n.* E19.

funambulo /fjuːˈnambjʊləʊ/ *n.* Long *arch.* Pl. **-o(e)s**. E17. [Sp. or It., f. L *funambulus*: see prec.] = prec.

funckia *n.* var. of FUNKIA.

functi officio *pred. a. phr.* see FUNCTUS OFFICIO.

function /ˈfʌŋ(k)ʃ(ə)n/ *n.* M16. [(O)Fr. *fonction* f. L *functio(n-)*, f. *funct-* pa. ppl stem of *fungi* perform: see -ION.] **1** The activity proper or natural to a person or thing; the purpose or intended role of a person or thing; an office, duty, employment, or calling. Also, a particular activity or operation (among several); an organizational unit performing this. M16. **b** An official duty. Orig. usu. in *pl.* M16. †**c** An order or class (of people). L16–M18. **d** *Chem.* (The characteristic mode of reaction of) a functional group. M19. **e** *Computing.* Any of the basic operations in a computer; *esp.* one that corresponds to a single instruction. Freq. *attrib.* M20. **2** The action of functioning; performance (*of*). L16. †**3** Activity, action. L16–E17. **4a** Orig. *RC Ch.* A religious ceremony. Now *rare.* M17. **b** A public ceremony or occasion; a formal or important social gathering. M19. **5** *Math.* A variable quantity regarded in relation to one or more other variables in terms of which it may be expressed or on which its value depends; a mathematical expression containing one or more variables. Also *transf.*, (with *of*) something dependent on (another factor or factors). L18.

1 G. MURRAY The chief function of poetry is the criticism of life. J. G. COZZENS The function of ice was to melt. A. STORR The obsessional's habitual disgust with bodily functions, especially with those of excretion. *Times* The smooth . . running of our centralised cashier function. *Marketing* Finance is shaking off its grey, dowdy image. It is becoming a creative, dynamic function. b J. MARQUAND The door was opened . . by the door keeper, . . ready to perform that function at any hour of the day. 2 P. PARISH The function of the liver, kidneys and brain may all be impaired. *Belle* (*Australia*) Opening up paths of communication so essential to effective office function. 3 SHAKES. *Macb.* Function is smother'd in surmise. 4b L. WHISTLER Selfconscious and unconfident, I . . made few interesting friends, and went to few functions. 5 R. M. PIRSIG The time spans of scientific truths are an inverse function of the intensity of scientific effort. *Nature* Functions are considered . . as mappings between sets. W. GOLDING What men believe is a function of what they are. *complementary function*: see COMPLEMENTARY *a.* 2. *wave function*: see WAVE *n.* ZETA *function.*

Comb.: **function space** *Math.* a topological space the elements of which are functions; **function word** *Ling.* a word expressing a formal or grammatical purpose.

functionate *v.i.* (*rare*) = FUNCTION *v.* M19. **functionless** *a.* M19.

function /ˈfʌŋ(k)ʃ(ə)n/ *v.i.* M19. [f. the n., after Fr. *fonctionner.*] Fulfil a function; perform a duty or role; act, operate.

A. KOESTLER The wash-basin . . had no plug, but the tap functioned. N. O. BROWN Criticism . . functioning as a mask for moral prejudice. *function on all cylinders*: see CYLINDER 3.

functional /ˈfʌŋ(k)ʃ(ə)n(ə)l/ *a.* & *n.* M17. [f. FUNCTION *n.* + -AL[1].] **A** *adj.* **1** Of, pertaining to, or serving a function, office, or purpose; relating to activity rather than to structure or form. M17. **b** *Med.* Of a disorder (esp. mental): not caused by discernible organic disease. M19. **c** *spec.* Of architecture etc.: designed only or primarily with a view to its purpose; practical, utilitarian. M20. **2** *Math.* Of or pertaining to a function (FUNCTION *n.* 5). E19.

1 *Times Lit. Suppl.* In a good poem imagery and rhythm are functional, not merely decorative. R. F. CHAPMAN Even if there is no anatomical differentiation of the midgut there may be functional differentiation. **functional group** *Chem.* an atom or group of atoms present in a molecule of an organic compound which confers characteristic chemical properties on the compound. c *Illustrated London News* The outside of this building is functional and severe. 2 **functional calculus** *Logic* = *predicate calculus* s.v. PREDICATE *n.*

B *n. Math.* A function the value of which is a scalar depending on the whole form of another function. E20.

functioˈnality *n.* L19. **functionally** *adv.* E19.

functionalise *v.* var. of FUNCTIONALIZE.

functionalism /ˈfʌŋ(k)ʃ(ə)n(ə)lɪz(ə)m/ *n.* E20. [f. prec. + -ISM.] **1** *Social Sciences.* The study or interpretation of phenomena in terms of the functions which they fulfil (esp. within an overall system). E20. **2** Consideration for the function and purpose of a building etc. as regulating its design. M20.

functionalist *n.* & *a.* (*a*) *n.* an adherent or student of functionalism; (*b*) *adj.* exhibiting or pertaining to functionalism: E20. **functionaˈlistic** *a.* E20.

functionalize /ˈfʌŋ(k)ʃ(ə)n(ə)lʌɪz/ *v.t.* Chiefly *US.* Also **-ise**. M19. [f. as prec. + -IZE.] Assign to or place in some function or position; organize according to function.

functionaliˈzation *n.* E20.

functionary /ˈfʌŋ(k)ʃ(ə)n(ə)ri/ *n.* L18. [f. FUNCTION *n.* + -ARY[1], after Fr. *fonctionnaire.*] A person having a duty or function to perform; an official.

functionarism *n.* (now *rare*) administration by functionaries; officialism: M19.

functionary /ˈfʌn(k)ʃ(ə)n(ə)ri/ *a.* E19. [f. FUNCTION *n.* + -ARY[2].] Of or pertaining to a function, functional; *esp.* official.

functor /ˈfʌŋktə/ *n.* M20. [f. FUNCTION *n.* + -OR, after *factor* etc.] **1** *Logic.* A function, an operator. M20. **2** *Ling.* = *function word* s.v. FUNCTION *n.* M20.

funcˈtorial *a.* M20.

functus officio /ˌfʌŋktəs əˈfɪʃɪəʊ/ *pred. a. phr.* Pl. ***functi officio*** /ˈfʌŋktʌɪ/. M19. [L = having discharged an office.] *Law.* Free from further obligations, having discharged its (or their) duty.

fund /fʌnd/ *n.* M17. [L *fundus* bottom. Partly refash. of FOND *n.* after this.] †**1** The bottom, the lowest part. M17–M18. †**2** Basis, foundation. L17–M18. **3** A source of supply, a permanent stock ready to be drawn upon. (Now chiefly of immaterial things.) L17. **4a** A stock or sum of money, esp. as set apart for a particular purpose. L17. **b** In *pl.* The money at a person's disposal; financial resources. E18. **5** *spec.* †**a** A portion of revenue set apart as security for specified payments. L17–E19. **b** In *pl.* (exc. in *comb.*). *The* stock of the National Debt as a mode of investment; government securities. *arch.* E18. **6** = FOUNT *n.*[2] L17.

3 A. UTTLEY He had . . a fund of good humour and laughter. DAY LEWIS A certain fund of calm within myself. 4a A. C. BOULT He . . organized a fund to give concerts in hospitals. b R. CAMPBELL All my funds ran out but I got a job. A. EDEN My mother's effort to raise funds to build a cottage hospital. 5b C. S. LEWIS He wore the expression of a nineteenth-century gentleman with something in the Funds.

Phrases: *Consolidated Fund*: see CONSOLIDATE *v.* 1. **in funds** having money to spend. †**in the fund** at bottom. *sinking fund*: see SINKING *vbl n.* *trust fund*: see TRUST *n.*

Comb.: **fund-holder** *arch.* a person who has money invested in the stock of the national debt; **fund-raiser, -raising** (a person engaged in) persuading individuals or organizations to provide financial support for a cause, enterprise, etc.

fund /fʌnd/ *v.t.* L18. [f. the n.] **1** Orig., provide a fund (FUND *n.* 5b) for the regular payment of the interest on (a national debt). Now, convert (a floating debt) into a more or less permanent debt at a fixed rate of interest. Freq. as *funded* pa. ppl a. L18. **b** Invest money in the stock of the national debt. *arch.* M19. **2** Put into a fund or store; collect or store (something immaterial). E19. **3** Supply with funds, finance (a person, position, or project). E20.

2 R. FORD Every day . . we are unconsciously funding a stock of treasures . . of memory. 3 *Science Journal* A system in which research projects are funded by grants.

fundable *a.* able to be funded L19. **funding** *n.* (*a*) the action of the vb; (*b*) financial support: L18.

fundal /ˈfʌnd(ə)l/ *a.* L19. [f. FUNDUS + -AL[1].] *Med.* Of or relating to the fundus of an organ, esp. the uterus or the eyeball.

fundament /ˈfʌndəm(ə)nt/ *n.* ME. [(O)Fr. *fondement* f. L *fundamentum*, f. *fundare* FOUND *v.*[1]: see -MENT.] †**1** The foundation or base of a wall, building, etc. Also, the action of founding a building, institution, etc.; the building itself. ME–L17. †**2** The ground, basis, or principle on which anything is founded. ME–L17. **3** The buttocks, the anus. ME. **4** *Geogr.* The landscape as it appeared before humans began to modify it by their activities. E20.

fundamenta divisionis, relationis *n. phrs.* pls. of FUNDAMENTUM DIVISIONIS, RELATIONIS.

fundamental /fʌndəˈmɛnt(ə)l/ *a.* & *n.* LME. [Fr. *fondamental* or late L. *fundamentalis*: see prec., -AL[1].] **A** *adj.* **1** Of or pertaining to the basis or groundwork; going to the root of the matter. LME. **2** Serving as the base or foundation; essential or indispensable. Also, primary, original; from which others are derived. LME. †**3** Of or pertaining to the foundation(s) of a building. E17–M18. **4** Of or pertaining to the fundament (sense 3). *joc.* M18. **5** Of a stratum: lowest, lying at the bottom. L18.

1 M. PATTISON The fundamental question of what is a University. J. MICHIE Is it that you simply aren't willing, Or have you a fundamental moral objection to killing? 2 GEO. ELIOT The ideas of strict law and order were fundamental to all his political teaching. S. WEINBERG The hadrons are . . composites of more fundamental particles, known as 'quarks'.

Special collocations: **fundamental bass** a supposed bass line consisting of the roots of a series of chords. **fundamental note** (*a*) *Mus.* the lowest note of a chord in its original (uninverted) form; (*b*) = *fundamental tone* below. **fundamental particle** = *elementary particle* s.v. ELEMENTARY *a.* 4. **fundamental tone**: produced by vibration of a sonorous body acting as a whole (opp. *harmonic*).

B *n.* **1** A basic or primary principle, rule, or article, which serves as the groundwork of a system; an essential part. Usu. in *pl.* M17. **2** A fundamental note or tone. E18.

fundamenˈtality *n.* (*rare*) E18. **fundamentally** *adv.* LME.

fundamentalism /fʌndəˈmɛnt(ə)lɪz(ə)m/ *n.* E20. [f. prec. + -ISM.] The strict maintenance of traditional orthodox religious beliefs or doctrines; *esp.* belief in the inerrancy of Scripture and literal acceptance of the creeds as fundamentals of Protestant Christianity.

fundamentalist *n.* & *a.* (*a*) *n.* an adherent of fundamentalism; (*b*) *adj.* of or pertaining to fundamentalism or fundamentalists: E20.

fundamentum divisionis /fʌndəˌmɛntəm dɪvɪʒɪˈəʊnɪs, dɪvɪz-/ *n. phr.* Pl. ***fundamenta divisionis*** /fʌndəˌmɛntə/. M19. [L = foundation or basis of division.] *Logic.* The principle or basis of logical division of a genus into its constituent species.

fundamentum relationis /fʌndəˌmɛntəm rɪˌleɪʃɪˈəʊnɪs/ *n. phr.* Pl. ***fundamenta relationis*** /fʌndəˌmɛntə/. M19. [L = foundation of the relation.] *Logic.* Those elements of the objective world that constitute the terms of a relation.

fundatrix /fʌnˈdeɪtrɪks/ *n.* Pl. **-trices** /-trɪsiːz/. M16. [mod.L fem. of L *fundator*, f. *fundat-*: see FOUNDATION, -TRIX.] †**1** A foundress. Only in M16. **2** *Entomol.* The founding female of a colony of aphids, producing young parthogenetically. E20.

fundi /ˈfʌndi/ *n.*[1] M19. [W. Afr. name.] = HUNGRY *rice*.

Fundi /ˈfʌndi, *foreign* ˈfʊndɪ/ *n.*[2] Pl. **-is**, **-ies**. L20. [G, abbrev. of *Fundamentalist* fundamentalist.] A radical member of the Green movement; *gen.* a fundamentalist.

fundi *n.*[3] pl. of FUNDUS.

fundiform /ˈfʌndɪfɔːm/ *a.* Now *rare.* M19. [mod.L *fundiformis*, f. L *funda* sling: see -FORM.] *Anat.* Sling-shaped; *spec.* designating ligaments (*a*) on the front of the ankle enclosing tendons of the extensor muscles of the leg, and (*b*) forming a loop enclosing the root of the penis.

fundus /ˈfʌndəs/ *n.* Pl. **fundi** /-dʌɪ/. M18. [L = bottom.] *Anat.* The more broadly rounded extremity of a hollow organ, usu. that part opposite to the external aperture; *spec.* (*a*) the upper extremity of the uterus; (*b*) the part of the interior of the eyeball opposite to the pupil.

funduˈscopic *a.* of, pertaining to, or involving funduscopy M20. **funˈduscopy** *n.* ophthalmoscopy of the fundus of the eye M20.

funebrial /fjuːˈniːbrɪəl/ *a.* Now *rare.* L16. [f. L *funebris*, f. *funus* funeral: see -IAL.] = FUNEREAL.

Also **funebrious** *a.* M17.

funeral /ˈfjuːn(ə)r(ə)l/ *n.* LME. [OFr. *funeraille* collect. fem. sing., f. med.L *funeralia* neut. pl. of late L *funeralis*: see next.] **1** *sing.* & †*in pl.* (treated as *sing.*). The ceremonies connected with the burial or cremation of a dead body; a burial or cremation with its attendant ritual; obsequies. LME. †**2** In *pl.* Funeral expenses. L15–E17. †**3** Death; a grave or monument. *poet.* L16–E18. **4** *sing.* & †*in pl.* A funeral sermon or service. Now *US.* E17. **5** A procession of mourners accompanying the corpse to the place of burial or cremation. L17. **6** *fig.* With *possess.*: one's own (unpleasant) concern, of which one must accept the consequences. *slang* (orig. *US*). M19.

1 *walking funeral*: see WALKING *ppl a.* 6 M. GORDON It's your funeral I mean . . it's up to you.

funeral /ˈfjuːn(ə)r(ə)l/ *a.* (now usu. regarded as *attrib.* use of the n.). LME. [OFr., f. late L *funeralis* f. L *funus*, *funer-* funeral, death, corpse: see -AL[1].] **1** Of or pertaining to the ceremonial burial or cremation of the dead; concerned with a funeral or funerals. LME. **2** = FUNEREAL. Now *rare.* LME.

1 *funeral expenses*, *funeral oration*, *funeral procession*, *funeral service*, etc. **funeral director** an undertaker. *funeral escutcheon*: see ESCUTCHEON 1b. **funeral home** = *funeral parlour* below. *funeral honours*: see HONOUR *n.* **funeral parlour** an undertaker's establishment. **funeral pile**, **pyre** a pile of wood etc. on which a corpse is burnt. **funeral urn**: holding the ashes of a cremated body. 2 BYRON The raven flaps her funeral wing.

funeralize /ˈfjuːn(ə)r(ə)lʌɪz/ *v.* Also **-ise**. M17. [f. FUNERAL *a.*, *n.* + -IZE.] †**1** *v.t.* Make sad or melancholy. Only in M17. **2** *v.t.* & *i.* Hold a funeral for (a dead person or animal). Chiefly *US.* M19.

funerary /ˈfjuːn(ə)r(ə)ri/ *a.* L17. [Late L *funerarius*, f. L *funus*, *funer-*: see FUNERAL *a.*, -ARY[1].] Esp. *Archaeol.*: of or pertaining to a funeral or burial; connected with a funeral or funerals.

funereal /fjuːˈnɪərɪəl/ *a.* E18. [f. L *funereus* f. *funus*, *funer-* see FUNERAL *a.*] Of, pertaining to, or appropriate to a funeral; gloomy, dark, dismal, mournful.

R. CHANDLER Along the empty halls through the big silent . . funereal living-room. O. MANNING The voice rose into a funereal wail.

funereally *adv.* M19.

funest /fjuːˈnɛst/ *a.* M17. [(O)Fr. *funeste* f. L *funestus*, f. *funus*: see FUNERAL *a.*] Causing or portending death or evil; fatal, disastrous; dreadful.

Also †**funestal** *a.*: only in M16.

fungaceous /fʌŋˈgeɪʃəs/ *a.* L19. [f. L FUNGUS + -ACEOUS.] Of the nature of a fungus or fungi.

fungal /ˈfʌŋg(ə)l/ *a.* & *n.* M19. [f. FUNGUS + -AL[1].] A *adj.* Of or pertaining to a fungus; of the nature of or resembling a fungus. M19. B *n.* A fungus. Now *rare* or *obs.* M19.

fungate /ˈfʌŋgeɪt/ *v.i.* M19. [f. FUNGUS + -ATE[3].] *Med.* Esp. of a tumour: grow outwards from a surface, with a fungoid appearance.

funˈgation *n.* E20.

†**funge** *n.* LME. [OFr. *fonge* f. L FUNGUS.] **1** A fungus. Only in LME. **2** [After L *fungus*.] A soft-headed person; a fool. M16–E17.

fungi *n.pl.* see FUNGUS.

fungi- /ˈfʌndʒi, ˈfʌŋgi/ *comb. form* of FUNGUS: see -I-.

fungiform *a.* (chiefly *Anat.*, of papillae on the tongue) having the form of or resembling a fungus or mushroom E19. **fungiˈstasis** *n.* inhibition of the growth of fungi M20. **fungiˈstatic** *a.* inhibiting the growth of fungi E20. **fungiˈstatically** *adv.* in a fungistatic manner, so as to inhibit the growth of fungi M20. **fungiˈtoxic** *a.* poisonous to fungi M20. **fungitoˈxicity** *n.* toxicity to fungi M20. **fungivorous** /fʌnˈdʒɪv(ə)rəs/ *a.* feeding on fungi or mushrooms E19.

fungible /ˈfʌndʒɪb(ə)l/ *n.* & *a.* L17. [med.L *fungibilis*, f. *fungi* 'perform, enjoy' with sense as in *fungi vice* 'take the place of': see -IBLE.] A *n.* *Law* (chiefly *Sc.*). A thing which precisely or acceptably replaces or is replaceable by another. L17. B *adj.* Chiefly *Law.* Precisely or acceptably replacing or replaceable by another item, mutually interchangeable: esp. of goods etc. contracted for, when a particular item is not specified. E19.

fungiˈbility *n.* E20. **fungibly** *adv.* M20.

fungic /ˈfʌndʒɪk/ *a.* Now *rare.* E19. [f. FUNGUS + -IC.] Of or pertaining to fungi, fungal.

fungicide /ˈfʌndʒɪsʌɪd, ˈfʌŋgɪ-/ *n.* L19. [f. FUNGI- + -CIDE.] An application or chemical for destroying fungi.

fungiˈcidal *a.* of the nature of, acting as, or characteristic of a fungicide E20.

†**fungite** *n.* L17–M18. [f. FUNGUS + -ITE[1].] *Palaeont.* = *mushroom-coral* s.v. MUSHROOM *n.* & *a.*

fungo /ˈfʌŋgəʊ/ *n.* *US.* Pl. **-oes**. M19. [Origin unkn.] *Baseball.* A fly ball hit in the air for practice. Also (in full *fungo bat*), a lightweight practice bat.

fungoid /ˈfʌŋgɔɪd/ *a.* & *n.* M19. [f. FUNGUS + -OID.] A *adj.* Of, pertaining to, resembling, or of the nature of a fungus. M19. B *n.* A fungus; a growth resembling a fungus. L19.

fungology /fʌŋˈgɒlədʒi/ *n.* Now *rare.* M19. [f. FUNGUS + -OLOGY.] The branch of science that deals with fungi; mycology.

fungoˈlogical *a.* L19. **fungologist** *n.* M19.

fungous /ˈfʌŋgəs/ *a.* Also (now *rare*) **fungose** /-əʊs/. LME. [f. L *fungosus*, f. FUNGUS: see -OUS, -OSE[1].] **1** Of or pertaining to a fungus or fungi; resembling or of the nature of a fungus. Also, affected by fungal growth. LME. **b** *Med.* Of a tumour etc.: like a fungus in form or growth. M17. **2** Growing or springing up suddenly like a mushroom or toadstool; not durable or substantial. M18.

funˈgosity *n.* the quality or condition of being fungous; a fungous growth: E18.

fungus /ˈfʌŋgəs/ *n.* Pl. **fungi** /ˈfʌŋgi, -gʌɪ, ˈfʌndʒi, -dʒʌɪ/, **funguses**. LME. [L, prob. f. Gk *sphoggos*, *spoggos* SPONGE *n.*[1]: cf. FUNGE.] **1** Any of a large division of organisms, including mushrooms, toadstools, moulds, rusts, yeasts, and constituents of lichens, which lack chlorophyll, reproduce as cryptogams, and grow on and obtain nutriment from organic matter; *esp.* a mushroom, toadstool, or similar kind. Also *collect.*, a growth formed by such organisms. LME. **b** *fig.* Something growing rapidly or extensively. M18. **2** *Med.* A growth of soft or spongy diseased tissue on a surface, as a tumour etc. L17. **b** A skin disease in fish. L19. †**3** An excrescence of lampblack etc. on a wick. L18–E19. **4** A growth of facial hair, a beard. *slang.* E20.

1 S. SPENDER A tree . . rotted by kidney-shaped fungus on the bark. *bracket fungus*: see BRACKET *n.* b T. PAINE Aristocracy . . a kind of fungus growing out of the corruption of society. 4 H. HOBSON In addition to the chin-fungus he'd put on a little weight.

Comb.: **fungus-garden** a growth of a fungus cultivated by ants or termites as a source of food; **fungus-gnat**, **-midge** a small fly of the family Mycetophilidae, the larvae of most of which feed on fungi.

¶ Fungi have usu. been classified as plants but are sometimes regarded as constituting a distinct kingdom.

funicle /ˈfjuːnɪk(ə)l/ *n.* M17. [Anglicized f. FUNICULUS.] †**1** = FUNICULUS 1. Only in M17. **2** Any of certain filamentary anatomical structures; *spec.*: (*a*) *Entomol.* a section of an insect's antenna, supporting the club; (*b*) *Bot.* the stalk attaching a seed or ovule to the placenta. M19.

funicular /fjʊˈnɪkjʊlə, fəˈnɪk-/ *a.* & *n.* M17. [f. as next + -AR[1].] A *adj.* **1** Of or pertaining to a funiculus or funicle; of the nature of a funiculus; filamentary, cordlike. M17. **2** Of or pertaining to a rope or its tension; depending on or worked by a rope. E19.

Special collocations: **funicular polygon** a figure assumed by a cord supported at its extremities and having weights attached at various points. **funicular railway**: a cable railway with ascending and descending cars counterbalanced.

B *n.* A funicular railway. E20.

funiculus /fjʊˈnɪkjʊləs/ *n.* Pl. **-li** /-lʌɪ, -liː/. M17. [L, dim. of *funis* rope: see -CULE.] **1** A thin rope or filament; *spec.* a hypothetical filament of matter postulated to support the column of mercury in Torricelli's experiment (which actually demonstrated atmospheric pressure). *obs.* exc. *Hist.* M17. **2** = FUNICLE 2. E19.

funiform /ˈfjuːnɪfɔːm/ *a.* M19. [f. L *funis* rope + -FORM.] Shaped like a rope or cord.

funipendulous /fjuːnɪˈpɛndjʊləs/ *a.* E18. [f. L *funis* rope + PENDULOUS.] Hanging from a rope; connected with a hanging rope. Chiefly *joc.*

†**funis** *n.* LME. [L *funis* rope.] *Anat.* **1** One of the veins of the arm. Only in LME. **2** The umbilical cord. M18–M19.

†**funk** *n.*[1] ME–L19. [MDu. *vonke* (Du. *vonk*); cf. PUNK *n.*[2], SPUNK *n.*] A spark; something used as tinder, touchwood. Latterly only *dial.*

funk /fʌŋk/ *n.*[2] & *v.*[1] E17. [Origin uncertain: perh. Fr. dial. *funkier* vb = OFr. *funkier*, *fungier*, f. pop.L wd repr. also by It. *fumicare*, f. late L *fumigare*, f. L *fumus* smoke.] A *n.* **1** A strong smell or stink, *esp.* of tobacco smoke. Now chiefly *US.* E17. **2** Funky music. *slang.* M20.

2 *attrib.*: A. J. AUGARDE Very popular with their loony, disjointed brand of funk rock.

B *v.* Now *rare* or *obs.* **1** *v.t.* Blow smoke on (a person); annoy with smoke. L17. **b** Smoke (a pipe, tobacco). E18. **2** *v.i.* Smoke. Also, cause a smell. L17.

funk /fʌŋk/ *n.*[3] & *v.*[2] *slang.* M18. [Origin uncertain; perh. = FUNK *n.*[2]] A *n.* **1** Cowering fear; a state of panic or terror. M18. **2** A person who funks; a coward. M19.

1 W. BOYD A blind funk seized him and he felt . . he wouldn't be able to go through with it. *blue funk*: see BLUE *a.*

Comb.: **funk-hole** a place of safety, *esp.* in wartime, a dugout; *fig.* an employment used as a pretext for avoiding military service; **funkstick**(s) a coward.

B *v.* **1** *v.i.* Flinch or shrink through fear; show cowardice. Now *rare.* M18. **2** *v.t.* Frighten. Now *rare.* E19. **3** *v.t.* Fight shy of, wish or try to avoid through fear; be afraid of. M19.

3 E. NESBIT Now it was Albert's turn . . but he funked it. E. WAUGH Had arranged to go to Pixton. Funked train and took taxi.

funker *n.* M19.

funkia /ˈfʌŋkɪə/ *n.* Also **funckia**. M19. [mod.L *Funkia* former genus name (obs. synonym of *Hosta*), f. H. C. *Funck* (1771–1839), Prussian botanist: see -IA[1].] = HOSTA.

funkster /ˈfʌŋkstə/ *n. slang* (chiefly *US*). M20. [f. FUNK *n.*[2] + -STER.] A performer or fan of funky music.

funky /ˈfʌŋki/ *a.*[1] *slang.* L18. [f. FUNK *n.*[2] + -Y[1].] 1 Smelling strong or bad; musty, mouldy. Chiefly *US.* L18. 2 Of jazz or other popular music: down-to-earth and uncomplicated; soulful and bluesy, freq. with a syncopated rhythm. Also, fashionable, trendy. M20.

funkily *adv.* L20. **funkiness** *n.*[1] M20.

funky /ˈfʌŋki/ *a.*[2] *slang.* M19. [f. FUNK *n.*[3] + -Y[1].] In a funk; frightened, nervous, timid.

funkiness *n.*[2] L19.

funnel /ˈfʌn(ə)l/ *n.* & *v.* LME. [App. f. OFr. (repr. also in Breton *founilh*), f. Prov. *fonilh*, *enfonilh*, f. L *infundibulum*, (late) *fundibulum*, f. (*in*)*fundere* pour (in).] A *n.* 1 A cone with a small hole or tube at the apex for guiding liquid (orig. esp. wine), powder, etc., through a narrow opening. LME. 2 A tube or shaft for lighting or ventilating; *esp.* the chimney of a steam engine or ship. M16. b The flue of a chimney. L17. 3 *Naut.* A cylindrical band of metal; *esp.* as fitted to the head of a mast, to which the rigging is attached. L17. 4 Anything funnel-shaped; *Zool.* a funnel-shaped organ; a funnel-shaped opening or shaft in rocks etc. E18.

Comb.: **funnel beaker** *Archaeol.* a pottery vessel with a flaring neck (*Funnel Beaker Culture*, a prehistoric culture of northern Europe characterized by the use of funnel beakers); **funnel-web** (*a*) a spider's web with a funnel shape; (*b*) *Austral. colloq.* = *funnel-web spider* (a) below; **funnel-web spider** a spider which builds a funnel-shaped web: (*a*) of the family Dipluridae, *esp.* the highly venomous *Atrax robustus* of eastern Australia; (also **funnel-web tarantula**); (*b*) of the family Agelenidae.

B *v.* Infl. **-ll-**, ***-l-**. 1 *v.i.* Issue (*out*) or rise (*up*) (as) from a funnel or in a funnel-shaped cloud; move (as) through a funnel. L16. 2 *v.t.* Cause to move (as) through a funnel; direct, channel. E20.

1 S. PLATH From between two hills a sudden wind funnels at me. 2 *Scientific American* Three magnetic spectrometers, which funnel the electrons into a system of detectors. D. ARKELL Could he funnel those bursting energies down narrow scholastic paths?

funnelled, ***-eled** *ppl a.* (*a*) provided with a funnel or funnels; funnel-shaped; (*b*) directed (as) through a funnel: L18.

funny /ˈfʌni/ *n.*[1] *arch.* L18. [Origin uncertain; perh. f. the adj.] A light, narrow rowing boat.

funny /ˈfʌni/ *a.*, *n.*[2], & *adv.* M18. [f. FUN *n.* + -Y[1].] A *adj.* 1 Producing fun; comical, amusing. M18. 2 Not quite in good health or good order; slightly unwell, nauseous, deranged, disordered, etc. Formerly also, tipsy. *colloq.* M18. 3 Curious, queer, odd. *colloq.* E19. b Underhand, tricky, deceitful; unorthodox. L19.

1 CONAN DOYLE Excuse my amusement . . but it is really funny to see you trying to play a hand with no cards in it. HENRY MILLER A comedienne of the first water, the only really funny woman I ever met. 2 J. GRENFELL You let him in . . . I feel funny. B. BAINBRIDGE Bernard probably needed exercise on account of his funny hip. 3 V. S. REID Funny thing, but when Father is vexed he looks more like white man than brown. B. EMECHETA There was something funny with that ear, it was definitely bigger than the other. b P. G. WODEHOUSE He is far too scared of our hostess to try any funny stuff on her.

Special collocations & *comb.*: **funny-bone** the part of the elbow over which the ulnar nerve passes, a blow on which can produce a tingling sensation. **funny business** *slang* jesting, comic behaviour; messing about; deception, underhand behaviour. **funny column**: (in a newspaper etc.) containing humorous matter. **funny farm** *slang* a mental hospital. **funny-ha-ha** *colloq.* = sense 1 above. **funny man** a clown or jester. **funny money** *colloq.* (*a*) money reduced in value by rapid inflation; (*b*) counterfeit currency; (*c*) finances amassed by dubious methods. **funny paper** a newspaper etc. containing humorous matter. **funny-peculiar** *colloq.* = sense 3 above.

B *n.* A joke; (usu. in *pl.*) the comic strip(s) in a newspaper etc. M19.

C *adv.* Funnily. *colloq.* M19.

C. M. YONGE They speak so funny, I can't hardly make them out.

funnily *adv.* in a funny manner; amusingly; oddly: E19. **funniment** *n.* (*joc.*, now *rare* or *obs.*) comicality; something comical: M19. **funniness** *n.* M19. **funniˈosity** *n.* (*joc.*) [-OSITY] comicality; something or someone comic: L19.

funster /ˈfʌnstə/ *n. colloq.* L18. [f. FUN *n.* + -STER.] A person who makes fun, a joker.

fur /fəː/ *n.*[1] & *a.* ME. [f. FUR *v.*[1]] A *n.* 1 The dressed coat of any of various animals, or fabric imitating this (now freq. in *pl.*); a trimming, lining, or garment made of this; *esp.* a piece of fur worn around the neck. ME. b Fur worn as a mark of office or state, or as a badge of certain degrees. M17. 2 The short, fine, soft hair of certain animals as distinct from the longer coarser hair. LME. b In *pl.* Animal skins with the fur on them. M16. c *collect.* Furred animals. E19. 3 *Her.* A tincture representing animal skins or portions of skins as if sewn together. M16. 4 Something resembling fur or adhering to a surface like fur; *esp.* (*a*) a coating formed on the tongue in ill health; (*b*) the deposit formed by hard water in a kettle, pipe, etc. L17.

1 W. HOLTBY Muffled in furs to the nose, she did not feel cold. 2 LONGFELLOW Cold would the winter be, for thick was the fur of the foxes. P. H. JOHNSON The cat . . jumped down, leaving . . clouds of fur upon her skirt. **make the fur fly** (orig. *US slang*) make a disturbance, stir up trouble. b W. IRVING Mr. Clarke . . packed all his furs on twenty-eight horses. c **fur and feather** game animals and birds. 4 DICKENS Empty wine bottles with fur and fungus choking up their throats. S. O'FAOLÁIN The fur of mildew and green damp.

Comb.: **fur-seal** any of several eared seals constituting the genera *Arctocephalus* and *Callorhinus*, with thick fur on the underside (the source of sealskin for garments).

B *attrib.* or as *adj.* Made of fur. ME.

A. SILLITOE Her brown coat with its fur collar.

fur *n.*[2] see FURROW *n.*

fur /fəː/ *v.*[1] Infl. **-rr-**. Cf. FURRED, FURRING. ME. [AN, alt. of OFr. *forrer* (mod. *fourrer*) line, encase, sheathe, f. *forre*, *fuerre* sheath f. Gmc.] 1 *v.t.* Line, trim, or cover (a garment etc.) with fur. ME. b Serve as a lining or trimming for. L16. 2 *v.t.* Clothe or adorn (a person) with fur or furs. LME. b In *pass.* Be covered with fur. M17. 3 *v.t.* Cover or coat with a deposit of fur (cf. FUR *n.*[1] 4). M16. 4 *v.i.* Become covered or coated (as) with fur. M16. 5 *v.t. Carpentry.* Fix a timber strip to (uneven joists etc.) to make a plane surface. L17.

1 H. AINSWORTH A robe of violet-coloured velvet, furred with . . ermine. b T. POWELL As many fox-skins as will fur his . . gowne. 2 SIR W. SCOTT Miss Mannering was furred and mantled up to the throat. 3 N. GORDIMER The bath . . was furred with putty-coloured lime like an old kettle. *fig.*: W. GOLDING We are so furred up with the growth of . . laborious knowledge. 4 OED This kettle soon furs.

fur *v.*[2] see FURROW *v.*

†furacan *n.* see HURRICANE.

furacious /fjʊ(ə)ˈreɪʃəs/ *a.* Now *rare.* L17. [f. L *furax*, *furac-* (f. *furari* steal) + -IOUS: see -ACIOUS.] Given to thieving, thievish.

furacity *n.* the inclination or tendency to steal E17.

furaldehyde /fjʊəˈraldɪhʌɪd/ *n.* E20. [f. FURFURALDEHYDE.] *Chem.* Either of two isomeric aldehydes, $C_4H_3(CHO)O$, derived from furan; *esp.* (more fully *2-furaldehyde*) = FURFURALDEHYDE.

furan /ˈfjʊəran/ *n.* L19. [f. FURFURAN.] *Chem.* An unsaturated heterocyclic compound, $(CH)_4O$, which has a planar five-membered ring in its molecule and is a colourless volatile liquid; any substituted derivative of this.

furanose *n.* a sugar with a molecular structure containing the five-membered (C_4O) ring present in furan E20. **fuˈranoside** *n.* a glycoside of a sugar in the furanose form M20.

furbelow /ˈfəːbɪləʊ/ *n.*, *a.*, & *v.* L17. [Alt. of FALBALA.] A *n.* 1 A gathered or pleated strip or border on a skirt or petticoat; a flounce, a ruffle; (in *pl.*, *derog.*) showy ornamentation or trimming on a garment (usu. a woman's). L17. 2 In *pl.* (treated as *sing.*). A seaweed, *Saccorhiza polyschides*, with large frilly fronds divided into ribbons at the ends. M19.

1 L. M. MONTGOMERY Those dresses are good, sensible, serviceable dresses, without any frills or furbelows about them.

B *attrib.* or as *adj.* Having or suggestive of a furbelow or furbelows. L17.

C *v.t.* Ornament with (something resembling) a furbelow or furbelows. Chiefly as *furbelowed* pa. pple. E18.

A. UTTLEY Cold chickens and galantines, all white-frilled and furbelowed.

furbery *n.* var. of FOURBERY.

furbish /ˈfəːbɪʃ/ *v.* & *n.* LME. [OFr. *forbiss-* lengthened stem of *forbir* (mod. *fourbir*) f. Gmc (repr. by OHG *furben*): see -ISH[2].] A *v.t.* 1 Remove the rust from, burnish, polish *up* (a sword, armour, etc.). LME. 2 Clean *up*, renovate, revive, give a new look to, (something dirty, faded, or old). L16.

1 GEO. ELIOT Old arms duly furbished. 2 E. BOWEN Artificial forget-me-nots . . to furbish up country summer hats.

B *n.* An act of furbishing. E19.

¶ Now less common than *refurbish*.

furbisher *n.* a person who furbishes LME.

furca /ˈfəːkə/ *n.* Pl. **-cae** /-siː, -kiː/. E17. [L = FORK *n.*] 1 *Rom. Antiq.* A gallows. Now *rare* or *obs.* E17. 2 *Entomol.* etc. a An apodeme or process in the thorax of many insects. L19. b A pair of diverging processes at the end of the abdomen in certain crustaceans. Also = FURCULA 3. E20.

furcal *a.* furcate; of or pertaining to a furca: M19.

furcate /ˈfəːkeɪt, -kət/ *a.* E19. [Late L *furcatus* cloven, f. L FURCA: see -ATE[2].] Forked, branched.

furcate /ˈfəːkeɪt, fəːˈkeɪt/ *v.i.* M19. [f. prec.: see -ATE[3].] Fork, divide.

furˈcated *a.* = FURCATE *a.*: E19.

furcation /fəːˈkeɪʃ(ə)n/ *n.* M17. [f. L FURCA + -ATION, prob. extracted from BIFURCATION.] The action or an act of forking or branching; a forklike division or branch.

furciferous /fəːˈsɪf(ə)rəs/ *a. rare* (*joc.*). E19. [f. L *furcifer* fork-bearer, (w. ref. to the 'fork' or yoke used to restrain criminals) rascal, jailbird: see -FEROUS.] Rascally.

furcraea /fəːˈkriːə/ *n.* Also **-croea**. E19. [mod.L, f. A. F. de *Fourcroy* (1755–1809), Fr. chemist.] Any of various tropical American plants of the genus *Furcraea*, allied to the agaves.

furcula /ˈfəːkjʊlə/ *n.* Pl. **-lae** /-liː/. M19. [L, dim. of FURCA: see -CULE.] 1 *Ornith.* The wishbone of a bird, consisting of the united clavicles. M19. 2 *Embryol.* A process from which the epiglottis is developed. L19. 3 *Entomol.* The forked appendage at the end of the abdomen in springtails, by which the insect jumps. E20.

furcular /ˈfəːkjʊlə/ *a.* M16. [OFr. *furculaire* f. L FURCULA; later f. prec.: see -AR[1].] †1 Of or pertaining to the collar-bone. Only in M16. 2 Of or pertaining to the furcula of a bird. M19.

furculum /ˈfəːkjʊləm/ *n.* M19. [mod.L, incorrectly formed dim. of FURCA.] = FURCULA 1.

furfur /ˈfəːfə/ *n. arch.* Pl. **-res** /-riːz/. LME. [L = bran.] (A particle of) dandruff or scurf.

furfuraceous /fəːf(j)əˈreɪʃəs/ *a.* M17. [f. late L *furfuraceus*, f. L FURFUR: see -ACEOUS.] Scurfy, scaly, flaky; *Bot.* covered with scales resembling bran.

furfural /ˈfəːf(j)əral/ *n.* L19. [f. FURFUROL + -AL[2].] *Chem.* = next.

furfuraldehyde /fəːf(j)əˈraldɪhʌɪd/ *n.* L19. [f. as prec. + ALDEHYDE.] *Chem.* 2-Furaldehyde, $C_4H_3O \cdot CHO$, a colourless liquid used in synthetic resin manufacture, orig. obtained by distilling bran.

furfuran /ˈfəːf(j)əran/ *n.* L19. [f. as prec. + -AN.] *Chem.* = FURAN.

furfurol /ˈfəːf(j)ərɒl/ *n.* Now *rare* or *obs.* M19. [f. L FURFUR + -OL.] *Chem.* = FURFURALDEHYDE.

furfurous /ˈfəːf(j)ərəs/ *a.* Now *rare.* LME. [f. L FURFUR + -OUS.] Branlike; containing bran or particles resembling bran.

furfuryl /ˈfəːf(j)ərʌɪl, -rɪl/ *n.* L19. [f. FURFUROL + -YL.] *Chem.* = FURYL.

furiant /ˈf(j)ʊərɪənt/ *n.* L19. [Czech.] *Mus.* A type of Bohemian dance in alternating duple and triple time; a piece of music for this dance.

furibund /ˈfjʊərɪbʌnd/ *a.* L15. [Orig. f. (O)Fr. *furibond*; later f. L *furibundus*, f. *furere* to rage.] Furious, raging.

†**furicano** *n.* see HURRICANE.

furied /ˈfjʊərɪd/ *a. rare.* E17. [f. FURY + -ED².] Furious.

furiosity /fjʊərɪˈɒsɪti/ *n.* LME. [OFr. *furiosité* or late L *furiositas* fury, (in med.L) fury, madness, f. L *furiosus*: see FURIOUS, -ITY.] 1 Fury, rage; agony. Now *rare.* LME. 2 Insanity, madness. Long only *Sc. Law* (now *Hist.*). LME.

furioso /fjʊərɪˈəʊzəʊ, *foreign* furiˈoːso/ *n.*, *a.*, & *adv.* M17. [It. f. L *furiosus* FURIOUS.] A *n.* Pl. **-os.** A furious person. Now *rare.* M17. B *adj.* & *adv. Mus.* (A direction:) furious(ly), wild(ly). E19.

furious /ˈfjʊərɪəs/ *a.* LME. [OFr. *furieus* (mod. *-eux*) f. L *furiosus*, f. *furia* FURY: see -OUS.] 1 Full of fury, very angry, raging; resulting from or showing fury; violent, frantic. Formerly also, (of pain etc.) agonizing. LME. 2 (Violently) mad or insane. Long only *Sc. Law* (now *Hist.*). LME. †b Foolish, absurd. *rare.* E16–E17. 3 Excessive; extravagant. *rare.* M17.

1 R. GRAVES Caligula was furious with the knight.. and gave him a good beating. O. MANNING He swung away from them and ran at a furious speed down the stairs. 3 DE QUINCEY Without a suspicion of his own furious romancing.

Phrases: **fast and furious** rapid(ly), hectic(ally), uproarious(ly).

furiously *adv.* LME. **furiousness** *n.* E16.

furison /ˈfjʊərɪz(ə)n/ *n. obs.* exc. *Her.* M16. [MDu. *vuurijzen*, *-ijzer*, f. *vuur* FIRE *n.* + *ijzen*, *ijzer* IRON *n.*] The steel used to strike fire from a flint.

furl /fəːl/ *v.* & *n.* L16. [(O)Fr. *ferler*, earlier *ferlier*, *fermlier*, f. *fer(m)* FIRM *a.* + *lier* bind (f. L *ligare*).] A *v.* 1 *v.t.* Roll up and secure neatly (a sail, flag, umbrella, etc.). Also foll. by *up.* L16. †b Make undulations on (a surface); ruffle, wrinkle. L17–M18. c Swathe or envelop *in* or *with* something folded or twisted. Now *rare.* E18. 2 *v.i.* Be rolled or gathered up or *up* in a twisted form. L17. 3 *v.i.* Roll away, vanish. Foll. by *off*, *from.* Now *rare.* E19.

1 *fig.*: R. LOVELACE All the hopes of your reward you furl.

B *n.* 1 A roll or fold of something furled. M17. 2 The action of furling; the state or manner of being furled. M19.

furlong /ˈfəːlɒŋ/ *n.* [OE *furlang*, f. *furh* FURROW *n.* + *lang* LONG *a.*¹] 1 Orig., the length of the furrow in a common field (regarded as a square of 10 acres), usu. understood to be equal to 40 poles; also, (equal to the Roman *stadium*), the eighth part of a Roman mile. Now, the eighth part of an English mile, 220 yards (201.168 m). OE. †b A running track. LME–E16. 2 An area of land equal to one square furlong; *gen.* an indefinite area of land, a field; the boundary of such an area. Now *dial.* OE.

furlough /ˈfəːləʊ/ *n.* & *v.* Also †**-low**, (earlier as n.) †**forloff.** E17. [Du. *verlof*, modelled on G *Verlaub*, f. *ver-* FOR-¹ + WGmc. base of LEAVE *n.*¹ The stress on the first syll. seems to show infl. of synon. Du. *oorlof* = G *Urlaub* (military or civilian) leave.] A *n.* 1 (A permit for) leave of absence, esp. as granted to a soldier, missionary, etc. E17. †2 A passport; a permit. M17–E19.

1 WELLINGTON Officers not on furlough .. are to join their corps without delay. M. J. BRUCCOLI To arrange .. for Zelda to have three or four months of furlough a year in the company of a nurse.

B *v.* Chiefly *US.* 1 *v.t.* Grant (a person) a furlough; give leave of absence to. L18. 2 *v.i.* Spend a furlough. L19.

furmety *n.* var. of FRUMENTY.

furnace /ˈfəːnɪs/ *n.* & *v.* ME. [OFr. *fornais(e)* (mod. *fournaise*), f. L *fornax*, *fornac-*, f. *fornus*, *furnus* oven.] A *n.* 1 An apparatus or structure consisting of a combustion chamber in which minerals, metals, etc., may be subjected to continuous intense heat. Formerly also, an oven or chamber for producing a low continuous heat (as for incubation). ME. b *fig.* A place of intense heat; a severe test or trial. ME. c (The fires of) a volcano. *rhet.* or *poet.* M17. 2 A boiler, a cauldron. *obs.* exc. *dial.* ME. 3 A closed fireplace for heating a building by means of hot-water pipes etc. L17. 4 (Usu. **F-**.) *The* constellation Fornax. Orig. *the Chemist's Furnace.* M19.

1 A. KOESTLER The sky was like a furnace and the sun its open door. *blast furnace, electric arc furnace, open-hearth furnace*, etc. b AV *Isa.* 48:10 I haue chosen thee in the fornace of affliction.

B *v.* 1 *v.t.* & *i. fig.* Exhale or issue as from a smoking furnace. Long *rare* or *obs.* L16. 2 *v.t.* Subject to the heat of a furnace. E17.

furnage /ˈfəːnɪdʒ/ *n.* L15. [OFr. *fornage* (mod. *fournage*), f. *forn* (mod. *four*), f. L *furnus* oven; in med.L *furn-*, *fornagium*: see -AGE.] *Hist.* The price paid for baking; in *Feudal Law*, the fee paid to the lord by tenants bound to bake in the lord's oven, for permission to use their own.

furner /ˈfəːnə/ *n.* Long *obs.* exc. *dial.* LME. [OFr. *fornier* f. late L *furnarius*, f. L *furnus* oven: see -ER².] A baker.

†**furniment** *n.* M–L16. [OFr. *fornement* (mod. *fourniment* f. It. *fornimento*), f. *fornir* (mod. *fournir*) FURNISH *v.*: see -MENT.] Decoration, fitting out; in *pl.*, fittings, furnishings.

furnish /ˈfəːnɪʃ/ *n.* E16. [f. the vb.] Orig., a provision or supply of anything. Now only *spec.*, the materials from which paper is manufactured.

furnish /ˈfəːnɪʃ/ *v.t.* LME. [OFr. *furniss-* lengthened stem of *furnir* (mod. *fournir*) f. Proto-Romance f. WGmc vb = promote, accommodate, f. base of FRAME *v.*, FROM: see -ISH².] 1 Provide or supply *with* something necessary, useful, or desirable; also foll. by †*in*, †*of.* Formerly also, (foll. by *of*, *with*) fill, occupy (a place) with people. LME. †b Provide for (a need or occasion). LME–M17. 2 Provide, supply, yield (something). LME. 3 Orig., supply with what is necessary, as prepare or equip (a person, ship, etc.) for work or service. Now only, fit up (a house, room, etc.) with (all) the necessary (*esp.* movable) furniture and accessories; equip *with* furniture of a specified kind. LME. †b Accomplish, complete, fulfil, (a task). L15–M16. †c Decorate, adorn. L16–L17.

1 W. S. CHURCHILL A system which .. had for long furnished mankind with its brightest dreams. G. HEYER I could furnish you with the names of at least three of Stavely's mistresses. 2 J. W. KRUTCH To furnish reliable evidence of his desires, tastes, .. and even prejudices. P. F. BOLLER Virginia, New York, Massachusetts, and Ohio have furnished most of the nation's Chief Executives. 3 A. J. CRONIN It had only one room and was .. sparsely furnished. L. DURRELL The interior was .. furnished with chairs of wicker. **furnished house, rooms**, etc., premises let with furniture. c SHAKES. *Much Ado* I'll show thee some attires, and have thy counsel Which is the best to furnish me to-morrow.

With advs. in specialized senses: **furnish forth** *arch.* (*a*) supply or equip with or *with* what is necessary; (*b*) provide (something). **furnish out** (now *rare*) (*a*) supply what is lacking, complete; (*b*) provide adequately for.

furnisher *n.* (*a*) a provider or supplier; *spec.* a furniture supplier; (*b*) a brush or roller supplying colour in fabric printing: E16. **furnishment** *n.* (*a*) the action of furnishing; the state of being furnished; (*b*) (in *pl.*, now *rare*) supplies, munitions: M16.

furnishing /ˈfəːnɪʃɪŋ/ *n.* LME. [f. prec. + -ING¹.] 1 Material or equipment necessary for some purpose. Now only *spec.* (usu. in *pl.*) furniture and other (decorative) accessories (as curtains, carpets, etc.) for a room, house, etc. LME. b (A) decoration; a clothing accessory. L16. †c In *pl.* Superficialities. *rare* (Shakes.). Only in E17. 2 The action of FURNISH *v.*; *arch.* an instance of this. L15.

1 *soft furnishing(s)*: see SOFT *a.*

furniture /ˈfəːnɪtʃə/ *n.* E16. [Fr. *fourniture* (OFr. *forneture*, AL *furnitura*), f. *fournir* FURNISH *v.*] †1 The action of furnishing; (a) decoration. E16–L17. 2 The condition of being equipped or prepared in body or mind (*esp.* for military action etc.); mental cultivation or culture. *arch.* M16. 3†a *sing.* & in *pl.* Personal belongings; dress, apparel; armour. M16–M18. b *sing.* & (*rare*) in *pl.* The harness, housings, trappings, etc., of a horse or other animal. M16. c *sing.* & †in *pl.* Apparatus, tools, military equipment and weaponry; *fig.* mental equipment or apparatus. Now chiefly *Naut.*, the movable equipment of a ship, as the rigging, sails, tackle, etc. M16. 4 *sing.* & †in *pl.* Accessory equipment. Now *spec.* the finger-plate, handle, and lock of a door; the plate, handle, etc., of a coffin; the mountings of a rifle. M16. b *Printing.* The pieces of wood, metal, etc. placed round or between the type to make blank spaces and fasten the matter in the chase. L17. 5 Something to fill or occupy a space, vessel, etc.; contents. Formerly also, a stock or supply of anything; stores, provisions. Now *rare.* M16. 6 (The predominant sense.) The movable (functional) articles in a room, house, etc.; such articles in general. Also (now *rare*), ornamental hangings or drapery, bedlinen. L16. b *fig.* Something or someone regarded merely as filling a vacant space in a room etc. (cf. *part of the furniture* below); *esp.* well-bound books intended to fill and adorn bookshelves. E20. 7 *Mus.* A powerful mixture stop in an organ. L17.

1 SHAKES. *1 Hen. IV* There shalt thou know thy charge, and there receive Money and order for their furniture. RBT JOHNSON They adorne themselves with plumes and feathers .. and such like furnitures. 2 J. MASON A Thing that hath been often attempted by Men of mean Furniture. 5 J. RAY The Earth remaining without any Furniture or Inhabitants. T. BEST Fishes .. make a considerable addition to the furniture of the table. 6 G. B. SHAW The trade in sham antique furniture. J. G. COZZENS The living-room .. had almost no furniture—two chairs, a card-table. **part of the furniture** *colloq.* a person or thing taken for granted. b B. FRIEDAN The need .. that makes husbands 'furniture' in their own homes.

Comb.: **furniture beetle** a small wood-boring beetle of the family Anobiidae (cf. WOODWORM); esp. *Anobium punctatum*; **furniture polish**: for the woodwork of furniture; **furniture van** a large van used to move furniture from one house to another; a removal van.

furnitureless *a.* L19.

furor /ˈfjʊərɔː/ *n.* LME. [L *furor*, f. *furere* to rage: see -OR.] 1 Fury, rage; madness. Now *rare* or *obs.* LME. 2 The inspired frenzy of artists and prophets; an excited mood. L16. 3 = FURORE. Now chiefly *N. Amer.* E18.

1 T. WYATT What rage is this? What furor? 2 With defining adj. in L, as *furor academicus, furor poeticus, furor scribendi*, etc. GEO. ELIOT They were written in a furor. S. FOOTE I am afraid the poetic Furor may have betray'd me into some Indecency. 3 R. MAY What a furor is made over kissing a girl.

furore /fjʊ(ə)ˈrɔːri, fjʊ(ə)ˈrɔː/ *n.* L18. [It., f. as prec.] 1 Enthusiastic admiration; a craze or rage. L18. 2 (An) uproar, (a) disturbance, (a) fuss M20.

2 H. CARPENTER Chester's critiques were causing a furore because of their outspokenness.

furosemide *n.* see FRUSEMIDE.

furphy /ˈfəːfi/ *n. Austral. slang.* E20. [*Furphy* carts, water and sanitary carts manufactured by the Furphy family at Shepparton, Vict., during the 1914–18 war.] A false report or rumour; an absurd story.

D. CUSACK Don't tell me you boys believe *that* old furphy?

furred /fəːd/ *a.* ME. [f. FUR *n.*¹, *v.*¹: see -ED¹.] 1 Made of, lined or trimmed with fur. ME. 2 Covered or coated with a deposit of fur (cf. FUR *n.*¹ 4). E16. 3 Of an animal: having fur. M16. 4 Wearing fur; wrapped or clothed in furs. L16.

furrier /ˈfʌrɪə/ *n.*¹ ME. [OFr. *forreor* (mod. *fourreur*), f. *forrer* FUR *v.*¹; later alt. after CLOTHIER.] A dealer in or dresser of fur or furs.

furriery *n.* †(*a*) (*collect.*) furs; (*b*) the process of dressing and making up furs; the business of a furrier: L18.

†**furrier** *n.*² var. of FOURRIER.

furrin /ˈfʌrɪn/ *a. dial.* or *joc.* L19. [Repr. a pronunc.] = FOREIGN *a.*

furriner *n.* = FOREIGNER M19.

furring /ˈfəːrɪŋ/ *n.* LME. [f. FUR *n.*[1], *v.*[1] + -ING[1].] **1** The action of clothing or adorning with fur; a lining or trimming of fur; fur or furs collectively. LME. **2** The state of being or process of becoming furred or crusted; a coating of fur (FUR *n.*[1] 4). E17. **3a** *Shipbuilding.* (A piece of timber used in) the action or process of double planking a ship's side. E17. **b** *Carpentry.* The fixing of timber strips to uneven joists etc. to make a plane surface. L17. **4** The business of trading in furs or hunting furred animals. L18.

furrow /ˈfʌrəʊ/ *n.* Also (*obs.* exc. *Sc.* or *dial.*) **fur.** [OE *furh* = OFris. *furch*, MLG, MDu. *vore* (Du. *voor*), OHG *furuh* (G *Furche*), ON *for* trench, drain, f. Gmc f. IE base repr. also by L *porca* ridge between furrows.] **1** A narrow trench made in the earth by a plough, esp. for seed. OE. **b** Arable land; ploughed land; cornfields. *poet.* LME. **c** A ploughing. Now only *Sc.* E17. **2** A trench, a drain. ME. †**3** A piece of land having the length and breadth of a furrow. ME–L15. **4** Something resembling a furrow; a rut or track, a groove, a long narrow depression or indentation. LME. **b** A deep wrinkle on the face (esp. on the brow). L16. **c** Any of the grooves in the face of a millstone. E19.

1 *plough a lonely furrow*: see PLOUGH *v.* **b** SHAKES. *Temp.* Sun-burnt sicklemen, of August weary, Come hither from the furrow and be merry. 2 N. GORDIMER Make some more furrows, then the water runs away. 4 R. HOOKE Great and deep scratches, or furrows. **b** S. O'FAOLÁIN The little angry furrow between her eyebrows.

Comb.: **furrow-slice** the slice of earth turned up by the mould-board of a plough.

furrowless *a.* M19. **furrow-like** *a.* M19. **furrowy** *a.* full of furrows or wrinkles E17.

furrow /ˈfʌrəʊ/ *v.* LME. [f. the n.] **1** *v.t.* Make furrows in (the earth) with a plough; plough. LME. **2** *v.t.* Make grooves, tracks, or indentations in. LME. **b** Make a track through (water). LME. **c** Make wrinkles in (the face, the brow); (of tears) make a path or mark across. E16. **d** Of a river: excavate (a channel), force (its way) along a channel. E17. **3** *v.i.* Make furrows with a plough; make a track through water. L16. **4** *v.i.* Become furrowed; wrinkle. M20.

2 J. FORBES A hard . . surface, furrowed by linear marks. **b** E. BOWEN A swan furrowed the water. **c** BYRON Fair cheeks were furrowed with hot tears. J. L. WATEN A frown furrowing his swarthy face. 4 C. RAYNER Charles's brow furrowed as he . . politely obeyed his host.

furrowed *ppl a.* having furrows, ploughed; wrinkled, grooved: L16.

furry /ˈfʌri/ *n. dial.* L18. [Origin uncertain: perh. conn. w. FAIR *n.*[1], L *feria*.] A festival held annually at Helston, Cornwall on the eighth of May; (more fully *furry dance*) a distinctive communal dance performed at this (also called *floral dance*).

furry /ˈfəːri/ *a.* L17. [f. FUR *n.*[1] + -Y[1].] **1** Of or consisting of fur; made of, lined or trimmed with fur. L17. **2** Covered with or wearing fur. L17. **3** Resembling fur; coated (as) with fur (cf. FUR *n.*[1] 4). M18.

2 G. C. DAVIES A furry little water-rat swimming along. 3 T. HARDY Cushions of furry moss. W. GOLDING The rock was furry with coloured growths.

furriness *n.* E20.

furthcoming *vbl n.* see FORTHCOMING *vbl n.*

further /ˈfəːðə/ *n. obs.* exc. *Sc.* E16. [f. the vb.] = FURTHERANCE.

further /ˈfəːðə/ *a.* See also FARTHER *a.* [OE *furþra* = OFris. *fordera*, OS *furþ(i)ro*, *forþro*, OHG *fordaro*, f. Gmc base of FORTH: see -ER[3]. Cf. FURTHER *adv.*] †**1** That is before another in position, order, or rank. OE–E19. **2** More extended, going beyond what exists or has been dealt with, additional. ME. **3** More distant or advanced, remoter; *esp.* the remoter of two. Cf. earlier FARTHER *a.* 3. L16.

2 T. HARDY She refrained from further speech. J. CONRAD He shuffled uneasily, but took no further notice. E. BOWEN He wrote for booklets containing further particulars. **further education** formal education, but not usu. university education, provided for people who have left school. **until further notice** or **orders** until explicitly changed. 3 J. CONRAD The passage leading beyond was dark at the further end. **Further India** the regions between the Indian subcontinent and China, i.e. the south-east peninsula of Asia.

¶See note s.v. FARTHER *adv.* & *a.*

further /ˈfəːðə/ *v.* See also FARTHER *v.* [OE *fyrþr(i)an* f. *furþor*, *-þra* FURTHER *adv.*, *a.*] **1** *v.t.* Help on, assist; promote, favour (an undertaking, movement, cause, etc.). OE. **2** *v.i.* Go on, continue; make progress. *obs.* exc. *Sc.* ME. †**3** *v.t.* Honour. *rare.* Only in LME.

1 C. CHAPLIN We went to a school for the week . . which did little to further my education. A. BLOND By furthering and enhancing his author's causes, he became highly successful.

furtherer *n.* a person who or thing which helps something forward; a promoter, a supporter: LME.

further /ˈfəːðə/ *adv.* See also FARTHER *adv.* [OE *furþor*, *-ur*, corresp. to OFris. *further*, OS *furþor* (early mod.Du. *voorder*), OHG *furdar*, *-ir*, f. Gmc base of FORTH: see -ER[3]. Cf. FURTHER *a.*] **1** To or at a more advanced point in space or time; = FARTHER *adv.* I. OE. **2** Beyond the point reached, to a greater extent, more. OE. **3** In addition, additionally; moreover (esp. used when introducing a fresh consideration in an argument). ME. **4** To or at a greater distance; by a greater interval. LME.

1 T. HARDY Instead of coming further she slowly retraced her steps. 2 J. MITCHELL His influence was spread even further than his name. M. KEANE He knew she was right so he didn't take the matter further. 3 K. GRAHAME And further, in addition thereto, you shall give me . . breakfast. **further to** following on from (esp. an earlier letter etc.). 4 B. JOWETT There is nothing further from his thoughts than scepticism. **I'll see you further first** used as a strong refusal of a request.

¶See note s.v. FARTHER *adv.* & *a.*

furtherance /ˈfəːð(ə)r(ə)ns/ *n.* LME. [f. prec. + -ANCE.] The fact of being helped forward; the action of helping forward; advancement, aid, assistance.

H. H. WILSON In furtherance of this project, she kept her son in a state of ignorance.

furtherly /ˈfəːðəli/ *adv.* & *a.* ME. [f. FURTHER *adv.*, *a.*: see -LY[1].] **A** *adv.* = FURTHER *adv.* ME. **B** *adj.* Favourable, advanced, flourishing. E16.

furthermore /fəːðəˈmɔː/ *adv.* ME. [f. FURTHER *adv.* + MORE *adv.*] †**1** = FURTHER *adv.* I, 2. ME–M16. **2** = FURTHER *adv.* 3. ME.

furthermost /ˈfəːðəməʊst/ *a.* See also FARTHERMOST. LME. [f. FURTHER *a.* + -MOST.] †**1** Foremost, first. Only in LME. **2** Most distant or remote, furthest. L15.

2 E. B. PUSEY He . . sets himself to flee to the then furthermost West.

furthersome /ˈfəːðəs(ə)m/ *a.* E17. [f. FURTHER *v.*, *adv.* + -SOME[1].] **1** Adapted to further or help forward; advantageous, helpful. E17. **2** Rash, inclined to go forward. M18.

1 CARLYLE Two little pieces of advice which may prove furthersome to him.

furthest /ˈfəːðɪst/ *a.* & *adv.* See also FARTHEST. LME. [Formed as superl. to FURTHER *a.*, *adv.*: see -EST[1].] **A** *adj.* **1** Most advanced in any direction; (as superl. of FAR *a.*) most remote, farthest. LME. **2** Most remote in time. *obs.* exc. as below. M16.

1 SWIFT The furthest corner of Naboth's vineyard. 2 **at (the) furthest** at the greatest distance, at the latest, at most.

B *adv.* To or at the greatest distance, farthest. LME.

D. C. MURRAY Even when his thoughts wandered furthest, he was mechanically accurate.

furtive /ˈfəːtɪv/ *a.* E17. [(O)Fr. *furtif*, *-ive* or L *furtivus*, *-iva*, f. *furt-* in *furtum* theft: see -IVE.] **1** Done by stealth; secret, clandestine, surreptitious. E17. **b** Stealthy, sly. M19. **2** Stolen; taken by stealth. Now *rare* exc. as passing into sense 1. E18. **3** Thievish. E19.

1 T. C. WOLFE The students made furtive drawings, or passed notes. D. HAMMETT There was nothing furtive about his going in: he entered boldly and directly. **b** CONAN DOYLE A serious change came over the Professor. He became furtive and sly. 2 M. PRIOR Do they [planets] . . Dart furtive beams, and glory not their own? 3 R. F. BURTON The Highlander could not be . . trusted to withhold his furtive hand from the flocks.

furtively *adv.* L15. **furtiveness** *n.* L19.

furuncle /ˈfjʊərʌŋk(ə)l/ *n.* LME. [L *furunculus* lit. 'petty thief', dim. of *fur* thief: see -UNCLE.] *Med.* A boil.

fuˈruncular, **fuˈrunculous** *adjs.* of, pertaining to, or characterized by boils; of the nature of a boil: M19.

furunculosis /fjʊˌrʌŋkjəˈləʊsɪs/ *n.* Pl. **-loses** /-ˈləʊsiːz/. L19. [f. as prec. + -OSIS.] **1** *Med.* A condition marked by the occurrence of multiple and often recurrent boils. L19. **2** A bacterial disease of salmonid fishes, marked by ulcers resembling boils. E20.

fury /ˈfjʊəri/ *n.* LME. [(O)Fr. *furie* f. L *furia*, f. *furiosus* FURIOUS, f. *furere* to rage: see -Y[3].] **I 1** (A fit of) fierce passion, madness, wild anger, or frenzied rage. LME. **2** Impetuosity or violence, esp. in battle. M16. **3** Inspired frenzy; (artistic) inspiration. Now *rare* or *obs.* M16. **4** Violence of weather, disease, or other agency. L16.

1 F. NORRIS One of those furies of impotent grief and wrath . . suddenly took possession of him. S. RUSHDIE In cold fury my uncle hurled his son from the room. 2 R. W. EMERSON To hunt with fury . . all the game that is in nature. 3 POPE A sacred fury fires My ravish'd breast, and all the Muse inspires. 4 E. STILLINGFLEET These waters falling down with so much fury and violence.

II 5 An avenging or tormenting infernal spirit; *spec.* (freq. **F-**) each of the three Greek or Roman goddesses of vengeance and punishment. Freq. in *pl.* LME. **6** A person resembling an avenging fury; *esp.* an angry or malignant woman, a virago. LME.

5 T. ARNOLD All prayed that the furies of her father's blood might visit her with vengeance. 6 DRYDEN Remember, sir, your fury of a wife.

furyl /ˈfjʊərʌɪl, -rɪl/ *n.* E20. [f. FURFURYL.] *Chem.* A radical, $\cdot C_4H_3O$ (of which two isomers exist), derived from furan. Usu. in *comb.*

furze /fəːz/ *n.* [OE *fyrs*: ult. origin uncertain.] **1** = GORSE. OE. **2** *fig.* A beard; a bushy growth of hair. E17.

1 *needle furze*: see NEEDLE *n.*

furzy *a.* of or like furze; overgrown with furze; bushy; fuzzy: E17.

fusain /ˈfjuːzeɪn, *in sense 1 also foreign* fyzɛ̃ (*pl. same*)/ *n.* L19. [Fr. = spindle tree, charcoal.] **1** Artists' charcoal (from the wood of the spindle tree); a charcoal drawing. L19. **2** *Geol.* Coal resembling wood-charcoal. Now *spec.* one of the lithotypes of coal: a dull, friable, porous material. L19.

fusarium /fjʊˈzɛːrɪəm/ *n.* E20. [mod.L (see below), f. L *fusus* spindle.] A mould of the large genus *Fusarium*, members of which are responsible for various wilting diseases of plants; infestation with any of these or related moulds.

fusarole /ˈfjuːzərəʊl/ *n.* M17. [Fr. *fusarolle* f. It. *fusaruola*, ult. f. L *fusus* spindle: see -OLE[1].] *Archit.* A semicircular beaded moulding usu. placed under the echinus in the Doric, Ionic, and Corinthian orders.

†**fusby** *n. slang. derog.* E18–L19. [Prob. alt. of FUBSY.] A (fat) woman.

fusc *a.* var. of FUSK.

fuscous /ˈfʌskəs/ *a.* M17. [f. L *fuscus* dusky + -OUS.] Of a dark or sombre colour; dusky.

fuse /fjuːz/ *n.*[1] Also ***fuze**. M17. [It. *fuso* spindle, f. L *fusus*.] **1** Orig., a tube, casing, cord, etc., filled or saturated with combustible matter for igniting a bomb, blasting-charge, etc. Now also more widely, any device or component designed to detonate the explosive charge in a bomb, mine, warhead, etc., after an interval of time, or under set circumstances such as impact. M17. **2** Prepared material of which fuses may be made by cutting it into lengths. M18.

1 I. MURDOCH He felt like someone who had lit a long fuse to a barrel of gun powder. *Guardian* Bombs equipped with photo cells, magnetic and proximity fuses, and vibration detectors that would set off the charge if you so much as looked at it. *short fuse*: see SHORT *a.*

fuse /fjuːz/ *n.*² L19. [f. FUSE *v.*¹] (A safety device containing) a strip or wire of easily-melted metal which, when incorporated in an electric circuit, will melt and so interrupt the circuit if the current increases beyond a set magnitude.

blow a fuse (cf. BLOW *v.*¹ 16) cause or undergo the failure of a fuse; *fig.* react with sudden anger or consternation, be incapacitated by exertion or shock.

Comb.: **fuse-box** a small cupboard or box containing the fuses for the circuits in a house etc. **fuse-wire** (a length of) wire suitable for use as a fuse (of given current rating).

fuse /fjuːz/ *v.*¹ L16. [L *fus-* pa. ppl stem of *fundere* pour, melt; cf. FOUND *v.*²] **1a** *v.t.* & (later) *i.* Melt or undergo melting by means of intense heat. L16. **b** *v.t.* Liquefy, thin (the blood). *arch.* E18. **2** *v.t.* & (later) *i.* Blend, unite, or bond (together) as one whole (as) by melting; be blended etc. thus. M17. **b** *v.i.* Of anatomical structures, groups of atoms, etc.: coalesce, join. Chiefly as *fused* ppl a., congenitally joined, forming one structure. L19.

1 B. TAYLOR As by fierce heat, the chains be fused apart. 2 E. TEMPLETON All the other evenings . . had fused together in her memory into one indistinguishable whole. E. JOHNSON No writer so intimately fuses the familiar and the strange as he does. **fused participle** *Gram.* a participle grammatically analysed as being joined with a preceding noun or pronoun where there is no clear indication of the nominal or verbal use of the participle (as *we heard them playing*), rather than as a gerund requiring the possessive (as *we heard their playing*). b ST G. J. MIVART In Tortoises all the trunk vertebræ are fused.

fuse /fjuːz/ *v.*²*t.* Also ***fuze**. E19. [f. FUSE *n.*¹] Provide (a bomb etc.) with a fuse; set by means of a fuse. Chiefly as *fused* pa. pple.

L. DURRELL The bomb, placed in a cinema and fused to go off during a charity performance.

fuse /fjuːz/ *v.*³ E20. [f. FUSE *n.*²: sense 2 partly use of FUSE *v.*¹] **1** *v.t.* Equip with a fuse. Chiefly as *fused* pa. pple. E20. **2a** *v.i.* Of an electric light, appliance, etc.: fail or cease to function owing to the melting of a fuse. M20. **b** *v.t.* Cause (an appliance etc.) to fail or cease to function thus. M20.

fusee /fjuːˈziː/ *n.*¹ Also **fuzee**. L16. [Fr. *fusée* spindleful, ult. f. L *fusus* spindle.] †**1** A spindle-shaped figure. Only in L16. **2** A conical pulley or wheel; *esp.* the wheel of a clock or watch on which the chain is wound and which equalizes the power of the mainspring. E17. **3** = FUSE *n.*¹ I. L17. **4** A large-headed match for lighting a cigar or pipe in the wind. M19.

fusee /fjuːˈziː/ *n.*² *obs.* exc. *Hist.* Also **fuzee**. M17. [Fr. *fusil*: see FUSIL *n.*²] = FUSIL *n.*² 2.

fuselage /ˈfjuːzəlɑːʒ, -lɪdʒ/ *n.* E20. [Fr., f. *fuseler* shape like a spindle, f. *fuseau* spindle: see FUSIL *n.*¹, -AGE.] The elongated body section of an aeroplane, containing the crew and passengers or cargo.

fusel oil /ˈfjuːz(ə)l ɔɪl/ *n. phr.* M19. [G *Fusel* bad brandy etc.; cf. *fuseln* FOOZLE *v.*] A mixture of several alcohols, esp. amyl alcohol, which is a by-product of alcoholic fermentation and can sometimes make alcoholic liquors harmful or poisonous.

†**fusht** *int. Sc.* & *dial.* L18-E19. [Repr. Sc. dial. pronunc. of WHISHT.] Hush!

fusible /ˈfjuːzɪb(ə)l/ *a.* LME. [(O)Fr., or med.L *fusibilis*, f. *fus-* (see FUSE *v.*¹) + *-ibilis* -IBLE.] Able to be melted.

fusible plug a metal plug in the skin of a boiler, designed to melt and allow escape of pressure if the contents reach too high a temperature.

fusiˈbility *n.* E17.

fusidic /fjʊˈsɪdɪk/ *a.* M20. [f. mod.L *Fusidium* (see below), f. L *fusus* spindle: see -IC.] Biochem. *fusidic acid*, an antibiotic steroid obtained from a strain of the fungus *Fusidium coccineum* and used esp. to treat staphylococcus infection.

fusiform /ˈfjuːzɪfɔːm/ *a.* M18. [f. L *fusus* spindle + -I- + -FORM. Cf. Fr. *fusiforme*.] Chiefly *Bot.* & *Zool.* Tapering at both ends, spindle-shaped.

fusil /ˈfjuːzɪl/ *n.*¹ LME. [OFr. *fu(i)sil*, *fusel* (mod. *fuseau*), f. Proto-Romance dim. of L *fusus* spindle.] *Her.* A charge in the form of an elongated lozenge.

fusil /ˈfjuːzɪl/ *n.*² L16. [Fr., ult. f. L FOCUS *n.* hearth (in pop.L fire).] †**1** A flint in a tinder-box. Only in L16. **2** *Hist.* A light musket. L17.

fusile /ˈfjuːsʌɪl, -zʌɪl, -zɪl/ *a.* Also **fusil** /ˈfjuːzɪl/. LME. [L *fusilis* molten, f. *fus-*: see FUSE *v.*¹, -ILE.] **1** Formed by melting or casting, cast. LME. **2** Able to be melted; molten. Now *rare*. E17.

fusilier /fjuːzɪˈlɪə/ *n.* Also ***-eer**. L17. [Fr., f. *fusil* FUSIL *n.*²: see -IER.] Orig. (now *Hist.*), a soldier armed with a fusil. Now, a member of any of several British regiments orig. armed with fusils (usu. in *pl.*, in regimental titles).

fusillade /fjuːzɪˈleɪd, -ˈlɑːd/ *n.* & *v.* E19. [Fr., f. *fusiller* shoot: see -ADE.] **A** *n.* (Wholesale slaughter by) a simultaneous or successive discharge of firearms; *fig.* a sustained outburst or barrage of criticism etc. E19. **B** *v.t.* Shoot down or assault by a fusillade. E19.

fusilly /ˈfjuːzɪli/ *a.* LME. [OFr. *fuselé*, f. *fusel* FUSIL *n.*¹] *Her.* Of a field: covered with a pattern of fusils.

fusimotor /ˈfjuːzɪməʊtə/ *a.* M20. [f. L *fusus* spindle + MOTOR *a.*] *Anat.* Of, pertaining to, or designating the motor neurons with slender fibres which innervate muscle spindles.

fusion /ˈfjuːʒ(ə)n/ *n.* M16. [Fr., or L *fusio(n-)*, f. *fus-* pa. ppl stem of *fundere* pour: see FUSE *v.*¹, -ION.] **1** The action or process of melting by means of intense heat; the state of fluidity as a result of being heated. M16. **b** A fused mass. E19. **2** The union, blending, or bonding together as one whole of different things (as) by melting. L18. **b** The coalition of political parties or factions. M19. **c** *Physiol.* & *Psychol.* [tr. G *Verschmelzung*.] A blending of separate stimuli (e.g. on each eye) into a unitary experience; the process whereby a succession of similar stimuli produces a continuous effect. L19. **3** *Physics.* The union of atomic nuclei to form a heavier nucleus, usu. with release of energy; this process as a source of energy. M20. **4** Music in which elements of more than one popular style are combined. L20.

2 J. ROSENBERG As in all his greatest works, one feels here a fusion of the real with the visionary. F. HOYLE There were widespread fusions which eventually formed the pieces into a single continent.

Comb.: **fusion bomb** a bomb deriving its energy from nuclear fusion; *spec.* a hydrogen bomb; **fusion weld**: made by melting and joining the metal without the application of pressure.

fusional *a.* of or pertaining to fusion; *spec.* in *Ling.* (of a language) inflecting: E20. **fusionist** *n.* & *a.* (*a*) *n.* a person who strives for coalition between political parties, factions, etc.; (*b*) *adj.* of or pertaining to fusionists; supporting political fusion: M19.

fusk /fʌsk/ *a.* Now *rare*. Also **fusc**. LME. [L *fuscus*.] Dark brown, dusky.

Also **fusky** *a.* E17.

fusogenic /fjuːzəˈdʒɛnɪk/ *a.* L20. [f. FUS(ION + -GENIC.] *Biochem.* Causing or promoting the fusion of membranes.

ˈ**fusogen** *n.* a fusogenic agent L20.

fusoid /ˈfjuːzɔɪd/ *a.* L19. [f. L *fusus* spindle + -OID.] = FUSIFORM.

†**fuss** *n.*¹ M17-E18. [Abbrev.] = FUSSOCK I.

fuss /fʌs/ *n.*² & *v.* E18. [Origin uncertain: perh. Anglo-Ir.] **A** *n.* **1** A (disproportionate or excessive) commotion or display of concern (*about* something); ostentatious or officious activity; the treatment of trifling matters as important; abundance of petty detail. Also (*colloq.*), a sustained protest or dispute. E18. **2** A state of (usu. excessive) concern or anxiety. E18. **3** A person who is continually making a fuss. *colloq.* M19.

1 MALCOLM X I would cry out and make a fuss until I got what I wanted. B. BAINBRIDGE The brain specialist had kicked up an almighty fuss about it, to no avail. **make a fuss of, over,** †**with** pamper, treat with an excessive display of affection or attention. 2 J. VANBRUGH Why, here's your Master in a most violent fuss.

B *v.* **1** *v.i.* Make a fuss (*about, over*); busy oneself excessively with trivial matters etc., bustle (*about*). L18. **2** *v.t.* Agitate, worry, bother (a person). E19.

1 A. F. LOEWENSTEIN She fussed around, showing how the door locked itself and how to set the alarm clock. K. MOORE Roberta had fussed over her and adored her as a rare little creature.

Comb.: **fussbudget, fusspot**, etc. = sense A.3 above.

fuˈssation *n.* the action or practice of fussing; a fuss: L18. **fusser** *n.* a person who fusses L19. **fussifiˈcation** *n.* = FUSSATION: M19. **fussify** *v.i.* bustle (*about*), make a fuss M19.

fussock /ˈfʌsək/ *n.* L17. [Origin unkn.] **1** A fat unwieldy woman. *dial.* (orig. *slang*). L17. **2** An untidy mass or bundle. *Sc.* M19.

fussocking *a.* (now *dial.*) unwieldy, fat L18.

fussy /ˈfʌsi/ *a.* M19. [f. FUSS *n.*² + -Y¹.] **1** Inclined to fuss; fastidious. M19. **b** Of a place: bustling. *dial.* & *US.* M19. **2** Of a dress etc.: having excessive detail or ornamentation. M19.

1 B. PYM He's fussy, so I had to pick out all the least greasy of the fried potatoes for him.

¶Earlier in UNFUSSY.

fussily *adv.* E19. **fussiness** *n.* M19.

fust /fʌst/ *n.*¹ L15. [OFr. (mod. *fût*) f. L *fustis* cudgel: cf. FOIST *n.*¹] **1** A wine cask. *obs.* exc. *Hist.* L15. **2** A musty smell. M18.

fust /fʌst/ *n.*² *arch.* M17. [It. *fusto* shaft, trunk, f. L *fustis* cudgel.] *Archit.* The shaft of a column or pilaster.

fust /fʌst/ *v.i.* L16. [f. FUST *n.*¹ Cf. FOIST *v.*²] Become mouldy or stale-smelling. Now chiefly *fig.*

A. S. BYATT Frederica's determination to . . not sit in a house and let her talents . . fust in her unused.

fustanella /fʌstəˈnɛlə/ *n.* M19. [It., f. mod.Gk *phoustani*, *phoustanela*, Albanian *fustan*, prob. f. It. *fustagno* FUSTIAN.] A full stiff white kilt worn by men in Greece and Albania.

fustet /ˈfʌstɪt/ *n.* E19. [(O)Fr. f. Prov. = Sp. *fustete*, an etymologizing corruption (as if dim. of Prov. *fust*, Sp. *fuste* stick) of the Arab. source of FUSTIC.] = *young fustic* s.v. FUSTIC.

fustian /ˈfʌstɪən/ *n.* & *a.* ME. [OFr. *fustaigne* (mod. *futaine*) repr. med.L *fustaneum*, (*tela*) *fustanea*, (*pannus*) *fustaneus* = cloth of *Fostat* suburb of Cairo, city in Egypt.] **A** *n.* **1** Orig., a napped fabric of a mixture of linen and cotton or wool. Now also, any of various coarse twilled cotton fabrics with a short nap. Formerly also, a blanket made of such material. ME. **2** Pompous or inflated speech or writing; bombast; drivel. Formerly also, gibberish, jargon. L16.

2 J. JONES Karamazov's powerful fustian about the whole God business.

B *adj.* **1** (Of language) pompous, inflated, (formerly) jargonistic; (of a person etc.) worthless, pretentious. E16. **2** Made of fustian. M16.

1 SHAKES. *2 Hen. IV* For God's sake thrust him down stairs; I cannot endure such a fustian rascal. V. NABOKOV A dismal exchange of . . fustian jokes.

fustianed *a.* dressed in fustian M19.

fustic /ˈfʌstɪk/ *n.* LME. [Fr. *fustoc* f. Sp. f. Arab. *fustuk* f. Gk *pistakē* pistachio tree.] Any of several kinds of wood yielding a yellow dye; *esp.* (more fully *old fustic*) that of the tropical American tree *Chlorophora tinctoria*, of the mulberry family, or (more fully *young fustic*) that of the Venetian sumac, *Cotinus coggygria*. Also, the dye obtained from any of these woods.

fustigate /ˈfʌstɪgeɪt/ *v.t.* Now *joc.* M17. [Late L *fustigat-* pa. ppl stem of *fustigare* cudgel to death, f. *fustis* cudgel: see -ATE³.] Cudgel, beat.

fustigation /fʌstɪˈgeɪʃ(ə)n/ *n.* Now *joc.* L16. [Late L *fustigatio(n-)*, f. *fustigat-*: see prec., -ATION.] The action of cudgelling or beating.

†**fustilarian** *n. rare* (Shakes.). Only in L16. [Origin uncertain: perh. a comic formation on next (see -ARIAN).] = next.

fustilugs /ˈfʌstɪlʌgz/ *n. obs.* exc. *dial.* M16. [App. f. next + LUG *n.*³] A fat slatternly person.

fusty /ˈfʌsti/ *a.* L15. [OFr. *fusté*, f. as FUST *n.*¹ + -Y⁵.] **1** Of bread, corn, (now *dial.*) liquor, etc.: stale-smelling, musty. Of a room etc.: close, stuffy, smelling of dust, damp, etc. L15. **2** Marked by age or neglect; old-fashioned or antiquated in appearance or behaviour. E17.

1 C. P. SNOW The smell of the chapel—earthy, odorous from wood, wax, fusty books. 2 *City Limits* One of the most venerable British companies has managed to shake off its fusty image.

fustily *adv.* L19. **fustiness** *n.* E16.

futah /ˈfuːta/ *n.* E17. [Arab. *fūṭa.*] In Arabic-speaking countries: a long piece of cloth used as a garment, esp. a loincloth, made from fabric of a kind orig. from India.

futchel /ˈfʌtʃ(ə)l/ *n.* Also **-ll**. L18. [Origin unkn.] Each of the pieces of timber carrying or supporting the shafts, pole, or splinter-bar of a carriage.

futhorc /ˈfuːθɔːk/ *n.* Also **-ark** /-ɑːk/. M19. [f. the first six letters, *f, u, þ, o* or *a, r, k.*] The runic alphabet.

futile /ˈfjuːtʌɪl/ *a.* M16. [L *futilis, futtilis* that easily pours out, leaky, f. *fut-*, app. f. *fundere* pour: see -ILE.] 1 Incapable of producing any result; useless, vain. M16. b Occupied with worthless or trivial matters; frivolous, lacking in purpose. M18. 2 Talkative, unable to keep silent. Long *rare.* M16.

1 CONAN DOYLE Our speculations are futile until we have all the facts. A. STORR His whole life has been a futile striving after the impossible.

futilely *adv.* L19. **futileness** *n.* (now *rare*): E18. **futilize** *v.t.* make futile M18.

futilitarian /ˌfjuːtɪlɪˈtɛːrɪən/ *n.* & *a. joc.* E19. [f. next after UTILITARIAN.] (A person) devoted to futile pursuits.

futilitarianism *n.* E20.

futility /fjʊˈtɪlɪti/ *n.* E17. [Fr. *futilité* or L *futilitas*, f. *futilis*: see FUTILE, -ITY.] 1 The quality of being futile; uselessness, pointlessness, ineffectiveness. E17. b Tendency to be occupied with worthless or trivial matters; frivolity. L17. 2 A futile person or thing. M17. †3 Talkativeness, inability to keep silent. M–L17.

1 *New York Times* For us to be instructing people in Central America in.. terrorism is an exercise in futility. 2 E. F. BENSON The futilities in which Aunt Elizabeth's days were passed.

†futilous *a.* E17–E18. [f. FUTILE + -OUS.] Futile.

futon /ˈfuːtɒn/ *n.* Also **futong**. L19. [Jap.] Orig. in Japan, a cotton-stuffed mattress rolled out on the floor for use as a bed; more widely, such a mattress that can be used as a seat when folded up.

futtah *n.* var. of WHATA.

futtock /ˈfʌtək/ *n.* ME. [Origin uncertain: perh. f. FOOT *n.* + HOOK *n.* or f. MLG, but cf. PUTTOCK *n.*[2]] *Naut.* Any of the timber pieces forming a ship's frames or ribs.

Comb.: **futtock plate** each of the metal plates by which the upper ends of the futtock shrouds are secured to the lower mast-top; **futtock shroud** each of the small ropes or metal rods supporting the top on a lower mast and running from the futtock plates downwards and inwards towards the lower mast.

futural /ˈfjuːtʃ(ə)r(ə)l/ *a.* E20. [f. next + -AL[1].] Of or pertaining to the future; *spec.* (*Gram.*) having a future sense.

future /ˈfjuːtʃə/ *a.* & *n.* LME. [(O)Fr. *futur(e)*, f. L *futurus, -ura*, future pple of *esse*, f. *fu-*: see BE.] A *adj.* 1 That is to be, become, or happen; intended, prospective. LME. 2 Of or pertaining to time to come; *spec.* in *Gram.* (of a participle or tense) expressing an action yet to happen. LME. 3 Subsequent. E17.

1 LYTTON I wish I were the future Lady Vargrave. I. MURDOCH Plans for future work. 3 W. L. SARGANT This rhapsody will not be intelligible to those unacquainted with St. Simon's future history.

B *n.* 1 *The* time to come. LME. 2 What will happen in time to come. Orig. in *pl.*, future events. LME. 3 The prospective condition (*spec.* a successful, prosperous one) of a person, country, etc. M19. 4 *Comm.* In *pl.* Goods and stocks bought and sold for future delivery; contracts to sell or buy on these terms. M19. 5 *Gram.* (A word or form in) the future tense. L19.

1 E. M. FORSTER She could look into the future and plan for her child. *personified*: T. S. ELIOT And what is spoken remains in the room, waiting for the future to hear it. **for the future, in future** from now onwards. *the wave of the future*: see WAVE *n.* 2 W. R. INGE To predict the future.. is.. the most important part of the work of an historian. 3 G. SANTAYANA She saw before her a desolate future. H. CARMICHAEL There's no future in being an accessory after the fact in a murder case.

Comb. & *special collocations*: **future contingent** *Philos.* a proposition which concerns the future and is therefore neither verifiable nor falsifiable in the present; **future life** existence after death, esp. as an object of belief; *future perfect*: see PERFECT *a.* 9, *n.* 3; **future shock** a state of distress or disorientation due to rapid social or technological change; **future state** = *future life* above.

futureless *a.* M19. **†futurely** *adv.* in future, hereafter; later: E17–L18. **futureness** *n.* E19. **futurize** *v. rare* (*a*) *v.i.* (*Gram.*) form the future tense; (*b*) *v.t.* make future: M19.

futurism /ˈfjuːtʃərɪz(ə)m/ *n.* E20. [f. FUTURE + -ISM, after It. *futurismo*, Fr. *futurisme.*] A movement in art, literature, music, etc., originating in Italy, characterized by violent departure from traditional forms so as to express movement and growth. Also more widely, futuristic tendencies in any sphere; belief or interest in human progress.

futurist /ˈfjuːtʃərɪst/ *n.* & *a.* M19. [f. FUTURE + -IST.] A *n.* 1 A person who is concerned with or studies the future; a believer in human progress. M19. 2 *Theol.* A person who believes that eschatological prophecies are still to be fulfilled. M19. 3 [Cf. It. *futuristo*, Fr. *futuriste.*] An adherent of futurism in art etc. E20. B *adj.* Of futurists or futurism; futuristic. L19.

futuristic /fjuːtʃəˈrɪstɪk/ *a.* E20. [f. prec. + -IC.] Having the characteristics of futurism; ultra-modern; of, pertaining to, or predicted for the future.

S. NAIPAUL H. G. Wells' futuristic fantasy.. in which the hero transports himself to the year 802,700. R. FRAME We had lunch at a round futuristic building beside the autobahn called the Sputnik-Sporthotel.

futurition /fjuːtʃəˈrɪʃ(ə)n/ *n.* Now *rare.* M17. [med.L *futuritio(n-)*, irreg. f. L *futurus*: see FUTURE, -ION. Cf. Fr. *futurition.*] *Philos.* 1 Existence or occurrence in the future; a future event or existence. M17. 2 The fact of something having a future existence. M17.

futurity /fjʊˈtjʊərɪti, -tʃ-/ *n.* E17. [f. FUTURE + -ITY.] 1 Future time. E17. 2 *sing.* & in *pl.* Future events. M17. b (A) future condition or state; (an) existence after death. M18. 3 = FUTURITION 2. *rare.* M17.

Comb.: **futurity stakes** a horse-race etc. held long after entries or nominations are made.

futurology /fjuːtʃəˈrɒlədʒi/ *n.* M20. [f. FUTURE + -OLOGY.] The systematic forecasting of the future esp. by the study of present trends in society etc.

futuroˈlogical *a.* L20. **futurologist** *n.* M20.

futz /fʌts/ *v.i. N. Amer. slang.* M20. [Origin uncertain: perh. alt. of Yiddish *arumfartzen* fart about.] Waste time, loaf or mess *around* (*with*).

fu yung /fuː ˈjʌŋ/ *n. phr.* Also **foo yong** /fuː ˈjɒŋ/. M20. [Chin. (Cantonese) *foō yung* lit. 'hibiscus'.] A Chinese dish or sauce made with eggs mixed and cooked with other ingredients.

fuze *n.*, *v.* see FUSE *n.*[1], *v.*[2]

fuzee *n.*[1], *n.*[2] vars. of FUSEE *n.*[1], *n.*[2]

fuzz /fʌz/ *n.*[1] L16. [Prob. of L Du. origin; cf. Du. *voos*, LG *fussig* spongy.] 1 In full and now only *fuzz-ball*. A puffball fungus. L16. 2 A light fluffy mass of particles or fibres; fluffy or frizzy hair; a blur on a photograph etc. L17.

2 *fig.*: B. PLAIN There was a fuzz of confusion in his mind right now.

Comb.: **fuzzbox** a device which imparts a buzzing quality to the sound of an electric guitar etc.; **fuzzword** a deliberately confusing or imprecise term; a piece of jargon.

fuzz /fʌz/ *n.*[2] *slang* (orig. *US*). E20. [Origin unkn.] *collect. The* police; police officers. Less commonly as *sing.*, a police officer.

fuzz /fʌz/ *v.*[1]*i.* Long *obs.* exc. *dial.* L17. [Imit.] Make a fizzing or popping noise.

fuzz /fʌz/ *v.*[2] E18. [f. FUZZ *n.*[1]] 1 *v.t.* & *i.* Make or become fluffy, blurred, or indistinct. E18. 2 *v.t.* Cover with fuzz. M19.

1 R. COOVER When he tried to picture it in his mind, it fuzzed into a big blur. 2 T. O'BRIEN His chest was fuzzed with black hair.

fuzzle /ˈfʌz(ə)l/ *v.t.* E17. [Origin uncertain: cf. FUZZ *n.*[1], FUDDLE *v.*] Intoxicate, confuse.

fuzzy /ˈfʌzi/ *a.* & *n.* E17. [f. FUZZ *n.*[1] + -Y[1].] A *adj.* 1 Not firm, spongy. *obs.* exc. *dial.* E17. 2 Frayed into loose light fibres; covered with fuzz; fluffy; (of hair) frizzy. E18. 3 Blurred, indistinct; imprecise, vague. L18. b *Computing* & *Logic.* Defined so as to allow for imprecise criteria of set-membership. M20.

3 *Philosophical Transactions* Venus appeared very dim and fuzzy. H. ROBBINS Rocco answered the phone; his voice was fuzzy with sleep. A. LURIE Escapism and fuzzy thinking; absorbing bogus ideas. b **fuzzy logic**: dealing with fuzzy sets and concepts.

B *n.* = FUZZY-WUZZY. *slang* (usu. considered *racially offensive*). L19.

fuzzily *adv.* M19. **fuzziness** *n.* E17.

fuzzy-wuzzy /ˈfʌzɪwʌzi/ *n. slang* (usu. considered *racially offensive*). L19. [Redupl. of prec.] A Black person, *esp.* one with tightly curled hair; *spec.* †(*a*) a Sudanese soldier; (*b*) *Austral.* a native of New Guinea.

-fy /fʌɪ/ *suff.* Also (see below) **-ify**. [f. or after F *-fier* f. L *-ficare* (cf. -FICATION) and *-facere* (cf. -FACTION).] Used, usu. w. intermediate -I-, to form vbs: (i) f. ns. w. the senses 'make, produce' (*pacify, satisfy, speechify*), 'make into' (*deify, petrify*), 'make like' (*countrify*); (ii) f. adjs. w. the sense 'bring or come into a certain state' (*Frenchify, sanctify, solidify*); (iii) f. L vbs w. causative sense (*horrify, stupefy*).

fyke /fʌɪk/ *n.*[1] *Sc.* E17. [f. the vb.] 1 A restless movement, a twitch or fidget. Formerly also, something causing this, *esp.* an itch. Now *rare.* E17. 2 (A) fuss; commotion, excitement. Formerly also, (a) flirtation. E18.

fyke /fʌɪk/ *n.*[2] *US.* M19. [Du. *fuik* fish-trap.] A bag-net for catching fish. Also *fyke-net*.

fyke /fʌɪk/ *v.* Also **fike**. Chiefly *Sc.* & *north.* ME. [ON (MSw.) *fikja* move briskly, be restless or eager.] 1 *v.i.* Move restlessly, bustle, fidget. ME. †2 *v.t.* Vex, trouble. L16–M19.

fylfot /ˈfɪlfɒt/ *n.* L15. [Origin uncertain: perh. f. *fill-foot* a pattern for filling the foot of a painted window.] A swastika.

fyrd /fəːd, fɪəd/ *n.* [OE *ferd, fierd, fyrd* = OFris. *ferd*, OS *fard*, OHG *fart* (G *Fahrt*) ON *ferð*, f. Gmc base of FARE *v.*] *Hist.* The English militia before the Norman Conquest; the duty to serve in this.

fytte *n.* var. of FIT *n.*[1]

G

G, g /dʒiː/, the seventh letter of the modern Eng. alphabet and of the ancient Roman one, orig. corresp. to a differentiated form of C. In early L the letter represented the voiced velar plosive consonant /g/; subsequently bef. front vowels it was pronounced as a palatal or palato-alveolar affricate /dʒ/, its representation in the Romance languages being the same as the L consonant I, which developed into the same sound. G in mod. Eng. has the following values. (i) G has the 'hard' sound /g/ bef. *a, o, u*, in a number of wds bef. *e, i, y*, bef. a consonant, and when final. (ii) G has the 'soft' sound /dʒ/ bef. *e, i, y*. (iii) *gh* is silent in many wds but in a few represents /f/. (iv) G is silent in *gn* at the beginning or end of a wd and in some wds medially. (v) In *ng* finally, and in many wds medially, the *g* is silent, serving to give the *n* the value of velar /ŋ/. Pl. **gees, G's, Gs.**

I 1 The letter and its sound. **2** The shape of the letter.

II Symbolical uses. **3** Used to denote serial order; applied e.g. to the seventh group or section, sheet of a book, etc. **4** *Mus.* (Cap. G.) The fifth note in the diatonic scale of C major. Also, the scale of a composition with G as its keynote. **5** The seventh hypothetical person or example. **6** Designating the seventh-highest class (of academic marks etc.). **7** (Italic *g*.) The acceleration due to gravity (about 9.81 metre/second^2). Also (cap. G), a force resulting from this amount of acceleration; *Astron.* the gravitational constant. **8** *Physics.* [G *gerade* even.] (Usu. italic *g*.) Designating functions, esp. wave functions, which do not change sign on inversion through the origin, and atomic states etc. represented by such functions. Cf. U, U 6.

4 G clef the treble clef. **7** *zero G*: see ZERO *n.* & *a.*

III 9 Abbrevs.: (A small selection only is given here. Those all in caps. or small caps. also occur with a full stop after each letter; some of those all in caps. also occur (i) with initial cap. only, (ii) in small caps.) **G** = general (*US* denoting films suitable for unrestricted viewing); (*Physics*) (as *pref.*) giga-; (*N. Amer. colloq.*) grand (a thousand dollars). **GA** = Georgia (in the US). **Ga** = (*Chem.*) gallium; Georgia (in the US). **Gal.** = Galatians (New Testament). **gal.** = gallon(s). **GATT** = General Agreement on Tariffs and Trade. **GB** = Great Britain. **GBE** = Knight (or Dame) Grand Cross (of the Order) of the British Empire. **GBH** = grievous bodily harm. **GC** = George Cross. **GCB** = Knight (or Dame) Grand Cross (of the Order) of the Bath. **GCE** (*Hist.*) = General Certificate of Education. **GCHQ** = Government Communications Headquarters. **GCIE** = Knight Grand Commander (of the Order) of the Indian Empire. **GCMG** = Knight (or Dame) Grand Cross (of the Order) of St Michael and St George. **GCSE** = General Certificate of Secondary Education. **GCSI** = Knight Grand Commander (of the Order) of the Star of India. **GCVO** = Knight (or Dame) Grand Cross of the Royal Victorian Order. **Gd** (*Chem.*) = gadolinium. **Gdn(s).** = Garden(s). **GDP** = gross domestic product. **GDR** = German Democratic Republic. **Ge** (*Chem.*) = germanium. **Gen.** = General; Genesis (in the Bible). **Geo.** = George. **Ger.** = German. **GeV** = gigaelectronvolt. **G5**, (*US*) **G-5** = Group of Five. **GG** = Governor-General. **GHQ** = General Headquarters. **GHz** = gigahertz. **Gib.** = Gibraltar. **GIFT** /gɪft/ = gamete intrafallopian transfer (the transfer of sperm and ova directly into the Fallopian tubes of a woman to facilitate conception). **GIGO** /ˈgʌɪgəʊ/ (*Computing*) = garbage in, garbage out. **Glam.** = Glamorgan(shire). **GLC** (*Hist.*) = Greater London Council. **Glos.** = Gloucestershire. **GM** = George Medal. **gm.** = gram(s). **GMT** = Greenwich Mean Time. **GMWU** = General and Municipal Workers' Union. **GNP** = gross national product. **Gnr.** = Gunner. **gns.** = guineas. **GOC** = General Officer Commanding. **GOM** = Grand Old Man (*spec.* William Ewart Gladstone). **GOP** (*US*) = Grand Old Party (the Republican Party). **Gov.** = Government; Governor. **Govr.** = Governor. **Govt.** = Government. **GP** = general practitioner; Grand Prix. **Gp. Capt.** = Group Captain. **GPI** = general paralysis (of the insane). **GPMU** = Graphical, Paper and Media Union (formed by the merger of the NGA and SOGAT). **GPO** = General Post Office; (*US*) Government Printing Office. **GR** = [L] *Georgius Rex* King George. **gr.** = grain(s); gram(s); grey; gross. **gs.** = guineas. **G7** = Group of Seven. **g.s.m.** = grams per square metre. **GT** = [It.] *gran turismo* (of a high-performance car designed for touring). **Gt.** = Great. **G10**, (*US*) **G-10** = Group of Ten. **GUI** /ˈguːi/ (*Computing*) = graphical user interface. **GUT** (*Physics*) = grand unified theory. **GW(R)** (*Hist.*) = Great Western (Railway). **Gy** (*Physics*) = gray (the unit).

Ga /gɑː/ *n.* & *a.* Pl. same, **-s**. M19. [Afr. name.] (Designating) a Black people of Ghana or their language.

gab /gab/ *n.*[1] ME. [OFr. = mockery, idle vaunt, f. ON *gabb*.] †**1** Mockery, derisive deception; a lie, deceit. Only in ME. **2** A piece of bravado; a boast. M18.

gab /gab/ *n.*[2] E18. [Var. of GOB *n.*[2]] **1** The mouth. *Sc.* E18. **2** The action of gabbing or talking; talk, prattle, twaddle. *colloq.* E18.

Phrases: **gift of the gab** a talent for speaking; fluency of speech. **stop your gab** be silent.

gab /gab/ *n.*[3] L18. [Origin uncertain: cf. Flem. *gabbe* notch, gash.] *Mech.* A hook or notch in a rod or lever which engages with a pin or spindle.

gab /gab/ *v.*[1] *arch.* Infl. **-bb-**. ME. [(O)Fr. *gaber* mock, deride, vaunt oneself, f. *gab* GAB *n.*[1]] †**1** *v.t.* Reproach, accuse. Only in ME. †**2** *v.i.* Speak mockingly, scoff. (Foll. by *on, upon*.) ME–L16. †**3** *v.i.* & *t.* Lie (to), tell lies (to). ME–L15. **4** *v.i.* Boast, brag. E19.

gab /gab/ *v.*[2]*i.* *colloq.* Chiefly *Sc.* Infl. **-bb-**. E18. [Perh. abbrev. of GABBLE *v.*] Talk glibly; chatter, prattle.

W. MARCH I'm not like you who's gabbing all the time and won't let nobody get a word in edgeways.

gabardine *n.* var. of GABERDINE.

gabbart /ˈgabət/ *n.* L15. [Fr. *gabarre* (now *gabare*), f. Prov. *gabarra* perh. (w. metathesis) f. late L *carabus* coracle.] **1** A sailing vessel for inland navigation; a sailing barge, a lighter. L15. **2** A support used in erecting a scaffold. L19.

gabber /ˈgabə/ *n.* L18. [f. GAB *v.*[2] + -ER[1].] A chatterer, prattler.

gabber /ˈgabə/ *v.t.* E18. [f. GAB *v.*[2] + -ER[5]. Cf. JABBER *v.*, GIBBER *v.*] Talk volubly, jabber.

gabble /ˈgab(ə)l/ *n.* E17. [f. the vb.] **1** Voluble confused unintelligible talk; an instance of this. E17. **2** The inarticulate noises made by some animals. E17.

1 H. E. BATES Forrester heard him shouting, the words simply a gabble of incoherent horror.

gabble /ˈgab(ə)l/ *v.* L16. [MDu. *gabbelen*, of imit. origin.] **1** *v.i.* Speak incoherently; chatter, jabber, prattle. L16. **2** *v.i.* Of a goose: gaggle. L17. **3** *v.t.* Utter rapidly and unintelligibly. M18.

3 E. M. FORSTER Freddy gabbled a grace, and they drew up their heavy chairs and fell to.

gabblement *n.* gabbling, rapid unintelligible noise M19. **gabbler** *n.* E17.

gabbro /ˈgabrəʊ/ *n.* Pl. **-os**. M19. [It. (Tuscan) f. L *glaber, glabr-* smooth.] A dark coarse-grained igneous rock of crystalline texture resembling dolerite and granite, and consisting largely of pyroxene (often as diallage), plagioclase feldspar, and often olivine.

gaˈbbroic, gabbroˈitic *adjs.* L19.

gabbroid /ˈgabrɔɪd/ *a.* & *n.* E20. [f. prec. + -OID.] *Petrogr.* **A** *adj.* Resembling gabbro; *spec.* belonging to the group of rocks including dolerites and gabbros, which contain a high proportion of ferromagnesian minerals. E20. **B** *n.* A gabbroid rock. E20.

gaˈbbroidal *a.* M20.

gabby /ˈgabi/ *a.* Orig. *Sc.* E18. [f. GAB *n.*[2] + -Y[1].] Garrulous, talkative.

gabbiness *n.* M20.

gabelle /gaˈbɛl/ *n.* LME. [Fr. f. It. *gabella* corresp. to Sp. ALCAVALA.] Chiefly *Hist.* A tax, *esp.* a foreign tax; *spec.* the salt-tax imposed in France before the Revolution.

gaberdine /gabəˈdiːn, gabəˈdiːn/ *n.* & *a.* Also (the usual form in senses A.3, B.) **gabardine**. E16. [OFr. *gauvardine, gallevardine*, perh. f. MHG *wallevart* pilgrimage.] **A** *n.* **1** *Hist.* A loose long upper garment, such as formerly worn by Jews, almsmen, beggars, and others. E16. **2** *transf.* & *fig.* Dress, covering, protection. *arch.* L16. **3** A twill-woven cloth, of fine worsted or cotton, freq. waterproofed. E20. **B** *adj.* Made of gabardine. M20.

gaberlunzie /gabəˈlʌnzi, -nji/ *n.* *Sc.* E16. [Origin unkn.] A beggar, a mendicant.

gabfest /ˈgabfɛst/ *n.* *slang* (chiefly *N. Amer.*). L19. [f. GAB *n.*[2] + FEST.] A gathering for talk; a spell of talking; a prolonged conference or conversation.

gabion /ˈgeɪbɪən/ *n.* M16. [Fr. f. It. *gabbione* augm. of *gabbia* CAGE *n.*] A cylinder of wicker or woven metal bands to be filled with earth or stones for use in engineering or (*Hist.*) fortification.

gabioˈnade *n.* a line of gabions E18. **gabionage** *n.* gabions collectively M19.

gable /ˈgeɪb(ə)l/ *n.* & *v.* LME. [(OFr. f.) ON *gafl*: corresp. wds in the other Gmc langs. mean 'fork'.] **A** *n.* **1** The vertical triangular piece of wall at the end of a ridged roof, from the level of the eaves to the summit. LME. **b** Any architectural member having the form of a gable, as a gable-shaped canopy over a window or door. M19. **2** The triangular-topped end wall of a building; a gable-end. LME.

Comb.: **gable-end** a gable-topped wall; **gable-topped** *a.* topped by a gable; having a gable-shaped top; **gable-window** a window in the gable or gable-end of a building.

B *v.* **1** *v.i.* Form a gable. M19. **2** *v.t.* End (a roof) in a gable. L19.

gabled *a.* furnished with a gable or gables M19.

gablet /ˈgeɪblɪt/ *n.* LME. [AN.: see GABLE *n.*, -ET[1].] A small gable, *esp.* one constructed as an ornament.

gablock /ˈgablək/ *n.* L17. [Var. of GAVELOCK.] **1** *Hist.* A metal spur for a fighting cock. L17. **2** An iron crowbar. *dial.* M18.

Gaboon /gəˈbuːn/ *n.* Also **g-**. E20. [A province (now the State of Gabon) and river in W. Africa.] **1** In full *Gaboon mahogany*. A hardwood from the W. African tree *Aucoumea klaineana* (family Burseraceae). E20. **2** *Gaboon adder, viper*, a venomous African snake, *Bitis gabonica*, largest member of the viper family. E20.

gaby /ˈgeɪbi, *dial.* ˈgɔːbi/ *n.* *colloq.* & *dial.* L18. [Origin unkn.] A simpleton.

gad /gad/ *n.*[1] ME. [ON *gaddr* goad, spike, sting = OHG *gart*, Goth. *gazds* f. Gmc: rel. to YARD *n.*[2]] 1 A sharp spike of metal. *obs.* exc. *Hist.* ME. †b A small rod for writing, a stylus. Only in L16. 2 A bar of metal; an ingot. Now *rare.* ME. b *Mining.* A steel wedge; an iron punch. L17. 3 A pointed rod or stick used for driving oxen etc.; a goad. ME. †4 A measuring rod for land; a measure of length differing in various districts; a division of open pasture. LME–L18. 5 A spear. Long *obs.* exc. *Hist.* M16. 6 A rod, a wand, *esp.* a fishing-rod; a stake, a stout stick. *dial.* M16.

3 †**upon the gad** *rare* (Shakes.) as if pricked with a gad, suddenly.

gad /gad/ *n.*[2] Also **G-**. L15. [Alt. of GOD *n.*: cf. AGAD, BEGAD, EGAD.] = GOD *n.*: chiefly as int. & in exclamatory phrs. corresp. to those s.v. GOD *n.* 5.

by gad!, gad!, gadsbodikins, GADZOOKS.

gad /gad/ *n.*[3] E17. [f. GAD *v.*[1]] The action of gadding or rambling about. Only in *on, upon the gad*, on the move, going about.

gad /gad/ *n.*[4] *Anglo-Ir.* & *Mil.* E18. [Ir. & Gael.] A band or rope made of twisted fibres of tough twigs.

gad /gad/ *v.*[1]*i.* Infl. **-dd-**. LME. [Back-form. f. GADLING *n.*[1]] 1 Wander from place to place; rove about idly or in search of pleasure. (Foll. by *about, abroad, out.*) LME. b Esp. of cattle: rush madly about. *obs.* exc. *dial.* M16. 2 *fig.* Wander or go astray in thought or desire. Now *rare.* L16. †3 Of an inanimate object: move about. L16–E17. 4 Of a plant: grow in a spreading or wayward manner, straggle. M17.

1 L. M. MONTGOMERY You're not going to begin gadding about to concerts and staying out all hours of the night.

gadder *n.* M16.

gad /gad/ *v.*[2]*i.* Infl. **-dd-**. M18. [f. GAD *n.*[1]] *Mining.* Use a gad.

gadabout /ˈgadəbaʊt/ *a.* & *n.* E19. [f. GAD *v.*[1] + ABOUT *adv.*] A *adj.* Gadding, roving. E19. B *n.* A person who gads about. M19.

Gadarene /ˈgadəriːn/ *a.* E19. [Late L *Gadarenus*, f. Gk *Gadarēnos*, inhabitant of Gadara (see below).] Of or pertaining to Gadara, a town of ancient Palestine, near the sea of Galilee; *esp.* (w. ref. to *Matt.* 8:28) involving or engaged in a headlong or suicidal rush or flight.

gadbee /ˈgadbiː/ *n.* M16. [f. GAD *n.*[1] + BEE *n.*[1]] A gadfly.

gaddi /ˈgʌdiː/ *n.* Also **gadi** /ˈgɑːdiː/. M19. [Panjabi *gaddī*, Marathi *gādī*, Bengali *gādi*, lit. 'cushion'.] A throne, *esp.* the cushioned throne of an Indian ruler. Also *transf.*, the position of ruler, ruling power.

gade /geɪd/ *n.* M19. [mod.L *gadus* cod f. Gk *gados*. Cf. Fr. *gade.*] A fish of the genus *Gadus*; a codfish.

gadfly /ˈgadflʌɪ/ *n.* L16. [f. GAD *n.*[1] or (esp. sense 2) *v.*[1] + FLY *n.*[1]] 1 A horsefly, bot-fly, or other fly which bites and irritates cattle. L16. †2 A person who gads about. E17–M18. 3 *fig.* A person who irritates or harasses another. Also, an irresistible impulse. M17.

1 D. L. SAYERS Kirk shook his massive head, like a bull teased by gadflies.

gadget /ˈgadʒɪt/ *n.* L19. [Origin unkn.] 1 Orig. *Naut.* A small device, mechanism, or fitting in a piece of machinery etc.; *local* (a vessel equipped with) a winch or small crane. L19. 2 *gen.* An accessory, an adjunct; a knick-knack, a gewgaw. E20.

gadgeˈteer *n.* a person who uses or invents gadgets M20. **gadgetry** *n.* gadgets collectively; the use of gadgets: E20. **gadgety** *a.* M20.

Gadhelic /gəˈdɛlɪk, ga-/ *a.* & *n.* Also (earlier) †**Gath-**. E16. [(med.L *gathelicus*, f. *gathelus* f.) Ir. *Gaedheal*, pl. *Gaedhil* (OIr. *Goidel* GOIDEL): see -IC.] (The language) of the Scottish, Irish, and Manx Celts.

¶The later form *Gadhelic* is a literary formation dating from L18.

gadi *n.* var. of GADDI.

gadid /ˈgeɪdɪd, ˈga-/ *n.* & *a.* L19. [mod.L *Gadidae* (see below), f. *gadus*: see GADE, -ID[3].] A *n.* Any fish of the teleost family Gadidae, which includes cod, haddock, and pollack. L19. B *adj.* Of, pertaining to, or designating this family. E20.

Gaditan /ˈgadɪt(ə)n/ *a.* & *n.* Also **-tane** /-teɪn/. Pl. same, **-s**. E17. [L *Gaditanus* (Sp. *Gaditano*) f. *Gades* Cadiz (see below): see -AN, -ANE.] (A native or inhabitant) of Cadiz, a port in SW Spain.

Gaditanian /gadɪˈteɪnɪən/ *a.* & *n.* M19.

†**gadling** *n.*[1] & *a.* [OE *gædeling* = OS *gaduling*, OHG *gateling*, Goth. *gadiliggs* cousin, f. Gmc base repr. also by OE *gæd* fellowship, *gegada* companion, rel. to GATHER *v.*] A *n.* 1 A companion, a fellow. OE–LME. 2 A base low-born person, a scoundrel. Also, a wanderer, a vagabond. ME–M16. B *adj.* Wandering, straggling. Formerly also, base, low-born. LME–E18.

gadling /ˈgadlɪŋ/ *n.*[2] L16. [f. GAD *n.*[1] + -LING[1].] *Hist.* Any of the metal spikes on the knuckles of a gauntlet.

gadman /ˈgadmən/ *n.* Chiefly *Sc.* Pl. **-men**. LME. [f. GAD *n.*[1] + MAN *n.*] *Hist.* A man or boy using a gad or goad to direct a team of animals, esp. in ploughing.

gadoid /ˈgeɪdɔɪd, ˈga-/ *a.* & *n.* M19. [f. mod.L *gadus* (see GADE) + -OID.] A *adj.* Of or pertaining to the order Anacanthini, which includes marine soft-finned fish such as the gadids and hake. M19. B *n.* A gadoid fish. M19.

gadolinite /ˈgad(ə)lɪnʌɪt, gəˈdəʊlɪnʌɪt/ *n.* E19. [f. Johan *Gadolin* (1760–1852), Finn. mineralogist + -ITE[1].] *Min.* A monoclinic silicate of iron, beryllium, yttrium, and other rare earth elements, occurring as black or brown crystals.

gadolinium /gadəˈlɪnɪəm/ *n.* L19. [f. prec. + -IUM.] A metallic chemical element of the lanthanide series, atomic no. 64, which is strongly magnetic below room temperature. (Symbol Gd.)

gadroon /gəˈdruːn/ *n.* L17. [Fr. *godron*, prob. rel. to *goder* pucker, crease: see -OON.] Any of a series of convex curves or arcs joined at their extremities and forming a decorative edge, like the inverted fluting on silverware etc. Usu. in *pl.*

gadrooned *a.* ornamented with gadroons M18.

gadso /ˈgadsəʊ/ *int. arch.* L17. [Var. of CATSO, infl. by GAD *n.*[2]] = GADZOOKS.

gadwall /ˈgadwɔːl/ *n.* M17. [Origin uncertain: perh. imit.] A greyish-brown freshwater duck, *Anas strepera*, widespread in the northern hemisphere.

gadzooks /gadˈzuːks/ *int. arch.* L17. [f. GAD *n.*[2] + *zooks* of unkn. origin.] Expr. asseveration, annoyance, surprise, etc.

SMOLLETT 'Gadszooks!' said he, 'What business had you with that?'

gadzookery *n.* the exaggeratedly exclamatory dialogue used in some historical novels M20.

gaed *v.* see GO *v.*

Gaekwar /ˈgʌɪkwɑː/ *n.* Also †**Guickwar**. E19. [Marathi *gāekwāḍ* lit. 'cowherd'.] *Hist.* (The title of) the native ruler of Baroda, a State in India until 1960, when it became part of Gujarat.

Gael /geɪl/ *n.* M18. [Gael. *Gael*, *Gàidheal*, corresp. to Ir. *Gael*, *Gaedheal* f. OIr. *Goidel* GOIDEL.] A Scottish Celt; a Gaelic-speaking Celt.

Gaeldom *n.* the land of the Gaels; Gaelic culture or civilization; the Gaelic people: M19.

Gaelic /ˈgeɪlɪk, ˈgalɪk/ *a.* & *n.* M18. [f. GAEL + -IC.] A *adj.* Of or pertaining to the Gaels or Celtic inhabitants of Scotland. Also more widely, of or pertaining to the Scottish, Irish, and Manx Celts. M18.

Gaelic coffee: see COFFEE *n.* **Gaelic football** an Irish game involving two teams of 15 players who can kick, punch, or bounce the ball in order to try and get it into the net or over the bar of the goal. **Gaelic League** a movement founded in 1893 to revive Irish language and culture.

B *n.* The Gaelic language, a member of the Celtic branch of the Indo-European language family consisting *spec.* of Scots Gaelic or, more widely, of Scots and Irish Gaelic and Manx. M18.

Gaelicize *v.t.* make or treat as Gaelic E19.

Gaeltacht /ˈgeɪltəxt/ *n.* E20. [Ir.] Any or all of the areas of Ireland where Irish is commonly spoken.

Gaetulian *a.* & *n.* var. of GETULIAN.

gaff /gaf/ *n.*[1] ME. [Prov. *gaf*, whence also Fr. *gaffe* boat-hook.] 1 A hook; a stick etc. with a hook. Now usu. a barbed fishing-spear, a stick with a hook for landing large fish. ME. b *Hist.* A metal spur for a fighting cock. L17. 2 *Naut.* A spar situated on the after side of a mast and supporting the head of a fore-and-aft sail. M18.

Comb.: **gaff-rigged** *a.* having a gaff on the mainsail; **gaff topsail** small sail having its foot on a gaff.

gaff /gaf/ *n.*[2] *slang.* M18. [Origin unkn.] 1 A fair. Now *rare* or *obs.* M18. 2 Any public place of amusement, *esp.* (also *penny gaff*) a popular theatre, a music hall. Now *rare.* E19. 3 A house, flat, shop, or other building. M20.

gaff /gaf/ *n.*[3] *slang.* E19. [Origin unkn.] 1 Noise; humbug, pretence. E19. 2 *blow the gaff*, reveal or let out a plot or secret. E19. 3 *the gaff*, rough treatment, criticism. Chiefly in *give, stand, take, the gaff. US.* L19.

1 R. SCRUTON I don't want you coming in here with that phoney crap . . I don't need all this gaff. 3 W. M. RAINE Neil has got to stand the gaff for what he's done.

gaff *n.*[4] var. of GAFFE.

gaff /gaf/ *v.*[1] L18. [f. GAFF *n.*[1]] Seize or strike (a fish) with a gaff; draw *out* or *up* with a gaff.

gaff /gaf/ *v.*[2] *slang.* E19. [Origin unkn.] 1 *v.i.* Gamble; *esp.* toss up. E19. 2 *v.t.* Deceive, trick; make (a game or device) crooked or dishonest. Orig. *US.* M20.

gaffe /gaf/ *n.* Also **gaff**. E20. [Fr.] A blunder, a clumsy or indiscreet act or remark.

Blackwood's Magazine I had obviously said the wrong thing, committed a gaffe. C. P. SNOW He gave her a piece of jewellery, and by a clerical gaffe the bill went to his wife.

gaffer /ˈgafə/ *n.* L16. [Prob. contr. of GODFATHER, w. *ga-* by assoc. w. *grandfather*. Cf. GAMMER.] 1 Used as an honourable title usu. preceding a name or as a simple form of address: master, sir; good fellow, old fellow. L16. 2 An elderly rustic; an old fellow; a fellow. L16. 3 A master, a boss; *esp.* the leader or foreman of a group of workmen. M17. b *spec.* The chief electrician of a film crew. M20.

1 SIR W. SCOTT You have marred my ramble, Gaffer Glover. J. H. NEWMAN My good old gaffer, you're one of the old world. 2 P. L. FERMOR Peasant girls, bewildered gaffers with tangled beards. 3b T. BARR As the crew chief, the gaffer is responsible for . . the . . equipment.

gaffle /ˈgaf(ə)l/ *n. obs.* exc. *Hist.* L15. [Origin uncertain: in sense 1 perh. f. Du. *gaffel* fork.] 1 A steel lever for bending a crossbow. L15. 2 A metal spur for a fighting cock. L17.

gaffled *a.* (*rare*) equipped with gaffles or spurs L18. †**gafflet** *n.* = GAFFLE 2 E–M18.

gag /gag/ *n.*[1] M16. [f. GAG *v.*[1]] 1 Something thrust into or held over the mouth to prevent speech or outcry, or to hold it open for an operation. M16. b Closure of a debate in a legislative assembly, guillotine. Orig. *US.* M19. 2 An actor's interpolations in a dramatic dialogue, an ad lib; a carefully prepared comic effect or business introduced into a music hall sketch, a stage-play, etc. Also (*gen.*) a joke; a humorous situation, action, etc. M19.

1 J. STEINBECK She put her thumb in her mouth for a gag and she cried silently. A. CLARE A gag is inserted in the patient's mouth to prevent him biting his tongue. 2 P. G. WODEHOUSE Some rotten little . . play . . without one good laugh or . . gag in it.

Comb.: **gag-bit** a powerful bit used to control a restive horse; **gag man** a writer of gags; a comedian; **gag-rein**: used to make a bit more powerful.

gagster *n.* [-STER after *punster*] a writer of gags, a comedian M20.

gag /gag/ *n.*[2] E19. [f. GAG *v.*[3]] An invented story; a deception, an imposture, a lie.

gag /gag/ *n.*[3] L19. [Local name.] Any of various large edible groupers found off the coasts of the southern US, esp. *Mycteroperca microlepis*.

gag /gag/ *v.*[1] Infl. **-gg-**. ME. [Origin uncertain; perh. imit. of choking sound, or rel. to ON *gaghāls* with the neck thrown back.] **1** †**a** *v.t.* Strangle, suffocate. Only in ME. **b** *v.i.* & *t.* Choke; (cause to) retch. E18. **2** *v.t.* Stop the mouth of (a person) to prevent speech or outcry; put a gag into or over (a person's mouth). E16. **b** Keep the mouth of (a patient, an animal) open with a gag. L16. **c** Deprive of the power or freedom of speech; stop the mouth of. E17. **3** *v.t.* Apply a gag-bit to the mouth of (a horse); confine unduly the mouth of (a horse). M19. **4** *v.i.* Orig. *Theatr.* Make gags or jokes. Also, ad lib. M19.

1b T. KENEALLY A dozen people were gagging or comatose from swallowing cyanide. G. KEILLOR A repulsive gelatinous fishlike dish that . . gave off an odor that would gag a goat. *fig.*: CLIVE JAMES Even Mozart . . would gag at so much worship. 2 JONSON Gag him, we may have his silence. c LD MACAULAY The time was not yet come when eloquence was to be gagged and reason hoodwinked.

gagger *n.*[1] E17.

†**gag** *v.*[2] L16. [Origin unkn.] **1** *v.t.* Jerk; strike sharply; prick. L16–E17. **2** *v.i.* Project, stick out. L16–L19.

gag /gag/ *v.*[3]*t.* & *i. slang.* Now *rare* or *obs.* Infl. **-gg-**. L18. [Origin uncertain: perh. fig. use of GAG *v.*[1] in sense of thrusting something down the throat of a credulous person.] Hoax, trick, deceive (a person).

gagger *n.*[2] L18. **gaggery** *n.* the practice of gagging E19.

gaga /ˈgɑːgɑː, ˈgagə/ *a.* & *n. slang.* Also **ga-ga**. E20. [Fr.] **A** *adj.* Senile; mad, crazy; foolish, fatuous. E20.

C. P. SNOW Hiding behind his smoke-screen of platitudes like an amiable old man already a bit ga-ga. D. LODGE This Dempsey character is gaga about computers.

B *n.* A senile or foolish person. M20.

gagaku /ˈgagakuː/ *n.* M20. [Jap., f. *ga* refined, graceful, noble + *gaku* music.] A traditional type of (chiefly ceremonial) Japanese music.

†**gagate** *n.* OE–E18. [L *Gagates* f. Gk *Gagatēs*, f. *Gagai* a town in Lycia in Asia Minor.] = JET *n.*[1]

gage /geɪdʒ/ *n.*[1] ME. [(O)Fr. f. Proto-Romance, f. Gmc base of WED *n.*: see WAGE *n.*] **1** A valued thing or person deposited as a guarantee of good faith; a pledge, surety, security. Formerly also, payment, ransom. ME. **2** A pledge, esp. a glove, thrown down as a symbol of a challenge to do battle; a challenge. Esp. in *gage of battle*. ME.

1 W. RALEIGH He also left Philip . . for the gage of his promises to Pelopidas. **in gage** as a pledge or deposit. 2 LD BERNERS Caste downe your gage in that quarell, and ye shall fynde him that shall take it vp.

gage /geɪdʒ/ *n.*[2] LME. [Var. of GAUGE *n.*] **I 1** A quart pot. Long *rare* or *obs.* LME. **2** A pipe; a pipeful (orig. of tobacco, now chiefly of marijuana). Hence, marijuana. *slang.* L17. **II** See GAUGE *n.*

gage /geɪdʒ/ *n.*[3] M19. [Abbrev.] = GREENGAGE.

gage /geɪdʒ/ *v.* LME. [(O)Fr. *gager* or aphet. of ENGAGE *v.*] †**1** *v.t.* Pledge, pawn; mortgage the revenues of; pledge oneself to (battle). LME–E17. †**2** *v.t.* Bind (as) by a formal promise. L15–E17. **b** Bind or entangle *in. rare* (Shakes.). Only in L16. **3** *v.t.* Stake, wager; risk; offer as a guarantee or forfeit. *arch.* E16. **4** *v.i.* Assert or guarantee *that. arch.* E19.

gage d'amour /gaːʒ damuːr/ *n. phr.* Pl. ***gages d'amour*** (pronounced same). M18. [Fr.] A pledge of love; a love-token.

gaggie *n.* var. of GEGGIE.

gaggle /ˈgag(ə)l/ *v.* & *n.* ME. [Imit.: cf. MHG *gāgen*, *gāgern* cry like a goose; Du. *gaggelen* gabble; ON *gagl* gosling; OHG *gackizōn*, *gackazzen* (G *gacksen*, also *gackeln*, *gackern*). Cf. GABBLE *v.* 2, CACKLE *v.*] **A** *v.* **1** *v.i.* Of a goose etc.: cackle. ME. **b** Make a noise like a goose; chatter. Now chiefly as *gaggling* ppl a. & vbl n. LME. †**2** *v.t.* Utter or express with noisy chatter like a goose. L16–M17.

1 C. S. LEWIS Crowing cocks and gaggling ducks.

B *n.* **1** A flock (of geese); *derog.* a group (of women). LME. **b** A (usu. disorderly or untidy) group of people or things; *slang* a group of aircraft. M20. **2** Noisy chatter; gabble. LME.

1b *Listener* There is hardly a modern skyscraper . . that does not have its gaggle of sightseers. 2 P. QUENNELL Shouting in unison with a gaggle of harsh sound.

gag-toothed /gagˈtuːθt/ *a.* L16. [f. GAG *v.*[2] + TOOTHED.] Having a projecting or prominent tooth or teeth.

gah /gɑː/ *int.* E20. [Natural exclam.] Expr. impatience or exasperation.

gahnite /ˈgɑːnʌɪt/ *n.* E19. [f. J. G. *Gahn* (1745–1818), Swed. chemist + -ITE[1].] *Min.* An oxide of zinc and aluminium, which crystallizes in the cubic system, and usu. occurs as dark green octahedra.

Gaia /ˈgʌɪə/ *n.* L20. [Gk *gaia* (the) earth.] The earth regarded as a self-regulating system in which living matter collectively defines and maintains the conditions for the continuance of life; (more fully *Gaia hypothesis*) the hypothesis that the earth is such a system.

Gaian *a.* & *n.* (*a*) *adj.* of or pertaining to Gaia or the Gaia hypothesis; (*b*) *n.* an advocate of this hypothesis: L20.

gaieté de coeur /gete də kœːr/ *n. phr.* E18. [Fr.] Light-heartedness, playfulness.

gaiety /ˈgeɪəti/ *n.* Also ***gayety**. M17. [(O)Fr. *gaieté* (mod. also *gaîté*), f. *gai* GAY *a.*: see -TY[1], -ITY.] **1** Cheerfulness, mirth; frivolity. M17. **2** Merrymaking, festivity; (now *rare*) a festive occasion, an entertainment. M17. **3** Cheerful or bright appearance or decoration; showiness. M17.

1 D. M. DAVIN He was full of gaiety, laughing, eyes shining, waving to my wife. **the gaiety of nations** (freq. *iron.* or *hyperbol.*) general gaiety or amusement. 2 A. RADCLIFFE He was allured by the gaieties of Paris. 3 J. G. MURPHY They . . lay aside all gaiety in dress.

Comb.: **Gaiety Girl** a chorus girl or performer in a musical show, orig. and esp. at the Gaiety, a former London theatre famous for its musicals.

gaijin /gʌɪˈdʒɪn/ *n.* & *a.* M20. [Jap., contr. of *gaikoku-jin*, f. *gaikoku* foreign country + *jin* person.] **A** *n.* Pl. same. In Japan: a foreigner, an alien. M20. **B** *attrib.* or as *adj.* Foreign, alien, (to the Japanese). M20.

gaillardia /geɪˈlɑːdɪə/ *n.* L19. [mod.L (see below), f. *Gaillard* de Marentonneau, 18th-cent. Fr. amateur botanist: see -IA[1].] Any of various plants of the American genus *Gaillardia*, of the composite family, several of which are cultivated for their showy flowers. Also called *blanket flower*.

gaily /ˈgeɪli/ *adv.* Also (now *rare*) **gayly**. ME. [f. GAY *a.* + -LY[2].] **1** In a gay manner; brightly, splendidly, smartly; cheerfully, joyously; jauntily. ME. **2** Fairly; pretty well. Chiefly *Sc.* & *dial.* M16.

1 D. WELCH 'Don't forget my party to-night' she called out . . gaily. E. BOWEN Her dear little table lamp, gaily painted with spots . . like a toadstool. 2 DE QUINCEY It's gaily nigh to four mile.

gain /geɪn/ *n.*[1] Long *obs.* exc. *north.* ME. [ON *gagn*, *gegn* adj. used as n.: see GAIN *a.*] Advantage, use, benefit; help.

gain /geɪn/ *n.*[2] L15. [OFr. *ga(a)in* (mod. *gain*) masc., *ga(a)igne* (mod. *gagne*) fem., f. *ga(a)ignier* (mod. *gagner*): see GAIN *v.*[2]] †**1** Booty, spoil. L15–M16. **2** Increase of possessions, resources, or advantages; an instance of this; profit, improvement; *spec.* the acquisition of wealth. (Opp. *loss.*) L15. **b** In *pl.* Sums acquired by trade etc.; emoluments, winnings. M16. **c** An increase in amount, magnitude, or degree. M19. **d** *Electronics.* An increase in power, voltage, or current, produced esp. in an amplifier, expressed as the ratio of the increased quantity to the original quantity or (more commonly) as the logarithm of this. E20. **3** The action of acquiring a possession, winning a battle, etc. *rare.* L16.

2 JOSEPH HALL (After long fightyng) bothe parties departed without either greate gain or losse. LD MACAULAY Greedy as they were of gain, they seldom became rich. *capital gain*: see CAPITAL *a.* & *n.*[2] b H. CECIL A thief, about to put his illgotten gains on a horse. c J. CARLYLE I was weighed yesterday and found a gain of five pounds. d *ride the gain*: see RIDE *v.*

gainless *a.* (now *rare*) M17.

gain /geɪn/ *n.*[3] *techn.* M19. [Origin unkn.] A mortise or notch esp. for a timber or connecting piece.

gain /geɪn/ *a. obs.* exc. *dial.* LOE. [ON *gagn*, *gegn* straight, direct, favourable, helpful, f. Gmc.] **1** Of a road or direction: near, straight. Esp. in superl., as *the gainest way*. LOE. **2** (Of a person) willing, kindly; (of a thing) available, useful, convenient. ME.

gain /geɪn/ *v.*[1]*i.* Long *obs.* exc. *Sc.* ME. [ON *gegna* meet, encounter, (hence) be meet, fit, or suitable, f. *gegn* (adj. & adv.) against, opposite (to): cf. GAIN *a.*] Be suitable, useful, or advantageous; help; suffice.

gain /geɪn/ *v.*[2] E16. [OFr. *ga(a)ignier* (mod. *gagner*) f. Proto-Romance, f. Gmc vb repr. also in OHG *weidenen* graze, pasture, forage, hunt, fish, f. n. repr. also in OHG *weida* fodder, pasture, hunting, OE *wāþ*, ON *veiðr* hunting.] **1** *v.t.* Obtain, secure, or acquire (esp. something desired or advantageous). E16. **b** Get *to be*, *to do. rare.* M17. **2** *v.t.* Obtain or receive (a sum of money) as profit or personal benefit; earn or obtain (a living). M16. **b** Obtain (a quantity or amount of anything) as an addition or increment. E17. **3** *v.t.* Acquire or win (land, a victory, a legal judgement, etc.) as the result of a contest or battle; be victorious in (a battle etc.). M16. **b** *v.t.* Acquire or reclaim (land) from the sea etc. M17. **4** *v.i.* Make a gain or profit; advance; receive a personal benefit. L16. **b** Foll. by *on*, *upon*: win favour with (now *rare*); get closer to (a person or thing pursued); (esp. of the sea) encroach upon. M17. **c** Improve or advance *in* some respect. M19. **d** Be enhanced *by* comparison or contrast. M19. **5** *v.t.* Win over or *over* to one's own opinion or interests; persuade, bribe. L16. **6** *v.t.* Arrive at, reach (a desired place); *rare* accomplish (a certain distance). E17. **7** Of a clock etc.: **a** *v.i.* become fast, so as to indicate a time ahead of the correct time. M19. **b** *v.t.* run fast by (a specified period). M19.

1 I. FLEMING The dull, flat voice gained a trace of animation. W. GOLDING His ideas on Church Reform . . gained him a good deal of respect. E. GELLNER Psychoanalysis . . can gain access to the contents of the Unconscious. 2 OED He gains a hundred a year by his change of employment. b B. SPOCK If he loses weight during an illness, he gains it back promptly. 3 W. COWPER A meaner than himself shall gain the prize. I. WATTS Either I shall gain the cause or lose it. 4 SHAKES. *Com. Err.* He gains by death that hath such means to die. R. C. HUTCHINSON My mind began to gain in its struggle against the weight of torpor. c R. W. EMERSON Popular theology has gained in decorum and not in principle. d LD MACAULAY The English Liturgy . . gains by being compared . . with those . . Liturgies from which it is taken. 5 J. H. NEWMAN He did not try to gain him over by smooth representations. E. BOWEN Ralph's charm so gained his father-in-law . . that he left Mount Bruis to Ralph and Mary. 6 E. WAUGH She . . led him across the yard. . . They gained the verandah. 7a M. TWAIN My beautiful new watch had run eighteen months without losing or gaining.

Phrases: *gain a march on*: see MARCH *n.*[3] **gain ground** (orig. *Mil.*), conquer territory belonging to an adversary; *fig.* make progress, advance, acquire ascendancy. **gain ground on, upon** make progress at the expense of; get closer to (someone or something pursued). *gain the ear of*: see EAR *n.*[1] *gain one's colours*: see COLOUR *n.* **gain the wind of** *Naut.* arrive on the windward side of (another vessel). **gain time** obtain a delay by pretexts, deliberate slowness, etc.

gainable *a.* (now *rare*) E17. **gainer** *n.* M16.

gain- /geɪn/ *pref.* (not productive). LOE. [f. GAIN *a.*] Chiefly in vbs & vbl derivs. (now all *obs.*, *arch.*, or *literary*) w. the sense 'against, in opposition to', as *gainsay*; formerly also 'reciprocal, in return' as *gain-giving*.

gainful /ˈgeɪnfʊl, -f(ə)l/ *a.* M16. [f. GAIN *n.*[2] + -FUL.] **1** Productive of (esp. financial) gain or profit; (of employment) paid, useful. M16. **2** Bent on making gain or profit. *rare.* M17.

1 M. R. MITFORD She . . speedily established a regular and gainful trade in milk.

gainfully *adv.* M16. **gainfulness** *n.* M17.

gain-giving /ˈgeɪngɪvɪŋ/ *n.* Long *arch.* LME. [f. GAIN- + GIVING *vbl n.*] †1 A giving in return. Only in LME. 2 A misgiving. E17.

gaining /ˈgeɪnɪŋ/ *n.* M16. [f. GAIN *v.*[2] + -ING[1].] 1 The action of GAIN *v.*[2] M16. 2 A thing gained; profit. Usu. in *pl.* M16.

gainly /ˈgeɪnli/ *a.* ME. [f. GAIN *a.* + -LY[1].] 1 Suitable, fitting. *obs.* exc. *Sc. dial.* ME. 2 Graceful, shapely; tactful. M19.

gainly /ˈgeɪnli/ *adv. obs.* exc. *dial.* ME. [f. GAIN *a.* + -LY[2].] 1 Suitably, fittingly, readily. ME. †2 Thoroughly, very. LME–M17.

gainsay /geɪnˈseɪ/ *v.* & *n.* Now chiefly *literary.* ME. [f. GAIN- + SAY *v.*[1]: prob. modelled on ON *gagnmæli* gainsaying.] A *v.t.* Pa. t. & pple **-said,** (*rare*) **-sayed,** /-ˈsɛd, -ˈseɪd/. 1 Deny, contradict, (a statement etc.). ME. 2 Refuse (a thing). *rare.* ME. 3 Speak or act against; oppose; hinder. LME.

1 J. LOCKE And that certainly you may think safely . . without fear of being gain-said. E. A. FREEMAN Facts which cannot be gainsaid. 3 P. LIVELY He had insisted on providing hospitality and would not be gainsaid.

B *n.* Contradiction. Now *rare.* M16.

ˈ**gainsayer** *n.* LME.

Gainsborough hat /geɪnzb(ə)rə ˈhat/ *n. phr.* L19. [Thomas *Gainsborough* (1727–88), Eng. painter.] A large broad-brimmed hat such as is worn by women in certain of Gainsborough's portraits.

gainst /geɪnst/ *prep. poet.* Also **'gainst.** L16. [Aphet.] = AGAINST.

gainstand /geɪnˈstand/ *v.t.* Long *arch.* ME. [f. GAIN- + STAND *v.*] Withstand, resist.

gainstander *n.* an opposer, an opponent L15.

†**gainstrive** *v.* M16. [f. GAIN- + STRIVE *v.*] 1 *v.t.* Strive against, oppose. M–L16. 2 *v.i.* Make resistance. L16–E17.

†**gairfowl** *n.* var. of GAREFOWL.

gaishen /ˈgeɪʃ(ə)n/ *n. dial.* E19. [Origin unkn.] A skeleton; a silly-looking person; an obstacle.

gait /geɪt/ *n.* Also †**gate.** See also GATE *n.*[2] LME. [A spec. use of GATE *n.*[2] The spelling *gait* was orig. Sc.] I 1 Manner of walking or stepping, carriage. Also *transf.* manner of forward movement of a vehicle etc. LME. b In *pl.* Esp. of a horse: paces. L17. 2 Chiefly *US.* Rate of movement, pace. M20.

1 SPENSER Scarse thy legs uphold thy feeble gate. D. M. THOMAS She walked with an awkward gait, bending forward from the waist. **go one's own gait** pursue one's own course.

II See GATE *n.*[2]

gaited *a.* having a (specified) gait or number of gaits L16.

gait /geɪt/ *v.t. dial.* or *techn.* M19. [App. f. GATE *n.*[2]] Put in working order; fix up.

gaita /ˈgaita/ *n.* M19. [Sp. & Port.] A kind of bagpipe played in northern Spain and Portugal.

gaiter /ˈgeɪtə/ *n.*[1] *obs.* exc. *dial.* Also **gatten** /ˈgat(ə)n/, **gatter** /ˈgatə/. OE. [Based on OE *gāte trēow* goat's tree.] In full *gaiter-tree.* Dogwood, *Cornus sanguinea.*

gaiter /ˈgeɪtə/ *n.*[2] & *v.* E18. [Fr. *guêtre,* †*guietre,* †*guestre,* perh. repr. metath. alt. of Gmc base of WRIST.] A *n.* 1 A covering of cloth, leather, etc., for the ankle, or ankle and lower leg. Also, a covering for a part of a machine etc. E18. 2 In full *gaiter boot, shoe.* A shoe or overshoe which extends to the ankle or above. Chiefly *US.* L18.

1 F. O'CONNOR He wore a small cloth hat and big gaiters over his long pants. *Mail on Sunday* The rubber gaiter on the gear lever slipped down into the box. (*all*) *gas and gaiters*: see GAS *n.*[1]

B *v.t.* Dress or provide with gaiters. M18.

gal /gal/ *n.*[1] *slang* & *dial.* Now chiefly *N. Amer.* L18. [Repr. a pronunc.] = GIRL *n.*

gal /gal/ *n.*[2] E20. [Abbrev. of *Galileo*: see GALILEAN *a.*[2]] A unit of gravitational acceleration equal to one centimetre per second per second.

gala /ˈgɑːlə, ˈgeɪlə/ *n.* E17. [Fr. or its source in It. f. Sp. f. OFr. *gale* merrymaking: see GALLANT *a.* & *n.*] 1 Fine or showy dress. Now only in *in gala.* E17. †2 Festivity, rejoicing. E18–E19. 3 A festive occasion; a festival characterized by finery and show. M18.

Comb.: **gala day** a day of festivity, finery, and show; **gala dress** a dress for a gala; festal attire; **gala night** a night or evening of festivity, finery, and show.

galabiya /gəˈlɑːbɪjə, galəˈbiːjə/ *n.* Also **galabieh, gallabiya,** & many other vars. E18. [Egyptian var. of Arab. *jallābiyya*: see JELLABA.] A long loose garment worn in Arabic-speaking Mediterranean countries, esp. in Egypt.

galactagogue /gəˈlaktəgɒg/ *a.* & *n.* M19. [f. GALACTO- + Gk *agōgos* leading, eliciting.] A *adj.* Inducing a flow of milk. M19. B *n.* A galactagogue agent. L19.

galactan /gəˈlaktan/ *n.* L19. [f. GALACTOSE + -AN.] *Biochem.* A polysaccharide whose constituent monosaccharides are galactoses.

galactase /gəˈlakteɪz/ *n.* L19. [f. GALACTO- + -ASE.] *Biochem.* A proteolytic enzyme present in the milk of many animals.

galactic /gəˈlaktɪk/ *a.* M19. [f. Gk *galaktias* var. of *galaxias* GALAXY + -IC.] *Astron.* Of or pertaining to the Galaxy or the Milky Way; of or pertaining to another galaxy or galaxies in general.

galactic equator a great circle passing as nearly as possible through the middle of the Milky Way. **galactic latitude, longitude, pole,** etc.: measured or fixed relative to the galactic equator (and some reference point on it).

galacto- /gəˈlaktəʊ/ *comb. form.* Bef. a vowel **galact-.** [f. Gk *gala, galakt-* milk + -O-.] 1 With the sense 'of milk'. 2 With the sense 'of galactose'. 3 With the sense 'of the Galaxy or of a galaxy'.

galactocele *n.* (*Med.*) a milk-filled swelling in the breast due to a blocked milk duct M19. **galactoˈcentric** *a.* with respect to the centre of the Galaxy M20. **galacˈtophorous** *a.* conveying milk M18. **galactopoiˈesis** *n.* [Gk *poiesis* production] production of milk M19. **galactopoiˈetic** *a.* [Gk *poietikos* capable of producing] tending to produce milk M17. **galactoˈrrhoea** *n.* excessive or inappropriate production of milk M19. **galactuˈronic** *a.*: *galacturonic acid,* the uronic acid derived from galactose, present esp. in pectins E20.

galactonic /galakˈtɒnɪk/ *a.* L19. [f. GALACTOSE + -ONIC.] Chem. *galactonic acid,* an acid, $CH_2OH(CHOH)_4COOH$, derived from galactose by oxidation of the latter's aldehyde group.

galactosaemia /gəlaktə(ʊ)ˈsiːmɪə/ *n.* Also ***-semia.** M20. [f. GALACTOS(E + Gk *haima* blood: see -IA[1].] *Med.* The presence of galactose in the blood; an inherited metabolic disorder of which this is a sign.

galactose /gəˈlaktəʊz, -s/ *n.* M19. [f. GALACTO- + -OSE[2].] A hexose sugar which is a common component of natural polysaccharides, notably lactose.

galactoside *n.* any glycoside containing galactose M19.

galactosemia *n.* see GALACTOSAEMIA.

galago /gəˈleɪgəʊ/ *n.* Pl. **-os.** M19. [mod.L.] A bushbaby; *spec.* one of the genus *Galago.*

galah /gəˈlɑː/ *n.* M19. [Aborig.] 1 A very common small Australian cockatoo, *Eolophus roseicapillus,* with a pink breast and grey back. Also called *rose-breasted cockatoo.* M19. 2 A fool, a simpleton. *Austral. slang.* M20.

Galahad /ˈgaləhad/ *n.* L19. [The noblest knight of the Round Table in Arthurian legend.] A person characterized by nobility, courtesy, integrity, etc.

galanga /gəˈlaŋgə/ *n.* LME. [med.L: see GALINGALE.] = GALINGALE.

galangal *n.* var. of GALINGALE.

galant /galɑ̃, gəˈlɑːnt/ *a.* L19. [Fr. & G: see GALLANT *n.* & *a.*] *Mus.* Designating or pertaining to a light and elegant style of 18th-cent. music.

galanterie /galɑ̃tri, (*in sense 2 also*) gal(ə)ntəˈriː/ *n.* Pl. ***-ries*** (pronounced same), (in sense 2 also w. G pl.) ***-rien*** /-ˈriːn/. E17. [Fr. or (sense 2) G: see GALLANTRY.] †1 = GALLANTRY 1. Only in E17. 2 *Mus.* A light non-essential movement in an early 18th-cent. classical suite. E20. 3 Courtesy, politeness, esp. to women. E20.

galantine /ˈgal(ə)ntiːn/ *n.* ME. [(O)Fr., alt. of *galatine* f. med.L *galatina.*] †1 A kind of sauce for fish or fowl. ME–M17. 2 A dish of white meat boned, cooked, pressed, and served cold with aspic, etc. E18.

galanty show /gəˈlantɪ ʃəʊ/ *n. phr.* Now *Hist.* E19. [Perh. It. *galanti* pl. of *galante* GALLANT *n.*] A shadow pantomime produced by throwing shadows of puppets on to a wall or screen.

galatea /galəˈtiːə/ *n.* L19. [HMS *Galatea,* a vessel commanded in 1867 by the Duke of Edinburgh.] A strong cotton material, usu. with blue and white stripes, orig. used for making children's sailor suits.

Galatian /gəˈleɪʃ(ə)n/ *n.* & *a.* M16. [f. *Galatia* (see below) + -AN.] A *n.* A native or inhabitant of Galatia, an ancient country of central Asia Minor. In *pl.* (treated as *sing.*), St Paul's Epistle to the Galatians, a book of the New Testament. M16. B *adj.* Of or pertaining to Galatia or its people. M19.

galax /ˈgalaks/ *n.* E19. [mod.L: cf. Gk *galaxias* GALAXY.] An evergreen plant, *Galax urceolata* of the family Diapensiaceae, native to the US and having white flowers and shiny leaves.

galaxy /ˈgaləksi/ *n.* LME. [(O)Fr. *galaxie* f. med.L *galaxia,* late L *galaxias* f. Gk *galaxias* (sc. *kuklos* circle), f. *gala, galakt-* milk: see -Y[3].] 1 The Milky Way. LME. b *Astron.* Any of the numerous vast systems of stars, gas, and dust that exist separately in the universe and together contain nearly all of its visible matter; *spec.* (often **G-**) that spiral system to which the earth belongs and whose disc of maximum star density is visible as the Milky Way. M19. 2 *transf.* & *fig.* A brilliant assembly esp. of beautiful or talented people. L16.

1 H. MOSELEY The Galaxy, or Milky-way, passes through the heavens like an irregular zone. 2 C. CHAPLIN The fruit-shop was a galaxy of colour. S. MORLEY A galaxy of stars from Herbert Marshall . . to Charles Laughton.

galbanum /ˈgalbənəm/ *n.* ME. [L f. Gk *khalbanē,* of Semitic origin (cf. Heb. *helbĕnāh* Exod. 30:34).] 1 A gum resin obtained in the Middle East from a ferula, esp. *Ferula galbaniflua,* and having medicinal uses. ME. 2 *fig.* Bosh, humbug. Now *rare* or *obs.* M18.

galbe /galb/ *n.* L19. [Fr.] A contour, an outline, a profile.

Galbraithian /galˈbreɪθɪən/ *a.* & *n.* M20. [f. *Galbraith* (see below) + -IAN.] A *adj.* Of, pertaining to, or characteristic of the opinions or writings of the N. American economist and diplomat John Kenneth Galbraith (b. 1908). M20. B *n.* A person who supports or is influenced by the writings of J. K. Galbraith. M20.

gale /geɪl/ *n.*[1] [OE *gagel, gagelle* = MDu. *gaghel,* Du. & G *gagel*: the present form is unexpl.] Bog myrtle, *Myrica gale.* Also *sweet gale.*

gale /geɪl/ *n.*[2] M16. [Origin uncertain: perh. orig. an adj. in *gale wind* and, in spite of the late date, of Scand. origin and to be conn. w. MSw., Norw. *galen* bad (of weather), ON *galenn* mad, frantic.] 1 A strong wind; *spec.* (on the Beaufort scale) one of force 8 and 9, or with a speed of between 34 and 47 knots; *Naut.* a storm. M16. b A gentle breeze. *poet.* & *rhet.* L17. 2 *transf.* & *fig.* a An outpouring, an outburst, esp. of laughter. Now usu. in *pl.* E17. b A state of excitement. *US.* M19.

1 F. CHICHESTER The seas were very rough . . with a gale south-west by west. E. ARDIZZONE By this time it was blowing a gale. **near gale**: with a speed of between 34 and 40 knots (8 on the Beaufort scale). **strong gale**: with a speed of between 41 and 47 knots (9 on the Beaufort scale). 2a W. MARCH She went into gales of merriment, her laughter resounding through the department.

gale /geɪl/ *n.*[3] M17. [Contr. of GAVEL *n.*[1]] 1 A periodical payment of rent; the amount of rent so paid. M17. 2 In the Forest of Dean, a royalty paid for a plot of land and for the right to mine on this land; land granted for this purpose. L18.

gale /geɪl/ *v.*[1]*i.* Now *rare.* L17. [f. GALE *n.*[2]] *Naut.* Sail *away* as if before a gale.

gale /geɪl/ *v.*[2]*t.* M19. [f. GALE *n.*[3]] Grant or take the gale of (a mine).

galea /ˈgeɪlɪə/ *n.* M19. [L = helmet.] *Bot.*, *Zool.*, & *Anat.* Any of various structures resembling a helmet in shape, function, or position.

galeate /ˈgalɪeɪt, -ɪət/ *a.* E18. [L *galeatus*, f. *galea* helmet: see -ATE².] = GALEATED 1.

galeated /ˈgalɪeɪtɪd/ *a.* E17. [f. as prec. + -ED¹.] 1 Wearing a helmet, helmeted. E17. 2 Chiefly *Bot.* & *Zool.* Shaped like a helmet; furnished with a galea or similar structure. L17.

1 H. PHILLIPS The galeated head of Minerva.

†galeche *n.* see CALASH.

galeeny /gəˈliːni/ *n.* Now *dial.* L18. [Sp. *gallina* (*morisca*) '(Moorish) hen' (so in Port. & It.) f. L *gallina*: see -Y⁶.] A guinea-fowl.

galega /gəˈliːgə/ *n.* L15. [mod.L, of unkn. origin.] A Eurasian leguminous plant, *Galega officinalis*, sometimes grown in gardens, with pinnate leaves and racemes of mauve or white flowers; goat's rue. Also, a medicinal preparation of this plant.

Galen /ˈgeɪlən/ *n. joc.* L16. [Anglicized f. L *Galenus* f. Gk *Galēnos* Galen: see below.] With allusion to Galen, a Pergamene physician and writer at the court of Marcus Aurelius in the 2nd cent. AD: a physician.

galena /gəˈliːnə/ *n.* L17. [L *galena* lead at a certain stage of smelting.] Lead sulphide, PbS, the principal ore of lead, found as grey, usu. cubic crystals with a metallic lustre.

galenic /gəˈlɛnɪk/ *a.* M17. [f. GALEN + -IC.] Of or pertaining to Galen, his followers, or his principles and practice; *esp.* (of a medicine) being a vegetable as distinct from a synthetic preparation.

Galenian *a.* L17.

galenical /gəˈlɛnɪk(ə)l/ *a.* & *n.* M17. [f. as prec.: see -ICAL.] A *adj.* = prec. M17. B *n.* A galenic or vegetable remedy; a simple. M18.

galenically *adv.* (now *rare*) with galenical or vegetable remedies L17.

Galenist /ˈgeɪlənɪst/ *n.* L16. [f. GALEN + -IST.] A follower of Galen.

Galenism *n.* the medical principles or system of Galen E18.

galère /galɛːr/ *n.* Pl. pronounced same. M18. [Fr. = galley, used fig. in Molière's *Scapin*.] A coterie; a (usu. undesirable) group of people; an unpleasant situation.

galette /gəˈlɛt/ *n.* L18. [Fr.] A broad thin cake usu. of pastry.

Galgenhumor /ˈgalgənhuːmɔr/ *n.* Also **g-**. E20. [G, f. *Galgen* gallows + *Humor* humour.] Grim, ironical humour. Cf. *gallows-humour* s.v. GALLOWS *n.*

Galibi /gəˈliːbi/ *n.* & *a.* Pl. of n. same, **-s**. L19. [Carib, lit. 'strong man'.] Of or pertaining to, a member of, a S. American Indian people of French Guiana; (of) the Carib language of this people.

Galician /gəˈlɪsjən/ *n.*¹ & *a.*¹ LME. [f. *Galicia* in the north-western corner of the Iberian peninsula + -AN.] A *n.* A native or inhabitant of Galicia, a medieval Castilian kingdom, subsequently a Spanish province. Also, the language of Galicia, closely related to Portuguese. LME. B *adj.* Of or pertaining to Galicia or its inhabitants. E19.

Galician /gəˈlɪsjən/ *a.*² & *n.*² M19. [f. *Galicia* in east central Europe + -AN.] A *adj.* Of or pertaining to Galicia, a former province of the Austro-Hungarian empire now divided between Poland and Ukraine, or its inhabitants. M19. B *n.* A native or inhabitant of Galicia. Also (*Canad.*, now *rare*) an immigrant from central Europe. E20.

Galilean /galɪˈliːən/ *n.* & *a.*¹ M16. [f. L *Galil(a)ea* (Gk *Galilaia*) Galilee (see below) + -AN.] A *n.* A native or inhabitant of Galilee; *contempt.* Jesus Christ. Also, a Christian. M16.

AV *Acts* 2:7 Are not all these which speake, Galileans?

B *adj.* Of or pertaining to Galilee, in Palestine. Also, Christian. M17.

MILTON The pilot of the Galilean lake. YEATS Galilæan turbulence.

Galilean /galɪˈliːən/ *a.*² E18. [f. *Galileo* Galilei (1564–1642), It. astronomer + -AN.] 1 Discovered, developed by, or characteristic of Galileo. E18. 2 *Physics.* Pertaining to an inertial frame of reference; designating a transformation between such frames. E20.

Special collocations: **Galilean moon, satellite** each of the four largest moons of Jupiter (Io, Europa, Ganymede, and Callisto). **Galilean telescope** a simple refracting telescope with convergent objective and divergent eyepiece.

galilee /ˈgalɪliː/ *n.* LME. [OFr. *galilée* f. med.L *galilea*, a use of the place-name *Galilee*: see GALILEAN *a.*¹ & *n.*] A porch or chapel at the entrance of a church.

galimatias /galɪˈmatɪəs, -ˈmeɪʃəs/ *n.* M17. [Fr., of unkn. origin.] Confused language, meaningless talk, gibberish.

W. H. AUDEN A tongue With . . no resemblance To the galimatias of nursery and bedroom.

galingale /ˈgalɪŋgeɪl/ *n.* Also **galangal** /ˈgal(ə)ŋgal/. LOE. [OFr. *galingal* f. Arab. *ḵalanjān* (Pers. *ḵūlinjān*, Skt *kulañjana*) perh. f. Chin. *gāoliángjiāng*, f. *gāoliáng* a district in Guangdong Province, China + *jiāng* ginger. Cf. med.L, med.Gk, It. *galanga* (Fr. *galangue*), GALANGA.] 1 The aromatic rhizome of certain east Asian plants of the genera *Alpinia* and *Kaempferia*, of the ginger family, used as a spice. LOE. 2 A sedge, *Cyperus longus*, having an aromatic root. Also more fully, *English* or *sweet galingale*. L16.

†galion *n.* var. of GALIUM.

galiot *n.* var. of GALLIOT.

galipot /ˈgalɪpɒt/ *n.* L18. [Fr. *galipot*, †*garipot*: cf. Prov. *garapot* pine-tree resin.] A kind of hardened turpentine formed on the stem of the cluster pine.

galium /ˈgeɪlɪəm/. *n.* Also (earlier) **†galion**. M16. [mod.L, or Gk *galion* bedstraw.] = BEDSTRAW 2.

galjoen /xalˈjʊn/ *n. S. Afr.* M19. [Afk. & Du. = galleon.] Each of two deep-bodied marine fishes belonging to the genus *Coracinus*, esp. *C. capensis*.

gall /gɔːl/ *n.*¹ [OE *ġealla*, OS *galla* (Du. *gal*), OHG *galla* (G *Galle*), ON *gall*, f. Gmc. Cogn. w. Gk *kholē*, *kholos*, L *fel* bile.] 1 The secretion of the liver, bile (exc. in certain combs. now only of the lower animals). Also, the type of an intensely bitter substance. OE. b *fig.* Bitterness; anything bitter. ME. 2 The gall bladder and its contents. ME. 3 Bitterness of spirit, asperity, rancour (supposed to have its seat in the gall bladder). ME. †b Spirit to resent injury or insult. LME–E18. 4 Assurance, impudence. *slang.* Orig. *US.* L19.

1 E. MANNIN The taste in his mouth was as bitter as gall. b W. IRVING The gall of disappointment. 3 GIBBON The bitterness of religious gall. 4 J. UPDIKE She had the gall to grin right in my face.

Phrases etc.: **†break someone's gall** break the spirit of, cow. **dip one's pen in gall** write with virulence and rancour. **gall of the earth** any of various bitter plants, esp. centaury or (*US*) a rattlesnake-root, *Prenanthes trifoliata*. *glass gall*: see GLASS *n.*

Comb.: **gall bladder** the organ which stores bile after its secretion by the liver; **gall-sickness** *S. Afr.* any of several diseases affecting the livers of livestock.

gall-less *a.* without gall or bitterness LME.

gall /gɔːl/ *n.*² [OE *ġealle* MLG, MDu. *galle* (Du. *gal*), (M)HG *galle*, ON *galli* (MSw. *galle*) fault, flaw; perh. identical w. GALL *n.*¹ Later forms f. MLG, MDu.] 1 Orig., a painful swelling, pustule, or blister, esp. in a horse (cf. *wind gall* s.v. WIND *n.*¹). Later, a sore produced by rubbing or chafing. OE. 2 A bare or barren spot in a field, coppice, etc. ME. b A place rubbed bare; an unsound spot, a fault or flaw. Now only *techn.* M16. 3 *fig.* A person or thing which irritates, vexes, or harasses. L15.

1 P. V. WHITE The old horse . . with girth galls, and saddle sores. 3 SPENSER They . . have left a perpetuall gall in the myndes of that people.

¶The sense has been influenced by GALL *v.*¹ (see note).

gall /gɔːl/ *n.*³ LME. [(O)Fr. *galle* f. L *galla* oak-apple, gall.] An excrescence produced on a tree (esp. the oak) or other plant by the action of a fungus, bacterium, an insect, etc.

Comb.: **gall-apple** = GALL *n.*³; **gallberry** *US* either of two hollies, *Ilex glabra* and *I. coriacea* (the large or sweet gallberry); **gall-fly** any of various insects which cause galls by laying their eggs in plant tissues; *spec.* any fly of the dipteran family Tephritidae; **gall-gnat, -midge** any gall-forming insect of the dipteran family Cecidomyidae; **gall-nut** = GALL *n.*³; **gall-wasp** any gall-forming insect of the hymenopteran superfamily Cynipoidea.

gall /gɔːl/ *v.*¹ ME. [Back-form. f. GALLED *ppl a.*] 1 *v.t.* Make (an animal, a person) sore by rubbing or chafing. ME. b Injure or damage (something) by rubbing or contact. E17. 2 *v.t.* Harass in warfare, esp. w. arrows or shot. L15. 3 *v.t. fig.* Irritate, annoy; vex, humiliate. L16. 4 *v.i.* Become sore or chafed. Now *rare.* E17.

1 W. COWPER The snorting beast began to trot, Which gall'd him in his seat. *fig.* J. MORSE Long and heavily did the Tartar yoke gall the neck of Russia. b C. MARSHALL Tie the tree . . with a firm hay band that it may not easily get galled. 2 M. ARNOLD The surrounding multitudes galled them . . with a cloud of arrows. 3 E. JONES It galled him that only very seldom could he give her even a meagre present.

¶The sense appears to have been infl. by assoc. w. OFr. *galler* scratch, rub.

gallingly *adv.* in a galling manner E19.

gall /gɔːl/ *v.*²*t.* L16. [f. GALL *n.*³] *Dyeing.* Impregnate with a decoction of galls.

gall- *comb. form* see GALLO-².

Galla /ˈgalə/ *n.* & *a.* L19. [Origin unkn.] A *n.* Pl. **-s**, same. A member of a Hamitic people inhabiting mainly parts of Ethiopia and Kenya; the language of this people, belonging to the Cushitic branch of the Afro-Asiatic language family. L19. B *adj.* Of or pertaining to this people. L19.

gallabiya *n.* var. of GALABIYA.

gallack /ˈgalək/ *a. dial.* E18. [Origin unkn.] Left. Chiefly in *gallack-handed*, left-handed, clumsy.

gallamine /ˈgaləmiːn/ *n.* L19. [f. GALLO-² + AMINE.] 1 Chem. *gallamine blue*, a blue gallocyanine dye. L19. 2 *Pharm.* In full *gallamine triethiodide*. A quaternary ammonium salt, $C_6H_3[\cdot O\cdot(CH_2)_2\cdot N(C_2H_5)_3]_3I_3$, used as a muscle relaxant, esp. in anaesthesia. M20.

gallanilide /gaˈlanɪlʌɪd/ *n.* L19. [f. GALLO-² + ANILIDE.] *Chem.* An anilide of gallic acid, $C_6H_2(OH)_3\cdot CONH\cdot C_6H_5$, used in dye manufacture.

gallant /ˈgal(ə)nt, (*esp. in senses A.4 & B.2*) gəˈlant/ *a.* & *n.* LME. [(O)Fr. *galant* pres. pple of *galer* make merry, make a show, f. *gale* merrymaking, rejoicing: see -ANT¹.] A *adj.* 1 Finely or splendidly dressed; smart, showy. Formerly also, (of a woman) attractive, fine-looking; (of language) ornate. *arch.* LME. †b Suited to fashionable society and its customs; courtly; polished in manners or behaviour. E16–M17. 2 Brave, heroic; chivalrous. LME. b Of a Member of Parliament: having served in the Armed Forces. L19. 3 Excellent, fine, (w. mixture of senses 1 and 2) splendid, noble. Now *rare* exc. of a ship or horse. M16. 4 Markedly polite and attentive to women; (now *rare*) concerned with (sexual) love, amatory. L17.

2 E. WAUGH The gallant stand he was making for the decencies of family life. A. GUINNESS She was an old lady by then, suffering acutely from arthritis but remarkably gallant and cheerful. 3 J. FRENCH A few drops . . put into any Wine giveth it a gallant relish. W. H. PRESCOTT A more gallant and beautiful armada never before quitted the shores of Spain. 4 E. WELTY Major Bullock shot his umbrella open and held it over Laurel in gallant fashion.

B *n.* 1 A (usu. dashing) man of fashion and pleasure (formerly also, a woman of this type); a (fine) gentleman. LME. 2 A man who pays court to women, a ladies' man; a suitor; a lover. LME.

1 SHAKES. *1 Hen. VI* Good morrow, gallants! Want ye corn for bread? 2 S. SPENDER He had ideas of himself as a gallant, so all through dinner he was markedly attentive to her.

gallantly *adv.* M16. **gallantness** *n.* (now *rare*) LME.

gallant /gəˈlant, ˈgal(ə)nt/ *v.* E17. [f. the adj.] 1 *v.i.* & †*t.* w. *it.* Cut a dash, make a show. *rare.*

E17. 2 *v.t.* Pay court to or flirt with (a woman); *esp.* attend or act as an escort to (a woman); escort or conduct (a person). L17. †b Use (a fan) flirtatiously. L17–M18. 3 *v.i.* & †*t.* w. *it.* Flirt (*with*). M18.

2 GEO. ELIOT Laidlaw gallants her about sometimes. 3 G. A. SALA The macaroni-cynic of Strawberry Hill is gallanting in the Mall with Lady Caroline Petersham.

gallantize /ˈgaləntʌɪz/ *v.* Now *rare.* Also **-ise**. E17. [f. GALLANT *a.* & *n.* + -IZE. Cf. Fr. *galantiser* treat with gallantry.] 1 *v.i.* & *t.* (w. *it*). = GALLANT *v.* 1. E17. 2 *v.t.* Court, flirt with (a woman). E18.

gallantry /ˈgaləntri/ *n.* L16. [Fr. *galanterie*, f. *galant*: see GALLANT *a.* & *n.*, -ERY.] †1 Splendour, magnificence; (an) ornamentation; (a) display (of elegance etc.). L16–E19. b A knick-knack, a trinket. L17–E18. †2 Fashionable people, gentry. Only in 17. 3 Bravery, nobility, dashing courage. Formerly also, a brave or noble deed. M17. 4 The behaviour of a gallant. M17. 5 Marked politeness or courteousness towards women; an instance of this. L17. 6 Sexual intrigue or flirtation. Formerly also, an instance of this. L17.

1 R. WELTON In whatever gallantry a man appears upon the stage, he must retire, and be undress'd. 2 SHAKES. *Tr. & Cr.* Hector.. and all the gallantry of Troy. 3 M. LOWRY And for it, or gallantry connected with it, he had received the British Distinguished Service Order. 4 POPE The men of pleasure, dress, and gallantry. 5 P. H. GIBBS He took Patricia's hand and raised it to his lips with old-fashioned gallantry. 6 BYRON What men call gallantry, and gods adultery.

gallate /ˈgaleɪt/ *n.*[1] L18. [f. GALLIC *a.*[2] + -ATE[1].] *Chem.* A salt or ester of gallic acid.

gallate /ˈgaleɪt/ *n.*[2] M20. [f. GALLIUM + -ATE[1].] *Chem.* A salt containing oxyanions of gallium.

gall bladder /ˈgɔːl bladə/ *n. phr.* L17. [f. GALL *n.*[1] + BLADDER.] A muscular sac, attached to the right lobe of the liver, in which bile is stored after secretion by the liver.

Galle *n.* see GAUL.

galleas *n.* var. of GALLIASS.

galled /gɔːld/ *a.* OE. [Orig. f. GALL *n.*[2] + -ED[2], but later as if f. GALL *v.*[1] + -ED[1].] 1 Suffering from galls; sore from chafing (freq. w. instrument specified as *saddle-galled*). OE. 2 *fig.* Irritated, distressed. E17. 3 Of land: eroded; sterile through exhaustion. Chiefly *US.* E19.

Gallegan /galˈjeɪg(ə)n/ *a.* & *n.* M19. [f. next + -AN.] = GALICIAN *a.*[1] & *n.*[1]

Gallego /galˈjeɪgəʊ/ *n.* Also **g-**. Pl. **-os**. E17. [Sp.] Orig. a ship from Galicia in Spain. Now = GALICIAN *n.*[1]

galleon /ˈgalɪən/ *n.* E16. [Either f. MDu. *galjoen*, f. (O)Fr. *galion* augm. of *galie* GALLEY, or f. Sp. *galeón*: see -OON.] *Hist.* A type of ship, shorter than a galley but usu. with 3 or more decks and masts, mainly square-rigged and having a high forecastle and poop (in (chiefly Spanish) use from 15th to 18th cent., orig. as a warship, later for trading between Spain and America).

galleria /galəˈriːə/ *n.* L19. [It.: see GALLERY.] A shopping arcade in an Italian city or designed in imitation of one of these.

gallerian /gəˈlɪərɪən/ *n.* M17. [Fr. *galérien*, f. *galère* slave-galley.] *Hist.* A galley-slave.

gallery /ˈgal(ə)ri/ *n.* & *v.* LME. [(O)Fr. *galerie*, f. It. *galleria* gallery, †church porch, f. med.L *galeria*, perh. alt. of *galilea* GALILEE by dissimilation of *l* to *r*.] A *n.* 1 A covered passageway, partly open at the side or having the roof supported by pillars; *US* a porch, a veranda. LME. 2 A long narrow balcony constructed on the outside of a building, at some elevation from the ground and open at the front apart from a railing, balustrade, etc. LME. b *Naut.* A balcony built outside the body of a ship, at the stern or the quarters. E17. c *Archit.* A long narrow passage built into the thickness of a wall or supported on corbels, open towards the interior of a building. M18. †d A passenger car like a basket attached to a hot-air balloon. L18–E20. 3 A long narrow room, sometimes one providing access to other parts of a house; a room or building devoted to the exhibition (and sale) of paintings, sculptures, etc. E16. b A more or less horizontal underground passage (*Mil.* & *Mining*); a passage made by an animal, now only underground or through a rock. M17. c = *shooting-gallery* s.v. SHOOTING *vbl n.* M19. 4 A platform or balcony projecting from the inner wall of a church, courtroom, hall, etc. serving e.g. to provide extra room for an audience or reserved for musicians etc.; *spec.* in a theatre, the highest of such balconies, containing the cheapest seats. L16. b The part of a meeting-house of the Society of Friends occupied by the elders. E19. c The control room of a television studio. M20. 5 *sing.* & †in *pl.* The people occupying the gallery in a theatre etc.; *fig.* the least refined part of an audience. M17. b A group of spectators at a golf match etc. L19. 6 *Real Tennis.* Each of eight openings beneath the side penthouses of the court, backed by netting to catch balls and protect spectators. L17. 7 An ornamental rim or railing edging a table, shelf, etc. M19.

1 H. HUNTER There is in the gallery of the Tuilleries, on the right as you enter the gardens, an Ionic column. W. A. PERCY Well-wishers.. drove him home, and deposited him.. in the swing on his own front gallery. 3 I. MCEWAN She was picking her way slowly through a long gallery of treasures, heirlooms. *fig.*: P. USTINOV His war tales of the provinces, of a gallery of powerful women and indeterminate men. b J. G. FARRELL The distance between the ends of the branch galleries should be such that the enemy cannot burrow between them unheard. 4 T. HARDY Her sight Swept the west gallery, and caught its row Of music-men. F. RAPHAEL When I was a girl there wasn't a gallery for the women at the synagogue. H. ROSENTHAL I could have got into the back of the gallery for 6d. 5 H. IRVING That same gallery which at first roared itself hoarse, while the play went on. **play to** or **for the gallery** appeal to unrefined tastes. b *Golf Monthly* Sandy Lyle acknowledges the cheers of the huge gallery on the last green.

Comb.: **gallery forest** a forest restricted to the banks of a river or stream; **gallery grave** *Archaeol.* an underground megalithic burial chamber which may be divided into sections but has no separate entrance passage; **gallery play** showy or ostentatious play designed to gain applause; **gallery tray** a silver tray with a raised rim, used to carry glasses etc.

B *v.t.* Provide with a balcony or gallery. E17.

galleried *a.* provided with a gallery M16. **galleryite** *n.* a member of the audience in the gallery of a theatre L19.

gallet /ˈgalɪt/ *n.* & *v.* E18. [Fr. *galet* rounded pebble on the beach, stone chip, f. OFr. *gal* pebble, stone.] *Building.* A *n.* A chip or splinter of stone inserted into wet mortar. E18. B *v.t.* Insert gallets into the mortar or joints of (a wall etc.). M19.

galley /ˈgali/ *n.* ME. [OFr. *galie* (mod. *galée*), f. med.L *galea*, med.Gk *galea*, of unkn. origin, but rel. to Fr. *galère*, ON *galeið*, med.L *galera*, *galeda*, *-ida*.] I 1 *Hist.* A low flat single-decked ship with sails and oars, usu. rowed by slaves or criminals and used chiefly in the Mediterranean; *esp.* such a ship with one or more banks of oars used by the ancient Greeks and Romans in war. ME. 2 *Hist.* A large open rowing boat esp. as used by the captain of a man-of-war, or on the Thames by customs officers or the press-gang. L16. 3 The kitchen of a ship, aircraft, etc. M18. II 4 *Printing.* [Fr. *galée*.] a A usu. metal oblong tray open at one end for holding set type. Now chiefly *Hist.* M17. b A proof in the form of long single-column strips (as orig. from type on a galley), not in sheets or pages; *loosely* a proof from a phototypesetter. L19.

Phrases: **in this galley** [after Molière: see GALÈRE] in this (usu. unpleasant) situation or group of people.

Comb.: **galley-packet** a made-up story, a lie; **galley proof** = sense 4b above; **galley-slave** a person condemned to row in a galley; (*fig.*) a drudge; **galleyworm** a millipede, esp. of the genus *Julus.* **galley-yarn** = *galley-packet* above.

†**galley-tile** *n.* E17–M18. [f. GALLEY + TILE *n.*: see GALLIPOT.] A glazed tile used for wall decoration.

galley-west /ˈgalɪwest/ *adv. colloq.* (orig. & chiefly *US*). L19. [Alt. of COLLY-WEST.] *knock galley-west*, knock sideways or askew; confuse; defeat, dispose of completely.

galliambic /galɪˈambɪk/ *n.* & *a.* M19. [f. L *galliambus* a song of the *Galli* or priests of Cybele (f. *Gallus* + IAMBUS) + -IC.] *Pros.* A *n.* A metre consisting of two catalectic iambic dimeters; (a) verse written in this metre. M19. B *adj.* Pertaining to or composed of galliambics. L19.

galliard /ˈgalɪəd/ *n.*[1] L19. [Origin unkn.] *Geol.* A local (Yorkshire) term for close-grained siliceous sandstones.

galliard /ˈgalɪɑːd, -ɪəd/ *a.* & *n.*[2] LME. [(O)Fr. *gaillard*, perh. f. Proto-Romance = strength, power, of Celt. origin (cf. Ir. *gal* valour, Welsh *gallu* (have) power): see -ARD.] A *adj.* 1 Valiant; sturdy. *arch.* LME. 2 Lively, brisk, full of high spirits; bright or colourful in appearance. *arch.* LME. B *n.* 1 Orig. a valiant man. Now only, a lively man of fashion and pleasure. LME. 2 *Hist.* A quick and lively dance for couples in triple time; a piece of music for this dance. M16.

¶ Earlier as a surname.

galliardize /ˈgalɪədʌɪz/ *n. arch.* Also **-ise**. L16. [Fr. *gaillardise*, f. *gaillard*: see GALLIARD *a.* & *n.*[2]] Gaiety, mirth, revelry; (an) entertainment.

galliass /ˈgalɪəs/ *n.* Also **galleas**. M16. [OFr. *gal(l)easse* (mod. *galéace*) f. It. *galeaza* augm. of *galea* GALLEY.] *Hist.* A large type of galley, chiefly used as a warship during the 16th and 17th cents.

Gallic /ˈgalɪk/ *a.*[1] L17. [L *Gallicus*, f. *Gallus*, *Gallia* Gaul: see -IC.] 1 (Typically) French. Freq. *joc.* L17. 2 Of or pertaining to Gaul or the Gauls. L18.

1 P. D. JAMES He spread his hands in a Gallic gesture of resignation.

gallic /ˈgalɪk/ *a.*[2] L18. [f. L *galla* oak-gall + -IC.] Chem. *gallic acid*, a crystalline acid, $C_6H_2(OH)_3COOH$, prepared from the oak-gall and other vegetable products, and used as a tanning agent and in dyes and inks; 3, 4, 5-trihydroxybenzoic acid.

gallic /ˈgalɪk/ *a.*[3] M20. [f. GALLIUM + -IC.] *Chem.* Of or containing gallium in the trivalent state.

gallica /ˈgalɪkə/ *n.* M19. [f. L *Gallicus*: see GALLIC *a.*[1]] A rose, *Rosa gallica*, ancestral to many cultivated varieties and native to southern Europe and western Asia.

Gallican /ˈgalɪk(ə)n/ *a.* & *n.* LME. [Either f. Fr. = †French, pertaining to the Church of France, or f. L *Gallicanus*, f. *Gallicus*: see GALLIC *a.*[1], -AN.] A *adj.* = GALLIC *a.*[1] (now *rare* in *gen.* sense); *Eccl.* Of or characteristic of the ancient Church of Gaul or France; of or pertaining to Gallicanism. LME. B *n.* An advocate or supporter of Gallicanism. L19.

Gallicanism *n.* (*Eccl.*) the doctrine that asserts the right of the Roman Catholic Church esp. in France to be in certain respects free from papal control M19. **Gallicanist** *n.* = GALLICAN *n.* E18.

gallice /ˈgalɪsi/ *adv. rare.* L19. [L, f. *Gallicus*: see GALLIC *a.*[1], -ICE[1].] In French.

gallicise *v.* var. of GALLICIZE.

Gallicism /ˈgalɪsɪz(ə)m/ *n.* M17. [Fr. *gallicisme*, f. L *Gallicus*: see GALLIC *a.*[1], -ISM.] 1 A French word, idiom, or grammatical feature, esp. one which is used in another language but which remains distinctively French in construction or meaning. M17. 2 A (typically) French characteristic, custom, or outlook. E18.

gallicize /ˈgalɪsʌɪz/ *v.t.* & *i.* Also **-ise**. L18. [f. L *Gallicus* (see GALLIC *a.*[1]) + -IZE.] Make or become French in speech, customs, characteristics, etc.

gallicizer *n.* M19.

galligaskins /galɪˈgaskɪnz/ *n.pl.* L16. [Prob. ult. f. Fr. †*garguesque* var. of †*greguesque*, f. It. *grechesca* use as n. of fem. of *grechesco*, f. *greco* Greek; but the origin of *galli-* remains unkn.] 1 A kind of wide loose hose or breeches worn in the 16th and 17th cents.; later (*joc.*), loose breeches or trousers in general. L16. 2 Leggings, gaiters. Chiefly *dial.* M19.

gallimaufry /galɪˈmɔːfri/ *n.* M16. [Fr. *galimafrée* (OFr. *calimafrée*), of unkn. origin.] 1

A varied miscellaneous jumble or medley; (chiefly *dial.*) a dish made up of minced (esp. leftover) meat etc., a hash, a ragout. M16. 2 A person of many accomplishments or qualities. Freq. *contempt.* Now *rare.* E17.

1 J. I. M. STEWART The canvas is an amazing gallimaufry of allegorical references.

gallinaceous /galɪˈneɪʃəs/ *a.* L18. [f. L *gallinaceus* (f. *gallina* hen f. *gallus* cock) + -OUS: see -ACEOUS.] Of or pertaining to the order Galliformes, which comprises domestic fowls, turkeys, grouse, pheasants, partridges, etc.

gallinacean *a.* & *n.* (*a*) *adj.* = GALLINACEOUS; (*b*) *n.* a gallinaceous bird: M19.

gallinazo /galɪˈneɪzəʊ/ *n.* Pl. **-os.** M18. [Sp., f. L *gallina* hen.] In Latin America: a turkey buzzard or other vulture.

gallinipper /ˈgalɪnɪpə/ *n.* Chiefly *US.* Also (earlier) †**gurnipper.** M17. [Origin unkn.] Any biting or stinging insect; *spec.* a very large American mosquito, *Psorophora ciliata*, whose bite results in a painful swelling.

gallinule /ˈgalɪnjuːl/ *n.* L18. [mod.L *Gallinula* genus name, dim. of L *gallina* hen: see -ULE.] Any of various aquatic birds of the rail family, esp. of the genera *Porphyrio* and *Porphyrula*.

common gallinule *N. Amer.* the moorhen, *Gallinula chloropus. purple gallinule*: see PURPLE *a.*

Gallio /ˈgalɪəʊ/ *n.* Pl. **-os.** M19. [A Roman proconsul of Achaia (*Acts* 18:17).] An indifferent easy-going person.

Galli'onic *a.* having the characteristics of a Gallio E20.

galliot /ˈgalɪət/ *n.* Also **galiot.** ME. [(O)Fr. *galiote* (in sense 2 through Du. *galjoot*), f. It. *galeotta* (Sp. & Port. *galeota*) dim. of med.L *galea* GALLEY: see -OT¹.] 1 *Hist.* A small fast (esp. Spanish or Mediterranean) single-masted galley. ME. 2 A Dutch single-masted cargo boat or fishing boat. Also (more fully *galliot* †*hoy, yacht*) any of various small vessels resembling this boat. M17.

Gallipoli /gaˈlɪp(ə)li/ *n.* E19. [A town in Apulia, Italy.] 1 *Gallipoli soap*, soap made from Gallipoli oil. E19. 2 *Gallipoli oil*, a type of olive oil produced in Gallipoli. M19.

gallipot /ˈgalɪpɒt/ *n.* LME. [Prob. f. GALLEY (as being brought in galleys from the Mediterranean) + POT *n.*¹] 1 A small pot of glazed earthenware or metal, esp. as used by apothecaries or pharmacists for ointments and medicines. LME. 2 An apothecary. *joc.* or *derog. arch.* L18.

Gallithumpian /galɪˈθʌmpɪən/ *n. dial.* L18. [Origin unkn.] †1 A heckler or troublemaker at parliamentary elections. Only in L18. 2 *Hist.* A member of a society of social reformers. L18.

gallium /ˈgalɪəm/ *n.* L19. [f. L *Gallia* France + -IUM.] A soft bluish-white metallic chemical element, atomic no. 31, which melts just above room temperature. (Symbol Ga.)

gallivant /ˈgalɪvant, galɪˈvant/ *v.i. colloq.* E19. [Origin uncertain: perh. alt. of GALLANT *v.*] Go out or *off* in search of pleasure or entertainment; gad about; flirt.

M. SHADBOLT Since Ned didn't drink or gallivant, he saved money. D. STOREY Your mother ill and me at work, and you go gallivanting off.

gallivat /ˈgalɪvat/ *n.* M18. [Port. *galeota*: see GALLIOT.] *Hist.* A large boat with oars and a triangular sail, used in the Indian subcontinent.

galliwasp /ˈgalɪwɒsp/ *n.* L17. [Origin unkn.] Any of various lizards of the Central American genus *Diploglossus*; esp. *D. monotropis* of the W. Indies.

Gallo- /ˈgaləʊ/ *comb. form*¹. [f. L *Gallus, Gallia* Gaul: see GAUL, -O-.] Forming adj. and noun combs. w. the sense 'of Gaul or France; Gallic or French and', as *Gallo-Celtic, Gallo-German.* Cf. FRANCO-.

Gallo'maniac *n.* & *a.* (a person) excessively devoted to France or things French E19. **Gallophil(e)** *n.* a lover of France or things French L19. **Gallophobe** *n.* & *a.* (a person) who is affected with Gallophobia L19. **Gallo'phobia** *n.* intense fear or hatred of France or what is French E19. **Gallo-'Roman** *a.* & *n.* (an inhabitant or the language) of Gaul when under Roman rule M19. **Gallo-Ro'mance** *n.* & *a.* (of or pertaining to) the hypothetical Romance language presumed to represent the Latin spoken in Gaul; (of or pertaining to) the group of chiefly northern and Provençal French dialects presumed to represent this: M20.

gallo- /ˈgaləʊ/ *comb. form*². Bef. a vowel also **gall-.** [f. GALLIC *a.*² + -O-.] Used in *Chem.* to form names of substances derived from or related to gallic acid.

gallo'cyanine *n.* any of a group of bluish-violet oxazine dyes derived from gallic acid L19. **gallo'tannin** any of a class of naturally occurring tannins which yield gallic acid on hydrolysis L19.

galloglass /ˈgalə(ʊ)glɑːs/ *n.* Also **gallowglass.** L15. [Ir. *gallóglach*, f. *gall* foreigner + *óglach* youth, servant, warrior, f. *óg* young + *-lach* abstract suff.] *Ir. Hist.* A member of a special class of soldiers or retainers maintained by Irish chiefs.

gallon /ˈgalən/ *n.* ME. [AN *galon*, var. of OFr. *jalon*, f. Proto-Romance, f. base of med.L *galleta* (whence OFr. *jaloie* liquid measure), *galletum* (whence OE *ġellet* dish, basin, OHG *gellita*, G *Gelte* bucket), perh. of Celt. origin.] 1 A measure of liquid or (in Britain) dry capacity, containing 4 quarts or 8 pints: in Britain (more fully *imperial gallon*) equivalent to 277.42 cu. in. (4.55 litres), in the US (more fully *US gallon*) equivalent to 231 cu. in. (3.79 litres). ME. 2 *sing.* & (usu.) in *pl. hyperbol.* A vast amount of a liquid etc. *colloq.* L16.

1 *Winchester gallon*: see WINCHESTER 1. 2 F. CLUNE The terrific heat made me sweat gallons.

gallonage *n.* the quantity in gallons of a liquid produced or sold E20.

galloon /gəˈluːn/ *n.* Also **galon** /gəˈlɒn/. E17. [Fr. *galon*, f. *galonner* trim with braid (of unkn. origin): see -OON.] (A piece of) narrow ornamental fabric, esp. close-woven silk braid or a strip of lace, used to trim or finish costume or upholstery.

gallooned *a.* trimmed with galloon M19.

gallop /ˈgaləp/ *n.* E16. [OFr. *galop*, f. *galoper*: see next. Cf. WALLOP *n.*] 1 The fastest pace of a horse or other quadruped, in which all four feet are off the ground together in each stride. E16. b A ride at this pace. E17. 2 A track or ground where horses are exercised at a gallop. M19.

1 **(at a) full gallop** as fast as possible. **at a gallop** (of a horse etc.) at its fastest pace, galloping. †**false gallop** a canter. *snail's gallop*: see SNAIL *n.* 1.

gallop /ˈgaləp/ *v.* E16. [OFr. *galoper*: see WALLOP *v.*] I 1 *v.i.* Of a horse or its rider: move at a gallop. E16. b Move or progress rapidly (*lit.* & *fig.*). L16. c *fig.* Foll. by *through*, (rare) *over*: read, recite, execute, etc., at great speed. *colloq.* L18. 2 *v.t.* Make (a horse etc.) go at a gallop. M16. 3 *v.t.* Traverse (a space) at a gallop. Long *rare.* L16. 4 *v.t.* Transport at a gallop or at great speed. L19. II 5 *v.i.* Dance the galop. Now *rare.* E19.

1b **galloping consumption** a consumptive disease that progresses at a rapid pace. c J. W. CROKER Do not gallop through my letter . . but read it over and over again. 3 SHAKES. *Tit. A.* The golden sun . . Gallops the zodiac in his glistering coach.

gallopade /galəˈpeɪd/ *n.* & *v.* Also **galop-.** M18. [Fr. *galopade*, f. *galoper* to gallop: see prec., -ADE. Cf. GALOP.] A *n.* 1 A short sidelong or curveting kind of gallop. M18. 2 A lively ballroom dance in 2/4 time; a piece of music for this dance. Cf. GALOP *n.* M19. B *v.i.* Dance a gallopade. M19.

galloper /ˈgaləpə/ *n.* L16. [f. GALLOP *v.* + -ER¹.] 1 A rider, esp. a huntsman, who gallops. L16. 2 A horse with special powers of galloping. M17. b A wooden etc. horse on a roundabout; a roundabout with such horses. M20. 3 *transf.* & *fig.* A person who proceeds at speed. Also, a gadabout. L17. 4 Chiefly *Hist.* A light field-gun. Also *galloper-gun.* M18. 5 Chiefly *Hist.* A military orderly. L19.

gallous /ˈgaləs/ *a.* & *adv.* Also **gallus,** (now less usu.) **gallows** /ˈgaləʊz/. LME. [(Var. of) attrib. use of GALLOWS *n.*] A *adj.* 1 Fit only to be hanged; wicked, atrocious. Now usu. in milder sense, high-spirited, dashing; full of mischief, cheeky, impish. Now *dial., Sc.,* & *Anglo-Ir.* LME. 2 Extremely great, fine, or handsome. *dial.* & †*slang.* L18.

1 R. BURNS An' plunder'd o' her hindmost groat By gallows knaves. KEATS An Irishman likes to be thought a gallous fellow.

B *adv.* Extremely, very. *dial.* & †*slang.* E19.

H. KINGSLEY The pleece come in, and got gallus well kicked about the head.

gallousness *n.* M19.

Gallovidian /galəˈvɪdɪən/ *a.* & *n.* M17. [f. med.L *Gallovidia* Galloway (see GALLOWAY) + -AN.] (A native or inhabitant) of Galloway in SW Scotland.

†**gallow** *n.* see GALLOWS *n.*

†**gallow** *v.* var. of GALLY *v.*

Galloway /ˈgaləweɪ/ *n.* L16. [An area of SW Scotland, comprising the former counties of Kircudbrightshire and Wigtownshire.] 1 A small strong horse of a breed originating in Galloway; any small-sized horse, *esp.* one suitable for riding. Also *Galloway mare, nag,* etc. L16. 2 (An animal of) a breed of sturdy hornless cattle originating in Galloway, black or (*belted Galloway*) black with a broad white stripe. M18.

Gallowegian *n.* & *a.* var. of GALWEGIAN.

gallowglass *n.* var. of GALLOGLASS.

gallows /ˈgaləʊz/ *n.sing.* & (orig.) †*pl.* Pl. **-es** /-ɪz/. Orig. sing. †**gallow.** See also GALLUS *n.* [OE *ġ(e)alga*, OFris. *galga*, OS, OHG *galgo* (Du. *galg*, G *Galgen*), reinforced by ON *gálgi*, also *gálgatré* gallows-tree, all from Gmc.] 1 A structure, usu. consisting of two upright posts and a crosspiece, for the hanging of criminals. Formerly also *pair of gallows.* OE. b Execution by hanging. L15. 2 Any of various frameworks consisting of two or more supports and a crosspiece as one for athletic exercises or *Austral.* for hanging the carcasses of slaughtered animals. LME. 3 A person who deserves hanging. L16. 4 *sing.* & (usu.) in *pl.* = GALLUS *n. dial., Sc.,* & *US.* M18.

1 A. WOOD A gallowes being erected before Temple gate. J. SULLIVAN That all our liberty-poles will soon be converted into gallowses. b *Proverb*: Save a thief from the gallows and he will cut your throat. **have the gallows in one's face** & vars., look like a person destined for, or deserving of, hanging. *pit and gallows, gallows and pit*: see PIT *n.*¹ 3 DICKENS 'Now, young gallows!' This was an invitation for Oliver to enter.

Comb.: **gallows-bird** a person who deserves to be, or (less freq.) has been, hanged; **gallows-humour** = GALGENHUMOR; **gallows-tree,** †**gallow-tree** = sense 1 above.

gallows *a.* & *adv.* see GALLOUS *a.* & *adv.*

gallstone /ˈgɔːlstəʊn/ *n.* M18. [f. GALL *n.*¹ + STONE *n.*] A calculus or hard mass of bile pigments, cholesterol, and calcium salts, formed in the gall bladder or bile ducts.

Gallup poll /ˈgaləp pəʊl/ *n. phr.* M20. [G. H. *Gallup* (1901–84), US statistician.] (Proprietary name for) an assessment of public opinion by the questioning of a representative sample, esp. as a basis for forecasting votes.

gallus /ˈgaləs/ *n. dial., Sc.,* & *US.* M19. [Var. of GALLOWS *n.*] *sing.* & (usu.) in *pl.* A pair of braces to support the trousers. Also *sing.*, a single trouser-brace.

gallus *a.* & *adv.* var. of GALLOUS *a.* & *adv.*

gally /ˈgɔːli/ *a.*¹ Now *rare* or *obs.* LME. [f. GALL *n.*¹ + -Y¹.] Bitter as gall.

gally /ˈgɔːli/ *a.*² *obs.* exc. *dial.* LME. [f. GALL *n.*² + -Y¹.] †1 Having galls or sores. Only in LME. 2 Full of bare or wet places. E17.

gally /ˈgali/ *v.t.* Chiefly *dial.* & *Whaling.* Also †**gallow.** E17. [Origin uncertain: perh. repr. OE *āgǣlwan* terrify, of unkn. origin.] Frighten, scare.

SHAKES. *Lear* The wrathful skies Gallow the very wanderers of the dark And make them keep their caves.

Comb.: **gally-beggar, -crow** *dial.* a scarecrow.

Galois /ˈgalwɑː/ *n.* L19. [Évariste *Galois* (1811–32), Fr. mathematician.] *Math.* Used *attrib.* to designate various concepts arising from Galois's work.

Galois field a field with a finite number of elements. **Galois theory** a method of applying group theory to the solution of algebraic equations.

Ga'loisian *a.* L19.

galon *n.* var. of GALLOON.

galoot /gəˈluːt/ *n. slang* (chiefly *N. Amer.* & *derog.*). E19. [Origin unkn.] Orig. (*Naut.*), an inexperienced marine. Later *gen.*, a clumsy or stupid person.
M. TWAIN He could lam any galoot of his inches in America. D. HEWETT Why doncha look where you're goin', y' great galoot.

galop /ˈgaləp, gəˈlɒp/ *n.* & *v.* M19. [Fr.: see GALLOP *n.*] A *n.* A lively ballroom dance in 2/4 time; a piece of music for this dance. Cf. GALLOPADE *n.* 2. M19. B *v.i.* Dance a galop. M19.

galopade *n.* var. of GALLOPADE *n.*

galopin /ˈgaləpɪn/ *n. Sc.* Now *rare* or *obs.* M16. [Fr., f. *galoper* GALLOP *v.*] †1 A scullion or page in a great house. M16–E19. 2 A street-urchin. M19.

galore /gəˈlɔː/ *adv., postpositive a.,* & *n.* E17. [Ir. *go leor* (Gael. *gu leòr*) to sufficiency.] A *adv.* & *postpositive adj.* In plenty, abundant(ly). E17.
Sport He has scored goals galore with the Essex side.
B *n.* A plentiful supply (*of*). Chiefly *dial.* M19.
W. CARLETON The best of aiting and dhrinking is provided ... and indeed there was galore of both there.

galosh /gəˈlɒʃ/ *n.* & *v.* Also **gol-**. LME. [(O)Fr. *galoche* repr. (with abnormal phonet. development) late L *gallicula* dim. of L *gallica* use as n. (sc. *solea* shoe) of *Gallicus* GALLIC *a.*] A *n.* 1 Orig., a clog or wooden sole attached by a strap to a shoe of more delicate material. Now, an overshoe of rubber or other waterproof material. Usu. in *pl.* LME. 2 An edging of leather or other material attached to a boot or shoe for protection or decoration. Now *rare.* M19. B *v.t.* Provide (a boot or shoe) with a galosh. Chiefly as *galoshed* ppl a. E19.

†galp *v.* ME. [Perh. alt. of GAPE *v.* Cf. GAWP.] 1 *v.i.* Yawn, gape. ME–L16. 2 *v.t.* Vomit *forth.* E–M16.

galpon /galˈpəʊn/ *n.* L19. [Amer. Sp. *galpón* f. Nahuatl *calpulli* large hall.] A large building like a barn on a S. American farm.

Galsworthian /gɔːlzˈwəːðɪən/ *a.* E20. [f. *Galsworthy* (see below) + -AN.] Relating to or characteristic of the English novelist and dramatist John Galsworthy (1867–1933) or his work.

galt /gɔːlt/ *n.*[1] *obs.* exc. *dial.* LME. [ON *gǫltr*, *galti* boar: cf. OHG *galza*, *gelza* a sow (MHG *galze*, *gelze*, G *Gelze*). Rel. to GILT *n.*[1]] A boar, a male pig.

galt *n.*[2] var. of GAULT.

Galton /ˈgɔːltən/ *n.* L19. [Sir Francis *Galton* (1822–1911), Eng. scientist.] 1 *Biol.* (now *Hist.*). *Galton's law*, either of two laws propounded by Galton: (*a*) the theory that parents contribute on average half the genes of their offspring, grandparents together a quarter, etc.; (*b*) the theory that offspring of outstanding parents tend to regress to, or below, the average for the species. L19. 2 *Galton('s) whistle*, a whistle producing a variable note of high frequency, used to test the upper limit of hearing. L19.
Galˈtonian *a.* of or relating to Galton or his work L19.

galumph /gəˈlʌmf/ *v.i.* L19. [Portmanteau wd combining *gallop* and *triumph*, coined by Lewis Carroll in *Through the Looking-Glass.*] Orig., advance exultantly with irregular bounds. Now chiefly, move in a noisy, ponderous, or clumsy way. Freq. as *galumphing* ppl a.
D. LODGE Shrieking and gasping ... they galumphed across the yard. *transf.*: D. WILKINSON The statement .. may .. give the impression that atoms are large, ungainly galumphing things.

galvanic /galˈvanɪk/ *a.* L18. [Fr. *galvanique*, f. *Galvani*: see GALVANISM, -IC.] 1 Of, pertaining to, or resulting from galvanism or (more widely) direct-current electricity; voltaic (as opp. to faradaic). L18. 2 *fig.* a Resembling the effects of galvanism; convulsive, spasmodic. M19. b Having an effect like that of galvanism; dynamic, electrifying, stimulating. E20.
2a H. STURGIS She embraced the whole party with a last galvanic effort at cheerful enthusiasm. b P. ROTH So galvanic is the word 'panties' that the trajectory of my ejaculation reaches .. new heights.
Special collocations: **galvanic battery**, **cell** an early form of electrical cell in which plates of alternate dissimilar metals are separated by pads moistened with an electrolyte. **galvanic electricity**: produced by chemical action. **galvanic pile** a galvanic battery with many plates. **galvanic skin response** a change in the electrical resistance of the skin caused by strong emotion, measurable with a sensitive galvanometer, e.g. in lie-detector tests.
galvanical *a.* M19. **galvanically** *adv.* M19.

galvanise *v.* var. of GALVANIZE.

galvanism /ˈgalvənɪz(ə)m/ *n.* Now *arch.* or *Hist.* L18. [Fr. *galvanisme*, f. Luigi *Galvani* (1737–98), It. physiologist: see -ISM.] 1 Electricity produced by chemical action. L18. 2 The therapeutic use of galvanic or other direct-current electricity (cf. FARADISM). E19.
galvanist *n.* an expert in galvanism E19.

galvanize /ˈgalvənʌɪz/ *v.t.* Also **-ise**. E19. [Fr. *galvaniser*, f. *Galvani*: see GALVANISM, -IZE.] 1 Apply galvanism to; stimulate (a muscle or nerve) by a galvanic current. Now chiefly *fig.*, stir into violent activity etc. by shock or excitement. (Foll. by *into*, *to*.) E19. 2 Coat with metal, orig. by means of electrolysis; *esp.* coat (iron) with zinc as a protection against rust, usu. without the use of electricity. M19.
1 P. KURTH A report from Dr Eitel .. galvanized Zahle into further action. H. CARPENTER What Macdonald found in that library galvanized his imagination.
galvaniˈzation *n.* M19. **galvanizer** *n.* M19.

galvano- /ˈgalv(ə)nəʊ/ *comb. form* of GALVANIC, GALVANISM: see -O-.
galvanoˈcautery *n.* electrocautery (see ELECTRO-) L19.

galvanometer /galvəˈnɒmɪtə/ *n.* E19. [f. GALVANO- + -METER.] An instrument for detecting and measuring small electric currents, usu. by the deflection of a magnetic needle by the current in a magnetic field.
BALLISTIC *galvanometer.*
galvanoˈmetric, **-ˈmetrical** *adjs.* of or pertaining to galvanometers or galvanometry M19. **galvanometry** *n.* the detection and measurement of small electric currents (by means of galvanometers) L19.

galvanoplasty /ˈgalv(ə)nə(ʊ)plasti/ *n.* L19. [f. as prec. + -PLASTY.] The process of electroplating a substance with metal; *esp.* the making of an electrotype.
galvanoplastic *a.* M19. **galvanoplastically** *adv.* M19.

galvanoscope /ˈgalv(ə)nəskəʊp/ *n.* M19. [f. as prec. + -SCOPE.] A galvanometer; *spec.* one acting by the deflection of a magnetic needle in the magnetic field produced by the current to be detected.
galvanoˈscopic *a.* of, pertaining to or acting as a galvanoscope M19.

galvanotaxis /galv(ə)nə(ʊ)ˈtaksɪs/ *n.* L19. [f. as prec. + -TAXIS.] *Biol.* Movement of an organism in response to the direction of an electric current or field.
galvanotactic *a.* of or pertaining to galvanotaxis E20.

galvanotropism /galv(ə)nə(ʊ)ˈtrəʊpɪz(ə)m/ *n.* L19. [f. as prec. + -TROPISM.] *Biol.* Growth or orientation of an organism or part of one in response to the direction of an electric current or field.
galvanotropic /-ˈtrəʊpɪk, -ˈtrɒpɪk/ *a.* L19.

galvo /ˈgalvəʊ/ *n.* Pl. **-os**. M20. [Abbrev. of GALVANOMETER, GALVANIZE: see -O.] 1 A galvanometer. *colloq.* M20. 2 Galvanized iron. *Austral. slang.* M20.

Galwegian /galˈwiːdʒ(ə)n/ *n.* & *a.* Also **Gallowegian** /galəˈwiːdʒ(ə)n/ L18. [f. *Galloway*, after *Norroway*, *Norway*, *Norwegian*.] = GALLOVIDIAN.

gam /gam/ *n.*[1] *slang.* L18. [Prob. var. of GAMB.] A leg. Now *esp.* a woman's shapely leg.
E. BIRNEY Daphne... Delectable child. Blonde... Lovely gams, adequate income.

gam /gam/ *n.*[2] & *v.* M19. [Origin unkn.] *Naut.* A *n.* 1 A school of whales, porpoises, or dolphins. M19. 2 A social meeting, orig. *spec.* of whalers at sea; a chat. M19. B *v.* Infl. **-mm-**. 1 *v.t.* & *i.* Meet (with) socially, exchange gossip (with): orig. of whalers at sea. M19. 2 *v.i.* Of whales etc.: gather together, form a school. L19. 3 *v.i.* Boast, brag. *slang.* M20.

gama grass /ˈgamə grɑːs/ *n. phr.* Also **-mm-**. M19. [Perh. alt. of GRAMA *n.*[1]] A tall strong fodder grass, *Tripsacum dactyloides*, grown in the southern and western US.

gamahuche /ˈgaməhuːʃ/ *v.* & *n. slang.* Also **gamaruche** /ˈgaməruːʃ/. M19. [Fr. *gamahucher*: perh. imit.] A *v.i.* & *t.* Perform fellatio or cunnilingus (with). M19. B *n.* An act of fellatio or cunnilingus. M19.

gamash /gəˈmaʃ/ *n.* Now chiefly *dial.* L16. [Fr. *gamache* f. mod.Prov. *gamacho*, *garamacho*, f. Sp. *guadamaci* a kind of ornamental leather, f. Arab. *ġadāmasī*, f. *Ġadāmas* (now *Ghadames* or *Ghudāmis*) a town in Libya where such leather was made.] In *pl.* & †*sing.* Leggings or gaiters, worn to protect the legs from mud and wet.

Gamay /ˈgameɪ/ *n.* M19. [A hamlet in Burgundy in eastern France.] A variety of black wine grape native to the Beaujolais district of France; a fruity red wine made from this grape; *US* (also *Gamay-Beaujolais*) any of several red wines with a similar flavour.

gamb /gamb/ *n.* Also **gambe**. M17. [ONFr. *gambe* var. of *jambe* JAMB.] *Her.* A charge representing the leg of an animal. Cf. JAMB 3b.

gamba /ˈgambə/ *n.*[1] Also **†gambo**. L16. [Short for VIOLA DA GAMBA.] 1 = VIOLA DA GAMBA I. L16. 2 An organ-stop resembling a violin or cello in tone. Also *gamba stop.* M19.

gamba /ˈgambə/ *n.*[2] M20. [Sp.] A kind of prawn, *Palaemon serratus*, as an article of food.

gambade /gamˈbeɪd/ *n.* & *v.* E16. [Fr., f. It. *gambata*, f. *gamba* leg: see -ADE. Cf. GAMBADO *n.*[2], GAMBOL *n.* & *a.*] A *n.* A leap or bound (of a horse); a caper, a frisk; a prank. E16. †B *v.i.* = GAMBOL *v.* E–M16.
¶Supplanted by variant GAMBOL during 16; readopted by Sir Walter Scott in E19.

gambado /gamˈbeɪdəʊ/ *n.*[1] Pl. **-o(e)s**. M17. [f. It. *gamba* leg + -ADO.] A leather boot or gaiter, orig. one attached to a saddle to protect the rider's legs from the weather. Usu. in *pl.*

gambado /gamˈbeɪdəʊ, -ˈbɑːd-/ *n.*[2] & *v.* E19. [Sp. *gambada*, f. *gamba* leg: see -ADO.] A *n.* Pl. **-o(e)s**. 1 A leap or bound of a horse. Usu. in *pl.* E19. 2 A fantastic movement, a caper; any sudden or fantastic action. Usu. in *pl.* M19.
1 SIR W. SCOTT The gambadoes of Sir Piercie and his prancing war-horse. 2 C. BRONTË Sending him a challenge or performing other gambadoes of the sort.
B *v.i.* Prance, caper. E19.

†gambaugium *n.* see GAMBOGE.

gambe *n.* var. of GAMB.

gambeson /ˈgambɪs(ə)n/ *n.* ME. [OFr., f. *gambais*, prob. f. OFrank. *wamba* belly (see WOMB *n.*).] *Hist.* A (padded) tunic of leather or thick cloth, worn orig. under the habergeon to prevent chafing, later as an outer (protective) garment.

†gambett *n.* see GAMBIT.

Gambia kino /ˈgambɪə ˈkiːnəʊ/ *n. phr.* L19. [f. *Gambia* (see GAMBIAN) + KINO.] Kino from W. Africa.

Gambian /ˈgambɪən/ *a.* & *n.* E20. [f. *Gambia* (see below) + -AN.] A *adj.* Of or pertaining to (The) Gambia, a country in W. Africa, or its inhabitants. E20. B *n.* A native or inhabitant of (The) Gambia. M20.

gambier /ˈgambɪə/ *n.* Also **-ir**. E19. [Malay *gambir*, name of the plant.] An astringent extract used in tanning, obtained from a tropical Asiatic climbing shrub, *Uncaria gambieri*, of the madder family. Also, the plant itself.

gambist /ˈgambɪst/ *n.* E19. [f. GAMBA *n.*[1] + -IST.] A performer on the viola da gamba.

gambit /ˈgambɪt/ *n.* Orig. **†gambett**. M17. [It. *gambetto* lit. 'tripping up', f. *gamba* leg; *-it* f. Fr. *gambit* f. Sp. *gambito*.] 1 *Chess.* An attack (usu. an opening) in which a chessman is sacrificed to gain an advantage; a (specified) play of this kind.

M17. 2 An opening move in a discussion etc.; a trick, a ruse, a device. M19.

1 *King's gambit*, *Queen's gambit*, etc. 2 J. R. ACKERLEY Taking Megan apart . . was one of her favourite opening gambits. P. LIVELY She searched for another gambit by which to escape.

¶The spelling *gambit* is not recorded bef. M18.

gamble /ˈgamb(ə)l/ *n.*[1] *obs.* exc. *dial.* E18. [Alt. of GAMBREL.] 1 = CAMBREL 2. E18. 2 = CAMBREL 3. L19.

gamble /ˈgamb(ə)l/ *n.*[2] E19. [f. the vb.] An act of gambling; a risky undertaking or attempt.

G. SAINTSBURY The real point is the chance, the uncertainty, the gamble.

gamble /ˈgamb(ə)l/ *v.* E18. [f. GAMEL or GAME *v.*: see -LE[3].] 1 *v.i.* Play games of chance for (a lot of) money; indulge in betting, esp. habitually; risk money, fortune, success, etc., on the outcome of an event. (Foll. by *on* an event or outcome, *that* a specified outcome will ensue.) E18. 2 *v.t.* Lose (money etc.) by gaming or betting. Freq. foll. by *away*. E19. b Bet (money etc.). L19.

1 D. H. LAWRENCE When they played cards, they always gambled. A. J. P. TAYLOR The British government had . . decided to gamble that Japan would remain neutral. F. RAPHAEL He gambled on the horses. 2 F. HUME He gambled away large sums at his club. b JOYCE Gambling every penny they have and losing it on horses.

gambler *n.* †(*a*) a gamester, a sharper; (*b*) a person who gambles, esp. habitually: M18. **gambling** *vbl n.* the action of the vb; *esp.* the risking of money on games of chance as a pastime or a sphere of human activity: L18.

gambo /ˈgambəʊ/ *n.*[1] *dial.* Pl. **-oes**. M19. [Origin unkn.] A simple farm cart, trolley, or sledge.

†**gambo** *n.*[2] var. of GAMBA *n.*[1]

gamboge /gamˈbəʊʒ, -ˈbuːʒ/ *n.* Also (earlier) in L form †**gambaugium** M17. [mod.L *gambaugium* var. of *cambugium* etc., f. *Cambodia* (= *Kampuchea*) a country in SE Asia.] A gum resin used as a bright yellow pigment and as a purgative, obtained from various eastern Asian trees of the genus *Garcinia* (family Guttiferae).

gambol /ˈgamb(ə)l/ *n.* & *a.* Also (earlier) †**-old**. M16. [Alt. of GAMBADE.] A *n.* 1 A caper, frisk, or frolic, esp. of a child or an animal; a playful action. Usu. in *pl.* M16. †2 A toy, a plaything. L16–M17.

1 SHAKES. *Wint. T.* A dance which the wenches say is a gallimaufry of gambols. S. RICHARDSON A silly poor girl, set up by the gambol of fortune for a May-game.

†B *attrib.* or as *adj.* Playful, sportive. L16–M17.

gambol /ˈgamb(ə)l/ *v.i.* Infl. **-ll-**. Also (earlier) †**-old**. E16. [f. as prec., after Fr. *gambader*.] Leap or spring in dance or play; frolic.

W. GOLDING The rats . . jumped and gambolled and played on the mud beach.

†**gambold** *n.*, *v.* see GAMBOL *n.* & *a.*, *v.*

gambrel /ˈgambr(ə)l/ *n.* Now chiefly *US* & *dial.* M16. [ONFr. *gamberel*, f. *gambier* forked stick, f. *gambe* var. of *jambe* leg: see JAMB, -REL. Cf. GAMBLE *n.*[1], CAMBREL.] 1 = CAMBREL 3. M16. 2 The joint in the upper part of a horse's hind leg, the hock; = CAMBREL 2. E17. b (The underside of) a person's thigh. M18. 3 A curved or hipped roof with a steep lower slope (also *gambrel roof*); a building with such a roof. M19.

gambroon /gamˈbruːn/ *n.* E19. [*Gambroon* (now *Bandar Abbas*), a seaport in Iran.] A twilled linen cloth used for linings; a cotton and worsted fabric used for men's coats etc.

game /geɪm/ *n.* [OE *gamen*, *gomen* = OFris. *game*, *gome*, OS, OHG, ON *gaman*; prob. identical with Goth. *gaman* fellowship (tr. Gk *koinōnia*), f. Gmc bases of Y-, MAN *n.*] I Amusement, fun, play. 1 Amusement, fun, mirth, pleasure. Now chiefly *dial.* OE. †2 Jest, as opp. to *earnest*. Also, a jest, a joke. ME–E17. b An object of ridicule, a laughing-stock. Also *laughing-game*. M16–L17. 3 An amusement, a diversion, a pastime. ME. 4 An amusing incident, a bit of fun, a lark. M19.

1 SHAKES. *L.L.L.* We have had pastimes here, and pleasant game. 2 SPENSER They . . crowned her twixt earnest and twixt game. 3 J. SULLY In their games children are actors, architects, and poets. 4 DICKENS I can't bear it; it is such a jolly game . . Oh, my eye, what a game!

II 5 Sport derived from the hunting, shooting, or catching of animals. *arch.* ME. 6 The object of a hunt; the quarry, the creature hunted. ME. 7 *collect.* Kinds of wild animals, birds, or fish now or formerly hunted for food or sport. ME. b The flesh of such animals and birds used as food. L18. 8 A flock or herd of animals kept for pleasure. Now only as *collect. n.* for swans. L15. 9 The spirit of a fighting cock; fighting spirit, pluck; a person or animal with this. Cf. GAME *a.*[1] M18.

5 DEFOE This [lion] was Game indeed to us, but this was no Food. 6 P. MATTHIESSEN A hill fox . . makes six pounces . . , four of them successful, though its game is small. 7 R. F. BURTON The country round is full of large game, especially elephants, giraffe, and zebras. b E. SHERIDAN Dick not yet arrived and what was worse some fish and game he had promised to bring was expected for dinner. 8 P. L. FERMOR An ornamental lake where a . . game of swans were reflected. 9 DICKENS They were thorough game and didn't make the least complaint.

III Competitive sport or pastimes. 10 A (form of) contest played according to rules and decided by skill, strength, or luck (as opp. *sport* esp. one in which opponents actively engage to defeat each other). ME. 11 A complete episode or period of play, usu. terminating in a definite result; in some contests, a single period of play forming a scoring unit. ME. 12 In *pl.* (occas. treated as *sing.*). a *Class. Hist.* (An event or entertainment made up of) various athletic, dramatic, or musical contests, gladiatorial displays, and other shows. LME. b (Also G-.) A (periodic) meeting consisting of various athletic and occas. other sporting contests. E19. c Athletics and sports as organized in a school or college. L19. 13†a The winning position in a contest. Also, the prize. LME–E17. b The course or outcome of a game. E19. 14 Now chiefly *Chess*. The position (of one side) in play. L17. 15 Esp. *Chess*. A method of play; a recognized sequence of moves. Also, a stage in play. M18. 16 A person's performance in a game; a person's normal standard or method of play. M19. 17 The score; *esp.* the number of points required to win; *Bridge* (a contract providing) a total of one hundred or more points below the line. M19. 18 The apparatus necessary to play a particular game, esp. a board game or computer game. L19.

10 M. PUZO He wandered through . . the huge gambling casino . . wondering what game to try next. A. PRICE Women's hockey is a tough game, I'm told. *board game*, *card-game*, *computer game*, *panel game*, *paper game*, *video game*, etc. 11 DAY LEWIS My father was talking . . in the club house after a game of golf. 12a L. WALLACE A Roman's love of games and bloody spectacles. M. TIPPETT The games were held in honour of Olympian Zeus. c J. BETJEMAN Greatest dread of all, the dread of games! 13b *fig.*: C. D. YONGE Napoleon . . said that in war the game is with him who commits the fewest faults. 14 BURKE The advantageous game which we have obtained. 15 H. GOLOMBEK He was quite outplayed in the early middle game. 16 F. GALE We had played . . together, and knew each other's game. 17 OED The game is four all.

IV *transf.* & *fig.* 19 An object of pursuit or attack. ME. 20 A proceeding, scheme, or intrigue carried out like a game. ME. b A simulation of a contest, battle, operation, etc., in order to test a strategy. E20. 21 Lovemaking (*spec.* sexual intercourse) viewed as a game or pastime. ME. 22 A person's policy, behaviour, or plan of action. LME. b A ruse, a dodge, a trick. Freq. in *pl.* M17. 23 A (specified) business or occupation. M20.

19 C. GIBBON She is game much too high for him. 20 W. H. PRESCOTT While this game of diplomacy was going on. J. LENNON It's the same game, nothing's really changed. b *attrib.*: M. LEAPMAN The best chance for Nato, according to the game planners, is to counterattack quickly. 21 G. GREENE What mattered was the game The two main characters made their stately progress towards the bed sheets. 22 E. CALDWELL Whatever his game is, it's a little bit more than just driving around . . looking at the sights. T. GUNN I was at my usual game of stealing what could be of use to me. 23 C. ODETS You're in the fighting game . . . what would you rather do than fight.

Phrases: *anybody's game*: see ANYBODY. **beat (someone) at his** (or **her**) **own game** outdo a person in his (or her) chosen procedure. **be in the game** have a chance of succeeding. *big game*: see BIG *a.* *compendium of games*: see COMPENDIUM 5a. *end-game*: see END *n.* **fair game** legitimately to be pursued or attacked. *fly at higher game*: see FLY *v.* *force the game*: see FORCE *v.*[1] *fun and games*: see FUN *n.* **game all** one game won by each side. *game is not worth the candle*: see CANDLE *n.* *game of chance*: see CHANCE *n.* **game, set, and match** final victory in a lawn tennis match; *fig.* complete and decisive victory. **give the game away** inadvertently reveal one's own or another's intentions. *great game*: see GREAT *a.* *guessing game*: see GUESS *v.* *Highland games*: see HIGHLAND. *laughing-game*: see sense 2b above. *losing game*: see LOSING *ppl a.* **make game of** make fun of, ridicule. *mug's game*: see MUG *n.*[6] I. **off one's game** playing badly. *Olympic games*: see OLYMPIC *a.* **on one's game** playing well. **on the game** *slang* (*a*) engaged in thieving or robbery; (*b*) engaged in prostitution. **one's (little) game** what one hopes to do undetected. **play a good** (or **poor**) **game of** be skilful (or not) at a (specified) game. **play games (with)** act dishonestly (towards), pretend. **play a person's game** advance a person's schemes unintentionally. **play the game** observe the rules or conventions; act correctly or honourably. *run a game* (*on*): see RUN *v.* **the game** †(*a*) cock-fighting; (*b*) a form of charades. **the game is up** the scheme is revealed or foiled; success is now impossible. *waiting game*: see WAITING *vbl n.* **what's the** (or **your**) **game?** what's going on?, what are you up to?

Comb.: **game act**, **law** (usu. in *pl.*): regulating the hunting and preservation of game; **gamebag**: for holding game killed by a sportsman or sportswoman; **game ball** *n.* & *a. phr.* (*a*) *n. phr.* the state of the game in fives etc. when one point may win; (*b*) *pred. a. phr.* (*Anglo-Ir. slang*) excellent, fine; **game-bird** a (kind of) bird now or formerly shot for sport *esp.* one of the order Galliformes, which includes the pheasants, grouse, etc.; **game-board** = BOARD *n.* 2b; **gamebook**: for recording a sportsman's or sportswoman's kill; **game chips** thin round potato chips served with game; **gamecock** a cock (of a kind) bred for fighting; **game-fish** a (kind of) fish caught for sport; **gamefowl** (a bird of) a kind bred for cock-fighting; **gamekeeper** a person employed to breed and manage game, prevent poaching, etc.; *game law*: see *game act* above; **game licence** a licence to hunt, or to deal in, game; **game park** an area set aside for the conservation of game species; **game-piece** (*a*) a piece or man used in a game; (*b*) a still-life painting including game; **game plan** a winning strategy worked out in advance for a particular game; *fig.* a plan of campaign, esp. in politics; **game-playing** the playing of games or sports; *fig.* insincere behaviour; **game point** a state of a game when one side needs only one point to win it; **game-preserver** a landowner etc. who breeds game and applies game laws strictly; **game reserve** = *game park* above; **game rhyme** a rhyme accompanying a (children's) game; **game show** a television light-entertainment programme in which people compete in a game or quiz, often for prizes; **games master**, **mistress**: in charge of sports and athletics in a school etc.; **game-tenant**: who rents the hunting, shooting, or fishing rights on an estate etc.; **game(s) theory** mathematical analysis of conflicts in war, economics, games of skill, etc.; **game-warden** a person locally supervising game and hunting.

game /geɪm/ *a.*[1] E18 [f. the n. (sense 9).] 1 Like a gamecock; full of fight; spirited, plucky. E18. 2 Having the necessary spirit or will *for*, *to do*; ready and willing. M19.

1 G. STEIN So game, nothing ever scared him. **die game** meet death resolutely; keep one's courage to the end. **game as Ned Kelly** *Austral. colloq.* very brave. 2 P. KURTH An avid tourist, tireless, inquisitive, and game for adventure. A. BROOKNER Mrs Pusey, although still game, suddenly looked rather old.

gamely *adv.* M19. **gameness** *n.* E19.

game /geɪm/ *a.*[2] L18. [Origin unkn. Cf. GAMMY.] Of a limb: crippled, lame.

M. SHADBOLT He had a game leg from the war.

game /geɪm/ *v.* [OE *gam(e)nian*, f. (as) GAME *n.*] 1 *v.i.* Play, sport, jest; amuse oneself. *obs.* exc. *dial.* OE. †b *v.t.* Amuse, please, give pleasure to. Only in ME. 2 *v.i.* Play at games of chance for money etc.; gamble. E16. b *v.t.* Throw *away* (money etc.), or while *away* time, by gambling. M17.

gamer *n.* (*a*) a person who plays a game; a gambler; (*b*) *rare* a person who hunts game: ME.

†**gameful** *a.* ME. [f. GAME *n.* + -FUL.] 1 Joyful, playful, sportive. ME–E18. 2 Having much game or wildlife that can be hunted. E17–E18.

gamel /ˈgam(ə)l/ *v.i.* Long *obs.* exc. *dial.* L16. [Frequent. of GAME *v.* or alt. of reflex of OE *gam(e)nian* GAME *v.*: see -LE[3]. Cf. GAMBLE *v.*] Play games; romp, frolic. Chiefly as *gameling* vbl n.

gamelan /ˈgamәlan/ *n.* E19. [Jav.] An Indonesian, esp. Javanese or Balinese, orchestra consisting mainly of percussion instruments.

gameless /ˈgeɪmlɪs/ *a.* M16. [f. GAME *n.* + -LESS.] †1 Yielding no fun or pleasure. Only in M16. 2 Containing no game (birds or animals). M19.

gamesman /ˈgeɪmzmәn/ *n.* Pl. **-men**. M20. [f. GAME *n.* + -S[1] + MAN *n.* Cf. next.] 1 A piece used in a game such as chess. *rare.* M20. 2 A person who takes part in games or sports; *spec.* one skilled in gamesmanship. M20.

gamesmanship /ˈgeɪmzmәnʃɪp/ *n.* M20. [f. GAME *n.* + -S[1] + -MANSHIP.] The art or practice of defeating an opponent by psychological or other questionable means; unsportsmanlike tactics.

S. POTTER The theory and practice of gamesmanship or the art of winning games without actually cheating.

gamesmen *n.* pl. of GAMESMAN.

gamesome /ˈgeɪms(ә)m/ *a.* LME. [f. GAME *n.* + -SOME[1].] Playful, merry, sportive.

gamesomely *adv.* LME. **gamesomeness** *n.* E18.

gamester /ˈgeɪmstә/ *n.* M16. [f. GAME *n.* + -STER.] 1 A gambler. *arch.* M16. 2 A player at any game. Also, an athlete. *arch.* L16. b A player at single stick or back-sword; a wrestler. *dial.* M19. †3 A merry, playful person. L16–E17. †4 A promiscuous person; a libertine, a whore. E–M17. 5 A keeper or owner of a game of swans. *obs.* exc. *Hist.* L19.

gamestress *n.* (now *rare* or *obs.*) a female gamester M17.

gametangium /gamɪˈtan(d)ʒɪәm/ *n.* Pl. **-ia** /-ɪә/. L19. [f. as next + Gk *aggeion* vessel + -IUM.] *Bot.* A specialized organ in which gametes are formed, esp. in algae and fungi.

gamete /ˈgamiːt/ *n.* L19. [mod.L *gameta* f. Gk *gametē* wife, *gametēs* husband, f. *gamos* marriage.] *Biol.* A mature haploid germ cell (male or female) which unites with another of the opposite sex in sexual reproduction to form a zygote.

Comb.: **gamete intrafallopian transfer** = *GIFT* s.v. G, G III.

gametic /gәˈmɛtɪk, -ˈmiː-/ *a.* E20. [f. prec. + -IC.] *Biol.* Of or pertaining to a gamete or gametes; of the nature of a gamete.

gametically *adv.* E20.

gameto- /gәˈmiːtәʊ/ *comb. form* of GAMETE: see -O-.

gametocyst *n.* a cyst containing gametes E20. **gametocyte** *n.* a cell that gives rise to gametes L19. **gametoˈgenesis** *n.* the formation of gametes E20. **gametoˈgenic** *a.* of or relating to gametogenesis; giving rise to gametes: E20. **gameˈtogeny**, **gameˈtogony** *ns.* = GAMETOGENESIS E20. **gametophore** *n.* (*Bot.*) a specialized filament or branch bearing sexual organs L19. **gametoˈphoric** *a.* (*Bot.*) of, pertaining to, or of the nature of a gametophore L19.

gametophyte /gәˈmiːtә(ʊ)fʌɪt/ *n.* L19. [f. prec. + -PHYTE.] *Bot.* In the alternation of generations, the gamete-producing (usu. haploid) phase in the life cycle of a plant (the dominant form in bryophytes) which forms the zygote from which the sporophyte arises. Cf. SPOROPHYTE.

gametophytic /-ˈfɪtɪk/ *a.* of, pertaining to, or of the nature of a gametophyte E20.

gamey *a.* var. of GAMY.

gamgee /ˈgamdʒi/ *n.* L19. [Joseph Sampson *Gamgee* (1828–86), Eng. surgeon.] A wound-dressing devised by Gamgee, consisting of a thickness of cotton-wool between two layers of gauze. Also *Gamgee tissue, pad*, etc.

gamic /ˈgamɪk/ *a.* M19. [Gk *gamikos*, f. *gamos* marriage: see -IC.] *Biol.* Of an organism: having a sexual nature; reproducing sexually, esp. as distinct from parthenogenetically.

gamin /ˈgamɪn, -mã; *foreign* gamɛ̃ (*pl. same*)/ *n.* & *a.* M19. [Fr.] A *n.* A street urchin, a waif; a street-wise or impudent child. M19. B *adj.* Of, pertaining to, resembling, or characteristic of a gamin. M19.

gamine /gaˈmiːn; *foreign* gamin (*pl. same*)/ *n.* & *a.* L19. [Fr.] A *n.* A female gamin; a small, attractively informal, mischievous, or elfish young woman. L19.

B *adj.* Of, pertaining to, resembling, or characteristic of a gamine. E20.

D. H. LAWRENCE He was fascinated by Lou's quaint aplomb . . her *gamine* knowingness.

gaminerie /gaminri/ *n.* E20. [Fr.] The behaviour or characteristics of a gamin or gamine.

gaminesque /gamɪˈnɛsk, -miː-/ *a.* E20. [f. GAMIN, GAMINE + -ESQUE.] Resembling or characteristic of a gamin or gamine.

gaming /ˈgeɪmɪŋ/ *vbl n.* LME. [f. GAME *v.* + -ING[1].] †1 Playing games; sport; merrymaking. *Sc.* LME–E17. 2 The action or habit of playing at games of chance for money; gambling. E16. †3 *Class. Hist.* In *pl.* Athletic or musical contests. L16–E17.

Comb.: **gaming-table** a table at which games of chance are played for money.

gamma /ˈgamә/ *n.* LME. [L f. Gk.] 1 The third letter (*Γ*, *γ*) of the Greek alphabet. LME. †2 *Mus.* Gamut. E17–E19. 3 Denoting the third in a numerical sequence: a *attrib. Sci.* Freq. written *γ*. (*a*) *Astron.* (preceding the genitive of the L name of the constellation) denoting the third brightest star in a constellation; (*b*) *Chem.* denoting the third of a number of isomeric forms of a compound, or of allotropes of an element, etc.; (*c*) designating high-energy electromagnetic radiation which consists of photons of wavelengths shorter than those of X-rays and is one of the three main types of decay product emitted by radioactive substances; also designating decay, emission, particles, etc., associated with such radiation. L17. b A third-class mark in an examination etc. M20. 4 More fully *gamma moth*. The silver Y, *Plusia gamma*. M19. 5 a A unit of magnetic field strength equal to 10^{-5} oersted. E20. b A unit of mass equal to 10^{-6} gram. M20. 6 *Photogr.* & *Television.* A measure of the contrast of an image compared with that of the scene represented. E20.

3a *gamma globulin*: see GLOBULIN. b **gamma plus, minus** rather better, worse, than the average third class.

gammadion /gaˈmeɪdɪәn/ *n.* M19. [Late Gk, f. GAMMA.] An arrangement of shapes of capital gamma (Γ), esp. of four, as a swastika or a hollow Greek cross.

gamma grass *n. phr.* var. of GAMA GRASS.

gammarid /ˈgamәrɪd/ *n.* & *a.* M19. [f. mod.L *Gammarus* (see below), f. L *g-*, *cammarus* f. Gk *kammaros* a sea-crab or lobster: see -ID[3].] *Zool.* A *n.* Any member of a large group of amphipod crustaceans typified by freshwater shrimps of the genus *Gammarus*. M19. B *adj.* Of or relating to this group. E20.

gammer /ˈgamә/ *n. arch.* L16. [Prob. contr. of GODMOTHER, w. *ga-* by assoc. w. *grandmother*. Cf GAFFER.] (A rustic title for) an old woman, corresp. to GAFFER.

R. D. BLACKMORE The rector having learned every gammer's alloverishness and every gaffer's rheumatics.

Gammexane /ˈgamɛkseɪn, gaˈmɛkseɪn/ *n.* M20. [f. alternative chemical name *gamma*-hexachlorocyclo*hexane*.] (Proprietary name for) the insecticide lindane.

gammon /ˈgamәn/ *n.*[1] L15. [ONFr. *gambon* (mod.Fr. *jambon*) ham, f. *gambe* leg: cf. JAMB.] †1 The ham or haunch of a swine. L15–E17. 2 The bottom piece of a flitch of bacon, including the leg. Also, ham cured like bacon. E16.

2 *gammon and spinach*: see GAMMON *n.*[3]

gammon /ˈgamәn/ *n.*[2] L17. [Perh. identical with prec., w. ref. to the tying up of a ham: cf. Fr. *gambes* (*de hune*) futtock shrouds.] *Naut.* The rope or ropes used to lash the bowsprit to the stem. Now usu. GAMMONING.

gammon /ˈgamәn/ *n.*[3] *slang.* E18. [Perh. f. as next.] 1 *give gammon* (*to*) give cover to or *to* a pickpocket etc.; *keep in gammon* distract (a victim) while a confederate carries out a robbery. *Criminals' slang.* E18. 2 Talk, chatter. L18. 3 Nonsense, humbug; deceit. Also as *int.*, rubbish! poppycock! E19.

2 **gammon and patter** talk, chatter, esp. between members of the same trade or profession; shop-talk. 3 **gammon and spinach** nonsense, humbug (with a pun on GAMMON *n.*[1]).

gammon /ˈgamәn/ *n.*[4] M18. [Perh. repr. reflexes of OE *gam(e)nian* GAME *v.* or *gamen* GAME *n.*] 1 The game of backgammon. Now *rare.* M18. 2 A victory in backgammon (carrying a double score) in which the winner removes all his or her pieces before the loser has removed any. M18.

gammon /ˈgamәn/ *v.*[1]*t.* L17. [f. GAMMON *n.*[4]] Beat at backgammon by a gammon; *fig.* beat decisively.

gammon /ˈgamәn/ *v.*[2]*t.* L17. [f. GAMMON *n.*[2]] *Naut.* Lash (the bowsprit) with ropes to the stem of a ship.

gammoning *vbl n.* (*a*) the action of the vb; (*b*) = GAMMON *n.*[2]: M19.

gammon /ˈgamәn/ *v.*[3] *slang.* L18. [f. GAMMON *n.*[3]] 1 *v.i.* Talk plausibly or persuasively. L18. 2 *v.i.* & *t.* Feign, pretend (*to do* or *to be*). E19. 3 *v.t.* Flatter, deceive, hoax. E19.

2 T. COLLINS He gammoned dead till we poured a pint of beer down his throat. 3 W. BLACK Gammon old Mackenzie into the belief that he can read poetry.

gammoner *n.* E19

gammon /ˈgamәn/ *v.*[4]*t.* M19. [f. GAMMON *n.*[1]] Cure (ham) by salting or smoking.

gammy /ˈgami/ *a.* M19. [Dial. var. of GAME *a.*[2]] 1 Bad; not good or genuine. *slang.* Now *rare* or *obs.* M19. 2 Disabled through injury or pain. Cf. GAME *a.*[2] L19.

2 M. KEANE He couldn't dance because of his gammy leg.

gamo- /ˈgamәʊ/ *comb. form.* [Gk, f. *gamos* marriage: see -O-.] Chiefly used in *Biol.* w. the sense 'of sexual reproduction' or in *Bot.* w. the sense 'of union of parts'.

gamoˈgenesis *n.* reproduction by union of gametes, sexual reproduction M19. **gamogeˈnetic** *a.* of, relating to, involving, or produced by gamogenesis M19. **gamoˈpetalous** *a.* (*Bot.*) having petals united along their margins to form a tubular corolla (opp. *polypetalous*) M19. **gaˈmophyllous** *a.* (*Bot.*) having the perianth segments fused L19. **gamoˈsepalous** *a.* (*Bot.*) having sepals united along their margins to form a tubular calyx (opp. *polysepalous*) M19.

gamont /ˈgamɒnt/ *n.* E20. [f. GAMETE + Gk *ont-*, *ōn* pres. pple of *einai* be, exist.] *Zool.* The sexual form of a protozoan displaying alternation of generations. Cf. SCHIZONT.

gamp /gamp/ *n.* M19. [Mrs *Gamp* (see below).] 1 A woman resembling Mrs Sarah Gamp, a monthly nurse in Dickens's *Martin Chuzzlewit*; *spec.* a drunken or disreputable sick nurse. Now *rare.* M19. 2 An umbrella, *esp.* a large untidy one such as that carried by Mrs Gamp. M19.

gamut /ˈgamәt/ *n.* LME. [Contr. of med.L *gamma ut*, f. GAMMA name of the symbol *Γ* (repr. in the Middle Ages a note one tone lower than A) + UT first of the six notes forming a hexachord.] I *Mus.* 1 *Hist.* The lowest note on the medieval sequence of hexachords, equal to modern G on the lowest line of the bass stave. LME. 2 *Hist.* A large scale (ascribed to Guido d'Arezzo), formed of seven hexachords or partial scales, and containing all the recognized notes used in medieval music. L15. 3 The full range of notes which a voice or instrument can produce. M17. 4 The major diatonic scale; the scale recognized by any particular people or in any period. E18.

II 5 *transf.* & *fig.* The whole range or scope of something. E17.

5 C. BEATON Her resonant voice covers the gamut from an emphatic whisper to an . . almost Rabelaisian roar.

gamy /ˈgeɪmi/ *a.* Also **gamey**. M19. [f. GAME *n.* + -Y[1].] 1 Having much game or wildlife that can be hunted; intent on game. M19. 2 Spirited, plucky. M19. 3 Having the flavour or smell of game, esp. when it is high; strong-tasting or smelling. M19. 4 Racy, spicy; scandalous, sensational; sexy. Chiefly *N. Amer.* M20.

2 J. M. SYNGE A fine, gamy . . lad the like of you. 3 P. ROTH Underwear athletically gamy. 4 D. ABSE Underweight women in the gamiest of skirts.

gaminess *n.* L19.

-gamy /gəmi/ *suff.* [f. Gk *gamos* marriage + -Y³] Appended to Gk stems to form ns. w. the senses 'marriage' or (*Biol.*) 'reproduction, fertilization' (*cleistogamy, endogamy, polygamy*, etc.).

Gamza /ˈgamzə, ˈgʌm-/ *n.* Also **Gum-**. M20. [Bulgarian.] A dark red Bulgarian grape; the wine made from this.

Gan /gan/ *n.* & *a.* Also **Kan** /kan/. M20. [Chin. *Gàn*.] A *n.* A Chinese dialect spoken in Jiangxi province. M20. B *adj.* Of or pertaining to this dialect. M20.

ganbei /ganˈbeɪ/ *int.* Also **kan-pei**. M20. [Chin. *gānbēi*, f. *gān* empty, dry + *bēi* glass, cup.] A Chinese toast, a call to drain one's glass.

ganbu /ˈganbuː/ *n.* Also ***kanpu*** /ˈkanpuː/. M20. [Chin. *gànbù*.] = CADRE *n.* 3b.

†ganch *n.* Also **gaunch**. E17. [Fr. †*ganche* f. mod.Prov. *ganche* hook, boathook, f. Sp. *gancho* or It. *gancio* hook.] 1 The apparatus used in execution by ganching; the punishment itself. E17–L18. 2 A gash or wound made by a wild boar's tusk. Only in E19.

ganch /gan(t)ʃ/ *v.t.* Also **†gaunch**. E17. [Fr. †*ganché* pa. pple of vb f. †*ganche*: see prec.] 1 Impale on sharp hooks or stakes as a means of execution. Now *rare*. E17. †2 Of a boar: tear or gash with the tusk. Usu. in *pass.* E17–L18.

gander /ˈgandə/ *n.* [Late OE *ganra, gandra*, corresp. to MLG *ganre* (LG, Du. *gander*), f. Gmc base also of GANNET.] 1 A male goose. LOE. 2 A dull or stupid person; a fool, a simpleton. M16. 3 A look, a glance. Esp. in *have, take, a gander at. slang.* E20.

1 *Proverb*: What is sauce for the goose is sauce for the gander.

Comb.: **gander-month, -moon** (long *rare*) the month after a wife's confinement.

gander /ˈgandə/ *v.i. dial.* & *US.* L17. [f. the n.] 1 Wander about aimlessly or foolishly. L17. b Stare, look inquisitively at or for something. L19. 2 Ramble in talk. M19.

gandharva /ganˈdɑːvə/ *n.* Also **-ba** /-bə/. L18. [Skt *gandharvās*. Perh. conn. w. Gk *kentauros* CENTAUR.] *Hindu Mythol.* Any of a class of minor deities or genii of the sky, often represented as celestial musicians, and depicted in a variety of presiding or attendant roles.

Gandhian /ˈgandɪən/ *a.* E20. [f. *Gandhi* (see below) + -AN.] Of, pertaining to, or characteristic of Mohandas Karamchand (known as Mahatma) Gandhi (1869–1948), Indian political leader and social reformer, or his principles, esp. those of non-violent social reform.

Gandhi'esque *a.* M20. **Gandhi-ism, Gandhism** *ns.* Gandhian principles or actions E20. **Gandhist** *n.* a follower of Gandhi E20.

Gandhi cap /ˈgandi kap/ *n. phr.* E20. [f. *Gandhi* (see prec.) + CAP *n.*¹] A close fitting white cap with a wide band encircling the head.

gandoura /ganˈdʊərə/ *n.* Also **-dourah, -dura(h)**. M19. [Algerian Arab. *gandūra*, classical Arab. *ḳandūra*.] A long loose gown worn mainly in the Near East and N. Africa.

gandy dancer /ˈgandɪ ˌdɑːnsə/ *n. phr. slang.* Chiefly *US.* E20. [Origin unkn.] A railroad maintenance worker. Also, a seasonal or itinerant worker.

gang /gaŋ/ *n.* OE. [ON *gangr* (masc.), *ganga* (fem.) walking motion, course (Sw. *gång*, Da. *gang* walk, pace, time) = OS, OHG (Du., G) *gang*, Goth. *gagg*, f. Gmc n. of action rel. to base of GO *v.*] I Action or manner of going. 1 A journey; a travelling, a journeying. *obs.* exc. *Sc.* OE. 2†a The power of going; the ability to go. OE–ME. b Manner of going; gait, carriage. *obs.* exc. *dial.* ME. 3 A way, a road, a passage. *obs.* exc. *dial.* OE. †b The course of a stream. OE–E19. c A pasture for cattle; the right of pasturing. *Sc.* & *north.* M16. 4 A turn or spell at any work or exercise. *rare. Sc.* & *dial.* M16. 5 A quantity (esp. of a liquid) that can be carried at one time. *Sc.* M16.

II A set of things or persons. 6 A set of articles that are usu. taken together. ME. b *spec.* A set of tools or instruments arranged to work in coordination. L18. 7 A band or group of people acting or going about together, esp. in a shared cause, or for disreputable or criminal purposes. LME. 8 A company of labourers. E17. b A company of slaves or prisoners. E18. 9 A herd of animals of the same species. *US.* M17.

6 G. SHELVOCKE I had fitted her with a gang of oars. b *Scientific American* The . . machine had a gang of cutter chains mounted . . on a swiveling head. 7 A. GIBBS Tomorrow's vote will surprise the old gang of professional politicians. A. PATON A gang of these youths attacked one of our own African girls. **gang of three, four**, etc., a political group or faction who are outspoken on a particular issue or who hold a minority view on something (orig. of the left-wing faction in the Chinese Communist Party accused of conspiracy after the death of Mao Zedong in 1976 and later discredited). 8 C. THUBRON A gang of labourers was shovelling rubble into a cart. b OUIDA A gang of . . captives would go by on foot and chained.

Attrib. & *comb.*: Designating various implements or pieces of equipment having a set of coordinating tools or instruments, as *gang drill, mower, plough, press*, etc. Special combs., as **gang-bang** *n.* & *v.* (*slang*) (*a*) *n.* an occasion on which several people copulate in turn with one other person; (*b*) *v.t.* & *i.* (of several people) copulate in turn with (one other person); **gangboard** (*a*) = GANGWAY 2; (*b*) = *gangplank* below; **gangbuster** a person who takes part in the aggressive breakup of criminal gangs; *transf.* an outstandingly successful person or thing; *go gangbusters* (US colloq.), do very well; do something energetically, enthusiastically, or extravagantly; **gang-cask** *Naut.* a water cask for carrying water to, or storing water on, a boat; **gangland** the domain of gangs or gangsters; gangs or gangsters collectively; **gang-man** a member of a gang; **gangplank** a movable plank usu. with cleats nailed on to it, for walking into or out of a boat etc.; **gang rape** the successive rape of one person by a group of other people; **gang-shag** *slang* = *gang-bang* (a) above; **gang war, warfare** fighting between rival groups of criminals, youths, etc.

gangdom *n.* the domain of gangs or gangsters, gangland E20.

gang /gaŋ/ *v.*¹*i.* Now only *Sc.* & *dial.* [OE *gangan, gongan* = OFris. *ganga, gunga*, OS, OHG *gangan*, ON *ganga*, Goth. *gaggan* f. Gmc.] Walk, go, proceed.

R. BURNS The best laid schemes o' mice an' men Gang aft a-gley. L. G. GIBBON Gang to your bed, lass, I'll tend to the rest. **gang one's gate** be on one's way, leave.

ganging *vbl n.* (*a*) the action or power of going or walking; (*b*) walking in procession (on gang-days): ME.

gang /gaŋ/ *v.*² M19. [f. GANG *n.* II.] 1 *v.t.* Arrange in a gang or band. M19. b Arrange (implements or instruments) in gangs. E20. 2 *v.i.* (Of a group) go together or as a company; (of an individual or a group) go in company *with*, act in conjunction *with*, join *up with*. L19. 3 *v.i.* Foll. by *up against, up on*: combine or form a gang against; torment, intimidate. E20.

2 R. PRICE The little knot of people that had ganged to listen. 3 J. BARZUN The . . resentment which makes the majority at school gang up on the bookish boy.

Comb.: **gang-up** *colloq.* an act of ganging up; a meeting of a gang.

ganga *n.* var. of GANJA.

gangan *n.* see GANG-GANG.

gang-days /ˈgaŋdeɪz/ *n.pl. obs.* exc. *Hist.* OE. [f. GANG *n.* + DAY *n.*; so called from the processions held on these days.] *Eccl.* The three days preceding Ascension Day, the Rogation days.

gange /gan(d)ʒ/ *v.t.* M19. [Origin unkn.] *Angling.* Protect (a fish hook or part of a fishing-line) with fine wire.

ganger /ˈgaŋə/ *n.*¹ *obs.* exc. *Sc.* & *dial.* LME. [f. GANG *v.*¹ + -ER¹.] 1 A person who goes on foot. LME. 2 A fast horse. E19.

ganger /ˈgaŋə/ *n.*² M19. [f. GANG *n.* or *v.*² + -ER¹.] A foreman or overseer in charge of a gang of labourers.

ganger /ˈgaŋə/ *n.*³ M19. [Perh. abbrev. of FOREGANGER.] *Naut.* One or more lengths of cable shackled to a sheet anchor.

Gangetic /ganˈdʒɛtɪk/ *n.* & *a.* L17. [L *Gangeticus*, f. *Ganges* (see below), f. Gk *Gaggēs*: see -IC.] †A *n.* In *pl.* Those who live on the banks of the Ganges. Only in L17. B *adj.* Belonging to the Ganges, a great river in the north of the Indian subcontinent, flowing from the Himalayas to the Bay of Bengal. M19.

gang-gang /ˈgaŋgaŋ/ *n.* Also (earlier) **gangan** /-gan/. M19. [Aborig.] A small grey cockatoo, *Callocephalon fimbriatum*, native to SE Australia and Tasmania, the male of which has a scarlet head and crest.

gangle /ˈgaŋg(ə)l/ *v.i.* M20. [Back-form. f. GANGLING.] Of a person: move the limbs loosely, appear awkward or gangling.

ganglia *n.pl.* see GANGLION.

gangliar /ˈgaŋglɪə/ *a.* L19. [f. as next + -AR¹.] Of, pertaining to, or of the nature of a ganglion or ganglia.

Also **ganglial** *a.* M19.

gangliated /ˈgaŋglɪeɪtɪd/ *a.* E19. [f. as next + -ATE³ + -ED¹.] Having ganglia.

gangliectomy /gaŋglɪˈɛktəmi/ *n.* E20. [f. as next + -ECTOMY.] Surgical removal of a ganglion; an instance of this.

gangliform /ˈgaŋglɪfɔːm/ *a.* Also (earlier) **-ioform** /-ɪəfɔːm/. L17. [f. GANGLION + -FORM.] Having the form of a ganglion or ganglia.

gangling /ˈgaŋglɪŋ/ *a.* E19. [f. GANG *v.*¹ + -LE³ + -ING². Cf. GANGLY, GANGREL.] (Of a plant) tall, straggling; (of a person) disproportionately tall and thin, lanky, loose-jointed.

C. P. SNOW He was tall . . slim, probably a trifle gangling.

ganglion /ˈgaŋglɪən/ *n.* Pl. **-lions, -lia** /-lɪə/. L17. [Gk *gagglion* tumour under the skin, on or near tendons or sinews, (Galen) complex nerve-centre.] 1 *Med.* A cystic swelling of unknown cause arising from the sheath of a tendon. L17. 2 *Anat.* A structure containing several nerve cells forming a swelling or knot on a nerve, or, within the central and automatic nervous systems, forming a well-defined mass. L17. 3 *fig.* A centre of force, activity, or interest. E19.

2 *basal ganglion*: see BASAL *a.* 1.

Comb.: **ganglion-blocking** *a.* that prevents the transmission of nerve impulses across the synapse in a ganglion.

ganglionated *a.* = GANGLIATED M19. **ganglio'nectomy** *n.* (*Med.*) = GANGLIECTOMY E20. **gangli'onic** *a.* relating to, composed of, or having ganglia E19.

ganglioside /ˈgaŋglɪəsʌɪd/ *n.* M20. [f. prec. + -OSIDE.] *Biochem.* Any of a group of glycolipids which are present in the grey matter of man and some animals and yield neuraminic acid on hydrolysis (cf. CEREBROSIDE).

gangly /ˈgaŋgli/ *a.* L19. [Alt. of GANGLING: see -Y¹.] = GANGLING.

G. GREENE His long gangly legs.

gangrel /ˈgaŋgr(ə)l/ *n.* & *a. dial.* & *arch.* ME. [App. f. GANG *n.* or *v.*¹ Cf. *haverel, wastrel*, etc.] A *n.* 1 A vagabond; a wandering beggar. ME. 2 A toad. *Sc.* & *north.* L15. 3 A lanky loose-jointed person. L16. 4 A child just beginning to walk. *Sc.* M18. B *adj.* Vagabond, vagrant. M16.

gangrene /ˈgaŋgriːn/ *n.* & *v.* M16. [Fr. *gangrène* f. L *gangraena* f. Gk *gaggraina* (cf. *goggros* growth on trees).] A *n.* 1 Localized death of body tissue, accompanied by putrefaction and usu. caused by obstructed circulation. M16. 2 *fig.* Moral corruption. E17.

1 **dry gangrene**: caused simply by lack of blood circulation. *gas gangrene*: see GAS *n.*¹ **moist gangrene**: caused by bacterial infection. 2 T. FULLER The Gangrene of that Heresy began to spread it self into this Island.

B *v.i.* & *t.* Become affected, affect, with gangrene. E17.

†gangrenate *v.i.* & *t.* = GANGRENE *v.* L16–M18.

gangrenous *a.* of the nature of or affected by gangrene M17.

gangsman /ˈɡaŋzmən/ *n.* Pl. **-men.** L18. [f. GANG *n.* + -S[1] + MAN *n.*] 1 A dock-porter. Now *rare.* L18. 2 A person in charge of a gang of labourers. M19. 3 = GANGSTER. E20.

gangster /ˈɡaŋstə/ *n.* L19. [f. GANG *n.* + -STER.] A member of a gang of violent criminals.

gangsterdom *n.* the domain of gangsters; gangsters collectively: E20. **gangsterish** *a.* resembling or characteristic of a gangster or gangsters M20. **gangsterism** *n.* the actions or methods of gangsters E20.

gangue /ɡaŋ/ *n.* E19. [Fr. f. G *Gang* way, course, vein or lode of metal: cf. GANG *n.*] The valueless or unwanted components of an ore deposit.

gangway /ˈɡaŋweɪ/ *n.* & *int.* [OE *gangweg*; later f. GANG *n.* + WAY *n.*] A *n.* 1 A road, thoroughfare, or passage of any kind. *obs.* exc. *dial.* OE. 2 *Naut.* a A passage or platform on a ship, *esp.* one connecting the quarterdeck and the forecastle. L17. b The opening in the bulwarks by which a ship is entered or left. Also (and now usu.), a movable bridge linking a vessel to the shore, or one vessel to another. L18. 3 A passage inside a building, *esp.* one that runs between rows of seats. E18. b *spec.* A cross-passage halfway down the British House of Commons which gives access to the back benches. M19. 4 *Mining.* A connecting passage or main level in a mine. L18. 5 *Building* A temporary arrangement of planks or steps for crossing muddy or difficult ground in a building site. E19.

3b above, below, the gangway (of a member of the House of Commons, according to which side of the gangway he or she sits on) more, less, closely associated with the policies of his or her party.

Comb.: **gangway seat** a seat at the end of a row, next to the gangway.

B *int.* Make way! Stand back! E20.

ganister /ˈɡanɪstə/ *n.* Also **-nn-**. E19. [Origin unkn.] A close-grained hard siliceous stone found in the lower coal measures of South Yorkshire, and used for furnace-linings etc.

ganja /ˈɡandʒə, ˈɡɑː-/ *n.* Also **ganga**. E19. [Hindi *gājā*.] A strong preparation of marijuana, used chiefly for smoking.

J. HEARNE The rest of them smoke ganja, the way you and I smoke tobacco.

gannet /ˈɡanɪt/ *n.* [OE *ganot* corresp. to MLG *gante*, Du. *gent*, MHG *ganiz*, *genz*, OHG *ganazzo*, MHG *ganze* gander f. Gmc base also of GANDER *n.*] 1 Each of three large gregarious sea birds of the genus *Sula* which capture fish by plunging, *S. bassana* of the N. Atlantic, *S. serrator* of Australasia, and (more fully *Cape gannet*) *S. capensis* of southern African waters. OE. 2 A greedy person. *slang.* E20.

gannetry *n.* a place where gannets breed; a colony of gannets: E20.

gannister *n.* var. of GANISTER.

ganoid /ˈɡanɔɪd/ *a.* & *n.* M19. [Fr. *ganoïde*, f. Gk *ganos* brightness: see -OID.] A *adj.* 1 Of a fish-scale: having a smooth shining surface, from being covered with a layer of enamel (esp. ganoin). M19. 2 Of a fish: having ganoid scales. Orig. designating an order of primitive bony fishes ('Ganoidei') possessing ganoid scales, mostly extinct but including the living garfishes, sturgeon, and bowfin, now classified as either chondrostean or holostean. M19. B *n.* A ganoid fish. M19.

ganoidal *a.* = GANOID *a.* 2 M19.

ganoin /ˈɡanəʊɪn/ *n.* Also **-ine** /-ɪn, -iːn/. M19. [f. Gk *ganos* brightness + -IN[1].] The hard shiny substance resembling enamel which forms the outer layer of ganoid fish-scales.

ganomalite /ɡəˈnɒməlʌɪt/ *n.* L19. [f. Gk *ganōma* brightness + -LITE.] *Min.* A lustrous silicate of lead and calcium, crystallizing in the hexagonal system and occurring massive or as colourless or grey tetragonal crystals.

ganophyllite /ɡəˈnɒfɪlʌɪt, ɡanəʊˈfɪlʌɪt/ *n.* L19. [f. Gk *ganos* brightness + *phullon* leaf: see -ITE[1].] *Min.* A monoclinic aluminosilicate of manganese, occurring foliated or as brown crystals.

ganosis /ɡəˈnəʊsɪs/ *n.* E20. [Gk *ganōsis*, f. *ganos* brightness, f. *ganoun* to polish.] The process of applying a wax polish to the white marble surface of a statue or occas. to some other surface in order to give warmth to its appearance.

gansel /ˈɡans(ə)l/ *n. obs.* exc. *dial.* LME. [OFr. *ganse aillie* garlic sauce.] A garlic sauce, used esp. with goose.

gansey /ˈɡanzi/ *n.* Chiefly *dial.* Also **gansie**, **ganzy**, & other vars. L19. [Repr. a pronunc. of GUERNSEY.] A jersey.

gant /ɡɑːnt/ *n.* & *v. Sc.* Also **gaunt** /ɡɔːnt/. L15. [Origin uncertain: perh. f. OE *ganian* yawn.] A *n.* A yawn, a gape. L15. B *v.i.* Yawn, gape. E16.

gantlet *n.* see GAUNTLET *n.*[2]

gantline /ˈɡantlʌɪn/ *n.* Orig. **girtline** /ˈɡəːtlʌɪn/. M18. [f. unkn. 1st elem. + LINE *n.*[2]] *Naut.* A line rove through a block near the masthead and used to hoist sails, rigging, etc.

gantlope /ˈɡantləʊp/ *n.* Now *rare.* M17. [Sw. *gatlopp*, f. *gata* lane, GATE *n.*[2] + *lopp* course.] *run* (or †*pass*) *the gantlope*, = *run* (or †*pass*) *the gauntlet* s.v. GAUNTLET *n.*[2]

gantry /ˈɡantri/ *n.* Also **gauntry** /ˈɡɔːntri/. LME. [Prob. f. GAWN + TREE *n.*] 1 A wooden stand for barrels. LME. 2 A supportive structure used esp. for a travelling crane, railway or road signals, or for equipment to prepare a rocket for launching. E19.

2 *Daily Telegraph* The train crashed into an overhead power gantry.

Gantt chart /ˈɡant tʃɑːt/ *n. phr.* Also **g-**. E20. [f. Henry Lawrence *Gantt* (1861–1919), Amer. management consultant + CHART *n.*] A chart in which a series of horizontal lines shows the amount of work done or production completed in certain periods of time in relation to the amount planned for those periods.

Ganymede /ˈɡanɪmiːd/ *n.* L16. [L *Ganymedes* f. Gk *Ganumēdēs* Zeus's cupbearer.] 1 A catamite. L16. 2 A cupbearer; *arch. joc.* a pot-boy. E17.

ganzy *n.* var. of GANSEY.

gaol *n.* & *v.* var. of JAIL.

gaoler *n.* var. of JAILER.

gaon /ˈɡɑːəʊn/ *n.* Pl. **gaons, geonim** /ɡeɪˈəʊnɪm/. L18. [Heb. *gā'ōn* excellence, pride.] (An honorific for) a head of a Jewish academy in Babylonia, Palestine, Syria, or Egypt, from the 6th to the 11th cents. Later, esp. in Spain, France, Italy, and Lithuania, an outstanding Talmudic scholar. Also *gen.*, a genius, a prodigy.

gap /ɡap/ *n.* ME. [ON = 'chasm' (Sw. *gap*, Da. *gab* open mouth, opening), rel. to ON *gapa* GAPE *v.*] 1 A breach in a wall, fence, hedge, etc., caused by violence or natural decay. ME. †b *fig.* An opening or breach by which an entry, attack, or escape may be effected. M16–M18. 2 A notch; a small break or opening in an edge or surface. Now *rare.* LME. 3 A break or opening in a range of mountains; a gorge, a pass. LME. b A hole or chasm in the ground. *rare.* L17. †4 A gash or wound in the body. L16–E17. 5 An unfilled space or interval; a blank; a break in continuity. E17. 6 A disparity, an inequality, an imbalance; a (usu. undesirable) divergence in sympathies, understanding, development, etc. M19. 7 *Aeronaut.* The vertical distance between the upper and lower wings of a biplane. E20.

1 M. MITCHELL There were wide gaps between the buildings .. where dwellings had been shelled or burned. J. T. STORY The path led me .. through a gap in a high elder hedge. 3 R. BOLDREWOOD One of those narrow rocky gaps .. over the line of ranges. 5 A. SILLITOE Through gaps in over-arching branches he could see the stars. B. EMECHETA The door opened a little, and someone peered at them through the small gap. *fig.*: V. WOOLF What vast gaps there were, what blank spaces .. in her knowledge. 6 D. H. LAWRENCE They always kept a gap, a distance between them. J. BARZUN The gap between words and experience in the .. world of professional educators. *Times Lit. Suppl.* The gap that has opened up .. between men of science and students of the humanities. *credibility gap*, *generation gap*.

Phrases: **bridge, close, fill, stop, a gap** make up a deficiency, supply a want, fill a space.

Comb.: **gap-toothed** *a.* having gaps between the teeth.

gappy *a.* full of gaps; full of deficiencies: M19.

gap /ɡap/ *v.* Infl. **-pp-**. M19. [f. the n.] 1 *v.t.* & *i.* Make or become notched, break at the edge. M19. 2 *v.t.* Make a gap or breach in or between. L19. 3 *v.i.* Have gaps; gape open. M20.

2 B. CABLE Eager hands tore down the sandbags to gap a passage for them.

gape /ɡeɪp/ *n.* E16. [f. the vb.] 1 An act of opening the mouth, a yawn. E16. 2 An open-mouthed stare; a gaze of wonder or curiosity. M17. 3 A rent or opening of any kind. M17. 4 The expanse of an open mouth or beak. M18. b The part of a beak which opens. M19. c A space between the edges of the closed valves of a bivalve mollusc. M19. 5 *the gapes*: a A disease of birds due to infestation with gape-worms (see below), in which frequent gaping is the symptom. L18. b *joc.* A fit of yawning. E19.

2 E. BLISHEN Sometimes evoking no response at all, sometimes an astonished gape.

Comb.: **gape-worm** a parasitic nematode worm of the family Syngamidae which infests the respiratory tract of birds, causing the gapes.

gape /ɡeɪp/ *v.* ME. [ON *gapa* (Sw. *gapa*, Da. *gabe*) = (M)Du. *gapen*, (M)HG *gaffen*.] 1 a *v.i.* Open the mouth wide, esp. in order to bite or swallow something. Also, (of the mouth) open wide. ME. b *v.t.* Open (the mouth) wide. *rare.* M17. 2 *v.i.* Stare open-mouthed; gaze at in wonder or admiration. (Foll. by *at*, *on*, *upon*.) ME. 3 *v.t.* & *i.* Be eager to obtain, have a longing for (something). (Foll. by *after*, *for*, †*at*, †*upon*.) Now *rare.* ME. b *v.i.* Desire eagerly *to do*. Now *rare.* ME. 4 *v.i.* Of earth, hell, etc.: be or become wide open; yawn. Also, of a wound, an oyster, etc.: split, part, open. LME. 5 *v.i.* Of a person: yawn, esp. from weariness. LME. †b Of a dead body: have the mouth open. LME–M16. †6 *v.i.* Gasp from pain, heat, etc. LME–L16. 7 *v.i.* Bawl, shout. *obs.* exc. *dial.* L16.

1a R. HOLME Such Fellows .. are fed .. as long as they can gape. 2 A. J. CRONIN She left the local inhabitants gaping by a display of trick riding. R. DAVIES They gaped at the curiosities of the World of Wonders. 4 B. GOOGE The ground gapes with the heate of the Sunne. TENNYSON A gulf that ever shuts and gapes. J. K. JEROME A clean-cut wound that gapes wide. *fig.*: R. MACAULAY When the years have all passed, there will gape the .. dark void of death.

gaping *n.* (*a*) the action of the vb; †(*b*) a deep opening or chasm in the earth: LME. **gapingly** *adv.* with open mouth, eagerly, amazedly L16.

gaper /ˈɡeɪpə/ *n.* LME. [f. prec. + -ER[1].] 1 †a A person who longs or gapes for something. LME–E17. b A person who stares or gazes in wonder or curiosity. L15. 2 A soft-shelled clam of the genus *Mya*, with a permanent opening between the valves through which the siphon protrudes. L18. 3 The comber fish, *Serranus cabrilla*, which gapes when dead. E19.

1b *Times Lit. Suppl.* Learned understanders and ignorant gapers.

gape-seed /ˈɡeɪpsiːd/ *n.* L16. [f. GAPE *n.* or *v.* + SEED *n.*] Something stared at by a gaping crowd. Also, the act of staring.

buy, seek, sow, gape-seed (*obs.* exc. *dial.*) stare gapingly at a fair or market instead of doing useful business.

gapped /ˈɡapt/ *a.* M16. [f. GAP *n.*, *v.*: see -ED[2], -ED[1].] 1 Having a notched or serrated edge. M16. 2 Broken through at intervals; full of holes or spaces. M19. 3 *Mus.* Of a scale or mode: having less than seven notes, *esp.* pentatonic. E20.

2 CARLYLE Closing his gapped ranks.

gar /ɡɑː/ *n.* M18. [Abbrev.] = GARFISH.

alligator gar: see ALLIGATOR.

gar /ɡɑː/ *v.t.* Chiefly *Sc.* & *north.* Infl. **-rr-**. Pa. t. & pple **garred, gart** /ɡɑːt/. ME. [ON *ger(v)a*, *gør(v)a* make, do = OE *gierwan* prepare, OS *garwian*, *gerwian*, OHG *garawen* (G *gerben* tan, curry, polish) f. Gmc: rel. to GEAR *n.*, YARE.] †1 Do, perform; make. *rare.* ME–M17. 2 Make, cause; *esp.* cause (*to*) *do* or *be*. ME.

2 R. BURNS He screw'd the pipes and gart them skirl.

Gar /gɑː/ *int.* L16. [Alt. of GOD *n.*] Expr. annoyance, surprise, impatience, etc. Cf. GAD *n.*[2]

garage /ˈgarɑː(d)ʒ, -ɪdʒ, gəˈrɑːʒ/ *n.* & *v.* E20. [Fr., f. *garer* to shelter.] **A** *n.* **1** A building or part of a building for keeping one or more motor vehicles when not in use. E20. **2** A commercial establishment which sells petrol, oil, etc., and freq. also repairs and services motor vehicles. M20. **3** A variety of house music influenced by soul music. L20.

1 *Oxford Times* Detached freehold House... Separate access to brick garage. 2 *Financial Times* Unleaded petrol has gone on sale at about 200 garages.

Comb.: **garage sale** (chiefly *Austral.* & *N. Amer.*) a sale of miscellaneous second-hand items, usu. held in the garage of a private house.

B *v.t.* Place or accommodate (a motor vehicle) in or at a garage. E20.

garaging *n.* (*a*) the action of the vb; (*b*) garage accommodation: E20.

garagist /ˈgarɑːʒɪst/ *n.* Also ***garagiste*** /garaʒist (*pl. same*)/. E20. [Fr. *garagiste*, f. as prec. + *-iste*: see -IST.] The proprietor or an employee of a commercial garage.

garam masala /gʌrəm məˈsɑːlə/ *n. phr.* M20. [Urdu *garam maṣālah*.] A spice mixture used in Indian cookery.

Garamond /ˈgarəmɒnd/ *n.* M19. [Claude *Garamond* (1499–1561), Fr. type-founder.] *Typogr.* A typeface modelled on those designed by or attributed to Garamond.

garancin /ˈgar(ə)nsɪn/ *n.* Also **-ine**. M19. [Fr., f. *garance* madder, of Gmc origin: see -IN[1], -INE[5].] A dye made by treating madder with dilute sulphuric acid, formerly much used in calico printing and to produce the scarlet cotton known as Turkey red.

Also ***garance*** /garɑ̃ːs/ *n.* L19.

Garand /ˈgar(ə)nd/ *n.* Also **g-**. M20. [John C. *Garand* (1888–1974), US gun designer.] In full *Garand rifle*. A type of semi-automatic rifle.

garb /gɑːb/ *n.*[1] *obs.* exc. *Her.* E16. [ONFr. *garbe* (OFr. *jarbe*, mod. *gerbe*) f. Frank.: see GERBE.] A wheatsheaf.

garb /gɑːb/ *n.*[2] L16. [Fr. †*garbe* (now *galbe*) f. It. *garbo* ult. f. Gmc (cf. OHG *garawī* adornment) f. base of GAR *v.*] †**1** Grace, elegance, esp. of manners or appearance. L16–L17. †**2** Style, manner, fashion; a prevailing custom, the current fashion. L16–L17. †**3** A person's outward bearing. E17–E18. **4** Dress, costume, esp. of a distinctive kind. Also, manner of dress. E17.

4 J. MAY Most of the people were dressed in buckskin or homespun peasant garb. *fig.*: MILTON Words cloath'd in reasons garb.

garbless *a.* (*rare*) without clothing M19.

garb /gɑːb/ *v.t.* L16. [f. GARB *n.*[2]] Clothe, dress.

L. M. MONTGOMERY A child .. garbed in a .. very ugly dress. *fig.*: S. DOBELL To garb with joy The naked soul of Grief.

garbage /ˈgɑːbɪdʒ/ *n.* LME. [AN, of unkn. origin.] †**1** The offal of an animal used as food. LME–M19. †**2** A mixture of straw etc. used as horse-feed. E16–E17. **3** Rubbish, filth; domestic waste, household refuse. L16. **4** *fig.* Anything worthless; *spec.* worthless literary matter. L16. **b** *Computing.* Incorrect or inappropriate input; data that is useless or no longer required. M20.

3 N. PEVSNER Antediluvian dust-carts scattering more garbage than they collect. 4 P. CAREY A lot of sentimental garbage was spoken on the subject. **b garbage in, garbage out** *Computing* incorrect or poor quality input will always produce faulty output (cf. *GIGO* s.v. G, G).

Comb.: **garbage can** *N. Amer.* a dustbin; **garbage collection** (*a*) *N. Amer.* the removal of household refuse; (*b*) *Computing* the removal from a memory of useless or unnecessary information; **garbage disposal unit, garbage disposer** a waste disposal unit.

garbanzo /gɑːˈbanzəʊ/ *n.* Pl. **-os**. M18. [Sp. = chick-pea: cf. CALAVANCE.] A chick-pea.

garble /ˈgɑːb(ə)l/ *n.* E16. [Prob. f. It. *garbello*, f. *garbellare*: see next.] †**1** Extraneous matter, *esp.* refuse of spices. E16–E19. †**2** Merchandise containing an element of waste. E–M17. **b** A mixture of base and precious metal; = ALLOY *n.* 3. Only in M19. **3** The process of garbling; selection, mutilation. Also, something garbled, distorted or mutilated information. E19.

3 G. KENDALL The screen .. was still filled with a garble of codes.

garbler *n.* (*a*) (*obs.* exc. *Hist.*) an official who garbled spices etc., a sifter; (*b*) a person who distorts or mutilates statements, stories, facts, etc.: LME.

garble /ˈgɑːb(ə)l/ *v.t.* LME. [AL & It. *garbellare* sift, sort, f. Arab. *ġarbala* sift, select, rel. to *ġirbāl* sieve, perh. f. late L *cribellare*, f. *cribellum*, dim. of L *cribrum* sieve.] †**1** Remove the extraneous matter or refuse from (spice etc.); sift (*out*), cleanse (*of*). LME–E19. **2** Select or sort out the best in (any thing or set of things). (Foll. by *out.*) Now *rare*. L15. †**b** *spec.* Select undesirable or unfit members for expulsion from (a body of people). M17–E19. **3** Make (usu. unfair or malicious) selections from (statements, facts, etc.); distort (a statement, story, theory, etc.) unintentionally; mutilate in order to misrepresent. Esp. as *garbled* ppl a. L17.

3 J. CLAVELL It was much better to hear the truth than a garbled version.

garbo /ˈgɑːbəʊ/ *n.* *Austral. slang.* M20. [f. GARBAGE + -O.] A dustman, a collector of rubbish.

garboard /ˈgɑːbɔːd/ *n.* E17. [Du. †*gaarboord*, perh. f. *garen* contr. of *gaderen* GATHER *v.* + *boord* BOARD *n.*] *Naut.* In full *garboard strake*. The first range of wooden planks or metal plates on the outer hull of a vessel next to the keel.

garboil /ˈgɑːbɔɪl/ *n.* *arch.* M16. [OFr. *garbouil(le)* f. It. *garbuglio*.] Confusion, tumult; a brawl, a disturbance.

garbologist /gɑːˈbɒlədʒɪst/ *n.* M20. [f. GARB(AGE + -OLOGIST.] **1** A dustman, a collector of rubbish. M20. **2** A person who studies and analyses the discarded rubbish of modern society. L20.

garbology /gɑːˈbɒlədʒi/ *n.* L20. [f. GARB(AGE + -OLOGY.] The study or investigation of the discarded rubbish of modern society, esp. regarded as an aspect of social science.

garcinia /gɑːˈsɪnɪə/ *n.* L19. [mod.L (see below), f. Laurent *Garcin* (1683–1751), Fr. botanist + -IA[1].] Any of various evergreen trees of the genus *Garcinia* (family Guttiferae), which are native to the tropics of Asia, Africa, and Polynesia, and include the mangosteen, *G. mangostana*.

garçon /garsɔ̃/ *n.* Pl. pronounced same. E17. [Fr.] A waiter, a male servant, esp. in a French hotel or restaurant.

garçonnière /garsɔnjɛːr/ *n.* Pl. pronounced same. E20. [Fr.] A bachelor's set of rooms or flat.

Garda /ˈgɑːdə/ *n.* Pl. **-dai** /-diː/, **-s**. E20. [Ir. *Garda Síochána* Civic Guard.] **1** The State police force of the Republic of Ireland. E20. **2** A member of the Garda; an Irish police officer. M20.

garde champêtre /gard ʃɑ̃pɛːtr/ *n. phr.* Pl. **-s -s** (pronounced same). E19. [Fr., lit. 'rural guard'.] In France: a rural police officer; a gamekeeper.

garde-du-corps /gardədykɔːr/ *n.* Pl. ***gardes-*** (pronounced same). M17. [Fr.] A bodyguard; a member of a bodyguard.

Garde Mobile /gard mɔbil/ *n. phr.* Pl. **-s -s** (pronounced same). M19. [Fr., lit. 'mobile guard'.] A French military force, now chiefly engaged in police activity; a member of this force.

garden /ˈgɑːd(ə)n/ *n.* ME. [ONFr. *gardin* var. of (O)Fr. *jardin*, f. Proto-Romance, f. Gmc: cf. YARD *n.*[1]] **1** A piece of ground (often enclosed) where fruits, flowers, herbs, or vegetables are cultivated; without specification *esp.* one adjoining a house or other residential building. With specifying n. *esp.* an area of this kind where the specified plants are grown, with the specified function or central feature, or in the specified place. ME. **b** *transf.* A region of great fertility. L16. **2** An enclosed piece of ground or (now, chiefly *US*) a large building where public entertainment is provided or where refreshments are served; *sing.* & in *pl.*, a park or grounds ornamented with plants and trees or with other displays or exhibits for public recreation. Usu. w. specification of the type of entertainment, refreshment, or display provided. L16. **3** (**G-.**) *sing.* & (usu.) in *pl.* A street, square, etc., with or near gardens, *esp.* one in which the buildings overlook private communal gardens. Freq. in proper names. M18.

1 V. BRITTAIN A gracious little garden where lilac and laburnum and pink hawthorn were already in flower. *flower garden*, *herb garden*, *kitchen garden*, *market garden*, *rock garden*, *roof garden*, *rose garden*, *water garden*, etc. 2 *bear garden*, *beer garden*, *botanic(al) garden(s)*, *tea garden*, *zoological garden(s)*, etc. 3 *Crown Gardens*, *Spring Gardens*, etc.

Phrases etc.: *common or garden*: see COMMON *a.* CULTIVATE *one's garden*. **everything in the garden is lovely** all is well. *garden of* EDEN. *lead up the garden*: see LEAD *v.*[1] **the Garden** (*a*) the area of Covent Garden in London; (*b*) the philosophy or school of Epicurus (Gk philosopher who taught in a garden). **the garden of England**: *spec.* (*a*) Kent; (*b*) the Vale of Evesham. *garden of* REMEMBRANCE. *winter garden*: see WINTER *n.*

Attrib. & *comb.*: Designating a plant, vegetable, etc. that is grown in the garden or cultivated (often opp. to 'wild') as *garden lettuce*, *thyme*, *rocket*, etc. Special combs., as *garden balsam*: see BALSAM *n.* 6. **garden carpet** (*a*) a grey and brown geometrid moth, *Xanthorhoe fluctuata*; (*b*) a Persian carpet with a formal design of plants and animals; **garden centre** a (usu. specialist) establishment where gardening tools, plants, etc., are sold; **garden chair**: for use in a garden; **garden city** a town or part of a town of limited size, located in or laid out systematically with spacious rural or landscaped surroundings; **garden cress** the cruciferous plant *Lepidium sativum*, grown for its pungent seedlings, which form one of the two components of mustard and cress; **garden flat** a flat which opens on to a garden, usu. a basement flat with access to a garden at the back; **garden gnome** a figure of a gnome used as a garden ornament; **garden-house** (*a*) a house situated in or having a garden; a suburban house; (*b*) a small building in a garden; a summer-house; **garden-party** a party or society event held on a lawn or in a garden; **garden path** a path in a garden; *lead up the garden-path*: see LEAD *v.*[1]; **garden pea** (*a*) any variety of pea cultivated for human consumption; (*b*) a pea canned or frozen when freshly picked; **garden-pot** †(*a*) a watering-can; (*b*) a plant-pot; **garden produce** vegetables etc. from a garden; **garden roller**: for use in a garden; **garden seat**: for use in a garden; **garden snail** *Helix aspersa*, commonly found in gardens; **Garden State** *US* the State of New Jersey; **garden stuff** garden produce; **garden suburb, village**: laid out like a garden city; **garden warbler** a small greyish-brown Eurasian warbler, *Sylvia borin*.

gardenage *n.* horticulture; garden produce: E17. **garde'nesque** *a.* resembling a garden or what belongs to a garden M19. **gardenful** *n.* as many or much as a garden can contain M19. **gardenist** *n.* a planner of gardens; an enthusiast for gardens: L18. **gardenless** *a.* without a garden or gardens M19.

garden /ˈgɑːd(ə)n/ *v.* L16. [f. the n.] **1** *v.i.* Cultivate a garden; work in a garden as a gardener. L16. **2** *v.t.* Cultivate as a garden. E17. **3** *v.t.* Provide with a garden or gardens. Now *rare*. E19. **4** *v.i.* *Cricket.* Of a batsman: smooth the pitch by cleaning away loose fragments, patting the ground flat, etc. L19.

1 E. FITZGERALD I .. read scraps of books, garden a little, and am on good terms with my neighbours.

gardening *n.* the action of the vb; horticulture; (freq. *attrib.*): L16.

gardener /ˈgɑːdnə/ *n.* ME. [AN var. of OFr. *gardinier* (mod. *jardinier*), AL *gardinarius*: cf. GARDEN *n.* see -ER[2].] A person who tends, cultivates, or lays out a garden; a person employed to tend and cultivate a garden. Also (more fully *jobbing gardener*), an employee who works periodically in a garden.

DAY LEWIS Keyes, the gardener, was digging potatoes or stooping amongst raspberry canes.

Comb.: **gardener-bird** any of a number of bowerbirds of the genus *Amblyornis*, which make 'gardens' of moss etc. in front of their bowers; **gardener's garters** ribbon-grass, *Phalaris arundinacea* var. *picta*.

gardenership *n.* (*rare*) the position or office of a gardener M16. **gardenery** *n.* (long *rare*) gardenership M16.

gardenia /gɑːˈdiːnɪə/ *n.* M18. [mod.L (see below), f. Alexander *Garden* (*c*1730–91),

Scottish-American naturalist + -IA[1].] Any of various evergreen trees and shrubs of the (sub)tropical African and Asiatic genus *Gardenia*, of the madder family, bearing large fragrant tubular white or yellow flowers; a flowering spray of such a shrub.

garderobe /ˈɡɑːdrəʊb/ *n. obs.* exc. *Hist.* LME. [Fr., f. *garder* keep + *robe* ROBE *n.*[1] Cf. WARDROBE.] A storeroom, esp. for clothing or armour; a wardrobe or its contents. Also, a private room, a bedroom.

gardes champêtres, ***gardes-du-corps***, ***Gardes Mobiles*** *ns.* pls. of GARDE CHAMPÊTRE etc.

gardie *n.* var. of GARDY.

gardy /ˈɡɑːdi/ *n. Sc.* Also **gardie**. E16. [Origin unkn.] An arm.

gardyloo /ɡɑːdɪˈluː/ *int.* & *n.* L18. [App. f. *gare de l'eau*, pseudo-Fr. for *gare l'eau* beware of the water. Cf. GARE *v.*] *Hist.* Beware of the water: a warning formerly shouted in Edinburgh before dirty water or slops were thrown from a window into the street; the act of throwing out such water or slops.

gare /ɡɛː/ *n.*[1] *rare.* M16. [AN, f. OFr *gard, jort.*] Coarse wool that grows on the legs of sheep.

gare /ɡaːr/ *n.*[2] Pl. pronounced same. M19. [Fr.] 1 A dock-basin on a river or canal. Also, a pier, a wharf. M19. 2 A railway station in France and French-speaking countries. L19.

gare /ɡaːr/ *v.i.* (*imper.*) M17. [Fr., imper. of *garer*: see GARAGE *n.*] Look out! Beware! Take care.

garefowl /ˈɡɛːfaʊl/ *n.* Also †**gairfowl**. L17. [ON *geirfugl* (Faroese *gorfuglur*, Sw. *garfogl*), perh. f. *geirr* spear + *fugl* bird, FOWL *n.* Cf. GYRFALCON.] The great auk (see AUK).

garfish /ˈɡɑːfɪʃ/ *n.* Pl. **-es** /-ɪz/, (usu.) same. Cf. GAR *n.*, GARPIKE. LME. [App. f. OE *gār* spear + FISH *n.*[1]] Any of various fishes of the family Belonidae, with slender bodies and long spearlike snouts (also called *needlefish*); esp. *Belone belone*, of the N. Atlantic Ocean and Mediterranean and Black Seas. Also, any of certain other fishes of similar form: (*a*) any of various mainly freshwater fishes of the genus *Lepisosteus* and family Lepisosteidae, found in Central and North America; (*b*) a half-beak.

garganey /ˈɡɑːɡ(ə)ni/ *n.* M17. [It. dial. *garganei*, imit.] A migratory Palaearctic duck, *Anas querquedula*, similar to the teal, the male of which has a broad white stripe above the eye.

gargantuan /ɡɑːˈɡantjʊən/ *a.* L16. [f. *Gargantua* the large-mouthed voracious giant in Rabelais's book of the same name + -AN.] Enormous, gigantic.

A. STORR These frugal periods alternated with gargantuan feasts.

gargarism /ˈɡɑːɡərɪz(ə)m/ *n.* Long *rare* or *obs.* LME. [Late L *gargarisma*, *-mum* f. Gk *gargarismos* gargle f. *gargarizein*: see GARGOYLE.] 1 A gargle. LME. †2 A disease of the throat which attacks swine. Only in 17.

garget /ˈɡɑːɡɪt/ *n.* ME. [OFr. *gargate*, *garguete* throat f. Prov. *gargata* rel. to L *gargarizare*: see GARGOYLE.] †1 The throat. Only in ME. 2 An inflammation of the head or throat in cattle, pigs, or poultry. *arch.* L16. 3 An inflammation of the udder (mastitis) in domestic animals; *esp.* persistent bovine mastitis with gross changes in the form and texture of the udder. E18. 4 In full *garget plant*, *garget root*. Pokeweed, *Phytolacca americana*. *US.* L18.

†**gargil** *n.* M16. [OFr. *gargouille* throat: see GARGOYLE.] 1 The gullet. M16–E18. 2 = GARGET 2. E17–M18. 3 = GARGET 3. M18–L19.

gargle /ˈɡɑːɡ(ə)l/ *n.* M17. [f. the vb.] 1 A liquid used for gargling. M17. 2 A sound (as) of gargling. M19. 3 An act of gargling; *slang* an act of drinking, a drink. L19.

2 *Guardian* With a throaty gargle of a laugh.

gargle /ˈɡɑːɡ(ə)l/ *v.* E16. [Fr. *gargouiller* gurgle, bubble, f. *gargouille* throat: see GARGOYLE.] 1 *v.t.* & *i.* Keep (a liquid) suspended and in motion in the throat by means of the breath, esp. for medicinal purposes. Also, wash (the throat or mouth) in this way. E16. 2 *v.t.* & *i.* Utter with or make a gargle or gargling sound. M17. b *v.i.* Drink. *slang.* L19.

1 W. COLES The decoction of mint gargled in the mouth, cureth the Gums. A. BURGESS She made me gargle with chloride of lime. 2 W. OWEN If you could hear . . the blood Come gargling from the froth-corrupted lungs.

gargouillade /ɡarɡujad/ *n.* Pl. pronounced same. M20. [Fr., f. *gargouiller*: see prec.] *Ballet.* A series of steps in which the left leg describes two circular movements in the air, before the left foot is drawn up to the right knee.

gargoyle /ˈɡɑːɡɔɪl/ *n.* ME. [OFr. *gargouille* throat, in a spec. sense from the water passing through the mouth of the figure, rel. to L *gargarizare* gargle, f. Gk *gargarizein*, of imit. origin.] A grotesque carving usu. in the form of a human or animal mouth, head, or body, projecting from the gutter of a building, esp. in Gothic architecture, and usu. acting as a spout to drain off rainwater.

Daily Telegraph Police talked him down from the roof of Amiens Cathedral. . . He had been balancing . . near a gargoyle. *transf.*: LONGFELLOW A tall brass candlestick with gruesome gargoyles carved on the base. C. RAINE An old tormented master . . screaming like a gargoyle.

gargoylism /ˈɡɑːɡɔɪlɪz(ə)m/ *n.* E20. [f. GARGOYLE + -ISM.] 1 Grotesqueness. *rare.* E20. 2 *Med.* = *Hurler('s) disease* s.v. HURLER *n.*[2] *arch.* E20.

gari *n.* var. of GARRI.

garibaldi /ɡarɪˈbɔːldi, -ˈbaldi/ *n.* Also **G-**. M19. [An It. patriot, general, and statesman (1807–82).] 1 A kind of loose blouse formerly worn by women and children, orig. of a bright red colour like the shirts worn by Garibaldi and his followers. M19. 2 A bright orange-red damselfish, *Hypsypops rubicundus*, of the Californian coast. L19. 3 More fully *garibaldi biscuit*. A thin biscuit containing a compressed layer of currants. L19.

Garibaldian /ɡarɪˈbɔːldɪən, -ˈbaldɪən/ *a.* & *n.* M19. [f. *Garibaldi* (see prec.) + -AN.] A *adj.* Of, pertaining to, or supporting Garibaldi (1807–82). M19. B *n.* A supporter of Garibaldi. M19.

garigue /ɡariɡ/ *n.* Also **-rr-**. Pl. pronounced same. L19. [Fr.] In the south of France: uncultivated land of a calcareous soil overgrown with low scrub; the vegetation found on such land.

garimpeiro /ɡarĩˈpeiru/ *n.* M19. [Port.] In Brazil: an independent prospector for diamonds, gold, etc.

garish /ˈɡɛːrɪʃ/ *a.* M16. [Origin unkn.] 1 Of dress, ornament, ceremonial, etc.: gaudy, overdecorated. M16. 2 Of colour or light: excessively bright, glaring. M16.

1 DICKENS All sorts of garish triumphal arches were put up. 2 *Successful Slimming* I tend to go for muted colours rather than anything garish.

garishly *adv.* L16. **garishness** *n.* L16.

garland /ˈɡɑːlənd/ *n.* ME. [OFr. *gerlande*, *garlande* of unkn. origin.] 1 A wreath of flowers, leaves, etc., worn on the head or around the neck, or hung about an object for decoration. ME. b A naturally growing loop or wreath of vegetation. M19. c Chiefly *Naut.* A wreath of ribbons. M19. 2 A wreath or coronet of gold, silver, or some other costly material. *obs.* exc. *Hist.* ME. 3†a A royal crown or diadem. ME–E17. b Orig., a wreath or crown conferred on a victor or hero, esp. in the games of ancient Greece or Rome. Now also more widely, a prize, a distinction. LME. †c *fig.* A person, thing, quality, etc., regarded as the glory or most prized part of something. L16–M17. 4 A circular object, *esp.* one which surrounds another object; *spec.* (*Archit.*) an ornamental band around a spire. L15. 5 a *Naut.* A band of rope or iron used as a securing device on a mast or spar. L15. b *Naut.* & *Mil.* A container for storing shot. L17. 6 A representation of a garland in metal, stone, etc. E16. b *Her.* A charge representing a ring of flowers, leaves, etc.; a chaplet. E19. 7 *fig.* A collection of short literary pieces, usu. poems and ballads; an anthology, a miscellany. *arch.* E17.

1 W. MORRIS Round about her shapely head A garland of dog-violet . . meetly had she set. M. CONEY Cat-girls had hung garlands of flowers around the captains' necks. *fig.*: TENNYSON Where Past and Present, wound in one, Do make a garland for the heart. *virgin's garland*: see VIRGIN *n.* b F. A. KEMBLE An ivy . . growing in profuse garlands from branch to branch. 3b **gain**, **win**, etc. **the garland** gain the victory. 6 H. PHILLIPS On the reverse a garland of olives encloses the words.

garlandry *n.* (*rare*) garlands collectively; decoration composed of or resembling garlands: M19.

garland /ˈɡɑːlənd/ *v.t.* LME. [f. the n.] 1 Form (flowers) into a garland. *rare.* LME. 2 Crown with a garland, deck with garlands. LME.

2 JONSON Their hair loose, and flowing, gyrlanded with sea grass. P. V. WHITE Green was garlanding the windows, the . . balconies, the . . gateways, in celebration. *transf.*: J. HERRIOT Spareribs, onions, liver and pork . . garlanded with those divine farm sausages.

garlanding *n.* (*a*) the action of the vb; (*b*) something which forms a garland: M19.

garled /ɡɑːld/ *a. obs.* exc. *dial.* E16. [App. f. OFr. *garre*, *garré* of similar meaning.] Chiefly of cattle: spotted, speckled.

garlic /ˈɡɑːlɪk/ *n.* [OE *gārlēac*, f. *gār* spear (w. ref. to the cloves of the plant) + *lēac* LEEK.] A bulbous plant of the lily family, *Allium sativum*, grown as a herb; the strong-smelling pungent-tasting bulb of this plant (divisible into cloves or smaller bulbs) much used as a flavouring. Also (w. specifying wd), any of various wild plants of the genus *Allium*.

bear's garlic, *crow garlic*, *field garlic*, *hedge-garlic*, *Spanish garlic*, etc. **wild garlic** any of various wild alliums, *esp.* ramsons, *Allium ursinum*.

Attrib. & *comb.*: In the sense 'made with or containing garlic', as *garlic butter*, *sausage*, etc. Special combs., as **garlic bread**: spread with garlic butter and heated; **garlic-mustard** a cruciferous plant, *Alliaria petiolata*, with white flowers and cordate leaves, common in shady places; also called *hedge-garlic*, *Jack-by-the-hedge*; **garlic pear** any of several tropical shrubs or trees of the genus *Crateva*, of the caper family, with a smell of garlic and pear-shaped fruit; **garlic press** a device for crushing a clove or cloves of garlic.

garlicky *a.* smelling or tasting of garlic L18.

garlits /ˈɡɑːlɪts/ *n.* Now *rare* or *obs.* L17. [Alt. of *Görlitz* a city in Germany and former centre of the textile industry.] A kind of linen cloth first imported from Germany.

garment /ˈɡɑːm(ə)nt/ *n.* & *v.* ME. [(O)Fr. *garnement* equipment, f. *garnir* GARNISH *v.*: see -MENT.] A *n.* 1 An article of dress; in *pl.*, clothes. ME. 2 *fig.* The outward and visible covering of anything. M16.

1 J. A. MICHENER He wore the plain sheepskin garment of a countryman. 2 M. L. KING Their rationalizations clothed obvious wrongs in the beautiful garments of righteousness.

B *v.t.* Dress, clothe. Chiefly as *garmented* ppl a. Usu. *rhet.* M16.

fig.: D. M. MOIR When the snow-mantle garments the land.

garmentless *a.* M19.

garn /ɡɑːn/ *n. north.* L15. [ON = OE *ġearn* YARN *n.*] Yarn.

garn /ɡɑːn/ *int. colloq.* L19. [Cockney alt. of *go on.*] 'Go on!': expr. disbelief, ridicule, etc.

garner /ˈɡɑːnə/ *n.* & *v.* ME. [AN *gerner*, OFr. *gernier* (mod. *grenier*) f. L *granarium* GRANARY: see -ER[2].] A *n.* A storehouse, a granary. Now *rare.* ME.

R. LLOYD Their garners bursting with their golden grain.

B *v.* 1 *v.t.* Store (corn etc.) in a garner. Now chiefly *literary.* LME. 2 *v.t.* Collect or deposit as in a garner; make a store of; harvest, gather. M16. 3 *v.i.* Accumulate, be stored up. *rare.* M19.

1 CARLYLE The harvest is reaped and garnered. TENNYSON The little pitted speck in garner'd fruit. 2 H. JAMES Any place where ancient prejudices are garnered up. B. PLAIN As for enemies, you could hardly get through life . . without garnering some. N. GORDIMER When her hands were full, she dropped what she had garnered. 3 TENNYSON On Death I wreak The wrath that garners in my heart.

garnet /ˈɡɑːnɪt/ *n.*[1] ME. [Prob. f. MDu. *gernate*, *garnate* f. (O)Fr. *grenat* f. med.L *granatus*, perh.

a transf. use of *granatum* POMEGRANATE. Cf. GRANATE *n.*[1]] Any of a large group of usu. red, yellow, or green silicate minerals which occur widely as components of rocks, crystallize in the cubic system, and have the general formula $A_3B_2(SiO_4)_3$, where A and B are respectively di- and trivalent metals; *esp.* a deep-red glassy form of this occurring as large crystals; a gem consisting of this.

garne'tiferous *a.* (of a rock) containing or yielding garnets M19.

garnet /ˈgɑːnɪt/ *n.*[2] Now *rare* or *obs.* exc. in CROSS-GARNET. ME. [Origin uncertain: perh. f. dim. of ONFr. *carne* hinge f. L *cardinem.*] = CROSS-GARNET.

garnet /ˈgɑːnɪt/ *n.*[3] L15. [Prob. f. Du. *garnaat*: ult. origin unkn.] *Naut.* A tackle used in a square-rigged ship for hoisting provisions and light cargo on board.

Garnet *n.*[4] var. of GARNETT.

Garnett /ˈgɑːnɪt/ *n.* & *v.* Also **-et** (as vb infl. **-tt-**). L19. [The surname *Garnett.*] A *n.* A carding-machine for the preparation of woollen waste. L19. B *v.t.* Prepare (woollen waste) by means of a Garnett. L19.

garnierite /ˈgɑːnɪərʌɪt, gɑːˈnɪərʌɪt/ *n.* L19. [f. Jules *Garnier* (?1839–1904), Fr. geologist + -ITE[1].] *Min.* A green amorphous mineral of the serpentine series, consisting of hydrated nickel magnesium silicate and constituting an important ore of nickel.

garnish /ˈgɑːnɪʃ/ *n.* LME. [f. the vb.] †1 A set of vessels for use at table. LME–L17. 2†a Trimming for articles of dress; material used for this. E–M16. b *gen.* Embellishment, decoration; a decoration, an ornament. Now usu. regarded as *fig.* use of sense 5 below. E17. †3 Outfit, dress. *rare* (Shakes.). Only in L16. 4 Money extorted from a new prisoner as a jailer's fee or a drink allowance for other prisoners. *slang. obs.* exc. *Hist.* L16. b Money extorted from a (new) labourer to pay for drink for other labourers. M18. 5 *Cookery.* A decorative or savoury addition to a prepared dish of food. Formerly also, a side dish. E17.

garnish /ˈgɑːnɪʃ/ *v.t.* LME. [(O)Fr. *garniss-* lengthened stem of *garnir, guarnir* f. Gmc vb prob. rel. to base of WARN *v.*[1]: see -ISH[2].] I Furnish, equip. †1 Equip (a place) with means of defence; garrison. LME–M19. †2 Equip or arm (oneself). LME–M18. †b In *pass.* Be provided *with* a retinue; be accompanied. L15–E17. 3 Fit out, esp. with something that beautifies; decorate, ornament, embellish. (Foll. by *with.*) Now usu. regarded as *fig.* use of sense 5 below. LME. †b Dress, clothe, esp. elegantly. E–M16. †4 Adorn with a commendable or excellent quality. LME–L16. 5 *Cookery.* Decorate (a dish of food) for presentation at table. L17.

3 SIR W. SCOTT An under tunic of dark purple silk, garnished with furs. D. L. SAYERS Uncle Delagardie made a speech, garnished with flowers of French eloquence. 5 H. GLASSE Garnish the dish with lemon, and send it to table.

II *Law.* 6 Serve notice on (a person) for the purpose of legally seizing money belonging to a debtor or defendant; legally seize (money owed by a debtor that is in the keeping of a third party). LME.

garnished *ppl a.* †(*a*) garrisoned; (*b*) equipped, decorated, ornamented; (*c*) *Her.* (of a charge) provided with decorations etc. of a different (specified) tincture: LME. **garnisher** *n.* (*rare*) a person who garnishes E16. **garnishing** *n.* (*a*) the action of the vb; (*b*) a furnishing, a decoration; a garnish: LME.

garnishee /gɑːnɪˈʃiː/ *n.* & *v.* E17. [f. GARNISH *v.* II + -EE[1].] *Law.* A *n.* 1 A third party required to surrender money belonging to a debtor or defendant in compliance with a court order obtained by the creditor or plaintiff. E17. 2 The legal process of recovering a debt by serving a garnishee order; an instance of this. E20.

Comb.: **garnishee order, proceedings**: requiring a garnishee to surrender money that he or she holds on behalf of or owes to a debtor.

B *v.t.* Pa. t. & pple **-sheed.** Recover a debt from (a person, his or her wages, etc.) by garnishee proceedings. L19.

garnishment /ˈgɑːnɪʃm(ə)nt/ *n.* E16. [f. GARNISH *v.* + -MENT.] 1 *Law.* A legal notice, *esp.* one seizing the money owed by a debtor and in the keeping of a third party. E16. 2 Ornament, decoration. M16.

garniture /ˈgɑːnɪtʃə/ *n.* L15. [Fr., f. *garnir* GARNISH *v.*] 1 Embellishment, decoration; *esp.* ornament or trimming of dress. L15. 2 Apparel, equipment, appurtenances. M16. b Trappings or harness of a horse etc. *rare.* L17. c Costume, dress. *rare.* E19. 3 *Cookery.* A garnish, a trimming for a prepared dish of food. E18.

1 F. NORRIS Minna's silk dress, with its garniture of lace, its edging of velvet.

garnwindle /ˈgɑːnwɪnd(ə)l/ *n. obs.* exc. *dial.* LME. [f. GARN *n.* + as WINDLE *n.*[1]] An appliance for winding yarn or thread.

Garo /ˈgɑːrəʊ/ *n.* & *a.* L19. [f. the *Garo* Hills, Assam.] A *n.* Pl. **-os**, same. 1 A member of one of a group of people of the Garo Hills, Assam. L19. 2 The Sino-Tibetan language of this people. L19. B *attrib.* or as *adj.* Of or pertaining to the Garos or their language. L19.

garotte *n.*, *v.* vars. of GARROTTE *n.*, *v.*

garpike /ˈgɑːpʌɪk/ *n.* L18. [f. GAR *n.* + PIKE *n.*[3]] = GARFISH.

garret /ˈgarət, -ɪt/ *n.* ME. [OFr. *garite* watch-tower (mod. *guérite*), f. *garir*: see GARRISON.] †1 A turret projecting from the top of a tower or from the parapet of a fortification; a watch-tower. ME–L16. 2 A (wretched) room or apartment on the top floor of a house, *esp.* one partly or wholly within the roof; an attic. ME. 3 The head. *slang.* Now *rare.* L18.

2 G. GISSING We . . lost everything, and we had to go and live in a garret. *attrib.*: R. COTGRAVE A garret window, or window in the roofe of a house.

garre'teer *n.* a person who lives in a garret; *esp.* an impecunious author or literary hack: E18. **garreted** *a.* having a garret or garrets M16.

garret /ˈgarət, -ɪt/ *v.t.* Infl. **-tt-.** M19. [Prob. alt. of GALLET *v.*] *Building.* = GALLET *v.*

garreting *n.* (*a*) the action of the vb; (*b*) = GALLET *n.*: M19.

garri /ˈgari/ *n.* Also **gari.** E20. [f. a W. Afr. lang.] In W. Africa, = CASSAVA 2.

garrigue *n.* var. of GARIGUE.

garrison /ˈgarɪs(ə)n/ *n.* & *v.* ME. [OFr. *garison* defence, safety, provision, store, f. *garir* defend, furnish, f. Gmc.] A *n.* †1 Store, treasure; a gift. Only in ME. †2 Defence; safety; a means of protection. ME–E17. 3 A body of troops stationed in a fortress, town, etc., esp. for defensive purposes. LME. 4 A place or building in which troops are quartered in a fortress, town, etc., esp. for defensive purposes; a garrison town. Formerly also, a fortress. LME.

3 S. RUSHDIE A string of border posts, each with its lonely garrison of six men. **in garrison** serving as (a member of) a garrison. 4 W. ROBERTSON Werk Castle, a garrison of the English.

Comb.: **garrison town**: having a permanent garrison.

B *v.t.* 1 Provide with or occupy as a garrison. M16. 2 Station (a body of troops) as a garrison; place on duty as a garrison. L16.

1 C. THIRLWALL He fortified the citadel and garrisoned the port. W. S. CHURCHILL Visiting the townships and posts garrisoned by the Spaniards. 2 SPENSER I would wish the chief power of the armye to be garrisoned in one countrey.

Garrisonian /garɪˈsəʊnɪən/ *a.* & *n.* M19. [f. W. L. *Garrison* (see below) + -IAN.] A *adj.* Of or pertaining to W. L. Garrison (1805–79) a leader in the American anti-slavery movement, or his views; abolitionist. M19. B *n.* A supporter of Garrison; an abolitionist. L19.

garrocha /gaˈrɒtʃa/ *n.* M19. [Sp.] A goad, *esp.* (in bullfighting) a short-pointed spear.

garron /ˈgarən/ *n.* M16. [Gael. *gearran*, Ir. *gearrán.*] (An animal of) a breed of small, sturdy workhorse originating in Ireland and Scotland.

garrotte /gəˈrɒt/ *n.* Also **garotte, *garrote.** E17. [Sp. *garrote* (orig.) cudgel, f. a base perh. of Celt. origin, repr. also in Prov. *garra* kneecap, Sp. *garra* claw.] †1 A stick used to twist and tighten a cord securing a load. *rare.* Only in E17. 2 A method of execution by strangulation, of Spanish origin, in which an iron or wire collar is tightened around the neck; strangulation by means of a wire, cord, etc.; the apparatus, a piece of wire, etc., used for this. E17. 3 *Hist.* Highway robbery in which the victim is throttled. M19.

garrotte /gəˈrɒt/ *v.t.* Also **garotte, *garrote.** M19. [Fr. *garrotter*, f. *garrot* stick, lever or Sp. *garrotear*, f. as prec.] 1 Execute by means of the garrotte. M19. 2 Throttle in order to rob. M19. 3 Strangle, choke. L19.

garrotter *n.* a person who garrottes someone M19. **garrotting** *n.* execution or robbery by garrotte M19.

garrulity /gəˈruːlɪti/ *n.* L16. [Fr. †*garrulité* f. L *garrulitas*, f. as next: see -ITY.] The quality of being garrulous or wordy; loquaciousness.

garrulous /ˈgarʊləs, -rjʊl-/ *a.* E17. [f. L *garrulus*, f. *garrire* chatter, prattle: see -ULOUS.] Talkative, esp. on trivial matters; loquacious; wordy, verbose.

W. BLACK The . . keeper might have kept up his garrulous talk for hours. P. G. WODEHOUSE A matter which called for silent meditation, not for chit-chat with a garrulous butler. *fig.*: TENNYSON Hear the magpie gossip Garrulous under a roof of pine.

garrulously *adv.* M19. **garrulousness** *n.* E18.

garrya /ˈgarɪə/ *n.* M19. [mod.L (see below), f. Nicholas *Garry* (see next) + -A[1].] Any of various N. American evergreen shrubs of the genus *Garrya* (family Garryaceae), allied to the cornels, with flowers in drooping clusters resembling catkins; esp. *G. elliptica*, native to California and Oregon. Also called *silk-tassel* (*bush*), *tassel-bush.*

Garry oak /ˈgari əʊk/ *n. phr.* E20. [Nicholas *Garry* (1781–1856), officer of the Hudson's Bay Company.] An oak, *Quercus garryana*, native to the Pacific coast of N. America. Also called *Oregon oak.*

Garryowen /garɪˈəʊɪn/ *n.* Also **g-.** M20. [An Irish rugby club in Limerick.] *Rugby Football.* An up and under.

†**garse** *n.*, *v.*, †**garsh**, *n.*, *v.* see GASH *n.*[1], *v.*

Garshuni /gɑːˈʃuːni/ *n.* Also **C-, K-.** M19. [(Arab. *karšūnī*) f. Syriac *garšūnī.*] Arabic written in Syriac characters.

garter /ˈgɑːtə/ *n.* Also (*Sc.*) **-ten** /-t(ə)n/. ME. [OFr. *gartier* var. of *jartier* (also *jartière*, mod. *jarretière*), f. *garet, jaret* bend of the knee, calf of the leg, prob. of Celt. origin: cf. GARROTTE *n.*] 1 A band worn round the leg to keep a sock or stocking up; *US* a suspender. ME. b In *pl.* Fetters, irons. *Naut. slang.* L18. 2 *The Garter*: the badge of the highest order of British knighthood, consisting of a dark blue velvet ribbon trimmed with gold, worn below the left knee by men and on the left arm by women; also, membership of this order; the order itself. LME. 3 *Her.* In full *Garter King of Arms.* (The title of) the principal King of Arms of the College of Arms. LME. 4 A band resembling a garter in shape or function. M16. b *spec.* The belt or band used in the cheating game of prick (in) the garter (see below); the game itself; a person who plays this game. M18. 5 *Her.* A bendlet; a charge representing a garter. M17. 6 = *garter-snake* below. L19.

1 E. LINKLATER Rosy, with shoes and garters already gone, was pulling off a stocking. **cast one's garter** *Sc.* (now *rare*) secure a husband. *have one's guts for garters*: see GUT *n.* 2 N. MITFORD His long thin legs in silk stockings and knee breeches, the Garter round one . . its ribbon across his shirt front. 4 *fly-the-garter*: see FLY *v.* b **prick (in) the garter** an old cheating game played with a stick and a belt or band; fast and loose; also, a con trick.

Comb.: **garter-belt** *N. Amer.* a suspender belt; **garter-blue** *n.* & *a.* (of) the colour (orig. pale, now dark blue) of the ribbon, worn by knights of the garter; **garter snake** (*a*) any of several harmless, viviparous, largely semi-aquatic colubrid snakes of the genus *Thamnophis*, often with more or less distinct longitudinal stripes on the back, widespread in N. America; (*b*) any of various banded venomous elapid snakes, of southern and tropical Africa; **garter stitch** the simplest knitting stitch, forming ridges in alternate rows, and orig. used in making garters; plain stitch; **garter-webbing** narrow elastic webbing used for garters.

garter /ˈgɑːtə/ *v.t.* Also (*Sc.*) **-ten** /-t(ə)n/. LME. [f. the n.] **1** Tie (*on, up*) with a garter; encircle with a garter. LME. †**2** Bandage tightly. L16–L17. **3** Fetter. Long *rare*. E17.

gartered /ˈgɑːtəd/ *a.* E17. [f. GARTER *n., v.*: see -ED², -ED¹ and cf. earlier UNGARTERED.] **1** Wearing a garter; *esp.* wearing the badge of the order of the Garter. E17. **2** That has been gartered; tied with a garter. M18. **3** *Her.* Surrounded by a garter. E19.

1 POPE In this hall .. have dined gartered knights and courtly dames.

gartering /ˈgɑːt(ə)rɪŋ/ *n.* E16. [f. GARTER *v.* + -ING¹.] **1** The action of GARTER *v.*; an instance of this. E16. **2** The material of which garters are made; in *pl.*, garters. L16.

garth /gɑːθ/ *n.*¹ Now *arch.* & *north.* ME. [ON *garðr* = OE *ġeard* YARD *n.*¹] **1** A small area of enclosed ground, esp. beside a house or other building, used as a yard, garden, or paddock. ME. **b** A cloister-garth. L19. **2** A fence, a hedge. Now chiefly *Hist.* ME. **3** A fishgarth. E17.

garth /gɑːθ/ *n.*² *north.* LME. [Alt. of GIRTH *n.*¹] **1** A saddle-girth. LME. **2** A (wooden) hoop, esp. for a barrel. LME. **3** Girth or measurement, esp. of a fighting cock. Now *rare* or *obs.* L17.

Gartner /ˈgɑːtnə/ *n.* L19. [Herman T. *Gartner* (1785–1827), Da. anatomist.] *Anat.* *Gartner's duct*, *duct of Gartner*, a vestigial part of the mesonephric duct present in some female mammals.

Gartnerian /gɑːtˈnɪərɪən/ *a.* (of a cyst) originating in Gartner's duct E20.

garuda /ˈgarʊdə/ *n.* L19. [Skt *garuḍa*.] *Indian Mythol.* A fabulous bird, half-eagle, half-man, ridden by the god Vishnu.

garum /ˈgɛːrəm/ *n.* L16. [L f. Gk *garon* earlier *garos*.] *Hist.* A sauce made from fermented fish, popular in ancient Rome; this sauce used as a medicine for horses.

gas /gas/ *n.*¹ Pl. **gases** /ˈgasɪz/. M17. [Invented by J. B. van Helmont (1577–1644), Belgian chemist, after Gk *khaos* chaos, Du. *g* representing Gk *kh*.] **1** An occult principle supposed to be contained in all bodies, and to represent an ultra-rarefied condition of water. Long *obs.* exc. *Hist.* M17. **2** Any airlike fluid that can change its volume indefinitely, *esp.* one that does not become liquid or solid at ordinary temperatures (cf. *vapour*); any substance normally existing in this state. E18. **3** *spec.* **a** Such a substance, usu. a hydrocarbon or hydrocarbon mixture, suitable for burning in order to provide heat, light, or power. L18. **b** Hydrogen, helium, or other substance used to fill a balloon or airship. L18. **c** *Mining.* An explosive mixture of firedamp (methane) and air. M19. **d** = *laughing-gas* s.v. LAUGHING *n.* L19. **e** Vapour generated in the alimentary canal; wind. Chiefly *N. Amer.* L19. **f** Any of various gases or vapours used in warfare to disable the enemy by poisoning, asphyxiation, irritation, etc. Also *poison gas*. E20. **4** A jet or jets of flammable gas, used for lighting, cooking, etc.; the supply of gas to a house etc. M19. **5a** Pointless idle talk; a chat; boasting, humbug, nonsense. *slang.* M19. **b** Fun; a joke. *Anglo-Ir. slang.* E20. **c** *A* person who or thing which is very attractive, exciting, impressive, etc. *slang.* M20.

2 *bottled gas, coal gas, exhaust gas, harassing gas, ideal gas, inert gas, marsh gas, mustard gas, natural gas, nerve gas, noble gas, producer gas, rare gas, tear-gas, town gas, water-gas*, etc. 3e P. BARRY Baby better. It was only gas. 5 R. W. EMERSON Lord Shaftesbury .. reads sermons to them, and they call it 'gas'. DAY LEWIS The sisters would sit .. shelling peas and having a great old gas. **(all) gas and gaiters** *slang* (*a*) a satisfactory state of affairs; (*b*) pomposity, verbosity. b B. BEHAN Someone was imitating my accent, and getting great gas out of it. c E. JONG Isn't that interesting? .. Isn't that a gas?

Attrib. & comb. In the sense 'using gas as a fuel', as *gas cooker, gas engine, gas fire, gas-lamp, gas motor, gas range* (N. Amer.), *gas stove, gas welding*, etc.; *gas-fired* adj. Special combs., as **gas alarm** an alarm device: (*a*) giving warning of the presence of esp. poisonous gas; (*b*) operated by gas; **gas black** a pigment made of carbon produced by the burning of gas; **gas bracket** a (usu. decorative) projecting metal pipe supporting and supplying a gas lamp or burner; **gas centrifuge** a centrifuge for partially separating gases (esp. gaseous compounds of different isotopes of the same element); **gas chamber** an airtight chamber used for killing people or animals by gas poisoning; **gas chromatography** a method of chromatography in which the moving phase is a carrier gas (cf. *gas-liquid chromatography* below); **gas coal** bituminous coal used in the manufacture of coal gas; **gas constant** (*Physical Chem.*) the constant of proportionality, R (= 8.314 joule kelvin^{-1} mole^{-1}), in the gas equation (see below); **gas-cooled** *a.* (of an engine, nuclear reactor, etc.) cooled by a current of gas; **gas engine** an internal-combustion engine using gas as fuel; **gas equation** (*Physical Chem.*) the equation of state of an ideal gas, $PV = nRT$, where P = pressure, V = volume, T = absolute temperature, R = the gas constant (see above), and n = the number of moles of gas; **gas-fitter** a person who installs and services gas fittings; **gas fittings** the apparatus used for heating etc. with gas; **gas gangrene**: resulting from infection by *Clostridium welchii* or a similar bacterium and characterized by the generation of gas; **gas gland**: secreting gas; **gas gun**: using gas as a propellant or as fuel; **gas helmet**: worn as protection against (poison) gas; **gasholder** a large structure for storing gas, a gasometer; **gas-house** (chiefly *US*) (a building forming part of) a gas-works; *gas kinetics*: see KINETICS 2; **gas laws** (*Physical Chem.*) a set of laws (e.g. Boyle's, Charles', Graham's laws) that describe the physical properties of gases; **gaslight** light given off by burning (esp. coal) gas; a jet of burning gas; a gas-lamp; **gas lighter** (*a*) a device for igniting gas; (*b*) a cigarette lighter with gaseous fuel; **gas-liquid chromatography** gas chromatography in which the stationary phase is liquid; **gas main** a main pipe supplying gas to a building or buildings; *gas-mantle*: see MANTLE *n.* 6; **gas mask** an appliance including a respirator worn over the face as a defence against poisonous gas; **gas meter** an apparatus recording the amount of gas consumed; **gas oil** petroleum distillate intermediate in viscosity and boiling point between paraffin (kerosene) and lubricating oils; **gas oven** (*a*) an oven heated by gas; (*b*) = *gas chamber* above; **gas-permeable** *a.* (of a contact lens) allowing the diffusion of gases into and out of the cornea; **gas plant** = FRAXINELLA; **gas poker** a perforated hollow poker through which gas flows to be ignited and so provide heat to kindle a fire; *gas producer*: see PRODUCER 3; **gas ring** a perforated hollow ring supplied with gas and on which a pan etc. can be heated; **gas thread** a standard form of screw-thread of relatively fine pitch, used on metal tubes; *gas trap*: see TRAP *n.*¹ 6c; **gas turbine**: driven by a flow of gas or by gas produced from combustion; **gasworks** a building or buildings where gas is manufactured.

gasless *a.* without gas; not lighted by gas: M19.

gas /gas/ *n.*² *N. Amer.* E20. [Abbrev.] = GASOLINE.

give it (or **her**) **the gas**, **step on the gas** accelerate a car etc. by pressing down on the accelerator; *fig.* hurry.

Comb.: **gas boat**: driven by a petrol engine; **gas guzzler** *N. Amer. slang* a motor vehicle, esp. a large car, that uses fuel extravagantly; **gas pedal** the accelerator in a car etc.; **gas station** a filling-station.

gas /gas/ *v.*¹ Infl. **-ss-**. M19. [f. GAS *n.*¹] **1** *v.t.* Pass (a fabric) through a gas-flame to remove superfluous fibres. M19. **2a** *v.t.* Deceive by idle or boastful talk. *colloq.* M19. **b** *v.i.* Talk idly or boastfully. *colloq.* M19. **c** *v.t.* Excite, thrill, impress. *slang* (orig. *US*). M20. **3** *v.t.* Supply with gas; *spec.* inflate (an airship) with gas. L19. **4** *v.t.* Expose to gas, esp. deliberately so as to cause death, injury, or unconciousness. (Earlier as GASSED *ppl a.* I.) E20. **5** *v.i.* Of a storage battery or dry cell: give off gas. E20.

2b M. GORDON All those others gassing on about volume and the picture plane. c L. ARMSTRONG Just the same the game gassed me. 4 H. WILLIAMSON Phillip wondered if he had been gassed, for his face was the colour of rotten eggs.

gas /gas/ *v.*²*t.* & *i.* *colloq.* (chiefly *N. Amer.*). Infl. **-ss-**. M20. [f. GAS *n.*²] Fill (*up*) the tank of (a car etc.) with petrol.

gasbag /ˈgasbag/ *n.* E19. [f. GAS *n.*¹ + BAG *n.*] **1** A bag for holding gas; *esp.* (the gas-container of) an airship or balloon. E19. **2** An empty or idle talker. *colloq.* L19.

2 S. BELLOW It's just as Thompson says. He's a big gasbag, but this time it's true.

Gascon /ˈgask(ə)n/ *n.* & *a.* ME. [(O)Fr. f. L *Vasco, -on-*, whence also BASQUE.] **A** *n.* **1** A native of Gascony, a former province in SW France. ME. **b** A braggart, a boaster. L18. †**2** Wine from Gascony. LME–M17. **3** The dialect of Gascony. E19. **B** *attrib.* or as *adj.* Of or pertaining to Gascony. LME.

gasconade /gaskəˈneɪd/ *n.* & *v.* M17. [Fr. *gasconnade*, f. *gasconner* talk like a Gascon, brag, f. as prec.: see -ADE.] **A** *n.* (An instance of) extravagant boasting. M17.

O. HENRY Whosoever entered it must sit .. and listen to the imp's interminable gasconade concerning his scandalous career.

B *v.i.* [Cf. Fr. *gasconner*.] Boast extravagantly. E18.

Listener Boyish, gasconading, gaily sincere, he talked easily.

gasconader *n.* a braggart M18.

gaseity /gaˈsiːɪti, -ˈseɪɪti, ˈgas-/ *n.* M19. [f. GASE(OUS + -ITY.] The state of being a gas.

gaselier /gasəˈlɪə/ *n.* Also **gasolier**. M19. [f. GAS *n.*¹ after CHANDELIER.] An ornamental frame to hold gas-burners, usu. hung from the ceiling of a room.

gaseosa /gaseˈosa, gasɪˈəʊsə/ *n.* E20. [Sp.] A fizzy drink; (a drink of) carbonated (mineral) water.

gaseous /ˈgasɪəs, ˈgeɪsɪəs/ *a.* L18. [f. GAS *n.*¹ after AQUEOUS: see -EOUS.] Of the nature or form of a gas; involving or relating to a gas or gases.

gaseousness *n.* M20.

gash /gaʃ/ *n.*¹ Also (earlier) †**garse**, †**garsh**. ME. [OFr. n. f. *garcer*, *jarcer* (mod. *gercer* chap, crack). For loss of *r* cf. BASS *n.*¹, DACE.] **1** A long deep cut or slash, esp. in the flesh; a cleft resembling this in any object. ME. **b** An act of making a gash. E19. **2** The mouth. *US slang.* M19. **b** The vulva. Also, a woman. *derog. slang.* L19.

1 R. DAHL He touched the gash that the axe had made in the wood. P. S. BUCK She cut a great gash in the beast's neck, and thus she severed its life. *fig.*: R. FRAME Under an early moon the water against the fields was like a gash of silver.

¶The mod. form is recorded from M16.

gash /gaʃ/ *n.*² Also **gashion** /ˈgaʃɪən/. *slang* (orig. *Naut.*). E20. [Origin uncertain: cf. GAISHEN.] Something superfluous or extra; waste, rubbish.

gash /gaʃ/ *a.*¹ L16. [Prob. rel. to GASHFUL and GASHLY.] Pale or dismal in appearance.

gash /gaʃ/ *a.*² *Sc.* E18. [Perh. f. Sc. pronunc. of *sagacious* w. short vowel.] **1** Sagacious, wise; dignified. E18. **2** Well-dressed, trim. L18.

gash /gaʃ/ *a.*³ *slang.* M20. [f. GASH *n.*²] Superfluous, extra, spare; free.

gash /gaʃ/ *v.* Also (earlier) †**garse**, †**garsh**. LME. [OFr. *garcer*: see GASH *n.*¹] **1** *v.t.* Make a deep cut or slash in (flesh, a garment, etc.); cut (a hole). LME. **2** *v.i.* Make a gash. L17.

1 V. WOOLF Any weapon that would have gashed a hole in his father's breast and killed him. J. L. WATEN The lofty walls of their bare rooms were gashed and punctured with .. cracks and holes. 2 *fig.*: B. GUTTERIDGE The chalk road gashed into the distance.

¶The mod. form is recorded from M16.

gashed *ppl a.* (*a*) slashed, cut; †(*b*) produced by gashing: L16.

gashful /ˈgaʃfʊl, -f(ə)l/ *a.* *obs.* exc. *dial.* E17. [Perh. alt. of GHASTFUL; cf. GASH *a.*¹, GASHLY.] Ghastly.

gashion *n.* see GASH *n.*²

gashly /ˈgaʃli/ *a.* & *adv.* *obs.* exc. *dial.* M17. [Perh. alt. of GHASTLY; cf. GASHFUL, GASH *a.*¹] Ghastly.

gasification /ˌgasɪfɪˈkeɪʃ(ə)n/ *n.* E19. [f. GAS *n.*¹ + -I- + -FICATION.] The process of converting into a gas. Also, treatment of a substance to yield a gaseous product; *esp.* distillation of coal to yield coal gas.

gasiform /ˈgasɪfɔːm/ *a.* E19. [f. GAS *n.*¹ + -I- + -FORM.] In a gaseous state.

gasify /ˈgasɪfʌɪ/ *v.t.* & *i.* E19. [f. GAS *n.*¹ + -I- + -FY.] Make or become gaseous. Also, subject (coal etc.) to gasification.

gasifiable *a.* L19. **gasifier** *n.* an apparatus for manufacturing gas L19.

gasket /ˈgaskɪt/ *n.* & *v.* As n. also **-kin** /-kɪn/, †**gassit**. E17. [Perh. alt. of Fr. *garcette* little girl, thin rope, dim. of *garce* fem. of *gars* boy.] **A** *n.* **1** *Naut.* A rope, plaited cord, or strip of canvas used to secure a sail when furled to a yard or boom. E17. **2** A strip of tow, plaited hemp, etc., for packing a piston or caulking a joint. E19. **3** A flat sheet or ring of rubber, asbestos, etc., inserted between two adjoining metal surfaces, esp. between the cylinder-head and the cylinder-block in an internal-combustion engine, in order to seal the joint against the pressure of gas or liquid. E20.

3 **blow a gasket** (*a*) cause or undergo the failure of a gasket; (*b*) *slang* lose one's temper.

B *v.t. Naut.* Fasten (a sail) with gaskets. L19.

gaskin /ˈgaskɪn/ *n.*[1] L16. [Perh. f. GALLIGASKINS or f. GASCON.] †**1** *sing.* & (usu.) in *pl.* = GALLIGASKINS 1. L16–M18. **2** The muscular part of the hind leg of a horse between the stifle and the hock. M17.

gaskin *n.*[2] see GASKET.

gasman /ˈgasman/ *n.* Pl. **-men**. E19. [f. GAS *n.*[1] + MAN *n.*] **1** A man employed in the manufacture or supply of gas; *esp.* a man who installs or repairs equipment for supplying household gas, reads gas-meters, etc. E19. †**2** A man who lights gas-lamps in the street; a man in charge of the gas-lights in a theatre. M–L19.

gasohol /ˈgasəhɒl/ *n.* L20. [f. GAS *n.*[2] + ALC)OHOL.] A mixture of petrol and ethyl alcohol used as fuel.

gasolene *n.* var. of GASOLINE.

gasolier *n.* var. of GASELIER.

gasoline /ˈgasəliːn/ *n.* Chiefly *N. Amer.* Also **-lene**. M19. [f. GAS *n.*[1] + -OL + -INE[5], -ENE.] Orig., a petroleum distillate used for heating and lighting; gas oil. Now usu. = PETROL.

gasometer /gaˈsɒmɪtə/ *n.* L18. [Fr. *gazomètre*, f. *gaz* gas + *-mètre* -METER.] **1** *Chem.* A vessel for holding and measuring gas. Now *rare* or *obs.* L18. **2** A large tank or reservoir in which gas is stored for distribution by pipes; a gasholder. E19.

gasometry /gaˈsɒmɪtri/ *n.* L18. [Fr. *gazométrie*, f. as prec.: see -METRY.] The science of measuring gases.

gasoˈmetric *a.* pertaining to gasometry M19.

gasp /gɑːsp/ *n.* L16. [f. the vb.] A convulsive catching of the breath from distress, exertion, surprise, etc.

last gasp the final attempt to draw breath before dying (*at the* or *one's last gasp*, at the point of death; *fig.* exhausted).

gasp /gɑːsp/ *v.* LME. [ON *geispa* yawn, (w. metathesis) f. base of *geip* idle talk, *geipa* talk idly.] **1** *v.i.* Catch the breath with open mouth, as from exhaustion or astonishment. LME. **2** *v.t.* Utter with gasps. (Foll. by *out*.) L16. **3** *v.i.* Pant or strain for air; *fig.* crave or long *for*. L16.

1 G. SWIFT She was gasping, her chest heaving, long jagged breaths came from her throat. 3 H. E. BATES Alex was quivering terribly all over as he gasped for his catarrh-choked breath.

Phrases: **gasp one's breath, life,** etc., **away** or **out** die. **gasp one's last** die.

gasper *n.* (*a*) a person who gasps; (*b*) *slang* a (cheap) cigarette: M19. **gaspingly** *adv.* in a gasping manner E19.

gaspacho *n.* var. of GAZPACHO.

gaspereau /ˈgaspərəʊ/ *n. Canad.* Pl. **-eaux** /-əʊ, -əʊz/, **-eaus**. E18. [Canad. Fr. *gaspareau*, *gasparot*.] = ALEWIFE 2.

gassed /gast/ *ppl a.* L19. [f. GAS *v.*[1] + -ED[1].] **1** Affected by poisonous gas. L19. **2** Drunk, intoxicated. *slang*. E20.

Gassendist /gaˈsɛndɪst/ *n.* L17. [f. *Gassendi* (see below) + -IST.] A follower of the French metaphysician Gassendi (b. 1592).

gasser /ˈgasə/ *n.* L19. [f. GAS *v.*[1] + -ER[1].] **1** A person who is employed in gassing fabric etc. L19. **2** An outstanding or highly successful person or thing. *slang*. M20. **3** A talkative or boastful person; an idle talker. *slang*. M20.

†**gassit** *n.* see GASKET.

gassy /ˈgasi/ *a.* M18. [f. GAS *n.*[1] + -Y[1].] **1** Full of or of the nature of gas. M18. **2** (Of a person) inclined to talk idly or boastfully; (of talk) pointless, verbose. *colloq.* M19.

gassiness *n.* L19.

†**gast** *n.* Long only *Sc.* LME–E20. [f. the vb.] A fright.

†**gast** *v.* & *a.* [OE *gǣstan*, f. Gmc base of GHOST *n.*] **A** *v.t.* Frighten, terrify. OE–E17.

SHAKES. *Lear* Or whether gasted by the noise I made, Full suddenly he fled.

B *adj.* Frightened, terrified. LME–L16.

Gastarbeiter /ˈgastɑːrbaɪtər/ *n.* Pl. **-s**, same. M20. [G, f. *Gast* guest + *Arbeiter* worker.] A person with temporary permission to work in another (esp. western European) country.

gaster /ˈgastə/ *v.t.* & *i. obs.* exc. *dial.* L16. [Frequent. of GAST *v.*: see -ER[5].] (Cause to) have fear.

gasteral *a.* var. of GASTRAL.

gasteromycete /ˌgast(ə)rəʊˈmʌɪsiːt/ *n.* Orig. only in pl. **-mycetes** /-ˈmʌɪsiːts, -mʌɪˈsiːtiːz/. L19. [Anglicized sing. of mod.L *Gasteromycetes* (see below), f. Gk *gastēr*, *gaster-* stomach + *mukētes* pl. of *mukēs* fungus.] *Mycol.* A fungus of the class Gasteromycetes of basidiomycetes, characterized by bearing spores in cavities in the fruiting body and not discharging them violently.

gasteromyˈcetous *a.* M19.

†**gastful** *a.* see GHASTFUL.

gasthaus /ˈgasthaʊs/ *n.* Pl. **-häuser** /-hɔyzər/. M19. [G, f. *Gast* GUEST *n.* + *Haus* HOUSE *n.*[1]] A small inn or hotel in a German-speaking country.

gasthof /ˈgasthoːf/ *n.* Pl. **-hofs, -höfe** /-høːfə/. M19. [G, f. *Gast* GUEST *n.* + *Hof* hotel, large house.] A German hotel, usu. larger than a *gasthaus*.

†**gastly** *a.* & *adv.* see GHASTLY.

†**gastness** *n.* LME–E17. [f. GAST *a.* + -NESS.] A threat; (a cause of) terror; terrified state or appearance.

SHAKES. *Oth.* Look you pale, mistress?—Do you perceive the gastness of her eye.

gastraea /gaˈstreɪə/ *n.* Also ***gastrea**. L19. [mod.L, f. Gk *gastēr*, *gaster-* stomach + L *-aeus*, Gk *-aios* adj. suff.] *Zool.* A hypothetical ancestral form of metazoan (multicellular animal) having two layers of cells, corresponding in organization to the gastrula in the embryonic development of living metazoans.

gastral /ˈgastr(ə)l/ *a.* Also **gasteral** /ˈgast(ə)r(ə)l/. E19. [f. as GASTRO- + -AL[1].] Chiefly *Zool.* = GASTRIC.

gastralgia /gaˈstraldʒə/ *n.* Now *rare* M19. [f. as GASTRO- + -ALGIA.] *Med.* Pain in the stomach.

gastralgic *a.* L19.

gastrectomy /gaˈstrɛktəmi/ *n.* L19. [f. GASTRO- + -ECTOMY.] Surgical removal of all or part of the stomach; an instance of this.

gastric /ˈgastrɪk/ *a.* M17. [mod.L *gastricus*, f. Gk *gastēr*, *gastr-* stomach: see -IC.] Of, pertaining to, or affecting the stomach.

gastric fever fever involving the stomach; now usu., an enteric fever or typhoid. **gastric flu**, (less commonly) **influenza** *colloq.* any intestinal disorder of unknown or supposedly viral cause. **gastric juice** the thin, clear fluid secreted by glands in the stomach wall, containing hydrochloric acid and enzymes such as pepsin, and important in digestion. **gastric mill** *Zool.* a masticatory apparatus in the gut; *esp.* (*a*) in malacostracan crustaceans, a framework of movable calcareous or chitinous pieces; (*b*) in birds and reptiles, the gizzard together with the small stones swallowed to aid its action.

gastrin /ˈgastrɪn/ *n.* E20. [f. GASTRIC + -IN[1].] *Physiol.* A polypeptide hormone which stimulates secretion of gastric juice, and is secreted into the bloodstream by the stomach wall in response to the presence of food.

gastritis /gaˈstrʌɪtɪs/ *n.* E19. [f. GASTRO- + -ITIS.] *Med.* Inflammation of the mucosa of the stomach.

gastro- /ˈgastrəʊ/ *comb. form* of Gk *gastēr*, *gaster-*, *gastr-* stomach, used esp. in *Med.*: see -O-. Bef. a vowel also **gastr-**.

gastrocele *n.* a hernia of the stomach E19. **gastroduodeˈnostomy** *n.* (an instance of) surgical connection of the stomach and the duodenum L19. **gastro-enˈteric** *a.* = GASTRO-INTESTINAL. **gastro-enteˈrostomy** *n.* (an instance of) surgical connection of the stomach and the intestine L19. **gastro-inteˈstinal** *a.* of or involving the stomach and intestines M19. **gastrojejuˈnostomy** *n.* (an instance of) surgical connection of the stomach and the jejunum L19. **gastrolith** *n.* a hard concretion in the stomach, usu. formed around foreign material which has been swallowed M19. **gaˈstropathy** *n.* any disease of the stomach M19. **gastropexy** *n.* (an instance of) the surgical attachment of the stomach to the abdominal wall L19. **gastroplasty** *n.* (an instance of) surgical correction of deformity of the stomach; *spec.* reduction by stapling as a treatment for obesity: M20. **gastroˈvascular** *a.* (*Zool.*) (of the body cavity of certain coelenterates) fulfilling both digestive and circulatory functions L19. **gastroˈzooid** *n.* (*Zool.*) in colonial hydrozoans and some colonial tunicates, a nutritive zooid L19.

gastrocnemius /gastrəʊˈkniːmɪəs/ *n.* Pl. **-mii** /-mɪʌɪ/. L17. [mod.L f Gk. *gastroknēmia* the calf of the leg, f. *gaster* stomach, belly + *knēmē* leg: so called from its 'bellying' or bulging form.] *Anat.* The chief muscle of the calf of the leg. Also *gastrocnemius muscle*.

gastrocnemial *a.* L19. **gastrocnemian** *a.* M19.

gastrocolic /gastrəʊˈkɒlɪk/ *a.* M19. [f. GASTRO- + COLIC *n.* & *a.*] *Med.* Pertaining to the stomach and colon.

gastrocolic fistula an abnormal passage between the stomach and the colon, resulting from disease. **gastrocolic reflex** a wave of peristalsis produced in the colon by introducing food into a fasting stomach.

gastro-enteritis /ˌgastrəʊɛntəˈrʌɪtɪs/ *n.* E19. [f. GASTRO- + ENTERITIS.] *Med.* Inflammation of the stomach and intestines, causing vomiting and diarrhoea.

gastro-enterology /ˌgastrəʊɛntəˈrɒlədʒi/ *n.* E20. [f. GASTRO- + ENTERO- + -LOGY.] The branch of medicine that deals with the diseases and abnormalities of the stomach and intestines.

gastro-enteroˈlogical *a.* E20. **gastro-enterologist** *n.* M20.

gastrology /gaˈstrɒlədʒi/ *n.* E19. [Gk *gastrologia*: see GASTRO-, -LOGY.] = GASTRONOMY.

gastrologer *n.* = GASTRONOME E19.

gastromancy /ˈgastrəmansi/ *n. obs.* exc. *Hist.* E17. [f. GASTRO- + -MANCY.] Divination by the belly; *spec.* divination by figures etc. seen in bellied glass vessels full of water or by sounds from, or signs on, the stomach.

gastronome /ˈgastrənəʊm/ *n.* E19. [Fr., back-form. f. *gastronomie* GASTRONOMY.] A connoisseur of good eating and drinking; a gourmet.

gastronomic /gastrəˈnɒmɪk/ *a.* E19. [Fr. *gastronomique*, f. as next: see -IC.] Of or pertaining to gastronomy.

gastronomical *a.* E19. **gastronomically** *adv.* M19.

gastronomy /gaˈstrɒnəmi/ *n.* E19. [Fr. *gastronomie*, f. Gk *gastronomia* alt. of *gastrologia* GASTROLOGY: see -NOMY.] The art and science of good eating and drinking.

gastronomer *n.* [after *astronomer*] = GASTRONOME E19. **gastronomist** *n.* = GASTRONOME E19.

gastropod /ˈgastrəpɒd/ *n.* & *a.* Also **gastero-** /ˈgast(ə)rə(ʊ)-/. E19. [Fr. *gastéropode* f. mod.L *Gasteropoda* (see below), f. as GASTRO-: see -POD.] **A** *n.* Any mollusc of the class Gastropoda (including snails, slugs, whelks, and limpets), typically having a flattened ventral foot for locomotion and a univalve shell. E19. **B** *adj.* gastropodous M19.

gaˈstropodan *a.* & *n.* = GASTROPOD L19. **gaˈstropodous** *a.* of, belonging to, pertaining to, or characteristic of the class Gastropoda E19.

gastroscope /ˈgastrəskəʊp/ *n.* L19. [f. GASTRO- + -SCOPE.] *Med.* An instrument for inspecting the interior of the stomach when passed into it via the mouth and oesophagus.

gastroscopy /gaˈstrɒskəpi/ *n.* M19. [f. GASTRO- + -SCOPY.] *Med.* **1** An examination of the abdomen. Now *rare*. M19. **2** (An) examination of the stomach by means of a gastroscope; the practice and technique of using a gastroscope. L19.

gastroˈscopic *a.* of or pertaining to the gastroscope or gastroscopy L19. **gastroˈscopically** *adv.* L19.

gastrostomy /ga'strɒstəmi/ *n.* M19. [f. GASTRO- + -STOMY.] A surgical operation involving the opening of the stomach for the introduction of food.

gastrotomy /ga'strɒtəmi/ *n.* M17. [f. GASTRO- + -TOMY.] Surgical cutting open of the abdomen, or (now usu.) of the stomach through the abdominal walls; an instance of this.
gastro'tomic *a.* M19.

gastrotrich /'gastrətrɪk/ *n.* M20. [f. GASTRO- + -TRICH.] Any minute aquatic multicellular animal of the phylum Gastrotricha, having a short wormlike body covered with cilia and bristles, thought to be related to the rotifers and nematodes.

gastrula /'gastrʊlə/ *n.* Pl. **-lae** /-liː/, **-las.** L19. [mod.L., f. Gk *gastēr*, *gastr-* stomach: see -ULE.] An embryo at the stage following inward migration of the cells of the blastula, typically consisting of a hollow cup-shaped structure having three layers of cells enclosing the archenteron. Cf. BLASTULA, MORULA *n.*[1]
gastrular *a.* M20. **gastru'lation** *n.* the process of formation of a gastrula L19.

gat /gat/ *n.*[1] E16. [App. f. ON *gat* (Sw., Da. *gat*) hole, opening, passage: see GATE *n.*[1]] **1** A hole in the ground. E16. **2** An opening between sandbanks; a channel, a strait. L16.

gat /gat/ *n.*[2] *slang.* Also **gatt.** E20. [Abbrev. of GATLING.] A revolver or other firearm.

gatch /gatʃ/ *n.* L19. [Pers. *gač.*] A type of plaster used in Iran for architectural decoration.

gate /geɪt/ *n.*[1] Also (*Sc.* & *north.*) **yett** /jɛt/. [OE *gæt*, *geat*, pl. *gatu*, corresp. to OFris. *gat* hole, opening, OS *gat* eye of a needle (LG, Du. gap, hole, breach), ON *gat* hole, opening, passage (cf. GAT *n.*[1]) f. Gmc. Forms w. *y-* remain in north. but *gate* has been standard since 16.] **1** An opening in the wall of a city, an enclosure, or a large building, made for entrance and exit, and able to be closed by a movable barrier. Also, the gateway over or around such an opening. OE. **2** A barrier which closes the opening across a wall, road, or passage; a wooden or iron framework either solid or consisting of bars or gratings, turning on pivots or hinges, or sliding, and used either singly or in pairs. OE. **b** A contrivance for stopping or regulating the passage of water in a lock etc. L15. **c** *spec.* A starting-gate. E20. **3** In biblical translations and allusions, a place of judicial assembly. OE. **4** *fig.* A means of entrance or exit. ME. **5** A mountain pass, *esp.* one providing entry to a country. LME. **6** A frame in which a saw or set of saws is stretched to prevent buckling. E19. **7** *Cricket.* The space between the bat and the batsman's body. Formerly also, the wicket. M19. **8** The total number of people entering through the gates to see a football match etc. L19. **b** The amount of admission money paid to see a football match etc. L19. **9** A device in a cine camera or projector which holds each frame of a film momentarily in position. E20. **10** An arrangement of slots through which the lever of a motor vehicle gearbox is moved to engage different gears. E20. **11** *Electronics.* **a** An electrical signal that causes or controls the passage of other signals in a circuit. M20. **b** A digital circuit producing one output signal that is determined by a combination of two or more input signals; *esp.* (in full *logic gate*) a logic circuit of this kind. M20. **c** The material in a unipolar transistor forming the electrodes to which the input signal is applied. M20. **12** A numbered place of access to an aircraft at an airport. M20. **13** The mouth. *slang.* M20. **14** [Perh. f. sense 4, or perh. abbrev. of *alligator.*] A person, *esp.* a jazz musician. *US slang.* M20.
1 B. GOOGE I made a square wall . . with a great gate, for the bringing in of my cariages. SHAKES. *Jul. Caes.* Brutus and Cassius Are rid like madmen through the gates of Rome. **2** E. F. BENSON Six . . steps led up from a small clanging gate to the front door. J. UPDIKE The gates were swung open, the mob laughingly pushed through. *floodgate*, *lich-gate*, *sluice-gate*, *starting-gate*, *tailgate*, *tide-gate*, *toll-gate*, *water-gate*, etc. *bull-at-a-gate*: see BULL *n.*[1] **c** T. FITZGEORGE-PARKER She spoilt three starts and then, when the gate went up, ran right out. **4** SHAKES. *Much Ado* For thee I'll lock up all the gates of love. **8** E. HEATH There was an enormous gate and the crowd was forthright in its advice.
Phrases: *creaking gate*: see CREAK *v.* 3. DECUMAN *gate*. *gate of horn*: see *ivory gate* below. **get the gate** *slang* be dismissed, rejected, or jilted. **give (someone) the gate** *slang* dismiss, reject, jilt. **ivory gate, gate of horn** in Greek legend, those gates through which false and true dreams respectively pass. **open a gate to** or **for** provide an opportunity for, make possible. *Pearly Gates*: see PEARLY *a. swing the gate*: see SWING *v.* **the gate(s) of death** the near approach of death.
Comb.: **gate array** (an electronic chip consisting of) a regular arrangement of logic gates; **gate-bill** formerly, at Oxford and Cambridge Universities, a record of the times at which a student returns to college after hours; a weekly account of the fines charged for this; **gate city** *US* a city located at the entrance to an administrative district; **gatecrash** *v.i.* & *t.* enter (a party etc.) as a gate-crasher; **gatecrasher** a person who enters a sports ground, private party, entertainment, etc., without an invitation or ticket; **gatefold** a folded oversize page or insert in a magazine etc.; **gatehouse** (*a*) a house at the gates or entrance of a park or other enclosure, a lodge; (*b*) *Hist.* a room over a city or palace gate, often used as a prison; **gatekeeper** (*a*) an attendant at a gate; (*b*) any of several Eurasian satyrid butterflies, esp. *Pyronia tithonus* (also called *hedge brown*), brownish orange with a black spot on the forewing; **gateleg(ged) table**: with a leg or legs in a frame resembling a gate, which may be swung round to allow the leaves to drop down; **gate-lodge** a lodge at the gate of the grounds of a country house etc.; **gateman** a man in charge of a gate, a gatekeeper; **gate-money** (*a*) = sense 8b above; (*b*) money charged on a gate-bill; **gate-net** a net hung loosely across a gateway in order to catch hares driven at night; **gatepost** a post on which a gate is hung or against which it shuts (*between you (and) me and the gatepost*: see BETWEEN *prep.* 3); **gate pulse** = sense 11a above; **gate receipts** = *gate-money* (a) above; **gate-stead** *rare* a gateway; **gate-table** a gateleg table; **gate-valve**: in which a sliding part controls the extent of the aperture; **gate-ward** *arch.* = *gatekeeper* (a) above.
gated *a.* having a gate or gates; *spec.* (of a road) having a gate or gates in order to control the flow of traffic: E17. **gateless** *a.* without a gate or gates E17.

gate /geɪt/ *n.*[2] Now only *Sc.* & *north.* Also **†gait.** See also GAIT *n.* ME. [ON *gata* = OHG *gazza* (G *Gasse* street, lane), Goth. *gatwō* f. Gmc.] **I1a** A way, a road, a path. ME. **b** A street. Freq. in street-names in Scotland and N. England, as Gallowgate, Kirkgate, etc. LME. **c** Length of way, distance. *obs.* exc. *Sc.* E16. **d** *Mining.* An underground passage. M18. **2** A going, a journey, a course. ME. **†b** The flight of a bird, esp. a hawk. ME–L17. **†c** *fig.* Proceeding. *rare* (Shakes.). Only in E17. **3** A way, manner, or method of doing or behaving; a peculiar habit. ME. **4** A right to a run or pasturage for a cow, horse, etc. *north.* L16. **II** See GAIT *n.*
Phrases: *gang one's gate*: see GANG *v.*[1] **take (the) gate** take the road, leave; follow a path or course. **this** or **that gate** this or that way; in this or that direction.
gateward(s) *adv.* on the road or way towards; by the direct road: E16.

gate /geɪt/ *n.*[3] L17. [Perh. same as GATE *n.*[1]: cf. synon. Du. *gietgat*, f. *gieten* pour, cast + *gat* opening = GATE *n.*[1]] *Founding.* **1** The opening or channel through which molten metal flows into a mould. L17. **2** The waste piece of metal cast in the gate. M19.

gate /geɪt/ *v.*[1]*t.* M19. [f. GATE *n.*[1]] **1** Confine (a student) to the precincts of a college or school either entirely or after certain hours. M19. **2** *Electronics.* Subject to the action of a gate; select parts of (a signal) that occur within a given time interval or range of amplitude; switch by means of a gate circuit. Chiefly as *gated* ppl a., *gating* vbl n. & ppl a. Cf. GATE *n.*[1] 11. M20.
1 G. SAINTSBURY He was . . gated for a fortnight for disobedience and contumacy.

gate /geɪt/ *v.*[2]*t.* & *i.* E20. [f. GATE *n.*[3]] *Founding.* Provide (a mould etc.) with a gate or gates.
gating *vbl n.* the action of providing gates; the arrangement of gates, runners, etc., provided: E20.

-gate /geɪt/ *suff.* [Extracted f. WATER)GATE.] Forming ns. denoting an actual or alleged scandal (and usu. an attempted cover-up) comparable in some way to the Watergate scandal of 1972, esp. with the name of the place associated with the scandal, as *Dallasgate*, *Irangate*.

gateau /'gatəʊ/ *n.* Also **gâ-.** Pl. **-eaux** /-əʊ(z)/, **-eaus.** M19. [Fr. *gâteau* cake.] **1** A large rich cake, *esp.* one with layers of cream or fruit. M19. **b** In full *gâteau de riz* /də riːz/ [= of rice]. A rich rice dessert in the shape of a cake. Now *rare.* M19. **2** Meat or fish baked and served in the form of a cake. Now *rare.* L19.

gateway /'geɪtweɪ/ *n.* M17. [f. GATE *n.*[1] + WAY *n.*] **1** An opening or passage that is or may be closed by a gate. Now *rare.* M17. **2** A frame or arch in which a gate is hung; a structure built at or over a gate. L18. **3** *transf.* & *fig.* A means of entrance or exit. M19. **b** = GATE *n.*[1] 5. L19. **4** *Computing.* A device used to connect two different networks. L20.
2 M. PATTISON A lofty massive front with three fortified and portcullised gateways. **3** *City Limits* Sutton, gateway to the Downs.

Gatha /'gɑːθɑː/ *n.* Also **g-.** M19. [Avest. *gāθā.*] Any of the seventeen poems which are the most ancient texts of the Avesta and are attributed to Zoroaster.

gather /'gaðə/ *n.*[1] M16. [f. the vb.] **1** An amount gathered. Long *rare* or *obs.* M16. **2** In *pl.* & (occas.) *sing.* Part of a garment or fabric which is gathered or drawn in. L16. **3** The action of gathering; a drawing together. L19. **4** *Glass-making.* A mass of molten glass on the end of a blowing-iron. M20.

†gather *n.*[2] LME–L18. [Prob. a spec. sense of prec.] The pluck (heart, liver, and lungs) of an animal.

gather /'gaðə/ *v.* [OE *gaderian* = OFris. *gaderia*, MLG *gadern*, (M)Du. *gaderen*, MHG *gatern* f. WGmc base of TOGETHER.] **I** *v.t.* **†1** Join, unite; put together. OE–ME. **2** Bring together, collect, assemble. Also foll. by *together*, *up.* OE. **†3** Collect or compile (literary matter) from various written or printed sources. OE–L17. **4** Collect or pick (flowers, fruit) from the place of growth. OE. **b** Collect (grain etc.) as harvest. Also foll. by *in.* OE. **c** Pick or pluck individually (a flower or fruit). L16. **5** Pick up, collect from the ground. Usu. foll. by *up.* ME. **b** *spec.* Catch (a ball) in rugby football or baseball as it moves through the air; pick up (a rolling ball) in cricket etc. when fielding. M19. **6** Of a material object: receive addition of, accumulate (something). ME. **7** Collect as a contribution (money etc.). *obs.* exc. *dial.* LME. **8** Make or scrape together (a living). *rare.* LME. **9** Bring into activity, summon up (strength, energy, one's thoughts, oneself) esp. for an effort. Also foll. by *together*, *up.* LME. **b** Gain or recover (breath). L15. **10** Acquire (knowledge) by observation and reasoning; infer, deduce. M16. **11** Draw together (a garment, the sails of a ship, etc.) in folds; bring into smaller compass. Also foll. by *up.* M16. **b** Draw up (a fabric, a garment, esp. a dress) along a thread which has been run through it. Also foll. by *up.* L16. **c** *Archit.* Contract, make narrower (a chimney, drain, etc.). E18. **d** Wrinkle, contract (one's brow). *rare.* L18. **12** Acquire by way of increase (a specified quality, condition, etc.), develop a higher degree of. L16. **13** Of a ship: gain on or draw nearer to, in following. Also foll. by *on.* E17. **14** *techn.* **a** *Bookbinding.* Collect and put in order (the leaves or sheets of a book). L17. **b** *Glass-making.* Collect (molten glass) on the end of a blowing-iron. M19.
2 R. LYND He would in time gather a great crowd round him. G. GREENE He had gathered up in his novels the two divided strands of Restoration fiction. **be gathered to one's fathers, to one's people** be buried with one's ancestors; die. **4** W. CATHER She had . . gone into the meadow to gather wild flowers. **5** H. KELLER I gathered up the fruit in my pinafore. N. SHUTE She gathered up her gloves and her bag. **6** *Proverb*: A rolling stone gathers no moss. **9** LEIGH HUNT It only made him gather up his determination. R. L. STEVENSON It was some time before either I or the captain seemed to gather our senses. D. H. LAWRENCE Ursula thought a moment, gathering her straying wits together. **10** T. HARDY Jim gathered from inquiries he made that he had come the wrong way. D. CUSACK She'd had a row with Rex . . something

about Portia, I gathered. 11 M. SINCLAIR She would look down at her shawl and gather it about her. b C. BRONTË A dress . . as full in the skirt as it could be gathered. 12 P. G. WODEHOUSE Horace . . pressed his foot on the accelerator and the Bingley gathered speed. †**gather ground** gain ground, make progress. **gather head** come to a head; grow stronger. **gather way** *Naut.* (of a ship) begin to move.

II *v.i.* 15 Of people: come together, congregate, assemble. OE. 16 Accumulate and come to a head; develop a purulent swelling. OE. 17†a Accumulate wealth. Only in ME. b Make a collection of money or other contributions. *obs.* exc. *dial.* M16. 18 Of things: collect, come together in a mass; form or increase by coming together. LME. 19 Contract; form folds or wrinkles. *rare.* M16. 20 *Naut.* Of a ship: make its way (towards something). L16.

15 G. VIDAL A crowd was beginning to gather. 16 E. NESBIT He had hurt his foot with a nail in his boot that gathered. *fig.*: SHAKES. *Temp.* Now does my project gather to a head. 18 SIR W. SCOTT It seemed as if a tear . . were gathering in his . . eye. T. COLLINS Dusk was gathering by this time. 19 J. L. WATEN Slowly a frown gathered on Mother's face.

With advs. in specialized senses: **gather out** select, pick out. **gather up** (*a*) draw up (one's limbs or person); (*b*) sum up, summarize, (something); (*c*) plough (land, a ridge) so that the earth is turned over towards the highest part of the ridge; (*d*) compose (one's features) *into* an expression; (see also senses 2, 5, 9, 11 above).

gatherable *a.* that may be gathered or inferred M16.

gatherer /ˈgað(ə)rə/ *n.* ME. [f. prec. + -ER[1].] 1 A person who gathers or collects something. Also foll. by *together, up.* ME. b *spec.* A collector of money. Now *rare.* LME. †c An accumulator of wealth, a miser. Only in 16. 2 *techn.* a *Bookbinding.* A person who or machine which collects and orders the leaves or sheets of a book. L17. b *Glass-making.* A person who accumulates molten glass or metal on the end of a blowing-iron. M19. 3 Each of the front teeth of a horse. L17.

gathering /ˈgað(ə)rɪŋ/ *n.* OE. [f. as prec. + -ING[1].] 1 *gen.* The action of GATHER *v.* I; collecting something. Also foll. by *together, up,* etc. OE. †b The action or practice of collecting wealth. ME–M16. c The action of drawing up the fabric in a garment; the gathers so formed. L16. 2 The action of GATHER *v.* II; coming together, uniting; a union, an accumulation. OE. 3 A bringing together or coming together of people; an assembly, meeting; *spec.* an (annual) assembly of dancing, piping, or sporting contests held in various parts of the Scottish Highlands. OE. b A signal to assemble, sounded on drums or pipes. Chiefly *Sc.* M17. 4 An accumulation of purulent matter; a suppurated swelling. OE. 5 That which is gathered or brought together. Now *rare* or *obs.* LME. 6 *techn.* a *Bookbinding.* The arrangement of the leaves or sheets of a book in proper order; a group of leaves or sheets brought together to form part of a book. L17. b *Glass-making.* = GATHER *n.*[1] 4. E20. 7 *Archit.* The narrowing or contracting of (esp. the wings of) a chimney. E18.

3 QUEEN VICTORIA We . . went . . to the Gathering at the *Castle of Braemar.* V. SACKVILLE-WEST They all thoroughly enjoyed their gatherings over the tea-table. 5 R. PALTOCK Some few new sorts of berries and greens were the gathering of that day. 6a E. DIEHL The book sections, or gatherings, were marked . . in order. 7 J. S. FOSTER The gathering over of the flue above the fire-place opening . . should be steep.

Comb.: **gathering coal** (chiefly *Sc.*) a large piece of coal put on the fire to keep it burning through the night; **gathering cry** (chiefly *Sc., Hist.*) a summons to assemble for war; **gathering ground** a region from which the feeding waters of a river or reservoir are collected; **gathering peat** (chiefly *Sc.*) a peat laid on the fire to keep it burning through the night; **gathering sound** *Hist.* = *gathering cry* above.

Gathic /ˈgɑːθɪk/ *a.* & *n.* E20. [f. GATHA + -IC.] A *adj.* Of or pertaining to the Gathas or the language in which they are written. E20. B *n.* The Gathic language, a more archaic form of the Avestan language. M20.

Gathaic /gɑːˈθɑːɪk/ *a.* (*rare*) = GATHIC *a.* L19.

Gatling /ˈgatlɪŋ/ *n.* M19. [R. J. *Gatling* (1818 1903), US inventor.] In full *Gatling gun.* An early type of machine-gun with clustered barrels into which cartridges were automatically loaded.

gator /ˈgeɪtə/ *n. colloq.* Chiefly *US.* Also **'gator.** M19. [Abbrev.] = ALLIGATOR.

Gatso /ˈgatsəʊ/ *n.* Pl. **-os.** L20. [f. Maurice *Gatso*nides, 20th-cent. Du. racing driver.] A camera which automatically takes a photograph of vehicles travelling over a certain speed (as measured by radar). Also *Gatso camera.*

gatt *n.* var. of GAT *n.*[2]

gatten *n.* see GAITER *n.*[1]

gatter /ˈgatə/ *n.*[1] *slang.* E19. [Origin unkn.] Beer; liquor in general.

gatter *n.*[2] var. of GAITER *n.*[1]

gattine /gaˈtiːn/ *n.* E19. [Fr.] A disease of the silkworm; = PÉBRINE.

gauche /gəʊʃ/ *a.* M18. [Fr., lit. 'left(-handed)'.] 1 Lacking in tact or ease of manner, awkward, blundering; lacking in subtlety or skill, crude, unsophisticated. M18. 2 *Math.* Skew, not plane. *arch.* L19. b *Chem.* Of a molecular conformation: skew, having two groups staggered along a central axis by (about) 60 degrees. M20.

1 C. CHAPLIN He was gauche in his attempt at conversation, asking inconsequential questions about my films. *Times* His illustrator scarcely ever achieves anything that is not gauche and lifeless.

gauchely *adv.* L19. **gaucheness** *n.* L19.

gaucherie /ˈgəʊʃ(ə)riː/ *n.* L18. [Fr., f. *gauche*: see prec., -ERY.] Gauche or awkward manner; a gauche action.

DISRAELI An elegant . . lad, with just enough of dandyism to preserve him from committing *gaucheries.* C. BAX Whitman uses rhyme . . with some awkwardness or, as he would have put it, gaucherie.

Gaucher's disease /ˈgəʊʃeɪz dɪˌziːz, gəʊˈʃeɪz/ *n. phr.* M20. [P. C. E. *Gaucher* (1854–1918), Fr. physician.] *Med.* An inherited lipid storage disorder, characterized by bone fragility, neurological disturbance, anaemia, and enlargement of the liver and spleen.

gaucho /ˈgaʊtʃəʊ, ˈgɔː-/ *n.* Pl. **-os.** E19. [Amer. Sp., prob. f. Araucanian *kauču.*] A mounted herdsman of the S. American pampas, usu. of mixed European and American Indian descent.

gaud /gɔːd/ *n.*[1] ME. [Perh. f. AN deriv. of OFr. *gaudir* f. L *gaudere* rejoice. In later senses infl. by GAUD *n.*[2]] 1 A trick; *esp.* a deceitful trick or pretence. Long only *Sc.* & *north.* Now *rare* or *obs.* ME. †b A piece of mockery, a jest. Also, an object of mockery. LME–M17. 2 A showy ornament, a piece of finery; a gewgaw. Now *rhet.* LME. 3 In *pl.*, showy ceremonies; *sing.* idle display. Now *rhet.* M17.

2 H. L. MENCKEN Their . . inclination to dress up, to strike the public eye with arresting gauds. 3 LYTTON The pomp, the gaud . . strongly contrasted the patriarchal simplicity which marked his justice court. C. C. FELTON Its bishops . . surrounded themselves with the pomps and gauds of this world.

gaud /gɔːd/ *n.*[2] *obs.* exc. *Hist.* LME. [AL *gaudium*, prob. based on med.L *quinque gaudia* the five 'joyful mysteries' of the rosary. Cf. AN *gaudes* in same sense.] Each of the large ornamental beads in a rosary, placed between the decades of aves.

†**gaud** *v.t.* LME. [f. GAUD *n.*[1] or *n.*[2]] 1 Equip (a rosary) with gauds. LME–M16. 2 Adorn, make showy. M16–E17.

2 SHAKES. *Coriol.* Their nicely gawded cheeks.

gaudeamus /gaʊdɪˈɑːməs, gɔːdɪˈeɪməs/ *n.* Chiefly *Sc.* Now *rare* or *obs.* E18. [First wd of the mod.L students' song *Gaudeamus igitur, juvenes dum sumus* 'Then let us be merry while we are still young'.] A convivial gathering, esp. of college or university students.

gaudery /ˈgɔːd(ə)ri/ *n.* E16. [f. GAUD *n.*[1] + -ERY.] †1 Trickery. Only in E16. 2 Gaudy decoration or show; a piece of finery. L16.

2 DRYDEN A plain suit . . Is better than to be by tarnished gawdry known.

gaudy /ˈgɔːdi/ *n.* LME. [L *gaudium* joy, f. *gaudere* rejoice, or *gaude* imper. of this vb.] †1 = GAUD *n.*[2] LME–M16. 2 (An instance of) rejoicing or making merry. Now *rare* or *obs.* M16. 3 A grand feast. Now usu., an annual celebratory dinner held by a college for old members. M17.

Comb.: **gaudy-day, -night** a gala day or night, *esp.* one on which a college gaudy is held.

gaudy /ˈgɔːdi/ *a.* Also †**gawdy.** L15. [In sense 3 perh. f. GAUDY *n.* In other senses f. GAUD *n.*[1]: see -Y[1].] 1 Brilliantly or (now chiefly) glaringly or vulgarly colourful or ornate; (excessively) showy, garish. L15. †2 Full of trickery. Only in E16. †3 Of food: luxurious. M16–E17. 4 Very good, splendid. Usu. in neg. contexts. *slang.* Now *rare* or *obs.* L19.

1 C. MCCULLERS The show was gaudy with coloured lights. E. CRISPIN Nice figure, and dressed well—plain . . clothes, nothing gaudy. *fig.*: *New Yorker* By pressuring [Nicaragua] . . to hold off from some of its more gaudy outrages. 4 M. TWAIN We played it to a hundred guests . . and had a perfectly gaudy time.

gaudily *adv.* E17. **gaudiness** *n.* E17.

gaudy-green /gɔːdɪˈgriːn/ *a.* & *n.* Long *arch.* LME. [f. (O)Fr. *gaude* weld (assim. to -Y[1]) + GREEN *n., a.*] (Of) a green dyed with the plant weld; (of) a yellowish green.

gauge /geɪdʒ/ *n.* Also (esp. *US* & in sense 2) **gage.** ME. [ONFr. var. of (also mod.) *jauge*: ult. origin unkn. For the pronunc. cf. *safe* /seɪf/ f. (O)Fr. *sauf.*] I A measure. 1 A standard measure or scale of measurement; *esp.* a measure of the capacity or contents of a barrel, of the diameter of a bullet, of the thickness of sheet metal, or of the fineness of a textile. ME. b *transf.* & *fig.* Extent, capacity, scope. E17. c *Physics.* In full *gauge function.* A function introduced as an additional term into a field equation, often for symmetry purposes, without altering the derived equations of observable physical quantities. Freq. in *comb.* (see below). E20. 2 *Naut.* (Usu. **gage.**) The position of one vessel relative to another and to the wind. L16. 3 *Building.* The length of projection of a tile or slate beyond that which overlaps it. E18. 4 The distance between the rails of a railway-track, tramline, etc. Also, the distance between the wheels at each end of the same axle of a railway vehicle. M19.

1b A. W. KINGLAKE His intellect . . was much above the low gauge which people used to assign to it. **take the gauge of** estimate, assess. 2 **have** or **keep the weather gauge of** be windward of; *fig.* get the better of. **have the lee gauge of** be leeward of. 4 *broad gauge*: see BROAD *a. narrow gauge*: see NARROW *a.*

II An instrument for measuring. †5 = *gauging-rod* s.v. GAUGE *v.* Also (*dial.*), a pair of connected rods dropped into a furnace to test whether it needs more fuel. M16–L18. 6 A graduated instrument for measuring a fluctuating quantity or force, as rainfall, tide, wind, a stream. L17. 7 An instrument for testing whether a tool, a machine part, wire, etc., conforms to standard dimensions. L17. 8 *fig.* A means of judging or assessing; a standard, a criterion. L17. 9 A carpenter's adjustable tool for making parallel lines. L17. 10 *Printing.* A strip of metal or other material used for measuring and controlling the depth of a margin, the length of a page, etc. Now chiefly *Hist.* L17. 11 A device attached or linked to a receptacle in order to indicate the extent, depth, condition, etc., of its contents. L18.

6 S. HAUGHTON The sea-waves were recorded on the self-registering tide gauges. 7 JAMES SMITH It is much easier to file correctly with the assistance of a guage than a pair of callipers. 8 M. HUNTER Duration of an emotion is no gauge of its intensity. 11 *fuel gauge, oil gauge, pressure gauge, tyre gauge,* etc.

Comb. (Physics): *gauge function*: see sense 1c above; **gauge invariance** the property of remaining unaltered under a gauge transformation; **gauge theory** a quantum field theory of subatomic particles and their interactions which makes use of gauge functions; **gauge transformation** the introduction of a gauge function into an equation.

gauge /geɪdʒ/ *v.t.* Also ***gage.** LME. [ONFr. *gauger*, var. of (also mod.) *jauger*: cf. prec.] 1 Measure or determine the exact dimensions, proportions, or amount of (esp. an object of standard size, as wire, a bolt, or a fluctuating force, as rainfall or wind); ascertain the exact depth of (a liquid). LME. 2 Find the capacity or content of (a cask or similar vessel) by measurement and calculation, esp. by means of a gauging-rod. LME. 3 Mark or measure off (a specified distance). LME. 4 *fig.* Evaluate, appraise; estimate, take the measure of; *esp.* assess the character, temperament, etc., of (a person). L16. 5 Cause to conform to standard dimensions; *spec.* cut (bricks or stones) to a uniform size. E17. 6 *Building.* Mix (plaster) in the proper proportions for quick drying. L17. 7 *Dressmaking.* Draw up (part of a garment) in a series of parallel gathers. L19.

1 LD BERNERS He gauged ye depnesse of the dyche with a speare. JOHN PHILLIPS I have gauged . . the river . . and obtained . . the quantity of water in cubic feet per day. P. WARNER The copper-tin alloy was not always accurately gauged. *Industry Week* Productivity is gaged by output per manhour. 4 G. ORWELL With no clocks and no daylight it was hard to gauge the time. G. GREENE Money was never the standard by which values were gauged. E. L. DOCTOROW Everyone talked around Freud, glancing at him . . to gauge his mood.

Comb.: **gauging-rod** an instrument for measuring the capacity or contents of casks.

gaugeable *a.* (*a*) *Hist.* (of a cask of liquor etc.) liable to be gauged for excise duty; (*b*) able to be measured or gauged: LME. **gauger** *n.* (*a*) a person who or an instrument which gauges; (*b*) *spec.* an official who measures the quantity of liquor in a cask; *esp.* (now *Hist.* & *Sc.*) an exciseman: ME.

gauk *a.* var. of GAWK *a.*

Gaul /gɔːl/ *n.* Also (earlier) †**Galle**. LME. [f. L *Gallus*, prob. f. Celtic. Cf. GALLIC *a.*[1]] 1 A native or inhabitant of ancient Gaul, a region roughly corresponding to the modern France and Belgium with parts of Germany and the Netherlands, and formerly including the northern part of Italy. LME. 2 A Frenchman, a Frenchwoman. *poet.* & *joc.* M17.

Gaulic *a.* (now *rare*) = GALLIC *a.*[1] 2 E17.

†**gaulding** *n.* var. of GAULIN.

gauleiter /ˈgaʊlʌɪtə/ *n.* M20. [G, f. *Gau* administrative district + *Leiter* leader.] A political official controlling a Nazi district; *transf.* an overbearing (local) official.

M. MCLUHAN Exclusive playgrounds for the *gauleiters* of big business.

gaulin /ˈgɔːlɪn/ *n. W. Indies.* Also (earlier) †**gaulding**. E18. [Origin unkn.] Any of various kinds of heron and egret.

Gaulish /ˈgɔːlɪʃ/ *a.* & *n.* M17. [f. GAUL + -ISH[1].] A *adj.* Of or pertaining to the ancient Gauls. Also (chiefly *poet.* & *humorous*) French. M17. B *n.* The language of the ancient Gauls. M17.

Gaullism /ˈgəʊlɪz(ə)m/ *n.* Also **de Gaull-** /də ˈgəʊl-/. M20. [Fr. *Gaullisme*, f. *de Gaulle* (see below): see -ISM.] (Adherence to) the nationalist principles of General Charles de Gaulle (1890–1970), French military and political leader.

Gaullist /ˈgəʊlɪst/ *a.* & *n.* Also **de Gaull-** /də ˈgəʊl-/. M20. [Fr. *Gaulliste*, f. as prec.: see -IST.] A *adj.* Supporting or pertaining to Gaullism. M20. B *n.* An adherent of Gaullism. M20.

gault /gɔːlt/ *n.* L16. [Origin unkn.] A thick heavy clay; *spec.* (*Geol.*, usu. **G-**) a series of clays and marls between the upper and lower greensand in S. England. Also *gault-clay*.

gaulty *a.* boggy and clayey L18.

gaultheria /gɔːlˈθɪərɪə/ *n.* M19. [mod.L, f. J.-F. *Gaultier* (*c* 1708–56), Canad. botanist: see -IA[1].] Any of various evergreen shrubs constituting the genus *Gaultheria*, of the heath family; *esp.* the checkerberry, *G. procumbens*, of N. America.

gaum /gɔːm/ *n.*[1] *obs.* exc. *dial.* Orig. †**gome**. ME. [ON *gaumr* care, heed = OS *gōma* OHG *gouma*, f. Goth. base repr. by *gaumjan* take notice of.] Heed, attention, notice; wit, understanding.

gaum *n.*[2] see GORM *n.*

gaum /gɔːm/ *v.*[1]*t. obs.* exc. *dial.* M17. [Origin unkn.] Pull about with the hands; handle improperly.

gaum /gɔːm/ *v.*[2]*i.* Chiefly *dial.* Also **gorm**. L17. [Origin unkn.] Stare vacantly or stupidly.

gaum /gɔːm/ *v.*[3]*t.* Also **gorm**. L18. [Cf. COOM *n.* 3.] Smear with a sticky substance; daub (something sticky) on a surface.

gaumless *a.* see GORMLESS.

gaumy /ˈgɔːmi/ *a.* Also **gormy**. L19. [f. GAUM *v.*[3] + -Y[1].] Of painting: coarsely executed, daubed. Also (*dial.*), sticky.

†**gaunch** *n.*, *v.* vars. of GANCH *n.*, *v.*

gaunt *n.* & *v.*[1] var. of GANT *n.* & *v.*

gaunt /gɔːnt/ *a.* & *v.*[2] LME. [Origin unkn.] A *adj.* †1 Not fat; slender, slim. LME–M18. 2 Abnormally lean, esp. from exhaustion or lack of nourishment; thin and angular in appearance. LME. 3 *transf.* Of an inanimate thing: desolate and forbidding in appearance or character. Formerly, of a sound: hollow. E19.

2 J. WAINWRIGHT He was a tall man and gaunt to the point of emaciation. 3 T. HARDY I am . . surrounded by gaunt realities. T. C. WOLFE The trees rose gaunt and stark.

B *v.t.* Make (excessively) lean or thin. Chiefly as *gaunted* ppl a. Now chiefly *US.* L16.

gauntly *adv.* M18. **gauntness** *n.* E17.

gauntlet /ˈgɔːntlɪt/ *n.*[1] LME. [(O)Fr. *gantelet* dim. of *gant* glove, f. Gmc base extant only in ON *vǫttr* glove (Sw., Da. *vante*): see -LET.] 1 A usu. leather-lined glove of mail worn as part of medieval armour. Also = CESTUS *n.*[2] LME. 2 A stout glove, reaching to the lower part of the arm, used in riding, fencing, falconry, wicket-keeping, etc. M19. b The part of a glove designed to cover the wrist. L19.

Phrases: **fling down, throw (down)**, etc., **the gauntlet** [from the medieval custom of throwing down a gauntlet when challenging someone to combat] *fig.* issue a challenge; show defiance. **pick up** or **take up the gauntlet** *fig.* accept a challenge; undertake the defence of a person or opinion.

gauntleted *a.* armed or equipped with a gauntlet E19.

gauntlet /ˈgɔːntlɪt/ *n.*[2] Also ***gant-** /ˈgɑːnt-/. M17. [Alt. of GANTLOPE, by assim. to prec.] *run* (or †*pass*) *the gauntlet*, run between two rows of people and be struck by them with sticks, knotted cords, etc., as a form of (orig. military or naval) punishment; *transf.* & *fig.* pass through a series of dangerous or unpleasant experiences.

gauntry *n.* var. of GANTRY.

gaup *v.* see GAWP.

gaupus *n.* var. of GAWPUS.

gaur /ˈgaʊə/ *n.* Also **gour**. E19. [Skt *gaura* f. base also of COW *n.*[1]] A large wild ox, *Bos gaurus*, found in forests from India to Malaysia. Also called *Indian bison*.

gauss /gaʊs/ *n.* L19. [K. F. *Gauss* (1777–1855) Ger. mathematician.] *Physics* Orig., a unit of magnetic field strength: = OERSTED. Later, a cgs unit of magnetic induction (equivalent to 10^{-4} tesla) equal to the flux density which exerts a force of one dyne per centimetre on a wire carrying one electromagnetic unit of current (ten amperes) perpendicular to the field.

Gaussian /ˈgaʊsɪən/ *a.* L19. [f. as prec. + -IAN.] Discovered or formulated by Gauss; *esp.* (*Statistics*) designating a curve, function, statistical process, etc., that is described mathematically by a function of the form (exp $[-(x-\mu)^2/2\sigma^2])/\sigma\sqrt{2\pi}$, where x is the variable, μ the mean, and σ^2 the variance. Cf. NORMAL *a.* 7.

Gaussian distribution a normal distribution.

gauze /gɔːz/ *n.* & *a.* M16. [Fr. *gaze*, perh. f. *Gaza* a town in Palestine.] A *n.* 1 A thin transparent fabric of silk, linen, cotton, etc. Also *Med.*, thin loosely woven material used for dressings and swabs. M16. 2 In full *wire gauze*. A very fine wire mesh. E19. 3 A thin transparent haze. M19.

3 T. HARDY A blue gauze of smoke.

B *adj.* Made of gauze. M18.

gauzelike *a.* resembling gauze, gauzy L18.

gauze /gɔːz/ *v.* L18. [f. the n.] 1 *v.t.* Cover (as) with gauze; give a gauzy appearance to. Chiefly as *gauzed* ppl a. L18. 2 *v.i.* Melt hazily *into.* E20.

1 E. BOWEN Midges gauzed the air.

gauzy /ˈgɔːzi/ *a.* L18. [f. GAUZE *n.* + -Y[1].] Of the nature of or resembling gauze; thin and transparent.

gauzily *adv.* E20. **gauziness** *n.* E19.

gavage /gaˈvɑːʒ/ *n.* L19. [Fr.] A method of forcible feeding by means of a force-pump and a stomach-tube.

gavel /ˈgav(ə)l/ *n.*[1] & *a.* Long *obs.* exc. *Hist.* [OE *gafol* f. Gmc, rel. to base of GIVE *v.*] A *n.* 1 †a Payment to a superior; tribute. OE–L15. b Rent. OE. †2 Interest on money lent; usury. OE–L15. B *attrib.* or as *adj.* Chiefly *Law.* Of or relating to payments or services exacted from a tenant. OE.

gavel /ˈgav(ə)l/ *n.*[2] *obs.* exc. *dial.* LME. [ONFr. *gavel* masc., *gavelle* fem. (mod. *javelle*).] A quantity of corn cut and ready to be made into a sheaf.

lie on the gavel (of corn) lie unbound.

gavel /ˈgav(ə)l/ *n.*[3] E19. [f. GAVEL(KIND.] *Hist.* A partition of land made among a whole tribe or sept on the death of the holder. Cf. GAVELKIND 3b.

Comb.: **Gavel Act, Law** a statute (1704) enforcing the practice of English gavelkind on Irish Catholics, but allowing the eldest son to inherit the whole estate if he conformed to the Church of Ireland.

gavel /ˈgav(ə)l/ *n.*[4] Orig. *US.* E19. [Origin unkn.] 1 A stonemason's mallet. E19. 2 An auctioneer's hammer; a small hammer used by a chairman, judge, etc., to call for order. M19.

2 R. P. WARREN Somebody snickered in the courtroom and the judge rapped with his gavel.

gavel /ˈgav(ə)l/ *v.*[1]*t. obs.* exc. *dial.* Infl. **-ll-**. LME. [f. GAVEL *n.*[2] Cf. (O)Fr. *javeler*, med.L *gavellare*.] Gather (mown corn) into heaps for loading.

gavel /ˈgav(ə)l/ *v.*[2]*t.* Infl. **-ll-**. E19. [f. GAVEL *n.*[3]] *Hist.* Divide and distribute (land) according to the practice of gavelkind.

gavel /ˈgav(ə)l/ *v.*[3] Chiefly *US.* Infl. **-ll-**, ***-l-**. E20. [f. GAVEL *n.*[4]] 1 *v.i.* Use a gavel. E20. 2 *v.t.* Bring (an assembly) to order or dismiss (a speaker) by use of a gavel. M20.

1 T. DREISER Gaveling for order and ordering the arrest of the offender. 2 *Time* He gaveled his Senate . . committee into session.

†**gavelet** *n.* ME–M18. [f. GAVEL *n.*[1] Cf. med.L *gavelettum.*] *Law.* A legal process against a tenant for non-payment of rent, esp. for lands held in gavelkind.

gavelkind /ˈgav(ə)lkʌɪnd, -kɪnd/ *n.* ME. [f. GAVEL *n.*[1] + KIND *n.*] *Hist.* 1 A kind of (chiefly Kentish) land-tenure (abolished in 1925) similar to socage but distinguished by the custom of dividing a deceased tenant's land equally among his sons. ME. 2 *gen.* The custom of dividing a deceased person's property equally among all (male) heirs. M16. 3 *transf.* a A Welsh system of property inheritance similar to the Kentish (see sense 1 above). M16. b More fully *Irish gavelkind*. A system of adding a deceased person's land to the common stock and re-dividing the whole area among all members of the tribe or sept. E17.

2 *fig.*: DONNE For God shall impart to us all a mysterious Gavel-kind, a mysterious Equality of fulness of Glory to us all.

Comb.: **Gavelkind Act** = *Gavel Act, Law* s.v. GAVEL *n.*[3]

gavelkinder *n.* (*rare*) a person holding land in gavelkind L16.

gaveller /ˈgav(ə)lə/ *n. obs.* exc. *Hist.* ME. [f. GAVEL *n.*[1] + -ER[1].] †1 A usurer. Only in ME. 2 In the Forest of Dean: an officer of the Crown who grants mining rights and collects dues. L17. 3 A person who pays gavel (GAVEL *n.*[1] 1b) for rented land. M19.

gavelock /ˈgav(ə)lɒk/ *n.* [OE *gafeluc* dim. of *gafol*, *geafel* fork: cf. GABLE *n.*] 1 A javelin, a dart. Long *obs.* exc. *Hist.* OE. 2 An iron crowbar or lever. Now *dial.* L15. †3 A metal spur for a fighting cock. Only in L17.

gavial *n.* var. of GHARIAL.

gavotte /gəˈvɒt/ *n.* & *v.* L17. [Fr. f. mod.Prov. *gavoto*, f. *Gavot* an inhabitant of the Alps.] A *n.* 1 A medium-paced dance popular in the 18th cent. L17. 2 A piece of music for this dance, composed in common time with each phrase beginning on the third beat of the bar; a piece of music in this rhythm, *esp.* one which forms a movement of a suite. E18. **B** *v.i.* Dance a gavotte. E19.

gavroche /gavrɔʃ/ *n.* Pl. pronounced same. L19. [Fr., a gamin in Victor Hugo's novel *Les Misérables*.] A gamin, gamine, or street urchin, esp. in Paris.

†**gaw** *v.i.* ME–E19. [ON *gá* heed.] Gape, stare; look intently.

Gawd /gɔːd/ *n. slang.* Also **g-**. L19. [Alt.] = GOD *n.*: chiefly as int. & in exclamatory phrs. corresp. to those s.v. GOD *n.* 5.

for Gawd's sake, Gawd knows.

Comb.: **Gawdelpus, Gawd-help-us** a helpless or exasperating person.

†**gawdy** *a.* var. of GAUDY *a.*

gawk /gɔːk/ *n.* L17. [In sense 1 perh. f. next; in sense 2 f. GAWK *v.*] **1** An awkward, stupid, or bashful person. L17. **2** A look, a glance. M20.

1 A. CARTER Great gawk of an ignorant black girl. 2 E. O'BRIEN I had a gawk at the letter she got.

gawkish *a.* awkward, bashful L19.

gawk /gɔːk/ *a. dial.* Also **gauk**. E18. [App. contr. of GALLACK.] Left. Chiefly in *gawk-handed*, left-handed.

gawk /gɔːk/ *v.i. colloq.* L18. [Perh. f. GAWK *n.* 1, but perh. an iterative f. GAW *v.* (with suff. as in *tal-k, wal-k, lur-k*).] Stare stupidly, gape.

K. KESEY I want you workin', not gawkin' around like some big useless cow! C. D. EBY Gawking in wonder at the falling bombs.

gawker *n.* M20.

gawky /ˈgɔːki/ *n.* & *a.* E18. [f. GAWK *n.* or *v.* + -Y[1].] **A** *n.* An awkward or stupid person; a lout. E18.

GEO. ELIOT Nothing makes a woman more of a gawky than . . showing tempers in public.

B *adj.* Of a person, occas. a thing: awkward, ungainly. M18.

G. GREENE The big boyish lover with his sulks . . and his gawky abandonment to joy and grief. *Sport* Are you fat and flabby? Or skinny and gawky?

gawkily *adv.* E19. **gawkiness** *n.* L19.

gawn /gɔːn/ *n.* Now *dial.* L15. [Contr. of GALLON.] **1** A gallon, a gallon measure. L15. **2** A bucket, *spec.* with one long stave serving as a handle. Also, a ladle. L17.

gawp /gɔːp/ *v.i.* Also (*arch.* & *dial.*) **gaup**, (*dial.*) **gorp**. L17. [Perh. alt. of GAPE *v.*: cf. GALP.] Yawn, gape; stare stupidly or in astonishment.

R. CAMPBELL Roaring mouths that gawp like cod. B. BAINBRIDGE It was raining heavily, but they stood there, gawping up at the windows.

gawper *n.* M20.

gawpus /ˈgɔːpəs/ *n. dial.* Also **gaupus**. L18. [f. prec.] A fool, a clumsy stupid lout.

¶Earliest in comb. *gilly-gawpus*, with 1st elem. of unkn. origin.

gay /geɪ/ *a.*, *adv.*, & *n.* ME. [(O)Fr. *gai*, of unkn. origin.] **A** *adj.* **1** Full of, disposed to, or indicating joy and mirth; light-hearted, carefree. ME. **b** Airy, offhand, casual. L18. **2** Given to pleasure; freq. *euphem.*, dissolute, immoral. LME. **b** Leading an immoral life; *spec.* engaging in prostitution. *slang.* E19. **3** Good, excellent, fine. Now chiefly *dial.* LME. **b** Of a woman: beautiful, charming, debonair. Long *arch.* & *poet.* LME. **c** In good health, well. *dial.* M19. **4** Showy, brilliant, brightly coloured. Also, brightly decorated *with*. LME. **b** Finely or showily dressed. Now *rare.* LME. †**c** Superficially attractive; (of reasoning etc.) specious, plausible. LME–L18. **5** Of a quantity or amount: considerable, reasonable, fair. (Cf. GEY *a.*) Chiefly *Sc.* L18. **6** Of an animal: lively, spirited, alert. E19. **b** Of a (dog's) tail: carried high or erect. E20. **7** (Of a person, sometimes *spec.* a man) homosexual; of or pertaining to homosexuals; (of a place etc.) intended for or frequented by homosexuals. Chiefly *colloq.* M20.

1 J. RHYS The music was gay but the words were sad. M. MOORCOCK This event lifted my spirits and I became quite gay. **b** O. SITWELL A gay, insouciant race of extroverts. 2 W. COWPER Silent and chaste she steals along, far from the world's gay busy throng. 3 M. TWAIN My business and your Law practice ought to make a pretty gay team. 4 E. PEACOCK Their costumes were gay with ribbons. **b** SHAKES. *Oth.* Never lack'd gold, and yet went never gay. 6 B. VESEY-FITZGERALD This terrier should impress with his fearless and gay disposition. 7 D. LODGE They thought Philip was gay because he had taken Charles Boon into his apartment.

Special collocations & phrases: **gay cat** *US slang* (*a*) a hobo who accepts occasional work; (*b*) a young tramp, *esp.* one in company with an older man. **gay dog** a man given to revelling or self-indulgence. **gay deceiver** (*a*) a deceitful rake; (*b*) in *pl.* (*slang*), shaped pads for increasing the apparent size of the female breasts. *gay Greek*: see GREEK *n.* 5. **Gay Lib, Liberation** (the advocacy of) the liberation of homosexuals from social stigma and discrimination. **gay plague** *colloq.* (sometimes considered *offensive*) Aids (so called because first identified amongst homosexuals). **get gay** *US slang* act in an impertinent or overfamiliar way. **the gay science** [Prov. *gai saber*] the art of poetry.

B *adv.* **1** Merrily, joyously; brightly, showily. Now chiefly with pres. and pa. pples, as *gay-chirping, -painted*, etc. *arch.* & *poet.* LME. **2** Very, considerably, somewhat. (Cf. GEY *adv.*) *Sc.* & *dial.* L17.

1 J. THOMSON Those gay-spent, festive nights. 2 SIR W. SCOTT I ken I'm gay thick in the head.

C *n.* **1** Anything bright or showy; an ornament, a child's toy. Now *dial.* LME. †**b** *fig.* A trifle, a childish amusement. L16–L17. **2** A picture, esp. in a book. Also, a picture-book. Now *dial.* M17. **3** A homosexual; sometimes *spec.* a male homosexual. Chiefly *colloq.* M20.

gaydom *n.* (chiefly *colloq.*) the realm or world of homosexuals L20.

gay /geɪ/ *v.* L16. [f. the adj.] **1** *v.t.* Make gay or pleasant, embellish, brighten *up*. L16. **2** *v.i.* Be gay; play. *obs.* exc. *dial.* M17.

1 *News Chronicle* The charming effect of houses gayed up with these flower-filled boxes.

gayal /gʌɪˈjɑːl/ *n.* L18. [Bengali.] A semi-domesticated ox, *Bos frontalis*, of India and SE Asia, which is black or brown with white legs, and possibly a variety of the gaur.

gayatri /ˈgɑːjətriː/ *n.* L18. [Skt, f. *ga* sing.] A Vedic metre comprising three octosyllabic lines; a hymn, verse, etc., composed in this metre, *esp.* the verse of the Rig-Veda repeated daily as a prayer by brahmins.

gayety *n.* see GAIETY.

gaylussite /geɪˈlʌsʌɪt/ *n.* E19. [f. J. L. *Gay-Lussac* (1778–1850), Fr. physicist + -ITE[1].] *Min.* A rare monoclinic hydrated carbonate of calcium and sodium occurring as white or yellowish crystals.

gayly *adv.* see GAILY.

gayness /ˈgeɪnɪs/ *n.* LME. [f. GAY *a.* + -NESS.] †**1** (A) delight, (a) pleasure; merriment. LME–E17. **2** Brilliant or showy appearance, brightness. Long *rare* or *obs.* LME. **3** Cheerfulness, mirth. L19. **4** Homosexuality. L20.

gaysome /ˈgeɪs(ə)m/ *a. arch.* & *poet.* E17. [f. GAY *a.* + -SOME[1].] Full of or giving rise to gaiety; merry, cheery, pleasant.

gazabo /gəˈzeɪbəʊ/ *n. slang* (freq. *derog.*). Chiefly *US.* Also **gazebo**. Pl. **-os**. L19. [Perh. f. Sp. *gazapo* a sly fellow.] A fellow, a guy.

B. PENTON Aw, leave the old gazabo He's drunk.

gazania /gəˈzeɪnɪə/ *n.* E19. [mod.L (see below), f. Theodorus *Gaza* (1398–1478), Greek scholar.] Any of various mostly southern African plants of the genus *Gazania*, of the composite family, with conspicuous orange, yellow, scarlet, etc., ray-florets; esp. *G. rigens* (also called *treasure-flower*), grown as an ornamental flower.

gaze /geɪz/ *n.* M16. [f. the vb.] **1** That which is gazed at; a spectacle, a sight. *obs.* exc. *dial.* M16. **2** The act of staring; a steady or intent look. M16.

1 A. M. BENNETT His father lolled in his coach, and was the gaze of the village. 2 F. TUOHY Witek watched her, with hurt love in his gaze. **at (†a, †the) gaze** gazing in wonder etc.; *spec.* in *Her.* (of a stag etc.) looking out of the shield, full-face. *meet a person's gaze*: see MEET *v.*

Comb.: **gaze-hound** a hound that hunts by sight.

†**gazeful** *a.* (*rare*, Spenser) gazing intently: only in L16. **gazement** *n.* (*rare*) a stare, a look; observation: L16.

gaze /geɪz/ *v.* LME. [Origin uncertain: perh. rel. to GAW.] **1** *v.i.* Orig., stare vacantly or curiously. Now usu., look intently or fixedly (*at, on, upon*, etc.). LME. **2** *v.t.* Look fixedly at, stare at. *poet.* L16.

1 J. STEINBECK He gazed about with mild, half-blind eyes. DAY LEWIS I would tag around . . content to gaze upon him idolatrously. *gaze at one's navel*: see NAVEL 1. 2 P. J. BAILEY Who dare gaze the sun.

Comb.: **gazing-stock** (now *rare*) a person on whom others gaze or stare.

gazer *n.* M16.

gazebo /gəˈziːbəʊ/ *n.*[1] Pl. **-o(e)s**. M18. [Perh. joc. f. GAZE *v.*, in imitation of Latin futures in *-ebo*.] **1** A building or structure (as a turret, lantern, summer-house, etc.) which commands a view. M18. **2** A projecting window or balcony. M19.

gazebo *n.*[2] var. of GAZABO.

gazelle /gəˈzɛl/ *n.* Also **-el**. Pl. same, **-s**. E17. [OFr. *gazel*, prob. f. Sp. *gacel* f. Arab. *ghazāl*.] Any of various small graceful soft-eyed usu. fawn and white antelopes of Africa and Asia, of the subfamily Antilopinae, *esp.* any of those of the genera *Gazella* and *Procapra*.

gazette /gəˈzɛt/ *n.* Also **G-**. E17. [Fr., or its source It. *gazzetta*, orig. Venetian It. *gazeta de la novità* i.e. a 'halfpennyworth of news', so called because sold for a *gazeta*, a Venetian coin of small value: see -ETTE.] **1** Orig., a news-sheet; a periodical publication giving an account of current events. Now, a newspaper, *esp.* (the title of) the official newspaper of an organization or institution. E17. **2** *spec.* (The title of) an official journal in Britain containing lists of government appointments, bankruptcies, and other public notices; an official journal of any government. M17.

1 R. KIPLING Far-off Calcutta papers, such as the *Indigo Planters' Gazette* 2 **be in the gazette** have one's bankruptcy published. *The Belfast Gazette, The Edinburgh Gazette, The London Gazette*, etc.

gazette /gəˈzɛt/ *v.t.* L17. [f. the n.] Publish in a gazette. Usu. in *pass.*, be the subject of an announcement in an official gazette, *esp.* be named as appointed *to* a post, command, etc.

W. S. CHURCHILL In March 1895 I was gazetted to the 4th Hussars. P. PORTER Though the crime is not gazetted Punishment is palpable and that's the same As Law.

gazetteer /gazɪˈtɪə/ *n.* & *v.* E17. [Fr. *gazettier* (now *gazetier*) f. It. *gazzettiere*, f. as GAZETTE *n.*: see -EER.] **A** *n.* **1** A journalist; *spec.* one appointed and paid by the Government. Now *Hist.* E17. **2** A geographical index or dictionary. E18. †**3** A newspaper. Only in M18. **B** *v.* **1** *v.i.* Write for a gazette or gazetteer. Now *rare.* L18. **2** *v.t.* Describe geographically in a gazetteer. *rare.* L19.

gazob /gəˈzɒb/ *n. Austral. slang.* E20. [Origin uncertain: perh. f. GAZABO.] A fool, a blunderer.

†**gazon** *n.* E–M18. [Fr. = grass, a piece of turf.] A wedge-shaped piece of turf used in fortification to line parapets etc. Usu. in *pl.*

gazoo *n.* var. of KAZOO.

gazook /gəˈzuːk/ *n. slang.* E20. [Origin unkn. Cf. GAZABO, GAZOB.] A fool, a stupid or unpleasant person.

gazoomph *v.* & *n.* see GAZUMP.

gazpacho /gəsˈpɑːtʃəʊ, *foreign* gaθˈpatʃo/ *n.* Also **gas-**. Pl. **-os**, /-əʊz, *foreign* -ɔs/. E19. [Sp.] A Spanish soup made from tomatoes, peppers, cucumber, garlic, etc., and served cold.

gazump /gəˈzʌmp/ *v.* & *n. colloq.* Also **-zoomph** /-zʊmf/, **-zumph** /-zʌmf/. E20. [Origin unkn.] **A** *v.t.* Swindle; *spec.* raise the price of a house etc. after accepting an offer from (an intending buyer). E20. **B** *n.* A swindle. M20.

gazunder /gəˈzʌndə/ *v.t. colloq.* L20. [f. GAZUMP + UNDER *adv.*] Of a house-buyer: reduce the value of an offer already accepted by (a seller) while threatening otherwise to withdraw.

gazunderer *n.* L20.

†**geal** *v.t.* & *i.* LME–E19. [(O)Fr. *geler* f. L *gelare* freeze.] Congeal.

gean /giːn/ *n.* M16. [OFr. *guine* (mod. *guigne*): ult. origin unkn.] The wild sweet cherry, *Prunus avium*. Also, the fruit of this tree.

geanticlinal /ˌdʒiːantɪˈklʌɪn(ə)l/ *n.* & *a.* L19. [f. Gk *gē* earth + ANTICLINAL.] *Geol.* A *n.* = next. Now *rare.* L19. B *adj.* Of, pertaining to, or of the nature of a geanticline. L19.

geanticline /dʒiːˈantɪklʌɪn/ *n.* L19. [Back-form. f. prec.] *Geol.* A large-scale upward flexure of the earth's crust; a broad anticline.

gear /gɪə/ *n.* & *v.* Also †**geer**. ME. [ON *gervi*, *gǫrvi* corresp. to OS *garawī*, *gar(e)wī* f. Gmc: rel. to GAR *v.*, YARE.] A *n.* I Equipment. 1 *collect. sing.* Items of personal wear; apparel, attire, esp. (*colloq.*) for young people. ME. †b In *pl.* Habits, manners. Only in ME. 2 Armour, arms, equipment for battle. *arch.* ME. 3a Harness for draught animals. Formerly usu. in *pl.* ME. b Accoutrements of a riding horse, or of the rider. Freq. w. specifying wd. LME.

1 WORDSWORTH Peasants in their homely gear. *Daily Mail* Prince William . . starts new fashions in toddler gear. 2 CARLYLE Of serviceable fighting-gear small stock. 3a S. JOHNSON She rises before the sun to order the horses to their geers. b J. YEATS The Egyptians were skilful manufacturers of riding gear.

II Apparatus. 4 Apparatus for a specified activity; appliances, implements, tackle, tools. ME. †b A set of heddles. E16–M19. 5 A combination of wheels, levers, and other mechanical appliances usu. for a given purpose; *esp.* the appliances or furnishings connected with the acting portions of any piece of mechanism. Freq. preceded by defining wd. E16. b Wheels working upon one another by means of teeth etc. E19. c In full *landing-gear.* The undercarriage of an aircraft. E20. 6 *Naut.* Rigging. M17. 7 The arrangements connecting a motor or engine with its work. E19. b Any of the several sets of gearwheels in a motor-vehicle, bicycle, etc., which can be used to alter the relation between the speed of the driving mechanism and of the driven part. Also, the particular state of adjustment of this relation. L19.

5 A. S. NEILL Another tried to put my lathe in screw-cutting gear when it was running. 7 **in gear** connected with the motor, working (*lit.* & *fig.*). **out of gear** with the connection with the motor interrupted or not working; *fig.* out of order. b J. GARDNER The grind of gears came, meaning he was halfway up the hill. *fig.*: *New Statesman* If Labour is to win the next election . . there now has to be a shift into a different gear. *bottom gear*: see BOTTOM *a.* **change gear** engage a different gear in a vehicle. *differential gear*: see DIFFERENTIAL *a.* 4. FIRST *gear. high gear*: see HIGH *a. low gear*: see LOW *a. reverse gear*: see REVERSE *a. top gear*: see TOP *a.*

III Stuff. 8 Goods, movable property, household utensils. LME. †b Objects of a specified kind. LME–E19. c Possessions in general, wealth, money. *Sc.* & *north. dial.* M16. 9a Discourse, doctrine, talk; *derog.* 'stuff', nonsense. Long *arch.* & *dial.* LME. b Doings, 'goings on'. Now *arch.* & *dial.* LME. c A matter, an affair, a business. *obs.* exc. *dial.* M16. 10 A material substance or stuff; *derog.* rubbish. *obs.* exc. *dial.* L15. b Corrupt matter, pus. M16–M17.

9 K. HULME The gear he spoke of is three suitcases and a forlorn carton of books. b A. S. SWAN That foolish, misguided sister of yours has married an old man for his gear! 10a DRYDEN Priests with prayers and other godly gear. b E. L. LINTON We shall have such fun! . . It will be good gear, I can tell you! c SIR W. SCOTT I understand this gear better than you do. 11 C. HEYDON That out of wheat there should spring vp darnell . . and smuttie geare. b HENRY MORE The wound of his throat gaping, but no gear or corruption in it.

Comb.: **gearbox**, **gearcase** (a box, case enclosing) the gearing of a motor vehicle etc.; **gear-change** (*a*) the action or an act of engaging a different gear in a vehicle; (*b*) *US* a gear lever; **gear lever** a lever employed to engage or change gear; **gear-shift** *N. Amer.* a gear lever; **gearwheel** a cog wheel, *esp.* one such in a bicycle which is driven directly by the pedals.

B *v.* †1 *v.t.* Adorn; array; dress. ME–L17. 2 *v.t.* Equip. *arch.* LME. 3 *v.t.* Harness (a draught animal). Also foll. by *up.* M17. 4a *v.i.* Be in gear, work smoothly *with.* M18. b *v.t.* Put (machinery) into gear; connect, link (as if) by gearing. M19.

4b *fig.*: *Spectator* An entire [ballet] production geared to the Bolshoi interpretation.

With advs. in specialized senses: **gear down** provide with a low gear, put into a lower gear. **gear up** (*a*) provide with a high gear, put into a higher gear; (*b*) set in readiness, prepare (usu. in *pass.*); (*c*) equip oneself, get ready.

geared *a.* †(*a*) equipped, armed; (*b*) having or provided with gears; (*c*) *Finance* having (high, low) gearing (GEARING *n.* 4): L15. **gearless** *a.* L19.

gearing /ˈgɪərɪŋ/ *n.* E19. [f. GEAR *n.* & *v.* + -ING[1].] 1 Equipment, working implements. *rare.* E19. 2 Harness. *dial.* M19. 3 The process of fitting with gears. Also, the set or arrangement of gears in a machine. M19. 4 *Finance.* The ratio of a company's total capital to its equity capital; the proportion of capital existing in the form of debt. M20.

3 *Footloose* Incredibly low gearing allowing the pedals to be turned quickly. 4 *Fortune* [Rupert] Murdoch operates with a phenomenal amount of debt, or gearing.

geason /ˈgiːz(ə)n/ *a.* [OE *gǣsne*, *gēsne* barren. Cf. OHG *keisinī* barrenness.] †1 Producing scantily, barren, unproductive. OE–LME. 2 Scantily produced; rare, scarce, uncommon. Long *obs.* exc. *dial.* LME. †3 Seldom encountered, extraordinary, amazing. Only in L16.

gebang /dʒɪˈbaŋ/ *n.* E19. [Malay *gebang.*] More fully *gebang palm.* A fan palm, *Corypha elata*, of tropical Asia, the fibre of whose leaf-petioles is used to make hats and ropes.

Gebrauchsmusik /gəˈbraʊksmuziːk/ *n.* M20. [G, f. *Gebrauch* use + *Musik* music.] Music intended primarily for practical use and performance; *esp.* music considered suitable for amateur groups and domestic playing.

gebur /gəˈbʊə/ *n.* [OE *ġebūr* = OS *gibūr*, OHG *gibūr(o)*: cf. BOOR, NEIGHBOUR *n.* & *a.*] *Hist.* A tenant-farmer in the pre-Conquest English community.

geck /gɛk/ *n.*[1] *obs.* exc. *dial.* E16. [Of LDu. origin: cf. MLG *geck*, MDu. *g(h)ec(k)*, Du. *gek* adj. & n.: rel. to *gecken* GECK *v.*] A fool, a simpleton; a butt, a dupe.

geck /gɛk/ *n.*[2] Chiefly *Sc.* E16. [Du. (= G) *geck* vbl n. corresp. to *gecken*: see GECK *v.*] A gesture of derision; an expression of scorn or contempt.

geck /gɛk/ *v. Sc.* & *north.* L16. [App. f. LG *gecken* = MDu. *ghecken*, Du. *gekken*, G *gecken*: see GECK *n.*[1]] †1 *v.t.* Mock, deceive, cheat. Only in L16. 2 *v.i.* Scoff *at*, use mocking language or gestures. E17. 3 *v.i.* & *t.* Toss (the head) scornfully; look proudly (at). E18.

gecko /ˈgɛkəʊ/ *n.* Also **gekko**. Pl. **-o(e)s**. L18. [Malay dial. *geko*, *gekok*, ult. imit. Cf. TOKAY *n.*[2]] Any of various small insectivorous usu. nocturnal lizards of the family Gekkonidae, widespread in warm regions, many being notable for adhesive pads on the feet enabling them to climb smooth or overhanging surfaces, and for their vocalizations.

Moorish gecko: see MOORISH *a.*[2] 1.

ged /gɛd/ *n. Sc.* & *north.* ME. [ON *gedda* rel. to *gaddr* GAD *n.*[1]] The pike (fish).

gedact /gəˈdakt/ *n.* M19. [G *gedackt*, obs. pa. pple of *decken* cover.] *Mus.* An organ flue-stop having its pipes closed at the top.

Gedankenexperiment /gəˈdaŋk(ə)n ɛˌkspɛrɪm(ə)nt/ *n.* M20. [G, f. *Gedanken* thought + *Experiment* experiment.] = *thought-experiment* s.v. THOUGHT *n.*[1]

geddit /ˈgɛdɪt/ *int. slang.* L20. [Alt. of (*do you*) *get it?* Cf. INNIT.] Do you understand?, do you see what I mean?

gee /dʒiː/ *n.*[1] *Sc.* & *north.* E17. [Origin unkn.] A fit of bad temper or sullenness.

gee /dʒiː/ *n.*[2] *colloq.* M19. [Orig. a child's wd, f. GEE *int.*[1] Cf. GEE-GEE.] A horse.

gee /dʒiː/ *n.*[3] *slang.* L19. [Origin unkn.: cf. GEE *n.*[4], GEE *v.*[2]] More fully *gee-man.* The assistant to a cheapjack or showman.

gee /dʒiː/ *n.*[4] *US slang.* E20. [f. the first letter of GUY *n.*[2]] A person, a fellow.

gee /dʒiː/ *n.*[5] *US slang.* M20. [f. the first letter of GRAND *n.*] A thousand dollars.

gee /giː, dʒiː/ *n.*[6] *slang* (orig. *US*). M20. [Origin uncertain, perh. rel. to GHEE.] Any of various narcotic drugs; *esp.* opium.

geed-up *a.* drugged. M20.

Gee /dʒiː/ *n.*[7] M20. [f. the first letter of GRID.] *Hist.* A British navigational radar designed to guide bombers to their targets, developed in the war of 1939–45.

gee /dʒiː/ *v.*[1]*i. slang.* Pa. t. & pple **geed**. L17. [Origin uncertain: perh. f. GEE *int.*[1]] 'Go', fit, suit, accord; (of people) behave as is desired, agree, get on well (together). Only in neg. phrases.

gee /dʒiː/ *v.*[2] Pa. t. & pple **geed**. E19. [f. GEE *int.*[1]] 1 *v.t.* a = JEE *v.* 2. E19. b Direct (a horse etc.) by the command 'gee'. M19. c *fig.* Incite or encourage (a person); cause (a person or animal) to move more quickly. Freq. foll. by *up.* L19. 2 *v.i.* = JEE *v.* 1. M19.

gee /dʒiː/ *int.*[1] E17. [Origin unkn.] A word of command used to a horse etc.: go on, go faster; occas., turn to the right.

gee /dʒiː/ *int.*[2] *slang* (orig. *US*). M19. [Perh. alt. of JESUS.] Expr. asseveration, discovery, enthusiasm, or surprise.

¶Earliest in phrs. as GEE WHILLIKINS etc.

geebung /ˈdʒiːbʌŋ/ *n.* E19. [Aborig.] (The edible fruit of) any of several chiefly Australian trees or shrubs of the genus *Persoonia* (family Proteaceae).

Geechee /ˈgiːtʃiː/ *n. US dial.* E20. [The *Ogeechee* River, Georgia, USA.] A dialect, comprising words of English and African origin, spoken originally by Black slaves in the region of the Ogeechee River, Georgia. Also *derog.*, a Black of the southern US.

geed *v.*[1], *v.*[2] pa. t. & pple of GEE *v.*[1], *v.*[2]

gee-gee /ˈdʒiːdʒiː/ *n. nursery* & *colloq.* Cf. GEE *n.*[2] M19. [Redupl. of GEE *int.*[1]] A horse.

gee-ho /dʒiːˈhəʊ/ *int.* & *v.* M17. [f. GEE *int.*[1] + HO *int.*[2]] A *int.* = GEE *int.*[1] M17. B *v.i.* = GEE *v.*[2] 1b. M17.

gee-hup *int.* see GEE-UP *int.*

geek /giːk/ *n. slang* (chiefly *US*). L19. [Var. of GECK *n.*[1]] A simpleton, a dupe; a person who is socially inept or boringly conventional or studious; *spec.* an assistant at a sideshow whose purpose is to appear as an object of disgust or derision.

geeky *a.* socially inept, boringly conventional or studious; strange, odd: L20.

geelbek /ˈxɪəlbɛk/ *n. S. Afr.* Also **-bec(k)**. Pl. **-s**, same. M19. [Afk., f. Du. *geel* YELLOW *a.* + *bek* BEAK *n.*[1]] 1 A large edible sciaenid fish, *Atractoscion aequidens*, which has bright yellow edges to the jaws and gill-covers and is found off the coasts of southern Africa and NE Australia. Also called *Cape salmon*, (Austral.) *teraglin.* M19. 2 = *yellowbill* (a) s.v. YELLOW *a.* M19.

geelhout /ˈxɪəl(h)əʊt/ *n. S. Afr.* L18. [Afk., f. Du. *geel* YELLOW *a.* + *hout* wood: see HOLT *n.*[1]] Any of several southern African trees of the genus *Podocarpus* (family Podocarpaceae), yielding yellow timber; the timber of such trees, used for furniture and in carpentry.

geelum *n.* see GUILLAUME.

†**geer** *n.* & *v.* var. of GEAR.

geese *n.* pl. of GOOSE *n.*

gee string *n. phr.* see G STRING.

gee-up /dʒiːˈʌp/ *int.* & *v.* Also **-hup** /-ˈhʌp/. M18. [f. GEE *int.*[1] + HUP *int.* (confused with UP *adv.*[1]).] A *int.* = GEE *int.*[1] M18. B *v.* Infl. **-pp-**. 1 *v.t.* Say 'gee-up' to; cause (a horse etc.) to move faster in this way. M18. 2 *v.i.* Say 'gee-up'; (of a horse etc.) move faster in response to such encouragement. E19.

gee whillikins /dʒiː ˈwɪlɪkɪnz/ *int.* Orig. *US.* M19. [Origin uncertain: rel. to GEE *int.*[2]] = GEE *int.*[2]

gee whiz /dʒiː ˈwɪz/ *int.* Orig. *US.* Also **-zz**. L19. [Rel. to prec.] = GEE *int.*[2]

Geez /ˈgiːɛz, gəˈɛz/ *n.* & *a.* Also **Ge'ez**. L18. [Ethiopic.] (Of or pertaining to) the ancient Semitic language of Ethiopia, now used only as a liturgical language. Cf. ETHIOPIC.

geez(e), **Geez(e)** *int.* var. of JEEZ.

geezer /ˈgiːzə/ *n. slang.* L19. [Repr. dial. pronunc. of GUISER.] A person, now usu. a man; an old fellow.

gefilte fish /gəˈfɪltə fɪʃ/ *n. phr.* Also **gefüllte fish.** L19. [Yiddish =stuffed fish, f. *gefilte* infl. pa. pple of *filn* FILL *v.*: see FISH *n.*[1]] A dish either of stewed or baked stuffed fish or of fish cakes boiled in a fish or vegetable broth.

Geg *n.* & *a.* var. of GHEG.

gegenschein /ˈgeɪgənʃʌɪn/ *n.* Also **G-.** L19. [G, f. *gegen* opposite + *Schein* shine, glow.] *Astron.* A patch of very faint nebulous light occurring in the ecliptic opposite the sun, thought to be the image of the sun reflected from gas and dust outside the atmosphere; = COUNTERGLOW.

geggie /ˈgɛgi/ *n. Sc.* Also **gaggie** /ˈgagi/. L19. [f. GAG *n.*[1]] A travelling theatrical show, *esp.* one held in a tent.

Geheimrat /gəˈhʌɪmraːt/ *n.* Pl. ***-räte*** /-rɛːtə/. M19. [G.] *Hist.* In Germany, a privy councillor (often as an honorific title).

Gehenna /gəˈhɛnə/ *n.* Also (earlier) in Fr. form **Gehenne.** L15. [Fr. *gehenne* or its source, eccl.L, f. Hellenistic Gk *geenna* f. Heb. *gē' hinnōm* hell, orig. the valley of Hinnom near Jerusalem where children were sacrificed (*2 Kings* 23:10).] 1 Hell; a place of burning, torment, and misery. L15. 2 A prison, esp. one where captives are tortured. Long *rare.* L16.

Geiger counter /ˈgʌɪgə kaʊntə/ *n. phr.* Also **g-, Geiger-Müller counter** /ˈmuːlə/. E20. [Hans *Geiger* (1882–1945), Ger. physicist; var. also f. W. *Müller*, 20th-cent. Ger. physicist.] An instrument for detecting and measuring ionizing radiation (e.g. from a radioactive substance or from cosmic rays) by means of the electrical discharges produced by the radiation in a gas-filled tube.

geiger tree /ˈgʌɪgə triː/ *n. phr.* L19. [John *Geiger*, 19th-cent. Amer. naturalist.] A Caribbean sebesten tree, *Cordia sebestena*, with orange or red flowers.

geikielite /ˈgiːkɪlʌɪt/ *n.* L19. [f. Archibald *Geikie* (1835–1924), Sc. geologist + -LITE.] *Min.* A trigonal magnesium titanate, which also contains ferrous iron and forms a series with ilmenite.

†**geir** *n.* M16–M19. [Du. *gier.*] A vulture. Also *geir-eagle.*

geisha /ˈgeɪʃə/ *n.* Pl. **-s**, same. L19. [Jap. *geisha* entertainer, f. *gei* (performing) arts + *sha* person.] A trained Japanese hostess who entertains men with conversation, dance and song, etc.; *loosely* a Japanese prostitute. Also *geisha girl.*

Geissler /ˈgʌɪslə/ *n.* M19. [Heinrich *Geissler* (1814–79), Ger. glass-blower.] *Geissler('s) tube*, a sealed glass or quartz tube with a narrow central section, filled with gas at low pressure, for the production of visible or ultraviolet light by electrical discharge (esp. for spectral analysis).

Geist /gaɪst/ *n.* L19. [G: see GHOST *n.*] The spirit of an individual or a group; intellectuality; intelligence.

Geisteswissenschaft /ˈgaɪstəsˌvɪsənʃaft/ *n.* Pl. ***-en*** /-ən/. E20. [G, f. as GEIST + *Wissenschaft* learning (f. *wissen* know).] Usu. in *pl.* The arts or humanities as opp. to the sciences.

geitonogamy /gʌɪtəˈnɒgəmi/ *n.* L19. [f. Gk *geitōn*, *geitono-* neighbour + -GAMY.] *Bot.* Fertilization of a flower by pollen from another flower on the same plant.

gekko *n.* var. of GECKO.

gel /dʒɛl/ *n.* & *v.* L19. [Abbrev. of GELATIN.] A *n.* 1 A semi-solid colloidal solution of a solid dispersed in a liquid, more or less elastic, and formed by the coagulation of a sol (colloidal liquid). L19. 2 A substance for setting or styling the hair, sold as a jelly. M20. 3 *Biochem.* A semi-rigid slab or cylinder of an organic polymer (e.g. starch, polyacrylamide) used as a medium for the separation of macromolecules. M20. B *v.i.* Infl. **-ll-.** Form a gel; *fig.* (of an idea etc.) take a definite form, achieve a sense of coherence, jell (see JELL *v.* 1b). L19.

gelada /dʒəˈlɑːdə/ *n.* M19. [Amharic *č'ällada.*] A gregarious, chiefly herbivorous baboon, *Theropithecus gelada*, of the Ethiopian mountains, having a long brownish coat and characterized by a bare red patch on the chest and (in the adult male) a heavy mane. Also *gelada baboon.*

Gelalaean /dʒɛləˈliːən/ *a.* Also **Jel-.** L18. [f. Pers. (Arab.) *Jalālī* pertaining to *Jalāl ad-Din* (formerly written *Gelal ed-din*) 'Glory of the Faith' or *Jalāl ad-Dawla* 'Glory of the Dynasty', titles of Malik-Shah, Seljuk Sultan of Khorasan and reformer of the Persian calendar.] Of or pertaining to (the calendar instituted by) Jalal ad-Din in 1079.

Gelasian /gəˈleɪzɪən/ *a.* L18. [f. *Gelasius* (see below) + -IAN.] Of or pertaining to Pope Gelasius I (492–6), or the liturgical books etc. attributed to him.

gelastic /dʒəˈlastɪk/ *a.* E18. [Gk *gelastikos*, f. *gelan* laugh: see -IC.] Of or pertaining to laughter. Also (*rare*), risible.

gelate /dʒəˈleɪt/ *v.i.* E20. [Back-form. f. GELATION *n.*[2]] Form a gel.

gelatification /dʒəˌlatɪfɪˈkeɪʃ(ə)n/ *n.* M19. [f. GELATIN + -FICATION.] Production of, or conversion into, gelatin or jelly.

gelatigenous /ˌdʒɛləˈtɪdʒɪnəs/ *a.* M19. [f. as prec. + -GENOUS.] Producing or developing gelatin.

gelatin /ˈdʒɛlətɪn/ *n.* Also **-ine** /-iːn/. E19. [Fr. *gélatine* f. It. *gelatina*, f. *gelata* JELLY *n.*[1]: see -IN[1], -INE[5].] 1 An amorphous yellowish or colourless transparent tasteless substance, brittle when dry, which is derived from collagen and obtained by prolonged boiling of animal skin, tendons, ligaments, etc., and is used in food preparation as the basis of jellies, in various photographic processes, and in glue; also, any of various substances containing or resembling gelatin. E19. 2 Any of various gelatinous explosives; *esp.* (more fully *blasting gelatin*) a high explosive chiefly consisting of a gel of nitroglycerine with added cellulose nitrate, used esp. under water. L19.

1 **vegetable gelatin** a constituent of gluten, identical with gelatin from animal sources.

Comb.: **gelatin dynamite** a powerful explosive containing blasting gelatin absorbed on to an inert base (cf. GELIGNITE); **gelatin paper**: coated with sensitized gelatin for photography.

geˈlatinase *n.* (*Biochem.*) an enzyme which liquefies gelatin, produced by certain bacteria, yeasts, etc.: E20. **geˈlatinoid** *a.* & *n.* (*a*) *adj.* gelatinous; (*b*) a substance resembling gelatin: M19.

gelatinate /dʒəˈlatɪneɪt/ *v.* Long *rare* or *obs.* L18. [f. GELATIN + -ATE[3].] 1 *v.i.* = GELATINIZE 1. L18. 2 *v.t.* = GELATINIZE 2. E19.

gelatiˈnation *n.* = GELATINIZATION *n.* L18.

gelatine *n.* var. of GELATIN.

gelatiniform /dʒɛləˈtɪnɪfɔːm/ *a.* M19. [f. GELATIN + -I- + -FORM.] Having the form, consistency, or appearance of gelatin.

gelatinize /dʒəˈlatɪnʌɪz/ *v.* Also **-ise.** E19. [f. as prec. + -IZE.] 1 *v.i.* Take the form of a jelly; become gelatinous. E19. 2 *v.t.* Make gelatinous or jelly-like. M19. 3 *v.t.* Coat with gelatin, apply gelatin to. L19.

geˈlatinizable *a.* (*rare*) E19. **gelatiniˈzation** *n.* conversion into a gelatinous state M19.

gelatinous /dʒəˈlatɪnəs/ *a.* E18. [Fr. *gélatineux*, f. as GELATIN + *-eux* -OUS.] 1 Having the character or consistency of a jelly; jelly-like. E18. 2 Of, pertaining to, or consisting of gelatin. L18.

gelatinously *adv.* L19. **gelatinousness** *n.* E20.

gelation /dʒɪˈleɪʃ(ə)n/ *n.*[1] M19. [L *gelatio(n-)*, f. *gelat-* pa. ppl stem of *gelare* freeze: see -ATION.] Solidification by freezing.

gelation /dʒəˈleɪʃ(ə)n/ *n.*[2] E20. [f. GEL + -ATION.] Formation of or conversion into a gel.

geld /gɛld/ *n.* Also †**gelt.** L15. [med.L *geldum* f. OE. *ġ(i)eld* (see YIELD *n.*). Cf. GILD *n.*[1], GUILD *n.*[2]] *Hist.* A tax paid to the Crown by English landholders before the Norman Conquest, and continued under the Norman kings.

geld /gɛld/ *a. obs.* exc. *dial.* ME. [ON *gelda* = OSw. *galder* (Sw. dial. *gall, gåll*, Da. *gold*), OHG *galt* (G *gelt*), f. Gmc. Cf. YELD.] Of a female animal, esp. a cow: barren.

geld /gɛld/ *v.*[1]*t.* Pa. t. & pple **gelded, gelt** /gɛlt/. ME. [ON *gelda*, f. *geldr* GELD *a.*] 1 Deprive (usu. a male animal) of the ability to reproduce; excise the testicles of; castrate. ME. b Excise the ovaries of; spay. M16. 2 *transf.* & *fig.* Deprive *of* some essential part; cut down the resources of; impair the strength or force of; weaken, enfeeble. Long *rare.* E16. †b Mutilate (a book etc.) by abridgement; expurgate. Also, (*rare*), edit *out.* M16–E18. 3a Cut (a plant); *esp.* prune or remove superfluous shoots from (a plant or tree). E16. †b Cut out the old comb from (a beehive); take out (the comb). L16–M17.

1 W. HOLTBY Treating his gelded toms with specially tender indulgence. 2 SHAKES. *Rich. II* Bereft and gelded of his patrimony. A. COOKE To geld a lively memory in the interests of good form.

gelder *n.* (long *rare*) LME.

geld /gɛld/ *v.*[2] Also †**gelt.** See also GILD *v.*[2] M19. [f. GELD *n.* Cf. med.L *geldare* pay geld, tax.] *Hist.* 1 *v.t.* Levy geld on. M19. 2 *v.i.* Pay geld. M19.

geldable *a.* liable to pay geld E17.

gelding /ˈgɛldɪŋ/ *n.* LME. [ON *geldingr*, f. as GELD *a.*: see -ING[3].] 1 A gelded person, a eunuch. Long *rare* or *obs.* LME. 2 A gelded animal; *esp.* a gelded male horse. LME.

Gelehrte /gəˈleːrtə, gəˈleːtə/ *n.* Also ***-ter*** /-tə(r)/. Pl. ***-ten*** /-tən, -t(ə)n/. M19. [G, f. *gelehrt* learned, *lehren* instruct.] A learned (German) person; a scholar; a savant.

gelid /ˈdʒɛlɪd/ *a.* E17. [L *gelidus*, f. *gelu* frost, intense cold: see -ID[1].] 1 Extremely cold, cold as ice, frosty. E17. 2 Cold, chill; cool. M17.

1 W. SCORESBY As the air passes over the gelid surface of the ice. *fig.*: W. STYRON Emmi had her father's voice, utterly gelid and remote. 2 J. THOMSON By gelid founts and careless rills to muse.

geˈlidity *n.* extreme cold, frigidity M17. **gelidly** *adv.* M19. **gelidness** *n.* E18.

gelignite /ˈdʒɛlɪgnʌɪt/ *n.* L19. [Prob. f. GEL(ATIN + L *l*)*ign-* wood + -ITE[1].] A powerful explosive containing nitroglycerine and cellulose nitrate in a base of potassium or sodium nitrate and (orig. & usu.) wood pulp.

gelly /ˈdʒɛli/ *n. slang.* Also **j-.** M20. [Abbrev.] = prec.

gelsemium /dʒɛlˈsiːmɪəm/ *n.* L19. [mod.L (see below), f. It. *gelsomino* JASMINE.] The rhizome of a twining shrub, *Gelsemium sempervirens* (family Loganiaceae) of southern N. America (also called *Carolina jasmine*); a preparation of this used medicinally, esp. in the treatment of neuralgia.

ˈgelsemine *n.* (*Chem.*) an indole-based alkaloid with depressant properties, present in gelsemium root L19.

gelt /gɛlt/ *n.*[1] Now only *slang.* E16. [G *Geld.*] Money.

gelt /gɛlt/ *n.*[2] Long *arch. rare.* L16. [Ir. *geilt* a frenzied person.] A mad person.

†**gelt** *n.*[3] var. of GELD *n.*

gelt *v.*[1] pa. pple: see GELD *v.*[1]

†**gelt** *v.*[2] var. of GELD *v.*[2]

gem /dʒɛm/ *n.* [OE *ġim(m)* f. L *gemma* bud, jewel; re-adopted or refash. in LME after (O)Fr. *gemme.*] 1 A precious stone of any kind, *esp.* when cut and polished for ornament; a jewel. Also *gemstone.* OE. b A precious or semiprecious stone, bearing an engraved design either in relief or intaglio. M17. 2 *fig.* A person or thing highly valued or of rare quality. ME. †3 A bud; *esp.* a leaf bud. Cf. GEMMA 1. LME–E19. 4 A common geometrid moth, *Orthonama obstipata*, found in Eurasia, Africa and America. M19. 5 A former size of type equal to about 4 points. L19.

1 K. CLARK A lot of gems—hyacinths, sapphires, rubies, topazes, emeralds. 2 MAX-MÜLLER Among the Hottentots . . we find the following gem of a fable.

Comb.: **gemfish** *Austral.* an edible marine fish, *Rexea solandri*; also called *hake.*

gemlike *a.* resembling (that of) a gem E19.

gem /dʒɛm/ *v.* Infl. **-mm-.** ME. [f. the n.] †1a *v.i.* Bud. Only in ME. b *v.t.* Put forth (a blossom, a fruit). M17–M18. 2 *v.t.* Adorn (as) with gems (*lit.* & *fig.*). Freq. as *gemmed* ppl a. ME. 3 *v.t.* Extract gems from; excavate to obtain gems. M19.

2 J. M. FAULKNER The lawns are gemmed with dew.

gemmer *n.* a person who seeks or digs for gems L19.

Gemara /gəˈmɑːrə/ *n.* E17. [Aram. *gĕmārā* completion.] The later of the two parts of the Palestinian or the Babylonian Talmud, consisting of a rabbinical commentary on the first part (the Mishnah).

Gemaric *a.* of, pertaining to, or concerned with the Gemara E18.

gematria /gɪˈmeɪtrɪə/ *n.* Also (earlier) Anglicized as †**gematry**. M17. [Aram. *gīmaṭrĕyā* f. Gk *geōmetria* GEOMETRY.] A cabbalistic method of interpreting the Hebrew Scriptures by computing the numerical value of words, based on those of their constituent letters.

Gemeinschaft /gəˈmaɪnʃaft/ *n.* M20. [G, f. *gemein* common, general + *-schaft* -SHIP.] *Sociol.* A form of social integration based on personal ties; community. Cf. GESELLSCHAFT.

gemel /ˈdʒɛm(ə)l/ *n.* & *a.* Also †**gemew**, †**gemow**. LME. [OFr. f. L *gemellus*, dim. of *geminus* twin. See also GIMMAL.] A *n.* †1 In *pl.* Twins; things associated in pairs. LME–E17. †2 *Her.* In *pl.* Bars or barrulets placed together as a couple. LME–M18. 3 A hinge. Now only in *gemel-hinge*, a hinge consisting of an eye or loop and a hook. LME. 4 Chiefly *Hist.* A kind of finger-ring, much worn in the 16th cent., which can be divided into two (rarely, three) rings. Also *gemel-ring*. Cf. GIMMAL. L15. B *attrib.* or as *adj.* Twin; double. Now only in *Her.* L15.

gemellion /dʒɪˈmɛlɪən/ *n.* L19. [med.L *gemellio*, f. L *gemellus* a twin.] Either of a pair of basins used for washing the hands, esp. for liturgical use; any decorative basin.

†**gemew** *n.* & *a.* var. of GEMEL.

geminal /ˈdʒɛmɪn(ə)l/ *a.* L20. [f. L *geminus* twin + -AL¹.] *Chem.* Of, pertaining to, or containing like atoms or groups attached to the same atom in a molecule. Cf. VICINAL.

geminate /ˈdʒɛmɪneɪt, -nət/ *a.* & *n.* LME. [L *geminatus* pa. pple of *geminare*: see next, -ATE².] A *adj.* Duplicated, combined in pairs, twin, binate. LME.

geminate leaves *Bot.* leaves springing in pairs from the same node, one leaf beside the other.

B *n.* A doubled consonant. L19.

geminate /ˈdʒɛmɪneɪt/ *v.t.* M17. [L *geminat-* pa. ppl stem of *geminare*, f. *geminus* twin: see -ATE³.] Double, duplicate; combine as a pair.

geminated *ppl a.* doubled, occurring in pairs E19.

gemination /dʒɛmɪˈneɪʃ(ə)n/ *n.* L16. [L *geminatio(n-)*, f. as prec.: see -ATION.] 1 A doubling, duplication, repetition. L16. 2 *Dentistry.* The union of contiguous teeth. M19. 3 *Ling.* a The doubling of an originally single consonantal sound. L19. b The doubling of a letter in the orthography of a word. L19.

ˈgeminative *a.* & *n.* (*a*) *adj.* characterized by gemination; (*b*) *n.* a geminated letter: L19.

Gemini /ˈdʒɛmɪnʌɪ, -ni/ *n.* & *int.* Exc. in sense A.1 also **g-**. OE. [L *gemini* pl. of *geminus* twin.] A *n.* 1 (The name of) a conspicuous constellation on the ecliptic between Auriga and Cancer, on the edge of the Milky Way; *Astrol.* (the name of) the third zodiacal sign, usu. associated with the period 21 May to 21 June (see note s.v. ZODIAC); the Twins (Castor and Pollux). OE. b = GEMINIAN. E20. †2 A couple, a pair (*of*); *esp.* in *pl.*, a pair of eyes. Now *rare.* L16.

1 TENNYSON When . . the starry Gemini hang like glorious crowns Over Orion's grave. *attrib.*: L. MACNEICE All astrologers agree that the Gemini type enjoys argument. 2 SHAKES. *Merry W.* Like a geminy of baboons.

B *int.* A mild oath or exclamation. Cf. JIMINY. M17.

Gemiˈnian *n.* a person born under the sign Gemini E20. **Geminid** *n.* any of an annual shower of meteors which appear to radiate from the constellation Gemini in December L19.

geminous /ˈdʒɛmɪnəs/ *a. rare.* M17. [f. L *geminus* twin + -OUS.] Double; occurring in pairs.

gemma /ˈdʒɛmə/ *n.* Pl. **gemmae** /ˈdʒɛmiː/. L18. [L = bud, jewel.] 1 *Bot.* A leaf bud, as distinct from a flower bud. Cf. GEM *n.* 3. Now *rare.* L18. 2 *Bot.* & *Zool.* A small, usu. cellular, asexual reproductive body which becomes detached from the parent organism and develops into a new individual, esp. in mosses, liverworts, some fungi, etc. M19.

gemman /ˈdʒɛmən/ *n. slang.* Now *rare.* Pl. **gemmen**. M16. [Contr.] = GENTLEMAN.

gemmary *n.*¹ var. of GEMMERY.

†**gemmary** *a.* & *n.*² LME. [Late L *gemmarius*, f. *gemma*: see GEM *n.*, -ARY¹.] A *adj.* Of or pertaining to gems; concerned with or skilled with gems. LME–L17. B *n.* A jeweller. Only in LME.

gemmate /ˈdʒɛmeɪt, -mət/ *a.* M19. [L *gemmatus* pa. pple of *gemmare*: see next, -ATE².] *Biol.* Possessing gemmae; gemmiparous.

gemmate /ˈdʒɛmeɪt/ *v.i.* E17. [L *gemmat-* pa. ppl stem of *gemmare* put forth buds, f. *gemma* bud, jewel: see -ATE³.] *Biol.* Produce gemmae; reproduce by gemmation.

gemmation /dʒɛˈmeɪʃ(ə)n/ *n.* M18. [Fr., f. *gemmer* form buds, f. *gemme* bud: see -ATION.] 1 *Bot.* The action of putting out buds. Also, the arrangement of buds on the stem, or of leaves within the bud. M18. 2 *Zool.* The production of gemmae; the mode of asexual reproduction in which a small growth from the parent organism (detaches and) develops into a new individual; budding. M19.

gemmen *n.* pl. of GEMMAN.

gemmeous /ˈdʒɛmɪəs/ *a.* E17. [f. L *gemmeus* (f. *gemma* GEM *n.*) + -OUS.] Of, pertaining to, of the nature of, or resembling a gem.

gemmery /ˈdʒɛməri/ *n.* Also **-ary**. M17. [f. GEM *n.* + -ARY¹.] †1 A jewel-house. M17–E18. 2 Gems as an object of connoisseurship. *rare.* M19.

gemmiferous /dʒɛˈmɪf(ə)rəs/ *a.* M17. [f. L *gemmifer* (f. *gemma* GEM *n.*) + -OUS: see -FEROUS.] 1 Yielding or containing precious stones. M17. 2 *Biol.* = GEMMATE *a.* E19.

gemmiparous /dʒɛˈmɪp(ə)rəs/ *a.* L18. [f. mod.L *gemmiparus* (f. *gemma* GEM *n.*) + -OUS.] *Biol.* 1 Producing offspring by gemmation. L18. 2 Of, pertaining to, or resulting from the process of gemmation. M19.

gemmiˈparity *n.* the condition or character of being gemmiparous M19. **gemmiparously** *adv.* M19.

gemmology /dʒɛˈmɒlədʒi/ *n.* E19. [f. L *gemma* GEM *n.* + -OLOGY.] The branch of geology or crystallography that deals with gems.

gemmoˈlogical *a.* M20. **gemmologist** *n.* M20.

gemmule /ˈdʒɛmjuːl/ *n.* M19. [Fr. f. L *gemmula* dim. of GEMMA bud, jewel: see -ULE.] 1 *Bot.* †a = PLUMULE *n.* 1. Only in M19. b A small gemma. L19. 2 *Zool.* A gemma; *spec.* a tough-coated cluster of cells produced in sponges for development in later more favourable conditions. M19. 3 *Biol.* (now *Hist.*). In the theory of pangenesis, a hypothetical minute hereditary particle transferred from the various cells in the body to the germ cells, to effect production of those cell types in the offspring. L19.

gemmuˈliferous *a.* bearing gemmules M19.

gemmy /ˈdʒɛmi/ *a.* LME. [f. GEM *n.* + -Y¹.] 1 Having many gems; covered or set with gems or something resembling gems. LME. 2 Resembling a gem; brilliant; glittering. L17.

gemot /gɪˈməʊt/ *n.* Also **gemote**. [OE *ġemōt*, f. *ġe-* Y- + *mōt* MOOT *n.*¹] *Eng. Hist.* A meeting; an assembly (in England before the Norman Conquest) for judicial or legislative purposes. See also WITENAGEMOT.

†**gemow** *n.* & *a.* var. of GEMEL.

gemsbok /ˈgɛmzbɒk/ *n.* Also **-bock**, **-buck** /-bʌk/. Pl. same, **-s**. L18. [Afk., f. Du. = chamois, f. *gems* chamois + *bok* buck.] A large antelope, *Oryx gazella*, of SW and E. Africa, having long straight horns and black markings on the face and flanks; *esp.* the southern form of this. Cf. BEISA, ORYX.

gemshorn /ˈgɛmzhɔːn/ *n.* E19. [G, lit. 'chamois horn'.] *Mus.* A light-toned organ-stop.

gemütlich /gəˈmyːtlɪç, -ˈmuːtlɪʃ/ *a.* M19. [G.] Pleasant, cheerful; cosy, snug, homely; genial, good-natured.

T. CAPOTE Their five-room apartment, with its *gemütlich* mélange of plump hassocks and squashy chairs.

Gemütlichkeit /gəˈmyːtlɪçkaɪt, -ˈmuːtlɪxkʌɪt/ *n.* M19. [G: cf. prec.] The quality of being *gemütlich*; geniality; cosiness; cheerfulness.

gen /dʒɛn/ *n.* & *v. slang* (orig. *Mil.*). M20. [Perh. f. first syllable of *general information.*] A *n.* Information; facts. M20.

J. RABAN The good navigator has to make the most of whatever gen he has to hand.

B *v.* (with *up*). Infl. **-nn-**. 1 *v.i.* Provide oneself with information; learn about something (hurriedly). M20. 2 *v.t.* Provide with information, 'put in the picture'. M20.

-gen /dʒ(ə)n/ *suff.* [Fr. *-gène* f. Gk *-genēs* -born, of a specified kind, f. *gen-* base of *gignesthai* be born, become, *genos* kind (n.), etc.] 1 *Sci.* (orig. *Chem.*). A substance that produces, as *hydrogen*, *oxygen* (the earliest wds so formed); *cyanogen*, *halogen*; *phellogen*; *allergen*, *androgen*. 2 *Bot.* A substance or plant that grows or is produced, as *acrogen*, *cultigen*.

gena /ˈdʒiːnə/ *n.* Pl. **-nae** /-niː/. E19. [L = cheek.] In an invertebrate, esp. an insect: either lateral part of the head below the level of the eyes.

genal *a.* L19.

genappe /dʒɪˈnap/ *n.* M19. [f. *Genappe* a town in Belgium, the orig. place of manufacture.] A smooth lustrous yarn used in the manufacture of braids, fringes, etc. Also *genappe yarn*.

gendarme /ˈʒɒndɑːm; *foreign* ʒɑ̃darm (*pl. same*)/ *n.* Pl. **gendarmes**, (now *Hist.*) ***gens d'armes*** /ʒɑ̃ darm/. M16. [Fr., a sing. f. the pl. (now *Hist.*) *gens d'armes* men of arms.] 1 In the older French army, a horseman in full armour, having several others under his command; later, a mounted trooper, esp. of the royal companies. Usu. in *pl. obs.* exc. *Hist.* M16. 2 In France and French-speaking countries: a police officer; orig. a member of a military force employed in policing. L18. b *gen.* A police officer. *slang.* E20.

¶ In Eng. and Fr., earliest in the form *gens d'armes*.

gendarmerie /ʒɒnˈdɑːməri; *foreign* ʒɑ̃darməri (*pl. same*)/ *n.* Also **-ery**. M16. [Fr., f. *gendarme*: see prec.] 1 *Hist.* A body of cavalry, esp. in the older French army (cf. GENDARME 1). M16. 2 In France and French-speaking countries: a body of police officers, a police force; orig. a military force employed as police. L18. b A headquarters or station of gendarmes; a police station. M20.

gender /ˈdʒɛndə/ *n.* LME. [OFr. *gendre* (mod. *genre*) f. Proto-Romance f. L *genus*, *gener-*: see GENUS.] †1 Kind, sort, class, genus. LME–L18. 2 *Gram.* Any of the classes (*masculine*, *feminine*, *neuter*, *common*) of nouns and pronouns distinguished by the modification which they require in words syntactically associated with them and roughly corresponding to the sex or sexlessness of the objects which they denote; the property of belonging to such a class; (of adjectives) the appropriate form for accompanying a noun of one such class; the classification of nouns and other words in this way, as a grammatical principle. LME. 3 The state of being male, female, or neuter; sex; the members of one or other sex. Now chiefly *colloq.* or *euphem.* LME. b Sex as expressed by social or cultural distinctions. M20.

2 C. ISHERWOOD Das Glueck, le bonheur, la felicidad—they have given it all three genders. *grammatical gender*: see GRAMMATICAL *a.* 3 M. W. MONTAGU Of the fair sex . . my only consolation for being of that gender has been the assurance . . of never being married to any one among them. b *attrib.*: A. OAKLEY Sex differences may be 'natural', but gender differences have their source in culture.

genderless *a.* (*Gram.*) without distinction of gender L19.

gender /ˈdʒɛndə/ *v.* ME. [OFr. *gendrer* f. L *generare* GENERATE *v.*] 1 *v.t.* & *i.* Of a parent or parents: beget, engender, produce (offspring). *arch.* ME. 2 *v.t.* †a Produce by natural processes, generate. LME–M17. b Give rise to, engender. *arch.* LME. 3 *v.i.* Esp. of animals: copulate. *arch.* LME.

gene /dʒiːn/ *n.* E20. [G *Gen*, f. *Pangen* PANGENE.] Each of the units of heredity which are transmitted from parent to offspring in gametes, usually as part of a chromosome, and control or determine a single characteristic in the offspring.

Comb.: **gene bank** a collection of living organisms maintained as a repository of genetic material, esp. for developing new breeds etc. or safeguarding the survival of existing ones; **gene flow** the movement of genes from one population to another as a result of interbreeding, hybridization, etc.; **gene pool** the stock of different genes in an interbreeding population; **gene splicing** the process of removing a chosen gene or sequence of genes from one organism and causing it to be integrated into the genetic material of another (usu. a bacterium, in order that it may produce the protein for which the gene codes); **gene therapy** the practice of introducing normal genes into cells in place of defective or missing ones in order to correct hereditary disorders.

¶Orig. defined as the ultimate units of mutation and recombination, genes are now regarded as sequences of nucleotides in a nucleic acid molecule each of which determines a single polypeptide.

-gene /dʒiːn/ *suff.* [f. (as) -GEN.] (A substance, structure, etc.) that is produced or formed, as *epigene*; *palaeogene*, *phosgene*.

gêne /ʒɛn, ʒɛːn/ *n.* E19. [Fr.] Constraint, embarrassment, discomfort.

gêné /ʒɛne/ *a.* Fem. **-née**. E19. [Fr., pa. ppl a. of *gêner* embarrass: rel. to prec.] Constrained, embarrassed, discomforted.

genealogic /dʒiːnɪəˈlɒdʒɪk, dʒɛn-/ *a.* M18. [Fr. *généalogique* f. Gk *genealogikos*, f. *genealogos* genealogist: see GENEALOGY, -IC.] = GENEALOGICAL.

genealogical /dʒiːnɪəˈlɒdʒɪk(ə)l, dʒɛn-/ *a.* L16. [f. as prec. + -AL[1].] Pertaining to genealogy, or the tracing of family descent.

A. EDEN An elaborate genealogical table tracing my descent to a saintly early Swedish king. **genealogical tree** a diagram, esp. one in the form of a tree with branches, which shows the different generations of a family and their members.

genealogically *adv.* M17.

genealogy /dʒiːnɪˈalədʒi, dʒɛn-/ *n.* ME. [(O)Fr. *généalogie* f. late L *genealogia*, f. Gk *genealogia*, f. *genealogos* genealogist, f. *genea* race, generation: see -LOGY.] 1 An account of a person's descent from an ancestor or ancestors, by enumeration of the intermediate people; a pedigree. ME. †2 Lineage, pedigree, family stock. ME–M16. †3 Progeny, offspring. E16–M18. 4 (The branch of knowledge that deals with) the investigation of the details of ancestry. E19. 5 The line of development of a plant or animal from earlier forms. L19.

1 C. H. PEARSON The early mention of genealogies in the Welsh laws is proof of the importance attached to noble birth. 4 A. TUCKER Genealogy and chronology can scarcely be called sciences.

genealogist *n.* a person who researches or studies genealogies E17. **genealogize** *v.t.* & *i.* (*a*) *v.t.* draw up a genealogy of; (*b*) *v.i.* trace the descent of people or families; make out genealogies: E17.

geneat /gɪˈniːt, jɛˈneɪat/ *n.* [OE *ġeneat*, f. *nēotan* enjoy, use.] *Hist.* A retainer, a vassal; a person who held lands in return for service or rent.

genecology /dʒɛnɪˈkɒlədʒi, dʒiːn-/ *n.* E20. [f. Gk *genos* kind, race + ECOLOGY.] The branch of science that deals with genetic differences between related species and populations in relation to their environment.

geneco'logic *a.* M20. **geneco'logical** *a.* E20.

genera *n.* pl. of GENUS.

generable /ˈdʒɛn(ə)rəb(ə)l/ *a.* L15. [L *generabilis*, f. *generare*: see GENERATE *v.*, -ABLE.] 1 Able to be generated or produced. L15. †2 Capable of generating. *rare.* L16–M17.

genera'bility *n.* (*rare*) E18.

general /ˈdʒɛn(ə)r(ə)l/ *a.*, *n.*, & *v.* ME. [(O)Fr. *général*, f. L *generalis*, f. *genus*, *gener-* class, race, kind: see GENUS, -AL[1].] A *adj.* 1 Including, involving, or affecting all or nearly all the parts of a (specified or implied) whole, as a territory, community, organization, etc.; completely or nearly universal; not partial, particular, local, or sectional. ME. †b Belonging or pertaining in common *to*. LME–M17. c With collect. or pl. n.: all, collective, whole. *obs.* exc. in *general body*. L16. 2 Chief, head; having unrestricted authority. LME. b *Mil.* Having superior rank and extended command; *spec.* (of an officer) above the rank of a colonel. L16. 3 Pertaining to or current among the majority; prevalent, widespread, usual, common. LME. 4 Not specifically limited in application; relating to a whole class of objects, cases, occasions, etc.; (of a rule, law, etc.) true for all or nearly all cases coming under its terms. LME. b Indefinite, imprecise; vague. E17. 5 Including the main features, elements, etc., and neglecting or ignoring unimportant details or exceptions. M16. b Of a name, term, concept, etc.: intended to include or cover those features common to the individuals of a class and neglect the differences. M16. 6 Not restricted to one field, class or area; not specialized; concerned with or skilled in all the branches of a particular business or activity (freq. used preceding an agent-n. esp. of employment). Formerly also, widely accomplished. M16.

1 G. ORWELL If it once became general, wealth would confer no distinction. W. PLOMER To the general agitation a particular one of my own was added. 3 C. IVES A matter nowadays of common impression or general opinion. 4 J. HERSEY On his first visit, he kept the conversation general, formal. ISAIAH BERLIN We must always avoid applying general principles but examine each case in its full individual detail. A. THWAITE He seemed to have a general grudge against writers. b H. JAMES A general conviction that it was horribly late and a particular objection to looking at my watch. F. FORSYTH He too was planning his campaign; not in detail like Shannon, but in general terms. 5 T. HARDY Their general likeness to each other . . suggested that . . they were brothers. G. VIDAL Each story varies a bit from the other but the general sense is as follows. b C. D. E. FORTNUM The general term . . Majolica, has long been . . applied to all varieties of glazed earthenware of Italian origin. 6 J. TYNDALL Never . . has this longing been more liberally responded to, both among men of science and the general public. R. HOGGART He has little call to move if he is a general labourer, . . hardly more if he is skilled.

Special collocations & phrases: **as a general rule** in most cases. *Attorney general*, *Attorney-General*: see ATTORNEY *n.* *consul general*: see CONSUL 5. *cook-general*: see COOK *n.* *General* AMERICAN. *general* ANAESTHESIA. *general anaesthetic*: see ANAESTHETIC *n.* **General Assembly** (*a*) the highest ecclesiastical court of various national churches, esp. the Church of Scotland; (*b*) the legislature of some states of the US. *general average*: see AVERAGE *n.*[2] 3. *General Certificate of (Secondary) Education*: see CERTIFICATE *n.* 2. **general confession** *Eccl.* (*a*) a confession to be made by the whole congregation; (*b*) a private confession of all past sins, including those previously confessed. *general court*: see COURT *n.*[1] **general dealer** a trader in many kinds of goods. **general delivery** *N. Amer.* a delivery of letters to personal callers at a post office who have e.g. no permanent address. *general* ELECTION. **general headquarters** *Mil.*: of a commander-in-chief. **general hospital** (*a*) a hospital not specializing in any particular field or restricted to patients of a particular age or sex; (*b*) a military hospital receiving sick and wounded from field hospitals. **general knowledge**: of miscellaneous facts, information, etc. **general meeting**: open to all members of a society. *general paralysis (of the insane)*: see PARALYSIS 1. **general post** (*a*) the first morning delivery; (*b*) an indoor game in which players are each given a place-name and exchange seats to evade the blindfolded 'postman'; *fig.* a general and rapid exchange of positions etc. **General Post Office** orig., the central office established in London with responsibility for the collection and dispatch of mail and later for the telephone system; now chiefly, the main post office in a town or city. **general practice** *Med.* the work of general practitioners. **general practitioner** *Med.* a doctor based in the community rather than a hospital and dealing with cases of all kinds in the first instance, as opp. to a consultant or specialist. *general* PUBLIC. **general reader**: of miscellaneous literature. **general staff**: assisting a military commander in planning and administration. **general store**: in which many kinds of goods are sold. **general strike** (*a*) a strike by all the workers of one industry; (*b*) a strike by the workers in all or most of the important trades; *spec.* that in Britain in 1926. *General Synod*: see SYNOD. *general warrant*: see WARRANT *n.*[1] **in a general way** ordinarily, usually. *Inquisitor General*: see INQUISITOR *n.* 2. *(Lord) Justice General*: see JUSTICE *n.* *minister general*: see MINISTER *n.* 2c. *Postmaster General*: see POSTMASTER *n.*[1] 1b. *Secretary-General*: see SECRETARY *n.* *Solicitor-General*: see SOLICITOR. *Surgeon General*: see SURGEON *n.*

B *n.* I A general thing or things collectively. 1 A general fact, truth, rule, etc. (usu. in *pl.*). Formerly also (esp. in *Logic*), a genus. Now *rare* exc. as opp. to *particulars*. LME. †b A quality or characteristic common to all. *rare* (Shakes.). Only in E17. †2 A neutral colour. LME–L17. 3 The public, the multitude. Formerly also *gen.*, the total or whole; the majority. *arch.* E17. 4 *Mil. Hist.* The first beat of the drum for the assembly of all the troops. E18.

1 I. MURDOCH We should start by considering art in general, and then move from the general to the particular. b SHAKES. *Tr. & Cr.* And in this fashion All our abilities, gifts, natures, shapes, Severals and generals exact. 3 F. BURNEY The general of people at his time of life are confined by infirmities. DISRAELI He . . understood all about . . sleepers and branch lines, which were then cabalistic terms to the general.

II A person of authority. 5 *Eccl.* The chief or head of a religious order. M16. 6 *Mil.* Orig., the commander of the whole army; later, the commander of a division. Now, an officer ranking next below a field-marshal; *US* a general of the army or air force. Also, by courtesy, a lieutenant general, a major-general. L16. †b *Naut.* An admiral. L16–E18. c The head of the Salvation Army; *spec.* (*the General*) its founder, General William Booth (1829–1912). L19. 7 A general servant. *arch. colloq.* L19.

Phrases: CAVIAR *to the general.* †**for the general** for the most part. **in general** †(*a*) in a body; universally, without exception; †(*b*) in all respects; (*c*) in general terms, generally; (*d*) as a rule, usually. **in the general** in general terms, generally.

C *v.t.* Infl. **-ll-**, ***-l-**. Lead or command like a general. M19.

D. L. EDWARDS This campaign, generalled by the inflexible Anselm.

generalate /ˈdʒɛn(ə)rəleɪt/ *n.* M17. [f. GENERAL *n.* + -ATE[1]. Cf. Fr. *généralat.*] The (period of) office of a military or ecclesiastical general.

generaless /dʒɛn(ə)rəˈlɛs/ *n. rare.* M17. [f. GENERAL *n.* + -ESS[1].] 1 The wife of a general. Chiefly *joc.* M17. 2 A female general. M19.

generalia /dʒɛn(ə)ˈreɪlɪə/ *n.pl.* M19. [Neut. pl. of L *generalis* GENERAL *a.*] General principles.

generalisation *n.* var. of GENERALIZATION.

generalise *v.* var. of GENERALIZE.

generalism /ˈdʒɛn(ə)rəlɪz(ə)m/ *n.* E19. [f. GENERAL *n.* + -ISM.] 1 A general statement or conclusion. E19. 2 The fact, quality, or action of generalizing; an instance of this. E20.

generalissimo /dʒɛn(ə)rəˈlɪsɪməʊ/ *n.* Pl. **-os**. E17. [It., superl. of *generale* GENERAL.] The commander of a combined military, naval, and air force, or of several armies.

fig.: *Times* Cricket does not lend itself, in the way that football may, to a generalissimo.

generalissima *n.* a female generalissimo M17.

generalist /ˈdʒɛn(ə)rəlɪst/ *n.* E17. [f. GENERAL *a.* + -IST.] A person trained or competent in several different fields or subjects. Opp. SPECIALIST *n.* 2.

Business Education Today These staff need to see themselves as generalists as well as bringing their areas of expertise to the team.

generality /dʒɛnəˈralɪti/ *n.* LME. [(O)Fr. *généralité* f. late L *generalitas*, f. *generalis* GENERAL: see -ITY.] 1 The quality or fact of being general; now *esp.* applicability to a whole class of instances; vagueness, lack of detail (in a statement etc.). Formerly also, prevalence, commonness. LME. 2 Something that is general; a general principle, law, point, or statement. Formerly also, a general class or category. Usu. in *pl.* LME. 3 The bulk, the greater part, the majority, (*of*). Formerly also, people in general. Now with *n.pl.* or *collect.* LME. 4 *Fr. Hist.* A fiscal and administrative division of the French kingdom. M17.

1 BURKE When an epitaph is very short, it is in danger of getting into a cold generality. E. E. KAY The subsequent words . . did not restrain the generality of the former words. 2 H. JAMES Mrs Vivian ventured upon nothing special; she contented herself with soft generalities. R. MACAULAY All generalities about human beings are nonsense. *glittering generality*: see GLITTER *v.* 3 L. VAN DER POST Once more he would have to isolate himself from the generality of men. D. LESSING I am talking of the generality, not of the rare individual.

generalization /dʒɛn(ə)rəlʌɪˈzeɪʃ(ə)n/ *n.* Also **-isation**. M18. [Fr. *généralisation*, f. *généraliser*: see next, -ATION.] 1 The action, the process, or an act of forming a general concept or proposition on the basis of induction; the result of this process. M18. 2 The process of becoming more general or widespread. L19.

1 J. HUTTON Here then is a generalization of many facts respecting light and heat. J. GATHORNE-HARDY What I am about to write . . are only generalisations; I could supply a mass of exceptions. **hasty generalization**: based on too few instances.

generalize /ˈdʒɛn(ə)rəlʌɪz/ *v.* Also **-ise**. LME. [f. GENERAL *a.* + -IZE. Cf. Fr. *généraliser*.] 1 *v.t.* Reduce to general laws; express in a general form; give a general character to; extend the application of. LME. 2a *v.t.* Infer (a conclusion, law, etc.) by induction; base a general law or conclusion on. L18. b *v.i.* Make general inferences or conclusions by induction; be inclined to make or express such inferences. L18. 3a *v.t.* Erode, soften, or blur the particulars or details of. L18. b *v.t.* & *i. Painting.* Portray only the typical or salient characteristics of (an object). E19. 4 *v.t.* Bring into general use; make common, familiar, or generally known; spread or extend. E19. 5 *v.i.* Of a law, theory, etc.: apply more generally; become extended in application *to*. L20.

generaliza'bility *n.* M20. **generalizable** *a.* M19. **generalized** *ppl a.* that has been generalized; *spec.* (*Med.*) (of a disease) that has extended to other parts of the body: M19. **generalizer** *n.* L18.

Général Jacqueminot /ʒeneral zakmino (*pl.* same), ˈdʒɛnər(ə)l ˈʒakmɪnəʊ/ *n. phr.* M19. [See JACQUEMINOT.] = JACQUEMINOT.

generally /ˈdʒɛn(ə)rəli/ *adv.* ME. [f. GENERAL *a.* + -LY[2].] 1 As a whole, collectively; universally, without exception. Now only in weaker sense, for the most part, on the whole; extensively. ME. 2 In a general sense or way, without reference to particulars or individuals. ME. 3 As a general rule; usually. LME.

generalness /ˈdʒɛn(ə)rəlnɪs/ *n.* Now *rare.* M16. [f. GENERAL *a.* + -NESS.] The state, quality, or fact of being general.

generalship /ˈdʒɛn(ə)rəlʃɪp/ *n.* L16. [f. GENERAL *n.* + -SHIP.] 1 (The discharge of) the office of general. Formerly also, the tenure of such an office. L16. 2 (Military) skill in command, strategy; tact, diplomacy. M18.

2 B. BEAUMONT His generalship and steadying influence were a great comfort to his team.

generant /ˈdʒɛn(ə)r(ə)nt/ *n.* M17. [L *generant-* pres. ppl stem of *generare*: see GENERATE *v.*, -ANT[1].] A thing which generates; *spec.* in *Math.* = GENERATRIX 2.

generate /ˈdʒɛn(ə)rət/ *ppl a.* LME. [L *generatus* pa. pple of *generare*: see next, -ATE[2].] Generated.

generate /ˈdʒɛnəreɪt/ *v.* E16. [L *generat-* pa. ppl stem of *generare* beget, f. *genus*, *gener-* stock, race: see -ATE[3].] 1 *v.t.* & *i.* Beget or reproduce (offspring). Now *rare.* E16. 2 *v.t.* Bring into existence, produce; cause to arise, give rise to; *Math.* (of a point, line, or surface) move and so notionally form (a line, surface, or solid). M16. b Produce (electricity, esp. electric current). L19. c *Math.* & *Ling.* Produce (a set, sequence, or string of items) by performing specified operations on or applying specified rules to an initial set. L19.

1 H. L. MENCKEN Man tries to protect himself against change even beyond the grave: he acquires property; he generates children. 2 T. H. HUXLEY Steam is generated from the water in the boiler. N. MOSLEY After he had gone the local enthusiasm he generated seemed to wane. *Times* The practice . . has the primary objective of generating commission income. J. KRANTZ The vast amount of publicity they generated was immediately reflected in sales. b **generating station** a building and site for generating electric current.

generation /dʒɛnəˈreɪʃ(ə)n/ *n.* ME. [(O)Fr. *génération* f. L *generatio(n-)*, f. as prec.: see -ATION.] I That which is generated. 1 The offspring of the same parent or parents regarded as a single step or stage in descent; such a step or stage. ME. †b Offspring, progeny; descendants. LME–E18. †c Family, race, stock; a class or kind of people or animals. LME–E18. d A kind or type, esp. of a computer, that is seen as representing a distinct advance on earlier kinds, or a recognized further stage of development. M20. 2 The whole body of people born and living at about the same time; later also, the average length of time in which children become ready to take the place of their parents, usu. reckoned at about thirty years. ME.

1 L. HELLMAN Nobody in his family had earned a living for three generations. d *Natural World* The M54, . . the first of a new generation of motorways. *first-generation*, *second-generation*, etc. 2 R. MACAULAY The last generation, the elderly people, were . . responsible for the unfortunate state. E. H. GOMBRICH Some two hundred years, scarcely more than six generations. B. PYM Like most girls of her generation and upbringing she had expected to marry.

II The action of generating. 3 The act or process of reproducing or being reproduced; procreation; propagation; *spec.* in *Theol.*, the origin of Christ from God the Father. LME. b Genealogy, lineage, pedigree. *rare.* LME. 4 The process of producing a substance, animal, plant, force, etc., by natural or artificial means; *spec.* the production of electricity. LME. b *Ling.* The process of deriving a sentence by the application of a rule or a series of rules which constitute the grammar. M20.

Phrases & comb.: *clogs to clogs in three generations*: see CLOG *n.* 3. **generation gap** differences in opinions, tastes, behaviour, etc. between those of different generations. *lost generation*: see LOST *a.*

generational *a.* L19. **generationism** *n.* (*Theol.*) the doctrine or belief that the soul as well as the body of a child is reproduced by the parents; traducianism: M19.

generative /ˈdʒɛn(ə)rətɪv/ *a.* LME. [(O)Fr. *génératif* or late L *generativus*, f. L *generat-*: see GENERATE *v.*, -IVE.] 1 Pertaining to generation or reproduction; able to generate or reproduce. LME. 2 Able to produce, productive. LME.

1 S. PEPYS We . . had very good discourse concerning the insects and their having a generative faculty as well as other Creatures. 2 R. G. COLLINGWOOD The generative act which produces that utterance is an act of consciousness. **generative grammar**: composed of rules which are able to generate all and only the permissible sequences of a language. TRANSFORMATIONAL-*generative*.

generatively *adv.* M17. **generativeness** *n.* E18. **generativism** *n.* (*Ling.*) the theory of the study of language on the basis of a generative grammar L20. **generativist** *n.* (*Ling.*) an adherent or practitioner of generativism M20.

generator /ˈdʒɛnəreɪtə/ *n.* M17. [L *generator*, f. *generat-*: see GENERATE *v.*, -OR. Later techn. uses directly f. GENERATE *v.*] 1 *gen.* A person who or thing which generates or reproduces. Now *rare.* M17. 2 A thing which generates or produces something; *spec.* (*a*) an apparatus for producing gases, steam, etc.; (*b*) a machine for converting mechanical into electrical energy, as a dynamo. L18. 3 *Mus.* The fundamental tone of a series of harmonics or of a chord. M19. 4 *Math.* A point, line, or surface regarded as moving and so notionally forming a line, surface, or solid respectively. Also called *generatrix.* M19. 5 *Math.* Each of a subset of elements in forms of which the other elements of the set can be represented. L19. 6 *Computing.* A routine that constructs other routines or subroutines using given parameters, for specific applications. M20.

generatrix /dʒɛnəˈreɪtrɪks/ *n.* Pl. **-trices** /-trɪsiːz/. M17. [L, fem. of *generator*: see prec., -TRIX.] †1 A female parent. Only *fig.* M17–E19. 2 *Math.* = GENERATOR 4. M19.

generic /dʒɪˈnɛrɪk/ *a.* & *n.* L17. [Fr. *générique*, f. L *genus*, *gener-* GENUS: see -IC.] A *adj.* 1 Characteristic of or belonging to a genus or class; applicable to (any individual of) a large group or class, general, non-specific. L17. 2 Of the name of a commercial product: not protected by legislation from general use; of a product, esp. a drug: not protected by a registered trade mark. Orig. *US.* L20.

1 ALDOUS HUXLEY The derisive individual in her . . repelled him, but the attraction of what was generic, . . the entire sex, was stronger. B. COTTLE Primitive languages have words for various trees but no generic term for 'tree'.

B *n.* Something generic; *spec.* (*a*) a general word as an element of a compound proper name; (*b*) (orig. *US*) a generic product. E19.

generical *a.* = GENERIC *a.* M17. **generically** *adv.* with reference to genus M17. **genericalness** *n.* (*rare*) E18. **genericness** *n.* generic quality or characteristics M20.

generification /dʒɪˌnɛrɪfɪˈkeɪʃ(ə)n/ *n.* M19. [f. L *genus*, *gener-* GENUS + -FICATION.] *Logic.* = GENERALIZATION I.

generosity /dʒɛnəˈrɒsɪti/ *n.* LME. [L *generositas*, f. *generosus*: see next, -ITY.] 1 Excellence or nobility of birth. *arch.* LME. 2 Orig., courage, nobility of conduct. Now only, magnanimity, willingness to forgive. Also (*rare*), an instance of this. E17. 3 Liberality in giving, munificence; *rare* an instance of this. L17.

2 R. BENTLEY His Judgment, like other mens Valour, has commonly the generosity to favour the weaker side. 3 R. DAVIES He gave away . . all sorts of stuff at every performance. . . What was all that generosity meant to conceal?

generous /ˈdʒɛn(ə)rəs/ *a.* L16. [(O)Fr. *généreux* f. L *generosus* noble, magnanimous, f. *genus*, *gener-*: see GENUS, -OUS.] 1 Of noble birth, high-born. Formerly also, (of an animal) of good stock. *arch.* L16. 2 Orig., characteristic of noble birth, gallant, courageous. Now only, noble-minded, magnanimous, free from meanness or prejudice. L16. 3 Ample, large; abundant, copious. E17. b Of wine etc.: rich and full. E17. 4 Free in giving, liberal, munificent. L17.

2 G. GREENE She had to be satisfied with that; one did not expect any generous response from an employer. H. KISSINGER He urged us to make concessions because great powers could afford a generous attitude. 3 A. EDEN Everything about Potter was of generous proportions, including his weight. *House & Garden* Curtains with swags and tails to match the splendour of the generous windows. 4 A. GUINNESS Ralph Richardson, always generous to a fault, gave me a number of presents.

generously *adv.* L16. **generousness** *n.* (now *rare*) E17.

genesis /ˈdʒɛnɪsɪs/ *n.* LOE. [L f. Gk = generation, creation, nativity, horoscope, name of the Old Testament book in Septuagint, hence in Vulgate, f. base of *gignesthai* be born or produced.] 1 (**G-**.) (The name of) the first book of the Bible, containing an account of the creation of the world. LOE. †2 *Astrol.* Nativity, horoscope. LME–M17. †3 Synthesis. Only in 17. 4 Origin, mode of formation or generation. E17.

1 T. H. HUXLEY The reconcilers of Genesis with science. 4 E. CLODD The theory of evolution must embrace the genesis and development of mind.

Gene'siacal *a.* (*rare*) = GENESITIC L19. **Gene'sitic** *a.* (*rare*) of or belonging to Genesis M19.

-genesis /ˈdʒɛnɪsɪs/ *suff.* [Repr. Gk GENESIS.] In compounds denoting modes of generation, as ABIOGENESIS, BIOGENESIS, PARTHENOGENESIS, etc.

genet /ˈdʒɛnɪt/ *n.*[1] Also **genette** /dʒɪˈnɛt/. LME. [OFr. *genete* (mod. *-ette*); cf. Arab. *jarnait*.] 1 †a In *pl.* Skins of the genet used as fur. LME–L17. b Fur obtained from genets; fur sold in imitation of this. L19. 2 Any of several small carnivorous catlike mammals constituting the genus *Genetta*, native to Africa and southern Europe and having spotted fur and long ringed bushy tails. L15.

genet /ˈdʒɛnət/ *n.*[2] L20. [f. GENET(IC after ORTET, RAMET.] *Biol.* A genetically distinct entity, such as may be produced by asexual reproduction from a single zygote. Cf. RAMET.

genet *n.*[3] var. of JENNET.

genethliac /dʒɛˈnɛθlɪak/ *n.* & *a.* Long *arch. rare.* L16. [Ult. f. Gk *genethliakos* belonging to one's birth or birthday (= *genethlios*, f. *genethlē*, f. base of *gignesthai*: see GENESIS).] A *n.* A person who calculates nativities or horoscopes, an astrologer. L16. B *adj.* = next. E17.

genethliacal /dʒɛnɪˈθlʌɪək(ə)l/ *a.* E17. [f. as prec. + -AL[1].] Relating to the calculation of nativities; relating to a birthday.

genethliacally *adv.* M17.

genethliacon /dʒɛnɪˈθlʌɪəkɒn/ *n.* Pl. **-ca** /-kə/. L16. [L f. Gk neut. sing. of *genethliakos* GENETHLIAC.] A birthday ode.

genethlialogy /dʒɛ,nɛθlɪˈalədʒi/ *n.* M17. [Gk *genethlialogia* f. *genethlialogein* cast nativities: see -LOGY.] The calculating or casting of nativities.

genetic /dʒɪˈnɛtɪk/ *a.* M19. [f. GENESIS after *antithesis*, *antithetic*, etc.] 1 Of, pertaining to, or involving origin; arising from a common origin. M19. b Of or pertaining to genetics or genes; hereditary. E20. 2 Generative; productive. *rare.* M19.

1 MAX-MÜLLER The only scientific and truly genetic classification of religions. b J. UPDIKE You shouldn't be drinking and smoking pot . . , you'll cause genetic damage. J. BRONOWSKI By some genetic accident, the wild wheat crossed with a natural goat grass and formed a fertile hybrid.

Special collocations: **genetic code** the basis on which genetic information is stored as sequences of nucleotides in chromosomal DNA or RNA, different groups of three consecutive nucleotides corresponding to different amino acids. **genetic counselling**: given to prospective parents concerning the chances of genetic disorders in a future child. **genetic drift** variation in the relative frequency of different genotypes in a small population owing to the chance disappearance of particular genes as individuals die or do not reproduce. **genetic engineering** the manipulation of genetic material in order to alter genes and hence the characteristics of the organism concerned. **genetic fingerprint** a set of genetic characteristics derived from the tissues or secretions of an individual and used to identify him or her. **genetic profile** a description listing the significant genetic characteristics of an individual and used for identification, the prediction of inherited disorders, etc.

-genetic /dʒɪˈnɛtɪk/ *suff.* [f. prec.] Forming adjs. corresp. to ns. in *-genesis* or *-geny*, as *biogenetic*, *phylogenetic*: = -GENIC 1, 2.

genetical /dʒɪˈnɛtɪk(ə)l/ *a.* M17. [f. as prec.: see -AL[1].] †1 Synthetic, as opp. to analytic. Cf. GENESIS 3. Only in M17. 2 = GENETIC. M19.

genetically /dʒɪˈnɛtɪk(ə)li/ *adv.* M19. [f. GENETIC or prec.: see -ICALLY.] 1 As regards origin. M19. 2 As regards genetics; by the agency of genes. E20.

geneticism /dʒɪˈnɛtɪsɪz(ə)m/ *n.* M20. [f. GENETIC + -ISM.] Orig., the theory that an individual's form and behaviour can be explained in terms of the history of both the individual and the race. Now (usu. *derog.*), the belief that human characteristics are genetically determined.

genetics /dʒɪˈnɛtɪks/ *n.* L19. [f. GENETIC + -S[1].] 1 The principles or laws of origination. Now *rare* or *obs.* L19. 2a The branch of science that deals with heredity and the variation of inherited characteristics in living organisms. E20. b The genetic characteristics of an organism or condition. M20.

2b *Nature* A world authority on the taxonomy and genetics of the cottons.

geneticist /-sɪst/ *n.* an expert in or student of genetics E20.

genetrix /ˈdʒɛnɪtrɪks/ *n.* Now *rare.* Also (earlier) †**-ice**. Pl. **-ices** /-ɪsiːz/. LME. [OFr *genitris* or L *genetrix*, *-itrix* fem. of GENITOR *n.*[2]: see -TRIX.] A female parent, a mother.

genette *n.*[1] var. of GENET *n.*[1]

genette *n.*[2] var. of JENNET.

Geneva /dʒɪˈniːvə/ *n.*[1] L16. [A city in Switzerland.] 1 Used *attrib.* to designate things found in, originating in, or associated with Geneva. L16. 2 Designating (a mechanism employing) a driving-wheel with a pin that engages with a radial slot or slots in a driven wheel for part of each revolution, so converting continuous motion into intermittent motion. L19.

1 **Geneva bands** clerical bands resembling those worn by the Swiss Calvinist clergy. **Geneva Bible**: the English translation first printed at Geneva in 1560; also called *Breeches Bible*. **Geneva Convention** an international agreement first made at Geneva in 1864 and later revised, governing the status and treatment of captured and wounded military personnel in wartime. **Geneva cross** a red cross (distinguishing hospitals, ambulances, etc., in war). **Geneva gown** a long loose black gown worn by (esp. Calvinist) clergy and academics. **Geneva Protocol**: any of various protocols drawn up in Geneva, *esp.* that of 1925 limiting chemical and bacteriological warfare. **Geneva watch** a Swiss-made watch. 2 **Geneva stop**: consisting of a pair of gears in which the driven wheel lacks cogs or slots on part of its circumference.

ˈ**Genevize** *v.i.* (now *rare*) imitate or introduce the practice or doctrines of the Genevan (Calvinist) church L17.

geneva *n.*[2] see GENEVER.

Genevan /dʒɪˈniːv(ə)n/ *n.* & *a.* Also (earlier) †**-vian**. M16. [f. GENEVA *n.*[1] + -AN.] A *n.* A native or inhabitant of the city of Geneva in Switzerland. Also (now *rare*), a person who follows the Calvinist doctrine associated with Geneva. M16. B *adj.* Of or pertaining to Geneva (orig. esp. to its ecclesiastical organization); (now *rare*) Calvinistic. L16.

genever /dʒɪˈniːvə, jəˈneɪvə/ *n.* Also (now *literary*) **-va**. E18. [Du. f. OFr. *genevre* (mod. *genièvre*) f. alt. of L *juniperus* JUNIPER. Var. assim. to GENEVA *n.*[1] See also GIN *n.*[2]] Dutch gin.

Genevese /dʒɛnəˈviːz/ *n.* & *a.* M17. [f. GENEVA *n.*[1] + -ESE.] A *n.* Pl. same. A native or inhabitant of the city of Geneva in Switzerland. M17. B *adj.* Of or pertaining to Geneva. E19.

†**Genevian** *n.* & *a.* see GENEVAN.

Genevois /ʒən(ə)vwa, ʒnɛv-/ *n.* & *a.* Pl. same. M16. [Fr. *genévois*.] = GENEVESE.

genial /ˈdʒiːnɪəl/ *a.*[1] M16. [L *genialis* nuptial, productive, joyous, f. GENIUS: see -AL[1].] 1 Of or pertaining to marriage, nuptial; of or pertaining to reproduction or procreation. Now *rare.* M16. †2 Festive. E17–M18. 3 Conducive to growth. Now chiefly of air, climate, sunshine, etc.: pleasantly warm, mild. M17. †4 Of or pertaining to natural disposition; natural. M17–M19. 5 Jovial, kindly, sociable; sympathetically cheerful. M18. 6 [Infl. by G *genial*, *-isch*.] Of, pertaining to or characterized by genius (GENIUS 6). Now *rare* or *obs.* E19.

1 SPENSER The bridal bowre and geniall bed. 2 DRYDEN In Winter shall the Genial Feast be made Before the Fire. 3 COLERIDGE Applause scarcely less genial to a poet, than the vernal warmth to the feathered songsters during their nest-building. 4 MILTON So much I feel my genial spirits droop. 5 V. S. PRITCHETT To find oneself among affectionate, genial and cultivated families . . must be heaven. O. SACKS He was a genial soul, very ready to talk and to answer any questions.

geniˈality *n.* E17. **genialize** *v.t.* (*rare*) make genial or agreeable M19. **genially** *adv.* M17. **genialness** *n.* (*rare*) geniality E18.

genial /dʒɪˈniːəl/ *a.*[2] M19. [f. Gk *geneion* chin, f. *genus* jaw: see -AL[1].] *Anat.* Of, pertaining to, or situated on the chin.

genic /ˈdʒiːnɪk, ˈdʒɛn-/ *a.* E20. [f. GENE + -IC.] Of or pertaining to a gene or genes.

genically *adv.* M20.

-genic /ˈdʒɛnɪk/ *suff.* [f. -GEN + -IC.] Forming adjs., mostly corresp. to ns. in *-gen*, *-genesis*, or *-geny*. 1 Producing, causing, as *carcinogenic*, *pathogenic*. 2 Caused by, originating in, as *iatrogenic*. 3 [After *photogenic*.] Well suited to: in adjs. referring to modes of dissemination or reproduction of information etc.

genicular /dʒɪˈnɪkjʊlə/ *a.* E19. [f. L *geniculum*: see next, -AR[1].] 1 = GENICULATE. *rare.* E19. 2 *Anat.* Of or pertaining to the knee or a genu. E20.

geniculate /dʒɪˈnɪkjʊlət/ *a.* M17. [L *geniculatus*, f. *geniculum* joint in a plant stem, small knee, dim. of *genu* knee: see -CULE, -ATE[2].] Bent at a sharp angle; *Anat.* situated at a sharp bend. Also, resembling a knee.

geniculate body *Anat.* either of two protuberances on each side of the inferior surface of the thalamus which relay auditory and visual impulses respectively to the cerebral cortex. **geniculate ganglion** *Anat.* a sensory ganglion at a bend of the facial nerve. **geniculate nucleus** *Anat.* = *geniculate body* above.

Also **geniculated** *a.* M17.

geniculation /dʒɪ,nɪkjʊˈleɪʃ(ə)n/ *n.* E17. [Late L *geniculatio(n-)*, f. *geniculare* bend the knee, f. L *geniculum*: see prec., -ATION.] †1 (A) genuflexion. E–M17. 2 The state of being geniculate. L19.

geniculum /dʒɪˈnɪkjʊləm/ *n.* Pl. **-lums**, **-la** /-lə/. E19. [L: see GENICULATE.] *Anat.* A small kneelike structure; a sharp bend; *Bot.* (*rare*) a joint in the stalk of a plant.

genie /ˈdʒiːni/ *n.* Pl. **genii** /ˈdʒiːnɪʌɪ/, **-s.** M17. [Fr. *génie* f. L GENIUS.] †1 = GENIUS 1. M17–E18. 2 A spirit or jinnee (in Arabian stories), esp. one trapped in or inhabiting a bottle, lamp, etc., and capable of granting wishes. Cf. GENIUS 2. M18.

2 S. RUSHDIE I just rub my jolly old lamp and out pops the genie bringing fame and fortune.

¶ See note s.v. GENIUS. *genie* was adopted in sense 2 by the Fr. translators of the *Arabian Nights' Entertainments* on account of its resemblance in both sound and sense to Arab. *jinnī*.

genii *n.* pl. of GENIE, GENIUS.

genin /ˈdʒɛnɪn/ *n.* E20. [Ending of SALIGENIN, SAPOGENIN.] *Chem.* Any of various steroids that occur as the non-sugar part of glycosides in some plants and toad venoms.

†**genio** *n.* E17–E18. [It. f. L GENIUS.] = GENIUS.

genio- /dʒɪˈnʌɪəʊ/ *comb. form* of Gk *geneion* chin: see GENIAL *a.*[2], -O-.

genioˈglossus (orig. †**-glosse**) *n.* a muscle which is inserted in the undersurface of the tongue and the hyoid and protrudes and retracts the tongue; also *genioglossus muscle*: M17. **genioˈhyoid** *n.* a muscle inserted in the hyoid which elevates the bone and draws it forward; also *geniohyoid muscle*: M19.

genip *n.* var. of GUINEP.

genipap /ˈdʒɛnɪpap/ *n.* E17. [Port. *jenipapo* f. Tupi *ianipaba*.] A tropical American tree, *Genipa americana*, which yields a dye used in tattooing; its fruit, resembling an orange in appearance.

Genist /ˈdʒiːnɪst/ *n.* E17. [Late L *Genistae* pl. f. Gk *Genistai*, prob. f. base of *gignesthai* be born.] A member of a sect of ancient Jews who claimed pure-blooded descent from Abraham.

genista /dʒɪˈnɪstə, dʒɛ-/ *n.* E17. [L = the plant broom.] Any of several yellow-flowered leguminous heathland shrubs belonging to or formerly included in the genus *Genista*; *esp.* dyer's greenweed, *G. tinctoria*, and petty whin, *G. anglica*.

genistein /dʒɪˈnɪstiːɪn/ *n.* E20. [f. prec. + -EIN.] *Chem.* A yellow isoflavone derivative, $C_{15}H_{10}O_5$, that occurs in subterranean clover and as an aglycone in dyer's greenweed, and is weakly oestrogenic.

genital /ˈdʒɛnɪt(ə)l/ *a.* & *n.* LME. [(O)Fr. *génital* or L *genitalis* (neut. sing. and pl. as n.), f. *genitus* pa. pple of *gignere* beget: see -AL[1].] A *adj.* Of or pertaining to the organs of reproduction; (now *rare*) pertaining to reproduction. LME. B *n.* The external organ or organs of reproduction, esp. of the male. Usu. in *pl.* LME.

genitalia /dʒɛnɪˈteɪlɪə/ *n.pl.* L19. [L, use as n. of neut. pl. of *genitalis*: see prec.] The interior or exterior reproductive organs (of male or female); the genitals.

genitival /dʒɛnɪˈtʌɪv(ə)l/ *a.* E17. [f. next + -AL[1].] †1 Of birth or reproduction. *rare.* Only in E17. 2 = GENITIVE *a.* 1. E19.

genitivally *adv.* L19.

genitive /ˈdʒɛnɪtɪv/ *a.* & *n.* LME. [(O)Fr. *génitif*, *-ive* or L *genitivus*, *-iva* (*gene-*), (sc. *casus* case), f. *genit-* pa. ppl stem of *gignere* beget, produce: see -IVE.] A *adj.* 1 Designating, being in, or pertaining to a case in inflected languages indicating relationship between nouns (in English corresponding to *of*, *from*, and other prepositions with a noun representing the source, possessor, etc.). LME. †2 Pertaining to reproduction. M16–M17.

B *n. The* genitive case; a word, form, etc., in the genitive case. LME.

genitive absolute a construction in Greek similar to the Latin ablative absolute.

genitor /ˈdʒɛnɪtə/ *n.*[1] LME. [(O)Fr. *géniteur* or L *genitor*, f. base of *gignere* beget: see -OR.] 1 A male parent, father; (in *pl.*) parents. *arch.* LME. 2 *Anthropol.* A person's biological as opp. to legal father. Cf. PATER 3b. M20.

†genitor *n.*[2] var. of GENITORY.

genitory /ˈdʒɛnɪt(ə)ri/ *n.* Now *rare.* Also **†-or.** LME. [(O)Fr. *génitoires* pl., suffix-variant (-ORY[1]) of synon. *†genitaire(s, †genitailles, génitures.*] A testicle. Usu. in *pl.*: testicles, (in later use) genitals.

genito-urinary /ˌdʒɛnɪtəʊˈjʊərɪn(ə)ri/ *a.* M19. [f. L *genitalis* GENITAL + -O- + URINARY.] Chiefly *Med.* = URINOGENITAL.

Daily Telegraph VD clinics, now designated genito-urinary clinics.

geniture /ˈdʒɛnɪtʃə/ *n.* LME. [(O)Fr. *géniture* or L *genitura*, f. base of *gignere* beget: see -URE.] 1 Begetting; birth. LME. †2 Offspring; product. LME–L17. †3 *Astrol.* Nativity, horoscope. E17–E19. †4 Animal semen. Only in 17.

1 QUILLER-COUCH A man's lineage and geniture being reckoned . . among the things he cannot reasonably be asked to amend.

genius /ˈdʒiːnɪəs/ *n.* Pl. **-ii** /-ɪʌɪ/, **-iuses.** LME. [L, f. base of *gignere* beget, Gk *gignesthai* be born, come into being.] 1 The tutelary or attendant spirit in classical pagan belief allotted to every person at birth, or to a place, institution, etc. Formerly also, an allegorical figure representing the moral instincts keeping passion within bounds. LME. b Esp. as *good* or *evil genius.* Either of the two mutually opposed spirits or angels supposed to attend each person. Hence a person who or thing which for good or bad powerfully influences another. L16. c The personification or embodied type of something immaterial. *rare.* L16. d *Astrol.* The combination of sidereal influences represented in a person's horoscope. M17. 2 A demon or spirit; *esp.* = GENIE 2. L16. 3†a Characteristic disposition, bent, or inclination; natural character or constitution. L16–E19. b Prevalent feeling, opinion, taste, or character (of a nation, age, etc.). M17. c The prevailing character or spirit, or characteristic method (of a law, language, etc.). M17. d The body of associations connected with or inspirations derived from a place. Cf. sense 5 below. E19. 4 Natural ability or tendency; attributes which fit a person for a particular activity. Passing into sense 6. E17. b Natural aptitude, talent, or inclination *for*, †*to* (something). M17. 5 *genius loci* /ˈləʊsʌɪ, ˈlɒkiː/ [L, of the place], the presiding god or spirit of a place. Also = sense 3d above. E17. 6 Inborn exalted intellectual power; instinctive and extraordinary imaginative, creative, or inventive capacity, freq. opp. to *talent*; a person having this. M17.

1 K. WHITE Kind genii of my native fields benign. c SHAKES. *2 Hen. IV* His dimensions . . were invisible. 'A was the very genius of famine. 2 G. BUCK Another kind of Genius, or *ignis fatuus.* 3a EVELYN Suitable to my rural genius, born as I was at Wotton, among the woods. b D. HUME The barbarous and violent genius of the age. c J. C. CALHOUN The genius of our constitution is opposed to the assumption of power. d C. LAMB Is the being shown over a place the same as . . detecting the genius of it. 4 B. FRANKLIN Different men have geniuses adapted to a variety of different arts and manufactures. b M. KEANE He had a genius for prolonging a visit if a house suited him. 5 N. PEVSNER The *genius loci*, . . in modern planning terms, is the character of the site. 6 H. SIDDONS Isaac was a good-dispositioned, industrious boy, but no genius. J. A. FROUDE A man of genius . . is a spring in which there is always more behind than flows from it.

¶The pl. *genii* is not usu. distinguishable from a pl. of GENIE. Ambiguous early examples have been regarded as belonging here.

genizah /gɛˈniːzə/ *n.* Also **-za.** L19. [Heb., lit. 'a hiding, hiding place', f. *gānaz* set aside, hide.] (The contents of) a storeroom for damaged, discarded, or heretical manuscripts and sacred relics, usu. attached to a synagogue.

gennel *n.* var. of GINNEL.

gennemic /dʒəˈnɛmɪk/ *a.* M20. [f. Gk *gennēma* product + -IC.] *Phonet.* Of or pertaining to speech sounds after they have been uttered.

geˈnnemically *adv.* M20.

gennet *n.* var. of JENNET.

geno- /ˈdʒɛnəʊ, ˈdʒiːnəʊ/ *comb. form.* [f. Gk *genos* offspring, race: see -O-.] Forming ns. and adjs. w. the senses 'gene' or 'genus'.

genophore *n.* (*Biol.*) a structure carrying genetic information in prokaryotes, viruses, and some organelles M20. **genoˈtoxic** *a.* (*Biol.* & *Med.*) designating a substance, esp. a carcinogen, that has a direct toxic effect on genetic material L20. **genotoxicity** /-tɒkˈsɪsɪti/ *n.* (*Biol.* & *Med.*) the property or degree of being genotoxic L20.

Genoa /ˈdʒɛnəʊə, dʒɛˈnəʊə/ *n.* L16. [A city and seaport of NW Italy.] †1 *paste of Genoa*, a baked sweet made of quince, spices, and sugar. L16–E17. 2 Used *attrib.* to designate things originating in or associated with Genoa. M17. b In full *Genoa velvet.* Velvet woven on a twilled ground. M18. c In full *Genoa cake.* A rich fruit cake topped with almonds. L19. d In full *Genoa jib.* A large jib with a low foot used on a racing yacht. M20.

Genoan *a.* & *n.* (now *rare* or *obs.*) = GENOESE E17.

genocide /ˈdʒɛnəsʌɪd/ *n.* M20. [f. GENO- + -CIDE.] The (attempted) deliberate and systematic extermination of an ethnic or national group.

genoˈcidal *a.* M20.

Genoese /dʒɛnəʊˈiːz/ *n.* & *a.* M16. [f. GENOA + -ESE after It. GENOVESE. Cf. GENOWAY.] A *n.* Pl. same, †-s. A native or inhabitant of Genoa; the dialect of Genoa. M16.

B *adj.* Of or pertaining to Genoa. M18.

Genoese sponge a sponge cake made of eggs, butter, and sugar beaten into a light, even batter.

genome /ˈdʒiːnəʊm/ *n.* M20. [f. GENO- + CHROMOSOME.] *Biol.* The complete set of genes or genetic material present in a cell, organelle, virus, etc., or in each cell of an organism. Also, (the genes in) a complete haploid set of chromosomes of a particular organism.

geˈnomic *a.* M20.

genotype /ˈdʒɛnətʌɪp, ˈdʒiːn-/ *n.*[1] Now *rare.* L19. [f. GENO- + -TYPE.] *Taxon.* The type species of a genus.

genotype /ˈdʒɛnətʌɪp, ˈdʒiːn-/ *n.*[2] & *v.* E20. [G *Genotypus*, f. as GENO-: see TYPE *n.*] A *n. Biol.* The genetic constitution of an individual, esp. as distinguished from the phenotype; the whole of the genes in an individual or group. E20. B *v.t. Med.* Investigate the genotype of. M20.

genotypic /-ˈtɪp-/ *a.* M20. **genotypical** /-ˈtɪp-/ *a.* E20. **genotypically** /-ˈtɪp-/ *adv.* E20.

-genous /dʒɪnəs/ *suff.* [f. -GEN + -OUS.] Forming adjs. 1 = -GENIC I, as *erogenous.* 2 = -GENIC 2, as *endogenous.*

Genovese /ˈdʒɛnəviːz/ *n.* & *a.* Now *rare.* E17. [It., f. *Genova* GENOA.] A *n.* Pl. same, †-s. = GENOESE *n.* E17. B *adj.* = GENOESE *a.* M17.

†Genoway *n.* & *a.* Also (earlier) **Jenoway.** LME–M17. [OFr. *Genoueis* f. It. *Genovese*: see prec.] = GENOESE.

genre /ˈʒɒ̃rə, ˈʒɒnrə/ *n.* E19. [Fr. = kind: see GENDER *n.*] Kind, type; *esp.* a style or category of painting, novel, film, etc., characterized by a particular form or purpose; *spec.* a style of painting depicting scenes of ordinary life.

T. MOORE Two very remarkable men . . but of entirely different genres. V. CRONIN Catherine particularly liked satirical comedies and encouraged two playwrights in this genre. *attrib.*: E. H. GOMBRICH Pictures in which the painters . . cultivated a certain . . kind of subject, particularly scenes from daily life . . became known as 'genre pictures'.

Genro /ˈgɛnrəʊ/ *n.* Pl. same. L19. [Jap. = principal elders, f. *gen* origin + *rō* old.] *Hist.* (A member of) a body of personal counsellors to the Japanese throne, who dominated the government from 1889 to the 1930s.

gens /dʒɛnz/ *n.* Pl. **gentes** /ˈdʒɛntiːz, -teɪz/. M19. [L, f. base of *gignere* beget.] 1 In ancient Rome: a group of families with a supposed common origin, a common name, and common religious rites. Also, a similar group of families in other cultures, e.g. in ancient Greece [tr. Gk *genos*]. M19. 2 *Anthropol.* A kinship group composed of people related through their male ancestors. L19.

gens d'armes *n. phr. pl.* see GENDARME.

gens de la robe /ʒɑ̃ də la rɔb/ *n. phr.* Also ***gens de robe.*** L17. [Fr., lit. 'folk of the long robe'.] Lawyers.

gent /dʒɛnt/ *n.* M16. [Abbrev.] 1 A gentleman. Now *slang, iron.,* & *commercial.* M16. 2 In *pl.* (treated as *sing.* & *pl.*). A public convenience for males, = GENTLEMAN 4d. M20.

1 S. LEWIS George's missus went into the gent's wear department . . to buy him some collars. I. MURDOCH 'He'll murder you.' 'Not he,' said Norman. . . 'He's a gent'.

†gent *a.* ME. [OFr. f. pop.L contr. of cl.L *genitus* born, hence well-born, noble. Cf. GENTLE *a.*] 1 Noble, high-born. Of a knight or warrior: brave and chivalrous. In later use, graceful in manners, polite. ME–L17. 2 Of the body or limbs, of a woman, child, etc.: slender, shapely; freq. *gent and small, fair and gent.* Also, tasteful, refined. ME–E19.

1 SPENSER The prowest and most gent, That ever brandished . . steele on hye! 2 R. GREENE Her middle was both small and gent. R. HOLME A Shooe of the Gentest fashion.

gentamicin /dʒɛntəˈmʌɪsɪn/ *n.* M20. [f. *genta-* of unkn. origin + alt. of -MYCIN.] A broad-spectrum antibiotic composed of sulphates of substances produced by the actinomycete *Micromonospora purpurea* and used esp. for severe systemic infections.

†gentee *a.* var. of GENTY.

genteel /dʒɛnˈtiːl/ *a., n.,* & *adv.* Orig. **†-tile.** L16. [Re-adoption of Fr. *gentil*, which had become GENTLE *a.*] A *adj.* 1 Fashionably elegant or sumptuous; stylish. *arch.* L16. b Of a person: suggestive of a gentleman or lady in appearance; stylishly dressed. Now *slang.* E17. 2 Of behaviour, manners, etc.: appropriate to or characteristic of a person of good social position. E17. 3 Of a person, family, etc.: of good social position. Cf. GENTLE *a.* I. *arch.* E17. 4 Qualified by manners or style of life to form part of good society. Formerly, polished, well-bred. E17. †b Liberal in money matters. Of a present etc.: handsome. E17–L18. †c Of behaviour: courteous, obliging. M17–E19. 5 Elegant or graceful in shape or appearance. Now *obs.* exc. with mixture of sense I. L17. †b Of an immaterial thing: refined, delicate. L17–M18. 6 In derog. use: cultivating the (supposed) manners or conventions of good society; marked by affected or excessive refinement, politeness, respectability, etc. L19.

1 V. KNOX The entertainment was sumptuous and genteel. A. TROLLOPE He was possessed of a genteel villa and ornamental garden. b GOLDSMITH Did I not work that waistcoat, to make you genteel? 2 W. TENNANT A genteel business, such as jewellery . . or perfumery. JOCELYN BROOKE He seemed, though not . . wealthy, to have more than a genteel sufficiency. J. FOWLES In those days a genteel accent was not the great social requisite it later became. 3 J. RAY All the Knights are of noble or gentile extraction. 4 L. RITCHIE A man . . might be rich without being genteel, and poor without being vulgar. T. HARDY The accomplishment was one which she did not care to profess in genteel company. 5 D. HUME His countenance beautiful; his limbs genteel and slender. 6 R. L. STEVENSON The parlour—a very genteel room, with Bible prints . . and a selection of dried grasses. G. B. SHAW We are much too pious and genteel to allow such things to be mentioned. J. B. PRIESTLEY She turned to Miss Trant and . . became very stiff and genteel 'I'm sure it's very kind of you.'

B *n.* A genteel person. L17.

T. D'URFEY Ye lofties, Genteels, who above us all sit.

C *adv.* In a genteel manner. Now *slang.* L18.

genteelish *a.* somewhat genteel M18. **genteelism** *n.* (a) genteel practice; *esp.* the substitution, for an everyday word or expression, of one considered socially more acceptable, e.g. *perspiration* for *sweat*; also, a word or expression so substituted: E20. **genteelly** *adv.* E17. **genteelness** *n.* genteel quality; an instance of this: M17.

genteelity *n.* see GENTILITY.

gentes *n.* pl. of GENS.

gentian /ˈdʒɛnʃ(ə)n/ *n.* & *a.* LME. [L *gentiana* (sc. *herba*), named, according to Pliny, after *Gentius*, king of Illyria: see -IAN.] **A** *n.* **1** Any of numerous plants of the genus *Gentiana* (family Gentianaceae), with four- or five-lobed corollas freq. of a brilliant deep blue, chiefly growing in damp alpine places; a flower or flowering stem of such a plant. Also, (a flower or stem of) any of a number of similar plants (esp. of the related genus *Gentianella*). LME. **2** A bitter tonic or (more fully *gentian brandy, spirit*) liqueur made from gentian root (see below). M19.

1 *autumn gentian, willow gentian*, etc.

Comb.: *gentian brandy*: see sense 2 above; **gentian root** the rhizome and root of the yellow-flowered *Gentiana lutea* of the Alps etc., used in pharmacy; *gentian spirit*: see sense 2 above; **gentian violet** a dye used as an antiseptic, esp. in the treatment of burns.

B *adj.* Having the blue colour of the gentian. E20.

gentianella /dʒɛnʃəˈnɛlə/ *n.* M17. [mod.L, dim. of *gentiana* GENTIAN.] Any of several dwarf plants belonging to the genus *Gentiana* or related genera; *esp.* the blue-flowered *G. acaulis* of the Alps.

¶In botanical L *Gentianella* is now recognized as a genus distinct from *Gentiana*, containing various species formerly included in the latter.

gentil *n., a.* see GENTLE *n., a.* & *adv.*

gentile /ˈdʒɛntʌɪl/ *n.* LME. [f. the adj.] **I** (Usu. **G-**.) In senses from Vulgate. **1** Among the Jews: a person not belonging to the Jewish people or faith. LME. **b** *transf.* A person not belonging to one's Church; *esp.* a non-Mormon. M17. **2** A pagan, a heathen. Now *rare*. LME. †**b** *spec.* A Hindu (opp. a Muslim). M16–E18. **II** In senses from classical L. **3** A word denoting nationality. E17. †**4** *Rom. Law.* A member of the same gens. Only in L19.

gentiledom *n.* the Gentile world; the state of being a Gentile in practice or belief: M17.

gentile /ˈdʒɛntʌɪl/ *a.* LME. [L *gentilis*, f. *gens*, *gent-* clan, race, f. base of *gignere* beget.] **I** (Freq. **G-**.) In senses from Vulgate. **1** Pagan, heathen. LME. **2** From a Jewish standpoint: non-Jewish. L17. **3** *transf.* (Pertaining to a person) that does not belong to one's Church; *esp.* non-Mormon. M19.

1 J. BRAND The basilicae of gentile Rome . . were converted into churches. 2 F. RAPHAEL Her friends were both Gentile and Jewish. 3 W. H. DIXON The Shakers . . smile at our Gentile ailments.

II In senses derived from classical L. **4** Pertaining to a nation or tribe. Now *rare*. E16. **5** *Gram.* Of a word: indicating nationality. E19. **6** Pertaining to a gens or clan. M19.

gentilesse /dʒɛntɪˈlɛs/ *n.* Long *arch.* LME. [(O)Fr. *gentillesse*, f. *gentil*: see GENTLE *a.*, -ESS[2].] Courtesy, good breeding; an instance of this.

gentilic /dʒɛnˈtɪlɪk/ *a.* E17. [f. L *gentilis* GENTILE *n.*, *a.* + -IC.] †**1** Pagan. Only in E17. **2** Belonging to a tribe or nation. L19.

gentilician *a.* var. of GENTILITIAN.

gentilise *v.*[1], *v.*[2] vars. of GENTILIZE *v.*[1], *v.*[2]

gentilism /ˈdʒɛntɪlɪz(ə)m/ *n.* L16. [OFr. or med.L *gentilismus*, f. eccl.L *gentilis* GENTILE *n.*, *a.*: see -ISM.] (A) heathen belief or practice.

gentilitial /dʒɛntɪˈlɪʃ(ə)l/ *a.* E17. [f. L *gentilicius* + -AL[1]. In sense 3, perh. f. med.L *gentilitia* GENTILESSE.] **1** Peculiar to a gens or clan. E17. **2** Peculiar to a nation or people; national. M17. **3** Gently born. E19.

gentilitian, -lician *a.* = GENTILITIAL I M17.

gentilitious /dʒɛntɪˈlɪʃəs/ *a.* E17. [f. as prec. + -OUS.] †**1** Characteristic of a Gentile or non-Christian; pagan. Only in E17. **2** = GENTILITIAL *a.* I. M17. **3** = GENTILITIAL *a.* 2. M17.

gentility /dʒɛnˈtɪlɪti/ *n.* Also (*Sc.*) **genteelity** /-ˈtiːl-/. ME. [In branch I f. (O)Fr. *gentilité*, f. *gentil*: see GENTLE *a.*, -ITY. In branch II, f. eccl. & med.L *gentilitas* paganism has at least been contributory.] **I** In senses rel. to GENTLE *a.*, GENTEEL *a.* **1** Gentle birth, honourable extraction. *arch.* ME. **b** People of gentle birth; *the* gentry. *obs.* exc. *Sc.* L16. **c** The rank or heraldic status of a gentleman. M17. †**2** Polite manners, courtesy. Only in L16. **3** Social superiority as shown by manners, behaviour, appearances, etc.; (an instance of) manners, behaviour, etc., displaying such superiority. Now chiefly *derog.*, genteel behaviour: see GENTEEL *a.* 6. M17. †**4** Elegance, refinement. M–L18.

1 J. COLLIER An ancient Gentility does not . . convey to us any Advantage . . of Body or Mind. b T. SMITH The Nobility, the rest of the gentilitie, & the yeomanrie. 2 SPENSER Such wilde woodes should far expell All civile usage and gentility. 3 J. RUSKIN Once get the wealthy classes to imagine that the possession of pictures . . adds to their gentility. GEO. ELIOT Let him forsake a decent craft that he may pursue the gentilities of a profession. J. GROSS No more staid men with sound views, no more suffocating gentility.

II In senses rel. to GENTILE *a.* †**5** Heathen belief or practice; paganism. Also, the pagan world. E16–M17. **6** Relationship between members of a gens. Formerly, the gens itself. L16.

gentilize /ˈdʒɛntɪlʌɪz/ *v.*[1]*t.* *arch.* Also **-ise**. L16. [f. Fr. *gentil* GENTLE *a.* + -IZE.] Turn into a person of breeding; make genteel.

gentilize /ˈdʒɛntɪlʌɪz, -tʌɪl-/ *v.*[2] Also **-ise**. L16. [f. GENTILE *n.* or *a.* + -IZE.] **1** *v.i.* Of a Jew: live like a Gentile. L16. **2** *v.t.* Make Gentile, i.e. non-Jewish or pagan. E19.

gentle /ˈdʒɛnt(ə)l/ *n.* Also (*obs.* exc. as in sense 3) **gentil**. LME. [f. the adj.] **1** A person of gentle birth or good social position. Usu. in *pl.* (formerly sometimes in polite address). Now mostly *arch.* LME. **2** A maggot, the larva of the flesh-fly or bluebottle, used by anglers. L16. **3** = *falcon-gentle* s.v. GENTLE *a.* 1b. L18.

gentle /ˈdʒɛnt(ə)l/ *a.* & *adv.* Also (*obs.* exc. *Falconry*) **gentil**. ME. [(O)Fr. *gentil* high-born (in mod.Fr. = pleasant, agreeable) f. L *gentilis* of the same clan, (Proto-Romance) belonging to a good family: see also GENTEEL, GENTILE *a.*, JAUNTY *a.*] **A** *adj.* **1** Of a person: well- (orig. nobly-) born; *spec.* entitled to bear a coat of arms. Formerly freq. as a vague epithet of commendation. *obs.* exc. in arch. phr. *gentle and simple*, and in comb. GENTLEFOLK, GENTLEMAN, etc. ME. **b** Of an animal: of excellent breed or spirit. Now only in *falcon-gentle, gentle falcon*, (the female of) the peregrine falcon, and TIERCEL-*gentle*. ME. †**c** Of a thing: noble, excellent. ME. **2** Of birth, family, etc.: distinguished, honourable. ME. **b** Of an activity or pursuit: suitable to a person of good social position; honourable, gentlemanly. L15. **3** Of a person: having the character appropriate to one of gentle birth; noble, courteous, chivalrous. *arch.* ME. **b** In complimentary address. Now only as a playful archaism, in *gentle reader*. LME. †**c** Of language, an action, etc.: courteous, polite. LME–M17. †**4** Graceful, slender, handsome. ME–E16. **5** Of a plant, fruit, etc.: having mild properties; cultivated. *arch.* LME. **b** Of an animal: quiet, tractable. M16. †**6** Not harsh to the touch; soft, pliant. M16–M18. **7** Moderate in action, effect, or degree; not violent, severe, or boisterous. M16. **b** Of a sound: low, soft. E17. **c** Of a slope etc.: gradual, not abrupt. L17. **8** Of a person, action, etc.: mild or benign in disposition; free from sternness or aggression. (Foll. by *to*, *with*.) M16. **9** Sacred to or haunted by fairies. See also *gentle people* below. *dial.* (chiefly *Anglo-Ir.*). E19.

1 J. FLETCHER I am as gentle as your self, as free born. b J. SKELTON A ientyll hownde shulde neuer play the kur. c J. MANDEVILLE Wyn . . that is fulle myghty and gentylle in drynkynge. 2 SIR W. SCOTT His birth being admitted as gentle, gave him access to the best society. b R. ADAMS Peasant girls, ignorant of gentle ways. 3 SIR T. MORE Sithe I am so gentle to graunt you so many things, I trust ye wyl grant me this one. b SHAKES. *Haml.* Thanks, Rosencrantz and gentle Guildenstern. A. THWAITE Such questions exercise the gentle reader Snug in his study. c B. YOUNG She gave him . . thanks for the gentle entertainment she had in his Castle. 5 B. JOWETT Tending the gentle shoots, and preventing the wild ones from growing. b W. FAULKNER To buy a good gentle horse. 7 A. REID Liquors . . evaporated by a gentle heat. E. O'NEILL She gives him a gentle shake. J. STEINBECK The brown algae waved in the gentle currents. b J. GRAHAME The murmuring So gentle of the brook. c P. PORTER I will not roll down this gentle bank. 8 H. JAMES A gentle pedagogue, prompting her with small caresses. H. ROBBINS Life had not been gentle with either of them. They had to fight for everything they got. *New York Times* Gentle persuasion is not going to make the Argentine Government give up what it has seized by force.

Special collocations: *falcon-gentle*: see sense 1b above. **gentle art** *the* sport of angling. **gentle craft** = *gentle art* above; formerly, *the* trade of shoemaking. *gentle falcon*: see sense 1b above. **gentle people** (*Ir.*) *the* fairies. **gentle-people** gentlefolk. NAVEW *gentle*. TIERCEL-*gentle*. *the gentle(r) sex*: see SEX *n.*

B *adv.* In a gentle manner. E17.

DYLAN THOMAS Do not go gentle into that good night.

gentle /ˈdʒɛnt(ə)l/ *v.* LME. [f. the adj.] †**1** *v.t.* Raise to a high social position; ennoble. LME–M17. **2** *v.t.* Make mild or gentle in character, manner, etc. M17. **b** *spec.* Make (an animal) docile or tractable. Also, stroke or massage gently. M18. **c** Soothe the feelings of, pacify (a person). L18. **3** *v.i.* Become mild or gentle. E20.

1 SHAKES. *Hen. V* Be he ne'er so vile, This day shall gentle his condition. 2 R. BROUGHTON A smile . . sweetening and gentling the . . sullenness of her face. *absol.*: E. HYAMS The gentling influence of the Atlantic allows . . trees to grow farther north. b W. HOLTBY He . . knelt by the kicking animal, . . gentling her head. E. FERBER A nice gentled riding pony. *fig.*: R. BRADBURY When you lay . . in your . . bed and were gentled to sleep by the sound. c J. LE CARRÉ He didn't get angry. . . He gentled him and smiled. 3 V. BUCHANAN-GOULD The African world gentled to soft femineity. P. BARKER Gradually . . the red gentles through purple and gold to rose.

gentlefolk /ˈdʒɛnt(ə)lfəʊk/ *n.pl.* Earlier **-folks** /-fəʊks/. L16. [f. GENTLE *a.* + FOLK.] People of gentle birth or good social position.

gentlehood /ˈdʒɛnt(ə)lhʊd/ *n.* M19. [f. GENTLE *a.* + -HOOD.] Position or character attaching to gentle birth.

gentleman /ˈdʒɛnt(ə)lmən/ *n.* Pl. **-men**. ME. [f. GENTLE *a.* + MAN *n.*, after OFr. *gentilz homme* (mod. *gentilhomme*).] **1** A man of gentle (orig. noble) birth. In later use, a man of good birth (according to heraldic interpretations, one entitled to bear arms) who is not a nobleman; (formerly sometimes placed as a title after a man's name). Now chiefly *Hist.* ME. **2** A man who demonstrates his gentle birth by appropriate behaviour or moral qualities, e.g. chivalrous conduct, consideration for others, sense of honour, etc.; *gen.* a man (of whatever rank) who displays such qualities. ME. **3** A man of gentle birth attached to the household of a monarch or other person of high rank. Freq. in titles, as *Gentleman of the Bedchamber*, *Gentleman of the Chapel Royal*, etc. See also *gentleman-at-arms*, *gentleman pensioner* below. LME. **b** A man (orig. of gentle birth) acting as personal attendant to a man of rank or quality. See also *gentleman's gentleman* below. LME. **4** Used as a courteous designation for a member of certain societies and professions, a fellow-member of the House of Commons or the House of Representatives, etc.; esp. *the gentleman from* (a specified constituency). M16. **b** In *pl.*, as a polite form of address to a group (esp. an audience) of men of whatever rank (corresp. to 'sir' in *sing.*). Formerly also *sing.*, as a polite form of address to one man. L16. **c** As a genteelism: a man, of whatever rank. E19. **d** *the gentlemen('s)* (treated as *sing.*), a public convenience for males. E20. **5** A man of superior social standing; a man with the refinement of manners, breeding, etc., that qualify him to mix in the best society. L16. **b** As a status: a man whose wealth frees him from the need to follow a trade or profession. Also (*joc.* & *dial.*), a man without employment. L18. **c** *Cricket* (now *Hist.*). A non-professional player (opp. PLAYER 2c). E19. **6** *euphem.* (*a*) = *gentleman of the road* below; (*b*) a smuggler. L18.

1 A. RADCLIFFE Pierre de la Motte was a gentleman descended from an ancient house of France. 2 P. G. WODEHOUSE Clarence is a gentleman He is incapable of insulting a woman. E. O'NEILL I give you my word as an officer and a gentleman. 3 C. V. WEDGWOOD The King was still accompanied by . . Thomas

Herbert, the gentleman in attendance, and three or four lower servants. b SMOLLETT I took the name from his gentleman, Mr. O'Frizzle. 4 W. S. CHURCHILL The hon. Gentleman opposite . . tries to suggest it is all some fake propaganda. c A. LOOS Gentlemen always seem to remember blondes. J. ORTON Miss Barclay, a gentleman wishes to see you. 5 R. L. STEVENSON In the steerage there are males and females; in the second cabin ladies and gentlemen. J. WAIN He was dressed in a quiet grey suit and looked . . every inch a gentleman. c *fig.*: H. GREENE Broadcasting is no longer a profession for gentlemen: the players have taken over.

Phrases etc.: COUNTRY *gentleman*. *fine gentleman*: see FINE *a.* **gentleman-at-arms** any of the forty gentlemen acting as bodyguard to the British monarch on ceremonial occasions. **gentleman of fortune** an adventurer. **gentleman of the road** (*a*) a highwayman; (*b*) a commercial traveller; (*c*) a Gypsy. *gentleman of virtu*: see VIRTU *n.* 1. **gentleman's agreement** (orig. *US*): binding in honour, but not enforceable at law. **gentleman's gentleman** a valet. **Gentleman's Relish** (proprietary name for) a highly seasoned anchovy paste. **gentlemen of the press** journalists. **gentlemen's agreement** = *gentleman's agreement* above. *ladies and gentlemen*: see LADY *n.* & *a.* **Old Gentleman** *the* Devil. *walking gentleman*: see WALKING *ppl a.*

Attrib. & *comb.*: Esp. in the sense 'practising a specified occupation as an amateur rather than for profit or pay', as *gentleman-adventurer*, *gentleman-farmer*, etc. Special combs., as **gentleman-commoner** *Hist.* (at Oxford and Cambridge) a member of a class of undergraduates enjoying special privileges; **gentleman friend** *arch. colloq.* a boyfriend, a beau; †**gentleman-pensioner** = *gentleman-at-arms* above; **gentleman-usher** a gentleman acting as usher to a person of superior rank.

gentlemanhood *n.* the position or character of a gentleman M18. **gentlemanlike** *a.* & *adv.* (*a*) *adj.* = GENTLEMANLY (a); †(*b*) *adv.* in the manner of a gentleman: M16. **gentlemanliness** *n.* gentlemanly quality L16. **gentlemanly** *a.* & *adv.* (*a*) *adj.* natural or appropriate to a gentleman; resembling a gentleman in appearance or conduct; (*b*) *adv.* (now *rare*) as befits a gentleman: LME.

gentleness /ˈdʒɛnt(ə)lnɪs/ *n.* ME. [f. GENTLE *a.* + -NESS.] †1 Gentle or noble birth. ME–L17. †2 Courteous or chivalrous nature. Only in LME. 3 Mildness of temper; freedom from sternness or aggression. M16. 4 Freedom from intensity, suddenness, steepness, etc.; moderateness. E17.

gentlewoman /ˈdʒɛnt(ə)lwʊmən/ *n.* Pl. **-women** /-wɪmɪn/. ME. [f. GENTLE *a.* + WOMAN *n.*] 1 A woman of good birth or breeding; a lady. Now *arch.* or *joc.* ME. 2 A woman (orig. of gentle birth) acting as attendant to a lady of rank. Now only *Hist.* LME.

gentlewomanhood *n.* the character appropriate to a gentlewoman M19. **gentlewomanlike** *a.* having the manners or appearance of a gentlewoman; appropriate to a gentlewoman: L16. **gentlewomanliness** *n.* gentlewomanly quality E19. **gentlewomanly** *a.* = GENTLEWOMANLIKE E19.

gently /ˈdʒɛntli/ *adv.* ME. [f. GENTLE *a.* + -LY[2].] 1 With gentleness of birth; only in *gently born*. Formerly, as befits a person of gentle birth; graciously, generously, etc. ME. 2 With moderate or subdued action; slowly, quietly, by easy stages. M16. 3 Without sternness or severity; mildly, benignly. M16.

2 J. BUCHAN A valley . . tilted up gently towards the west. J. STEINBECK Tom laid his hammer gently on the floor. 3 M. W. MONTAGU I can bear being told that I am in the wrong, but tell me gently.

Gentoo /dʒɛnˈtuː/ *n.*[1] & *a. Anglo-Ind.* (*obs.* exc. *Hist.*). M17. [f. Port. *gentio* GENTILE *n.*, *a.*] A *n.* 1 A non-Muslim inhabitant of Hindustan; a Hindu. Also *spec.*, a Telugu-speaking Hindu of southern India. M17. 2 The language spoken by Gentoos. L17. B *attrib.* or as *adj.* Of or pertaining to the Gentoos. L17.

gentoo /dʒɛnˈtuː/ *n.*[2] M19. [Perh. a use of prec.] A penguin, *Pygoscelis papua*, of the Falklands and other antarctic islands. Also *gentoo penguin*.

gentrice /ˈdʒɛntrɪs/ *n. obs.* exc. *Sc.* ME. [OFr. *genterise* var. of *gentelise*, f. *gentil* GENTLE *a.* + *-ise* -ICE[1].] 1 Superiority of birth or rank. ME. 2 Good breeding. Formerly, graciousness, magnanimity, etc. ME. 3 People of good birth or rank. LME.

gentrify /ˈdʒɛntrɪfʌɪ/ *v.t.* L20. [f. next + -FY.] Make genteel in character; *esp.* convert (a working-class or inner-city district) into an area of middle-class residence.

gentrifiˈcation *n.* L20.

gentry /ˈdʒɛntri/ *n.* LME. [OFr. *genterie*.] 1 Superiority of birth or rank; gentility. Formerly also occas. in neutral sense, quality of birth or rank. *obs.* exc. *Sc.* LME. 2 Conduct characteristic of a person of gentle birth; politeness of manners, good breeding. Formerly also, graciousness, magnanimity, etc. *obs.* exc. *Sc.* LME. 3 People of gentle birth or good breeding; *the* class composed of such people, *spec.* that below the nobility. L16. 4 People of a specified kind. *joc.* or *derog.* E18. 5 *The* fairies. *Anglo-Ir.* L19.

1 JONSON We haue raised Seianus from obscure, and almost vnknowne Gentry. ALAN ROSS 'Tis madness to presume too much upon our birth and Gentry. 3 G. B. SHAW The horrible condition of the working classes that underlies . . the prestige of the landed gentry and peerage. H. ARENDT The English gentry . . had assimilated the higher ranks of the bourgeoisie. 4 THACKERAY The light-fingered gentry pick pockets furiously. *transf.*: GEO. ELIOT The broken discourse of poultry and other lazy gentry in the afternoon sunshine.

genty /ˈdʒɛnti/ *a.* Also †**gentee**. M17. [Var. of GENTEEL, with attempt to render the sound of Fr. *gentil* more closely: see also JAUNTY *a.*] 1 Well-bred, genteel, courteous. Formerly, fashionably dressed. *obs.* exc. *Sc.* M17. 2 Dainty, graceful. *Sc.* E18.

gentiness *n.* L17.

genu /ˈdʒɛnjuː/ *n.* M19. [L.] 1 The knee. Chiefly *Med.*, in mod.L phrs. (see below). Also, a kneelike joint in invertebrates. M19. 2 A kneelike angle or bend. L19.

1 **genu valgum** [L VALGUS] knock-knee. **genu varum** [L VARUS *n.*[2]] bow-legs.

genual *a.* pertaining to the knee (or kneelike joint) M19.

genuant /ˈdʒɛnjʊənt/ *a.* L17. [f. L *genu* knee + -ANT[1].] *Her.* Kneeling.

genuflect /ˈdʒɛnjʊflɛkt/ *v.* M17. [eccl.L *genuflectere*, f. *genu* knee + *flectere* to bend.] †1 *v.t.* Bend (the knee). Only in M17. 2 *v.i.* Chiefly in Catholic or Anglo-Catholic ritual: lower one knee (or both knees simultaneously) momentarily to the ground, as an act of worship. (Foll. by *before*, *to*.) M19. b *fig.* Display servile obedience or deference *to*. L19.

2b JANET MORGAN The lower servants genuflected to those in higher authority.

genuflector *n.* a person who genuflects M19. **genuflectory** *a.* relating to genuflexion M19.

genuflexion /dʒɛnjʊˈflɛkʃ(ə)n/ *n.* Also **-flection**. LME. [eccl.L *genuflexio(n-)*, f. *genuflex-* pa. ppl stem of *genuflectere*: see prec., -ION.] An act of genuflecting.

genuine /ˈdʒɛnjʊɪn/ *a.* L16. [L *genuinus*, perh. f. *genu* knee, w. ref. to the Roman custom of a father acknowledging paternity of a newly born child by placing him or her on his knee.] †1 Natural or proper to a person or thing. L16–E18. 2 Having the character claimed for it; real, true, not counterfeit. M17. b Esp. of a literary or artistic work: really originating from its reputed author; authentic. M17. c Properly so called. L17. 3 Belonging to the original stock; pure-bred. E18. 4 Of a person: free from affectation or hypocrisy. M19. 5 Of a horse or greyhound: that does its honest best in races etc. L20.

1 WOODES ROGERS I . . keep to the Language of the Sea, which is more genuine, and natural for a mariner. 2 L.P. HARTLEY She didn't know if the delay was genuine, for sometimes her employer deliberately kept his clients waiting. LD BRAIN A psychological illness . . may be the result of very genuine worries. *genuine article*: see ARTICLE *n.* 10. b R. W. EMERSON The . . question concerning his reputed works—what are genuine, what spurious. c JAS. HARRIS The genuine pronoun always stands by itself. 3 E. A. FREEMAN The founder of a great name, whose genuine bearers soon passed away. 4 J. B. HILTON She used to . . tell her how grateful she was. Not smarmy, like; genuine.

genuinely *adv.* M17. **genuineness** *n.* M17.

genus /ˈdʒɛnəs, ˈdʒiːnəs/ *n.* Pl. **genera** /ˈdʒɛn(ə)rə/, **genuses**. M16. [L = birth, family, nation.] 1 *Logic.* A class of things containing a number of subordinate classes (called species) with certain common attributes; the first of the five predicables (PREDICABLE *n.*). M16. 2 *Biol.* A basic taxonomic grouping ranking below family and subfamily, which contains a number of related and morphologically similar species (or sometimes a single species). Formerly also used in the classification of minerals, chemical substances, etc. E17. b *gen.* A category, a kind. M17. 3 In ancient Greek music, each of the three kinds of tetrachord. M18.

1 K. DIGBY Rarity and Density . . can not change the common nature of Quantity, that is, their Genus. *middle genus*: see MIDDLE *a.* 2 T. THOMSON The genus sulphates contains several salts of . . importance. P. THEROUX There were spurges, plants of the genus euphorbia. *the genus Homo*: see HOMO *n.*[1] 2. *type genus*: see TYPE *n.* & *a.* b N. MITFORD I had never seen a slut before but recognized the genus . . as soon as I set eyes on this one.

-geny /dʒəni/ *suff.* [Corresp. to Fr. *-génie*, both repr. Gk *-geneia*, forming ns. f. adjs. in *-genēs*.] Forming ns. denoting '(mode of) generation', as in *biogeny*, *ontogeny*; = -GENESIS (which has tended to supersede it).

geo /gjəʊ, ˈdʒiːəʊ/ *n.* Orig. *Orkney* & *Shetland dial.* Also **gio**. Pl. **-os**. E17. [ON *gjá*.] A rocky gully or inlet in the coast (in Orkney and Shetland); *Physical Geogr.* a long, narrow steep-sided cleft formed by erosion in coastal cliffs.

geo- /ˈdʒiːəʊ/ *comb. form* repr. Gk *geō-* f. *gē* earth: see -O-.

geocoˈrona *n.* an envelope of gas (chiefly ionized hydrogen) forming the outermost layer of the earth's atmosphere and extending to the limit of the magnetosphere (also called *protonosphere*) M20. **geocoˈronal** *a.* of or pertaining to the geocorona M20. **geodyˈnamic(al)** *adjs.* of, pertaining to, or designating the (latent) forces of the earth L19. **geodyˈnamics** *n.* the branch of science that deals with geodynamic forces L19. **geoˈmembrane** *n.* a non-woven geotextile L20. **geophone** *n.* an instrument for detecting vibrations in the ground E20. **geophyte** *n.* (*Bot.*) a perennial plant which propagates by means of underground buds L19. **geoplaˈnarian** *n.* [L *planus* flat] a person who believes the earth to be flat M20. **geopoˈtential** *n.* the work that must be done against gravity to raise unit mass to a given point from sea level E20. **geosphere** *n.* (*a*) any of the more or less spherical concentric regions of the earth and its atmosphere; (*b*) the lithosphere: L19. **geoˈstrategy** *n.* strategy as applied to the problems of geopolitics; global strategy: M20. **geoˈtechnic** *a.* of or pertaining to geotechnics E20. **geoˈtechnical** *a.* geotechnic M20. **geoˈtechnics** *n.* the art of modifying and adapting the physical nature of the earth to the needs of man E20. **geotechˈnology** *n.* the application of technology to the utilization of the natural resources of the earth M20. **geotecˈtonic** *a.* = TECTONIC *a.* 2 L19. **geoˈtextile** *n.* an artificial material in the form of a woven or continuous sheet, used in combination with soil or rock in civil engineering, landscaping, etc. L20. **geotherˈmometer** *n.* (*a*) an instrument for measuring temperature within the earth; (*b*) a petrological phenomenon or property from which temperatures within the earth's crust can be inferred: M19.

geobotany /dʒiːəʊˈbɒtəni/ *n.* E20. [f. GEO- + BOTANY.] = PHYTOGEOGRAPHY.

geoboˈtanic *a.* E20. **geoboˈtanical** *a.* L19. **geoˈbotanist** *n.* E20.

geocentric /dʒiːə(ʊ)ˈsɛntrɪk/ *n.* & *a.* M17. [f. GEO- + -CENTRIC.] A *n.* Chiefly *Hist.* A person who believes that the earth is the centre of the universe. M17.

B *adj.* 1 Considered as viewed from the earth's centre; referred to the earth as centre. L17. 2 Having or representing the earth as the centre. Freq. opp. *heliocentric*. L17.

1 **geocentric latitude, longitude**: at which a planet etc. would appear if observed from the position of the earth's centre. 2 *fig.*: T. HARDY The geocentric view . . a zenithal paradise, a nadiral hell.

geocentrically *adv.* E18. **geocenˈtricity** *n.* the state of having the earth as centre or of being determined with reference to the centre of the earth M20. **geocentrism** *n.* (*Hist.*) the theory or belief that the earth is the centre of the universe L19.

geochemistry /dʒiːəʊˈkɛmɪstri/ *n.* E20. [f. GEO- + CHEMISTRY.] The chemistry of the earth; the science of the chemical composition of the earth.

geochemical *a.* L19. **geochemically** *adv.* M20. **geochemist** *n.* E20.

geochronology /dʒiːəʊkrəˈnɒlədʒi/ *n.* L19. [f. GEO- + CHRONOLOGY.] The chronology of the earth; the measurement of geological time and the ordering of geological events.

geochronoˈlogical *a.* M20. **geochronoˈlogically** *adv.* M20. **geochroˈnologist** *n.* M20.

geochronometry /dʒiːəʊkrəˈnɒmɪtri/ *n.* E20. [f. GEO- + CHRONOMETRY.] **1** Geometry extended to include time as the fourth dimension; a system of this. E20. **2** The measurement of geological time; absolute geochronology. M20.

geochronoˈmetric *a.* M20.

geocronite /dʒɪˈɒkrənʌɪt, dʒiːəʊˈkrəʊnʌɪt/ *n.* M19. [f. GEO- + Gk *Kronos* Saturn (in alchemy assoc. with lead) + -ITE[1].] *Min.* A grey to grey-blue orthorhombic sulphide of lead, antimony, and arsenic, usu. found as massive, granular, or earthy deposits.

geode /ˈdʒiːəʊd/ *n.* L17. [L *geodes* f. Gk *geōdēs* earthy, f. *gē* earth: see -ODE[1].] **1** A rock formation or a stone containing a cavity lined with crystals or other mineral matter. L17. **2** The cavity itself; the crystals within it. M19.

1 O. W. HOLMES An aphorism . . has been forming itself in one of the blank interior spaces of my intelligence, like a crystal in the cavity of a geode.

geˈodic *a.* of, pertaining to, or resembling a geode M19.

geodesic /dʒiːə(ʊ)ˈdɛsɪk, -ˈdiːsɪk/ *a.* & *n.* E19. [f. next + -IC.] **A** *adj.* Of or pertaining to geodesy; relating to the geometry of the earth's surface or, more generally, to curved surfaces; *spec.* designating, or built according to, constructional principles involving the use of spheres and geodesic lines (see below). Cf. GEODETIC. E19.

geodesic curve a geodesic line on a curved surface. **geodesic line** the shortest possible line on a surface between two points on that surface.

B *ellipt.* as *n.* A geodesic curve or line; a geodesic structure. L19.

geodesical *a.* = GEODESIC *a.* E19.

geodesy /dʒɪˈɒdɪsi/ *n.* L16. [mod.L *geodaesia* f. Gk *geōdaisia*, f. *daiein* divide: see GEO-, -Y[3].] Orig., land surveying. Now, the branch of mathematics that deals with the shape and area of the earth or of large parts of it.

geodesist *n.* M19.

geodetic /dʒiːə(ʊ)ˈdɛtɪk/ *n.* & *a.* L17. [f. Gk *geōdaitēs* land surveyor, f. *daiein* divide: see GEODESY, -IC.] **A** *n.* †**1** In *pl.* A cardinal number regarded as expressing an attribute, or as counting, rather than as an abstract quantity. Only in L17. **2** A geodesic line. L19. **B** *adj.* = GEODESIC. M19.

geodetical /dʒiːə(ʊ)ˈdɛtɪk(ə)l/ *a.* E17. [f. as prec. + -AL[1].] **1** Of or pertaining to geodesy; geodesic. E17. †**2** Math. *geodetical number*, = GEODETIC *n.* 1. L17–E18.

geodetically *adv.* L17.

geogeny /dʒɪˈɒdʒəni/ *n.* Now *rare.* M19. [f. GEO- + -GENY.] = GEOGONY.

geoˈgenic *a.* M19.

geognost /ˈdʒiːəgnɒst/ *n.* Now chiefly *Hist.* E19. [Fr. *géognoste*, f. Gk *gēo-* GEO- + *gnōtēs* a person who knows.] An expert in or student of geognosy.

geognosy /dʒɪˈɒgnəsi/ *n.* Now chiefly *Hist.* L18. [Fr. *géognosie*, f. Gk *gēo-* GEO- + *gnōsis* knowledge.] **1** The branch of science that deals with the structure and composition of the earth; *loosely* geology. L18. **2** The mineralogy of particular rocks (esp. in a region), together with the grouping, distribution and relations of those rocks. E19.

geogˈnostic(al) *adjs.* of or pertaining to geognosy L18. **geogˈnostically** *adv.* M19.

geogony /dʒɪˈɒgəni/ *n.* E19. [f. GEO- + -GONY.] The science or a theory of the formation of the earth.

geoˈgonic *a.* L19.

geographer /dʒɪˈɒgrəfə/ *n.* M16. [f. late L *geographus* (f. Gk *geōgraphos*: see GEO-, -GRAPH) + -ER[1]: see -GRAPHER.] An expert in or student of geography.

geographic /dʒɪəˈgrafɪk/ *n.* & *a.* E17. [Fr. *géographique* or late L *geographicus*, f. Gk *geōgraphikos*, f. *geōgraphos*: see prec., -IC.] **A** *n.* †**1** A treatise on geography. Only in E17. **2** In *pl.* = GEOGRAPHY 1. *rare.* M19. **B** *adj.* = GEOGRAPHICAL. M17.

geographical /dʒɪəˈgrafɪk(ə)l/ *a.* M16. [f. as prec.: see -ICAL.] Of, pertaining to, or of the nature of, geography.

geographical latitude the angle made with the plane of the equator by a perpendicular to the earth's surface at any point. **geographical mile** (*a*) a unit of length equal to one minute of longitude on the equator, or of latitude; = approx. 1850 metres; (*b*) the nautical mile of 1852 m. *geographical pole*: see POLE *n.*[2] 2.

geographically *adv.* E17.

geography /dʒɪˈɒgrəfi/ *n.* L15. [L *geographia* (partly through Fr.) f. Gk *geōgraphia*: see GEO-, -GRAPHY.] **1** The branch of knowledge that deals with the earth's surface, its form and physical features, natural and political divisions, climate, products, population, etc. L15. **2** A treatise on this. M16. **3** The subject matter of geography; (knowledge of) the features or arrangement of a region or (*colloq.*) a place, building, etc. M18.

1 DIALECT *geography*. **economic geography** the branch of geography that deals with the geographical distribution of economic resources. **human geography** the branch of geography that deals with the activities of humankind as they affect or are influenced by the earth's surface. LINGUISTIC *geography*. **mathematical geography**: studied using mathematical methods. *physical geography*: see PHYSICAL *a.* *plant geography*: see PLANT *n.* *social geography*: see SOCIAL *a.* 3 *transf.*: OED The geography of Mars. R. W. EMERSON We have seen the railroad and the telegraph subdue our enormous geography. **the geography (of the house)** *euphem.* the whereabouts of the lavatory.

geoid /ˈdʒiːɔɪd/ *n.* L19. [Gk *geoeidēs* adj., earthlike, f. GEO-: see -OID.] The earth's figure; a hypothetical solid figure the surface of which corresponds to mean sea level (and its imagined extension under land) and is perpendicular to the direction of gravity at all points.

geˈoidal *a.* L19.

geologic /dʒɪəˈlɒdʒɪk/ *a.* Now chiefly *US.* L18. [f. GEOLOGY + -IC.] = next.

geological /dʒɪəˈlɒdʒɪk(ə)l/ *a.* L18. [f. as prec. + -AL[1].] Of, pertaining to, or derived from geology.

geological map: showing the rock formations exposed at or underlying the surface of a region. **geological survey** detailed investigation of the geological features and resources of a region; an official body responsible for conducting such surveys. **geological time** the time which has elapsed since the earth's formation (up to the beginning of the historical period); time measured with reference to geological events.

geologically *adv.* E19.

geologize /dʒɪˈɒlədʒʌɪz/ *v.* Also **-ise**. E19. [f. GEOLOGY + -IZE.] **1** *v.t.* Examine (a place) geologically. E19. **2** *v.i.* Carry out geological investigations. M19.

geology /dʒɪˈɒlədʒi/ *n.* M18. [mod.L *geologia*, f. as GEO- + -LOGY.] †**1** The branch of science that deals with the earth in general. Only in M18. **2** The branch of science that deals with the physical structure and substance of the earth (or *transf.* of another planet etc.), the processes which act on these, and the earth's development since its formation. L18. **3** The geological features of a particular region. E19.

geologer *n.* (*rare*) = GEOLOGIST E19. †**geoˈlogian** *n.* = GEOLOGIST M–L19. **geologist** *n.* L18.

geomagnetism /dʒiːə(ʊ)ˈmagnɪtɪz(ə)m/ *n.* M20. [f. GEO- + MAGNETISM.] The branch of science that deals with the magnetic properties of the earth and related phenomena; terrestrial magnetism.

geomagˈnetic *a.* of or pertaining to geomagnetism E20. **geomagˈnetically** *adv.* M20. **geomagneˈtician** *n.* an expert in or student of geomagnetism M20. **geomagnetist** *n.* = GEOMAGNETICIAN E20.

geomancy /ˈdʒiːəmansi/ *n.* LME. [med.L *geomantia*, f. as GEO- + -MANCY.] (The art of) divination from the configuration of a handful of thrown earth or a number of random dots. Also, the art of siting cities, buildings, tombs, etc., auspiciously.

geomancer *n.* a person who practises geomancy LME.

geomantic /dʒiːə(ʊ)ˈmantɪk/ *a.* & *n.* L16. [f. as prec. + -IC: as n. f. med.L *geomanticus*.] **A** *adj.* Of or pertaining to geomancy. L16. †**B** *n.* A geomancer. Only in M17.

geoˈmantical *a.* = GEOMANTIC *a.* M16.

geometer /dʒɪˈɒmɪtə/ *n.* LME. [Late L *geometra* for cl.L *geometres* f. Gk = land-measurer, f. as GEO- + *metrēs* measurer.] **1** An expert in or student of geometry. LME. †**2** A surveyor. *US.* L18–E19. **3a** A moth caterpillar which moves by alternately hunching and stretching its body, as if measuring the ground; an inch-worm, measuring worm, or looper. E19. **b** = GEOMETRID *n.* M19.

geometric /dʒɪəˈmɛtrɪk/ *a.* M17. [(O)Fr. *géometrique* f. L *geometricus* f. Gk *geōmetrikos*, f. *geōmetrēs*: see prec., -IC.] **1** = next. M17. **2** *Archaeol.* (**G-**.) Designating or pertaining to a period of ancient Greek culture (*c* 900–*c* 700 BC) characterized by the use of geometrical decoration esp. for pottery. E20.

1 geometric mean (of *n* numbers) obtained by multiplying the numbers together and finding the *n*th root of their product.

geometrical /dʒɪəˈmɛtrɪk(ə)l/ *a.* LME. [f. as prec. + -AL[1].] **1** Of or pertaining to geometry; determined or constructed according to the methods of geometry. LME. **b** That works by the methods of geometry. L17. **c** *Archit.* (**G-**.) Designating or pertaining to an early style of English Decorated tracery, marked by the use of simple geometrical figures. E19. **2** Designating measures of length defined by geographical computation. *obs.* exc. *Hist.* M16.

Special collocations: *geometrical isomerism*: see ISOMERISM 1. **geometrical progression, series**: in which there is a constant ratio between successive quantities, as 1, 3, 9, 27, 81. **geometrical proportion** a proportion which involves an equality of ratio between its two parts, as 1 : 3 :: 4 : 12. *geometrical ratio*: see RATIO *n.* 2a. *geometrical series*: see *geometrical progression* above. **geometrical spider**: that constructs a web of geometrical pattern.

geometrically *adv.* in geometrical manner; according to geometry; by geometrical progression: M16.

geometrician /dʒɪəmɪˈtrɪʃ(ə)n/ *n.* L15. [OFr. *geometricien*, f. *geometrique*, L *geometricus*: see GEOMETRIC, -ICIAN.] **1** An expert in or student of geometry. L15. †**2** A person who measures the land; a surveyor. L16–L17.

geometrid /dʒɪˈɒmɪtrɪd/ *n.* & *a.* L19. [mod.L *Geometridae* (see below), f. *Geometra* genus name: see -ID[3].] **A** *n.* Any of various moths of the large family Geometridae, the caterpillars of which move by alternately hunching and stretching the body. Cf. GEOMETER 3. L19. **B** *adj.* Of, pertaining to, or designating this family. L19.

geomeˈtrideous *a.* (now *rare* or *obs.*) = GEOMETRID *a.* M19.

geometrize /dʒɪˈɒmɪtrʌɪz/ *v.* Also **-ise**. E17. [f. GEOMETRY + -IZE.] **1** *v.t.* Form geometrically; represent in geometric form. E17. **2** *v.i.* Work by geometrical methods. M17.

geometriˈzation *n.* E20.

geometry /dʒɪˈɒmɪtri/ *n.* ME. [(O)Fr. *géométrie* f. L *geometria* f. Gk, f. as GEO- + -METRY.] **1** The branch of mathematics that deals with the properties and relations of magnitudes (as lines, surfaces, solids) in space; a particular system describing these properties etc. ME. **b** The spatial arrangement of objects or constituent parts. M19. †**2** The art of measuring land; surveying. LME–E17.

1 D. R. HOFSTADTER The sum of the angles in a triangle is 180 degrees only in Euclidean geometry; it is greater in elliptic geometry. *fig.*: R. S. THOMAS You are old now; time's geometry Upon your face. †**hang by geometry** (of clothes) hang in a stiff, angular fashion. **b** B. LOVELL The epicyclic geometry of the Ptolemaic Universe. *Bicycle* The geometry of the Savoy gives reasonable manoeuvrability at low speed.

geomorphic /dʒiːə(ʊ)ˈmɔːfɪk/ *a.* L19. [f. Gk GEO- + *morphē* form + -IC.] Of or pertaining to the natural features of the earth's surface; geomorphological.

geomorphically *adv.* M20.

geomorphogeny /ˌdʒiːə(ʊ)mɔːˈfɒdʒəni/ *n.* L19. [f. GEO- + MORPHOGENY.] (The branch of geomorphology that deals with) the genesis of the physical features of the earth's surface.

geomorphoˈgenic *a.* L19.

geomorphology /ˌdʒiːə(ʊ)mɔːˈfɒlədʒi/ *n.* L19. [f. GEO- + MORPHOLOGY.] The branch of science that deals with the physical features of the earth's surface and their relation to the underlying geological structure. Also, the geomorphological features of a particular region.

geomorphoˈlogical *a.* of or pertaining to geomorphology L19. **geomorphoˈlogically** *adv.* M20. **geomorphologist** *n.* an expert in or student of geomorphology E20.

geomorphy /ˈdʒiːəmɔːfi/ *n.* L19. [f. Gk GEO- + *morphē* form.] = prec.

geonim *n.pl.* see GAON.

geophagy /dʒɪˈɒfədʒi/ *n.* M19. [f. GEO- + -PHAGY.] The practice of eating earth.

geophagist *n.* a person who eats earth L19.

geophysics /dʒiːə(ʊ)ˈfɪzɪks/ *n.* L19. [f. GEO- + PHYSICS.] The physics of the earth; geological investigation using the methods of physics.

geophysical *a.* L19. **geophysically** *adv.* E20. **geophysicist** *n.* E20.

geopolitics /dʒiːə(ʊ)ˈpɒlɪtɪks/ *n.* E20. [f. GEO(GRAPHY + POLITICS.] 1 Politics (esp. relations between States) as influenced by geographical factors; the branch of knowledge that deals with this. E20. 2 *Hist.* A theory developed in Nazi Germany which regarded the State as an organism with powers independent of and superior to those of its constituent groups or individuals. M20.

geopoˈlitical *a.* of or pertaining to geopolitics E20. **geopoˈlitically** *adv.* M20. **geopolitician** /-ˈtɪʃ(ə)n/ *n.* an expert in or student of geopolitics; *Hist.* an exponent or supporter of the theory of geopolitics: M20.

geoponic /dʒiːə(ʊ)ˈpɒnɪk/ *a.* Now *rare* or *obs.* M17. [Gk *geōponikos*, f. *geōponos* farmer: see -IC.] Of or pertaining to cultivation; agricultural.

geoponical *a.* = GEOPONIC M17. **geoponics** *n.* the science of agriculture; a treatise on this: E17.

Geordie /ˈdʒɔːdi/ *n.* & *a.* L18. [Dim. of GEORGE.] A *n.* 1 A guinea. Also *yellow Geordie.* Cf. GEORGE 3(b). *Sc.* & *north.* (now *Hist.*). L18. 2 A native or inhabitant of Tyneside in NE England; the dialect spoken on Tyneside. *colloq.* M19. b A coalminer; a miner's safety-lamp; a coal-ship. Chiefly *north.* L19. 3 A Scotsman. *Austral.* & *NZ colloq.* L19. B *attrib.* or as *adj.* Of or pertaining to Tyneside, its natives or inhabitants, or their dialect. *colloq.* M20.

George /dʒɔːdʒ/ *n.* E16. [Male forename.] I 1 A jewel bearing the image of St George, forming part of the insignia of the Order of the Garter. E16. 2 In interjectional phrs.: expr. surprise or asseveration; chiefly as *by George!* L16. 3 A British coin bearing the image of St George; *spec.* (*Hist.*) (*a*) a half-crown; (*b*) *slang* (also *yellow George*) a guinea (cf. GEORDIE *n.* 1). M17. 4 *Mil. slang.* a (A name for) an airman. *arch.* E20. b (A name for) an aeroplane's automatic pilot. M20. II In sense 5 chiefly, in senses 6 & 7 only, as *brown George* 5 A loaf of coarse brown bread; a hard biscuit. *obs.* exc. *dial.* L16. 6 A kind of wig, as worn by George III, king of Great Britain 1760–1820. *obs.* exc. *Hist.* M19. 7 A brown earthenware vessel. Now *dial.* M19.

Phrases & comb.: *brown George*: see branch II above. *by George!*: see sense 2 above. **George Cross, George Medal** decorations for gallantry in civilian life instituted by George VI, King of Great Britain 1936–52. **George-noble** *Hist.* an English gold coin worth one-third of a pound. **let George do it** (orig. *US*) let someone else do the work or take the responsibility. *yellow George*: see sense 3 above.

¶See also *St George's cross, day, mushroom* s.v. SAINT *n.* & *a.*

georgette /dʒɔːˈdʒɛt/ *n.* & *a.* E20. [f. Mme *Georgette* de la Plante (fl. c1900), French modiste.] (Made of) a thin plain-woven crêpe dress-material, usu. of silk.

R. WEST Pleated georgette—like chiffon but warmer.

Georgian /ˈdʒɔːdʒ(ə)n/ *n.*[1] & *a.*[1] LME. [f. *Georgia* (see below) + -AN.] A *n.* 1 A native or inhabitant of Georgia in the Caucasus (formerly a constituent republic of the USSR); the Caucasian language of this region. LME. 2 A native or inhabitant of the State of Georgia, USA. M18. B *adj.* 1 Of or pertaining to Georgia in the Caucasus, its inhabitants, or their language. E17. 2 Of or pertaining to the State of Georgia, USA. M18.

Georgian /ˈdʒɔːdʒ(ə)n/ *a.*[2] & *n.*[2] L18. [f. *George*, name of several kings of Great Britain + -IAN.] A *adj.* 1 *Georgian Planet*, = GEORGIUM SIDUS. *obs.* exc. *Hist.* L18. 2 Of, belonging to, or characteristic of the reigns of any of the first four Kings of Great Britain called George (1714–1830). M19. b *spec.* Designating, of or resembling the style of (esp. domestic) architecture characteristic of this period. L19. 3 Belonging to or characteristic of the reign of George V (1910–36) or George VI (1936–52), Kings of Great Britain; *spec.* designating the writers or literature of the early years of George V's reign. E20.

2 **Georgian green** a slightly yellowish green popular in the 18th and early 19th cents.

B *n.* 1 A person of the time of any of the Kings of Great Britain called George. E20. 2 *spec.* A writer of the early part of the reign of George V. E20.

Georgiˈana *n.pl.* articles or buildings of the Georgian period M20.

georgic /ˈdʒɔːdʒɪk/ *n.* & *a.* E16. [L *georgicus* f. Gk *geōrgikos*, f. *geōrgos* farmer: see -IC.] A *n.* A book or poem dealing with husbandry or other rural matters. Orig. & usu. in *pl.* (**G-**) as the title of a poetical treatise by Virgil. E16. B *adj.* Relating to agriculture. *obs.* exc. *joc.*, rustic, bucolic. E18.

georgical /ˈdʒɔːdʒɪk(ə)l/ *a.* Now *rare.* M17. [f. as prec. + -AL[1].] Rustic, agricultural.

Georgium Sidus /ˌdʒɔːdʒɪəm ˈsʌɪdəs/ *n. phr.* L18. [mod.L, lit. 'planet of George'.] *Hist.* The name given to the planet Uranus by its discoverer, William Herschel, in honour of King George III of Great Britain.

geostationary /dʒiːə(ʊ)ˈsteɪʃ(ə)n(ə)ri/ *a.* M20. [f. GEO- + STATIONARY.] Of an artificial satellite: that orbits the earth in exactly one day and hence always remains above the same point on the earth's surface. Of an orbit: (able to be) occupied by such a satellite.

geostrophic /dʒiːə(ʊ)ˈstrɒfɪk/ *a.* E20. [f. GEO- + Gk *strophē* a turning (f. *strephein* to turn) + -IC.] *Meteorol.* & *Oceanogr.* Of or pertaining to the Coriolis force; *esp.* (of a wind or ocean current) in which there is a balance between the Coriolis force and the horizontal pressure gradient. Cf. AGEOSTROPHIC.

geosynclinal /dʒiːəsɪŋˈklʌɪn(ə)l/ *n.* & *a.* L19. [f. GEO- + SYNCLINAL.] *Geol.* A *n.* = next. Now *rare.* L19. B *adj.* Of, pertaining to, or of the nature of a geosyncline. L19.

geosyncline /dʒiːə(ʊ)ˈsɪŋklʌɪn/ *n.* L19. [Back-form. f. prec.] *Geol.* A large-scale downward flexure of the earth's crust containing sedimentary and volcanic deposits of great thickness.

geotaxis /dʒiːə(ʊ)ˈtaksɪs/ *n.* L19. [f. GEO- + -TAXIS.] *Biol.* Movement related to the direction of the earth's gravity.

negative geotaxis: in which movement is upwards. **positive geotaxis**: in which movement is downwards.

geotactic *a.* of, pertaining to, or of the nature of geotaxis L19.

geothermal /dʒiːə(ʊ)ˈθəːm(ə)l/ *a.* L19. [f. GEO- + THERMAL.] Of, pertaining to, or derived from the internal heat of the earth.

Also **geothermic** *a.* L19.

geotropic /dʒiːə(ʊ)ˈtrəʊpɪk, -ˈtrɒpɪk/ *a.* L19. [f. next + -IC.] *Bot.* Pertaining to, marked by, or of the nature of geotropism.

geotropically *adv.* L19.

geotropism /dʒiːə(ʊ)ˈtrəʊpɪz(ə)m/ *n.* L19. [f. GEO- + Gk *tropē* turning + -ISM.] *Bot.* The growth of part of a plant in response to gravity.

negative geotropism tendency (of stems etc.) to grow upwards. **positive geotropism** tendency (of roots etc.) to grow downwards.

gephyrocercal /ˌdʒɛfɪrəʊˈsəːk(ə)l/ *a.* L19. [f. Gk *gephura* bridge + *kerkos* tail + -AL[1].] Of a fish: having the caudal tail formed by the meeting of dorsal and anal fins.

gerah /ˈgɪərə/ *n.* M16. [Heb. *gērāh.*] An ancient Hebrew coin and weight, the twentieth part of a shekel.

Geraldton wax /ˈdʒɛr(ə)l(d)tən waks/ *n. phr.* *Austral.* E20. [*Geraldton*, a town in W. Australia.] A western Australian evergreen shrub, *Chamaelaucium uncinatum*, of the myrtle family, with pink or white waxy flowers.

geranial /dʒɪˈreɪnɪəl/ *n.* L19. [f. as next + -AL[2].] *Chem.* The *trans* isomer of citral, a fragrant oil present in lemon-grass oil and used in perfumery.

geraniol /dʒɪˈreɪnɪɒl/ *n.* L19. [f. next + -OL.] *Chem.* A colourless oily unsaturated alcohol, $C_{10}H_{18}O$, with a fragrant odour, present in geranium oil and rose oil and used in perfumery.

geranium /dʒɪˈreɪnɪəm/ *n.* M16. [L f. Gk *geranion*, f. *geranos* crane: see -IUM.] 1 Any plant of the genus *Geranium* (family Geraniaceae); = *cranesbill* (a) s.v. CRANE *n.*[1] M16. 2 In popular use: any of various plants of the mostly southern African genus *Pelargonium*, which are related to true geraniums but with zygomorphic flowers and include many kinds grown as house or bedding plants for their showy scarlet, pink, etc., flowers or scented leaves. M18. 3 The colour of the scarlet pelargonium. M19.

2 *ivy geranium, lemon geranium, peppermint geranium*, etc.

gerardia /dʒɪˈrɑːdɪə/ *n.* E19. [mod.L (see below), f. John *Gerard* (1545–1612), Eng. herbalist + -IA[1].] Any of various purple- or yellow-flowered parasitic N. American plants of the figwort family, formerly referred to a genus *Gerardia* and now to the genera *Agalionis* and *Aureolaria* respectively.

†**gerate** *v.t.* L15–M19. [Origin unkn.] *Her.* Powder or strew with minor charges.

geratology /dʒɛrəˈtɒlədʒi/ *n.* L19. [f. Gk *gērat-*, *geras* old age + -OLOGY.] †1 The branch of biology that deals with the extinction of plant and animal species. Only in L19. 2 = GERONTOLOGY. M20.

gerbe /ˈdʒəːb/ *n.* L16. [Fr. = wheatsheaf f. Frank. *garbe* = OHG *garba* (G *Garbe*).] 1 Something resembling a wheatsheaf in form or appearance; *esp.* a kind of firework. L16. †2 A wheatsheaf. Only in E19.

gerbera /ˈdʒəːb(ə)rə, ˈgəː-/ *n.* L19. [mod.L (see below), f. T. *Gerber* (d. 1743), Ger. naturalist.] *Bot.* Any of several African and Asian plants of the genus *Gerbera*, of the composite family; *esp.* the Transvaal daisy, *G. jamesonii*, grown for its large daisy-like flowers in many shades.

gerbil /ˈdʒəːbɪl/ *n.* Also **gerbille, jerbil.** M19. [Fr. *gerbille* f. mod.L *gerbillus*, dim. of *gerboa* JERBOA.] Any of various mouselike burrowing rodents of African and Asian deserts, of the subfamily Gerbillinae (family Muridae); esp. *Meriones unguiculatus* of Mongolia, commonly kept elsewhere as a pet.

gerent /ˈdʒɪər(ə)nt, ˈdʒɛ-/ *n. rare.* L16. [L *gerent-* pres. ppl stem of *gerere* carry on, manage: see -ENT.] A manager, a ruler.

gerenuk /ˈgɛrənʊk/ *n.* L19. [Somali.] A long-necked antelope, *Litocranius walleri*, of E. Africa that is similar to the gazelles.

gerfalcon *n.* var. of GYRFALCON.

geriatric /dʒɛrɪˈatrɪk/ *a.* & *n.* E20. [f. Gk *gēras* old age + *iatrikos* (see IATRIC *a.*), after *paediatric.*] A *adj.* 1 Relating to geriatrics or to old people; designed for use by old people. E20. 2 Of a person: old; senile. *contempt.* M20.

2 *Times* Geriatric judges with 19th century.. prejudices only bring the rule of law into disrepute.

B *n.* 1 In *pl.* (treated as *sing.*). The branch of medical or social science that deals with the health and welfare of old people. E20. 2 An old person receiving geriatric care. Also *contempt.*, an old or senile person. L20. b Anything old or outdated. *colloq.* L20.

geriatrician /-ˈtrɪʃ(ə)n/, **geriˈatrist** *ns.* a doctor who specializes in geriatrics M20.

germ /dʒəːm/ *n.* & *v.* LME. [(O)Fr. *germe* f. L *germen* seed, sprout.] **A** *n.* **1** A part of a living organism which is capable of developing into a similar organism or part of one. LME. **2** *fig.* A thing from which something may spring or develop; an elementary principle; a rudiment. Usu. foll. by *of.* M16. **3**†**a** The ovary of a plant. M18–E19. **b** A plant seed. E19. **c** The embryo and scutellum of a plant seed, esp. of a grain of cereal. L19. **4** A micro-organism; *esp.* one which is supposed to cause disease. L19.

1 J. R. LOWELL A strong oak, doth from its boughs shed down The ripe germs of a forest. P. GALLICO The ageless germ of a patriarchal race ran in his bloodstream. 2 F. W. FARRAR His keen eye marked the germs of coming danger. C. S. LEWIS There is not even the germ of a feeling for design. **in germ** in a rudimentary form, not yet developed. 3c *Health Guardian* Natural sources are egg yolks, . . wheat germ and lecithin. 4 P. H. JOHNSON I picked up this wretched germ somehow—it's a virus pneumonia. E. O'BRIEN There's probably germs floating everywhere.

Comb.: **germ bomb**: containing germs, for use in germ warfare; **germ cell** a cell of a living organism that is specialized for reproductive purposes and ultimately gives rise to sperm cells and egg cells or (in plants) to spores; a sperm cell, an egg cell; cf. SOMATIC *cell*; **germ layer** *Biol.* each of the three layers of cells (ectoderm, mesoderm, and endoderm) that arise in the early stages of embryonic development; **germ line** a series of germ cells each descended or developed from earlier cells in the series, regarded as continuing through successive generations of an organism; **germ plasm** (*a*) *Hist.* the part of a germ cell which carries hereditary factors and is itself transmitted unchanged from generation to generation; (*b*) germ cells collectively; their genetic material; **germ theory** *Hist.*: that infectious diseases are caused by micro-organisms; **germ warfare** the spreading of disease germs among an enemy as a weapon of war.

B *v.i.* Germinate, sprout. Now only *fig.* L15.

germless *a.* L19. **germy** *a.* full of germs; unclean, polluted: E20.

†**germaine** *n.* see GERMEN.

German /ˈdʒəːmən/ *n.*[1] & *a.*[1] LME. [L *Germanus* used as n. and adj. to designate a group of related peoples of north and central Europe.] **A** *n.* **1** A native or inhabitant of Germany, a country in central Europe orig. consisting of a series of small States only fully united as one country in the mid 19th cent., and from 1945 divided into East Germany (the German Democratic Republic) and West Germany (the Federal Republic of Germany) until reunified in 1990. Formerly also, a member of any of the Germanic peoples of north and central Europe. LME. **b** A scholar of the German language. E19. **2** The principal language of Germany, spoken also in Austria and Switzerland and belonging to the West Germanic division. M17. **3** = *German cotillion* s.v. COTILLION *n.* 1. M19. **B** *adj.* **1** Of or pertaining to Germany or its inhabitants; native to or originating in Germany; characteristic of or attributed to Germans or Germany. M16. **2** Belonging to, written in, or spoken in the German language. E17.

Phrases (of adj. & n.): **East German** *Hist.* (*a*) of or pertaining to the German Democratic Republic; (*b*) a native or inhabitant of this State. **High German** (of or pertaining to) the variety of German orig. confined to 'high' or southern Germany, but now in literary or cultured use throughout Germany. **Low German** (*a*) (of or pertaining to) the dialects of Germany which are not High German, Plattdeutsch; (*b*) (of or pertaining to) all forms of West Germanic, including English and Dutch, except High German. *Old High German*: see OLD *a.* **West German** *Hist.* (*a*) of or pertaining to the Federal Republic of Germany; (*b*) a native or inhabitant of this State.

Special collocations & comb.: **German-American** *n.* & *a.* (*a*) *n.* an American of German extraction; (*b*) *adj.* of or pertaining to Americans of German extraction. **German band** a band of street musicians, properly of German extraction. *German* CATHOLIC. **German clock** an elaborately constructed clock, often with moving figures etc., of a type popular in the 16th and 17th cents. **German cockroach** a common indoor cockroach, *Blatella germanica*, found worldwide; also called *Croton bug*, *steam fly*. *German cotillion*: see COTILLION *n.* 1. **German ivy** a twining southern African plant, *Delairea odorata*, of the composite family, grown for its fragrant yellow flowers which appear in winter. *German* MADWORT. **German measles** a contagious virus disease that resembles a mild form of measles but can cause foetal malformations if caught by a woman early in a pregnancy, rubella. **German ocean** *arch.* the North Sea. **German sausage** a large sausage stuffed with partially cooked spiced meat. **German shepherd** (**dog**) a strong dog of a breed frequently used as guard dogs or for police work; an alsatian. **German silver** = *nickel silver* s.v. NICKEL *n.* **German sixth** *Mus.* a chord consisting of a major third, a perfect fifth, and an augmented sixth. **German-Swiss** *a.* & *n.* (*a*) *adj.* of or pertaining to the part of Switzerland where Schweizerdeutsch is spoken; (*b*) *n.* a native or inhabitant of the part of Switzerland where Schweizerdeutsch is spoken (cf. *Swiss-German*). *German* TAMARISK. **German wool** = BERLIN *wool*.

Germanify *v.t.* = GERMANIZE 2 M19. **Germanish** *a.* having German characteristics L18. **Germanist** *n.* (*a*) a person who has a knowledge of Germany and the German language; (*b*) an expert in Germanic philology; (*c*) a person influenced by Germanic thought: M19. **Gerˈmanity** *n.* (*a*) the characteristic qualities of Germany and the Germans; (*b*) devotion to German interests: M19. **Germanly** *adv.* L18.

german /ˈdʒəːmən/ *a.*[2] & *n.*[2] Also (now the only form in sense A.4) **germane** /dʒəːˈmeɪn/. ME. [(O)Fr. *germain* (in OFr. also 'brother') f. L *germanus* having the same parents, genuine (as ns. *germanus* brother, *germana* sister).] **A** *adj.* **I** Closely akin. **1** Having the same parents. *obs.* exc. in *brother german*, *sister german* (see BROTHER *n.*, SISTER *n.*). ME. **2** That is the child of one's uncle or aunt; that is one's first cousin. *obs.* exc. in COUSIN-GERMAN. ME. †**3** Closely related, akin. L15–M17. **4** Relevant, pertinent, (*to* a matter or subject). E17.

4 J. STEINBECK Any sound that was not germane to the night would make them alert. E. JONES Four considerations would appear to be germane here.

II 5 Genuine; true; thorough. *arch.* LME.

†**B** *n.* A close relative, *esp.* a sibling. L15–E18.

gerˈmanely *adv.* in a germane manner, pertinently M19. **gerˈmaneness** *n.* M20.

germander /dʒəˈmandə/ *n.* LME. [med.L *germandra*, *-drea* (cf. OFr. *gemandree*, Fr. *germandrée*), alt. of *gamandrea* (cf. G *Gamander*) ult. f. Gk *khamaidrus* lit. 'ground-oak', f. *khamai* on the ground + *drus* oak.] Any of certain plants with leaves thought to resemble the oak; *spec.* (more fully *wall germander*) a labiate plant, *Teucrium chamaedrys*, sometimes naturalized on old walls; also (w. specifying wd), any of several other plants of this genus.

water germander a rare marsh plant, *Teucrium scordium*. *wood germander*: see WOOD *n.*[1] & *a.*[1]

Comb.: **germander speedwell** a common hedge speedwell, *Veronica chamaedrys*, with bright blue flowers.

germane *a.* & *n.* see GERMAN *a.*[2] & *n.*[2]

Germanic /dʒəːˈmanɪk/ *a.*[1] & *n.* M17. [L *Germanicus* f. *Germanus* GERMAN *a.*[1]: see -IC.] **A** *adj.* **1** German; now *esp.* characteristic of or attributed to Germans or Germany. M17. **2** Of, pertaining to, or designating the former peoples of the Germanic-speaking areas of north and central Europe, *spec.* the Scandinavians, Anglo-Saxons, or Germans. L18. **b** Of, pertaining to, or designating the language of the Germanic peoples or any of its forms. E19.

1 J. UPDIKE Germanic thoroughness characterized . . the bibliographical rigor.

B *n.* A branch of the Indo-European language family including English, German, Dutch, Flemish, Frisian, the Scandinavian languages, and the earlier languages from which they have developed; *spec.* (and in this dictionary) Proto-Germanic. E19.

East Germanic (of or pertaining to) the now extinct division of Germanic represented chiefly by Gothic. **North Germanic** (of or pertaining to) the division of Germanic represented by the modern and ancient Scandinavian languages. **primitive Germanic** Proto-Germanic. **West Germanic** (of or pertaining to) the division of Germanic including English, German, Dutch, Flemish, Frisian, and the languages from which they have developed.

¶Cf. DUTCH *n.*[1], *a.* & *adv.*, TEUTONIC. See also PROTO-GERMANIC.

Germanical *a.* (*rare*) = GERMAN *a.*[1] 1 M16. **Germanically** *adv.* M19. **Germanicism** /-sɪz(ə)m/ *n.* a German characteristic, idiom, etc.; Germanic quality: E20.

germanic /dʒəːˈmanɪk/ *a.*[2] L19. [f. GERMAN(IUM + -IC.] *Chem.* Of, pertaining to, or containing germanium in the tetravalent state.

Germanise *v.* var. of GERMANIZE.

Germanism /ˈdʒəːmənɪz(ə)m/ *n.* E17. [f. GERMAN *a.*[1] + -ISM.] **1** A German idiom, *esp.* one used in some other language. E17. **2** Affectation of what is German. E19. **3** German ideas or attitudes; attachment to these. M19.

1 *American Speech* Germanisms are most numerous in eastern Pennsylvania.

germanium /dʒəːˈmeɪnɪəm/ *n.* L19. [f. L *Germanus* GERMAN *a.*[1] + -IUM.] A brittle metalloid chemical element, atomic no. 32, used as a semiconductor in solid-state electronic devices and as a constituent of alloys, phosphors, and infrared glasses. (Symbol Ge.)

Germanize /ˈdʒəːmənʌɪz/ *v.* Also **-ise**. L16. [f. GERMAN *a.*[1] + -IZE.] **1** *v.t.* Translate into the German language. L16. **2** *v.t.* Make German in character, appearance, etc. E17. **3** *v.i.* Adopt German manners or customs; become German in style, attitude, habits, etc. M17.

Germaniˈzation *n.* the action or process of Germanizing M19. **Germanizer** *n.* M19.

Germano- /dʒəːˈmanəʊ, ˈdʒəːmənəʊ/ *comb. form.* [f. GERMAN *n.*[1] & *a.*[1] + -O-.] Forming adjs. and ns. w. the sense 'German, of Germany'.

ˌ**Germano-Coleˈridgean** *a.* (*rare*) (of opinions) derived from German writers through Coleridge or from the Germans and Coleridge jointly M19. ˌ**Germanoˈmania** *n.* a craze or excessive liking for Germany and things German L19. **Gerˈmanophil(e)** *a.* & *n.* (a person who is) friendly towards Germany or fond of Germany and things German L19. ˌ**Germaˈnophilist** *n.* = GERMANOPHILE *n.* M19. **Gerˈmanophobe** *a.* & *n.* (a person who is) affected with Germanophobia E20. ˌ**Germanoˈphobia** *n.* dread or dislike of Germany and things German L19.

germanous /dʒəːˈmeɪnəs/ *a.* L19. [f. GERMAN(IUM + -OUS.] *Chem.* Of, pertaining to, or containing germanium in the divalent state.

Germantown /ˈdʒəːmәntaʊn/ *n. US.* Also **g-**. M19. [A suburb of Philadelphia.] Chiefly *Hist.* A one-horse covered vehicle used by farmers and other country people in the US.

germarium /dʒəːˈmɛːrɪəm/ *n.* Pl. **-ria** /-rɪə/. L19. [f. L *germen* seed, sprout, GERM *n.* + -ARIUM.] *Zool.* In certain invertebrates, the part of an ovary or testis where eggs and sperm are produced by germ cells.

germen /ˈdʒəːmən/ *n.* Also (earlier) †**germaine**. E17. [L *germen* seed, sprout, GERM *n.*] **1** The rudiment of an organism. Now only *fig.* (= GERM *n.* 2). E17. †**2** A shoot, a sprout. E17–L18. **3** *Bot.* The rudiment of a seed-vessel. M18.

germicide /ˈdʒəːmɪsʌɪd/ *n.* & *a.* L19. [f. GERM *n.* + -I- + -CIDE.] **A** *n.* A substance that kills germs, esp. ones which cause disease. L19. **B** *adj.* Germicidal. Now *rare*. L19.

germiˈcidal *a.* that has the effect of a germicide L19.

germin /ˈdʒəːmɪn/ *v.i. arch.* LME. [L *germinare*: see GERMINATE *v.*] Send out shoots; sprout, bud; begin to produce vegetation.

germinable /ˈdʒəːmɪnəb(ə)l/ *a.* L19. [f. GERMIN(ATE + -ABLE.] Capable of germinating.

germinaˈbility *n.* M20.

Germinal /ˈdʒəːmɪn(ə)l, *foreign* ʒɛrminal/ *n.* E19. [Fr., f. as next.] *Hist.* The seventh month of the French Republican calendar (introduced 1793) extending from 21 March to 19 April.

germinal /ˈdʒəːmɪn(ə)l/ *a.* E19. [L *germin-*, *germen* seed, sprout, GERM *n.* + -AL[1].] **1** *Anat.*, *Zool.*, & *Bot.* Of or belonging to a germ or germs; of the nature of a germ (GERM *n.* 1). E19. **2** *transf.* In the earliest stage of development; *joc.* rudimentary, undeveloped. E19. **3** Capable of development; productive of new ideas, influences, etc.; seminal. M20.

1 **germinal cell** = *germ cell* s.v. GERM *n.* **germinal vesicle** the enlarged nucleus of a maturing oocyte. 2

G. H. LEWES A forecasting tendency, germinal in animals and.. conspicuous in the civilized man. 3 *Music Teacher* Seven varied and contrasted pieces (chiefly constructed around germinal motives).

germinally *adv.* M19.

germinant /ˈdʒəːmɪnənt/ *a.* LME. [L *germinant-* pres. ppl stem of *germinare*: see next, -ANT[1].] Germinating, sprouting; capable of developing or producing life.

germinate /ˈdʒəːmɪneɪt/ *v.* L16. [L *germinat-* pa. ppl stem of *germinare*, f. *germin-*, *germen* seed, sprout, GERM *n.*: see -ATE[3].] **1 a** *v.t.* Cause (a seed, bud, etc.) to send out shoots or begin development; *fig.* cause to arise or develop. L16. **b** *v.i.* Send out shoots; sprout, bud; begin to develop. M17. **2** *v.i.* Of a salt etc.: effloresce. Now *rare* or *obs.* E17.

1a *Nature* Doku stated that he had germinated yam seeds. H. CAINE A crowd of people gathered in the street and germinated alarming rumours. **b** H. COLERIDGE From the first, or initiative idea.. successive ideas germinate. ANTHONY HUXLEY In the tropics seeds are apt to germinate immediately.

germinative *a.* (*a*) of or belong to germination; (*b*) capable of germinating: E18. **germinator** *n.* a thing which causes or promotes germination L19.

germination /dʒəːmɪˈneɪʃ(ə)n/ *n.* LME. [L *germinatio(n-)*, f. as prec.: see -ATION.] **1** The action or process, or an instance, of germinating; sprouting. LME. **2** Efflorescence. Now *rare* or *obs.* M17.

1 ANTHONY HUXLEY Pebble-like seeds which can float for.. years without losing their powers of germination.

germon /ˈdʒəːmən/ *n.* M19. [Fr.] A tunny, *esp.* the albacore, *Thunnus alalonga*.

gerocomy /dʒəˈrɒkəmi/ *n. rare.* E19. [Gk *gērokomia* care of the aged, f. *gēro-*, *gēras* old age + *komia* tending: see -Y[3].] = GERONTOLOGY.

†**gerocomical** *a.*: only in M17.

Geronimo /dʒəˈrɒnɪməʊ/ *int. US.* M20. [Name of an Apache Indian chief (1829–1909), adopted as a slogan in the war of 1939–45 by US paratroops.] Expr. exhilaration on performing a daring leap etc.

Geronomite /dʒəˈrɒnəmʌɪt/ *n.* M18. [Sp. or It. *geronomita*.] = HIERONYMITE *n.*

geront- *comb. form* see GERONTO-.

gerontic /dʒəˈrɒntɪk/ *a.* L19. [f. GERONT- + -IC.] Of or pertaining to old age; senile.

geronto- /dʒəˈrɒntəʊ, dʒɛrɒnˈtɒ/ *comb. form.* Bef. a vowel **geront-**. [f. Gk *geront-*, *gerōn* old man + -O-.] Old age.

gerontoˈmorphic *a.* of, pertaining to, or designating anatomical specialization most fully represented in the mature male of a species M20. **geˈrontophil(e)** *n.* & *a.* (a person) favouring old people, esp. old men; (a person) desiring sexual relations with old people: M20. **gerontoˈphilia** *n.* desire for sexual relations with old people E20. **gerontoˈphilic** *a.* = GERONTOPHIL(E) *a.* M20. **geronˈtophily** *n.* = GERONTOPHILIA M20.

gerontocracy /dʒɛrɒnˈtɒkrəsi/ *n.* M19. [f. GERONT-: see -CRACY.] Government by old people; a governing body consisting of old people.

geˈrontocrat *n.* a member of a gerontocracy M20. **geˌrontoˈcratic** *a.* of, pertaining to, or characteristic of (a) gerontocracy E20.

gerontology /dʒɛrɒnˈtɒlədʒi/ *n.* E20. [f. GERONT- + -OLOGY.] The branch of science that deals with old age, the ageing process, and the problems faced by old people.

geˌrontoˈlogical *a.* M20. **gerontologist** *n.* M20.

geropiga /dʒɛrəˈpiːgə/ *n.* Also **jeru-**. M19. [Port. *jeropiga*.] A grape juice mixture added in the making of port.

-gerous /dʒ(ə)rəs/ *suff.* [f. L *-ger* bearing (f. base of *gerere* bear, carry) + -OUS.] Forming adjs., usu. w. intermediate -I-, w. the sense 'bearing', as *cornigerous*, *frondigerous*, etc.

gerrymander /ˈdʒɛrɪmandə/ *n.* & *v.* E19. [f. Elbridge *Gerry* (1744–1814), US governor + SALA)MANDER *n.*, f. the supposed resemblance to a salamander of the outline of an electoral district in Massachusetts formed by Gerry in 1812 for party purposes.] **A** *n.* **1** The action of manipulating the boundaries of a constituency etc. so as to give an unfair advantage at an election to a particular party or class. E19. **2** A person elected by gerrymandering. E19.

1 H. EVANS His.. government.. retained power by a gerrymander giving two out of every three seats to the minority country voters.

B *v.t.* Subject (a constituency, voting area, etc.) to a gerrymander; *gen.* manipulate in order to gain an unfair advantage. E19.

gerrymanderer *n.* L19.

gersum /ˈgəːsəm/ *n.* Also (chiefly *Sc.*) **grassum**. [Late OE *gærsum*, *gersum* = ON *gersimi*, MSw. *görsam*.] **1** A treasure, a precious possession; a costly gift. *obs.* exc. *Hist.* LOE. **2** A sum paid to a feudal superior by a feuar on taking up a holding. Also, a sum paid or pledged to a landlord by a tenant on the receipt or renewal of a lease. Chiefly *Sc.* ME.

gertcha /ˈgəːtʃə/ *int. slang.* M20. [Repr. a joc. pronunc. of *get away* or *along with you*.] Expr. derisive disbelief.

gerund /ˈdʒɛrʌnd/ *n.* E16. [Late L *gerundium* f. *gerundum* var. of *gerendum* gerund of L *gerere* carry on.] A form of the Latin verb which is used as a noun but retains the syntactic relationships of the verb; a similar verbal form in other languages, *spec.* the English verbal noun, ending in *-ing*, esp. when used distinctly as part of the verb.

Comb.: **gerund-grinder** *arch.* a teacher of Latin, a pedantic teacher.

geˈrundial *a.* M19. **geˈrundially** *adv.* L16.

gerundive /dʒəˈrʌndɪv/ *n.* & *a.* LME. [Late L *gerundivus* (sc. *modus* mood), f. *gerundium* GERUND: see -IVE.] **A** *n.* **1** = GERUND. LME. **2** In Latin, the verbal adjective formed from the gerund stem and having the sense 'that can or must be done'; a similar grammatical form in other languages. E18. **B** *adj.* Of or like a gerund. E17.

gerundival *a.* L19. **gerundively** *adv.* M19.

gerusia /gɛˈruːzɪə/ *n.* M19. [L *gerusia* f. Gk *gerousia*, f. *gerōn* old man: see -IA[1].] *Hist.* An assembly of elders, *spec.* the senate in Sparta and other Dorian cities of ancient Greece.

Gervais /ʒɛrvɛ/ *n.* & *a.* Pl. same. L19. [Charles *Gervais* (1830–92), French cheese-maker.] (Proprietary name designating) a soft creamy cheese.

Gerzean /gəːˈziːən/ *a.* E20. [f. el-*Gerza* a district in Egypt + -AN.] *Archaeol.* Designating or pertaining to the later period (or middle period if the Semainean period is reckoned separately) of the ancient predynastic culture of upper Egypt.

Gesamtkunstwerk /gəˈzamtkʊnstˌvɛrk/ *n.* Pl. *-e* /-ə/. M20. [G, f. *gesamt* total + *Kunstwerk* work of art.] An ideal work of art in which drama, music, and other performing arts are integrated and each is subservient to the whole.

Gesellschaft /gəˈzɛlʃaft/ *n.* Also **g-**. L19. [G, f. *Gesell(e)* companion + *-schaft* -SHIP.] *Sociol.* A form of social integration based on impersonal ties; association. Cf. GEMEINSCHAFT.

†**gesine** *n.* ME–L18. [OFr., f. *gesir* to lie, f. L *jacere*.] Childbirth.

gesnera /ˈgɛsnərə, ˈdʒɛs-/ *n.* Also **gesneria** /-ˈnɪərɪə/. M19. [mod.L (see below), f. Conrad von *Gesner* (1516–65), Swiss naturalist + -IA[1].] Any of various tropical American plants of the genus *Gesneria* (family Gesneriaceae), grown elsewhere for their showy flowers.

Gesolreut /ˌdʒiːsɒlreɪˈʊt/ *n. obs.* exc. *Hist.* Also **G sol re ut**. ME. [f. *G* as a pitch letter + *sol*, *re*, *ut* designating tones in the solmization of Guido d'Arezzo (*c*990–1050).] *Medieval Mus.* The note G in Guido d'Arezzo's 2nd, 3rd, and 4th hexachords, where it was sung to the syllables *sol*, *re*, and *ut* respectively. Cf. ALAMIRE, CEFAUT, etc.

gesso /ˈdʒɛsəʊ/ *n.* Pl. **-oes**. L16. [It. f. L GYPSUM. Cf. YESO.] Gypsum, plaster of Paris, now only as prepared for use in painting and sculpture; any white substance that can be mixed with water to make a ground.

gessoed *a.* made of or covered with gesso M20.

gest /dʒɛst/ *n.*[1] Also †**jest**. See also JEST *n.* ME. [OFr. *geste*, *jeste* f. L *gesta* actions, exploits, use as n. of neut. pl. of pa. pple of *gerere* bear, carry, carry on, perform.] **I 1** A (heroic) deed or exploit, esp. as narrated or recorded; in *pl.*, actions, conduct. *arch.* ME. **2** Orig., a story, esp. a romance, in verse. Later also, a prose romance or tale. *obs.* exc. *Hist.* ME. †**II** See JEST *n.* II.

gest /dʒɛst/ *n.*[2] *arch.* Also **geste**. LME. [(O)Fr. *geste* f. L *gestus*, f. *gerere* bear, carry, carry on, perform.] **1** A gesture, a movement, an action. LME. **2** Bearing, carriage. E16.

†**gested** *a.* accompanied by gestures L16–M18.

†**gest** *n.*[3] M16. [Later form of GIST *n.*[1]] **1** In *pl.* The stages of a (royal) journey; the route followed or planned. M16–M18. **2** The time allotted for a halt or stay. *rare* (Shakes.). Only in E17.

†**gest** *v.* See also JEST *v.* LME. [f. GEST *n.*[1]] **1** *v.i.* Recite a romance or tale. Only in LME. **2** See JEST *v.*

gestagen /ˈdʒɛstədʒ(ə)n/ *n.* Also **gesto-**. M20. [f. GESTATION (+ -O-) + -GEN.] = PROGESTOGEN.

gestalt /gəˈʃtɑːlt, -ˈʃtalt/ *n.* Also **G-**. E20. [G = form, shape.] Chiefly *Psychol.* An integrated perceptual structure or unity conceived as functionally more than the sum of its parts.

Comb.: **gestalt psychology** a school of psychology maintaining that perceptions, reactions, etc., are gestalts.

gestaltism *n.* gestalt psychology M20. **gestaltist** *n.* an adherent or practitioner of the principles of gestalt psychology M20.

Gestapo /gəˈstɑːpəʊ/ *n.* Pl. **-os**. M20. [G acronym, f. *Ge*heime *Sta*ats*po*lizei Secret State Police.] *Hist.* (An officer of) the secret police of the Nazi regime in Germany.

gestate /dʒɛˈsteɪt/ *v.* M19. [L *gestat-*: see next, -ATE[3].] **1** *v.t.* & *i.* Carry and develop (offspring) in the womb. M19. **2** *v.i.* Develop in the womb; *fig.* undergo elaboration and refinement before being made public. M20.

2 *Times* The proposals.. have been gestating in the Department of Education and Science for the past year.

ˈgestative *a.* = GESTATIONAL E19.

gestation /dʒɛˈsteɪʃ(ə)n/ *n.* M16. [L *gestatio(n-)*, f. *gestat-* pa. ppl stem of *gestare* carry, carry in the womb, frequent. of *gerere* bear, carry: see -ATION.] **1** The action or an act of carrying or being carried (on horseback, in a carriage, etc.) as a form of exercise. Now *rare*. M16. **2** The action or process of carrying or being carried in the womb between conception and birth; the length of time for which an embryo or foetus has been developing in the womb. E17. **3** *fig.* The development of an idea, plan, etc., in the mind. L17.

gestational *a.* of or pertaining to gestation L19.

gestatorial /dʒɛstəˈtɔːrɪəl/ *a.* M19. [f. as next + -AL[1].] Designating a chair in which the Pope is carried on certain occasions.

gestatory /dʒɛˈsteɪt(ə)ri/ *a.* L17. [L *gestatorius*, f. *gestator* a person who carries, f. *gestare*: see GESTATION, -ORY[2].] †**1** Adapted for carrying or wearing. *rare.* L17–L19. **2** = GESTATIONAL. L19.

geste *n.* var. of GEST *n.*[2]

†**gesten** *v.* see GUESTEN *v.*

†**gestening** *n.* Also **gestning**. ME–L16. [Prob. ON: cf. OSw. *gestning*, *gist-*, *gäst-*, f. *gästa* lodge as a guest, f. *gäster* (mod. *gäst*) = ON *gestr* GUEST *n.*] Entertainment or lodging given to a guest; hospitality. Also, a feast, a banquet.

†**gester** *n.* var. of JESTER.

gestic /ˈdʒɛstɪk/ *a.* M18. [f. GEST *n.*[2] + -IC.] Of or pertaining to gestures; consisting or full of gestures.

gesticulant /dʒɛˈstɪkjʊl(ə)nt/ *a. rare.* L19. [L *gesticulant-* pres. ppl stem of *gesticulari* GESTICULATE: see -ANT[1].] Gesticulating.

gesticular /dʒɛˈstɪkjʊlə/ *a.* M19. [f. L *gesticulus* (see next) + -AR[1].] Of or pertaining to gesticulation.

gesticulate /dʒɛˈstɪkjʊleɪt/ *v.* E17. [L *gesticulat-* pa. ppl stem of *gesticulari*, f. *gesticulus* dim. of *gestus* action, gesture: see -ATE[3].] **1** *v.i.* Use lively and expressive movements of the limbs or body with or instead of speech. E17. 2 *v.t.* Convey or express by such movements. E17.

1 C. S. FORESTER It was natural when one spoke French to gesticulate, to indicate his men with a wave of the hand. M. ROBERTS A man . . gesticulating and coughing to catch her attention.

gesticulatingly *adv.* in a gesticulating manner; with gesticulations: L19. **gesticulative** *a.* given to or characterized by gesticulation L18. **gesticulator** *n.* L17. **gesticulatory** *a.* consisting or full of gesticulation L18.

gesticulation /dʒɛˌstɪkjʊˈleɪʃ(ə)n/ *n.* LME. [L *gesticulatio(n-)*, f. as prec.: see -ATION.] The action or an act of gesticulating.

gestion /ˈdʒɛstjən, -tʃ(ə)n/ *n.* L16. [L *gestio(n-)*, f. *gest-* pa. ppl stem of *gerere* carry, carry on: see -ION.] Performance, conduct, management. Formerly also, working order.

†gestning *n.* var. of GESTENING.

gestogen *n.* var. of GESTAGEN.

gesture /ˈdʒɛstʃə/ *n.* & *v.* LME. [med.L *gestura*, f. L *gerere* bear, carry, carry on, perform: see -URE.] A *n.* †1 Manner of carrying the body; carriage, deportment. LME–E19. b (A) position, posture, or attitude of the body, esp. in prayer or worship. M16–E18. 2 (A) movement of the body or limbs, now only as an expression of thought or feeling; the use of such movements as an expression of feeling or a rhetorical device. LME. 3 An action performed as a courtesy, formality, or symbol to indicate an intention or evoke a response. E20.

1 BURKE The fashion of the countenance and the gesture of the body . . is so correspondent to this state of mind. 2 A. MILLER With a gesture of his head he indicates the open country. D. M. DAVIN A first-rate raconteur who was able to act out his stories with gesture and mimicry. M. AMIS She crinkled her nose—a gesture which in her indicated uncertainty. 3 J. RABAN He had offered me a room to stay in; a characteristically kind and open-handed gesture. A. STORR This was clearly a gesture rather than a seriously intended attempt at suicide.

B *v.* †1 *v.t.* Order the position or carriage of (the body, oneself). M16–M17. 2 *v.i.* Make or use a gesture or gestures. M16. 3 *v.t.* Express or indicate (a thought or feeling) by a gesture or gestures. L16. 4 *v.t.* Direct (a person) by a gesture or gestures. L19.

2 C. HAMPTON Carlos gestures and one of the others lays his gun down . . and gags her. 4 F. RAPHAEL Alma gestured Julia to her place.

gestural *a.* E17. **gestureless** *a.* M19. **gesturer** *n.* L19.

gesundheit /ɡəˈzʊnthaɪt/ *int.* E20. [G = health.] Wishing good health, esp. to a person who has sneezed.

get /ɡɛt/ *n.*[1] See also GIT *n.*[1] ME. [f. GET *v.*] 1 a Offspring; descendants; a child. Now only of animals. ME. b A brat, a bastard (*Sc.* & *north.*); a contemptible person, a fool, an idiot, (*dial.* & *slang*). E16. 2 Begetting, procreation. Now only of animals. ME. 3 Gain, booty, earnings. Long *obs.* exc. *dial.* LME. 4 A getaway, a hasty retreat. Chiefly in *do* or *make a get*. *Austral.* & *NZ slang.* L19. 5 *Games.* An act of returning or retrieving a difficult ball; an act of making a difficult catch. E20.

get /dʒɛt/ *n.*[2] In senses 1 & 2 also **†jet**. ME. [OFr. *get* (mod. *jet*): see JESS *n.*] †1 Fashion, style, mode, manner. ME–E16. †2 A device, a contrivance. Only in LME. 3 A jess for a hawk. *rare.* E17.

get *n.*[3] var. of GETT.

get /ɡɛt/ *v.* Also (now chiefly *US dial.* exc. in sense 36) **git** /ɡɪt/. Pres. pple **getting**. Pa. t. **got** /ɡɒt/, (*arch.*) **gat** /ɡat/; perf. also (*colloq.*) **got** (= has or have got). Pa. pple **got**, (now *N. Amer.* & *dial.* exc. *arch.* & in comb., *rare* in branch IV) **gotten** /ˈɡɒt(ə)n/. ME. [ON *geta* obtain, beget, guess = base of OE *begietan* BEGET, *forgietan* FORGET *v.*, f. Gmc f. IE base also of L *praeda* booty, PREY *n.*, *praedium* estate, *praehendere* lay hold of, Gk *khandanein* (aorist *ekhadon*) hold, contain, be able.] I 1 *v.t.* Obtain as the result of effort or contrivance; procure, acquire for oneself or another; seek out and take, cause to come or be provided, fetch; prepare (a meal). (Foll. by indirect obj. or *for* a recipient or beneficiary.) ME. b *v.t.* Obtain in marriage, marry. Now *Sc.* & *north.* LME. c *v.i.* Acquire wealth or property. Now *rare.* L16. 2 *v.t.* Come into possession of; be the recipient of. ME. 3 *v.t.* Obtain as the proceeds of business or employment; earn; receive in payment. ME. b *v.i.* Earn money, make a living. Now *rare.* M16. 4 *v.t.* Win or earn (something immaterial, as love, credit, fame, etc.) by one's actions or character; obtain as a concession or favour; extract by insistence, entreaty, or inquiry. ME. 5 *v.t.* Achieve, attain, gain, come to have, (a position of superiority (in *get the better of, the upper hand of*, etc.); a desired state or quality; a feeling, an impression, etc.); (with n. of action) succeed in having (*a glance, a glimpse, (a) hold of*, etc.). ME. b Win (a victory). Now *rare.* LME. 6 *v.t.* Capture, get hold of, (a person, †a castle etc.). ME. †b Take hold of in one's hands. LME–L16. 7 *v.t.* Procure by hunting or fishing, catch; (orig. *US*) (deliberately) kill or injure, shoot. ME. 8 *v.t.* (Now usu. of an animal, esp. a stallion) beget, procreate, sire. ME. 9 *v.t.* Acquire by study or experience; learn (a lesson, †a language); commit to memory (esp. in *get by heart* or *rote*). LME. 10 *v.t.* Arrive at, reach. Now *rare* or *obs.* LME. 11 *v.t.* Have inflicted on one, suffer, (a fall, blow, defeat, etc.); receive by way of punishment or penalty. LME. 12 *v.t.* Obtain by way of profit; be benefited or advantaged to the extent of. L15. †b *v.i.* Derive profit, be a gainer (*by*). L16–M18. 13 *v.t.* Bring in as harvest; gather, carry home, (a crop). E16. 14 *v.t.* *Sports & Games.* Gain and be credited with, score, (a goal, points, runs, etc.); make as a score; take (a wicket in cricket). M16. 15 *v.t.* Obtain or ascertain as a result of calculation, logic, or experiment. M16. 16 *v.t.* Succeed in finding, locate; obtain an audible signal from, pick up (a broadcast signal); communicate with (a person or place) by telephone. E17. 17 *v.t.* Contract, catch, (an illness etc.). E17. 18 *v.t.* Obtain by mining, extract (coal etc.). M17. 19 *v.t.* a Puzzle, perplex, mystify, catch in argument. Chiefly in pa. t. or *pass. colloq.* M19. b Worry, annoy, exercise. *colloq.* M19. c Enthral, attract, appeal to; touch emotionally. *colloq.* E20. 20 *v.t.* Eat (a meal etc.). *colloq.* L19. 21 *v.t.* Understand (a person or thing). *colloq.* E20. b *v.i.* Grasp the point, understand. *colloq.* M20. 22 *v.t.* Take as transport, catch (a train, bus, etc.). M20. 23 *v.t.* Respond to, answer, (a telephone, door-bell, etc.). M20. 24 *v.t.* Notice or look at (a person), esp. to criticize or ridicule. Usu. in *imper. colloq.* M20.

1 R. W. EMERSON Men are not born rich; and in getting wealth the man is generally sacrificed. E. A. FREEMAN It was all honourably gotten and was designed to be honourably spent. B. T. WASHINGTON The news was usually gotten from the . . man who was sent to the post-office for the mail. J. CONRAD I ran back to the verandah to get my hat. D. H. LAWRENCE Mellors went into the country and got work on a farm. W. S. MAUGHAM I could have got all the women I wanted in London. J. C. POWYS He . . got his own breakfast. J. KEROUAC Dean got a table, bought drinks. I. MURDOCH I got myself a reasonably sound education. P. ROTH An Army friend . . had gotten us tickets for a Tchaikovsky extravaganza. 2 J. RHYS It's a great thrill getting your letters—so write again soon. 3 ADDISON Methods for getting a livelihood in this strange country. H. JAMES He got about two dollars a sitting. b WORDSWORTH Getting and spending, we lay waste our powers. 4 STEELE I knocked and called, but could get no answer. V. WOOLF Required and got in the end an effort of attention. N. MOSLEY You committed suicide for love; but you did not get love because you were dead. 5 T. SHADWELL It's nothing but a way of speaking, which young amorous fellows have gotten. D. HUME Their enemies . . had gotten possession of their sovereign's confidence. G. K. CHESTERTON For Rome was given to rule the world, And gat of it little joy. J. RHYS Get all the sleep you can my dear. G. VIDAL Occasionally they would come out . . to get a glimpse of me. A. BEATTIE I got the feeling he didn't like my prices. *get a grip on, a kick out of, a shot at*, etc. 6 SHAKES. *Coriol.* The plebeians have got your fellow tribune And hale him up and down. HOBBES And when the city Troy we shall have got. 7 E. GLYN She did not hit any rabbits, but she got a gardener in the leg. S. BELLOW The person who charges me with this cruelty is not without prejudice toward me, he is out to get me. 8 A. E. HOUSMAN Get you the sons your fathers got. T. FITZGEORGE-PARKER At stud, Hurry On . . got three Derby winners. 9 CHARLES CHURCHILL Without the least finesse of art He gets applause!—I wish he'd get his part. A. C. SWINBURNE In such wise I gat knowledge of the Gods. H. H. RICHARDSON The Getting of Wisdom. 11 V. WOOLF One got only a glare in the eye from looking at the line of the wall. R. K. NARAYAN Seven years . . is what one gets for murder only half-proved. *get the boot, the chop, the sack*, etc. 12 G. GREENE One never got anything for nothing. 15 L. CARROLL By taking *x* as subject, we get 'all *x* are *y*prime'. 16 M. LOWRY Hugh . . turned the radio dial back and forth, trying to get San Antonio. P. G. WODEHOUSE He took up the receiver. . . 'I hear you've been trying to get me.' 17 S. SONTAG He sickens . . , gets TB, and dies. J. MORTIMER Simeon Simcox got a dose of flu. 19a W. DE LA MARE 'Why was it mistaken?' He shook his head. . . 'That's got me, miss.' b *Scouting* It's the 'not knowing' that gets them. c *People* As soon as you enter any jazz club the atmosphere gets you. 21 T. DREISER Just what do you mean by that? . . I don't get you. J. HELLER You're doing a better job in your position than I'm doing in mine. Do you get what I mean? T. MALLON He got the jokes. b M. INNES Okay, okay. I get. 22 M. FORSTER She went to get the last train home and missed it. 24 *News Chronicle* If he is conceited, the girls mutter get *yew*!

II *v.t.* with compl. (see also specialized senses below). 25 With prep. or adv. (phr.). Succeed in bringing, sending, placing, or putting (another person, (*arch.*) oneself, a thing) *to, from, into, out of* a place, etc., *through, over* a space, etc.; succeed in bringing (another person, oneself, a thing) into or out of a specified position or state; incur or suffer the coming or bringing of (a person or thing) into a specified position or state. ME. 26 With inf. Induce or prevail on (a person) *to do* (†*do*); cause (a person) *to do*. LME. †b With pass. inf. Cause to undergo the specified action. *rare.* L16–M18. 27 With pa. pple. Cause or succeed in causing a specified action to be done to (a person or thing) or a specified result to happen to (a person or thing). E16. 28 With adj. Succeed in bringing (a person or thing) to be in the specified state. L16. 29 With pres. pple. Cause (a person or thing) to be *doing*. E20.

25 H. FIELDING Get you both about your business. B. JOWETT A difficulty into which I have got myself. SCOTT FITZGERALD We . . got her into a cold bath. DAY LEWIS Knos . . was always getting bees in her hair. 26 P. ROTH Lifting his voice so as to get Andrea to hear him. S. CHITTY Only by speaking to them like 'an angel' could Gwen John get them to go away. 27 T. JEFFERSON I got my right wrist dislocated. W. GOLDING Have you time to get your hair cut? 28 B. EMECHETA She was very slow in getting herself pregnant again. W. WHARTON Annastina's getting a bed ready for me.

III *v.i.* (chiefly with compl.: see also specialized senses below). 30 With prep. or adv. (phr.). Succeed in coming, going, or bringing oneself *to, from, into, out of* a place, etc., *through, over* a space, etc.; attain or come *to* an end aimed at or condition towards which progress has been made. ME. 31 With inf. Come or happen *to be, to do*; have or secure an opportunity *to do*; be allowed *to do*. L16. b With impers. *it* & *to be* (*so*) *that*: reach the point or stage where, be or become such that. Cf. sense 35 below. *N. Amer. colloq.* L19. 32 With adj. or equivalent. Become, succeed in becoming, make oneself; (with compar. & superl.) grow. L16. 33 With pa. pple. a With pple. of v.t. Cause a specified action or result to be done to oneself; have a specified action or result happen to oneself; come to be the object of a specified action. Freq. as pass.-forming aux. where a continuous state is not intended. M17. b With pple. of v.i. Accomplish or complete the specified action. Now *colloq.* E18. 34 With pres. pple. Come to be *doing*; *Sc.* find an opportunity for *doing*. E18. 35 With advb. cl. introduced by *so, so as* (*so's*), *so that, that, where*: reach the point or stage where, be or become such that. Cf. sense 31b above. *colloq.* (chiefly *N. Amer.*). M19. 36 Leave, go away. Freq. in *imper. colloq.*

(orig. *US*). M19. **37** Manage to go, make it. Chiefly *Sc.* L19.

30 T. JEFFERSON The scene has not yet got to its height. T. HARDY The cow had got out of the paddock. E. HEMINGWAY You have to get there on time. P. MORTIMER I got clumsily to my feet. **31** M. LAVIN It gets to be a habit with us fellows. L. KAUFMAN It isn't every day that an old man gets to meet his daughter's beau. *Wall Street Journal* If his salary doubles to $48,000, he gets to keep $18,074. K. VONNEGUT That is how you get to be a writer. A. BROOKNER One gets to fear one's own boredom. **32** SCOTT FITZGERALD The sun's getting colder every year. S. BRILL We're finished until we or some local prosecutor gets lucky. J. KEROUAC Terry and I.. got ready to hit the sack. J. GATHORNE-HARDY It got too much for them as they got older. *get clear of, rid of, shot of*, etc. **33** C. P. SNOW He had just got engaged. ISAIAH BERLIN Nothing ever gets articulated save enormous, sonorous generalisations. **34** J. RUSKIN I got thinking about the dry bed of the stream. **35** R. LARDNER I got so as I could beat him. SCOTT FITZGERALD My ambition is to get where I need write no more but only novels. J. STEINBECK Fella can get so he misses the noise of a saw mill. *Daily Telegraph* It is getting that you can't wear a badge . . for fear of being beaten up. **36** D. BUCKINGHAM I want you out of the way—so git. K. GILES Anybody in a room either gets or pays for another twenty-four hours.

IV Special perfect uses. **38** *has* or *have got* (colloq. simply *got*), has or have, possess(es). E17. **b** *has* or *have got to* (also simply *got to*), has or have to, must (*be*). Cf. GOTTA. *colloq.* M19.

38 V. WOOLF Why be always trying to bring up some feeling she had not got? E. BAGNOLD Got any boy friends? G. GREENE He hadn't got that courage. G. PALEY They got it in for men. **b** A. CHRISTIE Got to go up to Scotland to-night. J. P. DONLEAVY I've got to go and see my tutor.

Phrases: (A selection of cross-refs. only is included: see esp. other ns.) *get a person's goat*: see GOAT *n. get a person's gruel*: see GRUEL *n.* **get better** recover from illness. *get cracking*: see CRACK *v.* **get done (with)** have done (with), finish. **get going** (*a*) *v.phr.i.* begin; become talkative or animated; begin working or proceeding steadily, settle into a steady course; (*b*) *v.phr.t.* start; get (a person or thing) into a steady course; get (a person) excited. **†get ground** make progress, advance. **get hers, his** *slang* (of an individual) be killed (cf. *get theirs* below). *get hold of*: see HOLD *n.*[1] **get it** *spec.* (*a*) be successful, get what one wants, (freq. iron. in *I wish you may get it, don't you wish you may get it*); (*b*) understand a joke, grasp a point made; *get it in one*: see ONE *a., n. & pron.*; (*c*) be killed or injured; *get it in the neck*: see NECK *n.*[1]; (*d*) get into trouble; also *get it hot (and strong)*; (*e*) answer a telephone, doorbell, etc. *get knotted*: see KNOTTED. *get lost*: see LOST *a. get* NOWHERE. **get oneself gone** *arch.* go away, leave. *get religion*: see RELIGION. *get* STUFFED. **get theirs** *slang* (of two or more people) be killed. **get to know** become personally acquainted with (a person, place, etc.). **get well** recover from illness. **get with child** make pregnant. *give as good as one gets*: see GIVE *v.* **have got it bad(ly)** *slang* be infatuated, be in love. *have got something*: see SOMETHING *pron. & n. play hard to get*: see HARD *adv.*

With advs. in specialized senses: **get about** (*a*) go from place to place; visit many places; move about; begin to walk after an illness etc.; (*b*) (of a rumour, news, etc.) be circulated, esp. orally. **get abroad** *arch.* = *get about* (b) above. *get across*: see ACROSS *adv.* 2. **get ahead** make progress, meet with success. **get along** (*a*) proceed, progress, advance, meet with success; manage, cope, fare, (*well* etc., *without*); (*b*) coexist or communicate in a specified manner (*together, with*); live harmoniously, be or remain on good terms (*together, with*); (*c*) *get along with you!*, go away!, be off! nonsense! **get around** (*a*) get about, go round; (*b*) get round *to.* **get away** (*a*) escape, succeed in departing; manage to go away (*from, into, to* a place), esp. for rest or recreation; *get away from*, disregard, avoid the fact of, (usu. in neg. contexts); *get away from it all*, escape all demands and responsibilities, go away from one's everyday environment, tasks, and worries; (*b*) *get away (with you)!* (colloq.), expr. incredulity or astonishment; (*c*) *get away with*, succeed in winning or stealing; succeed in (an act) without detection, criticism, or punishment, accomplish with impunity; *get away with murder*, get away with anything, be able to do anything one wants; (*d*) *Cricket* hit (the ball) so as to make a run or runs; (*e*) begin; (of a plant) begin to grow vigorously or well. **get back** (*a*) return, arrive home; (of a statement etc.) come to the notice of an interested party etc. (foll. by *to* the person(s) concerned); (*b*) recover (something lost); *get (some of) one's own back* (*on*) (colloq.), get revenge (on), get even (with); (*c*) *get back at* (colloq.), retaliate against; (*d*) *get back to* (colloq.), contact (a person) again later. **get by** *colloq.* (just) manage or cope, be adequate, do enough; pass or be acceptable *as*; get away *with.* **get down** (*a*) succeed in coming or going down; alight; (esp. of a child) leave the table; (*b*) succeed in bringing or lifting down; swallow (food etc.); (*c*) record (something) in writing; (*d*) *get down to*, begin work on, turn one's attention seriously to, settle down to; consider the essentials or fundamentals of; (*e*) *colloq.* depress, weary; (*f*) *US slang* be successful, fulfil one's potential, participate fully, achieve mental harmony. **get in** (*a*) make one's way in; arrive at a destination, arrive home; gain entrance or admission; *slang* (of a man) have sexual intercourse; *get in there* (slang), take positive action, get to work; (*b*) succeed in bringing or placing (something) in; bring home, gather in, (a crop); collect (money owed); buy in, acquire a stock of; call in (a person, firm, etc.) to perform a specific function; gain admission or membership for; plant, sow; *get one's hand in*: see HAND *n.*; (*c*) *get in with*, become friendly with, gain intimacy or favour with, cultivate the acquaintance of; *Naut.* come close up to; (*d*) be elected to an office, parliament etc.; obtain membership of an institution; obtain a place at a college, university; (*e*) enter a vehicle; (*f*) succeed in doing, have time for (an activity); fit (work etc.) into a given time; succeed in delivering (a blow etc.); succeed in interposing (a comment etc.); *colloq.* allow or experience the lapse of (a period of time); *get a word in (edgeways)*: see WORD *n.*; (*g*) *get in bad, wrong* (slang), incur dislike, get or bring into disfavour or trouble (*with*); *get in good*, inspire liking, come or bring into favour (*with*). **get off** (*a*) escape, start (on a journey, in a race, etc.), succeed in leaving or setting off; *slang* stop having to use drugs etc.; *get off on the right* (or *wrong*) *foot*: see FOOT *n.*; *get off to a good, poor*, etc., *start*, begin well, poorly, etc.; (*b*) be acquitted or pardoned; be let off *lightly* etc., *with* or *for* a specified loss or penalty; procure acquittal, pardon, or a slight penalty for (a person); (*c*) get (a ship) under way; send off (on a journey, in a race, etc.); *arch. colloq.* marry off (a female dependant); dispatch, post, (a letter etc.); (*d*) remove, take off; (*e*) commit to memory, learn; (*f*) dismount from a horse, bicycle, etc.; alight or disembark from a bus, train, aeroplane, etc.; *tell a person where to get off, where he* or *she gets off* (colloq.), rebuke a person for interference or presumption; (*g*) succeed in uttering (esp. a joke); (*h*) (cause to) go to sleep; (*i*) *colloq.* become on friendly or amorous terms *with*, establish a romantic or sexual relationship *with*; (*j*) *Jazz slang* improvise skilfully; (*k*) *imper.* (colloq.) expr. incredulity or astonishment; (*l*) *slang* become intoxicated on drugs; achieve sexual satisfaction, experience an orgasm; *get off on*, be excited or aroused by, enjoy. **get on** (*a*) put on (clothes), don; *get one's skates on*: see SKATE *n.*[2]; (*b*) advance, make progress, prosper, succeed, (*with*); fare (*with*); pursue one's course, continue with or *with* one's activities; manage *without*; (*c*) be able to conduct relations (*together, with*) in a specified manner or to a specified degree; agree or live sociably (*together, with*); (*d*) acquire, display, (pace); *get a move on*: see MOVE *n.*; (*e*) *getting on for* (or *to*), approaching, coming close to, (a specified age, time, number, etc.); *getting on*, becoming old (more fully *getting on in years, life*, etc.), (of time) becoming late; (*f*) mount on to a bus, train, etc.; (*g*) *get on to* (colloq.) succeed in understanding, become aware of (a fact); get into communication with, get in touch with; begin or bring round to discussing (a subject); (*h*) *colloq.* take or bring oneself *off, up*, etc. (usu. in *imper.*); (*i*) *get it on* (US slang), give oneself up to an activity, enjoy oneself; become elated or intoxicated (*with*); have sexual intercourse (*with*). **get out** (*a*) leave a place of confinement, escape, leave one's house; become known; alight from a vehicle etc.; in *imper.* (*colloq.*) go away!, be off!, nonsense!; *get out from under*: see UNDER *adv.*; (*b*) take from a place of confinement or storage, take out, bring out; elicit (information); publish (a book etc.); succeed in uttering; succeed in solving or finishing (a puzzle etc.); *get one's finger out*: see FINGER *n.*; (*c*) dismiss or be dismissed at cricket; (*d*) *get out of*, issue or escape from, leave; alight from; go beyond (reach, sight, etc.); evade, avoid, (an act, *doing*); abandon (a habit) gradually; elicit, obtain, or extract from; *get a rise out of*: see RISE *n.*; *get out of bed on the wrong side*: see BED *n.*; *get out of hand*: see HAND *n.* **get outside of** = *get outside* below. **get over** (*a*) succeed in reaching or bringing to the other side; cross over; move over; (*b*) finish; bring (esp. a troublesome task) to an end; *get it over with*, perform a troublesome or unwelcome task, endure an unwelcome experience; (*c*) communicate successfully, get across; *US slang* be successful. **get round** (*a*) get about, go round; (*b*) *arch.* recover from illness, get well; (*c*) *get round to*, find the time or occasion for (an act, *doing*). **get through** (*a*) reach or bring to a destination; (of legislation) be passed by a legislative body; ensure the passage of (legislation etc.); (*b*) succeed in an examination or course; (*c*) make contact by radio or telephone; (*d*) *get through with*, succeed in accomplishing or enduring, finish with; (*e*) *get through to*, reach the attention or understanding of (a person). **get together** (*a*) collect (persons or things); gather together; meet, esp. to confer; (*b*) *slang* put in order, organize, harmonize; *get it together, get one's act together*, bring some order or purpose into one's life, start performing well; *get one's head together*, overcome emotional difficulties or inhibitions. **get up** (*a*) rise; raise oneself, esp. to a standing posture; rise from bed; climb up; mount, esp. on horseback; (of fire, wind, the sea) begin to be violent, increase in force; (of game) rise from cover; (of a cricket-ball) rise sharply from the pitch; *imper.* (as a command to a horse) go! go ahead! move more quickly! (see also GIDDAP); *get up and go* or (US) *get*, start moving quickly or acting energetically; (*b*) come close (*arch.*); come close *to*, come up *to*; (*c*) organize, set on foot; make ready; make presentable, arrange the appearance of (hair, oneself), produce (a play, a book, etc.) in a specified manner; (*d*) *arch.* make good, recover, (arrears etc.); (*e*) raise, lift up; produce or build up (speed etc.); work up, create in oneself, (a factitious emotion); acquire knowledge of (a subject) for a special purpose or by a special effort; *get a person's back up*: see BACK *n.*[1]; *get it up* (slang), get an erection of the penis, have sexual intercourse (*with* a woman); *get the wind up*: see WIND *n.*[1]; *get up steam*: see STEAM *n.*

With preps. in specialized senses: **get across —** *colloq.* annoy, get on the wrong side of. **get around —** circumvent, get round. **get at —** (*a*) reach, gain access to, get hold of; (*b*) find out, ascertain, learn; (*c*) *colloq.* attack, taunt, try to upset (a person); (*d*) *slang* tamper with, bribe, try to influence; (*e*) start work on, turn one's attention to; (*f*) *colloq.* imply, mean, try to say, (usu. w. *what* as obj.). **get by —** *colloq.* succeed in getting past. **get from —** †(*a*) escape from; (*b*) inherit (esp. a characteristic or habit) from, derive or develop in imitation of. **get inside —** penetrate, investigate closely; achieve a deep or intimate understanding of. **get into —** (*a*) come to be in, result in being in, (a specified state or condition); *get into one's stride*: see STRIDE *n.*; *get into the act*: see ACT *n.* 7c; *get into trouble*: see TROUBLE *n.*; (*b*) make one's way into, gain admittance to; (*c*) *colloq.* put on (boots, clothes); (*d*) become occupied, interested, absorbed, or involved in; (*e*) get knowledge of; (*f*) take possession of, cause to behave in an extraordinary way; (*g*) (of alcoholic drink) affect, confuse (one's head etc.); (*h*) have sexual intercourse with (a woman); (*i*) *get it into one's head that*, come to think, be convinced that. **get off —** (*a*) dismount from (a horse, bicycle, etc.); alight or disembark from (a bus, train, aeroplane, etc.); (*b*) obtain release from (an engagement etc.); (*c*) stop having to use (drugs etc.); (*d*) not remain on, remove oneself from on top of; leave, deviate from (a subject etc.); *get off a person's back*: see BACK *n.*[1]; *get off it* (colloq.), stop saying or doing such things, come off it; *get off the ground*: see GROUND *n.*; (*e*) remove or detach from; *get off one's chest*: see CHEST *n.* **get on —** (*a*) place oneself on, mount on to (a horse, bicycle, train, etc.); *get on a person's nerves, wick*: see NERVE *n.*, WICK *n.*[1]; *get on the (tele)phone*, make a telephone call; (*b*) rise on (one's feet or legs) to speak in public; (*c*) begin or bring round to discussing (a subject); get (a person) on to (a subject); (*d*) find out to the disadvantage or detriment of (a person); (*e*) lay or place (something) on; have or develop (something) on; *get one's hands on*: see HAND *n.*; *get on the brain*: see BRAIN *n.*; *get the jump on*: see JUMP *n.*[1] **get onto** *colloq.* = *get on to* above. **get outside —** *slang* eat, consume. **get over —** (*a*) overcome, surmount (a difficulty); cease to be troubled or surprised by; recover from (an illness, shock, loss, etc.); (*b*) travel over, cover, (a distance); (*c*) accomplish (a task); (*d*) *slang* take advantage of, circumvent. **get round —** (*a*) cajole, win round; (*b*) evade. **get through —** (*a*) bring to an end, reach the end of; spend (money); (*b*) (of a legislative bill etc.) be passed by (a legislative body); (*c*) while away (time etc.); (*d*) be successful in, pass, (an examination or course). **get to —** (*a*) reach, arrive at; *get to a* or *the point, place, where, get where* (US colloq.) = sense 35 above; *get to the bottom of*: see BOTTOM *n.*; (*not know* etc.) *where a person has got to*, (not know etc.) where an expected person is, what has happened to a person who should be present; (*b*) begin (an activity, *doing*), settle down to; (*c*) affect emotionally, upset; worry, depress; (*d*) *slang* tamper with, bribe, try to influence. **get upon —** = *get on* above. **get with —** *slang* become involved or absorbed in; become in tune with, reach harmony with. **†get within —** succeed in coming within the defences of (an adversary).

Comb.: **get-at-able** *a.* accessible, reachable, able to be got at; **get-rich-quick** *a.* concerned (esp. exclusively) with the rapid accumulation of wealth; **get-well** *a.* designating a card or message wishing a full recovery to a sick person.

geta /ˈgeɪtə/ *n.pl.* L19. [Jap.] Japanese wooden shoes with a thong to pass between the first (big) toe and the second toe.

Getae /ˈdʒɛtʌɪ, ˈgɛtʌɪ/ *n.pl.* E19. [L f. Gk *Getai.*] An ancient people inhabiting a region corresponding to parts of Bulgaria and Romania.

Getan /ˈdjɛt(ə)n, ˈgɛt(ə)n/ *a.* & *n.* L16. [f. as next + -AN.] A *adj.* = GETIC *a.* L16. B *n.* A member of the Getae. E20.

getaway /ˈgɛtəweɪ/ *n.* & *a.* M19. [f. *get away* s.v. GET *v.*] A *n.* An act of getting away; an escape, esp. after a crime. Freq. in *make a* or *one's getaway.* M19. B *adj.* Designating a vehicle, boat, etc., in which to get away or make a getaway. M20.

Gethsemane /gɛθˈsɛməni/ *n.* E20. [A garden on the Mount of Olives, scene of the agony of Christ (*Matt.* 26:36–46), late L (Vulgate) *Gethsemani*, Gk *Gethsēmanē*, f. Aram. *gaṯ šamnē* oil-press.] A scene or occasion of spiritual or mental anguish.

Getic /ˈdʒɛtɪk, ˈgɛtɪk/ *a.* & *n.* M17. [L *Geticus* f. GETAE: see -IC.] A *adj.* Of or pertaining to the Getae or their language; *loosely* Thracian. M17. B *n.* The language of the Getae. M20.

get-off /ˈgɛtɒf/ *n.* M19. [f. *get off* s.v. GET *v.*] 1 An evasion, a subterfuge. M19. 2 A take-off by an aeroplane etc. *rare.* E20. 3 A skilful improvisation or break in jazz. *slang.* M20.

get-out /ˈgɛtaʊt/ *n.* M19. [f. *get out* s.v. GET *v.*] 1 *as* or *like* (*all*) *get-out*, to the highest degree, with the utmost vigour. *slang.* M19. 2 A means of evasion; a withdrawal. *colloq.* L19. 3 *Theatr.* Orig., the ability of a touring company to pay all expenses and move on. Now usu., the total weekly cost of a production. M20.

gett /gɛt/ *n.* Also **get.** L19. [Heb.] A Jewish bill of divorce, in prescribed form; a divorce by such a bill.

gettable /ˈgɛtəb(ə)l/ *a.* M16. [f. GET *v.* + -ABLE.] That can be got.

getter /ˈgɛtə/ *n.* & *v.* LME. [f. GET *v.* + -ER[1].] A *n.* 1 A person who gets or obtains something, esp. wealth; a person who or (now only) an animal which begets offspring. Also with advs., *getter-in*, *-up*, etc., a person who gets in, up, etc. See also GO-GETTER. LME. 2 *spec.* A coal-miner who extracts the coal after a seam has been undercut. M19. 3 A substance used to remove residual gas from an evacuated vessel. E20. B *v.t.* Remove (gas) by means of a getter; evacuate (a vessel) by means of a getter. E20.

getting /ˈgɛtɪŋ/ *vbl n.* ME. [f. GET *v.* + -ING[1].] 1 The action of GET *v.* Also with advs., as *getting-in*, *-out*, *-up*, etc. ME. 2 *sing.* & (usu.) in *pl.* Acquisitions, gains, earnings. *arch.* LME.

get-together /ˈgɛt-təgɛðə/ *n. colloq.* E20. [f. *get together* s.v. GET *v.*] An informal social gathering, a sociable meeting.

get-togetherness *n.* tendency to get together, sociability M20.

Getulian /gɪˈtjuːlɪən/ *a.* & *n.* Also **Gaet-.** L16. [f. L *Gaetuli*, *Getuli* f. Gk *Gaitouloi* perh. f. a Berber base.] A *adj.* Designating or pertaining to an ancient nomadic Berber people inhabiting the desert region south and east of Numidia. L16. B *n.* A member of this people. E17.

get-up /ˈgɛtʌp/ *n.* M19. [f. *get up* s.v. GET *v.*] 1 A style of equipment or costume; an outfit. M19. 2 A style of production or finish, esp. of a book. M19. 3 Energy, enterprise, determination. Also *get-up-and-go*, (US) *get-up-and-get.* M19.

geum /ˈdʒiːəm/ *n.* M16. [mod.L (see below), var. of L *gaeum.*] Any of various plants of the genus *Geum*, of the rose family, which includes herb bennet, *G. urbanum*, and water avens, *G. rivale.*

gewgaw /ˈgjuːgɔː/ *n.* & *a.* ME. [Origin uncertain: perh. redupl. of OFr. *gogue* game, joke or f. GAW *v.*] A *n.* A (gaudy) plaything or ornament; *fig.* a (showy) worthless thing or person. ME.

J. P. HENNESSY A boutique, to sell gewgaws, bric-à-brac and imitation jewellery.

B *attrib.* or as *adj.* Resembling a gewgaw; *fig.* showy, worthless. M17.

gewgawed *a.* ornamented with gewgaws L19

Gewürztraminer /gəˈvʊətstrəˌmiːnə/ *n.* M20. [G, f. *Gewürz* spice + TRAMINER.] A variety of Traminer grape grown esp. in the Rhine valley, Alsace, and Austria; the mildly spicy white wine made from this grape.

gey /geɪ, gʌɪ/ *adv.* & *a. Sc.* E18. [Var. of GAY *a.* & *adv.* Cf. similar use of JOLLY *adv.*] A *adv.* Very; considerably. Also *gey and.* E18.

J. BUCHAN They'll be gey sick o' Antrobus by then.

B *adj.* (Of quantity) good, considerable; (of quality etc.) fine, excellent. E19.

L. G. GIBBON A gey man in Kinraddie, and maybe one of the gentry. A. RANSOME It's brought a gey lot down for me to clear.

geyser /ˈgiːzə, *in sense 1 also* ˈgʌɪ-/ *n.* L18. [Icel. *Geysir*, name of a particular hot spring in Iceland, rel. to *geysa* (ON *geysa*) gush.] 1 A hot spring (usu. in a volcanic area) which intermittently spouts steam and water; *fig.* a jet or stream of liquid etc. L18. 2 An apparatus connected to a bath, sink, etc., for rapidly heating water for washing. L19.

1 T. WILLIAMS The bottle cap pops off and a geyser of foam shoots up.

geyseric *a.* pertaining to or of the nature of a geyser L19.

geyserite /ˈgiːz(ə)rʌɪt, ˈgʌɪ-/ *n.* E19. [f. prec. + -ITE[1].] *Min.* A siliceous usu. opaline sinter occurring in thermal springs and geysers.

ghaffir /ˈgɑːfɪə/ *n.* E19. [Arab. dial. *ġafīr.*] In the Middle East: an Egyptian police officer; a guard, a watchman.

ghan /gan/ *n. Austral. slang.* E20. [f. AF)GHAN.] 1 An Afghan or Muslim immigrant to Australia, *esp.* one who drives or breeds camels. E20. 2 *the Ghan*, a train that runs between Adelaide and Alice Springs. M20.

Ghanaian /gɑːˈneɪən/ *n.* & *a.* M20. [f. *Ghana* (see below) + -IAN.] A *n.* A native or inhabitant of Ghana, a country on the coast of W. Africa known until 1957 as the Gold Coast. M20. B *adj.* Of, pertaining to, or characteristic of Ghana. M20.

ghap /gɑːp/ *n.* Also **guaap.** E19. [Nama.] Any of several succulent southern African plants of the genus *Trichocaulon* (family Asclepiadaceae), formerly used by the Nama as a thirst-quencher.

gharana /gəˈrɑːnə/ *n.* M20. [Hind. *gharānā* family.] *Indian Mus.* A school of players who practise a particular style of interpretation.

gharial /ˈgarɪɑːl, gʌrɪˈɑːl, ˈgɛːrɪəl/ *n.* Also **gavial** /ˈgeɪvɪəl/. E19. [Hind. *ghaṛiyāl*; form with *-v-* f. Fr., prob. alt. by scribal error.] A slender-snouted fish-eating crocodilian of the Indus and Ganges basins, *Gavialis gangeticus* (more fully *Indian gharial*); any slender-snouted crocodilian related to or resembling this, esp. *Tomistoma schlegeli* of SE Asia (more fully *false* or *Malayan gharial*).

gharry /ˈgɑːri, ˈgari/ *n.* E19. [Hind. *gāṛī.*] In the Indian subcontinent: a carriage, usu. horse-drawn and for hire.

Ghassulian /gaˈsuːlɪən/ *a.* & *n.* M20. [Fr. *Ghassoulien*, f. Teleilat el-*Ghassul* (see below): see -IAN.] *Archaeol.* A *adj.* Designating or pertaining to a chalcolithic culture of which remains have been found at Teleilat el-Ghassul, near Jericho in the Jordan valley. M20. B *n.* A person who belonged to this culture. M20.

ghast /gɑːst/ *a. arch.* or *poet.* E17. [Back-form. f. GHASTFUL or GHASTLY.] = GHASTLY *a.*

ghastful /ˈgɑːstfʊl, -f(ə)l/ *a. arch.* Orig. **†gastful.** LME. [f. GAST *v.* + -FUL. Cf. next.] 1 Full of fear, scared. LME. 2 Dreadful, terrible. LME.

†ghastfully *adv.* LME–E18. **†ghastfulness** *n.* LME–L16.

ghastly /gɑːs(t)li/ *a.* & *adv.* Orig. **† gastly.** ME. [f. GAST *v.* + -LY[1]. The spelling with *gh-* (after GHOST *n.*) became current after Spenser.] A *adj.* 1 Orig., causing real terror. Now, horrible, frightful; very unpleasant. ME. b Objectionable, shocking, tasteless. *colloq.* M19. 2 Like a ghost or corpse; deathly pale, wan; very ill; (of a smile, laugh, etc.) painfully forced. L16. †3 Full of fear. L16–M17.

1 J. WILSON The ghastly dreams, That haunt the parting soul. A. J. P. TAYLOR I had made a ghastly mistake. K. CROSSLEY-HOLLAND The ghastly rotting smell rose towards him. b A. BURGESS A ghastly metal model of Blackpool Tower. A. N. WILSON The ghastly little trade unionist . . whingeing and whining . . for more money. 2 J. M. COETZEE His face is ghastly . . his wounds plainly still cause him pain. A. THWAITE Feeling worn and ghastly after the steamer voyage. 3 SHAKES. *Temp.* Why are you drawn? Wherefore this ghastly looking?

B *adv.* 1 Frightfully, horribly. Formerly also, in a frightened manner. L16. 2 Deathly, deathlike. M17.

1 SHAKES. *2 Hen. VI* His eye-balls . . Staring full ghastly like a strangled man. 2 W. IRVING Her face was ghastly pale.

ghastlily *adv.* E19. **ghastliness** *n.* L16.

ghat /gɑːt, gɔːt/ *n. Indian subcontinent.* Also **ghaut.** E17. [Hind. *ghāṭ.*] 1 In *pl.* & †*sing.* Either of two mountain chains running parallel to the east and west coasts of southern India. E17. 2 A mountain pass. L17. 3 A flight of steps leading to a river-bank; a landing-place. L18. 4 In full *burning-ghat.* A level place at the top of a river ghat where Hindus cremate their dead. L19.

3 J. G. FARRELL The devout . . stood on the steps of the bathing ghat. 4 *fig.*: TIRESIAS We also pass several scrapyards and automobile ghats.

ghawazee *n.* pl. of GHAZEEYEH.

ghazal /ˈgazal/ *n.* Also **-el.** L18. [Pers. f. Arab. *ġazal.*] A usu. amatory Arabic, Turkish, Urdu, or (esp.) Persian lyric poem or song characterized by a limited number of stanzas and the recurrence of the same rhyme.

ghazeeyeh /gəˈziːjeɪ/ *n.* Pl. **ghawazee** /gəˈwɑːzi/. L18. [Arab. *ġāziya*, pl. *ġawāzī.*] In Egypt, a dancing girl. Usu. in *pl.*

ghazi /ˈgɑːzi/ *n.* Also (as a title) **G-.** Pl. **-is.** M18. [Arab. *al-ġāzī* act. pple of *ġazā* raid, invade, foray.] In the Middle East: a champion, esp. of Muslims against non-Muslims; a dedicated Muslim fighter. Freq. as an honorific title.

ghee /giː/ *n.* Also **ghi.** M17. [Hind. *ghī*, f. Skt *ghṛta* pa. pple of *ghṛ-* sprinkle.] Indian clarified butter made from the milk of a buffalo or cow.

Gheg /gɛg/ *n.* & *a.* Also **Geg.** E19. [Albanian *Geg.*] A *n.* Pl. **-s**, same. A member of a people of northern Albania; the language spoken by this people. E19. B *attrib.* or as *adj.* Of or pertaining to the Ghegs or their language. M19.

Ghent /gɛnt/ *a.* M19. [A city in Belgium (= Flem. *Gent*, Fr. *Gand*).] Designating any of a number of hybrid azaleas first raised at Ghent between 1804 and 1834.

†ghenting *n.* L17–M18. [f. prec. + -ING[1].] A kind of linen originally made in Ghent.

gherao /gɛˈraʊ/ *n.* & *v.* M20. [f. Hind. *gherna* surround, besiege.] A *n.* Pl. **-os.** In the Indian subcontinent: a form of protest or harassment in labour disputes whereby employers etc. are prevented by workers from leaving the place of work until their claims have been granted. M20. B *v.t.* Detain (a person) in this manner. M20.

gherkin /ˈgəːkɪn/ *n.* E17. [Du. (*au*)*gurkje* dim. of *a*(*u*)*gurk*, *gurk*, ult. f. Slav. wd repr. also by Pol. *ogórek*, Russ. *ogurets* cucumber, derivs. with dim. suff. of late Gk *aggourion* (mod. *aggouri*).] A young green, or a small kind of, cucumber used for pickling.

ghetto /ˈgɛtəʊ/ *n.* & *v.* E17. [Origin uncertain: perh. abbrev. of It. *borghetto* dim. of *borgo* BOROUGH, or f. It. *getto* foundry, where the first ghetto established in Venice, in 1516, was sited.] A *n.* Pl. **-o(e)s.** 1 *Hist.* The quarter in a city, chiefly in Italy, to which Jews were restricted. E17. 2 A densely populated slum area occupied by a minority group or groups, usu. as a result of social or economic pressures; an isolated or segregated social group or area. L19.

2 M. L. King In the ghettos of Chicago . . the problems of poverty and despair are graphically illustrated. *Nursery World* Our negotiators are pushing . . to break up the traditional 'women's work' ghettos.

Comb.: **ghetto blaster** *colloq.* a large and powerful stereo radio-cassette player.

B *v.t.* Put or keep (people) in a ghetto. M20.

fig.: *Listener* The narrow financial aspects ghettoed conveniently towards the back of newspapers or on late-night programmes.

ghettoize *v.t.* = GHETTO *v.* M20. **ghettoi'zation** *n.* the action of ghettoing; the state of being in a ghetto: M20.

ghi *n.* var. of GHEE.

Ghibelline /'gɪbɪlʌɪn/ *n.* & *a.* L16. [It. *Ghibellino*, supposedly f. G *Waiblingen*, an estate belonging to the Hohenstaufen family, said to have been used as a war cry by partisans of the Hohenstaufen emperor Conrad III at the battle of Weinsberg in 1140.] A *n.* A member of the emperor's faction in the medieval Italian States. Opp. GUELPH. L16. B *adj.* Of or adhering to the Ghibellines. E19.

Ghibellinism /-lɪn-/ *n.* (adherence to) the principles of the Ghibelline faction E19.

ghibli /'gɪbli/ *n.* Also **gi-**, **qi-**. E19. [Arab. *kiblī* southern.] A hot dry southerly wind of N. Africa.

ghilgai *n.* var. of GILGAI.

Ghilji *n.* see GHILZAI.

ghillie *n.* var. of GILLIE *n.*[1]

Ghilzai /'gɪlzʌɪ/ *n.* Also (earlier) **Ghilji**. E19. [Afghan name.] A member of one of the most famous of the Afghan tribes.

Ghiordes /gɪ'ɔːdəz/ *a.* E20. [*Gördes*, a town in western Turkey.] 1 Designating a fine type of Turkish rug. E20. 2 Designating a kind of double knot used in weaving some oriental rugs, made by twisting the knot around two warp threads and bringing both ends of the yarn on to the surface between them. E20.

gholam /gəʊ'lɑːm/ *n.* E19. [Arab. *gulām* boy, servant.] A courier, a messenger.

ghoont /guːnt/ *n.* Pl. **-s**, same. E17. [Hindi.] A Himalayan pony.

ghoor *n.* var. of GUR.

Ghoorkha *n.* & *a.* see GURKHA.

ghost /gəʊst/ *n.* [OE *gāst* = OFris. *gāst*, OS *gēst* (Du. *geest*) (O)HG *geist*, f. WGmc. The spelling with *gh-* (established in L16) is prob. f. Flem. *gheest*.] I 1 The soul or spirit as the source of life. *obs.* exc. in *give up the ghost*, *yield* (*up*) *the ghost* below. OE. †b Breath; a blast of wind. OE–E17. 2 The spiritual or immaterial part of a person, as distinct from the physical part; a person's emotional, mental, and moral nature. Now *rare* or *obs.* OE. b A person; *esp.* a wicked-looking person, a villain. OE–L16. 3 The Spirit or active essence of God; the Holy Spirit. *obs.* exc. in HOLY GHOST. OE. †4 An incorporeal being; a (good or evil) spirit. OE–E17. 5†a The soul of a dead person (later esp. of an ancestor), regarded as inhabiting the unseen world and freq. deified or revered. OE–L17. b The soul of a dead person which manifests itself to the living visibly (as a shadowy nebulous image), audibly, etc.; any apparition of a person or thing, a spectre. LME. †6 A corpse. ME–L16. 7 *fig.* An emaciated person. Long *rare.* L16.

II With ref. to the pale nebulous appearance attributed to ghosts (GHOST *n.* 5b). 8 A faint or unsubstantial mark; a slight trace or vestige. E17. 9 A spurious image in a photograph, a television or radar picture, or a spectrogram, caused usually by a defect in the image-forming system. M19. 10 A person who does creative or artistic work on behalf of another person who takes the credit; *spec.* = *ghost-writer* below. L19. 11 *Biol.* A wall or membrane of a cell that has lost its contents; *spec.* a red blood cell that has lost its cytoplasm. Also, a phage whose head end has lost its contents. L19. 12 A faint band on the surface of steel owing to the segregation of certain of its constituents. E20.

8 S. Sassoon He hadn't the ghost of an idea whether we could get through the Boche wire. D. Lodge A ghost of a smile hovered on Mrs Swallow's lips.

Phrases: **give up the ghost** die; *fig.* give up hope. **lay a ghost** cause a ghost to cease appearing. **not the ghost of a chance** no chance at all. **raise a ghost** cause a ghost to appear. **the ghost in the machine** *Philos.* the mind viewed as distinct from the body. **yield (up) the ghost** *arch.* = *give up the ghost* above.

Comb.: **ghostbuster** *colloq.* (*a*) a person who professes to banish ghosts, poltergeists, etc.; (*b*) *US* a person who investigates tax fraud; **ghost crab** a pale sand crab, *Ocypode albicans*, of W. Atlantic coasts; **ghost dance** *US Hist.* a 19th-cent. N. American Indian religious cult based on the performance of a dance to bring the dead to life and drive away White people; **ghost gum** *Austral.* a pallid smooth-trunked inland gum tree, *Eucalyptus papuana*; **ghost moth** a large moth, *Hepialus humuli* (family Hepialidae, the swifts), some of the males of which have pale wings; **ghost story** a story about ghosts or the supernatural; *fig.* an untrue statement or report; **ghost town** (orig. *US*) a town partially or completely devoid of inhabitants; **ghost train** (*a*) a train of cars at a funfair that travels through dark tunnels in which there are ghostlike effects; (*b*) a train run during the night to keep the track clear in periods of heavy snowfall or severe frost; **ghost word** a word originating in a writer's or printer's error or by popular etymology; **ghost-write** *v.t.* & *i.* write as a ghost-writer; **ghost-writer** a person who writes something on behalf of another person who takes the credit (cf. sense 10 above).

ghos'tess *n.* a female ghost M19. **ghosthood** *n.* the state of being a ghost L19. **ghostish** *a.* (*rare*) = GHOSTLY *a.* 3 E20. †**ghostishly** *adv.* in the manner of a ghost: only in L16. **ghostless** *a.* OE. **ghostlike** *a.* & *adv.* (*a*) *adj.* resembling a ghost or a place haunted by ghosts; (*b*) *adv.* in the manner of a ghost: E17. **gho'stology** *n.* the lore of ghosts E19. **ghostship** *n.* ghosthood; *joc.* (with possess. adj., as *his* etc. *ghostship*) a mock title of respect given to a ghost: E19.

ghost /gəʊst/ *v.* L16. [f. the n.] †1 *v.i.* Give up the ghost, die. L16–L17. 2 *v.t.* Haunt as a ghost. E17. 3 *v.i.* & (now *rare*) *t.* (w. *it*). Move like a ghost; *esp.* (of a boat) make good progress in very little wind. M19. 4 *v.t.* & *i.* Write as a ghost-writer. E20.

3 G. Green Clarke . . ghosted his way past three tackles across midfield. I. Murdoch His empty boat . . was found later ghosting along by itself. 4 A. Koestler I enjoyed fussing over her, ghosting her dispatches.

ghoster *n.* (*a*) a person or thing which ghosts; *Naut.* a lightweight sail for use in very light winds; (*b*) a person who does night-work as well as a day-time job: M20. **ghosting** *vbl n.* (*a*) the action of the vb; (*b*) the appearance of ghosts in a television picture: E19.

ghostly /'gəʊs(t)li/ *a.* OE. [f. GHOST *n.* + -LY[1].] 1 Pertaining to the soul or spirit; spiritual. *arch.* OE. †b Of a being: incorporeal, insubstantial. ME–L17. 2 Concerned with spiritual, sacred, or ecclesiastical matters. *arch.* OE. †b Devout. ME–L15. 3 Of, pertaining to, or resembling, a ghost; spectral, shadowy; (of a place) haunted by a ghost. OE.

1 Sir W. Scott Qualified to administer both worldly and ghostly comfort. 2 Tennyson Father . . bid call the ghostly man Hither, and let me shrive me clean. 3 A. P. Herbert The two quiet boats seemed to glide through the mist by some ghostly power.

ghostlily *adv.* M19. **ghostliness** *n.* ME.

ghostly /'gəʊs(t)li/ *adv.* Now *rare.* OE. [f. GHOST *n.* + -LY[2].] As a ghost. Formerly, in a spiritual manner or sense; in spirit.

ghosty /'gəʊsti/ *a.* M19. [f. GHOST *n.* + -Y[1].] Of or resembling a ghost or ghosts.

ghostily *adv.* M19. **ghostiness** *n.* L19.

ghoul /guːl/ *n.* L18. [Arab. *ġūl.*] In Arabic mythology, a desert demon preying on travellers; *gen.* an evil spirit or demon supposed to rob graves and devour corpses; a person unnaturally interested in death.

ghoulish *a.* resembling or characteristic of a ghoul M19. **ghoulishly** *adv.* M19. **ghoulishness** *n.* E20.

ghurry /'gʌri/ *n.* Also **ghuree**. M17. [Hind. *gharī* water-clock with a cycle of typically 24 minutes.] 1 In the Indian subcontinent, 24 minutes (a 60th of a day); among Anglo-Indians, an hour. M17. 2 The metal plate of a clock on which the hours are struck; a timepiece E19.

Ghuzz /guːz/ *n.* & *a.* M19. [Pers. *ġuz* f. Turkic OGHUZ.] A *n.* Pl. same. = OGHUZ *n.* M19. B *attrib.* or as *adj.* Of, pertaining to, or designating the Oghuz. M20.

ghyll *n.* see GILL *n.*[2]

GI /'dʒiːʌɪ, dʒiː'ʌɪ/ *a.* & *n.* M20. [Abbrev. of *government* or *general issue.*] A *adj.* For or pertaining to the US armed forces or servicemen. M20.

GI bride a foreign woman married to a US serviceman on duty abroad. **GI Joe** *colloq.* a US private soldier.

B *n.* A US private soldier. M20.

Giacobinid /dʒakə'bɪnɪd/ *n.* & *a.* M20. [f. Comet *Giacobini*-Zinner, (M. *Giacobini* (fl. 1900), It. astronomer): see -ID[3].] *Astron.* = DRACONID.

giallo antico /ˌdʒallo an'tiːko, ˌdʒaləʊ an'tiːkəʊ/ *n.* & *a. phr.* M18. [It., lit. ancient yellow.] (Made of) a rich yellow marble found among ruins in Italy, and used as a decoration.

giallolino /dʒiallo'liːno/ *n. rare.* E18. [It., now *giallorino*, dim. of *giallo* yellow.] The pigment Naples yellow.

giant /'dʒʌɪənt/ *n.* & *a.* ME. [(O)Fr. *géant*, †*jaiant* f. Proto-Romance var. of L *gigantem*, (nom.) *gigas*, f. Gk *gigas*, *gigant-*.] A *n.* 1 A mythical, pseudo-historical, or fictional being in human form but of superhuman size; *Gk Mythol.* a member of a race of such beings who fought against the gods. ME. b *fig.* An influence or agency of enormous power. M17. c *Econ.* A large or powerful industrial company; a business that dominates its market. M20. 2 An exceptionally large human being (freq. *hyperbol.*); any abnormally large creature or thing. M16. b *Astron.* Any of a class of large stars of high intrinsic luminosity and low mean density, as distinguished from the more common (dwarf) stars of the main sequence. Cf. SUPERGIANT. E20. 3 A person who has some notable quality to an extraordinary degree. M16. 4 *Mining.* A discharge-pipe used in washing ore. *US.* L19.

1 R. Eden The Gyaunte Atlas beareth the worlde on hys shoulders. c *Spectator* One of the soap giants, Unilever, is a British firm. 2 R. Dahl Their . . father, an amiable giant nearly seven foot tall. 3 J. H. Blunt The schoolmen were mental giants.

Phrases: **battle of the giants** a contest between two pre-eminent parties. *sleeping giant*: see SLEEPING *ppl. a.*

B *adj.* Of extraordinary size or force, gigantic, monstrous; (of species or varieties of plants or animals) much larger than the average of their kind; *colloq.* (of a packet, carton, etc.) extra large. LME.

Pope His giant voice the echoing region fills. E. Amadi Port Harcourt . . was a clean little town, cleaner by far than giant Kano.

Special collocations & comb.: **giant brain** *colloq.* an electronic computer. **giant-cell** *Biol.* any unusually large cell; *esp.* (*a*) a platelet-forming cell in the bone marrow; (*b*) a multinuclear cell formed by fusion of macrophages. *giant clam*: see CLAM *n.*[2] 1(b). **giant fibre** *Zool.* an enlarged or fused nerve fibre modified for rapid conduction of impulses, esp. in various invertebrates. **giant kangaroo** = FORESTER 3a(b). **giant-killer** a person who defeats a seemingly much more powerful opponent. **giant order** *Archit.* an order whose columns extend through more than one storey. *giant* PANDA. **giant petrel** either of two large petrels of the genus *Macronectes*, of southern oceans, which occur in dark and white morphs. **giant-powder** a kind of dynamite. **giant racer** a large switchback at a funfair. *giant* SEQUOIA. *giant* SLALOM. **giant('s) stride** a gymnastic apparatus consisting of a pole with a revolving head and hanging ropes enabling the user to take huge strides round the pole. **giant toad** = *cane toad* s.v. CANE *n.*[1]

giantess *n.* a female giant LME. **gianthood** *n.* the nature or characteristics of a giant; the race of giants: M19. **giantish** *a.* (*rare*) approaching the size of a giant; giant-like: M17. **giantize** *v.t.* (*rare*) give the appearance of a giant to E17. **giant-like** *a.* resembling a giant; like that of a giant; gigantic: L16. **giantly** *a.* (now *rare*) giant-like M16. **giantry** *n.* (*rare*) the race of giants; giants collectively: E17. **giantship** *n.* (*a*) the state of being a giant; (*b*) (with possess. adj., as *your* etc. *giantship*) a mock title of respect given to a giant: L17.

giantism /'dʒʌɪəntɪz(ə)m/ *n.* M17. [f. GIANT *n.* + -ISM.] 1 The quality of a giant; the state of being a giant. M17. 2 *Biol.* (Tendency to) abnormally large size; gigantism. L19.

giaour /ˈdʒaʊə/ *n. arch. derog.* M16. [Turk. *gâvur* f. Pers. *gaur* var. of *gabr*, prob. f. Arab. *kāfir* KAFFIR.] A non-Muslim, *esp.* a Christian.

giardia /dʒɪˈɑːdɪə/ *n.* Also G-. E20. [mod.L (see below), f. A. *Giard* (1846–1908), Fr. biologist: see -IA[1].] *Bacteriol.* A flagellate, *Giardia lamblia*, sometimes found in the mammalian gut; any member of the genus *Giardia*.

giardiasis /-ˈdʌɪəsɪs/ *n.* (*Med.*) infection of the gut with giardias E20.

gib /gɪb/ *n.*[1] Now *arch.* & *dial.* LME. [Abbrev. of the name *Gilbert*.] 1 (Orig. used as a familiar name for) a cat, *esp.* a male cat; *dial.* a cat that has been castrated. Now usu. more fully *gib-cat*. LME. †2 A woman, *esp.* an old woman. *derog.* E16–L17.

gib /gɪb/ *n.*[2] M16. [Origin unkn.] 1 Orig., an iron hook. Later, a hooked stick. Long *obs.* exc. *dial.* M16. 2 = KYPE. E19.

Comb.: **gib-staff** a quarterstaff; a hooked stick.

gib /dʒɪb, gɪb/ *n.*[3] L18. [Origin unkn.] 1 A piece of wood or metal used to keep some part of a machine etc. in place; a bolt, a pin, a wedge. L18. 2 *Mining.* A piece of wood used to support the roof of a coalmine. M19.

gib *v.*[1] var. of GIP.

gib *v.*[2] var. of JIB *v.*[2]

gibbed cat /gɪbd ˈkat/ *n. phr.* Long *rare* or *obs.* M17. [Orig. var. of *gib-cat* (GIB *n.*[1]), later taken as pa. pple of an assumed vb = geld + CAT *n.*[1]] A (male) cat; a castrated cat.

gibber /ˈgɪbə/ *n.*[1] *Austral.* L18. [Aborig.] A boulder, a (large) stone.

Attrib. & *comb.*: In the sense 'characterized by boulders and stones', as *gibber country* etc. Special combs., as **gibber gunyah** an Aboriginal cave-dwelling; **gibber-plain** (chiefly *Austral.*) a level area of desert covered with siliceous gravel or broken pebbles.

gibber /ˈdʒɪbə, ˈgɪbə/ *n.*[2] M19. [f. GIBBER *v.*] Rapid and inarticulate utterance.

ARNOLD BENNETT The mumbling toothless gibber of his shrill protesting.

gibber /ˈgɪbə/ *n.*[3] & *a.* M19. [L = hump.] *Bot.* A *n.* A hump or bulge. M19. B *adj.* = GIBBOUS. E20.

gibber /ˈdʒɪbə, ˈgɪbə/ *v.i.* E17. [Imit. Cf. GIBBERISH.] Speak rapidly and inarticulately; chatter, talk nonsense; (of an ape or monkey) utter a quick series of vocal noises.

H. MARTINEAU Monkeys . . hung by one arm from the boughs overhead, gibbering and chattering. A. HALEY To stare . . at the other naked men, most of them gibbering in their terror.

gibberellic /dʒɪbəˈrɛlɪk/ *a.* M20. [f. mod.L *Gibberella* (see below), dim. of *Gibbera* genus name, f. L *gibber* hump: see -IC.] *gibberellic acid*, one of the gibberellins, a tetracyclic lactonic acid first isolated from the fungus *Gibberella fujikuroi*, a parasite of cereals.

gibberellin /dʒɪbəˈrɛlɪn/ *n.* M20. [f. as prec + -IN[1].] Any of various tetracyclic compounds, e.g. gibberellic acid, present in many higher plants as growth hormones, promoting stem elongation, germination, flowering, etc.

gibberish /ˈdʒɪb(ə)rɪʃ, ˈgɪb-/ *n.* & *a.* E16. [Perh. rel. to GIBBER *v.* (but found earlier) + -ISH[1] as used in *Spanish*, *Swedish*, etc.] A *n.* Unintelligible speech belonging to no known language, a series of meaningless sounds; blundering or ungrammatical talk; nonsense. E16.

J. L. WATEN Martin and Benny were whispering together in some strange gibberish. E. H. GOMBRICH A language consisting only of new words and a new syntax would be indistinguishable from gibberish.

†B *adj.* Of or pertaining to gibberish, expressed in gibberish; unintelligible, unmeaning. L16–E19.

gibberose /ˈgɪbərəʊs/ *a.* E18. [f. L *gibberosus*, f. *gibber* hump: see -OSE[1].] *Bot.* = GIBBOUS.

gibbet /ˈdʒɪbɪt/ *n.*[1] ME. [OFr. *gibet* staff, cudgel, gallows, dim. of *gibe* staff, club, prob. ult. f. Gmc.] 1 *Hist.* Orig., a gallows. Later, an upright post with a projecting arm from which the bodies of criminals were hung after execution. ME. 2 The punishment of death by hanging. LME. 3a A chimney crane for hanging a pot over the fire. *Sc. rare.* L15. †b A short beam projecting from a wall, having a pulley fixed at the end. Only in 16. c The projecting arm of a crane; a jib. E18. †4 A cudgel. Only in 17.

1 GOLDSMITH There, the black gibbet glooms beside the way.

†**gibbet** *n.*[2] L16–M18. [Origin uncertain: cf. OFr. *juppet* the distance to which one can shout, f. *jupper*, *juper* whoop, cry out.] A note on a horn, a call or whistle as a signal to a dog or hawk.

gibbet /ˈdʒɪbɪt/ *v.* L16. [f. GIBBET *n.*[1]] †1 *v.i.* Hang as on a gibbet. Only in L16. 2 *v.t. fig.* Hold up to infamy or contempt. M17. 3 *v.t.* Put to death by hanging. E18. b Expose on a gibbet; hang up as on a gibbet. M18.

gibble-gabble /ˈgɪb(ə)lgab(ə)l/ *n.* E17. [Redupl. of GABBLE *n.* Cf. FIDDLE-FADDLE.] Senseless chatter.

gibbon /ˈgɪb(ə)n/ *n.* L18. [Fr., of unkn. origin.] Any of various small long-armed tailless arboreal apes of the SE Asian genus *Hylobates*.

Gibbonian /gɪˈbəʊnɪən/ *a.* L18. [f. Edward *Gibbon* (see below) + -IAN.] Relating to or resembling the style or opinions of the historian Edward Gibbon (1737–94).

gibbose /ˈgɪbəʊs/ *a.* L17. [Late L *gibbosus*, f. L *gibbus* hump: see -OSE[1].] = GIBBOUS.

gibbosity /gɪˈbɒsɪti/ *n.* LME. [(O)Fr. *gibbosité* hump or med.L *gibbositas* gibbosity, tumour, f. late L *gibbosus*: see next, -ITY.] 1 A swelling; a protuberance. LME. 2 The state, quality, or condition of being gibbose or gibbous. M16.

gibbous /ˈgɪbəs/ *a.* LME. [Late L *gibbosus*, f. L *gibbus* hump: see -OUS.] 1 Convex, rounded, protuberant. LME. b *Astron.* Of the moon or a planet: having the visible disc more than half but less than fully illuminated. L17. c *Bot.* Very convex or bulging, esp. of solid convexities. M19. 2 Of a person or an animal: hunch-backed; having a hump. Of a part of the body: hump-shaped. LME.

1b A. S. BYATT He . . through the window saw the irregular lump of a gibbous moon.

gibbously *adv.* M19. **gibbousness** *n.* (*rare*) L17.

gibbsite /ˈgɪbzʌɪt/ *n.* E19. [f. G. *Gibbs* (1776–1833), Amer. mineralogist + -ITE[1].] *Min.* A monoclinic hydrated aluminium oxide occurring as stalactitic incrustations, or more commonly as a major constituent of bauxite.

gibby /ˈgɪbi/ *n.* Chiefly *dial.* L18. [f. GIB *n.*[2] + -Y[6].] In full *gibby-stick*. A hooked stick; a stick with a bent handle.

gibe /dʒʌɪb/ *n.* Also j-. L16. [f. next.] A scoffing or sneering speech; a taunt, a jeer.

ISAIAH BERLIN Almost all Herzen's gibes and insults are directed against the hated Germans. A. BURGESS The 'mother's darling' gibe had come too late.

gibe /dʒʌɪb/ *v.*[1] Also j-. M16. [Origin uncertain: perh. f. OFr. *giber* handle roughly, (mod. dial.) kick (repr. in mod.Fr. by *regimber* buck, rear, cf. JIB *v.*[2]).] 1 *v.i.* Speak sneeringly or tauntingly; jeer, scoff. Usu. foll. by *at*. M16. 2 *v.t.* Speak scoffingly or sneeringly to; flout, taunt. L16.

giber *n.* M16. **gibingly** *adv.* in a gibing manner E17.

gibe *v.*[2] var. of JIBE *v.*[1]

†**gibecrack** *n.* see GIMCRACK.

gibel /ˈgiːb(ə)l/ *n. rare.* M19. [G *Giebel*, older sp. *Gibel*.] More fully *gibel carp*. = CRUCIAN *carp*.

Gibeonite /ˈgɪbɪənʌɪt/ *n.* LME. [f. *Gibeon* (see below) + -ITE[1].] *Hist.* A native or inhabitant of Gibeon (mod. Al-Jīb), a city in ancient Palestine north-west of Jerusalem which made a league with Joshua to avoid the fate of Jericho. Also *fig.* (w. ref. to *Josh.* 9:27), a menial, a drudge (long *rare*).

gibier /ˈdʒɪbɪə, *foreign* ʒibje/ *n.* Now *rare.* E16. [Fr.] Game; wildfowl.

giblet /ˈdʒɪblɪt/ *n.* ME. [OFr. *gibelet* game stew, perh. f. as prec. Cf. Walloon *giblè d'awe* goose giblets, Fr. *gibelotte* rabbit stew.] †1 An inessential appendage. Only in ME. †2 A piece of offal, garbage. Only in LME. 3 In *pl.* & (now *rare* exc. *attrib.*) *sing.* The edible parts of a goose or other fowl, as the liver, gizzard, etc., that are removed before cooking. M16. 4 *fig.* In *pl.* Things of little value, odds and ends. Now chiefly *dial.* M17.

3 D. BARTHELME Inside the Game Hens were the giblets in a plastic bag.

Comb.: **giblet pie**, **soup**: made with giblets.

gibli *n.* var. of GHIBLI.

Gibraltar /dʒɪˈbrɔːltə/ *n.* L16. [A fortified town and rocky headland at the S. tip of Spain, since 1704 a British colony.] †1 A monkey. L16–E17. 2 More fully *Gibraltar rock*. A kind of hard sweet; a piece of this. M19. 3 *fig.* Something impregnable. *rare.* M19.

Gibraltarian /dʒɪbrɔːlˈtɛːrɪən/ *n.* & *a.* (*a*) *n.* a native or inhabitant of Gibraltar; (*b*) *adj.* of or pertaining to Gibraltar or the Gibraltarians: L19.

Gibson /ˈgɪbs(ə)n/ *n.* E20. [A surname.] In full *Gibson cocktail*. A cocktail consisting of gin and vermouth garnished with pearl onions.

Gibson girl /ˈgɪbs(ə)n gəːl/ *n. phr.* L19. [Charles Dana *Gibson* (see below).] A girl typifying the fashionable ideal of the late 19th and early 20th cents., as represented in the work of Charles Dana Gibson (1867–1944), American artist and illustrator.

gibus /ˈdʒʌɪbəs/ *n.* M19. [*Gibus*, the 19th-cent. Fr. inventor of this kind of hat.] In full *gibus-hat*. A collapsible opera-hat.

gid /gɪd/ *n.* E17. [Back-form. f. GIDDY *a.*] (Usu. with *the*.) A fatal disease of sheep and goats, caused by larvae of the dog tapeworm *Taenia coenurus* encysted in the brain, and characterized by unsteady gait and loss of balance. Also called *staggers*, *sturdy*, & other names.

giddap /ˈgɪdap, gɪˈdap/ *int.* & *v. colloq.* Also -up /-ʌp/, **giddy-up** /ˈgɪdɪʌp, gɪdɪˈʌp/. E20. [Repr. a pronunc. of *get up*.] A *int.* A command to a horse etc.: go on!, go faster! E20. B *v.* Infl. -p-, -pp-. 1 *v.i.* Of a horse etc.: go on, go faster. M20. 2 *v.t.* Urge (a horse etc.) to go on or to go faster. M20.

giddify /ˈgɪdɪfʌɪ/ *v.t.* E17. [f. GIDDY *a.* + -FY.] Make giddy, daze (*lit.* & *fig.*).

giddily /ˈgɪdɪli/ *adv.* ME. [f. GIDDY *a.* + -LY[2].] In a giddy manner.

OUIDA It all swam giddily before my sight. J. GALSWORTHY He wondered giddily how old she was—she seemed so much more . . experienced than himself.

giddiness /ˈgɪdɪnəs/ *n.* ME. [f. GIDDY *a.* + -NESS.] 1 Thoughtless folly, flightiness; inconstancy, instability. Also (*rare*), an instance of this. ME. 2 The state of having a sensation of whirling and a tendency to fall, stagger, or spin round; dizziness. LME.

1 DICKENS The mincing vanities and giddinesses of empty-headed girls. WENDELL PHILLIPS A few mere giddiness hurries to ruin. 2 J. WAIN An attack of giddiness and a black-out.

giddup *int.* & *v.* var. of GIDDAP.

giddy /ˈgɪdi/ *n.* E17. [f. the adj.] = GID.

giddy /ˈgɪdi/ *a.* [OE *gidiġ* f. Gmc, f. base of GOD *n.* (the primary sense being 'possessed by a god'): see -Y[1].] 1†a Insane, mad, foolish, stupid. OE–ME. b Mad with anger, furious. *dial.* L17. 2 Having a sensation of whirling and a tendency to fall, stagger, or spin round (with sickness, pleasure, etc.); dizzy. LME. b Causing or apt to produce dizziness. L16. c Circling with bewildering speed. L16. d Of sheep: affected by the gid. M19. 3 Mentally intoxicated; incapable of attention; excitable; frivolous, flighty, inconstant. Also (*colloq.*), used as an (esp. iron.) intensive. Cf. earlier GIDDINESS 1. M16.

2 G. BERKELEY They seem to me drunk and giddy with a false notion of liberty. I. MURDOCH His head ached and when he sat up he felt giddy. b M. PRIOR The giddy precipice, and the dangerous flood. c POPE So whirls a wheel, in giddy circle toss'd. 3 J. BUCHAN A giddy lot Scudder's friends cared for peace and reform. K. TYNAN This Rosalind was a gay and giddy creature—loads of fun, game for any jape. *my giddy* AUNT. *play the giddy* GOAT, OX.

giddy /ˈgɪdi/ *v.* E17. [f. prec.] 1 *v.t.* Make giddy. E17. 2 *v.i.* Become giddy. M19.

giddy-up *int.* & *v.* var. of GIDDAP.

Gideon /ˈɡɪdɪən/ *n.* E20. [An Israelite leader: see *Judges* 6:11 ff.] A member of a Christian organization of American business people, founded in 1899.

Comb.: **Gideon bible** a bible purchased by this organization and placed in a hotel bedroom etc. for the occupant's use.

gidgee /ˈɡɪdʒiː/ *n.*[1] *Austral.* Also **gidgie**. M19. [Aborig. *giji.*] An Aboriginal spear.

gidgee /ˈɡɪdʒiː/ *n.*[2] Also **gidya, gidyea** /ˈɡɪdɪə/, & other vars. M19. [Aborig. *gijir.*] An Australian wattle, *Acacia cambagei*, the phyllodes of which give off a foul smell at the approach of rain.

†**gierfalcon** *n.* var. of GYRFALCON.

gif /ɡɪf/ *conj. Sc.* & *north.* LME. [Alt. of IF, prob. infl. by GIVE *v.* Cf. GIN *conj.*[2]] If (*that*).

giff-gaff /ˈɡɪfɡaf/ *n. Sc.* & *north.* M16. [Redupl. of GIVE *v.* Cf. MDu. *ghivegave.*] 1 Mutual giving, mutual help; give and take. M16. 2 Interchange of remarks; casual conversation. L18.

gift /ɡɪft/ *n.* ME. [ON *gipt* corresp. to OE *gift* payment for a wife, (in pl.) wedding, OFris. *jeft*, OS *sundargift* privilege, MDu *gift(e)* (Du. *gift* gift), OHG *gift* gift, (G *Gift* gift, Goth. *fragifts* espousal, f. Gmc base of GIVE *v.*] I Giving. 1 The action or an act of giving. ME. 2 *Law.* The voluntary transference of property without anything in return. L15.

1 H. REED Language always makes gift of its best wealth to a great poet. **in the gift of** (of a church living or other appointment) within the power or right of a specified person or institution to bestow. 2 **deed of gift** a deed by which property is conveyed from the donor to the donee without anything being given in return.

II Something given. 3 A thing given; a present, a donation. Also *fig.*, an accidental or unexpected opportunity or benefit. ME. 4 An offering to God or to a god. ME. 5 A faculty, power, or quality miraculously bestowed; a virtue or endowment looked on as an emanation from heaven. ME. b A natural endowment, faculty, ability, or talent. ME. †6 Something given with the intent to corrupt, a bribe. LME–E17. 7 A white speck on the fingernail, supposed to portend a gift. Now *dial.* E18. 8 An easy task etc. *colloq.* M19.

3 G. SWIFT My pet hamster, Sammy, a gift for my tenth birthday. JANET MORGAN To the press, the story of Agatha's disappearance was a gift. **as** (or *arch.* **at**) **a gift** even gratis (freq. in *would not have it* etc. *as a gift*). *free gift*: see FREE *a. Grecian gift*: see GRECIAN *a. Greek gift*: see GREEK *a.* 4 AV *Matt.* 5:24 Leaue there thy gift before the altar. 5 J. H. NEWMAN To obtain the gift of holiness is the work of a life. *the gift of tongues*: see TONGUE *n.* b D. ATHILL I knew in my bones that I had no gift for nursing. *gift of the gab*: see GAB *n.*[2] 6 AV 2 *Chron.* 19:7 There is no iniquitie with the Lord our God . . nor taking of gifts.

Comb.: **gift-book**: given or suitable for giving as a present; **gift coupon**: issued with certain commodities and entitling the holder of a specified number of such coupons to a free gift; **gift-horse**: given as a present (chiefly in *look a gift-horse in the mouth*, find fault with a gift); **gift shop**: dealing in articles suitable for gifts; **gift-token, voucher**: used as a gift and exchangeable for goods esp. at a specified shop etc.; **gift-wrap** *v.t.* wrap (a purchase etc.) attractively as a gift.

giftless *a.* LME.

gift /ɡɪft/ *v.t.* L16. [f. the n.] 1 Endow or provide with a gift or gifts; endow or present *with* as a gift. L16. 2 Bestow as a gift (foll. by *to*); give *away*. E17.

1 P. G. WODEHOUSE She was gifted with a sort of second sight. *Daily Telegraph* You can . . be gifted up to £90,000 before you become liable to tax. 2 J. C. LEES The Regent Murray gifted all the Church Property to Lord Sempill.

gifted /ˈɡɪftɪd/ *a.* M17. [f. GIFT *n.*, *v.*: see -ED[2], -ED[1].] 1 Endowed with a gift or gifts; *spec.* exceptionally talented or intelligent. M17. †2 Given, bestowed. Only in L17.

1 C. CONNOLLY There can have been few young writers as gifted. R. HOLMES Dr Labrunie regarded him as a brilliant and gifted child.

giftedly *adv.* M20. **giftedness** *n.* M17.

giftie /ˈɡɪfti/ *n. Sc.* L18. [f. GIFT *n.* + -IE.] = GIFT *n.* 5b.

R. BURNS O wad some Pow'r the giftie gie us To see oursels as others see us!

gig /ɡɪɡ/ *n.*[1] ME. [Prob. imit.] I †1 A flighty giddy girl. ME–L18. 2 An awkward, odd-looking, or boorish person; *dial.* a fool. Now *rare.* LME.

II 3 In full *gig-mill.* Orig., a building which housed rotary machines designed to raise the nap on fabric by the use of teasels, wire-cards, etc. Later, a machine employed in this process. M16. 4 A thing that whirls; *spec.* (*a*) (*obs.* exc. *dial.*) a whipping-top; †(*b*) a device consisting of an arrangement of feathers used to attract birds to a net by revolving. (Earlier in WHIRLIGIG.) L16.

III †5a A fancy, a joke, a whim. L16–E19. b Fun, merriment, glee. Now *arch.* & *dial.* L18.

5b **in high gig, on the** (**high**) **gig** in a state of boisterous hilarity.

giggish *a.* †(*a*) wanton; (*b*) *arch.* lively, flighty: E16.

gig /ɡɪɡ/ *n.*[2] E18. [Abbrev. of FISHGIG or FIZGIG *n.*[2]] 1 = FIZGIG *n.*[2] E18. 2 An arrangement of hooks set back to back and attached to a handline, used for catching fish by being dragged through a shoal. *US.* L19.

gig /ɡɪɡ/ *n.*[3] L18. [App. transf. sense of GIG *n.*[1] II.] 1 Chiefly *Hist.* A light two-wheeled one-horse carriage. L18. 2 A light narrow clinker-built ship's boat for rowing or sailing; a rowing boat chiefly used for racing. L18. 3 = KIBBLE *n.*[1] Also, a two-storied lift used by miners in ascending or descending a pit-shaft. L19.

Comb.: **gig-lamps** *arch. slang* spectacles.

gig /ɡɪɡ/ *n.*[4] *colloq.* E20. [Origin unkn.] (The engagement of a musician or musicians for) a performance of jazz, pop music, etc., esp. for one night only; the place of such a performance.

gig /ɡɪɡ/ *v.*[1]*t.* Infl. **-gg-**. L18. [Prob. f. GIG *n.*[1] 3.] Raise the nap of (fabric) with a gig.

gig /ɡɪɡ/ *v.*[2]*t.* Infl. **-gg-**. E19. [f. GIG *n.*[2]] Fish for with a gig.

gig /ɡɪɡ/ *v.*[3]*i.* & *t.* (w. *it*). Infl. **-gg-**. E19. [f. GIG *n.*[3]] Ride or travel in a gig.

gig /ɡɪɡ/ *v.*[4]*t.* Chiefly *US.* Infl. **-gg-**. L19. [Origin uncertain: perh. imit.] Move backwards and forwards; move *back* (the carriage of a sawmill) after a cut has been made.

gig /ɡɪɡ/ *v.*[5]*i. colloq.* Infl. **-gg-**. M20. [f. GIG *n.*[4]] Of a musician: perform at a gig or gigs.

giga- /ˈɡʌɪɡə, ˈɡɪɡə, dʒ-/ *comb. form.* M20. [f. Gk *gigas* giant.] Used in names of units etc. to denote a factor of 10^9 (one thousand million), as *gigahertz*, *gigametre*; also loosely, in some computing terms, used to denote a factor of 2^{30}, as *gigabit*, *gigabyte*. Abbrev. *G.*

gigaflop /ˈɡʌɪɡəflɒp, ˈɡɪɡə-, dʒ-/ *n.* L20. [f. GIGA- + acronym f. *fl*oating-point *op*erations per second (w. *-s* taken as pl. suff. -S[1]).] *Computing.* A unit of computing speed equal to one thousand million or 2^{30} floating-point operations per second.

gigantean /dʒʌɪɡanˈtiːən/ *a.* E17. [f. L *giganteus*, f. *gigant-*: see GIANT, -EAN.] = GIGANTIC *a.*

gigantesque /dʒʌɪɡanˈtɛsk/ *a.* E19. [Fr. f. It. *gigantesco*, f. *gigante* GIANT *n.*: see -ESQUE.] Having the characteristics of a giant; befitting a giant.

gigantic /dʒʌɪˈɡantɪk/ *a.* E17. [f. L *gigant-* (see GIANT) + -IC.] †1 Of, pertaining to, or characteristic of a giant or giants. E17–L18. 2 Having the proportions of a giant; giant-like in size, stature, etc.; abnormally large; huge, enormous. M17.

1 J. BRYANT He was the son of Uricus, and of the gigantic race. 2 HOR. WALPOLE Jeffery . . had many squabbles with the king's gigantic porter. D. ADAMS Three gigantic doors, maybe sixty feet high. J. M. ROBERTS A gigantic influence on the later development of Christian religion and civilisation.

gigantically *adv.* in a gigantic manner, to a gigantic degree L17.

giganticide /dʒʌɪˈɡantɪsʌɪd/ *n.* E19. [f. as prec. + -I- + -CIDE.] 1 A giant-killer. E19. 2 The action or an act of killing of a giant or giants. M19.

gigantise *v.* var. of GIGANTIZE.

gigantism /ˈdʒʌɪɡantɪz(ə)m, dʒʌɪˈɡantɪz(ə)m/ *n.* L19. [f. L *gigant-*, *gigas* GIANT + -ISM.] Abnormally large or excessive size; *spec.* (*a*) *Med.* excessive size of the entire body due to overproduction of growth hormone by the pituitary gland during childhood (cf. ACROMEGALY); (*b*) *Bot.* excessive size due to polyploidy. Also *fig.* Cf. GIANTISM.

gigantize /dʒʌɪˈɡantʌɪz/ *v.t.* Also **-ise**. M17. [f. as prec. + -IZE.] Cause to appear gigantic.

gigantology /dʒʌɪɡanˈtɒlədʒi/ *n. rare.* L18. [f. as prec. + -OLOGY.] The branch of study that deals with giants.

gigantomachy /dʒʌɪɡanˈtɒməki/ *n.* Also **gigantomachia** /ˌdʒʌɪɡantəˈmeɪkɪə/. L16. [Gk *gigantomakhia*, f. *gigas*, *gigant-* GIANT *n.*: see -O-, -MACHY.] In *Gk Mythol.*, the war waged by the giants against the gods; a contest resembling this.

Gigantopithecus /dʒʌɪɡantəˈpɪθɪkəs, -pɪˈθiːkəs/ *n.* M20. [mod.L, f. Gk *giganto-*, *gigas* giant + *pithēkos* ape.] A large fossil primate of the genus *Gigantopithecus*, sometimes considered hominid.

giggle /ˈɡɪɡ(ə)l/ *v.* & *n.* E16. [Imit.: cf. Du. *gi(e)chelen*, LG *giggeln*, MHG *gickeln*, Russ. *khikhikat'*.] A *v.* 1 *v.i.* Laugh in an affected, silly, or nervous manner; titter; give small bursts of half-suppressed laughter. E16. 2 *v.t.* Utter with a giggle or giggles. M17.

1 M. SPARK One or two . . giggled with hands to their helpless mouths.

B *n.* †1 A giggling girl. Only in E17. 2 A giggling laugh. Freq. in (*a fit of*) *the giggles*. L17. b An amusing person or thing; a joke; fun. *colloq.* M20. 3 A group (of girls). *colloq.* M20.

2 K. MANSFIELD Geraldine couldn't help a little giggle of amusement. b J. RATHBONE He enjoyed the course, which was mostly rather a giggle. **for a giggle** as a joke, not seriously, for fun.

Comb.: **giggle-house** *Austral.* & *NZ slang* a mental hospital; **giggle-water** *slang* intoxicating liquor.

giggler *n.* a person who giggles, esp. habitually M17. **giggliness** *n.* the state of being giggly L20. **gigglish** *a.* disposed to giggle L17. **giggly** *a.* much given to giggling M19.

giglet /ˈɡɪɡlɪt/ *n.* Also **-ot** /-ət/. ME. [Perh. f. GIG *n.*[1] and later assoc. with GIGGLE *v.*: see -LET.] Orig., a wanton woman. Later, a giggling girl.

gigman /ˈɡɪɡmən/ *n.* Pl. **-men**. M19. [f. GIG *n.*[3] + MAN *n.*] A person who keeps or uses a gig, esp. as a typical representative of the respectable unimaginative middle classes; a philistine.

gigmanic /ɡɪɡˈmanɪk/ *a.* of, pertaining to, or characteristic of a gigman or gigmanity L19. **gigmanity** /ɡɪɡˈmanɪti/ *n.* (*collect.*) respectable unimaginative middle-class people M19.

gigolo /ˈʒɪɡələʊ, dʒ-/ *n.* Pl. **-os**. E20. [Fr., formed as masc. of *gigole* dancehall woman.] A professional male dancing-partner or escort; a (usu. young) man supported by a (usu. older) woman in return for his attentions.

M. MOORCOCK Gigolos on the look-out for the wives or widows of self-satisfied merchants.

gigot /ˈdʒɪɡət/ *n.* E16. [Fr., dim. of dial. *gigue* leg, f. *giguer* hop, jump, of unkn. origin.] 1 A leg of mutton etc. E16. †2 A dish made from minced meat, a sausage. M16–M17. 3 More fully *gigot sleeve.* A leg-of-mutton sleeve. E19.

gigster /ˈɡɪɡstə/ *n.*[1] E19. [f. GIG *n.*[3] + -STER.] A horse suitable for drawing a gig.

gigster /ˈɡɪɡstə/ *n.*[2] M20. [f. GIG *n.*[4] + -STER.] A musician who performs at a gig or gigs.

gigue /ʒiːɡ/ *n.* L17. [Fr., f. JIG *n.*[1]] A lively piece of music in duple or triple time, often with dotted rhythms and forming the last movement of a suite.

Gila /ˈhiːlə/ *n.* Also **g-**. L19. [A river in New Mexico and Arizona.] In full *Gila monster.* A large carnivorous venomous lizard of Mexico and the south-western US, *Heloderma suspectum*, black with orange or pink markings.

gilbert /ˈɡɪlbət/ *n.* L19. [William *Gilbert* (1544–1603), English physician and natural philosopher.] *Physics.* An electromagnetic unit of magnetomotive force in the cgs system, equal to $10/4\pi$ ampere-turns.

Gilbertese /ɡɪlbəˈtiːz/ *n.* & *a.* E20. [f. the *Gilbert* Islands, f. the English adventurer

Thomas *Gilbert* who arrived there in 1788 + -ESE.] *Hist.* A *n.* (Pl. same.) A native or inhabitant of the Gilbert Islands in the mid-Pacific, formerly a British colony and since 1979 part of Kiribati. Also, the Micronesian language of the Gilbert Islands. E20. B *adj.* Of or pertaining to the Gilbert Islands or the Gilbertese. E20.

Gilbertian /gɪl'bəːtɪən, -bəːʃ(ə)n/ *a.* L19. [f. W. S. *Gilbert* (see below) + -IAN.] Of, pertaining to, or characteristic of W. S. Gilbert (1836–1911), librettist of the Gilbert and Sullivan operas, or his work; *esp.* resembling or reminiscent of a characteristically ludicrous or paradoxical situation in a Gilbert and Sullivan opera.

Daily Chronicle The Gilbertian question whether a Lord Chancellor could bring himself to justice for contempt of his own court.

Gilbertine /'gɪlbəːtiːn, -tʌɪn/ *a.* & *n.* M16. [med.L *Gilbertinus*, f. *Gilbertus* Gilbert of Sempringham (see below): see -INE[1].] *Hist.* A *adj.* Of or pertaining to St Gilbert of Sempringham (*c*1083–1189) or the English religious order for men and women founded by him. M16. B *n.* A member of the Gilbertine order. L17.

gild /gɪld/ *n.*[1] Also **guild**. E17. [med.L *gildum*, *geldum*: see GELD *n.* Cf. GUILD *n.*[1]] A payment, a tax.

gild *n.*[2] var. of GUILD *n.*[1]

gild /gɪld/ *v.*[1]*t.* Pa. t. & pple **gilded**, (now chiefly in lit. sense) **gilt** /gɪlt/. [OE *gyldan* (in pa. pple *gegyld*) = ON *gylla*, f. Gmc base of GOLD *n.*[1]] 1 Cover with a thin layer of gold, esp. as gold leaf. OE. b *transf.* Smear (with blood). Now *rare* or *obs.* L16. 2 Esp. of the sun: cover, tinge, or adorn with a golden colour or light. ME. †3 *Alch.* Impregnate (a liquid) with gold. L15–L17. 4 Supply with gold or money; make reputable or attractive by supplying with money. Now chiefly as passing into sense 5. L16. b Of money: make reputable or attractive. E17. 5 Give a (specious or illusory) brilliance or lustre to, esp. by the use of favourable or complimentary speech. L16. †6 Impart a brilliant colour or flush to (the face). *rare* (Shakes.). Only in E17.

1 R. CUMBERLAND Its magnificent owner . . had gilt and furnished the apartments with a profusion of luxury. b SHAKES. *Macb.* If he do bleed, I'll gild the faces of the grooms withal, For it must seem their guilt. 2 DRYDEN Stars . . shooting through the darkness, guild the Night With sweeping Glories, and long trails of Light. E. CRISPIN Gilded and warmed by the steady October sunlight. 4 C. MERIVALE The missions of proconsuls . . were gilded . . by gifts from states and potentates. 5 SHAKES. *1 Hen. IV* If a lie may do thee grace, I'll gild it with the happiest terms I have. 6 SHAKES. *Temp.* This grand liquor that hath gilded 'em.

Phrases, & with advs. in specialized senses: **gild over** cover with gilding, esp. to conceal defects (chiefly *fig.*). *gild the lily*: see LILY *n.* **gild the pill** make something unpleasant seem more acceptable.

†**gild** *v.*[2]*i. rare.* Also **guild**. M17–M18. [Var. of GELD *v.*[2] Cf. med.L *geldare*, *gildare* pay geld, tax.] Pay a tax or taxes.

gildable /'gɪldəb(ə)l/ *a.* & *n. obs.* exc. *Hist.* Also **guild-**. L15. [f. GILD *v.*[2] + -ABLE.] (An area) subject to taxation.

†**gildard** *n.* see GILDER *n.*[2]

gilded /'gɪldɪd/ *ppl a.* OE. [pa. pple of GILD *v.*[1]: see -ED[1]. Cf. GILT *ppl a.*] 1 That has been gilded; *spec.* overlaid wholly or partially with a thin coating of gold. OE. 2 Tinged with a golden colour. L16.

Special collocations: **gilded cage** a luxurious but restrictive environment. †**gilded spurs** = *gilt spurs* s.v. GILT *ppl a.* **gilded youth** = JEUNESSE DORÉE.

†**gilden** *a.* [OE *gylden* = OFris. *gulden*, *gelden*, OS *guldīn* (Du. *gulden*), OHG *guldīn* (G arch. *gülden*), ON *gullenn*, Goth. *gulþeins*, f. Gmc base of GOLD *n.*[1]: see -EN[4].] 1 Golden. OE–L16. 2 Gilded, gilt. (*rare* after M17.) M16–L19.

gilder /'gɪldə/ *n.*[1] ME. [f. GILD *v.*[1] + -ER[1].] A person who gilds something, *esp.* one who practises gilding as an art or a trade.

gilder /'gɪldə/ *n.*[2] *obs.* exc. *north.* In sense 2 also †**gildard**. ME. [ON *gildra* (fem.) a trap, *gildri* (neut.) the laying of a trap.] 1 A snare of horsehair etc., esp. for catching birds. ME. 2 A piece or section of an angler's line made of twisted horsehair; a tought. L17.

Gilderoy /'gɪldərɔɪ/ *n.* Chiefly *US colloq.* M19. [A Sc. robber said to have been hanged higher than other criminals on account of the wickedness of his crimes.] *higher than Gilderoy's kite* extremely high, out of sight.

gilding /'gɪldɪŋ/ *vbl n.* LME. [f. GILD *v.*[1] + -ING[1].] 1 The action or process of GILD *v.*[1] LME. 2 The golden surface produced by gilding; a thin layer (of gold) with which something is gilded. M17.

Comb.: **gilding metal** a copper-rich alloy formerly used to make objects to be gilded; now *esp.* brass containing 95 per cent copper and 5 per cent zinc.

gilet /ʒilɛ/ *n.* Pl. pronounced same. L19. [Fr.] A light often padded waistcoat, usu. worn for warmth by women.

gilgai /'gɪlgʌɪ/ *n. Austral.* Also **ghilgai**. M19. [Kamilaroi *gilgaay*.] A shallow depression between mounds or ridges, in which rainwater collects, probably formed by differential expansion in certain alluvial soils.

gilguy /'gɪlgʌɪ/ *n.* M19. [Origin unkn.] *Naut.* 1 A temporary guy for bearing up a boom or a derrick. M19. 2 A gadget, esp. of an unspecified kind. *slang.* L19.

gill /gɪl/ *n.*[1] ME. [ON (whence Sw. *gäl*, †*gel*, Da. *gjælle*), f. a base rel. to ON *gjǫlnar* pl. = gills of a fish (cf. ODa. *fiskegæln*), f. a base cogn. with Gk *khelunē* lip, jaw, *kheilos* lip.] 1 An organ of respiration in fish and some amphibians, in which oxygen is taken up into the blood from a current of water over vascular tissue within or connected to the wall of the pharynx or gullet. ME. b An organ of respiration in many aquatic invertebrates, variously situated and functioning as the gills of fish. E19. 2 *sing.* & (usu.) in *pl.* a The wattles on the neck of a fowl. E17. b The flesh below a person's jaw and ears. E17. 3 Usu. in *pl.* The radiating plates arranged vertically in the underside of the cap of mushrooms and other agaric fungi. E18. 4 In *pl.* The corners of a stand-up collar. *arch. slang.* E19.

2b C. SMITH 'My dear Sir!' replied Sir Appulby, in visible confusion, his fat gills quivering. **green** (or **yellow, white, blue**) **about the gills** miserable- or sickly-looking. **rosy about the gills** healthy-looking.

Comb.: **gill arch, bar** any of a series of bony or cartilaginous curved bars placed along the pharynx and supporting the gills of fish and amphibians; any of the corresponding rudiments in the embryos of higher vertebrates; **gill cleft** = *gill slit* below; **gill cover**: of skin protecting the gills of fish, usu. stiffened with bony plates; = OPERCULUM; **gill filament, lamella, leaflet** any of the vascular plates forming the gills of fish, molluscs, etc.; **gill maggot** a copepod of the genus *Salmincola*, the larvae of which are ectoparasitic on the gills of salmon; **gill-net**: hung vertically to trap fish by entangling the gills; **gill plate** = *gill filament* above; **gill pouch** (*a*) *Zool.* a pouch containing the gills (as in cyclostome fish) or into which they open (as in acorn worms); (*b*) *Embryol.* any of a series of paired indentations in the pharyngeal wall of all vertebrate embryos, which give rise to the gill slits of fish and amphibians; **gill raker** any of the processes on the inner side of a gill arch which prevent solid matter from entering the gill; **gill slit** any of a series of openings between the gill arches (e.g. of a fish) through which water passes from the pharynx to the exterior; any of the corresponding grooves in the embryos of higher vertebrates.

gill /gɪl/ *n.*[2] Also **ghyll**. ME. [ON *gil* deep glen, cogn. with *geil*. The spelling *ghyll* was introduced in L18 by Wordsworth.] 1 A deep cleft or ravine, usu. wooded and forming the course of a stream. ME. 2 A narrow mountain torrent. E17.

gill /dʒɪl/ *n.*[3] ME. [OFr. *gille*, *gelle*, in med.L *gillo*, *gillus*, *gellus*, late L *gello*, *gillo* water-pot.] 1 A measure of liquid or (in Britain) dry capacity, containing a quarter of a pint: in Britain (more fully *imperial gill*) equivalent to 8.67 cu. in. (0.142 litre), in the US (more fully *US gill*) equivalent to 7.22 cu. in. (0.118 litre). Also *local*, half a pint, esp. of wine, beer, etc. ME. 2 A container having the capacity for such a measure. *rare.* LME.

gill /dʒɪl/ *n.*[4] Also **j-**. LME. [Abbrev. of female forename *Gillian* f. Fr. *Juliane* f. L *Juliana*, orig. fem. adj. f. *Julius* name of a Roman gens: see -AN, -IAN.] 1 (Also **G-**.) A young woman. Freq. *derog.* LME. 2 In full *gill-creep-*, *go-*, etc., *by-ground*. Ground ivy. *dial.* L16. 3 A female ferret. *colloq.* M19.

1 *Jack and Jill*: see JACK *n.*[1]

gill /dʒɪl/ *n.*[5] Chiefly *dial.* Also **j-**. L18. [Origin unkn.] A two-wheeled machine used for the transport of timber.

gill /gɪl/ *n.*[6] E19. [Origin uncertain: perh. f. Fr. *aiguille* needle.] *Hist.* A device for preparing and combing flax etc., having a series of points used to divide the fibres into filaments.

gill /gɪl/ *v.*[1]*t.* LME. [f. GILL *n.*[1]] 1 Gut or clean (fish). LME. 2 Cut off the gills of (a mushroom). E18. 3 Catch (fish) in a gill-net. L19.

giller *n.* ME.

gill /gɪl/ *v.*[2]*t.* L19. [f. GILL *n.*[6]] *Hist.* Prepare (flax etc.) using a gill.

gillaroo /gɪlə'ruː/ *n.* L18. [Ir. *giolla ruadh*, f. *giolla* lad, fellow + *ruadh* red.] A trout, *Salmo trutta*, of a variety ('*stomachicus*') found locally in Ireland, having a part of the stomach toughened for crushing the shells of molluscs.

gilled /gɪld/ *a.* E19. [f. GILL *n.*[1], *v.*[1]: see -ED[2], -ED[1].] 1 Having gills (of a specified kind). E19. 2 That has been gilled. L20.

gillenia /dʒɪ'liːnɪə, gɪ-/ *n.* E19. [mod.L (see below), f. Arnold Gill or *Gillenius*, 17th-cent. Ger. botanist: see -IA[1].] Either of two N. American herbaceous plants of the genus *Gillenia*, of the rose family (also called *Indian physic*); the root of such a plant, used as an emetic.

gillery /'gɪl(ə)ri/ *n. obs.* exc. *dial.* Also †**guilery**. ME. [OFr. *g(u)ilerie*, f. *guiler*: see GUILE *v.*] Deception, deceit, trickery.

gill-flirt /'dʒɪlfləːt/ *n. arch. derog.* Also **j-**. M17. [f. GILL *n.*[4] + FLIRT *n.* or *v.* Cf. FLIRT-GILL.] A wanton; a girl or young woman of giddy character.

gillie /'gɪli/ *n.*[1] Orig. *Sc.* Also **ghillie, gilly**. L17. [Gael. *gille* = Ir. *giolla* lad, servant.] 1 *Hist.* An attendant on a Highland chief. Earliest in *gillie-wetfoot* (derog.), the servant who carried a chief across a stream. L17. 2 A man or boy attending a person hunting or fishing, esp. in Scotland. M19.

2 R. MACAULAY Sir Angus . . knew all their names, . . those of the ponies, the gillies, the keepers.

gillie /'dʒɪli/ *n.*[2] *Sc. rare.* L18. [f. GILL *n.*[3] + -IE.] A gill of liquor.

gillion /'gɪljən, 'dʒɪ-/ *n.* M20. [f. GI(GA- + MI)LLION.] A thousand million; a large number.

gilly *n.* var. of GILLIE *n.*[1]

gillyflower /'dʒɪlɪflaʊə/ *n.* Also (now *dial.*) **gilliver** /'dʒɪlɪvə/ & other vars. ME. [Alt. (by assim. to *flower*) of OFr. *gilofre*, *girofle* f. med.L *caryophyllum* clove f. Gk *karuophullon*, f. *karuon* nut + *phullon* leaf: cf. *clove-gillyflower* s.v. CLOVE *n.*[2] I.] †1 A clove. ME–E16. 2 Any of various cultivated flowers with a scent like that of cloves; *esp.* = CLOVE *n.*[2] 2. Also (*dial.*), the wallflower, *Erysimum cheiri*; (in full *stock-gillyflower*) the stock, *Matthiola incana*. LME.

gilpy /'gɪlpi/ *n.* & *a. Sc.* E18. [Origin unkn.] A *n.* A lively young girl. E18. B *adj.* Lively, sportive. M19.

gilravage /gɪl'ravɪdʒ/ *v.* & *n. Sc.* & *north.* M18. [Origin unkn.] A *v.i.* Feast or revel riotously or excessively. M18. B *n.* Riotous or lively behaviour; (an act of) romping. L18.

gilravager *n.* E19.

Gilsonite /'gɪlsənʌɪt/ *n.* Also **g-**. L19. [f. S. H. *Gilson*, 19th-cent. US mineralogist + -ITE[1].] *Min.* (Proprietary name for) the mineral uintaite.

gilt /gɪlt/ *n.*[1] ME. [ON *gyltr*.] A female pig; *spec.* a young sow.

gilt /gɪlt/ *n.*[2] LME. [f. GILT *ppl a.*] 1 = GILDING 2. LME. 2 Gold; money. *arch.* L16. b A gilt-edged security. Freq. in *pl.* M20.

1 **take the gilt off the gingerbread** strip something of its attractions.

†**gilt** *n.*^{3} *slang.* E17. [Origin unkn.] 1 A thief, a burglar. E17–L18. 2 A skeleton key, a picklock. L17–M19.

gilt /gɪlt/ *ppl a.* ME. [pa. pple of GILD *v.*^{1}: cf. GILDED.] Gilded.
silver gilt: see SILVER *n.* & *a.*
Comb. & *special collocations*: **gilt bronze**: gilded over fire with a gold-mercury amalgam, used for ornamental work (cf. ORMOLU); **gilt-edge** *a.* & *n.* (*a*) *adj.* = *gilt-edged* below; (*b*) *n.* a gilt-edged security; **gilt-edged** *a.* & *n.* (*a*) *adj.* having a gilt edge or edges; (of a security, esp. British government stock) having a high degree of reliability as an investment; high quality; (*b*) *n.* in *pl.*, gilt-edged securities; **gilt-head** any of several fishes having golden markings on the head; *esp.* an edible bream, *Sparus aurata*, of the Mediterranean and eastern Atlantic; **gilt spurs** *arch.*: as an emblem of knighthood; **gilt-tail** any of various yellowish maggots used for trout-fishing; **giltwood** *a.* made of wood and gilded; †**gilt youth** = GILDED *youth*.

gilt /gɪlt/ *v.*^{1}*t.* Now only *Sc.* & *north.* LME. [f. prec. by extension of the ppl form to the rest of the vb.] = GILD *v.*^{1}

gilt *v.*^{2} pa. t. & pple: see GILD *v.*^{1}

Gilyak /ˈgɪljak/ *n.* & *a.* M19. [Russ. *gilyak.*] A *n.* Pl. **-s**, same. A member of a people of the northern part of Sakhalin Island or the adjacent part of Siberia; the language of this people. M19. B *adj.* Of or pertaining to this people or their language. L19.

gim /dʒɪm/ *a. obs.* exc. *dial.* E16. [Origin uncertain: perh. var. of JIMP *a.*] Smart, spruce.

†**gimar** *n.* var. of JUMART.

gimbal /ˈgɪmb(ə)l, ˈdʒɪm-/ *n.* L16. [Var. of GIMMAL. Cf. GIMMER *n.*^{2}] †1 = GIMMAL 2. L16–M17. †2 = GEMEL 4. E17–E18. 3 *sing.* & (usu.) in *pl.* A contrivance (usu. of rings and pivots) for keeping instruments such as a compass and chronometer horizontal at sea, in the air, etc. L18.
Comb.: **gimbal-ring** = sense 3 above.
gimballed *a.* fitted or equipped with gimbals L19.

†**gimblet** *n.* & *v.* see GIMLET.

gimbri /ˈgɪmbri/ *n.* Also **gunibri** /ˈguːnɪbri/. L19. [Dial. var. of Arab. *ḳunbura* pomegranate.] A small Moorish guitar; a player of this instrument.

gimcrack /ˈdʒɪmkrak/ *n.* & *a.* Also (earlier) †**gibe-**. ME. [Origin unkn.] A *n.* †1 A kind of inlaid work in wood. Only in ME. 2 Orig., a contrivance, a device, a stratagem; a (fanciful) notion. Now, a useless ornament, a trumpery article, a knick-knack. LME. †3 An affected, showy, or worthless person. E17–E19. 4 A person adept at dealing with mechanical contrivances. Now *dial.* M18.
2 I. WALTON Nut-crackers, .. and Hobbyhorses, and many other gim-cracks .. that make a compleat Country Fair.
B *adj.* Trivial, worthless, showy and flimsy, trumpery. M18.
C. BEATON The lack of solidity and craftsmanship, the gimcrack way in which things are put together.
gimcrackery *n.* gimcrack articles collectively L18. **gimcracky** *a.* of a gimcrack nature E19.

gimlet /ˈgɪmlɪt/ *n.*, *a.*, & *v.* Also (now *rare* or *obs.* exc. in sense A.1) **gimblet** /ˈgɪmblɪt/. ME. [OFr. *guimbelet* dim. of *guimble*, f. Gmc base repr. also by WIMBLE *n.*] A *n.* 1 A kind of small boring-tool, usu. with a crosspiece handle and a screw at the pointed end. ME. 2 A cocktail of one part gin (occas. vodka) to one part lime-juice. E20.
B *attrib.* or as *adj.* Of an eye etc.: piercing, penetrating; *dial.* squinting. M18.
N. MITFORD With her gimlet eye nothing escaped her.
C *v.* 1 *v.t.* & *i. Naut.* Turn (an anchor) round by rotating the stock. Chiefly as *gimleting* vbl n. M18. 2 *v.t.* Pierce (as) with a gimlet. M19.
2 J. T. FARRELL Gimleting Studs with a searching eye-to-eye gaze.
gimlety *a.* (of an eye etc.) sharp, piercing L19.

gimmal /ˈdʒɪm(ə)l, ˈgɪ-/ *n.* M16. [Alt. of GEMEL. See also GIMBAL, GIMMER *n.*^{2}] †1 In full *gimmal song.* A duet. Only in M16. †2 In *pl.* & (*rare*) *sing.* Joints, links, or connecting parts in machinery, esp. for transmitting motion, as in clockwork. L16–M17. 3 = GEMEL 4. Now *rare.* L16. †4 = GIMBAL 3. E17–L18.
†**gimmalled** *a.* (*rare*) jointed: only in L16.

gimme /ˈgɪmi/ *v.* & *n. colloq.* L19. [Contr.: cf. LEMME.] A *v.t.* & *i.* (*imper.*). Give me; give (it) to me. L19.
R. BOLDREWOOD Gimme some grub. P. G. WODEHOUSE 'Will you have a whisky and soda, Uncle Donald?' .. 'Yes' said his relative, .. 'Gimme'
B *n.* 1 *sing.* & (usu.) in *pl.* Acquisitiveness, greed. Freq. in *have* or *get the gimmes.* E20. 2 *Golf.* A short easy putt, *esp.* one conceded without being played. E20.

gimmer /ˈgɪmə/ *n.*^{1} LME. [ON *gymbr* (Icel. *gimbur*, Da. *gimmerlam*): ult. origin unkn.] 1 A ewe-lamb between its first and second shearing. Orig. *Sc.* & *north.* LME. 2 A woman. *Sc. derog.* L18.
Comb.: **gimmer-hog** a ewe-lamb between weaning and first shearing; **gimmer-lamb** a ewe-lamb between birth and weaning.

gimmer /ˈdʒɪmə/ *n.*^{2} *obs.* exc. *dial.* E16. [Alt. of GIMMAL. Cf. GIMBAL.] 1 A hinge. E16. †2 = GIMMAL 2. L16–M17.

gimmick /ˈgɪmɪk/ *n.* & *v.* Orig. *US slang.* E20. [Origin unkn.] A *n.* A tricky or ingenious device (orig. in gambling or conjuring); *esp.* a contrivance, gadget, idea, etc., adopted for the purpose of attracting attention or publicity. E20.
I. BROWN Many comedians have their gimmicks, either as catch-phrase, theme-song, or bit of 'business'. *attrib.*: *Punch* Refuse to buy all goods with attached gimmick offers.
B *v.t.* Provide with a gimmick; alter or tamper with. M20.
D. BAGLEY I wasn't stupid enough to search Slade's luggage .. He would have gimmicked it so that he could tell.
gimmickry *n.* (*a*) the use of a gimmick or gimmicks; (*b*) gimmicks collectively: M20. **gimmicky** *a.* employing or characterized by a gimmick or gimmicks; designed to attract attention or publicity: M20.

gimp /gɪmp/ *n.*^{1} Also **guimp, gymp.** M17. [Du.: ult. origin unkn.] 1 A silk, worsted, or cotton twist, with a cord or wire running through it, used esp. as a trimming. M17. 2 A fishing-line of silk etc. bound with wire to strengthen it. E19. 3 The coarser thread which forms the outline of the design in some techniques of lace-making. M19.

gimp /gɪmp/ *n.*^{2} *rare.* M18. [Fr. *guimpe* repr. OFr. *guimple* WIMPLE *n.*] A neckerchief worn by a nun.

gimp /gɪmp/ *n.*^{3} *slang.* E20. [Origin unkn.] Courage.
J. POTTS She didn't even have the gimp to make the break herself.

gimp /gɪmp/ *n.*^{4} *slang* (orig. *US*). E20. [Origin uncertain: perh. alt. of GAMMY *a.*] A lame or crippled person or leg; a limp.
gimpy *n.* & *a.* (a person who is) lame or crippled E20.

gimp *a.* & *adv.* var. of JIMP *a.* & *adv.*

gimp /dʒɪmp/ *v.*^{1}*t. colloq.* (now *rare* or *obs.*). L17. [Origin unkn.] Give a scalloped or indented outline to.

gimp /gɪmp/ *v.*^{2}*t. rare.* M18. [f. GIMP *n.*^{1}] Trim or make with gimp.

gimp /gɪmp/ *v.*^{3}*i.* M20. [f. GIMP *n.*^{4}] Limp, hobble.

gin /dʒɪn/ *n.*^{1} ME. [Aphet. f. OFr. *engin* ENGINE *n.*] †1 Skill, ingenuity. Also, cunning, craft, artifice. ME–L15. †2 A scheme, a device; a trick. ME–E18. 3†a An instrument, a tool. ME–E17. b A mechanical contrivance or device, a machine. *arch.* LME. 4 A contrivance for catching game etc.; a snare, a net, a trap. ME. †5 An instrument of torture; *spec.* the rack. ME–L16. †6 A military machine for hurling stones or other missiles. ME–M16. 7 A device for fastening a door or window; a bolt, a bar. *obs.* exc. *dial.* ME. 8a A hoisting apparatus; *spec.* a three-legged crane or derrick. LME. b *Mining.* A horse- or wind-powered windlass for pumping, lifting, etc. L17. 9 A machine for separating cotton from its seeds. M18. 10 *Naut.* An all-metal tackle block with a skeleton frame. M19.

gin /dʒɪn/ *n.*^{2} E18. [Abbrev. of *geneva*, GENEVER.] 1 An alcoholic spirit distilled from grain or malt and flavoured with juniper berries; a drink of this. E18. 2 In full *gin rummy.* A form of rummy in which a player holding cards totalling ten or less may terminate play. M20.
1 G. GREENE He only felt his loneliness after his third gin. *gin and orange, gin and tonic*, etc. *gin and it*: see IT *n.* HOLLANDS *gin. pink gin*: see PINK *a.*^{2} 2 OKLAHOMA *gin.*
Comb.: **gin berry** the juniper berry; *gin-crawl*: see CRAWL *n.*^{2} 1b; **gin-mill** *US slang* a bar, a run-down or seedy nightclub; **gin-palace** a gaudily decorated public house; **gin pennant** *Naut.* a green and white flag hoisted to invite officers of other ships to come aboard for drinks; *gin rummy*: see sense 2 above; **gin sling** a sweetened and flavoured drink of gin and water; **gin-soaked, -sodden** *adjs.* soaked with gin, given to drinking large quantities of gin.
ginny *a.* affected by, addicted to, characterized by, or resembling gin L19.

gin /dʒɪn/ *n.*^{3} *Austral.* E19. [Aborig. *diyin.*] An Aboriginal woman.

gin /gɪn/ *v.*^{1} *arch.* Also **'gin.** Infl. **-nn-**. Pa. t. **gan** /gan/, (as aux. also) †**can.** ME. [Aphet. f. BEGIN or OE *onginnan.*] 1 *v.i.* Begin (*to*) *do.* In pa. t. formerly also in weakened sense as aux.: did *do.* ME. 2 *v.i.* Begin, commence; have or make a beginning. Also foll. by *at.* ME. 3 *v.t.* Begin (something). ME.
1 R. W. DIXON Forth from that evil house gin they proceed. 2 R. GREENE You shall to Henley .. 'Fore supper gin.

gin /dʒɪn/ *v.*^{2}*t.* Infl. **-nn-**. E17. [f. GIN *n.*^{1}] 1 Catch in a gin or trap; ensnare. E17. 2 Remove the seeds of (cotton) with a gin. L18.
1 M. E. G. DUFF Men are stationed with lassos to gin you dexterously.

gin /dʒɪn/ *v.*^{3}*i. colloq.* Infl. **-nn-**. L19. [f. GIN *n.*^{2}] Drink gin or other intoxicating liquor; become drunk. Usu. foll. by *up.*
ginned (**up**) *a.* drunk E20.

gin /gɪn/ *prep.* & *conj.*^{1} *Sc.* & *north.* M18. [Aphet. f. AGAIN *prep.* & *conj.*] A *prep.* By, before (a specified time); in view of a future event. M18.
D. S. MELDRUM He'll tak' me as a 'prentice gin summer.
B *conj.* Before, by the time that, when, until. M18.

gin /gɪn/ *conj.*^{2} *Sc.* & *dial.* E17. [App. rel. to GIF.] If; whether.
R. BURNS Ye shall gang in gay attire .. Gin ye'll leave your Collier Laddie.

ginep *n.* var. of GUINEP.

ging /gɪŋ/ *v.t.* Now *rare* or *obs.* M18 [Origin unkn.] *Mining.* Shore or wall up (a shaft). Also foll. by *up.*

gingall /ˈdʒɪŋg(ə)l/ *n.* Also **-gal, j-.** E19. [Urdu *janjāl.*] *Hist.* A heavy musket fired from a rest; a light swivel-gun.

ginger /ˈdʒɪndʒə/ *n.* & *a.*^{1} [Late OE *gingifer*(*e*), *ginġiber* conflated in ME with OFr. *gingi*(*m*)*bre* (mod. *gingembre*), both f. med.L *gingiber*, *zingeber* f. L *zingiber*(*i* f. Gk *ziggiberis* f. Pali *siṅgivera* f. Dravidian: cf. Tamil *iñci* ginger, *ver* foot (Skt *śṛṅgavera* infl. by *śṛṅga* horn from its antler-shaped root).] A *n.* 1 The hot spicy rhizome of the plant *Zingiber officinale*, used in cookery and medicine and candied as a sweet or preserved in syrup. LOE. 2 The monocotyledonous plant yielding this rhizome, *Zingiber officinale* (family Zingiberaceae), native to SE Asia. LME. 3 A fighting-cock with reddish-brown plumage. L18. 4 A light reddish-yellow colour; the sandy or reddish colour of a person's hair. M19. 5 *fig.* Mettle, spirit; stimulation. M19. 6 (Also **G-**.) (A nickname for) a person with red hair. *colloq.* L19.
2 H. ALLEN Next year he would .. put in indigo, cotton, sugar cane, and ginger. 4 J. MASTERS Red hair, a sort of dull ginger. 5 G. SANTAYANA This .. boy has no ginger in him, no fire.
Phrases: **black ginger** unscraped root of ginger. **green ginger** undried root of ginger, usu. in a preserve. *Jamaica ginger*: see JAMAICA 1. *root ginger*: see ROOT *n.*^{1} *stem ginger*: see STEM *n.*^{1} **white ginger** scraped root of ginger. *wild ginger*: see WILD *a.*, *n.*, & *adv.*

B *adj.* Of a light reddish-yellow colour; (of hair) sandy, reddish; (of a person) sandy- or red-haired. E19.

Comb. & special collocations: **ginger ale** an aerated ginger-flavoured drink; **ginger beer** (*a*) ginger ale; *spec.* an aerated drink made by fermenting sugar, water, and bruised or ground ginger; *ginger-beer plant*, a mixture of yeast and bacteria to ferment sugar solution in making ginger beer; (*b*) *slang* a homosexual man; **gingerbeery** *a.* frothy, lively; **ginger group** a group within an organization which stimulates or enlivens the main body; **ginger lily** any of various chiefly Indo-Malayan plants of the genus *Hedychium*, of the ginger family, grown for their spikes of showy fragrant flowers. **ginger-nob** *slang* (*a*) a red-haired person; (*b*) a head of ginger hair; **ginger-nut** (*a*) = GINGERBREAD *nut*; (*b*) a ginger-flavoured biscuit; **ginger-pop** *colloq.* ginger beer, ginger ale; **ginger-race** a root of ginger; **ginger-snap** a thin brittle ginger-flavoured biscuit; **ginger wine** a drink made from fermented sugar, water, and bruised ginger.

gingery *a.* (*a*) ginger-coloured, sandy; (*b*) spiced with or as with ginger: M19.

ginger /ˈdʒɪndʒə/ *a.*² Now chiefly *dial.* E17. [Back-form. f. GINGERLY *a.*] = GINGERLY *a.*

ginger /ˈdʒɪndʒə/ *v.t.* E19. [f. GINGER *n.*] **1** Flavour with ginger. E19. **2** Put ginger into a horse's anus to make it appear lively and spirited. E19. **3** *fig.* Enliven; stimulate, rouse *up*. M19.

3 M. KINGTON I just put her in to ginger things up.

gingerade /dʒɪndʒəˈreɪd/ *n.* M19. [f. GINGER *n.* after *lemonade*.] A sweet fizzy ginger-flavoured drink.

gingerbread /ˈdʒɪndʒəbrɛd/ *n.* & *a.* ME. [OFr. *gingembras*, *-brat* f. med.L *gingibratum*, *-etum*, f. *gingiber* GINGER *n.* & *a.*¹ + *-atum* -ATE¹; later assim. to *ginger*, *bread*.] **A** *n.* **1** Orig., ginger, *esp.* preserved ginger. Later, cake made with treacle and flavoured with ginger (formerly made into fancy shapes which were often gilded). ME. **2** Something showy or insubstantial. Now *esp.* elaborate carving or gaudy decoration on a building. E17. **3** Money. *slang.* Now *rare* or *obs.*. E18.

1 *take the gilt off the gingerbread*: see GILT *n.*² 2 *Caribbean Quarterly* Small wooden houses with much architectural gingerbread.

Comb.: **gingerbread man** a flat gingerbread cake cut out in a shape resembling the outline of the human figure with a head, arms, and legs; **gingerbread-palm** = DOUM; **gingerbread nut** a small button-like gingerbread cake; **gingerbread-plum** (the fruit of) the gingerbread tree; **gingerbread tree** a W. African tree, *Neocarya macrophylla* (family Chrysobalanaceae), with an edible starchy fruit.

B *adj.* Resembling the figures made of (gilded) gingerbread; *esp.* designating the ornate carved and gilded scrollwork on a ship or a building; showy, elaborate, gaudy. M18.

LADY BIRD JOHNSON A gingerbread bandstand decorated with . . bunting.

gingerly /ˈdʒɪndʒəli/ *a.* M16. [f. as or directly f. next: see -LY¹.] Orig., dainty, fastidious. Later, tentative, wary, reluctant.

MRS H. WOOD Tim treading with gingerly feet past his own door. T. ROETHKE Much too wary, much too gingerly in its approach to experience.

gingerliness *n.* (*rare*) L16.

gingerly /ˈdʒɪndʒəli/ *adv.* E16. [Perh. f. OFr. *gensor*, *genzor* pretty, delicate, compar. of *gent* graceful f. L *genitus* (well)-born: see -LY².] †**1** Elegantly, daintily; *derog.* mincingly. E16–E17. **2** Delicately, tentatively, with great caution. M16.

2 R. V. JONES Gingerly opening the box because it might easily have been a bomb.

gingham /ˈgɪŋəm/ *n.* & *a.* E17. [Du. *gingang* f. Malay *genggang* (orig. adj. = striped).] **A** *n.* **1** A plain-woven cotton cloth of dyed yarn, often striped or checked. E17. **2** An umbrella, *esp.* one covered with gingham. *colloq.* (now *rare* or *obs.*). M19. **B** *adj.* Of or pertaining to gingham; made of gingham. L18.

gingili /ˈdʒɪndʒɪli/ *n.* Also **gingelly**. E18. [Hind. & Marathi *jiñjalī* f. Arab. dial. *jonjolīn* f. Arab. *juljulān*.] Sesame, *Sesamum indicum*; oil from sesame seeds.

gingiv- *comb. form* see GINGIVO-.

gingival /dʒɪnˈdʒʌɪv(ə)l/ *a.* M17. [mod.L *gingivalis*, f. *gingiva* gum: see -AL¹.] (Of a consonant) alveolar; of or pertaining to the gums.

gingivitis /dʒɪndʒɪˈvʌɪtɪs/ *n.* L19. [f. L *gingiva* gum: see -ITIS.] *Med.* Inflammation of the gums.

gingivo- /ˈdʒɪndʒɪvəʊ, dʒɪnˈdʒʌɪvəʊ/ *comb. form* of L *gingiva* gums: see -O-. Bef. a vowel **gingiv-**.

gingiˈvectomy *n.* (an instance of) surgical removal of excess gum tissue L20. **ˌgingivostomaˈtitis** *n.* inflammation of the gums and the mucous lining of the mouth M20.

gingko *n.* var. of GINKGO.

†**gingle** *v.* & *n.* var. of JINGLE.

ginglymus /ˈgɪŋglɪməs/ *n.* Pl. **-mi** /-mʌɪ, -miː/. L16. [mod.L f. Gk *gigglumos* hinge.] *Anat.* A joint in the body resembling a hinge in having movement in only one plane, as the elbow.

ginglyform *a.* hinge-shaped M19. **ginglymoid** *a.* resembling a hinge M17.

gink /gɪŋk/ *n.* (Orig. *US*) *slang* (usu. *derog.*) E20. [Origin unkn.] A fellow, a man.

B. BROADFOOT Skinny little ginks, but men all the same.

ginkgo /ˈgɪŋkgəʊ, ˈgɪŋkəʊ/ *n.* Also **gingko** /ˈgɪŋkəʊ/. Pl. **-o(e)s**. L18. [Jap. *ginkyō* f. Chin. *yinxing*.] A freq. cultivated Chinese gymnospermous tree, *Ginkgo biloba*, with fan-shaped leaves and fleshy yellow fruit, the only living member of an order which flourished in Mesozoic times. Also called *maidenhair tree*.

ginnel /ˈgɪn(ə)l/ *n.* Chiefly *dial.* Also **gennel** /ˈdʒɛn(ə)l/. E17. [Perh. f. Fr. *chenel* CHANNEL *n.*¹] †**1** A channel, a gutter. E–M17. **2** A long narrow (roofed) passage between buildings; an alley. M17.

2 D. STOREY A figure came out of the ginnel at the end of the terrace.

ginormous /dʒʌɪˈnɔːməs/ *a. slang.* M20. [f. GI(GANTIC + E(NORMOUS.] Very large; impressively or shockingly big.

ginseng /ˈdʒɪnsɛŋ/ *n.* M17. [Chin. *rénshēn* (Wade–Giles *jên shên*), f. *rén* man + *shēn* kind of herb.] **1** A tuberous root credited, esp. in the Far East, with valuable tonic properties. M17. **2** The source of this root, any of several plants of the genus *Panax* (family Araliaceae), with palmate leaves and umbels of small greenish flowers; esp. *P. pseudoginseng*, of Korea and Manchuria, and *P. quinquefolius*, of eastern N. America. L17.

ginzo /ˈgɪnzəʊ/ *n.* & *a.* *US slang* (usu. *derog.*). Also **guinzo**. Pl. of n. **-os**. M20. [Perh. f. GUINEA 2b.] (Designating) an Italian or a person of Italian descent.

gio *n.* var. of GEO.

Gioconda /dʒɪəˈkɒndə/ *a.* E20. [*La Gioconda*, a portrait (also known as *Mona Lisa*) by Leonardo da Vinci of the wife of Francesco del Giocondo, noted for the sitter's enigmatic smile.] Of a smile etc.: enigmatic, reminiscent of the woman in the painting *La Gioconda*. Cf. MONA LISA.

L. PETERS Smith smiled again, putting a slightly mysterious, Gioconda quality into it.

giocoso /dʒəʊˈkəʊsəʊ/ *adv.* & *a.* E19. [It. = merry.] *Mus.* (A direction:) merrily, joyous(ly).

Giorgi /ˈdʒɔːdʒi/ *n.* E20. [Giovanni *Giorgi* (1871–1950), It. physicist.] *Giorgi system*, a system of units based on the metre, kilogram, second, and (usu.) ampere, which was expanded to form the SI system.

Giorgionesque /ˌdʒɔːdʒɪəˈnɛsk/ *a.* E20. [f. *Giorgione* (see below) + -ESQUE.] Resembling the style of the Italian painter Giorgione Barbarelli (1478–1510).

Giottesque /dʒɒˈtɛsk/ *a.* & *n.* M19. [f. *Giotto* (see below) + -ESQUE.] **A** *adj.* Resembling the style of the Italian painter Giotto di Bondone (*c*1267–1337). M19. **B** *n.* The style developed by Giotto; an artist of the school, or imitating the style, of Giotto. M19.

gip /gɪp/ *v.t.* Infl. **-pp-**. Also **gib** /gɪb/, infl. **-bb-**. E17. [Origin unkn.] Gut and clean (fish).

gipon /ˈdʒɪpɒn, dʒɪˈpɒn/ *n.* LME. [OFr. *gip(p)on* var. of *jup(p)on*: see JUPON. Cf. GIPPO *n.*¹] *Hist.* A close-fitting, padded tunic, usu. worn under a hauberk.

†**gippo** *n.*¹ Pl. **-o(e)s**. Only in 17. [Fr. †*jup(p)eau*, earlier *jupel*: cf. GIPON, JUPON.] A short tunic; *fig.* a scullion.

gippo /ˈdʒɪpəʊ/ *n.*² & *a.* *colloq.* (*derog.*). Also **gyp(p)o**, **G-**. E20. [Alt. of GIPPY: see -O.] **A** *n.* Pl. **-os**. **1** = GIPPY *n.* 1. E20. **2** = GIPPY *n.* 2. E20. **B** *attrib.* or as *adj.* = GIPPY *a.* 2. E20.

gippy /ˈdʒɪpi/ *n.* & *a.* *colloq.* (*derog.*). Also **gy-**, **G-**. L19. [f. GYPSY *n.* & *a.* infl. by EGYPTIAN: see -Y⁶. Cf. GIPPO *n.*² & *a.*] **A** *n.* **1** An Egyptian, *esp.* an Egyptian soldier. L19. **b** An Egyptian cigarette. E20. **2** A Gypsy. E20.

B *attrib.* or as *adj.* **1** Egyptian. E20. **2** Of or pertaining to a Gypsy or Gypsies. *rare.* E20.

1 **gippy tummy** diarrhoea suffered by visitors to hot countries.

†**gips** *n.pl.* var. of GIPSIES.

gipser /ˈdʒɪpsə/ *n. arch.* Also **-sire** /-sʌɪə/. LME. [OFr. *gibecier(e*, *gibessiere* purse, pouch, gamebag (mod. *gibecière*): ult. origin unkn.] A purse or small bag hung from a belt.

gipsies /ˈdʒɪpsɪz/ *n.pl.* Also †**gips**, †**vipseys**. ME. [Prob. f. or conn. w. the *Gypsey* Race, a river in Humberside, England.] Springs which flow only seasonally or intermittently.

Gipsify *v.* var. of GYPSYFY.

gipsire *n.* var. of GIPSER.

gipsy *n.* & *a.*, *v.* vars. of GYPSY *n.* & *a.*, *v.*

Gipsyfy *v.* var. of GYPSYFY.

giraffe /dʒɪˈrɑːf, -ˈraf/ *n.* Also †**giraffa**. L16. [Ult. f. Arab. *zarāfa* through Fr. *girafe*, It. *giraffa*, etc.] **1** A ruminant mammal, *Giraffa camelopardalis*, of the African savannah, the tallest living animal, beige with red-brown patches, having a very long neck and forelegs. L16. **2** (Usu. **G-**.) *The* constellation Camelopardalis. M19. **3** A tall upright piano of Viennese origin, ascending in height as the strings increase in length, popular in the early 19th cent. L19.

¶The animal was earlier called CAMELOPARD.

giraffid *a.* & *n.* of or pertaining to, any animal of, the artiodactyl family Giraffidae, comprising the giraffe, okapi, and related extinct forms L19. **giraffine** *a.* & *n.* = GIRAFFID E20. **giraffoid** *a.* = GIRAFFID *a.* L19.

girandola /dʒiˈrandola, dʒɪːr(ə)nˈdəʊlə/ *n.* M17. [It.: see next.] **1** = GIRANDOLE 2. M17. **2** = GIRANDOLE 1. L17.

girandole /ˈdʒɪr(ə)ndəʊl/ *n.* M17. [Fr. f. It. *girandola*, f. *girare* f. late L *gyrare* GYRATE.] **I 1** A kind of revolving firework; a discharge of rockets etc. from a revolving wheel. M17. **2** A revolving jet of water; a series of jets in an ornamental fountain. E19. **II 3** A branched support for candles or other lights which either stands on a surface or projects from a wall. M18. **4** An earring, a pendant, *esp.* one which has a large central stone surrounded by smaller ones. E19.

girasol /ˈdʒɪrəsɒl, -səʊl/ *n.* Also **-sole** /-səʊl/. L16. [Fr. *girasol* or It. *girasole*, f. *girare* (see prec.) + *sole* sun.] †**1** A sunflower. *rare.* Only in L16. **2** A variety of opal which reflects a reddish glow, a fire-opal. L16.

girba /ˈgəːbə/ *n.* L18. [Dial. var. of Arab. *kirba* waterskin.] A leather water-vessel used in N. Africa etc.

gird /gəːd/ *n.*¹ *obs.* exc. *north.* & *Sc.* ME. [Var. of GIRTH *n.*¹, perh. infl. by GIRD *v.*¹] **1** †**a** A girdle; a strap or band of any kind. ME–M17. **b** *spec.* A saddle-girth. L16. **2** A hoop for a barrel; a hoop used as a child's plaything. M16.

gird /gəːd/ *n.*² LME. [f. GIRD *v.*²] **1** A sharp stroke or blow. *obs.* exc. *dial.* & *Sc.* LME. **2** A sudden movement or jerk; a spurt of action. *obs.* exc. *dial.* M16. **3** A sharp or biting remark, a gibe, a dig. M16. **4** A spasm of pain, a sudden pang. *obs.* exc. *dial.* & *Sc.* E17.

gird /gəːd/ *v.*¹*t.* Pa. t. & pple **girded**, **girt** /gəːt/. See also GIRT *ppl a.* [OE *gyrdan* = OS *gurdian* (Du. *gorden*), OHG *gurten* (G *gürten*), ON *gyrða* f. Gmc. Cf. GIRDLE *n.*¹, GIRTH *n.*¹] **1** Surround, encircle (the waist), encircle the waist of (a person) with a belt or girdle, esp. in order to confine the clothes. Also foll. by *about*, *up*. OE. †**b** Bind (a horse) with a saddle-girth. ME–L17.

c *fig.* Prepare (oneself) for action; brace (oneself) *for, to, to do*; summon up (one's courage). Freq. foll. by *up*. LME. **2** *fig.* Invest *with* strength, power, or other attributes. *arch.* OE. **3a** Equip (oneself or another) *with* a sword suspended from a belt; invest *with* the sword of knighthood. OE. **b** Fasten or fasten *on* (a sword etc.) to one's person with a belt. (Foll. by *on* one's person, *to* one's side, etc.) OE. **4** Secure (clothing etc.) on one's body by means of a girdle, belt, etc. Also, secure (a belt etc.) firmly or tightly. ME. **5** Surround, encircle, enclose. ME. **b** Encircle (a town etc.) with or *with* an armed force or siege-works; besiege, blockade. M16. †**6** Surround as with a belt; tie firmly, confine. Usu. foll. by *up, in, about, together.* L16–L17.

1 DICKENS She girded herself with a white apron. G. K. CHESTERTON Girt round the waist with a red sash. M. M. KAYE A lean, bearded tribesman .. girt about with a bandolier. c S. LEACOCK A great nation .. was girding itself to join in the fight for .. democracy. D. M. FRAME Man's bleak condition obliges the noble humanist to ... gird up his soul to meet the ills of life. J. A. MICHENER Let every person .. gird his courage for the days ahead. 3a S. BUTLER Was I for this entitled Sir, And girt with trusty sword and spur. b DICKENS Girt to his side was the steel hilt of an old sword. T. H. WHITE Sir Ector girds on the sword. 4 W. IRVING His blanket being girt round his waist. W. GOLDING The women .. in their long robes of linen girt above the breast. 5 R. L. STEVENSON Girt about on every side by clocks and chimes. JOYCE A big hall girded at half its height by a gallery. S. HEANEY His silver watch chain girds him like a hoop.

Phrases: **gird (up) one's loins** surround one's loins with a belt, girdle, or other clothing; put on one's clothes, esp. for action; *fig.* gather or summon up one's courage.

girding *n.* (*a*) the action of the vb; (*b*) (now *rare*) that which girds; *spec.* a girdle, a saddle-girth: ME.

gird /gəːd/ *v.*^{2} ME. [Origin unkn. Cf. GRIDE *v.*] **1** *v.t.* Strike, smite, push. *obs.* exc. *dial.* & *Sc.* ME. †**2** *v.t.* Move or thrust hastily or roughly; pierce, stab. ME–M17. **3** *v.i.* Move suddenly or rapidly; rush, start, spring. *obs.* exc. *dial.* & *Sc.* LME. **4** *fig.* **a** *v.i.* Jeer or gibe *at*. M16. **b** *v.t.* Sneer or scoff at. Now *rare.* L16.

girder /ˈgəːdə/ *n.* & *v.* E17. [f. GIRD *v.*^{1} + -ER^1.] **A** *n.* **1** A main beam, orig. of wood but now often of steel or iron, used to support the joists of a floor. E17. **2** A latticed or other compound structure of esp. steel or iron used to form the span of a bridge, a roof, etc. M19.

1 ANTHONY HUXLEY Strong steel girders in a ferro-concrete building.

Comb.: **girder bridge**: with a superstructure of longitudinal girders.

B *v.t.* Support or strengthen with or as with a girder M20.

girdle /ˈgəːd(ə)l/ *n.*^{1} [OE *gyrdel* = MDu. *gurdel* (Du. *gordel*), OHG *gurtil, -ila* (G *Gürtel*), ON *gyrðill*, f. Gmc base of GIRD *v.*^{1}: see -LE^1.] **1** A belt or cord worn around the waist to secure the clothing or as a means of carrying a purse or weapon. OE. **b** A corset, *esp.* one which is elasticated and extends from the waist to the thighs. E20. **2** Something which surrounds like a girdle. OE. **b** Something which confines or binds in. E17. †**3** That part of the body round which a girdle is worn. ME–E18. **4** *spec.* **a** *Anat.* & *Zool.* The bony structure supporting (*a*) the arms, forelimbs, or pectoral fins (more fully *shoulder girdle, pectoral girdle*); (*b*) the legs, hind limbs, or ventral fins (more fully *hip girdle, pelvic girdle*). E17. **b** *Archit.* A small circular band around a column. E18. **c** The part of a cut gem dividing the crown from the base and embraced by the setting. E19. **d** A ring round the trunk of a tree made by removing the bark. E19.

1 E. LINKLATER A green dress and a girdle of twisted gold. J. HAWKES The gun and the gun's girdle—the holster, straps, strings—were visible. **girdle of chastity** a chastity belt. VENUS's *girdle*. †**put** etc. **a girdle about** go round, make a circuit of (the earth). †**turn one's girdle** (*rare*, Shakes.) make a challenge. **under one's girdle** in subjection, under one's control. b J. MASTERS She stood in the tiny bathroom .. struggling into her brassiere and girdle. 2 W. MACGILLIVRAY The horizon was bounded by a girdle of forest.

Comb.: **girdlestead** (long *arch. rare*) the part of the body round which a girdle is worn; the waist; **girdle-tailed lizard** any of various lizards of the family Cordylidae, esp. the genus *Cordylus*, which have the tail ringed with spiny scales and are found in southern Africa and Madagascar (also called *zonure*).

girdle /ˈgəːd(ə)l/ *n.*^{2} *north.* & *Sc.* LME. [Metath. alt. of GRIDDLE.] = GRIDDLE *n.* 2.

like a hen on a hot girdle in considerable unease or discomfort.

Comb.: **girdle-cake**: made on a girdle.

girdle /ˈgəːd(ə)l/ *v.t.* L16. [f. GIRDLE *n.*^{1}] **1** Surround with or as with a girdle. (Foll. by *about, in, round.*) L16. **2** Remove a ring of bark from (a tree, a branch) esp. as a means of killing or from (a branch) as a means of increasing a tree's fruitfulness. M17.

1 P. L. FERMOR Fragmentary walls .. girdled most of the little towns. K. CROSSLEY-HOLLAND A massive stronghold, girdled by flame and guarded by a giant.

girdler /ˈgəːdlə/ *n.* LME. [f. GIRDLE *n.*^{1}, *v.* + -ER^1.] **1** A maker of girdles. *arch.* exc. as a guild-name. LME. **2** A person who or animal which girdles something. Cf. *twig-girdler* s.v. TWIG *n.*^{1} L19.

giri *n.* pl. of GIRO *n.*^{1}

girl /gəːl/ *n.* See also GAL *n.*^{1} ME. [Perh. cogn. w. LG *gör* boy, girl.] †**1** A child or young person of either sex. Usu. in *pl.* Only in ME. †**2** A roebuck in its second year. L15–E18. **3** A female child; a young or relatively young woman. Also *gen.*, a woman. M16. **b** A female servant; a female employee, *esp.* a secretary or other assistant in an office, shop, factory, etc. (now freq. considered *offensive*). M17. **c** A sweetheart. Also, one's wife. M17. **d** A Black woman. *S. Afr.* & †*US* (now considered *racially offensive*). M19.

3 L. STRACHEY The child grew into the girl, the girl into the young woman. C. ODETS I like how you dress. The girls look nice in the summer time. *Guardian* A pretty, personable, and articulate 28-year-old girl. c U. SINCLAIR Each man would bring his 'girl' with him. M. FRENCH The men .. left the living room to the 'girls'.

Phrases etc.: **(all) girls together** *colloq.* on close friendly terms with another girl or girls. *be a big girl* (*now*): see BIG *a. best girl*: see BEST *a.* etc. *boy-meets-girl*: see BOY *n.* †**girl about town** a prostitute. †**girl of ease, of the town** a prostitute. *girls together*: see *all girls together* above. *hired girl*: see HIRED *ppl a.* **les girls** /leɪ/ [Fr. *les* (pl.) the] girls collectively; *spec.* chorus girls. *old girl*: see OLD *a. the girl next door*: see NEXT *a.* **the girls** *spec.* a group of women, esp. with similar interests; the grown-up daughters of a family. WORKING *girl*. ZIEGFELD *girl*.

Comb.: *girl Friday*: see FRIDAY *n.* 1; **girlfriend** a female friend, *esp.* a boy's or man's, or a lesbian's, usual or preferred female companion; *girl guide*: see GUIDE *n.*; *girl scout*: see SCOUT *n.*^{3}

girldom *n.* the domain or world of girls; girls collectively: M19. **girleen** *n.* (*Anglo-Ir.*) a young girl M19. **girlhood** *n.* the state of being a girl; the time during which one is a girl; girls collectively: L18. **girlless** *a.* (*rare*) without a girl or girls E20.

girl /gəːl/ *v.* M17. [f. the n.] **1** *v.t.* Provide with girls; *spec.* provide (a ship etc.) with girls as crew, workers, etc. *rare. joc.* M17. **2** *v.i.* Keep company or consort with women. L18.

girlie /ˈgəːli/ *n.* & *a.* Also **girly**. M19. [f. GIRL *n.* + -IE, -Y^6.] **A** *n.* (A term of endearment for) a girl, *esp.* a little girl. M19.

S. CONRAN Kate's father .. was delighted that his girlie was featuring so prominently in local life.

B *adj.* **1** Girlish. L19. **2** Of a publication, entertainment, etc.: featuring young women, usu. naked or semi-naked, in erotic contexts. M20.

2 P. ROTH The girlie magazines piled up in his barbershop.

girlish /ˈgəːlɪʃ/ *a.* M16. [f. GIRL *n.* + -ISH^1.] Of or pertaining to a girl or girlhood; characteristic of or like a girl.

R. GITTINGS Looking more girlish than her twenty years.

girlishly *adv.* E18. **girlishness** *n.* E17.

girly *n.* & *a.* var. of GIRLIE.

girly-girly /gəːlɪˈgəːli/ *a.* & *n.* L19. [Redupl. of prec.] **A** *adj.* Exaggeratedly or affectedly girlish; effeminate. L19. **B** *n.* A girl; a little girl. L19.

girn /gəːn/ *n.* Chiefly *Sc.* & *north.* Also **gurn**. E16. [Metath. alt. of GRIN *n.*^{2}] **1** The act of snarling or showing the teeth in rage, pain, disappointment, etc. E16. **2** The act of laughing or grinning. M17.

girn /gəːn/ *v.i.* Chiefly *Sc.* & *north.* Also (the usual form in sense 4) **gurn**. LME. [Metath. alt. of GRIN *v.*^{2}] **1** Show the teeth in rage, pain, disappointment, etc.; snarl. LME. **2** Show the teeth in laughing; grin. M16. **3** Whine, complain; be fretful or peevish. E18. **4** Distort the features; pull a hideous face. L18.

3 L. G. GIBBON Of a morning John Guthrie grumbled and girned at him. 4 *Sunday Times* Gordon Mattison .. won the world gurning championship .. by pulling the most hideous face.

girnel /ˈgəːn(ə)l/ *n.* & *v.* *Sc.* Also †**garnel**. LME. [Var. of GARNER *n.*] **A** *n.* A granary. Also, a large chest for meal. LME. †**B** *v.t.* Store up in a girnel. L15–E18.

giro /ˈdʒiːro, -əʊ/ *n.*^{1} Pl. ***-ri*** /-ri/ L17. [It. = round, circuit.] A tour, a circuit; a turn.

giro /ˈdʒʌɪrəʊ/ *n.*^{2} & *v.* L19. [G f. It. = circulation (of money).] **A** *n.* Pl. **-os**. **1** A system of credit transfer between banks, post offices, etc.; *spec.* (freq. **G-**) a system run by the British Post Office for the banking and transfer of money. Also *giro system*. L19. **2** In full *giro cheque, order*. A cheque or money order issued through the giro system; *spec.* in Britain, such a cheque used for unemployment benefit or social security payments. L20.

2 J. KELMAN All I'm fucking asking is regular giros and punctual counter clerks.

B *v.t.* Pay by giro. L20.

Gironde /dʒɪˈrɒnd, *foreign* ʒirɔ̃d/ *n.* L18. [A department of SW France.] *Fr. Hist.* The Girondist party.

Girondin /dʒɪˈrɒndɪn/ *n.* & *a.* M19. [Fr., f. prec. + *-in* -INE^4.] *Fr. Hist.* = GIRONDIST.

Girondism /dʒɪˈrɒndɪz(ə)m/ *n.* M19. [Fr. *Girondisme*, f. GIRONDE + *-isme* -ISM.] *Fr. Hist.* The doctrine or practice of the Girondists.

Girondist /dʒɪˈrɒndɪst/ *n.* & *a.* L18. [Fr. *Girondiste*, f. GIRONDE + *-iste* -IST.] *Fr. Hist.* **A** *n.* A member of the French moderate republican party, in power in France during the Revolution from 1791 to 1793, and so called because the party leaders came from Gironde. L18. **B** *adj.* Of or pertaining to the Girondists or their principles. E19.

girouette /ʒirwɛt/ *n.* Pl. pronounced same. E19. [Fr.] A weathercock.

girr /gəː/ *n.* *Sc.* M16. [Var. of GIRTH *n.*^{1}] A hoop for a barrel; a hoop used as a child's plaything.

girran /ˈgɪrən/ *n.* *Sc.* (now *dial.*). Also **gurrag** /ˈgʌrəg/, **gurry** /ˈgʌri/. E19. [Gael. *guirean* dim. of *gur* pimple.] A small boil, a pustule.

girse /gəːs/ *n.* *obs.* exc. *dial.* L16. [Var. of GIRTH *n.*^{1}, prob. f. pl. *girths*.] **1** A saddle-girth; = GIRTH *n.*^{1} 1. L16. †**2** A band, a hoop; = GIRTH *n.*^{1} 2. Only in L16.

girsh *n.* var. of QURSH.

girt /gəːt/ *n.* Now *rare.* M16. [Var. of GIRTH *n.*^{1} surviving in techn. uses, infl. by *girt* pa. pple of GIRD *v.*^{1}] **1** A saddle-girth; = GIRTH *n.*^{1} 1. *obs.* exc. *dial.* M16. **2** A girder. Latterly *US.* L16. **3** = GIRTH *n.*^{1} 3. Also (*techn.*), measurement across or around a surface which is not flat, as a moulded cornice, taking into account all elevations and depressions. M17. †**4** = GIRTH *n.*^{1} 5. Only in L17.

girt /gəːt/ *ppl a.* E17. [pa. pple of GIRD *v.*^{1}] **1** *Naut.* Of a ship: moored so tightly by its cables that it cannot swing about when the tide turns. E17. **2** That has been girt. Also *girt-up* etc. L18.

girt /gəːt/ *v.*^{1} Now *rare.* LME. [f. GIRT *n.*] **1** *v.t.* = GIRD *v.*^{1} LME. **2** *v.t.* Secure with a girth. M17. **3a** *v.t.* Surround with a measuring-line in order to ascertain the girth of. M17. **b** *v.i.* Take a measurement by leading a line round or across the object to be measured. E19. **4** *v.i.* Of a tree etc.: measure (so much) in girth. M18.

Comb.: **girting-place** (*a*) that part of a horse's body where the girth is worn; (*b*) that part of a tree-trunk which is girthed or measured.

girt *v.*[2] pa. t. & pple: see GIRD *v.*[1]

girth /gəːθ/ *n.*[1] ME. [ON *gjǫrð* girdle, girth, hoop, Goth. *gairda* girdle f. Gmc. See also GARTH *n.*[2], GIRD *n.*[1], GIRR, GIRSE, GIRT *n.*, and cf. GIRD *v.*[1], GIRDLE *n.*[1]] **1** A belt or band of leather or cloth tightened round the body of a horse or other beast of burden, so as to secure a saddle, pack, etc., on its back. Also *saddle-girth*. ME. **b** The part of a horse's body where the girth is fastened. M19. **2** A hoop of wood or iron, esp. for a barrel. *obs.* exc. *dial.* LME. **3** Measurement round the circumference of any more or less cylindrical object, as the trunk of a tree, the human body, etc. M17. **4** A horizontal beam or girder. *US.* E19. **5** *Printing.* Either of the two leather thongs or bands of webbing on the carriage of a hand printing-press by which it is moved back and forth. E19. **6** *transf.* Something that encircles; the area etc. encircled. E19.

1 W. HOLTBY Loosened her girth, pulled aside the saddle. 3 J. RUSKIN Walnuts, with trunks eight or ten feet in girth. V. NABOKOV Hip girth, twenty-nine inches; thigh girth . . seventeen. R. LOWELL He'd admire father's trim girth. 6 A. C. SWINBURNE That is girdled about with the round sea's girth As a town with its wall.

Comb.: **girth-web** woven material of which girths are made; a strong broad tape or band of this material.

girth *n.*[2] see GRITH.

girth /gəːθ/ *v.* LME. [f. the n.] **1** *v.t.* Gird, surround, encompass. LME. **2** *v.t.* Fit or bind (a horse etc.) with a girth. L16. **3** *v.t.* Secure (a saddle etc.) by means of a girth. Also foll. by *on*, *up*. E19. **4** *v.t.* & *i.* Draw (a string or measuring-line) close round or across a surface being measured. E19. **5** *v.i.* Measure (so much) in girth. M19.

1 SIR W. SCOTT The four seas that girth Britain.

girthing *n.* (*a*) the action of the vb; (*b*) material for making girths: LME.

girtline *n.* see GANTLINE.

Girtonian /gəːˈtəʊnɪən/ *n.* L19. [f. *Girton* (see below) + -IAN.] A student or former student of Girton College in Cambridge, orig. a women's college, but mixed since 1977.

gisarme /gɪˈzɑːm/ *n. obs.* exc. *Hist.* ME. [OFr. *g(u)isarme*, *wisarme* f. Frank. *wīs-arm* lit. 'guide-arm': cf. OS *wīsian* (= OE *wīsan*, OHG *wīsen*) show, teach.] A kind of battleaxe, bill, or halberd, having a long blade in line with the shaft, sharpened on both sides and ending in a point.

gise /dʒʌɪz/ *v. dial.* L17. [Var. of or back-form. f. GIST *v.*[2]] **1** *v.t.* Pasture (land) with cattle other than one's own. L17. **2** *v.t.* & *i.* Put (cattle) out to feed at a certain rate of payment. M19.

gisement /ˈdʒʌɪzm(ə)nt/ *n.*[1] Also (earlier) †**gistment**. E16 [Aphet. f. AGISTMENT.] Cattle taken on to one's land to remain and feed at a certain rate per head; the payment received for this.

¶ Current form recorded f. L17.

gisement /ʒizmɑ̃/ *n.*[2] *rare.* M19. [Fr.] The way in which something lies, position.

gism *n.* var. of JISM.

gismo /ˈgɪzməʊ/ *n. slang.* Chiefly *N. Amer.* Also **gizmo**. Pl. **-os**. M20. [Origin unkn.] A gadget, a gimmick.

Listener Electronic gismos for demagnetizing the heads of an audio tape-recorder.

gismondine /ˈgɪzm(ə)ndiːn/ *n.* E19. [f. C. G. *Gismondi* (1762–1824), It. mineralogist + -INE[5].] *Min.* A hydrated calcium aluminosilicate of the zeolite group occurring as whitish or purple crystals, esp. in Italian volcanic rocks.

Also **gismondite** *n.* L19.

†**gist** *n.*[1] ME–E18. [OFr. *giste* (mod. *gîte*) resting-place etc.; rel. to *gésir*, *gis-* lie. See GEST *n.*[3], GIST *n.*[3]] A stopping-place, a lodging.

gist /dʒɪst/ *n.*[2] *obs.* exc. *dial.* LME. [f. GIST *v.*[2]] The right of pasture for cattle at a certain rate of payment etc.; the payment made for this; agistment.

gist /dʒɪst/ *n.*[3] Also (earlier, & in sense 1 only) †**git**. E18. [OFr. (mod. *gît*), 3rd person sing. pres. indic. of *gésir* lie (f. L *jacere*), as in the Fr. legal phr. *cest action gist* this action lies.] **1** *Law.* The real ground or point of an action etc. E18. **2** The substance, essence, or main part of a matter. E19.

2 R. L. STEVENSON Making believe is the gist of his whole life. R. HUGHES Even though the words were unintelligible, their gist . . was not. E. BOWEN She had joined the sermon late and just got the gist of it.

†**gist** *n.*[4] & *v.*[1] see JOIST *n.* & *v.*

gist /dʒɪst/ *v.*[2] *obs.* exc. *dial.* L15. [Aphet. f. AGIST. Cf. GISE.] **1** *v.t.* = AGIST 2. L15. †**2** *v.i.* = AGIST 3. E16–E17.

†**gistment** *n.* see GISEMENT *n.*[1]

git /gɪt/ *n.*[1] *slang. contempt.* M20. [Var. of GET *n.*[1]] A worthless person.

Listener That bald-headed, moon-faced, four-eyed git.

†**git** *n.*[2] see GIST *n.*[3]

git *v.* see GET *v.*

gitana /dʒɪˈtɑːnə, *foreign* xiˈtana/ *n.* M19. [Sp., fem. of next.] A female (Spanish) Gypsy.

gitano /dʒɪˈtɑːnəʊ, *foreign* xiˈtano/ *n.* Pl. **-os** /-əʊz, *foreign* -ɔs/. M19. [Sp. repr. of pop.L = Egyptian, f. L *Aegyptus* Egypt + *-anus* -AN.] A male (Spanish) Gypsy.

gîte /ʒit/ *n.* Also ***gite***. Pl. pronounced same. L18. [Fr.: see GIST *n.*[1]] **1** A stopping-place, a lodging. Now *rare*. L18. **2** In France and French-speaking countries, a furnished holiday home usu. in a rural district. M20.

gith /gɪθ/ *n.* Now *rare* or *obs.* LME. [L *gith*, *git*, *gicti*, f. Semitic.] Any of various plants of the genus *Nigella*, of the buttercup family; *esp.* the fennel-flower, *N. sativa*.

gittern /ˈgɪtəːn/ *n.* LME. [OFr. *guiterne* (perh. through MDu. *giterne*), obscurely rel. to CITTERN and GUITAR.] An early plucked gut-stringed musical instrument of the guitar kind.

gitterner *n.* (long *rare*) a player on the gittern LME.

Giunta /ˈdʒʊntə/ *n.* L17. [It. (= Sp., Port. JUNTA), f. *giungere* join.] *Hist.* In the Venetian republic, a number of patricians chosen to act as advisers in special emergencies; later, the co-opted members of the council which ran the affairs of the State.

Giuoco Piano /dʒʊˌəʊkəʊ ˈpjɑːnəʊ, pɪˈɑːnəʊ/ *n. phr.* E19. [It. = quiet game.] *Chess.* An initially quiet opening in chess, formerly popular esp. among Italian players; *spec.* = *Italian opening* s.v. ITALIAN *a.*

†**giust** *n.* see JOUST *n.*

give /gɪv/ *n.* M19. [f. the vb.] Giving; *spec.* the quality of yielding to pressure, elasticity, flexibility.

Times If the weather stays fine we should have a fair surface with some give in it. P. ANGADI It was a one-way thing, this concern for one's children; all give and no take. *New Yorker* He's terribly conservative in things that matter. He has absolutely no give about them at all.

give /gɪv/ *v.* Pa. t. **gave** /geɪv/; pa. pple **given** /ˈgɪv(ə)n/. [OE *ġiefan*, *ġefan* = OFris. *jeva*, OS *geban* (Du. *geven*), OHG *geban* (G *geben*), ON *gefa*, Goth. *giban*, f. Gmc, with no certain IE cognates. Initial /g/ from Scand. in ME. See also GIMME.] (As *v.t.* where appropriate foll. by indirect obj. or *to*, (arch.) *unto* a recipient.) **I 1** *v.t.* Hand over as a present; transfer the possession of gratuitously; confer ownership on with or without actual delivery. OE. **b** *v.i.* Bestow alms or donations (*to*), give presents. ME. **c** *v.t.* *Law.* Bequeath, devise. Chiefly in *give and bequeath*, *give and devise*. LME. **d** *v.t.* Render (a benefit or service) without payment. E18. **2** *v.t.* Confer, grant, bestow, (favour, honour, etc., (of a higher power, esp. God) a physical or mental quality, a blessing, an advantage, etc.); grant *to be*, *to do*; accord to another (one's affection, confidence, etc.). OE. **b** *give me* — (imper.), I prefer or admire, I am in favour of. L16. **3** *v.t.* Sanction the marriage of (a daughter or female ward). Now chiefly in *give in marriage*. OE. **4** *v.t.* Deliver, hand over, (with no reference to ownership); put (food, drink) for a person to consume (also w. ellipsis of obj. (now *literary*) *give to eat*, *drink*); administer as a medicine or drug. OE. **b** Communicate or impart (a message, one's love, compliments, etc.) to a person. E17. **c** Connect telephonically with (a specified person or place). Usu. in *imper.* L19. **5** *v.t.* Commit, consign, entrust, (usu. *into the care, custody, hands*, etc., *of*); hand over as a pledge, assign as a guarantee. OE. **6** Make over in exchange or payment; exchange, buy, or sell *for* a price; pay (a price); (now *rare* exc. in biblical allusions) pay as due or demanded. ME. **b** *v.i.* In neg. contexts: care *a curse*, *a damn*, etc. *colloq.* L17. **7** *v.t.* Sacrifice, submit to the loss of for some object; dedicate, devote; apply or devote (oneself) exclusively *to*, †*to do*; *refl.* (esp. of a woman) yield (*to*) in sexual intercourse. ME. **8** *v.t.* Perform (an action), exert (an effort), esp. to affect another person or as a reaction or response; emit (a cry etc.). ME. **b** *v.i.* Deal a blow, make an attack or charge (*at*, *on*, *upon*). *obs.* exc. *Boxing.* LME. **c** *v.t.* Punish a person for (esp. an idea just expressed or words just uttered). *colloq.* E20. **d** *v.i.* *Jazz.* Play music excitingly or enthusiastically. Also foll. by *out*. M20. **9** *v.t.* Address (words) *to*; issue (a command etc.); pronounce (a blessing etc.); provide (information, evidence, etc.) verbally; [prob. f. ellipsis of *God* etc. in complimentary wishes] wish *good day* etc.; *colloq.* tell, offer, (esp. something unacceptable). ME. **b** *v.i.* Tell what one knows. *colloq.* M20. **10** *v.t.* Deliver (a judgement etc.) authoritatively; decide (a case, *it*) *for* or *against* a litigant; (of an umpire in cricket) declare a batsman etc. *out* or *not out*. ME. **11** *v.t.* As *given* pa. pple: (of a document) dated. LME. **12** *v.t.* Provide (a party, meal, etc.) as a host or benefactor or for the gratification of others; provide or conduct (a tour etc.) as a guide or helper. E16.

1 J. STEINBECK The little brown pennies he gave sparingly for alms. b C. M. YONGE She gave largely to hospitals. d OED He has charged only for the material; he has given his labour. 2 F. W. ROBERTSON It was given to the Apostle Paul to discern that this was the ground of unity. J. BRYCE Under such a charter the mayor is given power and opportunity to accomplish something. TENNYSON Sweet is true love tho' given in vain. b S. J. PERELMAN Give me home cooking every time. 3 V. WOOLF Prue Ramsay, leaning on her father's arm, was given in marriage. 4 H. T. LANE Often a child is simply given a rubber ring to bite. E. J. HOWARD He gave her the water, and stood beside her while she drank. *give the boot, the sack*, etc. 6 J. LOCKE He would give his Nuts for a piece of Metal. W. GOLDING It was just my size and I should have it for no more than he had given for it. b A. LURIE In his present mood he doesn't give a shit. 7 E. A. FREEMAN The Abbots . . had given their lives in the cause of England. M. J. GUEST He made a resolution to give to God the half of his services. R. MACAULAY Barbara . . gives herself to a young fisherman. O. MANNING She tried to give her attention to the menu. 8 E. WAUGH Lady Circumference gave a resounding snort of disapproval. A. SILLITOE He gave her a vicious clout across the face. E. WELTY He gave another imploring look. H. BASCOM The first mate . . gives a blast on the steamer's siren. *New Yorker* A novel I would need to give a final reading to. c M. ALLINGHAM 'The bear, perhaps,' he suggested. . . 'I'll give you bear,' the woman said. 9 DICKENS He heard them give each other Merry Christmas. R. TRAVERS He enlisted as a private . . , giving his name as John McKnight. *Daily Telegraph* The Ulster Defence Association gave warning yesterday that it will take 'appropriate' action against police officers. S. BELLOW He gave his okay. b P. LIVELY Come on then, give Where did you find him? 12 GOLDSMITH Intended that night giving the young ladies a ball. J. GALSWORTHY No Forsyte has given a dinner without providing a saddle of mutton.

II 13 *v.t.* Present, offer; hold out to be taken; expose to view or observation; show, indicate; state to be *at*; mention, include in a list. OE. †**b** Display as an armorial bearing, bear. M16–M17. **c** Represent, describe, report to be. Now *rare*. E17. **d** Propose as a sentiment or toast. E18. †**14** *v.t.* Of one's mind, conscience, etc.: suggest to one *that*; misgive; prompt one *to do*. ME–E19. **15** *v.t.* Read, recite, sing, or act in the presence of auditors or spectators; perform, produce, (a play etc.); deliver (a lecture etc.). LME.

13 DRYDEN All . . Give to the wanton Winds their flowing Hair. N. HAWTHORNE He holds out his hand;

she gives her own. OED Such words ought not to be given in a dictionary. *Times* The conclusions, details of which are given today. E. CRISPIN Radio Three gave rain. c TENNYSON What practice howsoe'er expert . . Hath power to give thee as thou wert? d R. DAVIES 'I give you the Devil!' He raised his glass. 15 THACKERAY Who will give us a song? A. S. NEILL I gave a lecture in the village hall. S. BRETT We worked together on a pantomime. . . *Cinderella*. You gave your Baron Hardup.

III 16 *v.t.* Allot, apportion, cause to have as one's share; assign, impose. OE. †**b** Appoint to an office or function. M16–E17. **c** Allow or predict (a period of time) for completion or accomplishment. M19. **17** *v.t.* Cause to have or receive; induce (a state etc.); impart, communicate, be the source or origin of. ME. **b** Cause *to do*. M16. **18** *v.t.* Supply, yield, furnish as a product; yield as the result of calculation or measurement. ME. †**b** Yield the conclusion *that*; signify. LME–L17. †**c** Be worth, fetch (a price). L16–L18. **19** *v.t.* Ascribe, attribute. L15. †**b** Consider to be, account as. Also *give for*. E17–M18. **20** *v.t.* Allow to have or take; concede. M16. **21** *v.t.* As *given* pa. pple: assigned or posited as a basis for calculation or reasoning; assuming as a fact. L16.

16 H. JAMES The amount of thought they give to their clothing. E. WAUGH She gave us the best room. c *Observer* The wiseacres . . gave Charles Chaplin and Oona O'Neill's marriage six months. It's lasted decades. A. F. LOEWENSTEIN She'll last a month. . . I give her till Thanksgiving. 17 M. PATTISON The Loire, its banks still clad with the broom which gives their title to the Plantagenets. W. S. MAUGHAM He gave her life an interest and excitement. J. FOWLES It gave . . the lovely illusion that one was the . . first man that had ever stood on it. *Daily Telegraph* He had accused her of . . having given him VD. 18 D. CARNEGIE A cow has to give milk. J. BARNES Orange on red gives dark brown. 19 M. J. GUEST Henry . . gave all the glory to God. 20 DRYDEN They give their Bodies due Repose at Night. J. PUDNEY He was a trier/I'll give him that, the Hun. *New Yorker* Winning . . by slightly more than a length from Sharp Gary, to whom he gave five pounds. 21 H. CARPENTER Childlike resilience was a distinct asset, given her domestic situation.

IV 22 *v.i.* Be affected, esp. detrimentally, by physical conditions; fade; deteriorate; become damp; shrink. M16. **23** *v.i.* Yield to pressure or strain; collapse, lose firmness (*lit.* & *fig.*); become relaxed; accommodate oneself or itself *to*; make concessions. L16. **b** Of weather: relax in severity, become milder, thaw. L17. **24** *v.i.* Afford a view or passage; look, lead, *into*, *on to*, (*up*)*on*, etc. M19. **25** *v.i.* Be happening. Chiefly in *what gives? colloq.* M20.

23 V. WOOLF It was her odious, weak, vacillating character again, always giving at the critical moment. I. MURDOCH Some stretched cord seemed to twang far away, something gave and broke. *Time Out* Thames have given and given over this but received no concessions from the other side. M. AMIS The heavy door at the top didn't give until the fifth push. 24 C. JACKSON The windows that gave on Seneca Street, six floors below. D. ADAMS Other corridors gave off it to the left and right.

Phrases: (A selection of cross-refs. only is included: see esp. other ns.) *give a back*: see BACK *n.*[1] *give a free hand*: see FREE *a. give a good account of*: see ACCOUNT *n. give a hand*: see HAND *n. give a horse its head*: see HEAD *n. give a miss*: see MISS *n.*[1] **give and take** exchange words, blows, or concessions. *give a person a hand*: see HAND *n. give a person beans*: see BEAN *n. give a person fits*: see FIT *n.*[2] **give a person furiously to think** [tr. Fr. *donner furieusement à penser*] set a person thinking hard; give a person cause for thought, puzzle. *give a person his* or *her colours*: see COLOUR *n. give a person his or her due*: see DUE *n.* 2. *give a person ideas*: see IDEA *n. give a person the air*: see AIR *n.*[1] 3. *give a person the gate*: see GATE *n.*[1] *give a person the hump*: see HUMP *n. give a person the push*: see PUSH *n.*[1] *give a person the slip*: see SLIP *n.*[3] 6. *give a person the wall*: see WALL *n.*[1] *give a piece of one's mind*: see MIND *n.*[1] **give as good as one gets** retort adequately in words or blows. *give a wide berth to*: see BERTH *n.* 1a. *give battle*: see BATTLE *n. give best*: see BEST *a.* etc. *give birth to*: see BIRTH *n.*[1] 1. *give chase* (*to*): see CHASE *n.*[1] 1. *give colour to*: see COLOUR *n. give credence to*: see CREDENCE 1. *give ground*: see GROUND *n. give guard*: see GUARD *n. give hell*: see HELL *n. give in charge*: see CHARGE *n.* 9. †**give into** yield to, give in to. **give it (hot, hot and strong) to** administer punishment to. *give mouth*: see MOUTH *n. give occasion to*: see OCCASION *n.* **give of oneself** act unselfishly, devote oneself to a specified person or thing. *give oneself airs*: see AIR *n.*[1] 10. *give one's hand*: see HAND *n. give one's heart to*: see HEART *n. give one's love to*: see LOVE *n. give one's mind to*: see MIND *n.*[1] *give one's word*: see WORD *n.* **give or take** *colloq.* add or subtract (a quantity etc.) in estimating. *give pause to*: see PAUSE *n. give place to*: see PLACE *n.*[1] *give rein* (*to*): see REIN *n.*[1] *give rise to*: see RISE *n.* **give something to cry about, for** chastise (esp. a child) for causeless crying. *give suck*: see SUCK *v. give thanks*: see THANK *n. give the Devil his due*: see DUE *n.* 2. *give the finger to*: see FINGER *n. give the gun*: see GUN *n. give the guy to*: see GUY *n.*[2] *give the lie to*: see LIE *n.*[1] *give the long handle*: see HANDLE *n.*[1] *give thought to*: see THOUGHT *n.*[1] **give to know** inform, assure. *give tongue*: see TONGUE *n.* **give to understand** inform, assure. *give vent to*: see VENT *n.*[2] 3. *give way*: see WAY *n.* **give what for** *slang* punish or scold (a person) severely. *not to give a hang*: see HANG *n.* **would give anything, one's ears, one's eyes, one's eye-teeth, the world**, etc., would make any sacrifice *for*, *if*, *to do*.

With advs. in specialized senses: **give about** *arch.* circulate (writings etc.), spread (a rumour etc.). **give again** (*obs.* exc. *dial.*) soften, yield. **give away** (*a*) transfer by gift, dispose of as a present; hand over (a bride) ceremonially to a bridegroom; *give away with a pound, a packet, of tea*, part with cheaply, regard as worthless; †(*b*) sacrifice (another's interest or rights); (*c*) betray or expose to ridicule or detection, let slip inadvertently; *give the game away*: see GAME *n.*; *give the* (*whole*) *show away*: see SHOW *n.*[1]; (*d*) distribute, present, (prizes etc.); (*e*) *Austral. slang* abandon, give up, stop, (chiefly in *give it away*); (*f*) (now *US*) give way. **give back** (*a*) return (a thing) to a previous owner or in exchange, return, restore; reflect, echo; †(*b*) retreat, fall back. **give down** (of a cow) let flow (milk), give milk. **give forth** (*a*) emit; (*b*) publish, report. **give in** (*a*) yield (*to*), concede defeat (*to*); stop fighting or arguing; (*b*) hand in (a document etc.) to a proper official. **give off** †(*a*) relinquish, leave off (something); cease, quit the field; (*b*) emit (a smell, vapour, etc., light, noise); (*c*) send out as a branch or other outgrowth. **give out** (*a*) announce, proclaim, profess, (*that*, *to be*); publish; (*b*) emit; (*c*) issue, distribute; (*d*) desist, now esp. through exhaustion or lack of patience; break down; run short, come to an end. **give over** (*a*) cease from (an action, *doing*); abandon (a habit etc.); cease, desist; (*b*) devote, surrender, hand over, (*to*); *arch.* = *give up* (h) below. **give up** (*a*) hand over, part with, resign, surrender; deliver (a fugitive etc.) into the hands of pursuers; abandon (oneself) *to* a feeling or influence; (*b*) relinquish the prospect of, cease to have to do with, cease from (an action, *doing*); (*c*) cease from effort, stop trying; succumb; (*d*) devote entirely *to* (chiefly *refl.* or in *pass.*); †(*e*) deliver (an account etc.); present (a petition etc.); (*f*) emit, breathe forth, (now only in *give up the ghost* s.v. GHOST *n.*); (*g*) divulge, reveal; (*h*) pronounce incurable or insoluble, abandon hope for or of; (foll. by *for*) abandon hope for as (dead, lost, etc.); (foll. by *on*) lose one's belief or trust in, forsake, abandon.

giveable *a.* (*rare*) capable of giving or yielding L19.

give and take /ɡɪv (ə)n(d) ˈteɪk/ *a.* & *n.* Also (esp. as adj.) **give-and-take**. M18. [f. *give and take* s.v. GIVE *v.*] **A** *adj.* (usu. *attrib.*). **1** *Hist.* Designating a horse race in which horses above a standard height carried more weight and those below the standard carried less. M18. **2** Involving give and take. E19. **B** *n.* **1** Mutual yielding, compromise. L18. **2** Exchange of words, repartee. M19.

giveaway /ˈɡɪvəweɪ/ *n.* & *a. colloq.* Also **give-away**. L19. [f. *give away* s.v. GIVE *v.*] **A** *n.* **1** The action or an act of giving a present etc. away; a free gift; a low price; a game in which the object is to make an opponent lose points, (in chess etc.) capture pieces, etc. L19. **2** The action or an act of giving a secret etc. away; an inadvertent betrayal; a person who or thing which betrays inadvertently. L19.

1 *Listener* A host of special offers and giveaways. *Bird Watching* The land giveaway may continue. 2 J. DIDION It was the giveaway, the proof of how she felt. **dead giveaway** a complete betrayal.

B *attrib.* or as *adj.* **1** Involving giving something away; given away, distributed free. L19. **2** That betrays someone or something inadvertently; revealing. M20.

1 *Times* Giveaway newspapers and free local directories are now Britain's fastest-growing media. 2 G. SWIFT It is impossible to climb those . . steps without a give-away medley of creaks.

giveback /ˈɡɪvbak/ *n.* Chiefly *US.* L20. [f. *give back* s.v. GIVE *v.*] A refund; a concession; *spec.* a giving up by workers in industry of benefits and conditions previously agreed or accepted.

given /ˈɡɪv(ə)n/ *ppl a.* & *n.* LME. [pa. pple of GIVE *v.*] **A** *ppl a.* **1** Usu. *attrib.* That has been given; handed over, conferred, or bestowed as a gift; assigned or posited as a basis for calculation or reasoning, fixed, specified. Also foll. by adv. LME. **b** Of a personal name: chosen for the particular individual and conferred at birth, baptism, etc. E19. **2** *pred.* Inclined, disposed, prone, *to* (or †*absol.*). LME.

1 DICKENS The second hand took the risk out of the given-out work. *Daily News* Given goods never prosper. B. MOORE How many there were on any given weekend. b P. ROTH One of the few remaining professors who address students . . as 'Mr.' and 'Miss', rather than by their given names. 2 E. WHARTON He . . was given to telling anecdotes about his children. J. RATHBONE Something of a blue-stocking, given to books. A. BROOKNER A type of emotional gangster, given to hijackings and other acts of terrorism.

B *n.* What is given; a known fact or situation. L19.

J. CARROLL He had no need to establish his standing. . . His standing was a given. E. JONG I feel . . as if I've been set adrift, as if all the givens of my life have suddenly changed.

givenness /-n-n-/ *n.* M19.

giver /ˈɡɪvə/ *n.* ME. [f. GIVE *v.* + -ER[1].] A person who gives. Freq. as 2nd elem. of comb. Also foll. by adv.

Indian giver: see INDIAN *a.*

give-up /ˈɡɪvʌp/ *n. US.* L19. [f. *give up* s.v. GIVE *v.*] **1** The action or an act of giving up; relinquishment; a concession. L19. **2** *Stock Exch.* A broker's revealing of the name of the principal in a transaction, who is obliged to complete the transaction. M20.

givey /ˈɡɪvi/ *a. dial.* & *colloq.* Also **givy**. E19. [f. GIVE *v.* + -Y[1].] Inclined to give or yield; pliable, springy, soft.

giving /ˈɡɪvɪŋ/ *vbl n.* LME. [f. GIVE *v.* + -ING[1].] **1** The action of GIVE *v.*; an instance of this. Also foll. by adv. LME. **2** A thing given, a gift. LME.

1 ADDISON Upon the first Giving of the Weather. W. ROBERTSON When the spirit of giving was substituted for the spirit of mere rivalry. *Daily News* The cruiser . . having broken down through the giving out of her cylinders.

Comb.: **giving-set** an apparatus for giving blood-transfusions, drips, etc.

givy *a.* var. of GIVEY.

gizmo *n.* var. of GISMO.

gizz /dʒɪz/ *n. Sc.* Now *rare* or *obs.* Also (earlier) †**jeezy**. L17. [Origin unkn.] A wig. Also, the face.

gizzard /ˈɡɪzəd/ *n.* LME. [OFr. *giser*, *gesier*, *juisier* (mod. *gésier*) f. Proto-Romance alt. of L *gigeria* n. the cooked entrails of a fowl.] **1** The thick-walled second region of a bird's stomach, in which food is ground, often together with small stones or grit. LME. **b** The muscular grinding stomach of some fishes, insects, molluscs, etc. L18. **2** *gen.* The stomach, the entrails; the throat. Freq. *joc.* M17.

2 K. S. MACQUOID Pick a quarrel and . . run him through the gizzard. **stick in one's gizzard** be distasteful, remain as something distasteful.

Comb.: **gizzard trout** = GILLAROO.

gjetost /ˈjɛtɒst/ *n.* E20. [Norw., f. *gjet*, *geit* goat + *ost* cheese.] A Norwegian cheese made from goat's milk.

glabella /ɡləˈbɛlə/ *n.* Pl. **-llae** /-liː/. E19. [mod.L use as n. of L adj., dim. of *glaber*: see GLABROUS.] **1** *Anat.* The smooth area of the forehead between the eyebrows; the underlying smooth projection of the frontal bone (used as a reference point in skull measurements). E19. **2** *Zool.* The smooth median portion of the cephalic shield of a trilobite. M19.

glabellar *a.* of or pertaining to the glabella E19.

glabrate /ˈɡleɪbrət, ˈɡlabreɪt/ *a.* M19. [L *glabratus* pa. pple of *glabrare* make bald, f. *glaber*: see GLABROUS, -ATE[2].] *Bot.* & *Zool.* Glabrous; glabrescent.

glabrescent /gleɪˈbrɛs(ə)nt, glə-/ *a.* M19. [f. L *glabrescere* become smooth, f. as next: see -ESCENT.] *Bot.* Of a surface: hairy when young but smooth when mature.

glabrous /ˈgleɪbrəs/ *a.* M17. [f. L *glabr-*, *glaber* hairless, smooth + -OUS.] Esp. of the skin or a leaf: free from hair or down, smooth.

D. OLIVER Foliage-leaves . . may be hairy, or nearly glabrous, that is, destitute of hairs. J. BARNES He was in his early forties, balding with a pinky glabrous complexion.

†glace *v.* see GLEASE.

glacé /ˈglaseɪ/ *a.* & *n.* M19. [Fr., pa. pple of *glacer* ice, give a gloss to, f. *glace* ice.] **A** *adj.* **1** Of cloth, leather, etc.: smooth, highly polished, glossy. M19. **2** Of fruit: covered with icing or sugar. Of icing: made with icing sugar and water. L19. **B** *n.* Glacé silk, glacé leather. M19.

glacial /ˈgleɪʃ(ə)l, -sɪəl/ *a.* & *n.* M17. [Fr., or L *glacialis* icy, f. *glacies* ice: see -AL^1.] **A** *adj.* **1** Of the nature of ice; (partly) consisting of ice; cold, icy, freezing (*lit.* & *fig.*). M17. **2** *Chem.* Crystalline (*arch.*); (esp. of pure acids) tending to form crystals resembling ice. Now chiefly in *glacial acetic acid.* M17. **3** *Geol.* Characterized or produced by the presence or agency of ice in the form of glaciers; pertaining to glaciers. M19. **4** Of movement, progress: resembling that of a glacier, very slow. E20.

1 W. GOLDING We were too angry . . for anything but the stiffest and most glacial farewell. C. THUBRON Central Siberia, bounded by the glacial waters of the Arctic Ocean. **3** J. MONTAGUE The only beauty nearby is a small glacial lake sheltering between drumlin moons of mountains. **glacial epoch, period**: during which glaciers covered a large part of the earth's surface, esp. the Pleistocene epoch. **4** D. ACHESON Negotiations with the Swiss moved at their glacial rate.

B *n.* A glacial epoch or period. M20.

glacialist *n.* a person who studies ice and esp. its action as a cause of certain geological phenomena M19. **glacially** *adv.* M19.

glaciarium /gleɪʃɪˈɛːrɪəm/ *n. rare* exc. *Hist.* M19. [f. L *glacies* ice + -ARIUM.] A skating-rink with artificially produced ice.

glaciate /ˈgleɪsɪeɪt/ *v.* E17. [L *glaciat-* pa. ppl stem of *glaciare* freeze, f. *glacies* ice: see -ATE^3.] **1** *v.t.* & *i.* Freeze. Long *rare* or *obs.* (chiefly in Dicts.). E17. **2** *v.t. Geol.* Mark or polish by the action of ice; cover with glaciers or ice sheets. Chiefly as *glaciated* ppl a. M19.

2 F. HOYLE Ice ages are not all-or-nothing affairs that glaciate the entire earth.

glaciˈation *n.* †(*a*) (a result of) the process of freezing; (*b*) *Geol.* the action, condition, or result of being covered by glaciers or ice sheets: M17.

glacier /ˈglasɪə, ˈgleɪs-/ *n.* M18. [Fr. (earlier *glacière*), f. *glace* ice, f. Proto-Romance alt. of L *glacies* ice: see -IER.] A slowly moving mass or river of ice formed by accumulation and compaction of snow on higher ground.

hanging glacier: see HANGING *a.*

Comb.: **glacier burst** the sudden release of water impounded by a glacier; **glacier mill** = MOULIN; **glacier snow**: at the upper end of a glacier, not yet compacted into ice.

glaciered *a.* covered with glaciers E19. **glacieˈret** *n.* a small alpine glacier L19. **glacieriˈzation** *n.* (*a*) *rare* conversion into a glacier; (*b*) the covering of land by an ice sheet; the state of being so covered: M19.

glacio- /ˈgleɪsɪəʊ, ˈgleɪʃɪəʊ/ *comb. form* of GLACIER: see -O-.

glacio-ˈeustasy *n.* = GLACIO-EUSTATISM M20. **glacio-euˈstatic** *a.* of or pertaining to glacio-eustatism M20. **glacio-ˈeustatism** *n.* changes in sea level caused by the waxing and waning of ice sheets M20. **glacioˈfluvial** *a.* = FLUVIOGLACIAL E20; **glaciolaˈcustrine** *a.* of or pertaining to a lake or lakes deriving water from the melting of ice E20.

glaciology /gleɪsɪˈɒlədʒi/ *n.* L19. [f. GLACIO- + -LOGY.] The science of the geological action of ice.

glacioˈlogical *a.* L19. **glaciologist** *n.* L19.

glacis /ˈglasɪs, -si/ *n.* Pl. same /-sɪz, -siːz/. L17. [Fr., f. OFr. *glacier* to slip, slide, f. *glace*: see GLACIER.] **1** A gently sloping bank; *spec.* in *Fortif.*, a natural or artificial bank sloping down from the covered way of a fort so as to expose attackers to the defenders' missiles etc. L17. **b** *fig.* A zone or area, *esp.* a small country, acting as a protective barrier or buffer between two (potentially) enemy countries. M20. **2** In full *glacis-plate.* A sloping armour-plate protecting an opening etc. in a ship. L19.

glad /glad/ *n.*^{1} OE. [f. the adj.] **†1** Gladness, joy (surviving as a first element in *gladful, gladless*, etc.) OE–E17. **2** = *the glad eye* s.v. GLAD *a.* E20.

glad /glad/ *n.*^{2} *colloq.* E20. [Abbrev.] = GLADIOLUS.

glad /glad/ *a.* & *adv.* [OE *glæd* = OS *glad* (only in *gladmōd*), ON *glaðr* bright, joyous, OHG *glat* (G *glatt*) smooth, f. Gmc base rel. to L *glaber* smooth, GLABROUS.] **A** *adj.* Compar. & superl. **-dd-**. **†1** Bright, shining, beautiful. (Cf. sense 6.) OE–L15. **2** Of a person: having a naturally cheerful or happy disposition; joyful, happy. *arch.* OE. **3** Orig., delighted, filled with joy by something particular. Now only (*pred.*) in weakened sense, made happy or pleased. (Foll. by *about*, (arch.) *at, for, of, that, to do.*) OE. **4** (Of a feeling, a look, an action, etc.) filled with, marked by, or expressing joy; (of news) causing joy. OE. **†b** Welcome, acceptable. L16–L17. **5** Of a door, bolt, etc.: working smoothly and easily. *dial.* M16. **6** Esp. of a natural object: full of brightness or beauty; cheering. M17.

2 WORDSWORTH Often, glad no more, We wear a face of joy, because We have been glad of yore. **3** H. JAMES It was a happy chance—he was uncommonly glad to see him. E. WAUGH Come in, come in. I'm very glad you've come. S. HILL I don't need them yet but when the weather gets colder . . I shall be pretty glad of them. R. CARVER He turned off the radio and was glad for the privacy. A. MUNRO He stopped saying such things and she was glad. **4** AV *Luke* 8:1 He went throughout euery citie and village preaching, and shewing the glad tidings of the kingdome of God. R. KIPLING He bought sweetmeats . . from a Hindu trader, and ate them with glad rapture. **6** LYTTON The glad sun rising gorgeously from the hills revived his wearied spirit. C. BRONTË What a living spring! What a warm, glad summer!

Phrases, special collocations, & comb.: **glad-hand** *v.t.* & *i.* greet or welcome (someone) cordially (freq. *iron.*). **glad rags** *colloq.* best clothes, evening dress. **the glad eye** *colloq.* an amorous glance. **the glad hand** (freq. *iron.*) a cordial handshake, greeting, or welcome (freq. in *give the glad hand*).

B *adv.* Compar. & superl. **-dd-**. Gladly. *poet.* ME.

glad /glad/ *v.* Infl. **-dd-**. [OE *gladian* = ON *glaða*, f. Gmc base of GLAD *a.*] **†1** *v.i.* Be or become glad; rejoice. Foll. by *on, in, of, for.* OE–E17. **2** *v.t.* Make glad; cause to rejoice. *arch.* or *poet.* OE.

gladden *n.* var. of GLADDON.

gladden /ˈglad(ə)n/ *v.* LME. [f. GLAD *a.* + -EN^5.] **1** *v.i.* Be or become glad, rejoice. Long *rare* bef. E19. LME. **2** *v.t.* Make glad. M16.

1 WORDSWORTH That all the Alps may gladden in thy might. **2** J. RUSKIN [An orchard] which was gladdened . . by flushes of almond and . . peach blossom.

gladdener *n.* L19.

gladdie /ˈgladi/ *n. Austral. colloq.* L20. [f. GLAD *n.*^{2} + -IE.] = GLAD *n.*^{2}

gladdon /ˈglad(ə)n/ *n.* Now chiefly *dial.* Also **gladden, gladwin, -wyn.** [OE *glædene* f. pop.L alt. of L GLADIOLUS.] A plant of the iris family, *Iris foetidissima*, of western Europe and N. Africa, having purplish flowers and an unpleasant odour when bruised (also called *stinking gladdon, stinking iris*). Formerly also, any of various plants with long, sword-shaped leaves, *esp.* yellow flag, sweet flag, or reed mace.

†glade *n.*^{1} ME–L18. [Perh. of Scand. origin: cf. Sw. dial. *gladas*, *gla(d)na* (of the sun) to set, Norw. dial. *gla* (of the sun and moon) to set.] *go to glade*, (of the sun) set.

glade /gleɪd/ *n.*^{2} LME. [Origin uncertain: cf. GLAD *a.* 1.] **1** A clear open space or passage between the trees in a wood, either naturally or artificially produced. LME. **†2** A clear or bright space between clouds in the sky; a flash or gleam of light. LME–M18. **3** A marshy area of low-lying grass-covered land. *US.* M17. **4** An unfrozen part or a break or opening in the ice of a stretch of water. *local* (*US*). L17.

Special collocations: **glade mallow** *US* a tall plant of the mallow family, *Napaea dioica*, of the eastern US, having small white flowers.

gladful /ˈgladfʊl, -f(ə)l/ *a. arch.* ME. [f. GLAD *n.*^{1} + -FUL.] Full of gladness, joyful.

¶Rare after L16.

gladfully *adv.* LME. **gladfulness** *n.* L16.

gladiate /ˈgleɪdɪət/ *a.* L18. [f. L *gladius* sword + -ATE^2.] *Bot.* Sword-shaped.

gladiator /ˈgladɪeɪtə/ *n.* LME. [L *gladiator*, f. *gladius* sword: see -ATOR.] **1** *Rom. Hist.* A man, usu. a slave or captive criminal, trained to fight with a sword or other weapon against other men similarly trained or wild animals, in combats freq. to the death, staged for public entertainment. LME. **†b** A professional swordsman or fencer. E17–M18. **2** A person who disputes with another esp. publicly in support of a political etc. cause. M17.

2 H. H. ASQUITH Huxley, the young gladiator of Evolution.

gladiaˈtorial *a.* (*a*) of or pertaining to a gladiator; (*b*) (of debate) contentious: M18. **†gladiatorian** *a.* of, pertaining to, or resembling a gladiator L17–M18. **gladiatorism** *n.* (now *rare*) gladiatorial fighting or arguing M19. **gladiatorship** *n.* the occupation or skill of a gladiator E19. **†gladiatory** *a.* = GLADIATORIAL E17–M18.

gladiolus /gladɪˈəʊləs/ *n.* Pl. **-li** /-lʌɪ, -liː/, **-luses.** Also **gladiole** /ˈgladɪəʊl/. OE. [L, dim. of *gladius* sword.] **1** Any of numerous plants constituting the genus *Gladiolus*, of the iris family, native to Eurasia and (chiefly) Africa, having erect sword-shaped leaves and spikes of (often brilliantly coloured) flowers, including many cultivars of mainly southern African origin; a flowering stem of such a plant. Formerly also, the gladdon. Cf. *corn-flag* s.v. CORN *n.*^{1} OE. **2** *Anat.* The large middle section of the sternum. L19.

gladius /ˈgleɪdɪəs/ *n.* E16. [L = sword.] **†1** A swordfish. Only in E16. **2** The horny, feather-shaped internal shell of a squid. Also called *pen.* L19.

gladless /ˈgladlɪs/ *a. rare.* E16. [f. GLAD *n.*^{1} + -LESS.] Joyless.

gladly /ˈgladli/ *a. arch.* OE. [f. as prec. + -LY^1.] **†1** Bright, beautiful, splendid. Only in OE. **2** Glad, joyful. OE.

gladly /ˈgladli/ *adv.* OE. [f. GLAD *a.* + -LY^2.] **1** With joy or pleasure. Freq. also in weakened sense, willingly, with alacrity. OE. **†2** Readily, easily; usually, regularly; habitually and with enjoyment. LME–L15.

1 SCOTT FITZGERALD I would gladly welcome any alienist you might suggest. P. LIVELY She could gladly hit him, lolling there complacent on the sofa. **2** CHAUCER Thise olde wommen, that been gladly wyse As is hir maistresse. CAXTON Where as ben corners there is gladly filth.

gladness /ˈgladnɪs/ *n.* OE. [f. GLAD *a.* + -NESS.] The state of being glad; (a) joy. Formerly also, alacrity.

gladsome /ˈglads(ə)m/ *a.* Now *poet.* or *arch.* LME. [Orig. f. GLAD *n.*^{1}; later regarded as f. GLAD *a.*: see -SOME^1.] **1** = GLAD *a.* 2, 3. LME. **2** = GLAD *a.* 4. LME. **3** = GLAD *a.* 6. E16.

gladsomely *adv.* LME. **gladsomeness** *n.* LME.

Gladstone /ˈgladst(ə)n/ *n.* M19. [William Ewart *Gladstone* (1809–98), Brit. statesman.] **1** *Hist.* Cheap French wine, imports of which greatly increased as a result of Gladstone's reduction in Customs duty. Also *Gladstone claret.* M19. **2** In full *Gladstone bag.* A light portmanteau opening into two equal compartments. L19.

Gladstonian /gladˈstəʊnɪən/ *a.* & *n.* M19. [f. prec. + -IAN.] **A** *adj.* Of, pertaining to, or characteristic of Gladstone or his policies. M19.

C. R. ATTLEE My father was a Gladstonian Liberal but the rest of the family was Conservative. A. J. P. TAYLOR Arthur Rowntree had a Gladstonian air and a Gladstonian way of speaking.

B *n. Hist.* A supporter of Gladstone or his policies. M19.

Gladstonianism *n.* the principles or policies of Gladstone, esp. as relating to the establishment of Home Rule in Ireland M19.

Gladstonism /ˈgladstənɪz(ə)m/ *n.* L19. [f. as prec. + -ISM.] = GLADSTONIANISM *n.*

Gladstonite *n.* = GLADSTONIAN *n.* L19.

gladwin, gladwyn *ns.* vars. of GLADDON.

glady /ˈgleɪdi/ *a.* L18. [f. GLADE *n.*[2] + -Y[1].] Full of glades; of, pertaining to, or resembling a glade.

Glagolitic /glagəˈlɪtɪk/ *a.* E19. [mod.L *glagoliticus*, f. Serbo-Croat *glagòljica* the Glagolitic alphabet f. Old Ch. Slav. *glagolŭ* word.] Of, pertaining to, or designating the Old Slavonic alphabet (ascribed to St Cyril and long superseded by Cyrillic), retained in the liturgy of some Roman Catholic Churches in Dalmatia, Montenegro, etc.

glaik /gleɪk/ *n. Sc.* E16. [Origin uncertain: cf. GLEEK *n.*[2]] †1 In *pl.* Tricks, pranks; mocking deceptions. E16–L19. 2 A foolish person. *contempt.* M16. †3 In *pl.* Interlocking pieces of wood, linked rings, etc., forming a puzzle or toy. L16–L19. †4 A dazzling flash of light. L18–E20.

glaikit /ˈgleɪkɪt/ *a. Sc.* & *north.* LME. [Rel. to prec.] Slow-witted, stupid. Also, thoughtless, flighty.

glaikitly *adv.* (*rare*) M19. **glaikitness** *n.* LME.

glair /glɛː/ *n.* & *v.* As n. also (earlier) **glaire**. ME. [(O)Fr. *glaire* f. med.L *glarea* f. var. of med.L use as n. of L *clarus* clear.] A *n.* 1 The white of an egg, esp. as used in various preparations; *spec.* in *Bookbinding*, an adhesive made from this applied before blocking or tooling in gold leaf. ME. 2 Any slimy viscous substance resembling egg-white. E16. B *v.t.* Orig., paint, daub. Later, smear with glair. M16.

glaireous *a.* of the nature of glair; slimy, viscous: M17. **glairy** *a.* (freq. in *Med.*) = GLAIREOUS M17.

glaistig /ˈglastɪk/ *n.* Also **glastick**. E20. [Gael.] A fairy with a variety of forms and characters, freq. appearing in the shape of a goat or as half-woman, half-goat, but also as a beautiful water-sprite.

glaive /gleɪv/ *n.* ME. [(O)Fr. (also †*glavie*) †lance, sword, app. f. L *gladius* sword.] †1 A weapon consisting of a blade or sharp point fixed to a long handle; a lance; a halberd. ME–L17. b A lance set up as the winning-post in a race and freq. given as a prize to the winner; *gen.* a prize. LME–M16. 2 A sword; *esp.* a broadsword. *arch.* or *poet.* L15. 3 A fish-spear. Chiefly *dial.* M17.

1 S. BUTLER Zeal, with aged clubs and gleaves Gave chase. 2 C. BOWEN [He] girds on the Achæan's glittering glaive. 3 G. SWIFT He would catch eels.. with a long, many-bladed spear called a glaive.

glam /glam/ *n.*[1] *obs.* exc. *dial.* LME. [ON *glam(m)* noise, din (Sw. *glam* merriment, loud mirth, Da. *glam* barking of dogs etc.), prob. of imit. origin.] A loud noise esp. of talking or merrymaking; a din, a clamour.

glam /glam/ *n.*[2] In sense 1 also **glaum**. L16. [Var. of CLAM *n.*[1] Cf. GLAND *n.*[3]] 1 In *pl.* The iron jaws of a vice; a clamp. *Sc.* L16. 2 The hand. *north.* M19.

glam /glam/ *n.*[3] *colloq.* M20. [Abbrev.] = GLAMOUR.

glam /glam/ *a. colloq.* M20. [Abbrev.] = GLAMOROUS.

glam /glam/ *v.*[1]*t. colloq.* Infl. **-mm-**. M20. [Abbrev.] = GLAMORIZE. (Foll. by *up.*)

glam *v.*[2] see GLAUM *v.*

glamorize /ˈglaməraɪz/ *v.t.* Orig. *US.* Also **-ise, -our-**. M20. [f. GLAMOUR *n.* + -IZE.] Make glamorous or attractive.

glamoriˈzation *n.* M20.

glamour /ˈglamə/ *n.* & *v.* Orig. *Sc.* Also ***-mor**. E18. [Alt. of GRAMMAR with the sense of GRAMARYE. For the form with *gl-* cf. med.L *glomeria* grammar, *glomerellus* a schoolboy learning grammar.] A *n.* 1 Magic, enchantment. E18. 2 (A) deceptive or bewitching beauty or charm; (a) mysteriously exciting or alluring physical attractiveness, esp. when artificially contrived. M19.

1 TENNYSON That maiden in the tale, Whom Gwydion made by glamour out of flowers. **cast the glamour over** enchant, bewitch. 2 F. RAPHAEL But Isidore's offences were sordid and commercial, quite without glamour. M. AYRTON He has an animal magnetism, or a glamour at once insupportable but compelling. *attrib.*: *Times* A glamour stock with large amounts of highly rated paper.

Comb.: **glamour boy, girl**: possessing glamour; **glamour puss** *slang* a glamorous person.

B *v.t.* 1 Enchant, bewitch. E18. 2 Glamorize. Foll. by *up. colloq.* M20.

1 R. GRAVES Woman and tree prove of a stuff Wholly to glamour his wild heart? 2 L. HOBSON It's lost some of the subtlety of the book.. and they've glamoured it up a little too much.

glamorous *a.* full of glamour L19. **glamorously** *adv.* L19.

glamoury /ˈglaməri/ *n.* Chiefly *Sc.* Also **-rie**. M18. [Var. of GLAMOUR *n.*; for ending cf. GRAMARYE.] = GLAMOUR *n.* 1.

glance /glɑːns/ *n.*[1] E16. [f. GLANCE *v.*] 1 A sudden movement producing a flash or gleam (of light); a flash, a gleam. E16. 2 A swift oblique movement or impact. Now *rare.* L16. b *Cricket.* More fully *leg glance.* A stroke made with the bat's face turned slantwise to deflect the ball. L19. 3 A brief or hurried look (*at, into, over,* etc.). Also, a gaze. L16. †4 An allusion or reference, *esp.* a satirical or jesting one. E17–E18.

1 SIR W. SCOTT The silver light, with quivering glance, Played on the water's still expanse. 2 H. L'ESTRANGE Though these speeches did not take their aime directly at his Majesty, yet did they by glance and obliquely deeply wound him. 3 R. MACAULAY Sir Gulliver's experienced eyes, in one glance, summed his daughter up. J. THURBER We exchanged a brief, knowing masculine glance of private understanding. R. INGALLS Flora's glance flickered lightly over the other people. **at a glance** immediately upon looking. *throw a glance*: see THROW *v.* 4 BACON Not knowing where to carp at him.. he gave a glance at his patience towards his wife.

glance /glɑːns/ *n.*[2] LME. [G *Glanz* (Du. *glans*) lustre: cf. Du. *glanserts* glance ore.] Orig. †*glance ore.* Any of various metallic ores, chiefly sulphides, with a grey or black lustre.

antimony glance, bismuth glance, copper glance, iron glance, lead glance, silver glance.

Comb.: **glance coal**: of high lustre (esp. anthracite); *glance ore*: see above; **glance pitch** a brilliant black variety of bitumen.

glance /glɑːns/ *v.* LME. [Prob. alt. of †*glace* vb (see GLEASE), infl. by GLENT *v.*, LANCE *v.*] 1 *v.i.* Of a weapon, tool, etc.: glide or slip *off* an object instead of striking it squarely. LME. 2 *v.i.* Move, usu. rapidly, in an oblique direction; go off at a tangent; spring *aside.* LME. 3 *v.i.* Orig., shine. Later, cause a flash of light by rapid movement; (of a bright object or light) flash, dart, gleam. M16. 4 *v.i.* Of a discussion, a speaker, etc.: pass quickly *over*, glide *off* or *from* a subject. L16. b Foll. by *at, (up)on,* †*against*: allude or refer to in passing, esp. sarcastically. L16. 5 *v.i.* Of the eye, a person looking: cast a swift brief look (*at*); look quickly or read hurriedly or cursorily *over* or *through.* L16. 6 *v.t.* Orig., allude to. Later, graze, barely touch. L16. 7 *v.t.* a Orig., turn (one's gaze) aside as when dazzled. Later, direct (one's eye) quickly *over* or *at* an object. Chiefly in *glance one's eye.* L16. b Survey with a glance or glances; catch a glimpse of. Now *rare* or *obs.* M17. c Convey with a glance or glances (of the eye). Now *rare.* E18. 8 *v.t.* Direct obliquely. Also, emit with a flash or gleam; reflect *back.* Now *rare.* M17. b *v.t.* & *i. Cricket.* Deflect (the ball) with the bat's face turned slantwise. Also, strike the ball in this way off (the bowler). L19.

1 SIR W. SCOTT The blow only glanced on the bone, and scarce drew blood. E. BIRNEY His axe glanced from a frosted branch and sank in his boot. 2 T. BLACKBURN Strange it is, since there's no fences, I do not take the path which glances Aside from this. 3 E. BOWEN The light glanced on Hilary's waved and burnished hair. 4 O. W. HOLMES I glanced off, as one often does in talk. b SWIFT Verses.. wherein he glanced at a certain reverend doctor. 5 J. CONRAD He sniffed from time to time, glancing out of the corners of his.. eyes. A. GUINNESS Down the Grand Canal in a gondola.. never once so much as glancing at the Venetian palaces. 8 W. DAMPIER Strike their Harpoons.. aside, or so glance them as to kill nothing.

glancer *n.* M16. **glancingly** *adv.* in a glancing manner M16.

gland /gland/ *n.*[1] Now *rare* or *obs.* LME. [Fr., or directly f. L *glans, gland-* acorn.] 1 An acorn or similar nut. Cf. GLANS 2. LME. 2 = GLANS 1. M19. 3 *Hist.* An acorn-shaped ball of lead used as a missile. M19.

gland /gland/ *n.*[2] L17. [Fr. *glande*, alt. of OFr. *glandre*: see GLANDER.] 1 *Anat.* & *Zool.* Any cell or organ which synthesizes and secretes some particular chemical substance or substances for use by the body or for excretion. Also (now *loosely*), an organ resembling a gland; *esp.* a lymph node. Cf. ENDOCRINE, EXOCRINE. L17. 2 *Bot.* Any of various (groups of) cells on or within a plant structure which secrete some particular substance or substances (e.g. oils, nectar, etc.). Also, any small protuberance like a gland. L18.

1 *mammary gland, monkey gland, scent gland, thyroid gland, Tyson's gland,* etc.

¶The glands were orig. characterized as extracting substances from the blood, a wider definition which included the lymph nodes. Cf. GLANDULE.

glandiform *a.* resembling a gland E19. **glandlike** *a.* = GLANDIFORM M19.

gland /gland/ *n.*[3] E19. [Prob. var. of GLAM *n.*[2]] A sleeve which fits around a piston rod or other shaft to form a seal, esp. by compressing a packing around the rod.

glander /ˈglandə/ *n.* L15. [OFr. *glandre* f. L *glandulae* pl., throat glands, swollen glands in the neck: see GLANDULE.] †1 A glandular swelling about the neck. L15–E16. 2 In *pl.* (treated as *sing.*; often with *the*). An infectious fatal disease of horses, donkeys, etc. (also transmissible to humans), caused by the bacterium *Actinobacillus mallei*, and characterized by inflammation or ulceration of the nasal mucous membranes and lymph nodes, and nodule formation in the lungs, spleen, etc. E16.

glandered *a.* affected with glanders M17. **glanderous** *a.* affected with, or of the nature of, glanders E18.

glandes *n.* pl. of GLANS.

glandiferous /glanˈdɪf(ə)rəs/ *a.* M17. [f. L *glandifer* (f. *glans, gland-* acorn) + -OUS: see -FEROUS.] Bearing acorns or similar fruit.

glandular /ˈglandjʊlə, ˈglan(d)ʒʊlə/ *a.* M18. [Fr. *glandulaire*, f. *glandule* GLANDULE: see -AR[1].] Of or pertaining to a gland; containing, bearing, or functioning as, a gland or glands.

glandular fever an infectious viral disease characterized by fever, inflammation of the lymph nodes, and abnormal lymphocytes; also called *infectious mononucleosis.*

glandulation /glandjʊˈleɪʃ(ə)n, glan(d)ʒʊ-/ *n.* M18. [f. as next: see -ATION.] *Bot.* The disposition of glandular cells or tissues in a plant.

glandule /ˈglandjuːl/ *n.* LME. [Fr., or directly f. L *glandula* (usu. in pl.) glands in the neck, tonsils (dim. of *glans, gland-* acorn): see -ULE.] †1 *Med.* & *Vet.* A gland; *esp.* a lymph node (usu. in *pl.*). LME–M18. †2 *Med.* & *Vet.* A swelling of the lymph nodes in the neck (usu. in *pl.*). Cf. GLANDER. LME–E17. †b *Med.* Any rounded swelling in the body. *rare.* LME–M19. 3 *Zool.* & *Bot.* A small gland, esp. in certain fungi and orchids. M18.

glanduˈliferous *a.* bearing glands or glandules E18.

glandulose /ˈglandjʊləʊs, ˈglan(d)ʒʊ-/ *a.* M19. [L *glandulosus*: see GLANDULOUS.] *Bot.* Bearing glands or formations like glands.

glandulous /ˈglandjʊləs, ˈglan(d)ʒʊ-/ *a.* LME. [(O)Fr. *glanduleux*, or directly f. L *glandulosus*, f. *glandula* GLANDULE: see -ULOUS.] 1 Of or pertaining to a gland or glandule; containing, bearing, or functioning as a gland or glands. LME. 2 *Bot.* Glandulose. L18.

glans /glanz/ *n.* Pl. **glandes** /ˈglandiːz/. M17. [L.] 1 *Anat.* A small conical or acorn-shaped structure, *esp.* that at the end of the mammalian penis (more fully *glans penis*) or clitoris (more fully *glans clitoridis*). M17. 2 *Bot.* A unicellular nut having the base enclosed in a cupule, as the acorn, beech mast, etc. E18.

glare /glɛː/ *n.*[1] LME. [f. the vb.] **1** Dazzling brilliance (of a light, the sun, etc.); a strong fierce light; *spec.* oppressive unrelieved sunshine. LME. **b** The glistening or shining of some surface. M17. **2** A fierce, esp. fixed, look or stare. M17. **3** Showy appearance; gaudiness; tawdry brilliance. E18.

1 A. B. EDWARDS A little before midday, when the heat and glare were becoming intolerable. S. LEACOCK I turned up the lights and the bright glare revealed . . the tattered figure. *fig.*: *Blitz* The 74-year-old GP scrupulously keeps himself away from the glare of publicity. 2 CONAN DOYLE His face turned upon us with a glare of baffled rage. R. HOLMES Eyes . . staring straight out at the onlooker with a glare of absolute defiance. 3 BYRON Maidens, like moths, are ever caught by glare.

glareless *a.* E19.

glare /glɛː/ *n.*[2] Now only *N. Amer.* M16. [Origin uncertain: perh. rel. to GLARE *n.*[1] 1.] Orig., frost, icy condition. Later, a sheet of ice.

glare /glɛː/ *a. N. Amer.* M19. [Prob. attrib. use of prec.] Esp. of ice: smooth and bright or translucent, glassy.

glare /glɛː/ *v.* ME. [MLG, MDu. *glaren* gleam, glare.] **1** *v.i.* Shine (esp. too) brilliantly or dazzlingly. ME. **b** Display oneself ostentatiously (now *rare*); be obtrusively evident or conspicuous. E18. **2** *v.i.* Look or stare fixedly and fiercely (*at*, (*up*)*on*). Cf. earlier GLARING *ppl a.* 1. E17. **3** *v.t.* Express or convey by staring fixedly and fiercely. M17. **4** *v.t.* Reflect dazzlingly. Also foll. by *back*. *rare*. L17.

1 CHAUCER Hyt is not al golde that glareth. J. T. STORY In the kitchen the bulb glared naked from its holder. b BOSWELL A writer . . whose ungenerous prejudice against the house of Stuart glares in misrepresentation. 2 H. A. VACHELL You needn't glare at me as if I'd left the old lady to burn on purpose. 3 H. H. MILMAN Two popes glaring defiance at each other. 4 T. SOUTHERNE The images Of a long mis-spent life were rising . . To glare a sad reflection of my crimes.

glareal /ˈglɛːrɪəl/ *a.* M19. [f. L *glarea* gravel + -AL[1].] *Bot.* Growing on dry, exposed soils. Cf. GLAREOUS 2.

glareose /glɛːrɪˈəʊs/ *a.* M19. [L *glareosus*: see next, -OSE[1].] *Bot.* = GLAREOUS 2.

glareous /ˈglɛːrɪəs/ *a.* LME. [f. L *glareosus*, f. *glarea* gravel: see -OUS.] †**1** Of soil: gravelly. LME–L17. **2** *Bot.* Growing on gravel. L19.

glaring /ˈglɛːrɪŋ/ *ppl a.* LME. [f. GLARE *v.* + -ING[2].] **1** Of the eyes: staring fiercely or wildly. LME. **2** That gives out or reflects a dazzling light; (of light, colour, etc.) vivid, dazzling, excessively bright. E16. **3** That displays itself openly; that is obtrusively evident and conspicuous. Freq. *derog.* E18.

1 DRYDEN And hissing, rowls his glaring Eyes around. 2 H. MARTINEAU Reflected in gleams upon the glaring white fronts of the houses. 3 A. N. WILSON Some of the mistranscriptions were so glaring that she thought they must have been mere typing errors.

glaringly *adv.* L16. **glaringness** *n.* M17.

glarney /ˈglɑːni/ *n.* M20. [Prob. alt. of GLASSY *n.*[1]] A glass marble.

glary /ˈglɛːri/ *a.*[1] Now *US.* L16. [f. GLARE *n.*[2] + -Y[1].] Smooth and slippery; icy.

glary /ˈglɛːri/ *a.*[2] M17. [f. GLARE *n.*[1] + -Y[1].] Full of glare; dazzling, glaring.

glariness *n.* M17.

glasnost /ˈglaznɒst, ˈglɑːs-/ *n.* L20. [Russ. *glasnost'* the fact of being public.] In the former USSR, the policy or practice of more open consultative government and wider dissemination of information.

glass /glɑːs/ *n.* & *a.* [OE *glæs* = OS *glas*, *gles*, (O)HG *glas*, f. WGmc var. of Gmc wd repr. by ON *gler* glass, prob. rel. to OE *glǣr*, MLG *glār* amber.] **A** *n.* **I 1** A substance, usu. transparent, lustrous, hard, and brittle, made by fusing soda or potash or both with other ingredients. OE. **2** Any of various other substances of similar properties or composition; any more or less rigid substance which has solidified from a molten state without adopting a regular internal (crystalline) structure. L16. **3** The substance thus obtained considered as the material from which articles for use or ornament are made; *collect. sing.* such articles. E17. **b** *spec.* in *Hort.* The main constituent of a greenhouse, frame, etc.; *collect.* greenhouses. M19.

1 H. M. ROSENBERG Many materials . . such as glass and cast iron, exhibit brittle fracture. 2 J. PINKERTON The volcanic glass called obsidian, appears in such quantities as to constitute rocks. 3 W. HOLTBY The array of glass and silver on the sideboard. b ANTHONY HUXLEY This plant prefers a very moist atmosphere under glass.

II 4 A glass vessel or receptacle. Also, the contents of such a vessel or receptacle. ME. **5** *spec.* A drinking-vessel made of glass; a beverage (esp. alcoholic) contained in such a vessel. LME. **6** A double-chambered glass receptacle containing sand etc. for the measurement of a specified unit of time. (Earlier in HOURGLASS.) M16. **b** Chiefly *Naut.* The time taken by the sand etc. of such a glass to run completely from the upper to the lower chamber; *esp.* a half-hour. L16. **c** *fig.* An allotted period of existence. *arch.* M17.

4 SWIFT Miss, will you reach me that Glass of Jelly? 5 J. FOWLES She had another glass, and drank it off in a minute. W. TREVOR Tippling away at glasses of sherry wasn't going to help the boy. 6 J. MILLER I will wait . . until Time he shall break his glass. c G. GROTE The glass of this worthless dynasty is run out.

III 7 A single sheet of glass made to form a transparent protective covering; *esp.* (*a*) *arch.* a window in a coach; (*b*) a plate of glass covering a picture; (*c*) a glazed frame for plants. LME. **8** A glass mirror. Formerly also, a mirror made of some other material. LME. **b** A mirror, crystal, etc., used in fortune-telling. Long *rare.* M16. **9** A piece of glass shaped for a special purpose, as a lens in a pair of spectacles, a convex glass disc covering the face of a watch, etc. (Earliest in *burning-glass* below.) E16. †**b** (The lens of) an eye. *poet.* L16–E17. **10** An optical instrument with a lens or lenses, used to aid sight esp. by magnifying; a telescope; (freq. in *pl.*) binoculars; *arch.* a microscope. E17. **b** A lens for correcting or assisting defective sight, an eyeglass; in *pl.*, spectacles. M17. **11** A barometer. Formerly also, a thermometer. M17.

7 T. HOOK Bang went the door, up went the glass. 8 D. LESSING She had put the dress on and was looking at herself in the long glass. b SHAKES. *Macb.* The eighth appears, who bears a glass which shows me many more. 9 SIR W. SCOTT Pleydell wiped the glasses of his spectacles. R. HUGHES I wiped the misty glass of my watch. b SHAKES. *Rich. II* Even in the glasses of thine eyes I see thy grieved heart. 10 H. B. TRISTRAM Even without a glass we could distinctly make out Jerusalem. R. MACAULAY I was on deck looking through glasses for the first sight of Trebizond. *field-glass*, *opera-glass*, etc. b W. COWPER With glass at eye, and catalogue in hand. J. WESLEY My eyes were so dim, that no glasses would help me. 11 H. ALLEN The fourth day of calm, with the glass still low but no change.

Phrases etc.: *aventurine glass*: see AVENTURINE 1. **burning-glass** a lens or concave mirror by which the rays of the sun may be concentrated on an object to burn it if combustible. *crown glass*: see CROWN *n.* *crystal-glass*: see CRYSTAL *n.* & *a.* *cut glass*: see CUT *ppl a.* *dark glasses*: see DARK *a.* *flint glass*: see FLINT *n.* 4a. **glass of antimony** a vitreous mixed oxide and sulphide of antimony formed in antimony refining. *ground glass*: see GROUND *ppl a.* HOURGLASS. LOOKING-GLASS *magnifying-glass*: see MAGNIFY 3. *musical glasses*: see MUSICAL *a.* *plate glass*: see PLATE *n.* *sand-glass*: see SAND *n.* *spy-glass*: see SPY *v.* STAINED *glass*. *Vaseline glass*: see VASELINE *n.* 2. *Venetian glass*: see VENETIAN *a.* VENICE *glass*. *vernal glass*: see VERNAL *a.* 1b. *Vita-glass*: see VITA *n.*[1] *volcanic glass*: see VOLCANIC *a.* *watch-glass*: see WATCH *n.* *water-glass*: see WATER *n.* *weather-glass*: see WEATHER *n.* *Wood's glass*: see WOOD *n.*[3] 1.

B *attrib.* or as *adj.* **1** Made of glass. OE. **2** Glazed, having pieces or panes of glass set in a frame. L16.

Comb. & special collocations: **glass ball** a ball made of glass, used esp. as an ornament; **glass-blower** a person who blows and shapes semi-molten glass; **glass-blowing** the action or an act of blowing and shaping semi-molten glass; **glass case** a case made chiefly of glass, for the exhibition and protection of its contents; **glass ceiling** *fig.* a barrier to personal advancement, esp. of a woman or members of ethnic minorities; **glass-cloth** (*a*) a linen cloth used for drying glassware etc.; (*b*) cloth covered with powdered glass, used for smoothing and polishing; (*c*) (without hyphenation) a woven fabric of fine-spun glass thread; **glass coach** (*obs.* exc. *Hist.*) a coach with glass windows as opp. to an unglazed one; **glass crab** the larva of any of various shrimps; **glass-cutter** a person who or thing which shapes or decorates glass by cutting; **glass-dust** powdered glass; **glass eye** †(*a*) = sense 10b above; (*b*) an artificial eye, *esp.* one made of glass; **glass-faced** *a.* (*rare*) having a face that reflects the looks of another; **glass fibre** (*a*) a filament of glass; (*b*) glass in the form of such filaments, as made into fabric or embedded as a reinforcement in plastic; **glass furnace**: in which the constituents of glass are fused; **glass gall** sandiver; **glass-gazing** *a.* (long *rare* or *obs.*) given to contemplating oneself in a mirror, self-regarding, vain; **glass-green** *a.* & *n.* (*poet.*) (of) a clear green colour; **glasshouse** (*a*) a building where glass is made; (*b*) a building made chiefly of glass; *esp.* a greenhouse, a conservatory; (*c*) *slang* a military prison or guard room; †**glass humour** the vitreous humour; **glass lizard** = *glass snake* below; **glass-making** the manufacture of glass; **glass-man** (now *rare*) a dealer in or maker of glass; **glass paper**: covered with powdered glass and used for polishing; **glass-rope sponge** a sponge of the genus *Hyalonema*, which roots itself to the seabed by a stem of twisted siliceous threads; **glass slipper** [mistr. Fr. *pantoufle en vair* fur slipper through confusion with *verre* glass] a slipper made of glass; *esp.* the one worn and lost by Cinderella in the fairy tale; **glass snail** a snail with a thin translucent shell; spec. *Retinella pura*; **glass snake** any of various snakelike lizards of the genus *Ophiosaurus*, of the southern US; **glass sponge** *Zool.* (*a*) any of various deep-water sponges of the class Hexactinellida, which often have a skeleton composed of fused six-pointed siliceous spicules; (*b*) = *glass-rope sponge above*; **glassware** articles made of glass; **glass wool** glass in the form of fine fibres for packing and insulation; **glass work** (*a*) (usu. in *pl.*) the works or factory where glass is manufactured; (*b*) the manufacture of glass and glassware, glazing; (*c*) glassware; **glasswort** a maritime plant of the goosefoot family rich in alkali and formerly used in the manufacture of glass: (*a*) any of various succulent jointed apparently leafless plants of the genus *Salicornia*, freq. dominant in salt-marshes; (*b*) (more fully *prickly glasswort*) prickly saltwort, *Salsola kali*.

glassful *n.* as much as a glass will hold E17. **glassless** *a.* E19. **glasslike** *a.* & *adv.* (*a*) *adj.* resembling glass, glassy, vitreous; (*b*) *adv.* (*rare*) in the manner of glass: E17.

glass /glɑːs/ *v.* LME. [f. the n.: cf. GLAZE *v.*[1]] **1** *v.t.* Fit or fill in with glass, glaze. Freq. in *pass.* LME. **2** *v.t.* Protect by a covering of glass; cover with a vitreous or glassy surface; encase in glass. Long *rare* or *obs.* L16. **3** *v.t.* Set (a person, freq. oneself, or thing) before a mirror or other reflecting surface so as to cause an image to be reflected; view the reflection of; see as in a mirror. L16. **b** Of a mirror or other reflecting surface: reflect, give back an image of. E17. **4** *v.t.* View or scan with field-glasses or other optical instrument. L18. **5** *v.t.* Dress leather with a device for smoothing and polishing. Also foll. by *out*. L19. **6** *v.i. esp.* in *Surfing.* Of water: become smooth and glassy in appearance. (Foll. by *off.*) L19.

1 JONATHAN ROSS Above the main doors a glassed-in bulb pushed out a sickly . . light. 2 WORDSWORTH A flower Glassed in a green-house. 3 BYRON Thou glorious mirror, where the Almighty's form glasses itself in tempests. b T. HARDY Both looked attractive as glassed back by the faithful reflector.

glassen /ˈglɑːs(ə)n/ *a.* Now *arch.* & *dial.* Also **glazen** /ˈgleɪz(ə)n/. [OE *glæsen*, f. as GLASS *n.* + -EN[4].] **1** Made of glass. OE. **2** Resembling glass; (of the eyes) glassy, glazed. LME.

glassen /ˈglɑːs(ə)n/ *v.t.* Long *obs.* exc. *dial.* Also **glazen** /ˈgleɪz(ə)n/. M16. [f. GLASS *v.* + -EN[5]. Cf. GLAZE *v.*[1]] **1** = GLAZE *v.*[1] 1. M16. **2** = GLAZE *v.*[1] 2. M17.

glassener *n.* a glazier L16.

glassichord /ˈglɑːsɪkɔːd/ *n. US. obs.* exc. *Hist.* M19. [f. GLASS *n.* after *harpsichord.*] = HARMONICA 1(b).

glassify /ˈglɑːsɪfʌɪ/ *v.t.* L20. [f. GLASS *n.* + -I- + -FY.] Vitrify (nuclear waste) for convenience of handling and storage.

glassifiˈcation *n.* L20.

glassine /ˈglɑːsiːn/ *n.* & *a.* E20. [f. GLASS *n.* + -INE[5].] (Designating or made of) a kind of glossy transparent paper.

Glassite /ˈglɑːsʌɪt/ *n.* & *a.* L18. [f. John *Glass* (see below) + -ITE¹.] *Hist.* **A** *n.* A member of the religious sect founded by Revd John Glass, a minister of the Established Church of Scotland (deposed in 1728). L18. **B** *adj.* Of or pertaining to this sect. M19.

glassy /ˈglɑːsi/ *n.*¹ L19. [f. GLASS *n.* + -Y⁶.] A glass marble.

glassy /ˈglɑːsi/ *n.*² M20. [f. the adj.] *Surfing.* (A stretch of) smooth water..

glassy /ˈglɑːsi/ *a.* LME. [f. GLASS *n.* + -Y¹.] **1** Having the properties of glass, vitreous; resembling or characteristic of glass; appearing to be made of glass. LME. †**b** Brittle or fragile like glass. L16–L18. **2** Of the eye etc.: having a fixed unintelligent look; lacking fire or life; dull. LME. †**3** Made or consisting of glass. LME–E19. **4** Of water etc.: lustrous and transparent as glass; having a smooth unruffled surface like glass. M16.

1 J. PINKERTON The glassy quartz retains its natural consistency. P. H. GOSSE The shell is glassy and colourless. B. HARTE The glassy tinkle of water. G. GREENE This unhappy man in all his curious glassy transparency. †**glassy humour** = VITREOUS *humour*; cf. GLAZY 1. **b** W. COWPER The glassy threads with which the Fancy weaves her brittle toils. **2** T. HEALD To approach . . with outstretched hand and glassy smile. H. BASCOM He stares glassy eyed and weeps. **3** G. CRABBE A glassy globe, in frame of ivory, prest. **4** C. MACKENZIE The strait was glassy calm. E. BOWEN The harbour . . lay glassy under the close sky.

glassily *adv.* E19. **glassiness** *n.* E17.

glastick *n.* var. of GLAISTIG.

Glastonbury /ˈglast(ə)nb(ə)ri/ *n.* L17. [A town in Somerset.] **1** *Glastonbury thorn*, a winter-flowering form of hawthorn, *Crataegus monogyna*, said to have originally sprung up at Glastonbury from the staff of Joseph of Arimathea. L17. **2** *Glastonbury chair*, a kind of folding armchair, supposedly designed after a chair owned by the last Abbot of Glastonbury (executed 1539). M19.

Glaswegian /glazˈwiːdʒ(ə)n, glas-, glɑːz-, glɑːs-/ *n.* & *a.* E19. [f. *Glasgow* (see below) after *Norwegian* etc.: see -IAN.] **A** *n.* A native or inhabitant of Glasgow, a city in Scotland. E19. **B** *adj.* Of or pertaining to (a native or inhabitant of) Glasgow. L19.

Glauber /ˈglɔːbə, ˈglaʊbə/ *n.* M18. [Johann Rudolf *Glauber*, Ger. chemist (1604–1668).] *Glauber('s) salt(s)*, crystalline (hydrated) sodium sulphate, used esp. as a laxative.

glauberite /ˈglaʊb(ə)rʌɪt/ *n.* E19. [f. as prec. + -ITE¹.] *Min.* A monoclinic sulphate of sodium and calcium occurring usu. as glassy white or faintly coloured dipyramidal crystals, esp. in salt lake deposits.

glaucescent /glɔːˈsɛs(ə)nt/ *a.* E19. [f. as GLAUCOUS: see -ESCENT.] Chiefly *Bot.* Somewhat glaucous.

glaucescence *n.* L19.

glaucodot /ˈglɔːkədɒt/ *n.* M19. [G *Glaukodot*, f. as Gk *glaukos* GLAUCOUS + *dotēr* giver.] *Min.* An orthorhombic arsenide and sulphide of cobalt and iron, occurring as greyish or reddish-white crystals with a metallic lustre.

glaucoma /glɔːˈkəʊmə/ *n.* M17. [Gk *glaukōma*, f. *glaukos*: see GLAUCOUS, -OMA.] *Med.* An eye condition characterized by increased pressure within the eyeball and a gradual impairment or loss of sight.

glauco'matic *a.* of or pertaining to glaucoma M19. **glau'comatous** *a.* of, pertaining to, or affected with glaucoma E19.

glauconite /ˈglɔːkənʌɪt/ *n.* M19. [G *Glaukonit*, f. as Gk *glaukon* neut. of *glaukos*: see GLAUCOUS, -ITE¹.] *Min.* A ferromagnesian clay mineral of the illite group. Also, a greenish earthy material consisting of pellets of this or similar minerals (also called *green earth*).

glauco'nitic *a.* M19.

glaucophane /ˈglɔːkəfeɪn/ *n.* M19. [G *Glaukophan*, f. Gk *glaukos* (see GLAUCOUS) + *-phanēs* shining.] *Min.* Any of a group of sodium-containing monoclinic amphiboles occurring esp. in schists and other metamorphic rocks.

glaucose /ˈglɔːkəʊs/ *a.* *rare.* E18. [f. as GLAUCOUS: see -OSE¹.] = GLAUCOUS.

glaucous /ˈglɔːkəs/ *a.* L17. [L *glaucus* f. Gk *glaukos* bluish-green, bluish-grey: see -OUS.] Of a dull greyish green or greyish blue; *esp.* in *Bot.*, covered with a powdery bloom as of grapes.

glaucous gull a large grey and white gull, *Larus hyperboreus*, of Arctic coasts.

glaucus /ˈglɔːkəs/ *n.* E16. [(mod.L f.) L: see prec.] †**1** A marine fish of uncertain identity. E16–E18. **2** = GLAUCOUS *gull*. Now *rare* or *obs.* L18. **3** A sea-slug (mollusc) of the genus *Glaucus*, usu. blue in colour and freq. floating in the open sea. M19.

glaum *n.* var. of GLAM *n.*²

glaum /glɔːm/ *v.i.* *Sc.* Also **glam** (infl. **-mm-**). L18. [Origin unkn.: cf. GLOM.] Snatch *at*; make threatening gestures.

glaver /ˈgleɪvə/ *n.* & *v.* Long *obs.* exc. *Sc.* & *north.* LME. [Origin unkn.] **A** *n.* Chatter; loud noise. LME. **B** *v.* **1** *v.t.* Flatter, deceive with flattery. LME. **2** *v.i.* Talk plausibly and deceitfully, flatter. LME.

glaze /gleɪz/ *n.* L17. [f. GLAZE *v.*¹] **1** A window. *arch. slang.* L17. **2** A coating or covering of ice; a stretch of ice. *US.* M18. **3** A smooth, lustrous, usu. transparent coating; *esp.* an edible coating of gelatin, sugar, egg, etc., on food; a smooth glossy surface. L18. **4** The vitreous substance fixed by fusion to the surface of pottery etc. and forming an impervious decorative coating. E19. **5** A thin top coat of transparent paint used to modify the tone of an underlying colour. M19.

2 E. K. KANE Old seasoned hummock, covered with a slippery glaze. **3** W. GREENER Dense hard powder will take a higher glaze than the softer kinds. **4** J. CLAVELL The . . glaze had run just short, leaving an uneven rim of bare porcelain. **5** J. MILLER With newly discovered glazes, painters take delight in showing the play of light on . . flesh.

glaze /gleɪz/ *v.*¹ LME. [f. GLASS *n.* as *graze* from *grass*: cf. MHG *glasen* and GLASS *v.*] **1** *v.t.* Fit or fill in (a window etc.) with glass; cover (a painting etc.) with glass; provide (a building) with glass windows. LME. **2** *v.t.* Cover (pottery etc.) with glaze; fix (glaze, paint) *on* pottery etc. by fusion. LME. **3** *v.t.* Cause to shine like glass; give a smooth glassy surface to, esp. by rubbing; polish. LME. **4** *v.t.* Overlay or cover with a smooth lustrous coating. Also, cover (the eyes) with a film (as of moisture etc.), dull. L16. **5** *v.t.* Cover (a painted surface) with glaze. Also, lay (a transparent colour) *over* another. E17. **6** *v.i.* Be or become glazed; *esp.* (of the eyes) take on a glassy or fixed appearance. M18.

1 BROWNING Somebody saw a portrait framed and glazed At Croisic. M. FRAYN The upper half of the door was glazed with dusty panes. **2** T. THOMSON The vessel now being baked, the paint is glazed on. **3** R. BOYLE Like polish'd Silver, or well glaz'd Arms. **4** SHAKES. *Rich. II* Sorrow's eye, glazed with blinding tears. V. WOOLF Little red and green vegetables glazed in sauce. **5** J. RUSKIN Red . . mixed with the pure blue, or glazed over it. **6** T. KENEALLY Harry tried to understand the point. His eyes glazed with the import of it.

glazed *ppl a.* (*a*) that has been subject to the action or an act of glazing; (*b*) *Metall.* having a smooth shining surface or fracture; (*c*) *glazed frost* = *silver thaw* s.v. SILVER *a.*: M16. **glazer** *n.* †(*a*) = GLAZIER 2; (*b*) a person who applies the glaze to pottery; (*c*) an implement for glazing; *esp.* a wheel used in polishing knives etc.: LME.

glaze /gleɪz/ *v.*²*i.* *obs.* exc. *dial.* E17. [Perh. blend of GAZE *v.* and GLARE *v.*] Stare.

glazen *a.* var. of GLASSEN *a.*

glazen *v.* var. of GLASSEN *v.*

glazier /ˈgleɪzɪə/ *n.* ME. [f. GLAZE *v.*¹ + -IER.] **1** A person whose trade is to glaze windows etc. ME. †**2** A person engaged in the manufacture of glass, a glass-maker. LME–L15. †**3** In *pl.* The eyes. *slang.* M16–L18. †**4** A thief, *esp.* one who broke a window etc. to steal. *slang.* L17–L18.

glaziery *n.* the work of a glazier M19.

glazing /ˈgleɪzɪŋ/ *n.* LME. [f. GLAZE *v.*¹ + -ING¹.] **1** The action of providing a building with windows or filling windows with glass; the trade or business of a glazier. LME. **b** Glass fixed in windows or frames. LME. **2** The action of polishing or burnishing. LME. **3** The operation of coating with a glaze, or of giving a smooth shiny surface. L17. **b** The substance used for producing a glaze or glossy surface; a glossy surface. E18. **4** The application of a thin top coat of transparent paint to modify the tone of the underlying colour; this paint. E18.

1b *double glazing*: see DOUBLE *a.* & *adv.*

glazy /ˈgleɪzi/ *a.* E17. [f. GLAZE *n.* or *v.*¹ + -Y¹.] †**1** *glazy humour*, the vitreous humour. *rare.* Only in E17. **2** Glassy, shining like glass; resembling or characteristic of a glaze or glazed surface. E18. **3** = GLASSY *a.* 2. M19.

glazily *adv.* M19. **glaziness** *n.* E18.

gleam /gliːm/ *n.*¹ & *v.*¹ [OE *glǣm* corresp. to LG *glēm*, OHG *gleimo* glow-worm, and rel. to OS *glīmo* brightness, OHG *glīmo*, MHG *glīmen* shine, glow. Cf. GLIMMER *v.*] **A** *n.* **1** Orig., a brilliant light. Now only, a subdued or transient light, *esp.* one that is reflected. OE. **b** *fig.* A bright or vivid manifestation of some quality. Now chiefly, a faint, transient, or intermittent appearance of this quality. ME. **c** A warm ray of sun; a bright warm interval between rain-showers. Long *dial.* E17. **2** Brilliance; radiant beauty. Long *dial.* OE. **b** A bright or joyous look. Long *rare.* M18.

1 F. M. FORD In the sunlight gleams come from . . the glass of windows; from the gilt signs. J. T. STORY Distantly, far beyond the sound, I saw the gleam of a torch. **b** T. KEN When first my Heart, thou Lord, didst melt, And of thy Love one Gleam I felt. N. MITFORD A gleam of amusement crossed Lady Patricia's sad face. *a gleam in one's eye*: see EYE *n.* **2** SPENSER Then was the faire Dodonian tree far seene . . to spred his gladsome gleame.

B *v.* **1** *v.i.* Emit a gleam or gleams; shine with esp. a reflected, subdued, or intermittent brightness; (of a quality) be indicated. ME. **2** *v.t.* Shine or reflect (a subdued or intermittent light). L16.

1 V. BRITTAIN A hundred lights gleamed like jewels against the deep cobalt of sky and water. R. WARNER I . . saw most vividly the candlelight gleaming on the mahogany table. G. VIDAL Eusebia's eyes gleamed with mischief. **2** SHAKES. *Lucr.* And dying eyes gleam'd forth their ashy lights.

gleaming *n.* the action of the vb; an instance of this, a gleam: LME. **gleamingly** *adv.* in a gleaming manner M19. **gleamless** *a.* L19.

gleam /gliːm/ *v.*² & *n.*² L16. [Var. of GLEIM *v.*] **A** *v.i.* Of a hawk: regurgitate gleam. Long *rare* or *obs.* L16. **B** *n.* The meat etc. regurgitated from the crop by a hawk. L19.

gleamy /ˈgliːmi/ *a.* L16. [f. GLEAM *n.*¹ + -Y¹.] **1** That gleams. L16. **2** That is lighted by a gleam or gleams; *esp.* (of weather) marked by intermittent sunshine. Now chiefly *dial.* L17. **3** Of light or colour: of the nature of a gleam; subdued, hazy. E18.

1 DISRAELI Fish, gleamy with prismatic hues. **2** WORDSWORTH And antique castles seen through gleamy showers. **3** J. INGELOW Stands by his fire, and dulls its gleamy light.

gleaminess *n.* M19.

glean /gliːn/ *n.* *obs.* exc. *dial.* LME. [OFr. *glene*, *glane*, f. *glener*: see GLEAN *v.*] **1** Something that has been gleaned; *esp.* a head of corn or other cereal. LME. **2** A bundle or sheaf of corn, hemp, etc. M17.

glean /gliːn/ *v.* ME. [OFr. *glener* (mod. *glaner*) f. late L *glen(n)are*, ult. f. Celt. base repr. by OIr. *do-glenn* (he) gathers.] **1** *v.t.* Gather or collect in small quantities, scrape together, (news, facts, etc.); find out or discover (something). ME. †**b** Gather or collect *into* a receptacle or mass. LME–M17. **2** *spec.* **a** *v.t.* & *i.* Gather or pick up (ears of corn or other produce) left by reapers or harvesters. LME. **b** *v.t.* Strip (a field etc.) thus. M16.

1 E. F. BENSON She would not . . read letters that were left about, but she constantly . . tried to glean their contents. R. H. MOTTRAM She was gleaning every scrap of information she could. **2a** J. CARY The field where we had been gleaning for our chickens. A. R. AMMONS The women glean remnant peas. **b** AV *Lev.* 19:10 Thou shalt not gleane thy vineyard.

gleaner *n.* LME. **gleaning** *n.* (*a*) the action or an act of the vb; (*b*) something that is gleaned (usu. in *pl.*): LME.

glease /gliːz/ *v.* Orig. †**glace**. ME. [OFr. *glacer*, *glacier* glide, slip, ult. f. L *glacies* ice.] †**1** *v.i.* Of a weapon: glance off, strike with a glancing blow. ME–L15. †**2** *v.t.* Glide, glance. Only in LME. **3** *v.t.* Glide or skim past, pass very close to. *dial.* L19.

gleba /ˈgliːbə/ *n.* Pl. **-bae** /-biː/. M19. [f. as next.] *Mycol.* The fleshy, spore-bearing tissue of certain fungi (Gasteromycetales and Tuberales), e.g. puffballs and stinkhorns.

glebe /gliːb/ *n.* LME. [L *gleba*, *glaeba* clod, land, soil.] **1** The soil of the earth; earth, land. Now *poet.* LME. **2** A piece of cultivated land, a field. Now *poet.* LME. **b** *spec.* A piece of land assigned as part of a parish clergyman's living. LME. †**3** A clod or mass of earth, ore, etc.; an earthy mineral. E16–M18.

1 T. CAMPBELL The glebe of fifty kingdoms shall be till'd To feed his . . train. 2 TENNYSON Many an . . upland glebe wealthy in oil and wine. b W. COBBETT This parish . . has a glebe, and a good solid house. 3 T. AMORY The glittering glebes of a gold colour found here.

Comb.: **glebe-house** (now *rare* or *obs.*) a parsonage; **glebe-land** = sense 2b above.

gleby *a.* (now *rare* or *obs.*) (of soil) rich, fertile, full of clods M16.

glebous /ˈgliːbəs/ *a. rare.* L17. [L *glebosus*, f. *gleba* GLEBE: see -OUS.] Earthy; full of clods.

gled /glɛd/ *n.* Now chiefly *north.* & *Sc.* Also **glede** /gliːd/. [OE *glida* corresp. to MLG *glede*, ON *gleða*, f. Gmc base of GLIDE *v.*] A bird of prey, *esp.* the kite.

gledge /glɛdʒ/ *v.* & *n.* *Sc.* E19. [Origin uncertain: cf. GLEG *n.* & *v.*, GLEY *v.*] **A** *v.i.* Squint; look sideways, esp. cunningly or slyly. E19. **B** *n.* A side-glance, a (sly) look. E19.

gleditsia /glɪˈdɪtsɪə/ *n.* Also **gleditschia** /-tʃɪə/. L18. [mod.L (see below), f. J. G. *Gleditsch* (1714–86), Ger. botanist + -IA[1].] Any of various usu. spiny Asian or American leguminous trees of the genus *Gleditsia* (e.g. the N. American honey locust, *G. triacanthos*), of which some species are cultivated as ornamentals, for the pods, or as hedges or timber.

glee /gliː/ *n.* [OE *glēo*, *glēow*, *glīw* = ON *glý*, f. Gmc.] †**1** Entertainment, play, fun; occas., mockery. OE–E17. **2** Musical entertainment; music, melody. Now *Sc.* (*arch.*) exc. in *gleeman* below. OE. **b** A part-song, *spec.* an unaccompanied one, for three or more (usu. adult male) voices and freq. consisting of contrasted movements. M17. **3** Mirth, joy. Now *esp.* triumphant or exuberantly displayed delight. ME. †**4** Bright colour, beauty. LME–L16.

3 J. HELLER Wintergreen crowed with malicious glee. J. G. FARRELL They shouted with laughter, held their sides, and even rolled in the dust in undignified glee.

Comb.: **glee club** a society for singing glees and other part-songs; **gleeman** *Hist.* a professional esp. musical entertainer; a minstrel.

gleeful *a.* L16. **gleefully** *adv.* M19. **gleefulness** *n.* M20. **gleesome** *a.* = GLEEFUL E17. **gleesomely** *adv.* M19. **gleesomeness** *n.* M19.

glee *v.* var. of GLEY *v.*

gleed /gliːd/ *n.* [OE *glēd* = OFris. *glēd*, OS *glōd*- (Du. *gloed*), OHG *gluot* (G *Glut*), ON *glóð*, ult. f. Gmc base of GLOW *v.*[1]] **1** An ember, a live coal; a (glowing) fire. Now *dial.* or *arch.* OE. **2** A spark or glimmer (of fire); a beam (of light). Now *dial.* M16. **3** In *pl.* Cinders; coke used as fuel. *dial.* M19.

gleek /gliːk/ *n.*[1] E16. [OFr. *glic*, *ghelicque*, perh. f. MDu. *ghelic* (mod. *gelijk*) LIKE *a.*] **1** *Hist.* A card-game for three people using forty-four cards, twelve being dealt to each player and eight forming a common stock. E16. †**2** A set of three court-cards of the same rank in one hand in the game of gleek; *transf.* a set of three, a trio. E17–E18.

gleek /gliːk/ *n.*[2] & *v.* M16. [Perh. dim. of GLEE *n.* Cf. GLAIK.] **A** *n.* †**1** A gibe, a jest; a joke, a trick. M16–E19. **2** A glance, *esp.* a coquettish one. *rare.* L16. **B** *v.* **1** *v.t.* Trick, outwit. *arch.* M16. **2** *v.i.* Make a jest, gibe (*at* a person). Now *arch. rare.* L16. **3** *v.i.* Look sideways, glance. *rare.* E17.

gleet /gliːt/ *n.* & *v.* Also (earlier, chiefly *north.* & *Sc.*) **glit** /glɪt/, **glet** /glɛt/, (infl. **-tt-**). ME. [(O)Fr. *glette* slime, filth, secretion, (now) litharge, of unkn. origin.] **A** *n.* **1** Mucus formed in the stomach, esp. of a hawk. *obs.* exc. *Sc.* ME. **2** Slimy, sticky, or greasy matter. *obs.* exc. *north.* & *Sc.* LME. **3** (A) watery discharge, now only *spec.* from the urethra, usu. as a result of chronic gonorrhoea. M16. **B** *v.* †**1** *v.i.* Esp. of a watery discharge: ooze, flow slowly. E16–E18. **2** *v.i.* & †*t.* Of a wound, the nose, etc.: discharge (a thin purulent matter). L17.

gleety *a.* (*a*) (*obs.* exc. *north.* & *Sc.*) slimy; (*b*) watery, purulent: LME.

gleg /glɛg/ *n.* & *v.* M17. [Origin uncertain: cf. GLEDGE, GLEY *v.*] **A** *n.* = GLEDGE *n. obs.* exc. *north.* M17. **B** *v.i.* = GLEDGE *v. dial.* L18.

gleg /glɛg/ *a.* & *adv.* *north.* & *Sc.* ME. [ON *gleggr*, *gløggr* clear, clear-sighted, corresp. to OE *glēaw* wise, clever, OS, OHG *glau* clever, f. Gmc base of Goth. *glaggwuba* (adv.) accurately.] **A** *adj.* **1** Quick or sharp in perception by any of the senses, esp. by sight. Chiefly in *gleg of the eye*, sharp-eyed. ME. **b** Of the eye, a blade, etc.: sharp, keen. E18. **2** Quick or clever *at* (doing) something; nimble; alert. M18. **3** Lively, cheery, happy. E19. **B** *adv.* = GLEGLY. E18.

glegly *adv.* quickly, cleverly, readily; brightly, clearly: M18. **glegness** *n.* M19.

glei *n.* see GLEY *n.*

Gleichschaltung /ˈglaɪçʃaltʊŋ/ *n.* Also **g-**. M20. [G.] The standardization of political, economic, and cultural institutions in authoritarian States.

gleification /ˌgleɪɪfɪˈkeɪʃ(ə)n/ *n.* M20. [f. GLEY *n.* + -FICATION.] *Soil Sci.* = GLEIZATION.

†**gleim** *v.* & *n.* LME. [Origin uncertain: cf. ON *kleima* daub corresp. to OE *clǣman* CLEAM *v.*, also GLEAM *v.*[2] & *n.*[2]] **A** *v.t.* Smear with a sticky substance; *fig.* in *pass.*, be attached *to* something. Only in LME. **B** *n.* A sticky or slimy substance; *spec.* rheum; *fig.* attachment, affection. LME–E16.

†**gleimy** *a.* LME–E18. [f. GLEIM *n.* + -Y[1].] Sticky, slimy.

gleization /gleɪˈzeɪʃ(ə)n, gleɪʌɪ-/ *n.* Also **gley-** /gleɪ-/. M20. [f. GLEY *n.* + -IZATION.] *Soil Sci.* The process of formation of a gley soil by waterlogging and chemical reduction of iron.

glen /glɛn/ *n.* & *a.* LME. [Gael., Ir. *gleann*, earlier *glenn* = Welsh *glyn*.] **A** *n.* A mountain valley, esp. narrow and steep-sided and forming the course of a stream or river. LME.

L. MACNEICE Three glens, each leading up to a loch in the mountains.

B *attrib.* or as *adj.* Designating any of various check fabrics, esp. the Glenurquhart check. LME.

glendoveer /glɛndəˈvɪə/ *n.* E19. [f. as GANDHARVA.] (In the artificial quasi-Hindu mythology of the poet Robert Southey) a member of a race of beautiful sprites.

glengarry /glɛnˈgari/ *n.* Also **G-**. M19. [f. *Glengarry* in Highland, Scotland.] A man's flat-sided cap, pointed at the front and back and usu. with a pair of ribbons hanging behind; chiefly worn as part of Highland dress.

Glenlivet /glɛnˈlɪvɪt/ *n.* E19. [*Glenlivet* in Grampian, Scotland, the place of production.] (Proprietary name for) a variety of Scotch whisky; a drink of this.

gleno- /ˈgliːnəʊ/ *comb. form* of GLENOID, used in *Anat.*: see -O-.

gleno'humeral *a.* of or relating to the shoulder joint M19.

glenoid /ˈgliːnɔɪd/ *a.* E18. [Fr. *glénoïde* f. Gk *glēnoeidēs*, f. *glēnē* ball or pupil of the eye: see -OID.] Anat. *glenoid cavity*, *fossa*, a socket or cavity on a bone into which another bone fits to form a joint; *esp.* that on the scapula articulating with the humerus.

glenoidal *a.* M19.

glent /glɛnt/ *v.* & *n.* Long *dial.* ME. [Prob. of Scand. origin: cf. Sw. dial. *glänta*, *glinta* slip, slide; shine, gleam. See also GLINT *v.*, *n.*[1]] **A** *v.i.* **1** Move quickly esp. in an oblique direction. ME. **b** Of a weapon, missile, blow, etc.: glance, strike obliquely. LME. **2** Look sideways, glance. ME. **3** Flash, gleam, shine; be reflected. LME. **B** *n.* **1** A look, a glance; a glimpse. ME. **2** A gleam, a flash. LME. **3** A sudden movement, a jump, a leap; a slip, a stumble. E16.

Glenurquhart /glɛnˈəːkət/ *n.* & *a.* E20. [*Glenurquhart*, a place in Highland, Scotland.] (Designating) a kind of Scottish plaid or check.

glet *n.* & *v.* see GLEET.

gletcher /ˈglɛtʃə/ *n.* Orig. (now *rare*) **Gletscher**. M18. [G *Gletscher* f. Swiss dial. = Fr. *glacier*.] A glacier.

glew /gluː/ *v.* Now *rare.* [OE *glēowian*, *glīwian*, f. *glēow*, *glīw* GLEE *n.*] **1** *v.i.* Make merry, jest, play music. OE. †**2** *v.t.* Entertain, make happy. ME–E16.

gley /gleɪ/ *n.* Also **glei**. E20. [Ukrainian *gleĭ* sticky bluish clay, cogn. w. CLAY *n.*] *Soil Sci.* A sticky blue-grey waterlogged soil or soil layer in which iron is reduced to the ferrous form; such a soil having brownish mottling due to oxidation during intermittent dry periods. Also *gley soil*.

gleyed *a.* turned into a gley M20. **gleying** *n.* = GLEIZATION M20.

gley /glʌɪ/ *v.i.* Also **glee** /gliː/. *obs.* exc. *north.* & *Sc.* ME. [Origin unkn. Cf. GLEDGE *v.* & *n.*, GLEG *n.* & *v.*] Squint, look sideways; have a cast in one or both eyes.

gleyd *a.* (*a*) having a cast in one or both eyes; squint-eyed; (*b*) crooked, twisted; wrong, awry: L15.

gleyde *n.* var. of GLYDE.

gleyzation *n.* var. of GLEIZATION.

glia /ˈglʌɪə, ˈgliːə/ *n.* L19. [Gk = glue.] *Anat.* The connective tissue of the nervous system, consisting of several different types of cell associated with neurons; = NEUROGLIA. Also *glia cell*, *glia tissue*.

glial *a.* of or pertaining to glia L19.

gliadin /ˈglʌɪədɪn/ *n.* Also **-ine** /-iːn, -ɪn/. M19. [Fr. *gliadine*, f. Gk *glia* glue: see -IN[1], -INE[2].] *Biochem.* Orig., any prolamine (plant protein soluble in aqueous alcohol). Now *spec.* a proline-rich protein, one of the components of cereal gluten.

glib /glɪb/ *n.* M16. [Ir.] *Ir. Hist.* A thick mass of matted hair worn hanging over the forehead and eyes.

glib /glɪb/ *a.* & *adv.* Compar. & superl. **-bb-**. L16. [Rel. to GLIBBERY.] **A** *adj.* **1** Smooth and slippery; offering no resistance to motion; moving easily; (of movement) unimpeded, easy. Now *arch.* & *dial.* L16. **2** Of an action etc.: easy, offhand. L16. **3** Of a speaker, speech, etc.: fluent, ready, more voluble than sincere or thoughtful. L16.

1 BROWNING The snow lies glib as glass and hard as steel. 2 B. RUBENS She hated herself for her glib and ready cruelty. 3 G. ALLEN The ordinary glib commonplaces of obituary notices. O. NASH Oh to be glib! Oh to be ever prepared with a plausible fib!

B *adv.* **1** Smoothly; easily. Now *rare.* L16. **2** Volubly; fluently. E17.

2 E. S. BARRETT You talked so glib of your great estates.

glibly *adv.* E17. **glibness** *n.* E17.

glib /glɪb/ *v.*[1] Infl. **-bb-**. L16. [f. the adj.] †**1** *v.t.* Make smooth or slippery. L16–E19. **2** *v.t.* Make fluent or plausible. *arch.* E17. **3** *v.i.* Talk glibly. *obs.* exc. *dial.* E17.

†**glib** *v.*[2]*t. rare.* Infl. **-bb-**. E–M17. [App. alt. of LIB *v.*[1]] Castrate, geld.

†**glibbery** *a.* E–M17. [Corresp. to Du. *glibberig*, MLG *glibberich*, LG *glibbrig*, f. Gmc base (cf. OHG *gleif* sloping): perh. ult. imit.] Slippery.

glidder /ˈglɪdə/ *n.* *Sc.* & *north.* L18. [Rel. to next.] A loose stone on a hillside.

glidder /ˈglɪdə/ *a.* & *v.* *obs.* exc. *dial.* [OE *glid(d)er*, f. wk grade of the base of GLIDE *v.*: see -ER[5].] **A** *adj.* Slippery. Long *rare.* OE. **B** *v.t.* Glaze over; cover with ice. E17.

gliddery *a.* slippery; *fig.* treacherous: M19.

glide /glʌɪd/ *n.* LME. [f. next.] **1** The action or an act of gliding. LME. **b** = GLANCE *n.*[1] 2b. L19. **c** A gliding dance step or dance. L19. **d** *Aeronaut.* The act of gliding; a flight in a glider. E20. **2** A shallow section of a stream. Formerly also, a stream. L16. **3** *Phonet.* A smoothly changing sound produced in passing from one position of the speech organs to another; a semivowel. M19. 4 *Cryst.* Plastic deformation of a crystal lattice by lateral displacement along an atomic plane. M20.

1 J. WILSON With a winged glide this maiden would rove. J. G. WHITTIER The dip of Indian oars, The glide of birch canoes.

Comb.: **glide bomb** a bomb fitted with aerofoils that enable it to glide towards its target when released from an aircraft; **glide path**, **glide slope** an aircraft's line of descent to land, esp. as indicated by ground radar.

glideless *a.* (*Phonet.*) unaccompanied by a glide E20.

glide /glʌɪd/ *v.* Pa. t. & pple **glided**, (*arch.*) **glode** /gləʊd/. [OE *glīdan* = OFris. *glīda*, OS *glīdan* (Du. *glijden*), OHG *glītan* (G *gleiten*), f. WGmc.] 1 *v.i.* Pass from one place to another or change position by a smooth continuous movement, esp. without effort or difficulty or perceptible means of locomotion. OE. b Of an aircraft: fly without engine-power. E20. 2 *v.i.* Move quietly or stealthily; steal *into*, *out of*, a place. ME. †3 *v.i.* Pass from one place to another, go, come. *poet.* ME–L16. 4 *v.i.* Slide; (now *dial.*) slide on ice as a sport. Formerly also, slip. ME. b Slip *away*, elude one's grasp. E16. 5 Of time, life, etc.: pass gently and imperceptibly *along*, *away*, etc. ME. 6 *v.t.* Cause to glide. M17. b Traverse in a glider. M20. 7 *v.i.* Pass lightly and without interruption *along* or *over* a surface. E19. 8 *v.i.* *Cryst.* Of units in a crystal: be displaced, esp. along an atomic plane. Also, of a crystal: undergo glide. Cf. GLIDE *n.* 4. L19. 9 *v.i.* & *t.* = GLANCE *v.* 8b. L19.

1 DRYDEN [The Snake] in some secret Cranny slowly glides. J. WILSON She glides away like a lambent flame. W. H. BARTLETT The little stream glided and rippled by. 2 D. G. MITCHELL He . . glides out stealthful as a cat. C. KINGSLEY A great dog-fox as red as the fir-stems through which he glides. 3 SPENSER Like sparke of fire that from the andvile glode. 4 J. SCHEFFER The Laplanders gliding upon the ice. b ADDISON It glided through the Fingers like a smooth Piece of Ice. 5 DISRAELI Two serene and innocent years had glided away. 6 A. C. GUNTER Ferdie glides the graceful Louise through the room in poetic motion. 7 GEO. ELIOT His hand glided from the face and rested on the young man's shoulder. *transf.*: C. LAMB Books of quick interest . . are for the eye to glide over only. **glide into** pass gradually into (a condition or state), pass unconsciously into (doing something). 8 **gliding-plane** = *glide-plane* below.

Comb.: **glide-plane** *Cryst.* (*a*) a plane in a crystal along which lateral deformation (slip) may occur; (*b*) a plane of symmetry such that reflection in the plane and translation parallel to it produce a lattice congruent with the original; **glide-twin** *Cryst.* a twin crystal produced by the gliding of adjacent layers of a crystal lattice over one another; **glide-twinning** the formation of glide-twins.

gliding *ppl a.* (*a*) that glides; *gliding possum* = *flying phalanger* s.v. FLYING *ppl a.*; (*b*) = GLISSANT: LME. **glidingly** *adv.* L18.

glider /ˈglʌɪdə/ *n.* LME. [f. GLIDE *v.* + -ER[1].] 1 A person who or thing which glides. Also, something that aids in gliding, a fitment that facilitates smooth continuous movement. LME. 2 An aeroplane designed to fly for long periods without power, and often having no engine. Also, a (skilled) user of such an aircraft. L19. 3 A long swing seat suspended from a vertical frame. *US.* M20. 4 Any of various small Australasian marsupials that glide from tree to tree; *spec.* a flying phalanger, a flying mouse. M20.

Comb.: **glider bomb** = *glide bomb* s.v. GLIDE *n.*

gliff /glɪf/ *v.* & *n.* Now only *Sc.* & *north.* ME. [Origin unkn.] A *v.* †1 *v.i.* Slip, glance aside; *fig.* make a slip in reading. Only in ME. †2a *v.i.* & (*rare*) *t.* Direct (the eyes) in a glance. Only in ME. b *v.i.* Shine suddenly, flash. LME–L16. 3 *v.t.* Frighten. E19. B *n.* 1 A passing view; a glance, a glimpse. ME. 2 A sudden fright; a scare. M18. 3 A short period of time. L18.

gliffing *n.* (*a*) the time required to give a glance, an instant; (*b*) a surprise, a fright: E19.

glim /glɪm/ *n.* LME. [Perh. abbrev. of GLIMMER *n.*[1] or GLIMPSE *n.*] †1 Brightness. *rare.* Only in LME. 2 Orig., a passing look, a glimpse. Later, as much as is seen at a glance; a scrap. *Sc.* E17. 3a A candle, a lantern, (*arch. slang*). Also, a faint light. L17. b An eye. *slang.* Now *rare* or *obs.* E19.

†**glimflashy** *a. slang.* L17–M19. [f. GLIM *n.* + FLASHY *a.*] Angry.

glimmer /ˈglɪmə/ *n.*[1] M16. [f. the vb.] †1 Fire. M16–M17. 2 A faint or wavering light, a shimmer, a sheen. L16. 3a Showiness of manner. Now *rare* or *obs.* E19. b A faint gleam (*of* hope, understanding, etc.); a glimpse, a half-view. M19.

2 TENNYSON In gloss of satin and glimmer of pearls. R. L. STEVENSON The men bustling to their places in the glimmer of the ship's lanterns. 3b E. A. FREEMAN Here we get the first glimmer of Austin canons. C. HAMPTON The man hasn't a glimmer of talent.

glimmerless *a.* without a glimmer L19. **glimmery** *a.* full of glimmer E20.

glimmer /ˈglɪmə/ *n.*[2] L17. [G, f. *glimmen* to glow.] *Min.* Mica.

glimmer /ˈglɪmə/ *v.i.* LME. [Prob. of Scand. origin (cf. Sw. *glimra*, Da. *glimre*, corresp. to (M)HG, Du. *glimmern*), f. Gmc. Cf. GLEAM *n.*[1] & *v.*[1]] †1 Shine brightly, glitter; (of the eyes) flash. LME–M16. 2 Shine faintly or intermittently. LME. 3 Look with half-closed eyes; see indistinctly. *rare.* L16.

2 T. GRAY Now fades the glimmering landscape on the sight. W. CATHER The light of a lamp glimmered through the cracks. *fig.*: GEO. ELIOT The idea of ever recovering happiness never glimmered in her mind for a moment. **go glimmering** *US slang* die away, die out, vanish.

glimmeringly *adv.* in a glimmering manner M16.

glimmering /ˈglɪm(ə)rɪŋ/ *n.* LME. [f. GLIMMER *v.* + -ING[1].] 1 The action of GLIMMER *v.*; an instance of this; the shining of a faint or intermittent light. LME. 2 A half-view; a glimpse, an inkling; a faint notion. LME.

1 R. ADAMS He could just perceive a glimmering of water. 2 G. B. AIRY It is only possible to give a glimmering of what I desire to convey.

glimpse /glɪm(p)s/ *n.* M16. [f. the vb.] 1 A faint and transient appearance. Formerly also, an occasionally perceptible resemblance; a trace (of a quality). M16. 2 A brief glance, a momentary and imperfect view (*of*). L16. 3 A momentary shining, a flash. Freq. in *the glimpses of the moon* below. Now *arch.* or passing into sense 2. E17.

1 MILTON In his face The glimpses of his Father's glory shine. 2 V. WOOLF A glimpse of the church through the trees. C. PRIEST Glimpses into other people's lives. *catch a glimpse of*: see CATCH *v.* 3 SIR W. SCOTT A glimpse of the moon showed the dark and huge tower. **the glimpses of the moon** [after Shakes. *Haml.*] the earth by night; sublunary scenes.

glimpse /glɪm(p)s/ *v.* ME. [f. the base of GLIMMER *v.*, perh. repr. OE = MHG *glimsen*, ult. f. WGmc.] 1 *v.i.* Shine faintly or intermittently; glimmer, glitter. ME. b Appear faintly; dawn. Now *poet.* or *arch.* E17. †2 *v.i.* Have imperfect vision. LME–E16. 3 *v.i.* Glance briefly. (Foll. by *at*, *upon*, etc.) LME. 4 *v.t.* Give a glimpse of. *rare.* M17. 5 *v.t.* Catch a glimpse of; see faintly or partly. L18.

1 A. MUNDAY Little glow-worms glimpsing in the dark. *fig.*: E. PAGITT The Law of God, which glimpsed in their hearts. b P. FLETCHER Then glimpst the hopefull morrow. 3 C. LAMB I read your letter, and glimpsed at your beautiful sonnet. 4 G. MACKENZIE The twilight of darkned reason glimpsing to man, that impressa of the divine Image. 5 I. MURDOCH He glimpsed her ahead, hurrying, and then she was gone. P. BROOK For a few rare flashes she glimpses her condition.

glint /glɪnt/ *n.*[1] M16. [f. the vb.] 1 A gleam; a faint appearance of light or of some lustrous object; a flash, a glitter, a sparkle. M16. b Shining appearance; shine. M19. 2 A passing look, a glance; a momentary view, a glimpse. Chiefly *Sc.* & *north.* E19.

1 H. WILLIAMSON She saw the glint of scales as the fish sped in zigzag course. *a glint in one's eye*: see EYE *n.* 2 W. BLACK I . . was having a glint at the newspaper.

glint /glɪnt/ *n.*[2] E20. [Da., Sw. *klint* cliff, rel. to Icel. *klettur* (ON *klettr*) rock, crag: cf. CLINT *n.*] *Physical Geogr.* A steep cliff or escarpment of almost horizontal strata, produced by erosion of adjacent rock.

Comb.: **glint-lake**: formed along a glint-line; **glint-line** an extensive glint or escarpment, *spec.* that at the boundary between an ancient shield (as the Baltic shield) and younger rocks.

glint /glɪnt/ *v.* LME. [Alt. of GLENT.] 1 *v.i.* = GLENT *v.* 1, 1b. Now *rare.* LME. 2 *v.i.* Shine with a flashing light; gleam, glitter. LME. b *v.t.* Make (something) shine flashingly. M19. 3 *v.i.* Peep, take a glance. L17.

1 LYTTON From the mirth of sunny Leofwine sorrow glints aside. 2 G. MACDONALD A few silvery threads glinted in his hair. J. BUCHAN The sun glinted on the metals of the line and the wet stones in the stream.

glioblastoma /ˌglʌɪə(ʊ)blaˈstəʊmə/ *n.* Pl. **-mas**, **-mata** /-mətə/. E20. [f. GLIA + -O- + -BLAST + -OMA.] *Med.* A fast-growing brain glioma.

glioma /glʌɪˈəʊmə/ *n.* Pl. **-mas**, **-mata** /-mətə/. L19. [f. Gk *glia* glue + -OMA. Cf. GLIA.] *Med.* Any malignant tumour of non-nervous cells (glia) in the nervous system.

gliomatous *a.* of the nature of a glioma L19.

gliosis /glʌɪˈəʊsɪs/ *n.* Pl. **-oses** /-ˈəʊsiːz/. L19. [f. GLIA: see -OSIS.] *Med.* Reparative or pathological proliferation of glial cells.

glirine /ˈglʌɪrʌɪn, ˈglɪ-/ *a.* M19. [f. L *glis*, *glir-* dormouse + -INE[1].] *Zool.* Orig., pertaining to rodents or lagomorphs (formerly grouped together in the order Glires). Now, pertaining to the family Gliridae of Palaearctic dormice.

glisk /glɪsk/ *n.* & *v.* L17. [Origin uncertain: perh. rel. to GLITTER.] A *n.* A glimpse; a glance; a gleam. *Sc.* L17. B *v.i.* 1 Glance *over*. *obs.* exc. *dial.* E18. 2 Glitter, shine. *dial.* M19.

gliss /glɪs/ *n.* E20. [Abbrev.] = GLISSANDO.

glissade /glɪˈsɑːd, -ˈseɪd/ *n.* & *v.* M19. [Fr., f. *glisser* slip, slide: see -ADE.] A *n.* 1 *Dancing.* A step consisting of a glide or slide in any direction, usu. a joining step. M19. 2 *Mountaineering.* The action or an act of sliding down a steep slope esp. of snow, usu. on the feet with the support of an ice-axe etc. M19. B *v.* 1 *v.i.* & *t.* (w. *it*). *Dancing.* Perform a glissade; progress by glissades. M19. 2 *Mountaineering.* Slide down a steep slope esp. of snow by means of a glissade. M19.

glissader *n.* M19.

glissando /glɪˈsandəʊ/ *n.* Pl. **-di** /-di/, **-dos**. L19. [It. f. Fr. *glissant* pres. pple of *glisser* slip, slide.] *Mus.* A continuous slide of adjacent notes upwards or downwards.

glissant /ˈglɪs(ə)nt/ *a.* M19. [Fr., pres. pple of *glisser* slip, slide: see -ANT[1].] *Her.* Of a serpent: shown moving forward in fess.

glissé /glise/ *n.* Pl. pronounced same. E20. [Fr., pa. pple of *glisser* slip, slide.] *Ballet.* More fully *pas glissé* /pɑ/. A sliding step in which the flat of the foot is often used.

glist /glɪst/ *v.* & *n.* ME. [App. abbrev. of GLISTEN *v.*] A *v.i.* Glisten. Now only *Sc.* ME. B *n.* †1 Mica. Only in 18. 2 A gleam, glistening. *rare.* M19.

glisten /ˈglɪs(ə)n/ *v.* & *n.* [OE *glisnian*, f. base of *glisian* (= OFris. *glisa*, MLG *glisen*), f. Gmc: see -EN[5]. Cf. GLISTER.] A *v.i.* Gleam, shine fitfully, glitter, sparkle (*lit.* & *fig.*). OE.

R. P. WARREN The pavements glistened in the quick sunlight that had followed a flurry of rain. T. WILLIAMS Her eyes are glistening with tears.

B *n.* Glitter; sparkle. M19.

D. H. LAWRENCE A glisten like sunshine refracted through crystals of ice.

glisteningly *adv.* in a glistening manner E17.

glister /ˈglɪstə/ *v.* & *n.* LME. [Corresp. to and prob. f. MLG *glistern*, (M)Du. *glisteren*, f. Gmc: see -ER[5]. Cf. GLISTEN.] A *v.i.* Shine, sparkle, glitter. Now *arch.* & *dial.* LME.

B *n.* A bright light; sparkle, glitter. M16.

C. E. CRADDOCK She caught a glimpse of . . the glister of a great lucent, tremulous star.

glisteringly *adv.* in a glistering manner L16. **glistery** *a.* full of glister E19.

glit *n.* & *v.* see GLEET.

glitch /glɪtʃ/ *n.* & *v. slang.* M20. [Origin unkn.: cf. *hitch* and Yiddish *glitsh* slippery place, *glitshik* elusive.] A *n.* A sudden irregularity or malfunction of equipment etc. M20.

W. GARNER We have a minor glitch I'd appreciate your help.

B *v.i.* Suffer a glitch. L20.
glitchy *a.* prone to malfunction L20.

glitter /ˈglɪtə/ *v.* & *n.* LME. [ON *glitra* = MHG, G *glitzern* sparkle, frequent. f. Gmc, in OS *glītan*, OHG *glīzan* (G *gleissen*) shine, ON *glita* glitter, Goth. *glitmunjan* (of clothes) shine bright: see -ER[5].] A *v.i.* 1 Shine with a brilliant tremulous light; gleam, sparkle. LME. 2 Esp. of a person: make a brilliant appearance or display; be showy or splendid. LME.
1 W. CATHER A diamond necklace glittered about her . . throat. G. ORWELL A high-ceilinged windowless cell with walls of glittering white porcelain. 2 BURKE I saw her [the Queen of France] . . glittering like the morning star. JAN MORRIS The social brilliance of Oxford . . when this was the most glittering university in Europe. **glittering generality** a platitude, a cliché, a superficially convincing but empty phrase, (usu. in *pl.*).
B *n.* 1 Brilliant tremulous light, (a) sparkle; brightness, brilliance; splendour, showiness. E17. 2 A powder consisting of tiny pieces of sparkling material used as a cosmetic or for decoration. M20.
1 M. MCCARTHY There was a glitter in his hollow, dark eyes. G. BORDMAN She is intrigued by the glitter of the big city.
Comb.: **glitter dust** = sense B.2 above; **glitter rock** rock music played by performers dressed in glittering costumes etc.
glitterer *n.* a person who or thing which glitters E19. **glitteringly** *adv.* in a glittering manner E17. **glitterless** *a.* devoid of glitter L19. **glittery** *a.* full of glitter M18.

glitterati /glɪtəˈrɑːti/ *n.pl. slang.* (orig. *US*). M20. [Punningly f. GLITTER *v.* & *n.* + LITERATI *n.pl.*] The fashionable and prominent people in the literary or show-business worlds.

glitz /glɪts/ *n. slang* (orig. *N. Amer.*). L20. [Back-form. f. GLITZY.] Extravagant but superficial display; ostentation; show-business glamour.

glitzy /ˈglɪtsi/ *a. slang* (orig. *N. Amer.*). M20. [Prob. f. GLITTER *n.* after RITZY *a.*: cf. G *glitzerig* glittering.] Characterized by glitter or extravagant show; tawdry, gaudy; glitteringly spectacular but in poor taste.
Listener The Oscars are . . a glitzy, vulgar affirmation that they're getting things right.
glitzily *adv.* L20. **glitziness** *n.* L20.

†**gloak** *n. slang.* L18–M19. [Origin unkn.] A man, a fellow.

gloam /gləʊm/ *n. poet.* E19. [Back-form. f. GLOAMING.] Twilight, gloaming.

gloam /gləʊm/ *v.i.* Chiefly *Sc.* E18. [f. as prec.] Darken, become dusk.

gloaming /ˈgləʊmɪŋ/ *n.* [OE *glōmung* f. *glōm* twilight, prob. f. Gmc base of GLOW *v.*[1]] 1 Evening twilight. OE. 2 Morning twilight. *rare.* M19.
1 S. DONALDSON Before the gloaming had thickened into darkness. *fig.*: J. M. BARRIE The help . . needed in the gloaming of their lives.
Comb.: **gloaming-shot** (*a*) a shot made in the twilight; (*b*) the beginning of twilight; **gloaming sight** (*a*) an indistinct view; (*b*) a front gun-sight for use in twilight.
¶From LME, chiefly *Sc.* In general literary use from E19.

gloat /gləʊt/ *n.*[1] M17. [f. GLOAT *v.*] †1 A side-glance; a furtive or sullen look. Only in M17. 2 An act of gloating; a look, feeling, or expression of triumphant satisfaction. L19.
2 A. HUNTER He was having a gloat over his gold.

gloat /gləʊt/ *n.*[2] *obs.* exc. *dial.* M18. [Origin unkn.] An eel.

gloat /gləʊt/ *v.i.* L16. [Origin uncertain: perh. of Scand. origin (cf ON *glotta* grin, Sw. dial. *glotta* peep, corresp. to (M)HG *glotzen* stare).] 1 Look with a furtive or sidelong glance. Also, appear sulky. *obs.* exc. *dial.* L16. 2 Shine, gleam; (of light) fall obliquely. *rare.* M17. †3 Cast amorous or admiring glances (*on*, *upon*). L17–E18. 4 Feast the eyes or mind lustfully, avariciously, malignantly, triumphantly, etc. Usu. foll. by *on*, *upon*, *over*. M18.
1 T. CREECH I . . with a squinting Eye glote o'er the Pit. 2 G. W. THORNBURY The light gloated on some strange-shaped glasses. 3 N. ROWE Teach . . her deluding Eyes to gloat for you. 4 P. H. GIBBS Our enemies are gloating over our ruin. A. TYLER She seemed to be gloating. She was . . so sure of her place.
gloatingly *adv.* in a gloating manner L17.

glob /glɒb/ *n.* E20. [Perh. a blend of BLOB *n.* and GOB *n.*[1]] A mass or lump of some liquid or semi-liquid substance; a dollop.
H. LAWSON A glob of mud on the sand. T. O'BRIEN Bullets struck . . exploding globs of flesh.

global /ˈgləʊb(ə)l/ *a.* L17. [f. GLOBE *n.* + -AL[1].] 1 Spherical, globular. *rare.* L17. 2 Pertaining to or embracing the whole of a group of items etc.; comprehensive, total; *spec.* pertaining to or involving the whole world, worldwide. L19.
1 H. BASCOM The gate with frosted global lights on the concrete pillars. 2 A. E. STEVENSON Global plans for solving all the world's problems by some master stroke. **global search** *Computing* a search through the whole of a computer file; a search for every occurrence of an item. **global variable** *Computing*: whose value is the same in all parts of a program. **global village** (orig. *N. Amer.*) the whole world considered as a single community brought together by high technology and international communications. **global warming** an increase in temperature at the surface of the earth supposedly caused by the greenhouse effect.
globalism *n.* internationalism M20. **globalist** *n.* & *a.* (a person) advocating a global approach to economic etc. issues M20. **globalization** *n.* the action or an act of globalizing M20. **globalize** *v.t.* make global M20. **globally** *adv.* M20.

globate /ˈgləʊbeɪt/ *a. rare.* M19. [f. GLOBE *n.* + -ATE[2].] Having the form of a globe; spherical.
globated *a.* given the form of a globe; made spherical: M18.

globe /gləʊb/ *n.* & *v.* LME. [OFr., or L *globus* spherical body.] A *n.* I 1 A spherical body. LME. 2a A planet, a star. Chiefly *poet.* M16. b *The* earth. L16. 3 A spherical representation of the earth (more fully *terrestrial globe*) or the constellations (more fully *celestial globe*). M16. 4 A golden orb as an emblem of sovereignty. E17. 5 An approximately spherical glass vessel, esp. a lampshade, a fish-bowl, an electric light bulb, etc. M17. 6 More fully *globe of the eye*. The eyeball. L18.
1 B. JOWETT In the form of a globe, round as from a lathe. 2a J. H. NEWMAN Some unknown globe in the heavens. b V. NABOKOV The gloom of yet another World War had settled upon the globe. 3 **use of the globes** *arch.* the learning or teaching of geography and astronomy by using terrestrial and celestial globes. 4 SIR W. SCOTT With crown, with sceptre, and with globe, Emblems of empery. 5 G. JONES An oil-lamp, the flame turned low in the frosted globe.
II 7 A compact body (of people etc.). *rare.* E17.
7 MILTON Him round A Globe of fierie Seraphim inclos'd.
Comb.: *globe amaranth*: see AMARANTH 1; *globe artichoke*: see ARTICHOKE 1; **globe daisy** any plant of the genus *Globularia* (family Globulariaceae), *esp.* the European *G. trichosantha* and *G. vulgaris*; **globe-fish** any of various chiefly tropical fishes with more or less rounded bodies; *esp.* = PUFFER 1b; **globe-flower** any of various plants of the genus *Trollius*, of the buttercup family, with large globular flowers composed of many overlapping yellow petaloid sepals; esp. *T. europaeus*, native to upland meadows; **globe lightning** = *ball lightning* s.v. BALL *n.*[1]; **globe-thistle** any of several thistles of the genus *Echinops*, esp. *E. sphaerocephalus*, grown in gardens for their globular heads of pale blue flowers; **globe-trot** *v.i.* go globe-trotting; **globe-trotter** a person who travels (orig., hurriedly, now usu., extensively) through countries, esp. for sightseeing; **globe-trotting** hurried or extensive travelling through countries, esp. for sightseeing; **globe tulip** any of certain mariposa lilies with nodding globular flowers.
B *v.* 1 *v.t.* Form into a globe; make globular. Usu. in *pass.* LME. 2 *v.i.* Be or become globular. M19.
1 *refl.*: TENNYSON The great stars that globed themselves in heaven.
globed *a.* (*a*) having the form of a globe, spherical; (*b*) having a globe, enclosed in a globe: E19.

globi *n.* pl. of GLOBUS.

globical /ˈglɒbɪk(ə)l, ˈgləʊb-/ *a.* E17. [f. GLOBE *n.* + -ICAL.] †1 Globular, spherical. Only in 17. 2 *Her.* Having the general outline circular. L17.

globigerina /ˌgləʊbɪdʒəˈraɪnə/ *n.* Pl. **-nae** /-niː/, **-nas**. M19. [mod.L (see below), f. L *globus*, *globi-* GLOBE + *-ger* carrying + -INA[2].] *Zool.* Any marine planktonic foraminiferan of the genus *Globigerina*, having a calcareous shell with globular chambers and spiny processes.
Comb.: **globigerina ooze** a deposit of soft pale mud over wide areas of the ocean floor, consisting largely of the shells of globigerinae.
gloˈbigerine *a.* pertaining to or derived from globigerinae M19.

globin /ˈgləʊbɪn/ *n.* L19. [Abbrev. of HAEMOGLOBIN.] *Biochem.* Any of various polypeptides forming the protein component of haemoglobin and related compound proteins.

globoid /ˈgləʊbɔɪd/ *a.* & *n.* L19. [f. GLOBE *n.* + -OID.] A *adj.* Approximately globe-shaped. L19. B *n. Bot.* A rounded mineral aggregate in the aleurone granules of plant seeds, consisting of amorphous phytin. L19.

globose /ˈgləʊbəʊs, gləʊˈbəʊs/ *a.* LME. [L *globosus*, f. *globus* GLOBE *n.*: see -OSE[1].] Globe-shaped; (approximately) spherical.
globosely *adv.* M19. **globoseness** *n.* (*rare*) E18. **gloˈbosity** *n.* the condition of being globose; a rounded part: M17.

globoside /ˈgləʊbəsaɪd/ *n.* M20. [f. GLOB(ULE + -OSIDE.] *Biochem.* A sphingolipid forming spherical globules, found in human erythrocytes.

globous /ˈgləʊbəs/ *a.* Now *rare.* E17. [Fr. †*globeux* or L *globosus*, f. *globus* GLOBE *n.*: see -OUS.] = GLOBOSE.

globular /ˈglɒbjʊlə/ *a.* M17. [f. L *globulus* (see GLOBULE) + -AR[1].] 1 Globe-shaped, spherical. M17. b Of a protein: having a relatively compact molecular structure with considerable folding. M20. 2 Composed of globules. M18.
Special collocations: **globular cluster** *Astron.* a large compact star cluster of spherical form, numbers of which surround the Milky Way and other galaxies. **globular lightning** = *ball lightning* s.v. BALL *n.*[1]
globuˈlarity *n.* the property of being globular E19. **globularly** *adv.* M19. **globularness** *n.* (*rare*) E18.

globule /ˈglɒbjuːl/ *n.* M17. [Fr., or L *globulus* dim. of *globus* GLOBE *n.*: see -ULE.] 1 A small spherical body or globe; a round drop (of liquid); *Biol.* (*arch.*) a blood corpuscle. M17. b *Bot.* The male reproductive structure of a charophyte (stonewort). Cf. NUCULE 2. M19. 2 A small pill. M19.

globulin /ˈglɒbjʊlɪn/ *n.* M19. [f. prec. (= blood corpuscle) + -IN[1].] *Biochem.* Any of a class of simple proteins with little or no solubility in water but soluble in salt solutions; *esp.* any of those forming the second largest electrophoretic fraction of blood plasma protein.
alpha, beta, gamma, globulin (any protein belonging to) each of the three fractions of blood plasma globulin distinguished by decreasing electrophoretic mobility from alpha to gamma. IMMUNOGLOBULIN, LACTOGLOBULIN.

globulite /ˈglɒbjʊlaɪt/ *n.* L17. [f. GLOBULE + -ITE[1].] 1 *gen.* A small globule. *rare.* L17. 2 *Petrogr.* A small spherical crystallite (in volcanic glass). L19.

globulous /ˈglɒbjʊləs/ *a.* Now *rare.* M17. [Fr. *globuleux*, f. as GLOBULE: see -ULOUS.] Globular in form; consisting of globules.

globus /ˈgləʊbəs/ *n.* Pl. **globi** /ˈgləʊbaɪ/. L18. [L = globe.] 1 *Med.* In full *globus hystericus* /hɪˈstɛrɪkəs/. A subjective sensation of a rounded object, esp. of a lump in the throat. L18. 2 *Anat.* Any of various spherical or rounded structures. Usu. w. specifying wd. M19.
2 **globus pallidus** /ˈpalɪdəs/ [L = pale globus] the median part of the lentiform nucleus in the brain.

globy /ˈgləʊbi/ *a.* L16. [f. GLOBE *n.* + -Y[1].] Globular, spherical.

glocalize /ˈgləʊk(ə)laɪz/ *v.i.* Also **-ise**. L20. [Blend of GLOBAL *a.* and LOCALIZE *v.*] *Comm.* Conduct business globally with adaptation to local conditions.
glocaliˈzation *n.* L20.

glochid /ˈgləʊkɪd/ *n.* L19. [Gk *glōkhis*, *glōkhid* arrowhead.] *Bot.* A glochidium or other barbed hair; *spec.* a barbed bristle on the areole of some cacti.

glochidia *n.* pl. of GLOCHIDIUM.

glochidiate /gləʊˈkɪdɪət/ *a.* E19. [f. as next + -ATE[2].] *Bot.* (Of a hair) barbed at the tip; (of a plant structure) bearing barbed hairs.

glochidium /glәʊˈkɪdɪәm/ *n.* Pl. **-dia** /-dɪә/. L19. [mod.L f. Gk. dim. of *glōkhis* arrowhead.] 1 *Zool.* The parasitic larva of certain freshwater mussels, which attaches to the fins or gills of fish by suckers or hooks. L19. 2 *Bot.* A barbed hair or bristle; *spec.* a barbed organ of attachment on the surface of a spore mass, as in the aquatic fern *Azolla.* L19.

glockenspiel /ˈglɒk(ә)nspiːl, -ʃpiːl/ *n.* E19. [G = bell-play.] *Mus.* 1 An organ-stop imitating the sound of bells. E19. 2 Any of several percussion instruments, *esp.* (*a*) a series of tuned metal bars mounted on a horizontal frame; (*b*) a series of bells or metal bars in a lyre-shaped frame carried in marching bands (also *lyra glockenspiel*). M19.

glode *v.* pa. t. & pple: see GLIDE *v.*

Gloger's rule /ˈglәʊgәz ruːl/ *n. phr.* M20. [f. C. L. *Gloger* (1803–63), Ger. zoologist.] *Zool.* The observation that races of an animal inhabiting warmer or more humid regions tend to be more heavily pigmented than those of cooler or drier regions.

glögg /glœg, glɒg/ *n.* Also **glugg** /glʌg/. E20. [Sw.] A Scandinavian winter drink, consisting of hot sweetened red wine with brandy, almonds, raisins, and spices.

gloire /glwaːr/ *n.* M19. [Fr.] In full *la gloire* /la/. Glory; *spec.* the national glory and prestige of France.

R. HOLMES The Napoleonic dreams of *La gloire.*

Gloire de Dijon /glwaːr dә diʒɔ̃/ *n. phr.* M19. [Fr. = glory of Dijon.] A yellow hybrid tea rose.

glom /glɒm/ *v.t.* & *i.* w. *on to. slang* (chiefly *US*). Infl. **-mm-**. E20. [Var. of GLAUM *v.*] Steal, grab.

Sunday Mail (Brisbane) She glommed . . cash and jewellery from the good doctor. W. SAFIRE Glomming on to a technical phrase and stretching its meaning.

glome /glәʊm/ *n.* M17. [L *glomus*: see GLOMERATE *v.*] †1 A skein or ball of yarn or thread. Only in M17. 2 *Bot.* A flower-head, a glomerule. *rare.* L18.

glomera *n.* pl. of GLOMUS.

glomerate /ˈglɒm(ә)rәt/ *a.* Now *rare.* L18. [L *glomeratus* pa. pple of *glomerare*: see next, -ATE².] Chiefly *Bot.* Compactly clustered; having the form of a rounded mass or cluster.

glomerate /ˈglɒmәreɪt/ *v.i.* & *t.* Now *rare* or *obs.* M17. [L *glomerat-* pa. ppl stem of *glomerare*, f. *glomus*, *glomer-* ball or clue of yarn etc.: see -ATE³.] Wind or twist about; wind into a ball, gather into a rounded mass.

gloˈmeration *n.* (*a*) the action or process of glomerating; (*b*) a compact cluster: E17.

glomerular /glɒˈmɛr(j)ʊlә/ *a.* L19. [f. GLOMERULUS + -AR¹.] Of or pertaining to glomeruli, esp. those of the kidney.

glomerule /ˈglɒmәruːl/ *n.* L18. [Fr. *glomérule* f. mod.L GLOMERULUS.] 1 *Bot.* A condensed cymose flower-head. Now *rare.* L18. 2 *Microbiol.* A small clump or cluster of cells or spores, esp. of algal cells in lichens. M19. 3 *Anat.* = GLOMERULUS 1. *rare.* M19.

gloˈmerulose *a.* (chiefly *Bot.*) bearing or occurring as glomerules L19.

glomeruli *n.* pl. of GLOMERULUS.

glomerulitis /glɒˌmɛr(j)ʊˈlʌɪtɪs/ *n.* L19. [f. GLOMERULUS + -ITIS.] *Med.* An inflammation of the renal glomeruli.

glomerulo- /glɒˈmɛr(j)ʊlәʊ/ *comb. form.* [f. GLOMERULUS + -O-.] *Med.* Of the glomeruli of the kidney.

glomeruloneˈphritis *n.* a disease of the kidneys, usually allergic in origin, resulting in acute inflammation L19.

glomerulus /glɒˈmɛr(j)ʊlәs/ *n.* Pl. **-li** /-lʌɪ, -liː/. M19. [mod.L dim. of L *glomer-*, *glomus* ball of thread: cf. -ULE.] 1 *Anat.* & *Zool.* A tuft or plexus of capillaries, nerve endings, etc.; *esp.* the network of capillaries in the end capsule of each tubule in the vertebrate kidney, where waste products are filtered from the blood. M19. 2 *Microbiol.* = GLOMERULE 2. M19.

glomus /ˈglәʊmәs/ *n.* Pl. **glomera** /ˈglәʊm(ә)rә/, (not after L) **glomi** /ˈglәʊmʌɪ/. M19. [L = ball of thread.] *Anat.* & *Zool.* A small body consisting of blood-vessels and associated tissue; *esp.* any of numerous small structures in the skin of the hands and feet involving a connection between a vein and an artery, and functioning in temperature regulation. Freq. w. specifying wd.

gloom /gluːm/ *n.*¹ L16. [In sense 1 f. GLOOM *v.*; in senses 2, 3 perh. back-form. f. GLOOMY.] 1 A sullen look; a frown, a scowl. *Sc.* L16. 2 Partial or total darkness; sombreness, obscurity. E17. b A dark place. *poet.* E18. 3 Melancholy, despondency. Also (*a fit of*) *the glooms.* M18.

2 N. MAILER In the gloom of the jungle each minute seemed more ominous. 3 *Daily Mirror* Got the glooms? . . How about an evening out? Just us two. **gloom and doom** pessimism, despondency.

gloomful *a.* (*rare*) melancholy, dark M19.

gloom /gluːm/ *n.*² Now *rare* or *obs.* L16. [Perh. repr. 1st elem. of GLOAMING.] †1 *hot gloom*, excessive heat (of the sun). L16–M18. 2 In full *gloom stove.* A drying oven used in making gunpowder. M19.

gloom /gluːm/ *v.* LME. [Origin unkn.] 1 *v.i.* Look sullen or displeased, frown, scowl; be or appear dejected or depressed. LME. b *v.t.* Express with gloom. M19. 2 *v.i.* Of the weather, sky, etc.: lour; be or become dull or threatening. LME. b Darken, become dusk. L16. 3 *v.t.* Make dark or sombre; cover with gloom. L16. b Make dismal or melancholy. M18. 4 *v.i.* Look dark or sombre; appear darkly or obscurely. L18.

1 *Century Magazine* I hate myself for glooming about the house in secret. E. BOWEN Marcelle . . who had lately quarrelled with her best friend . . gloomed at Sir Robert's right hand. b CARLYLE 'What interloping fellow is this?' gloomed Valori. 2 C. IVES It rains and darkens, and the sky glooms. b G. MACDONALD In the midst of the forest it gloomed earlier than in the open country. 3 G. MACBETH Then smoke . . gloomed the whole sky. 4 A. CARTER The shop gloomed behind its blinds.

glooming *n.* (*a*) the action or an instance of being or looking gloomy; (*b*) *poet.* = GLOAMING: LME.

gloomth /gluːmθ/ *n. rare.* M18. [f. GLOOM *n.*¹ or *v.* + -TH¹] = GLOOM *n.*¹ 2.

gloomy /ˈgluːmi/ *a.* L16. [f. GLOOM *n.*¹ 1 + -Y¹.] 1 Dark, unlighted, shadowy. L16. 2 Sullen, depressed, despondent. L16. 3 Causing gloom; dismal, disheartening. E18.

1 G. SWIFT He passed into the bedroom, gloomy behind the drawn curtains. 2 T. WRIGHT People of that gloomy character who never laugh. 3 W. K. KELLY A gloomy and forbidding spectacle.

gloomily *adv.* E18. **gloominess** *n.* E17.

gloop /gluːp/ *n. colloq.* L20. [Imit.: cf. GLOP *n.*] Unpleasantly viscid matter; slime.

gloopy *a.* L20.

glop /glɒp/ *n. slang* (orig. *US*). E20. [Imit.] A liquid or viscous substance or mixture; *spec.* inferior or unappetising food or drink.

fig.: *Newsweek* Metaphysical glop and heavy-breathing symbolism.

gloppy *a.* L20.

glop /glɒp/ *v.i. obs.* exc. *dial.* Infl. **-pp-**. LME. [Perh. abbrev. of GLOPPEN.] Stare, gaze in wonder or alarm.

gloppen /ˈglɒp(ә)n/ *v.* Long *obs.* exc. *dial.* ME. [ON *glúpna* be downcast.] 1 *v.t.* Startle, frighten, astound. Freq. as *gloppened* ppl a. ME. 2 *v.i.* Be distressed, downcast, or startled; stare in amazement. LME.

glore /glɔː/ *v.i.* Long *obs.* exc. *dial.* LME. [LG *glōren* or Scand. (cf. Icel. *glóra* gleam, stare) rel. to GLOW *v.*¹: see GLOWER.] 1 Shine, glitter, glisten. LME. 2 Gaze intently, stare, glower. LME.

gloria /ˈglɔːrɪә/ *n.* & *a.* In sense 1 **G-**. ME. [L *gloria* GLORY *n.*] A *n.* 1 Any of several Christian liturgical formulae, as *Gloria* (*Patri*) the doxology 'Glory be to the Father', *Gloria* (*tibi*) the response 'Glory be to thee', *Gloria* (*in excelsis*) the hymn 'Glory be to God on high', forming part of the Mass etc. ME. b The music to which any of these is set. L16. 2 An aureole, a nimbus. L18. 3 In France: (a drink of) coffee mixed with brandy or rum. M19. 4 A closely-woven fabric of silk and wool or cotton etc.; a garment made of this. L19. B *adj.* Made of the fabric gloria. E20.

gloriation /glɔːrɪˈeɪʃ(ә)n/ *n.* Now *rare* or *obs.* LME. [L *gloriatio(n-)*, f. *gloriat-* pa. ppl stem of *gloriari*: see GLORY *v.*, -ATION.] The action of glorying; boasting, triumphing.

gloriette /glɔːrɪˈɛt/ *n.* M19. [Fr.] A highly decorated chamber in a castle or other building.

glorification /ˌglɔːrɪfɪˈkeɪʃ(ә)n/ *n.* LME. [eccl.L *glorificatio(n-)*, f. *glorificat-* pa. ppl stem of *glorificare*: see next, -ATION.] 1 The action or an act of glorifying a person or thing, the condition of being glorified. LME. b *spec.* The exaltation of Christ or a human soul to heaven. LME. c Transformation to a more magnificent form; that which is transformed. L19. 2 A set form of worship; a doxology. M17. 3 The attribution of glory or praise to a person or thing; enthusiastic or extravagant praise. M19.

1 JER. TAYLOR They whose sins accidentally thus serv'd the glorification of God. b R. BAXTER His Ascension they beheld, and his Glorification they believed. c *Century Magazine* These houses . . are . . glorifications of the humble, early . . New England farm-house. 2 W. D. WHITNEY The songs are . . simple invocations and glorifications of the divinity. 3 H. J. LASKI His glorification of reason as the great key which is to unlock all doors.

glorified /ˈglɔːrɪfʌɪd/ *a.* ME. [f. prec. + -ED¹.] 1 *gen.* That has been glorified. ME. 2 Esp. of a common or inferior thing: that has been transformed into something more splendid. *colloq.* (freq. *iron.*). E19.

1 W. SPALDING Angels and glorified saints adore the Mother and her Son. 2 A. BURGESS A professional man, not a glorified foreman.

glorify /ˈglɔːrɪfʌɪ/ *v.* ME. [(O)Fr. *glorifier* f. eccl.L *glorificare*, f. late L *glorificus*, f. L *gloria*: see GLORY *n.*, -FY.] 1 *v.t.* Make glorious; *spec.* exalt (Christ, a human soul) to the glory of heaven. ME. b Invest with radiance. Formerly also, adorn, embellish. LME. c Transform into something more splendid; (try to) make (a common or inferior thing) seem unrealistically splendid. M19. 2 *v.t.* Advance the glory of (God, His name) by one's actions, suffering, etc.; ascribe glory or praise in adoration to (God). ME. 3 *v.refl.* & †*i.* Think oneself exceedingly fortunate, pride oneself, boast of one's good fortune. (Foll. by *in*, *to do*, *that*.) Now *rare.* ME. 4 *v.t.* Describe or represent as glorious; praise enthusiastically or extravagantly; extol. M16.

1 S. DANIEL Those righteous issues, which shall glorifie And comfort many Nations with their worth. b SHAKES. *Ven. & Ad.* The bright sun glorifies the sky. c J. F. CLARKE Burns, Wordsworth, Whittier . . have known how to glorify common life and every-day people. 2 G. PRIESTLAND Being religiously inclined, she or he is anxious to serve God and glorify him. 3 E. HOWARD For the which he glorified himself exceedingly. 4 J. A. FROUDE Cæsar, who was being so much praised and glorified.

glorifier *n.* LME.

gloriole /ˈglɔːrɪәʊl/ *n.* E19. [Fr. f. L *gloriola* dim. of *gloria* GLORY *n.*: see -OLE¹.] †1 A small measure of renown. Only in E19. 2 An aureole, a halo. M19.

glorious /ˈglɔːrɪәs/ *a.* ME. [AN *glorious*, OFr. *glorios*, *-eus* f. L *gloriosus*, f. *gloria* GLORY *n.*: see -OUS.] 1 a Having glory; renowned; illustrious; *spec.* designating a date or event considered particularly notable. ME. b Conferring glory; honourable. M16. 2 Magnificently beautiful, splendidly adorned. Formerly also, shining, lustrous. LME. b Splendid, magnificent, intensely delightful. Also (*joc.*) *hyperbol.* or *iron.* E17. 3 Boastful; proud, haughty, ostentatious. *obs.* exc. in VAINGLORIOUS. LME. †4 Eager for glory. E17–E18. 5 Ecstatically happy with drink, (happily) drunk. *colloq.* L18.

1a M. ARNOLD By nothing is England so glorious as by her poetry. *Glorious Fourth*: see FOURTH *n.* **Glorious Revolution** the expulsion of James II from England in 1688. *Glorious Twelfth*: see TWELFTH *n.* 1. b W. S. CHURCHILL The Indian Army, revived and reorganised, was to play a glorious part . . in two world wars. 2 H. POWER The Iris . . as vibrissant and glorious as a Cat's eye. G. MACDONALD The heavens were glorious with stars. b M. HOWITT What glorious afternoons and evenings have I spent at Phalerus! OED The glorious uncertainty of cricket. 3 R. NORTH After he was possessed of the Great Seal, he was in

Appearance the gloriousest Man alive. 4 T. HEARNE He always left such to Heroes as were purely Glorious. 5 E. HOWARD As fast as one man could be . . flogged into sobriety, another would become glorious.

gloriously *adv.* ME. **gloriousness** *n.* LME.

glory /ˈglɔːri/ *n.* ME. [AN, OFr. *glorie* f. L *gloria* fame, praise, renown.] 1 Exalted (now esp. merited) renown; honourable fame. ME. 2 Adoring praise and thanksgiving, esp. offered to God. ME. 3 The splendour and bliss of heaven. ME. 4 Resplendent majesty, beauty, or magnificence; a feature of resplendent beauty or magnificence, a splendour (freq. in *pl.*). Also, an effulgence of light; *fig.* an imagined unearthly beauty. LME. 5 Something which brings renown; a special distinction, a splendid ornament. LME. 6 Extreme vanity, boastfulness. *obs.* exc. in VAINGLORY. LME. 7 A state of exaltation, splendour, or prosperity. E17. 8 A circle of light, esp. as depicted around the head or whole figure of Jesus or a saint; a circle or ring of light; a halo. M17. **b** *spec.* A luminous halo projected on to a cloud or fog-bank by the sun; an anthelion. E19. 9 A representation of the heavens opening and revealing celestial beings. Now *rare* or *obs.* E18.

1 DEFOE You are to live here to the glory of Him that made you. P. SCOTT If . . not covered in warlike glory he was not covered in shame. 2 COLERIDGE Glory to Thee, Father of Earth and Heaven! 3 MILTON Thou, bright Saint, high sitt'st in glory. 4 WORDSWORTH There hath past away a glory from the earth. DISRAELI The scarlet glories of the *pyrus japonica*. 5 J. BUCHAN The little valleys which are the glory of the Oxford countryside. 6 P. MASSINGER A little glory in a soldier's mouth Is not uncomely. 7 W. IRVING They thought that the days of their ancient glory were about to return. 8 H. KINGSLEY Her own glorious golden hair, which hung round her lovely face like a glory. 9 R. CUMBERLAND The Holy Virgin is displayed in the center of the piece, above is a glory of Angels.

Phrases etc.: *crowning glory*: see CROWNING *ppl a.* 2. *death-or-glory*: see DEATH. **Glory Be** (esp. in Roman Catholic use) the *Gloria Patri*. **glory be (to God)!** expr. enthusiastic piety or (*colloq.*) surprise or delight. **glory-of-the-snow** = CHIONODOXA. **go to glory** go to heaven, die. GREENWELL'S *glory*. **in one's glory** in one's highest state; *colloq.* in a state of unbounded gratification or enjoyment. KENTISH *glory*. MORNING *glory*. *Old Glory*: see OLD *a.*

Comb.: **glory-box** *Austral.* & *NZ* a box for a woman's store of clothes and household linen in preparation for marriage; **glory-pea** = CLIANTHUS; **glory-tree** any of several trees or shrubs of the genus *Clerodendrum*, of the verbena family; esp. *C. thomsoniae* of tropical W. Africa, with clusters of crimson flowers.

glory /ˈglɔːri/ *v.* LME. [L *gloriari*, f. *gloria* GLORY *n.*] 1 *v.i.* Rejoice, exult, pride oneself. Freq. foll. by *in*, *to do*. LME. †2 *v.i.* & *t.* Boast (of). LME–L17. †3 *v.t.* Honour; make glorious, adorn. LME–L17.

1 H. MARTINEAU Cries . . which Archie always gloried in provoking. E. F. BENSON She gloried in it; she laughed with exultation at the thought of its success. 2 E. SYMMONS We have seen a glimpse of that perspicuity and modesty which is gloried to be in these annotations. 3 H. WOTTON Be ever gloried here Thy Soveraign Name.

glory-hole /ˈglɔːrɪhəʊl/ *n.* & *v.* E19. [Origin unkn.] **A** *n.* 1 An untidy small room, cupboard, drawer, etc., in which odds and ends are kept. E19. **b** Any of various small compartments on a ship, *esp.* one used for storage or as sleeping-quarters. *Naut. slang.* M19. **c** A small billet or dugout. *Mil. slang.* E20. 2 *Glass-making.* **a** A small furnace used in hand-working to keep the glass malleable. M19. **b** An opening in the wall of a furnace exposing the hot interior. L19. 3 A large cavernous opening into a mine; an open quarry. *N. Amer.* E20.

1 M. WILMOT A sort of play room or glory-hole for poor Wilmot to keep his rubbish. **b** R. BEDFORD I . . sneak out on the boat deck to sleep, the glory hole being so hot.

B *v.i.* Carry on surface mining. *N. Amer.* E20.

†**glose** *n.*, *v.* see GLOZE *n.*, *v.*[1]

gloss /glɒs/ *n.*[1] M16. [Refash. of GLOZE *n.* after med.L *glossa* explanation of difficult word f. Gk *glōssa* word needing explanation (also tongue, language: cf. GLOSSO-).] 1 A word inserted between the lines or in the margin in order to explain a foreign or otherwise difficult word in a text; a similar explanation of a word in a glossary or dictionary. Also (more widely), a comment, an explanation, an interpretation, a paraphrase. M16. 2 A collection of such words, a glossary. Also, an interlinear translation or series of annotations. L16. 3 A sophistical or disingenuous explanation; a misrepresentation of another's words. E17.

1 J. BARZUN Dewey . . should be read in the original, not in his followers' gloss. 3 V. GLENDINNING Some of the stories . . are . . untrue, fantastic glosses on a genuinely appalling situation.

glossist *n.* a writer of glosses, a commentator M17.

gloss /glɒs/ *n.*[2] M16. [Origin unkn.] 1 (A) superficial lustre. M16. 2 (A) deceptive external appearance, (a) plausible pretext. (Sometimes confused w. or merging into GLOSS *n.*[1] 3.) M16. 3 A layer of glowing matter, esp. in a fire. *rare.* M18. 4 = GLAZE *n.* 4. *rare.* E19. 5 In full *gloss enamel*, *paint*. An enamel or paint which contains varnish and dries to a bright glossy finish. E20.

1 F. RAPHAEL There was a gloss of tears in her large eyes. C. HAYES Some colours dry matt, others dry to a gloss. *fig.*: SHAKES. *Tr. & Cr.* Yet all his virtues . . Do in our eyes begin to lose their gloss. 2 J. WAINWRIGHT That which is difficult to describe still lurks beneath the gloss. G. S. FRASER An ambassador's business is not to lie but to set a polite gloss on the most awkward truth. 5 *Which?* A coat of primer, followed by two finishing coats of gloss.

gloss /glɒs/ *v.*[1] L16. [f. GLOSS *n.*[1]] 1 *v.i.* Write glosses; make (esp. unfavourable) comments or remarks. (Foll. by *on*, *upon*.) L16. 2 *v.t.* Insert glosses or comments in (a text etc.); comment on, explain (a word, a passage, etc.). L16. 3 *v.t.* Veil with glosses; read a different sense into. (Foll. by *away*, *over*.) M17.

1 SWIFT Those laws, which they assumed the liberty of interpreting and glossing upon. G. S. FRASER The poets are much less in need of illustration by . . quotation and glossing. 2 A. BURGESS Cornwall, which could be glossed as not really England.

glosser *n.*[1] a person who glosses a text; a glossator: E17.

gloss /glɒs/ *v.*[2]*t.* L16. [f. GLOSS *n.*[2], perh. infl. (esp. in sense 1b) by GLOSS *n.*[1]] 1 Give a deceptively fair appearance to. L16. **b** Veil or conceal (something), esp. with specious language or under a fair appearance; explain away. (Foll. by *over*.) M17. 2 Make bright and glossy, glaze; *spec.* coat with gloss paint. M18.

1b A. CARTER She tried to gloss over the humiliation of it. L. DEIGHTON The girl . . had been killed, but the inquiry had glossed over it. 2 SOUTHEY The moonlight fell, glossing the sable tide. *Options* Brickwork walls were painstakingly glossed in brilliant white.

glosser *n.*[2] a person who puts on a gloss M19.

glossal /ˈglɒs(ə)l/ *a.* E19. [f. Gk *glōssa* (see GLOSSO-) + -AL[1].] Of or pertaining to the tongue, lingual.

glossalalia *n.* var. of GLOSSOLALIA.

glossary /ˈglɒs(ə)ri/ *n.* LME. [L *glossarium*, f. *glossa*: see GLOSS *n.*[1], -ARY[1].] A collection of glosses; a list with explanations, often accompanying a text, of abstruse, obsolete, dialectal, or technical terms.

C. WILSON He . . . began making a glossary of basic alchemical terms.

gloˈssarial *a.* of, pertaining to, or of the nature of a glossary E19. **glossarist** *n.* a person who writes a gloss or compiles a glossary L18.

glossator /glɒˈseɪtə/ *n.* LME. [med.L *glossator*, f. *glossare*, f. L *glossa*: see GLOSS *n.*[1]] A writer of glosses; a commentator, esp. on the texts of civil and canon law.

glossaˈtorial *a.* of the nature of glosses L19.

glossematic /glɒsəˈmatɪk/ *n.* & *a.* M20. [f. GLOSSEM(E after Gk wds like *phōnēma*, *phōnēmatik-* and *thema*, *thematik-* and the names of sciences like *mathematics*: see -IC.] *Ling.* **A** *n.* In *pl.* (treated as *sing.*). A theory of language introduced by the Danish scholar Louis Hjelmslev (1899–1965), and concerned esp. with the reduction of language to minimal units (glossemes) and the distribution and mutual relationships of these units. M20. **B** *adj.* Of, relating to, or characteristic of glossematics. M20.

glossematician /-ˈtɪʃ(ə)n/, **gloˈssematist** *ns.* an expert in or student of glossematics M20.

glosseme /ˈglɒsiːm/ *n.* E20. [Gk *glōssēma* word requiring explanation, f. *glōssa*: see GLOSSO-, -EME.] *Ling.* In glossematics, a linguistic feature which carries meaning and cannot be broken down into smaller meaningful units.

glossic /ˈglɒsɪk/ *a.* & *n.* L19. [f. Gk *glōssa* (see GLOSSO-) + -IC.] (Designating) a phonetic alphabet or spelling system invented by A. J. Ellis (1814–90), in which each letter or digraph represents the sound it most commonly expresses in English.

glossitis /glɒˈsʌɪtɪs/ *n.* E19. [f. Gk *glōssa* (see GLOSSO-) + -ITIS.] *Med.* Inflammation of the tongue.

glosso- /ˈglɒsəʊ/ *comb. form.* [Gk *glōsso-* comb. form of *glōssa* tongue, language, word requiring an explanation (cf. GLOSS *n.*[1]): see -O-. Cf. GLOTTO-.] Forming adjs. and ns. w. the senses '(of) the tongue', '(of) glosses or glossaries.'

glosso-epiˈglottic *a.* pertaining to the tongue and to the epiglottis M19. **gloˈssographer** *n.* a writer of glosses or commentaries E17. **gloˈssography** *n.* the writing of glosses or commentaries; the compiling of glossaries: E17. **glosso-laˈryngeal** *a.* pertaining to the tongue and the larynx L19. **glosso-phaˈryngeal** *a.* & *n.* (*a*) *adj.* of or pertaining to the tongue and the pharynx or gullet; (*b*) *n.* either of the glosso-pharyngeal or ninth pair of cranial nerves, which supply these organs: E19. **glossoˈplegia** *n.* (*Med.*) paralysis of the tongue M19.

glossolalia /glɒsəˈleɪlɪə/ *n.* Also **glossa-**. L19. [f. GLOSSO- + -LALIA, w. allus. to *Acts* 10:46, *1 Cor.* 14:6, 23.] The gift of speaking with tongues (see TONGUE *n.* 6c).

glossolalic /-ˈlalɪk/ *a.* & *n.* (*a*) *adj.* of or pertaining to speaking with tongues; (*b*) *n.* a glossolalist: E20. **glossolalist** /-ˈleɪlɪst, -ˈlalɪst/ *n.* a person who speaks with tongues L19.

glossology /glɒˈsɒlədʒi/ *n.* Now *rare.* E18. [f. GLOSSO- + -LOGY.] 1 Orig., the study of a particular language or languages. Later, (comparative) philology. E18. 2 (The explanation of) the terminology used in any science. M19.

glossoˈlogical *a.* of or pertaining to glossology E18. **glossologist** *n.* (*a*) a person who defines and explains terms; (*b*) an expert in or student of language or languages: E19.

glossopetra /glɒsəˈpɛtrə/ *n. obs.* exc. *Hist.* L17. [mod.L f. L *glossopetra* a stone supposedly shaped like the human tongue f. Gk *glōssopetra*, f. *glōssa* (see GLOSSO-) + *petra* rock.] A kind of fossil tooth.

glossophagine /glɒˈsɒfədʒʌɪn/ *a.* & *n.* L19. [f. mod.L *Glossophaga* genus name, f. Gk *glōssa* (see GLOSSO-) + *phagein* eat: see -INE[1].] **A** *adj.* Of or pertaining to the subfamily Glossophaginae (family Phyllostomidae) of S. American bats, which feed on nectar by means of an extensible tongue. L19. **B** *n.* A glossophagine bat. L19.

glossopteris /glɒˈsɒpt(ə)rɪs/ *n.* L19. [Fr. f. Gk *glōssa* (see GLOSSO-) + *pteris* fern.] Any of various primitive angiosperms (orig. regarded as ferns) of the extinct genus *Glossopteris*, widespread as fossils.

glossy /ˈglɒsi/ *a.* & *n.* M16. [f. GLOSS *n.*[2] + -Y[1].] **A** *adj.* 1 Having a gloss; smooth and shining; highly polished. M16. 2 *fig.* Having a deceptively smooth and attractive external appearance. L17. 3 Of a type of paper: smooth and shiny; (of a magazine etc.) printed on such paper, expensive and attractive in appearance but sometimes lacking in depth or substance. L19.

1 W. GOLDING They had washed the pillars . . and painted the balcony glossy white. **glossy ibis** a cosmopolitan ibis, *Plegadis falcinellus*, with glossy wings. 2 H. S. RANDALL The smooth, glossy pretences of diplomacy. *Pan Am Clipper* The elegant shops and other glossy pleasures of Palm Beach. 3 A. S. BYATT The other woman . . . leafed through . . a heap of glossy magazines.

B *n.* A photograph with a glossy surface; a glossy magazine etc. M20.

A. WILSON The slightly too smart appearance, which the world of women's glossies had imposed upon her.

glossily *adv.* E18. **glossiness** *n.* L17.

glost /glɒst/ *n.* L19. [App. dial. alt. of GLOSS *n.*[2] 4.] *Ceramics.* A lead glaze used for pottery.
Comb.: **glost-fire** *v.t.* & *i.* fire (pottery etc.) after glazing; **glost oven** an oven in which glazed ware is fired.

glottal /ˈglɒt(ə)l/ *a.* M19. [f. GLOTT(IS + -AL[1].] Pertaining to or produced by the glottis.
J. HELLER The same splintered syllable, the same glottal stutter, kept coming out. **glottal catch, stop** a sound produced by the sudden opening or shutting of the glottis before or after an emission of breath or voice.
gloˈttalic *a.* relating to the glottis and its total or partial closure M20.

glottalize /ˈglɒt(ə)lʌɪz/ *v.t.* Also **-ise.** E20. [f. GLOTTAL + -IZE.] Articulate with total or partial closure of the glottis.
glottaliˈzation *n.* M20.

glottic /ˈglɒtɪk/ *a.*[1] & *n. rare.* E19. [Gk *glōttikos* of the tongue f. *glōtta*: see GLOTTO-, -IC.] A *adj.* Of or pertaining to language. E19. B *n.sing.* & (usu.) in *pl.* (treated as *sing.*). The branch of knowledge that deals with language. M20.
†**glottical** *a.*: only in M17.

glottic /ˈglɒtɪk/ *a.*[2] M19. [f. GLOTT(IS + -IC.] Of or pertaining to the glottis.

glottis /ˈglɒtɪs/ *n.* L16. [mod.L f. Gk *glōttis*, f. *glōtta*: see next.] *Anat.* & *Zool.* The upper aperture of the vertebrate larynx between the vocal cords, open during breathing but closed by the epiglottis during swallowing.

glotto- /ˈglɒtəʊ/ *comb. form.* M19. [Gk *glōtto-* comb. form of *glōtta* Attic form of *glōssa*: see GLOSSO-.] Forming adjs. and ns. w. the sense '(of) language or languages.'

glottochronology /ˌglɒtəʊkrəˈnɒlədʒi/ *n.* M20. [f. GLOTTO- + CHRONOLOGY.] *Ling.* The use of statistics to determine the degree of relationship between two or more languages and the chronology of their divergence from a common source.
glottochronoˈlogic(al) *adjs.* M20.

glottogonic /glɒtə(ʊ)ˈgɒnɪk/ *a.* L19. [f. GLOTTO- + Gk *gonikos* pertaining to production.] Relating to the origin of language or languages.

glottology /glɒˈtɒlədʒi/ *n.* Now *rare* or *obs.* M19. [f. GLOTTO- + -LOGY.] Philology, linguistics; *spec.* comparative philology.
glottoˈlogical *a.* M19.

Gloucester /ˈglɒstə/ *n.* L18. [A city in SW England.] A kind of cheese orig. made in Gloucestershire. Also *Gloucester cheese.*
double Gloucester (*cheese*): see DOUBLE *a.* & *adv. single Gloucester* (*cheese*): see SINGLE *a.* & *adv.*

Glou-morceau /gluːmɔːˈsəʊ/ *n.* Pl. **-ceaux** /-ˈsəʊ/. M19. [Fr. dial. = titbit.] A late-ripening variety of pear, producing fruit of high quality.

glout /glaʊt/ *v.* & *n.* Chiefly *dial.* LME. [Perh. var. of GLOAT *v.*] A *v.i.* Look sullen, frown, scowl. LME. B *n.* A frown, a sullen look. M17.

glove /glʌv/ *n.* [OE *glōf* corresp. to ON *glófi*, f. Gmc, perh. f. base of Y- + base of ON *lófi*, Goth. *lofa* hand.] 1 A covering for the hand to protect it or keep it warm, clean, or cool, usu. with separated fingers. OE. b A token of a pledge or of a challenge to battle. ME. 2 = *boxing glove* s.v. BOXING *vbl n.*[2] E18.
1 B. PYM She was wearing old black cotton gloves . . to protect her hands. **fit like a glove** fit or suit exactly. **go for the gloves** bet recklessly. *hand in* (or *and*) *glove*: see HAND *n. iron hand in a velvet glove*: see IRON *a. kid glove*: see KID *n.*[1] *oven glove*: see OVEN *n. velvet glove*: see VELVET *a.* b †**cast the glove** = *throw down the glove* below. **take up the glove** accept a challenge. **throw down the glove** issue a challenge. 2 ALBERT SMITH I . . put on the gloves . . and knocked him about. **take the gloves off** show no mercy, set to in earnest. *velvet glove*: see VELVET *n.* & *a.* **without gloves, with the gloves off**, etc., severely, without mercy.
Comb.: **glove box** (*a*) a box for holding gloves; (*b*) = *glove compartment* below; (*c*) a closed chamber with sealed-in gloves for handling radioactive or other material; **glove compartment** a recess in the dashboard of a motor vehicle for small articles like gloves etc.; **glove-fit** something that fits like a glove; **glove money** *Hist.* (*a*) a gratuity given to servants ostensibly to buy them gloves; (*b*) *Law* extraordinary rewards formerly given to officers of English Courts etc.; *spec.* money given by a sheriff to other officers in a county in which there were no offenders left for execution; **glove puppet** a puppet made to fit on the hand like a glove and operated by the fingers.
gloveless *a.* having or wearing no glove or gloves E19.

glove /glʌv/ *v.t.* LME. [f. the n.] Cover with or as with a glove; provide with gloves.
DAY LEWIS Her gloved hand holds a parasol.

glover /ˈglʌvə/ *n.*[1] ME. [f. GLOVE *n.* + -ER[1].] A person who makes or sells gloves.
gloveress *n.* a female glover ME.

glow /gləʊ/ *n.* LME. [f. the vb.] 1 The state or condition of glowing, esp. with heat or light. LME. 2 Brightness and warmth of colour; *esp.* a warm redness of the cheeks indicating youth or health. L16. 3 Warmth of feeling; ardour, passion. M18.
1 R. W. EMERSON Summer's scorching glow. A. MACLEAN On a dark night the glow from a torch can be seen from a considerable distance. **in a glow** hot, flushed. 2 G. STEIN The heat gave a pretty pink glow to her . . attractive face. 3 M. DRABBLE I went upstairs . . in a glow of contentment.
Comb. (partly f. the vb): **glow discharge** a sparkless electrical discharge, esp. in a low-pressure gas, producing a diffuse luminous glow; **glow-fly** a firefly; **glow-lamp** an electric lamp containing a high-resistance filament, esp. one in which most of the light is produced by the incandescence of an enclosed gas (usu. neon or argon); **glow-light** a glowing light; *spec.* a glow-lamp; **glow plug** an electrically heated plug used to ignite the gas in a gas turbine or diesel engine; **glow-worm** a beetle, *Lampyris noctiluca*, the wingless female and other stages of which emit light from the abdomen; any of numerous similar beetles constituting the family Lampyridae.

glow /gləʊ/ *v.*[1] [OE *glōwan* str. vb corresp. to the wk vbs OS *glōjan* (Du. *gloeien*), OHG *gluoen* (G *glühen*), ON *glóa*, f. Gmc. Cf. GLEED *n.*] 1 *v.i.* Be heated to incandescence; emit bright light and heat without flame. OE. 2 *v.i.* Shine, emit light, (as if) owing to intense heat. LME. 3 *v.i.* Be warm and bright in colouring. LME. b Pass *to* or *into* a glowing colour. L19. 4 *v.i.* Be excessively hot; be on fire, burn. LME. 5 *v.i.* Burn with or be indicative of bodily heat, esp. when accompanied by heightened colour. LME. 6 *v.i.* Burn with the fervour of emotion or passion. LME. †7 *v.t.* Make hot; heat. L16–L17.
1 S. JOHNSON I . . found it in ruins, with the fire yet glowing. 2 P. BOWLES The court glowed with reflected moonlight. D. LESSING There was a single . . electric-light bulb glowing down from the rafters. S. KING It had been treated with fluorescent paint so it would glow in the dark. 3 E. O. M. DEUTSCH Pictures teeming with life, glowing with colour. 4 *fig.*: E. SMITH Yawning Gulphs with flaming Vengeance glow. 5 W. C. SMITH Girls, all glowing with the flush of life. B. PYM Their skins glowed from the fresh air. 6 M. IGNATIEFF Not knowing whether to burn with shame or glow with pride.
glowing *ppl a.* that glows; *spec.* (of an account etc.) ardent, impassioned, expressing great pride or praise: OE. **glowingly** *adv.* E17.

glow /gləʊ/ *v.*[2]*i. obs.* exc. *dial.* LME. [Perh. a use of prec.; but cf. Sw., Da. *glo* stare, look sullen.] Stare.

glower /ˈglaʊə/ *v.* & *n.* L15. [Perh. Sc. var. of synon. GLORE or f. GLOW *v.*[2] + -ER[5].] A *v.i.* 1 Stare with wide open eyes; gaze, look. (Foll. by *at.*) Chiefly *Sc.* L15. 2 Look angrily or crossly; scowl. (Foll. by *at.*) E18.
2 R. F. HOBSON Sam sat rigidly . . and glowered at me—a picture of dumb insolence.
B *n.* The action of glowering; an intense look, a stare. Chiefly *Sc.* E17.

gloxinia /glɒkˈsɪnɪə/ *n.* E19. [mod.L (see below), f. P. B. *Gloxin*, 18th-cent. Ger. botanist.] Any of various tropical American plants of or formerly included in the genus *Gloxinia* (family Gesneriaceae); *esp.* any of the forms or hybrids of the Brazilian *Sinningia speciosa*, with large velvety trumpet-shaped corollas, grown as hothouse plants.

gloze /gləʊz/ *n.* Now *rare.* Also (earlier) †**glose.** ME. [(O)Fr. *glose* f. med.L *glosa, gloza*, for L *glossa*: see GLOSS *n.*[1]] 1 A marginal note, a comment. = GLOSS *n.*[1] 1. *arch.* ME. 2 Flattery, deceit; a flattering speech or comment. ME. 3 A pretence, a specious appearance. Also, a disguise. ME.

gloze /gləʊz/ *v.*[1] Also (earlier) †**glose.** ME. [(O)Fr. *gloser*, f. as prec.; in med.L *glossare.*] 1 *v.t.* Flatter, deceive with smooth talk or specious words. *arch.* ME. 2 *v.i.* Talk smoothly and speciously; use flattering language; fawn. *arch.* ME. 3 *v.t.* Veil with specious language; explain away, extenuate. (Foll. by *over*, †*out.*) LME. 4a *v.t.* Make glosses on; expound, interpret; comment on or about. LME. b *v.i.* Insert a gloss or explanation; comment. (Foll. by *on, upon*). Now *rare.* LME.
3 R. GLOVER It is not charity to gloze over the sins and sorrows of men. 4a E. CRISPIN Policemen whose activities he glozed and expounded.
†**glozer** *n.* (*a*) a person who writes glosses, a commentator; (*b*) a flatterer, a sycophant: LME–L18. **glozing** *n.* (*a*) the action of the vb; (*b*) flattery, specious talk: ME. **glozingly** *adv.* in a glozing manner LME.

gloze /gləʊz/ *v.*[2]*t.* & *i. rare.* E19. [Origin unkn.: cf. GLOSS *n.*[2]] (Cause to) shine, gleam, blaze.

gluc- *comb. form* see GLUCO-.

glucagon /ˈgluːkəg(ə)n, -gɒn/ *n.* E20. [f. GLUCO- + Gk *agōn* pres. pple of *agein* lead, bring.] A polypeptide hormone formed in the pancreas which promotes the breakdown of glycogen in the liver and thereby increases blood sugar.

glucan /ˈgluːkan/ *n.* M20. [f. GLUCO- + -AN.] Any polysaccharide composed chiefly of glucose residues, e.g. cellulose and starch.

glucaric /gluːˈkarɪk/ *a.* M20. [f. GLUCO- after SACCHARIC.] Chem. *glucaric acid*, a dibasic acid, $C_6H_{10}O_8$, formed by the oxidation of various sugars.

†**glucina** *n.* Also **-ine.** Only in 19. [mod.L (after *magnesia, soda*, etc.) f. Fr. *glucine*, f. as GLUCO-: see GLYCO-, -INE[5].] Beryllium oxide.

glucinum /gluːˈsʌɪnəm/ *n. obs.* exc. *Hist.* E19. [f. as prec.: cf. -IUM.] = BERYLLIUM.

gluck /glʌk/ *v.* & *n.* M19. [Imit.: cf. GLUG.] (Make) a light usu. repetitive gurgling sound as of liquid being poured from a bottle.

gluco- /ˈgluːkəʊ/ *comb. form.* Bef. a vowel also **gluc-** /gluːk/. [Fr. f. GLUCOSE and (later) Gk *glukus* sweet: see -O-. Cf. GLYCO-.] *Chem.* & *Biochem.* 1 Glucose; containing, related to, or yielding glucose; affecting the metabolism of glucose. 2 = GLYCO-.
glucoˈcorticoid *n.* any of a group of corticosteroids (e.g. hydrocortisone) which are involved in the metabolism of carbohydrates, proteins, and fats and have anti-inflammatory activity M20. **gluconeoˈgenesis** *n.* the formation of glucose in the body from non-carbohydrate precursors E20. **gluconeogeˈnetic, -ˈgenic** *adjs.* of or pertaining to gluconeogenesis M20. **glucoˈprotein** *n.* †(*a*) any of various amino acids or mixtures of amino acids to which were ascribed the empirical formula $C_nH_{2n}N_2O_4$, where *n* is between 6 and 12; (*b*) = GLYCOPROTEIN: L19. **glucoˈstatic** *a.* (*Physiol.*) pertaining to or designating a mechanism for maintaining a constant level of glucose in the blood, or a theory of metabolism that postulates such a mechanism M20.

†**glucogen** *n.* var. of GLYCOGEN.

gluconic /gluːˈkɒnɪk/ *a.* L19. [f. GLUCO- + -ONIC.] Chem. *gluconic acid*, an acid, CH_2OH-$(CHOH)_4COOH$, derived from glucose by oxidation of the latter's aldehyde group.
ˈ**gluconate** *n.* a salt or ester of gluconic acid L19.

glucosamine /gluːˈkəʊsəmiːn, -ˈkəʊz-/ *n.* L19. [f. GLUCO- after *glycosamine.*] *Chem.* A crystalline amino sugar, $CH_2OH(CHOH)_3CHNH_2CHO$, that is derived from glucose and is the principal constituent of chitin.

glucosan /ˈgluːkəsan/ *n.* M19. [Fr. *glucosane*, f. as GLUCOSE.] *Chem.* 1 Any of several isomeric anhydrides, $C_6H_{10}O_5$, of glucose. M19. 2 = GLUCAN. E20.

glucose /ˈgluːkəʊs, -z/ *n.* M19. [Fr. f. Gk *gleukos* sweet wine, rel. to *glukus* sweet: see -OSE[2].] 1 One of the hexose sugars, obtainable in dextro- and laevorotatory forms and as a racemic mixture; *spec.* the dextrorotatory form (also called D-*glucose, dextrose, grape sugar*), a white or colourless sweet-tasting solid which is an important energy source in living organisms and which occurs free in fruit juices and the blood and combined in glucosides, some oligosaccharides (e.g. sucrose), and some polysaccharides (e.g. cellulose and starch). M19. †2 Any of the hexoses, $C_6H_{12}O_6$; any monosaccharide. M19–E20. 3 A syrup containing D-glucose, maltose, dextrin, and water, obtained by the incomplete hydrolysis of starch and used in the food industry as a sweetener and thickener. Also *glucose syrup*. M19.

Comb.: **glucose phosphate** any phosphoric acid ester of glucose, esp. a monophosphate (*glucose-1-phosphate*, a phosphate formed in the body from glucose-6-phosphate in the synthesis of polysaccharides; *glucose-6-phosphate*, a phosphate formed in the body by the reaction of glucose with ATP in the initial step of glucose metabolism); **glucose tolerance test** a test for abnormal carbohydrate metabolism, esp. diabetes, in which glucose is given orally after a period of fasting and the blood sugar measured at intervals afterwards.

glu'cosic *a.* M19. **gluco'sinolate** *n.* [L *sinapis* mustard + *oleum* oil] any of a group of toxic glucosides produced by some brassicas and yielding mustard oil on ingestion M20.

glucosidase /gluːˈkɒsɪdeɪz, gluːkəˈsʌɪdeɪz/ *n.* E20. [f. next + -ASE.] *Biochem.* An enzyme, such as maltase, which hydrolyses a glucoside to form glucose.

glucoside /ˈgluːkəsʌɪd/ *n.* Also †**glyco-**. See also GLYCOSIDE. M19. [f. GLUCOSE + -IDE.] *Chem.* A glycoside in which the sugar is glucose.

gluco'sidal, -'sidic *adjs.* characteristic of a glucoside E20. **gluco'sidically** *adv.* M20.

glucuronic /gluːkjʊˈrɒnɪk/ *a.* E20. [f. GLUCO- after GLYCURONIC.] Chem. & Biochem. *glucuronic acid*, the uronic acid, HOOC·$(CHOH)_4$CHO, derived from glucose, which occurs naturally as a constituent of hyaluronic acid and other mucopolysaccharides, and in glucuronides.

glu'curonate *n.* a salt or ester of glucuronic acid E20. **glucu'ronidase** *n.* an enzyme which hydrolyses a glucuronide M20. **glu'curonide** *n.* any glycosidic compound formed by glucuronic acid; *esp.* one of those formed in the body by conjugation with another compound as part of the metabolic process by which the latter is excreted: M20. **glucuronyl** /gluːˈkjuːrənʌɪl, -nɪl/ *n.* the monovalent radical ·OC$(CHOH)_4$CHO derived from glucuronic acid M20.

glue /gluː/ *n.* ME. [(O)Fr. *glu* f. late L *glus*, *glut-*, f. L *gluten*.] 1 A hard brittle brownish gelatin made by boiling hides and bones and used in solution for sticking things together; the solution itself; any sticky or viscous substance used for the same purpose. ME. †2 A plant gum. LME–E19. †3 Birdlime. LME–E18. †4 Bitumen, pitch. Only in LME.

Comb.: **glueball** *Particle Physics* a bound state of two or more gluons; **glue ear** a condition in which a viscous fluid blocks the Eustachian tube and severely impairs hearing, occurring chiefly in children as a result of infection of the middle ear; **glue-pot** (*a*) a pot in which glue is heated, having an outer vessel which holds hot water; (*b*) *colloq.* an area of ground sticky because of wet or mud; **glue-sniffing** the inhalation of the fumes of plastic cement for their stimulating effects.

gluish *a.* (now *rare*) somewhat gluey LME. **gluelike** *a.* resembling glue E19.

glue /gluː/ *v.* LME. [(O)Fr. *gluer*, f. as GLUE *n.*] 1 *v.t.* Join or fasten (*to* something, *together*) with glue. Also foll. by *on*, *up*. LME. †**b** Involve or entangle in some sticky substance so as to impede free motion (*lit.* & *fig.*). LME–L17. **c** Seal (as) with glue; shut up tightly. Now only foll. by *up*. M17. 2 *v.t. fig.* Cause to adhere closely or firmly; apply or attach tightly or firmly; *esp.* apply (one's eyes or ears) closely *to* something in rapt attention (usu. in *pass.*). LME. 3 *v.i.* Admit of being fastened by glue. Formerly also, stick *together*, adhere (*lit.* & *fig.*). Long *rare*. LME. 4 *v.t.* Daub or smear with glue or some similar viscous substance. Now *rare* or *obs.* LME.

1 P. ROTH The saucer . . had broken neatly in two. . . 'She can glue it.' 2 SMOLLETT She now began to glue herself to his favour with the grossest adulation. C. BRONTË Her ear having been glued to the key-hole. N. MAILER They were all glued to the TV set. S. BRETT The . . chat-show . . kept millions glued to their armchairs every Saturday night. 3 EVELYN Oak will not easily glue to other Wood.

gluer *n.* L15.

gluey /ˈgluːi/ *a.* LME. [f. GLUE *n.* + -Y[1].] Resembling or of the nature of glue; viscous, glutinous; sticky.

gluily, glueily *adv.* E20. **glueyness** *n.* E17.

glug /glʌg/ *n.* & *v.* L17. [Imit.: cf. GLUCK.] **A** *n.* A hollow usu. repetitive gurgling sound as of liquid being poured from a bottle. L17. **B** *v.* Infl. **-gg-**. 1 *v.i.* Make a glug or glugs. Chiefly as *glugging* vbl n. & ppl a. L19. 2 *v.t.* Pour (liquid) so that it glugs. L20.

glugg *n.* var. of GLÖGG.

glühwein /ˈglyːvaɪn, ˈgluːvʌɪn/ *n.* Also **gluh-**. L19. [G, f. *glühen* mull, GLOW *v.*[1] + *wein* WINE *n.*] Mulled wine.

gluino /glʊˈiːnəʊ/ *n.* Pl. **-os**. L20. [f. GLUON + -INO.] *Particle Physics.* The supersymmetric counterpart of a gluon, with spin ½ instead of 1.

glulam /ˈgluːlam/ *n.* M20. [f. GLU(E *n.* + LAM(INATION.] A building material consisting of laminations of timber glued together.

glum /glʌm/ *n.* Long *obs.* exc. *dial.* E16. [f. GLUM *v.* or *a.* Cf. GLOOM *n.*[1]] A sullen look, a frown. Also, a glum person.

glum /glʌm/ *a.* Compar. & superl. **-mm-**. M16. [Rel. to GLUM *v.*] 1 Of a person or a person's expression: sullen, frowning; silent and morose; looking or feeling dejected or displeased. M16. 2 Of a thing: conducive to glumness; gloomy, dismal, depressing. Now only *fig.* from sense 1. M16.

2 THACKERAY We walked in the park . . surveying . . the glum old bridge.

glumly *adv.* E19. **glummy** *a.* (*rare*) †(*a*) gloomy; (*b*) glum: L16. **glumness** *n.* E18.

glum /glʌm/ *v.i.* *obs.* exc. *dial.* Infl. **-mm-**. LME. [Var. of GLOOM *v.*] Look sullen; frown, scowl.

glume /gluːm/ *n.* L18. [L *gluma* hull, husk rel. to *glubere* to shell, to peel.] *Bot.* Any of certain chaffy or membranous scales in the inflorescence of grasses or related plants: (*a*) (in grasses) either of the two empty bracts subtending the spikelet (more fully *empty* or *sterile glume*); also (now *rare*) = LEMMA *n.*[2] 2 (more fully *flowering glume*); (*b*) (in sedges and other plants of the Cyperaceae) the bract enclosing the flower.

glu'maceous *a.* resembling or having glumes; characterized by bearing glumes, as the grasses and sedges: E19. **'glumose** *a.* (now *rare*) having a glume or husk L18.

glump /glʌmp/ *v.* & *n.* *dial.* or (*rare*) *colloq.* M18. [Origin unkn.: cf. *glum*, *dump*, etc.] **A** *v.i.* Sulk; be glum or sullen. M18. **B** *n.* A sulky person. Also, in *pl.*, the sulks. M18.

glumpish *a.* = GLUMPY E19.

glumpy /ˈglʌmpi/ *a.* L18. [f. prec. + -Y[1]. Cf. GRUMPY.] Glum, sullen, sulky.

glumpily *adv.* M19.

glunch /glʌn(t)ʃ/ *v.*, *n.*, & *a.* *Sc.* E18. [Origin unkn.: cf. GLUM *a.*, CLUNCH *a.*] **A** *v.i.* Look sour or glum. E18. **B** *n.* A sour look. L18. **C** *adj.* Glum, sulky. E19.

†**glunimie** *n.* *Sc. derog.* M18–E19. [Perh. alt. of Gael. *glùineanach* (a person) wearing garters.] A Highlander.

gluon /ˈgluːɒn/ *n.* L20. [f. GLUE *n.*, *v.*, + -ON.] *Particle Physics.* Any of a hypothetical group of massless bosons that are thought to be the carriers of the colour force that binds quarks together in hadrons.

glu'onic *a.* L20.

glut /glʌt/ *n.*[1] Long *obs.* exc. *dial.* LME. [f. OFr. *gl(o)ut* greedy, gluttonous.] A glutton.

glut /glʌt/ *n.*[2] *obs.* exc. *dial.* M16. [OFr. *glout* gulp, rel. to *gloutir* GLUT *v.*[1]] A full draught; the amount of liquid swallowed at a gulp.

glut /glʌt/ *n.*[3] L16. [f. GLUT *v.*[1]] 1 The action of glutting or the condition of being glutted with food etc.; full indulgence in a pleasure to the point of satiety or disgust; a surfeit. L16. †**b** In *pl.* Excesses. L16–L17. 2 A supply of some commodity which greatly exceeds demand. L16. 3†**a** An excessive flow of saliva, bile, etc. L16–E18. **b** An excessive influx of water, rain, etc. Now *rare*. M17. 4 An excessive quantity or number. Foll. by *of*. Now *rare*. M17. †5 Something which chokes a channel. L17–E18.

1 J. MARSTON Even I have glut of blood. J. LONDON I knew what it was to sleep my full and to awake naturally from very glut of sleep. 2 W. LIPPMANN There is a scarcity of some goods and a glut of others.

glut /glʌt/ *n.*[4] M18. [Perh. alt. of dial. var. of CLEAT.] 1 A wedge. M18. 2 *Naut.* A piece of strengthening canvas sewn into the centre of a square sail at the bunt. M19. 3 A small brick or block, *esp.* one such placed in a building course to complete it. L19.

glut /glʌt/ *v.*[1] Infl. **-tt-**. ME. [Prob. f. OFr. *gloutir* swallow (with causative sense perh. developed in AN) f. L *gluttire* swallow: see GLUTTON *n.*] 1**a** *v.t.* Feed to repletion; indulge (appetite) to the utmost. ME. **b** *v.i.* Feed (*on*) to repletion. M17. 2 *v.t.* Overload with food (*lit.* & *fig.*); surfeit, cloy, or sicken with excess of something. LME. 3 *v.t.* Fill (a receptacle, channel, etc.) to excess, choke; saturate, impregnate thoroughly *with* some substance. Now *rare*. L15. 4 *v.t.* Gratify (esp. a ferocious or lustful desire) to the full. M16. **b** *v.i.* Take one's fill of thinking, gazing, etc., *on* something; long greedily *for*. *rare*. M17. 5 *v.t.* Overstock (a market) with goods. E17.

1a N. HAWTHORNE Destined to glut the ravenous maw of that detestable man-brute. P. V. WHITE The beasts were glutting themselves on dew and grass. 2 GOLDSMITH Swallowing their blood at large draughts, and seeming rather glutted than satiated. HAZLITT The ear is cloyed and glutted with warbled ecstasies. 3 E. L. DOCTOROW The sidewalks were glutted with shoppers. 4 J. R. GREEN His ambition was glutted . . with the rank of Cardinal. b T. CAREW Love doth with an hungry eye Glut on Beauty.

glut /glʌt/ *v.*[2]*t.* Now *rare*. Infl. **-tt-**. M16. [OFr. *gloutir* swallow: see prec. Cf. ENGLUT.] Swallow greedily; gulp down.

glutaei *n.pl.* see GLUTEUS.

glutaeo- *comb. form* var. of GLUTEO-.

glutaeus *n.* var. of GLUTEUS.

glutamate /ˈgluːtəmeɪt/ *n.* L19. [f. next + -ATE[1].] *Chem.* & *Biochem.* A salt or ester of glutamic acid, *esp.* a sodium salt used as a food additive to enhance flavour; the ion of glutamic acid, which is involved in nitrogen metabolism in man and other organisms.

MONOSODIUM *glutamate*.

glutamic /gluːˈtamɪk/ *a.* L19. [f. GLUT(EN + AM(INE + -IC.] Biochem. *glutamic acid*, an acidic amino acid, HOOC·$CH_2CH_2CH(NH_2)$COOH, which occurs in proteins and is the source of the glutamate ion.

glutamine /ˈgluːtəmiːn/ *n.* L19. [f. GLUT(AMIC + AMINE.] *Biochem.* A hydrophilic amino acid, H_2N·CO·$CH_2CH_2(NH_2)$COOH, which occurs in proteins and is an amide of glutamic acid, from which it is formed metabolically.

glutaric /gluːˈtarɪk/ *a.* L19. [f. GLUT(EN + TAR)TARIC.] *glutaric acid*, the crystalline acid $HOOC(CH_2)_3COOH$; pentanedioic acid.

glutathione /gluːtəˈθʌɪəʊn/ *n.* E20. [f. GLUTA(MIC + THIO- + -ONE.] *Biochem.* A tripeptide composed of glutamate, cysteine, and glycine which is important in metabolism, esp. as a coenzyme.

glutch /glʌtʃ/ *v.t.* & *i.* *dial.* E19. [Imit. or f. GULCH *v.* w. metathesis.] Swallow, gulp. Also foll. by *down*.

glutei *n.pl.* see GLUTEUS.

gluten /ˈgluːt(ə)n/ *n.* L16. [Fr. f. L *gluten* glue.] †1 = FIBRIN. L16–E19. 2 A sticky substance; a gum, a glue; a viscid secretion. *rare*. M17. 3 A substance present in flour, esp. flour of wheat, which is responsible for the elastic cohesion of dough and is a mixture chiefly of two proteins. E19.

Comb.: **gluten bread** bread with a high gluten content.

glutenin /ˈgluːtɪnɪn/ *n.* L19. [f. prec. + -IN[1].] *Biochem.* The chief protein present in wheat flour.

gluteo- /ˈgluːtɪəʊ/ *comb. form.* Also **-taeo-**. [f. GLUTEUS + -O-.] Pertaining to or designating the gluteus and —, as *gluteofemoral.*

glutethimide /gluːˈtɛθɪmʌɪd/ *n.* M20. [f. GLUT(ARIC + ETH(YL + IMIDE.] *Pharm.* A bicyclic compound with hypnotic properties, formerly used as an alternative to barbiturates.

gluteus /gluːˈtiːəs/ *n.* Also **-taeus**. Pl. **-t(a)ei**, /-ˈtiːʌɪ/. L17. [mod.L f. Gk *gloutos* buttock.] Each of three paired muscles of the buttocks (in full *gluteus maximus* /ˈmaksɪməs/ [L = largest], *gluteus medius* /ˈmiːdɪəs/ [L = middle], *gluteus minimus* /ˈmɪnɪməs/ [L = smallest]) which extend the thigh at the hip-joint. Also *gluteus muscle.*

gluteal *a.* L18. **glutean** *a.* (*rare*) E19.

†**glutinate** *v.t.* LME. [L *glutinat-* pa. ppl stem of *glutinare* glue together, close up (a wound), f. *glutin-*, *gluten*: see GLUTEN, -ATE³.] **1** *Med.* Close or heal (a wound); counter relaxation of (the bowels, veins, etc.). LME–M18. **2** Glue or stick together. Only in 17.

glutinize /ˈgluːtɪnʌɪz/ *v.t.* Also **-ise**. M18. [f. L *glutin-*, *gluten* glue + -IZE.] Make viscous or sticky.

glutinosity /gluːtɪˈnɒsɪti/ *n.* LME. [med.L *glutinositas*, f. L *glutinosus*: see next, -OSITY.] The quality or condition of being glutinous.

glutinous /ˈgluːtɪnəs/ *a.* LME. [(O)Fr *glutineux* or L *glutinosus*, f. *glutin-*, *gluten* glue: see -OUS.] Gluelike, sticky, viscid.

KEATS A glutinous pine. *fig.*: O. MANNING Priests . . trailed around all day in the glutinous heat.

glutinously *adv.* E17. **glutinousness** *n.* (long *rare*) M17.

glutton /ˈglʌt(ə)n/ *n.* & *a.* ME. [OFr. *gluton*, *gloton* (mod. *glouton*) f. L *glutto(n-)* rel. to *gluttire* swallow, *gluttus* greedy, *gula* throat.] **A** *n.* **1** A person who eats to excess, or who takes pleasure in immoderate eating; a greedy person. ME. **b** *fig.* A person who is inordinately fond (*of* a specified pursuit), or insatiably eager (*for* something). E18. †**2** A vile wretch; a rascal. ME–E16. **3** The wolverine, *Gulo gulo*. L17.

1 †**the rich glutton** the rich man of the biblical parable (Luke 16:19) whose fate is contrasted with that of the beggar Lazarus. **b** R. KIPLING He's honest, and a glutton for work. **a glutton for punishment** a person who is (apparently) eager to take on an onerous workload or an exacting task.

B *adj.* Gluttonous. Formerly also, villainous. Now *rare*. LME.

gluttoness *n.* (*rare*) a female glutton E17. **gluttonish** *a.* (*rare*) (somewhat) like a glutton, voracious LME. **gluttonize** *v.i.* (now *rare*) feed gluttonously (*on*) M17.

glutton /ˈglʌt(ə)n/ *v.* E17. [f. the n.] †**1** *v.i.* Feed voraciously or to excess (*on*). E17–E19. **2** *v.t.* = GLUT *v.*¹ 1a; swallow or devour greedily. *rare.* M17.

gluttonous /ˈglʌt(ə)nəs/ *a.* LME. [f. GLUTTON *n.* + -OUS.] Given to excess in eating; characterized by or of the nature of gluttony (*lit.* & *fig.*).

J. L. MOTLEY Philip the Prudent, as he grew older . . seemed to become more gluttonous of work. N. MONSARRAT Crumbs and a ring of milky white round his mouth betrayed the gluttonous boy.

gluttonously *adv.* LME.

gluttony /ˈglʌt(ə)ni/ *n.* ME. [OFr. *glutonie* etc. (mod. *gloutonnerie*), f. as GLUTTON *n.*: see -Y³.] Habitual (and culpable) greed or excess in eating and drinking; inordinate and uncontrolled desire for food. Also (*rare*), an instance of this.

glycan /ˈglʌɪkan/ *n.* M20. [f. GLYCO- + -AN.] *Chem.* = POLYSACCHARIDE.

glyceraldehyde /glɪsəˈraldɪhʌɪd/ *n.* L19. [f. GLYCER(IC + ALDEHYDE.] A sweet-tasting compound, CHO·CHOH·CH_2OH, that is an intermediate in the metabolic breakdown of glucose.

glyceria /glɪˈsɪərɪə/ *n.* E19. [mod.L (see below), f. Gk *glukeros* sweet: see -IA¹.] Any of several aquatic grasses of the genus *Glyceria*, relished by cattle for their succulent foliage. Also called *sweet-grass.*

glyceric /glɪˈsɛrɪk, ˈglɪs(ə)rɪk/ *a.* M19. [f. as next + -IC.] *Chem.* Of or pertaining to glycerol.

glyceric acid a syrup, HOOC·CH(OH)CH_2OH, produced by the action of nitric acid on glycerol.

glyceride /ˈglɪs(ə)rʌɪd/ *n.* M19. [f. GLYCERINE + -IDE.] *Chem.* An ester of glycerol, esp. with a fatty acid.

glycerin *n.* see GLYCERINE.

glycerinate /ˈglɪs(ə)rɪneɪt/ *v.t.* L19. [f. next: see -ATE³.] Preserve in or treat with glycerine or a glycerine-based liquid.

glyceriˈnation *n.* L19.

glycerine /ˈglɪs(ə)riːn, -ɪn/ *n.* Also ***-in** /-ɪn/. M19. [Fr. *glycerin* f. Gk *glukeros* sweet: see -INE⁵, -IN¹.] Glycerol.

Comb.: **glycerine tear** a drop of glycerine used in theatrical make-up to simulate a tear.

glycero- /ˈglɪs(ə)rəʊ/ *comb. form* of GLYCERINE and GLYCEROL: see -O-.

glyceroˈkinase *n.* (*Biochem.*) an enzyme in the liver that catalyses the reaction of glycerol and ATP to glycerophosphate and ADP M20. **glyceroˈphosphate** *n.* a salt or ester, or the ion, of glycerophosphoric acid, *esp.* the calcium or magnesium salts, given as tonics and dietary supplements M19. **glycerophosˈphoric** *a.*: *glycerophosphoric acid*, an acid, $C_3H_5(OH)_2{\cdot}H_2PO_4$, that is a colourless combustible liquid produced by the action of phosphoric acid on glycerol M19.

glycerol /ˈglɪs(ə)rɒl/ *n.* L19. [f. GLYCER(INE + -OL.] A colourless sweet viscous liquid, CH_2OH·CHOH·CH_2OH, that is an alcohol formed as a by-product in the manufacture of soap and used as an emollient and laxative and in the manufacture of many chemicals. Also called (esp. in non-*techn.* use) *glycerine.*

glycerole /ˈglɪs(ə)rəʊl/ *n.* Now *rare* or *obs.* M19. [f. as prec. + *-ole.*] A pharmaceutical preparation with glycerine as a vehicle.

glyceryl /ˈglɪs(ə)rɪl, -rʌɪl/ *n.* M19. [f. GLYCER(INE + -YL.] *Chem.* A radical derived from glycerol by the removal of one or more hydroxyl groups; *esp.* the trivalent radical C_3H_5≡.

Comb.: **glyceryl trinitrate** = NITROGLYCERINE.

glycin /ˈglʌɪsɪn/ *n.* L19. [f. next.] A crystalline derivative of glycine used as a photographic developer; *p*-hydroxyphenylglycine, HO·C_6H_4·-NH·CH_2COOH.

glycine /ˈglʌɪsiːn/ *n.* M19. [f. Gk *glukus* sweet + -INE⁵.] The simplest naturally occurring amino acid, H_2N·CH_2COOH, a sweet-tasting crystalline compound which occurs in proteins and is used in food technology; aminoacetic acid.

glyco- /ˈglʌɪkəʊ/ *comb. form.* [f. Gk *glukus* sweet + -O-.] *Chem.* & *Biochem.* Sugar; containing, related to, or yielding sugar; affecting the metabolism of sugar. Formerly also, glycerol. Cf. GLUCO-.

glycobiˈology *n.* the branch of science that deals with the role of sugars in biological processes L20. **glycocalyx** *n.* (*Biol.*) a layer on the outer surface of a plasma membrane, composed of carbohydrate chains of proteoglycans or glycoproteins M20. **glycocholic** /-ˈkɒl-/ *a.* (*Biochem.*) designating one of the principal acids in bile M19. **glycoˈlipid** *n.* (*Biochem.*) any compound in which a sugar or other carbohydrate is combined with a lipid M20. **glycoˈphorin** *n.* (*Biochem.*) a glycoprotein found in erythrocyte membranes L20. **glycophyte** *n.* (*Ecol.*) a plant whose growth is inhibited by saline soil M20. **glycophytic** /-ˈfɪtɪk/ *a.* (*Ecol.*) pertaining to or designating a glycophyte M20. †**glycoproteid** *n.* a glycoprotein L19–E20. **glycoˈprotein** *n.* a protein that has short side-chains of carbohydrate in its molecule E20. **glycotropic** /-ˈtrəʊpɪk, -ˈtrɒpɪk/ *a.* (*Biochem.*) antagonistic to insulin M20.

glycocoll /ˈglʌɪkəkɒl/ *n. obs.* exc. *Hist.* M19. [f. GLYCO- + Gk *kolla* glue.] = GLYCINE.

glycogen /ˈglʌɪkədʒ(ə)n/ *n.* Also †**gluc-**. M19. [f. GLYCO- + -GEN.] *Biochem.* A polysaccharide composed of glucose residues that is the form in which carbohydrate is stored in animals (corresponding to starch in plants) and is present esp. in liver and muscle.

glycoˈgenesis *n.* the metabolic formation of sugar, or of glycogen from sugar L19. **glycogeˈnetic** *a.* = GLYCOGENIC L19. **glycoˈgenic** *a.* of or pertaining to glycogenesis M19. **glycogeˈnolysis** *n.* the breakdown of glycogen to glucose in the body E20. **glycogenoˈlytic** *a.* of or pertaining to glycogenolysis E20.

glycol /ˈglʌɪkɒl/ *n.* M19. [f. GLYC(ERINE + -OL.] = ETHYLENE *glycol*; *Chem.* any diol.

glyˈcollate, **-ˈcolate** *n.* (*Chem.*) a salt or ester of glycollic acid M19. **glyˈcollic**, **-ˈcolic** *a.* (*Chem.*): *glycollic acid*, a crystalline acid, CH_2OH·COOH (also called *hydroxyacetic acid*), which occurs in sugar-cane syrup and has numerous industrial uses M19.

glycolyse /ˈglʌɪk(ə)lʌɪz/ *v.t.* Also ***-lyze**. M20. [Back-form. f. next.] *Biochem.* Metabolize in glycolysis.

glycolysis /glʌɪˈkɒlɪsɪs/ *n.* Pl. **-lyses** /-lɪsiːz/. L19. [f. GLYCO- + LYSIS.] *Biochem.* The breakdown of sugar; *esp.* the metabolic process in which sugar and other carbohydrates are broken down by enzymes in most living organisms to yield pyruvic acid or lactic acid.

glycoˈlytic *a.* L19. **glycoˈlytically** *adv.* M20.

Glyconean /glʌɪkəˈniːən/ *a. rare.* Also **Glyconian** /glʌɪˈkəʊnɪən/. E18. [f. late L *Glyconius* f. Gk *Glukōneios*, f. *Glukōn*: see next, -EAN, -IAN.] = GLYCONIC *a.*

Glyconic /glʌɪˈkɒnɪk/ *n.* & *a.* L17. [f. Gk *Glukōn* a Greek lyric poet + -IC.] **A** *n.* A Glyconic verse. L17. **B** *adj.* Of, pertaining to, or characterized by a metre in which there are three trochees and a dactyl in each line. L17.

glycosamine /glʌɪˈkəʊsəmiːn, -ˈkəʊz-/ *n.* L19. [f. *glycose*, obs. var. of GLUCOSE + AMINE.] *Chem.* **1** = GLUCOSAMINE. L19. **2** Any amino sugar in which an amino group replaces a hydroxyl group of a sugar other than the group attached to the first carbon atom. M20.

glycosaminoglycan /glʌɪˌkəʊsəmiːnəʊˈglʌɪkan/ *n.* M20. [f. prec. + -O- + GLYCO- + -AN.] *Biochem.* Any of a group of polysaccharides which contain amino-sugar residues, are often found in complexes with protein molecules as proteoglycans, and include heparin, chondroitin, hyaluronic acid, and the blood-group substances.

¶ See note s.v. MUCOPOLYSACCHARIDE.

glycoside /ˈglʌɪkəsʌɪd/ *n.* L19. [f. GLYCO- after GLUCOSIDE.] *Chem.* †**1** See GLUCOSIDE. L19. **2** Any of a class of sugar derivatives, many of which occur in plants, in which the hydroxyl group attached to the first carbon atom of a sugar is replaced by some other group, usually an alcohol or phenol. M20.

glycosidic /-ˈsɪd-/ *a.* of the nature of or characteristic of a glycoside E20. **glycosidically** /-ˈsɪd-/ *adv.* M20.

glycosuria /glʌɪkəˈsjʊərɪə/ *n.* M19. [Fr. *glycosurie*, †*gluco-* f. as GLUCOSE, -URIA.] *Med.* The presence of glucose in the urine.

glycoˈsuric *a.* pertaining to or exhibiting glycosuria L19.

glycosyl /ˈglʌɪkə(ʊ)sɪl, -sʌɪl/ *n.* M20. [f. GLYCO- + -OSE² + -YL.] *Biochem.* A monovalent radical derived from a sugar by removing a hydroxyl group from an anomeric carbon atom. Usu. in *comb.*

glyˈcosylate *v.t.* introduce a glycosyl group into (a compound) M20. **glycosyˈlation** *n.* M20.

glycuronic /glʌɪkjʊˈrɒnɪk/ *a.* L19. [Irreg. f. GLYCO- + Gk *ouron* urine + -IC.] *Chem.* & *Biochem.* = GLUCURONIC.

glycyl /ˈglʌɪsʌɪl, -sɪl/ *n.* E20. [f. GLYC(INE + -YL.] *Chem.* The monovalent radical H_2N·CH_2CO· derived from glycine.

glycyrrhizin /glɪsɪˈrʌɪzɪn/ *n.* M19. [f. late L *glycyrrhiza* f. Gk *glukurrhiza* LIQUORICE: see -IN¹.] *Chem.* A very sweet-tasting glycoside from liquorice root which has a triterpene as the aglycone and is used in the food and drug industries.

glyde /glʌɪd/ *n. Sc. arch.* Also †**gleyde**. M16. [Origin unkn.] An old worn-out horse.

glyoxal /glʌɪˈɒksal/ *n.* M19. [f. GLY(COL + OX(ALIC + -AL².] *Chem.* The compound $(CHO{\cdot})_2$, occurring as yellow crystals or a yellow liquid and used industrially.

glyoxylate *n.* a salt or ester, or the anion, of glyoxylic acid (*glyoxylate cycle*, a variant of the Krebs cycle in some micro-organisms) M19. **glyoxaline** *n.* = IMIDAZOLE M19. **glyoˈxylic** *a.*: *glyoxylic acid*, the acid CHO·COOH, a syrupy liquid, and its hydrated crystalline form $CH(OH)_2$·COOH, which is a metabolic intermediate and occurs esp. in unripe fruit M19.

glyph /glɪf/ *n.* L18. [Fr. *glyphe* f. Gk *gluphē* carving, rel. to *gluphein* carve.] 1 *Archit.* An ornamental groove or channel, usu. vertical. L18. 2 A sculptured character or symbol. E19.

glyphic *n.* & *a.* (*a*) *n.* (*rare*) an illustration, a glyph; (*b*) *adj.* carved, sculptured: E18.

glyphography /glɪˈfɒgrəfi/ *n.* Now *Hist.* M19. [f. Gk *gluphē* (see GLYPH) + -OGRAPHY.] A printing process in which a relief electrotype block is made from an image engraved through a coating of wax on a metal plate.

ˈ**glyphograph** *n.* a plate made by glyphography; an impression taken from such a plate: M19. **glyphographer** *n.* M19. **glyphoˈgraphic** *a.* pertaining to or produced by glyphography M19.

glyphosate /ˈglʌɪfəseɪt/ *n.* L20. [f. GLY(CINE + PHOS(PHO- + -ATE[1].] A non-selective systemic herbicide that is especially effective against perennial weeds.

glyptal /ˈglɪpt(ə)l/ *n.* Also *****G-**. E20. [Perh. f. GLY(CEROL + *phthalic*.] An alkyd resin, *esp.* one made from glycerol and phthalic anhydride or phthalic acid.

¶Proprietary name in the US.

glyptic /ˈglɪptɪk/ *n.* & *a.* E19. [Fr. *glyptique* or Gk *gluptikos*, f. *gluptēs* carver, f. *gluphein* carve: see -IC.] A *n.sing.* & in *pl.* (treated as *sing.*). The art of carving or engraving, esp. on precious stones. E19. B *adj.* Of or pertaining to glyptics. M19.

glyptical *a.* (*rare*) = GLYPTIC *a.* L19. **glyptically** *adv.* M20.

glyptodont /ˈglyptədɒnt/ *n.* Also **-don** /-dɒn/. M19. [f. as next + -ODONT.] An extinct mammal of Cenozoic times whose few teeth were grooved, related to the armadillos but much larger and with a bony shield round the body and tail.

glyptography /glɪpˈtɒgrəfi/ *n.* L18. [f. Gk *gluptos* carved + -OGRAPHY. Cf. Fr. *glyptographie*.] The art of engraving gems; the branch of knowledge that deals with engraved gems.

G-man /ˈdʒiːman/ *n.* Pl. **G-men** /-mɛn/. E20. [Prob. f. *G*overnment + MAN *n.*; in sense I perh. an arbitrary use of *G*.] 1 In Ireland, a political detective. E20. 2 A special agent of the Federal Bureau of Investigation. *US.* E20.

gnädige Frau /ˈgnɛːdɪgə fraʊ/ *n. phr.* M20. [G, lit. 'gracious lady': see FRAU.] A polite title or form of address for a German or German-speaking (esp. married) woman, corresp. to English *Madam*.

gnädiger Herr /ˈgnɛːdɪgər hɛː/ *n. phr.* E20. [G, lit 'gracious sir': see HERR.] A polite title or form of address for a German or German-speaking man, corresp. to English *Sir*.

gnamma hole /ˈnamə həʊl/ *n. phr. Austral.* Also **namma hole**. L19. [Aborig. *ŋama* + HOLE *n.*[1]] A natural hole in a rock, containing water; a water-hole.

gnap /nap/ *v.* & *n.* ME. [Imit.] A *v.i.* & *t.* Make a snapping bite (at). Now *Sc.* ME.

gnap at *fig.* find fault with.

B *n.* A bite, a morsel. *Sc.* M18.

gnar *n.* var. of KNAR.

gnar /nɑː/ *v.i.* Now *arch.* & *dial.* Infl. **-rr-**. Also **gnarr, narr**. LME. [Imit.: cf. MLG *gnarren*, G *knarren* creak, *knurren* snarl.] Snarl, growl.

gnarl /nɑːl/ *n.* E19. [Back-form. f. GNARLED. Cf. KNARL, KNURL *n.*] A contorted knotty protuberance, esp. on a tree.

gnarly *a.* [cf. KNURLY] = GNARLED E19.

†**gnarl** *v.*[1]*i.* L16–M19. [Frequent. of GNAR *v.*] Snarl.

gnarl /nɑːl/ *v.*[2]*t.* E19. [Back-form. f. GNARLED.] Contort, twist, make knotted and rugged like an old tree. Chiefly as *gnarled* pa. pple.

gnarled /nɑːld/ *a.* E17. [Var. of KNURLED.] Of a tree or a hand, person, etc.; covered with knotty protuberances; knobbly and rough, as with age and exposure to the weather.

C. MACKENZIE The old man held out his gnarled fist. M. RENAULT The oldest of the apple trees, too gnarled to bear.

¶Rare (Shakes.) bef. E19.

gnarr *v.* var. of GNAR *v.*

gnash /naʃ/ *v.* & *n.* In sense B.2 also **nash**. LME. [Origin uncertain: perh. imit., or alt. of GNAST.] A *v.* 1 *v.i.* (Of a person or animal) strike together or grind the teeth, esp. in rage; (of the teeth) strike together. LME. 2 *v.t.* Strike together or grind (the teeth), esp. in rage. L16. 3 *v.t.* Bite, gnaw. E18. B *n.* 1 A gnashing or snap of the teeth. *rare.* E19. 2 Biting remarks; insolent talk. *Sc.* E19.

gnasher *n.* †(*a*) a person who gnashes; (*b*) in *pl.* (*slang*) teeth, *esp.* false teeth: L15. **gnashing** *vbl n.* the action or an act of the vb GNASH L15. **gnashingly** *adv.* with gnashing teeth; in a way that makes one gnash one's teeth: E20.

†**gnast** *v.* ME. [f. base of ON *gnast(r)an* gnashing of teeth, *gneista* emit sparks, *gnesta* clatter.] 1 *v.i.* = GNASH *v.* 1. ME–M16. 2 *v.t.* = GNASH *v.* 2. Only in ME.

¶Perh. the source of GNASH *v.*

gnat /nat/ *n.*[1] [OE *gnætt* corresp. to LG *gnatte*, G dial. *Gnatze* rel. to MLG *gnitte*, G *Gnitze*.] 1 Any of numerous small mostly biting dipteran insects with long thin fragile legs, many of which are in the family Culicidae (cf. MOSQUITO *n.*[1]); spec. *Culex pipiens*, found near stagnant water. OE. 2 Something small and insignificant. OE.

2 *strain at a gnat* see STRAIN *v.*[1]

Comb.: **gnat-catcher** any of various tiny Old World warblers of the genus *Polioptila*, found in the warmer parts of N. and S. America; **gnat-eater** any of various small birds of the genus *Conopophaga*, related to the antbirds, which occur in the forests of northern and eastern S. America; **gnat-snap, -snapper** a bird that catches gnats; **gnat's piss** *slang* a very weak or poor quality drink.

gnatlike *a.* & *adv.* (*a*) *adj.* resembling (that of) a gnat; (*b*) *adv.* in the manner of a gnat: L19.

gnat /nat/ *n.*[2] *obs.* exc. *dial.* E17. [Var. of KNOT *n.*[2], prob. infl. by *gnat-snap, -snapper* (see prec.).] = KNOT *n.*[2]

gnathic /ˈnaθɪk, ˈneɪ-/ *a.* L19. [f. Gk *gnathos* jaw + -IC.] Of or pertaining to the jaws.

Also **gnathal** *a.* L19.

gnathion /ˈneɪθɪɒn/ *n.* L19. [f. as prec. + *-ion*, after *inion*.] *Anat.* The lowest point in the middle of the lower edge of the lower jaw.

†**gnatho** *n.* M16–E18. [L *Gnatho*: see GNATHONIC.] A parasite, a sycophant.

gnatho- /ˈneɪθəʊ/ *comb. form* of Gk *gnathos* jaw, forming terms chiefly in *Zool.*: see -O-.

gnathobase *n.* (*Zool.*) a process on the proximal part of a segmented limb in some arthropods which is used to bite or crush food L19. **gnathoˈbasic** *a.* (*Zool.*) of, pertaining to, or of the nature of a gnathobase E20. **gnathochiˈlarium** *n.* [Gk *kheilos* lip] *Zool.* a platelike structure in the floor of the mouth of a millipede L19. **gnathoˈstomatous** *a.* = GNATHOSTOME *a.* L19. **gnathostome** *n.* & *a.* (of, pertaining to, or designating) a vertebrate with fully developed upper and lower jaws E20.

gnathonic /neɪˈθɒnɪk/ *a.* Now *rare.* M17. [L *Gnathonicus*, f. *Gnatho(n-)* sycophantic character in Terence's *Eunuchus*, f. Gk *gnathōn* parasite, f. *gnathos* jaw: see -IC.] Sycophantic, toadying.

†**gnathonical** *a.* = GNATHONIC M16–M17. †**gnathonically** *adv.* L16–E17.

gnatling /ˈnatlɪŋ/ *n.* E17. [f. GNAT *n.*[1] + -LING[1].] A small gnat.

gnatoo /nəˈtuː, *foreign* ˈŋatuː/ *n.* E19. [Polynesian (now *gatu*).] A textile made in Tonga from the bark of the paper mulberry.

gnatter /ˈnatə/ *v.*[1]*t.* & *i. obs.* exc. *dial.* M18. [Origin unkn.] Nibble (at or *at*).

gnatter *v.*[2] & *n.* see NATTER.

gnatty /ˈnati/ *a.* M19. [f. GNAT *n.*[1] + -Y[1].] Resembling a gnat; infested with gnats.

gnaur *n.* var. of KNAR.

gnaw /nɔː/ *v.* & *n.* Pa. t. **gnawed**; pa. pple **gnawed, gnawn**. [OE *gnagan* = OS *gnagan*, OHG *(g)nagan* (G *nagen*), ON *gnaga*, of imit. origin.] A *v.* 1 *v.t.* (w. *away, off*, etc.) & *i.* (w. *at, into, on*). Bite (something) persistently so as to damage or remove parts of it; wear away by continued biting; make (a hole etc.) by gnawing. OE. 2 *v.t.* & *i.* (w. *at, into*, †*on*). Of a destructive agent, or a pain or emotion: corrode, eat away, consume; torture, torment. ME.

1 J. BUCHAN In the loft the rats had gnawed great holes in the floor. E. BLYTON He..sat down contentedly to gnaw the fine bone. A. CARTER Philip made a hearty meal and gnawed on the bones like Henry VIII. 2 J. LONDON The thought gnawed in his brain, an unceasing torment. A. MILLER She is almost content; she knows she might well be content but something gnaws at her.

B *n.* (A) gnawing. M18.

gnawable *a.* L19. **gnawer** *n.* a person who or thing which gnaws; *spec.* a rodent: L15. **gnawing** *vbl n.* the action of the vb; an instance of this: ME. **gnawing** *ppl a.* that gnaws; (of a worry, pain, etc.) persistent; worrying: M16. **gnawingly** *adv.* M19.

gneeve /gniːv/ *n. Anglo-Ir.* Now *rare.* M17. [Ir. *gníomh*.] The twelfth part of a ploughland.

gneiss /nʌɪs/ *n.* Also (earlier) †**kneiss**. M18. [G f. OHG *gneisto* (= OE *gnāst*, ON *gneisti*) spark.] A foliated usu. coarse-grained metamorphic rock in which bands of granular minerals alternate with bands of flaky or prismatic ones, and typically consisting of feldspar, quartz, and mica.

gneissic *a.* of the nature of or composed of gneiss; characteristic of gneiss: M19. **gneissoid** *a.* resembling gneiss M19. **gneissose** *a.* = GNEISSIC M19. **gneiˈssosity** *n.* gneissic character or structure E20. **gneissy** *a.* = GNEISSIC M18.

gnocchi /ˈn(j)ɒki, ˈgnɒki, *foreign* ˈɲɔkki/ *n.pl.* L19. [It., pl. of *gnocco*, f. *nocchio* knot in wood.] Small dumplings made with flour, semolina, or potato.

gnome /nəʊm, ˈnəʊmi/ *n.*[1] L16. [Gk *gnōmē* thought, judgement, opinion, *gnōmai* pl., sayings, maxims, f. *gnō-* base of *gignōskein* KNOW *v.*] A short pithy statement expressing a general truth; a maxim, an aphorism.

gnome /nəʊm/ *n.*[2] M17. [Fr. f. mod.L *gnomus* used by Paracelsus as a synonym of *Pygmaeus*.] 1 A member of a legendary subterranean race of diminutive beings, typically represented as bearded old men and supposedly guardians of the earth's treasure; a goblin, a dwarf. M17. 2 A statue or figure of a gnome, *esp.* one used as a garden ornament. M20. 3 An international, esp. Swiss, financier or banker, regarded as having sinister influence. Chiefly in *gnomes of Zurich*, *Zurich gnome*. *colloq.* M20.

gnomic /ˈnəʊmɪk/ *a.*[1] E19. [Gk *gnōmikos* (perh. through Fr. *gnomique*), f. as GNOME *n.*[1]: see -IC.] 1 Of, consisting of, or of the nature of gnomes or aphorisms; (of a writer) given to using gnomes or aphorisms. E19. 2 *Gram.* Of a tense: used to express a general truth without implication of time. M19.

1 N. FRYE Blake..is perhaps the finest gnomic artist in English literature. CLIVE JAMES Auden has for a long time been manufacturing gnomic utterances and quiddities of his own.

gnomical *a.* = GNOMIC *a.*[1] E17. **gnomically** *adv.* E17.

gnomic /ˈnəʊmɪk/ *a.*[2] M19. [f. GNOME *n.*[2] + -IC.] Of or resembling a gnome or dwarf.

gnomish /ˈnəʊmɪʃ/ *a.* E19. [f. GNOME *n.*[2] + -ISH[1].] Resembling a gnome or dwarf.

gnomist /ˈnəʊmɪst/ *n. rare.* E18. [f. GNOME *n.*[1] + -IST.] A gnomic poet or writer.

gnomology /nəʊˈmɒlədʒi/ *n.* M17. [Gk *gnōmologia*, f. as GNOME *n.*[1]: see -OLOGY.] 1 A collection of general maxims or precepts. M17. 2 The gnomic element in writing or a work. E19.

gnomoˈlogic *a.* (*rare*) = GNOMIC *a.*[1] M18. **gnomologist** *n.* (*rare*) = GNOMIST E19.

gnomon /ˈnəʊmɒn/ *n.* M16. [Fr., or L *gnomon*, f. Gk *gnōmōn* inspector, indicator, carpenter's square, f. *gnō-*: see GNOME *n.*[1]] 1 A pillar, rod, etc., which shows the time of day by casting its shadow on a marked surface; *esp.* the pin or triangular plate of a sundial. M16. b A column etc. used in observing the meridian altitude of the sun. E17. †2 The nose. *joc.* L16–E19. 3a *Geom.* The part of a parallelogram left after a similar parallelogram is taken away from one of its corners. L16. †b *gen.* Something shaped like a carpenter's square; an L-shaped bar. M17–L18. †4 A guide, an indicator; an indicating instrument. L16–M18. †5 A rule, a canon of belief or action. Only in 17.

gnomonic /nəʊˈmɒnɪk/ *a.* & *n.* E17. [L *gnomonicus* f. Gk *gnōmonikos*, f. *gnōmōn*: see prec., -IC.] A *adj.* 1 Of or pertaining to a gnomon or sundial or the measuring of time by this. E17. b Designating a map projection in which the centre of projection is the centre of the sphere being mapped. E18. 2 = GNOMIC *a.*[1] E18. †B *n.* = GNOMONICS. Only in M17.

gnomonical *a.* = GNOMONIC *a.* L16. **gnomonically** *adv.* E18.

gnomonics /nəʊˈmɒnɪks/ *n.* L17. [Pl. of GNOMONIC *n.*: see -ICS.] *Hist.* The art of using or constructing dials.

gnoscopine /ˈnɒskəpiːn/ *n.* L19. [f. Gk *gignōskein* know + OP(IUM + -INE[5].] Either of two isomeric alkaloids, $C_{22}H_{23}NO_7$, of which one occurs in opium.

gnosiology /nəʊzɪˈɒlədʒi/ *n.* Also **gnose-**. L19. [f. as next + -OLOGY.] The branch of knowledge that deals with cognition or the cognitive faculties.

gnosioˈlogical *a.* E20.

gnosis /ˈnəʊsɪs/ *n.* Pl. **gnoses** /ˈnəʊsiːz/. L16. [Gk *gnōsis* investigation, knowledge, f. *gno-*: see GNOME *n.*[1]] A special knowledge of spiritual mysteries; *spec.* in *Theol.*, the redemptive knowledge that the Gnostics claimed to have of God and of the origin and destiny of man.

gnostic /ˈnɒstɪk/ *n.* & *a.* L16. [eccl.L *gnosticus* f. Gk *gnōstikos*, f. *gnōstos* known, f. *gnō-*: see GNOME *n.*[1], -IC.] A *n.* (**G-**.) A member of a heretical Christian sect of the 1st to the 3rd cents. AD who claimed gnosis. Usu. in *pl.* L16. B *adj.* 1 Relating to knowledge; cognitive; intellectual. M17. †b Clever, knowing. *joc.* or *slang.* E-M19. 2 (**G-**.) Of or pertaining to the Gnostics; mystic, occult. M19.

gnostical *a.* = GNOSTIC *a.* E19. **gnostically** *adv.* E19. **Gnosticism, g-** *n.* (the principles of) the religious movement or beliefs of the Gnostics M17. **gnosticize** /-saɪz/ *v.t.* & *i.* (*a*) *v.i.* adopt or expound Gnostic principles; (*b*) *v.t.* give a Gnostic character to: M17.

gnotobiology /ˌnəʊtəʊbʌɪˈɒlədʒi/ *n.* M20. [f. as next + BIOLOGY.] = GNOTOBIOTICS.

gnotobiotic /ˌnəʊtəʊbʌɪˈɒtɪk/ *a.* M20. [f. Gk *gnōtos* known, f. *gnō-*: see GNOME *n.*[1], -O-, BIOTIC.] Of an animal or an environment: rendered free from the bacteria etc. normally present, or having only a few known organisms of this kind present.

gnotoˈbiote *n.* a gnotobiotic animal M20.

gnotobiotics /ˌnəʊtəʊbʌɪˈɒtɪks/ *n.* M20. [f. prec.: see -ICS.] The branch of knowledge that deals with producing and using gnotobiotic organisms.

gnu /nuː, njuː; gn-/ *n.* L18. [f. Khoisan, prob. through Du. *gnoe*.] = WILDEBEEST.

brindled gnu = *blue* WILDEBEEST. **white-tailed gnu** = *black* WILDEBEEST.

go /gəʊ/ *n.*[1] Pl. **goes**. L17. [f. the vb.] 1 The action or an act of going. L17. 2 An unforeseen turn of affairs, esp. causing embarrassment. *colloq.* L18. 3 A turn or attempt at something; a spell of something; a period of activity; *spec.* (*a*) a delivery of the ball or bowl at skittles etc.; (*b*) an attack of an illness; (*c*) a fight, an argument. L18. 4 A quantity of liquor, food, etc., served at one time. Formerly also, a vessel containing this quantity. *colloq.* L18. 5 *The* height of fashion, *the* rage. Now only in *be all* or *quite the go. colloq.* L18. 6 Mettle, spirit, dash, animation; *colloq.* vigorous activity. E19. 7 A success; a bargain, an agreement. L19.

2 K. AMIS 'Rum go, that,' said George when she had left. 3 R. DAHL It looked like a bad go of malaria. J. JOSEPH You can . . grow more fat And eat three pounds of sausages at a go. W. GOLDING Most of the pyramid collapsed in one go. 4 W. COBBETT Plates of beef and goes of gin. K. MOORE After consuming . . chocolate buns and a second go of sandwiches. 6 F. NORRIS There's no go, no life in me at all these days. A. BROOKNER It is all go here, a veritable whirl of activity. 7 U. SINCLAIR It's a go, then. I'm your man. A. WEST How any two people could make a go of a union that began with so much resentment and hostility.

Phrases: **give it a go** *colloq.* make an effort to succeed. *great go*: see GREAT *a.* **have a go** (*a*) make an attempt, act resourcefully; *spec.* take independent or single-handed action against a criminal or criminals; (*b*) (foll. by *at*) attack, find fault with. *little go*: see LITTLE *a.* **near go** *colloq.* a narrow escape. *no go*: see NO *a.* **on the go** *colloq.* †(*a*) on the verge of destruction or decline; (*b*) in constant motion, in a restless state. *open go*: see OPEN *a. square go*: see SQUARE *a.*

Comb.: **go-devil** *US* a movable contrivance used to clean the interior of pipes etc.; **go-fever** *colloq.* feverish restlessness or longing for movement.

go /gəʊ/ *n.*[2] L19. [Jap.] A Japanese board game of territorial possession and capture. Cf. WEI CH'I.

go /gəʊ/ *a.* E20. [f. the vb.] 1 Designating a gauge which must pass through or be passed through the piece. Cf. NO-GO, NOT-GO. E20. 2 Esp. of a device in a spacecraft: functioning properly; ready and prepared. *colloq.* M20. 3 Fashionable, progressive. *colloq.* M20.

go /gəʊ/ *v.* Pa. t. **went** /wɛnt/, (*Sc.* & *north.*) **gaed** /geɪd/, †**yede**, †**yode**; pa. pple **gone** /gɒn/, (*dial.*) **went**. 2 sing. pres. (*arch.*) **goest** /ˈgəʊɪst/; 3 sing pres. **goes** /gəʊz/, (*arch.*) **goeth** /ˈgəʊɪθ/. [OE *gān* = OFris. *gān*, *gēn*, OS *gān* (Du. *gaen*), OHG *gān*, *gēn* (G *gehen*), f. Gmc. The original pa. t. (OE *ēode*) was superseded in southern Eng. by forms f. WEND *v.*[1] from 15.] I Of movement, irrespective of point of departure or destination. †1 *v.i.* Walk; move on foot at an ordinary pace; (esp. of a horse) step in a specified manner. OE-M19. 2 *v.i.* Move or pass along, proceed, journey, travel, progress (by any means); *Hunting* ride to hounds. OE. b *v.t.* w. advb. obj. Travel over (a specified distance) or at (a specified speed); (with cognate obj.) go on (an errand, journey, etc.). Formerly also with direct obj.: go through (a tract of country etc.) or over (a river etc.). ME. 3 *v.i.* & *t.* w. advb. obj. Take a specified course (of movement or action). OE. b *v.i.* Be guided or regulated *by*; act in accordance or harmony *with*; judge or act (*up*)*on*; *colloq.* base a conclusion or course of action (*up*)*on*. L15. c *v.i.* Of a line etc.: lie, point in a specified direction. L19. 4 *v.i.* Be habitually or for a time in a specified state (now esp. of privation or disadvantage). Cf. sense 14 below. OE. 5 *v.i.* Of a female: be pregnant (more fully *go with child* etc.), esp. for a specified time. Now chiefly as *gone* ppl a. (see sense 34 below). ME. 6 *v.i.* Of time: pass, elapse. ME. 7 *v.i.* Be current or accepted; be known *by* or *under the name* etc. *of*. ME. 8 *v.i.* (Of events, a performance, activity, etc.) have a course or outcome of a specified kind, proceed or turn out *well* etc.; (of a contest, election, etc.) issue or result in a specified manner, result *for* or *against*; (of a constituency, voter, etc.) take a specified course or view. ME. b Be successful; *colloq.* be acceptable or permitted, be accepted without question. M18. 9 *v.i.* Be moving, acting, or working; (of a clock, watch, etc.) keep time in a specified manner; (of a bell, striking clock, gun, etc.) emit a sound in functioning; make a specified movement; (with imit. int. or vb-stem used advb.) make a specified sound or (audible) movement. ME. b *v.t.* Of a clock etc.: strike to indicate (a specified hour). Of an hour etc.: be struck (chiefly in *perf. tenses*, has been struck). E18. 10 *v.i.* Have ordinarily in degree or range of value or quality, be on average. LME. 11 *v.i.* Of a verse, song, etc.: be pleasingly or rhythmically constructed, proceed fluently; admit of being sung, or be usually sung, *to* a specified tune. L16. 12 *v.i.* Of a document, verse, tune, etc.: run, have a specified content, wording, or tenor. E17.

1 BUNYAN I have resolved to run when I can, to go when I cannot run, and to creep when I cannot go. DEFOE My horse went very awkwardly and uneasy. 2 T. HARDY The four went in one cab to Raye's lodgings. J. PUDNEY Our child now marches through the town, Bearing her own child as she goes. E. WELTY The train . . was going at eighty miles an hour. A. PRICE You'll have to go carefully. . . You'll need professional advice. ISAIAH BERLIN One cannot try and go up a staircase down which an army is trying to march. W. TREVOR High above them an aeroplane goes over. b SPENSER I went the wastefull woodes and forest wyde. L. MACNEICE Dials Professing to tell the distance We have gone, the speed we are going. 3 THOMAS HUGHES An exhortation to . . go outside of the barge which was coming up. M. CORELLI She will never go my way,—nor, I fear, shall I ever go hers. *go astray, wrong*, etc. b V. S. PRITCHETT You mustn't go by faces. P. ACKROYD If the editorials of *The Times* are anything to go by. P. ROTH They had nothing to go on but the most elemental manhood. 4 J. GATHORNE-HARDY I went for years thinking there was something wrong with me. P. ACKROYD At first he went hungry because he did not know how to beg. 6 R. C. HUTCHINSON There was still over half an hour to go before my day's work began. J. RATHBONE The next two hours or so went quickly. 7 DRYDEN Love is the only coin in heaven will go. LD MACAULAY The monk who . . sometimes went by the alias of Johnson. R. TRAVERS Butler in fact went under the name Newman. 8 SCOTT FITZGERALD Things went from bad to worse, until finally he had to give up his position. E. BOWEN How is your book going? A. TYLER The marriage wasn't going well and I decided to leave my husband. b M. ALLINGHAM Anything goes if it's done by someone you're fond of. 9 R. C. HUTCHINSON My fire was still going when I finished. D. MAHON The empty freighters . . In a fine rain, their sirens going. N. MAILER Boom! the waves would go against the wall. A. T. ELLIS She didn't go 'Aah' over babies and brides and the Princess of Wales. b K. HULME The clock's just gone eleven. 10 L. WOOLF As professional journalists go, Sharp was not a bad editor. 11 SHAKES. *Wint. T.* This is a passing merry one, and goes to the tune of 'Two maids wooing a man'. 12 DICKENS Those who are put in authority over me (as the catechism goes).

II With the point of departure prominent. 13 *v.i.* Move away, depart, leave; begin to move from a given point or state; begin an action. In *imper.*, used as a starter's word in a race. OE. 14 *v.i.* Get away *free*, *unpunished*, etc., (orig. from a court of justice etc.). Passing into sense 4. ME. 15 *v.i.* Be relinquished, dismissed, abolished, or lost; (of money) be spent (*in*, *on* a thing); be sold (*at*, *for* an amount). ME. 16 *v.i.* Die. LME. 17 *v.i.* Fail, give way, break down, crack; succumb to pressure or any deteriorating influence. M18.

13 J. CONRAD The last vestiges of youth had gone off his face. G. GREENE His anger went as quickly as it came. C. ODETS Pack up your clothes and go! Go! Who the hell's stopping you? I. MURDOCH At any sign of emotion he quietly went, leaving the room noiselessly like an animal. 14 T. TANNER It . . has not gone unnoticed—that her language is marked by a minimum of physical action. 15 M. J. GUEST Whatever money he got . . it all went in books. W. GOLDING His hair was gone on top except for a tiny black tuft. K. VONNEGUT The money was gone. S. CHITTY A small gouache of a girl in church . . went for £2,000. 16 D. LESSING You'll get what money I have when I go. 17 J. RHYS The fuse which lights the whole house has gone. M. DRABBLE She still thought that her brain might go or that her nerve might snap.

III With the direction or destination prominent, of self-originated movement. 18 *v.i.* Make one's way or proceed to or towards a specified place etc. or in a specified direction (in some contexts with the notion of an activity to be engaged in or way of life to be adopted uppermost); (of a road etc.) lead. (Foll. by *to*, *towards*, *into*, etc.) OE. b Urinate, defecate. *colloq.* M20. 19 *v.i.* Make one's way or proceed with a specified purpose (foll. by prep. phr., *to do*, *and do*, (now *colloq.* & *N. Amer.*) *do*). Foll. by *doing*, (arch.) *a-doing*: make an expedition to engage in the specified activity, *colloq.* be so foolish as to do the specified thing. OE. b (With n. compl.) Be employed as, go to be, become. Now only in *go bail*, act as bail (*for* a person). M17. 20 *v.i.* Proceed to some specified course of action or means of attaining one's object; have recourse, refer, appeal, *to*. ME. 21 *v.i.* & *t.* with *advb. obj.* Carry action to a specified point of progress or completeness; raise a bid or offering price to a specified level. L16. b *v.i.* Put or subject oneself *to* (trouble, expense). M19. c *v.t.* Venture as far as, go to the extent of; like to partake of or engage in (esp. in *I* etc. *could go a* —). M19. 22 *v.t.* Stake, wager, risk, adventure; bid, declare; *US* enter into a wager with (a person). E17.

18 J. STEINBECK She lighted a candle and went to the kitchen in her bare feet. P. ROTH Maria thought she'd have to go over to New York to buy the black underwear. 19 SHAKES. *Com. Err.* Our dinner done, and he not coming thither, I went to seek him. DONNE Goe and catch a falling starre. GOLDSMITH I was resolved not to go sneaking to the lower professors. R.

SUTCLIFF We went for picnics and for days out in the car. J. DAVIS Are you ready to go play golf? **20** J. S. BLACKIE You must go to Aristotle for that. **21** M. J. GUEST Strafford really went some way towards bringing his scheme to pass. H. JAMES My mother has not gone into details. E. WAUGH Twenty-five pounds. . . Thirty. I can't go higher than that. A. J. AYER He went so far as to quarrel with Gilbert Ryle. **b** A. T. ELLIS You needn't have gone to all this trouble our first night. **c** D. BALLANTYNE I could go a good feed of eels just now. **22** MARVELL This Gentleman would always go half a Crown with me. D. L. SAYERS He went three no trumps on the ace of spades singleton, five hearts to the king, queen.

IV With the direction or destination prominent, of imparted movement. **23** *v.i.* Be carried, moved, or impelled; penetrate, sink. Foll. by *to, towards, into*, etc. OE. **24** *v.i.* Be applied or appropriated *to, to do*; contribute *to* or *towards* a result, *to do*; conduce or tend *to, to do*. ME. **b** Amount together or be equivalent *to*. M19. **25** *v.i.* & *t.* with *advb. obj.* Reach, attain, extend, hold out, suffice, or last to a specified point. LME. **b** *v.t.* Yield, produce, (a specified amount). *US*. E19. **26** *v.i.* Pass into a specified condition; become, get to be; be transformed or reduced *to*. L16. **27** *v.i.* Be allotted or awarded *to*; pass by inheritance, succession, or otherwise *to*. E17. **28** *v.i.* Be able to pass *into, through*, etc.; be able to find room or fit *in, into*; (of a number) admit of being contained in another either without remainder or at all. L17. **b** Be usually placed or kept, belong, *in, on*, etc. E18.

23 I. MURDOCH The casement windows were open as wide as they could go. **24** W. COWPER There goes more to the composition of a volume than many critics imagine. T. JEFFERSON Those geographical schisms which go immediately to a separation. W. GOLDING Never let her know. . . It would just go to feed her vanity. **25** J. LOCKE No man's knowledge here can go beyond his experience. **26** E. WAUGH And he went to sleep for a little, with his head in her lap. M. PUZO Sandra noticed that her husband's face had gone red with flushing blood. A. BROOKNER She was recognizable, he saw thankfully, not gone to seed. **27** R. H. MOTTRAM Two of the sadly depleted companies went to adjacent farms, two remained on the premises. A. MCCOWEN Sometimes I was given a part that should perhaps have gone to another actor. **28** M. J. GUEST All the good we can find about him will go into a very few words. P. ROTH Eight from one doesn't go, so we must borrow one from the preceding digit.

V Special uses of *gone* pa. pple. See also GONE *ppl a.* **29**†**a** Ago, formerly. ME–M17. **b** Reckoned from the specified past date. M19. **c** (Of time) past; over the specified age. M19. **30** *be gone*, depart. Cf. BEGONE *v.*[1] L16. **31** Dead. Formerly also, unconscious. L16. **32** Lost; hopeless, ruined; failed. L16. **33** Infatuated. (Foll. by *on* a person.) L17. **34** Pregnant; having spent the specified period in gestation. (More fully *gone with child* etc.) L17. **35** *gone!*, just sold (an auctioneer's announcement). L18.

29c *Temple Bar* A man 'gone ninety years of age'. B. UNSWORTH He glanced at his watch. It was gone twelve. **32** SCOTT FITZGERALD It possessed the interest of a souvenir by representing a mood that was gone. J. BAYLISS With broken wing they limped across the sky / . . with their gunner dead, / one engine gone. **33** F. ASTAIRE Anything and everything about Phyllis was first and foremost with me. I was gone. S. BELLOW I was gone on her and . . gave her a real embrace. **34** J. CARY The woman was far gone with child. D. JACOBSON She must have been about five months gone. Even her face looked pregnant, somehow.

VI Special uses of *going* pres. pple (in senses 39, 40 orig. vbl n. after A *prep.*[1] 8: see GOING *n.* III). See also GOING *ppl a.* **36** *going to do, to be done*: orig., on the way to, preparing to, tending to; now usu., about to, intending or intended to, likely to. See also GONNA. LME. **37** *going (on, on for,* †*upon,* †*in,* †*of)* —, approaching the specified number (esp. of years of age), time, etc. E17. **38** *going!*, on the point of being sold (an auctioneer's announcement). L18. **39** Existing; to be had. L18. **40** In or into action or motion. E19. **41** *going for*, favourable or advantageous to, to be said in favour of. M20.

36 J. BUCHAN Listen, Sir Harry. . . You're a good fellow, and I'm going to be frank. *Observer* One man wrote and said he was going to kill me—but he gave his name and address. P. ROTH 'You are going to get yourself in trouble.' 'Not me.' **37** E. BOWEN At this hour, going on six o'clock. J. RABAN She had been five, going six. A. BURGESS How clever we are when we are seventeen going on eighteen. P. LIVELY The Lisa of today is an anxious busy woman going on for forty. **39** S. L. ELLIOTT There's a cup of cocoa going. V. GLENDINNING Ear trouble, eye trouble, bronchial trouble . . and every infection going. **40** W. J. KNOX-LITTLE She kept the conversation going. J. GARDNER Lit the new cigarette from the one he had going. **41** W. WHARTON The only thing a bird has going for it is that it can fly away. *Times* I think the plans . . seem excellent. The offer has a lot going for it.

Phrases etc.: (A selection of cross-refs. only is included: see esp. other ns.) *been (and gone) and* —: see BE *v. be gone*: see sense 30 above. *easy come, easy go*: see EASY *adv.* 1. *far gone*: see FAR *adv.* **from the word go** *colloq.* from the very beginning. *get going*: see GET *v. get oneself gone*: see GET *v. get up and go*: see GET *v.* **go a long way** = *go far* below. **go at it** *slang* copulate. *go bail*: see sense 19b above. **go big** *slang* be a big success, have a large sale. *go by the name* etc. *of*: see sense 7 above. †**go by the worse, worst** be worsted. **go for it** make an all-out attempt at something. *go gangbusters*: see GANG *n.* **go it** *slang* go at great speed, act rapidly, vigorously, or furiously; engage in reckless dissipation. *go it alone*: see ALONE 1. **go it strong** *slang* go to great lengths, use exaggeration. *go like hot cakes*: see CAKE *n. go near (to) doing, to do*: see NEAR *adv.*[2] *go off the handle*: see HANDLE *n.*[1] *go one better*: see BETTER *a.* etc. *go one's way(s)*: see WAY *n.* **go on the stage** *spec.* become an actor. **go on the streets** *spec.* become a prostitute. *go over big*: see BIG *adv. go* OVERBOARD. *go places*: see PLACE *n.*[1] *go public*: see PUBLIC *a.* & *n. go shares with*: see SHARE *n.*[2] *go short*: see SHORT *adv. go sick*: see SICK *a.* **go slow** *spec.* work at a deliberately slow pace. *go soft on*: see SOFT *a.* **go somewhere** *euphem.* go to the toilet. *go steady*: see STEADY *adv. go the distance*: see DISTANCE *n. go the pace*: see PACE *n.*[1] *go the vole*: see VOLE *n.*[1] **go the way of all the earth** [*1 Kings* 2:2, *Josh.* 23:14], **all flesh** die. *go the whole hog*: see HOG *n.* **go to a better place** or **world** die. **go to it** *colloq.* begin work (usu. in *imper.*). **go to one's account** die. **go to sea** (*a*) go on a sea voyage; (*b*) become a sailor. **go to show** serve as evidence or proof (*that*). **go to the bar** *spec.* become a barrister. *go under the name* etc. *of*: see sense 7 above. *go walkabout*: see WALKABOUT 1. *go west*: see WEST *adv. go with child*: see sense 5 above. *go without saying*: see SAYING *n.* 1. **go with the tide** or **times** do as others do. *have* SOMETHING *going. here goes!*: see HERE *adv.* **how goes it?, how is it going?, how are things going?** what progress is being made? how are things with you? *leave go*: see LEAVE *v.*[1] *let go*: see LET *v.*[1] **let it go at that** let that account etc. be accepted, let us say no more about it. **not go far** *esp.* be soon spent or used. *there you go*: see THERE *adv. the story goes*: see STORY *n.*[1] **to be going on with** to start with, for the time being. **to go** (chiefly *N. Amer.*) (of refreshments etc.) for taking away from the place of supply before consumption. *to hell and gone*: see HELL *n. touch-and-go*: see TOUCH *v.* **what has gone of —?** *arch.* what has become of —? what is the matter with —? **who goes there?**: a sentry's challenge.

With advs. in specialized senses: (See also Phrases above.) **go about** (*a*) move from place to place, circulate; (*b*) endeavour *to do*; be in the habit of *doing*; (*c*) *Naut.* change to the opposite tack. **go ahead** proceed without hesitation (*with*). **go aloft** *slang* die. **go along** (*a*) *go along with you!*: expr. dismissal, impatience, or derision; (*b*) proceed or travel in company *with*; go *with*. **go around** = *go round* below. **go away** depart, leave, esp. from home for a holiday; (of a problem etc.) cease to be an issue. **go back** (*a*) return (*to*); (*b*) turn one's thoughts backward in time (*to*); (*c*) extend backwards (in space or time), have a history going back *to*; (*d*) *go back on*: change one's mind about honouring (one's word etc.); prove disloyal to, betray; *go back from*: go back on (one's word etc.); (*e*) (of a clock, watch, etc.) be set to an earlier time representing a changed basis for national time-reckoning. **go by** (*a*) pass, go past; †(*b*) go unregarded. **go down** (*a*) proceed, move, or change to a lower place or condition; (of a ship etc.) sink, (of a person) be *on* a ship etc. that sinks; (of the sun etc.) set; (*b*) be continued *to* a specified point; (*c*) be overthrown, be defeated, be beaten, (foll. by *before* a conquering influence etc., *to* a conqueror); fail, deteriorate, decline in health or prosperity; (of a computer etc.) cease to function; fall ill *with* (a disease); (*d*) be recorded in writing; (*e*) be swallowed; (*f*) find acceptance *with*; be received in a specified manner; (*g*) leave a university or college, esp. permanently; *slang* be sent to prison; (*h*) *Bridge* fail to fulfil one's contract; (*i*) *slang* happen; (*j*) *go down* (slang), perform fellatio or cunnilingus (*on*). **go far** *fig.* (*a*) achieve much, be successful; (*b*) contribute greatly *towards*; (*c*) (of food, money, etc.) last long, suffice for long or for many, buy much. **go in** (*a*) enter as a competitor (*go in and win!*: expr. encouragement); (*b*) *Cricket* take or begin an innings; (*c*) (of the sun etc.) become obscured by cloud; (*d*) *go in for*: adopt as an object, pursuit, interest, style, or principle; enter as a candidate or competitor. **go off** (*a*) leave, depart, esp. suddenly; leave the stage; (*b*) (of a firearm etc.) explode, be discharged; (of an alarm etc.) sound, be activated; (*c*) die; gradually cease to be felt; (*d*) deteriorate; lose brightness, quality, or vigour; decay; (*e*) start *into* a sudden action, break *into* a fit of laughter etc.; pass suddenly *into* a state; (*f*) become unconscious in sleep, a faint, etc. (also *go off to sleep* etc.); (*g*) be disposed of by sale or (of a daughter, *arch.*) in marriage; (*h*) be received or accomplished in a specified manner, result in a specified way; (*i*) *go off at* (Austral. & NZ slang), reprimand, scold. **go on** (*a*) proceed on a journey or to another place; continue, persevere, persist, (*doing, with, in*); (*b*) proceed *to, to do* as one's next step; in *imper.* (*colloq.*) encouraging the overcoming of reluctance; (*c*) fare, manage, get on, (*arch.*); conduct oneself, behave, (esp. reprehensibly); (*d*) be in progress, happen, take place; (*e*) talk tediously or persistently (*about*) (also *go on and on*: continually, at tedious length); *colloq.* rail or grumble *at*; (*f*) appear on stage; *Cricket* begin bowling; (*g*) (of a garment etc.) be large enough for the wearer; (*h*) as *int.* (*colloq.*) expr. disbelief, ridicule, etc. (cf. GARN *int.*); (see also sense 37 above). **go out** (*a*) leave a room, house, or other building; (*b*) go on a military campaign, take to the field, (chiefly *Hist.*); depart to a battle-front; fight a duel; (*c*) be extinguished; cease to be lit; *colloq.* fall asleep, lose consciousness, (esp. in *go out like a light*); (*d*) (of the tide) recede; (*e*) (of a Government etc.) leave office; be defeated in or eliminated from a contest (foll. by *to* a victor); (*f*) (of a year) come to its end; (*g*) cease to be fashionable or popular; (*h*) depart *to* a colony etc.; (*i*) *arch.* (esp. of a girl or woman) find employment away from home; (*j*) mix in society, attend social engagements; keep company (*together, with*), esp. regularly in a romantic or sexual relationship; (*k*) (of workers) abandon work, go on strike; (*l*) be published, be issued, be broadcast; (*m*) (of the heart etc.) expand with love or sympathy *to* (a person); (*n*) play the first 9 holes in a round of golf (comprising 18 holes); (*o*) *Cards* be the first to dispose of one's hand. **go over** (*a*) change one's allegiance or religion (*to*); (*b*) communicate to an audience in a specified manner; be well received, be successful. **go round** (*a*) revolve, rotate; (of the head) reel, swim; (*b*) circulate, pass from person to person; move about; be regularly in company *with*; be in the habit of *doing*; (*c*) make a detour; pay an informal visit *to*; (*d*) be long enough to encompass the desired thing; (of food etc.) suffice for the whole party, satisfy need or demand. **go through** †(*a*) complete an enterprise or undertaking; (*b*) be approved, accepted, or carried; pass all stages to completion; (*c*) *go through with*, carry to completion, not leave unfinished; (*d*) *Austral. slang* desert, abscond. **go to** †(*a*) go about one's work; (*b*) in *imper.* (*arch.*) expr. remonstrance, incredulity, impatience, etc. **go together** (*a*) be concomitant or compatible, match; (*b*) go out together on a romantic or sexual basis. **go under** sink, fail, succumb, die. **go up** (*a*) proceed, move, or change to a higher place or condition; (of sound) become audible); (*b*) (*colloq.*, chiefly *US*) go to ruin, go bankrupt, die, be killed; (*c*) be raised, be erected, be reared; (*d*) begin to attend a university or college; (*e*) increase in price, number, or value; (*f*) explode; be consumed *in flames, smoke*. **to go** *US* (of food and drink) to be taken away for consumption, for taking away.

With preps. in specialized senses (see also Phrases above): **go about —** busy oneself about, set to work at, take in hand. **go against —** (*a*) result unfavourably to; (*b*) run counter to, oppose, militate against. **go at —** attack, take in hand energetically; (see also sense 15 above). **go before —** (*a*) precede in time or serial order; †(*b*) *rare* take precedence of, be superior to. †**go between —** act as mediator or messenger between. **go by —** †(*a*) neglect, pass without notice; (*b*) pass by; *US* call in at or on, visit; (see also sense 3b above). **go for —** †(*a*) set out for; (*b*) go to fetch or reach; go to become; (*c*) pass as or as equivalent to, be accounted or valued as, (now only *nothing, little*, etc.); (*d*) have as one's aim, strive to attain; (*e*) prefer, choose, like; (*f*) *colloq.* attack, assail, (physically or verbally); (*g*) be valid for, be applicable to; (see also senses 15, 41 above). **go into —** (*a*) become a member of, start a career in, (a profession, Parliament, etc.); frequent (society etc.); (*b*) join or take part in, be a part of; (of effort, resources, etc.) be invested in, be devoted to; †(*c*) agree to, accede to; (*d*) pass into (a state or condition), enter into (a process); allow oneself to pass into (hysterics etc.); (*e*) dress oneself in (mourning etc.); (*f*) investigate, examine or discuss minutely; (*g*) go to stay in, be admitted to, (hospital etc.); (see also senses 18, 23, 28 above). **go off** — (*a*) *rare* shirk, fail to fulfil; (*b*) begin to dislike. **go on** — †(*a*) take up (a subject) for discussion; begin, undertake, (an action); (*b*) become chargeable to (the parish, relief funds, etc.); (*c*) *colloq.* care for or concern oneself (*much* etc.) about (usu. in neg. contexts); (see also senses 3b, 15, 28b above). **go over** — (*a*) inspect the various parts or details of; (*b*) review, rehearse, repeat; (*c*) retouch; (*d*) *slang* search and rob. **go through** — (*a*) deal with the successive stages of; (*b*) discuss or examine in detail, scrutinize (successively); (*c*) perform (a ceremony, recitation, etc.), *spec.* at full length; (*d*) undergo, experience, suffer; (*e*) use up, spend (money), make holes in; (*f*) (of a book) be successively published in (so many editions); (*g*) *slang* search and rob, search. **go upon** — †(*a*) attack; †(*b*) (of a judicial authority) consider the case of; (*c*) *arch.* take in hand; (see also sense 3b above). **go with** — (*a*) accompany; *colloq.* go out with on a romantic or sexual basis; (*b*) be associated with, be a concomitant of; (*c*) take the same view as, side with; (*d*) harmonize with, match; (*e*) follow the drift of, understand; (see also sense 3b above). **go without** — not have, put up with the lack of, (something specified or (*absol.*) understood contextually).

Comb.: **go-ashore** *a.* & *n.* (*a*) *adj.* designating clothes worn or articles used by sailors when ashore; (*b*) *n.* (*NZ*) an iron cauldron with three feet and attachments for hanging it over a fire; **go-as-you-please** *a.* & *n.* (*a*) *adj.* unfettered by regulations; (*b*) *n.* absence of (concern for) regulations; **go-easy** *a.* easy-going, characterized by going easy; **go-in** *arch. colloq.* (foll. by *at*) an attack on, a spell of work on; **go-off** the action or an act of going off, a time of going off, a start, (esp. in *at the first go-off*); **go-round** *N. Amer.* (*a*) the action or an act of going round; (*b*) a fight, a beating, an argument; a bad experience; **go-slow** an industrial protest in which work is done at a deliberately slow pace; **go-to-meeting** *a.* (of a hat, clothes, etc.) fit or kept for going to church in.

Goa /ˈɡəʊə/ *n.*[1] L17. [A district on the west coast of India, or its seaport (now Panaji).] Used *attrib.* to designate things found in or associated with Goa.

Goa ball = *Goa stone* below. **Goa bean** (the seed of) a twining leguminous plant of tropical Asia and Africa, *Psophocarpus tetragonolobus*, grown esp. in SE Asia for its edible roots and four-winged seed-pods. **Goa butter** = KOKUM. **Goa powder** a bitter yellowish powder obtained from cavities in the wood of the Brazilian araroba-tree, containing the drug chrysarobin and used to treat skin diseases; also called *araroba*. **Goa stone** (*obs.* exc. *Hist.*) an amalgam of fever remedies in a hard ball.

goa /ˈɡəʊə/ *n.*[2] M19. [Tib. *dgoba*.] The Tibetan gazelle, *Procapra picticaudata*, with backward curving horns.

goad /ɡəʊd/ *n.* [OE *gād* = Lombard *gaida* arrowhead, f. Gmc.] **1** A pointed stick for driving cattle. OE. **b** *fig.* Anything which torments, excites, or stimulates. M16. **2** A linear measure, orig. the length of a goad. Also, a square measure of varying quantity. Long *obs.* exc. *dial.* LME.

1b E. P. THOMPSON Poverty was an essential goad to industry.

Comb.: **goad(s)man** a cattle-driver.

goad /ɡəʊd/ *v.t.* L16. [f. the n.] Urge on or drive with or as with a goad; spur, incite, torment.

D. H. LAWRENCE The blame was torture, like knives goading him. I. HAMILTON Recriminations simply goaded him into a deeper fury. J. A. MICHENER He galloped to the river's edge and goaded the beast to plunge in. P. USTINOV The inconstancy of a crowd goaded by rhetoric.

goaf /ɡəʊf/ *n.*[1] *obs.* exc. *dial.* LME. [ON *gólv* floor, apartment (Sw. *golv*, Da. *gulv* floor, bay of a house or barn).] Cf. GOAVE *v.*] A grain-stack made in one bay of a barn.

goaf /ɡəʊf/ *n.*[2] Also **goave** /ɡəʊv/. M19. [Origin uncertain: cf. GOB *n.*[3]] *Mining.* An empty space from which coal has been extracted, and where the roof has been allowed to fall in.

go-ahead /ˈɡəʊəhɛd/ *a.* & *n.* M19. [f. GO *v.* + AHEAD *adv.*] **A** *adj.* Enterprising, having energy and initiative. M19. **B** *n.* **1** Enterprise, energy and initiative. *US.* M19. **2** Permission to proceed. Chiefly in *the go-ahead*. M20.

go-aˈheadative *a.* (*US*) characterized by enterprise or energy and initiative M19. **go-aˈheadativeness** *n.* (*US*) M19. **go-aˈheadism** *n.* enterprise, energy and initiative M19.

goal /ɡəʊl/ *n.* ME. [Origin unkn.] †**1** A boundary, a limit. Only in ME. **2** In various games: the space between two posts, a net, basket, etc., into which a ball or puck is driven in order to score a point or points; a successful attempt to get the ball etc. into this area; the point or points scored. M16. **3** The finishing-point of a journey or race; something marking this. M16. **4** The object of one's ambition or effort; a desired end or result. E17. **b** *spec.* in *Psychol.* An end or result towards which behaviour is consciously or unconsciously directed. E20. **5** *Rom. Antiq.* **a** A conical column marking either of two turning-points in a chariot race. M17. **b** The starting-point of a race. *rare.* L17.

2 *keep goal*: see KEEP *v. own goal*: see OWN *a.* **3** *fig.*: E. YOUNG Crown'd with Laurels, fairly won, Sits smiling at the goal, while others run. **4** C. STEAD The ultimate goal—to get a rich husband.

Comb.: **goal average** the ratio of numbers of goals scored by and against a team in a series of matches; **goal difference** the difference between the number of goals scored and goals conceded by a team in a series of matches; **goalkeeper** a player whose duty is to prevent a ball etc. from entering a goal; **goal-kick** (*a*) *Soccer* a kick by a defending side after the attackers have sent a ball over the goal-line; (*b*) *Rugby Football* a kick at goal; **goal-mouth** the area between goalposts or immediately in front of a goal; **goal-line** the line between each pair of goalposts, extended to form the end-boundary of the field of play; **goal-minder** = *goal-tender* below; **goalpost** either of the two upright posts of a goal; **goal-tender** *N. Amer.* a goalkeeper in ice hockey.

goalie, **-ee** *n.* (*colloq.*) a goalkeeper E20. **goalless** /-l-l-/ *a.* (*a*) having no destination or purpose, aimless; (*b*) without a goal scored by either side: L19.

goal /ɡəʊl/ *v.t.* E20. [f. the n.] *Rugby Football.* Convert (a try) into a goal.

Goan /ˈɡəʊən/ *n.* & *a.* E20. [f. GOA *n.*[1] + -AN.] = next.

Goanese /ɡəʊəˈniːz/ *n.* & *a.* M19. [f. GOA *n.*[1] + -*n*- + -ESE.] **A** *n.* Pl. same. A native or inhabitant of Goa. M19. **B** *adj.* Of or belonging to Goa. M19.

goanna /ɡəʊˈanə/ *n.* *Austral.* & *NZ.* M19. [Alt. of GUANA.] Any of various lizards, esp. large monitors of the genus *Varanus*.

go-around /ˈɡəʊəraʊnd/ *n.* Chiefly *US.* E20. [f. *go around* s.v. GO *v.*] **1** The action of avoiding, evading, or slighting. Chiefly in *give the go-around to. colloq.* E20. **2** *Aeronaut.* The action of taking a circular flight-path, esp. after an aborted landing. M20. **3** A (hostile) confrontation. *colloq.* M20.

goat /ɡəʊt/ *n.* [OE *gāt* (pl. *gǣt*) = OS *gēt* (Du. *geit*), OHG *geiz* (G *Geiss*), ON *geit*, Goth. *gaits*, f. Gmc base rel. to L *haedus* kid.] **I1** Any of various agile, coarse-haired, hollow-horned ruminant mammals of the bovid genus *Capra*, native to rocky terrain of N. Africa and Eurasia; *esp.* any of the domesticated varieties of *C. aegragus*, reared worldwide for milk, wool, and meat. Orig. (in OE) *spec.* a female animal of this kind (cf. BUCK *n.*[1] 1). OE. **b** The flesh of this as food. ME. **c** Leather made from goatskin. L19. **2** Any of various horned bovids resembling *Capra*, esp. any of the same subfamily Caprinae, e.g. the chamois. Cf. *goat-antelope* below. ME.

1 *angora goat*, *Kashmir goat*, etc.

II3 The domestic goat as a symbol of a (damned) sinner (usu. in *pl.*, with ref. to *Matt.* 25:32, 33). Cf. SHEEP *n.* 2. OE. **b** A licentious man; a lecher. L16. **c** A scapegoat; a person who (rightly or wrongly) takes the blame. *US.* L19. **d** A fool. *colloq.* E20. **4** (Usu. **G-**.) *The* constellation and zodiacal sign Capricorn. LME.

Phrases etc.: **act the goat** = *play the* (*giddy*) *goat* below. *billy-goat*: see BILLY *n.*[2] 3. **get a person's goat** *colloq.* make him or her angry; annoy. **goat and bee jug** a moulded Chelsea porcelain jug with two goats and a small bee in relief. JUDAS *goat*. NANNY-GOAT. **play the (giddy) goat** frolic, fool about, act irresponsibly. ROCKY MOUNTAIN *goat*. **separate the sheep from the goats** (w. allus. to *Matt.* 25:32, 33) sort the good persons or things from the bad or inferior.

Comb.: **goat-antelope** a bovid of the subfamily Caprinae; *spec.* one of the tribe Rupicaprini of goats resembling antelopes, which includes the goral, serow, chamois, and Rocky Mountain goat; **goat-fig** any of various wild figs; **goatfish** orig., any of various fishes usu. having barbels below the mouth; now *spec.* (chiefly *US*), a red mullet; **goat-foot** a faun or satyr, the Greek god Pan; **goat-footed** *a.* (*a*) having cloven hoofs like a goat; (*b*) sure-footed, nimble; **goat-god** the Greek god Pan; **goathair** *a.* & *n.* (made of) the skin or hair of a goat; **goatherd** a person who tends goats; **goatherdess** (now *rare*) a female goatherd; **goat moth** any moth of the worldwide family Cossidae, having reduced mouthparts and often wood-boring larvae, *esp.* the large Eurasian *Cossus cossus*, whose caterpillar smells like a goat; **goat nut** = JOJOBA; **goat-rue** = *goat's rue* below; **goat's foot** a South African low-growing plant of the wood sorrel family, *Oxalis caprina*; **goat's horns** a South African dwarf succulent plant of the carpetweed family, *Cheiridopsis candidissima*; **goatskin** *a.* & *n.* (made of) the skin of a goat; **goat's-rue** (*a*) = GALEGA; (*b*) a N. American leguminous plant, *Tephrosia virginiana*, having pink and yellow flowers; **goat's-thorn** any of several spiny plants of the mainly north temperate leguminous genus *Astragalus*, of which some are a source of gum tragacanth; **goatsucker** (now chiefly *N. Amer.*) a nightjar; **goat tang** a red seaweed, *Polyides rotundus* (order Gigartinates), which grows around the low-water mark; **goat-weed** any of various tropical weeds with a goatlike odour, esp. *Ageratum conyzoides* of the composite family; **goat willow** a pussy-willow, *Salix caprea*.

goatish *a.* goatlike; *spec.* lecherous: E16. **goatishly** *adv.* M19. **goatishness** *n.* M19. **goatlike** *a.* resembling or characteristic of a goat L16. **goatling** *n.* a young goat, *spec.* between twelve months and two years old L19. **goaty** *a.* resembling or characteristic of a goat E17.

goatee /ɡəʊˈtiː/ *n.* & *a.* M19. [f. GOAT + -EE[2].] (Designating) a beard resembling that of a goat, a narrow chin-tuft.

D. CAUTE A man in a yachting blazer and a goatee beard.

goateed *a.* having a goatee M19.

goat's-beard /ˈɡəʊtsbɪəd/ *n.* Also ***goatsbeard**. M16. [f. GOAT + BEARD *n.*, tr. Gk *tragopōgon* or L *Barba Capri*.] **1** Any of various plants of the genus *Tragopogon*, of the composite family, native to Eurasia, esp. *T. pratensis*, which has yellow flowers (also called *Jack-go-to-bed-at-noon*). M16. †**2** Meadowsweet. L16–E17. **3** Any of several fungi of the genus *Clavaria*. L17. **4** A plant of the rose family of (esp. American) northern temperate and subarctic regions, *Aruncus dioicus*, cultivated for its long spikes of small white flowers. M19.

goave *n.* var. of GOAF *n.*[2]

goave /ɡəʊv/ *v.t.* Long *obs.* exc. *dial.* ME. [Rel. to GOAF *n.*[1]] Stack (grain) in a goaf.

go-away /ɡəʊəˈweɪ, ˈɡəʊəweɪ/ *n.* Also **go-way**. L19. [Imit.] In full *go-away bird*. Any of several turacos constituting the genus *Corythaixoides*.

gob /ɡɒb/ *n.*[1] LME. [OFr. *gobe*, *goube* mouthful, lump (mod. *gobbe* food-ball, pill), f. *gober* swallow, gulp, perh. f. Celt. Cf. GOB *n.*[2], GOBBET *n.*] **1** A mass, a lump. Now chiefly *US* & *dial.* LME. †**2** A large sum of money. M16–L17. **3** A lump or large mouthful of food, esp. raw meat, fat, or gristle. M16. **4** A lump or clot of any slimy or viscous substance. M16. **5** A lump of molten glass used to make a single bottle, jar, etc. E20.

1 W. A. PERCY English was my favorite course . . because of the huge undigested gobs . . I'd already read. **3** H. B. STOWE They . . swallows it as a dog does a gob o' meat. **4** J. DOS PASSOS Let fly towards the cuspidor with a big gob of phlegm.

gob /ɡɒb/ *n.*[2] *dial.* (chiefly *north.*) & *slang.* M16. [Perh. f. Gael. & Ir. = beak, mouth. Sense 2 may be a different wd. See also GAB *n.*[2] and cf. GOB *n.*[1]] **1** The mouth. M16. **2** = GAB *n.*[2] 2. L17.

Comb.: **gobsmacked** *a.* (*slang*) [f. the gesture of clapping a hand over the mouth] astounded, flabbergasted; speechless with amazement; **gobstick** (*a*) *dial.* a large spoon; (*b*) a device for freeing a hook from a fish's mouth; (*c*) *slang* a clarinet; **gob-stopper** a large hard sweet for sucking; **gobstruck** *a.* (*slang*) = *gobsmacked* above.

gob /ɡɒb/ *n.*[3] M19. [Perh. alt. of GOAF *n.*[2], infl. by GOB *n.*[1]] *Mining.* An empty space from which coal has been extracted. Also, the rubbish used to pack such a space.

gob /gɒb/ *n.*^{4} *slang* (orig. *US*). E20. [Origin uncertain: cf. GOBBY.] An American sailor or ordinary seaman.

gob /gɒb/ *v.*^{1}*i.* Infl. **-bb-**. M19. [Perh. f. GOB *n.*^{1}] Of a furnace: become choked or blocked.

gob /gɒb/ *v.*^{2}*i.* & *t.* Infl. **-bb-**. L19. [f. GOB *n.*^{1}] Expectorate, spit, cough *up*.

W. BOYD One particularly irate jaywalker went so far as to gob . . on his windscreen.

gobang /gəʊˈbaŋ/ *n.* L19. [Jap. *goban* board for playing the game of go.] A simplified form of the game of go played on a board marked with squares, each player seeking to place five counters in a row.

gobbet /ˈgɒbɪt/ *n.* ME. [OFr. *gobet* dim. of *gobe* GOB *n.*^{1}] **1** A piece, a portion, a fragment. ME. **b** *spec.* A piece of raw flesh. ME. **c** An extract from a literary or musical work; *spec.* a piece of text set for translation or comment in an examination. E20. **2** A lump or mass, now chiefly of viscous, congealed, or (semi-)liquid material. LME. **3** A lump or mouthful of food. LME. **b** A lump of half-digested food. M16.

1 *fig.*: K. DOUGLAS Snatching little gobbets of glory for the regiment wherever possible. **c** *Daily Telegraph* Embellished with bits of Greek and well-worn gobbets from Milton and Yeats. **2** D. WELCH Rolls . . spread thickly with . . gobbets of rich black cherry jam.

†gobbet *v.t.* LME. [Partly f. OFr. *gobeter*, f. *gobet* GOBBET *n.*, partly f. the n.] **1** Divide (esp. trout) into portions. LME–E18. **2** Swallow (*down*, *up*) as a gobbet or in gobbets. Only in 17.

gobbing /ˈgɒbɪŋ/ *n.* Also (chiefly *dial.*) **-in** /-ɪn/. M19. [f. GOB *n.*^{3} + -ING^1.] *Mining.* The packing of an excavated space with waste rock; the material used for this.

gobble /ˈgɒb(ə)l/ *n.*^{1} L18. [f. GOBBLE *v.*^{2}] A characteristic gurgling sound made in the throat by a turkeycock.

gobble /gɒb(ə)l/ *n.*^{2} Now *Hist.* M19. [Prob. f. GOBBLE *v.*^{1}] *Golf.* A rapid straight putt into a hole.

gobble /ˈgɒb(ə)l/ *v.*^{1} E17. [Prob. f. GOB *n.*^{1} + -LE^3.] **1** *v.t.* (foll. by *up*) & *i.* Eat hurriedly and noisily; consume greedily. E17. **2** *v.t.* Seize avidly, grab, snatch (*up*). Orig. & chiefly *N. Amer.* E19.

1 B. MALAMUD Gobbled it down in three bites. *fig.*: K. AMIS Mrs. Welch's bill would gobble up his bank-balance. **2** *Sunday Times* Greig hit his first ball . . for two and the next one was gobbled up at short square.

gobble /ˈgɒb(ə)l/ *v.*^{2}*i.* L17. [Imit., perh. infl. by prec.] Of a turkeycock: make a characteristic gurgling sound in the throat. Also (*rare*), of a person: make a similar sound when speaking.

gobbler *n.* a turkey M18.

gobbledegook /ˈgob(ə)ldɪguːk, -ʊk/ *n.* Orig. *US.* Also **-dy-**. M20. [Prob. imit., after GOBBLE *n.*^{1}] Official, professional, or pretentious verbiage or jargon.

†gobbon *n.* LME–L16. [OFr., app. rel. to *gobbe* and *gobet*: see GOB *n.*^{1}, GOBBET *n.* Cf. GUBBIN.] A piece, a slice, a gobbet; a gob of slimy material.

gobby /ˈgɒbi/ *n. slang.* L19. [Perh. f. GOB *n.*^{1} + -Y^2. Cf. GOB *n.*^{4}] A coastguard. Also (*US*), a sailor.

gobdaw /ˈgɒbdɔː/ *n. slang* (chiefly *Anglo-Ir.*). M20. [Perh. f. GOB *n.*^{2} + DAW *n.*, but cf. Ir. *gabhdán* gullible person.] A fool; a pretentious person.

Gobelin /ˈgəʊb(ə)lan, ˈgɒb-, -lɪn/ *a.* & *n.* Also (as n.) **Gobelins.** L18. [f. *Gobelins*, the French State-owned carpet and tapestry factory in Paris, named after its founders, the 15th-cent. Gobelin family, weavers and dyers.] **A** *adj.* Designating things obtained from or associated with the Gobelins. L18.

Gobelin blue a greenish blue typically used in Gobelin tapestry. **Gobelin stitch** a short upright embroidery stitch, sometimes worked over a padded backing, giving the effect of tapestry. **Gobelin tapestry** (an imitation of) a tapestry made at the Gobelins.

B *n.* (A) Gobelin tapestry. E19.

C. WILMOT The apartments were hung over with fine Gobelins.

gobemouche /ˈgɒbmuːʃ/ *n.* & *a.* E19. [Fr. *gobe-mouches* fly-catcher, f. *gober* swallow + *mouche* fly.] (Designating) a person who credulously accepts all news.

C. MACKENZIE A new swarm of rumours the gobemouche parishioners swallowed . . eagerly.

go-between /ˈgəʊbɪtwiːn/ *n.* L16. [f. GO *v.* + BETWEEN *adv.*] **1** An intermediary, a negotiator. L16. **2** A thing that connects two others. M19.

gobiid /ˈgəʊbɪɪd/ *n.* & *a.* L19. [mod.L *Gobiidae* (see below), f. as GOBY + -ID^3.] *Zool.* **A** *n.* Any fish of the family Gobiidae of gobies. L19. **B** *adj.* Of, pertaining to, or designating this family. E20.

gobioid /ˈgəʊbɪɔɪd/ *n.* & *a.* M19. [f. mod.L *Gobioides* (former family name), f. as GOBY + -OID.] *Zool.* **A** *n.* Any spiny-finned teleost fish of the perciform suborder Gobioidea, including the gobies and sleepers. M19. **B** *adj.* Of or pertaining to the suborder Gobioidea. E20.

goblet /ˈgɒblɪt/ *n.*^{1} LME. [(O)Fr. *gobelet* dim. of *gobel* cup: see -ET^1.] **1** A metal or glass drinking-vessel, bowl-shaped and without handles, usu. having a foot and sometimes a cover. Also *poet.*, any kind of drinking-cup. LME. **b** A glass or other vessel with a foot and a stem. L19. **2** A beverage contained in such a vessel; a gobletful. LME. **†3** A conical cup or thimble used by conjurors. E16–L17. **4** A thing resembling a goblet, as a goblet-shaped part of a flower. M19. **5** A goblet-shaped receptacle for food forming part of a food-blender or liquidizer. L20.

gobletful *n.* as much as a goblet will hold LME.

†goblet *n.*^{2} L15–M18. [Alt. of GOBBET *n.*: see -LET.] = GOBBET *n.*

goblin /ˈgɒblɪn/ *n.*^{1} ME. [Prob. AN (cf. L *gobelinus* an evil spirit which haunted Évreux, France in 12) and Fr. *gobelin*; prob. dim. of the name *Gobel* (now *Gobeau*), app. rel. to KOBOLD, COBALT.] A mischievous ugly demon.

gobliˈnesque *a.* resembling a goblin E20. **goblinize** *v.t.* (*rare*) change into a goblin E19. **goblinry** *n.* the practices of a goblin or goblins E19.

goblin /ˈgɒblɪn/ *n.*^{2} *slang* (*obs.* exc. *Hist.*). Also **o'goblin** /əʊˈgɒblɪn/. L19. [Abbrev. of *Jimmy O'Goblin* s.v. JIMMY *n.*^{2} 2.] A sovereign, twenty shillings.

gobo /ˈgəʊbəʊ/ *n.* Orig. *US.* Pl. **-os.** M20. [Origin unkn.] *Cinemat.* & *Photogr.* A portable screen used to shield a camera lens from light or a microphone from noise.

†gobonated *a.* L15–M19. [f. med.L *gobonatus* (f. as next) + -ED^1.] = next.

gobony /gɒˈbəʊni/ *a.* LME. [f. OFr. base of GOBBON + -Y^5.] *Her.* Divided into squares of alternate tinctures in a single row; compony.

goby /ˈgəʊbi/ *n.* M18. [L *gobius*, *cobius* f. Gk. *kōbios* some small fish; cf. GUDGEON *n.*^{2}] Any of numerous small fishes of the worldwide perciform family Gobiidae, of marine coastal and fresh water, having typically a sucker formed of the united pelvic fins. Also, any other gobioid.

go-by /ˈgəʊbʌɪ/ *n.* E17. [f. GO *v.* + BY *adv.*] **1** The action of passing, outstripping, leaving behind, eluding, evading, disregarding, or slighting. Chiefly in *give the go-by to*. E17. **2** *gen.* The action of going by. *rare.* L17.

1 THACKERAY Becky . . gave Mrs. Washington White the go-by in the Ring. R. L. STEVENSON A French ship . . gave us the go-by in the fog. H. JAMES Paul always gave the pleasantest go-by to any attempt to draw out his views.

go-cart /ˈgəʊkɑːt/ *n.* L17. [f. GO *v.* + CART *n.* See also GO-KART.] **1** A baby-walker. *arch.* L17. **2** A handcart. M18. **3** *Hist.* A kind of light open carriage. E19. **4** A pushchair. M19.

Goclenian /gɒˈkliːnɪən/ *a.* E20. [f. Rudolph *Goclenius* (1547–1628), Ger. logician who first formulated it: see -AN.] *Logic.* Designating a variety of the sorites in which the order of the premisses is reversed, the subject of each proposition being the predicate of the next, the conclusion being formed of the last subject and first predicate.

god /gɒd/ *n.* In branch II now usu. **G-**. [OE *god* (pl. *godu* neut., *godas* masc.) = OFris., OS (Du.) *god* masc., OHG *got* (G *Gott*) masc., ON *goð* neut. (as branch I), *guð* masc. and neut. (as branch II), Goth. *guþ* (pl. *guda* neut.), f. Gmc, prob. ult. f. IE, repr. by Skt *hū-* invoke the gods.] **I 1** A superhuman person regarded as having power over nature and human fortunes; a deity. Also, *the* deity *of* a specified area of nature, human activity, etc. OE. **2** An image or object (as a plant or an animal) worshipped as symbolizing or constituting the visible habitation of a divinity or as itself possessing divine power; an idol. OE. **3** *transf.* **a** An adored, admired, or supremely powerful person. OE. **b** An adored or worshipped object; something exercising great or supreme influence. L16. **4** *Theatr.* In *pl.* (The occupants of) the gallery. M18.

1 MILTON By combat to decide whose God is God, Thine or whom I with Israel's Sons adore. DAY LEWIS *Pietas*—a habit of respect for gods, ancestors, parents, country. D. CUPITT The gods have set bounds which cannot be overstepped with impunity. *Health Shopper* The Romans dedicated the garlic bulb to Mars, the god of war. **2** POPE Statues, dirty Gods, and Coins. R. GRAVES The Romans trusted to their own visible tutelary gods, the golden Eagles of their legions. **3a** SHAKES. *Rom. & Jul.* Swear by thy gracious self, which is the god of my idolatry. F. POLLOCK The ruling gods of the circulating libraries. **b** P. SIDNEY Like a man whose will was his God, and his hand his law. **4** H. ROSENTHAL It was a wonderful experience to be downstairs instead of in the gods.

II 5 *spec.* In Jewish and Christian theology, the supreme being, regarded as the creator and ruler of the universe. Freq. as int. & in exclamatory phrs. expressive (*a*) of a strong desire for the benefit or injury of a particular person or thing, as in *God bless, curse, damn, preserve*, etc. (*him, it* etc.); (*b*) of asseveration, as in *as God sees me*, *as God is my judge*, etc.; (*c*) of astonishment or shock, as in *God bless me*, *my God*, etc.; (*d*) of imprecation, as in *God blast* (*it*) etc.; (*e*) of outrage, pain, or anger, as in *good God*, *my God*, etc.; (*f*) of exasperation, as in *for God's sake* etc.; (*g*) of pleasure or relief, as in *God be thanked*, *thank God*, etc.; or (*h*) of (urgent) supplication, as in *God forbid*, *please God*, etc. Also in phrs. w. possessive combinations expressive of asseveration or adjuration, as in *God's blood!*, †(*by*) *God's bodikins*, *God's wounds*, etc., and formerly freq. with altered or fabricated wds not otherwise found, as in †(*by*) *God's sonties* etc. OE. **6** In any of various monotheistic systems of belief, a sole divine creator and ruler of the universe, *esp.* (and orig.) as opp. to deities exalted by other faiths. Also, such a being as seen in a particular aspect or function in relation to the universe. OE.

5 HOBBES God, in which is contained Father, King, and Lord. C. V. WEDGWOOD The idea that he could be tried and condemned by the people over whom God had placed him. *Times* According to Jewish custom, the name of the Deity is written G-d out of respect. **6** H. A. L. FISHER His Universal God was an Arab, and Mecca was his Holy City. C. H. COOLEY The actual God of many Americans . . is simply the current of American life.

Phrases etc. (see also sense 5 above): **act of God** (the result of) the operation of uncontrollable natural forces. **a feast, sight,** etc., (**fit**) **for the gods** something exquisite, a supremely pleasing prospect. *blind god*: see BLIND *a.* *by guess and by God*: see GUESS *n.* *find God*: see FIND *v.* **God-a-mercy** *int.* & *n.* (*arch.*) (*a*) *int.* may God reward you; (*b*) *n.* an expression of approval or gratitude. *God bless*: see BLESS *v.*^{1} *God bless the mark*: see MARK *n.*^{1} *God defend*: see DEFEND *v.* *God forbid*: see FORBID *v.* **god from the machine** = DEUS EX MACHINA. *God help* (*you, me*, etc.): see HELP *v.* *God is for the big battalions*: see BATTALION *n.* 1. *God knows*: see KNOW *v.* **God of the gaps** God as an explanation of the unaccountable. *God save the mark*: see MARK *n.*^{1} **God the Father, God the Son, and God the Holy Spirit** (or **Ghost**): the persons of the Trinity. **God willing** if Providence allows. **God wot** *arch.* God knows. *Greek god*: see GREEK *a.* *Hottentot god*: see HOTTENTOT *n.* & *a.* HOUSEHOLD *gods.* *house of God*: see HOUSE *n.*^{1} *in God's name*: see NAME *n.* **in the lap of the gods** beyond human control. *like the wrath of God*: see WRATH *n.* (*little*) *tin god*: see TIN *n.* & *a.* *Lord God*: see LORD *n.* 5. *Lord* (*God*) *of hosts*: see HOST *n.*^{1} *Mother of God*: see MOTHER *n.*^{1} **on the knees of the gods** beyond human control. **play God** seek to be or behave as if all-powerful. *so help me God*: see HELP *v*. *Son of God*: see SON *n*.[1] *thank God*: see THANK *v*. *the City of God*: see CITY 2. *the Scourge of God*: see SCOURGE *n*. 2. *the voice of God*: see VOICE *n*. **under God** excepting the power and agency of God. *wait on God*: see WAIT *v*. *walk with God*: see WALK *v*.[1] 6. **with God** dead and in heaven. **ye gods (and little fishes)** *int.* (*mock-heroic*) expr. amazement, disbelief, etc.

Comb.: **God-awful** *a.* (*slang*, orig. *US*) extremely unpleasant, frightful; **God-box** *slang* a church or other place of worship; **godchild** a person (usu. a child) sponsored at baptism by a godparent or godparents, esp. as considered in relation to his or her godparents; **god-daughter** a female godchild; **Godfearing** *a.* that fears God; deeply religious; **God-forsaken** *a.* devoid of all merit, dismal; **godmamma** (*nursery* & *colloq.*, esp. as a form of address) godmother; **godpapa** (*nursery* & *colloq.*, esp. as a form of address) godfather; **God's Acre** [G *Gottesacker* 'God's seed-field' in which the bodies of the dead are 'sown' (*1 Cor.* 15:36–44)] a churchyard; *God's blood!*: see BLOOD *n.*; *God's bodikins*: see sense 5 above; **God's book** the Bible; **God's country** = *God's own country* below; **God's earth** the whole earth; **God's gift** (freq. *iron.*) a godsend; **God slot** *slang* a period in a broadcasting schedule regularly reserved for religious programmes; **godson** a male godchild; **God's own country** an earthly paradise, esp. (freq. *joc.*) the US regarded as such; **God's penny** [tr. med.L *denarius Dei* (whence Fr. *denier à dieu*, Du *godspenning*, G *Gottespfennig*)] (now *dial.*) a small sum given as earnest-money; **God squad** *slang* (the members of) a religious organization, esp. an evangelical Christian group; *God's sonties*: see sense 5 above; *God's wounds*: see WOUND *n.*

goddize *v.t.* (long *rare*) make into or treat as a god, deify L16. **godkin** *n.* (now *rare*) = GODLING E19. **godlet** *n.* = GODLING L19. **godness** *n.* †(*a*) = GODHEAD; (*b*) *rare* divine element or nature: ME. **godship** *n.* (freq. *joc.*) the position or personality of a god (chiefly w. possess. pron.) M16. **Godward** *adv.* (*a*) in the direction of God, towards God; (*b*) in relation to God, with respect or reference to God: LME. **Godwards** *adv.* = GODWARD M16.

god /gɒd/ *v.t.* Now *rare*. Infl. **-dd-**. L16. [f. the n.] **1** Treat as a god; deify, worship. L16. **2** (Usu. **G-**.) Make partaker of the Divine nature *with God*. Chiefly as *Godded* ppl a. Long *rare* or *obs.* L16. **3** Foll. by *it*: behave as a god. L19.

God Almighty /gɒd ɔːlˈmʌɪti/ *n.* & *adv. phr.* OE. [f. GOD *n.* + ALMIGHTY *a.*] **A** *n. phr.* **1** = GOD *n.* 5. OE. **2** A person regarded as omnipotent; a person demanding an unreasonable degree of compliance and deference. Chiefly *joc.* & *derog.* L17.

B *adv. phr.* (Usu. with hyphen.) Extremely, excessively. *colloq.* E20.

D. H. LAWRENCE Why should people . . be so God-Almighty puffed up?

goddam /ˈgɒdam/ *n.*, *a.*, & *adv.* Also **-damn**, **G-**. M17. [Abbrev. of *God damn* (*me*): see GOD *n.*] **A** *n.* **1** An utterance of 'God damn (me)'; an imprecation, a curse. M17. **b** = DAMN *n.* 2. E20. †**2** A person given to swearing. M17–E18. **3** [After Fr., f. OFr. *godon.*] An Englishman; *esp.* an English soldier. *arch.* M19.

1 M. REID The 'sacre' and the English 'Goddam', were hurled at everything Mexican. b B. SCHULBERG I don't give a goddam if you never move your ass off this seat again. 3 G. B. SHAW If the goddams . . do not make an end of me, the French will.

B *adj.* Accursed, damnable, wretched; perverse, annoying. *colloq.* E20.

P. ROTH Stop looking for that goddam bus and listen to me. A. T. ELLIS Oh, what a goddam waste of time.

C *adv.* Extremely, to an excessive degree. *colloq.* M20.

L. ALTHER Do you have to be so goddam intense all the time?

goddamned *a.* (*colloq.*) = GODDAM *a.* M20.

goddard /ˈgɒdəd, -ɑːd/ *n. obs.* exc. *dial.* LME. [OFr. *godart*, app. rel. to GODET.] A drinking-cup, a goblet.

goddess /ˈgɒdɪs/ *n.* ME. [f. GOD *n.* + -ESS[1].] **1** A woman who is adored or worshipped, esp. by a particular admirer. ME. **2** A female god, esp. in any of various polytheistic systems of belief. LME. **3** A female occupant of a theatre gallery. Now *rare* or *obs.* E19.

1 L. GORDON His veneration for his second wife was less discerning. He made of her a goddess. 2 J. A. MICHENER Astarte, the tempting, rich-breasted goddess of fertility.

goddesshood *n.* the nature, character, or position belonging to a goddess; divine female personality: M18. **goddesslike** *a.* & *adv.* (*a*) *adj.* resembling a goddess; (*b*) *adv.* in the manner of a goddess: L16. **goddess-ship** *n.* goddesshood E17.

Gödel /ˈgəːd(ə)l/ *n.* M20. [Kurt *Gödel* (1906–78), Austrian-born US mathematician.] Math. & Philos. *Gödel's proof*, *theorem*, the demonstration that in logic and in mathematics there must be true but unprovable statements, and that the consistency of a system such as arithmetic cannot be proved within that system.

godemiche /ˈgɒd(ə)miːʃ/ *n.* L19. [Fr.] = DILDO 1.

godet /gəʊˈdɛt, ˈgəʊdeɪ/ *n.* ME. [(O)Fr. Cf. GODDARD.] †**1** A drinking-cup. ME–E17. **2** A triangular piece of material inserted into a dress, glove, or other garment. L19. **3** A driven roller or wheel around which the filaments of any of various man-made fibres are drawn during manufacture. E20.

godetia /gə(ʊ)ˈdiːʃə/ *n.* M19. [mod.L (see below), f. C. H. *Godet* (1797–1879), Swiss botanist + -IA[1].] Any of several N. American plants of the former genus *Godetia* (now included in *Clarkia*), of the willowherb family, much grown as summer annuals.

godfather /ˈgɒdfɑːðə/ *n.* & *v.* OE. [f. GOD *n.* + FATHER *n.* Cf. GAFFER.] **A** *n.* **1** A male godparent. OE. **b** A male sponsor at the consecration of a bell. L15. **c** A male sponsor at a confirmation. Long *rare.* M16. **2** *transf.* & *fig.* A person who sponsors or provides care or support for a person, project, etc.; a person who or thing which gives a name to another. L16. †**b** In *pl.* Jurors delivering a capital verdict. *joc.* L16–L17. **3** A person directing an illegal and esp. criminal organization; *spec.* any of the leaders of the American Mafia. *slang.* M20. **B** *v.t.* Act as a godfather to; take under one's care, make oneself responsible for; give a name to. L18.

godfatherhood *n.* the position of godfather L19. **godfathership** *n.* the status or position of godfather L17.

Godfrey /ˈgɒdfri/ *n. obs.* exc. *Hist.* L18. [Thomas *Godfrey* of Hunsdon, Hertfordshire, fl. early 18th cent.] In full *Godfrey's cordial*. A sweet flavoured tincture of opium, popular as a medicine in the 18th and 19th cents.

Godfrey /ˈgɒdfri/ *int. US slang.* M19. [Alt. and assim. of *God* to the name *Godfrey*.] Expr. strong feeling, surprise, etc.

by guess and by Godfrey: see GUESS *n.*

godhead /ˈgɒdhɛd/ *n.* ME. [f. GOD *n.* + -HEAD.] **1** The character or quality of being God or a god; divine nature or essence. ME. †**b** With possess. pron., as a title: divine personality. LME–E18. **2** (Usu. **G-**.) *The* supreme being, God. LME. **b** A god, a deity. Now *rare.* L16.

1 COLERIDGE He [Christ] on the thought-benighted sceptic beamed Manifest Godhead. B. JOWETT Do you mean that I do not believe in the godhead of the sun or moon? b POPE Supreme he sits: and sees . . Your vassal godheads grudgingly obey. 2 *Derby Diocesan News* The complex problem of sexuality in the Godhead.

godhood /ˈgɒdhʊd/ *n.* ME. [f. GOD *n.* + -HOOD.] In early use, = GODHEAD 1. Now chiefly, the state or rank of being God or a god.

godless /ˈgɒdlɪs/ *a.* E16. [f. GOD *n.* + -LESS.] Without a god; not recognizing or worshipping God; irreligious, ungodly. Also, undertaken without regard to God, impious, wicked.

THACKERAY Military men . . rushed thither . . to . . partake of all sorts of godless delights. *absol.*: MILTON Behold Gods indignation on these Godless poured.

godless florin = GRACELESS *florin*.

godlessness *n.* M16.

godlike /ˈgɒdlʌɪk/ *a.* & *adv.* LME. [f. GOD *n.* + -LIKE.] **A** *adj.* **1** Resembling God or a god in some quality, esp. in nature or disposition; divine. LME. **2** Fit for, appropriate to, or characteristic of God or a god. LME.

1 MILTON Thus the Godlike Angel answerd milde. D. HEWETT Brawny, godlike, brief-trunked young men. *absol.*: CARLYLE Is not a Symbol . . some dimmer or clearer revelation of the Godlike! 2 J. MACKINTOSH To forego his work of heroic, or rather godlike benevolence. N. SYMINGTON To tell a patient . . she needs psychoanalysis . . is a very godlike judgement.

B *adv.* In a godlike manner. Long *rare* or *obs.* M17.

DRYDEN Praise Him alone, who god-like formed thee free.

godlikeness *n.* M17.

godling /ˈgɒdlɪŋ/ *n.* Freq. *joc.* or *derog.* L16. [f. GOD *n.* + -LING[1].] A small or minor god; a representation of such a god.

R. KIPLING Till ye become little Gods again—Gods of the jungle— . . Godlings of the tree. *Times* Mark Hateley . . has become the new godling of Italian football.

godly /ˈgɒdli/ *a.* LME. [f. GOD *n.* + -LY[1].] **1** Of, pertaining to, or coming from God or a god; divine; spiritual. Long *arch.* LME. **2** Of a person or (*arch.*) conduct, speech, etc.: devoutly observant of the laws of God; religious; pious. LME.

1 S. ANDERSON Something like a halo of Godly approval hung over him. 2 J. FRITH That the unfaithful might see the godly and virtuous conversation of his faithful. E. F. BENSON There was a new cook . . , a very godly woman. *absol.*: LD MACAULAY Soon the world begins to find out that the godly are not better than other men.

godlily *adv.* (now *rare*) M16. **godliness** *n.* M16.

godly /ˈgɒdli/ *adv.* Now *rare.* E16. [f. GOD *n.* + -LY[2].] In a godly manner.

God-man /ˈgɒdman/ *n.* M16. [f. GOD *n.* + MAN *n.*, tr. eccl.Gk *theandros*, *theanthrōpos*, whence eccl.L *deus-homo*: cf. Fr. *homme-Dieu* (late L *homo-deus*), Du. *Godmensch*, G *Gottmensch*.] A person who is both God and man; Christ.

godmother /ˈgɒdmʌðə/ *n.* OE. [f. GOD *n.* + MOTHER *n.*[1] Cf. GAMMER.] **1** A female godparent. OE. **2** A female sponsor at the consecration of a bell. *rare.* M19.

1 FAIRY *godmother*.

godmothership *n.* the status or position of godmother L17.

godown /ˈgəʊdaʊn, gəʊˈdaʊn/ *n.* L16. [Port. *gudão* f. Tamil *kiṭaṅku*, Malayalam *kiṭaṅṅu*, Kannada *gadaṅgu* store, godown. Cf. Malay *gedong*, *gadong*, *gudang*.] In the Indian subcontinent and other parts of eastern Asia, a warehouse or store for goods.

go-down /ˈgəʊdaʊn/ *n.* M17. [f. GO *v.* + DOWN *adv.*] †**1** A draught or gulp of liquid, a drink; a drinking-match. M17–L19. **2** A cutting allowing animals access to a stream etc. *Western US.* L19.

godparent /ˈgɒdpɛːr(ə)nt/ *n.* M19. [f. GOD *n.* + PARENT *n.*, after *godfather*, *godmother*.] A person who, in various Christian Churches, traditionally takes responsibility for the Christian upbringing or education of a person being baptized, and (if the latter is a child) makes the promises on behalf of the child at the baptism ceremony; a godfather, a godmother. Also called *sponsor*.

godsend /ˈgɒdsɛnd/ *n.* E19. [f. *God's send*: see SEND *n.*[1]] **1** A person or thing of great value or usefulness, unexpectedly arriving or present. E19. **2** A wreck of a ship cast up on a shore. *dial.* E19.

1 E. F. BENSON You are going to be a perfect godsend to us all. W. STYRON The money was a godsend, bailing me out. A. S. BYATT For the sake of information . . Conrad's talkativeness was, in its way, a godsend. 2 SIR W. SCOTT It's seldom sic rich Godsends come on our coast.

Godspeed /gɒdˈspiːd/ *n.* Also **g-**. ME. [f. *God speed* (*you*) may God prosper (you): see SPEED *v.*] An utterance of 'God speed you' to a departing person; an expression of goodwill at parting.

E. K. KANE Three hearty cheers . . followed us,—a God-speed as we pushed off. P. L. FERMOR With his wishes for godspeed in my ears . . I set off. †**in the Godspeed** in the nick of time.

Godwinian /gɒdˈwɪnɪən/ *a.* & *n.* E19. [f. *Godwin* (see below) + -IAN.] **A** *adj.* Of, pertaining to, or characteristic of the English writer and social reformer William Godwin (1756–1836) or his political and social views. E19. **B** *n.* A follower or adherent of Godwin or his views. M20.

Godwinism /ˈgɒdwɪnɪz(ə)m/ *n.* L18. [f. as prec. + -ISM.] The doctrine or ideas of William Godwin (see prec.).

godwit /ˈgɒdwɪt/ *n.* M16. [Origin unkn.] Any of several large migratory wading birds constituting the genus *Limosa*, related to the curlews, having long legs and a long, straight or upcurved bill.

Godwottery /gɒdˈwɒt(ə)ri/ *n.* Also **g-**. M20. [f. *God wot* in a line from T. E. Browne's poem *My Garden* (1876): see -ERY.] An affected, fussily decorative, or overelaborate style of gardening or garden design. Also, archaic and affected language.

A. BURGESS The tiny gates which you could step over; the god-wottery in the toy gardens.

goer /ˈgəʊə/ *n.* ME. [f. GO *v.* + -ER¹.] **1** A person who or thing which goes. Formerly also foll. by adv. ME. **2** As 2nd elem. of comb.: a person who (regularly) goes to the specified place, event, etc. L17. **3** A lively or persevering person; a sexually promiscuous or unrestrained person, a profligate; a horse etc. that goes fast; a successful person or thing; *Austral. colloq.* a project, proposal, etc., likely to be accepted or to succeed. E19.

1 SWIFT The intervening officious impertinence of those goers between us. F. E. PAGET My watch is a perfect goer. *Manchester Examiner* All the comers and goers appear to be fairly well pleased. 2 *churchgoer, theatre-goer*, etc. 3 T. C. HALIBURTON He looks . . as if he'd trot a considerable good stick. . . I guess he is a goer. F. MUIR Lady Caroline had been a bit of a goer in her youth. *Bulletin (Sydney)* Does not think privatisation is a goer in political terms.

goes *v.* see GO *n.*¹, *v.*

goest *v.* see GO *v.*

goeth *v.* see GO *v.*

Goethean /ˈgəːtɪən/ *a.* M19. [f. Johann Wolfgang von *Goethe* (1749–1832), Ger. writer: see -IAN.] Of, pertaining to, or characteristic of (the writings of) Goethe.

Also **Goethian** *a.* M19.

goethite /ˈgəːtʌɪt/ *n.* E19. [f. as prec. + -ITE¹.] *Min.* A reddish or brown hydrated iron oxide occurring as orthorhombic crystals or in massive form.

goety /ˈgəʊɪti/ *n. arch.* M16. [Late L *goetia* f. Gk *goēteia* witchcraft, f. *goēs, goēt-* sorcerer.] Witchcraft or magic performed by the invocation and employment of evil spirits; necromancy.

goˈetic *a.* of or pertaining to goety E17.

gofer /ˈgəʊfə/ *n.*¹ *dial.* M18. [Fr. *gaufre* honeycomb: see GOFFER *v.*] A thin batter-cake stamped in a honeycomb pattern by iron plates between which it is baked.

gofer /ˈgəʊfə/ *n.*² *slang* (chiefly *N. Amer.*). Also **gofor**, (the usual form in sense 2) **gopher**. M20. [Alt. of *go for* repr. pronunc.: see GO *v.*] **1** A person who runs errands, esp. as a job on a film set or in an office; a general dogsbody. M20. **2** *Baseball.* In full *gofer ball*. A pitch that can be hit for a run, esp. a home run. M20.

goff /gɒf/ *n. obs.* exc. *dial.* L16. [App. f. Fr. *goffe* awkward, stupid f. It. *goffo* f. med.L *gufus*.] A dolt, a stupid fellow.

goffer /ˈgɒfə/ *v.t.* L16. [Fr. *gaufrer* stamp with a patterned tool, f. *gaufre* honeycomb, AN *walfre* f. MLG *wāfel*: see WAFFLE *n.*¹, WAFER *n.*] Make wavy, flute, or crimp (a lace edge, a frill, etc.) by the use of a heated iron or similar instrument.

goffering iron an iron tool heated and used to flute or crimp lace, frills, etc.

goffered *a.* (*a*) made wavy by goffering, fluted, crimped; (*b*) (of the edges of a book) embossed or stamped with repeated patterns: E18.

gofor *n.* var. of GOFER *n.*²

gog /gɒg/ *n.*¹ *obs.* exc. *dial.* ME. [Origin unkn.] A bog, a swamp.

gog /gɒg/ *n.*² *Sc.* E19. [Origin unkn.] An object forming a mark in a game of quoits, marbles, etc.

go-get /ˈgəʊgɛt/ *v.i. colloq.* E20. [f. GO *v.* + GET *v.*] Be ambitious and enterprising. Chiefly as *go-getting* ppl a. & vbl n.

go-getter /ˈgəʊgɛtə/ *n. colloq.* E20. [f. (as) prec. + -ER¹.] An ambitious and enterprising person.

goggie /ˈgɒgi/ *n. north.* & (now only) *Sc. dial.* L18. [Prob. alt. In Sc. use cf. Gael. *gogaidh*. Cf. GOOG.] (A child's name for) an egg.

goggle /ˈgɒg(ə)l/ *v.*¹, *a.*, & *n.* LME. [Prob. frequent. f. imit. base *gog* (cf. JOG *v.*, JOGGLE *v.*¹): see -LE³.] **A** *v.* **1** *v.i.* Of a person: (orig.) turn the eyes to one side or the other, squint; (later) look with wide open, bulging, or protruding eyes, esp. in bewilderment or surprise; roll the eyes about. LME. **b** Of the eyes: (orig.) turn to one side or the other, squint; (later) roll about, bulge, or protrude, esp. with an expression of bewilderment or surprise. M16. **2** *v.i.* Sway or roll about; move loosely and unsteadily. *obs.* exc. *dial.* LME. **3** *v.t.* Turn (the eyes) sideways or from side to side. L16.

1 S. BUTLER Which made him . . goggle like an Owl. G. GREENE She goggled hopelessly at the boy. b THACKERAY The frog's hideous large eyes were goggling out of his head. 3 T. L. PEACOCK The stranger goggled about his eyes in an attempt to fix them steadily on Taliesin.

B *adj.* Of the eyes: protuberant, full and rolling. Formerly also, squinting. (See also earlier GOGGLE-EYE.) M16.

THACKERAY His goggle eyes were always rolling about wildly.

C *n.* **1** In *pl.* Spectacles for protecting the eyes from glare, dust, etc., (esp. during a specified activity), often having side shields and coloured glass, wire gauze, etc. M16. **b** In *pl.* The eyes. *slang.* E18. **2** A person who goggles or stares. *rare.* E17. †**3** A goggling look, a squint; a leer; a stare. M–L17. **4** In *pl.* A disease of sheep; = GID. L18.

Comb.: **goggle-box** *slang* a television set; **goggle dive** an underwater dive by a person wearing goggles.

goggler *n.* †(*a*) a person with a squint; (*b*) *slang* an eye; (*c*) *US* = GOGGLE-EYE 2(b): LME. **goggly** *a.* (of the eyes) goggling, having a tendency to goggle L17.

goggle /ˈgɒg(ə)l/ *v.*² Long *rare* or *obs.* E17. [Imit.] **1** *v.t.* = GOBBLE *v.*¹ I. E17. **2** *v.i.* = GOBBLE *v.*² M19.

goggled /ˈgɒg(ə)ld/ *a.*¹ Now *rare.* E16. [f. GOGGLE *v.*¹ + -ED¹.] = GOGGLE *a.*

goggled /ˈgɒg(ə)ld/ *a.*² E20. [f. GOGGLE *n.* + -ED².] Equipped with or wearing goggles.

goggle-eye /ˈgɒg(ə)lʌɪ/ *n.* LME. [f. GOGGLE *v.*¹ or *a.* + EYE *n.*] †**1** A person with a squint. Also, the action or an act of squinting. LME–M19. **2** Any of various fishes with particularly large or prominent eyes, *esp.* (*a*) *Priacanthus hamrur*, a common tropical Indo-Pacific fish; (*b*) *US* (more fully *goggle-eye Jack*) *Selar crumenophthalmus*, a large carangid fish of shallow (sub)tropical waters worldwide. L19.

goggle-eyed /gɒg(ə)lˈʌɪd/ *a.* LME. [f. as prec. + -ED².] Having protuberant, staring, or rolling eyes, esp. fixed in an expression of bewilderment or surprise. Formerly also, squint-eyed.

E. PAUL The way in which the American male seemed to be pushed around by his womenfolk left Parisians goggle-eyed.

goglet /ˈgɒglɪt/ *n. Anglo-Ind.* L17. [Port. *gorgoleta*.] A long-necked usu. porous vessel for keeping water cool.

Gogo /ˈgəʊgəʊ/ *n.* & *a.* L19. [Perh. f. Nyamwezi.] **A** *n.* Pl. same, **-os**, WAGOGO *n.* A member of a Bantu-speaking people inhabiting central Tanzania; the language of this people. L19. **B** *attrib.* or as *adj.* Of or pertaining to the Gogo or their language. M20.

go-go /ˈgəʊgəʊ/ *a. colloq.* M20. [Redupl. of GO *v.*, perh. infl. by A GOGO, GO *a.*] Unrestrained, energetic; (of music etc.) full of verve, movement, and excitement; (of a dancer) performing rhythmic and usu. erotic dance routines; (of investment) speculative.

Goidel /ˈgɔɪd(ə)l/ *n.* L19. [OIr. *Goídel*: see GAEL.] A Gael; a member of the Scottish, Irish, or Manx Celts as opp. to the Welsh, Cornish, or Breton Celts.

Goiˈdelic *a.* & *n.* (*a*) *adj.* of or pertaining to the Goidels; (*b*) *n.* the language group Celtic comprising Irish, Gaelic, and Manx, = *Q-Celtic* s.v. CELTIC *n.*: L19.

going /ˈgəʊɪŋ/ *n.* ME. [f. GO *v.* + -ING¹.] **I 1** The action of GO *v.*; an instance of this. Also foll. by adv. (see also branch II). ME. **b** *spec.* Departure; an act or instance of departing. ME. †**c** The ability to walk. LME–M17. **2** †**a** A path, a road, a passage. ME–E18. **b** The width of a stairway or step. E18. †**3** Manner or style of going, gait; in *pl.*, paces (of a horse). LME–E19. **4** The condition of the ground for walking, riding, etc., esp. for horse-racing; advance or progress as helped or hindered by the condition of the ground or *fig.* circumstances, subject-matter, etc. M19.

1 SHAKES. *Macb.* Stand not upon the order of your going, But go at once. P. ACKROYD His hopes of perpetual comfort, of happiness, of 'going steady', were being dismantled. *attrib.*: *Family Circle* And I discovered, reluctantly, that the *real* test of success was the 'going-home' present. b A. MACLEAN To monitor the comings and goings of everybody in the hospital. 4 T. FITZGEORGE-PARKER The going is not too heavy for my horse. K. AMIS The going was ideal here, short turf, level surface, dry but not baked hard. P. THEROUX The canal was choked with hyacinths, so the going was slow. J. H. CUTLER Joe [Kennedy] made his children stay on their toes. . . He would bear down on them and tell them, 'When the going gets tough, the tough get going'. **heavy going** *fig.* something difficult to negotiate, slow or difficult progress. **while the going is good** *fig.* while conditions are favourable.

II Special uses w. advs. **5** *going down, going-down*, (†*going adown*), setting (of the sun), sunset. ME. **6** *going away*, departure, freq. *spec.* on one's honeymoon. LME. **7** *going over, going-over*: †**a** A passage over a stream. *US.* M17–L18. **b** A scolding, a dressing-down. *colloq.* (orig. *US*). L19. **c** An inspection, an examination, an overhaul. *colloq.* (orig. *US*). E20. **d** A beating, a thrashing. *slang* (orig. *US*). M20. †**8** *goings-out*, expenses, outgoings. E18–E19. **9** *goings-on*, (esp. questionable or reprehensible) actions or proceedings, frolics. L18.

6 *attrib.*: L. OLIVIER The time had come for the newly-weds to change into their 'going-away' clothes. 7b M. TWAIN I got a good going over in the morning . . on account of my clothes. A. BURGESS I gave him the worst going over in really dirty French that he must ever have had. c H. PINTER How do you think the place is looking? I gave it a good going over. J. GATHORNE-HARDY 'Nobody takes this headache seriously.' I said, 'OK, . . let's give you a good going over'. d A. ROSS 'Got a going over, did you?' 'Not much . . Want to see the bruises?' 9 G. PRIESTLAND There will be all sorts of cloak-and-dagger goings-on. LD DENNING A curtain which conceals the goings on of the directors and managers of a company.

III *a-going* [A *prep.*¹ 8, vbl n. later interpreted as pres. pple: see GO *v.* 39, 40]. Now *arch.* & *dial.* **10** *gen.* Going. E16. **11** In or into action or motion. L16. **12** Existing, to be had. E18.

going /ˈgəʊɪŋ/ *ppl a.* ME. [f. GO *v.* + -ING². For pred. uses see GO *v.* VI.] That goes; departing; working, in action or operation; currently valid.

B. I. LANE The classical theological, . . theatre-going, card-playing Reverend Gentleman. M. PUZO The going price was now two thousand dollars. **going concern** a business in operation and thriving.

goitre /ˈgɔɪtə/ *n.* Also ***goiter**. E17. [Fr., either (i) f. OFr. *goitron* f. Prov. f. Proto-Romance, f. L *guttur* throat, or (ii) back-form. f. Fr. *goitreux* goitred, f. L adj. f. *guttur*.] *Med.* A swelling of the neck due to enlargement of the thyroid gland, as caused by disease of the gland, iodine deficiency, etc.

exophthalmic goitre goitre accompanied by exophthalmos; Graves' disease.

goit(e)red *a.* afflicted with goitre M19. **goiˈtrigenous, goit(e)roˈgenic, goiˈtrogenous** *adjs.* causing goitre E20.

goitrous /ˈgɔɪtrəs/ *a.* L18. [f. Fr. *goitreux*: see prec., -OUS.] *Med.* Of, pertaining to, resembling, or affected with a goitre. Also, of a place: characterized by the prevalence of goitre.

go-kart /ˈgəʊkɑːt/ *n.* M20. [Alt. of GO-CART.] A low light racing car with a skeleton body.

go-karting *n.* racing go-karts M20.

goky /ˈgəʊki/ *n.* Long *rare* or *obs.* exc. *Sc.* LME. [Origin uncertain: perh. rel. to GOWK.] A fool, a simpleton.

gola /ˈgəʊlə/ *n.*¹ Also (earlier) **gula** /ˈgjuːlə/. M17. [It. = throat f. L *gula*.] *Archit.* = CYMA I.

Gola /ˈgəʊlə/ *n.*[2] & *a.* Also **Golah**, **Gora** /ˈgɔːrə/. L17. [Gola.] A *n.* Pl. same, **-s**. 1 A member of an agricultural people of Liberia and Sierra Leone. L17. 2 The Niger-Congo language of this people. E20. B *attrib.* or as *adj.* Of or pertaining to the Gola or their language. L17.

gola *n.*[3] var. of GOLAH *n.*[1]

golah /ˈgəʊlə/ *n.*[1] Also **gola**. M18. [Hindi *golā* round storage jar, granary, f. *gol* round.] In the Indian subcontinent: a storehouse or silo for grain, salt, etc.

Golah *n.*[2] var. of GOLA *n.*[2]

Golconda /gɒlˈkɒndə/ *n.* L19. [A city near Hyderabad, India, famous for its diamonds.] A mine, a rich source, *lit.* & *fig.*

New Yorker There is a veritable Golconda of guidebooks . . at the traveller's disposal.

gold /gəʊld/ *n.*[1] & *a.* [OE *gold* = OFris., OS, OHG *gold* (Du. *goud*, G *Gold*), ON *goll*, *gull*, Goth. *gulþ*, ult. f. IE base of YELLOW *a.*] A *n.* 1 A precious metal which is characterized by its yellowish colour, resistance to tarnishing and corrosion, and great malleability and ductility, and is a chemical element of the transition series, atomic no. 79 (symbol Au). Also (w. specifying wd), any of various substances containing, resembling, or imitating, this. OE. b = *gold medal* below. M20. 2 Gold as a valuable possession or as a medium of exchange; coin(s) made of gold, money in large sums; *gen.* wealth. OE. b *Finance.* A share in a gold-mining company. E20. c Marijuana. *slang.* L20. 3 Gold used to ornament textiles; thread or wire wholly or partly made of gold. Formerly also, fabric embroidered with or partly made of gold. OE. b Gold used as a pigment or coating; gilding. LME. 4 *fig.* Something precious, beautiful, or brilliant. ME. 5 The colour of gold. LME. 6 *Archery.* The gilt centre or bull's eye of a target. L19.

1 *fairy gold*, *fool's gold*, *mosaic gold*, *red gold*, *roman gold*, *white gold*, etc. b *Sunday Express* When British teams could only come second at best, our singular athletes kept on grabbing Golds. 2 A. HAILEY If I were an Arab I'd refuse paper dollars for my oil and demand gold. b *Times* Golds were a few cents down. 3 E. WILSON Various companies put out a gold you can sew with. 5 G. MACDONALD Gazing at the red and gold and green of the sunset sky.

B *adj.* 1 Made wholly or chiefly of gold. ME. 2 Coloured like gold. ME. 3 *Finance.* Of a currency: reckoned at its full undepreciated value according to a gold standard. E20.

1 A. MASON It was a small gold satyr, set with gems, supporting a sweetmeat tray. 2 ANNE STEVENSON Then the hills fill with gold wheat.

Phrases: **age of gold** a golden age. *as good as gold*: see GOOD *a.* *black gold*: see BLACK *a.* *cloth of gold*: see CLOTH *n.* 4. *coronary gold*: see CORONARY *a.* 2. **go gold** (of a piece of recorded music) achieve sales meriting a gold disc. *heart of gold*: see HEART *n.* **old gold** (of) the dulled yellow colour of old gold. *pot of gold*: see POT *n.*[1] **worth one's weight in gold** exceedingly valuable or useful.

Comb. & *special collocations*: **gold amalgam** an easily mouldable combination of gold with mercury; **gold-beater** a person who beats out gold into gold leaf; *gold-beater's skin*, an animal membrane used to separate the leaves of gold during beating and (formerly) to cover slight wounds; **gold bloc** the bloc of countries having a gold standard; **gold blocking** the stamping of a gold leaf design on a book cover using a block or heated die; **gold brick** (*a*) a brick made or apparently made of gold; *fig.* a thing with only a surface appearance of value, a sham, a fraud; (*b*) *US slang* a lazy person, a shirker; **gold-brick** *v.* (*a*) *v.t.* cheat, swindle; (*b*) *v.i.* shirk, have an easy time; *gold bridge*: see BRIDGE *n.*[1]; **gold bug** (chiefly *US*) (*a*) an advocate of a single gold standard; (*b*) a person favouring gold as an investment; **gold card** (proprietary name for) a preferential credit or charge card conferring special benefits on the holder; **gold certificate** *US* a certificate or note issued by the US Treasury to the Federal Reserve Banks and (now rarely) the public certifying that gold to the amount stated on the face of the certificate has been deposited and is redeemable; **goldcrest** a tiny olive-green Eurasian kinglet, *Regulus regulus*, having a bright yellow crown; **gold-dig** *v.t.* (*slang*) extract money from; **gold-digger** (*a*) a person who digs for gold; (*b*) *slang* a woman who flirts etc. with a man solely with intent to extract money from him; **gold disc** a framed golden disc awarded to a recording artist or group for sales of a recording exceeding a million in the US or 500,000 in Britain for a single, or 500,000 in the US or 250,000 in Britain for an album; **gold-dust** (*a*) gold in very fine particles; (*b*) either of two low-growing garden plants with many small yellow flowers, the alyssum *Alyssum saxatile* and the stonecrop *Sedum acre*; **gold-eye** an edible N. American freshwater fish, *Hiodon alosoides*, silvery-blue in colour with a conspicuous golden iris; **gold-fever** the rage for going in search of gold; **goldfinch** any of several finches of the genus *Carduelis* with yellow in the plumage, *esp.* the Eurasian *C. carduelis* and the N. American *C. tristis*; **goldfinny** = *goldsinny* below; **goldfish** a fish with golden coloration or markings; now *spec.* a small reddish-golden Chinese carp, *Carassius auratus*, freq. kept as an ornamental fish or as a pet; *goldfish bowl*, a usu. globe-shaped glass bowl for keeping goldfish; *fig.* a place or situation with no privacy; **gold foil** gold beaten into a thin sheet, slightly thicker than gold leaf; **gold fringe** a small pink and yellow pyralid moth, *Hypsopygia costalis*; **gold leaf** gold beaten into a fragile wafer-thin sheet, thinner than gold foil, and used esp. in gilding; **gold medal** a gold-coloured medal awarded for a first place in a contest, esp. the modern Olympic Games; **gold-mine** a mine from which gold is obtained; *fig.* a source of wealth, income, or profit; **gold of pleasure** a yellow cruciferous European weed, *Camelina sativa*, grown sometimes for its oil-rich seeds; **gold plate** (*a*) vessels made of gold; (*b*) material plated with gold; **gold record** = *gold disc* above; **gold reserve**: of gold coin or bullion held by a central authority, bank, etc.; **gold-rush**: to gold-fields in search of gold; **gold salt** a salt of gold; *esp.* in *Pharm.*, any of several compounds containing gold and sulphur used to treat rheumatoid arthritis and lupus erythematosus; **goldsinny** any of several small European wrasses, esp. *Ctenolabrus rupestris*; **goldsmith** a worker in gold, a manufacturer of gold articles, (formerly acting also as a banker); *goldsmith beetle*, any of various scarabaeid beetles having wing-cases with a metallic golden lustre; *esp.* (*a*) the rose chafer; (*b*) the N. American *Cotalpa lanigera*, a pest of deciduous forests; *gold standard*: see STANDARD *n.*; **Gold Stick** (the bearer of) the gilt rod borne on State occasions by the colonel of the Life Guards or their successors the Household Cavalry Regiment, or the captain of the Gentlemen-at-arms; **gold thread** (*a*) thread of silk etc. with gold wire wound round it; (*b*) (usu. as one wd) (the root of) a plant, *Coptis trifolia* of the buttercup family, native to Alaska and NE Asia, with thin yellow rhizomes used in medicines or dyes.

goldish *a.* somewhat golden LME. **goldless** *a.* without gold LME.

gold /gəʊld/ *n.*[2] *obs.* exc. *dial.* [OE *golde* rel. to prec.: cf. Du. *goudbloem*, G *Goldblume*, Sw. *guldblomma* lit. 'gold-flower'.] Corn marigold, *Chrysanthemum segetum*. Formerly also, the garden marigold.

goldarn /gɒlˈdɑːn/ *a.*, *adv.*, & *v.* *N. Amer. slang.* M19. [Alt. of GODDAM. Cf. GOLLY *n.*[1]] = DAMN *a.* & *adv.*, *v.*

goldarned *a.* = DAMNED *a.* M19.

Goldbach /ˈgəʊldbɑːx/ *n.* E20. [C. *Goldbach* (1690–1764), Ger. mathematician.] Math. *Goldbach's conjecture, hypothesis, theorem*, the hypothesis that every even number greater than two can be represented as the sum of two primes.

golden /ˈgəʊld(ə)n/ *a.* & *v.* ME. [f. GOLD *n.*[1] + -EN[4], superseding GILDEN.] A *adj.* 1 Made of gold. ME. 2 Yielding or containing much gold. LME. 3 Of the colour of gold; shining like gold. LME. 4 Resembling gold in value; precious, important, excellent; (of an opportunity) very favourable or propitious. LME. 5 Of a time or epoch: characterized by great prosperity and happiness; flourishing. LME. †6 Of or pertaining to the search or desire for gold. E17–E18.

1 G. VIDAL I prostrated myself at the golden footstool. *kill the goose that lays* or *laid the golden eggs*: see GOOSE *n.* 3 B. EMECHETA The sun rose, warm and golden. R. WEST Her golden hair was all about her shoulders. 4 H. KELLER The golden words that Dr. Howe uttered . . helped her on the road to usefulness. ARNOLD BENNETT He understood that there was no golden and magic secret of the building. 5 U. BENTLEY He had picked on this . . golden future in order to characterize, by contrast, his wretched present.

Special collocations & *comb.*: **golden age** (*a*) an idyllic past time of prosperity, happiness, and innocence; (*b*) the period of a nation's greatest prosperity or literary etc. merit. **golden ager** *N. Amer.* an old person. **golden alga**: of the family Chrysophyceae. **golden balls**: a pawnbroker's sign. **golden boy** a popular or successful boy or man. **golden calf** [*Exod.* 32] something, esp. wealth, as an object of excessive or unworthy worship. **golden chain** laburnum, *Laburnum anagyroides*. **golden-crested** *a.* that has a golden crest; *golden-crested wren* = *goldcrest* s.v. GOLD *n.*[1] & *a.* **Golden Delicious** a variety of eating apple, a form of Delicious with pale yellow skin. **golden disc** = *gold disc* s.v. GOLD *n.*[1] & *a.* **golden eagle** a large brown eagle, *Aquila chrysaetos*, of northern mountain regions, having golden feathers on the head and neck. **goldeneye** a diving duck of the genus *Bucephala*; spec. *B. clangula*, a migratory holarctic duck with a large dark head and bright yellow eyes. *Golden Fleece*: see FLEECE *n.* 1. **golden girl** a popular or successful girl or woman. *golden* HAMSTER. **golden handcuffs** benefits and esp. deferred payments provided by an employer to discourage an employee from taking employment elsewhere. **golden handshake** a gratuity given as compensation for dismissal or compulsory retirement. **golden hello** a substantial sum of money offered to an individual, esp. a director or senior executive, as an inducement to change employers, and paid in advance on acceptance of the post. *Golden Horde*: see HORDE 1. **Golden Horn** the harbour of Istanbul. *golden jackal*: see JACKAL *n.* 1. **golden jubilee** the fiftieth anniversary of a monarch's accession, etc. *Golden Legend*: see LEGEND *n.* *golden maidenhair*: see MAIDENHAIR 3. **golden mean** (*a*) the avoidance of extremes, moderation; (*b*) = *golden section* below. *golden mole*: see MOLE *n.*[2] 1. **golden-mouthed** *a.* eloquent. **golden number** the number of a year in the Metonic lunar cycle, calculated by adding 1 to the remainder after dividing the number of the year by nineteen, and of importance in fixing the date of Easter. **golden oldie** *colloq.* an old and well-known thing; *esp.* a still popular film, a former hit record. **golden opinions** high regard. *golden* ORFE. *golden* ORIOLE. **golden parachute** *colloq.* financial compensation guaranteed to executives of a company dismissed as result of a merger or takeover. **golden perch** a green and gold serranid game-fish, *Plectroplites ambiguus*, of Australian rivers; also called *callop*, *yellowbelly*. **golden pheasant** a golden-headed pheasant, *Chrysolophus pictus*, native to central China and feral in Britain. **golden plover** either of two plovers, the Eurasian *Pluvialis apricaria* and the N. American *P. dominica*, having golden brown plumage on the head, back, and wings. **golden retriever** a retriever dog with a thick golden-coloured coat. **goldenrod** any of various plants of the genus *Solidago*, of the composite family, with long panicles of small yellow flowers; *esp.* the N. American *S. canadensis* and *S. gigantea*, much grown for their autumn blossom, and the European *S. virgaurea*, of woods and heaths; *collect.* flowering stems of such a plant. *golden rose*: see ROSE *n.* **golden rule** (*a*) a basic principle of action; (*b*) [*Matt.* 7:12] the precept of 'do as you would be done by'. **golden samphire** a yellow-flowered plant, *Inula crithmoides*, of western European coasts, related to the fleabanes and having long fleshy leaves enclosing the stem. **golden saxifrage** either of two small plants of the saxifrage family, *Chrysosplenium oppositifolium* and *C. alternifolium*, with inconspicuous flowers surrounded by greenish-yellow bracts, forming mats in wet shady places. **golden seal** a N. American woodland plant, *Hydrastis canadensis*, of the buttercup family, with a bright yellow medicinal root. **golden section** (the proportion resulting from) the division of a straight line into two parts so that the ratio of the whole to the larger part is the same as that of the larger to the smaller part, equal to $\frac{1}{2}(\sqrt{5}+1)$ or 1.61803.... **golden share** a residual government share in a privatized company, enabling the holder to veto major changes such as takeovers. **Golden State** *US* the State of California. *golden syrup*: see SYRUP *n.* *golden* TETTIX. *golden triangle*: see TRIANGLE *n.* 2. **golden wattle** any of certain wattles with golden flowers; esp. *Acacia pycnantha*, the flowers of which are used as the Australian national emblem, and (more fully *Sydney golden wattle*) *A. longifolia*. **golden wedding** the fiftieth anniversary of a wedding.

B *v.t.* & *i.* Make or become golden in colour. *rare.* M19.

goldenly *adv.* (*a*) excellently, splendidly; (*b*) like or as with gold: E17. **goldenness** /-n-n-/ *n.* E19.

goldilocks /ˈgəʊldɪlɒks/ *n.* M16. [f. GOLDY *a.* + LOCK *n.*[1] + -S[1].] 1 A person with golden hair. Formerly also, golden hair. M16. 2 Any of several yellow-flowered plants, *esp.* †(*a*) a kind of helichrysum, *Helichrysum stoechas*; (*b*) a buttercup, *Ranunculus auricomus*, found in hedges and woods; (*c*) a rare yellow-flowered plant of the composite family, *Aster linosyris*, of limestone cliffs. L16.

goldwasser /'gəʊldvasə, *foreign* 'gɔldvasər/ *n.* E20. [G = gold water.] A liqueur containing particles of gold leaf, orig. made at Gdańsk in Poland.

Goldwynism /'gəʊldwɪnɪz(ə)m/ *n.* M20. [f. *Goldwyn* (see below) + -ISM.] A witticism involving contradictory words or statements uttered by or typical of the American film producer Samuel F. Goldwyn (1882–1974).

goldy /'gəʊldi/ *a.* LME. [f. GOLD *n.*[1] + -Y[1].] Of the colour or brilliance of gold; made of gold.

†gole *a.* [OE *gāl* = OS *gēl* (Du. *geil*), OHG, G *geil*, cogn. w. Goth. *gailjan* cheer, make glad, f. Gmc.] 1 Merry; wanton, lustful. OE–ME. 2 Of rank or luxuriant growth. Chiefly *dial.* L16–M19.

golem /'gəʊləm, 'gɔɪl-/ *n.* L19. [Yiddish *goylem* f. Heb. *gōlem* shapeless mass.] A human figure of clay etc. supernaturally brought to life; an automaton, a robot.

goles /gəʊlz/ *n.* Now *arch.* & *dial.* M18. [Alt. Cf. GOLLY *n.*[1]] God: used in oaths and exclams. Chiefly in *by goles!*

golf /gɒlf/ *n.* & *v.* LME. [Perh. rel. to Du. *kolf* club.] A *n.* An open-air game in which a small hard ball is struck with a club having a wooden or metal head into each of a series of (usu. 18 or 9) holes at varying distances apart and separated by fairways, rough ground, hazards, etc., the aim of the game being to complete the course using the fewest possible strokes. LME.

clock golf, miniature golf, etc.

Comb.: **golf-bag**: for carrying clubs and balls; **golf ball** (*a*) a small hard usu. rubber-cored ball used in golf; (*b*) a small spherical ball used to carry the type in certain kinds of electric typewriters; **golf cart** (*a*) a trolley for carrying golf clubs; (*b*) a motorized cart for transporting golfers and their equipment; **golf club** (*a*) a club used in golf; (*b*) (the premises of) an association for playing golf; *golf course*: see COURSE *n.*[1] 6b; *golf links*: see LINK *n.*[1] 2; **golf widow** a woman whose husband spends much of his spare time playing golf.

B *v.i.* Play golf. L17.

golfdom *n.* the realm of golf E20. **golfer** *n.* (*a*) a person who plays golf; (*b*) a cardigan: M17.

Golgi /'gɒldʒi, -gi/ *n.* L19. [Camillo *Golgi* (1844–1926), It. histologist.] *Biol.* Used *attrib.* and in *possess.* to designate structures studied by Golgi and methods which he introduced.

Golgi apparatus, body, complex a complex of membranous vesicles in the cytoplasm involved in secretion and intracellular transport. **Golgi method** a method of staining cells with silver salts or osmium tetroxide. **Golgi organ, spindle** a sensory apparatus in tendons responsive to tension. **Golgi stain** a metal compound used in the Golgi method of staining (see above).

golgotha /'gɒlgəθə/ *n.* E17. [Late L (Vulgate), f. Gk by metathesis f. Aram. *gōgoltā*, perh. under infl. of Heb. *gulgōleṯ*: see CALVARY.] 1 A place of interment; a graveyard, a charnel-house. E17. †2 The meeting place of the heads of university colleges or halls. *slang.* E18–E19.

goliard /'gəʊlɪɑːd/ *n.* L15. [OFr. = glutton, f. *gole* (mod. *gueule*) f. L *gula* gluttony: see -ARD.] *Hist.* Any of a class of educated jesters or buffoons specializing in the writing of satirical Latin verse, who flourished chiefly in the 12th and 13th cent. in Germany, France, and Britain.

goliardery *n.* the poetry of the goliards M19. **goliardic** *a.* of or pertaining to (the poetry of) the goliards L19.

Goliath /gə'lʌɪəθ/ *n.* Also **g-**. L16. [eccl.L = Heb. *golyaṯ* the giant slain by David (*1 Sam.* 17).] 1 A giant. Freq. w. allusion to the biblical story of David and Goliath. L16. 2 More fully *Goliath beetle.* Any of several very large arboreal scarabaeid beetles constituting the tropical genus *Goliathus*, up to 20 cm (8 inches) in length. E19. 3 More fully *Goliath crane.* A kind of powerful travelling crane. L19.

Comb.: *Goliath beetle*: see sense 2 above; *Goliath crane*: see sense 3 above; **Goliath frog** a giant frog, *Rana goliath*, of west central Africa; **Goliath heron** a very large reddish-brown and grey heron, *Ardea goliath*, of African coastal and inland water margins.

gollan /'gɒlən/ *n. obs.* exc. *dial.* Also **-and** /-ənd/. LME. [Perh. rel. to GOLD *n.*[2]] Any of various (meadow) plants with yellow flowers; *esp.* a corn or marsh marigold, or a crowfoot. Cf. GOWAN.

golliwog /'gɒlɪwɒg/ *n.* L19. [f. *Golliwogg* a doll character in books by B. Upton (d. 1912), US writer. Perh. suggested by GOLLY *n.*[1] and POLLIWOG.] A black-faced brightly dressed soft doll with fuzzy hair; *derog.* a person resembling such a doll.

gollop /'gɒləp/ *v.* & *n. dial.* & *colloq.* E19. [Perh. extended form of GULP *v.*, infl. by GOBBLE *v.*[1]] A *v.t.* Swallow greedily or hastily. Freq. foll. by *down* or *up.* E19. B *n.* A greedy or hasty gulp. M20.

golly /'gɒli/ *n.*[1] L18. [Alt. Cf. GOLES, GOLDARN, GORRY.] God: used in oaths and exclams.

by golly!, good golly!

golly /'gɒli/ *n.*[2] M20. [Abbrev.] = GOLLIWOG.

golosh *n.* & *v.* var. of GALOSH.

golpe /gɒlp/ *n.* M16. [Perh. f. Sp. = wound, blow: cf. HURT *n.*[2]] *Her.* A purple roundel.

goluptious /gə'lʌpʃəs/ *a. joc.* M19. [Perh. f. VOLUPTUOUS.] Luscious, delightful.

gom *n.* see GORM *n.*

Gomarist /'gəʊmərɪst/ *n.* L17. [f. *Gomar* (see below) + -IST.] An advocate of the views of Francis Gomar (1563–1641), a professor of divinity at Leiden University who defended orthodox Calvinism in opposition to the views of Arminius. Cf. ARMINIAN.

Also **Gomarian** /gəʊ'mɛːrɪən/ *n.* (*rare*) E17.

gomashta /gɒ'mɑːʃtə/ *n. Anglo-Ind.* Now *rare* or *obs.* M18. [Urdu, f. Pers. *gumāšta* appointed, delegated.] A non-European agent or factor; a clerk dealing with vernacular correspondence.

gombeen /gɒm'biːn/ *n.* & *a. Anglo-Ir.* M19. [Ir. *gaimbín.*] A *n.* Usury. M19.

Comb.: **gombeen-man, -woman** a usurer, a moneylender.

B *adj.* Selfishly materialist. M20.

Listener This whirlpool of *gombeen* capitalism.

gombroon /'gɒmbruːn/ *n.* L17. [f. *Gambroon* (now Bandar Abbas), a seaport in Iran.] A kind of white semi-transparent pottery made in Iran in imitation of Chinese porcelain; similar pottery made in England.

†gome *n.* see GAUM *n.*[1]

gomerel /'gɒm(ə)r(ə)l/ *n. Sc.* & *north.* E19. [Origin unkn.] A fool, a simpleton.

gompa /'gɒmpə/ *n.* E20. [Tib. *gōn-pa, gōm-pa* a solitary place, a hermitage.] A Tibetan temple or monastery.

gomphosis /gɒm'fəʊsɪs/ *n.* Pl. **-phoses** /-'fəʊsiːz/. L16. [Gk, f. *gomphoun* bolt together, f. *gomphos* bolt: see -OSIS.] *Anat.* & *Zool.* A form of joint in which one hard part (as a mammalian or crocodilian tooth) is immovably set into a cavity in another.

gomuti /gə'muːti/ *n.* Also **-ta** /-tə/. E19. [Malay *gemuti.*] More fully *gomuti palm.* A Malaysian feather palm, *Arenga pinnata*, cultivated in the tropics for palm sugar. Also (more fully *gomuti fibre*), a strong black fibre obtained from the leaf sheaths of this palm and used in rope-making etc.

-gon /g(ə)n, gɒn/ *suff.* [Gk *-gōnos* angled.] Forming ns. denoting plane figures with a specified number of angles; also (*rare*) forming adjs. w. the sense 'possessing a specified number of angles', as *septagon*. Usu. w. Gk comb. forms, as *hexagon, polygon*; also w. algebraic symbols or numerals, as *n-gon, 16-gon.*

gonad /'gəʊnad/ *n.* L19. [mod.L *gonas*, pl. *gonades*, f. Gk *gonē, gonos* generation, seed: see -AD[1].] *Biol.* An organ in an animal (as a testis or an ovary) that produces gametes.

gonadal /gə(ʊ)'neɪd(ə)l/ *a.* of or pertaining to the gonads M20. **gona'dectomy** *n.* (an instance of) surgical removal of a gonad E20. **gonadial** /gə(ʊ)'neɪdɪəl/, **gonadic** /gə(ʊ)'nadɪk/ *adjs.* gonadal E20.

gonadotrophic /ˌgəʊnədə(ʊ)'trəʊfɪk, -'trɒfɪk/ *a.* Also **-tropic** /-'trəʊpɪk, -'trɒpɪk/. M20. [f. GONAD + -O- + -TROPHIC, -TROPIC.] *Physiol.* Regulating the activity of the gonads; of or pertaining to gonadotrophins.

gonadotrophin, -tropin *ns.* any of several glycoprotein hormones secreted by the mammalian pituitary or placenta and controlling gonadal activity M20.

gonangium /gə(ʊ)'nandʒɪəm/ *n.* Pl. **-ia** /-ɪə/. L19. [mod.L, f. Gk *gonos* offspring + *aggeion* vessel.] 1 *Zool.* = GONOTHECA. L19. 2 *Mycol.* In lichens, a hyphal organ in which propagative cells develop. L19.

Gond /gɒnd, gəʊnd/ *n.* & *a.* E19. [f. Skt *gonḍa.*] A *n.* 1 A member of a Dravidian people of central India. E19. 2 The Dravidian language of this people. M19. B *attrib.* or as *adj.* Of or pertaining to the Gonds or their language. M19.

Gondi /'gɒndi/ *n.* & *a.* (of) the Gond language M19.

gondola /'gɒndələ/ *n.* M16. [(Venetian) It., f. Rhaeto-Romance *gondolà* to roll or rock.] 1 A light asymmetric flat-bottomed boat used on the Venetian canals, having a high pointed prow and stern and usu. propelled by a single oar at the stern. M16. 2 A large light flat-bottomed riverboat; a lighter, used also as a gunboat. *US.* L17. 3 A car or nacelle attached to the underside of a dirigible or airship; something resembling this. M19. 4 More fully *gondola-car, -wagon.* An open railway goods wagon with low sides. *US.* L19. 5 A car attached to a ski-lift. M20. 6 An island display counter in a self-service shop. M20.

1 H. JAMES A gondola passed along the canal with its slow rhythmical plash. 3 I. ASIMOV Balloons with sealed gondolas reach the stratosphere. 4 *Time* Hopping aboard slow-moving railroad gondolas to knock off a few chunks of coal. 5 *Skiing Today* Ride a chair or gondola a couple of thousand feet up into the heart of the . . mountains.

gondole /gɒn'dəʊl/ *v.t.* & *i.* row or travel in a gondola L19. **gondolet** *n.* a small (Venetian) gondola E17.

gondolier /gɒndə'lɪə/ *n.* & *v.* E17. [Fr. f. It. *gondoliere*, f. GONDOLA: see -IER.] A *n.* A person who rows a Venetian gondola. E17.

B *v.* 1 *v.i.* Be a gondolier. Chiefly as *gondoliering* vbl n. L19. 2 *v.t.* Convey in a gondola. M20.

2 F. CLUNE Albert gondoliered us across the stream.

Gondwana /gɒn'dwɑːnə/ *n.* & *a.* L19. [f. *Gondwána* a region in central north India, f. Skt *gonḍavana*, f. *gonḍa* GOND + *vana* forest.] *Geol.* A *n.* 1 Orig., any of a series of rocks in India, chiefly fluviatile shales and sandstones, of Upper Carboniferous to Cretaceous age. Later also, any similar rock systems in other countries with the same characteristic fossil flora. Also, the period of their formation. L19. 2 = GONDWANALAND. M20. B *attrib.* or as *adj.* 1 Of, pertaining to, or characteristic of the Gondwana systems or their period of formation. L19. 2 Of or pertaining to Gondwanaland. M20.

Gondwanaland /gɒn'dwɑːnəland/ *n.* L19. [f. prec. + LAND *n.*[1]] *Geol.* A supercontinent thought to have existed in the southern hemisphere in Palaeozoic times, comprising the present Africa, S. America, Australia, Antarctica, and the Indian peninsula. Also, these land masses collectively as they exist today.

gone /gɒn/ *a.* L16. [pa. pple of GO *v.* For pred. uses see GO *v.* V.] 1 That has gone (also foll. by adv.); departed; lost, hopeless; dead. L16. b *gone-by*, bygone, long gone. E19. 2 Excellent, inspired. *slang.* M20.

1 SIR W. SCOTT Up heart, master, or we are but gone men. DICKENS In the chair before the gone-out fire . . was the gentleman whom she sought. **gone coon** *US slang*, **gone goose, gosling** *colloq.* a person or thing beyond hope or help. 2 J. KEROUAC I have found the gonest little girl in the world.

goneness *n.* faintness, exhaustion M19.

gone *v.* pa. pple: see GO *v.*

goner /'gɒnə/ *n. slang.* M19. [f. prec. + -ER[1].] A person or thing which is doomed, ended, or irrevocably lost; a person or thing beyond hope or help.

W. H. AUDEN Rome will be a goner. E. JONG The minute he walked into a room and smiled at me, I was a goner. P. BAILEY I plunged in and swam to his rescue. He was a goner when I reached him.

gonfalon /ˈgɒnf(ə)lən/ *n.* L16. [It. *gonfalone* = Fr., later form of GONFANON.] A banner, often with tails or streamers, hung from a crossbar.

MILTON Standards, and Gonfalons .. Stream in the Aire.

gonfalonier /gɒnf(ə)ləˈnɪə/ *n.* L16. [Fr. (OFr. *gonfanonier*): see prec., -IER.] A standard-bearer; *spec.* (*a*) the Pope's standard-bearer; (*b*) *Hist.* any of various officials or magistrates in the Italian city-states.

gonfaloniership *n.* the office of a gonfalonier E18.

gonfanon /ˈgɒnfənɒn/ *n. obs.* exc. *Hist.* ME. [OFr. f. Frank. (= OE *gūþfana*, OHG *gundfano*, ON *gunnfani*) f. Gmc. Cf. FANON.] A gonfalon. Also, a small flag or pennant immediately below the head of a knight's lance.

gong /gɒŋ/ *n.* E17. [Malay *gong*, *gung*, of imit. origin.] **1** A metallic disc with an upturned rim which gives a resonant sound when struck, used esp. as a summons to a meal or in an orchestra. E17. **b** A saucer-shaped bell struck by a mechanical clapper, used as an alarm. M19. **c** A warning bell on a police car. *slang.* M20. **2** A medal; a decoration, an honour. *slang.* E20. **3** A narcotic drug, *spec.* opium. *US slang.* E20.

1 D. H. LAWRENCE The gong sounded for the luncheon. c P. LAURIE We turn on the light and gong and go. 2 *Evening Advertiser* (*Swindon*) Civil servants and military men who get these gongs merely for doing their normal job. 3 **beat** or **hit the gong**, **kick the gong (around)** smoke opium.

gonger *n.* (*US slang*) opium; an opium pipe: E20. **gonge'rine** *n.* (*US slang*) an opium pipe E20.

gong /gɒŋ/ *v.* E20. [f. the n.] **1** *v.i.* Sound a gong or warning bell; make a sound like that of a gong. E20. **2** *v.t.* Summon (a person) by sounding a gong; *slang* order (a driver) to stop by ringing the warning bell of a police car. M20.

gong-gong /ˈgɒŋgɒŋ/ *n.* L18. [Redupl. of Malay *gong*: see GONG *n.*] Any of various simple percussion instruments.

gongoozler /gɒŋˈguːzlə/ *n. dial.* & *slang.* E20. [Origin unkn.] A person who stares for prolonged periods at something unusual. Orig. & chiefly, an idler who watches activity on a canal.

J. GAGG The gongoozlers—the hangers-around that canals often attract. *New Yorker* To watch a game on one of three huge outdoor screens .. supplied for gongoozlers like me.

gongora /ˈgɒŋgərə/ *n.* E19. [mod.L (see below), f. Don Antonio Caballero y *Góngora* (fl. 1782), Viceroy of New Granada.] Any of various tropical American epiphytic orchids of the genus *Gongora*, sometimes cultivated as curiosities.

gongorism /ˈgɒŋgərɪz(ə)m/ *n.* E19. [f. *Góngora* (see below) + -ISM.] A Spanish literary style marked by inversion, antithesis, and classical allusion, introduced by the Spanish poet Luis de Góngora y Argote (1561–1627).

gongorist *n.* a person who writes in this style M19. **gongo'ristic** *a.* E20.

goniatite /ˈgəʊnɪətʌɪt/ *n.* M19. [f. mod.L *Goniatites* (see below), f. Gk *gōnia* angle: see -ITE[1].] *Palaeont.* Any ammonoid fossil of the genus *Goniatites* or a related genus, common in Devonian and Carboniferous rocks, and having simple usu. angular suture lines. Cf. AMMONITE, CERATITE.

gonia'titic /gəʊnɪəˈtɪtɪk/ *a.* L19.

gonidium /gə(ʊ)ˈnɪdɪəm/ *n.* Pl. **-ia** /-ɪə/. M19. [mod.L, f. Gk *gonos* offspring + L dim. *-idium*] *Bot.* An asexual reproductive cell in certain algae. Also (*arch.*), an algal cell in a lichen.

gonidial *a.* M19.

gonif(f) *n.* var. of GONOPH.

goniometer /gəʊnɪˈɒmɪtə/ *n.* M18. [Fr. *goniomètre*, f. Gk *gōnia* angle: see -METER.] Any of various instruments used for the measurement of angles, as in surveying, in crystallography, in radio direction-finding, in medicine (e.g. in the study of joints, and of balance), etc.

gonio'metric(al) *adjs.* of or pertaining to goniometry M19. **goniometry** *n.* the measurement of angles E19.

gonion /ˈgəʊnɪɒn/ *n.* L19. [Fr., f. Gk *gōnia* angle + *-ion*, after INION.] *Anat.* The outermost point on the angle of the lower jaw on each side.

gonioscopy /gəʊnɪˈɒskəpi/ *n.* E20. [f. Gk *gōnia* angle: see -O-, -SCOPE, -Y[3].] *Med.* Examination of the angle of the anterior chamber of the eye.

'gonioscope *n.* an instrument for gonioscopy E20. **gonio'scopic** *a.* E20.

gonk /gɒŋk/ *n. colloq.* M20. [Arbitrary.] An egg-shaped soft doll.

gonna /ˈgɒnə/ *v.* (*pres. pple*). *non-standard.* E20. [Repr. a pronunc.] Going to (see GO *v.* 36).

M. SHULMAN I'm gonna keep on yelling till you let me out.

gonnoff *n.* var. of GONOPH.

gono- /ˈgɒnəʊ, ˈgəʊnəʊ/ *comb. form* of Gk *gonos*, *gonē* generation, offspring, semen, etc.: see -O-. Bef. a vowel also **gon-**.

gonoduct *n.* (*Zool.*) in various invertebrates, a duct through which gametes are discharged from a gonad L19. **gonophore** *n.* (*a*) *Bot.* in certain flowers, an elongate structure bearing the stamens and pistil; (*b*) *Zool.* any structure bearing gonads; *esp.* in some colonial hydrozoans, a sessile medusoid polyp bearing gonads: M19. **gonopore** *n.* (*Zool.*) a small genital aperture L19. **gono'theca** *n.*, pl. **-thecae**, *Zool.* in colonial hydrozoans of the order Thecata, an extension of the perisarc into a capsule surrounding the gonophores M19. **go'notocont, -kont** *n.* (chiefly *Mycol.*) any cell or organ in which meiosis occurs E20. **gono'zooid** *n.* (*Zool.*) in colonial hydrozoans and some colonial tunicates, a zooid which performs a reproductive function L19.

gonococcus /gɒnəˈkɒkəs/ *n.* Pl. **-cci** /-k(s)ʌɪ, -ˈkɒk(s)iː/. L19. [f. GONO(RRHOEA + COCCUS.] *Med.* A spherical bacterium, *Neisseria gonorrhoeae*, the causative agent of gonorrhoea.

gonococcal /gɒnəˈkɒk(ə)l/ *a.* E20.

gonoph /ˈgɒnɒf/ *n. slang.* Also **gonnoff**, **gonif(f)**. M19. [f. Yiddish *ganev* f. Heb. *gannāḇ* thief.] A pickpocket, a thief; a swindler, a rascal.

gonorrhoea /gɒnəˈrɪə/ *n.* Also ***-rrhea**. E16. [Late L f. Gk *gonorrhoia*, f. *gonos* semen: see -RRHOEA.] A venereal disease caused by the gonococcus bacterium, characterized by purulent inflammation of the genital mucous membranes, and consequent pain during urination and discharge.

gonorrhoeal *a.* of, pertaining to, or affected with gonorrhoea E19.

gony /ˈgəʊni/ *n.* In sense 2 freq. **goon(e)y** /ˈguːni/. L16. [Origin unkn.] **1** A simpleton, a fool. Now *dial.* L16. **2** An albatross; *esp.* (*a*) the black-footed albatross, *Diomedea nigripes*, of the N. Pacific; (*b*) = LAYSAN *albatross. colloq.* (chiefly *US*). M19.

2 *attrib.*: R. ARDREY The albatross .. became known to all the American fleet as the gony bird.

-gony /gəni/ *suff.* [f. Gk *-gonia* generation, production + -Y[3].] Forming ns. denoting '(mode of) generation', as *cosmogony*, *heterogony*, *theogony*.

gonyaulax /gəʊnɪˈɔːlaks/ *n.* E20 [mod.L (see below), f. Gk *gonu* knee + *aulax* furrow.] A dinoflagellate of the genus *Gonyaulax*, toxic to marine life.

gonys /ˈgɒnɪs/ *n.* M19. [App. erron. f. Gk *genys* underjaw.] *Ornith.* The central ridge in the lower part of a bird's beak.

gonzo /ˈgɒnzəʊ/ *a.* & *n. slang* (orig. & chiefly *US*). L20. [Perh. f. It. = foolish, or Sp. *ganso* goose, fool.] **A** *adj.* Of, pertaining to, or designating a style of subjective journalism characterized by factual distortion and exaggerated rhetoric; *gen.* bizarre, crazy. L20. **B** *n.* Pl. **-os**. Gonzo journalism; a journalist writing in this style; *gen.* a crazy or foolish person. L20.

goo /guː/ *n. colloq.* E20. [Origin uncertain: perh. abbrev. of BURGOO.] A viscous or sticky substance; *fig.* sickly sentiment.

W. S. BURROUGHS Cat shit and nameless goo. *Times Lit. Suppl.* Subjects which .. have .. so embarrassingly degenerated into a mess of gush and goo.

goo /guː/ *v.i.* M20. [Imit.] Make an inarticulate cooing or gurgling sound like that made by a baby; converse affectionately.

goober /ˈguːbə/ *n. N. Amer.* M19. [Kikongo (& other w. central African langs.) *Nguba*.] The peanut.

good /gʊd/ *n.* Also (*Sc.*) **guid** /gɪd/. OE. [f. the adj.] **1** What is good or beneficial; well-being; profit or benefit; resulting advantage. OE. **b** The good part or aspect (of anything). L17. **2** A desirable object or end; something advantageous or worth attaining. OE. **†b** A good quality, virtue, grace. OE–M16. **†c** A good action. OE–E18. **3** Property or possessions; *esp.* movable property. Now only in *pl.* OE. **†b** Money. ME–M16. **†c** In *pl.* Livestock. L15–L18. **4** In *pl.* Saleable commodities; merchandise, wares. Also occas. in *sing.*, a type of merchandise. ME. **b** Items for transmission by rail etc. (freq. *attrib.* in *goods train*, *yard*, etc.). Also *ellipt.*, a goods train. M19. **5** *collect.* Virtuous people; *the* class of good people. Formerly also *sing.*, a good person. ME.

1 JONSON If he had employ'd Those excellent gifts .. Vnto the good, not ruin, of the State. N. ROWE What is the good of Greatness but the Power. W. S. TYLER A prayer-meeting .. has become a power for good in the College. W. S. JEVONS No good .. building docks unless there were ships to load in them. b J. B. NORTON The absence of necessity for the measure, its many evils, and its little good. 2 GEO. ELIOT Life .. is a doubtful good to many. 3 R. BAXTER Stay not to save your Goods or Clothes. 4 A. BURGESS Indian cotton goods .. competed .. with the products of our own Lancashire mills. *Times* The consumer .. being misled into thinking a good is British. 5 M. PRIOR Sought by the good, by the oppressor fear'd.

Phrases & comb.: **a bit of no good** a lot of harm. **all to the good** generally advantageous. **be any** (or **much**, **some**, **no**, etc.) **good** be of any etc. use. **be — to the good** have — as a profit, gain, or advantage. *bill of goods*: see BILL *n.*[3] *bit of goods*: see BIT *n.*[2] 6. *brown goods*: see BROWN *a.* *capital goods*: see CAPITAL *a.* & *n.*[2] **come to good** yield a good result. **come to no good** yield no good result; come to a bad end. *deliver the goods*: see DELIVER *v.* 6. **do any good** effect any good result; make progress, succeed. **do good** act rightly; show kindness *to*; be involved in charitable work; improve the condition of, be beneficial to. *do more harm than good*: see HARM *n.* *do one's heart good*: see HEART *n.* *dry goods*: see DRY *a.* *fancy goods*: see FANCY *a.* **for good (and all)** finally, permanently. **good-doer** a person who does good, a do-gooder; an animal or plant which thrives; *goods and chattels*: see CHATTEL 2. **have the goods on** *slang* have (information etc. giving one) a hold over (another). **highest** (or **first**, **chief**, etc.) **good** = SUMMUM BONUM. **in good** *colloq.* in favour *with*. *no good*: see NO *a.* **piece of goods** *joc.* a person. *soft goods*: see SOFT *a.* **the goods** (*a*) what is provided or required; the real thing; the genuine article; (*b*) stolen articles found in a thief's possession; clear evidence, positive proof. *the great and the good*: see GREAT *n.* *the unco guid*: see UNCO *adv.* **up to no good** up to mischief. *white goods*: see WHITE *a.*

good /gʊd/ *a.* Compar. BETTER *a.*, (*joc.*, *rare*) **gooder**; superl. BEST *a.*, (*joc.*) **goodest**. Also (*Sc.*) **guid** /gɪd/. [OE *gōd* = OFris., OS *gōd* (Du. *goed*), OHG *guot* (G *gut*), ON *góðr*, Goth. *gōþs*, f. Gmc, f. var. of base 'bring together, unite' repr. also in GATHER *v.*] **I1** Having (enough of) the appropriate qualities; adequate; satisfactory, effective. Occas., excellent. OE. **b** Of food or drink: fit for consumption; fresh. OE. **c** Of soil: fertile. LME. **d** Fine, worthy. Now only as a conventional epithet in *the good ship —*, *the good town of —*, etc. LME. **e** Of money: genuine, not counterfeit. Now usu., a proper or considerable amount of (money); (money) which might have been spent usefully elsewhere. L16. **2** Adapted to a purpose; useful, suitable. Foll. by *for*, †*to* (a function), *to* w. inf. OE. **3** Of a person: distinguished in moral worth, (formerly) in rank or valour. Now *rare* exc. in *as good as*, *good enough for*, *too good for*, (arch.) *good men and true*. OE. **b** As a conventional epithet used preceding titles of high rank; (*one's*) *good lord* or *lady* a patron(ess). Also, in forms of address, as *good my lord*, etc. Now *arch.* or *Hist.* OE. **c** In courteous, patronizing, ironically polite, or indignant address, esp. as *my good man*, *sir*, etc., *your good lady*, *self*, etc. Cf. GOODMAN, GOODWIFE. OE. **4** Commendable, desirable, right, proper; expedient. OE. **b** As *int.* expr. approval, pleasure, etc.: excellent, fine. LME. **5 a** Of birth, family, rank, etc.: elevated, not humble. OE. **b** (Of condition, health, etc.)

satisfactory, unimpaired; (of courage or spirits) not dejected. ME. c Of reputation: honourable. L15. d Of a quality: commendable, conducive to value or merit. L16. e Of appearance, a physical attribute: attractive. E17. **6** Having the characteristics or aptitudes necessary or suitable in a certain capacity or relationship. OE. b Competent, skilful, efficient, or clever *at*, *in*, *with*. LME. **7** Of a right, claim, contract, etc.: valid, sound, effectual. OE. **8** Sufficient in quantity or degree; ample; considerable. Also as intensifier. OE. **9** Not less than and usu. greater than (a specified quantity). OE. **10** Of an action or activity: adequate to the purpose; sufficient; thorough. ME. **11** Reliable, safe, sure; financially sound; able to meet one's liabilities; *spec.* in *Insurance*, (of a life) likely to be profitable to an insurer. E16.

1 W. BLIGH One half of us slept on shore by a good fire. M. PATTISON A good history of our foreign policy would be very useful. b OED In the cold chamber meat will keep good for an indefinite time. c G. BERKELEY The seed of the gospel sown in good ground. e J. CONRAD Father was earning good money. 2 F. MORYSON Like a Quince, requiring great cost ere it be good to eat. CARLYLE He was not now good for much; alas, it had been but little he was ever good for. 3 OED His wife is far too good for him. c I. BANKS We were heading for the good doctor's office. 4 MAX-MÜLLER It was not good to be without an ancestor. 5a DEFOE I was born in the Year 1632 . . of a good Family. b LD MACAULAY The health of the crews had . . been . . wonderfully good. J. CARLYLE I don't feel in such good heart about the Devonshire visit as I did. d OED The author's style is not without some good qualities. e A. N. WILSON A good chin, and a long swan-like throat. 6 DRYDEN Good Shepherds after shearing drench their sheep. DICKENS The Doctor, I believe, is a very good shot. b A. THWAITE He cared about children and was good with them. I. COLEGATE Few people like doing what they are not very good at. 7 F. MORYSON Having the Lawes . . together with a good cause on his side. 8 W. H. DIXON The composition of this work kept Penn at home a good part of the year. OED He writes a good bold hand. 9 GEO. ELIOT He . . played a good hour on the violoncello. 10 SHELLEY I have taken good care That shall not be. S. WALPOLE Society did not see anything unseemly . . in a man administering a good beating to his wife. 11 T. FULLER He is called . . a Good Man upon the exchange, who hath a responsible estate.

II 12 Morally excellent or commendable; virtuous. OE. **13** Kind, benevolent; gracious; friendly. (Foll. by *to*.) Formerly also, naively trusting. OE. **14** Pious, devout; spiritually edifying. OE. b Of a day or season: observed as holy. Now only in *Good Friday* below. LME. **15** Esp. of a child: well behaved, quiet, obedient. L17.

12 H. B. STOWE She is as good as she is beautiful. H. SPENCER If we call good every kind of conduct which aids the lives of others. 13 H. JAMES The lady with whom you were so good as to make me acquainted. G. GORDON Edward wanted to be thanked for his good intentions. In exclamations: *good God!*, *good gracious (me)!*, *good grief!*, *good heavens!*, (Austral.) *good iron!*, *good Lord!*; arch. also *good hallow!*, *good lack!*, *good me!* 15 W. CONGREVE Be a good Girl, don't perplex your poor Uncle.

III 16 Fortunate; welcome; *spec.* (of a wind) favourable. OE. **17** Pleasant to the senses or feelings; tasty, appetizing; agreeable; amusing, entertaining, witty. OE. **18** Beneficial; advantageous; wholesome. (Foll. by *for*, †*to*). OE. b Useful as a remedy (*for*, †*against*). LME. **19** Of an opinion or account: favourable, approving, laudatory. L16.

16 H. JAMES Bring the good news from Ghent to Aix. 17 W. HAY Wine, and good fare. J. CONRAD The young man laughed as if at a good joke. 18 G. GREENE Lime juice is very good for you . . It contains . . vitamins. 19 SHAKES. *Jul. Caes.* His silver hairs will purchase us a good opinion.

Special collocations, phrases, & comb.: In comb. denoting (i) a grandparent (*good-dame*, *-sire*), or (ii) a relation by marriage (= *-in-law*; rarely also = *step-*), (*good-brother*, *-daughter*, *-father*, *-mother*, *-sister*, *-son*). *Sc.* & *north.* Generally: *a good cry*: see CRY *n.* *a good day's work*: see WORK *n.* *a good* FEW. *a good field*: see FIELD *n.* **a good one** or **'un** *colloq.* an incredible lie or exaggeration; an excellent joke. **a good question** a difficult question; a question requiring careful consideration before answering. **a good way**, *dial.* **ways** a considerable distance. **all in good time** in due course; not immediately. *as good as*: see AS *adv.* etc. **as good as gold** extremely or angelically good (GOOD *a.* 15). **be as good as one's word** carry out one's promise fully. **be good** *joc.* (esp. said at parting) behave yourself. **be good enough to (do)** please (do). *be in one's good graces*: see GRACE *n.* **be so good as to (do)** please (do). *get in good*: see GET *v.* *give a good account of*: see ACCOUNT *n.* *give as good as one gets*: see GIVE *v.* **good-bad** *a.* good but of an inferior or second-rate type. *good book*: see BOOK *n.* **good breeding** courteous or correct manners (resulting from a good education). **good buddy** *slang* (chiefly *N. Amer.*) (among citizens' band radio operators) chum, pal. *good buy*: see BUY *n.* *good cause*: see CAUSE *n.* *good cheer*: see CHEER *n.*[1] 2, 5. *good* CONSCIENCE. *good creature*: see CREATURE 1C. **good debt**: which is sure to be paid. **good deed** a good or kind action; *esp.* (in *Scouting*) an act of service for another person. *good egg*: see EGG *n.* 3. **good fairy** a benefactor or benefactress; a fairy godmother. *good faith*: see FAITH *n.* **good for** (of a person) that may be relied on to pay (a sum); (of a promissory note etc.) drawn for (a sum); *gen.* capable of producing, valid for, able to accomplish (something); likely to live or last for (a period of time); acting as surety for (a person). *good form*: see FORM *n.* **good for nothing** worthless (cf. GOOD-FOR-NOTHING). **good for you (her**, etc.) *colloq.* well done. **Good Friday** the Friday before Easter Day, observed as the anniversary of Jesus' Crucifixion. **goodhap** *arch.* good fortune. **good-hearted** *a.* kindly, well-meaning. *good job*: see JOB *n.*[1] **Good King Henry** a herb of the goosefoot family, *Chenopodium bonus-henricus*. **good-liking** (now *rare* or *obs.*) friendly or kindly feeling towards a person; approval, goodwill. *good liver*: see LIVER *n.*[2] *good living*: see LIVING *n.*[1] **good-looker** an attractive or handsome person. **good-looking** *a.* attractive, handsome. **good looks** attractiveness, personal beauty. *good luck to you, it*, etc.: see LUCK *n.* **good man!** *colloq.* well done! *good name*: see NAME *n.* *good now* int.: see NOW *adv.* *good oil*: see OIL *n.* *good old*: see OLD *a.* **good on** knowledgeable and usu. helpful or informative about (a subject). **good on you (her**, etc.)! (chiefly *Austral.* & *NZ*) = *good for you* above. **good people** the fairies; occas., witches. *good Samaritan*: see SAMARITAN *n.* 2. *good sense*: see SENSE *n.* *good show!*: see SHOW *n.*[1] **good-tempered** *a.* having a good temper; not easily angered. *Good Templar*: see TEMPLAR *n.* 1C. *good thing*: see THING *n.*[1] **good-time** *a.* (of a person) recklessly pursuing pleasure; loose-living. **good times** a period of prosperity. *good turn*: see TURN *n.* 18. *good value*: see VALUE *n.* *good word*: see WORD *n.* **good works** charitable acts. *have a good mind*: see MIND *n.*[1] **have a good time** enjoy oneself. *have a good war*: see WAR *n.*[1] *hold good*: see HOLD *v.* **in good time** (*a*) with time to spare; punctual, without risk of being late; †(*b*) at the right moment; †(*c*) (as *int.*) to be sure! indeed! *in good voice*: see VOICE *n.* *in someone's good books*: see BOOK *n.* **make good** (*a*) *v.phr.t.* make up for, compensate for; supply (a deficiency), pay (an expense); (*b*) *v.phr.t.* fulfil, perform (a promise etc.); carry out, effect (a purpose); (*c*) *v.phr.t.* prove to be true or valid; substantiate; (*d*) *v.phr.t.* (*arch.*) make sure of; make secure, hold, retain; (*e*) *v.phr.t.* replace or restore (what is lost or damaged); (*f*) *v.phr.i.* & *t.* make (a surface) even or level; (*g*) *v.phr.i.* (orig. *US*) succeed; satisfy expectations; fulfil an obligation; (*h*) *v.phr.i.* (*Poker*) add enough to an ante or bet to make it equal the stake of the other player(s). **not good enough** *colloq.* unsatisfactory; not worth doing, accepting, etc. *of good family*: see FAMILY *n.* **one's good lady** one's wife. *stand good*: see STAND *v.* *take in good part*: see PART *n.* **too good to be true** incredibly good or pleasant. *very good*: see VERY *a.*[1] & *adv.* *walk good!*: see WALK *v.*[1] *well and good*: see WELL *a.* *while the going is good*: see GOING *n.* 4. *with a good grace*: see GRACE *n.* **your good self** or **selves** (as a polite form of address) you.

good /gʊd/ *v.* Long *obs.* exc. *Sc.* Also (*Sc.*) **guid** /gɪd/. OE. [f. the adj.] †**1** *v.i.* Become better, improve. OE–ME. †**2** *v.t.* Enrich, endow (a church etc.). OE–ME. **3** *v.t.* †**a** Make good; improve. ME–M17. **b** Improve (land) by manuring it. M16. †**4** *v.t.* Do good to, benefit (a person). ME–E17.

good /gʊd/ *adv.* Also (*Sc.*) **guid** /gɪd/. *colloq.* ME. [f. the adj.] Well, properly, thoroughly.

D. CROCKETT I . . shot him the third time, which killed him good. J. P. DONLEAVY My mother could never cook this good. **as good** as well. **good and —** *colloq.* (orig. *US*) thoroughly —, extremely —.

good afternoon /gʊd,ɑːftəˈnuːn/ *int.* & *n.* E20. [f. GOOD *a.* + AFTERNOON *n.*] (A conventional utterance) expr. good wishes on meeting or parting during the afternoon.

goodbye /gʊdˈbʌɪ/ *int.* & *n.* Also ***-by**. Pl. **-byes**, ***-bys**. L16. [Contr. of *God be with you*, with later substitution of GOOD *n.* for GOD *n.*, after GOOD DAY, GOOD NIGHT.] **A** *int.* Farewell. Cf. BYE *int.*, BYE-BYE *int.* L16. **B** *n.* A farewell, a saying goodbye. L16.

attrib.: T. W. HIGGINSON Her father would seize Annie for a good-bye kiss.

good day /gʊdˈdeɪ/ *n.* & *int.* OE. [f. GOOD *a.* + DAY *n.*] (A conventional utterance) expr. good wishes on meeting or parting during the daytime. Orig. in phrs. *God give you good day*, *have good day*, etc.

good-den *int.* & *n.* see GOOD-EVEN.

gooder, **goodest** *adjs.* see GOOD *a.*

good-even /gʊdˈiːv(ə)n/ *int.* & *n.* Now *dial.* or *arch.* Also (*dial.*) **good-den** /gʊˈdɛn/. LME. [f. GOOD *a.* + EVEN *n.*[1]] = GOOD EVENING. Formerly also = GOOD AFTERNOON. Orig. in *God give you good even*, etc.

good evening /gʊdˈiːvnɪŋ/ *int.* & *n.* M19. [f. GOOD *a.* + EVENING *n.*] (A conventional utterance) expr. good wishes on meeting or parting in the evening.

good fellow /gʊd ˈfɛləʊ/ *n. phr.* ME. [f. GOOD *a.* + FELLOW *n.*] **1** An agreeable or jovial companion, a convivial person; a reliable or true friend. ME. †**2** A thief. E–M17.

¶See also ROBIN GOODFELLOW.

good-fellowship *n.* conviviality; true friendship or companionship: LME.

good-for-nothing /ˈgʊdfənʌθɪŋ/ *a.* & *n.* E18. [The phr. *good for nothing* (see GOOD *a.*) used attrib. or as n.] **A** *attrib. adj.* Useless; worthless. E18.

BYRON A little curly-headed, good-for-nothing, And mischief-making monkey.

B *n.* A useless or worthless person or (formerly) thing. M18.

A. BIRRELL His brother was a good-for-nothing, with a dilapidated reputation.

good-for-nothingness *n.* M18. **good-for-nought** *a.* & *n.* = GOOD-FOR-NOTHING E19.

good humour /gʊd ˈhjuːmə/ *n. phr.* E17. [f. GOOD *a.* + HUMOUR *n.*] The state or disposition of amiable cheerfulness.

good-ˈhumoured *a.* characterized by good humour; in a good humour: M17. **good-ˈhumouredly** *adv.* M18.

goodie *n.* var. of GOODY *n.*[2]

gooding /ˈgʊdɪŋ/ *vbl n.* L15. [f. GOOD *v.* + -ING[1]. Sense 2 prob. f. GOOD *n.*] **1** The action of improving something (esp. land by manuring); manure. *obs.* exc. *Sc.* L15. **2** Orig., the practice of begging. Now only *local*, the custom of collecting alms on St Thomas's Day (21 December). M16.

goodish /ˈgʊdɪʃ/ *a.* M18. [f. GOOD *a.* + -ISH[1].] Somewhat good, fairly good.

DICKENS A goodish bit ago.

†**goodlike** *a.* M16–M19. [f. GOOD *a.* + -LIKE.] Goodly; good-looking.

goodly /ˈgʊdli/ *a.* [OE *gōdlić*: see GOOD *a.*, -LY[1].] **1** Good-looking, comely, attractive, handsome; well-proportioned. *arch.* OE. **2** Considerable in size or quantity. ME. **3** Of good quality, admirable, excellent. Also, convenient, suitable. *arch.* LME. †**4** Gracious, kindly. Only in LME.

3 *iron.*: SHAKES. *Oth.* Here's a goodly watch indeed!

†**goodlihead** *n.* comeliness, beauty; good character or personality: LME–M19. **goodliness** *n.* comeliness, beauty; goodness: LME.

goodly /ˈgʊdli/ *adv.* Now *rare* or *obs.* ME. [f. GOOD *a.* + -LY[2].] †**1** Beautifully, elegantly. ME–M16. †**2** Favourably, graciously; courteously, becomingly. ME–L17. **3** Excellently. ME. **4** Conveniently; with propriety. LME. †**5** In neg. contexts: easily, readily. LME–M17.

goodman /ˈgʊdmən/ *n.* Pl. **-men**. ME. [f. GOOD *a.* + MAN *n.*] **1** The master or male head of a household or other establishment; *esp.* a husband (in relation to his wife). Now chiefly *Sc. arch.* ME. **2** As a prefix to the surname (or occupation) of a man of humble birth or low rank: Mr. *obs.* exc. *Hist.* LME. **3** A man of substance, not of gentle birth, a guildsman, burgess; a yeoman; a Scottish laird. *obs.* exc. *Hist.* LME.

good morning /gʊd'mɔːnɪŋ/ *int.* & *n.* LME. [f. GOOD *a.* + MORNING *n.*] (A conventional utterance) expr. good wishes on meeting or parting in the morning.

good-morrow /gʊd'mɒrəʊ/ *int.* & *n. arch.* LME. [f. GOOD *a.* + MORROW *n.*] A *int.* Hello, goodbye (said during the morning). LME. B *n.* A hello or farewell (said during the morning). Formerly also, an idle or trivial saying, a trifling matter. M16.

good nature /gʊd 'neɪtʃə/ *n. phr.* LME. [f. GOOD *a.* + NATURE *n.*] Friendly or kindly disposition; *esp.* (unselfish) readiness to be imposed upon.

good-natured /gʊd'neɪtʃəd/ *a.* L16. [f. prec. + -ED².] Having a good nature.

good-naturedly *adv.* M18.

good neighbour /gʊd 'neɪbə/ *n. phr.* LME. [f. GOOD *a.* + NEIGHBOUR *n.*] 1 A friendly and helpful neighbour. Also, a good Samaritan. LME. 2 A country which has good relations with neighbouring countries. Chiefly *N. Amer.* E20.

1 †**the good neighbours** fairies; witches. 2 *attrib.*: *Listener* The shelving of a good neighbour policy in favour of the Dulles mania.

good-neighbourhood *n.* friendly or helpful disposition or behaviour L16. **good-neighbourliness** *n.* = GOOD-NEIGHBOURHOOD: L19.

goodness /'gʊdnɪs/ *n.* [OE *gōdnes*: see GOOD *a.*, -NESS.] 1 The quality or condition of being good; excellence in respect of some quality; moral virtue. OE. 2 Benevolence, beneficence (freq. that of God); kindness, generosity; clemency. OE. 3†a Advantage, profit. ME-L16. b A good act or deed. Long *rare* or *obs.* ME. 4 (Freq. with *the*.) That which is good in anything; the strength or essence of something. L16.

1 W. TEMPLE Goodness . . makes men prefer their Duty . . before their Passions. T. JEFFERSON Our superiority in the goodness, though not in the number of our cavalry. 2 G. BURNET Goodness is an inclination to promote the Happiness of others. J. WESLEY I sing the goodness of the Lord, the goodness I experience. L. STERNE Have the goodness, madam . . to step in. In various exclamatory phrases: *For goodness' sake!, Goodness!, Goodness gracious!, Goodness (only) knows, (I wish) to goodness!, Surely to goodness!, Thank goodness!*, etc. 4 *Times* The liquor in which canned vegetables are packed . . contains flavour and goodness from the vegetables.

good night /gʊd'naɪt/ *int.* & *n.* LME. [f. GOOD *a.* + NIGHT *n.*] (A conventional utterance) expr. good wishes on parting or going to bed at night. Orig. in phrs. *have good night, (God) give you good night*, etc.

attrib.: HARPER LEE Give me a good night kiss.

goodo /'gʊdəʊ, gʊd'əʊ/ *int., adv.,* & *a.* Also **good-oh**. E20. [f. GOOD *a.* + O, OH *ints.*] A *int.* Good! Excellent! E20. B *adv.* & *adj.* Excellent(ly); well; good. *Austral.* & *NZ.* E20.

goodwife /'gʊdwaɪf/ *n.* Pl. **-wives** /-waɪvz/. ME. [f. GOOD *a.* + WIFE *n.*] 1 The female head of a household, a housewife; *esp.* a wife (in relation to her husband). Now chiefly *Sc. arch.* ME. 2 As a prefix to the surname of a woman (usu. of low rank): Mrs. *obs.* exc. *Hist.* E16.

goodwill /gʊd'wɪl/ *n.* Also **good will**. OE. [f. GOOD *a.* + WILL *n.*¹] †1 Virtuous, pious, or honest disposition or intention. OE-E17. 2 Kindly feeling towards a person, cause, etc.; favour; benevolence. Freq. *attrib.*, as *goodwill mission, visit*, etc. OE. 3 Cheerful acquiescence or consent; heartiness, zeal. ME. 4 The established custom or popularity of a business etc.; (a sum paid for) the privilege, granted to the purchaser by the seller of a business, of trading as the recognized successor of the seller. L16.

2 LD MACAULAY Some pious men . . spoke of him, not indeed with esteem, yet with goodwill. E. WAUGH Every man of goodwill should devote all his powers to preserving the few good things remaining to us. 3 WORDSWORTH Horses have worked with right goodwill. T. BENN Capital can't do without the goodwill of labour. †**of, with,** or **by one's goodwill** voluntarily, freely. 4 T. LUNDBERG Goodwill is normally measured by reference to a percentage of . . turnover or by a multiple of . . pre-tax profit.

goodwives *n.* pl. of GOODWIFE.

goody /'gʊdi/ *n.*¹ M16. [Hypocoristic f. GOODWIFE; cf. HUSSY from HOUSEWIFE *n.*] 1 = GOODWIFE. *arch.* M16. 2 At Harvard University: a female servant, *esp.* a bedmaker. E19.

goody /'gʊdi/ *n.*² *colloq.* Also **-die**. M18. [f. GOOD *a.* + -Y⁶.] A good or attractive thing, esp. to eat; a sweet confection. Usu. in *pl.*

goody /'gʊdi/ *n.*³ *colloq.* Also **-die**. M19. [f. GOOD *a.* + -Y⁶.] A good person (*esp.* in a film, play, etc., as opp. BADDY); a goody-goody.

goody /'gʊdi/ *a. colloq.* E19. [f. GOOD *a.* + -Y⁶.] Goody-goody. Formerly also, pleasant.

goody two-shoes: see TWO.

goodiness, goodyness *n.* E19.

goody /'gʊdi/ *int.* L18. [f. GOOD *a.* + -Y⁶.] Expr. childish delight or surprise. Freq. redupl.

N. FREELING Buttered toast, and cherry cake, as well as Marmite. Goody, goody gumdrops.

goodyear /'gʊdjɪə/ *n. obs.* exc. *dial.* M16. [GOOD *a.* + YEAR *n.*¹, perh. ellipt. f. 'I hope for a good year.'] A more or less meaningless expletive, chiefly used in interrog. phr. *what the* (or *a*) *goodyear?*; [through equivalence with *devil*] a malevolent power, an evil spirit.

goodyera /gʊd'jɪərə, 'gʊdjərə/ *n.* E19. [mod.L (see below), f. John *Goodyer* (1592–1664), Eng. botanist.] Any of various orchids of the genus *Goodyera*, with creeping rhizomes and small chiefly whitish flowers; *esp.* (in full *creeping goodyera*) *G. repens*, native to moist pinewoods in northern temperate regions. Also called *creeping lady's tresses*.

goody-goody /'gʊdɪgʊdi/ *a.* & *n.* M19. [Redupl. of GOODY *a.* or *n.*³] (A person who is) sentimentally, primly, affectedly, or obtrusively virtuous.

E. J. WORBOISE I abominate your goody-goody, circumspect, infallibly-proper young lady. P. LEACH Four year olds often sound goody-goody as well as bossy.

Also **goody-good** *a.* & *n.* M19.

gooey /'guːi/ *a. colloq.* (orig. *US*). E20. [f. GOO *n.* + *-ey* (-Y¹).] Soft and viscous; *fig.* mawkishly sentimental.

News of the World Gooey chocolate gateau. *Daily Express* Her once tough father has gone positively gooey over Fawn.

gooeyly /'guːɪli/ *adv. colloq.* Also **gooily**. M20. [f. prec. + -LY².] In a gooey manner; mawkishly, sentimentally.

goof /guːf/ *n. slang.* E20. [Origin unkn.] 1 A person who is always making stupid blunders. E20. 2 A stupid blunder or gaffe, esp. by an entertainer. M20.

goof /guːf/ *v. slang* (chiefly *N. Amer.*). M20. [f. the n.] 1 *v.i.* Spend time idly or irresponsibly; *esp.* fool *about, around*, skive *off*. Also, watch in wide-eyed amazement. M20. 2 *v.i.* Make a stupid blunder. Also foll. by *off, up*. M20. 3 *v.t.* In *pass.* Be under the influence of drugs. Foll. by *up*. M20. 4 *v.t.* Foll. by *up*: bungle, mess up. M20.

1 M. PUZO He never . . goofed off into restaurants when he was on foot patrol. J. LENNON It was just ad libbing and goofing about. 2 M. AMSTERDAM The laundry sure goofed; they must have sent me the wrong shirt.

Comb.: **goof-ball** (*a*) a pill containing a narcotic drug, esp. a barbiturate; (*b*) a blundering or eccentric person; **goof-up** a stupid blunder; a cock-up, a goof.

goofer /'guːfə/ *n.*¹ *US.* Also **goopher**. L19. [Of African origin: cf. Mende *ngafa* spirit, devil.] A (magic) spell; a practitioner of magic.

Comb.: **goofer dust** a powder (esp. dust from a grave) used in casting spells.

goofer /'guːfə/ *n.*² E20. [f. GOOF *v.* + -ER¹.] A person who goofs.

go-off /'gəʊɒf/ *n. colloq.* M19. [f. *go off* s.v. GO *v.*] A commencement, a start. Chiefly (*at*) *first go-off*, at one's first attempt; *at one go-off*, at one go.

goofus /'guːfəs/ *n. obs.* exc. *Hist.* E20. [Prob. f. (as) GOOF *n.*] A variety of harmonica made in the form of a miniature saxophone.

goofy /'guːfi/ *a. slang.* E20. [f. GOOF *n.* + -Y¹.] 1 Stupid, fatuous, inane. E20. 2 Of teeth: protruding. L20.

1 P. G. WODEHOUSE He was lying back . . with his mouth open and a . . goofy expression in his eyes.

Special collocations: **goofy foot** *Surfboarding* a person who rides, the position of riding, with the right (instead of the left) foot forward.

goofily *adv.* E20. **goofiness** *n.* E20.

goog /gʊg/ *n. Austral. slang.* Also **googie** /'gʊgi/. E20. [Origin uncertain: cf. GOGGIE.] An egg.

full as a goog: see FULL *a.*

googly /'guːgli/ *n.* E20. [Origin unkn.] *Cricket.* An off-break ball bowled with apparent leg-break action; *fig.* a disconcertingly awkward question etc.

googly /'guːgli/ *a.* E20. [Cf. GOO-GOO *a.*] Of the eyes: round and staring. Also, of a person: casting amorous looks.

googol /'guːgɒl/ *n.* M20. [Arbitrary.] Ten raised to the hundredth power (10^{100}).

¶This word and its deriv. are not in formal mathematical use.

googolplex *n.* [cf. *-plex* in *multiplex*] ten raised to the power of a googol M20.

goo-goo /'guːguː/ *a.* & *n. slang.* E20. [Perh. rel. to GOGGLE *a.* & *v.*¹] A *adj.* Of the gaze: amorously adoring. Usu. in *goo-goo eyes*. E20. B *n.* An amorous look. E20.

gooily *adv.* var. of GOOEYLY.

gook /guːk, gʊk/ *n.* & *a. slang* (orig. & chiefly *US*). *derog.* & usu. considered *racially offensive*. E20. [Origin unkn.] A *n.* A foreigner, *esp.* a member of an Asian or Pacific people; *spec.* a Filipino; a Korean; a Vietnamese. E20. B *adj.* Foreign, *esp.* oriental; made in a foreign country. M20.

gool /guːl/ *n.* ME. [AN *gole, goule*, spec. use of OFr. *gole, goule* throat: cf. GULL *n.*³] 1 A small channel, a ditch; an outlet for water. Chiefly *dial.* ME. 2 Chiefly *Law.* A breach in a sea wall or embankment. M17.

goolie /'guːli/ *n. slang.* Also **gool(e)y**. E20. [Cf. Hind. *golī* ball, bullet.] 1 A small stone, a pebble. *Austral.* E20. 2 A testicle. Usu. in *pl.* M20.

goombah /'guːmbɑː/ *n.*¹ *W. Indies.* Also **-bay** /-beɪ/. L18. [W. Indian creole: cf. Kikongo *ŋkumbi* a kind of drum, Twi *gumbe* drum music.] Any of various types of drum played with the fingers (rather than with sticks).

goombah /guːm'bɑː/ *n.*² *US slang.* M20. [Prob. f. It. dial. alt. of *compàre* godfather, friend, accomplice.] A close friend or associate, a crony; a patron; occas. *spec.*, a godfather.

goon /guːn/ *n. slang.* M19. [Perh. f. *goon(e)y* var. of GONY, but in part infl. by name of Alice the *Goon*, a subhuman creature invented by US cartoonist E. C. Segar (1894–1938).] †1 A simple affectionate person. *rare*. Only in M19. 2 A stolid or stupid person; a booby, a dolt. Orig. & chiefly *N. Amer.* E20. 3 A bully-boy, a thug; orig., one hired to terrorize workers. Orig. & chiefly *N. Amer.* M20. 4 Among prisoners-of-war in the war of 1939–45: a German guard. *derog.* M20. 5 (**G-**.) Any of the members of the cast of a British radio show of the 1950s and 1960s, the Goon Show, noted for its zany and surrealist humour; *transf.* a person who exhibits similar humour. M20.

goonery *n.* zany humour typical of the Goons M20. **goonish** *a.* typical of or resembling a goon E20.

goonda /'guːndə/ *n.* Also **-ah**. E20. [Hindi *guṇḍā* rascal.] In the Indian subcontinent: a hired bully.

goondie /'guːndi/ *n. Austral.* Also **gundy**. L19. [Kamilaroi *gunday* stringy-bark.] An Aboriginal hut; = GUNYAH.

goon(e)y *n.* see GONY.

goop /guːp/ *n. slang* (orig. *US*). E20. [Arbitrary formation: cf. GOOF *n.*] A fatuous or stupid person.

goopy *a.* fatuous, silly; *esp.* amorous in a silly way: E20.

goopher *n.* var. of GOOFER *n.*¹

goor *n.* var. of GUR.

Goorkha *n.* & *a.* see GURKHA.

gooroo *n.* var. of GURU.

goosander /guːˈsandə/ *n.* E17. [Prob. f. GOOSE *n.* + 2nd elem. of BERGANDER.] A Eurasian saw-billed duck, *Mergus merganser*.

goose /guːs/ *n.* Pl. **geese** /giːs/, (sense 5) **gooses**. [OE *gōs* = OFris., MLG *gōs*, (M)Du., OHG (mod.G) *gans*, ON *gás*, f. Gmc, f. IE base also of L *anser*, Gk *khēn*, Skt *haṃsá* masc., *haṃsī* fem.] 1 Any of various large web-footed birds, intermediate between ducks and swans in size, belonging to the genera *Anser*, *Branta*, or related genera of the family Anatidae; *spec.* the domesticated form of the greylag goose, *Anser anser*. See also SOLAN *goose*. OE. b *spec.* The female bird (the male being the *gander*). ME. c The flesh of the (usu. domestic) goose. M16. 2 A foolish person, a simpleton. LME. †3 In full (*royal*) *game of goose*. A game played with counters on a board divided into sections, some of which had a goose depicted on them. L16–E19. †4 In full *Winchester goose*. A venereal infection. L16–E18. 5 A tailor's smoothing-iron (so called from the resemblance of the handle to a goose's neck). E17. 6 A hissing sound like that of a goose; *spec.* (*Theatr. slang*) one expressing disapproval of an actor's performance. E19.

1 *barnacle goose, brent goose, Canada goose, Hawaiian goose, pink-footed goose, snow goose*, etc. *green goose*: see GREEN *a.* c *colonial goose*: see COLONIAL *a.* 1.

Phrases: *can't say boo to a goose*: see BOO *int.* & *n.*[2] *cook someone's goose*: see COOK *v. fox and geese*: see FOX *n.* 1. *game of goose*: see sense 3 above. *gone goose*: see GONE *a.* 1. **kill the goose that lays** (or **laid**) **the golden eggs** sacrifice long-term advantage to short-term gain. **turn geese into swans** exaggerate the merits of people. *Winchester goose*: see sense 4 above.

Comb.: **goose barnacle** [see note s.v. BARNACLE *n.*[1]] any of various stalked barnacles of the genus *Lepas*; **goose-bumps** *N. Amer.* = GOOSE-FLESH; **goose-cap** *arch.* a simpleton, a fool; **goose-egg** (*a*) the egg of a goose; (*b*) *transf.* (*N. Amer.*) a zero score in an athletic contest etc.; **goose-fair**: held at certain English towns (still at Nottingham) about Michaelmas, when geese are in season; **goose-girl**: employed to tend geese; **goosegrass** any of several plants, *esp.* (*a*) silverweed, *Potentilla anserina*; (*b*) cleavers, *Galium aparine*; **goose-neck** (*a*) *Naut.* a metal fitting at the end of a boom, connecting it to a metal ring round the base of the mast; also, a davit; (*b*) a pipe or piece of iron etc. curved like a goose's neck; **goose-pimples** = GOOSE-FLESH; **goose quill** a quill pen made from a goose's feather; **goose-skin** = GOOSE-FLESH; **goose-step** a marching step, esp. associated with Nazi Germany, in which the legs are advanced alternately without bending the knees; also, a form of drill in which the soldier balances alternately on either leg and swings the other leg; **goose-step** *v.i.* do the goose-step; **goose-winged** *a.* (*Naut.*) (of a sail in a square-rigged ship) with only the goose-wings spread; (of a fore-and-aft rig) with two working sails boomed out, one on either side; **goose-wings** *n.* (*Naut.*) in a square-rigged ship, the clews of a course or topsail spread for scudding under when the wind is strong, the bunt of the sail being hauled up to the yard; in a fore-and-aft rigged ship, having the sails goose-winged.

gooselike *a.* resembling (that of) a goose M16.

goose /guːs/ *v.t.* M17. [f. the n.] 1 Press (clothes) with a tailor's smoothing-iron. M17. 2 Express disapproval of (a play, an actor, etc.) by hissing. M19. 3 Poke or tickle in a sensitive part of the body; *esp.* poke between the buttocks. Also = FUCK *v.* 2. *slang* (chiefly *US*). L19. 4 In *pass.* Be ruined or done for. *slang.* E20.

gooseberry /ˈgʊzb(ə)ri, ˈguːs-/ *n.* M16. [1st elem. perh. alt. (by unexpl. assim. to GOOSE *n.*) of forms such as Fr. dial. *groser*, *gozell*, repr. remotely (O)Fr. *groseille*, †*grozelle*; but perh. f. GOOSE *n.* + BERRY *n.*[1]] 1 An acid green or red-tinged freq. hairy edible berry, the fruit of the European thorny shrub *Ribes uva-crispa* and related species or hydrids; the shrub producing this berry. M16. †b The berry of other species of *Ribes*; a (red, black, etc.) currant. L16–M17. c With specifying wd.: (the fruit of) any of various shrubs resembling the gooseberry. M19. 2 Gooseberry wine. Also (*joc.*), inferior champagne. M18. 3 *old gooseberry*, the Devil; esp. in *play old gooseberry*, create havoc. *slang.* L18. 4 A chaperon; an unwanted third party. Freq. in *play gooseberry*. *slang.* M19.

1c **Barbados gooseberry** (the edible fruit of) *Pereskia aculeata*, a West Indian vine of the cactus family. *Cape gooseberry*: see CAPE *n.*[1] *Chinese gooseberry*: see CHINESE *a.* OTAHEITE *gooseberry*. 4 G. SWIFT Her husband . . a clumsy gooseberry to this scene of painful intimacy.

Comb.: **gooseberry-bush** a shrub producing gooseberries, *esp.* as a supposed place where (in coy explanations of the human reproduction) newly born babies are found; **gooseberry eyes**: dull grey; *gooseberry fool*: see FOOL *n.*[2]; **gooseberry season** the time when gooseberries are ripe (*big gooseberry season* (arch.) = SILLY *season*).

goose-flesh /ˈguːsflɛʃ/ *n.* LME. [f. GOOSE *n.* + FLESH *n.*] 1 The flesh of a goose. LME. 2 A rough pimply state of the skin produced by cold, fear, etc. E19.

gooseflesby *a.* exhibiting goose-flesh L19.

goosefoot /ˈguːsfʊt/ *n.* Pl. (in sense 1) **-feet**, (in sense 2) **-foots**. E16. [f. GOOSE *n.* + FOOT *n.*] 1 Something made or arranged in the shape of a goose's foot; *esp.* (*a*) a three-branched hinge; (*b*) a number of roads radiating from a common point. E16. 2 [f. the shape of the leaf in some species] Any of various plants of the genus *Chenopodium* (family Chenopodiaceae), chiefly mealy weeds with spikes of inconspicuous greenish flowers. E16.

goosegog /ˈgʊzgɒg, ˈguːsgɒg/ *n. dial.* & *colloq.* E19. [Alt. of GOOSEBERRY; the 2nd elem. is alt. of GOB *n.*[1]] A gooseberry.

gooseherd /ˈguːshəːd/ *n.* Also **gozzard** /ˈgɒzəd/. ME. [f. GOOSE *n.* + HERD *n.*[2]] A person who tends a flock of geese.

goosery /ˈguːsəri/ *n.* M17. [f. GOOSE *n.* + -ERY.] 1 Silliness such as is attributed to geese. *rare.* M17. 2 A place where geese are kept; a collection of geese. E19.

goosey /ˈguːsi/ *n.* Also redupl. **goosey-goosey**. Also **goosie**, **goosy**. E19. [f. GOOSE *n.* + -Y[6].] 1 *goosey(-goosey) gander*, (a pet name for) a gander. E19. 2 A silly person. Also *goosey-gander*. M19.

goosey *a.* var. of GOOSY *a.*

goosish /ˈguːsɪʃ/ *a.* LME. [f. GOOSE *n.* + -ISH[1].] Resembling a goose, silly.

goosishness *n.* M19.

goosy *n.* var. of GOOSEY *n.*

goosy /ˈguːsi/ *a.* Also **goosey**. E19. [f. GOOSE *n.* + -Y[1]. In sense 3, cf. GOOSE *v.* 3.] 1 Resembling a goose; *fig.* foolish, silly. E19. 2 Exhibiting goose-flesh (GOOSE-FLESH *n.* 2). M19. 3 Sensitive to being goosed, ticklish, nervous. *US slang.* E20.

goosiness *n.* L19.

gopak /ˈgəʊpak/ *n.* E20. [Russ. f. Ukrainian *hopak*.] A lively Ukrainian dance in 2/4 time.

gopher /ˈgəʊfə/ *n.*[1] E17. [Heb. *gōper*.] The (unidentified) tree from whose wood Noah's ark was made. Chiefly as *gopher-wood* (see below).

Comb.: **gopher-wood** (*a*) the wood of the gopher; (*b*) *US* (the wood of) the yellow-wood, *Cladrastis lutea*.

gopher /ˈgəʊfə/ *n.*[2] L18. [Origin uncertain: perh. f. Canad. Fr. *gaufre* lit. 'honeycomb', w. ref. to the animals' burrowing habits.] 1 In full *gopher tortoise*. Any of several N. American burrowing land tortoises of the genus *Gopherus*, esp. *G. polyphemus* of the south-eastern US. L18. 2 In full *pocket gopher*. Any of various burrowing rodents belonging to the family Geomyidae, which are native to N. and Central America, and have external food-pouches on the cheeks. E19. 3 A chipmunk, ground-squirrel, or prairie dog. *N. Amer.* M19. 4 [W. allus. to sense 2 or 3 above.] (A nickname for) a native or inhabitant of Minnesota or (formerly) Arkansas. M19.

Comb.: **gopher-hole** the opening of a gopher's burrow; a hole dug in small-scale or haphazard mining; **gopher snake** (*a*) = *bull-snake* s.v. BULL *n.*[1]; (*b*) = *indigo snake* s.v. INDIGO *n.*; **Gopher State** *US* the State of Minnesota.

gopher *n.*[3] var. of GOFER *n.*[2]

gopher /ˈgəʊfə/ *v.i. N. Amer.* L19. [f. GOPHER *n.*[2]] Burrow like a gopher; *spec.* carry out small-scale or haphazard mining operations.

gopi /ˈgəʊpiː/ *n.* Also **G-**. L18. [Skt.] *Hindu Mythol.* Any of the milkmaids of Brindavan, companions of Krishna.

gopura /ˈgəʊpʊrə/ *n.* Also **-ram** /-rəm/. M19. [Skt *gopura* city gate, f. *go* cow, cattle + *pura* city, quarter.] In southern India: the great pyramidal tower over the entrance-gate to a temple precinct.

gorah /ˈgɔːrə/ *n.* Also **goura** /ˈgʊərə/. L18. [Prob. f. Nama or San.] A musical instrument of indigenous southern African peoples, consisting of a string stretched along a stick, and played by blowing on a piece of quill attached to these.

goral /ˈgɔːr(ə)l/ *n.* Also **gur-** /ˈgʊə-/. M19. [Local (Himalayan) name.] A goat-antelope, *Nemorhaedus goral*, which inhabits montane forest from Myanmar (Burma) and northern India to Siberia.

Gorbachevian /gɔːbəˈtʃɛvɪən/ *a.* Also **Gorbachovian** /gɔːbəˈtʃəʊvɪən/. L20. [f. *Gorbachev* (see below) + -IAN.] Of, pertaining to, or characteristic of Mikhail Sergeyevich Gorbachev (b. 1931), General Secretary of the Communist Party of the Soviet Union (1985–90) and later its President, or his policies.

gorbelly /ˈgɔːbeli/ *n.* E16. [Origin uncertain: perh. f. GORE *n.*[1] + BELLY *n.*; cf. Sw. dial. *går-bälg*.] †1 A protuberant stomach. E16–L18. 2 A person with a protuberant stomach. *obs.* exc. *dial.* M16.

gorbellied *a.* (long chiefly *dial.*) corpulent E16.

gorblimey /gɔːˈblʌɪmi/ *int.*, *n.*, & *a. slang.* L19. [Alt. of *God blind me*: cf. BLIMEY.] A *int.* Expr. surprise, amazement, etc. L19.

B *n.* A soft unwired service cap. Chiefly *Mil.* E20.

C *attrib.* or as *adj.* 1 Designating such a cap, or any loud clothing. E20. 2 Of a person or thing: common, ordinary; vulgar. M20.

2 *ellipt.*: *Daily Telegraph* Descending from the sublime to the gorblimey.

gorbuscha /gɔːˈbʊʃə/ *n.* L18. [Russ. *gorbusha*, f. *gorb* hump.] = *humpback salmon* s.v. HUMPBACK *a.*

†**gorce** *n.* Also **gort** & other vars. L15. [AN *gortz* pl. of *gort* (OFr. *gord*, *gourt*) f. L *gurges*, *gurgit-* whirlpool.] 1 A whirlpool. L15–E17. 2 Any form of obstruction in a river, as a weir, dam, etc. E18–L19.

gorcock /ˈgɔːkɒk/ *n. Sc.* & *north.* E17. [Origin unkn.] The male of the red grouse.

gorcrow /ˈgɔːkrəʊ/ *n.* Now chiefly *dial.* E17. [f. GORE *n.*[1] + CROW *n.*[1]] The carrion crow.

Gordian /ˈgɔːdɪən/ *n.* & *a.* M16. [f. L *Gordius* or *Gordium* (see sense B.1) + -AN.] A *n.* †1 = *Gordian knot* below. M16–E18. 2 A native or inhabitant of Gordium in Phrygia. *rare.* E17.

B *adj.* 1 *Gordian knot*, an intricate knot tied by Gordius, king of Gordium, Phrygia, and cut through by Alexander the Great in response to the prophecy that only the future ruler of Asia could loosen it; *fig.* or *allus.*, an extremely difficult problem or task, an indissoluble bond. L16. 2 Resembling the Gordian knot; intricate, convoluted, involved. E17.

1 **cut the Gordian knot** solve a problem by force or by evading the conditions.

Gordon /ˈgɔːd(ə)n/ *n.* M19. [f. Alexander *Gordon*, 4th Duke of Gordon (1743–1827), who promoted the breed.] In full *Gordon setter*. A breed of black and tan setter, used as a gun dog; an animal of this breed.

Gordon Bennett /gɔːd(ə)n ˈbɛnɪt/ *int.* L20. [Prob. alt. of GORBLIMEY *int.* after James *Gordon Bennett* (1841–1918), US publisher and sponsor of sporting events.] Expr. surprise, incredulity, or exasperation.

gore /gɔː/ *n.*[1] [OE *gor* = (M)Du. *goor* mud, filth, OHG, ON *gor* cud, slimy matter, rel. to OIr. *gor*, Welsh *gôr* matter, pus.] 1 Dung, faeces; dirt of any kind; slime, mucus. *obs.* exc. *dial.* OE. 2 Blood shed and thickened or clotted; (chiefly *poet.*) blood shed in carnage. M16.

2 V. NABOKOV Hands . . black and bloody . . anointed with his thick gore. †**in a gore of blood** bathed in or besmeared with blood.

gore /gɔː/ *n.*[2] [OE *gāra* = OFris. *gāra*, MDu. *ghēre* (Du. *geer*), OHG *gēro* (G *Gehre*), ON *geiri* prob. rel. to OE *gār* spear.] 1 Orig., a promontory, a corner of land. Now, (long *dial.*) a wedge-shaped piece of land on the side of an asymmetric field; (chiefly *US*) a small strip or tract of land lying between larger divisions such as parishes, townships, etc. OE. 2 A wedge-shaped or triangular piece of cloth used to adjust the width of a garment where required, esp. to narrow a dress or skirt at the waist. Formerly also, *gen.* a skirt or the lower part of a gown or robe. ME. b Any of several triangular or lune-shaped pieces used to form the surface of a hot-air balloon, umbrella, dome, globe, etc. L18. c *Naut.* A piece of canvas cut at an angle to increase the breadth or depth of a sail; an angular piece of plank used to fill up the planking of a wooden vessel where necessary. L18. 3 *Her.* A charge formed by two concave curved lines meeting in the fesse-point, the one drawn from the sinister or dexter chief corner of the shield and the other from the base point. M16.

gore /gɔː/ *v.*[1]*t.* LME. [Origin unkn.] 1 Cut, pierce, or stab deeply with a sharp weapon, spur, etc. Now *rare* exc. as sense 2. LME. 2 Of an animal: pierce or stab with the horns or (rarely) tusks. E16.

1 J. DICKEY I wondered if I should tell whatever doctor dressed it that I had gored myself on my own arrow. 2 W. S. MAUGHAM His hired man had been gored by a bull and was in hospital. *absol.*: ADAM SMITH The dog that bites, the ox that gores.

†**gore** *v.*[2] LME. [f. GORE *n.*[1]] 1 *v.i.* Of a wound: fester. Only in LME. 2 As *gored* pa. pple: covered (as) *with* or *in* gore or blood. M16–M17.

gore /gɔː/ *v.*[3] M16. [f. GORE *n.*[2]] 1 *v.t.* Cut or shape into a gore; shape using a gore or gores. M16. 2 *v.i.* Plough a gore. Chiefly as GORING *n.*[2] *obs.* exc. *dial.* L18.

goree /gɒˈriː/ *n.* Also **gori**. M19. [Nyanja *goli.*] Chiefly *Hist.* A forked stick used by Arabs to fasten slaves together by the neck. Also *goree-stick*.

gorge /gɔːdʒ/ *n.*[1] LME. [(O)Fr. = throat f. Proto-Romance alt. of L *gurges* whirlpool.] I 1 The external throat; the front of the neck. *arch.* LME. 2 The internal throat. Now only *rhet.* LME. 3 Orig. in *Falconry*, (the contents of) the crop of a hawk. Now *gen.*, the contents of the stomach (chiefly in phrs. below). LME. 4 A meal, *esp.* (in *Falconry*) for a hawk. Long *rare.* LME. II *transf.* 5 *Fortif.* The neck of a bastion or other outwork; the rear entrance to the platform or body of a work. M17. 6 *Archit.* A hollow or concave moulding. E18. 7 A narrow opening between hills or mountains, *esp.* one with rocky walls and a stream. M18. 8 The groove of a pulley. E19. 9 A mass of ice obstructing a narrow passage, esp. a river. M19. 10 *Angling.* A bait intended to ensure capture of the fish when swallowed. Also *gorge-bait*, *-hook*. M19.

Phrases: **cast the gorge at** reject with loathing. **cast (up) (the) gorge** *Falconry* = GLEAM *v.*[2] *heave the gorge*: see HEAVE *v.* **one's gorge rises at** one is sickened or disgusted by.

gorge /gɔːdʒ/ *n.*[2] M19. [f. next.] An act of gorging oneself; a glut (of food, wine, etc.).

gorge /gɔːdʒ/ *v.* ME. [(O)Fr. *gorger*, f. as GORGE *n.*[1]] 1a *v.i.* Orig. *spec.* of a bird of prey: fill the gorge. Now *gen.* of a person or animal: feed greedily (*on*, *upon*). ME. b *v.t.* (freq. *refl.*) Stuff with food (also foll. by *with*, (*up*)*on*); satiate (the appetite); (now *rare*) fill the gorge of (a hawk). L15. 2a *v.t.* Fill full, distend; choke up. Chiefly as *gorged* pa. pple. Cf. ENGORGE 1b. LME. b *v.i.* Of ice: become fixed so as to form an obstruction. *US.* M19. 3 *v.t.* Gobble up, devour greedily. E17.

1a J. WAIN Robert gorged like a man driven insane by hunger. D. M. FRAME Some men gorged while others . . . starved. b R. LINDNER She would be seized by an overwhelming compulsion to gorge herself, to eat almost continuously. *fig.*: P. DE VRIES She would gorge herself on the outrage a moment or two. 2a C. DARWIN During excessive laughter . . the head and face become gorged with blood. 3 P. G. WODEHOUSE Half a century of gorging food and swilling wine. *Times* The deal with CCF is better than being gorged by one of the financial giants.

gorger *n.* a person or animal that gorges E19.

gorgeaunt /ˈgɔːdʒ(ə)nt/ *n.* Long *obs.* exc. *Hist.* LME. [Fr., pres. pple of *gorger* GORGE *v.*] A boar in its second year.

gorged /gɔːdʒd/ *a.* E17. [f. GORGE *n.*[1] + -ED[2].] *Her.* Having the gorge or neck encircled with a coronet, collar, etc.

gorgeous /ˈgɔːdʒəs/ *a.* L15. [OFr. *gorgias* fine, stylish, elegant, of unkn. origin; assim. in ending to wds in -EOUS.] 1 Richly or brilliantly coloured, sumptuous, magnificent, (esp. in attire); dazzling. L15. 2 Wonderful, splendid, delightful. *colloq.* L19.

1 H. L. MENCKEN The gorgeous tricolor baldrics, sashes and festoons of the Légion d'Honneur. J. I. M. STEWART The college organist (in the most gorgeous of all Oxford's robes).

gorgeously *adv.* E16. **gorgeousness** *n.* M16.

gorgeret /ˈgɔːdʒərɪt/ *n.* Now *rare* or *obs.* M18. [Fr., f. as GORGE *n.*[1]: see -ET[1].] *Surg.* = GORGET *n.*[2]

gorgerin /ˈgɔːdʒərɪn/ *n.* M17. [Fr. = gorget, frieze of a Doric capital, f. as GORGE *n.*[1]] 1 *Archit.* = HYPOTRACHELIUM. M17. 2 = GORGET *n.*[1] 1. M19.

gorget /ˈgɔːdʒɪt/ *n.*[1] LME. [OFr. *gorgete*, f. as GORGE *n.*[1]: see -ET[1].] 1 A piece of armour for the throat. *obs.* exc. *Hist.* LME. b A woman's wimple, covering the head, neck, and shoulders. *obs.* exc. *Hist.* M16. c A collar. E17. 2 An ornament for the neck; a necklace, a decorative collar, etc.; *Mil. Hist.* a gilt crescent-shaped badge worn on a chain round the neck by officers on duty. L15. 3 In *pl.* A type of pillory consisting of a hinged iron collar worn about the neck. *Sc. obs.* exc. *Hist.* M17. 4 A patch of colour on the throat or breast of an animal, esp. a bird E19.

gorget /ˈgɔːdʒɪt/ *n.*[2] M18. [Alt. of GORGERET.] *Surg.* An instrument with a wide longitudinal groove or channel used in the removal of stones from the bladder.

Gorgio /ˈgɔːdʒɪəʊ/ *n.* Pl. **-os**. M19. [Romany *gorjo.*] Among Gypsies: (a name for) a non-Gypsy.

gorgon /ˈgɔːg(ə)n/ *n.* & *a.* Also **G-**. LME. [L *Gorgo*, *Gorgon-* f. Gk *Gorgō*, f. *gorgos* terrible.] A *n.* 1 *Gk Mythol.* Each of three sisters, Stheno, Euryale, and Medusa (the only mortal one), who had snakes for hair and whose gaze, on meeting that of another, turned the beholder to stone. LME. †b = DEMOGORGON. *rare* (Spenser). Only in L16. 2 A person resembling a gorgon in manner or appearance; *esp.* an ugly or terrifying woman. E16.

B *attrib.* or as *adj.* Petrifying, terrible. L16.

J. FOWLES Other passengers . . were rebuffed by that Gorgon stare . . the English have so easily at command.

gorgoneion /gɔːgəˈnʌɪən/ *n.* Pl. **-neia** /-ˈnʌɪə/. M19. [Gk *gorgoneion* neut. of *gorgoneios* of or pertaining to a GORGON.] A representation of a gorgon's head.

gorgonia /gɔːˈgəʊnɪə/ *n.* Pl. **-ias**, **-iae** /-iiː/. M18. [mod.L *Gorgonia* (see below), fem. of *gorgonius*, f. L *Gorgo* GORGON: so named from its petrifaction.] = GORGONIAN *n.*; *esp.* a member of the genus *Gorgonia*.

gorgonian /gɔːˈgəʊnɪən/ *n.* & *a.*[1] M19. [f. as prec. + -IAN.] A *n.* Any of various horny corals of the order Gorgonacea, with upright, plantlike forms. M19. B *adj.* Belonging to or characteristic of this order. L19.

gorgonian /gɔːˈgəʊnɪən/ *a.*[2] L16. [f. GORGON + -IAN.] Of or pertaining to a gorgon; resembling a gorgon in effect or appearance.

gorgonize /ˈgɔːg(ə)nʌɪz/ *v.t.* Also **-ise**. E17. [f. GORGON + -IZE.] Petrify as by the gaze of a gorgon; stare at like a gorgon.

Gorgonzola /gɔːg(ə)nˈzəʊlə/ *n.* L19. [f. *Gorgonzola* a village near Milan, Italy, where originally made.] A type of Italian blue cheese usu. made from cow's milk.

gorgy /ˈgɔːdʒi/ *a.* L19. [f. GORGE *n.*[1] + -Y[1].] Full of gorges or ravines.

gorilla /gəˈrɪlə/ *n.* M19. [mod.L (see below), f. an alleged African wd (= wild or hairy man) found in accus. pl. fem. *gorillas* in the Gk account of the voyage of the Carthaginian Hanno.] 1 A large powerful anthropoid ape, *Gorilla gorilla*, inhabiting forest in parts of central Africa. M19. 2 A person resembling a gorilla in appearance; *colloq.* a heavily-built thug. L19.

2 S. BELLOW The union guy called off his gorillas and they came to position round him.

gorily /ˈgɔːrɪli/ *adv.* M19. [f. GORY *a.* + -LY[2].] In a gory manner.

goring /ˈgɔːrɪŋ/ *n.*[1] L15. [f. GORE *v.*[1] + -ING[1].] The action of GORE *v.*[1]; an instance of this; (a) stabbing, (a) piercing.

goring /ˈgɔːrɪŋ/ *n.*[2] E17. [f. GORE *v.*[3] or *n.*[2] + -ING[1].] 1 The cutting out or fitting of gores. E17. b *Naut.* A piece of cloth used as a gore. M18. 2 The action of ploughing a gore. Also = GORE *n.*[2] 1. Chiefly *dial.* M19.

gorm /gɔːm/ *n.* Also (earlier) **gaum**, (*Anglo-Ir.*) **gom** /gɒm/. M19. [Cf. GAUM *v.*[2], GORMLESS: Irish use may represent an independent wd (cf. Ir. *gamal* stupid-looking person).] A fool; a stupid lout.

gorm /gɔːm/ *v.*[1]*t.* M19. [Alt. of (*God*) *damn.*] = DAMN *v.* 3.

gorm *v.*[2], *v.*[3] see GAUM *v.*[2], *v.*[3]

gormandize /ˈgɔːm(ə)ndʌɪz/ *n.* Also **-ise**; **gourmandise** /*usu.* gʊəmɒ̃ˈdiːz/. LME. [Fr. *gourmandise*, f. GOURMAND.] Orig., gluttony. Now chiefly, indulgence or connoisseurship in good eating.

J. GLASSCO The chilled wine was a coarse Niersteiner. . . Joyce sipped it with gormandise.

gormandize /ˈgɔːm(ə)ndʌɪz/ *v.* Also **-ise**; **gour-** /*usu.* ˈgʊəmɒ̃dʌɪz/. M16. [f. the n.] 1 *v.i.* Eat greedily; indulge in good eating. M16. 2 *v.t.* Devour greedily. E17. †3 *v.t.* Satiate. E17–L18.

1 Y. MENUHIN One of my clearest memories . . is of gormandizing at a luncheon given in the park. 2 *fig.*: C. D. WARNER Taken all the best seats . . with the intention of gormandizing the views.

gormandizer *n.* a glutton L16.

gormless /ˈgɔːmlɪs/ *a.* *colloq.* (orig. *dial.*). Also (earlier) **gaumless**. M18. [f. GAUM *n.*[1] + -LESS.] Slow-witted, stupid, lacking sense.

gormlessly *adv.* M20. **gormlessness** *n.* M19.

gormy *a.* var. of GAUMY.

gorp *v.* see GAWP.

gorry /ˈgɒri/ *int.* & *n.* M19. [Alt. of GOD *n.* Cf. GOLLY *n.*[1]] God. Chiefly in *by gorry*.

gorse /gɔːs/ *n.* [OE *gors*, *gorst*, f. IE base meaning 'rough, prickly', repr. in L *hordeum* barley, rel. to OHG *gersta* (G *Gerste*) barley.] Any of several spiny yellow-flowered leguminous shrubs of the genus *Ulex* (esp. *U. europaeus*), characteristic of heathy places. Also called *furze*, *whin*.

gorsy *a.* overgrown with gorse; characteristic of gorse: E16.

Gorsedd /ˈgɔːsɛð/ *n.* L18. [Welsh = mound, throne, assembly, Gorsedd.] A meeting of Welsh bards and druids; *esp.* the assembly that meets to announce the next Royal National Eisteddfod and at certain times during this festival.

†**gort** *n.* var. of GORCE.

gory /ˈgɔːri/ *a.* LME. [f. GORE *n.*[1] + -Y[1].] 1 Covered with gore, stained with blood, bloody. LME. †b Of blood: clotted. M–L16. c Resembling blood in colour. *rare.* E19. 2 = BLOODY *a.* 3. L16.

1 SIR W. SCOTT Away the gory axe he threw. 2 A. GHOSH It is a gory history in parts; a story of greed and destruction.

gos /gɒs/ *n.* *colloq.* L18. [Abbrev.] = GOSHAWK.

gosain /gə(ʊ)ˈsʌɪn/ *n.* L18. [Hind. *gosāī̃* f. Skt *gosvāmin* 'lord of cows', f. *go* COW *n.*[1]] A Hindu who professes a life of religious mendicancy.

gosh /gɒʃ/ *n.* & *int.* M18. [Alt.] (In mild exclamations and other expressions substituted for) God.

New Yorker My gosh, we're so up to here in church activities.

Comb.: **goshawful** *a.* (*colloq.*) = *God-awful* s.v. GOD *n.* **gosh-darned** *a.* = GODDAM *a.*

goshawk /ˈgɒshɔːk/ *n.* [OE *gōshafoc*, f. *gōs* GOOSE *n.* + *hafoc* HAWK *n.*[1]: cf. ON *gáshaukr*.] Any of various large short-winged hawks; spec. *Accipiter gentilis*, occurring widely throughout the northern hemisphere.

chanting goshawk any of a number of grey hawks of the genus *Melierax*, native to Africa, notable for the melodious calls of the male in the breeding season.

Goshen /ˈgəʊʃ(ə)n/ *n.* E17. [Heb., the fertile land allotted to the Israelites in Egypt, in which (*Exod.* 10:23 implies) there was light during the plague of darkness.] A place of plenty or of light.

gosling /ˈgɒzlɪŋ/ *n.* ME. [ON *gæslingr* (Sw. *gäsling*, Da. *gæsling*), f. *gás* GOOSE *n.*; assim. to Eng. *goose*: see -LING[1].] 1 A young goose. ME. 2 *fig.* A foolish, inexperienced person. Now *rare.* E17. 3 A catkin or blossom on a tree. E18.

Comb.: **gosling-green** *n.* & *a.* (of) a pale yellowish green.

go-slow /gəʊˈsləʊ, ˈgəʊsləʊ/ *n.* M20. [f. GO *v.* + SLOW *adv.*] A form of industrial protest in which employees work at a deliberately slow pace. Cf. CA'CANNY.

gospel /ˈgɒsp(ə)l/ *n.* [OE *gōdspel*, i.e. *gōd* GOOD *a.*, *spel* news, tidings (see SPELL *n.*[1]), rendering of eccl.L *bona annuntiatio*, *bonus nuntius*, used as literal renderings of eccl.L *evangelium*, Gk *euaggelion* EVANGEL *n.*[1] Later assoc. with *God*, as in all the forms adopted in the Gmc langs. of peoples evangelized from England, viz. OS *godspell*, OHG *gotspell*, ON *guð-*, *goðspjall*.] 1 The 'good news' preached by Jesus; the religious doctrine of Christ and his apostles; the Christian revelation, religion, or dispensation. OE. b *gen.* Any revelation from heaven. L15. c (A term used by Protestants for) the doctrines of Protestantism; the doctrine of salvation according to Puritans or Evangelicals. M16. 2 (G-.) The record of Jesus' life and teaching, contained in the first four books of the New Testament. OE. b One of these books (of the Four Evangelists: Matthew, Mark, Luke, and John), or of some other texts of doubtful authenticity. ME. †c The Holy Scriptures generally. LME–L15. 3 *the Gospel* (*for* or *of the day*): the portion from one of the four Gospels read at the Eucharist in various Christian denominations. (Cf. EPISTLE *n.* 2b.) OE. 4 A thing regarded as undoubtedly true. ME. 5 A principle that one acts upon, believes in, or preaches. M17. 6 In full *gospel music.* A type of fervent or evangelical singing performed mostly by US Blacks. M20.

1 W. IRVING To spread the light of the gospel in that far wilderness. c OED 'Why don't you go to church?' 'Because the Gospel is not preached there'. *social gospel*: see SOCIAL *a.* 4 M. WEBB He'll take it for gospel that Gideon writes the letters. 5 P. G. WODEHOUSE Physical fitness was her gospel.

Comb.: *gospel music*: see sense 6 above; **gospel oath**: sworn on the Gospels; **gospel-sharp** *US colloq.* a Christian minister of religion; **Gospel side** *Chr. Ch.* the north end of an altar, from which the Gospel is traditionally read; **gospel-singer**: of gospel music; **gospel-song** (one performed in the style of) gospel music; **gospel truth** (*a*) the truth or truths contained in the Gospel; (*b*) something as true as the Gospel.

gospel /ˈgɒsp(ə)l/ *v.* Infl. **-ll-**, ***-l-**. [OE *gōdspellian*, f. the n., repr. eccl.L *benenuntiare*, Gk *euaggelizesthai*.] 1 *v.i.* Preach the gospel. *rare.* OE. †2 *v.t.* Preach the gospel to; evangelize. M16–M17.

gospeler *n.* see GOSPELLER.

gospelize /ˈgɒspəlʌɪz/ *v.t.* Also **-ise**. E17. [f. GOSPEL *n.* + -IZE.] 1 = EVANGELIZE 3. E17. †2 Impart the spirit of the gospel to. Only in M17.

gospeller /ˈgɒsp(ə)lə/ *n.* Also ***-eler**. OE. [f. GOSPEL *n.* or *v.* + -ER[1].] 1 Each of the four evangelists. OE. 2 A book containing the Gospels. Now *rare.* LME. 3 A person who reads the Gospel at a Eucharist. E16. 4 A person who professes the faith of the gospel, or who claims personally or for a sect the exclusive possession of gospel truth. M16. 5 A preacher of the gospel; a missionary. *rare.* L16.

Phrases: **hot gospeller** a fervent gospel preacher; a zealous puritan, a rabid propagandist.

goss /gɒs/ *n.*[1] *slang.* M19. [Origin unkn.] *give, get goss*, give, receive punishment.

Goss /gɒs/ *n.*[2] E20. [f. W. H. *Goss* (1833–1906), Eng. china manufacturer.] In full *Goss china.* A kind of china orig. manufactured by Goss, and later made esp. as mementoes of places, events, etc.

gossamer /ˈgɒsəmə/ *n.*, *a.*, & *v.* ME. [App. f. GOOSE *n.* + SUMMER *n.*[1]; perh. f. the time of year (around 'St Martin's Summer') when geese were eaten, which is when gossamer tends to be most seen. Cf. G *Mädchensommer*, *Altweibersommer*.] A *n.* 1 A fine filmy substance, consisting of cobwebs spun by small spiders, which is seen esp. in autumn, floating in the air or spread over a grassy surface. Also, a thread or web of this. ME. b *transf.* & *fig.* Something light and flimsy. LME. 2a A light make of silk hat; *joc.* a hat generally. *arch.* M19. b A very light kind of waterproof. *US.* L19. 3 A rich silk gauze used for veils and dresses. L19.

1 H. WILLIAMSON Gossamers glinted across the stubbles.

B *adj.* 1 Made of gossamer. E19. 2 *fig.* Light and flimsy as gossamer; frivolous, volatile. E19.

2 A. LEWIS The rain . . a gossamer stream Too light to stir the acorns.

C *v.t.* Coat (as) with gossamer. Chiefly as *gossamered* ppl a. M19.

gossamery *a.* made of or like gossamer; flimsy, unsubstantial: L18.

gossan /ˈgɒz(ə)n/ *n.* L18. [Origin unkn.] *Geol.* & *Mining* (orig. *Cornish*). A ferruginous secondary deposit, largely consisting of oxides, occurring at an outcrop of a metallic ore.

gossip /ˈgɒsɪp/ *n.* [Late OE *godsibb*, corresp. to ON *guðsifi* godfather, *guðsiffa* godmother, f. as GOD *n.* + SIB *a.*, denoting the spiritual affinity of the baptized and their sponsors.] 1 A godfather or godmother; a sponsor. *obs.* exc. *Hist.* or *dial.* LOE. 2 A familiar acquaintance, a friend. (Now only of women.) *arch.* ME. b *spec.* A female friend invited to be present at a birth. *arch.* L16. 3 A person who habitually indulges in idle talk, esp. the spreading of rumours and discussion of the private concerns of others. M16. 4 Idle talk; groundless rumour; tittle-tattle; informal, unrestrained talk or writing, esp. about people or social incidents. E19.

2 C. BRONTË The old duenna—my mother's gossip. 3 E. F. BENSON Edgar is a dreadful gossip . . I recommend you never tell him anything private. 4 G. SANTAYANA Talk . . was chiefly gossip, and gossip encouraged a morbid interest in matters that didn't concern one.

Comb.: **gossip column** a section of a newspaper devoted to social news; **gossip-columnist** a person who regularly writes a gossip column; **gossip-monger** a person who habitually passes on confidential information, or spreads rumours.

gossipdom *n.* gossips as a class; the realm of gossip: L19. **gossiphood** *n.* (now *rare*) †(*a*) spiritual relationship; (*b*) a body of gossips: E16. **gossipy** *a.* inclined to gossip; characterized by or full of gossip: E19.

gossip /ˈgɒsɪp/ *v.* L16. [f. the n.] †1 *v.i.* Act as a familiar acquaintance; take part (in a feast); make oneself at home. L16–M17. †2 *v.t.* Be a sponsor to; give a name to. E17–E18. 3 *v.i.* Indulge in gossip; talk idly or lightly; write in a gossipy style. E17. 4 *v.t.* Tell or discuss like a gossip; communicate by gossip. E17.

3 O. MANNING He imagined they were gossiping about him.

gossiper *n.* a person who gossips M16. **gossiping** *n.* †(*a*) a meeting of gossips; orig. a christening-feast, or a meeting of friends at a birth; (*b*) the action of the vb; idle talking, tattling: M16. **gossipingly** *adv.* in a gossiping manner E19.

gossipred /ˈgɒsɪprɛd/ *n. obs.* exc. *Hist.* ME. [f. GOSSIP *n.* + -RED.] 1 The relationship of gossips (see GOSSIP *n.* 1, 2); spiritual affinity. ME. †2 = GOSSIP *n.* 4. Only in 19.

gossipry /ˈgɒsɪpri/ *n.* E16. [f. GOSSIP *n.* + -RY.] 1 Spiritual relationship; = GOSSIPRED 1. *obs.* exc. *Hist.* E16. 2 The practice of gossiping; small talk, gossip. E19. b A body of gossips. M19.

gossoon /gɒˈsuːn/ *n.* Chiefly *Anglo-Ir.* L17. [(O)Fr. *garçon* boy.] A youth, a boy; a servant-boy.

gossypol /ˈgɒsɪpɒl/ *n.* L19. [f. mod.L *Gossypium* genus name of the cotton-plant, f. L *gossypinum*, *-pion* cotton-plant (ult. origin unkn.): see -OL.] *Chem.* A toxic crystalline phenolic compound, $C_{30}H_{30}O_8$, present in cottonseed oil.

got /gɒt/ *ppl a.* L16. [pa. pple of GET *v.* Cf. GOTTEN *ppl a.*] 1 = GOTTEN *ppl a.* 1. Now *rare.* L16. 2 *got-up*, artificially produced or adorned to impress or deceive. E19.

got *v.* pa. t. & pple: see GET *v.*

gotcha /ˈgɒtʃə/ *v. perf. non-standard.* Also **gotcher**. M20. [Repr. a pronunc.] (I) have got you (see GET *v.* 37).

gote /gəʊt/ *n.* Chiefly *north.* LME. [f. *got-* wk base of OE *ġēotan* pour; cf. MLG, MDu. *gote* (Du. *goot*) of similar meaning. See GOUT *n.*[3]] 1 A watercourse; a channel for water; a stream. LME. 2 A sluice. LME.

Goth /gɒθ/ *n.* [OE *Gota*, usu. in pl. *Gotan*, superseded in ME by adoption of late L *Gothi* pl. = Gk *Gothoi*, *Gotthoi* pl. f. base of Goth. *Gutþiuda* the Gothic people.] 1 A member of a Germanic tribe which invaded the Eastern and Western Empires between the 3rd and the 5th cents. and founded kingdoms in Italy, France, and Spain. OE. 2 A person who behaves like a barbarian, esp. in the destruction or neglect of works of art; a rude, uncivilized, or ignorant person. Cf. VANDAL. M17. b = GOTHICIST. M19. 3 (A performer or fan of a) style of rock music derived from punk, characterized by mystical lyrics and associated with a sombre style of punk dress; a person dressed in this style. L20.

Gothish *a.* resembling something Gothic, looking like a Goth; barbarous: E17. **Gothism** *n.* barbarism, bad taste E18.

Gotham /ˈgɒθəm, ˈgəʊθəm, -t-/ *n.* LME. [English place-name.] 1 The name of a village proverbial for the folly of its inhabitants. LME. 2 New York City. *US colloq.* E19.

1 **wise man of Gotham** a fool.

¶Allusion to Gotham in Nottinghamshire is not certain.

Gothamite *n.* (*a*) a simpleton; (*b*) *US colloq.* a New-Yorker: L16.

Gothic /ˈgɒθɪk/ *a.* & *n.* Also **g-**, (*pseudo-arch.*) **-ck**. L16. [Fr. *gothique* or late L *Gothicus*, f. *Gothi*; see GOTH, -IC.] A *adj.* 1 Of or pertaining to the Goths or their language. L16. b = MOZARABIC. M19. 2†a = GERMANIC *a.*[1] 2. M17–M19. b Designating the style of handwriting used in Western Europe from the 13th cent. and the typefaces derived from it, such as Fraktur and, formerly, black letter. M17. 3 Designating the style of architecture prevalent in western Europe from the 12th to the 16th cent., of which familiar features include the pointed arch and the flying buttress; (of a building, an architectural detail, ornamentation, etc.) in this style. Also, of the Gothic revival (see below). M17. 4 Belonging to or (supposedly) characteristic of the Middle Ages; medieval, romantic. Orig. & freq. *derog.*, redolent of the Dark Ages, portentously gloomy or horrifying. L17. 5 Barbarous, crude, uncouth. *arch.* E18. 6 Of or pertaining to the rock music of Goths. L20.

3 M. ROBERTS The attic floor of a decaying gothic mansion in North Oxford. 4 W. COWPER Tedious years of Gothic darkness. R. BARBER The ideals of chivalry . . flourish best in a gothic and romantic climate. *Nature* A large sunken arena, with gothick grottos around the edges. 5 J. T. HEWLETT Dinner . . at the gothic hour of one o'clock.

Special collocations: **Gothic novel**: of a style popular in the 18th and 19th cents., with a complex plot characterized by supernatural or horrifying events. *Gothic revival*: see REVIVAL 1c.

B *n.* 1 Gothic architecture, or ornamentation; Gothic style in literature etc. Also (*rare*), a Gothic building. M17. 2 *Typogr.* Gothic type. Also (*US*), sanserif, grotesque. L17. 3 The East Germanic language of the Goths. M18.

1 *collegiate Gothic*: see COLLEGIATE *a.* *Victorian Gothic*: see VICTORIAN *a.*[2] 3 CRIMEAN *Gothic.*

gothically *adv.* M19. †**gothicly** *adv.*: only in L18. **gothicness** *n.* M19.

Gothicise *v.* var. of GOTHICIZE.

Gothicism /ˈgɒθɪsɪz(ə)m/ *n.* E18. [f. GOTHIC + -ISM.] 1 Barbarism, crudity; absence of polish or taste; an instance of this. *arch.* E18. 2 Conformity or devotion to the Gothic style, esp. of architecture. M18.

Gothicist *n.* a person who uses or is familiar with the Gothic style, esp. in architecture M19.

Gothicize /ˈgɒθɪsʌɪz/ *v.* Also **-ise** M18. [f. GOTHIC + -IZE.] †1 *v.i.* Indulge one's taste for something Gothic. *rare.* Only in M18. 2 *v.t.* a Give an architecturally Gothic character to. L18. b Give a medieval look or character to; make Gothic (GOTHIC *a.* 4). E19.

Gothick *a.* & *n.* see GOTHIC.

Gothonic /gɒˈθɒnɪk/ *a.* & *n.* Now *rare.* E20. [f. L *Gothones* Goths + -IC.] A *adj.* Of or belonging to the primitive Germanic stock. E20. B *n.* The common language of this stock. E20.

gotra /ˈgəʊtrə/ *n.* L19. [Skt *gotra.*] Amongst Hindus of brahmin caste, any of the group of families supposedly descended from the seven mythical sages.

gotta /ˈgɒtə/ *v. perf. colloq.* E20. [Repr. a pronunc.] = *has* or *have got to* s.v. GET *v.* 38b.

gotten /ˈgɒt(ə)n/ *ppl a.* LME. [pa. pple of GET *v.*: see -EN[6]. Cf. GOT *ppl a.*] 1 Acquired, obtained, won, esp. in a specified manner. Now *rare* exc. in *ill-gotten.* LME. †2 Begotten. LME–M17.

gotten *v.* pa. pple: see GET *v.*

Götterdämmerung /ˈgœtərˌdɛmərʊŋ; gɒtəˈdamərʊŋ, gəːt-, -ˈdɛm-/ *n.* E20. [G, lit. 'twilight of the gods', (esp. as title of opera by Wagner).] In Germanic mythology, the twilight of the gods; *gen.* a cataclysmic downfall of a régime, institution, etc. Cf. RAGNAROK.

gouache /guˈɑːʃ, *foreign* gwaʃ/ *n.* L19. [Fr., f. It. *guazzo.*] A method of opaque watercolour painting, in which the pigments are bound by a glue to form a sort of paste; a painting executed in this way; the pigments thus used.

Gouda /ˈgaʊdə/ *n.* M19. [A town in the Netherlands.] In full *Gouda cheese.* A flat round cheese orig. made at Gouda.

Goudy /ˈgaʊdi/ *n.* & *a.* M20. [F. W. *Goudy* (1865–1947), US typographer.] (Designating) any of a number of typefaces introduced by Goudy.

gouge /gaʊdʒ, guːdʒ/ *n.* LME. [(O)Fr. f. late L *gubia, gulbia,* perh. of Celt. origin (cf. OIr. *gulba* beak, Welsh *gylf* sharp-pointed instrument, beak).] 1 A chisel with a concave blade for cutting rounded grooves or holes. Also, a surgical chisel for removing portions of bone. LME. b *Bookbinding.* A tool for impressing a curved line or segment of a circle on the leather; such a marking itself. L19. 2 An act of gouging; a groove or mark made by gouging. M19. 3 A swindle. *US colloq.* L19.

Comb.: **gouge-bit** a bit shaped at the end like a gouge.

gouge /gaʊdʒ, guːdʒ/ *v.* L16. [f. the n.] 1 *v.t.* Cut or make holes in with or as with a gouge. L16. b *v.i.* Work with a gouge. M19. 2 *v.t.* Cut, hollow, scoop, or force (*out*) with or as with a gouge. E17. 3 *v.t.* & *i.* Force out the eye of (a person); force out (a person's eye). L18. 4 *v.t.* & *i.* Cheat, steal, impose upon. *N. Amer. colloq.* M19. 5 *v.i.* In opal-mining, make an exploratory search to locate worthless material; dig for opal generally. *Austral.* M20.

2 P. P. READ The torrent . . had gouged out the earth from the bank.

gouger *n.* L18.

goujon /ˈguːdʒ(ə)n, *in sense 2 foreign* guʒɔ̃ (*pl. same*)/ *n.* L19. [Fr., f. as GUDGEON *n.*[2]] 1 The flathead catfish, *Pylodictis olivaris. US.* L19. 2 *Cookery.* In *pl.* Narrow, deep-fried, strips of fish, esp. sole, or of chicken. M20.

Goulard /guˈlɑːd/ *n. obs.* exc. *Hist.* E19. [Thomas *Goulard* (1720–90), Fr. surgeon.] A solution of lead acetate used as a lotion in cases of inflammation. Also *Goulard lotion, water,* etc.

goulash /ˈguːlaʃ/ *n.* M19. [Hungarian *gulyás(hús),* f. *gulyás* herdsman + *hús* meat.] 1 A stew or ragout of meat and vegetables highly seasoned. M19. 2 *Bridge.* A fresh deal of unshuffled cards, usu. three or more at a time, after the hands have been thrown in without bidding. E20.

goum /guːm/ *n.* Also **G-**. M19. [Fr. f. Arab. *ḳūm* dial. var. of *ḳawm* tribe, troop.] 1 A group of N. African tribesmen; a contingent of N. African soldiers (in French service). M19. 2 Such a tribesman or soldier. M19.

†**gound** *n.* OE–L17. [OE *gund* = Goth. *gund,* OHG *gunt.*] Foul matter, pus, *esp.* that secreted in the eye.

¶ Survived in BARNGUN.

gour *n.* var. of GAUR.

goura /ˈgʊərə/ *n.*[1] M19. [Name in New Guinea.] = *crowned pigeon* s.v. CROWNED 5.

goura *n.*[2] var. of GORAH.

gourami /gʊ(ə)ˈrɑːmi, ˈgʊərəmi/ *n.* L19. [Malay *gurami.*] A large perciform freshwater food fish, *Osphronemus goramy* (family Osphronemidae), native to SE Asia. Also, any of various fishes belonging to related families, often kept as aquarium fish.

kissing gourami: see KISSING *ppl a.*

gourbi /ˈgʊəbi/ *n.* M18. [Algerian Arab. *gurbī* (straw) hut.] In N. Africa, a hovel or hut.

gourd /gʊəd, gɔːd/ *n.* ME. [AN *gurde,* (O)Fr. *gourde,* repr. ult. L *cucurbita.*] 1 The fleshy, often large fruit of any of various trailing or climbing plants of the family Cucurbitaceae; *spec.* (also *bottle-gourd*) that of *Lagenaria siceraria,* native to the Old World tropics. Also, any of certain similar fruit from unrelated plants. ME. b The plant producing such a fruit. LME. 2 The dried, empty rind of such a fruit, used as a bottle, float, etc. Formerly also, a bottle or vessel of any kind. ME. b A gourdful. M18. 3 *Her.* A charge representing such a fruit. E16. 4 The head. Freq. in *out of one's gourd* crazy. *US slang.* M19.

Phrases etc.: *bitter-gourd*: see BITTER *a.* & *adv. bottle gourd*: see sense 1 above *out of one's gourd*: see sense 4 above. *snake-gourd*: see SNAKE *n. sour gourd*: see SOUR *a.*

gourdful *n.* as much as a gourd will hold M19.

†**gourdy** *a.* M16. [OFr. *gourdi* swollen, pa. pple of *gourdir* swell (mod. *s'engourdir* grow numb).] 1 Swollen with stuffing. Only in M16. 2 *Vet. Med.* (Of a horse's legs) swollen; (of a horse) with swollen legs. E18–E19.

†**gourdiness** *n.* E18–E19.

gourmand /ˈgʊəmənd, ˈgɔː-; *foreign* gurmɑ̃ (*pl. same*)/ *n.* & *a.* Occas. fem. **-mande** /-mɑːnd; *foreign* gurmɑ̃ːd (*pl. same*)/. LME. [(O)Fr., of unkn. origin.] A *n.* 1 A person who is overfond of eating; a glutton. LME. 2 A person who is fond of, or a judge of, good food; a gourmet. M18. B *adj.* Gluttonous, greedy; fond of eating. M16.

gourmandism *n.* E19.

gourmandise *n., v.* var. of GORMANDIZE *n., v.*

gourmet /ˈgʊəmeɪ, ˈgɔː-, *foreign* gurmɛ (*pl. same*)/ *n.* & *a.* E19. [Fr., formerly = wine-merchant's assistant, wine-taster, infl. in sense by GOURMAND.] A *n.* A connoisseur in eating and drinking; a judge of good food. E19. B *attrib.* or as *adj.* Of the nature of a gourmet; of a kind or standard suitable for gourmets. E20.

gousty /ˈgaʊsti/ *a. Sc.* & *north.* E16. [Origin unkn.] Large and empty or hollow; dreary, desolate; (of a sound) hollow.

gout /gaʊt/ *n.*[1] ME. [OFr. *gote, goute* (mod. *goutte*) or med.L *gutta* lit. 'drop' (w. ref. to the medieval theory of a flowing down of bodily humours).] 1 A disease in which defective metabolism of uric acid characteristically causes arthritis, esp. in the smaller bones of the feet, deposition of chalk-stones, and episodes of acute pain. Also (*arch.*), a painful attack of this disease. ME. †2 A disease of hawks or other birds, *esp.* a swelling on the feet. L15–E17. 3 Infestation and destruction of wheat etc. by the larva of a dipteran fly, *Chlorops pumilionis,* which causes swollen stems. E19.

1 SPENSER Eke in foote and hand A grievous gout tormented him full sore. H. ALLEN A round of high living at Paris . . was not calculated to help the gout. G. HEYER Thin fingers . . twisted by gout.

Comb.: **gout-fly** the fly whose larva causes gout in wheat (see sense 3 above); **goutweed** ground elder, *Aegopodium podagraria* (formerly used to treat gout).

gout /gaʊt/ *n.*[2] LME. [OFr. *gote* (mod. *goutte*) f. L *gutta.*] Orig., a drop, esp. of blood or (*Sc.*) medicine. Now usu. a splash, streak (of blood or other fluid, smoke, flame, etc.).

DAY LEWIS Fuchsia bushes which splash its white wall with blood-red gouts. CLIVE JAMES The huge machine . . belching gouts of flame from the exhausts.

gout /gaʊt/ *n.*[3] *obs.* exc. *dial.* L16. [Prob. aphet. f. Fr. *égout* sewer.] A water channel; a sluice; a covered drain or culvert. Cf. GOTE.

gout /gaʊt/ *v.i.* & *t.* L19. [f. GOUT *n.*[2]] Spurt, pour.

S. HASSEL The hail of bullets throws him backwards. . . Gouting blood he slides down from the tank. *fig.*: M. AYRTON My fears returned, first gouting in my belly and then dribbling . . to my brain.

goût /guː/ *n.* Also ***gout***. L16. [Fr., earlier *goust* f. L *gustus* taste. Cf. GUST *n.*[1], GUSTO.] 1 Liking, relish, fondness (*for*). L16. 2 The ability to perceive and discriminate between flavours, smells, etc.; the faculty of aesthetic appreciation or judgement; (good) taste. E18. 3 Style or manner; *esp.* a prevailing or fashionable style. E18. 4 Flavour, savour, taste. M18.

1 A. BURN Relished a dish of fine-flavoured tea with as high a goût as . . any man ever did. 2 H. FIELDING This last opera . . is too light for my goût. 3 *Times* Dubious furniture in the goût *Rothschild.*

goûter /guːte/ *n.* Pl. pronounced same. L18. [Fr., f. *goûter* to taste.] A light afternoon meal; five-o'clock tea.

†**goutify** *v.t.* M18–M19. [f. GOUT *n.*[1] + -I- + -FY.] Make gouty; afflict with gout.

goutish /ˈgaʊtɪʃ/ *a.* LME. [f. GOUT *n.*[1] + -ISH[1].] 1 Of a person: somewhat gouty, predisposed to gout. LME. 2 Of, pertaining to, or of the nature of gout. E18.

goutte /guːt/ *n.* LME. [Fr. Cf. GUTTÉ.] *Her.* A charge shaped like a drop of liquid.

gouty /ˈgaʊti/ *a.* LME. [f. GOUT *n.*[1] + -Y[1].] 1 Affected by or subject to gout. LME. 2 Swollen or bulging; out of shape, ill-proportioned; distorted, esp. with swellings. L16. b Full of knots or knobs. *obs.* exc. *dial.* L16. 3 Of, pertaining to, or resembling, gout. E17. b Used during an attack of gout. *obs.* exc. *Hist.* M18. c (Supposedly) predisposing to gout. E19. 4 Of land: boggy. *obs.* exc. *Sc.* & *dial.* L17.

1 M. IGNATIEFF Nursing a gouty foot. 2 **gouty-stem** *Austral.* the Australian baobab, *Adansonia gregorii.* 3 S. RICHARDSON The torture of a gouty paroxysm. b HOR. WALPOLE Wheeled into the room in gouty chairs. c T. BEDDOES The weaker wines of France are reputed more gouty than those in common use among the English.

goutily *adv.* M19. **goutiness** *n.* M17.

gouvernante /guːvəˈnɒnt, *foreign* guvɛrnɑ̃t/ *n.* Now *rare* or *obs.* Pl. pronounced same. Also (earlier) Anglicized as †**governante**. L16. [Fr., use as n. of fem. pres. ppl a. of *gouverner* GOVERN.] 1 A female governor or ruler. L16. 2 A chaperon; a governess, a female teacher. M17. 3 A housekeeper (usu. to a single man). M17.

gove /gəʊv/ *v.i. Sc.* ME. [Origin unkn.] Gaze, stare (esp. stupidly).

govern /ˈgʌv(ə)n/ *v.* ME. [OFr. *governer* (mod. *gouverner*) f. L *gubernare* steer, direct, rule f. Gk *kubernan* steer.] 1 *v.t.* & *i.* Rule with authority, conduct the policy, actions, and affairs of (a State, subjects), constitutionally or despotically; regulate the proceedings of (a corporation etc.); be in military command of (a fort, town). ME. b Direct and control, have under protective guardianship. Now *rare* or *obs.* ME. 2 *v.t.* Control, influence, regulate, or determine (a person, another's action, the course or issue of events). ME. †b Guide, direct, lead (*in* some course, *to* or *towards* an object). LME–M18. †c Master, prevail over. *rare* (Shakes.). Only in L16. 3 *v.t.* Conduct (oneself) in a particular way; restrain, curb, bridle (oneself, one's feelings). ME. 4 *v.i.* Hold sway; have or be the predominating or decisive influence. LME. †5 *v.t.* Administer, manage (an undertaking, an establishment, etc.). LME–M18. †6 *v.t.* Attend to, look after (a person), esp. with reference to health; tend (a plant). LME–L17. †7 Work or manage (a ship, the sails, the helm). LME–L17. 8 *v.t.* Regulate the working of, manage, manipulate, operate, control (an implement, machine, etc.). LME. 9 *v.t. Gram.* Esp. of a verb or preposition: have (a noun, pronoun, etc., or a case) depending on it; require a dependent word to be in (a certain case). LME. 10 *v.t.* Constitute a law, rule, standard, or principle for; serve to decide (a legal case). E19.

1 J. A. FROUDE The country had been governed by a succession of ecclesiastical ministers. C. KINGSLEY When God has to govern a nation because it cannot govern itself. M. PATTISON The throne was occupied by a minor.. whose mother.. governed as regent. **governing body** the body of managers of a hospital, school, etc. 2 STEELE Ordinary Minds are wholly governed by their Eyes and Ears. R. NIEBUHR He is governed far more by imagination than by reason. G. VIDAL We.. govern our days by clocks and watches. b R. CORBET A straying starr.. governd those wise-men to Christ. c SHAKES. *Ven. & Ad.* She.. govern'd him in strength, though not in lust. 3 BURKE I have no doubt of the principles on which you govern yourself. DICKENS I appeal to you to govern your temper. 4 E. POUND The same laws govern, and you are bound by no others. 5 EVELYN My Lord Sandwich.. always govern'd his affaires with successe. 6 I. WALTON His pensions.. were given to a woman that governed him. 8 *Which Micro?* If you have two joysticks.. you can set them both to govern different controls. 10 W. CRUISE The case of Peacock v. Spooner having been decided by the House of Lords, must govern this case. Y. WINTERS We assume that constant principles govern the poetic experience.

governable /ˈgʌv(ə)nəb(ə)l/ *a.* M17. [f. prec. + -ABLE.] Able to be governed, amenable to being governed.

governaˈbility *n.* L19. **governableness** *n.* L18. **governably** *adv.* M19.

†**governail** *n.* ME. [OFr. (mod. *gouvernail*) f. L *gubernaculum*, pl. *-la* rudder, f. *gubernare* GOVERN.] 1 A ship's rudder. Also, steering. ME–M16. 2 Government, authority. Also, a person who governs; the community governed. LME–L16. b Behaviour, self-control. LME–L16. c Management; treatment. L15–L16.

governance /ˈgʌv(ə)nəns/ *n.* ME. [OFr. (mod. *gouvernance*) f. *governer* GOVERN: see -ANCE.] 1 The action, manner, or fact of governing; government. ME. b Controlling or regulating influence; control, mastery. LME. †c The state of being governed; good order. LME–L16. 2 The function or power of governing; authority to govern. LME. †b A governing person or body. M16–M17. †3 Conduct of life or business; behaviour. LME–M17.

1 BROWNING I have submitted wholly.. to your rule and governance. b P. GAY Bentham saw man as an animal under the governance of the pleasure principle. c SPENSER Whose countries he.. shortly brought to civile governaunce. 2 J. PAYNE The king invested him with the governance of one of the provinces. 3 W. LAMBARDE Men.. learned in the Lawe and of good gouernance.

†**governante** *n.* see GOUVERNANTE.

governess /ˈgʌv(ə)nɪs/ *n.* Also †**governeress**. LME. [OFr. *governeresse* fem. of *governëo(u)r*: see GOVERNOR, -ESS[1].] 1 A female governor or ruler. Formerly also, a presiding goddess or tutelary. Now *rare* or *obs.* LME. 2 A female teacher, usu. of children in a private household. Formerly also, a woman in charge of a (young) person. LME. 3 The wife of a Governor. Now only *joc.* L17.

Comb.: **governess cart** (*Hist.*) a light two-wheeled tub-shaped cart with a rear entrance and side seats face-to-face.

governessy *a.* having the characteristics of a governess; *esp.* prim: L19.

governess /ˈgʌv(ə)nɪs/ *v.* E19. [f. the n.] 1 *v.i.* Work as a governess (GOVERNESS *n.* 2). E19. 2 *v.t.* Act as governess to; teach. M19.

1 M. R. MITFORD Sixteen years of governessing.. tamed that romantic imagination. 2 C. M. YONGE She has been governessed and crammed till she is half sick of all reading.

government /ˈgʌv(ə)nm(ə)nt, -vəm(ə)nt/ *n.* & *a.* LME. [OFr. *governement* (mod. *gouvernement*), f. as GOVERN: see -MENT.] A *n.* 1 The action of governing; continuous exercise of authority over subjects; authoritative direction or regulation; control; chiefly *spec.* the action of governing the affairs of a State; political rule and administration. LME. b Guidance (in action). *arch.* E18. †2 The manner in which a person's action is governed; demeanour; conduct. LME–M17. 3 The function of governing; authority to govern. LME. †b An appointment as governor. E17–E19. 4 The (freq. specified) system by which a nation, community, etc., is governed. LME. 5 The fact that a particular person governs. M16. b (Freq. **G-**.) Period of governing, tenure of office. E17. 6 *Hist.* The area ruled over by a governor; a subdivision of a kingdom or empire (esp. in France or Russia). E17. 7 (Freq. **G-**.) The governing power in a State; the body or successive bodies of people governing a State; the State as an agent; an administration, a ministry. E18. b In *pl.* Government securities. L19. 8 *Gram.* The influence of one word over another in determining the case of a noun, the mood of a verb, etc. M18.

1 J. BENTHAM The business of government is to promote the happiness of the society by punishing and rewarding. TENNYSON They [horses].. felt Her low firm voice and tender government. b L. MURRAY Examples.. which may serve as some government to the scholar. 3 SPENSER The first.. Of all the house had charge and governement, As Guardian and Steward. 4 T. GRAY Three sorts of government, Despotism, the limited Monarchy, and the Republican. G. BANCROFT Government, in early times, was very imperfectly organized. *civil government, coalition government, constitutional government, local government, military government, republican government*, etc. 5 W. ROBERTSON The government of a Queen was unknown in Scotland. b MARVELL God.. bless your Majesty with a long and happy Government. 6 C. WHITWORTH In 1710, the Czar.. divided the Empire into eight governments. 7 SOUTHEY Government are acting like themselves. W. S. CHURCHILL The Government advise the House, and the House decides. **form a government** (of a Prime Minister etc.) establish an administration esp. after a general election.

Comb.: **government house**, **Government House** the official residence of a governor; **government man** (*a*) *Austral. Hist.* a convict; (*b*) a government official; **Government paper**, **securities** bonds or other promissory certificates issued by a government; **government stroke** *Austral.* (*a*) *Hist.* a convict's work rate; (*b*) *slang* lazy or leisurely work rate; **government surplus** unwanted equipment sold by the government through retailers (freq. *government-surplus* attrib.).

B *attrib.* or as *adj.* Of or pertaining to government esp. of a State. L18.

govern'mental *a.* of or pertaining to a government, esp. of a State: M18. **govern'mentally** *adv.* L19.

governmentese /gʌv(ə)nmənˈtiːz/ *n.* M20. [f. GOVERNMENT + -ESE.] Long-winded or obscure language held to be characteristic of government departments.

governor /ˈgʌv(ə)nə/ *n.* ME. [AN *governour*, OFr. *governëo(u)r* (mod. *gouverneur*) f. L *gubernator*, f. *gubernare*: see GOVERN, -OR.] †1 A steersman, pilot, or captain of a ship. ME–E17. 2 A person who governs or exercises authoritative control over subjects etc.; a ruler. ME. 3 (Freq. **G-**.) An official appointed to govern a province, country, town, etc.; a representative of the Crown in a Commonwealth country or colony that regards the British monarch as head of State; the executive head of each State of the US. ME. b The officer commanding a fortress or garrison. M17. †4 The commander of a company, esp. an armed force. ME–E17. 5 The head, or one of the governing body, of an institution, establishment, etc.; *spec.* the official in charge of a prison. LME. †6 A person in charge of a young man's education; a tutor. M16–L18. 7 *colloq.* Cf. GUV, GUVNER. a An employer. E19. b One's father. E19. c As *voc.*: Sir; Mister. M19. 8 An automatic regulator of the supply of fuel, steam, water, etc., to a machine, ensuring uniform motion or limiting speed. E19. 9 *Angling.* A type of fly. M19.

2 SHAKES. *Merch. V.* Her gentle spirit Commits itself to yours to be directed, As from her lord, her governor, her king. R. CUDWORTH The Deity.. which is the supreme Governour of all things. 5 W. HOLTBY Carne alone among the governors had opposed her appointment to the High School. 6 J. LOCKE The great Work of a Governour is to.. form the Mind. 7a DICKENS Tell your governor that Blathers.. is here. b C. BEDE The bills will come in some day.. but the governor will see to them. c DICKENS 'My youngest died last week'. 'I'm sorry for it, governor, with all my heart.' 8 *Which?* Nearly all diesel engines have a 'governor' which prevents the engine being revved too fast.

governorate *n.* the residence or office of a governor; the area ruled by a governor: L19. **governorship** *n.* (the exercise or tenure of) the office of governor M17.

governor-general /gʌv(ə)nəˈdʒɛn(ə)r(ə)l/ *n.* L16. [f. prec. + GENERAL *a.*] A governor having authority over deputy- or lieutenant-governors.

governor-generalship *n.* the (term of) office of a governor-general M19.

gowan /ˈgaʊən/ *n. Sc.* & *north.* M16. [Prob. alt. of GOLLAN.] A yellow or white field flower; *spec.* a daisy.

gowany *a.* covered with gowans E18.

gowk /gaʊk/ *n.* & *v.* Orig. & chiefly *Sc.* & *north.* ME. [ON *gaukr* = OE *ġēac*, OFris., OS *gāk*, OHG *gouh* (G *Gauch* cuckoo, fool) f. Gmc, of imit. origin.] A *n.* 1 A cuckoo. ME. 2 A fool; a halfwitted or awkward person. L16.

2 L. G. GIBBON He would stand staring like a gowk for minutes on end.

B *v.i.* Stare foolishly. L15.

gowl /gaʊl/ *v.* & *n.* Chiefly *Sc.* & *north.* ME. [ON *gaula*, perh. from a base meaning 'to bark', but cf. YOWL *v.*] A *v.i.* Of a person, animal, the wind: howl, yell, cry. ME. B *n.* A howl or yell. E16.

gown /gaʊn/ *n.* & *v.* ME. [OFr. *goune*, *gon(n)e* f. late L *gunna* fur garment (cf. Byzantine Gk *gouna* fur, fur-lined garment).] A *n.* 1 A loose flowing outer robe indicating the wearer's office, profession, or status, esp. as worn by a lawyer, alderman, or judge, or by a member of the clergy or of a university, college, or school. ME. b The office, profession, or status denoted by the wearing of a gown; *collect.* the members or holders of this. E17. c *spec.* (*collect.*) The resident members of a university. Now chiefly in *town and gown*, non-members and members of a university in a particular place. M17. 2 Orig., a long loose upper garment for everyday wear by men or women. Now, a woman's (long, formal, or elegant) dress. LME. b *ellipt.* A nightgown; a dressing-gown. L16. 3 A Roman toga, or similar garment. LME. 4 A protective garment worn in a hospital by a staff member during surgery, or (more fully *hospital gown*) by a patient. E20.

1 SHAKES. *Twel. N.* Put on this gown and this beard; make him believe thou art.. the curate. W. M. PRAED A scholar, in my cap and gown. b DRYDEN The Cut-throat Sword and clamorous Gown. J. POTTER I have now taken the gown [holy orders]. c C. BEDE When Gown was absent, Town was miserable. 2 A. LURIE No mini-dresses.. it was all long gowns of chiffon, lace and watered satin. *blue gown*: see BLUE *a. dressing-gown, nightgown*, etc. b DEFOE I came down.. in my gown and slippers. 3 R. GRAVES His patrician's gown was disgracefully stained.

Comb.: **gownsman**, †**gownman**, a person who wears a gown, esp. as an indication of status, office, or profession; a member of the legal profession, a clergyman, a member of a university.

B *v.* 1 *v.t.* Attire in a gown. Freq. as *gowned* pa. pple or ppl a. LME. 2 *v.i.* Put on a gown. Chiefly in *gown up*, put on a protective overall, esp. in an operating theatre. L19.

1 A. LEVY Gorgeously gowned and bejewelled women.

gowpen /ˈgaʊp(ə)n/ *n. Sc.* & *north.* ME. [ON *gaupn* (Norw. dial. *gaupn*, Sw. *göpen*, etc.) = OHG *coufana* (MHG *goufen*). Cf. YEPSEN.] 1 The two hands held together to form a bowl; as much as they can hold, a double handful. ME. 2 *Law.* A perquisite of grain or flour allowed to a miller's servant. *obs.* exc. *Hist.* M18.

gowpenful *n.* as much as can be held in both hands cupped together L17.

goy /gɔɪ/ *n.* Pl. **goyim** /ˈgɔɪɪm/, **goys**. M19. [Heb. *gōy* people, nation, pl. *gōyīm*.] Among Jews: a non-Jew, a Gentile.

goyˈish *a.* M20.

Goyaesque /gɔɪəˈɛsk/ *a.* Also **Goyesque** /gɔɪˈɛsk/. M20. [f. *Goya* (see below) + -ESQUE.] Of, pertaining to, or characteristic of the Spanish painter Francisco de Goya y Lucientes (1746–1828) or his work.

goyal /ˈgɔɪəl/ *n. dial.* Also (earlier) **goyle**. E17. [Origin unkn.] A deep gully, a ravine.

Goyesque *a.* var. of GOYAESQUE.

goyim *n.pl.* see GOY.

goyle *n.* var. of GOYAL.

gozzard *n.* var. of GOOSEHERD.

gra /grɑː/ *n. Anglo-Ir.* Long *rare*. E18. [Ir. *a ghráidh* my dear.] Freq. as form of address: dear. Also, affection, love.

Graafian /ˈgrɑːfɪən/ *a.* M19. [f. R. de *Graaf* (1641–73), Du. anatomist + -IAN.] Anat. *Graafian follicle, vesicle*, any of the small sacs in the mammalian ovary in which ova are matured.

†**graal** *n.* var. of GRAIL *n.*[2]

grab /grab/ *n.*[1] L17. [Arab. *ġurāb* light galley.] A large coasting-vessel, built with a prow and usually two-masted, formerly in use in the waters around the Indian subcontinent.

grab /grab/ *n.*[2] L18. [f. GRAB *v.*] **1** Something which is grabbed. *Sc.* L18. **2** A quick sudden clutch or grasp; an attempt to seize. E19. **b** The action or practice of grabbing; *esp.* rapacious proceedings in business or commerce. L19. **3** A person who grabs; *spec.* a body-snatcher, a bailiff, a police officer. Now *rare* or *obs.* E19. **4** A mechanical device or implement for clutching or gripping (and usu. also lifting) objects. M19. **5** A children's card-game resembling snap in which cards of equal value may be snatched from the table. L19.

2 DE QUINCEY The chairman . . made a grab at it. **b up for grabs** *slang* open to offer; easily obtainable; inviting capture. 4 PETERSEN GRAB.

Comb.: **grab-bag** *N. Amer.* a lucky dip; **grab handle, rail**, a handle, rail, to steady passengers in a moving vehicle; **grab-hook** a hook used for gripping or clutching; *grab rail*: see *grab handle* above.

grab /grab/ *v.* Infl. **-bb-**. L16. [MLG, MDu. *grabben*, perh. f. modification of the base of GRIP *v.*[1], GRIPE *v.*[1], GROPE *v.*] **1** *v.t.* Grasp or seize suddenly and eagerly; snatch up; appropriate rapaciously or unscrupulously; *colloq.* obtain. L16. **2** *v.t.* Capture or arrest (a person). E19. **b** Attract the attention of, make an impression on. *slang*. M20. **3** *v.i.* Make a sudden snatch *at, for*. M19. **4** *v.i.* Of the brakes of a motor vehicle: act harshly or jerkily. E20.

1 W. WHARTON He grabs my shovel and pushes me aside. G. BOYCOTT A situation where batsmen . . must grab every opportunity to score a run. D. LODGE I'll grab another sherry while there's still time. **grab hold of** seize. *smash-and-grab*: see SMASH *v.*[1] 2 H. NISBET A very dangerous young criminal . . whom I reckon we won't be able to grab in a hurry. **b** *Grimsby Evening Telegraph* Hoping that the book will grab so many people that something will eventually be done.

grabbable *a.* E19.

grabber /ˈgrabə/ *n.* M19. [f. GRAB *v.* + -ER[1].] A person who or thing which grabs.

land-grabber: see LAND *n.*[1]

grabble /ˈgrab(ə)l/ *v.* & *n.* L16. [Prob. f. Du., LG *grabbeln* scramble for a thing, frequent. of *grabben*: see GRAB *v.*, -LE[3].] **A** *v.* **1** *v.i.* Feel or search with the hands, grope about. L16. **b** *v.t.* Feel (one's way). E17. †**2** *v.t.* Handle rudely or roughly. L17–L18. **3** *v.i.* Sprawl or tumble about; scramble (for money etc.). M18. **4** *v.t.* Seize, appropriate. L18. **b** *v.i.* Grab *at* (something). M19. **5** *v.i.* Grapple *with*. *rare*. M19. **B** *n.* **1** A grapple or struggle. *rare*. L16. **2** A device to catch or grab. Chiefly in *fish on the grabble* fish with a line held down by a plummet so that the hook-link is in the water. E18.

grabby /ˈgrabi/ *n. slang*. M19. [Origin unkn.] A foot-soldier.

grabby /ˈgrabi/ *a. colloq.* E20. [f. GRAB *v.* + -Y[1].] Having a tendency to grab; greedy, grasping; arresting.

J. H. VANCE Nice when they don't steal my copra. Some people are pretty grabby. *Oxford Mail* A grabby front page headline.

graben /ˈgrɑːb(ə)n/ *n.* Pl. **-s**, same. L19. [G., orig. = ditch.] *Geol.* A depression in the earth's surface between faults, a rift valley.

grace /greɪs/ *n.* ME. [OFr. (mod. *grâce*) f. L *gratia*, f. *gratus* pleasing: cf. GRATEFUL.] **I 1** The quality of pleasing, attractiveness, charm, *esp.* that associated with elegant proportions or ease and refinement of movement, action, expression, or manner. ME. **b** Seemliness, becomingness; favourable or creditable aspect. Freq. w. specifying wd, as in (*with*) *a good, bad, ill*, etc., *grace* below. L16. **2** An attractive or pleasing quality or feature; an agreeable accomplishment. Freq. in *pl.* ME. **b** Something that imparts beauty; an ornament; the part in which the beauty of a thing consists. Long *rare*. L16. **c** A mode of behaviour, attitude, etc., adopted with a view to elegance or refinement. *obs.* exc. in *airs and graces* below. E17. **3** *Class. Mythol.* (**G-**.) Each of the three beautiful sister-goddesses, Aglaia, Thalia, and Euphrosyne, regarded as the bestowers of beauty and charm. L16. **4** *Mus.* In full *grace-note*. An additional note (often printed smaller than the others) introduced as an embellishment not essential to the harmony or the melody of a piece. M17. **5** In *pl.* with *the* (treated as *sing.*). A game in which a player holds a hoop on a pair of slender rods and by drawing one rod rapidly across the other impels the hoop into the air. Long *rare*. M19.

1 STEELE It gives new Grace to the most eminent Accomplishments. G. ORWELL In spite of the bulkiness of his body there was a remarkable grace in his movements. **b** H. MARTINEAU As soon as she could with any grace leave the company. 2 SMOLLETT Possess'd of ev'ry manly grace. JOHN BROOKE George I lacked the graces and never became an English gentleman. P. G. WODEHOUSE A fellow lacking in the softer social graces. **b** DRYDEN A spreading laurel stood, The grace and ornament of all the wood. 3 TENNYSON The Muses and the Graces, group'd in threes. *transf.*: A. S. BYATT Attendant nymphs and graces. 4 *transf.*: J. BRAINE The extra refinement, the grace-note, was Jack's waving away of my offer to buy the drinks.

II 6 Favour; favourable or kindly regard or its manifestation (now only on the part of a superior); unconstrained good will as a ground of concession. ME. **7** An instance or manifestation of favour; a favour conferred on or offered to another. Also (*obs.* exc. *Hist.*), an exceptional favour granted by someone in authority, a privilege, a dispensation. ME. †**b** Permission to do something, leave. Only in ME. †**8** The share of favour allotted to one by Providence; fate, destiny; luck, fortune. Freq. w. specifying wd. ME–L16. **9** *Theol.* **a** The free and unmerited favour of God as manifested in the salvation of sinners and the bestowing of blessings. ME. **b** The divine regenerating, inspiriting, and strengthening influence. Freq. w. specifying wd. ME. **c** An individual virtue or excellence, divine in origin; a divinely given talent etc. ME. **d** The condition of a person under such divine influence. LME. **10** †**a** In a thing: beneficent virtue or efficacy. ME–E17. **b** In a person: virtue; an individual virtue; a sense of duty and propriety. M16. **11** Mercy, clemency; pardon, forgiveness. *arch.* ME. **12 a** A royal or noble personage, designated in the complimentary periphrasis *his, her, my lord's, the king's*, etc., *grace*. *arch.* ME. **b** Now usu. **G-**. The designation of a duke, duchess, or archbishop, used as a form of address. Formerly also, the designation of a king or queen. E16. **13** The condition or fact of being favoured. Now only in (*a person's*) *good graces*: below. LME. **14** Orig., a dispensation from some of the statutory conditions required by a university for a degree. Now, permission to take a university degree; a dispensation from the University statutes; at Cambridge University, a decree of the Senate or Regent House. LME. **15** Favour shown by granting a delay in the performance of an action, or the discharge of a duty, or immunity from penalty during a specified period. E18.

6 SIR W. SCOTT The marks of grace which Elizabeth . . shewed to young Raleigh. B. EMECHETA But for God's grace he would have been a dead person by now. 7 DRYDEN But, to return and view the chearful skies, . . To few great Jupiter imparts this Grace. TENNYSON Do me this grace my child, to have my shield In keeping. 8 SIR T. MORE Elizabeth, whose fortune and grace was after to bee Quene. **9a** S. PURCHAS Holding that they are saved by Merit, without Law or Grace. **b** SHAKES. *1 Hen. VI* Chosen from above By inspiration of celestial grace. WORDSWORTH Blest Is he who can, by help of grace, enthrone The peace of God within his single breast! **c** E. WHITE A general acknowledgement of worldly virtues as Christian graces. **d** W. LITHGOW The flying from evil, is a flying to grace. **10a** SHAKES. *Rom. & Jul.* Mickle is the powerful grace that lies In plants. **b** SIR W. SCOTT He blushes again, which is a sign of grace. 11 MILTON To bow and sue for grace With suppliant knee. 15 J. P. HOPPS Your long day of grace is gone. M. CORELLI I give you a day's grace to decide.

III †**16** In *pl.* Thanks, thanksgiving. ME–M16. **17** (Orig. chiefly *pl.*, treated as *sing.*, now only *sing.*) A short prayer uttered as a thanksgiving before or after eating. ME.

16 LD BERNERS I . . gyue great graces to my goddes of my good happe. 17 TINDALE *Matt.* 26:30 When they had sayd grace they went out. DAY LEWIS Family prayers and grace before meals were taken for granted.

Phrases: **act of grace** (*a*) a privilege or concession that cannot be claimed as a right; (*b*) (*Act of Grace*) a formal pardon, esp. a free and general pardon, granted by Act of Parliament. *actual grace*: see ACTUAL *a.* 1. **airs and graces** behaviour displaying an affected elegance of manner designed to attract or impress. **be in one's good graces** have one's favour, liking, and sympathy. **by the grace of God** through God's favour, *esp.* [tr. L *Dei gratia*] appended to the formal statement of a monarch's title, and formerly to that of some ecclesiastical dignitaries. *Covenant of Grace*: see COVENANT *n.* **days of grace** the period of time allowed by law for the payment of a bill of exchange or an insurance premium after it falls due. †**do (a person) grace** reflect credit on, embellish, do honour *to*. *effectual grace*: see EFFECTUAL *a.* **efficacious grace** *RC Ch.* a divine influence which inspires its recipient to effect some good act. *expectative grace*: see EXPECTATIVE *a.* **fall from grace** lapse from a state of grace into sin; *loosely* lapse from good behaviour into disgrace. *free grace*: see FREE *a.* **grace-and-favour** *a.* designating a house or other residence occupied by permission of the British monarch, the British Government, or other owner. *grace expectative*: see EXPECTATIVE *a. herb-grace, herb of grace*: see HERB *n.* **have the grace to** be sufficiently conscious of duty or decency to. *means of grace*: see MEAN *n.*[1] *prevenient grace*: see PREVENIENT *a.* 1. *saving grace*: see SAVING *ppl a.* **state of grace** the condition of a person who is generally subject to the divine regenerating, inspiriting, and strengthening influence. **sufficient grace** *RC Ch.* a divine influence which renders its recipient capable of some good act. *take etc. heart of grace*: see HEART *n. Throne of Grace*: see THRONE *n.* **with a bad, an ill, grace** with a display of unwillingness, reluctantly and ungraciously. **with a good grace** with a show of willingness, pleasantly and readily. **year of grace** *arch.* a year as reckoned from the birth of Jesus.

Comb.: **grace-cup** a cup of wine etc. passed round after grace has been said; the last drink before going to bed, a parting drink; *grace-note*: see sense 4 above; **grace-wife** (long *obs.* exc. *dial.*) a midwife.

gracy *a.* (long *obs.* exc. *Sc. rare*) full of grace, devout M17.

grace /greɪs/ *v.t.* ME. [Partly (in sense 1) f. OFr. *gracier* thank, partly f. GRACE *n.*] †**1** Thank. Usu. in *pass.* Only in ME. †**2** Show favour or be gracious to; countenance. L15–E17. **3** Lend or add grace to; adorn, embellish, set off; enhance *with*. L16. **b** *Mus.* Embellish with grace-notes or similar detail. E17. **4** Confer honour or dignity on, honour *with* a title or dignity. Also, do honour or credit to. L16. †**b** W. compl.: name or designate honourably. *rare* (Milton). Only in M17. †**5** Give pleasure to, gratify, delight. L16–E18. **6** Address by the courtesy title of 'your grace'. Long *rare* or *obs.* E17. **7** Endow with divine grace. Long *rare*. M17.

graced /greɪst/ *ppl a.* L16. [f. GRACE *n.* or *v.*: see -ED[1], -ED[2].] Endowed with grace; favoured; having a grace or graces; embellished.

SHAKES. *Rich. II* After a well-grac'd actor leaves the stage.

graceful /ˈgreɪsfʊl, -f(ə)l/ *a.* LME. [f. GRACE *n.* + -FUL.] †**1** Full of divine grace; (of a person) holy. LME–E17. 2 Orig. pleasant, possessed of pleasing and attractive qualities. Now chiefly (of form, movement, expression, or action) elegant; (of actions, esp. acts of courtesy, etc.) aptly timed, well chosen, happy. LME. †3 Conferring grace or honour. Only in L16. †4 Of a person: possessed of graces of character, virtuous. E17–E18. 5 Favourable, friendly. *rare* (Shakes.). Only in E17.

1 SHAKES. *Wint. T.* You have a holy father, A graceful gentleman. 2 P. GAY His gift for graceful exposition. H. BASCOM The plane glides and sails .. in a graceful descent.

gracefully *adv.* L16. **gracefulness** *n.* L16.

graceless /ˈɡreɪslɪs/ *a.* LME. [f. GRACE *n.* + -LESS.] 1 Not in a state of grace, unregenerate; depraved, wicked, ungodly, impious. Also, unseemly, uncouth, improper. Now chiefly *arch.* or *joc.* LME. †2 Lacking favour. LME–L16. †3 Merciless, unfeeling, cruel, pitiless. LME–M17. 4 Lacking charm or elegance. M17.

4 C. P. SNOW A big, broad-shouldered woman, .. physically graceless apart from her smile. J. LE CARRÉ The graceless tower .. posturing against the racing clouds.

Special collocations: **graceless florin** a florin, minted in 1849, from which the words 'Dei gratia' were omitted.

gracelessly *adv.* LME. **gracelessness** *n.* L16.

gracile /ˈɡrasɪl, ˈɡrasʌɪl/ *a.* E17. [L *gracilis*.] Slender, thin, lean. Now also, gracefully slender.

graˈcility *n.* (*a*) slenderness; (*b*) unornamented simplicity of literary style: E17.

gracilis /ˈɡrasɪlɪs/ *n.* E17. [L, see prec.] *Anat.* A superficial muscle on the medial side of the thigh, passing from the hip-bone to the tibia. Also *gracilis muscle*.

graciosity /ɡreɪʃɪˈɒsɪti, ɡreɪs-/ *n.* L15. [Fr. *gracieuseté* or late L *gratiositas*, f. *gratiosus*: see GRACIOUS, -ITY.] The quality or state of being gracious; graciousness.

gracioso /ɡreɪʃɪˈəʊzəʊ/ *n.* Pl. **-os**. M17. [Sp. = GRACIOUS *a.*] †1 A court favourite. M–L17. 2 In Spanish comedy, a buffoon. M18.

gracious /ˈɡreɪʃəs/ *a.* & *int.* ME. [OFr. (mod. *gracieux*) f. L *gratiosus*, f. *gratia*: see GRACE *n.*, -OUS.] A *adj.* 1 Of a character likely to find favour; agreeable, pleasing. *arch.* or *poet.* ME. †b Endowed with grace or charm of appearance; graceful, elegant. LME–M17. 2 Characterized by or exhibiting kindness or courtesy; kindly, courteous. *poet.* ME. 3 Of exalted people: kind, indulgent, and beneficent to inferiors (freq. also *joc.* or *iron.*); *esp.* and orig., as a polite epithet of royal persons, their actions, etc. ME. 4 Of God etc.: disposed to show or dispense grace, merciful, benignant. ME. 5 Characterized by or inspired by divine grace; godly, righteous, regenerate. Long *arch. rare.* ME. †6 Enjoying favour; in good standing, acceptable, popular. Also (of an action), winning favour or goodwill. LME–E19. 7 Happy, fortunate, prosperous. Long *obs.* exc. *Sc.* LME. †8 Given as an indulgence or a mercy. Only in E18.

1 HOR. WALPOLE The body .. was found almost entire, and emitted a gracious perfume. M. ARNOLD How gracious is the mountain at this hour! b EVELYN His person is not very gracious, the small-pox having put out one of his eyes. 2 TENNYSON Sir Lancelot .. Was gracious to all ladies. 3 SWIFT When I am fixed anywhere .. I may be so gracious to let you know. G. B. SHAW Your most gracious majesty's desire To see some further triumphs. P. ROTH A warm and gracious letter from the famous writer. 5 BUNYAN All the holy and truly gracious Souls that are with him on the Mount Zion. 6 J. RAY Which renders persons gracious and acceptable in the eyes of others. 7 SHAKES. *Wint. T.* Go; fresh horses. And gracious be the issue!

Special collocations: **gracious living** an elegant style of life distinguished by a particular observance of standards of propriety and comfort.

B *int.* (Orig. *ellipt.* for *gracious God!*). Expr. surprise, dismay, or indignation. Freq. as *good gracious!, gracious me!* E18.

graciously *adv.* ME. **graciousness** *n.* LME.

grackle /ˈɡrak(ə)l/ *n.* L18. [mod.L *Gracula* (see below) f. L *graculus* jackdaw.] Any of various New World orioles belonging to the genus *Quiscalus* and related genera, esp. *Q. quiscula* with glossy purplish-black plumage. Also, any of various Asian mynahs of the genus *Gracula*.

grad /ɡrad/ *n.*[1] L19. [Abbrev.] A graduate. Also, an undergraduate. Cf. UNDERGRAD, POSTGRAD.

grad /ɡrad/ *n.*[2] E20. [f. GRADE *n.*] = GRADE *n.* 1b.

grad /ɡrad/ *n.*[3] E20. [Abbrev.] *Math.* = GRADIENT *n.* 2b.

gradal /ˈɡreɪd(ə)l/ *a. rare.* L19. [f. L *gradus* degree + -AL[1].] Of or pertaining to degree.

gradate /ɡrəˈdeɪt/ *v.* M18. [Back-form. f. GRADATION.] 1 *v.t.* & *i.* (Cause to) pass by imperceptible degrees from one shade of colour to another. M18. 2 *v.t.* Arrange in steps or grades. Usu. in *pass.* M19.

1 J. RUSKIN Take the two extreme tints and carefully gradate the one into the other.

gradatim /ɡrəˈdeɪtɪm/ *adv.* Now *rare* or *obs.* L16. [L, f. *gradus* step.] Step by step, gradually.

gradation /ɡrəˈdeɪʃ(ə)n/ *n.* M16. [L *gradatio(n-)*, f. *gradus* step: see GRADE *v.*, -ATION.] 1 A series of successive conditions, qualities, events, or (formerly) locations, forming stages in a process or course. M16. b *Rhet.* = CLIMAX *n.* 1. M16. 2 In *pl.* Stages of transition, advance, development, or (formerly) gradual movement. L16. †3 *Alch.* = EXALTATION 4. E17–E18. 4 In *pl.* Degrees of rank, merit, intensity, etc., constituting a series between two extremes. E17. †b *sing.* Position in a scale, relative rank. E17–E19. 5 A scale or series of degrees of rank, merit, intensity, or divergence from a standard; arrangement in such a scale. L17. †6 In *pl.* Steps, tiers; anything resembling these. L17–E19. 7 *spec.* A gradual passing from one colour, shade, or tone, to another. E18. 8 The action of arranging in a series of grades. M19. 9 *Philol.* = ABLAUT. Also *vowel gradation.* L19.

1 C. CIBBER One continual gradation of political errors. 4 L. MACNEICE Gradations of puddles and pools for the young seals, who do not take easily to swimming. 7 QUILLER-COUCH Their leaves .. knew no gradations of red and yellow, but turned at a stroke to brown.

gradational *a.* pertaining to or characterized by gradation M19. **gradationally** *adv.* M19.

gradatory /ˈɡreɪdət(ə)ri/ *n.* L17. [med.L *gradatorium* flight of steps, f. *gradatio(n-)*: see GRADATION, -ORY[1].] A flight of steps, *esp.* those leading from the cloisters to the choir of a church.

gradatory /ˈɡreɪdət(ə)ri, ɡrəˈdeɪt(ə)ri/ *a. rare.* L18. [f. GRADATION + -ORY[2].] Proceeding by steps or gradations.

grade /ɡreɪd/ *n.* E16. [Fr., or L *gradus* step.] 1 *Math.* †a A unit of angular measurement, the ninetieth part of a right angle; a degree. Only in 16. b In the centesimal system: a hundredth part of a right angle. E19. 2 A crossbred animal; *spec.* (one of) a variety produced by crossing native stock with a superior breed. Freq. *attrib.* L18. 3 A step or stage in a process. L18. 4 A degree in rank, proficiency, quality, intensity, or value. E19. b *Philol.* The position in an ablaut series occupied by a particular form. L19. c A mark (usu. alphabetical) indicating an assessment of the year's work, examination papers, etc., of a student. L19. 5 A class of persons or things of a similar degree of ability, rank, or quality. E19. b A class or form in a school, usu. numbered from first up to twelfth according to age. *N. Amer.* M19. c *Zool.* A group of species held to represent a similar level of development or organization. L19. 6 The rate of ascent or descent of a slope; the gradient. Chiefly *N. Amer.* E19. b A slope, an ascent or descent on a railway, road, etc. E19. c A length of (made or improved) road, esp. in a hilly district. *US.* M19. 7 Of a surface: a degree of altitude, a level. M19. 8 *Physical Geogr.* The condition or profile of a river in which there is a state of equilibrium between river-bed erosion and sedimentation. E20.

2 *attrib.*: C. WILSON Grade animals .. can be made .. as productive as thorough-breds. 4 F. C. SELOUS The ore was of such low grade that it would not pay to work it. R. V. JONES A promotion of only one grade, to Principal Scientific Officer. b *low grade, strong grade, weak grade, zero grade*, etc. c S. BRILL His grades were not terribly good, but he managed to get into .. Law School. 5 J. GATHORNE-HARDY There seem to have been five grades of patient in the class-conscious thirties. b *Scientific American* The study .. involved 4,500 schoolgirls between the fifth and the 12th grade. 6 G. A. SHEEHAN A .. long hill with a fairly steep grade. b J. DOS PASSOS The train began going fast down long grades.

Phrases: **at grade** (*a*) *US* on the same level; (*b*) *Physical Geogr.* (of a river) at equilibrium between erosion and sedimentation. **grade** (also **Grade**) **A** of the highest grade or quality; (*colloq.*) excellent, first-rate; hence **grade B, C**, etc., lower grades. *grade of comparison*: see COMPARISON 4. **make the grade** *colloq.* reach the proper standard, be successful. **on the up** (or **down**) **grade** ascending (or descending); *fig.* getting better (or worse).

Comb.: **grade cricket** *Austral.* club cricket with teams competing in various grades; **grade-crossing** *US* a place where a road and a railway, or two railways, cross each other at the same level; **grade line** a prescribed or notional line to which a road or railway is built; **grade school** *US* = *elementary school* (b) s.v. ELEMENTARY *a.*

grade /ɡreɪd/ *v.* M16. [f. (as) the n.] †1 *v.t.* Admit to a (specified) university degree. Only in M16. †2 *v.t.* Lay out (a map etc.) by degrees of latitude and longitude. Only in E17. 3 *v.t.* Arrange or categorize according to quality, merit, rank, intensity, etc. M17. 4 *v.t.* Reduce (the line of a road, railway, etc.) to levels or practicable gradients. E19. 5 *v.t.* Erode the surface of so as to produce or alter a slope. M19. 6 *v.i.* Be of good or specified quality; reach a required or expected standard. L19. 7 *v.t.* Blend with other things so as to affect the grade or quality. L19. 8 *v.t.* Cross (cattle, etc.) with some better breed. Foll. by *up*: improve (stock) by so doing. L19. 9 *v.t.* & *i.* (Cause to) shade or pass gradually (*up, down*) from one grade into another. L19. 10 *v.t. Philol.* In *pass.*: be altered by gradation or ablaut. L19. 11 *v.t.* Give a grade to (a student, his or her work). M20.

3 S. BELLOW Neuroses might be graded by the inability to tolerate ambiguous situations. 6 **grade up with** *US* be equal or comparable to, measure up to. 8 F. FRANCIS Turning in a good bull and grading up your stock. 9 V. NABOKOV That silky shimmer above her temple grading into bright brown hair. 11 *American Poetry Review* If anyone will tell me how to grade creative writing, I'll be grateful.

grader *n.* a person who or a machine which grades; *spec.* a wheeled machine for levelling the ground in road-making: M19.

gradeability /ɡreɪdəˈbɪlɪti/ *n.* M20. [f. GRADE *n.* + -ABILITY.] The ability of a vehicle to climb a gradient at an efficient speed.

graded /ˈɡreɪdɪd/ *ppl a.* M19. [f. GRADE *n.*, *v.*: see -ED[1].] 1 Formed like a flight of steps. Now chiefly *fig.*, proceeding by degrees, graduated. M19. 2 Divided or arranged according to grades of rank or quality. M19. 3 Of a road etc.: levelled or reduced to easy gradients. M19. 4 Of livestock: improved by crossing with superior stock. L19. 5 *Physical Geogr.* Of a river: that has attained grade (GRADE *n.* 8). L19.

2 **graded school** = *grade school* s.v. GRADE *n.*

gradely /ˈɡreɪdli/ *a.* & *adv.* Now *dial.* ME. [ON *greiðligr*, f. *greiðr* GRAITH *a.* & *adv.*: see -LY[1].] A *adj.* 1 Excellent, noble; fine, suitable. ME. 2 Decent, respectable, worthy. M18. 3 Real, proper. M19. 4 Healthy, well. M19. B *adv.* †1 Promptly, readily, willingly. ME–L15. 2 Exactly, carefully, properly; quite, really, well. ME.

Gradgrind /ˈɡradɡrʌɪnd/ *n.* M19. [Thomas *Gradgrind*, character in Charles Dickens's novel *Hard Times*.] A person resembling Gradgrind; a person lacking warm feelings and interested only in facts.

Gradgrindery *n.* E20.

gradience /ˈɡreɪdɪəns/ *n.* M20. [f. GRADIENT *n.*: see -ENCE.] *Ling.* (An instance of) the property of being continuously variable between two values or categories.

gradient /ˈɡreɪdɪənt, -djənt/ *n.* M19. [Prob. f. GRADE *n.* after *salient*.] 1 The degree of slope of a road, railway, etc.; amount of inclination to the horizontal. M19. b An inclined part of a road etc.; a slope. M19. 2 An increase or decrease in the magnitude of a property, e.g. temperature, pressure, concentration, etc., observed in passing from one point to another; the rate of such a change. L19. **b** *Math.* The vector formed by the operator ∇ (see DEL) acting on a scalar function at a given point in a scalar field. E20. **3** *Math.* The degree of steepness of a graph at any point. Hence, the first derivative of a function (cf. DERIVATIVE *n.* 3). L19.

1 F. HOYLE Slopes with gradients up to about 18°. b D. M. THOMAS They were soon crawling up the steep gradient—their train pushed by two engines. 2 R. F. CHAPMAN Water passes directly from the midgut to the hindgut along an osmotic gradient. T. PYNCHON A gradient of . . 50° between the wind at their backs and the warmth in front. 3 A. BARTON A line whose gradient is zero is parallel to the *x*-axis.

Comb.: **gradient post**: beside a railway line, indicating a change of gradient; **gradient wind** *Meteorol.* a (hypothetical) wind having the direction of the geostrophic wind but with calculated speed allowing for centrifugal effects arising from the curved path of the wind.

gradient /ˈɡreɪdɪənt, -djənt/ *a.* M17. [L *gradientem* pres. pple of *gradi* proceed, walk, f. *gradus* step: see -ENT.] Of an animal: adapted for walking, ambulant; *Her.* in a walking attitude.

gradine /ɡrəˈdiːn/ *n.* Also **gradin** /ˈɡreɪdɪn/. M19. [It. *gradino* dim. of *grado* step.] **1** Each of a series of low steps or seats raised one above the other. M19. **2** A shelf or ledge at the back of an altar. L19.

gradiometer /ɡreɪdɪˈɒmɪtə/ *n.* L19. [f. GRADIENT *n.* + -OMETER.] **1** Any of various surveying instruments used for setting out or measuring the gradient of a slope. L19. **2** An instrument for measuring the gradient of a field, esp. the horizontal gradient of the earth's gravitational or magnetic field. E20.

gradual /ˈɡradʒʊəl/ *n.* LME. [med.L *graduale* use as n. of neut. of *gradualis*: see next, and cf. GRAIL[1].] **1** A service book containing various sung parts of the Mass. LME. **2** An antiphon sung between the Epistle and the Gospel at the Eucharist. M16.

gradual /ˈɡradʒʊəl/ *a.* & *adv.* LME. [med.L *gradualis*, f. *gradus* step: see -AL[1].] **A** *adj.* †**1** Having or arranged in degrees; graduated. LME–M18. †**2** Of or pertaining to degree. M17–E18. **3** Taking place by degrees, slowly progressive; (of a slope) gentle, not steep or abrupt. M17. **b** Tapering, gently sloping; moving or changing slowly. *poet.* M18.

3 KEATS Isabel By gradual decay from beauty fell. b E. B. BROWNING Back to the gradual banks and vernal bowers.

Special collocations: **gradual psalms** Psalms 120–34 (f. the title of each, rendered *Song of Degrees* (AV), *of Ascents* (RV)).

B *adv.* Little by little, by degrees. *poet.* M18.

G. WHITE The distant view, That gradual fades till sunk in misty blue.

graduˈality *n.* the quality or condition of being gradual M17. **gradually** *adv.* M17. **gradualness** *n.* M19.

gradualism /ˈɡradʒʊəlɪz(ə)m/ *n.* M19. [f. prec. + -ISM.] The principle or method of gradual as opp. to immediate or abrupt change, esp. in politics; belief in gradual change.

gradualist (*a*) *n.* a person who believes in or advocates gradualism; *Biol.* a person who views evolution as a process of continuous gradual change; (*b*) *adj.* of or pertaining to gradualists or gradualism: M19. **graduaˈlistic** *a.* E20.

graduand /ˈɡradʒʊand, -dj-, -ənd/ *n.* Chiefly *Sc.* & *Canad.* L19. [med.L *graduandus* gerundive of *graduare* GRADUATE *v.*: see -AND.] A person about to receive a degree or other academic qualification.

graduate /ˈɡradʒʊət, -djʊət/ *n.* & *a.* LME. [med.L *graduatus* pa. pple (used as n.) of *graduari* GRADUATE *v.*: see -ATE[1], -ATE[2].] **A** *n.* **1** A person holding a degree or other academic qualification; *N. Amer.* a person who has completed a course at high school; a former student *of* a place of learning; *loosely*, one who has successfully completed any course of education or training. LME. **2** An experienced or proficient person in any art or occupation. Now *rare.* L16. **3** A graduated vessel, *esp.* a chemist's measuring-glass. L19.

1 P. NORMAN She was no recent learner, no stumbling graduate from beginners' bars, but someone to whom movement on skates was inborn. 2 T. WALL A graduate in ungraciousness.

B *adj.* **1** That has graduated; having a university degree. Now only *attrib.* LME. **2** Arranged by steps or degrees. Now *rare.* E17.

Comb. & *special collocations*: **graduate nurse** *US* a trained nurse; **graduate school** *N. Amer.* a department of a university for advanced work by graduate students.

graduateship *n.* (*a*) the condition of being a graduate; †(*b*) the period during which one is a graduate: M17.

graduate /ˈɡradʒʊeɪt, -djʊeɪt/ *v.* LME. [med.L *graduat-* pa. ppl stem of *graduare* take a degree, f. L *gradus* degree, step: see -ATE[3].] **I 1** *v.t.* Confer a degree, diploma, or other academic qualification on; send (a person) *from* a place of learning with an academic qualification. Usu. in *pass.* Now *US.* LME. †**2** *v.t.* Be sufficient to qualify (a person) for a degree or other distinction. E17–E19. **3** *v.i.* Take a university degree or (*N. Amer.*) high school diploma; successfully complete a course of education or training. E19. **b** *v.i.* Qualify (as); train in order to qualify. E19. **4** *v.i.* Progress to a more advanced or more extreme activity or position. E20.

1 D. ACHESON Our daughter-in-law was being graduated with honors from Bryn Mawr College. 3 J. CHEEVER Russell had graduated from the local high school and gone off to college. 4 G. GREENE I had already graduated into the position of the old friend.

II 5 *v.i.* Change gradually or step by step. LME. **6** *v.t.* Arrange in a series or according to a scale. LME. **b** Mark out in degrees or portions. L16. †**7** *v.t.* Improve the grade or quality of; *spec.* in *Alch.*, transmute to a higher grade. Only in M17.

5 D. CECIL Eight long-tailed ponies whose colour graduated from dark to pale brown.

graduator *n.* a person or thing which graduates E19.

graduated /ˈɡradʒʊeɪtɪd, -djʊ-/ *ppl a.* M17. [f. GRADUATE *v.* + -ED[1].] **1** Having successfully completed a course of education or training; qualified. M17. **2** Arranged in grades or gradations; advancing or proceeding by degrees. L17. **3** Marked with lines to indicate degrees, grades, or quantities. M18.

2 G. GORER The respondents . . choose one of a graduated series of answers—always, often, occasionally, never. 3 L. DURRELL A huge register graduated and squared.

Special collocations: **graduated filter** *Photogr.* a lens filter that increases in colour density from one edge to the opposite edge; **graduated pension**: paid on a scale related to one's previous earnings. **graduated response** = *flexible response* s.v. FLEXIBLE *a.* 4.

graduation /ɡradʒʊˈeɪʃ(ə)n, -djʊ-/ *n.* LME. [f. GRADUATE *v.* + -ATION.] **I 1** The receiving or (*US*) conferring of an academic degree, diploma, etc. Also, the ceremony of conferring degrees. LME. **II 2** The action or process of dividing into degrees or other proportionate divisions on a graduated scale. (*rare* bef. M19.) LME. **b** Each or all of the marks on a vessel, instrument, etc., which indicate degrees of a quantity; a gradation on a scale; a line of latitude or longitude on a map. Usu. in *pl.* L16. **c** The manner in which something is graduated. M17. **3** Arrangement by degrees or gradations; a gradation. L15. **b** Progression or elevation by degrees; a step in the process. M17. †**4** *Alch.* The process of tempering or refining a substance. L15–L17. †**5** The process of grading a railway etc.; a gradient. *US.* Only in M19.

gradus /ˈɡreɪdəs/ *n.* M18. [L *gradus* step(s) in *Gradus ad Parnassum* 'Step(s) to Parnassus', the title of a manual of Latin prosody. Cf. VULGUS *n.*[2]] *Hist.* A manual of classical prosody used in schools to help in writing Greek and Latin verse.

Graecise *v.* var. of GRAECIZE.

Graecism /ˈɡriːsɪz(ə)m, ˈɡrʌɪ-/ *n.* Also **Grecism** /ˈɡriːsɪz(ə)m/. L15. [Fr. *grécisme* or med.L *Graecismus*, f. *Graecus* Greek: see -ISM.] †**1** The *Graecismus*, a grammatical treatise in Latin, of the early 13th cent. Only in L15. **2** A Greek idiom, grammatical feature, etc., *esp.* one as used in some other language. L16. **3** Greek spirit, style, mode of expression, etc.; adoption or imitation of any of these. E17.

2 ADDISON Milton . . has infused a great many . . Graecisms . . into the Language of his Poem.

Graecize /ˈɡriːsʌɪz, ˈɡrʌɪ-/ *v.* Also **Grecize** /ˈɡriːsʌɪz/, **-ise.** L17. [L *Graecizare* imitate the Greeks, f. *Graecus* Greek: see -IZE.] **1** *v.t.* Give a Greek cast, character, or form to. L17. **2** *v.i.* **a** Favour the cause of the Greeks. *rare.* M19. **b** Become like the Greeks; adopt Greek expressions, idioms, modes of life, etc. L19.

Graeco- /ˈɡriːkəʊ, ˈɡrʌɪ-/ *comb. form.* Also **Greco-** /ˈɡriːkəʊ, ˈɡrɛ-/. [f. L *Graecus* GREEK *n.* + -O-.] Forming: (*a*) adjs. w. the senses 'relating to Greek settlements or states established abroad' as *Graeco-Asiatic* or 'Greek and' as *Graeco-Latin*; (*b*) adjs. and ns. w. the sense 'Greek, of Greece'.

Graecoˈmania *n.* a craze or excessive liking for Greece and things Greek E19. **Graecophil(e)** *n.* & *a.* (a person who is) friendly towards Greece or fond of Greece and things Greek L19. **Graeco-Roman** *a.* Greek and Roman; *spec.* (of a style of wrestling) like that of the Greeks and Romans, attacking only the upper part of the body: L19. **Graecotrojan** *a.* relating to the Greeks and the Trojans M17.

Graf /ɡrɑːf/ *n.* M17. [G: see GRAVE *n.*[2]] A German nobleman corresponding in rank to a European count or British earl. (Chiefly in titles.)

graff /ɡrɑːf/ *n.*[1] *arch.* LME. [OFr. *grafe*, *grefe*, (also mod.) *greffe* f. L *graphium* f. Gk *graphion*, *grapheion* stylus, f. *graphein* write.] = GRAFT *n.*[2] 1, 2.

¶ Superseded by GRAFT *n.*[2]

graff /ɡrɑːf/ *n.*[2] Long *dial.* E16. [Perh. var. of GRAFT *n.*[1]] **1** = GRAFT *n.*[1] 2. Usu. *spade('s) graff.* E16. **2** = GRAFT *n.*[1] 3. L19.

graff /ɡrɑːf/ *n.*[3] *obs.* exc. *Hist.* M17. [Prob. f. MDu. *grave* = GRAVE *n.*[1] Cf. GRAFT *n.*[1]] A trench serving as a fortification; a ditch; a moat.

graff /ɡrɑːf/ *v. arch.* LME. [f. GRAFF *n.*[1]] **1** *v.t.* = GRAFT *v.*[1] 1. LME. †**b** = GRAFT *v.*[1] 1b, 4. LME–M17. **2** *v.i.* = GRAFT *v.*[1] 4. L15. **3** *v.t.* = GRAFT *v.*[1] 3. M16.

¶ Superseded by GRAFT *v.*[1]

†**graffer** *n.* = GRAFTER *n.*[1] LME–L17.

graffiti *n.* see GRAFFITO.

graffiti /ɡrəˈfiːti/ *v.t.* L20. [f. pl. of next.] Apply graffiti to; write as graffiti.

graffito /ɡrəˈfiːtəʊ/ *n.* Pl. (freq. used as *sing.*) **-ti** /-ti/. M19. [It., f. *graffio* scratching.] **1** A drawing, writing, or scribbling on a wall etc., orig. *spec.* on an ancient wall, as at Rome and Pompeii. Usu. in *pl.* M19. **2** A method of decoration or design produced by scratching through a plaster layer to reveal a different colour below. L19.

1 J. BARNES The concrete bus-shelters were still unstained by damp or graffiti.

graffitist *n.* a person who writes graffiti M20.

graft /ɡrɑːft/ *n.*[1] Now *dial.* ME. [ON *groftr* action of digging, f. Gmc: cf. GRAVE *v.*[1], GRAFF *n.*[2] Perh. reinforced f. MDu. *graft*, f. *graven* dig. Cf. GRAFF *n.*[3]] **1** A ditch, a moat. ME. **2** The depth of earth that may be thrown up at once with a spade. Also *spade('s) graft.* E17. **3** A kind of spade for digging drains L19.

graft /ɡrɑːft/ *n.*[2] L15. [Alt. of GRAFF *n.*[1], perh. due to confusion of *-ff* and *-ft* at the end of wds.] **1** A shoot or scion inserted into a slit made in another plant or stock, from which the shoot receives sap and on which it grows. L15. †**2** A twig, shoot, or scion for use in grafting; *gen.* a branch, plant. L16–E17. **3** The place in a stock where a scion is inserted. E19. **4** The process of grafting; an instance of grafting. M19. **5** A piece of living tissue surgically transplanted to another place on the same organism, or to another organism, so that it might adhere and grow; the process of transplanting tissue for this purpose. L19.

graft /ɡrɑːft/ *n.*[3] *colloq.* M19. [Origin uncertain: perh. dial. extension of GRAFT *n.*[1] w. the sense 'digging'.] 1 Work, *esp.* hard work. M19. 2 A trade, a craft. *rare.* L19.

1 F. S. ANTHONY Twenty-six bob for a day's graft. M. DUFFY When it comes to the hard graft they're not so keen.

graft /grɑːft/ *n.*[4] *colloq.* M19. [Perh. a use of GRAFT *n.*[3] or perh. rel. to GRAFT *n.*[2] with the additional notion of 'excrescence'.] Illicit gain, esp. in connection with politics or business; the practices used to secure this, *esp.* bribery, blackmail, or the abuse of one's power or influence.

C. ACHEBE The excesses of the last regime, .. its graft, oppression and corrupt government. S. BELLOW A business agent who takes graft from him.

graft /grɑːft/ *v.*[1] L15. [Alt. of GRAFF *v.*] 1 *v.t.* Insert (a shoot or scion from one plant) as a graft into another plant. (Foll. by *in, into, on, upon, together.*) L15. b *gen.* Plant, implant. Now *rare.* M16. 2 *v.t. fig.* a Insert or fix in or on so as to produce a vital or indissoluble union. Foll. by *in, into, on, upon.* M16. b *v.t. spec.* Join together (two unfinished or broken pieces of knitting) by weaving an extra row of stitches between the pieces. M19. 3 *v.t.* Fix a graft or grafts on (a stock). Also, produce (fruit) by grafting. E17. 4 *v.i.* Insert a graft or grafts; use grafts as a method of propagation. E17. 5 *v.t. Naut.* Cover (the end of a rope, a block-stoop etc.) with a weaving of small yarns to form a decorative finish. E19. 6 *v.t.* Transplant (a piece of living tissue) surgically to another place on the same organism, or to another organism. M19.

1 P. V. PRICE The Spaniards in Mexico actually grafted European vines on to native vine stocks, as a protection against phylloxera. **grafting-clay, -wax** a composition for covering the united parts of graft and stock. 2a R. G. COLLINGWOOD That kind of collaboration in which one artist grafts his own work upon that of another. R. V. JONES The Germans seemed simply to have grafted their radar stations on to their existing Observer Corps network. 6 G. GREENE Dr Gogol grafted the hands of a guillotined murderer on to the smashed stumps of .. the great pianist.

grafter *n.*[1] †(*a*) a tree from which a shoot is taken for grafting; (*b*) a person who grafts trees etc.; (*c*) a tool for grafting: L16.

graft /grɑːft/ *v.*[2]*i. colloq.* M19. [f. GRAFT *n.*[3]] Work, *esp.* work hard.

Radio Times My father was a miner, hard-working... He grafted.

grafter *n.*[2] a person who works (hard); a steady worker: E20.

graft /grɑːft/ *v.*[3]*i. colloq.* M19. [f. GRAFT *n.*[4]] Practise graft; obtain profit or make money by shady or dishonest means.

J. FLYNT They make their living, such as it is, by grafting. U. SINCLAIR The bosses grafted off the men, and they grafted off each other.

grafter *n.*[3] a person who makes gains by shady or dishonest means; *spec.* a politician or other public figure who abuses his or her position to make dishonest gains: L19.

Graham /ˈgreɪəm/ *a.* Chiefly *N. Amer.* Also **g-**. M19. [Sylvester *Graham* (1794–1851), US advocate of dietary reform.] Designating wholewheat flour; (of bread, biscuits, etc.) made from wholewheat flour in accordance with the vegetarian principles of Graham.

Grahamism *n.* the vegetarian principles advocated by Graham M19. **Grahamite** *n.* a follower of Graham M19.

Graham's law /ˈgreɪəmz lɔː/ *n. phr.* M19. [Thomas *Graham* (1805–69), Sc. chemist.] *Chem.* A law stating that the rates of diffusion and effusion of a gas are inversely proportional to the square root of the density of the gas.

grail /greɪl/ *n.*[1] *arch.* ME. [OFr. *grael* f. med.L *gradale* for *graduale* GRADUAL *n.*] = GRADUAL *n.* 1, 2.

Grail /greɪl/ *n.*[2] Also **g-**, (earlier) †**greal**, †**graal**. ME. [OFr. *graal, grael, greel, greil* f. med.L *gradalis* dish, of unkn. origin.] More fully *Holy Grail.* In medieval legend, the cup or platter used by Christ at the Last Supper, and in which Joseph of Arimathea received Christ's blood at the Cross; this cup or platter as the object of long quests by many knights; *fig.* the (elusive) object of a long and difficult quest.

J. A. BAKER For ten years I followed the peregrine... It was a grail to me. *Sunday Times* The holy grail for the ceramics industry is the ceramic engine.

grail /greɪl/ *n.*[3] *poet.* L16. [Perh. contr. of GRAVEL *n.*] Gravel.

grail /greɪl/ *n.*[4] L17. [Fr. *grêle*, f. *grêler* make slender, taper and smooth (the teeth of a comb).] A comb-maker's file.

grain /greɪn/ *n.*[1] ME. [OFr. *grain, grein* (mod. *grain*) f. L *granum* grain, seed, exc. Branch III f. OFr. *graine* f. Proto-Romance base of pl. of L *granum.*] I Seed; corn. 1†a A single seed of a plant, *esp.* one which is small, hard and roundish. Later, the stone or pip of a fruit. ME–E19. b The fruit or seed of a cereal. LME. 2 *collect.* Wheat or the other cereal grasses; the fruit or seeds of these plants; corn. ME. b A particular kind of corn; a cereal. LME. 3 In *pl.* a In full *grains of Paradise.* The capsules of *Aframomum melegueta*, a W. African plant of the ginger family, used as a spice and in medicine. ME. b Refuse malt after brewing or distilling. E16. 4†a A berry, a grape. ME–L17. b Any of the parts of a collective fruit. *rare.* L17.

2 R. GRAVES Nor could he starve Naples out, since it was plentifully supplied with grain. *attrib.*: J. STEINBECK Fruit trees took the place of grain fields.

II *transf.* from sense 1. †5 A bead; *esp.* any of the beads on a rosary. Also, a pearl. ME–M17. 6 A small, hard, usu. roundish particle of sand, gold, salt, incense, etc. ME. b A particle of gunpowder, or of solid fuel for rockets, of a definite size. M17. c Any of the usu. small discrete particles or crystals in a rock or metal. E19. 7 The smallest unit of weight in the avoirdupois, troy, and apothecaries' systems (orig. the average weight of a grain of wheat) being $^1/_{7000}$ pound avoirdupois or (equivalently) $^1/_{5760}$ pound troy or apothecaries' (approx. 0.0648 gram). LME. 8 *fig.* The smallest possible quantity. Freq. in neg. contexts. LME.

6 DEFOE Gold-dust, Guinea grains. V. WOOLF He ground the grains of sugar against the wall of his cup. 7 J. G. FARRELL Every half hour he gave pills of calomel (half a grain), opium and capsicum (of each one-eighth of a grain). 8 H. JAMES She has treated me without a grain of spite. P. G. WODEHOUSE I have ceased to expect intelligence in a man, and I am grateful for the smallest grain.

III With ref. to dyeing. 9 *Hist.* Kermes, cochineal; the dye made from either of these. ME. 10 Dye; *esp.* a fast dye; colour, hue. Now only *poet.* ME.

10 *fig.*: J. TRUMBULL Crimes of blackest grain.

IV Texture. 11 Roughness of surface, giving an appearance of small grains or roundish particles side by side; granular appearance or texture. LME. b *Photogr.* A granular appearance in a photograph or negative. L19. 12a The longitudinal arrangement of fibres or particles in wood, flesh, paper, etc., which often form a pattern and along which such substances can more easily be cut. M16. b The lamination or plane of cleavage in coal, stone, etc. M16. 13 The rough or wrinkled surface of leather or any similar artificially-produced material. M16. b In full *grain-side.* The side of a skin on which the hair originally grew. M19. c In full *grain-leather.* Leather dressed with the grain-side outwards. M19. 14a A textured internal substance, usu. visible in a cross-section or fracture. Now *rare.* L16. b Texture; the arrangement and size of the constituent particles of any substance, esp. of flesh, wood, stone, or metal. E17. 15 *fig.* Nature, temper, quality; tendency. M17.

11b *Listener* Faster films .. suffer more from grain. 12a BETTY SMITH She brought her eyes close to the .. desk and examined the patterned grain of the wood. 14a R. HAKLUYT The graine of the bone is somewhat more yellow than the Ivorie. b J. SMEATON A large flat stone, of a close grain. DICKENS His hands .. were of a rough coarse grain. 15 GEO. ELIOT Hatred of innocent human obstacles was a form of moral stupidity not in Deronda's grain. G. S. HAIGHT Her mind was of much finer grain than her husband's.

Phrases: **against the grain** contrary to one's inclination. *dyed-in-(the-)grain*: see DYE *v.* 1. *fine grain*: see FINE *a.* *grains of Paradise*: see sense 3 above. **in grain** fast-dyed; *fig.* thorough, genuine, by nature, downright; indelible, ingrained. *take with a grain of salt*: see SALT *n.*[1]

Comb.: **grain colour** (*a*) scarlet dye; (*b*) a fast colour; a cloth dyed with this; **grain-cradle** = CRADLE *n.* 7; **grain-elevator** = ELEVATOR 2, 2b; **grain-gold** †(*a*) gold dust; (*b*) gold formed into grains by heat; *grain-leather*: see sense 13c above; *grain-side*: see sense 13b above; **grain whisky**: made mainly from unmalted barley and maize or rye; cf. *malt whisky* s.v. MALT *n.*[1] & *a.*

grainless *a.* without a grain or grains L19.

grain /greɪn/ *n.*[2] In sense 4b also **grane**. ME. [ON *grein* division, distinction, branch (Sw., Da. *gren*), of unkn. origin.] 1 In *pl.* The fork of the body, the lower limbs. *obs.* exc. *dial.* ME. 2a A fork in a river valley; a valley branching out from another. *obs.* exc. *Sc.* & *dial.* ME. b An arm of the sea; a branch of a stream. *obs.* exc. *Sc.* LME. †3 An edge, a blade. Only in ME. 4 Each of the prongs of a fork. *obs.* exc. *dial.* & *Sc.* L15. b Freq. in *pl.* (treated as *sing.*). A fish-spear or harpoon with more than one prong. L18. 5 A tree branch or bough; the fork between two boughs. *obs.* exc. *dial.* & *Sc.* E16.

grain *n.*[3] see GRAINE.

grain /greɪn/ *v.*[1] LME. [f. GRAIN *n.*[1]] 1 *v.i.* Yield grain; (of corn) form grains. Long *rare.* LME. b *v.t.* Feed with grain. *US.* M19. 2 *v.t.* Dye in grain. M16. 3 *v.t. Tanning.* Remove the hair from (a skin); soften and raise the grain of (leather etc.). M16. 4 *v.t.* & *i.* (Cause to) deposit or form grains of any substance. L17. 5 *v.t.* Paint in imitation of the grain of wood or marble. L18. 6 *v.t.* Give a granular surface to. L19.

grainer *n.* a person who or thing which grains; *spec.* a vat or device for graining leather: E19. **grainering** *n.* the preparation of hides with a grainer M19.

grain /greɪn/ *v.*[2]*t. rare.* M17. [f. GRAIN *n.*[2]] †1 *refl.* Branch, divide. Only in M17. 2 Spear (fish) with a grains. L19.

grainage *n.* var. of GRANAGE.

graine /greɪn/ *n.* Also **grain.** M19. [Fr.] The eggs (formerly, an egg) of the silkworm.

grained /greɪnd/ *a.*[1] LME. [f. GRAIN *v.*[1] + -ED[1]] 1 Dyed in grain. LME. 2 Of leather: without hair; softened, raised. E18. 3 Painted to imitate the grain of wood or marble. L18. 4 Of sugar etc.: formed into grains. E19.

grained /greɪnd/ *a.*[2] LME. [f. GRAIN *n.*[1] + -ED[2].] 1 Of wood, stone, leather, flesh, etc.: having a grain, or a granular structure or texture. LME. 2 Having grains, seeds, or particles. *obs.* exc. in *large-grained, small-grained*, etc. E17.

1 R. C. HUTCHINSON Features which testified to his actual age—the grained skin, the crevices about the eyes. *coarse-grained, fine-grained*, etc.

grained /greɪnd/ *ppl a.*[3] *obs.* exc. *dial.* E16. [f. GRAIN *n.*[2] + -ED[2].] Having prongs or grains. Also *two-grained, three-grained.*

graining /ˈgreɪnɪŋ/ *vbl n.* LME. [f. GRAIN *v.*[1] + -ING[1].] 1 The action of GRAIN *v.*[1]; the result of this action. LME. 2 A ring of grooves round the edge of a coin, or (formerly) of other similar marks in relief; milling. M17.

grainy /ˈgreɪni/ *a.* LME. [f. GRAIN *n.*[1] + -Y[1].] 1 Resembling grain in composition, texture, appearance, etc.; granular. LME. b Of a voice or other sound: rough, gritty. M20. 2 Full of grain or corn. M18.

1 A. TYLER Little old grainy newspaper picture, heap of grey dots nobody'll recognize. R. CARVER He smoothed his fingers over the grainy wood. M. DRABBLE Lady Henrietta's grey, diminutive, pinched, grainy features.

graininess *n.* E20.

graip /greɪp/ *n. Sc.* & *north.* LME. [ON *greip* corresp. to OE *grāp* grasp.] A three- or four-pronged fork used as a dung-fork or for digging.

graith /greɪθ/ *n.* Now only *Sc.* & *dial.* ME. [ON *greiði* wk masc., cogn. w. OE *ġerǣde* str. neut., = trappings, equipage, f. Gmc bases of Y-, READY *a.* Cf. GEAR.] †1 A state of preparation, readiness. Only in ME. 2 Personal equipment; attire, apparel. ME. b Armour. LME. c Harness; the harness and tackle of a plough. M16. 3 Possessions; wealth. ME. 4 Apparatus, gear, tackle; a structure, a contrivance. LME. 5

Material, stuff (for a particular purpose); *spec.* (*Sc.*) soapy water. LME.

†graith *a.* & *adv.* ME. [ON *greiðr* = OE *gerǣde* ready, f. as prec. Cf. GRADELY.] A *adj.* 1 Ready. ME–L15. 2 (Of a road) direct; (of a measure) exact; (of a sign, truth, etc.) clear, plain. Only in ME. B *adv.* Readily; clearly, plainly. Only in ME.

graith /greɪθ/ *v. obs.* exc. *Sc.* & *dial.* ME. [ON *greiða*, f. *greiðr* ready: see prec.] 1 *v.t.* Make ready, prepare. Also, procure. ME. †b *refl.* Prepare oneself, get ready. ME–M17. 2 *v.t.* Equip, furnish; array; fit out. ME. †3 *v.t.* Make up, compose; constitute; set *up*. Only in ME.

graithing *vbl n.* (*a*) the action of the vb; (*b*) furniture, attire: ME.

grallatorial /graləˈtɔːrɪəl/ *a.* M19. [f. mod.L *grallatorius*, f. L *grallator* walker on stilts, f. L *grallae* stilts: see -ATOR, -IAL.] *Ornith.* Belonging or pertaining to the group of long-legged wading birds (formerly comprising the order Grallatores).

gralloch /ˈgralək/ *n.* & *v.* Also **-ck**. M19. [Gael. *grealach* entrails.] A *n.* 1 The viscera of a dead deer. M19. 2 An act of gralloching. L19. B *v.t.* Disembowel (a deer etc.). M19.

gram /gram/ *n.*[1] E18. [Port. *grão*, †*gram* f. L *granum* GRAIN *n.*[1]] (The seed or fruit of) any of several kinds of pulse grown esp. in the Indian subcontinent and other parts of Asia, *spec.*: (*a*) (in full *Bengal gram*) the chick-pea, *Cicer arietinum*; (*b*) (in full *black gram*) *Vigna mungo*, which has small black or green seeds; (*c*) (in full *green gram*) *Vigna radiata*, which has small green or golden seeds. Cf. MUNG *n.*[1]

gram /gram/ *n.*[2] Also **gramme**. L18. [Fr. *gramme* f. late L *gramma* small weight f. Gk.] A unit of mass or (*loosely*) weight in the metric system, orig. defined as the mass of a cubic centimetre of pure water at the maximum density, now defined as a thousandth part of a kilogram.

Comb. & *phrases*: **gram-atom** the quantity of a chemical element whose mass in grams numerically equals its atomic weight; **gram-force** a unit of force (or weight) equal to the weight of a mass of one gram under standard gravity; **gram-equivalent** (*Chem.*) the equivalent of an element expressed in grams (see EQUIVALENT *n.* 3); **gram-molecule** the quantity of a chemical compound whose mass in grams numerically equals its molecular or formula weight; **gram-weight** = *gram-force* above; *fluid gram*: see FLUID *a.*

gram /gram/ *n.*[3] *colloq.* L19. [Abbrev.] 1 = TELEGRAM. L19. 2 = GRAMOPHONE. M20.

Gram /gram/ *n.*[4] L19. [H. C. J. *Gram* (1853–1938), Da. physician.] 1 Used *attrib.* and in *possess.* to designate a method of staining bacteria first employed by Gram, and the iodine solution used in this method. L19. 2 *Gram-positive, -negative*, adjs., (of bacteria) stained, not stained, by Gram's method (a test used as a broad initial classification of bacteria). E20.

-gram /gram/ *suff.* [Repr. Gk *gramma, -atos* thing written, letter of the alphabet, f. *graphein* write.] Forming ns. w. the sense 'a thing written', as *chronogram, ideogram*; *esp.* w. the sense 'a (written) message', as *telegram, cablegram*, whence in recent use in the names of special types of humorous greetings message sent through commercial agencies and delivered by their representatives, as *kissogram*.

grama /ˈgramə/ *n.*[1] Also **gramma**. E19. [Sp. = grass.] Any of various low grasses of the genus *Bouteloua* of the western US. Also *grama grass*.

grama /ˈgrɑːmə/ *n.*[2] E19. [Skt *grāma*.] Either of two octave scales in Indian music consisting of an ascending series of seven notes.

gramarye /ˈgraməri/ *n.* Long *arch.* ME. [AN *gramarie* = OFr. *gramaire* GRAMMAR: cf. Fr. *grimoire* book of magic, earlier †*gramoire* (dial. var. of *grammaire*) †Latin grammar.] †1 Grammar; learning. ME–L15. 2 Occult learning; magic, necromancy. L15.

gramash /grəˈmaʃ/ *n. Sc.* Now *rare* or *obs.* L17. [Var. of GAMASH.] = GAMASH.

gramdan /ˈgrɑːmdɑːn/ *n.* M20. [f. Skt *grāma* village + *dāna* gift.] In India, the pooling by villagers of their land for the collective good, esp. as advocated by Vinoba Bhave (1895–1982). Cf. BHOODAN.

grame /greɪm/ *n.* Long *arch.* [OE *grama*.] †1 Anger. OE–E17. 2 Grief, sorrow; harm. OE.

gramercy /grəˈməːsi/ *int.* & *n. arch.* ME. [OFr. *grant merci* (God give you) great reward: see GRAND *a.*[1], MERCY.] A *int.* 1 Thank you kindly. Formerly also *gramercies*. ME. †b Foll. by *dat.* of agent or instrument, later *to*: by the instrumentality of, thanks to. LME–M18. 2 As an exclam. of surprise: mercy on us! E17.

1 R. H. BARHAM Gramercy for thy benison! 2 COLERIDGE Gramercy! They for joy did grin.

B *n.* An expression of thanks. Now *rare* or *obs.* L15.

gramicidin /gramɪˈsʌɪdɪn/ *n.* M20. [f. GRAM *n.*[4] + -I- + -CIDE + -IN[1].] *Pharm.* Any of various polypeptide antibiotics obtained from the bacterium *Bacillus brevis* and active esp. against Gram-positive bacteria. Cf. TYROTHRICIN.

graminaceous /gramɪˈneɪʃəs/ *a.* M19. [f. L *gramen, -min-* grass + -ACEOUS.] = next.

gramineous /grəˈmɪnɪəs/ *a.* M17. [f. L *gramen, -min-* grass: see -EOUS.] Of, pertaining to, or resembling grass; *spec.* belonging to the Gramineae or grass family.

graminivorous /gramɪˈnɪv(ə)rəs/ *a.* M18. [f. L *gramin-, -men* grass + -VOROUS.] Feeding on grass, cereals, etc.

graminology /gramɪˈnɒlədʒi/ *n. rare.* L19. [f. as prec. + -OLOGY.] The branch of botany that deals with grasses.

graminous /ˈgramɪnəs/ *a.* Now *rare* or *obs.* M17. [L *graminosus*, f. as prec.: see -OUS.] = GRAMINEOUS. Also, covered with grass.

gramma *n.* var. of GRAMA *n.*[1]

grammalogue /ˈgraməlɒg/ *n.* M19. [Irreg. f. Gk *gramma* written character + *logos* word, on the analogy of *catalogue* etc.: see -LOGUE.] A word represented in shorthand by a single sign. Also, a letter or character representing a word; a logogram.

grammar /ˈgramə/ *n.* LME. [AN *gramere*, OFr. *gramaire* (mod. *grammaire*) ult. f. L *grammatica* f. Gk *grammatikē* use as n. (sc. *tekhnē* art) of fem. of *grammatikos* relating to letters, f. *grammat-, gramma* letter, written character.] 1 The branch of language study or linguistics which deals with the means of showing the relationship between words in use, traditionally divided into the study of inflections (or morphology) and of the structure of sentences (syntax) accidence, and often including also phonology. LME. †2 Latin. Cf. *grammar school* below. LME–L16. 3 A treatise or book on grammar. M16. 4 A person's manner of using grammatical forms; speech or writing judged as good or bad according as it conforms to or violates the rules of grammar. Also, what is correct according to these rules. L16. 5 (Usu. **G-**.) (The name of) a class in a Roman Catholic school, college, or seminary, now only *spec.* the fourth class, immediately above Rudiments and below Syntax, in certain Jesuit schools. E17. 6 *transf.* The basic rules or principles of an art or science; a book embodying these. E17. 7 The system of inflections and syntactical forms characteristic of a language. M19. 8 = *grammar school* below. *colloq.* M20. 9 *Computing.* A set of rules governing what strings are valid or allowable in a language or text. M20.

1 *case grammar, comparative grammar, generative grammar, historical grammar, philosophical grammar, prescriptive grammar, transformational grammar, universal grammar*, etc. 4 DRYDEN *Varium et mutabile semper Femina* . . . the adjectives are neuter, and *animal* must be understood to make them grammar. J. BRODSKY If her sayings were dark, it wasn't due to her grammar. 6 J. H. NEWMAN An Essay in aid of a Grammar of Assent. *Daily Telegraph* The fact is that the grammar of television demands movement. 7 **have little** or **no grammar** (of a language) be sparingly inflected.

Comb.: **grammar-school** (*a*) any of a class of (usu. endowed) English schools founded in or before the 16th cent. orig. for teaching Latin, later secondary schools with a 'liberal' curriculum which included languages, literature, history, and the sciences; after the Education Act of 1944, any of the secondary schools offering a similar curriculum and taking only pupils selected for their ability; (*b*) *US* = *elementary school* (b) s.v. ELEMENTARY *a.*; formerly, a school intermediate between a primary school and a high school.

grammarless *a.* ignorant of grammar; (of a language) not having a highly inflected structure: E19.

grammarian /grəˈmɛːrɪən/ *n.* LME. [OFr. *gramarien* (mod. *grammairien*), f. *gramaire* GRAMMAR: see -IAN.] 1 A person expert in grammar or linguistics; *spec.* the author of a grammar (GRAMMAR *n.* 3). LME. †2 A pupil at a grammar-school. L16–L18. 3 A member of the class called Grammar in a Roman Catholic school, college, or seminary, now only *spec.* in certain Jesuit schools. L17.

grammatic /grəˈmatɪk/ *a.* L16. [(OFr. *gramatique* f.) L *grammaticus* f. Gk *grammatikos*: see GRAMMAR, -IC.] = GRAMMATICAL *a.*

grammatical /grəˈmatɪk(ə)l/ *a.* & *n.* E16. [Fr., or late L *grammaticalis*, f. as prec.: see -AL[1], -ICAL.] A *adj.* 1 Of, relating to, or based on grammar. E16. b *Logic.* Relating to the mere arrangement of words in a proposition, as opp. to its logical structure. L19. 2 Conforming to the rules of grammar or (*transf.*) of an art or science. M18. 3 Of a language: relying more on diversity of inflections than on richness of vocabulary. M20.

Special collocations: **grammatical change** *Philol.* (in Germanic languages) the system of contrasting consonants found in the strong verb, exemplifying Verner's Law. **grammatical gender**: determined by the form of a word, not by the real or attributed sex. **grammatical meaning** the meaning of a word or inflection as judged by its function in a sentence; opp. *lexical meaning*.

†B *n.* In *pl.* The subjects taught in a grammar-school. L17–E19.

grammatiˈcality *n.* (*Ling.*) conformity with grammatical rules M20. **grammatically** *adv.* LME. **grammaticalness** *n.* M17.

grammaticalize /grəˈmatɪk(ə)lʌɪz/ *v.t.* Also **-ise**. M20. [f. prec. + -IZE.] Express by or adopt in grammar; *spec.* (*Ling.*) change (an element) from being one having lexical meaning into one having a largely grammatical function.

grammaticaliˈzation *n.* M20.

grammaticaster /grəmatɪˈkastə/ *n. derog.* E17. [med.L, f. L *grammaticus*: see GRAMMATIC, -ASTER.] A petty grammarian.

grammaticise *v.* var. of GRAMMATICIZE.

grammaticism /grəˈmatɪsɪz(ə)m/ *n.* Now *rare.* E17. [f. GRAMMATIC + -ISM.] A point or principle of grammar.

grammaticize /grəˈmatɪsʌɪz/ *v.* Also **-ise**. L17. [f. as prec. + -IZE: cf. med.L *grammatizare*.] 1 *v.i.* Discuss grammatical points. *rare.* L17. 2 *v.t.* Reduce to grammatical rules; make grammatical. Also = GRAMMATICALIZE. L17.

grammatist /ˈgramətɪst/ *n.* L16. [(Fr. *grammatiste* f.) L *grammatista* f. Gk *grammatistēs*, f. *gramma, grammat-* letter: see -IST.] A student of grammar (usu. *derog.*). Also, in Gk sense, a teacher of reading and writing.

grammatolatry /graməˈtɒlətri/ *n.* M19. [f. Gk *gramma grammat-* letter + -O- + -LATRY.] The worship of letters; *spec.* rigid adherence to the letter of Scripture.

gramme *n.* var. of GRAM *n.*[2]

Grammy /ˈgrami/ *n.* Orig. *US.* M20. [f. GRAM *n.*[3] after EMMY.] (Proprietary name for) any of several annual awards given by the American National Academy of Recording Arts and Sciences for outstanding achievements in the record industry.

gramophile /ˈgraməfʌɪl/ *n. arch.* E20. [f. GRAMOPHONE *n.* + -PHILE.] = DISCOPHILE.

gramophone /ˈgraməfəʊn/ *n.* & *v.* L19. [Inversion of elems. of PHONOGRAM.] A *n.* An instrument (orig. driven by clockwork, later by electricity) for reproducing recorded sound by the vibrations of a stylus travelling in an irregular spiral groove in a disc rotating on a turntable. Now *arch.* or *Hist.* (the later electrically driven model being usu. called a *record-player*). L19.

Comb.: *gramophone record*: see RECORD *n.* 5a.

B *v.t.* Play on or record for the gramophone. Now *arch. rare.* E20.

gramophonic /-ˈfɒnɪk/ *a.* of, relating to, or of the nature of a gramophone or gramophone record E20. **gramoˈphonically** *adv.* E20.

gramp /gramp/ *n. dial.* & *colloq.* Also **grampy** /-pi/. L19. [Contr. of GRANDPAPA.] = GRANDFATHER.

grampus /ˈgrampəs/ *n.* E16. [Alt. (through assim. to GRAND *a.*[1]) of GRAPEYS.] **1** Any of various blowing, spouting, blunt-nosed cetaceans of the family Delphinidae; *esp.* (*a*) Risso's dolphin, *Grampus griseus*; (*b*) the killer whale, *Orcinus orca.* E16. **2** A person given to puffing and blowing. M19.

grampy *n.* var. of GRAMP.

gran /gran/ *n. colloq.* M19. [Abbrev.] = GRANDMOTHER.

grana *n.* pl. of GRANUM.

granadilla /granəˈdɪlə/ *n.* Also **gren-** /grɛn-/. L16. [Sp. dim. of *granada* pomegranate.] **1** (A fruit of) any of various tropical kinds of passion-flower. L16. **2** A W. Indian leguminous tree, *Brya ebenus*, yielding cocus-wood; the timber itself. Chiefly as *granadilla-tree.* M17.

1 purple granadilla = *passion fruit* s.v. PASSION *n.*

Granadine /ˈgranədiːn/ *a.* M19. [Sp. *Granadino*, f. *Granada* (see below) + *-ino* -INE[1].] Of or pertaining to Granada, a province of southern Spain.

granage /ˈgranɪdʒ/ *n.* Long *obs.* exc. *Hist.* Also **grain-** /ˈgreɪn-/. L16. [AN, formally corresp. to OFr. *grenage* duty on grain, f. *grain* GRAIN *n.*[1] + -AGE. The AN sense is unaccounted for.] A duty formerly levied by the City of London on salt imported by foreigners.

granary /ˈgran(ə)ri/ *n.* L16. [L *granarium* (usu. pl. *-ia*), f. *granum* GRAIN *n.*[1]: see -ARY[1].] **1** A storehouse for threshed grain. L16. **2** *fig.* A country or region producing a large amount of grain; esp. such a region considered as the supplier of another region. L16.

1 F. FITZGERALD The French and Japanese administrations had neglected to fill the emergency rice granaries. 2 BOSW. SMITH Palestine was the granary of Tyre, supplying it with corn and oil. J. RABAN The rest of Arabia had looked to the fertile soil of the plateau to provide a granary for the subcontinent.

Comb.: **Granary bread** (proprietary name for) a type of brown bread containing whole grains of wheat.

†granate *n.*[1] LME–E19. [med.L *granatus*: see GARNET *n.*[1]] = GARNET *n.*[1] Also, a deep red colour.

granate /ˈgranɪt/ *n.*[2] Long *rare* or *obs.* LME. [med.L (*pomum*) *granatum*, OFr. (*pome*) *grenate* (mod. *grenade*): see POMEGRANATE.] A pomegranate.

grand /grand/ *a.*[1] & *n.* LME. [AN *graunt*, OFr. *grand*, *grant* masc. and fem. (mod. *grand(e)*), f. L *grandis* fully grown, big, great, which in Proto-Romance superseded L *magnus* in all its uses.] **A** *adj.* **†1** — *the Grand*: designating a famous country, city, or person. Cf. GREAT. LME–E16. **2** Of a personal designation: pre-eminent, chief, leading. Formerly also, eminent, great. Cf. ARCH- 2. Now *rare* or *obs.* E16. **b** Designating a (now only foreign) monarch or an official who is senior to others of the same general rank. Now chiefly *Hist.* L16. **3** Great, large; main or principal by virtue of greatest size. Now only, (of a specified part of a large building) main or principal by virtue of size and magnificence. E16. **b** Comprehensive, complete. *obs.* exc. in *grand total* below. L16. **4** *Law.* (Of a tribunal etc.) of great importance, chief, principal; (of a crime) serious, on a large scale. Cf. PETTY *a.* Now chiefly *Hist.* E16. **5** Of most or great importance, value, or scope; great, vital. L16. **6** (Esp. of architecture, a natural object, etc.) imposing, impressive, magnificent; (of an idea, style, design, etc.) lofty and dignified in conception or expression. E18. **7** (Of a person) stately, dignified; now *esp.* imposing, superior, haughty; (of appearance) rich, splendid. M18. **8** Of a ceremony, occasion, etc.: conducted with great solemnity and splendour esp. on a large scale. M18. **9** Splendid, excellent; (of a person) in good health, well. *colloq.* E19.

1 CAXTON He was . . borne in grece not ferre fro Troye the graunt. 2 MILTON To conquer Sin and Death, the two grand Foes. 3 LD MACAULAY The Swedish minister alighted at the grand entrance. 5 H. JAMES She rose . . with an indescribable grand melancholy of indifference and detachment. G. SAINTSBURY Defoe had done a great deal; but nothing in the direction of his two grand achievements. 6 E. H. GOMBRICH The grand classical manner of narrative painting died a natural death in the eighteenth century. G. GORDON Realizing that he'd outlined his entire grand plan. A. N. WILSON The dome of the Oratory, . . grand and black against the pale English sky. 7 E. FEINSTEIN She is very grand in such matters, and has always believed herself far above domestic work. 8 JANET MORGAN Five-course dinners were prepared daily by Jane . . with a professional cook and butler hired for grand occasions. M. DRABBLE He thought a grand finale would be her kind of thing, better wrap it up in style, he said. 9 E. COXHEAD You don't look too grand . . Are you sure you're all right? J. O'FAOLAIN It'll mean you'll be with all blood relatives. Isn't that grand? M. BINCHY He's in Africa, he's grand, he's got a lovely English friend.

Special collocations & phrases: **grand air** a distinguished appearance or bearing; an affected dignity. *grand* CLIMACTERIC. *Grand Cross*: see CROSS *n.* 12. **Grand Fleet** *Hist.* (*a*) in the 18th cent., the British fleet based at Spithead; (*b*) the British battle fleet operating in the North Sea 1914–16. *grand horizontal*: see HORIZONTAL *n.* 4. *grand inquest*: see INQUEST 2. *grand inquistor*: see INQUISITOR *n.* 2. **grand jury** *Hist.* & *US Law* a jury selected to examine the validity of an accusation prior to trial. **grand lama** = DALAI LAMA. *grand* LARCENY. *Grand Lodge*: see LODGE *n.* 7. **grand manner** a style suited to noble or stately matters. *Grand Mufti*: see MUFTI *n.*[1] *Grand National*: see NATIONAL *n.* 4. **grand old man** a venerated person esp. in a specified field or profession. **Grand Old Party** *US* the Republican Party (now usu. abbrev. *G.O.P.*). **grand opera** serious opera without spoken dialogue. **grand passion** an intensely passionate and overwhelming love or love affair. **grand piano** a usu. large, harp-shaped, full-toned piano with horizontal strings. **grand scale** a very large or magnificent scale (of activity etc.). **Grand Seignior** *Hist.* the Sultan of Turkey. *grand slam*: see SLAM *n.*[1] *grand Sophy*: see SOPHY 1. **grand style** = *grand manner* above. **grand total** the sum or final amount after the adding together of all other totals. **grand tour** a tour of major cities and places of interest esp. in Europe, formerly undertaken as part of a person's education; any extensive tour or journey. *grand* UNIFIED (*field*) *theory*. *grand* VIZIER.

B *n.* **†1** = GRANDEE. E–M17. **2** With *the*: that which is grand, impressive, or magnificent. M18. **3** A Freemason official whose title is qualified by 'grand'. M18. **4** A grand piano. M19. **5** *sing.* & (occas.) in *pl.* A thousand pounds or dollars. *slang.* E20.

4 Y. MENUHIN The piano was a small grand of blond wood. *baby grand*: see BABY *a.* 5 M. GEE Bozo's getting over two hundred grand as an advance.

grand /grɑ̃, grɒ̃; *bef. a vowel* grɑ̃d, grɒnd/ *a.*[2] [Fr.: see prec. Cf. GRANDE.] The Fr. (masc.) for 'great', occurring in various phrases used in Eng.

grand battement /batmɑ̃, ˈbatmɒ̃/, pl. *-s -s* (pronounced same), a battement executed with the moving leg stretched M19. ***grand coup*** /ku, kuː/, pl. *-s -s* (pronounced same), (*a*) a bold or important stroke or effort; (*b*) *Whist* & *Bridge* the deliberate disposal of a superfluous trump by ruffing a winning card from the opposite hand: E19. *grand* CRU. *grand* JETÉ. ***Grand Marnier*** /marnje, ˈmɑːnɪeɪ/ [*Marnier*-Lapostolle, manufacturer's name] an orange-flavoured cognac-based liqueur; a drink of this: E20. ***grand monarque*** /mɔnark, mɔˈnɑːk/, pl. *-s -s* (pronounced same), a supreme and absolute ruler; *spec.* an epithet of Louis XIV of France (1638–1715): L17. ***grand monde*** /mɔ̃d, mɒnd/ = BEAU MONDE E18. ***grand seigneur*** /sɛɲœːr, seɪnˈjəː/, pl. *-s -s* (pronounced same), a great nobleman E17. ***grand siècle*** /sjɛkl, sɪˈɛk(ə)l/ [lit. 'great century *or* age'] a classical or golden age; *esp.* the reign of Louis XIV (1643–1715) in France: M19.

grand- /grand/ *comb. form.* ME. [Fr., use of prec.] With the names of family relationships denoting the second degree of ascent or descent from the relationship specified.

grand-aunt great-aunt. **grand-nephew** the son of a person's nephew or niece. **grand-niece** the daughter of a person's nephew or niece. **grand-uncle** a great-uncle. See also GRANDCHILD, GRANDDAUGHTER, GRANDFATHER, etc.

grandad /ˈgrandad/ *n. nursery* & *colloq.* Also (earlier) **grand-dad.** L18. [f. GRAND- + DAD *n.*[1]] Grandfather.

grandaddy /ˈgrandadi/ *n.* Also (earlier) **grand-daddy.** M18. [f. as prec. + DADDY.] **1** Grandfather. *nursery* & *colloq.* M18. **2** A superlative or the largest example *of. colloq.* M20.

2 M. BEADLE The grandaddy of all electrical storms dumped a cloudburst.

Comb.: **grandaddy-long-legs** *US* a daddy-long-legs. Earlier **grandada** *n.* L17.

grandam /ˈgrandam/ *n.* Also (exc. in sense 1b) **-dame** /-deɪm/. ME. [f. GRAND- + DAM *n.*[2]] **1** = GRANDMOTHER 1. *arch.* ME. **b** The dam of an animal's dam. M19. **†2** Great-grandmother. *Sc.* LME–M17. **3** An old woman. *arch.* M16. **4** = GRANDMOTHER 2. *arch.* E17.

grandchild /ˈgran(d)tʃʌɪld/ *n.* Pl. **-children** /-tʃɪldrən/. L16. [f. GRAND- + CHILD *n.*] A child of one's son or daughter.

grand-dad(dy) *ns.* vars. of GRANDAD(DY).

granddaughter /ˈgrandɔːtə/ *n.* E17. [f. GRAND- + DAUGHTER.] A daughter of one's son or daughter.

Comb.: **granddaughter clock** a small grandfather clock.

grand-ducal /gran(d)ˈdjuːk(ə)l/ *a.* M18. [f. GRAND *a.*[1] + DUCAL.] Of, pertaining to, or characteristic of a grand duke or grand duchess.

grand duchess /gran(d) ˈdʌtʃɪs/ *n. phr.* M18. [f. GRAND *a.*[1] + DUCHESS.] A female ruler of a grand duchy; the wife or widow of a grand duke. Also (*Hist.*), a daughter of a Russian tsar.

grand duchy /gran(d) ˈdʌtʃi/ *n. phr.* M19. [f. GRAND *a.*[1] + DUCHY.] A territory ruled over by a grand duke or grand duchess.

grand duke /gran(d) ˈdjuːk/ *n. phr.* L17. [f. GRAND *a.*[1] + DUKE *n.*, after F. *grand duc.*] **1** A male ruler of any of various territories whose monarch is or was considered to have royal or noble status one degree below that of king or queen. Also (*Hist.*), a son of a Russian tsar. L17. **2** [tr. Fr. *grand duc.*] The eagle owl, *Bubo bubo.* M19.

grande /grɑ̃d/ *a.* [Fr.: see GRAND *a.*[1] Cf. GRAND *a.*[2]] The Fr. (fem.) for 'great', occurring in various phrases used in Eng.

grande amoureuse /amurøːz/, pl. *-s -s* /grɑ̃dz amurøːz/, a passionate or amorous woman E20. ***grande dame*** /dam/, pl. *-s -s* (pronounced same), a woman of high rank or eminence and dignified bearing M18. *grande* HORIZONTALE. ***grande passion*** /pɑsjɔ̃/, pl. *-s -s* (pronounced same), = *grand passion* s.v. GRAND *a.*[1] E19. ***grande sonnerie*** /sɔnri, ˈsɒnəri/ a system of clock chiming in which the hour and the quarter is struck each quarter M20. ***grande tenue*** /təny/ full dress; *esp.* full military costume: M19.

grandee /granˈdiː/ *n.* L16. [Sp., Port. *grande*, use as n. of *grande* (adj.) grand, the ending assim. to -EE[1].] A Spanish or Portuguese nobleman of the highest rank; *gen.* a person of high rank, position, or eminence.

A. WEST Sir Hugh Rigby was the titled medical grandee called in to give the second opinion. M. IGNATIEFF He made the rounds . . . dispensing rewards and punishments like an Asiatic grandee.

grandeeship *n.* the office or rank of a grandee L18.

grandeur /ˈgrandjə, -(d)ʒə/ *n.* E16. [(O)Fr., f. *grand* great, GRAND *a.*[1] + *-eur* -OR.] **†1** Height; tall stature. *rare.* E16–M17. **2** Great power, rank, or eminence. Now *rare.* E17. **3** Greatness or nobility of character; dignity or stateliness in conduct, attitude, etc. Formerly also, haughtiness, arrogance. M17. **4** The quality of being grand; magnificence, splendour, majesty of appearance, style, composition, etc.; an instance or example of this. M17.

3 CLIVE JAMES His grandeur really *was* grandeur, not grandiloquence. *delusions of grandeur*: see DELUSION 2. 4 LONGFELLOW Switzerland . . outbids the imagination by its grandeurs and surprises. H. A. L. FISHER Many of these buildings . . impress the traveller with a sense of grandeur and force. J. RABAN Ordinary courtesies in

Arabic take on a quality of Miltonic grandeur when translated directly into English.

grandeval /granˈdiːv(ə)l/ *a. rare.* M17. [f. L *grandaevus* aged, f. *grandis* great + *aevum* age: see -AL[1].] Old, ancient.

grandezza /granˈdɛddza/ *n.* Long *rare.* Also ***grandeza*** /granˈdeθa/. E17. [It., also Sp. *grandeza*, f. *grande* grand: see -ESS[2].] Grandeur, greatness, magnificence; stateliness. Formerly also, an instance of this.

grandfather /ˈgran(d)fɑːðə/ *n.* & *v.* LME. [f. GRAND- + FATHER *n.*, after (O)Fr. *grandpère.*] A *n.* 1 The father of one's mother or father. LME. 2 = GRANDSIRE 2. Long *rare.* E17. 3 The founder or originator *of*; a superlative example *of. colloq.* E17. 4 [After the title of a popular song by H. C. Work (1876).] In full *grandfather clock*, (now rare) *grandfather's clock*. A weight-and-pendulum clock in a tall wooden case, a long-case clock. L19. 5 *Computing.* A tape of data two versions earlier than the one currently being processed. Cf. FATHER *n.* 7. M20.

3 P. BARRY There's been the grandfather of a mix-up somewhere.

Comb.: **grandfather clause** *US colloq.* a legislative clause exempting certain pre-existing classes of people or things from the requirements of a regulation; *grandfather('s) clock*: see sense A.4 above.

B *v.t.* 1 Be excessively deferential or flattering to. Foll. by *up. rare.* M18. 2 Fix the status of grandfather or (*fig.*) originator of (a person or thing) *on. rare.* L19. 3 Exempt by means of a grandfather clause. *US colloq.* M20.

grandfatherhood *n.* the condition of being a grandfather M19. **grandfatherless** *a.* without a grandfather LME. **grandfatherly** *a.* of, pertaining to, resembling, or characteristic of a grandfather E19.

grandfer *n.* var. of GRANFER.

grandfilial /gran(d)ˈfɪlɪəl/ *a.* E20. [f. GRAND- + FILIAL.] Of or due from a grandchild.

Grand Guignol /grɒn giːˈnjɒl, *foreign* grɑ̃ giɲɔl/ *n. phr.* E20. [Fr. (= Great Punch), the name of a theatre in Paris.] A dramatic entertainment in which short horrific or sensational pieces are played successively. Cf. GUIGNOL.

Grand Guignolesque *a.* pertaining to, characteristic of, or of the nature of Grand Guignol E20.

grandiflora /grandɪˈflɔːrə/ *a.* E20. [mod.L (freq. used in the specific names of large-flowered plants), f. L *grandis* great + *flos flor-* flower + fem. adj. suff. *-a.*] Bearing large flowers.

grandiloquent /granˈdɪləkwənt/ *a.* L16. [f. L *grandiloquus*, f. *grandis* great + *loquus* speaking, f. *loqui* speak; ending assim. to that of ELOQUENT.] Characterized by a pompous or boastful manner or quality, esp. in speech or writing.

K. VONNEGUT A grandiloquent coda not entirely in keeping with the facts.

grandiloquence *n.* the quality of being grandiloquent; the use of pompous or boastful language: L16. **grandiloquently** *adv.* M19. **grandiloquous** *a.* = GRANDILOQUENT L16.

grandiose /ˈgrandɪəʊs/ *a.* M19. [Fr. f. It. *grandioso*, f. *grande* grand: see -OSE[1].] 1 Impressive or imposing on account of grandeur or extravagance of appearance, manner, design, etc. M19. 2 Of speech, manner, etc.: characterized by (esp. affected) grandeur or stateliness; pompous, arrogant. M19.

1 D. MORRIS Despite our grandiose ideas and our lofty self-conceits, we are still humble animals. E. REVELEY The whole . . was built on an absurdly grandiose scale, avenues wide as air strips, colossal white monuments. 2 E. JOHNSON Forster was so grandiose that Fitzgerald half complained to Dickens about his intolerable condescension.

grandiosely *adv.* M19. **grandiˈosity** *n.* the quality of being grandiose; an instance or example of this: M19.

grandioso /grandiˈoːso/ *adv.*, *a.*, & *n.* L19. [It.: see GRANDIOSE.] *Mus.* A *adv.* & *adj.* (A direction:) in a grand or imposing manner. L19. B *n.* Pl. **-si** /-si/. A movement or passage played in this way. L20.

grandisonant /granˈdɪs(ə)nənt/ *a. rare.* L17. [f. late L *grandisonus*, f. *grandis* GRAND *a.*[1] + *sonus* sounding: see -ANT[1].] Stately-sounding.

Also **grandisonous** *a.* L17.

Grandisonian /grandɪˈsəʊnɪən/ *a. literary.* E19. [f. Sir Charles *Grandison*, the eponymous hero of Samuel Richardson's novel (1754) + -IAN.] Of manner, bearing, etc.: resembling that of Sir Charles Grandison; stately, courteous, magnanimous.

†**grandity** *n.* L16–M19. [L *granditas*, f. *grandis*: see GRAND *a.*[1], -ITY.] Grandeur, stateliness.

grandly /ˈgrandli/ *adv.* M17. [f. GRAND *a.*[1] + -LY[2].] In a grand manner; magnificently, splendidly, grandiosely.

grandma /ˈgran(d)mɑː/ *n. nursery* & *colloq.* Also **granma** /ˈgranmɑː/. L18. [f. GRAND- + MA.] Grandmother.

grand mal /grɒn ˈmal, *foreign* grɑ̃ mal/ *n. phr.* L19. [Fr., lit. 'great sickness'.] General convulsive epilepsy, with loss of consciousness. Cf. PETIT MAL.

grandmamma /ˈgran(d)məmɑː/ *n. nursery* & *colloq.* (now *arch.*). Also **-mama**. M18. [f. GRAND- + MAMMA *n.*[2]] Grandmother.

grand master /grand ˈmɑːstə/ *n. phr.* In sense 3 usu. **grandmaster**. M16. [f. GRAND *a.*[1] + MASTER *n.*[1]] †1 The chief officer of a royal household. M16–M18. 2 (**G- M-**.) The head of a military order of knighthood (as the Templars), or of the Freemasons or other similar society. M16. 3 (A title accorded to) a chess-player of the highest class; usu. one who has achieved a stipulated level of performance in international tournaments. M19.

grandmasterly *a.* (*Chess*) M20. **grandmastership** *n.* the office or position of grand master M18.

grandmaternal /gran(d)məˈtəːn(ə)l/ *a.* L18. [f. GRAND- + MATERNAL.] Of, pertaining to, or characteristic of a grandmother; grandmotherly.

grandmother /ˈgran(d)mʌðə/ *n.* & *v.* LME. [GRAND- + MOTHER *n.*[1], after (O)Fr. *grandmère.*] A *n.* 1 The mother of one's mother or father. LME. 2 An ancestress, *spec.* as a designation of Eve. Long *rare.* E16. 3 = GRANDFATHER *n.* 3. E17. 4 In full *grandmother clock*. A clock resembling a grandfather clock but with a smaller case. E20.

Phrases: **Grandmother's (foot)steps** a children's game in which one player turns around often and without warning with the aim of catching (and sending back) the other players stealthily creeping up to touch him or her on the back. **my** (or **your**) **grandmother!** *int.* expr. disagreement with preceding word or phrase. **teach one's grandmother to suck eggs** presume to advise someone who is more experienced.

B *v.t.* Take care of or behave towards (a person) as a grandmother. E20.

grandmotherhood *n.* the condition or state of being a grandmother M19. **grandmotherless** *a.* LME. **grandmotherly** *a.* of, pertaining to, resembling, or characteristic of a grandmother M19.

grandness /ˈgran(d)nɪs/ *n.* E18. [f. GRAND *a.*[1] + -NESS.] The state or quality of being grand. Also, a grand action.

grandpa /ˈgran(d)pɑː/ *n. nursery* & *colloq.* L19. [f. GRAND- + PA *n.*[2]] Grandfather.

grandpapa /ˈgran(d)pəpɑː/ *n. nursery* & *colloq.* (now *arch.*). Also **-pappy** /-papi/. M18. [f. GRAND- + PAPA *n.*[2]] Grandfather.

Also **grandpop** *n.* L19.

grandparent /ˈgran(d)pɛːr(ə)nt/ *n.* M19. [f. GRAND- + PARENT *n.*] A parent of either of one's parents.

ˈ**grandparentage** *n.* the state or condition of being a grandparent; descent from grandparents: L19. **grandpaˈrental** *a.* of, pertaining to, or characteristic of a grandparent E20.

grandpaternal /gran(d)pəˈtəːn(ə)l/ *a.* M19. [f. GRAND- + PATERNAL.] Of, pertaining to, or characteristic of a grandfather; grandfatherly.

Grand Prix /grɒ̃ ˈpriː/ *n. phr.* Pl. **Grands Prix** (pronounced same). M19. [Fr. = great prize.] 1 In full *Grand Prix de Paris* /də paˈriː/. An international horse race for three-year-olds run annually in June at Longchamps, Paris. M19. 2 The highest prize awarded in a competition or exhibition. L19. 3 Any of a series of motor or motorcycle races forming the World Championship, held in various countries under international rules. Also, a very important competitive event in various other sports. E20.

grandsire /ˈgran(d)sʌɪə/ *n.* ME. [f. GRAND- + SIRE *n.*] 1 a = GRANDFATHER *n.* 1. *arch.* & *dial.* ME. b The sire of an animal's sire. L19. 2 A forefather, a male ancestor. *arch.* ME. †3 A great-grandfather. *Sc.* E16–E20. 4 An old man. *arch.* L16. 5 *Campanol.* A basic method of change-ringing using an odd number of bells. L17.

grandson /ˈgran(d)sʌn/ *n.* L16. [f. GRAND- + SON *n.*[1]] A son of one's son or daughter.

grandstand /ˈgran(d)stand/ *n.* & *v.* M19. [f. GRAND *a.*[1] + STAND *n.*[1]] A *n.* The principal stand for spectators at a racecourse or other sporting venue. M19. B *v.i.* Perform with a view to getting applause from spectators in the grandstand; seek to attract favourable public or media attention. Chiefly as *grandstanding* vbl n. E20.

Comb.: **grandstand finish** a close or exciting finish in a race or competition; **grandstand play** *US* a way of performing with a view to getting applause. **grandstand view** a very good view of events such as is afforded by a seat in a grandstand.

grandstander *n.* (*a*) a spectator in a grandstand; (*b*) a person who grandstands: L19.

grane *n.* see GRAIN *n.*[2]

granfer /ˈgranfə/ *n. dial.* Also **grandfer**. L19. [Contr.] = GRANDFATHER.

grange /greɪn(d)ʒ/ *n.* ME. [(O)Fr., or AN *graunge*, f. med.L *granica* (fem.) pertaining to grain, used as n. (sc. *villa*), f. L *granum* GRAIN *n.*[1]] 1 A granary, a barn. *arch.* ME. 2 A farm; *esp.* a country house with farm-buildings attached. ME. b *Hist.* An outlying farmstead with tithe-barns etc. belonging to a monastery or feudal lord. LME. 3 A country house (for recreation). Now only in house names. M16. 4 *US Hist.* (Also **G-**.) (A local branch of) the 'Patrons of Husbandry', a national association of agriculturists. L19.

granger /ˈgreɪn(d)ʒə/ *n.* ME. [AN *graunger* = OFr. *grangier*, f. prec.: see -ER[2].] 1 *Hist.* The steward of a grange. ME. 2 *US Hist.* (Also **G-**.) A member of a grange (see GRANGE 4). L19. b In *pl.* = *granger shares* below. *US.* L19. 3 A farmer. Chiefly *joc.* or *derog. N. Amer.* L19.

Comb.: **granger (rail)road** *US Hist.* a railway carrying grain etc. from the western States; **granger shares** *US Hist.* shares in a granger road.

grangerize /ˈgreɪn(d)ʒərʌɪz/ *v.t.* Also **-ise**. L19. [f. James *Granger* (1723–76), Eng. biographer + -IZE.] Illustrate (a book) by later insertion of material, esp. prints cut from other works (Granger's *Biographical History of England* had blank pages to allow for this).

grangerism *n.* the practice of grangerizing L19. **grangerite** *n.* = GRANGERIZER L19. **grangeriˈzation** *n.* L19. **grangerizer** *n.* a person who grangerizes L19.

graniferous /graˈnɪf(ə)rəs/ *a.* M17. [f. L *granum* GRAIN *n.*[1] + -FEROUS.] Producing grain or seed resembling grain.

graniform /ˈgranɪfɔːm/ *a.* L18. [f. as prec. + -I- + -FORM.] Formed like a grain or as if made of grains.

granita /graˈniːtə, *foreign* graˈniːta/ *n.* Pl. **-te** /-ti, *foreign* -te/. M19. [It.] A coarse water-ice or sherbet; a drink made with crushed ice.

granite /ˈgranɪt/ *n.* & *a.* M17. [It. *granito* lit. 'grained, granular', pa. ppl formation on *grano* GRAIN *n.*[1]] A *n.* 1 Any of a broad class of granular crystalline plutonic rocks, consisting essentially of quartz, orthoclase, feldspar, and mica or hornblende, often used for building. M17. 2 *fig.* This as the type of something solid, hard, or unyielding; unyielding quality. M19. 3 = GRANITA. *US.* L19.

1 **bite on granite** *fig.* waste pains, persist in vain. *graphic granite*: see GRAPHIC *a.*

B *attrib.* or as *adj.* 1 Consisting or made of granite. E18. 2 *fig.* Like granite; hard, stern, unfeeling. E20.

1 **the Granite City** Aberdeen, Scotland. **the Granite State** *US* the State of New Hampshire. 2 *Daily Chronicle* His countenance expressed neither the . . tenderness of the saint nor the granite severity of the prophet.

Comb. & special collocations: **granite-porphyry** any porphyritic hypabyssal rock of granitic composition; **graniteware** (*a*) speckled pottery imitating the appearance of granite; (*b*) a kind of enamelled ironware.

†**granitell** *n.* L18–L19. [Fr. *granitelle* f. It. *granitello*, dim. of *granito* GRANITE.] *Geol.* Any granular crystalline rock having two principal components.

granitic /graˈnɪtɪk/ *a.* L18. [f. GRANITE + -IC.] 1 Of, pertaining to, or of the nature of granite; composed of or containing granite. L18. 2 *fig.* Hard, rigid, unimpressionable. M19.

2 F. C. L. WRAXALL The granitic solidity of certain celebrated prose.

Also **granitical** *a.* (now *rare*) L18.

granitize /ˈgranɪtʌɪz/ *v.t.* Also **-ise**. L19. [f. as prec. + -IZE.] *Geol.* Alter so as to give a granitic character to. Chiefly as *granitized* ppl a.

granitiˈzation *n.* L19.

granitoid /ˈgranɪtɔɪd/ *n.* & *a.* L18. [f. as prec. + -OID.] *Geol.* (A rock) resembling granite in having a granular crystalline texture.

granivorous /graˈnɪv(ə)rəs/ *a.* M17. [f. L *granus* GRAIN *n.*[1] + -VOROUS.] Feeding on grain.

granma *n.* var. of GRANDMA.

grannam /ˈgranəm/ *n. obs.* exc. *dial.* Also **-num**. L16. [Repr. colloq. pronunc. of GRANDAM.] A grandmother, an old woman.

grannie *n.* var. of GRANNY.

grannom /ˈgranəm/ *n.* L18. [Origin unkn.] A caddis-fly (spec. *Brachycentrus subnubilus*), or an imitation of this, used in fly-fishing.

grannum *n.* var. of GRANNAM.

granny /ˈgrani/ *n.* Also **grannie**. M17. [f. GRANNAM + -Y[6], -IE.] 1 Grandmother. Also, any elderly woman. *colloq.* M17. 2 More fully *granny woman*. A nurse, a midwife. *US colloq.* & *Canad. dial.* L18. 3 More fully *granny('s) knot*. A reef-knot incorrectly tied and therefore insecure or easily jammed. M19. 4 A stupid or fussy person (of either sex). *colloq.* & *dial.* L19.

1 MAX-MÜLLER Stories . . for which we are indebted to the old grannies in every village. **your granny!** *int.* expr. disagreement with preceding word or phr. 3 A. RANSOME Oh gosh! He's tied my legs with a granny and it's stuck.

Attrib. & comb.: designating garments etc. resembling those (formerly) typical of old women, worn by young people, as *granny bonnet, dress, shoe*. Special combs., as **granny annexe** a detached part of a property designed as self-contained accommodation for an elderly relative; **granny bashing, battering** violence towards an elderly person, esp. a member of one's family; **granny bond** (*colloq.*) an index-linked National Savings certificate originally available only to those of pensionable age; **granny's bonnet** *colloq.* columbine, aquilegia; **granny flat** part of a house made into self-contained accommodation for an elderly relative; **granny glasses** round steel-rimmed spectacles; *granny('s) knot*: see sense 3 above; **granny-sit** *v.i.* look after or stay with an elderly person while the usual carer is out; **granny-sitter** a person engaged to granny-sit; *granny woman*: see sense 2 above.

Granny Smith /granɪ ˈsmɪθ/ *n. phr.* L19. [Maria Ann *Smith* (*c*1801–70): see below.] An (orig. Australian) variety of bright green eating and cooking apple, first propagated in Australia by Maria 'Granny' Smith.

granodiorite /granə(ʊ)ˈdʌɪərʌɪt/ *n.* L19. [f. GRANITE + -O- + DIORITE.] *Geol.* Any of a class of coarse-grained quartz-containing plutonic rocks intermediate between granite and diorite in composition, with plagioclase forming at least two-thirds of the total feldspar content.

granola /graˈnəʊlə/ *n. N. Amer.* E20. [f. *gran-* repr. GRAIN *n.*[1] or GRANULAR + -OLA.] Orig., a proprietary name for a breakfast cereal. Now, a kind of breakfast cereal resembling muesli.

granolithic /granəˈlɪθɪk/ *a.* & *n.* L19. [f. L *grano-* (irreg. comb. form of *granum* GRAIN *n.*[1]) + Gk *lithos* stone + -IC.] (Designating or made of) a kind of concrete containing crushed granite.

granophyre /ˈgranə(ʊ)fʌɪə/ *n.* L19. [G *Granophyr*, f. *Granit* GRANITE + -O- + *Porphyr* PORPHYRY.] *Geol.* Any of a class of porphyritic plutonic rocks of granitic composition characterized by a medium- to fine-grained groundmass of intergrown feldspar and quartz.

granoˈphyric *a.* L19.

grant /grɑːnt/ *n.* ME. [f. the vb.] †1 Consent, permission. ME–M17. b A promise. LME–L16. c Admission, acknowledgement. E16–L17. 2 The action of granting (a request etc.). LME. 3 A formal gift or legal assignment of money, privilege, etc. LME. b The thing granted; *esp.* a sum of money given for a specific purpose. E19. 4 *Law.* A transfer of (real) property by deed or other written instrument. L16. 5 A piece of land occupied by a specified person. Chiefly *US*, in place-names; spec. ((*New Hampshire*) *Grants* (US Hist.) the area now forming the State of Vermont. E18.

2 *Law Times* The grant or refusal of an injunction upon a matter of law is appealable. 3 R. STUART Fifty years after the grant of the patent. LD MACAULAY He obtained a grant of all the lands . . belonging to Jesuits. b A. HAILEY Our company does give grants for academic research. *direct grant*: see DIRECT *a.* J. WAIN Till I go to college and my student grant comes through.

Comb.: **grant-aid** *v.* & *n.* (*a*) *v.t.* give financial assistance to (a school etc.); (*b*) *n.*= *grant-in-aid* below; **grant-aided** *ppl a.* (of a school etc.) assisted by an allowance from government or official funds; **grant-in-aid** a sum given as a grant, *esp.* by an authority or institution to support research or education.

grant /grɑːnt/ *v.* ME. [OFr. *gra(a)nter, greanter* alt. of *creanter* guarantee, assure f. Proto-Romance, f. L *credent-* pres. ppl stem of *credere* believe, trust.] †1 *v.i.* Consent to a request; agree *to* (*do*). ME–E18. 2 *v.t.* Agree to, promise, undertake; consent *to do, that. obs.* exc. *Law.* ME. 3 *v.t.* Accede to, consent to fulfil (a request etc.). ME. 4 *v.t.* Concede as an indulgence, bestow as a favour; allow (a person) to have. ME. b In pa. pple *granted*, as a polite rejoinder to an apology. E20. 5 *v.t.* Give or confer (a possession, a right, etc.) formally; transfer (property) legally. ME. †6 *v.t.* Yield, give up. ME–E17. 7 *v.t.* Admit, acknowledge. Now usu., concede (a proposition) as a basis for argument. Freq. as *granted* pa. pple. ME. b With compl.: admit (a person) to be. *rare.* LME.

1 SHAKES. *3 Hen. VI* The soldiers should have toss'd me . . Before I would have granted to that act. 2 W. CRUISE A. covenanted, granted, and agreed that B. should have the land. 3 T. HARDY This entreaty he granted; but on her asking for yet another, he was inexorable. 4 N. EZEKIEL God grant me privacy. P. ROTH He . . granted no public interviews. **take for granted** regard as necessarily true or certain to happen; cease to appreciate through familiarity. b H. CALVIN She yawned a great yawn and said, 'Sorry.' 'Granted,' I said. 5 L. STEFFENS The charters were granted on June 5. *Soldier* He was granted the BEM for his services. 7 A. WHITE And, granted the initial assumptions . . I think it stands the test. E. BOWEN I do grant . . it's a good deal to ask. b SIR W. SCOTT I grant him brave, But wild.

grantable *a.* possible to grant M16. **granˈtee** *n.* the person to whom a grant or conveyance is made LME. **granter** *n.* a person who grants LME. **grantor** *n.* (*Law*) a person who makes a grant or conveyance E17.

Granth /grʌnt/ *n.* Also **Grunth**. L18. [f. Skt *grantha* tying, literary composition, f. *granth* tie.] Any of the sacred scriptures of the Sikhs. Also (more fully *Adi Granth* /ˈɑːdi/ [*ādigrantha* lit. 'first book']), these collectively.

Grantha /ˈgrʌntə/ *n.* Also **-am** /-(ə)m/. L19. [Skt: see prec.] A southern Indian alphabet used by the Tamil brahmins for the Sanskrit transcripts of their sacred books.

gran turismo /gran tuˈrizmo, tʊəˈrɪzməʊ/ *n.* & *a. phr.* M20. [It., lit. 'great touring'.] (Designating) a comfortable high-performance model of motor car. Abbrev. *GT*.

I. FLEMING He had . . a white convertible Lancia Gran Turismo.

†**granula** *n.* Pl. **-lae**. M17–M19. [mod.L, irreg. dim. of *granum*, = late L *granulum* GRANULE.] = GRANULE.

granular /ˈgranjʊlə/ *a.* L18. [f. as GRANULE + -AR[1].] 1 Consisting of grains or granules. L18. 2 Having a granulated surface or structure. M19. 3 Of the nature of a granule or granules. M19.

granuˈlarity *n.* L19. **granularly** *adv.* E20.

granulate /ˈgranjʊlət, -leɪt/ *a.* L18. [f. as GRANULE + -ATE[2].] Chiefly *Bot.* & *Zool.* = GRANULATED 2.

granulate /ˈgranjʊleɪt/ *v.* M17. [f. as GRANULE + -ATE[3].] 1 *v.t.* & *i.* Form into or take the form of granules or grains; make or become granular. M17. 2 *v.t.* Raise in granules; roughen the surface of. L17. 3 *v.i. Med.* Of a wound, tissue, etc.: form multiple small prominences, as the beginning of the process of healing or joining. M18.

granulator *n.* an apparatus for making granules of a substance M19.

granulated /ˈgranjʊleɪtɪd/ *ppl a.* L17. [f. prec. + -ED[1].] 1 Of a solid material: formed into or consisting of granules. L17. 2 (Of a surface) raised in small projections; having a surface roughened in this manner. Also, mottled so as to appear granular. L17. 3 *Med.* Displaying granulation. M19.

1 *ellipt.* as *n.*: D. FRANCIS 'Sugar?' He had a two-pound bag of granulated, and a . . spoon. 2 *Times* A granulated gold pendant.

granulation /granjʊˈleɪʃ(ə)n/ *n.* E17. [f. as GRANULE + -ATION.] 1 The action or process of forming into granules or grains; the condition of being granulated. Also (in *pl.*), granules. E17. 2 *Med.* (The process of healing by) the formation of multiple small prominences on the surface of injured tissue, as part of the growth of new connective tissue. Also (in *pl.*), the prominences so formed. M18. 3 *gen.* The formation or existence of small granular projections or bodies on the surface or in the substance of an object. Also, the structure, or (in *pl.*) the granules, so formed. L18.

Comb.: **granulation tissue** connective tissue newly grown at the site of a wound etc.

granule /ˈgranjuːl/ *n.* M17. [Late L *granulum* dim. of L *granum* GRAIN *n.*[1]: see -ULE.] A small grain or compact particle, usu. larger than a particle of a powder; a prominence resembling a grain on a surface.

G. F. CHAMBERS Granule is the best word to describe the luminous particles on the Sun's surface. M. DRABBLE Nescafé . . in those days came not in granules in jars but in powder in tins.

granuliform /granˈjuːlɪfɔːm/ *a.* M19. [f. as prec. + -I- + -FORM.] Having a granular structure.

granulite /ˈgranjʊlʌɪt/ *n.* M19. [f. GRANULE + -ITE[1].] *Geol.* Any of a class of fine-grained granulose metamorphic rocks in which the main component minerals are usu. feldspars and quartz.

granulitic /-ˈlɪtɪk/ *a.* L19.

granulo- /ˈgranjʊləʊ/ *comb. form.* M19. [f. as GRANULE + -O-.] Forming ns. and adjs. w. the sense 'of granules, having granules' or (*rare*) adjs. w. the sense 'granular and —'.

granulocyte /ˈgranjʊləsʌɪt/ *n.* E20. [f. prec. + -CYTE.] *Physiol.* A cell containing or developing conspicuously granular cytoplasm; *spec.* any of a class of leucocytes which show a granular appearance of the cytoplasm when stained.

granulocytic /-ˈsɪtɪk/ *a.* E20. **granulocytoˈpenia** *n.* [Gk *penia* poverty] the presence of abnormally small numbers of granulocytes in the blood M20. **granulocyˈtosis** *n.* the presence of abnormally large numbers of granulocytes in the blood M20.

granuloma /granjʊˈləʊmə/ *n.* Pl. **-mas**, **-mata** /-mətə/. M19. [f. as GRANULE + -OMA.] *Med.* A mass of granulation tissue produced in any of various disease states, usu. in response to infection, inflammation, or the presence of a foreign substance.

granuloma inguinale /ɪŋgwɪˈnɑːli/ [mod.L = inguinal granuloma] (the granulomatous formation characteristic of) donovanosis.

granulomaˈtosis *n.*, pl. **-toses** /-ˈtəʊsiːz/, any condition marked by the growth of granulomas E20. **granulomatous** *a.* of, pertaining to or of the nature of a granuloma L19.

granulometric /ˌgranjʊlə(ʊ)ˈmɛtrɪk/ *a.* E20. [Fr. *granulométrique*, f. as GRANULO- + -METRIC.] Relating to the size distribution of grains of sand or other materials; relating to or involving the measurement of grain sizes.

granulose /ˈgranjʊləʊs/ *a.* M19. [f. GRANULE + -OSE[1].] Granular; *spec.* (*Petrogr.*) (of a rock structure) marked by the presence of granular minerals, usu. in streaks and bands.

granulous /ˈgranjʊləs/ *a.* LME. [f. med.L *granulosus* (see -ULOUS); later directly f. GRANULE + -OUS.] Granular.

granum /ˈgrɑːnəm, ˈgreɪnəm/ *n.* Pl. **grana** /ˈgrɑːnə, ˈgreɪnə/. L19. [G f. L *granum* grain.] *Bot.* Any of the stacks of thylakoids in a chloroplast.

grape /greɪp/ *n.* ME. [OFr. (mod. *grappe* bunch of grapes), prob. vbl n. f. *graper* gather (grapes), f. *grap(p)e* hook, f. Proto-Romance f. Gmc (OHG *krāpfo*) hook, rel. to CRAMP *n.*[1]] †1 A bunch of grapes. Chiefly *wine-grape*. ME–L15. 2 Each of the small oval berries, usu. green, purple, or black, growing in clusters on a vine and eaten fresh or dried as fruit or used for making wine. With specifying wd: a variety of this. ME. b The (fermented) juice of the grape; wine. M17. 3 The berry or fruit of any of various other plants. Now only w. specifying wd as in sense 4. LME. 4 A climbing plant of the genus *Vitis* (family Vitaceae), on which grapes grow; a vine. Also (w. specifying wd), any of various other fruit-bearing plants resembling the vine. LME. 5 In *pl.* A diseased growth resembling a bunch of grapes on the pastern of a horse etc., or on the pleura in cattle. E17. †6 More fully *grape-paper*. A size of paper. E17–L19. 7 *Hist.* Small cast-iron balls grouped several together to make a scattering charge for cannon. Orig. in *pl.*; now only *collect.* or as *grapeshot*. L17.

2 *black grape, muscat grape, seedless grape, white grape*, etc. **sour grapes** [alluding to Aesop's fable of 'The Fox and the Grapes'] an expression or attitude of deliberate disparagement of a desired but unattainable object.

Comb.: **grape-brandy** brandy distilled solely from grapes or from wine; *grape* HYACINTH; **Grape-Nuts** (proprietary name for) a breakfast cereal, a preparation of maize or wheat in a crisp granular form; *grape-paper*: see sense 6 above; *grape* PHYLLOXERA; **grape-scissors** (*a*) clippers used for thinning grapes on the vine; (*b*) scissors used for dividing a bunch of grapes at table; *grapeshot*: see sense 7 above; **grape-stone** (*a*) the seed of a grape; (*b*) *Geol.* a cemented cluster of calcareous or other particles in a sedimentary deposit; **grape-sugar** dextrose; **grape tree** (*a*) = *seaside grape (tree)* s.v. SEASIDE; (*b*) a grapevine.

grapelet *n.* a small grape E17. **grapelike** *a.* resembling (that of) a grape or grapes E17. **grapery** *n.* a greenhouse etc. in which grapes are grown; a plantation of vines; a vinery: E19.

grapefruit /ˈgreɪpfruːt/ *n.* Pl. same. E19. [f. GRAPE *n.* + FRUIT *n.*: prob. from the fruits being borne in clusters.] A large round yellow-skinned citrus fruit having pale yellow, occas. pink, juicy acid pulp. Also (usu. *grapefruit tree*), the tree bearing this fruit, *Citrus paradisi*, a hybrid or mutation of the shaddock, *C. maxima*, of W. Indian origin.

grapevine /ˈgreɪpvʌɪn/ *n.* M18. [f. GRAPE *n.* + VINE.] 1 A vine which bears grapes. M18. 2 An unofficial means of transmission of information (often of a secret or private nature) or rumour. Orig. (*US colloq.*) as *grapevine telegraph*. M19. 3 A skating figure in which both feet are on the ice together and form interlacing lines. M19. 4 A hold in wrestling. L19.

2 T. HEALD Contacts who had heard, on the grapevine, that he was looking for work. J. HELLER The grapevine says I'm finished. *Bird Watching* The 'grapevine' is a loose association of active birders who keep in touch by passing on news of rare and interesting birds.

grapey *a.* var. of GRAPY.

†**grapeys** *n.* Only in ME. [OFr. *grapois, graspeis* (also *craspois*) f. med.L *craspiscis*, f. L *crassus* thick + *piscis* fish.] The flesh of the grampus.

graph /grɑːf, graf/ *n.*[1] & *v.* L19. [Abbrev. of *graphic formula*: see GRAPHIC *a.*] A *n.* 1 A diagram showing the relation between two variable quantities each measured along one of a pair of axes usu. at right angles. L19. 2 *Math.* A symbolic diagram in which connections between items are represented by lines. Now also in abstract terms, a finite non-empty set of elements together with a set of unordered pairs of these elements. L19.

1 *fig.*: A. COOKE Somewhere along the falling graph of our allegiance to authority.

B *v.t.* Plot or trace on a graph; represent by means of a graph. L19.

I. JEFFRIES Anybody graph the survival rates against the day of admission? *fig.*: *Listener* The book graphs . . the hostility between generations.

Comb.: **graph paper**: printed with a network of lines to assist the drawing of graphs; **graph theory** the mathematical theory of the properties and applications of graphs (sense 2).

graph /grɑːf, graf/ *n.*[2] M20. [Gk *graphē* writing.] *Ling.* A visual symbol representing a phoneme or cluster of phonemes or some other feature of speech; *esp.* a letter or a combination of letters.

-graph /grɑːf, graf/ *suff.* [f. or after Fr. *-graphe* f. L *-graphus* f. Gk *-graphos* written, writing.] Forming ns. w. the sense 'something written, drawn, etc., in a specified way,' as *autograph, photograph, pictograph*, etc., or w. the sense 'an instrument that records something or by some means,' as *heliograph, seismograph, telegraph*, etc.

grapheme /ˈgrafiːm/ *n.* M20. [f. GRAPH *n.*[2] + -EME.] *Ling.* The class of letters and other visual symbols that represent a phoneme or a cluster of phonemes; a feature of written expression that constitutes a minimal distinctive unit.

grapheˈmatic, **graˈphemic** *adjs.* of or relating to graphemes or graphemics M20. **graˈphemically** *adv.* M20. **graˈphemics** *n.* the branch of knowledge that deals with systems of written symbols in relation to spoken language: M20.

-grapher /grəfə/ *suff.* [f. or after Gk *graphos* writer + -ER[1].] Forming ns. (usu. corresp. to ns. in -GRAPH, -GRAPHY) w. the sense 'a person skilled in a style or method of writing, drawing, etc.', as *calligrapher, stenographer*, etc.; w. the sense 'a person who writes (about) (something denoted by the first element)', as *hagiographer, historiographer*; w. the sense 'a person skilled in a particular descriptive science or the use of a recording instrument' as *bibliographer, geographer, radiographer*, etc.

graphic /ˈgrafɪk/ *n.* L19. [f. the adj.] I In *pl.*, usu. treated as *sing.* 1 The technical use of diagrams and figures as an aid to mathematical calculation or to engineering or architectural design. L19. b The use of computers linked to VDUs to generate and manipulate visual images. More fully *computer graphics*. M20. 2 Design and decoration involving or accompanying typographic work; the production of pictures, diagrams, etc., in association with text. M20. II *sing.* (with *pl.*). 3 A product of the graphic arts or of graphic design. M20. 4 A diagram, picture, or other visual image produced by means of a computer. In *pl.* also *computer graphics*. M20.

graphic /ˈgrafɪk/ *a.* M17. [L *graphicus* f. Gk *graphikos*, f. *graphē* drawing, writing: see -IC.] †1 Drawn with a pencil or a pen. Only in M17. 2 Producing by words the effect of a clear pictorial representation; vividly descriptive; conveying all (esp. unpleasant or unwelcome) details, clear, unequivocal. M17. 3 Relating to or producing pictorial representations; of or pertaining to drawing, painting, engraving, etching, etc. M18. 4 Of or pertaining to handwriting etc.; *occas.* suitable for writing on. L18. b Of a mineral: showing marks like writing on the surface or in fracture. E19. 5 Pertaining to or involving diagrams, graphs, or similar figures; graphical. M19.

2 H. B. STOWE Expressions, which not even the desire to be graphic in our account shall induce us to transcribe. C. DARWIN A graphic description of the face of a young Hindoo at the sight of castor-oil. 3 G. STEINER Brilliant, instantaneous graphic devices—the photograph, the poster, the moving picture. 4 E. R. CONDER Letters, hieroglyphics, or any kind of graphic symbol.

Special collocations: *graphic arts*: see ART *n.*[1] **graphic equalizer** a device enabling the quality of an audio signal to be varied by adjusting its strength in each of a series of frequency bands independently, usu. by means of slides. **graphic granite** *Petrogr.* a pegmatite with intergrown crystals of feldspar and quartz producing a pattern resembling cuneiform script. **graphic novel** a full-length story in the form of a comic strip, published as a book.

graphicness *n.* M19.

-graphic /ˈgrafɪk/ *suff.* [Partly f. or after Gk *graphikos*, (see prec.), partly f. ns. in -GRAPH(Y) + -IC.] Forming adjs. (usu. corresp. to ns. in -GRAPH, -GRAPHY) w. the sense 'of or pertaining to or by a style or method of writing, drawing, etc.', as *calligraphic, photographic*, etc.; w. the sense 'of or pertaining to the writing of or about (something denoted by the first element)', as *hagiographic, historiographic*; w. the sense 'of or pertaining to a descriptive science or method of instrumental recording', as *geographic, bibliographic, radiographic*, etc.

graphicacy /ˈgrafɪkəsi/ *n.* M20. [f. GRAPHIC *a.* after *literacy, numeracy*.] The ability to understand maps, graphs, etc., or to present information by means of diagrams.

graphicate *a.* [after *numerate*] possessing or displaying graphicacy M20.

graphical /ˈgrafɪk(ə)l/ *a.* E17. [f. as GRAPHIC *a.*: see -ICAL.] †1 Clearly drawn or traced. Only in E17. 2 = GRAPHIC *a.* 3. Formerly also, skilled in drawing. E17. 3 = GRAPHIC *a.* 2. Now *rare*. M17. 4 Of or pertaining to writing; consisting of letters. M17. 5 = GRAPHIC *a.* 5. L18.

graphicalness *n.* L19.

-graphical /ˈgrafɪk(ə)l/ *suff.* [f. as *-graphic* + -ICAL.] = -GRAPHIC.

graphically /ˈgrafɪk(ə)li/ *adv.* L16. [f. GRAPHIC *a.* or prec.: see -ICALLY.] 1 As in a clear pictorial representation; in a vividly descriptive manner; so as to convey all (esp. unpleasant or unwelcome) details; clearly, unequivocally. L16. 2 Orig., in the manner of writing. Now, by means of or in respect of written signs. E17. †3 By means of drawing, painting, etc. *rare*. Only in M17. 4 By the use of diagrams, linear figures, or symbolic curves; by the construction of diagrams or graphs. L18.

1 D. W. GOODWIN The . . study makes this point graphically clear. . . Those who came back for booster sessions did better. 2 OED The verbs *read* and *rede* differ only graphically; in etymology and pronunciation they are the same word. 4 *Which Micro?* You can . . display figures graphically.

graphite /ˈgrafʌɪt/ *n.* L18. [G *Graphit*, f. Gk *graphein* write (from its use as pencil 'lead'): see -ITE[1].] A grey electrically conducting allotropic form of carbon, with a crystalline structure containing layers of carbon atoms.

graphited *a.* lubricated with graphite; containing added graphite: E20. **graphitoid** *a.* = GRAPHITOIDAL L19. **graphiˈtoidal** *a.* having the appearance or structure of graphite M19.

graphitic /grəˈfɪtɪk/ *a.* M19. [f. prec. + -IC.] Of, pertaining to, or of the nature of graphite.

graphitization /ˌgrafɪtʌɪˈzeɪʃ(ə)n/ *n.* Also **-isation**. L19. [f. as prec. + -IZATION.] 1 Conversion of carbon (wholly or partially) into the form of graphite. Also, graphitic character. L19. 2 *Metall.* a The formation of graphite from combined carbon in a ferrous alloy. E20. b Corrosion of grey cast iron in which the metallic iron constituents are lost leaving a soft porous residue largely of graphite. E20.

graphitize /ˈgrafɪtʌɪz/ *v.t.* & *i.* Also **-ise**. L19. [f. as prec. + -IZE.] (Cause to) undergo graphitization.

graphology /grəˈfɒlədʒi/ *n.* M19. [f. Gk *grapho-* comb. form f. *graphē* writing + -LOGY.] 1 *Ling.* The branch of knowledge that deals with written and printed symbols and of writing systems. M19. 2 The branch of knowledge that deals with handwriting, esp. as used to infer a person's character etc. from his or her handwriting. L19.

graphoˈlogical *a.* L19. **graphoˈlogically** *adv.* M20. **graphologist** *n.* L19.

graphomania /grafəˈmeɪnɪə/ *n.* Now *rare*. M19. [f. as prec. + -MANIA.] A mania for writing.

graphomaniac *n.* E19.

graphometer /grəˈfɒmɪtə/ *n.* L17. [Fr. *graphomètre*, f. as prec. + -METER.] A semicircle used in measuring angles in surveying.

graphotype /ˈgrafə(ʊ)tʌɪp/ *n.* Now *Hist.* M19. [f. as GRAPHOLOGY + -TYPE.] A printing process in which a stereotype or electrotype copy is made from a drawing which has been put in relief; the block or plate produced by this means.

graphy /ˈgrafi/ *n.* M20. [Fr. *graphie* system of writing.] = GRAPH *n.*[2]

-graphy /grəfi/ *suff.* [Fr., G *-graphie* f. L f. Gk *-graphia* writing.] Forming ns. (freq. w. -O-: see -OGRAPHY) w. the sense 'a style or method of writing, drawing, etc.,' as *calligraphy*, *lithography*, *stenography*; w. the sense 'the writing of or about (something denoted by the first element)', as *hagiography*, *historiography*; w. the sense 'the branch of knowledge relating to a particular descriptive science or instrumental recording technique,' as *bibliography*, *geography*, *radiography*.

grapnel /ˈgrapn(ə)l/ *n.* LME. [AN, f. OFr. *grapon* (mod. *grappin*) f. Gmc base of GRAPE *n.*: see -EL[2].] **1** A grappling-iron. Also, a small anchor with several flukes. LME. **2** = GRAPPLE *n.* 2. L19.

grappa /ˈgrapə/ *n.* L19. [It.] A brandy distilled from the refuse of grapes after wine-making.

grappier /ˈgrapɪə, *foreign* grapje (*pl. same*)/ *n.* L19. [Fr., f. *grappe* (*de la chaux*) cluster (of lime).] A hard lump of unslaked material left in hydraulic lime after slaking.

Comb.: **grappier cement**: made by pulverizing grappiers.

grapple /ˈgrap(ə)l/ *n.* ME. [Branch I f. OFr. *grapil* f. Prov. f. *grapa* hook f. Gmc base of GRAPE *n.*; branch II f. the vb.] **I 1** A grappling-iron. ME. **2** Any of various contrivances or implements for clutching and grasping. L16. **3** A small anchor with several flukes. *obs.* exc. *dial.* E17. **II 4** The action or an act of grappling (*with*); the state of being grappled. Also, the grip or close hold (as) of a wrestler; a contest at close quarters. E17.

grapple /ˈgrap(ə)l/ *v.* M16. [f. the n.] **1** *v.t.* Seize or hold with a grappling-iron (*lit.* & *fig.*); fasten *to* something by this means. M16. **2** *v.i.* **a** Fasten oneself firmly (*to* an object) by means of a grapple (*lit.* & *fig.*). Now *rare.* M16. **b** Foll. by *for*: seek to locate or retrieve by means of a grapnel. L18. **3** *v.t.* Take hold of with the hands; seize; grip firmly; come to close quarters with. L16. **4** *v.i.* Take a firm grip, esp. in wrestling; get a tight grip of another person or thing; contend in close fighting. L16. **5** *v.i.* Make movements with the hands as if to grasp something; grope. Also foll. by *after*, *at*, *for*, *to*. Long *rare* exc. *Sc.* L16.

1 P. WARNER The English . . grappled their own boats to the French with hooks and chains. *Daily Telegraph* To locate the wreck, grapple it and fix its position. *fig.*: BURKE Never to be torn from thence, but with those holds that grapple it to life. 2 F. SMITH The Piece of Ice we grappled to had a Pond upon it. 3 T. PRINGLE Grappling its antagonist by the throat with its fore-paws. R. L. STEVENSON I've seen him grapple four, and knock their heads together. 4 P. PEARCE The two boys were grappling in real fight. 5 SIR W. SCOTT Their hands oft grappled to their swords.

Phrases: **grapple with** (*a*) contend or struggle with, esp. at close quarters; (*b*) grip as in wrestling; seize with the hands and arms, close with bodily; (*c*) *Naut.* make one's ship fast to (an enemy) with grappling-irons; come to close quarters with; (*d*) *fig.* try to overcome, accomplish, or deal with.

†**grapplement** *n.* (*rare*) a grappling, a close grasp in fighting: only in L16. **grappler** *n.* (*a*) a person who or thing which grapples; *spec.* a grappling-iron, a grapnel; (*b*) *slang* (*rare*) a hand: E17.

grappling /ˈgraplɪŋ/ *n.* L16. [f. GRAPPLE *v.* + -ING[1].] **1** Orig. *collect.*, instruments for grappling. Now, a grappling-iron (see below). Also = GRAPPLE *n.* 3. L16. **2** The action of GRAPPLE *v.* E17. †**3** A place where a vessel could be grappled. Only in 18.

Comb.: **grappling-hook**, **grappling-iron** an iron-clawed instrument intended to be thrown with a rope attached in order to get a firm hold on an object such as a wall or an enemy ship, or to be used when dragging a river.

grapsoid /ˈgrapsɔɪd/ *a.* M19. [f. mod.L *Grapsus* (see below: cf. Gk *grapsaios* crab) + -OID.] Of or pertaining to a large cosmopolitan family of crabs, Grapsidae, typified by the genus *Grapsus*, with a quadrilateral carapace.

graptolite /ˈgraptəlʌɪt/ *n.* M19. [f. Gk *graptos* painted or marked with letters + -LITE; in sense 1 f. mod.L *graptolithus*.] †**1** A stone showing a resemblance to a drawing. Only in M19. **2** Any member of a group of fossil hemichordates remains of which (esp. of their tubular skeletons) are widely distributed in rocks of Lower Palaeozoic age. M19.

grapto'litic *a.* of or pertaining to graptolites (sense 2); rich in graptolite fossils: M19.

grapy /ˈgreɪpi/ *a.* Also **grapey**. LME. [f. GRAPE *n.* + -Y[1].] †**1** Designating the choroid coat of the eye. LME–L17. **2** Of or pertaining to grapes or the vine; composed or savouring of grapes. L16.

grasp /grɑːsp/ *v.* & *n.* LME. [Origin uncertain: perh. ult. f. Gmc base parallel to that of GROPE *v.*, or of LG origin (cf. LG, EFris. *grapsen*).] **A** *v.* **1 a** *v.i.* Make clutches with the hand, grope, try (usu. successfully) to seize. Now only foll. by *at*: also *fig.*, accept eagerly or greedily. LME. †**b** *v.i.* Grapple *with*. L16–M18. **c** *v.t.* Seize or clutch at greedily. M17. **2** *v.t.* Seize and hold firmly (as) with the hand or fingers, grip. L16. †**b** Clasp or hold firmly in or *in* the arms, embrace. E17–M18. **3** *v.t.* Get a mental hold of, comprehend fully. L17.

1a LD MACAULAY By grasping at too much, the government would lose all. *grasp at a straw* or *straws*: see STRAW *n.* c *absol.*: DRYDEN Like a miser 'midst his store, Who grasps and grasps 'till he can hold no more. 2 G. GREENE His small steely hand grasped hers, like one half of a handcuff. E. CALDWELL She was grasped by her arm and pulled into the hall. **grasp the nettle** *fig.* tackle a difficulty or danger with courage or boldness. 3 W. TREVOR He frowned, . . unable to grasp immediately what was being implied. P. ROTH I cannot grasp it—I don't understand what has happened *at all*.

B *n.* **1** Something that is fitted or designed to grasp or be grasped. Now only *Naut.*, the handle of an oar. M16. **2** The action of grasping; a grip or firm hold; *fig.* control, mastery. Formerly also, an embrace. L16. **3** Mental hold; *esp.* comprehension, mastery (of a subject). L17.

2 W. OWEN The burying-party, picks and shovels in their shaking grasp, Pause over half-known faces. 3 J. ARCHER How well the French speak our language compared with our grasp of theirs.

Phrases: **beyond one's grasp** (*a*) out of one's reach or control; (*b*) beyond one's mental hold or comprehension. **within one's grasp** (*a*) close enough to be grasped; (*b*) within one's mental hold or comprehension.

graspable *a.* (earlier in UNGRASPABLE) E19. **grasper** *n.* †(*a*) a grappling-iron; (*b*) a person who or thing which grasps: M16. **grasping** *a.* that grasps; *fig.* avaricious, greedy: LME. **graspingly** *adv.* M19. **graspingness** *n.* M18. **graspless** *a.* (*a*) without grasp or grip; loose, relaxed; (*b*) unable to be grasped: L18.

grass /grɑːs/ *n.* [OE *græs*, *gærs* = OFris. *gres*, *gers*, OS (Du.), OHG, G, ON, Goth. *gras*, ult. f. Gmc base of GREEN *a.*, GROW *v.*] **1** Herbage of which the blades or leaves and stalks are eaten by cattle, sheep, horses, etc.; low-growing plants (chiefly as in sense 4b below) blanketing the ground. OE. **b** The blade stage of growth (formerly esp. of corn); young shoots esp. of the carnation. OE. **2** Pasture or grazing, esp. as sufficient for the animal(s) specified; land on which grass is the permanent crop, pasture-land. OE. **b** The time or season when grass grows, spring and early summer; grazing-time. *arch.* & *dial.* L15. **3** Grass-covered ground; a lawn in a public or private garden. ME. **b** The ground (*slang*); *Mining* the earth's surface, the pit-head. E17. **c** A fuzzy appearance along the time base-line of a cathode-ray tube display due to random fluctuating deflections caused by electrical noise. M20. **4** †**a** A small herbaceous plant; a (medicinal) herb. ME–L16. **b** Any of the plants which form grass (sense 1); *gen.* any plant of the large cosmopolitan family Gramineae (including cereals, reeds, and bamboos besides the characteristic plants of pasture-land), members of which typically have erect jointed stems (culms) bearing narrow bladelike leaves and insignificant flowers. Also, any of various plants resembling the members of Gramineae in appearance. M16. **5** An individual plant of grass (formerly also, of corn). Long only in *pl.* LME. **6** = SPARROW-GRASS. Now *arch.* & *dial.* M18. **7** Marijuana, esp. as smoked. *slang* (orig. *US*). M20. **8** A police informer. Cf. GRASSER. *slang.* M20.

1 JONSON Her treading would not bend a blade of grasse! R. S. THOMAS The ewes starve Milkless, for want of the new grass. **cut the grass from under a person's feet** foil or thwart a person. **not let the grass grow under one's feet** be quick to act or seize an opportunity. 2 J. ROBERTSON They have not only a house, but . . a cow's grass to afford milk to their families. **at grass** at pasture. **(out) to grass**: to pasture; *fig.* redundant, in retirement, on holiday. b M. R. MITFORD She is five years old this grass. 3 DICKENS Two men . . seated in easy attitudes upon the grass. **keep off the grass** *fig.* do not take liberties, interfere, encroach. **b go, send to grass** be knocked, knock down. 4b *arrow-grass*, *bluegrass*, *cotton-grass*, *couch grass*, *crab-grass*, *goose-grass*, *hair-grass*, *knot-grass*, *lemon grass*, *meadow-grass*, *pampas-grass*, *quaking grass*, *ryegrass*, *scurvy-grass*, *tore grass*, *velvet grass*, etc. *grass of Parnassus*: see PARNASSUS 2. 5 B. EMECHETA They gave the . . white women long grasses tied together for sweeping.

Comb.: **grass-bird** any of various birds associated with grass; *spec.* (*a*) a southern African warbler, *Sphenoeacus afer* (more fully *Cape grass-bird*); (*b*) any of a number of Australasian warblers of the genus *Megalurus*; **grass box** the receptacle on a lawnmower for collecting the cut grass; **grass carp** a Far Eastern river fish, *Ctenopharyngodon idella*, sometimes introduced to control aquatic vegetation, on which it feeds; **grass-cloth** a cloth resembling linen, woven from ramie etc.; **grass-comber** *Naut.* (*arch.*, *derog.*) a landlubber, esp. a farm worker; **grass court** a grass-covered tennis-court; **grass-eating**, **-feeding** *adjs.* graminivorous; **grass-finch** any of various finches associated with grassland, *esp.* of the Australian genus *Poephila*; **grass frog** the common frog, *Rana temporaria*, esp. as found in Continental Europe and Asia; **grass hockey** *Canad.* hockey played on grass, as opp. to *ice hockey*; **grass hook** a sickle for cutting grass; **grassland** (an area of) land covered with grass, esp. as used for grazing; **grass moth** any of numerous small pyralid moths of the subfamily Crambinae, whose larvae feed on grasses; **grass parakeet**, **parrot** *Austral.* any of various small parrots frequenting grassland, esp. of the genus *Neophema*; **grass pea** (the edible seed of) a leguminous plant, *Lathyrus sativus*, cultivated esp. as a fodder crop in the Middle East and Indian subcontinent; **grass-plat**, **-plot** a piece of ground covered with turf, sometimes ornamented with flower-beds; *grass poly*: see POLY *n.*[1] 2; **grassquit** any of various neotropical finches of the genera *Tiaris*, *Volatinia*, and *Loxipasser*; **grass roots** *fig.* (*a*) the fundamental level or source; (*b*) the ordinary people as representative of a basic viewpoint etc.; *esp.* in *Polit.*, the voters themselves; **grass sickness** an equine disease which can occur when a horse is put on to certain pastures and is usu. fatal; **grass ski** a short ski mounted on wheels or rollers used for skiing down grass- or straw-covered slopes; **grass skiing** skiing with grass skis; **grass skirt**: made of long grass and leaves fastened to a waistband, orig. worn by the hula dancers of some Pacific islands; **grass snake** any of various colubrid snakes; *esp.* (*a*) a common Eurasian snake, *Natrix natrix*, generally greenish brown or greenish grey with a yellow collar; (*b*) *N. Amer.* the smooth green snake, *Opheodrys vernalis*; (*c*) *S. Afr.* either of two spotted or striped mildly venomous snakes of the genus *Psammophylax*; **grass staggers**, **tetany** *Vet. Med.* a disease of livestock caused by magnesium deficiency, occurring esp. when there is a change from indoor feeding to outdoor grazing; **grass-tree** any of various Australasian woody plants with grasslike leaves in tufts at the top of the trunk; *esp.* (*a*) *Austral.* = *blackboy* (b) s.v. BLACK *a.*; (*b*) *NZ* the cabbage tree, *Cordyline australis*; **grass warbler** *Austral.* the gold-capped fantail warbler, *Cisticola exilis*; **grass-wrack** eel-grass, zostera; **grass-wren** any of several Australian wrens of the genus *Amytornis* (family Maluridae).

grasslike *a.* resembling (that of) grass L17.

grass /grɑːs/ *v.* LME. [f. the n. Cf. GRAZE *v.*[1]] **1** *v.t.* & (now *rare*) *i.* Cover or become covered with grass. LME. **2** *v.t.* Provide with pasture; (of land) yield enough grass for. Formerly also, graze (cattle etc.). L15. **3** *v.t.* Spread out (flax etc.) on the grass or ground for bleaching. M18.

4 *v.t.* Put down on the grass; *esp.* knock or bring down, fell (an opponent). E19. **b** Bring (a fish) to bank; bring down (game) by a shot. M19. **5** *v.i. Printing.* Of a compositor: do casual work. L19. **6** *v.t.* & *i.* (w. *on*). Betray (someone); inform the police about (someone). *slang.* M20.

1 T. HARDY The gardeners were beginning to grass down the front. C. THUBRON The vegetable plots . . . were grassed in years ago. 4 *Times* In Rugby football . . players were not tackled but grassed. 6 J. R. ACKERLEY So it looked bad for me, like as if I'd grassed 'im. F. DHONDY The Kray brothers hired a tank to attack a lad that grassed on them.

grassed *a.* (*a*) covered with grass; †(*b*) *Golf* (of a club or driver) with a slightly filed-back face: LME. **grasser** *n.* (*slang*) = GRASS *n.* 6 M20. **grassing** *n.* (*a*) the action of the vb; an instance of such action; (*b*) *Sc.* the privilege of grazing in a particular place; the place for grazing or cutting turfs: E16.

†**grassant** *a.* M17–M18. [L *grassant-* pres. ppl stem of *grassari* lie in wait: see -ANT[1].] Roaming about or lurking with evil intent.

grasserie /'gras(ə)riː/ *n.* M19. [Fr., f. *gras* fat.] A virus disease of silkworms, characterized by yellowing of the skin and liquefaction of the internal tissues.

grass-green /grɑːs'griːn, 'grɑːsgriːn/ *a.* & *n.* OE. [f. GRASS *n.* + GREEN *a.*] **A** *adj.* **1** Green as grass; of the colour of grass. OE. **2** Green with grass. E17.

2 TENNYSON Two graves grass-green beside a gray church-tower.

B *n.* The colour of grass. M17.

†**grasshop** *n.* OE–E17. [OE *gærshoppa, -e*, Orm *gresshoppe* (f. *gærs* GRASS *n.* + *hoppa*, agent-n. of *hoppian* HOP *v.*[1]), perh. after OSw. *gräshoppare* or LG *grashüpper* (G *Grashüpfer*); cf. synon. OS *feldhoppo.*] A grasshopper, a locust.

grasshopper /'grɑːshɒpə/ *n.* & *v.* LME. [Extended form of prec.] **A** *n.* **1** Any orthopterous insect of the families Acrididae (locusts) and Tettigoniidae (bush-crickets), characterized by having legs adapted for jumping, and the ability of the males to make chirping sounds. LME. **2** *fig.* A person held to resemble a grasshopper in character or behaviour; an inconstant, flighty, or frivolous person. L16. **3** *Music.* = HOPPER *n.*[1] 8. E19. **4** An artificial bait for fish. M19. **5** = COPPER *n.*[2] *rhyming slang.* L19. **6** *Watchmaking.* More fully *grasshopper escapement.* A type of recoil escapement equipped with springs and requiring no lubrication. L19. **7** A small light aircraft for observation or liaison. *US slang.* M20.

1 **knee-high to a grasshopper** *colloq.* very small or very young. 5 B. BEHAN Put the paper inside your shirt, so . . that old bastard of a grass-'opper won't tumble it.

Comb.: *grasshopper escapement*: see sense 6 above. **grasshopper mouse** any of a number of mice of the genus *Onychomys*, native to N. America and Mexico; **grasshopper sparrow** a N. and Central American sparrow, *Ammodramus savannarum*; **grasshopper warbler** any of various warblers of the genus *Locustella*, spec. *L. naevia*, characterized by prolonged buzzing calls.

B *v.i.* **1** Live in a frivolous, improvident manner. E19. **2** Of a riverboat: move *over* sand bars or shallow waters with the aid of poles. *US.* L19. **3** Jump like a grasshopper. Chiefly *fig.* M20.

1 A. GILBERT [We] enjoy ourselves . . by working. We shouldn't get any fun out of grasshoppering. 3 J. FOWLES My mind travelled up to the Bonnards, and grasshoppered from them to Alison.

grasshoppery *a.* like a grasshopper E20.

grassless /'grɑːslɪs/ *a.* LME. [f. GRASS *n.* + -LESS.] Without grass, bare of grass.

Grassmann's Law /'grɑːsmənz lɔː/ *n. phr.* L19. [Hermann *Grassmann* (1809–77), Ger. mathematician and polymath.] A phonetic law stating that where two aspirated plosives occurred in neighbouring syllables in Indo-European, dissimilation took place and the first of the two lost its aspiration in Greek and Sanskrit.

grassum *n.* see GERSUM.

grass widow /grɑːs 'wɪdəʊ/ *n. phr.* E16. [f. GRASS *n.* + WIDOW *n.*[1] Cf. MLG *graswedewe*, Du. *grasweduwe*, Sw. *gräsenka*, Da. *graesenke*; also G *Strohwitwe* 'straw widow'.] **1** An unmarried woman who has cohabited with one or more men, or has had an illegitimate child. *obs.* exc. *dial.* E16. **2** A woman living apart from her husband (temporarily or permanently). M19.

grass widower *n. phr.* a man living apart from his wife (temporarily or permanently) M19. **grass-widowhood** *n.* L19.

grassy /'grɑːsi/ *a.* LME. [f. GRASS *n.* + -Y[1].] **1** Covered with grass, having much grass. LME. **2** Resembling grass in colour, form, or smell. M16. **3** Of or pertaining to grass; consisting of or containing grass. E17.

1 D. H. LAWRENCE The upper road is all grassy, fallen into long disuse. 2 H. CRANE A marvelous stillness and grassy perfume pervade the district.

grassiness *n.* E18.

grate /greɪt/ *n.* ME. [OFr, or Sp. *grada* hurdle, corresp. to It. *grata* grate, gridiron, hurdle (cf. med.L *grata* hurdle), perh f. Proto-Romance f. L *cratis.*] **1** = GRATING *n.*[2] 1. Now chiefly *N. Amer.* ME. **2** The railing round a monument, building, etc. *obs.* exc. *Hist.* LME. †**3** A (barred) prison or cage (for people or animals). M16–L18. **4** A frame of metal bars for holding the fuel in the recess of a fireplace or furnace; the fireplace itself. E17. **5** *Mining.* = GRATING *n.*[2] 2. L18.

1 K. KESEY And got his finger stuck . . in the grate . . over the drain at the bottom of the pool. 3 J. HOWARD Every debtor that lies in the common grate. 4 G. CHARLES Whoever sees a fire these days; real living flames? You hardly see a grate any more!

†**grate** *a.* E16. [L *gratus.* Cf. earlier INGRATE.] **1** Pleasing, agreeable. E16–M17. **2** Thankful, grateful. M–L16.

grate /greɪt/ *v.*[1] LME. [OFr. *grater* (mod. *gratter*) f. Proto-Romance, f. Gmc (rel. to OHG *krazzōn*, G *kratzen* scratch).] **1** *v.t.* Scrape, file, abrade; wear *away, down, to nothing*, etc., by abrasion. Now *rare.* LME. **2** *v.t.* Reduce (esp. food) to small particles by rubbing against a grater. LME. †**3a** *v.t.* Cause (a weapon) to strike *on.* Only in LME. **b** *v.i.* Of a weapon: strike. E16–L17. †**4** *v.i.* Dwell querulously or harp (*up*)*on* a subject. M16–L17. **5** *v.t.* Affect painfully, as if by abrasion; irritate, annoy. Now *rare.* M16. **6** *v.i.* Have an irritating effect (*on, upon*). Formerly also, oppress with exactions (*up*)*on.* M16. **7** *v.t.* Make a harsh grinding noise by rubbing against (something) roughly; grind (the teeth). Also, utter in a harsh voice. M16. **8** *v.i.* Rub *against, upon*, etc., with a harsh, grinding noise; move creakingly; make a harsh noise. L16.

1 T. NASHE Some of them have grated . . theyr smooth tender skinnes, with hayre shirts. 2 G. H. NAPHEYS A little nutmeg grated over the surface. J. AIKEN They were all on a low diet of lemon-juice, olives, grated carrot and tomatoes. 5 W. BLACKSTONE With sounds uncouth, and accents dry, That grate the soul of harmony. 6 L. DURRELL The falseness of his gestures . . grated disagreeably. A. CARTER The voices that grated daily on her nerves. 7 SPENSER Thereat the feend his gnashing teeth did grate. KEATS His galley now Grated the quay-stones. G. GREENE She . . grated a greeting in a voice full of discords. 8 A. RADCLIFFE A Key grated in the lock. TENNYSON Lest the harsh shingle should grate underfoot.

gratingly *adv.* in a grating manner L17.

grate /greɪt/ *v.*[2] Now *rare* or *obs.* LME. [f. GRATE *n.*] Provide with a grate or grating. Formerly also, confine behind bars.

EVELYN A well . . grated over with iron.

grateful /'greɪtfʊl, -f(ə)l/ *a.* M16. [f. GRATE *a.* + -FUL.] **1** Feeling gratitude; actuated by or showing gratitude; thankful. M16. **2** Pleasing, agreeable, *arch.* welcome. M16.

1 LYNDON B. JOHNSON I told him how grateful I was for his counsel and his support. 2 E. DARK Two trees gave a sparse but grateful shade.

gratefully *adv.* M16. **gratefulness** *n.* L16.

grater /'greɪtə/ *n.* LME. [Partly f. OFr. *grateor, -our*, partly f. GRATE *v.*[1]: see -ER[1], -ER[2].] **1** An instrument with a rough surface for grating or scraping; *spec.* a kitchen utensil with a rasping surface formed by sharp protuberances, used for grating cheese, carrot, nutmeg, etc. LME. †**2** A person who or thing that grates. Chiefly *fig.* LME–E17.

†**gratia dei** *n. phr.* LME. [med.L = grace of God.] **1** Any of various medicinal herbs; *esp.* hedge hyssop, *Gratiola officinalis.* LME–M19. **2** A salve or plaster. LME–M17.

graticulation /grətɪkjʊ'leɪʃ(ə)n/ *n.* E18. [Fr., f. *graticuler* divide into squares, f. as next: see -ATION.] The drawing or provision of a network of lines or graticule on a surface; such a network, a graticule.

graticule /'gratɪkjuːl/ *n.* L19. [Fr. f. med.L *graticula* for (also cl.L) *craticula* small gridiron, dim. of L *cratis* hurdle.] **1** A network of lines representing meridians and parallels, on which a map or plan can be represented. L19. **2** A series of fine lines or fibres incorporated in a telescope or other optical instrument as a measuring scale or an aid in locating objects; a plate etc. bearing this. E20.

gratification /ˌgratɪfɪ'keɪʃ(ə)n/ *n.* L16. [(O)Fr., or L *gratificatio(n-)*, f. *gratificat-* pa. ppl stem of *gratificari*: see next, -ATION.] **1** The action of gratifying, satisfaction; the giving of pleasure or doing of a favour. L16. **b** The satisfaction or indulgence of, or compliance with a feeling, desire, etc. E17. **2** Something given to gain favour; a reward, recompense, gratuity; a bribe. Now *rare.* L16. **3** The state of being gratified or pleased; enjoyment, satisfaction. E18. **b** An instance of being gratified; a thing that gratifies; a source of pleasure or gratification. Usu. in *pl.* E18.

1 H. T. BUCKLE Men, in the pursuit of wealth, consider their own gratification oftener than the gratification of others. b E. STILLINGFLEET The pleasure of humane life lies in the gratifications of the senses. 2 LD MACAULAY Six thousand guineas was the smallest gratification that could be offered. 3 A. STORR He obtains gratification from having a number of patients who turn to him. b S. JOHNSON That insatiable demand of new gratifications, which seems . . to characterize the nature of man.

gratify /'gratɪfʌɪ/ *v.t.* LME. [Fr. *gratifier*, or its source L *gratificari* do a favour to, make a present of, f. *gratus* GRATE *a.* + -I- + -FY.] †**1** Make pleasing or acceptable; grace. LME–L17. **2** Reward, esp. financially, (a person, a service, etc.); recompense, remunerate; bribe. Formerly also, show gratitude to or for. *arch.* M16. †**3** Express pleasure at, welcome. M16–E17. **4** Please, satisfy; oblige; *esp.* please by compliance; give free rein to, indulge, satisfy (a feeling, desire, etc.). M16.

2 W. S. CHURCHILL His rewards were princely; . . and the chief personalities were gratified with rich presents. 4 W. CATHER It gratified him to hear these gentlemen admire his fine stock. E. TEMPLETON It is always gratifying to have one's suspicions confirmed by others. D. CECIL It is clear that Jane Austen enjoyed . . a chance to gratify her taste and talent for nonsense and comic fantasy.

gratifier *n.* M16. **gratifyingly** *adv.* in a gratifying manner E19.

†**gratility** *n. rare. joc.* E17–E19. [Alt. of GRATUITY.] = GRATUITY.

gratin /gratɛ̃, 'gratã(ŋ)/ *n.* M17. [Fr., f. *gratter*, earlier *grater* GRATE *v.*[1]] **1** A method of cooking, or a dish cooked, with a crisp brown crust, usu. of grated cheese or breadcrumbs. Cf. AU GRATIN. M17. **2** The highest class of society. M20.

1 *attrib.*: *Daily Chronicle* Drain and turn into a gratin dish, . . cover with fine breadcrumbs. 2 S. PAKENHAM One of the most famous Paris salons, where all but the very highest gratin of the French nobility congregates.

gratiné /gratine (*pl. same*), 'gratɪneɪ/ *n.* & *a.* Also ***-ée.*** E20. [Fr., pa. ppl a. of *gratiner* cook *au gratin.*] *Cookery.* (A dish) cooked with a crisp topping or stuffing of breadcrumbs or grated cheese.

gratinéed *a.* = GRATINÉ *a.* L20.

grating /'greɪtɪŋ/ *n.*[1] LME. [f. GRATE *v.*[1] + -ING[1].] **1** The action of breaking something into small particles by rasping or rubbing; the product of this. LME. **2** The action of rasping against something; a harsh grinding noise so produced; *fig.* irritation. E17.

grating /'greɪtɪŋ/ *n.*[2] E17. [f. GRATE *n.* + -ING[1].] **1** A framework of parallel or crossed bars, usu. preventing access through an opening while permitting communication, ventilation, the draining away of liquid, etc. Formerly esp. *Naut.*, an open woodwork cover for the hatchway. E17. 2 *Mining.* A perforated plate used for separating large from small ore. M19. 3 *Optics.* A set of equally-spaced parallel wires, or a surface ruled with equally-spaced parallel lines, used to produce spectra by diffraction. Also *diffraction grating.* L19.

1 F. RAPHAEL The only fresh air came from a window which opened up to a pavement grating. B. BAINBRIDGE The first time I saw him through a grating in the door.

gratiola /grəˈtʌɪələ/ *n.* L16. [mod.L, f. *gratia* grace. Cf. GRATIA DEI.] Hedge hyssop, *Gratiola officinalis*; a medicinal preparation of this. Now only as mod.L genus name.

gratis /ˈgratɪs, ˈgrɑː-, ˈgreɪ-/ *adv.* & *a.* LME. [L *gratis* contr. of *gratiis* out of favour or kindness, abl. pl. of *gratia* grace, favour.] A *adv.* 1 Freely, for nothing, without return made or expected; without charge, cost, or pay. LME. †2 Without a reason; gratuitously, unjustifiably. L16–E19.

1 E. JONES Take low fees, treat a good many people gratis. *free, gratis, and for nothing*: see FREE *adv.*

B *adj.* Given or done for nothing; free; gratuitous. M17.

E. TEMPLETON I once saw him . . squeeze out a gratis consultation.

gratitude /ˈgratɪtjuːd/ *n.* LME. [Fr., or L *gratitudo*, f. as GRATE *a.*: see -TUDE. Cf. earlier INGRATITUDE.] 1 The quality or condition of being grateful or thankful; the appreciation of and inclination to return kindness; gratefulness. LME. b An instance or expression of gratefulness. Long *rare.* LME. 2 A gift, gratuity, or reward; *esp.* (*Sc.*) a grant of money made to the monarch. Long *rare.* L15. †3 Grace; a favour. Chiefly *Sc.* E–M16.

1 N. EZEKIEL Express your gratitude By giving what you have to give. B. EMECHETA Every living being had to be able to contribute something, . . in gratitude for being alive.

grattage /grəˈtɑːʒ/ *n.* L19. [Fr. = scraping.] *Surg.* The scraping or rubbing of a surface to remove excessive granulation tissue and promote healing.

grattoir /ˈgratwɑː/ *n.* L19. [Fr. = stratcher, scraper.] *Archaeol.* = *end-scraper* s.v. END *n.*

gratuitous /grəˈtjuːɪtəs/ *a.* M17. [(OFr. *gratuiteus*, Fr. †*-eux*) f. L *gratuitus* freely given, spontaneous: see -OUS.] 1 Given or obtained for nothing; not earned or paid for; free. M17. 2 Uncalled for, unwarranted, unjustifiable; done or acting without a good or assignable reason; motiveless. L17.

1 R. L'ESTRANGE We are given to Mistake the Gratuitous Blessings of Heaven, for the Fruits of our Own Industry. G. S. HAIGHT Except for her teaching, which was gratuitous, Marian had not found the literary work she was hoping for. 2 *Daily Telegraph* I should be held up to execration as . . a gratuitous liar. P. GAY Killing animals for sport . . came to seem gratuitous, coarse, indecent, inhuman.

gratuitously *adv.* L17. **gratuitousness** *n.* E18.

gratuity /grəˈtjuːɪti/ *n.* L15. [OFr. *gratuité* or med.L *gratuitas* gift, f. as GRATE *a.*: see -ITY.] †1 Graciousness, favour; *esp.* God's grace or favour; a favour, a kindness. L15–M17. 2 A gift (usu. of money) of an amount decided by the giver. Now usu. = TIP *n.*[5] M16. †b Payment, wages. M17–M19. 3 A bounty given to service personnel on discharge etc. E19. 4 Gratuitousness. *rare.* M19.

2 OED: The attendants . . are forbidden to receive gratuities. 3 W. S. CHURCHILL The subject of gratuities and other release benefits for members of the Forces.

gratulant /ˈgratjʊl(ə)nt/ *a. rare.* L15. [L *gratulant-* pres. ppl stem of *gratulari*: see GRATULATE *v.*, -ANT[1].] Pleased, joyful, satisfied; congratulatory.

†**gratulate** *a. rare.* L15–E17. [L *gratulatus* pa. pple of *gratulari*: see next, -ATE[2].] Pleasing, to be rejoiced at.

gratulate /ˈgratjʊleɪt/ *v.t.* Now *arch.* or *poet.* M16. [L *gratulat-* pa. ppl stem of *gratulari*, f. as GRATE *a.*: see -ATE[3].] 1 Welcome, hail; greet joyfully, salute. M16. 2 = CONGRATULATE *v.* 1, 2a. L16. †3 Be grateful or show gratitude for or to. L16–L17. †4 Gratify, please. L16–E19.

gratulation /gratjʊˈleɪʃ(ə)n/ *n.* Now *arch.* or *poet.* L15. [OFr., or L *gratulatio(n-)*, f. as prec.: see -ATION.] 1 A feeling of gratification or joy, inward rejoicing. Now with mixture of sense 4 below, self-congratulation. L15. †2 (An) expression of gratitude. L15–L17. 3 Expression of delight; an instance of expressing delight. M16. 4 (A) compliment, felicitation, or congratulation. M16. †5 A welcome; a joyful greeting. L16–M17.

gratulatory /ˈgratjʊlət(ə)ri/ *a.* M16. [Late L *gratulatorius*, f. as GRATULATE *v.*: see -ORY[2].] †1 Expressing gratitude; thankful. M16–M18. 2 Congratulatory, complimentary. L16.

gratulatorily *adv.* E17.

graunch /grɔːn(t)ʃ/ *v.* & *n. colloq.* (orig. *dial.* & *NZ*). L19. [Imit.] A *v.t.* & *i.* (Cause to) make a crunching or grinding noise, esp. with resulting damage; damage (a mechanism) thus. L19.

Observer Many people graunch their gears.

B *n.* A crunching or grinding sound, esp. one associated with damage. M20.

Autosport An ominous graunch came from the rear wheel.

graupel /ˈgraʊp(ə)l/ *n.* L19. [G.] *Meteorol.* Soft hail, small snow pellets with a fragile ice crust.

Grauwacke *n.* see GREYWACKE.

gravamen /grəˈveɪmɛn/ *n.* Pl. **-mens, -mina** /-mɪnə/. E17. [Late L *gravamen* physical inconvenience, (in med.L) grievance, f. L *gravare* weigh on, oppress, f. *gravis* GRAVE *a.*[1]] 1 a In the Anglican Church, a memorial from the Lower House of Convocation to the Upper House representing the existence of disorders and grievances within the Church. E17. †b A formal complaint or accusation. M17–L19. 2 A grievance. M17. 3 The essential or most serious part of an accusation; the part that bears most heavily on the accused. M19.

†**gravaminous** *a.* M17–E19. [f. L *gravamen*, *-min-* (see prec.) + -OUS.] Grievous, annoying, distressing.

†**gravative** *a.* L16–E18. [f. L *gravare*: see GRAVAMEN, -ATIVE.] *Med.* Designating a sensation of pain accompanied by that of pressure.

grave /greɪv/ *n.*[1] [OE *græf* = OFris. *gref*, OS *graf*, OHG *grap* (G *Grab*), f. WGmc, parallel to N & EGmc base repr. by ON *grǫf*, Goth. *graba*; ult. f. base of GRAVE *v.*[1]] 1 A place of burial; an excavation made to receive a corpse; the monument etc. raised over it. Formerly also, a mausoleum or the like. OE. b A grave-mound. M19. 2 The condition or state of being buried; the state of being dead; death. LME. 3 An excavation of any kind; a pit, a trench. Now chiefly *Sc.* E16. 4 Anything that is, or may become, a receptacle for what is dead. Freq. with specifying wd. M16.

1 H. ASQUITH A skull, torn out of the graves nearby. M. MITCHELL The new grave lying by the three short mounds of her little brothers. *bloody grave*: see BLOODY *a.* & *adv.* **dig the grave of** *fig.* cause the downfall of. *have one foot in the grave*: see FOOT *n.* **secret as the grave** kept as a close secret. **someone walking on my grave** an explanation of an otherwise unaccountable shivering. **turn in one's grave** (of a deceased person) supposedly react thus through extreme outrage at an action or an event. *watery grave*: see WATERY 7. 2 SWIFT I shall carry the Mark to my Grave. A. MASON Those who put their faith in Joshua's return from the grave would themselves survive death. *on this side (of) the grave*: see SIDE *n.* 4 C. KINGSLEY They had only just escaped a watery grave. **grave of reputations** a place where many reputations have been lost. *white man's grave*: see WHITE *a.*

Comb.: **grave-cloth** a pall; **grave-clothes** the clothes or wrappings in which a corpse is buried; **gravedigger** (*a*) a person who digs graves, esp. as a form of employment (*lit.* & *fig.*); (*b*) *colloq.* an insect that buries prey or carrion in the ground as food for its larvae; *esp.* a burying-beetle; **grave-goods** (esp. valuable) objects deposited with corpses in ancient graves; **grave-mound** a hillock constructed over the site of an interment; **graveside** the edge of a grave; the ground immediately adjacent to a grave; **gravestone** a stone placed at the mouth of a tomb or over a grave; *esp.* an inscribed headstone; **grave-trap** *Theatr.* a trapdoor sited approximately in the centre of the stage.

graveless *a.* E17. **graveward** *a.* & *adv.* (leading) towards the grave M19. **gravewards** *adv.* L19.

grave /greɪv/ *n.*[2] ME. [Sense 1 f. ON *greifi* f. OLG *grēve*; sense 2 f. OLG *grēve* rel. to MHG *grâve* (G GRAF).] 1 Orig., a steward. Later, each of a number of elected administrative officials in townships in certain parts of Yorkshire and Lincolnshire. *obs.* exc. *Hist.* ME. 2 A foreign nobleman, a count; *spec.* a Count of Nassau. Earlier and now only as 2nd elem. in *burgrave*, *landgrave*, *margrave*, etc. E17.

grave /greɪv; *in sense 5 and as n.* grɑːv/ *a.*[1] & *n.*[3] L15. [(O)Fr., or L *gravis* heavy, important.] A *adj.* †1 Of a wound: serious, severe. (Cf. sense 6b below.) Only in L15. 2 Physically ponderous, heavy. Long *arch.* or *poet. rare.* E16. 3 Dignified in behaviour or delivery; solemn; serious as opp. to mirthful or jocular. E16. b Expressive of or befitting serious feelings; solemn, serious; slow-moving. L16. †4 Of people, their writings, etc.: having weight or importance; influential; respected; authoritative. M16–M18. 5 Of a sound: low-pitched, deep (*Phonet.* a classificatory feature opp. *acute*). M16. 6 Of a matter: weighty, significant; requiring serious consideration. M16. b Of a fault, difficulty, responsibility: highly serious, formidable. Of a symptom: threatening a serious or fatal outcome. E19. 7 Of dress, colour, etc.: sombre, plain; not striking or showy. L16.

2 WORDSWORTH The mountains against the heaven's grave weight Rise up. 3 G. BERKELEY The nation ought to be too grave for such trifles. I. MURDOCH His grave frowning gaze betrayed weighty thoughts. b DICKENS The children had ancient faces and grave voices. 4 SHAKES. *Coriol.* Most reverend and grave elders. 5 A. BEDFORD The Verse was also mixt with acute and grave Sounds. **grave accent** the mark ` placed over letters in some languages to show quality, vowel length, pronunciation, etc. 6 SIR W. SCOTT When our council is assembled, we will treat of graver matters. b OED Grave news from the front. 7 GEO. ELIOT The folds of his . . garment . . hang in grave unbroken lines from neck to ankle.

B *n.* A grave accent. Formerly also, a grave note. E17.

gravely *adv.* in a grave manner M16. **graveness** *n.* the quality or state of being grave, sobriety, gravity: L16.

grave /greɪv/ *v.*[1] Pa. t. **graved**; pa. pple **graven** /ˈgreɪv(ə)n/, **graved.** [OE *grafan* str. vb (also in *begrafan* bury) = OLFrank. *gravan* (Du. *graven*) dig, OHG *graban* dig, carve (G *graben* dig, *begraben* bury), ON *grafa* dig, bury, Goth. *graban* dig, f. Gmc: cf. GRAVE *n.*[1], GROOVE *n.*] I 1 *v.i.* Dig. *obs.* exc. *dial.* OE. 2 *v.t.* Dig (out), excavate; form by digging. Also foll. by *out*, *up*, †*away*. Long *rare* exc. *dial.* OE.

2 COVERDALE *Jer.* 18:14 Maye the springes off waters be grauen awaye.

II 3 *v.t.* Form by carving; carve; sculpt. *obs.* exc. *poet.* OE. †4 *v.t.* Cut into (a hard material) (*lit.* & *fig.*). Also, mark by incisions; ornament by incised marks; engrave. ME–L17. 5 *v.t.* Engrave (an inscription, figure, etc.) on a surface; engrave (a surface) *with* letters etc. Also, record by engraved or incised letters. *arch.* ME. b *fig.* Impress deeply, fix indelibly (*on*, *in* the mind etc.). LME. †6 *v.t.* Portray or copy in an engraving. M17–E19.

3 MILTON Affirming it thy Star new graven in Heaven. H. PHILLIPS I graved for thee a silver god. 4 SHAKES. *Ven. & Ad.* Being steel'd, soft sighs can never grave it [thy heart]. 5 R. D. BLACKMORE My name . . graven on that very form. C. BOWEN Graved on the doors is the death of Androgeos.

III 7 *v.t.* Deposit (a corpse) in the ground or in a tomb; bury; inter. Long *arch.* ME. †b Deposit or hide underground. Only in ME. †c Swallow up (as) in a grave. ME–E17.

7 JAS. GRANT Dead too and graved in yonder kirk. c SHAKES. *Timon* Ditches grave you all!

grave /greɪv/ *v.*[2]*t.* LME. [Prob. f. dial. Fr. *grave* (OFr. = GRAVEL *n.*), var. of (O)Fr. *grève* shore f. Celt. base = gravel, pebbles, repr. by Breton *grouan* GROWAN.] Clean (a ship's bottom) by burning off accretions and tarring while aground or in dry dock. Now *Hist.* exc. in *graving dock* s.v. DOCK *n.*[3]

grave /grɑːv, 'grɑːveɪ/ *adv.* & *a.*[2] L16. [Fr. or It., = GRAVE *a.*[1]] *Mus.* A direction: with slow and solemn movement.

†gravedo *n.* E18–L19. [L *gravedo* heaviness (in the limbs or head), f. *gravis* heavy.] *Med.* A cold in the head; coryza.

gravel /'grav(ə)l/ *n.* ME. [OFr. *gravel* masc., *gravel(l)e* fem., dim. of OFr. *grave* gravel, coarse sand: see GRAVE *v.*[2], -EL[2].] †1 Sand. ME–E18. 2 Coarse sand and small water-worn or pounded stones, sometimes with an intermixture of clay, used for laying paths and roads. ME. b A stratum of this; formerly *esp.* one containing gold. M19. 3 *Med.* Aggregations of visible calculi in the urinary tract; a disease marked by these. LME.

Comb.: **gravel-blind** *a.* almost completely blind (orig. *joc.* 'more than sand-blind', with reference to Shakes. *Merch. V.*); **gravel court** a tennis-court with a surface of gravel; **gravel culture** a hydroponic method of plant cultivation, using beds of gravel supplied with nutrient solutions; **gravel-pit** an excavation from which gravel is or has been obtained; **gravel-rash** abrasions caused by a fall on a gravelly or rough surface; **gravel voice** a deep rough-sounding voice; **gravel-voiced** *a.*; **gravel-walk** an alley or path laid with gravel.

gravelish *a.* M16.

gravel /'grav(ə)l/ *v.t.* Infl. **-ll-**, ***-l-**. LME. [f. the n.] 1 Lay or cover (a path etc.) with gravel or sand. Freq. (earlier) as *gravelled* ppl a. LME. †b Choke or block (*up*) with gravel or sand. Only in 17. 2 *fig.* Bring to a standstill, confound, embarrass, nonplus, perplex, puzzle. Also (chiefly *US* & *dial.*), irritate, be uncongenial to. M16. †3 Bury in gravel or sand; overwhelm with gravel; *fig.* suppress, stifle. L16–L17. †4 Run (a ship) aground. Usu. in *pass.* L16–L17. 5 Cause (a horse) to suffer from gravelling (see below). Usu. in *pass.* L16. 6 *gravelled voice*, = *gravel voice* s.v. GRAVEL *n.* M20.

2 R. BURNS These English songs gravel me to death. E. P. WHIPPLE We might hear.. Sophocles gravel a sophist with his interrogative logic. 4 *fig.*: J. HEALEY Graueled in the quick-sands of erroneous ignorance.

graveller *n.* (*rare*) something which perplexes or puzzles, a 'poser' L17.

gravelling /'grav(ə)lɪŋ/ *n.*[1] Also **graveling**. E16. [f. GRAVEL *v.* + -ING[1].] 1 Injury to a horse caused by particles of gravel forced between the shoe and the hoof. E16. 2 The action of GRAVEL *v.* L16.

gravelling /'grav(ə)lɪŋ/ *n.*[2] Also **graveling**. L16. [Origin unkn.] A parr; a young salmon or trout.

gravelly /'grav(ə)li/ *a.* LME. [f. GRAVEL *n.* + -Y[1].] 1 Full of gravel; consisting of or containing gravel; strewn with gravel; resembling gravel. Formerly also, containing much sand, sandy. LME. 2 *Med.* Of the nature of gravel (GRAVEL *n.* 3); characterized by or arising from the presence of gravel. LME. †3 Containing gritty particles. M17–E18. 4 Of a voice: deep and rough-sounding. M20.

†gravelous *a.* LME–M18. [(O)Fr. *graveleux*, f. as GRAVEL *n.*: see -OUS.] Gravelly; granular.

graven /'greɪv(ə)n/ *ppl a.* LME. [pa. pple of GRAVE *v.*[1]] 1 Sculptured, hewn. LME. 2 Carved on a surface; engraved. E19.

1 **graven image** an idol (esp. in allusion to *Exod.* 20:4). 2 L. DURRELL The mason's signature upon the graven iron plaque.

graven *v.* pa. pple: see GRAVE *v.*[1]

Gravenstein /'grɑːv(ə)nstʌɪn/ *n.* E19. [G form of *Graasten*, a village in Denmark formerly in Schleswig-Holstein, Germany.] A variety of eating apple, which has large fruit with yellow, red-streaked skin.

graveolent /grə'vɪəl(ə)nt/ *a.* M17. [L *graveolent-*, f. *grave* use as adv. of neut. of *gravis* heavy (see GRAVE *a.*[1]) + *olent-*, *-ens* pres. pple of *olere* have a smell: see -ENT.] Having a rank offensive smell; fetid.

†graveolency *n.* (*rare*) E17–E18.

graver /'greɪvə/ *n.* OE. [f. GRAVE *v.*[1] + -ER[1].] 1 Orig., a sculptor. Later, a carver, an engraver. Now *rare*. OE. 2 A person who digs, or digs up turf. Long *obs.* exc. *dial.* ME. 3 Any of various tools for cutting and shaving; now *esp.* an engraver's tool, a burin. LME.

Graves /grɑːv/ *n.*[1] Pl. same /grɑːvz/. E17. [Fr. (see below).] A white or red wine produced in the Graves district of SW France.

graves *n.*[2]*pl.* var. of GREAVES.

Graves' disease /'greɪvz dɪˌziːz/ *n. phr.* M19. [f. Robert J. *Graves* (1796–1853), Ir. physician.] *Med.* A disease caused by excessive thyroid secretion, characterized by weight loss, a nervous tremor, staring eyes, and a swollen neck; exophthalmic goitre.

Gravette /grə'vɛt/ *n.* Also **g-**. E20. [La *Gravette*, a site in SW France.] *Archaeol.* Used (usu. *attrib.*) to designate a type of long narrow knifelike flint characteristic of the Gravettian culture (see below).

Gravettian *a.* & *n.* (*a*) *adj.* designating or pertaining to an upper palaeolithic culture represented by remains found at La Gravette; (*b*) *n.* (a person of) *the* Gravettian culture: M20.

graveyard /'greɪvjɑːd/ *n.* L18. [f. GRAVE *n.*[1] + YARD *n.*[1]] A burial ground.

fig.: D. W. GOODWIN The history of medicine is a graveyard of treatments that were worthless but flourished.

Comb.: **graveyard cough** = *churchyard cough* s.v. CHURCH *n.* **graveyard shift** (chiefly *N. Amer.*) (the relay of workers on duty during) the work period between midnight and 8 a.m.; **graveyard watch** *Naut.* the middle watch between midnight and 4 a.m.

gravid /'gravɪd/ *a.* L16. [L *gravidus* laden, pregnant, f. *gravis* heavy: see GRAVE *a.*[1], -ID[1].] Of an animal or (now *literary*) a woman: pregnant, heavy with young.

†gravidation *n.* the condition or fact of being pregnant L15–E18. **gra'vidity** *n.* the state of being gravid, pregnancy M17.

gravida /'gravɪdə/ *n.* M20. [L, use as n. of fem. of *gravidus* GRAVID.] *Med.* A woman who is pregnant; (with preceding or following numeral) a woman who had had the specified number of pregnancies, including a present one.

Lancet Born to a 36-year-old gravida 7, para 5 mother by vaginal delivery.

gravific /grə'vɪfɪk/ *a.* E19. [Fr. *gravifique* f. L *gravis* heavy + *-fique* -FIC.] That makes heavy or produces weight.

gravimeter /grə'vɪmɪtə/ *n.* L18. [Fr. *gravimètre*, f. L *gravis* heavy: see -METER.] 1 A kind of hydrometer for measuring the relative density of solid or liquid bodies. L18. 2 (Now the usual sense.) Any instrument designed to measure the variation in the force of gravity from one place to another. M20.

gravimetric /gravɪ'mɛtrɪk/ *a.* L19. [f. prec. + -METRIC.] Of or pertaining to gravimeters or gravimetry.

gravimetric analysis quantitative chemical analysis based on the weighing of reagents and products.

gravimetrical *a.* = GRAVIMETRIC L19. **gravimetrically** *adv.* M19.

gravimetry /grə'vɪmɪtri/ *n.* M19. [f. as prec. + -METRY.] The measurement of weight; *esp.* the use of a gravimeter to measure gravitational force.

graving /'greɪvɪŋ/ *n.* ME. [f. GRAVE *v.*[1] + -ING[1].] 1 Digging. *obs.* exc. *dial.* ME. †2 Burial. Only in ME. 3†a Carving, sculpturing; incision of ornamental lines etc. in stone, metal, or other material. LME–E18. b Something cut or carved; a carving, a sculpture; an inscription. *arch.* LME. 4 The engraving of a design, picture, etc. on metal or wood. *arch.* M17.

Comb.: **graving tool** (*a*) = GRAVER 3; (*b*) (*dial.*, *rare*) a spade used in making drains etc.

gravitas /'gravɪtɑːs, -tas/ *n.* E20. [L.] Solemn demeanour; seriousness.

gravitate /'gravɪteɪt/ *v.* M17. [mod.L *gravitat-* pa. ppl stem of *gravitare*, f. L *gravitas* gravity: see -ATE[3].] †1 *v.i.* Exert weight or pressure, press *on*. Of a heavy body: (tend to) move downward by its own weight. M17–E19. 2 *v.i.* Be affected by gravitation; move or tend to move by the force of gravity (*towards* etc.). L17. b Sink or fall (as) by gravitation; tend to reach a low level; settle down. E19. c *v.t.* Cause to descend or sink by gravitation. *rare*. L19. 3 *v.i.* Move or tend to move towards a certain point or object as a natural goal or destination; be strongly attracted to some centre of influence. Freq. foll. by *to*, *towards*. L17.

2 J. N. LOCKYER Systems of bodies which gravitate round a central body. T. HARDY That natural law of physics which causes lesser bodies to gravitate towards the greater. b F. W. ROBERTSON The soul gravitates downward beneath its burden. 3 G. F. KENNAN Governmental power in Russia gravitated increasingly to the left. D. M. DAVIN I gravitated of an evening to the Wheatsheaf. J. LE CARRÉ Gravitating by instinct towards Cambridge Circus.

gravitation /gravɪ'teɪʃ(ə)n/ *n.* M17. [mod.L *gravitatio(n-)*, f. as prec.: see -ATION.] 1 The action or process of gravitating; the falling of bodies to earth; movement, or tendency to move, towards a centre of attractive force. M17. 2 The attractive force exerted by each particle of matter on every other particle. M17. 3 *transf.* & *fig.* Attraction or tendency to move towards a centre of influence; natural tendency (*to*, *towards*). M17.

1 D. BREWSTER The moon.. kept in her orbit by gravitation to the earth. 2 S. WEINBERG Galaxies.. slowing down under the influence of their mutual gravitation. **law of gravitation** the law according to which the force of gravity acting between two bodies is directly proportional to the product of their masses and inversely proportional to the square of the distance between them. 3 W. COWPER That low And sordid gravitation of his pow'rs To a vile clod.

gravitational /gravɪ'teɪʃ(ə)n(ə)l/ *a.* M19. [f. prec. + -AL[1].] Of, pertaining to, or caused by gravitation.

gravitational constant the constant of proportionality in the equation relating the strength of the gravitational attaction between two bodies to their masses and their separation, equal to 6.67×10^{-11} N m^2 kg^{-2} approx. (symbol *G*). **gravitational lens** *Astron.* a region of space containing a massive body whose gravitational field acts like a lens on electromagnetic radiation. **gravitational mass** the mass of a body as measured by the force exerted on the body by a gravitational field. **gravitational radiation** gravitational waves (sense a below). **gravitational system (of units)** a system of units based on a fundamental unit of weight rather than a unit of mass. **gravitational wave** (*a*) a periodic variation in gravitational field-strength which is propagated through space; (*b*) = *gravity wave* s.v. GRAVITY.

gravitationally *adv.* L19.

gravitative /'gravɪteɪtɪv/ *a.* L18. [f. GRAVITATE + -IVE.] = prec.

gravitino /gravɪ'tiːnəʊ/ *n.* Pl. **-os**. L20. [f. next + -INO.] *Particle Physics.* The supersymmetric counterpart of a graviton, with spin 3/2 instead of 2.

graviton /'gravɪtɒn/ *n.* M20. [f. GRAVIT(ATION + -ON.] *Particle Physics.* A hypothetical subatomic particle supposed to propagate the gravitational force.

gravity /'gravɪti/ *n.* L15. [(O)Fr. *gravité* or L *gravitas*, f. *gravis* GRAVE *a.*[1]: see -ITY.] I 1 Grave or serious character or nature; importance; seriousness. L15. 2 Dignity, solemnity, serious and dignified formality; solemn conduct or demeanour, staidness. Now *esp.* seriousness as opp. to levity or gaiety. E16. 3†a Weight, influence, authority. M16–M18. b Something grave; a grave or serious subject, speech, or remark. Formerly also as a respectful title. *arch.* E17.

1 J. PARKER Great questions should be considered in a spirit worthy of their gravity. 2 LD MACAULAY The gravity and pomp of the whole proceeding. H. CAINE She grew uneasy at the settled gravity of his face. 3b GIBBON Your Gravity, Your Excellency, Your Eminence. GEO. ELIOT Books of German science, and other gravities.

II 4†a The quality of having weight; tendency to downward motion. Only in 17. b Weight, heaviness. Now chiefly in *centre of gravity*, *specific gravity* below. M17. 5 Lowness of pitch of sound. M17. 6 The attractive force by which bodies are drawn towards the centre of the earth or of another celestial object; the degree of intensity of this measured by the acceleration produced; gravitational force. L17.

4b *centre of gravity*: see CENTRE *n. specific gravity*: see SPECIFIC *a.* 6 BURKE If I were to explain the motion of a body falling to the ground, I would say it was caused by gravity. P. DAVIES Stars so massive that their gravity even traps their own light. *zero gravity*: see ZERO *n.* & *a.*

Comb.: **gravity-fed** *a.* supplied with material by gravity feed; **gravity feed** a supply system that makes use of gravity to maintain the flow of material; the supply of material in this way; **gravity wave** (*a*) a wave on a liquid surface in which the dominant force is gravity; (*b*) = GRAVITATIONAL *wave* (a).

gravure /grəˈvjʊə/ *n.* L19. [Abbrev.] = PHOTOGRAVURE.

gravy /ˈgreɪvi/ *n.* ME. [Perh. f. misreading as *gravé* of OFr. *grané*, prob. f. *grain* spice (cf. OFr. *grenon* stew): see GRAIN *n.*[1], -Y[5].] **1** A kind of dressing used for white meats, fish, and vegetables, comprising broth, milk of almonds, spices, and (usu.) wine or ale; a sauce. Long *obs.* exc. *Sc.* ME. **2** The fat and juices that exude from meat during and after cooking; a dressing for food made from these and other ingredients. L16. **b** Laughter readily obtained from an audience; good comic lines. *Theatr. slang.* M19. **c** Money easily acquired; an unearned or unexpected bonus; a tip. *slang* (orig. *US*). E20.

Comb.: **gravy-boat** a boat-shaped vessel for serving gravy; **the gravy train** (*slang*) a source of easy financial benefit.

Gray /greɪ/ *n.*[1] M20. [F. *Gray* (1887–1969), US physicist.] Used *attrib.* with ref. to a code in which consecutive integers are represented by binary numbers differing in only one digit.

gray /greɪ/ *n.*[2] L20. [L. H. *Gray* (1905–65), English radiobiologist.] *Physics.* The SI unit of absorbed dose of ionizing radiation, corresponding to the absorption of one joule of energy per kilogram of irradiated material. (Symbol Gy.)

gray *n.*[3], *a.*, *v.* see GREY *n.*, *a.*, *v.*

grayling /ˈgreɪlɪŋ/ *n.* ME. [f. *gray* var. of GREY *a.* + -LING[1].] **1** A European freshwater salmonid fish, *Thymallus thymallus*, with a long, high dorsal fin. Also (in full *Arctic grayling*), a related holarctic fish, *T. arcticus*. ME. **b** A silvery freshwater fish of the genus *Prototroctes*, superficially resembling a trout, native to Australia and New Zealand. L19. **2** A brown Eurasian satyrid butterfly, *Hipparchia semele*, with grey undersides to its wings. Also, a similar, related N. American butterfly, *Cercyonis pegala*. E19.

†graymill *n.* M16–M18. [Alt. of Fr. *grémil* GROMWELL after GRAY *a.*] = GROMWELL.

graywacke *n.* see GREYWACKE.

grazable *a.* var. of GRAZEABLE.

graze /greɪz/ *n.* L17. [f. GRAZE *v.*[2]] **1** An act or instance of (esp. shot) grazing or touching lightly. L17. **2** A superficial wound or abrasion. M19.

graze /greɪz/ *v.*[1] [OE *grasian*, f. GRASS *n.*; cf. MDu., MHG *grasen* and GRASS *v.*] **1** *v.i.* Of an animal: feed on growing grass or other herbage. OE. **b** Of a person: eat small quantities of food at frequent intervals in the course of other activities. Chiefly *US.* L20. **2** *v.t.* & *i.* Put (an animal) to feed on growing grass; tend (an animal) while so feeding. M16. **3** *v.t.* (Of an animal) feed on (grass etc.); (of a person) put cattle to feed on (grass, land). E17. **4** *v.i.* Of land: produce grass; be suitable for grazing. *obs.* exc. *dial.* E17.

1 J. A. MICHENER A few goats grazed among the scattered boulders. *fig.*: *Times* Anyone who grazes . . off the front page of *The Times*. 2 J. R. MCCULLOCH Great numbers of cattle . . are grazed in the fens. 3 S. JOHNSON You may graze the ground when the trees are grown up. *Sunday Express* Cattle grazed meadows which flooded regularly in the spring.

grazer *n.* an animal or person that grazes E18. **grazing** *n.* (*a*) the action of the vb; (*b*) pasture-land, pasture: LME.

graze /greɪz/ *v.*[2] L16. [Perh. a spec. use of prec., as if 'take off the grass close to the ground'; cf. G *grasen* browse, pasture, scythe, glance off, Sw. *gräsa* (of a shot) graze, Da. *græsse* pasture, (of a bullet) ricochet.] **1** *v.i.* Touch lightly in passing, esp. so as to produce a slight abrasion. Formerly also, (of a bullet) ricochet. Usu. foll. by *against*, *along*, *by*, *past*, etc. L16. **2** *v.t.* Touch (a surface) lightly in passing; abrade (skin etc.) in rubbing past; suffer a slight abrasion of (a part of the body). E17.

1 H. BASCOM Wharf timbers creak . . as a tethered steamer grazes and pounds against them. 2 M. STOTT I was always falling over and grazing my knee. M. IGNATIEFF She leans over him, her hand grazing the back of his head.

grazeable /ˈgreɪzəb(ə)l/ *a.* Also **grazable**. M17. [f. GRAZE *v.*[1] + -ABLE.] Of land: that may be grazed, suitable for grazing.

grazet /grəˈzɛt/ *n. obs.* exc. *Hist.* or *poet.* L17. [Perh. f. Fr. *grisette* a cheap grey woollen fabric] A silk and worsted dress material.

grazier /ˈgreɪzɪə/ *n.* ME. [f. GRASS *n.*: see -IER. Formerly assoc. with Fr. *graissier* fattener.] A person who grazes or feeds cattle for the market; *Austral.* a sheep-farmer.

graziery *n.* the occupation or business of a grazier M18.

grazioso /gratsiˈoːzo/ *a.* & *adv.* E19. [It. = gracious, graceful.] *Mus.* A direction: graceful(ly).

†greal *n.* var. of GRAIL *n.*[2]

grease /griːs/ *n.* ME. [AN *grece*, *gresse*, (O)Fr. *graisse* f. Proto-Romance f. L *crassus*: see CRASS.] **1 †a** *gen.* The fat part of the body of an animal; fatness. ME–L17. **b** *Hunting.* The fat of a game animal. ME. **2** Melted fat of a (usu. specified) dead animal; *gen.* oily or fatty matter, esp. in semi-solid state as a lubricant. ME. **b** Butter. *dial.* & *slang.* L18. **c** The oily matter in wool; uncleansed wool. M19. **3** = GREASY *heels.* L17. **4** Money given as a bribe, or as protection money. (Cf. GREASE *v.* 3). *slang.* L18.

1b **in grease**, **in prime** or **pride of grease** fat and fit for killing. 2 J. MORTIMER A pole's covered with grease and you have to try and climb it but of course you can't. B. LOPEZ The husband wiped seal grease from his fingers with a ptarmigan wing. **c in the grease** that has not been cleansed after shearing.

Comb.: **grease-ball** *N. Amer. slang, derog.* (*a*) a foreigner, esp. of Mediterranean or Latin American origin; (*b*) = GREASER 3c; **grease-band** *n.* & *v.* (*a*) *n.* a band of sticky material applied to a tree-trunk, as a barrier against insects; (*b*) *v.t.* apply such a band to (a tree); **grease cup**: from which machinery is supplied with grease; *grease-gun*: see GUN *n.* 5. **grease monkey** *slang* a mechanic; **greasepaint** a waxy substance used as make-up by a stage performer; **greaseproof** *a.* (esp. of paper) impervious to the penetration of grease; **grease-trap** an appliance for catching grease in drains; **greasewood** any of various dwarf resinous shrubs of the goosefoot family, esp. *Sarcobatus vermiculatus*, which grow in dry alkaline valleys in the western US.

grease /griːs, -z/ *v.* LME. [f. the n. Cf. Fr. *graisser*.] **1** *v.t.* Smear or anoint with grease. LME. **b** *v.t.* & *i.* Apply a salve of tallow and tar to (sheep). Now *rare.* LME. **c** *v.t.* Make greasy; soil with grease or fat. E17. **2** *v.t.* Lubricate with grease. LME. **3** *v.t.* Ply with money, bribe. Chiefly in *grease a person's hand* or *palm.* E16. **4** *v.t.* Cause (a horse) to contract the disease greasy heels. E18.

1 *like greased lightning*: see LIGHTNING *n.* 1. 2 D. W. JERROLD Silently went the window up . . as though greased by some witch. **grease the wheels** *fig.* make things run smoothly; provide the entertainment, pay the expenses. 3 **grease the fat pig** or **sow** give to a person needing nothing.

greaser /ˈgriːsə, -z-/ *n.* M17. [f. prec. + -ER[1].] **†1** A person who greases sheep. Only in M17. **2** A person who cleans and lubricates machinery with grease; *spec.* an engineer on a ship. M19. **3** A Latin American; *spec.* a Mexican. *US slang.* (*derog.* & usu. considered *racially offensive*). M19. **b** An objectionable person; a sycophant. *slang.* E20. **c** A member of a gang of (typically long-haired) motorcyclists. *slang.* M20. **4** A machine used to separate diamonds from the material in which they are found. E20. **5** A smooth or gentle aircraft landing. *slang.* L20.

greasy /ˈgriːsi, -zi/ *a.* E16. [f. GREASE *n.* + -Y[1].] **1** Smeared, covered, or soiled with grease. E16. **†b** Esp. of language: obscene. L16–E19. **2** Composed of or containing grease; of the nature of grease; *spec.* (of food or diet) containing too much grease. L16. **b** *spec.* Of wool: containing natural grease, uncleansed. L16. **3** Having the appearance or feel of containing or being covered with grease. E18. **b** Of a road, path, etc.: slippery with moisture or mud. E19. **c** Of the weather or the sky: threatening, stormy. E19. **4** Of a horse: suffering from greasy heels (see below). E18. **5** Of manner or expression: disagreeably unctuous. M19.

1 V. WOOLF I hate your greasy handkerchiefs—you will stain your copy of *Don Juan*. O. MANNING A waiter . . producing from an inner pocket a greasy, food-splashed card. *Practical Hairstyling & Beauty* If your hair tends to get greasy after a week without washing—that's normal. 2 T. HOOD When a German dish is not sour it is sure to be greasy. 3 T. SHARPE Their foreheads greasy with perspiration. b DICKENS Just enough damp gently stealing down to make the pavement greasy. 5 THACKERAY With a . . greasy simper—he fawns on everybody.

Special collocations: **greasy heels** a chronic inflammation of the skin and sebaceous glands of a horse's heels. **greasy pole**: greased for difficult climbing or walking on in sports. **greasy spoon** (**restaurant**) *slang* a cheap inferior café or restaurant.

greasily *adv.* L16. **greasiness** *n.* M16.

great /greɪt/ *a.*, *n.*, & *adv.* [OE *grēat* = OFris. *grāt*, OS *grōt* (Du. *groot*), OHG *grōz* (G *gross*), f. WGmc, of unkn. origin.] **A** *adj.* **I** Thick, coarse, massive, big. **1** Composed of large particles; coarse of grain or texture. Formerly also, (of diet) coarse, not delicate. *obs.* exc. *Sc.* OE. **2** Thick; massive, big, bulky; stout, corpulent. *obs.* exc. *Sc.* OE. **3** Pregnant; far advanced in pregnancy. Foll. by *with*. Now *arch.* & *dial.* ME. **4** Esp. of the heart: full of emotion, esp. grief; angry, grieved, proud. *obs.* exc. *Sc.* ME. **5** (Of the sea) high, stormy; (of a river) swollen, in flood. *dial.* LME.

3 *fig.*: SHAKES. *Per.* I am great with woe, and shall deliver weeping.

II Highly placed in a scale of measurement or quantity. **6** Of relatively large or above average size, extent, duration, quantity, number, degree, or intensity. OE. **†b** A great number or quantity of; many, much. LME–L17. **c** *attrib.* in compar. *Greater.* (Of a city etc.) including adjacent urban areas; (of a country) including dependencies. E17. **7a** Of an object: big, large, (now usu. w. implied surprise, admiration, contempt, indignation, etc.). Freq. preceding a partly synon. adj. w. intensive force. ME. **b** *attrib.* Designating the larger or largest of things of the class specified; forming names of animals (esp. birds), towns, rivers, streets, districts, etc., that are larger or more important, earlier established, etc., than another or others of that name. Opp. LITTLE *a.* 1b. LME. **c** Of a letter: capital. *arch.* M16. **d** Of a specified part of a building or a particular building etc.: main, principal. L16. **e** *attrib.* in compar. *greater*. Designating the larger of two similar or related plants, animals, anatomical parts, or places. Opp. LESSER *a.* 2a. L18. **†8** Of an animal, esp. above a particular age: full-grown, mature. L15–L18.

6 LD MACAULAY To raise a great army had always been the King's first object. T. HARDY I feel it a great relief, Farfrae, to tell some friend o' this. E. WAUGH Soon everyone was eating and drinking at a great pace. I. MURDOCH These matters had occupied Christopher for a greater part of the night. G. GORDON What he had in mind would cost a great deal. *Southern Rag* They played a great variety of songs and tunes. A. THWAITE He had no great hopes of immortality and his reputation certainly suffered . . after his death. E. AMADI Right now my greatest desire is to patch up this quarrel. c *Listener* Apart from Greater London and Greater Birmingham all the conurbations were . . increasing their population. 7a S. RICHARDSON A great over grown, lank-haired, chubby boy. J. STEINBECK There it lay, the great pearl, perfect as the moon. L. P. HARTLEY It was a great big thing, the size of a small haystack. E. ARDIZZONE A gale was blowing and the great waves were crashing on the beach. b *great mullein*, *great reed warbler*, *great tit*, *great willowherb*, etc.; *Great Malvern*, *Great Ouse*, *Great Portland Street*, etc. c *Church Times* Canon Gore will lecture . . in the Great Hall of the Church House. e *greater celandine*, *greater horseshoe bat*, etc.

III Important, elevated, distinguished. 9 Of more than ordinary importance; weighty; distinguished; pre-eminent; famous. ME. **b** Of a time, day, etc.: having important results; critical. LME. †**c** Distinguished or impressive in appearance. L16–L17. **10** (Of a person) eminent by reason of birth, rank, wealth, or power; (of a thing) of or pertaining to such a person. ME. **b** — *the Great*: designating a person, esp. a monarch, as pre-eminent amongst those of that name. LME. **c** Designating an official who is senior to others of the same general rank. *obs.* exc. in *Lord Great Chamberlain*. M16. **11** Of a person: extraordinary or remarkable in ability, genius, or achievement in some specific or specified activity. ME. **b** *gen.* Eminent in (esp. mental) achievement or moral worth; having integrity or nobility of character. E18. **c** Of the soul, ideas, etc.: lofty, magnanimous, noble. E18. **12** *attrib.* Being or having the quality of the n. indicated to a high degree; (of an agent) that does the action indicated habitually or extensively. ME. **b** *pred.* Having considerable knowledge of a specified subject; skilled in doing something specified. Foll. by *at*, *on*, *colloq.* E17. **13** Intimate, familiar, friendly, *with* (now only *Sc.* & *dial.*); much in use, high in favour *with* (now *rare*). LME. **14** Excellent, very good, fine, admirable. *colloq.* E19.

9 J. BUCHAN I felt that great things, tremendous things, were happening. DAY LEWIS In youth, I thought it great and glorious to be a Poet. P. V. PRICE When the Cabernet Sauvignon makes a good wine, it is so good that it verges on great. I. MURDOCH Would he be called upon to make great choices, world-altering decisions? R. HUNTFORD Dulwich was not exactly one of the great public schools with aristocratic connections. b LD MACAULAY The great day of the Exclusion Bill. 10 LD MACAULAY The great man, at whose frown, a few days before, the whole kingdom had trembled. R. H. TAWNEY None are too mean to be beneath or too great to be above it [religion]. R. GRAVES Aren't you someone greater than Jove? b J. H. BURTON Napoleon was little, so was Frederic the Great. 11 *Law Times* If he was great as an advocate, he was still greater as a judge. M. LOWRY She might under other conditions have become a really first-rate, even a great artist. T. S. ELIOT He was a great financier—And I am merely a successful one. b SCOTT FITZGERALD He had been told Lincoln was a great man whom he should admire. M. KLINE Pascal was great in many fields. c A. THWAITE I tried to open up so many eyes To the great minds of all humanity. 12 SHAKES. *Twel. N.* I am a great eater of beef. J. FORBES Epicures esteem the black pomfret a great dainty. H. JAMES Are you and he such great friends? SCOTT FITZGERALD I was just as beautiful as the great beauties. T. WOGAN My beloved cockatiel . . was in his day a great pecker of . . fingers. b THACKERAY He was great at cooking many of his Virginian dishes. 14 P. KAVANAGH It was such nice sweet land, . . great for growing potatoes and oats. G. SWIFT Great! I'm glad you've got it all so worked out! A. TYLER I play a great guitar. P. ROTH 'I want you to work with me.' 'Oh, great.'

Special collocations & *phrases*: **a great one for** a habitual doer of, an enthusiast for. *go great guns*: see GUN *n. great Argus*: see ARGUS 3. **great attractor** *Astron.* a large aggregation of galaxies several hundred million light-years away that is thought to be the cause of the deviation of nearer galaxies from uniform recession. *great* AUK. *Great Bear*: see BEAR *n.*[1] 2. **Great Bible** the English version of the Bible by Coverdale (1539). **great blue heron** a large grey-blue heron, *Ardea herodias*, which is found in N. and Central America. *Great Britain*: see BRITAIN *n.*[1] **Great British Public** (*joc.* or *iron.*) the British people. *great* CALORIE. *great* CASSINO. *Great Charter*: see CHARTER *n. great circle*: see CIRCLE *n. Great Council*: see COUNCIL *n. great cry and little wool*: see CRY *n. Great Dane*: see DANE 2. **great day** *arch.* (*a*) the Day of Judgement; (*b*) an important feast- or fast-day. *great deal*: see DEAL *n.*[1] **Great Deliverer**: William III of Great Britain (1650–1702). *Great Dipper*: see DIPPER 5a. *great divide*: see DIVIDE *n. Great Dog*: see DOG *n.* 5. *great egret*: see *great white egret* below. *Great Entrance*: see ENTRANCE *n. Greater* BAIRAM. *greater diesis*: see DIESIS 1. *Greater Doxology*: see DOXOLOGY 2. *greater* PANATHENAEA. **Great Fire**: which destroyed much of London in September 1666. **great game** (*a*) golf; (*b*) spying. **great go** *arch. slang* the final examination for the degree of BA at the Universities of Oxford and Cambridge. *great grief!*: see GRIEF *n.* **great gross** twelve gross, 1,728. *great gun*: see GUN *n.* **great horse** *Hist.* a war-horse, *spec.* that of a knight in armour. **great house** the large house belonging to the person of highest social standing of a locality. *great hundred*: see HUNDRED *n.* 5. *great inquest*: see INQUEST 2. **great insertion** the section of St Luke's Gospel, 9:51–18:14, which is independent of St Mark. **great kangaroo** = FORESTER 3a (b). **Great Lakes** a group of large lakes along the boundary of US and Canada, comprising Superior, Huron, Michigan, Erie, and Ontario. **great laurel** an evergreen shrub of the heath family, *Rhododendron maximum*, of the eastern US. **Great Leap (Forward)** an unsuccessful attempt, begun in 1958, to modernize China rapidly by introducing advanced techniques into industry. **great-line** a long line used in deep-sea fishing for cod, ling, etc. *great northern diver*: see DIVER 1. **great omission** the section of St Mark's Gospel, 6:45–8:26, which is omitted in St Luke's. **great organ** the chief manual in a large organ, with its related pipes and mechanism. **Great Power** a nation of considerable economic or military strength and so playing an important part in international relations. †**great pox** syphilis. *great primer*: see PRIMER *n.*[1] 3. **Great Russian** *n.* & *a.* (*a*) *n.* a member of one of the principal ethnic groups in central Asia; the language of this group; (*b*) *adj.* of or pertaining to the Great Russians or Great Russian. **Great Scott!** *int.* expr. surprise, exasperation, etc. *Great Seal*: see SEAL *n.*[2] †**great ship** a man-of-war, a warship. **Great Spirit** [tr. Ojibwa *kitchi manitou*] the supreme god in the traditional religion of many N. American Indians. **great thought** (freq. *iron.*) a maxim, an apophthegm. **great toe** big toe. *great vassal*: see VASSAL *n.* 1. *great vowel shift*: see VOWEL *n.* **Great War** (*a*) the French Revolutionary and Napoleonic wars (1792–1815), jointly; (*b*) the war of 1914–18. **Great Week** = *Holy Week* s.v. HOLY *a. great white chief*: see CHIEF *n.* **great (white) egret** a large white egret, *Egretta alba*, which has a yellow bill and black legs and occurs worldwide. **great white heron** (*a*) = *great (white) egret* above; (*b*) *US* a white variety of the great blue heron, *Ardea herodias*, found in Florida. **great white shark** = *white shark* s.v. WHITE *a.* **Great White Way** [with ref. to the brilliant street illumination] Broadway in New York City. **great year** *Hist.* = *Platonic year* s.v. PLATONIC *a.* 1. *Lord Great Chamberlain*: see sense 10c above. *the great — in the sky*: see SKY *n. the great assize(s)*: see ASSIZE *n.* 3. *the great Author*: see AUTHOR *n.* 1. **the great majority** (*a*) by far the most (*b*) the dead; *join the great majority*, die. **the great outdoors** the open air; outdoor life. *the Great Rebellion*: see REBELLION. *the great unwashed*: see UNWASHED 2. **to a great extent** largely.

B *n.* †**1** Thickness. *rare*. OE–ME. **2** Great, eminent, or distinguished people. (Now usu. w. *the*.) ME. **b** Something great. Now only (*US colloq.*), a great part or amount, a great deal. ME. **c** That which is great; great things collectively. Formerly also, great quantity. M16. **3** A great, eminent, or distinguished person. ME. **4** (**G-**.) In *pl.* The final examination for the degree of BA at Oxford University. Now *spec.* (the final examinations for) an honours course in classics and philosophy. *colloq.* M19.

2 LD MACAULAY The masques which were exhibited at the mansions of the great. 3 J. WALSH Statues and paintings of the greats of French science and literature. L. ARMSTRONG I had hit the big time. I was up North with the greats.

Phrases: **by the great** (*a*) (now *dial.*) (of work done) at a fixed price for the whole amount; by the piece; †(*b*) in large quantities, wholesale. *modern Greats*: see MODERN *a.* †**in great** for the whole amount; wholesale; on a large scale. **the great and the good** (freq. *iron.*) worthy people. **the greatest** *colloq.* the best, the most wonderful, (person or thing).

C *adv.* **1** In a great degree; to a great extent; much; very. *obs.* exc. *dial.* ME. †**2** In a distinguished manner; imposingly. L17–M18. **3** Well, successfully. *colloq.* M20.

3 *New Yorker* 'How is Charlotte?' Vivian and I asked. 'Doing great,' Barry said.

greaterness *n.* (now *rare*) the condition or quality of being greater M16. **greatish** *a.* somewhat great M19.

great- /greɪt/ *comb. form.* M16. [Use of prec.] With the names of family relationship denoting one degree further removed in ascent or descent: repeatable according to the number of degrees to be expressed, as *great-great-grandfather*, *great-great-great-grandmother*, etc.

great-aunt a father's or mother's aunt. **great-grandchild** a grandchild's child. **great-granddaughter** a grandson's or granddaughter's daughter. **great-grandfather** a grandfather's or grandmother's father. **great-grandmother** a grandfather's or grandmother's mother. **great-grandson** a grandson's or granddaughter's son. **great-nephew** a nephew or niece's son. **great-niece** a nephew or niece's daughter. **great-uncle** a father's or mother's uncle.

greatcoat /ˈgreɪtkəʊt/ *n.* L17. [f. GREAT *a.* + COAT *n.*] A large heavy overcoat; a topcoat.

greatcoated *a.* wearing a greatcoat M18. **greatcoatless** *a.* L19.

greaten /ˈgreɪt(ə)n/ *v. arch.* LME. [f. GREAT *a.* + -EN[5].] †**1** *v.i.* Become pregnant. Only in LME. **2** *v.t.* Make great or greater in size or amount. E17. **3** Make eminent, prominent, distinguished, or important. E17. **b** Exalt mentally or spiritually; elevate (the mind). M17. **4** *v.i.* Become great or greater in size or extent. E18.

great-hearted /greɪtˈhɑːtɪd, ˈgreɪthɑːtɪd/ *a.* LME. [f. GREAT *a.* + HEARTED.] Magnanimous; having a noble or generous spirit.

great'heartedness *n.* E19.

greatly /ˈgreɪtli/ *adv.* ME. [f. GREAT *a.* + -LY[2].] **1** To a great extent; in a great degree; much; very. ME. **2** In a great manner; grandly. *arch.* LME. **3** On a large scale; in large numbers. Now *rare* or *obs.* L17. **b** For the most part; mainly. *rare.* M18. **4** In or to a high rank or position. *rare.* E19.

1 R. KIPLING Careless and lazy is he, Greatly inferior to Me. J. CONRAD 'It looks queer to me,' burst out Jukes, greatly exasperated. J. KOSINSKI Yours is the spirit which this country so greatly needs. 4 J. AUSTEN You encourage her to expect to marry greatly.

greatness /ˈgreɪtnɪs/ *n.* OE. [f. GREAT *a.* + -NESS.] †**1** Thickness, coarseness; stoutness. OE–M16. †**b** Pregnancy. LME–M17. **2** The quality of being great in size, extent, or degree. ME. †**b** Magnitude, size. LME–M18. **3** Great or high rank; eminence, distinction, importance. ME. †**b** With possess. adj. (as *your* etc. *greatness*): an honorific title given to a person of high rank or importance. L16–M18. **4** Inherent nobility or dignity (of mind, character, action, or expression). L16. †**5** Intimacy, familiarity. E17–L19.

3 LD MACAULAY Nothing in the early existence of Britain indicated the greatness which she was destined to attain.

greave /griːv/ *n.*[1] *obs.* exc. *dial.* [OE *grǣfa*, *grǣfe*, f. Gmc. Cf. GROVE.] †**1a** Brushwood. Only in OE. **b** A branch, a twig. LME–E17. **2** A thicket; a grove. OE.

greave /griːv/ *n.*[2] ME. [OFr. *greve* calf of the leg, shin, armour (mod.Fr. dial. *grève*, *graive* upper part of the leg) = Sp. *greba*, of unkn. origin.] A piece of armour for the leg below the knee, esp. the shin. Usu. in *pl.*

greaved *a.* equipped with greaves M19.

greaves /griːvz/ *n.pl.* Also **graves** /greɪvz/. E17. [LG *greven* pl. (whence also Da. *grever*) corresp. to OHG *griubo*, *griobo* (G *Griebe* refuse of lard or tallow), of unkn. origin: orig. a whaler's term.] The fibrous refuse of tallow, used as dog-food, fish-bait, etc.

grebe /griːb/ *n.* M18. [Fr. *grèbe*, of unkn. origin.] **1** Any of various long-necked aquatic birds constituting the family Podicipedidae (and order Podicipediformes), having unwebbed lobate toes and able to dive and swim under water. Cf. *sun-grebe* s.v. SUN *n.*[1] M18. **2** The plumage of a grebe. Now *rare*. M19.

1 *great crested grebe*, *little grebe*, *Slavonian grebe*, etc.

grebo /ˈgriːbəʊ/ *n.* Pl. **-os**. L20. [Perh. f. GREASER + *-bo* after *dumbo* etc.] (A member of) an urban youth cult favouring heavy metal and punk rock music and freq. characterized by long hair and antisocial attitudes.

grece /griːs/ *n. obs.* exc. *dial.* & *Her.* Also **grice**, (Her.) **griece**. ME. [OFr. *gres*, *grez*, *greis* pl. of *gré* GREE *n.*[1]] A set or flight of stairs; a step, a stair; in *pl.*, steps, stairs, a stairway.

Grecian /ˈgriːʃ(ə)n/ *a.* & *n.* LME. [OFr. *grecien* or med.L, f. L *Graecia* Greece: see -IAN.] **A** *adj.* Of or pertaining to Greece or its inhabitants; Greek. Now *rare* exc. w. ref. to architecture or facial outline. LME.

TENNYSON A Gothic ruin and a Grecian house. **Grecian bend** an affected way of walking in which the body is bent forward from the hips, prevalent in the late 19th cent. **Grecian gift** = *Greek gift* s.v. GREEK *a.* **Grecian knot** a way of dressing the hair at the back of the head in imitation of the ancient Greeks. **Grecian nose** a straight nose which continues the line of the forehead. **Grecian plait** an elaborate plait of hair made from about 13 strands. **Grecian slipper** a soft slipper with low-cut sides.

B *n.* **1** A native or inhabitant of Greece; a Greek. Long *arch.* LME. **b** [tr. Gk *Hellēnistēs*.] A Greek Jew, a Hellenist. *Hist.* E17. **2** A person skilled in Greek; a Greek scholar. M16. †**3** A member of the Greek Orthodox Church. M16–M18. **4** An Irish person; = GREEK *n.* 6. *slang.* M19.

1 SHAKES. *All's Well* Was this fair face the cause.. Why the Grecians sacked Troy?

Grecianize *v.t.* make Grecian or Greek E17.

grecing /ˈɡriːsɪŋ/ *n. obs.* exc. *dial.* LME. [f. GRECE *n.* + -ING¹.] In *pl.*, the stairs in a flight; flights of stairs. In *sing.* (*rare*), a step.

Grecism *n.*, **-ize** *v.*, **Greco-** *comb. form* vars. of GRAECISM etc.

grecque /ɡrɛk/ *n.* M19. [Fr., fem. of *grec* GREEK *n.*.] *Archit.* A Greek fret.

gree /ɡriː/ *n.*¹ *obs.* exc. *Sc.* & *dial.* ME. [OFr. *gré* f. L *gradus* step: cf. GRECE.] **1** = DEGREE *n.* 1a. ME. †**2** *fig.* = DEGREE *n.* 5. ME–L16. †**3** = DEGREE *n.* 2. ME–E17. **4** Pre-eminence; mastery; victory in battle. Also, the prize for a victory. ME. **5** = DEGREE *n.* 3. LME. †**6** = DEGREE *n.* 6. LME–M16.

gree /ɡriː/ *n.*² *arch.* ME. [(O)Fr. *gré* pleasure, goodwill, will f. L *gratum* use as n. of neut. of *gratus* pleasing. Cf. MAUGRE.]. **1** Favour, goodwill. Long *rare* exc. *Sc.* ME. **2** Satisfaction. Chiefly in phrs. ME. †**3** (One's) good pleasure; will, desire; consent. ME–M18.

1 in gree with goodwill or favour, in good part. **2 do** or **make gree** give satisfaction for an injury. **make one's gree** make one's peace *with*, give satisfaction *to*.

gree /ɡriː/ *v. obs.* exc. *Sc.* & *dial.* Pa. t. & pple **greed**. LME. [Aphet. f. AGREE *v.* or f. GREE *n.*² Cf. OFr. *gréer* which may be the direct source.] **1** *v.t.* Please, make pleased; reconcile (people); settle (a matter). LME. **2** *v.i.* Consent, accede, agree. LME. **3** *v.i.* Come into or be in accord or harmony; agree. LME.

greement *n.* agreement, consent, accord LME.

greed /ɡriːd/ *n.* L16. [Back-form. f. GREEDY.] Intense or inordinate longing, esp. for wealth or food; avarice, covetous desire.

P. GALLICO He saw the naked greed and possessive desire come into her eyes.

¶Orig. *Sc.*

greed /ɡriːd/ *v.*¹ *rare.* L17. [f. the n.] **1** *v.i.* Indulge one's greed; be avaricious. L17. **2** *v.t.* Long for. M19.

greed *v.*² pa. t. & pple of GREE *v.*

greedily /ˈɡriːdɪli/ *adv.* OE. [Partly OE *grǣdelīce*, f. base also of ON *gráðr*; partly OE *grǣdi(ġ)līce*, f. as GREEDY: see -LY².] **1** With keen appetite; hungrily, ravenously, voraciously. OE. **2** Avariciously, covetously, rapaciously. OE. **3** Keenly, eagerly. Formerly also, zealously, fervently. ME.

1 J. MITCHELL Shrieve found Jumbo there, munching greedily from a plate. 2 J. R. GREEN The eyes of the feudal baronage turned greedily on the riches of the Church.

greediness /ˈɡriːdɪnɪs/ *n.* [OE *grǣdignes*, f. as GREEDY: see -NESS.] **1** Excessive longing for wealth or gain; avarice, greed. OE. **2** *gen.* Eagerness, keenness. ME. **3** Excessive longing for food or drink; gluttony, voracity. LME.

2 R. BOYLE A Greediness of Knowledge, that is impatient of being confin'd.

greedy /ˈɡriːdi/ *a.* [OE *grēdiġ*, *grǣdiġ* = OS *grādag*, OHG *grātac*, ON *gráðugr*, Goth. *grēdags*, f. Gmc, f. base meaning 'hunger, greed', of unkn. origin.] **1** Having an intense desire or inordinate appetite for food or drink; voracious, gluttonous. Formerly also, hungry. (Foll. by *of*.) OE. **2** Eager for gain, wealth, etc.; avaricious, covetous, rapacious. (Foll. by *of*, *for*.) OE. **3** Keen, eager; intensely desirous *of*, †*to do*. ME.

1 W. BOYD Three sausages! You greedy thing! 2 P. LIVELY Jasper is greedy; he has to have money for its own sake.

Comb.: **greedy-gut(s)** *colloq.* a voracious eater, a glutton.

greegree /ˈɡriːɡriː/ *n.* Also **gris-gris**. L17. [f. Fr. *grigri*, *grisgris*, of W. African origin.] An African charm, amulet, or fetish.

Greek /ɡriːk/ *n.* & *a.* [OE *Grēcas* pl. (so for the most part until 16) corresp. to MLG *Grēke*, MDu. *Grieke*, G *Grieche*, ON *Grikkir* pl., of which the earliest forms are OE *Crēcas*, OHG *Chrēch*, Goth. *Krēks*, f. Gmc f. L *Graecus* (applied by the Romans to the people who called themselves *Hellēnes* (see HELLENE)) f. Gk *Graikos* adj. (according to Aristotle a prehistoric name of the Hellenes).] **A** *n.* **I** A person. **1** A native or inhabitant of Greece, a country in SE Europe occupied by Greek-speaking peoples since about 2000 BC; a person of Greek descent. OE. **2** A member or adherent of the Greek Orthodox Church. LME. †**3** = GRECIAN *n.* 1b. LME–L17. **4** A cunning or wily person; a cheat, a card-sharper. *arch.* E16. **5** In full *merry, mad, gay Greek*. A roisterer; a dissolute person. Long *rare*. M16. **6** An Irish person. *slang.* E19.

4 THACKERAY He was an adventurer, a pauper, a blackleg, a regular Greek.

II [absol. use of the adj.] Language. **7** The language of Greece or the Greeks, a member of the Hellenic branch of the Indo-European language family; *spec.* Ancient Greek (see *ancient Greek* (a) below). OE. **8** Unintelligible speech or language, gibberish. E17.

7 L. DURRELL I asked in Greek and was answered in English. 8 DICKENS I am a stranger and this is Greek to me.

B *adj.* [Infl. by L *Graecus*, Fr. *grec* adjs.] **1** Of or pertaining to Greece or its inhabitants; native to or originating in Greece; characteristic of or attributed to Greece or the Greeks; *spec.* ancient Greek (see *ancient Greek* (b) below). LME. **2** Belonging to, written in, or spoken in the language of Greece. M16. **3** Designating or pertaining to the national church of Greece, the Greek Orthodox Church. M16.

2 MILTON Wretched barbarizing against the Latin and Greek idiom, with their untutored Anglicisms.

Special collocations & phrases: **ancient Greek** (*a*) (also **A-**) (of or pertaining to) the earliest form of Greek, consisting of the Aeolic, Arcadic, Doric, and Ionic (including Attic) dialects, and surviving until about 300 BC; (*b*) of or pertaining to, a native or inhabitant of, Greece from about 2000 to 300 BC. **Greek chorus** (*a*) the chorus in Greek drama; (*b*) *transf.* conduct imitative of this chorus, consisting of open wailing or wise sympathetic comments. **Greek cross** an upright cross with limbs of equal length. *Greek Cypriot*: see CYPRIOT. **Greek Fathers** the Fathers of the Church who wrote in Greek. *Greek fire*: see FIRE *n.* 2c. *Greek fret*: see FRET *n.*² 3. **Greek gift** a gift given with intent to harm (w. allus. to Virgil's *Aeneid* ii. 49). **Greek god** (*a*) *fig.* a paragon of male beauty; (*b*) a hairstyle with short curls all over the head. *Greek key*: see KEY *n.*¹ *on, at or till the Greek Calends*: see CALENDS 3. **Greek valerian** the plant Jacob's ladder, *Polemonium caeruleum*.

Greekdom *n.* (*a*) the Greek world; a Greek State or community; (*b*) *arch.* the fraternity of card-sharpers: M19. **Greekery** *n.* (*rare*) practices attributed to Greeks; *spec.* (*arch.*) cheating at cards: L17. **Greekess** *n.* (*rare*) a female Greek M19. **Greekless** *a.* without knowledge of Greek L19. **Greekly** *adv.* in a Greek fashion, in the Greek language LME. **Greekness** *n.* M19.

Greek /ɡriːk/ *v.* E17. [f. the n. Cf. L *Graecari*.] †**1** *v.t.* (w. *it*). Follow the practice of the Greeks; play the Greek scholar. E17–L18. †**2** *v.i.* Cheat at cards. *slang.* Only in E19. **3** *v.t. Computing.* (Usu. **g-**.) Print or reproduce with random or arbitrary characters in place of the actual ones, so as to give an impression of the appearance of a page etc. L20.

Greekish /ˈɡriːkɪʃ/ *a.* OE. [In branch I repr. OE *Crēcisć*, *Grēcisć*, f. *Crēcas*, *Grēcas* (see GREEK *n.* & *a.*); in branch II f. GREEK *n.* or *a.*: see -ISH¹.] **I** †**1** = GREEK *a.* 2. OE–M17. **2** Of or pertaining to Greece or the Greeks. *arch.* ME. †**3** = GREEK *a.* 3. E–M17.

2 R. CUDWORTH The very Names of many of the Greekish Gods were originally Egyptian.

II 4 Somewhat Greek; resembling Greek persons or things; characteristic of a Greek or Greeks. M16.

4 R. BURNS There, Learning, with his Greekish face, Grunts out some Latin ditty.

Greekling /ˈɡriːklɪŋ/ *n.* M17. [f. GREEK *n.* + -LING¹, after L *Graeculus* (Juvenal) dim. of *Graecus* Greek.] A little Greek; a degenerate contemptible Greek.

green /ɡriːn/ *n.* In sense 9 also **G-**. OE. [The adj. used ellipt. or absol.] **1** That which is green; the green part of something; *spec.* a thing distinguished by green colour, as green tea, the green ball in snooker, a green signal, a green bird, etc. OE. **2** Green colour; a shade of this (freq. w. specifying wd). ME. **b** A pigment of a green colour. Freq. w. defining wd. E17. **c** The emblematic colour of Ireland. L18. **3** Green clothing or dress; green fabric; in *pl.*, green clothes esp. as uniform. ME. **4** Verdure, vegetation. Formerly also, a tree, a herb, a plant (usu. in *pl.*). ME. **b** *fig.* Vigour, youthfulness, vitality. LME. **5** Grassy ground; a grassy area. Now chiefly, a piece of public or common grassy land in the centre of a village or town; a grass plot used for some specified purpose. ME. **b** *Golf.* A putting-green; a fairway. Also, a golf course. M18. **6** In *pl.* †**a** The green parts of a plant or flower. Only in E17. **b** Freshly cut branches or leaves for decoration. Now *US.* L17. **c** The (boiled etc.) leaves and stems of various plants, esp. certain vegetables, for eating; *slang* sexual intercourse. E18. **7** *sing.* & in *pl.* Money. Cf. GREENBACK *n.* 2. *slang* (orig. *US*). E20. **8** Marijuana of poor quality. *slang* (orig. *US*). M20. **9** A supporter of environmentalism; a conservationist; a member or supporter of an ecological political party. Cf. GREENIE 3. L20.

1 *Cue World* Chambers wrapped up the first frame.. after missing a straightforward green. 2 E. M. FORSTER The main colour was an agricultural green. G. HEYER In a dressing-gown.. of.. material dyed every shade of green. b *Brunswick green*, *Paris green*, *Scheele's green*, etc. 3 T. O'BRIEN Harvey wore his dress greens. 4 H. BASCOM A vast clearing of felled trees.. in an immeasurably vaster carpet of green. 5 J. WYNDHAM A small village.. disposed neatly about a triangular green. *bleaching-green*, *bowling-green*, *putting-green*, etc. 6c L. MACNEICE Fruits and greens are insufficient for health. G. GREENE Why not go after the girl?.. She's not getting.. what is vulgarly called her greens. *collard greens*, *spring greens*, etc.

Phrases & comb.: **green-fee** the charge for playing one round on a golf course. **green in one's eye** signs of gullibility or inexperience. **greenkeeper** the keeper of a golf course. **green spot** the spot on which the green ball is placed in snooker. **in the green** in the period of youthful growth or vigour. **on the green** on the stage (cf. GREENGAGE). **the long green** *slang* money. **through the green** *Golf* between the tee and the putting-green. VERDIGRIS *green*. *wigs on the green*: see WIG *n.*³

green /ɡriːn/ *a.* & *adv.* [OE *grēne* = OFris. *grēne*, OS *grōni* (Du. *groen*, OHG *gruoni* (G *grün*), ON *grœnn*, f. Gmc, f. base of GRASS *n.*, GROW *v.*] **A** *adj.* In sense 2d also **G-**. **I 1** Of the colour of grass, foliage, an emerald, etc., between blue and yellow in the spectrum. OE. **b** Designating the green-coloured light in a set of lights which when illuminated gives permission to proceed in railway or road traffic signals. L19. **2** Covered with herbage or foliage; (of a tree) in leaf. OE. **b** (Of a season of the year) characterized by much verdure; (of a winter, Christmas, etc.) mild, without snow. LME. **c** Consisting of green plants or vegetables. LME. **d** Of, pertaining to, or supporting environmentalism, esp. as a political issue; belonging to or supporting an ecological political party. Also, (of a product etc.) not harmful to the environment. L20. **e** *Econ.* Designating a currency unit of account or the exchange rate according to which national currencies are translated, used for the payment of agricultural produce in the European Community. L20. **3** Of fruit, a plant, etc.: unripe; young and tender; flourishing; retaining the natural moisture, not dried. OE. **4** Having or designating a pale sickly complexion; *fig.* full of jealousy or envy. ME.

1 *apple-green*, *bottle-green*, *dark green*, *grass-green*, *light green*, *olive-green*, *sea-green*, etc. 2 J. RABAN In a green

country it is almost impossible to communicate the . . price . . put on vegetation in the desert. A. Mason They were green hills, not the bare stony highlands of the south. **d** *Scientific American* Non-polluting 'green chemicals', detergents, and . . bio-degradable plastics. **e** *Times* The effect . . will be qualified . . by a 4 per cent devaluation of the green pound. **3** R. Brautigan Take green walnuts before the shell is formed. P. V. Price The berries develop quite rapidly, passing from green to ripe. C. Conran Fresh or green pepper is soft and subtle. **4** B. Plain He looked sallow and faintly green. M. Roberts She stops, hearing her voice green with jealousy and envy.

II *transf.* & *fig.* of sense 3. **5** Not prepared or treated; (of wood etc.) undried, unseasoned; (of meat or fish) uncured, undried, raw; (of hide) untanned; (of pottery, bricks, etc.) unfired. OE. **b** Fresh, new; (of a fire) recently kindled (now chiefly *Sc.*); (of a wound) recent, unhealed, *arch.* ME. **6** Full of vitality; vivid, not faded or worn out; (now only *Sc.*) youthful. OE. **7** (Of a thought, plan, etc.) not fully developed or elaborated; (of a person) immature, inexperienced, naive, gullible; (of an animal) untrained. ME.

6 R. L. Stevenson To lead an adventurous and honourable youth, and to settle . . into a green and smiling age. G. Greene My memory was green and retentive. **7** H. Robbins I might be green in the picture business, but I'm not so dumb as you think. Sloan Wilson They had been green troops, . . boys who had never been on a combat jump before. M. Gee Her green hopes sprouting in darkness.

Special collocations, comb., & *phrases*: **be not so green as one is cabbage-looking** *colloq.* be less of a fool than might be assumed. *green about the gills*: see GILL *n.*[1] 2. **green alga** an alga of the division Chlorophyta, members of which typically have two types of chlorophyll, cellulose cell walls, and starch grains, as in land plants. *green alkanet*: see ALKANET 2. *green amaranth*: see AMARANTH I. **green baize** baize of a green colour, used for covering esp. office or card tables; such a table. **green bean** any bean plant, *esp.* the French bean, *Phaseolus vulgaris*, grown for its edible young pods rather than for its seeds; the pod of such a plant (usu. in *pl.*). **green belt** an area of countryside usu. enclosing a built-up area and officially designated as not to be built on. **Green Beret** *colloq.* a British or American commando. **green-blind** *a.* affected with green-blindness. **green-blindness** = DEUTERANOPIA. **greenbottle** any of various green bodied dipteran flies of the genus *Lucilia*, esp. *L. caesar*. *green brier*: see BRIER *n.*[1] **green card** (*a*) a card to be filled in by a person seeking an interview with an MP at the Houses of Parliament; (*b*) an international insurance document for motorists taking their cars abroad; (*c*) *US* a permit enabling a foreign national to live and work permanently in the US. **green carder** a holder of a US green card. **green channel** at a port, airport, etc., the channel through which passengers should pass who have no goods to declare. **green cheese** (*a*) whey cheese; (*b*) cheese coloured green with sage; (*c*) unripened or unmatured cheese. *green* COPPERAS. **green crop**: used for fodder while in a green or unripe state rather than as hay etc. **Green Cross code** a kerb drill esp. taught to children. *green dragon*: see DRAGON *n.* 9. *green drake*: see DRAKE *n.*[1] 4. **green earth** = GLAUCONITE. **green eye** (*a*) an eye with a green iris; (*b*) *fig.* jealousy. **green-eyed** *a.* with green eyes; *fig.* jealous (*green-eyed monster*, jealousy). *green fallow*: see FALLOW *n.* **green fat**: of a turtle, esteemed by gourmets. **greenfeed** (chiefly *Austral.* & *NZ*) forage grown to be fed fresh to livestock. **greenfield** *a.* designating a site with no previous (similar) building development, or (*fig.*) a business with only the prospect rather than the record of profitability. **greenfinch** any of a number of green-plumaged Old World finches of the genus *Carduelis*; *spec.* a common Eurasian and N. African finch, *Carduelis chloris*, with green and yellow plumage. **green fingers** *colloq.* skill in making plants grow. **greenfly** a green aphid; *collect.* green aphids. *green ginger*: see GINGER *n.* **green goose** (now chiefly *dial.*) a young goose, *esp.* one killed under four months old. **greenhead** (*a*) (now *rare*) an inexperienced or ignorant person; (*b*) *N. Amer.* a green-eyed biting tabanid fly, esp. *Tabanus nigrovittatus*. (*c*) an Australian ant, *Ectatomma metallicum*, with a painful sting. **greenheart** a tall evergreen tree of northern S. America, *Ocotea rodiaei*, of the laurel family (also called *bebeeru*, *sipeera*); its strong dark green wood, used for shipbuilding etc. *green* HELLEBORE. **green heron** either of two small herons with greenish upperparts, the pantropical *Butorides striatus* and the N. American *B. virescens* (often considered conspecific). **greenhorn** an inexperienced person, a novice, a raw recruit; an ignoramus, a simpleton. **greenhouse** (*a*) a transparent glass or plastic building for rearing or hastening the growth of plants; *greenhouse effect*, the heating of the surface and lower atmosphere of a planet due to the greater transparency of the atmosphere to visible radiation from the sun than to infrared radiation from the planet; *greenhouse gas*, carbon dioxide or another gas contributing to the greenhouse effect; (*b*) *slang* the cockpit of a plane. **green lane** a permanent untarred lane giving access to woodland, fields, etc. *green leek*: see LEEK 3. **green light** *fig.* permission to proceed on a project. **greenlight** *v.t.* & *i.* give (a person) permission to proceed on a project etc. **green linnet** *arch.* the common greenfinch, *Carduelis chloris*. **green man** (*a*) (chiefly *Hist.*) a man dressed up in greenery to represent a wild man of the woods or seasonal fertility; †(*b*) an inexperienced sailor on a whaling vessel; (*c*) *colloq.* a symbol of a walking figure illuminated green on some types of pedestrian crossing to indicate a time to cross. **green manure** growing plants ploughed into the soil as fertilizer. *green* MEALIE. *green meat*: see MEAT *n.* **green monkey** the common African savannah monkey, *Cercopithecus aethiops*; *spec.* one of a dark-faced W. African race, often tamed (cf. VERVET). **Green Mountain State** *US* Vermont. **Green Paper** a tentative report of British government proposals without any commitment to action. **Green Party** (in the UK) an ecological political party. *green plant*: see PLANT *n.* 2. **green plover** the lapwing, *Vanellus vanellus*. **green porphyry** *Petrogr.* = *greenstone* (a) below. **green pound** the exchange rate for the pound for payments for agricultural produce in the European Community. **green revolution** greatly increased crop production in developing countries through the introduction of modern farming methods and higher-yielding seeds. **green road** a permanent untarred road, esp. a farm road, giving access to fields etc. **green-room**: in a theatre for actors and actresses who are not on-stage. **green salad**: chiefly composed of green ingredients such as lettuce, chicory, cucumber, watercress, etc. **greensand** (*a*) = GLAUCONITE; (*b*) a kind of sandstone consisting largely of grains of quartz and glauconite; *esp.* (**G-**) as forming strata in the Cretaceous System in Southern England. **green sandpiper** a migratory Eurasian sandpiper, *Tringa ochropus*, with dark greenish-brown upperparts. **green sauce** a savoury sauce with a sharp taste made with sorrel or with herbs and vinegar. **greenshank** an elegant green-legged Eurasian sandpiper, *Tringa nebularia*. **greensick** *a.* (now *rare*) affected with greensickness. **greensickness** = CHLOROSIS *n.* I. **greenstick** *a.* designating a type of bone-fracture, esp. in children, in which one side of the bone is broken and one only bent. **greenstone** (*a*) any igneous rock of dark-green appearance, esp. containing chlorite, epidote, hornblende, etc.; (*b*) nephrite, esp. of New Zealand origin. **greenstuff** (*a*) vegetation; (*b*) in *pl.*, green vegetables. **greensward** *arch.* grassy turf; an expanse of this. **green tea**: made from steam-dried rather than fermented leaves (cf. *black tea* s.v. BLACK *a.*). **green thumb** *colloq.* = *green fingers* above. *green tobacco*: see TOBACCO 2. **green turtle** a turtle, *Chelonia mydas*, with a brown or olive carapace, found in warm seas worldwide. *green* VITRIOL. **greenweed** a low-growing yellow-flowered leguminous shrub of rough pastures, *Genista tinctoria*, formerly used to make a green dye (also *dyer's greenweed*); also, any of several other shrubs of this genus. **greenwood** a wood or forest in leaf, esp. as the typical scene of medieval outlaw life. **green woodpecker** a large European woodpecker, *Picus viridis*, with largely green and yellow plumage and a red crown. **greenyard** (chiefly *dial.*) an enclosure for stray animals, a pound. *little green man*: see LITTLE *a.* *wear the green willow*: see WILLOW *n.*

B *adv.* *run green*, (of a racehorse etc.) be easily upset or distracted during a race through lack of experience. L19.

Sporting Life She ran very green and didn't seem to know what racing was about until the final two furlongs.

green /griːn/ *v.*[1] [OE *grēnian*, f. *grēne*: see prec.] **1** *v.i.* Become green; *esp.* become covered (*over*) with verdure. OE. **2 a** *v.t.* Colour or stain green; cover (*over*) with verdure. Also foll. by *up*. L16. **b** *v.t.* & (*rare*) *i.* Turn (oysters) green in the gills by putting them in pits. M17. **3** *v.t.* Hoax, take in. *slang.* L19. **4** *v.t.* **a** Make (an urban area) more verdant by tree-planting etc.; reclaim (desert); *fig.* rejuvenate. M20. **b** Cause to adopt policies or behaviour beneficial to the environment. L20.

1 M. Sarton Slowly the grass has been greening over. D. Dunn The first leaves are greening. **2a** T. Hardy The . . white frock . . which she had so carelessly greened . . on the damping grass. S. Naipaul Elephantine limbs, greened with moss, spread . . high above their heads.

green /griːn/ *v.*[2]*i.* *Sc.* LME. [Perh. (w. metathesis) f. ON *girna* = OE *giernan*, (Northumb.) *giorna*: see YEARN *v.*[1]] Desire earnestly; yearn *after*, *for*.

greenback /ˈgriːnbak/ *n.* L18. [f. GREEN *a.* + BACK *n.*[1]] **1** An animal, bird, fish, or other creature with a green back. L18. **2** A monetary note issued by the US Government; *gen.* the US dollar; in *pl.*, money. Cf. GREEN *n.* 7. M19. **3** A book with a green cover. L19. **4** A disease of tomatoes, often due to potassium deficiency, shown by hard green patches on the calyx side of the fruit. E20.

2 S. Bellow A check? Hell with a check. Get me the greenbacks. *Times* Every currency heaved in the wake of the mighty greenback.

green cloth /griːn ˈklɒθ/ *n. phr.* In sense I also **G- C-**. LME. [f. GREEN *a.* + CLOTH *n.*, w. ref. to the green-covered table at which business was orig. transacted.] **1** A board or department of the royal household, consisting of the Lord Steward and his staff and controlling various financial, legal, and judicial matters within the sovereign's household. LME. **2** (The green woollen material covering) a billiard, pool, etc., table. L19.

Greeneian /ˈgriːnɪən/ *a.* Also **Greenian**. M20. [f. Graham *Greene* (1904–91), Eng. writer + -IAN.] Typical or characteristic of the style or matter of the works of Graham Greene. Cf. next.

Greeneland /ˈgriːnlənd/ *n.* M20. [f. as prec. + LAND *n.*[1]] The seedy politically unstable and dangerous world said to be the typical setting for the characters in the novels of Graham Greene.

greener /ˈgriːnə/ *n.*[1] *slang.* L19. [f. GREEN *a.* + -ER[1]. Cf. Yiddish *griner* greenhorn.] An inexperienced or naive person.

N. Algren He's over there shakin' down the greenhorns 'n the biggest greener on his beat is his own brother.

Greener /ˈgriːnə/ *n.*[2] & *a.* L19. [W. *Greener* (1806–69) or his son, W. W. *Greener*, gunsmiths and authors.] **A** *n.* A gun made by or according to the designs of W. or W. W. Greener. L19. **B** *adj.* Designating guns, rifles, cartridges, etc., made by or according to the designs of W. or W. W. Greener. L19.

greenery /ˈgriːn(ə)ri/ *n.* L18. [f. GREEN *a.* or *n.* + -ERY.] **1** Green foliage or vegetation; this used for decoration. L18. **2** A place where plants are reared, kept, or exhibited. Now *rare*. M19.

1 A. Mason The dense greenery which clothed the banks on either side was rank and tangled jungle. A. Munro There is a hot tub surrounded by windows and greenery.

greenery-yallery /ˌgriːn(ə)rɪˈjal(ə)ri/ *a.* *colloq.* L19. [f. GREEN *a.* + *yaller* var. of YELLOW *a.* + -Y[1], w. redupl. suff.] Of, pertaining to, or affecting the colours green and yellow, after the style of the late 19th-cent. aesthetic movement; *transf.* affected.

B. Pym The advance copy has a springlike or greenery-yallery cover. Clive James Greenery-yallery fin de siècle lyricism.

greeney *n.* see GREENIE.

greengage /ˈgriːngeɪdʒ/ *n.* E18. [f. GREEN *a.* + Sir William *Gage* (1657–1727), who introduced it to England.] **1** Any of several round green-fleshed fine-flavoured kinds of plum; the tree bearing this fruit. E18. **2** The stage; in *pl.*, wages. *rhyming slang.* M20.

greengrocer /ˈgriːngrəʊsə/ *n.* E18. [f. GREEN *n.* or *a.* + GROCER.] A retail dealer in fruit and vegetables.

greengrocery *n.* the business of or the goods sold by a greengrocer E19.

Greenian *a.* var. of GREENEIAN.

greenie /ˈgriːni/ *n.* Also (exc. in sense 3) **green(e)y**. E19. [f. GREEN *a.* + -IE.] **1** A green-coloured bird; *spec.* (*dial.*) a greenfinch. E19. **2** A greenhorn. *colloq.* M19. 3 A conservationist. Cf. GREEN *n.* 9. *colloq.* (chiefly *Austral.*). L20.

greening /ˈgriːnɪŋ/ *n.* E17. [Prob. f. MDu. *groeninc* (Du. *groening*) kind of apple: see GREEN *a.*, -ING[3].] Orig., a kind of pear. Now, a kind of apple which is green when ripe (also *Rhode Island greening*).

greenish /ˈgriːnɪʃ/ *a.* LME. [f. GREEN *a.* + -ISH[1].] Somewhat green.

Greenland /ˈgriːnlənd/ *a.* L17. [A large island in the Arctic Ocean.] Designating animals, plants, etc., native to or associated with Greenland.

Greenland dove: see DOVE *n.* 1b. **Greenland (right) whale** a large right whale, *Balaena mysticetus*, of Arctic seas; also called *bowhead*. **Greenland shark** a shark of the northern N. Atlantic, *Somniosus microcephalus*; also called *gurry-shark*, *sleeper shark*. *Greenland whale*: see *Greenland right whale* above.

Greenlander *n.* (*a*) a native or inhabitant of Greenland; †(*b*) a type of small sailing ship used in war: L17. **Greenˈlandic** *a.* & *n.* (*a*) *adj.* of or pertaining to Greenland, its inhabitants, or its (Eskimo) language or dialect; (*b*) *n.* the language or dialect of Greenland: E19. **Greenlandish** *a.* & *n.* (*a*) *adj.* characteristic of Greenland; (*b*) *n.* = GREENLANDIC *n.*: L18.

greenless /ˈgriːnlɪs/ *a.* E17. [f. GREEN *n.* + -LESS.] Without greenness or verdure.

greenlet /ˈgriːnlɪt/ *n.* M19. [f. GREEN *a.* + -LET: app. formed to render the etym. sense of L *vireo*.] = VIREO; *spec.* a member of the S. and Central American genus *Hylophilus*.

greenling /ˈgriːnlɪŋ/ *n.* ME. [f. GREEN *a.* + -LING[1].] 1 A fish of the family Gadidae, *esp.* a pollack. *local.* ME. 2 A food fish, *Hexagrammos duagrammus*, of the N. Pacific. E20.

greenly /ˈgriːnli/ *adv.* L16. [f. GREEN *a.* + -LY[2].] 1 With a green colour; with green vegetation. L16. 2 In an inexperienced or untrained manner; unskilfully. *arch.* exc. in *run greenly* below. L16. 3 Freshly, vigorously; vividly. M17.

1 J. MITCHELL Primrose Hill rose greenly above the surrounding roofs. 2 **run greenly** = *run green* s.v. GREEN *adv.*

greenmail /ˈgriːnmeɪl/ *n.* L20. [f. GREEN *a.* + BLACK)MAIL *n.*: cf. GREEN *n.* 7.] *Stock Exch.* The practice of purchasing enough shares in a company to threaten a takeover, thereby forcing the owners to buy them back at a higher price in order to retain control of the business.

greenmailer *n.* L20.

greenness /ˈgriːnnɪs/ *n.* OE. [f. GREEN *a.* + -NESS.] 1 Green colour; green vegetation. OE. 2 Vigour; vitality; youth. ME. b Freshness, newness. Long only *Sc.* M16. 3 Unripeness of fruit etc. Now *rare.* LME. b *fig.* Immaturity; inexperience; gullibility, naïvety. LME. 4 Awareness of ecological issues; commitment to environmental conservation. L20.

greenockite /ˈgriːnəkʌɪt/ *n.* M19. [f. Charles Murray Cathcart, Lord *Greenock*, later Earl Cathcart, (1783–1859), Sc. general + -ITE[1].] *Min.* Native cadmium sulphide, which crystallizes in the hexagonal system and usu. occurs as a yellow crust on zinc ores.

greenth /ˈgriːnθ/ *n. literary.* M18. [f. GREEN *a.* + -TH[1].] Verdure.

Greenwell /ˈgriːnwɛl/ *n.* L19. [Revd William *Greenwell* (1820–1918), Eng. archaeologist and angler.] In full *Greenwell's glory*. A fishing-fly designed by Greenwell.

Greenwich /ˈgrɛnɪtʃ, -ɪdʒ/ *n.* M19. [*Greenwich* in London, the former site of the Royal Observatory.] 1 *Greenwich* (*Mean*) *Time*, the mean solar time on the meridian of Greenwich, used as an international basis of time-reckoning. M19. 2 *Greenwich meridian*, the prime meridian, passing through Greenwich. L19.

greeny *n.* see GREENIE.

greeny /ˈgriːni/ *a.* L16. [f. GREEN *a.* + -Y[1].] †1 Green, verdant; vigorous. L16–L17. 2 = GREENISH. E19.

greeshoch /ˈgriːʃɔx/ *n. Sc.* E19. [Gael. *griosach* embers, f. *grios*, *gris* heat.] (A fire of) hot embers.

greet /griːt/ *n. obs.* exc. *Sc.* ME. [f. GREET *v.*[2]] Weeping, lamentation; a cry of sorrow.

greet /griːt/ *v.*[1] [OE *grētan* = OFris. *grēta* salute, complain, OS *grōtian* call upon (Du. *groeten* salute), OHG *gruozzen* address, attack (G *grüssen* salute, greet), f. WGmc.] †1 *v.t.* Approach; begin on, begin to treat or handle. Only in OE. †2 *v.t.* Assail, attack. OE–LME. 3 *v.t.* Accost or address with a salutation customary on meeting; send one's own or another's regards to (a person) (now chiefly *literary*). OE. b Salute *with* words or gestures; receive on meeting or arrival *with* some speech or action (friendly or otherwise). OE. †c Offer congratulations on (an achievement etc.). *rare* (Spenser). Only in L16. †d Gratify, please. L16–E17. 4†a *v.i.* Meet *with*. *rare*. Only in L16. b *v.t.* Receive or meet with demonstrations of welcome. E17. 5 *v.t.* Orig., of a thing: present itself to. Now only, of sights or sounds: meet, become apparent to or noticed by. L17. 6 Of a response: be addressed to (a person) or evoked by (an action etc.); hail. L19.

3 P. BOWLES She . . rose . . to greet him. 'Mr. Tunner! How delightful!' J. HELLER He greeted Milo jovially each time they met. *absol.*: DRYDEN None greets, for none the greeting will return. b V. SACKVILLE-WEST They greeted her arrival always with beaming smiles. M. L. KING He forgot to greet me with the usual 'hello.' G. GREENE He greeted his mother with an exaggerated hug. K. MILLER When the doctor arrived to deliver Frost, the father greeted him with a revolver. d SHAKES. *Per.* It greets me as an enterprise of kindness Perform'd to your sole daughter. 4b LD MACAULAY The cavalcade . . was greeted two miles from the city by the bishop and clergy. 5 J. FRYER The Sea on one side greets its Marble Walls. H. I. JENKINSON A wide extent of sea greets the eye. 6 J. R. GREEN Shouts of assent greeted the resolution. A. S. NEILL The contemptuous glance that usually greets the man who blows his own horn. B. EMECHETA The laughter that greeted this remark was unreal.

greeter *n.*[1] LME.

greet /griːt/ *v.*[2] Now *Sc.* & *north.* OE. [Partly OE (Anglian) *grētan* = OS *grātan*, MHG *grāzen* cry out, rage, storm, ON *gráta*, Goth. *grētan* f. Gmc, orig. redupl. str. vb rel. to prec.; partly OE *grēotan* (= OS *griotan*) perh. f. Gmc base of Y- + vb repr. by synon. OE *rēotan*.] 1 *v.i.* Weep, cry, lament, grieve. OE. †b *v.t.* Shed (tears). ME–E18. †2 *v.t.* Weep for, lament, bewail. OE–ME. †3 *v.i.* Cry or call out in supplication or anger. ME–E16.

greeter *n.*[2] (*rare*) E19. **greety** *a.* (*rare*) inclined to shed tears, tearful LME.

greeting /ˈgriːtɪŋ/ *n.* OE. [f. GREET *v.*[1] + -ING[1].] The action of GREET *v.*[1] Also, an instance of this, a salutation, (freq. in *pl.*).

H. JAMES They had exchanged greetings. J. BARTH I met Col. Morton . . and tipped my hat in greeting.

Comb.: **greetings card** a (usu. folded) card having a decorated outer cover and inside a message of goodwill etc. for a particular anniversary etc.

greffier /ˈgrɛfɪə/ *n.* L16. [Fr. f. med.L *graphiarius* registrar, f. *graphium* register: see GRAFF *n.*[1]] A registrar or notary, esp. in the Channel Islands.

gregal /ˈgriːg(ə)l/ *a.* M16. [L *gregalis*, f. *grex*, *greg-*: see -AL[1].] 1 Pertaining to a flock or to the common people. *rare*. M16. †2 = GREGARIOUS 1. E–M17.

gregale /greɪˈgɑːleɪ/ *n.* E19. [f. It. *grecale*, app. repr. late L n. f. L *Graecus* Greek.] A strong north-east wind blowing in the Mediterranean.

gregarian /grɪˈgɛːrɪən/ *a.* Long *rare* or *obs.* M17. [f. L *gregarius* (see GREGARIOUS) + -AN.] Of or pertaining to flocks or crowds, common.

gregarine /ˈgrɛgərʌɪn/ *n.* & *a.* M19. [f. mod.L *Gregarina* genus name, f. L *gregarius*: see next, -INE[1].] A *n.* Any of numerous vermiform protozoans of the sporozoan subclass Gregarinidia (or Gregarina), internal parasites chiefly of insects, annelids, and other invertebrates. M19. B *adj.* Of or relating to this subclass. L19.

gregarious /grɪˈgɛːrɪəs/ *a.* M17. [f. L *gregarius*, f. *grex*, *greg-* flock, herd + -OUS: see -ARIOUS.] 1 Of kinds of animal: tending to live in flocks or loosely organized communities. M17. b Of a person: inclined to associate with others, fond of company. L18. 2 *Bot.* Growing in open clusters or (*Ecol.*) in pure associations. E19. 3 Of or pertaining to a flock or community; characteristic of or affecting people gathered together in a crowd. M19.

1b R. COBB Edward was naturally gregarious, always in need of a wide audience of friends. M. MEYER Strindberg in his gregarious way was to enjoy many . . contacts. 3 DICKENS An instance of the gregarious effect of an excitement.

gregariously *adv.* L17. **gregariousness** *n.* E19.

gregarization /grɛgərʌɪˈzeɪʃ(ə)n/ *n.* Also **-isation**. M20. [f. mod.L *gregaria* swarming form of locust + -IZATION.] *Entomol.* The development of swarming behaviour and morphology in locusts.

grège /grɛʒ/ *a.* & *n.* Also **greige** /greɪʒ/. E20. [Fr., in *soie grège* raw silk, f. It. *greggio* raw, crude, unprocessed.] (Of) a colour between beige and grey.

grego /ˈgreɪgəʊ/ *n.* Pl. **-os**. M18. [f. some Proto-Romance alt. of L *Graecus* GREEK *a.*] A coarse jacket with a hood, worn in the eastern Mediterranean region. Also (*arch. slang*) a rough greatcoat.

Gregorian /grɪˈgɔːrɪən/ *a.* & *n.* L16. [Partly f. med.L *Gregorianus* (in sense 2 *cantus Gregorianus*) f. late L *Gregorius* f. Gk *Grēgorios*; partly f. the Eng. name *Gregory*: see -IAN.] A *adj.* 1 Of, pertaining to, or established by Pope Gregory XIII (1502–85). L16. 2 Of or pertaining to Pope Gregory I (*c* 560–604); *esp.* designating or according to the plainsong ritual music or chant founded on the Antiphoner attributed to him. L16. †3 *Gregorian tree*, the gallows. (Cf. GREGORY 2.) M17–L18. 4 Designating a kind of reflecting telescope, invented by J. Gregory (1638–75), Scottish mathematician, in which light reflected from a secondary mirror passes through a hole in the primary mirror. M18.

1 **Gregorian calendar** the modified form of the Julian calendar, established by Pope Gregory XIII in 1582 and adopted in Britain in 1752. 2 **Gregorian tones** in the RC Ch., the eight plainsong melodies prescribed for the psalms.

B *n.* †1 A variety of wig worn in the 16th and 17th cents. and supposedly named after its inventor, a Strand barber. L16–M17. 2 A member of a society (often classed with the Freemasons) which existed in England in the 18th cent. *obs.* exc. *Hist.* M18. 3 A Gregorian chant. L19.

gregory /ˈgrɛg(ə)ri/ *n.*[1] Also **G-**. L16. [The Eng. name *Gregory* in various applications.] †1 A gentleman of fashion. *rare*. Only in L16. †2 A hangman. (Cf. GREGORIAN *a.* 3.) Only in M17. 3 A feast, a party; *esp.* one held on St Gregory's day (12 March). *Anglo-Ir.* E19.

Gregory /ˈgrɛg(ə)ri/ *n.*[2] L19. [James *Gregory* (1758–1822), Sc. physician.] In full *Gregory('s) powder*. A laxative powder containing rhubarb, ginger, and magnesium carbonate.

greisen /ˈgrʌɪz(ə)n/ *n.* L19. [G, prob. dial. f. *greis* grey with age.] *Petrogr.* A light-coloured rock containing quartz, mica, and fluorine-rich minerals, produced by the pneumatolysis of granite.

greisening, **greiseniˈzation** *ns.* the pneumatolytic alteration of granite by fluorine-rich vapour E20.

greking /ˈgriːkɪŋ/ *n.* Long *obs.* exc. *Sc.* ME. [Corresp. to MDu. *griekinge*, prob. f. base of ON *grýja* to dawn.] Daybreak, dawn.

Grelling /ˈgrɛlɪŋ/ *n.* M20. [Kurt *Grelling* (1886–1942), Ger. logician.] Philos. *Grelling's paradox* (or *antinomy*), a semantic paradox concerning the applicability of the word 'heterological' to itself.

gremial /ˈgriːmɪəl/ *n.* & *a.* M16. [med.L *gremialis* alumnus, *gremiale* bishop's apron, f. L *gremium* lap, bosom: see -IAL.] A *n.* 1 A resident member (of a university or society). *obs.* exc. *Hist.* M16. 2 A silk apron placed on a bishop's lap when celebrating Mass or conferring orders. E19. B *adj.* 1 Of or pertaining to the bosom or lap; *fig.* (of a friend etc.) intimate. *obs.* exc. in *gremial veil* = sense A.2 above. M17. 2 Living within a university or society, resident. Also, designating ordinary or full members of a society as opp. to honorary members. *obs.* exc. *Hist.* M18.

gremlin /ˈgrɛmlɪn/ *n.* E20. [Prob. after *goblin*.] 1 Orig., a menial, a dogsbody. Now, a mischievous sprite alleged to cause mechanical or other faults, esp. in aircraft. *colloq.* E20. 2 A young surfer. Also, a troublemaker who frequents the beaches but does not surf. *Surfing slang.* M20.

gremmie /ˈgrɛmi/ *n.* *Surfing slang.* Also **gremmy**. M20. [f. GREM(LIN: see -IE, -Y[6].] = GREMLIN 2.

Grenache /grəˈnaʃ/ *n.* M19. [Fr.] (The black grape producing) a sweet dessert wine from the Languedoc-Roussillon region of France.

Grenadan /grɪˈneɪd(ə)n/ *n.* & *a.* M20. [f. as GRENADIAN + -AN.] = GRENADIAN.

grenade /grəˈneɪd/ *n.*[1] M16. [Fr. (16), alt. of (O)Fr. (*pome*) *grenate* POMEGRANATE after Sp. *granada*.] †1 A pomegranate. M16–M17. 2 A small explosive shell designed to be thrown by hand or launched mechanically. L16. 3 A glass receptacle thrown to break and disperse chemicals etc. for testing drains, extinguishing fires, etc. L19.

2 *hand-grenade, rifle-grenade*.

Comb.: **grenade-launcher** a device for launching grenades.

grenade /grəˈneɪd/ *n.*[2] Long *rare.* E18. [Perh. f. Fr. *grain* GRAIN *n.*[1] w. the sense 'something spiced' (cf. OFr. *grané* mentioned s.v. GRAVY). Cf. GRENADINE *n.*[1]] A dish consisting of pieces of larded veal braised with pigeons.

grenade /grəˈneɪd/ *v.t.* M19. [f. GRENADE *n.*[1]] Attack with a grenade or grenades.

Grenadian /grɪˈneɪdɪən/ *n.* & *a.* E20. [f. *Grenada* (see below) + -IAN.] A *n.* A native or inhabitant of Grenada, an island in the W. Indies. E20. B *adj.* Of or pertaining to Grenada or its inhabitants. M20.

grenadier /grɛnəˈdɪə/ *n.* L17. [Fr., f. as GRENADE *n.*[1]: see -IER.] 1 Orig., a soldier who threw grenades. Later, each of a company formed from the tallest men in a regiment. Now, a member of the Grenadier Guards (see below). L17. 2 Any of several African weaver-birds or waxbills, usu. with red in the plumage; *esp.* (more fully *common grenadier*) *Uraeginthus granatina*, and the red bishop, *Euplectes orix*. M18. b A notably tall person. E19. c A rat-tail (fish). L19.

1 **Grenadier Guards** (in the British army) the first regiment of household infantry.

grenadilla *n.* var. of GRANADILLA.

grenadine /ˈgrɛnədiːn/ *n.*[1] E18. [Fr. *grenadin*: cf. GRENADE *n.*[2]] A dish of veal or of poultry fillets, trimmed, larded, and glazed.

grenadine /ˈgrɛnədiːn/ *n.*[2] & *a.* M19. [Fr. (formerly *grenade*) silk of a grained texture, f. *grenu* grained, f. *grain* GRAIN *n.*[1]: see -INE[4].] (Of) a fabric of loosely woven silk or silk and wool.

grenadine /ˈgrɛnədiːn/ *n.*[3] L19. [Fr. (*sirop de*) *grenadine* f. *grenade* GRENADE *n.*[1]] A cordial syrup made from pomegranates; a drink of this.

grenado /grɪˈneɪdəʊ/ *n.* *arch.* Pl. **-o(e)s**. E17. [Sp. *granada*: see GRENADE *n.*[1], -ADO.] = GRENADE *n.*[1] 2.

grenat /grəna/ *n.* & *a.* M19. [Fr.: see GARNET *n.*[1]] (Of) a deep red colour, like that of a garnet.

Grenfell /ˈgrɛnfɛl/ *a.* E20. [Sir Wilfred Thomason *Grenfell* (1865–1940), Eng. medical missionary who founded the Labrador Medical Mission in 1893.] Proprietary name designating (clothing made from) a type of tough closely-woven windproofed cotton fabric.

Grenzbegriff /ˈgrɛntsbəgrɪf/ *n.* L19. [G, f. *Grenze* limit, boundary + *Begriff* concept.] In Kantian philosophy, a concept showing the limitation of sense-experience, a limiting concept; *gen.* a conception of an unattained ideal.

Grepo /ˈgrɛpəʊ/ *n.* Pl. **-os**. M20. [G *Gre(nz)po(lizei* frontier police.] *Hist.* An East Berlin border guard.

grès /grɛ/ *n.* L19. [Fr.] Stoneware. Chiefly in *grès de Flandres* /də flɑ̃ːdr/, Flemish ware.

Gresham's law /ˈgrɛʃ(ə)mz lɔː/ *n. phr.* M19. [Sir Thomas *Gresham* (d. 1579), Eng. financier and founder of the Royal Exchange.] *Econ.* The tendency for money of lower intrinsic value to circulate more freely than money of higher intrinsic and equal nominal value.

gressible /ˈgrɛsɪb(ə)l/ *a.* Long *rare* or *obs.* E17. [Late L *gressibilis* f. L *gress-* pa. ppl stem of *gradi* proceed, walk: see -IBLE.] Able to walk.

gressorial /grɛˈsɔːrɪəl/ *a.* M19. [f. mod.L *gressorius*, f. *gress-* (see prec.) + -AL[1].] *Zool.* Walking; adapted for walking.

Gretchen /ˈgrɛtʃ(ə)n/ *n.* L19. [*Gretchen* (see below).] A girl held to resemble Gretchen, the heroine seduced by Faust in Goethe's play; a typically German girl or woman. Freq. *attrib.*

Gretna Green /grɛtnə ˈgriːn/ *a. phr.* E19. [A village in Scotland, close to the border with England.] *Hist.* Designating or pertaining to a marriage contracted by an eloping couple from England immediately after entering Scotland, where parental consent was not necessary.

†greund *n.* LME–M19. [App. contr.] A greyhound.

grevillea /grɪˈvɪlɪə/ *n.* M19. [mod.L (see below), f. Charles Francis *Greville* (1749–1809), Sc. horticulturist.] Any of various chiefly Australian trees and shrubs of the genus *Grevillea* (family Proteaceae), bearing conspicuous but petalless flowers with prominent styles.

Grevy's zebra /ˌgrɛvɪz ˈziːbrə, ˈzɛbrə/ *n. phr.* Also **Grévy's** /ˌgreɪvɪz/. L19. [f. F. P. Jules *Grévy* (1807–91), Fr. president.] An endangered zebra, *Equus grevyi*, which has narrow stripes, a white belly, and prominent broad ears, and is found on arid steppe from Ethiopia to Kenya.

grew /gruː/ *n.* & *a.* ME. [OFr. *griu* f. L *Graecus* GREEK *n.* & *a.* In sense A.2 abbrev. of *grew-hound*.] A *n.* †1 The Greek language; a Greek. ME–M16. 2 A greyhound. *Sc.* & *north.* M16. B *adj.* Greek. Long *obs.* exc. *Sc.* in *grew-hound* [alt. of GREUND], a greyhound. LME.

grew *v.* pa. t.: see GROW *v.*

grex /grɛks/ *n.* M20. [L = flock.] *Mycol.* A cohesive, often mobile clump of amoeboid cells formed during the migratory phase of the life cycle of some cellular slime moulds. Also called *slug*.

grey /greɪ/ *n.* Also ***gray**. ME. [The adj. used ellipt. or absol.] 1 Grey clothing or fabric. ME. b The uniform of the Confederate troops in the American Civil War. *US.* M19. c Unbleached fabric. L19. d In *pl.* Grey flannel trousers. *colloq.* M20. †2 (The fur or dressed skin of) a badger; *gen.* grey fur. ME–L19. 3 An animal distinguished by grey colour, as a grey whale, a grey squirrel, etc.; *spec.* a grey or white horse. (Earliest in DAPPLE GREY *n.*) LME. 4†a A grey-haired person, an old man. LME–E16. b A white-skinned person. *Black slang.* M20. c A dull, anonymous, or nondescript person. M20. 5 A grey or subdued light; the cold sunless light of the morning or evening twilight. L16. 6 In *pl.* In full *the Scots Greys*. A regiment in the British army raised in 1681 as the Royal Regiment of Dragoons and now the 2nd Dragoons, orig. wearing a grey uniform. M18. 7 Grey colour; a shade of this; greyness. E19. b A pigment of a grey colour. Freq. w. specifying wd. L19. 8 A coin with two heads or two tails. *arch. slang.* E19.

1 G. DOWNES A blind old man, dressed in grey. 3 R. GRAVES Pituazes's men, all mounted on greys, came at him. 5 W. PIKE The first grey of dawn being the favourite time of attack. 7 J. A. SYMONDS The colour of the olive tree is delicate. Its pearly greys . . in no wise interfere with the lustre. *fig.*: D. BAGLEY A world in which black and white merged into an indeterminate grey, where bad actions were done for good reasons and good actions were suspect. *ash-grey, dapple grey, iron-grey, pearl-grey, silver-grey*, etc. *French grey*: see FRENCH *a.*

greyers *n.pl.* (*arch. colloq.*) = GREY *n.* 1d E20.

grey /greɪ/ *a.* Also ***gray**. [OE *grǣg* = OFris. *grē*, MDu. *grau*, *gra* (Du. *grauw*), OHG *grāo* (G *grau*), ON *grár*, f. Gmc.] 1 Of the colour intermediate between black and white; of the colour of the sunless sky, ash, lead, etc.; *spec.* (of a horse) of this or a white colour. Freq. prefixed w. specifying wd denoting some particular shade of grey. OE. b Of fabric: unbleached, untreated. M19. c Of a person: white-skinned. *Black slang.* M20. 2 Of hair: turning white with age, grief, etc. Of a person: having grey hair. OE. b *fig.* Ancient, immemorial; belonging to old age; experienced, wise. E17. 3 Of weather etc.: dull, sunless; clouded, overcast. ME. b *fig.* Not bright or hopeful; dismal, gloomy, sad, depressing. E18. c Esp. of a person: dull, anonymous, nondescript, without distinction. M20. d Less extreme than 'black'; indeterminate, not clearly defined. M20. 4 [f. the colour of the habit.] Designating a Cistercian monk, a Franciscan friar, or a sister of the third order of St Francis. ME.

1 BROWNING Down the grass path grey with dew. G. GREENE He dusted the ashes from his white trousers, leaving one more grey smear. *ash-grey, dapple grey, iron-grey, pearl-grey, silver-grey*, etc. 2 W. H. PRESCOTT He had grown grey in the service of the court. J. GALSWORTHY Her hair . . was going grey. b W. SHENSTONE Herbs for use, and physic, not a few Of grey renown. L. MORRIS Gray wisdom comes with time and age. 3 J. TYNDALL In the gray light of the evening. B. EMECHETA The bright night gradually gave way to a grey, damp morning. b E. F. BENSON Without seeing anything that broke the endless grey monotony of my days. J. GROSS He represented everything . . most at enmity with joy, everything grey, ponderous, drearily rationalistic. c *Times* The identity of these grey men of politics should be revealed. G. PRIESTLAND The grey fellowship of the depressed is wider than it knows. d *Guardian* As for the over-prescribing doctors, it was not just the black sheep we had to worry about. It was the grey sheep too.

Special collocations & comb.: *grey* ANTIMONY. **grey area** (*a*) a situation or subject not clearly or easily defined or categorized, or not clearly covered by existing rules etc.; (*b*) *S. Afr.* a residential area where Blacks and Coloureds live illegally alongside Whites by tacit consent. **grey-back** (*a*) *Hist.* (*US colloq.*) a Confederate soldier in the American Civil War; (*b*) *dial.* & *US colloq.* a louse; (*c*) (chiefly *local*) any of various grey-backed birds or animals, as the hooded crow, the scaup, etc. **greybeard** (*a*) a man with a grey beard; (freq. *derog.*) an old man; (*b*) a large earthenware or stoneware jug or jar for spirits; (*c*) *dial.* traveller's joy, *Clematis vitalba*, in seed. **greybearded** *a.* having a grey beard. **grey birch** a small birch, *Betula populifolia*, with light-coloured bark, found in eastern N. America; also called *old-field birch* (US), *wire birch* (Canad.). **grey box** any of various Australian eucalypts, esp. *Eucalyptus moluccana*. **grey cells** *colloq.* = *grey matter* below. **grey-coat** a person wearing grey clothing; *spec.* (*Hist.*) a Cumberland yeoman. **grey crow** = HOODED *crow*. *grey drake*: see DRAKE *n.*[1] 4. **grey duck** an Australasian duck, *Anas superciliosa*, with mainly grey-brown plumage and a striped head. **grey economy** the part of the economy that is not accounted for in official statistics. **grey eminence** = ÉMINENCE GRISE. **grey eye** an eye with a grey iris. **grey-eyed** *a.* having grey eyes; *poet.* designating the early morning. **grey fowl** (a) grouse in winter plumage. **grey fox** a greyish American fox, *Vulpes cinereoargenteus*, noted for an ability to climb trees. **Grey Friar** [f. the colour of the order's habit] a Franciscan friar. **grey goose** any goose of the genus *Anser* with predominantly grey plumage; *esp.* the greylag. **grey groat** *arch.* a groat; *fig.* something of little value. **grey gurnard** a small gurnard, *Trigla gurnardus*. **greyhen** the female black grouse. **grey jay** a fluffy long-tailed jay, *Perisoreus canadensis*, which has dark grey upperparts and a whitish face, and is found in Canada and the north-western US (also called *Canada jay*). **grey kangaroo** either of two large woodland kangaroos, the eastern *Macropus giganteus* and the western *M. fuliginosus*. **greymail** *colloq.* (*US*) [after *blackmail*] (a ploy involving) the threat by the defence, esp. in a spy trial, to expose government secrets unless charges are dropped. **grey mare** (*a*) a mare with a grey coat; (*b*) *fig.* a wife who dominates her husband. **grey market** [after *black market*] (a place of) traffic of questionable status in officially controlled goods or in commodities in short supply; *spec.* trading in a security not yet quoted on the Stock Exchange. **grey marketeer** one engaged in dealing in the grey market. **grey marketeering** dealing in the grey market. **grey matter** (*a*) the greyish unmyelinated tissue in the vertebrate central nervous system containing nerve cell bodies, dendrites, and glial cells, and forming the cortex of the cerebrum and cerebellum and the core of the spinal cord (cf. *white matter* s.v. WHITE *a.*); (*b*) *colloq.* intelligence, brains. **grey mullet** any of various thick-bodied detritus-feeding fish of the worldwide family Mugilidae, esp. of inshore and estuarine waters, many of which are important food fish. **grey nurse** a large Australasian shark, *Odontaspis arenarius*. **grey oak** any of several N. American oaks, esp. *Quercus coccinea* and *Q. borealis*. **grey-out** *n.* & *v.i.* (*Aeronaut.*) (suffer from) a dimming of the vision, less severe than a blackout. **grey parrot** a parrot, *Psittacus erithacus*, of western equatorial Africa, which has red tail-feathers and is often kept as a pet for its mimicking abilities. *grey partridge*: see PARTRIDGE *n.* 1. **grey phalarope** a northern holarctic phalarope, *Phalaropus fulicarius*, which has grey upperparts in winter and chestnut red underparts in its breeding plumage. **grey pine** any of several N. American pines, esp. the jack pine, *Pinus banksiana*. **grey scale** a range of tones from white to black. **grey seal** a common seal, *Halichoerus grypus*, of the N. Atlantic and Baltic. **grey squirrel** a common squirrel of eastern N. America, *Sciurus carolinensis*, introduced into the British Isles in the late 19th cent. **grey tin** the alpha allotrope of tin, which is a brittle form to which white tin slowly changes at temperatures below 18 degrees C. **grey trout** (*a*) the sea trout; (*b*) *US* the lake trout, *Salvelinus namaycush*; (*c*) *US* the weakfish, *Cynoscion regalis*. *grey wethers*: see WETHER. **grey whale** a baleen whale, *Eschrichtius robustus*, of N. Pacific coastal waters. **grey willow** any of several kinds of willow with leaves hoary beneath, esp. *Salix cinerea* and (*N. Amer.*) *S. sericea*. *grey wolf*: see WOLF *n.* 1.

greyish *a.* somewhat grey M16. **greyly** *adv.* E19. **greyness** *n.* L15.

grey /greɪ/ *v.* Also ***gray**. LME. [f. the adj.] 1 *v.i.* Become or grow grey. LME. 2 *v.t.* Make grey. M19.

1 S. R. CROCKETT It was already greying for the dawn. E. FEINSTEIN Tsvetayev was forty-five, a greying, slightly stooped figure. 2 F. MACLEOD He is a man whose hair has been greyed by years and sorrow. P. PEARCE The green of the garden was greyed over with dew.

greyhound /ˈgreɪhaʊnd/ *n.* [OE *grīghund* (= ON *greyhundr*) f. Gmc base also of ON *grey* bitch (ult. origin unkn.) + *hund* HOUND *n.*[1]] 1 (An animal of) a tall slender long-legged and keen-sighted breed of dog capable of high speed and used in racing and hare-coursing. OE. 2 The figure or representation of this, esp. used as a badge of office. LME. 3 *Hist.* More fully *ocean greyhound*. An ocean steamship specially designed for great speed. L19.

Comb.: **greyhound-racing** a sport in which a mechanical hare is coursed by greyhounds on a track.

greylag /ˈgreɪlag/ *n.* Also (earlier) **grey lag**. E18. [Prob. f. GREY *a.* + LAG *n.*[3]] A large, grey-brown and white Eurasian goose, *Anser anser*, ancestor of the farmyard goose. Also *greylag goose*.

greywacke /ˈgreɪwakə/ *n.* Also ***gray-**; earlier in G form ***Grauwacke*** /ˈgraʊvakə/, pl. ***-wacken*** /-vakən/. L18. [G *Grauwacke*, f. *grau* grey + WACKE.] *Petrogr.* Any coarse-grained, usu. dark sandstone containing angular mineral and rock fragments in a fine-grained clayey matrix.

gribble /ˈgrɪb(ə)l/ *n.*[1] *obs.* exc. *dial.* L16. [Perh. rel. to dial. var. of CRAB *n.*[2]] A young crab tree or blackthorn; a stick made from it. Also, the stock of a crab tree used for grafting on.

gribble /ˈgrɪb(ə)l/ *n.*[2] L18. [Perh. cogn. w. GRUB *v.*] A wood-boring marine isopod crustacean, *Limnoria lignorum*.

grice /grʌɪs/ *n.*[1] Now *Sc.* & *arch.* Pl. **-s**, (long *rare* or *obs.*) same. ME. [ON *griss* (Sw., Da. *gris*) young pig, pig.] A pig; *esp.* a young pig.

grice *n.*[2] var. of GRECE.

gricer /ˈgrʌɪsə/ *n. colloq.* M20. [Origin unkn.] A railway enthusiast; *esp.* a person who seeks out and photographs unusual trains etc.

gricing *n.* the activity of a gricer M20.

grid /grɪd/ *n.* M19. [Back-form. f. GRIDIRON *n.*] 1 An arrangement of parallel bars with openings between them; a grating. Formerly also = GRIDIRON *n.* 1. M19. **b** *Naut.* = GRIDIRON *n.* 2c. M19. **c** *Theatr.* = GRIDIRON *n.* 2d. L19. **d** An electrode (orig. a wire mesh) placed between the cathode and anode of a thermionic valve or cathode-ray tube, and serving to control or modulate the flow of electrons. Also *control grid*. E20. 2 A network of lines, esp. of two series of regularly spaced lines crossing one another at right angles; *spec.* such a network on a map, numbered to enable the precise location of a place, feature, etc. E20. **b** = GRIDIRON *n.* 2f. E20. **c** Esp. in *Motor Racing*. A pattern of lines painted on a racetrack at the starting-point to indicate the starting positions. M20. **d** The layout of a town divided into roughly equal blocks by streets at right angles to each other. Usu. *attrib.* as *grid plan*, *grid system*, etc. M20. 3 A bicycle. *slang.* E20. 4 A network of high-voltage transmission lines by which electrical power from a number of generating stations is distributed throughout a country or region; a similar distribution network for gas or water supply. E20.

Comb.: **gridlock** a traffic jam affecting a network of streets caused by continuous queues of intersecting traffic; *grid plan*, *system*: see sense 2d above.

gridded /ˈgrɪdɪd/ *a.* E20. [f. prec. + -ED[2].] Covered with, forming, or containing a grid.

griddle /ˈgrɪd(ə)l/ *n.* & *v.* ME. [OFr. *gredil*, *gridil* gridiron (mod. *gril*) f. Proto-Romance dim. of L *cratis*: see CRATE *n.*, GRATE *n.* Cf. GRILLE.] **A** *n.* 1 = GRILL *n.*[1] ME. 2 A usu. circular flat metal (esp. iron) plate heated for baking, toasting, etc. LME. 3 *Mining.* A sieve for separating ore. L18.

Comb.: **griddle cake**: cooked on a griddle.

B *v.t.* 1 Cook on a griddle. LME. 2 Sieve *out* with a griddle. L18.

gride /grʌɪd/ *v.* Chiefly *poet.* LME. [Metath. alt. of GIRD *v.*[2]: adopted by Spenser f. Lydgate.] 1 *v.t.* Pierce with a weapon; wound. Now *rare*. LME. 2 *v.i.* Pierce *through*; cut, scrape, or graze *along*, *through*, etc., with a grating sound or a rasping pain. L16. 3 *v.t.* (Cause to) clash or grate against. E19.

gridelin /ˈgrɪdəlɪn/ *n.* & *a.* Now *rare*. E17. [Fr. *gridelin*, *gris-de-lin* lit. 'grey of flax'.] (Of) a pale purple or greyish-violet colour.

gridiron /ˈgrɪdʌɪən/ *n.* Also (earlier) †**gridire**. ME. [Alt. of GRIDDLE *n.*, with assim. of 2nd syll. to IRON *n.* Cf. ANDIRON.] 1 A cooking utensil of parallel metal bars for boiling or grilling; a grill; *Hist.* a similar but larger structure used as an instrument of torture. ME. 2 An object resembling a gridiron; *esp.* the flag of the US. ME. **b** *Hist.* In full *gridiron pendulum*. A compensation pendulum made of parallel rods of different metals. M18. **c** *Naut.* An open framework of parallel beams for supporting a ship in dock. M19. **d** *Theatr.* An open framework of beams above a stage from which scenery or lights can be hung. L19. **e** = GRID 2d. L19. **f** An American football field, with parallel lines marking out the area of play; the game of American football. L19.

1 **on the gridiron** *arch.* in a state of anguish or uneasiness.

gridiron /ˈgrɪdʌɪən/ *v.t.* M19. [f. the n.] Mark with parallel lines or in a gridiron pattern.

griece *n.* see GRECE.

grief /griːf/ *n.* ME. [AN *gref*, OFr. *grief* (mod. *grief* grievance, injury, complaint), f. *grever* GRIEVE *v.*] 1 Orig. *gen.*, mental anguish or sorrow. Now *spec.* deep sorrow caused esp. by bereavement, or bitter regret or remorse. Also, *colloq.* trouble, annoyance. ME. **b** The cause or subject of grief. E16. †2 (A kind or cause of) hardship or suffering. ME–E18. †3 Hurt, harm, damage, or injury, done or caused by another. ME–L16. **b** = GRIEVANCE 3. LME–M19. †4 Anger, displeasure; offence. ME–L16. †5 Physical pain or discomfort; a physical injury or illness. ME–E18.

1 A. BRINK The woman lost her husband. She was shattered with grief. QUILLER-COUCH I got some grief on that because it took three days to do Maxwell's Silver Hammer. **b** COVERDALE *Prov.* 17:25 An indiscrete sonne is a grefe unto his father.

Phrases & comb.: **bring to grief** bring to disaster. **come to grief** meet with disaster, fail. **good** (or great) **grief!** *int.* expr. surprise, alarm, etc. **grief-stricken** *a.* overcome by grief.

griefful *a.* painful; full of grief, sorrowful: LME. **griefless** *a.* M16. **grieflessness** *n.* (now *rare*) L16.

grievance /ˈgriːv(ə)ns/ *n.* ME. [OFr. *grevance*, *grievance*, f. *grever*: see GRIEVE *v.*, -ANCE.] †1 The infliction of wrong or hardship; (a cause of) injury or oppression. ME–M18. †2 The state or fact of being oppressed, injured, or distressed; trouble, distress, pain. ME–L16. 3 A (real or imagined) wrong or ground of complaint. ME. †4 Displeasure, indignation, offence. ME–E16. †5 A disease, an ailment. LME–M18.

3 G. A. BIRMINGHAM A letter to *The Times*, the usual resort of an Englishman with a grievance. V. CRONIN He listened personally to any grievances and when justified put them right.

grieve /griːv/ *n.* [OE (Northumb.) *grǣfa* = WS *ġerēfa*: see REEVE *n.*[1]] 1 A governor of a province, town, etc. Now only *Hist.*, a sheriff. OE. 2 The manager, overseer, or bailiff on a farm. *Sc.* & *north.* L15.

grieveship *n.* a district under the charge of a grieve LME.

grieve /griːv/ *v.* ME. [OFr. *grever* burden, encumber f. Proto-Romance alt. of L *gravare*, f. *gravis* GRAVE *a.*[1]] †1 *v.t.* Harass, trouble, oppress; do wrong or harm to (a person). ME–M19. **b** Cause harm or damage to (a thing). ME–L16. †2 *v.t.* & *i.* Do bodily or material injury (to). ME–E19. †3 *v.t.* Affect with pain or disease. (Cf. GRIEVED *a.* 2.) ME–L16. 4 *v.t.* Affect with grief or deep sorrow. Also, trouble, annoy, cause pain or anxiety to. ME. †5 *v.t.* Make angry; offend. ME–M16. 6 *v.i.* Feel grief or distress; sorrow deeply *at*, *for*, *about*, *over*, *to do*. ME. **b** *v.t.* Feel or show grief or regret at or for. Chiefly *poet.* L16.

4 H. B. STOWE It really grieves me to have you be so naughty. I. MURDOCH I . . was grieved to see his tools so idle. 6 A. ALVAREZ She began to sob, weeping for her father as she had never grieved before.

grievingly *adv.* with grief E17.

grieved /griːvd/ *a.* LME. [f. GRIEVE *v.* + -ED[1].] †1 Annoyed, made angry. Only in LME. †2 Afflicted with pain or disease. L16–E18. 3 Affected with grief; distressed, troubled. L16. †4 Harassed, oppressed, harmed; having a grievance. E17–E19.

griever /ˈgriːvə/ *n.* LME. [f. GRIEVE *v.* + -ER[1].] †1 A person who harms or wrongs another or is the cause of a grievance. LME–M17. 2 A person who feels or shows grief. E19.

grievous /ˈgriːvəs/ *a.* & *adv.* ME. [Fr. *grevos*, *-eus*, f. *grever*: see GRIEVE *v.*, -OUS.] **A** *adj.* 1 Burdensome, oppressive; heavy, severe. *obs.* exc. as passing into sense 4. ME. †**b** Arduous, difficult; troublesome, annoying. LME–E17. 2 Bringing serious trouble; injurious. ME. 3 Serious, grave; (of a wound, pain, etc.) severe; (of a fault, crime, etc.) atrocious, heinous. ME. 4 Causing mental pain or distress, exciting grief; *rare* full of grief, sorrowful. LME.

1 LD MACAULAY The High Commission . . the most grievous of the many grievances under which the nation laboured. 2 G. VIDAL It had been a grievous mistake for Sparta to join the enemies of our family. 3 SHAKES. *1 Hen. IV* The complaints I hear of thee are grievous. R. L. STEVENSON His wounds were grievous indeed, but not dangerous.

Special collocations: **grievous bodily harm** (orig. *Law*) (the act of causing) serious physical injury.

†**B** *adv.* Grievously. *rare* (Shakes.). Only in L16.

grievously *adv.* ME. **grievousness** *n.* ME.

griff /grɪf/ *n.*[1] *Anglo-Ind.* E19. [Abbrev.] = GRIFFIN *n.*[2]

griff /grɪf/ *n.*[2] *slang.* L19. [Abbrev.] = GRIFFIN *n.*[3]; a tip (in betting etc.); a hint, a signal; news, reliable information.

griff *n.*[3] var. of GRIFFE *n.*[1]

griffaun /grɪˈfɔːn/ *n. Anglo-Ir.* L18. [Ir. *grafán*, f. *grafaim* scrape, grub.] A sturdy hoe for cutting turf.

griffe /grɪf/ *n.*[1] Also **griff**. LME. [OFr. *grif* (mod. *griffe*), f. *griffer* seize as with a claw, or f.

Frank.] A claw; *esp.* in *Archit.* a claw-shaped decoration at the base of a column.

¶Rare bef. E19.

griffe /grɪf/ *n.*[2] *US* (*obs.* exc. *Hist.*). M19. [Fr., f. Sp. *grifo* curly, frizzy.] A mulatto; *spec.* a person having one Black and one mulatto parent.

griffin /ˈgrɪfɪn/ *n.*[1] Also †**griffon, gryphon**. See also GRIFFON. ME. [OFr. *grifoun* (mod. *griffon*) f. Proto-Romance augm. of late L *gryphus*, f. *gryps, gryph-* f. Gk *grups, grup-*.] **1** A mythical creature usu. represented as having the head and wings of an eagle and the body of a lion; a representation of this. ME. **2** See GRIFFON.

griffiˈnesque *a.* in the style of a griffin M19. **griffiness** *n.* (*rare*) a female griffin M19.

griffin /ˈgrɪfɪn/ *n.*[2] *Anglo-Ind.* L18. [Perh. fig. use of prec. Cf. GRIFF *n.*[1]] A European newly arrived in India; a novice, a newcomer, a greenhorn.

griffinage *n.* the state of being a griffin E19. **griffinhood** *n.* = GRIFFINAGE M19. **griffinish** *a.* M19.

griffin /ˈgrɪfɪn/ *n.*[3] *slang.* L19. [Origin unkn.: cf. GRIFF *n.*[2]] A tip (in betting etc.); a hint, a signal; news, reliable information. Freq. abbrev. GRIFF *n.*[2]

A. N. LYONS 'This is the Straight Griffin, Fred,'.. 'the absolute straight Tip'.

griffon /ˈgrɪfən/ *n.* In sense 2 also †**-in**. ME. [f. as GRIFFIN *n.*[1] In sense 3 f. mod.Fr.] **I 1** See GRIFFIN *n.*[1] ME.

II 2 A vulture; now (also called *griffon vulture*) any of several vultures of the chiefly Eurasian genus *Gyps*, esp. *G. fulvus*. LME. **3** (An animal of) any of various European breeds of coarse-haired dog similar to terriers. L18.

3 Brussels griffon a small (variety of) griffon with a flat face and reddish-brown hair.

griffonage /grɪfəˈnɑːʒ/ *n.* Now *rare*. E19. [Fr., f. *griffonner* to scrawl.] Scrawl, scribble.

grift /grɪft/ *n.* & *v.* *US slang.* E20. [Perh. alt.] A *n.* = GRAFT *n.*[4] E20. **B** *v.i.* = GRAFT *v.*[3] E20.

grifter *n.* = GRAFTER *n.*[3] E20.

grig /grɪg/ *n.*[1] LME. [Origin unkn.] †**1** A small person; a dwarf. LME–E17. **2** A young or small eel in fresh water. E17. **3** A merry, lively, etc., person. Freq. in *as merry as a grig* or w. pleonastic adj. M17. **b** A grasshopper, a cricket. *dial.* M19. **4** A farthing; in *pl.*, money, cash. *slang.* Now *rare* or *obs.* M17.

griggish *a.* (*rare*) merry, happy L19.

grig /grɪg/ *n.*[2] Chiefly *dial.* L17. [Welsh *grug*.] Heather, *Calluna vulgaris*.

grig /grɪg/ *v.t.* Now *Anglo-Ir.* & *US.* M16. [Origin unkn.] Irritate, annoy.

griggle /ˈgrɪg(ə)l/ *n.*[1] *dial.* E19. [Origin uncertain: perh. f. GRIG *n.*[1]] A small apple left on the tree by a gatherer. Usu. in *pl.*

Grignard /ˈgriːnjɑː, -jɑːd, *foreign* griɲaːr/ *n.* E20. [f. Victor *Grignard* (1871–1934), Fr. chemist.] Chem. *Grignard('s) compound, reagent*, any of a class of organometallic magnesium compounds of formula RMgX (R = alkyl, X = halogen), widely used in organic syntheses.

Grignolino /grɪnjəˈliːnəʊ/ *n.* L19. [It.] An Italian wine grape grown in Piedmont; red wine made from this.

gri-gri *n.* var. of GRUGRU.

grihastha /grɪˈhʌstə/ *n.* L19. [Skt *gṛhastha* a married Hindu householder.] A brahmin in the second stage of life, which entails social obligations such as marriage and parenthood.

grike /grʌɪk/ *n.* Orig. *north.* Also **gryke**. L18. [Origin unkn.] A crack in rock, or between flagstones; a ravine in a hillside; now chiefly *spec.* in *Geol.*, a fissure enlarged by rainwater dissolution between limestone clints.

grill /grɪl/ *n.*[1] L17. [(O)Fr. *gril*, earlier *grail, greïl* masc. form (cf. GRIDDLE *n.*) based on fem. *grille*: see GRILLE.] Orig., a gridiron. Now, a device on a cooker for the downward emission of heat, used for cooking food on one side at a time.

Successful Slimming All the meals can be cooked under the grill.

grill /grɪl/ *n.*[2] M18. [f. GRILL *v.*] **1** (A dish of) grilled food. M18. **2** A period of grilling. M19. **3** In full *grill-room*. A restaurant or eating-place specializing in grilled food. L19.

1 MIXED *grill*.

grill *n.*[3] see GRILLE.

grill /grɪl/ *v.* M17. [Fr. *griller*, f. *gril* (*grille*) GRILL *n.*[1]] **1** *v.t.* Cook under a grill or on a gridiron. M17. **b** Subject to severe questioning or interrogation. L19. **2** *v.i.* Be cooked under a grill or on a gridiron. M19.

1 *fig.*: J. HILTON Midday sunlight, blazing on the roof of the cabin, grilled the air inside. **b** *New Yorker* He is grilled by a police detective. **2** *fig.*: R. CURZON Malta.. was cool in comparison to the fiery furnace in which we were at present grilling.

griller *n.* a person who or thing which grills M19.

grillade /grɪˈleɪd, -ˈjɑːd, ˈgriːɑːd/ *n.* M17. [Fr., f. as GRILL *v.*: see -ADE.] (A dish of) grilled food; a grill.

grillage /ˈgrɪlɪdʒ/ *n.* L18. [Fr., f. as GRILLE: see -AGE.] *Engin.* A heavy framework of cross-timbering, sometimes resting on piles, providing a foundation for building on unstable soil.

grille /grɪl/ *n.* & *v.* As n. also (earlier) **grill**. M17. [(O)Fr., earlier *graïlle* f. med.L *graticula, crat-* = L *craticula* dim. of *cratis*: see CRATE *n.*, GRATE *n.* Cf. GRIDDLE.] **A** *n.* †**1** Each of the bars in the visor of a helmet. Only in M17. **2** A framework of parallel or crossed bars or a structure of open metalwork dividing one area from another, esp. to allow discreet communication or vision etc., but not entry or exit; a grating. L17. **b** A similar structure positioned in front of the radiator in a motor vehicle, providing protection without preventing the flow of air over it. Also *radiator grille*. M20. **3** *Real Tennis.* A square opening in the end wall adjacent to the hazard side, backed by a wooden board or grating. E18. **4** A rectangular pattern of small dots impressed on some issues of postage stamps. L19.

2 D. F. CHESHIRE A private supper-room in the gallery, looking down on the hall through a grille. A. TYLER All the shops were locked behind iron grilles.

Comb.: **grille-work** open or lattice work.

B *v.t.* Equip with a grille; fence *off* with a grille. M19.

L. NKOSI I sit at a small wooden table by the grilled window of my cell.

grillo /ˈgrɪləʊ/ *n.* Pl. **-os**. M19. [It. & Sp. f. L *gryllus* f. Gk *grullos*.] A cricket.

grilse /grɪls/ *n.* LME. [Origin unkn.] A young salmon that has returned to fresh water after one year in the sea.

grim /grɪm/ *a.* & *adv.* Compar. & superl. **-mm-**. [OE *grim* = OFris., OS (Du.), OHG *grim* (G *grimm*), ON *grimmr*, f. Gmc.] **A** *adj.* **1** Orig., fierce, cruel, savage. Later, formidable, of fierce, frightening, or forbidding appearance or aspect. Formerly also, fiercely angry. OE. **b** Of a situation, scene, etc.: repellent, uninviting. ME. **2** Stern, unrelenting, merciless; resolute, uncompromising. OE. **3** Extremely painful or unpleasant; severe, unremitting. Now passing into senses 1 and 2. OE. **4** Of a smile or laughter: mirthless. Of humour: dealing with a ghastly or painful subject. M17. **5** Dreadful, ominous, sinister. L19.

1 J. THOMSON Bony, and gaunt, and grim, Assembling wolves in raging troops descend. DICKENS With a grim and ghastly stare. *the Grim Reaper*: see REAPER 1. **b** J. BUCHAN Grey Yorkshire moors, grim at first sight. **2** I. MURDOCH Together, like a grim tribunal, they looked disapprovingly down upon their stepfather. *like grim* DEATH. **3** W. HOLTBY The grim hand of poverty lay upon them. C. CHAPLIN The war was now grim Ruthless slaughter and destruction were rife over Europe. **4** SIR W. SCOTT One of those grim smiles, of which it was impossible to say, whether it meant good or harm. **5** J. BRODSKY The financial situation in our family was grim. B. LOPEZ The grim news—three ships.. were lost, crushed in the ice.

B *adv.* In a grim manner or mood. Now *rare* and only in *comb.*, as *grim-frowning, grim-set*, etc. OE.

grimful *a.* (long *rare*) full of grimness, fierce, terrible ME. **grimness** *n.* OE.

grim /grɪm/ *v.* Infl. **-mm-**. LME. [Sense 1 f. Du. *grimmen*, f. *grim* GRIM *a.*; sense 2 f. GRIM *a.*] **1** *v.i.* Be angry; have or take on a fierce appearance. Long *rare*. LME. **2** *v.t.* Make grim or fierce; give a grim look to. E18.

2 J. BARLOW Grimm'd by the horrors of the dreadful night.

grimace /grɪˈmeɪs, ˈgrɪməs/ *n.* & *v.* M17. [Fr., earlier †*grimache* f. Sp. *grimazo* caricature, f. *grima* fright.] **A** *n.* **1** A distortion of the face expressing annoyance, pain, etc. or intending to cause laughter; a wry face. M17. **2** Affectation, pretence, sham. Now *rare*. M17. **3** An affected look or (formerly) gesture; the use of this. L17.

1 D. JACOBSON His lips twist into a crabbed, enigmatic grimace. I. MURDOCH His face was distorted in a grimace of mingled fear and annoyance. **2** LD MACAULAY It was natural for them to consider all piety as grimace. **3** GEO. ELIOT Too well-bred to have.. the grimaces and affected tones that belong to pretentious vulgarity.

B *v.i.* [Perh. f. Fr. *grimacer*.] Make a grimace; pull a face. M18.

P. ACKROYD He.. stood up, grimacing at a pain in his back.

grimacer, -ier *ns.* a person who grimaces E19.

Grimaldi /grɪˈmaldi/ *n.* E20. [See below.] *Archaeol.* Used *attrib.* to designate (remains of) a group of upper palaeolithic hominids known from discoveries in the Grimaldi caves in Liguria, Italy.

Grimaldian *a.* of, pertaining to, or characteristic of Grimaldi man M20.

grimalkin /grɪˈmalkɪn, -ˈmɔːl-/ *n.* *arch.* L16. [f. GREY *a.* + MALKIN.] (A name for) a cat, esp. an old she-cat; *transf.* an unpleasant old woman.

Grimbarian /grɪmˈbɛːrɪən/ *n.* L19. [f. *Grimsby* + -ARIAN w. unexpl. loss of *-s-*.] A native or inhabitant of the town of Grimsby in NE England.

grime /grʌɪm/ *n.* ME. [f. as next.] Soot, coal-dust, etc., on or ingrained in a surface; dirt, filth.

U. LE GUIN The ends of the sleeves were black with grime. *Glaswegian* Glasgow has cast off the grime of its industrial past.

grime /grʌɪm/ *v.t.* LME. [MLG, MDu. (cf. Flem. *grijmen*, LG *gremen*). Cf. BEGRIME.] Blacken with grime; dirty.

TED HUGHES Comes home dull with coal-dust deliberately To grime the sink and foul towels.

grimgribber /ˈgrɪmgrɪbə/ *n.* L18. [f. *Grimgribber*, an imaginary estate invented by a sham lawyer in Richard Steele's play *The Conscious Lovers* (1722).] Legal jargon; learned gibberish.

J. H. TOOKE The grimgribber of Westminster-Hall is a more fertile source of imposture.

grimly /ˈgrɪmli/ *a.* Now *rare* or *obs.* OE. [f. GRIM *a.* + -LY[1].] Grim-looking; grim in appearance or nature.

grimliness *n.* (*rare*) LME.

grimly /ˈgrɪmli/ *adv.* OE. [f. GRIM *a.* + -LY[2].] **1** With stern or cruel action, intention, or feelings. Also, rigidly, doggedly. OE. †**2** Dreadfully, terribly, hideously. Only in ME. **3** With a grim look or air. ME. **b** So as to produce a grim appearance. *rare*. LME.

1 J. CONRAD 'I haven't any half-crowns to spare for tips', he remarked grimly. E. ARDIZZONE It was a long, long row.. but he kept grimly on. **3** POPE Grimly frowning with a dreadful look. F. SWINNERTON She sat grimly still, shoulders contracted, and brain busy. **b** S. LEWIS His face was as grimly creased as the mask of tragedy.

Grimm's Law /ˈgrɪmz lɔː/ *n. phr.* M19. [Jacob *Grimm* (1785–1863), Ger. philologist.] A set of rules specifying regular differences in the consonants of related words in different Indo-European languages, primarily accounting for the separation of the Germanic languages from other Indo-European languages.

grimoire /grɪmˈwɑː/ *n.* M19. [Fr., alt. of *grammaire* GRAMMAR.] A manual of black magic supposedly used to cast spells, invoke demons, etc.

H. AINSWORTH A witch with a Bible! It should be a grimoire.

grimpen /ˈgrɪmpən/ *n.* M20. [f. the *Grimpen* Mire in Conan Doyle's *The Hounds of the Baskervilles*.] A marshy area.

T. S. ELIOT On the edge of a grimpen, where is no secure foothold.

Grim the Collier /grɪm ðə ˈkɒlɪə/ *n. phr.* E17. [A character in *Grim the Collier of Croyden*, a comedy by William Haughton (*c* 1575–1605).] A kind of hawkweed, *Hieracium aurantiacum*, grown in gardens, with orange or red flowers and calyces covered with black hairs.

grimthorpe /ˈgrɪmθɔːp/ *v.t.* L19. [Sir Edmund Becket, first Lord *Grimthorpe* (1816–1905), restorer of St Albans Cathedral.] Restore (an ancient building) with lavish expenditure rather than skill and taste.

Daily Chronicle The parish church, which despite of vigorous 'grimthorping' still shows .. its old Norman architecture.

grimy /ˈgrʌɪmi/ *a.* E17. [f. GRIME *n.* + -Y[1].] 1 Covered with grime, begrimed, dirty. E17. 2 *fig.* Unpleasant, mean. L19.

grimily *adv.* L19. **griminess** *n.* M17.

grin /grɪn/ *n.*[1] *obs.* exc. *dial.* OE. [Origin unkn.] 1 A snare made of cord, wire, etc. with a running noose; *transf.* & *fig.* a trap, a pitfall. OE. 2 A noose; a halter. OE.

grin /grɪn/ *n.*[2] M17. [f. GRIN *v.*[2]] An act of grinning. Now usu., a broad smile.

H. ROBBINS Her smile broadened to a mischievous grin. A. S. BYATT He had a nice, frank grin, friendly, not cheeky.

grin /grɪn/ *v.*[1]*t. obs.* exc. *dial.* Infl. **-nn-**. OE. [f. GRIN *n.*[1]] Catch in a noose, ensnare; choke, strangle.

grin /grɪn/ *v.*[2] Infl. **-nn-**. [OE *grennian* rel. to OHG *grennan* mutter (MHG *grennen* wail, grin), ON *granōn* grunt, ON *grenja* howl, OSw. *gränia* roar, gnash the teeth, f. Gmc. Cf. GROAN *v.*, GIRN *v.*] 1 *v.i.* Draw back the lips and reveal the teeth in pain or (formerly) anger. OE. 2 *v.i.* Smile broadly usu. showing the teeth. (Now the usual sense.) L15. b *v.t.* Form the mouth into, give, (a grin, a broad smile). M17. 3 *v.t.* Express by grinning. L17. 4 *v.i.* Of a surface: show gaps, gape; show through a covering. M19.

1 SIR W. SCOTT Here grins the wolf as when he died. 2 W. SOYINKA They were grinning, laughing at me. b T. HEGGEN He just stood and grinned the widest and most foolish grin Billings had ever seen. 3 G. GRANVILLE He grins defiance at the gaping crowd. SMOLLETT The surgeon grinned approbation. 4 R. A. FREEMAN When you have drilled the holes, .. put a drop of walnut stain in each, or else they 'grin'. *Times* Cheaper ones have a tendency to 'grin' .., that is, to show the backing through the all-too-sparse pile.

Phrases: **grin and bear it** take pain, adversity, etc., stoically. *grin like a Cheshire cat*: see CHESHIRE 2. **grin through a horse-collar** (in rustic sports) put one's head through a horse-collar and grimace (cf. GIRN *v.*).

grinner *n.* LME.

grinagog /ˈgrɪnəgɒg/ *n.* Chiefly *dial.* M16. [Fanciful formation f. GRIN *v.*[2]] A person who is always grinning, esp. foolishly and without cause.

†grincome *n.* var. of CRINKUM.

grind /grʌɪnd/ *n.* ME. [f. the vb.] 1 *gen.* The action or an act of grinding. ME. 2 Hard monotonous work or study; a dull and laborious task. *colloq.* M19. 3 A walk taken for exercise; a steeplechase. *Univ. slang.* M19. 4 Intensive study or tuition for an examination etc.; an instance of this. *slang.* M19. 5 A hard-working student; a swot. *US slang.* L19. 6 A ferry. *Cambridge Univ. slang.* L19. 7 (An act of) sexual intercourse. *slang.* L19. b The action of rotating the hips or pelvis in a dance etc. Also in *bump and grind*. *slang.* M20. 8 The size of the particles of a powder or other ground substance, *spec.* of ground coffee. E20.

1 D. DU MAURIER The grind of the gate itself, as it scraped the stone beneath and was opened. T. GUNN Dry rough/substance encountered the grind / of my teeth. 2 CONAN DOYLE He .. settled down to rest after a life of ceaseless grind. **the daily grind** *colloq.* one's usual day's work. 3 N. ANNAN The pair of them pounded the last ten miles of the grind back to Cambridge. 4 A. HIGGINS He was giving grinds in mathematics to the clergyman's two .. sons. 5 E. JONG Just because you were a grub and a grind and did well in school. 7 J. WAINWRIGHT A grind with a cheap scrubber? 8 W. H. UKERS A mixture of a very fine with a coarse grind gives the best results in the cup.

Comb.: **grind (movie) house** *US slang* a cinema showing a continuous programme with no intermissions.

grind /grʌɪnd/ *v.* Pa. t. & pple **ground** /graʊnd/, **†grinded**. [OE *grindan*, of which there are no Gmc cognates. Cf. L *frendere* rub away, gnash.] 1 *v.t.* & *i.* Reduce to small particles or powder by crushing between millstones, the teeth, etc. Also foll. by *down*, & w. other advs. or advb. phrs. OE. b *v.t.* Produce by grinding. LME. 2 *v.i.* Scrape or rub on or against something; make a harsh or grating sound. Also, proceed noisily and laboriously, with or by means of friction. OE. b *v.t.* Rub (one thing) roughly or gratingly against or upon another (foll. by *against*, *into*, *upon*, etc.). Also make (one's way) laboriously. M17. 3†a *v.i.* Gnash with the teeth. OE–L16. b *v.t.* Rub (the teeth) together with a grating sound. ME. 4 *v.t.* Sharpen (a tool, weapon, etc.) by friction. ME. b Make smooth or reduce to the required size or shape by friction. M17. c *spec.* Make (a machine part, esp. a valve) fit its seat or housing by moving it to and fro in place with a suitable abrasive. Foll. by *in* (adv. & prep.), *into*, *on to*. L19. 5 *v.t. fig.* a Afflict, torment. Now chiefly *US*, annoy. LME. b Crush, oppress, exploit. Also foll. by *down*. E17. 6 *v.i.* & *t.* Copulate (with). *slang.* M17. b *v.i.* Rotate the hips or pelvis in a suggestive manner, esp. in a dance. *slang.* M20. 7 *v.i.* & *t.* Produce (music) on a barrel-organ etc.; *esp.* produce or bring *out* laboriously or monotonously. L18. 8 *v.t.* Teach (a subject, a pupil) in a steady laborious manner. E19. 9 *v.i.* Work (*away*, *on*) doggedly *at*; *spec.* study hard. M19. b Study hard with a tutor or grinder. *arch.* M19.

1 LONGFELLOW Though the mills of God grind slowly, yet they grind exceeding small. N. MAILER What we did not .. devour we could grind away in the electric Disposall beneath the sink. W. WHARTON A bird needs sharp gravel to grind food in its crop. 2 J. BETJEMAN No lorries grind in bottom gear Up steep and narrow lanes. R. WEST The voices of my father and mother grinding quietly against each other in an interminable argument. **grind to a halt** (freq. *fig.*) be brought to a standstill by pressure or friction. b W. GOLDING I ground the cigarette out in the ashtray. 3b E. O'BRIEN He was in a .. temper and I could see him grind his false teeth. 4 SHAKES. *Per.* I have ground the axe myself: Do you but strike the blow. *grind an axe*, *have an axe to grind*: see AXE *n.*[1] b I. NEWTON Good Workmen who can grind and polish Glasses truly spherical. c *Boy's Own Paper* To make the valves fit tight you should grind them .. with .. fine emery and oil. 5b *New Yorker* I see the economic system grinding people down .. the poor are getting poorer. **grind the faces of** = sense 5b above. 6 H. R. BROWN Her breath smells bad, but she sure can grind. 7 A. JESSOPP A half-starved organ grinder comes and delights my heart by grinding for half an hour. L. GORDON All through Virginia's childhood .. her father was grinding out immense numbers of biographies. 9 A. BURGESS I ground away at Pliny's Letters and Virgil Book Six.

Comb.: **grinding-stone** a grindstone; **grinding-wheel** (*a*) a wheel adapted for grinding or polishing; (*b*) a building in which cutlery or tools are ground.

grindaˈbility *n.* the extent to which a material is easily ground or pulverized M20. **grindable** *a.* able to be ground M17.

grinder /ˈgrʌɪndə/ *n.* OE. [f. GRIND *v.* + -ER[1].] 1 A person who grinds corn etc. in a mill; a miller. OE. b A person who grinds cutlery, tools, glass, etc. LME. c A person who works a barrel-organ, a winch on a yacht, etc. E19. 2 A molar tooth. In *pl.* also (*colloq.*), the teeth. LME. 3 A machine or implement for grinding. L17. 4 A person who prepares students for examinations; a crammer. *slang.* E19. b A diligent student. *US slang.* M19. 5†a A person who works for another. *rare.* Only in E19. b An employer of sweated labour. M19. 6 More fully *scissor(s)-grinder*. The restless flycatcher, *Myiagra inquieta*. *Austral.* M19. 7 A derisive gesture made by putting the thumb to the nose and working the little finger like the handle of a coffee-mill. *slang.* M19. 8 A large sandwich or filled roll usu. with several fillings. *US slang.* M20.

1b *New York Times* Jewellery. Grinders and Polishers. Experienced only. 2 W. GOLDING They were the grinders of old age. Worn away. M. GEE He spluttered with irritation as one of his treacle toffees stuck to his grinders. 4 M. EDGEWORTH A clever grinder .. would soon cram the necessary portion of Latin and Greek into him.

grindery /ˈgrʌɪnd(ə)ri/ *n.* E19. [f. GRIND *v.* + -ERY.] 1 Materials, tools, etc. (orig. only the whetstone) used by shoemakers and other leather-workers. E19. 2 A place for grinding tools, weapons, etc. L19.

grinding /ˈgrʌɪndɪŋ/ *ppl a.* OE. [f. GRIND *v.* + -ING[2].] 1 That grinds. OE. b Of a sound: grating, strident. E19. 2 Crushing, exacting, oppressive. L16. 3 Of pain etc.: excruciating, racking, wearing. L16.

1 **come to a grinding halt** = *grind to a halt* s.v. GRIND *v.* 2. b E. K. KANE You become conscious of a sharp, humming, grinding murmur. 2 *Times* Civil strife fuelled by grinding poverty has continued to flare. 3 **grinding pains**: in the first stage of childbirth.

grindingly *adv.* E19.

grindle /ˈgrɪnd(ə)l/ *n.*[1] Long *obs.* exc. *dial.* LME. [Origin unkn.] A narrow ditch or drain.

grindle /ˈgrɪnd(ə)l/ *n.*[2] *US.* E18. [G *Gründel*, f. *Grund* GROUND *n.*, bottom.] = *bowfin* s.v. BOW *n.*[1]

grindle stone /ˈgrɪnd(ə)l stəʊn/ *n. phr. obs.* exc. *dial.* ME. [Prob. f. instrumental n. f. GRIND *v.* + STONE *n.*, & already in OE.] 1 A grindstone. ME. †2 A piece, or kind, of stone suitable for making grindstones. E16–E18.

grindstone /ˈgrʌɪn(d)stəʊn/ *n.* ME. [f. GRIND *v.* + STONE *n.*] 1 A millstone. Long *rare.* ME. 2 A thick revolving stone disc used for grinding, sharpening, or polishing. ME. 3 A kind of stone suitable for making grindstones. Also *grindstone grit*. E18.

2 **hold** or **keep a person's nose to the grindstone** †(*a*) oppress, grind down; (*b*) cause to work hard and incessantly.

gringo /ˈgrɪŋgəʊ/ *n.* & *a.* Usu. *derog.* Pl. **-os**. M19. [Sp. = foreign, foreigner, gibberish.] A *n.* A (male) foreigner, esp. British or American, in a Spanish-speaking country. M19.

B *adj.* Of or pertaining to a gringo or gringos; foreign. L19.

High Times From Belize to Bolivia flows a growing trickle of gringo tourists in pursuit of the primitive.

gringa /-gə/ *n.* & *a.* (of or pertaining to) a female gringo M20.

griot /ˈgriːəʊ/ *n.* E19. [Fr.] A member of a class of travelling poets, musicians, and folk-historians, in North and W. Africa; a praise-singer.

grip /grɪp/ *n.*[1] OE. [Partly OE *gripe* grasp, clutch, corresp. to OHG *grif-* in comb., MHG *grif* (mod. *Griff*) grasp, handle, claw, ON *grip* grasp, clutch, and partly OE *gripa* handful, sheath, both f. weak base of *grīpan* GRIPE *v.*[1]] 1 A firm hold or grasp; the action of gripping, grasping, or clutching, esp. with the hand or claw; grasping power; ability to maintain contact, esp. by friction. Cf. HANDGRIP. OE. b A way of grasping or clasping hands, esp. as a means of recognition by members of a secret society such as the Freemasons. M18. c A way or style of grasping or holding something, as a racket, club, bat, etc. L19. 2 As much as can be seized in the hand; a handful. *obs.* exc. *dial.* OE. 3 A seizure or spasm of pain. *obs.* exc. *Sc.* LME. 4 *fig.* A firm or tenacious hold, grasp, or control; power, mastery; *spec.* oppressive power, irresistible force. L15. b An intellectual hold; power to understand or master a subject. M19. c The quality in a drink which gives it a lasting taste or other sensation on the palate. L19. 5 Something which grips or clips; *spec.* (*a*) *Sc.* in *pl.*, bonds, fetters; (*b*) *techn.* a device or machine part which grips, clips, or secures; (*c*) a hairgrip. M18. 6 That which is gripped or grasped; *esp.* the part of a weapon or handle of an implement etc. by which it is held; the cover of such a part, enabling it to be held more firmly. M19. 7 *Theatr.*, *Cinemat.* A stage-hand; a member of a camera crew responsible for moving and setting up equipment. L19. 8 In full *grip car*. A tramcar linked to a cable by a grip; a cable-car. *US.* L19. 9 A travelling bag; a piece of hand luggage. Orig. *US.* L19. 10 A job, an occupation. *Austral. slang.* E20.

1 D. Lodge Melanie smiled . . and attempted to disengage her arms from his grip. K. Laing His teeth had a sharper grip of it than his hands. M. Ignatieff He held on to his blanket with a grip no one could loosen. *What Car?* We were impressed by the excellent grip of the tyres. b F. O'Brien Hands were extended till they met, the generous grip of friendship. 4 S. King His mother was in the grip of a religious mania. J. M. Roberts The grip of the emperors at Constantinople and Ctesiphon was already loosened. b J. I. M. Stewart I kept a grip on the facts as they came together. 5 *hair-grip*, *kirby-grip*, etc. 6 W. van T. Clark It was a long, blue-barrelled Colt six-shooter with an ivory grip.

Phrases: **at grips** in close combat. **come to grips with** come into close quarters or into combat with. **get a grip on oneself** keep or recover one's self-control. **get to grips with** approach with determination, get control of. **lengthen one's grip** hold one's bat, club, etc. further from the point of impact. **lose one's grip** *fig.* lose control. **shorten one's grip** hold one's bat, club, etc., nearer to the point of impact. **take a grip on oneself** = *get a grip on oneself* above.

Comb.: *grip car*: see sense 8 above; **gripman** *US* a cable-car operator; **gripsack** = sense 9 above.

gripless *a.* having no grip or hold E17.

grip /grɪp/ *n.*^{2} Now chiefly *dial.* or *Hunting*. Also (*dial.*) **gripe** /grʌɪp/. [OE *grypa*, *-e* rel. to *grēop* burrow, MLG *grüppe*, MDu. *grippe*, *greppe*, f. Gmc base meaning 'hollow out'.] A small open furrow or ditch, esp. for carrying off water; a trench, a drain, a channel.

grip /grɪp/ *v.*^{1} Infl. **-pp-**. [OE (late Northumb.) *grippa* corresp. to MHG *gripfen*.] 1 *v.t.* Grasp, seize, or hold firmly or tightly, esp. with the hand, claw, etc. OE. b Of a disease: afflict strongly. E19. 2 *v.t. gen.* Seize, catch; obtain hold or possession of. *obs.* exc. *Sc.* LME. b *spec.* Seize or encroach on (land). *Sc.* E17. 3 *v.i.* Take firm hold, maintain contact, esp. by friction; grasp something, get a grip. LME. 4 *v.t.* Join firmly *to*. L19. 5 *v.t. fig.* Compel the attention or interest of; take hold of (the mind, the emotions, etc.). L19.

1 S. R. Crockett He . . held it [his weapon] gripped between his knees as he rowed. J. Buchan I . . gripped his arm, for I thought he was going to faint. 3 T. Boston Like a bird on the side of a wall gripping with its claws. 5 P. G. Wodehouse It gripped him from the first page. F. Herbert Deathly stillness gripped the arena. T. Sharpe A sense of righteous anger gripped him.

gripper *n.* a person who or thing which grips; *spec.* any contrivance or implement used to hold or secure an object: L16. **gripping** *a.* that grips, clutches, or clips tightly; *fig.* that compels the attention: E16. **grippingly** *adv.* M20. **grippy** *a.* (*a*) that grips or holds; *spec.* that holds the attention; (*b*) *Sc.* grasping, avaricious: E19.

grip /grɪp/ *v.*^{2}*t.* Now *dial.* Infl. **-pp-**. Also (*dial.*) **gripe** /grʌɪp/. L16. [f. GRIP *n.*^{2}] Make furrows or grips in; ditch, trench.

†**gripe** *n.*^{1} ME. [OFr. *grip* griffin, corresp. to med.L *grypus*, *-is*, *gripes*, *grippis*, *gripa* griffin, vulture, vars. of *gryphus* f. L *gryps*, *gryph-* (*gryphus*) f. Gk *grups*, *grup-*: see GRIFFIN *n.*^{1}] 1 A griffin. ME–M17. 2 A vulture. ME–M18.

Comb.: **gripe's egg** a large egg, supposedly that of a gripe; *transf.* an oval-shaped vessel or cup.

gripe /grʌɪp/ *n.*^{2} LME. [f. GRIPE *v.*^{1}] 1 The action of gripping, clutching, or grasping, esp. with the hand, arm, claw, etc. LME. b *fig.* Grasp, hold, control, grip. LME. c *Surg.* An act of compressing an artery etc. with the fingers. Now *rare*. L17. 2 *transf.* & *fig.* a The clutch or pinch of something painful. Formerly also (in *pl.*), spasms of pain, pangs of grief. Now *rare* or *obs.* M16. b An intermittent spasmodic pain in the bowels. Usu. in *pl.*, colic pains. E17. †3 The hand held in a grasping or clutching position. M16–L18. 4 A handful or other specified quantity. *local.* L16. †5 a A shrewd gambler who places or leads bets. *slang.* L16–E17. b A grasping covetous person, a usurer. *slang.* Only in 17. 6 Something which grasps or clutches; *spec.* something which restrains, a brake. L16. 7 Something which is held or grasped; the handle of an implement, the hilt of a sword. E17. 8 *Naut.* In *pl.* Lashings securing a boat on a deck or hanging in davits. M18. 9 A complaint, a grumble. Freq. in *pl. slang.* M20.

1 Sir W. Scott Rescue me from the gripe of this iron-fisted . . clown. 2b J. Baxter Excess of green food, sudden exposure to cold, are . . occasional causes of gripes. 9 *Observer* It is a perpetual gripe from spectators that the toilet facilities are inadequate.

Comb.: **Gripe Water** (proprietary name for) a carminative, esp. for babies.

gripe /grʌɪp/ *n.*^{3} L16. [Du. *greep*, later assim. to GRIPE *n.*^{2}] *Naut.* The piece of timber etc. terminating the forward part of the keel. Also *gen.*, = FOREFOOT 2.

gripe *n.*^{4} see GRIP *n.*^{2}

gripe /grʌɪp/ *v.*^{1} [OE *grīpan* = OFris. *grīpa*, OS *grīpan* (Du. *grijpen*), OHG *grīfan* (G *greifen*), ON *grípa*, Goth. *greipan*, f. Gmc. Cf. GRIP *n.*^{1}, GROPE *n.*, *v.*] 1 *v.i.* Grasp or clutch something; seek to get a hold. Long *rare*. OE. 2 *v.t.* Lay hold of, seize; get into one's power or possession. *arch.* OE. 3 *v.t.* & *i.* Clutch or grip with the hand, claw, etc. *arch.* ME. †b *v.t.* Embrace, encircle tightly. LME–M18. †4 *v.t. fig.* Apprehend. comprehend. ME–M18. 5 *v.t.* Grieve, distress, annoy. Now chiefly *Sc.* & *N. Amer.* M16. 6 *v.t.* Produce spasmodic pain in (the bowels); affect with gripes or colic. Now chiefly as *griped* pa. pple. E17. b *v.i.* Produce pain in the bowels as if by constriction or contraction; cause gripes. E18. 7 *Naut.* a *v.i.* Of a ship: turn to face the wind in spite of the helm. E17. b *v.t.* Secure (a boat) with gripes. M19. †8 *v.t.* Close (the fingers) tightly; clench (the fist). *rare.* M17–E18. 9 *v.t.* & *i.* Oppress (someone) by miserly or penurious treatment; pinch, squeeze. *arch.* M17. 10 *v.i.* Complain, grumble, grouse. *colloq.* M20.

3 Milton Let each . . gripe fast his orbed Shield. 9 Dickens He feeds the poor baby when he himself is griped with want. 10 W. Wharton Lotte's griping because I'm dividing her place.

griper *n.* (*a*) a thing which gripes; (*b*) a person who oppresses others by extortionate or miserly means; (*c*) *colloq.* a person who complains or grumbles: L16. **griping** *ppl a.* that gripes, that clutches tightly; grasping; painful, distressing: M16. **gripingly** *adv.* E17. **gripingness** *n.* L17.

gripe *v.*^{2} see GRIP *v.*^{2}

†**griph** *n.* M17–L19. [L *griphus* f. Gk *griphos* creel, (fig.) riddle.] A puzzling question; a riddle; an enigma.

griphite /ˈgrɪfʌɪt/ *n.* L19. [f. Gk *griphos* riddle (on account of its complex composition) + -ITE^{1}.] *Min.* A basic phosphate of manganese and other elements, which crystallizes in the cubic system and usu. occurs as brown or black masses.

grippe /grɪp, *foreign* grip/ *n.* L18. [Fr.] Influenza.

grippé /gripe/ *a.* affected with grippe L19.

†**gripple** *n. rare.* M16. [f. GRIP *n.*^{1}, GRIPE *v.*^{1}: see -LE^{1}. Cf. GRAPPLE *n.*] 1 A hook to seize things with. Only in M16. 2 Grasp. *rare* (Spenser). Only in L16.

gripple /ˈgrɪp(ə)l/ *a. obs.* exc. *dial.* [OE *gripul*, f. *grip-* weak base of *grīpan* GRIPE *v.*^{1}: see -LE^{1}.] 1 Miserly, niggardly, usurious. OE. 2 Gripping, tenacious. E16.

grippleness *n.* avarice, greed, niggardliness L16.

Griqua /ˈgriːkwə/ *n.* & *a.* M18. [Nama.] A *n.* A member of a Coloured people of mixed Nama and European descent, native to East and West Griqualand in the Cape Province of South Africa. M18. B *adj.* Of or pertaining to this people. E19.

grisaille /grɪˈzeɪl, -li; *foreign* grizaːj (*pl. same*)/ *n.* & *a.* M19. [Fr., f. *gris* grey + *-aille* -AL^{1}.] A *n.* A method of painting in grey monochrome, used to represent objects in relief or to decorate stained glass; a stained-glass window or other work of this kind. M19. B *adj.* Executed in grisaille. M19.

grisard /ˈgrɪzɑːd/ *a.* & *n. rare.* E17. [(O)Fr., f. *gris* grey: see -ARD.] †A *adj.* Greyish. Only in E17. B *n.* A grey-haired man. L19.

Griselda /grɪˈzɛldə/ *n.* Also (*arch.*) **Grizel** /ˈgrɪz(ə)l/. LME. [*Grisilde*, the heroine in Chaucer's *Clerk's Tale*, typifying a meek, patient wife.] A meek patient woman or wife.

griseofulvin /ˌgrɪzɪə(ʊ)ˈfʊlvɪn/ *n.* M20. [f. mod.L (*Penicillium*) *griseofulvum* (species name), f. med.L *griseus* grey + L *fulvus* reddish-yellow.] *Pharm.* An anti-fungal antibiotic produced by moulds of the genus *Penicillium* and used to treat ringworm and other fungal infections.

griseous /ˈgrɪzɪəs/ *a.* E19. [f. med.L *griseus* + -OUS.] Chiefly *Bot.* & *Zool.* Grey; pearl-grey; greyish; mottled with grey.

grisette /grɪˈzɛt/ *n.* & *a.* E18. [Fr., f. *gris* grey: see -ETTE.] A *n.* 1 A cheap grey dress fabric, formerly worn by working girls in France. E18. 2 A young working-class Frenchwoman. E18. B *adj.* Made of grisette. E18.

gris-gris *n.* var. of GREEGREE.

griskin /ˈgrɪskɪn/ *n.* L17. [Obscurely f. GRICE *n.*^{1} + -KIN.] The lean part of a loin of pork.

grisly /ˈgrɪzli/ *a.* [Late OE *grislić*, f. weak base of *-grīsan* (in *āgrīsan* terrify) = MLG, MDu. *grīsen*: see -LY^{1}.] 1 Causing horror, terror, or superstitious fear; causing unpleasant feelings; grim, ghastly. LOE. †2 Full of fear, inspired by fear. LOE–L17. 3 Ugly. *dial.* L17.

1 A. Jessopp The tangible memories of grisly conflict. J. Gathorne-Hardy Hare suddenly thought of . . selling the body . . . the grisly tale is well known but still grips.

grisliness *n.* ME.

grisly /ˈgrɪzli/ *adv. arch.* ME. [f. weak base of OE *-grīsan* (see prec.) + -LY^{2}.] Horribly, terribly; grimly.

grison /ˈgrɪz(ə)n, ˈgrʌɪs(ə)n/ *n.* L18. [Fr., use as n. of adj. f. *gris* grey: see -OON.] Each of three carnivorous mustelid mammals of the genus *Galictis*, of Central and S. America, which are grey with black legs, face, and underparts.

grissino /grisˈsiːno, grɪˈsiːnəʊ/ *n.* Pl. **-ni** /-ni/. M19. [It.] A long thin stick of crisp bread. Usu. in *pl.*

grist /grɪst/ *n.*^{1} & *v.* [OE f. Gmc, f. as GRIND *v.*] A *n.* 1 The action or an act of grinding. OE. 2 Corn to be ground. Also, a batch of such corn. ME. 3 Corn that has been ground. L15. 4 Malt crushed or ground for brewing. E19. 5 A lot, a large number or quantity. *US.* M19.

2 *fig.*: E. Baynard This grinds life's grist, yet takes small tole. **grist for, to, the mill** useful experience, knowledge, material, etc.

B *v.t.* Grind (corn). E19.

Comb.: **grist-mill** a mill for grinding corn.

grist /grɪst/ *n.*^{2} Now chiefly *Sc.* E18. [Perh. rel. to GIRD *v.*^{1}] The size or thickness of a yarn or rope.

gristle /ˈgrɪs(ə)l/ *n.* [OE *gristle* = OFris., MLG *gristel*, *gerstel*, OHG *chrustila*, MHG *krustel* rel. to OE *grost* gristle: ult. origin unkn.] 1 Cartilage, or a cartilaginous structure: now chiefly when occurring in meat. OE. b *fig.* The unformed or initiatory stage of anything (w. ref. to the cartilaginous nature of the bones in infancy). Now *rare*. L18. †2 *fig.* A tender or delicate person. M16–M17.

gristly /ˈgrɪsli/ *a.* LME. [f. GRISTLE *n.* + -Y^{1}.] 1 Pertaining to or of the nature of gristle; consisting or full of gristle; cartilaginous. LME. 2 Having a texture like gristle, tough. E17.

1 M. Mackenzie A piece of gristly meat one inch in length.

†**grisy** *a.*^{1} L16–M19. [f. as GRISLY *a.* + -Y^{1}.] Horrible, grim, grisly.

†**grisy** *a.*^{2} *rare.* L16–E17. [f. Fr. *gris* grey + -Y^{1}.] Grey, grizzled.

grit /grɪt/ *n.*^{1} [OE *grēot* = OS *griot*, OHG *grioz* (G *Griess*), ON *grjót*, f. Gmc base also of next.] 1 *collect.* Formerly, sand, gravel, small stones. Now, minute particles of stone or sand, *spec.* as causing discomfort, clogging machinery, etc. OE. b A grain of sand. *rare.* E17. 2 Coarse sandstone. ME. 3 Earth, soil, mould; the ground. *obs.* exc. *dial.* ME. 4 The grain or texture of a stone; the fineness, coarseness, etc., of a stone. E16. 5 Strength of character; pluck, endurance, stamina. Also *clear grit*, *true grit*. *colloq.* E19. b *Canad. Polit.* (now *Hist.*). More fully *clear grit*. Orig., a supporter of the Clear Grit party, a 19th cent. liberal reform group which ultimately merged with the Liberal Party. Later, a liberal, a radical. M19.

1 *Soldier* The road . . is unmetalled and covered in grit. 5 G. STEIN She had grit and endurance and a vital courage.

Phrases & comb.: *clear grit*: see senses 5, 5b above. **grit-blast** *v.t.* & *i.* clean and roughen (a surface) by using a directed stream of abrasive particles; sandblast. **gritstone** = sense 2 above. MILLSTONE *grit*. **the clear grit** *slang* the real thing, the genuine article. *true grit*: see sense 5 above.

gritless *a.* (*rare*) L19.

grit /grɪt/ *n.*[2] Now *dial.* & *US*. [OE *grytt(e)* = MLG, Du. *grutte*, OHG *gruzzi* (G *Grütze*) f. WGmc, f. Gmc base also of prec., GROATS, GROUT *n.*[1]] †1 Bran, chaff, mill-dust. OE–ME. 2 In *pl.* (treated as *sing.* or *pl.*). Coarse oatmeal. Also (*US*), any coarsely ground grain, esp. when made into a kind of porridge. L16.

2 *Orlando (Florida) Sentinel* Eat Real Jail Food, such as cold grits and fried bologna.

grit /grɪt/ *v.* Infl. **-tt-**. LME. [f. GRIT *n.*[1]] 1 *v.i.* Produce or move with a grating sound, such as is caused by the crushing of grit. LME. b *v.t.* Cause to make such a sound. M19. 2 *v.t.* Grind or clench (the teeth). L18. b *v.t.* Utter through gritted teeth. E20. 3 *v.t.* Cover with grit or sand; spread grit on (an icy road etc.). M19.

1 E. GASKELL A slate-pencil gritting against a slate. 2 A. HALEY Gritting her teeth to keep from crying out.

gritter *n.* a machine or vehicle for spreading grit on roads etc. M20.

grith /grɪθ/ *n. obs.* exc. *Hist.* Also (esp. in sense 1b) **girth** /gəːθ/. LOE. [ON *grið* domicile, home, (pl.) truce, peace, pardon, quarter.] 1 †a Guaranteed security; protection, defence; safe conduct. LOE–M17. b A place of protection; a sanctuary, an asylum. ME. 2 *Law* (now *Hist.*). In Anglo-Saxon England, security, peace, or protection guaranteed under specific limits of time or place; (more fully *church-grith*) sanctuary, security within the precincts of a church. LOE. †3 Peace. LOE–LME. †4 Mercy, quarter, esp. in battle. ME–L15.

Comb.: **grithbreach** breach of the peace; the penalty for this; **grith-man** a man, esp. a criminal, who has taken sanctuary.

gritty /ˈgrɪti/ *a.*[1] L16. [f. GRIT *n.*[1] + -Y[1].] 1 Of the nature of or resembling grit; containing, consisting of, or covered with grit; sandy. Also, (of sound) low and rough, gravelly. L16. 2 *spec.* Containing minute hard particles which impair or make unpleasant the substance harbouring them. E17. b *fig.* Of literary style: difficult to read through, tedious. L19. 3 Having strength of character; plucky, courageous. *colloq.* M19.

1 R. SHAW He saw that their . . bodies were gritty from the ashes of the fires. O. MANNING A hot and gritty wind blew through the streets. A. TYLER The gritty click of heels on the sidewalk. 2 W. S. LANDOR These young bakers make their bread very gritty. 3 *USA Today* The kind of people who made it from nothing—gritty and gutsy people.

grittily *adv.* E20. **grittiness** *n.* E17.

gritty /ˈgrɪti/ *a.*[2] Long *rare*. L15. [Origin unkn.] *Her.* Of a field: composed equally of a metal and a colour.

grivet /ˈgrɪvɪt/ *n.* M19. [Fr., of unkn. origin.] The common African savannah monkey, *Cercopithecus aethiops*; *spec.* one of a race with long white facial hairs found in Ethiopia and Sudan. Cf. *green monkey* s.v. GREEN *a.*, VERVET.

Grizel *n.* see GRISELDA.

grizzle /ˈgrɪz(ə)l/ *a.* & *n.*[1] ME. [OFr. *grisel*, f. *gris* grey: see -EL[1].] A *adj.* Of grey colour; grey, grizzled. Formerly also, (of a horse) roan. ME. B *n.* †1 (A nickname for) a grey-haired old man. ME–L17. 2 A grey animal; *esp.* a grey or (formerly) roan horse. ME. 3 Grey hair; a sprinkling of grey hair. E17. b A grey wig. M18. 4 Grey colour; the colour grey. E17. 5 A second-class stock brick, so called from its grey colour. M19.

grizzle /ˈgrɪz(ə)l/ *v.*[1]*t.* & *i.* M18. [f. GRIZZLE *a.*, or back-form. f. GRIZZLED.] Make or become grey or grey-haired.

A. T. ELLIS The old wolf-coloured woods, grizzled with snow.

grizzle /ˈgrɪz(ə)l/ *v.*[2] & *n.*[2] M18. [Origin unkn.] A *v.i.* 1 Show the teeth; grin, laugh. *dial.* M18. 2 Fret, sulk, grumble; (esp. of a child) whine or cry fretfully. *colloq.* M19.

2 M. DUFFY The baby beside her . . had grizzled hungrily. *Times Lit. Suppl.* Fat and fractious babies strapped in their high-chairs and grizzling for attention.

B *n.* 1 A person who grizzles or frets. Chiefly *dial.* L19. 2 A bout of grumbling or sulking; a bout of whining or fretfulness. *colloq.* E20.

grizzler *n.* (*dial.* & *colloq.*) a person who grumbles or frets E20.

grizzled /ˈgrɪz(ə)ld/ *a.* LME. [f. GRIZZLE *a.* + -ED[2].] 1 Grey; *spec.* (of hair) greyish, sprinkled with grey. LME. 2 Having grey or greying hair. E17.

1 A. J. P. TAYLOR He was a fine figure of a man . . with a grizzled beard. 2 W. C. WILLIAMS A wonderful man, a tough grizzled old primitive.

grizzly /ˈgrɪzli/ *n.*[1] E19. [f. GRIZZLY *a.*[1]] A grizzly bear.

grizzly /ˈgrɪzli/ *n.*[2] *US* & *S. Afr.* L19. [Origin unkn.] *Mining.* A grating of parallel iron bars for screening off larger stones from finer material.

grizzly /ˈgrɪzli/ *a.*[1] M16. [f. GRIZZLE *a.* + -Y[1].] 1 Grey; greyish; grey-haired; grizzled. M16. 2 *grizzly bear*: a A large brown bear (*Ursus arctos*) of a race found in western N. America, distinguished by having brown fur with white-tipped hairs. E19. b A jazz dance in which the hug and walk of the grizzly bear are imitated. E20.

1 DICKENS He had a grizzly jagged beard of some three weeks' date.

grizzly /ˈgrɪzli/ *a.*[2] *colloq.* E20. [f. GRIZZLE *v.*[2] + -Y[1].] Inclined to grizzle, grumble, or whine fretfully.

groan /grəʊn/ *n.* ME. [f. the vb.] An act of groaning. Also, a deep inarticulate vocal sound expressing esp. pain, distress, complaint, or disapproval.

SIR W. SCOTT A low groan went through the assembly. D. WELCH We gave mock groans to show what a dreary old joke we thought it was. T. MO A groan escapes from Gideon's lips. *transf.*: N. ROWE In hollow Groans the falling Winds complain.

groanful *a.* (*rare*) full of groans or groaning; lugubrious: L16.

groan /grəʊn/ *v.* [OE *grānian* f. Gmc, whence also OHG *grīnan* grin with laughing or weeping (G *greinen*), MHG *grinnen* gnash the teeth (G *grinsen* laugh, weep); cf. MDu. *grinsen* (Du. *grijnsen*) grin. Cf. GRIN *v.*[2]] 1 *v.i.* Breathe with a deep-toned murmur; make a deep inarticulate sound expressing esp. pain, distress, complaint, or disapproval. OE. b *v.t.* Breathe (one's life, soul, etc.) *out*, *away*, with a groan or groans. M17. †2 *v.i.* Of a buck: utter a characteristic call in the rutting season. L15–L17. 3 *v.i.* Make a deep harsh sound resembling a groan. E16. 4 *v.i.* Express earnest longing (as if) by groans; yearn or long *for*, *to do*. Now *rare*. M16. 5 *v.t.* Utter with groans; say miserably or despairingly. E17. 6 *v.i.* Be oppressed or overloaded (as) to the point of groaning. Foll. by *beneath*, *under*, *with*. E17. 7 *v.t.* Express disapproval of by groans. *rare*. L18.

1 G. STEIN The pain came hard . . . and he groaned. **groan inwardly** feel but not express or display misgiving, dismay, distress, etc. b J. EATON Christ groaned out his blood and life upon the Crosse. 3 W. COWPER He heard the wheels . . Groan heavily along the distant road. KEATS The key turns, and the door upon its hinges groans. 4 SHAKES. *Jul. Caes.* This foul deed shall smell above the earth With carrion men, groaning for burial. 5 J. CONRAD He groaned, 'Oh, my leg!' R. GRAVES My father whispered, 'She read my letter?' 'Before I did myself,' groaned my uncle Tiberius. 6 JAS. MILL The injustice under which he appeared to himself to groan. D. M. THOMAS At the dinner table which groaned with flowers, silver and cut glass. 7 A. SEWARD They would be hissed, groaned, and cat-called.

groaner *n.* (*a*) a person who groans or complains; (*b*) *US local* a whistling buoy: LME. **groaning** *vbl n.* (*a*) the action of the vb; (*b*) (long *obs.* exc. *dial.*) a lying-in: OE. **groaningly** *adv.* in a groaning manner M16.

groat /grəʊt/ *n.* LME. [MDu. *groot*, MLG *grōte*, use as n. of the adj. (= GREAT) in the sense 'thick' (cf. MHG *grōze* (later *grosse*) *pfennige* 'thick pennies', GROSCHEN).] 1 A denomination of coin issued from the 13th cent. in any of various European countries, having from the 14th cent. a theoretical value equal to that of 1/8 oz. of silver but varying in actual intrinsic value. Long *obs.* exc. *Hist.* LME. 2 *Hist.* An English silver coin issued 1351–1662, in value equal to four pennies. Later also, a fourpenny piece. LME. †b A denarius; a drachma. Only in 16. 3 A small sum or amount. *arch.* E16.

3 CHESTERFIELD I do not care a groat what it is.

Phrases: *grey groat*: see GREY *a.* *Harry groat*: see HARRY *a.* & *n.*[2]

groats /grəʊts/ *n.pl.* [Late OE *grotan* (pl.) rel. to GROT *n.*[1], GRIT *n.*[1], *n.*[2], GROUT *n.*[1]] Hulled (sometimes also crushed) grain, esp. oats.

Grobian /ˈgrəʊbɪən/ *n.* E17. [G, or its source med.L *Grobianus* an imaginary typical German boor (15–16), f. G *grob* coarse, rude, GRUFF *a.*] A coarse slovenly person.

grocer /ˈgrəʊsə/ *n.* ME. [AN *grosser*, OFr. *grossier* f. med.L *grossarius*, f. *grossus* GROSS *a.*] †1 A person buying and selling in large quantities; a wholesale dealer or merchant. ME–L17. 2 A dealer in esp. dried and preserved foods and other miscellaneous household provisions. LME.

2 **grocer's itch** eczema caused by prolonged contact with material, e.g. flour or animal feeds, contaminated by acarid mites. **grocer's port, sherry, wine** cheap port, sherry, wine of low quality (supposedly) bought from a grocer's shop.

grocerdom *n.* (*rare*) the realm or world of grocers E19. **grocering** *n.* the trade or occupation of a grocer L19.

grocery /ˈgrəʊs(ə)ri/ *n.* LME. [f. prec. + -Y[3]: see -ERY.] 1 In *pl.* & (now *rare*) *collect. sing.* Goods sold by or bought from a grocer. LME. 2 The trade of a grocer. L17. †3 Small change. *slang.* E18–E19. 4 A grocer's shop; *dial.* a bar, a public house. *US.* E19.

1 *attrib.*: A. TOFFLER In a grocery store . . milk turns over more rapidly than, say, canned asparagus.

groceteria /grəʊsɪˈtɪərɪə/ *n. N. Amer.* E20. [f. prec. after *cafeteria*.] A self-service grocer's shop.

grockle /ˈgrɒk(ə)l/ *n. SW dial.* & *slang* (freq. *derog.*). M20. [Origin unkn.] A holiday-maker or summer visitor (esp. in Devon).

grody /ˈgrəʊdi/ *a. US slang.* Also **groaty**. M20. [f. GROT(ESQUE + -Y[1] with regular US change of intervocalic *t* to *d*. Cf. GROTTY.] Disgusting, revolting; slovenly, squalid.

grody to the max unspeakably awful.

Groenendael /ˈgrəːnəndeɪl, ˈgruːn-, -dɑːl/ *n.* E20. [A town in Belgium where the breed was developed.] (An animal of) a breed of black smooth-coated Belgian sheepdog.

grog /grɒg/ *n.* M18. [App. abbrev. of GROGRAM: first as a nickname of Admiral Vernon (1684–1757), who wore a grogram cloak, afterwards applied to the mixture he ordered to be served out to sailors instead of neat rum.] 1 A drink consisting of spirits (orig. rum) and water. M18. b (An) alcoholic drink of any kind, *esp.* (a) beer. *Austral.* & *NZ colloq.* M20. 2 Pulverized burnt clay or pottery mixed with ordinary clay to increase its heat resistance. L19.

Comb.: **grog-shanty** (*Hist.*, chiefly *Austral.* & *NZ*) a shanty serving as a public house; **grog-shop** *arch.* a public house.

groggery *n.* (*arch.*) a public house E19.

grog /grɒg/ *v.* Infl. **-gg-**. M19. [f. the n.] 1 *v.i.* Drink grog. M19. 2 *v.t.* Extract spirit from (an empty cask) by pouring hot water into it and letting it stand. L19.

groggy /ˈgrɒgi/ *a.* L18. [f. GROG *n.* + -Y[1].] 1 Intoxicated, drunk. *arch.* L18. 2 Dazed, muzzy, weak, unsteady; (of a horse) unsteady or tottering due to weakness in the forelegs. E19.

2 B. BETTELHEIM A heavy blow on the head . . led to a loss of blood that left me groggy. E. AMADI He felt groggy from loss of sleep.

groggified *a.* (*colloq.*, now *rare* or *obs.*) affected by grog, tipsy L18. **groggily** *adv.* L19. **grogginess** *n.* E19.

grognard /grɔɲaːr/ *n.* Pl. pronounced same. E20. [Fr., lit. 'grumbler'.] A member of Napoleon's Old Guard; *transf.* a veteran soldier.

grogram /ˈgrɒgrəm/ *n.* & *a.* M16. [Fr. *gros grain* lit. 'coarse grain': see GROSS *a.*, GRAIN *n.*[1] & cf. GROSGRAIN. For the change of final *n* to *m* cf. *buckram*, *vellum*.] **A** *n.* **1** A coarse fabric of silk, or of mohair and wool, or of a mixture of all these, often stiffened with gum. M16. **2** A garment made of grogram. M17. **B** *adj.* Made or consisting of grogram. L16.

groin /grɔɪn/ *n.*[1] *obs.* exc. *dial.* ME. [OFr. *groign* (= med.L *grugnum*) mod. *groin* f. late L *grunium*, *grunia*, med.L *grunnium* snout, f. L *grunnire* grunt like a pig (cf. GROIN *v.*[1]). In sense 2 alt. of Sp. *La Coruña*.] **1** The snout of an animal, esp. a pig. ME. †**2** (**G-**.) *The* port of Corunna in NW Spain. *Naut. slang.* LME–E19.

groin /grɔɪn/ *n.*[2] Orig. †**grynde**. LME. [Origin uncertain: perh. repr. OE *grynde* depression.] **1** The fold or depression on either side of the body between the abdomen and the upper thigh; *colloq.* the (esp. male) genitals. LME. **2** *Archit.* The edge formed by the intersection of two vaults; the rib or fillet of stone or wood covering this; the arch supporting a vault. Cf. earlier GROINING. E18. **3** A ring. *slang.* E20.

groin *n.*[3] see GROYNE.

groin /grɔɪn/ *v.*[1]*i.* ME. [OFr. *grognir*, (also mod.) *grogner* f. L *grunnire*: see GROIN *n.*[1]] **1** Of an animal: grunt, growl. Long *obs.* exc. *Sc.* ME. †**b** Of a buck: utter a characteristic call in the rutting season. L15–E18. †**2** Of a person: grumble, murmur. ME–L16.

groin /grɔɪn/ *v.*[2]*t.* E19. [f. GROIN *n.*[2] Cf. earlier GROINING.] *Archit.* Form into or provide with groins; build with groins.

groin *v.*[3] see GROYNE.

groined /grɔɪnd/ *a.* L18. [f. GROIN *n.*[2], *v.*[2]: see -ED[2], -ED[1].] *Archit.* Built or provided with groins.

groining /ˈgrɔɪnɪŋ/ *n.* M17. [f. GROIN *n.*[2] or *v.*[2]: see -ING[1].] *Archit.* A groin or an arrangement of groins; groined work.

grok /grɒk/ *v.* *US slang.* Infl. **-kk-**. M20. [Invented by Robert Heinlein (1907–), US author.] **1** *v.t.* Understand intuitively or by empathy; establish rapport with. M20. **2** *v.i.* Empathize or communicate sympathetically (*with*). Also, experience enjoyment. M20.

1 R. A. HEINLEIN Smith had been aware of the doctors but had grokked that their intentions were benign. 2 *New Yorker* We ought to get together somewhere . . and grok about our problems.

Grolier /ˈgrɒljeɪ, ˈgrəʊlɪə/ *a.* & *n.* E19. [Jean *Grolier* de Servin (see below).] **A** *adj.* Designating (a book decorated with) the interlacing geometrical designs adorning the bindings of books bound for the French book-collector Jean Grolier de Servin, Vicomte d'Aiguisy (1479–1565). E19. **B** *n.* (A book in) a Grolier binding. L19.

gromel(l) *n.* see GROMWELL.

grommet /ˈgrɒmɪt/ *n.*[1] Also **grummet** /ˈgrʌmɪt/. E17. [Fr. †*grom(m)ette*, *gourmette* curb chain, f. *gourmer* to curb, to bridle, of unkn. origin.] **1** *Naut.* A ring or wreath of rope, usu. consisting of a single strand laid three times round, and used as a fastening, a wad in a gun, or a substitute for a rowlock. Also, an eyelet of metal. E17. **2** A washer used to insulate electric conductors passing through a hole in a conducting material. M20. **3** A stiffener used inside a cap worn by a member of the Armed Forces. M20. **4** *Med.* A small tube passed through the eardrum in surgery to make a communication with the middle ear. M20.

grommet /ˈgrɒmɪt/ *n.*[2] *slang* (chiefly *Austral.*). Also **-it**. L20. [Origin unkn. Cf. GRUMMET *n.*[1]] A young surfer or skateboarder.

gromwell /ˈgrɒmw(ə)l/ *n.* Also (earlier) **gromel(l)** /ˈgrɒm(ə)l/. ME. [OFr. *gromil*, *grumil* (mod. *grémil*), prob. f. med.L collocation meaning 'crane's millet'.] Any of several related plants of the borage family with polished stony nutlets and white or blue flowers in bracteate cymes; *esp.* (more fully *common gromwell*) *Lithospermum officinale*, of bushy places, and (more fully *corn* or *field gromwell*) *L. arvense*, a weed of arable land.

groof /gruːf/ *n.* & *adv.* *obs.* exc. *Sc.* & *north.* Also **grufe**. LME. [ON *grúfa*, in *á grúfu* face downwards. Cf. GROVELLING.] **A** *n.* The face, the front. Chiefly in *on* (*one's*) *groof*, *a-groof*, face downwards, in a prone position. LME. †**B** *adv.* On the face, prone. LME–E18.

groo-groo *n.* var. of GRUGRU.

groom /gruːm/ *n.*[1] ME. [Origin uncertain: cf. AN *gromet*, AL *gromus*, *grometus* in sense 3.] †**1** A male child, a boy. ME–L17. **2** A male adult, a man. *arch.* ME. **3** A man of low position or birth, a male servant or attendant (*arch.*); in later use *spec.* a person employed to take care of horses. ME. **4** *spec.* (Also **G-**.) Any of various officers of the royal household. Freq. with defining prepositional phr. LME. **5** = BRIDEGROOM. E17.

1 C. COTTON To bring him Plums and Mackaroons Which welcome are to such small Grooms. 2 WORDSWORTH What sprinklings of blithe company! Of lasses and of shepherd grooms. 3 SHAKES. *Rich. II* I was a poor groom of thy stable. C. KINGSLEY Your nephew's lands are parted between grooms and scullions. A. HIGGINS She saw . . a groom in hobnail boots leading out a docile roan mare. 4 *Pall Mall Gazette* Sir Henry was a Groom-in-Waiting to Her Majesty. 5 R. HOGGART A bride must not see her groom before the ceremony on her wedding-day.

Comb.: **groom-porter** (*obs.* exc. *Hist.*) in the royal household, the holder of an office (abolished under George III) whose principal function was to regulate gaming; **groomsman** a male friend officially attending the bridegroom at a wedding; *esp.* the best man.

groomish *a.* (*rare*) characteristic of a groom M19. **groomless** *a.* (*rare*) L19. **groomship** *n.* (*rare*) the office or condition of a groom L17. **groomy** *a.* (now *rare*) of, pertaining to, or characteristic of a groom M19.

groom /gruːm/ *n.*[2] *dial.* L18. [Origin uncertain: perh. rel. to CROME.] A forked stick used in thatching.

groom /gruːm/ *v.t.* E19. [f. GROOM *n.*[1]] **1** Clean or brush the coat of and generally attend to (esp. a horse); (of an ape or monkey) clean and comb the fur of (its fellow) with the fingers. E19. **2** Attend to carefully; give a neat, tidy, or smart appearance to. M19. **3** *fig.* Prepare (a person) as a political candidate; *esp.* prepare or coach (a person) for a particular career, activity, etc. Orig. *US.* L19.

2 N. GORDIMER A white woman lawyer so perfectly groomed she appeared to be under glaze. J. LE CARRÉ His grey hair was groomed with military correctness. 3 P. G. WODEHOUSE A man whom the committee were grooming for the amateur championship. C. MCCULLOUGH They could simply have earmarked Senator Hillier for the job and begun to groom him.

groop /gruːp/ *n.* Now *dial.* ME. [MDu. *groepe* (Du. *groep*) = OFris., LG *grōpe*; cf. also Icel. *gróp* groove, Norw., Sw. *grop* hollow, cavity, Da. dial. *grob* ditch.] **1** A small trench, a ditch, an open drain; *spec.* the drain or gutter in a stable or cowhouse. ME. **2** A groove, a mortice. Long *obs.* exc. *Sc.* LME.

groop /gruːp/ *v.t.* Long *obs.* exc. *dial.* ME. [Cf. Icel. *grópa* make a groove; Faeroese *grópa* dig (a hole).] †**1** Dig (a trench). Only in ME. **2** Make a groove in, hollow out, incise. Long *obs.* exc. *Sc.* LME.

groose /gruːz/ *v.i.* *Sc.* & *north.* L17. [App. f. GRUE *v.*] Shiver, shudder.

groot /gruːt/ *n.* *obs.* exc. *dial.* LME. [Origin uncertain: rel. to GRIT *n.*[1], GROUT *n.*[1]] Mud, soil, earth; sediment, refuse.

groot /gruːt/ *v.i.* & *t.* *obs.* exc. *Sc.* E19. [App. f. GROOT *n.* Cf. earlier GROUT *v.*[1]] = GROUT *v.*[1]

groove /gruːv/ *n.* ME. [Du. †*groeve* furrow, ditch (now *groef*) = OHG *gruoba* (G *Grube* pit, ditch), ON *gróf*, Goth. *grōba*, f. Gmc, rel. to base of GRAVE *n.*[1], *v.*[1]] **1** A mining shaft; a mine, a pit. Now *dial.* ME. **2** A channel or furrow cut by artificial means in metal, wood, etc.; *esp.* one made to direct motion or to receive a corresponding ridge. M17. **b** *Theatr. Hist.* A wooden channel permitting a piece of scenery to be moved easily onstage and offstage. M19. **c** The spiral cut in a gramophone record (or a phonographic cylinder) to form a path for the stylus or needle. E20. **3** A channel or furrow of natural formation, as in a plant or animal structure, a rock, etc. L18. **4** *fig.* A fixed routine; a narrow limited unchanging course; a rut. M19. **5** A style of playing jazz, esp. particularly well; a style of doing anything well or in a favoured way. *slang* (orig. *US*). M20.

2 W. GREENER He formed a number of circular grooves on the cylindrical part of the bullet. *Practical Woodworking* A drawer side needs a groove for the runner. 3 A. GEIKIE Its rocks covered with ruts and grooves. W. VAN T. CLARK Heavy lines under the eyes . . and heavy, unhappy grooves down from her mouth. 4 A. HELPS His ideas were wont to travel rather in a groove. R. LEHMANN But folk are apt to get in a groove as they grow older. 5 *Melody Maker* The rhythm team . . developed a very propulsive rhythmic groove.

Phrases & comb.: **groove cast** *Geol.* a ridge on the lower surface of a layer of sandstone corresponding to a groove on underlying mudstone. **in the groove** *slang* = GROOVY 3.

grooveless *a.* M19.

groove /gruːv/ *v.* L15. [f. the n.] **1** *v.i.* Sink a mining shaft, mine. *dial. rare.* L15. **2** *v.t.* Cut a groove or grooves in, provide with grooves. L17. **3** *v.t.* Cut in the form of a groove or channel; excavate (a channel). M19. **4** *v.t.* & *i.* (Cause to) settle *in*(*to*) a groove (chiefly *fig.*). M19. **5** *v.i.* Play esp. jazz music with ease and brilliance; dance or listen *to* such music with enjoyment; please; get on well *with*. M20. **b** *v.t.* Play (esp. jazz music) well; please (someone). M20.

2 R. HOLME In these holes are threads of Screws grooved inwards. S. BELLOW What a face he saw, how grooved with woe and age. 4 J. A. FROUDE Morality . . grooved into habits of action creates strength. 5 *Melody Maker.* The rhythm section . . grooves along in true Basie manner. *Listener* Let's move and groove to this latest gas group from Croydon.

groover *n.* (*a*) (now *dial.*) a miner; (*b*) a tool for making grooves, a gouge; (*c*) *slang* a person who is groovy: E17.

grooved /gruːvd/ *a.* L18. [f. GROOVE *n.*, *v.*: see -ED[2], -ED[1].] Provided with or having a groove or grooves.

grooved ware *Archaeol.* a late neolithic pottery ware characterized by a flat base, vertical or outsloping walls, and decoration including grooves made in the clay before firing.

groovy /ˈgruːvi/ *a.* M19. [f. GROOVE *n.* + -Y[1].] **1** Resembling a groove. M19. **2** Of a person: having a tendency to adhere to a narrow limited unchanging course; in a rut. *colloq.* (now *rare*). L19. **3** (Capable of) playing esp. jazz music with ease and brilliance; *gen.* fashionable, sophisticated; very good, excellent. *slang* (orig. *US*). M20.

3 *Sunday Express* Thinking back, I must have looked like hell. But I thought I looked ever so groovy.

groovily *adv.* L20. **grooviness** *n.* M19.

grope /grəʊp/ *n.* [OE *grāp* = OHG *greifa* fork, f. Gmc ablaut var. of base of GRIP *n.*[1] In sense 2 f. GROPE *v.*] †**1** A hold, a grasp. OE–ME. **2** The action or an act of groping. E16.

grope /grəʊp/ *v.* [OE *grāpian* = OHG *greifōn* f. WGmc, f. Gmc base of GRIPE *v.*[1]] †**1** *v.i.* Use the hands in feeling, touching, or grasping; handle or feel something. OE–M16. **2** *v.i.* Attempt to find something by feeling about esp. with the hand as if blind or in the dark (also foll. by *for*, *after*); feel about in order to find one's way; move *along* etc. in this manner. OE. **b** *fig.* Search for mentally with hesitation or uncertainty; have difficulty in finding. (Foll. by *for*, *after*.) ME. **c** Try to catch fish by feeling in the water. Foll. by *for*. E17. **3** *v.t.* Touch or examine with the hands or fingers; handle, feel; grasp, seize. Now chiefly *spec.* (*colloq.*), feel or fondle (a person) clumsily for sexual pleasure. OE. †**4** *v.t.* *fig.* Examine or sound out (a person, the conscience, etc.); investigate (a matter). ME–M17. **b** Perceive, understand, (something, *that*). LME–M17.

2 S. SASSOON We were groping and stumbling along a deep ditch. R. C. HUTCHINSON His hand groped in the deep pocket of his coat for the coin. b F. HERBERT

Paul groped for words, could find nothing to say. D. W. WINNICOTT The scientist . . gropes towards a facet of the truth. 3 C. PHILLIPS Michael pushed the key into the door, opened it and groped the wall. T. WOGAN The girlish giggles of typists being groped in the safe. 4 D. CALDERWOOD Davie gropped their mindes, how they were affected to the banished lords. b D. ROGERS When you might have felt and groped the Lord in his manifest providence.

Phrases: **grope one's way** find one's way by groping; proceed in this manner. **grope out** find by groping, search out, (chiefly *fig.*).

gropingly *adv.* in a groping manner, blindly M16.

groper /ˈɡrəʊpə/ *n.*[1] M16. [f. prec. + -ER[1].] 1 A person who gropes. M16. 2 A West Australian. Also more fully *sand-groper*. *Austral.* (*joc.*). L19.

groper /ˈɡrəʊpə/ *n.*[2] *Austral.* & *NZ*. L19. [Var. of GROUPER.] 1 Any of several serranid fishes; esp. (*a*) (more fully *Queensland groper*) a large voracious Indo-Pacific grouper, *Promicrops lanceolatus*; (*b*) the hapuku. L19. 2 More fully *blue groper*. Any of various large Australasian wrasses, esp. *Achoerodus gouldii*. L19.

gros /ɡro/ *n.* Pl. same. M18. [Fr., use as n. of *gros* GROSS *a.*] †1 *gros du soie*, a heavy silk fabric. Only in M18. 2 A silk fabric orig. from or associated with a specified city etc., as *gros de Londres* /də lɔ̃:dr/, *gros de Lyons* /də ljɔ̃/, *gros de Naples* /də napl/, etc. L18.

grosbeak /ˈɡrəʊsbiːk/ *n.* L17. [Fr. *grosbec*, f. *gros* GROSS *a.* + *bec* BEAK *n.*[1]] Any of various finchlike birds with heavy bills, esp. (*a*) finches of the genera *Coccothraustes* and *Pinicola*; (*b*) cardinals (CARDINAL *n.* 2).

evening grosbeak, *pine grosbeak*, *sociable grosbeak*, *song grosbeak*, etc.

gros bleu /ɡro blø/ *n.* & *a. phr.* L19. [Fr. = dark blue.] (Of) a deep blue used to paint china.

groschen /ˈɡrəʊʃ(ə)n/ *n.* Pl. same. E17. [G (Bohemian) alt. of late MHG *gros(se)*, f. med.L *denarius grossus* thick penny: see GROSS *a.*, GROAT.] 1 *Hist.* A small German silver coin of low denomination; the sum represented by this. E17. 2 A German 10-pfennig piece. *colloq.* E20. 3 A monetary unit of Austria, equal to one-hundredth of a schilling; a small coin representing this. E20.

groser /ˈɡrəʊzə/ *n. obs.* exc. *Sc.* & *north.* E16. [Fr. *groseille*.] = next.

groset /ˈɡrəʊzɪt/ *n. Sc.* L18. [Alt. of prec.] A gooseberry.

grosgrain /ˈɡrəʊɡreɪn; *foreign* ɡroɡrɛ̃ (*pl. same*)/ *n.* & *a.* M19. [Fr: see GROGRAM.] (Made of) any of various heavy ribbed fabrics, esp. silk or rayon.

Gros Michel /ɡrəʊ mɪˈʃɛl/ *n. phr.* L19. [Fr.] A variety of banana originating in the W. Indies.

gros point /ɡro pwɛ̃/ *n. phr.* M19. [Fr. = large stitch.] 1 More fully *gros point de Venise* /də vəniːz/. A type of lace, originally from Venice, worked in bold relief. M19. 2 Any of various embroidery stitches worked over two or more horizontal and vertical threads of the canvas. M20.

gross /ɡrəʊs/ *n.*[1] Pl. same. LME. [Fr. *grosse* use as n. (sc. *douzaine* dozen) of fem. of *gros* great: see next and cf. Sp. *gruesa*, Port., It. *grossa*.] A quantity of twelve dozen.

Phrases: **by the gross** in large quantities, wholesale. *great gross*: see GREAT *a.*

gross /ɡrəʊs/ *n.*[2] LME. [f. the adj.] 1 The gross or coarse part of something; the dregs, dross; sediment. *obs.* exc. *dial.* LME. 2 The greater part, the majority, the bulk; *esp.* the main body of a military force. *arch.* LME. †b A large body, a mass. Chiefly *Mil.* Only in 17. 3 The sum, sum total; now *esp.*, the whole amount earned. L16.

2 BURKE This denial of landed property to the gross of the people has further evil effect. 3 G. BORDMAN Disappointing grosses on the road . . warned that show would not prove . . long-lasting.

Phrases: †**by gross** in large quantities, wholesale. **in** (**the**) **gross** (*a*) (now *rare*) generally, without going into particulars; on the whole; †(*b*) in a body; †(*c*) in bulk, wholesale; †(*d*) in full; (*e*) *Law* (*in gross*) absolute and independent.

†**gross** *n.*[3] M16–E18. [Repr. Fr. *gros*, It. *grosso*.] Any of various coins of low denomination in various currencies, as the German groschen.

gross /ɡrəʊs/ *a.* ME. [(O)Fr. *gros*, fem. *grosse* f. late L *grossus* (freq. in late L (Vulgate)), of similar formation to *bassus* BASE *a.*, *crassus* CRASS.] **I** 1 †a Thick, stout, massive, bulky. Also (of printed or written letters), large. ME–L18. b Of a shoot or stalk: bulky, esp. as a result of abnormal growth; luxuriant, rank. L16. †2 Of conspicuous magnitude; plain, evident, obvious, easy to understand. LME–L18. 3 Overfed, bloated, repulsively fat; (now *dial.*) big-bodied, burly. M16. 4 As an intensive: flagrant, glaring, complete. L16.

1 DRYDEN Your finger is more gross than the great monarch's loins. 2 DEFOE We should . . give him up for a Magician in the grossest acceptation of the word. 3 LONGFELLOW He was a gross, corpulent fellow. M. GEE She knew he looked heavy. Now she realised he must have looked gross. S. MORLEY I was so gross . . that I actually sent off for . . a fat dissolvent. 4 A. TROLLOPE [He] had in his opinion made a gross fool of himself. A. TREW There must be gross inefficiency on board.

II 5 Concerned with a large area or mass; general, not particular or in detail. LME. b *Med.* Visible to the naked eye, not microscopic. L19. 6 Entire, total, whole. Now *spec.* (of an amount, value, weight, etc.), without deductions, not net. E16. †b Main; the great majority of. L16–L18. †7 Of a denomination of value or weight: relatively large; containing lower denominations. Of a method of calculation: using large units. M16–E19.

5 G. WINOKUR There is no gross or microscopic abnormality of the brain. 6 LD MACAULAY The gross receipt was about seventy thousand pounds. J. UPDIKE Gross sales are down about eleven per cent over last year. **gross domestic product** the annual total value of goods produced and services provided in a country excluding transactions with other countries. **gross national product** the annual total value of goods produced and services provided in a country. b N. LUTTRELL Admirall Russell with the grosse fleet arrived at Torbay.

III 8a Dense, thick, (now only of air, vapour, darkness, etc.). Now *arch.* & *poet.* LME. b Material, perceptible to the senses; not spiritual or ethereal. E16. †9 Of a body of armed men: compact, solid. L16–L17.

8a LONGFELLOW Through the gross vapours, Mars grows fiery red. b M. ELPHINSTONE Each soul is invested with a subtile body, which again is clad in a grosser body. 9 F. VERE The enemy, seeing no grosse troop to follow them, began to take heart.

IV †10 Consisting of comparatively large parts or particles; lacking in fineness or delicacy of texture, etc. LME–L18. b Of a file, whetstone, etc.: coarse, rough. Only in 17. 11 Orig. (chiefly of food), plain, not delicate; coarse; inferior. Now (of food or diet), coarse, greasy, unwholesome. *arch.* LME. 12†a Of workmanship, a method of work etc.: rough, improvised, clumsy. L15–M17. †b Not clear or definite; approximate, general. L15–E19. c Of a sense or faculty or (formerly) a person: dull, stupid, lacking in perception. (Now chiefly after *Matt.* 13:15.) *arch.* E16. 13 Of a person: uneducated, ignorant. Formerly also (of a dialect, word, etc.) uncultivated, barbarous. Now *rare*. E16. 14 Of a person, behaviour, language, etc.: extremely coarse; brutally lacking in refinement or decency; *slang* repulsive, disgusting. M16.

11 DEFOE Dealing only in fish and oil, and such gross commodities. E. W. LANE Their diet is extremely gross. 12a J. WILKINS But this would have been too grosse a way for so excellent an artificer. b DRYDEN The crowd cannot be presumed to have more than a gross instinct, of what pleases . . them. c J. RAY Our Eyes and Senses . . are too gross to discern the Curiosity of the Workmanship of Nature. 13 S. PURCHAS The Inhabitants were so grosse . . , that they knew not the use of fire. GIBBON The vulgar dialect of the city was gross and barbarous. 14 J. HYAMS 'She really thinks he's gross, huh?' . . 'The pits,' said Freda. D. M. THOMAS The gross expressions which her illness has dredged up from this normally shy and prudish girl. P. THEROUX I don't want to be gross, but sometimes they eat their prisoners.

grossen *v.t.* (*rare*) make coarse or gross L19. **grossy** *a.* (long *obs.* exc. *dial.*) somewhat gross M17.

gross /ɡrəʊs/ *v.* LME. [f. the adj.] †1 *v.t.* Foll. by *up*: = ENGROSS 1. LME–E16. 2†a *v.t.* Foll. by *up*: = ENGROSS 3, 4. LME–M16. b *v.i.* Save, amass wealth. *dial.* L18. †3a *v.i.* Become gross, increase. Only in M16. b *v.t.* Make gross or coarse. Only in M17. 4 *v.t.* Make a gross profit of; earn a total of. L19. b Foll. by *up*: count or add as part of the total; increase (a net amount) to its value before deductions. M20. 5 *v.t.* Foll. by *out*: Disgust or shock, esp. by repulsive or obscene behaviour. *N. Amer. slang.* M20.

4 H. ROBBINS This picture looks like it will gross a quarter of a million dollars. *Bookseller* Ghostbusters, currently the biggest grossing movie in the States. 5 A. LURIE Some of the jokes told by grownups . . really gross Vinnie out. T. O'BRIEN Let us discuss obesity. You porkers gross me out.

Comb.: **gross-out** *a.* & *n.* (*N. Amer. slang*) (designating) something repulsive or obscene.

grosser *n.* (*a*) (*obs.* exc. *dial.*) a person who amasses wealth (orig. by buying up land etc.); (*b*) a film etc. that brings in a (*big* etc.) sum of money: M16.

grossly /ˈɡrəʊsli/ *adv.* L15. [f. GROSS *a.* + -LY[2].] †1 Plainly, obviously; in plain or understandable terms. L15–L18. 2 Indelicately, unrefinedly, coarsely, indecently. L15. †3 Stupidly, clumsily, unskilfully. E16–E18. 4 Roughly, generally, without regard to detail (*arch.*); *Med.* by visual inspection. M16. †5 Densely, thickly. M16–E18. †6 Of grinding, milling, etc.: coarsely, as opp. to finely. L16–E19. †7 Materially, as opp. to spiritually. L16–E17. 8 Excessively; glaringly, flagrantly; to a shocking degree. L16.

4 *Nature* The bones were examined grossly, by radiography, and histologically. 8 J. MITCHELL The official inquiry . . found them grossly exaggerated. I. MURDOCH The eyelids of both eyes were so grossly red and swollen with weeping.

grossness /ˈɡrəʊsnɪs/ *n.* LME. [f. GROSS *a.* + -NESS.] †1 Bigness, bulkiness. LME–M17. 2 Thickness, denseness, materiality. Now *rare*. LME. 3 Lack of education, ignorance; dullness, stupidity. M16. 4 Coarseness, lack of delicacy, decency, or refinement. M16. 5 Exaggerated or flagrant character, excessiveness. L16.

grosso modo /ɡrosso ˈmɔːdo, ɡrɒsəʊ ˈməʊdəʊ/ *adv. phr.* M20. [It.] Roughly, approximately.

grossular /ˈɡrɒsjʊlə/ *n.* E19. [mod.L *grossularia* (former specific epithet of) gooseberry.] A garnet containing calcium and aluminium, occurring in grey, pinkish, or yellow-green crystals and used as a gemstone. Also (when green) called *gooseberry garnet*.

grossularite *n.* = GROSSULAR M19.

Gros Ventre /ɡrəʊ ˈvɒntrə/ *n.* & *a. phr.* Pl. **Gros Ventres** (pronounced same). E19. [Fr., lit. 'big belly'.] 1 = HIDATSA. E19. 2 = ATSINA. M19.

†**grot** *n.*[1] OE–M18. [Rel. to GROATS, GROUT *n.*[1]] A fragment, a particle.

grot /ɡrɒt/ *n.*[2] Now chiefly *poet.* E16. [Fr. *grotte* f. It. *grotta* f. Proto-Romance vars. of L *crypta* f. Gk *kruptē* vault, CRYPT.] 1 = GROTTO 1. E16. 2 = GROTTO 2. M17.

grot /ɡrɒt/ *a.* & *n.*[3] *slang.* M20. [Abbrev.] **A** *adj.* = GROTTY. M20.

Listener What with grot hotels . . and general anxiety, I had not had what I would call a meal since leaving Khartoum.

B *n.* Something or someone grotty; *esp.* rubbish, dirt. M20.

Civil Service Motoring Old cars . . may be coated with a couple of decades worth of grot.

grotesque /ɡrəʊˈtɛsk/ *n.* & *a.* M16. [Fr. *crotesque* f. (with assim. to OFr. *crote* (mod. *grotte*) GROT *n.*[2]) It. *grottesca* ellipt. use (for *opera* or *pittura grottesca* work or painting resembling a grotto) of fem. of *grottesco*, f. *grotta*; finally assim. to Fr. *grotesque*: see -ESQUE.] **A** *n.* Also (esp. in sense 1b) in It. form ***grottesco*** /ɡrotˈtesko, ɡrəʊˈtɛskəʊ/, pl. ***-schi*** /-ski/. 1 A style of decorative painting or sculpture consisting of a fantastic interweaving of human and animal forms with flowers and foliage. M16. b A work of art, a figure or design in this style (usu. in *pl.*); *loosely* a comically distorted figure or design. M17. 2 A grotesque person or thing. M17. b That which is grotesque. E19. 3 *Typogr.* A sanserif type. L19.

1 EVELYN The foliage and grotesque about some of the compartments are admirable. b C. G. LELAND Adorned with fifteenth century grotesques. 2 M. AYRTON The sting-ray, that flat, long-tailed sea grotesque. b C. PETERS The grotesque is rare in his mature work.

B *adj.* **1** *Archit.* In the style of a grotesque. E17. **2** Comically or repulsively distorted; unnatural, bizarre. M17. †**b** Of landscape: romantic, picturesquely irregular. M17–M18. **3** Ludicrous from incongruity; fantastically absurd. M18.

1 R. W. EMERSON Let there be grotesque sculpture about the gates and offices of temples. 2 H. BASCOM The hammock, distorted by his body, casts a grotesque shadow. b R. DODSLEY The more pleasing parts of this grotesque and hilly country. 3 LYTTON O'Carroll gave a grotesque sort of signal between a wink and a beckon. M. IGNATIEFF Cabinet discussions which took on an increasingly grotesque and surreal character.

grotesquely *adv.* M18. **grotesqueness** *n.* L18. **grotesquerie** /grəʊˈtɛskəri/ *n.* grotesque objects collectively; grotesque quality; an example of grotesqueness: L17.

Grotian /ˈgrəʊʃɪən/ *a.* & *n.* M19. [f. *Grotius* (see below) + -AN.] **A** *adj.* Of or pertaining to the Dutch lawyer, statesman, and theologian Hugo Grotius (1583–1645), esp. as the founder of the modern science of international law. M19. **B** *n.* An adherent of the tenets or policies of Grotius. M20.

Grotianism *n.* the views or policies of Grotius E20.

grotteschi *n.pl.*, ***grottesco*** *n.* see GROTESQUE *n.*

grotto /ˈgrɒtəʊ/ *n.* Pl. **-o(e)s**. E17. [It. *grotta*: see GROT *n.*[2]] **1** A cave or cavern, *esp.* one which is picturesque or forms a pleasant retreat. E17. **2** An ornamental room, structure, etc., adorned with shells etc. in imitation of a cave and serving as a pleasant retreat. E17. **3** *Hist.* A structure of oyster-shells in the form of a grotto, erected and exhibited by London street-boys on the 5th of August, the feast of St James of Compostella. M19.

grottoed *a.* ensconced in a grotto; formed into a grotto: M18. **grottoˈesque** *a.* resembling a grotto M19.

grotty /ˈgrɒti/ *a. slang.* M20. [f. GROT(ESQUE + -Y[1].] Unpleasant, dirty, nasty, ugly; generally displeasing or disagreeable.

grottiness *n.* L20.

grouch /graʊtʃ/ *n.*[1] *colloq.* L19. [Var. of GRUTCH *n.*] **1** A fit of grumbling, bad temper, or the sulks; (a cause for) a complaint. L19. **2** A (habitual) grumbler. E20.

2 *Listener* I am probably a humourless old grouch.

Comb.: **grouch bag** a hidden pocket or purse for concealing money or valuables; hidden money.

†**grouch** *n.*[2] var. of KURUS.

grouch /graʊtʃ/ *v.i.* & *t. colloq.* E20. [Var. of GRUTCH *v.*] Grumble, complain.

H. L. FOSTER The tourists . . all came back to the train at a painfully slow walk . . and grouched all the way home.

grouchy /ˈgraʊtʃi/ *a.* L19. [f. GROUCH *n.*[1] or *v.* + -Y[1].] Grumbling; sulky, irritable, bad-tempered.

H. ROBBINS You've been grouchy as a bear the last month.

grouchily *adv.* E20. **grouchiness** *n.* E20.

ground /graʊnd/ *n.* [OE *grund* = OFris., OS *grund* (Du. *grond*), OHG *grunt* (G *Grund*), f. Gmc. No cognates outside Gmc are known.] **I** The lowest or deepest part. **1** The bottom or the depths of a hole, a well, or a container of any kind. Long *obs.* exc. *Sc.* OE. **b** *Theol.* The Godhead as the source of all being. Also, the divine essence of the soul. LME. **2** The seabed. Now only *Naut.* OE. **b** The bottom of shallow water; the point where a vessel may run aground. Now chiefly in phrs. below. L16. **3** In *pl.* **a** Solid particles, now esp. of coffee, forming a residue; dregs, lees, sediment. ME. **b** Refuse; refuse particles or scraps (of meal, wool, etc.). *rare.* E17.

1 *fig.*: J. WESLEY We praised God from the ground of the heart. 2 SHAKES. *1 Hen. IV* Or dive into the bottom of the deep, Where fathom-line could never touch the ground.

II Base, foundation. †**4** The base or (in *pl.*) foundations of a building or other structure. OE–E18. **b** The basic constituent or essential part of a substance or object. L16–E18. **5** The basis or foundation of a system, institution, or state of affairs. Now *rare.* ME. †**b** A fundamental principle; in *pl.*, the elements of a branch of knowledge. M16–M18. **6** The basis of an opinion or argument, the reason or motive for an action, (now freq. in *pl.*). In *pl.* also, sufficient reason or reasons *for*, *that*. ME. **7a** A piece of cloth on which embroidery etc. is worked. In *Lace-making*, the mesh on which the pattern is constructed. LME. **b** A first coat of paint or colouring serving as a base for further colouring or as background for a design; a part left undecorated; the prevailing colour or tone. LME. **c** *Mus.* The melody on which a descant is raised. L16. **d** *Etching.* An acid-resistant coating applied to a plate, through which the design is traced with a fine point. E18. **e** A piece of wood embedded in the surface of a wall, to which a skirting-board etc. may be attached. Usu. in *pl.* E19.

6 K. CLARK Have we grounds for thinking that landscape painting will continue to be a dominant form of art? S. UNWIN An action was brought on the ground that the name and occupation were the same. A. J. AYER Russell's family disapproved of the engagement, partly on social grounds. T. BENN They operate in secrecy on the grounds that secrecy is inseparable from security. 7b B. JOWETT Dyers first prepare the white ground and then lay on the dye of purple. V. WOOLF White letters upon a blue ground.

III The earth, land. **8** The earth as distinguished from heaven. Chiefly in *on (the) ground.* Now *rare* exc. as passing into sense 10. OE. †**9** The earth as distinguished from the sea; dry land. OE–L17. **10** The earth's surface, on which human, animal, and plant life exists; a part of this. In *Aeronaut.*, the earth as distinguished from the air. OE. †**b** The pit of a theatre. (Cf. GROUNDLING 2.) L16–E17. **c** The floor. M19. **11** (The) soil; earth, mould. OE. †**b** A kind or variety of soil. LME–L18. **c** = EARTH *n.*[1] 7. Chiefly *N. Amer.* L19. †**12** A region, a land, a country. *rare.* OE–E17. **13** In *pl.*, a large enclosed area of land surrounding or attached to a house or other building. Also *sing.*, a piece of (cultivated) land (*obs.* exc. *dial.*). LME. **14** Area or distance (usu. of a specified extent) on the face of the earth; land. LME. **b** *fig.* Subject matter; object(s) of study or discourse. L18. **15** The area or piece of land owned or occupied by a particular person. LME. **16** An area of (specified) extent or character. Now *spec.* a piece of land or other area or expanse used for a specific or specified purpose; the place of action of a sporting or other contest. LME. **b** *Cricket.* The space within which a player is allowed to stand while taking a particular part in the game; *esp.* that of the batsman behind the popping-crease. L18.

10 E. CRANKSHAW When the shooting stopped some 200 lay dead on the ground. c A. CHRISTIE We . . forced the door open. Mrs. Allen was lying in a heap on the ground. 11 S. HEANEY When the spade sinks into gravelly ground. 13 W. H. PRESCOTT Extensive grounds were also laid out around the palace. 14 S. PEPYS I have a mind to buy enough ground to build a coach-house and stable. 15 SHAKES. *Merry W.* Like a fair house built on another man's ground. 16 E. BLISHEN We played on a ground lent to us by a local club. *New Yorker* They fish in deep water, and stay out on the grounds several days at a time. *cricket ground, fishing-ground, football ground, parade-ground*, etc.

Phrases: **above ground** (*a*) alive; (*b*) dead but not yet buried. **below ground** dead and buried. *bite the ground*: see BITE *v.* *blue ground*: see BLUE *a.* *break (the) ground*: see BREAK *v.* **cover much ground** (of an inquiry, report, etc.) be wide-ranging. **cover the ground** deal adequately with the subject. **cut the ground from under a person's feet** anticipate and defeat his or her arguments or plans. **down to the ground** *colloq.* completely. *fall to the ground*: see FALL *v.* **forbidden ground** a subject which should be avoided. **from the ground up** *colloq.* completely. *fruits of the ground*: see FRUIT *n.* 1. *gain ground (on, upon)*: see GAIN *v.*[2] *get ground*: see GET *v.* **get in on the ground floor** be admitted to a project, company, etc. as one of the initiators or in the early stages. **get off the ground** start successfully. **give ground** recede, retire, retreat. **go to ground** (of an animal) go into a burrow; (of a person) withdraw from public notice. *happy hunting-ground*: see HAPPY *a.* *have one's feet on the ground*: see FOOT *n.* **hold one's ground** hold one's own. **into the ground** to exhaustion, to a standstill. **lose ground** fall back, fall behind, decline. *middle ground*: see MIDDLE *a.* **on firm** or **solid ground** using soundly-based reasoning. **on one's own ground** on one's own territory or subject, on one's own terms; freq. in *meet on one's own ground.* **on the ground** on the spot, in practical conditions; (see also sense 8 above). *run into the ground*: see RUN *v.* **run to ground** = *run to earth* s.v. EARTH *n.*[1] **shift one's ground** change one's line of argument. **smell the ground** (of a ship) steer erratically as a result of being in shallow water. *stand one's ground*: see STAND *v.* **take the ground** run aground. *thick on the ground*: see THICK *a.* *thin on the ground*: see THIN *a.*

Comb.: **ground-ash** (a stick made from) an ash sapling; **ground-bait** *n.* & *v.* (*Angling*) (*a*) *n.* bait thrown into the water to attract fish; (*b*) *v.t.* prepare (a fishing-ground) with ground-bait. **ground ball** *Sports & Games* a ball hit along the ground; **ground bass** *Mus.* a short passage usu. in the bass, constantly repeated with varying melody and harmony; *fig.* a constant background or undertone; **ground-breaking** *a.* pioneering, innovative; **ground-cedar** = *ground-pine* (b) below; **ground-cherry** (chiefly *US*) = PHYSALIS; **ground-colour** (*a*) the first coat of paint; (*b*) the prevailing colour of any object; **ground control** (*a*) the directing of an aircraft's landing from the ground; (*b*) the personnel and equipment for monitoring and controlling an aircraft or spacecraft from the ground; **ground cover** plants covering the surface of the earth; *spec.* (*Hort.*) low, rapidly spreading plants grown to suppress weeds; **ground dove** a pigeon of terrestrial habits, *spec.* (in full *scaly-breasted ground dove*) *Columbina passerina* of the southern US, Central America, and parts of S. America; **ground effect** the aerodynamic effect of the ground on a vehicle, aircraft etc. travelling close to it; **ground elder** an umbelliferous plant, *Aegopodium podagraria*, troublesome as a garden weed; also called *goutweed*; **ground-fielding** *Cricket* fielding or stopping a cricket ball near the ground; **ground-fish**: that lives at the bottom of the water; **ground floor** the storey of a building approximately level with the ground; **ground frost**: which forms on the surface of the ground or in the top layer of the soil; **ground game** ground-dwelling game animals, as rabbits and hares; **ground-hemlock** a N. American yew, *Taxus canadensis*, growing as a low straggling shrub; **ground-ice**: formed below the surface of the water and esp. adhering to the bed of a river, lake, etc.; **ground itch** the presence of small blisters which itch intensely, usu. on the feet or legs, as a result of the penetration of the skin by hookworm larvae; **ground ivy** a common early-flowering hedge plant, *Glechoma hederacea*, with blue-purple flowers in the axils of kidney-shaped leaves; **groundkeeper** *US* = *groundsman* below; **ground-landlord** the owner of land which is leased for building on; **ground-laurel** = ARBUTUS 2; **ground level** (*a*) the level of the ground, *spec.* that outside a building; (*b*) *Physics* (the energy level of) a ground state; **ground loop** a violent uncontrolled movement of an aircraft while landing, taking off, or taxiing; **groundmass** *Petrogr.* the compact basic material of a porphyritic rock, in which larger grains (phenocrysts) are embedded; **ground moraine**: situated underneath a glacier; **groundnut** (*a*) (the edible tuber of) a N. American wild bean, *Apios americana*; (*b*) (the fruit of) the peanut, *Arachis hypogaea*; **ground parrot** a parrot of terrestrial habits; *spec.* (*a*) *Pezoporus wallicus* of the Australian and Tasmanian coast; (*b*) = KAKAPO; **ground-pine** (*a*) a rare yellow-flowered labiate weed, *Ajuga chamaepitys*, reputedly so called from its resinous smell; (*b*) *N. Amer.* any of several clubmosses resembling miniature conifers, esp. *Lycopodium obscurum* and *L. tristachyum*; **ground-plan** a plan of the ground floor of a building; the outline or general plan of anything; **ground-plate** the lowest horizontal timber in a framing; **ground-rent**: payable to the owner of the land on which a building stands; **ground robin** *US* = TOWHEE; *ground roller*: see ROLLER *n.*[2]; **ground rule** a fundamental precept, a basic principle; **groundsheet** a waterproof sheet spread on the ground to give protection from moisture; *ground-sill*: see GROUNDSEL *n.*[2]; **ground sloth** any of various extinct terrestrial edentates from the Tertiary and Pleistocene of S. America, esp. of the genera *Megatherium* and *Mylodon*, and often of very large size; **groundsman** a person employed to maintain a sports ground; **ground speed** an aircraft's speed relative to the ground; **ground squirrel** any of several rodents resembling squirrels in build but of terrestrial habits, *esp.* a spermophile; **ground staff** (*a*) the non-flying members of an airline or airport staff; (*b*) a paid staff of (now esp. promising young) players kept by a cricket club; **ground state** *Physics* the state of lowest energy of an electron, atom, molecule, etc.; **ground stroke** *Tennis* a stroke played near the ground after the ball has bounced; **ground-swell** (*a*) a large or extensive swell of the sea; (*b*) an apparently spontaneous movement or build-up of or *of* feeling, opinion, etc., in a group of people, esp. the public; **ground tackle** the equipment (cable, anchor, etc.) used to anchor or moor a boat or ship; **ground thrush** any of various Old World thrushes of the genus *Zoothera*, most of which are ground-feeders in forests; **groundwater** water held in the soil or in pores, crevices, etc., in rock, *esp.* that below the water table; any underground water; **ground wave** a radio wave reaching a receiver directly from the transmitter or by some other means that does not involve reflection by the ionosphere; **ground zero** (*a*) the ground under an exploding (nuclear) bomb; (*b*) *US colloq.* the (very) beginning, the starting point.

ground /graʊnd/ *ppl a.* LME. [pa. pple of GRIND *v.*] **1** Reduced to fine particles by grinding or crushing. Also foll. by *down*. LME. **b** *fig.* Foll. by *down*: exhausted, worn out. E20. **c** Of meat: minced. Chiefly *N. Amer.* E20. **2** Shaped or sharpened by grinding; having the surface abraded or polished by grinding. L16.

Special collocations & comb.: **ground-down** a short thick pointed sewing-needle; **ground glass** (*a*) powdered glass; (*b*) glass made semi-opaque by having its surface roughened; **ground wood** wood pulp.

ground /graʊnd/ *v.*[1] ME. [f. the n.] **I** †**1** *v.t.* Lay the foundations of (a house etc.); found, establish firmly. ME–E17. **2** *v.t.* Establish, base (an institution, principle, or belief) *on*, *upon*, or *in* some fact or authority. Now usu. in *pass.* LME. **b** In *pass.* Of a conjecture, fear, etc.: be (*well* or *ill*) founded. M18. **3** *v.t.* Establish or settle (a person) in respect of his or her position, beliefs, etc. Foll. by *in*, *of*. Long *obs.* exc. *dial.* LME. †**4** *v.refl.* & *i.* Rest or rely *upon*, esp. in argument. LME–E19. **5** *v.t.* Foll. by *in*: instruct (a person) thoroughly in the rudiments of a subject; in *pass.*, be (*well* or *ill*) acquainted with a subject. LME. **6** *v.t.* Provide with a ground or basis for painting, embroidery, etc. LME. **7** *v.t.* Form or supply grounds or a reason for. *rare.* M17.

2 H. L. MENCKEN A large part of altruism, . . is grounded upon the fact that it is uncomfortable to have unhappy people about. P. FULLER Culture itself is grounded in man's highly specific psycho-biological nature. 5 C. RYCROFT My father grounded his sons in the first principles of mathematics.

II 8 *v.t.* Bring to the ground, knock down. ME. **9** *v.t.* & *i. Naut.* (Cause to) run aground; in *pass.* be beached or stranded. LME. **10** *v.t.* & *i. Naut.* (Cause to) sink to the bottom. M17. **11** *v.t.* Place or set (esp. a weapon) on the ground; put down. M17. **b** *v.i.* Come to or strike the ground; land. M18. **c** *v.i. Baseball.* Hit a ground-ball to the infield; be thrown *out* at first base as a result of this. E20. **12** *v.t. Electr.* Connect with the soil as a conductor; earth. Chiefly *N. Amer.* L19. **13** *v.t.* Prevent or prohibit (an aircraft, pilot, etc.) from flying. Also *transf.* curtail the actions or activities of (a person), esp. as a punishment. M20.

8 *fig.*: J. N. ISBISTER His theories had well and truly grounded the old enemy, religion. 9 *Lifeboat* Launched to help a Grimsby steam trawler, . . which had grounded on a reef. 10 J. SMEATON We proceeded lowering till our anchor was grounded. 11 R. ADAMS Each man grounded his spear and laid it beside his belt. **ground arms** lay down one's weapons, esp. in surrender. 13 *Daily Telegraph* Three . . jets were grounded by mechanical faults and an accident. T. K. WOLFE Slayton's problem was that the Air Force had decided to ground him altogether.

Comb.: **groundout** *Baseball* a play in which a batter grounds out.

ground *v.*[2] pa. t. & pple of GRIND *v.*

groundage /ˈgraʊndɪdʒ/ *n.* LME. [f. GROUND *n.* + -AGE.] A toll, a tax; *spec.* a duty levied on vessels lying in harbour. Cf. TERRAGE.

grounded /ˈgraʊndɪd/ *a.* LME. [f. GROUND *n.*, *v.*[1]: see -ED[2], -ED[1].] †**1** Thoroughly instructed or proficient in a branch of knowledge. Also, deeply imbued with certain principles. LME–E19. **2** Firmly fixed or established; on a sound basis. Also with advs.: *well*, *ill*, etc., founded. L15. **3a** Of lace: having the spaces in the pattern filled with plain stitches. Now *rare.* L17. **b** Having a ground of a specified colour. M18. **4** Placed on or brought to the ground; run aground, stranded. L18. **5** Having an electrical connection with the soil; earthed. Chiefly *N. Amer.* L19. **6** Of an aircraft, pilot, etc.: prevented or prohibited from flying. Also *transf.* having one's actions or activities curtailed, esp. as a punishment. M20.

2 J. KRANTZ I wish I didn't have so much common sense. I get so tired of being grounded in reality. 6 S. BELLOW My flight is grounded. *New Yorker* Can I go out? Am I still grounded?

groundedly *adv.* (now *rare*) fundamentally, deeply, thoroughly; with good reason: M16. **groundedness** *n.* (*rare*) the quality or condition of being well grounded or firmly established E17.

grounder /ˈgraʊndə/ *n.* LME. [f. GROUND *v.*[1] + -ER[1].] **1** A person who or thing which founds, establishes, or causes, something. Long *spec.* a foundation stone of a wall. *obs.* exc. *dial.* & *Archaeol.* LME. **2** *Sports & Games.* A ball passed or hit along the ground. M19. **3** A person who applies background colour, *spec.* to wallpaper. L19.

1 *Antiquity* The walls consist of huge 'grounders', whose triangular interstices are filled with smaller stones. 2 R. COOVER I never wanted to be just an ordinary ballplayer, stooping for grounders.

groundhog /ˈgraʊndhɒg/ *n.* L18. [f. GROUND *n.* + HOG *n.*] **1** A woodchuck. *N. Amer.* L18. **2** A caisson worker. Also, the brakeman of a train. *US slang.* E20.

Comb.: **groundhog case** *US* a desperate or urgent affair; **Groundhog Day** *N. Amer.* a day (in most areas 2 February) which, if sunny, is believed to indicate wintry weather to come.

grounding /ˈgraʊndɪŋ/ *vbl n.* LME. [f. GROUND *v.*[1] + -ING[1].] **1** The action or an act of founding or establishing something; the basis or foundation of something. Now *rare.* LME. **2** The preparation or laying of a ground on which a design is to be worked. LME. **3** Instruction in or knowledge of the rudiments or fundamental principles of a subject. M17. **4** The beaching of a ship for inspection or repair; (accidental) running aground. L17.

3 A. N. WILSON He was indebted to his teachers for giving him a thorough grounding in the classics. 4 *Independent* As the general standard of those ships declines, so the prospect of collisions and groundings increases.

groundless /ˈgraʊndlɪs/ *a.* OE. [f. GROUND *n.* + -LESS.] †**1** Bottomless, unfathomable. OE–E17. **2** Without basis, authority, or support; unfounded. E17.

2 R. BAXTER A groundless fiction that cannot be proved.

groundlessly *adv.* M17. **groundlessness** *n.* M17.

ground-line /ˈgraʊndlʌɪn/ *n.* LME. [f. GROUND *n.* + LINE *n.*[2] Cf. Du. *grondlijn*, G & Sw. *grundlinie* (in senses 2 and 3).] **1** A line used for bottom-fishing. Long *rare* or *obs.* LME. **2**†**a** *Geom.* A line to which a perpendicular is drawn. M16–M17. **b** A line in a drawing, diagram, etc., that represents the ground or the horizon. M19. **3** In *pl.* Outlines, bases, foundations. E17. **4** *Equestrianism.* The (actual or notional) line at the base of a jump from which a horse judges its take-off point. M20.

groundling /ˈgraʊndlɪŋ/ *n.* E17. [f. GROUND *n.* + -LING[1]. Cf. MDu. *grundelinck* (Du. *grondeling*), MHG *grundelinc* (G *Gründling*) gudgeon.] **1** Any of various small bottom-dwelling freshwater fishes, *esp.* a gudgeon or a loach. E17. **2** A frequenter of the pit of a theatre (see GROUND *n.* 10b); an ignorant or undiscerning spectator or reader. Chiefly *literary.* E17. **3** A creeping or low-growing plant. E19. **4** A person on the ground, as opp. to one in an aircraft or spacecraft. M20.

2 J. A. SYMONDS The soliloquies of Hamlet . . must have been lost upon the groundlings of Elizabeth's days. 4 *Guardian* Of the R.A.F.'s courage and skill it would be almost presumptuous for any mere groundling to speak.

groundsel /ˈgraʊn(d)s(ə)l/ *n.*[1] [OE *grundeswylige*, earlier *gundæswelg(i)æ*, prob. f. *gund* pus + base of SWALLOW *v.*, with ref. to its use in poultices.] A common weed, *Senecio vulgaris*, of the composite family, with small rayless heads and lobed leaves. Also (w. qualifying adjs.), any of several related plants.

Comb.: **groundsel tree** a N. American coastal shrub, *Baccharis halimifolia*, of the composite family, with axillary panicles of rayless flowers.

groundsel /ˈgraʊn(d)s(ə)l/ *n.*[2] Also **ground-sill** /ˈgraʊn(d)sɪl/. LME. [App. f. GROUND *n.* + SILL *n.*[1], but the 2nd elem. early became a mere termination.] **1** The lowest horizontal timber in a (wooden) building; the foundation or lowest part of any structure. LME. **b** *fig.* An underlying principle. Now *rare* or *obs.* E17. **2** The bottom timber of a door-frame; a door-sill, a threshold. E16.

groundward /ˈgraʊndwəd/ *adv.* M16. [f. GROUND *n.* + -WARD.] Towards the ground.

Also **groundwards** *adv.* L19.

groundwork /ˈgraʊndwəːk/ *n.* LME. [f. GROUND *n.* + WORK *n.* Cf. MDu. *gront-werck* (mod. *grondwerk*), G *Grundwerk*.] **1** The basis or foundation of a (now chiefly immaterial) thing; preliminary work, preparation. LME. **2** The base on which a design is worked in various crafts; the background of a painting etc. M17. **3** Exercises or movements performed on the ground. E20.

1 K. ISHIGURO A case of laying the groundwork for the real negotiations.

group /gruːp/ *n.* Also (earlier) †**groupe**. L17. [Fr. *groupe* f. It. *gruppo* f. Gmc: rel. to CROP *n.* The etymological sense is app. 'lump' or 'mass'.] **1** Two or more people, animals, or things standing or positioned close together so as to form a collective unity; a knot or cluster (of people, animals, or things); *spec.* in *Art*, two or more figures or objects forming (a part of) a design. L17. **b** *Mus.* = GRUPPETTO. Cf. earlier GRUPPO. E18. **c** A set of letters, figures, etc., used in coding. E20. **d** A cluster or set of hits made by a series of shots fired at a target. Also *shot-group.* E20. **2** A number of people or things regarded as forming a unity or whole on the grounds of some mutual or common relation or purpose, or classed together because of a degree of similarity. E18. **b** *Chem.* Any combination of atoms bound together within a molecule, which behaves as a unit and is regarded as a distinct entity; a radical. M19. **c** (Also **G-**.) Any of the constituent bodies of the Oxford Group Movement (see OXFORD *a.*). E20. **d** A division of an air force, esp. the Royal Air Force, comprising a number of wings. E20. **e** A number of commercial companies together with the holding company controlling them. M20. **f** A number of musicians or singers performing esp. popular music together. M20. **g** *Polit.* A unit smaller than a party. L20. **3** *Biol.* An assemblage of organisms or classificatory division of unspecified rank; *esp.* a set of closely related species not formally recognized as a subgenus. E19. **b** *Geol.* Formerly, any of various categories into which rocks were classified, corresponding to modern geological time-units. Now, a stratigraphic unit consisting of two or more formations. M19. **c** *Chem.* (*a*) In qualitative analysis, a set of ions or radicals which are characterized by common behaviour during specific tests; (*b*) any of several sets of elements having (similar electronic structure and hence) similar chemical and physical properties, commonly represented as the columns of the periodic table. M19. **d** = *blood group* s.v. BLOOD *n.* E20. **4** *Math.* Orig., a set of elements, together with a binary operation, which is closed with respect to the operation. Now *spec.* such a set in which the operation is associative, and which contains an inverse for each element and an identity element. M19.

1 CONAN DOYLE I found that a little group of wondering folk had gathered round it. A. J. CRONIN Men were standing in groups around the cafes. N. MITFORD The great steep Gothic double staircase . . meeting at a marble group. 2 A. STORR When men form groups, . . it may be on a basis of common interest or shared background. F. WELDON Phillip belonged to a reform group who were trying to legalise

. . cannabis. C. PRIEST We were the same age group—she was thirty-one, two years older than myself. *Times* The Group of five finance ministers of the biggest industrial market economies . . have been meeting at No 11. *attrib.*: J. M. ROBERTS For almost the whole of history . . clothes have been signs of group membership. *primary group*: see PRIMARY *a.* e *pop group*, *rock group*, etc. g *Times* Svecia Antique is a recently formed company, backed by a large multinational group. 4 M. BÔCHER The positive and negative integers with zero form a group if the rule of combination is addition.

Comb.: **group assurance** = *group life assurance* below; **group captain** a rank in the Royal Air Force next below air commodore and equivalent to colonel in the army; **group dialect** (a) distinctive language used by members of a group identified as such by a common occupation or interest; **group dynamics** a branch of social psychology that deals with the interactions of people in groups; **group genitive** the construction in English whereby the genitive ending is added to the last element in a noun phrase; **group insurance** = *group life insurance* below; **group language** = *group dialect* above; **group life assurance** or **insurance** (chiefly *N. Amer.*) the assurance or insurance of a group of lives at reduced premiums; *group marriage*: see MARRIAGE; **group practice** a medical practice consisting of several doctors; **group rate** a reduced rate (of the charge for entry, travel, shipment, etc.) for a group of people or things; **group sex** sexual activity in which more than two people take part; **group theory** the branch of algebra that deals with the properties of groups and their applications, esp. in physics; **group therapy**: in which patients having a similar problem meet together to help each other psychologically; **group velocity** *Physics* the speed at which the energy of a wave travels; **groupware** *Computing* software designed to facilitate collaborative working by a number of different users; **group work**: done by a group working in close association.

groupist *n.* an adherent of a group, esp. (**G-**) of the Oxford Group Movement L19. **grouplet** *n.* a small group M19.

group /gruːp/ *v.* E18. [f. the n., or f. Fr. *grouper*.] 1 *v.t.* Esp. in *Art* & *Photogr.* Arrange (figures, colours, etc.) into a well-proportioned and harmonious whole. E18. 2 *v.t.* Form into a group; place in a group *with*. Also foll. by *together*. M18. b *v.i.* Form a group; gather into a group or groups. E19. c *v.i.* (Of shots from a firearm) cluster about a point (on a target); (of a firearm or marksman) fire shots which do this. E20. 3 *v.i.* Belong to a group; harmonize *with*. E19. 4 *v.t.* Arrange in groups according to some common feature or property; classify. M19. b *Med.* Assign to a particular blood group; determine the blood group of. M20.

1 *Studio Week* The central panels are grouped within easy reach. 2 A. SCHLEE Unconsciously they had grouped themselves in a semi-circle facing the door. b W. GOLDING Tourists walk through. Conducted parties group to listen.

groupage *n.* the arrangement of objects in a group or groups M19. **grouping** *vbl n.* (*a*) the action of the vb; (*b*) a formation resulting from this action: M18. **groupment** *n.* (*a*) a group; (*b*) the action of placing in groups: L19.

†groupe *n.* see GROUP *n.*

grouper /ˈgruːpə/ *n.* See also GROPER *n.*[2] E17. [Port. *garoupa*, prob. f. a S. Amer. name. For the alt. of form cf. BREAKER *n.*[2]] 1 Any of numerous large marine serranid fishes of warm and tropical seas; *esp.* any of those of the genera *Epinephelus* and *Mycteroperca*. Cf. GROPER *n.*[2] 1. E17. 2 Locally, any of various large marine fishes; *esp.* (*a*) the Californian rockfish, *Sebastes paucispinis*; (*b*) the triple-tail, *Lobotes surinamensis*. L19.

groupie /ˈgruːpi/ *n.* In sense 2 also **-py**. M20. [f. GROUP *n.* + -IE.] 1 = *group captain* s.v. GROUP *n. RAF slang.* M20. 2 A fan of a pop group or groups; *esp.* a (female) fan following a group on tour and providing sexual favours; *gen.* a fan, a follower. M20.

2 J. LENNON If we couldn't get groupies, we would have whores. G. KAUFMAN I do not mean . . I have become a cinema groupie, attaching myself to film-makers.

groupism /ˈgruːpɪz(ə)m/ *n.* M20. [f. GROUP *n.* + -ISM.] 1 (**G-**.) The principles of the Oxford Group Movement. M20. 2 The principle of arranging or dividing into groups, or thinking as or conforming to the social behaviour of a group. M20.

groupuscule /ˈgruːpəskjuːl, *foreign* grupyskyl (*pl. same*)/ *n.* M20. [Fr., dim. of *groupe*: see -CULE.] A small political group; an extremist splinter group.

grouse /graʊs/ *n.*[1] Pl. same. E16. [Origin uncertain: perh. orig. pl. of form rel. to med.L *gruta*, or OF *grue*, L *grus* crane.] 1 Any of various stocky feather-footed birds of the gallinaceous family Tetraonidae, of which several are valued as game-birds; *esp.* in Britain (more fully *red grouse*), a moorland game-bird conspecific with the willow grouse, *Lagopus lagopus*, but lacking white plumage in winter. E16. 2 The flesh of one of these birds, eaten as food. L18.

1 *black grouse*, *hazel grouse*, *pinnated grouse*, *willow grouse*, etc.

grousey *a.* (*a*) having many grouse; (*b*) having the flavour of grouse: M19.

grouse /graʊs/ *n.*[2] *colloq.* E20. [f. GROUSE *v.*[2]] A grumble, a complaint; a reason for grumbling.

G. BOYCOTT Our team meeting for general discussion . . , the grouses and grumbles as well as the good points.

grouse /graʊs/ *n.*[3] & *a. Austral.* & *NZ slang.* E20. [Origin unkn.] (Something) good or excellent.

grouse /graʊs/ *v.*[1]*i.* L18. [f. GROUSE *n.*[1]] Shoot grouse. Chiefly as *grousing* vbl n.

grouser *n.*[1] M19.

grouse /graʊs/ *v.*[2]*i. colloq.* E19. [Origin unkn. Cf. GROUCH *v.*, *n.*[1]] Grumble, complain.

H. T. LANE It's no good grousing about things you don't like.

grouser *n.*[2] L19.

grout /graʊt/ *n.*[1] [OE *grūt* corresp. to MDu. *grūte*, *gruut* coarse meal, peeled grain, malt, yeast, (Du. *gruit* dregs), MHG *grūz* (G *Grauss*) grain, small beer, f. Gmc var. of base of GRIT *n.*[1], *n.*[2], GROATS. Cf. GROOT *n.*] 1 Coarse meal, peeled grain. In *pl.*, = GROATS. Now *rare.* OE. b A kind of coarse wholemeal porridge. Now *rare* or *obs.* L16. 2 The infusion of malt before and during fermentation. Also, small beer. OE. 3 Orig., slime, mud. Now, sediment; in *pl.*, dregs, lees, grounds. LME.

3 DICKENS Old women might have told fortunes in them, better than in grouts of tea. A. E. COPPARD When he coughed . . his insides come up out of him like coffee grouts.

grout /graʊt/ *n.*[2] M17. [Perh. a use of prec., but cf. Fr. dial. *grouter* grout a wall.] Orig., a fluid mortar used to fill gaps or interstices, esp. in stonework. Now also, a waterproof cement-based paste used to fill gaps between wall or floor tiles.

grout /graʊt/ *v.*[1] E18. [f. GROUT *n.*[1] or var. of GROOT *v.*] 1 *v.i.* Of a pig: turn up the ground with the snout; root. E18. 2 *v.t.* Turn *up* with the snout. L19.

1 *fig.*: N. ANNAN Jowett . . encouraged his undergraduates to grout among the pearls that he cast before them.

grout /graʊt/ *v.*[2]*t.* M19. [f. GROUT *n.*[2]] Fill up or finish with grout; cement.

grouting *n.* (*a*) the action of the vb; (*b*) = GROUT *n.*[2]: L18.

grout /graʊt/ *v.*[3]*i. US.* M19. [Origin unkn.] Grumble, sulk.

groutiness *n.* crossness, sulkiness L19. **grouty** *a.* cross, sulky M19.

grouter /ˈgraʊtə/ *n.*[1] *Austral. slang.* E20. [Origin unkn.] An unfair advantage. Esp. in *come in on the grouter*.

grouter /ˈgraʊtə/ *n.*[2] M20. [f. GROUT *v.*[2] + -ER[1].] 1 An instrument or tool for grouting a wall etc. M20. 2 A person who grouts a wall etc. M20.

grove /grəʊv/ *n.* [OE *grāf* rel. to *grǣfa* brushwood, thicket, f. Gmc. Cf. GREAVE *n.*[1]] A (small) wood; a group of trees, esp. giving shade, often deliberately planted as an avenue, walk, etc.; an orchard, esp. of olives, citrus fruit, etc.

ALDOUS HUXLEY The orange groves gave place . . to huge fields of alfalfa. J. THURBER The avenue dwindled to a wood road that led into a thick grove of oak and walnut trees. *fig.*: N. GORDIMER The baby . . making its way through a grove of legs.

¶Used in biblical translations to render Heb. *'ăšērāh* (see ASHERAH) and *'ēšel*, now understood to mean 'sacred tree' and 'tamarisk' respectively.

groved *a.* having or planted with a grove or groves; encircled by a grove: E19. **groveless** *a.* M19. **grovet** *n.* (*obs.* exc. *dial.*) [-ET[1]] a little grove E16. **grovy** *a.* (now *rare*) of, pertaining to, or resembling a grove; situated in a grove, provided with groves: L16.

grovel /ˈgrɒv(ə)l, ˈgrʌv-/ *n. colloq.* L19. [f. the vb.] The action or an act of grovelling.

Daily Telegraph A telephone call . . advises that a grovel is owed to the M.P.

grovel /ˈgrɒv(ə)l, ˈgrʌv-/ *v.i.* Infl. **-ll-**, ***-l-**. LME. [Back-form. f. GROVELLING.] Lie or move in a prone position or with the face downwards, esp. in abject humility; *fig.* humble oneself, behave obsequiously, esp. in seeking favour or forgiveness.

G. ORWELL He saw himself grovelling on the floor, screaming for mercy. P. LIVELY Sylvia . . drops the packet, grovels for it on the floor.

groveller *n.* L18.

grovelling /ˈgrɒv(ə)lɪŋ, ˈgrʌv-/ *adv.* (now regarded as *pres. pple*) & *a.* Also ***groveling**. ME. [f. GROOF: see -LING[2], -LIN(G)S.] A *adv.* Also **†grovellings**. Face downward; in or to a prone or prostrate position. ME.

E. A. FREEMAN The Earl . . bowed himself to the ground, and lay grovelling.

B *adj.* 1 Having the face or front of the body on or towards the ground; prone. LME. 2 Abject, base; low, mean. E17.

1 S. BUTLER Nature gave Man an erect Figure, to raise him above the groveling Condition of . . the Beasts. 2 H. T. BUCKLE Some of the most powerful minds were still corrupted by . . grovelling superstition.

grovellingly *adv.* M16.

grow /grəʊ/ *n. obs.* exc. *Sc.* M16. [f. the vb.] The process or result of growing; growth.

grow /grəʊ/ *v.* Pa. t. **grew** /gruː/, (*dial.* & *colloq.*) **growed** /grəʊd/. Pa. pple **grown** /grəʊn/, (*dial.* & *colloq.*) **growed** /grəʊd/. [OE *grōwan* = OFris. *grōwa*, *grōia*, MDu. *groeyen* (Du. *groeien*), OHG *gruoan*, ON *gróa*, f. Gmc str. vb f. base also of GRASS *n.*, GREEN *a.*] I *v.i.* 1 Orig. (of a plant), show vigorous life, put out foliage, flourish. Now only, (of land), produce vegetation. *rare.* OE. 2 Develop or exist as a living plant (in a specified habitat or with a specified characteristic). OE. b Orig. (of a mineral), be native to a certain place. Now (*gen.*, *joc.*), be found or available in a certain place. LME. 3 Germinate, sprout, spring up; be produced. OE. 4 Of an immaterial thing: come naturally into existence; arise, originate, develop (as from a seed). (Foll. by *from*, *out of*.) OE. 5 Of (the hair, nails, etc. of) a living thing: increase gradually in size, length, or height by natural development. (Orig. only of plants: cf. WAX *v.*[1]) OE. 6 With compl. (esp. adj.): become by degrees; *esp.* become increasingly. ME. b Come or pass by degrees (*in*)*to* some state or condition; develop gradually (*in*)*to*. LME. †c Arrive at, come to, (an agreement, conclusion, etc.). Foll. by *to*, *upon*. L16–M17. 7 Of a thing: increase gradually in magnitude, power, quantity, or degree. LME. 8 Increase *in* some specified quality or property. *arch.* LME. 9 a *grow up*. Esp. of a person: develop to maturity. Freq. as GROWN-UP *ppl a.* M16. b Of a custom, condition, etc.: arise gradually, come into existence. L16. c Be sensible or mature. Freq. in *imper.* M20. 10 Become gradually fixed *in*(*to*) or united *to* something. Esp. in *grow into one*, *together* etc. coalesce, become united. *arch.* or *poet.* L16.

1 I. MURDOCH The garden could be begun . . , and grow with the membership of the community. 2 DRYDEN Green Beds of Parsley near the River grow. J. FOWLES Trees . . grew more thickly there than anywhere else. b HOR. WALPOLE All the tables and chairs and conveniences . . which he seems to think don't grow out of England. 3 SHAKES. *Oth.* Men whose heads Do grow beneath their shoulders. F. BROOKE Sugar-canes grow without planting. A. URE There grew upon the oak in Africa . . a small excrescence like a bird. 4 TENNYSON As months ran

on and rumour of battle grew. 5 J. CONRAD His red-gold pair of horizontal moustaches had grown to really noble proportions. T. S. ELIOT You were always getting yourself measured To prove how you had grown since the last holidays. 6 G. K. CHESTERTON Evening was closing in, and the room had grown darker. G. GREENE Married people grow like each other. D. ABSE He grew older, fatter, greyer, balder. B. PYM Tom was beginning to grow tired of her. H. CRANE I have grown accustomed to an 'ivory tower' sort of existence. b G. GREENE I had grown to love the place. *Grimsby Gazette* She watches her own chosen dress grow from just a drawing . . into a beautiful gown. 7 C. S. FORESTER A yellow light grew until the ship there was wrapped in flame. C. P. SNOW He felt that niggle of disquiet growing. 8 MILTON They . . In mean estate live moderate, till grown In wealth and multitude, factious they grow. 9a B. JOWETT His children, one of whom is growing up. b LD BRAIN A strong friendship grew up between the two men. c A. WESKER Oh, grow up, Ronnie. You should know that by now. 10 SHELLEY Clasp me till our hearts be grown Like two lovers into one.

II *v.t.* 11 Produce (plants, fruit, wool, etc.) by cultivation; (of land, plants, etc.) bring forth. (*rare* bef. 19.) LME. b Develop, enlarge. (*rare* bef. 20.) L15. c Let (beard etc.) develop or increase in length etc. E19. d *Cryst.* Bring about formation of (a crystal); cause (a crystal) to increase in size. E20. 12 In *pass.* Be covered (*up* or *over*) with growth. LME.

11 W. S. MAUGHAM. On the plantation . . we'd have grown rice and rye and corn and kept pigs. B. PATTEN The trees outside her window have grown leaves. b *Observer* We've grown our sterling turnover to 18 per cent. c G. GREENE With the years he had grown a small pot-belly under a double-breasted waistcoat. 12 J. DICKEY We came out among some fields grown up six or seven feet high in grass.

Phrases: *grow on trees*: see TREE *n.* *grow whiskers, have grown whiskers*: see WHISKER *n.* *not let the grass grow under one's feet*: see GRASS *n.* 1.

With advs. & preps. in specialized senses: **grow away** develop (well). **grow down(wards)** (*a*) extend downwards; (*b*) diminish. **grow on** keep (seedling plants) in situations or conditions conducive to development. **grow on —** become more appealing to or acquire gradually more influence over (a person). **grow out** become obliterated by growth. **grow out of —** (*a*) be the result or development of; (*b*) become too large to wear (a garment etc.); (*c*) become too mature to retain (a childish habit etc.). **grow to —** †(*a*) come into existence to the benefit or injury of (a person etc.); †(*b*) be an integral part of; (*c*) see sense 10 above. *grow up*: see sense 9 above.

growable *a.* L19. **growingly** *adv.* increasingly M18.

growan /ˈgraʊən/ *n. Cornish dial.* Also **grouan**. M18. [f. base of MCorn. *grow* sand, cogn. w. Welsh *graean*, Breton *grouan*: see GRAVE *v.*[2]] The soft gravelly decomposed granite overlying a tin vein. Also *soft growan*

hard growan solid granite.

grower /ˈgraʊə/ *n.* LME. [f. GROW *v.* + -ER[1].] 1 A person who or commercial company which grows esp. a specified type of produce. LME. 2 A plant that grows in a specified way. M16.

1 *fruit-grower, rose-grower*, etc. 2 *free grower, slow grower*, etc.

growing /ˈgrəʊɪŋ/ *n.* LME. [f. GROW *v.* + -ING[1].] 1 The action of GROW *v.* LME. †2 (A) growth. LME–E18. †3 Advance, progress. *rare* (Shakes.). Only in E17.

Comb.: **growing bag**: containing peat-based potting compost in which plants may be grown; **growing pains** neuralgic pains popularly attributed to growth; *fig.* early difficulties in the development of a project etc.; **growing point** the point at which growth originates; *spec.* (*Bot.*) the primary meristematic region at the apex of a plant shoot at which continuous cell division and differentiation occur; **growing season**: when rainfall and temperature allow plants to grow; **growing stock** *Forestry* the total quantity of trees in an area; **growing zone** the region in an annelid or tapeworm in which growth of new parts occurs.

growl /graʊl/ *v.* & *n.* M17. [Prob. imit. Perh. continuous with GURL *v.*, but more likely an independent formation.] A *v.* 1 *v.i.* Of an animal: make a low guttural sound, expressive of (rising) hostility. M17. b Of a person: speak in a low and angry voice. E18. c Of thunder, a storm, etc.: rumble. M18. 2 *v.t.* Of a person: utter with a growl or in a growling manner. Freq. foll. by *out*. M18. 3 *v.i.* Esp. *Jazz*. (Of a wind instrument) make a low rasping sound; (of a musician) make such a sound on an instrument. M20.

1 W. IRVING The bear . . turned, reared, showed his teeth, and growled. b F. BURNEY Though he pretended to growl, he was evidently delighted. c *Observer* The big jets of . . BOAC growl in and out daily on their way round the world. 2 S. JOHNSON She growls out her discontent.

B *n.* 1 A low hostile guttural sound made by an animal. E18. b A low angry expression of complaint etc. uttered by a person or group of persons. E19. c A rumble (of thunder, gunfire, etc.). M19. 2 Esp. *Jazz*. A deep rasping sound made on a wind instrument. M20.

1 LD MACAULAY The growl of a fierce watch-dog but half-aroused from sleep. b M. MCCARTHY 'Shut up,' came a furious growl from her other side.

growlingly *adv.* in a growling manner E19. **growly** *a.* like a growl; in a growling mood or manner: L19.

growler /ˈgraʊlə/ *n.* M18. [f. GROWL *v.* + -ER[1].] 1 A person who or an animal or thing which growls. M18. 2 A four-wheeled cab. *colloq. obs.* exc. *Hist.* M19. 3 A small iceberg showing very little above the water. M19. 4 A container for fetching beer. *US slang.* L19. 5 *Electr.* An electromagnet with two poles designed to test for short circuits in the windings of an armature. E20.

growlery /ˈgraʊləri/ *n.* M19. [f. GROWL *v.* + -ERY.] 1 Growling. Now *rare.* M19. 2 [After Dickens's use in *Bleak House.*] A place to growl or be grumpy in; a private sitting-room or study. M19.

Growmore /ˈgrəʊmɔː/ *n.* M20. [f. GROW *v.* + MORE *adv.*] Orig. *National Growmore.* Vegetable fertilizer of a standard kind.

grown /grəʊn/ *ppl a.* LME. [pa. pple of GROW *v.*] 1 Advanced in growth; increased in size, quantity, etc. Now *rare.* LME. b Of a crystal: artificially produced by growing. E20. 2 Adult, grown-up. LME. 3 Of the sea: running high. E17. 4 Of corn: that has sprouted in the ear after reaching maturity. L17.

2 J. CHEEVER Theresa had been too young . . for her to have, as a grown person, any clear memories.

grownness /-n-n-/ *n.* (now *rare*) the state or condition of being (esp. excessively) increased in size etc. L16.

grown-up /ˈgrəʊnʌp, grəʊnˈʌp/ *ppl a.* & *n.* Also **grown up**. LME. [f. prec. + UP *adv.*[1]] A *ppl a.* 1 Having reached the age of maturity; adult. LME. 2 Suitable for or characteristic of an adult; sensible, worthwhile. M19.

1 A. KOESTLER People who have learnt the alphabet late, when already grown-up. 2 C. M. YONGE As to books, all the real good grown-up ones are down in Mr. Lyddell's library.

B *n.* A grown-up person; an adult. E19.

J. WAIN I have absolutely no need to talk *down* to you, as a grown-up to a kid.

grown-upness *n.* the state of being grown-up M19.

growth /grəʊθ/ *n.* & *a.* LME. [f. GROW *v.* + -TH[1].] A *n.* 1 The action, process, or manner of growing; development; increase in size or value. LME. b A crop or yield of grapes, esp. as used in the classification of quality; a wine of a specified (*first, second*, etc.) crop or classification of quality. Cf CRU. E18. c More fully *economic growth*. The increase per head in the production of goods and services over a stated period of time; the rate of expansion of national income. M20. 2 Something which grows or has grown; produce, product; *spec.* (*Med.*) a tumour. LME. 3 A stage in the growing process; size or stature attained by growing. Now *rare* exc. *Sc.* and in *full growth* below. M16. 4 Production and development by cultivation. M17.

1 J. YEATS Barley, oats, and rye may be measured in their daily growth. 2 H. BELLOC A thick growth of low chestnuts with here and there a tall silver birch. G. ORWELL The half-conscious belief that language is a natural growth. D. M. THOMAS She had recently had a breast removed because of a growth. 3 W. COWPER Pride has attained its most luxuriant growth, And poisoned every virtue in them both. 4 R. BOLDREWOOD A yeoman class . . could use these great levels for the growth of certain semi-tropical crops.

Phrases: *classed growth*: see CLASS *v.* 3. **full growth** the size ultimately attained. **of foreign** etc. **growth** grown or originating abroad etc.

B *attrib.* or as *adj.* Of or pertaining to growth. M17.

Special collocations & comb.: **growth area** an area of or designated for economic growth. **growth curve** a line representing growth by showing how some quantity varies with time. **growth factor** *Biol.* any substance required by an organism in minute amounts to maintain its growth. **growth industry**: developing faster than most other industries. **growth point** (*a*) = *growth area* above; (*b*) = GROWING *point*. **growth regulator** *Biol.* any natural or synthetic substance, such as a hormone or auxin, which regulates growth. **growth ring** *Biol.* a layer (of wood, shell, etc.) developed during a single period of growth, esp. an annual ring in wood. **growth stock**: tending to increase in capital value rather than yield a high income. **growth zone** (*a*) = *growth area* above; (*b*) = GROWING *zone*.

groyne /grɔɪn/ *n.* & *v.* Also ***groin**. L16. [Transf. use of GROIN *n.*[1]] A *n.* A (timber) framework or low broad wall run out into the sea to check the drifting of sand etc. and so stop encroachment of the sea; a breakwater. L16. B *v.t.* Provide (a beach) with groynes. L19.

groyning *n.* the erection of groynes; a system of groynes: M19.

grozing-iron /ˈgrəʊzɪŋʌɪən/ *n.* LME. [f. as MDu. *gruis-* stem of *gruizen* trim glass, crush, f. MDu. *gruus, gruis* fragments, + IRON *n.*] 1 *Hist.* Nippers used for cutting glass. LME. 2 *Hist.* A tool heated to smooth solder joints on pipes. E19.

grub /grʌb/ *n.* LME. [Prob. f. the vb.] 1 The larva of an insect, esp. of a beetle; a caterpillar, a maggot; (now *dial.*) a worm. LME. 2 *derog.* †a A short person. LME–E18. b A person of low ability; a drudge; *US* an industrious student. Now *rare* or *obs.* M17. 3 Food. *colloq.* M17. 4 An acne pimple. Now *rare* or *obs.* M18. 5 A root left in the ground after clearing; a stump. *US.* L18. 6 *Cricket.* A ball bowled underarm along the ground. L19.

1 *Sunday Express* He was talking about some grubs he'd dug up in a crocodile swamp. *bardee grub, white grub, witchetty grub*, etc. 3 A. MOOREHEAD We were not long in getting out the grub . ., and we made a good supper. **grub up!** *colloq.* the food is ready.

Comb.: **grub-kick** *Rugby Football* = GRUBBER 6; **grub-screw** a small headless screw with a recess at one end to receive a screwdriver or key; **grubstake** *n.* & *v.* (*N. Amer. colloq.*) (*a*) *n.* rations etc. granted to a prospecting miner in return for a share in any find or profits; (*b*) *v.t.* supply with grubstake; **grubstaker** a prospector supplied with a grubstake; the supplier of a grubstake; **grub-worm** = sense 1 above; *fig.* (*derog.*) an unpleasant person.

grubhood *n.* (now *rare*) the condition of being a grub or larva M19.

grub /grʌb/ *v.* Infl. **-bb-**. ME. [Origin uncertain: cf. OHG *grubilōn* dig, search closely, MDu. *grobben* scrape together, Du. *grobbelen* root out, f. Gmc base rel. to base of GRAVE *n.*[1], *v.*[1]] 1 *v.t.* (foll. by *up*) & *i.* Dig superficially, break up the surface of, (the ground); clear (ground) of roots and stumps. ME. †b *v.t.* Dig round the roots of (a plant). LME–E16. c *v.i.* Of an animal: root, search for something in the earth etc. Now *esp.* (of a person) search in an undignified or grovelling manner; rummage. M17. d *v.i.* Plod, toil, (*along, away, on*). M18. 2 *v.t.* Extract by digging; uproot. Foll. by *up, out.* LME. 3 [Prob. f. the n.] a *v.i.* Feed, eat. *slang.* E18. b *v.t.* Provide with food. *slang.* E19.

1 J. RABAN Children dressed in cast-offs grubbed in the dirt. A. S. BYATT The bulldozers were grubbing up pastureland to make the new university. c R. CAMPBELL We used to grub about for arrowheads, ancient beads, and other things. R. ADAMS Along the foot of a tilted, red rock a porcupine came nosing and grubbing. d A. MILLER If I have to grub for money all day long at least at evening I want it beautiful. S. MIDDLETON Like your inspector grubbing away until the truth's revealed. 2 A. CARTER He was crouching on the ground grubbing up plants with a small spade.

grubber /ˈgrʌbə/ *n.* ME. [f. GRUB *v.* + -ER[1].] 1 A person who digs; a searcher; a laborious worker. ME. 2 An implement for digging etc. L16. 3 Now usu. more fully *money-grubber*. A person who is sordidly intent on amassing money. L16. 4 An eater, a feeder. *arch. colloq.* M19. 5 *Cricket* = GRUB *n.* 6. M19. 6 *Rugby Football.* In full *grubber kick.* A forward kick of the ball along the ground. M20.

grubbery /ˈɡrʌbəri/ *n.* L18. [f. GRUB *n.* or *v.* + -ERY.] †1 A room for hard work or study. *rare.* Only in L18. 2 Food; a dinner; a place where one eats. *slang.* E19. 3 Sordid or sleazy way of life. *rare.* M19.

grubble /ˈɡrʌb(ə)l/ *v.* L17. [Var. of GRABBLE *v.*, infl. by GRUB *v.*] †1 *v.i.* & *t.* Grope; gather up or *up.* L17–E18. 2 *v.i.* = GRUB *v.* 1c. *rare.* M19.

grubby /ˈɡrʌbi/ *a.* E17. [f. GRUB *n.* + -Y[1].] 1 Stunted, dwarfish. Now *dial.* E17. 2 Infested with grubs. E18. b Of the nature of a grub or larva. M19. 3 Dirty, grimy, slovenly. (The usual sense.) M19.

3 T. E. LAWRENCE I then washed my very grubby hands.

grubbily *adv.* M20. **grubbiness** *n.* M19.

Grubean /ˈɡrʌbɪən/ *a. joc.* E18. [f. GRUB (STREET) + -EAN.] = GRUB STREET *a. phr.*

Grübelsucht /ˈɡryːbəlzʊxt/ *n.* L19. [G, f. *grübeln* to brood + *Sucht* mania.] A form of obsession in which even the simplest facts are compulsively queried.

Grub Street /ˈɡrʌb striːt/ *n.* & *a. phr.* Also **Grubstreet**. M17. [A street in London (later Milton St., Moorgate) where many needy and struggling authors lived.] (Pertaining to or typical of) the world or class of needy authors or literary hacks.

SWIFT Till of late Years, a Grubstreet Book was always bound in Sheepskin. V. S. PRITCHETT If we have one foot in Grub Street we write to be readable.

grudge /ɡrʌdʒ/ *n.* LME. [f. GRUDGE *v.* or var. of GRUTCH *n.*] †1 Discontent, complaint, grumbling, reluctance. LME–E17. 2 Uneasiness of the conscience or mind; doubt, misgiving; an instance of this. Long *obs.* exc. *Sc.* L15. 3 Orig., ill will or resentment due to some special cause. Now only, a particular, esp. enduring, instance of such resentment. (Foll. by *against.*) L15. †4 Injury, injurious influence or effect. *rare.* L15–M17.

3 P. BOWLES Adelkader was very sorry to hear of his death. He bore him no grudge, you know. A. S. NEILL If . . a man succeeds in sending a reluctant wife to be analysed, she quite naturally goes with a grudge. D. JACOBSON Say it was a grudge I had against all David's children for having so many advantages over me. D. NOBBS She wasn't one to hold a grudge just because you had called her mother a hippopotamus.

Comb.: **grudge fight** a fight based on personal antipathy.

grudgeful *a.* (*rare*) resentful L16.

grudge /ɡrʌdʒ/ *v.* LME. [Var. of GRUTCH *v.*] 1 *v.i.* Murmur; grumble, complain; be discontented. (Foll. by *against, with, at, of, that.*) *obs.* exc. *Sc.* LME. †2 *v.t.* (in *pass.*) & *i.* Be seized or suffer *with* a disease or disability; have the first symptoms of a fever. LME–M16. †3 *v.t.* & *i.* Trouble or vex (a person, the conscience); (of the conscience) be troubled. LME–E17. 4 *v.t.* Be unwilling to give, grant, or allow, (a thing, *to do*); begrudge. Usu. w. person as indirect obj. L15.

4 H. A. VACHELL He never grudged the time spent in showing his wares to non-buyers. D. H. LAWRENCE The women made way for them, but barely sufficient, as if grudging to yield ground. E. AMADI He did not grudge the expatriate engineers their fatter pay-packets.

grudgement *n.* (*rare*) envy, resentment M19. **grudger** *n.* M16. **grudgingly** *adv.* in a grudging manner; with reluctance: M16. **grudgingness** *n.* the quality of being grudging E19.

†**grue** *n.*[1] LME–L19. [Origin unkn.] A particle, a whit. Usu. in neg. contexts.

grue /ɡruː/ *n.*[2] Chiefly *Sc.* & *north.* L18. [Origin unkn.] Ice, esp. in pieces, on the surface of a body of water.

grue /ɡruː/ *n.*[3] Chiefly *Sc.* & *north.* E19. [f. GRUE *v.*] Shivering, shuddering; a shiver, a shudder.

grue /ɡruː/ *v.i.* Chiefly *Sc.* & *north.* ME. [f. Scand. wd repr. by OSw. *grua*, ODa. *grue* (= OHG *ingrūēn* shudder, G *grauen* be awed, Du. *gruwen* abhor).] Feel terror or horror; be troubled; shrink from something; shiver, shudder.

gruel /ˈɡrʊəl/ *n.* ME. [OFr. (mod. *gruau*) f. Proto-Gallo-Romance dim. (repr. by med.L *grutellum*), f. Frank.: see -EL[2].] 1 Flour, meal, or other farinaceous substance. *obs.* exc. *dial.* ME. 2 Oatmeal or similar food boiled in water or milk (sometimes with the addition of other ingredients), esp. as part of an invalid's diet. LME. 3 Punishment, defeat. *arch.* L18.

gruelly *a.* resembling gruel M19.

gruel /ˈɡrʊəl/ *v.t.* Infl. **-ll-**, ***-l-**. E19. [f. the n.] 1 Feed with gruel. *rare.* E19. 2 Exhaust, punish, tax severely. Chiefly as GRUELLING *a.* M19.

grueller *n.* †(*a*) a person who feeds on gruel; (*b*) (chiefly *dial.*) a difficult problem; an ordeal: L17.

gruelling /ˈɡrʊəlɪŋ/ *n.* Also ***grueling**. L19. [f. GRUEL *v.* + -ING[1].] A harsh or exhausting experience; (a) punishment or defeat.

gruelling /ˈɡrʊəlɪŋ/ *a.* Also ***grueling**. M19. [f. GRUEL *v.* + -ING[2].] Exhausting, extremely demanding, severe.

Tennis Lendl's training programme is so gruelling that few people could keep up with it.

gruellingly *adv.* L20.

gruesome /ˈɡruːs(ə)m/ *a.* L16. [f. GRUE *v.* + -SOME[1].] 1 Inspiring fear or horror; horrific, grisly; repulsive, disgusting. L16. 2 Full of or inspired by fear. *rare.* M19.

1 F. SMYTH It was a particularly gruesome killing, for . . he had been shot twice more through each eye.

gruesomely *adv.* L19. **gruesomeness** *n.* L19.

gruff /ɡrʌf/ *a.* & *v.* L15. [Flem., Du. *grof* coarse, rude = MLG *grof*, OHG, G *grob*, f. WGmc.] A *adj.* 1 Coarse-grained; containing coarse particles. *obs.* exc. *Sc.* L15. b Of an immaterial thing: rough, rude, unrefined. *Sc.* L17. 2 Rough, surly, or sour in manner or aspect; curt, awkwardly taciturn; (of speech or the voice) characterized by hoarse or guttural sounds. L17.

2 H. READ A gruff country man, not conscious of, and therefore not ashamed of, his provinciality. V. WOOLF Speaking in the gruff voice of deep emotion. S. RAVEN Then a hearty handshake, a resumption of the usual gruff manner.

B *v.* †1 *v.t.* Treat gruffly. Only in E18. 2 *v.i.* Grunt, snore. *dial.* M18. 3 *v.t.* Say or utter gruffly. E20.

3 J. T. FARRELL Young Horn said hello to him. He gruffed a reply.

gruffish *a.* somewhat gruff E19. **gruffly** *adv.* in a gruff manner, with a gruff voice E18. **gruffness** *n.* L17. **gruffy** *a.* (*obs.* exc. *Sc.*) gruff L18.

gruft /ɡrʌft/ *n. dial.* E19. [Origin unkn.] Particles of soil which are washed up by rain among the grass.

grufted *a.* dirty L19.

grugru /ˈɡruːɡruː/ *n.* Also **groo-groo**, **gri-gri**. L18. [Amer. Sp. (Puerto Rican) *grugrú* f. Carib.] 1 More fully *grugru palm.* Any of various spiny tropical American palms of the genus *Acrocomia*; esp. *A. totai* of northern Argentina and Paraguay, an important source of palm kernel oil. L18. 2 More fully *grugru grub*, *grugru worm.* The edible larva of any of various S. American insects, esp. weevils of the genus *Rhyncophorus*, which feeds on the pith of palms and sugar cane. L18.

gruiform /ˈɡruːɪfɔːm/ *a.* L19. [mod.L *Gruiformes*, f. L *grus*, *grui-* crane + -FORM.] *Ornith.* Belonging or pertaining to the order Gruiformes, which includes the cranes and rails.

grum /ɡrʌm/ *a.* Now *rare.* E17. [Prob. blend of GRIM *a.* and GLUM *a.* Cf. Da. *grum* cruel.] Gloomy, surly, glum.

grumly *adv.* E18. **grumness** *n.* L17.

grumble /ˈɡrʌmb(ə)l/ *v.* & *n.* L16. [Frequent. of GRUMME + *-b-* -LE[1]. Cf. (M)Du. *grommen*, MLG *grommelen*; f. imit. Gmc.] A *v.* 1 *v.i.* Of a person or animal: utter low inarticulate sounds; growl faintly; mutter, murmur. L16. b Of thunder etc.: rumble, esp. faintly or as from a distance. E17. 2 *v.i.* Utter murmurs of discontent; complain, esp. in a repetitive ineffectual way. (Foll. by *about, at, over, that.*) L16. 3 *v.t.* Express or utter complainingly. (Foll. by *out.*) E19.

1 D. ABSE Bluebottles grumbling up and down the window-pane. b J. I. M. STEWART Thunder had been grumbling in the distance. 2 D. H. LAWRENCE They grumble a lot, but they're not going to alter anything. A. S. BYATT Her ghosts only grumbled, they did not threaten. **grumbling appendix** *colloq.* an appendix that causes intermittent discomfort without developing appendicitis. 3 B. EMECHETA There were murmurs and grumbled protests.

B *n.* 1 An act of grumbling; a complaint; a rumble (of thunder etc.). L16. b In *pl. The* sulks. *colloq.* M19. 2 In full *grumble and grunt* [rhyming slang] = CUNT. Esp. in *a bit of grumble*, a sexually desirable woman. *slang.* M20.

1 B. PYM The dull routine, the petty grumbles and the shared irritation of the men. *Blackwood's Magazine* The thunder . . fading at last to a distant grumble.

grumbler *n.* a person who habitually grumbles M17. **grumblesome** *a.* grumbling, complaining E20. **grumbling** *vbl n.* the action or an act of the vb E17. **grumblingly** *adv.* (*a*) in a grumbling manner; †(*b*) mumblingly: L17. **grumbly** *a.* (*colloq.*) (*a*) resembling a grumble; (*b*) inclined to grumble: M19.

Grumbletonian /ɡrʌmb(ə)lˈtəʊnɪən/ *n.* & *a.* L17. [f. GRUMBLE *v.* after *Muggletonian* etc.] A *n.* †1 Orig., a member of the Country Party in 17th-cent. English politics, allegedly motivated by dissatisfied personal ambition. Later, a supporter of the Opposition. *derog.* L17–M19. 2 A grumbler. L18. †B *attrib.* or as *adj.* Of, pertaining to, or characteristic of a Grumbletonian or Grumbletonians. L17–M18.

grume /ɡruːm/ *n.* Now *rare* or *obs.* M16. [L *grumus* little heap. Cf. Fr. †*grume* (now *grumeau*) clot.] †1 A lump. Only in M16. 2 *Med.* A blood clot; a clotted fluid, esp. blood. E17.

†**grumme** *v.i.* LME–L16. [Origin uncertain: cf. Du. *grommen.*] Grumble.

grummel /ˈɡrʌm(ə)l/ *n. obs.* exc. *dial.* M16. [Origin unkn.: cf. Sw. *grummel.*] Mud, sediment; in *pl.*, dregs, coffee-grounds.

grummet /ˈɡrʌmɪt/ *n.*[1] *obs.* exc. *Hist.* L16. [OFr. *gro(u)met* servant, valet, shop-boy, wine-merchant's assistant (see GOURMET) = Sp. *grumete* ship's boy.] A ship's boy; a cabin-boy.

grummet *n.*[2] var. of GROMMET *n.*[1]

grumose /ˈɡruːməʊs/ *a. rare.* M18. [f. GRUME + -OSE[1].] Chiefly *Med.* & *Bot.* Formed of clustered grains or clots. Cf. GRUMOUS.

grumous /ˈɡruːməs/ *a.* M17. [f. GRUME + -OUS.] 1 Of a fluid, esp. blood: clotted, viscid. M17. 2 *Bot.* Of a root etc.: granular, knotty. L17. 3 *Geol.* Of a rock: formed of clustered or aggregated granules or grains. L20.

grump /ɡrʌmp/ *n.* E18. [Imit. of a sound expr. displeasure.] †1 A slight, a snub. Chiefly in *humps and grumps.* E–M18. 2 A bad mood; in *pl.*, the sulks. M19. 3 A gruff or grumpy person. *colloq.* E20.

2 L. M. ALCOTT Hannah had the grumps, for being up late. Never did suit her. *Expression!* I knew that sitting in the crowd could put her in a real grump. 3 A. TYLER You always were a grump when you weren't feeling well.

grump /ɡrʌmp/ *v.i.* L19. [f. the n.: cf. GLUMP *v.*] Sulk, be grumpy.

grumph /ɡrʌmf/ *n.* & *v.* Chiefly *Sc.* M18. [Imit.: cf. GRUNT *v.*, GRUMP *n.*] A *n.* A grunt. M18. B *v.i.* & *t.* Grunt or utter with a grunt. E19.

grumphie *n.* (a name for) a pig L18. **grumphy** *a.* grumpy M19.

grumpish /ˈɡrʌmpɪʃ/ *a.* L18. [f. GRUMP *n.* + -ISH[1].] Grumpy.

grumpishly *adv.* L20.

grumpy /ˈɡrʌmpi/ *a.* L18. [f. GRUMP *n.* + -Y[1].] Surly, ill-tempered.

F. BURNEY You were so grumpy you would not let me.

grumpily *adv.* L19. **grumpiness** *n.* M19.

Grundy /ˈɡrʌndi/ *n.* L18. [The surname of a character in T. Morton's play *Speed the Plough* (1798).] *Mrs Grundy*, a person embodying conventional propriety and prudery.

H. JAMES It was anything but Bohemia—it was the very temple of Mrs. Grundy.

Grundyish *a.* prudish L19. **Grundyism** *n.* the principles of Mrs Grundy, conventionalism M19. **Grundyite** *n.* a stickler for propriety M19.

grunerite /ˈɡruːnəraɪt/ *n.* Also **grünerite**. M19. [G *Grünerit*, f. E. L. Gruner (1809–83), Fr.

geologist + -ITE[1].] *Min.* A monoclinic iron silicate of the amphibole group, also containing magnesium.

grunge /grʌn(d)ʒ/ *n.* M20. [Rel. to next.] **1** A repugnant, unpleasant, or dull person or thing. *slang* (chiefly *N. Amer.*). M20. **2** A style of rock music characterized by a raucous guitar sound and lazy delivery. L20.

grungy /ˈgrʌn(d)ʒi/ *a. slang* (chiefly *N. Amer.*). M20. [App. arbitrary formation after GRUBBY *a.*, DINGY *a.*, etc.: cf. prec. and GUNGY *a.*] **1** Grimy, dirty; of poor quality, unappealing; unpleasant, repugnant. M20. **2** Of music: of the nature of or resembling grunge. L20.

grunginess *n.* L20.

grunion /ˈgrʌnjən/ *n.* E20. [Prob. f. Sp. *gruñón* grunter.] A small silverside fish of Californian coasts, *Leuresthes tenuis*, which comes ashore to spawn.

grunt /grʌnt/ *n.* & *a.* M16. [f. the vb.] **A** *n.* **1** A low guttural sound made esp. by pigs; a similar sound made by humans to indicate approval or disapproval. Formerly also, a groan. M16. **2** Any of numerous tropical marine fishes of the family Haemulidae, which produce a grunting sound by grinding together the pharyngeal teeth; *esp.* (*a*) (more fully *blue-striped grunt*) *Haemulon sciurus*, (*b*) (more fully *French grunt*) *H. flavolineatus.* Cf. GRUNTER 2. L17. **3a** A junior assistant to a worker on electricity or telephone lines; *gen.* an unskilled or low-ranking assistant, a dogsbody. *US slang.* E20. **b** An infantry soldier. *N. Amer. slang.* M20.

1 DICKENS With a deprecatory grunt, the jackal again complied. B. EMECHETA He.. answered their questions with grunts. 3b *Times Lit. Suppl.* The first Vietnamese film to try and tell the story like it was for the ordinary American grunt.

Phrases: grumble and grunt: see GRUMBLE *n.* 2.

B *attrib.* or as *adj.* Of an occupation or task: suitable for a low-ranking worker, menial, tedious. *colloq.* L20.

grunt /grʌnt/ *v.* [OE *grunnettan* = OHG *grunnizōn* (G *grunzen*), intensive formation on imit. Gmc base (whence also OE *grunian* grunt) which has an analogue in L *grunnire* grunt).] **1** *v.i.* Of an animal, esp. a pig, or a person: utter a grunt or grunts. OE. **b** Utter a grunt or grunts expressing discontent, dissent, effort, etc.; grumble. ME. †**c** Groan. ME–E17. **2** *v.t.* Utter or express with a grunt; breathe or speak *out* with a grunt. E17.

1 W. IRVING Sleek unwieldy porkers were grunting in the repose and abundance of their pens. b A. MACLEAN An ill-advised move that made him grunt with pain. 2 W. SOYINKA He grunted a response to the greeting of a passer-by.

grunting *vbl n.* the action or an act of the vb ME. **gruntingly** *adv.* in a grunting manner E17.

grunter /ˈgrʌntə/ *n.* LME. [f. prec. + -ER[1].] **1** An animal or person that grunts; *esp.* a pig. LME. **2** Any of various marine or freshwater fishes which emit a grunting noise when caught. Cf. CROAKER, GRUNT *n.* 2. E18.

Grunth *n.* var. of GRANTH.

gruntle /ˈgrʌnt(ə)l/ *n. Sc.* E16. [f. the vb.] **1** The snout of a pig or other animal; *transf.* a person's face. E16. **2** A little or subdued grunt. L17.

gruntle /ˈgrʌnt(ə)l/ *v.*[1]*i.* Now chiefly *dial.* LME. [f. GRUNT *v.* + -LE[3]. Cf. DISGRUNTLE.] **1** Chiefly of a pig: utter a little or subdued grunt. LME. **2** Grumble, murmur, complain. L16.

gruntle /ˈgrʌnt(ə)l/ *v.*[2]*t. colloq.* E20. [Back-form. f. DISGRUNTLE *v.*] Please, satisfy, make content. Chiefly as *gruntled* ppl a.

gruntling /ˈgrʌntlɪŋ/ *n.* L17. [f. GRUNT *v.* + -LING[1].] A young pig.

gruppetto /grupˈpetto, grʊˈpɛtəʊ/ *n.* Pl. ***-tti*** /-t(t)i/, ***-ttos*** /-təʊz/. M19. [It., dim. of *gruppo.*] *Mus.* A melodic ornament consisting of a group of three, four, or five notes, comprising the principal note and the notes one degree above and below it; a turn.

gruppo /ˈgruppo/ *n.* Long *rare.* Pl. ***-ppi*** /-ppi/. L17. [It.] = prec.

Grus /grʊs/ *n.* E18. [L *grus* crane (bird).] (The name of) a small constellation of the southern hemisphere, south of Piscis Austrinus; the Crane.

grush /grʌʃ/ *v.t. obs.* exc. *Sc.* LME. [Var. of CRUSH *v.*] Crush. Formerly also, make a deep wound in, gash.

grushie /ˈgrʌʃi/ *a. Sc.* L18. [Origin unkn.] Healthy, thriving.

grutch /grʌtʃ/ *n.* LME. [f. the vb. Cf. GROUCH *n.*[1], GRUDGE *n.*] †**1** = GRUDGE *n.* 1. LME–M16. **2** = GRUDGE *n.* 3. *obs.* exc. *Sc.* & *US.* M16.

grutch /grʌtʃ/ *v.* Long *dial.* & *arch.* ME. [OFr. *groucier*, *grouchier* grumble, murmur, of unkn. origin. Cf. GROUCH *v.*, GRUDGE *v.*] **1** *v.i.* = GRUDGE *v.* 1. ME. **2** *v.t.* = GRUDGE *v.* 4. LME. †**3** *v.i.* Make a jarring or grating sound; gnash one's teeth. LME–E16.

†**grutchingly** *adv.*: only in ME.

Gruyère /ˈgruːjɛː, *foreign* gryjɛːr/ *n.* & *a.* E19. [A town in Switzerland.] (Designating) a firm pale cows'-milk cheese with many cavities.

gryke *n.* var. of GRIKE.

gryllotalpa /grɪləˈtalpə/ *n.* L18. [f. L *gryllo-* comb. f. *gryllus* cricket + *talpa* mole.] A mole-cricket, of the orthopteran family Gryllotalpidae. Now only as mod.L genus name.

gryphite /ˈgrɪfʌɪt/ *n.* L18. [mod.L *gryphites*, f. late L *gryphus*: see GRIFFIN *n.*[1]] *Palaeont.* A kind of fossil oyster.

gryphon *n.* see GRIFFIN *n.*[1]

grysbok /ˈgrʌɪsbɒk, ˈxreɪs-/ *n.* Also **-buck** /-bʌk/. Pl. same, **-s**. L18. [Afk., f. Du. *grijs* grey + *bok* BUCK *n.*[1]] Either of two small reddish-brown straight-horned antelopes, *Raphicerus melanotis* and *R. sharpei*, of central and southern Africa.

G string /ˈdʒiː strɪŋ/ *n. phr.* In sense 2 also **g(ee) string.** M19. [f. G, G + STRING *n.*] **1** *Mus.* The string on a violin etc. tuned to the note G. M19. **2** A strip of cloth etc. covering the pubic area, attached to a narrow waistband or string; *esp.* a similar garment of minimal extent worn e.g. by striptease artists. L19.

G-suit /ˈdʒiːsuːt/ *n.* Also **g-**. M20. [f. G, G + SUIT *n.*] A garment equipped with inflatable areas, designed to enable the wearer to withstand high acceleration.

guaap *n.* var. of GHAP.

guaca *n.* see HUACA.

guacamole /gwɑːkəˈməʊli/ *n.* Also **guaco-**. E20. [Amer. Sp. f. Nahuatl *ahuacamolli*, f. *ahuacatl* avocado + *molli* sauce.] A Mexican dish made from mashed avocados, onions, tomatoes, chillies, and seasoning.

guacharo /ˈgwɑːtʃərəʊ/ *n.* Pl. **-os.** E19. [Sp. *guácharo*, of S. Amer. origin.] = *oil-bird* s.v. OIL *n.*

guaco /ˈgwɑːkəʊ/ *n.*[1] Pl. **-os.** M19. [Amer. Sp.] **1** Any of several tropical American plants used as antidotes to snake-bites; esp. *Mikania guaco*, of the composite family, and *Aristolochia maxima* (family Aristolochiaceae). Also, the medicinal substance obtained from the plant. M19. **2** = *Rocky Mountain bee plant* s.v. BEE *n.*[1]; a black pigment obtained from this, used by Pueblo Indians to decorate pottery. M19.

guaco *n.*[2] var. of HUACO.

guacomole *n.* var. of GUACAMOLE.

Guadalupe /ˈgwɑːdəluːp, -pi/ *n.* L19. [A Mexican island situated off the coast of California.] Used *attrib.* in the names of plants and animals found there.

Comb.: **Guadalupe palm** an ornamental palm, *Brahea edulis*, bearing edible pulpy fruit.

Guadeloupian /gwɑːdəˈluːpɪən/ *n.* & *a.* M20. [f. *Guadeloupe* (see below) + -IAN.] **A** *n.* A native or inhabitant of Guadeloupe, a group of islands in the Lesser Antilles. M20. **B** *adj.* Of or pertaining to Guadeloupe or its inhabitants. M20.

Also **Guadeloupean** *a.* & *n.* M20. **Guadeloupan** *a.* & *n.* L20.

guaiac /ˈgwʌɪək/ *n.* M16. [Anglicized. f. GUAIACUM. Cf. Fr. *gaïac.*] Guaiacum; *esp.* = GUAIACUM 2, 3.

Comb.: **guaiac test** = GUAIACUM *test.*

guaiacol /ˈgwʌɪəkɒl/ *n.* M19. [f. next + -OL.] A liquid with a penetrating aromatic odour obtained by the fractional distillation of wood tar and the dry distillation of gaiacum resin; *o*-methoxyphenol, $OH{\cdot}C_6H_4{\cdot}OCH_3$, the principal constituent of this, a yellow crystalline solid or oily liquid used as a synthetic flavouring.

guaiacum /ˈgwʌɪəkəm/ *n.* M16. [mod.L f. Sp. *guayaco*, *guayacan*, f. Taino *guayacan.*] **1** Any of various trees and shrubs of the genus *Guaiacum* (family Zygophyllaceae), native to the W. Indies and tropical America, esp. *G. officinale* and *G. sanctum.* M16. **2** The hard very heavy wood of such a tree; lignum vitae. M16. **3** A resin obtained from such a tree, formerly used to treat gout and rheumatism, now as a flavouring; a drug prepared from it. Also *gum guaiacum.* M16.

Comb.: **guaiacum test** *Med.*: for the absence of blood from urine or faeces, involving guaiacum.

Guaicuru *n.* & *a.* var. of GUAYCURU.

guajira /gwaˈxira/ *n.* E20. [Cuban Sp., fem. of next.] A Cuban song and dance tune whose rhythm shifts from 6/8 to 3/4 time.

guajiro /gwaˈxiro/ *n.* Pl. **-os** /-ɔs/. M19. [Cuban Sp. = rustic, rural.] A Cuban agricultural worker.

guan /gwɑːn/ *n.* L17. [f. Amer. Sp. f. Miskito *kwamu.*] Any of various game-birds of tropical America of the genus *Penelope* or other genus of the family Cracidae (which also contains the curassows).

guana /ˈgwɑːnə/ *n.* E17. [Aphet. f. IGUANA.] **1** An iguana. E17. **2** A goanna. Latterly *Austral.* & *NZ.* Now *rare* or *obs.* L17.

guanaco /gwəˈnɑːkəʊ/ *n.* Pl. **-os.** E17. [Sp. f. Quechua *huanacu.*] A mammal of the Andean foothills, *Lama guanicoe*, which belongs to the same family as the llama, vicuña, and camels and has a coat of soft pale brown hair used for wool.

guanay /ˈgwɑːneɪ/ *n.* M19. [Amer. Sp. *guanae.*] A cormorant, *Phalacrocorax bougainvillei*, of the coasts of Chile and Peru. Also *guanay cormorant.*

Guanche /ˈgwɑːntʃi/ *n.* L16. [Sp.] Any of the aboriginal inhabitants of the Canary Islands who were absorbed by the Spanish on their conquest of the islands in the 15th cent.

guanethidine /gwəˈnɛθɪdiːn/ *n.* M20. [f. GUANIDINE by insertion of ETH(YL.] *Pharm.* A derivative of guanidine that is used esp. to treat moderate to severe hypertension.

guango /ˈgwaŋgəʊ/ *n. W. Indies.* Pl. **-os.** L19. [Amer. Sp., of unkn. origin.] = *rain-tree* (b) s.v. RAIN *n.*[1]

guanidine /ˈgwɑːnɪdiːn/ *n.* M19. [f. GUANO + -IDE + -INE[5].] *Chem.* A strongly basic compound, $NH_2{\cdot}C(NH){\cdot}NH_2$, used in organic synthesis.

guanidino /gwɑːnɪˈdiːnəʊ/ *a.* M20. [f. prec. + -O-.] *Chem.* Containing or designating the group $H_2N{\cdot}C(NH){\cdot}NH{\cdot}$ derived from guanidine. Used bef. a n.

Also **ˈguanido** *a.* M20.

guanine /ˈgwɑːniːn/ *n.* M19. [f. GUANO + -INE[5].] *Biochem.* A derivative of purine that occurs in guano, fish scales, etc., and is also one of the four constituent bases of nucleic acids, paired with cytosine in double-stranded DNA; 6-oxy-2-aminopurine, $C_5H_5N_5O$.

guano /ˈgwɑːnəʊ/ *n.* & *v.* E17. [Sp., or S. Amer. Sp. *huano*, f. Quechua *huanu* dung.] **A** *n.* Pl. **-os.** **1** The excrement of sea birds as found esp. on the islands off Peru and Chile and used as fertilizer. E17. **b** A sea bird which produces guano. Now *rare* or *obs.* L17. **2** More fully *fish guano.* An artificial fertilizer resembling natural guano, *esp.* one made from fish. M19. **B** *v.t.* Fertilize with guano. M19.

guanophore /ˈgwɑːnəfɔː/ *n.* E20. [f. GUAN(INE + -O- + -PHORE.] *Zool.* A chromatophore containing crystals of guanine, found in the skin of fishes and reptiles.

guanosine /ˈgwɑːnəsiːn/ *n.* E20. [f. GUANINE by insertion of -OSE[2].] *Biochem.* A nucleoside composed of guanine linked to ribose.

guanylic /gwɑːˈnɪlɪk/ *a.* L19. [f. as prec. + -YL + -IC.] Biochem. *guanylic acid*, a nucleotide composed of a phosphoric acid ester of guanosine, present in most DNA and RNA.

guar /gwɑː/ *n.* L19. [Hind. *guār*.] **1** A drought-resistant leguminous plant, *Cyamopsis tetragonoloba*, grown esp. in the Indian subcontinent as a vegetable and fodder crop and as a source of guar gum. L19. **2** More fully *guar flour, gum.* A fine powder obtained by grinding the endosperm of guar seeds and used in the food, paper, and other industries. M20.

guara /ˈgwɑːrə/ *n.* Now *rare.* E17. [(Port. *guará* f.) Tupi *agwa'rá.*] The scarlet ibis, *Eudocimus ruber.*

guaracha /gwəˈratʃə/ *n.* M19. [Sp.] A lively Cuban song and dance in 3/4 and 6/8, or 2/4, time; a ballroom dance resembling this.

guarache *n.* var. of HUARACHE.

guarana /gwəˈrɑːnə, ˈgwɑːrənə/ *n.* M19. [Port. f. Tupi *guaraná.*] A Brazilian liana, *Paullinia cupana*, of the soapberry family; a paste prepared from the seeds of this shrub, used as a food or medicine and esp. to make a drink resembling coffee.

†**guarand** *n.* L17–E18. [Prob. f. Fr. *garant*: see GUARANTEE.] = GUARANTEE *n.* 1.

Guarani /gwɑːrəˈniː; *in sense 3* ˈgwɑːrəni/ *n.* In sense 3 **g-.** L18. [Sp., f. *Guarini.*] **A** *n.* Pl. same, **-s.** **1** A member of a S. American Indian people of Paraguay and adjacent regions. L18. **2** The language of this people, one of the main divisions of the Tupi-Guarani language family. E20. **3** (**g-**.) A monetary unit of Paraguay, equal to 100 centimos. M20. **B** *attrib. or as adj.* Of or pertaining to the Guarani or their language. L19.

¶ See also TUPI-GUARANI.

guarantee /gar(ə)nˈtiː/ *n.* & *v.* Also (earlier, as n.) **garanté.** L17. [Prob. orig. f. Sp. *garante* = Fr. *garant* WARRANT *n.*[1]; later infl. by Fr. *garantie* GUARANTY.] **A** *n.* **1** = GUARANTOR. L17. **2** = GUARANTY *n.* 1. L18. **3** A thing, esp. a document from a manufacturer etc., given or existing as security for the fulfilment (esp. by a product, service, etc.) of certain conditions. M19. **4** A person to whom a guaranty is given. M19.

3 C. FRANCIS The proximity of the shore is no guarantee of safety.

Comb.: **guarantee fund** a sum pledged as a contingent indemnity for future loss.

B *v.t.* **1** Be a guarantee for; undertake to be responsible for the fulfilment of (a contract), the nature of (a product), etc.; secure the persistence or existence of; ensure *that*; engage *to do.* L18. **2** Secure (a person or thing) *against* or *from* risk, injury, etc., or *in* the possession of something. E19. **3** Secure the possession of (something) *to.* M19.

1 N. SHUTE If I didn't stop drinking . . he couldn't guarantee my life for longer than a year. P. GOODMAN A ten-foot drop to a concrete pavement, guaranteed to break both ankles. D. CAUTE You will personally guarantee our safety?

guarantor /gar(ə)nˈtɔː/ *n.* M19. [f. GUARANT(EE *v.* + -OR, after WARRANTOR.] A person who makes or gives a guarantee.

guaranty /ˈgar(ə)nti/ *n.* & *v.* E16. [AN *guarantie*, (O)Fr. *garantie* use as n. of fem. pa. pple of *g(u)arantir* to guarantee, f. Proto-Romance (whence *guarant*: see WARRANT *n.*[1]). Cf. WARRANTY.] **A** *n.* **1** The action of securing, warranting, or guaranteeing; *spec.* a written undertaking to answer for the payment of a debt or the performance of an obligation by another person liable in the first instance to such payment or obligation. E16. **2** Something which secures or guarantees the existence or permanence of a thing. L17. **B** *v.* = GUARANTEE *v.* Now *rare.* M18.

guard /gɑːd/ *n.* LME. [(O)Fr. *garde* f. Proto-Romance f. WGmc, whence also WARD *n.*] †**1** Care; keeping, guardianship, custody. LME–E18. **b** A precaution. Formerly also, caution. Now *rare.* L16. **2** A keeper, a protector, a defender; a sentry; *N. Amer.* a prison warder. Freq. also w. defining wd, as *coastguard.* LME. **b** *Astron.* Either of two stars in Ursa Minor that are the next brightest in it after the polestar; either of the two stars in the Plough which form a line indicating the direction of the polestar. Chiefly as *the Guards.* L16. **c** An official in general charge of a train or (*Hist.*) a stagecoach. L18. **d** Either of two players in basketball or American football responsible for offensive play and defensive marking. L19. **e** = GARDA 2. M20. **3** A body of soldiers etc. appointed to protect a person or position or to act as a sentry or escort; a separately designated section of an army. LME. **b** (**G-**.) In *pl. The* household troops of the British army, consisting of the Foot Guards, the Horse Guards, the Life Guards, and by extension some (orig. seven) regiments of the Dragoon Guards. (These, with the exception of the Foot Guards, are now merged in the Household Cavalry Regiment.) L17. **4** Something which protects or defends; a protection, a defence; *esp.* a device to prevent injury, damage, or an accident; *spec.* (*a*) the part of a sword-hilt that protects the user's hand; (*b*) a metal device protecting the trigger of a gun; (*c*) a reinforcing slip of paper inserted between the pages of a book for the attachment of additional leaves; (*d*) a piece of protective sports equipment. LME. **b** An ornamental binding or trimming on a garment. *obs.* exc. *Hist.* E16. **5** A defensive posture or motion in fencing, boxing, etc.; the position in which a cricket bat is held to defend the wicket. M16. **6** Protection, defence. *arch.* L16. **7** The condition or fact of protecting or defending; watch, vigilance; sentry duty. Freq. in phrs. (see below). L16. †**8** A guardroom or guardhouse. E17–L18. **9** *Curling.* A stone delivered so as to lie directly in front of another so that it protects it from an opponent's play. E19.

2 P. BOWLES The main gate . . was locked at night so that no guard was necessary. R. ELLISON Armoured cars with alert guards went by. E. ARDIZZONE Sail it alone to the coastguard station and tell the guards to come and help us. 3 *home guard, Swiss guards, Varangian Guard*, etc. b *Grenadier Guards*, etc. *attrib.*: *Guards battalion, officer, tie*, etc. 4 SHAKES. *Tr. & Cr.* There is between my will and all offences A guard of patience. *fire-guard, leg-guard, mudguard, watch-guard*, etc. 5 C. S. LEWIS After being knocked down sufficiently often I began to know a few guards and blows. H. WILLIAMSON Blows, which wove . . through the almost static guard of his right arm. C. FRANCIS Night is the time when your guard is down and your reactions slow. 6 GIBBON The rivals . . , had withdrawn the greatest part of their forces from the guard of the general frontier. 7 T. HARDY It was characteristic of Ethelberta's jealous motherly guard over her young sisters. E. AMADI The crunch crunch of the boots of the soldier on guard outside.

Phrases: **give guard** *Cricket* (of an umpire) indicate to a batsman the position of the bat with respect to the wicket. **guard of honour** a body of usu. uniformed people appointed to receive a person of distinction or perform a special ceremonial duty. *hanging guard*: see HANGING *a.* **keep guard** act as a sentry, keep watch. **off (one's) guard** unprepared against attack, surprise, etc. **on (one's) guard** prepared for attack, surprise, etc.; cautious. **mount guard** take up sentry duty. **relieve guard** take another's place on sentry duty. **take guard** *Cricket* (of a batsman) take up position before the wicket, esp. by requesting the umpire to give guard. **stand guard** = *keep guard* above. *Yeoman of the Guard*: see YEOMAN.

Comb.: **guard band** (*a*) a narrow frequency band left vacant in order to prevent interference between communication bands on either side of it; (*b*) an unrecorded strip separating neighbouring recording tracks on magnetic tape; **guard-boat** (*a*) a boat detailed to ensure that a good watch is kept by officers of a fleet in harbour; (*b*) an official harbour boat enforcing quarantine or customs regulations; **guard-book**: arranged for the reception of additional leaves, cuttings, etc.; **guard cell** *Bot.* each of the pair of cells bordering a stoma, which becomes larger or smaller according to the turgor of the cells; **guard-chain**: for securing a watch, brooch, etc.; **guard dog** a watchdog; **guard hair** any of the hairs forming the coarse outer fur of an animal; **guardhouse**: accommodating a military guard or securing prisoners; **guard-rail**: preventing a fall, derailment, etc.; **guard ring** (*a*) a ring preventing another ring from slipping off a finger etc.; (*b*) *Physics* a plate placed round and close to a disc electrode so that the field of the latter is not made irregular by edge effects; **guardroom**: for accommodating a military guard or securing prisoners; **guardsman** a soldier belonging to a guard or the Guards.

guard /gɑːd/ *v.* L15. [f. the n. or (O)Fr. *garder*, †*guarder* f. Proto-Romance f. WGmc whence also WARD *v.*] **1** *v.t.* Trim or ornament (a garment) with braid, lace, etc. *arch.* L15. **2** *v.t.* Keep safe; protect, defend, (*against, from*); stand guard over, esp. to control entry or exit through (a door, passage, etc.). L15. **b** Accompany or escort as a guard *to* a place. *arch.* L16. **c** *Chess & Cards.* Protect or support (a piece, a card) with another. E17. **d** *Cricket.* Defend or protect (the wicket). M18. **e** *Curling & Bowls.* Defend (a stone, a bowl) by placing another between it and another player. L18. **3** *v.i.* Stand on guard; take up a defensive position, esp. in fencing; *esp.* be on one's guard, take precautions *against.* L15. **4** *v.t.* Keep watch over, keep in check, control, (thoughts, speech). L16. **5** *v.t.* Provide with a guard (chiefly *techn.*); *fig.* protect against misunderstanding by stipulation or explanation. L19. **6** *v.t.* Supply (a guard-book) with guards; insert into a guard-book. L19.

2 L. DURRELL The talisman which . . guards a house against the evil eye. P. S. BUCK To his uncle's wife he said nothing, guarding his purpose from her. A. MACLEAN The entrance . . was sealed off by a . . gate guarded by heavily armed soldiers. 3 J. BARNES Her mother was always telling her to guard against over-excitement. 4 W. COWPER Guard what you say.

guardable *a.* L16. †**guardage** *n.* (*rare*) keeping, guardianship: only in E17. **guarder** *n.* a keeper, a protector; a guard: M16. **guarding** *n.* (*a*) the action of the vb; (*b*) a binding or trimming (*Hist.*); *Sc.* a border on a herring net: M16. **guardingly** *adv.* in a guarding manner E19.

guarda-costa /gwardaˈkosta, gɑːdəˈkɒstə/ *n.* M18. [Sp., f. *guarda-* stem of *guardar* to guard + *costa* coast.] *Hist.* A Spanish ship used for protecting the coast.

guardant /ˈgɑːd(ə)nt/ *a.* & *n.* L16. [Fr. *gardant* pres. pple of *garder*: see GUARD *v.*, -ANT[1].] **A** *adj.* **1** *Her.* Of an animal: depicted in profile or with the face turned towards the spectator. L16. **2** Guarding, protecting. *arch.* E17. **B** *n.* A guardian, a protector. Long *rare* or *obs.* L16.

guarda-roba /gwardaˈrɔːba, gwɑːdəˈrəʊbə/ *n.* *arch.* E17. [It., f. *guarda-* stem of *guardare* to guard + *roba* clothes.] A wardrobe.

guarded /ˈgɑːdɪd/ *a.* E16. [f. GUARD *v.*, *n.*: see -ED[1], -ED[2].] **1** Trimmed, ornamented. *arch.* E16. **2** Defended, protected; having a guard or sentry. L16. **3** On one's guard; *esp.* (of speech, behaviour, etc.) careful, cautious, unrevealing, non-committal. E18. **4** *techn.* Provided with a guard or guards. L19.

2 E. JOHNSON Dickens's friends knew about Ellen, although he kept her as closely guarded a secret as possible. 3 M. RENAULT. A suitable smile which, without being exactly guarded, revealed nothing whatever. P. ACKROYD He sounded guarded—whether out of suspicion or embarrassment, it was impossible . . . to tell.

guardedly *adv.* cautiously (earlier in UNGUARDEDLY) L18. **guardedness** *n.* cautiousness E19.

guardee /gɑːˈdiː/ *n. colloq.* E20. [f. GUARD *n.* + -EE[2].] A guardsman, esp. as representing smartness or elegance.

guardful /ˈgɑːdfʊl, -f(ə)l/ *a.* Now *rare* or *obs.* exc. *dial.* E17. [f. GUARD *n.* + -FUL.] Watchful; careful.

guardfully *adv.* E17.

guardia civil /gwarˌdia θiˈbil/ *n. phr.* Pl. ***guardias civiles*** /gwarˌdias θiˈbiles/. M19. [Sp. = civil guard.] (A member of) a police force in Spain organized on military lines.

guardian /ˈgɑːdɪən/ *n.* LME. [AN *gardein*, OFr. *garden*, earlier *gardenc* (mod. *gardien*, w. assim. of suff. to *-ien* -IAN, which was followed in Eng.), f. Frank., f. Gmc base of WARD *n.* Cf. WARDEN *n.*[1]] **1** A keeper, a defender, a protector; *Hist.* (in full *Guardian of the Poor*) a member of a board elected to administer the poor laws in a parish or district. LME. **2** *spec.* in *Law.* A person who has custody of the person or property of a minor or other person deemed incapable of managing his or her own affairs; *esp.* one who has been given this by legal appointment. LME. 3 In various official titles, now superseded by WARDEN *n.*[1] *obs.* exc. *Hist.* LME. 4 The superior of a Franciscan convent. LME. 5 *Astron.* = GUARD *n.* 2b. Chiefly as *the Guardians* (*of the Pole*). M16.

1 F. WARNER So we, the guardians of Mosaic Law, .. Have killed the prophets? 2 V. NABOKOV Alabama prohibits a guardian from changing the ward's residence without an order of the court.

Comb.: **guardian angel** an angel conceived as watching over or protecting a particular person or place.

guardia'ness *n.* a female guardian E17. **guardianless** *a.* E17.

guardianship /ˈɡɑːdɪənʃɪp/ *n.* M16. [f. prec. + -SHIP.] 1 The condition or fact of being a guardian. M16. 2 Keeping, protection. M17.

guardias civiles *n. phr.* pl. of GUARDIA CIVIL.

guardless /ˈɡɑːdlɪs/ *a.* E17. [f. GUARD *n.* + -LESS.] 1 Undefended, unprotected. E17. 2 Off one's guard; careless. M17. 3 Esp. of a sword: having no guard. L19.

guardo /ˈɡɑːdəʊ/ *n.* Pl. **-os.** M19. [f. GUARD *n.* + *-o*, in imitation of Sp. wds.] *US Hist.* A receiving ship for enlisted men who are to be drafted to seagoing vessels.

guardship /ˈɡɑːdʃɪp/ *n. rare.* E17. [f. GUARD *n.* + -SHIP.] = GUARDIANSHIP.

guardy /ˈɡɑːdi/ *n. colloq.* M19. [f. GUARD *n.* + -Y[6].] = GUARDIAN 2.

guarea /ˈɡwɑːrɪə/ *n.* M20. [mod.L (see below) f. Cuban Sp. *guara.*] Any of various tropical hardwood trees of the genus *Guarea*, esp. the mainly W. African *G. cedrata* and *G. thompsonii*, which yield a pale timber like mahogany; this timber.

guariba /ɡwəˈriːbə/ *n.* M18. [(Port. & Sp. f.) Tupi *waˀriwa.*] A howler monkey.

†guarish *v.t.* L15–L16. [OFr. *g(u)ariss-* lengthened stem of *g(u)arir* (mod. *guérir*) f. Frank. vb cogn. w. WERE *v.*[1]: see -ISH[2]. Cf. GARRISON *n.*] Cure, heal.

Guarnerius /ɡwɑːˈnɪərɪəs/ *n.* M19. [*Guarnerius*, latinized form of Joseph *Guarnieri* del Gesù. Cf. JOSEPH 3.] A violin or cello made by a member of the Guarnerius family of Cremona, Italy, during the 17th and 18th cents.

guarri /ˈɡwari/ *n. S. Afr.* L18. [Nama *um-gwali.*] (The small succulent fruit of) any of various trees and shrubs of the genus *Euclea*, of the ebony family, esp. *E. undulata* and *E. crispa* var. *crispa.*

Guatemalan /ɡwɑːtəˈmɑːl(ə)n, ɡwa-/ *n.* & *a.* E19. [f. *Guatemala*: see below, -AN.] A *n.* A native or inhabitant of Guatemala, the northernmost country of Central America, bordering Mexico. E19. B *adj.* Of or pertaining to Guatemala. L19.

guava /ˈɡwɑːvə/ *n.* M16. [Sp. *guayaba, -abo*, of S. Amer. origin.] 1 Any of various tropical American evergreen trees and shrubs of the genus *Psidium*, of the myrtle family; esp. *P. guajava*, widely cultivated in tropical and subtropical regions for its edible fruit and freq. naturalized. M16. 2 The yellow pink-fleshed fruit of the guava, used to make jams, jellies, etc. M16.

Guaycuru /ɡwʌɪkʊˈruː/ *n.* & *a.* Also **Guai-.** E19. [Sp. f. Tupi, lit. 'fast runners'.] A *n.* Pl **-s**, same. 1 A member of a S. American Indian people inhabiting the Gran Chaco in Paraguay. E19. 2 The language of the Guaycurus or the language group of which their language is the principal member. M20. B *attrib. or as adj.* Of or pertaining to the Guaycurus or their language. L19.

Guaycuruan *n.* & *a.* (of or pertaining to) the language or language group Guaycuru E20.

guayule /ɡwʌɪˈuːli/ *n.* E20. [Amer. Sp. f. Nahuatl *cuauhuli.*] A silvery-leaved shrub of Mexico and Texas, *Parthenium argentatum*, of the composite family, formerly used as a source of rubber.

gubbin /ˈɡʌbɪn/ *n.* M16. [Var. of GOBBON.] 1 a A fragment. Usu. in *pl.*, shavings, fragments, esp. (formerly) of fish. *obs.* exc. *dial.* M16. b In *pl.* Unspecified articles; equipment, gear. Also (treated as *sing.*), a piece of equipment, a gadget. *slang.* E20. 2 In *pl.* (A *derog.* nickname for) the people living near Brent Tor, Dartmoor, formerly reputed to be like savages. *obs.* exc. *Hist.* M17. 3 In *pl.* (treated as *sing.*). A fool. *slang.* E20.

Gubbio /ˈɡʊbɪəʊ/ *a.* M19. [A town in Umbria, Italy.] Designating the majolica (esp. a ruby-lustred type) made in the 16th cent. at Gubbio.

gubble /ˈɡʌb(ə)l/ *v.i.* E20. [Imit.] Make an inarticulate gurgling or murmuring sound like 'gub'.

gubernaculum /ɡjuːbəˈnakjʊləm/ *n.* Pl. **-la** /-lə/. M17. [L = steering-oar, f. *gubernare* steer, govern: see GOVERN, -CULUM.] †1 Some part of an insect. Only in M17. 2 *Anat.* Each of a pair of fibrous strands in the male foetus that connect the testes to the scrotum and guide their descent into it. L18. 3 *Anat.* A band of fibrous tissue joining a permanent tooth follicle to the gum during the early development of the tooth. M19.

gubernacular *a.* L19.

gubernation /ɡjuːbəˈneɪʃ(ə)n/ *n.* Now *rare.* LME. [OFr., or L *gubernatio(n-)*, f. *gubernat-* pa. ppl stem of *gubernare* steer, govern: see prec., -ATION.] The action of controlling; government.

gubernative /ˈɡjuːbənətɪv/ *a.* Now *rare.* LME. [(OFr. *gubernatif, -ive* f.) late L *gubernativus*, f. L *gubernat-*: see prec., -IVE.] Concerned with government.

gubernator /ˈɡjuːbəneɪtə/ *n. rare.* E16. [L, f. *gubernat-*: see GUBERNATION, -ATOR.] A ruler, a governor.

gubernatorial /ɡjuːbənəˈtɔːrɪəl/ *a.* Chiefly *US.* M18. [f. as prec. + -AL[1].] Belonging to a governor (esp. the Governor of an American state) or the office of governor.

guddle /ˈɡʌd(ə)l/ *v.* Chiefly *Sc.* M17. [Origin unkn.] 1 *v.i.* Grope in the water for fish, as under the stones or banks of a stream. M17. 2 *v.t.* Catch (a fish) by groping in the water. E19.

guddler *n.* L19.

gudgeon /ˈɡʌdʒ(ə)n/ *n.*[1] ME. [OFr. *goujon* dim. of *gouge* GOUGE *n.*] 1 A device attached to a gate etc. incorporating a ring or socket into which the pin or hook on the post fits so as to form a hinge. ME. 2 A metallic pin or other device for screwing together slabs of stone. ME. 3 A pivot, usu. of metal, fixed on or let into the end of a beam, spindle, axle, etc., and on which a wheel turns, a bell swings, or the like. LME. 4 *Naut.* The socket in which the pintle of a rudder turns. M16.

gudgeon /ˈɡʌdʒ(ə)n/ *n.*[2] LME. [OFr. *goujon* f. L *gobio(n-)*, f. *gobius* GOBY.] 1 A small European freshwater fish, *Gobio gobio*, used as bait. LME. †b = GOBY *n.* L16–M19. 2 *fig.* A person easily imposed on; a dupe. L16. 3 A thing that is swallowed greedily or credulously; a bait. Chiefly *fig.*, esp. in *gape for gudgeons, swallow a gudgeon.* L16.

gudgeon /ˈɡʌdʒ(ə)n/ *v.* L18. [f. GUDGEON *n.*[2]] †1 *v.i.* Become a dupe. *slang.* Only in L18. 2 *v.t.* Defraud *of*; delude *into.* L18.

Guebre /ˈɡiːbə, ˈɡeɪbə/ *n.* L17. [Fr. *guèbre* f. Pers. *gabr*: see GIAOUR.] A Zoroastrian, a Parsee.

guelder rose /ˈɡɛldə rəʊz/ *n. phr.* L16. [Du. *geldersche roos*, f. *Gelderland* Dutch province, or its capital *Gelders.*] (The flower of) a deciduous shrub, *Viburnum opulus*, of the honeysuckle family, with leaves like those of the maple and cymes of creamy-white flowers, the outer of which are larger and sterile. Orig. *spec.*, the snowball tree, *V. opulus* var. *roseum.*

Guelph /ɡwɛlf/ *n.* & *a.* Also **Guelf.** L16. [It. *Guelfo* f. MHG *Welf*, (the founder of) one of the two great rival dynasties in the Holy Roman Empire.] A *n.* A member of the papal faction in the medieval Italian States. Opp. GHIBELLINE. L16. B *adj.* Of or adhering to the Guelph faction. M19.

Guelphic *a.* of the family or faction of the Guelphs E19.

guemal /ˈɡweɪm(ə)l/ *n.* Also **huemal** /ˈhweɪ-/. E19. [Sp. f. Araucanian *güemul, hüemul.*] Either of two small S. American deer, *Hippocamelus bisulcus* and *H. antisiensis*, with simply forked antlers.

guenon /ɡəˈnɒn/ *n.* M19. [Fr., of uncertain origin.] Any of a group of African monkeys with characteristic long tails and hind limbs, mostly belonging to the genus *Cercopithecus* and including the vervet.

guerdon /ˈɡəːd(ə)n/ *n.* & *v.* Now *poet.* & *literary.* LME. [OFr. *guer(e)don* f. Proto-Romance (med.L) *widerdonum* f. WGmc (= OHG *widarlōn*, OE *wiþerlēan*, f. *wiþer* again + *lēan* payment), with 2nd elem. assim. to L *donum* gift.] A *n.* A reward, a recompense. LME.

M. BEERBOHM The true conjurer finds his guerdon in the consciousness of work done perfectly.

B *v.t.* Reward; make compensation for. LME.

TENNYSON Him we gave a costly bribe To guerdon silence.

guerdonless *a.* LME.

guereza /ˈɡɛrɪzə/ *n.* M19. [Prob. Afr.] The eastern black and white colobus, *Colobus guereza*, a black monkey with a white patch on each side and at the tip of the tail that is found in parts of central Africa.

guéridon /ˈɡɛrɪd(ə)n, *foreign* ɡeridɔ̃/ *n.* M19. [Fr.] A small ornamental table or stand, usu. round, with a single central pedestal, and ornately carved.

guerilla *n.* var. of GUERRILLA.

guérite /ɡerit/ *n.* E18. [Fr.: see GARRET *n.*] *Hist.* A wooden or stone turret or box for a sentry.

Guernsey /ˈɡəːnzi/ *n.* L16. [The second largest of the Channel Islands. Cf. GANSEY.] I *attrib.* 1 Used *attrib.* to designate things found in or associated with Guernsey. L16.

1 **†Guernsey coat** = sense 2a below. **Guernsey cow** an animal of a breed of usu. brown and white dairy cattle that originated in Guernsey. **†Guernsey frock** = sense 2a below. **Guernsey lily** a southern African amaryllis, *Nerine sarniensis*, with umbels of red lily-like flowers, once believed to be naturalized in Guernsey. **†Guernsey shirt** = sense 2a below.

II *ellipt.* 2a (Also **g-.**) A close-fitting woollen sweater, *esp.* a navy blue one worn by sailors. E19. b (**g-.**) A usu. sleeveless shirt worn by an Australian Rules player. M20. 3 A Guernsey cow. M19.

2b get (or **draw**) **a guernsey** *Austral.* be selected for a team; *fig.* be successful; gain recognition; get mentioned, included, etc.

guerrilla /ɡəˈrɪlə/ *n.* & *a.* Also **guerilla.** E19. [Sp. dim. of *guerra* war: introduced into France and England during the Peninsular War (1808–14).] A *n.* 1 A person taking part in an irregular war waged by small bands operating independently (freq. against a stronger more organized force) with surprise attacks etc. E19. 2 A war waged by guerrillas. Now *rare.* E19.

1 *urban guerrilla*: see URBAN *a.*

B *attrib.* or as *adj.* Of fighting: carried on by small irregular bands. Of a person: taking part in such fighting. E19.

guerrillero /ɡɛrɪˈlɛːrəʊ/ *n.* Also **gueri-.** E19. [Sp., f. GUERRILLA.] = GUERRILLA *n.* 1.

Guesdist /ˈɡeɪdɪst/ *n.* L19. [f. *Guesde* (see below) + -IST.] A follower of the principles of revolutionary Marxism advocated by the French political leader Jules Guesde (1845–1922).

Guesdism *n.* the policy or principles of the Guesdists M20.

guess /ɡɛs/ *n.* Also **†ghess.** ME. [f. GUESS *v.*: cf. MDu. *gisse* (Du. *gis*).] The action or an act of guessing; an opinion not based on certain knowledge or exact calculation; a conjecture.

J. BUTLER Mere guess, supposition and possibility, when opposed to historical evidence, prove nothing. M. SHADBOLT I don't need three guesses to know what you're talking about.

Phrases: *anybody's guess*: see ANYBODY. **at a guess, by (one's) guess** at a rough estimate. **by guess and by God** (or **Godfrey**) *slang* (orig. *Naut.*) (to steer) blind, without the guidance of landmarks. **have (got) another guess coming** *colloq.* be destined to have one's expectations disappointed. **miss one's guess** *US* be mistaken in one's assumption. **my guess is** I am tolerably sure (*that*).

guess /gɛs/ *a.* (*attrib.*). *arch.* & *dial.* E19. [Use as independent wd of *-guess* in *anotherguess* s.v. ANOTHER, OTHERGUESS.] Kind or sort of.
Blackwood's Magazine He had no guess-idea of what bemused his vision.

guess /gɛs/ *v.* Also †**ghess**. ME. [Perh. orig. naut. and f. vars. with *-e-* of MLG, MDu. (Du., Fris.) *gissen*, or OSw. *gissa*, ODa. *gitse*, all ult. f. base of GET *v.* (cf. ON *geta* guess). The sps. with *gu-* and *gh-* date from 16: cf. GUEST *n.*] **1** *v.t.* Form a rough estimate of (an amount, size, distance, etc.) without actual measurement or calculation. ME. †**2** *v.i.* Take aim (foll. by *to*); purpose *to do*. ME–M16. †**3** *v.t.* (w. compl.). Consider to be; regard *as*. Only in ME. **4** *v.t.* Suppose, think; think it likely, believe. Foll. by cl. as obj. Long *obs.* exc. in *N. Amer. colloq.* in 1st person sing. (*I*) *guess*. LME. **5** *v.t.* & *i.* Form an opinion (about), or form the opinion *that*, on the basis of uncertain indications or none; hazard an opinion as to *why*, *who*, *whether*, etc.; estimate *to be*; conjecture. Also foll. by subord. cl., & †w. obj. & compl. LME. **6** *v.i.* Indulge in conjecture or speculation. Foll. by *at*: (attempt to) solve or discover by conjecture. LME. **7** *v.t.* & *i.* Conjecture rightly; solve (a riddle etc.), divine the nature of (a thing), by guesswork. M16.
1 J. TYNDALL The eye being liable to be grossly deceived in guessing the direction of a perpendicular. T. HARDY Guess my surprise when . . I received a mysterious note. 4 R. MACDONALD 'May I come in for a minute?' 'I guess so.' W. WHARTON Joe knows everybody, everywhere. I guess that's part of being a cop. M. CALLAGHAN There's no harm in you talking to Mother if you want to, I guess. 5 SHAKES. *1 Hen. VI* Discover . . what cause that was, For I am ignorant and cannot guess. G. A. BIRMINGHAM I should guess the island to be about two miles around. E. O'NEILL Guess which one of Mamie's charmers I picked. J. UPDIKE Nelson guesses she's three or four years younger than he is. J. RATHBONE I did not need to listen, for already I had guessed her tale. I. WALLACE Dilman guessed that there must be more than three thousand persons present. 6 J. RABAN People could only guess at the total amounts involved. V. WOOLF Lye seemed to hold infinite possibilities she had never guessed at. A. BURGESS Laurence had a great capacity to see into things, to guess and be proved right. 7 H. BUSHNELL But which is worse . . it is not difficult, I think, to guess. DICKENS Sure enough it's Barnaby—how did you guess? G. GREENE The others had to guess his wish by asking questions.
Phrases: **guessing game** a game in which much of the playing consists of guessing; *fig.* a situation in which one is kept constantly in the dark. **keep a person guessing** *colloq.* (orig. *US*) keep a person in a state of uncertainty about one's feelings, future intentions, etc.
guessable *a.* E19. **guesser** *n.* LME. **guessingly** *adv.* by guesswork E17.

guess-rope *n.* var. of GUEST-ROPE.

guesstimate /*as n.* ˈgɛstɪmət, *as vb* ˈgɛstɪmeɪt/ *n.* & *v.* Orig. *US*. Also **guest-**. M20. [f. GUESS *n.*, *v.* + ESTIMATE *n.*, *v.*] **A** *n.* An estimate based more on guesswork than calculation. M20. **B** *v.t.* & *i.* Form a guesstimate (of). M20.

guess-warp /ˈgɛswɔːp/ *n.* L15. [f. unkn. 1st elem. + WARP *n.*: cf. GUEST-ROPE.] **1** A rope carried to a distant object in order to warp a vessel towards it, or make fast a boat. L15. **2** = GUEST-ROPE 2. M19.

guess work /ˈgɛswəːk/ *n.* E18. [f. GUESS *n.* + WORK *n.*] (Procedure based on) guessing, as opp. to knowledge or reasoning.

guest /gɛst/ *n.* ME. [ON *gestr*, superseding OE *ġiest*, *gest* = OS, OHG (Du., G) *gast*, Goth. *gasts*, f. Gmc, f. an IE base repr. also by L *hostis* enemy, (orig.) stranger. The spelling *gu-* (L16) marks the hard *g*, like the earlier var. with *gh*: cf. GUESS *v.*] **1** A person staying in another's house etc. at his or her invitation; a person having a meal at the expense of another. ME. †**2** A stranger. ME–L16. **3** A person having (temporary) accommodation in a hotel, inn, or boarding-house. ME. **4** A person (of a specified kind), a fellow. Long *obs.* exc. *dial.* ME. **5** An object regarded as an omen of an approaching stranger. *local.* E18. **6** A parasitic organism. M19. **7** An occasional performer appearing by special invitation with a company other than his or her regular one. E20.
1 E. WAUGH Father Aelred Watkin came to stay. A very agreeable guest. P. H. JOHNSON She took out her purse to pay the bill, forgetting she was my guest. **be my guest!** *colloq.* you are welcome (to take the action indicated)! **guest of honour** the chief guest at a dinner or other function. **paying guest** a lodger.
Attrib. & *comb.*: In the sense 'reserved or suitable for the use of guests in a house', as *guest-chamber*, *-hall*, *-room*, *-towel*; in the sense 'performing or appearing as a guest (sense 7)', as *guest artist*, *conductor*, *star*; 'involving such a performer', as *guest appearance*. Special combs., as **guest-house** a house where strangers are accommodated; now usu., a (superior) boarding-house, esp. one catering for holiday-makers; **guest list** a list of the people invited to a function; **guest-master** a member of a monastery or other religious establishment who looks after guests; **guest-night**: on which members of a club, college, mess, etc., bring guests to dinner; **guest speaker** a public speaker entertained to a dinner at which he or she gives an address; **guest-worker** [tr. G *Gastarbeiter*] a person with temporary permission to work in another country, esp. Germany.
guestless *a.* having no guests; [tr. Gk *axenos*] inhospitable: L16. **guestship** *n.* the status of a guest M19.

guest /gɛst/ *v.* ME. [f. the n.] **1** *v.t.* Receive as a guest. ME. **2** *v.i.* Lodge or enjoy hospitality as a guest. *rare.* LME. **3** *v.i.* Appear in a show or programme as a guest performer or star. M20.
3 *Melody Maker* Ian Carr guested with the Roy Budd Trio . . on Saturday.

guesten /ˈgɛst(ə)n/ *a.* *arch.* L15. [Perh. repr. ME genit. pl. of GUEST *n.*] Reserved for guests. Only in *guesten chamber*, *hall*.

guesten /ˈgɛst(ə)n, ˈgɛs(ə)n/ *v.t.* & *i.* Long *arch.* *rare.* Orig. †**gesten**. ME. [f. GUEST *n.* + -EN[5] or back-form. f. GESTENING.] = GUEST *v.* 1, 2.

guestimate *n.* & *v.* var. of GUESSTIMATE.

guest-rope /ˈgɛstrəʊp/ *n.* Also **guess-rope**. E17. [The first elem. may be a var. of *guess-* in GUESS-WARP, to which *guest-rope* may be a later parallel formation.] **1** A second rope, fastened to a boat in tow, to keep it steady. E17. **2** A stout rope slung outside a vessel fore and aft (formerly also fastened to the end of a boom) to give a hold for boats coming alongside. L18.

guestwise /ˈgɛstwʌɪz/ *n.* & *adv.* Now *rare* or *obs.* LME. [f. GUEST *n.* + -WISE.] †**A** *n.* *in*, *on guestwise* = sense B. below. LME–M17. **B** *adv.* As a guest. L16.

gueux /gø/ *n.pl.* E17. [Fr., pl. of *gueux* ragamuffin, beggar.] *Hist.* The Dutch nobles who in 1566 petitioned Margaret, Governess of the Netherlands, on behalf of Protestants; the Dutch and Flemish Protestant partisans who subsequently fought against Spain in the wars of the 16th cent.

Guevarist /gɪˈvɑːrɪst/ *a.* & *n.* M20. [f. *Guevara* (see below) + -IST.] **A** *adj.* Of, pertaining to, or characteristic of the S. American revolutionary and guerilla leader Ernesto ('Che') Guevara (1928–67) or his beliefs. M20. **B** *n.* A follower of Guevara. M20.
Guevarism *n.* the political principles or actions of Guevara or his followers M20.

gufa /ˈgʊfə/ *n.* Also †**kuphar**. E19. [Arab., dial. var. of *quffa* large basket.] A Mesopotamian round boat made of straw and palm branches.

guff /gʌf/ *n.* E19. [Imit.: cf. Norw. dial. *gufs* puff of wind, *guffa* blow softly.] **1** A whiff, esp. of a bad smell; a puff of wind, vapour, etc. *Sc.* E19. **2** Empty or meaningless verbiage. *colloq.* (orig. *US*). L19.

guffaw /gəˈfɔː/ *n.* & *v.* Orig. *Sc.* E18. [Imit.] **A** *n.* A coarse or boisterous laugh. E18. **B** *v.* **1** *v.i.* Laugh coarsely or boisterously. E18. **2** *v.t.* Say with a guffaw. M19.

guffer /ˈgʌfə/ *n.* *Sc.* E19. [Origin unkn.] The viviparous blenny, *Zoarces viviparus*.

guga /ˈguːgə/ *n.* *Sc.* M19. [Gael.] A young gannet.

gugelhupf /ˈguːgəlhʊpf/ *n.* Also ***gugl-***; ***kugel-*** /ˈkuːgəl-/. Pl. **-e** /-ə/. L19. [G; the form w. *k* is f. dial.] A light Austrian cake baked in a ring-shaped mould.

Guggenheim /ˈgʊg(ə)nhʌɪm/ *a.* & *n.* M20. [John Simon *Guggenheim*, in whose memory his father Simon Guggenheim (1867–1941), US Senator and industrialist, established the Guggenheim Foundation in 1925.] **A** *adj.* Designating any of the fellowships awarded annually by the John Simon Guggenheim Memorial Foundation for creative work in the arts and for advanced study and research. M20. **B** *n.* A Guggenheim fellowship or award. M20.

guggle /ˈgʌg(ə)l/ *n.* L17. [f. the vb.] **1** The windpipe. *obs.* exc. *dial.* L17. **2** A guggling sound. E19.

guggle /ˈgʌg(ə)l/ *v.* E17. [Imit.] **1** *v.i.* Make a sound like that of liquid pouring from a small-necked bottle; flow with such a sound. E17. **2** Bring *up* or pour *forth* with a guggling sound. M18.

guglhupf *n.* var. of GUGELHUPF.

guglia /ˈguːljə/ *n.* Also **-glio** /-ljəʊ/, pl. **-os**. M17. [It., aphet. var. of *agulia*, lit. 'needle'. Cf. med.L *aculea*.] An obelisk, esp. in Italy.

guhr /guːr, gʊə/ *n.* L18. [G dial., lit. 'ferment'.] A loose earthy deposit from water found in the cavities of rocks.

Guianese /gʌɪəˈniːz, gɪə-/ *n.* & *a.* M19. [f. *Guiana* (see below) + -ESE. Cf. GUYANESE.] **A** *n.* Pl. same. A native or inhabitant of Guiana, a tropical region in north-eastern S. America. M19. **B** *adj.* Of or pertaining to Guiana. L19.
Guianan /gʌɪˈanən, gɪˈɑːnən/ *n.* & *a.* (*a*) *n.* a Guianese; (*b*) *adj.* = GUIANESE *a.*: M19. **Guianian** /gɪˈɑːnɪən/ *n.* & *a.* = GUIANAN E17.

guib /gwɪb/ *n.* L18. [Wolof.] = *bushbuck* s.v. BUSH *n.*[1]

guichet /ˈgiːʃeɪ/ *n.* M19. [Fr.] A wicket, a hatch; *esp.* one through which tickets are sold.

guid *n.*, *a.*, *v.*, *adv.* see GOOD *n.*, *a.*, etc.

guidance /ˈgʌɪd(ə)ns/ *n.* M16. [f. GUIDE *v.* + -ANCE.] **1** The action of guiding; leadership, direction; *spec.* counselling or advice about marriage problems, career decisions, etc. M16. **b** The control of a missile or spacecraft in its course. M20. **2** Something which guides. E18.
1 R. ELLMANN He looked to Ruskin for spiritual guidance. N. SYMINGTON With guidance from Winnicott the family was able to cope with his need. b *attrib.*: *Listener* The shuttle had been given four separate guidance computers.

guide /gʌɪd/ *n.* LME. [(O)Fr., alt. of OFr. †*guie* (whence GUY *n.*[1]), f. *guider* GUIDE *v.*] **I 1** A person or thing which shows the way; *spec.* (*a*) a person who conducts less experienced mountaineers; (*b*) a person (usu. hired) who indicates and gives information on objects of interest in a city, building, etc., to a tourist. LME. **b** *Mil.* A person employed to give information to an invading army about the enemy's country; a member of a reconnaissance group; a soldier, vehicle, or ship whose movements are taken as a guide for the movement and formation of others. M16. **c** (Usu. **G-**.) A member of an organization of girls similar to the Scouts, known as the Guides Association. Orig. *Girl Guide*. E20. **2** An adviser, a director; a directing principle or standard. Formerly also, a ruler, a leader. LME. **b** *Spiritualism.* = CONTROL *n.* 4b. M19. **3a** A manual or book of instruction on a specified subject. E17. **b** A book of information on a city, building, etc., for the use of tourists. Also *guidebook*. M18. **4a** An object which steadies or guides by physical contact the motion of a tool or machine part. L17. **b** *Sci.* A linear structure or a surface along or over which an electromagnetic wave is propagated and to which it is confined; *spec.* a waveguide. L19. **5** Something which marks a position or guides the eye. L19.
1 R. KIPLING He was an agreeable guide, ever keen to point out the beauties of his royal master's domain. E. BAKER A pretty, uniformed guide . . told him the tours didn't begin until ten o'clock. **c King's** or **Queen's Guide** a Guide who has reached the highest rank of proficiency. *Ranger Guide*: see RANGER *n.* 4. *Queen's Guide*: see *King's Guide* above. 2 A. MASON

He was looking for a guide, a teacher. 4 R. CARVER He threaded the line through the guides of his rod.

II 6 The action of GUIDE *v.*; direction, guidance. Now *rare*. E16.

6 SHAKES. *Timon* Pray entertain them; give them guide to us.

Comb.: **guide-board** a sign in a road indicating the way; *guidebook*: see sense 3b above; **guide dog**: trained to lead a blind person; **guide fossil** = *index fossil* s.v. INDEX *n.*; **Guide Law** a code of conduct enjoined on a Guide to which a member must promise obedience; **guideline** a line for guiding; *fig.* a directing or standardizing principle laid down as a guide to procedure, policy, etc.; **guidepost** a signpost; **guide-rope** (*a*) a small rope attached to the load of a crane, by which its movement may be guided; (*b*) a rope trailed by a balloon or small airship to assist in maintaining a constant altitude by the drag of part of the rope on the ground; (*c*) any of several ropes used to steady an airship before flight; **Guide's honour** the oath taken by a Guide, used as a protestation of honour and sincerity; **guideway** a groove, a track.

guideless *a.* L15.

guide /gʌɪd/ *v.t.* LME. [(O)Fr. *guider* alt. of †*guier* (whence GUY *v.*[1]), f. Proto-Romance f. Gmc, f. alt. of base of WIT *v.*] 1 Act or serve as a guide to; go with or before to lead the way. LME. 2†a Lead, command, (an army, soldiers). LME–M16. b Manage, control, (money, property, a process). Now *Sc.* LME. c Manage the affairs of (a household, a state). Long *rare*. LME. 3 Lead or direct in a course of action, the formation of opinions, etc.; influence; advise; be the principle, motive, or ground of (an action, judgement, etc.). LME. 4 Direct the motion or course of (something inanimate). LME. 5 Treat or handle (a person) in a specified way. *Sc.* & *north.* E18.

1 R. H. MOTTRAM She dropped her things, and, guided by George's voice, found the bedroom. N. SHUTE He took her arm to guide her through the Saturday evening crowds. **guided tour**: led by or having a guide in charge. 2b SIR W. SCOTT Them that sells the goods guide the purse—them that guide the purse rule the house. 3 O. SITWELL Policy is guided by feeling, not by cold reason. M. MCCARTHY She wanted to guide Dottie to discover her own real feelings. 4 J. B. PRIESTLEY Long rows of sewing machines worked by electric power but guided by hand. R. V. JONES Bosch was to design the radio beam system that guided some of the V-2 rockets. **guided missile**: operating by remote control or as directed automatically by equipment inside it. **guiding telescope** a visual telescope fixed to a photographic telescope so that the latter can be manually made to follow a star etc. kept in position in the field of view of the former during an exposure.

guidable *a.* L17.

guider /ˈgʌɪdə/ *n.* LME. [In sense 1 f. GUIDE *v.*, in sense 2 f. GUIDE *n.*: see -ER[1].] 1 A person who or thing which guides someone or something. LME. 2 (**G-**.) An adult leader of the Guides (GUIDE *n.* 1c). Orig. *Girl Guider*. E20.

guidguid *n.* var. of HUET-HUET.

guiding /ˈgʌɪdɪŋ/ *n.* LME.[In sense 1 f. GUIDE *v.*, in sense 2 f. GUIDE *n.*: see -ING[1].] 1 The action or practice of GUIDE *v.* LME. 2 The characteristic activity and occupation of a Guide (GUIDE *n.* 1c). Also the Guide movement itself. E20.

guidon /ˈgʌɪd(ə)n/ *n.* M16. [Fr. f. It. *guidone*, f. *guida* guide: see -OON.] 1 A pennant narrowing to a point or fork at the free end, esp. as used as the standard of a regiment or (*US*) a troop of cavalry. M16. 2 An officer who carries a guidon. L16.

Guidonian /gwɪˈdəʊnɪən/ *a.* E18. [f. *Guidon-* taken as stem of *Guido* (see below) + -IAN.] *Mus.* Of or pertaining to the 11th-cent. Italian musician Guido d'Arezzo, the reputed inventor of the system of hexachords. Chiefly in *Guidonian hand*, a drawing of the left hand marked with the degrees of the scale and the solmization according to the system devised by Guido.

guige /giːʒ/ *n.* LME. [(O)Fr.] *Hist.* A strap passing over the neck or shoulder and serving as an additional support for a medieval soldier's shield.

Guignet's green /ˈgiːnjeɪz ˈgriːn/ *n. phr.* M19. [C. E. *Guignet*, 19th-cent. Fr. chemist.] = VIRIDIAN *n.*

Guignol /giːˈnjɒl/ *n.* L19. [Fr. = Punch.] In France, (a) marionette drama resembling Punch and Judy. Also = GRAND GUIGNOL.

guignoˈlesque *a.* resembling or characteristic of (Grand) Guignol M20.

guild /gɪld/ *n.*[1] Also (in sense 1) **gild**. LOE. [Prob. f. MLG, MDu. *gilde* (Du. *gild*) f. Gmc; rel. to OE *gi(e)ld* payment, offering, sacrifice, idol, (also) guild (continued in ME as *ȝild*, *yeld*), OFris. *geld*, *ield* money, OS *geld* payment, sacrifice, reward, OHG *gelt* payment, tribute (Du., G *Geld* money), ON *gjald* payment and *gildi* guild, payment, Goth. *gild* tribute, f. Gmc.] 1 An organization formed for the mutual aid and protection of its members, or for the furtherance of some common purpose; *esp.* (occas. **gild**) a medieval association of craftsmen or merchants. LOE. b *gen.* A company, a fellowship. M17. †2 The meeting-place of a guild; the home of a religious guild. LOE–M17. 3 *Ecol.* A group of species which have similar roles in the same community. E20.

Comb.: **guild-brother** a man who belongs to a guild; **guildhall** a hall in which a medieval guild met; a town hall; (*Guildhall*) the building in the City of London used by the Corporation of the City for meetings, banquets, etc.; **guild socialism** an economic system in which the resources, methods, and profits of each industry are controlled by a council of its members.

guildry *n.* (*Sc.*) (*a*) the municipal corporation of a Scottish royal burgh; †(*b*) = GUILDSHIP 2: E16.

guild *n.*[2] var. of GILD *n.*[1]

†**guild** *v.* see GILD *v.*[2]

guildable *a.* & *n.* see GILDABLE.

guilder /ˈgɪldə/ *n.* LME. [Alt. of Du. GULDEN.] Orig., a gold coin of the Netherlands and parts of Germany; now, the basic monetary unit of the Netherlands, the Netherlands Antilles, and Suriname, equal to 100 cents or a note or coin of the value of this.

guildship /ˈgɪldʃɪp/ *n.* [OE *gieldscipe*, f. as GUILD *n.*[1], -SHIP.] 1 = GUILD *n.*[1] 1. OE. 2 Membership of a guild. M16.

guile /gʌɪl/ *n.* ME. [OFr. f. ON: see WILE *n.*] 1 Insidious cunning, deceit, treachery. ME. †2 An instance of this, a trick, a stratagem. ME–M18.

1 B. PYM Was he being sarcastic? . . he was too nice a man for that, too lacking in guile.

guile /gʌɪl/ *v.t.* *arch.* ME. [(O)Fr. *guiler*, f. as prec. Cf. WILE *v.*] Beguile, deceive.

guileful /ˈgʌɪlfʊl, -f(ə)l/ *a.* Now *literary*. ME. [f. GUILE *n.* + -FUL.] Full of guile; deceitful.

guilefully *adv.* LME. **guilefulness** *n.* LME.

guileless /ˈgʌɪllɪs/ *a.* E18. [f. GUILE *n.* + -LESS.] Devoid of guile; artless, innocent.

guilelessly *adv.* E18. **guilelessness** *n.* E18.

†**guiler** *n.* ME–L16. [OFr. *guileor*, *gyllour*, f. as GUILE *v.*: see -OUR, -ER[2].] A beguiler, a deceiver.

†**guilery** *n.* var. of GILLERY.

Guillain-Barré syndrome /gijanˈbareɪ ˈsɪndrəʊm/ *n. phr.* M20. [f. G. *Guillain* (1876–1961) and J. *Barré* (1880–1967), Fr. physicians, two of those who first described the disease.] *Med.* An acute infectious form of polyneuritis, with temporary paralysis.

guillaume /ˈgiːləm, *foreign* gijoːm/ *n.* Also (*Sc.*) **geelum** /ˈgiːləm/. E19. [Fr. = William.] A rabbet plane.

guillem /ˈgɪləm, ˈgwɪ-/ *n.* E17. [Welsh *Gwilym* William, (as common n.) guillemot. Cf. next.] = next.

guillemot /ˈgɪlmɒt/ *n.* L17. [Fr., dim. of *Guillaume* William.] Any of several diving sea birds of northern latitudes constituting the genera *Uria* and *Cepphus*, of the auk family, with black (or brown) and white plumage and pointed bills; *spec.* (also *common guillemot*) *Uria aalge*. Cf. MURRE.

black guillemot *Cepphus grylle*, with less white than the common guillemot. BRÜNNICH'S GUILLEMOT.

guilloche /gɪˈləʊʃ, -ˈlɒʃ/ *n.* M19. [Fr. *guillochis* guilloche, or *guilloche* the tool used in making it.] An architectural or metalwork ornament imitating braided or twisted ribbons.

guillotine /ˈgɪlətiːn, gɪləˈtiːn/ *n.* L18. [Fr., f. Joseph-Ignace *Guillotin*, Fr. physician (1738–1814) who suggested its use for executions in 1789.] 1 An instrument for beheading consisting of a weighted blade with a diagonal edge which is allowed to drop between two tall grooved uprights, used in France esp. during the Revolution. L18. b *the guillotine*, execution by means of a guillotine. M19. 2 A surgical instrument with a blade that slides in a long groove, suitable for excising tonsils etc. M19. 3 A machine with a long blade for cutting paper; a machine for cutting other material. L19. 4 A method used in a legislative assembly for preventing obstruction or delays by fixing the times at which different parts of a bill must be voted on. L19.

guillotine /ˈgɪlətiːn, gɪləˈtiːn/ *v.t.* L18. [Fr. *guillotiner*, f. as prec.] 1 Behead by means of a guillotine. L18. 2 Cut with a guillotine; *fig.* cut short. L19.

guilt /gɪlt/ *n.* [OE *gylt*; ult. origin unkn.] †1 A failure of duty, an offence, a sin. OE–LME. †2 Responsibility for an action or event; the fault *of*. OE–L17. †3 Desert (*of* a penalty). OE–E17. 4 The fact or state of having (wilfully) committed, or of being guilty of, a crime or moral offence; guiltiness, culpability. OE. b An instance, kind, or degree of guilt. *rare*. LME. c A feeling or sense of being guilty. L17. d Conduct involving guilt; sin; crime. E18.

4 H. H. WILSON Positive proof of his guilt could not be adduced. **guilt by association** guilt ascribed to a person not because of any evidence but because of his or her association with an offender. c C. G. WOLFF The guilt Wharton felt in fighting free of Lucretia . . cannot easily be dismissed.

guiltless /ˈgɪltlɪs/ *a.* & *n.* ME. [f. GUILT + -LESS.] A *adj.* 1 Free from guilt; innocent. (Foll. by *of*.) ME. 2 Having no knowledge or experience *of* something. M17.

1 T. GRAY Some Cromwell, guiltless of his country's blood. 2 L. CARR Distinguishing it from other farmhouses, which were guiltless of that special ornamentation.

B *absol.* as *n.* Guiltless people as a class. Now only with *the*. ME.

guiltlessly *adv.* LME. **guiltlessness** *n.* L16.

guilty /ˈgɪlti/ *a.* & *n.* [OE *gyltiġ*, f. as GUILT: see -Y[1].] A *adj.* 1 That has incurred guilt; deserving punishment; criminal, culpable. Formerly also, that has offended or been at fault. OE. 2 That has committed a particular offence or crime, or is justly chargeable with a particular fault. (Foll. by *of*.) ME. †3 Foll. by *of*: culpably responsible for, to blame for. ME–E18. †4 Deserving *of*, liable *to*, (a penalty). LME–M17. 5 Of an action or condition: involving guilt, culpable, criminal. L16. 6 Conscious of or prompted by guilt. L16. †7 Conscious, cognizant, (*of*, *to*). L16–L17.

1 WOODES ROGERS We put ten of the Mutineers in Irons . . . Others less guilty I punish'd and discharg'd. *transf.*: BYRON He hangs his guilty head. 2 H. JAMES I indignantly protest that I am never guilty of *that* clumsiness. *Sunday Express* An Old Bailey jury found Patrick Reilly . . not guilty. 6 P. H. GIBBS 'I feel a little guilty in eating cream buns,' said Maria Theresa. *guilty* CONSCIENCE.

B *absol. as n.* 1 Guilty people as a class. Now only w. *the*. LME. †2 A guilty person. Usu. w. *the*. M16–E18.

guiltily *adv.* L16. **guiltiness** *n.* the condition, quality, or state of being or feeling guilty; an instance of this: LME.

guimauve /gɪˈməʊv, *foreign* gimoːv/ *n.* E19. [Fr.] The marsh mallow, *Althaea officinalis*; a medicinal preparation made from the root of this.

guimp *n.* var. of GIMP *n.*[1], GUIMPE.

guimpe /gɪmp, *foreign* gɛ̃ːp/ *n.* Also **guimp**. M19. [Fr.: cf. GIMP *n.*[2], WIMPLE *n.*] A high-necked chemisette; a blouse designed for wearing under a low-necked dress.

Guinea /ˈgɪni/ *n.* M16. [Orig. a region bordering part of the west coast of Africa; now a State on that coast.] I Also **g-** in certain combs. 1 Used *attrib.* to designate persons or things from Guinea or W. Africa. M16. 2a A Black person, *esp.* one recently arrived from Africa. *US* (now

Hist.). E19. b An immigrant of Italian or Spanish origin. *US slang. derog.* L19.

1 **Guinea corn** any of several varieties of sorghum, *Sorghum bicolor*, esp. durra. **guinea-fowl** any of numerous gallinaceous birds of sub-Saharan Africa of the subfamily Numidinae (family Phasianidae), with wattles and a head and neck largely bare of feathers; *spec.* (also *helmeted guinea*) *Numida meleagris*, a species domesticated throughout the world. **Guinea grass** a tall African grass, *Panicum maximum*, grown as fodder, esp. in tropical America. **guinea-hen** †(*a*) a turkey, *esp.* a female; (*b*) a guinea-fowl, *esp.* a female; †(*c*) *slang* a prostitute. *Guinea* LINSANG **Guineaman** (*a*) *Hist.* a ship trading to the Guinea coast; a slave ship; (*b*) (a man descended from) a Black man from Guinea. **Guinea Negro** = sense 2a. *Guinea peach*: see PEACH *n.*[1] 2(a). **Guinea pepper**: see PEPPER *n.* **Guinea worm** a nematode worm, *Dracunculus medinensis*, up to several feet long, which lives under the skin (usu. of the legs) of infected people in rural parts of tropical Africa and Asia.

II **g-**. 3 *Hist.* A British gold coin with a nominal value of a pound first struck in 1663 for the African trade, and from 1717 legal tender in Britain with a value fixed at 21 shillings. M16. 4 A sum of money equal to 21 shillings or £1.05. Now only used in stating professional fees, auction prices, etc. L17.

Comb.: **guinea flower** any of various Australian shrubs of the genus *Hibbertia* (family Dilleniaceae), with flat golden or white flowers.

Guinean /ˈgɪnɪən/ *n.* & *a.* L16. [f. GUINEA + -AN.] A *n.* A native or inhabitant of Guinea or a country whose name contains 'Guinea'. L16. B *adj.* Of or pertaining to such a region or country. E17.

guinea-pig /ˈgɪnɪpɪg/ *n.* M17. [f. GUINEA + PIG *n.*[1]] 1 A tailless dumpy rodent, *Cavia porcellus*, now found only in captivity as a pet or a subject for biological research, but related to the wild cavies of S. America. M17. b A person who or thing which is used as a subject for experiment or to test something. E20. 2 A midshipman on board an East Indiaman (*Hist.*); a young or inefficient seaman. M18. 3 A recipient of a fee, esp. one of a guinea; *spec.* a director of a company appointed chiefly because of the prestige of his or her name or title. *colloq.* E19. 4 An evacuee or billetee in the war of 1939–45. *colloq.* (now *Hist.*). M20.

guinep /gɪˈnɛp/ *n.* Also **genip** /gɛˈnɪp/, **ginep**, **kinep** /kɪˈnɛp/. M18. [Amer. Sp. *quenepo* guinep tree, *quenepa* its fruit, both f. Arawak.] (The fruit of) the W. Indian tree *Melicoccus bijugatus* (family Sapindaceae). Also called *Spanish lime*.

guinguette /gɛ̃gɛt/ *n.* Pl. pronounced same. M18. [Fr.] Chiefly *Hist.* A garden where public entertainment, esp. drinking and dancing, is provided.

†**guiniad** *n.* var. of GWYNIAD.

Guinness /ˈgɪnɪs/ *n.* M19. [Family name.] (Proprietary name for) a brand of stout manufactured by the firm of Guinness; a bottle or glass of this.

guinzo *n.* var. of GINZO.

guipure /gɪˈpjʊə/ *n.* M19. [Fr., f. *guiper* cover with silk, wool, etc., f. Gmc base meaning 'wind round'.] A kind of openwork lace in which the motifs are connected by brides.

guira /ˈgwʌɪrə/ *n.* M19. [Amer. Sp. f. Tupi *wiʼra* bird.] In full *guira cuckoo*. A non-parasitic cuckoo, *Guira guira*, of eastern S. America.

guiro /ˈgwʌɪrəʊ/ *n.* L19. [Sp. = gourd.] A gourd with an artificially serrated surface which gives a rasping sound when scraped with a stick, used (orig. in Latin America) as a musical instrument.

guisard /ˈgʌɪzəd/ *n.* & *v.* E17. [f. GUISE *v.* + -ARD.] = GUISER.

guise /gʌɪz/ *n.* & *v.* ME. [(O)Fr. f. Proto-Romance f. Frank. (= OS *wīsa*) f. Gmc base repr. also by WISE *n.*[1]] A *n.* †1 Manner, method; style. ME–L18. †2 Custom, habit, practice. ME–E18. 3 Behaviour, conduct. ME. 4 Style or fashion of dress or personal appearance; costume, garb. *arch.* ME. 5 External appearance, aspect; assumed appearance, pretence. ME. 6 A disguise, a mask. Hence, a masquerade, a show. *Sc.* E16.

1 W. COWPER And thus unto the Calender In merry guise he spoke. 4 BYRON Thou know me? in this guise Thou canst not know me. 5 W. S. CHURCHILL This was a peace proposal in martial guise. W. C. WILLIAMS The witch . . . made these weird visits to the sufferer, in the guise of a cat. A. BURGESS Sex and violence under the guise of a lesson in morality.

B *v.* Also **guize**. 1 *v.t.* Dress, esp. fantastically; dress up. LME. 2 *v.t.* Disguise. *Sc.* & *north.* E16. 3 *v.i.* Go about in disguise or fantastic dress. Chiefly *Sc.* & *north.* M19.

guising *n.* the action of the vb; a masquerade, a mummery: M16.

guiser /ˈgʌɪzə/ *n.* & *v.* Also **guizer**. L15. [f. GUISE *v.* + -ER[1].] A *n.* A masquerader, a mummer. Cf. GUISARD. L15.

G. PRIESTLAND The guisers would come round performing the play of St. George and the Dragon.

B *v.i.* Masquerade; go mumming. E20.

Guisian /ˈgiːzɪən/ *n.* & *a.* M16. [f. Fr. (*duc de*) *Guise* + -IAN.] *Hist.* A *n.* A supporter of the faction led by the Catholic Ducs de Guise in 16th-cent. France. M16. B *adj.* Of or pertaining to the Guisians. L16.

guitar /gɪˈtɑː/ *n.* & *v.* Also (earlier) †**guitarra**. E17. [Orig. f. Sp. *guitarra*, later f. Fr. *guitare* (superseding OFr. *guiterne* GITTERN) f. Sp. *guitarra* f. Gk *kithara* (adopted in L as *cithara*, whence Prov. *cedra*, It. *cetera*, OHG *cithara* (G *Zither*)): cf. CITHERN, CITOLE, ZITHER.] A *n.* A usu. six-stringed musical instrument, orig. and often still with a waisted body, played with the fingers or with a plectrum. E17.

bass guitar, *classical guitar*, *folk guitar*, *metal guitar*, etc. *electric guitar*: see ELECTRIC *a.* *Hawaiian guitar*: see HAWAIIAN *a.* *Spanish guitar*: see SPANISH *a.*

Comb.: **guitar-fish** any fish of the family Rhinobatidae, comprising bottom-dwelling cartilaginous fishes of tropical and subtropical oceans, like rays with fiddle-shaped bodies.

B *v.i.* Play the guitar. E19.

guitarist *n.* a person who plays the guitar L18.

guiver *n.* var. of GUYVER.

guize *v.*, **guizer** *n.* vars. of GUISE *v.* etc.

Gujarat /guːdʒəˈrɑːt, gʊ-/ *n.* Also **-jer-**. L16. [Hind. *Gujarāt*: see next.] = GUJARATI *n.* 1.

Gujarati /guːdʒəˈrɑːti, gʊ-/ *a.* & *n.* Also **-jer-**. E19. [Hind. *Gujarātī* (Skt *Gurjara*): see -I[2].] A *adj.* Of or pertaining to Gujarat, a State in western India, its people, or their language. E19. B *n.* Pl. same, **-s**. 1 A native or inhabitant of Gujarat. M19. 2 The Indo-Aryan language of Gujarat. M19.

Gujerat *n.*, **-ati** *a.* & *n.* vars. of GUJARAT, -ATI.

gul /gʊl/ *n.* E19. [Pers.] 1 A flower; *esp.* a rose. Freq. in *gardens of gul*. *poet.* E19. 2 A large geometrical motif derived from the shape of the rose that forms part of the design of a Turkoman rug. E20.

gula /ˈgjuːlə/ *n.*[1] LME. [L = throat, appetite. Cf. GULE *n.*[1]] †1a The external throat; the gullet. Only in LME. b An animal's gullet. *rare.* Only in M17. †2 Gluttony. Only in LME. 3 A sclerite on the lower middle part of an insect's head, between the two genae. E19.

gula *n.*[2] see GOLA *n.*[1]

Gulag /ˈguːlag, *foreign* guˈlak/ *n.* Also **g-**. M20. [Russ. acronym, f. *Glavnoe upravlenie ispravitelʼno-trudovykh lagereĭ* Chief Administration for Corrective Labour Camps.] 1 A department of the Soviet secret police that administered corrective labour camps and prisons between 1934 and 1955. *rare.* M20. 2 The Soviet network of labour camps; a camp or prison within it; *fig.* an oppressive environment. L20.

gular /ˈgjuːlə/ *a.* & *n.* E19. [f. GULA *n.*[1] + -AR[1].] A *adj.* Of, pertaining to, or situated on the throat of an animal, esp. a reptile, fish, or bird. E19. B *n.* A plate, scale, etc., on the throat of a reptile or fish. L19.

gulch /gʌltʃ/ *n.*[1] Long *obs.* exc. *Sc.* & *dial.* L16. [f. GULCH *v.*] A glutton, a drunkard.

gulchin *n.* a (little) glutton; a fat or greedy person: L17.

gulch /gʌltʃ/ *n.*[2] Long *obs.* exc. *dial.* L17. [Perh. imit.] A heavy fall.

gulch /gʌltʃ/ *n.*[3] Chiefly *N. Amer.* M19. [Perh. f. GULCH *v.*] A narrow deep steep-sided ravine, often forming the course of a torrent; *esp.* one containing gold.

gulch /gʌltʃ/ *v.t.* Long *obs.* exc. *Sc.* & *dial.* ME. [Imit.: cf. Norw. *gulka*, Sw. dial. *gölka*.] 1 Swallow or devour greedily. Also foll. by *down*, *in*, *up*. ME. 2 Foll. by *out*: expel (as) by vomiting. ME.

gulden /ˈgʊld(ə)n/ *n.* Pl. **-s**, same. L15. [Du. & G, use as n. of adj. corresp. to GILDEN. Cf. GUILDER.] Orig., any gold coin, esp. of Germany or the Netherlands. Later, a guilder.

†**gule** *n.*[1] ME. [L GULA *n.*[1]] 1 Gluttony. ME–M16. 2 The gullet. M17–M18.

gule /gjuːl/ *n.*[2] *arch.* Also **G-**. M16. [OFr. *g(o)ule*, med.L *gula Augusti*, of unkn. origin.] *the gule of August*, 1 August, Lammas Day.

gules /gjuːlz/ *n.* & *a.* ME. [OFr. *go(u)les* (mod. *gueules*) pl. of *gole* throat (mod. *gueule* mouth), used like med.L pl. *gulae* for pieces of red-dyed fur used as a neck ornament.] (Of) the heraldic tincture red; *poet.* & *rhet.* red.

gulf /gʌlf/ *n.* & *v.* Also †**-ph**. LME. [(O)Fr. *golfe* f. It. *golfo* f. Proto-Romance f. Gk *kolpos*, (late) *kolfos* bosom, fold, gulf.] A *n.* I 1 A portion of the sea, proportionally narrower at the mouth than a bay, partly surrounded by the coast. LME. 2 A profound depth (in a river, the sea); the deep. *poet.* LME. 3 A yawning chasm or abyss, esp. one produced by an earthquake; a vast ravine or gorge. LME. b [After *Luke* 16:26.] An impassable gap; a wide difference of feelings, opinions, etc. M16. 4 An eddy that sucks things from the surface; a whirlpool; *fig.* something which devours or swallows up anything. *arch.* L15. b A voracious appetite. Also, the stomach. *arch.* M16. 5 A large deposit of ore in a lode. *obs.* exc. *dial.* L18.

1 *the Gulf* (*of Mexico*), *the* (*Persian*) *Gulf*, etc. 2 *transf.*: LONGFELLOW The headlong plunge through eddying gulfs of air. 3 MILTON The Gulf of Tartarus, which . . opens wide His fiery Chaos. b M. DRABBLE The gulf between them had widened with the years.

II [f. the vb.] †6 = GULP *n.* M17–L18.

Comb.: **Gulf Country** *Austral.* the hinterland of the Gulf of Carpentaria, in the northern part of Queensland and the Northern Territory; **Gulf State** a State bordering the Persian Gulf or the Gulf of Mexico; **Gulf Stream** (*a*) a warm ocean current flowing north along the N. American coast from the Florida Straits (or Cape Hatteras) to the Grand Banks of Newfoundland; (*b*) *colloq.* the warm North Atlantic Drift, flowing from where the Gulf Stream proper ends north-eastwards to (esp. northern) Europe; **Gulf War** either of two wars waged against Iraq, the one by Iran from 1980 to 1988 and the other by a multinational force in 1991; **gulfweed** any brown alga of the genus *Sargassum*, members of which form dense floating masses in the Gulf Stream.

B *v.* 1 *v.i.* Move swiftly and strongly like a whirlpool; eddy, swirl. Long *rare.* M16. 2 *v.t.* Engulf, swallow up (*lit.* & *fig.*). Also foll. by *down*, *in*, *up*. E19.

gulfy *a.* (*a*) full of eddies or whirlpools, like a whirlpool; †(*b*) deep as an abyss; (*c*) full of hollows or depths: L16.

gulix /ˈgjuːlɪks/ *n.* L17. [Du. *Gulik* = Jülich in Germany.] A kind of fine linen. Also *gulix Holland*.

gull /gʌl/ *n.*[1] LME. [Brit.: cf. OCorn. *guilan*, Welsh *gwylan*, Breton *gouelan*, *gwelan* (whence Fr. *goéland*).] Any of numerous birds of the family Laridae, related to the terns, comprising long-winged gregarious mainly coastal birds that occur worldwide and are usually white with a grey or black mantle and a bright bill; *colloq.* a tern, a skua.

herring gull, *ivory gull*, *Ross's gull*, *wagel gull*, etc.

Comb.: **gull-wing** *n.* & *a.* (*a*) *n.* an aeroplane wing composed of a shorter part sloping upwards from the fuselage and a longer part more nearly horizontal; (*b*) *adj.* designating a car door that opens upwards.

gull-like *a.* resembling a gull L19.

gull /gʌl/ *n.*[2] Now *dial.* LME. [Prob. use as n. of GULL *a.*] An unfledged bird; *esp.* a gosling.

gull /gʌl/ *n.*[3] LME. [AN *gule, gole*, OFr. *gola, gole* (mod. *gueule* mouth) f. L GULA *n.*[1]. Cf. GOOL] †1 The throat, the gullet. LME–M17. 2 A breach or channel made by a stream or torrent, a gully, (now *dial.*); (now *dial.*) a chasm, a fissure; *Geol.* a fissure in rock produced by tension and filled with rock fragments. M16.

gull /gʌl/ *n.*[4] L16. [Perh. f. GULL *a.* In sense 2 also infl. by GULL *v.*[1]] 1 A credulous person; a dupe, a fool. L16. 2 A trick, a deception, a fraud. Long *obs.* exc. *Sc.* L16. 3 A trickster, a cheat; an impostor. *arch. slang.* E17.

†**gull** *a.* ME–L16. [ON *gulr* (Da., Sw. *gul*) ult. f. IE base of YELLOW *a.*] Yellow, pale.

gull /gʌl/ *v.*[1]*t.* M16. [Rel. to GULL *n.*[4]] 1 Dupe; trick (*into*); deceive. M16. †2 Deprive *of* by trickery or deception; cheat *out of*. E17–L18.
gullable *a.* = GULLIBLE E19.

gull /gʌl/ *v.*[2]*t.* & *i.* Long *rare* exc. *dial.* L16. [f. GULL *n.*[3]] (Of water) make channels (in); wear by friction; wear *down*; sweep *away*.

Gullah /ˈgʌlə/ *a.* & *n.* *US.* M18. [Origin uncertain: perh. abbrev. of *Angola*, or f. GOLA *n.*[2]] A *adj.* Pertaining to or designating Blacks living on the sea-islands and tidewater coastline of South Carolina. M18. B *n.* 1 The dialect spoken by Gullah Blacks. L19. 2 A Gullah Black. M20.

gullery /ˈgʌləri/ *n.*[1] Now *rare* or *obs.* L16. [f. GULL *v.*[1] + -ERY.] Deception, trickery, a deception, a trick.

gullery /ˈgʌləri/ *n.*[2] M19. [f. GULL *n.*[1] + -ERY.] A place where gulls breed; a colony or roost of gulls.

gullet /ˈgʌlɪt/ *n.* & *v.* LME. [OFr. *goulet* dim. of *go(u)le*: see GULES, -ET[1].] A *n.* 1 The passage in the neck by which food passes from the mouth to the stomach. LME. b The throat; the neck. M17. †2 A piece of armour or part of a hood covering the neck. LME–L15. 3 A water channel; a narrow, deep passage through which a stream flows; a strait; an estuary. Now *local.* LME. 4a A long narrow piece of land. *dial.* M16. b A gorge, a pass; a gully, a ravine; a narrow passage. Now chiefly *dial.* E17. 5 A hollow in front of each tooth of a saw, on alternate sides. M19. B *v.t.* Make gullets in (a saw). L19.
gulleting *n.* †(*a*) swallowing, guzzling; (*b*) the action of the vb; (*c*) a groove in a rudder post to receive the rudder: M17.

gullible /ˈgʌlɪb(ə)l/ *a.* E19. [f. GULL *v.*[1] + -IBLE.] Easily cheated or duped; credulous.
gulli'bility *n.* L18. **gullibly** *adv.* L19.

gulli-gulli *n.* var. of GULLY-GULLY.

gullish /ˈgʌlɪʃ/ *a.* L16. [f. GULL *n.*[4] + -ISH[1].] Of the nature of a gull; foolish, credulous.

gully /ˈgʌli/ *n.*[1] & *v.* M16. [Fr. *goulet*: see GULLET.] A *n.* †1 The gullet. Only in M16. 2 A channel or ravine worn in the earth by water, esp. on a mountain or hillside. M17. 3 A deep narrow artificial watercourse; a deep gutter, drain, or sink. M18. 4 A river valley. *Austral.* & *NZ.* M19. 5 *Cricket.* (The position of) a fieldsman between point and the slips. E20.
Comb.: **gully-hole** an opening from a street into a drain or sewer.
B *v.t.* Make gullies in. M18.

gully /ˈgʌli/ *n.*[2] *Sc.* & *north.* M16. [Origin unkn.] A large knife. Also *gully-knife*.

gully-gully /ˈgʌlɪˌgʌli/ *int.* Also **gulli-gulli**. M20. [Origin unkn.] A conjuror's catch word.

gulose /ˈgjuːləʊz, -s/ *n.* L19. [Alt. of GLUCOSE.] *Chem.* An artificial hexose that is a stereoisomer of glucose.

gulosity /gjʊˈlɒsɪti/ *n.* Now *rare.* L15. [Late L *gulositas*, f. *gulosus* gluttonous, f. as GULA *n.*[1]: see -ITY.] Gluttony, greediness, voracity.

gulp /gʌlp/ *n.* L15. [f. the vb.] 1 The action or an act of gulping. L15. b An effort to swallow; the noise caused by this; a choke. L19. 2 As much as is swallowed at a gulp; a mouthful. E17.

gulp /gʌlp/ *v.* LME. [Prob. f. MDu. *gulpen* swallow, guzzle: ult. origin imit.] 1 *v.t.* & *i.* Swallow hastily or greedily, esp. in large draughts or pieces. Freq. foll. by *down.* LME. b *v.t.* Keep in or suppress as if by swallowing. Freq. foll. by *back.* M17. 2 *v.i.* Swallow only with difficulty; gasp, choke. M16.
1 S. LEWIS He gulped a cup of coffee in the hope of pacifying his stomach. E. BOWEN The girl answered . . by making a bee line for the spring-water crock . . and thirstily gulping straight from the dipper. *fig.*: SIR W. SCOTT The worthy knight fairly gulped down the oaths. 2 C. MACKENZIE The sergeant-major gulped in embarrassment.
gulper *n.* M17. **gulpin** *n.* [prob. f. GULP *v.* + IN *adv.*] (*a*) a credulous person, a simpleton; (*b*) *Naut. colloq.* a marine: E19. **gulpingly** *adv.* in a gulping manner, with a gulp E18. **gulpy** *a.* marked by gulps or choking M19.

gum /gʌm/ *n.*[1] [OE *gōma*, corresp. to OHG *guomo* gum, ON *gómr* roof or floor of the mouth, fingertip, rel. to OHG *goumo* (G *Gaumen* roof of the mouth).] †1 *sing.* & in *pl.* The inside of the mouth or throat. OE–M18. 2 In *pl.*, the firm flesh at the base of the teeth; *sing.* the part of this next to any one tooth. ME. 3 Impertinent talk, chatter. *obs.* exc. *dial.* M18.
Comb.: **gumboil** a small abscess on the gums; **gum-shield** a pad worn to protect the teeth and gums, esp. by boxers.

gum /gʌm/ *n.*[2] ME. [OFr. *gomme* f. Proto-Romance for L *gummi* var. of *cummi* f. Gk *kommi* f. Egyptian *kemai.*] I A substance. 1 A viscous secretion of some trees and shrubs that hardens on drying but unlike a resin is soluble in water; a kind of this. Now also, any of various natural or synthetic polymers which dissolve or swell in water. ME. b Such a substance used as a glue for paper etc., to stiffen textiles, and in food products, detergents, etc. LME. †c A product of gum employed as a drug or perfume, or for burning as incense. Freq. in *pl.* LME–L18. 2 The sticky secretion that collects in the inner corner of the eye. L16. 3 The viscous or waxy substance surrounding the filaments of raw silk. L18. 4 A mixture containing gelatin used for making sweets; a hard translucent sweet made from this. E19. 5 = *chewing-gum* s.v. CHEW *v.* *N. Amer.* M19. 6 A solid or semi-solid substance deposited by some petroleum products when stored for long periods or heated, formed by the oxidation of some constituents. E20.
1 KAURI *gum.* XANTHAN *gum.* 4 *fruit gum, wine gum,* etc.
II 7 In full *gum tree.* A tree that exudes gum; *esp.* = EUCALYPTUS 1. Freq. preceded by specifying wd. L17. b A hollowed-out or otherwise adapted log, esp. from a gum tree, used as a beehive, water-trough, or well-curb. *US.* E19. 8 = GUMMOSIS. E18. 9 A gumboot; a galosh. *US.* M19.
7 *bluegum, flooded gum,* etc. *black gum*: see BLACK *a.*
Comb.: *gum acacia*: see ACACIA 1c; *gum* ADRAGANT; *gum ammoniac*: see AMMONIAC *a.* 2; *gum* ANIMÉ; *gum arabic*: see ARABIC *a.* 1; **gumboot** a long rubber boot; *gum* COPAL; *gum* ELEMI; **gum ivy** the congealed juice of the stem of the ivy; **gum juniper** sandarac; **gum lac** an inferior grade of lac from Madagascar; *gum mastic*: see MASTIC *n.* 1; *gum* OLIBANUM; **gum resin** a vegetable secretion of resin mixed with gum, e.g. gamboge; *gum sandarac*: see SANDARAC 3; *gum storax*: see STORAX 1; *gum succory*: see SUCCORY 2; **gumsucker** *Austral.* [f. sense 1] (a nickname for) a native-born Australian, esp. a Victorian; *gum thus*: see THUS *n.*; *gum* TRAGACANTH; **gum tree** (*a*) see sense 7 above; (*b*) *up a gum tree* (colloq.), in a predicament, in great difficulties. **gum-water** a solution of gum arabic in water; **gum-wood** (the wood of) a gum tree.

gum /gʌm/ *n.*[3] Orig. *Sc.* L18. [Origin uncertain: perh. rel. to CULM *n.*[1], COOM] *Mining.* Coal-dust, fine coal; now *esp.* that produced by a coal-cutting machine.
gumming *n.* (*a*) the clearing away of gum during the operation of a coal-cutting machine; (*b*) in *pl.*, fine particles of gum: M20.

gum /gʌm/ *n.*[4] E19. [Alt.] God: used in oaths and exclams.
by gum!, my gum!, etc.

gum /gʌm/ *v.*[1] Infl. **-mm-**. LME. [f. GUM *n.*[2]] †1 *v.t.* Treat with aromatic gums. LME–L15. 2 *v.t.* Fasten or fix in position with gum or other sticky substance. Also foll. by *down, together, up.* L16. 3 *v.t.* Stiffen with gum; coat or smear with gum. E17. 4 *v.i.* a Of a fruit tree: exude gum as a result of disease. L18. b Of a petroleum product: turn into or deposit gum. Chiefly as *gumming* vbl n. L19. 5 *v.t.* Cheat, delude, humbug. *US slang.* M19. 6a *v.i.* Foll. by *up*: (of a machine) become clogged or obstructed with a viscous substance, such as dried oil. E20. b *v.t. fig.* Interfere with the smooth running of; spoil, wreck. Usu. foll. by *up*, esp. in *gum up the works*. Orig. *US.* E20.

gum /gʌm/ *v.*[2]*t.* Infl. **-mm-**. L18. [f. GUM *n.*[1]] Deepen and enlarge the spaces between the teeth of (a worn saw).

Gumban /ˈgʌmb(ə)n/ *a.* & *n.* M20. [f. Kikuyu *Gumba*, a race of diminutive people believed to have been former inhabitants of Kikuyu country: see -AN.] *Archaeol.* (Designating or pertaining to) a late Stone Age culture of E. Africa.

gumbo /ˈgʌmbəʊ/ *n.* *N. Amer.* E19. [Of Afr. origin: cf. Bantu (Angolan) *kingombo* (w. pref. *ki-*) okra.] 1 Okra. Also, a spicy chicken or seafood soup thickened with okra pods, rice, filé, etc. E19. 2 A fine clayey soil that becomes sticky and impervious when wet. Also, thick clinging mud. M19. 3 (**G-**.) A French-based creole language spoken in Louisiana. M19.
1 *chicken gumbo, shrimp gumbo.*
Comb.: **gumbo filé** (*a*) gumbo soup thickened with filé; (*b*) filé as used to thicken gumbo soup.

gumbo-limbo /gʌmbəʊˈlɪmbəʊ/ *n.* M19. [f. GUMBO *n.* + 2nd elem. of unkn. origin. Perh. alt. of *gum elemi.*] A deciduous tree of Florida, Central America, and the W. Indies, *Bursera simaruba* (family Burseraceae), a source of gum elemi.

gumbotil /ˈgʌmbətɪl/ *n.* E20. [f. GUMBO + TILL *n.*[3]] A leached grey clay, very sticky when wet and very hard when dry, formed in regions of poor drainage by the weathering of clay-rich till.

gum-gum /ˈgʌmgʌm/ *n.* Now *rare.* E18. [Prob. f. Malay. Cf. GONG-GONG.] A musical instrument consisting of an iron bowl which is struck with an iron or wooden stick; a series of these of different sizes and pitches.

gumlah /ˈgʌmlə/ *n.* M19. [Hind. *gamlā.*] In the Indian subcontinent, an earthenware water-jar.

gumly /ˈgʌmli/ *a.* *Sc.* & *dial.* Now *rare* or *obs.* L18. [Origin unkn.] Muddy, turbid; gloomy.

gumma /ˈgʌmə/ *n.* Pl. **-as**, **-ata** /-ətə/. E18. [mod.L f. L *gummi* GUM *n.*[2]] *Med.* A granulomatous lesion characteristic of tertiary syphilis, with a firm rubbery core of dead tissue.
gummatous *a.* of the nature of or resembling a gumma; characterized by gummas: L17.

gummed /gʌmd/ *a.*[1] ME. [f. GUM *n.*[2] or *v.*[1]: see -ED[2], -ED[1].] Mixed with gum; coated, smeared, or stiffened with gum.

gummed /gʌmd/ *a.*[2] E16. [f. GUM *n.*[1] + -ED[2].] That has gums (of a specified kind).

gummer /ˈgʌmə/ *n.*[1] *N. Amer.* M19. [f. GUM *v.*[2] + -ER[1].] A person who or machine which gums saws.

gummer /ˈgʌmə/ *n.*[2] L19. [f. GUM *v.*[1] + -ER[1].] A person who applies gum.

gummer /ˈgʌmə/ *n.*[3] E20. [f. GUM *n.*[3] + -ER[1].] A person who or machine which removes the gum from under a coal-cutting machine.

Gummidge /ˈgʌmɪdʒ/ *n.* & *v.* L19. [Mrs *Gummidge*, a character in Dickens's *David Copperfield.*] A *n.* Peevish, self-pitying, and pessimistic complaining; a person who indulges in this. L19. B *v.i.* Complain in this manner. L19.

gummite /ˈgʌmʌɪt/ *n.* M19. [f. GUM *n.*[2] + -ITE[1].] *Min.* A reddish-yellow hydrated uranium oxide that resembles gum.

gummosis /gəˈməʊsɪs/ *n.* L19. [f. GUM *n.*[2] + -OSIS.] The production and exudation of gum by a diseased tree; a disease of fruit trees marked by this.

†**gummosity** *n.* LME. [med.L *gummositas*, f. as GUMMOUS *a.*[2]: see -OSITY.] 1 A gummy substance, deposit, or concretion. LME–L17. 2 The quality of being gummy or resembling gum; *Alch.* a supposed attribute of metals. M17–E18.

gummous /ˈgʌməs/ *a.*[1] L16. [f. GUMMA + -OUS.] = GUMMATOUS.

gummous /ˈgʌməs/ *a.*[2] M17. [L *gummosus*, f. *gummi* GUM *n.*[2]: see -OUS.] Of the nature of gum, resembling gum.

gummy /ˈgʌmi/ *n.* & *a.*[1] L19. [f. GUM *n.*[1] + -Y[6].] **A** *n.* **1** A small shark, *Mustelus antarcticus*, with rounded teeth that is found off the south coasts of Australia and New Zealand, where it is fished commercially for food. Also *gummy shark*. L19. **2** A sheep that has lost or is losing some teeth. *Austral.* & *NZ.* L19. **3** A toothless person; an old person. *Austral. slang.* E20. **B** *adj.* Toothless. E20.

gummily *adv.* M20.

gummy /ˈgʌmi/ *a.*[2] LME. [f. GUM *n.*[2] + -Y[1].] **1** Of the nature of gum, resembling gum; sticky, viscid. LME. **2** Suffused with or exuding gum. LME. **3** Of an ankle or leg: puffy, swollen. M18.

2 TENNYSON I came and lay Beneath those gummy chestnutbuds. P. D. JAMES She looked . . at the eyes, still gummy with sleep.

gumminess *n.* (*a*) the quality or condition of being gummy; (*b*) something gummy: E17.

gummy /ˈgʌmi/ *a.*[3] M19. [f. GUMMA + -Y[1].] *Med.* Gummatous.

gump /gʌmp/ *n.*[1] *dial.* & *US.* Also **gumph** /gʌmf/. E19. [Origin unkn.] A foolish person, a dolt.

gump /gʌmp/ *n.*[2] *US slang.* E20. [Perh. same wd as prec.] A chicken.

gump /gʌmp/ *n.*[3] Also **gumph** /gʌmf/. E20. [Abbrev.] = GUMPTION I.

gumph *n.*[1] var. of GUMP *n.*[1]

gumph *n.*[2] var. of GUMP *n.*[3]

gumpheon /ˈgʌmfɪən/ *n. Sc.* Long *rare* or *obs.* E18. [Alt. of GONFANON or GONFALON.] A funeral banner.

gumption /ˈgʌm(p)ʃ(ə)n/ *n.* Orig. *Sc.* E18. [Origin unkn.] **1** Common sense; ready practical sense; initiative, enterprising spirit, courage. *colloq.* E18. **2** *Painting.* The art of preparing colours. Also, a vehicle for colours. Now *rare.* E19.

1 J. WAINWRIGHT If he'd any gumption he'd give himself up.

gumptionless *a.* E19.

gumptious /ˈgʌm(p)ʃəs/ *a.* Now *rare.* M19. [f. GUMPTION by assoc. w. *bumptious*.] Clever; vain, self-important.

gumshoe /ˈgʌmʃuː/ *n.* & *v.* M19. [f. GUM *n.*[2] + SHOE *n.*] **A** *n.* **1** A galosh. M19. **2** A stealthy action. *colloq.* E20. **3** A detective; a police officer. *N. Amer. colloq.* E20. **B** *v.i.* Move or act stealthily; act as a police officer or a detective. *colloq.* (orig. *US*). E20.

Gumza *n.* var. of GAMZA.

gun /gʌn/ *n.* ME. [Prob. f. application to ballistae etc. of pet-form (in Sw. dial. *Gunne*) of Scand. female name *Gunnhildr*, f. *gunnr* + *hildr* both meaning 'war'.] **I** †**1** Any large piece of equipment used in medieval warfare. ME–M16. **2** A weapon consisting of a large metal tube mounted on a carriage or fixed substructure from which missiles are expelled by the force of an explosion; a cannon. ME. **b** The firing of such a weapon as a salute or signal; the time of such a signal. E17. **3** Any portable firearm (formerly, excluding the pistol). LME. **b** *spec.* in *Athletics.* The starting pistol; the start of a race. E20. **4** A member of a shooting party; a gunner; *N. Amer.* a gunman. E19. **5** A hand-held device from which a substance can be discharged at will by means of compressed air etc. (freq. w. defining wd); *US slang* a hypodermic syringe used by drug addicts. L19. **6** = *electron gun* s.v. ELECTRON *n.*[2] E20.

2 J. G. FARRELL They had two camel guns, small cannons which could be . . fired from the backs of camels. **b** A. WEST Sleeping till the morning gun. 3b *Swimming Times* Andrew Jameson was going all out for gold as he led from the gun. 5 *grease-gun*, *popgun*, etc. *airgun*: see AIR *n.*[1]

II *transf.* **7** [Cf. GAWN.] A flagon of ale. *slang* & *dial.* (now *rare* or *obs.*). M17. **8** A tobacco-pipe. *slang* or *joc.* Now only *Sc.* E18. **9** A thief; a rascal. *slang.* M19. **10** [Cf. *big gun* s.v. BIG *a.*] An expert sheep-shearer. Also *gun shearer*. *Austral.* & *NZ.* L19. **11** In *pl.* A gunnery officer. *Naut. slang.* E20. **12** A large heavy surfboard used for riding big waves. M20.

Phrases: (**as**) **sure as a gun** beyond all question. **at gunpoint** under threat of injury from a gun. **beat the gun** = *jump the gun* below. *big gun*: see BIG *a.* *blow great guns*: see BLOW *v.*[1] **give her, it,** etc. **the gun** *colloq.* = GUN *v.* 5b. **go great guns** *colloq.* have a run of success; proceed rapidly or vigorously towards success. **great gun** †(*a*) a piece of ordnance, a cannon; (*b*) = *big gun* s.v. BIG *a.* **have the guns for** have the ability or strength for. **jump the gun** start before the signal is given; *fig.* act before the proper time. **son of a gun** *colloq.* a rogue; a chap, a fellow. **stick to one's guns** maintain one's position under attack (*lit.* & *fig.*). *sure as a gun*: see (*as*) *sure as a gun* above.

Comb.: **gun-carriage** a wheeled support of a gun; **gun-cotton** nitrocellulose, made by steeping cotton or wood pulp in a mixture of nitric and sulphuric acids; *esp.* a highly nitrated form used as an explosive and a smokeless powder for guns; **gun-deck** a deck of a ship on which guns are placed; *spec.* (*Hist.*) the lowest such deck on a ship of the line; **gun dog** a dog trained to retrieve etc. for a gamekeeper or the members of a shoot; a dog of a breed suited to such training; **gunfight** *colloq.* a fight with revolvers; **gunfighter** *colloq.* a person who frequently participates in gunfights; **gun-harpoon**: fired from a gun instead of being thrown by hand; **gun-layer** a person, esp. a soldier, whose task is to aim a large gun; *gunlock*: see LOCK *n.*[2] 3; *gun-lascar*: see LASCAR 2; **gunman** a man armed with a gun; an assassin who uses a gun; **gun-metal** (*a*) orig., a bronze used for guns; now, an alloy of copper, tin, and a small amount of zinc; (*b*) a dull bluish-grey colour (freq. *attrib.* or as *adj.*); **gun microphone**: with a number of parallel tubes of different length in front of the diaphragm to increase its directional property; **gun moll** *slang* (*a*) a gangster's mistress; (*b*) an armed woman criminal; **gun-pit** an excavation to protect guns and gun crews from enemy fire; **gunplay** (skill in) the use of firearms; a fight with firearms; **gunpower** the number and strength of guns available; **gun-range** (*a*) the range of a gun's fire; (*b*) a place where the firing of guns is practised; **gunroom** (*a*) a room in a house for keeping sporting guns etc.; (*b*) a compartment in a warship orig. occupied by the gun crew, but now fitted up for junior officers or as a lieutenants' mess-room; **gunrunner** a person engaged in gunrunning; **gunrunning** the smuggling or illegal transportation of firearms and ammunition into a country; **gunship** a heavily armed helicopter; **gunshot** (*a*) (a) shot fired from a gun; (*b*) the range of a gun (chiefly in *out of*, *within*, *gunshot*); **gun-shy** *a.* (esp. of a sporting dog) frightened by the report of a gun; **gun-site** an emplacement, usu. fortified, for guns; **gunslinger** = *gunman* above; *gun slip*: see SLIP *n.*[3] 4d; **gunsmith** a maker and repairer of small firearms; **gunstock** (*a*) the wooden mounting of a gun barrel; †(*b*) the support of a cannon on board ship; **gunstone** †(*a*) a cannon-ball; a bullet; (*b*) *Her.* an ogress, a pellet.

gun /gʌn/ *v.* Infl. **-nn-**. E17. [f. GUN *n.*] **1** *v.i.* Shoot with a gun; go shooting. E17. **2** *v.t.* Shoot at; *esp.* shoot *down*. L17. **3** *v.t.* Look at closely, examine. *colloq.* E19. **4** *v.i.* Foll. by *for*: go in search of with a gun; seek to attack, harm, or destroy; go determinedly or energetically after. L19. **5a** *v.t.* Accelerate (a vehicle); open the throttle of (an engine). M20. **b** *v.i.* Accelerate; drive or move *off* quickly. M20.

2 *Times* Police 'gunned down innocent man by mistake.' 4 B. FRIEDAN She doesn't realise how lucky she is—her own boss, . . no junior executive gunning for her job. 5a S. BELLOW He gunned his motor at the stoplight. **b** N. ALLEY We gunned into an easy takeoff.

guna /ˈguːnə/ *n.* E19. [Skt *guṇa*.] **1** *Skt Gram.* The middle grade of an ablaut series of vowels; the process of raising a vowel to the middle grade (considered to be produced by the prefixing of *a*). E19. **2** *Hinduism.* In Sankhya philosophy, each of the three dominating principles of nature. M19.

gunate *v.t.* (*Skt Gram.*) subject to the process of guna M19.

gunboat /ˈgʌnbəʊt/ *n.* L18. [f. GUN *n.* + BOAT *n.*] **1** A small vessel of shallow draught (fitted for) carrying relatively heavy guns. L18. **2** Large shoes; large feet. Usu. in *pl. US slang.* L19.

Comb.: **gunboat diplomacy**: supported by the use or threatened use of military force.

gundi /ˈgʌndi/ *n.* L18. [N.Afr. Arab.] Any rodent of the family Ctenodactylidae, the members of which resemble guinea-pigs and live on rock outcrops in the deserts of N. and E. Africa.

gundy *n.* var. of GOONDIE.

†**gundy-gut** *n.* L18–E20. [f. *gundy* of unkn. origin + GUT *n.* (cf. *greedy-guts*).] A fat paunch; in *pl.*, a greedy person.

gunfire /ˈgʌnfʌɪə/ *n.* E19. [f. GUN *n.* + FIRE *n.*] **1** The firing of a gun or guns, esp. rapidly and repeatedly; *Naut.* & *Mil.* the time of the morning or evening gun. E19. **2** An early morning cup of tea served to troops before going on first parade. *Mil. slang.* E20.

gunge /gʌn(d)ʒ/ *n.*[1] L18. [Pers. & Urdu *ganj* store, store-house, market.] An Indian market.

gunge /gʌn(d)ʒ/ *n.*[2] *colloq.* M20. [Origin uncertain: cf. GOO *n.*, GUNK.] A sticky or viscid mass; any messy clogging substance, esp. one considered otherwise unidentifiable.

gungy *a.* L20.

gung-ho /gʌŋˈhəʊ/ *a.* M20. [Chin. *gōnghé*, taken as 'work together', adopted as a slogan in the war of 1939–45 by the US Marines.] Enthusiastic, eager.

gunibri *n.* var. of GIMBRI.

gunite /ˈgʌnʌɪt/ *n.* E20. [f. GUN *n.* + -ITE[1].] *Building.* A mixture of cement, sand, and water applied through a hose.

gunk /gʌŋk/ *n.* Orig. *US.* M20. [Origin uncertain: cf. next.] **1** Proprietary name for a detergent used for heavy-duty cleaning. M20. **2** Any viscous or liquid substance. *colloq.* M20. **3** A person. *slang. derog.* M20.

gunk-hole /ˈgʌŋkhəʊl/ *n. colloq.* (chiefly *N. Amer.*). E20. [Origin unkn.] *Naut.* A shallow inlet or cove difficult or dangerous to navigate because of mud, rocks, etc.

gunkholing *n.* cruising around gunk-holes L20.

gunless /ˈgʌnlɪs/ *a.* M19. [f. GUN *n.* + -LESS.] Having no gun.

Gunn /gʌn/ *n.* M20. [J. B. *Gunn* (b. 1928), physicist.] Electronics. *Gunn effect*, an effect in some semiconductors in which a constant electric field greater than a threshold value, applied between opposite faces of a thin piece of the material, results in an oscillatory current with a frequency in the microwave region. Hence *Gunn diode*, a semiconductor diode in which the Gunn effect occurs.

gunned /gʌnd/ *a.* M17. [f. GUN *n.* + -ED[2].] Provided with guns. Chiefly w. qualifying adv.

gunnel /ˈgʌn(ə)l/ *n.*[1] L17. [Origin unkn.] Any of various small slender fishes of the family Pholidae, found along the Atlantic and Pacific coasts; *spec.* the butterfish, *Pholis gunnellus*, of Atlantic coastal and intertidal waters.

gunnel *n.*[2] var. of GUNWALE.

gunner /ˈgʌnə/ *n.* ME. [f. GUN *n.* after AN analogies: see -ER[2]. Cf. AL *gunnarius*.] **1** A person who operates a gun, esp. a large one. Now chiefly, an artillery soldier, *esp.* (in official use) a private. ME. **b** *Hist.* A warrant-officer in the navy in charge of the battery, ordnance stores, etc. L15. **c** A member of an aircraft crew who operates a gun. E20. **2** A gunsmith. *obs.* exc. *dial.* LME. **3** A person who shoots game. M18. **4** With number prefixed: a vessel carrying a specified number of guns. E19.

1 **Master Gunner** (*a*) orig., the chief gunner in charge of ordnance and ammunition; now only as an honorary title conferred on a distinguished soldier; (*b*) a Royal Artillery warrant-officer in charge of the stores and equipment in a fort or other armed place.

Comb.: **gunner's daughter** *joc.* the gun to which a sailor, esp. a boy serving on warship, was lashed for flogging.

gunnera /ˈgʌn(ə)rə, gʌˈnɪərə/ *n.* L18. [mod.L (see below), f. J. E. *Gunnerus* (1718–73), Norw. botanist.] Any of various plants of the genus *Gunnera* (family Gunneraceae); esp. *G. tinctoria* and *G. manicata*, gigantic S. American plants with palmate leaves, often grown as waterside ornamentals.

gunnery /ˈgʌnəri/ *n.* L15. [f. GUN *n.* + -ERY.] **1** Guns collectively. *rare.* L15. **2** The construction and management of guns, esp. large ones. E17. **3**

The firing of guns; the use of guns in hunting. E19.

gunnis /ˈɡʌnɪs/ *n.* Also **-ies**. L18. [Prob. f. Corn. *gonys* working.] *Mining*. A crevice; a space left by the working of a lode.

gunny /ˈɡʌni/ *n.* & *a.* E18. [Marathi *gōṇī* f. Skt *goṇī* sack.] A *n.* A coarse material made from jute or sunn fibre, used chiefly for sacking; a sack made of this. E18. B *adj.* Made of gunny. E19.

Comb.: **gunny bag, sack**: made of gunny or similar material.

gunpowder /ˈɡʌnpaʊdə/ *n.* & *a.* LME. [f. GUN *n.* + POWDER *n.*[1]] A *n.* 1 A low explosive powder consisting of a mixture of potassium nitrate, ground charcoal, and sulphur, used for fuses, fireworks, and blasting and in muzzle-loading guns. LME. 2 In full *gunpowder tea*. A fine kind of green tea, each leaf of which is rolled up into a pellet. L18.

Comb.: **Gunpowder Plot** *Hist.* the conspiracy to blow up James I and Parliament at Westminster on 5 November 1605. *gunpowder-tea*: see sense 2 above.

B *adj.* Easily angered, fiery. L16.

†**gunpowdered** *a.* (*a*) charged with gunpowder; (*b*) = GUNPOWDER *a.*; (*c*) begrimed with gunpowder: M16–E18. **gunpowdery** *a.* of, pertaining to, or characteristic of gunpowder; *fig.* fiery, easily angered: M19.

gunsel /ˈɡʌns(ə)l/ *n.* *US slang*. E20. [Yiddish *gendzel* = G *Gänslein* gosling, little goose; in sense 2 infl. by GUN *n.*] 1 A naive youth; a homosexual youth, *esp.* a passive one kept by a tramp. E20. 2 An informer; a criminal, a gunman. M20.

Gunter /ˈɡʌntə/ *n.* L17. [Edmund *Gunter* (1581–1626), Eng. mathematician.] 1 *Gunter's chain*, a surveyor's chain 66 feet long, the use of which gave rise to this distance as a unit of length (cf. CHAIN *n.* 6b). L17. 2 (Also **g-**.) A long ruler graduated on one side with trigonometrical and other functions and on the other side with the logarithms of these, formerly used in surveying and navigation. Also more fully *Gunter's scale*. E18. 3 *Naut.* Orig., a type of rig in which the topmast slides up and down the lower mast on rings. Now, a fore-and-aft sail whose spar is nearly vertical, so that the sail is nearly triangular. Also *Gunter rig*. L18.

gunwale /ˈɡʌn(ə)l/ *n.* Also **gunnel, gunwhale**. LME. [f. GUN *n.* + WALE *n.*[1], having formerly been used to support guns.] The upper edge of a ship's side; in large wooden vessels, the uppermost planking covering the timber-heads.

M. RULE I held on to my mask, sat on the gunwale and fell backwards into the sea. P. SCOTT She has ridden . . low, laden heavily to the gunwales.

Phrases: **gunwale to, under** level with, below, the surface of the water.

gunyah /ˈɡʌnjə/ *n.* *Austral.* E19. [Aborig.] An Aboriginal hut; a bush hut.

gunyang /ˈɡʌnjaŋ/ *n.* M19. [Aborig.] Any of several Australian shrubby nightshades of the genus *Solanum*, esp. *S. vescum*, with edible greenish berries.

Günz /ɡʊnts, *foreign* ɡynts/ *a.* & *n.* E20. [A river near the Alps in southern Germany.] *Geol.* (Designating or pertaining to) a middle Pleistocene glaciation in the Alps, preceding the Mindel and possibly corresponding to the Menapian of northern Europe.

Guomindang *n.* var. of KUOMINTANG.

gup /ɡʌp/ *n.* *colloq.* (orig. *Anglo-Ind.*). E19. [Urdu f. Pers. *gap*.] Gossip, chatter; silly talk, nonsense.

guppie /ˈɡʌpi/ *n.*[1] *colloq.* Also **-y**. L20. [Blend of GAY *a.* and YUPPIE *n.*] A homosexual yuppie.

guppie /ˈɡʌpi/ *n.*[2] *colloq.* Also **-y**. L20. [Blend of GREEN *a.* and YUPPIE *n.*] A yuppie who professes concern about the environment and ecological issues.

guppy /ˈɡʌpi/ *n.*[1] E20. [R. J. L. *Guppy*, a 19th-cent. Trinidadian clergyman who sent the first specimen to the British Museum.] A small topminnow, *Poecilia reticulata*, of the W. Indies and S. America, popular as an aquarium fish. Also called *millions* (*fish*).

guppy *n.*[2], *n.*[3] vars. of GUPPIE *n.*[1], *n.*[2]

Gupta /ˈɡʊptə/ *a.* & *n.* L19. [f. *Candragupta*, the founder of the dynasty.] (A member) of a dynasty which ruled in northern India from the 4th to the 6th cents.

gur /ˈɡʊə/ *n.* Also **ghoor, goor**. L17. [Hind. *gur*, Marathi *gūṛ* f. Skt *guḍa*.] In the Indian subcontinent: unrefined sugar, molasses.

gurdwara /ɡʊəˈdwɑːrə, ɡəːˈdwɑːrə/ *n.* E20. [Panjabi *gurduārā*, f. Skt GURU + *dvāra* door.] A Sikh temple.

gurge /ɡəːdʒ/ *n.* M17. [L *gurges*.] 1 A swirling mass of liquid; a whirlpool. Chiefly *poet.* M17. 2 *Her.* A charge representing a whirlpool, consisting of a spiral of two narrow bands, usu. blazoned argent and azure. M19.

gurge /ɡəːdʒ/ *v.i.* E16. [f. as prec.] Esp. of water: rise or swell turbulently.

gurgeons /ˈɡəːdʒ(ə)nz/ *n.pl.* Now *dial.* Also **grudgeons**. L15. [Origin uncertain: cf. Fr. †*grugeons* lumps of crystalline sugar in brown sugar, rel. to *gruger* to crunch.] Coarse meal; the coarse refuse from flour.

gurgeon stopper /ˈɡəːdʒ(ə)n ˈstɒpə/ *n. phr.* L19. [Origin of 1st elem. uncertain: cf. GURJUN. See STOPPER *n.* 5.] A hardwood tree, *Eugenia foetida*, of the myrtle family, occurring in Florida and the W. Indies.

gurges /ˈɡəːdʒiːz/ *n.* LME. [L.] 1 = GURGE *n.* 1. Also (*dial.*) a lake, a fish-pond. LME. 2 *Her.* = GURGE *n.* 2. LME.

gurgitate /ˈɡəːdʒɪteɪt/ *v.* M17. [Late L *gurgitat-* pa. ppl stem of *gurgitare*: see next, -ATE[3].] †1 *v.t.* Swallow, devour. *rare*. Only in M17. 2 *v.t.* & *i.* Discharge or be discharged with a swirling motion. E20.

gurgitation /ɡəːdʒɪˈteɪʃ(ə)n/ *n.* M16. [f. late L *gurgitat-*, pa. ppl stem of *gurgitare* engulf, f. as GURGES: see -ATION.] 1 The action of swallowing or absorbing. *rare*. M16. 2 Surging or swirling motion of a liquid etc. L19.

gurgle /ˈɡəːɡ(ə)l/ *n.* M16. [f. the vb.] †1 A gargle. Only in M16. 2 A gurgling sound or cry. M18.

gurgle /ˈɡəːɡ(ə)l/ *v.* LME. [Prob. imit., if not directly f. similarly formed wds such as MLG, Du. *gorgelen*, G *gurgeln*, med.L *gurgulare*, all ult. f. L *gurgulio* gullet.] I 1 *v.i.* Make a bubbling sound as of liquid escaping intermittently from a bottle or of water flowing among stones; flow with such a sound. LME. 2 *v.i.* Utter broken guttural cries. M18. 3 *v.t.* Utter with gurgling cries. E19.

1 T. SHARPE The radiators gurgled gently. E. FIGES He could hear fresh water gurgling through the sluice. 2 D. MORRIS A baby may gurgle and burble, but it does not laugh.

II †4 *v.i.* Gargle. M16–E17.

gurgler *n.* a person who or thing which gurgles; *spec.* (*Austral. colloq.*) a plughole (*down the gurgler*, = *down the drain* s.v. DOWN *prep.*): L20. **gurglingly** *adv.* in a gurgling way L19. **gurgly** *a.* characterized by gurgling L19.

gurjun /ˈɡəːdʒ(ə)n/ *n.* Also **-jan, -jon**. M19. [Bengali *garjan*.] Any of various large Indian trees of the genus *Dipterocarpus* (family Dipterocarpaceae) which are sources of gurjun oil.

Comb.: **gurjun balsam, oil** a viscid resin obtained from trees of the genus *Dipterocarpus* and formerly used as a varnish and medicinally.

gurk /ɡəːk/ *v.* & *n.* *colloq.* E20. [Imit.] A *v.i.* Emit a belch. E20. B *n.* A belch. M20.

Gurkha /ˈɡəːkə, ˈɡʊəkə/ *n.* & *a.* Also (*arch.*) **G(h)oorkha**. E19. [Name of locality f. Skt *gorakṣa* cowherd (f. *go* cow + *rakṣ-* protect) as epithet of patron deity.] A *n.* A member of the principal Hindu community in Nepal, renowned for its military prowess and forming special regiments in the British army. E19. B *attrib.* or as *adj.* Of or pertaining to the Gurkhas. E19.

Gurkhali /ɡəːˈkɑːli/ *n.* L19. [f. as prec.] 1 A Gurkha. Only in *pl.* L19. 2 The Indo-Aryan language of the Gurkhas. E20.

gurl /ɡəːl/ *a.* & *n.* E16. [Rel. to GURL *v.*] A *adj.* = GURLY 1. *Sc.* E16. B *n.* A growl; rough weather. Now *Sc.* M18.

gurl /ɡəːl/ *v.i.* Now *Sc.* LME. [Imit.: cf. prec., *growl*.] Of a dog etc.: growl. Of the stomach: rumble. Of the wind: roar, howl.

gurly /ˈɡəːli/ *a.* *Sc.* E18. [f. prec. + -Y[1].] 1 Of weather, the wind, etc.: rough, stormy. E18. 2 Surly, ill-tempered. E18.

Gurmukhi /ˈɡʊəmʊki/ *n.* & *a.* M19. [Panjabi, f. Skt GURU + *mukha* mouth.] A *n.* The script used by Sikhs; the Panjabi language as written in this script. M19. B *adj.* Of or designating this script or language. M19.

gurnard /ˈɡəːnəd/ *n.* Also **-net** /-nɪt/. Pl. **-s**, same. ME. [OFr. *gornart*, f. *gronir* by-form of *grondir* f. L *grundire*, *grunnire* GRUNT *v.*: see -ARD. Cf. AL *gurnardus*.] Any of various marine fishes of the genus *Trigla* or the family Triglidae, characterized by a large spiny head with mailed cheeks and by three free pectoral fins. Also, any of various related fishes.

fig.: SHAKES. *1 Hen. IV* If I be not ashamed of my soldiers, I am a sous'd gurnet. *red gurnard*: see RED *a.*

gurney /ˈɡəːni/ *n.* *US.* L19. [App. f. J. T. *Gurney* of Boston, Massachusetts, who patented a new cab design in 1883.] 1 *Hist.* In full *Gurney cab*. A two-wheeled horse-drawn cab with a rear door and lengthwise seating. Also, a similar vehicle used as a police wagon or ambulance. L19. 2 A wheeled stretcher used for transporting hospital patients. M20.

Gurneyite /ˈɡəːnɪaɪt/ *n.* & *a.* M19. [f. *Gurney* (see below) + -ITE[1]. Cf. WILBURITE.] A *n.* A follower of Joseph John Gurney (1788–1847), leader of an evangelical movement among English Quakers. M19. B *adj.* Of or pertaining to Gurney or his followers. M19.

†**gurnipper** *n.* see GALLINIPPER.

gurrag *n.* var. of GIRRAN.

gurrah /ˈɡʌrə/ *n.* E19. [Hind. *gharā* f. Skt *ghaṭa*.] In the Indian subcontinent, an earthen jar.

gurry /ˈɡʌri/ *n.*[1] Chiefly *US.* L18. [Origin unkn.] The mixture of blood, slime, etc., obtained in cutting up a whale and melting down its blubber for oil; fish offal; any mixture of dirt and grease.

Comb.: **gurry-shark** = GREENLAND *shark*.

gurry *n.*[2] var. of GIRRAN.

gurry sore /ˈɡʌri sɔː/ *n. phr.* L19. [f. *gurry* (prob. = GURRY *n.*[2]) + SORE *n.*[1]] A sore or boil caused by repeated exposure to salt water.

guru /ˈɡʊruː, ˈɡuːruː/ *n.* Also **gooroo**. E17. [Skt *guru* elder, teacher.] 1 A (Hindu) spiritual teacher. E17. 2 Anyone looked up to as a source of wisdom or knowledge; an influential leader or pundit. M20.

2 C. WILSON Jung suddenly became the guru of the Western World, a universal oracle. *Times* Wall Street guru Mr. Joe Granville predicted world stock markets were going to enter a bear market.

guruship *n.* the position of a guru M19.

Gurung /ˈɡʊrʊŋ/ *n.* & *a.* E19. [Nepali *gurung*, perh. f. Gurung.] A *n.* Pl. **-s**, same. 1 A member of a people of western Nepal. E19. 2 The Tibeto-Burman language of the Gurungs. L20. B *attrib.* or as *adj.* Of or pertaining to the Gurungs or their language. L19.

gush /ɡʌʃ/ *n.* L17. [f. the vb.] 1 A sudden copious emission of liquid; a torrent or flood *of* liquid so emitted. L17. 2 A gust *of* wind (now *dial.*); a burst *of* light, heat, sound, etc. E18. b An outburst of feeling or of expressive speech, gestures, etc. E18. c A strong smell, a whiff. *colloq.* M19. 3 Overeffusive or sentimental display of feeling, esp. in language. *colloq.* M19.

1 M. REID A red gush spurted over the garments of the Indian. 2 DICKENS The host of that tavern approached in a gush of cheerful light to help them to dismount. b M. HOLROYD She had always been swept upward by gushes of enthusiasm. 3 N. ANNAN The man who hated sentimentality and gush.

gush /ɡʌʃ/ *v.* LME. [Prob. of northern, imit. origin.] 1 *v.i.* Rush in a sudden copious stream, as water released from confinement, blood from a wound, etc. Freq. with *down*, *out*, *up*, etc. LME. 2 *v.i.* Of a person, a part of the body, etc.:

have a copious flow of blood, tears, etc. M16. 3 *v.t.* Emit in a copious stream. M16. 4 *v.i.* & *t.* Act, speak, or utter in an overeffusive manner. *colloq.* M19.

1 K. MANSFIELD The noise of water gushing out of a pump into a big pail. J. HELLER Statements gush from her in a high shriek. 2 S. RICHARDSON Father, not able to contain himself, . . gushed out into a flood of tears. 3 D. C. PEATTIE Spurge . . that gushes a spurt of milky juice upon the hands. 4 J. RUSKIN Few things he hated more than hearing people gush about particular drawings. C. MACKENZIE 'Oh, I'd love a cup of tea,' she gushed gratefully.

gusher *n.* (*a*) a person who speaks or behaves effusively; (*b*) a well from which oil flows profusely without being pumped: M19.

gushing /ˈɡʌʃɪŋ/ *ppl a.* L16. [f. GUSH *v.* + -ING².] That gushes; *esp.* given to effusive outbursts of feeling.

gushingly *adv.* E19. **gushingness** *n.* M19.

gushy /ˈɡʌʃi/ *a.* M19. [f. GUSH *n.* + -Y¹.] Gushing, overeffusive.

gushily *adv.* E20. **gushiness** *n.* M19.

gusle /ˈɡʊslə/ *n.* Also **-la**. E19. [Serbo-Croat.] A simple usu. one-stringed fiddle used in the Balkans, esp. to accompany the chanting of Slavonic epics.

guslar /ˈɡʊslɑː/ *n.*, pl. **-ri** /-ri/, a person who plays the gusle or accompanies epic ballads on it M19.

gusset /ˈɡʌsɪt/ *n.* LME. [(O)Fr. *gousset* dim. of *gousse* pod, shell, of unkn. origin.] 1 A (triangular) piece of material let into a garment to strengthen or enlarge some part. LME. 2 *Hist.* A piece of flexible material introduced in a coat of mail to fill up a space at the joints between two adjoining pieces of mail. LME. 3 *Her.* A charge formed by a line drawn from the dexter or sinister chief to a central point, from where the line is continued perpendicularly to the base of the escutcheon. Cf. GORE *n.*² 3. M16. 4 A triangular piece or corner of land. Chiefly, & now only, *Sc.* L16. 5 A flat bracket or angular piece fixed at an angle of a structure to give strength or firmness. M19.

gusseted *a.* having a gusset or gussets L19.

gussy /ˈɡʌsi/ *v.t. slang.* E20. [Perh. f. *Gussie* pet-form of male first name *Augustus*: see -Y⁶.] Smarten *up*. Usu. in *pass.*

gust /ɡʌst/ *n.*¹ *arch.* LME. [L *gustus* taste: cf. GOÛT, GUSTO.] 1 The sense of taste. Formerly also, an act of tasting. LME. 2 Flavour, taste (of food). LME. **b** Pleasing taste. M17. †3 Individual taste or preference. L16–M18. 4 Keen enjoyment; relish, zest. M17. †5 An experience or taste *of* something. M–L17.

1 T. HERBERT The fruit is somewhat unpleasant at first gust. 2 C. LAMB The whole vegetable tribe have lost their gust with me. 4 W. COWPER He drinks his simple beverage with a gust. **have a gust for, of** appreciate, have a taste for. 5 SIR T. BROWNE In seventy or eighty years, a man may have a deep gust of the world.

gust /ɡʌst/ *n.*² L16. [ON *gustr*, f. weak grade of base of ON *gjósa* gush.] 1 A sudden violent rush of or *of* wind. Formerly also, a whirlwind. L16. 2 A sudden burst of rain, fire, sound, etc. E17. 3 An outburst or sudden fit of feeling. E18.

2 P. H. GIBBS The inn door opened and there came out a gust of laughter. 3 H. JAMES Strether had . . been subject to sudden gusts of fancy . . . odd starts of the historic sense.

gust /ɡʌst/ *v.*¹*t.* LME. [f. GUST *n.*¹ or L *gustare*, f. *gustus* GUST *n.*¹] †1 Taste (food); taste with pleasure, relish. LME–M17. 2 *gust the mouth* or *gab*, give pleasure to the palate. *Sc.* LME.

gust /ɡʌst/ *v.*² L18. [f. GUST *n.*²] 1 *v.t.* Blast with sea-spray. *Sc.* L18. 2 *v.i.* Of wind etc.: blow or rise in gusts. E19.

2 D. BAGLEY The wind was now fifty miles an hour, gusting to sixty. P. THEROUX The dust whirled out of the corridor and gusted around the light-bulbs.

gustable /ˈɡʌstəb(ə)l/ *a.* & *n.* Now *rare.* L15. [Late L *gustabilis*, f. *gustare* to taste: see GUST *v.*¹, -ABLE.] **A** *adj.* 1 Able to be tasted; having a pleasant taste, appetizing. L15. 2 Of a quality: perceptible to the taste. M17. **B** *n.* A thing that can be tasted; *esp.* an article of food. Usu. in *pl.* M17.

gustation /ɡʌˈsteɪʃ(ə)n/ *n.* L16. [Fr., or L *gustatio(n-)*, f. *gustat-* pa. ppl stem of *gustare* to taste: see GUST *v.*¹, -ATION.] The action or faculty of tasting.

gustative /ˈɡʌstətɪv/ *a.* E17. [med.L *gustativus*, f. L *gustat-*: see prec., -IVE.] = next.

gustatory /ɡʌˈsteɪt(ə)ri, ˈɡʌstət(ə)ri/ *a.* L17. [f. L *gustat-*: see GUSTATION, -ORY².] Concerned with tasting or the sense of taste.

Also **gustaˈtorial** *a.* M20.

gustful /ˈɡʌstfʊl, -f(ə)l/ *a.* M17. [f. GUST *n.*¹ + -FUL.] 1 Tasty, appetizing; *fig.* delightful to the mind or feeling. M17. 2 Marked by relish or zest. *arch.* L17.

gustfully *adv.* M17. **gustfulness** *n.* L17.

gusto /ˈɡʌstəʊ/ *n.* Pl. **-o(e)s**. E17. [It. f. L *gustus* GUST *n.*¹] 1 An individual fondness or preference. *arch.* E17. 2 Keen enjoyment displayed in action or speech, esp. in eating or drinking; relish, zest. Freq. in *with* (*great* etc.) *gusto*. E17. 3 Style in which a work of art etc. is executed; esp. *great* or *grand gusto* (= It. *gran gusto*). *arch.* M17.

2 J. M. COETZEE Though it was no more than fish . . served with lettuce, I ate with gusto. H. WOUK His gusto for the work was evident. 3 J. JAMES The Designs . . are of very mean Gusto.

gusty /ˈɡʌsti/ *a.*¹ E17. [f. GUST *n.*² + -Y¹.] 1 Blowing in gusts; marked or accompanied by gusts of wind. E17. **b** Disturbed or blown by gusts of wind. E18. 2 Marked by sudden bursts of feeling or action. L17.

1 E. WAUGH A gusty night always brought down a litter of dead timber. **b** KEATS The long carpets rose along the gusty floor. 2 *New Yorker* Energetic, sociable, gusty of temperament.

gustily *adv.*¹ E19. **gustiness** *n.* E20.

gusty /ˈɡʌsti/ *a.*² Chiefly *Sc.* E18. [f. GUST *n.*¹ + -Y¹.] Tasty, appetizing.

gustily *adv.*² with taste or gusto E19.

gut /ɡʌt/ *n.* & *a.* [OE *guttas* pl., prob. f. base of OE *gēotan*, Goth. *giutan* pour.] **A** *n.* 1 In *pl.* The contents of the abdominal cavity, esp. (now) that of an animal; bowels, entrails. OE. **b** In *pl.* The entrails of animals as food; offal. E17. 2**a** *sing.* & †in *pl.* The intestine; intestinal tissue. LME. **b** The alimentary canal as a whole, *esp.* that of an animal; the enteron. LME. 3 *sing.* & in *pl.* The stomach, esp. as the seat of appetite or gluttony. Now *dial.* & *slang.* LME. **b** In *pl.* A corpulent or gluttonous person. L16. 4 A narrow passage; a lane; a channel of water, a strait. M16. 5 A material made from the intestines of animals for use in violin or racket strings, and in surgery. Formerly also, in *pl.*, the strings themselves. Cf. CATGUT. E17. **b** A silky fibrous material obtained from inside a silkworm about to spin, formerly used for fishing-lines. M19. 6 In *pl.* The physical contents of something; substance, substantial meaning or impact; the essential part, the heart, *of* something. M17. 7 In *pl.* Courage, force of character; energy, verve, staying power. *colloq.* L19. 8 In machine sheep-shearing, a flexible shaft which conveys the power from an overhead source to the shearer's handpiece. *Austral.* & *NZ.* M20.

1 P. MACGILL A cramp in my guts! . . It isn't 'arf giving me gyp! 2 *blind gut*: see BLIND *a.* *small gut, guts*: see SMALL *a.* 5 C. FORD Pass a loop of gut over the fingerboard from bass to treble. 6 R. L. STEVENSON It's got life to it and guts. K. AMIS Cliff . . peered for a moment into the guts of the ruined set. *New Yorker* To me, that's really the guts of it. 7 A. GIBBS Someone . . who's had the guts to appeal to the electorate on what he really thinks.

Other phrases: **bust** (or **rupture**) **a gut** *slang* exert oneself, make a great effort. *greedy-gut(s)*: see GREEDY *a.* *hate a person's guts*: see HATE *v.* **have a person's guts for garters** *slang*: a hyperbolical threat. **have no guts in it** *slang* be of no real value or force. *misery guts*: see MISERY **slog, sweat,** or **work one's guts out** *slang* work extremely hard; make a great effort.

Comb.: **gut-bucket** *n.* & *a.* (*slang*) (designating) a primitive, unsophisticated style of jazz; **gut instinct** a compellingly intuitive feeling; **gut-level** *a.* & *n.* (of or pertaining to) basic principles or a basic level; **gut-rot** *colloq.* unwholesome or unpalatable liquor or food; **guts-ache** *colloq.* stomach-ache; **gut-shoot** *v.t.* (*slang*) shoot in the stomach; **gut-tie** a condition in which a length of a bullock's bowel has become entangled with the spermatic cord.

B *attrib.* or as *adj.* (Of an issue) basic, fundamental; (of a feeling or reaction) instinctive and emotional rather than rational. M20.

Marxism Today This is a real gut issue. J. BRODSKY It wasn't so much a conscious choice as a gut reaction.

gutful, gutsful *n.* (*slang*) = BELLYFUL E20. **gutling** *n.* (long *obs.* exc. *dial.*) a great eater, a glutton L16.

gut /ɡʌt/ *v.* Infl. **-tt-**. ME. [f. the n.] 1 *v.t.* Take out the guts of (a fish); eviscerate. ME. 2 *v.i.* Eat voraciously or greedily. *slang.* E17. 3 *v.t.* **a** Clear out the contents or inside of; empty thoroughly; *esp.* remove or destroy the internal fittings of (a building etc.). (Foll. by *of*.) Now freq. in *pass.* L17. **b** Extract the essential contents or the important passages of (a book etc.) in reading or in a review or abridgement. E18. 4 Disappoint bitterly, make desolate, exasperate, disgust. Only as *gutted* ppl a. *slang.* L20.

3a R. HUGHES All nautical instruments gone, cabin stores—the saloon in fact gutted of everything. U. LE GUIN The shopfronts . . were all covered up . . , except for one which had been gutted by fire. 4 *Sun* I've heard nothing for four months. I'm gutted because I still love him.

Gutian /ˈɡuːtɪən/ *n.* & *a.* E20. [f. *Guti*, the tribe or *Gutium*, their country + -AN.] *Archaeol.* **A** *n.* A member of a people from the Zagros Mountains in western Iran who overthrew the Dynasty of Akkad in Mesopotamia in the late 3rd millennium BC. E20. **B** *adj.* Of or pertaining to this people. E20.

gutless /ˈɡʌtlɪs/ *a. colloq.* E17. [f. GUT *n.* + -LESS.] †1 Having no guts; disembowelled. Only in E17. 2 Lacking in energy, courage, or determination. E20.

gutlessly *adv.* L20. **gutlessness** *n.* M20.

Gutnish /ˈɡʊtnɪʃ/ *n.* & *a.* L19. [G *Gutnisch*, f. ON *gotneskr* adj., of Gotland.] **A** *n.* An East Norse dialect spoken on the island of Gotland, off SE Sweden in the Baltic Sea. L19. **B** *adj.* Of or pertaining to Gotland or its inhabitants. E20.

guts /ɡʌts/ *v.i.* & *t. colloq.* E20. [f. GUT *v.*] Eat greedily.

gutser /ˈɡʌtsə/ *n. Austral.* & *NZ colloq.* Also **gutzer**. E20. [f. GUT *n.* + -S¹ + -ER¹.] A heavy fall.

come, fetch, etc. **a gutser** come a cropper, make a mistake; *Air Force slang* crash.

gutsy /ˈɡʌtsi/ *a.* In sense 1 also **-sie**. E19. [f. GUT *n.* + -SY.] 1 Greedy, voracious. Chiefly *Sc.* E19. 2 Tough, spirited, courageous. *slang.* L19.

gutsily *adv.* E19. **gutsiness** *n.* E19.

gutta /ˈɡʌtə/ *n.*¹ Pl. **-tae** /-tiː/. LME. [L = drop. Cf. GOUT *n.*¹] †1 Gum; gum resin, *esp.* gamboge. LME–E18. 2 *Archit.* Each of a row of usu. conical projections resembling drops underneath the triglyph (and sometimes the mutule) of a Doric capital. M16. 3 *Pharm.* & *Med.* A drop of liquid. Now *rare* or *obs.* M16. 4 A roundish coloured dot on an insect's wing, *esp.* one of a light colour. E19.

Comb.: †**gutta rosacea, rosea** acne rosacea; †**gutta serena** = AMAUROSIS.

gutta /ˈɡʌtə/ *n.*² M19. [Malay *getah*: see next.] 1 = GUTTA-PERCHA. M19. 2 A gutta-percha golf ball. Cf. GUTTY *n.* M19.

gutta-percha /ɡʌtəˈpəːtʃə/ *n.* M19. [Malay *getah perca*, f. *getah* gum + *perca* strips of cloth (which it resembles); assim. to GUTTA *n.*²] 1 The coagulated latex of certain Malaysian trees, a hard tough thermoplastic substance consisting chiefly of a hydrocarbon isomeric with rubber and now used esp. in dentistry and for electrical insulation. M19. 2 Any of the trees, of the sapote family, which yield gutta-percha, esp. *Palaquium gutta*, a tall evergreen. M19.

guttate /ˈɡʌteɪt/ *a.* E19. [L *guttatus*, f. as GUTTA *n.*¹: see -ATE².] Having drops or marks resembling drops; in the form of or resembling drops.

guˈttated *a.* guttate; characterized by marks resembling drops E18.

guttatim /ɡʌˈteɪtɪm/ *adv.* Now *rare.* L17. [L, f. as GUTTA *n.*¹] Drop by drop.

guttation /gʌˈteɪʃ(ə)n/ *n.* L19. [f. GUTTA *n.*[1] + -ATION.] *Bot.* The secretion of droplets of water from the hydathodes.

gutté /gyte/ *a.* Also **gutty** L16. [AN = OFr. *gouté* spotted, f. *goute* (mod. *goutte*) drop (f. as GUTTA *n.*[1]) + *-é* -ATE[2].] *Her.* Powdered or spotted with drops of liquid.

gutter /ˈgʌtə/ *n.*[1] & *a.* ME. [AN *gotere*, OFr. *gotiere* (mod. *gouttière*) f. Proto-Romance f. as GUTTA *n.*[1]: see -ER[2].] **A** *n.* †**1** A watercourse. Orig. also, a downpour. ME–M19. **b** A furrow or track made by running water. L16–M19. **2** A shallow trough fixed below the eaves of a roof, or a channel at the side of a road, to carry off rainwater. ME. **b** A channel forming a receptacle for refuse or foul matter (*lit.* & *fig.*), a sink. Now *dial.* LME. **c** *sing.* & (usu.) in *pl.* Mud, filth. Chiefly *Sc.* E18. **d** *fig.* The milieu of very poor people or people without breeding. M19. †**3** A groove or elongated hollow in a living organism. LME–E18. **4** An artificial groove. Now only *techn.* M16. **5** A trough or pipe for the removal of fluid in an industrial process. M17. **6** *Printing* & *Typogr.* A piece of furniture separating adjacent pages in a forme (also *gutter-stick*); the space between facing pages of an open book etc. or (*loosely*) between columns on a page; the space between adjacent (rows and columns of) stamps on a sheet. M19.

2d *Times* Middle-class courtesans . . were always the toast of society when lower-class street walkers were considered the gutter.

B *adj.* Brought up in or appropriate to the gutter (sense 2d above); of a low or disreputable character. M19.

A. BURGESS Her beauty was marred by a gutter accent and vocabulary.

Comb. & *special collocations*: **gutter-blood** *Sc.* a person of low breeding; **gutter-crawling** kerb-crawling; **gutter journalism, press**: (considered as) fit only for the gutter; marked by sensationalism and vulgarity; **gutter-splint** a splint moulded to the shape of the limb; *gutter-stick*: see sense A.6 above; **gutter-tile** a tile used in the construction of gutters, or to line the valleys of a roof.

gutterling *n.* a person of low breeding M19.

gutter /ˈgʌtə/ *n.*[2] L16. [f. GUT *v.* + -ER[1].] **1** A person employed in gutting animals, esp. fish. L16. **2** A person who guts buildings. M18.

gutter /ˈgʌtə/ *v.* LME. [f. GUTTER *n.*[1]] **1** *v.t.* Make gutters or channels in; channel, furrow; cut grooves in. LME. **2** *v.i.* Flow in streams, stream *down.* L16. **3** *v.i.* Of water: form gutters or gullies. M17. **4** *v.i.* Of a candle: melt away rapidly by becoming channelled on one side. (Foll. by *down, out.*) E18.

4 JOYCE The porter halted on the stairs to settle his guttering candle.

guttering *n.* (*a*) the action of the vb.; (*b*) material used for making gutters, gutters collectively; (*c*) the melted tallow or wax which runs down a candle: LME.

guttered /ˈgʌtəd/ *a.* M16. [f. GUTTER *n.*[1], *v.*: see -ED[2], -ED[1].] **1** Furrowed, gullied. M16. **2** Having gutters. L18. **3** Esp. of a candle: that has guttered. M19.

guttersnipe /ˈgʌtəsnʌɪp/ *n.* & *a.* M19. [f. GUTTER *n.*[1] + SNIPE *n.*] **A** *n.* **1** A street urchin; a person of low breeding. M19. **2** A gatherer of refuse from street gutters. M19. **3** A person who deals in shares on the street. *US slang.* Now *rare* or *obs.*. M19.

B *attrib.* or as *adj.* Typical of a guttersnipe. E20.

L. OLIVIER Here was I, with guttersnipe rashness, chalking some rudeness upon Sir Barry Jackson's fine escutcheon.

guttery /ˈgʌtəri/ *n.* M19. [f. GUT *v.* + -ERY.] A place where fish are gutted or the offal of slaughtered animals is disposed of.

guttery /ˈgʌtəri/ *a.* M18. [f. GUTTER *n.*[1] + -Y[1].] **1** Of corn: grooved, channelled. Now *rare.* M18. **2** Miry, muddy. *Sc.* L18.

Gut-tide /ˈgʊttʌɪd/ *n.* Long *dial.* E17. [Alt. of *good tide.* Perh. also assoc. w. GUT *n.*] Shrove Tuesday; *gen.* a time of feasting.

guttiform /ˈgʌtɪfɔːm/ *a.* L19. [f. L GUTTA *n.*[1] + -I- + -FORM.] = GUTTATE, GUTTATED.

gutting /ˈgʌtɪŋ/ *n.* M17. [Origin unkn.] A kind of canvas.

guttle /ˈgʌt(ə)l/ *v.* M17. [f. GUT *n.* after *guzzle.*] **1** *v.i.* Eat voraciously. M17. **2** *v.t.* Devour or swallow greedily. (Foll. by *up, down.*) L17.

guttler *n.* E18.

guttur /ˈgʌtə/ *n.* Now *rare.* M16. [L: see next.] The throat of a person or an animal.

guttural /ˈgʌt(ə)r(ə)l/ *a.* & *n.* L16. [Fr., or med.L *gutturalis*, f. L *guttur* throat: see -AL[1].] **A** *adj.* **1** Of a sound: produced in the throat, or by the back of the tongue and the (soft) palate; of articulation: throaty, harsh-sounding. L16. **2** Chiefly *Anat.* Of or pertaining to the throat. E17.

1 C. S. FORESTER A portly, kindly gentleman with . . a deep guttural voice.

B *n.* A guttural sound. L16.

gutturalism *n.* guttural quality or characteristics L19. **guttuˈrality** *n.* guttural nature, gutturalism L18. **gutturalize** *v.t.* pronounce or utter gutturally; make (a sound) guttural in character: E19. **gutturally** *adv.* †(*a*) indistinctly; (*b*) in a guttural manner; with a guttural sound: M17.

gutturo- /ˈgʌt(ə)rəʊ/ *comb. form.* L18. [f. L GUTTUR + -O-.] *Anat.* Pertaining to the throat and —, as *gutturo-maxillary*; *Phonet.* guttural and —, as *gutturo-labial.*

guttus /ˈgʌtəs/ *n.* M19. [L.] *Archaeol.* A narrow-necked cruet or oil-flask of ancient Roman times.

gutty /ˈgʌti/ *n. Golfers' slang.* L19. [f. GUTTA *n.*[2] + -Y[6].] In full *gutty ball.* A gutta-percha golf ball. Cf. GUTTA *n.*[2] 2.

gutty /ˈgʌti/ *a.*[1] L18. [f. GUT *n.* + -Y[1].] **1** Corpulent, pot-bellied. Chiefly *Sc.* L18. **2** Earthy, primitive. *Jazz slang.* M20. **3** = GUTSY *a.* 2. *slang.* M20.

gutty *a.*[2] var. of GUTTÉ *a.*

gutzer *n.* var. of GUTSER.

guv /gʌv/ *n. slang.* L19. [Abbrev.] = GOVERNOR 7c. Cf. next.

guvner /ˈgʌvnə/ *n.* Also **guv'ner, guvnor, guv'nor.** M19. [Repr. non-standard or colloq. pronunc.] = GOVERNOR 7c. Cf. prec.

guy /gʌɪ/ *n.*[1] LME. [Sense 1 f. OFr. *guie* guide, f. *guier* GUY *v.*[1] Sense 2 prob. of LG origin, as are Du. *gei* brail, *geitouw* clew-garnet, *geiblok* pulley, G *Geitau* clew-line, (pl.) brails.] †**1** A guide; a conductor, a leader. *rare.* LME–E16. **2** In full *guy-rope.* A rope, chain, etc., used to guide, secure, or steady something, esp. on a ship; a line helping to hold a tent in place. LME.

guy /gʌɪ/ *n.*[2] E19. [*Guy* Fawkes (1570–1606), Eng. Catholic, who was hanged for his part in the Gunpowder Plot.] **1** An effigy of a man, usually a crude one in ragged clothes, which is burnt on a bonfire on or near 5 November, the anniversary of the Gunpowder Plot. Cf. GUY FAWKES. E19. **2** A person of grotesque appearance, esp. in dress. M19. **3** A man, a fellow; in *pl.* also (chiefly *N. Amer.*), people (of either sex). *colloq.* (orig. *N. Amer.*). L19. **4** An act of running off secretly. *slang.* L19.

1 PENNY *for the guy.* 3 B. SCHULBERG I never saw a guy work so hard for twelve bucks a week. *regular guy*: see REGULAR *a. tough guy*: see TOUGH *a. wise guy*: see WISE *a.* & *n.*[2] 4 **do a guy** run away. **give the guy to** give the slip to.

guy /gʌɪ/ *v.*[1]*t. obs.* exc. *Sc.* ME. [OFr. *guier*: see GUIDE *v.*] †**1** Control, direct, (a person, his or her action). ME–E16. †**2** Command (an army); govern (a country); manage (affairs). Cf. GUIDE *v.* 2. ME–E17. **3** = GUIDE *v.* 1. LME.

guy /gʌɪ/ *v.*[2]*t.* E18. [f. GUY *n.*[1]] Fasten or secure with a guy or guys. (Foll. by *down, out, up*, etc.)

Scientific American Hemp was woven into rigging and line that would guy the masts.

guy /gʌɪ/ *v.*[3] M19. [f. GUY *n.*[2]] **1a** *v.i.* Carry or exhibit a guy in the streets around 5 November. M19. **b** *v.t.* Exhibit (a person) in effigy. L19. **2a** *v.t.* Make fun of, ridicule by innuendo; trifle with (a theatrical part). M19. **b** *v.i.* Mock (*at*); play the fool. L19. **3** *v.i.* Run away or *off*; go away. *slang.* L19.

2a G. GREER Vociferous women are guyed in the press.

Guyanese /gʌɪəˈniːz/ *a.* & *n.* M20. [f. *Guyana* (see below) + -ESE. Cf. GUIANESE.] **A** *n.* Pl. same. A native or inhabitant of Guyana (until 1966 British Guiana), a country in north-eastern S. America. M20. **B** *adj.* Of or pertaining to Guyana. M20.

Also **Guyˈanan** *n.* M20.

Guy Fawkes /gʌɪ ˈfɔːks/ *n.* E19. [See GUY *n.*[2]] = GUY *n.*[2] 1. Chiefly in *Guy Fawkes day, night.*

Comb.: **Guy Fawkes day, night** 5 November, the anniversary of the Gunpowder Plot (cf. *Bonfire Night* s.v. BONFIRE *n.*).

guyot /ˈgiːəʊ/ *n.* M20. [A. H. *Guyot* (1807–84), Swiss geographer.] A seamount with a flat top.

guyver /ˈgʌɪvə/ *n. Austral.* & *NZ slang.* Also **gui-, gy-.** M19. [Origin unkn.] Talk intended to impress or deceive; affectation of behaviour. Freq. in *put on the guyver*

guz /gʌz/ *n.* L17. [Urdu & Pers. *gaz.*] In the Indian subcontinent and Iran, a measure of length varying between approximately 27 and 41 inches.

guze /gjuːz/ *n.* M16. [Origin uncertain: cf. Turk. *göz* eye.] *Her.* A roundel of a sanguine tincture.

guzzle /ˈgʌz(ə)l/ *n.* L16. [App. f. the vb.] **1** A gutter, a drain. *obs.* exc. *dial.* L16. **2** The throat. *dial.* M17. **3** Drink, liquor. L17. **4** A bout of excessive eating and drinking. M19.

Comb.: **guzzle-guts** *slang* a glutton.

guzzle /ˈgʌz(ə)l/ *v.* L16. [Perh. f. OFr. *gosillier* chatter, vomit, f. (O)Fr. *gosier* throat f. late L *geusiae* cheeks.] **1** *v.t.* Swallow (esp. drink) greedily or to excess. (Foll. by *down, up.*) L16. **2** *v.i.* Drink a large amount, drink greedily. L16. **3** *v.t.* Consume (time, money) in guzzling. Usu. foll. by *away, down.* M17. **4** *v.t.* Seize by the throat; choke, strangle. *slang* & *dial.* L19.

1 A. SILLITOE They were guzzling tea in the common room. 2 L. DEIGHTON Tequila . . or imported whisky, it's all the same to him once he starts guzzling.

guzzler *n.* E18. **guzzling** *ppl a.* that guzzles; drunken; gluttonous, greedy: M17.

gwan /gwɑːn/ *v.i. Ir. dial.* & *US* (*non-standard*). E20. [Repr. a pronunc.] Go on: esp. in expressions of impatience or encouragement.

gwely /ˈgwɛli/ *n.* L19. [Welsh.] *Hist.* A social unit formerly traditional in Wales, comprising four generations of one family in which the great-grandfather as head of the group had proprietary rights over landed property; the land held by the members of such a group.

Gwentian /ˈgwɛntɪən/ *n.* & *a.* M19. [f. *Gwent* (see below) + -IAN.] **A** *n.* A native or inhabitant of Gwent, formerly a Welsh principality and since 1974 a Welsh county formed from parts of the former counties of Monmouthshire (England) and Breconshire (Wales); the dialect of this region. M19. **B** *adj.* Of or pertaining to Gwent. M19.

gwine /gwʌɪn/ *v.* (*pres. pple*). *dial.* & *US* (*non-standard*). M19. [Repr. a pronunc.] Going.

gwyniad /ˈgwɪnɪad/ *n.* Also †**guin-.** E17. [Welsh, f. *gwyn* white.] The houting, *Coregonus lavaretus*, of a race occurring in Bala Lake, N. Wales. Cf. POWAN, SKELLY *n.* 1.

†**gybe** *n.*[1] *slang.* M16–E19. [Origin unkn.] A counterfeit pass or licence.

gybe /dʒʌɪb/ *n.*[2] Also ***jibe.** L19. [f. the vb.] *Naut.* The action or an act of gybing.

gybe /dʒʌɪb/ *v.* Also ***jibe.** L17. [Du. †*gijben* (now *gijpen*, whence G *geipen*). Cf. JIB *v.*[1]] *Naut.* **1a** *v.i.* Of a fore-and-aft sail or its boom: swing from one side of a vessel to the other (now, when the vessel is running before the wind). L17. **b** *v.t.* Cause (a fore-and-aft sail or its boom) to gybe. L19. **2a** *v.i.* Of a vessel or its crew: change course in such a way that the mainsail gybes. Cf. TACK *v.*[1] 7. L17. **b** *v.t.* Cause (a vessel) to gybe. L19.

gyle /gʌɪl/ *n.* ME. [MDu. *ghijl* (Du. *gijl*) rel. to *gijlen* ferment; ult. origin unkn.] *Brewing.* **1** Wort in the process of fermentation. (Earliest in *gyle-fat* below.) ME. **2** A brewing; the quantity of beer or ale brewed at one time. L16.

Comb.: **gyle-fat** *obs.* exc. *Sc.* & *dial.* = *gyle-tun* below; **gyle-kier** *obs.* exc. *dial.* a tub or other vessel for holding wort; the wort itself; **gyle-tun** a vat in which the wort is left to ferment.

gym /dʒɪm/ *n. colloq.* L19. [Abbrev.] A gymnasium; gymnastics. Freq. *attrib.*
Comb.: **gymslip**, **gym tunic** a schoolgirl's sleeveless usu. belted garment reaching from shoulder to knee.

gymkhana /dʒɪmˈkɑːnə/ *n.* Orig. *Anglo-Ind.* M19. [Alt. by assim. to GYM, GYMNASTIC of Urdu *gendḵānah* racket-court, f. Hind. *gēd* ball + Pers. *kānah* house.] Orig., a public place in India with facilities for athletics; later, an athletics display. Now *spec.* a meeting for competition between horse-riders or car-drivers.

gymnadenia /dʒɪmnəˈdiːnɪə/ *n.* E19. [mod.L (see below), f. Gk *gumnos* naked + *adēn*, *aden-* gland: see -IA[1].] Any of various orchids of the genus *Gymnadenia*; *esp.* the fragrant orchid, *G. conopsea*.

gymnasiarch /dʒɪmˈneɪzɪɑːk/ *n.* M17. [L *gymnasiarchus*, *-archa* f. Gk *gumnasiarkhos*, *-arkhēs*, f. *gumnasion* GYMNASIUM: see -ARCH.] **1** *Gk Hist.* An Athenian official whose duty was to superintend athletic schools and games. M17. **b** A leader among athletes, an expert athlete. E19. **2** A governor of a school, college, or academy, esp. a Continental gymnasium; a head instructor. L17.
gymnasiarchy *n.* the position or function of a gymnasiarch M19.

gymnasiast /dʒɪmˈneɪzɪast/ *n.* E19. [f. Gk *gumnasion* GYMNASIUM after G *Gymnasiast*.] **1** A student in a Continental gymnasium. E19. **2** A gymnast. M19.

gymnasium /dʒɪmˈneɪzɪəm/ *n.* Pl. **-iums**, **-ia** /-ɪə/. L16. [L f. Gk *gumnasion*, f. *gumnazein* exercise naked, f. *gumnos* naked.] **1** A place, room, or building, equipped for gymnastics or for indoor sports. L16. **2** Formerly, a high school, college, or academy in Continental Europe. Now *spec.* in Germany and some other Continental countries, a school of the highest grade, preparing pupils for universities. L17.
gymnasial *a.* of or pertaining to a gymnasium in Continental Europe M19.

gymnast /ˈdʒɪmnast/ *n.* L16. [Fr. *gymnaste* or Gk *gumnastēs* trainer of athletes, f. *gumnazein*: see prec.] A person skilled or trained in gymnastics.

gymnastic /dʒɪmˈnastɪk/ *a.* & *n.* L16. [L *gymnasticus* f. Gk *gumnastikos*, f. *gumnazein*: see GYMNASIUM, -IC.] **A** *adj.* **1** Pertaining to or concerned with gymnastics. L16. **2** *fig.* Pertaining to mental exercise, discipline, effort, or activity. E18. **3** Of an initial letter in an illuminated manuscript: decorated with human figures etc. which are represented climbing like gymnasts round the letter. M20. **B** *n.* **1** In *pl.* (now usu. treated as *sing.*) or (now *rare*) *sing.* The performance of athletic exercises and feats of physical agility, esp. in a place equipped for the purpose. L16. †**2** An authority on gymnastics. *rare.* L16–E17. **3** A gymnastic feat. *rare.* M19.
1 *fig.*: R. BROUGHTON It seemed an impossible feat in mental gymnastics to . . wrench his thoughts away.
gymnastical *a.* = GYMNASTIC *a.* L16. **gymnastically** *adv.* in a gymnastic manner; pertaining to gymnastics: M17.

gymnic /ˈdʒɪmnɪk/ *a.* & *n.* Now *rare.* E17. [L *gymnicus* f. Gk *gumnikos* pertaining to bodily exercises f. *gumnos* naked: see -IC.] **A** *adj.* = GYMNASTIC *a.* I. E17. **B** *n.* In *pl.* Gymnastics; gymnastic exercises. E17.
†**gymnical** *a.* = GYMNIC *a.* L16–M18.

gymno- /ˈdʒɪmnəʊ/ *comb. form.* [Gk *gumnos* naked: see -O-.] Bare, uncovered, naked.

gymnosophist /dʒɪmˈnɒsəfɪst/ *n.* Now *rare.* LME. [Fr. *gymnosophiste* f. L *gymnosophistae* pl. f. Gk *gumnosophistai* pl., f. as GYMNO- + *sophistēs* SOPHIST.] A member of a reputed Hindu sect, reported in ancient history, who wore very little clothing and were given to asceticism and contemplation; *transf.* an ascetic, a mystic.
gymnosophy *n.* (*rare*) the doctrine or system of gymnosophists E19.

gymnosperm /ˈdʒɪmnəspəːm/ *n.* M19. [mod.L *gymnospermus* f. Gk *gumnospermos*, f. as GYMNO- + *sperma* seed.] A woody plant belonging to the Gymnospermae, one of the two main divisions of seed plants, lacking flowers and with seeds unprotected by an ovary or fruit, and including conifers, cycads, and ginkgos.
gymnoˈspermous *a.* characteristic of or designating a gymnosperm E18.

gymnotus /dʒɪmˈnəʊtəs/ *n.* Pl. **-ti** /-tʌɪ/. L18. [mod.L *Gymnotus* (see below), f. as GYMNO- + Gk *nōton* back, w. ref. to the absence of dorsal fins.] An electric eel (formerly placed in the genus *Gymnotus*).

gymnure /ˈgɪmnjʊə/ *n.* L19. [mod.L *Gymnura* former genus name, f. Gk *gumnos* naked + *oura* tail.] *Zool.* Any of several ratlike nocturnal insectivores constituting the subfamily Galericinae of the hedgehog family, native to SE Asia. Also called *moon rat*.

gymp *n.* var. of GIMP *n.*[1]

gympie /ˈgɪmpi/ *n.* L19. [Aborig.] An Australian evergreen shrub, *Dendrocnide moroides*, of the nettle family, with leaves covered with stinging hairs.

gyn- *comb. form* see GYNO-.

gynae /ˈgʌɪni/ *n. colloq.* Also **gynie**. M20. [f. GYNAE(COLOGY etc.: see -IE.] Gynaecology; the gynaecology department of a hospital; a gynaecologist.

gynaeceum /dʒʌɪnɪˈsiːəm, g-/ *n.* Also **-cium**, †**-caeum**, ***-nec-**. E17. [L *gynaeceum* f. Gk *gunaikeion*, f. as next.] **1** *Hist.* The women's apartments in a household; any room or building set aside for women esp. in ancient Greece or Rome. E17. †**2** A textile factory under the Roman Empire. E17–L18. **3** *Bot.* See GYNOECIUM.

gynaeco- /gʌɪˈniːkəʊ, dʒ-/ *comb. form.* Also ***-nec-**. [Gk *gunaiko-*, f. *gunaik-*, *gunē* woman, female: see -O-.] Woman, women; female(s).
gynaecoˈmastia, †**-masty** *n.* the state in a man of having breasts like those of a woman, owing to hormone imbalance or hormone therapy M19. **gynaecoˈmazia** *n.* (now *rare* or *obs.*) = GYNAECOMASTIA M19.

gynaecocracy /gʌɪnɪˈkɒkrəsi, dʒ-/ *n.* Also ***-nec-** E17. [Fr. *gynécocratie* or mod.L *gynaecocratia* f. Gk *gunaikokratia*, f. as prec.: see -CRACY.] Government by a woman or women; female dominance; *derog.* petticoat government. Cf. GYNARCHY.
gynaecoˈcratic *a.* L19. **gynaecoˈcratical** *a.* M19.

gynaecoid /ˈgʌɪnɪkɔɪd, ˈdʒʌɪ-/ *a.* Also ***-nec-**. E20. [f. GYNAECO- + -OID.] **1** *Entomol.* Designating a worker ant that lays eggs. E20. **2** Resembling or characteristic of (that of) a female. M20.
2 R. GORDON Petunia appeared, in an evening gown nicely displaying her gynaecoid pelvis.

gynaecology /gʌɪnɪˈkɒlədʒi, dʒ-/ *n.* Also ***-nec-**. M19. [f. GYNAECO- + -OLOGY.] The branch of medicine that deals with the physiology and diseases of women and girls, esp. of their reproductive organs.
gynaecoˈlogic *a.* (*US*) M20. **gynaecoˈlogical** *a.* L19. **gynaecoˈlogically** *adv.* in accordance with gynaecology L19. **gynaecologist** *n.* L19.

gynander /dʒɪˈnandə, gʌɪ-/ *n.* E19. [f. as GYNANDROUS.] †**1** *Bot.* A gynandrous plant. *rare.* Only in E19. **2** = GYNANDROMORPH. M20.

gynandromorph /dʒɪˈnandrəmɔːf, gʌɪ-/ *n.* L19. [f. as GYNANDROUS + -O- + Gk *morphē* form.] An individual, esp. an insect, with some male and some female characteristics.
gynandroˈmorphic *a.* = GYNANDROMORPHOUS L19. **gynandroˈmorphism** *n.* the state of being a gynandromorph M19. **gynandroˈmorphous** *a.* pertaining to or designating a gynandromorph M19.

gynandrous /dʒɪˈnandrəs, gʌɪ-/ *a.* E19. [f. Gk *gunandros* of doubtful sex, f. *gunē* woman, female: see -ANDROUS.] **1** *Bot.* Having the stamens and pistils united in a column, as in orchids. E19. **2** Of people or animals: hermaphrodite. M20.

gynarchy /ˈgʌɪnɑːki, ˈdʒʌɪ-/ *n.* Now *rare.* Orig. †**gun-**. L16. [f. GYNO- + -ARCHY.] Government by a woman or women. Cf. GYNAECOCRACY.

gyne /dʒʌɪn/ *n.* E20. [Gk *gunē* woman, female.] A queen ant.

gyneco- *comb. form*, **gynecocracy** *n.*, etc.: see GYNAECO-, GYNAECOCRACY, etc.

gyneocracy /gʌɪnɪˈɒkrəsi/ *n. rare.* E17. [f. GYNO- + -CRACY.] = GYNAECOCRACY.

gynie *n.* var. of GYNAE.

gyno- /ˈgʌɪnəʊ, ˈdʒʌɪ-/ *comb. form.* Bef. a vowel **gyn-**. [f. Gk *gunē* woman, female + -O-.] Used in senses (*a*) woman, women; (*b*) female reproductive organ, esp. (*Bot.*) of a plant.
gynobase *n.* (*Bot.*) an enlargement of the receptacle that supports the gynoecium in some plants M19. **gynoˈbasic** *a.* (*Bot.*) pertaining to or having a gynobase M19. **gynodioecious** /-dʌɪˈiːʃəs/ *a.* (*Bot.*) having female and hermaphrodite flowers on separate individuals L19. **gynodioecism** /-dʌɪˈiːsɪz(ə)m/ *n.* = GYNODIOECY L19. **gynodioecy** /-dʌɪˈiːsi/ *n.* (*Bot.*) the condition of being gynodioecious M20. **gynoˈgenesis** *n.* (*Zool.*) reproduction in which a sperm penetrates an ovum but their nuclei do not fuse, and the embryo develops with maternal chromosomes only E20. **gynogeˈnetic** *a.* (*Zool.*) of the nature of, arising by, or involving gynogenesis E20. **gynomonoecious** /-məˈniːʃəs/ *a.* (*Bot.*) having female and hermaphrodite flowers on the same individual L19. **gynomonoecism** /-məˈniːsɪz(ə)m/ *n.* (*Bot.*) = GYNOMONOECY L19. **gynomonoecy** /-məˈniːsi/ *n.* (*Bot.*) the condition of being gynomonoecious M20. **gynoˈphobia** *n.* fear of women L19. **gynoˈphobic** *a.* pertaining to or affected with gynophobia L20. **gynophore** *n.* (*Bot.*) a stalk which in some plants supports the ovary etc. above the level of other parts of the flower E19. **gynostegium** /-ˈstiːdʒɪəm/ *n.* (*Bot.*) a united anther and stigma in certain plants L19.

gynocracy /gʌɪˈnɒkrəsi, dʒ-/ *n.* E18. [f. GYNO- + -CRACY.] = GYNAECOCRACY; a government of women; women as the ruling class.
gynoˈcratic *a.* M19.

gynoecium /gʌɪˈniːsɪəm, dʒ-/ *n.* Also ***-nec-**, †**gynaeceum**. Pl. **-ia** /-ɪə/. M19. [mod.L, f. GYNO- + Gk *oikos* house; *gynaecium* by alt., after L GYNAECEUM.] *Bot.* The female part of an angiosperm flower, which may consist of a single carpel, a number of unfused carpels (apocarpous), or a number of fused carpels (syncarpous).

-gynous /ˈdʒʌɪnəs/ *suff.* [f. mod.L *-gynus* f. Gk *-gunos*, f. as GYNO-: see -OUS.] **1** *Bot.* Having female reproductive organs of an indicated kind or number, as *androgynous*, *monogynous*. **2** Of or pertaining to women, as *androgynous*.

gyp /dʒɪp/ *n.*[1] M18. [Perh. abbrev. of GIPPO *n.*[1]] A college servant, esp. at the Universities of Cambridge and Durham.

gyp /dʒɪp/ *n.*[2] *colloq.* L19. [App. contr. of GEE-UP.] Only in *give a person gyp*, (*a*) (of a person) scold or punish a person severely; (*b*) (of a pain etc.) hurt a person very much.

gyp /dʒɪp/ *n.*[3] & *v. colloq.* L19. [Origin unkn.] **A** *n.* **1** A thief, a swindler. L19. **2** A fraudulent action, a swindle. E20. **B** *v.t.* Infl. **-pp-**. Cheat, swindle. (Foll. by *of*.) L19.

gyp /dʒɪp/ *n.*[4] *US.* L19. [Perh. abbrev. of GYPSY *n.* used as a proper name.] A bitch.

gypo *n.* & *a.* var. of GIPPO *n.*[2] & *a.*

gyppo *n.* & *a.* var. of GIPPO *n.*[2] & *a.*

gyppy *n.* & *a.* var. of GIPPY.

gyps /dʒɪps/ *n.* LME. [Anglicization.] Gypsum.

gypseous /ˈdʒɪpsɪəs/ *a.* LME. [f. late L *gypseus*, f. L GYPSUM: see -OUS.] **1** Resembling gypsum; hardened, calcified. LME. **2** Containing gypsum, composed chiefly of gypsum. L18.

gypsiferous /dʒɪpˈsɪf(ə)rəs/ *a.* M19. [f. GYPSUM + -I- + -FEROUS.] Containing or yielding gypsum.

Gypsologist *n.* var. of GYPSYOLOGIST.

gypsophila /dʒɪpˈsɒfɪlə/ *n.* L18. [mod.L (see below), f. Gk *gupsos* chalk, gypsum + *-philos* -loving.] Any of several plants constituting the genus *Gypsophila*, of the pink family; esp. *G. elegans* and *G. paniculata*, grown for their profusion of delicate white flowers.

gypsophilous /dʒɪpˈsɒfɪləs/ *a.* E20. [f. Gk *gupsos* chalk + -OUS.] *Ecol.* Growing on soils rich in gypsum or, formerly, on limestone.
ˈgypsophile *n.* a gypsophilous plant M20.

gypsous /ˈdʒɪpsəs/ *a.* M17. [f. GYPSUM + -OUS.] = GYPSEOUS.

gypsum /ˈdʒɪpsəm/ *n.* & *v.* LME. [L f. Gk *gupsos* chalk, gypsum.] A *n.* Hydrated calcium sulphate, a soft mineral that occurs as colourless, white, or grey monoclinic prismatic crystals in many sedimentary rocks and is used for making plaster of Paris and as a fertilizer. LME. B *v.t. Agric.* Dress with gypsum. E19.

gypsy /ˈdʒɪpsi/ *n.* & *a.* Also **gi-**, (orig.) **†gipcyan, †gipsen**. M16. [Aphet. f. EGYPTIAN, Gypsies having been orig. thought to have come from Egypt. Later form *gypsy* perh. f. L *Aegyptius*.] A *n.* 1 (Also **G-**.) A member of a travelling people in Europe and N. America who have dark skin and hair and came originally from India, their language (Romany) being related to Hindi; a person regarded as resembling one of this people in looks or way of life. M16. †2 An Egyptian. Only in E17. 3 A cunning, deceitful, or fickle woman (*derog.*); (a playful name for) a woman or girl. E17. 4 In full *gypsy moth*. A kind of tussock moth, *Lymantria dispar*, which has become a serious pest of trees in parts of N. America since it was introduced there from Europe. E19. 5 (In full *gypsy winch*) a small winch used on board ship; a toothed or recessed drum on the shaft of a windlass for taking an anchor chain; *US* a smooth drum used similarly to take a rope. L19. 6 An independent truck-driver. *US.* M20.

Phrases: **Gypsy's warning** a cryptic or sinister warning.

Comb.: **gypsy cab** *US* a taxi that is licensed only to respond to telephone calls to the company, *esp.* one that nevertheless cruises for prospective fares; *gypsy moth*: see sense 4 above; **gypsy rose** *dial.* the field scabious, *Knautia arvensis*; *gypsy winch*: see sense 5 above; **gypsywort** [from its reputed use by Gypsies to stain the skin] a labiate plant of watersides, *Lycopus europaeus*, with deeply cut leaves and whorls of small white flowers.

B *attrib.* or as *adj.* Of, pertaining to, or characteristic of a Gypsy or Gypsies; characteristic of Gypsies; (of a meal) taken outdoors. M17.

J. BUCHAN The traveller had a receptive ear for music . . from the operas of Rome and Paris to gypsy dances. D. WELCH He . . looked dark, Saturnine and rather gypsy with the bright colour.

Gypsydom *n.* (*a*) Gypsies collectively; (*b*) *rare* the state of being a Gypsy or living like a Gypsy: M19. **Gypsyhood** *n.* = GYPSYDOM M19. **Gypsyish** *a.* L19. **Gypsyism** *n.* the life and customs of Gypsies E17.

gypsy /ˈdʒɪpsi/ *v.i.* Also **gi-**. E17. [f. GYPSY *n.*] Live or behave like a Gypsy. Chiefly as *gypsying* vbl n. & ppl a.

Gypsyfy /ˈdʒɪpsɪfʌɪ/ *v.t.* Usu. **Gipsify, Gipsyfy**. E17. [f. GYPSY *n.* & *a.* + -FY.] Make like a Gypsy.

Gypsyologist /dʒɪpsɪˈɒlədʒɪst/ *n.* Also **Gypsol-** /dʒɪpˈsɒl-/. M19. [f. GYPSY *n.* + -OLOGIST.] A person who studies Gypsies and their ways.

gyral /ˈdʒʌɪr(ə)l/ *a.* E19. [f. GYRE *n.* + -AL[1].] Moving in a circle or spiral; of or pertaining to a gyre or gyrus.

gyrally *adv.* M18.

gyrase /ˈdʒʌɪreɪz/ *n.* L20. [f. GYRE *n.* + -ASE.] *Biochem.* An enzyme which removes supercoils from double-helix DNA.

gyrate /ˈdʒʌɪrət/ *a.* M19. [L *gyratus*, f. as GYRUS: see -ATE[2].] Chiefly *Bot.* Arranged in rings or convolutions; circinate.

gyrate /dʒʌɪˈreɪt/ *v.i.* E19. [Late L *gyrat-* pa. ppl stem of *gyrare*, f. L *gyrus*: see GYRUS, -ATE[3].] Move in a circle or spiral; revolve round a fixed point or axis; rotate, whirl.

V. WOOLF Twisting couples gyrating in time to the tune of the gramophone.

gyration /dʒʌɪˈreɪʃ(ə)n/ *n.* E17. [Late L *gyratio(n-)*, f. as prec.: see -ATION.] The action or process, or an act, of gyrating; rotation, whirling.

fig.: S. WADDINGTON The vortex of religious excitement . . kept him idly moving in its ceaseless gyrations.

gyrator /dʒʌɪˈreɪtə/ *n.* M19. [f. GYRATE *v.* + -OR.] 1 A person who or thing which gyrates. M19. 2 *Electr.* A passive circuit element with two pairs of terminals which introduces a 180-degree phase shift in one direction of propagation but none in the other. M20.

gyratory /dʒʌɪˈreɪt(ə)ri, ˈdʒʌɪrət(ə)ri/ *a.* E19. [f. GYRATE *v.* + -ORY[2].] Moving in a circle or spiral; rotating, whirling; (esp. of a road junction or road system) involving such movement.

gyre /ˈdʒʌɪə, ˈgʌɪə/ *n.* M16. [L *gyrus* f. Gk *guros*.] I Chiefly *poet.* & *literary.* 1 A circular movement or turn; a revolution, a gyration. M16. 2 A circle, a spiral; a vortex. L16.

1 S. O'FAOLÁIN I . . felt the new day come up . . and life begin once more its ancient, ceaseless gyre. 2 J. A. BAKER Seven hundred lapwings . . dwindled up in spiral tiers and widening gyres.

II 3 *Sci.* A circular pattern of surface currents round an ocean basin. M20.

gyre /ˈdʒʌɪə, ˈgʌɪə/ *v.* LME. [Late L *gyrare*: see GYRATE *v.*] 1 *v.t.* Turn or whirl round. *rare.* LME. 2 *v.i.* Turn round, rotate, gyrate, whirl. L16.

gyre-carline /gʌɪəˈkɑːlɪn/ *n. Sc.* (now *rare* or *obs.*). M16. [f. ON *gýgr* ogress, witch + CARLINE *n.*[1]] A witch, a hag.

gyrectomy /dʒʌɪˈrɛktəmi/ *n.* M20. [f. GYRUS + -ECTOMY.] Surgical removal of a gyrus of the brain; an instance of this.

gyrene /dʒʌɪˈriːn, ˈdʒʌɪriːn/ *n. US slang.* Also **-ine, ji-, jy-**. L19. [Origin uncertain: *-rene* f. alt. of MA)RINE.] A US marine.

gyrfalcon /ˈdʒəːfɔː(l)k(ə)n, -fɒlk(ə)n/ *n.* Also **ger-, †jer-, †gier-**, etc. ME. [OFr. *gerfaucon* (mod. *gerfaut*) f. Frank. (G *Gerfalke*) = ON *geirfálki*, prob. f. OHG *gêr* spear: see FALCON. Spelling *gyr-* by false etym. from L *gyrare* GYRATE *v.*] Orig., any large falcon, *esp.* one used to fly at herons. Now, a heavy, powerful falcon, *Falco rusticolus*, of cold northerly regions, occurring in a wide range of colour forms from almost pure white to dark brown.

gyrine *n.* var. of GYRENE.

gyrinid /dʒɪˈrɪnɪd/ *a.* & *n.* E20. [mod.L *Gyrinidae* (see below), f. *Gyrinus* genus name f. Gk *gurinos* tadpole, f. *guros*: see GYRO-, -ID[3].] (Of, pertaining to, or designating) a beetle of the family Gyrinidae, comprising the whirligig beetles.

gyro /ˈdʒʌɪrəʊ/ *n.*[1] Pl. **-os**. E20. [Abbrev.] 1 = GYROSCOPE. *colloq.* E20. 2 = GYROCOMPASS. *colloq.* E20.

Comb.: **gyro-horizon** = ARTIFICIAL *horizon*; **gyro-pilot** a gyrocompass used to provide automatic steering for an aircraft or ship; **gyro-stabilizer** a gyroscope kept continuously spinning and mounted so as to counter any tendency to roll on the part of a ship, aircraft, platform, etc.

gyro /ˈjɪərəʊ, ˈdʒɪə-, ˈdʒʌɪ-; *foreign* ˈjiro/ *n.*[2] *US.* Pl. **-os** /-əʊz, *foreign* -ɔs/. L20. [mod.Gk *guros* turning: see GYRO-.] A sandwich of pitta bread filled with slices of spiced meat cooked on a spit, tomatoes, onions, etc.

gyro- /ˈdʒʌɪrəʊ/ *comb. form* of Gk *guros* ring, circle, used also w. the sense 'rotation': see -O-.

gyrocopter *n.* a kind of autogiro, now *spec.* a small light single-seater one E20. **gyrofrequency** *n.* (*Physics*) the frequency with which a charged particle spirals about the lines of force of a magnetic field M20. **gyroplane** *n.* an aircraft in which lift is provided by aerofoils rotating in an approximately horizontal plane; *esp.* one in which these are not driven by an engine but rotate as a result of the aircraft's forward motion E20. **gyrostat** *n.* any of various forms of gyroscope L19. **gyro'static** *a.* of or pertaining to a gyrostat or the principle of the gyroscope L19. **gyro'statically** *adv.* = GYROSCOPICALLY L19. **gyro-the'odolite** *n.* a type of theodolite that incorporates a gyroscope as an aid to orientation M20. **gyrotiller** *n.* (*Agric.*) a cultivator in which tines rotate about an axis M20.

gyrocompass /ˈdʒʌɪrə(ʊ)kʌmpəs/ *n.* E20. [f. GYRO(SCOPE + COMPASS *n.*] A non-magnetic compass in which a continuously driven gyroscope is so mounted that its axis remains parallel to the earth's axis of rotation.

gyromagnetic /ˌdʒʌɪrəʊmagˈnɛtɪk/ *a.* E20. [f. GYRO- + MAGNETIC.] 1 *Physics.* Of or pertaining to the interaction between the spin of a charged particle and the magnetic moment that it causes. E20. 2 Designating a compass in which the reading is provided by a directional gyroscope whose gradual deviations are automatically corrected by a magnetic compass. M20.

1 **gyromagnetic ratio**: of the magnetic moment of a spinning charged particle to its angular momentum.

gyromancy /ˈdʒʌɪrəmansi/ *n.* M16. [(O)Fr. *gyromancie*, f. as GYRO-: see -MANCY.] *Hist.* Divination by inference from the point at which a person walking round and round a marked circle fell down from dizziness.

gyron /ˈdʒʌɪərən/ *n.* L16. [(O)Fr. *giron*, †*geron* gusset f. OFrank. equiv. of OHG *gēro*: see GORE *n.*[2]] *Her.* A triangular ordinary made by two lines drawn from the edge of the shield to meet in the fess point and occupying half of the quarter.

gyronny /dʒʌɪˈrɒni/ *a.* LME. [Fr. *gironné*, f. as prec.: see -Y[5].] *Her.* Of a shield: divided into gyrons by lines crossing at the fesse-point.

gyroscope /ˈdʒʌɪrəskəʊp/ *n.* M19. [Fr., f. as GYRO-, -SCOPE.] A wheel or disc mounted so that it can spin rapidly about an axis which itself can rotate about either of two other axes perpendicular to it and to each other; because the spin axis tends to maintain the same direction in space gyroscopes are used in different devices to provide stabilization or a reference direction, and to measure angular velocity and acceleration.

gyro'scopic *a.* of, pertaining to, or employing a gyroscope L19. **gyro'scopically** *adv.* by or with a gyroscope; in a gyroscopic manner: E20.

gyrose /ˈdʒʌɪrəʊs/ *a.* M19. [f. L *gyrus*: see GYRUS, -OSE[1].] *Bot.* Wavy; marked with wavy lines.

gyrous /ˈdʒʌɪrəs/ *a. rare.* L17. [f. L *gyrus*: see GYRUS, -OUS.] Circular; spiral.

gyrus /ˈdʒʌɪrəs/ *n.* Pl. **-ri** /-rʌɪ/. M19. [L f. Gk *guros* ring, circle.] *Anat.* A ridge or convolution of the brain; (now *rare*) a convolution or turn of another organ.

FASCIOLAR *gyrus*. *uncinate gyrus*: see UNCINATE *a.* 1.

gyte /gʌɪt/ *n. Sc. derog.* L19. [Perh. alt. of GET *n.*[1] Cf. GIT *n.*[1]] A child; a brat.

gyte /gʌɪt/ *a. Sc.* E18. [Origin unkn.] Mad.

gytrash /ˈgʌɪtraʃ/ *n.* Chiefly *north.* M19. [Origin unkn.] An apparition, usu. in the form of a large dog or other animal.

gyttja /ˈjɪtʃə/ *n.* L19. [Sw. = mud, ooze.] A usu. black sediment, rich in organic matter, deposited in productive lakes.

gyve /dʒʌɪv, gʌɪv/ *n.* & *v.* Now *arch.* or *poet.* ME. [Origin unkn.] A *n.* A shackle, orig. esp. one for the leg. Usu. in *pl.* ME. B *v.t.* Fasten (as) with gyves; fetter. ME.

gyver *n.* var. of GUYVER.

H

H, h /eɪtʃ/, the eighth letter of the modern Eng. alphabet and of the ancient Roman one, repr. a Semitic letter adopted by Gk as eta, orig. the eighth and later, after the omission of ϝ (see F), the seventh letter of the alphabet. In Semitic the letter represented a voiceless laryngeal fricative; in early Gk and subsequently in L the letter represented the voiceless glottal fricative /h/ (in later Gk H represented a long vowel). In the Gmc languages the letter represented /h/ initially, and a voiceless velar or palatal fricative medially and finally. In OE the letter occurred bef. vowels and bef. the consonants *l, n, r, w*, as in *hlāf* loaf, *hræfn* raven, *hwā* who. H in mod. Eng. has the following values. (i) H has the sound /h/ bef. *a, e, i, o, u, y*. (ii) H following the consonants *c, p, s, t*, forms the digraphs *ch* /tʃ; *occas.* x, ç/, *ph* /f/, *sh* /ʃ/, *th* /θ, ð/. Pl. **H's, Hs**. See also AITCH.

I 1 The letter and its sound. **2** The shape of the letter.

2 **H-block** an H-shaped building in the Maze prison in Northern Ireland. **H-iron** a girder of H-shaped section. **H-shaped** *a.* having a shape or a cross-section like the capital letter H; having two long side pieces with a right-angled crosspiece joining them at or near the middle.

II Symbolical uses. **3** Used to denote serial order; applied e.g. to the eighth group or section, sheet of a book, etc. **4** The eighth hypothetical person or example. **5** *Physics* etc. **a** (Cap. H.) Magnetic field strength. **b** (Cap. H.) The Hamiltonian function of classical mechanics; the Hamiltonian operator of quantum mechanics. **c** (Italic *h*.) Planck's constant. Also $\hbar = h/2\pi$. **d** (Cap. H.) Enthalpy.

III 6 Abbrevs.: (A small selection only is given here. Those all in caps. or small caps. also occur with a full stop after each letter; some of those all in caps. also occur (i) with initial cap. only, (ii) in small caps.) **H.** = hardness; hard (pencil-lead); (*Electr.*) henry(s). **H** = hydrogen. **h.** = (as *pref.*) hecto-; hour(s). **Ha** = hahnium. **ha.** = hectare(s). **Hab.** = Habakkuk (in the Bible). **HAC** = Honourable Artillery Company. **Hag.** = Haggai (in the Bible). **h. & c.** = hot and cold (water). **Hants.** = Hampshire. **HB** = hard black (pencil-lead). **Hb** (*Med.*) = haemoglobin. **HBM** = Her, His, Britannic Majesty('s). **HC** = Holy Communion; House of Commons. **h.c.** = HONORIS CAUSA. **HCF** = highest common factor; Honorary Chaplain to the Forces. **HCFC** = hydrochlorofluorocarbon. **HDTV** = high-definition television. **HE** = high explosive; His Eminence; Her, His, Excellency. **He** (*Chem.*) = helium. **Heb.** = Hebrew; Hebrews (New Testament). **HEFCE** = Higher Education Funding Council for England. **HEFCS** = Higher Education Funding Council for Scotland. **HEFCW** = Higher Education Funding Council for Wales. **Herts.** = Hertfordshire. **HEW** (*US*) = Department of Health, Education, and Welfare. **HF** = high frequency. **hf.** = half. **Hf** (*Chem.*) = hafnium. **HG** = Her, His, Grace; Home Guard. **hg.** = hectogram(s). **Hg** (*Chem.*) = [mod.L] *hydrargyrum* mercury. **HGV** = heavy goods vehicle. **HH** = Her, His, Highness; His Holiness; double-hard (pencil-lead). **hh.** = hands (units of 4 inches, the linear measure of a horse's height). **hhd.** = hogshead(s). **HI** (*US*) = Hawaii; the Hawaiian Islands. **HIH** = Her, His, Imperial Highness. **HIM** = Her, His, Imperial Majesty. **HIV** = human immunodeficiency virus. **HK** = Hong Kong; House of Keys. **HL** = House of Lords. **hl.** = hectolitre(s). **HM** = headmaster; headmistress; heavy metal (music); Her, His, Majesty('s). **hm.** = hectometre(s). **HMAS** = Her, His, Majesty's Australian Ship. **HMCS** = Her, His, Majesty's Canadian Ship. **HMG** = Her, His, Majesty's Government. **HMI** = Her, His, Majesty's Inspector (of Schools). **HMNZS** = Her, His, Majesty's New Zealand Ship. **HMS** = Her, His, Majesty's Ship. **HMSO** = Her, His, Majesty's Stationery Office. **HMV** = His Master's Voice (proprietary name). **HNC** = Higher National Certificate. **HND** = Higher National Diploma. **ho.** = house. **Ho** (*Chem.*) = holmium. **Hon.** = Honorary; Honourable. **Hon. Sec.** = Honorary Secretary. **Hos.** = Hosea (in the Bible). **h.p.** = hire purchase. **hp** = high pressure; horsepower. **HQ** = headquarters. **HR** (*US*) = House of Representatives. **hr.** = hour. **HRH** = Her, His, Royal Highness. **hrs.** = hours. **HRT** = hormone replacement therapy. **HSH** = Her, His, Serene Highness. **HT** = high tension. **HTLV** = human T-cell lymphotropic (or lymphocyte) virus. **Hunts.** (*Hist.*) = Huntingdonshire (a former county in England). **h.w.** = hit wicket. **HWM** = high-water mark. **Hy** = Henry. **Hz** = hertz.

ha /hɑː/ *v.i.* Also **hah**. E17. [f. HA *int.*] Utter 'ha' in hesitation. Esp. in *hum and ha*: see HUM *v.*[1] I.

ha /hɑː/ *int.* & *n.* Also **hah**. ME. [Natural exclam. Cf. AH *int.*, AHA *int.*, HE *int.*, HO *int.*[1]] **A** *int.* **1** Expr. surprise, joy, suspicion, indignation, etc. (Earlier in HA HA *int.*) ME. **2** Used as an interjectional interrogative, *esp.* one which follows a question; = EH 2. L16. **3** Expr. hesitation or interruption in speech. Cf. HAW *int.*[1], HUM *int.* E17. **B** *n.* This interjection, esp. as an expression of hesitation. Freq. in *hums and ha's*: see HUM *n.*[1] I. E17.

ha' *n.* see HALL *n.*

haaf /hɑːf, haf/ *n.* L18. [ON *haf* (Sw. *haf*, Da. *hav*) sea, high sea, ocean.] In Orkney and Shetland, the deep or main sea, esp. as used for deep-sea fishing.

haar /hɑː/ *n.* Chiefly *Sc.* & *north.* L17. [Perh. f. ON *hárr* hoar, hoary.] A wet mist or fog; *esp.* a cold sea-fog.

haarder *n.* var. of HARDER.

hab /hab/ *adv.* & *n. obs.* exc. *dial.* M16. [Repr. OE *hæbbe* pres. subjunct. of HAVE *v.*, w. corresp. neg. form *næbbe*. Cf. HOB *adv.* & *n.*[3], HOB-NOB *adv.*] (*by*) *hab or nab*, *by habs and nabs*, = HOB-NOB *adv.*

habanera /habəˈnɛːrə, ɑːb-/ *n.* L19. [Sp., short for *danza habanera* Havanan dance, fem. of *habanero* of Havana the capital of Cuba.] A slow Cuban dance and song in duple time.

habara /ˈhab(ə)rə/ *n.* Also **-ah, habra**. E19. [Arab. *ḥabara*.] In N. Africa, a woman's silk outdoor garment.

habdabs /ˈhabdabz/ *n.pl. slang.* M20. [Origin unkn.] Nervous anxiety, the heebie-jeebies. Freq. in *screaming habdabs*.

Habdalah /havˈdɑːlə/ *n.* Also **Hav-**. M18. [Heb. *habdālāh* separation, division.] A Jewish religious ceremony marking the end of the Sabbath; a prayer said at this ceremony.

habeas corpora /ˌheɪbɪəs ˈkɔːpərə/ *n. phr.* LME. [L = thou (shalt) have the bodies (*sc.* in court).] *Law* (now *Hist.*). A process formerly issued from the Court of Common Pleas, directing the sheriff to compel the attendance of reluctant jurors.

habeas corpus /ˌheɪbɪəs ˈkɔːpəs/ *n. phr.* LME. [L = thou (shalt) have the body (*sc.* in court).] *Law.* A writ requiring a person to be brought before a judge or into a court; *spec.* such a writ requiring the investigation of the legitimacy of a person's detention, by which his or her release may be secured.

Habeas Corpus Act an Act of Charles II in 1679, which greatly facilitated the use of such writs.

habendum /həˈbɛndəm/ *n.* E17. [L, lit. 'to be had, to be possessed', gerundive of *habere* have.] *Law* (now *Hist.*). The part of a deed determining the estate or quantity of interest granted by the deed.

haberdash /ˈhabədaʃ/ *n.* Long *rare.* LME. [Back-form. f. next or f. as next.] Small wares or merchandise.

haberdasher /ˈhabədaʃə/ *n.* ME. [Prob. f. unrecorded AN (cf. AL *habardasshator*) presumably f. recorded *hapertas*, of unkn. origin, perh. the name of a fabric: see -ER[2].] †**1** A dealer in a variety of household articles; *esp.* from the 16th cent., a dealer in hats and caps, a hatter. ME–E18. **2** A dealer in small articles related to dress, as thread, tape, ribbon, etc. Also (*N. Amer.*), a dealer in men's clothing and accessories. E17. **3** A drink-seller. *slang.* Now *rare.* E19.

haberdashery /ˈhabədaʃ(ə)ri/ *n.* LME. [f. as prec.: see -ERY.] **1** The goods and wares sold by a haberdasher. LME. **2** The shop or establishment of a haberdasher, esp. as a department in a store. E19.

1 R. BROUGHTON A whirlwind of haberdashery, Brussels lace, diamonds.

habergeon /ˈhabədʒ(ə)n, həˈbəːdʒ(ə)n/ *n.* ME. [(O)Fr. *haubergeon* f. OFr. *hauberc* (mod. *haubert*): see HAUBERK, -OON.] *Hist.* A sleeveless coat or jacket of mail or scale armour; a small hauberk.

habile /ˈhabɪl/ *a.* LME. [Var. of ABLE *a.*, conformed to mod.Fr. *habile* or L *habilis*.] **1 a** Suited; suitable; competent; = ABLE *a.* 2. *obs.* exc. *Sc.* LME. †**b** Manageable, easy to use; = ABLE *a.* 1. Only in M18. **2** Having the capacity or power (*to do*); = ABLE *a.* 4. Now *literary.* LME. **3** Handy, ready; skilful, adroit, dexterous. Now *literary.* L15.

habiliment /həˈbɪlɪm(ə)nt/ *n.* Also †**a-**. LME. [OFr. *abillement* (later & mod. *hab-*), f. *habiller* make fit, fit out (hence, by assoc. w. *habit*) clothe, dress, f. as prec.: see -MENT.] **1** Outfit, equipment, attire, dress. LME. †**2** In *pl.* Munitions, weapons, apparatus of war. LME–L17. **b** In *pl.* Pieces of armour, apparel of war. Also, the trappings of a horse. L15–E19. **3** In *pl.* The garments or apparel appropriate to any office or occasion. Also (*joc.*), ordinary clothes or dress. L15. †**4** Anything worn as an ornament; = BILIMENT. L15–E17. †**5** *fig.* Mental equipment or capacity; in *pl.*, abilities, faculties, powers. L16–M17.

1 S. ROGERS In rich habiliment Two Strangers at the Convent-gate. 3 A. B. JAMESON The Saviour is seen in the habiliments of a gardener.

habilimented *a.* (*arch.*) equipped, apparelled, dressed E17.

habilitate /həˈbɪlɪteɪt/ *v.* E17. [med.L *habilitat-* pa. ppl stem of *habilitare*, f. *habilitas* ABILITY: see -ATE[3].] **1** *v.t.* **a** Make capable, qualify. Now *rare.* E17. **b** Fit out (esp. the workings of a mine). *US.* E19. **2** *v.i.* [G *habilitieren.*] Qualify as a teacher in a German university. L19. **3** *v.t.* Clothe, dress. L19.

habili'tation *n.* the action of enabling; capacitation, qualification: E17.

hability /həˈbɪlɪti/ *n.* LME. [Var. of ABILITY. In sense 2 after Fr. *habileté*.] †**1** See ABILITY. LME. **2** The quality of being habile; readiness; adroitness. *rare.* M19.

habit /ˈhabɪt/ *n.* ME. [OFr. *abit* (later & mod. *habit*) f. L *habitus*, f. *habit-* pa. ppl stem of *habere* have, hold, (refl.) be constituted, be.] I Dress. 1 Bodily apparel or attire; clothing, dress. *arch.* ME. b A set or suit of clothes; a dress (of a specified kind). *arch.* LME. c A garment; a gown, a robe. Usu. in *pl. arch.* L15. d *transf.* & *fig.* Outward form or appearance; guise. M16. 2 *spec.* The dress or attire characteristic of a particular rank, profession, function, etc.; *esp.* the dress of a religious order. ME. 3 A costume designed to be worn by a woman on horseback, a riding-habit. L18.

1 H. J. LASKI Bolingbroke's Patriot King, dressed up in the habit of the elder Pitt. 2 L. DURRELL Her body lay shrouded in the habit of St Francis. *riding-habit* etc. 3 *Pony* Ready made side-saddle habits.

II Physical appearance or constitution. †4 Bearing, demeanour, deportment; posture. LME–L17. 5 Bodily condition or constitution. LME. †b The bodily system. L16–M18. †c The surface or outward appearance of the body. M17–E18. 6 *Biol.* & *Cryst.* The characteristic mode of growth and general external form of an organism (esp. a plant), mineral, etc. L17.

5 J. PRIESTLEY A being . . of a delicate tender habit. 6 *Scientific American* The pepper plant usually has a very leafy habit. *Photography* Controlling crystal habit (its shape) is closely determined by the sort of chemicals added to improve sensitivity.

III Mental disposition or constitution. 7 A person's mental or moral qualities; mental constitution, disposition, character. LME. 8 A settled disposition or tendency to act in a certain way, *esp.* one acquired by frequent repetition of the same act until it is almost involuntary; a customary practice or way of acting; (usu. in *pl.*) a characteristic action or mode of behaviour of an animal. LME. b Custom, usage. E17. c *spec.* A craving for or dependency on an addictive drug or drugs; the practice of taking such a drug or drugs. *colloq.* E19. d *Psychol.* An automatic reaction to a specific situation, acquired by learning or repetition. M19. †9 The condition of being accustomed to something; familiarity. L16–M19.

7 E. YOUNG You . . suit the gloomy habit of my soul. 8 J. THURBER Her habit of starting sentences in the middle bewildered him. T. A. COWARD The Red-footed Falcon . . shares with the Hobby one habit, that of hawking for crepuscular moths. c L. D. ESTLEMAN As innocent as a hooker with a heroin habit.

IV †10 *Logic.* The eighth of the ten categories or predicaments postulated by Aristotle: having, possession. M16–M19.

Phrases: **break the habit** stop doing a habitual thing, *esp.* give up an addictive or otherwise damaging practice. *creature of habit*: see CREATURE 5. **fall into the habit of** begin to do regularly. **from (force of) habit** because it is one's usual or customary behaviour. **get into the habit of** = *fall into the habit of* above. **get out of the habit of** cease to do regularly. **in the habit of**, **†in habits of** having the custom or regular practice of. **kick the habit** = *break the habit* above. **make a habit of** do regularly. **out of habit** = *from (force of) habit* above.

Comb.: **habit-forming** *a.* addictive; **habit-shirt** *Hist.* a kind of chemisette with a collar, formerly worn by women under an outer bodice; **habit-training** the training of a child in regular patterns of behaviour.

habit /ˈhabɪt/ *v.* LME. [(O)Fr. *habiter* f. L *habitare* have possession of, inhabit, f. *habit-*: see prec.] 1 †a *v.i.* Dwell, reside. LME–M17. b *v.t.* Dwell in, inhabit. *arch.* L16. 2 *v.t.* Dress, clothe, attire. LME. 3 *v.t.* Accustom, familiarize, habituate. *obs.* exc. *Sc.* & *dial.* E17.

2 M. INNES Two elderly women, habited in old-fashioned . . mourning.

habitable /ˈhabɪtəb(ə)l/ *a.* LME. [OFr. *abitable* (later & mod. *hab-*) f. L *habitabilis*, f. *habitare*: see prec., -ABLE.] Fit or suitable for habitation; that can be inhabited.

E. F. BENSON The house . . was habitable again after a period of prolonged neglect.

habitaˈbility *n.* E19. **habitableness** *n.* M17. **habitably** *adv.* E19.

habitacle /ˈhabɪtək(ə)l/ *n.* Now *rare.* LME. [(O)Fr. f. L *habitaculum* dwelling-place, f. *habitare*: see HABIT *v.*, -CULE.] 1 A dwelling-place, a habitation. LME. 2 A niche in the wall of a building. LME.

†habitance *n. rare* (Spenser). Only in L16. [OFr., f. as HABIT *v.*: see -ANCE.] A dwelling-place, a habitation.

habitancy /ˈhabɪt(ə)nsi/ *n.* L18. [f. next: see -ANCY.] 1 Residence as an inhabitant. L18. 2 Inhabitants collectively. E19.

habitant /ˈhabɪt(ə)nt/; *in sense A.2 & corresp. adj. foreign* abitɑ̃ (*pl. same*)/ *n.* & *a.* LME. [(O)Fr., pres. pple of *habiter*: see HABIT *v.*, -ANT[1].] A *n.* 1 A person who dwells or resides in a place; a resident, an inhabitant. LME. 2 (A descendant of) a French settler in Canada, *esp.* one who works the land. Also, a native of Louisiana of French descent. L18. B *adj.* Inhabiting, residing; of or pertaining to a habitant; used for habitation. M19.

habitat /ˈhabɪtat/ *n.* L18. [L, lit. 'it inhabits', 3rd person sing. pres. of *habitare*: see HABIT *v.*] 1 The natural environment characteristically occupied by a particular organism; an area distinguished by the set of organisms which occupy it. Also, such areas collectively. L18. 2 *gen.* One's dwelling-place; a habitation; usual surroundings. M19.

1 E. NEWMAN The Black Spleenwort . . occurs on rocks as a native habitat. ANTHONY HUXLEY Desert and mountain habitats. B. LOPEZ Bailey Point . . the best muskox habitat in the high Arctic. *Photography* The wood . . has a lot of varied habitat. 2 K. WATERHOUSE A transport café in the Huddersfield Road, her natural habitat.

habitate /ˈhabɪteɪt/ *v.* Long *rare.* E17. [L *habitat-* pa. ppl stem of *habitare*: see HABIT *v.*, -ATE[3].] 1 *v.t.* Accustom, habituate. E17. 2 *v.i.* Dwell. M19.

habitation /habɪˈteɪʃ(ə)n/ *n.* LME. [(O)Fr. f. L *habitatio(n-)*, f. as prec.: see -ATION.] 1 The action of dwelling in or inhabiting; occupancy by inhabitants. LME. 2 A place of abode, a dwelling-place; *spec.* a house, a home. LME. 3 A settlement. M16.

1 *Daily Chronicle* The premises to be closed . . until they were made fit for human habitation. 2 I. MURDOCH The only habitation near it was a farmhouse. W. SOYINKA If monster snakes had a choice, the bamboo clumps would be their ideal habitation.

Comb.: **habitation site** *Archaeol.* a site where there has been a settlement.

habitative /ˈhabɪteɪtɪv, -tət-/ *a.* L16. [f. as HABITATE: see -IVE.] Of or pertaining to habitation.

habitual /həˈbɪtʃʊəl, -tjʊəl/ *a.* & *n.* LME. [med.L *habitualis*, f. *habitus*: see HABIT *n.*, -AL[1].] A *adj.* †1 Belonging to the inward disposition; inherent or latent in the mental constitution. See HABIT *n.* 7. LME–M19. 2 Of the nature of a habit; fixed by habit; constantly repeated or continued; customary. E17. b Given to a specified habit; that habitually does or is what is denoted by the noun. E19. 3 Usual, constant, continual. M17.

2 K. AMIS He turned with his habitual abruptness and went into the room. b P. G. HAMERTON Almost all English people are habitual tea-drinkers. 3 O. SACKS Her migraines turned from habitual to occasional.

B *n.* †1 A latent disposition of the soul. *rare.* Only in M17. 2 A person who does something habitually; *esp.* a habitual criminal or drunkard. L19.

habituˈality *n.* E19. **habitualize** *v.t.* make habitual L18. **habitually** *adv.* †(*a*) with respect to habit; inherently; potentially; (*b*) in the way of habit or settled practice; usually, customarily: LME. **habitualness** *n.* M17.

habituate /həˈbɪtʃʊeɪt, -tjʊeɪt/ *v.t.* L15. [L *habituat-* pa. ppl stem of late L *habituare*, f. L *habitus*: see HABIT *n.*, -ATE[3].] 1 Settle (a person) in a habit; accustom *to*, familiarize *with.* L15. †2 Make (something) habitual; form into a habit. E–M17. †3 Settle as an inhabitant *in*. Only in 17. 4 Be in or visit frequently; frequent. *N. Amer.* L19.

1 R. DAVIES School had habituated Francis to shabbiness and discomfort and stinks.

habituation /həbɪtʃʊˈeɪʃ(ə)n, -tjʊ-/ *n.* LME. [Fr., or med.L *habituatio(n-)*, f. as prec.; in mod. use f. prec.: see -ATION.] 1 The action of making or becoming habitual; formation of habit; *spec.* the formation of a damaging or addictive habit as a dependency on a drug or drugs. LME. 2 The action of habituating or the condition of being habituated; *spec.* in *Psychol.*, the diminishing of an innate response to a frequently repeated stimulus. E19.

habitude /ˈhabɪtjuːd/ *n.* LME. [(O)Fr. f. L *habitudo*, f. *habit-*: see HABIT *n.*, -TUDE.] 1 Manner of being or existing; mental or bodily constitution; disposition; = HABIT *n.* 5, 7. LME. 2 A disposition to act in a certain way; a custom, a tendency; = HABIT *n.* 8. LME. b Custom, usage; = HABIT *n.* 8b. L16. †3 Familiar relation or acquaintance; familiarity. L15–L18. †4 Manner of being with relation to something else; relation, respect. M16–M18. †5 *Chem.* Chemical behaviour; reactions. L18–M19.

2 J. BUTLER Many habitudes of life, not given by nature, but which nature directs us to acquire. b H. ALLEN The orphan out of habitude from old times came close to the Virgin.

habiˈtudinal *a.* †(*a*) habitual, customary; (*b*) of or pertaining to habit: LME.

habitué /abitɥe (*pl. same*); həˈbɪtjʊeɪ/ *n.* E19. [Fr., pa. pple of *habituer* f. L *habituare*: see HABITUATE *v.*] A habitual visitor or resident (*of* a place).

E. WAUGH I stayed at the Cavendish once . . but I was never an habitué.

habitus /ˈhabɪtəs/ *n.* L19. [L.] Bodily constitution.

hab-nab *adv.* see HOB-NOB *adv.*

haboob /həˈbuːb/ *n.* L19. [Arab. *habūb* blowing furiously.] A violent and oppressive seasonal wind blowing in Sudan and bringing sand from the desert.

habra *n.* var. of HABARA.

habs-nabs *adv.* see HOB-NOB *adv.*

habutai /ˈhɑːbʊtʌɪ/ *n.* L19. [Jap. *habutae.*] Fine soft silk of a type orig. made in Japan. Also called *Japanese* (or *Jap*) *silk*.

háček /ˈhɑːtʃɛk, ˈha-/ *n.* M20. [Czech, dim. of *hák* hook.] A diacritic mark (ˇ) used chiefly in Baltic and Slavonic languages, esp. to indicate various types of palatalization.

hacendado /ɑːsɛnˈdɑːdəʊ, *foreign* aθenˈdaðo/ *n.* Also **hacien-** /ˌɑːsɪɛn-, *foreign* aθien-/. Pl. **-os** /-əʊz, *foreign* -os/. M19. [Sp.] The owner of a hacienda.

hachis /haˈʃiː, *foreign* aʃi/ *n.* Pl. same. M18. [Fr.] A hash, a mess.

hachure /haˈʃjʊə/ *n.* & *v.* M19. [Fr., f. *hacher* HATCH *v.*[2]: see -URE.] *Cartography.* A *n.* Any of a number of short lines of shading on a map running in the direction of a slope and indicating steepness by their closeness and thickness. Also *hachure line*. Usu. in *pl.* M19. B *v.t.* Shade (a map) with hachures. M19.

†hachy *n.* ME–M17. [(O)Fr. *haché* pa. pple of *hacher* to hash; later infl. by *hachis*. Cf. HASH *n.*[1], HACHIS.] = HASH *n.*[1]

hacienda /hasɪˈɛndə, *foreign* aθiˈenda/ *n.* M18. [Sp. f. L *facienda* things to be done, f. *facere* do.] In Spain and Spanish-speaking countries, an estate including a house; a large farm, a plantation; a rural factory.

O. HENRY Ranch supplies, bound on the morrow for some outlying hacienda.

hack /hak/ *n.*[1] ME. [Partly f. MLG *hakke*, f. *hacken* HACK *v.*[1]; partly f. HACK *v.*[1]] 1 An implement for breaking or chopping up, esp. used in agriculture and mining; *spec.* a two-pronged tool resembling a mattock. ME. 2 A cut, a notch; a gash, a wound, (esp. caused by a kick with the toe of a boot); a chap in the skin. LME. b *Curling.* A notch made in the ice, or a metal or wooden insert into the ice, used to steady the foot when delivering a stone. E19. 3 A hesitation in speech. Now *rare.* M17. 4 An act of hacking or chopping, a hacking blow; *fig.* (*N. Amer.*) a try, an attempt. M19. 5 A short dry hard cough. L19. 6 A spell of, or the action of, hacking on a computer. *colloq.* L20.

hack /hak/ *n.*[2] & *a.* Chiefly *colloq.* ME. [Abbrev. of HACKNEY *n.* & *a.*] A *n.* 1 A horse for ordinary riding. ME. b A horse let out for hire; *derog.* a worn-out horse, a jade. E18. †2 The driver of a hackney carriage. L17–M19. 3 A person hired to do esp. dull or routine work, a drudge; *esp.* a writer of poor or average quality literary or (esp.) journalistic work. L17. b A prostitute. M18. 4 A vehicle plying for hire; a taxi. Now *N. Amer.* E18. †5 Anything that is hackneyed or made commonplace by frequent indiscriminate use. Cf. sense B.2. E18–E19. 6 *Naut.* In full *hack watch.* A chronometer watch used on deck to take an astronomical sight for navigational purposes. M19.

1 *Illustrated London News* Sir Charles Knightley.. stuck to his road hack long after his neighbours had taken to post-horses. 3 C. CONNOLLY There are no pensions for literary hacks. J. CRITCHLEY The cluster of hacks..notebooks in hand..ready to transmit their ramblings to the nation.

B *attrib.* or as *adj.* 1 Of a person: employed as a hack; for hire. Of writing etc.: like that undertaken by a hack. M18. 2 Commonplace; hackneyed; trite. L18. 3 Of or pertaining to a hack or taxi. E19.

1 B. CASTLE The hack journalists of the right-wing press must be desperate..to discredit Harold. **hackwork** work, esp. literary work, (of a kind) which a person is hired to do; menial work. 2 BYRON When the old world grows dull And we are sick of its hack sounds and sights.

hack'ette *n.* (*colloq.*) a female journalist L20.

hack /hak/ *n.*^{3} In senses 2, 3 also **hake** /heɪk/. LME. [Var. (f. inflected forms) of HATCH *n.*^{1} Cf. HECK *n.*^{1}] †1 = HATCH *n.*^{1} I. Only in LME. 2 = HECK *n.*^{1} 2. *Sc.* & *north.* M16. 3 *Falconry.* A board on which a hawk's meat is laid (also *hack board*). Hence, the state of partial liberty of a young hawk. L16. 4 A wooden frame for drying cheeses, fish, bricks, etc. Also, a row of bricks laid out to dry. L17.

3 **at hack** (of a young hawk) given partial liberty.

hack /hak/ *v.*^{1} [OE (*tō*)*haccian* cut in pieces = OFris. (*tō*)*hakia*, MLG, MDu., (M)HG *hacken* (Du. *hakken*), ult. f. WGmc deriv. of imit. base: cf. synon. OE *hæċċan*, OHG *hecken*. Cf. HECK *v.*] I *v.t.* 1 Cut or chop with heavy blows in a rough or random fashion; mangle or mutilate by jagged cuts. (Foll. by *at*, *away*, *down*, *off*, etc.) OE. b *spec.* in *Agric.* Break or plough up the surface of (the ground); hoe *in* (seed); reap (a crop). Now *dial.* E17. c Of cold or frost: chap or crack the skin. *dial.* L17. †2 *fig.* Mangle (words) in utterance. L16–L17. 3 *Sport*, esp. *Football.* Kick the shin of (an opponent) intentionally with the toe of the boot. (Foll. by *over*, *up.*) M19. 4 *slang.* a Annoy; embarrass, disconcert, confuse. Also w. *off.* Freq. as *hacked(-off)* ppl a. *N. Amer.* L19. b Cope with, manage; tolerate, accept; comprehend. Freq. w. *it.* M20. 5 Gain unauthorized access to (a computer file or system or the data held in one). *colloq.* L20.

1 J. M. BARRIE Crichton and Treherne..hacking and hewing the bamboo..making a clearing. A. J. TOYNBEE To hack one's way with a machete through hundreds of miles of jungle. 3 M. SHEARMAN No hacking, or hacking over, or tripping up shall be allowed. 4a *Rolling Stone* I wouldn't be so hacked off about it if I didn't love country music. b *Newsweek* I had proved to the world during my four years in the Senate..that I can hack it. T. PARKER If you're going to be an officer, it's no use saying you can't hack something.

II *v.i.* 6 Make rough or random cutting or chopping blows. Freq. foll. by *at.* OE. b Massage by striking with the edge of the hand. Chiefly as *hacking* vbl n. L19. 7 Of the teeth: chatter. *obs.* exc. *dial.* OE. 8 Hesitate in speech; stammer. Cf. HACKER *v. obs.* exc. *dial.* M16. †b Hesitate, haggle. L16–L17. 9 Cough repeatedly with a short dry cough. Cf. HECK *v.* E19. 10 Use a computer purely for one's own satisfaction; gain unauthorized access *into* (a computer file, system, etc.). Freq. as *hacking* vbl n. *colloq.* L20.

6 H. INNES Engles and Keramikos were hacking away at the concrete flooring with pick and hammer. 9 **hacking cough** a short, dry, frequently repeated cough.

Comb.: **hack-and-slash** *a.* designating a game, film, etc., characterized by combat and violence; **hack-hammer** a tool resembling an adze but with a short handle, used in dressing stone; **hacksaw** a saw with a narrow blade set in a frame, used for cutting metal.

hacking *n.* (*a*) the action of the vb; (*b*) *dial.* a large Christmas pudding of sausage or mincemeat: LME. **hackster** *n.* (*obs.* exc. *dial.*) a cutthroat, a murderer L16.

hack /hak/ *v.*^{2} M18. [f. HACK *n.*^{2}] 1 *v.t.* Make trite or commonplace by overuse; = HACKNEY *v.* 2. M18. 2 *v.t.* Employ as a literary hack. E19. 3 *v.i.* & *t.* Use (a horse) for ordinary riding. Now *esp.* ride (a horse) in the country for pleasure. Cf. HACKNEY *v.* I. M19. 4 *v.i.* Ride in a hack or taxi. *US.* L19.

3 **hacking coat, jacket**: for use when riding, with slits at the sides or back and freq. tailored in tweed.

hack /hak/ *v.*^{3}*t.* L19. [f. HACK *n.*^{3}] 1 Place (bricks) in rows on a hack or drying frame. L19. 2 *Falconry.* Keep (a young hawk) at hack or in a state of partial liberty. L19.

hackamore /ˈhakəmɔː/ *n.* *US.* M19. [Perh. Sp. *jaquima*, formerly *xaquima* halter.] A type of bitless bridle with a hard oval noseband which allows pressure to be exerted on the nose by means of the reins attached just in front of a heavy counterbalancing knot. Also, a bitless bridle with a single rein.

hackberry /ˈhakb(ə)ri/ *n.* M18. [Var. of HAGBERRY.] 1 = HAGBERRY. *north.* M18. 2 Any of several N. American kinds of nettle-tree (genus *Celtis*), esp. *C. occidentalis*; the edible purplish-black fruit of such a tree, resembling that of the hagberry or bird cherry. M18.

hackbut /ˈhakbət/ *n.* Also **hag-** /ˈhag-/, (earliest) †**-bush.** L15. [(Fr. *haquebut*(*e* alt. of) *haquebusche* f. MDu. *hakebus*, *hagebus* (Du. *haakbus*), MLG *hakebusse*, f. *hake*(*n* HOOK *n.* + *bus*(*se* gun, firearm (cf. BLUNDERBUSS). Cf. HARQUEBUS.] = HARQUEBUS I.

¶Forms in *-but* recorded f. M16.

hackbu'teer *n.* (*Hist.*) = HACKBUTTER E17. **hackbutter** *n.* (*Hist.*) a soldier armed with a hackbut E16.

hackee /ˈhaki/ *n.* *N. Amer.* M19. [Prob. imit.] A chipmunk.

hacker /ˈhakə/ *n.* ME. [f. HACK *v.*^{1} + -ER^{1}.] 1 A person who or thing which hacks (something). ME. 2 *spec.* An enthusiastic computer programmer or user; a person who tries to gain unauthorized access to a computer or to data held in one. *colloq.* L20.

hackerdom *n.* the realm or world of computer hackers L20.

hacker /ˈhakə/ *v.i.* *dial.* L18. [Frequent. of HACK *v.*^{1}] Stammer, stutter.

hackery /ˈhak(ə)ri/ *n.* *Anglo-Ind.* L17. [Hind. *chakṛā* two-wheeled cart.] A bullock-cart; a carriage.

hackia /ˈhakɪə/ *n.* M19. [Guyanese name.] = GUAIACUM I, 2.

hackie /ˈhaki/ *n.* *US colloq.* Also **-ky.** M20. [f. HACK *n.*^{2} + -IE.] A taxi-driver.

hackle /ˈhak(ə)l/ *n.*^{1} [OE *hacele*, *hæcile*, corresp. (exc. in formative suff.) to OHG *hachul*, MHG *hachel*, ON *hǫkull*, Goth. *hakuls.*] †1 A cloak, a mantle, an outer garment; a chasuble. OE–ME. 2 A covering of any kind, as a bird's plumage, a snake's skin, etc. *obs.* exc. *dial.* LME. 3 A conical straw roof on a beehive. E17.

hackle /ˈhak(ə)l/ *n.*^{2} LME. [Var. of HATCHEL *n.* Cf. HECKLE *n.*] I 1 A long shining feather or a series of feathers on the neck or saddle of a domestic cock, peacock, pigeon, etc., which is erected in anger. LME. b A stickleback. *dial.* M17. 2 *Angling.* An artificial fly dressed wholly or chiefly with a hackle. Also *hackle fly.* L17. 3 A cockade of hackles in a Highland soldier's bonnet. L18. 4 *transf.* In *pl.* The erectile hairs along the back of a dog, which rise when it is angry or alarmed. L19. II 5 An instrument with parallel steel pins for splitting and combing the fibres of flax or hemp; a flax-comb. (Earlier as HECKLE *n.* I.) L15. b A tool with spikes used in wig-making for combing or carding skeins of hair. E20.

4 **make a person's hackles rise, raise a person's hackles** anger or annoy a person.

hackle /ˈhak(ə)l/ *v.*^{1}*t.* L16. [Dim. or frequent. of HACK *v.*^{1}: see -LE^{3}, cf. HAGGLE *v.*] = HACK *v.*^{1} I.

hackle /ˈhak(ə)l/ *v.*^{2}*t.* *obs.* exc. *dial.* E17. [f. HACKLE *n.*^{1}] Cover (a beehive) with a hackle.

hackle /ˈhak(ə)l/ *v.*^{3}*t.* L17. [f. HACKLE *n.*^{2} Cf. HECKLE *v.*] 1 Dress or comb (flax or hemp) with a hackle, in preparation for spinning. L17. 2 *Angling.* Dress (a fly) with a hackle. Chiefly as *hackled* ppl a. M19. 3 Dress (hair) in wig-making. M20.

hackler *n.* a flax-dresser M18.

hacklet /ˈhaklɪt/ *n.* *dial.* M19. [Origin unkn.] = KITTIWAKE.

hackly /ˈhakli/ *a.* L18. [f. HACKLE *v.*^{1} + -Y^{1}.] Rough, jagged; *esp.* (of a metal or mineral surface) having short sharp points.

hackman /ˈhakmən/ *n.* *US.* Pl. **-men.** L18. [f. HACK *n.*^{2} + MAN *n.*] A driver of a hack; a cabman.

hackmatack /ˈhakmətak/ *n.* L18. [Perh. f. Western Abnaki.] Any of several N. American coniferous trees; *esp.* the American larch or tamarack, *Larix laricina.*

hackney /ˈhakni/ *n.* & *a.* ME. [AN *hakeney*, AL *hakeneius*, prob. f. *Hackney* (formerly *Hakenei*) in London where horses were pastured.] A *n.* 1 Orig., a horse of medium size and quality, used for ordinary riding and frequently kept for hire. Now *spec.* (an animal of) a breed of light harness-horse with a compact body and a characteristic high-stepping striding trot. Also *hackney horse.* ME. †2 A person hired to do menial or servile work. M16–M19. b A prostitute. L16–L17. 3 A vehicle plying for hire. Now only in *hackney carriage*, (official term for) a taxi. M17.

1 SIR W. SCOTT He rode..a strong hackney for the road, to save his gallant warhorse. 2 S. PEPYS I should ..become the hackney of this office, in perpetual trouble and vexation. 3 W. CONGREVE If you won't lend me your Coach, I'll take a Hackney, or a Chair.

B *attrib.* or as *adj.* 1 Of, pertaining to, or designating a hackney. LME. †2 Trite, commonplace; hackneyed. L16–L18.

Special collocations & comb.: *hackney carriage*: see sense A.3 above. †**hackney-chair** a sedan chair, a bath chair for public hire. **hackney-chairman** the bearer, drawer, or keeper of a hackney-chair. **hackney-coach** *Hist.* a two-horse four-wheeled coach kept for hire. **hackney-coachman** the driver of a hackney-coach. *hackney horse*: see sense A.1 above.

hackney /ˈhakni/ *v.* Now *rare* exc. as HACKNEYED *ppl a.* L16. [f. HACKNEY *n.*] 1 *v.t.* Use (a horse) for ordinary riding. Cf. HACK *v.*^{2} 3. Long *dial.* L16. 2 *v.t.* Make trite or commonplace by overuse. (Foll. by *out*, *about.*) L16. b *v.i.* Make experienced *in* or (esp. excessively) familiar with. M18. †c Make vulgar or indelicate. L18–E19. †3 *v.t.* & *i.* Hasten, hurry. E17–L18. †4 *v.t.* Let *out* for hire. E17–M18.

hackneyed /ˈhaknɪd/ *ppl a.* M18. [f. prec. + -ED^{1}.] 1 Trite, uninteresting, or commonplace through familiarity or indiscriminate and frequent use. M18. 2 Experienced, habituated (sometimes with the idea of disgust or weariness). M18. †3 Hired; kept for hire. M18–E19.

1 D. PIPER Two of the most insistently reproduced, not to say hackneyed, images.

hackneydom *n.* a state of commonplaceness L19.

hacky *n.* var. of HACKIE.

had *v.* pa. t. & pple of HAVE *v.*

hadada /ˈhɑːdədɑː/ *n.* Orig. *S. Afr.* Also **-ah**, (esp. *S. Afr.*) **hadeda(h)** /ˈhɑːdɪdɑː/. L18. [Imit.] A greenish-brown ibis, *Hagedashia hagedash*, of sub-Saharan Africa, with a characteristic raucous cry. Also *hadada ibis.*

hadal /ˈheɪd(ə)l/ *a.* M20. [f. HADES + -AL^{1}.] Of, pertaining to, or designating the zone of the sea greater than 6000 metres in depth (chiefly oceanic trenches). Cf. ABYSSAL.

Hadassah /həˈdasə/ *n.* E20. [Heb. *hădassāh* myrtle, the name of the biblical character Esther (*Esther* 2:7).] An American Zionist women's organization, founded in 1912, which contributes to welfare work in Israel.

hadda /ˈhadə/ *v., pa. t. non-standard.* M20. [Repr. a pronunc.] Had to.

haddie /ˈhadi/ *n. Sc.* M17. [Dim. of HADDOCK: see -IE.] A haddock.

haddock /ˈhadək/ *n.* Pl. same. ME. [AN *hadoc* f. OFr. *(h)adot*, pl. *hadoz, haddos*, of unkn. origin.] A gadoid food fish, *Melanogrammus aeglefinus*, of the N. Atlantic; (with specifying wd) any of various other (edible) marine fishes. Also, the flesh of these fishes as food.

NORWAY *haddock*.

hade /heɪd/ *n.*[1] *obs.* exc. *dial.* E16. [Origin unkn.] A strip of land left unploughed as a boundary line and means of access between two ploughed portions of a field.

hade /heɪd/ *n.*[2] L18. [f. the vb.] *Mining & Geol.* The inclination of a mineral vein, fault, etc., from the vertical; the complement of the *dip*.

hade /heɪd/ *v.i.* L17. [Perh. a dial. form of HEAD *v.*, retaining the older pronunc. of that word.] *Mining & Geol.* Of a shaft, vein, fault, etc.: incline or slope from the vertical.

Hadean /ˈheɪdɪən, heɪˈdiːən/ *a.* M19. [f. next + -AN.] Of or pertaining to Hades.

Hades /ˈheɪdiːz/ *n.* L16. [Gk *haidēs* (orig. *aidēs*), of unkn. origin; in biblical Greek used as tr. Heb. *šĕʼōl*, the abode of departed spirits.] **1** *Gk Mythol.* The god of the dead, also called Pluto; *transf.* the kingdom of Hades, the underworld, the abode of the spirits of the dead. L16. **b** Used as a substitute for *hell* in imprecations etc. *colloq.* E20. **2** In biblical use (esp. in the New Testament), the state or abode of the spirits of the dead, esp. as a place of waiting before judgement. L16.

1 SIR T. BROWNE The dead seem all alive in the humane Hades of Homer.

Hadith /haˈdiːθ/ *n.* E18. [Arab. *ḥadīṯ* statement, tradition.] The body of traditions concerning the sayings and doings of the Prophet Muhammad, now considered to be second in authority to the Koran and to embody the Sunna.

hadj *n.* var. of HAJJ.

hadji *n.* var. of HAJJI.

Hadley cell /ˈhadlɪ sɛl/ *n.* M20. [f. G. *Hadley* (1685–1768), Eng. lawyer and scientific writer + CELL *n.*[1]] *Meteorol.* An atmospheric convection cell on a global scale, *spec.* each of two in which air rises at the equator and sinks at latitude 30° N. or S.

hadn't *v.* see HAVE *v.*

Hadrianic /heɪdrɪˈanɪk/ *a.* L19. [f. L *Hadrian(us)* (of) the Emperor Hadrian + -IC.] Of or pertaining to the Roman Emperor Hadrian (76–138).

hadrome /ˈhadrəʊm/ *n.* Now *rare.* L19. [G *Hadrom*, f. Gk *hadros* thick, bulky: see -OME.] *Bot.* The conducting tissue of the xylem, excluding fibres. Cf. LEPTOME.

hadron /ˈhadrɒn/ *n.* M20. [f. Gk *hadros* bulky + -ON.] *Particle Physics.* Any of a class of subatomic particle including baryons and mesons, which can take part in the strong interaction. Cf. LEPTON *n.*[2]

haˈdronic *a.* of or pertaining to hadrons M20.

hadrosaur /ˈhadrəsɔː/ *n.* L19. [mod.L *Hadrosaurus* genus name, f. Gk *hadros* thick, stout: see -SAUR.] Any of a family of bipedal herbivorous ornithischian dinosaurs of the Upper Cretaceous, which have beaked and often elaborately crested skulls.

hadroˈsaurian *a.* L20. **hadroˈsaurid** *n.* & *a.* (*a*) *n.* an animal of the family Hadrosauridae; (*b*) *adj.* of, pertaining to, or designating this family: L20. **hadroˈsaurine** *n.* & *a.* of or pertaining to, or an animal of, a group of largely crestless hadrosaurs L20.

hadst *v.* see HAVE *v.*

hae *v.* see HAVE *v.*

haecceity /hɛkˈsiːɪti, hiːk-/ *n.* M17. [med.L *haecceitas*, f. L *haec* fem. of *hic* this + *-itas* -ITY. Cf. QUIDDITY, SEITY.] *Philos.* The quality that makes a thing describable as 'this'; particular character, individuality.

Haeckelian /hɛˈkiːlɪən/ *a.* L19. [f. *Haeckel* (see below) + -IAN.] Of, pertaining to, or in accordance with the theories of the German biologist E. H. Haeckel (1834–1919), esp. relating to recapitulation of evolutionary development in embryos.

haem /hiːm/ *n.* Also **heme**. E20. [Back-form. f. HAEMOGLOBIN.] *Chem.* A coordination compound in which an iron atom is chelated within a porphyrin molecule; *esp.* (the original sense) that complex of ferrous iron and protoporphyrin forming the red non-protein constituent of haemoglobin.

haem- *comb. form* see HAEMO-.

haemagglutinate /hiːməˈgluːtɪneɪt/ *v.t.* Also ***hem-** /hiːm-, hɛm-/. E20. [f. HAEMO- + AGGLUTINATE *v.*] Cause (red blood cells) to coagulate.

haemaggluti'nation *n.* the action or process of haemagglutinating cells E20.

haemagglutinin /hiːməˈgluːtɪnɪn/ *n.* Also ***hem-** /hiːm-, hɛm-/. E20. [f. as prec. + AGGLUTININ.] Any substance that causes agglutination of red blood cells.

haemal /ˈhiːm(ə)l/ *a.* Also ***hem-**. M19. [f. Gk *haima* blood + -AL[1].] *Anat.* Of the blood or circulatory system; *esp.* belonging to, situated on, or towards that side of the body containing the heart and major blood-vessels, ventral. (Chiefly w. ref. to animals.)

haemangioma /ˌhiːmandʒɪˈəʊmə/ *n.* Also ***hem-** /hiːm-, hɛm-/. Pl. **-mas, -mata** /-mətə/. L19. [f. HAEMO- + ANGIOMA.] *Med.* A benign angioma, esp. forming a birthmark.

haemanthus /hiːˈmanθəs/ *n.* L18. [mod.L (see below), f. Gk *haima* blood + *anthos* flower.] Any of various bulbous plants of the genus *Haemanthus*, of the amaryllis family, of central and southern Africa, grown for their umbels of red, pink, or white flowers.

haemarthrosis /hiːmɑːˈθrəʊsɪs/ *n.* Also ***hem-** /hiːm-, hɛm-/. Pl. **-throses** /-ˈθrəʊsiːz/. L19. [f. HAEMO- + ARTHROSIS.] *Med.* Haemorrhage into a joint.

haemat- *comb. form* see HAEMATO-.

haematemesis /hiːməˈtɛmɪsɪs/ *n.* Also ***hem-** /hiːm-, hɛm-/. E19. [f. HAEMATO- + Gk *emesis* vomiting.] *Med.* Vomiting of blood.

haematic /hiːˈmatɪk/ *a.* Also ***hem-** /hiːm-, hɛm-/. M19. [Gk *haimatikos*, f. *haima, haimat-* blood: see -IC and cf. HAEMIC.] Of or containing blood. Also, acting on the blood.

haematin /ˈhiːmətɪn/ *n.* Also ***hem-** /ˈhiːm-, ˈhɛm-/. E19. [f. Gk *haima, haimat-* blood + -IN[1].] *Chem.* †**1** = HAEMATOXYLIN. E–M19. **2** A bluish-black oxidized derivative of haem, containing ferric iron. M19.

haemaˈtinic *n.* & *a.* (*a*) *n.* a medicine used to treat anaemia; (*b*) *adj.* of or relating to haematin: M19.

haematite /ˈhiːmətʌɪt/ *n.* Also ***hem-** /ˈhiːm-, ˈhɛm-/. Also in L form †**haematites**. LME. [L *haematites* f. Gk *haimatitēs* (*lithos*) lit. 'bloodlike (stone)', f. *haima, haimat-* blood: see -ITE[1].] Ferric oxide, Fe_2O_3, occurring as a dark-red, reddish-brown, or reddish-black mineral which crystallizes in the hexagonal system and constitutes an important ore of iron.

brown haematite = LIMONITE.

haemaˈtitic *a.* L18.

haemato- /ˈhiːmətəʊ/ *comb. form.* Bef. a vowel **haemat-**. Also ***hem-** /ˈhiːm-, ˈhɛm-/. [f. Gk *haima, haimat-* blood: see -O-.] Forming ns. etc. esp. in *Med.*, w. the sense 'of blood, containing blood'. Cf. HAEMO-.

haematiˈdrosis *n.* [Gk *hidrōsis* sweating] the secretion of sweat containing blood M19. †**haematoblast** *n.* a blood platelet: only in L19. **haematocele** *n.* [Gk *kēlē* tumour] a swelling containing extravasated blood M18. **haematocyst** *n.* a cyst containing blood M19. †**haematoglobulin** *n.* = HAEMOGLOBIN: only in M19. **haematomyˈelia** *n.* [Gk *muelos* marrow] haemorrhage into the tissue of the spinal cord L19. **haematopoiˈesis** *n.* = HAEMOPOIESIS M19. **haematopoiˈetic** *a.* = HAEMOPOIETIC M19. **haematoˈporphyrin** *n.* [Gk *porphuros* purple: see -IN[1]] a dark violet porphyrin obtained from haem by hydration in strong acid L19. **haematoˈsalpinx** *n.*, pl. **-pinges** /ˈpɪn(d)ʒiːz/, [Gk SALPINX: cf. SALPINGO-] (an) accumulation of menstrual blood in the Fallopian tubes L19. **haematoˈthorax** *n.* = HAEMOTHORAX M19.

haematocrit /ˈhiːmətə(ʊ)krɪt/ *n.* Also ***hem-** /ˈhiːm-, ˈhɛm-/. Also †**-krit**. L19. [f. prec. + Gk *kritēs* judge.] An instrument for determining the ratio of the volume of red cells to the total volume of a blood sample. Also, the measured ratio, usu. expressed as a percentage.

haematogenous /hiːməˈtɒdʒɪnəs/ *a.* Also ***hem-** /hiːm-, hɛm-/. M19. [f. as prec. + -GENOUS.] Having its origin in or carried by the blood.

haematoid /ˈhiːmətɔɪd/ *a.* Also ***hem-** /ˈhiːm-, ˈhɛm-/. M19. [Gk *haimatoeidēs*, f. as HAEMATO- + -OID.] Resembling blood; characterized by the presence of blood.

haematoidin /hiːməˈtɔɪdɪn/ *n.* Also ***hem-** /hiːm-, hɛm-/. M19. [f. as prec. + -IN[1].] *Med.* Bilirubin, esp. as formed from the breakdown of haemoglobin in extravasated blood.

†**haematokrit** *n.* var. of HAEMATOCRIT.

haematology /hiːməˈtɒlədʒi/ *n.* Also ***hem-** /hiːm-, hɛm-/. L17. [f. HAEMATO- + -LOGY.] The branch of medicine that deals with the blood, esp. its disorders.

haematoˈlogic *a.* M20. **haematoˈlogical** *a.* M19. **haematoˈlogically** *adv.* M20. **haematologist** *n.* E20.

haematoma /hiːməˈtəʊmə/ *n.* Also ***hem-** /hiːm-, hɛm-/. Pl. **-mas, -mata** /-mətə/. M19. [f. as prec. + -OMA.] *Med.* A swelling containing (coagulated) extravasated blood.

haematophagous /hiːməˈtɒfəgəs/ *a.* Also ***hem-** /hiːm-, hɛm-/. M19. [f. as prec. + -PHAGOUS.] Feeding or subsisting on blood.

haematosis /hiːməˈtəʊsɪs/ *n.* Now *rare* or *obs.* Also ***hem-** /hiːm-, hɛm-/. L17. [med. or mod.L f. Gk *haimatōsis*, f. *haimatoun* make into blood, f. as HAEMATO-: see -OSIS.] **1** = SANGUIFICATION. L17. **2** Oxygenation of the blood. M19.

haematoxylin /hiːməˈtɒksɪlɪn/ *n.* Also ***hem-** /hiːm-, hɛm-/. M19. [f. mod.L *Haematoxylum* genus name of logwood, f. as HAEMATO- + Gk *xulon* wood: see -IN[1].] *Chem.* A colourless crystalline polycyclic phenol, $C_{16}H_{14}O_6$, which is present in logwood, can be easily converted into a number of red, blue, or purple dyes, and is used as a biological stain.

haematuria /hiːməˈtjʊərɪə/ *n.* Also ***hem-** /hiːm-, hɛm-/. E19. [f. HAEMATO- + -URIA.] *Med.* The presence of blood in the urine.

haematuric *a.* pertaining to, characterized by, or affected with haematuria M19.

haemerythrin /hiːməˈrɪθrɪn/ *n.* Also ***hem-** /hiːm-, hɛm-/. E20. [f. HAEMO- + ERYTHRO- + -IN[1].] *Biochem.* A rare red respiratory pigment present in the blood of some invertebrates.

haemic /ˈhiːmɪk/ *a.* Also ***hemic**. M19. [f. Gk *haima* blood + -IC. Cf. HAEMATIC.] Of or pertaining to the blood.

haemin /ˈhiːmɪn/ *n.* Also ***hem-**. M19. [f. as prec. + -IN[1].] *Biochem.* The red, crystalline salt of haematin with hydrochloric acid.

haemo- /ˈhiːməʊ/ *comb. form.* Also ***hemo-** /ˈhiːməʊ, ˈhɛməʊ/. Bef. a vowel **h(a)em-**. [f. Gk *haima* blood + -O-.] Forming ns. etc., esp. in *Med.*, w. the sense 'of blood'. Cf. HAEMATO-.

haeˌmangioblaˈstoma *n.*, pl. **-mas, -mata** /-mətə/, a tumour of the blood-vessels E20. **haemochromaˈtosis** *n.* a hereditary disorder of iron metabolism in which excessive haemosiderin is deposited in the tissues, leading to bronze skin coloration, liver damage, and diabetes mellitus (also called *bronze diabetes*) L19. **haemocoel(e)** *n.* [Gk *koilos* hollow, cavity] *Zool.* the primary body cavity of metazoan invertebrates, containing circulatory fluid L19. **haemoconcenˈtration** *n.* an increase in the relative proportion of red cells in the blood M20. **haemoˈdialyser** *n.* a kidney dialysis machine M20. **haemodiˈalysis** *n.* purification of a patient's blood by dialysis (DIALYSIS 3) M20. **haemogram** *n.* the set of results of a number of tests on a blood sample E20. **haemolymph** *n.* the fluid analogous to blood or lymph which circulates in the body cavity of invertebrates L19. **haemoˈsiderin** *n.* [Gk *sidēros* iron] a brownish-yellow substance consisting of protein and iron salts, deposited in the body as a means of storing iron L19. **haemosideˈrosis** *n.* excessive deposition of iron (chiefly as haemosiderin) in the tissues E20. **haemoˈthorax** *n.* haemorrhage into or an accumulation of blood in the pleural cavities L19.

haemocyanin /hiːmə(ʊ)ˈsʌɪənɪn/ *n.* Also ***hem-** /hiːm-, hɛm-/. M19. [f. as prec. + CYAN- + -IN[1].] *Biochem.* A blue pigment present in blood. Now only *spec.*, a copper-containing respiratory protein (blue when oxygenated, colourless when deoxygenated), present in the blood of some crustaceans, molluscs, and arachnids.

haemocytometer /ˌhiːmə(ʊ)sʌɪˈtɒmɪtə/ *n.* Also ***hem-** /ˌhiːm-, ˌhɛm-/. L19. [f. HAEMO- + CYTO- + -METER.] *Biol.* A device for visual counting of the numbers of cells in a specimen of blood or other fluid under a microscope.

haemodynamic /ˌhiːmə(ʊ)dʌɪˈnamɪk/ *a.* Also ***hem-** /ˌhiːm-, ˌhɛm-/. E20. [f. HAEMO- + DYNAMIC.] Of or relating to the motion of the blood.

haemodynamically *adv.* L20. **haemodynamics** *n.* the science of the motion of the blood M19.

haemoglobin /hiːməˈgləʊbɪn/ *n.* Also ***hem-** /hiːm-, hɛm-/. M19. [Abbrev. of HAEMATOGLOBULIN.] The iron-containing pigment, resolvable into four subunits consisting of haem and a globulin, which is the oxygen-carrying substance present in the red blood cells of vertebrates, and is red when oxygenated and purple when deoxygenated.

haemoglobiˈnaemia *n.* the presence of free haemoglobin in blood plasma L19. **haemoglobiˈnometer, -metry** *ns.* an instrument for measuring, the measurement of, the concentration of haemoglobin in a blood sample L19. **haemoglobiˈnopathy** *n.* any of a group of hereditary conditions in which there is an abnormality in the production of haemoglobin M20. **haemoglobiˈnuria** *n.* the presence of free haemoglobin in the urine M19.

haemolysis /hiːˈmɒlɪsɪs/ *n.* Also ***hem-**. L19. [f. HAEMO- + -LYSIS.] The dissolution or lysis of red blood cells with the consequent liberation of their haemoglobin.

ˈhaemolyse, *hemolyze *v.t.* & *i.* (cause to) undergo haemolysis E20. **haemolysin** /hiːˈmɒlɪsɪn, hiːməˈlʌɪsɪn/ *n.* any substance which causes haemolysis E20.

haemolytic /hiːməˈlɪtɪk/ *a.* Also ***hem-** /hiːm-, hɛm-/. L19. [f. HAEMO- + -LYTIC.] Of, pertaining to, characterized by, or producing haemolysis.

haemolytic disease of the newborn: see ERYTHROBLASTOSIS.

haemolytically *adv.* E20.

†haemony *n. rare* (Milton). Only in M17. [f. Gk *haima* blood, after *agrimony*.] An imaginary plant having supernatural virtues.

haemophilia /hiːməˈfɪlɪə/ *n.* Also ***hem-** /hiːm-, hɛm-/. Also (earlier) Anglicized as **†haemophily**. M19. [f. HAEMO- + -PHILIA.] A hereditary disease in which the ability of the blood to coagulate is severely reduced owing to a deficiency of the coagulation factor VIII, the person concerned having a tendency to prolonged bleeding from even minor injuries.

haemophilia B a hereditary disease clinically identical to ordinary haemophilia but due to the absence of a different coagulation factor; also called *Christmas disease*.

haemophiliac *n.* & *a.* (*a*) *n.* a person with haemophilia; (*b*) *adj.* = HAEMOPHILIC *a.*: L19. **haemophilic** *a.* & *n.* (*a*) *adj.* of or pertaining to haemophilia; affected with haemophilia; (*b*) *n.* = HAEMOPHILIAC *n.*: M19.

haemopoiesis /ˌhiːməʊpɔɪˈiːsɪs/ *n.* Also ***hem-** /ˌhiːm-, ˌhɛm-/. E20. [f. HAEMO- + Gk *poiēsis* making. Cf. earlier HAEMATOPOIESIS.] The production of blood cells and platelets, which occurs in the bone marrow.

haemopoietic /-pɔɪˈɛtɪk/ *a.* of, pertaining to, or concerned with haemopoiesis L19.

haemoptysis /hiːˈmɒptɪsɪs/ *n.* Also ***hem-**. M17. [mod.L *hemoptysis*, f. as HAEMO- + Gk *ptusis* spitting.] *Med.* Expectoration of blood or bloody mucus.

haemorrhage /ˈhɛmərɪdʒ/ *n.* & *v.* Also ***hem-**. L17. [Alt. of HAEMORRHAGY.] A *n.* 1 An escape of blood from the blood-vessels; bleeding, esp. when profuse. L17. 2 *fig.* A damaging or uncontrolled outflow of something. M19.

2 D. H. LAWRENCE This haemorrhage of self-esteem tortured him to the end. *Washington Post* An economic hemorrhage threatening Israel's stability.

B *v.* 1 *v.i.* Undergo a haemorrhage. E20. 2 *v.t.* Dissipate or expend in large amounts. L20.

2 D. ADAMS He had been simply haemorrhaging money.

†haemorrhagia *n.* var. of HAEMORRHAGY.

haemorrhagic /hɛməˈradʒɪk/ *a.* Also ***hem-**. E19. [Gk *haimorrhagikos*, f. *haimorrhagia*: see next, -IC.] Pertaining to or of the nature of haemorrhage; accompanied by or produced by haemorrhage.

†haemorrhagy *n.* Also ***hem-**, & in L form **haemorrhagia**. LME–M19. [f. OFr. *emorogie* (mod. *hémorr(h)agie*), or its source L *haemorrhagia* f. Gk *haimorrhagia*, f. as HAEMO- + base of *rhēgnunai* break, burst.] = HAEMORRHAGE *n.*

haemorrhoid /ˈhɛmərɔɪd/ *n.* Also ***hem-**. LME. [OFr. *emeroyde*, later *hémorrhoides* f. L *haemorrhoida* f. Gk *haimorrhois*, -*oid*- discharging blood, pl. -*oides* (sc. *phlebes* veins) bleeding piles, f. *haimorrhoos*, f. as HAEMO- + -*roos* flowing. Cf. EMERODS.] In *pl.*, abnormally distended groups of veins in the region of the rectum and anus; piles. Also occas. *sing.* (usu. *attrib.*).

E. BAKER Norma . . could tell . . that his haemorrhoids were bothering him again. *attrib.*: M. PIERCY He had not taken his hemorrhoid medicine.

haemorrhoiˈdectomy *n.* (an instance of) surgical removal of haemorrhoids E20.

haemorrhoidal /hɛməˈrɔɪd(ə)l/ *a.* LME. [f. prec. + -AL[1].] 1 *Anat.* Of veins, nerves, etc.: distributed to the region of the rectum and anus. LME. 2 Of or pertaining to haemorrhoids. M17.

†haemorrhois *n.* LME–L18. [L f. Gk *haimorrhois*: see HAEMORRHOID.] A snake whose bite was fabled to cause unstanchable bleeding.

haemostasis /hiːmə(ʊ)ˈsteɪsɪs/ *n.* Also ***hem-** /hiːm-, hɛm-/. M19. [f. HAEMO- + STASIS.] *Med.* Stoppage of bleeding; stoppage or esp. prevention of the flow of blood.

haemostatic /hiːmə(ʊ)ˈstatɪk/ *n.* & *a.* Also ***hem-** /hiːm-, hɛm-/. E18. [f. HAEMO- + -STATIC.] A *n.* 1 A substance that arrests bleeding, a styptic. E18. †2 In *pl.* (treated as *sing.*). The hydrostatics of the blood. M18–M19. B *adj.* Having the property of arresting bleeding, styptic; serving to prevent the flow of blood. M19.

ˈhaemostat *n.* an instrument for preventing blood flow by compression of a blood-vessel E20.

haere mai /ˈhʌɪrə ˈmʌɪ, *foreign* ˈhaere ˈmai/ *int.* & *n. phr. NZ.* M18. [Maori, lit. 'come hither'.] (A Maori term expr.) welcome.

haet /heɪt/ *n. Sc.* Also **hate**. L16. [Contr. of *hae* (= *have*) *it*.] 1 *deil* (*a*) *haet*, *fiend* (*a*) *haet*, & vars. (in emphatic negatives) not a bit, nothing at all. L16. 2 A bit, a small quantity. Usu. in neg. contexts. E19.

haff /haf/ *n.* M19. [G, f. (M)LG *haf* sea, corresp. to ON *haf*, OE *hæf* sea.] A shallow freshwater lagoon found at a river mouth, esp. on the Baltic coast.

haffet /ˈhafɪt/ *n. Sc.* & *north.* E16. [Prob. f. OE *healfhēafod* the front part of the head, f. as HALF- + HEAD *n.*] The side of the head above and in front of the ear; the temple; the cheek.

Hafflinger *n.* see HAFLINGER.

hafiz /ˈhɑːfɪz/ *n.* M17. [Pers. f. Arab. *ḥāfiẓ* pres. pple of *ḥafiẓa* guard, know by heart.] A Muslim who knows the Koran by heart.

Haflinger /ˈhaflɪŋə/ *n.* Also (earlier) **Haffl-**. L19. [G, f. *Hafling*, a village in the Tyrol where the breed originated.] (An animal of) a breed of sturdy chestnut draught horse.

hafnium /ˈhafnɪəm/ *n.* E20. [f. *Hafnia* Latinized form of Da. *Havn* (= harbour), orig. name of Copenhagen, Dan. capital city: see -IUM.] A chemical element, atomic no. 72, which is one of the transition metals and occurs naturally in association with zirconium, which it resembles. (Symbol Hf.)

haft /hɑːft/ *n.*[1] Also (now chiefly *Sc.* & *dial.*) **heft** /hɛft/. [OE *hæft(e)* corresp. to MLG *hechte* (Du. *hecht, heft*), OHG *hefti* (G *Heft*), ON *hepti*, f. Gmc base of HEAVE *v.*: see -T[1].] The handle of a cutting or piercing instrument, as a knife, spear, etc.; the hilt of a sword, dagger, etc.

haft *n.*[2] var. of HEFT *n.*[2]

haft /hɑːft/ *v.*[1]*t.* Also (chiefly *Sc.* & *north.*) **heft** /hɛft/. LME. [f. HAFT *n.*[1]] Provide (a knife etc.) with a haft or handle.

hafter *n.* ME.

haft *v.*[2] var. of HEFT *v.*[1]

hag /hag/ *n.*[1] ME. [Perh. abbrev. of OE *hægtesse*, *hegtes* fury, witch = MDu. *haghetisse* (Du. *hecse*), OHG *hagazissa* (G *Hexe*), of unkn. origin. Cf. HEX *n.*[1]] 1 A woman supposed to have dealings with the devil; a witch; an evil woman; (now *dial.* or *arch.*) an evil spirit or demon in female form, a malicious fairy or goblin, a nightmare conceived of as caused by this. ME. 2 An ugly repulsive old woman, *esp.* a vicious or malicious one. Formerly also, an ugly repulsive man. LME. 3 Orig., a kind of hazy light or mist supposedly appearing about a horse's mane or a human head at night. Now only (*dial.*), a mist usually accompanying a frost. M16. 4 *ellipt.* A hagfish. E19.

1 SHAKES. *Macb.* How now, you secret, black, and midnight hags! 2 P. THEROUX The zone which turned lovely little girls into bad-tempered and rapacious hags.

hag /hag/ *n.*[2] *Sc.* & *north.* ME. [f. ON *hǫgg* gap, breach, cutting blow, f. *hǫggva*: see HAG *v.*[1] and cf. HEDGE *n.*] I †1 A break, gap, or chasm in a crag or cliff. Only in ME. 2 A soft marshy break in a moor resulting from peat-cutting or the flow of water; a firm turfy or heathery clump in a peatbog. M17. 3 An overhang of peat or turf. E19.

2 SIR W. SCOTT A small and shaggy nag, That through a bog, from hag to hag, Could bound.

II 4 A hack, a cut; a cutting or felling of a certain quantity of wood; a portion of a wood marked off for cutting. Earliest in place-names. ME. 5 The stump of a tree left after felling; an amount of firewood. E17.

hag /hag/ *n.*[3] *north.* L15. [ON *hagi* enclosed field, pasture, rel. to OE *haga*: see HAW *n.*[1]] †1 A hedge. Only in L15. 2 A wooded enclosure; a copse. E17.

hag *n.*[4] var. of HAKE *n.*[2]

hag /hag/ *v.*[1]*t.* & *i. Sc.* & *north.* Infl. **-gg-**. ME. [f. ON *hǫggva* strike with a sharp weapon, hack, hew = OE *heawan* HEW *v.*] Hack, cut, or hew (something).

R. L. STEVENSON That he should have a hand in hagging and hashing at Christ's Kirk.

hag /hag/ *v.*[2]*t.* Now *dial.* Infl. **-gg-**. M16. [Origin uncertain: sense 3 prob. f. HAG *n.*[1]] 1 Fatigue, tire out. M16. 2 Incite, urge. L16. 3 Torment, terrify; trouble. L16.

Haganah /hagaˈnɑː/ *n.* E20. [Heb. *hăgannāh* defence.] *Hist.* An underground defence force comprising a group of Jewish settlers in Palestine and playing a leading part in the creation of the State of Israel in 1948.

Hagarene /hagəˈriːn/ *n.* M16. [med.L *Agarenus*, *Hagarenus* f. *Agar* Hagar.] A reputed descendant of Hagar the concubine of Abraham and the mother of Ishmael (*Gen.* 16:3); a Saracen.

hagberry /ˈhagb(ə)ri/ *n. north.* Also **heck-** /ˈhɛk-/, **heg-** /ˈhɛg-/. See also HACKBERRY. L16. [Of Norse origin: cf. Da. *hæg(g)ebær*, Norw. *heggebær*, etc.] (The fruit of) the bird cherry, *Prunus padus*.

hag-boat /ˈhagbəʊt/ *n.* Now *rare* or *obs.* L17. [Origin unkn.] A large type of ship with a very narrow stern, used as a man-of-war and in the timber and coal trade.

hagfish /ˈhagfɪʃ/ *n.* Pl. same, **-es**. E17. [f. HAG *n.*[1] + FISH *n.*[1]] Any of various scavenging or predatory cyclostome fishes of the family Myxinidae, having an eel-like body without paired fins, slime glands, and a jawless mouth with movable toothed plates, found chiefly in oxygen-poor mud in deep cold seas and estuaries.

Haggadah /həˈgɑːdə, hagaˈdɑː/ *n.* Also **Agga-** /əˈgɑː-, agə-/. Pl. **-doth, -dot**, /-dəʊt/. M18. [Heb. *Haggādāh* tale, esp. an edifying one, f.

biblical Heb. *higgīd* declare, tell, expound.] 1 (A book containing) the text recited at the Seder, on the first two nights of the Passover. M18. 2 An illustrative legend or parable in the Talmud; the non-legal element of the Talmud. M19.

Haggadic(al) *adjs.* of, pertaining to, or of the nature of the Haggadah M19. **Haggadist** *n.* a writer or user of Haggadoth L19. **Haggadistic** *a.* of, pertaining to, or characteristic of a Haggadist M19.

haggard /ˈhagəd/ *n.*[1] Chiefly *Anglo-Ir.* & *dial.* ME. [Repr. ON *heygarðr*, f. *hey* hay + *garðr* GARTH *n.*[1]] A rickyard.

P. KAVANAGH The corn was gathered, and in one or two haggards the threshing mills were set up.

haggard /ˈhagəd/ *n.*[2] M16. [Absol. use of HAGGARD *a.*] A wild (usu. female) hawk caught in its adult plumage; *fig.* a wild intractable person.

M. FRENCH The oppressive, demanding wife.., the grim-faced haggard who did not understand.

†haggard *n.*[3] M17–E18. [f. HAG *n.*[1] + -ARD.] A hag, a witch.

haggard /ˈhagəd/ *a.* M16. [(O)Fr. *hagard*, perh. f. Gmc wd meaning 'hedge, bush'. Cf. HAG *n.*[3], HAW *n.*[1], HEDGE *n.*, & see -ARD. Later infl. in sense by HAG *n.*[1] (cf. HAGGARD *n.*[3]); cf. also HAGGED.] 1 Of a hawk: caught after having assumed its adult plumage; wild, untamed. Formerly also of a person: wild, perverse. M16. †b Of plumage: ragged. *rare.* E17–L18. 2 Of a person: half-starved, emaciated, gaunt. *obs.* exc. as in sense 3. M17. 3 Of a person: wild-looking; *esp.* having a worn or gaunt appearance as a result of fatigue, privation, worry, old age, etc. Formerly, of the eyes: having a wild expression. L17.

3 H. JAMES His face was haggard, his whole aspect was that of grim and hopeless misery. R. HOGGART Her face.. was well-lined but not haggard.

haggardly *adv.* L17. **haggardness** *n.* L16.

hagged /hagd, ˈhagɪd/ *a.* Now *dial.* L17. [f. HAG *v.*[2]; in sense 1 cf. HAGGARD *n.*[3] and prec.] 1 Gaunt, haggard, worn-out. L17. 2 Resembling a hag; (*rare*) bewitched. Long *rare* or *obs.* L17.

haggis /ˈhagɪs/ *n.* LME. [Prob. f. HAG *v.*[1]] 1 A dish consisting of the heart, lungs, and liver of a sheep etc. minced with suet, oatmeal, and onions, stuffed into the maw of the animal or into an artificial bag like a large sausage and usu. boiled. LME. 2 *fig.* A mixture, a hotchpotch; a mess. L19.

haggish /ˈhagɪʃ/ *a.* L16. [f. HAG *n.*[1] + -ISH[1].] Resembling or of the nature of a hag.

haggishly *adv.* M19. **haggishness** *n.* L19.

haggle /ˈhag(ə)l/ *v.* & *n.* L16. [f. as HAG *v.*[1] + -LE[3]. Cf. HACKLE *v.*[1]] A *v.* 1 *v.t.* & *i.* Hack or mangle (something) with repeated irregular or clumsy cuts. Now chiefly *Sc.* & *dial.* L16. 2 *v.i.* Advance with difficulty, struggle forward. Now chiefly *Sc.* L16. 3 *v.i.* Dispute or wrangle over a price, deal, etc. (Foll. by *about*, *over*.) E17. b *v.t.* Harass or weary (as) with haggling. Now *dial.* M17.

1 SHAKES. *Hen. V* Suffolk first died; and York, all haggled over, comes to him. 3 E. AMADI The wives of rich politicians.. hardly bothered to haggle over prices.

B *n.* A dispute, a wrangle. M19.

B. CHATWIN No one could be fiercer in a haggle over stock-prices.

haggler /ˈhaglə/ *n.* L16. [f. HAGGLE *v.* + -ER[1].] 1 A clumsy awkward worker. *obs.* exc. *dial.* L16. 2 A person who haggles over a price etc. E17. 3 An itinerant dealer, a pedlar. *obs.* exc. *dial.* E17.

haggy /ˈhagi/ *a.*[1] M17. [f. HAG *n.*[1] + -Y[1].] Of, pertaining to, or resembling a hag.

haggy /ˈhagi/ *a.*[2] Chiefly *Sc.* L18. [f. HAG *n.*[2] + -Y[1].] Boggy and full of holes.

hagi- *comb. form* see HAGIO-.

hagigah /haˈgiːgɑː, x-/ *n.pl.* Also **ch-**. M19. [Heb. *ḥăgīgāh*.] *Judaism.* The peace-offering brought by pilgrims to the Temple at the three great feasts of Passover, Pentecost, and Tabernacles.

hagio- /ˈhagɪəʊ/ *comb. form.* Before a vowel also **hagi-**. [f. Gk *hagios* holy, saintly: see -O-.] Of or pertaining to saints; saintly.

hagiarchy *n.* the hierarchy of saints E19. **hagiˈocracy** *n.* (a) government by people regarded as holy M19. **hagiˈolatrous** *a.* tending to hagiolatry M19. **hagiˈolatry** *n.* the worship of saints E19. **hagioscope** *n.* an opening in a chancel wall enabling worshippers in an aisle or side-chapel to see the altar M19.

Hagiographa /hagɪˈɒgrəfə/ *n.pl.* LME. [Late L f. Gk: see prec., -GRAPH.] One of the three canonical divisions of the Hebrew Scriptures, comprising Psalms, Proverbs, Job, Canticles, Ruth, Lamentations, Ecclesiastes, Esther, Daniel, Ezra, Nehemiah, and Chronicles, the other two divisions being the Law and the Prophets. Also called *Writings*, *Kethubim*.

hagiographal *a.* of or pertaining to the Hagiographa M17.

hagiographer /hagɪˈɒgrəfə/ *n.* M17. [f. late L *hagiographus* + -ER[1]: see HAGIO-, -GRAPHER.] 1 An author of sacred writings; *spec.* any of the writers of the Hagiographa. M17. 2 A writer of saints' lives. M19.

hagiographic /hagɪəˈgrafɪk/ *a.* E19. [f. as prec. + -IC.] 1 Of or pertaining to hagiography. E19. 2 Of or pertaining to the Hagiographa. L19.

hagiographical /hagɪəˈgrafɪk(ə)l/ *a.* L16. [f. as prec. + -AL[1].] 1 Of or pertaining to the Hagiographa or (formerly) other sacred writings. L16. 2 = HAGIOGRAPHIC 1. M19.

2 J. N. ISBISTER One-sided pictures of Freud abound—from the hagiographical to the derogatory.

hagiography /hagɪˈɒgrəfi/ *n.* E19. [f. HAGIO- + -GRAPHY.] †1 Holy Scripture; the Hagiographa. *rare.* Only in E19. 2 The writing of saints' biographies; saints' biographies as a branch of literature or legend; *transf.* the writing of an idealized biography of any person. E19.

2 J. UPDIKE Busch avoids hagiography as well as criticism.

hagiology /hagɪˈɒlədʒi/ *n.* E19. [f. HAGIO- + -LOGY.] 1 The literature dealing with the lives and legends of saints; a work on this subject; a catalogue of saints. E19. 2 The history of sacred writings. M20.

hagioˈlogic *a.* of or pertaining to hagiology E19. **hagioˈlogical** *a.* = HAGIOLOGIC L19. **hagiologist** *n.* a writer or student of hagiology E19.

hagridden /ˈhagrɪd(ə)n/ *a.* L17. [f. HAG *n.*[1] + RIDDEN *a.*] 1 Ridden by a hag (see RIDE *v.* 12), afflicted by a nightmare. L17. 2 Oppressed in mind, harassed. E18.

2 T. BANKHEAD As long as I can remember, I've been absolutely hagridden with ambition.

hag-ride /ˈhagrʌɪd/ *v.t.* Infl. as RIDE *v.* M17. [f. HAG *n.*[1] + RIDE *v.*] Afflict by nightmares; *esp.* harass or oppress mentally. Now chiefly as HAGRIDDEN.

hagship /ˈhagʃɪp/ *n.* E17. [f. HAG *n.*[1] + -SHIP.] (A humorous title for) a hag.

hag-taper /ˈhagteɪpə/ *n.* Now *dial.* Also **hag's taper** /ˈhagz teɪpə/. M16. [Second elem. TAPER *n.*[1]; first elem. unexpl.: cf. G *Kerzenkraut* lit. 'taperwort', MDu. *tortsecruyt* lit. 'torchwort'.] The great mullein, *Verbascum thapsus*, a plant of the figwort family.

hah *int.* & *n.*, *v.* vars. of HA *int.* & *n.*, *v.*

ha-ha /ˈhɑːhɑː/ *n.* Also **haw-haw** /ˈhɔːhɔː/. E18. [Fr., perh. from the cry of surprise on discovering the obstacle: cf. HA *int.*] A ditch with a wall on its inner side below ground level, forming a boundary to a garden or park without interrupting the view from within, being visible only from a close proximity.

ha ha /hɑː ˈhɑː/ *int.*, *v.*, & *n.* Also **ha ha ha**, **ha-ha(-ha)**, **hah hah**, etc. OE. [Natural exclam.: see HA *int.*] A *int.* Expr. hearty or open amusement or repr. laughter. *funny-ha ha*: see FUNNY *a.* OE.

New Yorker I thought I might want to be a teacher, ha, ha, ha.

B *v.i.* Laugh aloud. E17.

C *n.* A loud or open laugh; a joke. E19.

Times Lit. Suppl. Death-bed confessions from the forger's family who thought it a great 'Ha-ha' as it, sadly, was.

haham /ˈhɑːhəm/ *n.* Also **chacham** /ˈxɑːxəm/ & other vars. L17. [Heb. *ḥākām* wise.] A person learned in Jewish law; a wise man; *spec.* among Sephardic Jews, a rabbi; the spiritual head of a Sephardic community.

hahnium /ˈhɑːnɪəm/ *n.* L20. [f. Otto *Hahn* (1879–1968), Ger. physicist + -IUM.] (A name proposed for) the artificially produced transuranic chemical element of atomic no. 105. (Symbol Ha.)

haick *n.* var. of HAIK.

Haida /ˈhʌɪdə/ *n.* & *a.* Also **Haidah**, **Hydah**. M19. [Haida = people.] A *n.* 1 Pl. **-s**, same. A member of a N. American Indian people living on the Queen Charlotte Islands in British Columbia, and on Prince of Wales Island, Alaska. M19. 2 The language of this people. E20. B *attrib.* or as *adj.* Of or pertaining to the Haidas or their language. M19.

haidingerite /ˈhʌɪdɪŋərʌɪt/ *n.* E19. [f. W. K. von *Haidinger* (1795–1871), Austrian mineralogist + -ITE[1].] *Min.* An orthorhombic hydrated arsenate of calcium, occurring as minute white crystals.

haik /heɪk, ˈhɑːɪk/ *n.* Also **haick**. E18. [Arab. *ḥā'ik*.] In N. Africa, a large outer wrap, usu. white, worn by both sexes.

haikal /ˈhʌɪk(ə)l/ *n.* L19. [Arab. = temple.] The central chapel of three forming the sanctuary of a Coptic church.

Comb.: **haikal screen** a screen, often carved or decorated, which separates the haikal from the body of the church.

haiku /ˈhʌɪkuː/ *n.* Pl. same, **-s**. L19. [Jap., abbrev. of *haikai no ku* unserious or comic verse.] A short Japanese poem in three parts and usu. having 17 syllables; an English imitation of such a poem.

hail /heɪl/ *n.*[1] [OE *hagol*, *hægl*, corresp. to OFris. *heil*, OS, OHG *hagal* (Du., G *Hagel*), ON *hagl*, f. Gmc, rel. to Gk *kakhlēx* pebble.] 1 Frozen rain falling in a shower or storm of pellets. OE. 2 A shower or storm of hail. Now usu. *hail shower*, *hailstorm*. OE. 3 *transf.* & *fig.* A storm or shower of something falling like hail, as bullets, curses, questions, etc. LME.

1 J. C. OATES A harsh percussive rain hardened suddenly into hail. 3 M. LOWRY A continuous hail of golf balls flying out of bounds bombarded the roof. E. BAKER This hail of hissing accusations and threats.

Comb.: **hailstone** a pellet of hail; **†hail-shot** small shot which scatters like hail when fired; *hail shower*: see sense 2 above; *hailstorm*: see sense 2 above.

haily *a.* (now *rare*) consisting of or characterized by hail or hailstorms M16.

hail /heɪl/ *n.*[2] E16. [f. HAIL *int.* or *v.*[2]] 1 An exclamation of 'hail!'; a greeting, a salutation. E16. 2 An act of hailing someone or something; a shout of welcome; a call to attract attention. L17.

2 R. L. STEVENSON I could hear hails coming and going between the old buccaneer and his comrades.

Phrases: **within hail** within call, close enough to be hailed.

†hail *n.*[3] see HALE *n.*[1]

hail /heɪl/ *a.*[1] *obs.* exc. *Hist.* in *drink hail* (see DRINK *v.*). ME. [ON *heill* = OE *hāl* HALE *a.*, WHOLE *a.* See also WASSAIL *n.*] Sound, healthy, wholesome; = HALE *a.*

hail *a.*[2] see HALE *a.*

hail /heɪl/ *v.*[1] [OE *hagalian* = ON *hagla*. Repl. in ME by forms f. HAIL *n.*[1]] I *v.i.* 1 *impers.* in *it hails, it is hailing*, etc., hail falls, hail is falling, etc. OE. 2 Pour or send down hail. *rare.* LME. 3 Fall as or like hail. M19.

II *v.t.* 4 Pour down as hail; throw or send *down* or *upon* violently like hail in a storm. LME.

4 TENNYSON Walter hail'd a score of names upon her.

hail /heɪl/ *v.*[2] ME. [f. *hail* var. of HALE *n.*[1]] 1 *v.t.* Salute with 'hail!'; salute, greet; welcome. ME. 2 *v.t.* Call, shout, or wave to (a person, a ship, etc.) from a distance, in order to attract attention; signal to (a taxi, a bus, etc.) to stop and take one as a passenger. L15. 3 *v.i.* Call out in order to attract attention. L16. 4 *v.i.* Of a ship, a person: have come originally *from* a place. M19.

1 V. WOOLF Friends hailed each other in passing. I. WALLACE Her father had hailed her prestigious government job as the inevitable triumph of her

upbringing. 2 J. CONRAD Being hailed across the street he looked up. W. STYRON We hailed a taxi and headed back to the McAlpin. *within hailing distance*: see DISTANCE *n.* 4 *Golf Illustrated* Simpson is 31 and hails from San Diego.

hailer *n.* (*a*) a person who hails or calls to attract attention; (*b*) *loud-hailer*: see LOUD *a.*: L19.

hail /heɪl/ *int.* Now *arch.* or *rhet.* exc. in comb. ME. [f. HAIL *a.*[1] in expressions of good wishes as †*hail be thou* (cf. WASSAIL *n.*).] Used as an exclamation of greeting or salutation or of acclamation. Also foll. by *to*.

all hail: see ALL *a.*, *pron.*, *n.*, & *adv.*

Comb.: **hail-fellow(-well-met)** *a.* & *adv.* on most intimate terms (*with*), *esp.* overfamiliar(ly); **Hail Mary** = AVE MARIA I.

hain /heɪn/ *v.t.* Now *Sc.* & *dial.* ME. [ON *hegna* to hedge, fence, protect, f. Gmc.] 1 Enclose or protect with a fence or hedge; *esp.* preserve (grass) from cattle. ME. 2 Spare, save; refrain from using or spending. E16.

hair /hɛː/ *n.* [OE *hǣr*, *hēr* = OFris. *hēr*, OS, OHG *hār* (Du., G *Haar*), ON *hár*, f. Gmc. In branch II orig. OE *hǣre*, *hēre* reinforced in ME by OFr. *haire*, f. Frank., identified w. this.] I 1 Any of the numerous fine flexible keratinized filaments that grow from beneath the skin of a mammal, esp. from the head of a person; any fine filament growing from the integument of an animal. OE. 2 (*collect.* & (*arch.*) in *pl.*) All such filaments growing on an animal; *spec.* those growing on the head of a person. Also, hairs in a mass, as used in manufacture etc. OE. b *fig.* Something radiating, spreading, or trailing in the manner of hair, as the rays of the sun, the foliage of a tree, etc. L16. 3 A very small degree or quantity; the slightest thing; a jot, an iota. ME. †4 The distinctive type of something; sort, kind; stamp, character. LME–E17. 5 *transf.* Something resembling (a) hair in shape, appearance, or consistency. LME. 6 A fine elongated or filamentous plant structure, as a stamen or leaf-fibre; *spec.* in *Bot.*, any elongated outgrowth from the epidermis, as a root hair. L16.

1 J. WILSON And would not hurt a hair upon his head. 2 T. MORRISON His eyes were so wild, his hair so long and matted. 3 T. KENEALLY Anyone who has loaded weapons is only a hair away from savagery.

II 7 Cloth made of hair, haircloth; *esp.* a hair shirt worn next to the skin by ascetics and penitents. OE.

Phrases: **against the hair** contrary to the natural lie of an animal's hair; *fig.* contrary to inclination. **a hair in one's neck** *rare* a cause of trouble or annoyance. *curl a person's hair*: see CURL *v.* *get by the short hairs*: see SHORT *a.* **hair of the dog (that bit one)** an alcoholic drink taken to cure a hangover, so called because it is a cure consisting of a small amount of the cause. *hang by a hair*: see HANG *v.* *have by the short hairs*: see SHORT *a.* *head of hair*: see HEAD *n.* *hide nor hair*: see HIDE *n.*[1] **in one's hair** (*a*) (now *rare*) with the hair down; bareheaded; (*b*) *fig.* encumbering, persistently annoying, in one's way. **keep one's hair on** *slang* remain calm. **let one's hair down** (*a*) release one's hair from a style where it is secured against the head or tied back; (*b*) *fig.* (*colloq.*) cease to be formal, behave unconventionally or unrestrainedly. **lose one's hair** lose one's temper. *make a person's hair curl*: see CURL *v.* *neither hide nor hair*: see HIDE *n.*[1] **not turn a hair** show no sign of discomposure or exhaustion. **out of one's hair** not encumbering, out of one's way. **put up one's hair** arrange one's hair in a style where it is secured against the head, formerly a sign of the transition from girlhood to womanhood. **split hairs** make overfine distinctions. *tear one's hair*: see TEAR *v.*[1] **to a hair** exactly.

Comb.: **hair bag** (*a*) a bag made of hair; (*b*) a bag for keeping hair in; **hair-ball** a ball of hair which collects esp. in the stomach of various animals; **hairband** a band for securing the hair; **hairbreadth** *n.* & *a.* = *hair's breadth*, *hair's-breadth* below; **hairbrush** (*a*) a brush for smoothing and styling the hair; (*b*) a kind of hand-grenade; **hair-cell** *Anat.* any of the ciliated vibration-sensitive cells of the inner ear and (in fish etc.) the lateral-line system; **hair clip** a clip, often ornamental, for securing the hair; **haircloth** (*a*) a cloth or fabric of hair used for making tents, towels, shirts, etc., or in drying malt, hops, etc.; (*b*) an article made of this fabric; **hair-cord** (*a*) a finely striped fabric resembling hair in appearance; (*b*) a cord made of human hair; **hair crack** a hairline crack; **haircut** an act of cutting the hair; the shape or style into which the hair is cut; **hairdo** *colloq.* the process of styling the hair; a particular way in which the hair is styled; **hairdress** (*a*) a way of dressing the hair; (*b*) a head-dress; **hairdresser** a person whose occupation is the cutting or styling of hair; **hairdressing** (*a*) the action, process, or occupation of cutting or styling the hair; (*b*) a liquid preparation for the hair; **hair-drier** an electrical device for drying the hair by blowing warm air over it; *hair follicle*: see FOLLICLE *n.* I; **hair-grass** (*a*) any of various slender grasses, esp. of the northern temperate genera *Aira* and *Deschampsia*; (*b*) any of several thin-leaved aquatic plants used in aquaria, esp. of the genus *Eleocharis* (family Cyperaceae); **hairgrip** a grip for securing the hair, *esp.* one similar to a hairpin but with the ends close together; **hair lace** (now *rare*) a tie or net for securing the hair; **hair lacquer**: for holding the hair in place; **hair-lock** a lock of hair on or from the head; **hair mattress**: stuffed with hair; **hair moss**: of the genus *Polytrichum*; esp. *P. commune*, a large moss of damp or acid soils, with a hairy calyptra; **hairnet** a fine net for keeping the hair in place; **hair oil** cosmetic oil for dressing the hair; **hairpiece** a piece of false hair used to augment a person's natural hair; **hair-point** the fine tip of some moss leaves; **hair-powder** *Hist.* a scented powder for sprinkling on the hair or a wig; **hair-raising** *a.* fearsome, horrifying, exciting, esp. so as to make the hair stand on end; **hair-restorer** a substance used to promote the growth of esp. receding or thinning hair; **hair's breadth** the breadth of a hair; a minute distance; **hair's-breadth** *a.* extremely narrow or close; **hair seal** a seal without a thick fur undercoat; (cf. *fur-seal* s.v. FUR *n.*[1]); **hair shirt** a shirt made of haircloth, worn by penitents or ascetics; **hair-shirt** *a.* austere, harsh, self-sacrificing; **hair-sieve** (now *rare*) a sieve which has a base made of finely woven hair; *hair-slide*: see SLIDE *n.* 6; **hair-space** *Typogr.* a very thin space between letters or words; **hair-splitter** a person who splits hairs; **hair-splitting** *vbl n.* & *ppl a.* making overfine distinctions; **hairspray** spray-on hair lacquer; **hairspring** a fine spring which regulates the balance-wheel in a watch; **hairstreak** any of various lycaenid butterflies belonging to the genus *Thecla* and related genera, having fringed wings often with pale markings like streaks (*white-letter hairstreak*: see WHITE *a.*); **hair-stroke** a very fine stroke made in writing or drawing; **hairstyle** a particular way of dressing the hair; **hairstylist** a person who advises on and creates hairstyles for individual people; **hair-trigger** a secondary trigger in a firearm which releases the main trigger by very slight pressure; **hair-triggered** *a.* having a hair-trigger. **hair-worm** any of various long slender worms, *esp.* one whose larva is parasitic; *spec.* an aquatic worm of the class (or phylum) Nematomorpha (also called *horsehair worm*), whose larvae are parasites of arthropods, *esp.* one of the common freshwater species *Gordius aquaticus*.

hairlike *a.* resembling hair; finely drawn-out like hair: M17.

hair /hɛː/ *v.* M16. [f. the n.] †1 *v.t.* Edge with hair or fur. *Sc.* M–L16. 2 *v.t.* Free from hair; depilate. E19. 3 *v.i.* Produce or grow hair or a hairlike substance. L19.

haired /hɛːd/ *a.* LME. [f. HAIR *n.* + -ED[2].] Having hair; covered with hair or hairs. Freq. w. qualifying adj., as *black-haired*, *long-haired*, etc.

hairen /ˈhɛːrən/ *a.* Long *obs.* exc. *dial.* & *Sc.* [OE *hǣren* = OHG *hārīn*, f. Gmc. base of HAIR *n.*: see -EN[4].] Made or consisting of hair.

hairif /ˈhɛːrɪf/ *n.* Chiefly *dial.* Also **harif** /ˈharɪf/, **hayrif**. [OE *heġerife*, app. f. *heġe* HAY *n.*[2] + *rife*, of unkn. origin.] The plant cleavers, *Galium aparine*.

hairless /ˈhɛːlɪs/ *a.* M16. [f. HAIR *n.* + -LESS.] Without hair; bald.

hairlessness *n.* L19.

hairline /ˈhɛːlʌɪn/ *n.* L16. [f. HAIR *n.* + LINE *n.*[2]] 1 A line or rope made of hair. L16. 2 A fine line; *spec.* the upstroke in a written or printed letter. M19. 3 = *hair-cord* (a) s.v. HAIR *n.* M19. 4 The natural line on the head at which the hair stops growing. E20. 5 In full *hairline crack*. A very fine crack, *esp.* one which occurs in steel or other metals. E20. 6 A fine line on glass, plastic, paper, etc., often used as a measuring guide or a dividing line. M20. b *fig.* A very fine dividing line. M20.

4 L. C. DOUGLAS The forward curve of the hair-line on the temples. 6b *attrib.*: *Times* It looked a hairline decision indeed.

Comb.: *hairline crack*: see sense 5 above; **hairline fracture** *Med.* a very fine crack in a bone.

hairpin /ˈhɛːpɪn/ *n.* L18. [f. HAIR *n.* + PIN *n.*[1]] 1 A kind of pin used to secure the hair, *esp.* a long-legged U-shaped pin. L18. 2 A person, *esp.* a thin person. *joc. slang.* L19. 3 In full *hairpin bend*, *corner*. A sharp U-shaped bend in a road or track. E20.

2 J. O'FAOLAIN Maybe someone should give the old hairpin a bit of a fright. 3 P. KEMP Its sudden ascents and declivities, its blind curves and hairpin bends.

hairy /ˈhɛːri/ *a.* & *n.* ME. [f. HAIR *n.* + -Y[1].] A *adj.* 1 Having much hair; covered in hair. Also, having a rough appearance suggestive of hair(s). ME. 2 a Hairlike. Now *rare*. LME. b Made of hair. M16. 3 *Bot.* Pubescent, esp. with separately distinguishable hairs. L16. 4 *fig.* Difficult; unpleasant, frightening; crude, clumsy. *slang.* M19. 5 Uncouth, ill-mannered. *slang.* L19.

1 D. W. GOODWIN Maybe men can't see their bruises because of those hairy legs. 4 D. LODGE Landing at Genoa is a pretty hairy experience at the best of times.

Phrases, special collocations, & comb.: *great hairy willowherb*: see WILLOW. **hairy about, at, the heels** *slang* = sense 5 above. **hairy-heeled** *a.* (*slang*) = sense 5 above. **hairy frog** a W. African frog, *Trichobatrachus robustus*, the males having hairlike filaments on the sides and thighs. **hairy in the heels** *slang* = sense 5 above. **hairy woodpecker** a black and white N. American woodpecker, *Dendrocopos villosus*. *hairy* WOUBIT.

B *n.* A draught horse (from its hairy fetlocks). Also, a hairy person; an aggressive or unpleasant person. M19.

hairily *adv.* M19. **hairiness** *n.* LME.

hait /heɪt/ *int.* *obs.* exc. *dial.* Also **heit**. LME. [Cf. G *hott* go right.] Used to urge a horse forward.

haith /heɪθ/ *int.* *Sc.* L17. [Alt. of FAITH.] Used as an asseveration or oath.

Haitian /ˈheɪʃ(ə)n, hɑːˈiːʃ-, hʌɪˈiːʃ-; -tɪən/ *a.* & *n.* Also (now *rare*) **Haytian**. E19. [f. *Haiti* (see below) + -IAN.] A *adj.* Of or pertaining to Haiti, the French-speaking western portion of the Caribbean island of Hispaniola. E19.

Haitian creole the creolized French spoken in Haiti.

B *n.* A native or inhabitant of Haiti. Also, Haitian creole. E19.

hajeen *n.* var. of HYGEEN.

hajj /hadʒ/ *n.* Also **hadj**, **haj**. E18. [Arab. (*al-*)*ḥajj* (the Great) Pilgrimage.] The pilgrimage to the Sacred Mosque at Mecca undertaken in the twelfth month of the Muslim year and constituting one of the religious duties of Islam.

hajji /ˈhadʒiː/ *n.* Also (fem.) **hajja** /ˈhadʒə/; **-dj-**. E17. [Pers., Turk. *ḥājjī*, *ḥājī* pilgrim, f. as prec.] (The title given to) a person who has undertaken the hajj. Cf. AL-HAJJ.

haka /ˈhɑːkə/ *n.* M19. [Maori.] A ceremonial Maori dance accompanied by chanting.

hakama /ˈhakəmə, ˈhɑː-/ *n.* M19. [Jap.] Japanese loose trousers with many pleats in the front.

hake /heɪk/ *n.*[1] ME. [Perh. f. OE *haca* hook: cf. OE *hacod* pike.] 1 Any of various blue-grey and silver gadoid fishes of shallow temperate seas, of the genus *Merluccius* or the family Merlucciidae, having a rather elongate body with two dorsal fins, most species being commercially fished; *spec.* the European *M. merluccius*. Also, the flesh of these as food. ME. 2 a Either of two reddish-brown gadid food fishes, *Urophycis chuss* and *U. tenuis*, of the north-western Atlantic (both also more fully *red hake*, *squirrel hake*, *white hake*). *US.* L19. b = *gemfish* s.v. GEM *n.* *Austral.* M20.

hake /heɪk/ *n.*[2] *obs.* exc. *Hist.* Also **hag** /hag/. M16. [App. abbrev. of *haquebut*: see HACKBUT.] A short firearm used in the 16th cent.

hake *n.*[3] see HACK *n.*[3]

hakea /ˈhɑːkɪə, ˈheɪ-/ *n.* M19. [mod.L (see below), f. C. L. von *Hake* (1745–1818), Ger. patron of botany: see -IA[1].] Any of numerous xerophytic shrubs and small trees of the genus *Hakea*, of the protea family, endemic to Australia.

hakeem *n.* var. of HAKIM *n.*[2]

Hakenkreuz /ˈhaːkənkrɔyts/ *n.* Also **h-**. Pl. **-e** /-ə/. M20. [G, f. *Haken* hook + *Kreuz* cross.] A swastika, esp. as a Nazi symbol.

hakim /ˈhɑːkɪm/ *n.*[1] E17. [Arab. *ḥākim* ruler, governor, judge f. *ḥakama* pass judgement.] A judge, ruler, or governor in a Muslim country.

hakim /haˈkiːm/ *n.*[2] Also **hakeem**. M17. [Arab. *ḥakīm* wise man, philosopher, physician, f. as prec.] A physician in a Muslim country.

Hakka /ˈhakə/ *n.* & *a.* M19. [Chin. (Cantonese) *haàk ka*, lit. 'guest, stranger'.] A *n.* A member of a people of south-eastern China, esp. Canton, Taiwan, and Hong Kong; the form of Chinese, comprising a group of dialects, spoken by this people. M19. B *attrib.* or as *adj.* Of or pertaining to this people or this group of dialects. L19.

Halacha /halɑːˈxɑː, həˈlɑːkə/ *n.* Also **-chah**, **-kah**. M19. [Heb. *hă lākāh* law.] The body of Jewish law contained in the Mishnah and in later Jewish literature; the legal element of the Talmud; a legal ruling included as a binding part of this law.

Halachic *a.* M19.

Halafian /həˈlɑːfɪən/ *a.* M20. [f. Tell *Halaf* in NE Syria + -IAN.] *Archaeol.* Designating or pertaining to a culture (*c* 6000–5400 BC) which extended from northern Syria to eastern Iraq and the neighbouring parts of Iran and Turkey and was characterized by polychrome pottery first discovered at Tell Halaf.

Halakah *n.* var. of HALACHA.

halal /həˈlɑːl/ *a.*, *v.*, & *n.* Also **hallal**. M19. [Arab. *ḥalāl* according to religious law.] A *adj.* Killed or prepared in the manner prescribed by Islamic law. M19. B *v.t.* Kill (an animal) in this manner. M19. C *n.* An animal killed, or meat prepared, in this manner. M20.

halala /həˈlɑːlə/ *n.* Pl. **-s**, same. M20. [Arab.] A monetary unit of Saudi Arabia, equal to one-hundredth of a rial.

Halalcor /həˈlalkɔː/ *n.* M17. [Urdu *halāl-ḵōr*, f. Arab. HALAL & base of Pers. *ḵordan* eat.] A person of the lowest and poorest class in India, Iran, etc., to whom everything is lawful food.

halation /həˈleɪʃ(ə)n/ *n.* M19. [Irreg. f. HALO *n.* + -ATION.] The spreading of light beyond its proper boundaries to form a fog round the edges of a bright image in a photograph or on a television screen.

halawi /həˈlɑːwi/ *n.* M19. [Arab. *ḥalāwī*, pl. of *ḥalwā* HALVA.] = HALVA.

halberd /ˈhalbəːd/ *n.* Also **-ert** /-əːt/. L15. [Fr. *hallebarde*, †*alabarde* f. It. *alabarda* f. MHG *helmbarde* (G *Hellebarde*), f. *helm* handle, HELM *n.*[2] + *barde*, *barte* hatchet, rel. to *bart* beard (cf. ON *skeggja* halberd, lit. 'the bearded', f. *skegg* beard).] *Hist.* 1 A weapon, in use esp. during the 15th and 16th cents., consisting of a long handle ending in a combined spearhead and battleaxe. L15. 2 The rank of sergeant (from the right of a sergeant to carry a halberd). M18.

Comb.: **halberdman** a halberdier.

halberded *a.* armed with a halberd L18.

halberdier /halbəˈdɪə/ *n.* E16. [Fr. *hallebardier*, f. as prec.: see -IER.] A soldier armed with a halberd; a guardsman carrying a halberd as a badge of office.

halch /hal(t)ʃ/ *v.t. obs.* exc. *dial.* LME. [Var. of HALSE *v.*[1]] †1 Embrace, greet, salute. LME–M17. 2 Fasten, tie, knot. LME.

halcyon /ˈhalsɪən, ˈhalʃ(ə)n/ *n.* & *a.* LME. [L (*h*)*alcyon* f. Gk *alkuōn* kingfisher (also *halkuōn* by assoc. w. *hals* sea and *kuōn* conceiving), rel. to L *alcedo* kingfisher.] A *n.* 1 A bird said by the ancients to breed in a nest floating on the sea around the time of the winter solstice, and to charm the wind and waves so that the sea was calm for this purpose; *poet.* a kingfisher. LME. b Any of various brightly coloured tropical kingfishers of the genus *Halcyon*. L18. †2 Calm, quietude. M17–L18.

B *adj.* 1 Calm, peaceful; happy, prosperous, idyllic. L16. 2 Of or pertaining to the halcyon or kingfisher. E17.

halcyon days orig., fourteen days of calm weather supposed to occur when the halcyon was breeding; now, days of idyllic happiness or prosperity.

haldi /ˈhʌldi/ *n.* Also **huldee**. M19. [Hind. f. Skt *haridrā*.] The plant *Curcuma longa*, of the ginger family, whose powdered tubers yield turmeric. Also, turmeric itself.

haldu /ˈhalduː/ *n.* E20. [Hind.] A tree, *Adina cordifolia*, of the madder family, found in the Indian subcontinent, Myanmar (Burma), and Thailand; the yellowish hardwood obtained from it.

hale /heɪl/ *n.*[1] Long *rare*. Also †**hail**. ME. [ON *heill* health, prosperity, good luck, rel. to HEAL *n.*; assim. to HALE *a.*] 1 Health, safety, welfare. ME. †2 Luck, fortune: in *evil*, *ill*, etc., *hale*. ME–E16.

hale /heɪl/ *n.*[2] Long *rare* or *obs.* ME. [(O)Fr. *halle* covered market-place, f. Frank. = OS, OHG *halla*: see HALL *n.*] A place roofed over, but usu. open at the sides; a tent, a pavilion; a temporary shelter.

hale /heɪl/ *n.*[3] Now *rare* or *obs.* L15. [f. HALE *v.*[1]] 1 *hale and how*: an exclam. of sailors in hauling. L15. 2 An act of hauling. L17. 3 A haul of fish. Chiefly *Sc.* M18.

hale /heɪl/ *n.*[4] E17. [App. f. ON *hali*, Da. *hale* tail.] Either of the two handles of a plough or wheelbarrow. Usu. in *pl.*

hale /heɪl/ *a.* Also (*Sc.*) **hail**. OE. [North. dial. repr. of OE *hāl* WHOLE *a.* Cf. HAIL *a.*[1]] I Sound, healthy. 1 Free from injury; safe, unhurt. Now only *Sc.* & *north.* OE. 2 Free from disease, healthy; recovered from disease, healed. Now only *Sc.* & *north.* OE. 3 Esp. of an old person: free from infirmity; sound, robust, vigorous. Freq. in *hale and hearty*. E18.

II 4 Whole, entire, complete; unbroken, undecayed. Now only *Sc.* & *north.* ME.

4 *the hale ware*: see WARE *n.*[2]

¶In Sc. *hail* the *i* indicated a long vowel not a diphthong as in HAIL *a.*[1]

halely *adv.* ME. **haleness** *n.* ME.

hale /heɪl/ *v.*[1] ME. [(O)Fr. *haler* f. ON *hala* = OS *halon*, OHG *halōn*, *holōn* (Du. *halen*, G *holen* fetch): cf. OE *ġeholian* acquire & HAUL *v.*] 1 *v.t.* Draw, pull; *spec.* drag, tug, or haul forcibly. ME. 2 *v.t. fig.* Draw forcibly to, into, out of, a course of action, feeling, condition, etc. (Foll. by *to*, *into*, *out of*.) LME. 3 *v.i.* Pull, tug. LME. 4 *v.i.* †a Move along as if drawn or pulled; hasten, rush; *spec.* (of a ship) proceed before the wind with the sails set. LME–E18. b Flow, run, pour. *obs.* exc. *Sc.* & *north.* LME.

1 R. ELLMANN He was haled before the Vice-Chancellor's court in November 1877. 2 J. H. FRISWELL Garrick haled on one hand by Tragedy and on the other by Comedy.

hale /heɪl/ *v.*[2] *obs.* exc. *Sc.* ME. [f. HALE *a.*, or var. of HEAL *v.*[1] assim. to HALE *a.*] Make hale or whole; heal.

haler /ˈhɑːlə/ *n.* Pl. **haleru** /ˈhɑːləruː/, same. M20. [Czech *haléř* (genit. pl. *haléřů*) f. MHG *haller*: see HELLER *n.*[1]] A monetary unit of Bohemia, Moravia, and Slovakia, equal to one-hundredth of a koruna.

halesia /həˈliːzɪə/ *n.* M18. [mod.L (see below), f. Stephen *Hales* (1677–1761), Eng. plant physiologist: see -IA[1].] Any of several trees of the southern US constituting the genus *Halesia*, of the styrax family, with pendulous white flowers; esp. *H. tetraptera*, freq. grown for ornament. Also called *silver-bell tree*, *snowdrop tree*.

halesome /ˈheɪls(ə)m/ *a.* Chiefly *Sc.* ME. [f. HALE *a.* + -SOME[1]. Cf. HEALSOME.] Wholesome.

half /hɑːf/ *n.* Pl. **halves** /hɑːvz/, †**halfs**. [OE *healf* fem. = OFris. *halve*, OS *halba*, OHG *halba*, ON *hálfa*, Goth *halba* side (earliest sense), half; in sense 6 f. the adj.] †1 Side; either of the (two) sides of an object etc. as a specification of position or direction; the *right* or *left* side. OE–M16. †2 *fig.* Either of two opposing sides identified contextually, as two parties in a conflict, the representatives of male and female lines of descent, etc. OE–M16. b Side, part (as of each of the parties to a transaction). Freq. in *on my*, *this*, etc., *half*. OE–E16. 3 Either of two opposite, corresponding, or equal parts into which a thing is or may be divided; either of two equal parts into which a number or quantity is or may be divided. OE. b *spec.* Either of two equal periods of play, usu. separated by an interval, into which a game of football etc. is divided. L19. 4 Either of two divisions more or less approaching equality (freq. with preceding compar. adj.). Formerly also, each of three or more divisions. ME. †5 Either of two partners or sharers. Only in 16. 6 [Absol. use of the adj.] *colloq.* a A half-sized thing; a half quantity or division according to some specific measure. M17. b A school term (the school year formerly being divided into two portions). E19. c A half-pint of beer, lager, etc.; *Sc.* a half-gill of spirits (esp. of whisky). L19. d A half-back. Usu. w. specifying wd, as *fly-half*, *left-half*, etc. L19. e A fare or ticket at a reduced (usu. half) rate, esp. for a child. Also, a person entitled to travel at such a rate. M20. f *Amer. Football.* Half-time. Freq. with *the*. M20. 7 *Golf.* A halved hole. L19.

1 SIR T. MORE Then thou shalte see me on the backe halfe. 2 J. DOLMAN On princes halves the myghty god doth fyght. 3 AV *1 Kings* 3:25 Diuide the liuing childe in two, and giue halfe to the one, and halfe to the other. J. MCLEOD One of his attendants . . received . . about a dozen and a half blows with a flat bamboo. W. SCORESBY Of this number of whales, considerably above half have been taken by five ships. A. J. P. TAYLOR He had lost the return half of his ticket. D. PRATER Clara joined him . . for the first half of August. *Gentleman (Bombay)* The two halves of east and west . . joined by a common heritage. J. VIORST More than half of those with children under the age of six now go to work. b *Sporting Mirror* For most of the first half . . it seemed that only one end of the field was in use. 4 H. SPENCER The larger half of the phenomena. R. KIPLING Half of them were thin-legged, gray-bearded Ooryas from down country. 5 SHAKES. *Tam. Shr.* Son, I'll be your half. 6a N. ALGREN He found three halves, wrapped in a ten-dollar bill, in her apron. b A. POWELL I went to Eton in the summer half of 1919. c A. BURGESS Our men sat gloomily over their halves of washy bitter. e *New Statesman* Two adults and three halves, please. 7 *Daily Telegraph* He . . secured the necessary 5 for the half and the match.

Phrases: **and a half** *fig.* (*colloq.*) of an exceptional kind; and more. **by halves** imperfectly or incompletely (usu. in neg. contexts). **cry halves** claim an equal share. **go halves, go half and half, (on, in)** share equally (in something) (*with* a person). *one's better half*: see BETTER *a.* etc. *one's worse half*: see WORSE *a.*, *n.*, & *adv.* **other half** (*a*) *the* people having a different (esp. superior) social, cultural, or economic standing (chiefly in *how the other half lives*); (*b*) *colloq.* (freq. *joc.*) a person's spouse or boyfriend or girlfriend; (*c*) *slang the* second drink (esp. when bought in return for the first). **the half of it** the more significant or important part (usu. in neg. contexts). **too clever** etc. **by half** far more clever etc. than is satisfactory or desirable.

half /hɑːf/ *a.* (in mod. usage also classed as a *determiner*) & *adv.* [OE *half* (*healf*) = OFris., OS (Du.) *half*, (O)HG *halb*, ON *hálfr*, Goth. *halbs*, f. Gmc.] A *adj.* 1 Forming either of two equal parts or corresponding groups into which something is or may be divided; of an amount or quantity equal to a half. Following or (passing into HALF *n.* 3) preceding a determiner (article, demonstrative, or possessive adj.). OE. †2 Designating a half-unit less than the cardinal numeral that corresponds to the preceding or following ordinal numeral. OE–ME. 3 Falling short of the full or perfect amount, degree, type, etc.; partial, incomplete, imperfect. ME. 4 Half the length or breadth of. Now *rare* or *obs.* L15.

1 LD MACAULAY His victory . . had deprived him of half his influence. J. M. MURRY Keats spent half the year at his side. G. GREENE Sickness benefit; half wages; incapacity; the management regrets. W. BOYD The Norfolk was half a mile further on. *fig.*: A. TROLLOPE If you are half the woman I take you to be, you will understand this. 3 M. B. KEATINGE Contented with half views of things and truths. *UnixWorld* You can instruct the processor to run at half speed. 4 J. DAVIES Their hair . . hangs down over their shoulders to half their backs.

Phrases: **half a crown** = *half-crown* s.v. HALF-. **half a dozen** a half of a dozen, six. **half a minute** a half of a minute, thirty seconds. *half an eye*: see EYE *n.* **half an hour** a half of an hour, thirty minutes. *half the battle*:

see BATTLE *n. half the time*: see TIME *n. with half a heart*: see HEART *n.*

B *adv.* 1 To the extent or amount of half; *loosely* in part, partially, to a certain extent, in some degree, nearly. OE. 2 *not half*: not, not sufficiently (now *rare* exc. w. *enough* following adj.); *slang* not at all, rather the reverse of; also (*slang*) (as a mere intensive), in no small measure, certainly, undoubtedly, etc. L16. 3 *Naut.* a By the amount of half a point beyond a (preceding) specified compass point towards a (following) specified compass point. E18. b By the amount of half a unit more than the following specified number of fathoms in a sounding. E19. 4 By the amount of half an hour past (or *past*) the (following) specified hour. M18.

1 J. CONRAD They would . . address him half seriously as Rajah Laut. D. H. LAWRENCE His talk was fragmentary, he was only half articulate. J. BUCHAN They were only foolish people scared half out of their minds. B. PYM 'These men see . . His wonders in the deep', Julian said half to himself. O. MANNING Hugh found Simon prone, eyes half closed. H. SECOMBE Miss Thomas gave a little shriek which she half stifled with a gloved hand. L. GORDON Lying half asleep, half awake in her warm bed. J. ARCHER She only hoped that Raymond's remarks would be half as flattering. 2 V. WOOLF I could live on fifteen shillings a week . . It wouldn't be half bad. L. P. HARTLEY 'You don't half like getting your own way, do you?' grumbled Harold. A. WESKER He didn't half upset them. *Beano* Coo! Smashing film, eh, lads? . . Not half! P. BARKER They aren't half a price. 3a G. SHELVOCKE Bearing South East half East, distant six leagues. b F. MARRYAT We shall have *half four* directly, and after that the water will deepen. 4 M. AMSTERDAM This morning at half past three.

half /hɑːf/ *v.i.* & *t.* Chiefly *dial.* L19. [f. HALVE *v.*] Halve; go halves in (something).

half- /hɑːf/ *comb. form.* OE. [Repr. HALF *a.* & *adv.*] Forming combs. with ns., adjs., vbs, and advs. in various relations and senses, as 'forming a half' (*half-belt*, *half-share*); 'of an amount or quantity equal to a half' (*half-dozen*, *half-pound*); 'incomplete(ly), imperfect(ly), partial(ly)' (*half-thought-out*, *half-done*, *half-kill*). Can be written with or without a hyphen.

half-adder *Computing* a logic device which has two inputs (addend and augend) and generates two outputs (sum and carry digits). **half-and-half** *n., a.,* & *adv.* (*a*) *n.* something that is half one thing and half another; *spec.* (*arch.*) a mixture of ale and porter in equal quantities, (*US*) a mixture of milk and cream; (*b*) *adj.* that is half one thing and half another; (*c*) *adv.* in equal parts; half — and half not. **half-arse(d)**, **-ass(ed)** *adjs.* (*slang*) incompetent, inadequate. **half-back** *Football, Hockey*, etc. (the position of) a player playing between the forwards and the backs; *Amer. Football* (now *rare*) a flanker. **half-baked** *a.* (*fig.*) (*a*) not thorough, not thoroughly planned, not serious, incomplete; (*b*) stupid, halfwitted. **half-ball** *Billiards, Snooker*, etc. a stroke in which the cue is aimed through the cue-ball at the edge of the object-ball, and so covers half of it. **half-bap'tize** *v.t.* baptize privately or without full rites. **half-beak** any of various small, slender, mostly marine surface-skimming tropical fishes of the family Hemiramphidae, related to flying fish and typically having the lower jaw much longer than the upper. **half-'belt** a belt extending only halfway around the body, *esp.* one worn at the back of a garment. **half-binding** a style of bookbinding in which the back and corners are covered in one material and the sides in another, usu. less durable. **half-blood** (*a*) the relation between people having only one parent in common; (*b*) a person or group of persons related in this way; (*c*) a person of mixed descent. **half-blooded** *a.* of mixed descent. **half-blue** (the holder of) the colours awarded to the player who is second choice to represent his or her university (esp. Oxford or Cambridge) in inter-university contests or who plays a minor sport in such contests. **half board** accommodation at a hotel etc. providing bed, breakfast, and one main meal (usu. dinner) a day. **half-boot** a boot which reaches up to the calf. **half-bound** *a.* (of a book) bound with leather back and corners and cloth or paper sides. **half-bred** *a.* & *n.* (an animal, esp. (*Austral.* & *NZ*) a sheep) of mixed breed. **half-breed** (freq. *derog.* & considered *offensive*) a person with parents from different races, esp. (*N. Amer.*) with White and Black parents or with White and American Indian parents. **half-brother** a male related to one or more other persons (male or female) by having one biological parent in common. **half-butt** *Billiards* a cue of a length between an ordinary cue and a long butt. **half-cap** †(*a*) a half-courteous salute given by a slight movement of the cap; (*b*) *Hist.* a kind of woman's head-dress. **half-caste** *a.* & *n.* (freq. *derog.* & considered *offensive*) (designating or pertaining to) a person with parents of different races, *spec.* with a European father and an Indian mother. †**half-cheek** a face in profile. **half-circle** a semicircle. **half cock** the position of the cock of a gun when partly raised; freq. in *at half cock* (see COCK *n.*[1] 12). **half-cocked** *a.* (*a*) at half cock (*lit.* & *fig.*); (*b*) *dial.* partly drunk, tipsy; (*c*) incompletely prepared or realized. **half-court** *Tennis, Badminton*, etc. a section of the court demarcated by a line parallel with the sidelines, a service-court. **half-crown** *Hist.* a British silver (orig. gold) coin worth two shillings and sixpence; the amount represented by this. **half-crowner** *arch. colloq.* a person who paid a half-crown for admission etc. **half-cut** *a.* (*colloq.*) partly drunk, tipsy. **half-day** half a working day, esp. taken as holiday. **half-dead** *a.* in a state in which death seems as likely as recovery; in a state of extreme exhaustion or weakness. **half-deck** (*a*) a deck covering half the length of a ship or boat, fore and aft; *spec.* (*Hist.*) in a ship of war, a deck extending aft from the mainmast between the upper deck and the quarterdeck; (*b*) the quarters of cadets and apprentices on a merchant vessel. **half-dime** *US Hist.* a (silver) coin worth five cents; the amount represented by this. **half-dollar** in the US and other countries, a coin worth fifty cents; the amount represented by this. **half-door** a door of half the normal size, usu. with a space above it. **half-dozen** a half of a dozen, six. **half-dress** *Hist.* costume worn at day and informal evening functions during the late 18th and 19th cents. **half-eagle** *US Hist.* a gold coin worth five dollars; the amount represented by this. **half-ebb** the state or time of the tide halfway to its ebb. **half-face** (*a*) a half of a face; a face as seen in profile; a profile on a coin etc.; (*b*) *Mil.* an act or a position of facing halfway to the right or left. **half-'faced** *a.* (*a*) presenting a half-face or profile; (of a coin) stamped with a profile; (of a person) having a thin, pinched face; (*b*) with only half the face visible; (*c*) imperfect, incomplete, half-and-half; (*d*) *US* (of a camp or shelter) left open on one side. **half-flood** the state or time of the tide halfway to its flood. **half-frame** *a.* (*a*) designating reading-spectacles consisting of only the lower half of the frames and lenses; (*b*) *Photogr.* (taking) half the standard 35 mm picture size. **half-frames** half-frame spectacles. **half-galley** a galley of about half the full size. **half-god** a demigod. **half-groat** (*obs.* exc. *Hist.*) a British silver coin worth two old pence; the amount represented by this. **half-guinea** *Hist.* a British gold coin worth ten shillings and sixpence; the amount represented by this. **half-hardy** *n.* & *a.* (a plant) able to grow in the open air at all times except in severe frost. **half-headed** *a.* (*arch.*) deficient in intellect, stupid. **half-hearted** *a.* not having one's whole heart in a matter; lacking in courage, enthusiasm, or determination; feeble. **half-heartedly** *adv.* in a half-hearted manner. **half-heartedness** the state or condition of being half-hearted. *half-hitch*: see HITCH *n.* **half holiday** †(*a*) a day considered only half a holy day; a saint's day or holy day other than Sunday; (*b*) the (usu. latter) half of a working day used for recreation or esp. taken as holiday. **half-hose** socks. **half-hour** a half of an hour, thirty minutes. **half-hourly** *a.* & *adv.* (occurring) at intervals of half an hour. *half-*HUNTER. **half-inch** *n.* & *v.* (*a*) *n.* a unit of length half as long as an inch; (*b*) *v.t.* [rhyming slang for *pinch*] steal. **half integer** any member of the set of numbers obtained by dividing the odd integers by two. **half-integral** *a.* equal to half an odd integer. **half-jack** *Hist.* a counter made to resemble a half sovereign. *half-James*: see JAMES 1b. **half-joe** *Hist.* a Portuguese gold coin, formerly current in N. America, worth 3,200 reis; the amount represented by this. **half-landing** a landing halfway up a flight of stairs. *half lap*: see LAP *n.*[3] **half-leg** *US* half the height of a person's leg (chiefly in *half-leg high*). **half-length** a portrait of the upper half of a person. **half-life** (*a*) a life of half the full length; an unsatisfactory way of life; (*b*) the length of time in which a quantity (esp. of a substance) is reduced by half; *spec.* (i) the time in which half of any number of atoms of a given radioactive isotope will decay; (ii) the time required for half of a quantity of a given substance to be broken down chemically or otherwise lost in the body, the environment, etc. **half-lift** *Pros.* a half or secondary stress. **half-light** a dim imperfect light. **half-line** *Pros.* half of a line of verse, esp. as a structural unit in OE and related poetry. **half-man** (*a*) a being who is only half human, or deficient in humanity; (*b*) an effeminate man; a eunuch. **half-mark** (*obs.* exc. *Hist.*) an English money of account worth six shillings and eightpence. **half-mast** *n.* & *v.* (*a*) *n.* the half of a mast, half the height of a mast; *at half-mast*, *half-mast high* (of a flag) lowered towards the middle of the mast as a mark of respect for the dead; (*b*) *v.t.* hang at or lower to half-mast. **half measure** an inadequate or unsatisfactory compromise, policy, etc. (usu. in *pl.*). **half-mile** *n.* & *a.* (a race) extending to or covering half a mile. **half-miler** a runner who competes in a half-mile or whose preferred distance is half a mile. **half-minute** a half of a minute, thirty seconds. †**half-mourner** the marbled white butterfly, *Melanargia galathea*. **half-mourning** (*a*) the second stage or period of mourning after the expiry of full mourning; (*b*) (dress of) black relieved or replaced by grey, mauve, etc., in token of this. **half-move** *Computing* either of a pair of moves (one by each side) investigated by a chess-playing program during the course of a game. **half-naked** *a.* nearly naked. *half nelson*: see NELSON *n.*[2] **half-noble** (*obs.* exc. *Hist.*) an English or British gold coin equal to half a noble; the amount represented by this. **half-note** *Mus.* †(*a*) a semitone; (*b*) *N. Amer.* a minim. **half-part** (long *rare* or *obs.*) a half. **half-pass** a dressage movement in which the legs on the side to which the horse is moving pass and cross behind the outside legs. **half pay** (*a*) half of the full or usual wages or salary, *esp.* a reduced allowance made to an army etc. officer when retired or not in actual service; (*b*) (now *rare*) an officer on half pay. **half-pie** *a.* (*NZ slang*) [perh. Maori *pai* good] halfway towards, imperfect, mediocre. **half-pike** *Hist.* a small pike with a shaft about half the length of a full-sized one. **half-pint** (*a*) an amount of liquid equal to half a pint; (*b*) *fig.* a small, insignificant, or ineffectual person. **half-plane** *Math.* that part of a plane which lies to one side of a line in the plane. **half-plate** (a photograph reproduced from) a photographic plate 6½ by 4¾ inches. **half-price** *a.* & *n.* (at) half of the full or usual price. *half-relief*: see RELIEF *n.*[2] 1. **half-rhyme** an imperfect or near rhyme; *esp.* the rhyming of one word or syllable with another in consonants but not in vowels. **half-round** *a.* & *n.* (*a*) *adj.* semicircular, semicylindrical; (*b*) *n.* (now *rare*) a semicircle, a hemispherical figure. **half-seas-over** *adv.* & *a.* (*a*) *adv.* (*arch.*) halfway across the sea; *transf.* & *fig.* halfway towards a goal or destination or between one state and another; (*b*) *adj.* (*slang*) half-drunk. *half-*SHAVED. **half-sheet** (*a*) a size of paper equal to half a sheet; (*b*) a kind of printing in which all the pages of a signature are in one forme. **half-shell** half of the shell of an oyster etc., esp. as used for serving food (chiefly in *on the half-shell*). **half-shot** *Golf* a shot played with about half the full swing. **half-sibling** a half-brother or half-sister. **half-sister** a female related to one or more other persons (male or female) by having one biological parent in common. **half-slip** the lower half of a slip, a waist petticoat. **half-sole** *n.* & *v.* (*a*) *n.* the part of the sole of a boot or shoe extending from the shank to the toe; (*b*) *v.t.* provide (a boot or shoe) with a half-sole. **half-sovereign** *Hist.* a British gold coin worth ten shillings; the amount represented by this. **half-starved** *a.* having insufficient food; poorly fed; suffering from malnourishment. **half-step** *Mus.* a semitone. **half-stress** *Pros.* a secondary stress. **half-stuff** *Paper-making* partly prepared pulp. **half-term** a period about halfway through a school term, esp. taken as a short holiday. **half-tide** the state or time of the tide halfway between flood and ebb. **half-timber** *a.* (*a*) = *half-timbered*; (*b*) made of timber split in half. **half-timbered** *a.* (of a building) having walls with a timber frame and brick or plaster filling. **half-time** (*a*) half the usual or full time during which work is carried on; (*b*) the time at which half of a game or contest is completed; the interval then occurring. **half-title** (*a*) the title or short title of a book, printed on the recto of the leaf preceding the title-leaf or at the head of the first page; (*b*) the title of the section of a book printed on the recto of the leaf preceding it. **halftone** (*a*) *Mus.* (*US*) a semitone; (*b*) an image, produced by photographic or electronic means, in which an effect of continuous tone is simulated by dots of various sizes or lines of various thicknesses; the process which produces such an image; (*c*) *Art* an intermediate tone between the extreme lights and the extreme shades. **half-topped** *a.* (*Golf*) designating a stroke in which the ball is partly topped. **half-track** (a vehicle having) a propulsion system with the wheels at the front and endless driven bands at the back. **half-truth** a proposition or statement that (esp. deliberately) conveys only half the truth. **half-uncial** *a.* & *n.* (designating) writing which shares some of the features of both uncial and cursive; semi-uncial. **half-value** a value of a physical property, esp. intensity of radioactivity, that is half of an earlier value. **half-verse** = *half-line* above. **half-volley** *n.* & *v.* *Tennis, Football*, etc. (*a*) *n.* a stroke or shot in which a ball is hit or kicked immediately after it bounces on the ground; such a ball; (*b*) *v.t.* hit or kick (a ball) immediately after it bounces. **half-wave** *n.* & *a.* (*a*) *n.*

one half of a complete (electromagnetic) wave; (*b*) *adj.* using or involving half a wave or wavelength. **halfwit** a stupid or foolish person; an imbecile. **halfwitted** *a.* stupid, foolish; imbecile. **halfwittedness** the state or condition of being halfwitted. **half-word** a word that hints at or suggests something. **half-world** †(*a*) a hemisphere; (*b*) the *demi-monde*. **half-year** (*a*) a half of a year, six months; (*b*) (now *rare*) = HALF *n.* 6b. **half-yearly** *a.* & *adv.* (happening) every half-year or six months.

halfa *n.* var. of ALFA.

†halfen *a. pseudo-arch. rare* (Spenser). Only in L16. [Perh. f. next or irreg. f. HALF *a.*] Half.

halfendeal /ˈhɑːf(ə)ndiːl/ *n.* & *adv. obs.* exc. *dial.* [OE *þone healfan dǣl*, accus. case of *se healfa dǣl* the half part: see DEAL *n.*[1]] **A** *n.* A half; a half share. OE. **†B** *adv.* Half, by half. ME–L16.

half moon /hɑːf muːn/ *n. phr.* & *a.* As adj. usu. **half-moon**. LME. [f. HALF- + MOON *n.*] **A** *n.* **1** The moon when only half its disc is illuminated; the time when this occurs; *loosely* a crescent. LME. **2** Something shaped like a half moon or crescent; a semicircular object; *spec.* the white crescent-shaped mark at the base of a fingernail. L16. **3** *Fortif.* A demilune. M17. **B** *adj.* Shaped like a half moon or crescent; *spec.* designating spectacles with lenses shaped like half moons. L16.

half-mooned *a.* (long *rare*) shaped like a half moon, semilunate E17.

halfness /ˈhɑːfnɪs/ *n.* Now *rare.* M16. [f. HALF *a.* + -NESS.] The condition or quality of being half; incompleteness; irresoluteness.

half-pace /ˈhɑːfpeɪs/ *n.* M16. [Alt. of HALPACE after HALF *a.*] **1** A step or platform on which a throne, dais, etc. stands; *spec.* the platform at the top of steps on which an altar stands. M16. **2** A broad step or small landing between two half flights in a staircase. E17.

halfpenny /ˈheɪpni/ *n.* & *a.* Also **ha'penny**. Pl. **halfpennies** /ˈheɪpnɪz/, (see sense 1 below) **halfpence** /ˈheɪp(ə)ns/. ME. [f. HALF- + PENNY.] **A** *n.* **1** *Hist.* A British bronze (orig. copper) coin worth half a penny; (pl. **-pence**) the amount represented by this, *loosely* a very small amount of money. (Earlier in HALFPENNYWORTH.) ME. **b** A stamp costing a halfpenny. L19. †**2** A small fragment or piece. *rare* (Shakes.). Only in L16. **3** A form of earmark on cattle and horses. *US.* M17.

1 *Lancashire Evening Telegraph* Any judge . . would have . . awarded these sharks a halfpenny as their share of the compensation. **three halfpence** a penny and a halfpenny. *twopenny-halfpenny*: see TWOPENNY *a.* 1.

B *attrib.* or as *adj.* That costs a halfpenny; *fig.* worth no more than a halfpenny, of contemptible value, trumpery. LME.

D. H. LAWRENCE Oh carcase with a board-school mind and a ha'penny newspaper intelligence.

¶Earlier in HALFPENNYWORTH.

halfpennyworth /ˈheɪpəθ, ˈheɪpnɪwəθ/ *n.* Also **ha'p'orth** /ˈheɪpəθ/. [OE *healfpeniġwurþ*, f. as prec., WORTH *n.*[1]] As much as might be bought for a halfpenny; a very small amount.

Proverb: Do not spoil the ship for a ha'p'orth of tar.

halfway /hɑːfˈweɪ, ˈhɑːfweɪ/ *adv.*, *prep.*, *n.*, & *a.* Also **half-way**. ME. [f. HALF- + WAY *n.*] **A** *adv.* At or to half the way or distance; *loosely* partially. ME.

Times Higher Educ. Suppl. In science, there are fields which are a gift for any half-way decent PR Officer. A. GHOSH Bahram stopped only when he was halfway to his own house. *meet halfway*: see MEET *v.*

†B *prep.* Halfway up, down, along, etc. E17–E18.

I. WATTS Faint devotion panting lies, Half way th' ethereal hill.

C *n.* A point or position midway between two extreme points; a halfway place. Now *rare.* M17.

L. HUTCHINSON In the half-way between Owthorpe and Nottingham.

D *adj.* Midway or equidistant between two points; *fig.* midway between two states or conditions, half one thing and half another. L17.

HANNAH MORE Some half-way state, something between paganism and christianity. E. K. KANE My aim was to reach the half-way tent. **halfway house** (*a*) a house or esp. an inn midway between two towns or stages of a journey; (*b*) *fig.* a compromise; (*c*) the halfway point in a progression; (*d*) a centre for rehabilitating ex-prisoners, mental patients, or others unused to normal life. **halfway line** *Football, Hockey*, etc. a line midway between the two goals.

halgh *n.* var. of HAUGH.

halibut /ˈhalɪbət/ *n.* Also **hol-** /ˈhɒl-/. Pl. same, **-s**. LME. [Alt. of HOLY + BUTT *n.*[1] (from its commonly being eaten on holy days).] A very large flatfish of the N. Atlantic, *Hippoglossus hippoglossus*, fished intensively for food; any of several closely related fishes, *esp.* (more fully *Pacific halibut*) *Hippoglossus stenolepis* and (more fully *Greenland halibut*) *Reinhardtius hippoglossoides*. Also, the flesh of any of these as food.

halide /ˈheɪlʌɪd/ *n.* L19. [f. HAL(OGEN + -IDE.] *Chem.* A binary compound formed from a halogen and another element or a radical.

halidom /ˈhalɪdəm/ *n.* Long *rare* or *obs.* [OE *hāliġdōm* = MDu. *heilichdoem*, OHG *heilagtuom* (cf. ON *helgidómr*): see HOLY, -DOM.] †**1** Holiness, sanctity. OE–E17. **2** A holy place; a sanctuary. OE. **3** A holy thing, *esp.* a relic. Freq. in int. *by my halidom* expr. surprise, asseveration, etc. OE.

†halier *n.* see HALYARD.

halieutic /halɪˈjuːtɪk/ *n.* & *a.* Now *rare.* M17. [L *halieuticus* f. Gk *halieutikos*, f. *halieutēs* fisher: see -IC.] **A** *n.* In *pl.* (treated as *sing.*), the art or practice of fishing; *sing.* a treatise on fishing. M17. **B** *adj.* Of or pertaining to fishing. M19.

Halifax /ˈhalɪfaks/ *n. euphem.* M17. [The name of towns in W. Yorkshire, England and Nova Scotia, Canada.] Hell. Chiefly in *go to Halifax*.

haliotis /halɪˈəʊtɪs/ *n.* M18. [f. Gk *hals*, *hali-* sea + *ous*, *ōt-* ear.] A marine gastropod of the genus *Haliotis*, with an ear-shaped shell lined with mother-of-pearl; the shell of this.

halite /ˈhalʌɪt/ *n.* M19. [f. Gk *hals* salt + -ITE[1].] Rock-salt; sodium chloride, NaCl, as a mineral, crystallizing in the cubic system.

halitosis /halɪˈtəʊsɪs/ *n.* L19. [f. L HALITUS + -OSIS.] Foul-smelling breath.

halituous /həˈlɪtjʊəs/ *a.* E17. [f. as prec. + -OUS.] Resembling or characterized by breath or vapour.

halitus /ˈhalɪtəs/ *n. rare.* M17. [L, lit. 'breath', f. *halare* breathe.] A vapour, an exhalation.

hall /hɔːl/ *n.* Also (*Sc.*) **ha'** /hɔː/. [OE *hall*, *heall* = OS, OHG *halla* (Du. *hall*, G *Halle*), ON *hǫll*, f. a Gmc base meaning 'cover, conceal': cf. HELL *n.*] **1** A place, orig. *spec.* a large place, covered by a roof; in early use, any spacious roofed place; a temple, a palace, a court. *obs.* exc. as passing into specific senses below and w. specifying wd. OE. **2** A large residence, esp. of a landed proprietor; a mansion. Now chiefly in names or with *the* (referring to a specific local hall). OE. **3** A large public room in a mansion, palace, etc., used for receptions and banquets. ME. **4** A house or building belonging to a guild or fraternity. ME. **5** A large room or building for public gatherings. ME. †**b** A formal assembly called by the monarch, or by the principal officer of a town. M16–L17. **c** A music hall. Usu. in *pl.* M19. **6** At Oxford and Cambridge Universities: orig., any of the educational institutions including the colleges (now only *Hist.*, *arch.*, or *poet.*); later *spec.*, an educational institution which is not a corporate body and whose property is held in trust, as opp. to a college. LME. **b** A building, administered by a university, polytechnic, etc., in which students live (also *hall of residence*); an establishment of higher education in certain university towns, sometimes with (usu. restricted) affiliation to the university. L19. **7** In a college, university, polytechnic, etc.: the dining-room for all members of the institution. Hence, dinner in a hall. L16. **8** The entrance-passage or entrance-room of a house; a vestibule; (chiefly *N. Amer.*) a corridor, a passage. M17.

1 *banqueting-hall*, *city hall*, *dancehall*, *dining-hall*, *entrance-hall*, *guildhall*, *music hall*, *town hall*, *village hall*, etc. 2 A. TROLLOPE He would certainly sell Vavasor Hall in spite of all family associations. 3 T. HARDY Maryann . . show them in to me in the hall. 5 *Dumfries & Galloway Standard* The church would provide an elegant hall capable of seating approximately 250. c S. BRETT And then you toured the halls as a double-act? 7 THOMAS HUGHES You ought to dine in hall perhaps four days a week. Hall is at five o'clock. 8 S. SPENDER There was a stone-tiled hall . . out of which doors led.

Phrases: **†A hall! A hall!** *int.* Clear the way! Make room! (esp. for dancing). *bachelor's hall*: see BACHELOR. *Exeter hall*: see EXETER *n.* 2. **Hall of Fame** (chiefly *N. Amer.*) a building containing memorials etc. of famous people; *fig.* the class of those who are most celebrated (in a particular sphere). *hall of residence*: see sense 6b above. *liberty hall*: see LIBERTY *n. medical hall*: see MEDICAL *a.* **Servants' hall** a common-room or dining-room for servants in a house. *Tammany Hall*: see TAMMANY. **†the Hall** *spec.* Westminster Hall, formerly the seat of the High Court of Justice.

Comb.: **hall bedroom** *US* a small bedroom partitioned off the end of a hall; **hall boy** a page-boy, a call-boy in a hotel; **hall door** the door of a hall; the front door of a house; **hall house** a manor house; a house (esp. a medieval one) with a hall as a distinguishing feature; **hall porter** the porter in charge of the hall of a hotel and esp. responsible for the care of guests' luggage; **hall-stand** a piece of furniture for hanging coats etc. on, kept in an entrance-hall; **hall table** (*a*) a large table for a (dining-)hall; (*b*) a small table for an entrance-hall; **hall tree** *US* a hall stand; **hallway** an entrance-hall or corridor.

†hall *v.* see HAUL *v.*

hallabaloo *n.*, *int.*, & *v.* var. of HULLABALOO.

†hallage *n.* E17–E18. [(O)Fr., f. *halle* covered market: see -AGE.] A fee or toll paid for goods sold in a covered market.

hallal *a.*, *v.*, & *n.* var. of HALAL.

Hall effect /ˈhɔːl ɪfɛkt/ *n. phr.* E20. [Edwin H. *Hall* (1855–1938), US physicist.] *Physics.* The production of a potential difference across an electrical conductor when a magnetic field is applied in a direction perpendicular to that of the flow of current.

hallel /haˈleɪl, ˈhalɛl/ *n.* E18. [Heb. *hallēl* praise.] A portion of the service for certain Jewish festivals consisting of Psalms 113 to 118 inclusive.

hallelujah /halɪˈluːjə/ *int.* & *n.* Also **-luia**, **-luja**, **-luya(h)**. M16. [Heb. *hallĕlūyāh* praise Jah (God), f. imper. pl. of *hallēl* to praise: cf. prec.] **A** *int.* = ALLELUIA *int.* M16. **B** *n.* = ALLELUIA *n.* M17.

Comb.: **Hallelujah Chorus** a musical composition based on the word hallelujah, *esp.* that in the oratorio 'Messiah' by G. F. Handel (1685–1759), German-born musician; *hallelujah lass*: see LASS 3.

†haller *n.* see HELLER *n.*[1]

†hallier *n.*[1], *n.*[2] see HALYARD, HAULIER.

halling /ˈhalɪŋ/ *n.* M19. [Norw., f. *Hallingdal* a valley in S. Norway.] A Norwegian country dance in duple rhythm; a piece of music for this dance.

hallion /ˈhaljən/ *n. Sc.* & *north. derog.* L18. [Perh. rel. to Fr. *haillon* rag.] An idle or worthless person.

hallmark /ˈhɔːlmɑːk/ *n.* & *v.* E18. [f. HALL *n.* + MARK *n.*[1]] **A** *n.* **1** Any of various official marks used at Goldsmith's Hall and by the British assay offices for marking the standard of gold, silver, and platinum. E18. **2** *fig.* A mark or indication, esp. of excellence; a distinctive or striking feature. M19.

2 D. ADAMS And . . gives it that poignant twist which is the hallmark of the really great documentary. N. MOSLEY The . . image of ruthlessness that was the hallmark of Mussolini.

B *v.t.* Stamp with a hallmark. M19.

hallmote /ˈhɔːlməʊt/ *n.* Also **-moot**. OE. [f. HALL *n.* + MOOT *n.*[1]] *Hist.* The court of the lord of a manor; later also, the court of a trade guild.

hallo /həˈləʊ, ha-/ *v.*, *int.*, & *n.* Also **halloa**. L18. [Prob. var. of HOLLO *v.*, *int.* & *n.* with shifted stress. See also HELLO, HULLO.] **A** *v.i.* Say or shout 'hallo!'; call out to attract attention or in greeting. L18.

B *int.* Commanding or attempting to attract attention. Also = HELLO *int.* M19.

A. CHRISTIE Hallo, 'allo, 'allo, what's this?

C *n.* A shout of 'hallo!' L19.

hallock /ˈhalək/ *n. Sc.* E16. [Origin unkn.] A thoughtless or foolish person; *esp.* a flighty young woman.

hallockit /ˈhalәkɪt/ *a.* & *n. Sc.* Also (after Sir W. Scott) **hellicat** /ˈhɛlɪkәt/. L17. [f. prec. + Sc. adj. suff. *-it* -ED[2].] A *adj.* Esp. of a young woman: foolish, light-headed, flighty, reckless. L17. B *n.* = HALLOCK. Also, a mischievous person, a good-for-nothing. L17.

halloo /hәˈluː, ha-/ *v.* M16. [Prob. var. of HALLOW *v.*[2], HOLLO *v.* with shifted stress.] 1 *v.i.* Shout 'halloo!'; cry out or yell to attract attention, give encouragement, etc. M16. 2 *v.t.* Encourage (esp. dogs to the chase) by shouting. E17. 3 *v.t.* Shout out. E17.

halloo /hәˈluː, ha-/ *int.* & *n.* Also **hulloo** /hәˈluː, hʌ-/. L17. [Prob. var. of HOLLO *int.* & *n.* with shifted stress.] A *int.* Inciting dogs to the chase; calling attention, esp. at a distance; expr. surprise. L17. B *n.* A shout of 'halloo!' Cf. *view-halloo* s.v. VIEW *n.* E18.

hallow /ˈhalәʊ/ *n.*[1] [OE *halga* use as n. of definite form of *hāliġ* HOLY.] 1 A holy person, a saint. Usu. in *pl. obs.* exc. in ALL HALLOWS & in *comb.* below. OE. †2 In *pl.* The shrines or relics of saints; (the shrines of) heathen gods. ME–M16.

Comb.: **Hallow day** *Sc.* & *dial.* All Hallows' Day; a saint's day, a holiday; **Hallowmass** (now chiefly *Sc.*) Allhallowmass; **Hallowtide** Allhallowtide.

hallow /ˈhalәʊ/ *n.*[2] Now *rare.* LME. [f. HALLOW *v.*[2]] A loud shout or cry to encourage, esp. dogs in the chase, or to attract attention.

hallow /ˈhalәʊ/ *v.*[1]*t.* [OE *hālgian* = OS *hēlagon*, OHG *heilagōn* (G *heiligen*), ON *helga*, f. Gmc vb f. base of HOLY.] 1 Make holy; sanctify, purify. OE. 2 Consecrate or set apart as sacred; dedicate to a sacred or religious purpose; bless. OE. b Consecrate (a king, bishop, etc.) to an office. Long *obs.* exc. *Hist.* OE. 3 Honour as holy; regard and treat with reverence; observe (a day, festival, etc.) solemnly. OE.

1 J. P. HENNESSY Her death was tranquil and .. hallowed by a kind of beauty. H. WILSON This is a question hallowed by tradition.

hallowedness *n.* sanctity, blessedness E19.

hallow /ˈhalәʊ/ *v.*[2] Now *rare.* LME. [Prob. f. OFr. *halloer*, of imit. origin. See also HALLOO *v.*, HOLLO *v.*] 1 *v.t.* Pursue with shouting; urge on by shouting; call *in*, *back*, etc., by shouting. LME. 2 *v.i.* & *t.* Shout in encouragement, esp. of dogs in the chase; shout to attract attention. LME.

Hallowe'en /halәʊˈiːn/ *n.* Also **-ween.** L18. [Contr. of *All Hallow Even*: see ALL HALLOWS, EVEN *n.*[1]] The eve of All Saints, 31st October (the last night of the year in the early Celtic calendar).

halloysite /haˈlɔɪzʌɪt/ *n.* E19. [f. J. B. J. d'Omalius-d'*Halloy* (1783–1875), Belgian geologist + *-s-* + -ITE[1].] *Min.* Any of a number of clay minerals chemically resembling kaolinite but with a greater (although variable) water content.

Hallstatt /ˈhalʃtat/ *a.* M19. [A village in Upper Austria, site of a prehistoric burial ground.] Designating (the culture and products of) a phase of the early Iron Age in Europe.

hallucal /ˈhaljʊk(ә)l/ *a.* L19. [f. HALLUX + -AL[1].] *Anat.* Of or pertaining to the hallux or big toe.

hallucinant /hәˈluːsɪnәnt, -ˈljuː-/ *a.* & *n.* L19. [f. HALLUCIN(ATE + -ANT[1].] A *adj.* Producing or experiencing hallucinations. L19. B *n.* A person who experiences hallucinations; a drug which produces hallucinations. E20.

hallucinate /hәˈluːsɪneɪt, -ˈljuː-/ *v.* E17. [L *hallucinat-* pa. ppl stem of *hallucinari* late form of *alucinari* wander in thought or speech, f. Gk *alussein* be distraught or ill at ease: see -ATE[3].] 1 †a *v.t.* Deceive. Only in E17. b *v.t.* & *i.* Affect with hallucinations; produce false impressions in the mind (of). E19. 2 *v.i.* Orig., be deceived, suffer illusions. Now, have a hallucination or hallucinations. M17. 3 *v.t.* Experience a hallucination of. L20.

1b J. DIDION But Durango. The very name hallucinates. 2 D. W. GOODWIN After a day or two without drinking, the alcoholic coming off a bender may start hallucinating. 3 J. WAIN I'm imagining things, hallucinating a conversation with my .. sister, who's no longer alive.

hallucinative *a.* causing hallucinations L19. **hallucinator** *n.* M19. **hallucinatorily** *adv.* in a hallucinatory manner E20. **hallucinatory** *a.* characterized by, pertaining to, or resembling (a) hallucination M19.

hallucination /hәluːsɪˈneɪʃ(ә)n, -ljuː-/ *n.* E17. [L *hallucinatio(n-)*, f. as prec.: see -ATION.] 1 Esp. *Med.* & *Psychol.* The apparent perception of an external object or sense-datum when no such object or stimulus is present; an instance of this. E17. 2 The mental state of being deceived, mistaken, or deluded; an unfounded idea or belief, an illusion. M17.

1 F. KING Had her distracted mind produced an hallucination?

halluciné /hәˈluːsɪneɪ, -ljuː-/ *n. rare.* L19. [Fr.] A person who (regularly) has hallucinations.

hallucinogen /hәˈluːsɪnәdʒ(ә)n, -ˈljuː-/ *n.* M20. [f. HALLUCIN(ATION + -O- + -GEN.] Any substance which induces hallucinations when ingested.

hallucinoˈgenic *a.* M20.

hallucinosis /hәˌluːsɪˈnәʊsɪs, -ˌljuː-/ *n.* Pl. **-noses** /-ˈnәʊsiːz/. E20. [f. HALLUCINATION + -OSIS.] *Psychiatry.* A mental condition, associated esp. with alcoholism, marked by persistent hallucination, often auditory.

hallux /ˈhalәks/ *n.* Pl. **halluces** /ˈhaljʊsiːz/. M19. [mod.L alt. of med.L *allex*, L *(h)allus*.] *Anat.* & *Zool.* The big toe; the first or innermost digit on the hind foot of a tetrapod vertebrate, in birds (if present) often directed backwards.

halm *n.* & *v.* var. of HAULM.

halma /ˈhalmә/ *n.* L19. [Gk = leap.] A game played by two or four people on a chequer-board of 256 squares, with pieces advancing from one corner to the opposite corner by being moved over other pieces into vacant squares.

halo /ˈheɪlәʊ/ *n.* Pl. **-o(e)s.** M16. [med.L *halo* for L *halos* f. Gk = threshing-floor, disc of the sun, moon, or a shield.] 1 A circle of light, either white or prismatically coloured, seen round a luminous body and caused by the refraction of light through vapour; *spec.* that seen round the sun or moon, usu. of 22° or 46° radius, with the red end of the spectrum inside the circle. Cf. CORONA *n.*[1] 3a. M16. b A coloured ring surrounding a pustule etc. Also, the areola of a nipple. E18. c Any circle of light or other substance that serves to frame a thing. E19. 2 A disc of light shown surrounding or hovering over the head in representations of Jesus and the saints; *fig.* an aura of glory, sanctity, etc., with which a person or thing is surrounded. M17.

1c E. M. FORSTER The light of a candle-lamp, which threw a quivering halo round her hands. J. UPDIKE His hair, .. stood far out from his head in wiry rays, a halo of wool. 2 H. T. BUCKLE That halo which time had thrown round the oldest monarchy in Europe.

Comb.: **halo-brimmed** *a.* [cf. *halo-hat* below] (of a woman's hat) worn so that the brim frames the face; **halo effect** the tendency of a favourable (or unfavourable) impression created by an individual in one area to influence one's judgement of him or her in other areas; **halo hat** a woman's hat worn at the back of the head so that the brim frames the face.

halo /ˈheɪlәʊ/ *v.t.* L18. [f. the n.] Surround or invest (as) with a halo.

V. WOOLF The windows were blurred, the lamps haloed with fog.

halo- /ˈhalәʊ/ *comb. form* of Gk *hals*, *halos* salt, sea, and of HALOGEN: see -O-.

haˈlobiont *n.* [-BIONT] *Ecol.* an organism that lives in a saline environment E20. **halobiˈontic**, **halobiˈotic** *adjs.* (*Ecol.*) living in a saline environment E20. **haloˈcarbon** *n.* (*Chem.*) a compound in which the hydrogen of a hydrocarbon is replaced by halogens M20. **haloform** *n.* [after *chloroform*] *Chem.* = TRIHALOMETHANE M20. **haloˈmethane** *n.* (*Chem.*) a halogenated derivative of methane, with the general formula CH_nX_{4-n}, where X is a halogen M20. **haloˈmorphic** *a.* (*Soil Sci.*) (of a soil) containing, or developed in the presence of, large quantities of salts other than calcium carbonate M20. **haloˈperidol** *n.* [PI]PERID(INE] *Pharm.* a tricyclic compound used to treat psychotic disorders, esp. mania L20. **haloˈphosphate** *n.* (*Chem.*) any of various compounds containing both halide and phosphate ions, some of which are used as phosphors M20. **halophyte** *n.* (*Ecol.*) a plant adapted to growing in saline conditions, e.g. salt-marshes L19. **halophytic** /-ˈfɪtɪk/ *a.* of the nature of a halophyte L19.

halogen /ˈhalәdʒ(ә)n, ˈheɪl-/ *n.* M19. [f. Gk *hals*, *halo-* salt + -GEN.] *Chem.* Any of the group of elements fluorine, chlorine, bromine, iodine, and astatine (together forming group VIIA of the periodic table) which are typically gaseous or volatile, strongly electronegative non-metals readily forming binary compounds with metals.

quartz-halogen: see QUARTZ.

halogenate /hәˈlɒdʒ(ә)neɪt, ˈhalәdʒ(ә)neɪt/ *v.t.* L19. [f. prec. + -ATE[3].] *Chem.* Introduce one or more atoms of a halogen into (a compound or molecule), usu. in place of hydrogen. Freq. as *halogenated* ppl a.

halogeˈnation *n.* E20.

halon /ˈheɪlɒn/ *n.* M20. [f. HALO- + -ON, after *neon*, *argon*, etc.] Any of the compounds of carbon, bromine, and another halogen, many of which are gases noted for their lack of reactivity.

halophile /ˈhalәfʌɪl/ *n.* & *a.* E20. [f. HALO- + -PHILE.] *Ecol.* A *n.* An organism that grows in or can tolerate saline conditions. E20. B *adj.* = HALOPHILIC. E20.

haˈlophilous *a.* = HALOPHILIC L19.

halophilic /halәˈfɪlɪk/ *a.* E20. [f. as prec.: see -IC.] *Ecol.* Growing in or tolerating saline conditions.

halothane /ˈhalәθeɪn/ *n.* M20. [f. HALO- + E)THANE.] *Chem.* A halogenated derivative of ethane, $CF_3CHBr\ Cl$, which is a volatile liquid used as a general anaesthetic.

halotrichite /haləˈtrɪkʌɪt/ *n.* M19. [f. HALO- + -TRICH, after G *Haarsalz* 'hair salt': see -ITE[1].] *Min.* A monoclinic alum (hydrated double sulphate) containing aluminium and ferrous iron, usu. occurring as greenish- or yellowish-white fibrous masses.

halpace /ˈhalpәs/ *n.* Long *arch. rare.* Also **halpas.** E16. [Alt. of HAUT-PAS f. Fr. *haut pas* lit. 'high step'. Cf. HALF-PACE.] = HAUT-PAS, HALF-PACE I.

†halse *n.* see HAWSE *n.*[1]

†halse *v.*[1]*t.* [OE *halsian*, *healsian* = OHG *heilisōn* augur, expiate, ON *heilsa* hail, greet (with good wishes), f. Gmc base also of HEAL *v.*[1] Cf. HAUSE *v.*] 1 Call on in the name of something holy; adjure, implore. OE–M16. 2 Hail, greet. LME–L16.

†halse *v.*[2] see HAUSE *v.*

halt /hɔːlt/ *n.*[1] *arch.* L15. [f. HALT *v.*[1] or *a.*] A lameness, a limp.

halt /hɔːlt/ *n.*[2] Also **†alt**, (earlier) **†alto.** L16. [Orig. in phr. *make halt* (or *†alto*) f. G *halt machen* (or its Sp. version *alto hacer*): in the G phr. *halt* is prob. orig. based on the imper. ('stop', 'stand still') of *halten* HOLD *v.*] 1 Orig. *Mil.* A temporary stop on a march or journey; *gen.* a sudden suspension of movement or activity. L16. 2 A place where a halt is made; *spec.* a railway stopping-place, usu. on a local line, without the normal station buildings, staff, etc. E20.

1 TOLKIEN At last they could go no further without a halt. K. WILLIAMS The radio series came to a temporary halt in June. *call a halt (to)*: see CALL *v.* *grind to a halt*: see GRIND *v.* 2. 2 P. LEVI A lorry-drivers' halt .. that served bacon sandwiches until midnight.

halt /hɔːlt/ *a.* Now *arch.* & *literary.* [OE *halt*, *healt* = OFris., OS *halt*, OHG *halz*, ON *haltr*, Goth. *halts*, f. Gmc base of unkn. origin.] Lame, limping; crippled. Now usu. *absol.*

P. PORTER I'll never know with what halt steps You mounted to this plain eclipse. *absol.*: N. BARBER The halt and the maimed .. joined in as best they could.

halt /hɔːlt/ *v.*[1]*i. arch.* [OE *healtian* (corresp. to OS *halton*, OHG *halzēn*), f. the adj.] 1 Walk lamely; limp. OE. †2 Play false; deviate *from* the proper course. OE–E17. 3 Hesitate or waver (*between* alternatives). LME. 4 Of reasoning, verse, etc.: lack smooth progress; proceed awkwardly or defectively. LME.

3 AV *1 Kings* 18:21 How long halt ye between two opinions? 4 T. GRAY Where the verse seems to halt, it is very probably occasioned by the transcriber's neglect.

halt /hɔːlt/ *v.*[2] M17. [f. HALT *n.*[2]] **1** *v.i.* Stop momentarily on a march or journey; make a halt. Freq. in *imper.* as a mil. command. M17. **2** *v.t.* Bring to a halt or abrupt stop; stop the advance or continuation of. L18.

1 G. B. SHAW A sentry's voice westward: Halt! Who goes there? H. FAST He raced down the deck, halting to caress the rusty winches. 2 A. J. P. TAYLOR The German pursuit was halted. *Studio Week* Capitol Magnetics . . has halted production at its US factory.

Comb.: **halt sign** a former traffic sign requiring a driver or rider to halt before entering a major road; *fig.* a warning to desist from speech or action.

halter /ˈhɔːltə/ *n.*[1] [OE *hælfter, hælftre*, corresp. to OLG *helifṭra* (MLG *helchter*, MDu. *halfter, halter*), f. WGmc (with instr. suff.), f. base repr. also by HELVE.] **1** A cord or strap with a headstall or noose, for leading or fastening a horse or other animal. OE. **2** A rope with a noose for hanging a criminal; execution by this means. LME. **3** A strap by which the top of a dress etc. is fastened or held behind at the neck, leaving the back and shoulders bare. M20. **b** *ellipt.* = *halter top* below. M20.

Comb.: **halter-break** *v.t.* (orig. *US*) accustom (an animal) to the halter; **halter neck(line)** a type or style of neckline incorporating a halter (sense 3 above); **halter top** a blouse or top with a halter neck.

halter /ˈhɔːltə/ *n.*[2] *arch.* LME. [f. HALT *v.*[1] + -ER[1].] A cripple etc. who halts; *fig.* a waverer.

halter /ˈhɔːltə/ *v.t.* ME. [f. HALTER *n.*[1]] **1** Put a halter on (a horse or other animal); *fig.* hamper, restrain. ME. **2** Catch (a bird etc.) with a noose or lasso. L16. **3** Execute (a person) by hanging. L16.

haltere /halˈtɪə/ *n.* Pl. **halteres** /halˈtɪəriːz/. M16. [Gk *haltēres* pl. (sense 1), f. *hallesthai* to jump.] **1** In *pl.* Weights, like dumb-bells, held in the hand to give an impetus in jumping. M16. **2** *Entomol.* Either of the two knobbed filaments which in dipteran insects take the place of posterior wings. Also called *balancer, poiser.* Usu. in *pl.* E19.

haltered /ˈhɔːltəd/ *a.* E16. [f. HALTER *n.*[1] or *v.*: see -ED[2], -ED[1].] Having a halter on; fastened (as) with a halter.

halting /ˈhɔːltɪŋ/ *ppl a.* LME. [f. HALT *v.*[1] + -ING[2].] That halts; *esp.* lacking in smoothness of progress, fluency, or ease; stumbling, faltering.

F. TUOHY On the little dance-floor their progress was halting. W. M. SPACKMAN They all had to converse in halting Italian for some minutes.

haltingly *adv.* L16. **haltingness** *n.* L19.

halutzim /hɑːˈluːtsɪm, x-/ *n.pl.* Also **-luz-, ch-**. E20. [Heb. *ḥălūṣīm.*] *Hist.* Jewish pioneers who entered Palestine from 1917 onwards to build it up as a Jewish State.

halva /ˈhalvɑː, -və/ *n.* Also **halvah**, (earlier) †**hulwa**. M17. [(Yiddish *hal(a)va*, mod.Heb. *ḥalḇāh*, mod.Gk *khalbas*, Turk. *helva*, etc., f.) Arab. (& Pers.) *ḥalwā* sweetmeat.] A Middle Eastern sweet confection made of sesame flour and honey.

halve /hɑːv/ *v.* ME. [f. HALF *n.*] **1** *v.t.* Divide in two, share in two equal parts; reduce by a half. Formerly also, break in two. ME. †**2** *v.i.* Show divided loyalty. (Foll. by *with.*) Chiefly as *halving* vbl n. M16–L17. **3** *v.t. Golf.* Play (a hole) in the same number of strokes as another player; win the same number of holes as another player in (a match etc.). E19. **4** *v.t. Carpentry.* Join (timbers) together by cutting out half the thickness of each, so that one can be let into the other. Chiefly as *halving* vbl n. E19.

1 *Proverb*: A trouble shared is a trouble halved. 2 T. BROOKS God neither loves halting nor halving; he will be served truly and totally.

halver /ˈhɑːvə/ *n.* Now chiefly *Sc., north.,* & *US.* E16. [f. prec. + -ER[1].] **1** A half-share. Usu. in *pl.*; esp. in *go halvers (with).* Also *halvers!*, an exclam. by a child claiming half of something found. E16. †**2** A person who has a half-share in something; a partner. E17–L18.

halyard /ˈhaljəd/ *n.* Orig. †**hal(l)ier**. Also **halliard, haul-** /ˈhɔːl-/. LME. [f. HALE *v.*[1] + -IER, alt. in 18 by assoc. w. YARD *n.*[2]: cf. LANYARD.] *Naut.* A rope or tackle for raising or lowering a sail, yard, etc.

ham /ham/ *n.*[1] & *a.* [OE *ham, hom* = MLG *hamme*, OHG *hamma* (G dial. *Hamm*) rel. to synon. MLG *hame*, OHG *hama*, ON *ham*, f. Gmc vb. meaning 'be crooked.'] **A** *n.* **I 1** The hollow or bend of the knee. *arch.* OE. **2** The back of the thigh; the thigh and buttock collectively. Usu. in *pl.* L15. **3** The thigh of an animal (now usu. a pig) used as food; *esp.* (the meat from) a cured pig's thigh. Also, the hock of an animal. L15.

2 T. MO I believe I can sit again up on my bruised hams. 3 J. CARY Hams, and often whole sides of bacon, dangled from the blackened ceiling.

II [Cf. HAMFATTER.] **4** An inexpert performer; an inferior, amateurish, or excessively theatrical actor, actress, or performance. *slang* (orig. *US*). L19. **5** An amateur telegraph operator. Now *esp.* (more fully *radio ham*), an amateur radio operator. *slang* (orig. *US*). E20.

Comb.: **ham-bone** (*a*) the bone from a ham joint; such a bone with the meat still attached; (*b*) *N. Amer. slang* an inferior actor or performer, *esp.* one who uses a spurious Black accent.

B *attrib.* or as *adj.* **1** Esp. of an actor, actress, or a performance: inexpert; amateurish; excessively theatrical. *slang.* M20. **2** Clumsy, incompetent. Cf. HAM-FISTED, HAM-HANDED. *slang.* M20.

1 D. M. DAVIN The actor in him, too often ham, made him long to play God. 2 W. WHARTON Sasha punches me again, tough, thick, ham hands.

ham /ham/ *n.*[2] Long *dial.* [OE *ham(m), hom(m)* = OFris. *ham* a meadow enclosed with a ditch, LG *hamm* piece of enclosed ground.] A plot of (esp. enclosed) pasture or meadowland.

ham /ham/ *v.t.* & *i. slang.* Infl. **-mm-**. M20. [f. HAM *n.*[1] II.] Overact (a part, a scene, etc.). Freq. foll. by *up.*

M. DICKENS She had hammed her scene with the seducer at the final run through. S. MIDDLETON I have to act . . And the temptation to ham it up is constant.

hamada *n.* var. of HAMMADA.

Hamadan /ˈhamədan/ *n.* & *a.* E20. [A town in NW Iran.] (Designating) a heavy hard-wearing long-pile carpet or rug, often having brightly coloured animal designs.

hamadryad /haməˈdrʌɪəd, -ad/ *n.* Also (the usual form in sense 3) **-as** /-əs/, pl. **-ases**, †**-ades**. LME. [L *Hamadryas, -ad* f. Gk *Hamadruas, -ad*, f. *hama* together + *drus* tree.] **1** *Class. Mythol.* A wood nymph supposed to live and die with the tree she inhabited. LME. **2** The king cobra, *Ophiophagus hannah.* M19. **3** A large baboon, *Papio hamadryas*, of Ethiopia, Somalia, and southern Arabia, held sacred in ancient Egypt. Also *hamadryad baboon.* L19.

hamamelis /haməˈmiːlɪs/ *n.* M18. [mod.L (see below), f. Gk *hamamēlis* medlar.] Any of various ornamental N. American and eastern Asian shrubs of the genus *Hamamelis* (family Hamamelidaceae), with yellow flowers which appear in winter before the leaves; a witch hazel. Also, the medicinal lotion prepared from the leaves and bark of *H. virginiana.*

Haman /ˈheɪmən/ *n.* M17. [The chief minister of Ahasuerus, who was hanged on the gallows he prepared for the Jew Mordecai (*Esther* 7:10).] A person resembling Haman in behaviour or circumstance. Chiefly in *hang as high as Haman*, be well and truly hanged; be hoist with one's own petard.

Haman's ears fritters or cakes eaten at the Jewish festival of Purim.

hamartia /həˈmɑːtɪə/ *n.* L18. [Gk = fault, failure, guilt.] The fault or error leading to the destruction of the tragic hero or heroine of a play, novel, etc.

hamartiology /həmɑːtɪˈɒlədʒi/ *n.* L19. [f. as prec. + -OLOGY.] *Theol.* The doctrine of sin.

hamartoma /hamɑːˈtəʊmə/ *n.* Pl. **-mas, -mata** /-mətə/. E20. [f. Gk *hamartanō* go wrong + -OMA.] *Med.* A tumour-like mass resulting from the faulty growth or development of normal tissue.

hamate /ˈheɪmət/ *a.* E18. [L *hamatus* hooked, f. *hamus* hook: see -ATE[2].] Having hooks; hook-shaped; *spec.* (*Anat.*) designating one of the bones of the wrist, having an anterior hooked process.

Also **hamated** *a.* (now *rare* or *obs.*) L17.

Hamathite /ˈheɪməθʌɪt/ *n.* & *a.* E17. [f. *Hamath* the biblical name for Hama, a city in western Syria + -ITE[1].] **A** *n.* A native or inhabitant of the ancient Syrian city of Hamath. E17. **B** *adj.* Of or pertaining to Hamath; *spec.* designating an ancient script found in the Taurus Mountains (now usu. called *Hittite*). E17.

hamber-line *n.* see HAMBRO-LINE.

hamble /ˈhamb(ə)l/ *v.* Also **hammle** /ˈham(ə)l/. [OE *hamelian* = OHG *hamalōn*, ON *hamla*, f. Gmc adj. appearing as OHG *hamal* maimed, whence G *Hammel* castrated sheep. Cf. HAMEL *n.*[2]] **1** *v.t.* Mutilate, maim; dock; dehorn; *spec.* cut off the balls of the feet of (a dog) to prevent it from hunting. Also, hamstring. Now *dial.* or *Hist.* OE. **2** *v.i.* Walk lame, hobble. *dial.* E19.

hambro-line /ˈhambrəʊlʌɪn/ *n.* Also (now *rare*) **hamber-** /ˈhambə-/. L18. [f. alt. of next + LINE *n.*[2]] *Naut.* A three-stranded small-sized rope (esp. of tarred hemp) used for lashings, lacing sails, etc.

Hamburg /ˈhambəːg/ *a.* & *n.* LME. [A city in northern Germany.] **A** *adj.* (*attrib.*) †**1** Designating a type of barrel, chiefly used as a measure of salmon. *Sc.* LME–E16. **2** Designating a variety of parsley grown for its thick edible root like a turnip. L18. **3** *Hamburg grape* = sense B.1 below. L19. **4** *Hamburg steak*, a dish composed of flat cakes of chopped lean beef, mixed with beaten eggs, chopped onions, and seasoning, and fried. *US.* L19. **B** *n.* **1** More fully *Black Hamburg.* A black variety of grape of German origin, specially adapted to hothouse cultivation. M18. **2** A small variety of domestic fowl. M19.

hamburger /ˈhambəːgə/ *n.* E17. [G, f. as prec.] **1** (**H-**.) A native or inhabitant of Hamburg, a city in northern Germany. E17. **2** (A bread bun containing) seasoned minced beef formed into a round flat cake or patty, fried or grilled and usu. served with onion, relish, etc. Also (now *rare*), *hamburger steak.* Orig. *US.* L19.

2 *attrib.*: S. BELLOW She had kept the hamburger stand on Route 158. *Wimpy hamburger*: see WIMPY *n.* 1a.

hame /heɪm/ *n.*[1] ME. [MDu. (Du. *haam*), corresp. to MHG *ham(e)* fishing-rod, of unkn. origin.] Either of two curved pieces of iron or wood forming (part of) the collar of a draught horse. Usu. in *pl.*

D. HALL Your brute shoulders strained against collars, padding and steerhide over the ash hames.

hamel /ˈham(ə)l/ *n.*[1] *obs.* exc. *dial.* LME. [OFr. (mod. *hameau*), dim. of *ham* village, f. MLG *hamm*: see -EL[2].] = HAMLET *n.*[1]

hamel /ˈhɑːm(ə)l/ *n.*[2] *S. Afr.* M19. [Afk. = Du. *hamel*, G *Hammel.* Cf. HAMBLE *v.*] A castrated ram, a wether.

hamerkop /ˈhɑːməkɒp/ *n.* Also (earlier) **hammer-** /ˈhamə-/. M19. [Afk., f. *hamer* HAMMER *n.* + *kop* head.] = HAMMERHEAD 4.

hamesucken /ˈheɪmsʌk(ə)n/ *n. Hist.* & *arch.* [OE *hāmsōcn*, f. *hām* home, dwelling + *sōcn* seeking, visiting, attack, assault, ON *sókn* attack.] *Anglo-Saxon* & *Sc. Law.* (The crime of committing) an assault on a person in his or her own house or dwelling-place. Formerly also, the fine or penalty for this.

hametz /hɑːˈmets, ˈxɑː-/ *n.* Also ***cha-, cho-***. M19. [Heb. *ḥāmēṣ.*] Leaven or food mixed with leaven, prohibited during the Passover.

hamfatter /ˈhamfatə/ *n. US slang.* Also **hamfat.** L19. [Origin uncertain: perh. alt. of AMATEUR. Cf. HAM *n.*[1] II.] An inexpert or amateurish performer; *esp.* a mediocre jazz musician.

ham-fisted /ham'fɪstɪd/ *a.* E20. [f. HAM *n.*[1] + FISTED *a.*] Having large or clumsy hands; awkward, bungling.
Daily Mail A ham-fisted BBC driver locked the entire film crew out of their van.
ham-fistedly *adv.* M20. **ham-fistedness** *n.* M20.

ham-handed /ham'handɪd/ *a.* E20. [f. HAM *n.*[1] + HANDED *a.*] = prec.
J. GASKELL Old Ginger tailors . . but he's so ham-handed he always breaks his needles.
ham-handedly *adv.* M20. **ham-handedness** *n.* E20.

Hamiltonian /ham(ə)l'təʊnɪən/ *n.* & *a.* L18. [f. *Hamilton* (see below) + -IAN.] A *n.* In sense 2 also **h-**. 1 *US Polit.* A follower or adherent of the American statesman and Federalist leader Alexander Hamilton (1757–1804) or his doctrines. L18. 2 A Hamiltonian operator or function (see sense B.2 below). M20.
B *adj.* 1 Of or pertaining to the British language teacher James Hamilton (1769–1831) or his system of language teaching. E19. 2 Of, pertaining to, or invented by the Irish mathematician Sir W. R. Hamilton (1805–65); *esp.* designating certain concepts employed in the wave-mechanical description of particles. M19. 3 Of or pertaining to Alexander Hamilton or his doctrines. L19.
2 **Hamiltonian function** a function used to describe a system of particles in terms of their positions and momenta. **Hamiltonian operator** an operator that generates a Hamiltonian function when applied e.g. to a wave function.

Hamite /'hamʌɪt/ *n.* & *a.* M17. [f. *Ham* (formerly *Cham*), Gk *Ham*, L *Cham*, the second son of Noah (*Gen.* 6:10) + -ITE[1].] A *n.* †1 A follower of Ham. *derog. rare.* Only in M17. 2 A member of a people supposedly descended from Ham, as an Egyptian or other N. African. M19. B *adj.* = HAMITIC *a.* M19.

Hamitic /ha'mɪtɪk/ *a.* & *n.* M19. [f. prec. + -IC.] A *adj.* Of or pertaining to the Hamites; *spec.* of, pertaining to, or designating a group of northern African languages, formerly analysed as one of two branches of the Hamito-Semitic family, but now regarded as forming four separate groups: Egyptian, Berber, Chadic, and Cushitic. M19. B *n.* The Hamitic group of languages. L19.

Hamito-Semitic /ˌhamɪtəʊsə'mɪtɪk/ *n.* & *a.* L19. [f. HAMIT(IC + -O- + SEMITIC.] (Of, pertaining to, or designating) a language family spoken in the Middle East and northern Africa and divided into five groups, Semitic, Berber, Chadic, Cushitic, and Egyptian.

hamlet /'hamlɪt/ *n.*[1] ME. [AN *hamelet(t)e*, OFr. *hamelet*, dim. of *hamel*: see HAMEL *n.*[1], -ET[1].] A group of houses or a small village, *esp.* one without a church; the people living there.

Hamlet /'hamlɪt/ *n.*[2] E19. [A legendary prince of Denmark, the hero of a tragedy by Shakespeare.] 1 Used allusively (now chiefly as *Hamlet without the Prince* (*of Denmark*)) to refer to a performance or event taking place without the central figure, actor, etc. E19. 2 An anxious indecisive person. E20.
1 H. GRANVILLE I am not used to be newsmonger and perhaps I leave out Hamlet. L. STRACHEY The Catholic Church without . . the Pope might resemble the play of Hamlet without the Prince of Denmark.
Hamletish *a.* resembling or of the nature of Hamlet; anxious, indecisive: M19. **Hamletism** *n.* an attitude or attitudes characteristic of Hamlet; anxiety, indecision: M19. **Hamletize** *v.i.* (*rare*) soliloquize, meditate M19.

hammada /hə'mɑːdə/ *n.* Also **hamada**. M19. [Arab. *ḥammāda*.] A flat rocky area of desert blown free of sand by the wind, typical of the Sahara.

hammal /hə'mɑːl/ *n.* M18. [Arab. *ḥammāl*, f. *ḥamala* carry.] A Turkish or oriental porter.

hammam /'hamam, hə'mɑːm, 'hʌmʌm/ *n.* Also **hummum** /'hʌmʌm/. E17. [f. Turk. or its source Arab. *ḥammām* bath, f. *ḥamma* to heat.] An establishment where one may take a Turkish bath.

hammed /hamd/ *a.* E18. [f. HAM *n.*[1] + -ED[2].] Having hams (of a specified kind).
Farmer & Stockbreeder The boar in question was sound on his legs, well hammed and extremely robust.

hammer /'hamə/ *n.* [OE *hamor*, *hamer*, *homer* = OFris. *homer*, OS *hamur* (Du. *hamer*), OHG *hamar* (G *Hammer*), ON *hamarr* hammer, back of an axe, crag.] 1 A tool or instrument with a hard solid (now usu. steel) head set at right angles to the handle, used for beating, breaking, driving nails, etc.; a machine with a metal block serving the same purpose. OE. †2 A door-knocker. LME–E17. 3 In a flintlock gun, a piece of steel covering the flash-pan and struck by the flint; in a percussion-lock gun, a spring lever which strikes the percussion-cap to ignite the charge; in a modern gun, a part of the firing mechanism which either strikes the firing pin to ignite the cartridge or has the firing pin as an integral part. LME. 4 A lever with a hard head for striking a bell in a clock etc. M16. 5 *Anat.* = MALLEUS I. L16. 6 An auctioneer's mallet, used to indicate by a rap that an article is sold. E18. 7 *Mus.* A small padded mallet forming part of the mechanism for striking the strings of a piano; a small hand-held mallet for playing various percussion instruments, as the xylophone, dulcimer, etc. L18. 8 *Athletics.* A heavy metal ball attached to a flexible wire; the contest of throwing this as far as possible. L19.
1 J. GARDNER He was one with . . the hammer that sent nails in cleanly at two blows. 3 W. STYRON A white man standing over him with a musket, hammer cocked, ready to shoot. 4 W. W. SKEAT Within the gray church-tower The hammer strikes the midnight hour. 6 W. C. KETCHUM Upon the fall of the Auctioneer's hammer . . the item purchased remains at the purchaser's . . responsibility. 7 B. MASON The tuner saw a . . wad of chewing gum . . tugging the hammer.
Phrases: **be on a person's hammer** pursue, pester, bother, (a person). **come, go, under the hammer** be put up for sale at an auction. **hammer and sickle** an emblem of a crossed hammer and sickle symbolizing the industrial worker and the peasant respectively, used esp. on the national flag of the former USSR and to represent international Communism. **hammer and tongs** with great energy and noise.
Comb.: **hammer-action** (*a*) the action of a hammer, an action like that of a hammer; (*b*) the mechanism of a piano comprising and controlling the hammers; **hammerbeam**: projecting from the wall at the foot of a principal rafter in a roof; **hammer-blow** a stroke (as) with a hammer. **hammer-dressed** *a.* (of stone) roughly faced or smoothed by a hammer; **hammer drill**: having a bit which moves forwards and backwards whilst rotating; **hammer-harden** *v.t.* harden (a metal) by hammering; **hammerlock** a position in which a wrestler is held with one arm bent behind his or her back; **hammerman** a man who works with a hammer; *spec.* a smith or worker in metal, a blacksmith's assistant; **hammer price** (*a*) the actual price realized by an item sold by auction; (*b*) *Stock Exch.* the price realized for the shares of a hammered defaulter; **hammer-smith** = *hammerman* above; **hammer-toe**: permanently bent downwards; **hammer-work** (*a*) work performed with a hammer; (*b*) something constructed or shaped with a hammer.
hammerless *a.* (of a gun) having no hammer; having a concealed hammer: L19.

hammer /'hamə/ *v.* LME. [f. the n.] I *v.t.* 1 Strike, drive, beat (*out*), shape, (as) with the repeated blows or the force of a hammer. LME. b Fasten (as) with a hammer; nail *up*, *down*, *together*, etc. LME. 2 Devise laboriously, shape with effort, work hard or forcefully at (a task, plan, etc.); smooth out (difficulties etc.). Usu. foll. by *out*. L16. b Drive (an idea, a fact, etc.) into a person's head by means of repeated or forceful argument. Usu. foll. by *in*, *into*. E17. c Inflict heavy defeat(s) on in a war, game, etc.; beat up (a person); squash (a proposal etc.). *colloq.* E20. 3 *Stock Exch.* a Beat down the price of (a stock); depress (a market). *slang.* M19. b Declare (a person or firm) a defaulter with three taps of a hammer on the London Stock Exchange rostrum. L19.
1 D. H. LAWRENCE The man was hammering a piece of metal, with quick, light blows. *Lancashire Evening Telegraph* Mark Loram . . hammered in a stunning 14th minute goal. T. C. WOLFE The pianist began to hammer out a tune on the battered piano. b B. MALAMUD You work up a sweat sawing wood apart and hammering it together. TENNYSON All that long morn the lists were hammer'd up. 2 M. HUNTER A philosophy has to be hammered out, a mind shaped, a spirit tempered. A. BROOKNER Before they have hammered out the final details it is all arranged. b G. B. SHAW All the cognate tribal superstitions which are hammered into us in our childhood. **hammer home** make fully understood by means of repeated or forceful argument. c *City Limits* The social ownership strategy . . was hammered by the Campaign Group MPs. *Pot Black* Dennis Taylor . . hammered Cliff Thorburn 5–1 to reach the semi-finals.
II *v.i.* 4 Beat, strike, thump, (as) with the repeated blows or the force of a hammer. LME. †b Debate earnestly *at*, *of*, (*up*)*on*. L16–L17. c Of a thought, an idea, etc.: agitate, be persistently in one's mind. L16. d Work hard or toil (*at*); move quickly and forcefully. M18. 5 Stammer. Now *dial.* E17.
4 S. O'FAOLÁIN We hammered with our rifle butts on the door. J. M. COETZEE His legs were weak, his head hammered. b SHAKES. *Two Gent.* Whereon this month I have been hammering. c A. F. LOEWENSTEIN It was . . hard to concentrate with all the voices hammering at her. d L. STEPHEN He liked . . to hammer away at his poems in a study where chaos reigned supreme. J. HIGGINS He . . ran across the parkland . . he . . hammered along the grass verge of the main road.
hammerer *n.* a person who operates or works with a hammer E17.

hammer-cloth /'haməklɒθ/ *n.* LME. [f. elem. of unkn. origin + CLOTH *n.*] A cloth covering the driver's seat or box in a coach.

hammerhead /'haməhɛd/ *n.* M16. [f. HAMMER *n.* + HEAD *n.*] 1 The head or striking part of a hammer. M16. 2 A person's head (*derog.*); a stupid person, a blockhead. Now chiefly *US* & *dial.* M16. 3 Any of a number of sharks of the genus *Sphyrna*, with a flattened, laterally elongated head bearing the eyes and nostrils at the extremities. Also *hammerhead shark*. M19. 4 A long-legged African marsh-bird, *Scopus umbretta*, with a thick bill and an occipital crest. L19.
hammerheaded *a.* having a head shaped like that of a hammer; *fig.* stupid: M16.

Hamming /'hamɪŋ/ *n.* M20. [R. *Hamming* (b. 1915), US scientist.] Used *attrib.* to designate concepts in information coding.
Hamming code: in which errors are detected by multiple parity bits. **Hamming distance** the number of positions at which two words of equal length are different.

hammle *v.* var. of HAMBLE.

hammochrysos /hamə(ʊ)'krʌɪsɒs/ *n.* E18. [L f. Gk *hammokhrusos*, f. *hammos* sand + *khrusos* gold.] A legendary sparkling stone, usu. identified with a yellow micaceous sand.

hammock /'hamək/ *n.*[1] Orig. †**hamaca**. M16. [Sp. *hamaca* f. Taino *hamaka*; the ending has been assim. to -OCK.] 1 A hanging bed made from a large piece of canvas or netting suspended from supports by cords at each end, formerly used esp. on board ship. M16. 2 Something resembling a hammock, as a hanging nest, a cocoon, etc. M19.
1 **sling one's hammock** hang up one's hammock ready for sleeping in; *Naut. slang* have a period of time off-duty to get used to a new ship.
Comb.: **hammock chair** a folding reclining chair with canvas support for the body; a deck-chair.

hammock /'hamək/ *n.*[2] Also **hu-** /'hʌ-/. See also HUMMOCK. M16. [Orig. form of HUMMOCK.] †1 See HUMMOCK. M16. 2 A densely wooded area of ground rising above a plain or swamp. *US.* M16.

Hammond organ /hamənd 'ɔːg(ə)n/ *n. phr.* M20. [Laurens *Hammond* (1895–1973), Amer. mechanical engineer.] (Proprietary name for) a type of electric organ. Freq. *ellipt.* as *Hammond*.

hammy /'hami/ *a.* M19. [f. HAM *n.*[1] + -Y[1].] 1 Covered with ham. M19. 2 Resembling ham. L19. 3 Of, pertaining to, or characteristic of a ham actor or ham acting. *slang.* E20.
3 *Listener* Bela Lugosi's hammy Count Dracula.
hammily *adv.* M20.

hamous /'heɪməs/ *a.* Now *rare* or *obs.* M17. [f. L *hamus* hook + -OUS.] Having hooks, hooked.
Also **hamose** *a.* E18.

hamper /ˈhampə/ *n.*[1] ME. [Reduced form of AN HANAPER.] 1 Orig., any large case or casket for safe keeping. Now usu., a large basket or wickerwork packing-case with a cover, used esp. for packing or transporting food, drink, etc.; *transf.* a consignment of food, drink, etc., usu. as a present, in any type of case or box. ME. †2 = HANAPER 2b. LME–E18.

1 P. THEROUX It was like stocking a hamper for a two-day picnic. G. CLARE I can still see and smell in my memory the big hampers which Father sent.

hamper /ˈhampə/ *n.*[2] E17. [f. HAMPER *v.*[1]] 1 An impediment, a hindrance. Now *rare*. E17. 2 *Naut.* A necessary but cumbersome part of the equipment of a vessel. Earliest and chiefly in *top-hamper* s.v. TOP *a.* L18.

hamper /ˈhampə/ *v.*[1]*t.* LME. [Origin uncertain: cf. MHG, G *hemmen* restrain, hamper, -ER[5].] 1 Obstruct or prevent the movement of (a person or animal) by material obstacles or restraints; fetter, shackle; entangle, catch, (*in*). Now *rare* exc. as passing into sense 2. LME. b Restrain by confinement. Long only *Sc.* LME. c Interfere with the workings of (a lock, mechanism, etc.). Now *rare*. E19. 2 *fig.* Impede, hinder, burden. LME. 3 Pack together in a bundle, case, etc. Now *rare*. LME.

1 DEFOE He caused them to be hampered by ropes, and tied together. F. SMITH At five we engaged with Ice.. and were hampered in it until eleven. c R. A. FREEMAN It is useless to wrench at that key, because I have hampered the lock. 2 J. SYMONS The Club was hampered by lack of money from holding exhibitions. J. A. MICHENER If he had not been hampered by this irritating calf, he could have beaten back the wolves.

hamper /ˈhampə/ *v.*[2]*t.* & *i. obs.* exc. *dial.* E16. [Origin unkn.] Beat, strike.

hamper /ˈhampə/ *v.*[3]*t. joc.* E18. [f. HAMPER *n.*[1]] Load with hampers; present with a hamper.

Hampshire /ˈhampʃə/ *n.* M17. [A county in southern England.] I 1 Used *attrib.* to designate things from or associated with Hampshire, *esp.* (*a*) (an animal of) a breed of black pig with a white saddle and prick ears, (*b*) (more fully *Hampshire Down*) (an animal of) a breed of large hornless sheep with close wool and dark brown face and legs. M17.

1 **Hampshire hog** *fig.* (*colloq.* or *derog.*) a native or inhabitant of Hampshire.

II 2 In *pl.* (The soldiers of) the Royal Hampshire Regiment. E20. 3 A Hampshire pig. M20.

Hampstead /ˈham(p)stɪd/ *n. rhyming slang.* L19. [*Hampstead Heath*, a district in north London.] In *pl.* or *Hampstead Heath*. Teeth.

hamsin *n.* var. of KHAMSIN.

hamster /ˈhamstə/ *n.* E17. [G f. OHG *hamustro* = OS *hamustra* corn-weevil.] Any of various short-tailed ratlike burrowing rodents of the Eurasian subfamily Cricetinae (family Muridae), with cheek pouches used to carry grain etc. for storage.

golden hamster a mouselike, largely tawny Asian hamster, *Mesocricetus auratus*, much kept as a pet or laboratory animal.

hamstring /ˈhamstrɪŋ/ *n.* & *v.* M16. [f. HAM *n.*[1] + STRING *n.*] A *n.* In humans, apes, etc., each of the five tendons at the back of the knee; in quadrupeds, the great tendon at the back of the hock. M16.

B *v.t.* Pa. t. & pple **-strung** /-strʌŋ/, (now *rare*) **-stringed**. Lame or disable (a person or animal) by cutting the hamstrings; *fig.* destroy the activity or efficiency of. M17.

T. H. WHITE They were crawling along the roads on hands and knees, because they had been hamstrung. A. STORR I know of no creative person who was more hamstrung by his inability to write.

hamular /ˈhamjʊlə/ *a.* M19. [f. next + -AR[1].] Chiefly *Anat.* Of the form of a small hook, hooked.

hamulus /ˈhamjʊləs/ *n.* Pl. **-li** /-lʌɪ, -liː/. E18. [L *hamulus* dim. of *hamus* hook: see -ULE.] A small hook or hooklike part on a bone etc.

hamular *a.* of the form of a small hook, hooked M19.

hamza /ˈhamzə/ *n.* E19. [Arab., lit. 'compression'.] (A symbol in the Arabic script representing) the glottal stop.

Han /han/ *n.*[1] & *a.* M18. [Chin. *Hàn*.] (Designating or pertaining to) a dynasty which ruled China from the 3rd cent. BC to the 3rd cent. AD, a period noted for religious and cultural changes and technological developments.

han *n.*[2] var. of KHAN *n.*[2]

Hanafi /ˈhanəfi/ *n.* & *a.* M18. [Arab. *ḥanafī*, f. *Ḥanīfah* (see below).] A follower of, of or pertaining to, the school of Islamic law founded by the jurist Abū Ḥanīfa (*c* 699–767).

Hanafite /ˈhanəfʌɪt/ *n.* & *a.* M19. [f. as prec. + -ITE[1].] = prec.

hanap /ˈhanəp/ *n. obs.* exc. *Hist.* L15. [(O)Fr. f. Frank., = OE *hnæp*, OHG *hnapf* (G *Napf*).] A drinking-vessel, a wine-cup. Now *esp.* an ornate medieval goblet.

hanaper /ˈhanəpə/ *n. obs.* exc. *Hist.* ME. [AN = OFr. *hanapier* (AL *hanaperium*), f. as prec.: see -ER[2].] †1 A case or basket for a hanap or hanaps; a repository for plate or treasure. Only in ME. 2 The department of the Chancery into which fees were paid for the sealing and enrolment of charters etc. LME. b A (wicker) case or basket for keeping documents. M18.

hanaster /ˈhanəstə/ *n. obs.* exc. *Hist.* Also †**hanster**. ME. [f. HANSE + -ER[1] (= AL *hansterus, hanasterius*).] In the City of Oxford, a person who paid the entrance fee to the merchant guild and was admitted as a freeman.

Hanbali /ˈhanbəli/ *n.* M19. [Arab. *ḥanbalī*, f. *Ḥanbal* (see below).] A follower of the school of Islamic law founded by the jurist Ahmad Ibn Hanbal (780–855).

Hanbalite /ˈhanbəlʌɪt/ *n.* M19. [f. as prec. + -ITE[1].] = prec.

hance /hɑːns/ *n.* Also **-se**. M16. [AN, alt. of OFr. *hau(l)ce* (mod. *hausse*), f. *hau(l)cer* (mod. *hausser*), f. Proto-Romance base repr. also by ENHANCE.] 1 A lintel. *obs.* exc. *dial.* M16. 2 *Naut.* A curved ascent or descent from one part of a ship to another. M17. 3 *Archit.* The arc at the springing of an elliptical or many-centred arch. Also = HAUNCH 2. E18.

†**hanch** *n.* var. of HAUNCH.

hand /hand/ *n.* [OE (also *hond*) = OFris. *hānd, hōnd*, OS *hand*, OHG *hant* (Du., G *Hand*), ON *hǫnd*, Goth. *handus*, f. Gmc, of unkn. origin.] I The member; its use; its position; its symbolic representation. 1 The terminal part of the human arm beyond the wrist, consisting of the palm, fingers, and thumb; a similar (i.e. prehensile) member forming the terminal part of a limb of any animal, e.g. of all four limbs of a monkey; the forefoot of a quadruped. OE. †b The whole arm. E17–M18. 2 Possession, care, custody, authority, disposal. Chiefly in *in a person's hands* below. Usu. in *pl.* OE. 3 Action performed with the hand; agency, instrumentality; manual assistance. OE. b A part or share in an action. L16. c A turn in various games, as billiards, rackets, etc.; an innings in cricket. Cf. sense 19c below. L18. 4 Side, position, direction. (See also LEFT HAND, RIGHT HAND.) OE. 5 A pledge (of agreement or acceptance); *esp.* a promise of marriage. ME. 6 A round of applause. *colloq.* L16. 7 In *pl.* = HANDBALL *n.* 5. L19.

1 V. S. NAIPAUL She started to count off the fingers of her left hand. ALDOUS HUXLEY The hand he gave to Jeremy was disagreeably sweaty. M. AMIS His hands palm-upwards on its grained surface. 2 D. CUSACK The future of social morality is in the hands of women. S. SPENDER It was expected that Madrid would fall into their hands within a matter of hours. V. S. NAIPAUL The farm manager retired... The farm passed into new hands. 3 A. HALEY All of this had happened to her at the hands of Massa Waller. G. WINOKUR 15 per cent will die by their own hand. *Times* Listing all the troublespots attributed by the Americans to 'the hand of Moscow'. b K. AMIS I'm sorry it's happened, but I had no hand in it. R. RENDELL Wexford felt sure no true architect had had a hand in its building. 4 R. L. STEVENSON The bed of a stream, lined on either hand with sweet-smelling willows. J. MORTIMER At Doughty's right hand sat Grace. 5 J. AUSTEN When the dancing recommenced .. and Darcy approached to claim her hand. L. STRACHEY Various candidates for her hand were proposed—among others .. Prince Leopold of Saxe-Coburg. HENRY MILLER All I had to do was to ask her to marry me, ask her hand. 6 L. ARMSTRONG The kids gave me a big hand when they saw the gleaming bright instrument. F. ASTAIRE At the final exit of our closing dance number we received a sparse, sympathetic kind of hand.

II Something resembling the hand in size or form. 8 An image of or device shaped like a hand. OE. b *Typogr.* = FIST *n.*[1] 2b. Now *rare*. E17. 9 A pointer on a clock for indicating the divisions of the dial. M16. 10 A linear measure, now only used of a horse's height, equal to four inches; a hand-breadth. M16. b A measure of quantity of various commodities etc., as a cluster of bananas, a handful of tobacco leaves, or a palmate root of ginger. E18. 11 *Cookery.* A shoulder of pork or, formerly, of mutton. L17.

9 J. MASTERS The hands were very dim on its blurred white face. *hour-hand, minute hand, second(s)-hand.* 10 *Horse International* He .. already stands 16.3 hands after wintering out. b D. STUART Two hands of men, ten men, all proper men, had charge of them. H. BASCOM He .. took a hand of green plantains from off a bunch.

III As representing a person. 12a A performer of some action; *spec.* a performer, writer, etc., of some artistic or literary work. ME. b A manual worker; *spec.* a member of a ship's crew. M17. 13 A person as a source from which something originates or is obtained. Now only with ordinal numerals, as *first hand, second hand*, etc. LME. 14 A person of a specified skill, ability, or character. *colloq.* L18.

12a W. PALEY Everything about them indicates that they come from the same hand. *Proverb*: Many hands make light work. b W. SCORESBY All hands on board perished. BETTY SMITH The poor do everything with their own hands and the rich hire hands to do things. P. USTINOV The son of a stable hand. 13 W. BEDELL You have it but at the third, or fourth hand, perhaps the thirtieth or fortieth. W. COWPER I might .. serve your Honour with cauliflowers and broccoli at the best hand. J. W. CROKER I hear from a good hand that the King is doing much better. 14 V. WOOLF I was never a great hand at that. M. COX But you know I am no hand at expressing myself.

IV Capacity, performance. 15 Capacity for or skill in doing something with the hand; *gen.* skill, ability, knack. ME. b *Horsemanship.* Skill in handling the reins. LME. 16 Style of writing, esp. as belonging to a particular person, historical period, profession, etc. LME. b The signature of a person. M16. 17 Style of artistic execution; touch; handiwork. M17.

15 A. RADCLIFFE I had always a hand at carpentry. 16 F. O'CONNOR It was written in a drunken-looking hand. G. GREENE A message written in his clear slanting American hand. J. GARDNER An old almanac with notes in the margin, written in his father's childish hand. *Italian hand, round hand, running hand*, etc. b OED As witness the hands of the said A.B. and C.D. 17 HOR. WALPOLE By what I have seen of his hand, .. he was an admirable master. M. ARNOLD The compiler did not put his last hand to the work.

V Something held in the hand. 18 A handle. Now only *Sc.* LME. 19 The cards dealt to each player at the beginning of a card-game; the cards held at any stage of a game (esp. poker). L16. b The person holding the cards. L16. c A round of play with these cards. E17.

19 M. PIERCY You have to find out what kind of hand she's holding. *fig.*: I. MURDOCH She had been dealt a rotten hand by fate. c V. SACKVILLE-WEST She played an admirable hand at Bridge.

Phrases etc.: *a bird in the hand*: see BIRD *n.* **at hand** (*a*) near, close by; (*b*) near in time; †(*c*) at the start. *at* FIRST HAND. **at the hands of** from, through the action of. *bear a hand*: see BEAR *v.*[1] *bear in hand*: see BEAR *v.*[1] **bind hand and foot** bind completely. *bite the hand that feeds one*: see BITE *v. bloody hand*: see BLOODY *a.* & *adv.* **by hand** (*a*) with the hand or hands, by manual action or labour; (*b*) (of writing) not typed, printed, etc.; (*c*) (of a delivery etc.) by messenger, not posted. **by my, this, hand**: introducing a solemn oath. *cap in hand*: see CAP *n.*[1] **change hands** (*a*) pass to a different owner; (*b*) use opposite hands for a task, action, etc. *clean hands*: see CLEAN *a. come in foot and hand*: see FOOT *n.* **come to hand** turn up, come into one's possession; be received. *dab hand*: see DAB *n.*[3] *dead* *hand*: see DEAD *a.* etc. **do a hand's turn** do a stroke of work, make the slightest effort (usu. in neg. contexts). *eat out of a person's hand*: see EAT *v. fine-hand*: see FINE *a.* FIRST HAND. *force a person's hand*: see FORCE *v.*[1] **for one's own hand** for one's own benefit, on one's own account. *free hand*: see FREE *a.* **(from) hand to mouth** improvidently, precariously, with provision for immediate needs only. *full-hand*: see FULL *a.* **get one's hand in** get in practice. **get one's hands on** find, get hold of. *give a free hand*: see FREE *a.* **give (a person) a hand** help, lend assistance, (to a person). **give one's hand** present one's hand to be grasped to seal a bargain, make peace, etc. **hand and** or **in glove (with)** on intimate terms (with), in close association (with). **hand in hand** with hands mutually clasped; *fig.* together, in close association. **hand of glory** [tr. Fr. *main de gloire*, alt. of *mandegloire*, orig. *mandragore* mandrake] orig., a French charm made from a mandrake root; later, a charm made from the hand of an executed criminal. **hand of writ** *Sc.* handwriting. **hand over hand** or **fist** with each hand successively passing the other as in climbing a rope etc.; *fig.* with steady or rapid progress. **hands down** with ease, with little or no effort; esp. in *win hands down*. **hands off!** do not touch! do not interfere! (cf. *hands-off* below). **hands up!**: ordering a person or persons to raise one hand to signify assent or both hands to signify surrender. **hand to hand** (of fighting) at close quarters, man to man. *hand to mouth*: see *from hand to mouth* above. *have a free hand*: see FREE *a.* **have a hand in** have a share in, be involved in. **have one's hand in** be in practice. **have one's hand in the till** *fig.* steal, embezzle. **have one's hands full** be fully occupied. **have one's hands tied** *fig.* be powerless to act. *heel of the hand*: see HEEL *n.*[1] *helping hand*: see HELP *v. hidden hand*: see HIDDEN *a.* **hold a person's hand** *fig.* give close guidance or moral support to a person. **hold hands** be hand in hand. **hold one's hand** refrain from action, esp. punishment. **in a person's hands** to be dealt with by a person, subject to his or her control. **in hand** (*a*) held in the hand; (*b*) in actual possession, at one's disposal; to spare; (*c*) in process or preparation, receiving attention; (*d*) under control; †(*e*) led by the hand, a leash, etc.; †(*f*) in suspense. *in huckster's hands*: see HUCKSTER *n. in the hollow of one's hand*: see HOLLOW *n.*[1] **join hands** = *hold hands* above. **keep one's hand in** keep in practice. *kiss hands*: see KISS *v. know like the back of one's hand*: see BACK *n.*[1] *lay hands on*: see LAY *v.*[1] *lay hands on the ark*: see ARK 2. **lay one's hands on** = *get one's hands on* above. **lend (a person) a hand** = *give (a person) a hand* above. *light hand*: see LIGHT *a.*[1] *lone hand*: see LONE *a.* & *adv.* **make a (fine, good, etc.) hand** make a (fine, good, etc.) success or profit. **man of his hands** a practical or skilful person. **off one's hands** no longer one's responsibility or on one's hands. *old hand*: see OLD *a.* **on hand** (*a*) in one's possession, in one's charge or keeping; (*b*) in attendance. **on all hands, on every hand** on all sides, to or from every quarter. **on one hand** = *on the one hand* below. **on one's hands** resting on one as a charge or responsibility. **on the one hand**: introducing a point of view, fact, etc. (often followed by another which contrasts with it, introduced by *on the other hand*). **on the other hand**: introducing a point of view, fact, etc., contrasting with another previously mentioned (often introduced by *on (the) one hand*). **out of hand** (*a*) at once, immediately, without thinking; (*b*) out of control; (*c*) done with, dealt with. *play into the hands of*: see PLAY *v.* **put one's hands on** = *get one's hands on* above. **put one's hand to** set about, undertake. SECOND HAND. **serve, wait on,** etc., **hand and foot**: assiduously, servilely. *set in hand*: see SET *v.*[1] **set one's hand to** (*a*) = *put one's hand to* above; (*b*) write one's signature on, authorize by signing. *shake (a person's) hand, shake by the hand, shake hands (with)*: see SHAKE *v. show one's hand*: see SHOW *v. sit on one's hands*: see SIT *v. stay* one's own or another's *hand* see STAY *v.*[1] *strike hands*: see STRIKE *v.* **take hands** join hands, esp. in marriage. **take in hand** take the responsibility of; undertake (a task); *esp.* undertake the charge or care of (a person). *take one's courage in both hands*: see COURAGE *n.* 4. *throw in one's hand*: see THROW *v.* **tie hand and foot** = *bind hand and foot* above. *time on one's hands*: see TIME *n.* **to hand** (*a*) within reach, accessible; (*b*) (now *rare*) under control. **to one's hand** ready for one to deal with easily. *try one's hand*: see TRY *v.* **turn one's hand to** undertake for the first time. **under (one's) hand** with one's signature, properly signed. *upper hand*: see UPPER *a. wait on hand and foot*: see *serve hand and foot* above. *wash one's hands*: see WASH *v. wash one's hands of*: see WASH *v.* WEAKEN *the hands of. with a heavy hand*: see HEAVY *a. with a high hand*: see HIGH *a.* **with both hands** *fig.* with all one's might.

Attrib. & comb.: In the senses 'held or carried in the hand', as *hand-baggage, -camera, -microphone, -mirror,* 'operated by hand', as *handbrake, hand-drill, -press, -pump, -puppet*, or w. ref. to action performed by or with the hand, as opp. to by machine, as *hand-knitted, -painted, -sewn, -written* adjs., *hand-wash* vb. Special combs., as **hand-axe** an axe used or wielded with one hand; *spec.* in *Archaeol.*, a large bifacially worked stone cutting tool of stone, with no haft, typical of certain lower and middle palaeolithic industries; **handbag** (*a*) a small bag for holding personal articles such as a purse, wallet, diary, etc.; (*b*) a light travelling-bag; *hand-barrow*: see BARROW *n.*[3] 1; **handbell** a small bell rung by being swung in the hand; *spec.* each of a set of such bells specially designed for musical performance; **handbill** a printed notice delivered or circulated by hand; **hand('s)-breadth** a unit of linear measure (not now in technical use) based on the width of the average adult hand and equal to approx. four inches; **handcart**: drawn or pushed by hand; **handclasp** (chiefly *US*) = HANDGRIP 2; **hand cream** an emollient for the hands; **hand-gallop** an easy controlled gallop; **hand-grenade** a grenade designed to be thrown by hand; **handhold** a hold for the hand; a projection, crack etc., which one can hold on to in climbing; **handhorn** *Mus.* a natural horn played by stopping the bell with the hand; **hand-jam** *v.* & *n.* (*Mountaineering*) (*a*) *v.i.* wedge a hand in a crack as a handhold; (*b*) *n.* the action of hand-jamming; **handjob** *coarse slang* an act of (usu. male) masturbation; **hand-labour** manual labour; **handline** *n.* & *v.* (*Angling*) (fish using) a line worked or drawn by hand; **handlist**: of books etc. for easy reference; **handloom** a weaver's loom worked by hand as opp. to by machine; **handmade** *a.* made by hand as opp. to by machine; **handmaid(en)** (*arch.* exc. *fig.*), a female attendant or servant; **hand-mill** a mill consisting of one millstone turned on another by hand; a small mill for grinding coffee etc.; **hand-organ** a barrel-organ played by means of a crank turned by the hand; **handpicked** *a.* carefully chosen; **hand-press** a printing-press operated by hand; **handprint** the mark left by the impression of a hand; **handrail** a rail or railing used as support for the hand or as a guard along the edge of a platform, stairs, etc.; **handrunning** *adv.* (*dial.* or *colloq.*) consecutively, in a row; **hands-across-the-sea** promoting closer links, friendly. **handsaw** a saw used or worked with one hand; *know a hawk from a handsaw*: see HAWK *n.*[1]; *hand's-breadth*: see *hand-breadth* above; **handset** a telephone mouthpiece and earpiece as one unit; **hand signal** a manual indication by a cyclist or driver of a motor vehicle of his or her intention to stop, turn, etc.; **hands-off** *a.* & *adv.* [f. *hands off!* above] (*a*) *adj.* (of a policy, attitude, etc.) non-intervening, aloof; (of a flight) automatic; (*b*) *adv.* automatically. **hands-on** *a.* involving direct participation, practical, not theoretical; (of a person) having or willing to gain practical experience; **handspring** a gymnastic movement in which a performer moves forwards or backwards from a standing position on to the hands and completes a somersault, landing on the feet; **hand-staff** a handle resembling a staff; *esp.* that of a flail; **handstand** a gymnastic movement in which the body is supported vertically in an upside-down position by the hands alone; **hand-to-mouth** *a.* improvident, precarious, providing for immediate needs only (cf. *(from) hand to mouth* above); **hand-towel** a small towel for drying the hands after washing.

hand /hand/ *v.* LME. [f. the n.] **1** *v.t.* Touch, grasp, seize, with the hand or hands; manipulate, handle. *obs.* exc. *techn.* LME. **2** *v.t.* Help or conduct (a person) *up* or *down* a step, *over* an obstacle, *into* or *out of* a carriage, etc. M17. **3** *v.t.* Deliver, pass, or transfer with the hand or hands. Freq. foll. by *back, in, over*. M17. **b** *spec.* Offer, serve, or distribute (food) at a meal. Freq. foll. by *round*. E19. **4** *v.t.* Pass on, transfer, transmit. Now only w. advs. (see below). M17. **b** Give, impose; palm off. *N. Amer.* E20. **5** *v.t.* & *i. Naut.* Take in or furl (a sail). M17. **6** *v.t.* Join hand in hand, *spec.* in marriage. Only in *handed* ppl a. *rare.* M17.

1 SHAKES. *Temp.* If you can command these elements to silence, . . we will not hand a rope more. 2 A. TROLLOPE He handed her into the carriage. E. M. FORSTER Henry . . handed Margaret down the cellar-stairs. 3 A. CARNEGIE The five hundred dollars which I handed over to Mr. Scott. P. ACKROYD Monro handed the poem back to him. A. TYLER His waiter . . handed him a menu. M. DRABBLE Charles had raged, stormed, and handed in his resignation. **hand it to a person** *fig. colloq.* congratulate, acknowledge the merit of a person. b H. JAMES I wonder whether Verena hadn't better hand the cake. V. WOOLF Amelia Whatshername, handing round cups of tea. 4b T. MORRISON Don't hand me that mess. 5 E. LINKLATER Before they rounded the Horn Sam could hand, reef, and steer.

With advs. in specialized senses: **hand down** (*a*) pass on to a later generation or age; *spec.* pass on (an outgrown or unwanted garment) to another (esp. younger) member of one's family; (*b*) deliver or transmit (a verdict) from a superior court etc. **hand off** (*a*) *Rugby Football* push off (a tackling opponent) with the hand; (*b*) *Amer. Football* pass the ball by hand. **hand on** pass to the next in a series or succession (*hand on the torch*: see TORCH *n.*). **hand out** distribute, give out. **hand over** transfer; relinquish.

Comb.: **hand-in** *Real Tennis, Squash, & Badminton* the person who or side which is serving the ball (cf. HAND-OUT 1); **hand-me-down** *n.* & *a.* (designating) a second-hand garment or (*fig.*) idea; **hand-off** *Rugby Football* the action of pushing off an opponent.

handball /'han(d)bɔːl, *in sense A.5* -'bɔːl/ *n.* & *v.* LME. [f. HAND *n.* + BALL *n.*[1]] **A** *n.* **I 1** A ball for throwing with the hand; *spec.* (*a*) an inflated leather ball used in handball (sense 2 below); (*b*) a small hollow rubber ball used in handball (sense 3 below). LME. **2** A game similar to football in which the ball is thrown rather than kicked in the attempt to get it into the opposing team's goal. L16. **3** A game resembling fives in which a ball is hit with the hand in a walled court. L19. **II 4** *Austral. Rules Football.* = HANDPASS *n.* M19. **5** *Football.* A foul involving illegal handling of the ball. E20. **B** *v.t.* & *i. Austral. Rules Football.* = HANDPASS *v.* M20.

handbook /'han(d)bʊk/ *n.* OE. [f. HAND *n.* + BOOK *n.*, tr. med.L *manualis liber*, late L *manuale* (tr. Gk *egkheiridion*) MANUAL *n.*; the wd in current use was introduced, after G *Handbuch*, in the 19th cent.] †**1** The manual of medieval ecclesiastical offices and ritual. OE–L16. **2** A book containing concise information on a particular subject; a guidebook. E19. **3** A bookmaker's betting-book; a bookmaking establishment. Chiefly *US.* L19.

2 J. P. DONLEAVY Dignity in debt. A handbook for those just starting out. 3 S. BELLOW. He went to a handbook on Fifty-third Street to bet on horses.

handclap /'han(d)klap/ *n.* E19. [f. HAND *n.* + CLAP *n.*[1]] A clap of the hands; a round of applause; *fig.* an instant.

K. AMIS Cries of approval as well as handclaps followed the final triumphant chord. *slow handclap*: see SLOW *a.* & *adv.*

handclapping *n.* M19.

handcraft /'han(d)krɑːft/ *n.* & *v.* OE. [f. HAND *n.* + CRAFT *n.*] **A** *n.* = HANDICRAFT 1. OE.

Comb.: **handcraftsman** a handicraftsman; **handcraftsmanship** skilled craftsmanship with the hands.

B *v.t.* Make by handicraft. M20.

Belle (*Australia*) Moran features hand-crafted Mountain Ash hardwood frames.

handcuff /'han(d)kʌf/ *n.* & *v.* E17. [f. HAND *n.* + CUFF *n.*[1]] **A** *n.* †**1** = CUFF *n.*[1] 2a. E–M17. **2** *sing.* & (usu.) in *pl.* A pair of lockable metal rings, joined by a short chain or bar, which can secure both a prisoner's wrists together or one wrist to that of his or her captor. M17.

2 *golden handcuffs*: see GOLDEN *a.*

B *v.t.* Put handcuffs on, manacle. E18.

handed /'handɪd/ *a.* L15. [f. HAND *n.* + -ED[2]. See also earlier LEFT-HANDED, RIGHT-HANDED.] **1** Having a hand or hands; (as 2nd elem. of comb.) having hands of a specified kind or number. L15. **2** Of a tool or implement: specially designed for either right-handed or left-handed use. L20.

1 *empty-handed, free-handed, open-handed, two-handed*, etc.

handedness /'handɪdnɪs/ *n.* E20. [f. prec. + -NESS. See also earlier LEFT-HANDEDNESS, RIGHT-HANDEDNESS.] **1** The quality or state of being handed; *esp.* the tendency to use or the preference for the use of either the right or the left hand. E20. **2** That property of the configuration of a molecule, crystal, or other object (defined as *left-* or *right-handedness* by arbitrary convention), which distinguishes it from its mirror image. M20.

1 P. LEACH His handedness is controlled by the part of the brain that controls language. 2 *Listener* Proteins

..contain amino acids (all of one particular handedness) joined together.

Handelian /han'di:lɪən, -'deɪl-/ *n.* & *a.* M18. [f. *Handel* (orig. *Händel*) (see below) + -IAN.] **A** *n.* A person who favours or imitates the style of the German musician and composer Georg Friedrich *Handel* (1685–1759). M18.

B *adj.* Of, pertaining to, or characteristic of Handel or his style of composition. L18.

H. ROSENTHAL Handel's *Julius Caesar* in a performing edition that understandably upset Handelian experts.

hander /'handə/ *n.*[1] L17. [f. HAND *v.* + -ER[1].] A person who hands, delivers, or passes. Usu. w. *back*, *down*, *on*, *over*, etc.

LEIGH HUNT The hander down of his likeness to posterity.

hander /'handə/ *n.*[2] *colloq.* M19. [f. HAND *n.* + -ER[1].] A blow on the hand.

handfast /'han(d)fɑ:st/ *n.* M16. [App. f. HAND *n.* + FAST *a.*; sense 2 f. HANDFAST *v.*] †**1** (A) firm hold or grip with the hands. M16–M17. **2** A contract; *spec.* a betrothal or marriage contract, *esp.* such a contract sealed by a handshake. *obs.* exc. *Hist.* E17.

1 R. HAWKINS Such were the blowes he gave them.. as both left their hand-fast. 2 SHAKES. *Cymb.* And the remembrancer of her to hold the hand-fast to her lord. *attrib.*: *Daily Telegraph* The 'handfast' marriage by which a couple could marry by clasping hands and swearing their vows before witnesses.

handfast /'han(d)fɑ:st/ *a.* ME. [In senses 1, 2, orig. pa. pple of HANDFAST *v.*; in sense 3 f. HAND *n.* + FAST *a.*] **1** Contracted by the joining of hands; betrothed, espoused. *obs.* exc. *Hist.* ME. †**2** Bound; manacled. ME–M17. **3** Close-fisted (*lit.* & *fig.*). Now *rare* or *obs.* E17.

handfast /'han(d)fɑ:st/ *v.t.* LOE. [In sense 1 f. ON *handfesta* strike a bargain by joining hands etc.; in senses 2, 3 f. HAND *n.* + FAST *a.*] **1** Betroth (two people or one person *to* another); *esp.* contract (a person or two people) to cohabit with another or together for a trial period before marriage. *obs.* exc. *Hist.* LOE. **b** Of a man: become betrothed to, cohabit with (a woman). Long *rare.* L16. †**2** Grasp, seize firmly with the hand. M16–M17. †**3** Manacle, secure the hands of. L16–E17.

handfasting *n.* (*obs.* exc. *Hist.*) betrothal; the ceremony of contracting a trial period of marriage: L15.

handful /'han(d)fʊl, -f(ə)l/ *n.* OE. [f. HAND *n.* + FULL *a.* (in early use not inflected as from -FUL).] **1** A quantity that fills the hand; as much or as many as a hand can grasp or contain. OE. **b** A small number or amount. E16. †**2** = HAND *n.* 10. LME–M18. **3** A person, animal, or task that is troublesome or difficult to manage. *colloq.* M18. **4** A five-year prison sentence. *slang.* M20.

1 R. C. HUTCHINSON He put down the handful of crayons he was holding. D. PRATER He.. stooped now and then to gather great handfuls from the carpet of forget-me-nots. b R. SUTCLIFF The valiant handful of cavalry were struggling to keep clear the line of retreat. M. DRABBLE He studied Current Affairs, along with a handful of public schoolboys. 3 P. G. WODEHOUSE Bailey will find her rather a handful Does she ever sit still, by the way?

handglass /'han(d)glɑ:s/ *n.* L18. [f. HAND *n.* + GLASS *n.*] **1** A small portable glass frame for protecting or bringing on plants. L18. **2** A magnifying glass held in the hand. E19. **3** A small mirror with a handle. L19.

handgrip /'han(d)grɪp/ *n.* Also †**handygrip**. OE. [f. HAND *n.* + GRIP *n.*[1]; var. after HANDIWORK.] **1** Firm hold or grasp with the hand. OE. **2** *spec.* A grip or clasp of the hand in greeting or leave-taking. L19. **3** A part of something designed to be held or gripped; a handle, a hilt, etc. L19.

1 J. SYLVESTER Hee, that both Globes in his own hand-gripe holds. **at** or **in handgrips** (now *rare* or *obs.*) in close combat. 2 E. H. YATES With his warmest handgrip. 3 *Camera Weekly* The other.. change is in the hand-grip cover.

handgun /'han(d)gʌn/ *n.* ME. [f. HAND *n.* + GUN *n.*] Orig., a gun (with or without a rest) held and fired with the hand or hands, as opp. to a cannon. Now, a gun held and fired with one hand only.

handgunner *n.* a person who uses a handgun M16.

hand-habend /'handhɑ:bənd/ *a.* Long *arch. rare.* ME. [f. OE *æt hæbbendre handa* lit. 'at or with a having hand'.] *Law.* Of a thief: apprehended in the possession of stolen goods.

hand-held /'handhɛld/ *a.* & *n.* E20. [f. HAND *n.* + HELD *a.*] **A** *adj.* Held in the hand. E20. **B** *n.* A small hand-held computer for business or recreational use. L20.

handicap /'handɪkap/ *n.* & *v.* M17. [App. f. 'hand i' cap' or 'hand in the cap', referring to the drawing out of full or empty hands: see below.] **A** *n.* **1** *Hist.* A game in which a challenger laid claim to an article belonging to another person, offering something in exchange for it, the difference in the value of the two items being determined by an umpire who stood to gain the forfeit-money deposited by all three contestants if the other two parties both signified (by drawing out full or empty hands from a cap, pocket, etc.) their acceptance or rejection of his award (otherwise the one who accepted it won the forfeit-money). M17. **2** A horse-race in which an umpire determines, according to the horses' merits, what weights have to be carried by each in order to equalize their chances (also *handicap race*); any race or competition in which the chances of an inferior competitor are made more equal by some means, as by having a head start etc. L18. **3** The extra weight or other disadvantageous condition imposed upon a superior in favour of an inferior in a competition; *spec.* in *Golf*, the number of strokes by which a golfer normally exceeds the par for the course, used to equalize the chances between players by granting the inferior player or players an advantage based on the difference between handicaps as extra strokes. L19. **4** *fig.* An encumbrance, a hindrance; *spec.* a condition that markedly restricts a person's ability to function physically, mentally, or socially. L19.

2 *welter handicap*: see WELTER *n.*[3] 1b. 3 G. SANTAYANA He had intended to race in earnest, having given a generous handicap. 4 C. POTOK His sickness is quite a handicap. *National Trust Magazine* Those with a visual or physical handicap are asked to contact the property when planning a visit.

B *v.t.* Infl. **-pp-**. †**1** Draw out or gain (money) in a game of handicap. Only in M17. **2** Impose a handicap on (a competitor, *esp.* a racehorse). M19. **3** *fig.* Be a handicap to, hamper, disadvantage. M19.

3 E. HEMINGWAY He was handicapped by his short stature. *Look Now* Guilt.. handicaps the way we think.

handicapped *a.* & *n.* (*a*) *adj.* possessing a handicap; (*b*) *n. the* handicapped people as a class: E20. **handicapper** *n.* (*a*) the official who determines the weights the horses are to carry in a handicap; (*b*) a horse running in a handicap: M18.

handicraft /'handɪkrɑ:ft/ *n.* ME. [Alt. of HANDCRAFT after HANDIWORK.] **1** Manual skill. ME. **2** A manual art, trade, or occupation. Formerly also, a handicraftsman. M16.

Comb.: **handicraftsman** a person employed or skilled in a manual occupation, an artisan.

handicuffs /'handɪkʌfs/ *n.pl. arch.* Also **handy-**. E18. [f. HAND *n.* or HANDY *a.* + CUFF *n.*[2], app. after FISTICUFFS *n.*] Blows with the hand; fighting hand to hand.

handie-talkie /'handɪ,tɔ:ki/ *n.* M20. [f. HAND *n.* after WALKIE-TALKIE.] A light form of walkie-talkie two-way radio set, easily carried in the hand.

handily /'handɪli/ *adv.* E17. [f. HANDY *a.* + -LY[2].] In a handy manner; expertly; *N. Amer.* easily. Formerly also, manually.

T. O'BRIEN With Eddie as captain the Third Squad won handily.

handiness /'handɪnɪs/ *n.* M17. [f. as prec. + -NESS.] **1** The quality of being handy or expert. M17. **2** Manageableness; convenience. L19.

handiwork /'handɪwə:k/ *n.* Also (now *rare*) **handy-work**. [OE *handġeweorc*, f. *hand* HAND *n.* + *ġeweorc* collect. formation (see Y-) on *weorc* WORK *n.*; analysed in 16 as f. HANDY *a.* + WORK *n.*] **1** A thing or collection of things made by the hands. OE. **2** Work done by the hands or by direct personal agency. OE. **3** Working with the hands; practical work. M16. **4** Work of any kind; doing, performance, achievement. M19.

1 J. B. PRIESTLEY 'Ow's the repairs going, George?' He.. began to inspect the other's handiwork. B. BETTELHEIM Man is afraid of being robbed of his own humanity by his own handiwork the machine. 2 P. PEARCE He had drawn the creature.., and then was startled by his own handiwork. 3 E. H. GOMBRICH Artists had to insist that their real work was not handiwork but brain work. A. S. BYATT She came first in the theoretical paper.., but her handiwork let her down. 4 DICKENS That was your handiwork, Giles, I understand.

handkercher /'haŋkətʃə/ *n. dial.* & *slang.* M16. [f. HAND *n.* + KERCHER.] = next.

handkerchief /'haŋkətʃɪf/ *n.* Pl. **-chiefs**, **-chieves** /-tʃi:vz/. M16. [f. HAND *n.* + KERCHIEF.] A small square of cotton, linen, silk, or (now, more fully *paper handkerchief*) soft absorbent paper, used for wiping the nose, eyes, face, etc., and formerly also worn about the neck.

A. PATON He.. took out a large red handkerchief to wipe his face. J. BARTH He drew a handkerchief from his sweater pocket and blew his nose violently. *pocket handkerchief*: see POCKET *n.*

handle /'hand(ə)l/ *n.*[1] OE. [f. HAND *n.* + -LE[1].] **1** A part of a thing by which it is to be held in order to use, move, or carry it. OE. **2** *fig.* A fact or circumstance that may be taken advantage of; an opportunity, a pretext. M16. **3** A thing resembling a handle; *joc.* the nose. M17. **b** (The beer contained in) a glass with a handle; this as a measure of approx. one pint. *NZ colloq.* M20. **4** A title of rank or courtesy. Freq. in *a handle to one's name. colloq.* M19. **b** A name; *spec.* in *Citizens' Band Radio slang*, a call-sign. *slang.* E20.

1 D. LESSING He lifted the handles to propel the cart onwards. H. BASCOM Over his other arm a long umbrella.. hangs by an ornate handle. 2 L. STRACHEY Victoria's retirement gave an unpleasant handle to the argument. *Gainesville Daily Sun* The floodplain.. is vegetated by plants not on the old list, so we don't.. have a good handle on protecting it. 4b M. LAURENCE Got this real classy name. Alvin Gerald Cummings—some handle, eh?

Phrases: **fly** or **go off the handle** lose one's temper. **get a handle on** *colloq.* (chiefly *N. Amer.*) gain control over; acquire an understanding of. *go off the handle*: see *fly off the handle* above. *long handle*: see LONG *a.*[1] **up to the handle** *US colloq.* thoroughly, completely.

handle /'hand(ə)l/ *n.*[2] L19. [f. next.] The feel of goods, esp. textiles, when handled.

Belle (*Australia*) Wool has superior handle and resilience.

handle /'hand(ə)l/ *v.*[1] [OE *handlian* corresp. to OFris. *handelia*, OS *handlon*, OHG *hantalōn* (G *handeln*), ON *hǫndla* seize, treat: see -LE[3].] I Touch, take hold of, etc., with the hand; manage. **1** *v.t.* Touch or feel with the hand or hands; take hold of in or with the hand or hands; use the hands on. OE. **b** *v.i.* Have a specified feel when touched. Now *rare.* E18. **c** *v.t. Football* & *Cricket.* Touch (the ball) in contravention of the rules. L18. **2** *v.t.* Use, operate, manipulate, (a tool, machine, car, etc.) in a controlled manner. ME. **b** *Tanning.* Move (hides) up and down in the tannin infusion in which they are immersed. M19. **c** *v.i.* Of a tool, machine, car, etc.: react or behave in a specified way in response to use, operation, or direction. L19. **3** *v.t.* Manage, direct, control, cope with, (a thing or person). E16. †**b** Conduct *oneself*, behave. M16–M19.

1 G. GREENE I have.. been in the habit of wearing gloves when I handle the notes. B. EMECHETA There was an intrinsic satisfaction in handling and touching natural things. 2 R. HUNTFORD It was also the fastest and the most dangerous sailing ship to handle. A. BURGESS None of us could be trusted to handle a knife and a fork. c *Which?* The car won't handle as well in an emergency. *Shooting Life* The gun handles far too quickly for most people. 3 J. CARY I'd no idea you could handle a crowd like that. L. GOULD Extraordinary niceness in a man was one of those things she couldn't handle. K. ISHIGURO Women can't handle saké.

II Deal with, treat. 4 *v.t.* Deal with in speech or writing, discuss, (a theme, subject, etc.). OE. 5 *v.t.* Deal with; treat; *spec.* act towards in some specified way. ME. **b** Portray or represent (an artistic subject) in a specified way. M16. 6 *v.t.* Trade or deal in (goods). L16.

4 I. WATTS The very same theme may be handled .. in several different methods. 5 C. ODETS The job is to handle him gently. R. K. NARAYAN I had a small lawyer handling my case in the court. *Dumfries Courier* Complaints about new vehicles are handled by the trade association of the motor manufacturers. **b** C. KINGSLEY Our painting is only good when it handles landscapes and animals. 6 J. UPDIKE We only handle silver in the form of pre-'65 silver dollars.

handlea'bility *n.* ease of handling M20. **handleable** *a.* able to be (easily) handled E17.

handle /ˈhand(ə)l/ *v.*[2]*t.* Now *rare* or *obs.* E17. [f. HANDLE *n.*[1]] Provide with a handle.

handlebar /ˈhand(ə)lbɑː/ *n.* L19. [f. HANDLE *n.*[1] + BAR *n.*[1]] *sing.* & (usu.) in *pl.* A transverse bar, freq. curved at each end to form handles (usu. fitted with some form of grip) and fixtures for the brake-levers, connected to the front wheel of a bicycle, motorcycle, etc., and used to steer the vehicle.

DROP-HANDLEBAR(S). *dropped handlebar*: see DROPPED 2.

Comb.: **handlebar moustache** a long heavy moustache with curved ends.

handled /ˈhand(ə)ld/ *a.* L18. [f. HANDLE *n.*[1], *v.*[2]: see -ED[2], -ED[1].] Having a handle, esp. of a specified type or material, as *ivory-*, *long-*, *silver-handled*.

handleless /ˈhand(ə)llɪs/ *a.* L19. [f. HANDLE *n.*[1] + -LESS.] Without a handle.

W. WHARTON She hands me a big handleless cup of tea whenever I come.

handler /ˈhandlə/ *n.*[1] LME. [f. HANDLE *v.*[1] + -ER[1].] I 1 A person who handles esp. something specified. LME. 2 **a** A person who controls and incites a dog or gamecock in a fight. E19. **b** A person who shows the points of a dog at a trial. L19. **c** A person, esp. a police officer, who is in charge of a trained dog. M20. 3 *Boxing.* A person who trains and acts as a second to a boxer. E20.

1 *Times* These specially preposed dies .. are brought together .., the handlers wearing gloves. 2b *National Trust Magazine* Thirty-five collie dogs and their handlers .. competed on the hilly terrain. c N. GORDIMER Alsatian dogs strapped to their handlers kept passers-by back.

II 4 *Tanning.* A pit containing a weak tannin infusion in which hides are handled. L18.

handler /handlə/ *n.*[2] L16. [f. HANDLE *v.*[2] + -ER[1].] A person who fixes a handle to a vessel, tool, etc.

handless /ˈhandlɪs/ *a.* ME. [f. HAND *n.* + -LESS.] 1 Without hands. ME. 2 *fig.* Inept or incompetent, esp. with the hands. Now chiefly *dial.* LME.

2 J. M. BARRIE He is most terribly handless.

hand-off /ˈhandɒf/ *n.* E20. [f. *hand off* s.v. HAND *v.*] 1 *Rugby Football.* The action of pushing off an opponent with the hand. E20. 2 *Amer. Football.* The action or an instance of passing the ball by hand to another team member. M20.

hand-out /ˈhandaʊt/ *n.* L19. [f. *hand out* s.v. HAND *v.*] 1 *Real Tennis, Squash, & Badminton.* The person or side to whom the ball is served. L19. 2 That which is handed out; *spec.* a gift of food, clothes, or money to a beggar or other person in need. L19. 3 A prepared statement given out to the press or some other group of people; *spec.* a circular or pamphlet giving information, guidance, etc. E20.

2 A. T. ELLIS Government hand-outs can never be the same as simple generosity. S. BELLOW Eating your own meal .. is different from a hand-out.

handpass /ˈhan(d)pɑːs/ *n.* & *v.* M20. [f. HAND *n.* + PASS *n.*[2] or *v.*] *Austral. Rules Football.* **A** *n.* An act of handpassing. M20. **B** *v.t.* & *i.* Pass (the ball) by punching it with the fist. M20.

Hand-Schüller-Christian disease /hand ʃʊləˈkrɪstʃ(ə)n dɪziːz/ *n. phr.* M20. [f. Alfred *Hand* (1868–1949), US paediatrician, Artur *Schüller* (1874–1958), Austrian neurologist, and H. A. *Christian* (1876–1951), US physician.] *Med.* A pathological condition, often associated with diabetes insipidus, in which the bones, esp. of the skull, are invaded by lipid-laden histiocytes. Also called *Schüller-Christian('s) disease, syndrome.*

handsel /ˈhans(ə)l/ *n.* & *v.* Also **hansel**. ME. [Corresp. to late OE *handselen* delivery into the hand and ON *handsal* giving of the hand, esp. in a promise or bargain (OSw. *handsal*, Sw. *handsöl* money handed over, gratuity, Da. *handsel* earnest money); ult. f. as HAND *n.* + base of SELL *v.*] **A** *n.* †1 Luck, fortune; a token, omen or indication of (good or bad) luck. ME–L17. 2 A gift supposedly bringing good luck, given to mark the beginning of a new year, a new enterprise, the wearing of new clothes, etc. LME. 3 A first instalment of a payment; the first money taken by a trader in the morning; *gen.* anything given or taken as a pledge of what is to follow. LME. 4 The first use, experience, trial, etc., of anything; a foretaste. L16.

2 H. T. COCKBURN About the New Year .. every child had got its handsel, and every farthing of every handsel was spent there. 4 P. HOLLAND But this Perillus was the first himselfe that gaue the handsell to the engine of his own inuention.

B *v.t.* Infl. **-ll-**. 1 Give handsel to (a person). LME. 2 Inaugurate with some ceremony or gift; *gen.* inaugurate the use of, be the first to use, try, or test. E17.

2 M. DELANY Send in .. wine to your cellar at Welsbourne, by way of hanselling a new place. E. FITZGERALD If my Father's cook arrive .. she shall handsel her skill on my fowl.

handshake /ˈhan(d)ʃeɪk/ *n.* L19. [f. HAND *n.* + SHAKE *n.*] An act of handshaking, esp. in greeting or leave-taking; *fig.* an exchange of standardized signals between devices in a computer network regulating the transfer of data.

E. CRANKSHAW He preferred to surround himself with applauding sycophants, turning others away with a chilly handshake. *golden handshake*: see GOLDEN *a.*

handshake /ˈhan(d)ʃeɪk/ *v.i.* L18. [f. HAND *n.* + SHAKE *v.*] Participate in a handshake (*lit* & *fig.*). Orig. & chiefly as HANDSHAKING.

handshaker *n.* E20.

handshaking /ˈhan(d)ʃeɪkɪŋ/ *vbl n.* L18. [f. HAND *n.* + SHAKING *vbl n.*] The action of shaking hands with a person. Also (*Computing*), an exchange between a computer system and an external device or another computer, indicating that a process can be started after establishment of communication, is running properly, or is complete.

handsome /ˈhans(ə)m/ *a.*, *adv.*, & *n.* LME. [f. HAND *n.* + -SOME[1].] **A** *adj.* 1 †**a** Easy to handle, deal with, or use in any way. LME–L16. **b** Handy, convenient, suitable. Now *rare* exc. *dial.* M16. 2 Of an action, speech, agent, etc.: apt, skilled, clever. Now chiefly *US.* M16. 3 Orig. (of conduct, action, dress, etc.), fitting, proper, becoming. Now (only of conduct or action), generous, magnanimous. L16. 4 Now chiefly of a sum of money, a fortune, etc.: considerable; generous, ample. L16. 5 Of fine, impressive, or stately appearance; (esp. of a man) good-looking, attractive. L16.

2 H. FIELDING He determined to quit her, if he could but find a handsome pretence. 3 B. TARKINGTON George .. was doing .. a handsome thing in taking a risky job for .. his aunt. 4 C. S. FORESTER He had seen to it that the tip was handsome without being extravagant. J. GROSS They offered serious writers .. handsome rates of pay. 5 A. S. NEILL I saw some handsome lads and some pretty girls on that campus. N. MONSARRAT Her face, .. beautiful when young, markedly handsome in old age, betrayed nothing of her feelings. A. MUNRO The apartment and office are in a handsome old brick house.

B *adv.* = HANDSOMELY. Now *rare* exc. as below. LME.

handsome is as handsome does one is judged by behaviour not appearance. *high, wide, and handsome*: see HIGH *adv.*

C *n.* A handsome person. Used chiefly as a form of address. *colloq.* E20.

E. WAUGH Be a sport, handsome: no one's seen anything but you.

handsomeish *a.* (*rare*) somewhat handsome M18. **handsomely** *adv.* (*a*) in a handsome manner; (*b*) (now only *Naut.*) carefully, gradually, without haste: M16. **handsomeness** *n.* M16.

handspaik *n.* var. of HANDSPOKE.

handspike /ˈhan(d)spʌɪk/ *n.* & *v.* E16. [Du. †*handspaeke* (now *-spaak*), f. *hand* HAND *n.* + MDu. *spāke* pole, rod; assim. to SPIKE *n.*[2]] **A** *n.* A wooden lever usu. shod with iron, used chiefly on board ship and in artillery. E16. **B** *v.t.* Move or strike with a handspike. L18.

handspoke /ˈhan(d)spəʊk/ *n.* Chiefly *Sc.* Also **-spaik** /-speɪk/. E18. [f. HAND *n.* + SPOKE *n.*] A spoke or bar of wood held in the hand and used esp. for carrying the coffin at a funeral.

handwork /ˈhandwəːk/ *n.* OE. [f. HAND *n.* + WORK *n.*] †1 = HANDIWORK 1. OE–L19. 2 Working with the hands; work done by the hands, esp. as opp. to work done by or with machinery. OE.

handworked *a.* worked or made by hand not machine E19. **handworker** *n.* a manual worker M19.

handwrite /ˈhandrʌɪt/ *n.* *Sc.*, *Anglo-Ir.*, & *US.* Also (earlier) †**-writ**. ME. [f. HAND *n.* + WRITE *n.*] Handwriting.

handwrite /ˈhandrʌɪt/ *v.t.* Pa. t. **-wrote** /-rəʊt/, pa. pple **-written** /-rɪt(ə)n/. E19. [f. HAND *n.* + WRITE *v.*] Write by hand; write with one's own hand. Chiefly as *handwritten* ppl a.

handwriting /ˈhandrʌɪtɪŋ/ *n.* LME. [f. HAND *n.* + WRITING *n.*: cf. L *manuscriptum*, Gk *kheirographon.*] 1 Writing by hand with a pen or pencil, esp. as done by a particular person or characteristic of a particular country or historical period; *fig.* a distinctive, individually identifiable style of doing something, as painting, designing, etc. LME. 2 That which is written by hand; a written document etc. *arch.* M16.

1 J. MORTIMER Simcox has got such awful handwriting, he's going to copy it out neatly later. J. T. STORY I looked at the page of neat, close-written, feminine handwriting. 2 A. RADCLIFFE Adeline took it up, and opening it perceived a hand-writing.

Comb.: **handwriting expert** a person who studies handwriting in order to detect forgeries etc. or infer aspects of a person's character from his or her style of writing.

handwritten, **-wrote** *vs.* see HANDWRITE *v.*

handy /ˈhandi/ *a.* ME. [f. HAND *n.* + -Y[1]; in sense 2 after HANDIWORK.] 1 Clever with the hands; dexterous. ME. 2 Of or done by the hand; manual. *obs.* exc. *Sc.* M16. 3 Ready to hand, conveniently accessible. Usu. *pred.* M17. 4 Convenient to handle or use. L17.

1 K. GRAHAME I'll teach you to row, and .. swim, and you'll soon be handy on the water. N. PEVSNER The practical, handy, inventive Englishman who rather makes a thing himself than relies on others. 3 R. C. HUTCHINSON One keeps a coin handy for a cab-fare. A. T. ELLIS If .. I'd had a gun handy, I'd've widowed myself more than once. 4 A. CHRISTIE And I remember picking up the Mauser—it was a nice handy little gun.

Phrases: **come in handy** be (occasionally) useful. **handy for** *colloq.* conveniently situated for. **handy to** *dial.* & *N. Amer.* = *handy for* above.

Comb.: **handy-billy** *Naut.* a small tackle with one double and one single block which can multiply the power exerted by four times when required; **handyman** a person able to do various odd jobs esp. in house or building maintenance; **handy-sized** *a.* of a convenient size.

handycuffs *n.pl.* var. of HANDICUFFS.

handy-dandy /ˈhandɪdandi/ *n.* & *adv.* LME. [Redupl. rhyme f. HANDY *a.*] **A** *n.* †1 A covert bribe or present. Only in LME. 2 A children's game in which one player guesses which of the other players' hands conceals some object. Also as *int.*, the call offering the choice between the two hands. L16. **B** *adv.* †1 With bribery or other covert payment. Only in LME. 2 With change of places; alternately. Long *rare.* E16.

handygrip *n.* var. of HANDGRIP.

handy-work *n.* see HANDIWORK.

hanepoot /ˈhɑːnəpʊət/ *n.* *S. Afr.* L18. [Afk., f. Du. *haan* cock + *poot* foot.] 1 A variety of sweet muscat grape, often used for making wine or raisins. L18. 2 A sweet white wine made from these grapes. E19.

hang /haŋ/ *n.* L18. [f. the vb.] **1** The way in which a thing (esp. a garment) hangs or is poised. L18. **b** The hanging of pictures, esp. for an exhibition. M20. **2** The action of hanging, drooping, or bending down. Also, a downward inclination, a droop; a declivity. E19. **b** A slackening or suspension of motion. M19. **3** Something that hangs or is suspended, esp. a crop of fruit. E19. **4** A negligible amount. Chiefly in *not* (*care, give*) *a hang* below. *colloq.* M19.

1 A. BROOKNER The minute adjustments to .. the hang of a skirt. 2 LEIGH HUNT Never shall I forget her face .. with that weary hang of the head on one side. 3 A. JOBSON She had .. a nice hang of apples. 4 V. WOOLF They don't care a hang for the upper classes.

Phrases: **get the hang of** *colloq.* become familiar with the use of (a tool etc.); *fig.* come to understand or manage, get the knack of. **hang of a** *a.* & *adv.* (*Austral.* & *NZ colloq.*); (*a*) *adj. a* terrible, *a* big; (*b*) *adv.* terribly, extremely. **like hang** *Austral.* & *NZ colloq.* exceedingly. **not** (**care, give**) **a hang** *colloq.* not (care) at all.

hang /haŋ/ *v.* Pa. t. & pple **hung** /hʌŋ/, (*arch.* exc. in sense 2) **hanged**. [OE *hangian* v.i. = OFris. *hangia*, OS *hangon*, OHG *hangēn* (Du., G *hangen*), f. a WGmc wk vb; partly f. ON *hanga* v.t. = OE *hōn*, OFris. *hūa*, OS, OHG *hāhan*, Goth. *hāhan*, f. a Gmc redupl. vb.] **I** *v.t.* **1** Support or suspend (a thing) from above, allowing it otherwise to take the position determined by gravity or any external force; fasten or attach to an object above. OE. **b** Suspend (meat) in the air to mature or dry. L16. **2** Orig., crucify. Later, kill by suspending by the neck, esp. as a form of capital punishment; *colloq.* in imprecations as *hang it* (*all*), *hang me*, etc., expr. anger, contempt, irritation, etc. (cf. DAMN *v.* 3). OE. **b** *refl.* Commit suicide by suspending oneself by the neck. ME. **3** Cause or allow to droop, bend downward, or lean over. Freq. in *hang one's head* below. OE. **b** *Surfing.* Allow (a specified number of toes) to project beyond the nose of the surfboard. M20. **4** Attach so as to allow free movement about the point of attachment; attach in a well-balanced or poised position. LME. **5** Decorate or provide *with* (things suspended or fastened on); *esp.* attach (wallpaper) to a wall. Also, furnish (a gallery etc.) with pictures. Freq. in *pass.* LME. **6** Reduce to or keep in a state of indecision or inaction. Freq. in *hang a jury* below. Chiefly *US.* L18. **7** Catch or fasten in something; *esp.* hitch up (a horse). Chiefly *US.* M19.

1 P. MORTIMER In the next garden but one, a woman was hanging washing on the line. G. CHARLES Where did we finally decide to hang those two Broidal portraits ..? **b** J. GRIGSON Their butchers .. choose good animals, hang them properly and cut and present the meat well. 2 J. ARBUTHNOT Part with my country-seat .. I'll see him hanged first. R. S. SURTEES 'Hang the rain!' exclaimed Jawleyford. *Observer* I am hanged if I will ask a woman to offload 30 tons of peat. J. CARY This unsavoury Lothario killed his paramour .. ran away to London, was .. arrested and duly hanged. **b** W. LOWTHER You may regard it as only giving them rope to hang themselves! 4 W. WHARTON I build and hang the door. 5 *Listener* The National Gallery is most beautifully hung now. J. RATHBONE The walls were not hung with painted paper but whitewashed. 6 *Guardian* The lone juror who finally hangs the jury will not emerge .. unless .. his view has some support.

II *v.i.* **8** Be or remain fastened or suspended from above; dangle; swing loose. OE. **b** Be decorated or furnished with things suspended or attached. LME. **c** Of meat: be suspended in the air to mature or dry. M19. **9** Orig., be crucified. Later, be killed by being suspended by the neck, esp. as a form of capital punishment. OE. **b** In imprecations expr. anger, irritation, displeased surprise, etc. Esp. in *go hang* below. *colloq.* E17. **10** Lean or project (*over*); bend forward or downward. OE. **11** Rely *on* for support or authority; depend *on*, be dependent *on*. Also (now *rare* or *obs.*), remain or rely in faith or expectation, count confidently *on*. OE. **b** Consider attentively; listen with rapt attention. Freq. in *hang on a person's lips* or *words* below. ME. **12** Be attached or suspended so as to allow free movement or attachment; be attached in a well-balanced or poised position. ME. **13** Appear to be suspended; rest or float (in air etc.). ME. **b** *fig.* Esp. of something unpleasant: hover *over*, ready to fall; impend, be imminent. M16. **14** Attach oneself, esp. for support, cling (*up*)*on*; adhere, stick *on*, *to*, etc.; *arch.* be a hanger-on or dependant. ME. **b** Of the wind: remain persistently in a certain point of the compass. L17. **15** Cling or adhere as an encumbrance; (esp. of time) be a burden. LME. **16** Be or remain in suspense; be doubtful or undecided. LME. †**b** Remain unsettled or unfinished. L15–E18. **c** Of a jury: be unable to reach a verdict because of disagreement. Chiefly *US.* M19. **17** Of (a note in) music: be prolonged. L16. **18** Slacken motion perceptibly (esp. in *Cricket* & *Baseball*); remain with motion suspended. M17. **19** Stay as unwilling or unable to leave or move on, freq. as a parasitical attachment; loiter, linger, wait, *about*, *around*, etc. M19. **20** Of a horse: veer to one side. M20.

8 J. BUCHAN A flagstaff from which an enormous Union Jack hung limply in the still air. S. BARSTOW A suit hangs well on him when he lets it. DAY LEWIS A photograph that .. used to hang in dark corners or passages of the houses we occupied. 9 G. GREENE I found Marcel hanging from his own belt from the centre light. 10 E. A. FREEMAN The later castle, whose picturesque turrets and battlements hang so proudly over the river. *fig.*: S. ROGERS O'er infant innocence to hang and weep. 11 T. HARDY Everything now hung upon their mother's assent. J. BUCHAN My neck's safety was to hang on my own wits. **b** *Times Lit. Suppl.* Desdemona .. hung on to every detail in Othello's narrative. 12 C. PHILLIPS The gate still hung drunkenly from its hinges. 13 V. BRITTAIN The harvest moon hung like a Chinese lantern in the sky. **b** *fig.*: H. NICOLSON The dread of the ordeal .. had been hanging over me like a sullen cloud. R. INGALLS They ought to get rid of the duties first, so as not to have them hanging over their heads. 14 SHAKES. *Tam. Shr.* She hung about my neck, and kiss on kiss she vied so fast. I. MCEWAN. I hang on to the side of the boat. E. FEINSTEIN She hung on to her job for five and a half months. *fig.*: W. SOMERVILLE The patient Pack Hang on the Scent unweary'd. 15 SHELLEY Most heavy remorse hangs at my heart. W. PIKE Time did not hang at all heavily. 16 G. GREENE I hung between life and death .. for exactly five days. 19 H. JAMES He hung about, .. took up the time of busy people. W. SOYINKA The occasional kind-hearted guard who would .. let him hang outside for a while. R. INGALLS Trouble-maker .. who had the money and the time to hang around getting drunk.

Phrases, & with advs. & preps. in specialized senses: *every herring should hang by its own head*: see HERRING *n.* **go hang** *colloq.* go to hell; be dismissed or rejected. **hang about** loiter about, not move away or disperse. **hang a jury** (chiefly *US*) prevent a jury by disagreement from reaching a verdict. **hang a left, a right**, etc. (orig. *US*) turn left, right, etc. **hang around** = *hang about* above. *hang as high as* HAMAN. **hang back** resist advance esp. by inertia; show reluctance to act or move, keep to the rear. **hang by a hair, thread**, etc. (of a person's life etc.) be in a precarious state; be determinable either way by something still in doubt. **hang fire** (of a firearm) be slow in going off; *fig.* be delayed in action. **hang heavy** or **heavily** (of time) pass slowly. **hang in** *colloq.* (chiefly *N. Amer.*) persist in spite of adversity, hold out. *hang in the balance*: see BALANCE *n.* *hang it* (*all*): see sense 2 above. **hang it up** *slang* give credit. **hang loose** *colloq.* be casual or unconcerned. *hang me* etc.: see sense 2 above. **hang off** (*a*) *arch.* let go; (*b*) hesitate, hang back. **hang on** (*a*) linger, esp. with reluctance or inability to leave, wait for a short time (freq. as *imper.*, be patient! be reasonable!), *colloq.* (in telephoning) not ring off; (*b*) see sense 11 above; (*c*) attend closely to; (*d*) *hang on a person's lips* or *words*, listen attentively to a person; (*e*) stick or hold closely (*to*); (*f*) remain in office, stick to duty etc.; (*g*) *hang on to* (colloq.) retain, not let go of. **hang one on** (**someone**) *colloq.* deal (someone) a blow. **hang one's head** show shame, embarrassment, or despondency by letting one's head droop forward. **hang out** (*a*) (cause to) protrude downwards; *let it all hang out* (slang), be uninhibited; (*b*) suspend (a sign, colours, etc.) from a window on a projecting pole etc.; (*c*) suspend (washing etc.) from a clothes-line etc. outside (*to dry*); *hang one's bat out to dry* (Cricket), play an indecisive defensive stroke at a ball outside off stump, either missing or edging the ball; (*d*) *slang* reside, be often present; associate *with*; (*e*) (chiefly *Austral.* & *NZ*) endure, hold out. *hang the rap on*: see RAP *n.*[1] **hang together** (*a*) stick or adhere together loosely; (*b*) be coherent or consistent; make a coherent or consistent whole; (*c*) be associated, united, or mutually dependent; (of a person) keep body and soul together, survive. **hang up** (*a*) suspend (a garment, utensil, etc.) from a hook, rail, etc.; freq. in *hang up one's boots*, give up playing a sport, *hang up one's fiddle* (see FIDDLE *n.*), *hang up one's hat*, make one's home, *hang up one's sword, gun*, etc., lay aside, give up using, one's sword, gun, etc.; (*b*) (of a garment, utensil, etc.) be suspended from a hook, rail, etc.; (*c*) put aside, postpone indefinitely, hinder; (*d*) *Austral.* hitch up (a horse); (*e*) end a telephone conversation with someone (freq. foll. by *on*); (*f*) replace (a telephone receiver); (*g*) cause delay or difficulty or (*slang*, freq. in *pass.*) obsession to. *let it all hang out*: see *hang out* above.

Comb.: **hang-by** (*obs.* exc. *dial.*) (*a*) *derog.* a dependant, a hanger-on; (*b*) an appendage, an adjunct; **hang-fire** a delay in the igniting of a firearm or a blasting-charge; **hang-glider** a small glider from which the operator is suspended in a frame and which is controlled by movements of the body; **hang-gliding** the operation of a hang-glider, esp. as a sport; **hang-out** *slang* a place of residence or frequent visitation; **hang-up** a difficulty, an obsession, an inhibition.

hangable *a.* able or liable to be hanged; *esp.* (of an offence) punishable by hanging: L16. **hangworthy** *a.* (*rare*) worthy of being hanged L16.

hangar /ˈhaŋə/ *n.* L17. [Fr., of unkn. origin.] A shed, a shelter. Now *spec.*, a building for housing aircraft, spacecraft, etc.

¶ Rare bef. M19.

hangarage /ˈhaŋərɪdʒ/ *n.* M20. [f. HANGAR + -AGE] Accommodation for aircraft etc. in a hangar.

hangbird /ˈhaŋbəːd/ *n.* *N. Amer.* L18. [f. HANG *v.* + BIRD *n.*] A bird which builds a hanging nest; *esp.* the northern oriole *Icterus galbula*.

hangdog /ˈhaŋdɒɡ/ *n.* & *a.* L17. [f. HANG *v.* + DOG *n.*] **A** *n.* A despicable or degraded fellow; a sneaking shamefaced person. L17.

B *attrib.* or as *adj.* Of, pertaining to, or characteristic of a hangdog; degraded; sneaking, shamefaced, guilty; dejected. L17.

S. T. WARNER I am feeling hangdog and apprehensive. E. BLISHEN The headmaster was addressing a hangdog group of boys.

hanger /ˈhaŋə/ *n.*[1] [OE *hangra* deriv. of HANG *v.*: now identified with next.] A wood on the side of a steep hill or bank.

hanger /ˈhaŋə/ *n.*[2] LME. [f. HANG *v.* + -ER[1].] **1** A person who hangs (someone or something); *spec.*: **a** A person who kills or causes another to be killed by hanging, esp. as a form of capital punishment; one who advocates this. LME. **b** A person who causes a thing to be suspended or fastened on; *spec.* one who selects and hangs pictures for an exhibition. L18. **2** Something that hangs down or is suspended. LME. **3** A device by or on which something is hung; a support. E16. **b** A loop or strap on a sword-belt for hanging the sword from. *obs.* exc. *Hist.* L16. **c** A chain or rod in a fireplace for suspending a pot or kettle from by means of a pot-hook. Also, (a child's name for) a stroke with a double curve made in learning to write (chiefly in *pot-hooks and hangers*). L16. **d** A loop by which something, esp. a garment, is hung up. L17. **e** A coat-hanger. L19. **4** Something that overhangs; *Mining* the rock over a lode or vein. M17.

1a I. MCEWAN He decided to speak against the hangers in the annual punishment debate. 3 J. S. FOSTER Floor joists .. should preferably not be supported by metal hangers. *coat-hanger*. **e** P. ROTH Then from a hanger she took down a plaid hooded jacket.

Comb.: **hanger-back** a person who hangs back; **hanger-on** (freq. *derog.*) a follower, a dependant.

hanger /ˈhaŋə/ *n.*[3] LME. [Prob. identical with prec.: cf. early mod.Du. *hangher*, perh. the immediate source.] *Hist.* A type of short sword, orig. hung from the belt.

hangi /ˈhaŋi, ˈhɑːŋi/ *n.* Chiefly *NZ.* M19. [Maori.] An earth-oven in which food is cooked on heated stones; the food cooked in such an oven.

hangie /ˈhaŋi/ *n.* *Sc.* (now chiefly *arch.*). E18. [f. HANG *v.* + -IE.] A hangman; a worthless person. Also, the devil.

hanging /ˈhaŋɪŋ/ *n.* ME. [f. HANG *v.* + -ING[1].] **1** The action or an instance of hanging a person (esp. as a form of capital punishment); the fact of being hanged. ME. 2 The action of suspending; the fact of being suspended; suspension. LME. 3 Something that hangs or is suspended, *esp.* (usu. in *pl.*), tapestries etc. with which walls etc. are hung; something attached, an appendage. LME. 4 A downward slope or curve; *esp.* (now *local*) a steep slope or declivity of a hill. LME. 5 The state of being in suspense, left aside, or waiting for some time. M17.

3 J. S. FOSTER Solid wall covered externally with slate, tile or other hanging. A. S. BYATT The room had no character, and dark green silk hangings.

Comb.: **hanging committee**: to decide the hanging of pictures in an exhibition; **hanging day**: on which judicial hangings are carried out; **hanging matter** a matter likely to result in severe punishment; a serious matter; **hanging wardrobe**: designed for clothes hanging at full length.

hanging /'haŋɪŋ/ *a.* ME. [f. HANG *v.* + -ING².] 1 Leaning over; overhanging; steep, declivitous; *esp.* (of a wood, garden, etc.) so situated as to (appear to) hang. ME. †2 Remaining in suspense or abeyance; pending. LME–L16. 3 Supported or suspended from above; projecting downward; drooping. L15. 4 Gloomy or depressed-looking. L16. 5 That causes (people) to be hanged. Chiefly in *hanging judge* below. M19.

Special collocations: **hanging basket** a suspended basket or other container for growing decorative plants. **hanging bird** = HANGBIRD. **hanging bowl** *Archaeol.* a metal bowl of the Bronze Age or Anglo-Saxon period designed to be suspended. **hanging drop** a drop of liquid containing living cells or organisms, suspended from a cover glass to allow viewing in a microscope. **hanging glacier** a small glacier on a steep slope, from whose lower end ice may occasionally fall. **hanging guard** *Fencing* (chiefly *Hist.*) a type of defence. **hanging indent(at)ion** *Typogr.* the indentation of all lines but the first of a paragraph. **hanging judge** a judge who habitually sentences harshly, *esp.* one who is predisposed towards sentencing to death. **hanging lie** *Golf* the position of a ball lying on ground sloping downhill in the direction of play. **hanging paragraph** = *hanging indent(at)ion* above. **hanging pawn** *Chess* either of two advanced pawns, side by side with no adjacent pawns to support them. **hanging shelf** a suspended shelf. **hanging sleeve** a loose open sleeve hanging down from the arm, formerly worn by children. **hanging valley**: that is cut across by the side of a deeper valley (esp. one enlarged by glaciation) or by a sea-cliff. **hanging wall** (*a*) *Mining* the rock which hangs over a lode; (*b*) *Geol.* the fault block which lies above an inclined fault.

hangman /'haŋmən/ *n.* Pl. **-men.** ME. [f. HANG *v.* + MAN *n.*] 1 An executioner, *esp.* one who executes by hanging. Also, a worthless person. ME. 2 A word-game for two or more players, in which a tally of failed guesses is kept by drawing a gallows one stroke at a time. M20.

hangmanlike *a.* & *adv.* (*rare*) (in the manner) of a hangman L17. **hangmanship** *n.* (*rare*) the office or function of hangman E19.

hangment /'haŋm(ə)nt/ *n. obs.* exc. *dial.* LME. [f. HANG *v.* + -MENT.] Hanging; execution.

who, what, etc., **the hangment**: expr. surprise.

hangnail /'haŋneɪl/ *n.* L17. [Alt. of AGNAIL.] A piece of torn skin at the root of a fingernail or toenail; soreness resulting from this.

hang-nest /'haŋnɛst/ *n. N. Amer.* Now *rare.* L17. [f. HANG *v.* + NEST *n.*] A hangbird.

hangover /'haŋəʊvə/ *n.* L19. [f. HANG *v.* + OVER *adv.*] 1 A person or thing remaining, left over or behind; a remainder, a survival; an after-effect. L19. 2 *spec.* A set of unpleasant after-effects of (esp. alcoholic) overindulgence. E20. 3 *Electr.* Delay in the cessation of output, esp. of a loudspeaker. M20.

1 L. DENNY That easily inspired hatred of Germany remained as a hang-over in America. 2 P. PARISH Even moderate amounts of alcohol, and even a slight hangover, impair driving ability.

Hang Seng /haŋ 'sɛŋ/ *a.* M20. [A bank in Hong Kong.] Designating an index of selected securities on the Hong Kong Stock Exchange.

hangul /'haŋgʊl/ *n.*¹ M19. [Kashmiri *hãngul.*] A red deer, *Cervus elaphus*, of the Kashmiri subspecies.

hangul /'haŋgʊl/ *n.*² M20. [Korean, f. *Han* Korea + *kul* script, alphabet.] The Korean phonetic alphabet. Also called *onmun.*

hanif /ha'ni:f/ *n.* Also **haneef.** M18. [Arab. *hanīf*, an epithet applied to Abraham in the Koran.] Among Muslims, a follower of the original and true (monotheistic) religion.

haniwa /'hanɪwə/ *n.* Pl. same. M20. [Jap.] *Archaeol.* A clay image based on a cylindrical shape of a type placed outside Japanese tombs of the 5th to 7th cent.

hanjar, hanjee *ns.* vars. of KHANJAR, KHANJEE.

hank /haŋk/ *n.* ME. [ON *hǫnk*, genit. *hankar* (cf. *hanki* hasp, clasp; Sw. *hank* hank, withy-band, farrier's rowel, Da. *hank* handle, ear of a pot).] 1 A (circular) loop or coil of something flexible. ME. **b** A skein or coil of yarn, thread, etc.; *spec.* a definite length of cotton yarn (840 yards), worsted (560 yards), etc. E16. 2 A loop of string, wire, etc., used to fasten things together or hang a thing up; *spec.* a fastening for a gate. Chiefly *dial.* ME. **b** *Naut.* A hoop or ring of rope, iron, etc., for securing staysails to stays. E18. 3 The handle of a jug or pot. *dial.* M16. 4 A restraining hold, a power of restraint. Freq. in *have a hank on* or *over someone.* Now *rare* or *dial.* E17. 5 A propensity, an evil habit. Chiefly *dial.* E18. †6 A baiting of an animal. *slang.* L18–L19.

hank /haŋk/ *v.* ME. [ON *hanka* to coil, f. *hǫnk*: see prec. Sense 2 perh. f. as HANKER.] 1 *v.t.* Fasten by a loop; catch by a loop etc. (now *dial.*); *Naut.* fasten (staysails) to stays. ME. 2 *v.i.* = HANKER *v.* Now *dial.* L16. 3 *v.i.* Hang or remain fastened; catch. E17. 4 *v.t.* Make up (yarn etc.) in hanks. E19. †5 *v.t.* Bait (an animal). *slang.* Only in 19.

hanker /'haŋkə/ *v.* & *n.* E17. [Prob. rel. to HANG *v.*: cf. synon. Du. *hunkeren*, dial. *hankeren.* Cf. HANK *v.* 2.] **A** *v.i.* 1 Linger or loiter *about* in longing or expectation. Now *dial.* E17. 2 Have a longing or craving *after, for, to do.* E17.

1 JOYCE He hankered about the coffee-houses and low taverns. 2 SAKI Instead of the news she was hankering for, she had to listen to trivial gossip. N. MOSLEY The hankering after small boys seldom got beyond . . loitering romantically in passageways.

B *n.* A hankering. *rare.* E19.

hankerer *n.* M19. **hankering** *n.* (*a*) the action of the vb; (*b*) a craving, a longing: M17.

hanksite /'haŋksʌɪt/ *n.* L19. [f. H. G. *Hanks* (1826–1907), US mineralogist + -ITE¹.] *Min.* A hexagonal sulphate and carbonate of sodium, also containing potassium and chloride, occurring as white or yellow prisms.

†Hankton *n.* see YANKTON.

hanky /'haŋki/ *n. nursery* & *colloq.* Also **-kie.** L19. [Contr.: see -Y⁶, -IE.] A handkerchief.

hanky-panky /haŋkɪ'paŋki/ *n.* M19. [Rel. to HOCUS-POCUS, perh. with a suggestion of 'sleight of hand'.] Orig., juggling, conjuring. Later, trickery, underhand dealing; questionable behaviour, esp. surreptitious or illicit sexual activity.

E. H. YATES If there was any hanky-panky, any mystery I mean. *New Yorker* They were still 'courting' . . in Dr. Rounds' boarding house . . where . . no hanky-panky was permitted.

Hannibal /'hanɪb(ə)l/ *n.* Long *rare* or *obs.* L16. [*Hannibal* (247–182 BC), Carthaginian general.] A great general.

Hannibalic /hanɪ'balɪk/ *a.* L17. [f. prec. + -IC.] Of, pertaining to, or characteristic of Hannibal.

Hanoverian /hanə(ʊ)'vɪərɪən/ *a.* & *n.* E18. [f. *Hanover*, a N. German State, an electorate of the Empire ruled by the Guelph dynasty and subsequently a province of Prussia, or the N. German town of the same name, capital of Lower Saxony and formerly capital of the State of Hanover: see -IAN.] **A** *adj.* Of, pertaining to, or characteristic of (the House of) Hanover, the dynasty of British monarchs from George I (Elector of Hanover) to Victoria, reigning in the period 1714–1901. E18. **B** *n.* A native or inhabitant of Hanover; a member or an adherent of the House of Hanover. L18.

Hans /hans/ *n.* M16. [G & Du. abbrev. of *Johannes* John.] (A name for) a German, a Dutchman.

Hansard /'hansɑːd, -səd/ *n.*¹ ME. [f. HANSE + -ARD.] A merchant or citizen of a Hanseatic town.

Hansard /'hansɑːd, -səd/ *n.*² L19. [L. *Hansard*, Eng. printer (1752–1828): see below.] The official (verbatim) report of the proceedings of the British Parliament, (compiled by Messrs Hansard 1774–1892, now published by HMSO). Also, the official report of certain other legislative bodies.

Hansardize *v.t.* (now *rare*) confront (a member of Parliament) with his former statements recorded in Hansard; prove (a person) to have expressed a different opinion previously: M19.

Hanse /hans/ *n.*¹ Also **h-.** ME. [MLG *hanshūs* and med.L *hansa* f. OHG *hansa*, (M)HG *hanse* (whence MLG *hanse*) = OE *hōs* (instr. only) troop, company, Goth. *hansa* company, crowd, f. Gmc, whence also Finn. *kansa* people, company.] *Hist.* 1 A merchant guild. ME. **b** *spec.* (A merchant, citizen, or town of) the Hanseatic League. LME. 2 A membership fee payable to a merchant guild; a trading fee imposed on non-members of the guild. ME.

Comb.: **Hanse-house** a guildhall; **Hanse town** a town of the Hanseatic League.

hanse *n.*² var. of HANCE.

Hanseatic /hansɪ'atɪk/ *a.* E17. [med.L *Hanseaticus*, f. as HANSE *n.*¹ + -ATIC.] *Hist.* Designating, of, or pertaining to a political and commercial league of N. Germanic towns, established in the mid 14th cent.

hansel *n.* & *v.* var. of HANDSEL *n.* & *v.*

Hansen /'hans(ə)n/ *n.* E20. [G. H. A. *Hansen* (1841–1912), Norw. physician.] *Med.* 1 *Hansen('s) bacillus*, the causative agent of Hansen's disease, *Mycobacterium leprae.* E20. 2 *Hansen's disease*, a chronic bacterial disease of low infectivity, confined mainly to the tropics, affecting the skin, nerves, and mucous membranes and causing numbness, discoloration and lumps on the skin, and, in severe cases, disfigurement and deformity (now the most usual condition referred to as *leprosy*). M20.

hansom /'hans(ə)m/ *n.* M19. [Joseph Aloysius *Hansom* (1803–82) architect, who registered a Patent Safety Cab in 1834.] Chiefly *Hist.* In full *hansom cab.* A two-wheeled cabriolet for two inside, with the driver mounted behind and the reins going over the roof.

†hanster *n.* var. of HANASTER.

hantle /'hant(ə)l/ *n. Sc.* & *north.* L17. [Origin unkn.] A (large) number or quantity.

hantu /'hantuː/ *n.* E19. [Malay.] An evil spirit; a ghost etc.

Hanukkah /'hanʊkə, x-/ *n.* Also **Chanuk(k)ah** /'xan-/. L19. [Heb. *ḥănukkāh* consecration.] A Jewish festival, commemorating the purification and rededication of the Temple at Jerusalem in 165 BC by Judas Maccabaeus after its pollution by the Syrians. Also *festival of lights.*

Hanuman /hʌnʊ'mɑːn/ *n.* In sense 2 now usu. **h-.** E19. [Skt *hanumant*, nom. *hanumān* large-jawed.] 1 *Hindu Mythol.* (The name of) a semi-divine being represented as resembling a monkey with extraordinary powers. E19. 2 A common grey monkey of India, *Presbytis entellus*, venerated by Hindus. Also *hanuman langur.* M19.

hào /haʊ/ *n.* Pl. same, **-s.** M20. [Vietnamese.] A monetary unit of Vietnam, equal to one-tenth of a dong.

haoma *n.* var. of HOM.

haori /'hɑːɒri/ *n.* L19. [Jap.] In Japan, a short loose coat.

hap /hap/ *n. arch.* ME. [ON *happ* rel. to OE *ġehæp(lič)* fitting, convenient, orderly.] 1 The fortune (good or bad) that falls to a person; one's lot. ME. 2 A fortuitous occurrence, a happening; *esp.* an unfortunate event, a mischance. ME. †3 Success, prosperity, good fortune. ME–E19. 4 Chance considered as determining events. ME.

1 W. WARING It has not been my hap to meet with it elsewhere. 2 GEO. ELIOT All the 'haps' of my life are so indifferent. 4 *Quiver* By curious hap . . [she] was actually located at 'The Beeches'. **by** or **through hap** casually, by chance.

hap /hap/ *v.*[1]*i. arch.* & *dial.* Infl. **-pp-**. Pa. t. & pple **happed, hapt**. ME. [f. the n.: superseded by HAPPEN *v.*] 1 Of an event etc.: come about by chance. (Freq. w. impers. subj.; formerly also w. person affected as indirect obj.) ME. 2 Have the fortune or luck *to do*. LME. 3 Foll. by *on, upon*: meet with or find by chance. LME. †4 Have luck of a specified kind; fare (*well, ill*, etc.). LME–E17.

1 TENNYSON Never had huger slaughter of heroes . . Hapt in this isle. 2 J. GAY A maiden fine bedight he hapt to love. 3 A. B. GROSART [This book] I have not been fortunate enough to hap upon.

hap /hap/ *v.*[2]*t.* Now only *Sc.* & *dial.* Infl. **-pp-**. ME. [Prob. of Scand. origin] Cover; *esp.* cover with bedclothes or extra clothing, wrap up warmly, (foll. by *up*.).

hapax /'hapaks/ *n.* M20. [Abbrev.] = HAPAX LEGOMENON.

hapaxanthic /hapak'sanθɪk/ *a.* L19. [f. Gk *hapax* once + *anthein* to flower + -IC.] *Bot.* Of a plant: flowering and fruiting only once in its life; monocarpic.

Also **hapaxanthous** *a.* E20.

hapax legomenon /hapaks lɛ'gɒmənɒn/ *n. phr.* Pl. **hapax legomena** /-mənə/. M17. [Gk = (a thing) said only once.] A word, form, etc., of which only one recorded instance is known.

¶Used in Greek characters until L19.

haphazard /hap'hazəd/ *n., a.,* & *adv.* L16. [f. HAP *n.* + HAZARD *n.*, lit. 'hazard of chance'.] **A** *n.* 1 Mere chance, fortuitousness. Chiefly in *at* or *by haphazard*. L16. †2 A matter of chance. L16–L17.

1 *Spectator* The . . hereditary principle, with all its necessary haphazard.

B *adj.* Occurring, put together, etc., casually or without design; random. L17.

S. BELLOW It was a shuffle, all, all accidental and haphazard. K. MOORE The haphazard ways of the household harassed her.

C *adv.* Casually, at random. M19.

F. HARRISON This new social system did not come hap-hazard.

haphazardly *adv.* L19. **haphazardness** *n.* M19. **haphazardry** *n.* haphazard quality E20.

haphtarah /hɑːftɑː'rɑː/ *n.* Also **haf-, haphtorah** /hɑːf'təʊrə/. Pl. **-rot(h)** /-rəʊt/. E18. [Heb. *hap̄ṭārāh* lit. 'dismissal', f. *pāṭar* dismiss (because this once marked the end of the service).] *Judaism*. A lesson from one of the Former or Latter Prophets, read in synagogues after the parashah (the reading from the Law).

hapless /'haplɪs/ *a.* LME. [f. HAP *n.* + -LESS.] Ill-starred, luckless.

W. BOYD The Maseru hunt took off after some hapless hyena.

haplessly *adv.* E17.

haplo- /'hapləʊ/ *comb. form* of Gk *haploos* single, simple: see -O-. Cf. DIPLO-.

haplophase *n.* (*Biol.*) the phase of an organism's life cycle in which its cells are haploid E20.

haplography /hap'lɒgrəfi/ *n.* L19. [f. HAPLO- + -GRAPHY.] *Palaeogr.* The inadvertent writing of a letter, word, etc., once, when it should have been repeated. Opp. *dittography*.

haploid /'haplɔɪd/ *a.* & *n.* E20. [f. Gk *haploos* single + -OID.] *Biol.* **A** *adj.* (Of a cell) containing a single set of unpaired chromosomes, as in a gamete; (of an individual) composed of haploid cells; *Bot.* gametophytic. E20. **B** *n.* A haploid organism, a gametophyte. E20.

haploidy *n.* haploid condition E20.

haplology /hap'lɒlədʒi/ *n.* L19. [f. HAPLO- + -LOGY.] The utterance of one letter, syllable, or word instead of two (as *idolatry* for *idololatry*).

haplont /'haplɒnt/ *n.* E20. [f. HAPLOID + -ONT.] Chiefly *Bot.* A sexually reproducing organism at a stage in its life cycle when it is haploid; an organism which is haploid throughout its life except as a zygote.

ha'plontic *a.* E20.

haply /'hapli/ *adv.* Now *arch.* & *dial.* LME. [f. HAP *n.* + -LY[2].] By any chance; perhaps.

AV *Mark* 11:13 Hee came, if haply hee might find any thing thereon.

happen /'hap(ə)n/ *v.i.* LME. [f. HAP *n.* + -EN[5], superseding HAP *v.*[1]] 1 Of an event, experience, etc.: come about, occur. (Foll. by *to* the person or thing affected; also (*obs.* exc. *dial.*) with indirect obj.) LME. **b** With impers. subj.: occur, be the situation (*that*). LME. **c** Occur or come into existence by pure chance or spontaneously. M20. 2 Have the (good or bad) fortune *to do*. LME. 3 With pred. adj. or phr.: chance to be. *obs.* exc. *dial.* LME. 4 Foll. by *on, upon*: find or meet with by chance. M16. 5 Foll. by *along, around, by, in, into, over*, etc.: come or turn up in a place casually or as if by chance. Now chiefly *N. Amer.* M16. †6 Foll. by *to, unto*: fall to the lot of. L16–M18. 7 Of music, a player, etc.: succeed, come off, be effective, make an impression. *slang*. M20.

1 H. NELSON If anything happens to me, recollect that death is a debt we must all pay. E. S. BARRETT No harm shall happen you. G. VIDAL When we crossed into Gael, an interesting thing happened. P. ROTH I'm not someone who makes miracles happen. **b** T. BLOUNT Some of their party . . might quarter at the house (as had often hapned). W. CATHER It happened that none of the Captain's closest friends could come to his funeral. **c** L. MACNEICE As for my supporting symbols, they happened; I did not usually look for them. 2 G. GREENE He happened to be at the airport when they arrived. **do you happen to, you don't happen to** (in tentative requests), is it possible that you (have, know, etc.). 3 SIR W. SCOTT It's the only book thou canst not happen wrong in. 5 R. FROST I go nowhere on purpose: I happen by. P. MATTHIESSEN I . . set out binoculars in case wild creatures should happen into view. 6 J. WHITGIFT If temporal dominion or possession happen to the minister of the gospel. 7 *Down Beat* They were all trying to create . . but it didn't really happen.

happen /'hap(ə)n/ *adv. north.* & *Sc.* L15. [f. the vb.] It may be that; possibly, perhaps.

happenchance /'hap(ə)ntʃɑːns/ *n.* Chiefly *US*. M20. [Blend of HAPPENING and CHANCE *n.*] = HAPPENSTANCE.

happening /'hap(ə)nɪŋ/ *n.* & *a.* LME. [f. HAPPEN *v.* + -ING[1].] **A** *n.* 1 Occurrence (*of* an event). Formerly, chance. LME. 2 A (significant or unusual) event or occurrence. L16. 3 An improvised or spontaneous theatrical display, demonstration, etc. M20. **B** *attrib.* or as *adj.* Eventful, significant; fashionable. *slang*. L20.

happen-so /'hap(ə)nsəʊ/ *n.* Chiefly *US*. E20. [f. HAPPEN *v.* + SO *adv.*] A chance event.

happenstance /'hap(ə)nstans/ *n.* Chiefly *N. Amer.* L19. [Blend of HAPPENING and CIRCUMSTANCE *n.*] Chance; a chance event.

happi-coat /'hapɪkəʊt/ *n.* L19. [f. Jap. *happi* + COAT *n.*] A Japanese loose outer coat. Also, a fashion garment modelled on this.

happify /'hapɪfʌɪ/ *v.t.* Now chiefly *US*. E17. [f. HAPPY *a.* + -FY.] Make happy.

happily /'hapɪli/ *adv.* LME. [f. HAPPY *a.* + -LY[2].] 1 By chance, possibly. Long *arch.* LME. 2 By or with good fortune; fortunately. Freq. modifying a sentence. LME. 3 Appropriately, felicitously. L16. 4 With mental pleasure or contentment. L16.

2 *Sunday* (*Calcutta*) Happily for India, potentially profitable sites lie along the east and west coast.

happiness /'hapɪnɪs/ *n.* LME. [f. HAPPY *a.* + -NESS.] 1 Good fortune, success. LME. 2 Pleasant appropriateness, felicity. L16. 3 Deep pleasure in, or contentment with, one's circumstances. L16.

happy /'hapi/ *a.* LME. [f. HAP *n.* + -Y[1].] 1 Of a person: favoured by good fortune; fortunate, successful. Formerly also, blessed. Now chiefly *arch.* & *dial.* LME. **b** Of an event or period: marked by good fortune, auspicious; esp. (now largely assoc. w. sense 4) in greetings etc., as *happy birthday! happy New Year!* E18. 2 Of a chance, circumstance, etc.: involving, or occurring by, good fortune; lucky, fortunate. LME. 3 Of an action, speech, etc.: pleasantly appropriate to the occasion or circumstances; felicitous. Of a person: dexterous in hitting on the action, words, etc., appropriate to the circumstances. LME. 4 Feeling deep pleasure in, or contentment with, one's circumstances. Also, marked by or expressive of such feeling. E16. **b** (In weakened sense.) Pleased, glad (*at, that, to do*); satisfied (*with*). L18. **c** *euphem.* Mildly drunk. *colloq.* L18. 5 Of an organization etc.: marked by a pleasant spirit of harmony and mutual goodwill. Freq. in *happy ship* below. E20.

1 AV *John* 13:17 If yee know these things, happy are ye if ye doe them. C. MIDDLETON The happy seat of liberty, plenty, and letters. *Law Times* A testator in the happy position of having . . realty both in Lancashire and in America. 2 LD BERNERS It was happy for them that the wether was so fayre. W. CONGREVE What a happy Discovery. H. L. MENCKEN There is in writing the constant joy of sudden discovery, of happy accident. 3 R. BENTLEY English Translators have not been very happy in their Version of this Passage. J. S. MILL This happy thought was considered to get rid of the whole difficulty. 4 SCOTT FITZGERALD Happy . . bursts of laughter. S. HILL She would tell the people joyful things, cheer them up, make them happy. A. THWAITE The second marriage . . was a very happy one. *fig.*: S. M. GAULT The . . floribunds are not generally happy on chalk. **b** D. J. ENRIGHT The soldiers were happy to quit Vietnam. *South Oxfordshire Guardian* Chris . . says he's happy with the compensation from the Ministry of Defence.

Special collocations & phrases: **happy as a clam, a king, a sandboy**, & vars., blissfully happy. **happy couple** *the* bridal couple. **happy day** *the* day of a couple's wedding. **happy days!**: used as a drinking-toast. *happy dispatch*: see DISPATCH *n.* **happy dust** *slang* cocaine. **happy ending** an ending in a novel, play, etc., in which the leading characters acquire spouses, become rich, etc. **happy event** the birth of a child. **happy families** a game usu. played with special cards in sets of four, each set depicting the various members of a family, in which the object is to collect as many complete sets as possible. **happy family** (*a*) a group of (esp. diverse) people or creatures living together in harmony; (*b*) *Austral.* = APOSTLE-*bird*. **happy hour** (orig. *US*) a period during which a bar etc. sells drinks at reduced prices or offers free hors d'oeuvres. *happy hunting-ground*: see *hunting-ground* s.v. HUNTING *vbl n.* **happy land** a land of unusual prosperity; *spec.* heaven. **happy landings!**: used as a toast among aviators. **happy medium** = *golden mean* (a) s.v. GOLDEN *a.* **happy pair** = *happy couple* above. **happy pill** *slang* a tranquillizer. **happy release** release from misfortune; *esp.* death. **happy ship** a ship in which the crew work harmoniously together; *fig.* an organization marked by team spirit. **happy warrior** a person dauntless in the face of difficulty (esp. as a conventional designation of a good soldier). **many happy returns (of the day)**: a greeting to a person on his or her birthday.

happy /'hapi/ *v.t.* Now *arch. rare*. L16. [f. the adj.] Make happy.

-happy /'hapi/ *suff.* [f. HAPPY *a.*] Placed after ns. to form adjs. in senses (*a*) dazed or suffering stress as a result of exposure to something, as *bomb-happy*; (*b*) preoccupied with or overfree in the use of something, as *trigger-happy*.

happy-go-lucky /ˌhapɪgəʊ'lʌki/ *adv.* & *a.* L17. [f. HAPPY *a.* + GO *v.* + LUCKY *a.*] **A** *adv.* Just as it may happen; haphazardly. Now *rare* or *obs.* L17. **B** *adj.* Taking things as they come; easy-going. M19.

happy-go-luckiness *n.* L19.

hapten /'hapt(ə)n/ *n.* E20. [f. Gk *haptein* fasten.] *Immunol.* Any small molecule, itself non-allergenic, which when combined with a larger carrier molecule elicits production of an antibody specific to both free and complexed hapten.

hap'tenic *a.* M20.

hapteron /'haptərɒn/ *n.* Pl. **-ra** /rə/. L19. [mod.L, f. Gk *haptein* fasten.] *Bot.* An organ or structure of a cryptogamic plant which serves to anchor it to a support; *esp.* the holdfast of an alga (occas. *spec.*, one of the rootlike branches into which the holdfast may be divided).

haptic /'haptɪk/ *a.* L19. [Gk *haptikos*, f. *haptesthai* to grasp or touch, middle voice of *haptein* fasten.] Relating to the sense of touch; dependent on feeling by touch rather than seeing.

haptically *adv.* M20. **haptics** *n.* the branch of psychology or linguistics that deals with touch, esp. as a means of communication L19.

haptoglobin /haptə'gləʊbɪn/ *n.* M20. [f. Gk *haptein* fasten + -O- + GLOBIN.] *Biochem.* Any of several alpha globulins which form complexes with free haemoglobin which are then removed from the plasma.

haptotropism /haptə(ʊ)'trəʊpɪz(ə)m, -'trɒp-/ *n.* L19. [f. Gk *haptein* fasten + -O- + -TROPISM.] *Bot.* The tendency of parts of a plant (e.g. tendrils) to move in a particular direction in response to external contact.

hapu /'hɑːpuː/ *n.* *NZ.* [Maori.] A division of a Maori tribe.

hapuku /'hɑːpuːkuː, -kə/ *n.* *NZ.* Also **-ka** /-kə/. M19. [Maori.] A large marine serranid food fish, *Polyprion oxygeneios*.

haqueton /'hakt(ə)n/ *n.* *obs.* exc. *Hist.* ME. [Alt. of ACTON after OFr. *hocqueton* (mod. *hoqueton*).] = ACTON.

harai-goshi /harʌɪ'gɒʃi/ *n.* M20. [Jap., f. *harai* sweep + *koshi* waist, hips.] A type of sweeping hip throw in judo.

hara-kiri /harə'kɪri/ *n.* Also (corruptly) **hari-** /harɪ-/. M19. [Jap., f. *hara* belly + *kiri* cutting.] In Japan, a ritual form of suicide by disembowelling, formerly prescribed by a feudal superior to disgraced members of the samurai class as an alternative to execution. Also, suicide practised voluntarily from a sense of shame, as a protest, etc.

haram /hɑː'rɑːm/ *n.* & *a.* E17. [Arab. *ḥarām* forbidden. Cf. HAREM.] A *n.* A Muslim sacred place, forbidden to non-Muslims. E17. B *adj.* Of food: forbidden under Islamic law. Opp. HALAL *a.* E17.

harangue /hə'raŋ/ *n.* LME. [Fr., earlier †*arenge* f. med.L *harenga*, perh. ult. f. Gmc elems.] A speech addressed to an assembly; a long, loud, or impassioned address or monologue.

T. MALLON The volumes read like a lifelong harangue from Speaker's Corner in Hyde Park.

harangue /hə'raŋ/ *v.t.* & *i.* L17. [Fr. *haranguer*, f. as prec.] Deliver a harangue or long address (to).

COLERIDGE There is no subject, which men in general like better to harangue on than politics. P. LIVELY Madame Charlot harangues the cook, in an unbroken monologue that lasts five minutes.

haranguer *n.* M17.

haras /arɑ/ *n.* Pl. same. ME. [(O)Fr., of unkn. origin.] An enclosure or establishment in which horses are kept for breeding. Formerly, a herd of such horses.

¶Orig. a naturalized Eng. word, with Anglicized pronunc.

harass /'harəs/ *n.* M17. [f. the vb.] Harassment.

harass /'harəs, hə'ras/ *v.t.* E17. [Fr. *harasser* pejorative deriv. of *harer* set a dog on, f. *hare* cry used for this purpose.] 1 Trouble by repeated attacks. Now freq., subject to constant molesting or persecution. E17. †2 Lay waste, devastate. E17–E18. †3 Tire out, exhaust. E17–M18. 4 Overwhelm with cares, misfortunes, etc. Chiefly as *harassed* ppl a. M17.

1 F. PARKMAN The Indians unceasingly harassed their march. S. NAIPAUL The .. programme organized by the FBI .. to harass, discredit and destroy the radical movements. **harassing agent** or **gas** a gas designed to incapacitate enemy troops, rioters, etc., without being lethal. 4 D. M. THOMAS She helped a harassed woman .. who had four children to cope with.

harasser *n.* E18. **harassment** *n.* M18.

haratch *n.* see CARATCH.

harbinge /'hɑːbɪn(d)ʒ/ *v.* Also (earlier) †**harberge**. L15. [OFr. *herbergier*: see next, and cf. HARBOUR *v.* In sense 2 back-form. f. HARBINGER *n.*] †1 *v.t.* & *i.* Provide with or occupy lodgings. L15–E17. 2 *v.t.* Be a harbinger of. *rare.* M19.

harbinger /'hɑːbɪn(d)ʒə/ *n.* Also (earlier) †**herberger**, †**herbergeour**. ME. [AN, OFr. *herbergere* (obl. case *-geour*), f. *herbergier* provide lodging for, f. *herberge* lodging f. OS (= OHG) *heriberga* shelter for an army, f. *heri*, *hari* host, army (see HARRY *v.*) + Gmc base meaning 'protect' (see BOROUGH). For the intrusive *n* cf. *messenger*, *passenger*, etc.] †1 A person who provides lodging; an entertainer, a host. ME–E16. 2 A person sent in advance to procure lodgings for an army, a royal train, etc. Now only *Hist.*, and as title of an officer of the Honourable Corps of Gentlemen-at-Arms. LME. 3 A person sent to announce the approach of someone; a herald, a forerunner. Now chiefly *transf.* & *fig.*, a sign *of* some coming event or condition. M16.

3 L. GARFIELD The mad daughter of the mad father was come as harbinger of doom. J. UPDIKE The first few pimples, harbingers of messy manhood.

Comb.: **harbinger-of-spring** an early-flowering N. American umbelliferous plant, *Erigenia bulbosa*.

harbinger /'hɑːbɪn(d)ʒə/ *v.t.* M17. [f. the n.] Announce the approach of.

SOUTHEY The star that harbingers a glorious day.

harbor *n.*, *v.* see HARBOUR *n.*[1], *v.*

harborage *n.* see HARBOURAGE.

†**harborough** *n.*, *v.* vars. of HARBOUR *n.*[1], *v.*

harbour /'hɑːbə/ *n.*[1] Also ***harbor**, †**harb(o)rough**. [Late OE *herebeorg* corresp. to OS, OHG *heriberga* (Du. *herberg*, G *Herberge*), ON *herbergi*: see HARBINGER *n.*, -OUR.] 1 (A place of) shelter; (a) refuge, (a) lodging. Now *arch.* & *dial.* LOE. 2 A piece of sheltered seawater providing anchorage for ships; *esp.* one protected from rough water by piers, jetties, and other artificial structures; *spec.* such a place under statutory control as regards its use. ME. 3 The covert of a deer or other wild animal. L16. 4 A halting-place for tanks. M20.

1 P. HOLLAND That the legions from out of their winter harboroughs, should there meete together. DRYDEN For harbour at a thousand doors they knocked. W. COWPER Give harbour in thy breast on no account To after-grudge or enmity. **cold harbour** a roadside shelter from the weather (esp. as a place-name). 2 DYLAN THOMAS Its cobble streets and its little fishing harbour.

Comb.: **harbour-due(s)** a charge for the use of a harbour; **harbour-master** the official in charge of a harbour, responsible for allocating berths and collecting harbour-dues; **harbour seal** *N. Amer.* the common seal, *Phoca vitulina* (so called because it often frequents estuaries).

harbour *n.*[2] see ARBOUR.

harbour /'hɑːbə/ *v.* Also ***harbor**, †**harborough**. [Late OE *hereborgian* corresp. to (M)Du. *herbergen*, OHG *heribergōn*, ON *herbergja*, cogn. w. HARBOUR *n.*[1]] I *v.i.* 1 Occupy shelter or lodging, latterly esp. for concealment. Now *arch.* & *dial.* LOE. 2 Of an animal, *spec.* a stag: have its lair or covert. L15. 3 Of a ship etc.: take shelter in a harbour. L16. b Of tanks, military forces, etc.: shelter, halt for the night. M20.

1 Z. M. PIKE I was suspicious that possibly some party of Indians might be harboring round.

II *v.t.* 4†a Give lodging or temporary accommodation to; billet (troops). ME–L17. b *fig.* Cherish (an idea or feeling, freq. a suspicion or grudge) in the mind. ME. 5 Give shelter or refuge to. Now freq., give secret refuge to (a wanted criminal, a noxious animal, etc.). LME. †b Of a thing: contain, hold within itself. LME–L17. 6 Trace (a stag) to its lair or covert. LME. 7 Shelter (a ship) in a harbour. M16.

4a *fig.*: MILTON The anguish of my soul, that suffers not Mine eyes to harbour sleep. b LD MACAULAY He believed them to harbour the worst designs. L. ALTHER She still harbored a faint hope Diana would change her mind. 5 W. S. CHURCHILL Soon Canada was to harbour many refugees from the United States. E. HUXLEY Leeds .. harbours the largest ready-made clothing business in the world. E. BOWEN Crannied giltwork harboured more dust than energy could extract. *Blitz* The rural populace .. allegedly harbour terrorists. b R. BOYLE The Aeriall particles, that are wont to be harboured in the Pores of that liquor.

harbourage /'hɑːb(ə)rɪdʒ/ *n.* Also ***-bor-**. L15. [f. HARBOUR *n.*[1] + -AGE.] 1 *gen.* (A place of) shelter, (a) refuge. L15. 2 Shelter for ships in a harbour. L17.

1 SHAKES. *John* Your King .. Craves harbourage within your city walls.

harbourer /'hɑːb(ə)rə/ *n.* Also ***-bor-**. ME. [f. HARBOUR *v.* + -ER[1].] 1 A person who provides shelter or (formerly) lodging. ME. 2 A person whose office is to trace a stag to its covert. LME.

harbourless /'hɑːbəlɪs/ *a.* ME. [f. HARBOUR *n.*[1] + -LESS.] 1 Having no shelter or home. ME. 2 Without harbours for ships. E17.

†**harbrough** *n.* var. of HARBOUR *n.*[1]

hard /hɑːd/ *a.*, *adv.*, & *n.* [OE *h(e)ard* = OFris. *herd*, OS (Du.) *hard*, (O)HG *hart*, ON *harðr*, Goth. *hardus*, f. Gmc f. IE whence Gk *kratus* strong, powerful.] A *adj.* I 1 That does not yield to pressure; not easily penetrated, cut, or separated into particles; firm; compact in substance and texture. OE. b Of porcelain: made of hard paste. E19. c Of a tennis-court: surfaced with asphalt or other hard material as opp. to grass. L19. 2 Orig., courageous, bold. Later, not easily worn out or made to give way; capable of great physical endurance and exertion. OE. †b Firm, steadfast, unyielding, (*lit.* & *fig.*). ME–M17. †c Inured, obdurate. *rare* (Shakes.). Only in E17. 3 Not easily impressed or moved; unfeeling, callous; hard-hearted. OE. 4 Not easily persuaded to part with money; stingy, niggardly. Now chiefly *Sc.* ME. 5 Requiring effort or skill; occasioning trouble; difficult, laborious, fatiguing, troublesome. Foll. by *to do*, *of*. ME. b Not easily able or capable, having difficulty in doing something. *obs.* exc. in *hard of hearing* below. ME. 6 Difficult to understand or explain. LME. 7 Of the pulse: beating strongly because of high blood pressure. LME. 8 Difficult to manage, control, or resist. Now chiefly in *hard case* below. L16. b Of (a) fact: unable to be denied or explained away. L19. c Of news or information: factual, reliable, substantiated. Cf. SOFT *a.* 21. E20. 9 Of money: in specie as opp. to paper currency, or in currency as opp. to cheques etc. Cf. SOFT *a.* 19a. E18. 10 Not easily moved by sentiment; of a practical, shrewdly intelligent character. M18. b Not readily affected by alcohol. M19.

1 E. WAUGH The infantry: hard, bare feet rhythmically kicking up the dust. E. HARDWICK English muffins which had been toasted in the morning and were as hard as cement. 3 T. HARDY Allenville, cold and hard as he was, had some considerable affection for .. his daughter. 4 LD MACAULAY Many wondered that a man .. could be so hard and niggardly in all pecuniary dealings. 5 N. BAILEY Bread made of spelt is hard of digestion. L. STERNE I was hard to please. H. MARTINEAU It is a hard thing to manage. J. B. MOZLEY Often .. what we must do as simply right .. is just the hardest thing to do. J. LE CARRÉ The snow was blurring his glasses, he found it hard to see. b DICKENS I have been very hard to sleep too, .. last night I was all but sleepless. 6 J. W. BURGON To ask hard questions. H. HENDERSON Then I understood the meaning of the hard word '*pietas*'. 8b A. H. COMPTON The hard fact is that war, like business, reduces to a question of gain versus cost. c D. W. GOODWIN Will treatment .. improve the prognosis? .. There is little hard evidence. 9 J. BENTHAM Husbandmen, like other labourers, are paid in hard money by the week. 10 LYTTON My books don't tell me .. a good heart gets on in the world: it is a hard head.

II 11 Difficult to bear, endure, or consent to; involving undue or unfair suffering; severe, oppressive, cruel. OE. b Of the season or weather: severe, esp. frosty; rigorous, violent. M16. 12 Of a person: harsh or severe in dealing with someone. Freq. foll. by *on*, *upon*. OE. b Of a thing, action, etc.: characterized by harshness or severity; cruel. OE. c Of a bargain etc.: strict, without abatement or concession. E17. d *Polit.* Designating a strict or extreme faction at the wing of a political party. Esp. in *hard left*, *hard right*. Cf. SOFT *a.* 8d. L20.

11 W. HONE It is .. hard .. that I should have these .. compliments and .. reproaches at the same time. G. GREENE An old couple driven by hard times to live on their children. b R. BOYLE Very hard frost. Thames frozen. Carts went over. 12 A. TROLLOPE Felix began to perceive that he had been too hard upon her. b R. GARNETT She almost invariably took a hard view of persons and things. c N. WARD They never complain of me for giving them hard measure, or under-weight.

III †13 Intense in force or degree; strong, deep, profound. OE–E19. **14** Acting with, involving, or requiring great exertion, energy, or persistence; strenuous, unremitting. OE.

13 COVERDALE *Gen.* 2:21 The Lorde God caused an herde slepe to fall vpon man. 14 C. KINGSLEY The hardest rider for many a mile round. *Law Times* Every hard worker . . requires sufficient and regular holidays. E. AMADI His neatness and hard work had made him a favourite of the teachers.

IV 15 Harsh or unpleasant to the eye or ear; aesthetically unpleasing. (Earliest in *hard-favoured.*) E16. **16a** Of wine etc.: harsh or sharp to the taste; acid. L16. **b** Of water: having a high proportion of mineral (esp. calcareous) salts which make the use of soap difficult. Cf. SOFT *a.* 17. M17. **c** Strongly alcoholic, intoxicating; (of a drug) potent and addictive. L18. **17** *Phonet.* Of a consonant: velar, guttural; not palatalized; (now *rare*) voiceless, fortis. Cf. SOFT *a.* 3b. L18. **18** Of markets and prices: high, unyielding. M19. **19** *Physics.* **a** Of a vacuum: (almost) complete. Of a vacuum tube or valve: containing a hard vacuum. L19. **b** Of radiation: having great penetrating power. E20. **20** Of pornography: highly obscene. L20.

15 P. CAREY Painted in the colours of railway stations and schools: hard green and dirty cream. 16a P. V. PRICE Too high in elements that can make the wine hard, astringent and generally unpalatable. b N. G. CLARK Produce insoluble scums with hard water. c J. GARDNER You start on pot and . . you're mixing with people who've graduated to the hard stuff. *Dumfries & Galloway Standard* You should aim, therefore, to cut down on: . . soft drinks and hard alcohol. 17 N. WEBSTER When *a* is preceded by the gutturals hard *g* or *c*. 18 *Daily Telegraph* A widely held view that yields will be harder in a year's time.

B *adv.* **1** With effort or violence; strenuously, vigorously; fiercely; (now *US colloq.*) intensely, extremely. OE. **2** So as to bring or involve pain, difficulty, or hardship; cruelly, harshly. ME. **†b** At an uneven pace. L16–E19. **3** Firmly, securely; tightly; fast. Now *rare.* ME. **4** So as to be hard; to the point of hardness. ME. **b** On a hard surface, floor, etc. L16. **5** With difficulty, hardly; scarcely. ME. **6** In close proximity. LME. **b** *Naut.* To the full extent possible. M16.

1 M. SINCLAIR It had blown hard all day, and now the wind had dropped. E. WAUGH He had fought long and hard since then and won a DSO. C. PHILLIPS Father Daniels looked hard at them. 2 ADDISON I shall be very hard put to it to bring my self off handsomly. L. GORDON Any judgement worth having is hard won. b SHAKES. *A.Y.L.* He trots hard with a young maid. 3 SHAKES. *Haml.* He took me by the wrist, and held me hard. 4b E. TOPSELL That so he may lie soft and stand hard. 5 SIR W. SCOTT And hard his labouring breath he drew. 6 F. HALL Incongruity which trenches hard on nonsense.

C *n.* **1** That which is hard, something hard (*lit.* & *fig.*); hardship. ME. **†2** The hard part, the shell. *rare.* Only in ME. **b** An erection of the penis. Also *hard-on.* (*coarse slang.*) L19. **3** (A piece of) hard or firm ground. Long *obs.* exc. *Sc.* L16. **4** A firm beach or foreshore; a sloping esp. stone roadway or jetty across a foreshore. M19. **5** Tobacco in the form of a cake. M19. **6** = *hard labour* below. *slang.* L19.

1 *Daily Chronicle* She . . has given her life to nursing, and has gone through its hards. b R. PRICE When evening comes and I lay a-hold of Lois, I'll have up a hard. 4 DICKENS The Common Hard, a dingy street leading down to the dock-yard. F. CHICHESTER The yacht had looked powerful and tall standing on the hard of the river bank. 6 H. L. WILSON I would . . be . . left to languish in gaol, perhaps given six months' hard.

Phrases: *a hard act to follow*: see ACT *n.* 7c. *a hard nut to crack*: see NUT *n. a hard row to hoe*: see ROW *n.*[1] *as hard as nails*: see NAIL *n. bear hard*: see BEAR *v.*[1] **be hard put to do** have difficulty in accomplishing. **be hard put to it** be in difficulties. *die hard*: see DIE *v.*[1] *drive a hard bargain*: see DRIVE *v.* **go hard with** turn out to the disadvantage of (a person). **hard and fast** *a.* (*a*) *Naut.* (of a ship) on shore; (*b*) *gen.* (of a distinction made, a rule of behaviour, etc.) strict, inflexible. **hard at it** working hard. **hard by** close by, in close (local) proximity (to), very near (to). **hard of hearing** somewhat deaf. **hard to get** aloof, unapproachable, uninterested, (freq. in *play hard to get*). **hard up** (*a*) *Naut.* (of a tiller) put as far as possible to windward to turn the ship's head away from the wind (usu. as a command); (*b*) in want, esp. of money; at a loss *for. heavens hard*: see HEAVEN *n. hold hard*: see HOLD *v.* **put the hard word on** (a person) *Austral.* & *NZ slang* ask (a person) for a favour or a loan; *esp.* proposition (a woman). **run (a person) hard** pursue (a person) closely. **the hard way** by one's own unaided efforts, through bitter experience. *wink hard*: see WINK *v.*[1]

Special collocations & comb.: **hardbake** almond toffee. **hardball** *N. Amer.* (*a*) baseball; (*b*) rough uncompromising dealings or actions (esp. in a political context); chiefly in *play hardball.* **†hardbeam** the hornbeam, *Carpinus betulus.* **hardbitten** *a.* tough in fight etc.; hardened by experience, hard-headed, sceptical. **hardboard** *n.* & *a.* (made of) a stiff board of compressed and processed wood pulp fibre. **hard-boil** *v.t.* boil (an egg) so that the white and the yolk solidify. **hard-boiled** *a.* (*a*) boiled so as to be hard; *spec.* (of an egg) boiled so that the white and the yolk have solidified; (*b*) *fig.* tough, callous, shrewd; shrewdly practical. **hard-bound** *a.* (*a*) *rare* slow in action; (*b*) (of a book) bound in stiff covers. **hard bread** a kind of hard-baked cake or biscuit. **hard case** (*a*) a difficult or intractable person; (*b*) *Austral.* & *NZ* an eccentric or incorrigible person, a character; (*c*) an instance of hardship. *hard cash*: see CASH *n.*[1] **hard cheese** (*a*) any of various firm-textured cheeses; (*b*) *colloq.* bad luck, too bad. **hard chine** a join of the side and bottom of a ship which is angular as opp. to rounded. *hard clam*: see CLAM *n.*[2] 1. **hard coal** anthracite. **hard copy** a legible permanent record of material stored on microfilm etc., *esp.* (*Computing*) a printed record of data intended for output. **hard core** (*a*) heavy material, *spec.* rubble, forming the foundation of a road; (*b*) an irreduceable nucleus or residuum; *fig.* a stubborn, reactionary, or highly committed minority, something blatant or intractable; (*c*) (usu. *hardcore*) hardcore music or pornography. **hardcore** *a.* (*a*) blatant, uncompromising; stubborn, highly committed; (*b*) (of pornography) highly obscene; (*c*) (of popular music) experimental in nature and usually characterized by high volume and aggressive presentation. **hard cover** the stiff durable binding-case of a book. **hard currency** currency that is not likely to depreciate suddenly or fluctuate greatly in value. **hard disk** *Computing* a disk that is rigid and has a large storage capacity, as distinct from the smaller capacity floppy disk. **hard-done-by** harshly or unfairly treated. **hard-favoured** *a.* (*arch.*) having a hard or unpleasing appearance or look; ill-favoured, ugly. **hard-featured** *a.* having hard, harsh, or unpleasing features. **hard feeling(s)** resentment. **hard fern** a fern of heathy places, *Blechnum spicant*, with leathery simply pinnate fronds. **hard-fisted** *a.* stingy. **hard-grass** any of several tough-stemmed grasses; *esp.* (more fully *sea hard-grass*) either of two salt-marsh grasses, *Parapholis strigosa* and *P. incurva.* *hard* GROWAN. **hardhack** a low shrub, *Spiraea tomentosa*, of the rose family, common in eastern N. America, with dense panicles of rose-coloured or white flowers. **hard-handed** *a.* (*a*) having hard hands from manual labour; †(*b*) *rare* = *hard-fisted* above; (*c*) ruling with a firm or cruel hand, severe. **hard hat** (*a*) a hat made of hard or stiffened felt, a bowler hat; (*b*) (a person who wears) an article of protective headgear such as is worn on a building site; (*c*) a reactionary or conservative person. **hard-heart** *a.* (*arch.*) = HARD-HEARTED. **hard hit** *a.* severely stricken by misfortune, grief, or disaster, or by love. **hard-hitter** *Austral.* & *NZ colloq.* a bowler hat. **hard-hitting** *a.* vigorous, not sparing the feelings. **hard labour** compulsory physical labour by prisoners without privileges, formerly (until 1948) in Britain undertaken during the first few weeks of a sentence. **hard-laid** *a.* (of string, fabric, etc.) tightly twisted or woven. **hard landing** an uncontrolled landing in which a spacecraft etc. is destroyed. **hard line** an unyielding adherence to a hard or firm policy without abatement or concession. **hard-liner** a person who maintains a hard line habitually or on a specified issue. *hard lines*: see LINE *n.*[2] *hard luck*: see LUCK *n.* **hard-lying money** extra pay made to naval men serving in small craft. **hard-meat** (now *rare* or *obs.*) corn and hay used as fodder as opp. to grass; *at hard-meat* (*fig.*), in close confinement. **hard money** *US* coins. **hard-mouthed** *a.* (of a horse) not easily controlled by the bit; *fig.* self-willed, obstinate. **hard-nose** *a.* (*US slang*) = *hard-nosed* (b) below. **hard-nosed** *a.* (*a*) (of a dog used in hunting etc.) having little or no sense of smell; (*b*) *N. Amer. colloq.* (of a person) obdurate, realistic, uncompromising. *hard-on*: see sense C.2b above. **hard pad** a form of distemper of dogs etc., sometimes causing hardness of the pads of the feet. *hard palate*: see PALATE *n.* 1. **hardpan** (orig. *US*) a hard, impervious layer of clay, sand, or gravel; hard unbroken ground; *fig.* the lowest level or foundation, bottom, bedrock. **hard paste** the mixture of clay and water, fired at a high temperature, from which porcelain is made. **hard-pressed** *a.* closely pursued (*lit.* & *fig.*), hard-pushed. **hard-pushed** *a.* in difficulties, almost at the end of one's resources. **hard rock** *colloq.* rock music with a heavy beat. *hard roe*: see ROE *n.*[2] **hard rubber** ebonite. **hard sauce** a sweet relish made with butter and sugar and often with brandy etc. **hard-scrabble** *a.* & *n.* (*US*) (*a*) (land) that yields subsistence only with difficulty, barren land; (*b*) (requiring) a vigorous effort made with great difficulty. **hard sell** (an instance of) aggressive salesmanship or advertising. **hard set** *a.* set so as to be hard; (of an egg) that has been subjected to incubation; (of a person) hungry. **hard shoulder** a strip of land with a hard surface beside a motorway enabling vehicles to leave the road during an emergency. **hard soap** soap made with sodium compounds. *hard solder*: see SOLDER *n.* 1. **hard standing** an area of hard material for a vehicle to stand on when not in use. **hardstone** precious or semiprecious stone used for intaglio, mosaic work, etc. **hard stuff** strong alcoholic drink, *esp.* whisky. **hard swearing** unabashed perjury. **hard tack** ship's biscuit; *gen.* hard bread or biscuit (*lit.* & *fig.*). **hardtail** (*a*) *US* the blue runner, a carangid fish, *Caranx crysos*, of the west Atlantic; (*b*) *slang* a mule. **hard tick** a tick of the family Ixodidae, having a rigid dorsal shield. **hard ticket** *US slang* = *tough nut* (a) s.v. NUT *n.* **hardtop** the metal roof of a motor car; a car having such a roof. **hard-up** tobacco from cigarette-ends etc. **hardware** (*a*) small ware or goods of metal; ironmongery; (*b*) weapons, machines; (*c*) the physical components of a computer etc. (opp. *software*). **hard-wearing** *a.* able to stand a considerable amount of wear. **hard wheat**: with a hard grain rich in gluten. **hard-wired** *a.* (*Computing*) using or having permanently connected circuits designed to perform a specific unchangeable function. **hardwood** the wood of any non-coniferous tree (orig. that of the oak or other trees noted for their hardness); *ellipt.* a hardwood tree. **hard word** (*a*) (chiefly *dial.*) important or scandalous information; a hint, a password, a proposal, a refusal; (*b*) in *pl.*, words that are difficult to understand; (*c*) in *pl.*, angry talk. **hard-working** *a.* diligent.

hardish *a.* somewhat hard L16. **hardness** *n.* (*a*) the quality or condition of being hard; (*b*) an instance of this quality, a hardship: OE.

†hard *v.i.* & *t.* OE–E17. [OE *heardian* = OS *hardon*, OHG *hartēn*, *hartōn*, f. base of HARD *a.*] Make or become hard (*lit.* & *fig.*).

Hardanger /ˈhɑːdaŋə/ *a.* L19. [A district in W. Norway, the original place of manufacture.] **1** Designating a kind of folk violin strung with four stopped and four sympathetic strings. L19. **2** Designating a form of ornamental needlework characterized by a diamond or square pattern. E20.

hardback /ˈhɑːdbak/ *n.* & *a.* M18. [f. HARD *a.* + BACK *n.*[1]] **A** *n.* **1** A (flying) beetle. *W. Indies.* M18. **2** A book bound in stiff covers. M20.

2 in hardback in a hardback edition.

B *attrib.* or as *adj.* Of or pertaining to a hardback; *spec.* (of a book) bound in stiff covers. M20.

harden /ˈhɑːd(ə)n/ *n.* & *a.* LME. [f. HARD(S + -EN[4].] *Hist.* (Of) a coarse fabric made from hards.

harden /ˈhɑːd(ə)n/ *v.* ME. [f. HARD *a.* + -EN[5], after ON *harðna*: repl. HARD *v.*] **I** *v.t.* **1** Render or make hard. ME. **2** Make bold in action; embolden; incite to action. Long *obs.* exc. *dial.* ME. **†3** Maintain stiffly, affirm. Only in ME. **4** Make difficult to make an impression on; make callous or unfeeling. ME. **5** Make persistent or obdurate in a course of action or state of mind. LME. **6** Chiefly *Naut.* Make firm and tight. Freq. foll. by *in.* E16. **7** Make hardy, robust, or capable of endurance. L16. **b** Increase the resistance to attack of (a nuclear missile or base). M20.

1 J. R. GREEN The rise of a lawyer class was everywhere hardening customary into written rights. W. WHARTON The statues . . spotted black, green and yellow with clots of hardened moss. 4 LYTTON I hardened my heart against his voice. D. W. WINNICOTT We may become hardened, because the repeated losses of patients make us wary against getting fond of the newly-ill. 5 *Manchester Examiner* It would . . confirm and harden her in a policy of settled hostility. 7 R. HOLMES A hardened campaigner of forty-three . . limped from the effect of two leg

wounds. **harden off** inure (plants) to cold by gradually reducing the temperature of a hotbed or forcing-house or by increasing the exposure to wind and sunlight.

II *v.i.* 8 *gen.* Become hard. LME. 9 Become hard in feeling, emotion, constitution, etc. M17. 10 Of prices, markets, etc.: become higher and less yielding. L17.

8 TENNYSON That we might . . watch The sandy footprint harden into stone. *fig.*: GEO. ELIOT That cold dislike . . was hardening within him. 9 C. KINGSLEY He hardened into a valiant man. DAY LEWIS Her sadness at certain insensitivities of my father would have hardened into resentment. 10 *Economist* The hardening Yen knocked nearly 16% off Nissan's pre-tax profits in 1985.

hardena'bility *n.* (*Metall.*) the extent to which metal may be hardened M20.

harder /ˈhɑːdə/ *n. S. Afr.* Also **haarder**. M18. [Afk. f. Du.] Any of various grey mullets resembling herring, of South African waters, esp. *Mugil cephalus* and *Liza ramada*.

Harderian /hɑːˈdɪərɪən/ *a.* M19. [f. J. J. *Harder* (1656–1711), Swiss anatomist + -IAN.] Zool. *Harderian gland*, in many reptiles, birds, and mammals, a gland in the inner angle of the eye which lubricates the nictitating membrane or third eyelid.

hard-head /ˈhɑːdhɛd/ *n.* Also (esp. in sense 3) **hardhead**. E16. [f. HARD *a.* + HEAD *n.* In branch II alt. of some wd of unkn. origin.] I 1 A hard-headed person, *esp.* someone who is practical and unsentimental. Also, a stupid person. E16. b A person not easily affected by alcohol. M19. †2 A contest of head-butting. L17–M19. 3 *sing.* & in *pl.* A tough-stemmed kind of knapweed, *Centaurea nigra*, common in grassland, with heads of dense purple florets. L18. 4 Any of various fishes said to have hard heads; *spec.* (*Sc.*) the father-lasher, *Myoxocephalus scorpius*. E19. II 5 A Scottish copper coin of Mary and James VI of Scotland worth about three halfpence of English money. Long *obs.* exc. *Hist.* M16.

hard-headed /hɑːdˈhɛdɪd/ *a.* L16. [f. (as) prec. + -ED².] †1 Not easily led (*lit.* & *fig.*) or persuaded; obstinate; stubborn. L16–M17. 2 Not easily swayed by sophistry or sentiment; matter-of-fact, logical, practical. L18.

hard-headedly *adv.* L19. **hard-headedness** *n.* M19.

hard-hearted /hɑːdˈhɑːtɪd/ *a.* ME. [f. HARD *a.* + HEART *n.* + -ED².] Having a hard heart; incapable of being moved to pity or tenderness; unfeeling; unmerciful.

hard-heartedly *adv.* E19. **hard-heartedness** *n.* L16.

hardiesse /hɑːdɪˈɛs/ *n. literary.* ME. [(O)Fr., f. *hardi* HARDY *a.* + *-esse* -ESS².] Hardihood, boldness.

hardihead /ˈhɑːdɪhɛd/ *n. arch.* L16. [f. HARDY *a.* + -HEAD.] = HARDIHOOD 1.

hardihood /ˈhɑːdɪhʊd/ *n.* M17. [f. HARDY *a.* + -HOOD.] 1 Boldness, hardiness; audacity. M17. 2 Robust physique or constitution. *rare.* L18.

hardily /ˈhɑːdɪli/ *adv.* In sense 2 also †**hardly**. ME. [f. HARDY *a.* + -LY².] 1 Boldly; courageously; with audacity. ME. †2 It may be asserted; freely, certainly, by all means. ME–E17. †3 Robustly, not tenderly. *rare.* L17–L18.

hardiment /ˈhɑːdɪm(ə)nt/ *n. arch.* LME. [OFr. = act of daring, f. *hardier* attack, charge, harass + -MENT.] 1 Boldness, courage, daring, hardihood. LME. †2 A deed of daring, a bold exploit. LME–E17.

hardly /ˈhɑːdli/ *adv.*¹ ME. [f. HARD *a.* + -LY².] †1 With energy, force, or strenuous exertion; vigorously, forcibly, violently. ME–E19. †2 Boldly, daringly, hardily. ME–E17. †3 Firmly. ME–L16. 4 With severity or rigour; harshly. E16. 5 With trouble or hardship; uneasily, painfully. Now *rare.* M16. 6 Not easily, with difficulty. Long *rare* exc. as passing into sense 7. M16. 7 Barely, only just; almost not; not quite; scarcely. M16. 8 In close proximity, closely. *rare.* L16.

1 E. TOPSELL The Lamprey caught fast hold on his hand, biting hardly. 2 W. PAINTER Speake hardly thy minde. 4 R. KNOLLES The unconstant people . . now began to speak hardly of him. W. STEBBING The honour and loyalty of the hardly-used veteran. 5 LD MACAULAY What is made is slowly, hardly, and honestly earned. 6 A. S. BYATT His self-effacement was a little strained, his security too hardly achieved. 7 D. H. LAWRENCE It was hardly to be borne. I. MURDOCH I constantly try and hardly ever succeed! E. FEINSTEIN It is hardly likely that he was still ignorant of the Reiss murder. 8 R. KNOLLES They were so hardly pursued.

†**hardly** *adv.*² see HARDILY *adv.*

hards /hɑːdz/ *n.pl.* (also treated as *sing.*). Now *local.* Also **hurds** /həːdz/. [OE *heordan* wk fem. pl. corresp. to OFris., OLG *hēde* (Du. *heede*), ult. origin unkn.] The coarser parts of flax or hemp; tow.

hardshell /ˈhɑːdʃɛl/ *a.* & *n.* M19. [f. HARD *a.* + SHELL *n.*] A *adj.* Having a hard shell (*lit.* & *fig.*); (of a person) rigid and uncompromising in religious orthodoxy, *esp.* (*US*) belonging to a strict sect of Baptists of extreme Calvinist views. M19. B *n.* A hardshell Baptist. M19.

hardshelled *a.* E17.

hardship /ˈhɑːdʃɪp/ *n.* ME. [f. HARD *a.* + -SHIP.] †1 The quality of being hard to bear; painful difficulty. ME–L17. 2 Hardness of fate or circumstance; severe suffering or privation. Also, an instance of this. ME. †b A piece of harsh treatment. M–L18.

2 K. M. E. MURRAY For many scholars it is no hardship to sit indoors studying on a fine afternoon. N. ANNAN His body learnt to endure hardship. b BURKE I do not know that I have ever offered . . a hardship . . to the religious prejudices of any person.

hardy /ˈhɑːdi/ *n.* L19. [Prob. f. HARD *a.* or HARDY *a.*] A blacksmith's edged blade of hard iron for shaping metal on.

hardy /ˈhɑːdi/ *a.* ME. [(O)Fr. *hardi* pa. pple of *hardir* become bold, f. Gmc, f. base of HARD *a.*] 1 Bold, daring; reprehensibly audacious. ME. 2 Capable of endurance; physically robust, vigorous. M16. b Of a plant: able to grow in the open all the year. M17.

1 HOR. WALPOLE Art thou so hardy, as to dare my vengeance? J. W. KRUTCH Few . . are hardy enough openly to advocate starting a war. 2 A. SCHLEE The sudden cooling of the air had driven . . the less hardy into the cabin. *half-hardy*: see HALF-. **hardy annual** an annual plant that may be sown, or sows itself, in the open; *fig.* (*joc.*) a subject that comes up at regular intervals. **hardy perennial** a herbaceous plant with a perennial rootstock; *fig.* (*joc.*) a subject that comes up at regular intervals.

Hardyesque /hɑːdɪˈɛsk/ *a.* E20. [f. *Hardy* (see below) + -ESQUE.] Of, pertaining to, or characteristic of the English novelist and poet Thomas Hardy (1840–1928) or his work.

hare /hɛː/ *n.*¹ [OE *hara* = OFris. *hasa*, MDu. *haese* (Du. *haas*), OHG *haso* (G *Hase*), ON *heri*, f. Gmc.] 1 Any of various fast-running plant-eating mammals of the family Leporidae (order Lagomorpha), esp. of the genus *Lepus*, typically larger than rabbits, with longer ears and hind legs and a short tail. Also, the flesh of any of these as food. OE. 2 *fig.* A person likened to a hare in some way, as in swiftness or timidity, or in allusion to various phrasal or proverbial uses. ME. b The player in the game of hare and hounds who lays the 'scent' for the hounds to follow. Cf. HOUND *n.*¹ 2b. M19. c More fully *electric hare.* A dummy hare propelled by electricity, used to lead the dogs in greyhound racing. E20. 3 (Usu. **H-.**) *The* southern constellation Lepus. M16. 4 More fully *sea hare.* Any marine opisthobranch mollusc of the genus *Aplysia*, with tentacles resembling projecting ears. L16.

1 *Arctic hare, blue hare, brown hare, calling hare, mountain hare, snowshoe hare, varying hare*, etc. BELGIAN *hare.*

Phrases: **first catch your hare** [an instruction erron. ascribed to Mrs Glasse's *Art of Cookery* (1747)]: as the first step in trying to cook it, or (*fig.*) to do anything. *give a hare a turn*: see TURN *n.* **hare and hounds** a paper-chase. **hare and tortoise** [w. allus. to Aesop's fable] the defeat of ability by persistence. *hold with the hare and hunt with the hounds*: see *run with the hare and hunt with the hounds* below. *hunt the hare*: see HUNT *v.* (*mad as a*) *March hare*: see MARCH *n.*¹ **run** (or **hold**) **with the hare and hunt with the hounds** try to remain on good terms with both sides in a quarrel etc.; play a double role. *steady from hare*: see STEADY *a.* 6c. **start a hare** raise a topic of discussion.

Comb.: **harebell** either of two plants with nodding blue bell-shaped flowers: (*a*) orig., the bluebell or wild hyacinth, *Hyacinthoides non-scripta* (now *dial.*); (*b*) now usu. (orig. *north.*), a slender bellflower, *Campanula rotundifolia*, of dry grassy banks etc.; **hare-finder** (long *rare*) a person employed to find or sight a hare in its form; **harefoot** (*a*) (long *rare* or *obs.* exc. as an epithet for Harold I of England, d. 1040) a swift-footed person; (*b*) a long narrow foot found in some dogs; **hare-pipe** *Hist.* a trap for catching hares; **hare's-ear** (*a*) any of various umbelliferous plants of the genus *Bupleurum*, esp. thorow-wax, *B. rotundifolium*; (*b*) *hare's-ear mustard*, a cruciferous weed, *Conringia orientalis*, with broadly clasping leaves; **hare's foot** (*a*) the foot of a hare, esp. (*Theatr.*) as used to apply make-up to the face; (*b*) (more fully *hare's-foot trefoil*) a clover of sandy ground, *Trifolium arvense*, with pink flowers almost hidden by the hairy calyx-teeth; (*c*) *hare's-foot fern*, a Mediterranean fern, *Davallia canariensis*, the rhizome of which is covered in brown hairs; **hare's fur** a brown or black glaze streaked with silvery white or yellow used on some Chinese pottery; **hare's-tail** (*a*) *hare's-tail grass*, an ornamental grass, *Lagurus ovatus*, with softly hairy spikelike panicles; (*b*) *hare's tail cotton-grass*: see *cotton-grass* s.v. COTTON *n.*¹

harelike *a.* resembling (that of) a hare L16.

hare /hɛː/ *n.*² Long *rare* exc. in HAREWOOD. M17. [G dial. *Ehre* f. Proto-Romance f. L *acer* maple.] = HAREWOOD.

†**hare** *v.*¹*t.* E16. [Origin uncertain: perh. partly f. HARRY *v.* and partly f. HARE *n.*¹] 1 Harry, worry, harass. E16–L17. 2 Frighten, scare. M17–M18.

hare /hɛː/ *v.*² L19. [f. HARE *n.*¹] †1 *v.t.* (w. *it*). Double back like a hare. Only in L19. 2 *v.i.* & *t.* (w. *it*). Run or move with great speed. E20.

2 S. BARSTOW I'm . . haring down the hill to the bus stop.

hare-brain /ˈhɛːbreɪn/ *n.* Also **hair-**. M16. [f. HARE *n.*¹ (later app. also assoc. w. HAIR *n.*) + BRAIN *n.*] †A *n.* A hare-brained person. M16–L17. B *adj.* = HARE-BRAINED. M16.

hare-brained /ˈhɛːbreɪnd/ *a.* Also **hair-**. M16. [f. prec. + -ED².] Having or showing no more sense than a hare; reckless, rash.

G. CLARE This hare-brained scheme went too far.

Hare Krishna /harɪ ˈkrɪʃnə, hɑːreɪ/ *a.* & *n.* L20. [The wds (= 'O Vishnu Krishna') of a Skt devotional chant: see HARIJAN, KRISHNAISM.] Designating or pertaining to, a member of, a sect devoted to the worship of the Hindu god Krishna.

hareld /ˈhar(ə)ld/ *n. rare.* M19. [f. mod.L *Harelda* former genus name, alt. of *Havelda*, f. Icel. *haferla*, *hávella*.] The long-tailed duck, *Clangula hyemalis*.

harelip /hɛːˈlɪp/ *n.* M16. [f. HARE *n.*¹ + LIP *n.*] A congenital cleft in the upper lip on one or both sides of the centre, often associated with cleft palate; cleft lip.

¶The use of *harelip* for cleft lip is increasingly regarded as offensive.

hare-lipped *a.* E17.

harem /ˈhɑːriːm, hɑːˈriːm, ˈhɛːrəm/ *n.* M17. [Orig. (f. Turk *harem*) f. Arab. *ḥaram* (that which is) prohibited, (hence) sacred or inviolable place, sanctuary, women's apartments, wives, women, later also f. Arab. *ḥarīm* w. same meaning, both f. *ḥaruma* to be prohibited or unlawful.] 1 Separate women's quarters in a Muslim house, designed for the privacy and seclusion of the occupants. M17. 2 The occupants of such quarters collectively; *spec.* a Muslim's wives and concubines. L18. b A group of female animals of a single species sharing a mate. L19.

1 N. BARBER The old ladies of the harem . . could . . watch, unseen, as the men below listen to the music. 2 BYRON Were it less toil . . to head an army than to rule a harem? b R. DAWKINS Elephant seals win and hold on to their harems.

Comb.: **harem skirt** a (divided) skirt of a full billowy cut gathered into a narrow hem, supposedly resembling the costume traditionally worn by an inhabitant of a harem.

haremlik /həˈriːmlɪk, ˈhɛːrəm-/ *n.* E20. [Turk. *haremlık* f. HAREM + *-lık* place.] = HAREM 1.

harewood /ˈhɛːwʊd/ *n.* L17. [f. HARE *n.*² + WOOD *n.*¹] Stained sycamore-wood used in cabinet-making.

Hargrave /ˈhɑːgreɪv/ *a.* E20. [Lawrence *Hargrave* (see below).] Designating a kind of cellular box kite invented in 1894 by Lawrence Hargrave (1850–1915), an Australian pioneer in aeronautics.

haricot /ˈharɪkəʊ/ *n.* M17. [Fr., in sense 1 in *febves de haricot* (17), perh. f. Aztec *ayacotli*, in sense 2 OFr. *hericoq*, *hericot* (*de mouton*), prob. rel. to *harigoter* cut up.] 1 More fully *haricot bean*. A leguminous plant, *Phaseolus vulgaris*, native to tropical America but having numerous widely cultivated varieties; the edible pod or seed of this plant; *esp.* white varieties of the dried seed. Cf. BEAN *n.* 1b. M17. 2 A ragout, esp. of mutton or lamb. M17.

harif *n.* var. of HAIRIF.

Harijan /ˈhʌrɪdʒ(ə)n, ˈharɪdʒan/ *n.* & *a.* Also **h-**. M20. [Skt *harijana* person devoted to the Hindu god Vishnu, f. *Hari* Vishnu + *jana* person.] A *n.* Pl. **-s**, same. In the Indian subcontinent, a Hindu of a hereditary low caste, regarded as defiling by contact members of higher castes. Cf. UNTOUCHABLE *n.* M20. B *attrib.* or as *adj.* Of or pertaining to this caste. M20.

¶The term was adopted and popularized by Gandhi.

hariolate /ˈharɪəleɪt/ *v.i. arch.* M17. [L *hariolat-* pa. ppl stem of *hariolari*, f. *hariolus* soothsayer: see -ATE³.] 1 Prophesy, soothsay. M17. †2 Practise ventriloquism. M–L17.

hark /hɑːk/ *v.* & *n.* ME. [Corresp. to OFris. *herkia*, *harkia* rel. to MLG, MDu., Flem. dial. *horken*, OHG *hōrechen* (G *horchen*): cf. HEARKEN.] A *v.* 1 *v.t.* Listen to; hear with active attention. Now *arch.* or *poet.* ME. 2 *v.i.* Listen. (Foll. by *at*, *to*.) ME. 3 *v.i.* Speak in one's ear; whisper, mutter. *Sc.* & *north.* L16. 4 *Hunting.* a *v.i.* Go (*away*, *forward*, *off*, etc.). Chiefly in *imper.* E17. b *v.i.* Foll. by *back*: (of hounds) retrace the course taken to find a lost scent; *fig.* revert (*to* a subject). E19. c *v.t.* Urge (hounds) *on*, *forward*, with encouraging cries; call (hounds) *back*. E19.

1 J. MASEFIELD I've shaked to hark The peewits . . in the dark. 2 G. MORTIMER 'I can't trust you. . .' 'Hark at him!' laughed Mrs. Larpenti. S. SASSOON Hark! There's the big bombardment. 4b R. SUTCLIFF He harked back to an earlier point in their discussion.

B *n.* The action or an act of harking (*away*, *back*, etc.); an utterance of 'hark!'. M18.

harker *n.* (*rare*) E19.

harka /ˈhɑːkə/ *n.* E20. [Moroccan Arab. *ḥarka*: cf. literary Arab. *ḥaraka* movement, action, military operation.] A body of Moroccan irregular troops.

harken *v.* see HEARKEN.

harl /hɑːl/ *n.*¹ Also **harle**. See also HERL. M17. [App. = MLG *herle*, *harle*, etc., LG *harl*, EFris. *harrel* fibre of flax or hemp.] 1 A filament or fibre (of flax or hemp). M17. 2 A barb or fibre of a feather. L19.

harl /hɑːl/ *n.*² *Sc.* & *north.* E19. [f. HARL *v.*] 1 The action or an act of harling; something dragged or scraped together. E19. 2 A small quantity, a scraping (of something). (*lit.* & *fig.*) E19. 3 A composition of lime and gravel or sand; roughcast. M19.

harl /hɑːl/ *v.* *Sc.* & *north.* ME. [Origin unkn.] 1 *v.t.* Drag, usu. with friction or scraping of the ground. ME. 2 *v.i.* Drag or trail oneself, go with dragging feet. E16. b Come as if dragged off. *rare.* L18. 3 *v.t.* Roughcast with lime mingled with small gravel. L16. 4 *v.i.* Troll for fish. M19.

harle *n.* var. of HARL *n.*¹

Harleian /hɑːˈliːən, ˈhɑːlɪən/ *a.* M18. [mod.L *Harleianus* f. surname *Harley* (see below): see -AN, -IAN.] Of or belonging to Robert Harley, Earl of Oxford (1661–1724) and his son Edward Harley, and esp. designating or pertaining to their library of books and manuscripts now deposited in the British Library.

Harlem /ˈhɑːləm/ *n.* & *a.* M20. [A predominantly Black area in Manhattan, New York.] (Designating) a strongly swinging jazz style.

M. T. WILLIAMS The Harlem style of James P. Johnson and Fats Waller.

Harlemese /hɑːləˈmiːz/ *n.* & *a.* E20. [f. prec. + -ESE.] (Designating) a regional type of speech characteristic of the inhabitants of Harlem, New York.

Harlemite /ˈhɑːləmʌɪt/ *n.* L19. [f. as prec. + -ITE¹.] A person born in or residing in Harlem, New York.

harlequin /ˈhɑːlɪkwɪn/ *n.* & *a.* L16. [Obs. Fr. (mod. *arlequin* after It. *arlecchino*), later var. of *Herlequin* (also *Hellequin*, as in OFr. *maisnie Hellequin*, in med.L *familia Hellequini* or *Herlechini*) leader of a legendary nocturnal troop of demon horsemen, also called in med.L *familia Herlethingi*, perh. ult. rel. to OE *Herla cyning* king Herla. For the It. associations cf. COLUMBINE *n.*², PUNCH *n.*⁴ 3, ZANY *n.*] A *n.* 1 (Usu. **H-**.) A stock character of the witty servant in Italian comedy (and subsequently French light comedy). Also, a mute character in English pantomime, and a mischievous buffoon invisible to the clown and the pantaloon and usu. wearing a mask and particoloured tights. L16. b A buffoon. L19. 2 A dog of a black and white variety or breed. L18. 3 = *harlequin duck* below. M19. 4 An opal (variety) with a mosaic pattern of colours. L19. B *attrib.* or as *adj.* Of, pertaining to, or characteristic of (esp. the dress of) a harlequin; gaily coloured, *esp.* (of an animal, bird, etc.) having distinctively variegated markings. L18.

Special collocations & comb.: **harlequin beetle** a large S. American longhorn beetle, *Acrocinus longimanus*, having red, white, and black elytra. **harlequin bronzewing** the Australian flock pigeon, *Phaps histrionica*. **harlequin bug** (*a*) = *harlequin cabbage-bug* below; (*b*) either of two brightly coloured Australian heteropteran bugs, *Tectocoris diophthalmus*, a cotton pest, or *Dindymus versicolor*, a fruit pest. **harlequin cabbage-bug** a red and black stink bug of southern N. America, *Murgantia histrionica*, a pest of vegetables. **harlequin cup** each of a set of cups in which each cup is a different colour. **harlequin duck** a duck of northern coasts and rivers, *Histrionicus histrionicus*, the breeding males having deep grey-blue plumage with chestnut and white markings. **harlequin fish** (*a*) a small freshwater cyprinid fish of SE Asia, *Rasbora heteromorpha*, popular in aquariums; (*b*) *Austral.* any of several edible red rockfish. **harlequin quail** (*a*) a small nomadic African quail, *Coturnix delagorguei*; (*b*) any of several American quails of the genus *Cyrtonyx*. **harlequin ring**: set round with variously-coloured stones. **harlequin smiler** a perciform fish of Australian waters, *Merogymnus eximius* (family Opistognathidae).

harlequiˈnesque *a.* having the style of a harlequin L19. **harlequinism** *n.* the performance of a harlequin; an action characteristic of a harlequin: E19.

harlequin /ˈhɑːlɪkwɪn/ *v.* M18. [f. the n.] 1 *v.t.* Conjure *away*, as a harlequin in a pantomime. *rare.* M18. 2 *v.i.* Play the harlequin. *rare.* E19. 3 *v.t.* Colour, decorate, with contrasting colours. Chiefly as *harlequined* ppl a. M20.

3 D. FRANCIS She wore a black and white harlequined ski-ing jacket.

harlequinade /ˌhɑːlɪkwɪˈneɪd/ *n.* & *a.* L18. [Fr. *arlequinade*, f. *arlequin* HARLEQUIN *n.*: see -ADE.] A *n.* 1 A kind of pantomime; the part of a pantomime in which a harlequin plays the chief part. L18. b A piece of buffoonery. E19. 2 A piece of gaily-coloured variegated work. L19. B *attrib.* or as *adj.* Of, pertaining to, or characteristic of a harlequinade; gaily-coloured, variegated. M20.

C. BEATON Bright futuristic scarves of checkered or harlequinade triangles or squares.

harlequinade /ˌhɑːlɪkwɪˈneɪd/ *v.i.* L18. [f. the n.] Play the harlequin; act fantastically.

Harley Street /ˈhɑːli striːt/ *n. phr.* M19. [A street in London associated with eminent physicians and surgeons.] Medical specialists collectively.

attrib.: M. GILBERT Two Harley Street surgeons discussing a difficult case.

harlot /ˈhɑːlət/ *n.*, *a.*, & *v.* *arch. derog.* ME. [OFr. (*h*)*arlot*, *herlot* young fellow, knave, vagabond = Prov. *arlot*, med.L *harlotus*, *herlotus* vagabond, beggar: cf. also It. *arlotto*, med.L *arlotus*, *erlotus* glutton, OSp. *arlote*, *alrote* lazy, OPort. *alrotar* go about begging.] A *n.* †1 A vagabond, a beggar, a rogue, a low fellow, a knave. Also, a lecher. ME–M17. †2 An itinerant jester, buffoon, or juggler; a person who tells or does something to raise a laugh. ME–L15. †3 A male servant or attendant; a menial. Cf. KNAVE. ME–M16. †4 A fellow; *joc.* a good chap. LME–M17. †5 A kind of pointed boot or shoe worn in the 14th cent. LME–E17. 6a A promiscuous woman (*derog.*); a prostitute. LME. b A woman. Long *rare* or *obs.* L15.

6a E. AMADI Any woman in trousers is a harlot as far as they are concerned.

B *attrib.* or as *adj.* That is a harlot; of or pertaining to a harlot. ME.

C *v.i.* Behave as or like a harlot; prostitute oneself. M17.

harlotry /ˈhɑːlətri/ *n.* & *a.* *arch. derog.* ME. [f. HARLOT *n.* + -RY.] A *n.* †1 Buffoonery, jesting, ribaldry; obscene talk or behaviour. ME–E19. 2 (An act of) sexual immorality, promiscuity; the practice or trade of prostitution. LME. 3 A prostitute, a harlot. Now *rare* or *obs.* L16. 4 *fig.* Meretriciousness, showy but false attractiveness. M18. †B *attrib.* or as *adj.* Base, filthy, worthless, trashy. L16–M17.

harm /hɑːm/ *n.* & *v.* [OE *hearm* = OFris. *herm*, OS, OHG, G *harm*, ON *harmr* grief, sorrow, f. Gmc.] A *n.* 1 Hurt, injury, damage, mischief; an instance of this. OE. 2 (A) sorrow, (an) affliction. Long *obs.* exc. *Sc.* OE.

1 E. M. FORSTER She had done wrong . . ; she only hoped that she had not done harm. D. CUSACK Dora, you're too sweet to wish harm even to Hitler! **do more harm than good** make matters worse (despite good intentions). **do no harm** do no damage; *colloq.* be beneficial. GRIEVOUS *bodily harm.* **out of harm's way** in safety.

B *v.* 1 *v.t.* Do harm to; injure, damage. OE. †2 *v.i.* Do harm or damage. ME–M17.

1 B. EMECHETA The people of Shavi didn't plan to harm them. J. GATHORNE-HARDY Never give them anything likely to harm them.

harmala /ˈhɑːmələ/ *n.* Also **harmal**, **-el**, /-m(ə)l/. OE. [Late L f. Gk, prob. of Semitic origin (cf. Syriac *'armĕlā*, Arab. *ḥarmal*).] A Mediterranean plant, *Peganum harmala* (family Zygophyllaceae), having aromatic seeds containing various alkaloids and used locally for medicines, oil, and dye.

harmaline *n.* an alkaloid found in harmala seeds M19.

harman /ˈhɑːmən/ *n.* *arch. slang.* M16. [1st syll. unexpl.; 2nd syll. cf. DARKMANS, LIGHTMANS.] †1 In *pl.* The stocks. M16–E17. 2 In full *harman beck* [cf. BEAK *n.*²]. A constable, *esp.* a parish constable; a beadle. M16.

harmattan /hɑːˈmat(ə)n/ *n.* L17. [Twi *haramata*.] A parching dusty land-wind on the W. African coast from December to February. Also *harmattan wind*.

harmel *n.* var. of HARMALA.

harmful /ˈhɑːmfʊl, -f(ə)l/ *a.* ME. [f. HARM *n.* + -FUL.] Apt to cause harm; injurious, damaging.

A. J. CRONIN He had . . to *prove* that the dust was harmful, . . destructive to lung tissue.

harmfully *adv.* LME. **harmfulness** *n.* L16.

harmine /ˈhɑːmiːn/ *n.* M19. [f. HARMALA + -INE⁵.] *Chem.* An alkaloid drug derived from harmala seeds or by oxidation of harmaline.

harmless /ˈhɑːmlɪs/ *a.* ME. [f. HARM *n.* + -LESS.] 1 Free from injury or damage; unharmed. Now *rare.* ME. 2 Free from guilt; innocent. Now *rare* or *obs.* ME. 3 Free from liability to punishment or payment for damages. Now *rare.* LME. 4 Doing or causing no harm; inoffensive, innocuous. M16.

2 C. CLARKE She bears him harmless of all suspicion. 3 **hold** or **save harmless** indemnify. 4 D. W. GOODWIN Everything is either a poison or harmless depending on the dose. A. N. WILSON Chesterton, in reality the most . . harmless of men, loved to fantasise about battle.

harmlessly *adv.* M16. **harmlessness** *n.* L16.

harmonial /hɑːˈməʊnɪəl/ *a.* *rare.* M16. [f. L *harmonia* HARMONY + -AL¹.] = HARMONIOUS.

harmonic /hɑːˈmɒnɪk/ *a.* & *n.* L16. [L *harmonicus* f. Gk *harmonikos* (in neut. pl. *harmonika* used as n. = theory of music), f. *harmonia* HARMONY: see -IC.] A *adj.* 1 Relating to music, musical; (of ancient music) relating to melody as distinguished from rhythm. *obs.* in *gen.* sense. L16. 2a Sounding in harmony, harmonious. M17. b Relating to or marked by harmony, agreement, or concord. M18. 3 *Mus.* Relating to harmony; belonging to the combination of musical notes in chords. M17. 4 *Math.* a Designating or involving the relation of quantities whose reciprocals are in arithmetical progression, as in the series 1 + ½ + ⅓ + ¼ + ... E18. b Expressible in the form of sine and cosine functions. M19. 5 *Physics* & *Mus.* Designating or relating to tones produced by the vibration of the aliquot parts of strings etc. M19.

Special collocations: **harmonic analysis**: of a periodic function into simple trigonometrical components. **harmonic function**: that satisfies any of a class of differential equations including that of simple harmonic motion. **harmonic minor** a scale with the minor sixth and major seventh both ascending and descending. **harmonic motion** symmetrical oscillatory motion under a retarding force proportional to the displacement from the equilibrium position (more fully *simple harmonic motion*), like the projection of uniform motion in a circle on to a diameter; periodic motion having simple harmonic components. **harmonic progression** (the relation between) a series of quantities whose reciprocals are in arithmetical progression. **harmonic series** (*a*) *Math.* a series of quantities in harmonic progression; (*b*) *Acoustics* & *Mus.* the scale formed by the harmonics of a fundamental note.

B *n.* 1 In *pl.* & (occas.) *sing.* Musical sounds or intervals constituting a theory or system; acoustics as relating to music. *obs.* exc. *Hist.* E18. 2 *Physics* & *Mus.* A secondary tone produced by the vibration of an aliquot part of a string, reed, etc., usu. accompanying the fundamental tone produced by a vibrating body as a whole. L18. b *Physics.* A component or subsidiary (electromagnetic) wave or oscillation whose frequency is a multiple of the fundamental. L19. 3 *Math.* A harmonic function. M19.

harmonica /hɑːˈmɒnɪkə/ *n.* M18. [Use as n. of fem. sing. or neut. pl. of L *harmonicus*: see prec.] 1 Any of various musical instruments; *spec.* (*a*) a mouth-organ consisting of one or more rows of free reeds arranged in a case and vibrated by blowing and sucking; (*b*) more fully *glass harmonica*, an instrument consisting of a row of concentric glass bowls kept moist and played by finger-pressure or by means of a keyboard. M18. 2 Any of various organ-stops. M19.

harmonical /hɑːˈmɒnɪk(ə)l/ *a.* L15. [f. HARMONIC + -AL[1].] †1 Of sounds: harmonious, sweet-sounding, tuneful. L15–L18. 2 Marked by harmony or agreement. Now *rare.* M16. 3 = HARMONIC *a.* 4. M16. †4 Relating to the collation of parallel texts, esp. of the four Gospels. Only in 17. †5 Relating to music; musical. E17–M19. †6 Relating to the combination of notes in music. Only in 18.

harmonically /hɑːˈmɒnɪk(ə)li/ *adv.* L16. [f. HARMONIC or prec.: see -ICALLY.] †1 With harmony or concord (esp. of sounds); harmoniously. L16–L18. 2 *Math.* In a harmonic relation or proportion; in the manner of harmonic motion. L16. 3 *Mus.* In relation to harmony. L18.

harmonicon /hɑːˈmɒnɪk(ə)n/ *n.* M19. [Gk *harmonikon* neut. sing. of *harmonikos* HARMONIC.] *Hist.* = HARMONICA.

harmonious /hɑːˈməʊnɪəs/ *a.* M16. [f. HARMONY + -OUS.] 1 Tuneful, sweet-sounding; sounding together in harmony. M16. b Of a person: singing, playing, or speaking tunefully or pleasantly. M16. 2 Forming a consistent, orderly, pleasing, or agreeable whole. M17. 3 Free from dissent or ill feeling; amicable, cordial. E18.

2 F. L. WRIGHT No part of anything is of any great value in itself except as . . part of the harmonious whole. 3 LD MACAULAY No constitutional question had ever been decided . . with more harmonious consent. J. I. M. STEWART I believe I enjoy harmonious relationships with everybody.

harmoniously *adv.* E17. **harmoniousness** *n.* L17.

harmonisation *n.* var. of HARMONIZATION.

harmonise *v.* var. of HARMONIZE.

harmonist /ˈhɑːmənɪst/ *n.* L16. [f. HARMONY + -IST.] 1a *Gk Hist.* A member of a school of musical theorists in ancient Greece who founded the rules of music on the subjective effects of tones as opp. to their mathematical relations. L16. b A musician. *arch.* M18. c A composer skilled in, or an expert in the theory of, harmony. L18. 2 A collator of parallel or related texts, esp. of the four Gospels. E18. 3 A person who brings things into harmony or agreement. E19. 4 (**H-**.) A member of the Harmony Society, a 19th-cent. communistic Christian religious sect which settled in Pennsylvania. E19.

1b G. HUDDESFORD Ballads I have heard rehears'd By harmonists itinerant. c E. GURNEY Modern harmonists are unwilling to acknowledge that the minor triad is less consonant than the major.

harmonistic /hɑːməˈnɪstɪk/ *a.* & *n.* M19. [f. HARMONIST + -IC.] A *adj.* Of or pertaining to the collation and harmonizing of parallel or related texts, esp. of the four Gospels. M19. B *n.sing.* & in *pl.* The branch of biblical criticism which seeks to harmonize parallel or related texts, esp. the four Gospels. L19.

harmonistically *adv.* L19.

harmonium /hɑːˈməʊnɪəm/ *n.* M19. [Fr., f. L *harmonia* HARMONY or Gk *harmonios* harmonious.] A keyboard instrument in which reeds are made to vibrate by air from a pedal-operated bellows.

harmonization /ˌhɑːmənʌɪˈzeɪʃ(ə)n/ *n.* Also **-isation.** M19. [f. HARMONIZE + -ATION.] 1 The action or process of bringing into harmony or agreement; reconciliation, standardization. M19. 2 Agreement in colour; matching or blending of tones. L19. 3 The adding of harmony to a melody. L19.

harmonize /ˈhɑːmənʌɪz/ *v.* Also **-ise.** L15. [(O)Fr. *harmoniser*, f. as HARMONY: see -IZE.] 1 *v.i.* Sing or play in harmony. L15. 2 *v.i.* Be in harmony (*with*); accord, be agreeable, in artistic effect. E17. 3 *v.t.* a Bring into harmony, attune. E18. b Reduce to internal harmony; make agreeable in artistic effect. E18. c Bring into agreement (*with*), reconcile. M18. 4 *v.t.* & *i.* Add notes to (a melody) to form chords; add harmony (to). L18.

2 G. P. R. JAMES It harmonizes well with his general character. J. KRANTZ I . . pick out colors that harmonize with what I planted last year. 3a TENNYSON A music harmonizing our wild cries. c E. A. FREEMAN A harmonized narrative of the martyrdom.

harmonizer *n.* L17.

Harmon mute /ˈhɑːmən ˈmjuːt/ *n. phr.* M20. [Perh. f. HARMON(ICA + MUTE *n.*[2]] (Proprietary name for) a type of trumpet or trombone mute. Also called *wah-wah mute.*

harmonogram /hɑːˈmɒnəgram/ *n.* E20. [f. Fr. *harmonie* HARMONY: see -O-, -GRAM.] A figure or curve drawn with a harmonograph.

harmonograph /hɑːˈmɒnəgrɑːf/ *n.* L19. [f. as prec.: see -O-, -GRAPH.] An instrument for tracing curves representing sonorous vibrations.

harmonometer /hɑːməˈnɒmɪtə/ *n.* E19. [Fr. *harmonomètre*, irreg. f. *harmonie* HARMONY + *-mètre* (see -METER).] An instrument for measuring the harmonic relations of musical notes.

harmony /ˈhɑːməni/ *n.* LME. [(O)Fr. *harmonie* f. L *harmonia* agreement, concord f. Gk, f. *harmos* joint, *harmozein* fit together.] 1 Combination or adaptation of parts, elements, or related things, so as to form a consistent and orderly whole; agreement, accord, congruity. LME. 2 The combination of (simultaneous or successive) musical notes to produce a pleasing effect; music; tuneful sound; *gen.* pleasing combination of sounds, as in poetry etc.; sweet or melodious sound. LME. 3 *Mus.* The combination of (simultaneous) notes to form chords; the structure of a piece of music with regard to its chords; the branch of music that deals with these. Cf. MELODY *n.* 4. LME. 4 Agreement of feeling or sentiment; accord, peace. E16. 5 A collation of parallel narratives etc., esp. of the four Gospels. L16. 6 Combination of parts to produce an aesthetically pleasing effect; agreeable effect of apt arrangement of parts. M17.

1 SOUTHEY To heavenliest harmony Reduce the seeming chaos. H. MACMILLAN We should hold frequent consultations . . that our policies and purposes might be kept in harmony. *vowel harmony*: see VOWEL *n.* 2 R. DAHL There is a new exciting music being made, with subtle harmonies and grinding discords. *harmony of the spheres*: see SPHERE *n.* 2. 3 *Classical Music* An experienced teacher of A level Harmony, to take over all Sixth Form harmony. *close harmony*: see CLOSE *a.* & *adv.* *open harmony*: see OPEN *a.* 4 H. H. WILSON The harmony which had thus been re-established with the Court of Baroda. 5 *Church Times* A concordance or harmony of the Gospels, produced . . by slicing up similar editions of the Bible. 6 JAS. HARRIS How pleasing the harmony between hills and woods, between rivers and lawns.

harmost /ˈhɑːmɒst/ *n.* L18. [Gk *harmostēs*, f. *harmozein* fit, regulate.] *Hist.* Any of the governors sent out by the Spartans after the Peloponnesian War to control subject cities and islands.

harmotome /ˈhɑːmətəʊm/ *n.* E19. [Fr., f. Gk *harmos* joint + *-tomos* cutting (app. in ref. to the way the octohedral crystal divides).] *Min.* A monoclinic hydrated silicate of aluminium and barium, occurring often in cruciform twin crystals of various colours.

harness /ˈhɑːnɪs/ *n.* ME. [OFr. *harneis* military equipment (mod. *harnais*) f. ON = provisions for an army (w. assim. of the termination: cf. OFr. *harneschier* equip), f. *herr* army (see HARRY *v.*) + *nest* = OE, OHG *nest* provisions.] 1 Orig., the equipment of a horse for riding, driving, etc. Now *spec.* the equipment by which a horse or other draught animal may be fastened to a cart etc. and controlled; *fig.* working equipment. ME. b Any of various arrangements of straps etc. resembling a horse's harness, as, (*a*) one fitted to a dog in place of a collar, (*b*) one used for fastening a thing to a person, (*c*) one used for holding a person (esp. round a child and held by an adult) for safety or restraint. L19. 2 The armour of a foot-soldier or of a mounted soldier and his horse; a suit of mail. Now *arch.* or *Hist.* ME. †3 The baggage or portable equipment of an army, a party of travellers, etc. Only in ME. 4†a Household and personal equipment; furniture; clothing. ME–E17. b Formal clothing, uniform. *US slang.* L19. †5 The genitals. Also *privy harness.* LME–E16. 6 Tackle, gear, armament; the equipment or mounting of something. Now only *spec.* the mechanism by which a large bell is suspended and hung. LME. 7 The apparatus in a loom for shifting the warp-threads. L16. 8 *Aeronaut.* A system of engine ignition leads, esp. when screened to prevent interference with radio signals. M20.

1 *Lancashire Evening Telegraph* Thieves stole £400 worth of harness, including a horse collar and various straps. *double harness*: see DOUBLE *a.* & *adv.* **in harness** in the routine of daily work (*die in harness*: see DIE *v.*[1]). *single harness*: see SINGLE *a.* & *adv.* b C. G. BURGE Safety belts and safety harness have been specially designed for use in aircraft. J. P. PHILIPS She unbuckled the dog's harness. C. RYAN Without removing his harness, and dragging his parachute behind him, Raub rushed the Germans. 2 LONGFELLOW A single warrior, In sombre harness mailed.

Comb.: **harness bull** *US slang* a uniformed policeman; **harness cask** *Naut.* a cask of salt meat for current consumption; **harness cop** *US slang* = *harness bull* above; **harness-racing**: in which a horse pulls a two-wheeled vehicle and a driver.

harness /ˈhɑːnɪs/ *v.t.* ME. [OFr. *harneschier* equip, f. base of OFr. *harneis* (see prec.), or directly f. the n.] 1 Put a harness on (a horse etc.); fasten (a horse etc.) *to* a cart etc. with a harness. ME. b *fig.* Utilize (a river, a waterfall, natural forces) for motive power. L19. 2 Equip with armour, arm. Now *arch.* or *Hist.* LME. †3 Dress, clothe, array. LME–M19. †4 Equip, adorn, esp. with fittings of precious material. LME–L19.

1 J. CARY We harnessed the old sheep-dog to the sledge. *fig.*: V. GLENDINNING Neither sex can achieve much . . without harnessing the complementary attributes of the other. b A. E. STEVENSON The powers of the atom are about to be harnessed for ever-greater production.

harnessed /ˈhɑːnɪst/ *a.* LME. [f. HARNESS *n.* or *v.*: see -ED[2], -ED[1].] 1 Armed, in armour. Long *arch.* or *Hist.* LME. †2 Equipped; mounted with (precious) metal. LME–M16. 3 Yoked, in harness. L15.

Special collocations: **harnessed antelope**: of the genus *Tragelaphus* with white stripes across the back; *spec.* the bushbuck, *T. scriptus*.

haro *int.* var. of HARROW *int.*

haroseth /həˈrəʊsɛθ/ *n.* Also **ch-** /x-/; **-set** /-sɛt/. L19. [Heb. *ḥărōseṯ* f. *ḥeres* earthware.] A mixture of apples, nuts, spices, etc., eaten at the Passover Seder service to symbolize the clay mixed by the Israelites during their slavery in Egypt.

harp /hɑːp/ *n.* & *v.* [OE *hearpe* = OS *harpa* (Du. *harp*), OHG *harfa* (G *Harfe*), ON *harpa*, f. Gmc, whence also late L *harpa*.] A *n.* 1 A stringed musical instrument usu. consisting of a (roughly triangular) framework fitted with a series of strings of definite lengths, played by plucking with the fingers (esp. traditionally by those in heaven), now esp. in the form of a large vertical orchestral instrument resting on the floor and equipped with pedals to alter the pitch of the strings. OE. b A representation of a harp, esp. as the national device of Ireland. M17. c More fully *mouth-harp*. A mouth-organ, a harmonica. *US colloq.* L19. d A person of Irish origin or descent. *US slang.* E20. 2 (Usu. **H-**.) *The* constellation Lyra. M16. †3 Either of two Irish coins bearing the representation of a harp. Cf. HARPER *n.*[1] 2. M16–E17. 4 Any of various types of sieve. M17. 5 In full *harp-shell*. Any of various marine gastropods of the family Harpidae, having large ornate shells with a widely flared aperture, mainly found in the Indian and Pacific Oceans. M18. 6 More fully *harp-seal*. A light grey-brown seal with distinctive dark markings, *Phoca groenlandica*, of the north-west Atlantic, and the Barents and White Seas. L18.

1 *attrib.*: DAY LEWIS I . . sang . . to the harp accompaniment of Sidonie Goossens. *Aeolian harp*: see AEOLIAN 2. **double harp**: having two sets of strings differently tuned. *Irish harp*: see IRISH *a.* *Jew's harp*: see JEW *n.* **triple harp**: having three sets of strings differently tuned. *Welsh harp*: see WELSH *a.*

Comb.: *harp-seal*: see sense 6 above; *harp-shell*: see sense 5 above; **harp-string** any of the strings of a harp.

B *v.* 1 *v.i.* Play (on) a harp. OE. b *v.t.* Play (notes, music, etc.) on a harp. Now *arch. rare.* ME. 2 *v.i.* Dwell tediously *on* a subject in speech, writing, etc. E16. 3 *v.t.* Bring *out of*, *into*, etc., a place or state by playing the harp. E16. 4 *v.t.* Give voice to; guess. Now *rare* or *obs.* E17. 5 *v.i.* Make a sound like that of a harp. M17.

1 F. O'BRIEN A hunchback that harped for his living about the streets. 2 CARLYLE Harping mainly on the religious string. E. TAYLOR Still harping on the money she had lent him.

harper /ˈhɑːpə/ *n.*[1] OE. [f. HARP *n.* + -ER[1].] 1 A person who plays (on) the harp. OE. 2 Any of various Irish coins, esp. a shilling, bearing the figure of a harp. Cf. HARP *n.* 3. Long *obs.* exc. *Hist.* L16.

†**harper** *n.*[2] *rare.* Also **harpier**. L16–E17. [App. erron. f. HARPY.] A harpy.

harping /ˈhɑːpɪŋ/ *n.* Also (earlier) †**-pon**. LME. [OFr. *harpon* clamp: see HARPOON.] *Naut.* 1 Any of various pieces of timber for supporting and strengthening, esp. as used to hold the frames of a wooden vessel in place until the outside planking is done. Also, the forward part of the wales which encompass the bow of a ship and are fastened to the stem. Freq. in *pl.* LME. 2 In *pl.* In full *cat-harpings*. Ropes or cramps used to brace in the shrouds of lower masts behind their yards. E17.

†**harping-iron** *n.* LME–E19. [Perh. f. Fr. *harpin* boat-hook (f. *harper* grasp, grapple) + IRON *n.* Repl. by HARPOON *n.*] A barbed spear used for spearing whales and large fish; a harpoon.

harpist /ˈhɑːpɪst/ *n.* E17. [f. HARP *n.* + -IST.] A (professional) harper.

†**harpon** *n.* see HARPING.

harpoon /hɑːˈpuːn/ *n.* & *v.* E17. [Fr. *harpon*, f. *harpe* dog's claw, cramp-iron, clamp, f. L (also *harpa*) f. Gk *harpē* sickle.] A *n.* Orig., a barbed dart or spear. Later, a barbed spearlike missile with a cord attached to the shank, for catching whales and large fish. Cf. earlier HARPING-IRON. E17.

Comb.: **harpoon-gun**: for firing a harpoon.

B *v.t.* Strike or spear with a harpoon. L18.

harpoo'neer *n.* (now *rare* or *obs.*) a harpooner E17. **harpooner** *n.* a person who throws or fires a harpoon E18.

†**harpsical** *n.* E17–L18. [Alt. of HARPSICHORD, prob. after *virginal*.] A harpsichord.

harpsichord /ˈhɑːpsɪkɔːd/ *n.* E17. [Fr. †*harpechorde* = It. *arpicordo*, mod.L *harpichordium*, f. late L *harpa* HARP *n.* + *chorda* string (see CORD *n.*[1]), w. unexpl. intrusive *s*.] A keyboard musical instrument shaped like a grand piano, having strings in line with the direction of the keys and plucked by quill or leather points, esp. popular from the 16th to the 18th cent.

harpsichordist *n.* a person who plays the harpsichord L19.

harpuisbos /hɑːˈpœysbɒs/ *n.* Also ***-bosje*** /-bɒsi/, (in semi-Anglicized form) ***harpuis bush*** /hɑːˈpœys bʊʃ/. E19. [Afk., f. Du. *harpuis* resin + *bos* BUSH *n.*[1]] Any of various southern African shrubs of the genus *Euryops*, of the composite family, which bear yellow-rayed flowers and exude resin. Also called *resin-bush*.

harpy /ˈhɑːpi/ *n.* LME. [(O)Fr. *harpie* or its source L *harpyia*, pl. *-iae* f. Gk *harpuiai* snatchers, rel. to *harpazein* seize.] 1 *Class. Mythol.* Also **H-**. A rapacious monster covered in filth, having a woman's face and body and a bird's wings and claws, supposed to be a minister of divine vengeance. LME. b A representation of a harpy. L16. 2 A greedy, cruel or grasping person, *esp.* a rapacious woman. L15. 3 In full *harpy eagle*. A very large, powerful eagle, *Harpia harpyja*, of Central and S. America. M19.

harquebus /ˈhɑːkwɪbəs/ *n.* Also **arq-** /ˈɑːk-/. M16. [Fr. (*h*)*arquebuse*, ult. f. MLG *hakebusse* (mod. *Haakbus*) or MHG *hake*(*n*)*bühse* (mod. *Hakenbüchse*): see HACKBUT.] *Hist.* 1 An early type of portable firearm; *spec.* one supported on a tripod by a hook or on a forked rest. M16. 2 Soldiers armed with harquebuses collectively. Long *rare* or *obs.* L16.

harquebu'sier *n.* a soldier armed with a harquebus M16.

harquebusade /ˈhɑːkwɪbəseɪd/ *n. obs.* exc. *Hist.* Also **arq-** /ˈɑːk-/. M16. [Fr. (*h*)*arquebusade*, f. as prec.: see -ADE.] 1 A continuous discharge of harquebus shots, a fusillade. Formerly also, a single harquebus shot. M16. 2 Usu. **a-**. In full *harquebusade water*. A lotion used to treat gunshot and other wounds; a restorative. M18.

harr /hɑː/ *n.* Now chiefly *dial.* Also **harre**. [OE *heorr* corresp. to MDu. *herre*, *harre* (Du. *har*(*re*)), and *heorra* corresp. to ON *hjarri*, both f. Gmc.] The hinge of a door or gate; the part of a gate or door to which hinges are fastened.

harr /hɑː/ *v.i. obs.* exc. *dial.* LME. [Imit.] Make a rough guttural sound; snarl.

harrateen /ˈhɑːrətiːn/ *n.* & *a. obs.* exc. *Hist.* Also **hara-**. E18. [Origin unkn.] (Of) a linen fabric used for curtains, bed hangings, etc.

harre *n.* var. of HARR *n.*

Harri *n.* var. of HURRI.

Harrian *a.* & *n.* var. of HURRIAN.

harridan /ˈharɪd(ə)n/ *n. derog.* (orig. *slang*). L17. [Perh. alt. of Fr. *haridelle* old horse: ult. origin unkn.] A haggard or ill-tempered (old) woman.

P. BAILEY I have complained till I'm hoarse. They must not find me an impossible old harridan.

harrier /ˈharɪə/ *n.*[1] LME. [f. HARE *n.*[1] + -ER[1] after (O)Fr. *levrier*, repr. med.L *leporarius* greyhound, w. assim. to HARRIER *n.*[2]] 1 A kind of hound used for hunting hares. LME. b In *pl.* Such hounds as a pack with huntsmen etc. Also, cross-country runners as a group or club. L19. 2 Any of the pursuers in the game of hare and hounds. L19.

harrier /ˈharɪə/ *n.*[2] E16. [f. HARRY *v.* + -ER[1].] A person who harries, ravages, or lays waste.

harrier /ˈharɪə/ *n.*[3] Also (earlier) †**harrower**. M16. [f. HARROW *v.*[1] + -ER[1], assim. in 17 to HARRIER *n.*[2]] Any of a number of medium-sized, long-winged, slender-bodied hawks of the genus *Circus*.

hen-harrier, *marsh harrier*, *Montagu's harrier*, etc.

Comb.: **harrier-eagle** a serpent-eagle; **harrier-hawk** (*a*) = *forest falcon* s.v. FOREST *n.*; (*b*) either of two long-tailed, long-legged hawks of the genus *Polyboroides*, of sub-Saharan Africa and Madagascar.

Harriet Lane /harɪət ˈleɪn/ *n. slang* (chiefly *Naut.*). L19. [A murder victim: cf. FANNY ADAMS.] Preserved meat; *esp.* Australian tinned meat.

Harris /ˈharɪs/ *n.* L19. [The island of Lewis with *Harris* in the Outer Hebrides.] More fully *Harris tweed*. (Proprietary name designating) the hand-woven tweed produced in the Outer Hebrides, esp. on the island of Lewis with Harris.

Harrogate /ˈharəgət/ *n.* L18. [A borough in North Yorkshire.] 1 *Harrogate water*, a mineral water from springs in Harrogate. L18. 2 *Harrogate toffee*, (proprietary name for) a kind of toffee. L19.

Harrovian /həˈrəʊvɪən/ *n.* & *a.* E19. [f. mod.L *Harrovia* Harrow (see below): see -AN, -IAN.] A *n.* A past or present member of Harrow School, a public school at Harrow-on-the-Hill, Middlesex. E19. B *adj.* Of, pertaining to, or characteristic of Harrow School. M19.

harrow /ˈharəʊ/ *n.* ME. [f. ON *herfi*, *hervi* (Sw. *harf*, *härf*, Da. *harv*) obscurely rel. to MLG, MDu. *harke* (Du. *hark*) rake. Sense 3 f. HARROW *v.*[2]] 1 A heavy frame set with esp. iron teeth or tines, drawn over ploughed land to break up clods, root up weeds, cover seed, etc. ME. 2 *transf.* A similar contrivance used for other purposes. ME. 3 The action or an act of harrowing. L19.

1 *fig.*: L. STRACHEY The Napoleonic harrow passed over Saxe-Coburg. **under the harrow** in distress.

harrow /ˈharəʊ/ *v.*[1]*t.* ME. [By-form of HARRY *v.*] Harry, rob, spoil. Now chiefly of Christ: rescue the souls of the righteous from (hell).

J. CLAPHAM These Picts . . did oft-times harrow the borders.

harrow /ˈharəʊ/ *v.*[2]*t.* ME. [f. HARROW *n.*] 1 Draw a harrow over; break up, crush, or pulverize with a harrow. ME. 2 Lacerate, wound, (the body, the feelings, etc.); cause to suffer, distress. E16.

1 H. E. BATES Parker was harrowing ground for spring seed. **harrow in** cover (seed) by harrowing. 2 H. ACTON For fear of harrowing them by the spectacle of her agony. D. ADAMS The heavy movement and breath that had first so harrowed the Professor.

harrow /ˈharəʊ/ *int.* Now *rare*. Also **haro**. ME. [(O)Fr. *harou*, (also mod.) *haro*, imit.: cf. HARASS *v.*] Expr. distress or alarm.

cry harrow (on) denounce (a person).

Harrow drive /harəʊ ˈdraɪv/ *n. phr.* M19. [f. *Harrow* (see HARROVIAN) + DRIVE *n.*] *Cricket.* Orig., a drive through extra cover. Now, a mishit drive in which the ball deflects off the inside edge of the bat behind the wicket.

harrower /ˈharəʊə/ *n.*[1] ME. [f. HARROW *v.*[2] + -ER[1].] A person who or thing which harrows land, the body, feelings, etc.

†**harrower** *n.*[2] see HARRIER *n.*[3]

harrowing /ˈharəʊɪŋ/ *a.* E19. [f. HARROW *v.*[2] + -ING[2].] That harrows the feelings; acutely distressing or painful.

J. A. MICHENER The ordeal he had undergone . . was so much more harrowing.

harrowingly *adv.* L18. **harrowingness** *n.* (*rare*) L19.

harrumph /həˈrʌmf/ *n.*, *int.*, & *v.* M20. [Imit.]

A *n.* & *int.* (A guttural sound made by clearing the throat) expr. disapproval. M20.

B *v.* 1 *v.i.* Make a guttural sound, esp. expressing disapproval. M20. 2 *v.t.* Speak (words) in a guttural way, esp. expressing disapproval. M20.

1 J. A. MICHENER The old man harrumphed.

harry /ˈhari/ *n.*[1] *rare.* ME. [f. the vb.] The action or an act of harrying.

Harry /ˈhari/ *a.* & *n.*[2] L15. [Familiar by-form of the male name *Henry*.] A *adj.* Designating any of various coins of Henry VI, Henry VII, or Henry VIII. Long *rare* or *obs.* L15.

B *n.* 1 a (A name for) a country fellow, a rustic. Now *dial. rare.* L18. b (A name for) a young man of the lower classes. Now chiefly in *Flash Harry* below. L19. 2 In *pl.* Playing-cards of the second quality. *rare.* M19.

Phrases: **By the Lord Harry!** *int.* (*arch.*) expr. surprise or asseveration. **Flash Harry** an ostentatious, loudly-dressed and extrovert man; a show-off. **Old Harry** the Devil; esp. in *play Old Harry with*, play the devil with, work mischief on, ruin.

Special collocations & comb.: **Harry groat** a groat of Henry VIII; **Harry-long-legs** (now *dial.*) a crane-fly; **Harry noble** a gold coin of Henry VI.

harry /ˈhari/ *v.* [OE *hergian*, *herian* corresp. to OFris. *-heria*, OS *herion*, OHG *heriōn*, ON *herja*, f. Gmc, f. a base meaning 'host, army'. Prob. conflated with synon. OFr. *harier*, *her(r)ier*. Cf. HARROW *v.*[1]] 1 *v.i.* Make predatory raids. OE. b *v.t.* Plunder, carry off (cattle etc.) in a raid. *Sc.* LME. 2 *v.t.* Overrun (a territory) with an army; lay waste, pillage, spoil. ME. 3 *v.t.* Harass, persecute; despoil. ME. b Drive out deprived of house or possessions. *Sc.* M16. 4 *v.t.* Worry, goad, harass; ill-treat. ME. 5 *v.t.* Drag. *obs.* exc. *dial.* ME.

1 E. A. FREEMAN The Danes spread themselves over the country, harrying. 2 J. R. GREEN Pirate-boats were harrying the western coast of the island. 3 W. S. CHURCHILL American privateers . . continued to harry British shipping. 4 A. S. BYATT She had a reputation for driving and harrying her subordinates.

harsh /hɑːʃ/ *a.* Also (orig. & *north.*) **harsk** /hɑːsk/. ME. [MLG, G *harsch* rough, lit. 'hairy', f. *haer* (G *Haar*): see -ISH[1]. Cf. OSw. *harsk* (mod. *härsken*) rank, rancid and HASK.] 1 a Hard and rough to the touch; coarse-textured. ME. b Rough to the taste or smell; astringent. LME. c Rough to the ear; grating, jarring, discordant. M16. d Physically disagreeable; lacking any comfort; bleak, stark. E17. e Of a rough or forbidding appearance; inharmonious or unpleasant to the eye. L18. 2 Of an action, a person, etc.: severe, rigorous, cruel, unfeeling. L16. 3 Lacking smoothness; jarring or grating to the mind or one's taste. L16.

1a W. BOORER A few harsh-coated breeds need no trimming. b P. V. PRICE Such wines can be harsh rather than truly dry. c V. WOOLF It shattered the song of another bird with harsh discord. d R. P. JHABVALA There was a white glare in which everything looked very clean and harsh. *Sunday Express* These boots keep you warm in the harshest of conditions. e J. MASTERS The lights seemed harsh to me, coming in out of the soft night. C. P. SNOW A harsh red brick village interrupted the flow of fields. P. ROTH The harsh and rugged pioneer with that pistol in his pocket. 2 H. WOUK With difficulty Pug refrained from saying something harsh. J. M. ROBERTS They were so harsh, intransigent, cruel, uncompromising. *Practical Hairstyling & Beauty* Protect hair . . from the harsh drying effects of the sea and sun. 3 CAPT. J. SMITH Though the beginning may seeme harsh . . a pleasanter Discourse ensues. F. MYERS No harsh transitions Nature knows.

harshen *v.t.* make (more) harsh E19. **harshly** *adv.* LME. **harshness** *n.* LME.

harsh /hɑːʃ/ *v.* L16. [f. the adj.] †1 *v.i.* Make a harsh sound, creak. Only in L16. 2 *v.t.* Rub or crash roughly against. *rare.* L19.

harsk *a.* see HARSH *a.*

hart /hɑːt/ *n.* [OE *heort*, earlier *heorot* = OS *hirot* (Du. *hert*), OHG *hir(u)z* (G *Hirsch*), ON *hjǫrtr*, f. Gmc.] The male of the deer, esp. of the red deer; *spec.* a male deer after its fifth year.

hartal /ˈhɑːtɑːl, ˈhɑːtɑːl/ *n.* E20. [Hind. *hartāl*, *hartāl* for *haṭtal* lit. 'locking of shops' (Skt *haṭṭa* shop, *tāla* lock, bolt.).] In the Indian subcontinent, the organized closing of shops and offices as a mark of protest or as an act of mourning.

hartebeest /ˈhɑːtɪbiːst/ *n.* Also (earlier) †**hartbeest**. Pl. same, **-s**. L18. [Afk. (now *hartebees*) f. Du. *hert* hart + *beest* beast.] A large African antelope, *Alcelaphus buselaphus*, with a long head, a sloping back, and hooked horns, of which there are several races, including the kongoni (now extinct), the bubal, and the tora. Also, any of several related antelopes, esp. *Sigmoceros lichtensteinii* and members of the genus *Damaliscus* (as the hirola and the tsessebi).

bastard hartebeest = TSESSEBI. BUBAL *hartebeest*. **Cape hartebeest** a red hartebeest of the southern African race. **northern hartebeest** = BUBAL. *red hartebeest*: see RED *a.* TORA *hartebeest*.

Hartleian /ˈhɑːtlɪən, hɑːtˈliːən/ *a.* Also **Hartleyan**. E19. [f. David *Hartley* (see below): see -AN, -IAN.] Of or pertaining to the doctrines of the English psychologist David Hartley (1705–57), regarded as the founder of English associationist psychology.

hartshorn /ˈhɑːtshɔːn/ *n.* OE. [f. HART + -'S[1] + HORN *n.*] 1 The horn or antler of a hart; the substance obtained by rasping, slicing, or calcining this, formerly the chief source of ammonia. OE. 2 The aqueous solution of ammonia from any source. Also *spirit of hartshorn*. Now *arch.* or *Hist.* L17.

hart's tongue /ˈhɑːts tʌŋ/ *n. phr.* ME. [tr. med.L *lingua cervi*: so named from the shape of the fronds. Cf. G *Hirschzunge*, Da. *hertstong*, Fr. *langue de cerf*, etc.] An evergreen fern, *Phyllitis scolopendrium*, of shady places, with long strap-shaped undivided fronds. Also *hart's tongue fern*.

hartwort /ˈhɑːtwəːt/ *n.* Also (earlier) †**hert-**. LME. [f. var. of HEART *n.* + WORT *n.*[1], from the heart-shaped form of the leaves or seeds.] †1 A plant resembling bugle, perhaps self-heal, *Prunella vulgaris*. Only in LME. †2 The plant birthwort, *Aristolochia clematitis*. M16–E17. 3 An umbelliferous plant, *Tordylium maximum*. Formerly, any of various plants of the related genus *Seseli*. M16.

harum-scarum /hɛːrəmˈskɛːrəm/ *adv.*, *a.*, & *n. colloq.* L17. [A rhyming comb., app. f. HARE *v.*[2] + SCARE *v.*] A *adv.* Recklessly, wildly. Now *rare* or *obs.* L17.

J. PORTER I should not like a son of mine to run harum-scarum through my property.

B *adj.* Reckless, wild. M18.

V. WOOLF The manner of a harum-scarum Irish hostess.

C *n.* A reckless person; reckless action or behaviour. L18.

HOLME LEE His reminiscences of Basil as a handsome harum-scarum.

harum-scarumness *n.* M19.

haruspex /həˈrʌspɛks/ *n.* Orig. †**a-**. Pl. **-spices** /-spɪsiːz/. L15. [L *(h)aruspex*, *-spicem*, f. a base appearing in Skt *hirā* artery + L *-spex*, f. *specere* look at.] *Rom. Hist.* A person who inspected the entrails of sacrificial victims in order to foretell the future.

haruspical /həˈrʌspɪk(ə)l/ *a.* M17. [L *(h)aruspicalis*, f. as prec.: see -ICAL.] Of, pertaining to, or having the function of a haruspex.

haruspication /hərʌspɪˈkeɪʃ(ə)n/ *n. rare.* L19. [Late L *haruspicatio(n-)*, f. as HARUSPEX: see -ATION.] = next.

haruspicy /həˈrʌspɪsi/ *n.* Orig. †**a-**. M16. [L *haruspicium*, f. as HARUSPEX.] *Rom. Hist.* Divination by inspection of the entrails of sacrifices.

Harvardian /hɑːˈvɑːdɪən/ *n.* E18. [f. *Harvard* College, Cambridge, Mass., now part of *Harvard* University.] A student or graduate of Harvard University.

Harveian /ˈhɑːvɪən, hɑːˈviːən/ *a.* M18. [f. William *Harvey* (see below): see -AN, -IAN.] Of, pertaining to, or commemorating the English physician William Harvey (1578–1657), who discovered how the blood circulated.

harvest /ˈhɑːvɪst/ *n.* & *v.* [OE *hærfest* = OFris., (M)Du. *herfst*, OHG *herbist* (G *Herbst* autumn, (dial.) fruit harvest), ON *haust*, f. Gmc, f. IE base repr. by L *carpere* pluck, Gk *karpos* fruit.] A *n.* 1 The third season of the year, autumn. *obs.* exc. *dial.* or passing into sense 2. OE. 2 (The season for) the cutting and gathering in of ripened grain and other produce. ME. 3 The crop of ripened grain. ME. b *gen.* The season's yield of any natural product. E17. 4 *fig.* The product of any action or effort. LME.

1 M. MACKENZIE Toward the End of Harvest, when the Days are turning short. 2 MILTON Seed time and Harvest, Heat and hoary Frost Shall hold thir course. M. IGNATIEFF It was the season of the grape harvest. 3 A. GHOSH Bhudet Roy . . had a magnificent harvest that year. b J. G. FARRELL At one time this orchard alone must have provided a great harvest of fruit. 4 SHAKES. *Rich. III* To reap the harvest of perpetual peace. R. S. THOMAS Your eyes betray The heart's rich harvest.

Comb.: **harvest-bug** = *harvest-mite* below; **harvest festival** a Christian church service giving thanks for the completion of the harvest, for which the church is usu. decorated with grain, fruit, etc.; **harvest field** a field in the process of being harvested; *harvest maiden*: see MAIDEN *n.* 7a; **harvestman** (*a*) a reaper, a harvester; (*b*) any arachnid of the order Opiliones, characteristically with very long legs and a small rounded waistless body; **harvest mite** any of various mites, or their biting larvae, which are common at harvest-time; esp. (in Great Britain and Ireland) *Trombicula autumnalis*; **harvest moon**: full within a fortnight of the autumnal equinox (22 or 23 September) and rising at almost the same time for several nights, at points successively further north on the eastern horizon; **harvest mouse** (*a*) a small Eurasian mouse, *Micromys minutus*, which builds a nest above ground in the stems of growing grain or other vegetation; (*b*) any of various small Central and N. American mice of the genus *Reithrodontomys*, that resemble brownish house mice; **harvest queen** a doll made from or decorated with sheaves of corn or a young woman chosen from the reapers, representing the goddess of agriculture and crops and given a place of honour at the harvest home; **harvest-spider** = *harvestman* (b) above.

B *v.* 1 *v.t.* & (later) *i.* Reap and gather in (ripe grain or other produce). LME. b *v.t.* Remove (cells) from a culture; remove (cells, tissues, organs) from a person or animal for experimental or transplantation purposes. M20. c *v.t.* Kill or remove (wild animals) for food, sport, or population control. M20. 2 *v.t. fig.* Gather up, collect, (and store); receive as the consequence of previous actions. L19.

1 C. MORGAN All the barley was not yet harvested. E. O'BRIEN Fields that have been mown, others that have been harvested. b *Nature* Macrophages were harvested from the peritoneal cavity 10 days after the second immunization. *British Medical Journal* They could harvest skin 24 hours after irreversible asystole and transplant it. 2 S. NAIPAUL He . . looked forward contentedly to harvesting a decent Second at the end of his three years. *transf.*: B. NEIL She went back to the sitting-room and harvested her scattered clothes.

harvestless *a.* devoid of harvests; sterile: M19.

harvester /ˈhɑːvɪstə/ *n.* L16. [f. HARVEST *v.* + -ER[1].] 1 A person who reaps and gathers in the harvest. L16. 2 A machine for reaping and esp. also for binding up the sheaves. Cf. *combine harvester* s.v. COMBINE *n.* 3. M19. 3 A harvestman (arachnid); a harvest-mite. L19.

harvest home /hɑːvɪst ˈhəʊm/ *n. phr.* L16. [f. HARVEST *n.* + HOME *adv.*] 1 The fact, time, or occasion of bringing in the last of the harvest; the festival (now rarely held) celebrating this. L16. 2 A song of rejoicing on this occasion. M17.

1 SHAKES. *1 Hen. IV* His chin new reap'd Show'd like a stubble-land at harvest-home. 2 SIR W. SCOTT Harvest-home hath hush'd the clanging wain.

Harvey /ˈhɑːvi/ *n.* M17. [f. surname *Harvey* (see below).] 1 [Prob. f. Gabriel *Harvey* (?1545–1630), English writer.] A variety of cooking and cider apple. M17. 2 [Peter *Harvey* (fl. 1760), English publican.] More fully *Harvey('s) sauce*. (Proprietary name for) a savoury sauce or relish for accompanying meat or fish. E19. 3 *Harvey wallbanger*, a cocktail made from vodka or gin and orange juice. Orig. *US*. L20.

harveyize /ˈhɑːvɪʌɪz/ *v.t.* Also **-ise**. L19. [f. H. A. *Harvey* (1824–93), US manufacturer + -IZE.] *Metall.* Case-harden (steel, esp. for armour-plating) by means of a cementation process invented by Harvey.

harzburgite /'hɑːtsbəːgʌɪt/ *n.* L19. [f. (Bad) *Harzburg*, a town in Germany + -ITE[1].] *Geol.* A rock of the peridotite group consisting largely of orthopyroxene and olioine.

has *v.* see HAVE *v.*

has-been /'hazbiːn/ *n. colloq.* E17. [f. *has* 3 sing. pres. indic. of HAVE *v.* + *been* pa. pple of BE.] A person who or thing which has lost a quality or proficiency formerly possessed; an out-of-date person or thing.

I. WALLACE A doddering and reactionary has-been who ought to have been interred long ago.

hasenpfeffer /'hɑːz(ə)n(p)fɛfə/ *n.* L19. [G, f. *Hasen* hare's + *Pfeffer* pepper.] A highly seasoned hare stew.

hash /haʃ/ *n.*[1] M17. [f. the vb, replacing earlier HACHY.] **1** Something cut up into small pieces; *spec.* a dish of chopped (esp. previously cooked) meat heated with gravy, potatoes, etc.; *fig.* old matter served up in a new form (now chiefly passing into sense 3). M17. **2** A stupid person, one who is careless or muddled in speech or action. *Sc.* M17. **3** A (spoiled) mixture of jumbled incongruous things; a mess, a muddle. Freq. in *make a hash of* below. M18. **4** Noise in a received signal due to imperfect equipment; *gen.* radio noise. M20. **5** *Computing.* An act or the action of hashing. M20. **6** In full *hash sign.* The symbol #, esp. used before a numeral that is a number in a series. L20.

Phrases: **make a hash of** spoil in attempting to deal with, make a mess of. **settle a person's hash** *colloq.* silence or subdue a person.

Comb.: **hash browns** (chiefly *N. Amer.*) a dish made of chopped cooked potatoes and onions (sometimes shaped into a patty), fried until brown; **hash-house** *colloq.* (chiefly *N. Amer.*) a cheap eating-house; *hash sign*: see sense 4 above.

hashy *a.* of the nature of a hash; muddled, careless: L19.

hash /haʃ/ *n.*[2] *colloq.* M20. [Abbrev.] = HASHISH.

attrib.: *Daily Telegraph* All claimed that they were unaware of any hash smuggling operation.

hash /haʃ/ *v.* L16. [(O)Fr. *hacher*, f. *hache* HATCHET *n.*] **1** *v.t.* Cut (esp. meat) up or *up* into small pieces; make into a hash, serve up as a hash; hack about, mangle (now only *fig.* exc. *Sc.* & *dial.*). L16. **2** *v.t.* Talk *over*, discuss exhaustively. *colloq.* M20. **3** *v.t.* & *i.* *Computing.* Apply an algorithm to (a character string, esp. a record key) in order to obtain a number, esp. as an address for a record. M20.

1 *fig.*: SCOTT FITZGERALD The things .. they had hashed and rehashed for many a frugal conversational meal. *New Socialist* People are offered the same view hashed up as 'left' culture. **2** *New Yorker* Asked him in to hash over a point or two.

Hashemite /'haʃmʌɪt/ *n.* & *a.* Also **Hashimite**. L17. [f. *Hashim*, great-grandfather of Muhammad + -ITE[1].] **A** *n.* A member of an Arabian princely family claiming descent from Hashim. L17. **B** *adj.* Of, pertaining to, or characteristic of the Hashemites. L19.

Hashimoto /haʃɪ'məʊtəʊ/ *n.* M20. [H. *Hashimoto* (1881–1934), Japanese surgeon.] Med. *Hashimoto's disease, goitre, thyroiditis*, an autoimmune disease causing chronic inflammation and consequential failure of the thyroid gland.

hashish /'haʃiːʃ, -ʃɪʃ, ha'ʃiːʃ/ *n.* L16. [Arab. *ḥašīš* dry herb, hay, powdered hemp-leaves, intoxicant made from this.] = CANNABIS 2.

R. OWEN A drive against the growing use of drugs in Georgia, mainly hashish and opium.

Hasid /'hasɪd/ *n.* Also **Cha(s)sid** /'xa-/, **Hassid**. Pl. **-im** /-ɪm/. E19. [Heb. *ḥāsīḏ* pious, pietist.] A member of a Jewish sect founded in the 18th cent. by Israel Baal Shem Tov and emphasizing joy in the service of God. Also = ASSIDEAN.

Ha'sidic *a.* of or belonging to the Hasidim E20. **Hasidism** *n.* the tenets of the Hasidim L19.

hask /hɑːsk/ *a.* Long *dial.* LME. [Alt. of *harsk*: see HARSH *a.*] Rough and hard to the touch or taste, esp. from lack of moisture.

hasky *a.* dry, rough, coarse M17.

haslet /'heɪzlɪt, 'hazlɪt/. *n.* Also **harslet** /'hɑːslɪt/. LME. [OFr. *hastelet* (mod. *hâtelet(te)*) dim. of *haste* (mod. *hâte*) spit, roast meat (cf. Du. *harst* sirloin) = OHG *harst*: see -LET.] Orig., a piece of meat for roasting; *esp.* a pig's pluck. Now chiefly, a meat loaf made from cooked minced and seasoned pig's pluck, usu. served cold.

Hasmonean /hazmə'niːən/ *n.* & *a.* Also **As-** /az-/. E17. [f. mod.L *Asmonaeus*, f. Gk *Asamonaios* = *ḥašmonāy*, the reputed grandfather of Mattathias, the head of the Maccabee family of priests: see -AN, -EAN.] **A** *n.* A member of a Jewish dynasty established by the Maccabees. E17. **B** *adj.* Of, pertaining to, or designating this dynasty. E17.

hasp /hɑːsp/ *n.* [OE *hæpse*, *hæsp* corresp. to MLG *haspe*, *hespe*, OHG *haspa* (G *Haspe*), ON *hespa*, rel. further to MLG., Du. *haspel*, OHG *haspil*.] **1** A contrivance for fastening a door or lid; *esp.* a hinged metal plate with a hole which fits over a staple and is secured by a pin or padlock; in a trunk or case, a similar metal plate with a projecting piece which is secured by the lock. OE. **b** Any of various similar simple devices for fastening a door, window, etc. L18. **2** A clasp or catch for fastening two parts of a garment, the covers of a book, etc. ME. **3** A hank or skein of yarn or thread; a definite quantity of yarn, the fourth part of a spindle. Now *dial.* LME.

hasp /hɑːsp/ *v.t.* OE. [f. the n.] **1** Fasten (as) with a hasp. OE. †**b** Confine, imprison; lock *up*. L17–E18. †**2** Clasp, embrace. LME–E17.

Hassid *n.* & *a.* var. of HASID.

hassle /'has(ə)l/ *v.* & *n.* L19. [Origin uncertain: perh. blend of HAGGLE *v.* and TUSSLE *v.*] **A** *v.* **1** *v.t.* Hack or saw at. *dial.* L19. **2** *v.t.* & *i.* Bother, pester, harass (a person); quarrel or wrangle *over* (something). *colloq.* M20.

2 W. WHARTON I hassle a guy into moving his truck.

B *n.* A problem, a difficulty; a quarrel, an argument; fuss, bother. *colloq.* M20.

K. AMIS Since the end of the legal hassle, we had not met more than a couple of times. A. BLOND To write a book without having the hassle of having to sell it too.

hassock /'hasək/ *n.* OE. [Origin unkn.] **1** A firm tuft or clump of grass etc., esp. as occurring in boggy ground. OE. **b** A shock of hair. *Sc.* M18. **2** A thick firm cushion, formerly freq. stuffed with straw, used to rest the feet on or, esp. in church, to kneel on. E16. **3** The soft calcareous sandstone separating the beds of ragstone in Kent. E18.

hassocky *a.* (*a*) (of a marsh or bog) having many hassocks; (*b*) of the nature of or consisting of calcareous sandstone: M17.

hast *v.* see HAVE *v.*

hasta la vista /'asta la 'vista/ *int.* M20. [Sp.] Goodbye, *au revoir*.

hastate /'hasteɪt/ *a.* L18. [L *hastatus*, f. *hasta* spear: see -ATE[2].] Shaped like a spearhead, narrowly triangular; *Bot.* (of a leaf) triangular with basal corners laterally projecting.

Also †**hastated** *a.* M–L18.

haste /heɪst/ *n.* ME. [OFr. (mod. *hâte*) f. Gmc (whence OE *hǣst* violence, fury, ON *heifst*, *heipt* hate, revenge, Goth. *haifsts* strife; OE *hǣste* violent, OFris. *hāste*, OHG *heisti* powerful), of unkn. origin.] **1** Quickness or speed of motion or action, esp. as prompted by urgency or pressure. ME. **2** Quickness of action without due consideration; rashness, precipitancy. ME. **3** Eagerness to do something quickly; impatience, hurry. LME.

1 A. J. CRONIN His haste was desperate, a frantic race against her ebbing strength. R. C. HUTCHINSON Without haste .. he turned and went away. **2** W. COWPER Friends, not adopted with a schoolboy's haste. **3** P. V. WHITE Such was his haste, he scarcely paused for his due reward. E. O'BRIEN The men and women .. seemed to be devoid of fret or haste.

Phrases: **in haste** (*a*) quickly; (*b*) hurriedly. **make haste** move or act quickly. **more haste, less speed** best results are obtained by proceeding with deliberation.

hasteful *a.* (*arch.*) full of haste; hurrying, hurried: E17. **hastefully** *adv.* (*rare*) L19.

haste /heɪst/ *v. arch.* ME. [OFr. *haster* (mod. *hâter*), f. as prec. Superseded by HASTEN.] **1** *v.t.* = HASTEN 1. ME. **2** *v.i.* & *refl.* = HASTEN 2. ME.

1 SHAKES. *Coriol.* Let's hence, And with our fair entreaties haste them on. **2** C. BRONTË The hour is hasting but too fast.

hasten /'heɪs(ə)n/ *v.* M16. [f. prec. + -EN[5].] **1** *v.t.* Cause to move more quickly; urge on; quicken, hurry. M16. †**b** Send in haste. E17–M18. **2** *v.i.* Make haste (*to do*); come or go quickly; hurry. M16.

1 D. L. SAYERS How easy it would be .. to hasten Mrs. Wrayburn's death a trifle. **2** W. S. CHURCHILL Parliament hastened to send the exiled Charles a large sum of money. J. G. FARRELL The Major hastened along the corridor, up the stairs three at a time.

hastener *n.* L16.

hastilude /'hastɪljuːd/ *n. obs.* exc. *Hist.* L16. [med.L *hastiludus*, *-dium*, f. L *hasta* spear + *ludus* play.] A kind of joust or tournament; spear-play.

hastily /'heɪstɪli/ *adv.* ME. [f. HASTY *a.* + -LY[2].] **1** Quickly, speedily; now usu., hurriedly. Formerly also, soon; suddenly. ME. **2** Rashly, inconsiderately, precipitately; in sudden anger. Formerly also, violently, fiercely. ME.

1 J. B. PRIESTLEY She withdrew her hand, though not hastily. J. SIMMS I hastily did my utmost to reassure him. **2** ADDISON That the Reader may not judge too hastily of this Piece of Criticism. M. KEANE She gave in hastily, 'if you must you must'.

hastiness /'heɪstɪnɪs/ *n.* ME. [f. as prec. + -NESS.] †**1** Quickness; suddenness. ME–L16. **2** Hurriedness; precipitancy, rashness; quickness of temper. ME.

hasting /'heɪstɪŋ/ *n.* & *a.* M16. [f. HASTE *v.* + -ING[2] (prob. orig. as ppl a.).] **A** *n.* †**1** In *pl.* People making haste or hurrying. M16–L17. **2** An early-ripening fruit or vegetable; *spec.* a variety of early pea. *obs.* exc. *local.* L16. **B** *adj.* †**1** Of a fruit or vegetable: ripening early. L16–M18. **2** That hastens or hurries. Now *rare* or *obs.* L16.

†**hastive** *a.* Also **hastif**. ME. [OFr. *hastif*, *-ive*: see next.] **1** = HASTY 1, 2, 3. ME–L15. **2** = HASTY 1C. Only in E18.

hasty /'heɪsti/ *a.*, *v.*, & *adv.* ME. [OFr. *hasti(f)* (mod. *hâtif*), f. as HASTE *n.*; see -Y[7]. Superseded HASTIVE (cf. TARDY *a.*).] **A** *adj.* **1** Speedy or quick, esp. in movement or action. *arch.* exc. as in sense 1b. ME. **b** Speedy or quick due to pressure of time; hurried; made or done in haste. LME. †**c** Of a fruit or vegetable: that ripens early. Cf. HASTIVE 2. LME–L17. **2** Rash, precipitate; quick-tempered; (of speech or action) said or done in anger or without due consideration. ME. †**3** Eager or impatient (*to do*). LME–M18.

1 S. BELLOW Walking quickly there, back and forth in his hasty style. **b** J. KRANTZ She gave them .. a hasty kiss before she was finally free to dash away. **2** S. O'CASEY You're a bit hasty at times .. an' say things you shouldn't say. A. THWAITE Philip .. cautioned him not to be hasty in committing himself. R. DAVIES I don't like to make hasty judgements.

Special collocations: **hasty pudding**: of wheat flour or (*US*) maize flour stirred to a thick batter in boiling milk or water.

B *v.t.* & *i.* = HASTEN. *obs.* exc. *Sc.* ME.

†**C** *adv.* Hastily. LME–M16.

hat /hat/ *n.* [OE *hætt* corresp. to ON *hǫttr* hood, cowl, f. Gmc, f. base of HOOD *n.*[1]] **1** A covering for the head worn by either sex; *esp.* one with a horizontal brim round the part covering the head (freq. w. specifying wd). OE. **2** A hat as showing the wearer's rank or office; *spec.* (in full *red hat*) the hat or dignity of a cardinal. ME. **3** A person's official capacity; one's status. Freq. in *wear one's — hat*, *wear two hats*, below. M20.

1 DAY LEWIS The .. beautiful face is shadowed by a perfectly enormous hat. E. WELTY A stylish hat with a quill slanting up from the crown. *bowler hat*, *Cossack hat*, *Gainsborough hat*, *hard hat*, *high hat*, *opera hat*, *sailor hat*, *stove-pipe hat*, *straw hat*, *top hat*, *Zulu hat*, etc. **3** J. D. WATSON The hat he now displayed was that of the chairman of a committee.

Phrases: *at the drop of a hat*: see DROP *n.* 7. **bad hat** *dated slang* a rascal, a ne'er-do-well. *cock one's hat*, *cocked hat*: see COCK *v.*[1] 6b. *hang (up) one's hat*: see HANG *v.* **hats off to —**: a call to acknowledge the outstanding qualities of a person or thing. **I'll eat my**

hat if — *colloq.* I shall be greatly astonished if (a predicted event does not take place). **in a** (or **the**) **hat** *slang* in trouble, in a fix. **keep under one's hat** keep secret or confidential. **my hat!** expr. surprise. **old hat** *slang* (something regarded as) old-fashioned or tediously familiar. **pass round the hat** (*lit.* & *fig.*) solicit donations by personal appeal. **pick out of a hat** *fig.* select completely at random. **pull one** etc. **out of the hat** bring off an unexpected trick in an apparently desperate situation. **raise one's hat** (of a man) lift the hat a short distance above the head, as a respectful salutation (foll. by *to* the person saluted). **send round the hat** = *pass round the hat* above. **take off one's hat** (*a*) (of a man) doff the hat, as a salutation or sign of respect; (*b*) *fig.* (foll. by *to*) acknowledge the outstanding qualities of. *talk through one's hat*: see TALK *v.* **throw one's hat into the ring** announce one's intention of entering a contest. **touch one's hat** (of a man) touch the brim of the hat with the hand, as a respectful greeting (*to* a person). **wear one's — hat** operate in one's — capacity. **wear two hats** operate in two capacities simultaneously. **whose hat covers his** (or **her**) **family** (& vars.) who has only himself (or herself) to provide for. *Yellow Hat*: see YELLOW *a.*

Comb.: **hatband** (*a*) a narrow ribbon worn round a hat above the brim (*gold hatband* (Hist.), a gentleman commoner at a university); (*b*) a band of crape worn round a hat as a sign of mourning; **hatbox** a box to hold a hat, esp. for travelling; **hat-check boy, girl** *N. Amer.* a cloakroom attendant; **hat-money** a gratuity paid by a merchant to the master of a ship; primage; **hatpin** a long pin usu. with an ornamental head, used to secure a woman's hat to her hair; **hatstand** an upright stand with hooks for hanging hats etc. on; **hat-tree** *US* = *hatstand* above; **hat trick** (in cricket) the feat of taking three wickets with three successive balls; *gen.* the achievement of three (consecutive) successes in any other sport or activity.

hatful *n.* as much as a hat will hold; a large quantity: M17. **hatless** *a.* not having or wearing a hat LME. **hatlessness** *n.* L19.

hat /hat/ *v.t.* Infl. **-tt-**. LME. [f. the n.] Provide or equip with a hat.

hatable /ˈheɪtəb(ə)l/ *a.* Also **hateable**. LME. [f. HATE *v.* + -ABLE.] That deserves to be hated; odious.

hatch /hatʃ/ *n.*^{1} [OE *hæċċ, heċċ*, corresp. to MLG *heck*, MDu. *hecke* (Du. *hek*), f. Gmc. Cf. HACK *n.*^{3}, HECK *n.*^{1}] **1** The lower half of a divided door, which may be closed while the upper half is open. Also (now *dial.*), a small gate or wicket. OE. **b** An opening in a wall through which dishes etc. may be passed between a kitchen and a dining area. Also *serving-hatch*. E18. **2** *Naut.* (The trapdoor or grated framework covering) a hatchway. Formerly (usu. in *pl.*), a movable planking forming a kind of deck; the permanent deck. ME. **b** *transf.* (The trapdoor covering) an opening in the floor of a timber-shed or other building. L19. †**3** = HACK *n.*^{3} 2, 4. Only in ME. **4** A floodgate, a sluice. Also = HECK *n.*^{1} 1. LME. **5** An opening or door in an aeroplane or spacecraft. M20.

1b M. SCAMMELL His better rations, which he now received from a different hatch in the canteen. **2** J. HAWKES Midships were three hatches, two battened permanently shut. **down the hatch** *slang*: a call to drink up. **under hatches** below deck; *fig.* in a state of servitude or adversity.

Comb.: **hatchback** (a car having) a sloping rear door hinged at the top, usu. giving access to storage space; **hatch-boat** a half-decked fishing boat with hatches through which the fish are passed into the hold; **hatchway** *Naut.* an opening in a ship's deck through which cargo is lowered into the hold; one leading to a lower deck.

hatch /hatʃ/ *n.*^{2} E17. [f. HATCH *v.*^{1}] The action or an act of hatching, (an) incubation. Also, a set of young birds etc. hatched, a brood.

C. DARWIN Two hybrids from the same parent but from different hatches. **hatches, matches, and dispatches** *joc.* (the notices in a newspaper etc. of) births, marriages, and deaths.

hatch /hatʃ/ *n.*^{3} M17. [f. HATCH *v.*^{2}] An engraved line or stroke; *esp.* one used to represent shading in an engraving.

†**hatch** *n.*^{4} E18–E19. [Fr. *hache*.] A hatchet.

hatch /hatʃ/ *v.*^{1} ME. [Rel. to MHG *hecken*, Sw. *häcka*, Da. *hække*, of unkn. origin.] **1** *v.t.* & *i.* Produce (young birds etc.) from an egg by incubation. Also foll. by *out*. ME. **b** *v.t. gen.* Bring into existence, generate (an animal, a plant). ME. **2** *v.t.* Cause (an egg) to break open when incubation is complete. LME. **3** *v.t. fig.* Devise (a plot etc.) by secret scheming. Also foll. by *up*. M16. **b** *v.i.* Of a plot etc.: be in the process of being devised. Only in *be hatching*. M17. **4** *v.i.* (Of a young bird etc.) emerge from an egg after incubation; (of an insect) emerge from a chrysalis. Freq. foll. by *out*. L16. **5** *v.i.* Of an egg: break open when incubation is complete, so as to release the young bird etc. inside. Also foll. by *out*. E18.

1 T. D'URFEY My Hen has hatched today. J. CONRAD A strange bird is hatched sometimes in a nest in an unaccountable way. *count one's chickens before they are hatched*: see CHICKEN *n.*^{1} **b** W. BARTRAM Serving as a nursery bed to hatch . . the infant plant. **3** E. O'BRIEN Perhaps it was then I hatched my revenge. **b** C. MIDDLETON The great dangers and plots, that were now hatching against the state. **4** A. HARDY In about 10 days' time the first little herrings began to hatch. C. MILNE Caterpillars, . . you can keep them until they finally hatch into moths.

hatchaˈbility *n.* capacity (of an egg) to hatch; ability (of a bird etc.) to produce eggs that will hatch: E20. **hatcher** *n.* (*a*) a person who or thing which hatches; *spec.* an incubator; (*b*) *fig.* a secret deviser *of* plots etc.: L16.

hatch /hatʃ/ *v.*^{2}*t.* L15. [(O)Fr. *hacher*, f. *hache* axe: see HATCHET *n.*] **1** Inlay with or *with* gold, silver, or other metal in narrow strips. Formerly, inlay (metal) *on* a surface. L15. **2** Mark (a surface) with (close parallel) lines, esp. to represent shading in engraving. L16.

2 hatched moulding *Archit.*: formed by two series of oblique parallel incisions crossing each other.

†**hatch** *v.*^{3} L16–E17. [f. HATCH *n.*^{1}] Close (a door) with a hatch.

fig.: P. SIDNEY While sleepe begins with heauy wings To hatch mine eyes.

hatchel /ˈhatʃ(ə)l/ *n.* & *v.* Also (earlier, now *dial.* & *US*) **hetchel** /ˈhɛtʃ(ə)l/. Infl. **-ll-**, ***-l-**. ME. [Ult. f. WGmc base repr. also by HOOK *n.*: cf. HACKLE *n.*^{2}, HECKLE *n.*, *v.*] **A** *n.* = HACKLE *n.*^{2} 5. ME. **B** *v.t.* **1** = HACKLE *v.*^{3} 1. ME. **2** *fig.* Harass, persecute. E19.

hatcheller *n.* a flax-dresser E17.

hatchery /ˈhatʃəri/ *n.* L19. [f. HATCH *v.*^{1} + -ERY.] A place for the artificial hatching of eggs, esp. of fish or poultry.

hatchet /ˈhatʃɪt/ *n.* ME. [(O)Fr. *hachette* dim. of *hache* axe f. med.L *hapia*, f. Gmc (OHG *happa, heppa* sickle-shaped knife): see -ET^{1}.] **1** A small or light short-handled axe, adapted for use with one hand. ME. **2** A N. American Indian tomahawk, esp. as used as a symbol of war. M17.

1 sling or **throw the hatchet** *slang* (now *rare* or *obs.*) spin yarns, talk in an exaggerated way. **throw the helve after the hatchet**, [by confusion] **throw the hatchet after the helve** risk adding fresh loss to that already incurred. **2 bury the hatchet** (now chiefly *fig.*) cease hostilities and resume friendly relations. **dig up** or **take up the hatchet** (now *Hist.*) renew hostilities.

Comb.: **hatchet-face** a narrow sharp face; **hatchet-faced** *a.* having a hatchet-face, grim-looking; **hatchet fish** either of two kinds of fish with broad strongly compressed bodies and slender tails: (*a*) any of various deep-sea fishes of the family Sternoptychidae; (*b*) any of various tropical American flying freshwater fishes of the family Gasteropelecidae, often kept in aquariums; **hatchet job** a piece of hatchet work (freq. in *do a hatchet job on*); **hatchet-man** (orig. *US*) (*a*) a hired (orig. Chinese) assassin; (*b*) a person, esp. a journalist, used to destroy another's reputation; (*c*) a person employed to coerce or intimidate others; **hatchet work** (orig. *US*) journalistic or other criticism designed to destroy a person's reputation.

hatchet /ˈhatʃɪt/ *v.t.* E17. [f. the n.] †**1** Cut or destroy with a hatchet. E17–M18. **2** Perform hatchet work on. M20.

hatchettite /ˈhatʃɪtʌɪt/ *n.* M19. [f. Charles *Hatchett* (1765–1847), Eng. chemist + -ITE^{1}.] *Min.* Naturally occurring paraffin wax or mineral tallow.

Also **hatchettine** *n.* E19.

hatchety /ˈhatʃɪti/ *a.* M19. [f. HATCHET *n.* + -Y^{1}.] Esp. of the face: resembling a hatchet-blade; thin and sharp.

hatching /ˈhatʃɪŋ/ *n.* M17. [f. HATCH *v.*^{2} + -ING^{1}.] The drawing of parallel lines so as to produce the effect of shading; a series of lines so drawn; *Her.* a system for identifying tincture in monochrome by lines and dots.

hatchling /ˈhatʃlɪŋ/ *n.* L19. [f. HATCH *n.*^{2} + -LING^{1}.] A fish, bird, etc., just hatched (esp. artificially) and not yet able to take care of itself.

hatchment /ˈhatʃm(ə)nt/ *n.* E16. [Prob. f. Fr. †*hachement* f. OFr. *acesmement* adornment.] An escutcheon or armorial device; *esp.* a square or diamond-shaped panel or canvas with a deceased person's armorial bearings, affixed to his or her house during mourning or placed in a church.

hate /heɪt/ *n.*^{1} [OE *hete* = OS *heti*, OHG *haz* (G *Hass*), ON *hatr*, Goth. *hatis*, superseded in ME by ON *hatr* or after HATRED.] **1** Hatred. OE. **2** An object of hatred. Chiefly *poet.* exc. (*colloq.*) in *one's chief, pet*, etc., *hate*. L16. **3** An artillery bombardment. *arch. slang.* E20.

1 M. O. W. OLIPHANT Generations which succeeded each other in the same hates and friendships. QUILLER-COUCH A look of cold hate. **2** *Nature* One of his particular hates is the fallacy that the Church impeded the progress of Science. **3** E. J. THOMPSON He was watching a spasmodic 'hate' of some violence.

Attrib. & *comb.*: In the sense 'expressive of hate', as *hate literature, message*; 'designed to stir up hate', as *hate campaign*. Special combs., as **hate mail** letters sent (often anonymously) in which the senders express their hostility towards the recipient.

hateless *a.* L16.

hate *n.*^{2} var. of HAET.

hate /heɪt/ *v.t.* [OE *hatian* = OFris. *hatia*, OS *haton* (Du. *haten*), OHG *hazzōn*, *-ēn* (G *hassen*), ON *hata*, Goth. *hatan*, f. Gmc, f. base of HATE *n.*^{1}] **1** Have feelings of hostility or strong antipathy towards. OE. **2** In weakened sense: have a (strong) distaste for, be unable to endure. Freq. foll. by *to do, doing*. ME.

1 G. GREENE I hated him for the very quality which had once helped my love. P. ROTH You hate them and wish they were dead. **hate a person's guts** hate a person intensely. **2** T. HARDY Stephen's wife hated the sea . . and couldn't bear the thought of going into a boat. G. B. SHAW Don't you hate people who have no character . . ? W. S. MAUGHAM You know how I hate to interfere in other people's business. G. VIDAL I hate being called by my first name by strangers.

hater *n.* LME.

hateable *a.* var. of HATABLE.

hateful /ˈheɪtfʊl, -f(ə)l/ *a.* LME. [f. HATE *n.*^{1} + -FUL.] **1** Full of hatred; malignant. *arch.* LME. **2** Exciting hate; odious, repugnant. LME.

1 SHAKES. *2 Hen. VI* Ah, Gloucester, hide thee from their hateful looks. **2** J. PRIESTLEY No vice is universally so hateful as ingratitude. W. SOYINKA A hateful job this, hardly time for leisure.

hatefully *adv.* LME. **hatefulness** *n.* M16.

hath *v.* see HAVE *v.*

hatha yoga /hʌtə ˈjəʊgə, hatə/ *n. phr.* E20. [Skt, f. *haṭha* force + YOGA.] A system of physical exercises and breathing control used in yoga.

hatha yogi /ˈhʌtə ˈjəʊgi, ˈhatə/ *n. phr.* M20. [Skt, f. as prec. + YOGI.] A person who practises hatha yoga.

Hathor /ˈhaθɔː/ *n.* Also **Ath-** /ˈaθ-/. L18. [Gk *Hathōr* f. Egyptian *Ḥet-Ḥeru* house of Horus.] The Egyptian goddess of love, a representation of whose head (depicted with a cow's ears and horns) was used to ornament columns.

Haˈthoric *a.* relating to Hathor E20.

hatred /ˈheɪtrɪd/ *n.* ME. [f. HATE *v.* + -RED.] A feeling of hostility or strong aversion towards a person or thing; active and violent dislike.

G. GREENE He had a hatred of undressing before another man. E. FEINSTEIN She disliked the old man's bigoted hatred of all minorities.

hatted /ˈhatɪd/ *a.* M16. [f. HAT *n.*, *v.*: see -ED^{2}, -ED^{1}.] Wearing a hat.

P. LIVELY Women in silk and crêpe-de-chine, gloved and hatted. **hatted kit** [KIT *n.*^{1}] a preparation of buttermilk and warm milk, which forms a creamy top.

hatter /ˈhatə/ *n.* ME. [f. HAT *n.* + -ER^{1}.] **1** A maker of or dealer in hats. ME. **2** A person (orig. a miner) who works or lives alone; a solitary bushman. *Austral.* & *NZ.* M19.

1 as mad as a hatter wildly eccentric.

hatter /ˈhatə/ *v.t.* Now *Sc.* & *north.* LME. [Perh. of imit. origin, with frequent. ending: cf. *batter*, *shatter*, etc.: see -ER[5].] 1 Knock about, batter. LME. 2 Exhaust with fatigue or drudgery. (Foll. by *out.*) L17.

2 DRYDEN He's hattered out with penance.

hattery /ˈhatəri/ *n.* E19. [f. HAT *n.* + -ERY.] A place where hats are made or sold. Also, hats collectively.

Hatti /ˈhati/ *n.* Also **Kh-**. L19. [Assyr. & Hittite.] 1 *collect. pl.* A pre-Hittite people of Anatolia. L19. 2 = HATTIC *n.* L20.

Hattic /ˈhatɪk/ *a.* & *n.* E20. [f. HATTI + -IC.] A *adj.* Of or pertaining to the Hatti. E20. B *n.* The (non-Indo-European) language spoken by the Hatti. M20.

Hattian *a.* & *n.* (*a*) *adj.* = HATTIC *a.*; (*b*) *n.* the Hattic language; a member of the Hattic race: E20.

hatti-sherif /ˌhatɪʃəˈriːf/ *n.* L17. [Pers. *ḵaṭṭ-i-šarīf*, f. Arab. *khaṭṭ* writing + *i* (Pers.) connective + Arab. *šarīf* noble.] *Hist.* A decree bearing a Sultan's personal mark and so made irrevocable.

hattock /ˈhatək/ *n.* E16. [f. HAT *n.* + -OCK.] 1 A little (esp. fairy) hat. Chiefly in *horse and hattock*, orig. a supposed call by witches to be on their way. *Sc.* E16. 2 A shock of standing sheaves of corn, the tops of which are protected by two sheaves laid along them in such a way as to carry off the rain. *dial.* L17.

hau /haʊ/ *n.* M19. [Haw. & Marquesan.] A bushy tree of tropical coasts, *Hibiscus tiliaceus*, the bast of which yields a valuable fibre. Also *hau tree*.

hauberk /ˈhɔːbəːk/ *n.* ME. [OFr. *hau(s)berc*, *holberc*, f. Frank. (= OHG *halsberc*, OE *healsbeorg*, ON *halsbjǫrg*), f. base of HAUSE *n.* + Gmc base meaning 'protect'.] *Hist.* A piece of defensive armour, orig. for the neck and shoulders, but early developed into a long coat of mail or military tunic.

haubitz *n.* var. of HOWITZ.

hauerite /ˈhaʊərʌɪt/ *n.* M19. [f. Franz von *Hauer* (1822–99), Austrian geologist + -ITE[1].] *Min.* Native manganese disulphide, a cubic mineral crystallizing in the cubic system and usu. occurring as octahedral or cubo-octahedral reddish-brown crystals.

haugh /hɔː, hɑːx/ *n.* *Sc.* & *north.* Also (*north.*) **halgh**. ME. [Prob. repr. OE *healh* corner, nook, rel. to *holh* HOLLOW *n.*[1]] A piece of flat alluvial land by the side of a river, forming part of the floor of the river-valley.

haught /hɔːt/ *a.* *arch.* Also (earlier) †**haut**. LME. [Fr. *haut(e)* (OFr. *ha(u)lt*) high f. L *altus* high, infl. by Gmc base of HIGH *a.*] 1 Haughty. LME. †2 High-minded. L15–L16. †3 High-ranking, high-born. L15–E17.

haughtonite /ˈhɔːt(ə)nʌɪt/ *n.* L19. [f. Samuel *Haughton* (1821–97), Ir. scientist + -ITE[1].] *Min.* An iron-rich variety of biotite.

haughty /ˈhɔːti/ *a.* M16. [Extension of HAUGHT *a.* with -Y[1].] 1 High in one's own estimation; lofty and disdainful. M16. b *fig.* Imposing, grand, stately, dignified. L16. 2 Of exalted character, style, or rank. *arch.* M16. †3 *lit.* High, lofty. L16–E17.

1 A. BURGESS They were a haughty lot who found Manchester inferior to Hamburg. HENRY MILLER Look at his haughty air of pride and arrogance!

haughtily *adv.* L16. **haughtiness** *n.* M16.

Hau Hau /ˈhaʊ haʊ/ *n.* *NZ.* Pl. **-s**, same. M19. [Maori.] A follower of the Pai-Marire religion during the 19th-cent. Maori wars.

Hau-hauism *n.* L19.

haul /hɔːl/ *n.* L17. [f. the vb.] 1 The act of hauling; a pull; *spec.* the draught of a fishing net. L17. b The distance over which something is hauled; a journey; *fig.* a project, a task. Freq. in *long haul*, *short haul*. L19. 2a A quantity of yarn for rope-making. L18. b (The quantity of) a draught of fish. M19. 3 *fig.* The making of a substantial gain; an amount gained, seized, stolen, etc. L18.

1b R. SUTCLIFF An aged ferry steamer whose normal run was only the short haul between Malta and Syracuse. 3 *Cricket World* A career best haul of eight wickets for 107 runs.

haul /hɔːl/ *v.* Also (earlier) †**hall**. M16. [Var. of HALE *v.*[1]] 1 *Naut.* a *v.t.* Trim the sails etc. of (a ship) so as to sail closer to the wind; *haul one's* (or *the*) *wind*, sail closer to the wind, change course (*lit.* & *fig.*). M16. b *v.i.* Sail closer to the wind; sail in a specified direction; change course (*lit.* & *fig.*). Also *haul to* (or *upon*) *the wind*. L16. 2 *v.t.* Pull or draw with force; drag, tug. L16. †b *v.t.* Worry, torment, pester. *colloq.* L17–M18. c *v.t.* Transport by cart or other conveyance. M18. d *v.t.* Bring *up* for a reprimand, call to account. *colloq.* L18. e *v.i.* Of a bachelor seal: come out of the water to rest on the hauling-grounds. M19. 3 *v.i.* Pull, tug, (*at* or *on* something). M18. 4 *v.i.* Of the wind: change direction; *spec.* (more fully *haul forward*) shift to a direction nearer the bow of a boat. M18.

2 V. WOOLF She clutched the banisters and hauled herself upstairs. *haul ass*: see ARSE *n.* 1. *haul down one's colours*: see COLOUR *n.* d G. SWIFT In Quinn's office you are the luckless schoolboy hauled before the headmaster. *haul over the coals*: see COAL *n.* 3 J. DICKEY Lew and Bobby pulled the canoes up the bank . . hauling on the bow ropes.

With advs. in specialized senses: **haul off** (*a*) *v.phr.t.* & *i.* (*Naut.*) trim the sails etc. of (a ship) so as to sail closer to the wind; (*b*) *v.phr.i.* (chiefly *N. Amer. colloq.*) withdraw a little in preparation; *haul off and* —, proceed to —. **haul out** *v.phr.i.* (*US*) go out, depart.

Comb.: **haulabout** *US* a vessel like a barge used for coaling ships; **hauling-ground** a place where bachelor seals congregate.

haulage /ˈhɔːlɪdʒ/ *n.* E19. [f. HAUL *v.* + -AGE.] 1 The action or process of hauling; the conveyance of a load in a vehicle; the practice of conveying loads as a business. E19. 2 The expense of or charge for the transport of goods. M19.

hauler /ˈhɔːlə/ *n.* L17. [f. HAUL *v.* + -ER[1].] A person who or thing which hauls; a haulier.

haulier /ˈhɔːlɪə/ *n.* Also (earlier) †**hall-**. LME. [f. HAUL *v.* + -IER.] 1 A person employed in hauling. Formerly *spec.*, a person who transported coal in tubs in a mine. LME. 2 A firm or a person engaged in road transport of goods. E20.

haulm /hɔːm/ *n.* & *v.* Also **halm** /hɑːm/. [OE *halm* (*healm*) = OS, OHG (Du., G) *halm*, ON *hálmr*, f. Gmc, f. IE base repr. also by L *culmus*, Gk *kalamos* reed.] A *n.* 1 *collect. sing.* The stems of various cultivated plants, esp. peas, beans, vetches, hops, potatoes, etc., or (now less commonly) corn or grass, esp. as left after gathering the crop and used for litter or thatching; straw. OE. 2 A single stalk or stem (of a bean, potato, grass, etc.). OE. B *v.t.* Lay (straw or haulm) straight for thatching. M17.

haulyard *n.* var. of HALYARD.

haunch /hɔːn(t)ʃ/ *n.* Also †**hanch**. ME. [(O)Fr. *hanche* = Prov., Sp., It. *anca* of Gmc origin (cf. LG *hanke* hind leg of a horse).] 1 In humans and quadrupeds, the part of the body between the ribs and the thigh; in the horse, the part of the hindquarters between the reins or back to the hock or ham. ME. b The leg and loin of a deer, sheep, or other animal as a joint of meat for cooking and eating. L15. †c The pelvis as containing the womb. L16–M17. †d *fig.* The last part of anything. Only in L16. 2 *Archit.* The underside of an elliptical arch immediately above the springing; the corresponding part of any arched figure. Cf. HANCE 3. E18. 3 The end of a tenon reduced in width. E20. 4 The side of a made-up road. M20.

1 GEO. ELIOT A fine black retriever . . sat on his haunches, and watched him.

Comb.: **haunch-bone** the ilium or the innominate bone of which it forms part.

haunched *a.* (of a tenon) having its end reduced in width L19. **haunching** *n.* (*a*) the parts of an arch belonging to the haunch collectively; (*b*) a recess in a style for the end of a tenon: L19. **haunchy** *a.* having prominent haunches M19.

haunt /hɔːnt/ *n.* Also (now only in sense 4) **hant, ha'nt**. ME. [f. the vb.] 1 Habit, wont, custom. Now *Sc.* & *dial.* ME. †b Habitual practice or use. LME–L16. †2 The act or practice of frequenting a place. ME–E18. 3 A frequented place, an abode, (esp. of a specified person); the habitation or feeding-place of particular animals. ME. 4 A spirit supposed to haunt a (specified) place. M19.

3 G. ORWELL He frequented the Chestnut Tree Café, haunt of painters and musicians.

haunt /hɔːnt/ *v.* ME. [(O)Fr. *hanter* f. Gmc vb (repr. by OE *hāmettan* provide with a home, house, ON *heimta* get home, recover), f. base of HOME *n.*] I *v.t.* †1 Practise or employ habitually or frequently. ME–L16. 2 Frequent (a place); associate habitually with (a person). ME. 3 *transf.* & *fig.* a Of a thought or feeling: occur to or affect frequently, esp. as a cause of trouble. LME. b Of a ghost, a spirit, etc.: visit frequently, with manifestations of its presence. L16.

2 D. CAUTE The despondent Gilson had begun to haunt the bars. 3a D. WIGODER An awful and unforgettable memory which still haunts me. b G. GREENE The Glowrie ghost, who is condemned to haunt an impoverished castle in the Highlands.

II *v.i.* †4 Be accustomed. ME–M16. 5 Be present habitually (in a specified place); associate (with a specified person). ME. †6 Go *to*. ME–M17.

haunted *a.* much visited by a ghost, a spirit, etc.; much resorted to; (*obs.* exc. *dial.*) practised, habituated: ME. **hauntedness** *n.* the state of being haunted L19. **haunter** *n.* LME.

haunting /ˈhɔːntɪŋ/ *a.* LME. [f. HAUNT *v.* + -ING[2].] That haunts (esp. the thoughts or memory); evocative.

E. WAUGH One of his most haunting impressions. R. HUNTFORD A haunting fear of being left behind. *Studio Week* A single which . . was quite a haunting tune.

hauntingly *adv.* †(*a*) frequently, customarily; (*b*) so as to haunt (esp. the thoughts or memory): LME.

haurient /ˈhɔːrɪənt/ *a.* L16. [L *haurient-* pres. ppl stem of *haurire* draw (water etc.): see -ENT.] *Her.* Of a fish borne as a charge: placed palewise or upright with the head in chief (as if to draw in air).

Hausa /ˈhaʊsə/ *n.* & *a.* E19. [Hausa.] A *n.* Pl. **-s**, same. A member of a people of northern Nigeria and adjacent regions; the Chadic language of this people, widely used in W. Africa. E19. B *attrib.* or as *adj.* Of or pertaining to the Hausas or their language. M19.

hause /hɔːs/ *n.* *Sc.* & *north.* Also **hawse**. [OE *hals*, *heals* = OFris., OS, OHG, ON *hals*, f. Gmc base rel. to L *collum* neck. Cf. HAWSE *n.*[1]] 1 The neck. OE. 2 *transf.* A narrow neck of land or channel of water; a col or narrow ridge joining two summits. ME. 3 The throat, the gullet. LME.

hause /hɔːs/ *v.t.* Now only *Sc.* & *north.* Also **hawse**, (earlier) †**halse**. ME. [f. HAUSE *n.*, or use of HALSE *v.*[1] assoc. with it.] Clasp, embrace.

hausen /ˈhaʊz(ə)n/ *n.* Pl. same. M18. [G f. OHG *hūso*.] The beluga, *Huso huso*.

hausfrau /ˈhaʊsfraʊ/ *n.* Pl. **-s, -en** /-ən/. L18. [G, f. *Haus* house + *Frau* wife, woman.] A (German) housewife; a person who embodies housewifely qualities.

S. BELLOW I am not just another suburban hausfrau.

hausmaler /ˈhaʊsmɑːlə/ *n.* M20. [G, f. *Haus* house + *Maler* painter.] A person who paints undecorated china at home or in a private workshop.

hausmannite /ˈhaʊsmənʌɪt/ *n.* M19. [f. J. F. L. *Hausmann* (1782–1859), Ger. mineralogist + -ITE[1].] *Min.* A mixed-valence oxide of manganese, Mn_3O_4, usu. occurring as brownish-black pseudo-octahedral crystals belonging to the tetragonal system.

hausse /oːs, həʊs/ *n.* Pl. pronounced same. L18. [Fr., f. *hausser* raise.] A type of sight for the breech of a cannon.

hausse-col /oskɔl, ˈhəʊskɒl/ *n.* Pl. pronounced same. E19. [Fr., f. *hausser* raise + *col* neck.] *Hist.* A gorget of chain-mail, or (later) of plate-armour.

Haussmannize /ˈhaʊsmənʌɪz/ *v.t.* Also **-ise**. M19. [f. Baron Eugène-Georges *Haussmann*, who, when prefect of the Seine (1853–70), remodelled a great part of Paris: see -IZE.] Widen and straighten (a street); rebuild (a district) to a more open plan.

Haussmani'zation *n.* M19.

haustella *n.* pl. of HAUSTELLUM.

haustellate /ˈhɔːstələt, -leɪt/ *a.* M19. [mod.L *haustellatus*, f. as next + -ATE².] *Zool.* **1** Esp. of an insect: provided with a mouth adapted for sucking (rather than mastication); provided with a haustellum (rather than mandibles). M19. **2** Of a mouth or mouthparts: adapted for sucking, suctorial. M19.

haustellum /hɔːˈstɛləm/ *n.* Pl. **-lla** /-lə/. E19. [mod.L dim. of *haustrum* bucket, scoop, f. *haust-* pa. ppl stem of *haurire* draw (water).] *Zool.* The sucking organ or proboscis of an insect or crustacean.

haustorium /hɔːˈstɔːrɪəm/ *n.* Pl. **-ia** /ɪə/. L19. [f. L *haustor* agent-n. f. *haurire* to draw, to drain: see -ORIUM.] A slender projection from the root of a parasitic plant, such as a dodder, or from the hyphae of a parasitic fungus, enabling the parasite to penetrate the tissues of its host and absorb nutrients from it.

haustorial *a.* of or pertaining to a haustorium M20.

haustrum /ˈhɔːstrəm/ *n.* Pl. **-stra** /-strə/. L19. [mod.L: see HAUSTELLUM.] *Anat.* Each of the small sacs enclosed by folds in the colon.

haustral *a.* E20.

haut *a.* see HAUGHT.

hautboy /ˈ(h)əʊbɔɪ/ *n. arch.* Also (now usual in sense 2) **hautbois**, (now *rare*) **hoboy**. M16. [Fr. *hautbois*, f. *haut* high + *bois* wood. Cf. OBOE.] **1** = OBOE 1. *arch.* M16. **b** = OBOE 2. E18. **2** More fully *hautboy strawberry*. A central European strawberry, *Fragaria muricata*, formerly grown for its fruit. M18.

hautboyist *n.* M19.

haute *a.* see HAUGHT.

haute Bohème /ot bɔɛm, əʊt bəʊˈɛm/ *n. phr.* E20. [f. Fr., lit. 'high Bohemia' (coined by M. Baring after next).] A fast or upper-class Bohemian set of people.

haute bourgeoisie /ot burʒwazi, ˌəʊt bʊəʒwɑːˈziː/ *n. phr.* L19. [Fr. lit. 'high bourgeoisie': see BOURGEOISIE.] The upper middle class.

haute couture /ot kutyːr, əʊt kuːˈtjʊə/ *n. phr.* E20. [Fr., lit. 'high dressmaking': see COUTURE.] High fashion; the leading dressmakers and fashion houses or their products collectively.

haute cuisine /ot kɥizin, əʊt kwɪˈziːn/ *n. phr.* E20. [Fr., lit. 'high cooking': see CUISINE.] High-class (French) cooking.

haute école /ot ekɔl, əʊt eɪˈkɒl/ *n.* & *a. phr.* M19. [Fr., lit. 'high school'.] (Of or pertaining to) the more difficult feats of horsemanship, or *transf.* of music or other arts.

haute noblesse /ot nɔblɛs, əʊt nəʊˈblɛs/ *n. phr.* L18. [Fr., lit. 'high nobility': see NOBLESSE.] The upper stratum of the aristocracy.

hauteur /əʊˈtəː, *foreign* otœːr/ *n.* E17. [Fr., f. *haut* high + *-eur* -OR.] Haughtiness of manner.

B. TARKINGTON In their hearts they must be humiliated by his languid hauteur.

haute vulgarisation /ot vylgarizasjɔ̃, ˌəʊt vʌlgəraɪˈzeɪʃ(ə)n/ *n. phr.* M20. [Fr., lit. 'high vulgarization': see VULGARIZATION.] The popularization of abstruse or complex matters.

haut-goût /ogu, ˈəʊguː/ *n.* M16. [Fr., lit. 'high flavour'. See also HOGO.] **1** A strong flavour or relish, seasoning, (*lit.* & *fig.*). M16. **†2** A highly flavoured or seasoned dish. M17–E19. **3** A slightly rotten flavour; a taint. L17.

haut monde /o mɔ̃d, əʊ ˈmɒnd/ *n. phr.* M19. [Fr., lit. 'high world'.] The fashionable world. Cf. BEAU MONDE.

haut-pas /opɑ/ *n.* Pl. same. LME. [Fr., lit. 'high step'.] A dais raised one or more steps above the level of the rest of the floor.

¶ Formerly fully naturalized.

haut-relief /orəljɛf, əʊrɪˈliːf/ *n.* M19. [Fr., lit. 'high relief'.] = ALTO-RELIEVO.

haut ton /o tɔ̃/ *n. phr.* Now *rare.* E19. [Fr., lit. 'high tone'.] (People of) high fashion.

haüyne /ˈhaʊiːn/ *n.* E19. [f. René Just *Haüy* (1743–1822), Fr. crystallographer + -(I)NE⁵.] *Min.* A blue feldspathoid mineral of the sodalite group containing calcium and sulphur.

Also **haüynite** *n.* M19.

Havana /həˈvanə/ *n.* E19. [The capital of Cuba.] **1** In full *Havana cigar*. A cigar made in Cuba, or from Cuban tobacco. E19. **2** In full *Havana brown*. The shade of brown of a Havana cigar. Freq. *attrib.* E19. **3** In full *Havana rabbit*. (An animal of) a variety of domestic rabbit, orig. from the Netherlands, bred for meat and its dark brown fur. E20.

have /hav/ *n.* & *a.* ME. [f. the vb.] **A** *n.* **1** Possession. Long *rare.* ME. **2** A person, country, etc., that possesses wealth or resources. Usu. in *pl.*, contrasted w. *have-nots*. *colloq.* M18. **B** *attrib.* or as *adj.* Designating a 'have'. *colloq.* M20.

have /hav, *unstressed* həv/ *v.* Pres. indic.: 1 **have**, (*Sc.*) **hae** /heɪ, ha/; 2 **have**, (*arch.*) **hast** /hast/; 3 **has** /haz, həz/, (*arch.*) **hath** /haθ, həθ/; *pl.* **have**, (*Sc.*) **hae**. Past indic.: **had** /had, həd/; 2 *sing.* also (*arch.*) **hadst** /hadst/. Pres. subjunct.: **have**. Past subjunct.: **had**. Imper.: **have**. Pa. pple: **had**. Informal abbrev. forms: **'d** = *had*; **'s** = *has*; **'ve** = *have*; **hadn't** /had(ə)nt/ = *had not*; **hasn't** /haz(ə)nt/ = *has not*; **haven't** /hav(ə)nt/ = *have not*; (*joc.* & *colloq.*) **ain't** = *have not*; (*arch.*) **an't** = *have not*. [OE *habban* = OFris. *hebba*, OS *hebbian* (Du. *hebben*), OHG *habēn* (G *haben*), ON *hafa*, Goth. *haban*, f. Gmc base prob. rel. to HEAVE *v.* In ME the *habb-* forms were reduced by levelling to *hav-*; the *haf-* forms (in OE in past indic. and 2nd & 3rd person sing. pres. indic.) lost their *f* bef. the following consonant to give *ha-th*, *ha-s*, etc.] **I** *v.t.* Possess. **1** Hold in possession as one's property or as something at one's disposal. OE. **2** Possess in a certain relationship. OE. **3** Possess or contain as a part or adjunct. OE. **4** Possess as an attribute, function, position, etc.; be characterized by. OE. **5a** Experience, be affected with; enjoy; suffer. OE. **b** Hold, or allow to be present, in the mind; be the subject of (a feeling). OE. **c** Possess with the mind; understand; know. LME. **6** Possess as a thing to be done or to happen. Foll. by obj. & inf. OE. **b** Be under an obligation *to do*; be necessitated by circumstances *to do*. L16. **7** Hold or keep *in* some relation to oneself. Now chiefly in certain set phrs. OE. **8** Hold in a specified estimation; regard as. (Foll. by *in*, †*at*.) *arch.* OE. **9** Engage in, carry on, (an activity); organize and bring about (a meeting, party, etc.). OE. **10** Exercise (a personal attribute or quality) or show the presence of (a feeling) by one's action or attitude, esp. towards a person. ME. **†11** *refl.* Behave. LME–M16. **12** Assert, maintain; claim, allege, (*that*). Chiefly w. *it*. LME. **b** Foll. by obj. & inf. without *to*. Represent (a person) as doing, esp. in a work of fiction. *colloq.* E20.

1 J. STEINBECK You have only ragged overalls and no hat. W. GOLDING They had more toys than they wanted. **2** T. HERBERT They used to have their Wives in common. R. C. HUTCHINSON He had no brothers or sisters. **3** C. P. SNOW She had a large, blunt, knobbly nose. SCOTT FITZGERALD Every cross has just a date on it, and the word 'Unknown'. **4** H. JAMES If he hadn't a sense of beauty he had after all a sense of justice. J. BUCHAN The air . . had the strangest effect on my spirits. W. GOLDING The universe had a beginning. **5a** R. RENDELL Mr Knightow had a shock. He went white. J. RHYS I am having one devil of a time. B. NEIL Did people like Ben have athlete's foot and piles? **b** B. JOWETT They have the feelings of old men about youth. J. H. SHORTHOUSE I have no doubt the Italian is at the bottom of all this. **c** V. WOOLF I had all Shakespeare by heart before I was in my teens. I. MURDOCH He knew Latin and Greek . . , I had only a little French. **6** J. H. NEWMAN He had nothing special to say for himself. *Strand Magazine* Her contract . . had two years more to run. **b** R. C. HUTCHINSON I had to make a mental effort to remember where I was going. Q. CRISP I have to go back to work. R. RENDELL She got pregnant and . . Adam had to marry her. **7** *have in mind*, *have in one's possession*, *have in safekeeping*, *have in sight*, etc. **9** P. ROTH Shuki apologized for being unable to have dinner with me. R. HUNTFORD Shackleton and Elspeth Beardmore were having an affair. *have a go*, *look*, *try*, etc. **10** I. MURDOCH I'm still a rational being, so have the decency to address me as one. *have a care*, *have mercy*, etc.; *have patience with*, *regard to*; *have the goodness*, *impudence*, etc., *to do*. **12** W. GOLDING The scurvy politician, as my favourite author would have it. M. MILNER *Tradition* has it that this is the place where the heathen used to sacrifice their children.

II *v.t.* Obtain, get. **13** Possess by obtaining or receiving; get, obtain; take and imbibe (a drink) or eat (food, a meal); conceive (an idea); have obtained (a qualification). OE. **b** Give birth to. LME. **c** In imper. Cheers! (as a drinking toast). *dial.* & (with *to you*) *arch.* LME. **14** With obj. & compl. **a** With pres. or pa. pple or inf. Experience or suffer the specified action happening to or being done to (a thing or person). ME. **b** With adj. or adv. (phr.). Bring into a specified condition or state. ME. **c** With pa. pple or inf. (now usu. without *to*). Cause or oblige (a person or thing) to be subject to a specified action or to carry out a specified action. LME. **15** With *will*, *would*. Wish, will, or require (a person) to (arch. *to*) *do* or (a deed) to be *done*; (with *it*) wish or require the doing of (a deed) or the occurrence of (an event, situation, etc.). ME. **b** With *will not*, *would not*: not permit or tolerate. Foll. by obj., or obj. & pple or inf. (without *to*). L16. **16** Cause to come or go; bring; take. *arch.* ME. **17** Have got into one's power or at a disadvantage; *colloq.* get the better of in an argument etc. L16. **18** Have sexual intercourse with. *slang.* L16. **19** Outwit; deceive; cheat. *slang.* E19.

13 G. ROSE If Lord Spencer returns he must have the Admiralty. *Times Lit. Suppl.* All these books may be had of any bookseller. G. S. HAIGHT Mary Ann asked to have her letters back. **b** G. ORWELL I'm thirty-nine and I've had four children. I. MURDOCH A spider . . which lives in a burrow and has its young in the late summer. **14a** T. HARDY You would rather have me die than have your equatorial stolen. **b** E. WAUGH She can't print *that*. She'll have us all in prison. **c** J. P. DONLEAVY I can call the police and have you thrown out. B. MOORE She had him bring the car up to the entrance. E. BOWEN I'm going . . to have my hair cut. K. HULME For a moment . . you had me worried. **15** SHAKES. *Two Gent.* What would your Grace have me to do in this? G. BERKELEY Those who will have us judge of distance by lines and angles. I. FLEMING As luck would have it, there were no vacancies and I had to turn him down. I. COLEGATE He was a village boy, though his mother would have it he was something better. **b** TENNYSON O my friend, I will not have thee die! V. WOOLF She would have none of it. **16** R. L. STEVENSON A little later he was had to bed. **17** *New Yorker* 'How many other politicians would take a chance on asking this question?' he asked . . —and he had them there. **19** M. E. BRADDON If you've advanced money on 'em, you've been had.

III *v.i.* **†20** Of a person: go; come *over* here. LME–M19. **21** Foll. by *at* (or, *arch.*, other preps.): go at, esp. aggressively; attack; make an attempt at. Usu. in *imper.* LME.

21 J. BUCHAN Sit down, sir, and have at that pie.

IV Idiomatic uses. **22** *had* (pa. subjunct.), †*have* (pres. indic.), would: in expressions of preference, desirability, or obligation. Foll. by adjs. (or advs.) in compar., superl., or positive w. *as*. Now esp. in *had better* below, *had rather*. ME. **23** With subj. duplicated by pers. or refl. pron. as indirect (dative) obj. Provide or get for oneself; indulge oneself with. *colloq.* (chiefly *N. Amer.*). E20.

22 J. B. MOZLEY You must give way; and you had as well do so voluntarily. W. H. MALLOCK I had best not give her any. **23** O. LA FARGE He had himself two good highballs. *New Yorker* I got to have me one of them.

V As aux. vb w. pa. pple of another vb, forming past tenses of the latter expressing action already completed at the time indicated. **24a** Pres. tense. OE. **b** Pa. tense. OE. **c** Compound tenses. ME. **d** In compound tenses w. redundant *have* or *had*. Now *US dial.* LME.

24a E. BOWEN You could have run the world. **b** J. C. POWYS Three months had passed. J. CONRAD The carpenter had driven in the last wedge. **c** SHELLEY Before the whirlwind wakes I shall have found My inn of lasting rest. C. M. KIRKLAND I thought I never should have got out. **d** J. F. WILSON 'If the fire hadn't have gone out,' he mused.

Phrases: (A selection of cross-refs. only is included: see esp. other ns.) **had better** *colloq.* would find it wiser to; ought to. **have a nice day** (orig. *US*) (a wish expressed on saying) goodbye. *have a person's guts for garters*: see GUT *n.* *have a wolf by the ears*: see WOLF *n.*

have got: see GET *v.* 38. **have (got) to be** *colloq.* must be (expr. certainty). **have had —** *colloq.* have had enough of, be tired of or discontented with. **have had it** *colloq.* (*a*) have lost one's chance, have no chance; (*b*) be past one's prime or past its best; (*c*) have been killed, defeated, exhausted, etc. **have it** (*a*) gain a victory or advantage; win (esp. a vote); (*b*) *colloq.* receive a beating, punishment, etc. (chiefly in *let a person have it*); (*c*) have thought of the answer, a solution, etc.; (*d*) *have it away* (slang) = *have it off*, sense (i) below; (*e*) *have it both ways*, choose now one, now the other of alternatives or contradictories to suit one's argument etc.; (*f*) *have it coming to one*: see COME *v.*; (*g*) *have it in for* (colloq.), intend revenge on; seek to harm; (*h*) *have it in one*, have the capacity (*to do*); (*i*) *have it off* (slang), have sexual intercourse (*with*); (*j*) *have it off* (Criminals' slang), commit a robbery; (*k*) *have it on, over*, have the advantage of; be superior to; (*l*) *have it out*: see *have out* below; (*m*) *have it so good* (colloq.), possess so many advantages, esp. of a material kind; usu. in neg. contexts; (see also sense 12 above). **have nothing on —** (*a*) have no advantage or superiority over; (*b*) know nothing discreditable or incriminating about. *have sex* (*with*): see SEX *n.* 4b. *have to wife*: see WIFE *n.* *have way*: see WAY *n.* *have words*: see WORD *n.* 7. **to have and to hold** have or receive and continue to keep. WHAT *have you*.

With advs. in specialized senses: **have on** *colloq.* hoax, deceive jocularly; (see also ON *adv.*). **have out** (*a*) *colloq.* bring (a contentious matter) to a resolution by discussion or argument; (*b*) get (a tooth, appendix, etc.) taken out. **have up** bring before a court of justice; call to account.

haveless /ˈheɪvlɪs/ *a.* [OE *hafenlēas*, *hæfen-*, f. *hæfen* property, f. *haf-*, *hæf-* stem of *habban* HAVE *v.*: see -LESS.] †**1** Destitute. OE–LME. **2** Not resourceful; shiftless. *Sc.* & *dial.* M19.

havelock /ˈhav(ə)lɒk/ *n.* Chiefly *US.* M19. [Sir Henry *Havelock* (1795–1857), major-general of the British army in India.] A cloth covering for a military cap, with a neck-flap to give protection from the sun.

haven /ˈheɪv(ə)n/ *n.* LOE. [ON *hǫfn* (genit. *hafnar*) = MLG, MDu. *havene*, Du. *haven* (whence G *Haven*).] **1** A place providing good sheltered mooring for ships; a port, a harbour. Now chiefly *literary.* LOE. **2** A place of shelter, safety, or retreat; a refuge. ME.

1 N. MONSARRAT For wandering sailors a safe haven was bound to be the crucial magnet of their lives. 2 *Encounter* San Francisco, which 'is already a haven for wandering psychotics'. A. BROOKNER Reaching the haven of her room, closing the door behind her.

havenage *n.* harbour-dues M19. **havener** *n.* a harbour-master ME. **havenless** *a.* having no haven or shelter LME.

haven /ˈheɪv(ə)n/ *v.* LME. [f. the n.] †**1** *v.i.* Go into or shelter in a haven. LME–E17. **2** *v.t.* Put (a ship etc.) into a haven. Now chiefly *fig.*, give shelter to, protect. E17.

2 KEATS Blissfully haven'd both from joy and pain.

have-not /havˈnɒt/ *n.* & *a.* *colloq.* M18. [f. *have not* neg. of HAVE *v.*: see NOT *adv.*] **A** *n.* A person, country, etc., that has little wealth or resources. Usu. in *pl.*, contrasted w. *haves*. M18. **B** *attrib.* or as *adj.* Designating a 'have-not'. M20.

haven't *v.* see HAVE *v.*

haver /ˈhavə/ *n.*[1] Chiefly *Sc.* & *north.* ME. [ON *hafr* = OS *habero*, MLG, MDu. *haver(e)* (Du. *haver*), OHG *habaro* (G dial. *Haber*, *Hafer* f. LG).] Oats.

Comb.: **haver-cake** oatcake.

haver /ˈhavə/ *n.*[2] LME. [f. HAVE *v.* + -ER[1].] A person who has or possesses; *spec.* in *Sc. Law*, the holder of a document required as evidence in court.

SHAKES. *Coriol.* It is held That valour is the chiefest virtue and Most dignifies the haver.

haver /ˈheɪvə/ *n.*[3] *Sc.* & *north.* Also **haiver**. L18. [Origin unkn. Cf. HAVER *v.*] *sing.* & (usu.) in *pl.* Foolish talk, idle chatter. Also as *int.*, nonsense!

haver /ˈheɪvə/ *v.i.* E18. [Origin unkn. Cf. HAVER *n.*[3]] **1** Talk foolishly, babble. *Sc.* & *north.* E18. **2** Vacillate, hesitate, dither. Orig. *Sc.* M19.

1 W. MCILVANNEY Tom havered on, the certainties growing more empty, the promises wilder. 2 A. FRASER Still the Scots havered. Their army lurked uncertainly west of Fife.

haverel *n.* & *a.* (*Sc.*) (a person) given to foolish chattering L18.

haversack /ˈhavəsak/ *n.* M18. [Fr. *havresac* f. G †*Habersack* orig. = bag in which cavalry carried oats for their horses, f. *Haber* (see HAVER *n.*[1]) + *sack* SACK *n.*[1]] A strong bag for provisions carried on the back or over the shoulder by a soldier, traveller, hiker, etc.

M. PATTISON Every private in the French army carries in his haversack the bâton of a marshal.

Haversian /həˈvəːsɪən/ *a.* M19. [f. Clopton *Havers* (d. 1702), Eng. anatomist + -IAN.] *Anat.* Designating or pertaining to the ramifying system of minute cylindrical passages (*Haversian canals*) in bone, through which blood-vessels pass.

haversine /ˈhavəsʌɪn/ *n.* Also **-sin**. L19. [Contr. of *half versed sine.*] Half of the versed sine of an angle.

havier /ˈheɪvjə/ *n.* L17. [Origin unkn.] A gelded deer.

havildar /ˈhavɪldɑː/ *n.* L17. [Urdu *hawildār* f. Pers. *ḥawāl(a)dār* charge holder, f. *ḥawāl*, f. Arab. *ḥawāl(a)* charge, assignment + Pers. *-dār* holding, holder.] An Indian non-commissioned officer equivalent to a sergeant.

having /ˈhavɪŋ/ *n.* ME. [f. HAVE *v.* + -ING[1].] **1** A possession. Freq. in *pl.*, property, belongings. ME. **2** The action or condition of having; possession. LME. **3** *sing.* & in *pl.* Behaviour, manners, deportment. Chiefly *Sc.* LME.

having /ˈhavɪŋ/ *a.* ME. [f. HAVE *v.* + -ING[2].] **1** Possessing property. Long *rare* or *obs.* ME. **2** Covetous, grasping. *obs.* exc. *dial.* L16.

haviour /ˈheɪvjə/ *n.* Also †**havour**. LME. [AN *aver* = OFr. *aveir*, (also mod.) *avoir* possession, property, use as n. of inf. *aveir*, *avoir* have (infl. by HAVE *v.*) f. L *habere*: see -OUR. Cf. BEHAVIOUR.] †**1** The fact of having, possession; a possession, wealth. LME–E17. **2** Bearing, behaviour, manner. Also in *pl.*, manners. *obs.* exc. *dial.* E16.

havoc /ˈhavək/ *n.* LME. [AN *havok* alt. of OFr. *havo(t)* pillage: ult. origin unkn.] **1** Used as a signal-cry to an army etc. to seize spoil. Only in *cry havoc*, give this cry. Now *rare* or *obs.* exc. as *fig.* (usu. after Shakes., and assoc. w. sense 2), predict imminent disaster. LME. **2** Devastation, destruction; (now freq.) confusion, disorder. L15.

1 SHAKES. *Jul. Caes.* And Caesar's spirit, Shall . . Cry 'Havoc!' and let slip the dogs of war. 2 B. LOPEZ A place of spiritual havoc, the abode of the Antichrist. **cause, make,** or **wreak havoc** devastate, cause damage (*to*), throw into chaos or confusion. **play havoc (with)** damage, impair; confound. *wreak havoc*: see *cause havoc* above.

havoc /ˈhavək/ *v.t.* Infl. **-ck-**. L16. [f. the n.] Devastate, lay waste; bring into confusion or chaos.

†**havour** *n.* var. of HAVIOUR.

haw /hɔː/ *n.*[1] *obs.* exc. *Hist.* [OE *haga* corresp. to OS *hago*, MDu. *hage*, *haghe* (Du. *haag*), ON *hagi*, f. Gmc base also of HAG *n.*[3], HAY *n.*[2], HEDGE *n.*] A hedge or fence enclosing a dwelling or piece of land; what is enclosed, a yard, a close, an enclosure.

haw /hɔː/ *n.*[2] [OE *haga* prob. same wd as prec.] **1** A hawthorn-berry. (Formerly used as a symbol of something valueless.) OE. **2** A hawthorn. E19.

Comb.: **hawfinch** a large Eurasian and N. African finch of deciduous woodland, *Coccothraustes coccothraustes*, with a heavy, strong beak.

haw /hɔː/ *n.*[3] LME. [Origin unkn.] †**1** A morbid excrescence in the eye. LME–L17. **2** The nictitating membrane of the eye of a horse, dog, or other animal. E16.

haw /hɔː/ *n.*[4] & *int.*[1] L17. [Imit. Cf. HAW-HAW.] (A slight inarticulate vocal sound) expr. hesitation. Freq. in *hums and haws*: see HUM *n.*[1] 1.

haw /hɔː/ *n.*[5] & *int.*[2] Chiefly *dial.* & *N. Amer.* L17. [Origin unkn. Cf. HAW *v.*[2]] (A call) directing a draught animal or team to turn to the left.

haw /hɔː/ *v.*[1]*i.* M17. [Imit. Cf. HAW *n.*[4] & *int.*[1]] Utter 'haw', esp. as an expression of hesitation. Freq. in *hum and haw*: see HUM *v.*[1] 1.

H. FIELDING Don't stand humming and hawing, but speak out.

haw /hɔː/ *v.*[2] Chiefly *dial.* & *N. Amer.* M19. [Origin unkn. Cf. HAW *n.*[5] & *int.*[2]] **1** *v.i.* Of a draught animal or team: turn or move left. M19. **2** *v.t.* Direct (a draught animal or team) to move or turn left. M19.

Hawaiian /həˈwʌɪən/ *a.* & *n.* Also **-waian**. E19. [f. *Hawaii* (see below) + -AN.] **A** *adj.* Of or pertaining to the island of Hawaii in the N. Pacific, or the archipelago of which it is part, now the American state of Hawaii. E19.

Hawaiian goose = NENE. **Hawaiian guitar** a steel-stringed instrument, usu. held horizontally, in which a characteristic glissando effect is produced by sliding a metal bar along the strings as they are plucked. **Hawaiian shirt** a highly coloured and gaily patterned shirt.

B *n.* A native or inhabitant of Hawaii; the Austronesian language of Hawaii. M19.

hawbuck /ˈhɔːbʌk/ *n.* Chiefly *dial.* E19. [f. HAW *n.*[1] or *n.*[2] + BUCK *n.*[1]] A country bumpkin, an oaf.

Hawcubite /ˈhɔːkəbʌɪt/ *n.* E18. [Origin unkn.] *Hist.* A member of a band of violent young men frequenting the London streets in the early 18th cent. Cf. MOHOCK.

haw-haw /ˈhɔːhɔː/ *n.*, *a.*, & *v.* M19. [Imit. Cf. HAW *n.*[4] & *int.*[1], HAW *v.*[1]] **A** *n.* (A repeated slight inarticulate vocal sound) expr. hesitation or affected pausing in speech. Also, (repr.) a loud or boisterous laugh. Also as *int.* M19.

B *adj.* Resembling or imitating so-called upper-class speech or manner; affected. M19.

Daily News One of those haw-haw officers, who look down on men like me. *Times* Declaring that BBC announcers were 'too haw-haw' in their diction. R. C. HUTCHINSON You think I wanted him for his haw-haw accent or his old school tie.

C *v.* **1** *v.i.* Utter 'haw-haw'; laugh loudly and boisterously. M19. **2** *v.t.* Laugh at. M19.

hawk /hɔːk/ *n.*[1] [OE *hafoc*, *heafoc*, earlier *haebuc*, *habuc* = OFris. *havek*, OS *habuk* (Du. *havik*), OHG *habuh* (G *Habicht*), ON *haukr*, f. Gmc.] **1** A bird of prey used in falconry; any diurnal bird of prey. Now *esp.* any of the smaller or moderate-sized birds of the family Accipitridae with relatively short, rounded wings. Cf. FALCON. OE. **2** A rapacious, aggressive, or ruthless person. M16. **b** A person who advocates an uncompromising or warlike policy. (Opp. *dove*.) M20.

1 *black hawk*, *blue hawk*, *Cooper's hawk*, *goshawk*, *sharp-shinned hawk*, *sparrowhawk*, *Swainson's hawk*, etc. *ignoble hawk*: see IGNOBLE *a.* **know a hawk from a handsaw** or **heronshaw** have ordinary discernment (now chiefly in allusion to Shakes. *Haml.*). *noble hawk*: see NOBLE *a.*

Comb.: **hawkbill (turtle)** = *hawksbill* below; **hawkbit** [f. *hawk(weed* (see below) + *devil's bit* s.v. DEVIL *n.*] any of several plants constituting the genera *Leontodon*, of the composite family, with heads of yellow ligulate florets and leaves in rosettes; *esp.* autumnal hawkbit, *L. autumnalis*, a common late-flowering plant of grassland; **hawk-cuckoo** any of various south and east Asian cuckoos of the genus *Cuculus*, of somewhat hawklike appearance, esp. the brain-fever bird, *C. varius*; **hawk-eagle** any of various tropical or subtropical eagles of the genus *Spizaetus*; **hawk-eye** (*a*) a keen-sighted or perceptive person; (*b*) *US colloq.* a native or inhabitant of Iowa; *the Hawkeye State* (US colloq.) Iowa; **hawk-eyed** *a.* keen-sighted; **hawk-faced** *a.* sharp- or hard-faced; **hawkmoth** any of various large, swift-flying moths constituting the family Sphingidae, with elongated forewings; **hawk-nose** a nose curved like a hawk's bill, an aquiline nose; **hawk-nosed** *a.* having a hawk-nose; **hawk-owl** †(*a*) the short-eared owl, *Asio flammeus*; (*b*) a somewhat long-tailed, partly diurnal owl, *Surnia ulula*, of northern coniferous woodland; **hawk's-beard** any of various plants constituting the genus *Crepis*, of the composite family, allied to the hawkweeds; **hawksbill (turtle)** a small sea turtle, *Eretmochelys imbricata*, with hooked jaws, found in tropical seas; **hawkweed** any of the numerous microspecies of the genus *Hieracium* and *Pilosella*, of the composite family, plants of banks, rocks, etc., with heads of usu. yellow ligulate florets.

hawkish *a.* (*a*) resembling a hawk in appearance or nature; (*b*) inclined to favour uncompromising or warlike policies: M19. **hawkishness** *n.* M20. **hawklike** *a.* resembling (that of) a hawk E17.

hawk /hɔːk/ *n.*[2] LME. [Origin unkn.] A rectangular board with a handle underneath, used by a plasterer or bricklayer to hold wet plaster or mortar.

hawk /hɔːk/ *n.*[3] E17. [f. HAWK *v.*[3]] An effort made to clear the throat; the noise thus made.

hawk /hɔːk/ *v.*[1] ME. [f. HAWK *n.*[1]] **1** *v.i.* Hunt game with a trained hawk. ME. **2** *v.i.* Hunt on the wing. LME. **b** *v.t.* Hunt (prey) on the wing. E19. **3** *v.i.* Foll. by *at*: attack as a hawk does, fly at; (of a person) fly a hawk at. LME. †**4** *v.i.* Foll. by *after*, *for*: pursue; try to catch or gain. E16–E18.

2 R. JEFFERIES A dragon fly, hawking to and fro on the sunny side of the hedge. 3 SHAKES. *Macb.* A falcon, tow'ring in her pride of place, Was by a mousing owl hawk'd at and kill'd.

hawk /hɔːk/ *v.*[2] L15. [Back-form. f. HAWKER *n.*[2]] **1** *v.t.* Carry *about* from place to place and offer for sale. L15. **2** *v.i.* Travel around touting or selling one's wares. M16.

1 R. W. CLARK The quacks who hawked medicines at fairgrounds. C. FRANCIS He hawked his idea around England, France and Portugal. *hawk one's mutton*: see MUTTON. 2 J. ARBUTHNOT To go hawking and peddling about the streets, selling knives, scissors, and shoe-buckles.

hawk /hɔːk/ *v.*[3] L16. [Prob. imit.] **1** *v.i.* Clear the throat noisily or with an effort. L16. **2** *v.t.* Bring *up* (phlegm etc.) from the throat with an effort. L16.

1 N. BAWDEN My mother coughed. She hawked, with a disgusting liquid noise.

hawked /hɔːkt/ *a.*[1] *Sc.* & *north.* Also **hawkit** /ˈhɔːkɪt/. L15. [Origin unkn.] Of cattle: spotted, streaked.

hawked /hɔːkt/ *a.*[2] L16. [f. HAWK *n.*[1] + -ED[2].] Curved like a hawk's beak; aquiline.

hawker /ˈhɔːkə/ *n.*[1] OE. [f. HAWK *n.*[1] + -ER[1].] A person who breeds, trains, or hunts with, hawks; a falconer.

hawker /ˈhɔːkə/ *n.*[2] E16. [Prob. of LDu. origin (cf. MLG *hoker*, LG *höker*, Du. *heuker*): see HUCKSTER *n.*] A person who travels about selling goods (esp. with a horse and cart or a van).

hawker /ˈhɔːkə/ *n.*[3] M20. [f. HAWK *v.*[1] + -ER[1].] A dragonfly whose flight behaviour is characterized by patrolling a particular area; *spec.* any of the family Aeschnidae.

Hawking radiation /ˈhɔːkɪŋ reɪdɪˌeɪʃ(ə)n/ *n. phr.* L20. [Stephen *Hawking* (b. 1942), Eng. physicist.] *Physics.* The radiation emitted by a black hole.

hawkit *a.* var. of HAWKED *a.*[1]

hawkshaw /ˈhɔːkʃɔː/ *n.* Also **H-**. E20. [A detective in *The Ticket-of-Leave Man*, a play by Tom Taylor (1817–80), Eng. dramatist; also in the comic strip *Hawkshaw the Detective* by Augustus Charles ('Gus') Mager (1878–1956), Amer. cartoonist.] A detective.

hawse /hɔːz/ *n.*[1] Earlier †**halse**. LME. [Prob. f. ON *hals* neck, ship's bow, tack of a sail, rope's end (= OE *heals* neck, prow). Cf. HAUSE *n.*] *Naut.* **1** A ship's bow; now *spec.* the part through which the anchor cables pass. Also in *pl.*, the hawse-holes. LME. †**2** A cable, a hawser. L16–M17. **3** The arrangement of cables when a ship is moored with port and starboard forward anchors; the space between the head of a moored vessel and its anchor(s). L16.

1 **ride hawse-full**, †**-fallen** sail in a rough sea with the water coming into the hawse. 3 **athwart-hawse**, **athwart** or †**thwart the hawse** transversely in front of an anchored ship.

Comb.: **hawse-hole** the hole through which the anchor cable passes; **hawse-piece** a plank or plate through which a hawse-hole is cut; **hawse-pipe** a metal pipe fitted in the hawse-hole of a wooden ship to prevent wear by the cable; **hawse-plug** a plug fitted into a hawse-hole to keep water out.

hawse *n.*[2], *v.* vars. of HAUSE *n.*, *v.*

hawser /ˈhɔːzə/ *n.* ME. [AN *haucer*, *-eour* (in AL *haucerus*, *ausorus*, *auncerus*) f. OFr. *haucier* (mod. *hausser*) hoist, f. Proto-Romance, f. L *altus* high: see -ER[2]. Assoc. from an early period w. HAWSE *n.*[1]] *Naut.* A large rope or small cable used for mooring or anchoring.

Comb.: **hawser-laid** *a.* = *cable-laid* s.v. CABLE *n.*

hawthorn /ˈhɔːθɔːn/ *n.* [OE *hagaþorn*, *hagu-* (= MDu. *hagedorn* (Du. *haagdoorn*), MHG *hage(n)dorn* (G *Hagedorn*), ON *hagþorn*) f. *haga* HAW *n.*[1] + THORN *n.*] Any of various thorny shrubs or low trees of the genus *Crataegus*, of the rose family, with white or pink blossom (may) and usu. red berries (haws); *esp.* (*a*) (more fully *common hawthorn*) the Eurasian *C. monogyna*, much used for hedging; (*b*) (more fully *midland hawthorn*) the European *C. laevigata*, found in woodlands. Also, any of several related shrubs.

Yeddo hawthorn: see YEDDO *n.*

Comb.: **hawthorn china** a kind of oriental porcelain with a pattern of plum-blossom on a dark blue ground.

Hawthorne effect /ˈhɔːθɔːn ɪˈfɛkt/ *n. phr.* M20. [f. the *Hawthorne* plant of the Western Electric Company in Chicago, Ill., where first observed in the 1920s.] *Psychol.* The alteration of behaviour by the subjects of a study due to their awareness of being observed.

hay /heɪ/ *n.*[1] [OE *hēġ*, *hīeġ*, *hīġ* = OFris. *hā*, *hē*, OS *hōi*, OHG *hewi*, *houwi* (Du. *hooi*, G *Heu*), ON *hey* (whence the native wd was reinforced), Goth. *hawi*, f. Gmc = cut down, HEW *v.*] Grass mown or cut and dried for fodder. Also (now *rare*), grass ready or kept for mowing.

J. GALSWORTHY A machine drawn by a grey horse was turning an early field of hay. *a roll in the hay*: see ROLL *n.*[2] 2f. *hit the hay*: see HIT *v.* (*look for*) *a needle in a bottle of hay*: see NEEDLE *n.* **make hay** mow grass and turn it over for exposure to the sun; *make hay of*, throw into confusion; *make hay* (*while the sun shines*), seize opportunities for advantage, pleasure, etc. **not hay** *US colloq.* a large amount of money. **roll in the hay** *colloq.* make love.

Comb.: **hay asthma** = *hay fever* below; **haybag** *derog. slang* a woman; **hay-band** a rope of twisted hay used to bind up a truss or bundle of hay; **hay-barn** a barn for the storage of hay; **haybox** (*a*) *dial.* a hayloft; (*b*) a box stuffed with hay, in which heated food may be left to continue cooking; **haycock** a conical heap of hay in a field; **hay fever** an allergic reaction to the airborne pollen of grasses or other plants, manifested in early summer and causing sneezing, nasal congestion, conjunctival irritation, and in some cases asthmatic symptoms; **hayfield** a field where hay is being or is to be made; **hay-fork** a long-handled fork for turning over or loading hay; **hay-home supper** *Hist.* a meal to celebrate the successful bringing home of the hay (cf. HARVEST HOME); **hayloft** a loft or storing-place for hay over a stable or barn; **haymaker** (*a*) a person employed in making hay, *esp.* one who lifts, tosses, and spreads hay after mowing; (*b*) a machine for shaking and drying hay; (*c*) *colloq.* a swinging blow or punch; (*d*) *Cricket* a sweeping stroke with the bat; **haymaking** the action or process of making hay (*lit.* & *fig.*); **haymow** a stack etc. of hay; hay stored in a barn; the part of a barn for the storage of hay; **hayrick** a haystack; **hayride** *US* a pleasure ride in a wagon carrying hay; **hay-scales** *US* a public weighing-machine for weighing loads of hay or other produce; **hayseed** (*a*) the grass seed from hay; (*b*) *N. Amer.*, *Austral.*, & *NZ colloq.* a rustic; **haystack** a regular pile of hay built in the open air and having a ridged or pointed top; *look for a needle in a haystack*: see NEEDLE *n.*

hay /heɪ/ *n.*[2] Now *arch.* & *dial.* [OE *heġe* f. Gmc base of HAG *n.*[3], HAW *n.*[1], HEDGE *n.*] **1** A hedge, a fence. OE. **2** An enclosed space; an enclosure; a park. ME. †**3** *Mil.* An extended line of men. L17–M19.

Comb.: †**hayhove** [OE *hōfe* w. same meaning: cf. ALE-HOOF] ground-ivy, *Glechoma hederacea*; **hayward** an officer of a parish etc. in charge of fences and enclosures. Also, a herdsman in charge of cattle etc. grazing on common land.

hay /heɪ/ *n.*[3] Long *obs.* exc. *dial.* LME. [AN *haie*, prob. an extension of HAY *n.*[2] or of the equiv. (O)Fr. *haie*: cf. OFr. *haier.*] More fully *hay-net*. A net used for catching wild animals, esp. rabbits.

hay /heɪ/ *n.*[4] Also **hey**. E16. [Fr. †*haie* a kind of dance.] (A figure in) a country dance with interweaving steps.

dance the hay(s) *arch.* perform winding movements (around numerous objects); *fig.* go through varied stages of development.

†**hay** *n.*[5] Only in L16. [It. *hai* you (sing.) have (it). Cf. L *habet* = he has (it), exclaimed when a gladiator was wounded.] A home thrust.

hay /heɪ/ *n.*[6] L19. [tr. Fr. *foin.*] The choke of an artichoke.

hay /heɪ/ *v.* M16. [f. HAY *n.*[1]] **1** *v.i.* Make hay. M16. **2** *v.t.* Provide or supply with hay; put (land) under grass for hay. E18. **3** *v.t.* Make (grass) into hay. L19.

haybote /ˈheɪbəʊt/ *n.* ME. [f. HAY *n.*[2] + BOTE. Cf. HEDGEBOTE.] Chiefly *Law.* Wood or thorns for the repair of fences; the right of a tenant to take such material from a landlord's estate.

†**haye** *n.* Also (earlier) **-en**. E17–M19. [Du. *haai*, WFlem. *haaie* rel. to Sw. *haj*, G *Hai*: cf. ON *hár(r)* dogfish, *há-* shark.] A shark.

haylage /ˈheɪlɪdʒ/ *n.* M20. [f. HAY *n.*[1] + SI)LAGE *n.*] Silage made from grass which has been partially dried.

hayrif *n.* var. of HAIRIF.

Haytian *a.* & *n.* see HAITIAN.

haywire /ˈheɪwʌɪə/ *n.* & *a.* E20. [f. HAY *n.*[1] + WIRE *n.*] **A** *n.* Wire for binding bales of hay, straw, etc. E20.

B *adj.* **1** Poorly or roughly contrived (w. ref. to the practice of using wire for baling hay to effect makeshift repairs). E20. **2** Of a person: in an emotional state, distracted, crazy. Of circumstances: tangled, in disorder, confused. *colloq.* (orig. *US*). M20.

1 *Listener* A haywire, unpredictable, one-man business. 2 J. O'HARA A married man . . and absolutely haywire on the subject of another woman. E. C. R. LORAC The time element's all haywire. **go haywire** go wrong, become confused or crazy.

hazan *n.* var. of HAZZAN.

hazard /ˈhazəd/ *n.* ME. [(O)Fr. *hasard* f. Sp. *azar* f. colloq. Arab. *az-zahr* f. *az-* AL-[2] + Pers. *zār* gaming die or Turk. *zar* die, dice, chance.] **1** A dice game in which the chances are complicated by arbitrary rules. ME. **2** Risk of loss or harm; (a source of) danger, jeopardy. M16. **3** *Real Tennis.* Each of the various openings or galleries around the court; *spec.* those which are not winning openings. M16. **4** Chance, venture; a chance. L16. †**5** Something risked or staked. *rare.* Only in L16. **6** *Billiards.* †**a** Any of the holes or pockets in the sides of a billiard table. L16–M18. **b** A stroke by which one of the balls is driven into a pocket. Freq. in *losing*, *winning*, *hazard* below. L18. **7** *Golf.* An obstruction in playing a shot such as a bunker, water, a road, etc. M18.

2 T. O'BRIEN People were asking one another about the hazards of nuclear fallout. 4 LYTTON On what hazards turn our fate!

Phrases: **at all hazards** despite all risks. **at hazard** *arch.* (*a*) at random; (*b*) at risk. **losing hazard** *Billiards* the pocketing of one's own ball off another. OCCUPATIONAL *hazard*. **winning hazard** *Billiards* the striking of the object-ball into a pocket.

Comb.: **hazard** (**warning**) **light** a flashing light used to warn that a vehicle is stationary or decelerating unexpectedly, usu. each of a vehicle's direction indicators operating simultaneously (usu. in *pl.*); **hazard side** *Real Tennis* the side of the court into which the ball is served.

hazard /ˈhazəd/ *v.* L15. [Fr. *hasarder*, f. as prec.] **1** *v.i.* Play at hazard. Chiefly as *hazarding* vbl n. *rare.* L15. **2** *v.t.* Put (a thing) to the risk of being lost in a game of chance etc.; stake; expose to hazard. M16. **3** *v.t.* Run the risk of (a penalty, a misfortune). Also foll. by *to do.* M16. †**4** *v.t.* Endanger. L16–L18. †**5** *v.t.* Get by chance or luck; chance on. L16–M17. **6** *v.t.* Take the chance or risk of; venture on (an action, statement, guess, etc.); venture *to do.* L16. †**7** *v.t. Billiards.* Strike (a ball) into a pocket. *rare.* Only in L17.

2 F. FORSYTH The general cargo business is too risky for a rich man . . to hazard money on it. 6 P. BAILEY If I were ordered to put a date on it, I'd hazard a guess.

hazarder *n.* (now *rare*) a player at hazard or dice; a person who hazards: ME.

†**hazardize** *n. rare* (Spenser). Only in L16. [f. HAZARD *n.* after *merchandise* etc.] A hazardous position, a condition of peril or risk.

hazardous /ˈhazədəs/ *a.* M16. [f. Fr. *hasardeux*, f. as HAZARD *n.*: see -OUS.] **1** Fraught with hazard, risky. M16. †**2** Tending to take risks; venturesome. M16–M17. **3** Dependent on chance; casual, fortuitous. Now *rare.* L16.

hazardously *adv.* E17. **hazardousness** *n.* L17.

hazardry /ˈhazədri/ *n.* Long *rare* or *obs.* ME. [OFr., f. as HAZARD *n.*: see -ERY. Cf. AL *hasarderia*.] **1** The playing of hazard; dicing; gambling. ME. †**2** The incurring of risk; venturesomeness. Only in L16.

haze /heɪz/ *n.* E18. [Prob. back-form. f. HAZY. Cf. HAZE *v.*[2]] **1** Orig., fog, hoar-frost. Now, (an) obscuration of the atmosphere near the earth, esp. by fine particles of water, smoke, or dust, tending to make distant objects indistinct. E18. **2** *fig.* Mental obscurity or confusion. L18.

1 E. HARDWICK A steamy haze blurred the lines of the hills. 2 A. J. P. TAYLOR I moved in a haze and have not the slightest recollection what the examination papers were about.

haze /heɪz/ *v.*[1] L17. [Origin uncertain: cf. Fr. †*haser* tease, anger, insult.] **1** *v.t.* Frighten; scold; punish by blows. *Sc.* & *dial.* L17. **2** *v.t.* *Naut.* Harass with overwork. M19. **3** *v.t.* Bully; try to disconcert. *US.* M19. **4** *v.i.* Frolic, lark. *US.* M19. **5** *v.i.* Loaf, roam, *about.* M19. **6** *v.t.* Drive (cattle etc.) while on horseback. L19.

hazer *n.* L19. **hazing** *n.* (*a*) the action of the vb; (*b*) *rare* a sound beating, a thrashing: E19.

haze /heɪz/ *v.*[2] L17. [Prob. back-form. f. HAZY. Cf. HAZE *n.*] **1** *v.i.* Drizzle. *dial.* L17. **2** *v.t.* Make hazy. E19.

hazel /ˈheɪz(ə)l/ *n.*[1] & *a.*[1] [OE *hæsel*, corresp. to MDu. *hasel* (Du. *hazelaar* hazel-tree, *hazelnoot* hazelnut), OHG *hasal*, *-ala* (G *Hasel*), ON *hasl*, f. Gmc, f. an IE base repr. also by L *corylus*.] **A** *n.* **1** Any of various deciduous shrubs and low trees constituting the genus *Corylus*, of the birch family, bearing edible nuts enclosed in leafy involucres; *esp.* the European hazel, *C. avellana*, and its N. American counterpart, *C. americana*. Also *hazel bush*, *hazel tree*, etc. OE. **b** With specifying wd: any of several trees thought to resemble the hazel in some respect. (Earlier in WITCH HAZEL.) L19. **2a** The wood of the hazel. LME. **b** A stick made from a hazel branch. E17. **3** The light (reddish- or greenish-)brown colour of a ripe hazelnut. L18.

1b **Australian hazel** either of two Australian trees, *Pomaderris apetala* and *P. lanigera*, of the buckthorn family. **Chile** or **evergreen hazel** a Chilean evergreen tree, *Guevina avellana* (family Proteaceae), the seeds of which taste like hazelnuts.

Comb.: **hazel-grouse**, **-hen**, a brown speckled grouse of European woodland, *Bonasa bonasia*; **hazelnut** the fruit of the hazel, a round hard-shelled nut.

B *adj.* Esp. of the eyes: of a hazel colour. L16.

hazel /ˈheɪz(ə)l/ *a.*[2] & *n.*[2] Chiefly *dial.* Also **hazle.** E17. [Origin unkn. Cf. HAZELLY *a.*[1]] **A** *adj.* Consisting of a mixture of sand, clay, and earth; loamy; easily worked. E17. **B** *n.* A kind of freestone. *local.* L18.

hazeled /ˈheɪz(ə)ld/ *a.* M17. [f. HAZEL *n.*[1] + -ED[2].] Covered with hazels. Formerly, hazel-coloured.

hazelly /ˈheɪz(ə)li/ *a.*[1] Chiefly *dial.* L16. [f. as HAZEL *a.*[2] & *n.*[2] + -Y[1].] = HAZEL *a.*[2]

hazelly /ˈheɪz(ə)li/ *a.*[2] L18. [f. HAZEL *n.*[1] + -Y[1].] Full of or covered with hazel bushes.

hazelwort /ˈheɪz(ə)lwəːt/ *n.* Now *rare* or *obs.* L16. [G *Haselwurz*, f. *Hasel* HAZEL *n.*[1] + *Wurz* herb, WORT *n.*[1]] (A herbalists' name for) the plant asarabacca, *Asarum europaeum*.

hazle *a.* & *n.* var. of HAZEL *a.*[2] & *n.*[2]

Hazlittian /hazˈlɪtɪən/ *a.* & *n.* Also **-ean.** E20. [f. William *Hazlitt* (see below) + -IAN, -EAN.] **A** *adj.* Of, pertaining to, or characteristic of the English critic William Hazlitt (1778–1830) or his work. E20. **B** *n.* An admirer or student of Hazlitt or his writing. M20.

hazy /ˈheɪzi/ *a.* E17. [Origin unkn.] **1** Orig., foggy. Later, characterized by the presence of haze; misty; not distinctly visible. E17. **2** *fig.* Vague, indistinct, uncertain. E19. **b** Slightly drunk. *arch. colloq.* E19.

1 A. S. BYATT The room was hazy with soft smoke. 2 R. MACAULAY I was becoming pretty hazy about right and wrong.

hazily *adv.* M19. **haziness** *n.* E18.

hazzan /xəˈzɑːn, ˈhɑːz(ə)n/ *n.* Also **chaz(z)an, hazan.** Pl. **-im** /-ɪm/. M17. [Heb. *ḥazzān* beadle, cantor, prob. f. Assyr. *hazannu* overseer or governor.] = CANTOR 1b.

he /hiː, *unstressed* ɪ/ *pers. pron.*, *3 sing. masc. subjective* (*nom.*), *n.*, & *a.* [OE *he*, *hē* = OFris. *hi*, *he*, OS *hi*, *he*, *hie*, f. Gmc demonstr. stem repr. also in OHG (Franconian) *er*, *her*, *hē* he, dat. *himo*, ON (*h*)*inn* him, Goth. *himma* to him, *hina* (direct objective) him. Cf. HIM, HIS *pron.*[1] & *a.*, UN *pron.*[1]] **A** *pron.* **1** The male person or animal, or the person or animal of unknown or unspecified sex, previously mentioned or implied or easily identified. OE. **2** The thing personified or conventionally treated as male (as a mountain, a river, a tree, the sun) or (in early use) the thing grammatically masculine, previously mentioned or implied or easily identified. ME. **3** The or any male person *who* (or *that*); the or any person *who* (or *that*); (with prep. phr., now *arch.* or *literary*) the (male) person *of*, *with*, etc. ME. **4** *he and he*, this and that, the one and the other, both. *arch.* ME. **5** The player who has to catch others in a children's game, 'it'. Cf. sense B.3 below. E19.

1 DRYDEN He first, and close behind him followed she. LONGFELLOW The skipper he stood beside the helm. T. HARDY Anne thought, 'Perhaps that's he, and we are missing him.' L. STEFFENS The business man has failed in politics as he has in citizenship. J. STEINBECK When Danny came home from the army he learned that he was an heir. W. S. MAUGHAM When someone . . wants to write the story . . he'll find all the material ready. G. GREENE Perhaps she . . fought his doubts (she was more a fighter than he). I. MURDOCH You and he were appointed her joint guardians. P. ACKROYD Of course he, Sir Frederick, would not stand for their bullying tactics. 2 TENNYSON Tonight I saw the sun set: he set and left behind The good old year. T. HARDY The Bear had swung round it . . he was now at a right angle with the meridian. 3 SHAKES. *Merry W.* He in the red face had it. J. CONRAD He who loves the sea loves also the ship's routine.

B *n.* **1** The male; a male. OE. **2** A person, a man. LME. **3** A children's chasing game in which one player is 'he' (see sense A.5 above). E20.

1 J. MAPLET It is also carefull in laying vp store for Winter, both the Hee and Shee. B. JOWETT Do we divide dogs into hes and shes, and take the masculine gender out to hunt? 2 BUNYAN He has shewed as much honesty . . as any he in Mansoul.

C *adj.* (Usu. hyphenated w. following n.) Male. Now chiefly of animals. ME.

he-goat etc. **he-man** a particularly strong, masterful, or virile man. **he-oak** *Austral.* any of various trees of the genus *Casuarina* (family Casuarinaceae), esp. *C. stricta*.

he /hiː/ *int.* OE. [Natural exclam. Cf. HA *int.*, HO *int.*[1], etc.] Repr. laughter, usu. affected or derisive. Chiefly in conjunction w. other similar ints. & redupl. HE HE.

head /hɛd/ *n.* & *a.* [OE *hēafod* = OFris. *hāved*, *hād*, OS *hōbid* (Du. *hoofd*), OHG *houbit* (G *Haupt*), ON *haufuð*, *hǫfuð*, Goth. *haubiþ*, f. Gmc, the relation of which with L *caput*, Gk *kephalē*, Skt *kapāla* skull is not clear.] **A** *n.* **I 1** The foremost part of the body of an animal or the upper part of the human body, separated from the rest of the body by a more or less distinct neck, and containing the mouth, the sense-organs, and the brain. OE. **b** The length of a head as a measure. M16. **c** A headache. Usu. w. specifying wd. L18. **2a** A part essential to life; life. OE. **b** The seat of intellect and imagination. Also, a natural mental aptitude or talent *for.* LME. **3** The hair on the head. Cf. *head of hair* below. *obs.* exc. *dial.* OE. **4** The hair dressed in a particular style. *arch.* ME. **5a** A person with a head of a specified kind; an individual. Also (freq. w. specifying wd prefixed) a drug addict. ME. **b** An individual animal of cattle, game, etc. (usu. treated as *pl.* following a numeral); *collect.* cattle, game. Also, an indefinite number *of* animals. E16. **6** A representation of a head, esp. as the image on the obverse of a coin; in *pl.*, this side turned upwards after a toss. LME. **b** A postage stamp (bearing the monarch's head). *arch. colloq.* M19. **7** The antlers of a deer. LME.

1 R. INGALLS Kelsoe . . had had his head . . torn from his body. J. MASTERS The only starers were the glass eyes of a pair of buffalo heads. b E. LINKLATER He topped Nikitin by half a head. c J. WADE I get one of those blinding heads. 2a L. MACNEICE Charles Edward lost Culloden, hid near Arnish in Lewis, thirty thousand pounds on his head. b *Times Lit. Suppl.* He had a head for figures. M. L. KING Only through the bringing together of head and heart—intelligence and goodness—shall man rise. R. G. COLLINGWOOD The bridge exists only in his mind, or (as we also say) in his head. 3 TENNYSON I curl'd and comb'd his comely head. 4 ADDISON At my toilette, try'd a new head. 5a *Times Educ. Suppl.* Wise heads . . are counselling against opening up the . . list. W. WHARTON They have a movie at ten cents a head. *acid-head*, *hophead*, *pot-head*, etc. b A. HIGGINS A Kildare farmer . . had lost thirteen head of cattle. *Coarse Fishing* 18 years ago my favourite water contained a very small head of pike. 6 J. FOWLES A penny . . with all but that graceful head worn away. G. PRIESTLAND The penny is still spinning; heads for war, tails for peace. 7 G. MARKHAM Stags yearly cast their Heads in March, April, May or June.

II 8 A compact mass of leaves, flowers, etc., at the top of a plant's stem; *esp.* = CAPITULUM (b). Also, a compound bulb (of garlic). OE. **b** The rounded leafy top of a tree or shrub. E16. **9** The upper end of something, as: the end of a lake at which a river enters it; the end of a bed, grave, etc., at which a person's head rests; the end of a table at which the host sits. OE. **10** The part of an object which resembles a head in form or position, as: the cutting, striking, etc., end of a weapon, tool, etc.; the knobbed end of a nail, pin, screw, etc.; the rounded part of a musical note; the flat surface of a cask, drum, etc.; the hood of a carriage, roof of a motor car, etc.; the pommel of a saddle; the closed end of a cylinder of a pump or (esp. an internal-combustion) engine. ME. **11** The top or upper end of something, as of a pile, a mast, a staircase, etc. ME. **12** The fully developed part of a spot, boil, etc., where it tends to break. ME. **13** The foremost part or end of something; *esp.* the front of a procession, army, etc. Also, the front part of a plough holding the share. ME. **14** The source of a river or stream. Also *fig.*, a source, the origin (now chiefly in *fountain-head*). ME. **15** A promontory. Now usu. in place-names. ME. **16**†**a** The beginning of a word, passage, etc. Latterly only *Astrol.*, the point at which the sun enters a sign of the zodiac. LME–E19. **b** *Phonet.* The first accented element or elements in a sequence of sounds before the nucleus. E20. **c** *Ling.* An element that has the same functions as the larger structure of which it is part and is therefore regarded as central to that structure. M20. **17** The top of a page, passage of text, etc. Also, a title etc. appearing there, a heading. LME. **b** The top of a book. E17. **c** A headline in a newspaper. E20. **18** An end or extremity of something having greater length than breadth. Now *rare.* LME. **19** A body of water or other liquid kept at a height in order to provide a supply (e.g. for a mill); the height of such a body or the pressure it exerts. L15. **b** = BORE *n.*[2] 2. L16. **c** The pressure of a confined body of steam etc. M19. **20** The bows of a ship. Also *spec.*, (now chiefly *Hist.*) any part of the structure forward of the stern, *esp.* a figurehead. L15. **b** *Naut. sing.* & in *pl.* A seamen's latrine (orig. in a ship's bows). Also (*N. Amer.*), a lavatory ashore. M18. **21** (A layer of) foam on the top of liquor, esp. beer. Also, (a layer of) cream on the top of milk. M16. **22** A measure of flax etc. M16. **23** = HEADING 7. M17. **24** *Curling*, *Bowls*, etc. A playing of one end in a game to its conclusion. E19. **25** A component in an audio, video, information, etc., system by which information is transferred from an electrical signal to the recording medium, or vice versa. M20.

8 V. WOOLF Laying the flowery heads of the grasses together. G. SANTAYANA Plenty of bread and cheese and a nice fresh head of lettuce. b T. MORRISON Shadrack stood . . watching the heads of trees tossing. 9 P. LIVELY Mother sits at the head of the table. *National Trust Magazine* This embraces 5,000 acres of mud-flats at the head of the lough. 10 J. CARY Rake-handles waiting for new heads. O. NASH When you go to strike a match the head dissolves on the box. 11 SHAKES. *Haml.* The skyish head of blue Olympus. F. BURNEY I then accompanied her to the head of the stairs. 12 DRYDEN To lance the Sore, And cut the

Head. **13** A. W. KINGLAKE The head of the vast column of troops. E. AMADI The head of the comet-like procession turned right. **14** A. DAY I will go to the head of the matter. I. WATTS Jordan beheld their march and fled with backward Current to his Head. **15** LD MACAULAY High on St. Michael's Mount it shone: it shone on Beachy Head. **17** ADDISON Without seeing his name at the head of it. **18** LD MACAULAY As that great host . . Rolled slowly towards the bridge's head. **19** W. FAIRBAIRN The head of the water is 132 feet. **20** G. GROTE They were moored by anchors head and stern. **25** *read/write head, record(ing) head*, etc.

III 26 A person to whom others are subordinate; a ruler, a chief. OE. **b** The master etc. of a college; a headmaster, a headmistress. M16. **27** Position of leadership or supreme command. ME. **28** Result; culmination, crisis; strength, force. Chiefly in *come to a head, bring to a head, gather head*, etc. ME. †**29** A force gathered esp. in insurrection. L15–M17. **30** A main division in a discourse, a category. E16. **31** Advance against opposing force; resistance, insurrection. Chiefly in *make head, keep head against*. L16. **32** A hunted animal's backward change of course to elude pursuit. Now *rare* or *obs.* E17.

26 S. KINGSLEY President ain't a good title for the head of the United States. P. CAREY You are the head of this household. *transf.*: AV *Isa.* 7:8 The head of Syria is Damascus. **b** D. CUSACK She'll make a splendid head Such an inspiring influence for the girls. **27** LD MACAULAY He was placed at the head of the administration. **28** J. WESLEY Vice is risen to such a head, that it is impossible to suppress it. R. F. HORTON But it is time to draw to a head this somewhat lengthened discussion. **29** S. PEPYS Some talk to-day of a head of Fanatiques that do appear about Barnett. **30** ISAIAH BERLIN The main issues between my serious critics and myself may be reduced to four heads.

Phrases. *a bone in one's head*: see BONE *n.* **above one's head** = *over one's head* below. *bang one's head against a brick wall*: see WALL *n.*[1] *bite a person's head off*: see BITE *v. break one's head*: see BREAK *v. by the head*: see BY *prep. comb a person's head with a three-legged stool*: see COMB *v.* 1. *come into one's head*: see COME *v.* **come to a head** (*a*) (of a boil etc.) suppurate; (*b*) *fig.* reach a climax or crisis. **count heads** (merely) determine the number present, voting, etc. *crowned head*: see CROWNED 1. *do one's head*: see DO *v. eat its head off*: see EAT *v. enter one's head*: see ENTER *v.* 1b. **from head to foot, heel, toe** all over a person. *get it into one's head that*: see GET *v. get one's head together*: see GET *v.* **give (a horse) its head** allow it to go freely; *fig.* allow (a person) to act without restraint or guidance. **go to a person's head** (*a*) intoxicate; (*b*) make vain or proud. *greenhead*: see GREEN *a. hang one's head*: see HANG *v. have one's head screwed on the right way*: see SCREW *v.* **head and front** (*a*) *rare* (Shakes.) the highest extent; (*b*) *arch.* the essence *of* an offence, the leader *of* an action. *head first*: see FIRST. **head for heights** the ability to be close to the edge of a high cliff, roof, etc., without giddiness. **head of hair** the hair on a person's head, esp. as a noticeable feature. **head of the river** (the boat, crew, etc. holding) the leading position in a series of boat races; a regatta in which crews attempt to gain this position. *head over ears*: see EAR *n.*[1] **head over heels** topsy-turvy, so as to turn completely over in a somersault etc. **heads I win, tails you lose** I win in any event. **heads will roll** *fig.* there will be some people dismissed or disgraced. **head to head** *colloq.* (orig. *US*) a conflict or contest (between two adversaries) at close quarters; a confrontation. *hide one's head*: see HIDE *v.*[1] *hit the nail on the head*: see HIT *v. hold one's head high*: see HOLD *v.* **keep one's head** remain calm. *keep one's head above water*: see WATER *n.* **keep one's head down** avoid distraction or danger. *knock one's head against a brick wall*: see WALL *n.*[1] *knock on the head*: see KNOCK *v. laugh one's head off*: see LAUGH *v.* **lay their heads together** consult one another. **let (a horse) have its head** = *give (a horse) its head* above. *like a bear with a sore head*: see BEAR *n.*[1] **lose one's head** (*a*) be beheaded; (*b*) become agitated or confused. †**make a head** raise a body of troops. **make head** make progress, advance or make resistance *against*. **make head or tail of** understand in any way (usu. in neg. contexts or interrog.). **need one's head examined** *joc. colloq.* be foolish, be crazy. *need (something) like a hole in the head*: see HOLE *n.*[1] **off one's head** *colloq.* crazy. **off the top of one's head** *slang* impromptu. **of one's own head** (now *rare* or *obs.*) by one's own decision, of one's own accord. **of the first head** (of a deer) at the age when the antlers are first developed; *fig.* of the first importance. **on one's (own) head** (of vengeance, guilt, responsibility, etc.) falling on one. **out of one's head** (*a*) from one's own invention; (*b*) forgotten by one; (*c*) *N. Amer. colloq.* crazy. *over head and ears*: see EAR *n.*[1] **over one's head** (*a*) above one, *esp. fig.* (of impending danger) threatening one; (*b*) beyond one's comprehension; (*c*) (of another's promotion, involvement, etc.) when one has a prior or stronger claim; (*d*) *arch.* (of time) past, over; (*e*) out of one's depth (*lit.* & *fig.*). **put a pistol to one's head** commit suicide by shooting. **put a pistol to someone's head**: (chiefly *fig.*) coerce someone by this means. *put ideas into a person's head*: see IDEA *n.* **put into a person's head** suggest to a person. **put their heads together** = *lay their heads together* above. *run one's head against a brick wall*: see WALL *n.*[1] *show one's head*: see SHOW *v. snap a person's head off*: see SNAP *v.* 3. **take it into one's head** conceive a notion (*that, to do*). *talk a person's head off*: see TALK *v.* **to one's head** (*obs.* exc. *dial.*) to one's face, directly. *turn a person's head*: see TURN *v. wash a person's head (without soap)*: see WASH *v. wash one's head*: see WASH *v. wet the baby's head*: see WET *v.* **win by a head** *Racing* win by the length of the horse's head. *wiping head*: see WIPE *v. wolf's head*: see WOLF *n.*

B *attrib.* or as *adj.* **1** In the position of command or superiority; chief, principal, capital. OE. **2** Situated at the top or front. Also, coming from the front, meeting one directly in front. LME.

Comb. & *special collocations*: **headband** (*a*) a band worn round the head; (*b*) an ornamental band of silk etc. fastened to the inner back of a bound book at the head and tail; (*c*) (long *rare* or *obs.*) a band round the top of a pair of trousers etc.; **headbanding** (the action or process of fastening) the headbands of a book; **headbanger** (*a*) a person who practises headbanging; (*b*) *colloq.* an enthusiast for loud music; **headbanging** (*a*) violent rocking of the body and shaking or knocking of the head, associated with mental disorder in adults; (*b*) vigorous head-shaking in time to heavy metal music etc.; **headboard** a board forming the head of a bed etc.; **headborough** *Hist.* = BORSHOLDER; **head boy** the senior male pupil in a school; **head-butt** *v.t.* & *n.* (attack with) a forceful thrust with the top of the head into another's chin or body; **head case** *colloq.* a crazy person; **head cheese** *N. Amer.* brawn made from a pig's head etc.; **head-chief** the paramount chief of a N. American Indian people; **head-cloth** a cloth or covering for the head; **head-court** *Hist.* a chief court (of justice); **head-dress** a covering (esp. ornamental attire worn by women) for the head; **head-dresser** (*a*) a hairdresser; †(*b*) a maker of head-dresses; **headfast** a rope or chain securing the head of a vessel to the quay etc.; **headgear** (*a*) something worn on the head, as a hat, cap, head-dress, etc.; (*b*) machinery etc. at the top of a mine shaft; **head girl** the senior female pupil in a school; **head-hunt** *v.t.* (seek to) obtain by head-hunting; **head-hunter** (*a*) a person who head-hunts (another); (*b*) *spec.* an employment agent or agency specializing in the recruitment for an organization etc. of skilled personnel already employed elsewhere; **head-hunting** (*a*) the practice of collecting the heads of one's enemies as trophies; (*b*) the action or practice of seeking to recruit on behalf of an organization etc. skilled personnel already employed elsewhere; **headkerchief** *arch.* a kerchief for the head; **headlamp** (*a*) a headlight; (*b*) a lamp carried on the front of a bicycle; **headland** (*a*) a strip of land left unploughed at the edge of a field; (*b*) a high point of land projecting into the sea etc., a promontory; **headlight** (the beam from) a powerful lamp carried on the front of a locomotive, motor vehicle, etc.; **headlock** a wrestling hold in which the arm is round an opponent's head; **head louse** a louse of the form infesting the hair of the human head; **headman** (*a*) a chief man, the chief of a tribe, etc.; †(*b*) *rare* = HEADSMAN 2; **headmaster** the principal master of a school; **headmastership** the office or position of a headmaster; **headmistress** the principal mistress of a school; **head-money** a fee paid by or for each person; **head-note** (*a*) *Law* a summary giving the principle of the decision and an outline of the facts prefixed to the report of a decided case; (*b*) *Mus.* a note produced in a high register of the voice; (*c*) a note or comment inserted at the head of a page, document, etc.; **head noun** the noun which other words in a noun phrase qualify; **head office** the principal office of a business organization constituting the centre for administration, policy-making, etc.; **headphone** a radio, telephone, etc., earphone held by a band fitting over the head; **headpiece** (*a*) a helmet; (*b*) (now *rare*) a cap etc.; (*c*) *arch.* the head, the skull; (*d*) the intellect; (*e*) a person of intellect; (*f*) a halter, a headstall; (*g*) the top part of something; **head-race** the part of a mill-race bringing water to the wheel; **headrest** a support for the head attached to the seat of a motor vehicle etc.; **head restraint** a head-rest that prevents the head from jerking back suddenly; **headroom** overhead space; **head-rope** †(*a*) one of the stays of a mast; (*b*) the part of a bolt-rope sewn on to the upper edge of a sail; a small rope for hoisting an attached flag to the masthead etc.; (*c*) a rope along the top of a fishing net; (*d*) a rope for leading or tethering a horse etc.; **head-sail** a sail on the foremast or bowsprit; **headscarf** a scarf worn instead of a hat; **head sea** waves from a forward direction; **headset** an attachment for fitting earphones and microphone to the head; **head-shrinker** (*a*) a head-hunter who preserves and shrinks the heads of enemies; (*b*) *slang* a psychiatrist; **headspring** a fountain-head, a source (*lit.* & *fig.*); **headsquare** a (square) scarf for the head; **headstall** the part of a bridle or halter that fits round a horse's head; **head start** (*a*) an advantage at the start of a race (*lit.* & *fig.*); (*b*) *spec.* (w. cap. initials) an educational and welfare programme in the US; *head-stave*: see STAVE *n.* 2; **headstock** (*a*) the bearings or supports of revolving parts in various machines; (*b*) the horizontal end members in the underframe of a railway vehicle; **headstone** (*a*) the chief stone in a foundation, the cornerstone of a building (*lit.* & *fig.*); (*b*) a gravestone; **head tax** *US* a poll tax; **head-teacher** the principal teacher or administrator of a school; a headmaster, a headmistress; **head-tie** a head-cloth; **head-tire** (now *arch.* & *dial.*) covering for the head; a head-dress; **head-up** *a.* (of the instrument-readings in an aircraft, vehicle, etc.) shown so as to be visible without lowering one's eyes from the view ahead; **head-voice** a high register of the voice in speaking or singing; **headwater(s** the part of a river or stream closest to the head or source; **head wind** a wind blowing from directly in front; **headword** (*a*) a word forming a heading (of an entry in a dictionary etc.); (*b*) *Ling.* a word that is the head (sense 16c above) of a syntactic group; **headwork** mental work; **head-yard** any of the yards on the foremast of a sailing ship.

headage *n.* the number of animals in question M20. **headlet** *n.* (*obs.* exc. *dial.*) a little head L16. **headship** *n.* the position or office of a head or principal; leadership; supremacy: L16.

head /hɛd/ *v.* ME. [f. the n.] **I 1** *v.t.* Cut off or remove the head of; *esp.* (*arch.*) behead (a person). ME. **2** *v.t.* Lop off the upper part or branches of (a plant or tree). Also foll. by *down*. E16.

1 SHAKES. *Meas. for M.* If you head and hang all that offend that way. **2** J. JAMES The willow . . is headed every three or four years.

II 3 Put a head on; provide with a head. LME. **b** Close *up* (a cask etc.) by fitting the head on; enclose in a cask etc. by this means. E17. **c** Form the head of. M17. **4** *v.i.* Form a head; come, grow to a head. Also foll. by *out, up*. LME. **5** *v.i.* Of a stream: have its source, rise. Chiefly *US*. M18. **6** *v.t.* Foll. by *up*: collect (water) to form a head (*lit.* & *fig.*). E19. **7** *v.t.* Provide with a heading; place a title, name, etc., at the head of (a chapter, list, etc.). Also, form the heading of. M19.

3 DRYDEN Whet the shining Share . . Or sharpen Stakes, or head the Forks. **4** G. WASHINGTON All my early wheat . . was headed and heading. **5** H. M. BRACKENRIDGE The Kansas, a very large river . . heads between the Platte and the Arkansas. **6** ISAAC TAYLOR Religious knowledge long . . accumulated and headed up above the level of the plains of China. **7** TENNYSON Heaven heads the count of crimes with that wild oath. M. MEYER Heading his letters with the month but not the date.

III 8 *v.t.* Be the head or ruler of; be or put oneself at the head of. Also (chiefly *N. Amer.*) foll. by *up*. LME. **9** *v.t.* Go in front or at the head of; lead, precede; *fig.* surpass. E18.

8 W. S. CHURCHILL Essex soon headed the war party in the Council. B. T. BRADFORD He thinks you're ideally suited to head up a wholesale supply company. A. J. P. TAYLOR I found our house full of Thompson relatives, headed by my grandmother. **9** J. DAVIDSON And he tossed his branching antlers high/As he headed the hunt.

IV 10 *v.i.* Face in a specified direction. E17. **11** *v.t.* Go round the head of (a stream or lake). M17. **12** *v.t.* Move forward so as to meet, advance in opposition to the course of; confront (*lit.* & *fig.*). *arch.* L17. **b** Get in front of so as to turn back or aside. Freq. foll. by *off*. E18. **13** *v.i.* Move towards (a particular point); proceed (in a specified direction); make *for*. M19.

10 C. C. ADLEY Two strong veins . . heading on in the direction of the main lode. **11** T. H. HUXLEY It is shorter to cross a stream than to head it. 12 M. E. BRADDON He has to cover his face with a muffler, and head the driving snow. b R. H. SAVAGE To head my rival off I indulged in a tremendous flirtation. 13 P. ROTH Beside me in the taxi heading away from the sea. P. BAILEY A great articulated lorry heading straight in their direction.

V 14 *v.t.* Chiefly *Football.* Strike (esp. the ball) with the head; score (a goal) thus. L18.

-head /hɛd/ *suff.* [Var. of -HOOD.] Forming ns. of condition or quality or grouping f. ns. and adjs. Now chiefly repl. by *-hood* exc. in *godhead*, *maidenhead*.

headache /ˈhɛdeɪk/ *n.* OE. [f. HEAD *n.* + ACHE *n.*[1]] 1 A continuous pain (usu. dull and deep-seated) in the head. OE. b *fig.* A troublesome or annoying situation etc., a worry. *colloq.* M20. 2 A wild poppy (so called from the effect of its odour). *dial.* E19.

1 *sick headache*: see SICK *a.* b *Yachting World* Freak weather conditions are a constant headache for skippers.

headachy *a.* (*a*) suffering from or subject to headache; (*b*) accompanied by or causing headache: L18.

head and shoulders /hɛd ən(d) ˈʃəʊldəz/ *n.*, *adv.*, & *a. phr.* L16. [f. HEAD *n.* + AND *conj.*[1] + SHOULDER *n.*] A *n. phr.* 1 *by head and shoulders*, by force, violently. Now *rare.* L16. 2 A head and shoulders portrait. L19. B *adv. phr.* (*Taller* etc.) by the measure of the head and shoulders; *fig.* considerably. M19. C *adj. phr.* Designating a portrait etc. in which only the head and shoulders are shown. M19.

headed /ˈhɛdɪd/ *a.* ME. [f. HEAD *n.*, *v.*: see -ED[2], -ED[1].] 1 Having a head (of a specified kind); furnished with a head; having heads (of a specified number). ME. 2 That has come to a head or matured (*lit.* & *fig.*). *rare.* E17. 3 Furnished with a (written or printed) heading. M19.

1 T. SCOTT All the arrowes they shoote . . are both headed and feathered. *clear-headed*, *light-headed*, *many-headed*, etc. *half-headed*: see HALF-. 2 SHAKES. *A.Y.L.* All th' embossed sores and headed evils. 3 *Daily News* A letter on the headed notepaper of a firm in New Bond-Street.

header /ˈhɛdə/ *n.* LME. [f. HEAD *v.* or *n.* + -ER[1].] 1 A person or thing which removes the head; *esp.* a reaping-machine which cuts off the heads of grain. LME. 2 A brick or stone laid at right angles to the face of a wall. Cf. STRETCHER *n.* 3. L17. 3 A person who puts heads on casks etc. M18. 4 A person who heads a party etc., a leader. *rare.* E19. 5 A dive or plunge head first. *colloq.* M19. 6 *Football.* A ball which is headed; the action or an act of heading the ball. Also, a player who heads the ball. E20. 7 = *heading dog* s.v. HEADING *n.* M20. 8 A line of information appearing at the top of each page of a document, containing the date, the chapter-heading, etc. L20.

5 **take a header** fall head first.

¶ See also *double header* s.v. DOUBLE *a.* & *adv.*

heading /ˈhɛdɪŋ/ *n.* ME. [f. HEAD *v.* + -ING[1].] I 1 *gen.* The action of HEAD *v.* ME. 2 The action or an act of facing or moving in a particular direction; *spec.* the course of a ship, aircraft, etc. E17. 3 *Football.* The action of striking the ball with the head. L19.

1 F. ROBERTSON The heading up of the water. *Athenaeum* Plots and rumours of plots, with their consequences of headings and hangings. 2 C. A. LINDBERGH A degree or two change in heading could easily cause a crash. *Scientific American* The Pacific plate . . switched to that course from a more northerly heading about 40 million years ago.

II 4 †a A bank, a dam. M17–M19. b *gen.* A distinct or separate part forming the head, top, or front of something. L17. 5 Material for making cask-heads. L17. 6 A top layer or covering. L18. 7 A horizontal passage driven in preparation for a tunnel; a drift. E19. 8 A title etc. at the head of a page etc.; (the title of) a category. M19.

8 P. LEVI His business letter heading carried a wonderful rigmarole of which I was very proud. J. O'HARA Joe Montgomery could be classified under many headings.

Comb.: **heading-course** a course of bricks consisting of headers; **heading dog** *NZ* & *Austral.* a dog trained to round up etc.

headless /ˈhɛdlɪs/ *a.* OE. [f. HEAD *n.* + -LESS.] 1 Without a head, beheaded; having no head. OE. 2 Having no chief or leader. ME. 3 Lacking in brains or intellect; senseless, stupid. Long *rare.* M16.

headline /ˈhɛdlʌɪn/ *n.* & *v.* LME. [f. HEAD *n.* + LINE *n.*[2]] A *n.* 1 *Naut.* A line making a sail fast to the yard. Also, a strengthening line sewn on the upper edge of a flag. LME. 2 A baseline used in surveying. Long *rare.* M17. 3 *Typogr.* †a The notional upper line that bounds a small letter. Only in L17. b The line at the top of a page containing the title etc.; a title or subtitle in large type in a newspaper etc. Also (usu. in *pl.*), a summary of main items given during a broadcast news bulletin. E19. 4 A fold in the palm of the hand regarded in palmistry as significant of a person's abilities. M19. 5 A line etc. attached to the head of something; *spec.* a line fastening a vessel's head to the shore. L19.

3b G. HUNTINGTON He studied the headlines of the *Corriere della Sera. attrib.*: R. OWEN Yalta is again headline-news rather than the stuff of faded documents. **hit** or **make the headlines** be very important news, come suddenly to public notice. *running headline*: see RUNNING *a.*

B *v.* 1 *v.t.* Provide with a headline; display in a headline. L19. 2 *v.i.* & *t.* Appear as the chief performer (at). L20.

1 *Listener* The answer . . faithfully reported and perhaps headlined the next day in the local press. 2 *Sounds* Siouxsie and the Banshees . . will be headlining the Ostend Festival.

headliner *n.* (*US*) a star performer L19. **headliˈnese** *n.* the elliptical style of language characteristic of (esp. popular) newspaper headlines E20.

headlong /ˈhɛdlɒŋ/ *adv.* & *a.* Orig. †**-ling.** LME. [f. HEAD *n.* + -LING[2], assim. in LME to -LONG.] A *adv.* 1 Head foremost (in falling etc.); head downmost. LME. 2 With an unrestrained forward motion, precipitately (*lit.* & *fig.*). LME.

1 J. CONRAD Shaw was thrown headlong against the skylight. 2 B. JOWETT He amongst us who would be divine . . should not rush headlong into pleasures. J. B. MORTON Hastily collecting his things he runs headlong from the room.

B *adj.* 1 Rushing forward without restraint; impetuous; precipitate (*lit.* & *fig.*). E16. 2 Of a height etc. from which a person might fall headlong; precipitous. Now *rare.* M16. 3 Plunging downwards head foremost as in falling etc. L16.

1 BYRON Like a tower upon a headlong rock. 2 LD MACAULAY Wild mountain passes . . torn by headlong torrents. W. STYRON Plunging in panicky headlong flight toward the fields and the woods beyond. R. MACAULAY What a child she was for enthusiasms and ideas and headlong plans. 3 M. KINGSLEY Taking a headlong dive into the deep Atlantic.

headlongness *n.* (*rare*) headlong quality or speed, precipitateness (*lit.* & *fig.*) E18. **headlongs** *adv.* (*obs.* exc. *dial.*) = HEADLONG *adv.* LME.

headmost /ˈhɛdməʊst/ *a.* E17. [f. HEAD *n.* & *a.* + -MOST.] 1 Foremost (esp. of a ship). E17. 2 Topmost. Chiefly *dial.* L18.

head-on /*as adv.* hɛdˈɒn, *as adj.* ˈhɛdɒn/ *adv.* & *a.* Orig. *US.* M19. [f. HEAD *n.* + ON *adv.*] A *adv.* With the head pointed directly towards an object (*lit.* & *fig.*). M19. B *adj.* Involving the (violent) meeting of two vehicles head to head, or of the head of a vehicle with a stationary object; *fig.* with direct opposition. E20.

headquarter /ˈhɛdkwɔːtə/ *v.t.* E20. [f. next.] Provide with headquarters (at a specified location). Usu. in *pass.*

headquarters /hɛdˈkwɔːtəz/ *n.* (treated as *sing.* or *pl.*). M17. [f. HEAD *n.* + QUARTER *n.* + -S[1].] 1 *Mil.* The quarters of the officer commanding an army, a corps, a division, etc.; the officers stationed there. M17. 2 A central or chief place of business etc.; a centre of operations. L18.

head-rail /ˈhɛdreɪl/ *n.*[1] L18. [f. HEAD *n.* + RAIL *n.*[2]] 1 In *pl.* The teeth. *slang.* L18. 2 A rail at the head of a ship. L18.

head-rail /ˈhɛdreɪl/ *n.*[2] M19. [f. HEAD *n.* + RAIL *n.*[1]] *Hist.* A woman's head-dress of the OE period.

headsman /ˈhɛdzmən/ *n.* Pl. **-men.** LME. [f. HEAD *n.* + -'S[1] + MAN *n.*] 1 A chief, a headman. Now *rare.* LME. 2 An executioner who beheads. E17. 3 *Hist.* The commander of a whaling boat. M19. 4 A miner who moves loads of coal etc. from the workings into position for transport to the surface. M19.

headstrong /ˈhɛdstrɒŋ/ *a.* LME. [f. HEAD *n.* + STRONG *a.*] 1 Violently self-willed, obstinate. LME. 2 Proceeding from wilfulness or obstinacy. L16.

1 R. W. EMERSON They are testy and headstrong through an excess of will and bias. V. S. PRITCHETT The parentless boy would tend to run wild, to resemble his headstrong father. 2 R. ELLIS Should . . humour headstrong Drive thee wilfully . . to such profaning.

headstrongly *adv.* (long *rare* or *obs.*) M17. **headstrongness** *n.* E17.

headward /ˈhɛdwəd/ *n.*, *a.*, & *adv.* LME. [f. HEAD *n.* + -WARD.] †A *n. to the headward*, towards the head; *Naut.* ahead. LME–L17. B *adj.* That is in the region or direction of the head; *esp.* (of erosion) occurring along the course of a stream etc. in an upstream direction. M17. C *adv.* Towards or in the direction of the head. L18.

Also **headwards** *adv.* M19.

headway /ˈhɛdweɪ/ *n.* E18. [f. HEAD *n.* + WAY *n.*] I 1 *Mining.* A narrow passage or gallery connecting broad parallel passages. E18. 2 *Archit.* Headroom; the clear height of a door, tunnel, etc. L18. 3 The interval of time between successive buses etc. on a route. L19.

II 4 A ship's movement ahead or forward; rate of progress; *gen.* advance, progress (*lit.* & *fig.*). M18.

4 M. SCAMMELL Solzhenitsyn was too naïve and inexperienced to make much headway. *Ships Monthly* The ship was losing headway, the engines stopped.

heady /ˈhɛdi/ *a.* LME. [f. HEAD *n.* + -Y[1].] 1 Headlong, impetuous, violent; passionate; headstrong. LME. 2 Apt to intoxicate (*lit.* & *fig.*). L16. 3 Headachy. *colloq.* L19.

1 SHAKES. *Hen. V* Never came reformation in a flood, With such a heady currance, scouring faults. S. JOHNSON Passions by which the heady and vehement are seduced and betrayed. 2 M. HOLROYD The heady cosmopolitan world of Montparnasse intoxicated him. A. S. BYATT The fruit salad had been heady with some dark and potent wine. 3 E. HILLARY I felt thick and heady and a sharp cough rasped my sore throat.

headily *adv.* LME. **headiness** *n.* LME.

†**heal** *n.* Also **hele.** [OE *hǣlu*, *hǣl*, corresp. to OS *hēli*, OHG *heili*, f. *hāl* adj.: see HALE *a.*, WHOLE *a.*] 1 Sound bodily condition; health. In later use *Sc.* OE–E20. b Healing, recovery. ME–L17. 2 Welfare, prosperity. OE–E17. 3 Spiritual health or healing. OE–L16.

heal /hiːl/ *v.*[1] [OE *hǣlan* = OFris. *hēla*, OS *hēlian* (Du. *heelen*), (O)HG *heilen*, ON *heila*, Goth. *hailjan*, f. Gmc, f. base repr. also by WHOLE *a.*] 1 *v.t.* Free (a person) from disease or ailment, restore to health (now chiefly by miraculous, spiritual, or psychic means). (Foll. by (*arch.*) *of* a disease.) OE. b *fig.* Restore to a sound condition; save from sin, danger, etc. OE. c *spec.* Of a monarch: touch for the 'king's evil'. *obs.* exc. *Hist.* E16. 2 *v.t.* Make whole (a wound); cure (a disease). (Foll. by *over*, *up.*) OE. b *fig.* Repair, correct (an undesirable condition, esp. a breach of relations). ME. 3 *v.i.* Of a wound, a part of the body, etc.: become whole or sound again, esp. by the growth of new tissue; become cured. LME.

2 J. KOSINSKI Whatever had been broken by the butt of the Kalmuk's rifle was now healed. b G. GREENE I will make you a bet . . that . . relations are healed and the American Ambassador returns. 3 B. EMECHETA One of his feet had a nasty scar that had healed badly. M. AMIS Father's ankle had healed . . he now claimed to be fleeter of foot.

Comb.: **heal-all** (*a*) a universal remedy, a panacea; (*b*) any of various plants with reputed healing powers; *esp.* rose-root, *Sedum rosea*, and (chiefly *US*) self-heal, *Prunella vulgaris*.

healer *n.* a person who or thing which heals; *spec.* a faith-healer: ME. **healing** *ppl a.* that heals; *esp.* having therapeutic or curative properties: LME. **healingly** *adv.* M19.

heal *v.*^{2} var. of HELE *v.*

heald /hiːld/ *n.* [OE *hefel, hefeld*, OS *hevild*, ON *hafald*, f. base meaning 'raise': see HEDDLE.] *Weaving.* †1 The warp and weft. OE–L15. 2 = HEDDLE. M18.

heald *v.* var. of HIELD.

healsome /ˈhiːls(ə)m/ *a. obs.* exc. *Sc.* LME. [f. HEAL *n.* + -SOME^{1}: cf. HALESOME.] Wholesome, healthy.

health /hɛlθ/ *n.* [OE *hǣlþ* = OHG *heilida*, f. WGmc, f. Gmc base repr. also by WHOLE *a.*: see -TH^{1}.] 1 Sound condition of body; freedom from disease. OE. †2 Healing, cure. OE–M16. 3 Spiritual or moral soundness. Also, salvation. *arch.* OE. †4 Welfare, safety; deliverance. ME–E17. 5 Condition of body in respect of its vigour and soundness. Freq. w. qualifying adj., as *good, bad, delicate health.* M16. 6 A toast drunk in a person's honour. L16.

1 S. SPENDER This .. period of alternating health and illness. J. GATHORNE-HARDY Dr. Wasing's astonishment .. as M and B swept his pneumonia patients to health. *fig.*: *Community Librarian* The revenue from this source is essential for the continuing health of our journal. **to your (good) health!** expr. a wish for another's well-being uttered by a person drinking. 3 E. LYALL As you value the health of your own souls. 4 G. CHAPMAN There is no mercy in the wars, your healths lie in your hands. 5 V. GLENDINNING He was .. nervous about his health and suffered from asthma. *bill of health*: see BILL *n.*^{3} **mental health** condition of a person or group in respect of the functioning of the mind. **not for one's health** *colloq.* (orig. *US*) for serious (financial) motives. 6 T. S. ELIOT Now I'll propose a health Can you guess whose health I'm going to propose?

Comb.: **health camp** *NZ* an outdoor camp for children of poor physique; **health care** the maintenance and improvement of personal health; **health centre** a local headquarters of medical facilities; *spec.* one containing the surgery and offices of a group practice; **health club** an establishment providing facilities for gymnastic exercises, massage, etc.; **health farm** (orig. *US*) a place where visitors stay for an intensive course of dieting etc.; **health food** food, usu. produced by non-artificial methods, eaten for its supposed health-giving properties; **health insurance** insurance against loss of earnings through illness or to cover the cost of medical treatment; **health officer**: charged with the administration of health laws and sanitary inspection; **health physics** the branch of radiology that deals with the health of those working with radioactive materials; **health resort** a place, such as a spa, resorted to by visitors for the benefit of their health; **health salts** magnesium sulphate or other salts taken in effervescent form as a mild laxative; **health service** the aggregate of public medical facilities available to members of a community; **health visitor** a trained person who visits people, esp. expectant mothers and the elderly, in their homes to give them advice on their health.

healthful /ˈhɛlθfʊl, -f(ə)l/ *a.* LME. [f. prec. + -FUL.] 1 Wholesome, salubrious. LME. 2 Of a person etc.: full of or marked by moral, intellectual, or (now *rare*) physical health; healthy. LME.

healthfully *adv.* LME. **healthfulness** *n.* M16.

healthless /ˈhɛlθlɪs/ *a.* Now *rare.* M16. [f. as prec. + -LESS.] 1 Lacking physical or spiritual health; unhealthy. M16. 2 Not conducive to health; unwholesome. M17.

healthsome /ˈhɛlθs(ə)m/ *a.* Now *rare.* M16. [f. as prec. + -SOME^{1}.] 1 Wholesome, salutary. M16. †2 Enjoying good health; healthy. M16–M17.

healthy /ˈhɛlθi/ *a.* M16. [f. HEALTH + -Y^{1}.] 1 Possessing good health; sound in body, free from disease. M16. 2 Conducive to health, salubrious; *fig.* salutary in effect. M16. b In ironical use: safe, prudent. M19. 3 Indicative or characteristic of good health or sound condition (*lit.* & *fig.*). Opp. *morbid.* L16. 4 Of a quantity etc.: gratifyingly or impressively large. *colloq.* L19.

1 P. ROTH Men .. young and healthy enough to make a rapid physical recovery from bypass surgery. *fig.*: J. GROSS The infected areas of his work cannot simply be cordoned off from the healthy. 2 W. S. CHURCHILL London was a healthier place to live in than rural Prussia. J. KRANTZ Raspberries sounded very healthy to both Dolly and Lester. *Oxford Mail* The fall [in the market] is a healthy reminder that the small print in the unit trust advertisements .. is true. b G. D. BREWERTON It would not have been 'healthy' .. for Major Clarke to have entered the place. 3 STEELE With a fresh, sanguine, and healthy Look. H. M. STANLEY An interchange of small gifts served as a healthy augury for the future. E. O'NEILL Now I'm going to give an honest healthy yell. K. ISHIGURO People .. need to express their views openly and strongly—now that's a healthy thing. 4 G. BORDMAN The healthy salaries stars were beginning to draw. *Keyboard Player* Output from the monitor speakers is a healthy 20 watts.

healthily *adv.* M17. **healthiness** *n.* (earlier in UNHEALTHINESS) L17.

heap /hiːp/ *n.* [OE *hēap* = OFris. *hāp*, OS *hōp* (Du. *hoop*: cf. FORLORN HOPE), OHG *houf* (rel. to MLG *hūpe*, OHG *hūfo*, G *Haufen*), f. WGmc.] 1 A collection of objects or material piled up so as to form a high (freq. conical) mass. Cf. PILE *n.*^{3} OE. †2 A large company (esp. of people); a crowd, a host. OE–L16. 3 *sing.* & in *pl.* A large number or quantity; a great deal, a lot. Foll. by *of. colloq.* ME. b Without preceding *a*, as *adv.* in representations (now freq. *joc.*) of N. American Indian speech: very (much); esp. *heap big.* M19. 4 A heaped measure of capacity. LME. 5 A slovenly woman. Usu. w. qualifying adj. *colloq.* (orig. *dial.*). E19. 6 A battered old car. *colloq.* (orig. *US*). E20.

1 K. MANSFIELD An old gardener .. was sweeping the path, brushing the leaves into a neat little heap. *compost heap, dust-heap, scrap heap, slag-heap*, etc. 2 SHAKES. *Rich. III* Among this princely heap, if any here, By false intelligence or wrong surmise, Hold me a foe. 3 W. BESANT He got into trouble a heap of times. J. B. MORTON There are heaps of candidates. b E. WHARTON We'd be heaps hotter up where Miss Mellins is. A. LURIE I've got a heap to tell you.

Phrases: **a heap sight** *US colloq.* to a considerable degree or extent. **(at the) bottom of the heap** *colloq.* in a losing, inferior, or disadvantaged position. **(at the) top of the heap** *colloq.* in a winning, pre-eminent, or advantageous position. †**by** or **in heaps** in great numbers, in crowds. *heap big*: see sense 3b above. **knock (a person) all of a heap** = *strike (a person) all of a heap* below. †**on a heap, on heaps** in a prostrate mass. **strike (a person) all of a heap** knock (a person) prostrate, esp. (*hyperbol.*) with surprise or dismay. *top of the heap*: see *at the top of the heap* above.

heap /hiːp/ *v.* [OE *hēapian* (corresp. to OHG *houfōn*), f. prec.] 1 *v.t.* Form into a heap; pile (*up*). OE. b *fig.* Bestow in large quantities (*up*)*on.* L16. 2 *v.t.* Cover or fill with or *with* objects or a substance piled high. ME. b *fig.* Overwhelm *with* large quantities of something (e.g. praise, blame). LME. 3 *v.i.* Become piled up, form a heap. Now *US.* LME.

1 M. PATTISON Generations of antiquaries have heaped together vast piles of facts. J. TYNDALL The snow had been heaped in oblique ridges across my path. J. WAIN Canvases, dirty crockery, and clothes .. had been heaped on to this [table] in a kind of unsteady mound. *heap coals (of fire) on a person's head*: see COAL *n.* b L. DEIGHTON The miseries that airline companies heap upon their clients. P. ROTH The ridicule he'd heaped upon them all in that book. *heap praises on*: see PRAISE *n.* 2 G. MACDONALD A side-table, heaped up with books and papers. *Harper's Magazine* That is stinted measure. I heap my cup, before emptying. b C. KINGSLEY We are received with open arms, and heaped with hospitality. 3 *Harper's Magazine* Fallen avalanches heap whitely at intervals below.

heaped *ppl a.* that has been heaped; *esp.* having its contents piled above the brim instead of being levelled: LME. **heaper** *n.* L15. **heaping** *ppl a.* (*N. Amer.*) heaped above the brim M19.

heapy /ˈhiːpi/ *a. rare.* M16. [f. HEAP *n.* + -Y^{1}.] Full or consisting of heaps.

hear /hɪə/ *v.* Pa. t. & pple **heard** /hɜːd/. [OE *hēran*, (WS) *hīeran* = OFris. *hēra, hōra*, OS *hōrian* (Du. *hooren*), OHG *hōren* (G *hören*), ON *heyra*, Goth. *hausjan*, f. Gmc.] I 1 *v.t.* Perceive with the ear (a sound etc., someone or something *do* (pass. *to do*), *doing, done*). (See also *hear say, hear tell* below.) OE. b *v.i.* Possess or exercise the faculty of perceiving sounds. OE. 2 *v.t.* & *i.* Listen (to) with attention or understanding. OE. b *v.t.* Listen to (a play, religious service, etc.) as a member of an audience or congregation. ME. c *v.t.* Listen to someone reciting (something learned by heart). Also (*arch.*) w. indirect obj. E19. 3a *v.t.* Chiefly in scriptural and liturgical use: listen to with favour; grant (a prayer). OE. b *v.i.* Foll. by *of*, (US) *to*: entertain the notion of. Usu. preceded by *will* (*would*) and neg. L16. 4 *v.t.* (orig. w. indirect obj.). Be obedient to. Long *arch.* OE. 5a *v.t.* Get to know (a fact etc.) by hearing; learn, be told. (Foll. by subord. cl., advb. obj.) OE. b *v.i.* Be told *about*; learn, get knowledge, *of.* ME. 6 *v.t.* Listen to in a court of law; consider judicially. ME. †7 *v.i.* With advs. [after Gk *eu, kakōs akouein*, L *bene, male audire*]: be spoken (favourably or unfavourably) of. L16–E18. 8 *v.i.* Receive a communication *from*; receive a warning or reprimand *from.* E17.

1 T. HARDY He heard at that moment the noise of wheels behind him. SCOTT FITZGERALD I heard the phone taken up inside. A. CHRISTIE In the stillness you could have heard a pin drop. T. FRISBY You could hear that drummer half-way down the street. A. SHAFFER The front door is heard to close. ANNE STEVENSON Listen and you can hear them bustling in my lost rooms. b B. JOWETT [He] whispered .. so that Menexenus should not hear. 2 F. MORYSON There is a Chamber [in the Vatican] .. wherein Ambassadours are heard. D. H. LAWRENCE Madame and Max heard in silence. R. MACAULAY Father Chantry-Pigg was hearing confessions. E. WAUGH They talk entirely for their own pleasure. Nothing they say is designed to be heard. B. ENGLAND I should be interested to hear your reasoning. P. O'BRIAN I hear what you say. I think that you are probably mistaken. b H. HALLAM Many persons were sent to prison for hearing Mass. G. B. SHAW He actually took me to hear his performance. c R. D. BLACKMORE Three pupils, and not a lesson have I heard them. 3a AV *Ps.* 116:1. I loue the LORD: because hee hath heard .. my supplications. b O. WILDE Constance's doctor .. won't hear of her going out tonight. E. POOLE When I tried .. to turn our talk .., at first she would not hear to it. 4 M. PRIOR The fiery Pegasus disdains To mind the Rider's Voice, or hear the Reins. 5a SCOTT FITZGERALD I've just heard the most amazing thing. E. WAUGH Nina, I hear you're engaged. J. LE CARRÉ 'Mundt .. found it quite easy.' 'So I hear'. E. WELTY So you're the young man we've heard so much about. b M. SINCLAIR Roucliffe was coming to dinner. Such a thing had never been heard of. L. HUGHES I heard on the radio about the Freedom Train. E. JOHNSON He was saddened to hear of the death of his old friend. 6 H. H. WILSON Three Judges were appointed to the special duty of hearing appeals from the courts below. J. LE CARRÉ We shall hear evidence as we think fit. D. M. WALKER Only very exceptionally .. can a criminal case be heard 'in camera'. 7 JOSEPH HALL Aristotle himself is wont to hear ill for his opinion of the soul's mortality. 8 *Fraser's Magazine* You shall hear from my attorney. A. BROOKNER When the telephone rang .. she had not expected to hear from anyone.

II Special uses of the imp. 9 *hear! hear!* (orig. †*hear him!* (*hear him!*)), an exclam. calling attention to a speaker's words, e.g. in the House of Commons, and now usu. expressing enthusiastic assent, occas. ironical derision. L17.

Phrases, & with advs. in specialized senses: **be unable** etc. **to hear oneself think** be unable etc. to think clearly for the noise. **do you hear?** *colloq.*: a phr. appended by way of emphasis to an impatient request, a warning, etc. **hear of it** *colloq.* be called to account over a matter. **hear out** listen to (a person, something said) to the end. †**hear rather** prefer to be called. **hear say** *arch.* be informed. **hear tell** (now *colloq.* & *dial.*) learn, be informed (*of, that*). *hear the last of*: see LAST *n.*^{5} 8. **hear things** have auditory hallucinations. **like to hear oneself speak** or **talk** be fond of talking. **you hear?** *colloq.* = *do you hear?* above.

Comb.: **hear-hear** *n.* & *v.* (*a*) *n.* a cheer expressed in the words 'hear! hear!'; (*b*) *v.i.* & *t.* utter or cheer with cries of 'hear! hear!'; †**hear-him** a cry of 'hear him!' (see sense 9 above).

hearable /ˈhɪərəb(ə)l/ *a.* LME. [f. prec. + -ABLE.] Able to be heard; audible.

heard *v.* pa. t. & pple of HEAR.

hearer /ˈhɪərə/ *n.* ME. [f. HEAR *v.* + -ER^{1}.] 1 A person etc. who hears; a listener. ME. 2 A person who receives oral instruction or attends lectures etc.; *Sc.* a member of the congregation *of* a particular minister. L17. 3 [tr. L *audiens*] *Eccl. Hist.* A person admitted to readings of the Scriptures and to instruction, but not to church worship; a catechumen or a penitent of the second order. L17.

hearing /ˈhɪərɪŋ/ *n.* ME. [f. HEAR *v.* + -ING[1].] **1** The action or faculty of perceiving sounds by the ear. ME. **b** Earshot; esp. *out of, within, hearing.* LME. **2** The action or an act of listening; an opportunity to be listened to. ME. **3** (A piece of) news, (a) report. Now *dial.* ME. **4** The action or process of listening to evidence etc. in a court of law or before an official; *spec.* a trial before a judge without a jury. L16. **5** A scolding. *Sc.* E19.

1 *Daily Telegraph* Mr Betts was left with impaired sight and hearing. **come to someone's hearing** become known to one through report. *hard of hearing*: see HARD *a.* **in one's hearing** in such a way as to be heard by one. 2 C. IVES When a new . . work is accepted as beautiful on its first hearing. R. P. GRAVES The Liberal speakers were not given a fair hearing. 3 DICKENS This is a pleasant hearing I thank Heaven for it. A. CHRISTIE Miss Marple smiled at him and said that that was a good hearing. 4 P. HOWARD In February 1897 a Select Committee of the House of Commons began its hearings.

Comb.: **hearing-aid** a small sound-amplifier worn by people who are hard of hearing.

hearken /ˈhɑːk(ə)n/ *v.* Also ***harken**. [OE *hercnian, heorcnian*: see HARK, -EN[5]. The spelling with *-ea-* is due to assoc. w. HEAR.] **1** *v.i.* Listen. Freq. foll. by *to* (OE & ME *dat.*). *arch.* & *literary.* OE. **b** Listen with compliance or sympathy *to.* ME. **c** Listen as an eavesdropper (*to*). *obs.* exc. *Sc.* LME. **2** *v.t.* Hear with attention, listen to (a person, words, etc.). Now *poet.*, *dial.*, & *Sc.* OE. †**3** *v.i.* Enquire *after*; seek news *of.* ME–M19. **4** *v.i.* Wait, lie in wait. *obs.* exc. *dial.* L16. †**5** *v.t.* Usu. foll. by *out*: search out or get to hear of by enquiry. L16–E18. **6** *v.t.* & *i.* Whisper in one's ear. *obs.* exc. *Sc.* E17.

1 SHAKES. *Ven. & Ad.* She hearkens for his hounds and for his horn. **b** A. FRASER Their determination not even to be seen to hearken to outside pleadings. 2 W. DE LA MARE Sadly that music she hearkened. 4 SHAKES. *Tam. Shr.* The youngest daughter, whom you hearken for, Her father keeps from all access of suitors.

hearkener *n.* ME.

hearsay /ˈhɪəseɪ/ *n.* LME. [Orig. in phr. *by hear say*, tr. OFr. *par oüir dire* (now *ouï-dire*), i.e. *par* by, *oüir* hear, *dire* say.] That which one hears or has heard someone say; report, rumour, common talk. Also (*arch.*), an instance of this, a piece of gossip.

J. I. M. STEWART Not many people knew of the scandal other than by hearsay.

Attrib. & comb.: In the senses 'of the nature of hearsay', 'founded on hearsay', as *hearsay account, knowledge, report*; 'speaking by hearsay', as *hearsay witness* etc. ; Special combs., as **hearsay evidence** evidence in support of an allegation based not on the witness's direct knowledge but on what he or she has heard others say.

hearse /həːs/ *n.*[1] Also (in branch I formerly, in branch II usu.) **herse**. ME. [(O)Fr. *herse* lit. 'harrow' f. med.L *erpica* f. L (*h*)*irpex* kind of harrow, f. Samnite (*h*)*irpus* wolf, w. ref. to the teeth.] **I** Applied to things associated with funerals and other religious rites. **1** A structure placed over the bier or coffin of a distinguished person while it rested in church: orig., a latticework canopy bearing many lighted tapers; later, a wooden structure resembling a pagoda decorated with banners, heraldic devices, and lighted candles, sometimes bearing complimentary verses attached by friends. *obs.* exc. *Hist.* ME. **b** A permanent framework of iron or other metal placed over a tomb to support rich coverings. M16. **c** A light wooden framework for supporting the pall over the body at funerals. M16. **2** A harrow-shaped triangular frame designed to hold candles and used in Holy Week at the Tenebrae service. Also, a triple candlestick used in the Holy Saturday rite. *obs.* exc. *Hist.* LME. †**3** A funeral pall. M16–E17. †**4** A corpse. M16–M17. **5** A bier, a coffin; vaguely, a tomb. *arch.* L16. †**6** A funeral obsequy; any solemn religious ceremony. *rare* (Spenser). Only in L16. **7** A carriage or car for conveying the coffin at a funeral. (The current use.) M17.

1 A. COWLEY Be this my latest Verse With which I now adorn his Herse. 5 LONGFELLOW Decked with flowers a simple hearse To the churchyard forth they bear.

II In other contexts. **8** A portcullis. *obs.* exc. *Hist.* LME. †**9** A harrow, used in agriculture or to perform the function of chevaux de frise. L15–M18. **10** A kind of battle formation. *obs.* exc. *Hist.* E16.

Comb.: **hearse-cloth** a black cloth used to cover a bier or coffin; a funeral pall.

†**hearse** *n.*[2] var. of HEARST.

hearse /həːs/ *v.t.* L16. [f. HEARSE *n.*[1]] **1** Place (a corpse) on a bier or in a coffin; bury with funeral rites. Now usu., convey to the grave in a hearse (HEARSE *n.*[1] 7). L16. **2** *fig.* Provide with something suggestive of a hearse. M17.

1 SHAKES. *Haml.* Tell why thy . . bones, hearsed in death, Have burst their cerements. 2 LONGFELLOW The hill-top hearsed with pines.

hearst /həːst/ *n.* Also †**hearse**. L17. [Origin unkn.] *Hunting.* A hind of the second or third year.

heart /hɑːt/ *n.* [OE *heorte* = OFris. *herte*, OS *herta* (Du. *hart*), OHG *herza* (G *Herz*), ON *hjarta*, Goth. *hairtō*, f. Gmc, f. IE base repr. also by Gk *kēr*, *kardia*, L *cor*, *cord-*.] **I** The bodily organ. **1** The hollow muscular organ which in vertebrates keeps up the circulation of the blood by rhythmic contraction and dilatation; an organ of analogous function in some invertebrates. OE. **b** A diseased condition of this organ. *colloq.* M19. **2** The heart as the centre of vital bodily functions; (the seat of) life. Long *arch.* OE. **3** The region of the heart in man; the breast, bosom, chest. ME. **4** The stomach. Orig. in *next the heart*, on an empty stomach. *obs.* exc. *dial.* ME.

1 *attrib.*: A. MUNRO The gray-faced people in his waiting room, the heart cases. **b** W. HAGGARD He's got a heart, by the way, and I'm afraid this might finish him. 2 W. RALEIGH That the king . . had granted my heart under the Great Seal. 3 H. S. CUNNINGHAM He pressed her to his heart.

II The seat of feeling and thought. **5** The mind, intellect; *esp.* (the seat of) one's inmost thoughts and secret feelings; the soul. OE. **6** (The seat of) perception, understanding, or (rarely) memory. *obs.* exc. in *by heart*, by rote, in or from memory. OE. **7** (The seat of) the emotions, esp. love, as opp. to reason. Freq. contrasted w. *head.* OE. **b** Susceptibility to emotion; feeling, sensitivity. Also, kindliness, cordiality. M17. **8** Purpose, inclination, desire. *obs.* exc. in *after one's own heart*, just such as one likes or desires. OE. **9** (The seat of) courage, spirit. OE. **b** (The source of) energy, enthusiasm, or ardour. L18. **10** Disposition, temperament, character. ME. **11** Conscience. Now only in *one's* etc. *heart smote one* etc. *arch.* ME.

5 H. CONWAY Capable of any villainy that the heart of man could devise. H. BASCOM Deep down in his heart he wants to go back. 7 A. MASON The religion of his childhood . . retains its hold on his heart. F. WARNER She had my adolescent heart, and I Had her entire devotion. **b** MRS ALEXANDER Which would have been pain and humiliation to a woman of real heart and delicacy. 9 B. STOKER I plucked up what heart I could and said that we had better hasten. W. SOYINKA He had lost heart since the failure of that nation-wide movement. **b** W. VAN T. CLARK He had no heart in his effort. 10 A. E. HOUSMAN And many the handsome of face and the handsome of heart. N. MOSLEY It's a poor heart that never rejoices.

III Substituting for the person. **12** As a term of endearment, usu. qualified with *dear, sweet*, etc.: a loved one. Cf. SWEETHEART. ME. **13** A man of courage or spirit. E16.

12 TENNYSON Dear heart, I feel with thee the drowsy spell. 13 W. COWPER History . . Tells of a few stout hearts that fought and died.

IV A central part; a vital or essential part. **14** The centre, middle, or innermost part of anything. Often passing into sense 16. ME. **b** The part of a time or season when its character is most intense; the height, depths. L16. **15** *esp.* A central part of distinct conformation or character, e.g. the white tender centre of a cabbage, lettuce, etc. LME. **b** The dense inner wood of a tree, hardened by age and lacking functioning vascular tissue. Also called *heartwood.* LME. **16** The vital, essential, or working part of something. Also, the best or most important part. Cf. sense 14 above. M16. **17** Vigour, fertility (of soil etc.). L16.

14 SHAKES. *Merch. V.* A goodly apple rotten at the heart. *Grimsby Gazette* A site for their information office in the heart of the town. **b** DISRAELI It was the heart of the London season. 15 C. CONRAN Cook the artichokes whole, to conserve the full flavour of the hearts. 16 R. HOGGART The living-room is the warm heart of the family. *fig.*: E. AMADI The heart of the dance was in the flutes and the huge bass drum. 17 W. RYE The heart of the land was so improved that Coke began to sow wheat.

V Something heart-shaped. **18** A representation of the human heart, usu. a conventional symmetrical figure with two equal curves meeting in a lower point and an upper cusp; an object of this shape. LME. **19** *Cards.* In *pl.* (occas. treated as *sing.*), one of the four suits into which a pack of playing-cards is divided, distinguished by representations of hearts in red; in *sing.*, a card of this suit. E16. **b** (*Hearts.*) A card-game of which the object is to avoid taking a trick containing a heart or any other penalty card. L19. **20** *Naut.* A kind of deadeye with only one hole, for a lanyard. M18.

Phrases: *after one's own heart*: see sense 8 above. **at heart** in one's inmost feelings or true character; inwardly, really. *bless his, her*, etc., *my, heart*: see BLESS *v.*[1] **break someone's heart** overwhelm someone with sorrow. *by heart*: see sense 6 above. **change of heart** conversion to a different frame of mind. **close one's heart (to)** keep one's feelings or thoughts secret (from); refuse to feel sympathy (for) or consider. **cross my heart (and hope to die)** I promise or guarantee. *cry from the heart*: see CRY *n.* **cry** (or other vb) **one's heart out** cry etc. violently or exhaustingly or to an extreme degree. **(dear) heart** *int.* (long *rare*) expr. surprise, dismay, etc. **do one's heart good** cheer one, make one happy. *eat one's heart (out)*: see EAT *v. enlarge the heart*: see ENLARGE *v. find (it) in one's heart*: see FIND *v.* **from (the bottom of) one's heart** with the sincerest or deepest feeling. **give one's heart (to)** fall in love (with). **go to one's** or **the heart** deeply touch or grieve one. **have a heart** *colloq.* be merciful; freq. in *imper.*: be reasonable, have some pity. **have at heart** be deeply interested in; have in mind. **have one's heart in** be deeply involved in or committed to. **have one's heart in one's boots** be afraid or dejected. **have one's heart in one's mouth** be very alarmed or apprehensive. **have one's heart in the right place** have good intentions, mean well. **have the heart** be courageous or strong enough (*to do*); (esp. w. *neg.*) be hard-hearted enough. **heart and dart** a common noctuid moth, *Agrotis exclamationis*, so called from the black markings on the forewing. **heart and soul** (with) all one's energies and affections. **heart of gold** a kind or generous nature. **heart of oak** (a person with) a strong, courageous nature. **hearts and minds** emotional and intellectual support; complete approval. **heart-to-heart** a sincere, frank, and usu. intimate conversation (freq. *attrib.*). *hole in the heart*: see HOLE *n.*[1] *hollow heart*: see HOLLOW *a.* **in (good etc.) heart** in (good etc.) spirits; (of soil etc.) in (good etc.) condition. **in (one's) heart** = *at heart* above. **lay to heart** (now *rare*) = *take to heart* below. LEARN *by heart. lift up the heart of*: see LIFT *v.* **lose heart** be discouraged. **lose one's heart (to)** = *give one's heart (to)* above. **near(est) one's** or **the heart** dear to one, affecting one most deeply. *next the heart*: see sense 4 above. **one's heart breaks** one is extremely upset. **one's heart goes out to** one feels strong attraction to or sympathy for. **one's heart of hearts** one's inmost thoughts or feelings. *one's* or *the heart bleeds*: see BLEED *v.* 1. *one's* etc. *heart smote one*: see sense 11 above. **open one's heart (to)** reveal one's feelings or thoughts (to), confide (in); feel sympathy for; consider. **out of heart** in low spirits, discouraged; (of soil etc.) in poor condition. **put one's heart into** apply oneself to with enthusiasm. *Sacred Heart*: see SACRED *a. set one's heart on*: see SET *v.*[1] **shut one's heart (to)** = *close one's heart (to)* above. **take heart** pluck up courage. **take** etc. **heart of grace** = *take heart* above. **take to heart** take seriously, be much affected or upset by. *the cockles of one's heart*: see COCKLE *n.*[2] **to one's heart's content** to the full extent of one's desires. **wear one's heart on one's sleeve** allow one's feelings to be obvious. **with (all one's, one's whole) heart** with sincerity or devotion; with great goodwill. **with half a heart** with divided enthusiasm, half-heartedly.

Comb.: **heartache** †(*a*) a form of dyspepsia, heartburn; (*b*) distress of mind, esp. from a disappointment in love; **heart attack** a sudden severe failure of the heart to function normally; **heartbeat** a beat of the heart; *transf.*, a very brief space of time; **heart-block** (a) failure of the parts of the heart to beat synchronously; **heartbreak** overwhelming sorrow or distress; **heartbreaker** a person who or thing that causes emotional turmoil or great distress; **heartbreaking** *a.* causing (overwhelming) sorrow or distress; **heartbreakingly** *adv.* in a heartbreaking manner; **heartbroken,** (*arch.*) **heart-broke** *adjs.* affected by (overwhelming) sorrow or grief; **heartbrokenly** *adv.* in a heartbroken manner; **heart-cherry** a heart-shaped cultivated sweet cherry; **heart cockle** a bivalve mollusc, *Glossus humanus*, the shell of which is heart-shaped when seen laterally; **heart-disease** (a) disease affecting the heart; **heart failure** severe derangement of the functioning of the heart, esp. as a cause of death; **heartfelt** *a.* (of emotion etc.) sincere, genuine; **heartland** the central or most important part of an area; **heart-lung** *attrib. a.* involving the heart and lungs; *heart-lung machine*: providing the means to bypass these organs in blood circulation during an operation; **heart-moth** a noctuid moth, *Dicycla oo*, with heart-shaped markings on the forewing; **heart-piercing** *a.* that pierces or is capable of piercing the heart; *fig.* that appeals sharply to the emotions; **heartquake** palpitation of the heart; *fig.* sudden and violent emotion; **heart-rending** *a.* very distressing; **heart-rendingly** *adv.* very distressingly; **heart-root** *arch.* (*a*) the bottom of the heart, the seat of deepest emotion and most genuine feelings (freq. in *pl.*); (*b*) a sweetheart; **heart rot** any disease causing decay in the heart of a tree, or of a root vegetable; **hearts-and-flowers** extreme sentimentality, cloying sweetness (freq. *attrib.*); **heart('s)-blood** blood from the heart, lifeblood; life; **heart-searching** *a.* & *n.* (*a*) *adj.* that closely examines one's own feelings; (*b*) *n.* close examination of one's own feelings; **heart-shaped** *a.* shaped like a heart (see sense 18 above); **heartsick** *a.* depressed, despondent, miserable; **heartsickness** the condition of being heartsick; **heartsome** *a.* (chiefly *Sc.*) †(*a*) courageous; (*b*) cheering, heartening; cheerful, merry; **heartsore** *n.* & *a.* (*a*) *n.* mental anguish; (*b*) *adj.* grieved; characterized by grief; **heart sounds** sounds of the working of the heart, heard in auscultation; **heart-spoon** (*obs.* exc. *dial.*) (*a*) the depression at the base of the breastbone; (*b*) the pit of the stomach, the midriff; **heart-stricken** *a.* = *heart-struck* (a) below; **heart-strings** †(*a*) the tendons or nerves formerly supposed to brace the heart; (*b*) *fig.* one's deepest emotions (often w. allusion to stringed musical instruments); **heart-struck** *a.* (*a*) affected by mental anguish; †(*b*) affecting the heart; **heartthrob** (*a*) a heartbeat; (*b*) *colloq.* an extremely attractive (male) person, esp. an actor or other celebrity; a (male) lover; **heart-urchin** a sea urchin of the order Spatangoida, with a heart-shaped body; **heart-warming** *a.* emotionally moving and encouraging; **heartwater** *Vet. Med.* a rickettsial disease of livestock, occurring esp. in southern Africa, producing an accumulation of fluid in the pericardium of the heart; **heart-whole** *a.* (*a*) (now *rare*) undismayed, unafraid; (*b*) not emotionally attached, not in love; (*c*) wholehearted, sincere, genuine; **heartwood** (*a*) see sense 15b above; (*b*) *Austral.* (the timber of) Tasmanian ironwood, *Notelaea ligustrina*; **heart-worm** (disease caused by) a parasitic nematode worm which infests the hearts of some carnivores;

heartful *n.* & *a.* (*a*) *n.* as much as a heart will hold (chiefly *fig.*); (*b*) *adj.* characterized by deep emotion or sincere affection: LME. **heartfully** *adv.* LME. **heartfulness** *n.* E17. **heartlike** *a.* resembling (that of) a heart E17. †**heartling** *n.* (*rare*, Shakes.) dear heart (only in int. *'ods heartlings*): only in L16. **heartwise** *adv.* in the shape of a heart E18.

heart /hɑːt/ *v.* [OE *hiertan*, f. prec.: superseded by HEARTEN.] **1** *v.t.* Give heart to; inspire with confidence, encourage. *obs.* exc. *poet.* OE. **2** *v.t.* Take to heart. Long *rare* or *obs.* E17. **3** *v.t.* Fill up the central space in (a piece of masonry) with rubble etc. L18. **4** *v.i.* Of cabbage, lettuce, etc.: form a heart (HEART *n.* 15) or close compact globe of leaves. M19.

heartburn /ˈhɑːtbəːn/ *n.* & *v.* ME. [f. HEART *n.* + BURN *n.*[2]] **A** *n.* †**1** Fire of passion. *rare.* Only in ME. **2** A form of dyspepsia felt as a pain in the chest, caused by acid regurgitation into the oesophagus. L16. **3** Rankling jealousy or hatred. Now *rare* or *obs.* E17. †**B** *v.t.* Make jealous or full of hatred. M16–M17.

heart-burning /ˈhɑːtbəːnɪŋ/ *n.* & *a.* LME. [f. HEART *n.* + *burning* vbl n. & pres. pple of BURN *v.*] **A** *n.* **1** Rankling jealousy or hatred; anger, bitterness; in *pl.*, feelings of this kind, grudges. LME. †**2** = HEARTBURN *n.* 2. LME–M18. **B** *adj.* That angers or consumes one; distressing. *poet.* L16.

hearted /ˈhɑːtɪd/ *a.* ME. [f. HEART *n.*, *v.*: see -ED[2], -ED[1].] **1** Having a heart, esp. one of a specified kind. ME. **2** Fixed or established in the heart. E17. **3** Heart-shaped. M19.

1 *faint-hearted, free-hearted, full-hearted, half-hearted, hard-hearted, heavy-hearted*, etc. (hence *faint-heartedly, -heartedness*, etc.)

hearten /ˈhɑːt(ə)n/ *v.* E16. [f. HEART *v.* + -EN[5]: superseding HEART *v.*] **1** *v.t.* Give heart to; inspire with confidence, encourage; rouse to energy or enthusiasm; animate, cheer. (Foll. by *to* + inf., *on*, *up*.) E16. †**2** *v.t.* Give physical strength or stimulus to. L16–L18. **3** *v.refl.* & *i.* Cheer (oneself) *up*. E18.

1 M. STOTT We..feel heartened and even exhilarated by their enthusiasm. *refl.*: G. STANHOPE Let us hearten our selves with their Assistance against Temptations.

hearth /hɑːθ/ *n.* [OE *heorþ* = OFris. *herth, herd*, OS *herþ* (Du. *haard*), OHG *hert* (G *Herd*), f. WGmc.] **1** The floor of a fireplace; the area in front of a fireplace. OE. **2** *transf.* The home or household. Freq. in alliterative phr. *hearth and home*, home and its comforts. OE. **3** The floor or bottom of a furnace; the fireplace of a forge. ME.

3 open-hearth process: for making steel in a shallow reverberatory furnace; hence *open-hearth furnace*.

Comb.: **hearth-money** *Hist.* a tax on hearths, esp. a 17th-cent. tax of two shillings per year on every hearth in England and Wales; **hearth-penny** *Hist.* = *Peter's pence* s.v. PETER *n.*[1]; **hearthrug** a rug laid in front of a fireplace (to protect the carpet or floor); **hearthstead** a fireplace, hearth; hence, a home, a homestead; **hearthstone** *n.* & *v.* (*a*) *n.* a flat stone forming a hearth; a material used to whiten hearths, doorsteps, etc.; (*b*) *v.t.* whiten (a hearth etc.) with hearthstone; **hearth-tax** = *hearth-money* above.

heartless /ˈhɑːtlɪs/ *a.* ME. [f. HEART *n.* + -LESS.] **1** Lacking courage or spirit; disheartened. ME. **b** Without warmth or zeal; not heartfelt. M17. †**2** Stupid, foolish. LME–E17. **3** *lit.* Having no heart; (of a tree) lacking heartwood; (of a vegetable) not forming a heart. L16. **4** Unfeeling, pitiless; callous, unkind. (Now the usual sense.) L16. **5** Of land: unfertile. L16. **6** Of food etc.: lacking sustaining or stimulating power. M17.

heartlessly *adv.* E17. **heartlessness** *n.* L16.

heartsease /ˈhɑːtsiːz/ *n.* Also **heart's-ease**. LME. [f. HEART *n.* + -'S[1] + EASE *n.*] **1** Peace of mind, content, freedom from cares or trouble. LME. **2** A pansy; *esp.* the wild pansy, *Viola tricolor*. M16.

hearty /ˈhɑːti/ *a.*, *adv.*, & *n.* LME. [f. HEART *n.* + -Y[1].] **A** *adj.* **1** Orig., courageous, bold. Now, zealous in support of a person, cause, etc.; energetic, enthusiastic. Also, of the nature of a hearty (sense C.2 below). LME. **b** Giving unrestrained expression to the feelings; vehement, vigorous. M17. **2** Heartfelt, genuine, sincere. Also, kindly, affectionate; genial. LME. **b** Of or pertaining to the inner feelings. *rare.* M16. **3** In good health; robust, hale. M16. **b** Of soil: fertile. L16. **c** Of timber: strong, durable; consisting of heartwood. E17. **4** Of food: nourishing, invigorating. Of a meal: satisfying to the appetite, ample. L16.

1 LD MACAULAY Two of the allied powers..were hearty in the common cause. P. ROTH I knew about Palestine and the hearty Jewish teenagers there reclaiming the desert. **b** K. AMIS Rarely in the past could the theatre have rung with so much happy, hearty laughter. **2** LYTTON No hearty welcoming smile on his face. B. T. WASHINGTON I received very hearty congratulations. **3** R. C. SHERRIFF He is a big hearty man; ..full of vigour. **4** SPENSER Ech drunk an harty draught. G. VIDAL It is Rusty's favourite restaurant for the food is profoundly hearty.

B *adv.* Heartily. *non-standard.* M18.

C *n.* **1** A hearty or vigorous person. M19. **2** *spec.* An extrovert, outgoing person involved in sport and social activities; an athlete as opp. to an aesthete. Orig. *Univ. slang.* E20.

2 A. POWELL Militarily moustached, bluff in demeanour, apparently a hearty of hearties.

heartily *adv.* ME. **heartiness** *n.* M16.

heat /hiːt/ *n.* [OE *hǣtu* = OFris. *hēte*, MDu. *hēte*, OHG *heizi*, f. WGmc, f. base of HOT *a.*: also OE *hǣte*.] **I** In literal use. **1** The quality which is felt as the opposite of cold and is expressed by temperature; the quality of being hot; *esp.* a perceptible degree of this quality, (high) temperature, warmth. OE. **b** More fully *vital* etc. *heat*. The normal high temperature of a living warm-blooded animal. ME. **2a** Hot weather or condition of the atmosphere; a hot spell. OE. **b** A hot environment. *arch.* LME. **3** (An instance of) abnormally high body temperature; the hot or burning sensation which this gives rise to. Freq., high temperature caused by sickness or fever. OE. **b** An eruption of the skin, accompanied by a hot sensation. OE. **4a** An exposure to warmth or heat. Now only *Sc.*, esp. in *give oneself* or *get a heat*, warm oneself. ME. **b** A single operation of heating, as of metal in a furnace; the amount of metal etc. heated in one operation. L16. †**5** In medieval physiology: heat as one of the four fundamental qualities of 'elements', bodily humours, etc.: see HOT *a.* 2. Cf. COLD *a.*, DRY *a.*, MOIST *a.* ME–E17. **6** *Physics.* Heat regarded as a form of energy arising from the random motion of molecules and capable of transmission by conduction, convection, or radiation: formerly held to be an elastic material fluid (*caloric*). Also, the amount of energy in this form required to bring about a process or involved in a process. E17.

1 A. REID Liquors..evaporated by a gentle heat. B. MALAMUD He was being boiled alive in the smothering heat of the small..cell. W. WHARTON The fire starts burning but it's not giving off enough heat. **2a** A. P. STANLEY The chief resorts of the Bedouin tribes during the summer heats. E. LANGLEY An hour when ..the clay of the roads is burning and sickly with the heat. **3** M. DRAYTON Her heat to cool, She bathes her in the pleasant Pool. J. CONRAD The essence of her tremors, her flushes of heat, and her shudders of cold. **4b** J. MOXON If it be not..thoroughly welded at the first Heat, you must reiterate your Heats.

II *transf.* & *fig.* **7** Vehemence of feeling, passion; an instance of this. Formerly, an angry dispute. OE. †**b** Passionateness of temperament, excitability. L17–E18. **8** Sexual excitement or desire. Now only, (the period of) a female animal's readiness for mating; esp. *on* or (chiefly *US*) *in heat*. ME. **9** Hotness or pungency of flavour. LME. **10** *The* (most) intense or violent stage of an activity. Also, *the* excitement or pressure generated by an activity or event. L16. **11** A single course or round in a race or other contest. Also (more fully *trial heat*), one of a series of preliminary contests in which inferior competitors are successively eliminated before the final contest. M17. †**12** A run given to a racehorse as exercise before a race. L17–E18. **13** A state of intoxication induced by drink or drugs; esp. *have a heat on*. *US slang.* E20. **14** A pistol. *slang* (orig. *US*). E20. **15** (Pursuit or intense activity by) the police; *gen.* pressure, harassment. Chiefly in *the heat is on* (or *off*), *turn on the heat*, and similar phrs. *slang* (orig. *US*). M20.

7 WELLINGTON To keep alive heats and animosities: L. RITCHIE A lady, who spoke with some heat, and great volubility. G. A. BIRMINGHAM A mere heresy can be settled without heat or unpleasantness by a few scholars sitting round a table. **9** M. JAFFREY If you want the flavour of chillies without their heat. **10** W. H. PRESCOTT In the very heat of the war against the insurgent Catalans. *Practical Gardening* In the heat of the programme-making, he left it in the boot of his car. **15** *Toronto Life* The heat is on to..reinvent the family.

Phrases: **at a (single) heat** in a single operation, at a go. ATOMIC *heat*. *black heat*: see BLACK *a*. *dead heat*: see DEAD *a*. etc. *get, give oneself, a heat*: see sense 4a above. *have a heat on*: see sense 13 above. **in heat** in a hotbed; see also sense 8 above. **in the heat of the moment** without pause for thought, as a result of the vigorous action etc. then in progress. LATENT *heat*. *mechanical equivalent of heat*: see EQUIVALENT *a*. MOLECULAR *heat*. *on heat*: see sense 8 above. PRICKLY *heat*. RADIANT *heat*. *red heat*: see RED *a*. *specific heat*: see SPECIFIC *a*. **take (the) heat** *N. Amer. slang* be at the receiving end of people's resentment, get the blame. *the heat is on, turn on the heat*: see sense 15 above. *trial heat*: see sense 11 above. *vital heat*: see sense 1b above. *waste heat*: see WASTE *n*. *white heat*: see WHITE *a*.

Comb.: **heat barrier** the limitation of the speed of an aircraft etc. by heat resulting from friction with the air; **heat capacity** thermal capacity; **heat death** *Physics* a state of uniform distribution of energy to which the universe is thought to be tending as a corollary of the second law of thermodynamics (that entropy must always increase); **heat-drop** (*a*) a drop of rain ushering in a hot day; (*b*) a drop of sweat; **heat engine** any device for producing motive power from heat; **heat-exchanger** a device for the transfer of heat from one medium to another; **heat exhaustion** fatigue and collapse resulting from prolonged exposure to excessive or unaccustomed heat; **heatproof** *a*. & *v*. (*a*) *adj*. able to resist great heat; (*b*) *v.t.* make heatproof; **heat pump** a device in which mechanical energy is used to force the transfer of heat from a colder area to a hotter area, as in a refrigerator; **heat rash** = *prickly heat* s.v. PRICKLY; **heat-resistant** *a*. = *heatproof* adj. above; **heat-seeker** (a missile incorporating) a heat-seeking device; **heat-seeking** *a*. (of a missile etc.) that detects and homes on infrared radiation emitted by a target; **heat shield** a device for protection from excessive heat, esp. to protect a spacecraft during re-entry to the earth's atmosphere; **heat sink** a device or substance for absorbing excessive or unwanted heat; **heatstroke** a condition marked by fever and often by unconsciousness, due to the failure of the body's temperature-regulating mechanism in circumstances of excessive exposure to heat; **heat treatment** (*a*) the use of heat to modify the properties of a material, esp. in metallurgy; (*b*) the therapeutic use of heat in various forms; **heat wave** a prolonged period of hot weather.

heat /hiːt/ *v*. Pa. t. & pple **heated**, †**heat**; pa. pple also (now *dial*.) **het** /hɛt/. See also HET. [OE *hǣtan* = (M)Du. *hēten*, OHG *heizzen*, *heizen* (G *heizen*), ON *heita*, f. Gmc, f. base repr. also by HOT *a*.] **I** *v.t.* **1** Expose to heat; make hot or warm. Freq. foll. by *up*. OE. **b** Cause to feel hot or warm. LME. **2** *fig*. Inflame with passion; excite. ME.

1 B. PYM I'll just go and heat up the soup. E. FEINSTEIN Their flat was heated by a small, sooty stove. **b** W. WARBURTON Men heated with wine. **2** LD MACAULAY Officers who heated each other into fury by talking against the Dutch.

II *v.i.* **3** Rise in temperature; become hotter or warmer. (Foll. by *up*.) OE. **b** Have or get a sensation of heat, grow hot. ME. **4** *fig*. Become excited or impassioned. Of a condition (usu. foll. by *up*): intensify. OE.

3 S. PURCHAS They set a kettle of water over the fire to heat. **4** J. BARNES He seemed to calm down as quickly as he had heated up. *Newsweek* Now competition is heating up.

heated *ppl a*. (*a*) that has been made or become hot (*heated term* (*US*), the hot season of the year); (*b*) fevered, inflamed; impassioned, animated, angry: L16. **heatedly** *adv*. in an impassioned or angry manner M19.

heater /ˈhiːtə/ *n*. L15. [f. HEAT *v*. + -ER[1].] **1** A person or thing which heats. L15. **2** *spec*. Any of various devices for imparting heat; *esp*. (*a*) a piece of iron made hot and placed in the cavity of a flat-iron; (*b*) a stove, hot-air blower, or other gas or electric device for warming the air in a room, car, etc.; (*c*) = IMMERSION *heater*; (*d*) *Electronics* a conductor used for indirect heating of the cathode of a thermionic valve. M17. **3** A firearm. *N. Amer. slang*. E20.

Comb.: **heater-shaped** *a*. (of a medieval shield) having the shape of a flat-iron heater, i.e. triangular with curved sides.

heath /hiːθ/ *n*. [OE *hǣþ*, corresp. to OS *hēþa*, MLG, MDu. *hēde*, MHG *heide* (Du. *heide*, *hei*, G *Heide*), ON *heiðr*, Goth. *haiþi*, f. Gmc.] **1** (An area of) open uncultivated ground, esp. on acid sandy or peaty soil and covered by heather or related plants (see sense 2 below). OE. **2** Any of various dwarf shrubs of the family Ericaceae characteristic of heathland or moor; esp. *Erica cinerea* (more fully *fine-leaved heath*) and *E. tetralix* (more fully *cross-leaved heath*), common in dry and in boggy heath respectively. Also (now chiefly *dial*.), heather, *Calluna vulgaris*. OE. **b** In biblical lang., in renderings of *Jer*. 17:6, 48:6: a desert plant of uncertain identity, perh. a tamarisk, or savin, *Juniperus sabina*. M16. **c** With specifying wd. Any of various plants resembling ericas and freq. growing in the same habitat. E17. **d** *Austral*. More fully *Australian heath*, *Tasmanian heath*. Any of various heathlike plants of the genus *Epacris* (family Epacridaceae). L19. **3** Either of two satyrid butterflies of the genus *Coenonympha*: *C. pamphilus* (the small heath), of rough grassland, and *C. tullia* (the large heath), of moors and bogs. E19.

1 A. YOUNG An uninteresting flat, with many heaths of ling. **native heath** native country or territory.

Comb.: **heath-bell** (the blossom of) any of several plants with bell-shaped flowers growing in heath; *esp*. harebell, *Campanula rotundifolia*; **heath-berry** any of several berry-bearing shrubs growing in heath; *esp*. bilberry or crowberry; **heath-bird** = *heath-fowl* below; **heath-cock** the male black grouse; **heath-cropper** a sheep or pony that grazes on open pasture or down; a person who inhabits a heath; **heath-fowl** *arch*. the black grouse, *Tetrao tetrix*; **heath-grass** a low-growing grass of acid soils, *Danthonia decumbens*; **heath-hen** the female black grouse; *N. Amer*. a variety of prairie chicken, now extinct; **heathland** heathy country; **heath-poult** the female or young of the black grouse; **heath speedwell** a creeping lilac-flowered speedwell, *Veronica officinalis*, of heaths and turfy pastures in Eurasia; **heath-thrush** the ring ouzel, *Turdus torquatus*.

heathlike *a*. resembling (that of) heath or a heath M19

heathen /ˈhiːð(ə)n/ *a*. & *n*. [OE *hǣþen* = OFris. *hēthin*, OS *hēþin* (Du. *heiden*), OHG *heidan* (G *heide*), ON *heiðinn*, in Goth. repr. by *haiþnō* Gentile woman: gen. regarded as a specific Christian use (perh. as a loose rendering of L *paganus*, and orig. in Gothic) of a Gmc adj. meaning 'inhabiting open country, savage', repr. by the ethnic and pers. names Gk *Khaideinoi* a people of W. Scandinavia (Ptolemy), OE *Hǣþnum* (dat.), ON *Heinir* (f. *Heiðnir*), OHG *theidanrīh*, f. Gmc base of HEATH *n*.: see -EN[4]. Cf. PAGAN.] **A** *adj*. **1** Of an individual or people: holding religious beliefs of a sort that are considered unenlightened, now esp. ones of a primitive or polytheistic nature; *spec*. not of the Christian, Jewish, or Muslim faiths. *derog*. OE. **2** Of a thing: belonging to heathen people or races or their beliefs and customs. OE. **3** *transf*. Resembling heathen people in their (supposed) beliefs, behaviour, etc.; unenlightened, barbarous. M19.

1 T. MO Bring spoons, you heathen devil. **2** J. A. MICHENER The villagers were convinced that it honored a heathen goddess. **3** R. W. EMERSON A country of extremes—dukes and chartists, Bishops of Durham and naked heathen colliers.

B *n*. **1** A heathen person: see sense A.1 above. *derog*. OE. **b** *collect*. (usu. preceded by def. article). Heathens as a group. In biblical language: those who do not worship Israel's God, idolaters. OE. **2** *transf*. An unenlightened, barbarous, or uncivilized person. E19.

1 SWIFT I was sorry to find more mercy in an heathen than in a brother Christian. **b** AV *Ps*. 33:10 The Lord bringeth the counsell of the heathen to nought. E. O'NEILL Like a missionary converting the heathen. **2** DICKENS My ideas of civility were formed among Heathens.

heathendom *n*. (*a*) heathenism; (*b*) heathen people or countries collectively: OE. **heathenism** *n*. heathen or (*transf*.) unenlightened beliefs or practices E17. **heathenize** *v.t.* & *i*. make or become heathen(ish) L17. **heathenly** *adv*. in the manner of the heathen LME. **heathenry** *n*. = HEATHENDOM L16.

heathenesse /hiːðəˈnɛs/ *n*. *arch*. [OE *hǣþennes*, *-nys*, f. HEATHEN + -NESS: because one of the two *n*'s was often omitted, sometimes interpreted as formed with -ESS[2].] = HEATHENDOM.

heathenish /ˈhiːð(ə)nɪʃ/ *a*. [OE *hǣþenisć*, OHG *heidanisc*, ON *heiðneskr*. In mod. use prob. a new formation f. HEATHEN *a*. & *n*. + -ISH[1].] **1** = HEATHEN *a*. 2. Now *rare*. OE. †**2** = HEATHEN *a*. 1. M16–E18. **3** Unworthy of a Christian, barbarous, uncivilized; *colloq*. objectionable, beastly. L16.

3 R. KIPLING The Gunner maps up a heathenish large detail for some hanky-panky in the magazines.

heathenishly *adv*. M16. **heathenishness** *n*. L16.

heather /ˈhɛðə/ *n*. [OE *hadre*, (*h*)*eddre* (in place-names), of unkn. origin: assim. to HEATH.] A dwarf shrub of the heath family, *Calluna vulgaris*, with terminal spikes of small purple flowers, freq. dominant over large areas of heathland and moor; ling. Also, any of several related or similar plants.

bell-heather: see BELL *n*.[1] **take to the heather** *Sc. Hist*. become an outlaw.

Comb.: **heather-bell** (the bell-shaped flower of) either of the heaths, *Erica tetralix* and *E. cinerea*; **heather-bleat**(**er** [perh. orig. alt. of OE *hæfer-blǣte* lit. 'goat-bleater'] *Sc*. & *north*. the snipe; **heather honey** a much-prized honey from the nectar of heather; **heather mixture** (a suit or garment made from) a fabric of interwoven varicoloured fibres suggestive of heather on a moor.

¶Orig. a Sc. and Border counties word, corresp. to *ling* of Yorkshire etc. and the southern & midland dial. *heath*; it is now the most general name for *Calluna vulgaris*.

heathered *a*. covered with heather M19.

heathery /ˈhɛð(ə)ri/ *a*. L15. [f. prec. + -Y[1].] Covered with or composed of heather.

Heath Robinson /hiːθ ˈrɒbɪns(ə)n/ *a*. & (*rare*) *n*. E20. [W. *Heath Robinson* (1872–1944), Brit. humorous artist, whose illustrations often depicted such contraptions.] (A contraption) having absurdly elaborate and ingenious machinery for performing some simple function. Cf. RUBE GOLDBERG.

Also **Heath-Robinsonish** *a*. M20.

heathy /ˈhiːθi/ *a*. LME. [f. HEATH *n*. + -Y[1].] Covered with heath; of the nature of heath.

heating /ˈhiːtɪŋ/ *n*. LME. [f. HEAT *v*. + -ING[1].] The action of HEAT *v*.; equipment for heating a building, room, etc.

CENTRAL *heating*.

Comb.: **heating engineer** a person who installs and maintains (central) heating systems.

heaume /həʊm/ *n*. *obs*. exc. *Hist*. L16. [Fr. f. OFr. *helme*: see HELM *n*.[1]] A massive helmet reaching to the shoulders, worn in the 12th and 13th cents.

heave /hiːv/ *n*. L16. [f. the vb.] **1** An act of heaving; an effort made to lift or move something; a swelling; a rhythmical rising that alternates with sinking; an utterance of a sigh with a deep breath or effort; a retch. L16. **2** In *pl*. A disease of horses characterized by laborious breathing. Cf. HOOVE, HOVEN *a*. & *n*. L18. **3** A horizontal displacement of a mineral vein or rock stratum. E19.

1 B. CABLE And with . . a heave flung the officer out over the front parapet. *New Yorker* The doctors who had watched the mysterious disease . . had felt a heave of fear. **heave of the sea** the force exerted by the swell of the sea on a ship's course.

heave /hiːv/ *v*. Pa. t. **heaved** /hiːvd/, (esp. *Naut*.) **hove** /həʊv/. Pa. pple **heaved**, (esp. *Naut*.) **hove, hoven** /ˈhəʊv(ə)n/. [OE *hebban* = OFris. *heva*, OS *hebbian* (Du. *heffen*), OHG *heffen* (G *heben*), ON *hefja*, Goth. *hafjan*, f. Gmc wd rel. to L *capere* take.] **I** *v.t.* **1** Lift or raise up. Now only (exc. *arch*. & *dial*.), lift, raise, or move with effort or force. Freq. foll. by *up*, *down*, etc. OE. **b** *Naut*. Haul up, raise, pull, cause (a ship) to move in a specified direction, by means of a rope; weigh (anchor); pull on (a rope). E17. **2** *fig*. Raise, lift. Formerly also, exalt, lift up, elevate, in dignity, station, etc. OE. †**3** *spec*. (Of a sponsor at baptism) lift (a child) from the font; *fig*. stand sponsor to; baptize, christen. ME–L16. **4**†**a** Lift and take away, carry off; remove; *Criminals' slang* rob. ME–L17. **b** Throw, fling, hurl (esp. something heavy requiring effort). Now only *Naut*. & *colloq*. L16. **c** Of a mineral vein or rock stratum: move away or displace (an intersecting vein or stratum). E18. **5a** Cause to swell or rise; *spec*. cause bloat in (livestock). Now *dial*. LME. **b** Cause to rise repeatedly. E17. **6** Utter (a sigh, groan, etc.) with effort or with a deep breath which causes the chest to rise; draw (a breath) with effort. L15.

1 POPE Her trembling hand she heaves To rend her hair. S. MIDDLETON The congregation heaved itself to its feet. E. CRISPIN Fen went and heaved the motorcycle in to the side of the lane. P. FITZGERALD Heaving up the two volumes of the *Shorter Oxford Dictionary*. **b**

Lifeboat Martin first thought he might be able to heave the lifeboat in closer. 2 MILTON For the prevention of growing schisme the Bishop was heav'd above the Presbyter. W. IRVING The resolution . . heaved a load from off my heart. 4b C. KINGSLEY Tom was . . hiding behind a wall, to heave half a brick at his horse's legs. 5b SIR W. SCOTT The death-pangs of long-cherished hope . . Convulsive heaved its chequered shroud. 6 P. DE VRIES I heaved a long, defeated sigh, blowing out my cheeks. J. HARVEY He only sat . . heaving long shuddering breaths.

II *v.i.* 7 Make an effort to lift or move something; push or pull with force. Formerly also, foll. by *at*: aim at, *fig.* strive after. ME. b *Naut.* Pull or haul *at* (a rope); move a ship, (of a ship) move, in a specified direction by such means. E17. 8 Rise, rear up or *up*. Now *rare* exc. as below. ME. 9 Rise up above the general surface, expand; (now *dial.*) swell up. E17. 10 Rise in alternation with sinking, as waves, or the chest in deep breathing. E17. b Pant; gasp *for* breath. L17. 11 Make an effort to vomit, retch, gag. E17.

7 L. DEIGHTON He heaved desperately on the stick with one hand. J. UPDIKE They heaved at the snow in their driveways. b *transf.*: S. BECKETT Nothing will induce her to throw herself down till he actually heaves into view. 8 E. K. KANE This ice seems to heave up slowly against the sky. 9 *Daily Telegraph* So violently did the soil heave when frozen after it was so damp. 10 D. H. LAWRENCE The sea heaved with a sucking noise inside the dock. R. P. JHABVALA Her chest . . was heaving . . with heavy sobs. M. PIERCY The ceiling above them heaved like a bullfrog's throat. 11 M. SCAMMELL A meatless, saltless, fatless, evil-smelling nettle soup that made his stomach heave.

Phrases, & with advs. in specialized senses: **heave down** turn (a ship) over on one side for cleaning, repairing, etc. **heave in sight** (*Naut.* & *colloq.*) become visible. **heave the gorge** retch, gag. *heave the log*: see LOG *n.*[1] **heave to** *v.phr.t.* & *i.* (*a*) *v.phr.t.* bring (a vessel) to a standstill without anchoring; (*b*) *v.phr.i.* (of a vessel) be brought to a standstill in this way. **heaving line** *Naut.* a line, usu. five to ten fathoms long and weighted at one end, used to cast a heavier line to another vessel or to the shore when coming alongside.

heave-ho /hiːvˈhəʊ/ *int.*, *n.*, & *v.* LME. [App. f. HEAVE *v.* (imper.) + HO *int.*[1]] A *int.* Expr. effort in heaving on a rope etc. Formerly used esp. by sailors. LME. B *n.* 1 A cry of 'heave-ho!' LME. 2 A dismissal or rejection. Chiefly in *give* (a person, thing) *the* (*old*) *heave-ho. slang* (orig. *US*). M20. C *v.* 1 *v.i.* Cry 'heave-ho!' M19. 2 *v.t.* Move or lift with effort. *colloq.* M20.

heaven /ˈhɛv(ə)n/ *n.* [OE *heofon*, earlier *hefen*, *heben*, corresp. to OS *heban*, ON *himinn* (inflected stem *hifn-*), Goth. *himins*; parallel formations with *l-* suff. are OFris. *himul*, OS, OHG *himil* (Du. *hemel*, G *Himmel*); ult. origin unkn.] 1 The expanse in which the sun, moon, and stars are seen, having the appearance of a vast vault arched over the earth (now usu. in *pl.* exc. *poet.*); *fig.* an immense height, distance, extent, etc. OE. b *transf.* & *fig.* A canopy; the covering over a stage. L15. 2 The part of the atmosphere in which the clouds float, the winds blow, and the birds fly. Chiefly *poet.* OE. b The condition of this; the climate. Chiefly *poet.* L16. 3 The region of space beyond the clouds or the visible sky. Chiefly in *heaven and earth* the universe. OE. b *Hist.* Each of the celestial spheres into which the regions of space were divided by medieval astronomers and cosmographers, the number varying from seven to eleven. ME. 4 *sing.* & (now *rare*) *pl. Chr. Theol.* The abode of God, the angels, and the beatified spirits, usu. regarded as beyond the sky; a state or condition of being or living with God after death; everlasting life. OE. b In Islamic theology, each of seven stages of blessed life after death. In Jewish religious thought, each of seven celestial regions. OE. c The abode of any of various non-Christian gods. LME. 5 (Usu. **H-**.) *sing.* & in *pl.* God, Providence; the gods. Freq. in exclamatory phrs. (see below). OE. 6 A place or state of supreme bliss. ME.

1 R. L. STEVENSON After the sun is down . . , the heavens begin to fill with shining stars. W. WHARTON Trucks . . go . . up the hills, are diesel and stink to heaven. b SHELLEY Under a heaven of cedar boughs. 2 H. BELLOC Clouds of a . . hurrying sort ran across the gentle blue of that heaven. DAY LEWIS I can still see the bubbles I blew . . towards the blue heaven. b DRYDEN Not tho' beneath the Thracian Clime we freeze; Or Italy's indulgent Heav'n forego. 3 TENNYSON All heaven bursts her starry floors. 4 AV *Luke* 11:2 Our Father which art in heaven, Halowed be thy Name. W. C. WILLIAMS Is it any better in Heaven, my friend Ford, Than you found it in Provence? 5 P. S. BUCK Each farmer felt that for once heaven was doing the work in the fields. 6 D. HEWETT It was heaven to get the weight off her legs. E. O'NEILL He'll go back to the Broadway he thinks is heaven.

Phrases & comb.: **by heaven** introducing a solemn or avowed declaration. *crystalline heaven*: see CRYSTALLINE *a.* 1. *for heaven's sake*: see SAKE *n.*[1] *good heavens*: see GOOD *a.* **heaven-born** *a.* of divine origin or design. *Heaven defend*: see DEFEND *v. Heaven forbid*: see FORBID *v. Heaven forfend*: see FORFEND *v. Heaven help you, me*, etc.: see HELP *v. Heaven knows*: see KNOW *v.* **heaven of heavens** = *seventh heaven* below. **Heavens above** or **alive!** expr. surprise, astonishment, exasperation, etc. **heaven-sent** *a.* providential. **heavens hard** etc. (*colloq.*) extremely hard etc. **heavens to Betsy!** *N. Amer.* expr. astonishment, dismay, exasperation, etc. *host(s) of heaven*: see HOST *n.*[1] *in Heaven's name*: see NAME *n.* **move heaven and earth** make every possible effort (*to do*). **seventh heaven** the highest of the seven Islamic heavens; *in the seventh heaven* in a state of extreme delight or exaltation. *thank heaven(s)*: see THANK *v. tree of heaven*: see TREE *n.*

heavenless *a.* (*rare*) having (no part of or place in) heaven M17. **heavenlike** *a.* divine M16.

heaven /ˈhɛv(ə)n/ *v.t.* E17. [f. the n.] Transport into heaven; make supremely happy; beatify.

heavenly /ˈhɛv(ə)nli/ *a.* & *n.* [OE *heofonlić*, f. as prec. + -LY[1].] A *adj.* 1 Of, in, or belonging to heaven, the abode of God; of or from God; divine, sacred, holy. OE. b Of, in, or belonging to heaven, the abode of non-Christian gods. LME. 2 Of or belonging to the sky. Now chiefly in *heavenly body* below. ME. 3 Of more than earthly or human beauty or excellence; *colloq.* wonderful, delightful. LME.

1 J. CONRAD As though I had got a heavenly mission to civilize you. C. CAUDWELL This Kingdom of Heaven was to be achieved by non-resistance, by heavenly forces and a general change of heart. b SHAKES. *Merch. V.* If two gods should play some heavenly match, And on the wager lay two earthly women. 2 L. BINYON The stars . . Moving in marches upon the heavenly plain. 3 I. MURDOCH After the first few heavenly puffs the cigarette began to lose its charm. J. KRANTZ The sound of her heavenly chortling mingled with Billy's half-repressed yelps.

Special collocations: *heavenly body*: see BODY *n. the Heavenly City*: see CITY 2. *heavenly host*: see HOST *n.*[1]

Comb.: **heavenly-minded(ness)** devout(ness)

B *n.* In *pl.* [tr. Gk *tois epouraniois* (Eph. 1:3, 3:10)] Heavenly places or things. M19.

heavenliness *n.* M16.

heavenly /ˈhɛv(ə)nli/ *adv.* OE. [f. as prec. + -LY[2].] 1 From or by heaven; divinely (usu. modifying an adj.). OE. †2 To the extent of heaven. Only in *heavenly wide.* L16–L17.

heavenward /ˈhɛv(ə)nwəd/ *adv.* & *a.* ME. [f. HEAVEN *n.* + -WARD.] A *adv.* Towards heaven. ME. B *adj.* Moving or directed towards heaven. L18.

Also **heavenwards** *adv.* M17.

heaver /ˈhiːvə/ *n.* L16. [f. HEAVE *v.* + -ER[1].] A person who or thing which heaves something; *spec.* (*a*) a labourer who lands goods at a dockyard; (*b*) a lever; a wooden bar for twisting or tightening a rope or strap on board ship.

heavily /ˈhɛvɪli/ *adv.* OE. [f. HEAVY *a.* + -LY[2].] 1 With heavy or laborious movement; without animation. OE. 2 Forcibly, violently; strongly; severely; to a heavy degree. OE. b To a large amount; extensively. E19. 3 With sorrow, grief, or displeasure. *arch.* OE. 4 (As) with weight; massively, thickly, ponderously; oppressively. ME.

1 P. ROTH He came heavily to his feet; slowly and heavily, like an elephant. A. BROOKNER She breathed heavily, her hand once more to her chest. 2 A. TREW Rain was falling more heavily now and the sky had darkened. W. WHARTON She's conscious but still heavily sedated. *New Statesman* They are . . all heavily into courgettes. P. ROTH Where the woman's English is heavily accented, Sisovsky's is only mildly flawed. b D. H. LAWRENCE He drank heavily now and again. G. GREENE They were noisy and heavily made-up and rather unconvincing. Z. MEDVEDEV Stalin had decided . . to invest heavily in Soviet science. J. VIORST I have drawn heavily on my own personal experiences. 3 CLARENDON Berkley . . took this refusal very heavily. R. LEHMANN 'Darling, you must do as you like,' he said heavily. 4 M. BARING A young woman dressed in black and heavily veiled. J. B. PRIESTLEY It bumped heavily against something. G. GREENE Time for a few days was hanging . . heavily on my hands. A. J. P. TAYLOR At six foot tall and heavily built, he was by no means beautiful. *bear heavily*: see BEAR *v.*[1]

heaviness /ˈhɛvɪnɪs/ *n.* [OE *hefignes*, f. as prec.: see -NESS.] 1 Weight; weightiness; oppressiveness. OE. 2 Oppressed condition of the body or mind; torpor, drowsiness; absence of animation. OE. 3 Dejectedness. Formerly also, sadness; anger, displeasure. ME. 4 Severity; force of impact. ME.

1 V. S. NAIPAUL Brenda's heaviness, in hips and thighs, had . . suggested someone spoilt. 2 A. BROOKNER At this the heaviness lifted from his face. 3 P. S. BUCK He thought of her with sadness that was not sorrow but only heaviness of memory.

Heaviside layer /ˈhɛvɪsʌɪd ˌleɪə/ *n. phr.* E20. [Oliver *Heaviside* (1850–1925), Eng. physicist.] = *E-layer* s.v. E, E II.

¶Also called KENNELLY LAYER, *Kennelly-Heaviside layer.*

heavisome /ˈhɛvɪs(ə)m/ *a. obs.* exc. *dial.* LME. [f. next + -SOME[1].] Doleful; dull, gloomy.

heavy /ˈhɛvi/ *a.* & *n.* [OE *hefiġ* = OS *hebig* (Du. *hevig*), OHG *hebīg*, ON *hǫfugr*, *hǫfigr*, f. Gmc (repr. by OE *hefe* weight), f. base of HEAVE *v.*] A *adj.* I Physically weighty. 1 Of great weight. OE. b Weighty because of the quantity present; abundant; in large quantity or amount. LME. c That does what is specified to excess. E19. 2 Of great relative density; dense. OE. b Of bread, pastry, etc.: not properly risen; dense, compact. E19. 3 Weighed down; laden *with*. Formerly foll. by *in*. ME. b At an advanced stage of pregnancy; heavily pregnant. LME. 4 (Of a class of goods, breed of animal, etc.) of more than a defined or usual weight; concerned with the manufacture, transport, etc., of these; (of ordnance) of the larger kind. E17. b Of an army division etc.: carrying heavy arms or equipment. M19.

1 DAY LEWIS There was a fire lit in my bedroom and a too heavy eiderdown. D. BAGLEY Mrs. Warmington collapsed on top of her, a warm, dead weight, flaccid and heavy. R. MACDONALD The heavy brown grocery bag was beginning to slip out of her arms. b G. GREENE The evidence was heavy against the teacher. B. W. ALDISS Saturday morning traffic into town was heavy. *Music Week* Hello Again has been picking up heavy Radio Two airplay. c M. PUZO Hagen's father, a heavy drinker, had become a hopeless drunkard. G. KEILLOR He was a heavy reader. He subscribed to four newspapers. 3 T. GUNN For the grass is heavy / with water and meets over / the bright path he makes. W. HOLTBY The days were long, heavy with pain and weariness. W. BOYD The atmosphere in the compartment was heavy with tension. 4 *Daily News* In heavy woollens . . there is a little more doing. D. FRASER The British Army of 1915 . . was short of heavy and medium artillery. *Horse International* She . . turned her attention away from ponies towards the heavy horses.

II Weighty in importance etc. 5 Weighty, important, serious. OE. b (Of a theatrical part or production) sombre, serious, tragic; (of a person, speech, etc.) ponderously dignified, sternly repressive. E19. c Of a newspaper: serious in tone. L19. 6 Grave, severe; marked, extensive; serious, intense, profound. OE.

5 *Australian Business* In his tough voice normally reserved for heavy negotiations. K. ISHIGURO It had not been my intention to make heavy talk at the supper table. W. A. PERCY An opera new to New Orleans called *Lohengrin*, which . . was *very* heavy. b K. AMIS Alexander's tone and manner were entirely respectful, neither heavy nor frivolous. 6 B. WEBB Sidney came down for good last week with a heavy cold. M. PUZO She had a heavy Italian accent. J. LENNON Anybody that sings with a guitar and sings about something heavy. J. UPDIKE Little shops heavy on macramé and batik.

III That weighs on or oppresses the senses or feelings. 7 Hard to bear or endure; grievous; causing sorrow, sad, distressing. OE. b

Troublesome, annoying; *esp.* violent. Now chiefly *colloq.*, in *heavy man, mob* below, or passing into sense 5. OE. 8 Hard to perform or accomplish; requiring much effort or exertion. ME. 9 Oppressive; overpowering. LME.

7 DEFOE This was a heavy piece of news to my nephew. W. SOYINKA Her sins had become heavy. B. EMECHETA He did not know why ones parents should be such a heavy responsibility. *New York Review of Books* The Depression was heavy on the country. b G. F. NEWMAN The more experienced protesters realised things might get heavy when they . . saw police transit vans. 8 *Boxing News* World-rated cruiserweight Spenser Chavis made heavy work of outpointing Joey Parker. 9 B. ENGLAND The night air was stiflingly heavy, the earth cold against his stomach. M. MOORCOCK The heavy scent of stocks and dying lilac ascended from the square.

IV Mentally weighed down. 10 Weighed down by sorrow or grief; saddened, despondent; (of the face, music, etc.) expressing grief, doleful. ME. 11 Sleepy, drowsy, weary; dulled. LME.

10 R. POLLOK Who farther sings, must change the pleasant lyre To heavy notes of woe. S. RUSHDIE The power of lifting the heaviest hearts and making one think that nothing was insoluble. 11 H. BASCOM His eyelids are heavy and he remembers a friend . . using matchsticks to keep his eyes propped open. A. MUNRO Her throat feels slightly raw and her head heavy.

V Having the slow or clumsy action of something physically heavy. 12 Acting or moving slowly, clumsily, or with difficulty; slow, laboured, sluggish. ME. b *spec.* in *Comm.* Characterized by declining prices. M19. 13 Of a person: intellectually slow, lacking vivacity. ME. 14 Esp. of an artistic or literary production: lacking vivacity, dull; tedious, uninteresting. E17.

12 TENNYSON If Time be heavy on your hands, Are there no beggars at your gate? D. H. LAWRENCE He heard Dawes's heavy panting, like a wild beast's. *Which?* Steering fairly heavy when parking or cornering hard. 13 STEELE A Set of heavy honest Men, with whom I have passed many Hours with much Indolence. 14 SWIFT It may still be a wonder how so heavy a book . . should survive to three editions.

VI Expressing the action of something physically heavy. 15 Having great momentum or force; striking or falling with force or violence. LME. b *spec.* of rock, jazz, etc., music: having a strong or forceful beat. M20. 16 Of food: difficult to digest, rich. Of wine, beer, etc.: containing much alcohol. LME. 17 Of soil, ground, etc.: clayey, cloggy; difficult to travel over. L16.

15 D. PRATER Despite high winds and heavy rain, he was on deck for the whole crossing. b *Sounds* Vocalist and Bassist for heavy but melodic band. 16 J. BUCHAN He . . ate a . . heavy tea about half-past four.

VII Having the appearance or sound of heaviness. 18 Having a loud and deep sound. LME. b (Of a syllable) stressed; *spec.* (of a line in Old English verse) containing more than the normal number of stressed elements. L19. 19 Of the sky: overcast, gloomy, threatening rain, snow, etc. L16. 20 Having the appearance of heaviness; thick, substantial; coarse, lacking grace, delicacy, or elegance. E19.

18 SHELLEY Listen well If you hear not a deep and heavy bell. 20 F. L. SHAW With heavy renaissance porch and wide spreading flight of granite steps. M. PIERCY The black eyes glinted anger under the heavy lids. P. ROTH A large man, . . wearing heavy tortoise-shell glasses.

Phrases, special collocations, & comb.: *as heavy as lead*: see LEAD *n.*[1] **heavier-than-air** *a.* (of an aircraft) weighing more than the air it displaces. **heavy-armed** *a.* bearing heavy weapons or armour. **heavy bag** a punch-bag. *heavy chemicals*: see CHEMICAL *n.* **heavy-duty** *a.* (of material etc.) designed to be unusually resistant to stresses in use. **heavy-footed** *a.* ponderous. *heavy going*: see GOING *n.* 4. **heavy-headed** *a.* (*a*) having a large head; (*b*) sleepy, dull; stupid. **heavy-hearted** *a.* sad, melancholy, doleful. **heavy hydrogen** deuterium. **heavy industry**: concerned with the production of metal, machines, etc. **heavy man** *colloq.* a criminal, a ruffian. **heavy metal** (*a*) a metal of high density; (*b*) a type of loud vigorous rock music with a strong (usu. fast) beat and a harsh or clashing musical style, freq. spectacularly performed. **heavy mob** *colloq.* (freq. w. *the*) violent gangsters; a bunch of hired ruffians. **heavy oil** any oil of a high relative density; orig., such an oil obtained from coal tar by distillation. **heavy petting** non-coital physical contact between two people involving stimulation of the genitals. **heavy sleeper**: difficult to rouse. **heavy spar** barytes. **heavy swell** (*a*) a strong swell of the sea; (*b*) *arch. slang* an exceedingly fashionable or stylish person. **heavy type** printed characters with unusually thick strokes. **heavy water** deuterium oxide, or a mixture of this with ordinary water. **heavy wet** *slang* malt liquor. *lie heavy*: see LIE *v.*[1] 10. *make heavy weather of*: see WEATHER *n.* *sit heavy on*: see SIT *v.* **with a heavy hand** oppressively (cf. HEAVY-HANDED).

B *n.* 1 (Strong) beer or ale. Cf. *heavy wet* above. *slang.* E19. 2 a In *pl.* Heavy cavalry; heavy artillery. M19. b A heavy bomber. M20. 3 Anything particularly large and heavy of its kind. M19. 4 A serious or tragic theatrical part. L19. b In *pl. The* serious newspapers or journals. M20. 5 A heavily built person of violent disposition, a thug. Also, an important person. M20.

1 *Truck & Driver* A pint of heavy costs 85p for drivers, 90p in the public bar. 3 *Truck & Driver* Wet trailer curtains were strapped down and the heavies began pulling out. *Strength Athlete* Bodyweight divisions . . range from the lightest . ., to the super heavies. 4 S. FORD It's as good as playin' leading heavy in 'The Shadows of a Great City'. b *Punch* To be subsequently published in one of the glossies or . . in one of the heavies. 5 J. WAINWRIGHT One Saturday night, the heavies from some other outfit started to throw muscle. *Australian Business* BT Australia's heavies were on hand to celebrate BT Innovation's first 12 months of activity.

heavy /ˈhɛvi/ *adv.* [OE *hefiġe* = OHG *hefīgo, hevīgo*, f. as prec.] = HEAVILY. Freq. qualifying adjs., as *heavy-laden, -pulling*, etc.

heavy-handed /hɛvɪˈhandɪd/ *a.* M17. [f. HEAVY *a.* + HANDED *a.*] 1 Having heavy or weary hands. Now chiefly *transf.*, clumsy; lacking subtlety. M17. 2 Oppressive; overbearing. L19.

1 K. CLARK Those critics who have maintained that he was a clumsy or heavy-handed painter. *Face* The heavy-handed irony of some sequences. 2 *City Limits* Camden . . is becoming so heavy-handed in dealing with the attendant problems.

heavy-handedness *n.* L19.

heavyweight /ˈhɛvɪweɪt/ *n.* & *a.* M19. [f. HEAVY *a.* + WEIGHT *n.*] A *n.* 1 A person (esp. a jockey), animal, or thing of more than the average weight. M19. 2 A weight at which boxing etc. matches are made, above middleweight (or cruiserweight) and usu. the heaviest weight, in the amateur boxing scale now being above 81 kg, though differing for professionals, wrestlers, and weightlifters, and according to time and place; a boxer etc,. of this weight. L19. 3 A person of importance and influence. L19.

1 W. HOLTBY Thundering round the ring at agricultural shows on his huge heavyweights. 3 *TV Guide* (*Canada*) Casting heavyweights Charlton Heston and Barbara Stanwyck to help win viewers.

B *adj.* Particularly heavy of its kind; (of a boxer etc.) that is a heavyweight, of or pertaining to heavyweights. L19.

Times Heavyweight American and Continental trucks and buses.

Phrases: **light heavyweight** (of) a weight in boxing and some other sports above middleweight, in the amateur boxing scale now being between 75 and 81 kg; (designating) a boxer etc. of this weight; also called *cruiserweight*.

hebdomad /ˈhɛbdəmad/ *n.* Also (now *rare*) **-ade** /-eɪd/. M16. [Late L f. Gk *hebdomas, -ad-*, the number seven, period of seven days, f. *hepta* seven: see -AD[1], -ADE.] †1 The number seven viewed collectively; a group of seven. M16–M19. 2 The space of seven days, a week, esp. w. ref. to *Dan.* 9:24–7. E17. 3 In Gnosticism etc., a group of seven superhuman beings. Also, a title of the Demiurge. M19.

hebdomadal /hɛbˈdɒməd(ə)l/ *a.* & *n.* E17. [Late L *hebdomadalis*, f. *hebdomas, -ad-*: see prec., -AL[1].] A *adj.* †1 Consisting of or lasting seven days. E–M17. 2 Meeting or occurring once a week; weekly. E18.

2 **Hebdomadal Council** the representative board of Oxford University, which meets weekly.

B *n.* A periodical appearing once a week; a weekly. *joc.* M19.

hebdomadally *adv.* E19.

hebdomadarian /hɛbdɒməˈdɛːrɪən/ *n.* L19. [f. next + -IAN.] = HEBDOMADARY *n.*

hebdomadary /hɛbˈdɒməd(ə)ri/ *n.* & *a.* Also **H-**, (earlier) †**eb-**. LME. [Late or eccl.L *hebdomadarius*, f. as HEBDOMADAL: see -ARY[1].] A *n.* *RC Ch.* A member of a chapter or convent, who takes his or her weekly turn in performing the sacred offices of the Church. LME. B *adj.* Weekly; doing duty for a week. E17.

hebdomary *n.* = HEBDOMADARY *n.* LME.

hebdomade *n.* see HEBDOMAD.

Hebe /ˈhiːbi/ *n.*[1] E17. [Gk *hēbē* youthful beauty, *Hēbē* the Greek goddess of youth and spring, daughter of Zeus and Hera, and cupbearer of Olympus.] 1 A young woman resembling Hebe; a waitress. E17. 2 (**h-**.) Any of numerous New Zealand evergreen shrubs constituting the genus *Hebe* (formerly included in *Veronica*), of the figwort family, with spikes of blue, white, mauve, etc., flowers. M20.

Hebe /hiːb/ *n.*[2] *derog.* Also **h-**. E20. [Abbrev. of HEBREW *n.* 1.] A Jew.

†**hebenon** *n.* var. of HEBONA.

hebephrenia /hiːbɪˈfriːnɪə/ *n.* L19. [f. HEBE *n.*[1] + Gk *phrēn* mind + -IA[1].] Orig., a form of insanity which occurs during puberty. Now, a form of schizophrenia characterized by incoherence, silliness, and inappropriate emotions.

hebephrenic /-ˈfrɛnɪk/ *a.* & *n.* (a person) affected by hebephrenia E20. **hebephreniac** *n.* a person affected by hebephrenia L19.

Heberden's node /ˈhɛbəd(ə)nz nəʊd/ *n. phr.* L19. [William *Heberden* (1710–1801), Eng. physician.] *Med.* A nodular enlargement of a terminal joint of a finger, due to osteoarthritis. Usu. in *pl.*

hebetate /ˈhɛbɪteɪt/ *v.t.* & *i.* L16. [L *hebetat-* pa. ppl stem of *hebetare*, f. *hebes, hebet-* blunt, dull: see -ATE[3].] Make or become dull or inert.

hebeˈtation *n.* E17.

hebete /ˈhɛbiːt/ *a.* *rare.* M18. [L *hebet-, hebes* blunt, dull.] Dull, stupid, obtuse.

hebetude /ˈhɛbɪtjuːd/ *n.* *literary.* E17. [Late L *hebetudo*, f. as prec.: see -TUDE.] Dullness, bluntness, lethargy.

hebona /ˈhɛbənə/ *n.* Long *rare.* Also †**hebenon.** L16. [Origin unkn.] A poisonous juice or substance.

SHAKES. *Haml.* Upon my secure hour thy uncle stole, with juice of cursed hebona in a vial.

hebra /ˈhɛbrə/ *n.* Also **chevra** /ˈxɛvrə/. Pl. **-ras, -roth** /-rəʊt/. L19. [Heb. *ḥeḇrāh* association, society.] A small group formed by members of a Jewish community for religious and charitable purposes.

Hebraean /hɪˈbreɪən, -ˈbriːən/ *n.* *rare.* Also **Hebrean.** E16. [f. L *Hebraeus*: see HEBREW, -AN.] †1 A Jew. Only in E16. †2 A Hebrew scholar. M17–E19. 3 A member of a Dutch religious sect whose beliefs were based on the meanings of hidden truths in Hebrew. *obs.* exc. *Hist.* L19.

Hebraic /hɪˈbreɪɪk/ *a.* LME. [Chr.L *Hebraicus* f. late Gk *Hebraikos*, f. *Hebra-* based on Aram. *ʿibray*: see HEBREW, -IC.] Pertaining or relating to the Hebrews or to their language; Hebrew.

Hebraical *a.* (now *rare*) E17. **Hebraically** *adv.* in Hebrew fashion; in the manner of the Hebrews or their language, *spec.* w. ref. to the fact that Hebrew is written from right to left: E18. †**Hebraician** *n.* = HEBRAIST 1 E17–E18.

Hebraise *v.* var. of HEBRAIZE.

Hebraism /ˈhiːbreɪɪz(ə)m/ *n.* L16. [Fr. *hébraïsme* or mod.L *Hebraismus* = late Gk *Hebraismos*: see HEBREW, -ISM.] 1 A Hebrew idiom or expression, esp. one as used in some other language. L16. 2 A quality or attribute of the Hebrew people; Hebrew character or nature; the Hebrew system of thought or religion. M19.

Hebraist /ˈhiːbreɪɪst/ *n.* M18. [f. Gk *Hebra-* stem of HEBRAIC + -IST.] 1 A Hebrew scholar; a person skilled in Hebrew. M18. 2 A person who maintains that the New Testament was written in Greek with Hebrew idioms. M19. 3 An adherent of Hebrew thought or religion. L19. 4 *Hist.* A Palestinian Jew, as opp. to a Hellenistic or Grecian Jew. L19.

Hebraˈistic *a.* M19.

Hebraize /ˈhiːbreɪʌɪz/ *v.* Also **-ise**. M17. [Late Gk *Hebraizein* speak Hebrew, imitate Jews, f *Hebra-*: see HEBRAIC, -IZE.] **1** *v.i.* Use a Hebrew idiom or expression. M17. **2** *v.t.* Make Hebrew; give a Hebrew character to. E19.

Hebrean *n.* var. of HEBRAEAN.

Hebrew /ˈhiːbruː/ *n.* & *a.* ME. [OFr. *ebreu*, *ebrieu* (mod. *hébreu*) f. med.L *Ebreus* f. L *Hebraeus* f. late Gk *Hebraios* f. Aram. *ʿibrāy*, for Heb. *ʿibrī* interpreted as 'one from the other side (of the river)', as if f. *ʿēber* the region on the other or opposite side, f. *ʿābar* cross or pass over.] **A** *n.* **1** A member of a Semitic people living in ancient Palestine and having a descent traditionally traced from Abraham, Isaac, and Jacob; an Israelite, a Jew. In *pl.* (treated as *sing.*), the Epistle to the Hebrews, a book of the New Testament traditionally (but probably not rightly) included among the epistles of St Paul. ME. **2** The Semitic language spoken by the Hebrews, in which most of the books of the Hebrew Scriptures were written. Also, a modern form of this revived in the 19th cent.; the official language of the State of Israel. ME. **b** Unintelligible speech. Cf. GREEK *n.* 8. *colloq.* E17.

B *adj.* **1** Belonging to, written in, or spoken in the language of the Hebrews. ME. **2** Of, belonging to, or characteristic of the Hebrews; Jewish. L15.

2 *Hebrew Scriptures*: see SCRIPTURE 1a.

Hebrewdom *n.* the Hebrew community; the quality of the Hebrew people: M19. **Hebrewess** *n.* (*rare*) a female Hebrew, a Jewess M16. **Hebrewism** *n.* (now *rare*) = HEBRAISM E17.

Hebrician /hiːˈbrɪʃ(ə)n/ *n.* Now *rare* or *obs.* M16. [f. as HEBRAIC + -ICIAN.] †**1** A Hebrew. M–L16. **2** A Hebrew scholar; a person skilled in Hebrew. L16.

Hebridean /hɛbrɪˈdiːən/ *a.* & *n.* Also **-ian**. E17. [f. *Hebrides* (see below) + -AN, -EAN.] **A** *adj.* Of or pertaining to the Hebrides, a group of islands off the west coast of Scotland. E17. **B** *n.* A native or inhabitant of the Hebrides. M17.

Also (*poet.*, *rare*) **ˈHebrid** *a.* = HEBRIDEAN *a.* M18.

Hecate /ˈhɛkəti/ *n.* L16. [Gk *Hekatē* fem. of *hekatos* 'far-darting' (an epithet of Apollo), in Gk mythol. name of a goddess of Thracian origin identified with Artemis and the moon, and also with Persephone, the goddess of the infernal regions, and accordingly regarded as presiding over magic and witchcraft.] A hag, a witch.

SHAKES. *1 Hen. VI* I speak not to that railing Hecate.

¶In Shakes. usually disyllabic (/ˈhɛkət/).

hecatomb /ˈhɛkətuːm/ *n.* & *v.* L16. [L *hecatombe* f. Gk *hekatombē*, f. *hekaton* hundred + *bous* ox.] **A** *n.* **1** A great public sacrifice, strictly of a hundred oxen, among the ancient Greeks and Romans; *gen.* a religious sacrifice; a large number of animals set apart for sacrifice. L16. **2** *transf.* & *fig.* A sacrifice of many victims. L16.

2 T. PARNELL A hecatomb of reputations was that day to fall for her pleasure.

B *v.t.* Provide with a hecatomb. *rare.* M18.

hecatomped /hɛkəˈtɒmpɪd/ *a.* E18. [Gk *hekatompedos*, f. *hekaton* hundred + *ped-* ablaut var. of *pous*, *pod-* foot.] Measuring a hundred feet (30.48 m) in length and breadth; that is a hundred feet square.

hecatompedon *n.* (*rare*) a temple of hecatomped dimensions (as the Parthenon at Athens) L18.

hecatontarchy /hɛkəˈtɒntɑːki/ *n.* M17. [Late Gk *hekatontarkhia* post or command of a centurion, f. *hekatont(a)-* comb. form, f. *hekaton* hundred: see -ARCHY.] Government by a hundred rulers.

heck /hɛk/ *n.*[1] Chiefly *Sc.* & *north.* ME. [Var. (f. inflected forms) of HATCH *n.*[1] Cf. HACK *n.*[3]] **1** A grating or frame of parallel bars in a river used to obstruct the passage of fish or solid bodies without obstructing the flow of water. Also = HATCH *n.*[1] 3. ME. **2** A rack of parallel spars used to hold fodder. ME. **3** The lower half of a divided door; a half-door, a gate, a wicket; = HATCH *n.*[1] 1. LME. **b** A passage in a house; *esp.* one forming a screen or division. E19. **4** = HACK *n.*[3] 4. *obs.* exc. *Sc.* LME. **5** A movable board at the back of a cart. E19. **6** A piece in a spinning-wheel or warping-mill by which the yarn or thread is guided to the reels. E19.

2 **at heck and manger** in comfortable circumstances, in plenty.

heck /hɛk/ *n.*[2] *colloq. euphem.* L19. [Alt. of HELL *n.*] **1** In exclamatory or imprecatory phrs. (in which *hell* can always be substituted) expr. anger, annoyance, incredulity, dismay, etc., or merely emphatic. L19. **2** As *int.* An exclam. of anger, annoyance, dismay, etc. M20.

1 M. RENAULT What the heck does he want? *Guardian* Sometimes he sings for sheer fun and the heck of it. D. WESTHEIMER It's a heck of a responsibility.

heck /hɛk/ *v.i.* Now *rare.* M17. [Imit.: cf. HACK *v.*[1]] Make a short dry cough; = HACK *v.*[1] 9. Chiefly in *hecking cough.*

heckberry *n.* var. of HAGBERRY.

heckelphone /ˈhɛk(ə)lfəʊn/ *n.* Also **-phon**. E20. [G *Heckelphon*, f. Wilhelm *Heckel* (1856–1909), Ger. instrument-maker + -PHONE.] A baritone oboe.

heckle /ˈhɛk(ə)l/ *n.* LME. [North. & East Anglian form of HACKLE *n.*[2]] **I 1** = HACKLE *n.*[2] 5. LME. **2** = HACKLE *n.*[2] 1. LME. **3** *Angling.* = HACKLE *n.*[2] 2. E19. **II** [Prob. f. the vb.] **4a** = HECKLER *n.* 2. L18. **b** The action of heckling. See HECKLE *v.* 2. E20.

heckle /ˈhɛk(ə)l/ *v.* ME. [f. the n. Cf. HACKLE *v.*[3], HATCHEL.] **1** *v.t.* Dress (flax or hemp) with a heckle, to split and straighten out the fibres for spinning; = HACKLE *v.*[3] 1. ME. **2** *v.t.* & *i.* Interrupt (a public speaker) with aggressive questions or abuse, esp. in order to undermine the speaker or to weaken his or her argument. M17. **3** *v.t.* Chastise, scold. *dial.* E19.

2 W. E. GOSSE On the hustings, Lord John Manners was a good deal heckled. B. EMECHETA They started to heckle and jeer.

heckler /ˈhɛklə/ *n.* LME. [f. HECKLE *v.* + -ER[1].] **1** A dresser of flax or hemp. LME. **2** A person who interrupts a public speaker in an abusive or aggressive manner. See HECKLE *v.* 2. E19.

2 N. CHOMSKY The speakers . . were drowned out by hecklers and counterdemonstrators.

hecogenin /hɛkəʊˈdʒɛnɪn/ *n.* M20. [f. mod.L *Hechtia* genus name of a source plant + -O- + GENIN.] *Biochem.* A steroid glycoside present in various plants and obtained commercially from sisal waste, used in the manufacture of cortisone and related steroids.

hectare /ˈhɛktɛː, -ɑː/ *n.* E19. [Fr., irreg. f. Gk *hekaton* hundred + ARE *n.*[2]: see HECTO-.] A metric unit of square measure equal to 100 ares (10000 m^2), or 2.471 acres.

hectarage *n.* extent of hectares; hectares collectively: L20.

hectic /ˈhɛktɪk/ *a.* & *n.* Also (earlier) †**etik**. LME. [OFr. *etique* f. late L *hecticus* f. Gk *hektikos* habitual, hectic, consumptive, f. *hexis* habit, state of body or mind: see -IC. Assim. to L, or mod.Fr. *hectique.*] **A** *adj.* **1** *Med.* Belonging to or symptomatic of the bodily state or condition; *spec.* characteristic of or associated with tuberculosis or other wasting disease; showing tubercular symptoms such as flushed cheeks and hot dry skin. LME. **2** *fig.* a Wasting, consuming. *rare.* E17. **b** Flushed, bright red. E19. †**3** Habitual, constitutional. Only in M17. **4** (Now the usual sense.) Stirring, exciting, disturbing; characterized by a state of feverish excitement or activity. E20.

1 C. KINGSLEY A pretty, hectic girl of sixteen. E. LYALL The hectic beauty of one dying of consumption. **hectic fever** a fever (often of regular daily occurrence) which accompanies tuberculosis or other wasting diseases. *hectic flush*: see FLUSH *n.*[2] 4. **2b** F. KING A high cheekbone hectic with rouge. **4** GODFREY SMITH Long periods of boredom broken by hectic spells of chaos. A. BROOKNER The streets now hectic with traffic and confusion.

B *n.* **1** A hectic fever. LME. **b** *fig.* A consuming disturbance or obsession of the mind. LME. **2** A person affected with hectic fever. LME. **3** A hectic flush; *gen.* a flush, heightened colour. M18.

hectical *a.* (*arch.*) E17. **hectically** *adv.* M18.

hecto- /ˈhɛktəʊ/ *comb. form.* [Fr., contr. of Gk *hekaton* hundred.] Used w. the sense 'one hundred', esp. to form units in the metric system, as *hectogram*, *hectolitre*, etc. Abbrev. *h.*

hectocotylus /hɛktəʊˈkɒtɪləs/ *n.* Pl. **-li** /-lʌɪ, -liː/. Also Anglicized as **-cotyl**. M19. [mod.L (see note below), f. as HECTO- + Gk *kotulē* cup, hollow thing.] *Zool.* A modified arm in male dibranchiate cephalopods which is adapted for the transfer of sperm to the female, in some species becoming detached and remaining in the body of the female.

¶Mod.L *Hectocotylus* was orig. proposed as a genus name by Cuvier in the mistaken belief that the detached structures were parasites.

hectocotyliˈzation *n.* the process of forming a hectocotylus L19. **hectocotylize** *v.t.* (in *pass.*) become modified into a hectocotylus L19.

hectogram /ˈhɛktə(ʊ)gram/ *n.* Also **-gramme**. L18. [Fr. *hectogramme*, f. as HECTO- + GRAM *n.*[2]] A weight of 100 grams.

hectograph /ˈhɛktə(ʊ)grɑːf/ *n.* & *v.* L19 [f. HECTO- + -GRAPH.] **A** *n.* An apparatus used for copying documents by means of a gelatin plate; the process of making copies with this apparatus. L19. **B** *v.t.* Reproduce by means of a hectograph. L19.

hectoˈgraphic *a.* L19.

hectolitre /ˈhɛktə(ʊ)liːtə/ *n.* Also **-liter**. E19. [Fr., f. as HECTO- + LITRE.] A volume of 100 litres.

hectometre /ˈhɛktə(ʊ)miːtə/ *n.* Also **-meter**. E19. [Fr. *hectomètre*, f. as HECTO- + METRE *n.*[2]] A length of 100 metres.

hector /ˈhɛktə/ *n.* Also **H-**. LME. [L *Hector*, Gk *Hektōr* son of Priam and Hecuba, a Trojan hero, use as n. of adj. *hektōr* holding fast, f. *ekhein* to hold.] **1** A valiant warrior. LME. **2** A swaggering fellow, a braggart, a bully. M17.

hector /ˈhɛktə/ *v.* M17. [f. the n.] **1** *v.i.* Play the bully; brag, bluster, domineer. M17. **2** *v.t.* Intimidate by bluster or threats; domineer over; bully *out of*, *into*, etc. M17.

hectoringly *adv.* in a blustering or intimidatory manner E20.

heddle /ˈhɛd(ə)l/ *n.* E16. [App. ult. f. OE alt. of *hefeld* HEALD *n.*] Any of the sets of small cords or wires between which the warp is passed in the loom before going through the reed, dividing the warp threads to allow the passage of the shuttle with the weft. Freq. in *pl.*

hedenbergite /ˈhɛd(ə)nbəgʌɪt/ *n.* E19. [f. Ludwig *Hedenberg*, 19th-cent. Swedish mineralogist + -ITE[1].] *Min.* A black calcium- and iron-containing mineral of the clinopyroxene group.

heder /ˈhɛdə, x-/ *n.* Also **cheder**. Pl. **-darim** /-ˈdɑːrɪm/, **-rs**. L19. [Heb. *ḥēder* room.] A school for Jewish children in which Hebrew and religious knowledge are taught.

hedge /ˈhɛdʒ/ *n.* [OE *heġġ* = EFris. *hegge*, MDu. *hegghe* (Du. *heg*), OHG *hegga*, *hecka* (G *Hecke*) f. Gmc base rel. to HAG *n.*[2], HAW *n.*[1], HAY *n.*[2]] **1** A closely planted line of bushes, small trees, or dead wood, esp. forming a boundary of a field, garden, road, etc. Also occas., a similar boundary of turf, stone, etc. OE. **b** *transf.* Any line of objects forming a barrier, boundary, or partition. E16. **2** A barrier; a means of protection or defence. ME. **b** *spec.* An act or means of hedging or protecting a bet or speculation. Cf. HEDGE *v.* 7. M18. **3** A fishing weir. LME.

1 W. BOYD An ornamental rose garden separated from the lawn by a neat briar hedge. b H. MARTINEAU Hedges of police from our little street to the gates of the Abbey. **2** *Atlantic Monthly* Last year you wanted some extra money as a hedge against hard luck. **b** *Punch* A good unit trust group . . provides . . a hedge against inflation.

Attrib. & *comb.*: In the senses 'living, working, occurring, etc., at the roadside; done under a hedge or clandestinely; inferior, paltry,' as *hedge-doctor*, *hedge-inn*, *hedge-lawyer*, *hedge-marriage*, *hedge-parson*, *hedge-poet*, etc. Special combs., as **hedge-bill** = *hedging-bill* s.v. HEDGING; *hedge bindweed*: see BINDWEED 1. **hedge-bird** (*a*) a bird that inhabits or frequents hedges; (*b*) a person born or brought up on or frequenting the roadside; a vagrant; a footpad; **hedge-clippers**: for trimming a hedge; **hedge-creeper** (now *rare* or *obs.*) a vagrant; a thief; a peeping tom; **hedge-fence** a hedge serving as a fence; **hedge-garlic** = GARLIC-*mustard*; **hedge-hop** *v.i.* & *t.* fly at a low altitude (over); **hedge-hyssop** any of various low-growing N. American marsh plants of the genus *Gratiola*, of the figwort family; earlier, a similar plant of central Europe, *G. officinalis*, once valued for its medicinal properties; *hedge maple*: see MAPLE *n.* 1; **hedge-mustard** a cruciferous roadside weed, *Sisymbrium officinale*, with small yellow flowers and adpressed pods; **hedge-parsley** any of several umbelliferous plants of the genus *Torilis*; *esp.* (in full *upright hedge-parsley*) *T. japonica*, a common plant of hedgerows; **hedge-pig** a hedgehog; **hedge-priest** *derog.* (*Hist.*) an illiterate priest of low status; **hedge-school** *Hist.* (orig.) an open-air school, esp. in Ireland; (later) an inferior type of school; **hedge-side**: of a hedge (freq. *attrib.*); **hedge sparrow** the dunnock, *Prunella modularis*; *hedge trimmer*: see TRIMMER *n.*; **hedge-wood** trees or bushes suitable for growing as hedges.

hedgeless *a.* E19.

hedge /hɛdʒ/ *v.* LME. [f. the n.] **1** *v.t.* Surround or enclose with a hedge or fence as a boundary or defence. (Foll. by *in*, *about*.) LME. **b** Make into a hedge or barrier. M18. **2** *v.i.* Construct a hedge or hedges. LME. **3** *v.t.* Surround or enclose as with a hedge or fence. LME. **b** Hem in, confine, restrict. M16. **4** *v.t.* Obstruct (as) with a hedge. M16. **5** *v.i.* Avoid committing oneself, refuse to face an issue, evade the question. Formerly also, turn from the direct path; leave a way of retreat. L16. †**6** *v.t.* With *in*: include within the limits of something else; *spec.* secure (a debt) by including it in another for which better security is obtained. E17–M18. **7** *v.t.* Secure oneself against total loss on (a bet or speculation) by making similar transactions on the other side. L17. **b** *v.t.* & *i. spec.* Insure (one's commercial activities) against risk or loss by entering into contracts which balance one another. E20.

3 SHAKES. *Haml.* There's such divinity doth hedge a King. b *fig.*: I. D'ISRAELI The King was hedged in by the most thorny difficulties. 5 P. CUSHING The miller hedged and dodged, but being pressed hard he finally admitted the truth. 7 *absol.*: LD MACAULAY He had betted too deep on the Revolution and .. it was time to hedge.

hedger *n.* (*a*) a person who lays or trims hedges; (*b*) a person who hedges (senses 5 & 7 above): ME. **hedgingly** *adv.* in an evasive or non-committal manner L19.

hedgebote /ˈhɛdʒbəʊt/ *n.* ME. [f. HEDGE *n.* + BOTE.] *Law.* = HAYBOTE.

hedgehog /ˈhɛdʒ(h)ɒg/ *n.* LME. [f. HEDGE *n.* + HOG *n.*] **1** Any of various spiny nocturnal insectivorous mammals of the family Erinaceidae (esp. the western European *Erinaceus europaeus*), noted for the ability to roll up into a ball when alarmed. LME. †**2** *fig.* A person who disregards the feelings of others. L16–M17. **3** Any of various other spiny animals; *esp.* (*US*) the porcupine; *sea hedgehog*, (*a*) a sea urchin; (*b*) the porcupine-fish, *Diodon hystrix*. L16. **4** Any of various objects held to resemble a hedgehog in shape, appearance, etc., as (*a*) a type of dredging-machine; (*b*) a pudding or cake shaped like a hedgehog; (*c*) a small self-contained fortified position bristling with defences on all sides; (*d*) a type of ship-borne multi-barrelled mortar firing a pattern of depth-charges. L17. **5** *sing.* & in *pl.* (The fruits of) any of several plants with prickly seed-vessels, esp. *Ranunculus arvensis*. E18.

Comb.: **hedgehog holly** a cultivated form of holly with leaves prickly on the upper surface.

hedgehoggy *a.* resembling a hedgehog; prickly; (of a person) difficult to get on with: M19.

hedgerow /ˈhɛdʒrəʊ/ *n.* OE. [f. HEDGE *n.* + REW, assim. to ROW *n.*[1]] A hedge, esp. as used as the boundary of a field or road.

hedging /ˈhɛdʒɪŋ/ *vbl n.* LME. [f. HEDGE *v.* + -ING[1].] **1** The laying, repairing, or trimming of hedges. LME. **2** (The trees, bushes, etc., forming) a hedge. LME. **3** The securing of, or limiting the possible loss on, a bet or financial speculation. M17. **4** Evasion; refusal to commit oneself. E18.

Comb.: **hedging-bill** a long-handled bill for cutting and trimming hedges.

hedgy /ˈhɛdʒi/ *a.* L16. [f. HEDGE *n.* or *v.* + -Y[1].] †**1** Pertaining to or of the nature of a hedge. Only in L16. **2** Characterized by or having many hedges. M17. **3** Marked by hedging; evasive, non-committal. E20.

hedonic /hiːˈdɒnɪk, hɛ-/ *a.* & *n.* M17. [Gk *hēdonikos*, f. as next: see -IC.] **A** *adj.* **1** Of or pertaining to pleasure; (chiefly *Psychol.*) of, pertaining to, or involving pleasurable or painful sensations or feelings, considered as affects. M17. **2** *Zool.* Designating or relating to glands in reptiles and amphibians which serve to attract members of the opposite sex for mating. E20.

1 **hedonic tone** the degree of pleasantness or unpleasantness associated with an experience or state, esp. as referred to a continuum extending from pleasure to pain.

B *n.* †**1** A Cyrenaic. Only in L17. **2** In *pl.* The science of pleasure; that part of ethics which refers to pleasure. Now *rare*. M19.

hedonism /ˈhiːd(ə)nɪz(ə)m, ˈhɛ-/ *n.* M19. [f. Gk *hēdonē* pleasure + -ISM.] The doctrine or theory of ethics in which pleasure is regarded as the chief good or the proper aim. Freq. now also, devotion to or pursuit of pleasure.

hedonist /ˈhiːd(ə)nɪst, ˈhɛ-/ *n.* M19. [f. Gk as prec. + -IST.] A person who regards pleasure as the chief good or the proper aim. Now *freq.*, a pleasure-seeker.

D. ATHILL Deliberately frivolous as he was, a hedonist, an opportunist.

hedoˈnistic *a.* M19. **hedoˈnistically** *adv.* L19.

hedonometer /hiːdɒˈnɒmɪtə, hɛ-/ *n. joc.* E19. [f. Gk *hēdonē* + -METER.] A (hypothetical) device for measuring pleasure.

-hedral /ˈhiːdr(ə)l, ˈhɛd-/ *suff.* [f. (as) next + -AL[1].] Forming adjs. (usu. corresp. to ns. in -HEDRON) in sense 'having or involving a specified number or kind of plane surfaces or faces' (*anhedral*, *dihedral*, *dodecahedral*, *rhombohedral*).

-hedron /ˈhiːdrən, ˈhɛd-/ *suff.* Pl. **-hedra** /ˈhiːdrə, ˈhɛd-/, **-hedrons**. [f. Gk *hedra* seat, base, after OCTAHEDRON etc.] Forming ns. denoting geometrical solid figures or objects with various numbers or shapes of faces (*dodecahedron*, *rhombohedron*).

hedrumite /ˈhɛdrəmʌɪt/ *n.* L19. [f. *Hedrum* a village in Norway + -ITE[1].] *Geol.* A hypabyssal porphyritic igneous rock having a trachytic texture and consisting essentially of a potash-feldspar with some pyribole and (usu.) nepheline.

hedychium /hɪˈdɪkɪəm/ *n.* E19. [mod.L *Hedychium* genus name, f. Gk *hēdus* sweet + *khiōn* snow, w. ref. to the fragrant white flowers of one species.] = *ginger lily* s.v. GINGER *n.*

heebie-jeebie /hiːbɪˈdʒiːbi/ *n. slang* (orig. *US*). Also **heeby-jeeby**. E20. [Origin unkn.] *sing.* or (usu.) in *pl.*, with *the*: a state of nervous depression or apprehension; delirium tremens. Also formerly, a type of dance.

Weekly Dispatch Does this work never give you the heebie-jeebies? Does it never depress you?

heed /hiːd/ *n.* ME. [f. the vb.] **1** Careful attention, observation, regard. Now chiefly in phrs. below. ME. †**2** That which is heeded. *rare* (Shakes.). Only in L16.

1 T. HERBERT Swimming so without heed, that some were in apparant danger. **give, pay, heed to** pay attention to. **take heed (of)** take care, attend (to).

heedful *a.* careful, attentive, mindful, cautious M16. **heedfully** *adv.* M16. **heedfulness** *n.* M16. †**heedily** *adv.* carefully, with attention L16–M17. †**heediness** *n.* attentiveness, caution L16–E17. **heedless** *a.* careless, inattentive, regardless, reckless L16. **heedlessly** *adv.* L17. **heedlessness** *n.* L16. †**heedy** *a.* attentive, cautious M16–M17.

heed /hiːd/ *v.* [OE *hēdan* = OS *hōdian* (Du. *hoeden*), OHG *huoten* (G *hüten*), f. WGmc base of OFris., MLG *hōde*, OHG *huota*, G *Hut* care, keeping.] **1** *v.i.* Have a care, pay attention, take notice. Now chiefly *dial.* OE. **2** *v.t.* Concern oneself about, take notice of, regard. ME.

1 R. MACAULAY I did my best to warn her, but she wouldn't heed. **never heed** *dial.* do not worry, never mind. 2 V. WOOLF Mrs Ambrose alone heeded none of this stir. C. CHAPLIN When the fates deal in human destiny, they heed neither pity nor justice. K. CROSSLEY-HOLLAND My advice will help you if you heed it.

hee-haw /ˈhiːhɔː/ *n.* & *v.* E19. [Imit.] **A** *n.* **1** (A representation of) a donkey's bray. E19. **2** A loud, coarse laugh. M19. **B** *v.i.* Utter a hee-haw, bray. E19.

heel /hiːl/ *n.*[1] [OE *hēla*, *hǣla* corresp. to OFris. *hēla*, MDu. *hiele* (Du. *hiel*), ON *haell*, f. Gmc base of OE *hōh* heel: see HOUGH *n.*] **1** The hinder part of the human foot below the ankle. OE. **b** The corresponding part of the foot or hind limb of an animal; *esp.* (*a*) the hinder part of the hoof; (*b*) a hind foot of a quadruped; (*c*) the hinder toe or hallux of a bird. OE. **c** The foot as a whole. ME. **2** The heel or foot as an instrument of kicking, trampling, or oppression. OE. **b** The armed, booted, or spurred heel, esp. as used in horsemanship. LME. **c** *Rugby Football.* A heeling of the ball from the scrummage. Cf HEEL *v.*[2] 6. M20. **3** The part of a sock or stocking which covers the heel; the part of a boot or shoe which supports or raises the heel. Also, in *pl.*, high-heeled shoes. ME. **b** Either of the raised extremities of a horseshoe; a calkin. M19. **4** (The heels as) the hindmost part of a person or animal, esp. one pursued; hence, the means of flight. LME. **5** The remains or end part of anything, as the crust of a loaf, the rind of a cheese, etc. LME. **6** The concluding part of anything, as a period of time, a book, etc. L16. **7** The lower or handle end of anything, as the handle end of a violin bow, the inner end of the head of a golf club, the lower part of a ship's mast or rudder, etc. L16. **8a** The part of a bivalve shell which bears the hinge. L17. **b** The vertical timber of a gate which bears the hinges. M19. **9** The broadest or thickest part of a wedge-shaped object. L19. **10** A projection resembling a heel in shape or position, as (*a*) a small piece of older wood taken off with a cutting; (*b*) the small projecting part at the back of the bowl of a spoon. L19.

1 E. LINKLATER A muslin wrapper which fell loosely from her shoulders to her heels. M. FRAYN He .. raised himself on his toes, and let himself sink .. back on to his heels. c M. PRIOR He .. was carried off to bed: John held his heels, and Nan his head. 2 H. GEORGE Those classes upon whom the iron heel of modern civilisation presses. 3 C. BEATON She wore .. white satin shoes whose Spanish Spike heels were fully six inches high. P. MATTHIESSEN I wear my .. socks upside down so that the hole in the heel sits on the top of my foot. *New York Times* 'Take off those heels,' my aunt says. 4 N. BAILEY One Pair of Heels is worth two Pair of Hands, that is, it is better to run for it. 5 D. L. SAYERS The heel of a stale loaf. P. V. PRICE The bottle heel or dregs can be filtered and used in cooking. 6 S. O'FAOLÁIN It was so fine in the heel of the day. 10 *Practical Gardening* Cuttings of young side-shoots .. preferably with a tiny heel of wood attached to each.

Phrases: *Achilles heel*: see ACHILLES. **at heel** = *to heel* below. **at one's heels, at the heels of** close behind, in close pursuit of or attendance on. **back on one's heels** into a state of discomfiture or astonishment. *beef to the heel(s)*: see BEEF *n.* **bring, come, to heel** make or come to walk at heel; bring or come under control. *dig in one's heels*: see DIG *v.* **down at (the) heel** (*a*) (of a shoe) having the heels worn down; worn carelessly with the heel part crushed under the foot; (*b*) (of a person) wearing down-at-heel shoes; destitute, slovenly. *hairy about, at, the heels*: see HAIRY *a.* *head over heels*: see HEAD *n.* **heel-and-toe** (*a*) with proper walking action, esp. as required in race-walking; (*b*) *Motoring* with the action of heeling-and-toeing (see HEEL *v.*[2]). **heel of Italy** the SE extremity of Italy (which country resembles a leg and foot in shape) **heel of the hand** the part of the palm nearest the wrist. **heels over head** (*arch.*) = *head over heels* s.v. HEAD *n.* **his heels** (*Cribbage*) a score of two points by a dealer turning up a jack. *hot on the heels of*: see HOT *a.* **kick one's heels** be kept waiting. **lay by the heels** fetter, arrest, confine; *fig.* overthrow, disgrace. *neck and heels*: see NECK *n.*[1] **on one's heels, on the heels of** = *at one's heels* above. **out at heels** with shoes worn out at the heel; destitute, in trouble or distress. **run heel** = HEEL *v.*[2] 8. **set by the heels** = *lay by the heels* above. *show a clean pair of heels*: see CLEAN *a.* **take to one's**

heels run away. **to heel** of a dog: following closely and obediently. **turn on one's heel** turn sharply round. **under the heel of** dominated by. **upon one's heels, upon the heels of** = *at one's heels* above. *wedge-heel*: see WEDGE *n.* 5(f).

Comb.: **heelball** (*a*) a polishing mixture of hard wax and (usu. black) colouring used by shoemakers; (*b*) this or a similar composition used to make rubbings of monumental brasses etc.; **heel bar** a shop or stall where shoes are mended while the customer waits; **heel-bone** the calcaneum; **heel bug** a harvest mite, *Trombicula autumnalis*; skin disease in horses due to this; **heel cup** a (usu. soft rubber) insert in a sports shoe to prevent or alleviate bruising of the heel; **heel grip** (*a*) a stud or cleat on the heel of a boot etc. to give footing on slippery ground; (*b*) (freq. adhesive) padding inside a shoe-heel to prevent it slipping or chafing; **heel-lift** any of the layers of leather etc. which make up the heel of a shoe; **heel-piece** *n.* & *v.* (*a*) *n.* a piece attached to or forming the heel of anything, as a shoe, a ship's mast, etc; *fig.* an end-piece or conclusion; (*b*) *v.t.* put a heel-piece on (a shoe); **heel-plate** (*a*) the plate on the butt end of a gun stock; (*b*) a metal plate protecting the heel of a shoe; (*c*) a plate to support the heel of a skating boot; **heel-post** (*a*) the post to which a door or gate is fixed; (*b*) *Shipbuilding* a post supporting the outer end of a propeller shaft; **heel-rope** a rope attached to the heel of anything, as a spar or rudder; a hobble for a horse etc.; **heeltap** (*a*) = *heel-lift* above; (*b*) liquor left in the bottom of a glass after drinking; **heel-tap** *v.* (*a*) *v.t.* add a piece of leather etc. to a shoe-heel; (*b*) *v.i.* delay, dawdle.

heelless /-l-l-/ *a.* having no heel; not using the heel: M19.

heel /hiːl/ *n.*[2] M18. [f. HEEL *v.*[1]] *Naut.* An act (on the part of a ship) of heeling or inclining to one side; a lurch; extent of this measured from the vertical.

heel /hiːl/ *n.*[3] *slang* (orig. *US*). E20. [Prob. f. HEEL *n.*[1]] An untrustworthy or despicable person.

L. P. HARTLEY She's lost her fiancé . . he was a heel and she's well rid of him.

heel /hiːl/ *v.*[1] L16. [Prob. f. HIELD *v.*, the *d* being taken as a pa. ppl suff.] 1 *v.i.* Of a ship etc.: lean to one side; lean or fall *over*, capsize, topple. L16. 2 *v.t.* Cause (a vessel) to incline thus. Formerly also, lay (a vessel) on its side for hull repairs etc. L16.

1 G. K. CHESTERTON The whole tree heeled over like a ship, smashing everyone in its fall. *Motor Cruiser* The boat . . heels until the . . tube is immersed. 2 E. K. KANE The Rescue was heeled over considerably by the floes.

heel /hiːl/ *v.*[2] E17. [f. HEEL *n.*[1]] 1 *v.i.* & (*rare*) *t.* Perform (a dance etc.) involving tapping the ground rhythmically with the heels. E17. 2 *v.t.* a Provide (a shoe, sock, etc.) with a heel or heel-piece. E17. b Arm (a gamecock) with a gaff or spur; (*slang*, orig. *US*) provide (a person) with something, esp. a weapon. M18. 3 *v.t.* Catch or tether by the heel; bind the heels of. M17. 4 *v.i. Shipbuilding.* Rest or be placed with the heel or lower end *on* something. M19. 5a *v.t.* Urge (a horse etc.) *on* with the heels. M19. b *v.t. Golf.* Strike (the ball) with the heel of the club. M19. 6 *v.t.* & *i. Rugby Football.* Send (the ball) out at the back of the scrummage with the heel. L19. 7a *v.i.* Of a dog: follow obediently at a person's heels. Freq. in *imper.* L19. b *v.t.* Of a dog: chase or drive (cattle etc.) by running or nipping at their heels. Foll. by *up*: nip the heels of. L19. 8 *v.i.* Of hounds: follow a scent in the direction from which the quarry has come. L19.

Phrases: **heel and toe** (*a*) *Dancing* touch the ground with the heel and toe alternately; (*b*) *Motoring* operate the accelerator and brake pedals with one foot simultaneously in contact with both.

heeling *n.* (*a*) the action of the verb; (*b*) the heel-piece of a stocking; the (square) lower end of a ship's mast: L16.

heel *v.*[3] see HELE *v.*

heelaman *n.* var. of HIELAMAN.

heeled /hiːld/ *a.* M16. [f. HEEL *n.*[1] or *v.*[2]: see -ED[1], -ED[2].] 1 Having a heel or similar projection; having a (specified) kind of heel, as *high-heeled*, *stiletto-heeled*, etc. M16. 2 *slang* (orig. *US*). a Provided, equipped; armed. M19. b Provided with money. Usu. preceded by *well*. L19.

2b G. MCINNES Dr. Crapp was a prominent dentist. . . He was therefore obviously well heeled.

heeler /ˈhiːlə/ *n.*[1] M17. [f. HEEL *v.*[2] or *n.*[1] + -ER[1].] 1 A person who puts heels on shoes. M17. b A person who fits spurs to a fighting cock. M19. 2 A person who trips up, undermines, or supplants another. M17. 3 A gamecock that uses its spurs in fighting. L18. 4 A fast runner; one who shows a clean pair of heels. E19. b A light, fast sailing ship. E20. 5 A person who follows a leader; a (disreputable) follower of a politician. *US.* L19. 6 A working dog which urges animals on by nipping at their heels. Also, a nip on the heels. *Austral.* L19. 7 *Rugby Football.* A player who heels the ball out of the scrummage. L19.

4 A. B. PATERSON Some horses, real heelers . . Beat our nags and won our money. 5 H. G. WELLS The specialist demagogue, sustained by his gang and his heelers, his spies and secret police. 6 *blue heeler*: see BLUE *a.*

heeler /ˈhiːlə/ *n.*[2] *colloq.* L19. [f. HEEL *v.*[1] + -ER[1].] A lurch (of a vessel) to one side; a vessel inclined to lurch.

heemraad /ˈhɪəmrɑːt, ˈheɪm-, -rɑːd/ *n.* Also **H-**, **-rad**. Pl. **-ra(a)den** /-rɑːd(ə)n/. L18. [Du., f. *heem* village, home + *raad* council.] *Hist.* A local court or council in South Africa and also formerly in the Netherlands. Also, a member of such a body.

heeze /hiːz/ *n. Sc.* & *north.* Also **heize**. E16. [f. the vb.] An act of hoisting or raising; a lift.

Also **heezy** /ˈhiːzi/ *n.* E18.

heeze /hiːz/ *v.t. Sc.* & *north.* Also **heize**. E16. [Var. of HOISE *v.*] Hoist, raise; push or pull *up*.

heffalump /ˈhɛfəlʌmp/ *n. nursery* & *joc.* E20. [Alt.] = ELEPHANT.

A. A. MILNE He and Piglet had fallen into a heffalump trap. *Guardian* Hannibal's heffalumps can hardly have had any such protection against the weather.

heft /hɛft/ *n.*[1] LME. [Prob. f. HEAVE *v.* on the analogy of *cleave/cleft*, *weave/weft*, etc.] I 1 Weight, heaviness. Now *dial.* & *N. Amer.* LME. 2 The bulk, mass, or main part. *N. Amer. colloq.* E19.

1 H. ROTH He was more on the lean side than supplied with heft. *Scientific American* Go ahead, pick it up. The heft tells you it's solid sterling silver. 2 J. PICKERING A part of the crop of corn was good, but the heft of it was bad.

II †3 A heave, a strain. *rare* (Shakes.). Only in E17. 4 The act of lifting; a lift, a push. *dial.* L19.

4 R. D. BLACKMORE The . . parson . . gave the stuck wheel such a powerful heft, that the whole cart rattled.

heft /hɛft/ *n.*[2] *Sc.* & *north.* Also **haft** /hɑːft/. M18. [Rel. to HEFT *v.*[1]] 1 A fixed place of residence. Now *rare* or *obs.* M18. 2 (The sheep in) a settled or accustomed pasturage. L18.

Heft /hɛft/ *n.*[3] Pl. ***Hefte*** /ˈhɛftə/. L19. [G.] A number of sheets of paper fastened together to form a book; *spec.* a part of a serial publication, a fascicle.

heft *n.*[4] see HAFT *n.*[1]

heft /hɛft/ *v.*[1] *Sc.* & *north.* Also **haft** /hɑːft/. L16. [Prob. of Scand. origin (cf. ON *hefða* gain possession by long occupation), infl. by HAFT *n.*[1], *v.*[1]] 1 *v.t.* Fix, establish, settle; now chiefly *spec.*, accustom (sheep, cattle) to a pasturage. L16. 2 *v.i.* Become established; (of sheep, cattle) become accustomed to a pasturage. E18.

heft /hɛft/ *v.*[2] M17. [f. HEFT *n.*[1]] 1 *v.t.* Lift, hoist up; pick up and carry. M17. 2 *v.t.* Lift or hold in order to feel the weight or balance of. E19. 3 *v.i.* Weigh, have weight. M19.

1 N. BAWDEN I develop . . lumbago from hefting my baggage at airports. P. CAREY He hefted the sledgehammer on to his shoulder. 2 R. MACDONALD I lifted one of the pistols and hefted it in my hand. It was so light and so well balanced. 3 C. M. YONGE I do believe it is [gold]. Brass never would heft so much.

heft *v.*[3] see HAFT *v.*[1]

Hefte *n.* pl. of HEFT *n.*[3]

hefty /ˈhɛfti/ *a. colloq.* M19. [f. HEFT *n.*[1] + -Y[1].] 1 Weighty, heavy; brawny, strong. Also *fig.*, great, considerable. M19. 2 Rough, violent. *US* & *dial.* L19. 3 Easy to lift or handle. *rare.* L19.

1 P. H. GIBBS A . . hefty man who . . might have been a professional pugilist. A. MACLEAN A hefty tot of rum all round. *TV Times* One of these entitles you to some hefty reductions on the trains.

heftily *adv.* L20. **heftiness** *n.* E20.

hegberry *n.* var. of HAGBERRY.

Hegelian /heɪˈgiːlɪən, hɪ-, -ˈgeɪl-/ *a.* & *n.* M19. [f. *Hegel* (see below) + -IAN.] A *adj.* Of or pertaining to Georg Hegel, German philosopher (1770–1831), or his philosophy of objective idealism. M19. B *n.* A person who believes in or advocates Hegel's philosophy. M19.

Hegelianism *n.* the philosophical system of Hegel M19. **Hegelianize** *v.t.* make hegelian L19. **Hegelism** /ˈheɪg(ə)lɪz(ə)m/ *n.* Hegelianism M19.

hegemon /ˈhɛgɪmɒn, ˈhiː-, -dʒɪ-/ *n.* E20. [Gk *hēgemōn* leader, f. *hēgeisthai* to lead.] A leading or paramount power; a dominant state or person.

Public Opinion Japan . . asserting her ambition to become hegemon of a Far East on which white influence shall be reduced. *Observer* Peace talks crucial to Peking's plans to contain the 'hegemons' in the Kremlin almost stalled.

hegemonic /hɛdʒɪˈmɒnɪk, hɛgɪ-/ *a.* & *n.* M17. [Gk *hēgemonikos* capable of command, f. *hēgemōn*: see prec., -IC.] A *adj.* Ruling, supreme, dominant. M17. B *n.* The supreme part; the master principle. L17.

Also **hegemonical** *a.* = HEGEMONIC *a.* E17.

hegemony /hɪˈdʒɛməni, -ˈgɛ-/ *n.* M16. [Gk *hēgemonia*, f. *hēgemōn*: see HEGEMON, -MONY.] 1 Leadership or predominance, esp. by one member of a confederacy or union (orig. of the States of ancient Greece); a State etc. having this. M16. 2 Dominance or undue influence exercised by a country (*spec.* the former USSR) over its weaker neighbour(s). L20.

1 H. H. ASQUITH Attempting . . to secure for the Papal State the political hegemony of Italy. A. BRIGGS A new working-class hegemony, . . an attempt to build a paradise for the poor. 2 *Daily Telegraph* In Third World terms 'hegemony' has come generally to mean Soviet domination.

hegemonist *n.* an advocate of a particular form of hegemony L19.

hegira /ˈhɛdʒɪrə/ *n.* Also **H-**, **-jira**, **hijra** /ˈhɪdʒrə/. L16. [med.L f. Arab. *hijra* departure from one's home and friends, f. *hajara* separate, emigrate.] 1 The emigration of Muhammad from Mecca to Medina in 622; the Muslim era reckoned from this. L16. 2 Any exodus or departure. M18.

hegumen /hɪˈgjuːmən/ *n.* Also **-nos** /-nɒs/. M17. [(Late L *hegumenus* f.) Gk *hēgoumenos*, use as n. of pres. pple of *hēgeisthai* lead, command.] In the Greek Orthodox Church, the head of a religious house, corresponding to an abbot or prior; the leader of any religious community.

heh /heɪ/ *int.* LME. [Natural exclam. Cf. HE *int.*, HEIGH.] Expr. emotion, inquiry, or surprise.

he he /hiː ˈhiː/ *int.* & *v.* As vb also **he-he**. [OE: see HE *int.*] A *int.* Repr. laughter, usu. affected or derisive. Also **he he he** etc. OE. B *v.i.* Laugh aloud (affectedly or derisively). M19.

†hei *int.* & *n.* see HEIGH.

Heian /ˈheɪən/ *a.* L19. [Jap., f. *Heian-kyō* (now Kyoto), former capital of Japan.] Of, pertaining to, or designating a period in Japanese history from the late 8th to the late 12th cent.

heiau /ˈheɪaʊ/ *n.* E19. [Haw.] An ancient pagan temple (in Hawaii).

Heidelberg /ˈhʌɪd(ə)lbəːg/ *n.* E20. [A city in SW Germany.] Used *attrib.* to designate a prehistoric jaw found at Mauer near Heidelberg in 1907, or the type of prehistoric man (*Homo heidelbergensis*) indicated by this jaw.

heifer /ˈhɛfə/ *n.* [OE *heahfore*, *heafru*, *-fre*, of unkn. origin.] 1 A young cow that has had no more than one calf; a female calf. OE. 2a A wife. Now *rare* or *obs.* E17. b A woman, a girl. *slang. derog.* M19.

heigh /heɪ/ *int.* & *n.* Also (earlier) **†hei**. ME. [Natural exclam. Cf. HE *int.*, HEH, HEY *int.* & *n.*[2]] A *int.* Expr. encouragement or inquiry. Formerly also, expr. challenge, anger, derision, or concern. ME.

J. WESLEY Now, heigh for the Romans!

B *n.* An exclamation of *heigh!* L16.

heigh-ho /heɪˈhəʊ/ *int.*, *n.*, & *v.* Also (earlier) **hey-**. LME. [f. HEIGH, HEY *ints.* + HO *int.*[1]] **A** *int.* Expr. boredom, weariness, disappointment, etc. Also (orig.), a meaningless refrain. LME.

D. CUSACK Heigho, it's a damn silly world. *Sunday Express* Two more butlers welcomed us aboard.. Heigh ho.

B *n.* An utterance of 'heigh-ho!'; a loud or audible sigh. L16.

C *v.i.* Utter 'heigh-ho!'; sigh audibly. E19.

height /hʌɪt/ *n.* Also †**-th**. [OE *hēhþu*, (WS) *hīehþu* = MDu. *hogede, hoochte* (Du. *hoogte*), OHG *hōhida*, Goth. *hauhiþa* f. Gmc. Cf. HIGH *a.*, -TH[1], -T[2].] **I 1** The highest part *of* anything; the top, summit. Now *rare*. OE. **2** The highest point of something immaterial; the extremity, summit, zenith. OE. **3** The heavens. *obs.* exc. *Sc.* OE. **4** A piece of high or rising ground; an eminence. LME. **5** A high point or position. M16.

2 D. BAGLEY The hurricane reached its height at eleven in the morning. M. SEYMOUR-SMITH He was now at the height of his fame. E. P. THOMPSON The price of wheat reached impossible heights. 4 M. MILNER The grey cliff bordering the valley.. that slopes down from the city's heights. 5 F. WELDON Mr. Allbright added golden syrup from a height, for the delight of seeing it fall.

II 6 Distance or measurement from the base to the top; altitude; stature (of a person); the elevation of an object above the ground or a recognized level, esp. sea level. ME. **b** *Astron.* Angular distance above the horizon; = ALTITUDE I. Long *rare*. LME. **c** *Typogr.* The distance from the foot of a piece of type to its face. Also *height to paper*. L17. **7** Great or considerable altitude or elevation. Now *rare*. ME. †**8** Exalted rank or estate. ME–E18. **9** Haughtiness, pride. Also, loftiness of mind, magnanimity. *arch.* ME. †**10** The diameter of a bullet; the bore of a gun. L16–L17. †**11 a** *Geogr.* = LATITUDE. L16–L17. **b** More *gen.*, position at sea alongside of or *off* some place. E17–M18. **12** High degree of any quality. *arch.* E17. **13** *Her.* Each of the rows of feathers into which a plume of more than one row of feathers is arranged. M19.

6 A. PATON The maize hardly reaches the height of a man. *fig.*: MILTON To attaine The highth and depth of thy Eternal wayes. 9 O. CROMWELL A very resolute answer, and full of height. 12 T. STANLEY Heighth of ambition causeth many men to go astray.

Phrases: **at its height** at its highest degree. *head for heights*: see HEAD *n.* **height of land** *N. Amer.* a watershed, a ridge of high land dividing two river basins. *height to paper*: see sense 6c above. †**in height** (*rare*, Shakes.) = *at its height* above. †**in the height** (*rare*, Shakes.) in the highest degree. †**on height** (*a*) on high, aloft; (*b*) aloud. **the height of** the utmost degree of (fashion, folly, luxury, etc.). **to the height** (*obs.* exc. *literary*) to the highest or utmost degree. †**upon height** = *on height* above. VIRTUAL *height*. *x-height*: see X, X I.

height /hʌɪt/ *v.t.* Now *rare* exc. *Sc.* LME. [f. the n.] **1** Raise in amount, degree, quality, etc.; increase, augment; elevate, exalt. LME. **2** Make high, heighten; raise aloft or on high. L15.

heighten /ˈhʌɪt(ə)n/ *v.* LME. [f. HEIGHT *n.* or *v.* + -EN[5].] †**1** *v.t.* Exalt; elate, excite; beautify. LME–L17. **2** *v.t.* Make high or higher; give or add height to; *fig.* increase or augment in amount or degree. E16. **b** *spec.* Make (a colour) more luminous or more intense. L16. **c** Strengthen or augment the details of (a description, a story). M18. **3** *v.i.* Become high or higher; increase in height. Now chiefly *fig.* increase in amount or intensity. M16.

2 E. A. FREEMAN That church.. had been simply repaired and heightened. M. M. KAYE The severity of the headgear only served to heighten the beauty of her features. D. WIGODER The atmosphere of suspicion.. was heightened by the theft. b J. GALSWORTHY His pleasant colour was heightened by exercise. J. BARNES A pen-and-ink drawing.. in sepia, heightened with white. 3 E. B. PUSEY Obadiah's description heightens as it goes on.

heightened *ppl a.* (*a*) raised, intensified, increased; (*b*) *spec.* (in *Her.*) having another charge placed higher in the field: M17. **heightener** *n.* M17. **heightening** *n.* (*a*) the action of the vb; (*b*) a colouring which highlights or intensifies another colour: L16.

†**heighth** *n.* var. of HEIGHT *n.*

heil /hʌɪl/ *int.*, *n.*, & *v.* E20. [G, lit. 'well-being'.] **A** *int.* Used as an exclamation of greeting, salutation, or acclamation, esp. during or w. ref. to the Nazi regime in Germany. E20.

heil Hitler! used by the Germans or their supporters during the Nazi regime as a greeting or an acclamation of the supremacy of Hitler.

B *n.* An exclamation of 'heil!' M20.

C *v.* **1** *v.i.* Make a Nazi salute. M20. **2** *v.t.* Greet or hail esp. with a Nazi salute. M20.

Heilsgeschichte /ˈhaɪlsgəʃɪçtə/ *n.* M20. [G.] *Theol.* Sacred history; *spec.* the history of the salvation of humankind by God; history seen as the working out of this salvation.

heimin /ˈheɪmɪn/ *n.* L19. [Jap., f. *hei* level, ordinary, common + *min* people.] In Japanese feudal society, the common people, including peasants and traders, as opp. to the court aristocracy and samurai.

heimisch /ˈheɪmɪʃ/ *a.* M20. [Yiddish *heymish* domestic, homelike.] In Jewish speech: homely, unpretentious.

Heimweh /ˈhaɪmveː/ *n.* E18. [G.] Homesickness.

Heimwehr /ˈhaɪmveːr/ *n.* M20. [G, f. *Heim* home + *Wehr* defence.] *Hist.* The German or Austrian Home Defence Force which existed between 1919 and 1938.

Heinie /ˈhʌɪni/ *n.* *N. Amer. slang.* Also **Hiney**. E20. [f. the German male name *Heinrich*.] A German, a German soldier.

heinous /ˈheɪnəs, ˈhiːnəs/ *a.* LME. [OFr. *haïneus* (mod. *haineux*), f. *haïne* (mod. *haine*) f. (O)Fr. *haïr* f. Frank., rel. to HATE *v.*: see -OUS.] **1** Of a crime, an offence, or its perpetrator: highly criminal or wicked, utterly odious or atrocious. LME. **b** *transf.* Of an accusation or charge: relating to a highly wicked person or deed. LME. †**2** Of words, feelings, etc.: full of hate, expressing hatred. LME–L16. †**3** Grievous, grave, severe. M16–L17.

1 R. JEBB Heinous offenders, whose crimes afford proof of an incorrigibly bad disposition. E. HUXLEY To refuse a stranger.. food and shelter is a heinous crime.

heinously *adv.* LME. **heinousness** *n.* M16.

heir /ɛː/ *n.* ME. [OFr. *eir*, *heir* (later *hoir*) f. arch. and late L *herem* for reg. *heredem*, accus. of *heres* heir.] **1** A person receiving or entitled by law to receive property or rank as the successor or legal representative of the former owner. ME. **2** *transf.* & *fig.* A person possessing or entitled to possess any gift or quality, orig. in succession to another. Now usu., a person to whom something, as joy, punishment, etc., is morally due. ME. †**3** *fig.* An offspring, product. LME–L16.

1 J. BERGER On 2 June 1914 Francis Ferdinand, heir to the Hapsburg throne, was shot dead. R. DAVIES He never married & leaves no direct heirs. 2 J. GILBERT The first born of the human race became the heir of failure.

Phrases & comb.: *expectant heir*: see EXPECTANT *a.* *heir apparent*: see APPARENT *a.* 2. **heir-at-law** a person who succeeds by right of blood; *esp.* (in English Law bef. 1926 and Scots Law bef. 1965) a person who succeeds in this way to an intestate's real property. **heir designate** a person who has been designated another's heir. **heir female** an heiress or an heir (male or female) whose rights are derived completely through the female line. **heir-general** an heir-at-law, *spec.* one who can be an heir female as distinct from exclusively an heir male. **heir in tail** a person who succeeds to an entailed estate by virtue of the deed of entail. **heir male** a male heir whose rights are derived completely through the male line. **heir of one's, the, body** an heir who is a direct descendant. *heir-portioner*: see PORTIONER I. *heir presumptive*: see PRESUMPTIVE I.

heirdom *n.* succession by right of blood; the state or dignity of an heir; an inheritance: L16. **heirless** *a.* without an heir LME. **heirship** *n.* the state, condition, or rights of an heir; right of inheritance: LME.

heir /ɛː/ *v.t.* ME. [f. the n.] Inherit; be or make heir to; acquire by inheritance or succession.

heiress /ˈɛːrɪs, ɛːˈrɛs/ *n.* M17. [f. HEIR *n.* + -ESS[1].] A female heir.

B. T. BRADFORD Paula, Daisy's daughter, was.. heiress to her enormous retailing empire.

heiress-ship *n.* the state or position of an heiress M19.

heirloom /ˈɛːluːm/ *n.* LME. [f. HEIR *n.* + LOOM *n.*[1]] A chattel which under a will or by custom is inherited by an heir in the same way as real estate. Also, any piece of personal property or any quality, name, etc., which has been in a family for generations.

R. B. SHERIDAN Learning that had run in the family like an heirloom! H. I. JENKINSON A glass cup.. a precious heirloom, and a harbinger of the family's fortunes.

heirmos *n.* var. of HIRMOS.

Heisenberg /ˈhʌɪz(ə)nbəːg/ *n.* M20. [Werner *Heisenberg* (1901–76), Ger. physicist.] Physics. *Heisenberg('s)* (*uncertainty* etc.) *principle*, = UNCERTAINTY *principle*.

heist /hʌɪst/ *v.* & *n.* *slang.* Chiefly *N. Amer.* M19. [Repr. US local pronunc. of HOIST *v.*[1] or *n.* Cf. HIST *v.*[2]] **A** *v.t.* Rob, hold up; steal. M19.

B *n.* A hold-up, a robbery. M20.

Superman We pulled off a heist in Smallville and got away with it!

heister *n.* a robber, a thief, a hijacker E20.

heit *n.* var. of HAIT.

hei-tiki /heɪˈtɪki/ *n.* *NZ.* M19. [Maori, f. *hei* hang + TIKI.] A greenstone human-shaped neck-ornament worn by Maoris.

heize *n.*, *v.* vars. of HEEZE *n.*, *v.*

hejira *n.* var. of HEGIRA.

hekistotherm /hɪˈkɪstəθəːm/ *n.* L19. [Fr. *hékistotherme*, f. Gk *hēkisto-s* least + *thermē* heat.] *Bot.* A plant capable of growing at very low temperatures, such as the Arctic and Antarctic mosses and lichens.

hekte /ˈhɛkti/ *n.* Pl. **-tae** /-tiː/. L19. [Gk *hektē* the sixth (of a stater), fem. of *hektos* sixth.] A Greek silver coin.

HeLa /ˈhiːlə/ *n.* M20. [f. *He*nrietta *La*cks, patient from whom the orig. tissue was taken.] *Med.* In full *HeLa strain*. A strain of human epithelial cells maintained in tissue culture and derived orig. from cervical carcinoma tissue.

hélas /elɑːs/ *int.* LME. [Fr., later form of *ha las*, *a las* ALAS.] Expressing grief, sadness, regret, etc.

¶Formerly naturalized, but now only in representations or affectations of French.

held /hɛld/ *ppl a.* L16. [pa. pple of HOLD *v.*] That is or has been held; (of breath) kept in; (of a note) sustained.

held *v.* pa. t. & pple of HOLD *v.*

Heldentenor /ˌhɛldənteˈnoːr/ *n.* Pl. ***-tenöre*** /-teˈnøːrə/. E20. [G = hero tenor.] A singer with a powerful tenor voice suited to heroic roles, esp. in Wagnerian opera.

†**hele** *n.* var. of HEAL *n.*

hele /hiːl/ *v.* Also **heal**, (now usual in sense 2(a)) **heel**. [OE *helian* = OS *bihellian*, OHG *bihellen*, f. WGmc causative vb f. Gmc base meaning 'conceal', rel. to L *celare*, Gk *kaluptein*.] **1** Conceal, hide; keep secret. *obs.* exc. *Sc.* OE. **2** Cover over or in; *spec.* (*a*) (esp. foll. by *in*) cover (roots, seeds, etc.) with earth; (*b*) cover with slates or tiles, roof. ME.

heling *n.* (*a*) the action of the vb; (*b*) a covering; *esp.* (the materials of) a roof: ME.

helenium /hɛˈliːnɪəm/ *n.* LME. [mod.L (see below), f. Gk *helenion*, perh. commemorating Helen of Troy.] †**1** The herb elecampane, *Inula helenium*. LME–E17. **2** Any of various N. American plants of the genus *Helenium*, of the composite family, freq. grown for their yellow- or orange-rayed flowers. L18.

heli- /ˈhɛli/ *comb. form* of HELI(COPTER *n.*

heliborne *a.* carried by helicopter M20. **helibus** *n.* a helicopter with room for a large number of passengers M20. **helipad** *n.* a landing pad for helicopters M20. **heliport** *n.* an airport or landing-place for helicopters M20.

heliac /ˈhiːlɪak/ *a.* L18. [Late L *heliacus* f. Gk *hēliakos*, f. *hēlios* sun: see -AC.] = next.

heliacal /hɪˈlʌɪək(ə)l/ *a.* M16. [f. med.L *heliacus* (f. Gk *hēliakos*, f. *hēlios* sun) + -AL[1].] Relating to the sun. Chiefly, in ancient astronomy: *heliacal rising*, the first rising of a star after a period of invisibility due to conjunction with the sun (in a given year); *heliacal setting*, the last setting of a star before a period of invisibility due to conjunction with the sun.

heliacally *adv.* M16.

helianthemum /hiːlɪ'anθɪməm/ *n.* E19. [mod.L (see below), f. Gk *hēlios* sun + *anthemon* flower.] Any of various chiefly Mediterranean shrubs and herbs constituting the genus *Helianthemum* (family Cistaceae), which includes the common rock rose, *H. nummularium.*

helianthus /hiːlɪ'anθəs/ *n.* L18. [mod.L, f. Gk *hēlios* sun + *anthos* flower.] Any of various plants constituting the genus *Helianthus,* of the composite family, which includes the common sunflower, *H. annuus.*

helical /'hɛlɪk(ə)l, 'hiː-/ *a.* L16. [f. L HELIX + -AL[1].] Having the form of a helix; spirally coiled.

helically *adv.* M17.

helices *n.pl.* see HELIX.

helichrysum /hɛlɪ'krʌɪsəm/ *n.* Also (now only *Art* etc.) **-son** /-sɒn/, **-sos** /-sɒs/. M16. [L (see below), also *helichrysos,* f. Gk *helikhrusos,* f. HELIX + *khrusos* gold.] 1 A yellow-flowered Mediterranean plant known to the ancient Greeks, perhaps the helichrysum (sense 2) *Helichrysum stoechas.* M16. 2 Any of various plants with persistent flower-heads (everlastings) constituting the genus *Helichrysum,* of the composite family, and found esp. in Australia and southern Africa. M17.

helicity /hiː'lɪsɪti/ *n.* M20. [f. L *helic-* HELIX + -ITY.] 1 *Physics.* The projection of the spin angular momentum of a subatomic particle on the direction of its linear momentum. M20. 2 Chiefly *Biochem.* Helical character. M20.

helicograph /'hɛlɪkə(ʊ)grɑːf/ *n.* M19. [f. L *helic-* HELIX + -O- + -GRAPH.] An instrument for drawing spirals.

helicoid /'hɛlɪkɔɪd, 'hiː-/ *n.* & *a.* L17. [Gk. *helikoeidēs,* f. HELIX: see -OID.] A *n.* 1 An object of spiral shape. *rare.* L17. 2 *Geom.* A surface generated by moving a straight line in the direction of an axis about which it simultaneously rotates. M19.

B *adj.* Esp. of a shell, inflorescence, etc.: having the form of a helix; spirally coiled. E18.

†**helicoid parabola** = *parabolic spiral* s.v. PARABOLIC *a.* 2.

heli'coidal *a.* = HELICOID *a.* M19. **heli'coidally** *adv.* M20.

Helicon /'hɛlɪk(ə)n/ *n.* L15. [L f. Gk *Helikōn* a mountain in Boeotia, Greece, formerly sacred to the Muses, often confused by 16th- and 17th-cent. writers with the springs of Aganippe and Hippocrene which rose in it. In sense 2 assoc. w. HELIX.] 1 A source, region, etc. of poetic inspiration. L15. 2 (**h-**.) A large kind of bass tuba made in spiral form. L19.

1 *Bookman* Any question of his precise place in England's Helicon.

Heliconian /-'kəʊnɪən/ *a.* of Helicon or the Muses M16.

helicopter /'hɛlɪkɒptə/ *n.* & *v.* L19. [Fr. *hélicoptère,* f. Gk HELIX + *pteron* wing.] A *n.* An aircraft deriving both lift and propulsive power from horizontally revolving, usu. engine-driven, blades or rotors and capable of ascending and descending vertically. L19. B *v.t.* & *i.* Transport or fly by helicopter. E20.

helictite /hɛ'lɪktʌɪt/ *n.* L19. [f. Gk *heliktos* twisted, after *stalactite.*] A distorted form of stalactite resembling a twig.

Heligoland trap /'hɛlɪgə(ʊ)land trap/ *n. phr.* M20. [*Heligoland,* an island in the North Sea off the NW German coast, site of the earliest bird observatory.] A long funnel-shaped enclosure of wire netting into which birds are driven for ringing.

helio /'hiːlɪəʊ/ *n.*[1] & *v. colloq.* L19. [Abbrev.] A *n.* Pl. **-os.** = HELIOGRAPH *n.* 4, 4b. L19. B *v.t.* = HELIOGRAPH *v.* I. L19.

helio /'hiːlɪəʊ/ *n.*[2] & *a. colloq.* L19. [Abbrev.] (Of) the colour heliotrope.

helio- /'hiːlɪəʊ/ *comb. form* of Gk *hēlios* sun: see -O-.

heliocentric /ˌhiːlɪə(ʊ)'sɛntrɪk/ *n.* & *a.* M17. [f. prec. + -CENTRIC.] †A *n.* A person who believes that the sun is the centre of the universe. Only in M17. B *adj.* 1 Considered as viewed from the centre of the sun; referred to the sun as centre. L17. 2 Having or representing the sun as the centre. Freq. opp. *geocentric.* M19.

1 **heliocentric latitude, longitude**: at which a planet etc. would appear if observed from the position of an observer at the sun's centre.

heliocentrically *adv.* as viewed from the centre of the sun E18. **heliocentricism** *n.* a heliocentric theory of the universe M19.

heliodon /'hiːlɪədɒn/ *n.* E20. [f. HELIO- + Gk *hodos* way, path.] A mechanical apparatus for demonstrating the apparent motion of the sun.

heliodor /'hiːlɪədɔː/ *n.* Also **-dore.** E20. [G, f. HELIO- + Gk *dōron* gift.] A golden-yellow variety of beryl found in Namibia.

Heliogabalus /ˌhiːlɪə'gab(ə)ləs/ *n.* L16. [Alt. of *Elagabalus* (f. *Elah-Gabal* Syrian deity), the name assumed by Varius Avitus Bassianus, Roman Emperor 218–222, with assim. to HELIO-.] A person resembling the emperor Elagabalus (Heliogabalus) in dissoluteness or moral depravity.

Heliogabalian /-gə'beɪlɪən/ *a.* pertaining to or characteristic of Heliogabalus; highly dissolute: M19.

heliogram /'hiːlɪə(ʊ)gram/ *n.* L19. [f. HELIO- + -GRAM.] A message signalled by heliograph (HELIOGRAPH *n.* 4).

heliograph /'hiːlɪə(ʊ)grɑːf/ *n.* & *v.* M19. [f. HELIO- + -GRAPH.] A *n.* 1 A photograph or engraving made by heliography (sense 2). *obs.* exc. *Hist.* M19. 2 A photographic telescope for photographing the sun. M19. 3 An instrument for measuring the intensity of sunlight. M19. 4 An apparatus for signalling by means of a movable mirror which reflects flashes of sunshine. L19. b A message sent by heliograph. L19. B *v.* 1 *v.i.* & *t.* Signal by means of a heliograph. L19. 2 *v.t.* Photograph by heliography. *obs.* exc. *Hist.* L19.

heli'ographer *n.* L19.

heliography /hiːlɪ'ɒgrəfi/ *n.* M18. [f. HELIO- + -GRAPHY.] 1 (A) description of the sun. M18. 2 An early photographic process using iodine-sensitized silver plate and an asphalt or bitumen varnish. *obs.* exc. *Hist.* M19. 3 Signalling by means of a heliograph (HELIOGRAPH *n.* 4). L19.

helio'graphic *a.* pertaining to heliography; *heliographic latitude (longitude),* the latitude (longitude) of points on the sun's surface, referred to the sun's equator and a meridian passing through the node of this with the ecliptic: E18. **helio'graphically** *adv.* by means of heliography L19.

†**heliogravure** *n.* Only in L19. [Fr. *héliogravure,* f. as HELIO- + *gravure* engraving.] = PHOTOGRAVURE.

heliolithic /ˌhiːlɪə'lɪθɪk/ *a. obs.* exc. *Hist.* E20. [f. HELIO- after *eolithic* etc.] Of a (supposed) civilization: marked by megaliths and sun-worship.

heliometer /hiːlɪ'ɒmɪtə/ *n.* M18. [f. HELIO- + -METER.] *Astron.* A refracting telescope with a split objective lens, used to measure angular distances between stars etc. (orig. to measure the sun's apparent diameter).

helio'metric(al) *adjs.* L19. **helio'metrically** *adv.* L19. **heliometry** *n.* L19.

helion /'hiːlɪɒn/ *n.* M20. [f. HELIUM + -ON.] *Nuclear Physics.* The nucleus of a helium atom: either (*a*) of the normal isotope ^{4}He, an alpha-particle, consisting of two protons and two neutrons, or (*b*) of the isotope ^{3}He, consisting of two protons and one neutron.

helioscope /'hiːlɪəskəʊp/ *n.* L17. [f. HELIO- + -SCOPE.] (A telescope fitted with) an apparatus for observing the sun without harm to the eyes, by means of smoked glass, reflectors, etc.

helio'scopic *a.* L19.

heliostat /'hiːlɪəstat/ *n.* M18. [mod.L *heliostata* or Fr. *héliostat,* f. HELIO- + Gk *statos* standing.] An apparatus containing a movable mirror, used to reflect the sun's light in a fixed direction.

heliotherapy /ˌhiːlɪə(ʊ)'θɛrəpi/ *n.* E20. [f. HELIO- + THERAPY.] The use of sun-baths as a therapeutic treatment.

heliotrope /'hiːlɪətrəʊp, 'hɛl-/ *n.* & *a.* Also (earlier) †**eliotropus** and other classical forms. OE. [L *heliotropium,* med.L also *eliotropus, -ius,* etc., f. Gk *hēliotropion,* f. *hēlios* sun + *-tropos* turning, *trepein* to turn.] A *n.* 1 Orig., any of several plants whose flowers turn towards the sun, e.g. the sunflower, the marigold. Now, any plant of the genus *Heliotropium,* of the borage family, with cymes of small blue, purple, or white flowers; esp. *H. arborescens,* a S. American shrub grown for its fragrant flowers. OE. b A scent imitating that of the heliotrope. M19. c A bluish-purple colour like that of the heliotrope. L19. 2 A green variety of chalcedony with veins of red jasper; bloodstone. LME. 3 An ancient kind of sundial, showing when the sun had reached the solstice. M17. 4 An apparatus with a telescope and a movable mirror for reflecting the sun's rays, used for signalling, esp. in geodesic operations. Cf. HELIOGRAPH *n.* 4. E19.

1 *winter heliotrope*: see WINTER *n.*

B *adj.* Of a heliotrope colour: see sense 1c above. L19.

heliotroper *n.* a person who operates a heliotrope (HELIOTROPE *n.* 4) M19.

heliotropic /ˌhiːlɪə(ʊ)'trəʊpɪk, -'trɒpɪk/ *a.* L19. [f. HELIOTROPISM + -IC.] *Bot.* Exhibiting heliotropism; growing towards the light.

heliotropically *adv.* L19.

heliotropin /ˌhiːlɪə'trəʊpɪn/ *n.* L19. [f. prec. + -IN[1].] = PIPERONAL.

heliotropism /ˌhiːlɪə(ʊ)'trəʊpɪz(ə)m/ *n.* M19. [f. HELIO- + Gk *-tropos* turning + -ISM.] *Bot.* The property of growing in a given direction in response to sunlight; *esp.* (in full *positive heliotropism*) growth towards the light. Also *negative heliotropism,* growth away from the light; *transverse heliotropism,* growth in a direction at right angles to the light.

heliotype /'hiːlɪətʌɪp/ *n.* L19. [f. HELIO- + -TYPE.] *Hist.* (A print made by) a variety of the collotype process.

heliozoan /ˌhiːlɪə'zəʊən/ *n.* & *a.* L19. [f. mod.L *Heliozoa* n.pl. (see below), f. Gk *hēlios* sun + *zōion* animal: see -AN.] A *n.* Any of the chiefly freshwater protozoans constituting the class Heliozoa, related to radiolarians and having spherical cells with long slender radial pseudopodia and often a siliceous test. L19. B *adj.* Of or pertaining to the class Heliozoa. L19.

helipterum /hɪ'lɪpt(ə)rəm/ *n.* M19. [mod.L (see below), f. Gk *hēlios* sun + *pteron* wing, w. ref. to the feathery pappus.] Any of various Australian and southern African shrubs and herbs constituting the genus *Helipterum,* of the composite family, grown as everlastings.

helium /'hiːlɪəm/ *n.* L19. [f. Gk *hēlios* sun + -IUM: the element was inferred to exist from an emission line in the sun's spectrum.] A colourless odourless gaseous chemical element, atomic no. 2, which is the lightest of the noble gases and is present in traces in the earth's atmosphere. (Symbol He.)

helix /'hiːlɪks/ *n.* Pl. **helices** /'hɛlɪsiːz, 'hiː-/, **helixes.** M16. [L *helix helicis* f. Gk *helix helikos.*] 1 Chiefly *Archit.* A spiral ornament, a volute; *spec.* each of the eight smaller volutes under the abacus of a Corinthian capital. M16. 2 An object of coiled form, either round an axis (like a corkscrew) or, less usually, in one plane (like a watchspring); *Geom.* a three-dimensional curve on a (notional) conical or cylindrical surface which becomes a straight line when the surface is unrolled into a plane. E17. 3 *Anat.* The curved fold which forms the rim of the exterior ear. Cf. ANTHELIX. L17. 4 *Zool.* Any spiral-shelled mollusc of the genus *Helix,* which includes the garden snail, *H aspersa.* E19.

2 *double helix*: see DOUBLE *a.* & *adv.*

hell /hɛl/ *n.* [OE *hel(l)* = OFris. *helle,* OS *hell(j)a* (Du. *hel*), OHG *hella* (G *Hölle*), ON *hel,* Goth. *halja* f. Gmc base meaning 'cover, conceal': see HELE *v.*] 1 The abode of the dead; the place of departed spirits; the infernal regions regarded as a place of existence after death, the kingdom of Hades. OE. 2 The infernal regions regarded as a place of torment or punishment;

the abode of devils and condemned spirits. Freq. in exclamatory or imprecatory phrs. expr. anger, annoyance, incredulity, dismay, etc., or merely emphatic (cf. HECK *n.*[2]). OE. **b** As *int.* Expr. anger, annoyance, dismay, etc. L20. **3a** The infernal regions regarded as a living being. Chiefly *poet.* OE. **b** The kingdom or power of hell; *collect.* the inhabitants, wicked spirits, or powers of hell. ME. **c** A devilish assembly. Long *rare.* L16. †**4** A part of a building etc. compared to hell because of its darkness, discomfort, etc.; a place of confinement or punishment. ME. **5** A place or state of wickedness, suffering, or misery; a place of turmoil and discord. LME. **6** The den or base to which captives are carried in the games barley-break and prisoners' base. M16. **7** A place in a tailor's shop into which shreds or offcuts of material are thrown; a similar place or receptacle used for the disposal of waste material in other trades. L16. **8** A gaming-house; a gambling-booth. L18.

Phrases: **a hell of a —** *colloq.* an infernal or an exceedingly bad, great, etc., —. **all hell let loose** utter pandemonium. **as hell** very, exceedingly. **beat, knock,** etc., **hell out of** thrash, pound heavily; *fig.* achieve supremacy over. **for the hell of it** for amusement, for fun. **get hell** be severely reprimanded. **get the, to, hell out (of)** make a hasty retreat (from). **give (a person) hell** make him or her uncomfortable, give him or her a difficult time. **go to hell** (chiefly *int.*) go away, make off. **hell and, or, high water** any great obstacle or problem. **hell and Tommy** = *merry hell* below. **hell for leather** at breakneck speed. **hell on wheels** a terrible person or thing, *esp.* one of great speed or ferocity. **hell to pay** great trouble, discord, pandemonium, esp. as a result of previous action. *knock hell out of*: see *beat hell out of* above. *like a bat out of hell*: see BAT *n.*[3] **like hell** very much, exceedingly; recklessly, desperately; *iron.* not at all, on the contrary. **merry hell** a disturbance, an upheaval; great trouble, great pain. **not a chance, hope,** etc., **in hell** no likelihood, no possibility. *not a snowball's chance in hell*: see SNOWBALL *n.* 1. **play (merry) hell (with)** upset, confuse; cause trouble (for); make a fuss. **raise hell** cause trouble, create chaos. **the hell of a —** = *a hell of a —* above. **the hell you say**: expr. surprise or disbelief. **till, until, hell freezes (over)** until some date in the impossibly distant future; forever. **to hell and gone** a great distance; endlessly, for ever. **to hell with it** or **you** away to perdition; go away. *until hell freezes (over)*: see *till hell freezes (over)* above. **what, who,** etc., **in, the, hell?** (*a*) as an intensive: expr. incredulity, amazement, annoyance, etc., cf. *who* etc. *on earth* s.v. EARTH *n.*[1]; (*b*) also simply *what the hell*, expr. dismissal of a difficulty etc. **when hell freezes (over)** at some date in the impossibly distant future; never. *who in, the, hell*: see *what in, the, hell* above.

Comb.: **hellbender** a large, grotesque N. American salamander, *Cryptobranchus alleganiensis*; **hell-bent** *a.* recklessly determined *for* or *on*; **hell-born** *a.* born of hell, of infernal origin; **hell-box** *Printing* a box for holding damaged or discarded type; **hell-bred** *a.* bred or engendered in hell; **hell-broth** *rare* a broth of infernal character or for an infernal purpose; **hell-cat** a spiteful or furious (esp. female) person; **hell-diver** *US* the pied-billed grebe, *Podilymbus podiceps*; **helldog** = HELL-HOUND; **hell-driver** *slang* a person who drives a vehicle in a fast or daredevil manner; **hell-gate(s)** the portal or entrance of hell; **hell-hag** a diabolical or vile woman; **hell-hole** an oppressive place; **hell-kite** *rare* a kite of hell; a person of hellish cruelty; **hell-raiser** a person who causes trouble or creates chaos; *hell's angel*: see ANGEL *n.* 2b; **hell's bells** an excl. of anger, annoyance, etc.; **hell's delight** pandemonium; **hell-ship**: with a reputation for cruelty and tyranny among the crew; *hell's kitchen*: see KITCHEN *n.*; **hellweed** (*obs.* exc. *dial.*) dodder.

hellful *n.* as many as hell can hold M17. **hell-like** *a.* M16.

hell /hɛl/ *v.* Now chiefly *slang.* E17. [f. the n.] †**1** *v.t.* Place in or as in hell; condemn to suffer. E-M17. **2** *v.i.* Hurry, rush; *spec.* rush *around* or conduct oneself in an irresponsible or high-spirited way. L19. **3** *v.t.* Make or turn into chaos or an inferno. E20. **4** *v.t.* Cause trouble for, annoy. E20.

hellacious /hɛˈleɪʃəs/ *a.* & *adv. US slang.* M20. [f. HELL *n.* + *-acious* perh. after BODACIOUS.] Terrific(ally), tremendous(ly), enormous(ly).

Helladic /hɛˈladɪk/ *a.* & *n.* E19. [Gk *Helladikos*, f. *Hellas, Hellad-* Greece: see -IC.] **A** *adj.* **1** Pertaining or relating to Greece or to Greek culture. E19. **2** *Archaeol.* Designating or pertaining to the Bronze Age cultures of Greece, lasting from *c*2800–*c*1200 BC. E20. **B** *n. Archaeol.* The (period of) Bronze Age culture in Greece. E20.

hellebore /ˈhɛlɪbɔː/ *n.* Also in L form **-rum** /-rəm/, **-rus** /-rəs/. OE. [(OFr. *ellebre, elebore* f.) med.L *eleborus*, L (*h*)*elleborus* f. Gk *helleboros*: refash. in 16 after prevailing Gk form.] Orig., (the root of) either of two poisonous and purgative plants reputed in classical times to cure insanity, *Helleborus orientalis* and related species (more fully *black hellebore*) and *Veratrum album* (more fully *white hellebore*; cf. *false hellebore* below). Now, any of various early-flowering plants constituting the Eurasian genus *Helleborus*, of the buttercup family, with palmately divided leaves and petaloid sepals; esp. *H. viridis* (in full *green hellebore*) and *H. foetidus* (in full *stinking hellebore*), both green-flowered plants of calcareous woodland.

false hellebore any of various plants of the genus *Veratrum* of the lily family (see VERATRUM).

helleborism *n.* [Gk *helleborismos*] the treatment of insanity etc. by means of hellebore (*Hist.*); the (excessive) ingestion of hellebore: E17.

helleborine /ˈhɛlɪbəriːn, -rʌɪn/ *n.* L16. [Fr., or L (*h*)*elleborine* f. Gk *helleborinē* a plant like hellebore: see -INE[1].] Any of various mainly woodland orchids of the genus *Epipactis*, chiefly with greenish sometimes self-fertilized flowers, and of the related genus *Cephalanthera*, with larger white or pink flowers.

Hellene /ˈhɛliːn/ *n.* M17. [Gk *Hellēn* a Greek.] A Greek: an ancient Greek of genuine Grecian descent; a subject of the modern nation of Greece.

Hellenian /hɛˈlɛnɪən, hɛˈliː-/ *n.* & *a. rare.* E17. [Gk *Hellēnios*, f. as HELLENIC: see -IAN.] **A** *n.* A member of an ancient Thessalian tribe, an ancient Hellene. E17. **B** *adj.* = HELLENIC *a.* E19.

Hellenic /hɛˈlɛnɪk, hɛˈliː-/ *a.* & *n.* M17. [Gk *Hellēnikos*, f. *Hellēn* HELLENE: see -IC.] **A** *adj.* Of or pertaining to the Hellenes or the Greeks; native to or originating in Greece; characteristic of or attributed to Greece or to the Hellenes. M17. **B** *n.* **1** The Greek language. M19. **2** In *pl.* Writings on Greece or things Greek. M19.

Hellenicize *v.t.* make Greek, Graecize M19.

Hellenise *v.* var. of HELLENIZE.

Hellenism /ˈhɛlɪnɪz(ə)m/ *n.* E17. [Gk *Hellēnismos*, f. *Hellēnizein* Hellenize: see -ISM.] **1** A particular feature of the Greek language; a Greek phrase, idiom, or construction, esp. one as used in some other language; a Graecism. E17. **2** Conformity to Hellenic speech and ideas; imitation or adoption of Greek characteristics, esp. by the Jews of the Diaspora or the later Romans. M19. **3** Greek character or nature; Grecian culture. M19. **4** Greek nationality; the Hellenic race or world as a political entity. L19.

1 I. D'ISRAELI When Greek was first studied .. it planted many a hellenism in our language.

Hellenist /ˈhɛlɪnɪst/ *n.* E17. [Gk *Hellēnistēs*, f. *Hellēnizein*: see prec., -IST.] **1** A person who uses the Greek language, but is not a Greek; *esp.* a Greek-speaking Jew of the Diaspora. E17. **2** A person skilled in Greek language or literature; a Greek scholar. L17.

Hellenistic /hɛlɪˈnɪstɪk/ *a.* E18. [f. prec. + -IC.] Of or pertaining to the Hellenists: using the Greek language or following Greek modes of thought or life; *spec.* of, pertaining to, or designating the period of Greek history and language from the death of Alexander the Great (323 BC) to the defeat of Antony and Cleopatra (31 BC).

Helleˈnistical *a.* M17. **Helleˈnistically** *adv.* M17.

Hellenize /ˈhɛlɪnʌɪz/ *v.* Also **-ise**. E17. [Gk *Hellēnizein* speak Greek, make Greek, f. *Hellēn* HELLENE: see -IZE.] **1** *v.i.* Use the Greek language; adopt Greek habits; live as or become a Hellenist. E17. **2** *v.t.* Make Greek or Hellenistic in form or character. L18.

Helleniˈzation *n.* L19. **Hellenizer** *n.* M19.

Hellenophile /ˈhɛlmə(ʊ)fʌɪl/ *a.* & *n.* Also **-phil** /-fɪl/. L19. [f. HELLENE + -O- + -PHIL, -PHILE.] (A person who is) friendly towards or fond of Greece and things Greek.

heller /ˈhɛlə/ *n.*[1] Also (earlier) †**haller**. L16. Pl. **-s**, same. [G f. MHG *häller, haller*, f. (*Schwäbisch*) *Hall*, a town in Germany where this coin was first minted: see -ER[1].] An old German or Austrian coin of low value. Also, = HALER.

heller /ˈhɛlə/ *n.*[2] *slang* (chiefly *US*). L19. [f. HELL *v.* + -ER[1].] A troublesome, reckless, or aggressive person; a hellion.

Hellespont /ˈhɛlɪspɒnt/ *n.* L16. [Gk *Hellēspontos*, ancient name for the Dardanelles, the strait linking the Aegean Sea and the Sea of Marmara, f. *Hellē*, daughter of Athamas, said to have drowned there + *pontos* sea.] Something which separates two lovers (w. allusion to Leander's feat of swimming the Hellespont to be with Hero).

Helleˈspontine *a.* of, pertaining to, or situated on the Hellespont M19.

hell-fire /ˈhɛlfʌɪə/ *n.* & *a.* OE. [f. HELL *n.* + FIRE *n.*] **A** *n.* **1** The fire or fires of hell. OE. **2** (**H-**.) A member of a Hell-fire club (see below). *obs.* exc. *Hist.* E18.

1 *transf.*: A. MACLEAN Breathing hell-fire and brimstone in all directions.

B *attrib.* or as *adj.* **1** Hist. *Hell-fire club*, any of a number of clubs of reckless young men, popular at the beginning of the 18th cent. E18. **2** Esp. of preaching: concerned with or emphasizing the damnation of souls and the eternal punishments of hell. M20.

2 R. CAMPBELL The hell-fire sermons of the local priest.

hell-fired *a.* subjected to hell-fire; chiefly *fig.* (*slang*) damned, confounded: E18.

hellgrammite /ˈhɛlgrəmʌɪt/ *n. US.* Also **helg-**. M19. [Origin unkn.] The aquatic larva of an insect, *spec.* of the dobsonfly, *Corydalus cornutus*, used as bait by anglers.

hell-hound /ˈhɛlhaʊnd/ *n.* OE. [f. HELL *n.* + HOUND *n.*[1]] **1** A hound or dog of hell; *esp.* in *Class. Mythol.*, Cerberus, the watchdog of Hades. OE. **2** A fiend, a fiendish person. LME.

hellicat *a.* & *n.* see HALLOCKIT.

hellier /ˈhɛljə/ *n.* Now *dial.* LME. [f. HELE *v.*: see -IER.] A slater, a tiler.

hellion /ˈhɛljən/ *n. colloq.* Chiefly *N. Amer.* Also **-yon**. M19. [Prob. var. of HALLION, assim. to HELL *n.*] A troublesome or disreputable person; a mischievous child.

hellish /ˈhɛlɪʃ/ *a.* & *adv.* M16. [f. HELL *n.* + -ISH[1].] **A** *adj.* **1** Of or pertaining to hell; infernal. M16. **b** Belonging to Hades. L16. **2** Of the nature or character of hell; worthy of hell; diabolical, fiendish. M16. **3** Exceedingly bad, long, fast, etc. *colloq.* L18. **B** *adv.* Infernally, devilishly; *colloq.* exceedingly. E17.

hellishing *a.* & *adv.* (*slang*, chiefly *Austral.* & *NZ*) = HELLISH *a.* 3, *adv.* M20. **hellishly** *adv.* (*a*) in a hellish manner, infernally, devilishly; (*b*) *colloq.* exceedingly, very much: L16. **hellishness** *n.* L16.

hellite /ˈhɛlʌɪt/ *n.* E19. [f. HELL *n.* + -ITE[1].] **1** The proprietor of a hell or gaming-house. E19. **2** An inhabitant of hell. *rare.* M19.

hello /həˈləʊ, hɛ-/ *int.*, *n.*, & *v.* L19. [Var. of HALLO. Cf. HULLO.] **A** *int.* Greeting or expr. surprise on encountering; beginning a telephone conversation. L19.

B *n.* Pl. **-os**. A shout of 'hello!'; an utterance of 'hello!' L19.

golden hello: see GOLDEN *a.*

C *v.i.* Infl. **-oes, -oed**. Say or shout 'hello!' L19.

helluo /ˈhɛljʊəʊ/ *n.* Pl. **-os**. L16. [L *helluo, heluo*.] A glutton, a gormandizer; *fig.* a greedy devourer.

helluva /ˈhɛləvə/ *a. non-standard.* E20. [Repr. a pronunc.] = *a hell of a —* s.v. HELL *n.*

C. E. MULFORD I got money—helluva lot of money. *Times* It's very unfortunate looking like him: he must have a helluva life.

hellward /ˈhɛlwəd/ *adv.* & *a.* LME. [f. HELL *n.* + -WARD.] **A** *adv.* Towards hell; downward, towards the centre of the earth; towards the place of final punishment. LME. B *adj.* Heading to hell. E19.

helly /ˈhɛli/ *a.* & *adv.* *obs.* exc. *poet.* OE. [f. HELL *n.*: see -LY[1], -LY[2], -Y[1].] A *adj.* Of or belonging to hell; of the nature of hell; hellish, infernal, devilish. OE. †B *adv.* Hellishly, infernally. E17–M18.

hellyon *n.* var. of HELLION.

helm /hɛlm/ *n.*[1] [OE *helm* = OFris, OS, OHG (Du., G) *helm*, ON *hjalmr*, Goth. *hilms*, f. Gmc, f. IE base meaning 'cover, conceal': see HELE *v.* Cf. HEMMEL.] 1 Armour for the head; a helmet. *arch.* OE. †b *transf.* A knight. ME–M16. c = HELMET *n.* 1b. M19. †2 Jesus' crown of thorns. OE–LME. 3 The top or summit of something. *obs.* exc. *dial.* OE. b The head or cap of an alembic or retort. *obs.* exc. *Hist.* L16. 4 A roofed shelter for cattle etc. *north.* E16. 5a More fully *helm cloud.* In the Lake District, a cloud forming over a mountain top before or during a storm. L18. b In full *helm wind.* A violent wind associated with a helm cloud. L18.

helmless *a.*[1] E17.

helm /hɛlm/ *n.*[2] [OE *helma* corresp. to MLG *helm* handle, OHG *helmo*, *halmo*, ON *hjalmvǫlr* rudder-stick: prob. rel. to HELVE.] 1 *Naut.* The tiller or wheel by which the rudder is controlled. OE. b Use of the helm; the space through which the helm is turned. L19. 2 *fig.* The position of leadership or government. OE.

1b A. MACLEAN Naseby gave the rudder maximum helm to port. 2 *fig.*: A. L. ROWSE Chamberlain, who had succeeded Baldwin at the helm of the drifting country.

Phrases: **down (with the) helm** place the helm so as to bring the rudder to windward. **lee helm** helm put down. *put the helm* APORT. *right the helm*: see RIGHT *v.* 8. **take the helm** control the direction of a boat; *fig.* assume control. **up (with the) helm** place the helm so as to bring the rudder to leeward. **weather helm** helm put up.

helmless *a.*[2] without a helm or rudder E19. **helmsman** *n.* the steersman E17. **helmsmanship** *n.* the function or practice of a helmsman L19. **helmswoman** *n.* a female steersman L19.

helm /hɛlm/ *v.*[1]*t.* *arch.* or *poet.* [OE *helmian*, f. HELM *n.*[1]] Provide or cover with a helm.

helmed *ppl a.* wearing a helm, helmeted ME.

helm /hɛlm/ *v.*[2]*t.* E17. [f. HELM *n.*[2]] Steer or guide (as) with a helm.

Irish Press Local boats helmed by Jack Roy and Roger Bannon set the pace. *Evening Press (Eire)* Mark Lester was finally signed to helm the movie.

helmet /ˈhɛlmɪt/ *n.* & *v.* LME. [OFr. f. *helme*, ult. f. as HELM *n.*[1]: see -ET[2].] A *n.* 1 A piece of (usu. metal) armour for the head. LME. b A representation of a helmet; *esp.* in *Her.*, one placed above the shield in an achievement and supporting the crest, used to denote rank. E17. c Any of various types of protective headgear as worn by police officers, fire-fighters, divers, motorcyclists, sportsmen, etc.; a felt or pith hat worn in hot climates. M19. 2 = HELM *n.*[1] 3b. *obs.* exc. *Hist.* L16. 3 A kind of fancy pigeon having distinctively coloured head plumage. L17. 4 In full *helmet shell.* (The large thick shell of) any of various marine gastropods of the family Cassididae. M18. 5 *Bot.* The arched upper part of the calyx of certain flowers, esp. of labiates and orchids; = GALEA. L18.

Comb.: **helmet-crest** (*a*) the crest of a helmet; (*b*) (in full *bearded helmet-crest*) a crested hummingbird, *Oxypogon guerinii*, of northern S. America; *helmet shell*: see sense 4 above.

B *v.t.* Equip with a helmet. Chiefly as *helmeted* ppl a. M16.

helmeted CURASSOW.

helmetless *a.* L19. **helmet-like** *a.* resembling (that of) a helmet L19.

Helmholtz /ˈhɛlmhəʊlts/ *n.* M20. [H. L. F. von *Helmholtz* (1821–94), Ger. physicist.] Used *attrib.* to designate devices and concepts introduced by Helmholtz.

Helmholtz resonator a simple acoustic resonator consisting of a straight tube open at one end, with the other end connected to an enclosed cavity.

helminth /ˈhɛlmɪnθ/ *n.* M19. [Gk *helmins*, *helminth-* intestinal worm.] Any of a diverse group of worms which are internal parasites of man and animals, as nematodes, flukes, etc.

helmin'thiasis *n.*, pl. **-ases** /-əsiːz/, infestation by helminths of any kind E19. **hel'minthic** *n.* & *a.* †(*a*) *n.* an anthelmintic substance; (*b*) *adj.* of or pertaining to, or caused by helminths: E18.

helminthology /hɛlmɪnˈθɒlədʒi/ *n.* E19. [f. prec. + -OLOGY.] The branch of zoology or medicine that deals with helminths and the diseases they cause.

helmintho'logic(al) *adjs.* E19. **helminthologist** *n.* E19.

helophyte /ˈhɛləfʌɪt/ *n.* E20. [f. Gk *helos* marsh + -PHYTE.] *Ecol.* A marsh plant; *spec.* one whose perennating buds are situated in the mud at the bottom of a pond, lake, etc.

helot /ˈhɛlət/ *n.* L16. [L *Helotes* pl. f. Gk *Heilōtes* (pl. of *Heilōs*), also *Hilotae* f. Gk *Heilōtai* (pl. of *Heilōtēs*): usu. derived from *Helos* a town in Laconia whose inhabitants were enslaved.] *Gk Hist.* 1 (**H-**.) A member of a class of serfs in ancient Sparta, intermediate in status between slaves and citizens. L16. 2 *transf.* & *fig.* A serf, a slave. E19.

1 **drunken Helot**: forced to appear in a drunken state as a dreadful warning to Spartan youths. 2 P. D. JAMES Dalgliesh's helot, whose role was to take unobtrusive notes.

helotage *n.* = HELOTISM (a) M19. **helotism** *n.* (*a*) a system under which a class of the community is treated as inferior or subjugated; the condition of a helot; (*b*) *Biol.* a form of symbiosis in which one organism is held to make use of another as if it were a slave; *esp.* the relationship of ants and aphids, or of fungus and alga in a lichen: E19. **helotize** *v.t.* reduce to the condition of a helot M19. **helotry** *n.* (*a*) helots collectively; (*b*) the condition of a helot, slavery: E19.

help /hɛlp/ *n.* [OE *help* = OFris. *helpe*, OS *helpa*, OHG *helfa*, ON *hjálp*, f. Gmc base of HELP *v.*] 1 The action of helping or being helped; the useful supplementing of action or resources; aid, assistance. OE. b An act of helping, an aid or assistance. Now *rare* exc. as passing into sense 2. ME. 2 A person who or thing that provides help; a source or means of assistance. OE. b A domestic servant or employee; *collect.* servants, hired workers; the labour of hired workers. Formerly, an assistant, an ally. ME. 3 Cure, remedy. Now chiefly in *there is no help for it* there is no way of avoiding it. OE. 4 A portion of food, a helping. E19.

1 K. VONNEGUT They . . have a tough job . . and they need all the help they can get. *Dumfries & Galloway Standard* It's an advanced communications system which summons help in an emergency. D. WIGODER They must all think me crazy and beyond help. b R. L. STEVENSON I'll ask you, later on, to give us a help. 2 AV *Ps.* 46:1 God is our refuge and strength: a very present helpe in trouble. J. S. BLACKIE Books are no doubt very useful helps to knowledge. b G. PALEY I was going to organize the help You know, the guards, the elevator boys. P. LIVELY She has taught herself to cook . . since the defection of the last of the village helps. 3 DICKENS Poor Catherine and I are not made for each other, and there is no help for it. 4 P. V. WHITE He agreed . . to accept another help of mutton.

Comb.: **helpline** a telephone service providing help with problems; **help-mate** *Chess* a type of problem in which Black must assist White to give mate in a certain number of moves.

help /hɛlp/ *v.* Pa. t. **helped,** (*arch.* & *US dial.*) **holp** /həʊlp/. Pa. pple **helped,** (*arch.* & *US dial.*) **holpen** /ˈhəʊlp(ə)n/. [OE *helpan* = OFris. *helpa*, OS *helpan* (Du. *helpen*), OHG *helfan* (G *helfen*), ON *hjalpa*, Goth. *hilpan*, f. Gmc.] 1 *v.t.* & *i.* Provide (a person etc.) with what is needed for a purpose; aid, assist. Also, supply the needs of, succour. Freq. in *imper.*, expr. a need for assistance. OE. b With inf., with or without direct obj.: give help or assistance to *do* etc. or *to do* etc. ME. 2 *v.t.* Benefit, do good to; be of use or service to; profit. OE. b *v.i.* Be of use or service; avail. OE. c *v.t.* Make (an action, process, etc.) more effective; assist in achieving; promote, further. LME. 3 *v.t.* Relieve or cure (a disease etc.); remedy, amend. Long *arch.* OE. b Succour in distress or misfortune; deliver, save (*from*, *of*); *spec.* cure of a disease. ME. 4 *v.refl.* Make an effort on one's own behalf; do what is needed for oneself; extricate oneself from a difficulty. ME. 5 *v.t.* Assist (a person etc.) to progress in a specified direction. ME. b Foll. by *with.* Assist (a person) to put, take, or get something (esp. an article of clothing) *on*, *off*, etc. ME. c Give assistance in dealing *with.* E19. 6 *v.t.* Avoid, obviate, prevent, remedy; cause to be otherwise; refrain from, forbear. LME. b With neg. omitted after a neg. expressed or implied. Be unavoidable. *colloq.* M19. 7 *help* (*a person*) *to.* Assist (a person) in obtaining; provide, present with. Also *help oneself* (*to*) provide oneself (with), take for oneself; *euphem.* take without permission, steal. Cf. sense 8. LME. 8 *v.t.* Serve (a person) with food etc. (foll. by *to*); serve (food etc.). L17.

1 G. GREENE He felt as though he were in a strange country without any maps to help him. DAY LEWIS Help! I've a bee in my hair! **God, Heaven,** etc. **help you, me,** etc. *int.* expr. pity, anxiety, etc. **so help me (God)** (in an invocation or oath) as I keep my word, as I speak the truth, etc. (cf. SWELP ME). b POPE He help'd to bury whom he help'd to starve. *Punch* Sir Kingsley Wood . . asked the House for £1,000,000,000 to help pay for the . . war. T. F. POWYS Someone had . . appeared to help Lord Bullman to open the gate. R. INGALLS Help me look for that one. 2 J. WESLEY Mustard, and Juice of Scurvy Grass, help in a cold Scurvy. b T. MORRISON She actually wanted to help, to soothe. c J. R. GREEN The troubles of the time helped here as elsewhere the progress of the town. 4 F. W. ROBINSON I don't think that I shall require your assistance, or that I shall be unable to help myself. 5 A. HIGGINS Leaning out the conductor helped her down, his hand at her elbow. J. STEINBECK He helped Curley out the door. **help out, through**: *spec.* assist in completing or enduring something, or out of a difficulty; supplement, eke out. c A. D. SEDGWICK If he sat there . . not helping with the water-cans, . . it was because he . . wanted to watch her. **help the police (in** or **with their enquiries)** be questioned (usu. as the chief suspect for a crime) by the police. 6 J. BARZUN A man cannot help being intelligent, but he can easily help becoming intellectual. b C. H. SPURGEON I did not trouble myself more than I could help. 8 G. GREENE I helped him to a glass of rum and awaited an explanation. *refl.*: I. MURDOCH Cheese and biscuits are on the table, so do help yourselves if you want any.

Comb.: **helping hand** *fig.* an act of assistance; **help-yourself** *a.* self-service.

helpable *a.* able to be helped L16. **helper** *n.* (*a*) a person who or thing that helps; (*b*) a person employed as an assistant; *spec.* a groom's assistant in a stable; *colloq.* an assistant minister (in Methodist and Scottish churches): ME. **helping** *n.* (*a*) the action of the vb; (*b*) *spec.* the action of serving food etc.; a portion of food, esp. as served at one time (cf. HELP *n.* 4): ME.

helpful /ˈhɛlpfʊl, -f(ə)l/ *a.* LME. [f. HELP *n.* + -FUL.] Giving or productive of help; useful, profitable.

helpfully *adv.* M19. **helpfulness** *n.* (earlier in UNHELPFULNESS) M17.

helpless /ˈhɛlplɪs/ *a.* ME. [f. HELP *n.* + -LESS.] 1 Lacking help or assistance; needy. Often passing into sense 2. ME. 2 Unable to help oneself; incapable. ME. †3 That cannot be helped or remedied. ME–L16. 4 Unhelpful. Now *rare* or *obs.* LME.

1 *Which?* Some . . parts of a car are designed so that even if they do go wrong you aren't left helpless. 2 P. CAMPBELL Bill was so helpless with laughter that he missed me with the ruler altogether.

helplessly *adv.* L16. **helplessness** *n.* M18.

helpmate /ˈhɛlpmeɪt/ *n.* E18. [f. HELP *n.* or *v.* + MATE *n.*[2]; prob. infl. by next.] A companion who is a help or who gives help; a partner, esp. a husband or wife.

helpmeet /ˈhɛlpmiːt/ *n.* L17. [f. *help meet* (two wds) in *Gen.* 2:18, 20 (AV), 'an help meet for him' (HELP *n.* 2 + MEET *a.* 3), taken as one wd.] A suitable helper; = HELPMATE.

helter-skelter /hɛltəˈskɛltə/ *adv.*, *n.*, & *a.* L16. [A rhyming comb.; cf. *harum-scarum.*] A *adv.* In disordered haste. *colloq.* L16.

S. BELLOW I've been writing letters helter-skelter in all directions.

B *n.* 1 Disordered haste; a hurried flight. *colloq.* E18. 2 A tower-shaped structure at a funfair etc., with an external spiral track down which one may slide on a mat. E20.

C *attrib.* or as *adj.* Characterized by disorderly haste or confusion. *colloq.* L18.

helve /hɛlv/ *n.* & *v.* [OE *helfe*, (WS) *hielfe*, corresp. to OS *helfi* (MDu. *helf*, *helve*), OHG *halp* f. WGmc, whence also HALTER *n.*[1]: cf. HELM *n.*[2]] **A** *n.* **1** A handle or shaft of a weapon or tool. OE. **2** In full *helve-hammer*. A tilt-hammer, the helve of which oscillates on bearings, so that it is raised by a cam carried by a revolving shaft, and falls by its own weight. M19.

1 *throw the helve after the hatchet* (or *the hatchet after the helve*): see HATCHET *n.*

B *v.t.* Provide or fit with a helve. Now *rare*. LME.

Helvetian /hɛlˈviːʃ(ə)n/ *a.* & *n.* M16. [f. L *Helvetia* Switzerland, f. *Helvetius* pertaining to the Helvetii: see -IAN.] **A** *adj.* Of or pertaining to the Helvetii; of or pertaining to Switzerland, Swiss. M16. **B** *n.* One of the Helvetii; a native or inhabitant of Switzerland, a Swiss. M16.

Helvetic /hɛlˈvɛtɪk/ *a.* E18. [L *Helveticus* pertaining to the Helvetii: see prec., -IC.] Swiss.

helvolic /hɛlˈvɒlɪk/ *a.* M20. [f. L *helvola* lit. 'yellowish', name of the mutant variety of fungus from which the acid was isolated: see -IC.] Biochem. *helvolic acid*, an antibiotic acid produced by some strains of the fungus *Aspergillus fumigatus*.

helxine /hɛlkˈsʌɪni/ *n.* L19. [mod.L former genus name f. Gk *helxinē* pellitory.] A small creeping mat-forming plant of the nettle family, *Soleirolia soleirolii*, native to the western Mediterranean islands and grown elsewhere in rockeries. Also called *mind-your-own-business*, *mother of thousands*.

hem /hɛm/ *n.*[1] [OE *hem* corresp. to OFris. *hemme* enclosed land.] **1** The border or edge of a piece of cloth or clothing; (long *dial.*) the border or edge of anything. OE. **2** *esp.* A border made on a piece of cloth by doubling or turning in the (usu. cut) edge and sewing it down; used for strengthening or preventing fraying. M17.

1 P. THEROUX Hetta . . was striding, lifting the hem of her coat with her knees. **2** N. GORDIMER She was putting safety pins round the torn hem of a skirt.

Comb.: **hemline** the edge of a skirt, coat, etc.; the height of this from the ground.

hem /həm, hɛm/ *n.*[2] M16. [f. the int.] An utterance of 'hem'.

C. BRONTË I heard a hem close at my elbow.

†hem *pron.* See also 'EM *pron.* OE–M17. [OE *him*, *hiom*, *heom* dat. pl. in all genders of HE *pers. pron.*; later supplanting the accus. *hi*; finally itself displaced by THEM.] Them.

hem /hɛm/ *v.*[1] Infl. **-mm-**. LME. [f. HEM *n.*[1]] **1** *v.t.* Edge or border (cloth, a garment), esp. decoratively. Long *rare*. LME. **2** *v.t.* & *i.* Turn and sew down the edge of (a garment or piece of cloth). M16. **3** *v.t.* Enclose, confine, shut *in*. Also foll. by *round*, *up*. M16.

1 SPENSER All the skirt about Was hemd with golden fringe. **2** T. HOOD One used to stitch a collar then, Another hemmed a frill. **3** G. GREENE Two one-armed men and three one-legged men hemmed him round. M. IGNATIEFF Hemmed in on one side by older brothers . . and on the other by this father. D. WIGODER I couldn't physically escape from the grim walls which hemmed me in.

hem /hɛm/ *v.*[2] Infl. **-mm-**. L15. [Imit.] **1** *v.i.* Utter a hem, clear the throat; hesitate in speech esp. through indecision, disagreement, etc. Chiefly in *hem and haw*. L15. **†b** *v.t.* Drown *out* (speech) with a cough. Also foll. by *over*. M16–L17. **2** *v.t.* Clear *away* with a cough. *rare*. E16.

1 HENRY MILLER He began to hem and haw, not knowing really what he wanted to say. I. WALLACE He hemmed and hawed, weaseling all the way. **2** SHAKES. *A.Y.L.* These burs are in my heart . . . Hem them away.

hem /həm, hɛm/ *int.* E16. [Imit.: see HEM *v.*[2]] Expr. hesitation or a desire to attract attention by a slight cough or clearing of the throat.

DICKENS Gardens are—hem—are not accessible to me.

hemagglutinate *v.*, **hemal** *a.*, **hematite** *n.*, **hemato-** *comb. form*, etc.: see HAEMAGGLUTINATE etc.

heme *n.* var. of HAEM.

hemelytron /hɛˈmɛlɪtrɒn/ *n.* Pl. **-tra** /-trə/. E19. [f. HEMI- + Gk *elutron* sheath.] *Entomol.* The forewing of a heteropteran insect, thickened at the base and membranous at the end.

hemeralopia /hɛmərəˈləʊpɪə/ *n.* E18. [mod.L, f. Gk *hēmeralōps*, f. *hēmera* day + *alaos* blind + *ōps* eye: see -IA[1]. Cf. NYCTALOPIA.] **1** Chiefly *Med.* A defect of vision (usu. congenital) in which there is poor vision in good light but comparatively good vision in poor light. Also called *day blindness*. E18. **2** [By confusion.] = NYCTALOPIA I. Now *rare*. E19.

hemeralopic *a.* affected with hemeralopia L19.

hemerobaptist /hɛm(ə)rə(ʊ)ˈbaptɪst/ *n.* L16. [eccl.L *Hemerobaptista* f. Gk *hēmerobaptistai* pl., f. *hēmera* day + *baptistēs* baptist.] *Hist.* A member of a Jewish sect which practised daily baptism as a means of ritual purification.

hemerocallis /hɛm(ə)rə(ʊ)ˈkalɪs/ *n.* M17. [Gk *hēmerokallis* a lily that flowers for one day only, f. *hēmera* day + *kallos* beauty.] = *day lily* s.v. DAY *n.*

hemerythrin *n.* see HAEMERYTHRIN.

hemi- /ˈhɛmi/ *pref.* [Gk *hēmi-* comb. elem. corresp. to L *semi-* SEMI-, f. IE base also of OE *sam-* (cf. SAND-BLIND), OS *sām-*, OHG *sāmi-*.] Used in wds adopted (ult.) f. Gk, or as a productive prefix (esp. in scientific and technical subjects) in new formations usu. w. Gk roots, w. the sense 'half-, affecting one half, partial.' Cf. SEMI-.

hemi-ˈacetal *n.* (*Chem.*) any of a class of compounds of formula R·CH(OH)(OR′), differing from acetals in having a hydroxyl instead of one alkoxy-group L19. **hemibranch** *n.* (*Ichthyol.*) an incomplete gill, having lamellae on one side only L19. **hemiˈcellulose** *n.* any of various polysaccharides of simpler composition than cellulose which occur as constituents of the cell walls of plants L19. **hemiˈchordate** *n.* & *a.* (*a*) *n.* any member of the phylum Hemichordata of wormlike marine invertebrates, including the acorn worms and pterobranchs and orig. classified as chordates; (*b*) *adj.* of or pertaining to this phylum: L19. **hemicircle** *n.* a semicircle E17. **hemicoˈlectomy** *n.* (an instance of) surgical removal of the right or left half of the colon E20. **hemiˈcryptophyte** *n.* (*Bot.*) a plant having perennial shoots and buds at ground level or within the surface layer of soil E20. **hemicyˈlindrical** *a.* having the form of half a cylinder M19. **hemiˈhedral** *a.* (*Cryst.*) (of a crystal or crystal class) having half of the maximum number of faces or symmetry planes possible for a given crystal system M19. **hemiˈhedron** *n.* (*Cryst.*) any hemihedral crystal M19. **hemiˈhedry** *n.* (*Cryst.*) the property of being hemihedral M19. **hemiˈhydrate** *n.* (*Chem.*) a hydrate containing half a mole of water per mole of the compound L19. **hemiˈparasite** *n.* (*Bot.*) a parasitic plant which can also live as a saprophyte (as certain fungi), or which also photosynthesizes (as mistletoe) L19. **hemiparaˈsitic** *a.* pertaining to or of the nature of a hemiparasite E20. **hemipaˈresis** *n.* = HEMIPLEGIA L19. **hemipaˈretic** *a.* = HEMIPLEGIC *a.* L19. **hemipenis** *n.* (*Zool.*) each of the paired eversible copulatory organs in snakes and lizards E20. **hemisect** *v.t.* bisect esp. longitudinally or into right and left halves L19. **hemiˈsection** *n.* the action or process of hemisecting L19. **hemispasm** *n.* a spasm affecting one side of the body only L19. **†hemitone** *n.* a semitone L17–M18. **hemiˈzygote** *n.* (*Biol.*) a hemizygous organism M20. **hemiˈzygous** *a.* (*Biol.*) having a single unpaired allele at a particular genetic locus E20.

hemianopsia /ˌhɛmɪəˈnɒpsɪə/ *n.* L19. [f. HEMI- + Gk AN-[5] + *opsis*: see -IA[1].] Blindness covering one half of the normal field of vision.

hemianopia /-ˈnəʊpɪə/ *n.* [-OPIA] = HEMIANOPSIA L19. **hemianopic** *a.* & *n.* (*a*) *adj.* of, pertaining to, or characterized by hemianopia; (*b*) *n.* a person with hemianopia L19.

hemic *a.* see HAEMIC.

hemicrania /hɛmɪˈkreɪnɪə/ *n.* LME. [OFr. *emigraine* or med.L *emigrania* f. late L *hemicrania* f. Gk *hēmikrania*, f. as HEMI- + *kranion* skull: see -IA[1], MEGRIM *n.*[1], and MIGRAINE.] A migraine; a headache, esp. one confined to one side of the head.

hemicycle /ˈhɛmɪsʌɪk(ə)l/ *n.* L15. [Fr. *hémicycle* f. L *hemicyclium* f. Gk *hēmikuklion*, f. as HEMI- + *kuklos* circle.] A semicircle; a semicircular structure.

J. ARCHER The hemicycle is a round bank of seats inside the theatre.

hemi-demi-semi- /ˈhɛmɪdɛmɪsɛmi/ *pref.* Also as adj. **hemi-demi-semi**. E20. [f. HEMI- + DEMI- + SEMI-, after next.] Half-half-half-, an eighth of; slight(ly), insignificant(ly).

hemidemisemiquaver /ˈhɛmɪdɛmɪˌsɛmɪkweɪvə/ *n.* M19. [f. HEMI- + DEMISEMIQUAVER.] *Mus.* A note of half the value of a demisemiquaver, represented as a quaver with four hooks.

hemidesmus /hɛmɪˈdɛsməs/ *n.* L19. [mod.L (see below), f. HEMI- + Gk *desmos* bond, w. ref. to the partial fusion of the stamens.] An Indian twining shrub, *Hemidesmus indicus* (family Asclepiadaceae), whose root is used as a substitute for sarsaparilla; a syrup prepared from this root.

hemimetabolous /ˌhɛmɪməˈtab(ə)ləs/ *a.* L19. [f. HEMI- + Gk *metabolos* changeable: see -OUS.] *Entomol.* Of an insect: that undergoes incomplete metamorphosis, with no pupal stage in the transition from larva to adult. Cf. HOLOMETABOLOUS.

hemimorphic /hɛmɪˈmɔːfɪk/ *a.* M19. [f. HEMI- + Gk *morphē* shape + -IC.] *Cryst.* Of a crystal: having unlike planes at the ends of the same axis.

hemimorphism *n.* the property of being hemimorphic L19.

hemimorphite /hɛmɪˈmɔːfʌɪt/ *n.* M19. [f. prec. + -ITE[1].] *Min.* An orthorhombic hydrated zinc silicate, usu. occurring as white flattened prisms, one of the forms of calamine (cf. SMITHSONITE).

hemin *n.* see HAEMIN.

hemina /həˈmʌɪnə/ *n.* Long *rare*. Also (earlier) **†emina**. E17. [L *hemina* f. Gk *hēmina*, f. as HEMI-.] A measure of corn; a liquid measure of approx. half a pint.

Hemingwayesque /ˌhɛmɪŋweɪˈɛsk/ *a.* M20. [f. Ernest *Hemingway* (1898–1961), US novelist + -ESQUE.] Characteristic or in the style of the works of Hemingway.

Also **Hemingˈwayan** *a.* M20.

hemiola /hɛmɪˈəʊlə/ *n.* Also **-lia** /-lɪə/. LME. [med.L *hemiolia* f. Gk *hēmiolia*, *-lios* in the ratio of one and a half to one, f. as HEMI- + *holos* whole.] In early music, an interval of a fifth (produced by shortening the string to two-thirds of its length); the substitution of three imperfect notes for two perfect ones. In modern music, the performance of two bars in triple metre as if they were notated as three bars in duple metre.

hemiopsia /hɛmɪˈɒpsɪə/ *n.* E19. [f. HEMI- + Gk *opsis* sight: see -IA[1].] = HEMIANOPSIA.

hemiopia /-ˈəʊpɪə/ *n.* [-OPIA] = HEMIANOPSIA M19. **hemiopic** *a.* = HEMIANOPIC *a.* L19.

hemiplegia /hɛmɪˈpliːdʒə/ *n.* E17. [mod.L f. Gk *hēmiplēgia*, f. as HEMI- + *plēgē* stroke: see -IA[1]. Cf. DIPLEGIA, PARAPLEGIA.] Paralysis of one side of the body.

hemiplegiac *n.* & *a.* = HEMIPLEGIC L18. **hemiplegic** *n.* & *a.* (a person) affected with hemiplegia E19. **ˈhemiplegy** *n.* (*rare*) = HEMIPLEGIA M18.

hemipode /ˈhɛmɪpəʊd/ *n.* M19. [mod.L *Hemipodius* former genus name, f. Gk HEMI- + *pous*, *podos* foot.] = *button-quail* s.v. BUTTON *n.*; *Andalusian hemipode*, the little button-quail, *Turnix sylvatica* (as occurring in Iberia).

Hemiptera /hɪˈmɪpt(ə)rə/ *n.* E19. [mod.L, neut. pl. of *hemipterus*, f. as HEMI- + Gk *pteron* wing (w. ref. to the partly hardened forewings of bugs): see -A[3].] (Members of) a large order of insects characterized by having piercing and sucking mouthparts, and comprising two suborders, Heteroptera (bugs in the narrower sense) and Homoptera (cicadas, leafhoppers, aphids, scale insects, etc.).

hemipteran /hɪˈmɪpt(ə)rən/ *a.* & *n.* L19. [f. prec. + -AN.] **A** *adj.* Of, pertaining to, or characteristic of the Hemiptera. L19. **B** *n.* A hemipteran insect. L19.

hemipterous *a.* = HEMIPTERAN *a.* E19.

hemisphere /ˈhɛmɪsfɪə/ *n.* LME. [OFr. *emisp(h)ere* (mod. *hémisphère*) and also L *hemisphaerium*, f. Gk *hēmisphairion*, f. as HEMI- + *sphaira* sphere.] **1** a Half the celestial sphere, now *esp.* as divided by the equinoctial or the ecliptic. Formerly *esp.* that half of the celestial sphere seen above the horizon, the sky. LME. **b** Either of the halves of the earth, esp. as divided by the equator (*Northern, Southern hemisphere*) or longitudinally (*Eastern, Western hemisphere*: see below). M16. **2** *fig.* A realm of thought, action, etc. E16. **3** *gen.* A half sphere. M16. **4** A map of half the earth or the celestial globe. M17. **5** *Anat.* Each of the halves of the cerebrum. More fully *cerebral hemisphere.* E19.

1a R. S. BALL The number of stars in the northern hemisphere alone is . . three hundred thousand. b J. D. MACDONALD The normal pattern in this hemisphere is for a storm to start near the equator. V. S. NAIPAUL A man from another hemisphere, another background. **Eastern hemisphere**: containing Europe, Asia, and Africa. **Western hemisphere**: containing America. 2 P. E. DOVE To surmise the possibility, as beyond the hemisphere of my knowledge. 3 A. R. AMMONS The dune thistle . . / opening thorny hemispheres / of yellow florets. A. GRAY The chamber was a perfect hemisphere. MAGDEBURG HEMISPHERE.

hemi'spheral *a.* (*rare*) M19. **hemisphe'rectomy** *n.* (an instance of) surgical removal of a cerebral hemisphere M20. **hemisphered** *a.* (*rare*) shaped like a hemisphere M17.

hemispherical /hɛmɪ'sfɛrɪk(ə)l/ *a.* E17. [f. prec. + -ICAL.] **1** Of the nature of or resembling a hemisphere; of or pertaining to a hemisphere. E17. **2** Concerned with, relating to, or extending over a hemisphere of the earth. L19.

hemispheric *a.* = HEMISPHERICAL L16. **hemispherically** *adv.* M19.

hemispheroid /hɛmɪ'sfɪərɔɪd/ *n.* E18. [f. HEMI- + SPHEROID.] A half spheroid; a figure approaching a hemisphere.

hemisphe'roidal *a.* having the form of a hemispheroid E18.

hemistich /'hɛmɪstɪk/ *n.* L16. [Late L *hemistichium* f. Gk *hēmistikhion*, f. as HEMI- + STICH.] Esp. in Old English verse, a half of a line of verse or a line of less than the usual length.

hemitrope /'hɛmɪtrəʊp/ *a.* & *n.* Now *rare* or *obs.* E19. [f. HEMI- + Gk *-tropos* turning.] *Cryst.* **A** *adj.* Of a crystal: twinned. E19. **B** *n.* A twinned crystal. E19.

hemitropic /-'trəʊpɪk, -'trɒpɪk/ *a.* L19. **hemi'tropism** *n.* M19. **he'mitropy** *n.* L19.

hemlock /'hɛmlɒk/ *n.* & *v.* [OE *hymlic(e, hemlic*, of unkn. origin. For the LME alt. of the final syll. to *-lock*, cf. *charlock.*] **A** *n.* **1** A highly poisonous umbelliferous plant, *Conium maculatum*, with glaucous spotted stems, white flowers, and finely divided leaves; also (chiefly *US*) *poison-hemlock*. Also *loosely*, any of several superficially similar tall umbellifers. OE. **b** A draught prepared from hemlock, reputedly the poison given to Socrates. E17. **2** More fully *hemlock spruce*. Any of various N. American coniferous trees of the genus *Tsuga*, with drooping branches recalling the leaves of *Conium maculatum*; *esp.* (in full *western hemlock*) *T. heterophylla*, of western N. America. M17.

1 *water hemlock*: see WATER *n.* b KEATS A drowsy numbness pains My sense, as though of hemlock I had drunk. 2 MOUNTAIN *hemlock*.

Comb.: *hemlock spruce*: see sense 2 above; **hemlock water dropwort** a poisonous umbellifer of marshy places, *Oenanthe crocata*.

B *v.t.* Poison with hemlock. M19.

L. ABERCROMBIE And with this stew Hemlock'd the wine of Heaven.

hemmel /'hɛm(ə)l/ *n. north.* E18. [Var. of HELM *n.*[1]] A (partly covered) cow-shed.

hemmer /'hɛmə/ *n.* ME. [f. HEM *v.*[1] + -ER[1].] **1** A person who hems. ME. **2** A hemming attachment for a sewing machine. M19.

hemming /'hɛmɪŋ/ *n.* LME. [f. HEM *v.*[1] + -ING[1].] The action of HEM *v.*[1] Formerly also, a hem, a border.

hemo- *comb. form*, **hemoglobin** *n.*, **hemophilia** *n.*, **hemorrhage** *n.* & *v.*, etc.: see HAEMO- etc.

hemp /hɛmp/ *n.* [OE *henep, hænep* = OS *hanap* (Du. *hennep*), OHG *hanaf* (G *Hanf*), ON *hampr*, f. Gmc wd rel. to Gk *kannabis* (whence L *cannabis*; cf. CANVAS *n.*[1]).] **1** A herbaceous plant, *Cannabis sativa* (family Cannabaceae), native to central Asia, cultivated for its valuable fibre and the drug marijuana (see *Indian hemp* s.v. INDIAN *a.*). OE. **2** The cortical fibre of this used for making rope and strong fabric. ME. **b** *joc.* or *allus.* A rope for hanging a person. M16. **3** With specifying wd: any of various plants related to hemp or producing a similar fibre; the fibre produced by such a plant. L16. **4** The drug marijuana. L19.

2 C. FRANCIS Hemp is strong, but it stretches a good deal when new and shrinks when wet. b SHAKES. *Hen. V* And let not hemp his windpipe suffocate. 3 *African hemp, bowstring hemp, Manila hemp, sisal hemp*, etc.

Comb.: **hemp agrimony** the plant *Eupatorium cannabinum*, of the composite family, found in damp bushy places and with heads of dull purplish flowers; **hempland** (now chiefly *dial.*) a piece of land on which hemp is or was grown; **hemp-nettle** any of several labiate weeds of the genus *Galeopsis*, with leaves like those of nettles; *esp.* the common *G. tetrahit*, which has purple, white, or vari-coloured flowers. **hempseed** (*a*) the seed of hemp; †(*b*) (*rare*, Shakes.) a gallows-bird.

hempen *a.* of, pertaining to, or resembling hemp LME.

hempy /'hɛmpi/ *a.* & *n.* Also (*Sc.* & *north.*) **hempie**. LME. [f. HEMP + -Y[1].] **A** *adj.* **1** Hempen. LME. **2** Mischievous, naughty; deserving to be hanged. *joc.* (*Sc.* & *north.*). M18. **B** *n.* A hempy person, esp. a girl. *joc.* (*Sc.* & *north.*). E18.

hemstitch /'hɛmstɪtʃ/ *n.* & *v.* M19. [f. HEM *n.*[1] + STITCH *n.*[1]] **A** *n.* In *Embroidery*, an ornamental stitch in drawn-work involving drawing bundles of thread together and used esp. to hem a piece of work; *gen.* a stitch used to hem a garment etc. involving small widely-spaced diagonal stitches designed to be invisible from the right side. M19. **B** *v.t.* Hem using this stitch. M19.

hen /hɛn/ *n.* [OE *henn* = OFris., MLG *henne*, OHG *henna* (G *Henne*), f. WGmc deriv. of Gmc base of OE *hana* cock, rel. to L *canere* sing.] **1** A female bird; *esp.* the female of the domestic fowl; in *pl.* also, domestic fowls of both sexes. OE. **2** *fig.* a A wife, a woman: *spec.* (*Sc.*) as a familiar form of address to a woman or girl. *colloq.* E17. **b** A coward. L19. **3** Any of various bivalve molluscs; *esp.* (more fully *hen-clam*) a large clam, *Spisula solidissima*, of the N. American Atlantic coast. Chiefly *N. Amer.* E17. **4** A female fish or crustacean. M18.

Phrases: **as scarce as hen's teeth** very scarce. *like a hen on a hot girdle*: see GIRDLE *n.*[2] **like a hen with one chicken** absurdly fussy.

Comb.: **hen and chickens** (*a*) (in full *hen-and-chickens daisy*) a freak form of the daisy, sometimes cultivated, in which smaller flower-heads grow from the edge of the main flower-head; (*b*) a kind of houseleek, *Sempervivum soboliferum*, with numerous offsets; (*c*) a kind of childrens' game; **hen-and-egg** *a.* = *chicken-and-egg* s.v. CHICKEN *n.*[1]; **henbane** a plant of the nightshade family, *Hyoscyamus niger*, with amber purple-streaked flowers, noted for its poisonous and narcotic properties; the drug obtained from this plant; **henbit** either of two low-growing weeds with roundish shallowly lobed leaves: †(*a*) (more fully *small hen*) the ivy-leaved speedwell, *Veronica hederifolia*; (*b*) (more fully *hen dead-nettle*, formerly *great hen*) a kind of dead-nettle, *Lamium amplexicaule*; *hen-clam*: see sense 3 above; **hen-coop**: for keeping fowls in; **hencote** (now *dial.*) a hen-house; **hen-egg** a hen's egg; **hen-fruit, hen's fruit** (chiefly *US slang*) eggs; **hen-harrier** a harrier, *Circus cyaneus*, inhabiting open country and moorland across much of the Palaearctic and New World; **hen-hawk** *US local* any of various large raptors reputed to attack poultry; †**hen heart** = sense 2b above; **hen-hearted** *a.* lacking courage; **hen-house** a small shed for fowls to roost in; *fig.* an establishment inhabited chiefly by women; **hen-party** *colloq.* (orig. *derog.*) a social gathering of women only, *esp.* one held in honour of a woman about to marry; **hen-roost** a place where fowls roost at night; **hen-run** an enclosure for fowls; **hen-scratch** *v.i.* & *t.* scratch in the manner of a hen; **hensure** *a.* (*joc.*) [after COCKSURE] = COCKSURE *a.* 4; **henwife** (chiefly *Sc.*, *arch.*) a woman who keeps fowls; **hen yard** = *hen-run* above.

hennery *n.* an establishment or place where hens are reared or kept M19. **henny** *a.* & *n.* (*a*) *adj.* of, pertaining to, or resembling a hen; (*b*) *n.* a male fowl resembling a hen: M19.

hen /hɛn/ *adv.* Long *obs.* exc. *dial.* [OE *heonan(e)* = OS, OHG *hinan(a)* (G *hinnen*); also OE *hina, heona* = MLG, MDu. *hēne* (Du. *heen*), OHG *hina* (G *hin*): WGmc formations on the Gmc pronominal base of HE *pers. pron.*] = HENCE *adv.*

†**henad** *n.* L17–L18. [Gk *henas, henad-* unit, f. *hen* one: see -AD[1].] In Platonic philosophy: a unit, a monad.

hence /hɛns/ *adv.*, *pron.*, & *n.* ME. [f. HEN *adv.* + -S[3]. The spelling *-ce* is phonetic, to retain the unvoiced sound denoted in the earlier sp. by *-s*. Cf. THENCE, WHENCE.] **A** *adv.* **I** Of place. **1** (Away) from here; to or at a distance from here; away. ME. **2** *spec.* From this world, from this life. ME. †**b** In the next or another world. LME–E17. **3** *ellipt.* As a command: go hence. L16.

2 **go hence** die. 3 SHAKES. *Temp.* Hence! Hang not on my garments. **hence with** — go away with —, take — away.

II Of time. **4** From this time forward. *arch.* & *poet.* LME. **b** (At some time in the future) from now. L16.

4b H. JAMES He wished he might see her ten years hence.

III Of result or consequence. **5** From this, as a source. L16. **6** For this reason, therefore. L16. **7** (As a result) from this fact or circumstance. E17.

6 D. LARDNER Hence, the surface of the entire sphere is equal to the surface of the entire cylinder. 7 A. BURGESS I was seven now, and hence had arrived at the age of reason. *Sunday Express* He is a member of the Upper House of Parliament (hence the Hon.).

B *pron.* & *n.* **1** *from* (or †*of*) *hence*, from this place; from this world; from now on; from this circumstance. LME. **2** The other world; the future. *US.* L19.

2 E. W. NYE One who is now in the golden hence. F. LYNDE Developments may be safely predicted in the immediate hence.

henceforth /hɛns'fɔːθ, 'hɛnsfɔːθ/ *adv.* & *pron.* LME. [f. prec. + FORTH *adv.*] Also (arch.) *from henceforth*. From now onwards.

M. SINCLAIR But that resource would henceforth be denied him.

henceforward /hɛns'fɔːwəd/ *adv.* ME. [f. as prec. + FORWARD *adv.*] = HENCEFORTH.

henceforwards *adv.* = HENCEFORWARD *adv.* LME.

henchman /'hɛn(t)ʃmən/ *n.* Pl. **-men**. ME. [f. OE *heng(e)st* stallion, gelding + MAN *n.*] **1** *Hist.* A squire or page of honour to a person of great rank. ME. **2** The chief personal attendant of a Highland chief; *gen.* a trusty attendant of a leader. M18. **b** A (political) supporter; a partisan. Freq. *derog.* M19.

2b D. JACOBSON To have your enemies killed off by your henchmen, as any other tyrant would.

henchwoman *n.* L19.

†**hend** *v.t.* ME–L16. [Prob. f. OE *gehendan* handle, take hold of, f. HAND *n.* Cf. ON *henda*.] Seize, take; grasp, hold.

hendeca- /'hɛndɛkə, hɛn'dɛkə/ *comb. form.* Bef. a vowel **hendec-**. Also **en-** /ɛn-/. [Gk *hendeka* eleven.] Having or consisting of eleven; elevenfold; in *Chem.* (now *rare*) = UNDECA-.

hen'decagon *n.* a plane figure with eleven sides and angles E18. **'hendecarchy** *n.* (*rare*) government by eleven people M17.

hendecasyllabic /ˌhɛndɛkəsɪ'labɪk, hɛnˌdɛk-/ *a.* & *n.* Also **en-** /ɛn-/. E18. [f. L *hendecasyllabus* (see next) + -IC, after *disyllabic, trisyllabic.*] **A** *adj.* Of a line of poetry: consisting of eleven syllables. E18. **B** *n.* A hendecasyllabic line. Usu. in *pl.* M19.

hendecasyllable /ˌhɛndɛkə'sɪləb(ə)l, hɛnˌdɛkə-/ *n.* Also **en-** /ɛn-/. E17. [Alt. (after SYLLABLE *n.*) of L *hendecasyllabus* f. Gk *hendekasullabos* use as n. (sc. *stikhos* row, line of verse) of adj. = eleven-syllabled, f. as HENDECA- + *sullabē* SYLLABLE *n.*] *Pros.* A verse or line of eleven syllables.

hendiadys /hɛn'dʌɪədɪs/ *n.* L16. [med.L, f. Gk *hen dia duoin* 'one through two'.] A figure of speech in which a single complex idea is expressed by two words usu. connected by *and* (e.g. *nice and warm* for *nicely warm*).

heneicosane /hɛˈnʌɪkəseɪn/ *n.* L19. [f. Gk *hen-*, *heis* one + *eikosi* twenty + -ANE.] *Chem.* Any saturated hydrocarbon of formula $C_{21}H_{44}$, of which numerous isomers exist; *spec.* the unbranched isomer (also called n-*heneicosane*).

henequen /ˈhɛnɪkɛn/ *n.* Also **-quin**. E17. [Sp. *jeniquen*, *geniquen*, f. the Mexican name.] A Mexican agave, *Agave fourcroydes*, grown for its leaf fibre; the fibre obtained from this plant.

henge /hɛn(d)ʒ/ *n.*[1] M18. [f. STONE)HENGE.] †1 A stone that is suspended overhead or overhangs. Only in M18. 2 *Archaeol.* Any large circular monument usually of later neolithic date, comprising a bank and internal ditch which may enclose stone or wooden structures. M20.

†**henge** *n.*[2] var. of HINGE *n.*

Henle /ˈhɛnli/ *n.* M19. [F. G. J. *Henle* (1809–85), Ger. anatomist.] *Anat.* Used in *possess.* to designate structures described by Henle.

Henle's layer, layer of Henle a layer of cubical cells in the inner root sheath of the hair follicle. **Henle's loop, loop of Henle** the part of a kidney tubule forming a loop within the renal medulla.

henna /ˈhɛnə/ *n.* & *v.* E17. [Arab. *hinnā'*: cf. ALCANNA, ALKANET.] A *n.* A shrub of the purple loosestrife family, *Lawsonia inermis*, native from N. Africa to India; a preparation of its powdered leaves and shoots, used to stain the hair and, in the east, the fingernails etc. a reddish-yellow colour. E17. B *v.t.* Dye or stain with henna. Chiefly as *hennaed* ppl a. E20.

Henoch /ˈhiːnɒx/ *n.* L19. [E. H. *Henoch* (1820–1910), Ger. paediatrician.] *Med.* 1 *Henoch's purpura*, a form of Henoch–Schönlein purpura associated esp. with gastrointestinal symptoms. Cf. SCHÖNLEIN 1. L19. 2 *Henoch–Schönlein purpura, syndrome*, a form of purpura affecting mainly young children, esp. boys, involving a characteristic rash and gastrointestinal or rheumatic symptoms. M20.

henotheism /ˈhɛnəʊˌθiːɪz(ə)m/ *n.* M19. [f. Gk *heno-* stem of *heis* one + *theos* god + -ISM.] Belief in a single god of e.g. one's tribe, without assertion that there is only one god.

henotheist *n.* L19. **henotheˈistic** *a.* L19.

henpeck /ˈhɛnpɛk/ *v.* & *n.* *colloq.* L17. [(Back-form.) f. next.] A *v.t.* Of a wife: domineer over (her husband). Usu in *pass.* L17.

N. BAWDEN Always the gentleman, hen-pecked by his harridan wife.

B *n. rare.* 1 A henpecked husband; a domineering wife. M18. 2 Domineering by a wife. M19.

henpeckery *n.* (*rare*) the state or condition of being henpecked M19.

henpecked /ˈhɛnpɛkt/ *a.* *colloq.* L17. [f. HEN *n.* + PECKED *ppl a.* (alluding to the plucking of the domestic cock by his hens).] Domineered over or ruled by a wife.

D. H. LAWRENCE A little red-faced man, rather beery and hen-pecked looking.

Henrician /hɛnˈrɪʃɪən, -ʃ(ə)n/ *n.* & *a.* L16. [med.L *Henrician-*, f. *Henricus* Henry: see -IAN.] *Hist.* A *n.* A follower of any of various people named Henry; *spec.* (*a*) a follower of Henry of Lausanne, a religious and moral reformer of the 12th cent.; (*b*) a supporter of the ecclesiastical policy of Henry VIII, king of England (1509–47). L16. B *adj.* Of or pertaining to Henry (see above) or the Henricians. L19.

Henri Deux /ɑ̃ri dø/ *a. phr.* M19. [Fr. = Henri II (see below).] Designating (the style of) Renaissance art or architecture developed in France during the reign of Henri II, king of France 1547–59; *esp.* designating the purest style of the French Renaissance.

Henrietta /hɛnrɪˈɛtə/ *n. obs.* exc. *Hist.* M19. [Female name.] In full *Henrietta cloth*. A lightweight dress fabric, sometimes with a silk warp.

Henry /ˈhɛnri/ *n.*[1] M19. [Benjamin Tyler *Henry* (1821–98), Amer. inventor.] Used *attrib.* to designate (parts of) a breech-loading magazine rifle introduced by Henry. See also MARTINI *n.*[1]

henry /ˈhɛnri/ *n.*[2] Pl. **-ries, -rys.** L19. [Joseph *Henry* (1797–1878), US physicist.] *Physics.* The SI unit of inductance, equal to the inductance of a circuit in which an electromotive force of one volt is produced by a current changing at the rate of one ampere per second. (Symbol H.)

Henry Clay /hɛnri ˈkleɪ/ *n.* M19. [*Henry Clay* (1777–1852), US statesman.] A type of cigar.

Henry's law /ˈhɛnrɪz lɔː/ *n. phr.* L19. [William *Henry* (1774–1836), Eng. chemist.] *Chem.* The statement that the amount of a gas dissolved in a given quantity of liquid in conditions of equilibrium is directly proportional to the pressure of the gas in contact with the liquid.

†**hent** *n.* E16. [f. the vb.] 1 The act of seizing; a grasp. Only in E16. 2 Something grasped in the mind; an idea. Only in E17.

hent /hɛnt/ *v. arch.* & *dial.* Pa. t. & pple same. [OE *hentan*, f. Gmc weak grade of base of HUNT *v.*] 1 *v.t.* Seize, grasp; move; take (*away*, *off*, etc.), put (*on*). OE. †2 *v.t.* Arrive at, reach, occupy. ME–E17. †3 *v.t.* Get, take, receive, meet with; experience, suffer; apprehend. ME–L16. †4 *v.t.* Seize, affect (as an influence or condition). ME–E17. 5 *v.i.* Go, depart. L16.

Hentenian /hɛnˈtiːnɪən/ *a.* E20. [f. *Henten* (see below) + -IAN.] Designating editions of the Vulgate prepared at Louvain by John Henten or Hentenius (1499–1566), theologian of the Dominican order.

hentriacontane /ˌhɛntrʌɪəˈkɒnteɪn/ *n.* L19. [f. Gk *hen-*, *heis* one + *triakonta* thirty + -ANE.] *Chem.* Any of a series of saturated hydrocarbons (alkanes) with the formula $C_{31}H_{64}$; *spec.* (also n-*hentriacontane*) the unbranched isomer, CH_3-$(CH_2)_{29}CH_3$, found in paraffin wax.

heortology /hɪɔːˈtɒlədʒi/ *n.* E20. [G *Heortologie*, Fr. *héortologie*, f. Gk *heortē* feast: see -OLOGY.] The branch of knowledge that deals with the religious feasts and seasons of the Christian year.

heortologist *n.* E20.

hep /hɛp/ *n.*[1] *slang.* E20. [f. the adj.] The state of being hep; something that is hep.

hep *n.*[2] var. of HIP *n.*[2]

hep /hɛp/ *a. slang.* E20. [Origin unkn. Cf. HIP *a.*, *v.*[3]] = HIP *a.*

S. SELVON Tall Boy, I always thought you was hep, that you on the ball. **hep-cat** = *hip-cat* s.v. HIP *a.*

hepster *n.* = *hep-cat* above (cf. HIPSTER *n.*[1]) M20.

hep /hɛp/ *v.t.* Infl. **-pp-**. M20. [f. the adj.] Pep *up*.

hepped *ppl a.* (*a*) pepped *up*; (*b*) (foll. by *on*) enthusiastic about: M20.

hep /hɛp/ *int.* M19. [Perh. f. the initials of L *Hierosolyma Est Perdita* ('Jerusalem is destroyed').] Usu. redupl. *hep! hep!* Used by (German) persecutors of Jews in the 19th cent.

hepar /ˈhiːpɑː/ *n. obs.* exc. *Hist.* L17. [Late L f. Gk *hēpar* liver.] Any of various sulphur compounds, generally of a reddish-brown colour and often in (former) medicinal use.

Comb.: **hepar sulphur(is)** (*a*) a preparation containing potassium sulphide; (*b*) in *Homoeopathy*, calcium sulphide.

heparin /ˈhɛpərɪn/ *n.* E20. [f. as prec. + -IN[1].] *Biochem.* A sulphur-containing polysaccharide with anticoagulant properties, present in the blood and various bodily organs and tissues.

heparini'zation *n.* the process of heparinizing M20. **heparinize** *v.t.* treat with heparin so as to inhibit blood clotting M20.

hepat- *comb. form* see HEPATO-.

hepatic /hɪˈpatɪk/ *a.* & *n.* LME. [L *hepaticus* f. Gk *hēpatikos*, f. *hēpar*, *hēpat-* liver: see -IC.] A *adj.* I †1 Affected with a liver complaint. Only in LME. 2 Of or pertaining to the liver. L16. 3 Acting on the liver, good for the liver. L17. II 4 Of the colour of liver; dark reddish-brown. LME. 5 Sulphurous; containing sulphur. Cf. HEPAR. *arch.* M17. B *n.* 1 A medicine that acts on the liver. L15. 2 = LIVERWORT. L19.

hepatical *a.* (now *rare*) = HEPATIC *a.* E17.

hepatica /hɪˈpatɪkə, hɛ-/ *n.* Pl. **-cas**, (in sense 1) **-cae** /-kiː/. LME. [med.L (sc. *herba*) plant with liver-shaped parts or used for liver diseases, use as n. of fem. of L *hepaticus*: see prec.] 1 = LIVERWORT 1. Orig., (a herbalist's name for) the liverwort *Marchantia polymorpha*. LME. 2 Any of several spring-flowering European and N. American woodland plants of the genus *Hepatica*, allied to the anemone, with three-lobed leaves thought to resemble the liver. L16.

hepatiˈcologist *n.* a person who studies liverworts L19.

hepatico- /hɪˈpatɪkəʊ/ *comb. form* of HEPATIC: see -O-. = HEPATO-.

hepatiˈcostomy *n.* (the surgical formation of) an opening in the main bile duct; an instance of this: E20.

hepatisation *n.* var. of HEPATIZATION.

hepatitis /hɛpəˈtʌɪtɪs/ *n.* E18. [mod.L, f. Gk *hēpar*, *hēpat-* liver + -ITIS.] *Med.* Inflammation of the liver; any of several diseases in which this occurs.

hepatitis A infectious hepatitis. **hepatitis B** serum hepatitis. **infectious hepatitis** a viral form of hepatitis transmitted in food, causing fever and jaundice. SERUM *hepatitis*.

hepatization /hɛpətʌɪˈzeɪʃ(ə)n/ *n.* Also **-isation**. L18. [f. Gk *hēpar*, *hēpat-* liver + -IZATION.] †1 *Chem.* Treatment with hydrogen sulphide. Cf. HEPATIC *a.* 5. Only in L18. 2 *Med.* Consolidation of lung tissue into a solid mass resembling liver tissue, occurring in lobar pneumonia. E19.

†**hepatize** *v.t.* (*Chem.*) treat with hydrogen sulphide L18–M19.

hepato- /ˈhɛpətəʊ/ *comb. form* of Gk *hēpar*, *hēpat-* liver: see -O-. Bef. a vowel also **hepat-**. Cf. HEPATICO-.

hepaˈtectomy *n.* (an instance of) surgical removal of all or part of the liver: E20. **hepatoˈcellular** *a.* of or pertaining to the cells of the liver M20. **hepaˈtoma** *n.*, pl. **-mas, -mata** /-mətə/, a carcinoma of the epithelial cells of the liver E20. **hepatomeˈgalia** *n.* = HEPATOMEGALY L19. **hepatoˈmegaly** *n.* abnormal enlargement of the liver E20. **hepatoˈpancreas** *n.* (*Zool.*) a glandular organ of digestion in most crustaceans L19. **hepaˈtoscopy** *n.* divination by examination of the liver of an animal E18. **ˌhepatoˌsplenomeˈgalia, -ˈmegaly** *ns.* abnormal enlargement of the liver and spleen M20. **hepatoˈtoxic** *a.* toxic to liver cells M20. **hepatotoˈxicity** *n.* hepatotoxic character M20. **hepatoˈtoxin** *n.* any substance toxic to the liver E20.

hepatolenticular /ˌhɛpətəʊlɛnˈtɪkjʊlə/ *a.* E20. [f. prec. + LENTICULAR (as affecting the lenticular (lentiform) nuclei of the basal ganglia of the brain).] Med. *hepatolenticular degeneration*, = *Wilson's disease* s.v. WILSON *n.*[2]

Hephaestian /hɪˈfiːstɪən/ *a.* M17. [f. *Hephaestus* (see below) + -IAN.] Of, belonging to, or made by Hephaestus, Greek god of fire, identified by the Romans with Vulcan.

hephthemimer /hɛfθɪˈmɪmə/ *n.* Also (earlier) in L form **-meris** /-mərɪs/. E18. [Late L *hephthemimeres* (*-is*) f. Gk *hephthēmimerēs* containing seven halves, f. *hepta* seven + *hēmi-* half + *meros* part, *-merēs* -partite.] *Class. Pros.* A group of seven half-feet; the part of a hexameter line preceding the caesura when this occurs in the middle of the fourth foot.

hepthemimeral *a.* L19.

hepialid /hɪːpɪˈalɪd/ *a.* & *n.* L19. [mod.L *Hepialidae* (see below), f. *Hepialus* genus name f. Gk *hēpiolos* moth, perh. alt. by confusion with *ēpialos* nightmare: see -ID[3].] *Entomol.* A *adj.* Of, pertaining to, or designating the family Hepialidae, comprising the swift moths. L19. B *n.* A moth of this family. L19.

Hepplewhite /ˈhɛp(ə)lwʌɪt/ *n.* L19. [George *Hepplewhite* (d. 1786), Eng. cabinet-maker.] Used *attrib.* to designate an English style of furniture of the late 18th cent., characterized by lightness, delicacy, and graceful curves.

hepta- /ˈhɛptə/ *comb. form.* Bef. a vowel **hept-**. [Gk *hepta* seven.] Having seven, sevenfold.

heptachlor *n.* a chlorinated hydrocarbon, $C_{10}H_5Cl_7$, used as an insecticide M20. **heptaˈhydrate** *n.* (*Chem.*) a hydrate containing seven moles of water per mole of the compound L19. **heptahyˈdrated** *a.* (*Chem.*) hydrated with seven moles of water per mole of the compound L19. **heptamer** *n.* (*Chem.*) a compound whose molecule is composed of seven molecules of monomer M20. **heptaˈmeric** *a.* (*Chem.*) of the nature of a heptamer, consisting of a heptamer or heptamers L20. **hepˈtangular** *a.* having seven angles E18. **heptastich** *n.* a group of seven lines of verse L19. **heptasyˈllabic** *n.* & *a.* (a metrical line) of seven syllables L18. **heptaˈtonic** *a.* (*Mus.*) consisting of seven notes L19. **hepta'valent** *a.* (*Chem.*) having a valency of seven L19.

heptachord /'hɛptəkɔːd/ *a.* & *n.* E18. [In senses A, B.1 f. Gk *heptakhordos* seven-stringed f. HEPTA- + *khordē* string (see CORD *n.*[1]). In sense B.2, 3 f. HEPTA- + CHORD *n.*[1]] *Mus.* †A *adj.* Seven-stringed. E–M18. **B** *n.* **1** Any musical instrument of seven strings. M18. **2** The interval of a seventh. M18. **3** A scale of seven notes; the modern major or minor scale. L18.

heptacosane /hɛptə'kəʊseɪn/ *n.* Also (earlier) †**heptaicosane**. L19. [f. HEPTA- + Gk *eikosi* twenty + -ANE.] *Chem.* Any of a series of saturated hydrocarbons (alkanes) with the formula $C_{27}H_{56}$; *spec.* (also n-*heptacosane*) the unbranched isomer, $CH_3(CH_2)_{25}CH_3$.

heptad /'hɛptad/ *n.* M17. [Gk *heptad-*, *heptas*, f. *hepta* seven: see -AD[1].] **1** A group of seven. M17. **2** *spec.* = HEBDOMAD 2. L19. †**3** *Chem.* A heptavalent element or group. Only in L19.

heptadecane /hɛptə'dɛkeɪn/ *n.* L19. [f. HEPTA- + Gk *deka* ten + -ANE.] *Chem.* Any of a series of saturated hydrocarbons (alkanes) with the formula $C_{17}H_{36}$; *spec.* (also n-*heptadecane*) the solid unbranched isomer, $CH_3(CH_2)_{15}CH_3$.

heptadeca'noic *a.* = MARGARIC L19.

heptaglot /'hɛptəglɒt/ *n.* & *a.* L17. [f. Gk *hepta* seven + *glōtta* tongue, *glōttos* tongued, prob. after POLYGLOT.] (A book) in seven languages.

heptagon /'hɛptəg(ə)n/ *n.* L16. [Fr. *heptagone* or med.L *heptagonum* use as n. of neut. sing. of late L *heptagonus* adj. f. Gk *heptagonos* seven-cornered, f. as HEPTA-: see -GON.] *Geom.* A plane figure with seven straight sides and seven angles.

heptagonal /hɛp'tag(ə)n(ə)l/ *a.* having the form of a heptagon; having seven sides: E17.

heptahedron /hɛptə'hiːdrən, -'hɛd-/ *n.* Pl. **-dra** /-drə/, **-drons**. L17. [f. HEPTA- + -HEDRON.] A solid figure or object with seven plane faces.

heptahedral *a.* having the form of a heptahedron; having seven faces: M18. †**heptahedrical** *a.* = HEPTAHEDRAL: M–L17.

†**heptaicosane** *n.* var. of HEPTACOSANE.

heptamerous /hɛp'tam(ə)rəs/ *a.* M19. [f. HEPTA- + Gk *meros* part + -OUS.] Having seven parts.

heptameter /hɛp'tamɪtə/ *n.* L19. [Late L *heptametrum* f. Gk *heptametron*, f. *hepta-* HEPTA- + *metron* measure, metre.] *Pros.* A line of seven metrical feet.

hepta'metrical *a.* E19.

heptane /'hɛpteɪn/ *n.* L19. [f. HEPTA- + -ANE.] *Chem.* Any of a series of saturated hydrocarbons with the formula C_7H_{16}; *esp.* (also n-*heptane*) the unbranched isomer, $CH_3(CH_2)_5CH_3$.

hepta'noic *a.* = OENANTHIC E20.

heptarch /'hɛptɑːk/ *n.* L17. [f. HEPTA- + -ARCH, after TETRARCH *n.*] †**1** A seventh king (see *Rev.* 17:9–11). Only in L17. **2** A ruler of one of seven divisions of a country; *esp.* any of the rulers of the Anglo-Saxon Heptarchy. E19.

heptarchy /'hɛptɑːki/ *n.* L16. [f. HEPTA- + -ARCHY, after TETRARCHY.] Government by seven rulers; an aggregate of seven districts, each under its own ruler; *spec.* the supposed seven kingdoms of the Angles and Saxons in Britain in the 7th and 8th cents.

hep'tarchal *a.* M19. **hep'tarchic** *a.* L18. **hep'tarchical** *a.* M19.

heptateuch /'hɛptətjuːk/ *n.* L17. [Late L *heptateuchus* f. Gk *heptateukhos*, f. *hepta* seven + *teukhos* book.] A volume consisting of seven books; *the Heptateuch*, the first seven books of the Bible. Cf. PENTATEUCH.

heptathlon /hɛp'taθlɒn, -lən/ *n.* L20. [f. HEPTA- + Gk *athlon* contest.] An athletic contest, usu. for women, comprising seven different events for the competitor.

heptathlete *n.* a competitor in the heptathlon L20.

heptode /'hɛptəʊd/ *n.* M20. [f. HEPTA- + -ODE[2].] *Electronics.* A thermionic tube with seven electrodes.

heptoic /hɛp'təʊɪk/ *a.* L19. [f. HEPTA- + -OIC.] *Chem.* = OENANTHIC.

heptose /'hɛptəʊz, -s/ *n.* L19. [f. HEPTA- + -OSE[2].] *Chem.* Any monosaccharide sugar with seven carbon atoms in its molecule.

heptyl /'hɛptʌɪl, -tɪl/ *n.* M19. [f. HEPTA- + -YL.] *Chem.* A radical, C_7H_{15}·, derived from a heptane. Usu. in *comb.*

her /həː, *unstressed* ə/ *pers. pron.*[1], *3 sing. fem. objective* (*dat.* & *accus.*), & *n.* [OE *hire* dat. of *hīo*, *hēo* HOO *pron.*, = OFris. *hiri*, MDu. *hare*, *haer*, *hore*, Du. *haar*, with inflection parallel to OS *iru*, OHG *iru*, *iro* (G *ihr*), Goth. *izai*.] **A** *pron.* **I 1** Objective (direct & indirect) of SHE *pron.* (orig. of HOO *pron.*): the female person or animal, or the animal conventionally regarded as female (as a cat, a hare, a rabbit), or the thing personified or conventionally treated as female or (in early use) grammatically feminine, previously mentioned or implied or easily identified. OE. **b** Herself: direct (*arch.* exc. after preps.) & indirect (*arch.* exc. *US dial.*) objective. OE. **2** Subjective: she. Esp. pred. after *be* & after *than*, *as*. *colloq.* L17.

1 TENNYSON He stoops—to kiss her—on his knee. J. MASEFIELD All I ask is a tall ship and a star to steer her by. J. RHYS To get in the dig that will make him or her feel superior. E. BOWEN Suspiciousness made him send her frequent bunches of flowers, and post her . . little letters. J. BETJEMAN The Morris eight. . . Put her in reverse. O. MANNING Harriet looked uneasily about her. J. BALDWIN I love America . . and . . I insist on the right to criticize her. **her indoors** *colloq.* (freq. *joc.*) one's wife, the woman with whom one lives. **herseems**, **-seemeth**, (pa. t. **-seemed**) *v.i. impers.* (long *arch.*) it seems, seemed, to her (modifying a sentence or parenthetically). b C. KINGSLEY Then peevishly she flung her on her face. 2 OED I am sure it was her that told me. **not quite her** (of a garment etc.) that does not suit her.

II 3 Repr. the Eng. of Welsh or Gaelic speakers: he, him, his. E16.

B *n.* The female; a female. *colloq.* M17.

her /həː, *unstressed* ə/ *possess. pron.*[2] & *a.* (in mod. usage also classed as a *determiner*), *3 sing. fem.* [OE *hiere*, *hire* genit. of *hīo*, *hēo* HOO *pron.*, = OFris. *hiri*, MDu. *hare*, Du. *haar*, with inflection parallel to OS *ira*, *iro*, *iru*, *ire*, OHG *ira*, *iro*, MHG *ire*, *ir* (G *ihr*), Goth. *izōs*. Cf. HERN *pron.*, HERS *pron.*] †**A** *pron.* **1** Genit. of HOO *pron.*; of her. OE–ME. **2** = HERS. Only in ME.

B *adj.* (*attrib.*) **1** Of her; of herself; which belongs or pertains to her(self). OE. **b** In titles (as *Her Ladyship*, *Her Majesty*): that she is. LME. **2** After a n. (esp. a personal name): substituting for the genit. inflection or possess. suff. -'s[1]. *arch.* OE.

1 J. CONRAD It does not matter much to a ship having all the open sea before her bows. J. BUCHAN London at the turn of the century had not yet lost her Georgian air. E. WAUGH Then she went on her way to the scoutmaster's. P. KAVANAGH With her left hand she poked the fire with a long pot-stick and her handling of that pot-stick showed better than her talk her annoyance with her son. SCOTT FITZGERALD Her name was Irene Scheerer, and her father was one of the men who . . believed in Dexter. I. MURDOCH Laura was looking her most energetic and eccentric. *her own*: see OWN *a.* & *pron.* *her watch*: see WATCH *n.* 2 H. L'ESTRANGE The Excellency of our Church her burial office.

Heracleid /'hɛrəklʌɪd/ *n.* M19. [Gk *Hērakleidēs* (pl. *-dai*), L *Heraclides* (pl. *-dae*).] Any of the descendants of Heracles (Hercules) from whom the Dorian aristocracy of the Peloponnese claimed descent. Usu. in *pl.*

Hera'cleidan *a.* of or pertaining to a Heracleid or the Heracleids E19.

Heracleitean *a.* & *n.* var. of HERACLITEAN.

Heracleonite /hɛrə'kliːənʌɪt/ *n.* M16. [f. *Heracleon* (see below) + -ITE[1].] A member of a sect of Gnostics founded by Heracleon (fl. AD 145–80), a disciple of Valentinus.

heracleum /hɛrə'kliːəm, hɛ'raklɪəm/ *n.* L18. [mod.L, f. Gk *hērakleia* a plant named after Heracles.] Any of various tall umbelliferous plants constituting the genus *Heracleum*, which includes the cow parsnip or hogweed, *H. sphondylium*.

Heraclitean /hɛrəklʌɪ'tiːən/ *a.* & *n.* Also **-cleit-**. E18. [f. (L *Heracliteus* f.) Gk *Hērakleiteios*, f. *Hērakleitos* Heraclitus (see below): see -AN.] **A** *adj.* Of or pertaining to (the theories of) the Greek philosopher Heraclitus of Ephesus (fl. *c* 500 BC), who maintained that all things are in a state of flux. E18. **B** *n.* A follower of Heraclitus. L19.

Heracliteanism *n.* L19. **Hera'clitic** *a.* = HERACLITEAN *a.* L17.

herald /'hɛr(ə)ld/ *n.* ME. [OFr. *herau(l)t* (mod. *héraut*) f. Gmc bases of HERE *n.*[1] and WIELD *v.*] **1** *Hist.* An official employed to make a ruler's proclamations and carry ceremonial messages between heads of state, or in tournaments, to convey challenges, marshal combatants, etc. or at Court, to arrange various State ceremonies, regulate the use of armorial bearings, settle questions of precedence, etc. Formerly also *herald of* (or *at*) *arms*. ME. **2** *transf.* & *fig.* **a** A messenger, an envoy. Also in titles of newspapers. LME. **b** A person who or thing which precedes and announces the approach of another; a precursor. L16. **3** Any of the members of the College of Arms (COLLEGE *n.* 1) or (in Scotland) of the Court of the Lord Lyon directly senior to the pursuivants. M16. **b** An expert in heraldry. E19.

1 C. THIRLWALL A herald came to demand an armistice. A. SETON The King's heralds had galloped throughout the country proclaiming the great tournament. *Windsor herald*: see WINDSOR *a.* 1. 2a W. COWPER A herald of God's love to pagan lands. *Catholic Herald*, *Glasgow Herald*, etc. b T. H. HUXLEY Earthquakes are often the heralds of volcanic eruptions. 3 *Heralds' College*: see COLLEGE 1. **Heralds' Office** the office of the College of Arms.

Comb.: **herald-snake** a moderately venomous southern African snake, *Crotaphopeltis hotamboeia*, with red- or yellow-edged mouth.

herald /'hɛr(ə)ld/ *v.t.* LME. [OFr. *herauder*, *heraulder*, etc., f. as prec.] Proclaim the approach of; usher *in*. Chiefly *fig.*

B. EMECHETA An envelope . . one of those horrible khaki-coloured ones that usually herald the gas bill. A. PRICE Any . . distant noise which might herald Audley's return.

heraldic /hɛ'raldɪk/ *a.* L18. [f. HERALD *n.* + -IC: cf. Fr. *héraldique*.] Of, pertaining to, or represented in heraldry.

O. NEUBECKER Unlike its natural counterpart, the heraldic pelican has no bill pouch. *heraldic tyger*: see TIGER *n.* 3.

heraldical *a.* = HERALDIC E17. **heraldically** *adv.* E19.

heraldist /'hɛr(ə)ldɪst/ *n.* E19. [f. HERALD *n.* + -IST.] An expert in heraldry.

heraldry /'hɛr(ə)ldri/ *n.* L16. [f. HERALD *n.* + -RY.] **1** The art or science of a herald; *spec.* that of blazoning armorial bearings and deciding the rights of people to bear arms. L16. †**b** Heraldic law. *rare* (Shakes.). Only in E17. †**c** Heraldic rank or title. Also, the practice of buying and selling precedence in a list of cases to be heard. E17–M18. **2** A heraldic emblazonment; heraldic devices collectively. L16. **3** The office of herald or messenger. L16. **4** Ceremony characteristic of a herald. M17.

1b SHAKES. *Haml.* This Fortinbras; who by a Seal'd Compact, Well ratified by law and heraldry, Did forfeit . . all those his lands. c SHAKES. *All's Well* You are more saucy with lords . . than the commission of your birth and virtue gives you heraldry. 2 F. R. WILSON A series of panels filled alternately with heraldry and figures. 4 J. S. MILL A writer . . announced, with all the pomp and heraldry of triumphant genius, a discovery.

†**heraldy** *n.* LME–M18. [f. HERALD *n.* + -Y[3].] = HERALDRY.

Herat /hɛ'rɑːt/ *a.* E20. [A city in NW Afghanistan.] Designating a type of carpet or rug made at Herat, or the small close design of leaf and rosette patterns characteristic of this.

Herati *n.* & *a.* (*a*) *n.* a Herat carpet or rug; (*b*) *adj.* = HERAT: E20.

herb /həːb/ *n.* ME. [OFr. *erbe* (mod. *herbe*) f. L *herba* grass, green crops, herb. The spelling with *h* is recorded from the earliest times, but a pronunc. without initial aspirate was regular till E19.] **1** A plant whose stem does not become woody and persistent (as in a shrub or tree) but remains soft and succulent, and dies (completely or down to the root) after flowering. ME. **2** A (freq. aromatic) plant used for flavouring or scent, in medicine, etc. ME. 3 *collect.* Herbage. In later use *poet.* LME. †4 The leafy part of a (herbaceous) plant, esp. as distinct from the root. M17–L18.

2 R. INGALLS She sprinkled some herbs and salt on the top. 3 W. OWEN Soon they topped the hill, and raced . . Over an open stretch of herb and heather.

Comb.: **herb beer** a drink made from herbs; *herb bennet*: see BENNET *n.*[1]; **herb Christopher** [tr. med.L *herba Christophori* herb of St Christopher, early martyr] (*a*) a baneberry, *esp.* a common Eurasian baneberry, *Actaea spicata*; †(*b*) royal fern, *Osmunda regalis*; **herb-doctor** (chiefly *N. Amer.*) a doctor who treats diseases with herbs instead of conventional remedies; **herb Gerard** [named after St *Gerard* of Toul (*c*935–94), formerly invoked against gout] the plant ground elder, *Aegopodium podagraria*; *herb-grace*: see *herb of grace* below; *herb mastic*: see MASTIC *n.* 3; **herb of grace, herb-grace** (now *arch.* & *dial.*) [app. after the formal coincidence of the name *rue* with RUE *v.*, *n.*[1] repent, repentance] the herb rue, *Ruta graveolens*; *gen.* any herb of valuable properties; **herb Paris** [tr. med.L *herba paris*, prob. lit. 'herb of a pair', from the resemblance of the four leaves to a true-lover's knot] a woodland plant, *Paris quadrifolia* (of the lily family), bearing a single greenish flower at the top of the stem, and just beneath it four large ovate leaves in the form of a cross; **herb Robert** [tr. med.L *herba Roberti*: variously referred to Robert Duke of Normandy, to St Robert, and to St Rupert] a wild cranesbill common in hedges, *Geranium robertianum*, with bright pink flowers, reddish stems, and finely cut leaves; **herb tea** an infusion of herbs; **herb tobacco** a mixture of herbs smoked as a substitute for tobacco; **herb Trinity** *arch.* the hepatica, *Hepatica nobilis*, so called from its three-lobed leaves; *herb* TWOPENCE; **herb water** = *herb tea* above.

†herba *n.* L16–E19. [It. (now *erba*), lit. 'grass'.] A sort of grass-cloth formerly imported from India.

herbaceous /həːˈbeɪʃəs/ *a.* M17. [L *herbaceus* grassy, f. *herba* HERB: see -ACEOUS.] 1 Of the nature of a herb (HERB 1); *esp.* not forming a woody stem but dying down to the root each year. M17. 2 *Bot.* Resembling a leaf in colour or texture. Opp. *scarious.* L18.

1 **herbaceous border** a garden border containing esp. perennial flowering plants.

herbage /ˈhəːbɪdʒ/ *n.* LME. [OFr. *erbage* (mod. *herbage*) f. med.L *herbaticum*, *-us* (also *herbagium*), f. L *herba* HERB.] 1 Herbaceous vegetation; *esp.* grass and other low-growing plants used as pasture. LME. 2 *Law.* The natural herbage of a piece of land as a species of property distinct from the land itself; the right of grazing one's cattle on another person's land. LME. 3 The green succulent parts of a herbaceous plant. E18.

herbaged *a.* covered in herbage E18.

herbal /ˈhəːb(ə)l/ *n.* E16. [med.L *herbalis* (sc. *liber*), f. L *herba*: see -AL[1].] 1 *Hist.* A book containing descriptions of plants, together with accounts of their properties and medicinal uses. E16. 2 A collection of herbs; *esp.* an album or collection of botanical specimens. Now *rare* or *obs.* L16.

herbal /ˈhəːb(ə)l/ *a.* E17. [(Fr. †*herbal* f.) med.L *herbalis*: see prec.] Pertaining to, consisting of, or made from a herb or herbs.

herbalist /ˈhəːb(ə)lɪst/ *n.* L16. [f. HERBAL *n.* + -IST.] 1 A collector of or writer on plants or herbs. Now *spec.* an early botanical writer. L16. 2 A dealer in medicinal herbs; a person who prepares herbal remedies. Also, a person who practises or advocates the use of herbs to treat disease. L16. b In S. Africa, a practitioner of traditional medicine. L16.

herbalism *n.* †(*a*) botany; (*b*) the use of herbs to treat disease: M17. **herbalize** *v.i.* (*arch.*) search for plants, esp. medicinal herbs L17.

herbarise *v.* var. of HERBARIZE.

herbarist /ˈhəːbərɪst/ *n. obs.* exc. *Hist.* L16. [f. L *herbaria* botany (see HERBARIUM) + -IST.] An expert on herbs or plants.

†herbarism *n.* botany L16–M19.

herbarium /həːˈbɛːrɪəm/ *n.* L18. [Late L *herbarium*, use as n. of adj. repr. by L *herbarius* botanist, *herbaria* (sc. *ars*) botany.] A collection of dried botanical specimens systematically arranged for reference. Also, a room or building housing such a collection.

herbarize /ˈhəːbərʌɪz/ *v.i. arch.* Also **-ise.** L17. [f. as HERBARIST + -IZE.] = HERBALIZE, HERBORIZE.

herbariˈzation *n.* L17.

Herbartian /həːˈbɑːtɪən/ *a.* & *n.* L19. [f. *Herbart* (see below) + -IAN.] A *adj.* Pertaining to the German philosopher J. F. Herbart (1776–1841) or the system of psychology and teaching originated by him. L19. B *n.* A follower of Herbart. L19.

herbary /ˈhəːbəri/ *n.* M16. [In sense 1 f. L *herbarius*, in sense 2 f. late L *herbarium*, in sense 3 f. med.L *herbarius*, *-um*, all f. L *herba* HERB: see -ARY[1].] †1 A herbalist. Only in M16. 2 A herbarium. Now *rare* or *obs.* L16. 3 A herb garden. *arch.* M17.

herbed /həːbd/ *a.* L20. [f. HERB *n.* + -ED[2].] Flavoured with herbs.

herber *n.* see ARBOUR.

herbicide /ˈhəːbɪsʌɪd/ *n.* L19. [f. L *herba* HERB + -CIDE.] A substance toxic to plants and used to destroy unwanted vegetation, esp. weeds.

herbiˈcidal *a.* M19.

herbivore /ˈhəːbɪvɔː/ *n.* M19. [f. as next or f. Fr. *herbivore*.] An animal, esp. a mammal, that feeds naturally on plants.

herbivorous /həːˈbɪv(ə)rəs/ *a.* M17. [mod.L *herbivorus*, f. L *herba* HERB: see -I-, -VOROUS.] Of an animal, esp. a mammal: feeding naturally on plants.

herˈbivory *n.* herbivorous nature or habits M20.

herbless /ˈhəːblɪs/ *a.* L17. [f. HERB *n.* + -LESS.] Devoid of herbage.

herblet /ˈhəːblɪt/ *n.* E17. [f. HERB *n.* + -LET.] An insignificant herb or herbaceous plant.

herborise *v.* var. of HERBORIZE.

herborist /ˈhəːbərɪst/ *n. arch.* L16. [Fr. *herboriste*, f. *herbe* HERB by assoc. w. L *arbor* tree: cf. next, ARBOUR & see -IST.] An expert on herbs or plants.

herborize /ˈhəːbərʌɪz/ *v.i. arch.* Also **-ise.** M17. [Fr. *herboriser*, f. as prec. by assoc. w. *arboriser* collect plants: see -IZE.] †1 Tend herbs; garden. *rare.* Only in M17. 2 Search for plants, esp. medicinal herbs. M18.

herboriˈzation *n.* a botanizing excursion L17.

herbose /həːˈbəʊs/ *a.* E18. [L *herbosus*, f. *herba* HERB: see -OSE[1].] Having much herbage.

herbous /ˈhəːbəs/ *a.* E18. [L *herbosus*: see prec., -OUS.] Pertaining to or of the nature of a herb (HERB 1, 2).

herby /ˈhəːbi/ *a.* M16. [f. HERB + -Y[1].] 1 Covered with herbage or grass, having much herbage. M16. 2 Of the nature of or pertaining to a herbaceous plant or the leafy part of it. M16. 3 Flavoured with or redolent of (aromatic) herbs. L19.

Hercegovinian *a.* & *n.* var. of HERZEGOVINIAN.

hercogamy /həːˈkɒɡəmi/ *n.* Also **herk-.** L19. [f. Gk *herkos* fence + -GAMY.] *Bot.* A condition in which the stamens and stigmas of a flower are separated by physical barriers, so preventing self-pollination.

hercoˈgamic, hercogamous *adjs.* L19.

Herculean /həːkjʊˈliːən, həːˈkjuːlɪən/ *a.* Also **h-.** L16. [f. L *Herculeus* (f. as next) + -AN: see -EAN.] 1 Of or pertaining to Hercules, the superhuman hero of classical mythology; resembling Hercules in strength etc., immensely powerful or vigorous. L16. 2 Of a task: as hard to accomplish as were Hercules's twelve labours; immensely arduous. E17.

1 Q. BELL A man of Herculean stature. K. WILLIAMS We . . made a herculean effort . . to put in all the new moves and dialogue. *transf.*: H. POWER The first (which is the main and Herculean-Argument). 2 *Horse & Rider* Such Herculean tasks aren't beyond it.

Hercules /ˈhəːkjʊliːz/ *n.* ME. [L *Hercules* alt. of Gk *Hēraklēs*, f. *Hēra* wife of Zeus + *kleos* glory, lit. 'having or showing the glory of Hera'.] 1 *Class. Mythol.* A hero of superhuman strength, usu. depicted as carrying a club, who was celebrated for accomplishing twelve extraordinary tasks or 'labours' imposed on him by Hera and who after death was ranked among the gods. ME. b A representation of Hercules or a strong man. M17. 2 An exceptionally strong or muscular man. M16. 3 (The name of) a faint constellation of the northern hemisphere, between Draco and Ophiuchus. M16. 4 Any of several powerful machines; *esp.* a heavy weight used like the ram in a pile-driving machine. L18. 5 More fully *Hercules beetle.* A very large S. American scarabaeid beetle, *Dynastes hercules.* E19.

Phrases & comb.: *Hercules beetle*: see sense 5 above. **Hercules braid** a heavily corded worsted braid, used for trimmings. **Hercules' club** either of two tall prickly shrubs or small trees of the US: (*a*) the southern prickly ash, *Zanthoxylum clava-herculis*, of the rue family; (*b*) the angelica tree, *Aralia spinosa*. **Hercules' Pillars** *arch.* = *Pillars of Hercules* below. **Hercules powder** *US* a powerful explosive used in mining. *labour of Hercules*: see LABOUR *n.* **Pillars of Hercules** the rocks (now Gibraltar and Ceuta) on either side of the Straits of Gibraltar, believed by the ancients to mark the western limits of the habitable world.

Hercynian /həːˈsɪnɪən/ *a.* L16. [f. L *Hercynia* (sc. *silva* wood) = Gk *Herkunios drumos*: see -AN.] 1 In ancient Greek and Roman writers, designating a vaguely defined area of forest-covered mountains between the Rhine and the Carpathians. L16. 2 *Geol.* a Designating or pertaining to one of the Devonian formations of the Harz Mountains. L19. b Designating or pertaining to an episode of mountain-building in Europe in late Carboniferous and early Permian times. Also called *Armorican.* L19.

hercynite /ˈhəːsɪnʌɪt/ *n.* M19. [f. as prec. + -ITE[1].] *Min.* A black mineral of the spinel group consisting essentially of ferrous iron and aluminium oxides, usu. found as granules.

herd /həːd/ *n.*[1] [OE *heord* = MLG *herde*, OHG *herta* (G *Herde*), ON *hjǫrð*, Goth. *hairda*, f. Gmc.] 1 A company of domestic animals, now esp. cattle, kept together. OE. 2 A company of animals feeding and travelling together. ME. 3 A large number of people, a crowd; a rabble. Now *derog.* LME.

1 M. SHADBOLT He got stuck into the milking, and had the herd finished before dark. *flocks and herds*: see FLOCK *n.*[1] **ride herd on** *US* keep watch on. 2 B. LOPEZ Herds of musk oxen graze below a range of hills in clusters of three or four. 3 C. THIRLWALL The legitimate chief was distinguished from the vulgar herd . . by his robust frame. SAKI That world where people are counted individually and not in herds. **the herd instinct** gregariousness and mutual influence as a psychological factor.

Comb.: **herd-book** a pedigree-book of cattle or pigs; **herd-grass, herd's-grass** *US* any of various grasses grown for hay or pasture, *esp.* timothy, *Phleum pratense*, and the red-top grass, *Agrostis capillaris*.

herd /həːd/ *n.*[2] [OE *hirdi*, (WS) *hierde* = OS *hirdi*, *herdi*, OHG *hirti* (G *Hirte*), ON *hirðir*, Goth. *hairdeis*, f. Gmc base of prec.] 1 A keeper of herds, a herdsman. Now usu. as 2nd elem. of comb. OE. 2 A spiritual shepherd, a pastor. Long *obs.* exc. *Sc.* OE. †3 A keeper, a guardian. OE–L16.

1 *cowherd, swineherd,* etc.

herd /həːd/ *v.*[1] ME. [f. HERD *n.*[2]] †1 *v.t.* Keep safe, shelter. ME–M16. 2 *v.t.* & (*rare*) *i.* Tend (sheep, cattle, etc.). LME. 3 *v.t.* Drive (an animal, a person) in a particular direction. Passing into HERD *v.*[2] 3. L19.

3 D. MORRIS They were particularly adept at herding and driving prey during hunting manoeuvres. J. A. MICHENER They had herded nearly three thousand longhorns thirteen hundred miles. J. M. COETZEE They herd the captives along.

herder *n.* (now chiefly *N. Amer.*) a herdsman ME.

herd /həːd/ *v.*[2] LME. [f. HERD *n.*[1]] 1 *v.i.* Go in a herd, form a herd; move (*about, along,* etc.) as a herd; *derog.* (of people) live together, associate with. Freq. foll. by *together, with.* LME. b Of things: gather, be assembled. *rare.* E18. 2 *v.i.* Join oneself to a company etc., go in company *with. arch.* LME. 3 *v.t.* Place in or among a herd; gather (*together*) as a herd. Passing into HERD *v.*[1] 3. L16.

1 GOLDSMITH These animals are in general fond of herding and grazing in company. R. INGALLS They all

herded forward over a bridge. 2 THACKERAY Ethel herded not with the children of her own age. 3 JONSON The rest, However great we are . . Are herded with the vulgar. B. TAYLOR Our mules had scattered far and wide . . and several hours elapsed before they could be herded. T. DREISER A sharp, almost January wind that herded the fallen leaves into piles.

herd-boy /ˈhəːdbɔɪ/ *n.* L18. [f. HERD *n.*[1], *n.*[2] + BOY *n.*] A boy who tends sheep, cattle, etc.; *US* a cowboy.

herderite /ˈhəːdərʌɪt/ *n.* E19. [f. S. A. W. von *Herder* (1776–1838), Ger. mining official + -ITE[1].] *Min.* A monoclinic phosphate and fluoride of beryllium and calcium, usu. occurring as colourless, yellowish, or greenish prisms or fibrous aggregates.

herdic /ˈhəːdɪk/ *n. US* (now *Hist.*). L19. [f. Peter *Herdic* (1824–88), Amer. inventor.] A kind of small cab or carriage for public transport.

†herdman *n.* Pl. **-men.** OE–M17. [f. HERD *n.*[2] + MAN *n.*] A herdsman.

herdsman /ˈhəːdzmən/ *n.* Pl. **-men.** LME. [Alt. of HERDMAN after *craftsman* etc.] 1 An owner or keeper of herds. LME. 2 (Usu. **H-**.) *The* constellation Boötes. L17.

herdsmanship *n.* L19.

herdswoman /ˈhəːdzwʊmən/ *n.* E19. [f. as prec. + WOMAN *n.*] A female owner or keeper of herds.

Herdwick /ˈhəːdwɪk/ *n.* ME. [f. HERD *n.*[2] + -WICK.] †1 (Usu. **h-**.) A pasturage. ME–E19. 2 (An animal of) a hardy breed of sheep originating in Cumbria, NW England. Also *Herdwick sheep*. E19.

here /ˈhɛrə/ *n.*[1] Long *obs.* exc. *Hist.* [OE *here* = OFris., OS, OHG *heri* (Du., G *Heer*), ON *herr*, Goth. *harjis*, f. Gmc. Cf. HARRY *v.*, HARBOUR *n.*[1], HERIOT.] A host, a multitude; an army; *esp.* the Danish invaders of England during the Anglo-Saxon period.

here /hɪə/ *adv.*, *n.*[2], & *pron.* [OE *hēr* = OFris., OS *hēr*, OHG *hiar* (Du, G *hier*), ON *hér*, Goth *hēr* (beside OFris., OS *hīr*), app. f. Gmc base meaning 'this' (see HE *pron.*). Cf. YERE.] A *adv.* I 1 In this place or position. OE. b Indicating the presence of something: in unemphatic use, chiefly preceding *is*, *was*, etc. LME. c Imparting emphasis preceding a n. qualified by *this*, *these*. *dial.* & *colloq.* M18. 2 In this world; in this life; on earth. Long *rare* exc. in *here below*. OE. 3 At this point in an argument, a situation, etc.; at this juncture. OE. 4 In the matter in question, in this case. ME. 5 To this place or position. ME.

1 OED My brother, here, is ready to give information. E. HARDWICK Dearest M.: Here I am in Boston, . . looking out on a snowstorm. b MRS ALEXANDER I says, 'here's your tea, sir', but he made no answer. c DICKENS 'Now, with regard to this here robbery, master', said Blathers. 'What are the circumstances?' 2 J. MONTGOMERY There is no union here of hearts, That finds not here an end. 3 *Book of Common Prayer* In Quires and Places where they sing, here followeth the Anthem. J. B. PRIESTLEY Here she was stopped by a cough. 4 STEELE Here can then be no Injustice, where no one is injured. J. MORLEY Here more than anywhere else you need to give the tools to him who can handle them. 5 V. WOOLF When we got back here we found the room full of people. J. GATHORNE-HARDY A Hungarian who came over here to escape from Hitler in the late thirties.

II As *int.* 6 I am present. OE. 7 Calling attention or introducing a command or a remonstration. M17.

6 SHAKES. *Mids. N. D.* Francis Flute, the bellows-mender. . . Here, Peter Quince. 7 OED John! here! quick! J. KRANTZ Here, I almost forgot, . . your Christmas present.

Phrases: **here and now** *adv.* & *n. phr.* (*a*) *adv. phr.* at this very moment, immediately; (*b*) *n. phr. the* present reality. **here and there** in various places. **here below** in this life. **here goes!** expr. an intention to begin a bold act. *here lies our, your way*: see WAY *n. here's how*: see HOW *adv. here's looking at you*: see LOOK *v. here's mud in your eye!*: see MUD *n.*[1] **here's to —** I drink to the health of —. **here, there, and everywhere** in many different places. **here today, gone tomorrow** short-lived, merely transient. **here we are** *colloq.*: said on arrival at one's destination. **here we go again** *colloq.* the same, usu. undesirable, events are recurring. **here you are**: said on handing something to somebody. *look here*: see LOOK *v.* **neither here nor there** of no importance or relevance. *same here*: see SAME *pron.* & *n. see here*: see SEE *v.*

Comb.: **hereabout, -abouts,** *advs.* †(*a*) about or concerning this thing etc.; (*b*) about or near this place; in the neighbourhood; **hereat** *adv.* †(*a*) at this place; (*b*) *arch.* as a result of this; **hereaway, -aways,** *advs.* (now *dial.* & *US*) (*a*) hereabouts; (*b*) to this place, hither; **herefrom** *adv.* (now *rare* or *obs.*) (*a*) from this place, from here; (*b*) from this circumstance, from this source; **hereon** *adv.* (long *rare* or *obs.*) †(*a*) herein; †(*b*) to this place, on here; (*c*) on this matter etc., on this basis; (*d*) = *hereupon* (b) below; **hereout** *adv.* (long *rare* or *obs.*) (*a*) out of this place; †(*b*) from this source; **hereunder** *adv.* (*formal*) below (esp. in a book, document, etc.); **hereunto** *adv.* (*arch.*) to this document etc.; **hereupon** *adv.* †(*a*) on this subject, matter, etc; (*b*) after this, in consequence of this; **herewith, †-withal** *advs.* (*a*) with this (esp. of an enclosure in a letter etc.); †(*b*) on this, with these words etc.; (*c*) *rare* by means of this, hereby.

B *n.* & *pron.* This place or position. E17.

SHAKES. *Lear* Thou losest here, a better where to find. DICKENS You would rather not leave here till to-morrow morning. JOYCE Go away from here, he said rudely.

hereness *n.* the fact or condition of being here L17.

hereafter /hɪərˈɑːftə/ *adv.*, *n.*, & *a.* [OE *hērǣfter*, f. HERE *adv.* + AFTER *adv.*] A *adv.* 1 After this in order or position. OE. 2 At a future time, later on. ME. 3 In the world to come. LME.

1 W. CRUISE In consequence of the statute . . which will be stated hereafter. 2 B. JOWETT We cannot . . anticipate the details which will hereafter be needed. J. P. DONLEAVY Things could be different. Must control myself hereafter. 3 P. LIVELY You do not merely believe but *know* that there is a life hereafter.

B *n.* 1 The future. M16. 2 The world to come. E18.

1 SYD. SMITH Leave hereafter to the spirit and the wisdom of hereafter. 2 V. BRITTAIN I knew now that death was the end. . . There was no hereafter.

C *adj.* To come, future. Now *rare.* L16.

A. SEWARD Claims . . to hereafter compensation.

hereby /hɪəˈbʌɪ/ *adv.* ME. [f. HERE *adv.* + BY *prep.*] †1 By or near this place, close by. ME–M17. 2 As a result of this, by this means. ME.

1 SHAKES. *L.L.L.* Hereby, upon the edge of yonder coppice. 2 O. WILDE I hereby agree to assign you the rights in my play.

hereditable /hɪˈrɛdɪtəb(ə)l/ *a.* LME. [Fr. †*héréditable* or med.L *hereditabilis*, f. eccl.L *hereditare*: see next, -ABLE.] That may be inherited.

heˌreditaˈbility *n.* (*rare*) M19. **hereditably** *adv.* (now *rare*) L15.

hereditament /hɛrɪˈdɪtəm(ə)nt, hɪˈrɛdɪt-/ *n.* LME. [med.L *hereditamentum*, f. eccl.L *hereditare* inherit, f. *heres, hered-* HEIR *n.*: see -MENT.] 1 *Law.* Property that can be inherited; real property. LME. 2 Inheritance. E16.

hereditary /hɪˈrɛdɪt(ə)ri/ *a.* & *n.* LME. [L *hereditarius*, f. as HEREDITY: see -ARY[1].] A *adj.* 1 Descending by inheritance. LME. 2 Transmitted from one generation to another. LME. b Identical with or similar to what one's parents or precursors had. E17. 3 Holding one's position by inheritance. M17. 4 Of or pertaining to inheritance. L18.

1 T. HARDY If knighthood were hereditary, . . from father to son, you would be Sir John now. A. MUNRO The ruler . . , not through hereditary right but through force of personality. 2 *Practical Hairstyling & Beauty* It is a hereditary trait which cannot be controlled. b E. YOUNG Long burnt a fixt hereditary hate, Between the crowns of Macedon and Thrace. 3 R. HOGGART These . . belong to the hereditary aristocracy of the neighbourhood. G. VIDAL The magians are the hereditary priests of the Medes and the Persians. 4 R. N. KHORY Abnormal structures are the most obvious instances of hereditary transmission.

B *n.* A person who holds a position by inheritance. *rare.* M19.

herediˈtarian *n.* a person who considers that heredity has the primary influence on a person's or a group's development L19. **hereditarily** *adv.* E17. **hereditariness** *n.* M17.

heredity /hɪˈrɛdɪti/ *n.* M16. [(O)Fr. *hérédité* or L *hereditas*, f. as HEIR *n.*: see -ITY.] †1 Hereditary succession; an inheritance. Only in M16. 2 *Law.* Hereditary character, quality, or condition. Now *rare* or *obs.* L18. 3 The tendency of like to beget like; the property of organic beings by which offspring have the nature and characteristics of their parents and ancestors; the genetic constitution of an individual. M19.

2 *Athenaeum* The heredity and independence of the fiefs . . shown to have commenced in . . the tenth century. 3 B. MACDONALD Gammy was a strong believer in heredity, particularly the inheritance of bad traits. R. MACDONALD Their basic trouble was genetic, and there's still not much we can do about heredity.

Hereford /ˈhɛrɪfəd/ *a.* & *n.* E19. [f. *Hereford* a city and county in the west of England where the breed originated.] A *adj.* Designating, of, or pertaining to a breed of red and white beef cattle. E19. B *n.* (An animal of) the Hereford breed of cattle. E19.

†Herefordshire *a.* = HEREFORD *a.* L18–M19.

heregeld /ˈhɛrɪɡɛld/ *n.* Long *obs.* exc. *Hist.* [OE *hereġield*, f. HERE *n.*[1] + *ġield* payment (see GELD *n.*).] The tribute paid by the Anglo-Saxons to the Danish army; Danegeld.

herein /hɪərˈɪn/ *adv. formal.* OE. [f. HERE *adv.* + IN *adv.*, *prep.*] 1 In this place; *esp.* in this book, document, etc.; into this place. OE. 2 In this matter, case, etc.; in this particular. ME.

1 J. RAY Herein were many vaulted or arched walks hewn out of the Rock. *Atlantic Monthly* 'Read this shit, man,' an attached note said. 'Essential knowledge herein'. 2 I. S. LEADAM He insists strongly that the king can be sued, herein opposing Bracton.

Comb.: **hereinafter** below (in this document etc.); **hereinbefore** in a preceding part (of this document etc).

herem *n.* var. of CHEREM.

†heremite *n.* var. of HERMIT.

herenach /ˈhɛrɪnɑːk/ *n.* Also **er-** /ˈɛr-/. E17. [Alt. of Ir. *airchinneach*, OIr. *airchinnech* chief man, principal, prince, leader, f. *a(i)r* over + *ce(a)nn* head, cogn. w. Welsh *arbennig*.] *Hist.* In the ancient Irish Church, a lay superintendent of church lands; the hereditary warden of a church.

hereof /hɪərˈɒv/ *adv. formal.* OE. [f. HERE *adv.* + OF *prep.*] 1 Of this, concerning this. OE. †2 From this, from here. ME–L16.

hereright /hɪəˈrʌɪt/ *adv. obs.* exc. *dial.* ME. [f. HERE *adv.* + RIGHT *adv.*] Straightway.

Herero /hɛˈrɛːrəʊ, həˈrɪə-/ *n.* & *a.* M19. [Bantu. Cf. OVAHERERO.] A *n.* Pl. same, **-os.** 1 The Bantu language of any of several Negroid peoples of Namibia, Angola, and Botswana. M19. 2 A member of any of these peoples. L19. B *attrib.* or as *adj.* Of or pertaining to the Herero or their language. M19.

heresiarch /hɛˈriːzɪɑːk/ *n.* M16. [eccl.L *haeresiarcha* f. eccl.Gk *hairesiarkhēs* leader of a sect (Gk = leader of a school), f. as HERESY + -ARCH.] A leader or founder of a heresy.

heresiography /ˌhɛrɪsɪˈɒɡrəfi/ *n.* M17. [f. Gk *hairesis* HERESY + -O- + -GRAPHY.] A treatise on or the description of heresies.

heresiologist /ˌhɛrɪsɪˈɒlədʒɪst/ *n.* E18. [f. as prec. + -O- + -LOGIST.] An expert in or student of heresies.

heresiology *n.* the branch of knowledge that deals with heresies M19.

heresy /ˈhɛrɪsi/ *n.* ME. [OFr. *(h)eresie* (mod. *hérésie*) f. Proto-Romance f. eccl.L *haeresis* (L = school of thought) f. eccl.Gk *hairesis* heretical sect (Gk = choice), f. Gk *haireomai* choose f. *hairein* take.] 1 Opinion or doctrine contrary to the orthodox doctrine of the Christian Church; an instance of this. ME. 2 Opinion or doctrine contrary to the accepted doctrine of any subject; an instance of this. LME. 3 Opinion or doctrine characterizing a particular individual or group; a school of thought, a sect. Now *rare.* LME.

1 R. MACAULAY [She] was a partial-diluvian, . . a heresy that the flood had not covered the whole earth. D. CUPITT Priscillian and a number of his followers were executed for heresy at Trier. 2 *Sunday Express* If winning is the name of the game, why is it heresy to suggest a soccer team to represent Great Britain?

heretic /ˈhɛrɪtɪk/ *n.* & *a.* ME. [(O)Fr. *hérétique*, f. eccl.L *haereticus* a. & n., f. eccl.Gk *hairetikos* heretical (Gk = able to choose) f. Gk *haireomai*:

see prec.: see -IC.] A *n.* 1 A person who holds an opinion or a doctrine contrary to the orthodox doctrine of the Christian Church. ME. 2 A person who holds an opinion or a doctrine contrary to the accepted doctrine of any subject. L16.

1 K. CLARK The northern heretics were insulting the Virgin, desecrating her sanctuaries. 2 SHAKES. *Much Ado* Thou wast ever an obstinate heretic in the despite of beauty.

B *attrib.* or as *adj.* = HERETICAL. *rare.* LME.

heretical /hɪˈrɛtɪk(ə)l/ *a.* LME. [med.L *hereticalis*, f. as prec.: see -ICAL.] Of or pertaining to heresy or heretics; of the nature of heresy.

heretically *adv.* E17. **hereticalness** *n.* (long *rare* or *obs.*) L17.

hereticate /hɪˈrɛtɪkeɪt/ *v.t.* E17. [med.L *hereticat-* pa. ppl stem of *hereticare*, f. *haereticus*: see HERETIC, -ATE[3].] 1 Pronounce (a person, a doctrine, etc.) to be heretical. E17. 2 Make a heretic of: esp. (*derog.*, now *Hist.*) denoting the ceremony of deathbed inauguration said to have been practised by the Albigenses. M18.

heretiˈcation *n.* M18.

hereto /hɪəˈtuː/ *adv. formal.* ME. [f. HERE *adv.* + TO *prep.*] 1 To this place. Long *rare* or *obs.* ME. 2 To this matter, subject, etc.; with regard to this point. ME. 3 Up to this time. Long *rare* or *obs.* ME. 4 (Annexed) to this document etc. M16.

heretofore /hɪətʊˈfɔː/ *adv.*, *a.*, & *n. formal.* LME. [f. HERE *adv.* + TOFORE.] A *adv.* Before this time, formerly. LME. B *adj.* Former, previous. Now *rare.* L15. C *n.* Time past; the past. *rare.* E19.

heretoforetime *adv.* (*rare*) = HERETOFORE *adv.* L15.

heretoga /hɛrɪˈtəʊgə/ *n.* [OE *heretoga* = OFris. *hertoga*, OS *heritogo* (Du. *hertog*), OHG *herizogo* (G *Herzog*), ON *hertogi*, f. HERE *n.*[1] + *-toga*, f. Gmc base of TEAM *n.*] *Hist.* The leader of an army; the commander of the militia of a shire etc.

heriot /ˈhɛrɪət/ *n.* [OE *hereġeatwa*, *-ġeatwe* (whence med.L *herietum -otum*, AN *heriet*), f. HERE *n.*[1] + *ġeatwa* (ON *gǫtvar* pl.) trappings.] *Hist.* A tribute, orig. the return of military equipment, later the best live beast or dead chattel or a money payment, made to a lord on the death of a tenant.

heriotable *a.* subject or liable to the payment of heriots E17.

herisson /ˈhɛrɪs(ə)n/ *n.* L16. [Fr. *hérisson*: see URCHIN.] †1 A hedgehog. L16–E17. 2 *Fortif.* A barrier consisting of a revolving beam set with iron spikes. E18.

herit /ˈhɛrɪt/ *v.t. rare.* LME. [OFr. *heriter* f. eccl.L *hereditare*.] Inherit.

heritable /ˈhɛrɪtəb(ə)l/ *a.* LME. [(O)Fr. *héritable*, f. *heriter* f. eccl.L *hereditare*: see HEREDITABLE.] 1 Able to be inherited; *esp.* in *Sc. law* (now *Hist.*) designating property which devolved on the heir at law as opp. to an executor (opp. *movable*). LME. b *Sc. Law.* Pertaining to or connected with heritable property. M16. 2 Transmissible from parent to offspring, hereditary. LME. 3 Capable of inheriting. LME.

heritaˈbility *n.* M19. **heritably** *adv.* LME.

heritage /ˈhɛrɪtɪdʒ/ *n.* ME. [OFr. (*h*)*eritage* (mod. *héritage*), f. *hériter*: see prec., -AGE.] 1 That which is or may be inherited; *fig.* the portion allotted to a specified person, group, etc. ME. b *Sc. Law* (now *Hist.*). Property consisting of land etc. that devolved on the heir at law as opp. to an executor. E16. †2 The fact of inheriting; hereditary succession. ME–M16. 3 A gift which constitutes a proper possession; *spec.* God's chosen people; the ancient Israelites; the Church. ME. 4 Inherited circumstances or benefits. E17.

1 SIR W. SCOTT Lord of a barren heritage. N. EZEKIEL God's love remains your heritage. 3 AV *1 Pet.* 5:3 Neither as being lords over Gods heritage. 4 LYNDON B. JOHNSON My Texas background or my Southern heritage. J. BRODSKY She was carrying the heritage of her predecessors into the art of this century.

Attrib. & *comb.*: In the senses 'forming part of a national or cultural heritage', as *heritage highway*, *train*, etc.; 'concerned with the conservation and use of the national or cultural heritage', as *heritage group*, *industry*, etc. Special combs., as *heritage coast* a section of the UK coastline designated as aesthetically or culturally important and therefore protected from development; *heritage trail* a route linking places of historic interest.

heritance /ˈhɛrɪt(ə)ns/ *n.* LME. [OFr., f. *heriter*: see HERITABLE, -ANCE.] Inheritance; heirship (*lit.* & *fig.*).

heritor /ˈhɛrɪtə/ *n.* LME. [AN *heriter* = (O)Fr. *heritier*, f. as HEREDITARY, assim. to wds in -OR.] 1 A person who inherits. LME. 2 *Sc. Law.* The proprietor of a heritable subject, esp. one who is liable for parochial dues. L15.

heritress *n.* an heiress, an inheritress M16. **heritrix** *n.* an heiress, a female heritor E16.

herkogamy *n.* var. of HERCOGAMY.

herky-jerky /ˈhəːkɪdʒəːki/ *a. slang.* L20. [f. JERKY *a.*] Of a movement: occurring at an irregular rate, spasmodic.

herl /həːl/ *n.* LME. [Alt.] = HARL *n.*[1]

herling /ˈhəːlɪŋ/ *n. Sc. local.* L17. [Origin unkn.] A salmon.

herm /həːm/ *n.* Also (now *rare*) **herma** /ˈhəːmə/, pl. **-mae** /-miː/. L16. [L *Herma*, f. Gk *Hermēs*: see HERMES II.] *Class. Antiq.* A squared pillar surmounted by a head or bust (usu. that of Hermes), used as a boundary-marker, signpost, etc.

Hermaic /həːˈmeɪɪk/ *a.* L17. [Gk *Hermaikos* of or like Hermes: see HERMES, -IC.] 1 = HERMETIC. L17. 2 Of the nature of or resembling a herm. E19.

hermandad /ermanˈdað/ *n.* Pl. ***-es*** /-es/. M18. [Sp. = brotherhood.] *Hist.* In Spain, a resistance group against oppression by the nobility; *spec.* a voluntary organization later reorganized as regular national police.

hermaphrodism /həːˈmafrədɪz(ə)m/ *n.* Now *rare.* E19. [Fr. *hermaphrodisme*, irreg. f. *hermaphrodite*, f. as next: see -ISM.] = HERMAPHRODITISM.

hermaphrodite /həːˈmafrədʌɪt/ *n.* & *a.* LME. [L *hermaphroditus* f. Gk *hermaphroditos*, orig. in Gk mythol. the name of the son of Hermes and Aphrodite, who became joined in one body with the nymph Salmacis.] A *n.* 1 A human being or animal combining characteristics of both sexes. LME. b *fig.* A person or thing combining two opposite qualities or functions; *Naut.* a ship having the characters of two kinds of vessel, *esp.* a hermaphrodite brig. LME. c A homosexual; an effeminate man. Long *rare.* L16. 2 An animal having normally both male and female sexual organs, as many snails and earthworms. E18. 3 A flower in which both stamens and pistils are present; a plant having such flowers. E18.

1 J. BRONOWSKI Males and females of the same species do not produce sexual monsters or hermaphrodites. b T. KEN He acts the Hermaphrodite of Good and Ill, But God detests his double Tongue and Will.

B *adj.* 1 Combining the characteristics of or consisting of both sexes; combining two opposite qualities. L16. 2 Of the nature of or being a hermaphrodite. E17.

1 *hermaphrodite brig*: see BRIG *n.*[1] 1. 2 B. TRAPIDO With my almost non-existent breasts and my narrow hips, I looked alluringly hermaphrodite.

hermaphroˈditic(-al) *adjs.* = HERMAPHRODITE *a.* E17. **hermaphroˈditically** *adv.* L17.

hermaphroditism /həːˈmafrədɪtɪz(ə)m/ *n.* E19. [f. HERMAPHRODITE + -ISM.] The state or condition of being hermaphrodite.

hermeneut /ˈhəːmɪnjuːt/ *n.* L19. [Gk *hermēneutēs* agent-n. f. *hermēneuein* interpret, f. *hermeneus* interpreter.] An interpreter, esp. in the early Christian Church.

Listener It is, he argues, not just medieval exegetes, rabbinic hermeneuts or Princeton professors who interpret.

hermeneutic /həːmɪˈnjuːtɪk/ *a.* L17. [Gk *hermēneutikos*, f. as prec.: see -IC.] Of or pertaining to (theories of) interpretation.

Journal of Theological Studies Augustine holds Paul's conversion as the hermeneutic key to Pauline theology.

hermeneutical *a.* = HERMENEUTIC *a.* L18. **hermeneutically** *adv.* E19.

hermeneutics /həːmɪˈnjuːtɪks/ *n.pl.* (also treated as *sing.*). M18. [mod.L *hermeneutica* f. Gk *hermēneutikē* use as n. of fem. sing. of adj. *hermēneutikos*: see prec., -ICS.] The branch of knowledge that deals with (theories of) interpretation, esp. of Scripture.

D. CUPITT Those who had sought the historical Jesus, .. had somehow assumed that exegesis was hermeneutics.

†**Hermes** *n.* L15. [L, Gk *Hermēs*: see below.] I [L *Hermes Trismegistus* irreg. tr. of 'Thoth the very great', the Egyptian god regarded as the founder of alchemy, astrology, etc., and more or less identified with the Greek god Hermes: see branch II.] Used *attrib.* in *Alch.* 1 *Hermes tree*, the mixture of substances acted upon by acids in the third stage of calcination. Only in L15. 2 *Hermes seal*, a hermetic seal. E17–M18. II [Gk *Hermēs* Hermes, the son of Zeus and Maia in Gk mythol., represented as the god of science, commerce, etc., and the messenger of the gods; identified by the Romans with *Mercury*.] 3 The metal mercury. *rare* (Milton). Only in M17.

hermetic /həːˈmɛtɪk/ *a.* & *n.* M17. [mod.L *hermeticus*, f. (prob. after *magnes*, *magneticus* MAGNET) *Hermes Trismegistus*: see HERMES I.] A *adj.* 1 Of or pertaining to Hermes Trismegistus or the theosophical etc. writings ascribed to him; *esp.* of, pertaining to, or concerned with occult science, esp. alchemy. M17. 2 Airtight, hermetically sealed; *fig.* protected from outside agencies, esoteric, recondite. E18. 3 (**H-**.) Of or pertaining to the god Hermes. L19.

1 K. A. PORTER A hermetic society, with ritual greetings, secret handgrips .. and a jargon. 2 E. BOWEN Her house was hermetic against the storm. C. THUBRON The Soviet Union was so vast and hermetic that it comprised all the conceivable world. **hermetic seal** an airtight closure of a vessel by fusion, soldering, etc., orig. as used by alchemists. 3 J. R. LOWELL [The Elizabethans] had the Hermetic gift of buckling wings to the feet of their verse.

B *n.* 1 A person skilled in hermetic science. L17. 2 In *pl.* Hermetism. *rare.* M19.

1 T. LEARY The ancient wisdom of gnostics, hermetics, sufis, Tantric gurus, yogis, occult healers.

hermetical *a.* = HERMETIC *a.* 1, 2 E17. **hermetically** *adv.* by means of a hermetic seal; *fig.* closely, tightly: E17. **hermeticism** /-sɪz(ə)m/ *n.* = HERMETISM *n.* E20.

hermetism /ˈhəːmɪtɪz(ə)m/ *n.* L19. [f. HERMET(IC *a.* + -ISM.] Hermetic or theosophical philosophy.

hermetist *n.* M19.

hermit /ˈhəːmɪt/ *n.* Also (now chiefly *Eccl. Hist.*) **eremite** /ˈɛrɪmʌɪt/, †**heremite**. ME. [OFr. (*h*)*ermite*, *eremite* (mod. *ermite*) or late L *eremita* (med.L *her-*) f. Gk *erēmitēs* f. *erēmia* desert, f. *erēmos* solitary, deserted.] 1 A person (esp. a man) who from religious motives has retired into solitary life; *esp.* an early Christian recluse. ME. b A person who falsely claims to be a recluse; a beggar. *obs.* exc. *Hist.* LME. †c A beadsman. L16–L17. 2 A member of any of various monastic orders. LME. 3 A person who lives in solitude or shuns human society from any motive; an animal, esp. a sheep, of solitary habit. M17.

1 H. MAUNDRELL Hermits retiring hither for Penance and Mortification. c SHAKES. *Tit. A.* As perfect As begging hermits in their holy prayers. 3 G. GORER The old and poor .. choose their own company; and these hermits are represented in every category. D. PRATER He was by no means a hermit, and went from time to time into town.

Comb.: **hermit crab** any soft-bodied decapod crustacean of the family Paguridae, members of which occupy cast-off mollusc shells as protection for their hind parts; **hermit ibis** = WALDRAPP; **hermit thrush** a migratory N. American thrush, *Catharus guttatus*.

hermitess *n.* a female hermit M17. **hermithood** *n.* E20. **hermitish** *a.* resembling or befitting a hermit E17. **hermitism** *n.* the state of being a hermit; the hermitic life: L19. †**hermitress** *n.* = HERMITESS E17–E19. **hermitry** *n.* the mode of life of a hermit L19. **hermitship** *n.* E19.

hermitage /ˈhəːmɪtɪdʒ/ *n.* Also †**eremitage**. ME. [OFr. *(h)ermitage* (mod. *ermitage*), f. as prec.: see -AGE.] 1 The dwelling-place of a hermit; a monastery. ME. b The condition of a hermit. L16. 2 A solitary or secluded dwelling-place. M17. 3 A French wine produced near Valence. L17.

2 Y. MENUHIN For a few years it was an idyllic summer holiday hermitage. 3 D. L. SAYERS Mellow with Hermitage and cigars.

Hermitian /həːˈmɪʃ(ə)n/ *a.* E20. [f. Charles *Hermite* (1822–1905), Fr. mathematician + -IAN.] *Math.* Designating, pertaining to, or taking the form of, a matrix in which pairs of elements symmetrically placed with respect to the principal diagonal are complex conjugates.

hermitic /həːˈmɪtɪk/ *a.* Also (earlier, now chiefly *Eccl. Hist.*) **ere-** /ɛrɪ-/. L15. [OFr. *heremitique*, f. as HERMIT: see -IC.] Of, pertaining to, or characteristic of a hermit.

hermitical /həːˈmɪtɪk(ə)l/ *a.* Also (now chiefly *Eccl. Hist.*) **ere-** /ɛrɪ-/. L16. [f. (as) prec.: see -ICAL.] = prec.

hermodactyl /həːməˈdaktɪl/ *n. obs.* exc. *Hist.* LME. [med.L *hermodactylus* f. Gk *hermodaktulos* lit. 'Hermes' finger', f. as HERMES II + -O- + DACTYL.] The dried bulbous root of some eastern plant, prob. of the genus *Colchicum*, formerly used in medicine; the plant itself. Usu. in *pl.*

hern *n.* see HERON.

hern /həːn/ *possess. pron.* Long *obs.* exc. *dial.* ME. [f. HER *pron.*[2] after *my* and *mine*, *thy* and *thine*, etc.] = HERS.

¶ See note s.v. HERS.

hernia /ˈhəːnɪə/ *n.* Pl. **-ias**, **-iae** /-iːː/. LME. [L.] *Med.* An abnormal displacement and protrusion of an organ or tissue through an aperture in the wall of the cavity which contains it, esp. through the wall of the abdomen; a rupture.

SLIDING *hernia*. *strangulated hernia*: see STRANGULATED 1.

hernial *a.* LME. **herniary** *a.* M18. **herniˈated** *a.* affected with or protruding as a hernia L19. **herniˈation** *n.* protrusion as a hernia L19.

hernio- /ˈhəːnɪəʊ/ *comb. form* of prec.: see -O-.

hernioˈrrhaphy *n.* (an instance of) surgical repair of a hernia and suturing of the opening E20. **herniˈotomy** *n.* (an instance of) surgical enlargement of the opening through which a strangulated hernia has protruded, to allow its reduction; *gen.* any operation on a hernia: E19.

hernsew, **-shaw**, **-shew** *ns.* vars. of HERONSHAW.

hero /ˈhɪərəʊ/ *n.* Pl. **-oes**. M16. [L *heros*, (pl.) *heroes* f. Gk *hērōs*, (pl.) *hērōes*.] 1 *Gk Hist.* A man of superhuman strength, courage, or ability, favoured by the gods; a demigod. M16. 2 A man, now also a woman, distinguished by the performance of extraordinarily brave or noble deeds; an illustrious warrior. L16. 3 A man, now also a woman, admired and venerated for his or her achievements and noble qualities in any field. M17. 4 The chief male character in a poem, story, play, etc. L17. 5 In full *hero sandwich*. A sandwich made with a large roll or small loaf and filled with meat, cheese, and mixed salad. *N. Amer.* M20.

1 H. ALLEN Perhaps there were even gods and giants, heroes and demi-gods . . buried there. 2 M. LOWRY He was an extremely brave man, no less than a hero. A. S. NEILL A hero is a man who can change his fear into positive energy. 3 JILLY COOPER He still identifies with David Bailey as a great working-class hero. A. GHOSH Edison became one of his heroes. 4 J. BARTH I recall once reading a story that ended with the hero dead on the floor. *Star & Style* (Bombay) It wasn't clear as to who the real hero of the film was.

Comb.: *hero sandwich*: see sense 5 above; **hero's welcome** a rapturous welcome, like that given to a successful warrior; **hero-worship** *n.* & *v.* (*a*) *n.* the idealization of an admired person; *Gk Hist.* worship of the ancient heroes; (*b*) *v.t.* worship as a hero, idolize; **hero-worshipper** a person engaging in or given to hero-worship.

†**heroess** *n.* = HEROINE E17–E18. **heroify** /hɪˈrəʊɪfʌɪ/ *v.t.* [cf. DEIFY] make a hero of, venerate as a hero E19. **heroˈology** *n.* (*rare*) a history of heroes L17. **heroship** *n.* L18.

heroa *n.* pl. of HEROON.

Herodian /hɛˈrəʊdɪən/ *n.* & *a.* LME. [eccl.L *Herodianus*, f. eccl.Gk *Hērōdianos*, pertaining to Herod, *Hērōdianoi* pl. followers of Herod (*Mark* 3:6): see -IAN.] A *n. Hist.* A member of a Jewish political party supporting the dynasty of Herod, esp. Herod Antipas (4 BC–AD 39). LME. B *adj.* Of or pertaining to Herod, King of Judaea (38–4 BC), or members of his family of the same name. M17.

Herodotean /hɛrɒdəˈtiːən/ *a.* M19. [f. *Herodotus* (see below): see -AN, -EAN.] Of, pertaining to, or characteristic of (the work of) Herodotus, Gk historian of the 5th cent. BC.

heroic /hɪˈrəʊɪk/ *a.* & *n.* LME. [(O)Fr. *héroïque* or L *heroicus* f. Gk *hērōikos* pertaining to heroes, f. *hērōs*: see HERO, -IC.] A *adj.* 1 Of an action, a quality, etc.: of, pertaining to, or characteristic of a hero; bold, daring, attempting great things; fit for a hero. LME. 2 Of a person: having the qualities of a hero. L16. 3 Of or pertaining to the heroes of (esp. Greek) antiquity; (of poetry etc.) dealing with heroes and their deeds, epic. L16. 4 Of language: grand; high-flown, exaggerated. L16. 5 (Of a statue) of a size between life-size and colossal; unusually large or great, extravagant. L18.

1 J. MASTERS He stood in a heroic posture, his legs braced and his revolver arm steady. M. PIERCY He didn't like shopping any better than she did, so his trip verged on the heroic. A. S. BYATT The heroic transatlantic crossings of certain butterflies. 2 B. WEBB She is heroic: as . . chieftain she would have led her people into battle and died fighting. E. FEINSTEIN She could distinguish no single heroic figure among the rebels—only a mob. 3 **the heroic age** the period in Greek history before the return from Troy. 5 CLIVE JAMES A flyover of heroic ugliness . . was built over Circular Quay. E. FERBER Himself of heroic stature, he fitted well into the gorgeous and spectacular setting.

Special collocations: **heroic couplet**: of rhyming iambic pentameters. **heroic verse** (a) verse used in heroic poetry, esp. the hexameter, the iambic pentameter, or the alexandrine.

B *n.* 1 A heroic verse. Usu. in *pl.* L16. †2 A heroic man; *esp.* a demigod. Only in 17. 3 In *pl.* High-flown or extravagant language; extravagantly or recklessly bold behaviour. E18.

3 J. FIELD No extravagant expressions of emotion were tolerated. 'Scenes' and heroics were alike taboo. A. MACLEAN The only thing that heroics will get us is an early and watery grave.

heroical /hɪˈrəʊɪk(ə)l/ *a.* LME. [f. as prec.: see -ICAL.] †1 = HEROIC *a.* 1. LME–E19. 2 = HEROIC *a.* 3. LME. 3 = HEROIC *a.* 2. M16. 4 = HEROIC *a.* 5. L18.

heroicalness *n.* (now *rare*) M17.

heroically /hɪˈrəʊɪk(ə)li/ *adv.* L16. [f. HEROIC *a.* or prec.: see -ICALLY.] In a heroic manner; by heroic means.

M. SEYMOUR-SMITH He behaved heroically, . . and was even recommended for a Victoria Cross. P. ROTH His chin was not protruding heroically but slightly receding.

heroi-comical /hɪˌrəʊɪˈkɒmɪk(ə)l/ *a.* E18. [f. Fr. *héroï-comique* + -AL[1]: see HEROIC, COMICAL.] Combining the heroic with the comic.

POPE The Rape of the Lock. An Heroi-comical Poem.

Also **heroi-comic** *a.* M18.

heroin /ˈhɛrəʊɪn/ *n.* L19. [G, f. as HERO (from its effect on the user's perception of his or her personality) + -IN[1].] A morphine derivative, diacetylmorphine, which is a sedative addictive drug (illicitly) used to produce intense euphoria.

heroine /ˈhɛrəʊɪn/ *n.* M17. [Fr. *héroïne* or L *heroina* f. Gk *hērōinē* fem. of *hērōs* HERO: see -INE[3].] 1 A woman distinguished and venerated for her extraordinary courage, fortitude, or noble qualities. M17. 2 *Gk Hist.* A demigoddess. M17. 3 The chief female character in a poem, story, play, etc. E18.

1 E. FEINSTEIN Marina waited . . for an autograph from the great actress—she had found a new heroine. 3 R. ELLMANN In his first play, *Vera*, the heroine plans to kill the Czar.

Comb.: **heroine-worship** the idealization of an admired woman.

heroineship *n.* M18. **heroinism** *n.* the conduct or qualities of a heroine L18.

heroism /ˈhɛrəʊɪz(ə)m/ *n.* E18. [Fr. *héroïsme*, f. *héros* f. as HERO: see -ISM.] The conduct or qualities of a hero.

heroize /ˈhɪərəʊʌɪz/ *v.t.* Also **-ise**. M18. [f. HERO + -IZE.] Make a hero of; treat or represent as a hero; make heroic.

heroiˈzation *n.* M19.

herola *n.* var. of HIROLA.

heron /ˈhɛr(ə)n/ *n.* Also (*arch.*, *poet.*, & *dial.*) **hern** /həːn/. ME. [OFr. (also *hairon* (mod. *héron*)) f. Gmc (whence OHG *heigaro*; cf. ON *hegri*).] Any of various large long-legged long-necked wading birds of the family Ardeidae; in Great Britain and Ireland, *esp.* the grey *Ardea cinerea*, widespread in the Old World.

TENNYSON I come from haunts of coot and hern. *Goliath heron*, *green heron*, *night heron*, etc.

Comb.: **heron's-bill** (now chiefly *US*) = *stork's-bill* s.v. STORK *n.*

heronry *n.* a place where herons breed; a colony of herons: E17.

heronshaw /ˈhɛr(ə)nʃɔː/ *n.* Now *arch.* & *dial.* Also **hern-** /ˈhəːn-/, **-sew** /-sjuː/, **-shew** /-ʃuː/. LME. [OFr. *heronceau*, earlier *-cel* dim. of *heron* HERON.] A young or small heron; *gen.* a heron.

know a hawk from a heronshaw: see HAWK *n.*[1]

heroon /hɪˈrəʊɒn/ *n.* Pl. **-roa** /-ˈrəʊə/. Also (earlier) **heroum** /hɪˈrəʊəm/. L18. [L *heroum* f. Gk *hērōon*, f. *hērōios* of a hero, f. *hērōs* HERO.] Orig., a temple dedicated to a hero, often over his supposed tomb. Now, a sepulchral monument in the form of a small temple.

herpes /ˈhəːpiːz/ *n.* LME. [L = shingles f. Gk, lit. 'creeping', f. *herpein* creep.] Orig., any skin disease characterized by the formation of groups of vesicles. Now, (infection with) any of a small group of viruses affecting the skin and nervous system.

Comb.: **herpes simplex** (infection with) a herpesvirus causing usu. localized inflammation, as conjunctivitis, cold sore, oral or vaginal inflammation, etc. **herpesvirus** any of a small group of viruses causing herpes. **herpes zoster** /ˈzɒstə, ˈzəʊ-/ [L *zoster*, Gk *zōstēr* girdle, shingles] shingles; the herpesvirus causing this (and also chickenpox).

herpetology /həːpɪˈtɒlədʒi/ *n.* E19. [f. Gk *herpeton* creeping thing + -OLOGY.] The branch of zoology that deals with reptiles and amphibians.

herpetoˈlogic (chiefly *US*), **-ˈlogical** *adjs.* E19. **herpetoˈlogically** *adv.* L19. **herpetologist** *n.* E19.

herpolhode /ˈhəːp(ə)lhəʊd/ *n.* M19. [f. Gk *herpein* creep + *polos* pole + *hodos* way.] *Geom.* A curve traced on a fixed plane by the point of contact of an ellipsoid rolling on the plane about an internal axis. Cf. POLHODE.

Herr /hɛː/ *n.* Pl. **Herren** /ˈhɛːrən/ M17. [G, f. OHG *hērro* compar. of *hēr* exalted.] A title used in referring to or addressing a German or German-speaking man, corresponding to *Mr* or *sir*; a German or German-speaking man.

W. S. CHURCHILL But Herr Hitler is not thinking only of stealing other people's territories.

Herrenvolk /ˈhɛːrənfɒlk, ˈhɛr(ə)n-, -fəʊk/ *n.* M20. [G = master-race, f. as prec. + FOLK.] The German nation, viewed (esp. by the Nazis) as a race born to mastery; in extended usage, a group regarding itself as innately superior.

G. B. SHAW Nations each of which regards itself as The Chosen Race or Herrenvolk.

herriment /ˈhɛrɪm(ə)nt/ *n. Sc.* L18. [f. HARRY *v.* + -MENT.] Harrying, ravaging, devastation.

herring /ˈhɛrɪŋ/ *n.* Pl. same, **-s**. [OE *hǣring*, *hēring* = OFris. *hēreng*, MLG *hērink*, *harink* (Du. *haring*), OHG *hāring* (G *Hering*), f. WGmc.] Any of various chiefly marine fishes of the family Clupeidae, which includes several important food fishes; *spec.* a blue-backed silvery fish of the N. Atlantic, *Clupea harengus*, which forms shoals in coastal waters at spawning time. Also, the flesh of any of these fishes as food.

fall herring a herring of NW Atlantic coastal waters, *Alosa mediocris*. **lake herring** = CISCO. MATJE *herring*. RED HERRING. **round herring** a herring of NW Atlantic coastal waters, *Etrumeus teres*, with a slender body of round cross-section. SMIG *herring*.

Comb.: **herring-choker** *slang* (*a*) *Canad.* a native or inhabitant of the Maritime Provinces; (*b*) *US* a Scandinavian; **herring-gull** a large gull, *Larus argentatus*, widespread and common on Palaearctic coasts; **herring-gutted** *a.* (of a horse) being too narrow through the body behind the ribs; **herring-pond** *joc.* the sea, *esp.* the N. Atlantic.

herring-like *a.* E20.

herring-bone /ˈhɛrɪŋbəʊn/ *n.*, *a.*, & *v.* Also **herringbone**. L16. [f. HERRING + BONE *n.*] A *n.* 1 (A bone from) the skeleton of a herring. L16. 2 = *herring-bone stitch* below. M18. 3 A zigzag pattern or arrangement, as of the weave of a cloth, or of stones, bricks, or tiles; cloth woven in a zigzag pattern. M19. 4 *Skiing.* A method of climbing a slope by walking with the skis pointed outwards. E20. B *attrib.* or as *adj.* Resembling the bones of a herring; having a zigzag pattern; (of cloth) having a zigzag weave. M17.

Special collocations & *comb.*: **herring-bone banding** a decorative border on furniture consisting of two diagonally-grained strips of veneer laid side by side. **herring-bone coralline** a marine coelenterate of the genus *Halecium*, often growing on oyster-shells. **herring-bone gear** a gearwheel with two sets of teeth inclined at an acute angle to each other. **herring-bone parlour** a milking parlour in which the cows stand at an angle to a central operator's pit. **herring-bone stitch** an asymmetric cross-stitch used in embroidery or for securing an edge.

C *v.* 1 *v.t.* & *i.* Sew with herring-bone stitch. L18. 2 *v.t.* Mark with a herring-bone pattern; *Archit.* lay (stones, bricks, tiles etc.) in a herring-bone design. L19. 3 *v.i. Skiing.* Climb a slope by pointing the skis outward. E20.

Herrnhuter /ˈhɛːnhuːtə, ˈhɛːr(ə)n-/ *n.* M18. [G, f. *Herrnhut* (= the Lord's keeping) the first German settlement of the Moravian Church + -ER[1].] A member of the Moravian Church.

hers /həːz/ *possess. pron.* ME. [f. HER *pron.*[2] + possess. suff. -'S[1]. Cf. HERN *possess. pron.*] 1 Her one(s), that or those belonging or pertaining to her. ME. 2 *of hers*, belonging or pertaining to her. L15.

1 W. S. MAUGHAM Julia took his head in both her hands and pressed his lips with hers. E. BAKER Hers was the seventh folding chair in from the aisle. M. ROBERTS The garden is not hers . . but the landlord lets all the tenants use it. *get hers*: see GET *v. his and hers*: see HIS *pron.*[2] 1. 2 H. G. WELLS She asked me with that faint lisp of hers.

¶Orig. northern, the southern & midland equivalent being HERN *pron.*

†**hersall** *n. rare* (Spenser). Only in L16. [Abbrev.] = REHEARSAL.

Herschelian /həːˈʃɛlɪən/ *a.* L18. [f. Sir William *Herschel* (1738–1822), German-born Eng. astronomer and discoverer of the planet Uranus + -IAN.] *Astron.* Of a (reflecting) telescope: having a concave mirror slightly inclined to the axis.

herse *n.* see HEARSE *n.*[1]

herself /həːˈsɛlf/ *pron.* OE. [f. HER *pron.*[1] + SELF *a.* (but long interpreted as HER *a.* + SELF *n.*).] I *refl.* 1 Refl. form (indirect, direct, & after preps.) of HER *pron.*[1]: (to, for, etc.) the female person or animal, or the thing personified or conventionally treated as female or (in early use) grammatically feminine, in question. OE.

1 H. JAMES Something she admitted herself shy about. J. CONRAD If you mean her to come with credit to herself and you. E. WAUGH I hope Doris is making herself useful about the house. P. ACKROYD Her reality . . was known only to herself.

II *emphatic.* 2 In apposition to a personal n. (subjective or objective) or to a subjective pron.: that particular female person or animal, etc., the female person in question personally. ME. 3 (Not appositional.) a Subjective: she herself. Now *arch.* & *dial.* exc. *colloq.* after *be* & after *than*, *as* (cf. HER *pron.*[1] 2). ME. b Objective: the female person etc. in question herself. ME.

2 J. BRYCE The Saracen wasted the Mediterranean coasts, and sacked Rome herself. E. BLISHEN Mother herself was a Methodist. C. P. SNOW She told me herself she was old enough to know better than marry Max. I. MCEWAN Again, Caroline stared at Mary as though she herself could not be seen. 3a T. HARDY Mrs. Garland acknowledged her friendship for her neighbour, with whom Anne and herself associated. C. RAYNER She had imagined . . the women as well endowed with beauty as herself.

Phrases: **be herself** (*a*) act in her normal unconstrained manner; (*b*) feel as well as she usually does (usu. in neg. contexts). **by herself** on her own.

hership /ˈhəːʃɪp/ *n. Sc.* (now *arch.* or *Hist.*). LME. [f. HERE *n.*[1] or stem of OE *hergan* HARRY *v.* + -SHIP. Cf. ON *herskapr* warfare, harrying.] 1 Harrying, pillage, plunder, devastation. LME. 2 Distress, poverty, or famine, caused by pillage etc. LME. 3 Booty, plunder; *esp.* cattle forcibly driven off. M16.

herstory /ˈhəːst(ə)ri/ *n.* Orig. *US.* L20. [f. HER *pron.*[2] + STORY *n.*[1], by anal. with *history*.] History as written or perceived from a feminist or woman's point of view.

Hertfordshire kindness /ˌhɑː(t)fədʃə ˈkʌɪndnɪs/ *n. phr. arch.* M17. [An English county.] The returning of a toast by drinking to the person who has just toasted one.

†**hertwort** *n.* see HARTWORT.

Hertz /həːts/ *n.* In sense 2 **h-**, pl. same. L19. [H. R. *Hertz* (1857–94), Ger. physicist.] *Physics.* 1 *Hertz waves*, = *Hertzian waves* below. *obs.* exc. *Hist.* L19. 2 A unit of frequency equal to one cycle per second. Abbrev. *Hz.* E20.

Hertzian *a.* of or pertaining to Hertz or the phenomena discovered by him; *Hertzian waves* (*obs.* exc. *Hist.*), radio waves: L19.

Herzegovinian /hɛːtsəgəˈvɪnɪən, həːt-/ *a.* & *n.* Also **Herce-**. L19. [f. *Hercegovina* (see below) + -IAN.] Of or pertaining to, a native or inhabitant of, Herzegovina, a region in the Balkans now a part of Bosnia-Herzegovina.

Heshvan *n.* var. of HESVAN.

Hesiodic /hiːsɪˈɒdɪk/ *a.* E19. [f. *Hesiod* (Gk *Hēsiodos*), (see below) + -IC.] Of, pertaining to, or resembling the poetical style of Hesiod, a Greek epic poet of *c* 700BC, or of the school of poetry which followed him.

hesitance /ˈhɛzɪt(ə)ns/ *n.* E17. [f. as next: see -ANCE.] Hesitation.

hesitancy /ˈhɛzɪt(ə)nsi/ *n.* E17. [L *haesitantia* (in late L = hesitation, delay) f. *haesitant-*, f. as next: see -ANCY.] (An instance of) hesitation, vacillation, or indecision.

G. VIDAL After many soft hesitancies, she came to the point. *Observer* The new dawn saw him working as an accounts clerk . . , but only after some hesitancy.

hesitant /ˈhɛzɪt(ə)nt/ *a.* LME. [L *haesitant-* pres. ppl stem of *haesitare*: see next, -ANT[1].] Hesitating, irresolute, undecided; (of speech) stammering.

M. L. KING From a hesitant leader with unsure goals to a strong figure with deeply appealing objectives. M. DRABBLE Stephan's narrative style was hesitant, oblique, slightly stammering.

hesitantly *adv.* M17.

hesitate /ˈhɛzɪteɪt/ *v.* E17. [L *haesitat-* pa. ppl stem of *haesitare* stick fast, be undecided, stammer, f. *haes-* pa. ppl stem of *haerere* stick, hold fast: see -ATE[3].] 1 *v.i.* Pause irresolutely; show or speak with indecision (*about*, *over*); be reluctant *to do*; be deterred by scruples. E17. b Move in an indecisive or faltering manner. E20. 2 *v.i.* Stammer or falter in speech. E18. 3 *v.t.* Express with hesitation. M18.

1 L. STEFFENS The items are so incredible that I hesitate to print them. J. MARQUAND A time when it is better to do something, even if it is wrong, than to hesitate. W. SOYINKA They would not hesitate to put an end to my life. 3 W. GODWIN I hesitated a confused and irresolute answer. SIR W. SCOTT 'I am not sure,' hesitated Edith.

hesitative *a.* showing or given to hesitation L18. **hesitatively** *adv.* L19. **hesitatory** *a.* (now *rare* or *obs.*) hesitative M18.

hesitation /hɛzɪˈteɪʃ(ə)n/ *n.* E17. [L *haesitatio(n-)*, f. as prec.: see -ATION.] 1 The action or an act of hesitating; irresolute pausing or delay; a state of doubt with regard to action. E17. 2 Hesitancy in speech; stammering. E18.

1 LYNDON B. JOHNSON Any hesitation or wavering, any false step, any sign of self-doubt, could have been disastrous. H. BAILEY Vera had no hesitation about condemning what was going on. 2 R. WARNER The Air Vice-Marshal spoke without hesitation, . . in the manner of one who was delivering important instructions.

Comb.: **hesitation-form** *Ling.* (a form representing) a sound uttered when hesitating or faltering in speech; **hesitation-step** a step in ballroom dancing which takes up more than one beat; **hesitation waltz**: characterized by the hesitation step.

Hesped /ˈhɛspɛd/ *n.* M17. [Heb.] A funeral oration pronounced over the dead at a Jewish memorial service.

Hesper /ˈhɛspə/ *n. poet.* E17. [L HESPERUS.] = HESPERUS.

Hesperian /hɛˈspɪərɪən/ *a.* & *n.* L15. [L *hesperius*, Gk *hesperios*, f. *Hesperia* (poet.) land of the west, f. as HESPERUS: see -AN, -IAN.] A *adj.* 1 Western. *poet.* L15. 2 *Gk Mythol.* Of or pertaining to the Hesperides. L16. 3 = HESPERIID *a.* Now *rare.* M19. B *n.* 1 A native or inhabitant of a western land. *arch. rare.* E17. 2 = HESPERIID *n.* Now *rare.* M19.

hesperid *n.* & *a.* var. of HESPERIID.

Hesperides /hɛˈspɛrɪdiːz/ *n.pl.* L16. [Gk, pl. of *hesperis* (adj.) western, (n.) daughter of the west, land of the sunset, f. *hesperos*: see HESPERUS.] *Gk Mythol.* 1 (*The* islands containing) gardens with a tree of golden apples guarded by nymphs and popularly located beyond the Atlas mountains at the western border of Oceanus, the river encircling the world. L16. 2 The (three, four, or seven) nymphs, daughters of Hesperus (or, in earlier versions, of Night and Hades), who guarded the tree in these gardens. E17.

hesperidia *n.* pl. of HESPERIDIUM.

hesperidin /hɛˈspɛrɪdɪn/ *n.* M19. [f. as next + -IN[1].] *Chem.* A flavonoid glycoside obtained from the peel of citrus fruits.

hesperidium /hɛspəˈrɪdɪəm/ *n.* Pl. **-ia** /-ɪə/. M19. [f. as HESPERIDES + -IUM, w. ref. to the mythical golden apples of the Hesperides.] *Bot.* A form of berry with a tough leathery rind, as a citrus fruit.

hesperiid /hɛsˈpɛrɪɪd/ *n.* & *a.* Also **hesperid** /ˈhɛspərɪd/. L19. [mod.L *Hesperiidae* (see below), f. *Hesperia* genus name: see -ID[3].] *Entomol.* A *n.* Any of numerous small butterflies of the family Hesperiidae, somewhat like moths; a skipper. L19. B *adj.* Of, pertaining to, or designating this family. E20.

Hesperus /ˈhɛspərəs/ *n. poet.* LME. [L, f. Gk *hesperos* (adj.) western, (n.) the evening star.] The evening star.

Hessian /ˈhɛsɪən/ *a.* & *n.* Also **h-** (see below). L17. [f. *Hesse* (see below) + -IAN.] A *adj.* 1 Of or pertaining to the former grand duchy, or the region or State, of Hesse in Germany. L17. 2 (**h-**.) Made of hessian. M20.

Special collocations: **Hessian boot** a tasselled high boot fashionable in the early 19th cent., first worn by Hessian troops. **hessian fly** [thought to have been brought to N. America in bedding by Hessian troops, *c* 1776] a gall-midge, *Mayetiola destructor*, native to SE Europe and introduced elsewhere, whose larvae are destructive to wheat and other crops.

B *n.* 1 A native or inhabitant of Hesse; *Hist.* a Hessian soldier. M18. b A military or political hireling, a mercenary. *arch. US.* M19. 2 In *pl.* Hessian boots. E19. 3 (**h-**.) A strong coarse cloth made of hemp or jute. L19.

hessite /ˈhɛsʌɪt/ *n.* M19. [f. G. H. *Hess* (1802–50), Swiss-born Russ. scientist + -ITE[1].] *Min.* Silver telluride, crystallizing in the cubic system and usu. occurring as grey prisms with a metallic lustre.

hessonite *n.* var. of ESSONITE.

hest /hɛst/ *n.* [OE *hǣs*, f. Gmc base of OE *hātan* call (see HIGHT *v.*) assim. to ns. in *-t*.] 1 Bidding, a command, an injunction. *arch.* OE. †2 A vow, a promise. ME–L16. †3 Will, purpose, determination. LME–M19.

1 SIR W. SCOTT Christian or heathen, you shall swear to do my hest. CARLYLE Standing like a hackney-coach . . at the hest of a discerning public.

†**hestern** *a.* L16–E18. [L *hesternus*.] Of yesterday; yester-.

hesternal /hɛˈstəːn(ə)l/ *a.* Now *rare.* M17. [f. as prec. + -AL[1].] Of yesterday, of yesterday's standing or date.

Hesvan /ˈhɛsv(ə)n/ *n.* Also **Ches-** /ˈxɛs-/, **Hesh-** /ˈhɛʃ-/, & other vars. M19. [Heb. *ḥešwān* f. earlier *marḥešwān*, f. Akkadian *araḫ samna* eighth month.] In the Jewish calendar, the second month of the civil and eighth of the religious year, usu. coinciding with parts of October and November.

Hesychast /ˈhɛsɪkast/ *n.* M19. [Late Gk *hēsukhastēs* hermit, f. *hēsukhazein* be still, f. *hēsukhos* still, quiet.] *Eccl. Hist.* A member of a movement dedicated to the practice of interior prayer originating among the monks of Mount Athos in the 14th cent.

het /hɛt/ *ppl a.* LME. [pa. pple of HEAT *v.* (cf. LEAD *v.*[1], LED *v.*).] 1 Heated, hot. Long *dial.* LME. 2 Excited, agitated; upset. Foll. by *up* (exc. *dial.*). M19.

2 P. LIVELY Being overtired and overstrained and generally het up.

hetaera /hɪˈtɪərə/ *n.* Pl. **-ras, -rae** /-riː/. Also **hetaira** /hɪˈtʌɪrə/, pl. **-ras, -rai** /-rʌɪ/. E19. [Gk *hetaira* fem. of *hetairos* companion.] Esp. in ancient Greece: a mistress, a concubine; a courtesan, a prostitute.

hetaerism /hɪˈtɪərɪz(ə)m/ *n.* Also **hetairism** /hɪˈtʌɪrɪz(ə)m/. M19. [Gk *hetairismos* prostitution, f. *hetairizein* be a prostitute, f *hetaira*: see prec., -ISM.] 1 Concubinage as a recognized social system. M19. 2 *Anthropol.* Communal marriage as a social system. L19.

hetaerolite /hɪˈtɪərəlʌɪt/ *n.* L19. [f. Gk *hetairos* companion (from having been orig. found associated with chlorophanite) + -LITE.] *Min.* A black, tetragonal, mixed oxide of zinc and manganese, usu. occurring as octahedral crystals and isostructural with hausmannite.

hetaira *n.* var. of HETAERA.

hetairai *n.pl.* see HETAERA.

hetairism *n.* var. of HETAERISM.

†hetchel *n.* & *v.* see HATCHEL.

hetero /ˈhɛt(ə)rəʊ/ *n.* & *a. colloq.* Pl. of n. **-os.** M20. [Abbrev.] = HETEROSEXUAL *n.* & *a.*

hetero- /ˈhɛtərəʊ/ *comb. form.* Bef. a vowel also **heter-**. [f. Gk *heteros* the other of two, other: see -O-.] Used in wds adopted f. Gk and in Eng. wds modelled on these, and as a freely productive pref., w. the sense 'other, different'. Freq. opp. HOMO-, occas. opp. AUTO-[1], ISO-, ORTHO-.

heteracanth *a.* (*Ichthyol.*) having the spines of the dorsal and anal fins alternately broader on one side than on the other L19. **heterau'xesis** *n.* [Gk *auxēsis* growth] growth of different parts at unequal rates L19. **hetero-a'gglutinin** *n.* an agglutinin that causes agglutination of cells of a different blood group, animal species, etc. E20. **hetero-aggluti'nation** *n.* agglutination of cells brought about by a hetero-agglutinin E20. **heteroaro'matic** *a.* & *n.* (*Chem.*) (*a*) *adj.* heterocyclic and aromatic; (*b*) *n.* a heteroaromatic compound: M20. **'hetero-atom** *n.* (*Chem.*) an atom, other than a carbon atom, in the ring of a cyclic compound E20. **hetero'auxin** *n.* a growth-promoting hormone present in some plants and micro-organisms M20. **hetero'blastic** *a.* (*a*) *Bot.* characterized by a marked difference between immature and adult forms; (*b*) *Petrogr.* composed of grains of two or more distinct sizes: L19. **hetero'carpous** *a.* producing fruit of different kinds L19. **hetero'cercal** *a.* [Gk *kerkos* tail] *Ichthyol.* designating or possessing a tail with unequal lobes, esp. with the spine deflected into the upper lobe M19. **heterochla'mydeous** *a.* [Gk *khlamud-*, *khlamus* cloak] *Bot.* having the calyx and corolla of different colour or texture L19. **hetero'chromia** *n.* (*Med.*) a difference in colour between two parts (esp. the irises of the eyes) that are usually the same colour L19. **hetero'chromic** *a.* characterized by or exhibiting heterochromia E20. **hetero'chromous** *a.* (chiefly *Bot.*) of different colours M19. **hetero'chronic** *a.* occurring at different times; irregular; *esp.* (of a transplant) between individuals of different ages: M19. **heterocosm** *n.* a different or separate world M20. **heterocycle** *n.* (*Chem.*) a heterocyclic molecule or compound E20. **hetero'cyclic** *n.* & *a.* (*Chem.*) (a molecule or compound) containing a ring formed of atoms of more than one element L19. **heterocyst** *n.* a specialized cell of different structure present in certain algae and bacteria L19. **hetero'desmic** *a.* (*Cryst.*) containing chemical bonds of more than one kind M20. **heterodimer** *n.* (*Chem.*) a dimer composed of two different subunits L20. **hetero'duplex** *a.* & *n.* (*Biochem.*) (a molecule) containing or consisting of polynucleotide strands derived from two different parent molecules M20. **heteroecious** /hɛtəˈriːʃəs/ *a.* [Gk *oikia* house] (of a fungus etc.) parasitic on different hosts at different stages of its life cycle L19. **heteroecism** /hɛtəˈriːsɪz(ə)m/ *n.* the condition of being heteroecious L19. **heterograft** *n.* = HETEROTRANSPLANT *n.* E20. **hetero-i'mmune** *a.* immune to an antigen derived from a different species E20. **hetero'nuclear** *a.* (*Chem.* etc.) (*a*) (of substitution) taking place on different rings in a polycyclic molecule; (*b*) composed of atoms whose nuclei are unlike: E20. **hetero'phasia** *n.* [Gk *phasis* speech] the condition of saying or writing one word or phrase when another is meant, esp. as a result of brain damage etc. M19. **hetero'phoria** *n.* a latent squint L19. **hetero'phoric** *a.* pertaining to or exhibiting heterophoria L19. **hetero'polar** *a.* characterized by opposite or alternating polarity; *esp.* having armatures passing north and south magnetic poles alternately: L19. **heterosce'dastic** *a.* [Gk *skedastos* able to be scattered, f. *skedannunai* scatter] *Statistics* of unequal scatter or variation; having unequal variances: E20. **ˌheterosceda'sticity** *n.* (*Statistics*) unequal variance E20. **heterospe'cific** *a.* (*a*) of different blood groups; (of a pregnancy) in which the mother's serum would agglutinate the red blood cells of the foetus; (*b*) derived from an organism of a different species: E20. **hetero'sporic**, **hete'rosporous** *adjs.* (*Biol.*) producing two different kinds of spore L19. **hete'rospory** *n.* (*Biol.*) the condition of being heterosporous L19. **heterosu'ggestion** *n.* suggestion from another person (cf. AUTO-SUGGESTION) E20. **heterosy'llabic** *a.* belonging to a different syllable E20. **hetero'thallic** *a.* (*Mycol.*) (of a fungus) having an incompatibility system such that only genetically different strains can undergo nuclear fusion during sexual reproduction E20. **hetero'thallism** *n.* the state or condition of being heterothallic E20. **hetero'thally** *n.* = HETEROTHALLISM M20. **heterotherm** *n.* a heterothermic animal M20. **hetero'thermic** *a.* displaying homoiothermy and poikilothermy at different times L19. **heterothermy** *n.* heterothermic behaviour M20.

heterocaryotic *a.* var. of HETEROKARYOTIC.

heterochromatic /ˌhɛtərəʊkrə(ʊ)ˈmatɪk/ *a.* L19. [Sense 1 f. HETERO- + CHROMATIC; sense 2 f. next + -IC.] 1 Relating to or possessing more than one colour; pertaining to light or other radiation of more than one wavelength. L19. 2 Exhibiting heteropycnosis. M20.

heterochromatin /hɛtərə(ʊ)ˈkrəʊmətɪn/ *n.* M20. [f. HETERO- + CHROMATIN.] Heteropycnotic chromosome material.

heterochromatini'zation *n.* = HETEROCHROMATIZATION M20. **heterochromatinized** *a.* = HETEROCHROMATIZED M20.

heterochromatization /ˌhɛtərə(ʊ)krəʊmətʌɪˈzeɪʃ(ə)n/ *n.* Also **-isation**. M20. [f. HETEROCHROMAT(IN + -IZATION.] (The extent of) a change of state of chromosome material in which it becomes heterochromatic and the action of the genes is modified or suppressed.

hetero'chromatized *a.* having undergone heterochromatization M20.

heteroclite /ˈhɛtərə(ʊ)klʌɪt/ *a.* & *n.* Orig. **†ethroclite**. L15. [med.L *ethroclitus* & late L *heteroclitus* f. Gk *heteroklitos*, f. as HETERO- + *-klitos* bent, inflected, f. *klinein* to lean, bend, inflect: see -ITE[2].] A *adj.* 1 Deviating from the norm; abnormal, irregular, anomalous. L15. 2 *Gram.* Irregularly declined or inflected. M17. B *n.* 1 A heteroclite person or thing. L15. 2 *Gram.* A heteroclite word, esp. a noun. L16.

hetero'clitic *a.* & *n.* = HETEROCLITE M17. **†heteroclitical** *a.* = HETEROCLITE *a.* M17–L19.

heterodont /ˈhɛt(ə)rə(ʊ)dɒnt/ *a.* & *n.* L19. [f. HETERO- + -ODONT.] A *adj.* Having teeth of different kinds. L19. B *n.* A heterodont animal. L19.

heterodox /ˈhɛt(ə)rə(ʊ)dɒks/ *n.* & *a.* E17. [Late L *heterodoxus*, -*os* f. Gk *heterodoxos*, f. as HETERO- + *doxa* opinion.] †A *n.* An unorthodox opinion. Only in 17.

B *adj.* Of an opinion or a person: unorthodox. M17.

E. H. JONES Men . . tabooed by society because they were believed to be heterodox on questions of social policy.

heterodoxy /ˈhɛt(ə)rə(ʊ)dɒksi/ *n.* M17. [Gk *heterodoxia* error of opinion, f. as prec.: see -Y[3].] 1 A heterodox opinion. M17. 2 The quality of being heterodox; deviation from what is considered to be orthodox. M17.

heterodyne /ˈhɛt(ə)rə(ʊ)dʌɪn/ *a.*, *v.*, & *n.* E20. [f. HETERO- + Gk *dunamis* power.] A *adj.* Pertaining to, involving, or designating the production of beats by the combination of two oscillations of slightly different frequencies, esp. as a method of radio detection in which the incoming signal combines with an oscillation generated in the receiver, producing an audible signal. E20. B *v.* 1 *v.t.* Change the frequency of (a signal) by a heterodyne process. E20. 2 *v.i.* Combine in a heterodyne process. M20. C *n.* A heterodyne receiver or oscillator. Now *rare.* E20.

heterogamete /hɛt(ə)rə(ʊ)ˈgamiːt/ *n.* L19. [f. HETERO- + GAMETE.] *Biol.* Either of a pair of conjugating gametes that differ in form or character.

heterogametic /ˌhɛt(ə)rə(ʊ)gəˈmɛtɪk, -ˈmiː-/ *a.* E20. [f. HETERO- + GAMETIC.] *Biol.* Producing gametes that differ with respect to a sex chromosome.

ˌhetero'gamety *n.* the condition or state of being heterogametic M20.

heterogamic /hɛt(ə)rə(ʊ)ˈgamɪk/ *a.* E20. [f. HETEROGAMY + -IC.] *Biol.* Characterized by heterogamy.

heterogamous /hɛtəˈrɒgəməs/ *a.* M19. [f. HETERO- + Gk *gamos* marriage + -OUS.] 1 *Bot.* Having flowers of different sexual types (male, female, and/or hermaphrodite) in the same inflorescence. M19. 2 *Biol.* Characterized by the alternation of generations. L19. 3 *Biol.* Involving, being, or producing heterogametes L19.

heterogamy /hɛtəˈrɒgəmi/ *n.* L19. [f. HETERO- + -GAMY.] *Biol.* 1 Alternation of generations. L19. 2 The condition of producing heterogametes; heterogamous reproduction. L19. 3 *Bot.* Heterogamous condition. L19.

heterogene /ˈhɛt(ə)rə(ʊ)dʒiːn/ *a.* Long *rare* or *obs.* Orig. **†ethrogene**. LME. [Gk *heterogenēs*: see HETEROGENEOUS.] = HETEROGENEOUS.

heterogeneal /hɛt(ə)rə(ʊ)ˈdʒiːnɪəl, -ˈdʒɛn-/ *a.* & *n.* Now *rare.* E17. [f. as HETEROGENEOUS + -AL[1].] A *adj.* = HETEROGENEOUS. E17. †B *n.* A heterogeneous person or substance. Only in M17.

heterogeneity /ˌhɛt(ə)rə(ʊ)dʒɪˈniːəti/ *n.* M17. [med.L *heterogeneitas*, f. as next: see -ITY.] 1 The quality or condition of being heterogeneous. M17. 2 A heterogeneous element or constituent. Now *rare.* M17.

heterogeneous /hɛt(ə)rə(ʊ)ˈdʒiːnɪəs, -ˈdʒɛn-/ *a.* E17. [f. med.L *heterogeneus*, f. Gk *heterogenēs* of different kinds, f. as HETERO- + *genos* kind: see -OUS.] 1 Diverse in kind or nature; dissimilar, incongruous; *gen.* (now *rare*) anomalous, abnormal. E17. 2 Composed of different elements or constituents; not homogeneous. M17. b *Physical Chem.* Consisting of or involving more than one phase. L19. c Of a nuclear reactor: not having the fuel uniformly mixed with the moderator and/or coolant. M20. 3 *Math.* Of different kinds or degrees; consisting of terms of different dimensions. M17.

1 N. PODHORETZ An organization embracing people of such diverse and heterogeneous tastes. 2 I. COLEGATE Another sub-group in this apparently heterogeneous but in fact multifariously differentiated collection of men.

heterogeneously *adv.* L18. **heterogeneousness** *n.* M17.

heterogenesis /hɛt(ə)rə(ʊ)ˈdʒɛnɪsɪs/ *n.* M19. [f. HETERO- + -GENESIS.] *Biol.* 1 The origination or birth of an organism otherwise than from a similar organism as parent. M19. 2 *spec.* Alternation of generations. M19.

heterogenetic /ˌhɛt(ə)rə(ʊ)dʒɪˈnɛtɪk/ *a.* L19. [f. HETERO- + GENETIC.] *Biol.* 1 Of, pertaining to, or characterized by heterogenesis or heterogeny. L19. 2 = HETEROPHILE *a.* E20.

heterogenous /hɛtəˈrɒdʒɪnəs/ *a.* L17. [Alt. of HETEROGENEOUS; in sense 2 prob. directly f. Gk *genos* race.] 1 Heterogeneous. L17. 2 *Med.* †a = HOMOPLASTIC *a.* 2. Only in E20. b = HETEROPLASTIC *a.* 2. M20.

heterogeny /hɛtəˈrɒdʒəni/ *n.* M17. [In sense 1 app. f. HETEROGENE + -Y[3]; in senses 2 and 3 f. HETERO- + -GENY.] †1 Heterogeneousness. Only in M17. 2 A heterogeneous collection or group. M19. 3 *Biol.* a Spontaneous generation. M19. b Alternation of generations, esp. of a sexual and a parthenogenetic generation. L19.

heterogenist *n.* a supporter of the hypothesis of spontaneous generation L19.

heterogony /hɛtəˈrɒɡəni/ *n.* L19. [f. HETERO- + -GONY.] 1 = HETEROGENESIS. L19. 2 Allometry. E20.

heteroˈgonic *a.* E20. **heterogonous** *a.* L19.

heterography /hɛtəˈrɒɡrəfi/ *n.* L18. [f. HETERO- + -GRAPHY, after *orthography*.] Unconventional or incorrect spelling.

heteroˈgraphic *a.* of, pertaining to, or characterized by heterography M19. **heteroˈgraphically** *adv.* L18.

heterokaryotic /ˌhɛt(ə)rə(ʊ)karɪˈɒtɪk/ *a.* Also **-caryotic**. E20. [f. HETERO- + KARYO- + -OTIC.] Chiefly *Mycol.* Having two or more genetically different nuclei within a common cytoplasm.

heteroˈkaryon *n.*, pl. **-ya**, a heterokaryotic cell, structure, or organism M20. **heterokaryosis** *n.* the state or condition of being heterokaryotic E20.

heterological /hɛt(ə)rə(ʊ)ˈlɒdʒɪk(ə)l/ *a.* E20. [G *heterologisch*, f. as HETERO- + Gk LOGOS: see -ICAL.] Of a word: not having the property which it denotes. Opp. AUTOLOGICAL.

heterologous /hɛtəˈrɒləɡəs/ *a.* M19. [f. HETERO- + Gk *logos* relation, ratio: see LOGOS, -OUS.] Not corresponding; consisting of different elements; derived from or pertaining to different species, bodies, etc. Opp. HOMOLOGOUS.

heterology /hɛtəˈrɒlədʒi/ *n.* M19. [f. as prec. + -Y[3].] The quality or condition of being heterologous.

heterolysis /hɛtəˈrɒlɪsɪs/ *n.* E20. [f. HETERO- + -LYSIS.] 1 *Biol.* The dissolution of cells of one kind by an agent produced by cells of another kind. E20. 2 *Chem.* The splitting of a molecule into two oppositely charged ions. M20.

heteroˈlytic *a.* characterized by or of the nature of heterolysis E20.

heteromerous /hɛtəˈrɒm(ə)rəs/ *a.* E19. [f. HETERO- + -MEROUS.] 1 *Entomol.* Of, pertaining to, or designating a group of beetles (sometimes classed as Heteromera) which typically have a reduced number of tarsal joints in the posterior pair of legs. E19. 2 *Bot.* a Of a lichen: having the algal and fungal components in separate layers. L19. b Of a flower: having a different number of members in each whorl. Opp. *isomerous*. L19.

heteromorph /ˈhɛt(ə)rə(ʊ)mɔːf/ *a.* & *n.* L19. [f. as next.] (A thing that is) heteromorphous.

heteromorphic /hɛt(ə)rə(ʊ)ˈmɔːfɪk/ *a.* M19. [f. HETERO- + Gk *morphē* form: see -IC.] *Biol.* 1 Differing in form; occurring in differing forms, esp. at different stages of life. M19. 2 Resulting from heteromorphosis. L19.

heteromorphism /hɛt(ə)rə(ʊ)ˈmɔːfɪz(ə)m/ *n.* M19. [f. as prec. + -ISM.] The quality or condition of being heteromorphic.

heteromorphosis /hɛt(ə)rə(ʊ)ˈmɔːfəsɪs, ˌhɛt(ə)rə(ʊ)mɔːˈfəʊsɪs/ *n.* Pl. **-morphoses** /-ˈmɔːfəsiːz, -mɔːˈfəʊsiːz/. L19. [f. HETERO- + MORPHOSIS.] *Biol.* & *Med.* 1 Growth of abnormal tissue. L19. 2 Regeneration of an organ etc. different from that which has been damaged or lost. L19.

heteromorphous /hɛt(ə)rə(ʊ)ˈmɔːfəs/ *a.* E19. [f. as HETEROMORPHIC: see -OUS.] Of abnormal or irregular form.

heteronomous /hɛtəˈrɒnəməs/ *a.* E19. [f. HETERO- + Gk *nomos* law: see -OUS.] 1 Subject to different laws, *spec.* (*Biol.*) of growth. E19. 2 Subject to an external law. L19.

2 D. CUPITT Morality was heteronomous, in being a matter of keeping to a sacred Law imposed upon you by another.

heteronomously *adv.* E20.

heteronomy /hɛtəˈrɒnəmi/ *n.* L18. [f. as prec.: see -Y[3], -NOMY.] 1 Subjection to an external law or power. L18. 2 Presence of a different law or principle. E19.

heteronym /ˈhɛt(ə)rə(ʊ)nɪm/ *n.* L19. [f. HETERO- + -NYM.] 1 Each of two or more words identical in spelling but distinct in sound and meaning. Cf. HOMONYM, SYNONYM. L19. 2 A word in one language which is a translation of the designation in another language. Opp. PARONYM 2. L19.

heteronymous /hɛtəˈrɒnɪməs/ *a.* L17. [Gk *heterōnumos*, f. as prec.: see -OUS.] 1 Designating correlatives which are denoted by unlike or unrelated terms, as *husband*, *wife*. Cf. SYNONYMOUS. L17. 2 Having the character of a heteronym. L19. 3 *Zool.* Of animal horns: such that the right horn has a left-handed spiral core and vice versa. E20.

heteroousian /hɛt(ə)rəʊˈuːsɪən, -ˈaʊ-, -z-/ *n.* & *a.* Also **heterous-** /hɛtəˈruː-, hɛtəˈraʊ-/, (esp. as n.) **H-**. L17. [f. Gk *heter(o)ousios* (f. as HETERO- + *ousia* essence, substance): see -IAN. Opp. HOMOIOUSIAN and HOMOOUSIAN.] *Chr. Theol.* & *Eccl. Hist.* A *n.* A person who believed the first and second persons of the Trinity to be different in essence or substance. L17. B *adj.* Of different essence or substance (esp. of the first and second persons of the Trinity). Also, of or pertaining to the heteroousians. L17.

heterophile /ˈhɛt(ə)rə(ʊ)fʌɪl/ *a.* & *n.* Also (esp. as n.) **-phil** /-fɪl/. E20. [f. HETERO- + -PHIL(E).] A *adj.* Able to react immunologically with sera etc. from organisms of another species. E20. B *n.* A polymorphonuclear leucocyte found in mammalian blood, stained by both acid and basic dyes. M20.

heteroˈphilic *a.* = HETEROPHILE *a.* E20.

heterophony /hɛtəˈrɒf(ə)ni/ *n.* M20. [Gk *heterophōnia* difference in note, f. as HETERO-: see -PHONY.] A simultaneous performance of the same melody by different voices or instruments.

heteroˈphonic *a.* different in sound E20.

heterophyllous /hɛt(ə)rə(ʊ)ˈfɪləs/ *a.* E19. [f. HETERO- + Gk *phullon* leaf: see -OUS.] *Bot.* Bearing leaves of different forms on the same plant.

ˈheterophylly *n.* the condition of being heterophyllous L19.

heteroplasia /hɛt(ə)rə(ʊ)ˈpleɪzɪə/ *n.* M19. [f. HETERO- + -PLASIA. Cf. next.] Abnormal growth of tissue.

heteroplastic /hɛt(ə)rə(ʊ)ˈplastɪk/ *a.* M19. [f. HETERO- + PLASTIC *a.* & *n.*[3]] *Biol.* & *Med.* 1 Pertaining to or being an abnormal growth of tissue. M19. 2 Of a graft: between individuals of different species. L19.

heteroplastically *adv.* E20.

heteroplasty /ˈhɛt(ə)rə(ʊ)plasti/ *n.* M19. [f. HETERO- + -PLASTY.] *Biol.* & *Med.* 1 The grafting of tissues between individuals of the same species. M19. 2 The grafting of tissues between individuals of different species. E20.

heteroploid /ˈhɛt(ə)rə(ʊ)plɔɪd/ *a.* E20. [f. HETERO- + -PLOID.] *Biol.* Having a chromosome number other than that typical of the species.

heteroploidy *n.* heteroploid condition E20.

heteropod /ˈhɛt(ə)rə(ʊ)pɒd/ *n.* & *a.* M19. [mod.L *Heteropoda* pl., f. as HETERO- + -POD.] *Zool.* A *n.* Pl. **heteropods**, in L form **Heteropoda** /hɛtəˈrɒpədə/. Any of a group of free-swimming prosobranch gastropods having the foot adapted for swimming. M19. B *adj.* Of or pertaining to this group. L19.

heteropteran /hɛtəˈrɒpt(ə)rən/ *n.* & *a.* M19. [f. mod.L *Heteroptera* (see below), f. as HETERO- + Gk *pteron* wing: see -AN.] *Entomol.* A *n.* Any hemipteran insect of the suborder Heteroptera, which comprises the true bugs, i.e. those whose wings, where present, have hardened bases and membranous tips. Cf. HOMOPTERAN. M19. B *adj.* Of, pertaining to, or characteristic of the suborder Heteroptera. E20.

heteropterous *a.* = HETEROPTERAN *a.* L19.

heteropycnosis /ˌhɛt(ə)rə(ʊ)pɪkˈnəʊsɪs/ *n.* Also **-pyknosis**. E20. [f. HETERO- + Gk *puknos* thick: see -OSIS.] *Biol.* The condition in chromosome material of being more (or less) condensed than the majority of such material, and hence staining more (or less) intensely.

heteropycnotic *a.* M20.

heterosexism /hɛt(ə)rə(ʊ)ˈsɛksɪz(ə)m/ *n.* L20. [f. HETERO- + SEXISM.] Discrimination or prejudice by heterosexuals against or towards homosexuals.

heterosexist *a.* L20.

heterosexual /hɛt(ə)rə(ʊ)ˈsɛksjʊəl, -ʃʊəl/ *a.* & *n.* L19. [f. HETERO- + SEXUAL.] A *adj.* 1 Of, pertaining to, or characterized by sexual attraction towards the opposite sex; of, pertaining to, or involving sexual activity between members of the opposite sex. L19. 2 Pertaining to, characteristic of, or comprising both sexes. E20.

1 *Daily Telegraph* Co-educational schools probably tend to hasten heterosexual experimentation. 2 D. MORRIS The males . . find themselves in heterosexual groups instead of the old all-male parties.

B *n.* A heterosexual person. E20.

heterosexuˈality *n.* the condition of being heterosexual; heterosexual characteristics: E20. **heterosexually** *adv.* M20.

heterosis /hɛtəˈrəʊsɪs/ *n.* Pl. **-roses** /-ˈrəʊsiːz/. M19. [Gk *heterōsis* alteration, f. *heteros* different: see -OSIS.] 1 The use of one form of a noun, pronoun, etc., for another as a figure of speech. *rare*. M19. 2 *Genetics*. The tendency of a crossbred individual to show qualities superior to those of both parents; hybrid vigour. E20.

heterotic *a.* (*Genetics*) pertaining to or exhibiting heterosis E20.

heterosite /ˈhɛt(ə)rə(ʊ)sʌɪt/ *n.* M19. [f. Gk *heteros* different + -ITE[1].] *Min.* An orthorhombic hydrated phosphate of iron and manganese that occurs as dark violet to bright purple masses. Cf. PURPURITE.

heterostyled /ˈhɛt(ə)rə(ʊ)stʌɪld/ *a.* L19. [f. HETERO- + STYLE + -ED[2].] *Bot.* In which the styles of different individual plants differ in length relative to the stamens.

heteroˈstylism *n.* the condition of being heterostyled L19. **heteroˈstylous** *a.* = HETEROSTYLED L19. **ˈheterostyly** *n.* = HETEROSTYLISM L19.

heterotaxy /ˈhɛt(ə)rə(ʊ)taksi/ *n.* M19. [f. HETERO- + -TAXY.] 1 *Anat.* & *Bot.* Abnormal disposition of organs or parts. M19. 2 *Geol.* Lack of uniformity in stratification. L19.

heterotopia /hɛt(ə)rə(ʊ)ˈtəʊpɪə/ *n.* Also Anglicized as **heterotopy** /hɛtəˈrɒtəpi/. L19. [mod.L, f. as HETERO- + Gk *-topia*, f. *topos* place: see -IA[1], -Y[3].] *Biol.* & *Med.* The presence of an organ or other tissue at a site where it is not normally found.

heterotopic /hɛt(ə)rə(ʊ)ˈtɒpɪk/ *a.* L19. [f. as prec. + -IC.] 1 *Biol.* & *Med.* Of, pertaining to, or displaying heterotopia. L19. 2 *Ecol.* Occupying different environments; present in an environment different from that normally occupied. L19.

heterotopically *adv.* E20.

heterotransplant /*as n.* hɛt(ə)rə(ʊ)ˈtranspləːnt, -ˈtrɑːns-, -nz-; *as vb* -transˈplɑːnt, -trɑːns-, -nz-/ *n.* & *v.* E20. [f. HETERO- + TRANSPLANT *n.*] *Med.* & *Biol.* A *n.* A piece of tissue or an organ (to be) transplanted from one individual to another of a different species. Also, an operation in which such a transplantation is performed. E20. B *v.t.* Transplant from one individual to another of a different species. E20.

ˌheterotransplantaˈbility *n.* ability to be heterotransplanted M20. **ˌheterotransˈplantable** *a.* able to be heterotransplanted M20. **ˌheterotransplanˈtation** *n.* E20.

heterotroph /ˈhɛt(ə)rə(ʊ)trəʊf/ *n.* Also **-trophe**. E20. [f. HETERO- + Gk *trophos* feeder.] *Biol.* Any organism depending on an external energy supply contained in complex organic compounds.

heterotrophic /hɛt(ə)rə(ʊ)ˈtrəʊfɪk, -ˈtrɒfɪk/ *a.* L19. [f. HETERO- + -TROPHIC.] *Biol.* Of an organism: deriving its nourishment from outside; not autotrophic.

heterotrophically *adv.* M20. **heterotrophism** *n.* E20. **heterotrophy** /ˈhɛt(ə)rə(ʊ)trəʊfi/ *n.* L19.

heterousian *n.* & *a.* var. of HETEROOUSIAN.

heterozygote /hɛt(ə)rə(ʊ)ˈzʌɪɡəʊt/ *n.* & *a.* E20. [f. HETERO- + ZYGOTE.] *Biol.* A *n.* An individual having different alleles at one or more genetic loci. E20. B *adj.* Heterozygous. E20.

heterozy'gosity *n.* the state or condition of being heterozygous E20. **heterozy'gotic, -zygous** *adjs.* having different alleles at one or more genetic loci, or *for* a given gene E20.

†hethen *adv.* ME–L15. [ON *heðan* f. the Gmc pronominal base of HE *pers. pron.*] Hence.

hetman /'hɛtmən/ *n.* M18. [Pol., prob. f. G *Hauptmann* (earlier *Heubtman*) headman, captain.] A Cossack military commander. Cf. ATAMAN.

heuch *n.* var. of HEUGH *n.*

heuchera /'hɔɪkərə, 'hjuːk-/ *n.* L18. [mod.L, f. J. H. *Heucher* (1677–1747), Ger. botanist.] Any of various frequently cultivated plants of the N. American genus *Heuchera*, of the saxifrage family, with loose panicles of small esp. reddish flowers and heart-shaped leaves in basal tufts. Also called *alum-root*.

heugh /hjuːx/ *n. Sc.* & *north.* Also **heuch**. LME. [Var. of HOE *n.*[1]] **1** A precipice, a cliff. LME. **2** (The steep face of) an excavation or quarry; a mine. LME. **3** A ravine, a narrow glen. L15.

heugh /hjuː(x)/ *int.* Now *rare.* Also **†hewgh**. E17. [Natural exclam.] Expr. surprise.

heulandite /'hjuːləndʌɪt/ *n.* E19. [f. Henry *Heuland* (1777–1856), Eng. mineralogist + -ITE[1].] *Min.* A monoclinic hydrated silicate of aluminium and calcium belonging to the zeolite group, usu. occurring as elongated tabular crystals, white or faintly coloured with a pearly lustre.

heumite /'hjuːmʌɪt/ *n.* E20. [f. *Heum* locality in southern Norway + -ITE[1].] *Geol.* A brownish-black hypabyssal rock occurring as dikes and containing predominantly alkali feldspars, hornblende, and biotite.

heuretic /hjʊ(ə)'rɛtɪk/ *a.* & *n. rare.* L17. [Gk *heuretikos* inventive, f. *heuriskein* find: see -IC.] (Designating or pertaining to) the branch of logic which treats of discovery or invention.

heurige /'hɔyrɪɡə/ *n.* Also ***-ger*** /-ɡər/. Pl. ***-gen*** /-ɡən/. M20. [Southern G & Austrian G = new (wine); vintner's establishment.] **1** Esp. in Austria: wine from the latest harvest. M20. **2** An establishment where such wine is served. M20.

heurism /'hjʊ(ə)rɪz(ə)m/ *n.* E20. [f. HEURISTIC + -ISM.] The educational practice or principle of training pupils to discover things for themselves.

heuristic /hjʊ(ə)'rɪstɪk/ *a.* & *n.* E19. [Irreg. f. Gk *heuriskein* find, after wds in -ISTIC from vbs in *-izein* -IZE.] **A** *adj.* **1** Serving to find out or discover something. E19. **2** Of or pertaining to heurism in education. L19. **3** Esp. *Computing.* Designating or employing trial-and-error methods in problem-solving. M20. **B** *n.* **1a** Heuretic logic. E19. **b** A heuristic method for attempting the solution of a problem; a rule or item of information used in such a process. M20. **2** In *pl.* (treated as *sing.*). The study and use of heuristic techniques in data processing. M20.

heuristical *a.* = HEURISTIC *a.* 2 M19. **heuristically** *adv.* M20.

heurte *n.* var. of HURT *n.*[2]

hevea /'hiːvɪə/ *n.* L19. [mod.L, f. Quechua *hyeve*.] Any of various S. American trees of the genus *Hevea*, of the spurge family; esp. *H. brasiliensis*, whose milky sap is a major source of rubber.

†hew *n.* L16–E17. [f. the vb.] An act of hewing; hacking, slaughter; a cut, a gash.

hew /hjuː/ *v.* Pa. pple **hewn** /hjuːn/, **hewed**. [OE *hēawan* = OFris. *hawa, howa*, OS *hauwan* (Du. *houwen*), OHG *houwan* (G *hauen*), ON *hǫggva*, f. Gmc.] **1** *v.i.* Deal cutting blows (*at, among*, etc.). OE. **2** *v.t. gen.* Chop or cut, with an axe, sword, etc. Freq. in *pass.* OE. **3** *v.t.* Cut into shape with cutting or chopping blows of an axe etc. OE. **4** *v.t.* Chop or cut *down* etc.; fell (timber); cut (coal) from a seam. OE. **5** *v.t.* Sever (a part from the whole) with cutting blows, cut *away, off*, etc. OE. **6** *v.t.* Make or produce by hewing. (Foll. by *out, into*, etc.) OE. **7** *v.t.* Divide with cutting blows; chop (a thing) into pieces. Now chiefly (*arch.*) in *hew asunder, hew in* or *to pieces*, etc. LME. **†8** *v.t.* & *i.* Of a horse etc.: strike (a foot etc.) *against, upon* another foot etc. in going. Cf. CUT *v.* 30. E16–E19. **9** *fig.* Conform *to. N. Amer.* L19.

1 TOLKIEN In a fury he hewed at them with his sword. **2** C. KINGSLEY His casque and armour . . were hewn and battered by a hundred blows. **3** C. THUBRON Some of the stones are hewn smooth, others left jagged. *rough-hew*: see ROUGH *adv.* **4** G. K. CHESTERTON The invaders were hewn down horribly with black steel. G. L. HARDING Those who hewed the stone from the local quarries. **5** E. A. FREEMAN The fragments of rock left when the rest is hewn away. **6** B. MALAMUD Rough steps that had been hewn into the rocky hills. **hew one's way** make a way for oneself by hewing. **9** *New Yorker* Even Sandra Day O'Connor . . has not reliably hewed to the Reagan agenda.

hewer /'hjuːə/ *n.* OE. [f. HEW *v.* + -ER[1].] A person who hews (something); *spec.* one who cuts coal from a seam.

hewers of wood and drawers of water [*Josh.* 9:21] menial drudges; labourers.

hewgag /'hjuːɡaɡ/ *n. US.* M19. [Origin unkn.] A toy musical instrument, in which a piece of parchment etc. is vibrated by blowing.

†hewgh *int.* var. of HEUGH *int.*

hewn *v.* pa. pple: see HEW *v.*

hex /hɛks/ *n.*[1] Chiefly *N. Amer.* M19. [Pennsylvanian G f. G *Hexe*. Cf. HEX *v.*, HAG *n.*[1]] **1** A witch; a woman resembling a witch. M19. **2** A magic spell, a curse. E20.

hex /hɛks/ *n.*[2] M20. [Abbrev.] *Nuclear Technol.* Uranium hexafluoride, UF_6, as used in the separation of uranium isotopes by gaseous diffusion.

hex /hɛks/ *n.*[3] & *a.* L20. [Abbrev.] *Computing.* = HEXADECIMAL *a.* & *n.*

hex /hɛks/ *v.* Chiefly *N. Amer.* M19. [Pennsylvanian G *hexe* f. G *hexen*. Cf. HEX *n.*[1]] **1** *v.i.* Practise witchcraft. M19. **2** *v.t.* Bewitch, cast a spell on. M20.

hexa- /'hɛksə/ *comb. form.* Bef. a vowel **hex-**. [Gk *hex, hexa-* six.] Having six, sixfold.

hexacanth *a.* [Gk *akantha* thorn] *Zool.* having six spines, rays, or hooks L19. **hexa'chloraphane, -phene** *n.* a powder, $CH_2(C_6HCl_3OH)_2$, used as a disinfectant, esp. for the skin M20. **hexachloro'ethane, hexachlo'rethane** *n.* a toxic crystalline compound, $Cl_3C{\cdot}CCl_3$, used as an insecticide and anthelmintic and in smoke-producing mixtures L19. **hexa'dactylism** *n.* the condition of having six digits on each hand or each foot L19. **hexa'decane** *n.* (*Chem.*) any of a series of saturated hydrocarbons (alkanes) with the formula $C_{16}H_{34}$, *spec.* (also *n-hexadecane*) = CETANE L19. **hexa'decapole** *n.* (*Physics*) a multipole of order 4 L20. **hexadecimal** *a.* & *n.* (*Computing*) (*a*) *adj.* designating or pertaining to a system of numerical notation that uses 16 rather than 10 as a base; (*b*) *n.* the hexadecimal system; hexadecimal notation: M20. **hexa'decimally** *adv.* using hexadecimal notation M20. **he'xagonous** *a.* (*Bot.*) hexagonal in cross-section L19. **hexa'hydrate** *n.* (*Chem.*) a hydrate containing six moles of water per mole of compound E20. **hexahy'drated** *a.* (*Chem.*) hydrated with six molecules of water per molecule of compound L19. **hexa'hydric** *a.* (*Chem.*) containing six hydroxyl groups in the molecule L19. **hexamer** *n.* (*Chem.*) a compound whose molecule is composed of six molecules of monomer M20. **hexa'meric** *a.* (*Chem.*) of the nature of a hexamer, consisting of a hexamer or hexamers M20. **he'xamerism** *n.* (*Biol.*) the condition of being hexamerous E20. **he'xamerous** *a.* (*Biol.*) having parts arranged in groups of six M19. **hexameta'phosphate** *n.* a phosphate regarded as derived from an acid with the formula $(HPO_3)_6$; *spec.* a glassy sodium salt used industrially as a water softener: L19. **hexame'thonium** *n.* (*Pharm.*) a quaternary ammonium ion, containing six methyl groups; any of the salts of this ion, some of which have been used as ganglionic blocking agents in cases of severe hypertension: M20. **hexa'methylene** *n.* (*Chem.*) = CYCLOHEXANE L19. **hexamethylene'diamine** *n.* (*Chem.*) a crystalline compound, $H_2N(CH_2)_6NH_2$, used in making nylon L19. **hexamethylene'tetramine** *n.* (*Chem.*) a heterocyclic crystalline compound, $(CH_2)_6N_4$, used in making phenol-formaldehyde resins and antiseptics L19. **he'xandrous** *a.* having six stamens M19. **he'xangular** *a.* having six angles, hexagonal M17. **hexa'peptide** *n.* (*Biochem.*) a peptide with six amino acids in its molecule E20. **hexa'petalous** *a.* having six petals E18. **hexarch** *a.* (*Bot.*) (of a vascular bundle) having six strands of xylem, formed from six points of origin E20. **hexa'sepalous** *a.* having six sepals L19. **hexastich** /'hɛksəstɪk/ *n.* a group of six lines of verse L16. **hexastyle** *n.* & *a.* (a portico or façade) of six columns E18. **hexasy'llabic** *a.* of six syllables L19. **Hexateuch** *n.* the first six books of the Bible L19. **hexa'tomic** *a.* (*Chem.*, now *rare*) containing six replaceable hydrogen atoms or groups; hexavalent: M19. **hexatone** *n.* (*Mus.*) an octave of six pitches M20. **hexa'tonic** *a.* (*Mus.*) characterized by hexatones M20. **hexa'valent** *a.* (*Chem.*) having a valency of six L19.

hexachord /'hɛksəkɔːd/ *n.* L17. [f. HEXA- + CHORD *n.*[1]] *Mus.* **†1** The interval of a sixth. L17–M18. **2** A diatonic scale of six notes with a semitone between the third and fourth, used at three different pitches in medieval music. M18.

hexad /'hɛksad/ *n.* M17. [Gk *hexad-, hexas* a group of six, f. *hex* six: see -AD[1].] **1** The number six in the Pythagorean system; a series of six numbers. M17. **b** A group of six. L19. **†2** *Chem.* A hexavalent element or group. M–L19.

he'xadic *a.*

hexaemeron *n.* var. of HEXAMERON.

hexagon /'hɛksəɡ(ə)n/ *n.* L16. [Late L *hexagonum* f. Gk *hexagōnon* use as n. of *hexagōnos* six-cornered, f. as HEXA-: see -GON.] A plane figure with six straight sides and six angles.

hexagonal /hɛk'saɡ(ə)n(ə)l/ *a.* L16. [f. prec. + -AL[1].] **1** Of or pertaining to a hexagon; having six sides and six angles. L16. **2** Of a solid: having a section which is a hexagon; constructed on a hexagon as base. M17. **3** Designating or pertaining to a crystal system referred to three coplanar axes of equal length separated by 60° and a fourth axis at right angles to these and of a different length; (of a mineral) crystallizing in this system. M19.

hexagonally *adv.* E18.

hexagram /'hɛksəɡram/ *n.* M19. [f. HEXA- + -GRAM.] **1** Any of various figures composed of six straight lines; *spec.* one formed by two intersecting equilateral triangles whose angular points coincide with those of a hexagon. M19. **2** Each of 64 figures composed of six whole or broken parallel lines occurring in the ancient Chinese text *I Ching.* L19.

hexahedron /hɛksə'hiːdrən, -'hɛd-/ *n.* Pl. **-dra** /-drə/, **-drons**. L16. [Gk *hexaedron* neut. sing. of *hexaedros*, f. as HEXA-: see -HEDRON.] A solid figure or object with six plane faces.

hexahedral *a.* having the form of a hexahedron; having six faces: E19. **†hexahedrical** *a.*: only in L17.

hexakis- /'hɛksəkɪs/ *comb. form.* [Gk *hexakis* adv.] Six times (a number denoted by a second comb. form), as *hexakistetrahedron*.

hexameron /hɛk'sam(ə)r(ə)n/ *n.* Also **hexaem-** /hɛksə'iːm-, -'ɛm-/. L16. [Late L *hexaemeron* (the title of a work by Ambrose) = Gk use as n. of *hexaēmeros* adj., f. as HEXA- + *hēmera* day.] The six days of the Creation; an account (as contained in Genesis) of this period.

hexameter /hɛk'samɪtə/ *n.* & *a.* LME. [L, f. Gk *hexametros* of six measures, f. as HEXA- + -METER.] *Pros.* **A** *n.* A line of six metrical feet. LME.

dactylic hexameter: having five dactyls and a spondee or trochee, any of the first four feet, and sometimes the fifth, being replaceable by a spondee.

B *attrib.* or as *adj.* Hexametric. M16.

hexa'metric *a.* of or pertaining to a hexameter; consisting of six metrical feet; composed in hexameters: L18. **hexa'metrical** *a.* = HEXAMETRIC M18. **hexametrist** *n.* a person who composes or writes (in) hexameters L18. **hexametrize** *v.i.* & *t.* compose or write (in) hexameters L18.

hexamitiasis /hɛksəmɪ'tʌɪəsɪs/ *n.* Pl. **-ases** /-əsiːz/. M20. [f. mod.L *Hexamita* (see below), f. HEXA- + Gk *mitos* thread: see -IASIS.] Infection with, or a disease caused by, protozoa of the genus *Hexamita*; *esp.* an infectious, often fatal, enteritis of turkeys.

hexane /'hɛkseɪn/ *n.* L19. [f. HEXA- + -ANE.] *Chem.* Any of five isomeric liquid alkanes with the formula C_6H_{14}; *esp.* (also *n-hexane*) the unbranched isomer, $CH_3(CH_2)_4CH_3$.

hexa'noic *a.*: *hexanoic acid*, a fatty acid, $CH_3(CH_2)_4COOH$, that is an oily liquid occurring in milk fat and in coconut and palm oil (also called *caproic acid*) E20.

hexapla /ˈhɛksəplə/ *n.* Also **hexaple** /ˈhɛksəp(ə)l/. E17. [Gk (*ta*) *hexapla* (title of Origen's work) neut. pl. of *hexaplous* sixfold.] A sixfold text in parallel columns, esp. of the Old or New Testament.

hexaplar *a.* E19. **hexaˈplaric** *a.* L19.

hexaploid /ˈhɛksəplɔɪd/ *a.* & *n.* E20. [f. HEXA- + -PLOID.] *Biol.* A *adj.* (Of a cell) containing six sets of chromosomes; (of an individual) composed of hexaploid cells. E20. B *n.* A hexaploid individual. E20.

hexaploidy *n.* hexaploid condition E20.

hexapod /ˈhɛksəpɒd/ *n.* & *a.* M17. [Gk *heksapod-*, *hexapous*, f. as HEXA- + *pous* foot: see -POD.] *Zool.* A *n.* An animal with six feet, an insect; *spec.* an animal of the superclass Hexapoda, which comprises the true insects together with the Protura, Diplura, and Collembola treated as separate classes. M17. B *adj.* Having six feet; of or pertaining to the superclass Hexapoda. M19.

hexapody /hɛkˈsapədi/ *n.* M19. [f. as prec. + -Y[3], after *dipody*, *tetrapody*, etc.] *Pros.* A line of verse consisting of six feet.

hexestrol *n.* var. of HEXOESTROL.

hexite /ˈhɛksʌɪt/ *n.* L19. [f. HEXA- + -ITE[1].] 1 *Chem.* = HEXITOL. L19. 2 A kind of high explosive. M20.

hexitol /ˈhɛksɪtɒl/ *n.* L19. [f. HEX(OSE + -ITOL.] Any of a class of hexahydric alcohols closely related to the hexoses.

hexobarbital /hɛksə(ʊ)ˈbɑːbɪtal/ *n.* Chiefly *US.* M20. [f. as next + BARBITAL.] *Pharm.* = next.

hexobarbitone /hɛksə(ʊ)ˈbɑːbɪtəʊn/ *n.* M20. [f. HEXA- + -O- + BARBITONE.] *Pharm.* A short-acting barbiturate, $C_{12}H_{16}N_2O_3$, with hypnotic properties, used as a very short-acting anaesthetic.

¶A proprietary name for this drug is EVIPAN.

hexode /ˈhɛksəʊd/ *a.* & *n.* L19. [f. HEXA- + -ODE[2].] A *adj.* 1 Designating a mode of telegraphy in which six messages can be sent simultaneously. L19. 2 Of a radio valve: having six electrodes. M20. B *n.* A radio valve with six electrodes. M20.

hexoestrol /hɛkˈsiːstrɒl/ *n.* Also **hexest-**. M20. [f. HEX(ANE + OESTR(US + -OL.] A synthetic oestrogen, $C_{18}H_{22}O_2$, related to stilboestrol and used in hormone therapy.

hexogen /ˈhɛksə(ʊ)dʒ(ə)n/ *n.* E20. [G, f. as HEXA- + -GEN.] = CYCLONITE.

hexokinase /hɛksə(ʊ)ˈkʌɪneɪz/ *n.* M20. [f. HEXO(SE + KINASE.] *Biochem.* Any of various enzymes that catalyse the transfer of a phosphate group from ATP to a hexose as the first step in glycolysis.

hexon /ˈhɛksɒn/ *n.* M20. [f. HEXA- + -ON.] *Microbiol.* A capsomere of the kind forming the majority of those in the capsid of an adenovirus, each of which is surrounded by six other capsomeres.

hexone /ˈhɛksəʊn/ *n.* L19. [f. HEXA- + -ONE.] 1 In full *hexone base*. Each of the three basic amino acids arginine, histidine, and lysine. L19. 2 Methyl isobutyl ketone as used industrially. M20.

hexosamine /hɛkˈsəʊsəmiːn/ *n.* E20. [f. as next + AMINE.] *Chem.* Any derivative of a hexose in which a hydroxyl group is replaced by an amino group.

hexosan /ˈhɛksəsan/ *n.* L19. [f. HEXOSE + -AN.] *Chem.* A polysaccharide whose constituent monosaccharides are hexoses.

hexose /ˈhɛksəʊz, -s/ *n.* L19. [f. HEXA- + -OSE[2].] *Chem.* Any monosaccharide sugar with six carbon atoms in its molecule, e.g. glucose and fructose.

hexuronic /hɛksjʊˈrɒnɪk/ *a.* E20. [f. prec. + URONIC.] *hexuronic acid*: any of a class of uronic acids derived from a hexose; *spec.* ascorbic acid.

hexyl /ˈhɛksʌɪl, -sɪl/ *n.* M19. [f. HEXA- + -YL.] *Chem.* A radical, $C_6H_{13}\cdot$, derived from a hexose. Usu. in *comb.*

Comb.: **hexylresorcinol** a crystalline derivative, $(HO)_2{\cdot}C_6H_3{\cdot}(CH_2)_5CH_3$, of resorcinol used as an anthelmintic and urinary antiseptic.

hey *n.*[1] var. of HAY *n.*[4]

hey /heɪ/ *int.* & *n.*[2] ME. [Natural exclam. Cf. OFr. *hai*, *hay*, Du., G *hei*, Sw. *hej*. Cf. also HEIGH.] A *int.* Attracting attention; expr. joy, surprise, or inquiry, or enthusiastic approval *for*. Freq. in comb. w. redupl. wds to form a meaningless refrain, as, *hey-diddle-diddle*, *hey-nonny-nonny*, etc. ME.

C. GEBLER Hey mother, the water's running down the back of my neck. *hey* COCKALORUM. *hey jingo*: see JINGO *int.* 1. *hey presto*: see PRESTO *adv. hey, Rube!*: see RUBE 2.

B *n.* A cry of 'hey!' LME.

heyday /ˈheɪdeɪ/ *n.* L16. [f. HEY-DAY *int.*] 1 A state of high spirits or passion. Now *rare*. L16. 2 The full bloom, flush, (of youth, vigour, prosperity, etc.). M18.

2 E. WAUGH The liturgy composed in the heyday of English prose style.

hey-day /ˈheɪdeɪ/ *int. arch.* E16. [Cf. LG *heida*, also *heidi* hurrah!] Expr. joy, surprise, etc.

heyduck /ˈhʌɪdʊk, ˈheɪdʌk/ *n. obs.* exc. *Hist.* E17. [Czech, Pol., Serbo-Croat *hajduk*, in Hungarian *hajdú*, (pl.) *-dúk*.] In Hungary, a member of an ennobled military class; in Poland, a liveried personal follower of a noble. Also, a robber, a brigand.

hey-ho *int.*, *n.*, & *v.* see HEIGH-HO.

Hezbollah /hɛzbəˈlɑː/ *n.* Also **Hiz-** /hɪz-/, **-bullah**. M20. [Pers. *hezbollāh*, Arab. *ḥizbu-'llāh(i)* party of God, f. *ḥizb* party + *allāh* ALLAH.] A Shiite Muslim group, active esp. in Lebanon.

Hezbollahi *n.* a member or adherent of Hezbollah L20.

hi /hʌɪ/ *a. informal* (chiefly *commercial*). E20. [Repr. pronunc.] High: esp. in special collocations & combs.

hi-fi, *hi-hat*, *hi-liter*, *hi-tech*, etc.

hi /hʌɪ/ *int.* LME. [Natural exclam. Cf. HEY *int.*] 1 Attracting someone's attention, or expr. encouragement or enthusiasm. LME. 2 = HELLO *int.* M19.

hi-de-hi /hʌɪdɪˈhʌɪ/ *int.* greeting, encouraging, or expr. enthusiasm, esp. in a dance band, holiday camp, etc., (freq. answered with HO-DE-HO) M20. **hi-de-ho** /hʌɪdɪˈhəʊ/ *int.* & *n.* (an exclam.) expr. joy or enthusiasm, esp. in a jazz or dance band M20.

hiant /ˈhʌɪənt/ *a. rare.* E19. [L *hiant-* pres. ppl stem of *hiare* gape: see -ANT[1].] Chiefly *Bot.* Gaping, having a wide aperture.

hiaqua /ˈhʌɪəkwə/ *n.* E19. [Chinook Jargon *hykwa*, *haikwa*, f. Nootka *ḥi:xʷa:*.] An ornament or necklace of large dentalium shells, formerly used as money by the natives of the N. Pacific coast of N. America.

hiatus /hʌɪˈeɪtəs/ *n.* Pl. same, **-tuses**. M16. [L = gaping, opening, f. *hiare* gape.] 1 A physical break in continuity; a gaping chasm; an opening, an aperture. *rare* in *gen.* sense. M16. b *Anat.* Any of various natural openings or gaps. Usu. w. specifying wd. L19. 2 A gap or break in continuity, esp. in a series or an account; a missing link in a chain of events; *esp.* in *Geol.* (the time value of) a break or unconformity in the stratigraphic sequence. E17. b *Logic.* A missing link in a chain of argument, a gap in reasoning or evidence. M19. 3 *Gram.* & *Pros.* A break between two vowels which come together without an intervening consonant in successive words or syllables. E18.

2 M. SARTON There has been a long hiatus in this journal because I have had no days here alone. I. COLEGATE Lunch was a hiatus which separated the morning from the afternoon.

Comb.: **hiatus hernia** protrusion of an organ, esp. the stomach, through the oesophagal opening in the diaphragm.

hiatal *a.* of or pertaining to a hiatus E20.

hiawa *n.* var. of HYAWA.

hiawaballi *n.* var. of HYAWABALLI.

Hib /hɪb/ *n.* L20. [Acronym, f. *Haemophilus influenzae b* (see below).] *Med.* Infection with the bacterium *Haemophilus influenzae* type *b*, a cause of acute meningitis, esp. in babies and young children. Freq. *attrib.*

Hib infection, *vaccine*, etc.

hibachi /hɪˈbatʃi, ˈhɪbatʃi/ *n.* M19. [Jap., f. *hi* fire + *hachi* bowl, pot.] 1 In Japan, a large earthenware pan or brazier in which charcoal is burnt to provide indoor heating. M19. 2 A type of esp. outdoor cooking apparatus similar to a barbecue. M20.

hibakusha /ˈhɪbakuːʃə/ *n.* Pl. same. M20. [Jap., f. *hi* suffer + *baku* explosion + *sha* person.] A survivor of an atomic explosion, *esp.* in *pl.*, the survivors of the atomic explosions at Hiroshima and Nagasaki in 1945.

hibernacle /ˈhʌɪbənak(ə)l/ *n.* Also †**hy-**. E18. [L *hibernaculum*: see next.] A winter retreat, a hibernaculum.

hibernaculum /hʌɪbəˈnakjʊləm/ *n.* Also †**hy-**. Pl. **-la** /-lə/. L17. [L (usu. in pl. *-la*), f. *hibernare* HIBERNATE: see -CULE.] †1 A greenhouse for wintering plants. Only in L17. 2 *Bot.* & *Zool.* A structure which protects (part of) a plant or animal during hibernation. M18. 3 *Zool.* The place or nest in which an animal hibernates. L18.

hibernal /hʌɪˈbəːn(ə)l/ *a.* Also †**hy-**. E17. [Late L *hibernalis*, f. *hibernus* wintry: see -AL[1].] Of, pertaining to, or proper to winter; appearing in winter.

hibernate /ˈhʌɪbəneɪt/ *v.i.* Also †**hy-**. E19. [L *hibernat-* pa. ppl stem of *hibernare*, f. *hiberna* winter quarters, use as n. of neut. pl. of *hibernus* wintry: see -ATE[3].] 1 Spend the winter in a state or location which mitigates its effects; (of an organism, esp. a mammal) pass the winter in a state of dormancy or torpor; (of a person, esp. an invalid) pass the winter in a mild climate. E19. 2 *fig.* Remain in a torpid or inactive state; lie dormant. M19.

1 B. LOPEZ In winter, while the grizzly hibernates, the polar bear is out . . hunting. 2 SOUTHEY Inclination would lead me to hibernate during half the year.

hibernator *n.* an animal which hibernates L19.

hibernation /hʌɪbəˈneɪʃ(ə)n/ *n.* Also †**hy-**. M17. [L *hibernatio(n-)*, f. as prec.: see -ATION.] 1 The action of wintering or passing the winter, esp. in a suitable place or condition. M17. 2 The condition of dormancy or torpor in which many plants and (esp.) animals spend the winter. E19. 3 *fig.* A period of dormancy or suspended activity; dormant condition. E19.

Hibernian /hʌɪˈbəːnɪən/ *a.* & *n.* Also †**Hy-**, (earlier) †**Ib-**. E16. [f. L *Hibernia* Ireland alt. of *I(u)verna*, *Iuberna* f. Gk *I(w)ernē* f. Celt., whence also Ir. *Eriu*, (accus.) *Éirinn* Erin, later MIr. *Éri*, whence OE *Īraland* Ireland: see -AN, -IAN.] A *adj.* Of or belonging to Ireland; Irish. E16. B *n.* A native or inhabitant of Ireland; an Irishman, an Irishwoman. M16.

Hibernically /hʌɪˈbəːnɪk(ə)li/ *adv.* E19. [med. or mod.L *Hibernicus* Irish, f. *Hibernia*: see prec., -ICALLY.] In an Irish manner; *esp.* (w. ref. to speech) with an (apparent) illogicality or self-contradiction.

Hibernicise *v.* var. of HIBERNICIZE.

Hibernicism /hʌɪˈbəːnɪsɪz(ə)m/ *n.* M18. [f. as HIBERNIAN + -IC + -ISM.] 1 An idiom or expression characteristic of or attributed to Irish speech, *esp.* an Irish bull (see BULL *n.*[4] 1). M18. 2 The condition of being Irish; Irish nationality. *rare.* E19.

Hibernicize /hʌɪˈbəːnɪsʌɪz/ *v.t.* Also **-ise**. E19. [f. as prec. + -IC + -IZE.] Make Irish in form or character.

Hibernize /hʌɪˈbəːnʌɪz/ *v. rare.* Also **-ise**. L18. [f. as prec. + -IZE.] 1 *v.t.* = HIBERNICIZE. L18. 2 *v.i.* Act as an Irishman or Irishwoman. L18.

Hiberno- /hʌɪˈbəːnəʊ/ *comb. form.* E19. [f. med.L *Hibernus* Irish, f. as HIBERNIAN: see -O-.] Forming ns. and adjs. w. the sense 'Irish and' as *Hiberno-English*, *Hiberno-Latin*, *Hiberno-Saxon*, etc.

hibiscus /hɪˈbɪskəs/ *n.* E18. [L f. Gk *hibiskos*, identified by Dioscorides with *althaia* marshmallow, ALTHAEA.] Any of numerous chiefly tropical herbaceous plants, shrubs, and trees of the genus *Hibiscus*, of the mallow family, with showy brightly coloured flowers, freq. grown for ornament; a flowering stem of such a plant. Also called *rose-mallow*.

hic /hɪk/ *int.* L19. [Imit.] Repr. the sound of a hiccup, esp. when made by a drunk person.

hiccius doccius /ˌhɪkʃɪəs ˈdɒkʃɪəs/ *n.* & *a. phr.* Now *rare.* L17. [Perh. alt. of *hicce est doctus* 'here is the learned man', or a nonsense formula simulating Latin.] A *n. phr.* A formula uttered by a juggler when performing a trick; a feat of dexterity, a clever trick. L17. B *adj. phr.* Accompanied by the formula 'hiccius doccius', magical, skilful. M18.

hiccough *n.*, *v.* vars. of HICCUP *n.*, *v.*

hiccup /ˈhɪkʌp/ *n.* Also **-cough**. L16. [Imit.: cf. ON *hixti* n., *hixta* vb, Du. *hik*, *hikken*, Sw. *hicka*, Da. *hik(ke)*, Russ. *ikat'*, Fr. *hoquet*. The form *hiccough* is due to assim. to COUGH *n.* Cf. HICKET.] 1 An involuntary spasm of the respiratory muscles, consisting in a quick inspiratory movement of the diaphragm checked suddenly by closure of the glottis, producing a characteristic sound. Also (orig. *sing.*, now usu. in *pl.*: often w. *the*), affliction with a succession of such spasms. L16. 2 *fig.* A temporary minor setback or stoppage. M20.

1 P. P. READ The hiccups of suppressed laughter. 2 J. HIGGINS The nonsense over Tanya Voroninova had been an unfortunate hiccup in his career.

Comb.: **hiccup-nut** *S. Afr.* an ornamental scarlet-flowered shrub, *Combretum bracteosum* (family Combretaceae); its fruit, said to cause violent hiccups.

hiccupy *a.* marked by hiccups M19.

hiccup /ˈhɪkʌp/ *v.* Also **-cough**. L16. [f. the n.] 1 *v.i.* Make the sound (as) of a hiccup; suffer from hiccups. L16. 2 *v.t.* Express by or utter with hiccups, as a drunken person. (Foll. by *out.*) L18.

1 A. GHOSH She . . sat down again beside him, shivering and hiccuping.

hic jacet /hɪk ˈdʒeɪsɛt, ˈjakɛt/ *n. phr.* E17. [L, lit. 'here lies', the first two wds of a L epitaph.] An epitaph.

hick /hɪk/ *n.*[1] & *a. derog.* M16. [Familiar by-form of male forename *Richard*: see DICK *n.*[1] Cf. HOB *n.*[1], HODGE *n.*] A *n.* An ignorant countryman, a silly person. M16.

S. RUSHDIE He would pretend to be a hick just down from the villages.

B *adj.* Characteristic of a hick; unsophisticated, provincial. *colloq.* E20.

Listener Their books were freely available in the most hick little market town.

hick /hɪk/ *n.*[2] & *v.* Now *rare.* E17. [App. abbrev. of HICCUP *n.*, HICKET.] A *n.* A hiccup. Also, a hesitation in speech. E17. B *v.i.* Hiccup. E17.

hickery-pickery /ˌhɪk(ə)rɪ ˈpɪk(ə)ri/ *n. rare.* E19. [Alt. of HIERA PICRA.] = HIERA PICRA.

†**hicket** *n.* M16–L17. [f. as HICCUP *n.*: see -ET[1].] = HICCUP *n.*

hickey /ˈhɪki/ *n.* Chiefly *N. Amer.* E20. [Origin unkn.] 1 A small gadget or device. E20. b Something of little consequence. E20. 2 A pimple; a mark left by a love-bite. *colloq.* M20. 3 *Printing.* A spot of foreign matter appearing on a negative, a proof, or a final printed sheet. M20.

hickle *n.* var. of HICKWALL.

hickory /ˈhɪkəri/ *n.* & *a.* L17. [Abbrev. of POHICKORY.] A *n.* 1 Any of various N. American trees of the genus *Carya*, of the walnut family, which have tough heavy wood, pinnate leaves, and a fruit consisting of a fleshy husk which splits into four and encloses a freq. edible nut. L17. b In Australia: any of various trees with timber similar in quality to the N. American tree; *esp.* a kind of wattle, *Acacia implexa*. L19. 2 The wood of the American hickory. L17. b A stick, rod, etc., made from hickory wood. E19. 3 In full *hickory nut*. The nut of the American hickory. L17.

1 *pignut hickory*, *scaly-bark hickory*, *shagbark hickory*, etc.

B *adj.* 1 Made of or resembling the wood of the hickory; *fig.* hard, tough. M18. 2 Of a member of a religious sect: lacking in religious fervour or devotion, flexible. M19.

hickwall /ˈhɪkwɔːl/ *n. dial.* Also **hickle** /ˈhɪk(ə)l/, & other vars. LME. [Prob. imit. Cf. HIGH-HOLE, WITWALL, YAFFLE *n.*] A woodpecker; *esp.* the green woodpecker, *Picus viridis*.

hid /hɪd/ *ppl a.* Long *rare.* ME. [pa. pple of HIDE *v.*[1]] Hidden, concealed, secret.

hid *v.* pa. t. & pple: see HIDE *v.*[1]

hidage /ˈhʌɪdɪdʒ/ *n. obs.* exc. *Hist.* ME. [AL *hidagium*, f. *hida* HIDE *n.*[2]: see -AGE.] 1 A tax payable to the royal exchequer, assessed at a certain quota for each hide of land. ME. 2 The assessed value or measurement of lands on which this tax was levied. M19.

hidalgo /hɪˈdalgəʊ/ *n.* Pl. **-os**. L16. [Sp., formerly also *hijo dalgo* contr. of *hijo de algo* lit. 'son of something'. Cf. FIDALGO.] 1 In Spain, a member of the lower nobility. L16. 2 *transf.* A person resembling a hidalgo; *spec.* one who is suited to be or aspires to be a member of the nobility. E19.

Hidatsa /hɪˈdatsə/ *n.* & *a.* L19. [Hidatsa *hiratsa* = willow wood lodge.] A *n.* Pl. same, **-s**. A member of a Siouan Indian people living on the Missouri river; the Siouan language of this people. L19. B *attrib.* or as *adj.* Of or pertaining to the Hidatsa or their language. L19.

¶ Also called *Gros Ventre*

hidden /ˈhɪd(ə)n/ *ppl a.* M16. [pa. pple of HIDE *v.*[1]] 1 Concealed, secret; occult. M16. 2 *spec.* a *Mus.* Of a consecutive fifth or octave: suggested in part music when two parts separated by one of these intervals move in similar motion. M19. b *Pros.* Of the quantity of a vowel: unable to be determined by scansion on account of the placing of the vowel (usu. before two consonants) in a word. L19.

1 I. MURDOCH He had heard in her bantering voice the hidden whine of despair. B. EMECHETA The sound of . . tiny hidden insects harmonized with the landscape.

Special collocations: **hidden agenda** a concealed motive or reason behind the ostensible purpose of an action, statement, etc. **hidden hand** a secret or occult influence, esp. of a malignant character. **hidden reserves** extra profits, resources, etc., kept concealed in reserve.

hiddenly *adv.* in a hidden manner, secretly L16. **hiddenmost** *a.* most hidden or secret L19. **hiddenness** /-n-n-/ *n.* the condition or state of being hidden; secrecy: LME.

hidden *v.* pa. pple of HIDE *v.*[1]

hiddenite /ˈhɪd(ə)nʌɪt/ *n.* L19. [f. W. E. *Hidden* (1832–1918), US mineralogist + -ITE[1].] *Min.* A rare green variety of spodumene, prized as a gemstone.

hide /hʌɪd/ *n.*[1] [OE *hȳd* = OFris. *hēd*, OS *hūd* (Du. *huid*), OHG *hūt* (G *Haut*), ON *húð*, f. Gmc f. IE whence also L *cutis*, Gk *kutos*.] 1 The skin of an animal, raw or dressed; *esp.* (a) skin (as of one of the larger animals) which may be tanned into leather. OE. 2 The human skin. Now *joc.* OE. b *fig.* Impudence, effrontery, nerve. Chiefly *Austral.* & *NZ.* E20. 3 (A piece of) animal hide used as material for clothing, shoes, etc. ME. 4 A whip made of animal hide. M19.

1 C. FREEMAN The hides were sold for four dollars a skin to a tannery. 2 HENRY MILLER Huge spiked thongs that will flay the living hide off you.

Phrases & comb.: †**hide and hue** skin and complexion; the visible outer part of the body. **hide beetle** = *leather beetle* s.v. LEATHER *n.* & *a.* (**neither**) **hide nor hair** (**of someone**) nothing whatever (of someone). *save one's (own) hide*: see SAVE *v.* **tan a person's hide** thrash or flog a person.

hided *a.* (*a*) having a hide, esp. of a specified kind; (*b*) *rare* made of twisted hide: LME. **hideless** *a.* LME.

hide /hʌɪd/ *n.*[2] *obs.* exc. *Hist.* [OE *hīd* earlier *hīgid* f. *hīg-*, *hīw-* (in comb.) = OHG *hī-*, ON *hý-*, Goth. *heiwa-* rel. to L *civis* citizen and to a Gmc *n*-stem in OE *hīwan* (pl.), OFris. *hīuna* members of a household, OHG *hī(w)un*, ON *hjún* man and wife. See HIND *n.*[2]] A measure of land in Anglo-Saxon and early Norman times, used esp. to specify the amount of land needed to support one free family and varying in extent from 60 to 120 acres (approx. 24 to 49 hectares) according to locality.

hide /hʌɪd/ *n.*[3] ME. [f. HIDE *v.*[1]] †1 The action or an act of hiding; concealment. Only in ME. 2 A hiding-place; *esp.* a place for observing or hunting wildlife without being seen. ME. b *spec.* A cache. L19.

2 E. FIGES Having set an inviting trap, I lie in my hide, in wait.

hide /hʌɪd/ *v.*[1] Pa. t. **hid** /hɪd/; pa. pple **hidden** /ˈhɪd(ə)n/, (*arch.*) **hid.** [OE *hȳdan* = OFris. *hēda*, MDu. *hūden*, LG (*ver*)*hüen*, f. WGmc.] 1 *v.t.* Put or keep out of sight; conceal intentionally from the view or notice of others. OE. †b Conceal in order to shield or protect. ME–E17. 2 *v.i.* & *refl.* Put or keep oneself out of sight, conceal oneself. OE. 3 *v.t.* Keep (a fact or matter) from the knowledge or observation of others; keep secret. ME. 4 *v.t.* Keep (something) from view without intention of secrecy; cover up; obstruct the view of. ME.

1 S. BELLOW Hoards sugar and potatoes, hides money in his mattress. 2 N. SYMINGTON Little Carl hid behind a bush to listen to their conversation. 4 V. S. NAIPAUL The four days of rain and mist that hid my surroundings from me.

Phrases, & with advs. & preps. in specialized senses: †**all hid** hide-and-seek; the signal cry in hide-and-seek. **hide away** conceal (a person or thing). **hide one's face** (in biblical language) turn away, withdraw one's eyes, take no heed. **hide one's head** protect one's head, take shelter; keep out of sight, keep from shame. *hide one's light under a bushel*: see BUSHEL *n.* 3. **hide out** remain in concealment. **hide up** (*a*) = *hide away* above; (*b*) = *hide out* above.

Comb.: **hide-and-coop** *US* = *hide-and-seek* below; **hide-and-go-seek** *N. Amer.* = *hide-and-seek* below; **hide-and-seek** (*a*) a children's game in which one or more players seek a player or players in hiding; (*b*) a process or an attempt to find an evasive person or thing, or to evade a seeker; **hide-out** *colloq.* a hiding place;

hider *n.* LME.

hide /hʌɪd/ *v.*[2]*t.* M18. [f. HIDE *n.*[1]] 1 Remove the hide from; flay. *rare.* M18. 2 Beat the hide or skin of; flog, thrash. *colloq.* E19.

hideaway /ˈhʌɪdəweɪ/ *n.* & *a.* L19. [f. HIDE *v.*[1] + AWAY *adv.*] A *n.* 1 A person who hides himself or herself away; a fugitive. L19. 2 A small quiet restaurant etc.; a secluded place of entertainment. E20. 3 A place of concealment or retreat. M20.

3 V. GLENDINNING Rural and remote, her hideaway was the perfect setting for a rustic idyll.

B *adj.* That hides, that is hidden away. L19.

hidebind /ˈhʌɪdbʌɪnd/ *v.t.* Now *rare.* Pa. t. & pple **-bound** /-baʊnd/. M17. [f. HIDE *n.*[1] + BIND *v.*, after *hidebound*.] Make hidebound; confine, constrict.

hidebound /ˈhʌɪdbaʊnd/ *n.* & *a.* M16. [f. HIDE *n.*[1] + BOUND *a.*[2]] A *n.* Hidebound condition of cattle. Now *rare* or *obs.* M16.

B *adj.* 1 (Of a person) having the skin tightly stretched over the bones, esp. as the result of malnutrition; (of cattle) having the skin clinging close to the back and ribs as a result of bad feeding or ill health; (of a tree) having the bark so closely adherent and unyielding as to impede growth. L16. 2 *fig.* †a Of a person: stingy, niggardly, mean. L16–L17. b Of a person, a mind, etc.: restricted in view or scope; narrow, cramped; bigoted. E17. 3 Having an edging or binding of hide. *rare.* M19.

2b R. L. STEVENSON An excellent fellow . . but a hide-bound pedant for all that. V. WOOLF I shall be debased and hidebound by the bestial and beautiful passion of maternity.

hideland /ˈhʌɪdland/ *n. obs.* exc. *Hist.* L16. [f. HIDE *n.*[2] + LAND *n.*[1]] = HIDE *n.*[2]

hideling /ˈhʌɪdlɪŋ/ *a.* & *n.* Chiefly *dial.* M19. [App. a derived use of HIDLINGS (the ending being confused with vbl ns. & ppl adjs. in *-ing*), also infl. by ns. in *-ling* as *changeling*: see -LING[2].] A *adj.* Given to hiding or concealment. M19. B *n.* A person or thing in the habit of hiding. L19.

hideosity /hɪdɪˈɒsɪti/ *n.* LME. [f. next. + -ITY, after *curiosity* etc.] (An embodiment of) hideousness, a very ugly object.

hideous /ˈhɪdɪəs/ *a.* & *adv.* ME. [AN *hidous*, OFr. *hidos*, *-eus* (mod. *hideux*), earlier *hisdos* f. *hi(s)de* fear, ult. origin unkn.: see -EOUS.] A *adj.* 1 Frightful, repulsive, revolting, (to the senses or the mind), extremely ugly; *colloq.* unpleasant, displeasing. ME. 2 Terrifying on account of size; immense. Now *rare* or *obs.* ME.

1 A. POWELL The Loathly Damsel, a hideous young woman riding upon a mule. R. INGALLS This is a hideous and freakish thing to have occurred. V. SETH That calendar is hideous. 2 J. MORSE The great precipice below . . is so hideous.

†**B** *adv.* Hideously. M17–E18.

hideously *adv.* in a hideous manner; *colloq.* dreadfully, excessively: ME. **hideousness** *n.* (*a*) the quality of being hideous; †(*b*) horror, dread: ME.

hidey-hole /ˈhʌɪdɪhəʊl/ *n. colloq.* (orig. *Sc.*). Also **hidy-**. E19. [Alt. of *hiding-hole* s.v. HIDING *n.*[1]] A hiding place.

hiding /ˈhʌɪdɪŋ/ *n.*[1] ME. [f. HIDE *v.*[1] + -ING[1].] 1 The action of HIDE *v.*[1]; the condition of being or remaining hidden; concealment. ME. †2 A hidden or secret thing. *rare.* Only in ME. 3 A thing that hides; a means of concealment; a hiding place. LME.

1 H. BASCOM Apata comes out of hiding and sneaks past the posted sentry. **be in, go into, hiding** conceal oneself, esp. from the authorities.

Comb.: **hiding-hole** *rare* a hiding place; a place of concealment; **hiding place** a place of concealment; **hiding power** the capacity of paint or other colouring materials to obliterate certain surfaces.

hiding /ˈhʌɪdɪŋ/ *n.*[2] *colloq.* E19. [f. HIDE *v.*[2] + -ING[1].] The action of HIDE *v.*[2]; a flogging, a thrashing, a beating; a punishment.

P. FERGUSON If it had been me . . doing that, I'd have got a hiding for it. **on a hiding to nothing** in a position from which there can be no successful outcome.

hidlings /ˈhɪdlɪŋz/ *adv.*, *n.*, & *a. Sc.* & *north.* As adj. also **-ling** /-lɪŋ/. ME. [f. HID *ppl a.* + -LING[2].] **A** *adv.* In a hidden way, secretly. ME. **B** *n.* 1 *in hidlings*, in secret, secretly. LME. 2 *pl.* Hiding places, secret places. E16. 3 *pl.* Secret or clandestine operations. E19. **C** *adj.* Hidden, secret, underhand, clandestine. L18.

hidrosis /hɪˈdrəʊsɪs/ *n.* M19. [Gk *hidrōsis* sweating, f. *hidrōs* sweat: see -OSIS.] *Med.* (Excessive) sweating.

hidrotic /hɪˈdrɒtɪk/ *n.* & *a.* E18. [med.L *hidroticus* f. Gk *hidrōtikos*, f. *hidrōt-*, *hidrōs* sweat: see -IC.] *Med.* **A** *n.* A drug or other agent that causes sweating. E18. **B** *adj.* Of, pertaining to, or promoting sweating. E18.

¶Cf. earlier HYDROTIC.

hidy-hole *n.* var. of HIDEY-HOLE.

hie /hʌɪ/ *v.* Now *arch.* or *poet.* Pa. t. & pple **hied** /hʌɪd/; pres. pple **hieing, hying**, /ˈhʌɪɪŋ/. OE. [Origin unkn.] †1 *v.i.* Strive, exert oneself; pant. OE–ME. 2 *v.i.* & *refl.* Hasten, hurry, go quickly, (*to*). ME. †**b** Advance quickly; make progress; prosper. ME–E17. †3 *v.t.* Cause to hasten; urge on; bring quickly; drive *away*. ME–L16. 4 *v.t.* Make *one's way* quickly. ME.

2 J. GRENFELL Now let us hie ourselves to the Low Countries. ALAN BENNETT Let us hie hence in yon Aston Martin.

hielaman /ˈhiːləmən/ *n. Austral.* Also **heela-**. M19. [Aborig. *yiliman*.] A narrow shield made of bark or wood.

hield /ˈhiːld/ *v. obs.* exc. *dial.* Also **heald**. [OE *hieldan* = OS *ofheldian*, MDu. *helden* (Du. *hellen*), f. WGmc base of OE *heald* inclined, OHG *halda* (G *Halde*), ON *hallr* slope: cf. HEEL *v.*[1]] **I** *v.i.* 1 Bend downwards or to one side; lean, incline, slope; go down. OE. 2 Incline *to*; favour. ME. **II** *v.t.* †3 Cause to incline; bend, bow *down*. OE–LME. 4 Pour (liquid) by tilting the vessel that contains it. ME.

hiemal /ˈhʌɪɪm(ə)l/ *a.* Now *rare.* Also **hye-**. M16. [L *hiemalis*, f. *hiems* winter: see -AL[1].] Of or belonging to winter.

hiemate /ˈhʌɪɪmeɪt/ *v.i.* Now *rare.* Also **hye-**. E17. [L *hiemat-* pa. ppl stem of *hiemare*, f. *hiems* winter: see -ATE[3].] Winter, hibernate.

hier- *comb. form* see HIERO-.

Hieracite /ˈhʌɪrəsʌɪt/ *n.* L16. [Late L *hieracita*, f. *Hierax* (see below) + -ITE[1].] *Eccl. Hist.* A follower of the teachings of Hierax (fl. *c* AD 300), an Egyptian ascetic who denied bodily resurrection and believed in the necessity of celibacy for Christian perfection.

hieracium /hʌɪˈreɪʃɪəm/ *n.* Pl. **-ia** /-ɪə/, **-iums**. M16. [L f. Gk *hierakion*, f. *hierax* hawk: see -IUM.] = *hawkweed* s.v. HAWK *n.*[1]

hiera picra /hʌɪrə ˈpɪkrə/ *n. phr.* LME. [med.L f. Gk, f. *hiera* sacred (name of many medicines) + *pikra* fem. of *pikros* bitter.] *Pharm.* A purgative drug composed mainly of aloes and canella bark. Cf. HICKERY-PICKERY.

hierarch /ˈhʌɪrɑːk/ *n.* Also (esp. in sense 2) **H-**. LME. [med.L *hierarcha* f. Gk *hierarkhēs* high priest, f. *hieros* sacred + *-arkhēs* -ARCH.] 1 A person who has authority in sacred matters; an ecclesiastical ruler or potentate; a chief priest; an archbishop. LME. 2 An archangel; Christ as commander of the celestial hierarchy. M16.

1 MILTON Their great Hierarch the Pope. 2 H. H. MILMAN Subject to the Hierarch of the Celestial Hierarchy.

hieˈrarchal *a.* hierarchic M17.

hierarchic /hʌɪˈrɑːkɪk/ *a.* L17. [med.L *hierarchicus* f. eccl.Gk *hierarkhikos*, f. *hierarkhēs* HIERARCH: see -IC.] Of or belonging to a hierarch or a hierarchy.

hierarchical /hʌɪˈrɑːkɪk(ə)l/ *a.* L15. [f. as prec. + -AL[1].] †1 Belonging to the celestial hierarchy. Only in L15. 2 Belonging to a priestly hierarchy or a body of ecclesiastical rulers. M16. 3 Belonging to or according to a regular gradation of orders, classes, or ranks. M19.

hierarchically /hʌɪˈrɑːkɪk(ə)li/ *adv.* E17. [f. HIERARCHIC or prec.: see -ICALLY.] In a hierarchical manner.

hierarchize /ˈhʌɪrɑːkʌɪz/ *v.t.* Also **-ise**. L19. [f. HIERARCH + -IZE.] Arrange in a hierarchy or gradation of orders.

hierarchy /ˈhʌɪrɑːki/ *n.* LME. [OFr. *ierarchie*, *gerarchie* (mod. *hiérarchie*) f. med.L (*h*)*ierarchia*, Gk *hierarkhia*, f. *hierarkhēs*: see HIERARCH, -Y[3]. Latinized forms usual from 16.] 1 In Christian theology, each of three divisions of angelic beings (each comprising three orders) in the ninefold celestial system described in a 4th-cent. work attributed to Dionysius the Areopagite; angels collectively, the angelic host. LME. **b** *transf.* Each of three divisions of other objects, esp. of heavenly bodies or beings. LME. 2 Rule or dominion esp. in sacred matters; priestly rule or government; a system of ecclesiastical rule. LME. 3 A body of ecclesiastical rulers; an organized body of priests or clergy in successive orders or grades. E17. 4 A body of people, animals, or things ranked (in grades, orders, or classes) one above the other, esp. with respect to authority or dominance; *spec.* in logical and scientific classifications, a system or series of (esp. more or less inclusive) terms of successive rank. M17.

3 A. BRIGGS The hierarchy of the Church—from bishops to parish priests—survived everywhere. 4 G. M. TREVELYAN At the top of the social hierarchy stood the Dukes.

hierarchism *n.* hierarchical practice and principles; hierarchical system: M19. **hierarchist** *n.* an adherent of a hierarchy or of hierarchical practice and principles M17.

hieratic /hʌɪˈratɪk/ *a.* M17. [L *hieraticus* f. Gk *hieratikos* priestly, sacerdotal, f. *hierasthai* be a priest, f. *hiereus* priest, *hieros* sacred: see -IC.] 1 Pertaining to or used by a priestly class; used in connection with sacred subjects; *spec.* designating a style of ancient Egyptian writing consisting of abridged forms of hieroglyphics. (Opp. *demotic.*) M17. **b** Appropriate to or characteristic of a sacred person or duty. M19. **c** Of a style of art, esp. of ancient Greece or Egypt: adhering to early methods as laid down by religious tradition. M19. 2 Priestly, sacerdotal. M19.

1 **hieratic paper** papyrus of highest quality used for sacred writings in ancient Egypt. c H. READ A hieratic art depending on a very exclusive priesthood.

hieratical *a.* hieratic E17.

hieratite /ˈhʌɪrətʌɪt/ *n.* L19. [f. *Hiera* ancient name of one of the Lipari Islands, now Vulcano: see -ITE[1].] *Min.* A greyish cubic phase of potassium hexafluorosilicate, K_2SiF_6, formed at high temperatures in volcanic vents.

hiero- /ˈhʌɪrəʊ/ *comb. form* of Gk *hieros* sacred, holy: see -O-. Bef. a vowel also **hier-**. Forming ns. and adjs. with the meaning 'holy', 'sacred'.

hieˈrogamy *n.* a sacred marriage L19. **hieˈrolatry** *n.* worship of saints; hagiolatry: E19.

hierocracy /hʌɪˈrɒkrəsi/ *n.* L18. [f. HIERO- + -CRACY.] 1 The rule of priests or religious dignitaries; government by priests or ecclesiastics. L18. 2 A body of ruling priests or ecclesiastics. E19.

hieroˈcratic *a.* M19.

hierodule /ˈhʌɪrədjuːl/ *n.* M19. [Late L *hierodulus* f. Gk *hierodoulos* (masc. and fem.), f. *hieron* (use as n. of neut. of *hieros* sacred) temple + *doulos* slave.] *Gk Hist.* A slave living in a temple and dedicated to the service of a god.

hieroglyph /ˈhʌɪrəglɪf/ *n.* & *v.* L16. [Back-form. f. HIEROGLYPHIC, or after Fr. *hiéroglyphe*.] **A** *n.* 1 Any of the characters of the ancient Egyptian writing system; a figure of an object standing for a word, syllable, or sound in a kind of writing, esp. in the writing found on ancient Egyptian monuments and records; a writing consisting of these characters. L16. 2 *transf.* & *fig.* A figure, device, or sign, with a hidden meaning; a secret or enigmatic symbol; an emblem. M17. **b** A piece of writing difficult to decipher. *joc.* L19. 3 A person who makes hieroglyphic inscriptions. *rare.* M19.

2 A. C. SWINBURNE On your brows is written a mortal sentence, An hieroglyph of sorrow.

B *v.t.* Represent by a hieroglyph; write in hieroglyphs. E17.

hieroglyphed *a.* written in or inscribed with hieroglyphs L19. **hieˈroglyphist** *n.* a writer of hieroglyphs; a person versed in hieroglyphs: E19.

hieroglyphic /hʌɪrəˈglɪfɪk/ *n.*, *a.*, & *v.* L16. [Fr. *hiéroglyphique* or late L *hieroglyphicus* f. Gk *hierogluphikos*, f. *hieros* (see HIERO-) + *gluphē* carving: see -IC. The adj. was used as n. by Plutarch *ta hierogluphika* (sc. *grammata*) letters, writing, whence *hieroglyphics*.] **A** *n.* 1 In *pl.* The characters or mode of writing used esp. by the ancient Egyptians and consisting of figures of objects directly or figuratively representing words, syllables, etc. Occas. *sing.*, such a character. L16. 2 A picture standing for a word or idea, *esp.* one symbolizing something which it does not directly depict; a figure, device, or sign having a hidden meaning; an enigmatic symbol. L16. **b** In *pl.* Characters or writing difficult to decipher. *joc.* M18.

B *adj.* 1 Of the nature of a hieroglyph, esp. an Egyptian one; written in or consisting of hieroglyphics. L16. 2 *transf.* & *fig.* Having a hidden meaning; symbolical, emblematic. M17.

1 G. DANIEL This was a bilingual inscription and . . the Demotic and hieroglyphic writing could be deciphered.

†**C** *v.t.* Represent by or express as a hieroglyphic. E17–E18.

hieroglyphical /hʌɪrəˈglɪfɪk(ə)l/ *a.* L16. [f. as prec. + -AL[1].] 1 Pertaining to or of the nature of hieroglyphics; *transf.* & *fig.* symbolical, emblematic. L16. 2 Difficult to decipher or make sense of. E17.

hierogram /ˈhʌɪrəgram/ *n.* E17. [f. HIERO- + -GRAM.] A sacred symbol; a hieroglyph.

hierograˈmmatic(al) *adjs.* of the nature of, relating to, or consisting of hierograms M17. **hieroˈgrammatist** *n.* a hierogrammate L17.

hierogrammate /hʌɪrə(ʊ)ˈgramət/ *n.* Also **-at**. M19. [Gk *hierogrammateus* sacred scribe, f. *hieros* (see HIERO-) + *grammateus* clerk, scribe.] A writer of sacred records; *spec.* a writer of hieroglyphics.

hierograph /ˈhʌɪrəgrɑːf/ *n.* M19. [f. HIERO- + -GRAPH.] A sacred inscription or symbol; a hieroglyph.

hierography /hʌɪˈrɒgrəfi/ *n.* M17. [f. HIERO- + -GRAPHY.] 1 A description of sacred things; a description of religions. M17. †2 Sacred writing; writing by hierograms. Only in M18.

hierology /hʌɪˈrɒlədʒi/ *n.* E19. [f. HIERO- + -LOGY.] †1 A discourse on sacred things. Only in E19. †2 Hieroglyphic lore; the branch of archaeology that deals with Egyptian records. Only in M19. 3 Sacred literature or lore; the literature embodying the religious beliefs of a country or people. M19. 4 The branch of knowledge that deals with the history of religions. L19. 5 = HAGIOLOGY. L19.

hieromonach /hʌɪrə(ʊ)'mɒnək/ *n.* Also **-monk** /-'mʌŋk/. L18. [Gk *hieromonakhos* holy monk: see HIERO-, MONK *n.*[1]] *Gk Orthodox Ch.* A monk who is also a priest; a regular as opp. to a secular cleric.

Hieronymian /hʌɪrə'nɪmɪən/ *n.* & *a.* M17. [f. *Hieronymus* (St Jerome, see below) + -IAN.] A *n.* = HIERONYMITE *n.* M17. B *adj.* Of or pertaining to St Jerome (d. 420), the author of the Latin Vulgate translation of the Bible and one of the Doctors of the Church. L19.

hieronymite /hʌɪ'rɒnɪmʌɪt/ *n.* & *a.* E18. [f. as prec. + -ITE[1].] A *n.* A hermit of an order of St Jerome. E18. B *adj.* Belonging to an order of St Jerome. M19.

hierophant /'hʌɪrə(ʊ)fant/ *n.* L17. [Late L *hierophanta*, *-es* f. Gk *hierophantēs*, f. *hieros* (see HIERO-) + *phan-* base of *phainein* reveal: see -ANT[1].] 1 *Antiq.* An official expounder of sacred mysteries or ceremonies, esp. in ancient Greece; an initiating or presiding priest. L17. 2 *gen.* An expounder of sacred mysteries; an interpreter of an esoteric principle. E19.

2 M. LOWRY What did.. the hierophants of science know of the fearful potencies of.. evil?

hiero'phantic *a.* L18.

hieroscopy /hʌɪ'rɒskəpi/ *n.* E18. [Gk *hieroskopia*, f. *hiera* sacrifices, victims + *-skopia* view.] Divination from the observation of objects offered in religious sacrifices, or from sacred things.

Hierosolymitan /hʌɪrə(ʊ)'sɒlɪmʌɪt(ə)n/ *n.* & *a.* M16. [Late L *Hierosolymitanus*, f. *Hierosolyma* = Gk *Hierosoluma* Jerusalem: see -AN.] Chiefly *Hist.* A *n.* A native or inhabitant of Jerusalem. M16. B *adj.* Belonging to Jerusalem. E18.

hierosolymite *n.* & *a.* Hierosolymitan M16.

hierurgy /'hʌɪrə:dʒi/ *n.* Long *rare.* L17. [Gk *hierourgia* religious service, f. *hierourgos* sacrificing priest. Cf. LITURGY.] A sacred performance; a religious observance or rite.

hi-fi /'hʌɪfʌɪ/ *a.* & *n. colloq.* M20. [f. HI *a.* + abbrev. of FIDELITY, repr. *high fidelity* s.v. HIGH *a.*] *Audio.* A *adj.* Of, pertaining to, or (esp.) designating equipment for the high-fidelity recording and reproduction of sound. M20. B *n.* (The design and use of) equipment for the high-fidelity recording and reproduction of sound; the use of such equipment as a hobby etc. M20.

higgle /'hɪg(ə)l/ *v.i.* M17. [Var. of HAGGLE.] 1 Dispute over terms, *esp.* try to gain the advantage in bargaining; haggle. M17. 2 Conduct the trade of a higgler; buy and sell; sell goods from door to door. L18.

higgling *vbl n.* (*a*) the action of the vb; (*b*) the occupation of a higgler: E18.

higgledy-piggledy /,hɪg(ə)ldi'pɪg(ə)ldi/ *adv.*, *n.*, & *a.* L16. [Rhyming jingle prob. based on PIG *n.*[1] w. ref. to swine herding together.] A *adv.* Without any order of position or direction; in utter confusion or disorder. L16.

J. L. WATEN The new-comers' wagon was piled higgledy-piggledy with stretchers, chairs, wooden boxes, pots and pans.

B *n.* A confusion; a disorderly jumble. M17.

C *adj.* Void of order or regular plan; confused, jumbled. M19.

L. EDEL The entire work.. offers us the data in higgledy-piggledy disorder.

higgler /'hɪglə/ *n.* M17. [f. HIGGLE *v.* + -ER[1].] A person who higgles in bargaining; an itinerant dealer, *esp.* one who buys poultry or dairy produce in exchange for small commodities.

Higgs /hɪgz/ *n.* L20. [P. W. *Higgs* (b. 1929), Eng. physicist.] *Physics.* In full *Higgs boson*, *particle.* A subatomic particle whose existence is predicted by the quantum theory of spontaneous symmetry-breaking.

high /hʌɪ/ *a.*, *adv.*, & *n.* [OE *hēah* (*hēag-*) = OFris. *hāch*, OS, OHG *hōh* (Du. *hoog*, G *hoch*), ON *há r*, Goth. *hauhs*, f. Gmc.] A *adj.* I 1 Of great or above average or (*pred.*) specified vertical extent or magnitude. OE. b Standing out from a surface, in relief. OE. c *spec.* in *Typogr.* Designating type which stands higher than the rest of the forme. L17. d Esp. of clothing: extending above the normal or average level. E19. 2 Situated far above the ground or a specified level; designating the upper or inland part of a country or district (chiefly in place-names). OE. b *pred.* Situated at a specified distance above some level. M17. 3 Of a physical action: extending to or from, or performed at, a considerable distance above the ground or some other level. L16. 4 Esp. of a river, lake etc.: above the usual vertical measurement; deep. L18. 5 *Phonet.* Of a sound: produced with part of the tongue raised close to the palate. M19.

1 SWIFT The common size of the natives is somewhat under six inches high. T. HARDY The granary.. stood on stone staddles, high enough for persons to walk under. E. WELTY Her high heels tilted her nearly to tiptoe. J. G. BALLARD To calculate the height of.. the highest building by pacing out its shadow on the ground. A. MUNRO The house we lived in had big, high rooms. 2 G. GREENE She had high prominent cheek-bones. J. STEINBECK The high slopes of this mountain were swaddled with pines. J. WAIN High up, but not at the top. b R. S. ROBINSON The limit of atmospheric air, supposed to be forty-five miles high. 3 *New Yorker* He climbed up the ladder to the high-diving platform.

II *fig.* 6 Of exalted rank, position, or quality; superior, noble; elevated; luxurious. OE. b Haughty, arrogant, overbearing; angry. Now chiefly *dial.* ME. c Important; serious, grave. ME. d Advanced, abstruse. *obs.* exc. in special collocations (see below). LME. e *Biol.* Having a highly developed or complex organization, *spec.* through evolutionary advance. Earlier in HIGHER *a.* 2b. L19. 7 Chief, principal, main. *obs.* exc. in special collocations (see below). ME. 8 (Of a quality, condition, etc.) great, intense; strong; violent; (of a quantity or value) greater than what is regarded as normal; (of a temperature) more likely to promote melting and the emission of radiation. Formerly also, (of a voice) raised, loud. ME. b Extreme in opinion; *spec.* = HIGH CHURCH *a. phr.* L17. c Expensive, costly; (of a card-game) played for large stakes. E18. d Of latitude: at a great distance from the equator. M18. e *Naut.* Of a ship or its head: pointing close to the wind. M19. 9 Of a time or season: far advanced, fully reached, at its peak of activity. ME. b *spec.* Of a period (in the past): remote in time, ancient, *esp.* at its peak of development. E17. c (Esp. of meat) smelling and beginning to go bad; (of game) slightly decomposed and so ready to cook. E19. 10 Of a voice, musical note, etc.: acute in pitch, shrill. LME. 11 Elated, merry (chiefly in *high spirits*, *high-spirited* below); *spec.* (*slang*) intoxicated by or *on* alcohol or drugs. E17.

6 F. NORRIS He now should follow his best, his highest, his most unselfish impulse. J. CONRAD I know the wife of a very high personage in the Administration. W. GOLDING My status there was not precisely as high as I had suggested. P. ROTH He loses his job.. because somebody high up wants to be rid of the stupid Vice-Minister. b D. JACOBSON He.. tried to take a high line with me, looking haughty and indifferent. c SIR W. SCOTT When tidings of high weight were borne To that lone island's shore. 8 E. WAUGH He played poker for high stakes. W. S. MAUGHAM He had high fever, and looked very much as if he were going to die. W. S. CHURCHILL In a time of high crisis he could play a decisive rôle. R. INGALLS Dorothy did not set the sound very high. J. GATHORNE-HARDY Diabetes is statistically high in Lincolnshire. b G. GREENE He learns the truth, takes a high moral line about deception. P. ACKROYD The services.. were as 'high' as possible without bearing the taint of Romanism. c G. SANTAYANA The thing was well worth the money, even if the tickets came rather high. 9 S. BEDFORD High time some of us were baptized. M. SHADBOLT It was a high hot summer before they got down to Telka. b A. BRIGGS The period from 1851–1867 was the period of high-Victorian England. c J. RABAN The room was high with the thin stink of their preservative. T. MO Disease from dead bodies, Sir. He'll be high by noon. 10 G. GREENE A saloon car with a high yapping horn. B. EMECHETA The high laughter of the Shavi women. 11 P. BOWLES You know, I think I'm getting quite high. J. HELLER She is at least a little bit high on wine or whiskey. *Midweek Truth* (*Melbourne*) She was high on heroin.

B *adv.* 1 At or to a great distance upward; in or into a high position; far up. OE. 2 In or to a high degree, rank, etc.; to a great extent; at or to a high price. Formerly also, loudly. ME. b Richly, luxuriously. E17. c At or to a high latitude; far from the equator. M17. †3 Haughtily, arrogantly, overbearingly. LME–M19. 4 At or to a high pitch in sound. LME. 5 Far back in time, early. Formerly also, far on in time, late. Now *rare.* E16.

1 M. ROBERTS She walks down the street as proud as a queen, holding her head high. H. BASCOM Twelve o'clock. The sun stands high. 2 LD MACAULAY Lewis consented to go as high as twenty-five thousand crowns. H. BELLOC A courtier who had risen high in the State by flattery and cowardice. B. EMECHETA Malaria would make a child's temperature run high. b R. CARVER He.. always had money and lived high. 4 R. DAHL The woman's voice, raised high in anger, or pain.

C *n.* 1 A high place or region; *spec.* an area of high barometric pressure. ME. 2 The highest card dealt or drawn. Chiefly in *high-low-jack* (*and the game*) = ALL FOURS 2. E19. 3 A high level exceeding that previously attained, a record. E20. 4 High school. *N. Amer. colloq.* E20. 5 High gear. E20. 6 A euphoric state (as) induced by the taking of a drug or drugs. *slang.* M20.

1 A. ALVAREZ The weather forecaster talked.. of a high over the Atlantic and continuing fine weather. 3 *St Louis Post-Dispatch* Kinloch's population has shrunk to 4,455 from a high of 10,000. 4 *New Yorker* I started playing drums in junior high. 6 J. GASKELL They think it's the smoke talking, and they feel it's the sign of a good high. J. O'FAOLAIN Yeats had managed to get a remarkable high out of his failures with women.

Phrases, special collocations, & comb.: **ace**, **King**, **Queen**, etc., **high** in card-games, having this card as the highest-ranking card. **a high old time** *colloq.* a most enjoyable time. *at high wish*: see WISH *n.* *blow high, blow low*: see BLOW *v.*[1] *friends in high places*: see FRIEND *n.* **from on high** from heaven or a high place. *hang as high as* HAMAN. *hell and high water*: see HELL *n.* **High Admiral** *Naut.* a chief officer of admiral's rank. **high altar** the principal altar of a church. **high and dry** (*a*) *fig.* out of the current of events; stranded; (*b*) *Naut.* (of a ship) out of the water. **high and low** *a.* & *n.* (people) of all conditions. **high and low** *adv.* everywhere, esp. in *search* etc. *high and low*. **high and mighty** (*a*) *colloq.* arrogant; (*b*) *arch.* of exalted rank. **high as a kite** intoxicated. **highbinder** *US* (*a*) a ruffian; an assassin; (*b*) a swindler; a fraudulent politician; (*c*) a member of a Chinese-American secret society resembling the Mafia. **highboard** *a.* of or relating to diving from a high diving-board. **high-born** *a.* of noble birth. **highboy** *N. Amer.* a chest of drawers on a stand or table with drawers. **high-brown** *n.* & *a.* (*US*) (a person) of mixed Black and White parentage, having a pale brown skin. **high camp** sophisticated camp (cf. CAMP *n.*[3]). **high card** a card that outranks others; *esp.* an ace or a court-card. **high chair** an infant's chair for use at meals, having long legs, and a tray acting as both table and restraint. **high-class** *a.* of high quality. *high* COCKALORUM. **high colour** a flushed or florid complexion. **High Commission** an embassy from one Commonwealth country to another. **High Commissioner** the head of such an embassy. *High Constable*: see CONSTABLE 4. **high country** *NZ* hilly country used for sheep-farming. *High Court of Chancery*: see CHANCERY 2. **High Court** (**of Justice**) the supreme court of justice for civil cases. *High Court of Justiciary*: see JUSTICIARY *n.*[2] **high day** a festal day. **high-definition** *a.* designating or providing a relatively clear or distinct image. *High Dutch*: see DUTCH *n.*[1], *a.* **high-end** *a.* of, pertaining to, or associated with the most expensive section of the market. **high enema**: delivered into the colon. **highest good** = SUMMUM BONUM. *high explosive*: see EXPLOSIVE *n.* **high farming** the extensive use of fertilizers in land cultivation. **high fashion** = HAUTE COUTURE. **high fidelity** *Audio* (the reproduction of) high-fidelity sound. **high-fidelity** *a.* (*Audio*) designating, pertaining to, or characterized by relatively accurate reproduction of sound with little distortion (cf. HI-FI). **high finance**: concerned with large sums. **high-five** *n.* & *a.* (*N. Amer. slang*) (*a*) *n.* a gesture of celebration or greeting in which two people slap each other's palms with their arms extended over their heads; (*b*) *v.t.* greet with a high-five. **high forest** a forest composed wholly or chiefly of trees raised from seed; *gen.* a forest composed of tall trees. **high frequency** *spec.* a frequency of vibration or oscillation having a relatively large number of cycles per second; in *Telecommunications* etc., a frequency in the range from 3 to 30 megahertz. **high gear** a gear of a motor vehicle providing a high ratio between the speed of the driven wheels and that of the driving mechanism and so a high speed to the vehicle itself. *High German*: see GERMAN *n.*[1] & *a.*[1] **high-grade** *a.* & *v.* (*a*) *adj.* of high quality; *spec.* (of ore) rich in metal value and commercially profitable; (*b*) *v.t.* & *i.* steal (high-grade ore). **high ground** (*a*) ground that is naturally elevated and therefore strategically advantageous; (*b*) *the* position of (esp. moral) superiority in a debate etc. **high-headed** *a.* proud, arrogant. **high-hearted** *a.* (*arch.*) courageous. **high heels** high-heeled shoes. **high holiday** the Jewish New Year or Day of Atonement. *high jinks*: see JINK *n.* 1. **high-jump** *n.* & *v.* (*a*) *n.* an athletic event consisting of jumping over a high bar without dislodging it; *for the high-jump*, on trial and likely to be sentenced to hanging, on a misdemeanour charge and likely to receive punishment, likely to be dismissed; (*b*) *v.i.* make or take part in a high-jump. **high-jumper** an athlete who performs or specializes in the high-jump. **high-jumping** the action of performing the high-jump. **high-key** *a.* (*Photogr.*) consisting of light tones. **high-keyed** *a.* of a high pitch; *fig.* tense, nervous. **high kick** a dancer's kick high in the air. **high-level** *a.* (*a*) (of negotiations etc.) conducted by high-ranking people; (*b*) (of a computer language) having each instruction corresponding to many instructions in machine code. **high life** (*a*) a luxurious existence ascribed to the upper classes; (*b*) a W. African type of dance music. **high living** = *high life* (a) above. *high mass*: see MASS *n.*[1] **high-melting** *a.* melting at a relatively high temperature. **high men** dice loaded to turn up high numbers. **high-octane** *a.* (of petrol etc.) having good antiknock properties. **high opinion** a favourable opinion *of*. **high-pitched** *a.* (*a*) (of a sound) high; (*b*) (of a roof) steep; (*c*) (of style etc.) elevated. **high point** the maximum or best state reached; a noteworthy or outstanding feature. **high polymer** a polymer having a high molecular weight. **high-powered** *a.* (*a*) having great power or energy; (*b*) *fig.* important, influential. **high pressure** (*a*) a high degree of activity, exertion, or coercion; (*b*) a condition of the atmosphere with the pressure above average. **high-pressure** *v.t.* pressurize. **high priest** (*a*) a chief priest, *esp.* (*Hist.*) a Jewish one; (*b*) the head of a cult. **high priestess** a chief priestess. **high profile** a conspicuous public image or way of behaving; exposure to attention or publicity. **high-profile** *a.* having a high profile. **high-ranking** *a.* of high rank, senior. **high-reaching** *a.* aspiring, ambitious. *high relief*: see RELIEF *n.*[2] 1. **high-rise** *a.* & *n.* (*a*) *adj.* (of a building) having many storeys; (*b*) *n.* a high-rise building, esp. a block of flats. **high-risk** *a.* involving or exposed to danger. **high road** (*a*) a main road; (*b*) a direct route *to*. **high roller** *N. Amer. slang* a person who gambles for high stakes or spends extravagantly. **high school** (*a*) a secondary school with a curriculum similar to that of a grammar school; *N. Amer.* a secondary school; (*b*) = HAUTE ÉCOLE. **high sea(s)** open sea(s), the sea(s) as not within any country's jurisdiction. **high season** the period of the greatest number of visitors at a resort etc. **high-set** *a.* (*arch.*) (of sound) high-pitched. *high sheriff*: see SHERIFF *n.* 1. **high sign** *US colloq.* a surreptitious gesture indicating that all is well or that the coast is clear. **high-sounding** *a.* (of speech etc.) pretentious, bombastic. **high-speed** *a.* (*a*) produced or able to operate at high speed; (*b*) (of steel) suitable for cutting tools even when red-hot. **high-spirited** *a.* vivacious; cheerful. **high spirits** vivacity; energy; cheerfulness. **high spot** *colloq.* a notable place or feature, an enjoyable moment or experience. **high-stepper** (*a*) a horse that lifts its feet high when walking or trotting; (*b*) a stately or high-class person. *High Steward*: see STEWARD *n.* **high-strung** *a.* = HIGHLY *strung*. **high table** a table on a platform at a public dinner, or for the fellows of a college. *high tea*: see TEA *n.* 5(b). **high tech** *n.* & *a.* (*a*) *n.* = *high technology* below; (*b*) *adj.* (of interior design etc.) imitating functional styles more usual in industry etc.; *gen.* involved in, employing, or requiring high technology. **high technology** advanced technological development or equipment, esp. in electronics. **high-tensile** *a.* (of metal) having great tensile strength. *high tension*: see TENSION *n.* 4. **high tide** the time or level of the tide at its flood. **high-toned** *a.* stylish; pretentious; dignified; superior. *high treason*: see TREASON *n.* 2a. **high-up** *colloq.* a person of high rank (cf. HIGHER *n.* 1). **high voltage** electrical potential causing some danger of injury or damage. **high water** (the time of) the tide at its fullest; *high-water mark*, the level reached at high water or in a flood, *fig.* the maximum recorded value or highest point of excellence. **high, wide, and handsome** in a carefree or stylish manner. **high wine**: containing a high percentage of alcohol. **high wire** a high tightrope. **highwood** a forest of tall trees. **high words** angry talk. **high yaller, yellow,** *US* (*derog.*) a person with one Black and one White parent and having a palish skin. *hold one's head high*: see HOLD *v. how is that for high*: see HOW *adv. in high feather*: see FEATHER *n. in high gig*: see GIG *n.*[1] **in the highest** (*a*) in the heavens; (*b*) in the highest degree. *King high*: see *ace high* above. *live high off* (or *on*) *the hog*: see HOG *n. Lord High Commissioner*: see COMMISSIONER 1. **on high** in or to heaven or a high place. *on one's high horse*: see HORSE *n. on the high gig*: see GIG *n.*[1] **play high** (*a*) play for high stakes; (*b*) play a card of high value. *Queen high*: see *ace high* above. *ride high*: see RIDE *v.* **run high** (*a*) (of the sea) have a strong current with high tide; (*b*) (of feelings) be strong. **the High** *colloq.* the High Street, esp. in Oxford. *the high(er) command*: see COMMAND *n.* 2b. **the Most High** God.

†high *v.* [OE *hēan*, f. as HIGH *a.* Cf. OHG *hōhen*, Goth. *hauhjan*.] **1** *v.t.* Make high or higher; raise, lift up, exalt. OE–M18. **2** *v.i.* Become high or higher; rise. ME–M17.

highball /ˈhʌɪbɔːl/ *n.* & *v.* *N. Amer.* L19. [f. HIGH *a.* + BALL *n.*[1]] **A** *n.* **1** A spirit (esp. whisky) and soda etc. served usu. with ice in a tall glass; a drink of this. L19. **2** A railway signal to proceed (orig. made by lifting up a ball); *gen.* a signal to go ahead, a clear way. Also *highball signal*. L19.

1 R. LARDNER Will you take yours straight or in a highball?

B *v.* **1** *v.i.* Signal a train to proceed. E20. **2** *v.i.* & *t.* (w. *it*). Go or travel at speed. Freq. foll. by *along*, *out*, etc. E20. **b** *v.t.* Drive (a vehicle) at speed. M20.

2 R. LINDNER The train highballed out of the city.

highbrow /ˈhʌɪbraʊ/ *n.* & *a.* *colloq.* (orig. *US*). L19. [Back-form. f. next.] **A** *n.* A person with (esp. consciously) superior intellectual or cultural interests. L19.

L. MACNEICE A fall in the standard of intellectual living And nothing left that the highbrow cared about.

B *adj.* Designed for, appealing to, or characteristic of a highbrow. L19.

F. SPALDING A highbrow seriousness that limits its appeal.

highbrowish *a.* E20. **highbrowism** *n.* intellectual superiority E20.

highbrowed /ˈhʌɪbraʊd/ *a.* M19. [f. HIGH *a.* + BROW *n.*[1] + -ED[2].] **1** Having a high forehead. M19. **2** = HIGHBROW *a.* E20.

High Church /hʌɪ ˈtʃəːtʃ/ *n.* & *a. phr.* E18. [f. HIGH *a.* + CHURCH *n.*, after next.] **A** *n. phr.* (The principles of) a section of the Church of England emphasizing ritual, priestly authority, and sacraments. E18. **B** *adj. phr.* Of, pertaining to, or characteristic of this section or its principles. E18.

High-ˈChurchism *n.* High Church principles, doctrine, or practice L18.

High Churchman /hʌɪ ˈtʃəːtʃmən/ *n. phr.* Pl. **High Churchmen**. L17. [f. HIGH *a.* + CHURCHMAN.] An advocate of High Church principles.

High-Churchmanship *n.* = HIGH-CHURCHISM L19.

higher /ˈhʌɪə/ *a.*, *adv.*, & *n.* [OE *hēr(r)a*, (WS) *hīer(r)a*, later conformed to HIGH *a.*: see -ER[3].] **A** *adj.* **1** Compar. of HIGH *a.* OE. **2** *spec.* Superior to the common or ordinary sort, passing beyond the ordinary limits. M19. **b** *Biol.* Of an organism or group: more advanced, complex in organization. M19.

Phrases & comb.: **higher court** *Law* a court that can overrule the decision of another. **higher education**: beyond school, at university, etc. **higher mathematics** advanced mathematics as taught at university etc. *higher orders*: see ORDER *n.* 5. *the higher command*: see COMMAND *n.* 2b. *the higher criticism*: see CRITICISM 2.

B *adv.* Compar. of HIGH *adv.* OE.

C *n.* **1** A person of higher rank; a superior. Chiefly (*colloq.*) in *higher-up* (cf. *high-up* s.v. HIGH *n.*). ME. **2** (**H-**.) (A pass in) an examination leading to the Scottish Certificate of Education, Higher Grade. E20.

highermost *a.* & *adv.* (*rare*) highest E17.

higher /ˈhʌɪə/ *v.t.* *rare* exc. *north.* E18. [f. prec.: cf. LOWER *v.*[1]] Make higher, raise.

highfalutin /hʌɪfəˈluːtɪn/ *a.* & *n.* *colloq.* Also **-ing** /-ɪŋ/. M19. [Perh. f. HIGH *a.* + *fluting* pres. pple of FLUTE *v.*] Absurdly pompous or pretentious (speech, writing, etc.).

Also **highfaluti'nation** *n.* M19.

high-flier *n.* var. of HIGH-FLYER.

high-flown /hʌɪˈfləʊn/ *a.* M17. [Orig. f. HIGH *adv.* + FLOWN *ppl a.*[2]; later assoc. with FLOWN *ppl a.*[1]] **1** Of language, style, etc.: extravagant, bombastic. M17. **†2** Extreme in opinion. L17–E18.

1 M. MEYER This powerful melodrama, written in high-flown prose. *Guardian* Many were irritated by the high-flown claims being made.

high-flyer /hʌɪˈflʌɪə, ˈhʌɪflʌɪə/ *n.* Also **-flier**. L16. [f. HIGH *adv.* + FLYER *n.*] **1** A person who or thing which flies high. L16. **2** An ambitious person; a person or thing with great potential for achievement. M17. **b** A person with extreme views. L17. **3** A high-class prostitute. *slang* (now *Hist.*). L17. **†4** A fast stagecoach. E–M19. **5** In full *high-flyer walnut*. A variety of walnut. Now *rare*. E19. **6** A moth of the genus *Hydriomena*. M19. **7** A speculative financial investment giving an above average return. *slang*. M20.

1 BROWNING All ye highfliers of the feathered race, Swallows and curlews! 2 P. LIVELY He's not headmaster . . for nothing, he knows a high-flyer when he sees one. 6 *July high-flyer*: see JULY *n.*[1] 7 *Fortune* Its stock was a highflier on the volatile Hong Kong Stock Exchange.

high-flying /ˈhʌɪflʌɪɪŋ, hʌɪˈflʌɪɪŋ/ *a.* L16. [f. HIGH *adv.* + FLYING *ppl a.*] **1** Reaching great heights; ambitious; having great potential. L16. **b** Extreme. L17. **2** That flies high. E17.

1 T. HEALD The general had tried to encourage high-flying state school applicants. *Times* The once high-flying shares of . . Britain's biggest housebuilder fell to a 1983/84 low yesterday.

Highgate resin /hʌɪgeɪt ˈrɛzɪn/ *n. phr.* E19. [See below.] A fossil resin similar to copal, found in clay at Highgate Hill, London.

high-handed /hʌɪˈhandɪd/ *a.* E17. [f. HIGH *a.* + HANDED *a.*] Overbearing; disregarding the feelings of others, imperious.

R. SUTCLIFF He was annoyed by the man's high-handed manner. K. ISHIGURO That there was something high-handed about these arrangements there was no denying.

high-handedly *adv.* L19. **high-handedness** *n.* L19.

high-hat /ˈhʌɪhat/ *n.*, *a.*, & *v.* In sense A.2 also **hi-hat**. L19. [f. HIGH *a.* + HAT *n.*] **A** *n.* **1** A tall hat; *esp.* a top hat; *fig.* a supercilious or snobbish person. L19. **2** A pair of foot-operated cymbals. M20.

B *adj.* Supercilious, snobbish, overbearing. E20.

H. ROBBINS Some people say you're getting very high-hat since you lived on Riverside Drive. A. COOKE Chaplin . . went at once into his act of the high-hat millionaire commanding empires.

C *v.t.* & *i.* Infl. **-tt-**. Assume or treat with a superior or condescending attitude. Chiefly *US*. E20.

C. E. MERRIAM Dever's dignity was mistaken by some for 'high-hatting.' T. K. WOLFE Some of the boys felt that rocket pilots . . were high-hatting them.

high-hole /ˈhʌɪhəʊl/ *n.* *US*. M19. [Cogn. of HICKWALL by pop. etymology.] = HICKWALL.

highland /ˈhʌɪlənd/ *n.* & *a.* OE. [f. HIGH *a.* + LAND *n.*[1]] **A** *n.* Orig., a high headland or cliff. Now chiefly (in *pl.*), an area of high land, a mountainous region of a country; spec. *the Highlands*, the mountainous northern region of Scotland. OE.

L. MACNEICE The Highlands and Islands had now a permanent focus for the age-old nostalgia of Gaeldom. *White Highlands*: see WHITE *a.*

B *adj.* Of or pertaining to high land or a mountainous region; *spec.* (**H-**) of, pertaining to, or characteristic of (the people of) the Scottish Highlands. LME.

R. BURNS There's naething here but Highland pride, And Highland scab and hunger. *New Yorker* In . . Bhutan . . rice—highland red rice, the highest-altitude rice on earth—is the staple. *the Highland clearances*: see CLEARANCE 1.

Special collocations & comb.: **Highland bonnet** a Scotch cap. **Highland cattle** (animals of) a small shaggy-haired breed of cattle with long spreading horns, developed in the Scottish Highlands (also called *West Highland cattle*, *kyloes*). **Highland dress** the kilt, sporran, plaid, etc. *Highland fling*: see FLING *n.* 2b. **Highland games** a meeting consisting of athletic events, piping, and dancing, orig. and esp. as held in various Highland centres, esp. Braemar. **Highlandman** a male native or inhabitant of the Scottish Highlands. **Highland terrier** = WEST HIGHLAND 2.

highlandish *a.* (*rare*) of the nature of high land; like the Scottish Highlands: M17.

highlander /ˈhʌɪləndə/ *n.* E17. [f. prec. + -ER[1].] **1** A native or inhabitant of high or mountainous land; *spec.* (**H-**) a native or inhabitant of the Scottish Highlands. Also (**H-**), a soldier of any of the Highland regiments of the British army. E17. **2** An animal of the Highland breed of cattle. L18.

highlight /ˈhʌɪlʌɪt/ *n.* & *v.* M17. [f. HIGH *a.* + LIGHT *n.*] **A** *n.* **1** A light area or one seeming to reflect the light in a painting, photograph, etc. Freq. in *pl.* M17. **2** A moment or detail of vivid interest or action; an outstanding feature. M19. **3** A bright (esp. artificial) tint in parts of the hair that catches the light. Usu. in *pl.* M20.

1 C. HAYES A neutral mid-tone into which both shadows and highlights could be painted. 2 *Times* Highlights from one of tonight's top soccer matches. D. PRATER At the end of the month was to come the highlight of the visit. 3 *City Limits* For my cut and highlights, I had a brief consultation with the women.

B *v.t.* **1** Bring into prominence; draw attention to; *spec.* mark with a highlighter. M20. **2** Tint or bleach (parts of the hair) so as to catch the light. M20.

1 E. HUXLEY Immigrants .. haven't really brought new problems with them, .. they've highlighted and sharpened up the problems we .. have. *Practical Householder* Wooden mouldings inside the ceiling perimeter can be highlighted in white gloss or strong colour. 2 *Hair* This tousled style is scrunch dried and highlighted to enhance the shape.

highlighter /ˈhʌɪlʌɪtə/ *n.* Also (earlier & as US proprietary name) **Hi-liter**. M20. [f. HIGHLIGHT *v.* + -ER[1].] A marker pen which emphasizes a printed word etc. by overlaying it with a transparent (usu. fluorescent) colour.

high-lone /ˈhʌɪləʊn/ *adv.* Now *obs.* exc. *US dial.* L16. [Alt. of ALONE, w. HIGH *adv.* as intensifier.] Quite alone, without support.

SHAKES. *Rom. & Jul.* For then she could stand high-lone.

highly /ˈhʌɪli/ *adv.* OE. [f. HIGH *a.* + -LY[2].] **1** In a high place; on high. Long *rare* or *obs.* OE. **2** In or to a high rank. Now *rare.* OE. **3** In or to a high degree, amount, or extent; greatly, extremely; at a high price or rate. Formerly also, loudly. OE. **b** To a high degree of artistic quality; elaborately. E18. **4** With high approval; favourably, honourably. ME. **5** With stateliness, solemnly; pompously, angrily. Formerly also, seriously, earnestly. Now *rare* or *obs.* ME.

2 G. MACKENZIE She is one of the Heads and highly situate. 3 E. BOWEN These two showed how highly they rated their fortune. M. AMSTERDAM A highly-publicized Hollywood 'sex-pot' was stopping at a New York hotel. K. VONNEGUT He was highly literate, well read, and the author of various pamphlets. M. DRABBLE Eating .. was to be a highly fashionable occupation, in the early 1980s. b W. PALEY The hinges in the wings of an earwig .. are as highly wrought as if the Creator had nothing else to finish. 4 E. WAUGH D'you read his paper? .. It's highly thought of. G. WINOKUR He was .. highly regarded and famous.

Comb.: **highly strung** *a.* very sensitive or nervous.

high-minded /hʌɪˈmʌɪndɪd/ *a.* E16. [f. HIGH *a.* + MINDED *a.*] **1** Haughty, arrogant. *arch.* E16. **2** Characterized by high principles; magnanimous. M16.

2 S. BELLOW He had a weakness for high-minded people, for people with moral principles. P. ROTH Two high-minded boys who were putting away their earnings for an education.

highmindedly *adv.* E19. **highmindedness** *n.* L16.

highmost /ˈhʌɪməʊst/ *a. obs.* exc. *dial.* L16. [f. HIGH *a.* + -MOST.] Highest.

high-muck-a-muck /ˈhʌɪmʌkəmʌk/ *n. N. Amer. colloq.* M19. [Prob. f. Chinook Jargon *hiyu muckamuck* plenty of food, f. Nootka *ḥayo* ten + *ma·ho·maq-* choice whalemeat, w. substitution of HIGH *a.*] A person of great self-importance.

highness /ˈhʌɪnɪs/ *n.* & *v.* OE. [f. HIGH *a.* + -NESS.] **A** *n.* **1** The quality or condition of being high. Formerly also a high place, a summit. Now *rare* exc. *fig.* OE. **b** *spec.* (**H-.**) An honorific title given to a person of royal etc. rank. (Chiefly modified by possess. adj.) LME. †**2** Haughtiness, arrogance. ME–M17.

1b *Imperial Highness, Royal Highness, Serene Highness*, etc.

B *v.t.* Address with the title of 'Highness'. *rare.* M17.

high street /ˈhʌɪ striːt/ *n.* & *a. phr.* OE. [f. HIGH *a.* + STREET *n.*] **A** *n. phr.* A main road; *esp.* the principal shopping street of a town. OE. **B** *attrib.* or as *adj.* Designed for, targeted at, or readily available to the general public. L20.

highstrikes /ˈhʌɪstrʌɪks/ *n.pl. joc. colloq.* M19. [Alt., after HIGH *a.* + STRIKE *n.*[1] + -S[1].] Hysterics.

hight /hʌɪt/ *n. obs.* exc. *Sc.* ME. [f. the vb.] †**1** A command, an order. Only in ME. **2** A promise, a vow. ME.

hight /hʌɪt/ *v. arch.* Long only as pa. t. & pple **hight**. [OE *hātan* = OFris. *hēta*, OS *hētan*, OHG *heizzan* (G *heissen* call, bid, be called), ON *heita*, Goth. *haitan*, f. a base repr. by L *ciere* summon, CITE *v.*] **1** *v.t.* Command, bid, order. Long *rare.* OE. **2** *v.t.* Promise, vow. *obs.* exc. *Sc.* OE. **3** *v.t.* Call, name. OE. **4** *v.i.* Be called, have as a name. OE. †**5** *v.t.* Direct; commit; designate; mean. *rare* (Spenser). Only in L16.

3 E. BIRNEY That sea is hight Time. 4 LONGFELLOW Father he hight.

hightail /ˈhʌɪteɪl/ *v.i.* & *t.* (w. *it*). *N. Amer. colloq.* E20. [f. HIGH *a.* + TAIL *n.*[1], w. allus. to the erect tails of animals in flight.] Move (away) at high speed.

highty-tighty *n.*, *a.*, & *int.* var. of HOITY-TOITY.

highveld /ˈhʌɪvɛlt, -f-/ *n.* L19. [Partial tr. Afk. *hoëveld*, f. *hoë* attrib. form of *hoog* high + VELD.] (A region of) veld situated at a high altitude; *spec.* the region in the Transvaal, South Africa, between 1200 and 1800 metres (4000 and 6000 feet) above sea level.

highway /ˈhʌɪweɪ/ *n.* OE. [f. HIGH *a.* + WAY *n.*] **1** A public road; *spec.* a main road forming the direct route between one town etc. and another. OE. **b** A main route by land or water; a well-used track. LME. **c** *Computing.* A main route or path along which signals from any of several sources travel to any of several destinations; a bus. M20. **2** *fig.* The ordinary or direct course of action; a course of conduct leading directly to some end. L16.

1 J. GARDNER There'd been a road through there, twenty .. years ago, but they'd moved the highway now. *Medway Extra* Kent County Council's highways department is carrying out carriageway reconstruction. DIVIDED *highway.* **King's** or **Queen's highway** a public road regarded as being under the monarch's protection. 2 B. JOWETT That state .. I perceive to be on the highway to ruin.

Comb.: **Highway Code** the official book of guidance for road-users; **highwayman** *Hist.* a (usu. mounted) man who robbed passengers on a highway.

higlif /iglif/ *n.* E20. [Repr. a Fr. pronunc. of *high life.*] English high society (seen from the point of view of the French or other Europeans).

hi-hat *n.* see HIGH-HAT.

hijack /ˈhʌɪdʒak/ *v.* & *n.* Also **hi-jack**. E20. [Origin unkn.] **A** *v.t.* Steal (goods, formerly *spec.* contraband etc.) in transit; seize control of (a means of transport, as a lorry with goods, an aircraft in flight, etc.) by force; reroute (an aircraft etc.) *to* a new destination in this way. E20.

A. W. SHERRING A stack of old banknotes leaves Central Post at three... The van will be hijacked. *transf.*: *Daily Telegraph* When a virus enters a cell it hijacks it, and makes it do what it wants. *Woman's Own* The charter companies have hi-jacked some of the trimmings they provide.

B *n.* The action or an act of hijacking. M20.

C. BONINGTON We were taking risks not just of hi-jacks but also of accidents.

hijacker *n.* a person who hijacks something E20.

hijra *n.* var. of HEGIRA.

hikayat /hɪˈkʌɪjat/ *n.* E19. [Malay f. Arab. *ḥikāya(t)* story, narrative.] In classical Malay literature, a prose narrative combining fact and romance.

hike /hʌɪk/ *v.* & *n. colloq.* (orig. *dial.*). E19. [Origin unkn.] **A** *v.* **1** *v.i.* Walk vigorously or laboriously; go for a long walk or walking-tour for pleasure or exercise. E19. **b** *v.t.* Traverse (a specified distance) in this way. M20. **2** *v.t.* Force to move, shove; hoist, pull; increase (a price etc.). Also foll. by *up.* M19. **b** *v.i.* Be or become hitched *up.* L19.

1 E. FEINSTEIN She .. spent some days hiking about the hills of France. *hitch-hike*: see HITCH *v.* b J. BARTH I walked out to the road and hiked two miles to a telephone. 2 E. BIRNEY Gilda .. hiked the strap of her shiny plastic bag higher on her shoulder. *Listener* Market restrictions .. have hiked the price of Japanese recorders. b *Saturday Evening Post* When I sit down, it hikes up.

B *n.* **1** A vigorous or laborious walk; a long walk or walking-tour undertaken for pleasure or exercise. M19. **2** An increase (in prices etc.). Chiefly *N. Amer.* M20.

1 H. L. WILSON What's the matter with him and Lon taking a swift hike down to New York? 2 *Scientific American* There will be no hikes in electricity rates until the 1990's.

hiker *n.* E20.

hila *n.* pl. of HILUM.

hilar /ˈhʌɪlə/ *a.* M19. [f. HILUM + -AR[1].] Of or pertaining to a hilum or hilus.

Hilaria /hɪˈlɛːrɪə/ *n.* M18. [L, neut. pl. of *hilaris*: see HILARITY, -IA[2].] *Class. Hist.* In ancient Rome etc., a festival in honour of Cybele celebrated at the vernal equinox.

hilarious /hɪˈlɛːrɪəs/ *a.* E19. [f. L *hilaris* (see next) + -OUS.] **1** Mirthful, joyous; causing merriment. E19. **2** Boisterously merry. M19.

1 SIR W. SCOTT In answer to my hilarious exhortations to confidence. O. MANNING Laughing as though Yakimov's speech had been one of hilarious impropriety. 2 B. PYM I was *very* happy and hilarious, cracking many jokes.

hilariously *adv.* M19. **hilariousness** *n.* M19.

hilarity /hɪˈlarɪti/ *n.* LME. [Fr. *hilarité* f. L *hilaritas*, f. *hilaris*, (-*us*) f. Gk *hilaros* cheerful: see -ITY.] **1** Cheerfulness; calm joy. LME. **2** Boisterous merriment. M19.

1 SOUTHEY The pleasure which they partake conduces .. to health and present hilarity. 2 C. STEAD There was wild hilarity, kind Bonnie and Jinny stuffing their hands into their mouths.

Hilary /ˈhɪləri/ *n.* LME. [f. *Hilarius*, bishop of Poitiers (d. 367), w. Anglican feast day 13 January.] In full *Hilary term.* A university etc. term beginning in January; a term or session of the High Court beginning in January.

Hilbert space /ˈhɪlbət speɪs/ *n.* E20. [f. D. *Hilbert* (1862–1943), Ger. mathematician + SPACE *n.*] *Math.* A normed space having an infinite number of dimensions with each point at a finite distance from the others.

Hildebrandine /ˈhɪldɪbrandʌɪn/ *a.* M17. [f. *Hildebrand* (see below) + -INE[1].] *Hist.* Of, pertaining to, or resembling the policy of Hildebrand (Pope Gregory VII 1073–85), who asserted the power of the papacy and hierarchy and insisted on clerical celibacy.

hilding /ˈhɪldɪŋ/ *n.* & *a.* Long *arch.* & *dial.* L16. [Origin unkn.] **A** *n.* †**1** A worthless or vicious animal, esp. a horse. L16–E19. **2** A contemptible or worthless person. L16. **B** *attrib.* or as *adj.* Of a person or an animal: worthless, contemptible. L16.

hili *n.* pl. of HILUS.

Hi-liter *n.* see HIGHLIGHTER.

hill /hɪl/ *n.* [OE *hyll* = OFris. *hel*, LG *hull*, MDu. *hille*, *hil*, *hul*, f. WGmc (of the LG area) f. IE base also of L *collis*, Gk *kolōnos*, *kolōnē* hill.] **1** A natural elevation of the earth's surface; a small mountain; *fig.* something not easily surmounted or overcome. OE. **2** A heap or mound of earth, sand, etc., raised by human or other agency. Freq. w. specifying wd. ME. **b** A heap formed round a plant by banking up soil. Also, a cluster of plants on level ground. Chiefly *US.* L16. **c**

The rising ground on which ruffs assemble at the breeding season; an assemblage of ruffs. L18. **d** *Her.* A charge representing a hill. E19.

1 MILTON About me round I saw Hill, Dale, and shadie Woods. L. GORDON From that hill, they could see both coasts of Cornwall. *fig.*: C. WESLEY O'er Hills of Guilt and Seas of Grief, He leaps. 2 W. COWPER The wain . . appears a moving hill of snow. *anthill, dunghill, molehill*, etc.

Phrases: *hill of beans*: see BEAN *n.* **old as the hills** very ancient. **over the hill** *colloq.* (*a*) past the prime of life; declining; (*b*) past the crisis. **the Hill** *N. Amer. colloq.* the US Senate; the Canadian federal parliament or government. **the hills** *Anglo-Ind.* the low mountains of the northern part of the Indian subcontinent, esp. as the location of hill-stations. **up hill and down dale** up and down in every direction, taking the country or (*fig.*) the situation as it comes. *up the wooden hill*: see WOODEN *a. watch hill*: see WATCH *n.* II.

Comb.: **hill and dale** *a.* (of a gramophone record) with undulations made by a cutting stylus that moved in a vertical plane (opp. *lateral-cut* s.v. LATERAL *a.*); **hillbilly** *US* (*a*) *colloq.* (freq. *derog.*) a person from a remote rural area in a southern State; (*b*) folk music of or like that of the southern US; **hill climb** the action or an act of climbing hills; *spec.* a race for motor vehicles over hilly ground; *Hill* DAMARA; **hill-folk** *arch.* hill-men; **hill-fort** a fort built on a hill, *esp.* a prehistoric hilltop fortification; **hill-man** (*a*) *gen.* an inhabitant or frequenter of hills or hilly country; (*b*) *Hist.* a Scottish covenanter, a Cameronian; (*c*) an elf, a troll; **hillside** the lateral slope of a hill; **hill-station** *Anglo-Ind.* a government settlement, esp. for holidays etc. during the hot season, in the low mountains of the N. part of the Indian subcontinent; **hilltop** the summit of a hill; **hillwalker** a person who engages in hillwalking; **hillwalking** the pastime of walking in hilly country.

hill /hɪl/ *v.*[1]*t. obs.* exc. *dial.* ME. [Corresp. to OE *behylian*, corresp. to OS *bihullean*, OHG *hullen* (G *hüllen*), ON *hylja*, Goth. *huljan*, f. Gmc weak grade of HELE *v.*] 1 Cover (up), protect. ME. †2 Cover from sight, conceal. Only in ME.

hilling *n.*[1] (*a*) covering; hiding; protection; (*b*) a covering: ME.

hill /hɪl/ *v.*[2] M16. [f. HILL *n.*, in branch II infl. by HILL *v.*[1]] **I** †1 *v.i.* Ascend; rise in or on a slope. Only in M16. 2 *v.t.* Form into a hill; heap up. L16. 3 *v.t.* Surround with hills; cover with hills. *rare.* E17. 4 *v.i.* Of ruffs: assemble on rising ground at the breeding season. L18. **II** 5 *v.t.* Bank *up* (plants) with soil. L16.

hillo /ˈhɪləʊ/ *int.* & *n.* Also **hilloa** /ˈhɪləʊ, hɪˈləʊ/. E17. [Var. of HOLLO *int.* & *n.*] **A** *int.* Commanding or attempting to attract attention. Also = HELLO *int.* E17. **B** *n.* A shout of 'hillo!' E19.

hillock /ˈhɪlək/ *n.* & *v.* ME. [f. HILL *n.* + -OCK.] **A** *n.* 1 A small hill. ME. 2 A small mound or heap. LME. †3 A protuberance; the raised portion of a surface. E16–M17. **B** *v.t.* Form into a hillock, heap up. Usu. in *pass.* Now *arch.* or *poet.* L18.

hillocky *a.* E18.

hilly /ˈhɪli/ *a.* LME. [f. HILL *n.* + -Y[1].] 1 Characterized by hills; having many hills. LME. 2 Resembling a hill; steep. LME. †3 Inhabiting or frequenting a hill or hills. Only in 17.

1 W. BLACK The hillier regions of Dumfriesshire. 2 G. CHARLES A hilly street with high, iron railings. T. MORRISON He could barely see the hilly outline of the island.

hilliness *n.* E17.

hilo /ˈhiːləʊ/ *n.* Pl. **-os.** M19. [Sp. = thread, f. L *filum.*] A thin vein of ore.

hilsa /ˈhɪlsə/ *n.* E19. [Hind.] An anadromous Indian food fish, *Alosa sapidissima*, of the herring family. Also called *Indian shad.*

hilt /hɪlt/ *n.* & *v.* [OE *hilt(e)*, corresp. to OS *hilte, helta*, MLG *hilte*, MDu. *helte*, OHG *helza*, ON *hjalt*, f. Gmc: ult. origin unkn.] **A** *n.* 1 The handle of a sword or dagger. (Formerly also in *pl.* w. sing. sense.) OE. 2 The handle of some other weapon or tool. LME.

1 P. L. FERMOR Their hands on the hilts of their broadswords tilted up the scabbards behind them. 2 A. W. KINGLAKE Unnecessary . . to shew even the hilt of his pistol.

Phrases: †**by these hilts**: expr. asseveration. **(up) to the hilt** completely.

B *v.t.* Provide with a hilt. E19.

hilted *a.* (*a*) furnished with a hilt; (*b*) *Her.* having a hilt of a different tincture from the corresponding blade: OE.

hilum /ˈhʌɪləm/ *n.* Pl. **-la** /-lə/. M17. [L *hilum* little thing, trifle, once thought to mean 'that which adheres to a bean'.] †1 A very minute thing. Only in M17. 2 *Bot.* The scar of a seed, marking the point where it was attached to the fruit by the funicle. M18. **b** A point in a starch granule around which the layers of starch are arranged. M19. 3 *Anat.* = HILUS. *rare.* L19.

hilus /ˈhʌɪləs/ *n.* Pl. **hili** /ˈhʌɪlʌɪ/. M19. [mod.L, alt. of prec.] *Anat.* An indentation in the surface of an organ, as the kidney or spleen, where blood-vessels, ducts, nerve fibres, etc., enter or leave it.

him /hɪm, *unstressed* ɪm/ *pers. pron., 3 sing. masc.* (& †*neut.*) *objective* (*dat.* & *accus.*), & *n.* [OE *him* = OFris. *him*, MDu. *hem*(*e*, *him* (Du. *hem*), f. Gmc base of HE *pron.*, with inflection parallel to OS, OHG *imu, imo* (G *ihm*), f. base also of L *is* he, *id* it, Goth. *is, ita*, OHG *er, ez*, G *er, es*. Cf. IT *pron.*, UN *pron.*[1]] **A** *pron.* 1 Objective (direct & indirect) of HE *pron.*: the (male) person or animal, or the thing personified or conventionally treated as male or (in early use) grammatically masculine, previously mentioned or implied or easily identified. OE. **b** Himself: direct (*arch.* exc. after preps.) & indirect (*arch.* & *US dial.*) objective. OE. †2 Objective of IT *pron.* ME–E17. 3 Subjective: he. Esp. pred. after *be* & after *than, as. colloq.* LME.

1 MILTON The Sun was sunk, and after him the Starr Of Hesperus. SCOTT FITZGERALD Dexter . . collected what money was due him . . and walked home. S. T. WARNER They sat on the lawn and watched him unpacking. J. BUCHAN The lover of gossip will find nothing to please him. I. MURDOCH God is . . important in Pattie's life and she is comforted when other people believe in Him. G. VIDAL Peter admired his father without liking him. R. P. JHABVALA I . . smartly boxed his ears for him. **himseems, -seemeth** (pa. t.) **-seemed** *v.i. impers.* (long *arch.*) it seems, seemed, to him (modifying a sentence or parenthetically). b BYRON He who hath bent him o'er the dead. D. H. LAWRENCE In the depths of him, he too didn't want to go. D. A. DYE If he could . . kill him a few gooks . . he'd shed the New Guy image. 3 S. JOHNSON No man had ever more discernment than him, in finding out the ridiculous. R. H. BARHAM Heedless of grammar, they all cried, 'That's him!'

B *n.* The male; a male; a man. *colloq.* L19.

W. S. GILBERT 'Mr F. shall introduce him' 'It ain't a him, it's a her.'

Himalayan /hɪməˈleɪən/ *a.* M19. [f. *Himalaya* mountains in Nepal (Skt, f. *hima* snow + *ālaya* abode) + -AN.] Of, pertaining, or belonging to the Himalayas; *fig.* enormous, vast.

Himalayan balsam: see BALSAM *n.* 6(b). *Himalayan* MONAL.

himation /hɪˈmatɪɒn/ *n.* M19. [Gk.] In ancient Greece, an outer garment worn over the left shoulder and under the right.

himbo /ˈhɪmbəʊ/ *n. joc. slang.* L20. [Blend of HIM + BIMBO *n.*] An attractive but unintelligent man.

himp /hɪmp/ *v.i.* Long *obs.* exc. *dial.* L16. [Corresp. to G dial. *humpen, hümpen, himpen*, Da. dial. *hompen* hobble.] Limp.

himself /hɪmˈsɛlf/ *pron.* OE. [f. HIM + SELF *a.* (but long interpreted as SELF *n.*: cf. HIS-SELF).] **I** *emphatic.* 1 In apposition to a personal n. (subjective or objective) or to a subjective pron.: that particular (male) person or animal, that particular thing personified or conventionally treated as male or (in early use) grammatically masculine; the (male) person in question personally. OE. 2 (Not appositional.) **a** Subjective: he himself (formerly also, it itself). Now *arch.* & *dial.* exc. *colloq.* after *be* & after *than, as*, (cf. HIM 3). OE. **b** Objective: the (male) person etc. in question himself. E16.

1 I. MURDOCH 'The great man himself!' said Nick Fawley. O. MANNING Yesterday he received a summons from the King himself. N. O. BROWN Freud himself added politics in his later writings. G. GREENE He never himself asked a question and his discretion seemed to rebuke our . . curiosity. E. HEATH He himself had been born in the North and come to the South. D. CECIL George Austen educated his sons himself. 2a TENNYSON The dagger which himself Gave Edith. G. GREENE He was full of the conventions of a generation older than himself. P. KAVANAGH Every evening himself and Eusebius went down the road. b J. C. POWYS That had been quite long enough for himself and Lady Val.

II *refl.* 3 Refl. form (indirect, direct, & after preps.) of HIM: (to, for, etc.) the (male) person in question himself. OE.

3 JOYCE His conversation was mainly about himself: what he had said . . to settle the matter. S. T. WARNER He had seen himself setting foot upon the island alone. O. MANNING He was going to prove himself the saviour of his country. R. P. JHABVALA The Nawab . . threw himself far back in his chair. C. P. SNOW Humphrey bought himself a second pint of bitter.

Phrases: **be himself** (*a*) act in his normal unconstrained manner; (*b*) feel as well as he usually does (usu. in neg. contexts). **by himself** on his own.

Himyarite /ˈhɪmjərʌɪt/ *n.* M19. [f. *Himyar*, a traditional king of Yemen + -ITE[1]. Cf. earlier HOMERITE.] A member of an ancient people in the southern part of the Arabian peninsula.

Himyaˈritic *a.* of or pertaining to the Himyarites or their language M19.

hin /hɪn/ *n.* Also **H-.** LME. [Biblical Heb. *hīn*.] A Hebrew liquid unit of capacity equal to approx. 5 litres, about one gallon.

†**hin** *pron.* see UN *pron.*[1]

hinaki /ˈhiːnakiː/ *n. NZ.* Pl. same. M19. [Maori.] A wicker eel-pot.

hinau /ˈhiːnaʊ/ *n.* M19. [Maori.] A New Zealand evergreen tree, *Elaeocarpus dentatus* (family Elaeocarpaceae), which yields a black dye.

Hinayana /hiːnəˈjɑːnə/ *n.* M19. [Skt, f. *hīna* lesser, little + *yāna* vehicle.] = THERAVADA.

hincty /ˈhɪŋkti/ *a. US slang.* E20. [Origin unkn.] Conceited, snobbish, stuck-up.

hind /hʌɪnd/ *n.*[1] [OE, corresp. to OS *hind*, (M)Du. *hinde*, OHG *hinta* (G *Hinde*), ON *hind*, f. Gmc f. IE base w. the sense 'hornless' repr. also by Gk *kemas* young deer.] 1 A female deer; *spec.* the female of the red deer, esp. in or after its third year. OE. 2 Any of several large edible groupers of the genus *Epinephelus* with spotted markings. M18.

hind /hʌɪnd/ *n.*[2] Also (earlier) †**hine.** [OE *hī(g)na* genit. pl. of *hīgan, hīwan* (cf. HIDE *n.*[2]), as in *hīna fæder* paterfamilias. For the parasitic *d* cf. SOUND *n.*[2]] †1 In *pl.* (Household) servants, domestics. OE–LME. 2 A servant, *esp.* an agricultural worker. Also, a bailiff, a steward. *arch.* ME. **b** A skilled farm-worker having a degree of responsibility and provided with tied accommodation. *Sc.* L16. 3 *transf.* A rustic; a boor. *arch.* ME. 4 A boy, a lad; a person, a fellow. Long *arch. rare.* ME.

hind /hʌɪnd/ *a.* & *n.*[3] ME. [Perh. abbrev. of OE *behindan* BEHIND. Cf. HINDER *a.* & *n.*] **A** *adj.* Situated behind or at the back; posterior, rear. Freq. opp. *front, fore.* ME.

T. ROETHKE The hind part of the worm wriggles the most. B. LOPEZ Ground sloths that stood as tall on their hind legs as modern giraffes. **on one's hind legs** *joc.* standing up to make a speech. *suck the hind tit* or *teat*: see SUCK *v. talk the hind leg(s) off a* DONKEY.

B *ellipt.* as *n.* A hind leg etc. L19.

D. L. SAYERS You know you've got a loose shoe on your rear hind.

Special collocations & comb.: **hindbrain** *Anat.* the part of the brain comprising the cerebellum, pons, and medulla oblongata; = RHOMBENCEPHALON. **hindgut** *Anat.* & *Zool.* the posterior part of the gut, in vertebrates including the large intestine. **hind-head** *arch.* the back of the head. **hindquarters** the hind legs and the adjoining parts of a quadruped. **hindside** the back part of something. **hindwing** either of the posterior wings of an insect.

hindward *adv.* & *a.* (*rare*) (*a*) *adv.* backward, to the rear; (*b*) *adj.* backward: ME.

hindberry /ˈhʌɪndb(ə)ri/ *n. obs.* exc. *north.* OE. [f. HIND *n.*[1] + BERRY *n.*[1]: so called because growing in woods and assumed to be eaten by deer.] The fruit of the (wild) raspberry, *Rubus idaeus.*

Hindenburg line /ˈhɪnd(ə)nbəːg lʌɪn/ *n. phr. Hist.* E20. [Paul von *Hindenburg* (1847–1934), German Field Marshal and statesman.] A line of fortifications in NE France constructed by the German forces in 1916–17.

hinder /ˈhʌɪndə/ *a.* & *n.* ME. [Perh. deduced f. OE *hinderweard* backward and taken as compar. of HIND *a.*] A *adj.* 1 Situated behind, at the back, or in the rear; posterior. ME. 2 Of (a period of) time: most recently past, last. *Sc.* LME. †3 Latter (opp. *former*). LME–M17.

1 H. READ The female of the species emitted a luminous glow from the hinder end of their bodies.

Special collocations: **hinder end** *Sc.* & *north.* (*a*) the latter end, esp. of life; (*b*) the rear or back of something.

B *n.* Usu. in *pl.* Hindquarters, buttocks; hind legs. M19.

hinderling *n.* †(*a*) a backward direction; †(*b*) a person at the rear; (*c*) *Sc.* (in *pl.*) the buttocks: OE. **hindermost** *a.* (*arch.*) = HINDMOST *a.* LME.

hinder /ˈhɪndə/ *v.* [OE *hindrian* = MLG, MDu. *hinderen*, OHG *hintarōn* (G *hindern*), ON *hindra*, f. Gmc, f. a base repr. by OE *hinder* below, OS *hindiro*, OHG *hintar*, Goth. *hindar* (prep.) beyond.] †1 *v.t.* Do harm to; injure, damage. OE–L18. b Disparage, slander, belittle. LME–L16. 2 *v.t.* Keep back, delay; impede, obstruct; prevent. (Foll. by *from*, *in*.) LME. 3 *v.i.* Delay or frustrate action; be an obstacle. LME.

2 S. PEPYS These pleasures do hinder me in my business. J. G. HOLLAND What's to hinder other people from liking one another? F. SPALDING Economic difficulties hindered the Labour Government's attempts at social reform. 3 CARLYLE It is not the dark place that hinders, but the dim eye.

hinderer *n.* LME. **hindersome** *a.* (*Sc.* & *north.*) tending to hinder, obstructive L16.

Hindi /ˈhɪndi/ *n.* & *a.* E19. [Urdu *hindī*, f. *Hind* India.] A *n.* A group of Indo-Aryan dialects of the northern part of the Indian subcontinent; a literary form of Hindustani with Sanskrit-based vocabulary and Devanagari script, one of the official languages of the Republic of India. E19. B *adj.* Of or pertaining to the northern part of the Indian subcontinent; of or pertaining to Hindi. E19.

Hindki /ˈhɪndkiː/ *n.* E19. [Origin unkn.] A member of a people of the north-western part of the Indian subcontinent and Afghanistan; the Indo-Aryan language of this people.

hindmost /ˈhʌɪn(d)məʊst/ *a.* LME. [f. HIND *a.* + -MOST.] 1 Furthest behind; last in position; most remote. LME. 2 Last in order or time. Chiefly *Sc.* LME.

1 C. M. YONGE The hindmost declared they would not stop till they were even with the front. *devil take the hindmost*: see DEVIL *n.* 2 J. M. BARRIE For the hinmost years o' his life.

Hindoo *n.* & *a.* see HINDU.

Hindooism *n.* see HINDUISM.

Hindoostanee *n.* & *a.* see HINDUSTANI.

hindrance /ˈhɪndr(ə)ns/ *n.* LME. [f. HINDER *v.* + -ANCE.] †1 Injury, damage, disadvantage. LME–L16. 2 (An) obstruction; an obstacle, an impediment. E16.

2 P. LARKIN Hardy built a private entrance . . so that he could enter and leave the house without hindrance. JANET MORGAN In discovering what happened . . the press is as much of a hindrance as a help. *let or hindrance*: see LET *n.*[1] STERIC *hindrance*.

hindsight /ˈhʌɪn(d)sʌɪt/ *n.* M19. [f. HIND *a.* + SIGHT *n.*] 1 Seeing what has happened and what ought to have been done after the event; wisdom after the event. (Opp. *foresight*.) M19. 2 The sight nearest the rear of a gun. M19.

1 G. F. KENNAN We can see today, with the advantage of hindsight, that the . . possibilities . . were extremely limited. A. MACLEAN Hindsight and bitter experience make for a splendid conductor to belated wisdom. 2 **knock** (or **kick**) **a person's hindsight**(s) **out** or **the hindsight(s) off a person** *US colloq.* dispose of or demolish completely.

Hindu /ˈhɪnduː, hɪnˈduː/ *n.* & *a.* Also (*arch.*) **-doo**. M17. [Urdu f. Pers. *hindū*, formerly *hindō*, f. *Hind* India.] A *n.* A native or inhabitant of (orig. the northern part of) the Indian subcontinent, *esp.* one adhering to Hinduism; an adherent of Hinduism. M17. B *adj.* Of, pertaining to, or characteristic of the Hindus or Hinduism. L17.

Hinduize *v.t.* make Hindu in appearance, customs, or religion M19.

Hinduism /ˈhɪndʊɪz(ə)m/ *n.* Also (*arch.*) **-dooism**. E19. [f. prec. + -ISM.] A system of religious beliefs and social customs, with adherents esp. in India, with a belief in reincarnation, the worship of several gods, and an ordained caste system, as the basis of society.

Hindustani /hɪndʊˈstɑːni/ *n.* & *a.* Also (*arch.*) **Hindoostanee**. E17. [Urdu f. Pers. *hindūstānī*, f. *hindū*, formerly *hindō*, + *-stān* country + adj. suff. *-ī*.] A *n.* 1 A language based on the Western Hindi dialect of the Delhi region with an admixture of Arabic, Persian, etc., current as the standard language and lingua franca in much of northern India and Pakistan; *arch.* Urdu. E17. 2 A native or inhabitant of (the N. part of) the Indian subcontinent. *arch.* E19. B *adj.* Of, pertaining to, or characteristic of the Hindustani language or the Hindustanis. E19.

†hine *n.* see HIND *n.*[2]

†hine *pron.* see UN *pron.*[1]

Hiney *n.* var. of HEINIE.

hing /hɪŋ/ *n.* L16. [Hindi *hīg* f. Skt *hiṅgu*.] = ASAFOETIDA.

hinge /hɪn(d)ʒ/ *n.* Also (earlier) **†henge**. ME. [f. base of HANG *v.*, cf. (M)LG *henge* hinge. Cf. HINGLE.] I 1 The movable joint or mechanism by which a door etc. is hung on its side post to permit opening and shutting; a similar mechanism providing for turning in other linked objects. ME. b A natural movable joint acting in a similar manner, *esp.* that of a bivalve shell. E18. c More fully *stamp-hinge*. A small piece of gummed transparent paper used for fixing a postage stamp in an album etc. L19. 2 The axis of the earth; the two poles about which the earth revolves; *loosely* (in *pl.*), the four cardinal points. Long *arch. rare.* LME. 3 The central principle, cardinal or critical point, on which everything turns or relies. E17.

1 A. CARTER The door swung silently inward on well-oiled hinges. 2 MILTON The winds . . rushed abroad From the four hinges of the world. 3 SWIFT We usually call reward and punishment the two hinges upon which all government turns. J. B. MARSDEN The nature of the sacraments . . was the hinge of the whole controversy with Rome.

II 4 Now *dial.* The pluck (heart, liver, and lungs) of an animal, as used for food. LME.

Comb.: **hinge-pin**: that fastens together the parts of a hinge.

hingeless *a.* E17.

hinge /hɪn(d)ʒ/ *v.* Pres. pple **hinging**, **hingeing**. E17. [f. the n.] 1 *v.t.* Bend (esp. the knee) as a hinge. *rare.* E17. 2 *v.i.* a Depend decisively *on*. E18. b Of a part of a structure: turn (as) on a hinge. L19. 3 *v.t.* Attach or hang (as) with a hinge. Cf. earlier HINGED. M18.

1 SHAKES. *Timon* Be thou a flatterer now, and . . hinge thy knee. 2a C. THIRLWALL The point on which the decision must finally hinge. b D. ATTENBOROUGH When the muscle contracts between these two attachment points, the limb hinges. 3 *fig.*: GOLDSMITH The vulgar . . whose behaviour . . is totally hinged upon their hopes and fears.

hinged /hɪŋ(d)ʒd/ *a.* E17. [f. HINGE *n.* or *v.*: see -ED[2], -ED[1].] Having a hinge or hinges; turning on a hinge or hinges.

hingle /ˈhɪŋg(ə)l/ *n.* Now *Sc.* & *dial.* ME. [f. base of HINGE *v.*: see -LE[1] and cf. MLG, MHG *hengel*, Du. *hengel* fishing-rod, handle, *hengsel* hinge, handle.] A hinge; *esp.* the part of a hinge attached to a door etc.

hinin /ˈhɪnɪn/ *n.* Pl. same. L19. [Jap.] A member of an outcast group in Japan. Cf. ETA *n.*[2]

hinnible /ˈhɪnɪb(ə)l/ *a. rare.* M17. [Late L *hinnibilis*, f. *hinnire* neigh: see -IBLE.] Capable of neighing.

hinnie *n.* var. of HINNY *n.*[2]

hinny /ˈhɪni/ *n.*[1] E17. [L *hinnus* f. Gk *hinnos*, *ginnos*: assim. to HINNY *v.*] An animal born of a mating between a female ass and a stallion.

hinny /ˈhɪni/ *n.*[2] *Sc.* & *north.* Also **hinnie**. E19. [Var. of HONEY *n.*] = HONEY *n.* 3.

singing hinny a currant cake baked on a griddle.

hinny /ˈhɪni/ *v.i.* LME. [(O)Fr. *hennir* f. L *hinnire* neigh (to which it was assim.).] Neigh, whinny.

hinoki /hɪˈnəʊki/ *n.* E18. [Jap.] (The timber of) a tall Japanese cypress, *Chamaecyparis obtusa*.

hint /hɪnt/ *n.* E17. [Prob. alt. of HENT *n.*] †1 An occasion, an opportunity. E17–E19. 2 A slight indication; a covert or indirect suggestion. (Foll. by *of*.) E17. b A small piece of practical information, a tip. L18.

1 SIR W. SCOTT It is my hint to speak. 2 G. VIDAL The hint of a sneer in his voice excited me. J. M. ROBERTS Trivial facts are often the best hints to what is going on. b R. MACAULAY Audrey gave them household hints.

Phrases: *broad hint*: see BROAD *a.* *drop a hint*: see DROP *v.* *take a hint*: see TAKE *v.*

hint /hɪnt/ *v.* M17. [f. the n.] 1 *v.t.* Give a hint of; suggest or indicate indirectly or covertly (*that*); express (something) by a hint or hints. M17. 2 *v.i.* Foll. by *about*, *at*, etc.: give a hint of; refer indirectly to. L17.

1 DICKENS 'I'm sure he is very rich, Fred,' hinted Scrooge's niece. E. M. FORSTER Already at Rome he had hinted to her that they might be suitable for each other. R. G. COLLINGWOOD Nothing was definitely said, but a great deal was hinted. 2 J. CONRAD A few books, with titles hinting at impropriety.

hinter *n.* M17.

hinterland /ˈhɪntəland/ *n.* L19. [G, f. *hinter-* behind + *Land* land.] The often deserted or uncharted district behind a coast or river's banks; an area served by a port or other centre; a remote or fringe area.

Guardian As Clydeside developed . . it attracted labour from its own hinterland and from . . Ireland. H. BASCOM The turbulence of the dangerous hinterlands of rivers and creeks. *fig.*: M. K. BRADBY Unexplored territories . . in the hinterland of their own minds.

hip /hɪp/ *n.*[1] [OE *hype* = MDu. *höpe*, *hüpe* (Du. *heup*), OHG *huf*, (pl.) *huffi* (G *Hüfte*), Goth. *hups*, (pl.) *hupeis*, f. Gmc base rel. to HOP *v.*[1]] 1 The projection of the pelvis and the upper part of the thigh in human beings and quadrupeds; *sing.* & in *pl.*, the circumference of the body at the buttocks. Also, the hip-joint. OE. 2 *Archit.* The arris of a roof from the ridge to the eaves; the triangular area of a sloping roof rising from the end of a rectangular building to meet a longitudinal ridge. LME.

1 W. WHARTON She stands at the edge of the water, with hands on hips. C. PHILLIPS People moved off . . the women walking as though their hips were on swivel joints. *attrib.*: B. BAINBRIDGE He's had a hip replacement. He's got a steel ball-and-socket thing. *hip and thigh*: see *smite hip and thigh* below. **on the hip** *arch.* at a disadvantage. (**smite**) **hip and thigh** (punish) unsparingly. 2 J. S. FOSTER The hip has an external angle greater than 180 degrees.

Comb.: **hip-bath** a bath in which a person can sit immersed up to the hips; **hip-bone** a bone forming the hip, *esp.* the ilium; **hip-boots**: reaching up to the hips; **hip-flask** a flask for spirits etc. (designed to be) carried in the hip-pocket; *hip girdle*: see GIRDLE *n.*[1] 4a; **hip-hole** a hollow dug in the ground to accommodate the hip, for greater comfort when sleeping on the ground; **hip-huggers** hip-hugging trousers; **hip-hugging** *a.* (of trousers etc.) fitting closely to the hips; **hip-joint** the articulation of the head of the thigh-bone with the ilium; **hip-length** *a.* (of a garment) reaching down to the hips; **hip-pocket** a pocket in trousers, a skirt, etc. just behind the hip; **hip-roof**: with the ends as well as the sides inclined; **hip-shot** *a.* having a dislocated hip; lame, disabled; **hip-tile**: specially shaped to be used at the hip of a roof.

hipless *a.* (*rare*) L19.

hip /hɪp/ *n.*[2] Also **hep** /hɛp/. [OE *hēope*, *hīope*, corresp. to OS *hiopo* (Du. *joop*), OHG *hiufa* (G *Hiefe*), f. WGmc.] The fruit of the (esp. wild) rose.

J. H. B. PEEL Country lanes are lined . . with hips and haws.

hip /hɪp/ *n.*[3] *arch. colloq.* Also **hyp**. Pl. **hipps**, **hips**. E18. [f. HYP(OCHONDRIA. Cf. HIP *v.*[3], HYPO *n.*[1]] *sing.* & in *pl.* Depression, low spirits.

C. JOHNSTON That . . sentimental strain gives me the hip.

hip /hɪp/ *n.*[4] & *int.* M18. [Origin unkn.] (A cry or shout) introducing a cheer, chiefly in *hip hip hurray*. Formerly also, (a cry or shout) attracting a person's attention.

hip /hɪp/ *a. slang* (orig. *US*). E20. [Origin unkn. Cf. HEP *a.*] Following the latest fashion in esp. popular and jazz music, clothes, etc., stylish; understanding, aware, (freq. foll. by *to*).
E. JONG He .. threw in a four-letter word to show how hip he was. S. NAIPAUL And now specially for you cool cats out there something real hip.
Comb.: **hip-cat** a person who is hip.
hipness *n.* M20.

hip /hɪp/ *v.*[1] Long *dial.* Infl. **-pp-**. ME. [Corresp. to MLG, Du. *huppen*, LG *hüppen*, (M)HG *hüpfen*, vars. of corresponding forms of HOP *v.*[1]] **1** *v.i.* Hop. ME. †**b** Limp, hobble. Only in LME. **2** *v.t.* Miss, skip, leave out. M18.

hip /hɪp/ *v.*[2]*t.* Infl. **-pp-**. E17. [f. HIP *n.*[1]] **1** Dislocate or injure the hip of (a person or an animal, esp. a horse). Usu. in *pass.* Now chiefly *dial.* Cf. earlier HIPPED *a.*[1] 2. E17. **2** Form (a roof) with a hip or sloping edge. Usu. in *pass.* Cf. HIPPED *a.*[1] 3. M17. **3** Carry on the hip. *US.* E19.

hip /hɪp/ *v.*[3]*t. arch. colloq.* Infl. **-pp-**. M19. [f. HIP *n.*[3] or back-form. f. HIPPED *a.*[2]] Depress, dispirit, sadden.

hip /hɪp/ *v.*[4]*t. rare.* Infl. **-pp-**. E19. [f. HIP *n.*[4]] Shout 'hip' at.
J. H. B. PEEL To hear the farmer yipping and hipping his collie.

hip /hɪp/ *v.*[5]*t. slang* (orig. *US*). Infl. **-pp-**. M20. [f. HIP *a.*] Make (a person) hip; inform, tell, (a person). Cf. earlier HIPPED *a.*[3]
J. KEROUAC Sand must have hipped him quietly .. what was happening with the lovers.

hipe /hʌɪp/ *n.* & *v.* E19. [Perh. f. HIP *n.*[1]] *Cumberland wrestling.* **A** *n.* A throw involving an opponent's being lifted over the thigh. E19. **B** *v.t.* Throw (an opponent) by such a move. E19.

hip-hop /ˈhɪphɒp/ *n.* Orig. *US.* Also **hip hop**. L20. [Redupl. of *hip* used as a jingling refrain: cf. HIP *a.*, BEBOP, HOP *n.*[2]] (The music associated with) a young people's subculture, of Black and Hispanic origin, comprising rap music, graffiti art, break-dancing, a distinctive style of dress, etc.

hip-hop /hɪpˈhɒp/ *adv.* L17. [f. HIP *v.*[1] + HOP *v.*[1]] With a hopping movement; with successive hops.

hipp- *comb. form* see HIPPO-.

hipparch /ˈhɪpɑːk/ *n.* M17. [Gk *hipparkhos*, f. *hippos* horse + *-arkhos* -ARCH.] *Gk Hist.* A commander of cavalry.

hippeastrum /hɪpɪˈastrəm/ *n.* E19. [mod.L, f. Gk *hippeus* horseman + *astron* star.] Any of various tropical American bulbous plants of the genus *Hippeastrum* (family Amaryllidaceae), with showy freq. bright red or crimson flowers. Also called *Barbados lily*.

hipped /hɪpt/ *a.*[1] LME. [f. HIP *n.*[1] + -ED[2].] **1** Of a person etc.: having hips (of a specified kind). LME. **2** Having the hip injured or dislocated. Now chiefly *dial.* M16. **3** Of a roof: constructed with a hip or hips. Cf. HIP *v.*[2] 2. E19.
1 A. TYLER Their wide-hipped khaki skirts. 3 M. GIROUARD The house is 'Queen Anne' in .. its .. hipped roof with gables.

hipped /hɪpt/ *a.*[2] *arch. colloq.* Also **hypped**, †**hypt**. E18. [f. HIP *n.*[3] + -ED[2].] Depressed, low-spirited.
LONGFELLOW What with his bad habits and his domestic grievances he became completely hipped.

hipped /hɪpt/ *a.*[3] E20. [f. HIP *a.* or *v.*[5]: see -ED[1].] Well-informed, knowing, up-to-date, *au fait*; enthusiastic about, keen, fond, (foll. by *on*).
R. MACDONALD He's been hipped on this subject for years.

hippety-hop /hɪpətɪˈhɒp/ *adv.* & *n.* Also (as adv.) **-hoppety** /-ˈhɒpəti/. E19. [f. HIP-HOP *adv.*, with fanciful ending. Cf. HOPPITY *adv.* & *a.*] **A** *adv.* = HIP-HOP *adv.* E19. **B** *n.* A small hop or skip. M20.

hippiatrics /hɪpɪˈatrɪks/ *n.pl. rare.* M17. [Gk *hippiatrikos* f. *hippiatros* veterinary surgeon, f. *hippos* horse + *iatros* healer, physician: see -ICS.] The treatment of diseases of horses.

hippic /ˈhɪpɪk/ *a. rare.* M19. [Gk *hippikos*, f. *hippos* horse: see -IC.] Of or pertaining to horses or (esp.) horse-racing.

hippie *n.* & *a.* var. of HIPPY *n.* & *a.*[1]

hippiedom /ˈhɪpɪdəm/ *n.* Also **hippy-**. M20. [f. *hippie* var. of HIPPY *n.* + -DOM.] The condition or fact of being a hippy; the domain of hippies.

hippish /ˈhɪpɪʃ/ *a. arch. colloq.* Also †**hy-**. E18. [f. HIP *n.*[3] + -ISH[1].] Depressed, low-spirited.
hippishness *n.* L18.

hippo /ˈhɪpəʊ/ *n. colloq.* Pl. **-os**. L19. [Abbrev.] = HIPPOPOTAMUS.

hippo- /ˈhɪpəʊ/ *comb. form* of Gk *hippos* horse: see -O-. Bef. a vowel **hipp-**. Forming ns. and adjs. w. the sense 'of or pertaining to horses'.
hiˈppologist *n.* a student of or expert on horses L19. **hiˈppology** *n.* (*rare*) the branch of knowledge that deals with horses M19. **hippomobile** *n.* (*Hist.*) a horse-drawn vehicle E20. **hiˈppophagy** *n.* the practice of eating horseflesh E19. **hippophil(e)** *n.* a lover of horses M19. **hippoˈphobia** *n.* fear of horses M19. **hiˈppotomist** *n.* a person skilled in horse anatomy M18.

hippoboscid /hɪpəˈbɒsɪd/ *n.* & *a.* L19. [mod.L *Hippoboscidae* (see below), f. HIPPO- + Gk *boskein* feed: see -ID[2].] **A** *n.* Any bloodsucking dipteran fly of the family Hippoboscidae, parasitic on mammals and birds. L19. **B** *adj.* Of, pertaining to, or designating this family. E20.

hippocamp /ˈhɪpəkamp/ *n.* Now *rare.* E17. [f. next.] = HIPPOCAMPUS 2.

hippocampus /hɪpə(ʊ)ˈkampəs/ *n.* Pl. **-pi** /-pʌɪ/. L16. [L f. Gk *hippokampos*, f. *hippos* horse + *kampos* sea-monster.] **1** A fish of the genus *Hippocampus*; a sea horse. L16. **2** A mythical sea-monster, half horse and half fish or dolphin, represented as drawing the chariot of Neptune etc.; a representation of this. E17. **3** *Anat.* A swelling on the floor of each lateral ventricle of the brain, containing folded cortical tissue and forming part of the limbic system. E18.
hippocampal *a.* of or pertaining to the hippocampus of the brain; *esp.* designating the part of the limbic system formed by the hippocampus and associated cortical tissue: M19.

hippocentaur /hɪpə(ʊ)ˈsɛntɔː/ *n.* E16. [L *hippocentaurus* f. Gk *hippokentauros*, f. *hippos* horse + *kentauros* CENTAUR.] = CENTAUR.

hippocras /ˈhɪpəkras/ *n.* LME. [OFr. *ipo-*, *ypocras*, forms of L *Hippocrates* (see next), used for med.L *vinum Hippocraticum* wine strained through a filter called 'Hippocrates' sleeve' (see next).] **1** *Hist.* Wine flavoured with spices. LME. †**2** In full *Hippocras bag.* = HIPPOCRATES' SLEEVE. Only in 17.
1 T. H. WHITE Would you like a glass of hippocras, or some perry?

†**Hippocrates' sleeve** *n. phr.* E17–L18. [tr. L *manica Hippocratis*, f. *Hippocrates* a Gk physician (*c*460–*c*377 BC).] A conical bag of cotton, linen, or flannel, used as a filter. Also called *Hippocras bag*.

Hippocratic /hɪpəˈkratɪk/ *a.* In sense 2 also **h-**. E17. [med.L *Hippocraticus*, f. *Hippocrates*: see prec., -IC.] †**1** *Hippocratic wine*, = HIPPOCRAS 1. Only in 17. **2** Of the face: shrunken and livid (as) on the point of death (as described by Hippocrates). E18. **3** Of or according to Hippocrates; *spec.* designating an oath stating the code of professional medical conduct and ethics, formerly taken by those beginning medical practice. M19.
Hippocratian /-ˈkreɪʃ(ə)n/ *a.* = HIPPOCRATIC M19. **Hippocratical** *a.* = HIPPOCRATIC E17.

Hippocrene /ˈhɪpəkriːn/ *n.* E17. [L *Hippocrene*, Gk *Hippokrēnē* or *Hippou krēnē* (lit. 'fountain of the horse'), a fountain on Mount Helicon sacred to the Muses, fabled to have been produced by a stroke of Pegasus' hoof.] Poetic or literary inspiration.
KEATS O for a beaker .. Full of the true, the blushful Hippocrene.

hippodame /ˈhɪpədeɪm/ *n.* Long *rare* or *obs.* L16. [Gk *hippodamos*, f. *hippos* horse + *damos* a tamer.] †**1** [By confusion.] = HIPPOCAMPUS 2. *rare* (Spenser). Only in L16. **2** A horse-breaker. E17.

hippodrome /ˈhɪpədrəʊm/ *n.* & *v.* L16. [(O)Fr., or L *hippodromus* f. Gk *hippodromos*, f. *hippos* horse + *dromos* race, course.] **A** *n.* **1** In ancient Greece and Rome, a course for chariot- or horse-races. Also, a modern circus. L16. **2** (**H-**.) (The name of) a theatre used for various stage entertainments. L19. **3** A race or contest in which the result is prearranged or fixed. *US slang.* L19. **B** *v.i.* Prearrange or fix the result of a race or contest. Chiefly as *hippodroming* vbl n. *US slang.* M19.

hippogriff /ˈhɪpə(ʊ)ɡrɪf/ *n.* Also †**-gryph**. M17. [Fr. *hippogriffe* f. It. *ippogrifo*, f. as HIPPO- + It. *grifo* griffin, f. late L *gryphus* GRIFFIN *n.*[1]] A mythical creature with the body and hindquarters of a horse and the wings and head of an eagle; a representation of this.
Also †**hippogriffin** *n.* M17–M19.

hippomanes /hɪˈpɒmənìːz/ *n.* E17. [Gk, f. as HIPPO- + *man-* base of *mainesthai* be mad.] A growth said to occur on the head of a newborn foal, used in antiquity as an aphrodisiac.

hippopotamus /hɪpəˈpɒtəməs/ *n.* Pl. **-muses**, **-mi** /-mʌɪ/. ME. [OFr. *ypotame*, med.L *ypotamus*, or its source L *hippopotamus* f. Gk *hippopotamos*, earlier *hippos ho potamios* horse of the river.] A very large heavy short-legged artiodactyl mammal of the family Hippopotamidae; spec. *Hippopotamus amphibius*, which lives in or near rivers and lakes in tropical African grassland and is a gregarious semi-aquatic herbivore having a wide tusked mouth and thick, almost hairless skin.
pygmy hippopotamus: see PYGMY *a.*
hippopoˈtamian *a.* of, belonging to, or suggestive of a hippopotamus M19. **hippopoˈtamic** *a.* = HIPPOPOTAMIAN L18. **hippopotamid** *n.* & *a.* (*Zool.*) (*a*) *n.* any animal of the family Hippopotamidae; (*b*) *adj.* of, pertaining to, or designating this family: L19. **hippopotamine** *a.* = HIPPOPOTAMIAN L19.

hipps *n.pl.* see HIP *n.*[3]

hippuric /hɪˈpjʊərɪk/ *a.* M19. [f. Gk *hippos* horse + *ouron* urine + -IC.] Biochem. *hippuric acid*, a benzoyl derivative of glycine, $C_6H_5CONHCH_2COOH$, found in urine (esp. of herbivores).

hippurite /ˈhɪpjʊrʌɪt/ *n.* E19. [f. mod.L genus name *Hippurites* f. Gk *hippouros* having a tail like a horse, f. *hippos* horse + *oura* tail: see -ITE[1].] = RUDIST *n.*

hippus /ˈhɪpəs/ *n.* L17. [mod.L f. Gk *hippos* tremor of the eyes.] *Ophthalm.* Spasmodic or rhythmic contraction of the pupil of the eye, a symptom of some neurological conditions.

hippy /ˈhɪpi/ *n.* & *a.*[1] Orig. *US colloq.* Also **hippie**. M20. [f. HIP *a.* + -Y[6], -IE. Cf. YIPPIE.] **A** *n.* A person of an unconventional appearance, typically with long hair, jeans, beads, etc., often associated with hallucinogenic drugs and a rejection of conventional values. M20.
T. LEARY Every visible hippy, barefoot, beflowered, beaded.
B *adj.* Of, pertaining to, or characteristic of a hippy or hippies. M20.
J. UPDIKE Hippie Ph.D's who've gone to work in the crafts to spite their fathers.
hippieness *n.* M20.

hippy /ˈhɪpi/ *a.*[2] E20. [f. HIP *n.*[1] + -Y[1].] Having large hips.

hippydom *n.* var. of HIPPIEDOM.

hipster /ˈhɪpstə/ *n.*[1] *slang* (orig. *US*). M20. [f. HIP *a.* + -STER.] A person who is hip.
P. GOODMAN The hipster will often boast: he knows the score, he is ahead of the game.

hipster /ˈhɪpstə/ *a.* & *n.*[2] M20. [f. HIP *n.*[1] + -STER.] **A** *adj.* Of a garment, esp. a pair of trousers: hanging from the hips rather than from the waist. M20. **B** *n.* In *pl.* Hipster trousers. M20.

Hirado /hɪˈrɑːdəʊ/ *a.* Also **-to** /-təʊ/. L19. [An island off the NW coast of Kyushu, Japan.] Designating a form of Hizen ware manufactured on Hirado.

hiragana /hɪrəˈɡɑːnə/ *n.* Also **-kana** /-ˈkɑːnə/. E19. [Jap., f. *hira* plain + KANA.] The form of kana normally used in Japanese, derived from the cursive style of writing. Cf. KATAKANA.

Hirato *a.* var. of HIRADO.

hircarra /hɜːˈkɑːrə/ *n.* Now *rare*. Also **-rah**. M18. [Pers. & Urdu *harkārah* messenger.] In the Indian subcontinent, a spy, a messenger.

hircine /ˈhɜːsʌɪn/ *a.* M17. [L *hircinus*, f. *hircus* he-goat: see -INE¹.] Of, belonging to, or resembling a goat; goatlike.

hircocervus /hɜːkə(ʊ)ˈsɜːvəs/ *n.* LME. [Late L, f. *hircus* he-goat + *cervus* stag.] A mythical animal, half goat, half stag; a representation of this.

hirdy-girdy /ˈhɜːdɪgɜːdi/ *n.* & *adv. Sc.* & *north.* E16. [Imit.: cf. HURDY-GURDY.] A *n.* Uproar, disorder. E16. B *adv.* In or into disorder. L16.

hire /ˈhʌɪə/ *n.* [OE *hȳr* = OFris. *hēre*, OS *hūria*, MLG, MDu. *hūre* (Du. *huur*), f. WGmc.] 1 Payment under contract for the use of something. OE. 2 Payment under contract for personal service; wages. ME. 3 *fig.* Reward, recompense, payment, (for work, service, etc.). ME. 4 The action of hiring or fact of being hired; engagement on agreed terms of payment for use, service, etc. E17.

1 D. WIGODER Regent's Park . . with its rowing boats for hire. *attrib.*: *Sunday Express* Avis . . has hire prices from about £15 per day. 2 AV *Luke* 10:7 The labourer is worthy of his hire. 4 OED To arrange for the hire of a horse.

Phrases: **for hire** available to be hired. **on hire** available to be hired, that has been hired.

Comb.: **hire-car**: available for hire; **hireman** (now only *Sc.*) a hired servant; **hire purchase, hire-purchase system**: by which something hired becomes the hirer's after a certain number of payments.

hireless *a.* (now *rare*) without hire; unhired: M17.

hire /ˈhʌɪə/ *v.* [OE *hȳrian* = OFris. *hēra*, MLG, MDu. *hūren* (Du. *huren*).] 1 *v.t.* Employ (a person) for wages; take on (an employee) for an agreed remuneration (now chiefly *N. Amer.*). OE. b Engage, induce, (a person) to do something by a (promise of) payment or reward; bribe. LME. c Borrow (money). *US.* L18. 2 *v.t.* Procure (*from* a person) the temporary use of (a thing) for stipulated payment. ME. 3 *v.t.* Grant (*out*, *to* a person) the temporary use or employment of (a thing, a person, etc.) for stipulated payment. LME. b *v.i.* Foll. by *out*: engage oneself as a servant for wages. *N. Amer.* M19.

1 W. S. CHURCHILL With his revenues he could hire Swiss infantry. N. MAILER Remind me to hire you if I need a lawyer. **hire and fire** engage and dismiss. b LD MACAULAY A popish priest was hired with the promise of the mitre of Waterford to preach . . against the Act. 2 V. GLENDINNING He and Martha hired a car in Naples. 3 TENNYSON He . . hired himself to work within the fields. b C. A. DAVIS I had hired out here this summer.

hir(e)able *a.* able to be hired M19. **hired** *ppl a.* (*a*) that has been hired; (*b*) *hired girl, man*, etc., (*N. Amer.*) a domestic servant (formerly a free person as opp. to a slave) esp. on a farm: ME. **hirer** *n.* LME.

hireling /ˈhʌɪəlɪŋ/ *n.* & *a.* Usu. *derog.* OE. [f. HIRE *n.* + -LING¹.] A *n.* 1 A person who serves for hire; one motivated chiefly by reward or material remuneration; a mercenary. OE. 2 A hired horse. L19.

1 BYRON Baser hirelings, who live by lies on good men's lives. A. DUGGAN I hoped that the infantry of the line would do better than our Arab hirelings.

B *attrib.* or as *adj.* Of or pertaining to a hireling; serving for hire; mercenary. L16.

¶Rare in OE; not recorded again until 16, when formed afresh, prob. after Du. *huurling*.

†**Hiren** *n.* L16–E17. [A character in Peele's play 'The Turkish Mahamet and Hyrin the fair Greek': alt. of *Irene*, Fr. *Irène*.] A seductive woman; a prostitute.

hirmos /ˈhɜːmɒs/ *n.* Also **heirmos**. Pl. **-moi** /-mɔɪ/, **-mi** /-miː/. M19. [Gk *heirmos* series, connection.] In the hymnology of the Orthodox Church, a model stanza forming a pattern for the other stanzas.

hirola /hɪˈrəʊlə/ *n.* Also **her-**. L19. [Galla.] A small antelope, *Damaliscus hunteri*, native to Kenya and Somalia. Also called *Hunter's hartebeest*.

hirondelle /hɪrɒnˈdɛl/ *n. obs.* exc. *Her.* E17. [Fr.] A swallow; a charge representing this.

hirple /ˈhɜːp(ə)l/ *v.i.* Chiefly *Sc.* & *north.* L15. [Origin unkn.] Walk or move with a gait between walking and crawling; walk lamely, hobble.

Hirschsprung's disease /ˈhɪəʃ(s)prʊŋz dɪˌziːz/ *n. phr.* E20. [f. Harald *Hirschsprung* (1830–1916), Danish paediatrician.] *Med.* Congenital absence of the ganglion cells in a segment of the colon and rectum, causing failure of peristalsis and colonic dilatation by faeces. Formerly also, any abnormal dilatation of the colon.

hirsel /ˈhɜːs(ə)l/ *n.* & *v.* Orig. *Sc.* & *north.* LME. [f. ON *hirzla* safe-keeping, f. *hirða* herd sheep f. Gmc base of HERD *n.*²] A *n.* 1 The collection of sheep under a shepherd's charge or on an individual farm; *fig.* a spiritual flock. *Sc.* & *north.* LME. 2 A company to look after; a collection of persons or things of one kind. *Sc.* & *north.* LME. 3 The ground occupied by a flock of sheep. E19.

3 *Punch* The Scottish hirsel (where the flock grazes all the year round on one hill).

B *v.t.* Form into a hirsel or hirsels. *Sc.* & *north.* L18.

hirsle /ˈhɜːs(ə)l/ *v. Sc.* & *north.* E16. [Origin unkn.] 1 *v.i.* Move or slide esp. with grazing or friction. E16. 2 *v.t.* Move (something) with much effort. E18.

hirst *n.* var. of HURST.

hirsute /ˈhɜːsjuːt/ *a.* E17. [L *hirsutus* rough, shaggy, rel. to synon. *hirtus*.] 1 Having rough or shaggy hair; hairy, shaggy; *transf.* & *fig.* rough, untrimmed. E17. 2 *Bot.* & *Zool.* Covered with long soft or moderately stiff hairs. E17. 3 Of or pertaining to hair; of the nature of or consisting of hair. E19.

1 A. S. BYATT Like many hirsute men he had thinned a little on top.

hirsuteness *n.* E17. **hirsutism** *n.* abnormal hairiness E20.

hirudin /hɪˈruːdɪn/ *n.* E20. [f. L *hirudo* leech + -IN¹.] An anticoagulant protein found in the saliva of leeches and in some snake venoms, which inhibits the action of thrombin in blood-clotting.

hirudinean /hɪrʊˈdɪnɪən/ *n.* M19. [f. mod.L *Hirudinea* (see below), f. *hirudo* leech: see -AN.] *Zool.* An annelid of the class Hirudinea, which comprises the leeches.

hirundine /hɪˈrʌndʌɪn/ *a.* & *n.* M19. [f. L *hirundo* swallow + -INE¹.] A *adj.* Of, pertaining to, or characteristic of a swallow. M19. B *n.* A bird of the swallow family Hirundinidae. L20.

his /hɪz, *unstressed* ɪz/ *possess. pron.*¹ & *a.* (in mod. usage also classed as a *determiner*), *3 sing. masc.* (& †*neut.*). [OE *his* genit. of HE *pron.*, IT *pron.*, with inflection parallel to OS, Goth. *is*, OHG *es* (cf. HIM). Cf. next, HISN.] †A *pron.* Genit. of HE *pron.*; of him. OE–LME.

B *adj.* (*attrib.*) 1 Of him; of himself; which belongs or pertains to him(self). OE. b In titles (as *His Lordship, His Majesty*): that he is. M16. 2 Its. Long *obs.* exc. in personification, passing into sense 1. OE. 3 After a n. (esp. a personal name): substituting for the genit. inflection or possess. suff. -'s¹. *arch.* OE.

1 KEATS The owl, for all his feathers, was a-cold. T. HARDY He went out and resumed his painting. G. GREENE He can't open his mouth without lying. J. C. POWYS Giants of his size were very rare among Mongolian Tartars. E. J. HOWARD He parked his car outside the mews in Hillsleigh Road. A. S. J. TESSIMOND For X is never annoyed Or shocked; has read his Jung and knows his Freud. G. GORDON He touched nothing that any other child had made, only his and Patrick's work. E. BLISHEN She remembered his making a doll's house for his daughters. *his own*: see OWN *a.* & *pron.* *his watch*: see WATCH *n.* 3 CARLYLE It were better for you . . to keep out of Pandarus his neighbourhood.

his /hɪz, *unstressed* ɪz/ *possess. pron.*² OE. [Absol. use of prec. Cf. HISN.] 1 His one(s), that or those belonging or pertaining to him. In early use also, its. OE. 2 *of his*, belonging or pertaining to him or, in early use, it. ME.

1 J. CONRAD His was the soul of obedience. E. WAUGH A tone of voice, . . a swift, epicene felicity of wit, . . these had been his. I. MURDOCH He took her ungloved hand in his. *get his*: see GET *v.* **his and hers** (a pair of matching items intending to be) a husband's and a wife's or a man's and a woman's.

hish /hɪʃ/ *v.i.* Now only *Sc.* & *dial.* LME. [Imit.: cf. HISS *v.*] Hiss, make a hissing noise (*at*).

hisn /ˈhɪz(ə)n/ *possess. pron.* Long *obs.* exc. *dial.* LME. [f. HIS *pron.*² after *my* and *mine*, *thy* and *thine*, etc.] His one(s), that or those belonging or pertaining to him.

Hispanic /hɪˈspanɪk/ *a.* & *n.* L16. [L *Hispanicus*, f. *Hispania* Spain: see -IC.] A *adj.* Of or pertaining to Spain (and Portugal); of or pertaining to Spain and Spanish-speaking countries. L16. B *n.* A Spanish-speaking person, esp. one of Latin American descent, living in the US. Usu. in *pl.* L20.

Hispanically *adv.* M19.

Hispanicise *v.* var. of HISPANICIZE.

Hispanicism /hɪˈspanɪsɪz(ə)m/ *n.* M19. [f. HISPANIC + -ISM.] A Hispanic idiom or characteristic.

Hispanicist /hɪˈspanɪsɪst/ *n.* M20. [f. as prec. + -IST.] = HISPANIST.

Hispanicize /hɪˈspanɪsʌɪz/ *v.t.* Also **-ise**. L19. [f. HISPANIC + -IZE.] Make Hispanic in form or character.

Hispanici'zation *n.* M20.

hispaniolize /hɪˈspanɪəlʌɪz/ *v.t.* Long *rare*. Also **-ise**. L16. [f. Sp. *españolar* make Spanish + -IZE, with assim. to L *Hispania* Spain.] = HISPANIZE.

hispanise *v.* var. of HISPANIZE.

Hispanism /ˈhɪspənɪz(ə)m/ *n.* M20. [f. L *Hispania* Spain + -ISM.] = HISPANICISM.

Hispanist /ˈhɪspənɪst/ *n.* M20. [f. as prec. + -IST.] An expert in or student of Spanish literature, language, and civilization.

hispanize /ˈhɪspənʌɪz/ *v.t.* Also **-ise**. E17. [f. L *Hispanus* Spanish, Spaniard + -IZE.] Make (esp. a person) Spanish in culture, speech, or sympathies.

hispani'zation *n.* M20.

Hispano- /hɪˈspanəʊ/ *comb. form.* [f. L *Hispanus* Spanish: see -O-.] Forming ns. and adjs. w. the sense 'Spanish and', as *Hispano-American*, *Hispano-Arab*, *Hispano-Arabic*, *Hispano-Gothic*, etc.

Hispanophile /hɪˈspanəfʌɪl/ *n.* Also **-phil** /-fɪl/. E20. [f. HISPANO- + -PHIL.] A lover of Spain and Spanish culture.

Hisperic /hɪˈspɛrɪk/ *a.* E20. [f. med.L *Hisperica* (see below). Cf. G *hisperisch*.] Designating a variety of medieval Latin, of which the group of documents entitled *Hisperica Famina* (probably of the 6th cent.) is a notable example, characterized by a highly artificial vocabulary, with many borrowed words.

hispid /ˈhɪspɪd/ *a.*¹ M17. [L *hispidus*: see -ID¹. Cf. (O)Fr. *hispide*.] Now chiefly *Bot.* Covered with short stiff hairs or bristles; bristly.

hi'spidity *n.* M17.

hispid /ˈhɪspɪd/ *a.*² & *n.* E20. [f. mod.L *Hispidae* (former family name), f. *Hispa* (genus name), f. as prec.: see -ID³.] *Entomol.* A *adj.* Of, pertaining to, or designating the subfamily Hispinae of leaf-beetles. E20. B *n.* A leaf-beetle of this subfamily. E20.

hi-spy *n. phr.* see I-SPY.

hiss /hɪs/ *n.* E16. [f. the vb.] 1 A sharp sibilant sound (as of *s*); *spec.* such a sound made to express disapproval or derision. E16. 2 *Phonet.* A sibilant. L19.

1 B. BAINBRIDGE The murmurings of their voices and the hiss of the gas fire merged. M. MEYER His first production there had been repeatedly interrupted by boos, hisses and cries.

hissy *a.* consisting of, accompanied by, or resembling a hiss E20.

hiss /hɪs/ *v.* LME. [Imit. Cf. HISH.] 1 *v.i.* Of a person, animal, or thing: make a sharp sibilant sound (as of *s*). Of a person: make such a sound to express disapproval or derision (foll. by *at*). LME. 2 *v.t.* Drive away by hissing. (Foll. by *away, down, off, out.*) E16. 3 *v.t.* Express disapproval of by hissing. L16. 4 *v.t.* Express by hissing or with a hiss. L18.

1 R. L. STEVENSON I saw snakes, and one . . hissed at me. W. VAN T. CLARK In the silence the fire crackled and hissed when the snow fell into it. *Independent* People in the public gallery have started to hiss when Barbie's defence counsel speaks. **hissing adder** *US* a hognose snake. 2 R. H. SHERARD The first performance of 'Faust', which was hissed off the stage. 4 F. HOWERD The orchestra leader hissed from the pit: 'Do something, or get off!'

hisser *n.* LME. **hissing** *n.* (*a*) the action of the vb; (*b*) *arch.* something that causes or is the object of expressed disapproval or scorn: LME. **hissingly** *adv.* in a hissing manner E17.

his-self /hɪz'sɛlf/ *pron.* Now *dial.* & *colloq.* ME. [f. HIS *a.* + SELF *n.* (reinterpreting *self* in HIMSELF).] = HIMSELF.

hist /hɪst/ *v.*[1] Now *poet.* E17. [f. the int.] 1 *v.t.* Incite, urge (*on*). E17. †2 *v.t.* Summon with the exclamation 'hist!'; summon silently. M17–L18. 3 *v.i.* Be silent. M19.

hist /hʌɪst/ *v.*[2]*t.* Chiefly *US.* Also **h'ist, hyst.** M19. [Var. of HOIST *v.*[1] Cf. HEIST *v.*] Raise aloft (= HOIST *v.*[1] 1); steal, hijack.

hist /hɪst/ *int.* L16. [Natural exclam. Cf. ST, WHISHT.] Calling attention, enjoining silence, inciting a dog etc.

Histadrut /'hɪstʌdruːt/ *n.* Also †**-druth.** E20. [mod.Heb. *ha-histaddĕrūṯ* the federation: in full *ha-histaddĕrūṯ ha-kĕlālīṯ šel hā-'ōbĕḏīm bĕ-'ereṣ Yiśrā'ēl* the general federation of workers in the land of Israel.] A labour organization in the State of Israel, the General Federation of Labour, founded in 1920, and having a large membership of industrial and agricultural workers.

histamine /'hɪstəmiːn/ *n.* E20. [f. HIST(IDINE + AMINE.] *Biochem.* A heterocyclic amine, $C_5H_9N_3$, widespread in animal and plant tissues, which is formed by decarboxylation of histidine, stimulates gastric secretion, smooth muscle contraction, and vasodilation, and is released by mast cells in response to wounding and in inflammatory, allergic, and anaphylactic reactions. Cf. ANTIHISTAMINE.

hister /'hɪstə/ *n.* L18. [mod.L (see below) f. L = actor (from the beetle's pretence of death when alarmed).] Any of numerous small carnivorous or scavenging beetles of the family Histeridae; *esp.* any of the genus *Hister.* Also *hister beetle.*

histerid *a.* & *n.* (*a*) *adj.* of or pertaining to the family Histeridae; (*b*) *n.* any beetle of this family: E20.

histidine /'hɪstɪdiːn/ *n.* L19. [f. Gk *histos* tissue, web + -IDINE.] *Biochem.* A weakly basic heterocyclic amino acid, $C_6H_9N_3O_2$, which occurs in proteins, often at catalytic sites, and is an imidazole derivative.

histiocyte /'hɪstɪəsʌɪt/ *n.* E20. [f. Gk *histion* dim. of *histos* tissue, web + -CYTE.] *Physiol.* A macrophage found in connective tissue and becoming motile when stimulated.

histio'cytic *a.* E20. **histiocy'tosis** *n.*, pl. **-toses** /-'təʊsiːz/, *Med.* any of a number of conditions involving proliferation of histiocytes E20.

histioid /'hɪstɪɔɪd/ *a.* Now *rare* or *obs.* M19. [f. Gk *histion* dim. of *histos* tissue, web: see -OID.] = HISTOID.

histo- /'hɪstəʊ/ *comb. form* of Gk *histos* tissue, web: see -O-.

histo'chemical *a.* of or pertaining to histochemistry L19. **histo'chemically** *adv.* by histochemical means M20. **histo'chemistry** *n.* the branch of science that deals with the chemical properties of tissues and cells, esp. by microscopic examination with staining; the histochemical properties *of* a thing: M19. **histocom'patibility** *n.* (*Med.*) compatibility between the tissue of different individuals, so that one accepts a graft from the other without giving an immune reaction M20. **histocom'patible** *a.* (*Med.*) exhibiting histocompatibility M20. **histo'genesis** *n.* the production and differentiation of organic tissue M19. **histoge'netic** *a.* of or pertaining to histogenesis M19. **histoge'netically** *adv.* as regards histogenesis L19. **hi'stogeny** *n.* = HISTOGENESIS M19. **hi'stolysis** *n.* the disintegration of organic tissue M19. **histo'lytic** *a.* of or pertaining to histolysis M19. **histopatho'logic** *a.* (chiefly *US*) = HISTOPATHOLOGICAL E20. **histopatho'logical** *a.* characterized by or characteristic of diseased tissue; of or pertaining to histopathology: M20. **histopatho'logically** *adv.* as regards histopathology; by histopathological means: E20. **histopa'thologist** *n.* an expert in or student of histopathology E20. **histopa'thology** *n.* the branch of medicine that deals with the tissue changes associated with disease; the tissue changes characteristic *of* a disease: L19. **histo'plasmin** *n.* (*Med.*) a sterile culture of the fungus *Histoplasma capsulatum*, used in skin tests for histoplasmosis M20. **histoplas'mosis** *n.* infection with *Histoplasma capsulatum* (a fungus found esp. in the droppings of birds and bats in humid areas), which may be a transient benign infection of the lungs or a disseminated usu. fatal disease of the reticulo-endothelial system E20. **Histosol** *n.* (*Soil Sci.*) a soil of an order comprising peaty soils, with a deep surface layer of purely organic material L20.

histogen /'hɪstə(ʊ)dʒ(ə)n/ *n.* E20. [f. prec. + -GEN.] *Bot.* Each of three layers (dermatogen, periblem, and plerome) supposedly distinguishable in an apical meristem, which is now usu. regarded as comprising tunica and corpus. Chiefly in *histogen theory.*

histogram /'hɪstəgram/ *n.* L19. [f. Gk *histos* mast, web + -GRAM.] A diagram consisting of a number of rectangles or lines drawn (usu. upwards) from a base line, their heights representing frequencies of a series of values (or value-ranges) of a quantity.

histoid /'hɪstɔɪd/ *a.* L19. [f. Gk *histos* tissue, web + -OID.] *Med.* Resembling (ordinary) tissue.

histology /hɪ'stɒlədʒi/ *n.* M19. [f. HISTO- + -LOGY. Cf. Fr. *histologie* (E19).] The branch of science that deals with the structure and composition of organic tissue, esp. on a microscopic scale; the histological properties *of* a thing.

histo'logic *a.* (chiefly *US*) L19. **histo'logical** *a.* M19. **histo'logically** *adv.* as regards histology M19. **histologist** *n.* M19.

histomap /'hɪstəmap/ *n.* M20. [f. HISTO(RY *n.* + MAP *n.*[1])] A diagram representing the historical development of a religion or a civilization.

histone /'hɪstəʊn/ *n.* L19. [G *Histon*, perh. f. Gk *histanai* arrest or *histos* web, tissue: see -ONE.] Any of a group of simple basic water-soluble proteins that occur associated with DNA in the cell nuclei of eukaryotes.

historian /hɪ'stɔːrɪən/ *n.* LME. [(O)Fr. *historien*, f. L *historia* after *logicien* etc.: see -AN, -IAN.] 1 A writer of history, *esp.* a critical analyst, as opp. to a chronicler or compiler; a person learned in history; a student of history. (Freq. w. specifying wd.) LME. †2 A storyteller. L16–M17.

1 R. SCRUTON Historians discuss the origins of the state. M. SEYMOUR-SMITH When literary historians come to record the development of modernism . . they ignore Graves. *ancient historian, economic historian, French historian, Marxist historian, medieval historian, modern historian, social historian*, etc.

historiated /hɪ'stɔːrɪeɪtɪd/ *a.* L19. [Repr. Fr. *historié* (in same sense) pa. pple of (O)Fr. *historier* †illustrate, f. med.L *historiare* as HISTORY *n.*: see -ATE[3], -ED[1].] Decorated with figures of people, animals, etc. Cf. FLORIATED, STORIATED.

historic /hɪ'stɒrɪk/ *a.* & *n.* E17. [Fr. *historique* or directly f. L *historicus* f. Gk *historikos*, f. *historia* HISTORY *n.*: see -IC.] A *adj.* 1 = HISTORICAL *a.* 1. *arch.* E17. 2 = HISTORICAL *a.* 3. L17. 3 Of great historical importance or fame; having a significance due to connection with historical events. L18. 4 *Gram.* Designating any of various tenses and moods used in the narration of past events, esp. the Latin and Greek imperfect and pluperfect, the Greek aorist, and the Latin perfect used in the sense of the latter. M19.

1 TENNYSON A hoard of tales that dealt with knights, Half-legend, half-historic. 2 M. EDWARDES The historic expectations of the motor industry worker who had grown used to seeing his income rise. *Times Lit. Suppl.* Russian artists . . were fixated by the historic genre. 3 P. GAY Certain historic acts—Napoleon invading Russia . . or Britain abandoning the gold standard in 1931. B. EMECHETA Asaba is . . an old and a very historic town. 4 **historic infinitive** the infinitive when used instead of the indicative. **historic present** the present tense when used instead of the past in vivid narration. *past historic*: see PAST *a.* & *n.*

B *n.* †1 A historian. Only in E17. 2 = HISTORICAL *n. rare.* M19.

historical /hɪ'stɒrɪk(ə)l/ *a.* & *n.* LME. [f. as prec.: see -ICAL.] A *adj.* 1 Of, belonging to, or pertaining to history, esp. as opp. to prehistory or to fiction or legend; of the nature of or in accordance with history. LME. 2 Relating to or concerned with (events of) history. E16. b (Of the study of a subject) based on history or an analysis of development in course of time; in connection with history, from the historian's point of view; belonging to the past, not to the present. L19. 3 Of a novel, a writer, etc.: dealing with events of history; depicting or describing events of history. L16. 4 = HISTORIC *a.* 3. M19. 5 = HISTORIC *a.* 4. *rare.* M19.

1 E. DOWDEN This historical Oldcastle is better known as Lord Cobham. *Sunday Express* The guide provides . . the historical background to the early English colonies. 2 J. B. MOZLEY By the historical imagination I mean the habit of realizing past time. b O. JESPERSEN Descriptive linguistics can never be rendered superfluous by historical linguistics. *American Speech* The utility of full-text data bases for historical-lexicographical research. *historical grammar*: see GRAMMAR *n.* 3 *Observer* Philip Woodruff's *Colonel of Dragoons* . . a very model of what historical fiction ought to be. 4 M. PATTISON It is the old historical lands of Europe that the lover of history longs to explore.

B *n.* A historical work etc.; *esp.* a historical novel. M17.

A. BLAISDELL Donaldson was yawning over a paper-back historical.

historicalness *n.* M17.

historically /hɪ'stɒrɪk(ə)li/ *adv.* M16. [f. HISTORIC or HISTORICAL: see -ICALLY.] In a historic or historical manner, *esp.* relatively to the past.

Economist The yields on copper shares are at historically high levels.

historicise *v.* var. of HISTORICIZE.

historicism /hɪ'stɒrɪsɪz(ə)m/ *n.* L19. [f. HISTORIC + -ISM: tr. G *Historismus.*] 1 The theory that social and cultural phenomena are determined by history. L19. 2 The belief that historical events are governed by laws. E20. 3 The tendency to regard historical development as the most basic aspect of human existence, and historical thinking as the most important type of thought. M20. 4 Excessive regard for the values or styles of the past. M20.

historicist *n.* & *a.* (*a*) *n.* an adherent of historicism; (*b*) *adj.* of or pertaining to historicism or historicists: M20.

historicity /hɪstə'rɪsɪti/ *n.* L19. [f. HISTORIC + -ITY, after *authenticity.*] Historic quality or character; *esp.* the historical genuineness or accuracy of an alleged event etc.

historicize /hɪ'stɒrɪsʌɪz/ *v.t.* Also **-ise.** M19. [f. as prec. + -IZE.] Make or represent as historical.

historicizer *n.* M20.

historico- /hɪ'stɒrɪkəʊ/ *comb. form.* [f. Gk *historikos* historic, historical: see -O-.] Forming adjs. and ns. w. the sense 'historically —', 'historical (and) —', as *historico-critical, historico-geographical, historico-philology.*

historied /'hɪst(ə)rɪd/ *a.* E19. [f. HISTORY *n.*, *v.*: see -ED[2], -ED[1].] 1 Having a history of a specified kind; recorded or celebrated in history. Chiefly *literary.* E19. 2 Decorated with figures, historiated. Cf. HISTORY *v.* 2. L19.

historiette /ˌhɪstɔːrɪ'ɛt/ *n.* Now *arch.* or *joc.* E18. [Fr. f. It. †*istorietta* (now *storietta*), f. †*istoria*, *storia* story: see -ETTE.] An anecdote, a short story or history.

historify /hɪ'stɒrɪfʌɪ/ *v.* L16. [f. HISTORY *n.*: see -FY.] 1 *v.t.* Relate the history of; record or celebrate in history. L16. 2 *v.i.* Write history; utter or write narrative. E17.

historio- /hɪ'stɔːrɪəʊ/ *comb. form.* [Gk, f. *historia* HISTORY *n.*: see -O-.] Forming adjs. w. the sense 'historical and —', as *historio-cultural, -patriotic, historiopoeic*, etc.

†**historiograph** *n.* LME–M18. [f. as HISTORIO-: see -GRAPH.] A historiographer.

historiographer /ˌhɪstɔːrɪ'ɒgrəfə, -stɒr-/ *n.* L15. [(O)Fr. *historiographe* or late L *historiographus* f. Gk *historiographos*, f. *historia* HISTORY *n.*: see -O-, -GRAPHER.] 1 A writer of history, *esp.* the official historian of a court etc. L15. 2 A person who describes or gives a systematic account of some natural object or objects; a writer of natural history. *arch.* M16.

historiographership *n.* the position of a historiographer E19.

historiography /ˌhɪstɔːrɪˈɒɡrəfi, -stɒr-/ *n.* M16. [med.L f. Gk *historiographia*, f. as HISTORIO-: see -GRAPHY.] The writing of history; written history; the study of history-writing.

historioˈgraphic *a.* pertaining to the writing of history E19. **historioˈgraphical** *a.* M17. **historioˈgraphically** *adv.* L19.

historiology /ˌhɪstɔːrɪˈɒlədʒi, -stɒr-/ *n.* L16. [f. HISTORY *n.* + -OLOGY.] The knowledge or study of history.

historize /ˈhɪstərʌɪz/ *v.* Now *rare* or *obs.* Also **-ise**. L16. [f. HISTORY *n.* + -IZE.] **1** *v.t.* Tell the history of; narrate as history. L16. **2** *v.i.* Compose history or narrative; act as a historian. M17.

history /ˈhɪst(ə)ri/ *n.* LME. [L *historia* f. Gk learning or knowing by enquiry, narrative, history, f. *histōr* learned, wise man, ult. f. IE base also of WIT *v.*] **1** A narration of (in later use, esp. professedly true) incidents; a narrative, a story. *obs.* exc. as passing into sense 2. LME. **2** *spec.* The continuous methodical record of important or public events, esp. those connected with a particular country, individual, etc. LME. **3** The branch of knowledge that deals with past events; the formal record or study of past events, esp. human affairs. Freq. w. specifying wd. LME. **4** Orig., a story represented dramatically. Later, a historical play. LME. **5** A story represented pictorially; a historical picture. LME. **6** A systematic account of natural phenomena etc. Now chiefly in *natural history* s.v. NATURAL *a.* M16. **7**†**a** A series of events (of which the story has been or might be told). L16–L17. **b** The whole train of events connected with a nation, person, thing, etc.; an eventful past career. M17. **c** The aggregate of past events; the course of human affairs. M17.

1 T. MEDWIN Some . . pairs of pistols, about most of which there were histories. 2 E. WILSON The first volume or two of Michelet's history, dealing with the early races of Gaul. 3 E. A. FREEMAN History is the science of man in his character as a political being. D. FRASER The name of Dowding . . was soon to take its place in history. C. HOPE Then you understand that history deceives us. *economic history, French history, medieval history, Marxist history, modern history, social history*, etc. 4 E. DOWDEN Both parts of *Henry IV* consist of a comedy and a history fused together. 5 *Listener* A race that . . converted the classical 'history' into a kind of privileged leg show. 7a A. LOVELL Many Figures in Bass Relief, representing several sacred Histories. b D. W. GOODWIN Women who give a history of 'heavy' drinking during pregnancy. J. VIORST People having strikingly similar histories may emerge from them in strikingly different ways. c ISAIAH BERLIN History alone—the sum of empirically discovered data—held the key.

Phrases: *ancient history*: see ANCIENT *a.* 1c. *case history*: see CASE *n.*[1] **drum-and-trumpet history** *derog.*: in which undue prominence is given to battles and wars. **go down in history** be recorded in history, be remembered. **make history** (*a*) influence the course of history; (*b*) do something memorable. *natural history*: see NATURAL *a.*

history /ˈhɪst(ə)ri/ *v.t.* Long *rare.* LME. [(O)Fr. *historier* f. med.L *historiare* (in both senses), f. L *historia* HISTORY *n.*, sense 2 partly through It. *istoriare, -ato.*] †**1** Relate in a history or narrative. LME–L16. **2** Decorate with figures, make historiated. Usu. in *pass.* Cf. HISTORIED 2. L16.

histrio /ˈhɪstrɪəʊ/ *n.* Long *arch. rare.* Pl. **-os.** M17. [L: see next.] = HISTRION.

histrion /ˈhɪstrɪən/ *n.* Now *rare.* M16. [Fr., or L *histrio(n-)* actor.] An actor.

histrionic /hɪstrɪˈɒnɪk/ *a.* & *n.* M17. [Late L *histrionicus*, f. L *histrio(n-)* actor: see -IC. Cf. next (earlier).] **A** *adj.* **1** Theatrical in character or style, dramatically exaggerated, stagy; hypocritical. M17. **2** Of or pertaining to actors or acting; dramatic. M18.

1 H. JAMES Madame Carré gave one of her histrionic stares, throwing back her head. 2 J. SYMONS His histrionic ability might have moved him to become an actor.

B *n.* **1** An actor. M19. **2** In *pl.* Theatricals, theatrical art; pretence, insincere actions done merely to impress others. M19.

2 L. NKOSI The exultant, most extravagant histrionics of the prosecution.

histrionicism *n.* histrionic action; histrionism: L19.

histrionical /hɪstrɪˈɒnɪk(ə)l/ *a.* M16. [f. (as) prec.: see -ICAL.] **1** = HISTRIONIC *a.* 1. M16. **2** = HISTRIONIC *a.* 2. L16.

histrionically /hɪstrɪˈɒnɪk(ə)li/ *adv.* M17. [f. HISTRIONIC *a.* or prec.: see -ICALLY.] In a histrionic manner.

histrionism /ˈhɪstrɪənɪz(ə)m/ *n.* L17. [f. HISTRION or directly f. L *histrio(n-)*: see -ISM.] Theatrical practice, action, or style; an instance of this.

hit /hɪt/ *n.* LME. [f. the vb.] **1** A blow; a shot etc. that hits its target; a stroke in many sports; a collision, an impact. LME. **b** A killing, a robbery. *slang* (orig. *US*). L20. **2** A stroke of sarcasm or censure (*at*). M17. **3** A stroke of good fortune; a lucky chance. M17. **4** *Backgammon.* A game; a win in which the loser has already borne off one or more men. Also, the act of hitting a blot (cf. HIT *v.* 11). L17. **5** An abundant crop of fruit. *dial.* L18. **6** A successful attempt; *esp.* a popular success in public entertainment. Freq. *attrib.* E19. **b** A striking or effective expression; a telling phrase. M19. **c** A successful guess. M19. **d** *Computing.* An instance of identifying an item of data which matches the requirements of a search. M20. **7** A dose of something, esp. a narcotic drug; the action of obtaining or administering such a dose. M20.

1 *base hit, safe hit, square hit*, etc. *direct hit*: see DIRECT *a.* b D. MACKENZIE I . . called the whole thing off. Someone else must have made the hit. 2 A. HELPS In Hudibras there is a sly hit at the sayings of the philosophers. 3 **look to** or **mind one's hits** *arch.* look to one's chances. 6 J. LE CARRÉ An elderly pianist was playing a medley of hits from the Fifties. D. PIPER As a theatrical spectacular there, it proved almost the smash hit of the century. *Melody Maker* Also, that nice Gary Kemp tells how to write light-operatic hit singles. **be** or **make a hit with** be successful or popular with. 7 *Daily Telegraph* In San Francisco's Haight-Ashbury district, the hippie Mecca, the price of one 'hit' has dropped. *Southerly* Somebody hands me a joint and I take a hit.

Comb.: **hit list** *slang* a list of prospective victims esp. of assassination or concerted action; **hit man** *slang* a hired assassin; **hit-mark** *slang* (orig. *US*) the scar from an injection of a drug, esp. a narcotic drug; **hit parade** *colloq.* a list of the best-selling records of popular music; **hit squad** a group of assassins or kidnappers.

†**hit** *pers. pron.* see IT *pers. pron.*

hit /hɪt/ *v.* Infl. **-tt-**. Pa. t. & pple **hit**. LOE. [ON *hitta* light upon, meet with (Sw. *hitta*, Da. *hitte*): ult. origin unkn.] **I 1** *v.t.* Come upon, light on, meet with, find. Now freq. (esp. *N. Amer.*) *colloq.*, go to, start or set out on. LOE. **2** *v.i.* Foll. by *on, upon*: come on, light on, meet with, find, esp. by chance. ME. **3** *v.i.* Attain a desired object, succeed; work out as intended. *obs.* exc. *dial.* LME. **b** Foll. by *off*: produce successfully; succeed in attaining or discovering. L17. **4** *v.t.* Suit, fit, be agreeable to. L16. †**b** *v.i.* Coincide or agree *with.* E17–E18. **c** *v.i.* Agree together. *obs.* exc. *dial.* E17. **5** *v.t.* Represent or imitate exactly. Freq. foll. by *off.* E17.

1 J. WAIN It was still night when I hit the outskirts of London. M. AMIS I hit a topless bar on Forty-Fourth. *New Yorker* You hit forty and have a couple of kids and a mortgage. 2 A. J. P. TAYLOR By chance I had hit on a good subject. 3 SHAKES. *Merch. V.* Hath all his ventures fail'd? What, not one hit? b M. A. KELTY You need to be rather au fait at hitting off a sonnet. *Sporting Magazine* The hounds again hit off the scent. 4 R. W. CHURCH In the hope . . of hitting her taste on some lucky occasion. b DEFOE The Scheme hit so exactly with my Temper. c T. NEVILE Believe me, contraries will never hit. 5 J. L. MOTLEY One of the most difficult things in painting is to hit the exact colour.

II 6 *v.i.* Give or direct a blow or blows; strike *at* or *out.* ME. **b** *v.t.* In various sports, strike (a ball etc.) with a bat, stick, etc., score (a goal) or make (a pass) by so doing; *Cricket* score (a number of runs) by batting (foll. by *off, up*); strike a ball from (the bowler). M19. **7** *v.t.* Strike (a person or thing) with a blow or missile; deliver (a blow or stroke); strike (a person etc. a blow etc.). ME. **b** Knock (a part of the body) *on* or *against* something. M17. **c** Kill, attack, rob. *slang* (orig. *US*). M20. **8** *v.t.* & *i.* Of a moving object: strike against or *against*, collide (with), crash (into). LME. **9** *v.t.* Cast, throw. *obs.* exc. *dial.* LME. **10** *v.t.* & *i. fig.* Affect the feelings, conscience, etc., of (a person), esp. deeply or painfully; hurt. LME. **11** *Backgammon.* Take (an opponent's unguarded piece) temporarily out of play by landing one's own piece on the same point, freq. in *hit a blot* (see BLOT *n.*[2]); *fig.* discover a weak point. L16. **12** *v.t.* & *i.* w. (*out*) *at.* Criticize, ridicule. M19. **13** *v.t.* Occur forcefully to (a person); affect in a particular way; have an impact on. L19. **14** *v.t.* Use (to excess), indulge in. Chiefly in phrs. below. *colloq.* (chiefly *US*). L19. **15** *v.t.* Ask (a person) for; beg. Also foll. by *up. N. Amer.* & *NZ slang.* E20. **16** *v.t.* & *i.* Give a drug, esp. a narcotic drug, or an alcoholic drink to (a person). M20.

6 E. WELTY Fay struck out with her hands, hitting at Major Bullock and Mr. Pitts and Sis. 7 DAY LEWIS I hit him a too effective blow during one of our rough-and-tumbles. H. KISSINGER Our bombing had accidentally hit four Soviet merchant ships. E. WELTY He reached out and without any warning hit Max in the jaw with his fist. b P. F. BOLLER The man fell, . . hit his head against the bar and was knocked unconscious. c D. E. WESTLAKE If they're cops, maybe it's not . . a good idea to have them hit. 8 B. HARRIS When we endeavour to shun one . . Sand-bank, we hit against another. R. INGALLS He didn't come back because he had been hit by a car. *fig.*: TENNYSON The sun, that now . . hit the Northern hills. 10 W. WHARTON Inflation's really hit hard here. H. BASCOM I understand how Uncle Joel's death must have hit you. 12 *Daily Express* He hit out at pay deals which were pushing up wages. 13 W. GASS Like something you see once and it hits you so hard you never forget it. W. SOYINKA I'm asking you what it sounded like. How did the words hit you? 14 *Daily Telegraph* The first thing I do is hit the tub. 15 R. INGALLS They may be planning to hit us for a little loan. 16 A. TYLER 'Hit me again,' the robber told the bartender, holding out his glass.

III 17 *v.t.* Set out for; set off in a particular direction. Now chiefly *US.* LME.

Phrases, & with advs. in specialized senses: *hard hit*: see HARD *adv. hit a blot*: see BLOT *n.*[2] **hit back** retaliate. **hit below the belt** (*a*) esp. in *Boxing*, give (a person) a foul blow; (*b*) *fig.* treat or behave unfairly. *hit for six*: see SIX *n.* 4. **hit home** make a salutary impression. **hit in** *Polo* hit the ball into the field of play. **hit it** (*a*) come to exactly the right place, point, or conclusion; (*b*) (now *rare*) agree or be congenial, get on; (*c*) *hit it off* (*with* or *together*), agree or be congenial, get on (*with, together*). *hit one in the eye*: see EYE *n.* **hit the booze, bottle**, etc., drink to excess. *hit the breeze*: see BREEZE *n.*[2] **hit the bricks** *US slang* go on strike. *hit the ceiling*: see CEILING *n.* **hit the deck** *colloq.* (*a*) go to bed; (*b*) land an aircraft; (*c*) fall to the ground; (*d*) get out of bed, get up. *hit the gong*: see GONG *n.* 3. **hit the hay** *colloq.* go to bed. *hit the headlines*: see HEADLINE 3b. **hit the jackpot** be remarkably lucky, esp. in winning a large prize. **hit the nail on the head** state the truth exactly. **hit the pipe** *US slang* smoke opium. **hit the road** *slang* (chiefly *US*) set off, depart. *hit the roof*: see ROOF *n. hit the sack*: see SACK *n.*[1] 1c. *hit the silk*: see SILK *n.* 6. **hit the trail** *slang* (chiefly *US*) = *hit the road* above. **hit wicket** *Cricket* be out by striking the wicket with the bat etc. in playing a stroke. **not know what hit one, wonder what hit one** be killed instantly, be knocked out or stunned; *fig.* be amazed.

Comb.: **hit-and-miss** *a.* (*a*) aimed or done carelessly, at random, or haphazardly; (*b*) designating ventilators etc. in which the flow of air etc. is controlled by the coincidence or otherwise of apertures in two plates which can move relative to each other; **hit-and-run** *a.* (*a*) designating a motor accident in which the vehicle involved does not stop, or a driver, vehicle, victim, etc., involved in such an accident; (*b*) designating an attack or attacker using swift action followed by immediate withdrawal; (*c*) *Baseball* with the departure of a runner from his or her base as soon as the pitcher begins to throw; **hit-in** *Polo* the hitting of the ball into the field of play; **hit-or-miss** *a.* = *hit-and-miss* above. **hit-out** (*a*) *Hockey* a pass awarded to a defending team to restart play after the ball has been sent over the goal-line (without a goal being scored) by the attacking team; (*b*) *Austral. slang* a brisk gallop.

hitch /hɪtʃ/ *n.* M17. [f. HITCH *v.*] **1** A short abrupt movement, pull, or push; a jerk. M17. **2** *Mining.* A slight fault or dislocation in strata. M17. **3** A limp, a hobble; a fault in a horse's gait. M17. **b** The act of hopping; a hop. *Sc.* & *dial.* L18. **4** An accidental or temporary stoppage; an interruption, an impediment. M18. **5** Any of various (specified) kinds of noose or knot used to fasten one thing temporarily to another. (Earliest in CLOVE HITCH.) M18. **b** A contrivance for fastening something; a catch. L19. **6** The action of catching or fastening in a temporary way. E19. **b** A method of harnessing a horse or team; a vehicle with its horse(s). *N. Amer.* L19. **7** A period of service (as in the armed forces); a spell, a term. *slang* (chiefly *N. Amer.*). M19. **8** = HITCHHIKE *n. colloq.* M20.

4 E. WAUGH The service passed off without a hitch. L. MACNEICE Loath to meet his fate, he cowers and prays For some last-minute hitch. *technical hitch*: see TECHNICAL *a.* 5 **half hitch** *Naut.* a knot formed by passing the end of a rope round its standing part and then through the bight. 6b *Horse International* Each pair of horses in the eight-horse hitch has a specific job. 7 J. KEROUAC Another hitch in prison and you'll be put away for life. 8 J. DOS PASSOS Getting hitches all over the place on graintrucks.

Comb.: **hitch and kick, hitch-kick** (*a*) *Gymnastics* a scissor-jump landing on the take-off foot; (*b*) *Athletics* a style of long jump in which the jumper makes two or more strides in the air before landing feet together.

hitch /hɪtʃ/ *v.* ME. [Origin unkn. Cf. HOTCH *v.*] **1** *v.t.* Move or lift *up* with a jerk; shift a little or aside. ME. **b** *v.i.* Move jerkily; shift one's position a little. Formerly also, jerk the body up and down. E16. **c** *v.t.* & *i. fig.* Move into some position; *spec.* insert or interpolate (a passage etc.) in a literary work, esp. in order to expose or ridicule. Also foll. by *in*, *into*. *arch.* M18. **2** *v.i.* Limp, hobble. Also (*Sc.* & *dial.*), hop. E16. **b** Of a horse: strike the feet together in going; brush. L17. **3** *v.i.* Catch on something; become caught or stopped by an obstruction. L16. **4** *v.t.* Catch as with a noose, loop, or hook; fasten, esp. temporarily and against force acting in one direction. E17. **5a** *v.i.* Foll. by *up*: harness a draught animal or team to a vehicle. E19. **b** *v.t.* Harness (a draught animal or team, a vehicle). Foll. by *up*. M19. **6** *v.t.* & *i.* Obtain (a lift, a ride) in or on (a vehicle); travel by this means, hitchhike. L19.

1 T. SHARPE Sir Godber hitched his chair forward. K. WILLIAMS I hitched up my sodden trousers and sat down. b E. WELTY 'I can see him coming . . ,' said Aunt Nanny, hitching forward in her rocker. c J. ADAMS If . . the letter should be caught and hitched into a newspaper. 2 *fig.*: *Examiner* A hitching verse or hobbling rhyme. 3 W. IRVING The lariat hitched on one of his ears, and he shook it off. *fig.*: SIR W. SCOTT Despatched all my sheriff processes, save one, which hitches for want of some papers. 4 R. OWEN Sometimes the crab hitches one of its claws into some crack or fissure. Z. GREY Several cowboy broncos stood hitched to a railing. 5a E. E. HALE He would hitch up at once and drive over to Elyria. *fig.*: J. O'FAOLAIN You never knew what class of customer Michael would hitch up with. b W. CATHER Old Ivar was hitching the horses to the wagon. 6 T. PYNCHON Let me hitch a ride with you guys. N. GORDIMER Don't send an air ticket or the train fare. I'll hitch.

Phrases: **get hitched (up)** *colloq.* get married **hitch horses (together)** *US colloq.* get on well together, act in harmony. **hitch one's wagon to a star** make use of powers higher than one's own.

Comb.: **hitching-post, -rail**, a fixed post, rail, for tethering a horse; **hitch pin**: to which the fixed end of a piano string is fastened.

hitcher *n.* (*a*) a person who or thing which hitches one thing to another; (*b*) a hitchhiker: M17.

Hitchcock /ˈhɪtʃkɒk/ *a.* E19. [L. H. *Hitchcock* (1795–1852), Amer. furniture manufacturer.] Designating a type of wooden chair, typically painted with stencilled decoration, as made in Hitchcock's factory at Barkhamsted, Connecticut.

Hitchcockian /hɪtʃˈkɒkɪən/ *a.* M20. [f. *Hitchcock* (see below) + -IAN.] Characteristic of or resembling Sir Alfred Hitchcock, British director of suspense films (1899–1980), or his work.

hitchhike /ˈhɪtʃhʌɪk/ *v.* & *n.* Orig. *US.* Also **hitch-hike**. E20. [f. HITCH *v.* + HIKE *v.*] **A** *v.i.* Travel, obtain transport, by begging a free ride in a passing vehicle. E20.

J. GATHORNE-HARDY I would . . hitch-hike and get a lift with someone I'd never seen before.

B *n.* A journey made by hitchhiking. E20.

hitchhiker *n.* E20.

hithe /hʌɪð/ *n.* Long *obs.* exc. *Hist.* & in place-names. Also **hythe**. [OE *hȳþ*, OS *hūþ*, MLG *-hude* (in place-names), of unkn. origin.] A port, a haven, *esp.* a small landing-place in a river.

hither /ˈhɪðə/ *adv.*, *a.*, & *v.* Chiefly *literary.* [OE *hider*, corresp. to ON *heðra* here, hither, Goth. *hidrē*, f. Gmc demonstr. base of HE *a.*, HENCE *adv.*, HERE *adv.*, + suff. appearing in L *citra* on this side. Cf. THITHER, WHITHER *adv.* etc.] **A** *adv.* **1** To or towards this place, here. OE. **b** To or on this side. *rare.* M19. †**2** Up to this point (of time, a discourse, etc.); thus far, hitherto. LME–E17. †**3** To this end or result; to this subject or category. M16–L17.

1 R. CROWLEY Come hither unto me. T. GRAY Till my return hither yesterday. *come-hither*: see COME *v.* **hither and thither, hither and yon**, this way and that, here and there, to and fro.

B *adj.* Situated on this side; the nearer (of two). ME.

Comb.: **hitherside** this side, the nearer side.

C *v.i.* Come hither. Chiefly in *hither and thither*, go to and fro. M19.

hithermost *a.* nearest M16.

hitherto /hɪðəˈtuː, ˈhɪðətuː/ *adv.* & *a.* ME. [f. HITHER *adv.* + TO *prep.*] **A** *adv.* **1** Up to this time, until now, as yet. ME. **2** Up to this point (in space, a discourse, writing, etc.); thus far. *arch.* ME. †**3** To this end or purpose; to this class or subject. E–M17.

1 HOBBES Except the vulgar be better taught than they have hetherto been. S. MORLEY Evening sing-songs produced some hitherto hidden talents. *Sunday* (*Calcutta*) The minimum time between . . issues would now be 24 months against 36 months hitherto. 2 S. JOHNSON Hitherto shall ye come and no further.

B *adj* Existing at or until this time. *rare.* L18.

hitherward /ˈhɪðəwəd/ *adv. arch.* LOE. [f. HITHER + -WARD.] **1** Towards this place, in this direction, hither. LOE. **b** On this side (*of*). M19. †**2** Up to this time, until now. ME–M16.

Also **hitherwards** *adv.* ME.

Hitler /ˈhɪtlə/ *n.* M20. [Adolf *Hitler* (1889–1945), leader of the Nazi Party and Chancellor of the German Reich. Cf. FÜHRER.] **1** Used *attrib.* and in *possess.* with ref. to Hitler's rule or personal characteristics. M20. **2** A tyrannical ruler or leader; a dictatorial person (freq. in *little Hitler*). M20.

1 **Hitler moustache** a small square moustache as worn by Hitler. **Hitler salute** = *Nazi salute* s.v. NAZI *a.* **Hitler's war** the war of 1939–45. **Hitler Youth (Movement)** the young persons' organization of the Nazi party, membership of which was compulsory under the Third Reich.

Hitlerian /hɪtˈlɪərɪən/ *a.* of, pertaining to, or characteristic of Hitler M20. **Hitlerism** *n.* the political principles or policy of the Nazi party in Germany M20. **Hitlerist** *n.* & *a.* (*a*) *n.* a follower of Hitler; (*b*) *adj.* resembling Hitler or his followers: M20. **Hitleˈristic** *a.* somewhat Hitlerist M20. **Hitlerite** *n.* & *a.* = HITLERIST M20.

Hittite /ˈhɪtʌɪt/ *n.* & *a.* M16. [f. Heb. *Ḥittī(m*, Hittite *Ḫatti* + -ITE[1].] **A** *n.* **1** In biblical use, a member of a Canaanite or Syrian tribe, perhaps a part of sense 2. M16. **2** A member of an ancient powerful (non-Semitic) people of Asia Minor or Syria, or of their subject peoples. L19. **b** The Indo-European language of this people. L19. **B** *adj.* Of or pertaining to the Hittites or their language. L19.

Hittiˈtologist *n.* an expert in or student of Hittite philology, archaeology, or history M20. **Hittiˈtology** *n.* the branch of knowledge that deals with Hittite philology, archaeology, or history M20.

hitty-missy /hɪtɪˈmɪsi/ *adv.* & *a.* Now *rare.* M16. [Perh. f. *hit I, miss I*: cf. WILLY-NILLY.] **A** *adv.* Hit or miss, haphazardly, at random. M16. **B** *adj.* Random, haphazard. L19.

hive /hʌɪv/ *n.* [OE *hȳf* f. Gmc base of ON *húfr* ship's hull: cf. L *cupa* barrel.] **I 1** An artificial structure to house a colony of bees. Also *beehive*. OE. **b** *fig.* A storehouse of sweet things. M17. **2** Something resembling this structure in (esp. domed) shape or design. M16. **3** A structure to house any gregarious livestock. *rare.* M17. **4** A place swarming with busy occupants. M17. **b** A place from which multitudes of people emerge. L18.

1 T. HOOPER Bees have been kept . . in earthenware pipes, straw skeps, wooden boxes and all types of hive. b G. HERBERT Must he leave that nest, that hive of sweetnesse. 4 J. HIGGINS The place was a hive of activity, workmen everywhere. b J. PRIESTLEY They no longer send forth those swarms of people . . which made them be called the northern hive.

II 5 Bees in a hive collectively. LME. **6** A swarm of people, a multitude. M19.

5 SHAKES. *2 Hen. VI* The commons, like an angry hive of bees That want their leader, scatter up and down.

hive /hʌɪv/ *v.* LME. [f. the n.] **1** *v.t.* House (bees) in a hive; place (a swarm) in a hive. LME. **b** Give shelter to, house snugly. L16. **2** *v.i.* Enter a hive; live together as bees in a hive. LME. **3** *v.t.* Hoard or store *up*, as honey in a hive. L16. **4a** *v.i.* Foll. by *off*: swarm off like bees; break away or separate from a group. M19. **b** *v.t.* Foll. by *off*: remove from a larger unit or group; form into or assign (work) to a subsidiary department or company; denationalize or privatize (an industry etc.). M20.

1 *Beekeeping* Smoke is used to subdue, . . bees . . when taking and hiving a swarm. b C. BRASCH I think of you Hived in another cell of this same House of pain and healing. 2 H. VAUGHAN Where bees at night get home and hive. POPE We are . . forc'd to . . get into warmer houses and hive together in cities. 3 BYRON And hiving wisdom with each studious year. 4a *Nature* Experimental psychology . . has hived off from physiology. b *Sunday Mail* (*Brisbane*) The ginger beer plant was preserved, and new ones could be hived off at this stage. *Fremdsprachen* The Arts Council itself cannot be hived off like British Telecommunications.

hives /hʌɪvz/ *n.* (treated as *sing.* or *pl.*). Orig. *Sc.* E16. [Origin unkn.] *Med.* Orig., any of various conditions, esp. of children, characterized by a rash. Now *spec.* urticaria.

hiya /ˈhʌɪjə/ *int. colloq.* Also **hi-ya, hiyah**. M20. [App. contr. of *how are you*, infl. by HI *int.* 2.] As a word of greeting: hello.

R. CHANDLER Hiya, babe. Long time no see.

Hizbollah, Hizbullah *ns.* vars. of HEZBOLLAH.

Hizen /hiːˈzɛn/ *n.* & *a.* L19. [A former province in the north-west of Kyushu in Japan.] (Designating) a class of high-quality porcelains characterized by rich decoration and delicate colouring, and including Hirado, Imari, and Nabeshima ware.

hizz /hɪz/ *v.i.* Now *rare.* L16. [Imit.: cf. HISS *v.*] = HISS *v.*

ho /həʊ/ *n.*[1] LME. [f. HO *int.*[1]] A cry of 'ho'.

ho /həʊ/ *n.*[2] Now *rare.* LME. [f. HO *int.*[2]] (A) halt; (a) pause; (a) limit.

SWIFT When your tongue runs, there's no ho with you.

Ho /həʊ/ *n.*[3] & *a.* Pl. of n. **Hos**. M19. [Ho, contr. of *horo* man.] Of or pertaining to, a member of, a people of the State of Bihar in India; (of) the language of this people, one of the principal dialects of central India, belonging to the Kolarian group.

ho /həʊ/ *int.*[1] See also HO HO. ME. [Natural exclam. Cf. HA *int.*, HOW *int.*[1], etc.] **1** Expr. surprise, admiration, triumph, or derision. ME. **2** Commanding or attempting to attract attention. LME. **b** Used after the name of a place or thing to which attention is called, esp. as a destination. L16. **3** Used as the 2nd elem. of other ints., as *heave-ho*, *heigh-ho*, *what ho*, etc. LME.

1 *Times Lit. Suppl.* If it be philistine to prefer gourmet dishes . . to a poetry reading . . , then ho for Philistia! 2 LD MACAULAY Ho! gunners, fire a loud salute. b C. KINGSLEY Thou too shalt forth, and westward ho, beyond thy wildest dreams. ALAN BENNETT They are rubbish, waste, junk. . . Dustbin ho!

ho-de-ho /həʊdɪˈhəʊ/ *int.* responding to the greeting HI-DE-HI M20.

ho /həʊ/ *int.*[2] Now *rare.* LME. [OFr. = halt! stop! Cf. WHOA.] Ordering or requesting a person or animal to stop.

wo ho, wo ho ho, wo ha ho: see WO *int.* 1.

Hoabinhian /həʊəˈbɪnɪən/ *a.* & *n.* M20. [f. *Hoabinh* a village in Vietnam where the first major site was found + -IAN.] (Designating or pertaining to) a mesolithic and neolithic culture of parts of SE Asia, characterized by stone tools.

hoactzin *n.* var. of HOATZIN.

hoagie /ˈhəʊgi/ *n.* *N. Amer.* M20. [Origin unkn.] A long loaf or roll filled with meat, cheese, salad, etc.

hoar /hɔː/ *a.*, *n.*, & *v.* [OE *hār* = OS, OHG *hēr* old, venerable (G *hehr* august, stately, sacred), ON *hárr* hoary, old f. Gmc, f. IE stem meaning 'shine'.] **A** *adj.* **1** Grey-haired or (of a thing) grey with age; ancient, venerable. OE. **2** Esp. of hair, or of a thing covered with frost: grey, greyish-white. OE. **3** Of a tree or wood: grey from absence of foliage or because covered in lichen. Long *arch.* & *poet.* ME. **4** Grey with mould; mouldy, musty. *obs.* exc. *dial.* LME.

1 R. JEFFERIES A very old hare, quite hoar with age. H. C. ADAMS To trace legends back to yet more hoar antiquity. **2** COLERIDGE Whose beard with age is hoar. W. DE LA MARE A northern wind had frozen the grass; its blades were hoar with crystal rime.

Comb.: **hoar-frost** frozen (in *Meteorol.*, distinctly crystalline) water vapour deposited in clear still weather on grass etc.; **hoarhead** *arch.* a hoary head; an old or grey-haired person; **hoar-headed** *a.* grey-haired; **hoarstone** an ancient stone, esp. as marking a boundary.

B *n.* †**1** A grey-haired person. OE–ME. **2** Hoariness; hoary appearance; hoar-frost. LME.

†**C** *v.t.* & *i.* Make or become hoary. OE–M18.

hoard /hɔːd/ *n.*[1] [OE *hord* = OS *hord*, *horþ* treasure, secret place, OHG *hort*, ON *hodd*, Goth. *huzd*, f. Gmc.] **1** A collection, esp. of valuable items, hidden or stored for preservation or future use; a stock, a store, esp. of money; an amassed stock of facts etc. OE. **2** A place in which items are hoarded; a hiding place; a treasury. *obs.* exc. *Hist.* ME.

1 D. WILSON A large hoard of coins was discovered. WORDSWORTH A hoard of grievances.

hoard /hɔːd/ *n.*[2] Now *rare* or *obs.* M18. [Prob. ult. f. AN *hourdis*, *hurdis* (taken as pl.) f. OFr. *hourd*, *hort* (f. Frank., = OHG *hurt* HURDLE *n.*) + *-is* f. L *-itius* (see -ICE[1]).] = HOARDING *n.*[2]

hoard /hɔːd/ *v.* OE. [f. HOARD *n.*[1]] **1** *v.t.* Collect and hide or store (esp. valuable items) for preservation, security, or future use; treasure *up* (esp. money); store in the mind etc. OE. **2** *v.i.* Hoard things. OE.

1 D. BOGARDE She hoards everything. Envelopes, string, elastic bands and so on. *fig.*: BURKE Revenge will be smothered and hoarded. **2** TENNYSON A savage race, That hoard, and sleep, and feed, and know not me.

hoarder *n.* †(*a*) the keeper of a hoard, a treasurer; (*b*) a person who hoards (esp. money): OE.

hoarding /ˈhɔːdɪŋ/ *n.*[1] L16. [f. HOARD *v.* + -ING[1].] **1** The action of HOARD *v.* L16. **2** In *pl.* Things hoarded. E18.

hoarding /ˈhɔːdɪŋ/ *n.*[2] E19. [f. HOARD *n.*[2] + -ING[1].] A temporary fence (of boards) round a building during erection or repair, often used for displaying advertisements or notices; a structure for displaying advertisements.

hoarse /hɔːs/ *a.* & *adv.* [OE *hās* = OFris. *hās*, MLG *hēs*, *hēsch* (Du. *heesch*), OHG *heis*(*i*, (M)HG *heiser*, f. Gmc: ult. origin unkn. Superseded in ME by forms with *-r-* f. ON cognate.] **A** *adj.* (Of a voice or (chiefly *poet.*) other sound) rough and deep-sounding, husky, croaking, harsh; having such a voice or sound. OE.

DICKENS Cloisterham, with its hoarse cathedral bell. OUIDA The hoarse sound of the sea surging amongst the rocks. L. M. MONTGOMERY She lay . . feverish and restless, while her hoarse breathing could be heard all over the house. I. COMPTON-BURNETT I have been calling until I am hoarse. R. OWEN He grins, and drinks wine to soothe a voice hoarse from poetry readings.

B *adv.* Hoarsely. *rare.* E18.

hoarsely *adv.* LME. **hoarseness** *n.* OE.

hoarse /hɔːs/ *v.i.* & *t.* *obs.* exc. *dial.* OE. [f. the adj.] Hoarsen. Latterly only foll. by *up*.

hoarsen /ˈhɔːs(ə)n/ *v.* M18. [f. HOARSE *a.* + -EN[5].] **1** *v.t.* Make hoarse. M18. **2** Be or become hoarse. L18.

hoary /ˈhɔːri/ *a.* LME. [f. HOAR *a.* or *n.* + -Y[1].] **1** (Of hair) grey or white with age; grey-haired; ancient, venerable. Also, old and trite. LME. **2** Grey, greyish-white, esp. with frost. L15. †**3** Mouldy, musty. M16–L17. **4** *Bot.* & *Zool.* Covered with short dense white or whitish hairs. L16.

4 hoary marmot a large stocky greyish-brown marmot, *Marmota caligata*, of mountains in north-western N. America (also called *siffleur*, *whistler*).

hoariness *n.* LME.

hoast /həʊst/ *n.* & *v.* Chiefly *Sc.* & *north.* ME. [ON *hóste* = MLG *hōste*, MDu. *hoeste*, OHG *huosto* (G *Husten*), f. Gmc.] **A** *n.* A cough. ME. **B** *v.* **1** *v.i.* Cough. LME. **2** *v.t.* Cough *up* or *out.* E16.

Hoastman /ˈhəʊstmən/ *n.* *local.* Pl. **-men.** E16. [f. HOST *n.*[2] II + MAN *n.*] Orig., a member of a guild in Newcastle-upon-Tyne who had the duty of receiving visiting merchants. Later, a member of a body controlling the sale of coal. Now, a member of the premier civic corporation.

hoatzin /həʊˈatsɪn/ *n.* Also (earlier) **hoactzin** /-kt-/. M17. [Amer. Sp. f. Nahuatl *uatzin*, prob. imit.] A large crested bird of S. American rainforests, *Opisthocomus hoazin*, of uncertain affinities, the young of which climb by means of claws on the wings.

hoax /həʊks/ *v.* & *n.* L18. [Prob. contr. of HOCUS *v.*] **A** *v.* **1** *v.t.* Deceive by way of a joke, play a trick or joke on. L18. **2** *v.i.* Perpetrate a hoax. E19.

B *n.* A mischievous or humorous deception; a trick, a joke. E19.

Sunday Express There was also a hoax involving a tailor's dummy dressed as a Russian officer. *attrib.*: R. INGALLS There had been a hoax call about a bomb at some large public building.

hoaxer *n.* E19.

hob /hɒb/ *n.*[1] LME. [f. *Hob* by-form of *Rob*, abbrev. of the names *Robert*, *Robin*: cf. HICK *n.*[1], HOBBY *n.*[1], HODGE *n.*] **1** (Also **H-**.) (A name for) a country fellow, a rustic. Now *dial.* LME. **2** A hobgoblin, a sprite; *spec.* (also **H-**) Robin Goodfellow. Now *rare.* LME. **3** A male ferret. Also *hob ferret.* L17.

Phrases: **play** or **raise hob** (chiefly *US*) cause mischief.

hob /hɒb/ *n.*[2] L16. [Alt. of HUB *n.*[1]] **I 1** A peg or pin used as a mark or target in games, esp. quoits. Also, a game using these. L16. **2** = HOBNAIL *n.* 1. L17. **3** The shoe of a sledge. L18. **4** A (rotating) cutting tool used for cutting gears, worm-wheels, etc. Also, a pattern for making a mould or die in cold metal. L19. **II 5** A side casing of a fireplace, having a surface level with the top of the grate. Cf. earlier HUB *n.*[1] 1. L17. **6** The top surface of a cooker or a separate cooking surface equipped with hotplates or burners. Also, a level support or set of supports on which a pan etc. is rested over a hotplate or burner on a cooker. M20.

hob /hɒb/ *v.*[1]*i.* Infl. **-bb-.** E17. [f. as HOB *adv.* & *n.*[3]] †**1** *3 sing. pres. subjunct.* Give (in *hob, nob*, give or take). *rare* (Shakes.). Only in E17. **2** *hob and* (or *or*) *nob*: **a** = HOBNOB *v.* 1. M18. **b** = HOBNOB *v.* 2. E19.

hob /hɒb/ *v.*[2]*t.* Infl. **-bb-.** M19. [f. HOB *n.*[2]] **1** Equip with hobnails. M19. **2** Cut or form by means of a hob (HOB *n.*[2] 4). L19.

hob /hɒb/ *adv.* & *n.*[3] M17. [Var. of HAB.] **1** See HOB-NOB *adv.* M17. **2** *hob and* (or *or*) *nob*: expr. good wishes to another person before drinking. *drink hob and* (or *or*) *nob*, drink to each other alternately, with clinking of glasses. *arch.* M18.

Comb.: **hob-and-nob** *a.* (*arch.*) companionable, on intimate terms; **hob-or-nob** *arch.* = HOB-NOB *n.* 2.

hobbadehoy *n.* var. of HOBBLEDEHOY.

Hobbesian /ˈhɒbzɪən/ *a.* L18. [f. *Hobbes* (see below) + -IAN.] Of or pertaining to the English political philosopher Thomas Hobbes (1588–1679) or his philosophy.

†**Hobbian** *a.* & *n.* L17. [f. *Hobb*(*es* (see prec.) + -IAN.] **A** *adj.* = HOBBESIAN. Only in L17. **B** *n.* = HOBBIST *n.* L17–M19.

†**Hobbianism** *n.* = HOBBISM M17–E18.

Hobbism /ˈhɒbɪz(ə)m/ *n.* L17. [f. *Hobb*(*es* (see HOBBESIAN) + -ISM.] The philosophy or principles of Thomas Hobbes.

Hobbist *n.* & *a.* (*a*) *n.* an advocate or follower of Hobbes's philosophy; (*b*) *adj.* = HOBBESIAN: L17.

hobbit /ˈhɒbɪt/ *n.* M20. [Invented wd: said by Tolkien to mean 'hole-builder'.] In the stories of J. R. R. Tolkien (1892–1973): a member of a fictional race related to humans, characterized by their small size and hairy feet.

hobble /ˈhɒb(ə)l/ *n.* E18. [f. the vb.] **1** The action of hobbling; an uneven, unsteady, or feeble gait. E18. **2** An awkward situation. Now *arch.* & *dial.* L18. **3** A rope, strap, block of wood, etc., used for hobbling a horse or similar animal. Usu. in *pl.* Cf. HOPPLE *n.* L18. **4** In full *hobble skirt.* A close-fitting skirt so narrow at or near the hem as to impede walking. E20.

1 SWIFT One of his heels higher than the other; which gives him a hobble in his gait. **2** B. FRANKLIN A fine Hobble they are all got into by their unjust and blundering Politics. **3** *fig.*: P. CAREY City women . . released from the hobble of high heels.

Comb.: **hobblebush** a N. American viburnum, *Viburnum alnifolium*, with clusters of white flowers and purple-black berries; **hobble chain** (chiefly *Austral.*) a chain used for hobbling a horse etc.; *hobble skirt*: see sense 4 above.

hobble /ˈhɒb(ə)l/ *v.* ME. [Prob. of LG origin (cf. early Du. *hobbelen* toss, rock from side to side, halt, stammer, frequent. of *hobben*). In sense 5 var. of HOPPLE *v.*] **1** *v.i.* Move unsteadily, esp. up and down; wobble. Formerly also (of a boat) rise and fall on the sea. Now *rare.* ME. **2** *v.i.* Walk with an uneven, unsteady, or feeble gait; limp. LME. **b** Dance, esp. clumsily. Now *rare* or *obs.* M16. **3** *v.i.* Proceed haltingly or lamely in action or speech. Now *rare.* E16. **4** *v.t.* Cause to hobble; *esp.* hinder, interfere with, foil, perplex. M18. **5** *v.t.* Tie or fasten together the legs of (a horse etc.) to prevent it straying, kicking, etc., or to regulate its pace in a race; tie or fasten together (the legs of a horse etc.) with this purpose. M18.

2 D. M. THOMAS An old and stooping nun had hobbled out with a basket of linen to wash. **4** A. COOKE The endless tedious chores that hobble the days and nights of royalty. *Nature* Progress on the clean-up is . . being hobbled by . . financial difficulties. **5** A. HALEY He remembered awakening . . and finding himself gagged, . . and his ankles hobbled with knotted rope.

hobblingly *adv.* in a hobbling manner E17.

hobbledehoy /ˈhɒb(ə)ldɪˌhɔɪ/ *n.* *colloq.* Also **hobbade-** /ˈhɒbədɪ-/ & other vars. M16. [Origin unkn.] A clumsy or awkward person, esp. a youth.

M. HARRIS Some of the town kids looked upon us as a bunch of hobbledehoys.

hobbledeˈhoydom *n.* the condition of a hobbledehoy, adolescence L19. **hobbledeˈhoyhood** *n.* = HOBBLEDEHOYDOM M19. **hobbledeˈhoyish** *a.* like a hobbledehoy E19. **hobbledeˈhoyism** *n.* = HOBBLEDEHOYDOM M19.

hobbler /ˈhɒblə/ *n.*[1] *obs.* exc. *Hist.* ME. [AN *hobeleor*, *-lour* = AL *hobellarius*, irreg. f. as HOBBY *n.*[1]: see -ER[2].] A retainer maintaining a small horse or pony for military service; a light horseman.

hobbler /ˈhɒblə/ *n.*[2] L16. [f. HOBBLE *v.* + -ER[1].] †**1** A child's top that wobbles or spins unsteadily. L16–M19. **2** A person who hobbles. *rare.* M17. **3** An unlicensed boatman or pilot, a hoveller. *obs.* exc. *Hist.* M19.

hobby /ˈhɒbi/ *n.*[1] LME. [By-form of *Robbie* abbrev. of the name *Robert*: cf. HOB *n.*[1]] **1** A small horse, a pony. *arch.* LME. **2** = HOBBY-HORSE *n.* 4. L17. **3** = HOBBY-HORSE *n.* 1. M18. **4** A favourite subject or occupation that is not one's main business; a spare-time activity followed for pleasure or relaxation. Cf. earlier

HOBBY-HORSE 5. E19. 5 *Hist.* = VELOCIPEDE 1. E19.

4 P. G. WODEHOUSE Kirk's painting had always been more of a hobby with him than a profession. M. IGNATIEFF Trade and industry were interesting hobbies but not serious vocations.

hobbyism *n.* pursuit of or devotion to a hobby or spare-time activity M19. **hobbyist** *n.* a person pursuing or devoted to a hobby or spare-time activity L19.

hobby /ˈhɒbi/ *n.*[2] LME. [OFr. *hobé*, *hobet* dim. of *hobe* falcon (cf. Fr. *hobereau*), prob. rel. to *hobeler* f. MDu. *hobbelen* turn, roll.] A migratory Old World falcon, *Falco subbuteo*, formerly used for hunting small birds. Also (w. specifying wd), any of a number of similar falcons.

hobby-horse /ˈhɒbɪhɔːs/ *n.* & *v.* ME. [f. HOBBY *n.*[1] + HORSE *n.*] **A** *n.* **1** A figure of a horse (made of wicker etc.) fastened around the waist or over the head of a performer in a morris dance, pantomime, etc. ME. †**2** = HOBBY *n.*[1] 1. L16–E17. †**3** A person who behaves in a ridiculous way; a jester, buffoon. Also, a lustful person; a prostitute. L16–E17. **4a** A toy consisting of a stick with a horse's head at one end, for a child to bestride. L16. **b** A horse on a merry-go-round; a rocking-horse. M18. **5** Orig., = HOBBY *n.*[1] 4. Now usu., a topic to which a person constantly recurs or in which he or she shows an obsessive interest. L17. **6** *Hist.* = HOBBY *n.*[1] 5. E19.

5 C. MCCULLOUGH He also had a tendency to be downright boring once he climbed aboard his hobbyhorse.

B *v.i.* Perform as a hobby-horse; move like a hobby-horse. E19.

hobby-ˈhorsical *a.* constantly recurring to the same topic, devoted to a hobby, crotchety, whimsical M18.

hobday /ˈhɒbdeɪ/ *v.t.* Also **H-**. M20. [F. T. *Hobday* (1869–1939), Brit. veterinary surgeon.] Operate on the larynx of (a horse) to improve its breathing.

hobgoblin /ˈhɒbgɒblɪn/ *n.*, *a.*, & *v.* M16. [f. HOB *n.*[1] + GOBLIN *n.*[1]] **A** *n.* A mischievous imp or sprite, *spec.* Robin Goodfellow; something to be feared superstitiously, a bogey, a bugbear. M16. **B** *attrib.* or as *adj.* Of, pertaining to, or resembling a hobgoblin. E17. **C** *v.t.* Terrify or pursue as a hobgoblin. Chiefly *joc.* E18.

hobnail /ˈhɒbneɪl/ *n.* & *v.* L16. [f. HOB *n.*[2] + NAIL *n.*] **A** *n.* **1** A nail with a large head and short tang, used to reinforce the soles of heavy boots and shoes. L16. **2** A person wearing hobnailed boots; a rustic, labourer. Now *rare.* M17.

Comb.: **hobnail liver** *Med.*: having many small knobbly projections due to cirrhosis.

B *attrib.* or as *adj.* Rustic, boorish. E17.

C *v.t.* Provide or reinforce with hobnails. M17.

hobnailed /ˈhɒbneɪld/ *a.* L16. [f. HOBNAIL *n.* or *v.*: see -ED[2], -ED[1].] **1** Rustic, boorish. Now *rare.* L16. **2** Provided or reinforced with hobnails. E17.

Special collocations: **hobnailed liver** = *hobnail liver* s.v. HOBNAIL *n.*

hobnob /ˈhɒbnɒb/ *v.* Also **hob-nob**. Infl. **-bb-**. E19. [f. *hob and* (or *or*) *nob*: see HOB *v.*[1] 2.] **1** *v.i.* Drink to each other, drink together. *arch.* E19. **2** *v.i.* & *t.* (w. *it*). Be on familiar terms (*with*); talk informally (*with*). M19.

2 C. S. FORESTER There were advantages .. in hobnobbing with generals.

hob-nob /ˈhɒbnɒb/ *n.* M18. [f. (as) HOBNOB *v.*] †**1** Any phrase or toast used in drinking together. M–L18. **2** A drinking to each other or together. *arch.* E19. **3** An intimate conversation, a tête-à-tête. L19.

hob-nob /ˈhɒbnɒb/ *adv. obs.* exc. *dial.* Also (earlier) **hab-nab** /ˈhabnab/, **habs-nabs** /ˈhabznabz/. L16. [See HAB.] However it may turn out, anyhow; in random fashion, by chance, by one means or another; hit or miss, succeed or fail.

hobo /ˈhəʊbəʊ/ *n.* & *v.* Chiefly *N. Amer.* L19. [Origin unkn.] **A** *n.* Pl. **-o(e)s**. A wandering workman or tramp. L19.

D. CARNEGIE He .. became a hobo, .. slept in haystacks, begged his food from door to door.

B *v.i.* & *t.* w. *it.* Be or behave like a hobo; wander. E20.

hobohemia /həʊbəʊˈhiːmɪə/ *n.* E20. [Blend of HOBO *n.* and *Bohemia.*] A community of hoboes; a district in which hoboes live.

hobohemian *a.* & *n.* (of, pertaining to, or resembling) a hobo E20.

hoboy *n.* see HAUTBOY.

Hobson-Jobson /hɒbs(ə)nˈdʒɒbs(ə)n/ *n.* L19. [Title of a famous collection (1886) of Anglo-Indian wds by Yule & Burnell, repr. alt. (by British hearers) of Arab. *Yā Ḥasan! Yā Ḥusayn!* O Hasan! O Husain!, a cry used by Muslims at the ceremonies held at Muharram.] Assimilation of adopted foreign words to the sound-pattern of the adopting language. Chiefly in *the law of Hobson-Jobson.*

Hobson's choice /hɒbs(ə)nz ˈtʃɔɪs/ *n. phr.* M17. [T. *Hobson* (1554–1631), a Cambridge carrier who gave his customers a choice between the next horse or none at all.] The option of taking what is offered or nothing; no choice.

Hobthrush /ˈhɒbθrʌʃ/ *n. obs.* exc. *dial.* Also **-thrust** /-θrʌst/, **-thurst** /-θəːst/. L16. [f. HOB *n.*[1] + THURSE with metathesis.] **1** A hobgoblin. L16. **2** A rustic. *derog.* L17.

hoc /hɒk/ *n. obs.* exc. *Hist.* Also **hock**. M17. [Fr., prob. f. L = this (neut.).] A card-game in which players may assign whatever value they choose to certain privileged cards.

hoch /hoːx/ *int.* & *n.* M19. [G, abbrev. of *hoch lebe* long live.] (An instance of the German exclamation) expr. loyal approval.

hocheur /hɒˈʃəː; *foreign* ɔʃœːr (*pl. same*)/ *n.* M19. [Fr., f. *hocher* nod + *-eur* -OR.] The spot-nosed monkey, *Cercopithecus nictitans*, of W. African rainforests, olive and black with a white spot on the nose. Also *hocheur monkey.*

hochgeboren /ˈhoːxgəboːrən/ *n.* & *a.* Pl. of n. same. E20. [G.] (A person who is) high-born.

hock /hɒk/ *n.*[1] Long *obs.* exc. in HOLLYHOCK. OE. [Origin unkn.] Any of various plants of the mallow family, *esp.* the common mallow, *Malva sylvestris*, and the hollyhock, *Alcea rosea.*

hock /hɒk/ *n.*[2] LME. [Var. of HOUGH *n.*] **1** The joint in the hind leg of a quadruped between the tibia and the metatarsus, the angle of which points backwards. LME. **2** A knuckle of meat, esp. pork. Cf. HOUGH *n.* 3. E18.

hock /hɒk/ *n.*[3] M16. [Perh. var. of HOOK *n.*] A rod, stick, or chain with a hook at the end.

hock /hɒk/ *n.*[4] E17. [Abbrev. f. as HOCKAMORE.] (A) white wine from the Rhine region (orig. from Hochheim on the River Main, Germany); *loosely* any dry white wine.

hock /hɒk/ *n.*[5] Chiefly *US.* M19. [Perh. abbrev. of HOCKELTY.] In faro, the last card remaining in the box after all the others have been dealt.

from soda (card) to hock from the top card to the last in the deal, from beginning to end.

hock /hɒk/ *n.*[6] *slang* (chiefly *N. Amer.*). M19. [Du. *hok* hutch, hovel, prison, (slang) credit, debt.] Pawn, pledge; debt. Also, prison. Chiefly in *in hock*

Collier's My cash was gone, and I was in hock for the next three years. G. CLARE There was never enough money to get her brooch out of hock again.

Comb.: **hock-shop** a pawnshop.

hock *n.*[7] var. of HOC.

hock /hɒk/ *v.*[1] *obs.* exc. *Hist.* LME. [f. HOCK-.] **1** *v.i.* Collect money (often by roughly humorous methods) for parish purposes at Hocktide; celebrate Hocktide. LME. **2** *v.t.* Tie up or otherwise beset (a person) to extract money at Hocktide. E18.

Comb.: **hocking ale**: brewed for the Hocktide festival.

hock /hɒk/ *v.*[2]*t.* L16. [f. HOCK *n.*[2]] Disable by cutting the tendons of the ham or hock; hamstring.

hock /hɒk/ *v.*[3]*t. slang* (chiefly *N. Amer.*). L19. [f. HOCK *n.*[6]] Pawn.

Hock- /hɒk/ *comb. form.* Now chiefly *Hist.* Also as separate wd. ME. [Origin unkn.] Designating days of or events connected with the beginning of the second week after Easter, formerly important for the payment of rents etc., the collection of money (often by roughly humorous methods) for parish purposes, and as the beginning of the summer half of the rural year.

Hock-day the second Tuesday after Easter Sunday; in *pl.* also, the second Monday and Tuesday after Easter Sunday. **Hock Monday** the second Monday after Easter Sunday. **Hock-money** money collected for parish purposes during Hocktide. **Hocktide** the period comprising the second Monday and Tuesday after Easter Sunday. **Hock Tuesday** the second Tuesday after Easter Sunday.

†**Hockamore** *n.* L17–M18. [Alt. of G *Hochheimer* (*Wein*) wine of Hochheim on the River Main, Germany.] = HOCK *n.*[4]

hock-cart /ˈhɒk-kɑːt/ *n. obs.* exc. *Hist.* M17. [Prob. f. elem. rel. to HOCKEY *n.*[2], HORKEY + CART *n.*] The cart which carried home the last load of a harvest.

hockelty /ˈhɒk(ə)lti/ *n.* Chiefly *US.* Now *rare.* Also **hocklety**, (earlier) **hockly** /ˈhɒkli/. E19. [Origin uncertain: 1st elem. perh. rel. to HOC.] In faro: the last card but one in the deal which forms part of the banker's gain; also = HOCK *n.*[5]

hocket /ˈhɒkɪt/ *n.* ME. [Fr. *hoquet* hiccup, in OFr. shock, sudden interruption, hitch.] †**1** A hitch, an obstacle; an interruption; a trick. Only in ME. †**2** *The* hiccups. Only in E17. **3** *Mus.* A device of medieval polyphony whereby a melody is divided between two or more contrapuntal voice parts which alternate with rests to produce a spasmodic effect. L18.

hockey /ˈhɒki/ *n.*[1] E16. [Origin unkn.] **I 1** An outdoor team game played with sticks hooked at one end with which the players drive a ball towards goals at opposite ends of the field. Also more fully (esp. in N. America to distinguish it from sense 2) *field hockey.* E16. **2** A variant of this game played on ice in skates with sticks hooked or (now usu.) angled at one end and a rubber disc or puck. Also more fully (esp. outside N. America to distinguish it from sense 1) *ice hockey.* L19. **II 3** A stick or club used in hockey. Chiefly *US.* M19.

Comb.: **hockey-stick** a stick hooked or angled at one end, used in hockey.

hockeyist *n.* (*N. Amer.*) a person who plays ice hockey L19.

hockey *n.*[2] var. of HORKEY.

hockey *n.*[3] see OCHE.

hocklety, hockly *ns.* see HOCKELTY.

hocus /ˈhəʊkəs/ *n.* M17. [Abbrev. of HOCUS-POCUS *n.* & *a.*] **I** †**1** A conjuror, a juggler. M–L17. †**2** A cheat, an impostor. Only in L17. **3** A stupid person. *Sc.* L18. **II 4** Jugglery, trickery, deception. *arch.* M17.

hocus /ˈhəʊkəs/ *v.t.* Infl. **-ss-**, **-s-**. L17. [f. the n.] **1** Play a trick on; hoax. L17. **2** Stupefy with drugs, esp. for a criminal purpose; drug (a drink). Cf. LOCUS *v.* M19.

hocus-pocus /həʊkəsˈpəʊkəs/ *n.* & *a.* E17. [f. pseudo-L *hax pax max Deus adimax*, used as magical formula.] **A** *n.* †**1** A conjuror, a juggler; a trickster. E17–M18. **2** (As *int.* used as) a formula of conjuring or magical incantation. E17. **3** A juggler's trick; conjuring; sleight of hand; trickery, deception. M17.

3 J. F. KENNEDY Englishmen, with their balanced budgets and sound economy, had watched the German financial hocus-pocus with amazement.

B *attrib.* or as *adj.* Juggling; cheating, tricky. Now *rare.* M17.

hocus-pocus /həʊkəsˈpəʊkəs/ *v.* Infl. **-ss-**, **-s-**. L17. [f. prec.] **1** *v.i.* Act the conjuror, juggle; play tricks, practise deception. L17. **2** *v.t.* Play tricks on; transform as if by jugglery. L18.

hod /hɒd/ *n.* L16. [Var. of HOT *n.*[1]] **1** A builder's open receptacle, now usu. a trough on a staff, for carrying mortar, bricks, or stones; the quantity that such a receptacle will contain, a hodful. L16. **2** A receptacle for carrying or holding coal; a coal-scuttle. E19.

Comb.: **hodman** a building worker who carries a hod; now chiefly *fig.*, an unskilled worker, a literary hack.

hodful *n.* the quantity that a hod will contain; *somewhat derog.* a large quantity: E19.

hod /hɒd/ *v.i. Sc.* Infl. **-dd-**. L18. [Imit.] Bob up and down in riding; jog.

hodad /ˈhəʊdad/ *n. Surfing slang.* M20. [Origin unkn.] An ill-mannered or boastful surfer.

hodden /ˈhɒd(ə)n/ *n.* & *a. Sc.* Now *arch.* or *Hist.* L16. [Origin unkn.] (Made of) woollen cloth of a coarse quality such as was made on hand-looms.

hodden grey (of) grey hodden made without dyeing from a combination of black and white fleeces, taken as typical rustic garb.

hoddy-doddy /ˈhɒdɪˌdɒdi/ *n.* & *a. obs.* exc. *dial.* In sense 3 also †**-dod**. M16. [Perh. nursery redupl. of *dod* in DODMAN.] A *n.* 1 A short and dumpy person. M16. †2 A cuckold; a henpecked man; a simpleton. L16–M17. 3 A small snail. E17. 4 A revolving light. *dial.* L18. B *adj.* 1 Confused; giddy; drunk. L18. 2 Short and dumpy; clumsy. E19.

hoddy-noddy /ˈhɒdɪˌnɒdi/ *n. rare.* E17. [Redupl. of NODDY *n.*[1] & *a.*: cf. prec.] A fool, a simpleton.

Hodegetria /həʊdɪˈgiːtrɪə/ *n.* L19. [Gk *hodēgētria* lit. 'the indicator of the way'.] An iconographical depiction of the Virgin and Child in which the Virgin with her right hand indicates the Child, who is on her left arm.

Hodge /hɒdʒ/ *n.* LME. [By-form of the male first name *Roger*: cf. HICK *n.*[1], HOB *n.*[1]] (A name for) a typical English agricultural labourer, a rustic.

hodgepodge /ˈhɒdʒpɒdʒ/ *n.*, *a.*, & *v.* Also (earlier) †**-potch**. LME. [Var. of HOTCHPOTCH, prob. w. assim. to prec. Cf. next, HOTCHPOT.] A *n.* 1 = HOTCHPOTCH *n.* 1. LME. b A clumsy mixture of ingredients. E17. 2 = HOTCHPOTCH *n.* 2. E17. B *attrib.* or as *adj.* = HOTCHPOTCH *a.* E17. C *v.t.* = HOTCHPOTCH *v.* M18.

hodgepot /ˈhɒdʒpɒt/ *n.* Long *rare.* LME. [Var. of HOTCHPOT, prob. w. assim. to HODGE. Cf. prec.] 1 = HOTCHPOTCH *n.* 2. LME. 2 = HOTCHPOT *n.* 3. E18.

†**hodgepotch** *n.* see HODGEPODGE.

†**hodge-pudding** *n. rare* (Shakes.). Only in L16. [f. HODGE(PODGE *n.* + PUDDING *n.*] A pudding made of a medley of ingredients.

Hodgkin's disease /ˈhɒdʒkɪnz dɪˌziːz/ *n. phr.* M19. [f. Thomas *Hodgkin* (1798–1866), Eng. physician.] *Med.* A malignant but often curable disease of the lymphatic system causing painless swelling of the lymph nodes, liver, and spleen.

hodiern /ˈhɒdɪəːn, ˈhəʊ-/ *a.* Long *rare.* E16. [L *hodiernus*, f. *hodie* today.] = next.

hodiernal /hɒdɪˈəːn(ə)l, həʊ-/ *a.* M17. [f. as prec. + -AL[1].] Of or belonging to the present day.

hodmandod /ˈhɒdmәndɒd/ *n. obs.* exc. *dial.* L16. [Redupl. var. of DODMAN: cf. HODDY-DODDY. In sense 2 alt. of HOTTENTOT.] 1 A snail; *fig.* a deformed person. L16. †2 A Nama. L17–E18.

hodograph /ˈhɒdəgrɑːf/ *n.* M19. [f. Gk *hodos* way + -GRAPH.] A curve constructed by extending from a fixed point lines representing in magnitude and direction the velocity of a moving particle, or some other vector quantity.

hodometer *n.* var. of ODOMETER.

hodometrical /hɒdəˈmɛtrɪk(ə)l/ *a.* M18. [f. Gk *hodos* way + *metrikos* metric + -AL[1].] *Naut.* Relating to the measurement of a ship's progress.

hodoscope /ˈhɒdəskəʊp/ *n.* E20. [f. Gk *hodos* way + -SCOPE.] 1 A form of microscope for examining light paths in a crystal. Now *rare* or *obs.* E20. 2 *Physics.* An array of particle detectors used for observing the paths of cosmic-ray and other particles. M20.

hoe /həʊ/ *n.*[1] Now only in place-names. [OE *hōh*, *hō* f. Gmc. Perh. same wd as HOUGH *n.* See also HEUGH *n.*] A projecting ridge of land, a promontory.

Plymouth Hoe etc.

hoe /həʊ/ *n.*[2] *obs.* exc. *dial.* Also †**how**. [OE *hogu* corresp. to OHG *hugu*, *hugi*, OS *hugi* (Du. *heug*), ON *hugr*, Goth. *hugs* thought, f. Gmc.] Care, anxiety, trouble.

hoe /həʊ/ *n.*[3] ME. [OFr. *houe* f. OFrank. = OHG *houwa* (G *Haue*) rel. to HEW *v.*] A tool consisting of a thin blade attached to a long handle, used for loosening the surface of the ground, digging up weeds, etc.

Dutch hoe: see DUTCH *a.* **draw-hoe** a hoe used with a pulling action.

Comb.: **hoe-cake** *US* a cake of maize flour of a type orig. baked on the blade of a hoe.

hoeful *n.* as much as can be lifted on a hoe M19.

hoe /həʊ/ *v.* LME. [f. HOE *n.*[3]] 1 *v.i.* Use a hoe; work with a hoe. LME. 2 *v.t.* Break or loosen (ground) with a hoe. Also foll. by *up*. M17. 3 *v.t.* Weed (crops) with a hoe; thin *out*, dig *up*, etc. (plants) with a hoe. L17.

Phrases, & with advs. & preps. in specialized senses: *a hard row to hoe*: see ROW *n.*[1] **hoe in** *Austral.* & *NZ slang* eat eagerly. **hoe into** *Austral.* & *NZ slang* attack (food, a person, a task).

hoer *n.* M18.

hoedown /ˈhəʊdaʊn/ *n.* Chiefly *N. Amer.* M19. [f. HOE *v.* + DOWN *adv.*] A lively folk-dance; a tune for such a dance; a social gathering for dancing hoedowns etc.

hoernesite /ˈhəːnəsʌɪt/ *n.* Also **hör-**. M19. [f. Moritz *Hörnes* (1815–68), Austrian mineralogist + -ITE[1].] *Min.* A monoclinic hydrated arsenate of magnesium, usu. occurring as groups of white crystals.

hoey /ˈhəʊi/ *n.* Now *rare* or *obs.* M19. [Chin. *hui* association, society, club.] A (secret) society or association of Chinese, esp. in an English-speaking community.

Hoffmann /ˈhɒfmən/ *n.* M18. [Ger. surname: in sense 1 Friedrich Hoffmann (1660–1742), physician; in sense 2 Johann Hoffmann (1857–1919), neurologist.] 1 Pharm. *Hoffmann's anodyne*, a mineral solution of alcohol and ether. M18. 2 Med. *Hoffmann's sign*, increased sensitivity of the sensory nerves to mechanical stimulation. E20.

Hofmann /ˈhɒfmən/ *n.* M19. [August Wilhelm von *Hofmann* (1818–92), Ger. chemist.] *Chem.* Used *attrib.* and in *possess.* to designate substances, methods, etc., discovered or devised by Hofmann.

Hofmann degradation (*a*) = *Hofmann reaction, rearrangement* below; (*b*) the pyrolysis of a quaternary ammonium hydroxide to yield a tertiary amine and an alkene. **Hofmann reaction**, **rearrangement** the elimination of a carbonyl group from an acid amide when heated in a solution of sodium hypochlorite or a similar compound, yielding a primary amine. **Hofmann's violet** any of a group of basic rosaniline dyes formerly used to dye fabrics.

hog /hɒg/ *n.* Also (now only in sense 4) **hogg**. LOE. [Perh. of Celt. origin: cf. Welsh *hwch*, Corn. *hoch* pig, sow.] I 1 A domesticated pig; *esp.* a castrated male reared for slaughter. LOE. 2 Any (wild) pig of the domesticated species, *Sus scrofa*. L15. 3 With specifying wd: any of various other animals of the pig family Suidae or otherwise held to resemble the pig. L16.

1 W. STYRON I could hear Travis's hogs grunting sleepily in their pen. 3 *groundhog, sea-hog, wart-hog, water-hog*, etc.

II 4 A young sheep, *esp.* one from the time it ceases to be a lamb until its first shearing. Now chiefly *Sc.* & *dial.* ME. b The first fleece shorn from such a sheep. Chiefly *dial.* M19. 5 Any of various farm animals of a year old; a yearling. Usu. more fully *hog-bull*, *-colt*, etc. L16.

4 *Yorkshire Post* Best Cheviot hogs and wethers are five per cent. cheaper.

III 6 A coarse, filthy, gluttonous, or inconsiderate person. Cf. ROAD-HOG. LME. 7 A shilling; *US* a ten-cent piece. *arch. slang.* L17. 8 *Naut.* A scrubbing-brush for cleaning a ship's bottom. M18. 9 *Curling.* A stone lacking sufficient impetus to carry it over the distance-line or hog-score; the distance-line itself. L18. 10 A machine for grinding (esp. refuse) wood into chips for fuel. L19. 11 A railway locomotive for hauling freight. *US slang.* L19.

6 SHAKES. *Rich. III* Thou elvish-mark'd, abortive, rooting hog.

Phrases: **go the whole hog** *colloq.* do a thing completely or thoroughly. **hog in armour** a person who is ill at ease. **hog on ice** *N. Amer. colloq.* an insecure person. **live high off** (or **on**) **the hog** *N. Amer.* live luxuriously.

Comb.: **hog-badger** a yellowish-grey badger, *Arctonyx collaris*, of east Asian forests, having an elongated mobile snout; **hog cholera** *US* swine fever; **hog-deer** a small, short-legged deer, *Cervus porcinus*, native to southern Asian grassland; **hog gum** a gum obtained from any of various West Indian trees, esp. *Rhus metopium* (family Anacardiaceae) and *Symphonia globulifera* (family Guttiferae); *hog-gum tree*, any of the trees producing this gum; **hog-head** *US slang* the driver of a locomotive; †**hogherd** a swineherd; **hog-killing** *US* the time when pigs are killed; *fig.* a time of special enjoyment; **hog-Latin** any incomprehensible language; esp. = *pig Latin* s.v. PIG *n.*[1]; **hog-line** = *hog-score* below; **hog louse** a woodlouse; cf. *pig louse* (a) s.v. PIG *n.*[1]; **hognose (snake)** any of several harmless colubrid snakes constituting the N. American genus *Heterodon*, which have an upturned snout and defensive behaviour including hissing, flattening the head, inflating the body, and feigning death; **hog-nosed** *a.* having a flattened or upturned snout suggesting that of a hog (*hog-nosed bat*, a tailless colonial bat, *Craseonycteris thonglongyai*, of west Thailand, the smallest known bat; *hog-nosed snake* = *hognose* above); **hognut** = *pignut* (a) s.v. PIG *n.*[1]; *hog peanut*: see PEANUT 1; **hog-pen** *N. Amer.* a pigsty; **hog plum** (the plumlike fruit of) any of several trees, esp. (*W. Indies*) *Spondias mombin* (family Anacardiaceae) and (*US*) *Ximenia americana* (family Olacaceae); **hog-score** *Curling* either of two lines drawn across each end of a rink at one-sixth of the rink's length from the tee, over which a stone must cross to count in the game; **hog's fennel** a tall umbelliferous plant, *Peucedanum officinale*, with yellowish flowers and finely divided leaves like those of fennel; **hogskin** *n.* & *a.* (made of) pigskin; **hog's pudding** the entrails of a hog, filled with either a sweet or savoury stuffing; **hog-sucker** any fish of the N. American genus *Hypentelium*; **hog-tie** *v.t.* (*N. Amer.*) secure by fastening the hands and feet or all four feet together; restrain, impede; **hog-tight** *a.* (of a fence) close or narrow enough to stop pigs forcing a way through; **hog-trough** a trough for hogs to feed out of; **hogwash** kitchen swill etc. for pigs; *fig.* worthless stuff, nonsense; **hogweed** any of various plants on which hogs feed or are fed; *spec.* (*a*) any of several coarse umbelliferous plants of the genus *Heracleum*, esp. cow parsnip, *H. sphondylium*; (*b*) *W. Indies* any of various plants of the genus *Boerhavia* (family Nyctaginaceae); **hog-wild** *a.* (*US colloq.*) absolutely wild or furious; **hog-yoke** a wooden frame for a hog's neck, used to prevent it from going through hedges.

hog /hɒg/ *v.* Infl. **-gg-**. M17. [f. the n.] I 1 *v.t. Naut.* Clean the bottom of (a ship) with a hog. Now *rare.* M17. 2 *v.t. Curling.* Play (a stone) without enough force for it to cross the hog-score. E19.

II 3 *v.t.* Cut (a horse's mane) short so that it stands up like a hog's bristles. M18. 4 *v.t.* Arch (the back); cause (a boat, plank, etc.) to rise archwise in the centre and sag at the ends as a result of strain. L18. b *v.i.* Arch the back; (of a ship) rise archwise in the centre. L18. 5 *v.t.* Appropriate greedily or selfishly; take an unduly large share of for oneself, monopolize. *colloq.* L19. b *v.t.* Eat (something) greedily. *colloq.* E20. c *v.t.* w. *it* & *i.* Behave as a road-hog, monopolize the road. E20.

4 WELLINGTON Draught bullocks ... stick in the mud, hog their backs, droop their heads and die. 5 A. BROOKNER My mother ... hogged all the attention at my wedding. *Brides & Setting up Home* Who hogs the duvet is no longer a problem. b C. THUBRON A modern restaurant where I hogged down two bowls of the meat soup.

III 6 *v.t.* Keep (a lamb) over winter for sale the following year. Now chiefly *Sc.* E19. 7 *v.t.* Feed swine on (a crop or crop-covered land). Also foll. by *down*, *off*. *US colloq.* M19.

Comb.: **hog-mane** a hogged mane; **hog-maned** *a.* having a hog-mane.

hogan /ˈhəʊg(ə)n/ *n.*[1] L19. [Navajo.] An American Indian (esp. Navajo) hut made from logs, earth, etc.

hogan *n.*[2] var. of HOGEN.

Hogan Mogan *n.* & *a.* var. of HOGEN MOGEN.

Hogarthian /həʊˈgɑːθɪən/ *a.* L18. [f. *Hogarth* (see below) + -IAN.] Of, pertaining to, or characteristic of the English satirical painter and caricaturist William Hogarth (1697–1764) or his style of painting.

hogback /ˈhɒgbak/ *n.* Also **hog's back** /ˈhɒgz bak/. M17. [f. HOG *n.* + BACK *n.*[1]] 1 A back like that of a hog. M17. 2 A thing shaped like a hog's back; *esp.* a sharply crested hill-ridge. E19. 3 A rectangular tomb with a curved or pitched roof. L19.

2 C. G. D. ROBERTS The lake lay . . sheltered . . by a high hog-back of dark green spruce.

hogbacked *a.* (*a*) having a back like that of a hog; (*b*) having a rise in the middle like a hog's back: M17.

hogen /ˈhəʊg(ə)n/ *n.* & *a.* Also **-an**. M17. [Abbrev. of next.] A *n.* Also **H-**. †1 A Netherlander. M–L17. 2 A strong type of beer. Cf. earlier HOGEN MOGEN *a.* 3. E18. †B *adj.* Excellent; high and mighty. L17–M18.

Hogen Mogen /ˌhəʊg(ə)n ˈməʊg(ə)n/ *n.* & *a.* Also **Hogan Mogan, h- m-**. M17. [f. Du. *Hoogmogendheiden* High Mightinesses, the title of the States General.] A *n.* Pl. same, **-s**. †1 The States General of the Netherlands; *pl.* the members of this. Also, any person, council, or authority affecting power. M17–E18. 2 A Netherlander. *derog.* Now *rare.* L17. B *adj.* 1 Dutch. *derog.* Now *rare.* M17. †2 Affecting power; high and mighty. M17–E18. †3 Of an alcoholic drink, esp. beer: strong. Cf. HOGEN *n.* 2. Only in M17.

hog-fish /ˈhɒgfɪʃ/ *n.* Pl. **-es** /-ɪz/, (usu.) same. L16. [f. HOG *n.* + FISH *n.*[1]] †1 A manatee. L16–E17. †2 A porpoise. Only in 17. 3a The orange scorpion fish, *Scorpaena scrofa*, of the Mediterranean and eastern Atlantic. Now *rare* or *obs.* E17. b Any of various fishes of American waters; *esp.* (*a*) a large edible wrasse, *Lachnolaimus maximus*; (*b*) a pigfish, *Orthopristis chrysoptera*. M18.

hogg *n.* see HOG *n.*

†**hoggaster** *n.* Also **hogster**. LME. [med.L *ho(c)gaster* (whence also AN *hogastre*), f. HOG *n.* + L -ASTER, as in late L *porcastra* young pig, med.L *porcaster* piglet.] 1 A boar in its third year. LME–M19. 2 A young sheep. E18–L19.

hogger /ˈhɒgə/ *n.* *US slang.* E20. [f. HOG *n.* + -ER[1].] A locomotive engineer.

hoggerel /ˈhɒg(ə)r(ə)l/ *n.* Now *dial.* M16. [f. HOG *n.*: see -REL. Cf. AL *hogerellus*.] A young sheep in its second year.

hoggery /ˈhɒg(ə)ri/ *n.* M17. [f. HOG *n.* + -ERY.] 1 A place where hogs are kept; a piggery. M17. 2 Hoggishness. *rare.* M19.

hogget /ˈhɒgɪt/ *n.* LME. [f. HOG *n.* + -ET[1]. Cf AL *hogettus*.] 1 A young boar in its second year. Now *rare* or *obs.* LME. 2 A yearling sheep; *esp.* (*NZ*) a lamb from when it is weaned to its first shearing. LME. 3 A year-old colt. *dial.* L18.

hoggin /ˈhɒgɪn/ *n.* M19. [Origin unkn.] A mixture of sand and gravel; sifted gravel.

hoggish /ˈhɒgɪʃ/ *a.* L15. [f. HOG *n.* + -ISH[1].] Of, pertaining to, or characteristic of a hog; filthy; gluttonous; selfish, mean.

hoggishly *adv.* L16. **hoggishness** *n.* E17.

hoglike /ˈhɒglʌɪk/ *a.* E19. [f. HOG *n.* + -LIKE.] Like (that of) a hog, hoggish.

hogling /ˈhɒglɪŋ/ *n.* LME. [f. HOG *n.* + -LING[1].] 1 A young or small pig. LME. 2 A kind of pastry turnover. *dial.* E19.

hogmanay /ˈhɒgmənеɪ, hɒgməˈneɪ/ *n.* *Sc.* & *north.* E17. [Corresp. in meaning and use to OFr. *aguillanneuf* last day of the year, (the cry for) new-year's gift, of which the Norman form *hoguinané* may be the immediate source of the Eng. wd.] (The celebration of) the last day of the year; (the cry for) the former customary gift of an oatmeal cake etc. demanded by children on this day.

hogo /ˈhəʊgəʊ/ *n.* Pl. **-os**. M17. [Anglicized f. Fr. HAUT-GOÛT.] †1 A strong or piquant flavour; a highly flavoured dish. M–L17. 2 An offensive smell; a stench, a stink. M17.

2 *Times* Amid the hogo of stale sweat and embrocation, Setter stretched himself back on a bench.

hog's back *n.* see HOGBACK.

hogshead /ˈhɒgzhɛd/ *n.* LME. [f. HOG *n.* + -'S[1] + HEAD *n.*, (for unkn. reason).] 1 A large cask; *spec.* one of a definite capacity, varying according to the commodity. LME. 2 A liquid or dry measure, varying according to the commodity; *esp.* (*a*) a liquid measure of beer equal to 54 imperial gallons or 63 US gallons; (*b*) a liquid measure of wine equal to 52.5 imperial gallons. LME. 3 A person resembling a hog in conduct or behaviour. *derog.* E16.

†**hogster** *n.* var. of HOGGASTER.

hohlflute /ˈhəʊlfluːt/ *n.* M17. [Partial tr. G *Hohlflöte* lit. 'hollow flute': see FLUTE *n.*[1]] An open 8-ft flute-stop in an organ, having a soft hollow tone.

ho ho /həʊ ˈhəʊ/ *int.* Also **ho ho ho, ho-ho(-ho)**. M16. [Redupl. of HO *int.*[1]] Expr. derision or repr. derisive laughter. Also, expr. surprise or triumph.

ho-ho bird /ˈhəʊhəʊ bəːd/ *n. phr.* E20. [f. Chin. *ho-ho* + BIRD *n.*] A mythical Chinese bird resembling a pheasant, freq. used as an emblem of courage.

Hohokam /həʊhəʊˈkɑːm/ *n.* & *a.* L19. [Pima *húhukam* old one.] A *n.* An extinct N. American Indian people; the culture of this people, characterized by irrigated agriculture and houses built in pits, and flourishing in Arizona after *c*450. L19. B *adj.* Of or pertaining to this people or culture. M20.

ho-hum /həʊˈhʌm/ *int.*, *n.*, & *a.* E20. [f. HO *int.*[1] + HUM *int.*, suggestive of a yawn.] A *int.* Expr. boredom. E20. B *n.* An utterance of 'ho-hum!'; a boring statement etc. M20. C *adj.* Dull, routine, boring. M20.

hoick /hɔɪk/ *v.*[1] & *n.* *slang.* Also **hoik**. L19. [Perh. var. of HIKE *v.*] A *v.t.* Lift or bring (*out* etc.), esp. with a jerk; yank. L19.

R. RENDELL Can you imagine him hoicking her out of bed.

B *n.* A jerky lift or pull; *Cricket* a jerky hoisted shot. L19.

J. HERRIOT The Hedwick lads . . gave a great hoick at the ball.

hoick *v.*[2] see next.

hoicks /hɔɪks/ *int.*, *n.*, & *v.* Also **hoick** /hɔɪk/. E17. [Origin unkn.: cf. YOICKS.] A *int.* Inciting a hound or hounds to the chase. E17. B *v.t.* & *i.* Incite with or cry 'hoicks!' M18. C *n.* A cry of 'hoicks!' L18.

hoik *v.* & *n.* var. of HOICK *v.*[1] & *n.*

hoi polloi /hɔɪ ˈpɒlɔɪ, pɒˈlɔɪ/ *n. phr.* M17. [Gk = the many.] The majority, the masses; the rabble. Freq. w. *the*.

Newsweek They're trying to get rid of the hoi polloi and make Venice into a country club for the wealthy.

¶Orig. in Gk characters; recorded in transliterated form f. M19.

hoise /hɔɪz/ *v.* *obs.* exc. *dial.* & after Shakes. Pa. t. & pple **hoised, hoist** /hɔɪst/. L15. [Prob. f. Du. †*hijschen* (now *hijsen*) or LG *hissen, hiesen* (whence also Fr. *hisser*), but recorded earlier. Cf. HEEZE *v.*] 1 *v.t.* = HOIST *v.*[1] 1. L15. †2 *v.i.* = HOIST *v.*[1] 4. M–L16. †3 *v.t.* Lift and move; remove. L16–M18. †4 *v.t.* Raise in degree, quality, or price. L16–M18.

Phrases (of pa. pple): **hoist with one's own petard** [after Shakes. *Haml.*] blown up by one's own bomb, ruined by one's own devices against others.

hoist /hɔɪst/ *n.* M17. [f. the vb. Cf. HEIST *n.*] I 1 An act of hoisting or raising something aloft; a lift (*up*), a raise. M17. 2 Orig., housebreaking. Now, shoplifting. Chiefly in (*on*) *the hoist. slang.* E19.

1 S. R. CROCKETT As one gets to the edge of a wall when a comrade gives a hoist up. *Sunday Times* Expect a big hoist in the dividend when Lonrho reports its full-year figures.

II 3 The middle part of a ship's mast; the perpendicular height of a sail or flag; the fore edge of a staysail; the part of a flag nearest to the mast or staff. M18. 4 Something hoisted; a group of flags raised as a signal. E19. 5 A device or mechanism for hoisting; a goods elevator. M19. b In full *rotary hoist*. A rotary clothes-drier. *Austral.* M20.

5 T. PYNCHON Turns out the only way down is by a cable, hooked to an overhead hoist. b A. LUBBOCK The . . washing blowing . . from the rotary hoists in their back gardens.

hoist /hɔɪst/ *v.*[1] See also HEIST *v.*, HIST *v.*[2] L15. [Alt. of HOISE *v.*, perh. after the pa. t. & pple.] 1 *v.t.* Raise aloft, lift or set up; raise by means of a rope or pulley and tackle, or other mechanical device. Also foll. by *up*. L15. b Chiefly *Hist.* Lift up (a person) on the back of another for a flogging. E19. †2 *v.t.* Lift and move; remove; carry *away*. M16–M18. 3 *v.t.* Raise in degree or quality; exalt, elevate. Now *rare.* M17. 4 *v.i.* Be raised, rise aloft. M17. 5 *v.t.* & *i.* Orig., break into (a building). Now, steal, esp. by shoplifting. (Cf. earlier HOISTER 1.) *slang.* L18.

1 W. WHARTON They hoisted the trees on top of their . . station wagon and drove off. D. BAGLEY They were hoisted up by the winch one at a time. J. G. BALLARD The Rising Sun was ceremonially hoisted to the mast of the USS *Wake*. 2 T. NASHE She saw her mistris . . hoysted away to hell or to heaven. 5 J. L. WATEN I know where we can hoist a car.

hoist *v.*[2] pa. t. & pple: see HOISE.

hoister /ˈhɔɪstə/ *n.* E18. [f. HOIST *v.*[1] + -ER[1]. Cf. HEISTER.] 1 Orig., a housebreaker. Now, a shoplifter, a pickpocket. *slang.* E18. 2 A person who hoists a flag etc., a contrivance for hoisting something. M19.

hoit /hɔɪt/ *v.i.* *obs.* exc. *dial.* L16. [Origin unkn.] 1 Indulge in riotous mirth; (of a woman) behave boisterously. L16. 2 Move clumsily; limp. *Sc.* L18.

hoity-toity /hɔɪtɪˈtɔɪti/ *n.*, *a.*, & *int.* Also **highty-tighty** /hʌɪtɪˈtʌɪti/. M17. [Redupl. of prec.; later infl. by *high, height*.] A *n.* 1 Orig., riotous or giddy conduct. Later, haughty behaviour, an assumption of superiority. *arch.* M17. 2 A frolicsome girl, a hoyden. Long *obs.* exc. *dial.* L17.

B *adj.* Orig. (*arch.*) frolicsome. Later, haughty, petulant. L17.

R. FRAME They don't like hoity-toity kids. . . Makes them sick. Stuck-up little madams.

C *int.* Expr. surprised protest at undue presumption, petulance, etc. L17.

H. FIELDING Hoity-toity! . . madam is in her airs, I protest.

hoity-toityness *n.* E19.

Hokan /ˈhəʊk(ə)n/ *n.* & *a.* E20. [f. Hokan *hok* approximate form of 'two' + -AN.] (Designating or pertaining to) a group of languages spoken by certain American Indian peoples of the west coast of the US.

hoke /həʊk/ *v.t.* *slang.* E20. [Back-form. f. HOKUM.] Overact (a part). Also foll. by *up*.

hokey /ˈhəʊki/ *n.* *slang.* Now *rare.* E19. [Origin unkn.] Only in *by (the) hokey, by the hokey fiddle*: expr. asseveration.

hokey /ˈhəʊki/ *a.* *slang* (chiefly *N. Amer.*). M20. [f. HOKE or HOKUM + -Y[1].] Involving hokum, sentimental, overacted.

hokey-cokey /həʊkɪˈkəʊki/ *n.* M20. [Origin unkn.] A kind of communal dance characterized by raising the hands in the air and shaking them while bowing and lowering them.

hokey-pokey /həʊkɪˈpəʊki/ *n.* *colloq.* M19. [In sense 1 alt. of HOCUS-POCUS *n.*; other uses of unkn. origin.] 1 Deception, trickery. M19. 2 A kind of cheap ice-cream sold by street vendors. L19. 3 A sweet resembling toffee. *NZ.* M20.

hokku /ˈhɒkuː/ *n.* Pl. same, **-s**. L19. [Jap. = 'opening verse (of a linked sequence of comic verses)'.] = HAIKU.

hokonui /ˈhɒkənuːi/ *n.* *NZ.* Also **H-**. M20. [Maori place-name.] Illicitly distilled spirits.

hokum /ˈhəʊkəm/ *n.* *slang* (orig. *US*). E20. [Origin unkn.] Sentimental, popular, sensational, or unreal situations, dialogue, etc., in a film or play etc.; bunkum.

CLIVE JAMES The ideal biographer's innocent nostrils have detected the odd whiff of hokum. *TV Times* Hard-to-swallow science fiction hokum about a mummy escaping from a sarcophagus.

hol- *comb. form* see HOLO-.

holarctic /həʊˈlɑːktɪk/ *a.* & *n.* Also **H-**. L19. [f. HOLO- + ARCTIC *a.*] A *adj.* Of, pertaining to, or (usu. **H-**) designating the biogeographical region which includes the cold and temperate zones of the northern hemisphere (i.e. both Nearctic and Palaearctic regions). Of an animal: inhabiting or (esp.) distributed throughout this region; circumpolar. L19. **B** *ellipt.* as *n.* (Usu. **H-**.) The Holarctic region. L20.

Holbein /ˈhɒlbʌɪn, ˈhəʊl-/ *a.* L19. [f. Hans *Holbein* (1497–1543), Ger. painter.] Designating or pertaining to a style of embroidery etc. embodying qualities or decoration characteristic of Holbein or his work.

Holbeinesque *a.* resembling the work of Holbein L19.

holcus /ˈhɒlkəs/ *n.* L18. [mod.L f. Gk *holkos* a kind of grass.] Any of various grasses of the genus *Holcus*, which includes the common pasture grass Yorkshire fog or meadow soft-grass, *H. lanatus*.

hold /həʊld/ *n.*[1] See also HOLT *n.*[2] OE. [Partly f. HOLD *v.*, partly f. ON *hald* hold, support, custody.] **I 1** †**a** The action or fact of keeping or guarding; occupation, possession; rule. OE–L16. **b** Tenure. (Earlier in senses of COPYHOLD, FREEHOLD.) *obs.* exc. *dial.* M17. **2** The action or an act of keeping something in one's hand or grasping; grasp (*lit.* & *fig.*), a controlling influence. Also, an opportunity of holding, something to hold by. ME. **b** *spec.* A manner of holding in wrestling etc. E18. **3** Confinement, custody, imprisonment. Long *arch. rare.* ME. **4**† **a** Retention, restraint. ME–L17. **b** A delay, a pause, a postponement. M20. **c** A facility whereby an incoming telephone connection is held automatically until a specified recipient can take the call; freq. in *on hold.* M20. †**5** Contention, struggle; resistance. E16–M17.

2 L. STEPHEN The hold was generally firm when the fissures were not filled with ice. L. GORDON Leslie Stephen's hold on his .. daughter's imagination was the result .. of the education he gave her. A. MCCOWEN My father .. tried to break the Conservative hold on the Royal Borough. *catch hold of*: see CATCH *v.* **get hold of** (*a*) take into one's grasp (*lit.* & *fig.*); (*b*) get possession of, obtain; (*c*) get into contact with (a person). *lay hold of* or *on*: see LAY *v.*[1] **take hold** (*a*) *take hold of*, take into one's grasp; (*b*) (of a custom or habit) become established. **b** (**with**) **no holds barred** (with) no restrictions, all methods being permitted. 3 J. BRAMHALL Father Oldcorne being in hold for the powder treason. 4 HENRY MORE And this is a good hold to the Church from relapsing into Heathenism again. **b** *New Scientist* Unless there has been a last-minute 'hold' .. the first .. *Mariner* spacecraft should .. be on its way. **c** D. E. WESTLAKE I put him on hold and called Mr Clarebridge. *fig.*: *Ottawa Journal* Our sex life is on hold until after the 10 p.m. sportscast. 5 E. JOHNSON Great hold and keepe there was about choice of Magistrates this yeare.

II †**6** A support, a defence. OE–ME. †**7** Property held, a holding; *spec.* a tenement. Cf. COPYHOLD, FREEHOLD, LEASEHOLD, etc. ME–L16. **8** A place of refuge or shelter; *esp.* an animal's lurking-place. ME. **9** A fortress, a stronghold. *arch.* ME. **10 a** A thing that holds something, a receptacle. E16. **b** Something which is grasped; something by or with which an object is grasped. L16. **11** *Mus.* A pause. Now chiefly *US.* L17. **12** A prison cell. E18. **13** The retention of an image in a film-shot. E20.

8 F. FRANCIS Reed or rush beds, .. all of which are favourite holds. 9 LYTTON A rude fortress .. out of the wrecks of some greater Roman hold. **10b** J. SPENCER To conclude it a falling cause which catcheth at such weak and unfaithful holds. F. MARRYAT Sharks .. watched with upturned eyes .. the snapping of the frail hold that supported me.

hold /həʊld/ *n.*[2] Long *obs.* exc. *Hist.* OE. [ON *hǫldr*, identified w. OE *hæleþ*, G *Held* hero, in Norse law a yeoman of higher rank, the owner of allodial land, (poet.) a man.] In the Anglo-Saxon period, a high-ranking officer in the Danelaw.

hold /həʊld/ *n.*[3] L16. [Alt., by assim. to HOLD *v.*, of HOLL *n.*, HOLE *n.*[1]] A compartment in a ship below the (lower) deck, where cargo is stored.

T. HEGGEN The ship was simultaneously unloading cargo from three holds.

hold /həʊld/ *v.* Pa. t. **held** /hɛld/; pa. pple **held** /hɛld/, (*arch.*) **holden** /ˈhəʊld(ə)n/. [OE *haldan* (*healdan*) = OFris. *halda*, OS *haldan* (Du. *houden*), OHG *haltan* (G *halten*), ON *halda*, Goth. *haldan*, f. Gmc orig. str. vb w. the senses watch (cf. BEHOLD), look after, pasture (cattle).] **I** *v.t.* †**1** Keep watch over (sheep etc.); rule (people). OE–ME. **2** Prevent from getting away; keep fast, grasp, have a grip on. Freq. w. advb. extension. OE. **b** *Cricket* etc. Catch (a ball), esp. particularly skilfully. M18. **c** *Sport.* Prove a match for; restrict (an opponent) *to* (a draw etc.). L19. **3** Keep from falling; support in or with the hands, arms, etc. OE. †**b** *fig.* Uphold, support. OE–E16. **c** Grasp so as to control (*lit.* & *fig.*). L16. †**d** Bear (a particular treatment). L16–M17. **4** Have or keep within it; contain or be able to contain; have the capacity for; (of a person) consume (liquor etc.) without undue intoxication. OE. **5** Have or keep as one's own; possess, be the owner, occupant, incumbent, or tenant of; have gained as a qualification or honour. OE. **b** Keep possession of (a place etc.) against attack. ME. **c** Be in (a place); retain possession or occupation of; dominate; engross, retain the attention of. ME. **6** Not let go; keep, retain; keep (a person etc.) in a specified place, condition, etc. (cf. sense II below); make (a person) adhere *to* (terms, a promise etc.). OE. †**b** Continue to occupy; remain in (a place); not leave. LME–L18. **c** Keep back, detain, delay. Also (orig. *US*) detain (a person) in custody. L19. **7** Keep together; keep in existence or operation, carry on; conduct (a meeting); observe, celebrate, (a festival etc.); engage in (a conversation); keep (company, silence, etc.); use (insolent etc.) language. OE. †**8** Keep unbroken or inviolate; abide by (a command, a promise, etc.). OE–E17. **9** Restrain, refrain from; *colloq.* withhold, cease, stop. OE. **10 a** Have in mind, entertain (a feeling, sentiment, etc.). *arch.* OE. **b** Accept the truth of (a belief, doctrine, etc.); think or believe *that*, believe to be or *to be*, regard *as*, (*arch.* also *for*). ME. **c** Have a specified feeling towards. ME. **d** Of a judge or court: lay down, decide. M17. **11** Keep (one's body, head, etc.) in a particular attitude or position. ME. **12** Oblige, constrain. Long *arch. rare.* ME. †**13** Offer or accept as a wager, bet. LME–M18.

2 E. AMADI Oyia held her in a vice-like grip. R. INGALLS She held his hand. *road-holding*: see ROAD *n.* **c** *Racing Post* Heiress Green .. held Another Earl by a head in the Coolmine Race. 3 *New Yorker* She was holding the baby. 'Would you like to hold him, Beverly?' M. AMIS I held the telephone at arm's length, and stared at it. **c** T. BIDDLECOMBE Going to the first fence there was no way I was going to hold the horse. **d** SHAKES. *Coriol.* Now humble as the ripest mulberry That will not hold the handling. 4 V. WOOLF Crumpling the bag which had held the cherries. S. LEWIS Their favourite motion-picture theatre was the Château, which held three thousand spectators. G. GREENE They were .. crushed at a small table, just large enough to hold three whiskies. D. BALLANTYNE It's Betty that can't hold the liquor. 5 P. MASSINGER I hold my dukedom from you, as your vassal. SIR W. SCOTT My Sovereign holds in ward my land. A. CARNEGIE We held the record and many visitors came to marvel at the marvel. C. HILL Arminians held all the best bishoprics and deaneries. N. SYMINGTON For the next three years he held posts in different hospitals. *Soldier* He also holds the Long Service and Good Conduct Medal. **b** SLOAN WILSON A very small island which the British had held for two months. **c** MILTON The star, that bids the shepherd fold, Now the top of heaven doth hold. J. R. SEELEY The intoxication of the Marengo campaign still held him. K. AMIS The journal held no more than half his attention. S. BELLOW He checked their smiles, holding them all with his serious, worn, blue gaze. R. CARVER He spent his time repairing things, now that he could no longer hold a job in the aerospace industry. *Stage & Television Today* Carr .. is a gifted, confident comedian who held the audience. 6 R. BUSH Vivienne held him to standards of emotional forthrightness he wished to but could not sustain. A. TREW A beam of light .. pierced the darkness, picked up the skimmer and held it. **b** W. A. OSBALDISTONE The hare will hold the highways more than at any other time. **c** J. RATHBONE There were no convictions, but she had been held for questioning on three occasions. J. CHEEVER I don't want you to hold dinner for me. 7 P. KAVANAGH Peter walked in the garden .. and there held commune with the spirits of wealth and influence. P. ACKROYD The seance was to be held near Ealing Common. 8 SHAKES. *Merry W.* To Master Brook you yet shall hold your word. 9 T. JEFFERSON The only restraining motive which may hold the hand of a tyrant. DICKENS I wish you'd hold your noise! **10a** H. W. TORRENS The first .. who acknowledged the .. theory and held great account of those who practised it. **b** J. CONRAD A kind of railway contractor .. who held the doctor for an ass. I. MURDOCH It may be relevant here to add that I hold no religious beliefs whatever. C. RYCROFT He also held that most of the dreams of adults express repressed erotic wishes. W. GOLDING Words I must ever hold sacred. A. BRIGGS Wives .. were held to be subordinate to their husbands. **c** T. S. ELIOT They hold these monkeys in peculiar veneration. **d** *Independent* The justices held that they could not grant a protection order. **11** W. C. RUSSELL She held her face averted. D. HAMMETT She held her small body stiffly erect. **12** S. WILLIAMS They could not view themselves as holden .. to submit. **13** T. D'URFEY I'll hold ye five Guineas to four.

II *v.i.* **14** Maintain one's position (against an adversary); (of a place) be held or occupied, hold out. OE. **15** Continue in a (specified) state or course; last. ME. **b** Be or remain valid, apply. ME. **c** Of the weather: continue fine. L19. **16** Maintain a hold, cling. ME. †**b** In *imper.* Here, take this. L15–E17. **c** Of a female animal: retain the seed of the male; conceive. E17. **d** *Boxing.* Grasp an opponent with the hands, in contravention of the rules. E20. **e** Be in possession of illicit drugs. *US slang.* M20. **17** Maintain an attachment *to*; adhere *to*, abide *by*, (a choice, purpose, etc.). ME. **18** Hold property by tenure; derive title to something (*of* or *from* a superior). Also *fig.*, (foll. by *of*, †*on*) depend on, belong or pertain to. ME. **19** Foll. by *with*: maintain allegiance to, side with; *colloq.* approve of (usu. in neg. contexts). ME. †**20** Avail, be of use. (Usu. in neg. & interrog. contexts.) Only in ME. **21** Keep going (in a specified direction); continue *on* (one's way etc.). ME. **22** Remain unbroken; not give way. LME. **23** Take place; occur, prevail. *arch.* LME. **24** Restrain oneself. *arch.* L16. **25** Have a capacity (now *rare*); *Hunting* (of a covert) contain game. L16.

14 SHAKES. *Ant. & Cl.* Our force by land Hath nobly held. **15** I. BANKS My luck holds. Miss Arrol is in. H. WEINZWEIG He could come back next week, to see if the tuning held. **b** H. R. MILL This law does not hold for gases. **c** L. WHISTLER The weather held, and with the may bushes lathered in blossom the scene grew unearthly. **16** TENNYSON There was no anchor, none, To hold by. **b** SHAKES. *Macb.* Hold, take my sword. **d** *Times* The referee had to speak to both men for holding. **17** J. BUCHAN In a pedestrian world he held to the old cavalier grace. P. GAY Freud persisted in holding to the cardinal ideas of psychoanalysis all his life. **18** W. LONGMAN Men holding by knight's service. W. S. LILLY No wonder, for genius holds of the noumenal. **19** M. HANMER Some there were, that held with both sides. *Cornhill Magazine* I don't hold with him buying flowers when his children haven't got enough to eat. **21** CONAN DOYLE I've held on my course when better men .. have asked me to veil topsails. *Field* Instead of holding to Oakhill Wood, the pack bore to the right. **22** *Illustrated London News* The helm was perfectly sound, and the lashings held bravely. **23** SHAKES. *Rich. II* What news from Oxford? Do these justs and triumphs hold? **24** SHELLEY 'Hold, hold!' He cried,—'I tell thee 'tis her brother!' **25** *Hounds* A cold, raw day with little scent and the coverts that normally hold were bare.

Phrases, & with advs. in specialized senses: (A selection of cross-refs. only is included: see esp. other ns.) **hold a candle to the devil** *arch.* serve or assist a wicked person, be active in wickedness. *hold a person's hand*: see HAND *n.* *hold a person's nose to the grindstone*: see GRINDSTONE *n.* *hold at bay*: see BAY *n.*[1] 2. *hold a torch for*: see TORCH *n.* *hold a wolf by the ears*: see WOLF *n.* **hold back** (*a*) impede the progress of; restrain; (*b*) keep (a thing) to or for oneself; (*c*) refrain or shrink (*from*). *hold cheap*: see CHEAP *a.* *hold court*: see COURT *n.*[1] *hold dear*: see DEAR *a.*[1] **hold down** (*a*) repress (*lit.* & *fig.*); (*b*) *colloq.* be competent enough to keep (one's job etc.). **hold everything!** cease action or movement. **hold forth** †(*a*) keep up, go on with; †(*b*) go on, proceed; (*c*) offer (an inducement etc.); (*d*) (usu. *derog.*) speak at length or tediously, preach. **hold good** be valid; apply. *hold hands*: see HAND *n.* **hold hard** (*a*) pull hard at the reins in order to stop a horse; (*b*) in *imper.* (*colloq.*) stop! wait! *hold harmless*: see HARMLESS 3. **hold in** (*a*) keep in check, confine; (*b*) continue in a particular state etc.; restrain oneself, refrain. *hold in* DEMESNE. **hold it!** = *hold everything!* above. **hold it against** regard it to the discredit of (*that*). **hold it good** think it advisable (*to do*). **hold off** *v.phr.t.* & *i.* delay; not begin; keep at a distance. **hold on** (*a*) *v.phr.t.* keep in place on something; †(*b*) *v.phr.t.* continue, keep up; (*c*) *v.phr.i.* keep one's grasp of something, not let go; (*d*) *v.phr.i.* continue, go on; (*e*) *v.phr.i.* (*colloq.*) wait a moment (freq. in *imper.*); (*f*) *v.phr.i.* (when telephoning) not ring off. *hold one's* BREATH. *hold one's ground*: see GROUND *n.* **hold one's head high** behave proudly and confidently. **hold one's horses** *colloq.* stop; slow down. *hold one's nose*: see NOSE *n. hold one's own*: see OWN *a.* & *pron. hold one's peace*: see PEACE *n.* **hold (one's) serve** or **service** win a game in which one is the server. *hold one's tongue*: see TONGUE *n. hold one's way*: see WAY *n. hold one's whistle*: see WHISTLE *n.* 2. **hold out** (*a*) *v.phr.t.* stretch out, proffer, (a hand etc.); offer (an inducement etc.); (*b*) *v.phr.t.* represent *to be*; (*c*) *v.phr.t.* (now *rare*) keep out, exclude; (*d*) *v.phr.t.* keep up, continue; formerly also, bear or sustain to the end; (*e*) *v.phr.t.* occupy or defend to the end; (*f*) *v.phr.i.* maintain resistance; persist, last; continue to make a demand *for*; (*g*) *hold out on* (*colloq.*), refuse something to (a person). **hold over** (*a*) *Law* remain in office etc. beyond the regular term; (*b*) keep for future consideration, postpone. **hold over (a person)** threaten (a person) constantly with. *hold serve* or *service*: see *hold one's serve* or *service* above. *hold the bag*: see BAG *n. hold the baby*: see BABY *n.* I. *hold the clock on*: see CLOCK *n.*[1] *hold the field*: see FIELD *n. hold the fort*: see FORT *n.* I. **hold the line** (*a*) not yield; (*b*) maintain a telephone connection. **hold the stage** dominate a conversation etc. **hold to bail** *Law* bind by bail. **hold together** (cause to) cohere. **hold to ransom** keep (a person) prisoner until a ransom is paid; demand concessions from by threats, esp. of industrial action. **hold true** = *hold good* above. **hold up** (*a*) maintain (the head etc.) erect; *fig.* support, sustain; (*b*) exhibit, display; subject openly to (contempt, derision, etc.); (*c*) let alone, give up; keep back, withhold; (*d*) stop and rob by violence or threats; (*e*) arrest the progress of, obstruct; (*f*) not fall, keep up; (*g*) hold out, endure; †(*h*) give in, surrender; (*i*) (of the weather) remain fine, not rain. **hold water** (*a*) not let water through or out; *fig.* (of reasoning) be sound, bear examination; (*b*) stop a boat by holding the blades of the oars flat against the boat's way. *not able* or *fit to hold a candle*: see CANDLE *n. hold wedlock*: see WEDLOCK *n.* I. **there is no holding him, her**, etc., he, she, etc., is restive, high-spirited, determined, etc. *too hot to hold one*: see HOT *a.*

holdall /ˈhəʊldɔːl/ *n.* M19. [f. HOLD *v.* + ALL *pron.*] A portable case or bag for miscellaneous articles.

hold-back /ˈhəʊl(d)bak/ *n.* L16. [f. HOLD *v.* + BACK *adv.*] 1 Something that holds one back, a hindrance. L16. 2 An iron or strap on the shaft of a horse-drawn vehicle to which the breeching of the harness is attached. M19.

hold-down /ˈhəʊl(d)daʊn/ *n.* L19. [f. HOLD *v.* + DOWN *adv.*] 1 A device to prevent material or apparatus from moving or shaking. L19. 2 A judo grip or move in which the opponent is held down on the ground. M20.

holden *v.* pa. pple: see HOLD *v.*

holder /ˈhəʊldə/ *n.*[1] ME. [f. HOLD *v.* + -ER[1].] **I** 1 A person who holds or grasps something. ME. 2 A person who occupies or possesses something; *spec.* (*a*) the occupant of a post, position, office, etc., the current possessor of a (hereditary) title; (*b*) *Sport* a person who has set a current record, the winner of a challenge-cup; (*c*) the owner of a bank account, credit card, company shares, etc. ME. 3a A canine tooth. *rare.* L17. b In various animals, an organ of attachment or for grasping. L18. 4 A contrivance for holding something. M19.

1 DICKENS The holder of a horse at Tellson's door. 2 E. ARBER The present holder of the farm. *Times* The effect on the players was clearly seen when L. Hoad, the holder, beat R. Bedard. *freeholder, householder, jobholder, smallholder,* etc. *account holder, cardholder, shareholder,* etc. 4 *cigarette-holder, kettle-holder, penholder,* etc.

II 5 Something of which hold is taken. L18.

Comb.: **holderbat** a type of bracket for fastening a pipe to a wall etc., consisting of two semicircular parts that are clamped round the pipe and a projection on one of the parts that is built into the wall.

holder /ˈhəʊldə/ *n.*[2] L15. [f. HOLD *n.*[3] + -ER[1].] A workman employed in a ship's hold.

holdfast /ˈhəʊl(d)fɑːst/ *a.* & *n.* M16. [f. HOLD *v.* + FAST *adv.*] **A** *adj.* That holds fast (*lit.* & *fig.*); persistent. M16. **B** *n.* 1 A thing affording a secure hold or support. M16. 2 The action or fact of holding fast; firm or secure grasp. M16. 3 A thing that holds something fast; a staple, bolt, clamp, etc., securing an object to a wall. L16. b A rootlike or disc-shaped organ of attachment in some algae (esp. seaweeds) and fungi. M19. 4†a A stingy person, a miser. L16–E18. b (A name for) a dog that holds tenaciously. Now chiefly in proverb *Brag is a good dog, but Holdfast is better.* L16.

holding /ˈhəʊldɪŋ/ *n.* ME. [f. HOLD *v.* + -ING[1].] **I** 1 The action of HOLD *v.* Also foll. by adv. ME. b *spec.* The tenure of land. LME. †c Consistency. *rare* (Shakes.). Only in E17. 2 Something which holds or lays hold; an attachment; a means of influencing. L18. **II** 3 An opinion held, a tenet. Now chiefly *US Law*, a ruling on a point of law. LME. †4 The burden of a song. L16–E17. 5a Property held, *esp.* stocks or shares. L16. b Land held by legal right. M17. c The hand held by a card-player. E20.

5b *smallholding*.

Comb.: **holding company** a company created to hold the shares of other companies, which it then controls; **holding ground** a bottom in which an anchor will hold; anchorage (*lit.* & *fig.*); **holding operation** a manoeuvre designed to maintain the status quo; **holding paddock** *Austral.* & *NZ* a paddock where sheep or cattle are kept until required for droving etc.

hold-out /ˈhəʊldaʊt/ *n.* L19. [f. HOLD *v.* + OUT *adv.*] 1 A card-sharper's mechanical device for concealing cards. *arch. slang.* L19. 2 The action of holding out for something; a person who holds out for something, esp. higher pay. Chiefly *N. Amer.* M20. 3 The ability of paint or ink to dry normally on an imperfect surface. M20.

hold-over /ˈhəʊldəʊvə/ *n.* L19. [f. HOLD *v.* + OVER *adv.*] 1 A person who remains in office etc. beyond the regular term. L19. 2 Something left over, a relic. *N. Amer.* E20.

hold-up /ˈhəʊldʌp/ *n.* M19. [f. HOLD *v.* + UP *adv.*[1]] 1 A check to progress; a stoppage or delay of traffic etc. M19. 2 A robbery, esp. with the use of violence or threats. L19.

hole /həʊl/ *n.*[1] [OE *hol* (repr. inflected forms w. lengthened vowel) = ON *hol*, orig. use as n. of neut. sing. of *hol* HOLL *a.* = OFris., OS, (M)Du., OHG *hol* (G *hohl*), ON *holr*, f. Gmc base repr. by OHG *hulī*, G *Höhle*, OE *hylu*, ON *hola* hollow, hole, *hylr* deep place, pool, ult. f. IE base meaning 'cover, conceal': see HELE *v.* Rel. also to HELL *n.*, HELM *n.*[1], HOLD *n.*[3], HOLL *n.*, HOLLOW *n.*[1], HOWE *n.*[2]] **I** A hollow place, a cavity. 1 An empty place or cavity in a solid body or in the ground; a pit; a cave; a deep place in a pond, stream, etc.; *spec.* an animal's den or burrow. OE. b A deep hollow in the surface of the body, as an eye socket. ME. 2a A secret place; a hiding-place. *obs.* exc. in *priest's hole* s.v. PRIEST. ME. b A dungeon, a prison-cell; *esp.* a cell used for solitary confinement. M16. c A small, unpleasant, dreary or dingy place. E17. 3a A valley. Chiefly in place-names. ME. b A small bay, a cove. *US* & *Sc.* M17. 4 The hold of a ship. (Earlier as HOLL *n.* 2.) Now *rare.* L15. 5 A cavity into which a ball etc. must be got in various games, esp. golf; each of the pockets of a billiard or pool table. L16. 6 *Golf.* Each of the divisions of a course from each tee to each green; the play on this; a point scored by a player driving the ball from one hole to another with the fewest strokes. M18. 7 An awkward situation, a fix, a scrape. *colloq.* M18. 8 *Chess.* A square no longer protected by a defender's pawns and so easily available to attacking pieces. L19. 9 *Physics.* A position from which an electron is absent, esp. in an energy band in a crystal lattice; such a vacancy regarded as a mobile carrier of a positive charge. E20.

1 DAY LEWIS I came to know . . the holes and corners, where each of them deposited her eggs. J. MILLER If you poke your tongue into a hole in . . your teeth, the hole feels enormous. B. EMECHETA Mendoza has seen to it that you have more water holes. 2c P. BOWLES Dahar's a filthy hole. S. MIDDLETON Nobody would want to live in a dead-and-alive hole like this. 7 B. BAINBRIDGE You got me out of a hole . . I'm very grateful.

II A perforation, an opening, etc. 10 An aperture passing through something; an opening, a perforation. OE. 11 The orifice of an organ or part of the body; *spec.* (*slang*) the mouth, the anus, the vagina; *transf.* sexual intercourse. ME.

10 G. ORWELL Large, dirty toes were sticking out of the holes in his socks. 11 L. COHEN Don't give me all this diamond shit, shove it up your occult hole. T. PARKER I never thought the day'd come when I'd pass by a chance to have a bit of hole.

Phrases: *a round peg in a square hole, a square peg in a round hole*: see PEG *n.*[1] *black hole*: see BLACK *a. burn a hole in one's pocket*: see BURN *v.* 9b. **hole in the heart** a congenital defect in the heart membrane. **hole in one** *Golf* a first shot from the tee that enters the hole. **hole in the wall** a small dingy place; *esp.* a business or (*US*) a place where alcoholic drinks are sold illegally. **in holes** worn so much that holes have formed. **in the hole** in debt. **make a hole in** use a large amount of. **make a hole in the water** commit suicide by drowning. **need like a hole in the head** have no need or desire at all for (something). **pick holes in** find fault with. **the hole** *slang* solitary confinement; (see also *in the hole* above). *toad in the hole*: see TOAD I. *white hole*: see WHITE *a.*

Comb.: **hole-and-corner** *a.* secret; underhand; **hole-card** in stud poker, a card which has been dealt face down; **hole-proof** *a.* (of a material) treated so as to be resistant to wear; **hole-saw** = *crown saw* s.v. CROWN *n.*

†hole *a.*, *n.*[2], *adv.*, & *int.* see WHOLE.

hole /həʊl/ *v.* [OE *holian* = OHG *holōn*, Goth. *-hulōn*, f. Gmc base of HOLL *a.*: see prec.] 1 *v.t.* Make a hole or holes in, hollow out; dig (the ground); *spec.* (*Naut.*) pierce the side of (a ship). OE. 2 *v.i.* Make a hole or holes; dig *through* from one mine-working to another. ME. 3 *v.i.* Become full of holes through wear. E17. 4 *v.i.* Go into a hole, esp. for hibernation; *esp.* (*N. Amer. colloq.*) hide oneself, lie in wait, seek shelter. Usu. foll. by *out, up.* E17. 5 *v.t.* Put into a hole; put in prison; hide. E17. 6 *v.t. Golf, Billiards*, etc. Drive (a ball) or play (a shot) into a hole or pocket. L17. b *v.i. Golf.* Drive the ball into the hole. Usu. foll. by *out.* M19. c *v.i. Cricket.* (Of a batsman) be dismissed by hitting a catch to a (usu. specified) fielder or position. Foll. by *out.* L20. 7 *v.t. Mining.* Sink (a shaft), drive (a tunnel) through; undercut (coal) in a seam. E18.

1 E. DIEHL After the boards have been cut to size, they are holed-out and laced onto the book. SNOO WILSON I've got to get him before we get holed by a Russian submarine. 4 E. BIRNEY Or you could hole out in Canada in an igloo or something. T. O'BRIEN I holed up in the bathroom. 6 JO GRIMOND His brother . . holed a putt of awkward length to win the Calcutta Cup. b N. BLAKE Holed out in one. *Golf Monthly* He . . gave a strong hint of . . greater things to come by holing for a birdie. c *Times* 47 runs were added in seven overs before Lloyds holed out to deep mid-wicket.

holeable *a.* (*Golf*) (of a stroke, esp. a putt) capable of sending the ball into the hole E20. **holer** *n.* a person who makes or bores a hole; *spec.* a collier who undercuts a coal seam: LME. **holing** *n.* (*a*) the action of the vb; (*b*) *Mining* a wedge-shaped section of a coal seam or floor removed to undermine or loosen it: LME.

holed /həʊld/ *a.* LME. [f. HOLE *n.*[1], *v.*: see -ED[2], -ED[1].] Having a hole or holes.

holey /ˈhəʊli/ *a.* ME. [f. HOLE *n.*[1] + -Y[1].] Full of holes.

J. RABAN Shoes which let the sand into their holey socks. **holey dollar** *Austral. Hist.* a coin originally worth 5s. current in parts of Australia from 1813 to about 1830, made by punching a circular piece out of the centre of a Spanish dollar.

Holi /ˈhəʊliː/ *n.* Also (earlier) **†Hoolee**. L17. [Hind. *holī*.] The Hindu spring festival in honour of Krishna the amorous cowherd.

holiday /ˈhɒlədeɪ, ˈhɒlɪ-, -di/ *n.* & *a.* [OE *hāligdæg*, late OE *hālidæg*, found beside *hālig dæg* HOLY DAY.] **A** *n.* 1 = HOLY DAY. Now *rare.* OE. 2 A day of festivity or recreation, on which no work is done; *sing.* & in *pl.*, a period of such recreation, a vacation. ME. b *gen.* Festivity, recreation. E16. 3 Chiefly *Naut.* A patch or area unintentionally left uncoated in painting etc. L18.

2 A. TROLLOPE Glomax thought that Tony had been idle, and had made a holiday of the day. A. S. BYATT He was sure she would find a nice holiday abroad very restorative. J. MORTIMER Separated at school the boys remained apart during the holidays. b T. KENEALLY To see the distinctive hills . . gave them an unwarranted sense of holiday.

Phrases etc.: *busman's holiday*: see *busman* s.v. BUS *n.* *blind-man's holiday*: see BLIND *a.* *half-holiday*: see HALF-. *high holiday*: see HIGH *a.* **make holiday** *arch.* have a break from work. **on holiday, on one's holidays** in the course of a holiday or vacation. *Roman holiday*: see ROMAN *a.* **take a holiday** have a break from work. *whole holiday*: see WHOLE.

Comb.: **holiday camp** a camp for holiday-makers with accommodation, entertainment, and facilities on site; **holiday centre** a place with many tourist attractions; **holiday home** a house or second home where people may spend holidays; **holiday loading** *Austral.* an addition to holiday pay to compensate for lost overtime earnings; **holiday-maker** a person on holiday; **holiday village** a complex for holiday-makers with cottages, shops, entertainment, etc., on site.

B *attrib.* or as *adj.* Of, pertaining to, or characteristic of a holiday; festive; idle, jesting. LME.

SHAKES. *A.Y.L.* They are but burs . . thrown upon thee in holiday foolery.

holiday /ˈhɒlədeɪ, ˈhɒlɪ-, -di/ *v.i.* M19. [f. prec.] Spend a holiday.

R. P. GRAVES He was holidaying in a hotel with a magnificent view.

holidayer *n.* L19.

holily /ˈhəʊlɪli/ *adv.* OE. [f. HOLY *a.* + -LY[2].] 1 With sanctity or devoutness; in a holy manner. OE. 2 Sacredly; solemnly. Now *rare* or *obs.* LME.

holiness /ˈhəʊlɪnɪs/ *n.* & *a.* OE. [f. HOLY *a.* + -NESS.] **A** *n.* 1 The quality of being holy; sanctity; saintliness. OE. †2 A holy place or thing. OE–ME. 3 (Usu. **H-.**) With possess. adj. (as *his* etc. *holiness*): a title of respect given to the Pope and (formerly) any of various high ecclesiastical dignitaries. LME.

1 P. ROTH In the old parables about the spiritual life, there were searches for a kind of holiness. 3 R. BOLT His present Holiness is . . a strikingly corrupt old person.

B *attrib.* or as *adj.* Designating or pertaining to any of various religious sects or Churches which emphasize sanctification, spiritual purity, and perfectionism. Chiefly *US.* L19.

holinight /ˈhɒlɪnʌɪt/ *n.* ME. [f. HOLY *a.* + NIGHT *n.*, after HOLIDAY *n.*] †1 The eve of a holy festival. Only in ME. 2 A night of festivity or pleasure. *rare.* E19.

holism /ˈhəʊlɪz(ə)m, ˈhɒl-/ *n.* E20. [f. HOLO- + -ISM. Cf. WHOLISM.] The theory or principle of a tendency in nature to form or produce organized wholes which are more than the mere sum of the component units; *spec.* the application of this theory in medicine, involving the treatment of the whole person rather than the physical symptoms alone.

hoˈlistic *a.* (*a*) of or pertaining to holism; (*b*) whole, complete, comprising or involving all parts, aspects, etc.: E20. **hoˈlistically** *adv.* as a whole E20.

†holk *v.* see HOWK.

holl /həʊl/ *n. obs.* exc. *dial.* See also HOWE *n.*[2] [OE *hol* HOLE *n.*[1], repr. orig. uninflected form w. short vowel (later w. diphthong). Cf. HULL *n.*[2]] 1 A hole, a hollow place, a dip, a valley. OE. †2 A ship's hold. ME–E17. 3 The middle or depth (of winter or night). *Sc.* & *north.* LME.

holl /həʊl/ *a. obs.* exc. *dial.* [OE *hol*: see HOLE *n.*[1]] 1 Hollow, concave, empty. OE. 2 Deeply excavated or dug; lying in a hollow. OE.

holla /ˈhɒlə/ *v.i.* & *t.* Pa. t. & pple **-aed, -a'd.** L16. [Partly var. of HOLLO *v.*, partly f. HOLLA *int.* & *n.*] = HOLLO *v.*

holla /ˈhɒlə, *occas.* hɒˈlɑː/ *int.* & *n.* E16. [Fr. *holà*, f. *ho* HO *int.*[2] + *là* there. Cf. HOLLO *int.* & *n.* etc.] **A** *int.* †1 Stop! Cease! E16–L17. 2 Commanding or attempting to attract attention. L16. 3 Expr. pleasure, satisfaction, encouragement, etc. E18. **B** *n.* A shout of 'holla!'. L16.

hollabaloo *n.*, *int.*, & *v.* var. of HULLABALOO.

holland /ˈhɒlənd/ *n.* & *a.* ME. [*Holland*, a former province of the Netherlands (now freq. also used as the name of the whole country), f. Du., earlier *Holtlant*, f. *holt* wood + *-lant* land, describing the Dordrecht district.] **A** *n.* Any smooth hard-wearing linen fabric, orig. a kind produced in the Netherlands (Holland). ME. **B** *attrib.* or as *adj.* 1 (**H-.**) Of, pertaining to, or produced in the Netherlands. LME. 2 Made of holland. M16.

Phrases: *brown holland*: see BROWN *a.*

hollandaise /hɒlənˈdeɪz, *attrib. also* ˈhɒləndeɪz/ *n.* & *a.* M19. [Fr. fem. of *hollandais* Dutch, f. *Hollande* Holland.] (Designating) a sauce made with butter, egg-yolks, vinegar or white wine, and lemon juice, usu. served with fish.

Hollander /ˈhɒləndə/ *n.* LME. [f. as HOLLAND + -ER[1].] 1 A native of the Netherlands (Holland); a Netherlander. Now chiefly *spec.*, a South African colonist or immigrant of Dutch birth or descent. LME. 2 *Hist.* A Dutch ship. L16. 3 A machine, invented in the Netherlands, for making paper pulp from rags. L19.

Hollands /ˈhɒləndz/ *n. arch.* L18. [f. Du. †*hollandsch genever* (now *hollands jenever*) Dutch gin: see GENEVER.] Dutch gin, genever. Also *Hollands gin.*

Hollantide /ˈhɒl(ə)ntʌɪd/ *n.* Now chiefly *Anglo-Ir.* L16. [Alt.] = *Hallowtide* s.v. HALLOW *n.*[1]

holler /ˈhɒlə/ *n.* Chiefly *dial.* & *N. Amer. colloq.* E19. [Partly var. of HOLLO *n.*, partly f. the vb.] A shout, esp. of protest or complaint; a protest, a complaint; a work-song of southern States of the US.

a whoop and a holler: see WHOOP *n.* 1.

holler /ˈhɒlə/ *v.i.* & *t.* Chiefly *dial.* & *N. Amer. colloq.* L17. [Var. of HOLLO *v.*] Cry out, shout, esp. in protest or complaint.

G. PALEY You always start hollering if I don't do what you tell me. J. BARTH 'Toddy!' one of my companions hollered from down a hallway. W. WHARTON With the sound of babies hollering to be fed . . it makes quite a racket.

Hollerith /ˈhɒlərɪθ/ *n.* L19. [Herman *Hollerith* (1860–1929), Amer. inventor.] Used *attrib.* to designate the system of using punched cards in accounting, statistics, etc., or such cards themselves.

hollin /ˈhɒlɪn/ *n.* Now *arch.* & *dial.* [OE *hole(g)n* rel. to OS, OHG *hulis* (MHG *huls*, G *Hulst*), OFrank. source of Fr. *houx*, and further to Welsh *celyn*, OIr. *cuilenn*, Gael. *cuilionn.*] Holly.

hollo /ˈhɒləʊ/ *v.* Also **holloa** /ˈhɒləʊ, hɒˈləʊ/, (now *rare*) **hollow.** LME. [Prob. var. of HALLOW *v.*[2] See also HALLO, HALLOO *v.*, HOLLER *v.*] 1 *v.i.* & *t.* Call out or yell to attract attention, express surprise, give encouragement, etc. LME. 2 *v.t.* Call after or to. E17. 3 *v.t.* Drive *away*, call *in*, *off*, etc., by holloing. E17.

hollo /ˈhɒləʊ/ *int.* & *n.* Also **holloa** /ˈhɒləʊ, hɒˈləʊ/, (now *rare*) **hollow.** L16. [Rel. to HOLLA *int.* & *n.* See also HALLO, HILLO, HOLLER *n.*] **A** *int.* Commanding or attempting to attract attention. Also expr. pleasure, satisfaction, encouragement, etc. L16. **B** *n.* A shout of 'hollo!'; a loud shout. L16.

holloa *v.*, *int.* & *n.* vars. of HOLLO *v.*, *int.* & *n.*

hollow /ˈhɒləʊ/ *n.*[1] [OE *holh* obscurely rel. to *hol* HOLE *n.*[1], HOLL *n.* Re-formed M16 f. the adj. (obs. f. early ME).] 1 A concave formation or place dug out or resembling one dug out; a depression on any surface; an internal cavity (with or without an opening), an empty space. OE. 2 *spec.* A depression on the earth's surface; a dip, a valley, a basin. ME. 3 *Bookbinding.* A strip of thick paper glued to the boards and back of a book in order to strengthen its spine. L19.

1 E. BOWEN A large double bed with a hollow in the middle. E. O'BRIEN The hollows in his face made him seem thinner than he actually was. **in the hollow of one's hand** *fig.* entirely subservient to one. 2 K. MANSFIELD Down below in the hollow the little cottages were in deep shade. 3 OXFORD *hollow.*

hollow *n.*[2] see HOLLO *n.*

hollow /ˈhɒləʊ/ *a.* & *adv.* ME. [f. HOLLOW *n.*[1]] **A** *adj.* 1 Having a hole or empty space inside; not solid. Formerly also, porous or open in texture or composition. ME. b Having an empty space below. M17. 2 Having a hole or depression on the surface; sunken, indented. ME. b Of the sea: having deep troughs. E17. 3 Empty; *transf.* having an empty stomach, hungry, lean. LME. 4 *fig.* Lacking substance or value; insincere, false; cynical. E16. 5 Of a sound: echoing, as if made in or on a hollow container. M16.

1 W. WHARTON The feather has a hollow shaft. *fig.*: L. GORDON Lily's very body felt stark and hollow with longing. 2 G. GREENE The men trudging to Castile for work . . , bony wrists and hollow chests, incredible rags. U. LE GUIN The stone plain was . . hollow, like a huge bowl full of sunlight. S. ROE She eats very little. . . Her cheeks are hollow. 3 SHAKES. *Merry W.* As jealous as Ford, that search'd a hollow walnut for his wife's leman. 4 C. G. WOLFF Raucous laughter pursues us . . hollow, mocking, derisive. K. MILLER The hollow enthusiasm which many people profess for music. *Times* If Seb had competed it would have been a hollow victory over him. 5 E. LANGLEY An emaciated boy with a hollow cough and that easy-going look of the consumptive. S. SASSOON A hollow cry of hounds like lonely bells.

B *adv.* 1 Hollowly. Now *rare* exc. in comb. & in *ring hollow*, sound insincere or unconvincing. L15. 2 Thoroughly, completely. *colloq.* M17.

2 GEO. ELIOT She beats us younger people hollow.

Special collocations & comb.: **hollow-eyed** *a.* with eyes (apparently) deeply sunken from fatigue etc. **hollow-ground** *a.* ground so as to have a concave surface. **hollow heart** a condition of potatoes in which a cavity is formed in the centre of the tuber by overrapid growth. **hollow horn** *US* listlessness and weakness in cattle erroneously believed to be due to hollow horns. **hollow square** *Mil. Hist.* a body of infantry drawn up in a square with a space in the middle.

hollow /ˈhɒləʊ/ *v.*[1] LME. [f. the adj.] 1 *v.t.* Make hollow or concave; form or bend into a hollow or concave shape. Also foll. by *out.* LME. 2 *v.t.* Form by making a hollow. Freq. foll. by *out.* M17. 3 *v.i.* Become hollow or concave. M19.

1 V. WOOLF The breeze blew out her match. Giles hollowed his hand and lit another. J. M. COETZEE The bowls we ate . . from were crude blocks of wood hollowed out by scraping and burning. 2 M. MEYER A huge natural cave hollowed into the rock. 3 K. ISHIGURO Kuroda's face . . had hollowed out around the cheekbones.

hollow *v.*[2] see HOLLO *v.*

hollow *int.* see HOLLO *int.*

holloware *n.* var. of HOLLOW-WARE.

hollow-hearted /hɒləʊˈhɑːtɪd/ *a.* M16. [f. HOLLOW *a.* + HEARTED *a.*] Insincere, false.

hollow-heartedness *n.* M16.

hollowly /ˈhɒləʊli/ *adv.* M16. [f. HOLLOW *a.* + -LY[2].] In a hollow manner; with a hollow sound or voice; insincerely.

J. WYNDHAM A louder voice echoing hollowly in the corridors.

hollowness /ˈhɒləʊnɪs/ *n.* LME. [f. HOLLOW *a.* + -NESS.] 1 The quality or condition of being hollow. LME. †2 A hollow formation or place. LME–E18.

hollow-ware /ˈhɒləʊwɛː/ *n.* Also **holloware.** L17. [f. HOLLOW *a.* + WARE *n.*[2]] Hollow articles of wood, china, or esp. metal, as pots, kettles, etc. Opp. *flatware.*

holluschickie /ˈhɒləstʃɪki/ *n.pl.* L19. [Russ. *kholostyaki* bachelors.] Young 'bachelor' male fur seals.

holly /ˈhɒli/ *n.* ME. [Reduced form of OE *hole(g)n* HOLLIN.] 1 Any of several evergreen shrubs or small trees of the genus *Ilex* (family Aquifoliaceae); *esp.* one of the common European species *I. aquifolium*, with tough dark green glossy leaves with indented edges usu. set with sharp stiff prickles at the points, and bearing small white flowers succeeded by red berries, much used for Christmas decoration. Also, the American holly, *I. opaca*, a similar tree of the US. Also *holly bush, tree.* ME. 2 Any of various plants resembling the holly in some way, esp. in having prickly leaves. Usu. w. specifying wd. ME.

2 *knee-holly*: see KNEE *n.* *sea holly*: see SEA *n.*

Comb.: **holly blue** a butterfly, *Celastrina argiolus*, whose caterpillars feed in spring on buds etc. of holly (the late summer brood feeding on ivy); **holly fern** a mountain fern, *Polystichum lonchitis*, having stiff glossy fronds with spine-tipped teeth; **holly-oak** = *holm-oak* s.v. HOLM *n.*[2] 2.

holly *adv.* see WHOLLY.

hollyhock /'hɒlɪhɒk/ *n.* ME. [f. HOLY *a.* + HOCK *n.*[1]: cf. the Welsh name (dating f. 16th cent.) *hocys bendigaid* lit. 'blessed mallow'.] Orig., the marsh mallow, *Althaea officinalis*, of the mallow family. Now, (a flowering stem of) a related garden plant, *Alcea rosea*, with very tall stout stems bearing numerous large blooms on very short stalks.

Hollywood /'hɒlɪwʊd/ *n.* & *a.* E20. [A district of Los Angeles in California, the principal centre of the US film industry.] A *n.* The American film industry or its products. E20.

H. G. WELLS There was a vast editor's desk, marvellously equipped, like a desk out of Hollywood.

B *adj.* Of, pertaining to, or characteristic of Hollywood. E20.

C. MORLEY Those black and white yachting shoes.. were definitely Hollywood.

Hollywoodean, -ian *adjs.* = HOLLYWOOD *a.* M20. **Hollywoodish** *a.* somewhat resembling or characteristic of a Hollywood film E20. **Hollywoodism** *n.* a style or idiom characteristic of Hollywood M20. **Hollywoodize** *v.t.* make typically Hollywoodian M20.

holm /həʊm/ *n.*[1] Also **holme**. OE. [ON *holmr* islet in a bay, lake, or river, meadow on the shore, corresp. to OS *holm* hill.] 1 An islet, esp. in a river or near the mainland. OE. 2 A flat low-lying piece of ground by a river, submerged in time of flood. ME.

holm /həʊm/ *n.*[2] ME. [Alt. of HOLLIN.] 1 The holly. *obs.* exc. *dial.* ME. 2 Now usu. more fully *holm-oak*. A kind of oak, *Quercus ilex*, common in Mediterranean countries, with dark evergreen sometimes spiny-toothed leaves. Also called *evergreen oak, ilex*. LME.

Comb.: *holm-oak*: see sense 2 above; **holm tree** (*a*) (*obs.* exc. *dial.*) the holly; (*b*) (now *rare*) the holm-oak.

holme *n.* var. of HOLM *n.*[1]

Holmesian /'həʊmzɪən/ *a.* E20. [f. *Holmes* (see below) + -IAN.] Of, pertaining to, or characteristic of Sherlock Holmes, the amateur detective in the stories of A. Conan Doyle (1859–1931).

C. WAUGH To uncover..plots with the aid of magnifying glass, pipe and Holmesian costume.

holmgang /'həʊmgaŋ/ *n.* M19. [ON *holmganga* 'going to the holm', on which a duel was fought.] *N. European Hist.* & *Mythol.* A duel to the death.

S. HEANEY That holmgang Where two berserks dub each other to death For honour's sake.

Holmgren /'həʊ(l)mgrən/ *n.* L19. [A. F. *Holmgren* (1831–97), Swed. physiologist.] *Holmgren's test*, a test for colour-blindness in which the subject is required to match differently coloured pieces of wool (*Holmgren's wools*).

holmium /'həʊlmɪəm/ *n.* L19. [f. *Holmia* Latinized form of *Stockholm*, Swed. capital city: see -IUM.] A soft silvery metallic chemical element of the lanthanide series, atomic no. 67. (Symbol Ho.)

holmia *n.* holmium oxide, Ho_2O_3, a pale yellow solid L19.

holmquistite /'həʊmkwɪstʌɪt, -kvɪst-/ *n.* E20. [f. Per Johan *Holmquist* (1866–1946), Swed. geologist + -ITE[1].] *Min.* A rare blue or violet orthorhombic amphibole containing lithium.

holo- /'hɒləʊ/ *comb. form.* Bef. a vowel also **hol-**. [Gk *holos* whole, entire.] Complete, whole; completely, wholly. Cf. HEMI-, MERO-[1].

ho'landric *a.* inherited solely in the male line (on the Y chromosome) M20. **holo-alpha'betic** *a.* containing the whole alphabet L20. **holo'axial** *a.* (*Cryst.*) (of a crystal class) having one or more (esp. all compatible) axes of symmetry, but no plane or centre of symmetry E20. **holo'benthic** *a.* (*Biol.*) living at the bottom of the sea at all stages of the life cycle E20. **holo'blastic** *a.* (of an ovum) undergoing complete cleavage L19. **holobranch** *n.* (*Ichthyol.*) a complete gill having lamellae on both sides E20. **holo'carpic** *a.* (*Mycol.*) designating a thallus the whole of which is transformed into a reproductive structure at maturity; possessing such a thallus: E20. **holo'cephalan, holoce'phalian** *ns.* & *adjs.* (*a*) *n.* a cartilaginous fish of the subclass Holocephali, which comprises the chimaeras or rat-fishes; (*b*) *adj.* of, pertaining to, or characteristic of (a fish of) the order Holocephali: M20. **holocrine** *a.* (*Physiol.*) of, pertaining to, or designating a gland in which secretion occurs by total disintegration of the cell E20. **holo'crystalline** *a.* (*Petrogr.*) wholly composed of (esp. large) crystals L19. **holoen'demic** *a.* (*Med.*) permanently affecting most or all of a population M20. **holo'enzyme** *n.* the active complex of an enzyme with its coenzyme M20. **hologamete** *a.* (*Biol.*) (in some protists) a gamete morphologically similar to an ordinary individual and not formed by special fission E20. **ho'logamous** *a.* (*Biol.*) (of certain unicellular organisms) reproducing by sexual fusion of two ordinary individuals acting as gametes E20. **ho'logamy** *n.* reproduction by hologamous fusion E20. **holo'hedral** *a.* (*Cryst.*) (of a crystal or crystal class) having the maximum possible symmetry for a given crystal system M19. **holo'hedron** *n.* (*Cryst.*) any holohedral crystal L19. †**holometer** *n.* a pantometer L17–M19. **holo'morphic** *a.* (*Math.*) (of a function of a complex variable) having a derivative at all points of the domain; analytic: L19. **holophote** *n.* [Gk *phōt-, phōs* light] an apparatus for making nearly all of the light from a lamp available (as in a lighthouse) M19. **holophy'letic** *a.* (*Biol.*) (of a taxon) including all descendants of the common ancestor (cf. MONOPHYLETIC) M20. **holophytic** /-'fɪtɪk/ *a.* (*Biol.*) of, pertaining to, or designating a plant or protozoan which obtains organic nutrients by photosynthesis L19. **holo'plankton** *n.* (*Biol.*) holoplanktonic organisms (cf. MEROPLANKTON) E20. **holoplank'tonic** *a.* (*Biol.*) (of aquatic organisms) passing all stages of the life cycle as plankton L19. **holopneustic** /hɒlə(ʊ)'pnjuːstɪk/ *a.* [Gk *-pneustos* breathing] *Entomol.* having eleven or (usu.) ten pairs of spiracles, all fully functional L19. **ho'loptic** *a.* (*Entomol.*) having the eyes meeting at the midline L19. **holose'riceous** *a.* (*Bot.* & *Entomol.*) wholly covered with a silky pubescence M19. **ho'lostean** *n.* & *a.* [Gk *osteon* bone] (*a*) *n.* any member of a group (Holostei) of bony fishes intermediate between chondrosteans and teleosts, and including the extant bowfin and gar pike, and many fossil forms; (*b*) *adj.* of, pertaining to, or characteristic of (a fish of) the group Holostei: L19. **holo'stylic** *a.* (*Zool.*) having the upper jaw fused to the cranium M20. **holosy'mmetrical, -syste'matic** *adjs.* = HOLOHEDRAL L19. **holo'zoic** *a.* (*Biol.*) of, pertaining to, or designating an organism which ingests organic nutrients from other organisms L19.

holocaine /'hɒləkeɪn/ *n.* L19. [f. HOLO- + -CAINE.] *Pharm.* = PHENACAINE.

holocaust /'hɒləkɔːst/ *n.* In sense 4 also **H-**. ME. [(O)Fr. *holocauste* f. late L *holocaustum* f. Gk *holokauston*, f. as HOLO- + *kaustos* var. of *kautos* burnt, f. *kau-* base of *kaiein* burn.] 1 A sacrifice wholly consumed by fire. ME. 2 A complete or large-scale sacrifice. L15. 3 A complete or wholesale destruction, esp. by fire; a great slaughter or massacre. L17. 4 spec. *The* (period of the) mass murder of the Jews (or *transf.* of other groups) by the Nazis in the war of 1939–45. M20.

3 W. STYRON His stable..burned to the ground in one horrid and almost instantaneous holocaust. B. CASTLE The bombing holocaust in Birmingham..has shaken the country. *nuclear holocaust*: see NUCLEAR *a.* 4 F. FORSYTH Yad Vashem,..the shrine to six million.. Jews who died in the holocaust. M. FRENCH My students..don't even care about World War II or the Holocaust.

holo'caustal *a.* (*rare*) = HOLOCAUSTIC E19. **holo'caustic** *a.* of the nature of or pertaining to a holocaust L19.

Holocene /'hɒləsiːn/ *a.* & *n.* L19. [Fr., f. as HOLO- + Gk *kainos* new, recent.] *Geol.* A *adj.* Of, pertaining to, or designating the most recent geological epoch, subsequent to the Pleistocene and forming with it the Quaternary period; = RECENT *a.* 4. L19. B *n.* The Holocene epoch; the series of rocks dating from this time. E20.

hologram /'hɒləgram/ *n.* M20. [f. HOLO- + -GRAM.] *Physics.* A pattern produced by interference between light reflected (or diffracted or transmitted) by an object and other light with the same or a related phase; a photograph of such a pattern, which can be illuminated so as to produce a spatial image of the object used.

holograph /'hɒləgrɑːf/ *n.* & *a.* E17. [Fr. *holographe* or late L *holographus* f. Gk *holographos*: see HOLO-, -GRAPH.] A *n.* A document etc. wholly written by hand by the person named as its author. E17. B *adj.* (Of a document etc.) wholly written by the hand of the person named as the author; *spec.* in *Sc.* & *US Law*, (of a will) written by the hand of and signed by the testator and thereby valid. E18.

holograph /'hɒləgrɑːf/ *v.t.* M20. [Back-form. f. HOLOGRAPHY, after PHOTOGRAPH *v.*, TELEGRAPH *v.*] *Physics.* Record as a hologram.

holographic /hɒlə'grafɪk/ *a.* E18. [f. HOLOGRAPH *n.*, HOLOGRAPHY + -IC.] 1 = HOLOGRAPH *a.* E18. 2 *Physics.* Of or pertaining to holography; produced by or involving holography. M20.

holographically *adv.* (*Physics*) by means of holography M20.

holography /hɒ'lɒgrəfi/ *n.* E19. [f. HOLO- + -GRAPHY; in sense 2 after *photography*, *telegraphy*, etc.] 1 Writing wholly by one's own hand. E19. 2 *Physics.* The process or science of producing and using holograms. M20.

holoku /hɒ'ləʊkuː/ *n.* L19. [Haw.] A long gown with a train, as worn in Hawaii.

holometabolous /,hɒləʊmə'tabələs/ *a.* L19. [f. HOLO- + Gk *metabolos* changeable: see -OUS.] *Entomol.* Of an insect: that undergoes complete metamorphosis to the adult from a morphologically distinct larval stage. Cf. HEMIMETABOLOUS.

holoparasite /hɒlə(ʊ)'parəsʌɪt/ *n.* L19. [f. HOLO- + PARASITE *n.*] *Biol.* An obligate parasite, unable to exist apart from its host.

holopara'sitic *a.* E20. **holo'parasitism** *n.* E20.

Holophane /'hɒləfeɪn/ *n.* Also **h-**. L19. [f. HOLO- + Gk *phanein* shine, appear.] (Proprietary name for) (a type of lampshade made of) glass specially fluted or ribbed to refract and reflect the light with little loss.

holophrase /'hɒləfreɪz/ *n.* L19. [f. HOLO- + PHRASE *n.*] A single word expressing a whole phrase or combination of ideas.

holophrasis /hɒlə(ʊ)'freɪsɪs/ *n.* Pl. **-phrases** /-'freɪsiːz/. M19. [f. HOLO- + Gk *phrasis* speech, phrase.] The use of a single word to express a whole phrase or combination of ideas.

holophrastic /hɒlə(ʊ)'frastɪk/ *a.* M19. [f. HOLO- + Gk *phrastikos*, f. *phrazein* tell: see -IC.] Of a particular language or a stage in language acquisition: characterized by holophrasis.

holothuria /hɒlə(ʊ)'θjʊərɪə/ *n.* Pl. **-iae** /-iːiː/, **-ias**. L18. [mod.L *Holothuria* genus name f. L *holothurion* some marine creature f. Gk, of unkn. origin.] *Zool.* A holothurian. Formerly also, any of several other elongate aquatic invertebrates. Now only as mod.L genus name.

holothurian /hɒlə(ʊ)'θjʊərɪən/ *n.* & *a.* M19. [f. as prec. + -AN.] *Zool.* A *n.* Any elongate, bilaterally symmetrical echinoderm of the class Holothuroidea, having a leathery integument and a diffuse skeleton of calcitic spicules; a sea cucumber. M19. B *adj.* Of or pertaining to the class Holothuroidea. L19.

holotype /'hɒlətʌɪp/ *n.* L19. [f. HOLO- + TYPE *n.*] *Taxon.* A single specimen chosen to represent a new species by the first author to describe it and with which the specific epithet remains associated during any taxonomic revision.

holo'typic *a.* M20.

holp *v.* pa. t.: see HELP *v.*

holpen *v.* pa. pple: see HELP *v.*

hols /hɒlz/ *n.pl. colloq.* E20. [Abbrev.] Holidays.

A. T. ELLIS He's going off on his hols for a couple of weeks.

Holstein /'hɒlstʌɪn/ *a.* & *n.* Chiefly *N. Amer.* M19. [A region in northern Germany.] = FRIESIAN.

Holsteinian /hɒl'stʌɪnɪən/ *a.* & *n.* M20. [f. prec. + -IAN.] *Geol.* (Designating or pertaining to) an interglacial stage of the Pleistocene in northern Europe, preceding the Saale glaciation.

holster /'həʊlstə, 'hɒl-/ *n.* & *v.* M17. [Corresp. to and contemporary with Du. *holster*, perh. ult. f. Gmc base of HELE *v.*: see -STER.] A *n.* A (usu. leather) case or holder for a pistol or occas. a larger gun, fixed to a saddle or worn on a belt or under the arm. Also, any such case designed for convenient holding or carrying, esp. of a piton hammer or ice axe in mountaineering. M17.

P. CAMPBELL The butt of an immense gun stood out from the holster strapped to his side. *Climber* Tools are slid into holsters, over-mitts removed and I pretend it's summer.

B *v.t.* Put (a pistol etc.) into a holster. Chiefly *US*. M20.

holt /həʊlt/ *n.*[1] [OE *holt* = OFris., OS, ON *holt*, MDu. *hout*, (O)HG *holz*, f. Gmc, f. IE base repr. by Gk *klados* twig.] **1** A wood, a copse. Now *arch.* & *dial.* OE. **b** A plantation, esp. of osiers. *local.* E17. **2** A wooded hill. M16.

holt /həʊlt/ *n.*[2] LME. [Var. of HOLD *n.*[1]] **1** Hold, grip. Now *dial.* & *US colloq.* LME. **2** The lair or den of an animal, esp. an otter or fish. L16.

holus-bolus /həʊləs'bəʊləs/ *adv.* Orig. *dial.* M19. [Origin uncertain: pseudo-L for 'whole bolus' or joc. repr. assumed Gk *holos bōlos* whole lump (see BOLUS).] All in a lump, altogether.

Times An insurance company can be swallowed holus-bolus like a sprat by a hungry predator.

holy /'həʊli/ *a.* & *n.* [OE *hāliġ*, *-eġ* = OFris. *hēlich*, OS *hēlag*, *-eg*, OHG *heilag* (Du., G *heilig*), ON *heilagr*, f. Gmc base of WHOLE.] **A** *adj.* **1** Of a thing, place, etc.: kept or regarded as sacred; set apart for religious use or observance; consecrated. OE. **2** Of a god or icon: (to be) held in religious veneration or reverence; *spec.* in the Christian Church, free from all contamination of sin and evil, morally and spiritually perfect (cf. sense 4). OE. **3** (Of a person) (regarded as) specially belonging to, empowered by, or devoted to God; (of a thing) pertaining to, originating from, or sanctioned by God or the Trinity. Formerly also, (of a person) religiously devoted *to* (anything). OE. **b** *gen.* Of surpassing excellence; having mysterious power. Also w. intensive force (*colloq.*), absolute, complete. L16. **4** Pious, devout; *esp.* of godly character and life, saintly, morally and spiritually clean; *colloq.* sanctimonious. OE. **5** Used w. following n. as an oath or expletive, as *holy cow!*, *holy mackerel!*, *holy Moses!*, *holy smoke!*, etc. M19.

1 G. VIDAL The holy capital of the Middle Kingdom. **2** AV *Ps.* 22:3 But thou art holy, O thou that inhabitest the praises of Israel. **3** S. MORLEY The players . . seemed . . to be regarding their work as a kind of holy calling. **b** G. KEILLOR If any of his children had done it he would have given them holy hell. **4** JONATHAN ROSS She said again, in that holy voice, [etc.]. *absol.*: T. ARNOLD For a moment it must overwhelm the mind of the holiest.

Special collocations & comb.: **holier-than-thou** *a.* (*colloq.*) self-righteous, characterized by an attitude of superior sanctity. **Holy Alliance** *Hist.* an alliance formed between Russia, Austria, and Prussia in 1815 on the basis of proposed common Christian principles of government. **holy basil** an Indian basil, *Ocimum sanctum*, regarded by Hindus as sacred to Vishnu. **holy bread** (*a*) the bread provided for the Eucharist; the bread consecrated in the Eucharist; (*b*) ordinary bread blessed and distributed after the Eucharist to non-communicants. *Holy Church*: see CHURCH *n.* **Holy City** (*a*) a city held sacred by the adherents of a religion, *esp.* Jerusalem; (*b*) Heaven. *Holy Communion*: see COMMUNION 5. **holy Cross** the Cross on which Jesus died; *Holy Cross Day*, the festival of the Exaltation of the Cross, 14 September. **Holy Family** the young Jesus with his mother and St Joseph (often with St John Baptist, St Anne, etc.) as grouped in pictures etc. *Holy Father*: see FATHER *n.* †**holy fire** erysipelas. *Holy Grail*: see GRAIL *n.*[2] **holy grass** a fragrant grass, *Hierochloe odorata*, which in Prussia was dedicated to the Virgin Mary and strewn on church floors. *Holy Innocents*: see INNOCENT *n.* **holy Joe** (orig. *Naut. slang*) a clergyman; a pious person. *Holy Lamb*: see LAMB *n.* **Holy Land** [tr. med.L *terra sancta*, Fr. *la terre sainte*] W. Palestine, esp. Judaea; a region similarly revered in religions other than Christianity. **holy laugh** a laugh by a person in a state of religious fervour. **holy loaf** (now *rare*) = *holy bread* above. **Holy Name** *RC Ch.* the name of Christ as an object of formal devotion. **Holy Office** *Hist.* the Inquisition. *holy orders*: see ORDER *n.* 2a. **holy place** the outer chamber of the sanctuary in a synagogue; in *pl.*, places to which religious pilgrimage is made. **holy roller** *slang* a member of a religious group characterized by frenzied excitement or trances. *Holy Roman Empire*: see ROMAN *a.* **Holy Rood** *arch.* (a representation of) the Cross of Jesus; *Holy Rood Day*, (*a*) the festival of the Invention of the Cross, 3 May; (*b*) = *Holy Cross Day* above. **Holy Saturday** Saturday in Holy Week. *Holy Scripture*: see SCRIPTURE. *Holy See*: see SEE *n.*[1] 2b. **holy souls** the blessed dead. **Holy Spirit** the third person of the Trinity; God as spiritually active; = HOLY GHOST 1; *God the Father, God the Son, and God the Holy Spirit*: see GOD *n.* *holy terror*: see TERROR *n.* 2b. **Holy Thursday** *Anglican Ch.* (*arch.* or *Hist.*) Ascension Day; *RC Ch.* Maundy Thursday. **holytide** *arch.* a holy day or season, a day or season of religious observance. *Holy Trinity*: see TRINITY. **holy war**: waged in support of a religious cause. **Holy Week** [after It. *la settimana santa*, Fr. *la semaine sainte*] the week before Easter Sunday. **holy Willie** a hypocritically religious person. *Holy Writ*: see WRIT *n.* 1. *Holy Write*: see WRITE *n.* 1. *the Holy Sepulchre*: see SEPULCHRE *n.* 1. *the holy table*: see TABLE *n.* 13(b).

B *n.* **1** That which is holy; a holy thing. OE. †**2** A holy person, a saint. LME–M17.

1 holy of holies (*a*) *Jewish Antiq.* the inner chamber of the sanctuary in the Jewish Temple, separated by a veil from the outer chamber; (*b*) an innermost shrine; a thing regarded as most sacred.

holy day /'həʊli deɪ/ *n. phr.* [OE *hāliġ dæġ*. Cf. HOLIDAY *n.* & *a.*] A day consecrated or set apart for religious observance, usu. in commemoration of some sacred person or event; a religious festival. Cf. HOLIDAY *n.* 1.

Holy Ghost /həʊli 'gəʊst/ *n. phr.* [OE *se hālga gāst*, *hāliġ gāst*, tr. eccl.L *spiritus sanctus*.] **1** *Chr. Theol.* = *Holy Spirit* s.v. HOLY *a.* OE. **2** A figure of a dove as a symbol of this. Long *rare* or *obs.* E16.

1 *God the Father, God the Son, and God the Holy Ghost*: see GOD *n.*

Comb.: **Holy Ghost flower** or **plant** a tropical American orchid, *Peristeria elata*, so called because part of the flower is thought to resemble a dove; also called *dove-flower*.

holystone /'həʊlɪstəʊn/ *n.* & *v.* E19. [Prob. f. HOLY *a.* + STONE *n.*, perh. so called because used while kneeling.] **A** *n.* A piece of soft sandstone used for scouring the decks of ships. E19.

B *v.t.* Scour with a holystone. E19.

T. MO He is on a deck holystoned white as any man-of-war's.

holy water /həʊli 'wɔːtə/ *n. phr.* [OE *hāliġwæter* tr. eccl.L *aqua benedicta* blessed water.] Water blessed by a priest and used in various rites etc. esp. of purification; water dedicated to holy uses.

Comb.: **holy-water sprinkle(r)** (*a*) an aspergillum; (*b*) *Hist.* a kind of club fitted with spikes.

hom /həʊm/ *n.* Also **haoma**, **homa**, /'həʊmə/. M19. [Pers. †*hōm*, *hūm* (Avest. *haoma*) = Skt *soma* SOMA *n.*[1]] (The juice of) the sacred plant of the ancient Persians and Parsees.

hom- *comb. form* see HOMO-.

homage /'hɒmɪdʒ/ *n.* ME. [OFr. (*h*)*omage* (mod. *hommage*) f. med.L *hominaticum*, f. L *homo*, *homin-* man: see -AGE.] **1** In *Feudal Law*, formal public acknowledgement of allegiance, by which a tenant or vassal declared himself the man of the king or lord from whom he held land, and bound himself to his service; *gen.* acknowledgement of a person's superior worth, rank, beauty, etc.; dutiful reverence. Freq. in *do*, *pay*, *render*, *homage* (*to*). ME. **2** A body of people owing allegiance; *spec.* the body of tenants attending, or the jury in, a manorial court. ME. **3** An act of homage; a payment of money etc. made as an acknowledgement of vassalage. L16.

1 N. MONSARRAT The crowd came forward to kneel in homage. E. FEINSTEIN Poets as disparate as Yevtushenko and Brodsky have paid homage to her. **3** J. UPDIKE Proust pens homages to such modern inventions as the railroad.

homage /'hɒmɪdʒ/ *v.* Now *rare*. LME. [f. the n.] **1** †**a** *v.i.* Pay homage. LME–M17. **b** *v.t.* Pay homage to. M17. †**2** *v.t.* Give or pay as a token of homage. L16–M17.

†**homageable** *a.* bound to pay homage M17–M18.

homager /'hɒmɪdʒə/ *n.* Now *arch.* or *Hist.* LME. [OFr. *homag(i)er*, f. as HOMAGE *n.*: see -ER[2].] A person who owes homage or holds land by it; *spec.* (*Eng. Law*, now *Hist.*) a manorial tenant.

fig.: SHAKES. *Ant. & Cl.* Thou blushest, Antony, and that blood of thine Is Caesar's homager.

homalographic *a.* var. of HOMOLOGRAPHIC.

hombre /'ɒmbreɪ, -bri/ *n.* M19. [Sp. = man, f. L *homo*, *homin-* human being: cf. OMBRE.] In Spain and Spanish-speaking countries, a man; *gen.* (chiefly *US slang*) a man, a guy.

American Speech Cowboys living a rough and hardy existence occasionally develop into 'tough hombres'.

Homburg /'hɒmbəːg/ *n.* L19. [*Homburg*, a town near Wiesbaden, western Germany.] In full *Homburg hat*. A soft felt hat with a curved brim and dented crown, first worn at Homburg.

home /həʊm/ *n.* & *a.* [OE *hām*, corresp. to OFris. *hām*, *hēm*, OS *hēm* (Du. *heem*), (O)HG *heim*, ON *heimr*, Goth. *haims*, f. Gmc.] **A** *n.* †**1** A collection of dwellings; a village, a town. OE–ME. **2** The place where one lives permanently, esp. as a member of a family or household; a fixed place of residence. Freq. without article or possessive, esp. as representing the centre of family life. OE. **b** The family or social unit occupying a home. Freq. w. descriptive adj., as *broken home*, *happy home*. L19. **c** The furniture or contents of a home. L19. **d** A private house, a dwelling-house. Chiefly *N. Amer.*, *Austral.*, *S. Afr.*, *NZ*. L19. **3** Usu. without article or possessive: (an affectionate term for) the country of one's origin; *esp.* Great Britain or England regarded as the mother country among citizens living abroad or (now *arch.* or *Hist.*) inhabitants of what were in the past its colonies or dependencies. ME. **4** A place or region to which one naturally belongs or where one feels at ease. Also *spiritual home*. M16. **5** A place where a thing flourishes or from which it originates. E18. **6** An institution looking after people etc. who need care or have no home of their own. M19. **b** *spec.* Such an institution for mentally ill or mentally handicapped people. *colloq.* M20. **7** *Sports & Games.* An area where a player is free from attack. Also, the point aimed at, the goal. M19. **8** *Lacrosse.* Each of the three players stationed nearest their opponents' goal. M19. **9** *ellipt.* A home win. L20.

2 G. B. SHAW When their business compels them to be away from home. LYNDON B. JOHNSON Every family in America deserves a decent home, whether a farmhouse or a city apartment. M. IGNATIEFF Home is the place we have to leave in order to grow up. G. STEIN Stray dogs and cats Anna always kept until she found them homes. *holiday home*, *mobile home*, *motor home*, etc. **d** N. MAILER Now he had a home instead of an apartment. **3** S. HARVESTER Members could . . sit quiet under lazy fans while they read the latest newspapers . . from home. **4** *Contemporary Review* In the Church of England he found a satisfying home. **5** M. ARNOLD Oxford . . . home of lost causes and forsaken beliefs! **6** G. STEIN They sent her where she would be taken care of, a home for poor consumptives. *convalescent home*, *dogs' home*, *mental home*, *nursing home*, *old people's home*, etc. **b** A. MCCOWEN His brain collapsed and he finished his days in a home.

Phrases: **at home** (*a*) in one's own home; one's neighbourhood, town, country, etc.; *arch.* in the mother-country, in Britain; (*b*) at ease as if in one's own home; well-informed, familiar (*in*, *on*, *with*); (*c*) available to callers; see also AT-HOME *n.*; (*d*) on a team's own ground (opp. *away*). **close to home** = *near home* below. *eat out of house and home*: see EAT *v.* *hearth and home*: see HEARTH *n.* **home away from home** *N. Amer.* & *Austral.* = *home from home* below. **home from home** a place other than one's home where one feels at home; a place providing homelike amenities. *house and home*: see HOUSE *n.*[1] *last home*: see LAST *a.* *long home*: see LONG *a.*[1] **near home** near one's home, country, etc.; *fig.* affecting one closely. *not at home*: see NOT *adv.* *second home*: see SECOND *a.* STARTER *home*. STATELY *home*. **to home** *dial.* & *US* at home. *walk home*: see WALK *v.*[1]

B *attrib.* (freq. hyphenated) or as *adj.* (not *pred.* except formerly in sense 3). **1** Of, relating to, or associated with (one's) home, domestic; used, performed, carried on, etc., at home. M16. **b** Adjoining or surrounding one's home, or the chief house on an estate. M17. **2** Relating to, produced or carried on in, originating from, one's country or nation. Opp. *foreign*. L16. **b** Dealing with the affairs of one's own country (opp. those of foreign countries) or (chiefly

Hist.) with the mother country (opp. its colonies). L18. **c** Of a team, player, etc.: belonging to the country, locality, etc., in which a sporting event takes place. Of a match, victory, etc.: played, experienced, etc., by a team on its own ground. L19. **3** That strikes home; searching, effective. (Passing into adv.) E17. **4** *Sports & Games.* Of, pertaining to, or situated at or near home (sense A.7 above); reaching or enabling a player to reach home. M19.

1 S. SMILES Its citizens had no true family or home life. I. NOVELLO Keep the home-fires burning. *home comforts, home computer, home cooking,* etc. **b** A. TROLLOPE An inner gate, leading from the home paddock, through the gardens. **2** *Time* Entente Cordiale . . was probably intended as French propaganda for home consumption. H. WILLIAMSON The least we civilians can do is to hold the Home Front. *home industry, home market, home produce,* etc. **b** *Listener* The Ministry of Defence is classified as a home rather than an 'overseas' department. **c** *Times* The biggest single event of the British season will bring together five home riders, four Danes, three Swedes. **3** HOR. WALPOLE That negociation not succeeding, the Duchess made a more home push.

Comb. & special collocations: With ppl adjs. in sense '(for use) at home', as *home-baked, home-based, home-born, home-brewed, home-cured* [CURE *v.* 8], *home-produced.* **home base** = *home plate* below; **home-bird, homebody** a person who likes to stay at home; **homeboy** (orig. & chiefly *Black English*) (*a*) a man coming from the same district, town, or community as the speaker; (*b*) a performer of rap music; **home-bred** *a.* (*a*) reared at home; indigenous; (*b*) *fig.* having no culture or breadth of experience; **home-brew** (*a*) beer or other alcoholic drink brewed at home; (*b*) *Canad.* a player of professional football etc. born or brought up where his team is based; **Home Counties** the counties (esp. Surrey, Kent, Essex, and formerly Middlesex) closest to London; **home economics** the study of household management, domestic science; **home economist** a student of or specialist in home economics; **home farm** a farm reserved and worked by the owner of an estate which contains other farms; **home-felt** *a.* felt intimately; **homefolks** *colloq.* (chiefly *US*) the people from or near one's home, one's family and neighbours; **homegirl** (orig. & chiefly *Black English*) (*a*) a woman coming from the same district, town, or community as the speaker; (*b*) a female performer of rap music; **home-grown** *a.* raised or cultivated on one's own land; *fig.* native, indigenous; **home guard** (a member of) a local volunteer force; *spec.* (w. cap. initials) (a member of) the British citizen army organized 1940–57 to defend the country against invaders; **home help** a person who helps with household work, *spec.* one deputed by a local authority to assist an elderly or infirm person; **home-keeping** *a.* that stays at or takes care of a home; **home key** *Mus.* the basic key in which a work is written; **homeland** (*a*) one's native land; *esp.* Great Britain; (*b*) *S. Afr.* an area reserved for members of a particular (indigenous African) ethnic or linguistic group (the official name for a Bantustan); **home language** one's native language; **home-leave** leave, esp. long leave, granted to officials etc. serving overseas; **home loan**: advanced to a person to assist in buying a house, flat, etc., to live in; **home-lot** *US* a building-plot; **home-made** *a.* made in one's own home or by one's own hands; crude or simple in construction; **home-maker** a person, esp. a housewife, who creates a (pleasant) home; **home-making** the activity of a home-maker; **home movie**: made at home or showing the activities of one's family circle; **Home Office** (the building used for) the British government department dealing with law and order, immigration, etc., in England and Wales; **home-owner** a person who owns his or her home; **home perm** a permanent hair-wave made with equipment for home use; *home plate*: see PLATE *n.* 15; **home port**: from which a ship sails or is registered; **home range** *Zool.* the area over which an animal regularly travels in search of food etc., and which may overlap with those of neighbouring animals of the same species (cf. TERRITORY 1d); **homeroom** *N. Amer.* a schoolroom where pupils of the same grade assemble at the beginning of school; **home rule** (a movement for) the government of a colony, dependent country, etc., by its own citizens; *spec.* (w. cap. initials) the movement advocating devolved government for Ireland, *c*1870–1914; **home run** *Baseball* a hit that allows the batter to make a complete circuit of the bases; **home science** (chiefly *NZ*) home economics, domestic science; **Home Secretary** (in Britain) the Secretary of State for the Home Department, the government minister in charge of the Home Office; **Home Service** *Hist.* one of the programme services of the BBC (renamed *Radio 4*); **homesick** *a.* depressed by a longing for home during an absence from it; **homesickness** the condition of being homesick; **home signal**: indicating whether or not a train may proceed into a station or to the next section of a line; **homesite** (chiefly *N. Amer., Austral.,* & *NZ*) a building-plot; **home straight** or (*N. Amer.*) **stretch** the concluding stretch of a racecourse; **home thrust** *Fencing* (now *rare*) a thrust which reaches the mark aimed at; *fig.* a direct remark or criticism which touches a person's feelings or consciousness; **home town**: of one's birth or early life or present fixed residence; **home truth** a wounding mention of a person's weakness; *home unit*: see UNIT *n.*[1] 7; **homework** work (to be) done at home; *esp.* lessons done at home by a schoolchild (*do one's homework* (fig.), brief oneself before a meeting etc.).

home /həʊm/ *v.* E17. [f. HOME *n.*, HOME *adv.*] †**1** *v.i. Naut.* Foll. by *in*: = *tumble home* (see TUMBLE *v.*). Only in E17. **2** *v.i.* Go home. Chiefly, of an animal: return by instinct to its territory after leaving it or being removed from it; (of a carrier pigeon) fly back to or arrive at its loft after being released at a distant point. M18. **b** *v.t.* Train (a pigeon) to fly home. E20. **3** *v.t.* Provide (esp. a pet) with a home. E19. **4** *v.i.* Have one's home, dwell. *poet.* M19. **5** *v.i.* (Of an aircraft, missile, etc.) be guided (*in*) by a landmark, radio beam, etc.; *fig.* direct one's attention, seek out. Foll. by *on, on to,* etc., the destination, target, object of attention, etc. E20.

3 *Maidenhead Advertiser* If we have a dog that has, perhaps, turned on a child, then we home it where there are no children. 5 *Daily Telegraph* The other helicopter located the dinghy by homing in on . . the emergency distress [call]. *New Scientist* Mexico's Professor S. F. Beltran homed in on education as a critical need. **homing device** an automatic device for guiding an aircraft, missile, etc.

home /həʊm/ *adv.* OE. [Orig. accus. of HOME *n.*, as the case of destination after a vb of motion.] **1** To one's home; to the house, district, country, etc., where one lives. Also, to one's family circle. OE. **b** To one's grave. E16. **c** With ellipsis of vb: go, drive, etc., home. L16. †**2** To one's normal or natural condition; to one's senses, right mind, etc. E16–M17. **3** To the mark aimed at, to the maximum extent of penetration etc., (esp. in *drive, hammer, press, ram,* etc., *home*). Freq. *fig.*, into a person's feelings or consciousness; formerly more *gen.*, fully, effectively. M16. **b** *Naut.* Directly to the shore. L18. **4** Expr. the result of motion: arrived at one's home after an absence. Also *fig.*, successfully arrived at, or within sight of, the end of a difficult enterprise, (more emphatically *home and dry* or (Austral. slang) *dried*). L16. **b** With no implication of motion: in one's home, at home. *N. Amer.* M19. **5** To or arrived in the mother country (from a colony or overseas possession). E17. **6** *Naut.* Towards or into the ship. Also, w. ref. to an anchor: away from its hold, so as to drag. E17. **7** *Sports & Games.* To or arrived at the home (HOME *n.* 7) or goal. L18.

1 D. H. LAWRENCE He worked automatically till it was time to go home. M. CALLAGHAN He liked to explain that he was doing well. He wrote home about it. **c** *Home, James, and don't spare the horses.* **2** F. QUARLES Call home thy selfe: Inspect thy selfe anew. **3** SHAKES. *Ant. & Cl.* Speak to me home; mince not the general tongue. DEFOE The witnesses swear so home against you. J. FOWLES I slammed the door and got the bolts home. P. ACKROYD She decided not to press home her advantage. *Survival Weaponry* Screw the magazine cap fully home. **4** E. BOWEN Elsie came in—home from a tennis party. **b** A. COOKE He would give his . . servants the sternest orders that he was home to nobody. **5** J. GAIRDNER The Regent Bedford . . wrote home to the government in England. **7** *Dumfries Courier* Hardy Lad is the new racing hero . . after romping home at 28–1 odds.

Phrases: **bring oneself home** recoup one's (financial) losses. **bring (something) home to** make (a person) fully aware of (something). **call home** *dial.* call the marriage banns of. **come home** = *bring oneself home* above. **come home to** (*a*) become fully realized by; (*b*) touch or affect intimately. *come home to roost*: see ROOST *n.*[1] †**come short home** fail to reach one's objective, come to grief. *down home*: see DOWN *prep. down-home*: see DOWN-. **go home** *spec.* (*dial.*) die. **nothing** etc. **to write home about** *colloq.* nothing etc. to boast about, nothing etc. special. *till the cows come home*: see COW *n.*[1] *tumble home*: see TUMBLE *v.* II. *when a person's ship comes home*: see SHIP *n.* I.

home-coming /ˈhəʊmkʌmɪŋ/ *n.* LME. [f. HOME *adv.* + COMING *n.*] A coming home, an arrival at home. Also, a reunion, *spec.* (*US*) of former students of a college or university.

homeish *a.* var. of HOMISH.

homeless /ˈhəʊmlɪs/ *a.* & *n.* E17. [f. HOME *n.* + -LESS.] **A** *adj.* **1** Of a person or (*transf.*) his or her condition etc.: having no home or permanent place to live in. E17. **2** Affording no home, inhospitable. *rare.* L18.

B *n.pl. The* people who are homeless as a class. M20.

Soldier Their first priority is housing the homeless.

homelessness *n.* M19.

homelike /ˈhəʊmlʌɪk/ *a.* E19. [f. HOME *n.* + -LIKE.] Resembling or suggestive of home; homely.

homeling /ˈhəʊmlɪŋ/ *n.* Long *arch. rare.* L16. [f. HOME *n.* + -LING[1].] A home-born inhabitant, a native.

homely /ˈhəʊmli/ *a.* ME. [f. HOME *n.* + -LY[1].] **1** Friendly, intimate; at home *with.* Long *arch.* & *dial. rare.* ME. †**2** Of or belonging to a home or household; domestic. LME–L16. **3** Kindly, sympathetic. Now *Sc.* LME. **4** Characteristic or suggestive of home, esp. in its cosiness, lack of formality, etc.; unsophisticated, plain, simple, unpretentious. LME. **5** Of a person, the features: plain or unattractive in appearance. Now *N. Amer.* LME.

1 R. W. EMERSON The end of friendship is a commerce, the most strict and homely that can be joined. 4 J. B. PRIESTLEY Her speech was far homelier . . and any suggestion of the great lady had completely vanished. A. WILSON She's a very nice, homely Lancashire body, but not stylish at all. M. MEYER The gift of making the place they lived in homely. **5** M. TWAIN She is not beautiful, she is homely.

homelily *adv.* (now *rare* or *obs.*) L15. **homeliness** *n.* ME.

†**homely** *adv.* ME. [f. HOME *n.* + -LY[2].] **1** Familiarly, intimately. ME–M17. **2** In a kindly manner. LME–L16. **3** Plainly, simply, unpretentiously. LME–L18. **4** Directly, without circumlocution. LME–L17.

homelyn /ˈhəʊmlɪn/ *n.* M17. [Origin unkn.] A coastal fish of the skate family, *Raja montagui.* Also called *spotted ray.*

homeo- *comb. form,* **homeopath** *n.*, etc., vars. HOMOEO- etc.

homeobox /hɒmɪə(ʊ)ˈbɒks, həʊm-/ *n.* Also **homoeo-**. L20. [f. HOMOEO(TIC + BOX *n.*[2] (as first discovered in homoeotic genes of *Drosophila* fruit flies).] *Genetics.* Any of a class of closely similar sequences which occur in various genes and are involved in regulating embryonic development in a wide range of species.

Comb.: **homeobox gene** a gene containing a homeobox.

homeostasis /hɒmɪəʊˈsteɪsɪs, həʊm-/ *n.* Also **homoeo-**. E20. [f. HOMOEO- + Gk *stasis* standing still, stationariness.] Maintenance of a dynamically stable state within a system by means of internal regulatory processes that counteract external disturbance of the equilibrium; the state so maintained; *spec.* in *Physiol.*, maintenance of relatively constant conditions in the body.

ˈ**homeostat** *n.* a system which maintains a steady state by internal processes M20. **homeostatic** *a.* of, pertaining to, or maintained by homeostasis E20.

homeothermic *a.* see HOMOIOTHERMIC.

homer /ˈhəʊmə/ *n.*[1] Also **cho-** /ˈkəʊ-/. M16. [Heb. *ḥōmer* lit. 'heap'.] A Hebrew measure of capacity equal to ten ephahs (about 400 litres). Also called *cor.*

homer /ˈhəʊmə/ *n.*[2] & *v.* M19. [f. HOME *v.* + -ER[1].] **A** *n.* **1** *Baseball.* A home run. M19. **2** A homing pigeon. L19. **3** A homing device. M20. **B** *v.i. Baseball.* Hit a home run. M20.

Homeric /həʊˈmɛrɪk/ *a.* E17. [L *Homericus* f. Gk *Homērikos*, f. *Homēros* Homer: see below, -IC.] **1** Of, relating to, or characteristic of Homer, the traditional author of two ancient epics, the *Iliad* and the *Odyssey*, the poems ascribed to him, or the age with which they deal; like or in the style of Homer. E17. 2 On a scale worthy of Homer; epic, tremendous. M20.

1 **Homeric laughter**: like that of Homer's gods as they watched lame Hephaestus hobbling. **Homeric question**: regarding the authorship of the *Iliad* and the *Odyssey*.

†**Homerical** *a.* = HOMERIC L16–L18. **Homerically** *adv.* M19. †**Homerican** *a.* = HOMERIC L17–E19.

Homerist /ˈhəʊmərɪst/ *n.* L16. [L *Homerista* f. Gk *Homēristēs*, f. *Homēros*: see prec., -IST.] An imitator of Homer; a Homeric scholar or rhapsodist.

Homerite /ˈhəʊmərʌɪt/ *n.* Now *rare* or *obs.* E17. [Gk *Homēritai* pl., f. as HIMYARITE: see -ITE[1].] = HIMYARITE.

Homerology /həʊməˈrɒlədʒi/ *n.* L19. [f. *Homer* (see HOMERIC) + -OLOGY.] The branch of knowledge that deals with Homer and the Homeric poems, their authorship, date, etc.

Homerologist *n.* L19.

homespun /ˈhəʊmspʌn/ *a.* & *n.* L16. [f. HOME *n.* + SPUN *ppl a.*] A *adj.* 1 Spun at home. L16. 2 *fig.* Simple, homely, unsophisticated, practical. E17.

2 J. P. MAHAFFY The plainest homespun morality. L. STEPHEN Crabbe was one of those simple, homespun characters.

B *n.* 1 A person who wears homespun cloth; a rustic. *arch.* L16. 2 Cloth made of yarn spun at home. Also, a material resembling this. E17. b *transf.* Something of plain or homely style. M19.

1 SHAKES. *Mids. N. D.* What hempen homespuns have we swagg'ring here. 2b *Athenaeum* Instead of being . . of superfine quality in one part, and arrant home-spun in another.

homestall /ˈhəʊmstɔːl/ *n.* Now *dial.* OE. [f. HOME *n.* + *steall* position, place.] 1 = HOMESTEAD *n.* OE. 2 A farmyard. M17.

homestead /ˈhəʊmstɛd/ *n.* & *v.* OE. [f. HOME *n.* + STEAD *n.*] A *n.* 1 Orig., the place in which a person or group lives; a settlement. In later use, a home. OE. 2 *N. Amer.* a A piece of land adequate for the residence and support of a family. M17. b A piece of land (usu. 160 acres, approx. 65 hectares) granted to a settler to live on, esp. (*US*) under the Homestead Act of Congress (1862). E19. 3 A house with its dependent buildings etc.; *esp.* a farmstead. L17. 4 In Australia and New Zealand: the owner's residence on a sheep or cattle station. Also (*NZ*), a place from which a run is worked. M19.

Comb.: **homestead exemption law** *US* a law exempting a homestead from seizure or forced sale for debt.

B *v.t.* & *i.* Settle, live on, (land) as a homestead. *N. Amer.* L19.

homesteader *n.* the holder of a homestead; *spec.* (*N. Amer.*) a person holding land acquired by settlement, esp. (*US*) under the Homestead Act of 1862: L19. **homesteading** *n.* (*a*) a farmstead; (*b*) *N. Amer.* the granting of land to settlers, esp. (*US*) under the Homestead Act of 1862; (*c*) settling or living on land as a homestead: M19.

homester /ˈhəʊmstə/ *n. rare.* M19. [f. HOME *n.* + -STER.] 1 A stay-at-home. M19. 2 A member of the home team in a sporting match. L19.

homeward /ˈhəʊmwəd/ *adv.* & *a.* OE. [f. HOME *n.* + -WARD.] A *adv.* In the direction of one's place of residence or native country; towards home. OE.

Comb.: **homeward-bound** *a.* (esp. of a ship) preparing to go home, on the way home.

B *adj.* Directed or going homeward. M16.

homewards /ˈhəʊmwədz/ *adv.* OE. [f. HOME *n.* + -WARDS.] = HOMEWARD *adv.*

homey /ˈhəʊmi/ *n. NZ slang.* Also **homie**. E20. [f. HOME *n.* + -Y[6], -IE.] A British immigrant, *esp.* one recently arrived.

homey /ˈhəʊmi/ *a. colloq.* Also **homy**. M19. [f. HOME *n.* + -Y[1].] Resembling or suggestive of home; homely.

D. ACHESON This homey chat between their shirt-sleeved diplomats at work.

homeyness /ˈhəʊmɪnɪs/ *n.* Also **hominess**. L19. [f. HOMY *a.* + -NESS.] The quality of being homey, homeliness.

homicidal /hɒmɪˈsʌɪd(ə)l/ *a.* E18. [f. next + -AL[1].] Of, pertaining to, or tending to homicide; having an impulse towards homicide; murderous.

homicidal mania insanity characterized by impulses to commit murder.

homiˈcidally *adv.* L19.

homicide /ˈhɒmɪsʌɪd/ *n.* ME. [(O)Fr., f. (sense 1) L *homicidium*, (sense 2) L *homicida*, both f. shortened stem of *homo homin-* human being: see -CIDE.] 1 The killing, by a human being, of a human being. ME. 2 A person who kills a human being. In early use often *spec.* a murderer. LME.

1 **excusable homicide**: incurring blame, but no criminal liability because in self-defence or by misadventure. **justifiable homicide**: incurring neither blame nor criminal liability because in the execution of one's duty. **unlawful homicide**: incurring criminal liability because done with malice aforethought or culpable neglect.

homie *n.* var. of HOMEY *n.*

homilete /ˈhɒmɪliːt/ *n. US.* L19. [Gk *homilētēs* disciple, scholar, f. *homilein*: see next.] = HOMILIST.

homiletic /hɒmɪˈlɛtɪk/ *a.* & *n.* M17. [Late L *homileticus* f. Gk *homilētikos*, f. *homilētos* vbl adj. of *homilein* consort or hold converse with, f. *homilos* crowd: see -IC.] A *adj.* Of the nature of or characteristic of a homily. M17. B *n.* In *pl.* & †*sing.* The art of preaching. M19.

homiletical *a.* †(*a*) relating to social intercourse; sociable; (*b*) = HOMILETIC *a.*: M17. **homiletically** *adv.* M19.

homiliary /hɒˈmɪlɪəri/ *n.* M19. [med.L *homiliarium*, *homiliarius* (sc. *liber* book), f. eccl.L *homilia* HOMILY: see -ARY[1]. Cf. OFr. *omiliaire.*] A book of homilies.

homilise *v.* var. of HOMILIZE.

homilist /ˈhɒmɪlɪst/ *n.* E17. [f. HOMILY + -IST.] A person who writes or delivers homilies; a preacher.

homilite /ˈhɒmɪlʌɪt/ *n.* L19. [f. Gk *homilia* association + -ITE[1].] *Min.* A black or brown monoclinic borosilicate of calcium also containing iron and magnesium.

homilize /ˈhɒmɪlʌɪz/ *v.i.* Also **-ise**. E17. [f. next + -IZE.] Preach, sermonize, discourse.

homily /ˈhɒmɪli/ *n.* LME. [OFr. *omelie* (mod. *homélie*) f. eccl.L *homilia* f. Gk = converse, discourse, (eccl.) sermon, f. *homilos* crowd: see -Y[3]. Finally assim. to L in 16.] 1 A religious discourse, a sermon. Now *spec.* a practical discourse aimed at the spiritual edification of a congregation (rather than an exposition of a point of doctrine). LME. 2 *transf.* A tedious (esp. moralizing) discourse; a lecture. L16.

2 J. BRAINE As each bottle [of wine] was brought out he treated me to a short homily on the reasons for his choice.

hominess *n.* var. of HOMEYNESS.

homing /ˈhəʊmɪŋ/ *a.* M19. [f. HOME *v.* + -ING[2].] That goes home; *spec.* (of a pigeon) trained to fly back to its loft from a distance, bred for long-distance racing.

hominid /ˈhɒmɪnɪd/ *n.* & *a.* L19. [mod.L *Hominidae* (see below), f. *homo*, *homin-* human being: see -ID[3].] A *n.* A primate of the family Hominidae, which includes human beings (*Homo sapiens*), and several fossil forms. L19. B *adj.* Belonging to or characteristic of a hominid or the Hominidae. E20.

hominine /ˈhɒmɪnʌɪn/ *a.* & *n.* L19. [f. L *homo homin-* human being + -INE[1]. Cf. ASININE.] A *adj.* Pertaining to human beings, zoologically considered; hominid; *spec.* designating larger-brained hominids (opp. smaller-brained australopithecines). L19. B *n.* A hominine primate. M20.

hominisation *n.* var. of HOMINIZATION.

hominivorous /hɒmɪˈnɪv(ə)rəs/ *a.* M19. [f. L *homin-*, *homo* human being + -VOROUS.] That feeds on human beings.

hominization /ˌhɒmɪnʌɪˈzeɪʃ(ə)n/ *n.* Also **-isation**. M20. [Fr. *hominisation*, f. L *homo homin-* human being: see -IZATION.] In evolution: the development of the higher characteristics that are thought to distinguish man from other animals.

hominoid /ˈhɒmɪnɔɪd/ *a.* & *n.* E20. [f. L *homo homin-* human being + -OID.] A *adj.* Of human (rather than apelike) form; *spec.* belonging to or characteristic of (a member of) the Hominoidea (see below). E20. B *n.* An animal resembling a human; *spec.* a primate of the superfamily Hominoidea, which includes man and the anthropoid apes. E20.

hominy /ˈhɒmɪni/ *n.* E17. [Contr. of Virginia Algonquian *uskatahomen*. Cf. ROCKAHOMINY.] Maize hulled and ground and prepared for food by being boiled with water or milk.

homish /ˈhəʊmɪʃ/ *a.* Also **homeish**. M16. [f. HOME *n.* + -ISH[1].] †1 Belonging to home; domestic. M–L16. 2 Homelike, homely. L18.

homishness *n.* M19.

homme /ɔm/ *n.* Pl. pronounced same. E18. [Fr.] The Fr. for 'man', occurring in various phrases used in Eng.

homme d'affaires /dafɛːr/, pl. ***hommes d'affaires*** (pronounced same), a businessman, an agent, a lawyer. ***homme moyen*** /mwajɛ̃/, pl. **-s -s** (pronounced same), an average man; ***homme moyen sensuel*** /sɑ̃sɥɛl/, the average sensual man.

homo /ˈhəʊməʊ, ˈhɒməʊ/ *n.*[1] Pl. **-os**. L16. [L = man.] 1 A human being. L16. 2 (**H-**.) The genus to which human beings and certain of their fossil ancestors belong. Also with Latin specific epithets in names of (proposed) species, and with Latin or mock-Latin adjs. (in imitation of zool. nomenclature) in names intended to personify some aspects of human life or behaviour. L18.

2 *Times* Symbolizing . . this concept of *homo turisticus*, the new Hilton hotel. *English Studies* An arraignment of Walter Pater in his quality of *homo aestheticus*. **homo faber** /ˈfeɪbə/ [L = maker] the human species regarded as makers of tools. **Homo sapiens** /ˈsapɪɛnz/ [L = wise] modern man regarded as a species. **the genus Homo** humankind.

homo /ˈhəʊməʊ/ *n.*[2] & *a. colloq.* (usu. *derog.*). Pl. of n. **-os**. E20. [Abbrev.] = HOMOSEXUAL *n.* & *a.*

homo- /ˈhɒməʊ, ˈhəʊməʊ/ *comb. form.* Bef. a vowel also **hom-**. [f. Gk *homos* same: see -O-.] 1 Used in wds adopted f. Gk and in Eng. wds modelled on these, and as a freely productive pref., w. the sense 'same, equal'. Freq. opp. HETERO-. 2 [Extracted f. HOMOLOGUE.] *Chem.* Forming names of compounds which are homologues (usu. by addition of $\cdot CH_2 \cdot$) of those whose names follow, as *homatropine*, *homocitrate*, *homoserine*, etc.

homacanth *a.* (*Ichthyol.*) having the spines of the dorsal and anal fins symmetrical L19. **homoˈcercal** *a.* [Gk *kerkos* tail] *Ichthyol.* designating or possessing a tail with equal lobes, esp. with the spine deflected into the upper lobe M19. **homochlaˈmydeous** *a.* [Gk *khlamud-*, *khlamus* cloak] *Bot.* having the outer and inner layers of the perianth alike, not differentiated into sepals and petals L19. **homoˈchromous** *a.* (chiefly *Bot.*) of uniform colour M19. **homochromy** *n.* (*Zool.*) cryptic coloration L19. **homoclime** *n.* (*Geogr.*) any of several places or regions having a similar climate E20. **homoˈcyclic** *a.* (*Chem.*) containing or designating a ring formed of atoms of a single element E20. **homoˈdesmic** *a.* (*Cryst.*) containing only a single kind of chemical bond M20. **homodimer** *n.* (*Chem.*) a dimer of two identical subunits L20. **homodont** *a.* (*Zool.*) of or possessing teeth all of the same type (as reptiles) L19. **homogeˈnetic** *a.* having a common descent or origin L19. **homogenˈtisic** *a.* (*Chem.*): *homogentisic acid*, an organic acid, intermediate in the metabolism of aromatic amino acids and excreted by persons with alkaptonuria; 2,5-dihydroxyphenylacetic acid: L19. **homograft** *n.* = HOMOTRANSPLANT *n.* E20. **homoˈlateral** *a.* (chiefly *Med.*) on or affecting the same side (of the body) E20. **homoˈlecithal** *a.* (of an egg or egg cell) having the yolk uniformly distributed throughout the cytoplasm L19. **homoˈnuclear** *a.* (*Chem.* etc.) (*a*) (of substitution) taking place on the same ring in a polycyclic molecule; (*b*) composed of atoms whose nuclei are identical: M20. **homoˈpolar** *a.* characterized by equal or constant polarity L19. **homosceˈdastic** *a.* [Gk *skedastos* able to be scattered, f. *skedannunai* scatter] *Statistics* of equal scatter or variation; having equal variances: E20. **homoscedaˈsticity** *n.* (*Statistics*) equal or constant variance E20. **hoˈmosporous** *a.* (*Biol.*) producing only one kind of spore L19. **hoˈmospory** *n.* (*Biol.*)

homosporous condition E20. **homo'thallic** *a.* (*Mycol.*) having self-fertile thalli E20. **homo'thallism** *n.* the state or condition of being homothallic E20. **homo'thally** *n.* = HOMOTHALLISM M20. **homotherm** *n.* = HOMOIOTHERM M20. **homo'thermic** *a.* = HOMOIOTHERMIC L19.

homocaryotic *a.* var. of HOMOKARYOTIC.

homocentric /hɒmə(ʊ)'sɛntrɪk, həʊm-/ *n.* & *a.*[1] E17.[mod.L *homocentricus*, f. as HOMO- + Gk *kentrikos*: see -CENTRIC.] †A *n.* *Astron.* A sphere or circle concentric with another or with the earth. Only in E17. B *adj.* 1 *Astron.* Concentric. *obs.* exc. *Hist.* L17. 2 *Physics.* Of rays: either parallel, or passing through a single focal point (or appearing to do so when extended). L19.

homocentric /həʊmə(ʊ)'sɛntrɪk, hɒm-/ *a.*[2] E20. [f. L HOMO *n.*[1] + -CENTRIC.] = ANTHROPOCENTRIC.

homocline /'hɒmə(ʊ)klʌɪn/ *n.* E20. [f. HOMO- + CLINE, as *anticlyne*, *syncline*, etc.] *Geol.* A set of strata dipping throughout in the same general direction. Cf. MONOCLINE.

homo'clinal *a.* of, pertaining to, or associated with a homocline E20.

homoe- *comb. form* see HOMOEO-.

Homoean /hɒ'miːən/ *a.* & *n.* M19. [f. mod.L *homoeus* f. Gk *homoios* like, similar + -AN.] *Eccl. Hist.* Designating or pertaining to, a member of, a group of Arians which developed *c*355 and repudiated both the Homoousion and the Homoiousion, maintaining simply that in the Trinity the Son is 'like' the Father.

homoeo- /'hɒmɪəʊ, 'həʊm-/ *comb. form* of Gk *homoios* like, similar: see -O-. Also **homeo-**, **homoio-**, bef. a vowel **homoe-**, **homoi-**.

homoeo'blastic *a.* (*Petrogr.*) (of metamorphic rocks) composed of grains equal in size E20. **homoeo'crystalline** *a.* (*Petrogr.*) composed of crystals of roughly equal size L19. **homoeo'geneous** *a.* [after HOMOGENEOUS] of a similar kind L19.

homoeobox *n.* var. of HOMEOBOX.

homoeomerous /hɒmɪ'ɒm(ə)rəs/ *a.* Also (in *Bot.* usu.) **homoi-** /hɒmɔɪ-/. L19. [f. HOMOEO- + Gk *meros* part: see -OUS.] Having or consisting of similar parts; *spec.* in *Bot.*, (of lichen) having the algal and fungal cells uniformly distributed (opp. *heteromerous*).

homoeomery /hɒmɪ'ɒm(ə)ri/ *n.* Also **homoi-** /hɒmɔɪ-/, **-omeria** /-ɒ'mɛrɪə/. L17. [f. L *homoeomeria* f. Gk *homoiomereia*, f. *homoiomerēs* consisting of like parts, f. *homoios* like + *meros* part: see -Y[3].] *Hist.* The theory (propounded by Anaxagoras) that the ultimate particles of matter are homogeneous. Also, in *pl.*, the ultimate particles of matter, regarded as homogeneous.

homoeomorph /'hɒmɪəmɔːf, 'həʊm-/ *n.* Also **homeo-**. L19. [f. HOMOEO- + Gk *morphē* shape, form.] A chemical substance, fossil species, or topological figure which exhibits homoeomorphism or homoeomorphy.

homoeomorphic /hɒmɪə(ʊ)'mɔːfɪk, həʊm-/ *a.* Also (in *Math.* usu.) **homeo-**. E20. [f. as prec. + -IC.] Of the same kind or form; homoeomorphous; *spec.* in *Math.*, topologically equivalent *to* another figure, space, etc.

homoeomorphism /hɒmɪə(ʊ)'mɔːfɪz(ə)m, həʊm-/ *n.* Also (in sense 2 usu.) **homeo-**. M19. [f. as prec. + -ISM.] 1 *Cryst.* The condition of being homoeomorphous; possession of similar crystal structures. M19. 2 *Math.* The condition of being homoeomorphic; topological equivalence. E20.

homoeomorphous /hɒmɪə(ʊ)'mɔːfəs, həʊm-/ *a.* Also **homeo-**. M19. [f. as prec. + -OUS.] 1 *Cryst.* Of chemical substances: having a similar crystal form and habit though different chemical composition. M19. 2 *Palaeont.* Exhibiting homoeomorphy; superficially similar. L19.

homoeomorphy /'hɒmɪəmɔːfi, 'həʊm-/ *n.* Also **homeo-**. L19. [f. as prec. + -Y[3].] *Palaeont.* A superficial or deceptive resemblance between two fossils or fossil species; *esp.* resemblance due to convergent evolution.

homoeopath /'həʊmɪəpaθ, 'hɒm-/ *n.* Also **homeo-**. M19. [G *Homöopath*: see HOMOEOPATHY.] A person who practises or advocates homoeopathy.

homoeopathic /həʊmɪə(ʊ)'paθɪk, hɒm-/ *a.* Also **homeo-**. M19. [G *homöopathisch*: see next, -IC.] 1 Of or pertaining to homoeopathy; practising or advocating homoeopathy. M19. 2 Extremely small, as the doses in homoeopathy. Chiefly *joc.* M19.

2 C. M. DAVIES The chapel was homœopathic in its dimensions.

homoeopathy /həʊmɪ'ɒpəθi, hɒm-/ *n.* Also **homeo-**, (earlier) †**-pathia**. E19. [G *Homöopathie*, f. Gk *homoios* like + *-patheia* -PATHY.] A system of medicine in which diseases are treated by the administration (usu. in extremely small doses) of salts, drugs, etc., which would in a healthy person cause the symptoms of the disease so treated.

homoeopathist *n.* = HOMOEOPATH M20.

homoeosis /hɒmɪ'əʊsɪs/ *n.* Also **homeosis**. Pl. **-oses** /-'əʊsiːz/. L19. [Gk *homoiōsis* a becoming like, f. *homoios* like.] *Biol.* In a segmented animal, the replacement of part of one segment by a structure characteristic of another segment, esp. in regeneration or by mutation. Also, an analogous process in plants.

homoeotic /-'ɒtɪk/ *a.* exhibiting, characterizing, or inducing homoeosis L19.

homoeostasis *n.* var. of HOMEOSTASIS.

homoeoteleuton /hɒ,miːətɪ'ljuːt(ə)n/ *n.* Also **homoi-** /,hɒmɔɪ-/. L16. [Late L f. Gk *homoioteleuton* (sc. *rhēma* word), f. *homoios* like + *teleutē* ending.] 1 A rhetorical figure consisting in the use of a series of words with the same or similar endings. *rare.* L16. 2 (An error in copying caused by) the occurrence of similar endings in two neighbouring words, lines, etc. M19.

homo-erotic /,hɒməʊɪ'rɒtɪk, 'həʊm-/ *a.* & *n.* E20. [f. HOMO- + EROTIC *a.* & *n.*] = HOMOSEXUAL.

homo-eroticism /-sɪz(ə)m/ *n.* M20. **homo-erotism** *n.* E20.

homogametic /hɒməgə'mɛtɪk, -'miː-; həʊm-/ *a.* E20. [f. HOMO- + GAMETIC.] *Biol.* Producing gametes that all have the same kind of sex chromosome.

homo'gamety *n.* the condition or state of being homogametic M20.

homogamous /hɒ'mɒgəməs/ *a.* M19. [f. HOMO- + Gk *gamos* marriage + -OUS.] *Bot.* 1 Of a plant: having all the florets of a capitulum or spikelet hermaphrodite, or of the same sex. M19. 2 Of a flower: having the anthers and stigmas maturing together, so as to permit self-fertilization. Cf. DICHOGAMOUS. M19.

homogamy /hɒ'mɒgəmi/ *n.* L19. [f. as prec. + -GAMY.] 1 *Bot.* The condition of being homogamous; the possession of homogamous flowers. L19. 2 *Biol.* Breeding between individuals similar in some characteristic; inbreeding. L19.

homo'gamic *a.* (*Biol.*) of or pertaining to homogamy E20.

homogene /'hɒmədʒiːn, 'həʊm-/ *a.* & *n.* Now *rare* or *obs.* M16. [Gk *homogenēs*: see HOMOGENEOUS.] A *adj.* Homogeneous. M16. B *n.* A homogeneous thing. E18.

homogeneal /hɒmə(ʊ)'dʒiːnɪəl, -'dʒɛn-; həʊm-/ *a.* & *n.* Now *rare.* E17. [med.L *homogenealis*, f. *homogeneus* (see HOMOGENEOUS) + *-alis* -AL[1].] A *adj.* Homogeneous. E17. B *n.* A homogeneous thing. M17.

homogeneate /hɒmə(ʊ)'dʒiːnɪeɪt, -'dʒɛn-; həʊm-/ *v.t.* *rare.* M17. [f. med.L *homogeneus* (see HOMOGENEOUS) + -ATE[3].] Make homogeneous.

homogeneity /,hɒmə(ʊ)dʒɪ'niːɪti, -'neɪti; ,həʊm-/ *n.* E17. [med.L *homogeneitas*, f. *homogeneus*: see next, -ITY.] The quality or condition of being homogeneous.

P. BOWLES The men . . all wore . . white turbans . . which lent the scene a strong aspect of homogeneity.

homogeneous /hɒmə(ʊ)'dʒiːnɪəs, -'dʒɛn-; həʊm-/ *a.* M17. [f. med.L *homogeneus*, f. Gk *homogenēs* of the same kind, f. as HOMO- + *genos* kind: see -OUS. See also HOMOGENOUS *a.*[2]] 1 Of the same kind, nature, or character; alike, similar, congruous. M17. 2 Consisting of parts or elements of the same kind; of uniform character throughout. M17. b *Physics.* Of light or other radiation: monochromatic. L18. c *Physical Chem.* Consisting of, or involving a single phase. L19. d Of a nuclear reactor: having the fuel uniformly mixed with the moderator. M20. 3 *Math.* Of the same kind or degree; consisting of terms of the same dimensions. L17.

3 **homogeneous coordinates**: replaced by their ratios such that equations in the system are homogeneous.

homogeneously *adv.* M17. **homogeneousness** *n.* M17.

homogenize /hə'mɒdʒənʌɪz/ *v.* Also **-ise**. L19. [f. HOMOGENE + -IZE.] 1 *v.t.* Make homogeneous or uniform; incorporate into a whole of uniform composition. L19. b Subject (milk, cream, or another emulsion) to a process by which suspended droplets are broken up and dispersed through the liquid, so preventing separation of the constituents. E20. c *Metall.* Render (an alloy) more uniform in composition by heating and slow cooling. E20. d Prepare a suspension of cell constituents from (tissue) by physical treatment (as grinding) in a liquid. M20. 2 *v.i.* Become homogeneous. M20.

homogenized *ppl a.* (*a*) that has been homogenized; *esp.* (of milk etc.) having the globules of fat reduced in size and distributed throughout the liquid; (*b*) (of abstract notions) not readily differentiated; similar in nature: E20. **homogenizer** *n.* a machine or apparatus designed to homogenize some material (as milk or tissue) L19.

homogenous /hə'mɒdʒɪnəs/ *a.*[1] *arch.* L19. [f. HOMO- + Gk *genos* race + -OUS.] Homogenetic.

homogenous /hə'mɒdʒɪnəs/ *a.*[2] M20. [Alt. of HOMOGENEOUS, prob. after *homogenize* etc.] Homogeneous.

homogeny /hə'mɒdʒəni/ *n.* E17. [In sense 1 f. mod.L *homogenia* f. Gk *homogeneia*, f. *homogeneus*: see HOMOGENEOUS, -Y[3]. In sense 2 f. HOMO- + -GENY.] †1 Homogeneity. Only in E17. 2 *Biol.* Correspondence of structure due to common descent. *rare.* L19.

homograph /'hɒməgrɑːf; 'həʊm-/ *n.* E19. [f. HOMO- + -GRAPH.] †1 A system of signalling. Only in E19. 2 Each of a set of words having the same written form but of different origin, meaning, or pronunciation. Also, a homonym. L19.

homographic /hɒmə'grafɪk, həʊm-/ *a.* M19. [f. HOMO- + -GRAPHIC, in sense 1 through Fr. *homographique*.] 1 *Geom.* Having the same anharmonic ratio or system of anharmonic ratios, as two figures of the same thing in different perspectives; belonging or relating to such figures. M19. 2 Designating or pertaining to a spelling-system having a one-to-one relationship between character and sound. M19. 3 Of, pertaining to, or consisting of homographs. L19.

homoi(o)- *comb. forms* see HOMOEO-.

homoiomerous *a.*, **-mery** *n.* vars. of HOMOEOMEROUS, -MERY.

homoiosmotic /,hɒmɔɪɒz'mɒtɪk/ *a.* Also **homeo-osmotic** /,hɒmɪəʊɒz'mɒtɪk/, **homoio-osmotic** /,hɒmɔɪəʊɒz'mɒtɪk/. M20. [f. HOMOIO- + OSMOTIC.] *Zool.* Maintaining a more or less constant concentration of solutes in the body fluids independent of variations of concentration in the surrounding medium.

homoiosmosis *n.* M20.

homoioteleuton *n.* var. of HOMOEOTELEUTON.

homoiothermic /,hɒmɔɪəʊ'θəːmɪk/ *a.* Also ***homeo-**, **homoeo-**, /,hɒmɪəʊ-/. L19. [f. HOMOIO- + THERMIC.] *Zool.* & *Physiol.* Maintaining an almost constant body temperature, independent of that of the surroundings. Opp. POIKILOTHERMIC *a.*

homoiotherm *n.* a homoiothermic animal L19. **'homoiothermy** *n.* M20.

homoiousian /hɒmɔɪ'uːsɪən, -'aʊ-, -z-/ *a.* & *n.* Also (esp. as n.) **H-**. L17. [f. eccl.L *homoeusius* f. Gk *homoiousios* of like essence, f. *homoios* like, similar + *ousia* essence, substance: see -IAN. Opp. HETEROOUSIAN and HOMOOUSIAN.] *Chr. Theol.* & *Eccl. Hist.* A *adj.* Of like but not identical essence or substance (esp. of the first and second persons of the Trinity). Also, of or pertaining to the homoiousians. L17. **B** *n.* A person who believed the first and second persons of the Trinity to be of like but not identical essence or substance; a semi-Arian. M18.

Homoiousion /hɒmɔɪ'uːsɪən, -'aʊ-, -z-/ *n.* M19. [eccl.Gk, neut. of *homoiousios*: see prec. Cf. HOMOOUSION.] *Chr. Theol.* & *Eccl. Hist.* *The* doctrine that the first and second persons of the Trinity are of like but not identical essence or substance.

homokaryotic /ˌhɒmə(ʊ)karɪ'ɒtɪk, ˌhəʊm-/ *a.* Also **-caryotic**. E20. [f. HOMO- + KARYO- + -OTIC.] Chiefly *Mycol.* Having two or more genetically identical nuclei within a common cytoplasm.

homo'karyon *n.*, pl. **-ya**, a homokaryotic cell, structure, or organism M20. **homokary'osis** *n.* the state or condition of being homokaryotic E20.

homolog *n.* see HOMOLOGUE.

homologate /hə'mɒləgeɪt/ *v.t.* Chiefly *Sc.* E16. [med.L *homologat-* pa. ppl stem of *homologare* agree, after Gk *homologein* confess, acknowledge: see -ATE[3].] Express agreement with; approve; acknowledge; confirm, ratify.

homolo'gation *n.* M17.

homological /hɒmə'lɒdʒɪk(ə)l, həʊm-/ *a.* M19. [f. HOMOLOGY + -ICAL.] **1** Homologous; pertaining to or characterized by homology. M19. **2** *Philos.* = AUTOLOGICAL *a.* M20.

homologically *adv.* M19.

homologize /hɒ'mɒlədʒʌɪz/ *v.* Also **-ise**. M18. [f. next + -IZE.] **1** *v.i.* Be homologous; correspond. M18. **2** *v.t.* Make or show to be homologous. E19.

homologizer *n.* (*rare*) E18.

homologous /hɒ'mɒləgəs/ *a.* M17. [f. med.L *homologus* f. Gk *homologos* agreeing, consonant, f. *homos* same + *logos* relation, ratio: see LOGOS, -OUS.] **I** *gen.* **1** Having the same relation, structure, relative position, etc.; corresponding. M17.

II *spec.* **2** *Math.* Of elements (as lines, points, terms, etc.): having similar or analogous positions or roles in distinct figures or functions. Also, of figures, expressions, etc.: showing one-to-one correspondence between elements; equivalent. M17. **3a** *Biol.* Of organs, parts, or traits: orig., having the same fundamental structure, organization, or mode of development. Now *esp.* having a common evolutionary origin. M19. **b** *Med.* Of a tumour: having the same form as normal tissue of the part. *obs.* exc. *Hist.* L19. **c** *Cytol.* Of chromosomes: pairing at meiosis and (usu.) identical in morphology and in arrangement of genetic loci. E20. **d** *Med.* & *Zool.* Derived from or involving conspecific organisms; *spec.* involving or containing antibodies and their specific antigens. E20. **4** *Chem.* Of a series of (esp. organic) compounds: differing successively by addition of some constituent (esp. $\cdot CH_2 \cdot$), and showing graded physical and chemical properties. M19.

3a E. C. MINKOFF The human arm, .. the bird's wing, and the pectoral fins of certain fishes are all homologous.

homolographic /hɒmələ'grafɪk/ *a.* Also **homalo-**. M19. [Alt. of Gk *homalos* even, level + -O- + -GRAPHIC: assim. to HOMO-.] *Geogr.* Designating a method of projection in which equal areas on the earth's surface are represented by equal areas on the map.

homologue /'hɒməlɒg/ *n.* Also ***-log**. M19. [Fr., f. Gk *homologos*: see HOMOLOGOUS.] A thing which is homologous; a homologous organ, compound, etc.

homology /hɒ'mɒlədʒi/ *n.* E17. [Late L *homologia* f. Gk *homologia* agreement, assent, f. *homologos*: see HOMOLOGOUS, -Y[3].] **1** The quality or condition of being homologous; sameness of relation; (an instance of) correspondence. E17. **2** *Biol.* **a** Orig., correspondence in fundamental structure of an organ, part, etc. Now chiefly, correspondence in evolutionary origin (of organs, parts, etc.). M19. **b** An instance of this. M19.

homolysis /hɒ'mɒlɪsɪs/ *n.* M20. [f. HOMO- + -LYSIS.] *Chem.* The splitting of a molecule into two neutral atoms or radicals.

homo'lytic *a.* of the nature of or involving homolysis M20.

homomorph /'hɒməmɔːf, 'həʊm-/ *n.* L19. [f. HOMO- + Gk *morphē* form.] A thing (as a letter, a word, a system) having the same form as another.

homomorphic /hɒmə(ʊ)'mɔːfɪk, həʊm-/ *a.* L19. [f. as prec. + -IC.] **I** *gen.* **1** Of the same or similar form; of, relating to, or consisting of things of the same or similar form. L19. **II** *spec.* **2a** *Biol.* Of organisms or organs: having external resemblance but not related in structure or origin. L19. **b** *Bot.* Designating (the self-fertilization of) flowers with stamens and pistils of equal length. L19. **c** *Entomol.* Having larvae resembling the adults; hemimetabolous. L19. **d** *Zool.* Of animal colonies: having the constituent individuals all alike. L19. **e** *Cytol.* Of homologous chromosomes: the same in size and form. E20. **3** *Math.* Relating to, produced by, or designating a homomorphism; giving rise *to* a second set by a homomorphism. M20.

homomorphism /hɒmə(ʊ)'mɔːfɪz(ə)m, həʊm-/ *n.* M19. [f. as prec.: see -ISM.] **1** Resemblance of form. *rare.* M19. **2** *Math.* A transformation of one set into another that preserves in the second set the relations between elements of the first. M20.

homomorphous /hɒmə(ʊ)'mɔːfəs, həʊm-/ *a.* M19. [f. as prec. + -OUS.] Of the same or similar form, homomorphic.

homonym /'hɒmənɪm/ *n.* L17. [L *homonymum* f. Gk *homōnumon* neut. of *homōnumos* HOMONYMOUS: see -NYM.] **1** Each of two or more words having the same written form but of different meaning and origin, a homograph. Also, a homophone. L17. **2** A person or thing having the same name as another; a namesake. M19. **3** *Biol.* A Latin genus name or binomial applied to more than one organism (the earlier use having precedence). L19.

homo'nymic *a.* M19. **homo'nymity** *n.* homonymy L20.

homonymous /hə'mɒnɪməs/ *a.* E17. [f. L *homonymus* f. Gk *homōnumos*, f. as HOMO- + *onuma* name: see -NYM, -OUS.] **1** Employing the same name for different things, equivocal, ambiguous. E17. **2** Having the same name. M17. **3** Having the same written or spoken form but differing in meaning and origin. L19. **4** *Zool.* Of animal horns: such that the right and left horns have right-handed and left-handed spiral cores respectively. E20.

homonymously *adv.* M18.

homonymy /hə'mɒnɪmi/ *n.* L16. [Late L *homonymia* f. Gk *homōnumia*, f. *homōnumos*: see prec., -Y[3].] The quality or state of being homonymous.

homoousian /hɒməʊ'uːsɪən, -'aʊ-, -z-; həʊməʊ-/ *n.* & *a.* Also **homousian** /hɒ'muː-, -'maʊ-/, (esp. as n.) **H-**. M16. [eccl.L *homousianus*, f. *hom(o)usius* f. Gk *hom(o)ousios*, f. as HOMO- + *ousia* essence, substance: see -IAN. Opp. HETEROOUSIAN and HOMOIOUSIAN.] *Chr. Theol.* & *Eccl. Hist.* **A** *n.* A person who believes the three persons of the Trinity to be of identical essence or substance; an orthodox Trinitarian. M16. **B** *adj.* Of identical essence or substance (esp. of the three persons of the Trinity). Also, of or pertaining to the homoousians. L17.

Homoousion /hɒməʊ'uːsɪən, -'aʊ-, -z-; həʊməʊ-/ *n.* L18. [eccl.Gk, neut. of *homoousios*: see prec. Cf. HOMOIOUSION.] *Chr. Theol.* & *Eccl. Hist.* *The* doctrine that the first and second persons of the Trinity are of identical essence or substance.

homoousios /hɒməʊ'uːsɪəs, -'aʊ-, -z-; həʊməʊ-/ *a.* M19. [Gk: see HOMOOUSIAN.] = HOMOOUSIAN *a.*

homophile /'hɒməfʌɪl, 'həʊm-/ *n.* & *a.* M20. [f. HOMO- + -PHILE.] = HOMOSEXUAL *a.* & *n.*

homophobia /hɒmə'fəʊbɪə, həʊmə-/ *n.*[1] *rare.* E20. [f. L HOMO *n.*[1] + -PHOBIA.] Fear or hatred of the male sex or humankind.

homophobia /hɒmə'fəʊbɪə, həʊmə-/ *n.*[2] M20. [f. HOMO(SEXUAL *a.* & *n.* + -PHOBIA.] Fear or hatred of homosexuals and homosexuality.

'**homophobe** *n.* a person who is afraid of or hostile to homosexuals and homosexuality L20. **homophobic** *a.* & *n.* (*a*) *adj.* afraid of or hostile to homosexuals and homosexuality; (*b*) *n.* = HOMOPHOBE: L20.

homophone /'hɒməfəʊn/ *a.* & *n.* E17. [Gk *homophōnos*, f. as HOMO-, -PHONE.] **A** *adj.* Pronounced the same. *rare.* E17.

B *n.* Each of a set of words pronounced the same but of different meaning, origin, or spelling. Also, each of a set of symbols denoting the same sound or group of sounds. E17.

homophonic /hɒmə'fɒnɪk, həʊm-/ *a.* L19. [f. as prec. + -IC.] **1** *Mus.* Characterized by having one melodic part, to which the other parts provide harmonic accompaniment. L19. **2** = HOMOPHONOUS 2. M20.

homophonous /hə'mɒf(ə)nəs/ *a.* M18. [f. as HOMOPHONE + -OUS.] **1** *Mus.* = HOMOPHONIC 1. M18. **2** Having the same pronunciation but differing in meaning, origin, or spelling. E19.

homophony /hə'mɒf(ə)ni/ *n.* M18. [Gk *homophōnia* unison f. as HOMOPHONE: see -PHONY.] **1** *Mus.* Homophonic music or style; a homophonic composition. M18. **2** The quality or state of being homophonous with regard to pronunciation. M19.

homoplastic /hɒmə(ʊ)'plastɪk, həʊm-/ *a.* L19. [f. HOMO- + Gk *plastos* moulded + -IC.] **1** *Biol.* Of a trait or character: having a similar structure but not a common origin; analogous. L19. **2** *Biol.* & *Med.* Of or involving tissue grafted from one individual to (the equivalent site in) another of the same species. E20.

'**homoplasty** *n.* homoplastic transplantation E20.

homoplasy /'hɒməpleɪsi, 'həʊm-/ *n.* L19. [f. as prec. + Gk *plasia*: see -PLASIA, -Y[3].] *Biol.* (An instance of) similarity of structure produced independently (as) by the operation of similar circumstances.

homopteran /hɒ'mɒpt(ə)rən/ *n.* & *a.* M19. [f. mod.L *Homoptera* (see below), f. as HOMO- + Gk *pteron* wing: see -AN.] *Entomol.* **A** *n.* Any hemipteran insect of the suborder Homoptera of chiefly plant-sucking bugs with wings of uniform texture, including aphids, scale insects, cicadas, etc. Cf. HETEROPTERAN. M19. **B** *adj.* Of, pertaining to, or characteristic of the suborder Homoptera. E20.

homopterous *a.* = HOMOPTERAN *a.* E19.

homorganic /hɒmɔː'ganɪk/ *a.* M19. [f. HOMO- + ORGANIC *a.*] *Phonet.* Produced by the same vocal organ or organs; sharing a specific place of articulation.

homosexual /hɒmə(ʊ)'sɛksjʊəl, -ʃʊəl; həʊm-/ *a.* & *n.* L19. [f. HOMO- + SEXUAL.] **A** *adj.* Sexually attracted to people of one's own sex; of, pertaining to, or characterized by sexual attraction between people of the same sex. L19. **B** *n.* A person who is sexually attracted (often exclusively) to people of his or her own sex. E20.

homosexualist *n.* a homosexual E20. **homosexually** *adv.* E20.

homosexuality /ˌhɒmə(ʊ)sɛksjʊ'alɪti, -kʃʊ-; həʊm-/ *n.* L19. [f. prec. + -ITY.] The quality or condition of being homosexual; homosexual character, behaviour, or activity.

homostyled /'hɒmə(ʊ)stʌɪld, 'həʊm-/ *a.* L19. [f. HOMO- + STYLE + -ED[2].] *Bot.* Having the styles in different individuals of the same length relative to the stamens.

homo'stylous *a.* homostyled L19. '**homostyly** *n.* the state or condition of being homostylous L19.

homotopic /hɒmə(ʊ)'tɒpɪk, həʊm-/ *a.* L19. [f. HOMO- + Gk *topos* place + -IC.] **1** Relating to corresponding parts or places. *rare.* L19. **2** *Math.* Related by a homotopy *to* another path, complex, etc. E20.

homotopy /'hɒmətəʊpi, hɒ'mɒtəpi/ *n.* E20. [f. as prec.: see -Y[3].] *Math.* (The property which characterizes) a mapping that deforms one path continuously into another, such that all intermediates lie within the topological space of which the two given paths are subspaces.

homotransplant /*as n.* hɒmə(ʊ)'transplɑːnt, -'trɑːns-, -nz-; həʊm-; *as vb* -trans'plɑːnt, -trɑːns-, -nz-/ *n.* & *v.* E20. [f. HOMO- + TRANSPLANT *n.*] *Med.* & *Biol.* A *n.* A piece of tissue or an organ (to be) transplanted from one individual to another of the same species. Also, an operation in which such a transplantation is performed. E20. B *v.t.* Transplant from one individual to another of the same species. M20.

homotransplan'tation *n.* E20.

homozygote /hɒmə(ʊ)'zʌɪgəʊt, həʊm-/ *n.* & *a.* E20. [f. HOMO- + ZYGOTE.] *Biol.* A *n.* An individual that has identical alleles at one or more genetic loci; a Mendelian hybrid that is not a heterozygote and so breeds true. E20. B *adj.* Homozygous. E20.

homozy'gosity *n.* (*a*) the state or condition of being homozygous; (*b*) the degree to which an individual is homozygous: E20. **homozy'gotic** *a.* of or pertaining to homozygosis; homozygous: E20. **homozygous** *a.* having identical alleles at one or more genetic loci, or *for* a given gene E20.

homuncio /hɒ'mʌnsɪəʊ/ *n.* Now *rare* or *obs.* Pl. **-o(e)s**. LME. [L, dim. of *homo* man.] = HOMUNCULUS.

homunculus /hɒ'mʌŋkjʊləs/ *n.* Pl. **-li** /-lʌɪ, -liː/. M17. [L, dim. of *homo* man: see -CULE.] A small or diminutive person, a dwarf; *Hist.* a foetus considered as a fully formed human being.

HENRY MORE There is an artificiall way of making an Homunculus, and . . the Fairies . . had some such originall. E. JONG An Herbal Remedy, swiftly swallow'd, which would loose the dread Homunculus from the womb.

homuncular *a.* diminutive, dwarfish E19. **homuncule** /hɒ'mʌŋkjuːl/ *n.* (now *rare*) = HOMUNCULUS L17.

homy *a.* var. of HOMEY *a.*

hon /hʌn/ *n. colloq.* E20. [Abbrev.] = HONEY *n.* 3 (chiefly as a form of address).

honcho /'hɒntʃəʊ/ *n.* & *v. slang.* Chiefly *N. Amer.* M20. [Jap. *hanchō* group leader.] A *n.* Pl. **-os**. The leader of a small group or squad; a person who is in a position of power; a strong leader. M20. B *v.t.* Oversee; be in charge of (a situation). M20.

honda /'hɒndə/ *n. US.* Also **-do** /-dəʊ/, pl. **-os**, **-du** /-duː/. L19. [Prob. f. Sp. *hondón* eyelet, infl. by Sp. *honda* sling.] The eye at the end of a lasso through which the rope passes to form a loop.

Honduran /hɒn'djʊər(ə)n/ *a.* & *n.* E20. [f. *Honduras* (see below) + -AN.] A *adj.* Of, pertaining to, or characteristic of the Central American country of Honduras or (formerly) of nearby British Honduras (now Belize). E20. B *n.* A native or inhabitant of Honduras or (formerly) British Honduras. M20.

Also **Honduranean, -ian** /hɒndjʊ'reɪnɪən/ *a.* & *n.* (now *rare*) L19.

hone /həʊn/ *n.* [OE *hān* = ON *hein*, f. Gmc.] †1 A stone, a rock. OE–ME. 2 A whetstone used for giving a fine edge to cutting tools. ME. 3 The stone of which whetstones are made. Also *hone stone*. E18.

hone /həʊn/ *v.*[2]*i. dial.* & *US.* LME. [OFr. *hogner, -ier* grumble.] 1 Whine or pine *for*; hanker *after*. LME. 2 Grumble, whine, moan. E17.

hone /həʊn/ *v.*[2]*t.* E19. [f. HONE *n.*] Sharpen on a hone or whetstone; *transf.* & *fig.* sharpen, streamline, focus. (Foll. by *up.*)

C. MCCULLOUGH Colonial axes had only one blade, honed to hair-splitting sharpness. A. PRICE Desperation honed up her wits to a razor edge.

honest /'ɒnɪst/ *a.* & *adv.* ME. [OFr. (*h*)*oneste* (mod. *honnête*) f. L *honestus*, f. *honos*, *honor* HONOUR *n.*] A *adj.* 1†a Of a person: held in honour; holding an honourable position; respectable. ME–L17. b Blameless but undistinguished. Chiefly *iron.* M16. 2 Of a thing, action, condition, etc.: bringing or deserving honour, honourable, decent, worthy, respectable; without disgrace or blemish. ME. 3a Of an action, one's feelings, etc.: showing sincerity of character or intention; fair, straightforward; free from fraud. ME. b Of a thing: exactly as it appears; genuine, unadulterated. L16. c Of money or gain: acquired by fair means; legitimate. L17. 4 Of a person: marked by uprightness or probity; fair and righteous in speech and act; fundamentally sincere, or truthful; not lying, cheating, or stealing. LME. †b *gen.* Of good moral character; virtuous, well-disposed. LME–E18. c Of a woman: chaste, virtuous. *arch.* LME. 5 Ingenuous; without disguise; open, frank, truthful. M17.

1b J. T. BROCKETT Now, my honest man, you have been convicted of felony. 2 *Globe & Mail* (*Toronto*) When the thermometer really plunges, this is an honest garment. G. GREENE Men who've never done a stroke of honest work, talkers, scribblers. 3a THACKERAY The very best and honestest feelings of the man came out in these artless pourings of paternal feeling. b U. BENTLEY It was not an honest gas fire, but one of those . . with coals fashioned out of fibre glass. 4 P. ROTH Far from being 'exploitive', I am just one of the few honest people around. 5 D. H. LAWRENCE Sam, seeing her look at him, distorted his honest features. J. O'HARA I went to the boxing match, and to be completely frank and honest, I enjoyed myself.

Phrases: **earn an honest penny** = *turn an honest penny* below. **make an honest woman of** *colloq.* marry (esp. a pregnant woman). **turn an honest penny** earn money by fair means, make one's livelihood by hard work.

Special collocations & comb.: **honest broker** an impartial mediator in international, industrial, etc., disputes (orig. *spec.* Otto von Bismarck, under whom Germany was united). *honest* INJUN. **Honest John** (*a*) an honest person; (*b*) *Hist.* an American missile designed to carry a nuclear warhead. **honest-to-God**, **honest-to-goodness** *adjs.* & *advs.* (*colloq.*) genuine(ly) real(ly).

B *adv.* Honestly; *esp.* (*colloq.*) really, genuinely, in truth. L16.

ARNOLD BENNETT 'But I'm not sarcastic!' he protested. 'Honest?' . . 'Honest!' he solemnly insisted.

honestly /'ɒnɪstli/ *adv.* ME. [f. prec. + -LY[2].] 1 In an honourable or respectful manner; worthily, decently. ME. †2 Chastely, virtuously. ME–L17. 3 With upright conduct; without fraud, by honest means; sincerely, fairly, openly. LME. b Really, genuinely, in truth. As *int.* also expr. exasperation. L19.

1 *Practical Woodworking* Honestly built in sound and suitable materials they have served several generations. 3 B. JOWETT He does not like honestly to confess that he is talking nonsense. b R. LEHMANN It isn't amusing to be poor, darling. You wouldn't like it, honestly. *Courier & Advertiser* (*Dundee*) Honestly, some of these drivers should have their heads seen to!

honesty /'ɒnɪsti/ *n.* ME. [OFr. (*h*)*onesté* f. L *honestas*, f. *honestus* HONEST *a.*: see -TY[1].] I The quality of being honest. †1 Honour gained or conferred; repute, respect; respectability. ME–E17. 2 Appropriateness; decency, decorum. *obs.* exc. *Sc.* LME. †3a Moral excellence; honourable character; *spec.* virtue, chastity, esp. of a woman. LME–M17. b Generosity, liberality, hospitality. LME–E19. 4 Integrity, uprightness, truthfulness, sincerity. L16.

4 E. M. FORSTER He had a strong regard for honesty, and his word, once given, had always been kept.

II 5 A cruciferous plant, *Lunaria annua*, much grown for its purple or white flowers and round semi-transparent seed-pods. L16.

Phrases: *in the way of honesty*: see WAY *n.*

honewort /'həʊnwəːt/ *n.* M17. [f. unkn. 1st elem. + WORT *n.*[1]] Orig., corn parsley, *Petroselinum segetum*. Now, the related plant *Trinia glauca*, a small European umbellifer found in limestone turf in SW England; *N. Amer.* a woodland plant of the same family, *Cryptotaenia canadensis*.

honey /'hʌni/ *n.* & *a.* See also HINNY *n.*[2] [OE *huniġ* = OFris. *hunig*, OS *honeg, -ig*, OHG *honag, -ang* (Du., G *Honig*), ON *hunang*, f. Gmc.] A *n.* 1 A sweet viscid fluid of various shades of yellow or gold, which is the nectar of flowers collected and worked up for food by insects, esp. by the honeybee. OE. b A colour resembling that of honey. E19. 2 A juice which has similar qualities to honey; nectar; the juice of dates etc. LME. 3 A term of endearment: sweetheart, darling. Also, a beloved person, a sweetheart. Now chiefly *N. Amer.* & *Anglo-Ir.* LME. b A good specimen of its kind; an excellent person or thing. *colloq.* L19. 4 *fig.* Sweetness, beauty, eloquence. L16. 5 A spoiled child; a person who is difficult to please. *US slang.* M20.

3 J. HELLER 'Be thankful you've got me,' she insisted. 'I am, honey'. *Blues & Soul* You can just curl up with your honey and listen to it. b M. HOWARD She will write him a honey of a book.

Phrases: *bees and honey*: see BEE *n.*[1] *milk and honey*: see MILK *n. palm honey*: see PALM *n.*[1] *sugar and honey*: see SUGAR *n.* 2b. **virgin honey** liquid honey that flows or is centrifugally extracted from the combs.

Comb.: **honey ant** = HONEY-POT 4; **honey-badger** = RATEL; **honey bag** a bag containing honey; *spec.* = *honey stomach* below; **honey-bear** (*a*) the kinkajou, *Potos flavus*; (*b*) the sloth-bear, *Melursus ursinus*; **honeybee** the common hive bee, *Apis mellifera*; **honey bucket** *N. Amer. slang* a container for excrement; **honey-bun, -bunch** *colloq.* = sense 3 above; **honey-buzzard** any of several hawks of the genus *Pernis*, *esp.* a migratory Eurasian hawk, *P. apivorus*, which feeds extensively on the contents of the nests of bees and wasps; **honey chile** /tʃʌɪl/ *Southern US* (*Black*) *colloq.* [repr. pronunc. of *child*] = sense 3 above; **honey-creeper** (*a*) any of various passerine birds of the family Drepanididae, native to the Hawaiian Islands; (*b*) any of various neotropical tanagers, esp. of the genera *Cyanerpes* and *Chlorophanes*, which feed on nectar; **honey drop** a drop of honey or of something sweet and delicious; **honey-eater** an animal etc. that feeds on honey; *esp.* any of various mainly Australasian passerine birds of the family Meliphagidae, with a long tongue used to take nectar from flowers; **honey-flow** (the period of) the secretion of honey or nectar by flowers; **honey-flower** any of various plants yielding abundant nectar; *esp.* (*a*) any of several southern African shrubs of the genus *Melianthus* (family Melianthaceae), grown for their fragrant flowers and handsome pinnate leaves; (*b*) an Australian shrub, *Lambertia formosa* (family Proteaceae); **honey-fungus** a fungus, *Armillaria mellea*, which attacks the roots of trees etc. and produces honey-coloured toadstools; **honey gilding** a dull gilding of gold leaf and honey used to decorate porcelain; the process of applying such gilding; **honeyguide** (*a*) any of various small tropical birds of the largely African family Indicatonidae, which feed on insects, honey, and beeswax, and can serve to reveal the location of bees' nests; (*b*) a marking on a flower which serves to direct pollinating insects to the nectaries; **honey-lipped** *a.* sweet or soft in speech; sweet talking, insincere; **honey-locust** a spiny N. American leguminous tree, *Gleditsia triacanthos*; †**honey-month** [after HONEYMOON] the first month after marriage; **honey mouse** = *honey possum* below; †**honey-mouthed** *a.* = *honey-lipped* above; **honey-myrtle** *Austral.* = MELALEUCA; **honey possum** a small nectar-eating marsupial, *Tarsipes spencerae*, of SW Australia; **honey sac, stomach** the crop of a bee, in which nectar is stored during conversion to honey; **honeystone** = MELLITE; **honeysucker** a honeyeater or other bird etc. that feeds on honey or nectar; **honey-sweet** *a.* & *n.* (*a*) *adj.* sweet as honey; (*b*) *n.* = sense 3 above; **honey-tongued** *a.* speaking sweetly, softly, or winningly; **honeywort** any of several plants of the genus *Cerinthe*, of the borage family, esp. *C. major*, with glaucous leaves and drooping bell-shaped flowers, grown as bee plants.

B *adj.* Resembling or of the nature of honey; sweet; honeyed; lovable, dear. LME.

honeyish *a.* (*rare*) somewhat like honey, rather sweet or pleasing M17. **honeyless** *a.* E17.

honey /'hʌni/ *v.* Pa. t. & pple **honeyed, honied**. LME. [f. the n.] 1 *v.t.* Make sweet with or as with honey; sweeten. LME. 2 *v.t.* Address as 'honey'; use endearing terms to. Chiefly *US.* E17. 3 *v.i.* Use honeyed or endearing words; talk fondly or sweetly, use flattery. E17. 4 *v.t.* Coax, cajole; flatter. E17.

honey-bird /'hʌnɪbəːd/ *n.* LME. [f. HONEY *n.* + BIRD *n.*] †1 A bee. LME–E17. 2 Any of various birds feeding on nectar or honey; *esp.* a honeyeater or a honeyguide. M18.

honeycomb /'hʌnɪkəʊm/ *n.* & *a.* OE. [f. HONEY *n.* + COMB *n.*[1]] A *n.* 1 A structure of wax containing two series of hexagonal cells separated by thin partitions, formed by bees for the reception of honey and their eggs; *fig.* a receptacle for sweet things. OE. †2 = HONEY *n.* 3. LME–M16. 3 A cavernous flaw in metalwork, esp. in a gun. M16. 4 The reticulum or second stomach of a ruminant. Also *honeycomb tripe*. E18. 5a Decorative or other work with a hexagonal or cellular arrangement like a honeycomb. M19. b A sturdy material consisting of a network of open-ended cells bonded together. M20.

B *attrib.* or as *adj.* Resembling or suggestive of a honeycomb; having a hexagonal or cellular pattern or arrangement. E18.

Special collocations & comb.: **honeycomb quilt**: with a raised hexagonal pattern; **honeycomb ringworm** = FAVUS. *honeycomb tripe*: see sense 4 above. **honeycomb wall** a wall with numerous small openings at regular intervals.

honeycomb /ˈhʌnɪkəʊm/ *v.* L18. [f. the n.] 1 *v.t.* & *i.* Make or become like a honeycomb with cells, cavities, or perforations; make or become cavernous, hollow, or insubstantial. L18. 2 *v.t. fig.* Penetrate throughout so as to make hollow, rotten, etc.; undermine. M19. 3 *v.t.* Mark with a honeycomb pattern. L19. 4 *v.t.* Build as a honeycomb wall. E20.

1 SLOAN WILSON They had honeycombed the island with tunnels and caves. 2 F. L. ALLEN The colleges were honeycombed with Bolshevism.

honeycombing *n.* (*a*) the action of the vb; (*b*) a defective condition of wood characterized by cracks and holes: L19.

honeycombed /ˈhʌnɪkəʊmd/ *a.* E17. [f. HONEYCOMB *v.*, *n.* + -ED[1], -ED[2].] 1 Having perforations, excavations, or cavernous parts like a honeycomb; *esp.* having numerous small cells. E17. 2 Marked with a honeycomb pattern. L19.

honeydew /ˈhʌnɪdjuː/ *n.* L16. [f. HONEY *n.* + DEW *n.*] 1 A sweet, sticky substance exuded by aphids, found on the leaves and stems of plants (orig. believed to be akin to dew). L16. 2 An ideally sweet or luscious substance; the nectar of flowers; honey. Now chiefly *poet.* E17. 3 A kind of tobacco sweetened with molasses. M19.

Comb.: **honeydew melon** a cultivated variety of the melon, *Cucumis melo*, with smooth ivory or pale yellow skin and sweet green flesh.

honeyed /ˈhʌnɪd/ *a.* Also **honied**. LME. [f. HONEY *n.* + -ED[2].] 1 Having much honey, laden with honey; consisting of or containing honey. LME. 2 *fig.* Sweet; sweet-sounding, mellifluous. LME.

honey-fuggle /ˈhʌnɪfʌg(ə)l/ *v. US colloq.* Also **-fugle** /-fjuːg(ə)l/. E19. [f. HONEY *n.* + FUGLE *v.*[1]] 1 *v.t.* Dupe, deceive, swindle. E19. b Obtain by duplicity or wheedling. E20. 2 *v.i.* Act in an underhand or indirect way in order to deceive or obtain by duplicity. M19.

honeymoon /ˈhʌnɪmuːn/ *n.* & *v.* M16. [f. HONEY *n.* + MOON *n.*, orig. w. ref. to waning affection, not to period of a month.] A *n.* 1 Orig., the first month after marriage. Now usu., a holiday spent together by a newly married couple. M16. 2 *transf.* (The period of) the first warmth of newly established friendly relations. L16.

2 *Guardian* The Government has had its honeymoon, free from captious criticism.

Comb. & *phrases*: **honeymoon couple** a newly married couple; **second honeymoon** a romantic holiday or trip taken by a couple who have been married for some time; *transf.* a period of renewed friendly relations.

B *v.i.* Spend a honeymoon. E19.

honeymooner *n.* L19.

honey-pot /ˈhʌnɪpɒt/ *n.* L15. [f. HONEY *n.* + POT *n.*[1]] 1 A pot in which honey is stored. L15. 2 The female external genitals. *slang.* E18. 3 In *pl.*, a children's game in which one player clasps hands under his or her thighs and is carried like a honey-pot by others; *sing.* the posture with the hands clasped under the thighs. E19. 4 More fully *honey-pot ant.* A worker ant distended with surplus food which can be regurgitated when needed by the colony; any of various kinds of ant which store food in this way. L19. 5 A person who or thing which tempts or attracts attention; *spec.* an attractive woman. E20.

honeysuck /ˈhʌnɪsʌk/ *n.* Long *obs.* exc. *dial.* OE. [f. HONEY *n.* + SUCK *v.*] = HONEYSUCKLE 1, 2.

honeysuckle /ˈhʌnɪsʌk(ə)l/ *n.* ME. [App. an extension of prec.] 1 *sing.* & in *pl.* The tubular flowers of certain plants, esp. red clover, *Trifolium pratense*, and white clover, *T. repens*, sucked for the nectar contained in them; any of the plants bearing these flowers. Now *dial.* ME. 2 A twining shrub of woods and hedges, *Lonicera periclymenum* (family Caprifoliaceae), with fragrant trumpet-shaped typically pale yellow pink-tinged flowers (also *common honeysuckle*; also called *woodbine*); *gen.* any plant of this or related genera. Also, the flower of these plants. LME. 3 Chiefly *Archit.* A design or ornament resembling a sprig or flower of honeysuckle. M16. 4 With or without specifying wd: any of various plants thought to resemble the honeysuckle (or clover), esp. in abundance of nectar; *esp.* (*a*) *Austral.* = BANKSIA; (*b*) *N. Amer.* a kind of columbine, *Aquilegia canadensis*; (*c*) *NZ* = REWAREWA. L16. 5 The colour of honeysuckle flowers, which combines pale yellow and pink. L19.

1 BACON Flowers that haue deepe Sockets, doe gather in the Bottome a kind of Honey; As Honeysuckles (both the Woodbine and the Trifoile). 2 T. KEN Sweet Honeysuckles round the Branches twin'd. **fly honeysuckle** either of two erect honeysuckles bearing flowers in pairs, the European *Lonicera xylosteum* and the N. American *L. canadensis*. **trumpet honeysuckle** a N. American climbing honeysuckle, *Lonicera sempervirens*, with evergreen foliage and scarlet flowers. 4 **French honeysuckle** an ornamental Italian leguminous plant, *Hedysarum coronarium*, with flowers like those of sainfoin. *swamp honeysuckle*: see SWAMP *n.*

honeysuckled *a.* overgrown or scented with honeysuckle M17.

hong /hɒŋ/ *n.* E18. [Chin. *háng*, (Cantonese) *hòhng* row, trade.] 1 In China, a series of rooms or buildings used as a warehouse, factory, etc. *esp.* one of the foreign factories formerly maintained at Canton. Also in Hong Kong, a trading establishment. E18. 2 *Hist.* The corporation of Chinese merchants at Canton who had a monopoly of trade with Europeans. L18.

honied *a.* var. of HONEYED *a.*

honied *v.* pa. t. & pple: see HONEY *v.*

Honiton /ˈhɒnɪt(ə)n, ˈhʌn-/ *a.* M19. [A town in Devon.] Designating or pertaining to a type of lace orig. made in Honiton consisting of floral sprigs hand sewn on to fine net or joined by bars of other lacework.

honk /hɒŋk/ *n.* & *v.* M19. [Imit.] A *n.* 1 The cry of the wild goose. M19. 2 Also redupl. **honk-honk**. The harsh sound of a motor horn. E20. B *v.* 1 *v.i.* Make or emit a honk. M19. 2 *v.t.* Utter with a honk; remove or drive away by a honk on a horn. E20.

honker /ˈhɒŋkə/ *n.* L19. [f. prec. + -ER[1].] 1 A wild goose. L19. 2 A person who makes a honking noise. L19. 3 The horn of a motor vehicle. E20. 4 A nose. *slang.* M20.

honkers /ˈhɒŋkəz/ *a. slang.* M20. [Origin unkn.] Drunk.

honky /ˈhɒŋki/ *n.* & *a. US Black slang. derog.* M20. [Origin unkn.] A *n.* A White person; *collect.* White people. M20. B *adj.* Of a person: White. L20.

honky-tonk /ˈhɒŋkɪtɒŋk/ *n.* & *a. colloq.* (orig. *US*). L19. [Origin unkn.] A *n.* 1 A tawdry drinking-saloon, dancehall, or gambling house; a cheap nightclub. L19. 2 Ragtime music or jazz of a type played in honky-tonks, esp. on the piano. M20. B *adj.* Of or pertaining to (a) honky-tonk; *esp.* (of a piano) tinny-sounding, out of tune. M20.

honnête homme /ɔnɛt ɔm/ *n. phr.* Pl. **-s -s** (pronounced same). M17. [Fr.] A decent, cultivated man of the world.

honor *n.*, *v.* see HONOUR *n.*, *v.*

honorable *a.* & *n.* see HONOURABLE.

†**honorance** *n.* ME–E18. [OFr., f. as HONOUR *v.*: see -ANCE.] The action of honouring.

honorand /ˈɒnərand/ *n.* M20. [L *honorandus* gerundive of *honorare* HONOUR *v.*: see -AND.] A person to be honoured, esp. with an honorary degree.

honorarium /ɒnəˈrɛːrɪəm/ *n.* Pl. **-iums**, **-ia** /-ɪə/. M17. [L *honorarium* gift made on being admitted to a post of honour, use as n. of neut. of *honorarius* HONORARY *a.*: see -ARIUM.] A (voluntary) fee, esp. for professional services nominally rendered without payment.

A. HAILEY Acceptance by one high-ranking FDA official of 'honorariums' totalling $287,000 from a drug firm source.

honorary /ˈɒn(ə)rəri/ *n.* Now *rare.* E17. [Orig. f. as prec; later f. next.] An honorarium; an honorary distinction; a holder of an honorary post.

honorary /ˈɒn(ə)rəri/ *a.* E17. [L *honorarius*, f. *honor* HONOUR *n.*: see -ARY[1].] 1 Of a title, position, etc.: conferred as an honour, esp. without the usual requirements, functions, etc. E17. 2 Of a person: holding an honorary title or position. E18. 3 Of an obligation etc.: depending on honour, not legally enforceable. L18.

1 DAY LEWIS The honorary membership of the Incorporated Society of Musicians which I was given. 2 R. P. JHABVALA He was, after all, only the paid secretary, whereas she was the honorary one.

Special collocations: *honorary alderman*: see ALDERMAN 3. *honorary canon*: see CANON *n.*[2] 2. *honorary degree*: see DEGREE *n.* **honorary secretary**, **treasurer**, etc.: serving without pay.

honoree /ɒnəˈriː/ *n.* Orig. *US.* M20. [f. HONOR *v.* + -EE[1].] A person who is honoured in some way.

honorer *n.* see HONOURER.

honorial /ɒˈnɔːrɪəl/ *a.* E19. [f. HONOR *n.* + -IAL.] Chiefly *Hist.* Of or pertaining to an honour (HONOUR *n.* 6); of or pertaining to an honorific title.

honorific /ɒnəˈrɪfɪk/ *a.* & *n.* M17. [L *honorificus*, f. *honor*: see HONOUR *n.*, -FIC.] A *adj.* Of a word, phrase, etc.: implying or expressing respect. M17.

A. BURGESS The honorific Mr was used, to the disgust of the NCOs.

B *n.* An honorific word or phrase. L19.

J. A. MICHENER His voluntary use of the Polish honorific proved the sincerity of his evaluation.

honorificabilitudinitatibus /ɒˌnɔːrɪfɪˌkɑːbɪlɪˌtjuːdɪnɪˈtɑːtɪbəs/ *n. rare* & *joc.* L16. [med.L.] Honourableness.

Also **honorificabilituˈdinity** *n.* M17.

honoris causa /ɒˌnɔːrɪs ˈkauzə/ *adv. phr.* E17. [L = for the sake of honour.] As a mark of esteem, esp. in reference to an honorary degree.

honorless *a.* see HONOURLESS.

honour /ˈɒnə/ *n.* Also ***honor**. ME. [AN *anur*, *anour*, OFr. (*h*)*onor*, (*h*)*onur*, earlier *enor* (mod. *honneur*), f. L *honor*, *honor-*: see -OUR.] 1 High respect, esteem, deferential admiration; an expression of this; glory, credit, reputation, good name. ME. b *spec.* The chastity or purity of a woman; a woman's reputation for this. LME. 2 Nobleness of mind or spirit; magnanimity; uprightness; adherence to what is due or correct according to some conventional or accepted standard of conduct. ME. b A promise, an assurance. *arch.* M17. 3 Exalted rank or position; distinction. ME. b (**H-**.) With possess.: a title of respect given to a County Court etc. judge, a US mayor, and (now only in Irish speech) to any person of rank. M16. 4 A thing conferred or done as a mark of respect or distinction, *esp.* a title of rank. ME. †b A bow or curtsy. M16–E19. c In *pl.* Civilities or courtesies rendered to a guest etc. Chiefly in *do the honours*. M17. d In *pl.* A special distinction for outstanding proficiency in an examination; in higher education, a degree or course of degree studies more specialized than that for an ordinary degree. L18. e A privilege, a special right; *spec.* in *Golf*, the right of driving off first. L19. 5 A source or cause of distinction; a person who or thing which does credit *to* another. ME. 6 *Law.* A seigniory of several manors under one baron or lord paramount. *obs.* exc. *Hist.* ME. 7 *Cards.* In whist, any of the ace, king, queen, and jack of trumps; in bridge, any of these and the ten also, or the four aces at no trumps. M17.

1 R. BOLT Your majesty does my house more honour than I fear my household can bear. M. IGNATIEFF Family honour could be rebuilt: father's debts could be paid off. b SHAKES. *Temp.* Till thou didst seek to violate The honour of my child. 3 S. MORLEY I must claim the honour of being one of his first stage directors. 4 R. L. FOX He was promptly recognised as a ruler of the Thessalians, a remarkable honour for an outsider. K. M. E. MURRAY It was almost the only royal Birthday honour of which the newspapers had approved. e E. CRANKSHAW His was the honour of discovering the young Turgenev in 1847. 5 I. MACLAREN You are an honour to our profession.

Phrases: *affair of honour*: see AFFAIR 1. **code of honour** the rules forming a conventional standard of conduct. *Companion of Honour*: see COMPANION *n.*[1] *debt of honour*: see DEBT *n. field of honour*: see FIELD *n.* **funeral honours** observances of respect at a funeral. *guest of honour*: see GUEST *n.* 1. **honour bright** *int.* (*colloq.*) protesting one's sincerity. **honours are even** the contest is equal. **honours of war** privileges granted to a capitulating force, e.g. that of marching out with colours flying. **in honour bound** under a moral obligation (*to do*). **in honour of** as a celebration of, as an expression of respect or admiration for. *lap of honour*: see LAP *n.*[3] **last honours** = *funeral honours* above. **law of honour** = *code of honour* above. *Legion of Honour*: see LEGION *n. maid of honour*: see MAID *n. matron of honour*: see MATRON *n.* **military honours** marks of respect paid by troops at the burial of a soldier, to royalty, etc. **on** (or **upon**) **my honour** *int.* protesting one's sincerity. **on one's honour** under a moral obligation (*to do*). *parole of honour*: see PAROLE *n.* & *a.* 2(a). *point of honour*: see POINT *n.*[1] *roll of honour*: see ROLL *n.*[1] *upon my honour*: see *on my honour* above. *word of honour*: see WORD *n.*

Comb.: **honour point** *Her.* the point halfway between the top of a shield and the fesse point; **honours course** a course at a university etc. leading to an honours degree; **honours degree** (a course leading to) a degree with honours; **honours list** (*a*) a list of successful candidates in an examination for an honours degree; (*b*) a list of people awarded honours by the British monarch, as at New Year; **honours school** a branch of study at a university etc. in which an honours degree may be taken; **honour system** a system of examinations etc. without supervision, relying on the honour of those concerned; **honour-trick** *Bridge* = *quick trick* s.v. QUICK *a.*

honour /ˈɒnə/ *v.t.* Also ***honor**. ME. [OFr. *onorer, onurer* (mod. *honorer*) f. L *honorare*, f. *honor-* HONOUR *n.*] †1 Pay respect or do honour to by some outward action; do homage to. ME–L17. 2 Regard with honour, respect highly, reverence. ME. 3 Confer honour upon; grace. ME. 4 Accept or pay (a bill or cheque) when due; fulfil (an obligation), abide by the terms of (an agreement). E18.

1 SHAKES. *Ven. & Ad.* Till I have honoured you with some graver labour. 2 E. WAUGH Women are naturally Bohemian, while men honour convention. A. BURGESS Honour thy father, though not necessarily thy stepfather. 3 K. AMIS Are you sure Alexander is to honour us with his company this evening. 4 B. MAGEE Necessary order should rest not on force but on consent and the honouring of agreements. J. C. OATES And there was some question about Goodheart's honouring their IOU.

honourable /ˈɒn(ə)rəb(ə)l/ *a.* Also ***honor-**. ME. [(O)Fr. f. L *honorabilis*, f. *honorare*: see prec., -ABLE.] A *adj.* 1 Worthy of being honoured; entitled to honour or respect. ME. †b Respectable in quality or amount; befitting a person of honour. ME–M17. 2 Characterized by honour; virtuous, upright, honest; bringing honour to the possessor. ME. b Consistent with honour. M16. 3 Holding a position of honour or rank. ME. b (**H-**.) Used as a title indicating eminence or distinction, given e.g. to the younger sons of Earls, children of Viscounts and Barons, Maids of Honour, Justices of High Court without higher title, Lords of Session, members of Government in Dominions, Colonies and Commonwealth States, to Members of Parliament by one another, and in the US to members of Congress, cabinet ministers, judges, etc. LME. 4 Showing or doing honour. LME.

1 B. JOWETT The soul which came from heaven is more honourable than the body which is earth-born. 2 SHAKES. *Two Gent.* The match Were rich and honourable. R. C. SHERRIFF An honourable man whose word was his bond. b J. STEINBECK She was surrounded, and there was no honourable way out save death. 3 LD MACAULAY This man, named Edward Petre, was descended from an honourable family. b **Most Honourable** the title of Marquesses, members of the Privy Council, and holders of the Order of the Bath. **Right Honourable** the title of Earls, Viscounts, Barons, Privy Counsellors, Lords (Justices) of Appeal, the Lord Mayor of London, York, or Belfast, Lord Provost of Edinburgh or Glasgow, etc. 4 BOSWELL An honourable monument to his memory.

Special collocations: **honourable discharge** *US* a discharge or release from the armed forces at the end of a period of honourable service. **honourable intentions** *colloq.*: to marry the woman one is courting. **honourable mention** an award of merit to a candidate in an examination, a work of art, etc., not entitled to a prize.

B *n.* An honourable person; *spec.* a person with the title Honourable. LME.

D. LESSING Marion's mother being the widow of a general, and her sisters all ladies or honourables.

honouraˈbility *n.* (*rare*) LME. **honourableness** *n.* M16. **honourably** *adv.* ME.

honourer /ˈɒnərə/ *n.* Also ***honor-**. ME. [f. HONOUR *v.* + -ER[1].] A person who honours someone or something. In early use also, a worshipper.

honourless /ˈɒnəlɪs/ *a.* Also ***honor-**. M16. [f. HONOUR *n.* + -LESS.] Lacking honour; unworthy of honour.

Honved /ˈhɒnvɛd/ *n.* M19. [Hungarian, f. *hon* home + *véd* defend.] (A member of) the Hungarian second-line formation during the revolutionary war of 1848–9, or later, the militia reserve.

honyock, honyocker *ns.* vars. of HUNYAK.

hoo /huː/ *n.*[1] Long *obs.* exc. *Sc.* Also **how** /haʊ/, (earlier) †**houve**. [OE *hūfe* = MLG, MDu. *hūve* (Du. *huif*), OHG *hūba* (G *Haube*), f. Gmc, f. base repr. also by HIVE *n.*] 1 A covering for the head; a cap, *spec.* a nightcap. OE. 2 A child's caul. M16.

hoo /(h)uː/ *pers. pron.* Long *obs.* exc. *dial.* [OE *hīo, hēo* fem. of HE *pron.*] = SHE *pers. pron.*

hoo /huː/ *int.*, *v.*, & *n.*[2] Also redupl. **hoo-hoo**. OE. [Partly natural exclam., partly imit. See also WHOO *v., int. & n.*] A *int.* 1 Expr. surprise or requesting attention etc. OE. 2 Repr. the hoot of an owl or the sough of the wind. L15. B *v.i.* Give a cry of 'hoo!'; (of an owl) hoot; (of the wind) sough. L18. C *n.* A call or cry of 'hoo!' M19.

hooch /huːtʃ/ *n.*[1] *colloq.* (chiefly *N. Amer.*). Also **hootch**. L19. [Abbrev. of HOOCHINOO.] Alcoholic liquor; *esp.* inferior or illicit alcoholic liquor.

D. LODGE 'Duty-free hooch,' said Morris Zapp, taking a half-bottle of Scotch from his . . pocket.

hooch /huːtʃ/ *n.*[2] *Mil. slang.* Also **hoochie** /ˈhuːtʃi/, **hootch**. M20. [Perh. f. Jap. *uchi* dwelling.] A dugout; a shelter, *esp.* a temporary or insubstantial one.

New York Times His decision to remove the United States Marines from their hooches at the Beirut airport.

Hoochinoo /ˈhuːtʃɪnuː/ *n.* In sense 2 also **h-**. L19. [Tlingit *xutsnu:wú* (place name) lit. 'brown bear's fort'.] 1 (A member of) a Tlingit Indian people of Admiralty Island, Alaska. L19. 2 = HOOCH *n.*[1] L19.

hood /hʊd/ *n.*[1] & *v.* [OE *hōd* = OFris. *hōd*, MDu. *hoet* (Du. *hoed*), OHG *huot* (G *Hut* hat), f. WGmc base rel. to that of HAT *n.*] A *n.* 1 A covering for the head and neck (sometimes also the shoulders) with an opening for the face, either forming part of a coat, cloak, etc., or separate. OE. 2 *spec.* A hood worn as a mark of official or professional dignity, usu. thrown back on the shoulders; *esp.* such a hood worn with an academic gown, coloured or ornamented to indicate degree, faculty, etc.; the ornamental attachment on the back of a cope, orig. shaped and used like a hood. ME. 3 The part of a suit of armour for covering the head, a helmet or a flexible covering worn under a helmet, (*obs.* exc. *Hist.*). Now also, a helmet-like covering for the entire head as protection against fumes, radiation, etc. ME. 4 A leather covering for a hawk's head to keep it quiet when not hunting. LME. 5 Something resembling a hood in shape or use; a covering, a protection; *spec.* (*a*) the cover of a carriage; *esp.* a folding waterproof cover of a pram, (convertible) motor car, etc.; (*b*) a canopy to remove fumes from a cooker etc. or to protect the user of machinery; (*c*) a tube attached to the front of a camera lens to protect it from strong or extraneous light; (*d*) (chiefly *N. Amer.*) the bonnet of a motor vehicle; (*e*) the upper part of the corolla or calyx in some flowers; (*f*) a flap of skin or a marking on the head of any of various animals, as the cobra. E17.

1 B. LOPEZ A movement of my head shifted the hood of my parka slightly. *three faces under* (or *in*) *a hood*: see THREE *a.* 2 D. L. SAYERS His surplice and Oxford hood over one arm. 3 *Observer* The burnproof transparent hood covers the entire head. 5 F. O'CONNOR He got out and opened the hood of the truck and began to study the motor. J. S. FOSTER Control of the . . air supply can be effected by a hood . . above the fire bed. P. LEACH Put the pram hood up and turn its back to the breeze.

Comb. **hood-end** *Naut.* the end of a plank fitting into the stem and stern rabbeting; **hood-mould, -moulding** *Archit.* a dripstone.

B *v.t.* Cover or protect (as) with a hood. ME.

W. WHARTON He listens, bright blue eyes hooded with fine red eyelashes. *New Yorker* Mrs. Wetten was forced into a car, hooded, taken to a cell.

hood /hʊd/ *n.*[2] *slang.* M20. [Abbrev. of HOODLUM.] A gunman, a gangster; a hoodlum.

J. DIDION She was sitting in a park watching some hoods rifling cars. D. CAUTE In my Bronx you were either a gangster or you fought the hoods.

hood /hʊd/ *n.*[3] *US slang.* Also **'hood**. L20. [Aphet.] = NEIGHBOURHOOD 2.

-hood /hʊd/ *suff.* [OE *-hād* = OS *-hēd*, (O)HG *-heit*, orig. a Gmc n. meaning 'person, sex, condition, rank, quality', repr. by OE *hād*, OS *hēd*, OHG *heit*, ON *heiðr* honour, worth, Goth. *haidus* kind, manner.] Forming ns. of condition or quality or indicating a collection or group f. ns. and adjs., as *childhood, falsehood, sisterhood*.

hooded /ˈhʊdɪd/ *a.* LME. [f. HOOD *n.*[1], *v.*: see -ED[2], -ED[1].] 1 Wearing a hood; covered (as) with a hood. LME. b Of a garment: having a hood attached to or forming part of it. L16. 2 *gen.* Having or provided with a hood or protective covering. E16. 3 *fig.* Covered, concealed. M17.

1 E. BLISHEN Mr. Trellis, gowned and hooded, was the first speechmaker. R. HUNTFORD A great bearded figure with high cheekbones and hooded, . . like a Viking chieftain. b *New Yorker* Hooded homespun cassocks. 2 D. WELCH Against one wall stood a huge Chinese bed hooded grimly in dark blue cotton. *Practical Gardening* Hooded flowers appear from April to June. *hooded crow*: see CROW *n.*[1] 1. **hooded seal** a seal, *Cystophora cristata*, of the Arctic and N. Atlantic Oceans, grey with black blotches, the male of which has inflatable nasal sacs used in display.

hoodie /ˈhʊdi/ *n.* L18. [f. HOOD *n.*[1] + -IE.] A hooded crow. Also *hoodie-crow*.

hooding /ˈhʊdɪŋ/ *n.* LME. [f. HOOD *n.*[1], *v.* + -ING[1].] †1 *collect.* Hoods as a mark of official or professional dignity. Only in LME. 2 The putting on or wearing of a hood. L16. 3 *Naut.* = *hood-end* s.v. HOOD *n.*[1] E17.

hoodless /ˈhʊdlɪs/ *a.* LME. [f. HOOD *n.*[1] + -LESS.] Without a hood.

hoodlum /ˈhuːdləm/ *n.* Orig. *US slang.* L19. [Origin unkn.] A street hooligan; a young thug.

J. K. TOOLE An old aunt had been robbed of fifty cents by some hoodlums. R. ELLMANN This childhood memory, in which a child dies and a hoodlum rises up in his place.

hoodlumism *n.* the conduct or methods of a hoodlum L19.

hoodman /ˈhʊdmən/ *n. arch.* Pl. **-men**. LME. [HOOD *n.*[1] + MAN *n.*] A hooded man; the blindfolded player in blind man's buff. Now only in *hoodman blind*, blindman's buff.

hoodoo /ˈhuːduː/ *n.*, *a.*, & *v.* Orig. *US.* L19. [App. alt. of VOODOO.] A *n.* 1 A person who practises voodoo. L19. 2 (A hidden cause of) bad luck; a person or thing supposed to bring bad luck. L19. 3 A fantastic pinnacle or column of rock formed by erosion or other natural agency. L19.

1 R. TALLANT I heard people say hoodoos was cannibals and used to eat babies. 2 L. VAN DER POST By nightfall everyone . . seemed convinced there was a permanent hoodoo on us. *Independent* McEvoy's hoodoo at the . . championship . . struck again—and . . he was knocked out.

B *adj.* Unlucky. L19.

C *v.t.* Bewitch; bring bad luck to. L19.

W. A. PERCY He had been hoodooed by a witch-doctor and was going to die.

hoodooism *n.* the practice of hoodoo rites L19.

hoodwink /ˈhʊdwɪŋk/ *v.* & *n.* M16. [f. HOOD *n.*[1] + WINK *v.*[1]] **A** *v.t.* **1** Cover the eyes (of a person) with a hood etc. to prevent vision; blindfold. *arch.* M16. **2** Cover up from sight. Long *rare.* L16. **3** Deceive, delude. E17.

3 W. H. AUDEN Expert impersonator and linguist, proud of his power To hoodwink sentries. P. HOWARD The rest of the Old Gang combining to hoodwink the public and turn a blind eye on Hitler.

B *n.* **1** A blindfold; *fig.* a deception. Now *rare.* L16. †**2** Blind man's buff. L16–E17.

hooer /ˈhuːə/ *n. Austral.* & *NZ colloq.* M20. [Repr. a pronunc. of WHORE *n.*] **1** A whore, a prostitute. M20. **2** A thoroughly unpleasant or contemptible person. M20.

hooey /ˈhuːi/ *n. colloq.* (orig. *US*). E20. [Origin unkn.] Nonsense, humbug.

W. WHARTON They give out reams of hooey about how *lucky* we are.

hoof /huːf/ *n.* Pl. **hoofs, hooves** /huːvz/. [OE *hōf* = OFris., OS *hōf* (Du. *hoef*), OHG *huof* (G *Huf*), ON *hófr*, f. Gmc base rel. to synon. Skt *śapha*, Avest. *safa*.] **1** (The horny casing of) the toe or foot of an ungulate mammal, esp. a horse. OE. **b** Horny or calloused skin on the hands etc. Long *dial.* LME. **c** The cloven hoof attributed to the Devil. M17. **2** A hoofed animal, as the smallest unit of a herd. M16. **3** The human foot. *joc.* or *derog.* L16.

1 E. LANGLEY I heard the little hard hooves of his mare come scuttling across the dry hill. 3 A. PRICE It's through the family that Danny has got his dirty little hoof into the door.

Phrases: *divide the hoof*: see DIVIDE *v.* 1. **on the hoof** (*a*) (of cattle) not yet slaughtered; (*b*) (of an action) extempore. *pad the hoof*: see PAD *v.*[1]

Comb.: **hoof-and-mouth disease** foot-and-mouth disease; **hoof-pick** a hooked implement for removing stones from a horse's hoof; **hoof stick** an instrument with a head shaped like a horse's hoof used for manicuring the nails.

hoofless *a.* E18.

hoof /huːf/ *v.* M17. [f. the n.] **1** *v.i.* & *t.* (w. *it*). Go on foot. M17. **2** *v.t.* Strike with the hoof; *slang* dismiss, expel, kick *out.* M19. **3** *v.i.* & *t.* (w. *it*). Dance, *spec.* tap-dance, esp. routinely or as a profession. E20.

1 W. WHARTON Marty, my daughter, lives near the garage so Billy and I hoof it over there. 2 D. L. SAYERS They'd hoof me out of the Club if I raised my voice beyond a whisper. *Rugby News* Mesnel kicked like the proverbial golfing gorilla, hoofing the ball as far as he could. 3 A. GILBERT A pretty nifty dancer himself . . and still able to hoof it quite neatly. W. ALLEN I was his best dancer . . The other girls just hoofed.

hoofer *n.* (*slang*) a dancer, *esp.* a professional dancer E20.

hoofed /huːft/ *a.* Also **hooved** /huːvd/. LME. [f. HOOF *n.* + -ED[2].] Having hoofs.

hoofy /ˈhuːfi/ *a.* L17. [f. HOOF *n.* + -Y[1].] Having a hoof or hoofs.

hoo-ha /ˈhuːhɑː/ *n. colloq.* Also **-hah**. M20. [Origin unkn.] A commotion, an uproar; trouble.

B. GOOLDEN I don't think Mummy will make much of a hoo-ha if she knows it's not for long. E. FAIRWEATHER One can imagine the hoo-ha if such an innovation were suggested here.

hoo-hoo *int., v., n.* see HOO *int., v.,* & *n.*[2]

hook /hʊk/ *n.* [OE *hōc* = OFris., MLG, MDu. *hōk* (Du. *hoek*) corner, angle, point of land, rel. to OE *haca* bolt, OS *haco* (MDu. *hake*, Du. *haak*) OHG *hāko* (G *Haken*) hook, ON *haki*.] **1** A piece of metal or other material bent back at an angle or with a round bend, for catching hold of things, or for hanging things on; such a hook attached to a pole etc. OE. **b** *spec.* A bent piece of thin wire, usu. barbed, attached to a fishing-line to carry bait (also *fish-hook*); *fig.* a baited trap, a snare, a lure. OE. **c** A small piece of bent and flattened metal or plastic used with a loop or 'eye' as a fastener or closure on a garment. Freq. in *hook and eye.* E16. **2** A curved sharp-edged cutting tool, esp. as used for reaping, mowing, and shearing. OE. **3** The pin in the fixed part of the hinge on which a door or gate is hung. ME. **b** Orig., a hook, now, a cradle on which a telephone receiver rests. L19. **4** The barb of an arrow; the fluke of an anchor. ME. **5** *Shipbuilding.* A curved piece of timber used to strengthen an angular framework. ME. **6** A sharp bend or angle in the length of something; *esp.* a bend in a river. Also, a projecting piece of land, a spit, a headland. Earliest in place-names. ME. †**7** A shepherd's crook, a bishop's crozier. LME–L17. **8** A ball or bowl's deviation from a straight line; the action or an act of hooking a ball (see HOOK *v.* 8). E17. **9** *Zool.* & *Bot.* Any recurved and pointed appendage in a plant or animal. M17. **10** A hook-shaped symbol or character, esp. in handwriting. M17. †**b** In *pl.* Brackets. Also, inverted commas. L17–E19. **c** *Mus.* A transverse line added to the stem of the ascender in the symbol for a quaver, semiquaver, etc. L18. **d** *Logic.* (A name for, or reading of) the sign ⊃, used as the implication sign. Also called *horseshoe.* M20. **11** A finger, a hand. Usu. in *pl. slang.* E19. **b** A thief, a pickpocket. *slang.* M19. **12** *Boxing.* A short swinging blow with the elbow bent. L19.

1 J. CARY The stable lantern hung from a bacon hook in the beam. *fig.*: *City Limits* The sociology becomes just a hook for some sly and witty observations. *boat-hook, coat-hook, flesh-hook, meat-hook, pot-hook*, etc. b T. WYATT Farewell, Loue . . Thy bayted hokes shall tangle me no more. 2 *grass-hook, pruning-hook, reaping-hook*, etc. 6 J. L. MOTLEY This narrow hook of land, destined . . to be the cradle of a considerable empire. 12 F. MUIR He . . let loose a right hook that would have felled an ox.

Phrases: **by hook or by crook** by one means or another, by fair means or foul. **hook, line, and sinker** entirely, without reservations. **get one's hooks into** or **on** get hold of; get a hold over. **off the hook** (*a*) *colloq.* no longer in difficulty or trouble; (*b*) (of a telephone receiver) not on its rest, thus preventing incoming calls. **off the hooks** *colloq.* dead; *pop off the hooks*, die. **on one's own hook** *slang* on one's own account; at one's own risk. **on the hook** *colloq.* ensnared; in someone's power or grasp; addicted. **put the hooks in** *Austral. slang* ask (someone) for a loan. **sling** or **take one's hook** *slang* leave, go away, make off.

Comb.: **hook-and-eye** *v.t.* fasten (as) with a hook and eye; **hook-and-ladder** *n.* & *a.* (*US*) (designating a fire engine etc. with) an apparatus of ladders and hooks used by fire-fighters; **hook-bill(ed)** (having) a curved bill; **hook-bolt**: with a hook at one end and threaded at the other; **hook-bone** the projecting upper part of the thigh bones of cattle near the hip-joint; **hook gauge**: for determining the surface level of water; **hook-ladder**: having hooks at one end by which it can be suspended; **hook-nose(d)** (having) an aquiline nose; **hook-pin**: having a hooked head, used to pin together the frame of a roof or floor; **hook-pot** *Naut.* a (tin) pot or mug designed to hang on the bars of the galley range; **hook rug** a rug made by pulling yarn, canvas, etc., through a canvas ground on a hook; **hook shop** *slang* a brothel; **hook shot** *Basketball* a twisting shot started with the player's back to the basket, and completed as he (or she) pivots round towards the basket; **hook stroke** *Cricket* a stroke played by hitting a short-pitched ball, after it has risen, round to leg with a horizontal swing of the bat; **hook-tip** any of various moths of the family Drepanidae having a curved point to the forewings; **hookworm** any of various nematode worms infesting the gut of people and animals, esp. in the tropics, and causing severe anaemia; the disease caused by hookworm infestation.

hookless *a.* L18. **hooklike** *a.* resembling (that of) a hook, shaped like a hook E17.

hook /hʊk/ *v.* ME. [f. the n.] **I 1** *v.t.* Make hooklike or hooked; bend, crook. *rare.* ME. **2** *v.t.* Catch (a fish) with a hook. ME. **b** *v.t. fig.* Catch, secure; captivate, ensnare. L17. **c** *v.i.* Solicit as a prostitute. *slang.* M20.

2 R. BRAUTIGAN I have lost every trout I ever hooked. b F. J. FURNIVALL A man trying to hook a well-off widow.

II 3 *v.i.* Have a hooked shape; bend or curve sharply. ME. **4** *v.i.* & *t.* (w. *it*). Make off, run away, esp. surreptitiously. (Foll. by *off, out.*) *colloq.* ME. **5** *v.i.* Attach oneself or be attached (as) with a hook; fasten (as) with a hook or hooks. (Foll. by *up.*) L16. **6** *v.t.* Catch hold of or grasp (as) with a hook; attach or secure (as) with a hook or hooks; connect or fasten together with hooks, or hooks and eyes. (Foll. by *in, on, up,* etc.) L16. **b** *v.t.* Make (a rug) using a hook to pull yarn, rag, etc., through a canvas ground. L19. **7** *v.t.* Snatch (as) with a hook; take by stealth; steal. E17. **8** *v.t.* & *i.* a Strike (a ball) so that it deviates from a straight line; *Golf* drive (the ball) wide in the direction of the follow-through; *Cricket* hit (a fast, short-pitched ball) round to leg from shoulder height with a horizontal or rising swing of the bat. M19. **b** *Rugby Football.* Secure and propel (the ball) backward with the foot in the scrummage. E20. **9** *v.t.* Provide with a hook. M19. **10** *v.t.* & *i.* *Boxing.* Strike (an opponent) with the elbow bent and rigid. L19.

3 W. HOLTBY A big pale face rather like Mussolini's—only his nose hooks a bit. 4 F. SARGESON If Ted saw her coming . . he'd hook off if he could before she got near. 5 THACKERAY He hooked on to my arm as if he had been the Old Man of the Sea. J. K. TOOLE The long red beard that hooked over his ears by means of wires. 6 E. BOWEN Hooking a stool towards her, she swung her feet up. A. TYLER He hooked his thumbs in his belt. C. PHILLIPS Bertram hooked both feet around the bar of his chair.

Comb.: **hook-up** *colloq.* a connection or link, esp. of radio or television broadcasting facilities.

hookah /ˈhʊkə/ *n.* M18. [Urdu f. Arab. *ḥukka* small box, container, pot, jar.] A pipe of oriental origin for smoking tobacco, marijuana, etc., with a long flexible tube connected to a container of water, through which the smoke is drawn from the tobacco etc.

Hooke /hʊk/ *n.* E19. [Robert *Hooke* (1635–1703), Eng. inventor and natural philosopher.] Used *attrib.* and in *possess.* to designate devices or concepts introduced by Hooke.

Hooke('s) coupling, Hooke('s) joint a kind of universal joint for transmitting rotary motion between shafts. **Hooke's law**: that the strain in an elastic solid is proportional to the applied stress producing it.

Hookean /-ɪən/ *a.* that obeys Hooke's law M20.

hooked /ˈhʊkt/ *a.* OE. [f. HOOK *n., v.*: see -ED[2], -ED[1].] **1** Shaped like a hook. OE. **2** Provided or equipped with a hook or hooks. ME. **3** Made, caught, etc., (as) with a hook. E17. **b** *pred.* Addicted, captivated. (Foll. by *on.*) E20.

1 A. MASON The black eyes were piercing, . . the nose hooked, dominant and uncompromising. 3b D. W. GOODWIN By now I was hooked . . I had been sneaking drinks for years. *Listener* Haunted by the death of his friends, and hopelessly hooked on drugs and drink.

hooker /ˈhʊkə/ *n.*[1] M16. [f. HOOK *v.* + -ER[1].] **I 1** A thief (orig., who snatched things using a hook). *slang.* M16. **2** A prostitute. *colloq.* M19. **3** *Rugby Football.* A player in the front row of the scrummage whose function it is to obtain the ball for his team by hooking it. E20. **II** *gen.* **4** A person who or thing which hooks. M19.

hooker /ˈhʊkə/ *n.*[2] M17. [Du. *hoeker*, f. *hoek* HOOK *n.* (in earlier *hoekboot*): see -ER[1].] Orig., a two-masted Dutch coasting or fishing vessel. Later also, a one-masted fishing smack from Ireland or SW England. Now usu., an old or fondly-regarded boat.

hooker /ˈhʊkə/ *n.*[3] *dial.* & *N. Amer. colloq.* M19. [Origin unkn.] A glass or drink of whisky, brandy, etc. Freq. in *stiff hooker.*

Hooker's green /ˈhʊkəz ˈɡriːn/ *n. phr.* M19. [William *Hooker* (1779–1832), botanical artist.] A bright green colour used in watercolour painting.

hookey /ˈhʊki/ *n. colloq.* (orig. *N. Amer.*). Also **hooky**. M19. [Perh. f. HOOK *v.* 4 + *-ey* -Y[6].] **1** Truanting. Chiefly in *play hookey*, play truant. M19. **2** In full *blind hookey.* A guessing-game using cards. M19.

1 P. G. WODEHOUSE He's played hookey from the choir so often.

Hookey /ˈhʊki/ *int. arch.* E19. [Origin unkn. Cf. WALKER *int.*] In full *Hookey Walker*. Expr. incredulity.

hooklet /ˈhʊklɪt/ *n.* M19. [f. HOOK *n.* + -LET.] A small hook.

hooky *n.* var. of HOOKEY *n.*

hooky /ˈhʊki/ *a.* M16. [f. HOOK *n.* + -Y[1].] Having a hook or hooks, full of hooks; hooked.

Hoolee *n.* see HOLI.

hooley /ˈhuːli/ *n.* Chiefly *Anglo-Ir.* L19. [Origin unkn.] A wild or noisy party.

hooligan /ˈhuːlɪg(ə)n/ *n.* L19. [Perh. f. *Hooligan* surname of a fictional rowdy Irish family in a music hall song, and a character in a cartoon.] A (young) ruffian or tough; *esp.* a member of a rowdy and vandalistic gang.

M. GIROUARD Local hooligans threw stones at the new schools.

hooliganism *n.* the behaviour or activity characteristic of hooligans; vandalism: L19.

hoolock /ˈhuːlɒk/ *n.* E19. [Perh. f. Bengali: imit. (from the animal's cry).] A gibbon of Assam and SE Asia, *Hylobates hoolock*, with white eyebrows and (in the male) black and (in the female) golden fur. Also called *white-browed gibbon*.

hooly /ˈhuːli/ *adv.* & *a. Sc.* & *north.* ME. [Prob. f. ON: cf. *hófligr* moderate, *hógligr* easy, gentle.] A *adv.* Gently, cautiously, slowly. ME. B *adj.* Gentle, cautious, slow. LME.

hoon /huːn/ *n.*[1] & *v. Austral. slang.* M20. [Origin unkn.] (Behave like) a lout or idiot.

hoon *n.*[2] var. of HUN *n.*[2]

hoop /huːp/ *n.*[1] [Late OE *hōp* = OFris. *hōp*, MDu. *hoop* (Du. *hoep*) f. WGmc, rel. to ON *hóp* small land-locked bay.] I 1 A measure for grain, salt, etc. *obs.* exc. *Hist.* LOE. 2 A circular band or ring of metal, wood, etc., esp. for binding together the staves of casks, barrels, tubs, etc. ME. †3 Each of the bands on a quart pot; the amount of liquor contained between two of these. L16–E17.

2 *fig.*: SHAKES. *Haml.* Those friends thou hast, .. Grapple them to thy soul with hoops of steel.

II 4 Anything having a structure or appearance that resembles a hoop; a circle, a ring, an arc. LME. 5 A finger-ring; a circular earring. E16. 6 Each of a set of circles of flexible material used to spread out a skirt; a hoop petticoat or skirt. M16. 7 A circle of wood, plastic, or metal rolled along as a toy or used in various exercises, esp. by children. M17. 8 A metal ring for holding cake mixture during baking. M18. 9 A circular wooden frame in which a cheese is moulded. L18. 10 A ring, often with paper stretched over it, through which acrobats or performing animals leap. L18. 11 A band in contrasting colour on a jockey's blouse, sleeves, or cap; *Austral.* a jockey. L19. 12 (The round metal frame of) the basket used in basketball. L19. 13 Each of the arches through which the ball must be driven in croquet. L19.

7 H. ALLEN He began to drive his hoop .. in skilful narrowing circles about the man. **10 be put, go,** or **jump through the hoop(s)** undergo an ordeal.

Comb.: **hoop-back** (a chair with) a hooped back; **hoop-iron**: in long thin strips for binding casks etc.; **hoop petticoat** (*a*) a petticoat spread out by hoops; (*b*) (in full *hoop-petticoat narcissus* or *daffodil*) a kind of narcissus, *Narcissus bulbocodium*, with long tubular corona and narrow reversed perianth segments; **hoop pine** an eastern Australian conifer, *Araucaria cunninghamii*, yielding a valuable timber; **hoop ring** a finger-ring; **hoop skirt**: spread out by hoops; **hoop-snake** an American snake popularly believed to roll like a hoop, usu. identified with the mud snake *Farancia abacura*.

†hoop *n.*[2] L15–E18. [Fr. *huppe*, f. L *upupa* HOOPOE.] A hoopoe; occas., by confusion, a lapwing.

hoop *n.*[3] & *int.* see WHOOP *n.*, *int.*

hoop /huːp/ *v.*[1]*t.* LME. [f. HOOP *n.*[1] Cf. earlier HOOPER *n.*[1]] Fasten round (as) with a hoop or hoops.

SHAKES. *Wint. T.* If ever henceforth thou .. hoop his body more with thy embraces. L. DURRELL A man hooping a barrel.

hoop *v.*[2] var. of WHOOP *v.*

Hoopa *n.* & *a.* var. of HUPA.

hooped /huːpt/ *a.* M16. [f. HOOP *n.*[1], *v.*[1]: see -ED[2], -ED[1].] Having or fastened with a hoop or hoops; made with a hoop; shaped like a hoop.

hooper /ˈhuːpə/ *n.*[1] ME. [f. HOOP *n.*[1] or *v.*[1] + -ER[1].] A person who makes hoops, or who fits hoops on barrels etc.; a cooper.

hooper *n.*[2] see WHOOPER.

hooping *vbl n.*, *ppl a.* see WHOOPING *vbl n.*, *ppl a.*

hoop-la /ˈhuːplɑː/ *n.*[1] E20. [f. HOOP *n.*[1] + LA *int.*, prob. after HOUP-LA.] A game in which rings are thrown in an attempt to encircle one of various prizes.

hoop-la *int.* & *n.*[2] var. of HOUP-LA.

hoopoe /ˈhuːpuː, -pəʊ/ *n.* M17. [Alt. of HOOP *n.*[2], after L *upupa* (imit., from the bird's cry).] A medium-sized, short-legged perching bird of Africa and Eurasia, *Upupa epops*, having a long, down-curved beak, a prominent crest, and pinkish-brown plumage with black and white striped wings and tail.

hooray /hʊˈreɪ; *attrib.* ˈhuːreɪ/ *n.*, *int.*, & *v.* Also **hurray**. L17. [Alt. of HURRAH. Cf. HURROO.] A *n.* A shout of 'hooray!', a cheer. L17. B *int.* 1 Expr. approval, encouragement, enthusiasm, or delight. L18. 2 Goodbye. *NZ* & *Austral. colloq.* L19.

C *v.i.* Shout 'hooray!'. L18.

Comb.: **Hooray Henry** a rich but ineffectual young man, *esp.* one who is fashionable, extroverted, and conventional.

hooroo *int.* see HURROO.

hooroosh /hʊˈruːʃ/ *n.* & *v.* **hurroosh**. M19. [Imit.] A *n.* A cry or noise of excitement or confusion. M19. B *v.i.* & *t.* Shoo. M19.

hoose /huːz/ *n.* & *v.* Also **hooze**. L18. [Perh. ult. f. base of WHEEZE.] A *n.* Chronic bronchitis in farm animals caused by parasitic nematodes; = HUSK *n.*[2] L18. B *v.i.* Cough, wheeze. *dial.* M19.

hoosegow /ˈhuːsgaʊ/ *n. US slang.* E20. [S. Amer. or Mex. Sp. *juzgao* = *juzgado* tribunal f. L *judicatum* pa. pple of *judicare* JUDGE *v.*] A prison.

W. WHARTON I found a corpse .. I thought .. I might spend the night in the hoosegow.

hoosh /huːʃ/ *int.* & *v.* L19. [Natural exclam. Cf. SHOO *int.* & *v.*] A *int.* Encouraging or inciting an animal etc. to move; shoo! L19.

T. HARDY Saying 'Hoosh!' to the cocks and hens when they go upon your seeds.

B *v.* 1 *v.t.* Drive (as) with the word 'hoosh!', shoo. (Foll. by *off*, *out*, etc.) E20. 2 *v.i.* Move rapidly. M20.

1 A. THIRKELL Oh, she's dressing, and Aunt Palmer hooshed me out.

hooshtah /ˈhuːʃtɑː/ *int.* & *v.* L19. [Natural exclam.] A *int.* Encouraging or ordering a camel to move, esp. to get down on its knees for mounting or dismounting. L19. B *v.t.* Direct with the word 'hooshtah!' E20.

Hoosier /ˈhuːʒɪə/ *n.* & *a. US.* E19. [Origin unkn.] A *n.* 1 (A nickname for) a native or inhabitant of the State of Indiana. E19. 2 An inexperienced, awkward, or unsophisticated person. M19. B *attrib.* or as *adj.* Of, pertaining to, or characteristic of Indiana. M19.

hoot /huːt/ *n.*[1] LME. [f. the vb.] 1 A loud inarticulate exclamation, a shout, *spec.* of derision or disapproval. LME. b A sound produced by a vehicle's horn, a siren, etc., esp. as a signal or warning. E20. c A shout of laughter; a joke, an amusing situation, person, or thing. M20. 2 An owl's cry. L18. 3 The smallest amount; a scrap, a whit. Chiefly in *not care*, *give*, *matter* etc. *a hoot* or *two hoots*. Cf. earlier HOOTER 2. L19.

1 C. G. LELAND I heard certain mutterings and hoots among the students. b H. GARNER A long hoarse hoot of the factory whistle announced the lunch break. c D. HALLIDAY Janey can imitate anybody. So can I. .. We'd have the whole form in hoots of laughter. 3 D. PARKER She paid no attention to her birthdays—didn't give a hoot about them.

Comb.: **hoot owl** any of various owls with a hooting call, as the tawny owl or (*US*) the barred owl.

hoot /huːt/ *n.*[2] *NZ slang* (now *rare*). E19. [Maori UTU.] Money, esp. paid as recompense.

hoot /huːt/ *v.* ME. [Perh. imit.] 1 *v.i.* Make loud expressive sounds, esp. of derision or disapproval; make a loud sound on a horn etc. ME. b Laugh loudly. *colloq.* E20. 2 *v.t.* Assail with shouts or sounds of derision, disapproval, or contempt; drive *out*, *away*, etc., by hooting. ME. 3 *v.i.* Of a bird, esp. an owl: make its natural cry, call. L15. 4 *v.t.* Vocalize or express by a hoot or hoots. L17. 5 *v.i.* Of a horn, siren, etc.: sound, emit noise as a signal or warning. L19. 6 *v.t.* Sound a hoot on (a horn etc.). M20.

1 W. IRVING A troop of strange children ran at his heels, hooting at him. C. MACKENZIE Visibility was hardly as much as twenty yards and he drove .. slowly, hooting almost continuously. W. WHARTON The whole crowd was hollering and hooting, whistling, throwing paper .. into the ring. b R. GITTINGS The class hooted with pleasure at the prospect of a free day. 2 LD MACAULAY His play had not been hooted from the boards. *Observer* In the shadiest lanes we were .. hooted out of the way. 3 H. BASCOM Outside, the owl hoots spookily from across the swamps. 5 R. KIPLING Through the yelling Channel tempest when the siren hoots and roars. R. C. HUTCHINSON An omnibus hooted as it passed the house.

hoot /huːt/ *int. Sc.* & *north.* M16. [Natural exclam.] = HOOTS.

hootch *n.*[1], *n.*[2] vars. of HOOCH *n.*[1], *n.*[2]

hootchy-kootchy /huːtʃɪˈkuːtʃi/ *n.* & *a.* Also **hootchie-kootchie**; **-cootchy**. L19. [Origin unkn.] A *n.* An erotic dance. L19. B *attrib.* or as *adj.* Erotic; indecent, suggestive. L19.

hootenanny /ˈhuːt(ə)nani/ *n. colloq.* Chiefly *US.* E20. [Origin unkn.] 1 A gadget. *rare.* E20. 2 An informal party, esp. with folk music. M20.

hooter /ˈhuːtə/ *n.* L17. [f. HOOT *v.* + -ER[1].] 1 A person or animal that hoots; *esp.* an owl. L17. 2 = HOOT *n.*[1] 3. *US colloq.* M19. 3 A siren, a steam whistle, esp. as a signal for work to begin or cease; a horn, esp. of a motor vehicle. L19. 4 A person's nose. *slang.* M20.

3 D. H. LAWRENCE They will hear far, far away the last factory hooter.

hoots /huːts/ *int. Sc.* & *north.* E19. [f. HOOT *int.* + -S[3].] Expr. dissatisfaction or impatience; contradicting or dismissing a statement.

hoove /huːv/ *n.* M19. [Alt.] = HOVEN *n.* Cf. HEAVE *n.* 2.

hooved *a.* var. of HOOFED.

Hoover /ˈhuːvə/ *n.* & *v.* Also (esp. as vb) **h-**. E20. [W. H. *Hoover* (1849–1932) Amer. industrialist.] A *n.* (Proprietary name for) a vacuum cleaner. E20.

B *v.t.* & *i.* Clean (a floor etc.) with a vacuum cleaner. E20.

fig.: *Rugby News* Judging by the amount of beer they hoovered up .. Worthing soon drowned their sorrows.

Hooverville /ˈhuːvəvɪl/ *n. US.* M20. [f. Herbert C. *Hoover* (1874–1964), US President 1929–33 + -VILLE.] (A name for) a shanty town.

¶From the temporary accommodation provided for unemployed workers in the economic depression of the early 1930s (during Hoover's presidency).

hooves *n.pl.* see HOOF *n.*

hooze *n.* & *v.* var. of HOOSE.

hop /hɒp/ *n.*[1] LME. [MLG, MDu. *hoppe* (Du. *hop*), in OS *feldhoppo* = late OHG *hopfo* (G *Hopfen*).] 1 In *pl.* & †*collect. sing.* The ripened conelike spikes of the female hop-plant (see sense 2 below), used to give a bitter flavour to malt liquors, and as a tonic and soporific. LME. b *sing.* & (usu.) in *pl.* Beer. Chiefly *Austral.* & *NZ slang.* M20. 2 A twining dioecious plant, *Humulus lupulus*, of the hemp family, with rough lobed leaves and small green flowers, the female becoming enlarged and conelike in seed, found in damp bushy places and much cultivated as a source of hops. Also *hop-plant.* M16. 3 A narcotic drug; *spec.* opium. L19.

Comb.: **hop-back** [BACK *n.*[2]] a vessel with a perforated bottom for straining off the hops in the manufacture of beer; **hop-bind, -bine** the climbing stem of the hop; **hopbush** any of various Australian shrubs of the genus *Dodonaea*, of the soapberry family; **hop-dog** a tool for drawing hop-poles out of the ground; **hop-fly** an aphid, *Phorodon humuli*, destructive to hops; **hop-garden, -ground** a piece of ground where hops are grown; **hophead** (*a*) *slang* (chiefly *US*) a drug addict; (*b*) *Austral.* & *NZ slang* a drunkard; *hop* HORNBEAM; **hop joint** *slang* an opium den; **hop-picker** a labourer or machine employed to pick hops; **hop-pillow**: stuffed with hops, to induce sleep; *hop-plant*: see sense 2 above; **hop-pole**: on which a hop plant is trained; **hop-sack(ing)** (*a*) (a sack or sacking for hops made from) a coarse material made from hemp etc.; (*b*) a coarse clothing fabric of a loose plain weave; **hop toy** *slang* a container used in smoking opium; **hop tree** a N. American shrub, *Ptelea trifoliata*, of the rue family, with bitter fruit which has been used in brewing as a substitute for hops; **hop trefoil** a yellow-flowered clover, *Trifolium campestre*, whose withered flower-heads resemble the cones of the hop; **hopyard** = *hop-garden* above.

hop /hɒp/ *n.*[2] E16. [f. HOP *v.*[1]] **1** An act or the action of hopping; a short spring or leap, esp. on one foot; a leap or step in dancing. E16. **b** A distance traversed in an aircraft or vehicle at one stretch; a stage of a flight or journey. E20. **c** *Radio.* A transmission path from one point on the earth to another that involves a single reflection from some region of the atmosphere. M20. **2** An informal dance. *colloq.* E18.

1b C. A. LINDBERGH The first hop was from Americus to Montgomery, Alabama. **2** *Listener* Taking a girl to the Saturday-night hop in my village.

Phrases: *Aztec hop*: see AZTEC *a.* **go on the hop** *slang* play truant. **hop, skip** (or **step**), **and jump** (*a*) the action of making these three (or similar) movements in succession, *spec.* as an athletic exercise or contest (= *triple jump* s.v. TRIPLE *a.*); (*b*) a short distance. *long hop*: see LONG *a.*[1] **on the hop** *colloq.* (*a*) unprepared (esp. in *caught on the hop*); (*b*) bustling about. **play the hop** = *go on the hop* above.

Hop /hɒp/ *n.*[3] *Austral. slang.* E20. [Rhyming slang for COP *n.*[4]] More fully *John Hop*. A police officer.

hop /hɒp/ *v.*[1] Infl. **-pp-**. Pa. t. & pple **hopped**, (*arch.*) **hopt**. [OE *hoppian*, corresp. to MHG (G dial.) *hopfen*, ON *hoppa*, f. Gmc base repr. also by OE *hoppetan*, G *hopsen*, a var. of which appears in HIP *v.*[1]] **1** *v.i.* Spring or leap a short distance once or in a succession of movements; *colloq.* make a quick change of position or location. OE. **b** *spec.* Of a small animal or bird: move by leaps with all feet at once, as opp. to walking or running. LME. **c** Of a person: spring or leap on one foot; move forward by a succession of leaps on one foot. E18. **d** Limp. E18. **e** With advb. extension: get lightly or quickly *in, into* (a motor vehicle etc.), *on, on to* (a bicycle, bus, etc.), *out, out of* (a motor vehicle etc.). *colloq.* E20. **2** *v.i.* Dance. Now *rare* or *obs.* ME. **3** *v.t.* Hop about, along, or over; pass quickly between each of a succession of. L18. **4** *v.t.* Jump on to (a moving vehicle); obtain (a ride, a lift) by jumping on to a moving vehicle; catch (a train etc.). *colloq.* E20.

1 *New Yorker* He used to be a pilot himself . . when he was a . . seed salesman and would hop about calling on prospects. **b** B. EMECHETA The . . parrots hopped about in their cages. **3** C. G. TURNER Twice daily [the cow] hopped the fence. *cloud-hopping, hedge-hopping*, etc. **4** J. KEROUAC I used to hop freights at least once a month.

Phrases, & with advs. in specialized senses: **hop into bed** have (casual) sexual intercourse (*with*). **hop it** *slang* go away. **hop off** (*a*) *slang* die; (*b*) depart, *spec.* in an aircraft; (*c*) *colloq.* get off a bicycle, bus, etc. **hop, skip** (or **step**), **and jump** make these three movements in succession, perform the triple jump. *hop the perch*: see PERCH *n.*[2] **hop the twig** or **stick** *slang* depart suddenly, die. **hop the wag** *slang* play truant.

Comb.: **hop-o'-my-thumb** [*o'* = on] a dwarf, a pygmy. **hop-toad** *US* a toad.

hop /hɒp/ *v.*[2] Infl. **-pp-**. L16. [f. HOP *n.*[1]] **1** *v.t.* Impregnate or flavour with hops. Usu. in *pass.* L16. **2** *v.i.* Pick hops. Chiefly as *hopping* vbl n. E18. **3** *v.i.* Of the hop-plant: produce hops. M19. **4** *v.t.* Foll. by *up*: stimulate or intoxicate with a narcotic drug. Cf. earlier HOPPED 2. *US slang.* M20.

hope /həʊp/ *n.*[1] [Late OE *hopa*, also *tōhopa*, corresp. to OLG *tōhopa*, OFris., MLG, MDu. *hope* (Du. *hoop*). Orig. belonging to LG areas, whence it spread to HG (MHG *hoffe*) and Scand. (Sw. *hopp*, Da. *haab*): of unkn. origin.] **1** Expectation of something desired, a feeling of expectation and desire combined (in *pl.* also w. sing. sense); *iron.* an expectation which has little or no chance of fulfilment. (Foll. by *of* (a thing, *doing*), *that, to do*.) LOE. †**b** Expectation (without implication of desire); prospect. LME–M16. **2** (A feeling of) trust or confidence. *arch.* LOE. **3** A person who or thing which gives cause for hope; an object or ground of hope; (a) probability; (a) promise. ME.

1 TENNYSON And still we follow'd . . In hope to gain upon her flight. V. BRITTAIN My hopes of ever escaping from provincial young-ladyhood were almost abandoned. B. EMECHETA After he had completely given up hope, a miracle . . happened. T. PYNCHON Always baiting his master in hopes of getting a . . stripe or two across those . . buttocks. C. EGLETON 'Make sure you get the right mix of weapons and explosives.' 'You've got a hope'. *personified*: HANNAH MORE Fair Hope, with smiling face but ling'ring foot. **2** G. MACDONALD Though the sky be dim, My hope is in the sky. **3** POPE Her tender mother's only hope and pride. SHELLEY Staking his very life on some dark hope.

Phrases: *hope against hope*: see HOPE *v.* 1. **not a hope** *colloq.* no chance at all (also *not a hope in hell*: see HELL *n.*). *pious hope*: see PIOUS *a.* 1. **some hope(s)!, what a hope!** *colloq.* little or no chance. *white hope*: see WHITE *a.*

Comb.: **hope chest** (chiefly *N. Amer.*) = *bottom drawer* s.v. BOTTOM *a.*

hope /həʊp/ *n.*[2] [Late OE *hop* = MLG *hop* (in place-names), MDu. *hop* bay: origin unkn.] **1** A piece of enclosed land. Now *rare* or *obs.* LOE. **2** A small valley, *esp.* one branching up from a main valley to higher ground. Chiefly *Sc.* & *north.* LME. **3** An inlet, a small bay; a harbour. Chiefly *Sc.* & *dial.* LME.

hope /həʊp/ *v.* [Late OE *hopian* = OFris. *hopia*, (M)Du. *hopen* (orig., like HOPE *n.*[1], belonging to LG areas), whence MHG, G *hoffen*.] **1** *v.i.* Entertain expectation of something desired. (Foll. by *for*.) LOE. †**b** Look for, expect (without implication of desire). Foll. by *to, for. rare.* ME–L16. **2** *v.i.* Trust, have confidence, (*in*). *arch.* LOE. **3** *v.t.* Expect and desire (a thing (*arch.*), *that, to do*); feel fairly confident *that*; intend, if possible, *to do*. LOE. †**4** *v.t.* Expect or anticipate (without implication of desire); suppose, think, suspect. ME–M17.

1 E. O'BRIEN She hoped, the way children hope, for a happy ending to this courtship. **hope against hope** cling to a mere possibility. **3** S. ROGERS With looks that asked yet dared not hope relief. C. P. SNOW He was hoping that Kate and Humphrey could go round to his house. I. MURDOCH Adelaide . . hoped to become a buyer. *cross my heart* (*and hope to die*): see HEART *n.*

hoped *ppl a.* expected with desire (now usu. *hoped-for*). L16. **hoper** *n.* LME. **hopingly** *adv.* (*rare*) with hope, hopefully E17.

hopeful /ˈhəʊpfʊl, -f(ə)l/ *a.* & *n.* ME. [f. HOPE *n.*[1] + -FUL.] **A** *adj.* **1** Full of hope; feeling or entertaining hope. ME. **b** Expressing hope. E17. **2** Inspiring hope, promising; *iron.* likely to disappoint hopes. M16.

1 T. HERBERT Hopeful of some reward. J. BUCHAN Gazing at his companion as a hopeful legatee might gaze at a lawyer engaged in reading a will. **b** J. B. PRIESTLEY In the original itinerary I sketched for myself . . there were hopeful references to places like Newmarket.

B *n.* A person, esp. (more fully *young hopeful*) a young person, likely to succeed or *iron.* to be disappointed; a person who hopes to achieve something. E18.

R. HUNTFORD Like many another hopeful, he was rushing to strike while the iron was hot.

hopefulness *n.* E17.

hopefully /ˈhəʊpfʊli, -f(ə)li/ *adv.* E17. [f. prec. + -LY[2].] **1** In a hopeful manner; with a feeling of hope; promisingly. E17. **2** (Modifying a sentence.) It is hoped (that). (Considered *erron.* by some.) E20.

1 V. GLENDINNING She was desperate to get *The Freewoman* re-established, and hopefully collected donations. **2** *Lebende Sprachen* Machines will hopefully enable the scientist to find quickly the information he needs. *Observer* Hopefully, they too will be pleasantly surprised.

hopeless /ˈhəʊplɪs/ *a.* M16. [f. HOPE *n.*[1] + -LESS.] **1** Having or feeling no hope; despairing. M16. **2** Admitting no hope, despaired of, irremediable. M16. **b** Ineffectual; incompetent, stupid. M19. †**3** Unhoped-for, unexpected. L16–E17.

1 G. GREENE He seemed too tired to hurry, too hopeless to have an object in hurrying. **2** C. G. WOLFF She . . fell so ill with typhoid fever that her case was considered hopeless. **b** C. S. FORESTER Only a couple of hands were necessary to show up Simpson as a hopeless whist player.

hopelessly *adv.* E17. **hopelessness** *n.* E19.

Hopi /ˈhəʊpi/ *n.* & *a.* L19. [Hopi.] **A** *n.* Pl. same, **-s**. A member of a group of N. American Indians living chiefly in NE Arizona; the Uto-Aztecan language of this people. L19. **B** *attrib.* or as *adj.* Of or pertaining to the Hopi or their language. E20.

Hopkinsian /hɒpˈkɪnzɪən/ *n.* & *a.* L18. [f. Samuel *Hopkins* (see below) + -IAN.] (An adherent) of the modified Calvinism of the New England theologian Samuel Hopkins (1721–1803).

Hopkinsianism *n.* the theological system of Samuel Hopkins E19.

hoplite /ˈhɒplʌɪt/ *n.* E18. [Gk *hoplitēs*, f. *hoplon* weapon, *hopla* arms: see -ITE[1].] A heavy-armed foot-soldier of ancient Greece.

hopo /ˈhəʊpəʊ/ *n.* Pl. **-os**. M19. [Of Afr. origin.] A trap for game, consisting of two converging hedges with a pit at the angle.

hopped /hɒpt/ *a.* M17. [f. HOP *n.*[1], *v.*[2]: see -ED[2], -ED[1].] **1** Impregnated, mixed, or flavoured with hops. M17. **2** Stimulated or intoxicated by a narcotic drug (usu. foll. by *up*). Foll. by *up* also, excited, enthusiastic, (of a motor vehicle etc.) modified to give improved performance. *US slang.* E20.

hopper /ˈhɒpə/ *n.*[1] ME. [f. HOP *v.*[1] + -ER[1]. Connection of sense 4 unkn.] **1** A person who hops, leaps, or dances. ME. **b** *Baseball.* A ball which having been struck rebounds from the ground. *US slang.* M20. **2** An animal characterized by hopping; *esp.* an insect that hops, as a grasshopper, a flea, a cheese-maggot, a young locust. ME. **3** In milling, a cone-shaped receptacle, orig. operated with a hopping motion, used to receive the material to be ground; any of various devices that resemble this in use or shape. ME. **4** A basket, *esp.* one used by a sower for carrying seed. Now only *Sc.* & *dial.* ME. **5** A barge which carries away mud or gravel from a dredging-machine and discharges it at sea through an opening in its bottom. M18. **6** A railway truck able to discharge coal, gravel, etc., through its floor. M19. **7** A funnel-shaped or conical hollow. M19. **8** A mechanism in a piano which regulates the movement of the hammer of a key. Also called *grasshopper*. M19.

Comb.: **hopper-barge** = sense 5 above; **hopper-car** = sense 6 above; **hopper-dredge(r)** a vessel combining the functions of a hopper and a dredger.

hopper /ˈhɒpə/ *n.*[2] E18. [f. HOP *v.*[2] + -ER[1].] A hop-picker.

hopperdozer /ˈhɒpədəʊzə/ *n. US.* L19. [f. HOPPER *n.*[1], perh. after *bulldozer*.] A device for catching and destroying insects, consisting of a movable pen or frame filled or smeared with a poisonous or glutinous substance.

hoppergrass /ˈhɒpəgrɑːs/ *n.* Chiefly *US dial.* E19. [Alt.] A grasshopper.

hoppet /ˈhɒpɪt/ *n.* Chiefly *north.* L17. [Origin uncertain: perh. f. HOPPER *n.*[1] + -ET[1].] **1** A basket, *esp.* a small hand-basket. L17. **2** A large bucket used for raising and lowering men and materials in a mine shaft. M19.

hoppety *adv.* & *a.* var. of HOPPITY *adv.* & *a.*

hopping /ˈhɒpɪŋ/ *n.* ME. [f. HOP *v.*[1] + -ING[1].] **1** The action of HOP *v.*[1] ME. **2** A dance; a festival with dancing. Now *dial.* ME.

hopping /ˈhɒpɪŋ/ *a.* & *adv.* L16. [f. HOP *v.*[1] + -ING[2].] **A** *adj.* **1** That hops. L16. **2** Very angry, furious, 'hopping mad'. L19. **3** Very active, busy, lively. *colloq.* (chiefly *N. Amer.*). E20.

1 BURKE The little shrivelled, meagre, hopping, though loud and troublesome insects of the hour. H. G. WELLS The hopping inconsecutiveness of English conversation. **Hopping Dick** *W. Indies* the common white-chinned thrush of Jamaica, *Turdus aurantius*. **hopping-john** in the southern US and W. Indies, a stew of rice with peas or bacon or other ingredients. **2**

W. HILDICK I was mad, real hopping! 3 N. MAILER You have two sons to take care of. That must keep you hopping. *Philadelphia Inquirer* The Devon Horse Show Grounds will be hopping.

B *adv.* So as to hop; extremely. Chiefly in *hopping mad*, very angry, furious. L17.

W. P. KELLER Building a hopping big fire to burn the rubbish.

hoppity /ˈhɒpɪti/ *n.* L19. [f. HOP *v.*[1]] = HALMA.

hoppity /ˈhɒpɪti/ *adv.* & *a.* Also **-ety**. Also redupl. **hoppity-hop, hoppity-hoppity**. E19. [f. HOP *v.*[1] Cf. HIPPETY-HOP.] A *adv.* In a hopping or limping manner, unevenly. E19. B *adj.* Hopping, full of movement; limping. L19.

hopple /ˈhɒp(ə)l/ *n.* M17. [f. the vb.] A device for hoppling animals; *transf.* a fetter; = HOBBLE *n.* 3.

hopple /ˈhɒp(ə)l/ *v.t.* L16. [Prob. of LG origin: cf. early Flem. *hoppelen* = MDu. *hobelen* jump, dance: see HOBBLE *v.*] Fasten together the legs of (an animal) to prevent straying; *transf.* fetter (a person); = HOBBLE *v.* 5.

Hoppo /ˈhɒpəʊ/ *n.* Pl. **-os**. E18. [Prob. f. Chin. *hùbù* the Ministry of Revenue in feudal China.] *Hist.* In China: the board of revenue or customs; (in full *Hoppo-man*) an officer of the customs.

Hoppus /ˈhɒpəs/ *n.* Also **h-**. L19. [Edward *Hoppus*, 18th-cent. Eng. surveyor.] Used *attrib.* and in *possess.* to designate a method of measuring the cubic content of round timber.

Hoppus foot a unit of timber volume equal to approximately 1.27 cu. ft (0.0360 cu. metre).

hoppy /ˈhɒpi/ *n.*[1] *US slang.* E20. [f. HOP *n.*[1] + -Y[6].] An opium addict; a hophead.

hoppy /ˈhɒpi/ *n.*[2] *colloq.* E20. [f. HOP *n.*[2] + -Y[6].] A lame person.

hoppy /ˈhɒpi/ *a.*[1] L19. [f. HOP *n.*[1] + -Y[1].] 1 Tasting or smelling of hops; beery. L19. 2 Of, pertaining to, or characterized by drugs or drug-taking. *US slang.* M20.

hoppy /ˈhɒpi/ *a.*[2] *colloq.* E20. [f. HOP *n.*[2] + -Y[1].] Characterized by or inclined to hopping; lively; limping, lame.

hopscotch /ˈhɒpskɒtʃ/ *n.* E19. [f. HOP *v.*[1] + SCOTCH *n.*[1]] A children's game involving hopping on one foot over lines or between compartments marked on the ground, over or into which a flat stone or similar object has been cast for retrieval.

J. L. WATEN I joined the . . game of hopscotch on white squares drawn in chalk on the footpath.

Also †**hop-scot** *n.* (*rare*): only in L18.

hopshackle /ˈhɒpʃak(ə)l/ *v.* & *n. obs.* exc. *dial.* E16. [Origin unkn.] A *v.t.* = HOBBLE *v.* 5. E16. B *n.* = HOBBLE *n.* 3. M16.

†**hopt** *v.* pa. t & pple: see HOP *v.*[1]

Hopton wood /ˈhɒptən ˈwʊd/ *n.* & *a. phr.* L19. [A wood and neighbouring quarries near Wirksworth, Derbyshire.] (Designating) a pale limestone used for building and decorative purposes.

hora /ˈhɔːrə/ *n.* Also **horah**. L19. [Romanian *horă*, Heb. *hōrāh*.] A Romanian and Israeli ring dance; a piece of music for this dance; a song to which it is performed.

horae /ˈhɔːriː/ *n.* L19. [L *horae* pl. of *hora* HOUR.] A book of hours.

horah *n.* var. of HORA.

horal /ˈhɔːr(ə)l/ *a.* E18. [Late L *horalis*, f. L *hora* HOUR: see -AL[1].] Of or pertaining to an hour or hours.

horary /ˈhɔːrəri/ *n. rare.* M17. [mod.L *horarium* book of hours, use as n. of neut. sing. of med.L *horarius*: see next.] †1 *Eccl.* A book containing the offices for the canonical hours. M17–L18. 2 An hourly account or narrative; a timed programme or plan. M19.

horary /ˈhɔːrəri/ *a.* E17. [med.L *horarius*, f. L *hora* HOUR: see -ARY[1].] 1 Occurring every hour, hourly. E17. †2 Lasting only for an hour, of a short duration. Only in 17. 3 Of, relating to, or indicating the hours. M17. 4 *Astrol.* Of or pertaining to observation of the sky and planets at a particular moment. M17.

4 **horary question**: the answer to which is obtained by erecting a figure of the sky and planets for the moment at which it is propounded.

Horatian /həˈreɪʃ(ə)n, -ʃɪən/ *a.* E17. [L *Horatianus*, f. Quintus *Horatius* Flaccus (see below): see -AN.] Of, pertaining to, or resembling the Roman poet Horace (Quintus Horatius Flaccus, 65–8 BC) or his work.

horchata /ɔrˈtʃata, ɔːˈtʃɑːtə/ *n.* Also **or-**. M19. [Sp.] In Spain and Latin American countries, an almond-flavoured soft drink.

horde /hɔːd/ *n.* M16. [Pol. *horda* (whence Fr., G, Du. *horde*, Sw. *hord*), corresp. to Russ. *orda*, It., Romanian *orda*, all ult. f. Turk. *ordu* (royal) camp: cf. URDU.] 1 A tribe or troop of Tartar or other nomads. M16. b *Anthropol.* A loosely knit social group consisting of about five families. L19. 2 A numerous company; a gang, a troop. Usu. *derog.* E17.

1 **Golden Horde** (a State established by) a Mongol and Turkish host under Mongol leadership which overran Asia in the 13th cent., and maintained control of the centre of the continent until the end of the 15th cent. 2 BURKE I hardly shall allow that with the horde of regicides we could . . obtain anything . . deserving the name of peace. DAY LEWIS He . . was . . inclined to separate himself from the horde of relations . . which littered Dublin.

hordeolum /hɔːdɪˈəʊləm/ *n.* Pl. **-la** /-lə/. E19. [Alt. of late L *hordeolus* sty, dim. of L *hordeum* barley.] *Med.* A sty on the eyelid.

horehound /ˈhɔːhaʊnd/ *n.* OE. [f. as HOAR + *hūne* the plant *Marrubium*, of unkn. origin. For the parasitic *d* cf. BOUND *a.*[1], SOUND *n.*[2]] 1 More fully *white horehound*. An aromatic labiate plant, *Marrubium vulgare*, with white flowers and cottony pubescence, formerly grown as a herb. Also, an extract or confection of this plant, used as a herbal remedy. OE. 2 *black horehound*, a fetid purple-flowered labiate plant, *Ballota nigra*, common by roadsides. M16.

Hori /ˈhɔːri/ *n. NZ. derog.* M20. [Maori form of the name 'George'.] A Maori.

horizon /həˈrʌɪz(ə)n/ *n.* & *v.* LME. [OFr. *orizon(te)* (mod. *horizon*) f. late L *horizon*, *horizont-* f. Gk *horizōn* use as n. (sc. *kuklos* circle) of pres. pple of *horizein* bound, limit, define, f. *horos* boundary.] A *n.* 1 The boundary of that part of the earth's surface visible from a given viewpoint; the line at which earth and sky appear to meet. Also (more fully *apparent*, *sensible*, or *visible horizon*), the circle where the earth's surface touches a cone whose vertex is at the observer's eye. LME. 2 *fig.* †a The dividing line between two regions of existence. Only in LME. b The boundary of any sphere of thought, action, etc.; the limit of mental perception, experience, interest, etc. Formerly also, the sphere so bounded or limited. E17. 3 *Astron.* More fully *celestial*, *rational*, or *true horizon*. A great circle of the celestial sphere, the plane of which passes through the centre of the earth and is parallel to that of the apparent horizon of a given place. LME. b The celestial hemisphere within the horizon of a place. L16. 4 A representation of the horizon; *esp.* the broad ring in which an artificial globe is fixed, the upper surface of which represents the plane of the rational horizon (see sense 3 above). L16. 5a *Geol.* A plane, interface between strata, or characteristic thin stratum, identifiable over a wide area and assumed originally continuous. M19. b *Soil Sci.* Any of several layers in the soil lying roughly parallel to the surface and having distinguishable physical and chemical properties. Also *soil horizon*. E20. c *Archaeol.* A level at which a particular group of remains is found, or which is taken as representing a particular culture or cultural period. E20. 6 *Embryol.* Any of a numbered sequence of stages in the development of the human embryo. M20. 7 In horizon mining, a system of approximately horizontal tunnels lying in the same horizontal plane; the plane containing these tunnels. M20.

1 K. GRAHAME The great ring of Downs that barred his vision . . his simple horizon. E. J. HOWARD He couldn't see the horizon, the sky just seemed to come down into the sea. **on the horizon** *fig.* (of an event etc.) just imminent or becoming apparent. 2b J. RUSKIN Their range necessarily includes the entire horizon of man's action. C. PRIEST Children lack a world perspective; their horizons are narrow. 3 T. HERBERT For the Æquator is Horizon to both Poles. b SIR W. SCOTT The burning Sun of Syria had not yet attained its highest point in the horizon. 4 *artificial horizon*: see ARTIFICIAL *a.* 2. 5b **A horizon** a surface horizon of mixed organic and mineral matter. **B horizon** a horizon of mineral material below the A (and E) horizons, in which certain minerals accumulate by illuviation. **C horizon** a horizon underlying the B horizon, consisting of unconsolidated or unaltered material. **E horizon** an eluvial horizon underlying the A horizon, with less organic matter.

Comb.: **horizon-blue** *n.* & *a.* [Fr. *bleu horizon*] (of) a light shade of blue, the colour of the French Army uniform during and after the war of 1914–18; **horizon glass** *Naut.* a small glass fixed on the frame of a quadrant or sextant, half of which is clear glass for direct observation of the horizon and half of which is silvered to bring the reflected image of an observed body into optical coincidence with the horizon; **horizon mining** a method of working inclined seams from systems of approximately horizontal tunnels lying in the same horizontal plane.

B *v.t.* Provide or bound with a horizon. Usu. in *pass.* L18.

horizonless *a.* M19.

horizontal /hɒrɪˈzɒnt(ə)l/ *a.* & *n.* M16. [Fr., or mod.L *horizontalis*, f. late L *horizon*, *horizont-*: see prec., -AL[1].] A *adj.* 1 Of or belonging to the horizon; at the horizon. M16. 2 Parallel to the plane of the horizon; at right angles to the vertical. M17. b Designating a device or structure which works or lies in a horizontal direction. L17. 3a Uniform; producing or based on uniformity. Chiefly *US.* M19. b Involving (the combining of) firms engaged in the same stage or type of production. E20. c Involving social groups of equal status etc. M20. 4 *Mus.* Involving the relationship of notes or chords as they are played, read horizontally. L19.

1 G. BERKELEY He will . . declare the horizontal moon shall appear greater than the meridional. 2 D. ATTENBOROUGH Their upright stems sprang from a horizontal one . . lying along the ground. b **horizontal bar** a round bar fixed horizontally some distance above the ground for gymnastic exercise. *horizontal pendulum*: see PENDULUM *n.* 3a *Congressional Globe* The Democratic bill made a horizontal cut of 20 per cent.

B *n.* †1 The horizon. *rare.* Only in M16. 2 A horizontal line, plane, etc. L17. 3 A Tasmanian evergreen tree, *Anodopetalum biglandulosum* (family Cunoniaceae), in which the stems and branches bend over into a horizontal position, so as to create an impenetrable mat. L19. 4 [tr. next.] More fully *grand horizontal* = next. *slang.* E20.

2 *Listener* Bonnard derived his use of horizontals and verticals within the picture from Gauguin.

¶In many senses opp. *vertical*.

horizontalism *n.* the quality of being, or of having some part, horizontal M19. **horizonˈtality** *n.* the condition or quality of being horizontal; horizontal position: M18. **horizontaliˈzation** *n.* the action or an act of making horizontal L19. **horizontalize** *v.t.* place in a horizontal position, make horizontal M19. **horizontally** *adv.* M17. **horizontalness** *n.* M19.

horizontale /ɔrizɔ̃tal/ *n. slang.* Pl. pronounced same. L19. [Fr.] More fully *grande horizontale* /grɑ̃ːd/ (pl. *grandes* /grɑ̃ːd/). A prostitute.

New Yorker He is over-shadowed . . by Aunt Augusta, the still unretired *grande horizontale* of seventy-three.

horkey /ˈhɔːki/ *n. dial.* (*obs.* exc. *Hist.*). Also **hockey** /ˈhɒki/. M16. [Origin unkn.] The festival of harvest home.

Horlicks /ˈhɔːlɪks/ *n.* Also **Horlick's**, (in sense 2) **h-**. L19. [f. W. *Horlick* (1846–1936), British-born Amer. industrialist, its first manufacturer + -'s[1].] 1 (Proprietary name for) a malted milk powder; the drink made from this. L19. 2 A mess, a muddle. Chiefly in *make a Horlicks of*. *slang.* L20.

horme /ˈhɔːmi/ *n.* Also **-mé**. L17. [Gk *hormē* impulse.] †1 A passion, an impulse. *rare.* Only in L17. 2 *Psychol.* Vital or purposeful energy. E20.

¶Introduced in current use by C. G. Jung.

hormic *a.* of, pertaining to, or characterized by horme E20.

hormogone /ˈhɔːməɡəʊn/ *n.* Also **-gon** /-ɡən/. L19. [f. next.] *Bot.* = next.

hormogonium /hɔːməˈɡəʊnɪəm/ *n.* Pl. **-nia** /-nɪə/. L19. [mod.L, f. Gk *hormos* chain, necklace + *gonos* generation.] *Bot.* In certain cyanobacteria, a short filament of rounded cells which detaches to form a new organism.

hormone /ˈhɔːməʊn/ *n.* E20. [f. Gk *hormōn* pres. pple of *horman* set in motion (f. *hormē* onset, impulse), assim. to -ONE.] *Physiol.* **1** Any of numerous organic compounds secreted into the body fluids (esp. the blood) of an animal by a specific group of cells, and regulating the activity of certain other cells; any synthetic compound having such an effect. E20. **2** Any of numerous organic compounds produced by plants which regulate growth and other physiological activities; any synthetic compound having such an effect. E20.

1 **hormone replacement** (**therapy**) treatment with oestrogenic hormones to alleviate certain menopausal symptoms.

hor'monal *a.* of, involving, acting as or effected by a hormone or hormones E20. **hor'monally** *adv.* M20. **hor'monic** *a.* (*rare*) = HORMONAL E20. **hormonize** *v.t.* treat with a hormone M20. **hormo'nology** *n.* (*rare*) endocrinology E20.

horn /hɔːn/ *n.* & *a.* [OE *horn* corresp. to OFris., OS, OHG, ON *horn* (Du., G *Horn*), Goth. *haurn*, f. Gmc, rel. to L *cornu*, Gk *keras*.] **A** *n.* **I 1** A non-deciduous bony outgrowth with (usu.) a keratinous sheath, often curved and pointed, found in pairs on the head of cattle, sheep, goats, and related mammals, and often used for display or combat. Also, the wholly keratinous outgrowth on the snout of a rhinoceros, found single or one behind another. OE. **b** A horned animal. Also (*sing.* & in *pl.*), cattle. Long *rare.* ME. **c** (The stars in) a part of the constellation Aries (the Ram) or of Taurus (the Bull). Long *rare.* LME. **2** An antler of a deer. OE. **3** In biblical and derived uses, a horn as a symbol of power and might or as a means of defence or resistance. OE. **4** A projection on the head of any of various animals, as, a snail's tentacle; an insect's antenna, the crest of the horned owl, etc. ME. **b** An erect penis; an erection. *coarse slang.* L18. **c** A person's nose. *joc.* M19. **5** (The representation of) an animal's horn as appearing on the head of a person, a supernatural (esp. evil) being, etc. LME. **6** A horn as fancifully said to be worn by a cuckold. LME. **7** The tusk of a narwhal. Formerly also, the tusk of an elephant. E17.

1 S. BECKETT A young boy holding a goat by a horn. **b** SHAKES. *L.L.L.* My lady goes to kill horns. 3 AV *2 Sam.* 22:3 Hee is my Shield, and the horne of my Saluation. 4 SHAKES. *L.L.L.* The tender horns of cockled snails. T. MEDWIN The beetle being somewhat restless, they pinioned down his horns . . to the ground. 5 P. THOMPSON Horns and a tail would not be more decisive to a frightened child at midnight. 6 J. BARTH When the horns on Harrison's brow were . . a few days old, . . I contrived to lengthen them a bit.

II 8 A vessel made out of or shaped like the horn of cattle or other animals, for holding liquid, powder, etc.; a drinking-vessel; a powder-flask. OE. **9** An animal's horn used as a wind instrument. Now usu. a wind instrument more or less resembling a horn in shape, played by lip-vibration and usu. made of brass (freq. w. specifying wd). OE. **b** An 8-foot reed-stop in an organ. *rare.* E18. **c** A trumpet; *gen.* a wind instrument. *Jazz slang.* M20. **d** The player of a horn. M20. **10** The wind instrument as used in forms of legal process, as the proclamation of outlawry. *obs.* exc. *Sc. Hist.* LME. **11** A cone-shaped apparatus (esp. part of an early gramophone etc.) for the collection or amplification of sound. L19. **b** *Radio.* A hollow waveguide expanded towards the open end to act as a transmitting or receiving aerial. M20. **12** An instrument for sounding a warning signal. E20. **13** A horn-shaped pastry case (to be) filled with cream etc. E20. **14** The telephone. Chiefly in *on the horn. US colloq.* M20.

8 T. H. WHITE The butler . . poured another horn, which Lancelot drained. 9 E. LINKLATER I hear the pizzicati of the strings under wood-wind and horns. *bugle-horn, hunting horn, post-horn*, etc. **c** G. AVAKIAN Each of these trio cuttings ends with Bix picking up his horn to play the coda. 11 J. MASTERS I remember their playing an old gramophone with a huge horn. 12 D. DELILLO A car came towards us, horn blowing. *fog-horn, motor horn*, etc. 14 D. C. COOKE I've been on the horn half the night trying to get you.

III 15 A horn-shaped projection at each corner of the altar in the Jewish Temple; *rare* either of the two outer corners of a church altar. OE. **16** Each of the extremities of the moon or other crescent; a cusp. OE. **b** Each tip or end of a bow. E17. **17** *Archit.* Orig. (*rare*) a pinnacle, a gable. Later, an Ionic volute, a projection of an abacus. OE. **18** Chiefly *Hist.* A horn-shaped appendage or ornament worn as (part of) a head-dress. ME. **19** Either of the two wings of an army. ME. **20** A pointed or tapering projection. ME. **b** *Aeronaut.* A projection from an aileron or other control surface, for attachment of a controlling wire, or to improve the balance of the surface. E20. **21** Either of two (or more) lateral projections; *esp.* an arm or branch of a bay, a river, etc. LME. **b** *Anat.* A cornu. LME. **22** *Naut.* Each of the extremities of a piece of rigging etc. L18. **23** In *pl.* The awns of barley. *dial.* E19. **24** Each of the curved projections of (part of) a particular mechanism, device, etc. L19. **b** *Electr.* Each of the conducting rods in a horn gap or horn arrester. E20.

15 AV *Exod.* 27:2 Thou shalt make an Altar . . and thou shalt make the hornes of it upon the foure corners thereof. 16 MILTON From the hornes Of Turkish Crescent. J. THOMSON The moon Wears a wan circle round her blunted horns. 19 E. DACRES Quintius seeing one of the hornes of his Army beginning to fayle. 20 *Athenaeum* The extreme western horn of Brittany. 21 W. MORRIS Within the long horns of a sandy bay. **b** J. M. DUNCAN The fœtus developed in a uterine horn.

IV 25 A hard, keratinous epidermal structure or growth, as a hoof, a nail, a corn, a callosity. LME. **26** The compacted keratinous material of which animals' horns are composed. LME. **27** A thing made from horn. L15. **b** The substance of which part of the face of a wooden golf club is made. M18.

26 *Horse & Hound* Oil feeds the hoof and helps to stimulate the growth of healthy horn. E. LINKLATER Faces behind heavy spectacles of tortoise-shell or horn. 27 E. TOPSELL To make hafts for knives, or else horns for Spectacles.

V 28 Either alternative of a dilemma. M16.

Phrases etc.: *bass-horn*: see BASS *a.* **draw in one's horns** (*a*) restrain one's ambition or ardour, draw back; (*b*) restrict one's expenditure. **English horn** the cor anglais. **French horn** an orchestral wind instrument with a coiled tube, valves, and wide bell, usu. made of brass. *gate of horn*: see GATE *n.*[1] *Golden Horn*: see GOLDEN *a. greenhorn*: see GREEN *a. hollow horn*: see HOLLOW *a.* **Horn of Africa** the peninsula of NE Africa separating the Gulf of Aden from the main part of the Indian Ocean. **horn of plenty** a cornucopia. **lift up the horn** *arch.* exalt oneself; offer resistance. *lock horns*: see LOCK *v.*[1] 4a. **on the horns of a dilemma** faced with a decision involving equally unfavourable alternatives. **pull in one's horns** = *draw in one's horns* above. **put to the horn** *Sc. Hist.* declare outlaw (by blowing three blasts on a horn). *shoehorn*: see SHOE *n. take the bull by the horns*: see BULL *n.*[1] 1. **the Horn** Cape Horn. *wear the horn(s)*: see WEAR *v.*[1] *Wiltshire Horn*: see WILTSHIRE 1. **wind a horn** *arch.* blow a horn.

B *attrib.* or as *adj.* Made of horn. LME.

Comb. & special collocations: **horn antenna** = sense A.11b above; **horn arrester** *Electr.* a horn gap designed to protect power lines from lightning arcs and other voltage surges; **horn-band** a band of musicians playing horns; **hornbeak** (now *dial.*) = *horn-fish* (a) below; **†horn-beast** an animal with horns; **horn beetle** a beetle with stout curved jaws or processes on the head, esp. (*a*) *US* a black woodland beetle, *Popilius disjunctus*; †(*b*) a stag beetle; **hornbill** any bird of the family Bucerotidae of tropical Asia and Africa, having a large down-curved bill with a ridge or elaborate casque along the top; **hornbook** *Hist.* a paper containing the alphabet, the Lord's Prayer, etc., orig. mounted on a wooden tablet with a handle, and protected by a thin plate of horn; **horn-bug** *US* = *horn beetle* above; **horn cell** *Anat.* (now *rare*) any of the ganglion cells of the cornua of the spinal cord; **horn-fish** (*a*) a garfish; †(*b*) *Canad.* a sauger; **horn-fly** a small black bloodsucking fly, *Haematobia irritans*, which hovers esp. around the heads of cattle; **horn gap** *Electr.* a pair of rod conductors diverging from a small gap, so as to attract and extinguish any electric arc struck across the gap; **horn-mad** *a.* (*arch.*) (*a*) (orig. of horned beasts) mad with rage; (*b*) *slang* lecherous; **horn-man** a man with a horn; *spec.* in Jamaica among the Maroons, a man who blew warning etc. signals on a horn; **horn-owl** = HORNED *owl*; **horn poppy** = HORNED *poppy*; **hornpout** the brown bullhead, *Ictalurus nebulosus*, introduced into western Europe from N. America in the 19th cent.; **horn-rimmed** *a.* (esp. of spectacles) having rims made of horn or a substance resembling it; **horn-rims** horn-rimmed spectacles; **horn-ring** a circular attachment to the steering-wheel of a motor vehicle by which the horn may be readily sounded; **horn silver** [tr. G *Hornsilber*] *Min.* native silver chloride, AgCl, crystallizing in the cubic system and having a dull lustre; cerargyrite; **horn-snake** an American snake with a spinelike tail; *esp.* the mud snake, *Farancia abacura*; **horn spectacles** = *horn rims* above; **hornstone** [tr. G *Hornstein*] (*a*) chert; (*b*) hornfels; **horntail** a woodwasp of the hymenopteran family Siricidae; **hornwork** (*a*) *Fortif.* an outwork consisting of two demi-bastions connected by a curtain and joined to the main work by two parallel wings; (*b*) work done in horn; articles made of horn; †(*c*) cuckoldry; **hornworm** *N. Amer.* any of several hawkmoth larvae having a hornlike spike on the tail, esp. the vegetable pests *Manduca sexta* (more fully *tobacco hornworm*) and *M. quinquemaculata* (more fully *tomato hornworm*); **hornwort** any of several submerged aquatic plants of the genus *Ceratophyllum* (family Ceratophyllaceae), with dense whorls of forked leaves; **hornwrack** any colonial bryozoan or sea mat (esp. *Flustra*) resembling seaweed and occasionally washed ashore.

hornen *a.* (long *obs.* exc. *dial.*) made of horn LME. **hornful** *n.* as much as a horn (esp. a drinking-horn) will hold E17. **hornless** *a.* without horns, destitute of horns LME. **hornlessness** *n.* L19. **hornlike** *a.* resembling horn or a horn L16.

horn /hɔːn/ *v.* LME. [f. the n.] **1** *v.t.* **a** Provide with horn or horns. LME. **b** Cuckold. Cf. HORN *n.* 4b. M16. **2** *v.t.* Put to the horn; outlaw. *obs.* exc. *Sc. Hist.* E16. **3** *v.t.* Butt or (esp.) gore with the horns. L16. **b** *v.i.* Foll. by *in*: intrude (*on*), interfere. *slang.* E20. **4** *v.t.* Adjust (the frame of a ship) at right angles to the line of the keel. M19. **5** *v.i.* Blow a horn; progress blowing a horn. L19.

hornbeam /ˈhɔːnbiːm/ *n.* LME. [f. HORN *n.* + BEAM *n.*] (The hard tough wood of) any of several trees of the genus *Carpinus*, of the birch family, resembling the beech, esp. the European *C. betulus* and the N. American *C. caroliniana*.

hop hornbeam either of two trees of the genus *Ostrya* (*O. carpinifolia* of southern Europe, *O. virginiana* of N. America) related to the hornbeam (so called from the resemblance of the ripe catkins to hops).

hornblende /ˈhɔːnblɛnd/ *n.* L18. [G, f. *Horn* HORN *n.* + BLENDE.] *Min.* A dark green or brown, monoclinic, basic aluminosilicate of calcium, sodium, magnesium, and iron, which is a mineral of the amphibole group and is a common constituent of igneous and metamorphic rocks, the crystals usu. being columnar prisms.

horn'blendic *a.* E19.

hornblendite /ˈhɔːnblɛndʌɪt/ *n.* Also **†-yte**. L19. [f. prec. + -ITE[1].] *Petrogr.* A granular rock composed largely or entirely of hornblende.

horned /hɔːnd/ *a.* ME. [f. HORN *n.*, *v.*: see -ED[2], -ED[1].] **1** Wearing or having a horn or horns, *spec.* designating animals and plants distinguished in this way. ME. **2** Crescent-shaped. LME. **3** Made of horn; provided or fitted with horn. LME.

1 H. W. TORRENS A peculiar horned or crested helmet. C. BOWEN Bull to the horned herd, and the corn to a fruitful plain. *yellow horned*: see YELLOW *a.* 2 W. HOLTBY She . . drove out, under a small horned moon.

Special collocations & phrases: **horned adder** = *horned viper* below. **horned cairn** *Archaeol.* a type of long barrow with an enclosed forecourt peculiar to Scotland and Ireland. **horned dace** *US* a small freshwater cyprinid fish, *Semotilus atromaculatus.* **horned frog** (*a*) = *horned toad* (a) below; (*b*) a S. American frog of the genus *Ceratophrys*, having hornlike projections on its eyelids. **horned grebe** (chiefly *US*) = *Slavonian grebe* s.v. SLAVONIAN *a.* 2. **horned helmet** a large gastropod mollusc, *Cassis cornuta*, or its shell, from which cameos are cut.

horned lark (*a*) a brown and white lark, *Eremophila bilopha*, having two black tufts on the head and found in N. African and Arabian deserts (also *Temminck's horned lark*); (*b*) (chiefly *N. Amer.*) = *shore lark* s.v. SHORE *n.*[1] **horned lizard** = *horned toad* below. **horned owl** an owl having hornlike feathers over the ears; now *esp.* a large American owl, *Bubo virginianus*. **horned pondweed** an aquatic plant, *Zannichellia palustris* (family Zannichelliaceae), with filiform leaves, small axillary flowers, and beaked achenes. **horned poppy** any of several glaucous poppies of the genus *Glaucium*, with very long curved capsules; *esp.* (more fully *yellow horned poppy*) *G. flavum*, a native of shingle beaches. **horned pout** = *hornpout* s.v. HORN *n.* **horned rattlesnake** = SIDEWINDER *n.*[2] **horned screamer** a large greenish-black screamer (bird), *Anhima cornuta*, of S. American tropical grasslands, having a hornlike quill on the forehead. **horned snake** (*a*) = *horn-snake* s.v. HORN *n.*; (*b*) = *horned viper* below. *horned sungem*: see SUN *n.*[1] †**horned syllogism** *Logic* the dilemma. **horned toad** (*a*) a small spiny American lizard of the genus *Phrynosoma*, esp. *P. cornutum*, sometimes kept as a pet; (*b*) any of several large Old World toads that have a fleshy 'horn' above the eye. **horned viper** a venomous N. African desert viper, *Cerastes cerastes*, having a spine over each eye. *Wiltshire Horned sheep*: see WILTSHIRE I.

horner /'hɔːnə/ *n.* ME. [f. HORN *n.* or *v.* + -ER[1].] 1 A maker of articles of horn, as spoons, combs, etc. ME. 2 A person who blows a horn. LME. †3 A person outlawed by being put to the horn. *Sc.* M–L16. †4 A person who has cuckolded another. L16–E18.

hornero /ɔː'nɛːrəʊ/ *n.* Pl. **-os**. L19. [Sp. = baker.] Any of various S. American birds of the genus *Furnarius*, esp. *F. rufus* (more fully *rufous hornero*). Also called *ovenbird*.

Horner's syndrome /'hɔːnəz ˌsɪndrəʊm/ *n. phr.* E20. [f. J. F. *Horner* (1831–86), Swiss ophthalmologist.] *Med.* A condition marked by a contracted pupil, drooping upper eyelid, and local inability to sweat on one side of the face, caused by damage to sympathetic nerves on that side of the neck.

hörnesite *n.* var. of HOERNESITE.

hornet /'hɔːnɪt/ *n.* [OE *hyrnet(u)* rel. to OHG *hornuz* (G *Hornisse*), OS *hornut*; later forms infl. by MDu., MHG *hornte*; perh. ult. f. base of HORN *n.*: see -ET[2].] 1 Any of various large social wasps of the family Vespidae, esp. the red and yellow European *Vespa crabro*, which has a severe sting. OE. 2 *transf.* & *fig.* A persistent and virulent attacker. Esp. in (*stir up*) *a hornets' nest, nest of hornets*, etc., (stir up) trouble or opposition. L16.

Comb.: **hornet clearwing** = *hornet moth* below; †**hornet fly** a robber fly; **hornet moth** either of two European wood-boring clearwing moths, *Sphecia bombeciformis* and *Sesia apiformis*, which resemble hornets.

hornfels /'hɔːnfɛls/ *n.* & *v.* M19. [G = horn rock.] *Geol.* A *n.* A dark, fine-grained, non-schistose rock composed mainly of quartz, mica, and feldspars, and formed by contact metamorphism. M19. B *v.t.* Metamorphose (a rock) into hornfels. E20.

hornify /'hɔːnɪfʌɪ/ *v.t.* E17. [f. HORNY: see -FY.] 1 Cuckold. Long *rare* or *obs.* E17. 2 Make horny or hornlike in texture. Usu. in *pass.* L17.

hornito /hɔː'niːtəʊ/ *n.* Pl. **-os**. M19. [Amer. Sp., dim. of *horno* (f. L *furnus*) oven, furnace.] *Geol.* A driblet cone formed by successive ejections through a vent in a lava flow.

hornpipe /'hɔːnpʌɪp/ *n.* LME. [f. HORN *n.* & *a.* + PIPE *n.*[1]] 1 *Hist.* A wind instrument made wholly or partly of horn. LME. 2 A lively and vigorous dance, usu. for one person, orig. to the accompaniment of the wind instrument, and esp. associated with the merrymaking of sailors. L15. 3 A piece of music for this dance. L18.

hornswoggle /'hɔːnswɒg(ə)l/ *v.t. slang* (orig. *US*). E19. [Origin unkn.] Get the better of; cheat, hoax; humbug.

horny /'hɔːni/ *a.* & *n.* LME. [f. HORN *n.* + -Y[1].] A *adj.* I 1 *gen.* Of or like horn; keratinous. LME. 2 Semi-opaque like horn. M17. 3 Hard as horn, callous. L17. b Sexually excited; lecherous. *slang.* L19. II 4 Wearing or having a horn or horns. M16.

Comb.: **horny-handed** *a.* having hands calloused by manual labour.

B *n.* 1 A police officer. *slang.* M18. 2 (With cap. initial, usu. **Hornie**.) The Devil. Chiefly *Sc.* (*colloq.*). L18. 3 A cow, a bullock. *Sc.* & *Austral. slang.* E19.

hornily *adv.* L19. **horniness** *n.* L19.

horography /hɒ'rɒgrəfi/ *n.* Now *rare.* E18. [Fr. *horographie*, f. Gk *hōra* time, season + *-graphia* -GRAPHY.] The art of making or constructing dials.

horologe /'hɒrəlɒdʒ/ *n. arch.* LME. [OFr. *or(i)loge* (mod. *horloge*) f. L *horologium* timepiece, f. Gk *hōrologion* dim. of *hōrologos*, f. *hōra* time, hour + *-logos* telling (see -LOGUE).] An instrument for telling the time; a dial, an hourglass, a clock.

horologer /hɒ'rɒlədʒə/ *n.* ME. [AN *orloger*, OFr. *orlogier*, f. as prec.: see -ER[2]. Reintroduced in 19, f. prec.] Orig., a person who proclaimed the time of day to others, or maintained a timepiece. Now, a clockmaker.

horologic /hɒrə'lɒdʒɪk/ *a.* M17. [Late L *horologicus* f. Gk *hōrologikos*, f. *hōrologos*: see HOROLOGE, -IC. Cf. next.] Of or pertaining to horology.

horological /hɒrə'lɒdʒɪk(ə)l/ *a.* LME. [f. as prec.: see -AL[1].] Of or pertaining to horology or (the use of) a horologe; measuring or recording time.

horologion /hɒrə'ləʊdʒɪən, -'lɒdʒ-/ *n.* E18. [Gk *hōrologion*: see HOROLOGE.] In the Orthodox Church, a liturgical book containing the offices for the canonical hours, corresponding more or less to the Western breviary.

horologist /hɒ'rɒlədʒɪst/ *n.* L18. [f. HOROLOGE or HOROLOGY *n.*[2] + -IST.] A person skilled in horology; a maker of clocks or watches.

horologium /hɒrə'ləʊdʒɪəm, -'lɒdʒ-/ *n.* M17. [L: see HOROLOGE.] 1 = HOROLOGE. M17. 2 = HOROLOGION. E18. 3 (Usu. **H-**.) (The name of) an inconspicuous constellation of the southern hemisphere, between Hydrus and Eridanus; the Clock. E19.

†**horology** *n.*[1] LME–M19. [f. HOROLOGIUM *n.*: see -Y[3].] = HOROLOGE.

horology /hɒ'rɒlədʒi/ *n.*[2] E19. [f. Gk *hōra* time, hour + -OLOGY.] The study or science of measuring time; the construction of clocks, watches, etc.

horometry /hɒ'rɒmɪtri/ *n.* L16. [f. as prec. + -METRY.] The measurement of time.

horo'metrical *a.* of or pertaining to horometry L17.

horopter /hɒ'rɒptə/ *n.* E18. [f. Gk *horos* limit + *optēr* a person who looks.] *Optics.* A line or surface containing all those points in space of which images fall on corresponding points of the retinas of the two eyes.

horoscopal /hɒ'rɒskəp(ə)l/ *a.* M17. [f. L *horoscopus* HOROSCOPE + -AL[1].] Of or pertaining to a horoscope.

horoscope /'hɒrəskəʊp/ *n.* & *v.* OE. [In early use f. L *horoscopus* f. Gk *hōroskopos* nativity, horoscope, etc., f. *hōra* time, hour + *scopos* observer (cf. SCOPE *n.*[1]); later f. (O)Fr.] A *n.* An observation of the sky and the configuration of the planets at a particular moment, esp. at a person's birth; a diagram showing such a configuration of the planets; a prediction of a person's future based on this. Formerly also *spec.*, the ascendant. OE.

R. DAVIES Request for my birth date and hour, as he would . . cast my horoscope.

B *v.t.* & *i.* Cast the horoscope of (a person). *rare.* E17.

horoscoper *n.* (now *rare*) an astrologer M16. **horo'scopic** *a.* M19. **horo'scopical** *a.* L18. **ho'roscopy** *n.* the casting of horoscopes M17.

horrendous /hɒ'rɛndəs/ *a.* Now *colloq.* M17. [f. L *horrendus* gerund. of *horrere* (see HORRIBLE) + -OUS. Cf. *tremendous*, *stupendous*.] Horrible, horrifying; awful, frightful.

B. GUEST The translations were mostly horrendous, . . stale and florid. S. MORLEY Niven had just lost his first wife in a horrendous fall down . . cellar stairs.

horrendously *adv.* M20. **horrendousness** *n.* L20.

horrent /'hɒr(ə)nt/ *a.* Chiefly *poet.* M17. [L *horrent-* pres. ppl stem of *horrere*: see HORRIBLE, -ENT.] 1 Of hair: standing on end, bristling. M17. 2 Shuddering; feeling horror. E18.

1 A. BURGESS Things went on in Manchester . . which would make our hair horrent.

horribile dictu /hɒˌrɪbɪleɪ 'dɪktuː, hɒˌriːbɪli/ *adv. phr.* M19. [mod.L, by analogy with MIRABILE DICTU.] Horrible to relate.

horribility /hɒrɪ'bɪlɪti/ *n.* Long *rare.* LME. [OFr. *horribleté*, f. *horrible*: see next, -ITY. Cf. med.L *horribilitas*. In mod. use f. next.] Horribleness. Formerly also, something horrible.

horrible /'hɒrɪb(ə)l/ *a.*, *n.*, & *adv.* ME. [OFr. *orrible*, (also mod.) *horrible* f. L *horribilis*, f. *horrere* (of hair) stand on end, tremble, shudder: see -IBLE.] A *adj.* Exciting, or likely to excite, horror; repulsive, hideous, shocking; *colloq.* excessive, frightful, unpleasant. ME.

V. WOOLF I should stand in a queue and smell sweat, and scent as horrible as sweat. J. F. LEHMANN It was horrible to me to imagine them being trained to kill young Englishmen. R. DAVIES The horrible children had become more tolerable since last he saw them. R. INGALLS The weather there was horrible.

B *n.* A horrible person or thing; that which is horrible. Formerly also, something exciting horror. LME.

H. MELVILLE Such a waggish leering as lurks in all you horribles! CONAN DOYLE There is but one step from the grotesque to the horrible.

C *adv.* Horribly. Now *rare.* LME.

horribleness *n.* (*a*) the quality of being horrible; †(*b*) a feeling of horror: LME. **horribly** *adv.* in a horrible manner; exceedingly: ME.

horrid /'hɒrɪd/ *a.* & *adv.* L16. [L *horridus*, f. *horrere*: see prec., -ID[1].] A *adj.* 1 Rough, bristling. *literary.* L16. 2 Exciting horror; repulsive, horrible, frightful. Now chiefly *colloq.*, disagreeable, objectionable. E17.

1 POPE Ye grots and caverns shagg'd with horrid thorn! 2 DRYDEN An horrid stillness first invades the ear, And in that silence we the tempest fear. P. G. WODEHOUSE You've grown a beard, and it looks perfectly horrid. R. WEST There have been a lot of horrid little boys since the world began.

B *adv.* Horridly. *colloq.* E17.

horridly *adv.* in a horrid manner, to a horrid degree, objectionably E17. **horridness** *n.* E17.

horridity /hɒ'rɪdɪti/ *n.* E17. [med.L *horriditas*, f. as prec.: see -ITY. Cf. Fr. †*horridité*.] †1 A shudder of horror. Only in E17. 2 The quality of being horrid; something horrid. *rare.* M17.

horrific /hɒ'rɪfɪk/ *a.* M17. [Fr. *horrifique* or L *horrificus*, f. *horrere*: see HORRIBLE, -FIC.] Exciting horror; horrifying.

J. GATHORNE-HARDY Dr Locking now recounted a horrific tale of *a whole year* devoted to Latin. N. SYMINGTON During this time she was also plagued by horrific nightmares.

horrifically *adv.* L17.

horrification /ˌhɒrɪfɪ'keɪʃ(ə)n/ *n.* E19. [f. next after *magnify*, *magnification* etc.: see -FICATION.] 1 A horrifying or objectionable thing. Now *rare.* E19. 2 The action of horrifying; the state of being horrified. L19.

horrify /'hɒrɪfʌɪ/ *v.t.* L18. [L *horrificare*, f. *horrificus*: see prec., -FY.] Excite horror in; shock, scandalize.

A. C. BOULT She was horrified one day to find three grand-daughters turning cartwheels across the room. J. HELLER She is . . ready to take chances that horrify even me.

horrifiedly *adv.* in a horrified manner E20.

horripilation /hɒˌrɪpɪ'leɪʃ(ə)n/ *n. literary.* M17. [Late L *horripilatio(n-)*, f. L *horripilat-* pa. ppl stem of *horripilare* become bristly or hairy, f. *horrere* (see HORRIBLE) + *pilus* hair: see -ATION.] Erection of the hairs on the skin caused by cold, fear, etc.; the condition of having goose-pimples.

ho'rripilate *v.t.* & *i.* (cause to) have bristling hairs or goose-pimples E17. **ho'rripilant** *a.* causing bristling hairs or goose-pimples M19.

horrisonant /hɒ'rɪs(ə)nənt/ *a.* L16. [f. L *horrere* (see HORRIBLE) + *sonant-* sounding, f. *sonare* to sound: see -ANT[1].] Having a horrible sound.

horror /'hɒrə/ *n.* & *a.* ME. [OFr. *(h)orrour* (mod. *horreur*) f. L *horror*, f. *horrere*: see HORRIBLE, -OR.] A *n.* 1 (A painful feeling of) intense loathing and fear; a terrified and revolted shuddering; a strong aversion or an intense dislike (*of*); *colloq.* dismay (*at*). ME. †**b** (A feeling of) awe. L16–E18. **2** The quality of exciting intense loathing and fear; a person who or thing which excites such feelings; *colloq.* a mischievous person, esp. a child. Also, a genre of literature etc. designed to excite pleasurable feelings of horror by the depiction of the supernatural, violence, etc. LME. **3a** An attack of shuddering or shivering, esp. as symptomatic of some disease. Now *rare.* LME. **b** *the horrors.* A fit of horror or depression, *spec.* as in delirium tremens. M18. **c** In *pl.* as *int.* Expr. shock, dismay, etc. L19. **4** Roughness, ruggedness. Now *poet.* L17.

1 V. BRITTAIN The older generation held up outraged hands in horror at such sacrilege. H. E. BATES I felt .. pure cold horror hit me more savagely than the wind. 2 E. HALL Took the horrors for a drive, and .. Sydney and Cornelia could not behave themselves. S. BELLOW Many of the things that terrified people lost their horror when a doctor explained them. E. AMADI Port Harcourt still bore the marks of the horrors of war. **Chamber of Horrors** a place full of horrors (orig., the room containing effigies of notorious murderers and their victims, methods of execution, etc., in Madame Tussaud's waxworks).

Comb.: **horror-stricken, -struck** *a.* horrified, shocked.

B *attrib.* or as *adj.* Of literature, a film, etc.: designed to excite pleasurable feelings of horror by the depiction of the supernatural, violence, etc. M20.

Variety Recently showed .. horror films and Sino-Japanese War cruelty shots. **horror comic** a periodical like a comic but with much violence and sensationalism.

horror vacui /hɒrə ˈvakjuːʌɪ/ *n. phr.* M19. [mod.L = the horror of a vacuum.] (A) fear or dislike of leaving empty spaces in an artistic composition etc.

E. LUCIE-SMITH Nudes .. fill the whole picture-space as if the artist suffered from horror vacui.

hors concours /ɔr kɔ̃kuːr/ *adv.* & *pred. a. phr.* L19. [Fr. = out of the competition.] Not competing for a prize; without a rival.

Tablet A work such as .. would, were it shown in the *Salon*, range him Hors Concours. V. NABOKOV Most husbands are fools, but that one was *hors concours.*

hors de combat /ɔr də kɔ̃bɑ/ *adv.* & *pred. a. phr.* M18. [Fr. = out of the fight.] Out of the fight; out of the running; in an injured or disabled condition.

hors d'oeuvre /ɔː ˈdəːv, ɔː ˈdəːvr(ə)/ *n. phr.* Pl. same, **hors d'oeuvres**. M18. [Fr., lit. 'outside the work'.] An extra dish served as an appetizer before or (occas.) during a meal; a starter; in *pl.* also, (usu. mixed) items of food served as such a dish.

horse /hɔːs/ *n.* Pl. **-s**, (see below) same. [OE *hors* = OFris. *hors, hars, hers,* OS *hros, hers* (MLG *ros, ors,* MDu. *ors,* Du. *ros*), OHG *(h)ros* (MHG *ros, ors,* G *Ross*), ON *hross,* f. Gmc. See also HOSS.] **I1** Pl. **-s**, (esp. after a numeral, now *rare*) same. A solid-hoofed perissodactyl ungulate mammal, *Equus caballus*, having a short coat and long mane and tail, native to central Asia but long domesticated as a draught animal and esp. for riding; *esp.* a member of a relatively large breed of this, *spec.* one of 15 hands or above (cf. PONY *n.* 1). Also (esp. in *Zool.*), any member of the family Equidae. OE. **b** The adult male of this; a stallion or gelding. LME. **2** A representation, figure, or model of a horse. ME. **3** In pl. *horse,* †*horses.* Cavalry soldiers. LME. **4** A person as resembling a horse in some way. Now chiefly as a familiar form of address in *old horse.* E16.

1 *Arab(ian) horse, cart-horse, draught horse, great horse, liberty horse, racehorse, saddle-horse, warhorse, wild horse,* etc. 2 F. WISE The Horse was the Standard which the Saxons used. *hobby-horse, rocking-horse,* etc. 3 E. LINKLATER Horse, foot, and guns they came, an army with banners. 4 SHAKES. *1 Hen. IV* If I tell thee a lie, spit in my face, call me horse.

II A thing. **5** Any of various devices on which a person rides or sits astride, used as conveyances, or for carrying or hauling; *spec.* (*a*) *Hist.* a wooden frame having a sharp ridge on which delinquent soldiers were made to sit; (*b*) a piece of gymnastic apparatus for vaulting over (also *vaulting horse*); (*c*) a board or seat on a rope on which a person is lowered down a shaft; (*d*) a low wooden stool used in various trades; (*e*) a tractor, a locomotive. LME. **6** Any of various small devices (chiefly wedges, vices, or clamps) used in various trades. LME. **7** *Naut.* Any of various ropes or bars; *spec.* (*a*) a rope or track on which a sail runs; (*b*) a rope or bar providing footing or protection for sailors, *spec.* a rope along the yards on which sailors stand when handling the sails. E17. **8** A frame or structure, usu. one with legs, on which something is mounted or supported. E18. **9** A lottery ticket hired out by the day. *obs.* exc. *Hist.* E18. **10a** *Mining.* An obstruction (as a mass of rock or earth) or fault in a vein. L18. **b** A shoal, a sandbank. Chiefly *dial.* E20. **11** Work charged for before it is carried out. *slang.* Now *rare* or *obs.* L18. **12** (A unit of) horsepower. *colloq.* M19. **13** = PONY *n.* 3. *US slang.* L19. **14** Heroin. *slang* (orig. *US*). M20.

8 C. MORFIT A horse .. formed of two uprights and two crossbars, solidly joined together. *clothes-horse, saw-horse,* etc. 12 *Motocross Rider* Judging an engine on how many horses escape from it. 14 J. BALDWIN His first taste of marijuana, his first snort of horse.

Phrases etc.: *back the wrong horse*: see BACK *v.* 5. *break a horse (to the rein)*: see BREAK *v.* **change horses in midstream** change one's ideas, plans, etc., in the middle of a project or process. *dark horse*: see DARK *a.* *dead horse*: see DEAD *a.* etc. *devil's coach-horse*: see DEVIL *n.* **eat like a horse** eat heartily or greedily. *Flemish horse*: see FLEMISH *a.* *flog a dead horse*: see DEAD *a.* etc. *Flying Horse*: see FLYING *ppl a.* **frighten the horses** cause consternation or dismay; shock. **from the horse's mouth** (of information etc.) from the person directly concerned or another authoritative source. *hitch horses together*: see HITCH *v.* *hold one's horses*: see HOLD *v.* *horse and hattock*: see HATTOCK *n.* **horse of another colour** a thing significantly different. **horses for courses** the matching of tasks and talents; *iron horse*: see IRON *a.* *light horse*: see LIGHT *a.*[1] *Little Horse*: see LITTLE *a.* *look a gift-horse in the mouth*: see GIFT *n.* *one-horse*: see ONE *a.* **on one's high horse** *colloq.* behaving with pretentiousness or arrogance. *put the cart before the horse*: see CART *n.* *sea horse*: see SEA *n.* **swap horses in midstream** = *change horses in midstream* above. **to horse** *imper.* mount your horses. *Trojan horse*: see TROJAN *a.* 1. *white horse*: see WHITE *a.* *wild horse*: see WILD *a., n.,* & *adv.* *wooden horse*: see WOODEN *a.* *workhorse*: see WORK *n.*

Comb.: **horse-and-buggy** *a.* (*N. Amer.*) old-fashioned, bygone; **horse ant** the large European wood ant, *Formica rufa*; **horse-balm** a lemon-scented labiate plant of N. America, *Collinsonia canadensis*; **horsebane** a poisonous umbelliferous plant of watery places, *Oenanthe aquatica*, also called *fine-leaved water-dropwort*; **horsebean** any of several leguminous plants grown as fodder, esp. *Vicia faba* and (in tropical America) *Canavalia ensiformis*; **horse-block** a small platform of stone or wood for mounting a horse; **horse-boat** (*a*) (chiefly *Hist.*) a ferry-boat for carrying horses or carriages; (*b*) *N. Amer. Hist.* a paddle-boat powered by horses working a treadmill; (*c*) a type of landing-craft; **horsebox** a closed vehicle for transporting a horse or horses; *horse brass*: see BRASS *n.* 2d; **horse-bread** *Hist.* bread fed to horses, made of beans, bran, etc.; **horse-breaker** (*a*) a person who breaks in horses; (*b*) *Hist.* a courtesan (freq. in *pretty horse-breaker*); **horse-car** *US* (chiefly *Hist.*) a horse-drawn tramcar or railway-car; **horse-cloth**: used to cover a horse, or as part of its trappings; **horse-collar** a thickly padded collar forming part of a draught horse's harness (*grin through a horse-collar*: see GRIN *v.*[2]); **horse-colt** a young male horse; **horse-comb** a comb for use on a horse, a curry-comb; **horse-coper** a dealer in horses; *horse-*CORSER; **horse cubes** concentrated food in pellet form for horses; **horse daisy** *dial.* = *ox-eye daisy* s.v. OX-EYE 1(c); **horse-doctor** a veterinary surgeon attending horses; **horse-drawn** *a.* (of a vehicle) pulled by a horse or horses; **horse-eye bean** (the seeds of) the W. Indian leguminous vine *Mucuna urens*, so called from the black hilum of the seeds; **horse fair** a (yearly) market for the sale of horses; **horsefeathers** *N. Amer. slang* nonsense; **horse-fish** any of various fishes having a horselike head, as the sea horse, the look-down; *spec.* a brownish fish with long joined dorsal spines, *Congiopodus torvus*, of deep southern African waters; **horsefly** any of various tabanid flies (esp. of the genus *Tabanus*), the females of which suck blood; also, any of various other bloodsucking flies, as the forest-fly *Hippobosca equina*; **horse-foal** a male foal; **horse-foot (crab)** *US* a horseshoe crab; **horse-gear** *collect.* harness or trappings for horses; **horse-godmother** *arch.* & *dial.* a large coarse-looking woman; **horse-head** (*a*) a horse's head; a head like that of a horse; (*b*) = *horse-fish* above; **horsehide** *n.* & *a.* (made of) leather made from the hide of a horse; **horse-hoe** *n.* & *v.* (*a*) *n.* an early horse-drawn cultivator; (*b*) *v.t.* & *i.* work with a horse-hoe; **horse-hoer** a person who horse-hoes; **horse-hoof** (now *dial.*) coltsfoot; **horse-jockey** (now *rare*) (*a*) a jockey in horse-races; (*b*) *US* a dealer in horses; **horse latitudes** a belt of calms in each hemisphere between the trade winds and the westerlies; **horse-laugh** a loud coarse laugh; **horseleech** a large predatory leech of the genus *Haemopis*; *fig.* = LEECH *n.*[2] 2; **horse-litter** (*a*) *Hist.* a litter hung on poles and carried between two horses, one in front, one behind; (*b*) straw etc. used as bedding for horses; this when soiled used as manure; **horse-load** (now *rare*) a quantity (formerly occas. a specific weight) constituting a pack load for a horse; *loosely* a large load or quantity; **horse-mackerel** (*a*) any of several large carangid fishes, *esp.* the scad, *Trachurus trachurus*; also *attrib.*, designating the family Carangidae; (*b*) (chiefly *N. Amer.*) any of various large tunnies or similar fishes; **horse manure** (*a*) horse dung and soiled straw etc. used as manure; (*b*) = *horse shit* below; **horse-master** a person who owns, manages, or breaks in horses; a person skilled in managing horses; **horse-mastership** skill in managing horses; **horse-meat** †(*a*) fodder for horses; (*b*) horse-flesh as food; **horse-mill** a mill driven by a horse or horses, usu. by one walking in a circle or in a wheel; **horsemint** any of several coarse spicate mints, esp. hairy variants and hybrids of spearmint, *Mentha spicata*; *US* = *wild bergamot* s.v. BERGAMOT *n.*[2] 3(b); **horse mushroom** an edible mushroom, *Agaricus arvensis*, larger and coarser than the field mushroom, *A. campestris*; **horse mussel** †(*a*) a freshwater mussel; (*b*) a large marine mussel of the genus *Modiolus*, esp. *M. modiolus*; **horse-nail** a nail for a horseshoe; **horse opera** *N. Amer. slang* a western film; **horse-pistol** a large pistol carried at the pommel of the saddle by a rider; **horseplay** †(*a*) play in which a horse is used or takes part, flamboyant horsemanship; (*b*) boisterous play; **horse-plum** (*a*) a coarse red variety of plum; (*b*) *US* either of two N. American wild plums, *Prunus americana* and *P. nigra*; **horse-pond** *n.* & *v.* (*a*) *n.* a pond for watering and washing horses, proverbial as a place for ducking obnoxious people; (*b*) *v.t.* (now *rare*) duck in or drag through a horse-pond; **horse-pox** a mild viral disease affecting horses; **horse-race** a race between horses with riders; **horse-racer** a person who participates in horse-racing; **horse-racing** the sport of conducting horse-races; **horse's ass** *N. Amer. slang* a fool; **horse sense** *colloq.* (orig. *US*) plain common sense; **horse shit** *fig.* (*N. Amer. slang*) nonsense, rubbish; **horse sickness** a usu. fatal viral disease of horses, esp. in southern Africa (also *African horse-sickness*); **horse's neck** (orig. *US*) a drink of ginger ale flavoured with lemon peel, usu. with whisky, brandy, or gin; **horse-soldier** a soldier mounted on a horse; **horse's tail** a hairstyle in which the hair is tied at the back and hangs down like a horse's tail, a pony-tail; **horse-trading** (*a*) *N. Amer.* dealing in horses; (*b*) shrewd bargaining; **horse-walker** a mechanically rotating arm to which horses are tied for the purpose of exercise; **horse-way** (now *rare*) a bridle-way; **horsewhip** *n.* & *v.* (*a*) *n.* a whip used in driving and controlling horses; (*b*) *v.t.* beat with a horsewhip; chastise.

horselike *a.* resembling (that of) a horse M16.

horse /hɔːs/ *v.* OE. [f. the n.] **1** *v.t.* Provide (a person, a vehicle) with a horse or horses. OE. **2** *v.i.* Mount or go on horseback. LME. **3a** *v.t.* Of a stallion: mate with (a mare). LME. **b** *v.i.* Of a mare: be in heat, desire the stallion. Freq. as *horsing* pres. pple. Chiefly *US dial.* & *Austral.* L16. †**4** *v.t.* Raise or hoist up. LME–M17. **5** *v.t.* Carry on a person's back; lift on someone's back in order to be flogged. *arch.* M16. †**6** *v.t.* Sit astride, bestride. *rare* (Shakes.). Only in E17. †**7** *v.t.* *Naut.* Of a tide or current: carry or sweep along. L17–E18. **8** *v.t.* Make fun of, ridicule, tease. *US.* E20. **9** *v.i.* Indulge in horseplay; fool *about* or *around.* Also, be promiscuous, sleep *around. colloq.* E20.

1 T. CORYAT Maron of Turin, who horsed our Company from Lyons to Turin. G. WASHINGTON We set out with less than thirty carriages .. all of them strongly horsed. 2 M. BRADBURY Two rodeo riders horsed showily down the street. 4 S. PURCHAS Three of them stole a horse .. but were therefore horsed on a Gibbet. 5 THACKERAY The biggest boy .. horsed me—and I was flogged. 7 G. SHELVOCKE We were in

eminent danger of being horsed by the current upon two rocks. 9 W. G. HARDY Peter horsed around and ducked Elise and she ducked him. S. KAUFFMANN It isn't as if I didn't love her. . . Then why do I have to go horsing around with dames?

horseback /ˈhɔːsbak/ *n.* & *adv.* LME. [f. HORSE *n.* + BACK *n.*[1]] **A** *n.* **1** A horse's back. Now only in *on horseback*, (*a*) mounted on a horse; (*b*) on to a horse. LME. **2** *Geol.* A low sharp ridge of gravel, sand, or rock, *esp.* an esker or kame. *US.* M19.

1 LD MACAULAY In an age when even princesses performed their journeys on horseback. OED He had some difficulty in climbing on horseback. *devils-on-horseback*: see DEVIL *n.*

Comb.: **horseback opinion** *US*: given without opportunity to consider the matter; **horseback-riding** (chiefly *N. Amer.*) horse-riding.

B *adv.* On horseback. E18.

M. AMSTERDAM I love to ride horseback.

horse chestnut /hɔːs ˈtʃɛsnʌt/ *n. phr.* L16. [f. HORSE *n.* + CHESTNUT *n.*, tr. mod.L †*Castanea equina*: cf. G *Rosskastanie*.] **1** Any of various trees constituting the genus *Aesculus* (family Hippocastanaceae), with large palmate leaves and panicles of white, pink, or red flowers; esp. *A. hippocastanum*, a widely planted tree, native to the Balkans. L16. **2** The hard shiny dark brown seed (enclosed in a prickly fruit) of the horse chestnut, resembling that of the sweet chestnut but with a coarse bitter taste. Also called (esp. by children) *conker*. E17.

horseflesh /ˈhɔːsflɛʃ/ *n.* LME. [f. HORSE *n.* + FLESH *n.*] **1** Horses collectively, esp. with regard to riding, driving, or racing. LME. **2** The flesh of a horse, esp. as food. M16. **3** In full *horseflesh mahogany*. The sabicu tree, *Lysiloma latisiliqua*, of the W. Indies; the wood of this tree. L18.

horse guard /hɔːs gɑːd/ *n. phr.* Also **horse-guard**. M17. [f. HORSE *n.* + GUARD *n.*] **I** *gen.* **1** A member of a body of cavalry selected for special guard duties. M17. **2** A person or persons set to guard horses. *N. Amer.* E19. **II** *spec.* (W. cap. initials.) **3** In *pl.* A cavalry brigade of the British Household troops, the Life Guards and (esp.) Royal Horse Guards (the Blues), now an armoured-car regiment providing a mounted squadron for ceremonial purposes, and merged with the Dragoon Guards in the Household Cavalry Regiment. M17. **4** In *pl.* & †*sing.* The headquarters of this brigade in Whitehall, London. M17. **5** In *pl.* The personnel of the office of the commander-in-chief of the British army and the military, as opp. to the civil, authorities. Now *arch.* or *Hist.* E19.

horsehair /ˈhɔːshɛː/ *n.* & *a.* ME. [f. HORSE *n.* + HAIR *n.*] **A** *n.* (A strand of) the hair of a horse's mane or tail. ME.

B *attrib.* or as *adj.* Of horsehair; stuffed with horsehair. L18.

horsehair worm, (*US*) **snake**, a hair-worm of the phylum Nematomorpha.

horseless /ˈhɔːslɪs/ *a.* L17. [f. HORSE *n.* + -LESS.] Having no horse.

horseless carriage *arch.* a motor car.

horseman /ˈhɔːsmən/ *n.* Pl. **-men**. ME. [f. HORSE *n.* + MAN *n.*] **1** A (skilled) rider on horseback. ME. **b** A mounted soldier. Now chiefly *Hist.* ME. **c** A knight. *obs.* exc. *Hist.* L16. **2** A stableman, a groom. LME.

1 JAS. HARRIS These Spanish Arabians . . were great horsemen, and particularly fond of their horses. b *light horseman*: see LIGHT *a.*[1] 2 RIDER HAGGARD The agricultural labourer . . works from six to six . . horsemen and cattlemen work longer.

horsemanship *n.* skill in riding or managing horses M16.

horse-marine /ˈhɔːsməriːn/ *n.* E19. [f. HORSE *n.* + MARINE *n.*] **1** In *pl.*, an imaginary corps of mounted marine soldiers (out of their natural element); *sing.* a person unsuited to the work in hand, a landlubber at sea. *joc.* E19. **2** A person who leads and attends to a barge-horse. M19. **3** A marine mounted on horseback; a cavalryman doing a marine's work. L19.

1 **tell that to the horse-marines** *colloq.*: indicating incredulity.

horsepower /ˈhɔːspaʊə/ *n.* Pl. same. E19. [f. HORSE *n.* + POWER *n.* (f. the supposed rate of work of a horse).] (Power as measured in terms of) a unit of rate of performing work, equivalent to 550 foot-pounds per second, (in the US) 746 watts or about 550 foot-pounds per second.

F. MARRYAT She . . preferred the three-horse power of the schuyt to the hundred-horse power of the steam-packet. *fig.*: R. W. EMERSON Enthusiasm is the leaping lightning, not to be measured by the horse-power of the understanding. **brake horsepower** the power available at the shaft of an engine, measurable by means of a brake. **indicated horsepower** the power produced within the cylinders of an engine, as shown by an indicator.

horseradish /ˈhɔːsradɪʃ/ *n.* L16. [f. HORSE *n.* + RADISH.] A white-flowered cruciferous plant, *Armoracia rusticana*, cultivated for its root; the thick pungent rootstock of this plant, which is scraped or grated as a condiment, and made into a sauce.

Comb.: **horseradish tree** an Indian tree, *Moringa oleifera* (family Moringaceae), with oil-yielding seeds (ben nuts) and a root smelling of horseradish; also called *drumstick tree*.

horseshoe /ˈhɔːsʃuː, -ʃʃ-/ *n.* & *a.* ME. [f. HORSE *n.* + SHOE *n.*] **A** *n.* **1** A shoe for a horse, now formed of a narrow band of iron etc. shaped to the outline of the hard part of the hoof and secured by nails driven through the hoof wall. Also, this or a representation of this as a good-luck charm. ME. **b** In *pl.* A game resembling quoits in which horseshoes are thrown at a peg. Chiefly *N. Amer.* E19. **2** Something shaped like a horseshoe or a circular arc larger than a semicircle. L15. **b** *Logic.* = HOOK *n.* 10d. E20. **3** = *horseshoe-vetch* below. Now *rare.* L16.

2 B. STOKER I read that every known superstition . . is gathered into the horseshoe of the Carpathians. *Road Racer* Spencer leapt away from the flag, and led round the first horseshoe.

B *attrib.* or as *adj.* Having the shape of a horseshoe. L18.

M. TWAIN The water cuts the alluvial banks of the 'lower' river into deep horseshoe curves. *Graphic* The delegates took their places . . at a horseshoe table.

Comb. & *special collocations*: **horseshoe bat** any of various mainly tropical Old World bats of the genus *Rhinolophus* and family Rhinolophidae, usu. having a horseshoe-shaped ridge on the nose; **horseshoe crab** any of several large marine arthropods, the only members of the chelicerate class Merostomata (subclass Xiphosura), having a horseshoe-shaped carapace and a long tail-spine, *esp.* the N. American *Limulus polyphemus*; a king crab; **horseshoe-vetch** a leguminous plant of calcareous grassland, *Hippocrepis comosa*, with heads of bright yellow flowers and pods breaking into horseshoe-shaped segments.

horse-shoe /ˈhɔːsʃuː, -ʃʃ-/ *v.* LME. [Partly f. prec., partly f. HORSE *n.* + SHOE *v.*] **1** *v.i.* Shoe horses; make horseshoes. Chiefly as *horse-shoeing* vbl n. LME. **2** *v.t.* Make horseshoe-shaped. *rare.* M19.

horse-shoer *n.* L16.

horsetail /ˈhɔːsteɪl/ *n.* ME. [f. HORSE *n.* + TAIL *n.*[1]] **1** The tail of a horse. ME. **b** This as formerly used in Turkey as a decoration, a military standard, or a symbol of a pasha's rank. E17. **c** A fine strong sewing silk. L19. **d** A pony-tail; = *horse's tail* s.v. HORSE *n.* M20. **2** Any of the flowerless plants constituting the nearly worldwide genus *Equisetum* (family Equisetaceae), which are related to the ferns and have hollow jointed grooved stems and leaves reduced to nodal sheaths. M16.

2 *rough horsetail*: see ROUGH *a.*

horsewoman /ˈhɔːswʊmən/ *n.* Pl. **-women** /-wɪmɪn/. L16. [f. HORSE *n.* + WOMAN *n.*] A (skilled) female rider.

horsewomanship *n.* a woman's skill in riding or managing horses M19.

horsey *n.*, *a.* vars. of HORSIE, HORSY.

horsfordite /ˈhɔːsfədʌɪt/ *n.* L19. [f. E. N. *Horsford* (1818–93), US chemist + -ITE[1].] *Min.* A brittle, silvery-white antimonide of copper.

horsiculture /ˈhɔːsɪkʌltʃə/ *n. derog.* L20. [f. HORSE *n.* + -CULTURE after *horticulture*.] The commercial development of farmland for the pasturing of horses or equestrian activities.

horsie /ˈhɔːsi/ *n. nursery* & *familiar.* Also **horsey**. E20. [f. HORSE *n.* + -IE, -Y[6].] A horse.

horst /hɔːst/ *n.* L19. [G = heap, mass.] *Geol.* A block of the earth's surface bounded by faults on some or all sides and raised relative to the surrounding land.

Horst Wessel /hɔːst ˈvɛs(ə)l/ *n.* M20. [Ger. writer of the words (1907–1930).] More fully *Horst Wessel lied, song*. The official anthem of the German Nazi party.

horsy /ˈhɔːsi/ *a.* Also **horsey**. L16. [f. HORSE *n.* + -Y[1].] **1** Of, pertaining to, or resembling a horse or horses. L16. **2** Concerned with or devoted to horses or horse-racing; affecting the dress and language of a groom or jockey. M19. **3** Of a mare: in heat, ready to mate. L19.

1 X. HERBERT Soon he heard a horsy snort and clink of hobbles. 2 P. LEVI Horsy people and hunting people seem to many of my friends painfully conventional.

horsily *adv.* L19. **horsiness** *n.* M19.

hortal /ˈhɔːt(ə)l/ *a. rare.* E18. [f. L *hortus* garden + -AL[1].] Of a plant: cultivated; of garden origin.

hortation /hɔːˈteɪʃ(ə)n/ *n.* M16. [L *hortatio(n-)*, f. *hortat-* pa. ppl stem of *hortari* exhort: see -ATION.] Exhortation.

hortative /ˈhɔːtətɪv/ *a.* & *n.* E17. [L *hortativus*, f. *hortat-*: see prec., -IVE.] **A** *adj.* Exhortative. E17.

J. MCPHEE When he is being pedagogical, the voice goes up . . , and becomes hortative and sharp.

B *n.* A hortative speech. E17.

hortatory /ˈhɔːtət(ə)ri/ *a.* L16. [Late L *hortatorius*, f. *hortat-*: see HORTATION, -ORY[2].] Exhortatory.

T. MO The vocabulary . . appears couched imperatively and in a hortatory tone.

hortensia /hɔːˈtɛnsɪə/ *n.* L18. [mod.L, f. *Hortense*, wife of J.-A. Lepaute (1720–*c*1787), French clockmaker.] A variety of the common hydrangea, *Hydrangea macrophylla*, in which all the flowers are of the sterile showy type.

horti conclusi *n. phr.* pl. of HORTUS CONCLUSUS.

horticulture /ˈhɔːtɪkʌltʃə/ *n.* L17. [f. L *hortus* garden, after AGRICULTURE.] The art of garden cultivation or management.

hortiˈcultural *a.* L18. **hortiˈculturalist** *n.* = HORTICULTURIST L20. **hortiˈculturally** *adv.* with regard to horticulture L19. **hortiˈculturist** *n.* a gardener, a specialist in horticulture E19.

horti sicci *n. phr.* pl. of HORTUS SICCUS.

hortulan /ˈhɔːtjʊlən/ *a.* Now *rare.* M17. [L *hortulanus*, f. *hortulus* dim. of *hortus* garden: see -ULE, -AN. Cf. ORTOLAN.] Of or pertaining to a garden or gardening.

hortus conclusus /ˌhɔːtəs kənˈkluːsəs/ *n. phr.* Pl. ***horti conclusi*** /hɔːtʌɪ kənˈkluːsʌɪ, -tiː -siː/. E17. [L = enclosed garden.] **1** An enclosed inviolate garden; freq., in spiritual and exegetical tradition, as symbolic of the soul, the Christian Church, or the virginity of Mary. E17. **2** A painting of the Madonna and Child in an enclosed garden. M19.

hortus siccus /ˌhɔːtəs ˈsɪkəs/ *n. phr.* Pl. ***horti sicci*** /hɔːtʌɪ ˈsɪkʌɪ, -tiː -kiː/. L17. [L = dry garden.] An arranged collection of dried plants; *fig.* a collection of uninteresting facts etc.

Horus /ˈhɔːrəs/ *n.* M19. [Late L f. Gk *Hōros* f. Egyptian *Hor*.] *Egyptian Mythol.* A sky god depicted as having the head of a hawk.

hosanna /həʊˈzanə/ *int.*, *n.*, & *v.* Also **-ah**. OE. [Late L (*h*)*osanna* f. Gk *hōsanna* f. Rabbinic Heb. *hōšaʿnā*, abbrev. of biblical *hōšīʿā-nnā* save, (we) pray (*Ps.* 118:25).] **A** *int.* Appealing for deliverance or praising God, *spec.* in Jewish liturgical or Christian use. OE. **B** *n.* A cry or shout of 'hosanna!'; a shout of praise or adoration. M17. **C** *v.t.* Address, applaud, or escort with cries of 'hosanna!' L17.

Comb.: **Hosanna Sunday** *arch.* Palm Sunday.

hose /həʊz/ *n.* Pl. **hose**, (in branch I, *arch.*) **hosen** /ˈhəʊz(ə)n/, (now only in branch II, where usual) **hoses**. [OE *hosa*, *-e* = OS, OHG, ON *hosa* (Du. *hoos* stocking, water-hose, G *Hose(n)* trousers), f. Gmc. In sense 3 prob. f. Du.] **I 1** In *pl.* & †*sing.*, an article of clothing for the leg, sometimes also covering the foot. Now *spec.* in *pl.*, stockings. OE. **b** *Hist.* In *pl.* Covering for the legs forming part of a suit of armour; greaves. ME. 2 *Hist.* In *pl.* Clothing for the legs and loins, breeches. LME.

1 H. WILSON Her hose had been laddered. *half-hose*: see HALF-.

II 3 A flexible tube or pipe used for the conveyance of water for watering plants, putting out fires, dispersing rioters, etc. ME. 4 A sheath or sheathing part; *spec.* the sheath enclosing an ear of corn, the sheath or spathe of an arum. *obs.* exc. *dial.* LME. †5 The bag at the lower end of a trawl-net etc. L15–M17. 6 A socket in a metal tool, golf club, etc., into which a handle or shaft is fitted. L16.

3 B. PYM Dulcie could see her neighbour .. watching her hose watering the lawn. *fire-hose, water-hose*, etc.

Comb. & phrases: **hose company** *US* a company in charge of a fire-hose; **hose-in-hose** *a.* & *n.* (*a*) *adj.* (esp. of a polyanthus or other primula) having a petaloid calyx, and so appearing to have one corolla within another; (*b*) *n.* a flower of this form; **hose-net** (chiefly *Sc.*, now *rare*) a kind of small net; *fig.* a situation from which escape is difficult; **hose-pipe** *n.* & *v.* (*a*) *n.* = sense 3 above; (*b*) *v.t.* spray with water etc. from a hose; *wear yellow hose*: see WEAR *v.*[1]

hoseless *a.* L16.

hose /həʊz/ *v.t.* ME. [f. the n.] 1 Provide with hose or stockings. ME. 2 Spray or drench with water etc. from a hose. Also foll. by *down*. L19.

2 H. FAST Jack Harvey had cleaned the deck and hosed it down.

hosen *n.pl.* see HOSE *n.*

hosier /ˈhəʊzə/ *n.* ME. [f. HOSE *n.* + -IER.] A person who makes or deals in hose or stockings, or in these and knitted or woven underwear. Occas. more widely, a men's outfitter, a haberdasher.

hosiery /ˈhəʊzɪəri, -ʒəri/ *n.* L18. [f. HOSE *n.* + -ERY.] 1 Hose collectively; the goods in which a hosier deals. L18. 2 The business or trade of a hosier. L18.

hospice /ˈhɒspɪs/ *n.* E19. [(O)Fr. f. L *hospitium* hospitality, lodging, f. *hospes, hospit-* HOST *n.*[2]] 1 A house of rest and entertainment for travellers or strangers, *esp.* one belonging to a religious order. E19. 2 A home for the destitute or sick; *spec.* a nursing-home for the care of the dying. L19.

hospitable /hɒˈspɪtəb(ə)l, ˈhɒspɪt-/ *a.* L16. [Fr., f. †*hospiter* receive a guest, f. med.L *hospitare*, f. L *hospes, hospit-* HOST *n.*[2]: see -ABLE.] 1 Offering welcome and entertainment to strangers; extending or disposed to extend a generous hospitality to guests and visitors. L16. 2 *transf.* Disposed to receive or welcome something readily, receptive *to*. M17.

1 E. TEMPLETON The English are very hospitable, they are bound to make you welcome. A. L. ROWSE In Elizabeth Mayer's hospitable house.

hospitableness *n.* E17. **hospitably** *adv.* E18.

hospitage /ˈhɒspɪtɪdʒ/ *n. rare.* L16. [med.L *hospitagium*, f. L *hospes, hospit-* HOST *n.*[2]: see -AGE.] †1 The position of a guest. Only in L16. †2 Lodging or entertainment as a guest. Only in E17. 3 A place of hospitality. M19.

hospital /ˈhɒspɪt(ə)l/ *n.* ME. [OFr. (mod. *hôpital*) f. med.L *hospitale* use as n. of L *hospitalis*: see next.] 1 *Hist.* A house for the reception and entertainment of pilgrims, travellers, or strangers; any of the establishments of the Knights Hospitallers. ME. 2 A charitable institution for the housing and maintenance of the needy; an asylum for the destitute, infirm, or aged. Now chiefly in surviving proper names. ME. †b *gen.* A place of lodging. Only in 16. †c A house for lodging students in a university; a hostel or hall. M16–E18. d A charitable institution for the education etc. of the young. Now only *Sc. Law* (*Hist.*) and in surviving proper names, (as *Christ's Hospital*, a public school formerly in London). M16. 3 An institution or establishment providing medical or surgical treatment for the ill or wounded. M16. b An establishment for the treatment of sick or injured animals. E17.

3 *cottage hospital, eye hospital, general hospital, isolation hospital*, etc. **in hospital**, (*US*) **in the hospital** receiving treatment, *spec.* as an in-patient, at a hospital. **to hospital** to a hospital for treatment. *walk the hospitals*: see WALK *v.*[1]

Comb.: **hospital ball** = *hospital pass* below; **hospital bed** (*a*) a bed for a patient in a hospital, usu. higher than an ordinary bed to facilitate nursing; (*b*) an available place for an in-patient at a hospital; **hospital blue(s)** the uniform worn by wounded soldiers in the wars of 1914–18 and 1939–45; **hospital corners** a way of tucking sheets, used by nurses; **hospital fever** typhus acquired in overcrowded, insanitary conditions in a hospital; **hospital gangrene**: caused by sepsis in a hospital; *hospital gown*: see GOWN *n.* 4; **hospital pass** in *Football* etc., a pass to a player likely to be tackled heavily as soon as it is received; **hospital ship**: to receive sick and wounded seamen, or to take sick and wounded soldiers home; **hospital train**: taking wounded soldiers from a battlefield.

†**hospital** *a.* LME–E19. [L *hospitalis* hospitable, f. *hospes, hospit-* HOST *n.*[2]: see -AL[1].] Hospitable; *spec.* (as an epithet of Jove) protecting the rights of hospitality.

hospitaler *n.* see HOSPITALLER.

hospitalise *v.* var. of HOSPITALIZE.

hospitalism /ˈhɒspɪt(ə)lɪz(ə)m/ *n.* M19. [f. HOSPITAL *n.* + -ISM.] The system of medical treatment in hospitals, esp. formerly in overcrowded and unhygienic conditions.

hospitality /hɒspɪˈtalɪti/ *n.* LME. [(O)Fr. *hospitalité* f. L *hospitalitas, -tat-*, f. *hospitalis*: see HOSPITAL *a.*, -ITY.] 1 The act or practice of being hospitable; the reception and entertainment of guests, visitors, or strangers; *transf.* receptiveness to new ideas etc. LME. †2 A hospitable institution or foundation; a hospital. M16–M18. †3 The quality of being hospitable. Only in E18.

1 P. ROTH Thanks to your hospitality we are getting nicely drunk here. **enjoy Her, His, Majesty's hospitality** *slang* spend time in prison.

Comb.: **hospitality room, suite** a room, suite, in a hotel or television studio set aside for the entertainment of guests.

hospitalize /ˈhɒspɪt(ə)lʌɪz/ *v.t.* Also **-ise**. M17. [f. HOSPITAL *n.* + -IZE.] Admit to or treat in a hospital.

¶App. not recorded between M17 and E20.

hospitaliˈzation *n.* E20.

hospitaller /ˈhɒspɪt(ə)lə/ *n.* Also *-aler. ME. [OFr. *hospitalier* f. med.L *hospitalarius* (also *-aris*), f. *hospitale*: see HOSPITAL *n.*, -ER[2].] 1 (H-.) More fully *Knight Hospitaller*. A member of a military religious order founded as the Knights of the Hospital of St John at Jerusalem in the 11th cent. Usu. in *pl.*, this order. ME. 2 *gen.* A member of a charitable religious order. LME. 3 In a religious house or hospice, the person with responsibility for receiving and attending to visitors, pilgrims, and strangers. LME. 4 In some London hospitals: formerly, the chief resident official, whose responsibilities included religious superintendence; now, the hospital chaplain. M16.

hospitia *n.* pl. of HOSPITIUM.

†**hospitious** *a.* L16–L18. [f. L *hospitium* (see HOSPICE) + -OUS.] Hospitable.

hospitium /hɒˈspɪʃɪəm/ *n.* Pl. **-tia** /-ʃɪə/. M17. [L: see HOSPICE.] = HOSPICE 1.

hospodar /ˈhɒspədɑː/ *n.* Also (as a title) **H-**. L16. [Romanian *hospodár*, f. Ukrainian *hospodar* = Russ. *gospodar'*, f. *gospod'* lord.] *Hist.* A lord: *spec.* the title of the former governors of Wallachia and Moldavia under the Ottoman Porte.

hoss /hɒs/ *n. dial.* & *US.* E19. [Repr. a pronunc. of HORSE *n.*] A horse.

host /həʊst/ *n.*[1] ME. [OFr. (*h*)*ost*, (*h*)*oost* f. L *hostis* stranger, enemy, (in med.L) army: cf. GUEST *n.*] 1 An armed company or multitude of men; an army. Now *arch.* & *literary*. ME. 2 *transf.* A great company; a multitude, a large number, (*of*). LME.

1 C. C. TRENCH Well might Marshal Noailles tremble when he saw the host arranged against him, commanded moreover by the King of England in person. 2 J. T. STORY We've got hosts of primroses. D. ACHESON Two long talks .. on a host of matters of common concern to us both.

Phrases: **be a host in oneself** be able to do as much as several ordinary people. **heavenly host, host(s) of heaven** (*a*) in biblical use, the angels that attend on God; (*b*) the sun, the moon, and the stars. **Lord (God) of hosts** God as Lord over earthly or heavenly armies.

host /həʊst/ *n.*[2] ME. [OFr. (*h*)*oste* (mod. *hôte*) f. L *hospis, hospit-* host, prob. f. *hostis*: see prec.] I 1 A person who lodges or receives and entertains another as a guest, esp. in his or her own home; a compère or presenter of a television programme. ME. 2 A person who lodges or entertains another for payment; a person who keeps a lodging-house; the landlord or landlady of an inn or public house. ME. 3 *Biol.* An animal or plant on or in which a parasite or commensal organism lives. M19. 4 a *Geol.* The rock or mineral mass of which a distinct substance such as an ore is a minor component. L19. b *Physics* & *Chem.* A crystal lattice or molecular structure that contains a foreign ion, atom, or molecule. M20. 5 *Biol.* & *Med.* An animal or person that is the recipient of tissue transplanted from another. E20. 6 In full *host computer*. A computer which mediates (usu. multiple) access to databases mounted on it or provides other services to a computer network. M20.

1 DAY LEWIS I feel more at home as a guest than as a host. P. F. BOLLER For eight years he acted as host and occasional star of .. a half-hour TV series. 2 W. HOLTBY These might be the new host and hostess of the Nag's Head. **mine host** the landlord or landlady of an inn or public house. **reckon without one's host** neglect a difficulty, opposition, etc.

II 7 A guest. Long *obs.* exc. in HOASTMAN & in *host-house* (dial.), an inn, a hostelry. ME.

hostless *a.* (*rare*) without a host; inhospitable: L16.

host /həʊst/ *n.*[3] ME. [OFr. (*h*)*oiste* f. L *hostia* sacrificial animal, victim, (in late L) eucharistic sacrifice. Cf. HOSTIE *n.*[1]] †1 A sacrificial victim; a sacrifice, *spec.* with reference to Christ. ME–M17. 2 *Eccl.* The bread consecrated in the Eucharist regarded as the body of Christ sacrificially offered; a wafer before or after consecration. ME.

†**host** *n.*[4] LME–L16. [Perh. f. OFr. (*h*)*osté* var. of (*h*)*ostel* HOSTEL *n.*] A place of lodging, an inn.

at host put up at an inn.

host /həʊst/ *v.*[1] ME. [f. HOST *n.*[1]] 1 *v.t.* Gather into a host; assemble in battle array, encamp. Long *obs.* exc. as HOSTING. ME. †2 *v.i.* Be assembled or gather in a host. LME–L18.

host /həʊst/ *v.*[2] LME. [f. HOST *n.*[2]] I 1 *v.t.* a Receive (a person) into one's house, town, or country and entertain as a guest. LME. b Be host at (a party, dinner, etc); compère, present, (a television show etc.). M20. 2 *v.i.* Play the host, be host. M19.

1a *John o' London's* A sense of deep and humble respect for the people and the country who had hosted them. b S. BRETT Alexander Harvey hosted the most successful chat-show in the country. D. DELILLO David was hosting a .. party at his house. 2 *Time* Critic John Crosby .. will host.

II †3 *v.i.* Be a guest; lodge. LME–M17.

hosta /ˈhɒstə/ *n.* E19. [mod.L, f. N. T. *Host* (1761–1834), Austrian physician: see -A[1].] Any plant of the genus *Hosta* of the lily family, comprising plants native to Japan and cultivated elsewhere for their broad often variegated leaves. Also called plantain lily.

hostage /ˈhɒstɪdʒ/ *n.*[1] ME. [(O)Fr. (*h*)*ostage* (now *otage*) f. Proto-Romance, f. late L *obsidiatus* hostageship, f. *obses, obsid-* hostage, f. *ob* OB- + base of *sedere* sit: see -AGE.] †1 (The state of a person or persons handed over in) pledge or security for fulfilment of an undertaking. Chiefly in *in, into, to hostage*. ME–E18. 2 A person given or seized and held as a pledge or security for fulfilment of an undertaking or imposed condition. ME. 3 A pledge, a security. ME.

2 M. PUZO Maybe Sollozzo figures to snatch you and hold you for a hostage to make a deal. J. CLAVELL Toranaga's war had begun when he was six and had been ordered as hostage into the enemy camp. **hold hostage** hold as a hostage (*lit.* & *fig.*). 3 **hostage to fortune** an acquisition, commitment, etc., regarded as endangered by unforeseen circumstances.

hostageship *n.* the condition of being a hostage M19.

†hostage *n.*[2] LME–M19. [OFr. *(h)ostage*, f. as HOST *n.*[2] + -AGE.] A hotel, a hostelry, an inn.

hostel /ˈhɒst(ə)l/ *n.* ME. [OFr. *(h)ostel* (mod. *hôtel* HOTEL) f. med.L *hospitale* HOSPITAL *n.*] **†1** A place to stay; a lodging. ME–E17. **†2** Lodging, entertainment. Only in ME. **3** A public house of lodging and entertainment for strangers and travellers; an inn, a hotel. *arch.* ME. **b** A youth hostel. E20. **4** A house of residence for students at a university or on a course, esp. at a non-residential college, or for some other special class of people. M16. **†5** A town mansion. L16–L17.

3 CONAN DOYLE After we had deposited our suit-cases at the ancient hostel. 4 C. HOPE The nearby hostel for homeless boys.

hostel /ˈhɒst(ə)l/ *v.* Infl. **-ll-**, ***-l-**. ME. [f. the n.] **†1** *v.t.* Provide with lodging. Only in ME. **2** *v.i.* Lodge (*at*). Long *obs.* exc. *dial.* ME. **3** *v.i.* Lodge at youth hostels, take a holiday lodging at youth hostels. Chiefly as *hostelling* vbl n. M20.

hosteler /ˈhɒst(ə)lə/ *n.* Also (esp. in sense 5) **-eller**. See also HOSTLER. ME. [AN, = OFr. *(h)ostelier* (mod. *hôtelier*), f. as prec.: see -ER[2]. In sense 5 f. HOSTEL *n.* or *v.* + -ER[1].] **1** A person who receives, lodges, or entertains guests and strangers, esp. in a religious house or monastery. *obs.* exc. *Hist.* ME. **2** A keeper of a hostelry or inn; an innkeeper. *arch.* LME. **†3** An ostler. LME–L15. **†4** A student who lives in a hostel. L16–M17. **5** A person who stays in a youth hostel; a person youth-hostelling. Also *youth-hosteler.* M20.

hostelry /ˈhɒst(ə)lri/ *n.* LME. [OFr. *(h)ostelerie* (mod. *hôtellerie*), f. *(h)ostelier*: see prec., -ERY.] **1** A house where lodging and entertainment are provided; an inn, a hostel. Now *arch.* or *literary.* LME. **2** The business of a hostel. *rare.* L16.

hostess /ˈhəʊstɪs, -ɛs, həʊˈstɛs/ *n.* & *v.* ME. [OFr. *(h)ostesse* (mod. *hôtesse*), f. *(h)oste* HOST *n.*[2]: see -ESS[1].] **A** *n.* **1** A woman who lodges or entertains guests; a woman who acts as a host. ME. **2** A woman who keeps a public place of lodging and entertainment; the landlady of an inn or public house. ME. **3** A woman employed to entertain customers at a nightclub etc.; *euphem.* a prostitute. M20. **4** A woman employed to attend to passengers on an aircraft (also *air-hostess*), train, etc. M20.

1 *Radio Times* The BBC was looking for two hostess-announcers for television. S. SPENDER She was a great hostess and patroness.

Comb.: **hostess apron**, **dress**, **pyjamas**, etc.: suitable for wearing to receive guests; **hostess trolley**: for holding (and keeping hot) food to be served at table.

B *v.i.* & *t.* Be the hostess of (a party etc.); act as hostess (at). E20.

hostessy *a.* pertaining to or typical of a hostess; hospitable: M20.

hostie /ˈhəʊsti/ *n.*[1] Now *arch. rare.* L15. [(O)Fr. f. L *hostia*: see HOST *n.*[3]] **†1** = HOST *n.*[3] 1. L15–L17. **2** = HOST *n.*[3] 2. L16.

hostie /ˈhəʊsti/ *n.*[2] *Austral.* & *NZ colloq.* M20. [f. HOSTESS: see -IE.] A hostess; *spec.* an air hostess.

hostile /ˈhɒstʌɪl/ *a.* & *n.* L16. [Fr., or L *hostilis*, f. *hostis* stranger, enemy: see -ILE.] **A** *adj.* **1** Of or pertaining to an enemy; pertaining to or engaged in hostilities. L16. **2** Of the nature or disposition of an enemy; unfriendly, antagonistic. L16. **b** Angry. *Austral.* & *NZ colloq.* M20. **3** Of a thing: contrary, adverse, opposed, (*to*). E19. **b** Of a takeover bid: liable to be opposed by the management of the target company. L20.

1 POPE Thus . . from the din of war, Safe he return'd without one hostile scar. WELLINGTON The operations of hostile armies. 2 J. STEINBECK Her hostile eyes glared at him. E. ROOSEVELT Their questions were so hostile as to give the impression that the witness had been . . prejudged a criminal. E. FEINSTEIN No good writer could be hostile to the Revolution. **hostile witness** *Law* a witness who appears hostile to the party calling him or her and therefore subject to cross-examination by that party. 3 W. LIPPMANN As industrial organization becomes bigger, it must become more inflexible, until . . it is hostile to invention, enterprise, competition, and change. b *Times* The low level of acceptances so far in the £160 million hostile bid . . shows that the shareholders recognize that the offer is without merit.

B *n.* A hostile person; *spec.* (*US Hist.*) a N. American Indian unfriendly to settlers. M19.

hostilely *adv.* E17.

hostilise *v.* var. of HOSTILIZE.

hostility /hɒˈstɪlɪti/ *n.* LME. [Fr. *hostilité* or late L *hostilitas*, f. *hostilis*: see HOSTILE, -ITY.] **1** The state of being hostile; hostile action exercised by one community, State, or power against another, *esp.* war; (a feeling of) unfriendliness, antagonism, or opposition. LME. **2** In *pl.* Hostile acts, *spec.* acts of war. E17.

1 N. MOSLEY His first wife . . had suffered much public hostility due to his politics. *New Republic* Nor does the new openness to religion signify a hostility to science. 2 L. STRACHEY Victoria's martial ardour was not to be side-tracked by hostilities against Lord Derby; hostilities against Russia were what she wanted.

hostilize /ˈhɒstɪlʌɪz/ *v.t. rare.* Also **-ise**. L18. [f. HOSTILE *a.* + -IZE.] Make hostile. Chiefly as *hostilized* ppl a.

hosting /ˈhəʊstɪŋ/ *n. obs.* exc. *Hist.* LME. [f. HOST *v.*[1] + -ING[1].] The raising of a host or armed multitude, hostile encounter or array; a military expedition, esp. in Ireland.

hostler /ˈ(h)ɒslə/ *n.* See also OSTLER. LME. [Syncopated form of HOSTELER.] **1** = OSTLER. LME. **2** A person in charge of locomotives when not in use. *US.* L19.

†hostry *n.* LME–L19. [OFr. *host(e)rie*, f. as HOST *n.*[2]: see -ERY.] = HOSTELRY.

hot /hɒt/ *n.*[1] *obs.* exc. *dial.* Also **hott**, (branch II) **†hutt**. ME. [(O)Fr. *hotte*, prob. of Gmc origin: cf. HOD *n.* Branch II may be a different wd.] **I 1** A kind of basket for carrying earth, sand, lime, manure, etc. *north.* ME. **2** A small heap (of dust, sand, etc.). *Sc.* & *north.* E18. **II †3** A padded sheath for the spur of a fighting-cock. E17–E19.

hot /hɒt/ *n.*[2] ME. [Absol. use of HOT *a.*] **1 a** Hot condition, heat. Now only (*dial.*), a spell of hot weather. ME. **b** *walk hots*, lead a horse around to cool it down after a race or exercise. M20. **2** Hot water. Chiefly in *hot and cold.* E20. **3** *the hots*, a strong sexual desire. Esp. in *have the hots for. slang.* M20.

hot /hɒt/ *a.* Compar. & superl. **-tt-**. [OE *hāt* = OFris., OS *hēt* (Du. *heet*), OHG *heiz* (G *heiss*), ON *heitr*, f. Gmc.] **1** Having or giving out a high degree of heat; of or at a high temperature, very warm. OE. **b** (Of food or drink) prepared by heating and consumed before it has time to cool; *fig.* recent, fresh in people's minds. ME. **c** Of metal, esp. iron: sufficiently high above melting point to flow readily. L19. **d** At a high voltage, live. E20. **e** Radioactive. Also, (of an atom, molecule, etc.) possessing extra energy in some form (nuclear, electronic, vibrational, etc.); excited. *colloq.* M20. **2** *Hist.* Designating a quality associated with heat and regarded in medieval and later times as one of the four qualities inherent in all things. Cf. *cold, dry, moist.* OE. **3** At a high emotional pitch; *esp.* enthusiastic (*for*), keen (*on*). Also, following closely in pursuit. OE. **b** Lustful, amorous, sexually aroused. Of a book, play, etc.: erotic, salacious. ME. **c** Very angry, indignant. Also = *hot-tempered* below. ME. **4** Attended with feverish or violent exertion; (of a contest, debate, etc.) fiercely contested, intense. Formerly also, of an epidemic: raging violently. OE. **5** Producing an effect as of heat or burning, esp. on the nerves of taste or on the mucous membrane; pungent, biting, acrid. ME. **6 a** Feeling an uncomfortable sensation of heat. Usu. *pred.* LME. **b** Producing or accompanied by (excessive) sensations of heat. M16. **7** Difficult or awkward to deal with; *spec.* (*a*) (of circumstances, a situation) uncomfortable, dangerous; (*b*) (of a hit, return, etc., in a ball-game) difficult for an opponent to cope with; (*c*) *Criminals' slang* (of property) stolen and hard to dispose of because easily identifiable; (of a person) wanted by the police; (*d*) (orig. *US*) (of goods, an area of work, etc.) affected by a trade-union dispute. E17. **8 a** *Hunting.* Of a scent: fresh, strong, intense. M17. **b** Of a participant in a children's seeking or guessing game: very close to finding or guessing what is sought. L19. **9** Of a shade of colour: (unpleasantly) intense. E19. **10** Exceptionally good, skilful, or successful. Freq. in neg. contexts. *colloq.* L19. **11 a** *Racing.* Of a favourite: strongly fancied. *slang.* L19. **b** Currently popular or in demand. M20. **12 a** Of information etc.: completely new; *esp.* novel and exciting. E20. **b** Of a treasury note: just issued. E20. **13** Of jazz etc.: strongly rhythmical and emotional. Opp. COOL *a.* 5. Orig. *US.* E20. **14** Of a motor vehicle or aircraft: fast or powerful, esp. in relation to its size. *colloq.* M20.

1 J. CONRAD A grey rock which smokes like a hot cinder after a shower. J. STEINBECK The hot sun beat on the earth. DAY LEWIS We were there during the phenomenally hot July of 1911. b E. O'BRIEN He had brought her some croissants hot from the oven. 3 R. BRAUTIGAN He ran around the house, . . with the dog hot after him. E. JONG 'Why are you a feminist?' I . . asked a guy . . who is very hot for the movement. JILLY COOPER The middle classes are obsessively hot on table manners. b F. M. COLBY A hot young satyr in pursuit of nymphs. *Music Week* No 'hot' videos required. c T. MORRISON More words were exchanged, hot words and dark. 4 DEFOE The Plague grows hot in the City. A. BURGESS The Stage Society was able, after months of hot argument, to agree. 5 H. DAY I had some curry . . which was so hot that it well nigh took the skin off my tongue. 6a C. PHILLIPS He began to feel hot as the climb became harder. b J. PURCELL Violent Hot Pains in the Lower-Belly. A. SILLITOE His uniform was too hot, and he unbuttoned the tunic. 7 G. F. KENNAN The place was well selected from the standpoint of making a getaway if things became hotter. 9 C. MCCULLERS His socks and tie were a hot red. 10 *Daily Express* The Deutsches have some pretty hot snipers. W. BOYD A pair of opera glasses . . that I use to see better—my eyesight's not too hot. 11b *Standard* Eddie Murphy has firmly established himself as America's hottest box office comedian. *Hairdo Ideas* One of the hottest trends this season are hair extensions. 12a B. SCHULBERG The idea is so hot I don't want to give anybody time to steal it. N. BARBER If you get onto something hot . . phone me.

Phrases etc.: **a bit hot** *Austral. slang* somewhat unreasonable. *blow hot and cold*: see BLOW *v.*[1] *boiling hot*: see BOILING *adv. get it hot* (*and strong*): see GET *v. give it hot* (*and strong*) *to*: see GIVE *v.* **go hot and cold** feel alternately hot and cold owing to fear etc. **hot and bothered** in a state of exasperated agitation. **hot and hot** *arch.* (of food) served piping hot. *hot dark matter*: see *dark matter* s.v. DARK *a.* **hot on the heels of** in close pursuit of. **hot under the collar** feeling anger, resentment, or embarrassment. *like a cat on hot bricks*: see CAT *n.*[1] **not so** (or **too**) **hot** *colloq.* only mediocre, indifferent in performance, health, etc. *piping hot*: see PIPING *adv. red-hot*: see RED *a.* **too hot to hold one** (of a place) not safe to remain in (because of past misconduct etc.). *white-hot*: see WHITE *a.*

Special collocations & *comb.*: **hot air** *fig.* (*colloq.*) pretentious or unsubstantial statements or claims. **hot-air** *a.* of or making use of heated air (esp. in *hot-air balloon*). **hot bath**: in hot water. **hot blast**: of heated air forced into a furnace. **hot-blooded** *a.* ardent, passionate. **hot bottle** = *hot-water bottle* below. **hotbrain** *arch.* = HOTHEAD. **hot-brained** *a.* (*arch.*) = HOTHEADED. **hot button** *US colloq.* (*a*) an emotionally or politically sensitive topic or issue; (*b*) a commercially attractive feature of a new product. **hot cake** (*a*) *US* a griddle-cake; (*b*) *go* or *sell like hot cakes*, be sold extremely fast, be a popular commodity. **hot cathode**: heated to emit electrons thermionically. *hot chisel*: see CHISEL *n.*[1] 1. **hot cockles** (*obs.* exc. *dial.*) a rustic game in which one player is blindfolded and has to guess which of the others struck him or her. *hot coppers*: see COPPER *n.*[1] 6. *hot cross bun*: see CROSS-. **hot cupboard** an airing cupboard; a cupboard in which crockery is made warm for a meal. **hot-dipped** *a.* coated in metal, either by being dipped in the molten metal or by being dipped hot in a bath of liquid. **hot flash**, **flush** a feeling of feverish heat, esp. as a menopausal symptom. *hot* GOSPELLER. **hot key** *Computing*: that initiates a complex operation. **hot laboratory**: designed for the safe handling of radioactive material. **hot line** a direct exclusive telecommunications link, esp. for use by heads of government in emergencies. **hot-metal** *a.* (*Printing*, chiefly *Hist.*) using metal type or slugs cast by a (Linotype, Monotype, etc.) composing-machine. **hot money** capital transferred from one country to another for the sake of high interest rates or to avoid the effects of currency devaluation. **hot pants** (*a*) *US slang* an uncontrollable sexual passion (esp. in *have* (*got*) *hot pants for*); (*b*) *slang* a sexually insatiable person; (*c*) brief shorts worn by young women, esp. as a fashion in the early 1970s. **hotplate** (*a*) a heated flat surface on a stove or electric cooker; (*b*) a low flat-topped portable device for keeping food warm. *hot potato*: see POTATO *n.* **hot-press** *n.* & *v.* (*a*) *n.* a press of glazed boards and hot metal plates for smoothing paper or cloth or making plywood; (*b*) *v.t.* press (paper etc.) in a hot-press. **hot-presser** a person who hot-presses paper etc. **hot pursuit** close pursuit, *spec.* of a criminal etc. across an international frontier. **hot rod** (*a*) a motor vehicle specially modified to give high power and speed; (*b*) = *hot-rodder* below. **hot-rod** *v.i.* drive a hot rod. **hot-rodder** a driver of a hot rod. **hot seat** *slang* (*a*) *US* the electric chair; (*b*) *fig.* a position of difficult responsibility. *hot-shoe*: see SHOE *n.* **hot-short** *a.* (of metal) brittle in its hot state (opp. *cold-short* adj.). **hot-shortness** hot-short quality or condition. **hot shower**: in hot water. **hot spot** (*a*) a small area in a surface or body that is at a higher temperature than its surroundings; (*b*) a lively nightclub; (*c*) a place of danger or military activity. **hot spring** a spring of naturally hot water. **hot-stove** *a.* (*N. Amer.*) designating a discussion about a favourite sport, esp. baseball, carried on during the off-season. **hot stuff** (*a*) sexually explicit material; (*b*) (a designation of) a woman reputed to be highly sexed; (*c*) (a designation of) a person or thing of outstanding quality. **hot tap**: dispensing hot water. **hot tear** *Metall.* a split produced in a casting as the hot metal cools. **hot-tempered** *a.* impulsively angry, short-tempered. **hot tip** *colloq.* an unusually reliable tip for the winner of a race etc. **hot tub** a wooden tub, freq. accommodating several people, filled with hot aerated water for recreation or physical therapy. **hot tube** in some early internal-combustion engines, a closed tube which projected from the cylinder and was heated externally by a flame, so that it ignited the mixture forced into it during the compression stroke. **hot war** an open war, involving active hostilities. **hot water** *fig.* (*colloq.*) trouble, difficulty (chiefly in *in, into, hot water*). **hot-water** *a.* using or containing heated water; *hot-water bottle* or (*US*) *bag*, a container, now usu. made of rubber, filled with hot water, esp. to warm a bed. **hot well** (*a*) = *hot spring* above; (*b*) a reservoir in a condensing steam engine. **hot wind**: heated by passing over plains or prairies. **hot-wire** *a.* operated by the expansion of heated wire. **hot-work** *v.t.* work (metal), e.g. by rolling, forging, etc., while it is still hot and above the temperature at which recrystallization takes place.

hotly *adv.* LME. **hotness** *n.* M16. **hottish** *a.* L16.

hot /hɒt/ *v.* Infl. **-tt-**. [OE *hātian*, f. *hāt* HOT *a.*: later formed afresh from the adj.] **1** *v.i.* Become hot or (*fig.*) intense, lively, dangerous, etc. Now only foll. by *up*. OE. **2** *v.t.* Make (esp. precooked food) hot; heat, warm up. Now usu. foll. by *up*. Now *colloq.* ME. **3** *v.t.* Foll. by *up*: make intense, lively, (unpleasantly) exciting, etc. E20. **4 a** *v.t.* Increase the power of (a car, engine, etc.) so that it is capable of higher speeds. Usu. in *pass.* E20. **b** *v.i.* Drive recklessly in a stolen car. Chiefly as *hotting* vbl n. L20.

1 E. MANNIN Immediately the day hotted up with the return of the sun. *Guardian* The . . takeover battle for control of John Waddington will hot up this week. 2 J. GALSWORTHY Let me hot up your stew. 3 J. CAREW The drummerboys hotted up the rhythm. *Guardian* The need to avoid actions which would 'hot up this cod war'.

¶Intrans. use long obs. bef. reintroduction in 20.

hot /hɒt/ *adv.* [OE *hāte* = OS *hēto*, OHG *heizo*: afterwards levelled with the adj.] Hotly; with or to great heat; eagerly, violently, angrily, etc.

SHAKES. *3 Hen. VI* The sun shines hot. BYRON Fast and hot Against them pour'd the ceaseless shot.

hotbed /ˈhɒtbɛd/ *n.* E17. [f. HOT *a.* + BED *n.*] **1** A bed of earth heated by fermented manure, for raising or forcing plants. E17. **2** *fig.* A place that favours the rapid growth of a (usu. undesirable) condition etc. M18. **3** A bed in a doss-house etc. which is slept in by two or more people in shifts; a doss-house. *US slang.* M20.

2 M. COX The monasteries were not hotbeds of crime and luxury.

hotch /hɒtʃ/ *v.* & *n.* *Sc.* & *north.* LME. [Corresp. to Du. *hotsen*, *hossen* to jog, to jolt, MHG & G dial. *hotzen* move up and down.] **A** *v.* **1** *v.i.* Jerk up and down; move forward in short leaps. Also, move impatiently, fidget. LME. **2** *v.i.* Swarm (*with*). L18. **3** *v.t.* Shake with a jerky motion. E19.

2 A. GRAY These nights the sky was just hotching with stars.

B *n.* A jerk, a jolt. E18.

hotcha /ˈhɒtʃə/ *a.* *slang* (now *rare*). M20. [Fanciful extension of HOT *a.*] **1** (Sexually) attractive. Also as *int.*, expr. enthusiastic approval. M20. **2** = HOT *a.* 13. M20.

Hotchkiss /ˈhɒtʃkɪs/ *a.* L19. [B. B. *Hotchkiss* (1826–85), US inventor.] Designating a revolving cannon, types of rifle, etc., invented by B. B. Hotchkiss, and a machine-gun developed by his successors.

hotchpot /ˈhɒtʃpɒt/ *n.* & *a.* LME. [AN, (O)Fr. *hochepot*, f. *hocher* to shake, prob. f. LG, + POT *n.*[1] Cf. next, HODGEPODGE.] **A** *n.* **1** = HOTCHPOTCH *n.* 1. LME. **2** = HOTCHPOTCH *n.* 2. LME. **3** *Eng. Law.* The reunion and blending together of properties in order to secure equality of division, esp. as practised in certain cases in the distribution of the property of an intestate parent. M16. **B** *attrib.* or as *adj.* = HOTCHPOTCH *a.* L16.

hotchpotch /ˈhɒtʃpɒtʃ/ *n.*, *a.*, & *v.* LME. [Alt., by rhyming assim., of prec. Cf. HODGEPODGE *n.*] **A** *n.* **1** A mixture of heterogeneous things, a confused medley. LME. **2** A dish containing a number of different ingredients; *spec.* a mixed stew, esp. of mutton and various vegetables. L16. **3** = HOTCHPOT *n.* 3. E17.

1 H. CARPENTER This final fantasy, with its . . hotchpotch of gnostic religions and sinister folklore.

B *attrib.* or as *adj.* Of the nature or composition of a hotchpotch; heterogeneous, confused, disorderly. L16.

C *v.t.* Make a hotchpotch of, mix up. L16.

hot dog /hɒt ˈdɒg/ *a.* & *n. phr.* Also **hot-dog**. L19. [f. HOT *a.* + DOG *n.*] **A** *adj. phr.* Outstandingly good, first-rate. Also as *int.*, expr. delighted approval. *N. Amer. slang.* L19. **B** *n. phr.* **1** A person outstandingly proficient in a sport etc., *esp.* one who gives a flamboyant display of his or her skill. *N. Amer. slang.* E20. **2** A hot frankfurter sandwiched in a soft roll. E20.

hotel /həʊˈtɛl, əʊ-/ *n.* Also **hôtel** /otɛl (*pl. same*)/. M17. [Fr. *hôtel*, later form of *hostel*: see HOSTEL *n.*] **1** In France and French-speaking countries: a *hotel-Dieu* /djø/, a hospital. M17. **b** *hotel de ville* /də vil/, a town-hall. M18. **c** *hotel garni* /garni/, a lodging-house providing bed and breakfast only; also, a furnished apartment. L18. **d** *hotel particulier* /partikylje/, a large privately owned town house or block of flats. M20. **2** A large town mansion of an (orig. French) aristocrat or person of position. Now only *Hist.* & in names of surviving mansions. L17. **3** An establishment, esp. of a comfortable or luxurious kind, where paying visitors are provided with accommodation, meals, and other services. M18. **4** A public house or other place serving alcoholic drink. *Canad.*, *Austral.*, & *NZ colloq.* E19.

3 *family hotel, private hotel, residential hotel, temperance hotel*, etc.

hoteldom *n.* the world of hotels E20.

hotelier /həʊˈtɛlɪeɪ, -ɪə/ *n.* E20. [Fr. *hôtelier*: see HOSTELER.] A person who owns or runs a hotel or group of hotels.

hotfoot /ˈhɒtfʊt/ *n.* M19. [Sense 1 f. the adv. Sense 2 f. HOT *a.* + FOOT *n.*] **1** Prompt or rapid action or movement; a quick escape. Chiefly in *do a hotfoot, give the hotfoot to. US slang.* M19. **2** An act of beating a person on the bare soles or of inserting a lighted match between the soles and uppers of the shoes, either to rouse from sleep or (in the latter case) as a practical joke. E20.

hotfoot /ˈhɒtfʊt, hɒtˈfʊt/ *adv.*, *v.*, & *a.* ME. [f. HOT *a.* + FOOT *n.*] **A** *adv.* With eager or rapid pace; in great haste. ME. **B** *v.i.* & *t.* (w. *it*). Go hotfoot, hasten. L19. **C** *adj.* Travelling hotfoot or in haste. E20.

hothead /ˈhɒthɛd/ *n.* M17. [f. HOT *a.* + HEAD *n.*] A hotheaded person.

hotheaded /hɒtˈhɛdɪd/ *a.* M17. [f. HOT *a.* + HEAD *n.* + -ED[2].] Having an impetuous or fiery temperament; impulsive, headstrong.

hotheadedly *adv.* L19. **hotheadedness** *n.* M19.

hothouse /ˈhɒthaʊs/ *n.*, *a.*, & *v.* E16. [f. HOT *a.* + HOUSE *n.*[1]] **A** *n.* †**1** A bath-house with hot baths, vapour-baths, etc. Also, a brothel. E16–M18. **2** A heated chamber or building for drying something. M16. †**3** A hospital for slaves etc. on a plantation. *W. Indies.* E18–M19. **4** A heated building with a glass roof and sides for growing plants out of season or in a colder climate. M18.

B *adj.* Characteristic of or raised in a hothouse. Freq. *fig.*, tender from overprotection; excessively artificial. E19.

J. S. MILL Modern German art . . appears to me a feeble, hothouse product. *Listener* Opera will never cease to be a hothouse plant in this country.

C *v.t.* Raise (as) in a hothouse; raise in an artificial environment; force the development of. M19.

A. S. NEILL Every child has been hothoused into an adult long before he has reached adulthood.

†**hoti** *n.* Pl. **hoties**. M17. [Gk = that, because.] **1** = DIOTI. Only in M17. **2** A statement of fact, a thing asserted. M17–M18.

Hotnot /ˈhɒtnɒt/ *n.* *S. Afr. slang* (*derog.* & usu. considered *racially offensive*). E20. [Afk. & Du., contr. of HOTTENTOT.] A Coloured person (COLOURED *a.* 4b).

hotpot /ˈhɒtpɒt/ *n.* L17. [f. HOT *a.* + POT *n.*[1]] **1** A hot drink composed of ale and spirits, or ale sweetened and spiced. *dial.* L17. **2** A stew of meat or fish and potatoes (and often other vegetables). Also, an oriental dish consisting of thinly-sliced meat, vegetables, etc., dipped in boiling soup by the diner. M19.

2 *Lancashire hotpot, Mongolian hotpot.*

hotshot /ˈhɒtʃɒt/ *n.* & *a.* L16. [f. HOT *a.* + SHOT *n.*[1]] **A** *n.* †**1** A reckless shooter with a firearm; a hothead. L16–M17. †**2** A ball of clay and coal, used as fuel. Also, a type of incendiary shell or bomb. L17–L19. **3** A fast or express goods train; a fast motor vehicle, aeroplane, etc. *US slang.* E20. **4** An important or exceptionally able person; a person who has gained sudden prominence. *colloq.* M20. **5** An exceptionally good shot or aim in a sport, as snooker, basketball, etc. *colloq.* M20.

4 S. BELLOW He's on the make everywhere and cultivates all the Chicago hot-shots. *Globe & Mail* (*Toronto*) He wasn't a showoff and didn't perceive himself to be a hotshot.

B *attrib.* or as *adj.* **1** Of a goods train etc.: fast, express, non-stop. *US slang.* M20. **2** Important; expert, exceptionally able; suddenly prominent. *colloq.* M20.

2 A. MILLER Let's face it: he's no hot-shot selling man. W. WHARTON I go to all the museums in Paris. I look at every hotshot object they have to show me.

hotspur /ˈhɒtspəː, -spə/ *n.* & *a.* LME. [f. HOT *a.* + SPUR *n.*[1]] **A** *n.* A person whose spur is hot with impetuous riding; *transf.* an impetuous or reckless person. Chiefly as the nickname of Sir Henry Percy (1364–1403), English rebel. LME. **B** *adj.* Fiery, impetuous. L16.

hotsy-totsy /hɒtsɪˈtɒtsi/ *a.* *slang* (orig. *US*). E20. [Fanciful formation f. HOT *a.*, by Billie De Beck, Amer. cartoonist.] Satisfactory, just fine.

Hottentot /ˈhɒt(ə)ntɒt/ *n.* & *a.* Now usu. considered *offensive* in reference to the people. L17. [Du., prob. orig. a repetitive formula in a Nama dancing-song, transferred by Dutch seamen to the people themselves.] **A** *n.* Pl. same, **-s**. **1** A member of the Nama people. L17. **2** An ignorant or savage person. Now *rare.* E18. **3** Any of several southern African marine fishes of the genus *Pachymetopon*, esp. *P. blochii.* M19. **4** The language of the Nama people, characterized by click consonants. M19.

B *attrib.* or as *adj.* Of or pertaining to the Nama people or their language. E18.

Special collocations & phrases: **Hottentot bread** = *elephant's foot* s.v. ELEPHANT. **Hottentot cherry** a southern African evergreen shrub or small tree, *Maurocenia frangularia*, of the spindle tree family. **Hottentot fig** a succulent plant, *Carpobrotus edulis*, of the mesembryanthemum family. **Hottentot fish** = sense A.3 above. **Hottentot god** a praying mantis (formerly venerated by the Nama people). **Hottentot's bread** = *Hottentot bread* above.

Hottentot's god = *Hottentot god* above. **Hottentot's tea** = *Hottentot tea* below. **Hottentot tea** a shrubby everlasting, *Helichrysum orbiculare*, infused as a drink by the Nama people.

hotter /ˈhɒtə/ *v.i. Sc.* & *north.* L18. [Perh. rel. to MDu. *hotten*, Flem. *hotteren* shake up: see -ER⁵.] 1 Vibrate, shake, rattle, clatter; totter. L18. 2 Cluster in a confused mass, swarm. E19.

hottie /ˈhɒti/ *n. colloq.* Also **hotty**. M20. [f. HOT *a.* + -IE, -Y⁶.] A hot-water bottle.

houbara /huːˈbɑːrə/ *n.* E19. [(mod.L f.) Arab. *ḥubārā*.] A kind of bustard, *Chlamydotis* (formerly *Houbara*) *undulata*, found in N. Africa and the Middle East.

Houdan /ˈhuːd(ə)n/ *n.* L19. [A town in the French department of Seine-et-Oise.] (A bird of) a French breed of fowl marked by black and white plumage, a heavy crest, and prolific laying.

Houdini /huːˈdiːni/ *a.* & *n.* E20. [Harry *Houdini*, professional name of Erich Weiss (1874–1926), US escapologist.] A *adj.* Characteristic or worthy of Houdini; involving ingenious escape. E20. B *n.* An ingenious escape; a person etc. clever at escaping. M20.

hougan *n.* var. of HOUNGAN.

hough /hɒk, hɒx/ *n.* Long chiefly *Sc.* See also HOCK *n.*² [OE *hōh* f. Gmc, shortened as 1st elem. of *hōhsinu* (= *hough-sinew* below). Cf. HOE *n.*¹] 1 Orig., a person's heel. Later, (the part of the thigh adjacent to) the hollow part behind a person's knee-joint. OE. 2 = HOCK *n.*² 1. LME. 3 A joint of meat consisting of the part extending from the hock some way up the leg. Cf. HOCK *n.*² 2. LME.

Comb.: †**hough-sinew** *n.* & *v.* [corresp. to ON *hásin*] (*a*) *n.* a person's hamstring, an animal's Achilles tendon; (*b*) *v.t.* hamstring.

hough /hɒk/ *v.t.* LME. [f. the n.] Disable by cutting a hamstring or hamstrings; hamstring.

hougher *n.* a person who hamstrings someone or something, *esp.* (*Ir. Hist.*) one who hamstrings cattle as an agrarian outrage: L16.

houghmagandie /hɒkməˈgandi, hɒx-/ *n.* Chiefly *Sc.* (now *rare*). Also **-gandy**. L17. [Fanciful formation, perh. f. HOUGH *n.* + CANTY *a.*] Fornication.

houhere /ˈhəʊhɛri/ *n.* L19. [Maori, f. *hou* bind together + *here* tie.] Any of several small New Zealand trees constituting the genus *Hoheria*, of the mallow family, whose bark supplies a fibre resembling raffia.

hoummos, houmous *ns.* vars. of HUMMUS.

hound /haʊnd/ *n.*¹ [OE *hund* = OFris., OS *hund* (Du. *hond*), OHG *hunt* (G *Hund*), ON *hundr*, Goth. *hunds*, f. Gmc, f. IE base repr. also by (O)Ir. *cú* (genit. *con*), Gk *kuōn* (genit. *kunos*).] 1 *gen.* A dog. *arch.* exc. *Sc.* OE. b *transf.* A detested, mean, or contemptible person. OE. 2 A dog used for hunting, *esp.* one that tracks by scent; *spec.* a foxhound. ME. b *transf.* A player in the game of hare and hounds who follows the 'scent' laid down. Cf. HARE *n.*¹ 2b. M19. 3 Orig. more fully †*hound-fish*. A small shark, a dogfish. Now only w. specifying wd (see below). LME. 4 The long-tailed duck, *Clangula hyemalis*, with a cry thought to resemble that of a pack of hounds. *Canad.* E17. 5 (As 2nd elem. of comb.) A person keen in the pursuit of the thing specified. Esp. *news-hound*. E20.

1 LONGFELLOW A traveller, by the faithful hound, Half-buried in the snow was found. b BROWNING Miserable hound! This comes of temporising, as I said! 2 *bloodhound, deerhound, foxhound, greyhound, otter-hound, Walker hound, Welsh hound*, etc. **the hounds** a pack of foxhounds; *follow the hounds*: see FOLLOW *v.*; *run (or hold) with the hare and hunt with the hounds*: see HARE *n.*¹ **ride to hounds** go foxhunting on horseback. 3 *nurse-hound*: see NURSE *n.*² *rough hound*: see ROUGH *a.* *smooth hound*: see SMOOTH *a.* & *adv.* 5 *City Limits* Camden Lock offers the best opportunity for the equipment hound.

Comb.: **hound-dog** *US colloq.* = sense 2 above; **hound-fish** †(*a*) see sense 3 above; (*b*) any of several garfish of the genus *Tylosurus*; †**houndsfoot** *n.* & *a.* (characteristic of) a rascal; **hound's-tongue** any of several plants of the genus *Cynoglossum*, of the borage family, esp. *C. officinale*, with dull red flowers and usu. bristly stems; also called *dog's-tongue*; **houndstooth** *n.* & *a.* (of) a check pattern with notched corners suggestive of a canine tooth.

houndish *a.* of the nature of or characteristic of a hound LME.

hound /haʊnd/ *n.*² L15. [Alt. (with parasitic *-d*, as in SOUND *n.*²) of earlier HUNE: infl. by HOUND *n.*¹] 1 *Naut.* Each of one or more wooden projections below a masthead, supporting (in smaller vessels) the shrouds by which a mast is stayed laterally, or formerly (in larger ships) the trestle-trees. Usu. in *pl.* L15. 2 Each of two or more wooden bars connecting the forecarriage of a springless carriage. *dial.* & *US.* M19.

hound /haʊnd/ *v.t.* LME. [f. HOUND *n.*¹] †1 *refl.* Of a dog: copulate. (Foll. by *on* the bitch.) Only in LME. 2 Hunt (as) with hounds; *spec.* (*US*) track or drive (a deer etc.) with hounds until it is brought under the hunter's gun. E16. 3 Set on (a dog); *transf.* incite (a person) to the attack. M16. 4 Harass or persecute relentlessly; drive *away*, *out*, etc., by persistent harassment. L16.

3 J. L. MOTLEY It was idle .. to hound the rabble upon them as tyrants and mischief-makers. 4 HARPER LEE Whoever breaks it is hounded from our midst as unfit to live with. R. INGALLS He was fed up with being hounded by reporters.

hounding /ˈhaʊndɪŋ/ *n.* M19. [f. HOUND *n.*² + -ING³, perh. after BUNTING *n.*², COAMING.] *Naut.* The lower part of a mast, below the hounds.

houngan /ˈhuːŋg(ə)n/ *n.* Also **hougan** /ˈhuːg(ə)n/ E20. [Fon *hun* vodun deity + *ga* chief.] A voodoo priest.

houp-la /ˈhuːplɑː/ *int.* & *n.* Also **hoop-la**. L19. [Fr. *houp-là!*, f. *houp* int. + *là* there.] A *int.* Accompanying or drawing attention to a quick or sudden movement. L19. B *n.* An exclamation of 'houp-la!'; *slang* a commotion, ballyhoo, pretentious nonsense. L19.

houppelande /ˈhuːplənd/ *n.* Also †**houpland**. LME. [Fr., of uncertain origin: cf. Sp. *hopalanda*.] *Hist.* A medieval tunic or gown, freq. with full sleeves and a long train.

hour /ˈaʊə/ *n.* ME. [AN *ure*, OFr. *ore*, *eure* (mod. *heure*) f. L *hora* f. Gk = season, time of day, hour.] 1 A space of time containing sixty minutes; the twenty-fourth part of a civil day. Formerly (more fully *planetary* or *unequal hour*), the twelfth part of a natural day, whatever its length. ME. b In *pl.* w. preceding numeral, denoting the number of hours that have elapsed between midnight and the following noon or between noon and the following midnight, and so indicating the time of day (chiefly *Sc.*, *arch.*). In recent use (chiefly *Mil.*), indicating the number of hours and minutes (usu. expressed in figures) past midnight, as measured on the twenty-four hour clock. LME. c The distance the sun moves above the horizon in an hour; the height of the sun a particular time after sunrise. *US.* M17. d The distance one can travel in an hour by a (stated or implied) means. Also, (as 2nd elem. of comb.) the amount of energy or work of the specified kind produced or done in an hour. L18. 2 A short indefinite period of the day, more or less than an hour; *esp.* one set aside for a specified activity. Freq. in *pl.* ME. b In *pl.* The part of a day during which a person has to work. E19. c In *pl.* The part of a day when a shop etc. is open, a doctor available for consultation, etc. Esp. in *after, during, out of, hours*. M19. d A scheduled radio or TV feature, orig. an hour long. Esp. in *children's hour* (see CHILD *n.*). M20. 3 The point of time at which each of the twelve or twenty-four hours measured by a timepiece ends and the next begins (in general or of each of a given succession of hours); the time on the clock; *gen.* any definite point in a day. ME. b In *pl.* One's habitual time of getting up or (esp.) going to bed. Usu. w. specifying adj., as *early, late, regular*. E17. 4 A particular moment when an event etc. occurs; *spec.* the moment of one's death. Also, *the* time to act etc. ME. b *The* present occasion, *the* time in question. Chiefly in *of the hour*. L19. 5 *Eccl.* In *pl.* The prayers or offices appointed to be said at certain stated times of day allotted to prayer. Also (usu. treated as *sing.*), a book containing these (more fully *book of hours*). ME. 6 *Mythol.* (**H-**.) Female divinities presiding over the changes of the seasons. E17. 7 *Astron.* & *Geogr.* An angular unit of right ascension or longitude equal to 1/24 of a great circle (15 degrees). L18.

1 SCOTT FITZGERALD We sped along .. at fifty miles an hour. M. DRABBLE A couple of hours of any party is enough for me. b J. K. HUNTER When it cam' near to ten hours at e'en. *Punch* It is 21.00 hours on the last day of our month's training. c M. H. NORRIS The sun was an hour high. d *New Yorker* Two years ago, .. I moved to a farm, an hour from Canada. *ampère-hour, horsepower-hour, man-hour, watt-hour*, etc. 2 E. DARWIN In dreams, we cannot compare them with our previous knowledge .., as we do in our waking hours. J. K. JEROME The boy does not .. prepare for the French or English hour any exhibition of homely wit. *lunch hour, office hours, school hours*, etc. b J. S. MILL A reduction of hours without any diminution of wages. 3 J. BUCHAN At the moment the clock .. struck the hour of seven. J. MARQUAND I looked at my watch and found .. that the hour was getting on to half-past eight. DAY LEWIS This took place every morning at a given hour. b R. B. SHERIDAN Their regular hours stupefy me—not a fiddle nor a card after eleven! 4 LD MACAULAY To hasten the hour of his own return. G. B. SHAW The law failed them in their hour of need. E. O'NEILL He knew .. his hour was near. b J. RUSKIN There are good books for the hour, and good ones for all time.

Phrases: **at all hours** at every hour of the day, no matter how early or late. **by the hour** for many hours at a time. *canonical hour*: see CANONICAL *a.* 1. ELEVENTH-*hour*. *evil hour*: see EVIL *a.* FORTY *hours*. *happy hour*: see HAPPY *a.* *one's finest hour*: see FINE *a.* **on the hour** (*a*) exactly at the hour named; (*b*) at the very beginning of every hour within a specified period. *planetary hour*: see sense 1 above. *small hours*: see SMALL *a.* *solar hour*: see SOLAR *a.*¹ *the wee (small) hours*: see WEE *a.* *the witching hour*: see WITCHING 2. **till all hours** until very late in the evening. *unequal hour*: see sense 1 above. *wait the hour*: see WAIT *v.* *zero hour*: see ZERO *n.* 5.

Comb.: **hour-angle** the angular distance measured westwards along the celestial equator from the observer's meridian to the hour-circle of a particular celestial object; **hour-circle** (*a*) any great circle of the celestial sphere passing through the poles; *esp.* any of 24 such marked on a globe etc. at intervals of one hour of right ascension; (*b*) a graduated circle on a globe, telescope, etc., marked with divisions of one hour of right ascension or longitude; **hour-hand** the short hand of a clock or watch, which indicates the hours; **hour-long** *a.* & *adv.* (*a*) *adj.* lasting for one hour; (*b*) *adv.* for one hour.

houred *a.* †(*a*) *rare* definite; (*b*) (as 2nd elem. of comb.) of the specified number of hours: L15.

hourglass /ˈaʊəglɑːs/ *n.* & *a.* E16. [f. prec. + GLASS *n.*] A *n.* A device for measuring time, consisting of two glass etc. bulbs joined by a narrow neck, the upper bulb containing grains of sand which travel into the lower bulb in the space of an hour; *fig.* (*arch.*) the space of an hour, a strictly finite period of time. E16. B *attrib.* or as *adj.* Shaped like an hourglass, constricted or narrowed in the middle. E19.

houri /ˈhʊəri/ *n.* M18. [Fr. f. Pers. *ḥūrī* f. Arab. *ḥūr* pl. of *ʼaḥwar*, fem. *ḥawrāʼ* having eyes with marked contrast of white and black.] Any of the virgins of the Muslim paradise, promised as wives to believers; *transf.* a voluptuously beautiful woman.

hourly /ˈaʊəli/ *a.* E16. [f. HOUR *n.* + -LY¹.] 1 Of an hour's duration; very brief. *rare.* E16. 2 Occurring, performed, etc., every hour; paid etc. by the hour. M16.

hourly /ˈaʊəli/ *adv.* L15. [f. HOUR *n.* + -LY².] 1 Every hour, by the hour. Also, very frequently, continually. L15. †2 For the duration of an hour, briefly, quickly. E–M16.

1 GIBBON The barbarians were hourly expected at the gates of Rome.

house /haʊs/ *n.*¹ & *a.* [OE *hūs* = OFris., OS, OHG (Du. *huis*, G *Haus*), ON *hús*, Goth. *-hūs* (only in *gudhūs* temple), f. Gmc: ult. origin unkn.] A *n.* Pl. **houses** /ˈhaʊzɪz/. 1 A building for human habitation, a dwelling, a home; *spec.* a self-contained unit having a ground floor and one or more upper storeys (as opp. to a bungalow, flat, etc.). OE. b A part of a building occupied by one tenant or family. *Sc.* & *dial.*

OE. c The living-room of a house. *dial.* L17. **2** (As 2nd elem. of comb. or with other specification.) A building accommodating or frequented by people that is other than an ordinary private dwelling; a building or place where a specified occupation, activity, etc., is pursued, or where refreshment of a specified kind is provided. OE. **b** *spec.* A building occupied by a religious community; a monastery, a convent; the religious community itself. ME. **c** A university college. Now *rare* exc. in *the House*, Christ Church, Oxford, *Peterhouse*, St Peter's College, Cambridge. M16. **d** A building in which a legislative or deliberative assembly meets; the assembly itself; *the* British House of Commons. M16. **e** A place of business; a business establishment, a firm; *spec.* a printing or publishing firm, a couture or fashion establishment. Also, *the* Stock Exchange. L16. **f** A building where public refreshment is provided; an inn, a tavern, a public house. Also as *int.*, demanding service at a bar, dining-table, etc. M17. **g** A theatre, a cinema; a performance or showing (usu. specified, as *first*, *second*, etc.) in a theatre or cinema; the audience in a theatre or cinema or at a (specified) performance or showing. M17. **h** A brothel. E19. **i** A boarding-house of a public school; a division of a school for organizational purposes, as for competitive games; the pupils in such a boarding-house or division. M19. **j** An establishment for gambling, a casino; the management of such an establishment (against which bets are placed). E20. **3** A place of worship (considered as the home of a god); a temple, a church. OE. **4** The natural habitation of an animal, a den, a burrow, a nest; *esp.* the shell of a snail, tortoise, etc. OE. **5** *fig.* & *gen.* A place of abode or rest. OE. **6** *collect.* The inhabitants of a house; a household, a family. OE. **7** The line of descent of a family; a dynasty, a lineage, *esp.* one of high rank or fame. OE. **8** (Chiefly as 2nd elem. of comb.) A building for the keeping of animals or plants or for the storage or protection of something; a building for the production of something specified. ME. **9** *Astrol.* **a** Each of the twelve divisions of the ecliptic fixed with respect to the horizon. Also *mundane house*. LME. **b** Any of the signs of the zodiac considered as the seat of the greatest influence of a particular planet. Cf. MANSION 5. LME. **10** †**a** Each square of a chessboard. M16–E19. **b** *Curling.* The space within the outermost circle drawn round either tee. L19. **11** Bingo, lotto, tombola, esp. as played for money; (the call announcing or the prize for) the winning of the game. E20. **12** A form of popular dance music characterized by the use of synthesized sounds and a fast beat. L20.

1 J. STEINBECK The rich people who lived in the stone and plaster houses of the town. *apartment house, council house, country house, doll's house, farmhouse, manor-house, mansion-house, town house, Wendy house,* etc. 2 *alehouse, almshouse, bakehouse, bath-house, bawdy-house, boarding-house, coffee-house, clubhouse, court-house, custom-house, doss-house, dwelling-house, eating-house, guardhouse, guest-house, lodging-house, madhouse, meeting-house, opera-house, playhouse, slaughterhouse, summer-house, wash-house, whore-house, workhouse,* etc. **d** *House of Commons, House of Delegates, House of Keys, House of Lords, House of Representatives, Lower House, Upper House,* etc. **f** J. P. DONLEAVY Can't serve you, sir, rules of the house, you've had enough to drink. **g** J. AGATE The play . . is being played to packed houses. 4 J. ALDAY Snayles . . beare with them their houses easely on their backes. 5 W. COWPER A heavenly mind May be indifferent to her house of clay. SIR W. SCOTT The peaceful house of death. 6 OED The whole house was down with influenza. 7 J. RUSKIN To read the shields, and remember the stories, of the great houses of England. *House of Hanover, House of Stuart,* etc. 8 *coach-house, coal-house, doghouse, glasshouse, greenhouse, henhouse, hothouse, ice house, lighthouse, outhouse, powerhouse, storehouse, warehouse, wheel-house,* etc.

Phrases: (**as**) **safe as houses** perfectly safe. *big house*: see BIG *a.* **bow down** (or **worship**) **in the house of Rimmon** [after *2 Kings* 5:18] pay lip-service to a principle; sacrifice one's principles for the sake of conformity. *bring down the house*: see BRING *v.* **clean house** *US* do housework; *fig.* wipe out corruption, inefficiency, etc. **daughter of the house** a daughter of the family. *dead house*: see DEAD *a.* etc. *disorderly house*: see DISORDERLY *a. free house*: see FREE *a. full house*: see FULL *a.* **go** (**all**) **round the houses** *fig.* beat about the bush; arrive at the point in a roundabout way. *great house*: see GREAT *a.* HALFWAY *house.* **house and home** *emphatic* home (*eat out of house and home*: see EAT *v.*). **house of call** *arch.* a place where carriers call for commissions, where a person may be heard of, etc.; a house one visits regularly. **house of cards** a structure built of playing-cards balanced together; *fig.* an insubstantial or precarious structure, an insecure or overambitious scheme. *house of correction*: see CORRECTION 3. **house of God** a church, a temple. **house of ill fame** or **repute** *arch.* a brothel. **house of office** *arch.* a privy, a lavatory. **house of prayer** a church, a temple. *house of* RELIGION. *house of the ascendant*: see ASCENDANT *n.* 1. *House of Windsor*: see WINDSOR *n.* 2. *Houses of Parliament*: see PARLIAMENT *n.* **keep a House** secure the presence of enough members for a quorum in the House of Commons. **keep house** maintain, provide for, or manage a household. **keep** (**to**) **the** or **one's house** not go outdoors, esp. because of illness. **like a house on fire** vigorously, fast; successfully, excellently. **make a House** = *keep a House* above. *man of the house*: see MAN *n. move house*: see MOVE *v.* **on the house** (esp. of a drink) at the publican's or management's expense, free. **open house** general hospitality (*keep open house*, provide this). **play house** play at being a family in its home. PUBLIC HOUSE. **put** (or **set**) **one's house in order** make necessary reforms; settle one's arrangements. *safe as houses*: see *as safe as houses* above. *set one's house in order*: see *put one's house in order* above. **set up house** begin to live in a separate dwelling. **son of the house** a son of the family. **the House** (*a*) see senses 2c, d, e above; (*b*) *euphem.* (*Hist.*) the workhouse. **the House of Windsor** the present British Royal Family. *the lady of the house*: see LADY *n.* **the Lord's house** a church, a temple. *throw the house out of the window*: see WINDOW *n. White House*: see WHITE *a. white house*: see WHITE *a. worship in the house of Rimmon*: see *bow down in the house of Rimmon* above.

B *attrib.* or as *adj.* (freq. w. hyphen). **1** *gen.* Of or pertaining to a house or a household; used or kept in or about a house; domestic. OE. **2** Of or pertaining to a house at a school. M19. **3** Of or pertaining to a commercial house or business establishment; (of a magazine etc.) published by a particular firm or society and dealing mainly with its activities; (of a wine etc.) selected and recommended by a restaurant etc. as a reasonable buy; (of a band, group, etc.) resident or regularly performing (in a club etc.). E20.

1 J. AUSTEN The loud noise of the house-bell. J. CARLYLE My house-money is utterly done. B. KIMENYE His house servant was away on leave, and the drawbacks of bachelorhood were making themselves acutely felt. R. LUDLUM His clumsy, long-haired house cat had knocked over a stray glass. 3 T. HILTON *The Germ* was the first house journal of a self-consciously avant-garde artistic group. O. LANCASTER The house burgundy at five bob a bottle.

Comb. & *special collocations*: **house-agent** an agent for the sale and letting of houses, an estate agent; **house arrest** detention in one's own house etc., not in prison; **house-arrest** *v.t.* put under house arrest; **houseboat** a boat fitted up for living in, usu. on inland waters; **housebote** [BOOT *n.*[1]] *Law* (a tenant's right to) timber from the landlord's estate for house repairs; **housebound** *a.* unable to leave one's house through illness etc.; **houseboy** a boy or man as a servant in a house, esp. in Africa; **house-burn** *v.i.* (of tobacco) become damaged or spoilt by disease during the curing process; **house call** a visit made to a patient in his or her own home by a doctor etc.; **housecarl** [CARL *n.*] *Hist.* (before the Norman Conquest) a member of the bodyguard of a Danish or English king or noble; **house church** (*a*) a charismatic Church independent of traditional denominations; (*b*) a group meeting in private houses as part of the activities of a Church; **house-clean** *v.t.* & *i.* clean (the interior of a house); **housecoat** a woman's informal coat-dress, esp. for wearing in the home; **house colours** a badge, cap, etc. awarded for representing a house of a school, esp. in a sporting event; **housecraft** (skill in) household management; **house detective** a private detective employed on the premises by a hotel, business, etc.; **house-dog** a dog kept as a pet or to guard a house; **house-father** the father of a household or family; a man in charge of a house, esp. of a home for children; **house-flag** a flag indicating to what firm a ship belongs; **housefly** the common fly of houses and farms, *Musca domestica*, a dipteran insect which lays its eggs in excrement and decaying organic matter, and spreads disease; **house-girl** a female domestic servant, formerly esp. a slave; **house guest**: staying in a private house; **house-heating** (*a*) the heating of a house; (*b*) (chiefly *Sc.*) a house-warming party etc.; **house-hunting** looking for a house to live in; **house-husband** a husband who carries out the household duties traditionally carried out by a wife; **house-lamb** (now *rare*) a lamb kept in or near a house as a pet or for fattening for the table; the meat from such a lamb; **houseleek** a plant of the stonecrop family, *Sempervivum tectorum*, with pink flowers and dense rosettes of fleshy leaves, formerly much planted on roofs as a protection against lightning; **house lights**: in the auditorium of a theatre; **house longhorn** a wood-boring beetle, *Hylotrupes bajulus*, of the family Cerambycidae; **house-lot** *N. Amer.* a building-plot; **house-manager** the manager of a theatre, cinema, club, etc.; **house-martin** an Old World swallow, *Delichon urbica*, which builds mud nests on house walls, rocky cliffs, etc.; **housemaster** a master of a house; *spec.* a male teacher in charge of a house in a school; **housemastership** the position or office of a housemaster; **housemate** a person who shares a house with another or others; **housemistress** a mistress of a house; *spec.* a female teacher in charge of a house in a school; **house-mother** the mother of a household or family; a woman in charge of a house, esp. of a home for children; **house mouse** a usually grey mouse, *Mus musculus*, which lives close to human habitation in most parts of the world and eats almost anything; **house music** = sense A.12 above; **house-officer** a (usu. resident) doctor of one of the more junior grades in a hospital; **house-parent** a house-mother or house-father; esp. of a home for children; **house party** (a gathering of) guests staying at a house; **house physician** a resident physician in a hospital, usu. of the most junior grade; **house-place** *dial.* a combined living-room and kitchen in a farmhouse etc.; **house-plant** a plant that is suitable for growing indoors; **house-proud** *a.* attentive to, or unduly occupied with, the care and appearance of the home; **house-raising** *US* (chiefly *Hist.*) a gathering of people to help a neighbour construct a house; **house-rent party** *US* (*a*) a party held to raise money to pay the rent of a house; (*b*) a jam session in a house or apartment; **houseroom** accommodation or space in a house (*not give houseroom to*, not tolerate having or keeping); **house row** *Hist.* a row or street of houses; **house-sitter** a person who temporarily lives in a house by arrangement during an absence by the usual occupant(s); **house snake** (*a*) any of several N. American colubrid snakes of the genera *Elaphe* and *Lampropeltis*; (*b*) a southern African colubrid snake of the genus *Boaedon*; (*c*) a snake kept as a household god; **house sparrow** the common sparrow, *Passer domesticus*, a small noisy gregarious bird native to Eurasia but now found close to human habitation in most areas other than the Far East; **house style** a particular printer's or publisher's etc. preferred way of presenting text, including rules for spelling, punctuation, etc.; the distinctive style, esp. in artistic presentation, of a firm etc.; **house-surgeon** a resident surgeon in a hospital, usually of the most junior grade; **house-to-house** *a.* visiting or performed in turn at each of a series of houses; **housetop** the top or roof of a house; *cry, proclaim,* etc., *from the housetops* [w. allus. to *Luke* 12:3], announce publicly, announce loudly; **housewares** (chiefly *N. Amer.*) utilitarian household items, esp. kitchen utensils; **house-warming** (*a*) the warming of a house; (*b*) a party or other entertainment celebrating a move to a new home (also *house-warming party* etc.); **housework** cleaning, cooking, and other domestic work undertaken in a house; **housewright** *arch.* a house-builder.

house /haʊs/ *n.*[2] Now *rare.* ME. [OFr. *houce* (mod. *housse*) f. med.L *hultia* f. Gmc (whence MDu. *hulfte* pocket for bow and arrow, MHG *hulft* covering).] A textile covering, *spec.* one attached to a saddle to cover the back and flanks of the horse. Cf. HOUSING *n.*[2]

house /haʊs/ *n.*[3] Orig. *US.* L20. [Prob. f. The Ware*house*, a Chicago nightclub.] In full *house music.* A type of popular music characterized by the extensive use of synthetic sounds produced electronically, sparse vocals, and a fast beat.

house /haʊz/ *v.*[1] [OE *hūsian* = MLG, MDu. *hūsen*, OHG *hūsōn* (Du. *huizen*, G *hausen*), ON *húsa*, f. Gmc base of HOUSE *n.*[1]] **I** *v.t.* **1** Take or put into a house; provide with a house or houses; keep or store in a house etc. OE. **b** *refl.* Enter a house; take shelter in a house. LME. †**c** Drive or pursue into a house. L16–E18. **2** Place or enclose as in a house; cover as with a roof; harbour, lodge; contain, as a house does; give shelter to. LME. 3 *Naut.* Place in a secure or sheltered position. M18. 4 Fix (a piece of wood, etc.) in a socket, joint, or mortise. M19.

1 A. J. P. TAYLOR He..housed us without a moment's fuss. b E. FEINSTEIN A small friendly square around which many Russians housed themselves. 2 L. DURRELL A small observatory which housed a telescope of thirty magnifications. K. TYNAN The difficulty of finding out what theatre is housing the play you want to see. *Antiquarian Horology* A clock-case which houses a clock by Thomas Fayrer of Lancaster. J. A. MICHENER The mound now housed a town of a hundred mud-brick houses.

II *v.i.* †5 Build a house or houses. ME–L15. 6 Live or take shelter (as) in a house. L16.

6 R. L. STEVENSON An old gentleman..housed with them for a while during our stay.

house /haʊz/ *v.*[2]*t.* Now *rare.* E16. [f. HOUSE *n.*[2]] Cover (a horse) with a textile house or housing.

housebreak /ˈhaʊsbreɪk/ *v.* Pa. t. (*rare*) **-broke** /-brəʊk/, pa. pple & ppl a. **-broken** /-brəʊk(ə)n/. ME. [f. HOUSE *n.*[1] + BREAK *v.*] 1 *v.i.* Break into a house with intent to steal etc. Chiefly as HOUSEBREAKING. ME. 2 *v.t.* = HOUSE-TRAIN. Freq. in *pass.* Chiefly *N. Amer.* E20.

housebreaker /ˈhaʊsbreɪkə/ *n.* LME. [f. HOUSE *n.*[1] + BREAKER *n.*[1]] 1 A person who breaks into a house with intent to steal etc. (in *Law* formerly in the daytime only: cf. BURGLAR). LME. 2 A person employed in demolishing houses. L19.

housebreaking /ˈhaʊsbreɪkɪŋ/ *n.* E17. [f. HOUSE *n.*[1] + BREAKING *n.*] The act of breaking into a house with intent to steal etc. (in *Law* formerly in the daytime only: cf. BURGLARY).

houseful /ˈhaʊsfʊl, -f(ə)l/ *n.* ME. [f. HOUSE *n.*[1] + -FUL.] As much or as many as a house will hold.

household /ˈhaʊshəʊld/ *n.* & *a.* LME. [f. HOUSE *n.*[1] + HOLD *n.*[1]] A *n.* 1 *collect.* The people living in a house, *esp.* a family in a house; a domestic establishment. LME. †2 The maintaining of a house or family; housekeeping. LME–L16. †3 *collect.* The contents of a house; household goods and furniture. LME–E18.

1 V. GLENDINNING The Fairfield household moved back to London. E. FEINSTEIN After his second wife's death, the household of Professor Tsvetayev split up. **the Household** *spec.* the royal household.

B *attrib.* or as *adj.* 1 Of or pertaining to a household; domestic. LME. 2 Intimate, homely. *arch.* LME.

2 L. STERNE Good plain household judgment.

Special collocations & comb.: **household appliance** a piece of equipment used in the house. **household book** a book for the keeping of household accounts. **household bread** *Hist.* bread of an ordinary quality for household use. **household effects** the movable contents of a house. **household franchise** *Hist.* the right of voting in elections consequent on being a householder. **household gods** (*a*) gods presiding over a household, *esp.* (*Rom. Hist.*) the lares and penates; (*b*) the essentials of home life. **household management** the management of domestic affairs, esp. as a subject of study. **household name** a well-known name. **household science** (chiefly *N. Amer.*) the study of household management, domestic science. **household stuff** *arch.* = *household effects* above. **household troops** (in Britain) troops nominally employed to guard the monarch. **household word** a well-known name or saying.

householdry *n.* (*arch.*) management of a household, housekeeping L16.

householder /ˈhaʊshəʊldə/ *n.* LME. [f. HOUSE *n.*[1] + HOLDER *n.*[1]] A person who owns or rents a house, flat, etc., as his or her own dwelling (*Hist.* with a type of occupancy bringing entitlement to the franchise); a head of a household or family.

householdership *n.* E19.

householding /ˈhaʊshəʊldɪŋ/ *n.* Now *rare.* LME. [f. HOUSE *n.*[1] + HOLDING *n.*] (Formerly) management or (later) occupancy of a house.

housekeep /ˈhaʊskiːp/ *v.i. colloq.* Pa. t. & pple **-kept** /-kɛpt/. M19. [Back-form. f. next or HOUSEKEEPING *n.* Cf. earlier HOUSEKEEPING *a.* 1.] Act as a housekeeper (*for*); keep house.

housekeeper /ˈhaʊskiːpə/ *n.* LME. [f. HOUSE *n.*[1] + KEEPER *n.*] †1 = HOUSEHOLDER. LME–M19. †2 With qualifying adj.: a *good* etc. person in offering hospitality. M16–E18. 3 A person in charge of a house, office, etc.; a caretaker. M16. †b A guard dog. Only in L17. 4 *spec.* A person, esp. a woman, who manages the affairs of a household (in a large establishment usu. including supervision of any female servants) or (now) the cleaning of a hotel etc.; (with qualifying adj.) a *good* etc. person at managing household affairs. Formerly also, a person engaged in a domestic occupation. L16. 5 A person who keeps to the house, or stays at home. *rare.* E18.

housekeeping /ˈhaʊskiːpɪŋ/ *n.* M16. [f. HOUSE *n.*[1] + KEEPING *n.*] 1 Maintenance of a household, keeping a house; management of household affairs, *transf.* management of an organization's finances etc. M16. †2 Hospitality. Usu. w. qualifying adj. M16–M19. 3 Money set aside or given for housekeeping expenses, housekeeping money. *colloq.* M20. 4 Those operations of a computer, an organization, etc., which make its work possible but do not directly constitute its performance, e.g. maintenance and record-keeping. M20.

1 C. ODETS We've set up housekeeping together, Joe. *Abingdon Herald* The Vale's financial strategy, based on continued good housekeeping and further capital investment. 3 J. PORTER If I ask you for a bit more housekeeping, that's a different story.

Comb. (see also HOUSEKEEPING *a.* 2): **housekeeping allowance, money**: set aside or given for housekeeping expenses.

housekeeping /ˈhaʊskiːpɪŋ/ *a.* M16. [Sense 1 f. HOUSE *n.*[1] + *keeping* pres. pple of KEEP *v.*; sense 2 the n. used attrib.] 1 That keeps a house or maintains a household. Now *rare.* M16. 2 Designating holiday or rented accommodation providing equipment for housekeeping; self-catering. *N. Amer.* M20.

housekept *v.* pa. t. & pple of HOUSEKEEP.

housel /ˈhaʊz(ə)l/ *n.* & *v. obs.* exc. *Hist.* [OE *hūsl* (whence ON *húsl*) = Goth. *hunsl* sacrifice, offering: ult. origin unkn.] A *n.* (The administration or receiving of) the Eucharist. OE. B *v.t.* Infl. **-ll-**, **-l-**. Administer the Eucharist to; in *pass.*, receive the Eucharist. OE.

houseling *n.* & *a.* (*a*) *n.* the action of the vb; (*b*) *adj.* (*attrib.*) used at the celebration of the Eucharist: OE.

houseless /ˈhaʊslɪs/ *a.* LME. [f. HOUSE *n.*[1] + -LESS.] Without a house; homeless.

houselessness *n.* E19.

housemaid /ˈhaʊsmeɪd/ *n.* & *v.* L17. [f. HOUSE *n.*[1] + MAID *n.*] A *n.* A female domestic servant, *esp.* one in charge of reception rooms and bedrooms. L17.

housemaid's closet, cupboard: where cleaning materials are kept. **housemaid's knee** swelling of the bursa in front of the kneecap, often the result of frequent kneeling.

B *v.t.* Look after in the manner of a housemaid; put in order. M19.

P. DEVLIN One of his [the trial judge's] jobs is to housemaid the case... To get the evidence as clean and tidy as he can.

houseman /ˈhaʊsmən/ *n.* Pl. **-men.** L18. [f. HOUSE *n.*[1] + MAN *n.*] 1 A married labourer on a Norwegian farm. *rare.* L18. 2 (**H-**.) A member of Christ Church, Oxford ('the House'). M19. 3 A man responsible for general duties in a house, hotel, etc. M19. 4 A house physician or house surgeon, in Britain now usu. a qualified junior doctor working under supervision in a hospital before being fully registered as an independent medical practitioner. M20.

housemanship *n.* the position of being a houseman in a hospital M20.

house-train /ˈhaʊstreɪn/ *v.t.* E20. [f. HOUSE *n.*[1] + TRAIN *v.*] Train (a domestic animal, an infant) to be clean in the house, teach where to urinate and defecate; *joc. colloq.* teach good manners or tidiness to. Usu. in *pass.*

housewife /ˈhaʊswʌɪf, *in sense 3 & dial.* ˈhʌzɪf/ *n.* Pl. **-wives** /-wʌɪvz/. Also (now only in sense 3) **hussive** /ˈhʌzɪv/, (esp. in sense 2) †**huswife.** ME. [f. HOUSE *n.*[1] + WIFE *n.* See also HUSSY.] 1 A (married) woman who looks after the domestic affairs of her household, esp. as her principal occupation; (with qualifying adj.) a *good* etc. domestic manager. ME. †2 = HUSSY 3. M16–E18. 3 A small case for sewing equipment. M18.

housewifeship *n.* (chiefly *Sc.* & *north.*) housewifery ME. **housewifish** *a.* housewifely M19.

housewife /ˈhaʊswʌɪf/ *v.* Now *rare.* M16. [f. the n.] 1 *v.i.* & *t.* (w. *it*). Be a (good) housewife; manage a household, esp. skilfully and economically. M16. 2 *v.t.* Manage as a (good) housewife, skilfully and economically. M17.

2 DEFOE I must housewife the money.

housewifely /ˈhaʊswʌɪfli/ *a.* LME. [f. as prec. + -LY[1].] Pertaining to or characteristic of a (good) housewife; skilful and economical in managing household affairs.

housewifeliness *n.* M16.

housewifery /ˈhaʊswɪfri/ *n.* LME. [f. as prec. + -RY.] 1 (Skill in) household management, housecraft; housekeeping. LME. †b Thrift, economy. M17–L18. †2 *collect.* Articles of household use. M16–E19.

housewives *n.* pl. of HOUSEWIFE *n.*

housey /ˈhaʊsi/ *n. colloq.* Also **housie.** M20. [Abbrev. of next.] = HOUSE *n.*[1] II.

housey-housey /haʊsɪˈhaʊsi/ *n.* Also **housie-housie.** M20. [f. HOUSE *n.*[1] + -Y[6].] = HOUSE *n.*[1] II.

housie(-housie) *ns.* vars. of HOUSEY(-HOUSEY).

housing /ˈhaʊzɪŋ/ *n.*[1] ME. [f. HOUSE *n.*[1] or *v.*[1] + -ING[1].] I 1 Shelter (like that of a house); lodging. ME. 2 Property consisting of houses; houses or buildings, collectively; *spec.* outbuildings attached to a house. LME. b A house, a building. Long *rare.* LME. 3 *Archit.* A canopied niche for a statue or other image. Long *obs.* exc. *Hist.* LME. 4 *Naut.* A covering or roofing for a ship. E19. 5 *Carpentry.* A recess or groove in one piece of timber etc. for another to fit into. E19. 6 A massive metal frame or pillar that supports one end of a set of rolls in a rolling-mill. M19. 7 A structure that supports and encloses the bearings at the end of an axle or shaft, a journal-box; a rigid casing that encloses and protects any piece of moving or delicate equipment. L19.

1 C. MATHER Their housing is nothing but a few mats tyed about poles fastened in the earth. 2 J. KRANTZ I'll never accept the idea that public housing can't be beautiful.

II 8 The action of HOUSE *v.*[1]; *esp.* provision of houses. LME.

Comb.: **housing association** an association aiming to provide housing at (relatively) low cost; **housing development** the act or process of planning and building a (large) group of houses; a housing estate; **housing estate** a residential area planned as a unit, and often having its own shops and other facilities; **housing list** a waiting-list for council houses; *housing project*: see PROJECT *n.* 6c; **housing scheme** a housing estate, esp. of council houses.

housing /ˈhaʊzɪŋ/ *n.*[2] LME. [f. HOUSE *n.*[2] or *v.*[2] + -ING[1].] A covering, esp. of cloth; *spec.* a covering put on a horse etc. for protection or ornament, trappings. Freq. in *pl.*

houstonia /huːˈstəʊnɪə/ *n.* E19. [mod.L (see below), f. William *Houston*, Sc. botanist (d. 1733): see -IA[1].] Any of various N. American plants of the former genus *Houstonia*, of the madder family, now included in the genus *Hedyotis*; *esp.* the bluets, *Hedyotis* (formerly *Houstonia*) *caerulea.*

houting /ˈhaʊtɪŋ/ *n.* L19. [Du. f. MDu. *houtic*, of uncertain origin.] Either of two whitefish, valued in places for food, either (*a*) the rare anadromous form *Coregonus oxyrhynchus*, of Baltic coasts and rivers, or (*b*) the variable freshwater form *Coregonus lavaretus*, which occurs in lakes of northern Europe and Asia. Cf. GWYNIAD, LAVARET, POWAN, SKELLY *n.* 1.

†**houve** *n.* see HOO *n.*[1]

houyhnhnm /ˈhʊɪnɪm, ˈhwɪnɪm/ *n.* E18. [The name (intended to suggest the neigh of a horse) of a fictional race of reasoning horses in Swift's *Gulliver's Travels.*] A horse considered as having human characteristics.

Hova /ˈhəʊvə, ˈhɒvə/ *n.* & *a.* M19. [Malagasy.] A *n.* Pl. **-s**, same. A member of the dominant people of the Malagasy Republic (formerly Madagascar); the dialect of Malagasy spoken by this people. M19. **B** *attrib.* or as *adj.* Of or pertaining to the Hovas or their dialect. L19.

hove /həʊv/ *v.*[1]*i.* Long *arch. rare.* ME. [Origin unkn.: superseded by HOVER *v.*] **1** Hover, as a bird etc. ME. **2** Wait, linger, stay, remain; *spec.* remain on horseback. ME. †**3** Float or soar *on* or *by*; move away; be borne (on horseback). ME–M17.

hove /həʊv/ *v.*[2] Now chiefly *Sc.* LME. [App. f. pa. t. & pple of HEAVE *v.*] †**1** *v.t.* Raise, lift. LME–L16. **2** *v.i.* Rise, swell up. L16. **3** *v.t.* Cause to swell up, inflate. E17.

hove *v.*[3] pa. t. & pple: see HEAVE *v.*

hovel /ˈhɒv(ə)l/ *n.*[1] LME. [Perh. of LG origin.] **1** An open shed or an outhouse used for sheltering cattle, storing grain, etc. Now chiefly *dial.* LME. **b** A stack of corn, a heap of hay, etc. Now *dial.* L16. **2** A simple, roughly constructed, or (esp.) squalid dwelling. LME. **3** *Archit.* A canopied niche for a statue or other image. Long *obs.* exc. *Hist.* LME. **4** A conical construction enclosing a kiln. E19.

hovel /ˈhɒv(ə)l/ *n.*[2] Now *rare.* L17. [MDu. *hövel*, Du. *heuvel*.] The bump on the top of a whale's head.

hovel /ˈhɒv(ə)l/ *v.t.* Infl. **-ll-**, ***-l-**. L16. [f. HOVEL *n.*[1]] **1** Shelter (as) in a hovel. L16. **2** Shape (a chimney) like a hovel or open shed. E19.

hoveller /ˈhɒv(ə)lə/ *n.* M18. [Origin unkn.] *Hist.* **1** An unlicensed boatman, esp. on the Kentish coast; *spec.* one who went out to wrecks. M18. **2** A boat used by a hoveller. M19.

hoven /ˈhəʊv(ə)n/ *a.* & *n.* M16. [pa. pple of HEAVE *v.*] **A** *adj.* Swollen, bloated. Now *dial.* M16. **B** *n.* Distension of the stomachs of cattle with gas, usu. owing to overfeeding on clover etc.; bloat. Cf. HEAVE *n.* 2, HOOVE. M19.

hoven *v.* pa. pple: see HEAVE *v.*

hover /ˈhɒvə/ *v.* & *n.* LME. [f. HOVE *v.*[1] + -ER[5].] **A** *v.* **I** *v.i.* **1** (Of a bird, esp. a hawk etc., or an insect) hang or remain suspended in the air by rapidly beating the wings; hang in the air with a wavering or fluttering movement. (Foll. by *over*, *about*.) LME. **b** Of a helicopter or other aircraft: maintain a stationary position in the air. L19. **c** Of a hovercraft: be supported, esp. in a stationary position, on the air-cushion. M20. **2** Be in an indeterminate or irresolute state, waver, (*between*); (*obs.* exc. *Sc.*) wait, delay, hesitate. LME. **3** Linger about or round (a person or place); move restlessly about. (Foll. by *about*, *round*.) L16.

1 HUGH WALPOLE A faint red glow hovered over the dark, heaving water. A. J. CRONIN He . . turned out the lamp, around which great moths were hovering in the languid air. B. HINES Persistently this time, hovering then dropping vertically in short bursts. **b** A. CARTER The whirring helicopter hovered over a crag where eagles nested. 2 P. G. WODEHOUSE He felt that he hovered on the brink of some strange revelation. TOLKIEN He lost count of time, hovering between sleep and waking. C. POTOK He hovered tenuously between life and death for three days. *Scientific American* A climate where the thermometer regularly hovers around 40 °C. 3 J. M. BARRIE He hovered around the table as if it would be unsafe to leave us. D. M. THOMAS Kolya was edging towards the door impatiently, but Lisa hovered, doubtful.

II *v.t.* **4** Cover, protect; *esp.* (of a bird) cover (the young) with its body. *arch.* LME. †**5** Of a bird: flap (the wings) in order to hang in the air. L16–L17. **6** Maintain (an aircraft) in a hovering state. M20.

6 *Daily Telegraph* It is feasible to fly a Sea Harrier and hover it to an accuracy of 2 ft.

B *n.* **1** Indecision; an instance or state of indecision. E16. **2** An overhanging shelter; *spec.* an overhanging stone or bank under which fish hide. Also, a shelter used in the brooding of chickens. Chiefly *dial.* E17. **3** An act or state of hovering. L19. **4** A floating island of vegetation or a bed of reeds. Chiefly *dial.* L19.

Comb.: **hovercraft** a vehicle or craft supported by a cushion of air ejected downwards against the surface (of land or sea); **hoverfly** any fly of the dipteran family Syrphidae, the members of which resemble wasps but are stingless and often hover in the air; **hover-mower** a lawnmower supported and moving on a cushion of air; **hoverport** a port used by hovercraft; **hovertrain** a train progressing along a concrete track on an air-cushion like a hovercraft.

hoverer *n.* E17. **hoveringly** *adv.* in a hovering manner E19.

how /haʊ/ *n.*[1] & *int.*[1] LME. [Natural exclam.] **1** (An utterance of the exclamation) attracting attention etc. *obs.* exc. *dial.* in *how way!*, come on! LME. **2** An exclamation of sailors in hauling. LME.

2 *hale and how*: see HALE *n.*[3]

how /haʊ/ *n.*[2] M16. [f. HOW *adv.*] (A question as to) the way or manner (of doing something).

W. GOLDING The Marxist is . . right to insist on the *how* of Utopia even if . . hazy about the what and when. R. F. HOBSON The 'how,' the manner of psychotherapy, can be prepared for.

how /haʊ/ *n.*[3] & *int.*[2] E19. [Cf. Sioux *háo*, Omaha *hou*.] Used in greeting or welcoming, by or in imitation of N. American Indians; an utterance of 'how!'.

†**how** *n.*[4] var. of HOE *n.*[2]

how *n.*[5] var. of HOO *n.*[1]

how *n.*[6], *n.*[7] see HOWE *n.*[1], *n.*[2]

how /haʊ/ *adv.* [OE *hū* = OFris. *hū*, *hō*, OS (*h*)*wō*, *hwuo* (MLG *woe*, Du. *hoe*), OHG *wuo*, f. WGmc. adv. f. base of WHO, WHAT.] An adverb primarily interrog., used also in exclams., and in conjunctive and relative constructions. **1** In what way or manner; by what means; in whatever way; by whatever means. Used in qualifying vbs in dependence on vbs of saying, asking, perceiving, etc., on ns. like *heed*, *care*, and related adjs., on preps., and following an infinitive. OE. **b** Used in weakened sense 'that' following vbs of saying, perceiving, etc. OE. **2** To what degree or extent. Used in qualifying adjs. or advs., or vbs of liking. OE. †**b** = HOWEVER 2. In later use, only correlative to *so*. ME–L19. †**c** As . . . as. LME–M18. **3** In what condition or state; in whatever condition or state. Used in qualifying vbs. ME. **4** *interrog.* What. Used esp. as a request for repetition of a question or statement. *arch.* & *US dial.* and in *how*(*'s*) *about* below. OE. **b** *interrog.* By what name; to what effect, with what meaning. Now chiefly, what, why (*colloq.*). ME. **5** At what rate or price. *arch.* LME.

1 T. HARDY He does not love you, but you love him—is that how it is? W. S. MAUGHAM She asked herself . . how on earth she was to endure the slow passing of the hours. SCOTT FITZGERALD Well, how can any one tell what's eccentric and what's crazy? J. KRANTZ No gigolo . . was going to tell him how to run his business. H. CARPENTER He wanted to understand machinery and to know how it worked. W. GOLDING What an audience wants to hear from a novelist is how he writes. P. ROTH Look at him! Look at how he dresses. *ellipt.*: E. BOWEN 'I say, *Father*, about tomorrow, how if I telephoned H.Q. for a lay reader?' A. MACLEAN 'A mistake, but easy enough to put right.' 'How?' *Independent* There is likely to be uncertainty . . over what to assess and how. **b** D. WELCH He told us how, as a child, he had once eaten swan for dinner. I. MURDOCH Did she show you her rings, how they were diamonds my father got for us? 2 T. HARDY Why, how late you are, Ethelberta, and how heated you look! W. S. MAUGHAM If he only knew how I adore him! M. SINCLAIR Her mother sat down to show how tired she was. I. MURDOCH How long are you planning to stay with us? K. VONNEGUT I suppose I should tell you how old I am too. **b** T. VENNER By how much the younger they are, by so much the moyster they are. W. GOODALL Cecil . . had all in readiness to be published how soon the Duke should be beheaded. 3 T. HARDY But I had a great wish to see you, and inquire how you were. R. LEHMANN How are you? . . You're looking awfully well. L. W. MEYNELL 'How's tricks?' he enquired. 'I'm fine. I slept like a top.' 4 A. PRICE How's that again, Elizabeth? . . This fellow you talked to—? **b** J. CONRAD How is it that you let Tait's people put us off with a defective lock? 5 SHAKES. *2 Hen. IV* 'How a score of ewes now?' . . . 'A score of good ewes may be worth ten pounds.'

Phrases & comb.: **and how!** *colloq.* (*iron.* or *emphatic*) very much so; and no mistake. *as how*: see AS *adv.* etc. **here's how!** I drink to your good health. *how about* (*that*): see ABOUT *prep.* 6. **how come?** *colloq.* how did (or does) it come about (*that*). **how do?** *colloq.* how do you do; hello. **how do you do?**, (*arch.* & *dial.*) **how do ye?** or **how d'ye?**: a formal greeting enquiring as to a person's health etc. **how-do-you-do, how-d'ye-do** (*a*) an enquiry of 'how do you do?'; (*b*) an awkward or embarrassing situation. *how goes it, how is it going, how are things going?*: see GO *v.* **how is that for high, queer**, etc.? *colloq.* isn't that amazing, surprising, etc.? **how many** what number. **how much** (*a*) what amount; (*b*) what price; (*c*) *joc.* what? pardon? **how now?** *arch.* how is it now? what is the meaning of this? *how say you?*: see SAY *v.*[1] **how so?** how can you show that that is so? **how — soever** to whatsoever degree or extent. *how's about*: see ABOUT *prep.* 6. **how's that?** (*a*) what is your opinion of that?; (*b*) *Cricket* (said to an umpire) is the batsman out or not? (cf. OWZAT). *how the other half lives*: see HALF *n.* *how the wind blows* or *lies*: see WIND *n.*[1] *how the world wags*: see WAG *v.* **how-to** *a.* (*colloq.*) instructive; of the nature of a manual.

howardite /ˈhaʊədʌɪt/ *n.* M19. [f. E. *Howard* (fl. 1802), Eng. chemist + -ITE[1].] **1** *Min.* A supposed silicate of iron and magnesium occurring in some meteorites. M19. **2** *Astron.* Any of a group of achondritic meteorites principally composed of hypersthene and anorthite. L19.

howbeit /haʊˈbiːɪt/ *adv.* & *conj.* Now *arch.* or *literary.* LME. [f. HOW *adv.* + BE + IT *pron.* (orig. as three wds w. pa. t. *how were it*).] **A** *adv.* Nevertheless; however. LME. †**B** *conj.* Though, although. LME–M17.

howdah /ˈhaʊdə/ *n.* L18. [Urdu *haudah* f. Arab. *hawdaj* a litter carried by a camel.] A seat for two or more, usu. with a canopy, carried on an elephant's back.

howdahed *a.* carrying a howdah E19.

howdie /ˈhaʊdi/ *n. Sc.* & *north.* Also **-dy**. L17. [Origin unkn.] A midwife.

howdy /ˈhaʊdi/ *n.*[1] & *int.* Chiefly *US. colloq.* E19. [Alt. of *how d'ye?* s.v. HOW *adv.*] (A greeting of) how do you do?; (a) hello.

T. MORRISON It was like talking to somebody's cousin who just stepped by to say howdy.

howdy *n.*[2] var. of HOWDIE.

howe /haʊ/ *n.*[1] Also (earlier, now only in sense 1) **how**. ME. [ON *haugr* mound, cairn, f. Gmc base of HIGH *a.*] **1** A hill. Now only in northern place-names. ME. **2** An artificial mound; *esp.* a tumulus, a barrow. M17.

howe /haʊ/ *n.*[2] *Sc.* & *north.* Also (earlier) **how**. LME. [Var. of HOLL *n.*] †**1** A hole. *rare.* LME–L16. †**2** = HOLL *n.* 2. E16–M17. **3** A hollow place; a depression. M16.

howe /haʊ/ *a.* & *adv. Sc.* & *north.* LME. [Var. of HOLL *a.*] Hollow(ly).

howe'er *adv.* see HOWEVER.

howel /ˈhaʊəl/ *n.* & *v.* E19. [Prob. of LG origin: cf. MLG *hövel*, LG *Höwel* plane.] **A** *n.* A plane with a convex sole, used by a cooper for smoothing the inside of a cask etc. E19. **B** *v.t.* Plane or smooth with a howel. M19.

however /haʊˈɛvə/ *adv.* Also contr. **-e'er** /-ˈɛː/. LME. [f. HOW *adv.* + EVER *adv.*] **I** **1** In whatever manner; by whatever means. Used in qualifyng vbs. LME. **2** To whatever degree or extent. Used in qualifying adjs. or advs. LME. †**3** In any case, at any rate. L16–M18. **4** For all that, nevertheless, notwithstanding; but; *arch.* however much, notwithstanding that. Used in qualifying a whole cl. or sentence. L16.

1 M. KEANE However she had done it, she had alerted the busy Abbot. 2 V. WOOLF I am sure however many years I keep this diary, I shall never find a winter to beat this. C. P. SNOW Whatever Sheriff did, however inconsequently he behaved, would only strengthen her love. E. FIGES Somebody was coming . . so however tired she felt, she would have to make an effort. L. GORDON However much Virginia criticised the Victorians . . she was nostalgic for their manners. 3 J. BUTLER Till we know the Whole, or, however, much more of the Case. 4 E. BOWEN However, to the left of the roadway, darker . . patches of growth were to be discerned. G. GREENE One must not exaggerate his knowledge, however. I. MURDOCH Under this cautionary rubric I shall however now attempt a general description of myself. *ellipt.*: M. WOODHOUSE 'Our component reliability was very high indeed during trials. However' 'Go on,' I said.

II *interrog.* **5** (Also as two wds.) Used w. emphatic force in place of *how* in a question. L19.

howff /haʊf/ *n.* & *v.* *Sc.* M16. [Origin unkn.] A *n.* 1 The main burial ground at Dundee (*Hist.*); *gen.* any cemetery. M16. 2 A favourite meeting-place, a haunt. E18. B *v.i.* Frequent, haunt. E19.

howgozit /haʊˈgəʊzɪt/ *n.* M20. [Alt. of *how goes it?* s.v. GO *v.*] A graph showing how much fuel an aircraft has left in relation to that needed to reach the destination or to return to the point of departure.

howish /ˈhaʊɪʃ/ *a.* *obs.* exc. *dial.* L17. [f. HOW *adv.* + -ISH[1].] Vaguely unwell; having a vague sense of illness.

†howitz *n.* Also **haubitz**. Pl. **-es**, same. L17–L18. [G *Haubitze*, †*Hau(f)enitz* f. Czech *houfnice* sling, catapult.] = next.

howitzer /ˈhaʊɪtsə/ *n.* L17. [Du. *houwitser* f. G *Haubitze*: see prec., -ER[1].] A short relatively light gun for the high-angle firing of shells at a low velocity.

howk /haʊk/ *v.* Now chiefly *dial.* Also (earlier) **†holk**. LME. [Cogn. w. MLG *holken*, LG *holken*, *hölken* hollow, f. base of HOLL *a.* + dim. formative *-k*, as in *talk* etc.] 1 *v.t.* Hollow out by digging; excavate; dig out or up; unearth. LME. 2 *v.i.* Dig; search about; find. E16.

1 B. MARSHALL Deep in their trenches the hairy men stood, howking out the brown earth. W. MCILVANNEY Ah canny see beyond the seam that Ah'm tryin' tae howk. 2 R. KIPLING Dan hiked and howked with a boat-hook (the brook was too narrow for sculls).

howl /haʊl/ *n.* L16. [f. the vb.] 1 A long loud doleful cry of a dog, wolf, etc.; a loud cry of pain, anguish, or laughter; a yell of derision. L16. 2 A wailing noise of an inanimate agent; *spec.* such a noise produced in a loudspeaker as a result of electrical or acoustic feedback. M19.

1 J. KRANTZ Dolly clutched her belly and gave a sudden grunting howl. P. HOWARD The attitude of *The Times* provoked howls of indignation.

howl /haʊl/ *v.* ME. [Corresp. to MLG, MDu. *hūlen* (Du. *huilen*), MHG *hiulen*, *hiuweln* (G *heulen*) rel. to OHG *hūwila* (MHG *hiuwel*) owl; perh. immed. f. OWL *n.* (cf. also L *ululare* howl, *ulula* owl, Gk *hulan* bark).] 1 *v.i.* (Of a dog, wolf, etc.) emit a long loud doleful cry; (of a person) utter a long loud cry of pain, derision, laughter, etc.; (esp. of a child) cry or weep loudly. Formerly also, (of an owl) hoot. ME. b Of an inanimate agent, esp. the wind or a storm: make a prolonged wailing noise. L17. 2 *v.t.* Utter (words) with howling. M16. 3 *v.t.* Foll. by *down*: prevent (a speaker, words) from being heard by howls of derision. L19.

1 C. CHAPLIN At night from my bedroom I would listen to the coyotes howling. V. S. PRITCHETT They were howling with grief, the tears drenched their faces as they rocked in . . sorrow. V. GLENDINNING The audience, after howling with derision during the first act, ended up applauding wildly. b T. C. WOLFE And the great winds howl and swoop across the land. I. BANKS The trains howl like lost souls. 2 SHAKES. *Macb.* But I have words That would be howl'd out in the desert air. 3 A. BURGESS There was no noise of disagreement save from myself, and I was easily howled down.

howler /ˈhaʊlə/ *n.* E19. [f. HOWL *v.* + -ER[1].] 1 More fully *howler monkey*. Any of several S. American cebid monkeys constituting the genus *Alouatta*, which have long prehensile tails and make loud howling noises. E19. 2 A person hired to cry or wail at a funeral or a person's death-bed. Now *rare*. M19. 3 A glaring blunder. *colloq.* L19.

3 E. JONG Herr Hummel . . spoke English well, but he made occasional howlers.

howlet /ˈhaʊlɪt/ *n.* *dial.* (chiefly *Sc.*). L15. [Dim. of OWL *n.* w. assim. to HOWL *v.*: see -ET[1]. Cf. OWLET.] An owl, an owlet.

howling /ˈhaʊlɪŋ/ *n.* LME. [f. HOWL *v.* + -ING[1].] 1 The action of HOWL *v.* LME. 2 *spec.* The production of a wailing noise in a loudspeaker by feedback. E20.

howling /ˈhaʊlɪŋ/ *a.* & *adv.* L16. [f. HOWL *v.* + -ING[2].] A *adj.* 1 That howls. L16. 2 Filled with howling; bleak, dreary. L16. 3 Extreme, glaring; great. *colloq.* M19.

1 **howling baboon** = HOWLER 1. *howling* DERVISH. **howling monkey** = HOWLER 1. 2 **howling wilderness** *biblical* a dreary wilderness. 3 *Times* The Frankie marketing campaign was a howling success. *Listener* If he wasn't guilty of (at best) howling incompetence, somebody in his administration was.

B *adv.* Extremely; completely. *colloq.* L19.

R. KIPLING He'll be howling drunk to-night.

howlingly *adv.* L16.

Howship /ˈhaʊʃɪp/ *n.* L19. [J. *Howship* (1781–1841), Eng. surgeon.] Anat. *Howship's lacuna*, †*lacuna of Howship*, each of the microscopic pits on the surface of bony tissue undergoing resorption.

howsoever /haʊsəʊˈɛvə/ *adv.* *arch.* Also contr. **-e'er** /-ˈɛː/. LME. [f. HOW *adv.* + SO *adv.* + EVER *adv.*] 1 = HOWEVER 1. LME. †2 = HOWEVER 3. L16–M17. †3 = HOWEVER 4. L16–E18. 4 = HOWEVER 2. L17.

howsomever /haʊs(ə)mˈɛvə/ *adv.* ME. [f. HOW *adv.* + SOME *adv.* + EVER *adv.*; parallel formation w. prec.] †1 = HOWEVER 1. ME–E17. 2 = HOWEVER 4. Now chiefly *dial.* & *N. Amer.* *colloq.* M16.

2 W. GOLDING Howsomever we must play our game as long as we can.

howtowdie /haʊˈtaʊdi/ *n.* *Sc.* E19. [Prob. f. OFr. *hétoudeau*, *estaudeau* a young chicken for the pot.] (A) boiled chicken served with spinach and poached eggs.

howzat *int.* var. of OWZAT.

†hox *n.* & *v.* LME. [Prob. abbrev. f. †*hough-sinew* s.v. HOUGH *n.*] A *n.* A hamstring. Only in LME. B *v.t.* Hamstring. LME–M18.

Hoxnian /ˈhɒksnɪən/ *a.* & *n.* M20. [f. *Hoxne*, a village in Suffolk + -IAN.] *Geol.* (Designating or pertaining to) an interglacial stage of the Pleistocene in Britain, preceding the Wolstonian glaciation and identified with the Holsteinian of northern Europe.

hoy /hɔɪ/ *n.*[1] ME. [MDu. *hoei* var. of *hoede*, *heude* (mod. *heu*), of unkn. origin.] *Hist.* A small sailing vessel, usu. rigged as a sloop, for carrying passengers and goods, esp. for short coastal journeys.

Comb.: **hoyman** a man in charge of a hoy.

hoy /hɔɪ/ *int.*, *v.*, & *n.*[2] LME. [Natural exclam. Cf. AHOY, OY *int.*[1], *n.*[2], & *v.*] A *int.* Attracting attention, driving animals; *Naut.* hailing or calling aloft. LME.

B *v.t.* Urge on, summon, with a cry or cries of 'hoy!' M16.

J. FOWLES He saw a man hoying a herd of cows away from a low byre.

C *n.* A cry of 'hoy!' M17.

hoya /ˈhɔɪə/ *n.* M19. [mod.L (see below), f. Thomas *Hoy*, Eng. gardener (d. 1821): see -A[1].] Any of various chiefly climbing or twining plants of the genus *Hoya* (family Asclepiadaceae), natives of southern Asia, Malaysia, and Australia, bearing dense umbels of fleshy or waxy pink, white, or yellow flowers. Also called *wax flower*, *wax plant*.

hoyden /ˈhɔɪd(ə)n/ *n.* & *a.* L16. [Prob. f. (M)Du. *heiden* HEATHEN, gypsy.] A *n.* †1 A rude or ignorant fellow. L16–E18. 2 A noisy, rude, or (esp.) boisterous girl or woman. L17.

2 B. GUEST She leaped over stiles in the fields, a hoyden, careless of her dress.

B *attrib.* or as *adj.* Pertaining to or characteristic of a hoyden. E18.

hoydenish *a.* behaving like or having the character of a hoyden; = HOYDEN *a.*: L18.

hoyden /ˈhɔɪd(ə)n/ *v.i.* Now *rare*. E18. [f. the n.] Behave like a hoyden.

hoyle /hɔɪl/ *n.*[1] Now *rare*. E17. [Origin unkn.] *Archery.* A short distance mark used esp. when shooting at rovers.

Hoyle /hɔɪl/ *n.*[2] E20. [Edmond *Hoyle* (1672–1769), Eng. author of several works on card-games.] A book of rules on card-games. Chiefly in *according to Hoyle*, according to the highest authority, in accordance with strict rules.

huaca /ˈwɑːkə/ *n.* Also (earlier) **†gua-**. E17. [Sp. *huaca*, *guaca* f. Quechua *waca* god of the house.] 1 The all-pervading spirit thought by some Peruvian Indians to be disseminated through the whole world; any material object thought to be the abode of such a spirit. E17. 2 A prehistoric Peruvian tomb or temple. M19.

huaco /ˈwɑːkəʊ/ *n.* Also **gua-** /ˈgwɑː-/. Pl. **-os**. M20. [Alt. of prec.] In Peru, Bolivia, and Chile, a piece of ancient Indian pottery.

huarache /waˈrɑːtʃi/ *n.* Also **gua-** /gwa-/. L19. [Mex. Sp.] A leather-thonged sandal, orig. worn by Mexican Indians.

Huastec /ˈwɑːstɛk/ *n.* Also **-teca** /-tɛkə/, **Huax-** /ˈwɑːks-/. Pl. **-s**, same. M19. [Sp. *huasteco*, *huaxteco*.] A member of an Indian people inhabiting parts of Mexico; the Mayan language of this people.

hub /hʌb/ *n.*[1] E16. [Origin unkn. Cf. HOB *n.*[2]] †1 = HOB *n.*[2] 5. E16. 2 The central solid part of a wheel, from which the spokes radiate, and which rotates on or with the axle. M17. 3 A bump in the ground. Now *US* & *dial.* M17. 4 *fig.* The central point of an activity, interest, etc. M19. 5 A cylindrical piece of steel on which the design for a coin is engraved in relief. M19.

2 **up to the hub** *US* as far as possible. 4 R. P. GRAVES The critic Edmund Gosse, who lived at the very hub of London's literary life.

Comb.: **hub brake**: that acts on the hub of a wheel; **hub-cap** a cover for the hub of a vehicle's wheel.

hubless *a.* L20.

hub /hʌb/ *n.*[2] E19. [Abbrev.] = HUBBY *n.*

hubba-hubba /ˈhʌbəhʌbə/ *int.* & *n.* *N. Amer.* *slang.* M20. [Origin unkn.] A *int.* Expr. approval, excitement, or enthusiasm. M20. B *n.* Nonsense; ballyhoo. M20.

Hubbard /ˈhʌbəd/ *n.* Chiefly *N. Amer.* M19. [Prob. a pers. name.] In full *Hubbard squash*. A large green or yellow variety of the winter squash (*Cucurbita maxima*).

Hubble /ˈhʌb(ə)l/ *n.* M20. [Edwin P. *Hubble* (1889–1953), US astronomer.] Used *attrib.* and in *possess.* to designate concepts arising from the work of Hubble.

Hubble('s) constant the ratio of the recessional speed of a galaxy to its distance; the reciprocal of this, interpretable as the time elapsed since the universe started to expand (at constant rate) from a single point. **Hubble('s) law**: that the redshifts in the spectra of distant galaxies (and hence their speeds of recession) are proportional to their distance.

hubble-bubble /ˈhʌb(ə)lbʌb(ə)l/ *n.* E17. [Imit. redupl. of BUBBLE *n.*] 1 A hubbub; confused talk; a bubbling sound. E17. 2 A rudimentary form of hookah, the water being held in a coconut shell or similar receptacle. M17.

hubbub /ˈhʌbʌb/ *n.* M16. [Perh. f. Ir.: cf. Ir. *ababú!* used in battle-cries, Gael. *ub! ub! ubub!* expr. aversion or contempt, *ubh ubh!* expr. disgust or amazement.] 1 A confused noise of a crowd shouting or talking; the shouting of a war cry; noisy turmoil; (a) confusion, (a) disturbance; a row. M16. 2 A game similar to dice, formerly played by American Indians in New England. *obs.* exc. *Hist.* M17.

1 P. MEDAWAR The hubbub that broke out after the publication of the Origin of Species.

hubbuboo, **-aboo** /ˈhʌbəbuː/ *n.* a confused yelling, esp. as a war cry; a tumult: L16.

hubby /ˈhʌbi/ *n.* *colloq.* L17. [Abbrev.] A husband.

hubby /ˈhʌbi/ *a.* *US.* Now *rare*. M19. [f. HUB *n.*[1] + -Y[1].] Of a road: full of bumps.

hübnerite /ˈhjuːbnərʌɪt/ *n.* Also ***hueb-**. M19. [f. A. *Hübner*, 19th-cent. Ger. miner + -ITE[1].] *Min.* Manganese tungstate, $MnWO_4$, occurring as a monoclinic mineral in red-brown crystals and forming a series with ferberite.

hubris /ˈhjuːbrɪs/ *n.* L19. [Gk.] Presumption, insolence, (orig. towards the gods); pride, excessive self-confidence.

ALDOUS HUXLEY Hubris against the essentially divine order of Nature would be followed by its appropriate nemesis.

huˈbristic *a.* insolent, contemptuous, proud M19. **huˈbristically** *adv.* with hubris; in a presumptuous manner: E20.

Hubshee /ˈhʌbʃiː/ *n.* & *a.* Now *rare*. Also **-shi**. E17. [Pers. & Urdu *ḥab(a)šī*, Arab. *ḥabašī*, f. *Ḥabaš(a)* (people of) Ethiopia.] A *n.* An Ethiopian, an Abyssinian. E17. B *adj.* Ethiopian, Abyssinian. L17.

huchen /ˈhuːk(ə)n, ˈhuːxən/ *n.* E20. [G.] A large slender salmonid fish, *Hucho hucho*, of the Danube river system.

†**hucho** *n.* [f. the L name] = HUCHEN: only in 19.

huck /hʌk/ *n. obs.* exc. *dial.* LME. [Origin uncertain: perh. rel. to MLG, MDu. *hūken*, *hukken* sit bent, crouch, f. Gmc base meaning 'be bent'.] The hip, the haunch.

Comb.: **huck-bone** = *huckle-bone* s.v. HUCKLE *n.*

¶Earliest in *comb.* Not recorded in isolation until L18.

huck /hʌk/ *v.i.* Long *obs.* exc. *dial.* ME. [Prob. ult. f. Gmc base also of HUCKSTER *n.*] Haggle, bargain.

huckaback /ˈhʌkəbak/ *n.* & *a.* L17. [Origin unkn.] (Made of) a strong linen or cotton fabric used for towels etc., having the weft threads thrown alternately up to form a rough surface.

hucker-mucker *n.*, *a.*, & *adv.* see HUGGER-MUGGER *n.*, *adv.*, & *a.*

huckle /ˈhʌk(ə)l/ *n.* E16. [Dim. of HUCK *n.*: see -LE[1].] The hip, the haunch.

Comb.: **huckle-back** a humpback; **huckle-backed** *a.* humpbacked; **huckle-bone** (*a*) the bone of the hip, or (occas.) the head of the femur; (*b*) the astragalus bone of the hock joint in a quadruped, used in games or divination; a knuckle-bone.

huckleberry /ˈhʌk(ə)lb(ə)ri/ *n.* L16. [Perh. f. HUCKLE *n.* + BERRY *n.*[1]] **1** Any of various low N. American shrubs of the genus *Gaylussacia*, esp. *G. baccata*, of the heath family, which are valued for their tart edible fruits; the fruit of such a plant. Also = *blueberry* s.v. BLUE *a.* L16. **2** In British use: the bilberry, *Vaccinium myrtillus.* M19.

¶Despite the lateness and paucity of the evidence for sense 2, it is likely that this was the original sense.

huckster /ˈhʌkstə/ *n.* ME. [Prob. of LG origin and rel. to HUCK *v.*: see -STER.] **1** A retailer in a small shop or at a stall; a pedlar, a hawker. ME. **2** A mercenary person ready to make a profit out of anything. LME. **3** A publicity agent or advertising copywriter, esp. for radio or television. *US.* M20.

1 L. DURRELL The hucksters set up their stalls in preparation for some familiar village fete.

Phrases: †**in huckster's hands** likely to be roughly used or lost.

hucksterdom *n.* L19. **hucksterism** *n.* (usu. *derog.*) the theory or practice of being a huckster M20. **huckstery** *n.* the trade or place of trade of a huckster; petty bargaining; in *pl.*, the goods of a huckster: LME.

huckster /ˈhʌkstə/ *v.* L16. [f. the n.] **1** *v.i.* Bargain, haggle. L16. **2** *v.t.* Deal in, retail, (esp. in small quantities); bargain over. M17.

hucksterer *n.* E18. **hucksteress, -tress** *n.* a female huckster E17.

hud /hʌd/ *n. obs.* exc. *dial.* LME. [Perh. f. Gmc base of HIDE *v.*[1]: cf. HUDDLE *v.*] The husk or covering of a seed; the pod of a legume.

†**hudder-mudder** *n.* LME–L16. [Redupl., w. 1st elem. prob. rel. to HUDDLE *v.*: cf. later HUGGER-MUGGER *n.*] Concealment; secrecy. Chiefly in *in hudder-mudder*, secretly, clandestinely.

huddle /ˈhʌd(ə)l/ *n.* L16. [Prob. f. the vb.] **1** A crowded or confused mass of people or things. L16. **2** Confusion; disorderly haste. E17. **3** A close or secret conference. Freq. in *go into a huddle. colloq.* E20. **b** *spec.* In any of various team games, esp. American football, a brief gathering of players during a game to receive instructions. M20. **4** *Bridge.* A pause during which a player considers his or her next call or play. M20.

1 B. MOORE In the distance, a huddle of slate rooftops. P. ROTH A huddle of graduate students waiting shyly . . to ask the writer serious questions. 3 F. ASTAIRE We immediately went into huddles . . to hear and discuss the material which they had written.

huddle /ˈhʌd(ə)l/ *v.* L16. [Perh. of LG origin and ult. f. Gmc base of HIDE *v.*[1]: cf. HUD.] **I** *v.t.* †**1** Hide; hush *up.* L16–E19. **2** Heap *up*, mix, or crowd *together* closely or in a disordered manner; push in a disorderly mass *into*, *out of*, *through*, etc.; put (clothes) on or *on* hurriedly or untidily. L16. **b** Hunch, coil, (oneself) *over*, *up*, etc. M18. **3** Hurry (*over*, *through*); hurry the completion of, botch *up* through haste. Now *rare* or *obs.* M17. **4** Hug. Now *dial.* M17.

2 SIR W. SCOTT The Friar . . had huddled a friar's frock over his green cassock. R. L. STEVENSON The bar-keeper led us upstairs to a room . . with . . chairs huddled into one corner. W. S. CHURCHILL They were huddling and clumping themselves together for mutual protection. b CONAN DOYLE I found him huddled up in his arm-chair with updrawn knees.

II *v.i.* **5** Gather or crowd closely or in disorder; hunch up; nestle closely in a hunched position. Freq. foll. by *together*, *up.* L16. †**6** Hurry in disorder or confusion. M17–M18.

5 H. ROTH They huddled together as if for protection. P. L. FERMOR Villages that huddled round the shingle roofs of churches. B. CHATWIN After dark, she would huddle over the fire.

huddlement *n.* huddled condition, huddling M19. **huddler** *n.* (*rare*) E17.

†**huddle** *adv.* & *a.* M16. [Rel. to the vb.] **A** *adv.* Confusedly; in a crowded mass; in disorderly haste. M16–E17. **B** *adj.* Huddled, confused, crowded. E17–E18.

hudibrastic /hjuːdɪˈbrastɪk/ *a.* & *n.* E18. [f. *Hudibras* (see below) after *fantastic* etc.] **A** *adj.* In the metre or manner of *Hudibras*, a mock-heroic satirical poem by Samuel Butler, published 1663–78. E18. **B** *n.* Hudibrastic language, verse, or style. M18.

hudibrastically *adv.* L19.

Hudson Bay /hʌds(ə)n ˈbeɪ/ *n. phr.* Also **Hudson's Bay** /ˈhʌds(ə)nz/. L19. [See next. Var. f. the Hudson's Bay Company.] In full *Hudson Bay blanket.* A durable woollen blanket of a kind orig. sold by the Hudson's Bay Company and freq. used as material for coats.

Hudsonian /hʌdˈsəʊnɪən/ *a.* M19. [f. *Hudson* Bay, f. its discoverer Henry *Hudson* (d. 1611), Eng. navigator: see -IAN.] Of or pertaining to Hudson Bay in Canada and the surrounding land; *esp.* designating the biogeographical zone represented by the territory around the bay (north of the tree line from Labrador to Alaska).

Hudsonian curlew *N. Amer.* a whimbrel, *Numenius phaeopus* (of the N. American subspecies). **Hudsonian godwit** a New World godwit, *Limosa haemastica*, breeding in NW Canada.

hue /hjuː/ *n.*[1] [OE *hēw*, *hēow*, *hīw*, *hīew* = ON *hý* down on plants (Sw. *hy* skin, complexion), Goth. *hiwi* form, appearance, f. Gmc base of unkn. origin.] **1** Form, shape, figure; appearance, aspect; species. Long *obs.* exc. *Sc.* OE. †**b** An apparition. OE–E17. **2** Colour. OE. **b** Variety, tint, or quality of a colour. M19. **c** That attribute of a colour by which it is recognized as a red, a green, etc., and which is dependent on its dominant wavelength, and independent of intensity or lightness. M19. **3** Complexion of the face or skin; *fig.* character, aspect. ME.

2 SLOAN WILSON The rocks were . . tinged with a dull red hue. B. BREYTENBACH Their cheeks have the hue of tomatoes. 3 ISAIAH BERLIN Muddle-headed men of good will and quacks and false prophets of every hue. *hide and hue*: see HIDE *n.*[1]

hueless *a.* colourless, pallid OE.

hue /hjuː/ *n.*[2] *obs.* exc. in HUE AND CRY. LME. [OFr. *hu*, f. *huer* HUE *v.*[2]] Outcry, shouting, clamour, esp. during battle or hunting.

hue /hjuː/ *v.*[1]*t.* OE. [f. HUE *n.*[1]] **1** Form, fashion, give an external appearance to; colour. Chiefly as *hued* ppl a. OE. †**2** Depict, describe vividly. Only in ME.

hue /hjuː/ *v.*[2] Now *local.* ME. [(O)Fr. *huer* shout as in battle or hunting: of imit. origin.] **1** *v.i.* Shout, make an outcry; *spec.* in hunting, and in guiding a seine-fishing operation. ME. **2** *v.t.* Assail, drive, or guide with shouts. L16.

huer *n.* M16.

hue and cry /hjuː (ə)n(d) ˈkraɪ/ *n.* & *v. phr.* Also **hue-and-cry**. LME. [Legal AN *hu e cri*, i.e. *hu* outcry, HUE *n.*[2], *e* and, *cri* CRY *n.*] **A** *n.* **1** *Law* (now *Hist.*). **a** An outcry calling for the pursuit of a felon; the pursuit of a felon with such an outcry. LME. **b** A proclamation for the capture of a criminal or the recovery of stolen property. E17. **c** An official publication in which details of offences committed and offenders sought are given. E19. **2** *gen.* A shout of pursuit or attack; a cry or general expression of alarm or opposition. L15.

1 W. COWPER They raised the hue and cry:—'Stop thief! stop thief!—a highwayman!' 2 H. EVANS There was, none the less, an immediate hue and cry in the press and Parliament.

B *v.* **1** *v.i.* Raise a hue and cry; make an outcry. M18. **2** *v.t.* Pursue with hue and cry. M19.

huebnerite *n.* see HÜBNERITE.

huegelite *n.* see HÜGELITE.

huerta /ˈhwɛːtə/ *n.* M19. [Sp.] In Spain and Spanish-speaking countries: a piece of irrigated land; an orchard.

huet-huet /ˈhuːɪthuːɪt/ *n.* Also **guidguid** /ˈgwɪdgwɪd/. M19. [Imit.] Either of two S. American birds of the tapaculo family, *Pteroptochos tarnii* and *P. castaneus.*

huff /hʌf/ *n.* L16. [f. the vb.] **1** A sudden rush *of* anger or arrogance. Now usu., a fit of pique or offended dignity. L16. †**2** A person puffed up with self-importance; a swaggerer, a bully. Also, (a display of) self-importance. E17–E18. **3** A puff of wind. *obs.* exc. in *huff and puff*, passing into sense 1. E17. **4** *Draughts.* The removal of an opponent's piece for missing or ignoring the opportunity to take one of one's own pieces (orig. accompanied by blowing on the piece). L19.

1 *Listener* It seems a pity that this new era . . should be accompanied by an international huff-and-puff over priorities. A. WEST The medical man . . leaves in a huff when his advice is turned down.

huff /hʌf/ *v.* L16. [f. as next.] **1** *v.i.* Blow, puff. *obs.* exc. in *huff and puff*, passing into sense 2. L16. **2** *v.i.* Puff or swell with pride or arrogance; speak arrogantly, bluster. Cf. earlier HUFFER *n.* L16. **b** *v.t.* Bully or scold (*into*, *off*, *to*, etc.); treat with arrogance or contempt. Now *rare* or *obs.* L17. **3a** *v.i.* Swell with anger or irritation; take offence. Now *rare.* L16. **b** *v.t.* Offend the dignity of; cause to take offence, put into a huff. L18. **4**†**a** *v.t.* Blow or puff (*up*); inflate, cause to swell. E17–E18. **b** *v.i.* Swell (up). *obs.* exc. *dial.* M17. **5** *v.t. Draughts.* Remove (an opponent's piece) for missing or ignoring the opportunity to take one of one's own pieces (orig. accompanied by blowing on the piece). L17.

1 W. D. SNODGRASS We huff like windy giants / scattering with our breath / gray-headed dandelions. *fig.*: A. F. DOUGLAS-HOME Tom Steele puffed and huffed and threatened to sue me. 3a W. BURKITT Some would have huffed at it as a rude affront.

huffingly *adv.* in a huffing manner E17.

†**huff** *int.* Also **huffa**. LME–E17. [Imit. of blowing or puffing: cf. PUFF *n.*, *v.*] Expr. a swaggering, boastful, or bullying personality (esp. on the theatrical stage).

huff-cap /ˈhʌfkap/ *a.* & *n. arch.* L16. [f. HUFF *v.* + CAP *n.*[1]] **A** *adj.* **1** Of drink: heady, strong. L16. **2** Blustering, swaggering. L16. **B** *n.* **1** (A drink made from) strong ale. L16. **2** A swaggering or blustering person. E17.

huff-duff /ˈhʌfdʌf/ *n.* M20. [f. initial letters of *h*igh-*f*requency *d*irection *f*inder.] *Hist.* (Equipment for) radio direction-finding (esp. in the war of 1939–45).

huffer /ˈhʌfə/ *n.* M16. [f. HUFF *v.* + -ER[1].] A person who huffs; formerly *esp.* a boastful or swaggering person.

huffish /ˈhʌfɪʃ/ *a.* M18. [f. HUFF *n.* + -ISH[1].] Arrogant; petulant, piqued.

huffishly *adv.* M18. **huffishness** *n.* M18.

huffkin /ˈhʌfkɪn/ *n. local.* L18. [Origin unkn.] A type of teacake made chiefly in Kent.

huffle /ˈhʌf(ə)l/ *v.t.* & *i. obs.* exc. *dial.* L16. [f. HUFF *v.* + -LE[3].] Blow; inflate, swell.

huffy /ˈhʌfi/ *a.* L17. [f. HUFF *n.* + -Y[1].] Quick to take offence or go into a huff; touchy.

N. BAWDEN I heard myself being huffy and whining and spiteful. J. UPDIKE I'm crazy about that huffy frozen look you get . . when you get defensive.

huffily *adv.* M19. **huffiness** *n.* L17.

hug /hʌg/ *n.* E17. [f. the vb.] **1** A squeezing grip in wrestling. Chiefly in *Cornish hug.* E17. **2** A tight embrace, usu. of affection; a rough grasp with the arms; the squeeze of a bear. M17.

2 C. Potok Manya . . smothered me with a hug that pushed the air from my lungs. *Independent* It was hugs, laughter and tears as they celebrated.

hug /hʌɡ/ *v.* Infl. **-gg-**. M16. [Prob. of Scand. origin: cf. ON *hugga* (Norw. *hugge*) comfort, console, rel. to *hugr* thought, feeling, interest, *hugða* interest, affection, *hugsa* think.] **1** *v.t.* Clasp in the arms, embrace, usu. affectionately; (of a bear etc.) squeeze with the forelegs. M16. **b** Show fondness for; *spec.* court in order to get patronage. Cf. HUGGERY. E17. **c** Cling emotionally or intellectually to (a belief etc.). M17. **2** *v.i.* Embrace tightly, cuddle. L16. **3** *v.refl.* Congratulate (oneself). E17. †**b** Cherish (oneself); make (oneself) comfortable. M17–M18. **4** *v.t.* Keep as close as possible to (a shore etc.). E19.

1 V. Woolf A son who was hugged to death by a bear. E. Caldwell Wayne put his arms around her and hugged her tightly against his chest. **hug-me-tight** a knitted close-fitting usu. sleeveless woollen wrap. c T. Moore Faith . . once wedded fast To some dear falsehood, hugs it to the last. 2 Pope Tis a Bear's talent not to kick but hug. 3 G. W. Le Fevre We hugged ourselves with the idea that we had done right. 4 C. Phillips This one road hugged the perimeter of the island. *Hairdo Ideas* Hair is scissored to hug the head.

huge /hjuːdʒ/ *a.* ME. [Aphet. f. OFr. *ahuge*, *ahoge*, *ahoege*: ult. origin unkn.] Very great, large, or big; immense, enormous, vast.

R. Lindner They were, he remembers, big people with heavy hands and huge feet. E. Reveley You seem to regard the—ah—gulf . . of your ignorance as so huge. *Star & Style (Bombay)* This was a big film with a huge cast.

hugely *adv.* LME. **hugeness** *n.* LME.

hügelite /ˈhjuːɡəlʌɪt/ *n.* Also ***huegelite**. E20. [f. G *Hügel* (family name) + -ITE^1.] *Min.* A brown or orange monoclinic hydrated arsenate of lead and uranium (orig. supposed a vanadate of lead and zinc).

hugeous /ˈhjuːdʒəs/ *a.* Now *rare.* LME. [f. HUGE + -OUS.] = HUGE.

hugeously *adv.* M17.

huggable /ˈhʌɡəb(ə)l/ *a.* L19. [f. HUG *v.* + -ABLE.] Such as invites hugging; cuddly.

hugger /ˈhʌɡə/ *n.* L17. [f. HUG *v.* + -ER^1.] A person who hugs.

hugger-mugger /ˈhʌɡəmʌɡə/ *n.*, *adv.*, & *a.* Also (earlier & now *dial.*) **hucker-mucker** /ˈhʌkəmʌkə/. E16. [Redupl., w. 1st elem. prob. rel. to HUDDLE *v.* and 2nd elem. to MUCKER *v.*^{1}: cf. earlier HUDDER-MUDDER.] **A** *n.* **1** Concealment, secrecy. Chiefly in *in hugger-mugger*, secretly, clandestinely. *arch.* E16. **2** Disorder, confusion; a muddle. L17.

1 S. Butler In Hugger-mugger hid. 2 *Times Lit. Suppl.* The . . Carthusians, revolting against the gregarious hugger-mugger of the older orders, were . . serious writers.

B *adv.* **1** Secretly, clandestinely. Now chiefly *dial.* E16. **2** In disorder or confusion, in a muddle. L19.

2 V. Glendinning Rich and poor lived here hugger-mugger, literally on top of one another.

C *adj.* **1** Secret, clandestine. L17. **2** Disorderly, confused; makeshift. M19.

1 A. Sillitoe There was no longer the hugger-mugger anecdote, or any juicy elbow-gripping gossip. 2 H. Nicolson It entailed . . living a rather hugger-mugger existence in Berlin.

hugger-mugger /ˈhʌɡəmʌɡə/ *v.* Now *rare.* E19. [f. prec.] **1** *v.t.* Keep secret or concealed. E19. **2** *v.i.* Proceed in a clandestine manner; behave in a confused or muddled way. E19.

huggery /ˈhʌɡ(ə)ri/ *n.* L18. [f. HUG *v.* or HUGGER: see -ERY.] The action or practice of hugging; *spec.* the action of a barrister in courting a solicitor etc. in the hope of employment.

huggle /ˈhʌɡ(ə)l/ *v.t.* & *i.* Now chiefly *dial.* L16. [Perh. iterative of HUG *v.*: see -LE^3.] Hug.

Hughie /ˈhjuːi/ *n.* *Austral.* & *NZ slang.* M20. [Dim. of male forename *Hugh*: see -IE, -Y^6.] The imaginary being responsible for the weather. Chiefly in *send her down, Hughie!*

Hugo /ˈhjuːɡəʊ/ *n.* Pl. **-os**. M20. [f. *Hugo* Gernsback (1884–1967), US science-fiction magazine editor.] Any of several awards presented annually to writers of the best new science fiction.

hugsome /ˈhʌɡs(ə)m/ *a.* L19. [f. HUG *v.* + -SOME^1.] = HUGGABLE.

Huguenot /ˈhjuːɡənəʊ, -nɒt/ *n.* & *a.* M16. [Fr., alt. (by assim. to the name of Besançon *Hugues* (*c* 1491–1532), Genevese burgomaster) of †*eiguenot*, pl. †*aignos*, †*hugenaulx*, f. Du. *eedgenot* f. Swiss G *Eidgnosse* confederate, f. *Eid* OATH *n.* + *Genoss* associate.] *Hist.* **A** *n.* A French Protestant of the 16th and 17th cents. M16. **B** *attrib.* or as *adj.* Of or pertaining to the Huguenots. L17.

Huguenotism *n.* French Protestantism in the 16th and 17th cents. E17.

†**hugy** *a.* LME–E19. [f. HUGE + -Y^1.] Huge.

huh /hʌ, hə/ *int.* E17. [Natural exclam.] Expr. surprise, derision, or enquiry.

W. Wharton Hey, Margolis, give us other guys a chance, huh? R. Jarrell Huh! . . I'll tell 'em.

huhu /ˈhuːhuː/ *n.* Chiefly *NZ.* M19. [Maori.] A common large New Zealand beetle, *Prionoplus reticularis*, or its larva (more fully *huhu grub*) found in decaying wood and eaten locally.

huh-uh *int.* & *adv.* var. of UH-UH.

hui /ˈhuːi/ *n.* M19. [Maori & Haw.] In New Zealand, a large social or ceremonial gathering; in Hawaii, a formal club or association.

huia /ˈhuːɪə/ *n.* M19. [Maori: imit.] A black New Zealand wattlebird, *Heteralocha acutirostris* (now extinct), having white-tipped feathers formerly prized by Maoris as marks of rank.

Huichol /wiˈtʃəʊl/ *n.* & *a.* E20. [Sp., f. Huichol.] **A** *n.* Pl. same, **-s**. A member of a Mexican Indian people; the language of this people. E20. **B** *attrib.* or as *adj.* Of or pertaining to the Huichol or their language. E20.

huitain /ˈwiːteɪn/ *n.* *rare.* L16. [Fr., f. *huit* eight + *-ain* -AN.] A set or series of eight lines of verse.

Huk /hʊk/ *n.* M20. [Abbrev. of Tagalog *Hukbalahap*, f. initial syllables of *hukbó* army + *bayan* people, country + *laban* against + *Hapón* Japanese (i.e. *hukbó ng bayan laban sa Hapón* people's army against the Japanese).] A guerrilla movement in the Philippines, orig. against the Japanese in the war of 1939–45, later popularly identified with Communism.

huke /hjuːk/ *n.* *obs.* exc. *Hist.* LME. [OFr. *h(e)uque*, in med.L *huca*, corresp. to MDu. *hūke*, *heuke* (Du. *huik*), MLG *hoike*, etc.: ult. origin unkn.] A kind of hooded cloak; later, a tight-fitting garment worn chiefly by women.

hula /ˈhuːlə/ *n.* & *v.i.* Also **hula-hula**. E19. [Haw.] (Perform) a Hawaiian dance with six basic steps and gestures symbolizing or imitating natural phenomena, historical events, etc.

Comb.: **hula hoop**, (US proprietary) **Hula-Hoop** a plastic or wooden hoop for spinning round the body by movement of the waist and hips; **hula skirt** a grass skirt as worn by a hula dancer.

hulan *n.* var. of UHLAN.

†**hulch** *a.* E17–M18. [Origin unkn.] Hunched; humpy. Freq. in *hulch-backed* adj.

huldee *n.* var. of HALDI.

hule /ˈuːli/ *n.* Also **ule**, **ulli**. E17. [Mex. Sp. *(h)ule* f. Nahuatl *ulli*, *olli*.] Any of several rubber-yielding trees of the tropical American genus *Castilla*, of the mulberry family, esp. *C. elastica* of Central America; the crude rubber obtained from such trees.

hulk /hʌlk/ *n.*^{1} [OE *hulc* prob. dim. formation f. wk grade of *helan*: see HULL *n.*^{1}] **1** A hut, a hovel. Long *obs.* exc. *dial.* OE. **2** The hull or husk of a fruit, grain, etc. Long *obs.* exc. *dial.* LME.

hulk /hʌlk/ *n.*^{2} [Late OE *hulc* (in AL *hulcus*), prob. reinforced in ME by MLG *hulk*, *holk(e*, MDu. *hulke*, *hulc* (Du. *hulk*) = late OHG *holko* (G *Hulk*, *Holk*), whence OFr. *hulque*); prob. of Mediterranean origin: cf. Gk *holkas* cargo ship.] **1** A large cargo or transport ship (*arch.*); any large unwieldy boat. LOE. †**b** The hull of a ship. M17–E19. **c** The body of a dismantled ship, esp. used as a storehouse or temporary quarters; *spec.* (*Hist.*) such a ship used as a prison. L17. **2** A big unwieldy person; a bulky or unwieldy mass. LME.

2 M. Gee Rawdon himself was there . . a hulk of a man with tall boots.

hulky *a.* = HULKING L18.

hulk /hʌlk/ *v.* L18. [f. HULK *n.*^{2}] **I 1** *v.i.* Behave in a clumsy or idle way. L18. **2** *v.i.* Appear like a hulk, be bulky or massive; rise *up* like a hulk. L19.

2 A. Tyler We . . came upon the car: hulking in the dark.

II 3 *v.t.* Accommodate (sailors) temporarily on a hulk. Formerly also, condemn to the hulks. E19.

hulking /ˈhʌlkɪŋ/ *a.* L17. [f. HULK *n.*^{2} + -ING^2.] Massive, bulky; unwieldy, clumsy due to bulk; idle.

P. Bowles Look at that hulking boy. He's never done a day's work in his life. J. Carey The hulking London footman making a darkness in the cabin as he stoops through it.

hull /hʌl/ *n.*^{1} [OE *hulu* f. wk grade of *helan* to cover, whence also OE *hylma*, OHG *hulla* mantle, head-covering (G *Hülle*) and Du. *huls*, OHG *hulsa* (G *Hülse* husk, pod): cf. HOLE *n.*^{1}, next.] **1** The outer covering, rind, shell, pod, or husk of any fruit or seed. OE. **b** Bran. *rare.* LME. **c** The calyx which persists at the base of some fruits, as strawberries. Also, the core of a fruit, as an apple, a raspberry, etc. L19. **2** A sty or pen for animals. Formerly also, a hut, a hovel. *Sc.* & *north.* ME. **3** Something that encases or encloses; a covering; *spec.* (now *rare*) the membrane enclosing the heart, the pericardium; in *pl.* (now chiefly *Sc.*), clothes. E17.

hull /hʌl/ *n.*^{2} LME. [Perh. var. of HOLL *n.* or same wd as prec.] The body or frame of a ship or boat, apart from the masts etc.; the frame of an airship, seaplane, etc.

hull down (of a ship) so far away that the hull is below the horizon; (of a tank) concealed apart from the gun-turret.

hull /hʌl/ *v.*^{1}*t.* LME. [f. HULL *n.*^{1}] Remove the hull, shell, or husk of; strip of the outer covering.

hull /hʌl/ *v.*^{2} M16. [f. HULL *n.*^{2}] †**1** *v.i.* Of a ship: move by the force of the wind or current on the hull alone; drift. M16–E18. **2** *v.t.* Strike (a ship) in the hull with cannon shot etc. E18.

hullabaloo /hʌləbəˈluː/ *n.*, *int.*, & *v.* Also **halla-**, **holla-**. M18. [Redupl. of HULLO, HALLO, etc.] **A** *n.* (An) uproar, (a) clamour; noisy confusion. M18.

J. Hersey A terrible hullabaloo of hammering, wedging, ripping, and splitting. W. Golding The excitement, the hullabaloo, the world interest of Tutankhamun's tomb.

B *int.* Used to attract attention. *rare.* M19.

C *v.i.* Make a hullabaloo. M19.

hullo /həˈləʊ, hʌ-/ *int.* Also **hulloa**, (*colloq.* & *joc.*) **'ullo** /əˈləʊ/. M19. [Var. of HALLO *int.*] = HELLO *int.*

Listener If, when you take off the receiver, you say 'Hullo!' . . . you might be saying 'Hullo!' to a total stranger.

†**hullock** *n.* M16–E18. [Origin unkn.] A small part of a sail let out in a gale to keep a ship's head to the sea.

hully gee /hʌlɪ ˈdʒiː/ *int.* Chiefly *US.* L19. [Alt. of *Holy Jesus*.] Expr. surprise or delight.

hully gully /hʌlɪ ˈɡʌli/ *n.* M20. [Origin unkn.] A dance that is a modification of the frug, popular in the 1960s.

hulver /ˈhʌlvə/ *n.* *obs.* exc. *dial.* ME. [ON *hulfr.*] Holly.

hulwa *n.* var. of HALVA.

hum /hʌm/ *n.*^{1} & *int.* LME. [Rel. to or f. as HUM *v.*^{1}] **A** *n.* **I 1** A slight inarticulate vocal sound usu. uttered in hesitation, embarrassment, approval, dissent, etc. Freq. in *hums and ha's* or *haws.* LME. **2** A low continuous non-sibilant sound (as) made by a bee, a spinning-top, working machinery, etc.; an indistinct sound produced by a blend of distant noises, a murmur; *transf.* a rumour. L16. **b** *Med.* In full *venous hum.* A continuous humming sound heard on auscultation of the jugular vein, esp. in some anaemic patients, due to increased blood flow. M19. c *Electronics.* Unwanted low-frequency variation in current or voltage (as from the alternating mains current) which causes a humming sound in a loudspeaker; the sound so produced. E20. 3 An instance of humming (a tune). M17.

2 N. BAWDEN I have found . . the persistent hum of the traffic . . remarkably soothing. R. INGALLS Her real conversion . . happened in semi-darkness, to the accompaniment of a low hum given off by the museum's slide projector. *Observer* All of a sudden . . a 'hum' goes round about some politician or other.

II †4 A type of strong ale. Cf. HUMMING 2b. E17–E18. 5 A bad smell, a stink. E20.

B *int.* Expr. hesitation, embarrassment, dissent, etc. Cf. HA *int.* 3. M16.

hum /hʌm/ *n.*[2] *slang.* M18. [Abbrev. of HUMBUG. Cf. HUMDUDGEON.] 1 A hoax, a sham. *arch.* M18. 2 A scrounger, a persistent borrower. *Austral.* E20.

hum /hʌm/ *n.*[3] E20. [Serbo-Croat.] *Physical Geogr.* A steep-sided hill, of roughly circular cross-section, characteristic of karst topography. Cf. MOGOTE, PEPINO.

hum /hʌm/ *v.*[1] Infl. **-mm-**. LME. [Imit.: cf. BUM *v.*[1], MHG (G dial.) *hummen*, G *summen*, *brummen*, Du. *brommen*.] 1 *v.i.* Utter 'hum' in hesitation, embarrassment, etc. Chiefly in *hum and ha* or *haw*. LME. 2 *v.i.* Make a low continuous non-sibilant sound. LME. b *v.i.* Emit or produce an indistinct noise; *colloq.* be in a state of activity. M18. 3 *v.t.* & *i.* Sing (a tune etc.) with closed lips and without articulation. L15. †b *v.t.* Express approval or disapproval of (a person or thing) by humming. M17–M18. c *v.t.* Bring (a person) into a specified state by humming. E19. 4 *v.i.* Smell unpleasant, stink. E20.

1 J. KELMAN They hummed and hawed and I could tell they weren't too interested. 2 E. L. DOCTOROW The car moved through the city, its motor humming in the warm afternoon. H. BASCOM Bullets like supersonic bees now hum through the darkness. b J. CONRAD The growling voices hummed steady amongst bursts of laughter. *Times* There was an initial shock . . but things are humming at the Mirror now. 3 W. WHARTON Doris starts humming to the music. E. O'BRIEN They glide through their own hallways, whistling or humming a familiar, guarded tune. c J. CLARE The busy bee hath humm'd himself to rest. 4 *Daily Telegraph* When the wind drops this stuff really hums.

hum /hʌm/ *v.*[2] *slang.* Infl. **-mm-**. M18. [Abbrev. of HUMBUG.] 1 *v.t.* Hoax, deceive, take in. Now *arch.* & *dial.* M18. 2 *v.t.* & *i.* Scrounge, cadge. *Austral.* E20.

huma /ˈhuːmə/ *n.* M19. [Pers. & Urdu *humā* phoenix.] A mythical bird similar to the phoenix, supposed to bring luck to any person over whom it hovers on its restless flights.

human /ˈhjuːmən/ *a.* & *n.* Also (earlier) †**humane**. See also HUMANE. LME. [(O)Fr. *humain(e)* f. L *humanus* rel. to *homo* man.] A *adj.* I 1 Of, pertaining to, or characteristic of humankind or people; belonging to humankind; of or belonging to the species *Homo sapiens*. LME. 2 *spec.* a Of, pertaining to, or characteristic of (the faculties of) human beings as opp. to gods or God; fallible; mundane. M16. b Of, pertaining to, or characteristic of the activities, relationships, etc., of human beings, esp. as distinct from those of lower animals, machines, mere objects, etc. M18. c Having or showing the (esp. better) qualities distinctive of or attributed to human beings. M19. 3 *Astrol.* Of a zodiacal sign: having the form of a man, woman, or child. M17.

1 V. WOOLF Now we wake the sleeping daws who have never seen a human form. I. ASIMOV Baley wondered if . . they would accept *anything* in human appearance as a man. M. AMSTERDAM There is definitely no human life on the planet, Mars. F. FITZGERALD Groups of students formed human roadblocks across the avenues leading into the city. R. WEST We obeyed that mysterious human impulse to smile . . at . . a fellow-creature occupied in baseness. M. GEE We have the cerebral cortex, the part that makes us human. *National Trust Magazine* Conservation . . is a key to the well-being of the human race. 2a POPE To err is humane, to forgive divine. J. GATHORNE-HARDY The GPs make a slip, they're only human. b *Observer* Much of British management does not seem to understand the human factor. c B. CASTLE I get very fond of my civil servants. . . The outside world has no idea how human they are. M. ESSLIN Bérenger, its hero, is a Chaplinesque little man, simple, awkward, but human.

II See HUMANE.

Special collocations: **human animal** the human being viewed as one member of the animal kingdom. **human being** a person; a man, a woman, a child; a member of the species *Homo sapiens*. *human* ECOLOGY. **human engineering** (the study of) the management of industrial labour, esp. concerning the relationships between machines and human beings. *human equation*: see EQUATION 4. *human* GEOGRAPHY. **human interest** reference to human experience and emotions etc., esp. in a news story etc. **human nature** the general characteristics and feelings attributed to human beings. **human race** the division of living creatures to which people belong; humankind. **human relations**: with or between people or individuals. **human resources** people (esp. personnel or workers) as a significant asset of a business etc. **human rights**: held to be justifiably claimed by any person. **human shield** a person or group of persons placed in a potential line of fire in order to deter attack.

B *n.* 1 A human being. M16. 2 That which is human. E20.

1 B. EMECHETA The centre apartment slept both the humans as well as the animals.

humanhood *n.* human character M19.

humanation /hjuːməˈneɪʃ(ə)n/ *n. rare.* M17. [Late L *humanatio(n-)*, f. *humanare* to incarnate, f. *humanus* HUMAN *a.*: see -ATION.] Incarnation.

humane /hjʊˈmeɪn/ *a.* & *n.* See also HUMAN. LME. [Earlier form of HUMAN.] A *adj.* I 1 See HUMAN. LME.

II 2 In early use, civil, courteous, or obliging towards others. Now only, characterized by sympathy with or consideration for others; compassionate; benevolent. (Earlier in HUMANELY.) E16. b Inflicting the minimum of pain. E20. 3 Of a branch of study: intended to civilize or refine; elegant. L17.

2 R. C. TRENCH It is just in man to be merciful . . to be humane is human. J. M. MURRY The humane and generous wisdom which seems to have been his birthright. b **humane killer** an instrument for the painless slaughter of animals.

†B *n.* See HUMAN. LME.

humanely /hjʊˈmeɪnli/ *adv.* Also †**humanly**. L15. [f. HUMANE *a.* + -LY[2].] In a humane manner, compassionately. Formerly also = HUMANLY.

humaneness /hjʊˈmeɪn-nɪs/ *n.* E19. [f. as prec. + -NESS.] Humane quality or condition; compassionateness.

humanics /hjʊˈmanɪks/ *n.* M19. [f. HUMAN *a.* & *n.* + -ICS.] The branch of knowledge that deals with human affairs.

humanify /hjʊˈmanɪfʌɪ/ *v.t.* E17. [f. HUMAN *a.* + -I- + -FY.] Make human.

humanifiˈcation *n.* L19.

humanise *v.* var. of HUMANIZE.

humanism /ˈhjuːmənɪz(ə)m/ *n.* E19. [In sense 1 f. HUMAN *a.* + -ISM; in other senses f. next.] †1 Belief in the humanity but not the divinity of Christ. Only in E19. 2 The quality of being human; devotion to human interests or welfare. M19. 3 Devotion to studies promoting human culture; literary culture, *esp.* that of the Renaissance humanists. M19. 4a *Philos.* & *Theol.* An outlook or system of thought concerned with human rather than divine or supernatural matters. M19. b *Philos.* A belief or outlook emphasizing common human needs and seeking solely rational ways of solving human problems, and concerned with humankind as responsible and progressive intellectual beings. E20.

humanist /ˈhjuːmənɪst/ *n.* & *a.* L16. [Fr. *humaniste* f. It. *umanista*, f. *umano* f. L *humanus*: see HUMAN, -IST.] A *n.* 1 A classical scholar, a Latinist (*arch.*); *spec.* (*Hist.*) a student of Roman and Greek literature and antiquities, esp. during the Renaissance. L16. 2 A person concerned with or interested in human affairs; a humanitarian. E17. 3 *Philos.* An adherent of humanism. E20. B *attrib.* or as *adj. Philos.* Of or pertaining to humanism. E20.

humanistic /hjuːməˈnɪstɪk/ *n.* & *a.* E18. [f. prec. + -IC.] A *n.* In *pl.* Classical studies. *rare.* E18. B *adj.* 1 *Hist.* Of or pertaining to the Renaissance humanists. M19. 2 *Philos.* Of, pertaining to, or characteristic of humanism. E20.

humanistical /hjuːməˈnɪstɪk(ə)l/ *a.* E18. [f. as prec. + -ICAL.] = HUMANISTIC *a.*

humanistically *adv.* L19.

humanitarian /hjʊˌmanɪˈtɛːrɪən/ *n.* & *a.* E19. [f. HUMANIT(Y + -ARIAN, after *equalitarian*, *unitarian*, etc.] A *n.* 1 A person believing in the humanity but not the divinity of Christ. Now *rare.* E19. 2 A person concerned with human welfare; a person advocating or practising humane action; a philanthropist. M19. 3 *Philos.* A person believing in the primary importance of the advancement or welfare of the human race. M19.

2 E. J. HOWARD He was regarded as a . . humanitarian, someone . . who cared what happened to society.

B *adj.* Of, pertaining to, or holding the views of a humanitarian. M19.

G. M. TREVELYAN This greater sensitiveness to evils . . was part of the general humanitarian movement.

humanitarianism *n.* humanitarian principles or practice M19.

humanitary /hjʊˈmanɪt(ə)ri/ *a. rare.* M19. [f. as prec. + -ARY[1]. Cf. Fr. *humanitaire*.] 1 Of or pertaining to the human race. M19. 2 Humanitarian, philanthropic. L19.

humanitas /hjʊˈmanɪtɑːs/ *n.* M20. [L *humanitas*.] Humanity.

humanity /hjʊˈmanɪti/ *n.* LME. [(O)Fr. *humanité* f. L *humanitas*, f. *humanus*: see HUMAN, -ITY.] I Rel. to HUMAN. 1 The quality, condition, or fact of being human. LME. b In *pl.* Human attributes. Also, human affairs. E19. 2 The human race; human beings collectively. LME.

1 *New York Voice* They denounced slavery as a sin, asserted the humanity of the blacks. 2 *Observer* Most of humanity is sensitive about apartheid because most of humanity is black. P. LIVELY The trams so loaded with humanity that they looked like a beeswarm.

II Rel. to HUMANE. 3 The quality of being humane; kindness, benevolence. LME. b An act of humanity. Usu. in *pl.* Now *rare.* L16. 4 Learning or literature concerned with human culture, *esp.* (now usu. in *pl.*) the branch of knowledge that deals with the Latin and Greek classics, esp. (in Scottish Universities, also *sing.*) the Latin ones. L15.

3 G. M. TREVELYAN The sentiment of humanity was now a great force in politics. T. KENEALLY For his humanity he had been honoured by the Israeli government. 4 R. HAYMAN Law students at Prague were obliged to devote one term to the humanities. Z. MEDVEDEV The humanities—philosophy, history, law, literature, linguistics, etc.—remained in the old university buildings.

humanize /ˈhjuːmənʌɪz/ *v.* Also **-ise**. E17. [Fr. *humaniser*, f. L *humanus*: see HUMAN, -IZE.] 1 *v.t.* Make human; give a human character to; represent in human form. E17. b *spec.* Render (cow's milk) more similar to human milk and hence more suitable for consumption by infants. L19. 2 *v.t.* Make humane; soften, refine, civilize. M17. b *v.i.* Become humane; cause humanization. L18.

1 *Times* Nash . . . was rendering a humanized version of a young lady goat with his usual facility.

humaniˈzation *n.* E19. **humanizer** *n.* L18.

humankind /hjuːmənˈkʌɪnd/ *n.* L16. [f. HUMAN *a.* + KIND *n.*, after MANKIND.] The human race; = MANKIND *n.* 1.

humanly /ˈhjuːmənli/ *adv.* See also HUMANELY. L15. [f. HUMAN *a.* + -LY[2].] 1 With human kindness or feeling. L15. 2 From a human point of view; within the range of human power; by human means; in accordance with human nature. L16.

1 J. R. LOWELL If he had not felt intensely and humanly. 2 B. BETTELHEIM A . . desire to destroy opposition is rationally understandable, though humanly we do not condone it. E. BOWEN By as soon

as was humanly possible after six o'clock she was back home.

humanness /'hjuːmən-nɪs/ *n.* E18. [f. as prec. + -NESS.] The quality, condition, or fact of being human.

humanoid /'hjuːmənɔɪd/ *a.* & *n.* E20. [f. HUMAN + -OID.] (An animal or thing) with human form or character.

New Scientist Evolving humanoids grew more intelligent at about the time they began using tools to hunt. *Sun* The humanoid robots familiar to us from fiction are worlds apart from today's industrial models.

humantin /hjʊ'mantɪn/ *n.* E20. [Fr., of unkn. origin.] A shark, *Oxynotus centrina*, of the Mediterranean Sea and Portuguese coasts, having high, angular, spiny dorsal fins.

humate /'hjuːmeɪt/ *n.* M19. [f. HUMIC + -ATE[1].] *Chem.* A salt of any of the humic acids.

hum-bird /'hʌmbəːd/ *n.* Now *US.* M17. [f. HUM *n.*[1] or *v.*[1] + BIRD *n.*] The hummingbird.

humble /'hʌmb(ə)l/ *a.*[1] & *v.*[1] ME. [OFr. *umble*, (also mod.) *humble* f. L *humilis* low, lowly, base, f. *humus* ground, earth, rel. to *homo* man.] A *adj.* 1 Having or showing a low estimate of one's own importance; (of an action, thought, etc.) offered with or affected by such an estimate; lacking assertion, deferential. ME. 2 Of lowly rank or condition; modest; (of a thing) of modest dimensions, pretensions, etc. LME. 3 Of a plant: low-growing (now chiefly *fig.* and passing into sense 1). Formerly also, (of land) low-lying. L16.

1 J. LONDON He was humble and meek, filled with self-disparagement and abasement. J. BUCHAN You're a great man. I offer you my humble congratulations. K. AMIS He muttered something and looked suitably humble, grateful and so on. 2 DAY LEWIS A love which had its humble beginnings in the harmonium at Monart. A. THWAITE Getting any . . place in the Civil Service, however humble, involved the exercise of patronage.

Phrases: **eat humble pie** [w. punning ref. to *umble pie* s.v. UMBLES as an inferior dish] make a humble apology; accept humiliation. **your humble** (**servant**) *arch.*: used in subscription of a letter or as a form of ironical courtesy.

B *v.* 1 *v.refl.* & †*i.* Lower oneself in respect or submission; bow. *arch.* LME. 2 *v.t.* Lower in dignity, position, etc.; abase; make humble in spirit. L15.

1 S. PURCHAS All the people did humble themselves, laying earth upon their heads. 2 BARONESS ORCZY She would crush her own pride, humble it before him.

humbleness *n.* LME. **humbler** *n.* E17. **humblingly** *adv.* in a humbling manner M19. **humbly** *adv.* LME.

humble *a.*[2], *v.*[2], & *n.* var. of HUMMEL.

humble-bee /'hʌmb(ə)lbiː/ *n.* LME. [Prob. f. MLG *hummelbē*, *homelbē*, f. *hummel* hum, buzz = (M)Du. *hommel*, OHG *humbal* (G *Hummel*) + *bē* BEE *n.*[1] Cf. BUMBLE-BEE.] = BUMBLE-BEE.

humble-jumble /'hʌmb(ə)ldʒʌmb(ə)l/ *n. rare.* M16. [A rhyming formation on JUMBLE *n.*[1]] = JUMBLE *n.*[1]

†**humblesse** *n.* LME–M18. [OFr. *(h)umblesse*, f. *(h)umble*: see HUMBLE *a.*[1] & *v.*[1], -ESS[2].] Humbleness, humility.

Humboldtian /hʌm'bəʊltɪən/ *a.* E20. [f. K. Wilhelm von *Humboldt* (see below) + -IAN.] Of, pertaining to, or characteristic of the German philosopher Wilhelm von Humboldt (1767–1835) or his work.

humboldtine /'hʌmbəʊltʌɪn/ *n.* E19. [f. F. H. A. von *Humboldt* (1769–1859), Ger. traveller + -INE[5].] *Min.* Ferrous oxalate, which forms yellow crystals of the monoclinic system.

humbug /'hʌmbʌg/ *n.* & *v.* M18. [Origin unkn.] A *n.* †1 A hoax, a trick. M–L18. 2 A deceiver; a fraud, a sham. M18. 3 Deception, pretence; nonsense, rubbish. E19. 4 A boiled sweet, usu. peppermint-flavoured, with a chewy centre and coloured stripes, and freq. pillow-shaped. E19.

2 G. K. CHESTERTON That old gentleman . . —that venerable humbug was not really a philosopher. M. SCHORER His announced purpose is, we admit, a pious humbug. 3 I. MURDOCH The theatre is humbug But who wants it to be like life, it's escape. A. L. ROWSE This was Hitler's propaganda line, bemusing the British with humbug about his pacific intentions.

B *v.* Infl. **-gg-**. 1 *v.t.* Delude (*into* doing); cheat or trick (*out of* something). M18. 2 *v.i.* Deceive, cheat; be a fraud or sham. M18. 3 Flounder *about*, make poor progress. Chiefly *local US.* M19.

1 J. M. SYNGE If it's not humbugging me you are, I'm thinking that I'll surely stay.

humbuggable *a.* E19. **humbugger** *n.* M18. **hum'buggery** *n.* the action or practice of humbugging M19.

humdinger /hʌm'dɪŋə/ *n.* E20. [Prob. f. HUM *v.*[1] + DINGER.] 1 A remarkable or outstanding person or thing; something exciting or thrilling. *slang* (orig. *US*). E20. 2 *Electronics* (chiefly *Hist.*). A voltage divider introduced into the heater circuit of a valve in order to reduce hum by biasing. M20.

1 J. L. CARR Anyway, this Roscoe was a humdinger, a truly Great American. *Gridiron Pro* The game was a humdinger, with the lead switching first one way, then the other.

humdrum /'hʌmdrʌm/ *a.*, *n.*, & *v.* M16. [Prob. redupl. of HUM *v.*[1]] A *adj.* 1 Lacking variety; routine; dull, monotonous. M16. †2 Undecided, irresolute. M17–E18.

1 J. F. LEHMANN The quiet, humdrum respectable façade of the neighbourhood dropped away. J. GATHORNE-HARDY They think it's going to be a glamorous life, and they find it's . . humdrum.

B *n.* 1 A humdrum person or thing. *arch.* L16. 2 Dullness, monotony. L16.

2 GEO. ELIOT She was living with some intensity, and escaping humdrum.

C *v.i.* & †*t.* w. *it.* Proceed or act in a humdrum manner. *arch.* M18.

hum'drummery *n.* = HUMDRUM *n.* 2 M19. **hum'drumness** *n.* = HUMDRUM *n.* 2 L19.

humdudgeon /hʌm'dʌdʒ(ə)n/ *n. colloq.* Now *rare.* L18. [Cf. HUM *n.*[2] and DUDGEON *n.*[2]] Bad temper, sulking; a fuss.

Humean /'hjuːmɪən/ *a.* & *n.* Also **Humian**. E19. [f. *Hume* (see below) + -AN, -EAN, -IAN.] A *adj.* Of or pertaining to the Scottish philosopher and historian David Hume (1711–76) or his philosophy. E19. B *n.* An adherent or student of the philosophy of Hume. L19.

Humism *n.* the philosophy or beliefs of Hume M19. **Humist** *n.* = HUMEAN *n.* L19.

humect /hjʊ'mɛkt/ *v.* Now *rare.* LME. [L *(h)umect-* pa. ppl stem of *(h)umectare*, f. *(h)umectus* moist, wet, f. *(h)umere* be moist.] 1 *v.t.* Moisten, make wet. LME. 2 *v.i.* Become moist or wet. Long *rare* or *obs.* LME.

humective *n.* (*rare*) a humectant LME.

humectant /hjʊ'mɛkt(ə)nt/ *a.* & *n.* M17. [L *(h)umectant-* pres. ppl stem of *(h)umectare*: see prec., -ANT[1].] A *adj.* 1 Moistening, wetting. Long *rare* or *obs.* M17. 2 That retains moisture. M20. B *n.* 1 A moistening agent. E19. 2 A substance, *spec.* a food additive, used to reduce the loss of moisture. M19.

humectate /hjʊ'mɛkteɪt/ *v.t.* Now *rare.* M17. [L *(h)umectat-* pa. ppl stem of *(h)umectare*: see HUMECT, -ATE[3].] = HUMECT 1.

humec'tation *n.* (*a*) the action of moistening, the condition of being moistened; †(*b*) liquefaction: LME.

humeral /'hjuːm(ə)r(ə)l/ *a.* L16. [Fr. *huméral* or mod.L *humeralis*, f. L HUMERUS: see -AL[1].] 1 Of or pertaining to the humerus of a human or other vertebrate. L16. 2 *Zool.* Of or pertaining to (the region of) the humerus of an insect or other invertebrate. See HUMERUS 2. E19. 3 Of or pertaining to the shoulder. M19.

3 **humeral veil** *RC Ch.* an oblong scarf worn on the shoulders by an officiant at the Eucharist.

humerus /'hjuːm(ə)rəs/ *n.* Pl. **-ri** /-rʌɪ/. LME. [L.] *Anat.* & *Zool.* 1 The bone of the upper arm or forelimb in man and other tetrapod vertebrates, articulating at the shoulder and elbow. LME. 2 Chiefly *Entomol.* Any of various structures in insects etc. involving or in the region of the posterolateral angle of the thorax, the anterolateral angle of the wing-case, the femur of the front leg, etc. E19.

†**humet** *a.* M17–M18. [Abbrev.] = HUMETTY.

humetty /hjʊ'mɛti/ *a.* L16. [OFr., dim. of *heaume* tiller of a rudder: see -ET[1], -Y[5].] *Her.* Designating an ordinary of which the extremities are cut off so as not to reach the sides of the shield.

humhum /'hʌmhʌm/ *n. obs.* exc. *Hist.* E17. [Origin unkn.] Any of various fabrics; *esp.* a coarse Indian cotton cloth.

Humian *a.* & *n.* var. of HUMEAN.

humic /'hjuːmɪk/ *a.* M19. [f. HUMUS + -IC.] Of, pertaining to, or contained in humus; rich in humus; derived from plant remains.

humic acid *Chem.* any of various complex organic acids formed in soil by decomposition of plant material. **humic coal**: derived from peat.

humicubation /ˌhjuːmɪkjʊ'beɪʃ(ə)n/ *n.* Now *rare.* M17. [mod.L *humicubatio(n-)*, f. L *humi* on the ground + *cubatio(n-)* (f. *cubare* lie down): see -ATION.] The action or an act of lying down on the ground, esp. as a sign of penitence or humiliation.

humid /'hjuːmɪd/ *a.* LME. [Fr. *humide* or L *(h)umidus*, f. *(h)umere* be moist: see -ID[1].] Slightly wet as with steam, mist, etc.; moist, damp.

D. BAGLEY The warm air rises, heavy and humid, full of water vapour. A. BROOKNER The warmth was humid, promising showers.

humidly *adv.* L19. **humidness** *n.* E18.

humidify /hjʊ'mɪdɪfʌɪ/ *v.t.* L19. [f. prec. + -I- + -FY.] Make humid, make or keep moist.

humidifi'cation *n.* the process of making the atmosphere etc. moist, esp. by means of a humidifier: L19. **humidifier** *n.* a machine or device for keeping the atmosphere moist: L19.

humidistat /hjʊ'mɪdɪstat/ *n.* E20. [f. HUMIDI(TY + -STAT.] A machine or device which automatically regulates the humidity of the air in a room or building.

humidity /hjʊ'mɪdɪti/ *n.* LME. [(O)Fr. *humidité* or L *humiditas*, f. *humidus* HUMID: see -ITY.] 1 The state or quality of being humid; moistness, dampness; *esp.* a specific degree of moisture in the atmosphere. LME. 2 Moisture, fluid, damp. LME. b In *pl.* The fluids of animal and plant bodies. Long *rare* or *obs.* LME.

1 J. S. FOSTER This detail should be used only in . . buildings . . not liable to high internal humidity. **absolute humidity** *Meteorol.*: measured as the mass of water vapour in a given volume of air, usu. expressed in grams per cubic metre. **relative humidity** *Meteorol.*: expressed as the ratio of the mass of water vapour in a volume of air to the value for saturated air at the same temperature. 2 *Practical Hairstyling & Beauty* Central heating and airconditioning . . takes humidity out of the air.

humidor /'hjuːmɪdɔː/ *n.* E20. [f. HUMID after *cuspidor*.] A box or room etc. for keeping cigars and tobacco moist.

humification /ˌhjuːmɪfɪ'keɪʃ(ə)n/ *n.* L19. [f. as HUMIFY *v.*[2]: see -FICATION.] The process by which plant remains are converted into humus; the resultant state of being humified.

humify /'hjuːmɪfʌɪ/ *v.*[1]*t. rare.* M17. [Late L *(h)umificare*, f. *(h)umificus*, f. *(h)umidus*: see HUMID, -FY.] = HUMIDIFY.

humify /'hjuːmɪfʌɪ/ *v.*[2] E20. [f. HUM(US: see -FY. Cf. earlier HUMIFICATION.] 1 *v.t.* Convert (plant remains) into humus. E20. 2 *v.i.* Of plant remains: be converted into humus. E20.

humiliate /hjʊ'mɪlɪeɪt/ *v.t.* M16. [Late L *humiliat-* pa. ppl stem of *humiliare*, f. *humilis* HUMBLE *a.*[1]: see -ATE[3].] 1 Make humble in position, state, or feeling; humble. Long *rare.* M16. 2 Injure the dignity or self-respect of. M18.

1 ROBERT BURTON How much we ought to . . examine and humiliate our selves. 2 J. GALSWORTHY It was humiliating to be treated like a child! R. P. GRAVES Housman was bitterly humiliated by his failure.

humiliatingly *adv.* in a humiliating manner L18. **humiliator** *n.* (*rare*) a person who humiliates another M19.

humiliation /hjʊˌmɪlɪ'eɪʃ(ə)n, ˌhjuːmɪlɪ-/ *n.* LME. [(O)Fr. f. late L *humiliatio(n-)*, f. as prec.: see -ATION.] The action or an act of humiliating; the state or condition of being humiliated. Formerly also, humility.

P. H. GIBBS Patricia had a sudden feeling of humiliation and shame and anger. A. CLARE Mentally ill patients . . have been exposed to the most extraordinary physical and mental humiliations.

humility /hjʊˈmɪlɪti/ *n.* ME. [(O)Fr. *humilité* f. L *humilitas*, f. *humilis* HUMBLE *a.*[1]: see -ITY.] **1** The quality of being humble; humbleness, meekness. ME. **b** An act of self-abasement. *rare.* E17. **2** Humble condition, rank, or position; unpretentiousness. E17. **3** Any of several snipe of the north-eastern US. *US (local).* M17.

1 P. G. HAMERTON The humility which acknowledges present insufficiency. R. PARK Out of her wickedness and pride had come tolerance, patience and humility. **2** C. LAMB I made a sort of apology for the humility of the fare.

humite /ˈhjuːmʌɪt/ *n.* E19. [f. A. *Hume* (1749–1838), Eng. scientist + -ITE[1].] *Min.* An orthorhombic silicate of magnesium, also containing fluoride and hydroxide; any of a group of magnesium silicates isomorphous with this.

humlie /ˈhʌmli/ *n. Sc.* E19. [f. HUMMEL + -IE.] A hornless cow.

hummable /ˈhʌməb(ə)l/ *a.* M20. [f. HUM *v.*[1] + -ABLE.] That may be hummed; suitable for humming, catchy.

hummel /ˈhʌm(ə)l/ *a.*, *v.*, & *n.* Chiefly *Sc.* & *north.* Also **humble** /ˈhʌmb(ə)l/. L15. [Corresp. to LG *hummel*, *hommel* hornless animal; prob. conn. w. HAMBLE *v.*] **A** *adj.* **1** Of barley etc.: awnless. L15. **2** Of a cow, stag, etc.: hornless. M16. **B** *v.t.* Infl. **-ll-**. **1** Deprive (cattle, stags, etc.) of horns. Chiefly as *hummelled* ppl a. L16. **2** Remove the awns from (barley etc.). M18. **C** *n.* A hornless stag. M19.

hummeller *n.* a machine for removing the awns from barley etc. L18.

hummer /ˈhʌmə/ *n.*[1] E17. [f. HUM *v.*[1] + -ER[1].] **1a** An insect that hums. Also, a hummingbird. E17. **b** A person who hums (a tune); a person who expresses doubt, hesitation, etc., by uttering 'hum'. M18. **2** A person or thing characterized by extreme activity, energy, etc. *colloq.* L17. **b** A person or thing of extraordinary excellence. *colloq.* L19.

hummer /ˈhʌmə/ *n.*[2] M18. [f. HUM *v.*[2] + -ER[1].] †**1** A hoaxer. M–L18. **2** A scrounger. *Austral. colloq.* E20. **3** False or mistaken arrest. *slang.* M20.

humming /ˈhʌmɪŋ/ *a.* E17. [f. HUM *v.*[1] + -ING[2].] **1** That hums or makes a low continuous murmuring sound. E17. **2** Of extraordinary activity, intensity, or magnitude; vigorous; striking. *colloq.* M17. **b** Of liquor: strong. Cf. HUM *n.*[1] 4. *arch. colloq.* L17.

1 hummingbird any of numerous small American birds of the family Trochilidae, having usu. long, thin bills and iridescent plumage, which feed from flowers while hovering. **humming-top** a spinning-top that makes a humming sound.

hummingly *adv.* E20.

hummock /ˈhʌmək/ *n.* Earlier †**hammock**. See also HAMMOCK *n.*[2] M16. [Origin unkn.] **1** Orig. (*Naut.*), a small eminence seen on the coast by approaching sailors. Later, any more or less rounded protuberance rising above the level of the surrounding ground; a hillock, a knoll. M16. **b** A coastal sand-hill. L18. **c** A mound or ridge in an ice-field. E19. **2** See HAMMOCK *n.*[2]

1 J. FOWLES The excavation of the harmless hummocks of earth that pimpled his three thousand Wiltshire acres. **c** JOHN ROSS We proceeded over . . the sea of ice, and, passing some hummocks, arrived at the . . cape.

hummocked *a.* formed into hummocks, hummocky M19.

hummocky /ˈhʌməki/ *a.* M18. [f. prec. + -Y[1].] **1** Having many hummocks, characterized by hummocks. M18. **2** Resembling a hummock. L18.

1 P. D. JAMES The garden, twenty yards of unmown grass, hummocky as a field. **2** J. GEIKIE Even the projecting masses of rock . . present a rounded hummocky aspect.

hummum *n.* var. of HAMMAM.

hummus /ˈhʊməs/ *n.* Also **hoummos**, **h(o)umous**. M20. [Arab. *ḥummuṣ*.] Ground chick-peas mixed with tahini, garlic, and lemon juice, freq. served as an hors d'oeuvre or dip.

humongous /hjuːˈmʌŋgəs/ *a. slang* (orig. *US*). Also **-mungous**. L20. [Origin unkn. Cf. HUGEOUS, MONSTROUS, STUPENDOUS, etc.] Extremely large, huge, enormous.

humor *n.*, *v.* see HUMOUR *n.*, *v.*

humoral /ˈhjuːm(ə)r(ə)l/ *a.* LME. [(O)Fr., or med.L *humoralis*, f. L *humor* HUMOUR *n.*: see -AL[1].] *Med.* (chiefly *Hist.*). **1** Of or relating to body fluids, esp. as opp. to cells. LME. **2** Of diseases: caused by or attributed to a disordered state of body fluids or (formerly) the bodily humours. M16. **3** Of or pertaining to the bodily humours. L18.

humored *a.* see HUMOURED.

humoresque /hjuːməˈrɛsk/ *n.* L19. [G *Humoreske*, f. *Humor* humour + *-eske* -ESQUE.] *Mus.* A short light capricious composition.

humorise *v.* var. of HUMORIZE.

humorism /ˈhjuːm(ə)rɪz(ə)m/ *n.* M19. [f. HUMOUR *n.* + -ISM.] **I 1** Humorous style or manner. *rare.* M19. **2** A humorous saying or remark. L19. **II 3** *Med. Hist.* The doctrine or theory of the relation of the bodily humours to temperament and disease. Cf. SOLIDISM. M19.

humorist /ˈhjuːm(ə)rɪst/ *n.* L16. [f. HUMOUR *n.* + -IST.] †**1** A person subject to humours or fancies; a whimsical person. L16–M19. **2** A witty or facetious person; a humorous talker, actor, or writer. L16. †**3** A person given to humouring or indulging himself or herself or another. Only in 17.

humoˈristic *a.* E19.

humorize /ˈhjuːm(ə)rʌɪz/ *v.* Also **-ise**. L16. [f. HUMOUR *n.* + -IZE.] †**1** *v.i.* Agree with the humour of a person or thing. Only in L16. **2** *v.i.* Speak or think humorously; make humorous remarks. E17. **3** *v.t.* Make (something) humorous. *rare.* L19.

humorous /ˈhjuːm(ə)rəs/ *a.* LME. [f. HUMOUR *n.* + -OUS.] †**1** Of, pertaining to, the bodily humours; humoral. LME–M19. †**2** Moist, humid, damp. L15–E17. **3** Subject to or influenced by humour or mood; fanciful, capricious, whimsical. Now *rare.* L16. †**b** Moody, peevish. E17–M19. **4** Full of, characterized by, or showing (a sense of) humour; facetious, comic, funny. E18.

humorously *adv.* L16. **humorousness** *n.* E17.

humorsome *a.* see HUMOURSOME.

humour /ˈhjuːmə/ *n.* Also *****-or**. ME. [AN (*h*)*umour*, OFr. (*h*)*umor*, *-ur* (mod. *humeur*) f. L (*h*)*umor*, f. (*h*)*umere*: see HUMID, -OUR.] **I 1** *Hist.* The body fluid of a plant or animal; *spec.* (also *cardinal humour*) each of the four fluids (blood, phlegm, choler, and melancholy) formerly (in Galen's theory) held to determine a person's physical and mental qualities. ME. **b** In *pl.* The qualities (of a specified kind) determined by these fluids. Long *arch.* E17. †**c** The particular constitution of a material substance. M17–E18. **2** Either of the transparent fluids which fill parts of the eyeball; the aqueous humour; the vitreous humour. LME. †**3** Moisture; vapour. LME–L17.

1 J. BRONOWSKI The Greek elements were also the four humours which the human temperament combines. **c** S. SWITZER To wonder how Sea-Water shall be thus stripped of its pristine humour. **3** SHAKES. *Jul. Caes.* To walk unbraced and suck up the humours Of the dank morning.

II 4 Mental disposition (orig. as held to have been determined by the bodily humours); temperament. L15. †**b** Character, style, or spirit (of a musical or literary composition etc.). L16–E18. **5** State of mind, mood. Formerly also, habitual frame of mind. E16. **b** An excited state of public feeling. Now *rare.* E17. **6** A particular inclination; a whim, a caprice. Also, (the state of mind characterized by) an inclination *for doing* or a fancy *to do* something. M16. **b** In *pl.* Moods or fancies exhibited in action; vagaries; odd or whimsical traits. Now passing into sense 7. M16. **7** A quality of action, speech, etc., which causes amusement; facetiousness, comicality; (more fully *sense of humour*) the faculty of perceiving and enjoying what is ludicrous or amusing; a sense of the ludicrous or amusing. L16.

4 SHAKES. *Tam. Shr.* Thus I'll curb her mad and headstrong humour. **5** P. BOWLES With all the venom of which a foul humour is capable. **b** CARLYLE Friedrich is deeply unaware of the humour he has raised against himself. **6** BURKE All which had been done . . was the effect not of humour, but of system. **b** N. HAWTHORNE Mariners . . who had come ashore to see the humors of Election Day. **7** SWIFT The priest . . shew'd some humour in his face. L. DEIGHTON Much of the book's humour came from its deadpan style. V. GLENDINNING She extracted surreal and sometimes ribald humour from the most unlikely situations.

Phrases: *aqueous humour*: see AQUEOUS 1. *cardinal humour*: see sense 1 above. *crystalline humour*: see CRYSTALLINE *a.* 1. *glassy humour*: see GLASSY *a.* 1. *glazy humour*: see GLAZY 1. **out of humour** displeased. *radical humour*: see RADICAL *a.* 2a. *sense of humour*: see sense 7 above. VITREOUS *humour*.

humourless *a.* devoid of humour M19. **humourlessness** *n.* L19.

humour /ˈhjuːmə/ *v.* Also *****-or**. L16. [f. the n.] **1** *v.t.* Comply with the humour of; gratify, indulge. L16. **2** *v.t.* Comply with the peculiar nature or exigencies of; adapt to; make concessions to. L16. †**3** *v.i.* Exercise one's fancy, imagine. Only in E17. **4** *v.t.* Give a particular character, style, or (now) turn or direction to. M17.

1 W. GERHARDIE He felt he wanted to humour them as one is inclined to humour . . , unreasonable children. **2** J. MOORE The path is continually winding to humour the position of the mountains. **4** R. L. STEVENSON The patroon humoured his boat nearer in.

humoured /ˈhjuːməd/ *a.* Also *****-or-**. L16. [f. HUMOUR *n.* + -ED[2].] Having a disposition of a specified kind. Now only in *comb.* as *good-humoured*, *ill-humoured*, etc.

humoursome /ˈhjuːməs(ə)m/ *a.* Also *****-or-**. M17. [f. HUMOUR *n.* + -SOME[1].] Capricious, peevish.

humoursomely *adv.* M17. **humoursomeness** *n.* M17.

humous *n.* var. of HUMMUS.

humous /ˈhjuːməs/ *a.* M19. [f. HUM(US: see -OUS.] Present in or of the nature of humus; rich in humus.

hump /hʌmp/ *n.* M17. [Prob. rel. to LG *humpe*, Du. *homp* lump, hunk. Branch II directly f. HUMPBACK.] **I** †**1** A complaint. Also, a slight, a snub (chiefly in *humps and grumps*). M17–M18. **II 2** A protuberance, esp. on the back, as a deformity or (in the camel etc.) as a natural feature. E18. **b** A humpbacked person. *rare.* E18. **c** The flesh of an animal's hump considered as food. E19. **3** *the hump*, a fit of depression or vexation. *slang.* E18. **4** A rounded raised mass of earth etc. E19. **b** A mound in a railway yard over which vehicles are pushed so as to run down the other side by gravity to a siding etc. E20. **c** A mountain barrier high enough to make land and air travel difficult. Chiefly *US.* E20. **d** The critical point in an undertaking, ordeal, etc. Chiefly in *over the hump*. E20. **5** A walk or hike with a load on one's back. *Austral.* & *NZ slang.* M19. **6** Copulation; a partner, esp. a woman, in copulation. *coarse slang.* M20.

Phrases: **get a hump on** *US colloq.* hurry. **give (a person) the hump** *colloq.* annoy, depress, (a person). **live on one's hump** be self-sufficient. **over the hump** over the worst, well begun. VISCERAL *hump*.

Comb.: **hump bridge** = HUMPBACK *bridge*; **hump-shouldered** *a.* (long *rare*) having a humped shoulder; **hump speed** *Aeronaut.* the speed of a seaplane or hovercraft at which the drag due to the water is a maximum.

humpless *a.* M19.

hump /hʌmp/ *v.* L17. [f. the n.] **1** *v.t.* & *i.* Make (oneself, one's back, etc.) humped or hump-shaped, esp. as a result of vexation; progress by assuming a humped form. L17. **2** *v.t.* & *i.* Copulate (with). *coarse slang.* L18. **3** *v.t.* Hoist up, shoulder, carry esp. on one's back, (a load, pack, etc.); transport with difficulty. Chiefly *Austral.* & *NZ slang.* M19. **4** *v.refl.* & *i.* Exert (oneself), make an effort; hurry. *slang.* M19. **5** *v.t.* Annoy, depress. *colloq.* M19.

1 S. R. CROCKETT Sal humped up the shoulder . . and turned sharply away from him. E. FIGES I was aware of . . coughing coming from humped bedclothes. **b** K. HULME Some kind of caterpillar with suckerfeet, humping up the wall. 2 R. PRICE Maybe he's the scoundrel that was humping that gal when you caught them, Macey? 3 K. WATERHOUSE I.. went downstairs, humping my parcel with me. K. CROSSLEY-HOLLAND They humped their boats overland on pine rollers. *hump bluey*: see BLUEY *n.* 2. 4 M. WOODHOUSE I.. humped myself into my coat. 5 A. BEARDSLEY Letter writing humps me dreadfully.

humper *n.* L19.

humpback /ˈhʌmpbak; *in sense A.1 also* hʌmpˈbak/ *n.* & *a.* L17. [Prob. f. as HUMP *n.* + BACK *n.*[1]: repl. earlier synon. *crump-back* and perh. infl. by *hunchback*.] A *n.* 1 A back with a hump; a humped back. L17. 2 A person with a humped back, a hunchback. E18. 3a = *humpback whale* below. E18. b = *humpback salmon* below. L19.

B *adj.* Having a back with a hump. E18.

humpback bridge a small bridge with a steep ascent and descent. **humpback salmon** a medium-sized migratory salmon, *Oncorhynchus gorbuscha*, of the Pacific and (more recently) Atlantic Oceans, the male of which has a humped back at spawning time; also called *gorbuscha*, *pink salmon*. **humpback sucker** *US* a freshwater fish, *Xyrauchen texanus*, of the Colorado basin. **humpback whale** a large black baleen whale with white-marked flippers, *Megaptera novaeangliae* (family Balaenopteridae), having a fleshy pad on the back and a complex mating call.

humpbacked *a.* having a humpback L17.

humped /hʌm(p)t/ *a.* E18. [f. HUMP *n.* + -ED[2].] Having a hump; hump-shaped; having a rounded back.

humph /hʌmf, *as int. also* h(ə)mf/ *int.*, *v.*, & *n.* M16. [Natural exclam.] A *int.* Expr. doubt or dissatisfaction. Formerly also, giving a warning. M16. B *v.i.* Utter 'humph'. L17. C *n.* An utterance of 'humph'. E19.

humpty /ˈhʌm(p)ti/ *a.* & *n.* E19. [App. irreg. f. HUMP *n.* or HUMPED *a.*, perh. also infl. by HUMPTY-DUMPTY *n.*[2]] A *adj.* Humped, hump-backed. E19. B *n.* A low padded cushion seat. E20.

humpty-dumpty /hʌm(p)tɪˈdʌm(p)ti/ *n.*[1] L17. [Origin uncertain: perh. rel. to HUM *n.*[1] 4.] A drink made from ale boiled with brandy.

Humpty-Dumpty /hʌm(p)tɪˈdʌm(p)ti/ *n.*[2] & *a.* L18. [Perh. f. HUMPY *a.* + DUMPY *a.*[2] & *n.*: -*t*- unexpl.] A *n.* A short dumpy person; (with reference to a nursery-rhyme character, whose name is taken to refer to an egg) a person who or thing which once overthrown cannot be restored; (with reference to a character of that name in Lewis Carroll's *Through the Looking-Glass*) a person who makes things mean what he or she chooses. L18. B *adj.* Short and fat; resembling or pertaining to the nursery-rhyme character Humpty-Dumpty. L18.

humpy /ˈhʌmpi/ *n.*[1] *Austral.* M19. [Aborig. *yumbi*, infl. by HUMP *n.*] A hut; *esp.* an Aboriginal hut.

humpy /ˈhʌmpi/ *n.*[2] *Austral. slang.* M20. [f. HUMP *n.* + -Y[6].] A camel.

humpy /ˈhʌmpi/ *a.* E18. [f. HUMP *n.* + -Y[1].] 1 Having a hump or humps; resembling a hump. E18. 2 Out of humour, annoyed, depressed. L19.

humpiness *n.* L19.

humstrum /ˈhʌmstrʌm/ *n.* Now *rare.* M18. [f. HUM *v.*[1] + STRUM *v.*] A roughly made or out of tune musical instrument; a hurdy-gurdy.

humulone /ˈhjuːmjʊləʊn/ *n.* Also **-on** /-ɒn/. E20. [f. mod.L *Humulus* genus name of the hop-plant after G *Humulon*: see -ONE.] *Chem.* A yellow crystalline cyclic ketone, $C_{21}H_{30}O_5$, that is one of the bitter-tasting constituents of hops and has antibiotic activity. Cf. LUPULONE.

humungous *a.* var. of HUMONGOUS.

humus /ˈhjuːməs/ *n.* L18. [L = soil.] The organic constituent of soil, formed by the decomposition of plant materials.

Hun /hʌn/ *n.*[1] [OE *Hūne*, *Hūnas* (pl.), corresp. to MHG *Hiunen* (G *Hunnen*), ON *Húnar*, *Hýnar*, f. late L *Hunni*, *Huni*, also *Chunni*, *Chuni* f. Gk *Hounnoi* f. Sogdian *xwn* (whence also Skt *Hūṇa*) = Chin. *Xiōngnú* (Wade-Giles *Hsiung-nu*).] 1 *Hist.* A member of a warlike nomadic people of Asian origin who invaded Europe *c*375 and who later, under their king Attila, overran and ravaged a great part of it. OE. 2 *transf.* A wanton destroyer of the beauties of nature or art; *gen.* a person of brutal conduct or character. E19. 3 Chiefly during the war of 1914–18: a German. *slang. derog.* E20.

1 *White Hun*: see WHITE *a.*

hun /huːn/ *n.*[2] Also **hoon**. E19. [Skt *hūna*.] *Hist.* In the Indian subcontinent: a gold coin, the pagoda.

Hunanese /huːnəˈniːz/ *a.* & *n.* M20. [f. *Hunan* (see below) + -ESE.] A *adj.* Of, pertaining to, or characteristic of the southern Chinese province of Hunan or the form of Chinese spoken there. M20. B *n.* Pl. same. 1 A native or inhabitant of Hunan. M20. 2 The form of Chinese spoken in Hunan. M20.

hunch /hʌn(t)ʃ/ *n.* M17. [f. the vb; in sense 3 app. inferred from HUNCHBACKED *a.* Sense 2 may be another wd: cf. HUNK *n.*[1]] 1 A push, a shove. *obs.* exc. *Sc.* M17. 2 A thick or clumsy piece; a hunk. L18. 3 A protuberance on the back etc.; a hump. E19. 4 A hint. *US colloq.* M19. 5 An intuitive feeling. *colloq.* (orig. *US*). L19.

5 HENRY MILLER I have a hunch as to who took that money, but I'm not absolutely sure. R. C. A. WHITE Jurors.. try cases according to the evidence and not on personal whims or hunches.

hunch /hʌn(t)ʃ/ *v.* L15. [Rel. to HUNCHBACK, HUNCHBACKED.] 1 *v.t.* Give a push to, shove, thrust. Now chiefly *dial.* & *US.* L15. b Nudge to attract the attention of. *US* (*obs.* exc. *dial.*). M19. 2 *v.i.* a Give a push, shove. *obs.* exc. *Sc.* L16. b Push or lunge forward. *US.* E20. 3 *v.t.* Thrust out or up (esp. the shoulders) to form a hump; arch convexly. Usu. in *pass.* L17. b *v.i.* Sit in or lower oneself into a bent or huddled position. Chiefly *N. Amer.* M20.

1 J. DICKEY Lewis.. tried to hunch the canoe free with his weight. 3 D. WELCH The others gathered round, bending their heads and hunching their shoulders like a rugger scrum. P. ACKROYD An engraving of Faust sitting hunched at his desk. b J. STEINBECK Lennie hunched down on the little barrel. A. TYLER Don't *hunch* Sit straight.

hunchback /ˈhʌn(t)ʃbak, *in sense A.1 also* hʌn(t)ʃˈbak/ *n.* & *a.* E18. [Back-form. f. next.] A *n.* 1 A hunched or protuberant back; *spec.* kyphosis. E18. 2 A person with such a deformity; a hunchbacked person. E18. B *adj.* Hunchbacked. M19.

hunchbacked /ˈhʌn(t)ʃbakt/ *a.* L16. [f. elem. of unkn. origin + BACK *n.*[1] + -ED[2].] Having a protuberant or crooked back; affected with kyphosis.

hunched /hʌn(t)ʃt/ *a.* M17. [f. HUNCH *n.*, *v.*: see -ED[2], -ED[1].] Having a hump, bowed into a hump, hunchbacked; *fig.* stuck-up, arrogant.

hundred /ˈhʌndrəd/ *n.* & *a.* (in mod. usage also classed as a *determiner*), (*cardinal numeral*). [Late OE *hundred* = OFris. *hundred*, OS *hunderod* (Du. *honderd*), MHG, G *hundert*, ON *hundrað*, f. Gmc, f. base meaning 'hundred' rel. to L *centum* + base meaning 'number' (cf. Goth. *raþjō* number, account).] A *n.* In senses 1 and 4 pl. now always same after a numeral and often after a quantifier, otherwise **-s**; as *sing.* usu. preceded by *a* (earlier *an*), in emphatic use *one*. 1 A number equal to ten times ten units *of* a specified category or group (now almost always definite, as *a hundred of the*, *those*, etc., *one hundred of her, his mother's*, etc.; orig. with *genit. pl.*); a number equal to ten times ten persons or things identified contextually, as years of age, pounds, dollars, points or runs in a game, chances (in giving odds), etc.; *pl.* after a quantifier, multiples of ten times ten such people or things. Usu. treated as *pl.* LOE. b In *pl.* without specifying wd: several hundred; *hyperbol.* large numbers. (Foll. by *of*.) ME. 2 A group or set of a hundred; *spec.* (*a*) a hundredweight; (*b*) (*obs.* exc. *dial.*) a hundred years, a century. LOE. 3 *Hist.* In England (and later Ireland): a subdivision of a county having its own court. Formerly also, such a court. Cf. WAPENTAKE. LOE. b A subdivision of a county in the State of Delaware, and in colonial times also in Virginia, Maryland, and Pennsylvania. E17. 4 Ten times ten as an abstract number, the symbol(s) or figure(s) representing this (100 in arabic numerals, c, C, in roman); *pl.* after a numeral, that number of multiples of ten times ten as an abstract number, the symbol(s) or figure(s) representing any such number (as 900). ME. b In *pl.* The digit denoting the number of hundreds. LME. c The hundredth of a set or series with numbered members, the one designated one hundred, (usu. *number one* (or *a*) *hundred*, or with specification, as *Psalm One Hundred*). E17. 5 In the sale of certain commodities, esp. herring and other fishes: a quantity greater than a hundred (*of*). Esp. in *great* or *long hundred*, six score, 120. LME. 6 In *pl.* The numbers from 100 to 109 (or 199) inclusive, esp. as denoting years of a decade or century or units of a scale of temperature. E20. 7 In *pl.* (After a numeral.) Used to represent the two noughts in a figure expressing the exact hour, in expressing time by the twenty-four hour clock, as *twenty hundred hours* = 20.00 hours, 8.0 pm. M20.

1 B. G. GERBIER About one hundred of Leagues. *Times* Tickets fabricated by the hundred. OED He lost several hundred of his men. E. O'NEILL I'll live to a hundred. J. LE CARRÉ They.. offered him six hundred a year. **a** (or **one**) **hundred per cent** (*a*) (orig. *US*) complete(ly), thorough(ly); (*b*) completely fit or well. *a hundred in the water-bag*: see WATER *n.* **a hundred to one** a very strong probability. FIVE *hundred*. *one hundred per cent*: see *a hundred per cent* above. b C. DARWIN For many, perhaps for hundreds of generations. SCOTT FITZGERALD Gatsby's notoriety, spread about by the hundreds who had accepted his hospitality. V. GLENDINNING Dame Rebecca had hundreds of friends. **hundreds and thousands** tiny coloured balls of sugar used chiefly for decorating cakes etc. 3 CHILTERN HUNDREDS. 6 SCOTT FITZGERALD The dark .. saloons of the faded-gilt nineteen-hundreds.

B *adj.* After an article, possessive, etc: ten times ten (a cardinal numeral represented by 100 in arabic numerals, c, C in roman); *hyperbol.* a great many. After a numeral or quantifier: multiples of ten times ten. LOE.

G. B. SHAW Anything from sixpence to several hundred guineas. E. O'NEILL Do you suppose I wouldn't prevent that—for a hundred reasons? E. WAUGH The whole place hummed from its hundred ventilators. S. HILL A house two hundred yards across the green. **a hundred and one** *hyperbol.* a countless number of. **not a hundred miles from** *joc.* very close to (this place etc.). **the Hundred Days** the period of the restoration of Napoleon Bonaparte, after his escape from Elba. **the Hundred Flowers** (the period of) an ideological movement in Communist China in the summer of 1957, when people were invited to voice their criticisms of the regime. **the Hundred Years** (or **Years'**) **War** the intermittent war between England and France from 1337 to 1453, arising out of the claim of the English kings to the French crown.

Comb.: Forming compound numerals (cardinal or ordinal) with numerals below 100, as *120* (read *a* (or *one*) *hundred and twenty*, (N. Amer.) also *a* (or *one*) *hundred twenty*), *120th* (read (*one*) *hundred and twentieth*), or (cardinals) with multiples of 1000, as *1200* (read *one thousand two hundred* or, esp. in dates, *twelve hundred*). Special combs., as **hundred-per-center** *N. Amer.* a thoroughgoing or uncompromising person; **hundred-pounder** a cannon throwing a shot that weighs one hundred pounds.

hundredal /ˈhʌndrəd(ə)l/ *a.* M19. [f. HUNDRED *n.* + -AL[1].] Relating to a territorial hundred.

hundredary /ˈhʌndrəd(ə)ri/ *n.* E18. [med.L *hundredarius*, f. as next + *-arius* -ARY[1].] = HUNDREDER *n.* 1.

hundreder /ˈhʌndrədə/ *n.* Also **-dor**. LME. [f. HUNDRED *n.* + -ER[2], -OR.] *Hist.* 1 The chief officer of a territorial hundred. LME. 2 An inhabitant of a territorial hundred, *esp.* one liable to be empanelled on a jury. E16.

hundredfold /ˈhʌndrədfəʊld/ *n.* & & *a.* OE. [f. HUNDRED + -FOLD.] A *n.* A hundred times the amount or number. Freq. used advb. OE. B *adj.* A hundred times as much or many. Now *rare* or *obs.* ME.

hundredor *n.* var. of HUNDREDER.

hundredth /ˈhʌndrətθ, -rədθ/ *a.* & *n.* ME. [f. HUNDRED + -TH[2].] A *adj.* Next in order after the ninety-ninth, that is number one hundred in a series, (represented by 100th). Also *one-hundredth*. ME.

K. VONNEGUT I am here to congratulate *The Cornell Daily Sun* on its one-hundredth anniversary.

hundredth part *arch.* = sense B.1 below.

B *n.* **1** Each of a hundred parts into which something is or may be divided, a fraction which when multiplied by one hundred gives one, (= *hundredth part* above). L18. **2** The hundredth person or thing in a category, series, etc., identified contextually; *spec.* in *Old Hundredth*, (the tune of) the hymn beginning 'All people that on earth do dwell', an early metrical version of Psalm 100 (99 in the Vulgate). M19.

hundredweight /ˈhʌndrədweɪt/ *n.* Pl. same (after numeral or quantifier), **-s**. E16. [f. HUNDRED + WEIGHT *n.*] An avoirdupois weight equal to 112 pounds, approx. 50.80 kg, (more fully *long hundredweight*) or (*US*) 100 pounds, approx. 45.36 kg, (more fully *short hundredweight*). Also, a metric weight equal to 50 kilograms, approx. 110.2 lb, (more fully *metric hundredweight*). Abbrev. *cwt.*

†hune *n.* ME–M18. [Orig. app. f. ON *húnn* knob at the top of a masthead; in later use prob. f. Fr. *hune* (f. Norse) in same sense: cf. HOUND *n.*[2]] = HOUND *n.*[2] 1.

hung /hʌŋ/ *a.* LME. [pa. pple of HANG *v.*] **1** Provided or decorated *with* hanging things. LME. **b** Of a male: having (esp. large) sexual organs. Chiefly w. qualifying adv. or phr., as *hung like a bull* (or *donkey*), *well hung*, etc. *slang.* M17. **2** Suspended, attached so as to hang. M16. **b** Of meat: suspended in the air to mature or dry. M17. **3a** Of a jury: unable to agree on a verdict. *US.* M19. **b** Of an elected body: in which no political party has an overall majority. L20. **4** Usu. *hung-over.* Suffering from the after-effects of excess alcohol or drugs, having a hangover. M20. **5** *hung up*: confused, bewildered; (foll. by *on*) obsessed or preoccupied with. *slang.* M20.

1 O. MANNING Tramway cars, hung with passengers like swarming bees. **5** E. JONG He was all hung up on Jewish girls. G. PRIESTLAND He was not one to . . get hung up on personal taboos.

†Hungar *n.* LME. [MHG *Ungar*, med.L *Hungarus*.] **1** A Hungarian. LME–E17. **2** A gold coin of Hungary. Also *Hungar-dollar*. L15–M18.

Hungarian /hʌŋˈgɛːrɪən/ *a.* & *n.* E16. [f. med.L *Hungaria* Hungary, f. (*H*)*ungarī*, *Ungrī*, *Ugrī* (cf. UGRIC), med.Gk *Ouggroi*, MHG *Ungar-n*, name applied to the Hungarians, who called themselves Magyars: see -AN.] **A** *adj.* **1** Of, pertaining to, or native to Hungary, a country in central Europe. E16. **†2** [With play on HUNGRY *a.*] Thievish, marauding; needy, beggarly. *slang.* L16–E17.

1 Hungarian cap the shell of a marine gastropod mollusc, *Capulus ungaricus*. **†Hungarian grass** = *Hungarian millet* below. **Hungarian millet** = FOXTAIL *millet*. **Hungarian turnip** (the swollen stem-base of) the kohlrabi, *Brassica oleracea* var. *gongylodes*. **2** SHAKES. *Merry W.* O base Hungarian wight! Wilt thou the spigot wield.

B *n.* **1** A native or inhabitant of Hungary, a Magyar. Also, a Hungarian horse. M16. **2** The Finno-Ugric language spoken by inhabitants of Hungary, and now its official language. M17.

Hungary /ˈhʌŋg(ə)ri/ *n.* LME. [See prec.] Used *attrib.* to designate things found in, obtained from, or associated with Hungary.

Hungary water a preparation distilled from rosemary flowers, formerly popular as a lotion and restorative.

hunger /ˈhʌŋgə/ *n.* [OE *hungor*, *-ur* = OS, OHG *hungar* (Du. *honger*, G *Hunger*), ON *hungr*, f. Gmc.] **1** The uneasy or painful sensation caused by lack of food; craving appetite. Also, the exhausted condition caused by lack of food. OE. **2** (A) famine. *arch.* OE. **3** *gen.* A strong desire or craving (*for* etc.); a hankering *after*. LME.

1 A. GRAY He had been foodless for two days and ached with hunger. **3** GEO. ELIOT This need of love—this hunger of the heart. T. KENEALLY He had a hunger for a thin, consumptive black girl called Tessie.

Comb.: **hunger-bitten** *a.* (*arch.*) pinched with hunger, famished; **hunger march**: undertaken by a body of the unemployed etc. to call attention to their condition; **hunger marcher** a person who goes on a hunger march; **†hunger-starve** *v.t.* famish, starve; **hunger strike** the refusal of food as a form of protest, esp. by a prisoner; **hunger striker** a person who takes part in a hunger strike; **hunger-weed** the buttercup *Ranunculus arvensis*.

hunger /ˈhʌŋgə/ *v.* [OE *hyngran*, *hyngrian* (= OS *gihungrian*, Goth. *huggrjan*), f. Gmc base of prec.; assim. in ME to the n.] **†1** *v.i. impers.* as in *me hungreth*, it hungers me, I am hungry. OE–LME. **2** *v.i.* Feel or suffer hunger through lack of food, be hungry. *arch.* OE. **†3** *v.t.* Have a hunger or craving for; desire with longing. OE–M16. **4** *v.i. gen.* Have a strong desire or craving *for*, *to do*; hanker *after*. LME. **5** *v.t.* Subject to hunger, starve; drive *out* by hunger, starve *out*. Now *rare*. L16.

4 E. WAUGH Basil is a Philistine and a crook . . and yet . . I hunger for his company. B. MALAMUD He hungered to explain who he was.

hungerer *n.* LME.

hungered /ˈhʌŋgəd/ *a.* *arch.* LME. [Partly aphet. f. AHUNGERED, partly pa. pple of HUNGER *v.*: see -ED[1].] Hungry; famished, starved.

hungerly /ˈhʌŋgəli/ *a.* Now *rare* or *obs.* LME. [f. HUNGER *n.* + -LY[1].] Having a hungry or famished look.

hungerly /ˈhʌŋgəli/ *adv.* Now *rare* or *obs.* M16. [f. HUNGER *n.* + -LY[2].] Hungrily, greedily.

hungry /ˈhʌŋgri/ *a.* [OE *hungriġ* = OFris. *hungerig*, OHG *hung(a)rag* (G *hungrig*), f. WGmc, f. base of HUNGER *n.*: see -Y[1].] **1** Feeling pain or discomfort from the lack of food; having a keen appetite. OE. **b** Indicating or marked by hunger; belonging to a hungry person. LME. **2** Having a strong desire or craving (*for*, *†after*); *spec.* eager for money, profits, etc.; *Austral.* & *Sc.* mean, stingy. ME. **3** Of a period, place, etc.: marked by famine or scarcity of food. Now *rare* exc. in *hungry forties* below. ME. **4a** Of air etc.: that produces a keen appetite. *rare*. LME. **b** Of a meal: eaten with a hearty appetite. Now *rare* or *obs.* M16. **5** Of food etc.: that does not satisfy the hunger. Now *rare*. M16. **6** Esp. of land, soil, etc.: deficient in nutrients, poor, infertile. Also, of a river: not supplying food for fish. L16.

1 I. MURDOCH She felt very hungry, having had no lunch. W. BRONK Yes, I'm hungry, I'll eat anything. **b** SHAKES. *Jul. Caes.* Yond Cassius has a lean and hungry look. **2** H. D. TRAILL The conveyance of prize-money . . into Charles's always hungry pocket. E. BOWEN She heard a great hum from the waiting plane hungry for flight. M. BINCHY He was hungry for every detail of her. **3** S. ROWLANDS When thou art hording vp thy foode, Against these hungry dayes. **6** M. B. KEATINGE Flat tracts of hungry pasture ground.

Special collocations: **hungry forties** the decade 1840–9 in Britain, a period of great distress and scarcity of food among the poor. **hungry rice** (the seed of) a kind of millet, *Digitaria exilis*, grown in arid areas of W. Africa; also called *fundi*.

hungrily *adv.* LME. **hungriness** *n.* M16.

hunk /hʌŋk/ *n.*[1] E19. [Prob. of LDu. origin: cf. WFlem. *hunke*. Cf. HUNCH *n.*] **1** A large piece cut off from a loaf, a cheese, etc.; a thick or clumsy piece. E19. **2** A large or solidly built person, esp. a man; a muscular or ruggedly handsome man, a sexually desirable man. *colloq.* M20.

hunk /hʌŋk/ *n.*[2] & *a.* *US.* M19. [Du. *honk*: cf. WFris. *honck(e)*, place of refuge.] **†A** *n.* In children's games (in New York): a position where a player is safe, the goal or 'home'. Esp. *be on hunk*, *reach hunk*. M–L19. **B** *adj.* (*slang.*) **1** = HUNKY-DORY. Now *rare*. M19. **2** Even, on even terms. In *get hunk* (*with*). M19.

hunk /hʌŋk/ *n.*[3] *N. Amer. slang. derog.* Now *rare*. L19. [Prob. alt. of HUNG(ARIAN. Cf. BOHUNK.] = HUNKY *n.*

hunker /ˈhʌŋkə/ *n.* *US.* Now *arch.* or *Hist.* Also **H-**. M19. [Origin unkn.] A member of a conservative faction of the Democratic Party (orig. that in New York in the 1840s); *transf.* (*colloq.*) a person of old-fashioned or conservative outlook.

hunkerish *a.* conservative, old-fashioned M19. **hunkerism** *n.* the views or policies of hunkers M19.

hunker /ˈhʌŋkə/ *v.i.* Chiefly *Sc.* & *N. Amer.* E18. [Cf. MDu. *hucken*, MLG *hūken* (Du. *huiken*, G *hocken*), ON *húka*.] **1** Squat (*down*) so that the haunches nearly touch the heels; crouch *down* for shelter or concealment. Also, station oneself in a hunched or huddled position. E18. **2** *fig.* Foll. by *down*. Apply oneself, knuckle down. Orig. *US.* E18.

1 K. TENNANT Kelly . . hunkered down by the sunny office wall. A. TYLER He played the drums intently . . sitting very straight instead of hunkering over.

hunkers /ˈhʌŋkəz/ *n.pl.* Orig. *Sc.* M18. [f. (as) prec.] The haunches, the hams.

on (or **upon**) **one's hunkers** in a squatting position; *fig.* in a desperate situation, on one's last legs.

hunkey, hunkie *ns.* vars. of HUNKY *n.*

hunks /hʌŋks/ *n.* *derog.* E17. [Origin unkn.] A surly cross-grained old person; a stingy person, a miser. Freq. in *old hunks*.

hunky /ˈhʌŋki/ *n.* *N. Amer. slang. derog.* Also **hunkey, hunkie**. E20. [f. (as) HUNK *n.*[3] + -Y[6], -IE. Cf. BOHUNK.] (A nickname given to) an immigrant to N. America from Hungary or the Slavonic countries of Europe, *esp.* one of inferior class.

†hunky *a.*[1] *US slang.* M19–E20. [f. HUNK *n.*[2] + -Y[1].] = HUNKY-DORY.

hunky /ˈhʌŋki/ *a.*[2] *colloq.* E20. [f. HUNK *n.*[1] + -Y[1].] Thickset, solidly built; *esp.* (of a man) ruggedly handsome, sexually desirable.

hunky-dory /hʌŋkɪˈdɔːri/ *a.* *slang* (orig. *US*). Also **-rey**. M19. [f. (as) HUNKY *a.*[1] + *dory* of unkn. origin.] In a safe or good position or condition; satisfactory, fine.

Hunnish /ˈhʌnɪʃ/ *a.* M17. [f. HUN + -ISH[1].] Of, pertaining to, or resembling the Huns; wantonly destructive.

hunsup *n.* see HUNT'S-UP.

†hunt *n.*[1] OE–E19. [OE *hunta* f. Gmc.] A hunter, a huntsman. In later use only in the title *common hunt*, an official appointed to look after a Lord Mayor's kennel.

¶ Surviving in the surname *Hunt*.

hunt /hʌnt/ *n.*[2] LME. [f. HUNT *v.*] **1** The action or an act of hunting game for sport or food. LME. **b** A diligent or energetic search or pursuit. E17. **c** *Teleph.* An automatic search for a free line. E20. **2a** A body of people (sometimes including their horses and hounds) engaged in hunting wild animals or game, esp. foxes. Also, a body of people meeting regularly to hunt. L16. **†b** Game pursued or killed in hunting. L16–E17. **c** The district over which a pack of hounds hunts. M19. **3** In change-ringing: a movement of bells through a fixed succession of positions. Formerly, the first or treble bell in a set of bells. L17. **4** An oscillatory motion. E20.

1b G. GORER The papers . . were much taken up with the hunt for the missing Coronation Stone. *Medway Extra* A twice-a-year hunt to recruit more staff. **2a** G. M. TREVELYAN Very few joined a Hunt who were not resident in the County. **c** *Field* Every landowner within the hunt should be careful to preserve foxes.

Comb.: **hunt ball** a ball or dance given by members of a hunt; **hunt saboteur** a person whose intention is to disrupt a hunt in the interests of animal welfare.

hunt /hʌnt/ *v.* [OE *huntian*, f. Gmc weak grade of base of HENT *v.*] **1** *v.i.* & *t.* Pursue (wild animals or game) for food or sport; *spec.* (chiefly in England) pursue (esp. foxes) with hounds; *N. Amer.* shoot (game). Also, of an animal: pursue (prey). OE. **2a** *v.i.* Make a diligent or energetic search, look *about*. (Foll. by *for*, *after*.) ME. **b** *v.t.* Make a diligent or energetic search for, look eagerly for. Now chiefly *US*. LME. **c** *v.i.* *Teleph.* Of a selector or switch: search automatically for a free line (and make connection with it). (Foll. by *for* a line, *over* lines.) E20. **3** *v.t.* Drive *away* or *from* a place, etc., by pursuit or harassment. ME. **b** *fig.* Pursue vexatiously; pester, dog. L16. **4** *v.t.* Scour (a district) in pursuit of game, esp. foxes. LME. **5** *v.t.* Follow up (a trail) in the manner of a hound. L16. **6** *v.t.* Direct (hounds) in a hunt; ride (a horse) in a hunt. E17. **7** *v.t.* & *i.* In change-ringing: alter the position of (a bell), (of a bell) have its position altered, through a fixed succession of changes. (Foll. by *up*, *down*.) L17. **8** *v.i.* (Of a generator, engine, etc.) run alternately too fast and too slow; *gen.* (of any machine, system, etc.) oscillate (undesirably) *about* a desired speed, position, or state. L19.

1 J. BUCHAN He used to hunt with the Pytchley. T. F. POWYS An old dog-fox who had been hunted many times before. J. RABAN The bustards .. were hunted with falcons. 2a E. M. FORSTER She hunted in the grass for her knitting-needle. C. STEAD She hunted high and low and found nothing but peanut-butter jars. b A. TYLER I'm hunting Oliver Jamison... You know him? 3b N. HAWTHORNE These pests had hunted the two travellers at every stage of their journey. 4 G. J. WHYTE-MELVILLE When he .. hunted the Cottesmore country. 5 J. TYNDALL I hunted the seams still farther up the glacier.

Phrases, & with advs. in specialized senses: **hunt away** *NZ* (of a dog) drive sheep forward. *hunt counter*: see COUNTER *adv.* **hunt down** (*a*) pursue or search for relentlessly until caught or apprehended; (*b*) *NZ* drive (sheep) down from higher ground. **hunt out** drive from cover by hunting; *fig.* bring to light by persistent searching. *hunt riot*: see RIOT *n. hunt the fox*: see FOX *n.* **hunt up** search energetically for until one finds.

Comb. (in names of various games): **hunt the hare** = *fox and hounds* s.v. FOX *n.*; **hunt the lady** a card-game of the whist family; **hunt the slipper** a game in which all the players but one sit in a ring and pass a slipper covertly from one to another, the remaining player having to find the player in possession of it; **hunt the thimble** a game in which one player hides a thimble which the other players then have to locate; **hunt the whistle** a game in which a player is blindfolded and is told to look for a whistle, which has actually been fastened to his or her own clothing.

huntable *a.* M19. **hunted** *a.* that is hunted; looking or behaving as if being pursued, worn and harassed: L16.

huntaway /ˈhʌntəweɪ/ *n. NZ.* E20. [f. *hunt away* s.v. HUNT *v.*] A dog trained to drive sheep forward.

hunter /ˈhʌntə/ *n.* ME. [f. HUNT *v.* + -ER[1].] **1** A person engaged in the pursuit of wild animals or game; a person who hunts. ME. **b** A person who searches or seeks diligently or energetically for something. Usu. in *comb.*, as *fortune-hunter.* LME. **2a** A dog good at or used in hunting. E17. **b** A horse bred for its stamina in hunting, its ability to jump, etc.; a horse used in hunting. L17. **3** An animal that hunts its prey; *spec.* (*a*) = *hunting spider* s.v. HUNTING *ppl a.*; (*b*) a Jamaican cuckoo, *Piaya pluvialis.* M17. **4** = *hunting-watch* s.v. HUNTING *n.* M19.

1 *White hunter*: see WHITE *a.* 4 **half-hunter** a watch with a hinged cover protecting the outer part of the glass.

Comb.: **hunter-gatherer** *Anthropol. & Archaeol.* a member of a people whose mode of subsistence is based on hunting land and sea animals and collecting wild plants, small land fauna, fish, and shellfish (freq. *attrib.*): **hunter-killer** *a.* (of a naval vessel or group of vessels) equipped to locate and destroy enemy vessels, esp. submarines; **hunterman** (*US, W. Indies*, etc.) = sense 1 above; **hunter's green** a dark slightly yellowish green; **hunter's moon** the next full moon after a harvest moon; **hunter trials** a competition for horses used in hunting, with obstacles to simulate the conditions of a hunt.

hunting /ˈhʌntɪŋ/ *n.* OE. [f. HUNT *v.* + -ING[1].] **1** The action of HUNT *v.*; *esp.* the action or sport of pursuing game; an act or instance of hunting, a hunt. OE. †**2** Game killed in hunting. ME-E17.

Comb. (partly also f. HUNTING *ppl a.*): **hunting-box** a small house or lodge for use during the hunting season; **hunting-case** a watch-case with a hinged cover to protect the glass (orig. against accidents in hunting); **hunting cat** = *hunting leopard* below; *hunting-crop*: see CROP *n.* 4; **hunting dog** (*a*) a dog used for hunting game; in *pl.* (*Hunting Dogs*) *the* constellation Canes Venatici; (*b*) a southern African animal of the dog family, *Lycaon pictus*, which hunts its prey in packs; **hunting-ground** a district or place where hunting or searching is carried on; *happy hunting-ground(s)*, (among N. American Indians) a fabled country full of game to which warriors go after death; *fig.* a fruitful place for collecting, making acquisitions, etc.; **hunting horn** (*a*) a straight horn blown to give signals in hunting; (*b*) = *leaping-horn* s.v. LEAPING *vbl n.* **hunting leopard** the cheetah, in Asia tamed and used for hunting; **hunting-lodge** a lodge for use during the hunting season; *hunting-pink*: see PINK *n.*[4]; **hunting-shirt** *US* an ornamented shirt orig. of deerskin, worn by trappers, hunters, etc.; **hunting-watch** a watch having a hunting-case to protect the glass.

hunting /ˈhʌntɪŋ/ *ppl a.* ME. [f. HUNT *v.* + -ING[2].] That hunts; that pursues game or prey.

Special collocations (see also HUNTING *n.*): **hunting spider** a spider that hunts its prey instead of lying in wait.

Huntingdonian /hʌntɪŋˈdəʊnɪən/ *a.* & *n.* L18. [f. *Huntingdon* (see below) + -IAN.] (A person) belonging to the Countess of Huntingdon's Connexion, a Calvinistic Methodist sect founded by Selina, Countess of Huntingdon (1707–91).

Huntington /ˈhʌntɪŋt(ə)n/ *n.* L19. [George *Huntington* (1851–1916), US neurologist.] Med. *Huntington's chorea, disease*, a hereditary disease with progressive brain-cell degeneration, causing spasmodic body movements and progressive dementia.

huntite /ˈhʌntʌɪt/ *n.* M20. [f. Walter F. *Hunt* (1882–1975), US mineralogist + -ITE[1].] *Min.* A mixed carbonate of magnesium and calcium, crystallizing in the trigonal system and usu. occurring as a white powder.

huntress /ˈhʌntrɪs/ *n.* LME. [f. HUNTER *n.* + -ESS[1].] **1** A woman (or goddess) who hunts. LME. **2** A mare used in hunting. M19.

huntsman /ˈhʌntsmən/ *n.* Pl. **-men**. M16. [f. HUNT *n.*[1] + -'S[1] + MAN *n.*] A man who hunts, a hunter; *spec.* a person in charge of a pack of hounds (esp. foxhounds), who directs the pursuit of wild animals and game.

Comb.: **huntsman's cup** = *pitcher-plant* s.v. PITCHER *n.*[1]; **huntsman spider** any of various spiders of the family Sparassidae, widespread in warmer regions of the world.

huntsmanship *n.* M17.

hunt's-up /ˈhʌntsʌp/ *n.* Now *rare* or *obs.* Also (long *dial.*) **hunsup** /ˈhʌnsʌp/. L16. [f. *The hunt is up*, the wds of an old song sung or (its tune) played to rouse huntsmen in the morning, and also as a dance.] **1** An early morning song, a song or tune to rouse sleepers. L16. **2** A disturbance, an uproar. E17.

huntswoman /ˈhʌntswʊmən/ *n.* Pl. **-women** /-wɪmɪn/. E17. [f. HUNT *n.*[1] + -'S[1] + WOMAN *n.*] A woman who hunts, a female hunter.

hunyak /ˈhʌnjak/ *n. US slang. derog.* Also **honyock** /ˈhɒnjɒk/, **honyocker** /ˈhɒnjɒkə/. E20. [Alt. of HUNGARIAN after *Polack*.] = HUNKY *n.*

Huon pine /ˈhjuːɒn ˈpʌɪn/ *n. phr.* E19. [A river in the south of Tasmania.] (The timber of) a large Tasmanian evergreen conifer, *Dacrydium franklinii.*

hup /hʌp/ *int.* & *v.* As int. also **hupp**. M18. [Cf. Du. *hop!* gee-up.] **A** *int.* Encouraging a horse etc. to go faster: gee-up. M18. **B** *v.* Infl. **-pp-**. **1** *v.i.* Shout 'hup!' E19. **2** *v.t.* Direct or turn (a horse) to the right. M19.

Hupa /ˈhuːpə, -pɔː/ *n.* & *a.* Also **Hoopa**. M19. [Yurok *hupō̜* the name for this people.] **A** *n.* Pl. **-s**, same. A member of an Athapaskan Indian people in California; the language of this people. M19. **B** *attrib.* or as *adj.* Of or pertaining to this people. L19.

hupp *int.* var. of HUP *int.*

hurcheon /ˈhəːtʃ(ə)n/ *n.* Long *obs.* exc. *Sc.* & *north.* ME. [ONFr. *herichon*: see URCHIN.] **1** A hedgehog. ME. **2a** A slovenly person; a hag. M18. **b** A mischievous person; an urchin. *rare.* L18.

hurdie /ˈhəːdi/ *n. Sc.* M16. [Origin unkn.] A buttock, a hip, a haunch. Usu. in *pl.*

hurdle /ˈhəːd(ə)l/ *n.* & *v.* [OE *hyrdel* f. Gmc, f. base repr. also by OS *hurþ*, MLG *hurt*, *hort*, (M)Du. *horde*, OHG *hurt* (G *Hürde*) hurdle, ON *hurð*, Goth. *haurds* door, f. IE (whence also Gk *kartalos* basket, L *cratis* hurdle): see -LE[1].] **A** *n.* **1** A portable rectangular frame strengthened by bars or withes, now esp. with horizontal bars, uprights, and a diagonal strengthening bar, used for temporary fencing or enclosure. OE. **2** A framework laid on marshy ground etc. to provide a path or bridge; a framework, often covered with earth etc., used to stop a gap in fortifications, or protect a position from enemy fire. ME. **3** *Hist.* A frame or sledge on which a traitor was drawn through the streets to execution. LME. **4** An upright frame to be jumped over in a race; in *pl.*, a race over hurdles (for athletes or horses). M19. **b** An obstacle, a difficulty. E20.

4b *Radio Times* Andrew Cooper describes the hurdles to be cleared .. to win .. a seat on the Board.

Comb.: **hurdle race** a race over hurdles; **hurdle racing** the sport of racing over hurdles.

B *v.* **1** *v.t.* Construct like a hurdle or with hurdles. Chiefly as *hurdled* ppl a. M16. **2** *v.t.* Enclose with hurdles; mark *off* etc. with hurdles. M17. **3** *v.i.* Run a race over hurdles; jump hurdles as an athletic activity. L19. **b** *v.t.* & *i.* Jump over (an obstacle) as if it were a hurdle. L19.

3 *Daily Mail* When Lord Burghley hurdled easily to victory. b B. HINES Long enough for Billy to hurdle the upturned settee.

hurdler /ˈhəːdlə/ *n.* ME. [f. prec. + -ER[1].] **1** A person who makes hurdles. ME. **2** A person who or horse which races over hurdles. L19.

hurdy-gurdy /ˈhəːdɪˌgəːdi/ *n.* M18. [Imit. of the sound of the instrument: cf. HIRDY-GIRDY.] **1** A musical instrument producing a droning sound, played by turning a handle, *esp.* one with a rosined wheel turned by the right hand to sound drone-strings, and with keys played by the left hand; *colloq.* a barrel-organ. M18. **2** In full *hurdy-gurdy wheel.* A wheel driven by a tangential jet of water under pressure, which strikes a series of buckets on the circumference. *US.* M19.

Comb.: **hurdy-gurdy girl** *N. Amer. Hist.* a dance hostess, esp. in a hurdy-gurdy house; **hurdy-gurdy house** *N. Amer. Hist.* a disreputable dancehall.

hure /hjʊə/ *n.* ME. [(O)Fr. = †hair of the head, †head of man or animal, (mod.) head of certain animals, corresp. to med.L *hura* rough cap: ult. origin unkn.] **1** A cap. Long *obs.* exc. *dial.* ME. **2** The head of a boar, wolf, or bear. *rare.* M19.

hurkle /ˈhəːk(ə)l/ *v.i.* Long *obs.* exc. *Sc.* & *dial.* ME. [Cf. (M)LG, Du. *hurken* to squat.] Draw the limbs closely together, esp. with pain or cold; shrink, cower, crouch; move in a crouching or cowering manner.

hurl /həːl/ *n.* LME. [f. the vb.] **1a** A rush or swirl of water; rushing water. *rare.* LME. **b** A noisy rush or fall, esp. of stones etc. down a slope. *Sc.* M16. †**2** Strife; commotion. LME-M17. **3** The action or an act of hurling; a violent throw or cast. M16. **4** A ride in a wheeled vehicle; a drive. *Sc.* E19.

hurl /həːl/ *v.* ME. [Prob. imit.: cf. LG *hurreln* toss, throw, push, dash.] **1** *v.i.* Move or be moved with violence or impetuosity. *arch.* exc. *Sc.* ME. **2** *v.t.* Move or drive with violence or impetuous force. ME. **b** *refl.* Throw or move oneself violently or impetuously. LME. **3** *v.t.* Throw or cast with violence; fling; throw down. ME. †**4** *v.t.* Drag or pull violently. ME-M17. †**5** *v.i.* Strive, contend. Only in LME. **6** *v.t.* Utter forcefully (words, abuse, etc.); dart (a glance, a ray or beam, etc.). M16. **7** *v.t.* & *i.* Drive (a vehicle), drive in (a vehicle); wheel (a barrow etc.). Earliest in *hurlbarrow*, a wheelbarrow. *Sc.* & *north.* M16. **8** *v.i.* Play hurley or hurling. L16.

1 J. THOMSON The very streams .. impatient, seem To hurl into the covert of the grove. 2 D. ADAMS Zaphod was .. hurled bodily backwards. b R. KIPLING Like .. a swimmer before sharks, who hurls himself half out of the water. 3 W. SOYINKA Her husband was about to be .. hurled from the church tower. G. SWIFT He hurls the bottle in a lofty, arcing trajectory into the river. 6 MILTON Hurling defiance toward the vault of Heav'n. H. E. MANNING The accusations that may be hurled at you. 7 A. GRAY Thaw and his mother .. sat in buses at night hurling through unseen country.

†**hurlbat** *n.* see WHIRLBAT.

hurler /ˈhəːlə/ *n.*[1] ME. [f. HURL *v.* + -ER[1].] **1** *gen.* A person who hurls something. ME. **2** A player at hurley or hurling. L16. **3** A pitcher at baseball. *N. Amer. slang.* E20.

Hurler /ˈhəːlə/ *n.*[2] M20. [G. *Hurler* (fl. 1894), Ger. paediatrician.] Med. *Hurler('s) disease, syndrome*, a form of mucopolysaccharidosis caused by the faulty metabolism of glycosaminoglycans, producing a characteristic facial appearance, short limbs, and a protruding abdomen. Also called *gargoylism*.

hurley /ˈhəːli/ *n.* E19. [f. HURL *v.* + *-ey*, -Y[6].] An Irish form of hockey; a broad stick (of the type) used in this. Cf. earlier HURLING 2a.

hurling /ˈhəːlɪŋ/ *n.* LME. [f. HURL *v.* + -ING[1].] **1** The action of HURL *v.*; throwing, casting, esp. with violence. LME. **2a** The game of hurley. LME. **b** *Hist.* A game, played esp. in Cornwall, in which two parties attempt to hurl or carry a ball to a distant goal. E17. †**3** Strife; commotion. LME–M17. †**4** (The sound of) the violent rushing of wind. LME–M17.

hurly /ˈhəːli/ *n.* Now *rare.* L16. [f. HURL *v.* + -Y[6].] Commotion, uproar; strife.

hurly-burly /ˈhəːlɪˌbəːli/ *n.*, *adv.*, *v.*, & *a.* ME. [Redupl. of HURL *v.*] **A** *n.* Commotion, uproar, confusion; struggle, strife; (now *rare*) an instance of this. ME.

SHAKES. *Macb.* When the hurlyburly's done, When the battle's lost and won. *House & Garden* Kitchen gadgetry remains indispensable to the hurly-burly of twentieth-century life.

†**B** *adv.* In commotion or confusion. M16–E18.

C *v.* †**1** *v.t.* Hurl about; throw into confusion. M16–L17. **2** *v.i.* Make an uproar. Now *rare.* L16.

D *adj.* Characterized by commotion, uproar, struggle, or confusion. L16.

Huron /ˈhjʊər(ə)n/ *n.* & *a.* M17. [Fr., f. as HURE.] **A** *n.* Pl. **-s**, same. A member of a N. American Indian people formerly inhabiting an area near Lake Huron; the Iroquoian language of this people. M17. **B** *attrib.* or as *adj.* Of, pertaining to, or characteristic of this people. L18.

hurr /həː/ *v.i. obs.* exc. *dial.* LME. [Imit.] Make or utter a vibrating or trilling sound; buzz, snarl.

hurrah /hʊˈrɑː/ *n.*, *int.*, *a.*, & *v.* Also **hurra**. See also HOORAY. L17. [Alt. of HUZZA.] **A** *n.* **1** A shout of 'hurrah!'; a cheer. L17. **2** *hurrah's nest*, a state of confusion or disorder. *US colloq.* E19.

1 *last hurrah*: see LAST *a.*

B *int.* Expr. approval, encouragement, enthusiasm, or delight. E18.

C *attrib.* or as *adj.* Characterized by loud cheering, (wildly or blindly) enthusiastic; expressing enthusiasm or joy. M19.

D *v.* **1** *v.i.* Shout 'hurrah!' M19. **2** *v.t.* Welcome or encourage with shouts of 'hurrah!' M19.

hurray *n.*, *int.*, & *v.* var. of HOORAY.

†**hurrer** *n.* Also **-ier**. LME–M18. [f. HURE *n.* I + -ER[1], -IER.] A maker of or dealer in hats and caps.

Hurri /ˈhʌri/ *n.* Also **Harri**, **Kh-**. Pl. same. E20. [Hittite & Assyr. *Ḫarri*, *Ḫurri*.] A member of a people, originally from Armenia, who settled in northern Mesopotamia and Syria in the second and third millennia BC and were later absorbed by the Hittites and Assyrians.

Hurrian /ˈhʌrɪən/ *a.* & *n.* Also **Harrian**, **Kh-**. E20. [f. prec. + -AN.] **A** *adj.* Of or pertaining to the Hurri or their language. E20. **B** *n.* **1** The language (written in cuneiform) of the Hurri. E20. **2** A member of the Hurri. M20.

hurricane /ˈhʌrɪk(ə)n, -keɪn/ *n.* & *v.* Also (earlier) †**furacan**, †**furicano**, †**hurricano**, (pl. **-o(e)s**), & other vars. M16. [Sp. *huracán* & Port. *furacão* prob. f. Taino *hurakán* god of the storm.] **A** *n.* **1** A tropical cyclone, *esp.* a W. Indian one; any violent and destructive storm; *Meteorol.* a wind of hurricane force. M16. **b** A space from which trees etc. have been cleared by a hurricane. M18. †**2** (As *hurricano*.) A waterspout. Only in E17. **3** A violent rush or commotion; a storm of words, noises, etc. M17. †**4** A large crowded assembly of fashionable people at a private house. M18–E19.

Comb.: **hurricane-bird** a frigate-bird; **hurricane-deck** a light upper deck on a ship etc.; **hurricane force** force 12 on the Beaufort scale, corresponding to a wind speed of 64 knots (about 74 m.p.h.); **hurricane-house** a shelter at the masthead or on deck; **hurricane-lamp**, **-lantern** a lamp designed to resist a high wind; **hurricane wind** a wind associated with a tropical cyclone; a wind of hurricane force.

B *v.i.* & *t.* Whirl like a hurricane. L17.

G. BOYCOTT A great swirl of dust . . , most of which seemed to hurricane into the Press box.

hurried /ˈhʌrɪd/ *a.* M17. [f. HURRY *v.* + -ED[1].] Carried along or performed with a rapidity due to pressure of circumstances, excitement, or lack of time; characterized by hurry; hasty.

O. MANNING He came over at a hurried trot. M. RULE Intriguing signs of hurried and makeshift alterations.

hurriedly *adv.* E19. **hurriedness** *n.* M19.

hurrier /ˈhʌrɪə/ *n.*[1] E17. [f. HURRY *v.* + -ER[1].] A person who or thing which hurries.

†**hurrier** *n.*[2] var. of HURRER.

hurroo /hʊˈruː/ *int.* & *n.* In sense 2 also **hooroo**. E19. [Alt. of HOORAY, HURRAH.] **1** *int.* & *n.* (A shout) expr. triumph or excitement. E19. **2** *int.* Goodbye. *Austral. colloq.* E20.

hurroosh *n.* & *v.* var. of HOOROOSH.

hurry /ˈhʌri/ *n.* E17. [Prob. ult. imit.: in sense 1 perh. alt. of HURLY. Cf. HURR *v.*, HURRY *v.*] **1** (An instance of) physical, social, or political disturbance; commotion. *obs.* exc. *Sc.* & *Ir.* E17. †**b** A confused crowd, a mob. E17–E18. †**2** (An instance of) mental agitation, excitement. E17–E19. **3** Rapidity due to pressure of circumstances, excitement, or lack of time; great haste; eagerness to get a thing done quickly; eagerness *for*, *to do*; an action or state characterized by this, a rush. M17. **b** (In neg. & interrog. contexts.) Need or reason for haste; urgency. M19.

1 J. WESLEY A poor man began to make some tumult . . . 'Constables, take him away.' They did so, and the hurry was over. 2 S. RICHARDSON I should not be admitted into her presence, till the hurries she was in had subsided. 3 LONGFELLOW A hurry of hoofs in a village street. M. BARING Coming down to dinner in a frantic hurry, thinking I was late. A. BURGESS The final issue . . lacked panache and it betrayed hurry. B. EMECHETA The hurry towards the kitchen had now begun. **not — in a hurry** *colloq.* not do the specified thing very soon, not do willingly or easily. b A. CHRISTIE There was no hurry now. The urgency had gone . . It only needed patience.

Comb.: **hurry call** a call for help in an emergency.

hurrygraph *n.* (*US*, now *rare*) a hurried sketch or impression M19.

hurry /ˈhʌri/ *v.* L16. [Imit.: cf. HURR *v.*, WHIRR *v.*; MHG, G *hurren* move quickly, Du. *herrie* agitation.] **1** *v.t.* Carry or take with great or undue haste, esp. because of pressure of circumstances, excitement, or lack of time. (Foll. by *away*, *into*, *into doing*, *out*, etc.) L16. **2** *v.i.* Move or act with great or undue haste or with an effort at speed. L16. **3** *v.t.* Agitate, disturb, excite; harass, worry. *obs.* exc. *dial.* E17. **4** *v.t.* Urge to greater speed; hasten (unduly) the action or progress of. E18. **5** *v.t.* Put *away*, *on*, *out*, etc., hurriedly. E19.

1 C. JOHNSTON My master was seized and hurried away to a prison. J. PITTS Drinking hurries Men on to the worst of Vices. 2 R. KIPLING Hurrying north on news of a job, and wasting no time by the road. J. STEINBECK The rabbits hurried noiselessly for cover. 3 ISAAC TAYLOR So under the influence of the imagination as to have their sleep hurried with visions. 4 R. FORD Nor is there any good to be got in trying to hurry man or beast in Spain. R. L. STEVENSON The motion and the close air . . hurried our departure. P. BARKER She tended . . to hurry Muriel along the road to recovery long before Muriel was ready. 5 L. M. MONTGOMERY 'He's gone . . for the doctor,' said Anne, who was hurrying on hood and jacket.

With advs. in specialized senses: **hurry along**, **up** *colloq.* (cause to) make haste, move or act faster.

hurryingly *adv.* in a hurry; by hurrying: M18.

hurry-scurry /ˈhʌrɪskʌri/ *adv.*, *a.*, *n.* & *v.* *colloq.* M18. [Redupl. of HURRY *v.*, perh. infl. by *scud*, or *scuttle*.] **A** *adv.* In disorderly haste, in hurry and confusion. M18.

E. ELMHIRST A whistling coal train drove these horsemen hurry-scurry out of its way.

B *adj.* Characterized by hurry and confusion. M18.

C *n.* Hurry and confusion; disorderly haste, rush. M18.

A. CARLYLE An alarm was beat in the camp, which occasioned a great hurry-scurry in the courtyard.

D *v.i.* & *t.* (Cause to) move or act in confusion and hurry; rush. L18.

W. COMBE She was among those busy wives, Who hurry-scurry through their lives.

hurry-up /ˈhʌrɪʌp/ *a.* & *n.* *colloq.* L19. [f. *hurry up* s.v. HURRY *v.*] **A** *adj.* (*attrib.*) Used or arising in an emergency; involving or requiring haste. *US.* L19. **B** *n.* An encouragement or demand to hurry up. M20.

hurst /həːst/ *n.* Also **hirst**. [OE *hyrst* f. base repr. also by OS, OHG *hurst*, (also mod.G) *horst*.] **I 1** A hillock, knoll, or bank, *esp.* a sandy one. OE. **b** A sandbank; a ford formed by a bed of sand or shingle. LME. **2** A wooded hillock or rise; a copse, a wood. OE. **II 3** The frame of a pair of millstones. L16.

hurt /həːt/ *n.*[1] ME. [OFr., f. as HURT *v.*] †**1** A knock or blow causing a wound, injury, or damage. ME–M19. **2** A physical injury, a wound; bodily or material damage. *arch.* ME. **3** An injury of any kind; harm, wrong. Now *spec.* mental pain, emotional distress. ME.

1 R. W. EMERSON You admire this tower of granite, weathering the hurts of so many ages. 2 LD MACAULAY He ordered his own surgeon to look to the hurts of the captive. 3 S. PEPYS But [I] do not think that all this will redound to my hurt. H. ROBBINS The sudden look of hurt that flashed across her face. D. PRATER His first act was to write . . expressing his deep hurt at this dismissal.

hurt /həːt/ *n.*[2] Also **heurte**. M16. [Fr. †*heurte*. Cf. GOLPE.] *Her.* A roundel azure (usu. held to represent a hurtleberry).

hurt /həːt/ *n.*[3] Now *dial.* M16. [Origin unkn. Cf. earlier HURTLEBERRY. See also WHORT.] = HURTLEBERRY.

hurt /həːt/ *v.* Pa. t. & pa. pple **hurt**, (*dial.*) **hurted**. ME. [OFr. *hurter* (mod. *heurter*) f. Proto-Gallo-Romance, perh. of Gmc origin.] **I** *v.t.* †**1** Knock, strike, dash, (when so as to wound or injure passing into sense 2). ME–M17. **2** Injure physically; inflict bodily pain on, wound; cause bodily or material damage to (a person or animal, *arch.* a thing). ME. **b** Of an injured limb etc.: be a source of pain to (a person or animal). M19. **3** Give mental pain to, cause emotional distress to; upset, offend, (a person, feelings, etc.). ME. **4** *gen.* Injure or harm in any way; be prejudicial or detrimental to; wrong. ME.

1 CAXTON Thone hurted the other soo harde thei felle doun. J. WINTHROP The Elizabeth Dorcas . . being hurt upon a rock . . lost sixty passengers at sea. 2 J. BERGER He has broken both his legs, but . . he isn't badly hurt otherwise. 3 DAY LEWIS He put on a hurt expression which . . succeeded in piercing me with guilt. J. HELLER He makes fun of me and often hurts my feelings. 4 E. NESBIT I don't think it hurts Albert to enjoy himself too. P. BOWLES It's fine old cognac. It won't hurt you. *Gentleman (Bombay)* Sanctions will hurt poor blacks more than rich whites.

II *v.i.* †**5** Strike or dash (*against* etc.); come into collision. ME–E17. **6** (Of a limb etc.) suffer injury or pain, be a source of pain; *US* (of a person) suffer pain or distress, have a dire need *for*. ME. **7** Cause hurt or pain; be injurious, damaging, or detrimental. LME.

6 C. POTOK My head doesn't hurt at all, and the wrist is a lot less sore. A. F. LOEWENSTEIN She was hurting bad, . . We just got that codeine into her. *Fortune* He knew the industry was hurting for trained personnel. 7 M. AMIS My shoes, they're too tight—they hurt more every day. *Company* It didn't hurt that his stepfather was . . a descendant of the founders of MGM studios.

hurter /ˈhəːtə/ *n.*[1] ME. [AN *hurt(o)ur* (in AL *hurtur(i)um*), f. as HURT *v.*: see -OUR, -ER[2].] **1** (A strengthening piece on) the shoulder of an axle, against which the nave of the wheel strikes. ME. **2** An attachment on a gun-carriage to restrict its movement or prevent it from damaging a parapet etc. E19.

hurter /ˈhəːtə/ *n.*[2] LME. [f. HURT *v.* + -ER[1].] A person who or thing which causes hurt or injury.

hurtful /ˈhəːtfʊl, -f(ə)l/ *a.* LME. [f. HURT *n.*[1] + -FUL.] Causing hurt; harmful, injurious; wounding to the feelings.

hurtfully *adv.* M16. **hurtfulness** *n.* E17.

hurtle /ˈhəːt(ə)l/ *n. literary.* L18. [f. the vb.] The action or an act of hurtling.

hurtle /ˈhəːt(ə)l/ *v.* ME. [f. HURT *v.* + -LE³.] **I** *v.t.* **1** Strike, knock, (a thing *against*, a thing †*down*, things *together*); strike against, collide with. Now *rare* exc. as passing into sense 2. ME. **2** Drive violently or swiftly; hurl, cast; *rare* brandish. LME.

1 LYTTON His emotions .. so hurtling one the other. 2 *Boy's Own Paper* Pieces of ice are being .. hurtled into the air.

II *v.i.* **3** Strike *against*, *together*, esp. with violence or noise; collide; clash. Now *rare* exc. as passing into sense 4. ME. **4** Move with a clattering or rattling sound; dash, rush, hurry, esp. noisily; move or travel rapidly. E16.

3 J. R. GREEN Where knights have hurtled together. 4 SHAKES. *Jul. Caes.* The noise of battle hurtled in the air. B. HECHT His streetcar .. had hurtled wildly through the streets. R. P. JHABVALA The mountains themselves crumble off in chunks which hurtle down.

hurtlingly *adv.* (*rare*) in a hurtling manner L19.

hurtleberry /ˈhəːt(ə)lb(ə)ri/ *n.* LME. [f. elem. of unkn. origin + BERRY *n.*¹: earlier than synon. HURT *n.*³ and WHORT, WHORTLEBERRY.] (The berry of) any of various dwarf shrubs of the genus *Vaccinium*, of the heath family, *esp.* (in Britain) the bilberry, *V. myrtillus*; *N. Amer.* = HUCKLEBERRY *n.* 1.

hurtless /ˈhəːtlɪs/ *a.* LME. [f. HURT *n.*¹ + -LESS.] **1** Unhurt. Now *rare*. LME. **2** Causing no hurt, harmless. M16.

hurtlessly *adv.* (*rare*) L16. **hurtlessness** *n.* (*rare*) L16.

hurtsome /ˈhəːts(ə)m/ *a.* Chiefly *Sc.* M16. [f. HURT *n.*¹ + -SOME¹.] Hurtful, injurious.

husband /ˈhʌzbənd/ *n.* LOE. [ON *húsbóndi* master of a house, husband, f. *hús* HOUSE *n.*¹ + *bóndi* occupier and tiller of the soil: see BOND *n.*¹] **I** †**1** The master of a house; the male head of a household. LOE–ME. **2** A married man esp. in relation to his wife. ME.

2 W. TREVOR Her husband .. had married her ... in the church of St. Cyril. *transf.*: E. TOPSELL A Bull is the husband of a Cow. COMPLAISANT *husband*.

II 3 The manager of a household or establishment; a steward. *obs.* exc. in *ship's husband* below. LOE. †**4** A tiller and cultivator of the soil, a farmer. Also, a manorial tenant (cf. HUSBANDLAND). ME–M18. **5** †**a** A good manager of his affairs. LME–L16. **b** With qualifying adj.: a *good*, *bad*, etc., manager of his affairs. *arch.* E16.

3 H. FINCH The King hath a proper Court... The Judges whereof are called Barons, or housebands. **ship's husband** an agent appointed by a ship's owners to see that a ship in port is well provided in all respects. 4 J. TULL Once in seven Years, the worst Husbands have the best Corn. 5b DEFOE I had been so good a husband of my rum that I had a great deal left. M. R. JAMES The next abbot was a bad husband to the Abbey.

husbandhood *n.* the state or position of a husband, the fact of being a husband LME. **husbandless** *a.* without a husband; unmarried; widowed: LME. **husbandlike** *a.* & *adv.* after the manner of a husband M16. **husbandom** *n.* (*rare*) = HUSBANDHOOD L19. **husbandship** *n.* (*a*) *rare* husbandly behaviour; (*b*) the fact or condition of being the husband *of*: L18.

husband /ˈhʌzbənd/ *v.t.* LME. [f. the n.] **I 1** Till (the ground); cultivate (plants). *arch.* LME. **2** Administer as a good steward; manage thriftily; use economically (*lit.* & *fig.*). LME.

1 L. MORRIS The grain scarce husbanded by toiling hands Upon the sunlit plain. 2 C. BRONTË Husbanding my monthly allowance. R. GITTINGS He had the sufferer's gift of husbanding his energy.

II 3 Provide (a woman) with a husband; mate. *arch.* M16. **4** Behave as a husband to, marry (a woman). *arch.* E17.

3 S. ROWLANDS I am husbanded with such a Clowne. 4 G. MEREDITH He had been ready to perform the duty of husbanding the woman.

husbander *n.* (*rare*) E17.

husbandland /ˈhʌzbəndlənd/ *n.* LME. [f. HUSBAND *n.* or ON *húsbóndi* freeholder + LAND *n.*¹] *Hist.* In N. England and Scotland, the holding of a manorial tenant; the land occupied and cultivated by the tenants of a manor as opp. to the demesne lands.

husbandly /ˈhʌzbəndli/ *a.* LME. [f. HUSBAND *n.* + -LY¹.] †**1** Thrifty, economical. LME–M18. **2**†**a** Of plants: cultivated. M–L16. **b** Pertaining or appropriate to a husbandman or husbandry. Now *rare* or *obs.* L16. **3** Pertaining or appropriate to a woman's husband; marital. L16.

1 O. BLACKALL He .. is nevertheless oblig'd to be frugal and husbandly. 3 *Daily Telegraph* Every mother with a daughter knows the husbandly potential of every other mother's son.

husbandly /ˈhʌzbəndli/ *adv.* Now *rare* or *obs.* L15. [f. as prec. + -LY².] Thriftily, economically.

husbandman /ˈhʌzbəndmən/ *n.* Pl. **-men**. ME. [f. HUSBAND *n.* + MAN *n.*] **1** A man who tills or cultivates the ground; a farmer. Formerly also, the holder of a husbandland. *arch.* ME. †**2** The male head or manager of a household. Only in ME. **b** A married man, a husband. *rare*. Only in LME.

husbandry /ˈhʌzbəndri/ *n.* ME. [f. HUSBAND *n.* + -RY.] †**1** The administration and management of a household; domestic economy. ME–M17. †**b** *gen.* Occupation, business. E–M17. **2** Tillage or cultivation of the ground; agriculture; farming. ME. †**3** Household goods; agricultural produce; land under cultivation; the body of husbandmen on an estate. ME–L17. **4a** Careful management, thrift, economy. LME. **b** With qualifying adj.: *good*, *bad*, etc., management of resources. M16.

1 SHAKES. *Merch. V.* Lorenzo, I commit into your hands The husbandry and manage of my house. 2 C. FRANCIS Good management and wise husbandry are the cornerstones of bountiful harvesting. Z. MEDVEDEV There are ... agricultural research institutes, one of which studies sheep and goat husbandry. **animal husbandry** the science of breeding and caring for farm animals. **crop husbandry** the science of growing and harvesting crops. 3 SHAKES. *Hen. V* All her husbandry doth lie on heaps, corrupting in it own fertility. 4a R. W. EMERSON Reform has no gratitude, no prudence, no husbandry. b BOLINGBROKE The excessive ill husbandry practiced from the very beginning of King William's reign.

†**huseau** *n.* LME–E18. [Fr. †*houseau* dim. of OFr. (& Fr. dial.) *house*, *heuse*, *husse* boot.] A boot, a legging.

hush /hʌʃ/ *n.*¹ E17. [f. HUSH *v.*¹] **1** An utterance of 'hush!' E17. **2** Suppression of sound; stillness; silence; an instance of this. L17. **b** Suppression of discussion, information, etc. L19. **3** *Phonet.* A palatal or palato-alveolar fricative (as /ʃ/ or /ʒ/). M20.

2 E. FIGES A hush fell as the conversation died. C. PHILLIPS The .. hush of a late afternoon in the Caribbean overtook him. b *attrib.*: T. E. LAWRENCE There is a 'Hush' policy over the Red Sea and Arabia.

Comb.: **hush money**: paid to prevent the disclosure of a discreditable affair.

hushful *a.* silent, still L19. **hushfully** *adv.* M19.

hush /hʌʃ/ *n.*² Chiefly *north.* E19. [f. HUSH *v.*³] A gush or rush of water, *esp.* one artificially produced.

hush /hʌʃ/ *a.* E17. [Alt. of HUSHT *a.*, also infl. by HUSH *v.*¹, *int.* In sense 2 merging w. attrib. use of HUSH *n.*¹] **1** Silent, still, quiet, hushed. *arch.* E17. **2** Secret. Cf. HUSH-HUSH *a.* *colloq.* M20.

1 LONGFELLOW Hush sat the listening bench. 2 J. WYNDHAM I don't know what goes on .. but I do know that it is very hush.

hush /hʌʃ/ *v.*¹ M16. [Prob. back-form. f. HUSHT *a.* regarded as a pa. pple: cf. prec. See also HUSH-HUSH *v.*] **I** *v.t.* **1** Make silent, quiet, or still. Also foll. by *up*. M16. **2** Calm (disturbance, disquiet, etc.); allay, lull, pacify. M17. **3** Suppress public mention of (an affair); keep (an event, news, etc.) from becoming known. Freq. foll. by *up*. M17.

1 T. O'BRIEN The child was talking .., then the young woman hushed her. G. CLARE Voices had to be hushed, movements subdued. **hush one's mouth** *US dial.* be quiet, stop talking. 2 H. MANN I do sincerely congratulate you, that the disturbance is hushed. 3 STEELE It had indeed cost him a Hundred Pounds to hush the affair. L. VAN DER POST Evil verily does not decrease by being hushed up as a non-reality.

II *v.i.* **4** Become silent, quiet, or still. Freq. in *imper.*: see HUSH *int.* Also foll. by *up*. M16.

4 A. SETON The crowd hushed and listened avidly. *New Yorker* Hush up! You want these bitches to hear you?

hush /hʌʃ/ *v.*²*t.* Now *dial.* E17. [Alt. of SH *int.* & *v.* Cf. SHOO, G *husch* shoo!] Shoo away (birds etc.).

hush /hʌʃ/ *v.*³*t.* Chiefly *north.* M18. [Imit.] Send or release (water) with a rush.

hush /hʌʃ/ *int.* E17. [Partly var. of HUSHT *int.*, partly imper. of HUSH *v.*¹] Demanding silence or quiet.

hushaby /ˈhʌʃəbʌɪ/ *int.* Also **-bye**. M18. [f. HUSH *v.*¹ or *int.* + *-a-* + *-by* as in BYE-BYE *int.* Cf. *lullaby*, *rock-a-bye*.] Lulling a child: hush and sleep.

hushed /hʌʃt/ *a.* E17. [(Alt. of HUSHT *a.* after) pa. pple of HUSH *v.*¹: see -ED¹.] Silenced, quieted, stilled.

hushedly /ˈhʌʃɪdli/ *adv.* in a hushed manner M19.

hush-hush /hʌʃˈhʌʃ/ *a.* *colloq.* E20. [f. redupl. of HUSH *int.*] (To be kept) highly secret.

A. S. BYATT I worked for British Intelligence, ... On some very hush-hush research.

hush-hush /hʌʃˈhʌʃ/ *v.t.* M19. [Redupl. of HUSH *v.*¹] Silence, quiet (by saying 'hush!' to).

hushion /ˈhʌʃ(ə)n/ *n.* *Sc.* L18. [Perh. f. HUSEAU: see -ION.] A stocking without a foot.

hush-puppy /ˈhʌʃpʌpi/ *n.* *US.* E20. [f. HUSH *v.*¹ + PUPPY *n.*] A kind of quickly fried maize bread.

husht /hʌʃt/ *a.* *arch.* LME. [Orig. f. HUSHT *int.*, later taken as a pa. pple (whence HUSH *v.*¹). See also HUSHED *a.*] Silent, still, quiet; made silent, hushed.

husht /hʌʃt/ *int.* Now *dial.* Also †**hust**. LME. [Natural exclam. Cf. HUSH, WHISHT, WHIST *ints.*] = HUSH *int.*

husk /hʌsk/ *n.*¹ LME. [Prob. f. LG *hūske* little house, core of fruit, sheath = MDu. *hūskijn* (Du. *huisken*) dim. of *hūs* HOUSE *n.*¹] **1** The dry outer covering of some fruits and seeds, esp. grain, nuts, etc.; *N. Amer.* the outer covering of an ear of maize. LME. †**b** The calyx of a flower. M16–E18. **2** The outside part of something, esp. when worthless. LME. **3** An insect's cocoon. Formerly, an elytron. *obs.* exc. *poet.* M16.

1 AV *Luke* 15:16 And he would faine haue filled his belly with the huskes that the swine did eate. D. ATTENBOROUGH It bears numerous seeds, .. that are easily plucked and winnowed from their husks. 2 J. R. LOWELL He .. gave us ravishing glimpses of an ideal under the dry husk of our New England. R. SUTCLIFF Some sitting like zombies. The husks of men, blind and leaden with exhaustion.

husk /hʌsk/ *n.*² E18. [Prob. partly f. HUSK *v.*², partly f. HUSK *n.*¹, HUSKY *a.*²] **1** Bronchitis in cattle, sheep, or swine caused by parasitic infestation, usu. marked by a husky cough. E18. **2** Huskiness. E19.

†**husk** *n.*³ see HUSS.

husk /hʌsk/ *v.*¹*t.* M16. [f. HUSK *n.*¹] Remove the husk or husks from.

husk /hʌsk/ *v.*² L16. [Prob. partly imit., partly f. HUSK *n.*¹, HUSKY *a.*²] **1** *v.i.* Of a farm animal: cough as when suffering from husk. *local.* L16. **2** *v.i.* Of the voice: be or become husky. E20. **3** *v.t.* Utter huskily. L20.

huskanaw /ˈhʌskənɔː/ *n.* & *v.* E18. [Virginia Algonquian.] *Hist.* **A** *n.* An initiation rite for American Indian youths at puberty involving solitary confinement and the use of narcotics. E18. **B** *v.t.* Cause to undergo this rite. E18.

huske /hʌsk/ *n.* Long *arch.* *rare.* L15. [Origin unkn.] A company of hares.

husked /hʌskt/ *a.* L16. [f. HUSK *n.*¹, *v.*¹: see -ED², -ED¹.] †**1** Provided or covered with a husk. L16–L17. **2** Stripped of the husk; hulled. E17.

husker /ˈhʌskə/ *n.* L18. [f. HUSK *v.*¹ + -ER¹.] A person who or thing which removes husks; *N. Amer.* a participant in a husking-bee.

huskie *n.* & *a.* var. of HUSKY *n.*¹ & *a.*¹

husking /ˈhʌskɪŋ/ *n.* L17. [f. HUSK *v.*¹ + -ING¹.] The action of HUSK *v.*¹; an instance of this; *N. Amer.* (more fully *husking-bee*) a gathering of neighbours etc. at a farm to remove husks from maize.

husky /ˈhʌski/ *n.*¹ & *a.*¹ Also **-ie**, **H-**. M19. Perh. ult. f. Cree *a:yaskime·w* or a related form: cf. ESKIMO.] **A** *n.* **1** The Eskimo language; an Eskimo. *colloq.* (now usu. *derog.*). M19. **2** =

ESKIMO *dog.* L19. **B** *adj.* Eskimo. *colloq.* (now usu. *derog.*) exc. in *husky dog,* = sense A.2 above. M19.

husky /ˈhʌski/ *a.*[2] & *n.*[2] M16. [f. HUSK *n.*[1] + -Y[1].] **A** *adj.* **1** Full of or consisting of husks; of the nature of a husk. M16. **2** Dry as a husk, arid (*lit.* & *fig.*). L16. †**3** Having or consisting of a cocoon. M17–M18. **4** Dry in the throat, hoarse; low-pitched and somewhat rough. E18. **5** Tough, strong, hefty. *colloq.* (orig. *N. Amer.*). M19.

1 R. GRAVES On the tree a husky fruit. 2 DISRAELI His translation is hard, dry, and husky, as the outside of a cocoa-nut. 4 L. DEIGHTON Jean's voice was husky, a bit edgy and rasplike. N. MAILER She had a rich husky voice. 5 D. DELILLO A husky blond Nebraskan.

B *n.* A strong stoutly built person; one whose appearance suggests strength and force. *N. Amer. colloq.* M19.

huskily *adv.* M19. **huskiness** *n.* L18.

huso /ˈhuːsəʊ/ *n.* Pl. **-os**. ME. [med.L *huso* f. OHG *hūso*. Cf. HAUSEN.] The beluga, *Huso huso*.

huspil /ˈhʌsp(ə)l/ *v.t.* Long *obs.* exc. *dial.* Also **-pel**. Infl. **-ll-**. LME. [Fr. *houspiller* maltreat by dragging about and shaking, alt. of earlier *hous(se)pigner*, f. *housse* (see HOUSE *n.*[2]) + *p(e)igner* to comb.] Treat with violence; maltreat; despoil; harass.

huss /hʌs/ *n.* Orig. †**husk**. LME. [Origin unkn.] A dogfish; *esp.* (*a*) (more fully *bull huss*) the nurse hound, *Scyliorhinus stellaris*; (*b*) (more fully *robin huss*) the lesser-spotted dogfish, *S. canicula*.

hussar /hʊˈzɑː/ *n.* M16. [Hungarian *huszár* †freebooter, light horseman f. OSerb. *husar, gusar, hursar* f. It. *corsaro* CORSAIR.] Orig., a Hungarian light horseman of the 15th cent. Later, a soldier of a light cavalry regiment.

Husserlian /hʊˈsəːlj(ə)n/ *a.* M20. [f. *Husserl* (see below) + -IAN.] Of, pertaining to, or characteristic of the German philosopher Edmund Husserl (1859–1938) or his work, esp. in phenomenology.

Hussite /ˈhʌsʌɪt/ *n.* & *a.* M16. [mod.L *Hussita* (usu. pl.) f. John Huss or Hus (see below), f. *Husinec* his native village: see -ITE[1].] **A** *n.* A follower of John Huss (*c* 1372–1415), a Bohemian religious reformer who became a national hero after being burned at the stake. M16. **B** *attrib.* or as *adj.* Of or pertaining to Huss, his beliefs, or his teachings. M19.

Hussitism *n.* L19.

hussive *n.* see HOUSEWIFE *n.*

hussy /ˈhʌsi, ˈhʌzi/ *n.* Also **huzzy** /ˈhʌzi/. LME. [Contr. of HOUSEWIFE *n.*: cf. GOODY *n.*[1]] †**1** = HOUSEWIFE *n.* 1. LME–E19. **2** = HOUSEWIFE *n.* 3. *obs.* exc. *dial.* E16. **3** A woman of light or worthless character; a pert girl. M17.

3 E. O'BRIEN She wished that her daughter had not grown into the cruel feelingless hussy . . she was.

†**hust** *int.* var. of HUSHT *int.*

husting /ˈhʌstɪŋ/ *n.* Pl. **hustings**. LOE. [ON *hūsþing* house of assembly (held by a king etc. with his immediate followers as opp. to a general assembly): see HOUSE *n.*[1], THING *n.*[2]] **1** A deliberative assembly, *esp.* one summoned by a king etc.; a council. Long *obs.* exc. *Hist.* LOE. **2** *sing.* & in *pl.* The most ancient and highest court in the City of London presided over nominally by the Lord Mayor and Sheriffs and actually by the Recorder of London. Formerly also (in *pl.* treated as *sing.*), the part of the Guildhall where this court was held. Also *Court of Husting.* LOE. **3** In *pl.* (now usu. treated as *sing.*). Orig. (now *Hist.*), the platform from which (before 1872) parliamentary candidates were nominated and electors addressed. Later, the proceedings of an election (for Parliament etc.). E18.

3 H. MARTINEAU The Church question was the leading one on the hustings. *Sunday (Calcutta)* At the hustings, her party somehow scraped through.

hustle /ˈhʌs(ə)l/ *n.* L17. [f. the vb.] **1** The action of shaking together. Chiefly in *pitch-and-hustle*, = *hustle-cap* s.v. HUSTLE *v.* Long *rare* or *obs.* L17. **2** The act of pushing or jostling roughly; forceful or strenuous activity; push, drive; bustle. E19. **3** A swindle, a means of deception or fraud. Also, a source of income, a paid job. *slang* (orig. *US*). M20.

2 E. AMADI She could not cope with all the hustle and pressures of business. **get a hustle on** *US* hurry up, get a move on. 3 MALCOLM X Hustles being used to avoid the draft. R. PHARR I got me a good hustle I write over $200 worth of numbers a day.

hustle /ˈhʌs(ə)l/ *v.* L17. [(M)Du. *husselen, hutselen* shake, toss, frequent. of *hutsen* = MHG *hutzen* (cf. *hussen* run, *hutschen* push), f. Gmc imit. base.] **I** *v.t.* †**1** Shake to and fro, shake about; toss (money) in the game of hustle-cap (see below). L17–M19. **2** Push roughly, jostle, esp. in order to rob; thrust (a person) *into, out of, through*, etc.; impel unceremoniously *into* an action etc.; cause to hurry. M18. **3** Obtain or produce by forceful action; steal, swindle. Also foll. by *up*. *US colloq.* M19. **4** Sell or serve (goods etc.), esp. aggressively. *N. Amer. slang.* L19.

2 SMOLLETT I was hussled by those rebellious rapscallions. R. K. NARAYAN Banks . . could not be hustled; they had their own pace of work. W. WHARTON He grabs me by the arm and hustles me down a tunnel. D. LESSING White clouds . . were being ripped and hustled and rolled across a mauve silk sky. *New Yorker* Transvestites hustled white men in business suits. 3 P. MANSFIELD Perhaps they can hustle up some coffee. 4 P. BOOTH I'm afraid they make poor Nixon look like he's hustling real estate.

II *v.i.* **5** Crowd together, jostle each other; push one's way; push roughly *against*. E19. **6** Move hastily, hurry, bustle. E19. **7** Engage in prostitution. *slang.* E20.

5 M. KINGSLEY The woman will accuse some man of having hustled against her. M. S. GATTY The tortoise began to hustle under the leaves and rubbish. 6 K. KESEY I'll have to hustle to catch up. 7 R. BRAUTIGAN She was hustling for a spade pimp.

Comb.: **hustle-cap** (now *rare* or *obs.*) a form of pitch-and-toss, in which the coins were shaken in a cap or hat before being tossed.

hustlement /ˈhʌs(ə)lm(ə)nt/ *n.* Long *obs.* exc. *dial.* LME. [OFr. *(h)ostillement* furniture, f. *hostiller* furnish, equip, f. *(h)ostil(le)* (mod. *outil*) tool: see -MENT.] **1** Household furniture. Usu. in *pl.*, household goods. LME. **2** Lumber; a miscellaneous collection; in *pl.*, odds and ends. M17.

hustler /ˈhʌslə/ *n.* E19. [f. HUSTLE *v.* + -ER[1].] A person who hustles; someone making a dishonest living, a thief, a pimp; (orig. *US*) an energetic person, *esp.* a (forcefully persuasive) salesman; *slang* a prostitute.

J. K. JEROME I don't want to appear a hustler, . . but it feels to me like hours since I asked you how the catastrophe really occurred. P. HOWARD Successful hustlers in modern methods of mass book-selling.

†**huswife** *n.* see HOUSEWIFE *n.*

hut /hʌt/ *n.* M16. [Fr. *hutte* f. (M)HG *hütte*.] **1a** *Mil.* A temporary wooden etc. house for troops. M16. **b** A small, simple, or crude house or shelter, *esp.* one made of mud, turf, etc., or constructed for temporary use; *Austral.* a dwelling for the use of stockmen, shearers, etc. M17. **2** The back end or body of the pin closing the breech of a musket. M19.

Comb.: **hut-circle** *Archaeol.* a ring of stones or earth or some other circular feature interpreted as the site of a prehistoric hut.

hut /hʌt/ *v.* Infl. **-tt-**. M17. [Fr. *(se) hutter* make a hut for one's lodging, f. as prec.] **1** *v.t.* Place (troops etc.) in a hut or huts; provide with a hut or huts. M17. **2** *v.i.* Lodge or take shelter in a hut or huts. L18.

hutch /hʌtʃ/ *n.* ME. [(O)Fr. *huche*, (dial.) *huge* f. med.L *hutica* (AN *hugia*): ult. origin unkn.] **1** A chest for storage, a coffer; *spec.* (*N. Amer.*) a (kitchen) sideboard with open shelves above for plates etc., a dresser. Now chiefly *N. Amer.* ME. **2** A cage; *spec.* a cage or box for small animals, a boxlike pen for rabbits etc. (also *rabbit-hutch* etc.). LME. **3** A hut, a cabin, a small house. *derog.* E17. **4** *techn.* Any of various boxlike devices or containers; *esp.* (*a*) a box for sifting flour etc. (also *bolting-hutch*); (*b*) a low carriage or wagon used in agriculture, mining, etc. E17. **b** A quantity (of coal, ore, etc.) held by a hutch. L17.

Comb.: **hutch table** *N. Amer.* a combination table and chest which converts into a chair or a settee.

hutch /hʌtʃ/ *v.* L16. [f. the n.] **1** *v.t.* Put or store in a hutch (*lit.* & *fig.*). L16. **2** *v.i.* & *t.* Crouch, squat; hunch, huddle, (*up*); lower (oneself) into or move with a crouching, bent, or huddled posture; hitch (one's chair etc.) forward. Chiefly *dial.* L19.

1 MILTON In her own loins She hutched the all-worshipped ore. 2 D. H. LAWRENCE Long smooth thighs Hutched-up for warmth. W. GOLDING He hutched to the very edge and let his legs hang over. B. HINES Billy hutched his chair up and leaned forward over his desk.

Hutchinson /ˈhʌtʃɪns(ə)n/ *n.* L19. [J. *Hutchinson* (1828–1913), Eng. surgeon.] *Med.* **1** *Hutchinson('s) tooth*, (the possession of) a permanent incisor with a narrow notched biting edge, found in children with congenital syphilis. Usu. in *pl.* L19. **2** *Hutchinson('s) triad*, Hutchinson's teeth, interstitial keratitis, and one form of deafness, jointly diagnostic of congenital syphilis. L19.

Hutchinsonian /hʌtʃɪnˈsəʊnɪən/ *a.* & *n.* M18. [f. *Hutchinson* (see below) + -IAN.] **A** *adj.* **1** *Eccl. Hist.* Of or pertaining to John Hutchinson (1674–1737), a writer on natural philosophy who interpreted the Bible mystically and opposed Newtonian philosophy. Also, of or pertaining to Anne Hutchinson (1591–1643), an antinomian teacher in New England. M18. **2** *Med.* (Also **h-**.) Designating an incisor notched in the manner of Hutchinson's teeth. E20. **B** *n.* *Eccl. Hist.* An adherent of John Hutchinson or of Anne Hutchinson. M18.

hutia /hʌˈtiːə/ *n.* M16. [Sp. f. Taino *huti, cuti*.] A rodent of the family Capromyidae, comprising W. Indian animals resembling cavies and related to the coypu.

hutment /ˈhʌtm(ə)nt/ *n.* L19. [f. HUT *v.* + -MENT.] Accommodation or lodging in huts; a hutted encampment.

hutt *n.* see HOT *n.*[1]

Hutterite /ˈhʌt(ə)rʌɪt/ *n.* & *a.* L19. [f. Jacob *Hutter* (d. 1536), a Moravian Anabaptist + -ITE[1].] *Chr. Ch.* **A** *n.* A member of an Anabaptist sect established in Moravia by Jacob Hutter, or of any of various N. American sects originating among immigrants holding similar beliefs. L19. **B** *adj.* Of, pertaining to, or holding the doctrines of, the Hutterites. M20.

Hutterian /hʌˈtɪərɪən/ *a.* = HUTTERITE *a.* E20.

Huttonian /hʌˈtəʊnɪən/ *a.* & *n.* E19. [f. *Hutton* (see below) + -IAN.] *Geol.* (now *Hist.*). **A** *adj.* Designating or pertaining to the ideas of James Hutton (1726–97), Scottish geologist, involving plutonism and uniformitarianism. E19. **B** *n.* An adherent of Hutton's views. E19.

Hutu /ˈhuːtuː/ *n.* & *a.* M20. [Bantu.] **A** *n.* Pl. same, **Bahutu** /bəˈhuːtuː/. A member of a Bantu-speaking people forming the majority of the population of Rwanda and of Burundi. M20. **B** *adj.* Of or pertaining to the Bahutu. M20.

hutung /ˈhʊtʊŋ/ *n.* E20. [Chin. (Pekingese) *hútòngr*.] In northern Chinese cities, a narrow side-street, an alley.

Huweitat /hʊˈweɪtɑːt/ *n.* & *a.* E19. [Arab. *(al-)Ḥuwayṭāt* Arab tribes in NW Saudi Arabia.] **A** *n.* (A member of) a Bedouin tribe of northern Saudi Arabia. E19. **B** *adj.* Of or pertaining to this tribe. M19.

Huxham /ˈhʌks(ə)m/ *n.* L18. [J. *Huxham* (1692–1768), Eng. physician.] *Pharm.* In full *Huxham's tincture (of bark)*. Compound tincture of cinchona bark, formerly used as a bitter tonic and febrifuge.

Huxleyan /ˈhʌksliən/ *a.* Also **-leian**. L19. [f. *Huxley* (see below): see -AN, -IAN.] **1** Of, pertaining to, or characteristic of T. H. Huxley (1825–95), Eng. Darwinian biologist, humanist, and educational reformer. L19. **2** Of, pertaining to, or characteristic of his grandson Aldous Huxley (1894–1963), Eng. novelist, or his work. M20.

Huygens /ˈhʌɪgənz/ *n.* Also **-ghens**. M19. [C. *Huygens* (1629–95), Du. physicist.] **1** *Huygens' principle*, a principle of wave propagation, that each point on a wave front can be regarded as a source of new waves, the overall effect of which constitutes the propagation of the wave front. M19. 2 *Huygens(') construction*, the geometrical construction for finding the position of a wave front using Huygens' principle. M19. 3 *Huygens(') eyepiece*, a negative eyepiece of an optical instrument, consisting of two planoconvex lenses with their plane side towards the observer. (Earlier called *Huygenian eyepiece.*) E20.

Huygenian /hʌɪˈɡiːnɪən/ *a.* E18.

huzoor /hʌˈzʊə, hʊ-/ *n. arch.* Also (as a title) **H-**. L18. [Pers. & Urdu *ḥuẓūr* f. Arab. *ḥuḍūr* presence, f. *ḥaḍara* be present.] An Indian potentate. (Chiefly a title used by Indians in respectful address.)

huzz /hʌz/ *v.i.* M16. [Imit.] Buzz.

huzza /hʌˈzɑː, hʊˈzɑː/ *n., int., & v. arch.* L16. [Perh. orig. a sailor's cry when hauling (see HOISE), but cf. also G *Hussa* a cry of pursuit and exultation. See also HURRAH.] A *n.* A shout of 'huzza!', a cheer. L16. B *int.* Expr. approval, encouragement, enthusiasm, or delight. L17. C *v.* 1 *v.i.* Shout 'huzza!' L17. 2 *v.t.* Welcome or encourage with shouts of 'huzza!' L17.

huzzy *n.* var. of HUSSY.

hyacinth /ˈhʌɪəsɪnθ/ *n.* Also †**hyacine** (Spenser). M16. [Fr. *hyacinthe* fr. L *hyacinthus* f. Gk *huakinthos*, of pre-Hellenic origin: cf. earlier JACINTH.] 1 Orig. (now *Class. Hist.*), a blue gem, perh. the sapphire. Now, the reddish-orange variety of zircon; also, a similar-coloured form of garnet or topaz. M16. 2 A flower whose dark markings were interpreted as the Gk word *aiai*, an exclamation of grief, and which was fabled to have sprung from the blood of Hyacinthus, a youth inadvertently killed by Apollo: variously identified with the martagon lily, a kind of iris, etc. Now *Class. Hist.* or *poet.* L16. 3 (A flowering stem of) any of various bulbous plants of the genus *Hyacinthus*, of the lily family, with dense racemes of bell-shaped flowers; esp. *H. orientalis*, native to SW Asia, much grown for its fragrant flowers. Also, any of various related or similar plants. L16. 4 A blue-black variety of the domestic pigeon with white markings. M19.

Phrases: **Cape hyacinth** = *summer hyacinth* below. **feather hyacinth** a sport of the tassel hyacinth in which all the flowers are sterile and divided into shreds. **grape hyacinth** any of various spring-flowering bulbs of the Mediterranean genus *Muscari*, of the lily family, much grown for their racemes of small ball-like blue flowers. **hyacinth of Peru** a bulbous plant of the lily family, *Scilla peruviana*, native to the Mediterranean, with dense racemes of blue-violet flowers. **Roman hyacinth** a smaller, earlier variant of *Hyacinthus orientalis*. **starch hyacinth** a kind of grape hyacinth with dark blue scented flowers. **summer hyacinth** a tall southern African plant of the lily family, *Galtonia candicans*, with fragrant white flowers. **tassel hyacinth** a kind of grape hyacinth, *Muscari comosum*, with a raceme of fertile brownish flowers bearing showy sterile purple-blue flowers at the top. **water hyacinth** a tropical American aquatic plant, *Eichhornia crassipes* (family Pontederiaceae), with large violet-blue flowers, a serious weed in waterways in warmer parts of the world. **wild hyacinth** either of two plants of the lily family: (*a*) (chiefly *Sc.*) the (English) bluebell, *Hyacinthoides non-scripta*; (*b*) *US* a meadow plant, *Camassia scilloides*, with starry pale blue flowers. **wood hyacinth** (chiefly *Sc.*) = *wild hyacinth* (a).

Comb.: **hyacinth bean** = LABLAB.

hyacinthine /hʌɪəˈsɪnθʌɪn/ *a.* M17. [L *hyacinthinus* f. Gk *huakinthinos*, f. *huakinthos*: see -INE[2].] 1 Of the colour of a hyacinth (the gem or the flower). Chiefly *poet.* & *rhet.*, as an epithet of hair. M17. 2 Consisting of or decorated with hyacinths (the flower). *poet.* L17.

Also **hyacinthian** *a.* E18.

Hyades /ˈhʌɪədiːz/ *n.pl.* LME. [Gk *Huades*, according to popular etym. f. *huein* to rain but perh. actually f. *hus* pig, SWINE (the L name being *Suculae* little pigs).] (The name of) a group of stars near the Pleiades in the constellation Taurus, the heliacal rising of which was once thought to foretell rain.

hyaena *n.* var. of HYENA.

hyaenid /hʌɪˈiːnɪd/ *n.* & *a.* M20. [mod.L *Hyaenidae* (see below), f. L HYAENA: see -ID[3].] A *n.* An animal of the family Hyaenidae, which comprises the hyenas and the aardwolf. M20. B *adj.* Of, pertaining to, or designating this family. L20.

hya-hya /hʌɪəˈhʌɪə/ *n.* M19. [Guyanese name.] A Guyanese evergreen tree, *Couma utilis*, of the dogbane family, with a drinkable latex.

hyaline /ˈhʌɪəlɪn, -iːn, -ʌɪn/ *a.* & *n.* In sense B.2 also **-in** /-ɪn/. M17. [L *hyalinus* f. late Gk *hualinos*, f. *hualos* glass: see -INE[2].] A *adj.* Transparent, translucent; glassy. *techn.* & *poet.* M17.

hyaline cartilage a translucent bluish-white kind of cartilage, present in joints and the respiratory tract and forming much of the foetal skeleton. **hyaline degeneration** hyalinization. **hyaline membrane disease** a condition in some babies, esp. premature ones, in which the lung spaces are lined with a membrane that inhibits adequate respiration.

B *n.* 1 A translucent substance such as the smooth sea or the clear sky. *poet.* M17. 2 *Anat.* & *Zool.* A clear translucent substance, such as that in hydatid cysts. M19.

2 *Zenker's hyaline degeneration*: see ZENKER *n.*[1]

hyalini'zation *n.* (*Med.*) a change of tissue into a homogeneous translucent often firm mass (also called *hyaline degeneration*) E20. **hyalinized** *a.* (*Med.*) having the appearance that results from hyalinization E20. **hyali'nosis** *n.*, pl. **-noses** /-nəʊsiːz/, *Med.* = HYALINIZATION L19.

hyalite /ˈhʌɪəlʌɪt/ *n.* L18. [f. Gk *hualos* glass + -ITE[1].] A clear colourless variety of opal occurring as globules.

hyalo- /ˈhʌɪələʊ/ *comb. form* of Gk *hualos* glassy: see -O-.

hyalo'clastite *n.* (*Geol.*) (a) material formed as a result of lava coming into contact with water, solidifying, and shattering M20. **hyalopi'litic** *a.* [Gk *pilos* felt] *Geol.* characterized by needle-like microlites in a glassy matrix L19. **hyaloplasm** *n.* (*Biol.*) the clear finely structured ground substance of cytoplasm L19.

hyaloid /ˈhʌɪəlɔɪd/ *a.* & *n.* M19. [Fr. *hyaloïde* or late L *hyaloïdes* f. Gk *hualoeidēs* like glass, f. *hualos* glass: see -OID.] *Anat.* A *adj.* Of, pertaining to, or designating a thin transparent membrane enclosing the vitreous humour of the eye. M19. B *n.* The hyaloid membrane. M19.

hyaluronic /ˌhʌɪəljʊəˈrɒnɪk/ *a.* M20. [f. prec. + URONIC.] *Biochem. hyaluronic acid*, a viscous glycosaminoglycan found in synovial fluid, vitreous humour, bacterial capsules, etc., and composed of glucosamine and glucuronic acid.

hya'luronate *n.* a salt of hyaluronic acid M20. **hyaluronidase** *n.* an enzyme which depolymerizes hyaluronic acid, so reducing its viscosity and making tissue containing it more permeable M20.

hyawa /ˈhʌɪəwə/ *n.* Also **hiawa**. E19. [Arawak *hayáawa*.] Any of several balsam-yielding trees and shrubs of Guyana, esp. *Protium heptaphyllum*, of the myrrh family.

hyawaballi /hʌɪəwəˈbali/ *n.* Also **hiaw-**. M19. [Arawak, f. as prec. + *-bali* suffix for a tree.] A Guyanese timber tree, *Tetragastris panamensis*, related to the hyawas.

†**hybernacle**, **-culum** *ns.*, †**hybernal** *a.*, †**hybernate** *v.*, **-ation** *n.*, †**Hybernian** *a.* & *n.* vars. of HIBERNACLE, HIBERNACULUM, etc.

Hyblaean /hʌɪˈbliːən/ *a.* Also **Hyblean**. E17. [f. L *Hyblaeus* (f. *Hybla*, Gk *Hublē*) + -AN: see -EAN.] Of or pertaining to Hybla in Sicily, famous in ancient times for its honey; *poet.* honeyed, sweet. Cf. HYMETTIAN.

hybodont /ˈhɪbədɒnt/ *n.* & *a.* M19. [f. Gk *hubos* hump, hump-backed + -ODONT.] (Of, characteristic of, or designating) an extinct elasmobranch fish of the family Hybodontidae or the order Hybodontiformes, from which present-day sharks are thought to be descended.

hybrid /ˈhʌɪbrɪd/ *n.* & *a.* E17. [L *hybrida*, (*h*)*ibrida*.] A *n.* 1 An animal or plant that is the offspring of individuals of different kinds (usually, different species). E17. 2 A person of mixed descent or mixed ancestry. Now usu. *derog.* M17. 3 A thing derived from heterogeneous sources or composed of incongruous elements; *Philol.* a word formed of elements from different languages; *Geol.* a hybrid rock. M19.

1 ANTHONY HUXLEY Showy man-made hybrids seen in florists' shops. 3 R. F. HOBSON A psychotherapist is a kind of hybrid . . : a quasi-scientist, a quasi-artist.

B *adj.* 1 Of mixed character, heterogeneous; derived from unlike sources; (of a parliamentary bill) treated in some respects as a public bill and in others as a private one; (of a computer) employing both digital and analogue methods; (of rock) formed by the mixing of two magmas, or by the incorporation of solid rock into magma. E18. 2 Bred or produced as a hybrid. L18.

Special collocations: **hybrid perpetual** any rose of a group of formerly popular garden hybrids, derived in part from the Bourbon rose. **hybrid swarm** *Ecol.* a variable population resulting from the hybridization of neighbouring species. **hybrid tea** any rose of a group of hybrids now much grown, evolved from crosses between hybrid perpetuals and the tea-rose, *Rosa*×*odorata*. **hybrid vigour** = HETEROSIS 2.

hybridism *n.* (*a*) the fact or condition of being hybrid; (*b*) the production of hybrids: M19. **hybridist** *n.* a hybridizer M19. **hy'bridity** *n.* = HYBRIDISM (a) M19.

hybridization /ˌhʌɪbrɪdʌɪˈzeɪʃ(ə)n/ *n.* Also **-isation**. M19. [f. next + -IZATION.] 1 The production of hybrids by crossbreeding or cross-fertilization. M19. 2 *gen.* The action or result of hybridizing something; *Biol.* the fusion of two somatic cells of different karyotypes to form a cell with nuclear material of both; *Biochem.* the process of combining into polymers complementary subunits of different but related substances, e.g. DNA and RNA. E20.

2 **Southern hybridization** = SOUTHERN BLOT.

hybridize /ˈhʌɪbrɪdʌɪz/ *v.* Also **-ise**. M19. [f. HYBRID + -IZE.] 1 *v.t.* Subject to crossbreeding, cause to produce hybrids. M19. b Combine (things of different kinds); combine *with* a thing of a different kind; subject to hybridization. M20. 2 *v.i.* Produce a hybrid; interbreed (*with*). M19.

1b *Listener* A new series . . hybridising chat show and fly-on-the-wall documentary. S. L. WOLFE Experiments in which RNA is hybridized with its DNA template.

hybridizable *a.* M19. **hybridized** *a.* obtained by hybridization; *techn.* hybrid: M19. **hybridizer** *n.* a person who produces hybrids, esp. plant hybrids M19.

hybridoma /hʌɪbrɪˈdəʊmə/ *n.* Pl. **-mas**, **-mata** /-mətə/. L20. [f. HYBRID + -OMA.] A culture of cells produced by hybridization; *spec.* one in which myeloma cells are hybridized with antibody-producing lymphocytes, used to produce monoclonal antibodies.

hybridous /ˈhʌɪbrɪdəs/ *a.* Now *rare* or *obs.* L17. [f. HYBRID *n.* + -OUS.] Hybrid.

hybris /ˈhʌɪbrɪs/ *n.* E20. [Gk HUBRIS.] = HUBRIS.

Hydah *n.* & *a.* var. of HAIDA.

hydantoin /hʌɪˈdantəʊɪn/ *n.* M19. [f. Gk *hudōr* water + ALL)ANTOIC + -IN[1].] *Chem.* & *Pharm.* A cyclic derivative of urea, used esp. in the synthesis of a class of anticonvulsants; glycolylurea, HN·CONH·$COCH_2$. Also, an anticonvulsant of this class.

hydathode /ˈhʌɪdəθəʊd/ *n.* L19. [f. Gk *hudat-*, *hudōr* water + *hodos* way: cf. -ODE[2].] A pore in a plant, esp. in a leaf, which exudes water.

hydatid /ˈhʌɪdətɪd/ *n.* L17. [mod.L *hydatid-*, *hydatis* f. Gk *hudatid-*, *-is* drop of water, watery vesicle, f. *hudat-*, *hudōr* water: see -ID[2].] Orig., a cyst containing watery fluid. Now, a fluid-filled cyst or a jelly-filled cluster of cysts produced by and containing a larva of the tapeworms *Echinococcus granulosus* or *E. multilocularis*, and occurring in dogs, sheep, etc., whence it is caught by humans; a tapeworm so encysted. Freq. *attrib.*

Comb.: **hydatid disease**: caused by a hydatid, with very variable symptoms and effects.

hyda'tidiform *a.* having the form of a hydatid; *hydatidiform mole*, (the condition of having) a cluster of fluid-filled vesicles in the womb as a result of the degeneration of chorionic tissue during pregnancy: M19. **hydati'dosis** *n.* hydatid disease E20.

Hyde /hʌɪd/ *n.* L19. [The evil personality assumed by Dr Jekyll in R. L. Stevenson's story 'Strange Case of Dr Jekyll and Mr Hyde'

(1886).] An unsuspected or hidden evil side to a person's character. Cf. JEKYLL.

hydel /ˈhʌɪdɛl/ *a.* M20. [Abbrev.] Hydroelectric.

Hyde Park /hʌɪd ˈpɑːk/ *a.* L19. [A park in London.] Designating or employing impromptu controversial oratory of a kind traditionally associated with Speakers' Corner in Hyde Park.

hydnocarpus /hɪdnə(ʊ)ˈkɑːpəs/ *n.* E20. [mod.L, f. Gk *hudnon* truffle + *karpos* fruit, from the appearance of the fruit.] Any of various tropical Asiatic trees of the genus *Hydnocarpus* (family Flacourtiaceae), several of which (esp. *H. pentandra* and *H. kurzii*) are a source of chaulmoogra oil. Also *hydnocarpus tree*.

hydnocarpate *n.* a salt or ester of hydnocarpic acid E20. **hydnocarpic** *a.*: *hydnocarpic acid*, an alicyclic acid, $C_5H_7(CH_2)_{10}COOH$, glycerides of which are the chief constituents of chaulmoogra oil and hydnocarpus oil E20.

hydr- *comb. form* see HYDRO-.

hydra /ˈhʌɪdrə/ *n.* & *a.* LME. [(OFr. *(h)ydre*, *idre* f.) L *hydra* f. Gk *hudra* water snake.] A *n.* 1 *Gk Mythol.* (Also H-.) A monster with many heads, which grew again as fast as they were cut off. LME. 2 (Usu. H-.) (The name of) a long faint constellation extending from Cancer to Centaurus; the Sea Serpent. Also *the Hydra*. Cf. HYDRUS 2. LME. 3 A thing or person likened to the mythological hydra in its baneful character, its multifarious aspects, or the difficulty of its extirpation. L15. 4 Any terrible serpent or reptile. *rhet.* M16. 5 A water snake. E17. 6 Any of several hydrozoans of the genus *Hydra* that live as solitary polyps attached to pond plants and reproduce by budding and sexually. L18.

Comb.: **hydra-headed** *a.* having many heads like the mythological hydra; chiefly *fig.*, having the character of a hydra (sense 3 above); **hydratuba** /-tjuːbə/ [L] the trumpet-shaped larva of certain jellyfishes.

B *attrib.* or as *adj.* As multifarious or as difficult to extirpate as the mythological hydra. L16.

M. ROBINSON They are the hydra assailants which return with every hour.

hydracid /hʌɪˈdrasɪd/ *n.* Also †**hydro-acid**. E19. [f. HYDRO- + ACID *n.*] *Chem.* Orig., an acid that contains hydrogen. Now, one that does not contain oxygen.

hydraelaeon *n.* var. of HYDRELAEON.

hydraemia /hʌɪˈdriːmɪə/ *n.* Also *-**remia**. M19. [f. HYDRO- + -AEMIA.] Thinness of the blood.

hydraemic *a.* L19.

hydraform *a.* var. of HYDRIFORM.

hydragogue /ˈhʌɪdrəgɒg/ *a.* & *n.* M17. [Late L *hydragogus* adj. f. Gk *hudragōgos* conveying water, f. *hudr-* HYDRO- + *agein* to lead.] (A medicine or drug) that causes accumulations of water or serum to disperse.

hydraˈgogic *a.* E18.

hydralazine /hʌɪˈdraləziːn/ *n.* Also -**ll**-. M20. [f. HYDRA(ZINE + PHTH)ALAZINE.] *Pharm.* A sympatholytic drug, $C_8H_5N_2NHNH_2$, used to treat hypertension.

hydramnios /hʌɪˈdramnɪɒs/ *n.* Also -**on** /-ɒn/. M19. [f. HYDRO- + AMNIOS, AMNION.] Excessive accumulation of amniotic fluid during pregnancy.

hydrangea /hʌɪˈdreɪn(d)ʒə/ *n.* M18. [mod.L *hydrangea*, f. as HYDRO- + Gk *aggeion* vessel, w. ref. to the cup-shaped seed-capsule.] Any of various ornamental shrubs, chiefly of Japanese and Chinese origin, of the genus *Hydrangea* (family Hydrangeaceae); esp. *H. macrophylla*, with large round clusters of blue, pink, etc., flowers.

hydrant /ˈhʌɪdr(ə)nt/ *n.* Orig. *US.* E19. [Irreg. f. HYDRO- + -ANT[1].] A pipe with a valve for drawing water directly from a main; *esp.* (also *fire hydrant*) one in the street etc. to which a fire-hose can be attached.

hydranth /ˈhʌɪdranθ/ *n.* L19. [f. HYDRA + Gk *anthos* flower.] *Zool.* A nutritive zooid in a colony of hydrozoans.

hydrapulper /ˈhʌɪdrəpʌlpə/ *n.* M20. [f. alt. of HYDRO- + PULPER.] A tank in which rotating vanes break up the fibres of wood pulp or other paper stock in water.

hydrarch /ˈhʌɪdrɑːk/ *a.* E20. [f. HYDR(O- + Gk *arkhē* beginning.] *Ecol.* Of a succession of plant communities: originating in a watery habitat.

hydrargyria /hʌɪdrɑːˈdʒɪrɪə/ *n.* Now *rare.* E19. [f. next + -IA[1].] Mercury poisoning.

hydrargyrum /hʌɪˈdrɑːdʒɪrəm/ *n.* Now *rare* or *obs.* M16. [mod.L f. L *hydrargyrus* f. Gk *hudrarguros* artificial quicksilver, f. *hudr-* HYDRO- + *arguros* silver.] Mercury (the element).

hydrase /ˈhʌɪdreɪz/ *n.* M20. [f. HYDRO- + -ASE.] *Biochem.* An enzyme which catalyses the addition of water to a substrate or its removal from it. Cf. HYDRATASE.

hydrastis /hʌɪˈdrastɪs/ *n.* M19. [mod.L, of unkn. origin.] (An extract of) the dried rhizome of golden seal, *Hydrastis canadensis*, formerly used as a stomachic and to control uterine bleeding; the plant itself.

hydrastine /-iːn/ *n.* the alkaloid that is the active constituent of hydrastis M19.

hydratase /ˈhʌɪdrəteɪz/ *n.* E20. [f. HYDRATE *v.* + -ASE.] = HYDRASE.

hydrate /ˈhʌɪdreɪt/ *n.* E19. [Fr., f. Gk *hudr-*, *hudor* water: see -ATE[2].] A compound in which water is chemically combined with another compound or an element.

hydrate /ˈhʌɪdreɪt, hʌɪˈdreɪt/ *v.* M19. [f. the n.] 1 *v.t.* Cause to combine chemically with water; cause to absorb water. M19. 2 *v.i.* Undergo hydration. E20.

hyˈdratable *a.* M20. **hyˈdration** *n.* the action of hydrating something; the condition of being hydrated: M19. **hydraˈtor** *n.* a hydrating agent M20.

hydrated /ˈhʌɪdreɪtɪd, hʌɪˈdreɪtɪd/ *a.* E19. [f. HYDRATE *n.*, *v.* + -ED[2], -ED[1].] Chemically combined with water or its elements; (of a mineral etc.) containing water of crystallization.

hydraulic /hʌɪˈdrɔːlɪk, -ˈdrɒl-/ *a.* & *n.* E17. [L *hydraulicus* f. Gk *hudraulikos*, f. *hudr-* HYDRO- + *aulos* pipe: see -IC. Cf. Fr. *hydraulique* (15).] A *adj.* 1 Involving or pertaining to water or other liquid conveyed through pipes or channels, esp. by mechanical means; of or pertaining to hydraulics. E17. 2 Of machinery or a mechanism: operated or controlled by water power or (more usually) by a liquid conveyed under pressure through pipes. E17. 3a Of cement or other material: that hardens under water. E19. b Of a liquid: used or suitable for use in hydraulic mechanisms. M20.

1 J. HUXLEY Squirted by hydraulic pressure out of the water-cushion in which it has grown to maturity. A. H. COMPTON His degree in hydraulic engineering. *Engineering* Experiments . . on the hydraulic transport of coal. 2 J. CRACE We . . bumped on the saloon's hydraulic suspension over the last few kilometres. A. TREW Gregorowski moved into the loader seat, checked the hydraulic controls. 3b *Drive* It is advisable to change hydraulic fluid every eighteen months or 24,000 miles.

Special collocations: **hydraulic brake** (*a*) a brake that uses a piston or rotor in a liquid-filled chamber to produce the slowing down; (*b*) a brake on a vehicle that is actuated hydraulically but operates through friction. **hydraulic intensifier** a device for obtaining an increase in pressure in a hydraulic system, by means of connected pistons with different areas. **hydraulic mining**: in which a powerful jet of water is used to wear down a bed of gravel etc. and carry the debris away for processing, or to extract coal from an underground seam. **hydraulic organ** = HYDRAULUS. **hydraulic press** a machine in which a force acting on a liquid, e.g. by means of a piston, produces elsewhere a larger force on a larger area of liquid. **hydraulic ram** (*a*) a device in which a falling body of water is brought to rest and its kinetic energy used to raise some of the water above its original level or produce water at increased pressure; (*b*) the larger or working piston of a hydraulic press.

B *n.* 1 †a A hydraulic organ. E–M17. b A hydraulic press or other machine. E18. 2 In *pl.* (treated as *sing.*). The branch of science and engineering that deals with the flow of liquids through pipes or channels, esp. as a source of mechanical force or control; hydrodynamics, fluid mechanics. L17.

†**hydraulical** *a.* = HYDRAULIC *a.* M17–L18. **hydraulically** *adv.* by hydraulic means L19. **hydraulician** /-ˈlɪʃ(ə)n/ *n.* an expert in hydraulics L19. **hydrauˈlicity** *n.* the property or quality of hardening under water M19.

hydraulic /hʌɪˈdrɔːlɪk, -ˈdrɒl-/ *v.t.* Infl. -**ic(k)**-. M19. [f. HYDRAULIC *a.* & *n.* For the inflection with *k* cf. *frolicking*, *trafficking*, etc.] Work or obtain by the methods of hydraulic mining.

hydraulis *n.* var. of HYDRAULUS.

†**hydraulo-pneumatical** *a.* M17–M18. [f. HYDRAULIC *a.* & *n.* + -O- + PNEUMATICAL.] Of or pertaining to hydraulics and pneumatics.

hydraulus /hʌɪˈdrɔːləs/ *n.* Also -**lis** /-lɪs/. L19. [L f. Gk *hudraulos*, *-lis*, f. *hudr-* HYDRO- + *aulos* pipe.] The pipe-organ of classical times, in which an even tone was ensured by using water pressure to maintain a constant airflow to the pipes. Also called *water-organ*.

hydrazide /ˈhʌɪdrəzʌɪd/ *n.* L19. [f. as next + -IDE.] *Chem.* Any compound of the formula RCO·HN·NH_2, where a hydrogen atom of hydrazine is replaced by an organic acid radical. Also, any substituted derivative of such a compound.

hydrazine /ˈhʌɪdrəziːn/ *n.* L19. [f. HYDRO- + AZO- + -INE[5].] *Chem.* A colourless fuming liquid, $H_2N{\cdot}NH_2$, used as a strong reducing agent and as a rocket propellant. Also, any substituted derivative of this.

hydrazinium /hʌɪdrəˈzɪnɪəm/ *n.* (*a*) the ion $H_2N{\cdot}NH_3^+$; (*b*) the ion $H_3N^+{\cdot}NH_3^+$: E20.

hydrazoic /hʌɪdrəˈzəʊɪk/ *a.* L19. [f. HYDRO- + AZO- + -IC.] Chem. *hydrazoic acid*, a colourless volatile explosive liquid, N_3H, with a foul smell.

hydrozoate *n.* an azide E20.

hydrazone /ˈhʌɪdrəzəʊn/ *n.* L19. [f. HYDRAZ(INE + -ONE.] *Chem.* Any compound containing the group $=N{\cdot}NH_2$ or the substituted groups $=N{\cdot}NHR$ or $=N{\cdot}NRR'$.

hydrazonium /hʌɪdrəˈzəʊnɪəm/ *n.* (*a*) = HYDRAZINIUM (a),(b); (*b*) an ion of the type $R{:}N{\cdot}NH_3^+$; a substituted derivative of such an ion: L19.

hydrelaeon /hʌɪdrəˈliːɒn/ *n.* Long *rare* or *obs.* Also **hydrae-**, -**leon**, -**laeum** /-ˈliːəm/, & other vars. M16. [Gk *hudrelaion*, f. *hudr-* HYDRO- + *elaion* oil.] A medicinal mixture of water and oil.

hydremia *n.* see HYDRAEMIA.

hydria /ˈhʌɪdrɪə, ˈhɪd-/ *n.* Pl. -**iae** /-iː/. ME. [(OFr. *idr(i)e* f.) L f. Gk *hudria*.] Formerly, a water-pot. Now (*Archaeol.*), a three-handled pitcher of ancient Greece.

hydric /ˈhʌɪdrɪk/ *a.*[1] Now *rare.* M19. [f. HYDR(OGEN + -IC.] *Chem.* Of or containing hydrogen in chemical combination.

hydric /ˈhʌɪdrɪk/ *a.*[2] E20. [f. HYDRO- + -IC.] *Ecol.* Of a habitat: containing plenty of moisture; damp.

hydride /ˈhʌɪdrʌɪd/ *n.* M19. [f. HYDRO- + -IDE.] *Chem.* Formerly = HYDRATE *n.* Now, a binary compound of hydrogen with another element, esp. a metal.

hyˈdridic *a.* (of a hydrogen atom) having a negative charge M20.

hydriform /ˈhʌɪdrɪfɔːm/ *a.* Also **hydra-** /ˈhʌɪdrə-/. E19. [f. HYDRA (+ -I-) + -FORM.] Having the form of a hydrozoan hydra or the hydra of mythology.

hydriodic /hʌɪdrɪˈɒdɪk, -drʌɪ-/ *a.* E19. [f. HYDR(OGEN + IOD(INE + -IC.] Chem. *hydriodic acid*, a colourless or pale yellow liquid that is an aqueous solution of the gas hydrogen iodide, HI, and a strong acid and reducing agent.

hydrion /ˈhʌɪdrʌɪən, -drɪɒn/ *n.* E20. [Contr. of *hydrogen ion.*] *Chem.* The hydrogen ion, the proton.

hydro /ˈhʌɪdrəʊ/ *n.*[1] Pl. -**os**. L19. [Abbrev. of *hydropathic.*] A clinic, hotel, etc., providing hydropathic treatment.

hydro /ˈhʌɪdrəʊ/ *n.*[2] Pl. -**os**. E20. [Abbrev. of *hydroelectric.*] Hydroelectric power, hydroelectricity; *Canad.* (a supply of, a company supplying) mains electricity.

hydro- /ˈhʌɪdrəʊ/ *comb. form.* Bef. a vowel also **hydr-**. [Gk *hudro-* comb. form of *hudōr* water: see -O-. In senses 3 & 4 partly f. the definientia, which are themselves f. Gk *hudro-*.] 1 Water; liquid. 2 *Med.* (An accumulation of) watery or serous fluid. 3 *Chem.* Hydrogen. 4 *Zool.* Hydrozoa, hydrozoan; hydroid.

hydro-aro'matic *a.* & *n.* (*Chem.*) (a compound) having one or more benzene rings which are partly or completely hydrogenated (reduced) E20. **hydrobio'logic** *a.* = HYDROBIOLOGICAL E20. **hydrobio'logical** *a.* of or pertaining to hydrobiology M20. **hydrobi'ologist** *n.* an expert in or student of hydrobiology E20. **hydrobi'ology** *n.* the branch of biology that deals with aquatic plants and animals E20. **hydro'borate** *n.* & *v.* (*Chem.*) (*a*) *n.* = BOROHYDRIDE; (*b*) *v.t.* add a boron compound to (another compound) by hydroboration: M20. **hydrobo'ration** *n.* (*Chem.*) a reaction of the type :BH + :C=C: → :B(C:)CH:, where a boron-hydrogen pair of atoms is added across a double or triple bond between a carbon atom and another atom; the process of subjecting to such a reaction: M20. **hydro'bromic** *a.* (*Chem.*): *hydrobromic acid*, a strong acid that is a colourless or pale yellow aqueous solution of the gas hydrogen bromide, HBr M19. **hydrocast** *n.* (*Oceanogr.*) a long cable with sampling bottles attached at intervals; an operation in which this is used: M20. **,hydrochloro'fluorocarbon** *n.* any of a class of partly chlorinated and fluorinated hydrocarbons, used as less ozone-destructive substitutes for CFCs (abbrev. *HCFC*) L20. **hydrochlor(o)'thiazide** *n.* (*Pharm.*) a sulphonamide drug, $C_7H_8ClN_3O_4S_2$, related to chlorothiazide and used to treat oedema and hypertension M20. **hydrochore** *n.* a hydrochoric plant E20. **hydrochoric** /-'kɔːrɪk/ *a.* [Gk *khōrein* spread] involving or characterized by the dispersal of plant seeds by water M20. **hydrochorous** /-'kɔːrəs/ *a.* hydrochoric E20. **hydro'colloid** *n.* & *a.* (designating) a substance that yields a gel on the addition of water, or the gel itself E20. **hydroco'lloidal** *a.* = HYDROCOLLOID *a.* E20. **hydrocool** *v.t.* dip (fruit or vegetables) in chilled water soon after harvesting and packing, in order to preserve their freshness M20. **hydrocooler** *n.* an apparatus for hydrocooling M20. **hydrocrack** *v.t.* crack (crude oil or a heavy distillate) by the action of a catalyst and hydrogen at a high temperature and pressure M20. **hydrocracker** *n.* an apparatus or plant where hydrocracking is carried out M20. **hydrodesulphuri'zation**, ***-sulf-** *n.* the removal of sulphur from crude oil or an oil product by the action of a catalyst and hydrogen at a moderately high temperature and pressure M20. **hydrode'sulphurize**, ***-'sulf-** *v.t.* subject to hydrodesulphurization M20. **hydrode'sulphurizer**, ***-'sulf-** *n.* an apparatus where hydrodesulphurization is carried out M20. **hydro-engi'neering** *n.* civil engineering as applied to the construction of dams, canals, etc. L20. **hydro-explosion** *n.* a volcanic explosion caused by hot magma or lava coming into contact with water and producing steam M20. **hydro-extract** *v.t.* dry in a hydro-extractor L19. **hydro-extraction** *n.* the process of spinning textiles etc. in a hydro-extractor L19. **hydro-extractor** *n.* an industrial machine for drying textiles etc. by spinning them in a perforated drum M19. **hydrofining** *n.* the process of stabilizing a petroleum product and reducing its sulphur content by the action of a catalyst and hydrogen at a relatively low temperature and pressure M20. **hydroflume'thiazide** *n.* (*Pharm.*) a drug, $C_8H_8F_3N_3O_4S_2$, analogous to hydrochlorothiazide and with similar uses M20. **hydroform** *v.t.* subject (petroleum naphtha) to a process in which paraffins and alicyclic compounds are converted to aromatic compounds by the action of a catalyst and hydrogen at a high temperature and moderate pressure M20. **hydro'formate** *n.* a petroleum product obtained by hydroforming M20. **hydroformer** *n.* an apparatus or plant where hydroforming is carried out M20. **hydroformy'lation** *n.* (*Chem.*) the catalytic addition of carbon monoxide and hydrogen to an olefin to produce an aldehyde M20. **hydrofracture** *v.t.* fracture (rock) by injecting water under pressure L20. **hydrofuge** *a.* & *n.* (a substance) that repels or is impervious to water M19. **hydrogasifi'cation** *n.* the production of methane directly from coal by treatment with hydrogen or hydrogen and steam at a high temperature and pressure. M20. **hydro'gasifier** *n.* an apparatus in which hydrogasification is carried out M20. **hydrogel** *n.* a gel or gelatinous precipitate in which the liquid constituent is water M19. **hydrogeo'logical** *a.* of or pertaining to hydrogeology L19. **hydroge'ologist** *n.* an expert in or student of hydrogeology M20. **hydroge'ology** *n.* the branch of geology that deals with the movement, effects, properties, etc., of underground water and surface water; the hydrogeological features *of* a thing: E19. **hydro'kineter** *n.* [Gk *kinētēs*, *-tēr* initiator, agitator] a device for heating water at the bottom of large boilers by injecting surplus steam L19. **hydroki'netic** *a.* pertaining to or involving the motion of liquids or a liquid L19. **hydrolith** *n.* calcium hydride, as a convenient source of hydrogen (evolved when water is added) E20. **hydromag'netic** *a.* = MAGNETOHYDRODYNAMIC M20. **hydromag'netics** *n.* = MAGNETOHYDRODYNAMICS M20. **hydro'mania** *n.* an abnormal craving for water; an enthusiasm about water: L18. **hydrome'chanical** *a.* of or pertaining to hydromechanics E19. **hydrome'chanics** *n.* the mechanics of liquids; hydrodynamics, esp. in relation to mechanical devices: M19. **hydrome'dusa** *n.*, pl. **-sae**, **-sas**, the medusoid phase in the life cycle of many hydrozoans L19. **hydrome'dusan** *a.* & *n.* (*a*) (of or pertaining to) a hydromedusa; †(*b*) (of or pertaining to) a hydrozoan (of a taxon Hydromedusae): L19. **hydrometa'llurgical** *a.* of or pertaining to hydrometallurgy L19. **hydrometallurgy** /-mɪ'tal-, -'mɛt(ə)l-/ *n.* metallurgical processes in which chemical reactions in water, such as leaching or precipitation, are used to extract or assay metals M19. **hydro'meteor** *n.* an atmospheric phenomenon or entity involving water or water vapour M19. **hydrometeoro'logical** *a.* of or pertaining to hydrometeorology L19. **hydrometeo'rology** *n.* (*a*) *rare* the branch of meteorology that deals with hydrometeors; (*b*) meteorology as it relates to or is applied to hydrological matters: M19. **hydrone'phrosis** *n.* distension of the renal pelvis with urine, usually as a result of an obstructed outflow M19. **hydrone'phrotic** *a.* of, characteristic of, or affected with hydronephrosis M19. **hydronym** *n.* a name of a body of water, such as a river or sea M20. **hydro'nymic** *a.* of, pertaining to, or designating a hydronym M20. **hy'dronymy** *n.* the branch of knowledge that deals with hydronyms; hydronyms collectively: M20. **†hydro-oxygen** *n.* oxy-hydrogen: only in M19. **hydroperi'cardium** *n.* (*Med.*) (the condition of having) an accumulation of watery fluid within the pericardium M19. **hydrope'roxide** *n.* (*Chem.*) any compound containing the hydroperoxyl group in its molecule E20. **hydrope'roxyl** *n.* (*Chem.*) the radical HO·O·; usu. *attrib.*: M20. **hydroplant** *n.* a hydroelectric generating station E20. **hydropneu'matic** *a.* (of apparatus) involving the action of both water and air; partly hydraulic and partly pneumatic: L18. **hydropower** *n.* hydroelectric power M20. **hydro'quinone** *n.* a substance formed by the reduction of quinone, used as a photographic developer; 1,4-dihydroxybenzene, $C_6H_4(OH)_2$: M19. **hydro'salpinx** *n.*, pl. **-salpinges** /-sal'pɪndʒiːz/, [Gk SALPINX: cf. SALPINGO-] *Med.* (the condition of having) an accumulation of watery fluid in the Fallopian tubes M19. **hydrosere** *n.* (*Ecol.*) a plant succession originating in a wet habitat E20. **hydroski** *n.* a hydrofoil on a seaplane or amphibious aircraft that skims the surface of the water during take-off and provides extra lift M20. **hydrosome** *n.* (*Zool.*) the body of a colonial hydrozoan M19. **hydrosphere** *n.* the waters of the earth's surface L19. **hydrospire** *n.* (*Zool.*) any of a number of respiratory tubes or pouches in blastoids M19. **hydro'theca** *n.* (*Zool.*) in some colonial hydrozoans, a cuplike extension of the perisarc that partly encloses a hydranth L19. **hydro'thorax** *n.* (*Med.*) (the condition of having) an accumulation of fluid in one or both of the pleural cavities L18. **hydrotreat** *v.t.* subject to hydrotreatment M20. **hydrotreater** *n.* an apparatus or plant where hydrotreatment is carried out M20. **hydrotreatment** *n.* the treatment of petroleum products with hydrogen in the presence of a catalyst, esp. at a higher temperature and pressure than in hydrofining M20. **hydrovane** *n.* (*a*) = HYDROPLANE *n.* 1; (*b*) = HYDROFOIL 1: E20. **hydrowire** *n.* a cable used for hydrocasts M20. **hydrozincite** *n.* (*Min.*) a monoclinic basic carbonate of zinc that is a secondary mineral occurring as light-coloured crusts on zinc deposits M19.

†hydro-acid *n.* var. of HYDRACID.

†hydro-aeroplane *n.* E-M20. [f. HYDRO- + AEROPLANE *n.*] A seaplane. Cf. HYDROPLANE *n.* 3.

hydrocarbon /hʌɪdrə(ʊ)'kɑːb(ə)n/ *n.* E19. [f. HYDRO- + CARBON *n.*] *Chem.* A compound that contains hydrogen and carbon only; a substituted derivative of such a compound.

Nature A much greater threat is posed by toxic chlorinated hydrocarbons such as DDT.

,hydrocarbo'naceous *a.* of the nature of or containing a hydrocarbon M19.

hydrocarbonate /hʌɪdrə(ʊ)'kɑːbəneɪt/ *n.* E19. [f. HYDRO- + CARBONATE *n.*] *Chem.* †1 A hydrocarbon, *spec.* methane. Only in E19. 2 A double salt consisting of a hydrate and a carbonate. Now *rare* or *obs.* M19. 3 A carbohydrate. *rare.* L19.

hydrocarbonous /hʌɪdrə(ʊ)'kɑːbənəs/ *a.* Now *rare* or *obs.* L18. [f. HYDRO- + CARBON *n.* + -OUS.] Hydrocarbonaceous.

†hydrocarburet *n.* E-M19. [f. HYDRO- + CARBURET *n.*] *Chem.* = HYDROCARBONATE 1.

†hydrocarburetted *a.* formed by the combination of hydrogen and carbon E-M19.

hydrocele /'hʌɪdrə(ʊ)siːl/ *n.* M16. [(Fr. *hydrocèle* f.) L *hydrocele* f. Gk *hudrokēlē*, f. *hudro-* HYDRO- + *kēlē* tumour.] 1 *Med.* An abnormal accumulation of fluid at a site in the body, esp. between the layers of serous membrane around a testicle. M16. 2 See HYDROCOEL.

hydrocephalus /hʌɪdrə'sɛf(ə)ləs, -'kɛf-/ *n.* L17. [mod.L f. Gk *hudrokephalon*, f. *hudr-* HYDRO- + *kephalē* head.] *Med.* A condition in which excessive cerebrospinal fluid accumulates in the cranial cavity, occurring esp. in young children, when it causes enlargement of the head and sometimes brain damage (also called *water on the brain*); the fluid accumulation itself.

hydroce'phalic *a.* & *n.* (*a*) *adj.* pertaining to, characteristic of, or affected with hydrocephalus; (*b*) *n.* a person with hydrocephalus: E19. **hydrocephaloid** *a.* designating a condition in which there are symptoms resembling those of hydrocephalus without any accumulation of cerebrospinal fluid M19. **hydrocephalous** *a.* M19.

hydrocephaly /hʌɪdrə'sɛf(ə)li, -'kɛf-/ *n.* L19. [f. HYDROCEPHALUS: see -Y³.] = HYDROCEPHALUS.

hydrochloric /hʌɪdrə(ʊ)'klɒrɪk, -'klɔːrɪk/ *a.* E19. [f. HYDRO- + CHLORIC.] Chem. *hydrochloric acid*, a colourless or faintly yellow liquid that is an aqueous solution of the gas hydrogen chloride, HCl, and a strong, highly corrosive acid; formerly called *muriatic acid*, *spirit of salt*.

†hydrochlorate *n.* a chloride; a hydrochloride: only in 19. **hydrochloride** *n.* a compound of hydrochloric acid with an organic base or (formerly) with an element E19.

hydrocoel /'hʌɪdrəsiːl/ *n.* Also **-coele**, **-cele**. L19. [f. HYDRO- + Gk *koilia* body cavity.] *Zool.* The water-vascular system of an echinoderm.

hydrocortisone /hʌɪdrə(ʊ)'kɔːtɪzəʊn/ *n.* M20. [f. HYDRO- + CORTISONE.] A glucocorticoid hormone, $C_{21}H_{30}O_5$, that is used to treat inflammatory and allergic conditions.

hydrocyanic /hʌɪdrə(ʊ)sʌɪ'anɪk/ *a.* E19. [f. HYDRO- + CYANIC.] Chem. *hydrocyanic acid*, a weak acid, HCN, that is a volatile colourless poisonous explosive liquid with a smell of bitter almonds and is used in many industrial processes. Also called *prussic acid*.

†hydrocyanate *n.* a cyanide E-M19.

hydrodictyon /hʌɪdrə(ʊ)'dɪktɪɒn/ *n.* M19. [f. HYDRO- + Gk *diktuon* net.] Any of the green algae of the genus *Hydrodictyon*, which combine in colonies of multinucleate cells to form pentagonal and hexagonal meshes on the surface of water; pop. called *water-net*.

hydrodynamic /,hʌɪdrə(ʊ)dʌɪ'namɪk/ *a.* E19. [mod.L *hydrodynamicus*, f. as HYDRODYNAMICS: see -IC.] Of or pertaining to hydrodynamics or its subject matter.

hydrodynamical *a.* = HYDRODYNAMIC M19. **hydrodynamically** *adv.* from the point of view of hydrodynamics; by means of hydrodynamic forces: M20.

hydrodynamician /,hʌɪdrə(ʊ)dʌɪnə'mɪʃ(ə)n/ *n.* E20. [f. as next + -ICIAN.] = HYDRODYNAMICIST.

hydrodynamicist /,hʌɪdrə(ʊ)dʌɪ'namɪsɪst/ *n.* M20. [f. next + -IST.] An expert in or student of hydrodynamics.

hydrodynamics /,hʌɪdrə(ʊ)dʌɪ'namɪks/ *n.* L18. [mod.L *hydrodynamica*, f. as HYDRO- + Gk *dunamikos* DYNAMIC: see -ICS.] The branch of physical science that deals with the motion of fluids, esp. liquids, and (in mod. use) with the forces acting on them and on bodies immersed in them.

hydroelectric /,hʌɪdrəʊɪ'lɛktrɪk/ *a.* E19. [f. HYDRO- + ELECTRIC.] †1 Of, pertaining to, or designating an electric current produced by a galvanic cell. E-M19. 2 Designating a machine for generating electricity by the friction of water or steam. *obs.* exc. *Hist.* M19. 3 Generating electricity by utilizing the energy of falling or flowing water; pertaining to such generation; (of electricity) generated in this way. L19.

3 *Daily Telegraph* Brazil wants to build a huge hydro-electric dam on . . the River Parana.

hydroelectrical *a.* = HYDROELECTRIC 3 E20. **hydroelectrically** *adv.* by hydroelectric means E20. **,hydroelec'tricity** *n.* †(*a*) galvanic electricity; (*b*) electricity generated hydroelectrically: E19.

hydrofluoric /hʌɪdrə(ʊ)ˈflʊərɪk/ *a.* E19. [f. HYDRO- + FLUORIC.] *Chem. hydrofluoric acid*, a colourless fuming liquid that is an aqueous solution of the gas hydrogen fluoride, HF, and is sufficiently corrosive to attack glass.

hydrofoil /ˈhʌɪdrə(ʊ)fɔɪl/ *n.* E20. [f. HYDRO- + FOIL *n.*[1] after *aerofoil.*] 1 A structure analogous to an aerofoil but attached underneath a boat to produce lift or to act as a stabilizer. E20. 2 A boat fitted with hydrofoils to lift its hull clear of the water at speed. Also more fully *hydrofoil boat.* M20.

hydrogen /ˈhʌɪdrədʒ(ə)n/ *n.* Also †**-gene**. L18. [Fr. *hydrogène*, f. Gk *hudr-* HYDRO-: see -GEN.] The simplest and lightest chemical element, atomic no. 1, a colourless flammable gas which is the commonest element in the universe and which occurs combined with oxygen in water and with carbon in organic compounds. (Symbol H.)

Comb.: **hydrogen bomb** an immensely powerful bomb in which hydrogen nuclei combine to form helium nuclei and release energy in an uncontrolled self-sustaining fusion reaction; also called an *H-bomb*; **hydrogen bond** *Chem.* a weak bond formed by the electrostatic attraction between a strongly electronegative atom and a hydrogen atom covalently linked to another electronegative atom; **hydrogen cyanide** hydrocyanic acid, esp. as a vapour; **hydrogen ion** the positive ion (a proton) formed when a hydrogen atom loses its electron; a solvated form of this, *esp.* the hydrated ion H_3O^+ (cf. HYDRONIUM); **hydrogen peroxide** a colourless viscous unstable liquid, H_2O_2, with both oxidizing and reducing properties; **hydrogen sulphide** (*a*) a colourless flammable poisonous gas, H_2S, which has a smell of rotten eggs and is produced by putrefying organic matter; (*b*) (also **hydrogensulphide**) = HYDROSULPHIDE.

hydrogen-like *a.* (of an atom) consisting of a nucleus to which is bound a single negatively charged particle; characteristic of such an atom: E20.

hydrogenase /hʌɪˈdrɒdʒəneɪz/ *n.* E20. [f. prec. + -ASE.] *Biochem.* An enzyme which catalyses the addition of hydrogen to an organic substrate, found esp. in some micro-organisms.

hydrogenate /hʌɪˈdrɒdʒəneɪt, ˈhʌɪdrədʒəneɪt/ *v.t.* E19. [f. as prec. + -ATE[3].] Cause to combine chemically with hydrogen.

hydroge'nation *n.* the state of being hydrogenated; the process of hydrogenating a substance: E19. **hydrogenator** *n.* a vessel or apparatus in which hydrogenation is carried out E20.

hydrogenic /hʌɪdrə(ʊ)ˈdʒɛnɪk/ *a.* M19. [Partly f. HYDRO- + -GENIC, partly f. HYDROGEN + -IC.] 1 *Geol.* (Of soil) formed with water as the dominant influence; (of rock etc.) = HYDROGENOUS 2. M19. 2 *Physics.* = HYDROGEN-LIKE. M20.

hydrogenite /hʌɪˈdrɒdʒənʌɪt/ *n.* E20. [f. as next + -ITE[1].] Either of two powders formulated to be convenient sources of hydrogen, one when water is added, the other when ignited.

hydrogenize /hʌɪˈdrɒdʒənʌɪz, ˈhʌɪdrə-/ *v.t.* Also **-ise**. E19. [f. HYDROGEN + -IZE.] = HYDROGENATE.

hydrogenolysis /hʌɪdrədʒəˈnɒlɪsɪs/ *n.* Pl. **-lyses** /-lɪsiːz/. M20. [f. as prec. + -O- + -LYSIS, after *hydrolysis.*] *Chem.* A reaction in which a bond to a carbon atom is broken and a hydrogen atom added to each of the previously bonded atoms.

,hydrogeno'lytic *a.* M20.

hydrogenosome /hʌɪdrə(ʊ)ˈdʒɛnəsəʊm/ *n.* L20. [f. as prec. + -O- + -SOME[3].] *Biol.* An organelle in some protozoans which oxidizes pyruvate anaerobically, producing hydrogen.

hydrogenous /hʌɪˈdrɒdʒɪnəs/ *a.* L18. [Partly f. HYDROGEN + -OUS, partly f. HYDRO- + -GENOUS.] 1 Containing or consisting of hydrogen. L18. 2 *Geol.* Of rock, mineral deposits, etc.: formed in or by water. L19.

hydrogenously *adv.* L20.

hydrograph /ˈhʌɪdrəgrɑːf/ *n.* L19. [f. HYDRO- + -GRAPH.] A graphical record showing the variation in a river's height, speed, or the like at a particular point.

hydrography /hʌɪˈdrɒgrəfi/ *n.* M16. [f. HYDRO- + -GRAPHY, after *geography.*] 1 The branch of science that deals with seas, lakes, rivers, etc., including the mapping of them, their currents and tides, and (formerly) the principles of navigation; a book in which such bodies of water are scientifically described. M16. 2 The hydrographic features *of* a region. M19.

hydrographer *n.* an expert in or student of hydrography; *esp.* a person who makes hydrographic surveys and charts of the sea and its currents: M16. **hydro'graphic** *a.* of or pertaining to hydrography M17. **hydro'graphical** *a.* = HYDROGRAPHIC L16. **hydro'graphically** *adv.* as regards hydrography or hydrographic features E18.

†**hydroguret** *n.* Only in 19. [f. HYDROG(EN after *sulphuret.*] *Chem.* A hydride.

†**hydroguretted** *a.* combined with hydrogen: only in E19.

hydroid /ˈhʌɪdrɔɪd/ *a.* & *n.* M19. [f. HYDRA + -OID.] *Zool.* A *adj.* 1 Designating or pertaining to any coelenterate of the hydrozoan order Hydroida, which has the polyp phase prominent. M19. 2 Of, pertaining to, or belonging to the polypoid phase in the life cycle of hydrozoans. L19. B *n.* A hydroid individual or colony. M19.

hydrol /ˈhʌɪdrɒl/ *n.* L19. [f. HYDRO- + -OL; sense 3 perh. f. HYDROLYSIS.] *Chem.* 1 Any substituted derivative of benzhydrol, *esp.* Michler's hydrol. L19. 2 A dark viscous liquid left as a mother liquor when starch is subjected to acid hydrolysis and dextrose is allowed to crystallize out. E20. 3 The simple water molecule, H_2O. E20.

hydrolase /ˈhʌɪdrəleɪz/ *n.* E20. [f. HYDROL(YSIS + -ASE.] *Biochem.* An enzyme which causes hydrolysis.

hydrolise, -ize *v.* see HYDROLYSE.

hydrology /hʌɪˈdrɒlədʒi/ *n.* L17. [mod.L *hydrologia*, f. as HYDRO- + -LOGY.] 1 The branch of medicine that deals with treatment by baths and waters. *rare.* L17. 2 The branch of science that deals with the water on and under the earth's surface and in the atmosphere; the hydrologic features *of* a region. L17.

hydro'logic *a.* of or pertaining to hydrology (*hydrologic cycle*, the continual movement of water between the different kinds of place in which it occurs, such as the atmosphere, rivers, seas, plants and animals, etc.) L19. **hydro'logical** *a.* = HYDROLOGIC L17. **hydro'logically** *adv.* as regards hydrology or hydrologic matters M20. **hydrologist** *n.* M19.

hydrolube /ˈhʌɪdrəl(j)uːb/ *n.* M20. [f. HYDRO- + *-lube* repr. *lubricant* (cf. LUBE).] Any of various non-flammable hydraulic fluids based on water and glycol.

hydrolysate /hʌɪˈdrɒlɪseɪt/ *n.* Also ***-lyz-** /-lɪz-/. E20. [f. next + -ATE[2].] *Chem.* A product of hydrolysis.

hydrolyse /ˈhʌɪdrəlʌɪz/ *v.* Also ***-lyze**, (*non-standard*) **-lise, -lize**. L19. [f. next after *analysis, analyse.*] *Chem.* 1 *v.t.* Subject to or decompose by hydrolysis. L19. 2 *v.i.* Undergo hydrolysis. E20.

hydrolysable *a.* E20.

hydrolysis /hʌɪˈdrɒlɪsɪs/ *n.* Pl. **-lyses** /-lɪsiːz/. L19. [f. HYDRO- + -LYSIS.] *Chem.* Any reaction in which a compound is decomposed and the hydrogen and hydroxyl of the water molecule become attached to separate products (AB + $H_2O \rightarrow AH + BOH$); an analogous decomposition of an organic compound by an acid or alkali; a reaction between a water molecule and an ion that gives a hydrogen or hydroxyl ion.

hydro'lytic *a.* L19. **hydro'lytically** *adv.* by means of or as regards hydrolysis E20.

hydrolyst /ˈhʌɪdrəlɪst/ *n.* Now *rare.* L19. [f. prec. after *analyse, analyst.*] *Chem.* A hydrolytic agent.

hydrolyze *v.* see HYDROLYSE.

hydromancy /ˈhʌɪdrəmansi/ *n.* LME. [(O)Fr. *hydromancie* or late L *hydromantia*, f. as HYDRO-: see -MANCY.] Divination by signs derived from water.

hydromantic /hʌɪdrəˈmantɪk/ *n.* & *a.* Now *rare* or *obs.* L16. [med.L *hydromanticus*, f. late L *hydromantia* HYDROMANCY: see -IC.] A *n.* †1 Hydromancy. Only in L16. 2 A person skilled in hydromancy. M17. B *adj.* Of or pertaining to hydromancy. M17.

hydromel /ˈhʌɪdrəmɛl/ *n.* LME. [L *hydromeli* (*-mel*) f. Gk *hudromeli*, f. *hudro-* HYDRO- + *meli* honey.] A mixture of honey and water; mead.

hydrometer /hʌɪˈdrɒmɪtə/ *n.* M18. [f. HYDRO- + -METER.] 1 An instrument for finding the relative density of a liquid (sometimes also that of a solid) and hence the strength of a solution or mixture. M18. 2 An instrument for finding the speed of a current or a boat. M18.

hydro'metric *a.* E19. **hydro'metrical** *a.* L18. **hydrometry** *n.* (the branch of hydrostatics that deals with) the measurement of relative density by means of a hydrometer E18.

hydronium /hʌɪˈdrəʊnɪəm/ *n.* E20. [f. HYDR(OX)ONIUM.] *Chem.* More fully *hydronium ion.* The hydrated hydrogen ion, H_3O^+. Cf. HYDROGEN *ion.*

hydropathy /hʌɪˈdrɒpəθi/ *n.* M19. [f. HYDRO- + -PATHY.] The treatment of disorders by the application of water, internally as well as externally.

'hydropath *n.* (*a*) = HYDROPATHIST; (*b*) = HYDROPATHIC *n.*: M19. **hydro'pathic** *a.* & *n.* (*a*) *adj.* of, pertaining to, or of the nature of hydropathy; practising hydropathy; (*b*) *n.* an establishment where hydropathy is offered: M19. **hydropathist** *n.* a person who practises or advocates hydropathy M19. **hydropathize** *v.i.* undergo hydropathy M19.

hydrophane /ˈhʌɪdrəfeɪn/ *n.* L18. [f. HYDRO- + Gk *-phanēs* apparent, *phanos* bright, clear, f. *phainein* to show.] A white variety of opal that absorbs water and becomes more translucent on immersion.

hy'drophanous *a.* becoming more translucent on immersion L18.

hydrophile /ˈhʌɪdrəfʌɪl/ *a.* Also **-phil** /-fɪl/. E20. [f. HYDRO- + -PHIL.] = HYDROPHILIC.

hydrophilic /hʌɪdrə(ʊ)ˈfɪlɪk/ *a.* E20. [f. HYDRO- + Gk *philos* loving + -IC.] Having an affinity for water; readily absorbing or wetted by water; (of a colloid) readily forming or remaining as a hydrosol.

hydrophilicity /-ˈlɪs-/ *n.* hydrophilic quality M20.

hydrophilous /hʌɪˈdrɒfɪləs/ *a.* M19. [f. HYDRO- + -PHILOUS.] 1 Fond of water; *spec.* growing or living in water. *rare.* M19. 2 Of a plant: pollinated by the agency of water. L19.

hydrophily *n.* pollination by the agency of water E20.

hydrophobe /ˈhʌɪdrəfəʊb/ *n.* & *a.* L19. [Fr. f. L *hydrophobus*, Gk *hudrophobos*, f. Gk *hudro-* HYDRO- + *phobos* fear.] A *n.* 1 A person with hydrophobia. *rare.* L19. 2 A hydrophobic substance. E20. B *adj.* = HYDROPHOBIC *a.* 2. E20.

hydrophobia /hʌɪdrə(ʊ)ˈfəʊbɪə/ *n.* LME. [Late L *hydrophobia* f. Gk *hudrophobia*, f. *hudrophobos*: see prec., -IA[1].] 1 A strong aversion to or fear of water arising from the spasms that a rabid person suffers when attempting to drink; rabies itself. LME. 2 *gen.* A fear or dislike of water; *fig.* madness. M18.

hydrophobial *a.* (now *rare* or *obs.*) M17. **hy'drophobous** *a.* (now *rare* or *obs.*) L17.

hydrophobic /hʌɪdrə(ʊ)ˈfəʊbɪk/ *a.* E19. [Late L *hydrophobicus* f. Gk *hudrophobikos*, f. *hudrophobia*: see HYDROPHOBIA, -IC.] 1 Of, pertaining to, or affected with hydrophobia. E19. 2 Tending to repel or not to absorb water; not readily wetted by water; (of a colloid) not readily forming or remaining as a hydrosol. E20.

¶ Recorded in LME as a n. in L form.

hydrophobical *a.* (long *rare* or *obs.*) = HYDROPHOBIC 1 M17. **hydrophobically** *adv.* in a manner that involves hydrophobic properties M20. **hydrophobicity** /-ˈbɪs-/ *n.* hydrophobic or water-repellent quality M20. **hy'drophobist** *n.* (*joc.*) a person who scorns non-alcoholic drinks M19.

hydrophone /'hʌɪdrəfəʊn/ *n.* M19. [f. HYDRO- + -PHONE.] 1 *Med.* A bag of water placed between a stethoscope and the patient's chest in order to intensify the sounds heard. Now *rare* or *obs.* M19. 2 A transducer which detects sound waves transmitted through water and produces corresponding electrical signals which can drive a loudspeaker etc. L19.

2 P. ZIEGLER Mountbatten claimed to have picked up traces of the U-boat on his hydrophone.

hydrophyte /'hʌɪdrəfʌɪt/ *n.* M19. [f. HYDRO- + -PHYTE.] A plant that grows in water or needs a waterlogged environment.

hydrophytic /-'fɪtɪk/ *a.* E20.

hydropic /hʌɪ'drɒpɪk/ *a.* & *n.* LME. [OFr. *ydropique, -ike* f. L *hydropicus* f. Gk *hudropikos*, f. *hudrops* HYDROPS: see -IC. In 16 conformed (along with Fr. *hydropique*) to L sp.] A *adj.* 1 Oedematous, dropsical. LME. †2 *fig.* Insatiable; very thirsty. LME–M18. 3 Containing a lot of water; swollen. M17. †4 That cures dropsy. L17–E18.

Special collocations: **hydropic degeneration**: in which a cell is swollen with so much excess water that its cytoplasm appears clear and homogeneous.

B *n.* 1 A person with dropsy. Formerly, *the* dropsical people as a class. Now *rare.* LME. 2 A medicine for curing dropsy. Long *rare* or *obs.* L17.

hydropical *a.* (now *rare* or *obs.*) = HYDROPIC *a.* 1,2,3 M16.

hydroplane /'hʌɪdrəpleɪn/ *n.* & *v.* E20. [f. HYDRO- + PLANE *n.*[3] (in sense 2 after *aeroplane*).] A *n.* 1 A movable horizontal vane (usu. one of several) projecting from the side of a submarine and used to steer it vertically and to provide stability. E20. 2 A motor boat with a specially shaped bottom to make it rise partly out of the water at speed. Also = HYDROFOIL 2. Also *hydroplane boat.* E20. 3 A seaplane. Cf. HYDRO-AEROPLANE. *obs.* exc. *Hist.* E20. B *v.i.* 1 Travel in a hydroplane boat. E20. 2 Of a boat or seaplane: rise out of the water at speed (without leaving it). E20. 3 Of a motor vehicle: aquaplane. Chiefly *US.* M20.

hydroponics /hʌɪdrə(ʊ)'pɒnɪks/ *n.* M20. [f. HYDRO- + Gk *ponos* work + -ICS.] The technique of growing plants without soil, in beds of sand, gravel, etc., flooded with nutrient solution.

hydroponic *a.* pertaining to or grown by hydroponics M20. **hydroponically** *adv.* M20. **hydroponicist** /-sɪst-/ *n.* a person who practises hydroponics M20. **hydroponicum** *n.* a place or structure in which hydroponics is practised M20.

hydropot /'hʌɪdrəpɒt/ *n.* E18. [mod.L *hydropota* f. Gk *hudropotēs* water-drinker, f. *hudro-* HYDRO- + *potēs* drinker.] A person who drinks only water; a teetotaller.

†**hydropotic** *a.* (*rare*): only in E17.

hydrops /'hʌɪdrɒps/ *n.* LME. [L f. Gk *hudrōps*, f. *hudr-*, *hudōr* water.] Oedema, dropsy. Now chiefly in *hydrops foetalis* below.

hydrops foetalis /fiː'tɑːlɪs/ [mod.L = of the foetus] the severest form of haemolytic disease of the newborn, in which the infant is grossly oedematous and anaemic and usually dies before birth or soon afterwards.

hydropsy /'hʌɪdrɒpsi/ *n.* Now *rare* or *obs.* ME. [OFr. *idropesie* f. med.L *(h)ydropsia*, for L *hydropisis* f. Gk *hudrōpiasis*, f. *hudrōps* HYDROPS: see -IASIS. Cf. DROPSY.] Oedema, dropsy.

hydroptic /hʌɪ'drɒptɪk/ *a. arch.* E17. [f. prec. after *epilepsy, epileptic*, etc.] = HYDROPIC *a.* 1,2,3.

hydroscope /'hʌɪdrəskəʊp/ *n.* L17. [Gk *hudroskopos* water-seeker, *hudroskopion* water-clock, f. *hudro-* HYDRO-: see -SCOPE.] †1 = HYGROSCOPE. Only in L17. 2 *Hist.* A water-clock consisting of a graduated cylinder from which water trickled through an aperture in the bottom. E18. 3 A tube closed with clear glass or plastic at one end for looking below the surface of water. E20.

hydroscopic /hʌɪdrə(ʊ)'skɒpɪk/ *a.* L19. [f. HYDRO- after *hygroscopic.*] = HYGROSCOPIC 3.

hydrosol /'hʌɪdrəsɒl/ *n.* M19. [f. HYDRO- + SOL(UTION.] A sol in which the liquid constituent is water.

hydrostat /'hʌɪdrəstat/ *n.* M19. [f. HYDRO- + -STAT.] 1 An apparatus for preventing the explosion of boilers. *rare.* M19. 2 An electrical device for detecting the presence of water. L19.

hydrostatic /hʌɪdrə(ʊ)'statɪk/ *a.* L17. [Prob. f. Gk *hudrostatēs* hydrostatic balance, (in med.Gk) fire-engine, f. *hudro-* HYDRO- + STATIC.] 1 Pertaining to the equilibrium of liquids or the pressure of stationary liquids; pertaining to hydrostatics. L17. 2 Involving or employing the pressure of water or other liquid. M18.

1 B. STEWART The hydrostatic pressure of the column of mercury. 2 **hydrostatic balance**: for finding the relative density of an object by weighing it in water. **hydrostatic press** = *hydraulic press* s.v. HYDRAULIC *a.*

hydrostatical *a.* (now *rare*) = HYDROSTATIC M17. **hydrostatically** *adv.* by hydrostatic means; as regards hydrostatics: M17.

hydrostatician /ˌhʌɪdrəʊstə'tɪʃ(ə)n/ *n.* M17. [f. next + -IAN.] An expert in or student of hydrostatics.

hydrostatics /hʌɪdrə(ʊ)'statɪks/ *n.pl.* (treated as *sing.* or †*pl.*). M17. [f. HYDRO- + STATICS or STATIC *n.*: see -ICS.] The branch of mechanics that deals with the properties and behaviour of stationary liquids.

†**hydrosulphate** *n.* Also **-sulf-*. Only in 19. [f. HYDRO- + SULPHATE *n.*] *Chem.* = HYDROSULPHIDE.

hydrosulphide /hʌɪdrə(ʊ)'sʌlfʌɪd/ *n.* Also **-sulf-*. M19. [f. HYDRO- = SULPHIDE *n.*] *Chem.* Any acid salt formed by replacing a hydrogen atom of hydrogen sulphide by a metal atom. Also called *hydrogensulphide*.

Also †**hydrosulphuret** *n.*: only in E19.

hydrosulphite /hʌɪdrə(ʊ)'sʌlfʌɪt/ *n.* Also **-sulf-*. L19. [f. HYDRO- + SULPHITE.] *Chem.* A salt of hydrosulphurous acid; *esp.* the sodium salt, $Na_2S_2O_6{\cdot}2H_2O$, used as a reagent.

†**hydrosulphuric** *a.* Also **-sulf-*. Only in 19. [f. HYDRO- + SULPHURIC.] Chem. *hydrosulphuric acid*, = SULPHYDRIC.

hydrosulphurous /hʌɪdrə(ʊ)'sʌlf(ə)rəs, -'sʌlfjʊr-/ *a.* Also **-sulf-*. M19. [f. HYDRO- + SULPHUROUS.] Chem. *hydrosulphurous acid*: an unstable acid, $H_2S_2O_4$, that is known only in solution and is a strong reducing agent; formerly, dithionic acid, $H_2S_2O_6$.

hydrotherapy /hʌɪdrə(ʊ)'θɛrəpi/ *n.* L19. [f. HYDRO- + THERAPY.] The treatment of disorders by the application of water, esp. externally by immersion.

ˌ**hydrothera'peutic** *a.* of or pertaining to hydrotherapeutics or hydrotherapy L19. ˌ**hydrothera'peutics** *n.* hydrotherapy; the branch of medicine that deals with this: M19. **hydrotherapic** *a.* L19.

hydrothermal /hʌɪdrə(ʊ)'θəːm(ə)l/ *a.* M19. [f. HYDRO- + Gk *thermos* hot + -AL[1].] Of, produced by, or designating naturally hot underground water that has geological effects.

F. H. POUGH Hydrothermal solutions, from which so many minerals are deposited. **hydrothermal vent** an opening in the sea floor out of which comes hot or warm water.

hydrothermally *adv.* by hydrothermal action M20.

hydrotic /hʌɪ'drɒtɪk/ *a.* & *n.* Long *rare* or *obs.* L17. [f. as HIDROTIC with spelling conformed to HYDRO-.] *Med.* A *adj.* = HIDROTIC *a.* L17. B *n.* = HIDROTIC *n.*; = HYDRAGOGUE *n.* L17.

hydrotical *a.* M17.

hydrotropic /hʌɪdrə(ʊ)'trəʊpɪk, -'trɒpɪk/ *a.* L19. [f. HYDRO- + -TROPIC.] 1 *Bot.* Exhibiting hydrotropism. L19. 2 *Chem.* Exhibiting, causing, or caused by hydrotropy. E20.

hydrotropically *adv.* (*a*) *Bot.* in a manner that results in movement towards moisture; (*b*) *Chem.* as regards hydrotropy: E20. **hy'drotropism** *n.* (*Bot.*) the property on the part of a plant root etc. of turning or bending under the influence of nearby moisture L19. **hy'drotropy** *n.* (*Chem.*) the phenomenon whereby a substance that is only slightly soluble in water will dissolve readily in certain aqueous solutions E20.

hydrous /'hʌɪdrəs/ *a.* E19. [f. Gk *hudr-* HYDRO- + -OUS.] Of a chemical or mineral: containing water.

hydroxide /hʌɪ'drɒksʌɪd/ *n.* M19. [f. HYDRO- + OXIDE.] *Chem.* A compound containing the hydroxyl group or the hydroxide ion.

Comb.: **hydroxide ion** the negatively charged ion OH^-.

hydroxo- /hʌɪ'drɒksəʊ/ *comb. form.* As attrib. adj. also **hydroxo.** E20. [f. HYDROX(YL + -O-.] *Chem.* Containing or designating a coordinated hydroxyl group; containing a hydroxide ion.

hydroxoco'balamin *n.* (*Biochem.*) an analogue of cyanocobalamin in which a hydroxide ion replaces the cyanide ion M20.

hydroxonium /hʌɪdrɒk'səʊnɪəm/ *n.* E20. [f. HYDRO- + OXONIUM.] *Chem.* More fully *hydroxonium ion.* = HYDRONIUM.

hydroxy- /hʌɪ'drɒksi/ *comb. form.* Also as attrib. adj. **hydroxy.** [f. HYDROXYL.] *Chem.* Containing the hydroxyl group, often in place of a hydrogen atom.

hydroxy'apatite *n.* a mineral of the apatite group that is rare in the ground but is the principal inorganic constituent of tooth enamel and bone E20. **hydroxyben'zoic** *a.* designating three acids, $HO{\cdot}C_6H_4{\cdot}COOH$, derived from benzoic acid in which a hydroxyl group is attached to the ring, *spec.* the *ortho* isomer (also called *salicyclic acid*) L19. **hydroxy'lysine** *n.* (*Biochem.*) an amino acid occurring chiefly as a constituent of collagen E20. **hydroxypro'gesterone** *n.* (*Pharm.*) any of various synthetic hydroxylated derivatives of progesterone, *esp.* one given to supplement a natural deficiency of progesterone M20. **hydroxy'proline** *n.* (*Biochem.*) any of various hydroxylated derivatives of proline, *esp.* one that is an imino acid and a constituent of collagen and elastin E20. **hydroxy'tryptamine** *n.* (*Biochem.*) any of various derivatives of tryptamine in which a hydroxyl group is attached to the benzene ring, *spec.* = SEROTONIN M20. **hydroxyu'rea** *n.* any of several compounds $CH_4N_2O_2$, *esp.* (*Pharm.*) one given orally in some forms of leukaemia E20. **hydroxyzine** /-ziːn/ *n.* (*Pharm.*) a derivative of piperazine given as a minor tranquillizer M20.

hydroxyl /hʌɪ'drɒksɪl, *uncombined also* -sʌɪl/ *n.* M19. [f. HYDRO- + OXY- + -YL.] *Chem.* More fully *hydroxyl group, radical.* The neutral or positively charged group ·OH. Also, the (negative) hydroxide ion.

Comb.: **hydroxylapatite** = HYDROXYAPATITE.

hydroxylase /-z/ *n.* (*Biochem.*) an enzyme which catalyses hydroxylation M20. **hydroxylate** *v.t.* & *i.* (*a*) *v.t.* introduce a hydroxyl group into; (*b*) *v.i.* accept a hydroxyl group: E20. **hydroxy'lation** *n.* the introduction of a hydroxyl group into a molecule or compound L19. **hydroxylic** /-drɒk'sɪlɪk/ *a.* of or containing a hydroxyl group L19.

hydroxylamine /hʌɪ'drɒksɪləˌmiːn, hʌɪˌdrɒksɪ'lamiːn, hʌɪdrɒk'sʌɪləmiːn/ *n.* M19. [f. prec. + AMINE.] A compound, NH_2OH, which forms unstable deliquescent crystals that detonate on heating and is used in stable solution as a reducing agent and reagent.

hydrozoan /hʌɪdrə(ʊ)'zəʊən/ *n.* & *a.* L19. [f. mod.L *Hydrozoa* (see below), f. HYDRO- + Gk *zōia* pl. of *zōion* animal.] *Zool.* A *n.* A coelenterate of the class Hydrozoa, comprising organisms that are mostly marine and colonial with polyp and medusoid stages in the life cycle. L19. B *adj.* Of or pertaining to the class Hydrozoa. L19.

hydrozoic *a.* M19. **hydrozoon** *n.*, pl. **-zoa,** = HYDROZOAN *n.* (usu. in *pl.*) M19.

†**hydruret** *n.* Only in 19. [f. HYDR(OGEN + -URET.] *Chem.* A hydride.

Hydrus /'hʌɪdrəs/ *n.* In sense 1 **h-**. M17. [L f. Gk *hudros* water snake.] 1 A mythical water snake or sea serpent. *rare.* M17. 2 (The name of) a constellation of the southern hemisphere between the star Achernar and the pole; the Water Snake. Cf. HYDRA *n.* 2. E18.

hyemal *a.* var. of HIEMAL.

hyemate *v.* var. of HIEMATE.

†**hyemnal** *a.* L17–L18. [f. HIEMAL, perh. after *autumnal*.] = HIEMAL.

hyena /hʌɪ'iːnə/ *n.* Also **hyaena.** ME. [(OFr. *hyene* f.) L *hyaena* f. Gk *huaina* use of fem. of *hus, hu-* pig, SWINE w. ending as in *leaina* lioness, etc.] 1a Any of several carnivorous scavenging animals somewhat resembling a dog, but with the hind limbs shorter than the forelimbs, and belonging to the genera *Hyaena* and *Crocuta* (family Hyaenidae). ME. **b** The thylacine, the Tasmanian wolf. Chiefly *Austral.* (now *rare*). E19. **2** *fig.* A person who is cruel, treacherous, and rapacious, or is otherwise likened to a hyena. E17. †**3** A mythical stone said to be taken from the eye of the hyena. E17–M19.

1a brown hyena *Hyaena brunnea*, of southern Africa. **laughing hyena** the spotted hyena; also (now *rare*), the striped hyena. **spotted hyena** *Crocuta crocuta*, of sub-Saharan Africa. **striped hyena** *Hyaena hyaena*, of Africa and SW Asia.

Comb.: **hyena-dog** = *hunting dog* (b) s.v. HUNTING *n.*

hyenaism *n.* behaviour characteristic of a hyena M19.

hyetograph /ˈhʌɪɪtəgrɑːf/ *n.* L19. [f. Gk *huetos* rain + -GRAPH.] **1** A chart or map of rainfall. L19. **2** A kind of recording rain-gauge. M20.

hyetoˈgraphic *a.* M19. **hyetoˈgraphical** *a.* L19.

hygeen /hɪˈdʒiːn/ *n.* Also **hajeen** /həˈdʒiːn/. E17. [Arab. *hajīn*.] A riding dromedary.

Hygeia /hʌɪˈdʒiːə/ *n.* E18. [Gk *hugeia* late form of *hugieia* health, *Hugieia* goddess of health, f. *hugiēs* healthy.] The personification of health; a system of sanitation or medical practice.

hygeian, H- *a.* pertaining to Hygeia, health, or sanitation; healthy: M18. **ˈhygeist, ˈHy-** *n.* an expert in hygiene E18.

hygiastic /hʌɪdʒɪˈastɪk/ *a.* L17. [Gk *hugiastikos* curative, f. *hugiazein* heal, f. *hugiēs* healthy: see -IC.] Relating to health, sanitary, hygienic.

hygiene /ˈhʌɪdʒiːn/ *n.* Orig. in L & Gk forms †**hygie(i)na**, †**hygieine**. L16. [(Fr. *hygiène* f. mod.L *hygieina* f.) Gk *hugieinē* (sc. *technē* art), use as n. of fem. of *hugieinos* healthful, f. *hugiēs* healthy.] The branch of knowledge that deals with the maintenance of health, esp. the conditions and practices conducive to it; the conditions and practices of a place or person in so far as they promote health.

A. GHOSH A campaign to teach people the principles of hygiene. *Which?* The standard of hygiene and efficiency in the salon generally—dirty towels, combs, and other equipment. *New York Times* Food service workers should follow established standards of good personal hygiene. *mental hygiene*: see MENTAL *a.*[1]

hyˈgienic *a.* pertaining to hygiene; conducive to health, clean and sanitary: M19. **hyˈgienically** *adv.* (earlier in UNHYGIENICALLY) in a hygienic manner; as regards hygiene: L19. **hyˈgienics** *n.* hygiene as a branch of knowledge M19. **hyˈgienist** *n.* (*a*) an expert in hygiene; (*b*) = DENTAL *hygienist*: M19.

hygro- /ˈhʌɪgrəʊ/ *comb. form.* [Gk *hugro-*, f. *hugros* wet, moist, fluid: see -O-.] Moisture.

ˈhygrograph *n.* an instrument that produces a graphical record of atmospheric humidity M19. **hyˈgrology** *n.* the branch of physics that deals with humidity and evaporation L18. **ˈhygrophile** *n.* a hygrophilous plant M19. **hyˈgrophilous** *a.* (of a plant) growing in damp environments M19. **ˈhygrophyte** *n.* a plant that grows in damp (but not aquatic) environments E20. **hygrophytic** /-ˈfɪtɪk/ *a.* designating or pertaining to a hygrophyte or hygrophytes M20. **ˈhygrostat** *n.* = HUMIDISTAT E20. **hygroˈthermograph** *n.* an instrument that produces a graphical record of atmospheric humidity and temperature E20.

hygroma /hʌɪˈgrəʊmə/ *n.* Pl. **-mas, -mata** /-mətə/. E19. [f. HYGRO- + -OMA.] *Med.* A sac, cyst, or tumour filled with watery fluid.

hygrometer /hʌɪˈgrɒmɪtə/ *n.* L17. [f. HYGRO- + -METER, or f. Fr. *hygromètre*.] An instrument for measuring the humidity of the air or other gas. Formerly also, a hygroscope.

hygrometric /hʌɪgrə(ʊ)ˈmɛtrɪk/ *a.* L18. [f. (as) prec.: see -IC.] **1** = HYGROSCOPIC 1. L18. **2** Pertaining to humidity or its measurement. E19. **3** = HYGROSCOPIC 3. M19.

hygrometrical *a.* = HYGROMETRIC L18. **hygrometrically** *adv.* E19. **hyˈgrometry** *n.* the branch of science that deals with the measurement of humidity L18.

hygroscope /ˈhʌɪgrə(ʊ)skəʊp/ *n.* M17. [f. HYGRO- + -SCOPE.] An instrument which gives a qualitative indication of atmospheric humidity without measuring it.

hygroscopic /hʌɪgrə(ʊ)ˈskɒpɪk/ *a.* L18. [f. (as) prec. + -IC.] **1** Of a substance: tending to absorb moisture from the air. L18. **2** Pertaining to humidity or its detection. L18. **3** Of water: present as moisture in soil as a result of humidity in the air to which it is exposed. M19.

hygroscopical *a.* L18. **hygroscopically** *adv.* E19. **hygroscopicity** /ˌhʌɪgrə(ʊ)skɒˈpɪsɪti/ *n.* hygroscopic quality; the property of a substance of retaining moisture: M19.

hying *v.* pres. pple of HIE *v.*

Hyksos /ˈhɪksɒs/ *n.* & *a.* E17. [Gk *Huksōs* f. Egyptian *heqa khoswe* foreign rulers.] **A** *n.pl.* A nomadic people of mixed Semitic and Asian descent who invaded Egypt in the 18th cent. BC and ruled it until the 16th cent. E17. **B** *adj.* Designating, of, or pertaining to the Hyksos. L19.

hyla /ˈhʌɪlə/ *n.* M19. [mod.L f. Gk *hulē*: see HYLE.] A tree frog of the genus *Hyla*.

†**hylarchic** *a.* L17–E18. [f. HYLE + -ARCH + -IC.] Ruling over matter.

hyle /ˈhʌɪliː/ *n.* LME. [Late L f. Gk *hulē* wood, timber, material, matter. Cf. OFr. *hyle*.] Matter, substance; *spec.* the primordial matter of the universe. Cf. YLEM.

hyleg /ˈhʌɪlɛg/ *n.* E17. [Pers. *haylāj* celestial indicator of the length of a newborn child's life.] *Astrol.* The giver of life in a nativity.

†**hylegial** *a.* M17–M18.

hylic /ˈhʌɪlɪk/ *a.* M19. [Late L *hylicus* f. Gk *hulikos*, f. *hulē* HYLE: see -IC.] Pertaining to matter, material.

hylicist /-sɪst/ *n.* a materialist L19.

hylo- /ˈhʌɪləʊ/ *comb. form.* [Gk *hulo-* comb. form of *hulē*: see HYLE, -O-.] **1** Wood; forest. **2** Matter.

hyˈlobatid *n.* [Gk *-batēs* walker] an animal of the family Hylobatidae, comprising the gibbons L20. **hyˈlology** *n.* a doctrine concerning matter; a branch of knowledge that deals with matter: M19. **hyloˈmorphic** *a.* (*Philos.*) of or pertaining to hylomorphism L19. **hyloˈmorphism** *n.* (*Philos.*) the doctrine that matter is the first cause of the universe and that physical objects result from the combination of matter with form L19. **hyˈlophagous** *a.* (of an insect) feeding on wood L19. **hyloˈtheism** *n.* the doctrine that God and matter are identical; material pantheism: E19. **hyloˈzoic** *a.* of, pertaining in, or advocating hylozoism L17. **hyloˈzoism** *n.* the doctrine that all matter has life, or that life is merely a property of matter L17. **hyloˈzoist** *n.* a person who advocates hylozoism L17. **hylozoˈistic** *a.* = HYLOZOIC L19.

hymen /ˈhʌɪmən/ *n.*[1] L16. [L f. Gk *Humēn* the god of marriage.] **1** (**H-**.) Marriage personified. L16. **2** (Usu. **H-**.) Marriage; a wedding. Now *rare*. E17. **3** = HYMENEAL *n.* 2. *rare*. E17.

hymen /ˈhʌɪmən/ *n.*[2] M16. [L f. Gk *humēn* membrane (also, seed-vessel of a plant).] A mucous membrane which partly closes the entrance to the vagina and is broken usu. at a woman's first experience of sexual intercourse.

hymenal *a.* = HYMENEAL *a.*[2] L19.

hymeneal /hʌɪməˈniːəl/ *a.*[1] & *n.* E17. [f. L *hymenaeus* f. Gk *humenaios*: see -AL[1].] **A** *adj.* Pertaining to marriage. E17. **B** *n.* **1** In *pl.* A wedding; nuptials. M17. **2** A wedding-hymn. E18.

hymeneally *adv.* M19.

hymeneal /hʌɪməˈniːəl/ *a.*[2] E20. [f. HYMEN *n.*[2] + -AL[1], perh. after HYMENEAL *a.*[1]] Of or pertaining to a woman's hymen.

hymenean /hʌɪməˈniːən/ *a.* & *n.* Now *rare*. E17. [f. as HYMENEAL *a.*[1] + -AN.] **A** *adj.* = HYMENEAL *a.*[1] E17. †**B** *n.* = HYMENEAL *n.* 2. Only in M17.

hymenial /hʌɪˈmiːnɪəl/ *a.*[1] E18. [f. HYMEN *n.*[1] + -IAL or alt. of HYMENEAL *a.*[1]] = HYMENEAL *a.*[1]

hymenial /hʌɪˈmiːnɪəl/ *a.*[2] L19. [f. next + -AL[1].] Of or pertaining to the hymenium of a fungus.

hymenium /hʌɪˈmiːnɪəm/ *n.* E19. [Gk *humenion* dim. of *humēn*: see HYMEN *n.*[2]] A spore-producing layer containing asci or basidia in some higher fungi.

hymenopter /hʌɪməˈnɒptə/ *n.* E19. [Fr. *hyménoptère* f. as next.] = HYMENOPTERAN *n.*

Hymenoptera /hʌɪməˈnɒpt(ə)rə/ *n.pl.* Also **h-**. L18. [mod.L f. neut. pl. of Gk *humenopteros* membrane-winged, f. *humen-*, *humēn* (see HYMEN *n.*[2]) + *pteron* wing: see -A[3].] (Members of) a large order of insects (including bees, wasps, and ants) characterized by two pairs of wings and in females an ovipositor adapted for stinging, piercing, or sawing.

R. F. CHAPMAN In some larval Diptera and Hymenoptera the antennae are very small.

hymenopterous *a.* of or pertaining to the Hymenoptera E19.

hymenopteran /hʌɪməˈnɒpt(ə)rən/ *n.* & *a.* M19. [f. prec. + -AN.] **A** *n.* A hymenopterous insect. M19. **B** *adj.* Hymenopterous. E20.

Hymettian /hʌɪˈmɛtɪən/ *a.* E17. [f. L *Hymettius*, f. *Hymettus*, Gk *Humēttos*: see -IAN.] Of or belonging to Mount Hymettus in Attica, famous in ancient times for its honey and marble; *poet.* honeyed, sweet. Cf. HYBLAEAN.

Hymie /ˈhʌɪmi/ *n.* *US slang* (*derog.* & usu. considered *racially offensive*). L20. [Colloq. abbrev. of Jewish man's name *Hyman*.] A Jew.

hymn /hɪm/ *n.* & *v.* OE. [(OFr. *ymne* f.) L *hymnus* f. Gk *humnos* song in praise of a god or hero, in Septuagint rendering various Heb. wds, and hence in New Testament and other Christian writings.] **A** *n.* **1** A song of praise to God; *spec.* a metrical composition sung during a religious service and consisting of something other than the text of the Bible. OE. **2** A song or other composition which praises a god or other exalted being or thing. LME.

1 W. SOYINKA Nothing but the sound of hymns at morning and evening prayers had been heard. 2 D. PRATER Since his admiration . . had first been awakened, Rilke's letters had contained many a hymn to Rodin. **hymn of hate** a tirade against a person or thing.

Comb.: **hymn-book** a book of hymns.

B *v.* **1** *v.t.* Praise or celebrate in a hymn. M17. **2** *v.t.* Sing as a hymn; express in a hymn. E18. **3** *v.i.* Sing a hymn or hymns. E18.

1 W. DE LA MARE Within the eternal peace of God they stood, Hymning his glory. O. NASH Some singers sing of ladies' eyes, . . coarse ones hymn their hips. 2 *British Medical Journal* It started in the 'fifties, hymning the praise . . of competition, and of private enterprise.

hymner /ˈhɪm(n)ə/ *n.* a singer of hymns E19. **hymnic** /ˈhɪmnɪk/ *a.* of, or of the nature of, a hymn or hymns L16. **hymnist** /ˈhɪmnɪst/ *n.* a composer of hymns E17. **hymnless** *a.* E19.

hymnal /ˈhɪmn(ə)l/ *n.* & *a.* L15. [f. L *hymnus* (see prec.) + -AL[1]. The n. use repr. a med.L *hymnale*.] **A** *n.* A hymn-book; a collection of hymns. L15. **B** *adj.* Of a hymn or hymns. M17.

hymnary /ˈhɪmnəri/ *n.* L19. [med.L *hymnarium*, f. as HYMN: see -ARY[1].] = HYMNAL *n.*

hymnody /ˈhɪmnədi/ *n.* E18. [med.L *hymnodia* f. Gk *humnōidia* singing of hymns: cf. PSALMODY.] **1** The singing or composition of hymns. E18. **2** Hymns collectively; the body of hymns belonging to a period, country, church, etc. M19.

2 *Presbyterian Herald* A massive tune—one of the finest things in all hymnody.

hymnodist *n.* a person who is skilled in hymnody; a hymnist: E18.

hymnographer /hɪmˈnɒgrəfə/ *n.* E17. [f. Gk *humnographos* hymn-writer + -ER[1]: see -GRAPHER.] A composer of hymns.

hymnography /hɪmˈnɒgrəfi/ *n.* M19. [f. (as) prec. + -GRAPHY.] The literary history and bibliography of hymns.

hymnology /hɪmˈnɒlədʒi/ *n.* M17. [Orig. f. Gk *humnologia* hymn-singing, med.L *hymnologia* praise in song, but in mod. usage f. HYMN *n.* + -OLOGY.] †**1** The singing of hymns. M17–M19. **2** The branch of knowledge that deals with hymns; hymns collectively or as a literary form. E19. **3** The composition of hymns. M19.

hymnoˈlogic(al) *adjs.* L19. **hymnoˈlogically** *adv.* as regards hymnology L19. **hymnologist** *n.* a composer of hymns; an expert in or student of hymnology: L18.

hyne /hʌɪn/ *adv.* Now *Sc.* & *dial.* LME. [Contr. of HETHEN.] Hence.

hyoid /ˈhʌɪɔɪd/ *a.* & *n.* E19. [Fr. *hyoïde* f. mod.L *hyoides* f. Gk *huoeidēs* shaped like the letter upsilon, f. *hu* (name of) the letter *υ*: see -OID.] *Anat.* & *Zool.* **A** *adj.* Designating a bone (U-shaped in man) or a group of bones which supports the tongue, being situated at its base above the thyroid cartilage. E19.

hyoid arch the second visceral arch in lower vertebrates and the embryos of higher vertebrates.
B *n.* The hyoid bone. L19.

hyoidean /hʌɪˈɔɪdɪən/ *a.* M19. [f. mod.L *hyoideus*, f. *hyoides*: see prec., -AN.] *Anat.* & *Zool.* Of or pertaining to the hyoid.

hyolithid /hʌɪəˈlɪθɪd/ *a.* & *n.* M20. [f. mod.L *Hyolitha*, f. Gk *huoeidēs* (see HYOID) + *lithos* stone: see -ID[3].] (Pertaining to or designating) a marine invertebrate of Palaeozoic times that was bilaterally symmetric with a conical shell and was probably a kind of mollusc.

hyomandibular /ˌhʌɪə(ʊ)manˈdɪbjʊlə/ *a.* & *n.* L19. [f. Gk *huoeidēs* (see HYOID) + MANDIBULAR.] *Anat.* & *Zool.* A *adj.* Pertaining to the hyoid bone or hyoid arch and the mandible. L19.

hyomandibular bone the dorsal component of the hyoid arch in vertebrates, which in fishes supports the jaws and in land animals is modified into an auditory ossicle.
B *n.* The hyomandibular bone. L19.

hyoscine /ˈhʌɪəsiːn/ *n.* L19. [f. HYOSC(YAMUS + -INE[5].] Scopolamine; *spec.* the naturally occurring laevorotatory isomer.

hyoscyamia /ˌhʌɪə(ʊ)sʌɪˈeɪmɪə/ *n.* Now *rare* or *obs.* E19. [f. as next after *ammonia*.] = next.

hyoscyamine /hʌɪə(ʊ)ˈsʌɪəmiːn/ *n.* M19. [f. next + -INE[5].] A poisonous alkaloid, $C_{17}H_{23}NO_3$; *spec.* the laevorotatory isomer, occurring in henbane and other solanaceous plants and used medicinally like atropine for its anticholinergic properties.

hyoscyamus /hʌɪə(ʊ)ˈsʌɪəməs/ *n.* E17. [mod.L f. Gk *huoskuamos*, f. *huos* genit. of *hus* swine + *kuamos* bean.] A medicinal extract or tincture of henbane.

hyp *n.* var. of HIP *n.*[3]

hyp- *comb. form* see HYPO-.

hypabyssal /hʌɪpəˈbɪs(ə)l/ *a.* L19. [f. HYP- + ABYSSAL.] *Geol.* Of igneous rock: formed from magma that has intruded into and solidified among other rocks not far below the earth's surface.

hypacusis /hʌɪpəˈk(j)uːsɪs/ *n.* Also **-cou-**, **-ku-**, **-usia** /-uːsɪə/. L19. [f. HYPO- + Gk *akousis* hearing.] Diminished acuteness of hearing.

hypaesthesia /ˌhʌɪpiːsˈθiːzɪə -pɛs-/ *n.* Also ***-pes-**. L19. [f. HYPO- + Gk *aisthēsis* sensation: see -IA[1].] Abnormally low sensitivity of the body or mind, esp. of the skin.
hypaesthetic *a.* M20.

hypaethral /hʌɪˈpiːθr(ə)l, hɪ-/ *a.* Also **-peth-**. L18. [f. L *hypaethrus* f. Gk *hupaithros*, f. as HYPO- + *aithēr* air, ETHER *n.*[1]: see -AL[1].] **1** *Archit.* Open to the sky; having no roof. Opp. CLEITHRAL. L18. **2** Open-air. L19.

hypakusis *n.* var. of HYPACUSIS.

hypalgesia /hʌɪpalˈdʒiːzɪə/ *n.* L19. [f. HYP- + Gk *algēsis* sense of pain + -IA[1].] Abnormally low sensitivity to pain.
hypalˈgesic *a.* characterized by or tending to produce hypalgesia E20.

hypallage /hʌɪˈpalədʒiː, hɪ-/ *n.* L16. [Late L *hypallage* f. Gk *hupallagē*, f. as HYPO- + *allag-* stem of *allassein* to exchange, f. *allos* other.] *Rhet.* A figure of speech in which there is a transposition of the natural relations of two elements of a proposition or a transference of an epithet.

Hypalon /ˈhʌɪp(ə)lɒn/ *n.* M20. [Origin unkn.] (Proprietary name for) a synthetic rubber consisting of chlorinated and sulphonated polyethylene.

hypanthium /hɪˈpanθɪəm, hʌɪ-/ *n.* M19. [mod.L, f. as HYPO- + Gk *anthos* flower + -IUM.] *Bot.* A cuplike or tubular enlargement of the receptacle, loosely surrounding the gynoecium (in a perigynous flower) or united with it (in an epigynous flower).
hypanthial *a.* L19.

hyparterial /hʌɪpɑːˈtɪərɪəl/ *a.* L19. [f. HYP- + ARTERIAL.] *Anat.* Of a branch of a bronchus: situated below the pulmonary artery.

hypaspist /hɪˈpaspɪst, hʌɪ-/ *n.* E19. [Gk *hupaspistēs* lit. 'shield-bearer', f. as HYPO- + *aspis* shield.] *Gk Hist.* A member of a distinguished body of troops in the Macedonian army that included the foot guards.

hypate /ˈhɪpətiː/ *n.* E17. [L f. Gk *hypatē* (sc. *khordē* string), fem. of *hupatos* uppermost, last.] In ancient Greek music, the fixed lowest note of a lower tetrachord.

hypaxial /hɪˈpaksɪəl, hʌɪ-/ *a.* L19. [f. HYP- + AXIAL.] *Anat.* & *Zool.* Situated on the lower or ventral side of the vertebral axis.

hype /hʌɪp/ *n.*[1] & *v.*[1] *slang* (orig. *US*). E20. [Origin unkn.] A *n.* **1** An instance of short-changing; a person who short-changes people. E20. **2** Cheating, deception; a confidence trick, a swindle; persuasive talk; promotional publicity, esp. of an extravagant or intensive nature. M20.
2 *Publishers Weekly* They carried off the biggest money-making hype in sports history. *Newsweek* Despite some media hype Frost insists his series really 'breaks some new ground'.
B *v.t.* **1** Short-change; cheat, deceive, esp. by persuasive talk. E20. **2** Promote with extravagant or intensive publicity. Also foll. by *up*. L20.
1 J. HYAMS His sales technique was to hype the kids. **2** *National Observer* (*US*) Scientists hype up low-tar tobacco.

hype /hʌɪp/ *n.*[2] & *v.*[2] *slang* (orig. *US*). E20. [Abbrev. of HYPODERMIC. Cf. HYPO *n.*[3] & *v.*] A *n.* **1** A drug addict. E20. **2a** A hypodermic injection. E20. **b** A hypodermic needle or syringe. M20. B *v.t.* Stimulate; excite, work up. Chiefly as *hyped* pa. pple & foll. by *up*. M20.

hyper /ˈhʌɪpə/ *n.*[1] L17. [Abbrev.] †**1** = HYPERCRITIC *n.* I. Only in L17. **2** = HYPER-CALVINIST. M19.

hyper /ˈhʌɪpə/ *n.*[2] *US slang.* E20. [f. HYPE *v.*[1] + -ER[1].] A person who gives short change.

hyper /ˈhʌɪpə/ *a.* *slang* (chiefly *US*). M20. [Abbrev. of HYPERACTIVE.] Hyperactive, excitable; very highly strung; extraordinarily energetic.

hyper- /ˈhʌɪpə/ *comb. form.* [Gk *huper-*, f. *huper* prep. & adv., over, beyond, overmuch, above measure.] **1** Over, beyond, above, (*lit.* & *fig.*). Chiefly in adjs., as *hyperconstitutional*, *hyperphysical*. **b** *Mus.* In names of modes, denoting (*a*) each of a set of modes in ancient Greek music which began at a definite interval above the ordinary Aeolian etc. modes; (*b*) the authentic (Aeolian etc.) modes in medieval music as contrasted with the plagal (Hypo-aeolian etc.) modes. **2** To excess, excessively; exceedingly. Chiefly in adjs. (& derived advs.) & ns., as *hyperaccurate*, *hypermodest*; *hyperconservatism*, *hyperscrupulosity*. **3** More than, greater than, as *hyperfocal*, *hypersonic*; (esp. *Med.*) more than normal, as *hyperacidity*. **b** *Chem.* In ns. denoting a compound in which a specified element is present in a higher proportion. Now largely superseded by PER-[1]. **c** *Math.* In ns. denoting an analogue in a space of four or more dimensions of a solid or figure of three-dimensional space.

hyperˈacid *a.* abnormally acid, characterized by hyperacidity L19. **hyperaˈcidity** *n.* a condition in which the gastro-intestinal tract, esp. the stomach, is too acid, causing a burning sensation L19. **hyperaˈcute** *a.* abnormally acute; *Med.* (of tissue rejection) occurring within 48 hours of grafting: L19. **hyperalgesia** /-ˈdʒiːzɪə/ *n.* abnormally great sensitivity to pain L19. **hyperalgesic** /-ˈdʒiːzɪk/ *a.* characterized by hyperalgesia L19. **hyperalgic** /-ˈaldʒɪk/ *a.* = HYPERALGESIC M20. **hyperalimenˈtation** *n.* (*Med.*) intravenous supply of nutrients to patients incapable of normal digestion M20. **hypercalˈcaemia** *n.* (*Med.*) an abnormally high concentration of calcium in the blood E20. **hypercalˈcaemic** *a.* (*Med.*) of or affected with hypercalcaemia M20. **hyperˈcapnia** *n.* [Gk *kapnos* smoke] *Med.* an abnormally high concentration of carbon dioxide in the blood E20. **hyperˈcapnic** *a.* (*Med.*) of, pertaining to, or affected with hypercapnia M20. **hypercaˈtharsis** *n.* (*Med.*) excessive or violent purging, esp. by means of drugs L17. **hyperˈcellular** *a.* (*Med.*) exhibiting hypercellularity M20. **hypercelluˈlarity** *n.* (*Med.*) an excessive number of cells at a site in the body E20. **hyperchlorˈhydria** *n.* (*Med.*) an abnormally high concentration of hydrochloric acid in the gastric juice L19. **hyperchlorˈhydric** *a.* (*Med.*) of, pertaining to, or characterized by hyperchlorhydria E20. **hypercholesteˈraemia** *n.* (*Med.*) = HYPERCHOLESTEROLAEMIA L19. **hypercholesteroˈlaemia** *n.* (*Med.*) an abnormally high concentration of cholesterol in the blood E20. **hypercholesteroˈlaemic** *a.* (*Med.*) of or affected with hypercholesterolaemia E20. **hypercoagulaˈbility** *n.* (*Med.*) an excessive tendency (of the blood) to coagulate M20. **hypercoˈagulable** *a.* (*Med.*) characterized by hypercoagulability M20. **hypercolour** *n.* (*Particle Physics*) a hypothetical quantized property of bosons which is thought to form a strong interaction, analogous to the colour force L20. **hypercolumn** *n.* (*Anat.* & *Zool.*) an array of columns of neurons in the visual cortex of the brain L20. **hyperˈcomplex** *a.* (*a*) *Math.* designating numbers such as quaternions that are generalizations of complex numbers for which multiplication is not commutative nor necessarily associative; (*b*) *Anat.* designating neurones of the visual cortex that respond only to visual stimuli satisfying certain conditions of orientation, size, etc.: L19. **hyperˈconjugated** *a.* (*Physical Chem.*) exhibiting hyperconjugation M20. **hyperconjuˈgation** *n.* (*Physical Chem.*) a direct attraction between the electrons of a methyl or substituted methyl group and the electrons of an adjacent conjugated system M20. **hypercoˈrrect** *a.* & *v.* (*Ling.*) (*a*) *adj.* (of a spelling, pronunciation, etc.) erroneous through being falsely modelled on an apparently analogous prestigeful form; (*b*) *v.t.* & *i.* alter by or practise hypercorrection: E20. **hypercoˈrrection** *n.* (*Ling.*) the use, or an instance, of hypercorrect spelling etc. M20. **hypercoˈrrectness** *n.* (*Ling.*) the use of hypercorrect spelling etc. M20. **hypercube** *n.* (*Math.*) an analogue in four or more dimensions of a cube in three dimensions E20. **hyperˈdiploid** *a.* & *n.* (*Genetics*) (*a*) *adj.* having one or a few chromosomes in excess of those of a diploid set; containing such cells; (*b*) *n.* a hyperdiploid individual: M20. **hyperdiploidy** *n.* (*Genetics*) the condition of being hyperdiploid M20. **hyperˈemesis** *n.* excessive vomiting, e.g. during pregnancy M19. **hyperenˈdemic** *a.* (*Med.*) permanently present in an area and affecting many individuals M20. **hypereuˈtectic** *a.* (of an alloy of iron) containing more carbon than the 4.3 per cent present in the eutectic composition E20. **hypereuˈtectoid** *a.* (of steel) containing more carbon than the 0.8 per cent present in the eutectoid composition E20. **hyperexcitaˈbility** *n.* the state or property of being hyperexcitable L19. **hyperexˈcitable** *a.* abnormally excitable L19. **hyperexˈtend** *v.t.* (*Med.*) bend (a limb, digit, etc.) so that it makes an abnormally great angle L19. **hyperextensiˈbility** *n.* (*Med.*) the property of being hyperextensible M20. **hyperexˈtensible** *a.* (*Med.*) able to be hyperextended M20. **hyperexˈtension** *n.* (*Med.*) the state of being hyperextended; the action or an act of hyperextending a limb etc.: L19. **hyperfine** *a.* (*Physics*) designating or pertaining to (the presence of) closely spaced groups of lines in atomic spectra produced by coupling between the magnetic moment of the nucleus and the electromagnetic field of the orbital electrons E20. **hyperˈfocal** *a.* designating or pertaining to the distance on which a camera must be focused for objects to be in focus over the greatest range of distances E20. **hyperform** *n.* (*Ling.*) a hypercorrect spelling or pronunciation M20. **hyperfunction** *n.* & *v.* (*Med.*) (*a*) *n.* overactivity or overproduction in a gland etc.; (*b*) *v.i.* exhibit hyperfunction: E20. **hyperˈfunctional** *a.* (*Med.*) exhibiting hyperfunction M20. **hypergamma,globuliˈnaemia** *n.* (*Med.*) an abnormally high concentration of gamma globulin in the blood M20. **hypergamma,globuliˈnaemic** *a.* (*Med.*) characterized by hypergammaglobulinaemia L20. **hyˈpergamous** *a.* (*Anthropol.*) of or pertaining to hypergamy L19. **hyˈpergamy** *n.* (*Anthropol.*) (the custom of) marriage to a person, esp. a husband, of superior standing L19. **hypergeoˈmetric** *a.* (*Math.*) designating or pertaining to a series of the kind $1, abx/c, a(a+1)b(b+1)x^2/2!c^2$, etc. L19. **hypergeoˈmetrical** *a.* (*Math.*) = HYPERGEOMETRIC E19. **hypergeusia** /-ˈgjuːzɪə, -sɪə/ *n.* [Gk *geusis* taste] *Med.* increased acuteness of the sense of taste L19. **hyperˈgluon** *n.* (*Particle Physics*) a hypothetical particle bearing the same relation to hypercolour that gluons do to colour L20. **hyperglyˈcaemia** *n.* (*Med.*) an abnormally high concentration of sugar in the blood L19. **hyperglyˈcaemic** *a.* (*Med.*) of, pertaining to, or characterized by hyperglycaemia E20. **hyperhiˈdrosis** *n.* (*Med.*) excessive sweating M19. **hyperinˈflation** *n.* a very high rate of monetary inflation M20. **hyperinˈflationary** *a.* of or pertaining to hyperinflation M20. **hyperinsuliˈnaemia** *n.* (*Med.*) an abnormally high concentration of insulin in the blood E20. **hyperinsuliˈnaemic** *a.* (*Med.*) characterized by hyperinsulinaemia M20. **hyperˈinsulinism** *n.* (*Med.*) excessive production of insulin by the pancreas; hyperinsulinaemia: E20. **hyperirritaˈbility** *n.* (*Med.*) abnormally high sensitivity to stimuli, esp. nervous stimuli E20. **hyper'irritable** *a.* (*Med.*) characterized by hyperirritability E20. **hyperka'laemia** *n.* [mod.L *kalium* potassium] *Med.* an abnormally high concentration of potassium in the blood M20. **hyperka'laemic** *a.* (*Med.*) characterized by hyperkalaemia M20. **hyperkera'tosis** *n.*, pl. **-toses** /-'təʊsiːz/, *Med.* †(*a*) staphyloma of the cornea; (*b*) a thickening of the outer layer of the skin: M19. **hyperkera'totic** *a.* (*Med.*) of or characterized by hyperkeratosis M20. **hyperki'nesia** *n.* (*Med.*) = HYPERKINESIS M19. **hyperki'nesis** *n.* (*Med.*) an abnormal degree of muscular or bodily activity; *spec.* (*a*) muscle spasm; (*b*) a disorder of children marked by hyperactivity and an inability to attend: M19. **hyperki'netic** *a.* (*Med.*) characterized by hyperkinesis L19. **hyperli'paemia** *n.* (*Med.*) an abnormally high concentration of fats or lipids in the blood L19. **hyperli'paemic** *a.* (*Med.*) of or characterized by hyperlipaemia M20. **hyperlipi'daemia** *n.* (*Med.*) = HYPERLIPAEMIA M20. **hyperlipi'daemic** *a.* (*Med.*) = HYPERLIPAEMIC M20. **hypermeta'bolic** *a.* of or involving hypermetabolism M20. **hyperme'tabolism** *n.* metabolism at a high rate M20. **hypermeta'morphic** *a.* (*Entomol.*) undergoing metamorphosis through two or more larval stages L19. **hyperm'nesia** *n.* [Gk *mnēsis* memory] unusual power of memory M19. **hyperm'nesic** *a.* pertaining to hypermnesia; accompanied by exceptionally vivid or detailed memories: M20. **hyper'mobile** *a.* characterized by or exhibiting hypermobility E20. **hypermo'bility** *n.* abnormally great freedom of movement or flexibility in a joint E20. **hyper'modern** *a.* excessively modern; *spec.* in *Chess*, of or pertaining to the strategy of controlling the centre of the board with pieces at a distance (first used in the early 20th cent.): E20. **hypermorph** *n.* (*Genetics*) an allele that is functionally more effective than a corresponding wild-type allele M20. **hyper'morphic** *a.* (*Genetics*) designating, of, or pertaining to a hypermorph M20. **hyperna'traemia** *n.* (*Med.*) an abnormally high concentration of sodium in the blood M20. **hyperna'traemic** *a.* (*Med.*) characterized by hypernatraemia M20. **hyper'oestrogenism** *n.* (*Med.*) excessive production of oestrogens by the body M20. **hyperosmo'lality** *n.* (*Med.*) = HYPEROSMOLARITY M20. **hyperos'molar** *a.* (*Med.*) accompanied by or characterized by hyperosmolarity M20. **hyperosmo'larity** *n.* (*Med.*) an abnormally high osmotic pressure of the blood serum of a person M20. **hyperpara'thyroid** *a.* (*Med.*) of, affected with, or accompanied by hyperparathyroidism M20. **hyperpara'thyroidism** *n.* (*Med.*) a condition in which there is an abnormally high concentration of parathyroid hormone in the blood, resulting in loss of calcium from the bones, which become soft E20. **hyperphagia** /-'feɪdʒɪə, -dʒə/ *n.* (*Med.*) an abnormally great desire for food; excessive eating: M20. **hyperphagic** /-'fadʒɪk/ *a.* (*Med.*) of or exhibiting hyperphagia M20. **hyperpha'langia, -pha'langism, -'phalangy** *ns.* (*Med.* & *Zool.*) the condition of having an additional digital phalanx, esp. in the absence of polydactyly L19. **hyper'phoria** *n.* (*Med.*) latent strabismus in which there is a tendency for one eye to be directed above (or below) the line of sight of the other L19. **hyper'phoric** *a.* (*Med.*) of or affected with hyperphoria L19. **hyperphospha'taemia** *n.* (*Med.*) an abnormally high concentration of phosphate (or other phosphorus compounds) in the blood E20. **hyperphospha'taemic** *a.* (*Med.*) pertaining to or characterized by hyperphosphataemia M20. **hyperpi'tuitarism** *n.* (*Med.*) increased hormone secretion by the pituitary E20. **hyperpi'tuitary** *a.* (*Med.*) of, pertaining to, or affected with hyperpituitarism E20. **hyperplane** *n.* (*Math.*) an analogue in four or more dimensions of a plane in three dimensions E20. **hyperploid** *a.* & *n.* (*Genetics*) (*a*) *adj.* having one or a few chromosomes in excess of those of a haploid or polyploid set; containing such cells; (*b*) *n.* a hyperploid individual: M20. **hyperploidy** *n.* (*Genetics*) the condition of being hyperploid M20. **hyperpolari'zation** *n.* (*Physiol.*) an increase in the potential difference across the membrane of a nerve fibre M20. **hyper'polarize** *v.* (*Physiol.*) (*a*) *v.t.* & *i.* produce hyperpolarization (in); (*b*) *v.i.* undergo hyperpolarization: M20. **hyperprolacti'naemia** *n.* (*Med.*) an abnormally high concentration of prolactin in the blood L20. **hyperprolacti'naemic** *a.* (*Med.*) of or characterized by hyperprolactinaemia L20. **hyperpy'retic** *a.* (*Med.*) of hyperpyrexia L19. **hyperpy'rexia** *n.* (*Med.*) fever marked by an exceptionally high temperature L19. **hyperpy'rexial** *a.* (*Med.*) hyperpyretic L19. **hyper'realism** *n.* = PHOTOREALISM L20. **hyper'realist** *n.* a person who practises hyperrealism L20. **hyper'rhythmical** *a.* = HYPERMETRIC E17. **hyper'saline** *a.* (of natural water) more salty than typical seawater M20. **hypersa'linity** *n.* the condition of being hypersaline M20. **hyperse'crete** *v.i.* (*Med.*) produce an increased amount of secretion (chiefly as *hypersecreting* ppl a.) E20. **hyperse'cretion** *n.* (*Med.*) increased secretion M19. **hyper'sexed** *a.* having an exceptionally strong sexual instinct M20. **hyper'sexual** *a.* exhibiting or associated with hypersexuality M20. **hypersexu'ality** *n.* a condition in which the sexual instinct is exceptionally strong E20. **hyper'somnia** *n.* a condition in which a person has abnormally long or frequent periods of sleep, or sleeps abnormally deeply L19. **hyper'somnic** *a.* causing hypersomnia; hypersomnolent: E20. **hyper'somnolence** *a.* = HYPERSOMNIA L20. **hyper'somnolent** *a.* of or affected with hypersomnia M20. **hypersphere** *n.* (*Math.*) an analogue in four or more dimensions of a sphere in three dimensions E20. **hyper'spherical** *a.* (*Math.*) of or pertaining to a hypersphere L19. **hyper'splenic** *a.* (*Med.*) of or characterized by hypersplenism M20. **hyper'splenism** *n.* (*Med.*) a condition in which there is a reduced number of circulating blood cells accompanied by an enlarged spleen E20. **hyper'static** *a.* (of an engineering structure) having more members or supports than the minimum required for stability M20. **hyper'telorism** *n.* [Gk *tēle* at a distance + *orizein* to separate from] *Med.* a developmental abnormality in which the eyes are abnormally far apart E20. **hyper'tensin** *n.* (*Biochem.*) = ANGIOTENSIN M20. **hyper'thyroid** *a.* (*Med.*) affected with or symptomatic of hyperthyroidism E20. **hyperthy'roidic** *a.* (*Med.*) = HYPERTHYROID E20. **hyper'thyroidism** *n.* (*Med.*) a condition in which the thyroid produces more hormone than normal, resulting in an increased rate of metabolism and often loss of weight, restlessness, and emotional instability E20. **hypertrichosis** /-trɪ'kəʊsɪs/ *n.* [TRICHO-[1]] excessive growth of hair L19. **hypertriglyceri'daemia** *n.* (*Med.*) an abnormally high concentration of triglycerides in the blood M20. **hypertriglyceri'daemic** *a.* (*Med.*) of or affected with hypertriglyceridaemia M20. **hyper'tropia** *n.* (*Med.*) strabismus in which one eye is directed above or below the line of sight of the other L19. **hyper'urban** *a.* exhibiting hyperurbanism E20. **hyper'urbanism** *n.* a manner of speech arising from an effort to avoid provincialism; a hypercorrect form of speech or phrase resulting from this effort: E20. **hyperuri'caemia** *n.* (*Med.*) an abnormally high concentration of uric acid in the blood L19. **hyperuri'caemic** *a.* (*Med.*) of or affected with hyperuricaemia M20. **hyperve'locity** *n.* a speed that is very great; usu. *attrib.*: M20. **hypervitami'nosis** *n.*, pl. **-noses** /-'nəʊsiːz/, *Med.* any condition caused by an excessive intake of a vitamin, esp. over a prolonged period E20. **hyper'weak** *a.* (*Physics*) designating a hypothetical fifth interaction M20.

hyperacousis *n.* var. of HYPERACUSIS.

hyperactive /hʌɪpər'aktɪv/ *a.* M19. [f. HYPER- + ACTIVE.] Abnormally active, very active; *spec.* (of a person, esp. a child) unable to relax or be quiet.

hyperac'tivity *n.* L19.

hyperacusis /hʌɪpərə'k(j)uːsɪs/ *n.* Also **-cou-, -ku-, -usia** /-uːsɪə/. E19. [f. HYPER- + Gk *akousis* hearing.] Abnormally acute hearing, often with pain from moderately loud sounds.

hyperaemia /hʌɪpər'iːmɪə/ *n.* Also ***-rem-**. M19. [f. HYPER- + -AEMIA.] The presence of more than the normal amount of blood in a part of the body.

hyperaemic *a.* M19.

hyperaesthesia /hʌɪpəriːs'θiːzɪə, -ɛs'θiː-/ *n.* Also ***-res-**. M19. [f. HYPER- + Gk *aisthēsis* sensation: see -IA[1].] Abnormally great sensitivity of the body or mind, esp. of the skin.

hyperaesthetic /hʌɪpəriːs'θɛtɪk, -ɛs'θɛ-/ *a.* Also ***-res-**. M19. [f. HYPER- + Gk *aisthētikos*: see AESTHETIC.] 1 Characterized by hyperaesthesia. M19. 2 Excessively aesthetic. L19.

hyperakusis *n.* var. of HYPERACUSIS.

†hyperaspist *n.* E17–M18. [Gk *huperaspistēs*, f. *huperaspizein* hold a shield over, f. as HYPER- + *aspis* shield.] A defender, a champion.

hyperbaric /hʌɪpə'barɪk/ *a.* M20. [f. HYPER- + Gk *baros* heavy + -IC.] 1 *Med.* Of a solution for spinal anaesthesia: denser than cerebrospinal fluid. M20. 2 Designating, employing, or pertaining to gas at a greater pressure than its partial pressure in the atmosphere, or at greater than atmospheric pressure. M20.

2 *Offshore* A new record for hyperbaric welding . . at a simulated depth of 300 metres. L. OLIVIER Two surgeons . . decided that the best thing for me would be hyperbaric oxygen irradiation.

hyperbaton /hʌɪ'pəːbətɒn/ *n.* M16. [L f. Gk *huperbaton* overstepping, f. *huperbainein*, f. as HYPER- + *bainein* walk.] *Gram.* & *Rhet.* A figure of speech in which the logical order of words or phrases is inverted, esp. for the sake of emphasis.

hyperbola /hʌɪ'pəːbələ/ *n.* Pl. **-las, -lae** /-liː/. M17. [mod.L f. Gk *huperbolē*: see next.] *Math.* A conic section consisting of two identical curves formed where a plane intersects a double cone and makes a smaller angle with the axis of the cone than the side of the cone makes; either of these curves individually, which consist of two infinitely long arms that are asymptotic to two straight lines that intersect midway between the two curves; a curve that is the graph of an equation of the type $x^2/a^2 - y^2/b^2 = 1$.

hyperbole /hʌɪ'pəːbəli/ *n.* LME. [L f. Gk *huperbolē* excess, exaggeration, f. as HYPER- + *ballein* to throw.] 1 A figure of speech consisting in exaggerated or extravagant statement, used to express strong feeling or produce a strong impression and not meant to be taken literally; an instance of this. LME. **b** *gen.* Excess, extravagance. *rare.* M17. **†2** = HYPERBOLA. L16–E18.

1 G. K. CHESTERTON Received with extravagant but dignified bows, and hyperboles of thanks. T. COLLINS The place was a residence, but by no stretch of hyperbole could you call it a home.

hyperbolic /hʌɪpə'bɒlɪk/ *a.* M17. [Late L *hyperbolicus* f. Gk *huperbolikos*, f. *huperbolē* HYPERBOLE: see -IC.] **1** = HYPERBOLICAL 1. M17. **2** Of, belonging to, or of the form of a hyperbola; related mathematically to the hyperbola. L17.

2 *hyperbolic* COSINE. **hyperbolic function** each of a set of functions that bear the same algebraic relation to a rectangular hyperbola as the trigonometric functions do to a circle. **hyperbolic geometry** a non-Euclidean geometry defined so that a line may have more than one parallel through a given point. **hyperbolic navigation**: in which the position of a receiver is on the intersection of two hyperbolas, each determined by the difference at the receiver between signals transmitted in synchronism by one or other of two pairs of radio stations. *hyperbolic sine*: see SINE 2. *hyperbolic tangent*: see TANGENT *n.* 1.

hyperbolicity /-'lɪsɪti/ *n.* the property of being hyperbolic M20.

hyperbolical /hʌɪpə'bɒlɪk(ə)l/ *a.* LME. [f. as prec. + -AL[1].] **1** Of the nature of, involving, or using hyperbole; exaggerated, extravagant (in language or expression). LME. **†b** Extravagant in character or behaviour; excessive; enormous. L16–M19. **2** = HYPERBOLIC 2. M16.

hyperbolically *adv.* with hyperbole or exaggeration M16.

hyperbolism /hʌɪ'pəːbəlɪz(ə)m/ *n.* M17. [f. as next + -ISM. In sense 2 f. mod.L *hyperbolismus*.] **1** The use of or fondness for hyperbole; (an instance of) exaggerated style. M17. **2** *Math.* A curve whose equation is obtained from that of another curve by substituting *xy* for *y*. Now *rare.* M19.

hyperbolist *n.* a person given to the use of hyperbole M17.

hyperbolize /hʌɪ'pəːbəlʌɪz/ *v.* Also **-ise**. L16. [f. HYPERBOLE + -IZE.] **1** *v.i.* Use hyperbole; exaggerate. L16. **2** *v.t.* Express or represent hyperbolically, exaggerate. Formerly also, praise extravagantly. L16.

hyperboloid /hʌɪ'pəːbəlɔɪd/ *n.* M18. [f. HYPERBOLA + -OID.] *Math.* A curved solid or surface for which the cross-sections parallel to one axis are hyperbolas and those parallel to either of the other two axes are ellipses or circles.

hyperbo'loidal *a.* L19.

†Hyperboreal *a. rare.* L16–L18. [f. HYPER- + BOREAL.] = HYPERBOREAN *a.* 1.

Hyperborean /hʌɪpəbɔː'riːən, -'bɔːrɪən/ *n.* & *a.* LME. [Late L *hyperboreanus* = cl.L *hyperboreus* f. Gk *huperbore(i)os*, f. as HYPER- + *boreios* northern, *boreas* BOREAS: see -AN.] **A** *n.* A member of a race of people who in Greek mythology lived in a land of sunshine and plenty beyond the north wind, worshipping Apollo; (also **h-**) a person who lives in the extreme north of the earth. LME. **B** *adj.* **1** (Also **h-**.) Of, pertaining to, or characterizing the extreme north of the earth or (*joc.* & *colloq.*) of a particular country. L16. **2** Of or pertaining to the Hyperboreans of mythology. E17.

hyper-Calvinist /hʌɪpəˈkalvɪnɪst/ *n.* M19. [f. HYPER- + CALVINIST.] *Theol.* A person who holds a doctrine (esp. of predestination) more Calvinistic than Calvin's own.
hyper-Calvinism *n.* L19. **hyper-Calviˈnistic** *a.* L19.

hypercatalectic /ˌhʌɪpəkatəˈlɛktɪk/ *n.* & *a.* E17. [Late L *hypercatalecticus* f. Gk *huperkatalēktos*, f. as HYPER- + *katalēktikos*: see CATALECTIC.] †**A** *n.* A hypercatalectic line, verse, or colon. Only in E17. **B** *adj. Pros.* Of a line, verse, or colon: having an extra syllable after the last complete dipody. Of a syllable: constituting such a syllable. E18.

hypercharge /ˈhʌɪpətʃɑːdʒ/ *n.* M20. [f. *hyper(onic) charge.*] *Particle Physics.* A property of hadrons that is conserved in strong interactions, represented by a quantum number *Y* whose value for each particle of a charge multiplet is equal to twice the average charge quantum number of the multiplet.

hyperchromasia /hʌɪpəkrəˈmeɪzɪə/ *n.* L19. [f. HYPER- + -CHROMASIA.] **1** *Med.* **a** Excessive pigmentation of the skin. L19. **b** = HYPERCHROMIA. E20. **2** *Cytol.* The presence of an abnormally large amount of chromatin in a cell or nucleus. M20.
hyperchromatic /-ˈmat-/ *a.* characterized by or exhibiting hyperchromasia; hyperchromic: L19.

hyperchromatosis /ˌhʌɪpəkrəʊməˈtəʊsɪs/ *n.* Pl. **-toses** /-ˈtəʊsiːz/. L19. [f. HYPER- + CHROMATO-, CHROMAT(IN + -OSIS.] **1** *Cytol.* The presence of an abnormally large number of chromosomes or amount of chromatin in a nucleus; hyperchromasia. L19. **2** *Med.* = HYPERCHROMASIA 1a. L19.

hyperchromia /hʌɪpəˈkrəʊmɪə/ *n.* M20. [f. as next + -IA[1].] *Med.* A hyperchromic condition of the blood.

hyperchromic /hʌɪpəˈkrəʊmɪk/ *a.* L19. [f. HYPER- + Gk *khrōma* colour + -IC.] **1** *Cytol.* Characterized by or exhibiting hyperchromasia. L19. **2** *Med.* Characterized by or designating red cells that contain more than the usual amount of haemoglobin and show little central pallor. E20. **3** Characterized by or exhibiting an increase in the extent to which light, esp. ultraviolet light, is absorbed. M20.
hyperchromicity /-ˈmɪs-/ *n.* the property of being hyperchromic M20.

hypercritic /hʌɪpəˈkrɪtɪk/ *n.* & *a.* L16. [mod.L *hypercriticus*, f. as CRITIC *n.*[1]: see HYPER-.] **A** *n.* †**1** Hypercriticism; a minute criticism; a critique. L16–M18. **2** A hypercritical person. Formerly, a master critic. M17. **B** *adj.* = HYPERCRITICAL. E19.

hypercritical /hʌɪpəˈkrɪtɪk(ə)l/ *a.* E17. [f. HYPER- + CRITICAL.] Apt to give excessive adverse criticism, esp. on trivial points; extremely or unduly critical.
hyperˈcritically *adv.* E18.

hypercriticism /hʌɪpəˈkrɪtɪsɪz(ə)m/ *n.* L17. [f. HYPER- + CRITICISM.] Excessive criticism; criticism that is unduly severe.

hypercriticize /hʌɪpəˈkrɪtɪsʌɪz/ *v.t.* & *i.* Also **-ise**. E18. [f. HYPER- + CRITICIZE.] Criticize excessively or unduly; be hypercritical.

hyperdisyllable /hʌɪpəˈdʌɪsɪləb(ə)l/ *n.* & *a.* L17. [f. HYPER- + DISYLLABLE. Cf. late Gk *huperdisullabos*.] (A word) consisting of more than two syllables.

hyperdrive /ˈhʌɪpədrʌɪv/ *n.* M20. [f. HYPER- + DRIVE *n.*, perh. suggested by HYPERSPACE, OVERDRIVE *n.*] In science fiction: a fictitious device by which a spaceship is enabled to travel to a distant point in a shorter time than light would take to reach it; the state of so travelling.

hyperdulia /hʌɪpədjʊˈlʌɪə/ *n.* M16. [med.L *hyperdulia*, f. as HYPER-, DULIA.] *RC Ch.* The veneration properly given to the Virgin Mary, higher than dulia but less than latria.
hyperdulic *a.* of the nature of hyperdulia M19. **hyperdulical** *a.* = HYPERDULIC M17.

hyperemia *n.* see HYPERAEMIA.

hyperesthesia *n.*, **-esthetic** *a.* see HYPERAESTHESIA etc.

hypergelast /hʌɪˈpəːdʒɪlast/ *n.* L19. [f. HYPER- + Gk *gelastēs* laugher, f. *gelan* to laugh.] A person who laughs excessively.

hypergol /ˈhʌɪpəgɒl/ *n.* M20. [G, prob. f. Gk *ergon* work + -OL.] A hypergolic rocket propellant.
hyperˈgolic *a.* (of a propellant) igniting spontaneously on contact with the oxidizer or another propellant M20.

hypericum /hʌɪˈpɛrɪkəm/ *n.* Also †**-con**. LME. [L *hypericum*, *-con* f. Gk *hupereikon*, f. *huper* over + *ereikē* heath.] **1** Any of various herbaceous plants or small shrubs of the genus *Hypericum* (family Guttiferae), with pentamerous usu. yellow flowers, stamens in bundles, and leaves usu. with glandular dots beneath. Also called *St John's wort, rose of Sharon.* LME. †**2** A medicinal preparation made from this plant. LME–L17.

hyperinosis /hʌɪpərɪˈnəʊsɪs/ *n.* Now *rare* or *obs.* Pl. **-noses** /-ˈnəʊsiːz/. M19. [f. HYPER- + Gk *inos*, *is* fibre + -OSIS.] *Med.* An abnormally high concentration of fibrinogen in the blood.
hyperinotic /-ˈnɒtɪk/ *a.* M19.

hypermarket /ˈhʌɪpəmɑːkɪt/ *n.* L20. [f. HYPER- + MARKET *n.* as tr. F *hypermarché*, f. *marché* market, after *supermarché* SUPERMARKET.] A very large self-service shop or complex of shops that sells a wide range of goods and is usually sited outside a town near a large car park.

hypermedia /hʌɪpəˈmiːdɪə/ *n.* M20. [f. HYPER- + MEDIA *n.*[2]] *Computing.* A method of structuring information in different media for presentation to a user (usu. via a workstation) whereby related items of information are interconnected. Cf. HYPERTEXT.

hypermetric /hʌɪpəˈmɛtrɪk/ *a.* M19. [f. HYPER- + METRIC *a.*[2]] *Pros.* (Of a verse or line) containing an extra syllable; designating such a syllable.
Also **hyperˈmetrical** *a.* M18.

hypermetropia /hʌɪpəmɪˈtrəʊpɪə/ *n.* M19. [f. Gk *hupermetros* beyond measure (f. as HYPER- + *metron* measure) + -OPIA.] The condition in which rays from distant objects are focused behind the retina instead of on it when the eye is relaxed, and the eye cannot be focused on objects near it; long-sightedness.
hyperˈmetrope *n.* a person with hypermetropia M19. **hypermetropic** /-ˈtrəʊpɪk, -ˈtrɒpɪk/ *a.* pertaining to or affected with hypermetropia M19.

hypernym /ˈhʌɪpənɪm/ *n.* L20. [f. HYPER- after *hyponym*.] *Ling.* A word whose meaning is implied by another and in terms of which the other word can be defined (e.g. *building* in relation to *house* or *hotel*).

hyperon /ˈhʌɪp(ə)rɒn/ *n.* M20. [f. HYPER- + -ON.] *Particle Physics.* A baryon other than a proton or neutron.
xi hyperon: see XI 2.
hypeˈronic *a.* M20.

hyperoodon /hʌɪpərˈəʊədɒn/ *n.* M19. [f. Gk *huperōios* superior or *huperōiē* palate + -ODON.] A bottlenose whale (genus *Hyperoodon*).

hyperopia /hʌɪpərˈəʊpɪə/ *n.* L19. [f. HYPER- + -OPIA.] = HYPERMETROPIA.
hyperope /ˈhʌɪpərəʊp/ *n.* = HYPERMETROPE M20. **hyperopic** /-ˈɒpɪk/ *a.* L19.

hyperostosis /hʌɪpərɒˈstəʊsɪs/ *n.* Pl. **-stoses** /-ˈstəʊsiːz/. M19. [f. HYPER- + Gk *osteon*, *osto-* bone + -OSIS.] A non-tumorous localized overgrowth of bone; excessive production of bone tissue.
hyperostotic /-ˈstɒtɪk/ *a.* M19.

hyperoxygenate /hʌɪpərˈɒksɪdʒəneɪt/ *v.t.* L18. [f. HYPER- + OXYGENATE.] Cause to contain or (now *rare*) combine with an increased proportion of oxygen; supersaturate (blood) with oxygen. Chiefly as *hyperoxygenated* pa. pple.
W. GOLDING The Dôle and the hyperoxygenated air did their work and I fell asleep.
hyperoxygeˈnation *n.* the action of hyperoxygenating something; the state of being hyperoxygenated: L18.

hyperparasite /hʌɪpəˈparəsʌɪt/ *n.* L19. [f. HYPER- + PARASITE *n.*] *Biol.* A parasite whose host is itself a parasite.
hyperparaˈsitic *a.* parasitic on or in a parasite M19. **hyperparasitism** *n.* the condition of being hyperparasitic L19.

hyperper /ˈhʌɪpəːpə/ *n.* L16. [med.L *hyperperum*, *-pyrum* f. Gk *huperpuron*, f. as HYPER- + *pur* FIRE *n.*] The Byzantine gold solidus.

hyperphysical /hʌɪpəˈfɪzɪk(ə)l/ *a.* E17. [f. HYPER- + PHYSICAL.] Above or beyond what is physical; supernatural.

hyperplasia /hʌɪpəˈpleɪzɪə/ *n.* M19. [f. HYPER- + -PLASIA.] *Med.* Enlargement of tissue (usu. abnormal but non-tumorous) as a result of an increase in the number of cells. Cf. HYPERTROPHY *n.*
hyperplastic /-ˈplastɪk/ *a.* exhibiting or accompanied by hyperplasia L19.

hyperpnoea /hʌɪpəpˈniːə/ *n.* Also ***-pnea**. M19. [f. HYPER- + Gk *pnoē* breathing: see -A[1].] Deep or rapid breathing.
hyperpnoeic *a.* of or exhibiting hyperpnoea E20.

hypersensitise *v.* var. of HYPERSENSITIZE.

hypersensitive /hʌɪpəˈsɛnsɪtɪv/ *a.* L19. [f. HYPER- + SENSITIVE.] **1** Sensitive to an abnormal or excessive degree; (of a person) easily hurt or offended, oversensitive. L19. **2** *Med.* Of an individual: having an adverse bodily reaction to a particular substance in doses that do not affect most individuals. L19. **3** Of a photographic film etc.: hypersensitized. M20.
hypersensitiveness *n.* L19. **hypersensiˈtivity** *n.* E20.

hypersensitize /hʌɪpəˈsɛnsɪtʌɪz/ *v.t.* Also **-ise**. L19. [f. HYPER- + SENSITIZE.] Make hypersensitive; *Photogr.* increase the speed of (a film etc.) by a special process before it is used.
ˌhypersensitiˈzation *n.* the action or process of hypersensitizing someone or something; the state of being hypersensitized: E20.

hypersonic /hʌɪpəˈsɒnɪk/ *a.* M20. [f. HYPER- + SONIC, after *supersonic*, *ultrasonic*.] **1** Designating, of, or pertaining to sound waves or vibrations with a frequency greater than about 1000 million Hz. M20. **2** Designating, involving, or pertaining to speeds greater than about five times the speed of sound; (of aircraft) able to fly at such speeds. Cf. SUPERSONIC. M20.
hypersonically *adv.* at a hypersonic speed L20. **hypersonics** *n.* the branch of science and technology that deals with hypersonic phenomena, esp. hypersonic flight M20.

hyperspace /ˈhʌɪpəspeɪs/ *n.* M19. [f. HYPER- + SPACE *n.*] **1** Space of more than three dimensions; any non-Euclidean space. M19. **2** *Sci. Fiction.* A hypothetical space-time continuum, through which motion and communication at effective speeds greater than that of light are supposed to be possible. Also called *subspace*. M20.
2 D. ADAMS An old drinking game that Ford learned to play in the hyperspace ports . . in the star system of Orion Beta.
hyperˈspatial *a.* of or occurring in hyperspace E20. **hyperspatiˈality** *n.* the property of being hyperspatial; travel in hyperspace: E20.

hypersthene /ˈhʌɪpəsθiːn/ *n.* E19. [Fr. *hyperstène*, f. as next, from its being harder than hornblende.] *Min.* A rock-forming orthorhombic silicate of magnesium and ferrous iron that is a member of the pyroxene group and is green, yellow, brown, or black in colour.
hypersthenite *n.* orig., norite; now, a pyroxenite composed almost wholly of hypersthene: M19.

hypersthenia /hʌɪpəsˈθiːnɪə/ *n.* M19. [f. HYPER- + Gk *sthenos* strength + -IA[1].] An abnormal degree of bodily strength or vitality.

hypersthenic /hʌɪpəsˈθɛnɪk/ *a.*[1] M19. [f. HYPERSTHENE + -IC.] *Min.* Pertaining to or containing hypersthene.

hypersthenic /hʌɪpəsˈθɛnɪk/ *a.*² L19. [f. HYPERSTHENIA + -IC.] Exhibiting or characterized by hypersthenia.

hypertely /hʌɪˈpəːtɪli, ˈhʌɪpətɛli/ *n.* L19. [G *Hypertelie*, f. Gk *huperteleios* beyond completeness, f. as HYPER- + *telos* end.] *Zool.* Extreme development of a characteristic beyond the degree to which it is apparently useful.
hyperˈtelic *a.* M20.

hypertension /hʌɪpəˈtɛnʃ(ə)n/ *n.* L19. [f. HYPER- + TENSION *n.*] **1** Abnormally or excessively high pressure of arterial blood or intra-ocular fluid, *spec.* the former. L19. **2** A state of great emotional or nervous tension. M20.
1 B. EMECHETA They were .. sending themselves to early graves with hypertension.
hypertensive *a.* & *n.* (*a*) *adj.* of, exhibiting, or associated with hypertension; tending to increase a person's blood pressure; (*b*) *n.* a person with (arterial) hypertension: E20.

hypertext /ˈhʌɪpətɛkst/ *n.* M20. [f. HYPER- + TEXT *n.*] *Computing.* A body of text, graphic material, etc., stored in a machine-readable form and structured in such a way that a reader can cross-refer between related items of information.
hyperˈtextual *a.* L20.

hyperthermia /hʌɪpəˈθəːmɪə/ *n.* L19. [f. HYPER- + Gk *thermē* heat + -IA¹.] The condition of having a body temperature substantially above the normal, whether through natural causes or artificially induced.
hyperthermic *a.* of or exhibiting hyperthermia L19.

hypertonia /hʌɪpəˈtəʊnɪə/ *n.* M19. [f. HYPER- + Gk *tonos* TONE *n.* + -IA¹.] *Med.* The condition of being hypertonic.

hypertonic /hʌɪpəˈtɒnɪk/ *a.* M19. [f. HYPER- + TONIC *a.*] **1** *Med.* (Of muscle) in a state of abnormally great tone or tension; of or characterized by muscle in such a state. M19. **2** *Physiol.* Having a higher osmotic pressure than some particular fluid (usually that in a cell, or a body fluid). L19.
hypertonicity /-ˈnɪsɪti/ *n.* the condition of being hypertonic; the extent to which a solution has a higher osmotic pressure than another: L19.

hypertonus /hʌɪpəˈtəʊnəs/ *n.* L19. [f. HYPER- + TONUS.] **1** Hypertension of the intra-ocular fluid. Now *rare*. L19. **2** = HYPERTONIA. E20.

hypertrophy /hʌɪˈpəːtrəfi/ *n.* & *v.* M19. [f. HYPER- + -TROPHY.] **A** *n.* Enlargement of tissue (usu. abnormal but non-tumorous), now *spec.* as a result of an increase in the size of cells (cf. HYPERPLASIA); *fig.* excessive development. M19.
I. DEUTSCHER We have here a historic hypertrophy of practice and an atrophy of thought.
B *v.* **1** *v.t.* Affect with hypertrophy. Now *rare*. M19. **2** *v.i.* Undergo hypertrophy. L19.
hypertrophic /-ˈtrɒfɪk, -ˈtrəʊfɪk/ *a.* of the nature of, affected with, or producing hypertrophy M19. **hypertrophically** /-ˈtrɒf-, -ˈtrəʊf-/ *adv.* in a hypertrophic manner, to a hypertrophic degree L19. **hypertrophied** *a.* affected with hypertrophy; *fig.* overgrown, excessive: M19. **hypertrophous** *a.* (now *rare*) affected with hypertrophy M19.

hyperventilate /hʌɪpəˈvɛntɪleɪt/ *v.* M20. [f. HYPER- + VENTILATE, or back-form. f. HYPERVENTILATION.] **1** *v.i.* Breathe deeply or rapidly. M20. **2** *v.t.* Produce hyperventilation in. M20.
ˌhyperventiˈlation *n.* an increased or excessive exposure of the lungs to oxygen, resulting in an increased loss of carbon dioxide from the blood; the action of bringing this about: E20.

hypethral *a.* var. of HYPAETHRAL.

hypha /ˈhʌɪfə/ *n.* Pl. **-phae** /-fiː/. M19. [mod.L f. Gk *huphē* web.] A filament in the mycelium of a fungus; any of the vertical unbranched filaments in the medulla of certain brown algae, believed to be conducting elements.
hyphal *a.* L19.

hyphaema /hʌɪˈfiːmə/ *n.* Also ***-phema**. L19. [f. HYPO- + Gk *haima* blood.] *Med.* The presence of blood in the anterior chamber of the eye, in front of the iris.

hyphen /ˈhʌɪf(ə)n/ *n.* & *v.* E17. [Late L f. late Gk *huphen* the sign ˘, use as n. of *huphen* together, f. *huph-*, *hupo* HYPO- + *hen* neut. of *heis* one.] **A** *n.* **1** A punctuation mark used to connect two words together, to indicate the division of a word between two successive lines, and to indicate a missing or implied element, and now represented as a short raised horizontal line. E17. **2** *transf.* A short pause between two syllables in speaking. M19. **3** A narrow connecting link or passage. M19.
1 DAY LEWIS I do not use the hyphen in my surname. *double hyphen*: see DOUBLE *a.* & *adv.* *soft hyphen*: see SOFT *a.*
B *v.t.* Join by a hyphen; write (a compound) with a hyphen. E19.
hyphenless *a.* M20.

hyphenate /ˈhʌɪfəneɪt/ *v.t.* L19. [f. HYPHEN + -ATE³.] = HYPHEN *v.*
hyphenated *ppl a.* (*a*) joined by a hyphen; (*b*) designating a person with dual nationality or mixed background or ancestry (describable by a hyphenated term such as *Anglo-American*), and any person whose patriotic allegiance is assumed to be divided: M19.

hyphenation /hʌɪfəˈneɪʃ(ə)n/ *n.* L19. [f. prec. + -ATION.] The use of the hyphen to join words or divide a word; *esp.* in printing, the division of words at the end of lines, marked with hyphens.

hyphenism /ˈhʌɪfənɪz(ə)m/ *n.* *US.* E20. [f. HYPHEN + -ISM.] The state of being a hyphenated American; the attitude or conduct implied by this.

hyphenize /ˈhʌɪfənʌɪz/ *v.t.* Also **-ise**. M19. [f. HYPHEN + -IZE.] = HYPHEN *v.*
hypheniˈzation *n.* = HYPHENATION M19.

hyphomycete /hʌɪfə(ʊ)ˈmʌɪsiːt/ *n.* Orig. only in pl. **-mycetes** /-ˈmʌɪsiːts, -mʌɪˈsiːtiːz/. M19. [Anglicized sing. of mod.L *Hyphomycetes* (see below), f. Gk *huphē* web + *mukētes* fungi.] *Mycol.* An imperfect fungus of the class Hyphomycetes, comprising filamentous moulds that bear naked asexual spores.
hyphomyˈcetous *a.* L19.

hypidiomorphic /hɪˌpɪdɪəˈmɔːfɪk/ *a.* L19. [f. HYP- + IDIOMORPHIC.] Of a rock texture or rock mineral: characterized by crystals that are incompletely developed.

hypinosis /hɪpɪˈnəʊsɪs/ *n.* Now *rare* or *obs.* Pl. **-noses** /-ˈnəʊsiːz/. M19. [f. HYP- + Gk *inos*, *is* fibre + -OSIS.] *Med.* An abnormally low concentration of fibrinogen in the blood.

hypna *n.* pl. of HYPNUM.

hypnagogic /hɪpnəˈgɒgɪk, -ˈgɒdʒɪk/ *a.* Also **hypno-**. L19. [Fr. *hypnagogique*, f. as HYPNO- + Gk *agōgos* leading, f. *agein* lead: see -IC.] That accompanies the process of falling asleep.

†hypnale *n.* LME–M18. [Late L *hypnale* f. Gk *hupnaleē* fem. of *hupnaleos* sending to sleep, f. *hupnos* sleep.] A snake whose bite was supposed to induce a fatal sleep.

hypno- /ˈhɪpnəʊ/ *comb. form* of Gk *hupnos* sleep, also used in the sense 'hypnosis, hypnotism': see -O-.
hypnoaˈnalysis *n.* psychoanalysis performed while the subject is hypnotized; = HYPNOTHERAPY *n.* below: E20. **hypnoanaˈlytic** *a.* of or involving hypnoanalysis E20. **hypnoˈanalyst** *n.* a person who uses hypnoanalysis M20. **hypnoˈgenic** *a.* producing hypnosis; producing sleep: L19. **hypˈnology** *n.* the science of the phenomena of sleep and hypnosis M19. **hypnoˈlogical** *a.* of or pertaining to hypnology M19. **hypˈnologist** *n.* an expert in hypnology M19. **hypnoˈpaedia** *n.* [Gk *paideia* education] learning by being exposed to spoken lessons while asleep; teaching by this method: M20. **hypnoˈpaedic** *a.* of or involving hypnopaedia M20. **hypnoˈpompic** *a.* [Gk *pompē* sending away] that accompanies the process of waking up E20. **hypnotheraˈpeutic** *a.* of or involving hypnotherapy L19. **hypnoˈtherapist** *n.* a person who uses hypnotherapy M20. **hypnoˈtherapy** *n.* psychotherapy that involves the use of hypnotism L19.

hypnogogic *a.* var. of HYPNAGOGIC.

hypnoid /ˈhɪpnɔɪd/ *a.* L19. [f. HYPNO- + -OID.] *Psychol.* Designating a state of consciousness marked by heightened suggestibility.
Also **hypˈnoidal** *a.* L19.

hypnosis /hɪpˈnəʊsɪs/ *n.* L19. [f. HYPNO- + -OSIS.] **1** A state of consciousness in which a person appears to lose all power of voluntary action or thought and to be highly responsive to suggestions and directions from the hypnotist. L19. **2** Artificially produced sleep or sleepiness. L19.
1 D. ADAMS You have been under hypnosis for a little less than an hour.

hypnotic /hɪpˈnɒtɪk/ *a.* & *n.* E17. [Fr. *hypnotique* f. late L *hypnoticus* f. Gk *hupnōtikos* putting to sleep, narcotic, f. *hupnoun* put to sleep, f. *hupnos* sleep: see -IC.] **A** *adj.* **1** Inducing sleep; soporific. E17. **2** Of, pertaining to, or of the nature of hypnosis; accompanied by or producing hypnosis. M19. **3** Susceptible to hypnotism; hypnotizable. L19.
2 D. DELILLO He bobbed his head, speaking in a soft hypnotic singsong. U. BENTLEY We all slowly came to out of a hypnotic trance.
B *n.* **1** An agent that produces sleep; *spec.* a sedative or soporific drug. L17. **2** A person under or open to the influence of hypnotism. L19.
hypnotically *adv.* in a hypnotic manner; by means of hypnotism: L17.

hypnotise *v.* var. of HYPNOTIZE.

hypnotism /ˈhɪpnətɪz(ə)m/ *n.* M19. [Orig. coined as *neuro-hypnotism*, f. NEURO- + HYPNOT(IC + -ISM, and shortened a year later.] **1** The action or process of hypnotizing a person; the branch of knowledge that deals with this and with the hypnotic state. M19. **2** = HYPNOSIS 1. M19. **3** = HYPNOSIS 2. M19.

hypnotist /ˈhɪpnətɪst/ *n.* M19. [f. as prec. + -IST.] A person who studies or practises hypnotism; a hypnotizer.

hypnotize /ˈhɪpnətʌɪz/ *v.t.* Also **-ise**. M19. [f. as prec. + -IZE.] **1** Put into a hypnotic state. M19. **2** Fascinate, beguile; capture the mind or fancy of; lead *into* something as if by hypnosis. L19.
2 A. COOKE The press was simply hypnotised by long habit into seeing .. no idiosyncrasy in the Royal Family. F. HOWERD Absolutely hypnotised by the fairyland magic of *Cinderella*.
hypnotizaˈbility *n.* L19. **hypnotizable** *a.* L19. **hypnotiˈzation** *n.* (now *rare*) the action or process of hypnotizing a person; the state of being hypnotized: L19. **hypnotizer** *n.* a hypnotist L19.

hypnum /ˈhɪpnəm/ *n.* Pl. **-na** /-nə/, **-nums**. M18. [mod.L (see below), f. Gk *hupnon* a kind of lichen.] Any of various pleurocarpous mosses of the genus *Hypnum* (order Hypnobryales), which form dense green mats on tree-trunks, in grassland, etc.

†hypo *n.*¹ E18–M19. [Abbrev. of HYPOCHONDRIA. Cf. HIP *n.*³] Depression, low spirits.

hypo /ˈhʌɪpəʊ/ *n.*² M19. [Abbrev. of HYPOSULPHITE.] Sodium thiosulphate as used as a fixer in photography.

hypo /ˈhʌɪpəʊ/ *n.*³ & *v.* *slang.* E20. [Abbrev. of HYPODERMIC. Cf. HYPE *n.*² & *v.*²] **A** *n.* Pl. **-os**. A hypodermic needle or injection; a drug addict. E20. **B** *v.t.* & *i.* Administer a hypodermic injection (to); *fig.* stimulate. E20.

hypo- /ˈhʌɪpəʊ/ *comb. form.* Bef. a vowel also **hyp-** /hʌɪp/. [Gk *hup(o)-*, f. *hupo* prep. & adv., under.] **1** Under, underneath, below; prepositionally, as *hypodermic* ('under the skin'); adverbially, as *hypoblast* ('a layer underneath'). **b** *Mus.* In names of modes, denoting (*a*) each of a set of modes in ancient Greek music which began at a definite interval below the ordinary Aeolian etc. modes; (*b*) the plagal modes in medieval music, which have a compass a fourth below that of the corresponding authentic modes. **2** Slightly, slight, partial; as *hypomania*, *hypoplasia*. **3** Less than, as *hypoploid*; (esp. *Med.*) less than normal, as *hypoacidity*; to a lesser degree, as *hyposensitize*. **b** *Chem.* In ns. and adjs. denoting a compound that contains an element in lower oxidation state or has a lower oxygen content, as *hypochlorous*.
hypoaˈcidity *n.* abnormally low acidity, esp. of gastric juice E20. **hypoˈactive** *a.* (*Med.*) exhibiting hypoactivity M20. **hypoacˈtivity** *n.* (*Med.*) diminished activity, *esp.* diminished secretory activity of a gland E20. **hypoaesˈthesia** *n.* = HYPAESTHESIA E20. **hypoalˈgesia** *n.* = HYPALGESIA E20. **hypoˈbaric** *a.* (*Med.*) (of a solution for spinal anaesthesia) less dense than cerebrospinal fluid M20. **hypoblast** *n.* (*Biol.*) endoderm, *esp.* that of an embryo L19. **hypoˈblastic** *a.* (*Biol.*) of or pertaining to the hypoblast L19. **hypoˈbranchial** *a.* (*Zool.*) situated below the gills M19. **hypoˈbromite** *n.* (*Chem.*) a salt of hypobromous acid M19. **hypoˈbromous** *a.* (*Chem.*): *hypobromous acid*, an unstable acid, HBrO, that has strong oxidizing

properties and is used as a bactericide M19. **hypocal'caemia** *n.* (*Med.*) an abnormally low concentration of calcium in the blood E20. **hypocal'caemic** *a.* (*Med.*) of or affected with hypocalcaemia M20. **hypo'capnia** *n.* [Gk *kapnos* smoke] *Med.* an abnormally low concentration of carbon dioxide in the blood E20. **hypo'capnic** *a.* (*Med.*) of, pertaining to, or affected with hypocapnia L20. **hypo'cellular** *a.* (*Med.*) exhibiting hypocellularity M20. **hypocellu'larity** *n.* (*Med.*) a diminution in the number of cells present at a site in the body M20. **hypochlor'hydria** *n.* (*Med.*) an abnormally low concentration of hydrochloric acid in the gastric juice L19. **hypochlor'hydric** *a.* (*Med.*) of, pertaining to, or characterized by hypochlorhydria E20. **hypocone** *n.* (*Zool.*) a cusp on the posterior lingual corner of the tribosphenic upper molar tooth L19. **hypo'conid** *n.* (*Zool.*) a cusp on the posterior buccal corner of the tribosphenic lower molar tooth L19. **hypocotyl** /-'kɒtɪl/ *n.* the part of the stem of an embryo plant beneath the stalks of the cotyledons and directly above the root L19. **hypodigm** /-dʌɪm, -dɪm/ *n.* [Gk *hupodeigma* example] *Taxon.* the material on which the description of a species is based M20. **hypo'diploid** *a.* & *n.* (*Genetics*) (*a*) *adj.* having one or a few chromosomes less than the number in a diploid set; containing such cells; (*b*) *n.* a hypodiploid individual: M20. **hypo'diploidy** *n.* (*Genetics*) the condition of being hypodiploid M20. **hypo'dorian** *a.* & *n.* (*Mus.*) (designating) a mode with a lower range than the Dorian but the same final M17. **hypoeu'tectic** *a.* (of an alloy of iron) containing less carbon than the 4.3 per cent present in the eutectic composition E20. **hypoeu'tectoid** *a.* (of steel) containing less carbon than the 0.8 per cent present in the eutectoid composition E20. **hypofunction** *n.* & *v.* (*Med.*) (*a*) *n.* diminished or insufficient activity or production in a gland etc.; (*b*) *v.i.* exhibit hypofunction: E20. **hypo'functional** *a.* (*Med.*) exhibiting hypofunction M20. **hypogamma,globuli'naemia** *n.* (*Med.*) an abnormally low concentration of gamma globulins in the blood M20. **hy'pogamous** *a.* (*Anthropol.*) of or pertaining to hypogamy M20. **hy'pogamy** *n.* (*Anthropol.*) (the custom of) marriage to a person, esp. a husband, of lower social standing M20. **hypogeusia** /-'gjuːzɪə, -sɪə/ *n.* [Gk *geusis* taste] *Med.* diminished acuteness of the sense of taste L19. **hypogly'caemia** *n.* (*Med.*) an abnormally low concentration of sugar in the blood L19. **hypogly'caemic** *a.* & *n.* (*Med.*) (*a*) *adj.* pertaining to or characterized by hypoglycaemia; (of a drug etc.) promoting the reduction of blood-sugar levels; (*b*) *n.* a hypoglycaemic person: E20. **hy'pognathous** *a.* (*a*) (of a bird or a bird's bill) having the lower mandible longer than the upper; (*b*) (of an insect) having the head ventral and the mouth directed ventrally: L19. **hypo'gonadal** *a.* (*Med.*) characterized by hypogonadism M20. **hypo'gonadism** *n.* (*Med.*) reduction or absence of gonadal activity, esp. of hormone secretion E20. **hypogonadotrophic** /-'trəʊfɪk, -'trɒfɪk/ *a.* (*Med.*) caused or characterized by a diminished secretion of gonadotrophic hormones M20. **hypoka'laemia** *n.* [mod.L *kalium* potassium] *Med.* an abnormally low concentration of potassium in the blood M20. **hypoka'laemic** *a.* (*Med.*) characterized by hypokalaemia M20. **hypoki'nesis** *n.* (*Med.*) an abnormally reduced amount of muscular or bodily activity L19. **hypoki'netic** *a.* (*Med.*) characterized by hypokinesis L19. **hypolem'niscus** *n.* a critical mark in the form of a lemniscus without its upper dot E18. **hypo'lydian** *a.* & *n.* (*Mus.*) (designating) a mode with a lower range than the Lydian mode but the same final E17. **hypomagne'saemia** *n.* (*Med.* & *Vet. Med.*) an abnormally low concentration of magnesium in the blood, important in cattle as the cause of grass tetany M20. **hypomagne'saemic** *a.* (*Med.* & *Vet. Med.*) caused or characterized by hypomagnesaemia M20. **hypo'mania** *n.* (*Psychiatry*) a mild form of mania, characterized by elation and quickness of thought and often occurring as part of the cycle of manic depressive illness of cyclothymia L19. **hypo'maniac** *n.* (*Psychiatry*) = HYPOMANIC *n.* below E20. **hypomanic** *a.* & *n.* (*Psychiatry*) (*a*) *adj.* of or affected with hypomania; (*b*) *n.* a hypomanic person: E20. **hypomixo'lydian** *a.* & *n.* (*Mus.*) (designating) a mode with a lower range than the mixolydian but the same final M18. **hypomorph** *n.* (*Genetics*) an allele that is functionally less effective than a corresponding wild-type allele M20. **hypo'morphic** *a.* (*Genetics*) designating, of, or pertaining to a hypomorph M20. **hypo'nastic** *a.* (*Bot.*) characterized by hyponasty L19. **hyponasty** *n.* [Gk *nastos* pressed] *Bot.* a tendency in part of a plant to grow more rapidly on the underside, so that it curves upwards L19. **hypona'traemia** *n.* (*Med.*) an abnormally low concentration of sodium in the blood M20. **hypona'traemic** *a.* (*Med.*) characterized by hyponatraemia M20. **hyponome** /'hɪpənəʊm/ *n.* [Gk *huponomē* underground passage] *Zool.* the funnel through which a cephalopod expels a jet of water as a means of locomotion L19. **hypopara'thyroid** *a.* (*Med.*) of, affected with, or accompanied by hypoparathyroidism E20. **hypopara'thyroidism** *n.* (*Med.*) a condition in which there is an abnormally low concentration of parathyroid hormone in the blood, resulting in hypocalcaemia and hypophosphataemia with consequent tetany and other signs of neuromuscular excitability E20. **hypopha'langism, -'phalangy** *ns.* (*Med.* & *Zool.*) the absence of one or more digital phalanges E20. **hypo'phoria** *n.* (*Med.*) latent strabismus in which there is a tendency for one eye to be directed below the line of sight of the other M20. **hypophospha'taemia** *n.* (*Med.*) an abnormally low concentration of phosphate (or other phosphorus compounds) in the blood M20. **hypophospha'taemic** *a.* (*Med.*) pertaining to or characterized by hypophosphataemia M20. **hypo'phosphate** *n.* (*Chem.*) a salt of hypophosphoric acid M19. **hypo'phosphite** *n.* (*Chem.*) a salt of hypophosphorous acid E19. **hypophos'phoric** *a.* (*Chem.*) designating an unstable tetrabasic crystalline acid, $H_4P_2O_6$ M19. **hypo'phosphorous** *a.* (*Chem.*) designating a monobasic acid, H_3PO_2, that is a colourless oily liquid or a deliquescent crystalline solid E19. **hypo'phrygian** *a.* & *n.* (*Mus.*) (designating) a mode with a lower range than the Phrygian but the same final M17. **hypopi'tuitarism** *n.* (*Med.*) diminished hormone secretion by the pituitary E20. **hypopi'tuitary** *a.* (*Med.*) of, pertaining to, or affected with hypopituitarism E20. **hypoploid** *a.* & *n.* (*Genetics*) (*a*) *adj.* having one or a few chromosomes missing from a haploid or polyploid set; containing such cells; (*b*) *n.* a hypoploid individual: M20. **hypoploidy** *n.* (*Genetics*) the condition of being hypoploid M20. **hypose'cretion** *n.* (*Med.*) diminished secretion E20. **hy'posmia** *n.* (*Med.*) a poor or non-existent sense of smell L19. **hypo'splenic** *a.* (*Med.*) of or characterized by hyposplenism M20. **hypo'splenism** *n.* (*Med.*) a condition in which there is hypofunction of the spleen and a changed blood picture E20. **hypostome** *n.* [Gk *stoma* mouth] *Zool.* any of several structures associated with the mouth in different invertebrates M19. **hypostyle** *a.* having a roof supported by pillars M19. **hypo'thallus** *n.* (*Bot.*) (*a*) the layer of filaments on which the thallus of a lichen is developed; (*b*) the sheetlike base of the fruiting body of a myxomycete: M19. **hypo'thecium** *n.* (*Bot.*) a mass of hyphae filling the lower part of the apothecium of a discomycetous fungus M19. **hypo'thyroid** *a.* (*Med.*) affected with or symptomatic of hypothyroidism E20. **hypothy'roidic** *a.* (*Med.*) = HYPOTHYROID E20. **hypo'thyroidism** *n.* (*Med.*) a condition in which the thyroid produces less hormone than normal, resulting in a reduced rate of metabolism and in severe cases cretinism (if congenital) or myxoedema (if acquired) E20. **hypotrichosis** /-trɪ'kəʊsɪs/ *n.* [TRICHO-[1]] partial or complete absence of hair L19. **hypotrichous** /hɪ'pɒtrɪkəs/ *a.* (*Zool.*) designating ciliates belonging to the order Hypotricha of the order Spirotricha, characterized by cilia largely restricted to the ventral surface L19. **hypo'trochoid** *n.* a curve traced by a point on a radius or extended radius of a circle that rolls inside another circle M19. **hypoventi'lation** *n.* a diminished or insufficient exposure of the lungs to oxygen, resulting in a reduced oxygen content or an increased carbon dioxide content of the blood M20. **hypovitami'nosis** *n.*, pl. **-noses** /-'nəʊsiːz/, *Med.* any condition caused by a vitamin deficiency in the diet E20. **hypovo'laemia** *n.* (*Med.*) a decreased volume of circulating blood in the body E20. **hypovo'laemic** *a.* (*Med.*) affected or associated with hypovolaemia M20. **hypo'xaemia** *n.* (*Med.*) an abnormally low concentration of oxygen in the blood L19. **hypoxanthine** /-'zanθiːn/ *n.* 6-hydroxypurine, $C_5H_4N_4O$, an intermediate in the metabolism of purines in animals which also occurs in plant tissues M19. **hy'poxia** *n.* (*Med.*) a deficiency of oxygen reaching the tissues M20. **hy'poxic** *a.* (*Med.*) of, pertaining to, or exhibiting hypoxia M20.

hypoacusis /hʌɪpəʊə'k(j)uːsɪs/ *n.* Also **-cou-**, **-ku-**. M20. [f. HYPO- + Gk *akousis* hearing.] = HYPACUSIS.

Also **hypoa'cusia** *n.* M20.

hypo-allergenic /,hʌɪpəʊalə'dʒɛnɪk/ *a.* M20. [f. HYPO- + ALLERGENIC.] Having little tendency to cause an allergic reaction; specially prepared or treated so as to cause no reaction in persons allergic to the normal product.

hypocaust /'hʌɪpə(ʊ)kɔːst/ *n.* L17. [L *hypocaustum* f. Gk *hupokauston* room or place heated from below, f. as HYPO- + *kau-*, *kaiein* to burn.] *Rom. Antiq.* In houses of Roman times, a hollow space under the floor where hot air was sent from a furnace to provide underfloor heating.

hypocausted *a.* provided with a hypocaust L19.

hypocentre /'hʌɪpə(ʊ)sɛntə/ *n.* Also ***-ter**. E20. [f. HYPO- + CENTRE *n.*] 1 The point within the earth where an earthquake originates. E20. 2 = *ground zero* (a) s.v. GROUND *n.* M20.

hypocentral *a.* M20.

hypochlorous /hʌɪpə(ʊ)'klɔːrəs/ *a.* M19. [f. HYPO- + CHLOROUS.] Chem. *hypochlorous acid*, an unstable weak acid, HOCl, that exists only in dilute aqueous solution, has strong oxidizing properties, and is used in bleaching and water treatment.

hypochlorite *n.* a salt of hypochlorous acid M19.

hypochonder /hʌɪpə(ʊ)'kɒndə/ *n.* Now *rare* or *obs.* Also **-dre**. M16. [(O)Fr. *hypocondre* f. late L *hypoc(h)ondria*: see next.] = HYPOCHONDRIUM.

hypochondria /hʌɪpə(ʊ)'kɒndrɪə/ *n.* See also HYPOCHONDRIUM. LME. [Late L *hypoc(h)ondria* pl. f. Gk *hupokhondria* pl., *-khondrion* sing., use as n. of *hupokhondrios* adj., f. as HYPO- + *khondros* gristle, cartilage, esp. that of the breastbone.] 1 The part of the abdomen lying under the ribs on either side of the epigastric region. Formerly also, the viscera situated there (the liver, gall bladder, spleen, etc.), regarded as the seat of melancholy and 'vapours'. LME. 2 Depression or low spirits for which there is no real cause. M17. b A person's unfounded belief that he or she is ill; persistent anxiety about or preoccupation with one's health. L19.

hypochondriac /hʌɪpə(ʊ)'kɒndrɪak/ *a.* & *n.* L16. [Fr. *hypocondriaque* f. Gk *hupokhondriakos* affected in the hypochondria, f. *hupokhondria*: see prec., -AC. Cf. med.L *hypochondriaca*.] A *adj.* 1 Affected with or disposed to hypochondria. L16. 2 (Of an illness or symptom) affecting the hypochondria; *arch.* of the nature of depression or low spirits. L16. 3 *Med.* Situated on or near a hypochondrium. E18.

B *n.* †1 = HYPOCHONDRIA 2. L16–L18. 2 A person affected with or disposed to hypochondria. M17.

2 C. P. SNOW He . . cherished his afflictions like a hypochondriac.

hypochondriacal /-'drʌɪ-/ *a.* (*a*) = HYPOCHONDRIAC *a.* 1, 2; (*b*) *rare* = HYPOCHONDRIAC *a.* 3: E17. **hypochondriacally** /-'drʌɪ-/ *adv.* in the manner of a hypochondriac; with hypochondria: E19. **hypochondriacism** /-'drʌɪ-/ *n.* = HYPOCHONDRIA 2 E18.

hypochondrial /hʌɪpə(ʊ)'kɒndrɪəl/ *a.* E17. [f. HYPOCHONDRIA + -AL[1].] *Med.* Situated on or near, or affecting, a hypochondrium.

Lancet The patient presented with a painful right hypochondrial mass.

hypochondriasis /,hʌɪpə(ʊ)kɒn'drʌɪəsɪs/ *n.* Pl. **-ases** /-əsiːz/. M18. [f. HYPOCHONDRIA + -IASIS.] Hypochondria, esp. as a pathological state.

hypochondric /hʌɪpə(ʊ)'kɒndrɪk/ *a. rare.* L17. [f. as prec. + -IC.] = HYPOCHONDRIAC *a.*

Also **hypochondrical** *a.* (long *rare* or *obs.*) M17.

hypochondrium /hʌɪpə(ʊ)'kɒndrɪəm/ *n.* Pl. **-ums**, HYPOCHONDRIA. M17. [Back-form. f. HYPOCHONDRIA.] The part of the hypochondria lying to the left or the right of the epigastric region.

Lancet A mass in his left hypochondrium suggested pseudocyst of pancreas.

†**hypochondry** *n.* Also **-condry**. LME. [f. as HYPOCHONDRIA: see -Y[3].] 1 = prec. Usu. in *pl.* LME–L17. 2 = HYPOCHONDRIA 2. M17–L19.

hypochoristic *a.* var. of HYPOCORISTIC.

hypochromasia /hʌɪpə(ʊ)krə'meɪzɪə/ *n.* E20. [f. HYPO- + -CHROMASIA.] *Med.* = HYPOCHROMIA 2.

hypochromatic /-'mat-/ *a.* (*a*) *rare* (of the skin) deficient in pigment; (*b*) = HYPOCHROMIC 1: L19.

hypochromatosis /,hʌɪpə(ʊ)krəʊmə'təʊsɪs/ *n.* E20. [f. HYPO- + CHROMATO-, CHROMAT(IN + -OSIS.] *Cytol.* The presence of an abnormally small number of chromosomes or amount of chromatin in a nucleus.

hypochromia /hʌɪpə(ʊ)ˈkrəʊmɪə/ *n.* L19. [f. as next + -IA[1].] *Med.* 1 Paleness of the skin. L19. 2 A hypochromic condition of the blood. M20.

hypochromic /hʌɪpə(ʊ)ˈkrəʊmɪk/ *a.* E20. [f. HYPO- + Gk *khrōma* colour, or prec., + -IC.] 1 *Med.* Characterized by or designating red cells that contain less than the usual amount of haemoglobin and show an increased central pallor. E20. 2 Characterized by or exhibiting a decrease in the extent to which light, esp. ultraviolet light, is absorbed. M20.

1 J. W. LINMAN Most hypochromic anemias are caused by iron lack.

hypochromicity /-ˈmɪsɪti/ *n.* the property of being hypochromic M20.

†**hypocistis** *n.* LME–M18. [med.L f. Gk *hupokistis*, f. as HYPO- + *kistos* CISTUS.] A former tonic and astringent consisting of the solidified juice of *Cytinus hypocistis*, a plant of southern Europe parasitic on cistus.

hypocoristic /ˌhʌɪpə(ʊ)kəˈrɪstɪk/ *a.* & *n.* Also **-chor-**. M18. [Gk *hupokoristikos*, f. *hupokorizesthai* play the child, f. as HYPO- + *korē* child: see -ISTIC.] A *adj.* Of the nature of a pet name; pertaining to the habit of using endearing or euphemistic terms. M18. B *n.* A pet name, a familiar name. L19.

hypocorism *n.* = HYPOCORISTIC *n.* M19. †**hypocoristical** *a.*: only in E17. **hypocoristically** *adv.* M17.

hypocrateriform /ˌhɪpə(ʊ)krəˈtɪərɪfɔːm/ *a.* M18. [mod.L *hypocrateriformis*, f. Gk *hupocratērion* stand of a large mixing-bowl, f. HYPO- + *cratēr* CRATER: see -FORM.] *Bot.* = SALVER-*shaped*.

hypocrise /ˈhɪpəkrʌɪz/ *v.i. rare.* L16. [Fr. *hypocriser* or back-form. f. HYPOCRISY.] Practise hypocrisy.

hypocrisis /hɪˈpɒkrɪsɪs/ *n.* ME. [L, see next.] Hypocrisy, dissembling, feigning; a false or deceitful show.

hypocrisy /hɪˈpɒkrɪsi/ *n.* ME. [OFr. *ypocrisie* (mod. *hypo-*), irreg. f. eccl.L *hypocrisis* f. Gk *hupokrisis* acting of a theatrical part, f. *hupokrinesthai* answer, play a part, pretend, f. as HYPO- + *krinein* decide, determine, judge. The etymol. sp. with *h* became current (as in Fr.) in 16.] The practice of falsely presenting an appearance of virtue or falsely professing a belief to which one's own character or conduct does not conform; dissimulation, pretence; an instance of this.

P. USTINOV The hypocrisy which permits selfish policies to be propounded in expressions of high-mindedness. R. H. TAWNEY To talk of holiness and to practise injustice is mere hypocrisy.

hypocrital /hɪˈpɒkrɪt(ə)l/ *a.* Now *rare.* M17. [f. next + -AL[1].] = HYPOCRITICAL.

hypocrite /ˈhɪpəkrɪt/ *n.* & *a.* ME. [OFr. *ypocrite*, *ipo-* (mod. *hypo-*) f. eccl.L *hypocrita* f. Gk *hupokritēs* actor, dissembler, pretender, f. *hupokrinesthai*: see HYPOCRISY.] A *n.* A person who falsely professes to be virtuously or religiously inclined or to have feelings or beliefs of a higher order than is the case; a person given to hypocrisy. ME. B *adj.* = HYPOCRITICAL. LME.

hypocritic /hɪpəˈkrɪtɪk/ *a.* M16. [med.L *hypocriticus* f. Gk *hypokritikos* pertaining to (an actor's) delivery, f. *hupokrisis*: see HYPOCRISY, -IC.] = HYPOCRITICAL.

hypocritical /hɪpəˈkrɪtɪk(ə)l/ *a.* M16. [f. as prec.: see -ICAL.] Of an action: of the nature of or characterized by hypocrisy. Of a person: given to hypocrisy, having the character of a hypocrite.

hypocritically *adv.* M16.

hypocycloid /hʌɪpə(ʊ)ˈsʌɪklɔɪd/ *n.* M19. [f. HYPO- + CYCLOID.] A curve traced by a point on the circumference of one circle as it rolls round the inside of another circle. Cf. EPICYCLOID.

hypocyˈcloidal *a.* L19.

hypoderma /hʌɪpə(ʊ)ˈdəːmə/ *n.* Pl. **-mata** /-mətə/. E19. [f. HYPO- + Gk *derma* skin.] †1 *Zool.* A membrane lining the underside of the elytra of Coleoptera. Only in E19. 2 *Bot.* = HYPODERMIS 1. L19.

hypodermal /hʌɪpə(ʊ)ˈdəːm(ə)l/ *a.* M19. [f. HYPODERMA, HYPODERMIS + -AL[1].] Of or pertaining to hypodermis.

hypodermatic /ˌhʌɪpə(ʊ)dəːˈmatɪk/ *a.* Now *rare* or *obs.* M19. [f. HYPO- + DERMATO- + -IC.] †1 *Anat.* = HYPODERMIC *a.* 2. Only in M19. 2 = HYPODERMIC *a.* 1. L19.

hypodermatically *adv.* L19.

hypodermic /hʌɪpə(ʊ)ˈdəːmɪk/ *a.* & *n.* M19. [f. HYPO- + Gk *derma* skin + -IC.] A *adj.* 1 Involving, pertaining to, or designating the introduction of a drug etc. by injection under the skin. M19. 2 *Anat.* Situated beneath the skin; pertaining to the region beneath the skin. L19.

1 *Times* Hospital waste such as blood samples and hypodermic needles..

B *n.* A hypodermic injection; a hypodermic syringe. L19.

hypodermically *adv.* M19.

hypodermis /hʌɪpə(ʊ)ˈdəːmɪs/ *n.* M19. [f. HYPO- + *-dermis*, after *epidermis*.] 1 *Bot.* A layer of cells immediately below the epidermis of a plant, *esp.* one of a different origin. Also, the inner layer of the capsule of mosses. M19. 2 *Zool.* A layer of cells below the cuticle of arthropods. L19.

hypogaeal *a.*, **hypogaeum** *n.* vars. of HYPOGEAL, -GEUM.

hypogastric /hʌɪpə(ʊ)ˈgastrɪk/ *a.* & *n.* M17. [Fr. *hypogastrique*, f. *hypogastre* hypogastrium f. as next: see -IC.] *Anat.* A *adj.* Pertaining to, situated in, or designating the region of the hypogastrium. M17. B *n.* †1 In *pl.* The hypogastric arteries. *rare.* Only in L18. 2 A hypogastric nerve (connecting the superior and inferior hypogastric plexuses). L19.

Also †**hypogastrical** *a.* (*rare*): only in E17.

hypogastrium /hʌɪpə(ʊ)ˈgastrɪəm/ *n.* L17. [mod.L f. Gk *hupogastrion*, f. as HYPO- + *gastr-*, *gastēr* belly: see -IUM.] *Anat.* The lowest part of the abdomen, below the navel; *esp.* the middle of this, between the iliac regions.

hypogea *n.* pl. of HYPOGEUM.

hypogeal /hʌɪpə(ʊ)ˈdʒiːəl/ *a.* Also **-gaeal**. L17. [f. as next + -AL[1].] = next.

Also **hypogeous** *a.* M19.

hypogean /hʌɪpə(ʊ)ˈdʒiːən/ *a.* M19. [f. late L *hypogeus* f. Gk *hupogeios* underground, f. as HYPO- + *gē* earth: see -AN.] Occurring or growing beneath the surface of the earth; underground.

hypogee /ˈhɪpədʒiː/ *n. rare.* M17. [Fr. *hypogée* or L *hypogeum* HYPOGEUM.] = HYPOGEUM.

hypogene /ˈhʌɪpədʒiːn/ *a.* M19. [f. HYPO- + -GENE.] *Geol.* Formed or occurring beneath the surface of the earth.

Also **hypoˈgenic** *a.* L19.

hypogeum /hʌɪpə(ʊ)ˈdʒiːəm/ *n.* Also **-gaeum**. Pl. **-g(a)ea** /-dʒiːə/. M17. [L *hypogeum*, *-gaeum* f. Gk *hupogeion*, *-gaion* use as n. of neut. sing. of *hupogeios*: see HYPOGEAN.] An underground chamber or vault.

hypoglossal /hʌɪpə(ʊ)ˈglɒs(ə)l/ *a.* & *n.* M19. [f. next + -AL[1].] *Anat.* A *adj.* Designating or pertaining to the twelfth pair of cranial nerves, which supply the muscles of the tongue. M19. B *n.* Either of the hypoglossal nerves. M19.

hypoglossus /hʌɪpə(ʊ)ˈglɒsəs/ *n. rare.* E19. [f. HYPO- + Gk *glōssa* tongue.] *Anat.* = HYPOGLOSSAL *n.*

hypogynous /hʌɪˈpɒdʒɪnəs/ *a.* E19. [f. mod.L *hypogynus*, f. as HYPO- + Gk *gunē* woman (used for 'pistil'): see -OUS.] *Bot.* Of a stamen, petal, or sepal: inserted on the receptacle below the gynoecium. Of a flower: having its parts so inserted. Cf. EPIGYNOUS, PERIGYNOUS.

hypogyny *n.* hypogynous condition L19.

hypoid /ˈhʌɪpɔɪd/ *a.* & *n.* E20. [Origin uncertain: perh. f. HYP(ERBOL)OID or *hy(perbolic parabol)oid*.] *Mech.* A *adj.* 1 Designating a gear similar to a spiral bevel gear but with the pinion offset from the centre-line of the wheel, to connect non-intersecting shafts. E20. 2 Suited for or employing a hypoid gear. M20.

2 *Practical Motorist* The rear final drive should be drained and refilled . . using hypoid API GLS oil.

B *n.* A hypoid gear. M20.

hypolimnion /hʌɪpə(ʊ)ˈlɪmnɪən/ *n.* Pl. **-nia** /-nɪə/. E20. [f. HYPO- + Gk *limnion* dim. of *limnē* lake.] The lower, cooler layer of water below the thermocline in a stratified lake.

hypolimˈnetic *a.* E20. **hypolimnial** *a.* M20.

hypomochlion /hɪpə(ʊ)ˈmɒklɪən/ *n. rare.* M17. [L f. Gk *hupomokhlion*, f. as HYPO- + *mokhlos*, *-lion* lever.] A fulcrum.

hyponitrous /hʌɪpə(ʊ)ˈnʌɪtrəs/ *a.* E19. [f. HYPO- + NITROUS.] Chem. *hyponitrous acid*, a weak unstable crystalline acid, $H_2N_2O_2$, which explodes when heated.

hyponitrite *n.* a salt of hyponitrous acid M19.

hyponym /ˈhʌɪpə(ʊ)nɪm/ *n.* E20. [f. HYPO- + -NYM.] 1 *Taxon.* A name made invalid by the lack of adequate contemporary description of the taxon it was intended to designate. E20. 2 *Ling.* A word whose meaning implies or is included in that of another (e.g. *scarlet* and *tulip*, in relation to *red* and *flower* respectively). M20.

hyponymy /hʌɪˈpɒnɪmi/ *n.* M20. [f. HYPO- after SYNONYMY.] *Ling.* The relation of a word to another word of which the former is a hyponym.

hypopharyngeal /ˌhʌɪpə(ʊ)fəˈrɪn(d)ʒɪəl, -far(ə)nˈdʒiːəl/ *a.* M19. [Partly f. HYPO- + PHARYNGEAL, partly f. HYPOPHARYNX.] 1 *Zool.* & *Anat.* Situated below the pharynx or in the hypopharynx. M19. 2 *Entomol.* Pertaining to the hypopharynx. L19.

hypopharynx /hʌɪpə(ʊ)ˈfarɪŋks/ *n.* E19. [Fr., f. as HYPO-, PHARYNX.] 1 *Entomol.* A sensory structure projecting from the labium of an insect and usually incorporating salivary apertures. E19. 2 *Anat.* The lower part of the pharynx (into which the larynx opens), between the epiglottis and the top of the oesophagus. E20.

hypophyllous /hʌɪˈpɒfɪləs/ *a.* E19. [f. HYPO- + Gk *phullon* leaf + -OUS.] *Bot.* Growing under, or on the underside of, a leaf.

hypophysectomy /ˌhʌɪpə(ʊ)fɪˈsɛktəmi/ *n.* E20. [f. as next + -ECTOMY.] Surgical removal of the hypophysis; an instance of this.

hypophyˈsectomize *v.t.* perform hypophysectomy on E20.

hypophysiotropic /ˌhʌɪpə(ʊ)fɪzɪəˈtrəʊpɪk, -ˈtrɒpɪk/ *a.* Also **-troph-** /-ˈtrəʊf-/. M20. [f. next + -O- + -TROPIC.] *Physiol.* Regulating the activity of the hypophysis.

hypophysis /hʌɪˈpɒfɪsɪs/ *n.* Pl. **-yses** /-ɪsiːz/. L17. [mod.L f. Gk *hupophusis* offshoot, outgrowth, f. as HYPO- + *phusis* growth.] †1 Cataract in the eye. *rare* (only in Dicts.). L17–L19. 2 *Anat.* The pituitary gland. Also, one or other lobes of this gland; both lobes together with the infundibulum. Also *hypophysis cerebri* /ˈsɛrɪbriː/. E19.

†**hypophysal** *a.*: only in L19. **hypophyseal**, **hypophysial** /hʌɪpə(ʊ)ˈfɪzɪəl, hʌɪpə(ʊ)fɪˈsiːəl/ *adjs.* L19.

hypoplasia /hʌɪpə(ʊ)ˈpleɪzɪə/ *n.* L19. [f. HYPO- + -PLASIA.] *Med.* Incomplete growth or development of a part.

hypoplastic /hʌɪpə(ʊ)ˈplastɪk/ *a.* L19. [f. HYPO(PLASIA + -PLASTIC.] *Med.* Of an organ or tissue: undersized or underdeveloped at maturity as a result of hypoplasia.

hypoplastic anaemia: due to an insufficient production of red blood cells.

hypopyon /hʌɪˈpəʊpɪən/ *n.* E18. [Gk *hupopuon* ulcer, neut. of *hupopuos* tending to suppuration, f. as HYPO- + *puon* pus.] *Med.* The presence of pus in the anterior chamber of the eye, in front of the iris.

hyporchem /ˈhɪpɔːkɛm, ˈhʌɪp-/ *n.* Also in L form **-chema** /-ˈkiːmə/. E17. [Gk *huporkhēma*, f. as HYPO- + *orkheesthai* to dance.] *Gk Hist.* A choral hymn to Apollo which was accompanied by dancing and pantomimic action.

hyposarca /hɪpə(ʊ)ˈsɑːkə, hʌɪp-/ *n. rare.* LME. [med.L f. Gk *hupo sarka* under the flesh.] = ANASARCA.

hyposcenium /hʌɪpə(ʊ)ˈsiːnɪəm, hɪp-/ *n.* M18. [mod.L, based, after *proscenium*, on Gk *huposkēnia* parts beneath the stage, f. as HYPO- + *skēnē* stage: see -IUM.] *Gk Antiq.* The low wall

For other words beginning with *hypo-* see the entry for **hypo-**

supporting the front of the stage in a Greek theatre.

hyposensitize /hʌɪpə(ʊ)'sɛnsɪtʌɪz/ *v.t.* Also **-ise.** M20. [f. HYPO- + SENSITIZE.] *Med.* Subject to hyposensitization.

ˌhyposensitiˈzation *n.* the process of reducing the sensitivity of a hypersensitive individual by special treatment; a state of reduced sensitivity so produced: E20.

hypospadias /hʌɪpə(ʊ)'speɪdɪəs, hɪp-/ *n.* E19. [Gk *hypospadias* person with hypospadias, app. f. as HYPO- + *span* to draw.] A congenital malformation of the penis in which the urethra opens on its underside.

hypospadiac *a.* M19. **hypospadial** *a.* L19.

hypostasis /hʌɪ'pɒstəsɪs/ *n.* Pl. **-ases** /-əsiːz/. Also (*rare*) Anglicized as †**hypostasy.** E16. [eccl.L f. Gk *hupostasis* sediment, foundation, subject-matter, (later) substance, existence, essence, personality, f. as HYPO- + *stasis* standing.] **1** *Theol.* A person; *spec.* (*a*) the single person of Christ, as opp. to his two natures, human and divine; (*b*) each of the three persons of the Trinity, which are of the same 'substance'. E16. **2** *Med.* **a** A sediment, esp. in urine. Long *rare* or *obs.* M16. **b** The accumulation of blood or other fluid in a dependent part of the body. M19. **3**†**a** A base or foundation on which something abstract rests. L16–E17. **b** *Philos.* An underlying reality, substance, as opp. to attributes ('accidents') or as distinguished from what is unsubstantial. E17. **c** Essence, essential principle. L17. **4** *Genetics.* [Back-form. f. HYPOSTATIC.] Inhibition of the expression of a gene by another at a different locus. E20. **5** *Ling.* The citing of a word, element, etc., as an example or model; the word etc. so cited. M20.

2b D. L. SAYERS The hypostasis produced by his having lain a whole week face downwards in the cellar.

hypostasize /hʌɪ'pɒstəsʌɪz/ *v.t.* Also **-ise.** E19. [f. prec. + -IZE.] Make into or represent as a substance or a concrete reality; embody, personify.

hypostasiˈzation *n.* L19.

hypostatic /hʌɪpə(ʊ)'statɪk/ *a.* L15. [med.L *hypostaticus* f. Gk *hupostatikos* pertaining to substance, substantial, personal, f. *hupostatos* set under, supporting.] **1** *Theol.* Of or pertaining to hypostasis (see HYPOSTASIS 1). Chiefly in *hypostatic union.* L15. **2** *Med.* Of the nature of or caused by hypostasis. M19. **3** *Genetics.* Of a gene: affected by hypostasis; not expressed owing to the effect of another gene at a different locus. E20.

hypostatical /hʌɪpə(ʊ)'statɪk(ə)l/ *a.* M16. [f. as prec. + -AL[1].] **1** *Theol.* = HYPOSTATIC 1. M16. †**2** Of a principle of matter: elemental. M17–E18.

hypostatically *adv.* in a hypostatic manner; in actual substance or personality: L16.

hypostatize /hʌɪ'pɒstətʌɪz/ *v.t.* Also **-ise.** E19. [f. Gk *hupostatos*: see HYPOSTATIC, -IZE.] = HYPOSTASIZE.

hypostatiˈzation *n.* hypostasization L19.

†**hyposulphate** *n.* Also ***-sulf-.** Only in 19. [f. HYPO- + SULPHATE *n.*] *Chem.* = DITHIONATE.

hyposulphite /hʌɪpə(ʊ)'sʌlfʌɪt/ *n.* Also ***-sulf-.** E19. [Fr., f. as HYPO-, SULPHITE.] **1** *Chem.* A thiosulphate, *esp.* sodium thiosulphate as used in photography. E19. **2** = HYDROSULPHITE. L19.

†**hyposulphuric** *a.* Also ***-sulf-.** Only in 19. [Fr. *hyposulphurique*, f. as HYPO-, SULPHURIC.] *Chem.* = DITHIONIC.

hyposulphurous /hʌɪpə(ʊ)'sʌlf(ə)rəs/ *a.* Also ***-sulf-.** E19. [f. HYPO- + SULPHUROUS.] †**1** = THIOSULPHURIC. -L19. **2** = HYDROSULPHUROUS. L19.

hypotaxis /hʌɪpə(ʊ)'taksɪs/ *n.* L19. [Gk *hupotaxis* subjection, f. *hupotassein* arrange under, f. as HYPO- + *tassein* arrange.] *Gram.* The subordination of one clause to another. Opp. PARATAXIS.

hypotactic *a.* of, pertaining to, or exhibiting hypotaxis; subordinate: L19.

hypotension /hʌɪpə(ʊ)'tɛnʃ(ə)n/ *n.* L19. [f. HYPO- + TENSION *n.*] Abnormally or excessively low pressure of arterial blood or intra-ocular fluid, *spec.* the former.

hypotensive *a.* of, exhibiting, or associated with hypotension; tending to reduce a person's blood pressure: E20.

hypotenusal /hʌɪˌpɒtɪ'njuːz(ə)l, -s(ə)l/ *a.* & *n.* Now *rare.* Also †**-then-.** L16. [Late L *hypotenusalis*, f. as next: see -AL[1].] **A** *adj.* Pertaining to or of the nature of a hypotenuse; forming a hypotenuse. L16. †**B** *n.* A hypotenuse. Only in M17.

hypotenuse /hʌɪ'pɒtɪnjuːz, -s/ *n.* Also †**-then-,** & in L form †**-tenusa.** L16. [L *hypotenusa* f. Gk *hupoteinousa* subtending (*sc.* line) fem. pres. pple of *hupoteinein* stretch under, f. as HYPO- + *teinein* to stretch.] The longest side of a right-angled triangle.

hypothalamus /hʌɪpə(ʊ)'θaləməs/ *n.* L19. [f. HYPO- + THALAMUS.] *Anat.* The lower part of the diencephalon in vertebrates, which in mammals controls autonomic functions such as temperature and hunger and regulates the hormonal activity of the adenohypophysis.

hypothalamic /-'θaləmɪk, -θə'lamɪk/*a.* L19. **hypothalamo-hypoˈphysial, -eal** *a.* of, pertaining to, or connecting the hypothalamus and the hypophysis M20.

hypothec /hʌɪ'pɒθɪk/ *n.* Also (now only w. ref. to Roman law) in L form **hypotheca** /hʌɪpə(ʊ)'θiːkə/. E16. [Fr. *hypothèque* f. late L *hypotheca* f. Gk *hupothēkē* deposit, pledge, f. *hupotithenai* deposit as a pledge, f. as HYPO- + *tithenai* to place.] In the law of Scotland, the Channel Islands, and ancient Rome: a creditor's right established over a debtor's property that continues in the debtor's possession.

hypothecal *a.* (now *rare* or *obs.*) = HYPOTHECARY E17.

hypotheca /hʌɪpə(ʊ)'θiːkə/ *n.*[1] L19. [f. HYPO- + THECA.] *Bot.* The inner of the two valves of a diatom.

hypotheca *n.*[2] see HYPOTHEC.

hypothecary /hʌɪ'pɒθɪk(ə)ri/ *a.* M17. [Late L *hypothecarius*, f. *hypotheca* HYPOTHEC: see -ARY[1].] *Rom.* & *Sc. Law.* Of, pertaining to, or of the nature of a hypothec.

hypothecate /hʌɪ'pɒθɪkeɪt/ *v.t.* E17. [med.L *hypothecat-* pa. ppl stem of *hypothecare*, f. *hypotheca*: see HYPOTHEC, -ATE[3].] **1** Give or pledge as security; pawn; mortgage. E17. **2** = HYPOTHESIZE 2. E20.

1 *Scientific American* It was proposed to collect the sum by hypothecating future tolls.

hypotheˈcation *n.* L17. **hypothecator** *n.* E19.

†**hypothenusal** *a.*, †**hypothenuse** *n.* vars. of HYPOTENUSAL etc.

hypothermia /hʌɪpə(ʊ)'θəːmɪə/ *n.* L19. [f. HYPO- + Gk *thermē* heat + -IA[1].] The condition of having a body temperature substantially below the normal, whether through natural causes or artificially induced.

hypothermic *a.* of or exhibiting hypothermia L19.

hypothesis /hʌɪ'pɒθɪsɪs/ *n.* Pl. **-theses** /-θɪsiːz/. L16. [Late L f. Gk *hupothesis* foundation, base, f. as HYPO- + *thesis* placing.] **1** A proposition put forward merely as a basis for reasoning or argument, without any assumption of its truth. L16. †**2** A subordinate thesis forming part of a more general one; a particular case of a general proposition; a detailed statement. L16–E18. **3** A supposition, an assumption; *esp.* one made as a starting-point for further investigation or research from known facts. E17. **4** A groundless assumption; a guess. E17. **5** An actual or possible situation considered as a basis for action. L18.

3 E. O'BRIEN The midwife . . repeated the hypothesis that if men had to give birth there would not be a child born. R. RENDELL That was what he thought had happened. It would do as a working hypothesis. G. A. BIRMINGHAM Have you any other hypothesis which meets the facts of the case better? *continuum hypothesis, Whorfian hypothesis, zeta hypothesis*, etc.

hypothesist *n.* a person who hypothesizes L18.

hypothesize /hʌɪ'pɒθɪsʌɪz/ *v.* Also **-ise.** M18. [f. HYPOTHES(IS + -IZE.] **1** *v.i.* Frame a hypothesis or supposition. M18. **2** *v.t.* Make a hypothesis of; put forward as a hypothesis; postulate, assume. M19.

2 M. T. TSUANG It has been hypothesized that the submissive twins may be . . more dependent on their parents. *Journal of Social Psychology* Hypothesizing an inverse relationship between task sophistication and conforming behavior.

hypothesizer *n.* M19.

hypothetic /hʌɪpə(ʊ)'θɛtɪk/ *a.* & *n.* L17. [L *hypotheticus* f. Gk *hupothetikos*, f. *hupothesis*: see HYPOTHESIS, -IC.] **A** *adj.* = HYPOTHETICAL *a.* L17. **B** *n.* †**1** A hypothetical statement, a hypothesis; a hypothetical proposition or syllogism. L17–E18. **2** In *pl.* The making of hypotheses; hypothesizing. L19.

hypothetical /hʌɪpə(ʊ)'θɛtɪk(ə)l/ *a.* & *n.* L16. [f. as prec. + -AL[1].] **A** *adj.* **1** Involving, based on, or pertaining to a hypothesis; *Logic* designating a proposition having the form *if p then q* or a syllogism containing such a proposition; *Gram.* expressing a conjective, supposition, or condition. L16. **2** Concerning which a hypothesis is made; supposed or assumed but not necessarily real or true. E17.

1 R. S. BALL The . . line which divides the truths that have been established . . from those parts of the science which . . [are] more or less hypothetical. R. B. LONG The verb forms used as hypothetical subjunctives are forms belonging to the four past tenses. **hypothetical imperative** *Ethics* a moral obligation that applies only if one desires the goal (opp. *categorical imperative*). **2** J. TYNDALL Any other obstacle will produce the same effect as our hypothetical post.

B *n.* **1** *Logic.* A hypothetical proposition or syllogism. M17. **2** *Gram.* A hypothetical word, phrases, or clause. M20.

hypothetically /hʌɪpə(ʊ)'θɛtɪk(ə)li/ *adv.* E17. [f. prec. + -LY[2].] In a hypothetical manner or form; by hypothesis; supposedly.

hypotheticate /hʌɪpə(ʊ)'θɛtɪkeɪt/ *v.t.* E20. [f. HYPOTHETIC(AL + -ATE[3].] = HYPOTHESIZE 2.

hypothetiˈcation *n.* L20.

hypothetico-deductive /hʌɪpəˌθɛtɪkəʊ dɪ'dʌktɪv/ *a.* E20. [f. HYPOTHETICAL + -O- + DEDUCTIVE.] *Philos.* Making use of or consisting in the testing of the consequences of hypotheses as a means of determining whether the hypotheses themselves are false or can be accepted.

hypothetico-deductively *adv.* M20. **hypothetico-deductivism** *n.* L20.

hypotonia /hʌɪpə(ʊ)'təʊnɪə/ *n.* Also Anglicized as **hypotony** /hʌɪ'pɒtəni/. L19. [f. HYPO- + Gk *tonos* TONE *n.* + -IA[1], -Y[3].] *Med.* **1** A state of reduced pressure of the intra-ocular fluid. L19. **2** The condition of being hypotonic. L19.

hypotonic /hʌɪpə(ʊ)'tɒnɪk/ *a.* L19. [f. HYPO- + TONIC.] **1** *Physiol.* Having a lower osmotic pressure than some particular fluid (usually that in a cell, or a body fluid). L19. **2** Of the eye: having a reduced intra-ocular pressure. E20. **3** *Med.* (Of muscle) in a state of abnormally low tone or tension; of or characterized by muscle in this state. E20.

hypotonically *adv.* with a hypotonic solution M20. **hypotonicity** /-'nɪsɪti/ *n.* the condition of being hypotonic; the extent to which a solution has a lower osmotic pressure than another: E20.

hypotonus /hʌɪpə(ʊ)'təʊnəs/ *n.* L19. [f. HYPO- + TONUS.] *Med.* = HYPOTONIA.

hypotony *n.* see HYPOTONIA.

hypotrachelium /ˌhɪpə(ʊ)trə'kiːlɪəm/ *n.* Also **-lion** /-lɪən/. M16. [L f. Gk *hupotrakhēlion*, f. as HYPO- + *trakhēlos* neck: see -IUM.] *Archit.* The lower part or neck of the capital of a column; in the Doric order, the groove or sinking between the neck of the capital and the shaft.

hypotyposis /hɪpətʌɪ'pəʊsɪs/ *n.* Pl. **-poses** /-'pəʊsiːz/. L16. [Gk *hupotupōsis* sketch, outline, pattern, f. *hupotupoun* to sketch, f. *tupos* TYPE *n.*: see -OSIS.] *Rhet.* (A) vivid description of a scene, event, or situation.

hypped, †**hyppish** *adjs.* vars. of HIPPED *a.*[2], HIPPISH.

hypsarrhythmia /hɪpsə'rɪθmɪə/ *n.* M20. [f. HYPSI-, HYPSO- + ARRHYTHMIA.] *Med.* (The condition of having) a grossly disturbed EEG pattern of the kind associated with infantile spasms.

hypsarrhythmic *a.* L20.

hypsi- /ˈhɪpsi/ *comb. form* repr. Gk *hupsi-* on high, aloft, used in senses 'high', 'height': see -I-.

hypsiceˈphalic *a.* (*Anthropol.*) having a skull that is high and broad in relation to its anteroposterior length L19. **hypsiconch** /-kɒŋk/, **-ˈconchic** *adjs.* (*Anthropol.*) in which the orbit of the eye is high in relation to its width E20. **hypsiconchous** /-ˈkɒŋk-/ *a.* (*Anthropol.*) = HYPSICONCH(IC) L19. **hypsiconchy** /-kɒŋki/ *n.* (*Anthropol.*) the condition of being hypsiconchic E20. **hypsiˈthermal** *a.* designating a period of the Holocene when the northern hemisphere was relatively warm, usually put at about 8000 to 1000 BC M20.

hypsilophodont /hɪpsɪˈlɒfədɒnt/ *a.* & *n.* L19. [f. Gk *hupsilophos* high-crested (f. as HYPSI- + LOPHO-) + -ODONT.] *Palaeont.* (Designating) any hypsilophodontid, *esp.* one of the genus *Hypsilophodon*, of Lower Cretaceous times.

ˌhypsilophoˈdontid *a.* & *n.* (designating) any of a family of ornithischian dinosaurs of Middle Jurassic to Late Cretaceous times which had powerful jaws and chisel-like teeth L20.

Hypsistarian /hɪpsɪˈstɛːrɪən/ *a.* & *n.* E18. [f. Gk *Hupsistarios*, f. *hupsistos* highest: see -AN.] *Eccl. Hist.* A *adj.* Belonging to a 4th-cent. sect which worshipped God under the name of 'Most High' rather than 'Father'. E18. B *n.* A member of this sect. E18.

Also †**Hypsistary** *n.*: only in E17.

hypso- /ˈhɪpsəʊ/ *comb. form* repr. rare Gk *hupso-* (= *hupsi-*: see HYPSI-) or *hupsos* height: see -O-.

hypsochrome *a.* & *n.* (*Chem.*) (*a*) = HYPSOCHROMIC; (*b*) *n.* a hypsochromic atom or group: L19. **hypsoˈchromic** *a.* (*Chem.*) causing or characterized by a lightening of colour or a shift of the absorption spectrum towards shorter wavelengths L19. **hypsodont** *a.* (of a tooth) having a high crown and short root L19. **hypsoˌdonty** *n.* the condition of being hypsodont or of having hypsodont teeth M20. **hypsoˈgraphic** *a.* of or pertaining to hypsography (*hypsographic curve*, a curve representing the proportion of the earth's surface, or of a specified part of it, that lies above each of a series of altitudes) L19. **hypsoˈgraphical** *a.* hypsographic L19. **hypˈsography** *n.* the branch of geography that deals with the relative altitudes of different parts of the earth's surface and with their determination L19. **hypˈsometer** *n.* an instrument for estimating height above sea level from the temperature at which water boils M19. **hypsoˈmetric** *a.* of or pertaining to hypsometry (*hypsometric curve*, a hypsographic curve) M19. **hypsoˈmetrical** *a.* hypsometric M19. **hypsoˈmetrically** *adv.* by hypsometric methods; with a hypsometer: M19. **hypˈsometry** *n.* the branch of science that deals with the measurement of altitude; the hypsometric features of a region: L16.

†**hypt** *a.* var. of HIPPED *a.*[2]

hyraces *n.pl.* see HYRAX.

hyraceum /hʌɪˈreɪsɪəm/ *n.* Also **-cium**. M19. [f. *hyrac-* comb. form of HYRAX.] A secretion of the African rock hyrax, *Procavia capensis*, formerly used as a fixative for perfume.

hyracotherium /hʌɪrəkə(ʊ)ˈθɪərɪəm/ *n.* M19. [mod.L, f. *hyraco-* comb. form of HYRAX + Gk *thērion* wild animal.] *Palaeont.* A member of the extinct Eocene genus *Hyracotherium*, which comprised small mammals ancestral to the horse.

hyrax /ˈhʌɪraks/ *n.* Pl. **hyraxes**, **hyraces** /ˈhʌɪrəsiːz/. M19. [mod.L f. Gk *hurax*, *hurak-* shrew-mouse.] A mammal of the order Hyracoidea, comprising small stumpy animals of Africa and the Middle East which resemble rodents but are actually related to ungulates and sirenians, having feet with nails like hoofs.

rock hyrax: see ROCK *n.*[1]

Hyrcan /ˈhəːk(ə)n/ *n.* & *a.* M16. [L *Hyrcanus* f. Gk *Hurkanos*.] A *n.* = HYRCANIAN *n.* M16. B *adj.* = HYRCANIAN *a.* L16.

Hyrcanian /həːˈkeɪnɪən/ *n.* & *a.* M16. [f. L *Hyrcania* f. Gk *Hurkania*: see -AN.] A *n.* A native or inhabitant of Hyrcania, an ancient region bordering the Caspian Sea which was noted for its wildness. M16. B *adj.* Of or pertaining to Hyrcania. L16.

hyson /ˈhʌɪs(ə)n/ *n.* M18. [Chin. *xīchūn* (Wade-Giles *hsī-ch'un*), lit. 'bright spring'.] A kind of Chinese green tea. Also *hyson tea*.

Hy-spy *n.* var. of I-SPY.

hyssop /ˈhɪsəp/ *n.* [OE (*h*)*ysope*, reinforced in ME by OFr. *ysope*, *isope*, later assim. to the source, L *hyssopus*, *-um* f. Gk *hussōpos*, *-on*, of Semitic origin (cf. Heb. *'ēzōb*).] 1 An aromatic bitter-tasting labiate herb, *Hyssopus officinalis*, native to the Mediterranean region, with spikes of small blue flowers. OE. b With specifying wd: any of various plants of the Labiatae and allied families thought to resemble hyssop. L16. 2 In biblical translations and allusions: a low-growing plant of uncertain identity, the twigs of which were used by the Hebrews for sprinkling in ritual purification; a bundle of these twigs. OE. b A holy-water sprinkler. M19.

1b **giant hyssop** any of various tall labiate plants of the Asian and N. American genus *Agastache*. *hedge-hyssop*: see HEDGE *n.* **water hyssop** a tropical aquatic plant, *Bacopa monnieri*, of the figwort family. 2 AV *Ps.* 51:7 Purge me with hyssope, and I shal be cleane.

hyst *v.* var. of HIST *v.*[2]

hysterectomy /hɪstəˈrɛktəmi/ *n.* L19. [f. HYSTERO- + -ECTOMY.] Surgical removal of the uterus; an instance of this.

J. ARCHER A hysterectomy prevented Arlene from bearing him any more children.

hysterectomize *v.t.* perform a hysterectomy on E20.

hysteresis /hɪstəˈriːsɪs/ *n.* Pl. **-reses** /-ˈriːsiːz/. L19. [Gk *husterēsis* short-coming, deficiency, f. *husterein* be behind, come late, f. *husteros* late.] The phenomenon whereby changes in some property of a physical system lag behind changes in the phenomenon causing it, *esp.* the lag of magnetization behind magnetizing force when the latter is varying; any dependence of the value of a property on the past history of the system.

Comb.: **hysteresis curve**, **loop**: showing how a property varies when the phenomenon causing it varies from one value to another and back again; **hysteresis loss** the energy dissipated as heat in a system as a result of hysteresis.

hysteresial *a.* L19.

hysteretic /hɪstəˈrɛtɪk/ *a.* L19. [Prob. f. prec. after *synthesis*, *synthetic*, etc., but cf. Gk *husterētikos* which comes on later.] Of, pertaining to, or exhibiting hysteresis.

hysteretically *adv.* by means or as a result of hysteresis E20.

hysteria /hɪˈstɪərɪə/ *n.* E19. [f. as next + -IA[1].] 1 A syndrome (formerly regarded as a disease peculiar to women) whose symptoms include shallow volatile emotions, overdramatic behaviour, susceptibility to suggestion, and amnesia, with physical symptoms such as anaesthesia, tremor, and convulsions that cannot be attributed to any physical pathology. E19. 2 Wild uncontrollable excitement or emotion. M19.

1 CONVERSION *hysteria*. **dissociative hysteria**: in which the principal manifestation is psychological symptoms (rather than physical ones). 2 *Observer* There is a war hysteria in this country now.

hysteric /hɪˈstɛrɪk/ *a.* & *n.* M17. [L *hystericus* f. Gk *husterikos* belonging to or suffering in the uterus, hysterical, f. *hustera* uterus (see -IC), hysteria being formerly regarded as a disease of women due to a disturbance of the uterus.] A *adj.* 1 = HYSTERICAL *a.* M17. †2 Of a medicine: good for hysteria or uterine disorders. L17–M18.

1 **hysteric passion** (now *rare* or *obs.*) hysteria.

B *n.* †1 A medicine that is good for hysteria or uterine disorders. L17–M18. 2 *sing.* & (now usu.) in *pl.* A hysterical fit or convulsion; *colloq.* overwhelming mirth; a display of uncontrolled laughter, sorrow, or anger. E18. 3 A person subject to or affected with hysteria. M18.

2 S. MIDDLETON When I get back home Irene's broken down, near hysterics. A. T. ELLIS I'm going to have hysterics. I'm going to stand in this stream and scream. D. LODGE She . . burst into uncontrollable hysterics and began throwing crockery at the wall.

hystericism /-sɪz(ə)m/ *n.* the condition of being hysterical; hysteria: E18.

hysterical /hɪˈstɛrɪk(ə)l/ *a.* & *n.* E17. [f. as prec. + -AL[1].] A *adj.* 1 Affected with hysteria or hysterics; of, pertaining to, or characteristic of hysteria. E17. 2 Extremely amusing. *colloq.* L20.

1 W. WHARTON We all get hysterical, start dancing around in the garden. B. T. BRADFORD Her hysterical tantrums and rivers of tears. 2 *Observer* All nuns are amusing but nuns who tap-dance are hysterical.

B *n.* †1 = HYSTERIC *n.* 1. M–L17. 2 In *pl.* Hysterics. *rare.* M19. 3 = HYSTERIC *n.* 3. L19.

hysterically /hɪˈstɛrɪk(ə)li/ *adv.* E18. [f. HYSTERIC *a.* or HYSTERICAL *a.*: see -ICALLY.] In a hysterical manner; in a fit of hysterics.

hysterica passio /hɪˌstɛrɪkə ˈpasɪəʊ/ *n. phr.* E17. [L *hysterica passio*, f. as HYSTERIC + *passio* passion.] = HYSTERIA 1.

hystericky /hɪˈstɛrɪki/ *a.* *US colloq.* E19. [f. HYSTERIC + -Y[1].] = HYSTERICAL *a.* 1.

hystero- /ˈhɪstərəʊ/ *comb. form* of Gk *hustera* uterus and of HYSTERIA: see -O-.

hystero-ˈepilepsy *n.* hysteria accompanied by epileptiform attacks L19. **hystero-epiˈleptic** *n.* & *a.* (a person) prone to hystero-epilepsy L19. **hysteroˈgenic** *a.* (now *rare*) designating an area of skin in some individuals pressure on which produces hysteria L19. **hysterosalˈpingogram** *n.* a radiograph of the uterus and Fallopian tubes L20. **hysterosalpinˈgography** *n.* radiography of the uterus and the Fallopian tubes following the injection of a radio-opaque fluid M20. **hysteroscope** *n.* a tubular instrument that can be inserted along the vagina into the uterus so that observations of its interior can be made or (now) operations performed on it E20. **hysteroˈscopic** *a.* of or pertaining to hysteroscopy M20. **hysteroˈscopically** *adv.* by means of hysteroscopy L20. **hysteˈroscopy** *n.* use of, or examination with, a hysteroscope M20. **hysterotome** *n.* an instrument for performing hysterotomy M19. **hysteˈrotomy** *n.* (an instance of) surgical incision into (or removal of) the uterus E19.

hysteroid /ˈhɪstərɔɪd/ *a.* & *n.* M19. [f. HYSTERIA + -OID.] A *adj.* Resembling (that of) hysteria. M19. B *n.* A person prone to hysteria. M20.

†**hysterology** *n.* E17–M19. [Late L *hysterologia* f. Gk *husterologia*, f. *husteros* later: see -OLOGY.] *Rhet.* Hysteron proteron. Also, anticlimax.

hysteron proteron /ˌhɪstərɒn ˈprɒtərɒn/ *n.*, *adv.*, & *a. phr.* M16. [Late L f. Gk *husteron proteron* latter (put in place of) former.] A *n. phr.* 1 *Rhet.* A figure of speech in which what should come last is put first. M16. 2 *gen.* Position or arrangement of things in the reverse of their natural or rational order. L16. †B *adv. phr.* In a topsy-turvy way. Only in E17. C *adj. phr.* Involving or employing hysteron proteron. M17.

hystricomorph /ˈhɪstrɪkə(ʊ)mɔːf/ *n.* L19. [mod.L *Hystricomorpha* (see below), f. L *hystric-*, *hystrix-* porcupine f. Gk *hustrix*: see -MORPH.] A rodent of the suborder Hystricomorpha, which includes the porcupines.

hystricoˈmorphic, **hystricoˈmorphine** *adjs.* E19.

hyte /hʌɪt/ *a.* *Sc.* E18. [Origin unkn.] 1 Mad, crazy. E18. 2 Excessively keen. L18.

hythe *n.* var. of HITHE.

hyther /ˈhʌɪθə/ *n.* E20. [f. HY(DRO- + THER(MO-.] *Climatology.* A quantity determined from temperature and humidity to represent the discomfort they jointly cause; a unit on a scale of 0 to 10 expressing this.

hythergraph /ˈhʌɪθəgrɑːf/ *n.* E20. [f. Gk *hy*(*etos* rain + *ther*(*mē* heat + -GRAPH.] A diagram in which temperature and either humidity or precipitation are shown for different occasions, esp. monthly throughout a year.

I

I, i /ʌɪ/, the ninth letter of the modern Eng. alphabet, repr. the Semitic consonant yod, which was adopted by Gk as iota, repr. a vowel. In L the letter represented both a high front vowel (long and short) and a palatal semi-vowel or continuant /j/; subsequently in Proto-Romance it also represented a palatal or palato-alveolar affricate /dʒ/, into which the semi-vowel had developed. In the 17th cent. a differentiation was made in the Roman alphabet, the consonant being represented by J, j (in its origin merely a variant form of I, i in certain positions), and the vowel by I, i. In Eng. the quality of the short vowel represented by I, i has not significantly changed since OE, but in the mod. period the long vowel has developed into a diphthong with a short high front vowel as its second elem.: for this and other values of this letter see the Key to the Pronunciation. Pl. **I's, Is, ies.**

I 1 The letter and its sound. **2** The shape of the letter.

1 *dot the i's (and cross the t's)*: see DOT *v.* 2 **I-beam** a girder of I-shaped section. **I-shaped** *a.* having a shape or cross-section like the capital letter I; having a long straight central piece with a right-angled crosspiece at each end.

II Symbolical uses. **3** Used to denote serial order; applied e.g. to the ninth group or section, sheet of a book, etc. **4** *Logic.* (Cap. I.) A particular affirmative proposition. **5** The ninth hypothetical person or example. **6** The roman numeral for 1. **7** *Math.* (Italic *i.*) The imaginary quantity $\sqrt{-1}$, the square root of minus one. Cf. J, J 6b. **8** *Anat.* & *Zool.* [Initial letter of *isotropic.*] *I band*, a light transverse band in a myofibril of striated muscle, which consists only of actin filaments and becomes narrower on contraction. Cf. A, A II.

6 **IV, IX** the roman numerals for 4, 9.

III 9 Abbrevs.: (A small selection only is given here. Those all in caps. or small caps. also occur with a full stop after each letter; some of those all in caps. also occur (i) with initial cap. only, (ii) in small caps.) **I.** = Institute; Institution; Island(s); Isle(s). **I** (*Chem.*) = iodine. **IA** = Institute of Actuaries; Iowa. **Ia.** = Iowa. **IAA** = indoleacetic acid. **IAEA** = International Atomic Energy Agency. **IATA** /ʌɪˈɑːtə/ = International Air Transport Association. **IBA** (*Hist.*) = Independent Broadcasting Authority. **IBM** = International Business Machines. **IBRD** = International Bank for Reconstruction and Development. **IC** = integrated circuit. **i/c** = in charge; in command; internal combustion. **ICAO** = International Civil Aviation Organization. **ICBM** = intercontinental ballistic missile. **ICC** (*US*) = Indian Claims Commission; Interstate Commerce Commission. **ICE** = Institution of Civil Engineers; internal-combustion engine. **I.Chem.E.** = Institution of Chemical Engineers. **ICI** = Imperial Chemical Industries. **ICS** (*Hist.*) = Indian Civil Service. **ICSU** = International Council of Scientific Unions. **ID** = Idaho; identification. **i.d.** = inner diameter. **IDA** = International Development Association. **IDB** = illicit diamond-buying. **IE** = Indo-European. **i.e.** = [L] *id est* that is to say. **IEE** = Institution of Electrical Engineers. **I.Eng.** = Incorporated Engineer. **IF** = intermediate frequency. **IFC** = International Finance Corporation. **Ig** (*Biochem.*) = immunoglobulin. **I.GasE.** = Institution of Gas Engineers. **IgG** (*Biochem.*) = gamma globulin, immunoglobulin G. **i.h.p.** = indicated horsepower. **IHS** [late L repr. Gk *IH(ΣΟΥ)Σ Iē(sou)s*, often taken as an abbrev. of various L wds] = Jesus. **IL** = Illinois; Institute of Linguists. **ILEA** /ˈɪlɪə/ (*Hist.*) = Inner London Education Authority. **Ill.** = Illinois. **ILO** = International Labour Organization. **ILR** = independent local radio. **IM** = intramuscular. **I.Mar.E.** = Institute of Marine Engineers. **IMCO** = Intergovernmental Maritime Consultative Organization. **I.Mech.E.** = Institution of Mechanical Engineers. **IMF** = International Monetary Fund. **I.Min.E.** = Institution of Mining Engineers. **IMM** = Institution of Mining and Metallurgy. **IMRO** = Investment Management Regulatory Organization. **IMS** (*Hist.*) = Indian Medical Service. **I.Mun.E.** = Institution of Municipal Engineers. **IN** = Indiana. **In** (*Chem.*) = indium. **in.** = inch(es). **Inc.** (*N. Amer.*) = Incorporated. **Ind.** = Independent; India; Indian; Indiana. **INF** = intermediate-range nuclear force(s). **INRI** = [L] *Iesus Nazarenus Rex Iudaeorum* Jesus of Nazareth, King of the Jews. **ins** = inches; insurance. **INSET** /ˈɪnsɛt/ = in-service education and training. **inst.** = institute; institution. **Inst.P.** = Institute of Physics. **int.** = interior; internal; international. **inter.** = intermediate. **internat.** = international. **I/O** (*Computing*) = input/output. **IOC** = International Olympic Committee. **IOM** = Isle of Man. **IOW** = Isle of Wight. **IPA** = International Phonetic Alphabet; International Phonetic Association. **IPCS** = Institution of Professional Civil Servants. **ips** = inches per second; (*Computing*) instructions per second. **IQ** = intelligence quotient. **IR** = infrared. **Ir** (*Chem.*) = iridium. **IRA** = Irish Republican Army; (*US*) individual retirement account. **IRBM** = intermediate-range ballistic missile. **IRO** = Inland Revenue Office; International Refugee Organization. **IRS** (*US*) = Internal Revenue Service. **Is.** = Isaiah (in the Bible); Island(s); Isle(s). **Isa.** = Isaiah (in the Bible). **ISBN** = international standard book number. **ISO** = (Companion of the) Imperial Service Order; International Organization for Standardization. **ISSN** = international standard serial number. **IT** = information technology. **It.** = Italian. **ITA** = Independent Television Authority. **i.t.a.** = initial teaching alphabet. **ital.** = italic (type). **ITC** = Independent Television Committee. **ITN** = Independent Television News. **ITO** = International Trade Organization. **ITU** = International Telecommunication Union. **ITV** = independent television. **IU** = international unit. **IUCD** = intrauterine contraceptive device. **IUD** = intrauterine (contraceptive) device; intrauterine death (of a foetus). **IUPAC** = International Union of Pure and Applied Chemistry. **IV** = intravenous(ly). **IVF** = *in vitro* fertilization. **IWW** = Industrial Workers of the World.

¶The dot over the lower-case *i* is derived from a diacritic mark, like an acute accent, used in Latin manuscripts to indicate the *i* in positions in which it might have been mistaken for part of another letter. The same cause led finally in Eng. to a kind of scribal canon that *i* must not be used as a final letter, but must in this position be changed to *y*, though in inflected forms, where the *i* was not final, it was retained (hence *city, cities, duty, dutiful*, etc.).

I /ʌɪ/ *pers. pron.*, 1 *sing. subjective (nom.)*, & *n.*[1] [OE *iċ* = OFris., OS (Du.) *ik*, OHG *ih* (G *ich*), ON *ek*, Goth. *ik*, f. Gmc, cogn. w. L *ego*, Gk *egō(n)*, Skt *aham*, Avest. *azəm*, Old Ch. Slav. *(j)azŭ* (Russ. *ya*), Lith. *eo*, Latvian, OPruss., Armenian *es*. Cf. ME *pron.*, MY *a.*] **A** *pron.* **1** Used by the speaker or writer referring to himself or herself, as the subject of predication or in attributive or predicative agreement with that subject. OE. **2** Objective: me. Esp. when separated from the governing vb or prep. by other wds. Now *colloq.* L16.

1 DRYDEN Wretched I, to love in vain. TENNYSON Her sweet 'I will' has made you one. D. BARNES So I, doctor Matthew Mighty O'Connor, ask you to think of the night the day long. E. BOWEN No one would be gladder than I would if things ran smoothly. G. GREENE He had been consulted as well as I. J. SIMMS I am saying, am I not, that I no longer loved Kiyoko. **I Am** God as self-existent; *loosely* an important or self-important person. 2 T. HARDY Nothing's known to poor I! *Oxford Mail* After showing photographer Bill Radford and I her stitching skill.

B *n.* **1** A self, a person identical with oneself. Chiefly in *another I*, a second self. Now *rare.* M16. **2** The pronoun 'I' as a word. L16. **3** *Metaphysics.* The subject or object of self-consciousness, *the* ego. E18. **4** The narrator of a work of fiction, appearing on his or her own account. M20.

4 G. GREENE Many readers assume . . that an 'I' is always the author.

†I *adv., int.,* & *n.*[2] see AYE *adv.*[2], *int.*, & *n.*[2]

i' *prep.* see IN *prep.*

†i- *pref.*[1] Repr. OE *ġe-* (see Y-), forming collective ns., deriv. adjs., advs., and vbs, esp. used with the pa. pple of vbs.

i- *pref.*[2] see IN-[3].

-i /*f. It.* i; *f.* L ʌɪ, iː/ *suff.*[1] Repr. L pl. ending of masc. ns. in *-us* and *-er* and It. pl. ending of masc. ns. in *-o* and *-e*, adopted unchanged as Eng. pl., as *foci, timpani, dilettanti*.

-i /i/ *suff.*[2] Repr. an adj. suff. in Semitic and Indo-Iranian langs., and forming adjs. and ns. f. the names of regions in or near the Middle East, as *Azerbaijani, Israeli, Pakistani*.

-i- /ɪ/ *comb. form (connective)*. Repr. L *-i-* as a stem-vowel or connective, adopted in Eng. through Fr. or directly f. L, forming the connecting vowel esp. of wds in -ANA, -FEROUS, -FIC, -FORM, -FY, -GEROUS, -VOROUS: cf. -O-.

-ia /ɪə/ *suff.*[1] Repr. Gk & L nom. sing. ending of fem. ns. (in Gk esp. freq. as the ending of abstract ns. f. adjs. in *-os*), adopted unchanged in Eng., as *hydrophobia, mania, militia*; hence in mod.L terms (as *utopia*), *spec.* (*a*) *Med.* in ns. denoting states and disorders, as *hysteria, diphtheria*; (*b*) *Bot.* & *Zool.* in names of genera, as *Dahlia, Latimeria*, and those of higher taxa also, as *Reptilia, Cryptogamia*; (*c*) in names of countries, as *Australia, India*; (*d*) (after *ammonia*) in names of alkaloids, as *morphia*: now superseded by -INE[5]. Cf. -A[1], -Y[3].

-ia /ɪə/ *suff.*[2] Repr. Gk pl. ending of neut. ns. in *-ion* and L pl. ending of neut. ns. in *-ium* or *-e*, adopted unchanged as Eng. pl. of collective ns., as *juvenilia, paraphernalia, regalia*, and (*Zool.*) in mod.L forming the names of classes, as *Mammalia, Reptilia*: cf. -A[3].

-ial /ɪəl/ *suff.* Repr. Fr. *-iel* or L *-ialis*, *-iale* in adjs. formed f. n. stems in *-io-*, *-ia-*, as *curialis, tibialis*; extensively used in med.L, Fr., and Eng. to form deriv. adjs. f. L adjs. in *-is*, *-ius*, as *celestial* f. L *caelestis*, *dictatorial* f. L *dictatorius*, etc.: cf. -AL[1].

iamb /ˈʌɪam(b)/ *n.* M19. [Anglicized f. IAMBUS.] = IAMBUS.

iambi *n.pl.* see IAMBUS.

iambic /ʌɪˈambɪk/ *a.* & *n.* M16. [Fr. *iambique* f. late L *iambicus* f. Gk *iambikos*, f. *iambos*: see IAMBUS, -IC.] *Pros.* **A** *adj.* **1** Consisting of, characterized by, or based on iambuses. M16. **2** Of a poet: using iambic metres. L16. **B** *n.* An iambic foot, verse, or poem. Usu. in *pl.* L16.

iambical *a.* (long *rare* or *obs.*) = IAMBIC *a.* L16. **iambically** *adv.* (*rare*) M19.

iambographer /ʌɪam'bɒgrəfə/ *n. rare.* E17. [f. Gk *iambographos*, f. *iambos*: see next, -O-, -GRAPHER.] A writer of iambics.

iambus /ʌɪ'ambəs/ *n.* Pl. **-buses, -bi** /-bʌɪ/. L16. [L f. Gk *iambos* iambus, lampoon, f. *iaptein* assail in words (the iambic trimeter having been first used by Gk satirists).] *Pros.* A metrical foot consisting of one short followed by one long syllable or (in English etc.) of one unstressed followed by one stressed syllable.

-ian /ɪən/ *suff.* 1 Repr. L *-ianus*, f. *-anus* -AN added to n. stems in *-i-*; in Eng. forming adjs. & ns. adopted or formed f. L, as *antediluvian*, *barbarian*, *equestrian*, *patrician*, and f. proper names of persons and places, as *Bostonian*, *Churchillian*, *Georgian*, *Oxonian*: see -I-, -AN. In some ns., as *theologian*, *-ian* is a refash. of Fr. *-ien*. 2 [f. MAGNES)IAN, MANGANES)IAN.] *Min.* Replacing the ending of Eng. or L names of elements to form adjs. w. the sense 'having a small proportion of a constituent element replaced by the element concerned'.

-iana /ɪ'ɑːnə/ *suff.* Repr. a euphonic var. of -ANA, after L wds ending in *-iana*: see -I-, -ANA.

Iapygian /ʌɪə'pɪdʒɪən/ *n.* & *a.* L18. [f. L *Iapygius*, f. *Iapyg-*, *Iapyx* a son of Daedalus said to have ruled over S. Italy: see -IAN.] A *n.* A member of a people inhabiting Iapygia, the name given by the ancient Greeks to the area comprising the peninsula of Apulia in S. Italy; the language of this people. L18. B *adj.* Of or pertaining to Iapygia or the Iapygians. M19.

-iasis /'ʌɪəsɪs/ *suff.* [f. -I- + L or Gk *-asis* used to form ns. of state or process.] Forming the names of diseases, as *elephantiasis*, *leishmaniasis*, *psoriasis*.

Iatmul /'jatmʊl/ *n.* & *a.* M20. [Iatmul.] A *n.* Pl. same. A member of a people of NW Papua New Guinea; the language of this people. M20. B *attrib.* or as *adj.* Of or pertaining to the Iatmul or their language. M20.

iatraliptic /ʌɪˌatrə'lɪptɪk/ *a.* & *n. rare.* M17. [L *iatraliptícus*, f. Gk *iatraleiptikos*, f. *iatraleiptēs*, f. *iatros* (see IATRO-) + *aleiptēs* anointer: see -IC.] A *n.* A physician who uses unguents to effect cures. M17. B *adj.* Consisting of the curative use of unguents. E18.

iatric /ʌɪ'atrɪk/ *a. rare.* M19. [Gk *iatrikos*, f. *iatros* physician: see IATRO-, -IC.] Of or pertaining to a physician or medicine; medical; medicinal.
iatrical *a.* L17.

iatro- /ʌɪ'atrəʊ/ *comb. form.* [Gk, f. *iatros* physician, f. *iasthai* heal: see -O-.] Of or pertaining to physicians or medicine.
iatro'chemical *a.* of, pertaining to, or advocating iatrochemistry M19. **iatro'chemist** *n.* an advocate of iatrochemistry M17. **iatro'chemistry** *n.* the theory or school of thought that was adopted by Paracelsus and others in the 16th and 17th cents., according to which medicine and physiology were to be understood in terms of chemistry M19.

iatrogenic /ʌɪˌatrə(ʊ)'dʒɛnɪk/ *a.* E20. [f. IATRO- + -GENIC.] (Of a disease, symptom, etc.) induced unintentionally by a physician's treatment, examination, etc.; of or pertaining to the inducing of disease etc. in this way.
British Medical Bulletin The epidemic of iatrogenic deaths in asthmatic children.
iatrogenically *adv.* M20. **iatrogenicity** /-'nɪsɪti/ *n.* iatrogeny M20. **ia'trogeny** *n.* the iatrogenic production of disease etc. E20.

iatromathematical /ʌɪˌatrə(ʊ)maθ(ə)'matɪk(ə)l/ *a.* E17. [f. mod.L *iatromathematicus* f. Gk *iatromathēmatikos*, f. as IATRO- + *mathēmatikos*: see MATHEMATIC, -AL[1].] *Hist. Sci.* †1 Practising medicine in conjunction with astrology. Only in E17. 2 Of, pertaining to, or advocating iatromathematics. M19.
iatromathematically *adv.* E17. **iatromathema'tician** *n.* an advocate or adherent of iatromathematics E18. **iatromathematics** *n.* †(*a*) a work on medicine and astrology; (*b*) a theory or school of thought that arose in Italy in the 17th cent., according to which medicine and physiology were to be explained in terms of mathematics and mechanics: M17.

iatromechanical /ʌɪˌatrə(ʊ)mɪ'kanɪk(ə)l/ *a.* M19. [f. IATRO- + MECHANICAL.] *Hist. Sci.* = IATROMATHEMATICAL 2.
iatromechanic, -mechanician /-mɛkə'nɪʃ(ə)n/ *ns.* an iatromathematician M19. **iatromechanics, -'mechanism** *ns.* iatromathematics L19. **iatro'mechanist** *n.* an iatromathematician M20.

iatrophysical /ʌɪˌatrə(ʊ)'fɪzɪk(ə)l/ *a.* L19. [f. IATRO- + PHYSICAL.] *Hist. Sci.* = IATROMATHEMATICAL 2.
iatrophysicist /-sɪst/ *n.* an iatromathematician L19. **iatrophysics** *n.* iatromathematics L19.

Iban /'iːban, iː'ban/ *n.* & *a.* E20. [Iban.] A *n.* A member of a people of Sarawak (also called *Sea Dyaks*); the Indonesian language of this people. E20. B *adj.* Of or pertaining to this people or their language. E20.

Ibanag /'iːbənɑːg/ *n.* & *a.* L19. [Ibanag.] A *n.* A member of a people inhabiting Luzon in the Philippines; the Austronesian language of this people. L19. B *adj.* Of or pertaining to this people or their language. M20.

Iberian /ʌɪ'bɪərɪən/ *a.* & *n.* E16. [f. L *Iberia* the country of the *Iberi* or *Iberes*, f. Gk *Ibēres*, (i) Spaniards, (ii) a people of the S. Caucasus: see -IAN.] A *adj.* 1 Of, pertaining to, or designating the peninsula of SW Europe occupied by Spain and Portugal or the (present or former) Iberians. E16. 2 Of or pertaining to ancient Iberia in Asia, a region approximately corresponding to modern Georgia. *rare.* L17. 3 Of or pertaining to the Iberians of neolithic Britain. L19. B *n.* 1 a A native or inhabitant of Spain or Portugal; a Spaniard, a Portuguese. E17. b A native or inhabitant of the Iberian peninsula in pre-Roman and Roman times. M19. c The language or languages spoken by the ancient Iberians. L19. 2 A native or inhabitant of ancient Iberia in Asia. Long *rare* or *obs.* E17. 3 An inhabitant of Britain in neolithic times regarded as belonging to a branch of the Iberians of Continental Europe. L19.

iberis /ʌɪ'bɪərɪs/ *n.* M18. [mod.L (see below), prob. f. Gk *ibēris* a kind of pepperwort.] Any of various low-growing cruciferous plants of the chiefly Mediterranean genus *Iberis*, bearing flattened heads of white, pink, or purple flowers and frequently grown as garden plants; = CANDYTUFT.

†**Ibernian** *a.* & *n.* see HIBERNIAN.

Ibero- /ʌɪ'bɪərəʊ/ *comb. form* of IBERIAN: see -O-.
Ibero-A'merican *a.* & *n.* (a) Spanish-American; (a) Latin American: E20. **Ibero-Cau'casian** *a.* & *n.* (of) a group of languages spoken in the region of the Caucasus and ancient Iberia in Asia (see IBERIAN *a.* 2) M20.

ibex /'ʌɪbɛks/ *n.* E17. [L.] A goat antelope, *Capra ibex*, with thick curved ridged horns and a chin beard and occurring chiefly in mountainous parts of NE Africa and central Asia. Also (in full *Spanish ibex*), a related animal of the Pyrenees, *Capra pyrenaica*.
Siberian ibex: see SIBERIAN *a.* WALIA *ibex*.

Ibibio /ɪbɪ'biːəʊ/ *n.* & *a.* E19. [Ibibio.] A *n.* Pl. same, **-os**. A member of a people of southern Nigeria; the Niger-Congo language of this people. E19. B *attrib.* or as *adj.* Of or pertaining to the Ibibio or their language. M19.

Ibicencan /ɪbɪ'θɛŋk(ə)n/ *n.* & *a.* M20. [f. Sp. *ibicenca* native or inhabitant of Ibiza + -AN.] A *n.* A native or inhabitant of Ibiza (see IBIZAN). M20.
B *adj.* Of or pertaining to Ibiza. M20.
Ibicencan hound = IVICENE *n.*

Ibicenco /ɪbɪ'θɛŋkəʊ/ *n.* & *a.* Pl. of n. **-os**. E20. [Sp. *ibicenco* pertaining to Ibiza (see IBIZAN).] = IBICENCAN.

ibid. /'ɪbɪd/ *adv.* M17. [Abbrev. of L: see next.] = IBIDEM.

ibidem /'ɪbɪdɛm, ɪ'bʌɪdɛm/ *adv.* M18. [L = in the same place, f. *ibi* there + demonstr. suff. *-dem*, as in *idem*, *tandem*, etc.] In the same book, chapter, passage, etc.

-ibility /ɪ'bɪlɪti/ *suff.* [Fr. *-ibilité* f. L *-ibilitas*.] Forming ns. f. adjs. in -IBLE, as *credibility*, *possibility*: see -ITY.

ibis /'ʌɪbɪs/ *n.* Pl. **ibises**; (now *rare*) **ibides** /'ʌɪbɪdiːz/, **ibes** /'ʌɪbiːz/. LME. [L (genit. *ibis*, *ibidis*, pl. *ibes*) f. Gk.] 1 Any of a group of gregarious wading birds of warm and tropical climates which have a long thin decurved bill, a long neck, and long legs, and which with the spoonbills constitute the family Threskiornithidae. LME. 2 *Angling.* Orig., a kind of artificial fly made with a feather dyed red. Now usu., such a feather. M19.
1 sacred ibis a white ibis, *Threskiornis aethiopica*, native to Africa and Madagascar and venerated by the ancient Egyptians. *scarlet ibis*: see SCARLET *a.*

Ibizan /ɪ'biːθ(ə)n/ *a.* & *n.* E20. [f. *Ibiza* (see below) + -AN.] A *adj.* Of or pertaining to Ibiza, the westernmost of the Balearic Islands in the western Mediterranean. E20.
Ibizan hound = IVICENE *n.*
B *n.* 1 The Catalan dialect of Ibiza. M20. 2 An Ibizan hound. L20.

-ible /ɪb(ə)l/ *suff.* [f. L *-ibilis* adj. suff., the form taken by the suff. *-bilis* (see -BLE) when added to L consonantal stems (vbl or ppl) and some *e-* and *i-* stems.] Forming adjs. w. the senses 'able to be, suitable for being', as *audible*, *compressible*, *edible*, and (formerly) 'able to, causing', as *horrible*, *passible*, *terrible*. Freq. displaced by -ABLE in wds that have come through Fr., or that are looked on as formed directly on an Eng. vb.

Iblis *n.* var. of EBLIS.

Ibo *n.* & *a.* var. of IGBO.

ibotenic /iːbəʊ'tɛnɪk/ *a.* M20. [f. Jap. *iboten(gutake* the mushroom *Amanita strobiliformis* from which the acid was first isolated, + -IC.] Biochem. *ibotenic acid*, an isoxazole found in certain mushrooms, used as an insecticide and as a selective neurotoxin.
ibotenate *n.* a salt of ibotenic acid L20.

Ibsenism /'ɪbs(ə)nɪz(ə)m/ *n.* L19. [f. *Ibsen* (see below) + -ISM.] The dramatic principles and aims of the works of the Norwegian dramatist and poet Henrik Ibsen (1828–1906) and his followers, in which social conventions are examined and criticized.
Ibsenish *a.* resembling events in Ibsen's plays L19. **Ibsenist** *n.* & *a.* (*a*) *n.* an admirer, student, or imitator of Ibsen; (*b*) *adj.* of or pertaining to Ibsenism or Ibsenists; typical of Ibsen's plays: L19. **Ibsenite** *n.* & *a.* = IBSENIST L19.

ibuprofen /ʌɪbjuː'prəʊf(ə)n/ *n.* M20. [f. I(SO- + BU(TYL + PRO(PIONIC + alt. of PHEN(YL, elems. of the systematic name (see below).] An anti-inflammatory and analgesic drug used to treat arthritis; 2-(4-isobutylphenyl)propionic acid, $C_{13}H_{18}O_2$.

-ic /ɪk/ *suff.* Also †**-ick**, †**-ique**. [Repr. Fr. *-ique*, its source L *-icus*, & its source Gk *-ikos*.] 1 In adjs. f. Fr., L (esp. late L), or Gk, as *civic*, *classic*, *historic*, or formed directly in Eng., as *artistic*, *Icelandic*, with the general sense 'of or pertaining to'. b Forming part of compound suffs., as -ATIC, -ETIC, -FIC, -OLOGIC. c *Chem.* In adjs. denoting a higher valence or degree of oxidation than those ending in *-ous*, as *ferric*, *sulphuric*. 2 In Gk, adjs. in *-ikos* were used absol. as ns., which in med.L gave wds in *-ica* which could be taken as fem. sing. or as neut. pl. In Eng. bef. 16 wds of this class had the sing. form, and in some, as *logic*, *magic*, *rhetoric*, the sing. has been retained; others have *-ic* after Fr. or G, as *dialectic*. More often such wds now end in -ICS. 3 In ns. that are Eng. adjs. used absol., as *cosmetic*, *emetic*; *epic*, *lyric*; *domestic*, *mechanic*, *rustic*.

icaco /ɪ'kɑːkəʊ/ *n.* Pl. **-o(e)s**. M18. [Sp. *(h)icaco* f. Taino *hikako*.] An evergreen tree, *Chrysobalanus icaco*, native to tropical America and the W. Indies and bearing white flowers; the fruit of this tree. Also called *coco-plum*.

-ical /ɪk(ə)l/ *suff.* 1 In adjs. f. late or med.L wds in *-icalis* (formed by adding *-alis* to ns. in *-icus* or *-ice*), as *clerical*, *grammatical*, or formed directly in Eng. from ns. in *-ic*, L adjs. in *-icus*, & Fr. adjs. in *-ique*, as *domestical*, *fanatical*, *philosophical*, *theoretical*: see -AL[1]. To many adjs. in *-ical* there corresponds another in *-ic*, that in *-ical* usually being the earlier and the more commonly used. 2 In compound suffs., as -OLOGICAL.

-ically /ɪk(ə)li/ *suff.* [f. -ICAL + -LY[2].] Forming advs. corresp. to adjs. in *-ic* and *-ical*.

Icarian /ɪˈkɛːrɪən/ *a.* M16. [f. L *Icarius* (= Gk *Ikarios*), f. as next: see -IAN.] Of, pertaining to, or characteristic of Icarus; rashly ambitious or presumptuous.

†**Icarian Sea** the Aegean Sea.

Icarus /ˈɪk(ə)rəs/ *n.* L16. [L *Icarus* (see below) f. Gk *Ikaros*.] A person who is rashly ambitious or presumptuous, or who resembles in some other way Icarus the son of Daedalus in Greek mythology, who flew so high that the sun melted the wax with which his wings were fastened, so that he fell to his death in the Aegean Sea.

ice /ʌɪs/ *n.* [OE *īs* = OFris., OS, OHG *īs* (Du. *ijs*, G *Eis*), ON *íss*, f. Gmc, with analogues in Iranian langs.] 1 Frozen water, a brittle transparent crystalline solid. OE. b A mass or body of ice. Usu. in *pl.* OE. 2 *the ice*, the sheet or layer of ice on something, esp. a pond, river, etc. ME. 3 *fig.* Complete absence of warm feeling; cold-heartedness; reserve. L16. 4a (An) ice-cream. E18. b Icing for cakes etc. E18. 5a Diamonds; jewellery. *slang.* E20. b Profit from the illegal sale of theatre, cinema, etc., tickets. *US slang.* E20. c Protection money. *slang.* M20.

1 MOUNTAIN *of ice.* 2 B. LOPEZ No ship . . had been able to breach the ice in Davis Strait. 3 M. IGNATIEFF She watched . . as the ice formed at the heart of her marriage.

Phrases: *as cold as ice*: see COLD *a.* *black ice*: see BLACK *a.* **break the ice** *fig.* make a beginning; break through reserve or stiffness. *cut ice*: see CUT *v.* *dry ice*: see DRY *a.* *fast ice*: see FAST *a.* *hog on ice*: see HOG *n.* *inland ice*: see INLAND *a.* **like ice** (of a room, one's extremities, etc.) very cold. **on ice** (*a*) (of an entertainment, sport, etc.) performed by skaters; (*b*) (of a bottle etc.) on or in ice to cool the contents; (*c*) *colloq.* held in reserve; postponed for attention at a later date. **on thin ice** in a risky situation. *skate on thin ice*: see SKATE *v.*

Comb.: **ice age** a glacial period, esp. one of those in the Pleistocene epoch, (*little ice age.*: see LITTLE *a.*); **ice-axe** a tool used by mountaineers for cutting footholds in ice; **ice-bag** an ice-filled rubber bag for medical use; **ice-bird** (*a*) any of several prions; (*b*) the little auk; *iceblink*: see BLINK *n.* 5a; **iceblock** (*a*) a block of ice; (*b*) *Austral.* & *NZ* an ice lolly; **ice-blue** a very pale blue; **ice-bolt** a bolt or dart of ice; an avalanche; *fig.* a sudden chill; **ice-bound** *a.* held fast or confined by ice; **icebox** (*a*) a box for holding ice; (*b*) a box kept cold by ice; (*c*) *US* a refrigerator; (*d*) a compartment in a refrigerator for making and storing ice; **ice bucket** = *ice pail* below; **ice-cap** (*a*) a permanent layer of ice covering a tract of land (esp. a polar region) or the top of a mountain; (*b*) a bag of crushed ice applied to the head; **ice chest** = *icebox* (a) above; **ice-cold** *a.* as cold as ice; **ice-cube** a small block of ice made in a refrigerator, used for chilling drinks; **ice-fall** (*a*) a steep part of a glacier resembling a frozen waterfall; (*b*) an avalanche of ice; **ice-field** an extensive flat expanse of ice, esp. in polar regions; **ice-fish** *n.* & *v.* (*a*) *n.* a capelin; (*b*) *v.i.* fish through holes in the ice on a lake or river (chiefly as *ice-fishing* vbl n.); *ice floe*: see FLOE; **ice-flower** a delicate pattern of ice crystals formed by frost, esp. on a window; **ice fog** fog in which the obscuring matter is minute ice crystals suspended in the air; **ice-foot** [Da. *isfod*] (*a*) a belt of ice on the sea next to the coast in Arctic regions; (*b*) the edge of an ice floe; **ice-front** the margin of a glacier, ice-shelf, or ice sheet; *ice hockey*: see HOCKEY *n.*[1] 2; **ice house** (*a*) a building, often partly or wholly underground, in which to store ice; (*b*) a small shelter built out of ice; *ice lolly*: see LOLLY *n.*[2] 1; **ice machine**: for making ice from water; **ice-master** a pilot or sailing-master who has experience of navigating among ice floes; **ice-pack** (*a*) (a mass of) pack ice; (*b*) a quantity of ice wrapped up and applied to the body for medical etc. purposes; **ice pail** a pail to hold ice for cooling bottles of wine; **ice pan** a small slab of floating ice; **ice-pick** (*a*) a needle-like implement with a handle for splitting table ice; (*b*) a mountaineer's pick; **ice-piton** a piton to assist climbing on ice; **ice plant** (*a*) any of various succulent plants of the mesembryanthemum family, native to southern Africa, esp. *Mesembryanthemum crystallinum*, whose leaves are covered with pellucid watery vesicles looking like ice crystals; (*b*) a tall freq. cultivated pink-flowered stonecrop, *Sedum spectabile*, with glaucous fleshy leaves; *ice rink*: see RINK *n.* 3; **ice sheet** a permanent layer of ice covering an extensive tract of land, esp. a polar region; **ice-shelf** a floating sheet of ice permanently attached to a land mass; **ice-show** an entertainment performed by skaters on ice; **ice-skate** *n.* & *v.* (*a*) *n.* a skate consisting of a boot with a blade beneath, for skating on ice; (*b*) *v.i.* skate on ice; **ice-skater** a person who skates on ice; **ice storm** a storm of freezing rain that leaves a deposit of ice; **ice-water**: obtained from or cooled by ice; **ice-wool** = EIS WOOL; **ice-work** (*a*) ornamentation executed in ice, or having the appearance of ice; frosted work; (*b*) work done by glaciers or icebergs; (*c*) (the technique of) climbing on icy surfaces; **ice-worm** a small oligochaete worm, *Mesenchytraeus solifugus*, found in N. American glaciers and ice-fields; **ice-yacht** a lightly built boat with runners and a sail for travelling at speed over ice.

iceless *a.* free of ice; not covered by ice: M19.

ice /ʌɪs/ *v.* LME. [f. the n.] 1 *v.t.* a Cover with ice. Foll. by *over*, *up*. Usu. in *pass.* LME. b Convert into ice. M17. 2 *v.t.* Cover or decorate (a cake etc.) with icing. E17. 3 *v.t.* Chill with ice; cool (esp. wine) by placing in ice. E19. 4 *v.t.* Make cold. Chiefly *fig.* E19. b Kill. *US slang.* M20. 5 *v.i.* Turn to ice; become covered with ice. Also foll. by *over*, *up*. M19.

1 *Times* A snowstorm was encountered and the aircraft became badly iced-up. 3 M. PIERCY Why don't you bring us iced tea? 5 C. A. LINDBERGH The turn indicator's icing up. E. JONG Pipes froze. The driveway iced over.

-ice /ɪs/ *suff.*[1] Forming (esp. abstract) ns. and repr. OFr. *-ice* (mod. *-ise*), of non-popular origin, f. L *-itia*, *-itius*, *-itium*; e.g. *avarice*, *novice*, *police*, *precipice*, *service*.

¶The ending has various other origins, partly through assim. to the above, as in *accomplice*, *apprentice*, *bodice*, *poultice*.

-ice /ɪsi/ *suff.*[2] Also **-icè**. In med.L forming advs. f. adjs., adopted esp. when f. names of peoples or languages, as *anglice*, *gallice*, and in Eng. occas. forming jocular nonce-words.

iceberg /ˈʌɪsbəːɡ/ *n.* L18. [(M)Du. *ijsberg*, whence also G *Eisberg*, Sw. *isberg*, Da. *isbjerg*: see ICE *n.*, BARROW *n.*[1]] †1 A glacier which comes close to the coast and is seen from the sea as a hill. L18–M19. 2 A very large mass of ice floating loose in the sea after becoming detached from a glacier or ice sheet. E19. 3 *fig.* An unfeeling or unemotional person. M19. 4 *fig.* Something of which the greater part is unknown or not recognized. M20.

4 **tip of the iceberg** a known or recognizable part of something (esp. a difficulty) evidently much larger.

Comb.: **iceberg lettuce** any of various crisp pale cabbage lettuces.

ice-boat /ˈʌɪsbəʊt/ *n.* & *v.* M18. [f. ICE *n.* + BOAT *n.*] A *n.* 1 A boat mounted on runners for travelling on ice; *spec.* an ice-yacht. M18. 2 = ICE-BREAKER 2. M19. 3 A fishing vessel with facilities for the refrigeration of fish. *US.* L19. B *v.i.* Travel in an ice-boat or ice-yacht. Chiefly as *ice-boating* vbl n. L19.

ice-boater *n.* E20.

ice-breaker /ˈʌɪsbreɪkə/ *n.* E19. [f. ICE *n.* + BREAKER *n.*[1]] 1 A thing which breaks up moving ice so as to diminish its impact; *spec.* a structure protecting the upstream end of a bridge-pier. E19. 2 A ship specially built or adapted for breaking a channel through ice. L19. 3 *fig.* Something that breaks the ice on a social occasion etc. L19.

ice-cream /ʌɪsˈkriːm/ *n.* M18. [Alt. of *iced cream* s.v. ICED 1.] A semi-solid or semi-liquid foodstuff made from sweetened and flavoured milk fat, stirred to incorporate air, and frozen; a portion of this.

Comb.: *ice-cream float*: see FLOAT *n.* 9; **ice-cream parlour** a cafe where ice-cream is sold.

iced /ʌɪst/ *a.* L17. [f. ICE *n.*, *v.*: see -ED[2], -ED[1].] 1 Covered or chilled with ice. L17. 2 Covered with icing; (of fruit) glacé. M19.

1 M. PIERCY Why don't you bring us iced tea? †**iced cream** ice-cream. *iced lolly*: see LOLLY *n.*[2] 1.

Iceland /ˈʌɪslənd/ *n.* Also †**Island**. M16. [See sense 2. Branch II directly f. ICE *n.* + LAND *n.*[1]] I 1 In full *Iceland dog*, (arch.) *cur*. A shaggy sharp-eared white dog, formerly in favour as a lap-dog in England. M16. 2 Used *attrib.* in the names of things associated with Iceland, an island republic in the N. Atlantic, near the Arctic Circle. L18.

2 **Iceland falcon** a usu. pale grey gyrfalcon from Iceland. **Iceland gull** a grey and white Arctic gull, *Larus glaucoides*. **Iceland lichen, moss** an Arctic and Alpine lichen, *Cetraria islandica*, which can be boiled to make an edible jelly. **Iceland poppy** an Arctic poppy, *Papaver nudicaule*, with leafless stems and white yellow-based petals; any of the garden poppies, with variously coloured flowers, derived from this or the related *P. alpinum* group, of European mountains. **Iceland spar** a transparent variety of calcite with strong double refraction.

II 3 (**i-**.) A country covered with ice; the realm of perpetual ice. M19.

Icelander *n.* a native or inhabitant of Iceland E17. **Iceˈlandish** *a.* Icelandic E18.

Icelandic /ʌɪsˈlandɪk/ *a.* & *n.* L17. [f. prec. + -IC.] A *adj.* Of or pertaining to Iceland or its people or language. L17.

B *n.* The Germanic language of Iceland. L18.

Old Icelandic: see OLD *a.*

iceman /ˈʌɪsmən/ *n.* Pl. **-men**. M19. [f. ICE *n.* + MAN *n.*] 1 A person skilled in traversing ice in Alpine or polar regions. M19. 2 A person responsible for looking after the ice on an ice rink. M19. 3 A person who deals in or sells ice. *N. Amer.* M19. 4 A person who makes ice-cream. L19.

icemanship *n.* skill in traversing ice L19.

Icenian /ʌɪˈsiːnɪən/ *n.* & *a.* L16. [f. L *Iceni* the Icenians + -AN.] A *n.* A member of a tribe of ancient Britons inhabiting the area of SE England represented by Norfolk and Suffolk and to which Boudicca belonged. L16. B *adj.* 1 Of or pertaining to the Icenians or the area they inhabited. M18. 2 *Geol.* Designating or pertaining to certain early Pleistocene beds of Norfolk and Suffolk. L19.

Iˈcenic *a.* = ICENIAN *a.* 1 L19.

ichabod /ˈɪkəbɒd/ *int.* E19. [W. allus. to *1 Sam.* 4:21, where Eli's daughter-in-law names her child Ichabod, saying 'The glory is departed from Israel.'] Expr. regret at former glories or higher standards.

ichneumon /ɪkˈnjuːmən/ *n.* L15. [L f. Gk *ikhneumōn* lit. 'tracker', f. *ikhneuein* to track, f. *ikhnos* track, footprint.] 1 The Egyptian mongoose, *Herpestes ichneumon*, found over much of Africa and parts of southern Europe, and noted for destroying crocodile eggs. L15. 2 More fully *ichneumon fly*. Any of the family Ichneumonidae of hymenopterous insects, which mostly lay their eggs in other insects, esp. caterpillars. M17.

ichneumoned *a.* infested with ichneumon flies M19.

ichnofossil /ˈɪknəʊfɒs(ə)l, -sɪl/ *n.* M20. [f. Gk *ikhnos* (see next) + FOSSIL *n.*] A trace fossil.

ichnography /ɪkˈnɒɡrəfi/ *n.* L16. [Fr. *ichnographie* or L *ichnographia* f. Gk *ikhnographia*, f. *ikhnos* track, footprint: see -GRAPHY.] A ground-plan; a plan, a map.

ichnoˈgraphic *a.* L17. **ichnoˈgraphical** *a.* L16.

ichnology /ɪkˈnɒlədʒi/ *n.* M19. [f. Gk *ikhnos* track, footprint + -LOGY.] The branch of palaeontology that deals with fossil footprints; the features of a region that belong to this.

ichnoˈlogical *a.* M19.

icho *n.* var. of ICHU.

ichoglan /ˈɪtʃəɡlan/ *n.* L17. [Obs. Turk., f. *īch* interior + *oğlan* young man.] *Hist.* A page-in-waiting in the palace of the Sultan of Turkey.

ichor /ˈʌɪkɔː/ *n.* M17. [Gk *ikhōr*.] 1 Blood; a liquid likened to the blood of animals. Now *literary*. M17. 2 *Med.* A watery discharge from a wound or sore. *arch.* M17. 3 *Gk Mythol.* A fluid supposed to flow like blood in the veins of the gods. L17. 4 *Geol.* An emanation from magma supposed by some to cause granitization. E20.

1 J. FULLER The sweat gathered . . as if some precious ichor of the spirit were being pressed.

†**ichorose** *a.* ichorous E–M18. **ichorous** *a.* of the nature of ichor; containing ichor: M17.

ichthammol /ˈɪkθəmɒl/ *n.* E20. [f. ICHTH(Y)OL w. insertion of AMM(ONIA.)] *Pharm.* A dark viscous liquid obtained by sulphonating ichthyol and neutralizing the product with ammonia, used to treat eczema.

ichthyic /ˈɪkθɪɪk/ *a.* M19. [Gk *ikhthuïkos* fishy, f. *ikhthus* fish: see -IC.] Of, pertaining to, or characteristic of a fish or fishes; piscine.

ichthyo- /ˈɪkθɪəʊ/ *comb. form* of Gk *ikhthus* fish: see -O-.

ichthyoˈdorulite *n.* [Gk *doru* spear] the fossil spine of a fish or fishlike animal M19. **ichthyolite** *n.* a fossil fish E19. **ichthyoˈlogic** *a.* ichthyological M19. **ichthyoˈlogical** *a.* of or pertaining to ichthyology E18. **ichthyˈologist** *n.* an expert in or student of ichthyology E18. **ichthyˈology** *n.* the branch of zoology that deals with fishes; the features or characteristics of a district that belong to this: M17.

ichthyocolla /ɪkθɪə(ʊ)ˈkɒlə/ *n.* E17. [Gk *ikhthuokolla*, f. as ICHTHYO- + *kolla* glue.] Fish glue, isinglass.

ichthyoid /ˈɪkθɪɔɪd/ *a.* & *n.* M19. [f. ICHTHYO- + -OID.] A *adj.* Resembling a fish. M19. B *n.* A fishlike vertebrate; an amphibian. Now *rare* or *obs.* M19.

Ichthyol /ˈɪkθɪɒl/ *n.* Also **i-**. L19. [f. ICHTHYO- + -OL.] (Proprietary name for) a brownish-yellow syrupy liquid obtained by the dry distillation of bituminous rocks containing the remains of fossil fishes, formerly used like ichthammol. Also = ICHTHAMMOL.

†ichthyophagan *n. rare.* L15–E17. [f. L *ichthyophagus* sing. of *ichthyophagi*: see next, -AN.] An ichthyophagist.

ichthyophagi /ɪkθɪˈɒfədʒʌɪ/ *n.pl.* M16. [L f. Gk *ikhthuophagoi* a fish-eating people, f. as ICHTHYO- + *-phagos* eating: see -PHAGOUS.] Eaters of fish.

ichthyophagian /ɪkθɪə(ʊ)ˈfeɪdʒɪən/ *n.* & *a. rare.* L15. [f. as prec. + -AN.] A *n.* An ichthyophagist. L15. B *adj.* Characterized by ichthyophagy. M19.

ichthyophagous /ɪkθɪˈɒfəgəs/ *a.* E19. [f. L *ichthyophagus* f. Gk *ikhthuophagos*, f. as ICHTHYO- + *-phagos* eating + -OUS.] That feeds on or eats fish.

ichthyophagy /ɪkθɪˈɒfədʒi/ *n.* M17. [Fr. *ichthyophagie* f. Gk *ikhthuophagia* fish diet, f. *ikhthuophagos*: see prec., -PHAGY.] The practice of feeding on or eating fish.

ichthyophagist *n.* an eater of fish E18.

ichthyornis /ɪkθɪˈɔːnɪs/ *n.* L19. [mod.L, f. ICHTHYO- + Gk *ornis* bird: the bird was orig. thought to have had teeth.] An extinct gull-like bird of Cretaceous times characterized by amphicoelous dorsal vertebrae like those of a reptile.

ichthyosaur /ˈɪkθɪəsɔː/ *n.* M19. [f. mod.L *Ichthyosauria* pl., f. as ICHTHYO-: see -SAUR.] Any of a group of extinct marine reptiles of Mesozoic times somewhat resembling porpoises, with paddle-like limbs and a caudal fin.

ichthyoˈsaurian *a.* & *n.* M19. **ichthyoˈsaurus** *n.*, pl. **-ri** /-rʌɪ, -riː/, an ichthyosaur, *spec.* one of the genus *Ichthyosaurus* M19.

ichthyosis /ɪkθɪˈəʊsɪs/ *n.* Pl. **-oses** /-ˈəʊsiːz/. E19. [mod.L, f. ICHTHYO- + -OSIS.] *Med.* A condition or disease in which the epidermis becomes dry, tough, and scaly.

ichthyotic /-ˈɒtɪk/ *a.* subject to or affected with ichthyosis L19.

ichu /ˈiːtʃuː/ *n.* Also ***icho*** /ˈiːtʃəʊ/. E17. [Quechua.] A coarse highland grass, *Stipa ichu*, of Central and S. America, used for thatching.

-ician /ˈɪʃ(ə)n/ *suff.* [(O)Fr. *-icien*, f. *-ique* -IC + *-ien* -IAN, or directly f. -IC, -ICS + -IAN.] Forming ns. denoting a person skilled in or practising an art or science whose name ends in *-ic(s)*, as *arithmetician*, *magician*, *politician*, *statistician*, etc. Occas. by analogy forming ns. from bases not ending in *-ic(s)*, as *geometrician*. Cf. also PATRICIAN.

icicle /ˈʌɪsɪk(ə)l/ *n.* ME. [f. ICE *n.* + ICKLE *n.*, after MSw. *isikil* (= MDa. *isegel*); cf. Norw. *isjøkel*, *-jokkel*.] 1 A hanging tapering length of ice produced by the freezing of successive drops of water trickling from the point of attachment. ME. 2 A stalactite. M17. 3 A needle-shaped crystal. E18.

1 E. O'BRIEN I watched the snow . . and saw the icicles extend from the roof. *fig.*: K. MANSFIELD I am writing with two icicles for fingers.

icicled *a.* (*a*) overhung with icicles; †(*b*) congealed, frozen: M17.

icily /ˈʌɪsɪli/ *adv.* M19. [f. ICY + -LY[2].] In an icy manner; coldly.

fig.: E. GASKELL A tone which he meant to be icily indifferent.

iciness /ˈʌɪsɪnɪs/ *n.* L16. [f. ICY + -NESS.] The quality or state of being icy; extreme cold; frigidity. Chiefly *fig.*

icing /ˈʌɪsɪŋ/ *n.* E18. [f. ICE *v.* + -ING[1].] 1 Sugar paste for coating or decorating cakes etc.; the process of making or applying such a paste; *fig.* (in full *icing on the cake*) an unlooked-for or incidental benefit. E18. 2 The process of chilling or preserving with ice. M19. 3 The (usu. unintended) formation of ice on a surface. Freq. foll. by *up*. L19.

1 *fondant icing*, *glacé icing*, *royal icing*, etc.

Comb.: **icing sugar** finely powdered sugar for making icing.

-icity /ˈɪsɪti/ *suff.* [Fr. *-icité* f. L *-icitat-*, *-tas* suff. combining *-tat-* (see -TY[1]) with adj. stems in *-ic(i)-*, as *rusticitas* f. *rusticus*.] Forming abstract ns., also, by analogy, from adjs. of any origin in *-ic*, as *electricity*, *publicity*, etc.

†-ick *suff.* var. of -IC.

icker /ˈɪkə/ *n. Sc.* E16. [Alt. of EAR *n.*[2]] An ear of corn.

ickle /ˈɪk(ə)l/ *n. obs.* exc. *dial.* [OE *gicel(a)* cogn. with ON *jǫkull* icicle, glacier f. Gmc. Cf. JOKUL.] An icicle.

ickle /ˈɪk(ə)l/ *a.* M19. [Hypocoristic form of LITTLE *a.*] In childish use: little.

P. HOBSON She changed her role. Now she was Daddy's ickle girl.

icky /ˈɪki/ *a. colloq.* E20. [Origin uncertain: perh. rel. to SICK *a.* and ICKLE *a.*] Distastefully sentimental or sweet; sickly; sticky; nasty, repulsive.

Harper's Bazaar Roast chestnuts or icky home-made fudge. B. T. BRADFORD Gran would have a fit because she'd consider it icky, bad form.

Comb.: **icky-boo** ill, sick.

†icod *int.* L17–L18. [f. as AGAD.] = EGAD.

icon /ˈʌɪkɒn, -k(ə)n/ *n.* Also **ikon**. M16. [L f. Gk *eikōn* likeness, image, similitude.] †1 *Rhet.* A simile. M16–L17. 2†a A portrait, a picture; *esp.* one of an animal or plant in a book of natural history. L16–E18. b *Eccl.* An image in traditional Byzantine style of Jesus or a holy person that is used ceremonially and venerated in the Orthodox Church. M19. c *Computing.* A small symbolic picture on a VDU screen, *esp.* one that may be selected with a cursor to exercise an option that it represents. L20. 3 A statue. L16. 4 A realistic description in writing. *rare.* L16. 5 *Philos.* A sign with some factor in common with the object it represents. E20.

iconic /ʌɪˈkɒnɪk/ *a.* M17. [L *iconicus* f. Gk *eikonikos*, f. *eikōn* ICON: see -IC.] Of, pertaining to, or resembling an icon; of the nature of an icon; *Art* designating ancient Greek statues of victorious athletes executed in a conventional style.

iconical *a.* (*rare*) = ICONIC M17. **iconically** *adv.* M20. **iconicity** /-ˈnɪsɪti/ *n.* the relation of similarity between a sign and its object M20. **iconize** *v.t.* represent pictorially L17.

iconism /ˈʌɪkɒnɪz(ə)m/ *n.* M16. [Late L *iconismus* f. Gk *eikonismos* delineation, f. *eikonizein* represent, f. *eikōn* ICON: see -ISM.] †1 Representation by an image; imagery. M16–L17. 2 *Philos.* The quality of being an icon. L20.

icono- /ˈʌɪkənəʊ/ *comb. form.* [Gk *eikono-*, f. *eikōn* ICON: see -O-.] Image; icon.

iconoˈdule *n.* = ICONODULIST L19. **iconoˈdulist** *n.* a person who venerates religious images or advocates their veneration E18. **iconoˈmetric** *a.* employing or forming part of iconometry L19. **iconoˈmetrical** *a.* iconometric E20. **iconoˈmetrically** *adv.* in or by means of iconometry E20. **icoˈnometry** *n.* the process of taking measurements from photographs of an area and using them to make a map of it L19. **iconophil(e)** *n.* & *a.* (*a*) *n.* a connoisseur or collector of book illustrations, engravings, etc.; *Eccl.* a person who uses or advocates the use of religious images or icons; (*b*) *adj.* designating an iconophile: L19. **iconoˈphobia** *n.* hatred of religious images or icons E20.

iconoclasm /ʌɪˈkɒnəklaz(ə)m/ *n.* L18. [f. next after *enthusiast*, *enthusiasm*, etc.] Destruction of or opposition to religious images; the action of an iconoclast.

iconoclast /ʌɪˈkɒnəklast/ *n.* & *a.* M17. [med.L *iconoclastes* f. eccl.Gk *eikonoklastēs*, f. as ICONO- + *klan* to break.] A *n.* 1 A destroyer or opponent of religious images or icons; *spec.* (*Hist.*) (*a*) a member of the movement against the use and veneration of images in the Orthodox Church in the 8th and 9th cents.; (*b*) a Puritan of the 16th or 17th cent. M17. 2 A person who attacks a cherished belief or respected institution. M19.

2 H. R. REYNOLDS Respectable vices . . need nothing so much as the stern iconoclast.

B *attrib.* or as *adj.* Iconoclastic. Now *rare.* L17.

iconoˈclastic *a.* of or pertaining to iconoclasts or iconoclasm M17. **iconoˈclastically** *adv.* M19.

iconography /ʌɪkəˈnɒgrəfi/ *n.* E17. [Gk *eikonographia* sketch, description, f. as ICONO-: see GRAPHY.] †1 A drawing, a plan. Only in 17. 2 The representation of a subject by illustrations; a book of illustrations; a collection of portraits of a particular subject. Also, the visual images and symbols of a work of art, a cult, etc.; (the interpretation of) the significance of these; iconology. L17.

2 D. PIPER It can be compared with other portraits of Prias, who has quite a rich iconography. *Library* An iconography of Don Quixote, 1605–1895.

iconographer *n.* an artist, an illustrator L19. **iconoˈgraphic(al)** *adjs.* of or pertaining to iconography; representing by visual images: M19. **iconoˈgraphically** *adv.* M20. **iconographist** *n.* (*rare*) an iconographer M19.

iconolatry /ʌɪkəˈnɒlətri/ *n.* E17. [eccl.Gk *eikonolatreia*, f. as ICONO-: see -LATRY.] The worship of religious images or icons.

iconolater *n.* a person who practises iconolatry M17.

iconology /ʌɪkəˈnɒlədʒi/ *n.* M18. [f. ICONO- + -LOGY.] 1 The branch of knowledge that deals with visual imagery and its symbolism and interpretation. M18. 2 Symbolism, symbolic representation. M19.

iconoˈlogical *a.* M19.

iconomachy /ʌɪkəˈnɒməki/ *n.* L16. [f. eccl.Gk *eikonomakhein* to fight against images, f. as ICONO-: see -MACHY.] A war against images; hostility to images, esp. their use in worship.

iconoscope /ʌɪˈkɒnəskəʊp/ *n.* M19. [f. ICONO- + -SCOPE.] †1 An optical instrument for giving an impression of relief when viewing flat images. M19–E20. 2 An early television camera tube in which an electron beam scanned a photoemissive surface bearing the optical image, the current from which varied according to the brightness of the various points on the surface. M20.

iconostas /ʌɪˈkɒnəstas/ *n.* M19. [Russ. *ikonostas* f. as next.] = next.

iconostasis /ʌɪkəˈnɒstəsɪs/ *n.* Pl. **-ases** /-əsiːz/. M19. [mod.Gk *eikonostasis*, f. as ICONO- + STASIS.] A screen separating the sanctuary or altar from the nave in some Orthodox churches and bearing icons.

icos- /ˈʌɪkɒs/ *comb. form.* Also **icosa-** /ʌɪˈkɒsə/, **icosi-** /ʌɪˈkɒsi/. See also EICOS-. [Gk *eikosi*.] Twenty.

iˌcosidodecaˈhedron *n.*, pl. **-dra**, **-drons**, a solid bounded by twenty equilateral triangles and twelve regular pentagons L16. **iˌcositetraˈhedron** *n.*, pl. **-dra**, **-drons**, a solid with 24 faces M19.

icosahedron /ˌʌɪkɒsəˈhiːdrən, -ˈhɛd-/ *n.* Also **†-drum**, **†eic-**. Pl. **-dra** /-drə/, **-drons**. L16. [Late L *icosahedrum* (med.L also *-hedron*) f. Gk *eikosaedron*, f. as ICOS-: see -HEDRON.] A solid figure or object with twenty plane faces; *esp.* (more fully *regular icosahedron*) one with twenty equal equilateral triangular faces.

icosahedral *a.* having the form of an icosahedron; having twenty faces: E19. **icosahedrally** *adv.* so as to form icosahedra L20.

icosane *n.* var. of EICOSANE.

icosi- *comb. form* var. of ICOS-.

-ics /ɪks/ *suff.* [f. -IC + -S[1], repr. Fr. *-iques*, med.L *-ica*, Gk *-ika*.] Forming ns. denoting a branch of knowledge (as *economics*, *ethics*) or a treatise on one, or a field or kind of activity (as *politics*, *acrobatics*).

¶ In earliest use in names of treatises.

ictal /ˈɪkt(ə)l/ *a.* M20. [f. ICTUS + -AL[1].] *Med.* Pertaining to or caused by an ictus.

icteric /ɪkˈtɛrɪk/ *a.* & *n.* L16. [L *ictericus* f. Gk *ikterikos*, f. *ikteros* jaundice: see -IC.] A *adj.* Associated with or caused by jaundice; affected with or by jaundice. L16. B *n.* A person with jaundice. Now *rare* or *obs.* M17.

icterical *a.* (now *rare* or *obs.*) M17.

icterine /ˈɪkt(ə)rʌɪn/ *a.* M19. [f. ICTERUS + -INE[1].] *Zool.* Yellow. Chiefly in *icterine warbler*, a yellow-breasted warbler, *Hippolais icterina*, of Continental Europe, found esp. in parks and gardens.

icteritious /ɪktəˈrɪʃəs/ *a.* E17. [f. late L *icteritia* jaundice (f. as ICTERUS) + -OUS.] Jaundiced.

icterogenic /ɪkt(ə)rə(ʊ)ˈdʒɛnɪk/ *a.* E20. [f. ICTERUS + -O- + -GENIC.] Causing jaundice.

icterus /ˈɪkt(ə)rəs/ *n.* E18. [L f. Gk *ikteros*.] 1 Jaundice. E18. 2 A yellow discoloration of normally green plant tissue. E19.

ictic /ˈɪktɪk/ *a. rare.* M19. [f. ICTUS + -IC.] 1 Of the nature of a sudden blow. M19. 2 Pertaining to or due to ictus or stress. L19.

ictus /ˈɪktəs/ *n.* E18. [L, f. *ict-* pa. ppl stem of *icere* to strike.] 1 *Med.* a The beat of the pulse. E18. b A stroke; a seizure, a fit; any sudden event involving the nervous system. L19. 2 *Pros.* Rhythmical or metrical stress. M18.

icy /ˈʌɪsi/ *a.* OE. [f. ICE *n.* + -Y[1].] 1 Characterized by ice, having much ice; covered with ice. OE. 2 Resembling ice; bitterly cold; slippery. L16. b *fig.* Cold in manner; unfriendly, hostile. L16. 3 Consisting of ice. E17.

2 P. S. BUCK A continual icy wind blew. b L. M. MONTGOMERY She passed him by with an icy contempt. *the icy* MITT.

¶ Not recorded in ME.

id /ɪd/ *n.*[1] *obs.* exc. *Hist.* L19. [f. Gk *idios* own, private, or contr. of IDIOPLASM.] *Biol.* In Weismann's theory of heredity: a unit of germ plasm.

id /ɪd/ *n.*[2] E20. [L = it, tr. G *es*.] *Psychoanalysis.* The inherited instinctive impulses of the individual, forming part of the unconscious and, in Freudian theory, interacting in the psyche with the ego and the superego.

L. TRILLING A plea being made on behalf of the anarchic and self-indulgent id.

id *n.*[3] var. of EID.

id. /ɪd/ *n.* & *adv.* L17. [Abbrev. of L *idem*.] = IDEM.

-id /ɪd/ *suff.*[1] (not productive). Repr. Fr. *-ide*, L *-idus*, forming adjs. chiefly f. vbs w. *e-* stems, as *acidus* ACID *a.* f. *acere* be sour; occas. f. vbs w. *i-* or consonant stems, and f. ns., as *fluidus* FLUID *a.* f. *fluere* flow, *morbidus* MORBID f. *morbus* disease.

-id /ɪd/ *suff.*[2] Corresp. to Fr. *-ide*, forming ns. derived f. L ns. in *-id*, *-is*, adopted f. Gk ns. in *-ida*, *-is*, as *carotid*, *chrysalid*, *pyramid*; in *Biol.* forming names of structural constituents, as *plastid*; in *Bot.* forming ns. denoting plants belonging to the family typified by a certain genus, as *amaryllid* from *Amaryllis* (family Amaryllidaceae).

-id /ɪd/ *suff.*[3] Corresp. to Fr. *-ide*, repr. L *-ides* (pl. *-idae*, *-ida*), f. Gk patronymic suff. *-idēs*. Forming ns. and corresp. adjs. w. the senses 'member of a specified family or dynasty,' as *Seleucid*, *Sassanid*; in *Zool.*, 'member of a specified family (in *-idae*) or class (in *-ida*),' as *canid*, *arachnid*; in *Astron.*, 'meteor in a group with its radiant in a specified constellation,' as *Leonid*, or 'star of a class like one in a specified constellation', as *cepheid*.

-id /ɪd/ *suff.*[4] [Arbitrary.] Used in nomenclature of mammalian teeth, to form names of structures in the teeth of the lower jaw, as *hypoconid*.

†-id *suff.*[5] see -IDE.

Idaean /ʌɪˈdiːən/ *a.* L16. [f. L *Idaeus* (f. *Ida*, *Ide*), Gk *Idaios* (f. *Idē*) + -AN.] Of, belonging to, or dwelling on Mount Ida in Asia Minor near the ancient city of Troy, or Mount Ida in Crete, the supposed birthplace of Zeus.

Idahoan /ˈʌɪdəhəʊən/ *n.* E20. [f. *Idaho* (see below) + -AN.] A native or inhabitant of Idaho, a State of the US.

id al-fitr *n.* var. of ID UL-FITR.

Idalian /ʌɪˈdeɪlɪən/ *a.* L16. [f. L *Idalius*, f. *Idalium* (see below) + -AN.] Of or belonging to the ancient town of Idalium in Cyprus, where the goddess Aphrodite was worshipped.

-idan /ɪdən/ *suff.* [f. -ID[3] + -AN.] *Zool.* Forming adjs. and ns. w. the senses 'of or pertaining to', 'a member of' a particular family (in *-idae*) or class (in *-ida*), as *arachnidan*, *carabidan*.

iddingsite /ˈɪdɪŋzʌɪt/ *n.* L19. [f. Joseph P. *Iddings* (1857–1920), US geologist + -ITE[1].] *Min.* A brownish mixture of silicates formed by alteration of olivine.

ide /ʌɪd/ *n.*[1] M19. [mod.L *idus*, f. Sw. *id*.] = ORFE *n.*

ide *n.*[2] see IDES.

-ide /ʌɪd/ *suff.* Also **†-id**. [f. OX)IDE.] *Chem.* Added to the (abbreviated) name of an element, radical, etc., to form ns. denoting binary compounds (*chloride*, *cyanide*, *halide*, *sulphide*), or other kinds of compound (*amide*, *anhydride*, *peptide*, *saccharide*) or element (*lanthanide*).

¶ In full names of binary compounds the suffix attaches to the more electronegative element (*sodium chloride*, *calcium carbide*).

idea /ʌɪˈdɪə/ *n.* Also (now *rare* exc. *dial.*) **idee** /ʌɪˈdiː/. LME. [L f. Gk = look, semblance, form, kind, nature, ideal form, model, f. base of *idein* see.] I An archetype, a pattern, a standard. 1 In Platonic philosophy: an eternally existing pattern of any class, of which the individual members are imperfect copies. LME. 2 The conception of something at its highest perfection or most complete stage of development; a standard of perfection, an ideal. L16. †b A person or thing as an ideal. L16–M17. 3 The conception of a standard to be aimed at; the plan or design according to which something is created or constructed. Now passing into sense 4. L16. †b A preliminary sketch or plan; a basic outline. M17–M18. 4 A conception of something to be done or achieved; an intention, a plan of action. L16.

2 E. B. BROWNING Thou [Lucifer] shalt be an Idea to all souls . . whence to mark despair. 3 F. MYERS The ground-plan of the Universe—the idea according to which it is. 4 D. L. SAYERS That was an ingenious idea nobody had yet thought of. W. S. BURROUGHS If you have your own ideas for a new model the designers will make it. W. MAXWELL He didn't think the party was at all a good idea.

†II Form, image, nature. 5 A likeness, an image, a representation; shape, form; nature, character. M16–M18.

III Mental image or conception. †6 A mental image of something previously seen or known and recalled by the memory. L16–M18. 7 Something imagined; a conception having no basis in reality; *gen.* a picture or notion of anything conceived in the mind. L16. 8 A product of mental activity existing in the mind; an item of knowledge or belief; a thought; a way of thinking. M17. b A vague or indefinite notion, belief, or opinion; a supposition, an impression. Also, a person's conception *of* an ideal, typical, or adequate example of the person or thing specified. E18.

6 H. FIELDING Though I despaired of possessing you . . I doted still on your charming idea. 7 C. DAY The idea of playing in public sent cold chills down Julie's back. A. LURIE The idea . . which seemed so lovely last autumn, has become a cold, exhausting reality. A. DAVIS The preview trip to the school completely shattered my ideas of what schools were . . like. 8 P. BOWLES 'I wonder if . . I'm a coward?' he thought. . . The idea saddened him. S. SPENDER The three great political ideas of our time—Fascism, Communism, and Liberal-Socialism. A. CLARE There is a poverty of ideas and mental imagery. b H. JAMES To sit on a balcony, eating ices—that's my idea of heaven. B. LOPEZ Even officers of the British whaling fleet had little idea where a meteorite might come from. A. MUNRO He . . had some idea of doing work in underdeveloped countries.

IV *Philos.* 9 In the philosophy of Descartes and Locke: whatever is in the mind and directly present to cognitive consciousness; the immediate object of thought or mental perception. M17. 10 (In the philosophy of Kant) a conception of reason transcending all experience, as opp. to a conception of the understanding which is confined by experience; (in the philosophy of Hegel) the absolute truth of which all phenomenal existence is the expression. M19.

Phrases: FIXED *idea*. **get** or **have ideas** *colloq.* be ambitious, rebellious, etc. **give a person ideas** (*a*) create a false impression of sexual promiscuity; (*b*) = *put ideas into a person's head* below. *have ideas*: see *get ideas* above. **have no idea** *colloq.* (*a*) not know at all; (*b*) be completely incompetent. **man of ideas** a resourceful man. **put ideas into a person's head** suggest ambitions etc. that he or she would not otherwise have thought of. **that's an idea** *colloq.* that proposal etc. is worth considering. **that's the idea!** *colloq.* you are beginning to understand how to proceed. **the big idea** (usu. *iron.*) the important intention or scheme. **the very idea!** *colloq.*: an exclamation of disapproval or disagreement. **woman of ideas** a resourceful woman.

idea'd *a.* having an idea or ideas, esp. of a specified kind M18. **idealess** *a.* lacking ideas; meaningless: E19.

ideal /ʌɪˈdɪəl, -ˈdiːəl/ *a.* & *n.* LME. [Late L *idealis*, f. L IDEA: see -AL[1]. Partly through Fr. *idéal*.] A *adj.* 1 In Platonic philosophy: pertaining to or existing as an archetype. LME. 2 Regarded as perfect or supremely excellent; representing a perfect example. E17. 3 Existing only as an idea, confined to the imagination, imaginary; visionary, not practical. E17. b *Math.* Of a number or quality: having no actual existence, but assumed for some purpose in a system of complex numbers; *spec.* in *Geom.*, introduced in order to do away with exceptions to generalizations. M19. 4 Of, pertaining to, or of the nature of an idea or conception; representing an idea. M17. b *Philos.* Regarding ideas as the only real entities; idealistic. M18.

2 K. AMIS This isn't the ideal time to ask you. I. MURDOCH You were a sort of ideal figure, and . . I never thought they were as good as you. 3 T. HARDY The doctor . . much preferred the ideal world to the real. 4 H. T. BUCKLE Starting from the so called nature of things, his first steps were ideal.

Special collocations: **ideal construction** *Philos.* a mental conception formed by abstracting properties found in experience and recombining or developing them. **ideal fluid** a hypothetical fluid that has no viscosity and is incompressible. **ideal gas** a hypothetical gas which consists of molecules occupying negligible space and exerting no mutual attraction, and therefore obeys simple laws. **ideal type** *Sociol.* a hypothetical construct made up of the essential features of a social or historical phenomenon or generalized concept and used in comparison or classification of what actually occurs.

B *n.* 1 A conception of something in its highest perfection, esp. as a thing to be aimed at; a perfect example or specimen; a standard of perfection or excellence. L15. b An actual thing as a standard for imitation. M19. 2 *Math.* A subring that contains all products of the form *rx* and *xr*, where *r* and *x* are elements of the ring and subring respectively. L19.

1 D. H. LAWRENCE We have an ideal of a perfect world. A. TOFFLER Maximum individual choice is regarded as the democratic ideal. b E. LANGLEY I should be to him the flawless love, the ideal of faithfulness. C. FRANCIS The Battle of Trafalgar . . the glorified ideal of everything that is brave . . in the fighting sailor.

idealise *v.* var. of IDEALIZE.

idealism /ʌɪˈdɪəlɪz(ə)m, -ˈdiːə-/ *n.* L18. [Fr. *idéalisme* or G *Idealismus*, f. as IDEAL: see -ISM.] 1 *Philos.* Any of various systems of thought in which the object of external perception is held to consist of ideas not resulting from any unperceived material substance. Opp. REALISM 1b. L18. 2 The representation of things in an ideal form; the practice of forming or pursuing ideals. E19. b An example of this practice; an ideal. E19.

2 *New York Times* Congress is an institution of compromises, and that's the antithesis of idealism.

idealist /ʌɪˈdɪəlɪst, -ˈdiːə-/ *n.* E18. [f. IDEAL + -IST.] 1 *Philos.* An advocate of a doctrine of idealism. E18. 2 A person who idealizes someone or something. E19. 3 A person who forms or pursues (esp. impractical) ideals. E19.

1 B. RUSSELL Idealists tell us that what appears as matter is really something mental. 2 E. BLISHEN He is not an idealist.. that chooses to invest life with a general cloudy glory. 3 A. G. GARDINER For the cynic is often the idealist turned sour. P. H. GIBBS We were the starry-eyed idealists talking peace when there was no peace.

ideaˈlistic *a.* of, pertaining to, or characteristic of an idealist E19. **ideaˈlistically** *adv.* L19.

ideality /ʌɪdɪˈalɪti/ *n.* E18. [f. IDEAL + -ITY.] †1 The faculty of forming ideas or archetypes. *rare.* Only in E18. 2 The faculty of imagining things. E19. 3 The quality of being ideal or imaginary; an imaginary or idealized thing. E19.

3 E. B. BROWNING I have had visions before.. and have called idealities realities all my life long. L. MUMFORD The belief in such ideality was almost a Quaker heresy.

idealize /ʌɪˈdɪəlʌɪz, -ˈdiːə-/ *v.* Also **-ise**. L18. [f. IDEAL + -IZE.] 1 *v.t.* & *i.* Represent or perceive (a person or thing) in an ideal form; exalt (a person or thing) to an ideal state of perfection. L18. 2 *v.i.* Form ideals. L18.

1 R. A. KNOX We.. differ from the animals in our capacity for idealizing.. the relations of the sexes. B. GUEST As long as H.D. lived she was idealized by Bryher as her heroine.

idealiˈzation *n.* the action of idealizing; an idealized thing: L18. **idealizer** *n.* E19.

ideally /ʌɪˈdɪəli, -ˈdiːəli/ *adv.* L16. [f. IDEAL *a.* + -LY[2].] 1 In the imagination, imaginarily. L16. 2 In relation to a general plan or archetype. M17. 3 In the highest conceivable perfection; in the most excellent way; as the best possible state of things. M19.

1 W. B. CARPENTER The unexpected conclusion.. that more than three dimensions in space are ideally possible. 3 J. KOSINSKI You are a man ideally suited to provide the country with an explanation. *Practical Health* Ideally, eat a lot at the start of the day.

ideate /ʌɪˈdɪət/ *n.* L17. [f. as next: see -ATE[1].] The external object of which an idea is formed.

ideate /ˈʌɪdɪeɪt/ *a.* E20. [f. as next: see -ATE[2].] 1 Produced by or deriving its existence from a Platonic idea. *rare.* E20. 2 Concerned with ideas as opp. to reality. M20.

ideate /ˈʌɪdɪeɪt/ *v.* E17. [med.L *ideat-* pa. ppl stem of *ideare* form an idea or conception of, f. L IDEA: see -ATE[3].] 1 *v.t.* Form an idea of, imagine. E17. 2 *v.i.* Form ideas, think. M19.

1 K. CLARK The arc whose ideated centre is a nodal point in the composition.

ideation /ʌɪdɪˈeɪʃ(ə)n/ *n.* E19. [f. IDEATE *v.* + -ATION.] The action of ideating; the formation of ideas or mental images.

ideational /ʌɪdɪˈeɪʃ(ə)n(ə)l/ *a.* M19. [f. prec. + -AL[1].] 1 Of or pertaining to ideation or the formation of ideas. M19. 2 *Sociol.* Designating a culture which emphasizes spiritual values and ideals above material values. Cf. SENSATE *a.* 4. M20.

ideationally *adv.* L19.

idee *n.* see IDEA.

idée fixe /ide fiks, iːdeɪ ˈfiːks/ *n. phr.* Pl. ***-s -s*** (pronounced same). M19. [Fr. = fixed idea.] An idea that dominates the mind, an obsession.

E. CRANKSHAW Rigid adherence to dogmatic principle degenerated into a series of *idées fixes.*

idée reçue /ide rəsy, ˌiːdeɪ rəˈsjuː/ *n. phr.* Pl. ***-s -s*** (pronounced same). M20. [Fr. = received idea.] A generally accepted notion or opinion.

idées fixes, reçues *n. phrs.* pls. of IDÉE FIXE, REÇUE.

idem /ˈɪdɛm, ˈʌɪ-/ *n.* & *adv.* LME. [L.] (In) the same author, work, etc.

idempotent /ʌɪdɛmˈpəʊt(ə)nt, ʌɪˈdɛmpət(ə)nt/ *a.* L19. [f. L *idem* same + POTENT *a.*[2]] *Math.* Of an element, matrix, etc.: unchanged in value after multiplication by itself. Also, (of a set) containing idempotent elements; (of a statement) expressing idempotency.

idemˈpotence, idemˈpotency *ns.* the property of being idempotent M20.

idem sonans /ʌɪdɛm ˈsəʊnanz/ *n.* & *a. phr.* M19. [L = sounding the same.] *Law* (chiefly *US*). A *n.* The occurrence in a document of a material word or name misspelt but having the sound of the word or name intended. M19. B *adj.* Homophonous *with.* M19.

-idene /ɪdiːn/ *suff.* [f. ETHYL)IDENE.] *Chem.* Forming names of divalent organic radicals in which both valencies derive from the same atom, as *propylidene.*

ident /ʌɪˈdɛnt/ *n. colloq.* M20. [Abbrev.] = IDENTIFICATION.

ident *a.* var. of EIDENT.

identic /ʌɪˈdɛntɪk/ *a.* M17. [med.L *identicus*, f. *ident-*: see IDENTITY, -IC.] 1 = IDENTICAL *a.* 1, 2. M17. 2 In diplomats' use: designating action or language in which two or more powers or countries agree to use precisely the same form in their relations with some other. M19.

2 **identic note**: containing a uniformly worded expression of opinion from two or more powers or countries to another.

identical /ʌɪˈdɛntɪk(ə)l/ *a.* & *n.* L16. [f. as prec.: see -AL[1], -ICAL.] A *adj.* 1 *Logic.* Designating a proposition whose terms express an identity or denote the same thing, as *man is man.* L16. 2 Of a thing or set of things viewed at different times: the very same. M17. 3 Of two or more separate things: agreeing in every detail. L17. 4 *Math.* Of the nature of or expressing an identity. L19.

2 B. H. MALKIN This is the very identical man. 3 C. SAGAN The inside of the Earth and the outside of Venus are alike but not identical. I. MURDOCH They began to sing, swaying.. in an identical rhythm, as if.. joined together. **identical twin**: developed from a single fertilized ovum and therefore of the same sex as and very similar to his or her sibling; a monozygotic twin.

B *n.* 1 An identical thing or feature. L17. 2 An identical twin. M20.

identically *adv.* M17. **identicalness** *n.* E18.

identifiable /ʌɪˈdɛntɪfʌɪəb(ə)l/ *a.* E19. [f. IDENTIFY + -ABLE.] Able to be identified.

identifiaˈbility *n.* L19.

identification /ʌɪˌdɛntɪfɪˈkeɪʃ(ə)n/ *n.* M17. [Orig. f. med.L *identificatio(n-)*, f. *identificat-* pa. ppl stem of *identificare* (see IDENTIFY); later f. IDENTIFY: see -FICATION.] 1 The action or an act of identifying, the fact of being identified. M17. 2 Documentary evidence, as a passport, driving licence, etc., serving to identify a person. M20.

1 N. ALGREN If you sent a man to prison on a wrong identification you're a criminal yourself. J. K. GALBRAITH Political identification with those of the lowest estate has anciently brought.. reproaches. *Lancashire Evening Telegraph* After formal identification of the body.., the inquest was adjourned. 2 *Globe & Mail (Toronto)* My driver's licence, draft card, student I.D., and all other identification I had on me.

Comb.: **identification bracelet, card, disc,** etc.: worn or carried and bearing a name, assigned number, etc., identifying the wearer or carrier; **identification parade** an assembly of people among whom a suspect is to be identified.

identificational *a.* of or involving identification M20. **identificatory** *a.* serving to identify M20.

identify /ʌɪˈdɛntɪfʌɪ/ *v.* M17. [med.L *identificare*, f. *ident-*: see IDENTITY, -FY.] 1 *v.t.* Regard or treat as identical (*with*). Now chiefly passing into sense 3b. M17. †b *v.i.* Be or become identical. L17–M19. 2 *v.t.* Establish the identity of; establish who or what a given person or thing is; recognize. M18. b *Taxon.* Refer (a specimen) to its proper species etc. L18. 3 *v.t.* & *i.* Foll. by *with*: regard (a person, oneself) as sharing the same characteristics, interests, principles, experiences, etc., with; feel (oneself) to be a part of; model (oneself) on. L18. b *v.t.* Associate (a person or thing) very closely or inseparably *with* (a person, event, etc.). Usu. in *pass.* M19.

1 GIBBON Osiris, whom he identifies with Serapis. 2 D. CUSACK She threw herself under a bus. We have to go—to identify her. R. LARDNER Rita.. identified Bob by the initials on his suitcase. B. EMECHETA She herself could not identify what it was that was unsettling her. 3 A. STORR Some depressives become expert at identifying themselves with others. D. LESSING She.. did not identify particularly with any aspect of being Jewish. b J. BUCHAN I identified appreciation with enjoyment. *Listener* The Mandelas are identified with the struggle of black people for rights in South Africa.

identifier *n.* (*a*) a person who or thing which identifies; (*b*) *Computing* a character or sequence of characters devised to identify or refer to a set of data, an element in a program, etc.: L19.

Identikit /ʌɪˈdɛntɪkɪt/ *n.* Also **i-**. M20. [Blend of IDENTITY and KIT *n.*[1]] (Proprietary name for) a reconstructed picture of a person (esp. a suspect sought by police) assembled from features described by a witness or witnesses; *transf.* an approximate image or conception of anything, comprising the basic or salient features. Freq. *attrib.*

CLIVE JAMES A letter.. evokes the identikit Wittgenstein whose components everybody knows. D. FRANCIS Yes, I would help him with an Identikit picture.

Identitätsphilosophie /idɛntiˈtɛːtsfilozoˌfiː/ *n.* M19. [G = identity-philosophy.] *Philos.* A system or doctrine that assumes the fundamental identity of spirit and nature.

identity /ʌɪˈdɛntɪti/ *n.* L16. [Late L *identitas*, f. L *idem* same, prob. after *entitas* ENTITY, but perh. assoc. w. *identidem* repeatedly: thus *ident-* was established as the comb. form of *idem.* Cf. IDENTIC, IDENTIFY.] 1 The quality or condition of being identical in every detail; absolute sameness; an instance or example of this. Also, the fact of being identified *with.* L16. 2 The condition or fact of a person or thing being that specified unique person or thing, esp. as a continuous unchanging property throughout existence; the characteristics determining this; individuality, personality. M17. 3 *Math.* a An equation which holds for all values of its variables. M19. b An element of a set which, if combined with another by a (specified) binary operation, leaves the second element unchanged. L19. c A transformation which gives rise to the same elements as those to which it is applied. E20. 4 In full *old identity.* A person long resident or well known in a place. *NZ & Austral.* M19.

1 H. FAWCETT There is no identity of interests between the employers and employed. D. MACDONALD The letter to Lang did express.. his feeling of identity with the masses. **mistaken identity** error as regards who a person is. 2 SAKI To disguise one's identity in a neighbourhood where one was entirely unknown seemed.. rather meaningless. H. ARENDT The Jews.. had been able to keep their identity through the centuries. *Sunday Express* The victory sparking off a new sense of pride in national identity. 4 *New Zealand Woman's Weekly* Havelock North identity Mrs C. E. Turner-Williams.. at 98 stitches happily on.

Comb.: **identity card** an identification card; **identity crisis** *Psychol.* a period of emotional disturbance in which a person has difficulty in determining his or her identity and role in relation to society, esp. as part of the maturing process; **identity element** = sense 3b above; **identity matrix** *Math.*: in which all the elements of the principal diagonal are ones and all other elements are zeros, so that its product with any matrix is identical with the latter; **identity parade** an identification parade.

ideo- /ˈʌɪdɪəʊ, ˈɪdɪəʊ/ *comb. form* of Gk IDEA: see -O-.

ideokiˈnetic *a.* (*Neurol.*) designating a form of apraxia in which an action cannot be performed on request despite retention of the necessary motor ability and understanding E20. **ideoˈmotor** *a.* (*Neurol.*) denoting or relating to a motor action stimulated by an idea; also, ideokinetic: L19. **ideophone** *n.* (*Ling.*) an onomatopoeic or sound-symbolic word or class of words L19. **ideoˈphonic** *a.* (*Ling.*) onomatopoeic, sound-symbolic M20. **ideoplasm** *n.* = ECTOPLASM 2 E20. **ideoplastic** *a.* designating physiological or artistic processes supposed to be moulded by mental impressions or suggestions; also *spec.*, ectoplasmic: E20.

ideogram /ˈɪdɪəgram, ˈʌɪd-/ *n.* M19. [f. IDEO- + -GRAM.] An ideograph.

ideoˈgrammic *a.* of the nature of an ideogram; expressed by symbols: E20.

ideograph /ˈɪdɪəgrɑːf, ˈʌɪd-/ *n.* M19. [f. IDEO- + -GRAPH.] A character symbolizing the idea of a thing without expressing the sequence of sounds in its name, as a numeral, any of various Chinese characters, etc.

ideo'graphic *a.* of the nature of an ideograph; pertaining to or composed of ideographs: E19. **ideo'graphical** *a.* ideographic M19. **ideo'graphically** *adv.* E19.

ideologist /ʌɪdɪ'ɒlədʒɪst, ɪd-/ *n.* L18. [Fr. *idéologiste*, f. as IDEO- + -LOGIST.] **1** A person who studies the origin and nature of ideas. *arch.* L18. **2** A theorist; a visionary, an idealist. M19. **3** A proponent or an adherent of an ideology. L19.

ideologue /'ʌɪdɪəlɒg, 'ɪd-/ *n.* E19. [Fr. *idéologue*, f. as IDEO- + -LOGUE.] A theorist, a visionary; a proponent or adherent of an ideology.

D. HALBERSTAM He was not an ideologue of the left, but he was sympathetic to it.

ideology /ʌɪdɪ'ɒlədʒi, ɪd-/ *n.* L18. [Fr. *idéologie*, f. as IDEO- + -LOGY.] **1** The branch of philosophy or psychology dealing with the origin and nature of ideas. *arch.* L18. **2** Ideal or abstract (esp. impractical) speculation. *arch.* E19. **3** A system of ideas or way of thinking pertaining to a class or individual, esp. as a basis of some economic or political theory or system, regarded as justifying actions and esp. to be maintained irrespective of events. Freq. w. specifying wd. E20.

3 A. KOESTLER Transformed the founders' once fluid ideas into rigid ideologies. E. P. THOMPSON The working-class ideology . . put an exceptionally high value upon . . personal liberty.

ideo'logical *a.* pertaining to or of the nature of an ideology L18. **ideo'logically** *adv.* M19. **ideologize** *v.t.* interpret ideologically; give an ideological character to: M19.

ides /ʌɪdz/ *n.pl.* Rarely in sing. **ide**. Also **I-**. LOE. [(O)Fr. f. L *idus* (pl.), of unkn. origin.] The eighth day after the nones in the ancient Roman calendar: the 15th day of March, May, July, and October, and the 13th of the other months.

id est /ɪd 'ɛst/ *adv. phr.* L16. [L = that is.] That is to say. Usu. abbrev. *i.e.*

-idin /ɪdɪn/ *suff.* [f. -IDE + -IN[1].] *Chem.* Forming names of anthocyanidins (*delphinidin*, *pelargonidin*).

-idine /ɪdiːn, ɪdɪn/ *suff.* [f. -IDE + -INE[5].] *Chem.* Forming names of usu. cyclic organic compounds containing nitrogen, esp. amino derivatives (*toluidine*, *guanidine*), heterocycles (*piperidine*, *pyridine*), and pyrimidine nucleosides (*thymidine*).

idio- /'ɪdɪəʊ/ *comb. form* of Gk *idios* own, personal, private, distinct: see -O-.

idio'glossia *n.* lallation; idiolalia: L19. **idiogram** *n.* (*Cytol.*) a diagram representing the chromosome complement of a cell or individual; a karyotype: E20. **idiograph** *n.* [Gk *idiographon*] one's signature or personal mark E17. **idio'graphic** *a.* concerned with the individual, pertaining to or descriptive of single and unique facts and processes (opp. NOMOTHETIC) E20. **idio'lalia** *n.* the speaking of an invented or private language M20. **idiophone** *n.* a percussion instrument that consists of elastic material (e.g. metal, wood), itself capable of producing sound M20. **idio'phoneme** *n.* (*Ling.*) a phoneme in individual speech M20. **idiopho'nemic** *a.* (*Ling.*) of or pertaining to an idiophoneme M20. **idioplasm** *n.* (*obs.* exc. *Hist.*) germ plasm, genetic material L19. **idio'r(r)hythmic** *n.* & *a.* [Gk *idiorruthmos*] (a member of a monastic institution) allowing freedom to the individual (opp. COENOBITIC) M19. **idiosome** *n.* †(*a*) a supposed ultimate unit of living matter; (*b*) = IDIOZOME: L19. **idioven'tricular** *a.* (*Med.*) (esp. of a rhythm) proper to the ventricle of the heart alone E20. **idiozome** *n.* [Gk *zōma* band, girdle, loincloth] *Cytol.* a rounded cytoplasmic structure in developing animal germ cells L19.

idioblast /'ɪdɪə(ʊ)blast/ *n.* L19. [f. IDIO- + -BLAST.] **1** *Bot.* A cell of distinctly different nature from the surrounding tissue. L19. **2** *Petrogr.* A mineral crystal which has grown with its own characteristic crystal faces in metamorphic rock. Opp. *xenoblast*. E20.

idio'blastic *a.* pertaining to, composed of, or of the nature of an idioblast or idioblasts E20.

idiocy /'ɪdɪəsi/ *n.* E16. [f. IDIOT (perh. partly after *lunacy*): see -CY. Cf. Gk *idiōteia* uncouthness, lack of education.] **1** The state or condition of being an idiot; extremely low intelligence (now *obs.* in *Med.* use); stupidity, foolishness. E16. **2** A stupid or foolish action, remark, etc. M20.

1 S. MORLEY An act of such wanton idiocy. **2** C. PETERS He is sharp, too, on the idiocies of historical novels.

idiolect /'ɪdɪəlɛkt/ *n.* M20. [f. IDIO- + DIA)LECT.] The linguistic system of an individual, differing in some details from that of all other speakers of the same dialect or language.

idio'lectal *a.* M20.

idiom /'ɪdɪəm/ *n.* L16. [Fr. *idiome* or late L *idioma* f. Gk = property, peculiar phraseology, f. *idiousthai* make one's own, f. *idios* own, private.] **1** The language of a people or country. Now usu., the language of a particular area or group of people, dialect. L16. **2** The specific character or property of a language or dialect; natural or individual manner of expression of a language or dialect. L16. **3** A form of expression, grammatical construction, phrase, etc., peculiar to a person or language; a phrase etc. which is understood by speakers of a particular language despite its meaning's not being predictable from that of the separate words. E17. **b** A characteristic mode of expression in music, art, writing, etc.; an instance of this. E20.

1 R. GODFREY The writings of Glauber, which were translated into the English Idiom. GIBBON On the spot I read . . the classics of the Tuscan idiom. *Idiom Neutral*: see NEUTRAL *n.* 4. **2** T. SHERLOCK To bring anything to light . . is . . in the Idiom of the English Tongue. *fig.*: LD MACAULAY Not so close as to destroy the idioms of national opinion and feeling. **3b** J. AGATE The music . . is written in a fascinating idiom. K. CLARK In his figure drawings he mastered . . the idiom of the time.

idiomatic /ɪdɪə'matɪk/ *a.* E18. [Gk *idiōmatikos* peculiar, characteristic, f. *idiōmat-*, *-ma*: see IDIOM, -ATIC.] **1** Peculiar to or of the nature of an idiom; conforming to idiom; vernacular, colloquial. E18. **2** Given to or distinguished by the use of idioms. M19.

1 JANET MORGAN It was from her that Agatha learnt her idiomatic and fluent French.

idiomatical *a.* (now *rare*) = IDIOMATIC E18. **idiomatically** *adv.* E18. **idioma'ticity** *n.* the quality or state of being idiomatic M20.

idiomorphic /ɪdɪə(ʊ)'mɔːfɪk/ *a.* L19. [f. IDIO- + -MORPH + -IC.] *Petrogr.* Of a crystal: euhedral. Of a rock: containing euhedral crystals.

idiomorphically *adv.* L19. **idiomorphism** *n.* the condition of being idiomorphic E20.

idiopathetic /ˌɪdɪə(ʊ)pə'θɛtɪk/ *a. rare.* M17. [f. as next after SYMPATHETIC.] = next.

idiopathic /ɪdɪə(ʊ)'paθɪk/ *a.* M17. [f. IDIO- + -PATHY + -IC.] *Med.* Of a disease: not consequent on or symptomatic of another disease; having no known cause.

idi'opathy *n.* (an) idiopathic disease L17.

idiosyncrasy /ɪdɪə(ʊ)'sɪŋkrəsi/ *n.* E17. [Gk *idiosugkrasia*, *-krasis*, f. *idios* IDIO- + *sugkrasis* commixture, tempering, f. *sun-* SYN- + *krasis* CRASIS.] **1** Orig., the physical constitution peculiar to an individual. Now only in *Med.*, abnormal individual sensitivity to a food or drug. E17. **2** A mental constitution, view, feeling, or mode of behaviour peculiar to a person, nation, etc.; something highly individualized or eccentric. M17. **3** A mode of expression peculiar to an author. M19.

2 C. BEATON The surprised eyebrows . . the bold gestures . . all of these idiosyncrasies are derived from Lina Cavalieri. C. RYCROFT The absence of imagery accompanying thought seems to be an idiosyncrasy common among scientists. R. STRANGE My intentions have been orthodox. Idiosyncrasy would be misplaced here.

idiosyncratic /ˌɪdɪə(ʊ)sɪn'kratɪk/ *a.* L18. [f. prec. (after Gk *sugkratikos* mixed together): see -ATIC.] Of, pertaining to, or of the nature of idiosyncrasy; characteristic of an individual.

M. N. COX Her idiosyncratic, peculiarly unrepeatable personal qualities. *Do-It-Yourself* An idiosyncratic choice, such as a black or scarlet suite.

idiosyncratical *a.* (now *rare*) idiosyncratic L17. **idiosyncratically** *adv.* in an idiosyncratic manner M17.

idiot /'ɪdɪət/ *n.* & *a.* ME. [(O)Fr. f. L *idiota* ignorant person f. Gk *idiōtēs* private person, plebeian, layman, ignorant person, f. *idios* private, peculiar. See also EEJIT.] **A** *n.* **1** A person with extremely low intelligence. *obs.* in *Med.*. ME. **b** A stupid person, a fool, a blockhead. *colloq.* LME. †**c** A person of weak intellect maintained as an amusement; a jester, a fool. E16–E18. †**2** An uneducated or ignorant person; a simple person. LME–E18. **b** A layman. LME–M17.

1 J. R. ACKERLEY The small blank eyes mooned stolidly at me . . it was like being gaped at by the village idiot. **b** E. M. FORSTER Charles clenched his fist and cried, 'The idiot, the idiot, the little fool!' P. G. WODEHOUSE She was incensed with this idiot who had flung himself before her car.

Comb.: **idiot board** a board displaying a television script to a speaker as an aid to memory; **idiot box** *colloq.* a television set; **idiot card** = *idiot board* above; **idiot light** *colloq.* a warning light that goes on when a fault occurs in a device; **idiot-proof** *a.* (*colloq.*) foolproof.

B *attrib.* or as *adj.* Of, pertaining to, or characteristic of an idiot or idiocy; idiotic. LME.

J. WAINWRIGHT The idiot woman rode her horse directly into my path. A. SILLITOE Baxter was whistling some idiot song.

idiotish *a.* (now *rare*) somewhat idiotic M16. **idiotize** *v.* (*a*) *v.i.* become idiotic; (*b*) *v.t.* make idiotic or into an idiot; make a fool of: L16. **idiotry** *n.* (*a*) *Sc. Law* idiocy; (*b*) idiotic behaviour: L15.

idiotic /ɪdɪ'ɒtɪk/ *a.* E18. [f. IDIOT, after Gk *idiōtikos* or L *idioticus* uneducated, ignorant, unskilful: see -IC.] Characteristic of an idiot or idiots; unintelligent; stupid, foolish.

V. WOOLF She was completely reckless; did the most idiotic things out of bravado. H. L. MENCKEN The army is so stupid as to be virtually idiotic.

idiotical /ɪdɪ'ɒtɪk(ə)l/ *a.* Now *rare.* M17. [f. as prec.: see -ICAL.] †**1** Uneducated, plain, ignorant. M17–E18. **2** Idiotic. M17.

idiotically /ɪdɪ'ɒtɪk(ə)li/ *adv.* M17. [f. (as) prec.: see -LY[2] .] In an idiotic manner.

idioticon /ɪdɪ'əʊtɪk(ə)n/ *n.* M19. [G f. Gk *idiōtikon* use as n. of neut. sing. of *idiōtikos* uneducated. Cf. IDIOT.] A dictionary, word-list, etc., of words and phrases peculiar to a dialect, a particular group of people, etc.

idiotism /'ɪdɪətɪz(ə)m/ *n.* L16. [Fr. *idiotisme* idiom, idiocy, f. L *idiotismus* common or vulgar manner of speaking f. Gk *idiōtismos*. In branch II partly f. IDIOT + -ISM.] **I** †**1** = IDIOM 1. L16–L17. †**2** = IDIOM 2. E17–M18. **3** = IDIOM 3. Now *rare* or *obs.* E17. **II 4** = IDIOCY. L16.

idiotope /'ɪdɪə(ʊ)təʊp/ *n.* M20. [f. IDIO- + Gk *topos* place.] *Immunol.* An antigenic determinant acting as (part of) an idiotype.

idiotype /'ɪdɪə(ʊ)tʌɪp/ *n.* M19. [f. IDIO- + -TYPE.] †**1** *Chem.* A substance of the same type as another. M–L19. **2** *Biol.* The set of all hereditary determinants of an individual. Formerly also, the genotype only. E20. **3** *Immunol.* A set of one or more antigenic determinants associated usu. with the binding region of an immunoglobulin and characteristic of a particular clone of antibody-producing cells. M20.

idiotypic /-'tɪp-/ *a.* of or pertaining to an idiotype M19.

-idium /'ɪdɪəm/ *suff.* Pl. **-idia** /'ɪdɪə/, **-idiums**. [mod.L dim. ending corresp. to -IUM (cf. Gk *-idion*).] *Biol.* Forming ns. denoting small structures, as *gonidium*, *nephridium*, etc.

idle /'ʌɪd(ə)l/ *n.* OE. [f. the adj. In branch II f. the vb.] **I** †**1** Something useless, vain, or frivolous. Freq. in *in idle*, in vain, without cause. OE–L15. †**2** Idleness. OE–L17. **3** An idle person. *rare.* M17. **II 4** An act of idling. L19. **5** Idling (of an engine); idling speed. Freq. *attrib.* M20.

idle /'ʌɪd(ə)l/ *a.* [OE *īdel* = OFris. *īdel*, OS *īdal* empty, worthless (Du. *ijdel* vain, useless, frivolous, trifling, conceited), OHG *ītal* empty, useless (G *eitel* bare, mere, worthless, vain), f. WGmc: ult. origin unkn.] †**1** Empty, vacant; void (*of*). OE–LME. **2** Of an action, thought, word, etc.: lacking worth or significance, useless; ineffective, vain, trifling. OE. **b** Baseless, groundless. L16. 3 Of a thing: useless. Now *rare*. OE. 4a Of a person: not working, doing nothing. OE. b Of time etc.: unoccupied; characterized by inaction or lack of occupation. ME. 5 Having a dislike for work or activity; lazy, indolent. ME. 6 Of a thing: inactive, unoccupied; not moving or in operation. LME. b Of money: out of circulation. M20.

2 SWIFT It is idle to propose remedies, before we are assured of the disease. A. TREW I'm sorry. It was just idle curiosity. b E. BOWEN Robert would never listen to idle gossip. 3 SHAKES. *Com. Err.* Usurping ivy, brier, or idle moss. 4a R. BURN They are idle for want of such work as they are able to do. M. ARGYLE There has been a decline of the old 'idle rich' . . living partly on unearned income. **idle and disorderly person** *Law* (now *Hist.*) an unlicensed pedlar, a common prostitute or beggar when walking the streets. b T. BROWN Persons . . that have a great deal of Idle Time lying upon their Hands. 5 S. LEACOCK 'Well, of all the idle creatures!' she exclaimed. 'Loafing here in the sand.' 6 I. WATTS Satan finds some mischief still For idle hands to do. JO GRIMOND If they are used for a month . . they must stand idle for eleven. U. BENTLEY The forces of convention . . had lain so idle for so long. **run idle** (of machinery) run without doing work or transmitting power.

Special collocations & comb.: **idleman** *rare* a man without occupation. **idle wheel** an intermediate wheel between two geared wheels, esp. to allow them to rotate in the same direction.

†**idleby** *n.* [-BY] an idle person. L16–E18. **idlehood** *n.* (*arch.*) idleness M16.

idle /ˈʌɪd(ə)l/ *v.* LME. [f. the adj.] †1 *v.t.* Make vain or worthless. Only in LME. 2 *v.i.* Move idly. L16. 3 *v.i.* Be idle; pass the time in idleness. M17. b *v.t.* Pass (time) in idleness. M17. 4 *v.t.* Cause to be idle. L18. 5 *v.i.* Of an engine: run while disconnected from a load or out of gear, so as to perform no external or useful work; run very slowly. Freq. as *idling* vbl n. E20. b *v.t.* Cause (an engine) to idle. E20.

2 W. D. HOWELLS A clear brown brook idles through the pastures. 3 J. FOWLES It seemed to him to explain all his previous idling through life. *New Yorker* The drugstore . . . where one could idle respectably. b R. HAYMAN Idling away the evenings on the hotel terrace. 4 O. WILDE I had better not come. . . You should be reading and I would idle you. 5 W. GOLDING Waiting at the traffic lights, the engine idling. **idling speed**: at which an engine idles. b M. ATWOOD At the dock he idled the motor and practically threw her onto the shore.

idleness /ˈʌɪd(ə)lnɪs/ *n.* OE. [f. IDLE *a.* + -NESS.] †1 Vanity, emptiness. Esp. in *in idleness*, in vain. OE–LME. 2 The state or condition of being idle or unoccupied; lack of occupation; habitual avoidance of work; inactivity, indolence; an instance of this. OE. 3 Groundlessness, worthlessness, triviality, futility. M17.

2 S. JOHNSON Unable to support any of his children . . in the hereditary dignity of idleness. *bread of idleness*: see BREAD *n.*[1]

idler /ˈʌɪdlə/ *n.* M16. [f. IDLE *v.* + -ER[1].] 1 A person who idles or is idle; a lazy indolent person. M16. 2 *Naut.* A person on a ship who is on constant day duty and so not liable for the night watch. L18. 3 A wheel or roller which transmits no power when in contact with a moving belt etc., but serves as a support or guide. L19. b = *idle wheel* s.v. IDLE *a.* L19.

1 A. MASON A crowd of rich young idlers . . gathered in a corner.

idlesse /ˈʌɪdlɛs/ *n. pseudo-arch.* & *poet.* L16. [f. IDLE *a.* + -ESS[2].] Idleness.

idli /ˈɪdli/ *n.* M20. [Malayalam, Kannada *iddali*.] A steamed cake of rice and black gram, popular in the southern part of the Indian subcontinent.

idly /ˈʌɪdli/ *adv.* OE. [f. IDLE *a.* + -LY[2].] 1 Vainly, uselessly; frivolously, carelessly, ineffectively. OE. 2 In an idle or lazy way; inactively; indolently. LME.

1 C. PHILLIPS He kicked idly at a ball of dust. 2 L. URIS British troops stood by idly.

Ido /ˈiːdəʊ/ *n.* E19. [Ido = offspring.] An artificial language based on Esperanto.

idocrase /ˈʌɪdəkreɪz, -s/ *n.* E19. [f. Gk *eidos* form + *krasis* mixture.] *Min.* = VESUVIANITE.

idol /ˈʌɪd(ə)l/ *n.*, *a.*, & *v.* ME. [(O)Fr. †*id(e)le*, *idole* f. L *idolum* image, form, apparition, (eccl.L) idol, f. Gk *eidōlon*, f. *eidos* form, shape.] A *n.* I From Jewish and Christian use. 1 An image or representation of a god or divinity used as an object of worship; a false god; *arch. derog.* a material object of worship in a Christian church. ME. 2 A person who or thing which is the object of extreme or excessive devotion. M16.

1 E. H. GOMBRICH Idols of which the Bible speaks: that people prayed before them. *Moorish idol*: see MOORISH *a.*[2] 2 S. BERINGTON Money, the Idol of other People, was the least of his Care. A. MCCOWEN My early idols were Jack Hulbert and Cicely Courtneidge. MATINÉE *idol*.

II From classical Greek and Latin use. †3 An image or representation of a person or thing; *esp.* a statue. M16–E17. b A likeness, an imitation. L16–M17. c A counterfeit, a sham; an impostor, a pretender. L16–M17. 4 An image without substance; a reflection, a phantom. Now *rare*. M16. 5 A fantasy, a fancy. Now *rare*. L16. b *Philos.* (now *Hist.*). A false mental image or conception; a false or misleading notion; a fallacy. L17.

5b **idols of the tribe**, **cave**, **market**, **theatre** four classes of fallacies referred by Bacon (1620) respectively to limitations of human mind, prejudices of idiosyncrasy, influence of words, philosophical and logical prepossessions.

B *attrib.* or as *adj.* Of, pertaining to, or resembling an idol. M16.

C *v.t.* Idolize. Now only *poet.* L16.

idola *n.* pl. of IDOLUM.

idolater /ʌɪˈdɒlətə/ *n.* Also **-tor**. LME. [f. (O)Fr. *idolâtre* (f. Proto-Romance (med.L) *idolatra* for *idololatra*, *-tres* f. Gk *eidōlolatrēs*: see -LATER; cf. IDOLATRY) + -ER[1], or f. IDOLATRY after *astronomer*, *astronomy*.] 1 A person who worships idols or images of deities or divinities. LME. 2 A person who idolizes or adores a person or thing. M16.

1 J. NORRIS Idolaters . . pay that Religious Worship . . to something else that is not God. 2 A. C. SWINBURNE The idolators of either [author] insisted . . on the superior claims of their respective favorite.

idolatress *n.* (now *rare*) a female idolater E17.

idolatric /ʌɪˈdɒlətrɪk/ *a. rare.* M17. [med.L *idolatricus*, f. *idolatria* IDOLATRY: see -IC.] Idolatrous.

†**idolatrical** *a.* M16–L18. [f. as prec. + -AL[1].] Idolatrous.

idolatrize /ʌɪˈdɒlətrʌɪz/ *v.* Also **-ise**. L16. [f. IDOLATRY + -IZE.] †1 *v.i.* Worship an idol or idols; practise idolatry. L16–E18. 2 *v.t.* Make an idol of, worship idolatrously; idolize. E17.

2 A. B. GROSART We are so used to idolatrize Shakespeare because of his simply incomparable genius.

idolatrous /ʌɪˈdɒlətrəs/ *a.* M16. [f. IDOLATER + -OUS.] 1 Of, pertaining to, or characteristic of idolatry; devoted to idolatry. M16. 2 Of a person: worshipping an idol or idols, worshipping false gods. E17.

1 T. FULLER He saw an idolatrous altar at Damascus. 2 MILTON The Philistines Idolatrous, uncircumcised, unclean.

idolatrously *adv.* L16. **idolatrousness** *n.* L16.

idolatry /ʌɪˈdɒlətri/ *n.* ME. [(O)Fr. *idolâtrie* f. Proto-Romance (med.L) *idolatria* for eccl.L *idololatria* f. Gk *eidōlolatreia*, f. *eidōlon* IDOL *n.*: see -LATRY.] 1 The worship of idols; the offering of divine honours to a created object. ME. 2 Excessive devotion to or veneration for a person or thing; adoration. LME.

2 R. MANNING I borrowed an idea from Dickens, whom I love this side idolatry.

idolise *v.* var. of IDOLIZE.

idolism /ˈʌɪd(ə)lɪz(ə)m/ *n.* E17. [f. IDOL *n.* + -ISM.] 1 Idolatry. E17. 2 = IDOL *n.* 5b. L17.

idolist *n.* a worshipper of idols, an idolater E17.

idolize /ˈʌɪd(ə)lʌɪz/ *v.* Also **-ise**. L16. [f. IDOL *n.* + -IZE.] 1 *v.t.* Make an idol of, worship idolatrously; adore or love to excess. L16. 2 *v.i.* Practise idolatry. *rare.* M17.

1 T. GALE The Moon is the same . . with Diana, which the Gauls greatly idolized. E. O'BRIEN The mother came to idolize the child, because it was quiet.

idolizer *n.* M17.

idoloclast /ʌɪˈdɒləklast/ *n.* E19. [f. IDOL *n.* after *iconoclast*.] A destroyer of idols; an iconoclast.

idolothyte /ʌɪˈdɒləθʌɪt/ *a.* & *n.* Now *rare* or *obs.* M16. [eccl.L *idolothytus* f. Gk *eidōlothutos* offered to idols, f. *eidōlon* IDOL *n.* + *thutos* sacrificed.] (A thing) offered to an idol.

idolum /ʌɪˈdəʊləm/ *n.* Pl. **-la** /lə/. E17. [L *idolum* f. Gk *eidōlon* IDOL *n.*] 1 An image without substance; a phantom; a mental image, an idea. E17. 2 = IDOL *n.* 5b. M17.

idoneous /ʌɪˈdəʊnɪəs/ *a.* Now *rare*. M16. [f. L *idoneus* fit, suitable + -OUS.] Apt, fit, suitable.

idoneity /ʌɪdəˈniːɪti, -ˈneɪɪti/ *n.* [late L *idoneitas*] fitness, suitability, aptness E17. **idoneousness** *n.* E18.

idrialin /ˈɪdrɪəlɪn/ *n.* Now *rare*. Also **-ine** /-iːn/. M19. [f. as next: see -IN[1], -INE[5].] *Chem.* & *Min.* Idrialite.

idrialite /ˈɪdrɪəlʌɪt/ *n.* M19. [f. *Idria* (now Idrija) in Slovenia, SE Europe + -LITE.] *Chem.* & *Min.* A colourless crystalline aromatic hydrocarbon, $C_{22}H_{11}$, which occurs naturally as a combustible mineral coloured brownish black by admixture with cinnabar, clays, etc.

idryl /ˈɪdrʌɪl, -rɪl/ *n.* M19. [f. as prec. + -YL.] *Chem.* A naturally occurring mixture of hydrocarbons including fluoranthene; fluoranthene.

id ul-fitr /ˈiːdʊlfɪtrə/ *n.* Also **id al-** /ˈiːdal-/. M18. [Arab. *ʿīd al-fiṭr*: cf. EID.] *Islam.* The feast of breaking the Ramadan fast.

Idumean /ɪdjʊˈmiːən, ʌɪd-/ *n.* & *a.* Also **-maean**. OE. [f. L *Idumaea* f. Gk *Idoumaia* f. Heb. *ʾĕdōm* Edom (see below) + -AN, -EAN.] *Hist.* A *n.* A member of a people inhabiting Idumaea or Edom, an ancient kingdom situated between Egypt and Palestine. OE. B *adj.* Of or pertaining to Idumaea or Edom. L17.

idyll /ˈɪdɪl, ˈʌɪd-/ *n.* Also **-yl**, in L form (earlier) †**idyllium**. L16. [L *idyllium*, f. Gk *eidullion* dim. of *eidos* form, picture.] 1 A short description in verse or (freq. more fully *prose idyll*) in prose of a picturesque scene or incident, esp. in rustic life. L16. 2 An episode suitable for treatment in such verse or prose, *esp.* a love-story. M19. 3 *Mus.* An instrumental composition on a pastoral or sentimental subject. L19.

2 L. STRACHEY If the . . elements of an idyll are happiness, love and simplicity, an idyll it was.

i'dyllian *a.* (*rare*) idyllic E18. **i'dyllic** *a.* of, pertaining to, or resembling an idyll; making a suitable subject for an idyll: M19. **i'dyllically** *adv.* L19. **idyllist** *n.* a writer of idylls L18. **idyllize** *v.t.* make into an idyll L19.

-ie /i/ *suff.* Var. (esp. *Sc.* & *Austral.*) of -Y[6], as in *birdie*, *doggie*, *roughie*, *sickie*; used also in independent formations, as *bookie*, *movie*.

-ier /ɪə/ *suff.* See also -YER. [Of varied origin in native wds; in wds f. Fr. repr. Fr. *-ier* f. L *-arius*: see -ARY[1]. Cf. -EER.] Forming ns. from ns., denoting a person whose employment, profession, etc., is concerned with a thing, also (rarely) agent-ns. from vbs in (i) ME words based chiefly on native words, in which the suff. is unstressed, as *clothier*, *collier*, *furrier*; (ii) later words of Fr. origin, in which the suff. is stressed, as *bombardier*, *cashier*.

ier-oe /ɪərˈəʊ/ *n. Sc.* E18. [Gael. *iar-ogha*, f. *iar* after + *ogha* grandchild.] A great-grandchild.

if /ɪf/ *conj.* & *n.* [OE *ġif*, *ġyf*, corresp. to OFris. *jef*, *ef*, *jof*, *of*, OS *ef*, *of* (Du. *of*), OHG *ibu*, *oba*, *ube*, also *niba*, *noba*, *nube* if not (G *ob* whether, if), ON *ef* if, Goth. *ibai*, *iba* whether, lest, *niba(i)* if not, *jabai* if, although: ult. origin unkn.] A *conj.* I 1 Introducing a condition where the question of, fulfilment or non-fulfilment is left open: given the hypothesis or proviso that, in the event that. (In *formal* or *archaic* lang. vb of *if* cl. may be in pres. subjunct.) OE. b With cl. reduced to *if* and a word or phr. Also, (often after *few*, *seldom*, etc.; introducing a more extreme term), or perhaps not even; *if not*, (often after *many*, *most*, etc.; introducing a more extreme term), or perhaps even. ME. c In rhetorical use, the main cl. expressing a proposition which is implied to be as true as that contained in the *if* cl. manifestly or self-evidently is: as truly as. Also, in comparing two situations:

whereas. ME. 2 With past subjunct. both in *if* cl. and principal cl., implying that the condition was not, is not, or will not be fulfilled: on the supposition that, supposing. OE. 3 With principal cl. suppressed and *if* cl. standing on its own, expr.: (*a*) a wish (now always *if only —!*); (*b*) an exclamation of surprise (the vb being qualified by *not*). OE. 4 Introducing a concession (the cl. often reduced to *if* and a word or phr.): while it is true that, though admittedly. Also, at the risk that, even if. ME.

1 J. CARLYLE I'll be hanged if I ever give you anything. F. W. CROFTS I'm blessed if I know. C. CLAIBORNE If the fish smells clean . . chances are it is fresh. O. NORTON I wasn't to worry if I found his tablets in the bathroom. b T. HERBERT Frogs are of great vertue, if physically used. *Bookman* [He] labours . . little, if at all, over the newspaper proofs. V. WOOLF I really must catch the first post if possible. M. KEANE Her reason if not now her life was in some danger. c P. LIVELY Dirty beggar . . , sixty if he was a day. V. S. PRITCHETT If a minute before he was drunkish, he was now sober. *Independent* It's a white poppy play if ever there was one. 2 R. MACAULAY I should get on better if I saw everything in black and white. G. B. SHAW Would you mind if I shewed him your draft? 3 V. WOOLF A fortnight already gone. . . If only one could sip slowly . . every grain of every hour! T. DREISER Well, by jing, if it ain't Tom. 4 F. W. CROFTS If he was not greatly liked in a personal capacity, he was respected as a sound business man. F. MUIR It foamed happily, if a bit glutinously. *Bodleian Library Record* Three interesting, if repetitious, publications.

II 5 Introducing a noun cl., chiefly as obj. of vbs such as *ask*, *doubt*, *know*, etc.: whether. OE. 6 In the hope or on the off chance that, to see whether. *arch.* ME.

5 *Law Times* He asked if his wife was there. SCOTT FITZGERALD It was doubtful if he knew who Andrew Jackson was. B. KEATON I went to New York, to see if I could get work there. A. BROOKNER Mummy was wondering if you would like to join us. 6 AV *Mark* 11:13 And seeing a figtree . . hee came, if haply hee might find any thing thereon.

Phrases: *and if*: see AND *conj.*[1] II. *as if*: see AS *adv.* etc. *be nothing if not*: see NOTHING *pron.* & *n.* **if and only if**: introducing a condition which is necessary as well as sufficient. **if and when** at the future time (if any) that. *if anything*: see ANYTHING *pron.* **if I were you** (in proffering advice) in your place. *if not*: see sense 1b above. *if only*: see sense 3 above. **if so be (that)** *arch.* & *dial.* if it should happen that, supposing. **if that** *arch.* supposing, if. *if you* PLEASE.

B *n.* An expression or condition of uncertainty; a proviso. E16.

ifs and ands or *ans*: see AND *n.*, AN *n.* *ifs and buts*: see BUT *n.*

Ife /ˈiːfi/ *n.* M20. [A town in western Nigeria, the religious centre of the Yoruba people.] Used *attrib.* to designate the art of the Yoruba people, esp. their bronzes and terracottas, the first examples of which were found at Ife.

-ifer *suff.* see -FER.

-iferous *suff.* see -FEROUS.

iff /ɪf ənd ˈəʊnlɪ ɪf/ *conj.* M20. [Written abbrev.] *Math.* & *Logic.* If and only if.

iffy /ˈɪfi/ *a. colloq.* M20. [f. IF *conj.* + -Y[1].] Full of or subject to conditions; doubtful, uncertain.

Also **iffish** *a.* L20.

-ific, -ification *suffs.* see -FIC, -FICATION.

-iform *suff.* see -FORM.

-ify *suff.* see -FY.

Igbo /ˈiːgbəʊ/ *n.* & *a.* Also **Ebo, Ibo,** /ˈiːbəʊ/. M18. [Afr. name.] A *n.* Pl. same, **-os.** 1 A member of a people of SE Nigeria. M18. 2 The Kwa language of this people. E19. B *adj.* Of or pertaining to this people or their language. M18.

iggerant *a.* see IGNORANT.

igloo /ˈɪgluː/ *n.* In sense 2 also **agloo, aglu,** /ˈagluː/. M19. [Eskimo (Inuit) *iglu* house.] 1 An Eskimo dome-shaped hut, usu. one built from blocks of snow. M19. b *transf.* Any similarly shaped building or structure used for storage, shelter, etc. M20. 2 A cavity in the snow above a seal's breathing-hole. M19.

Ignatian /ɪgˈneɪʃ(ə)n/ *a.* & *n.* E17. [f. *Ignatius* (see below) + -AN.] A *adj.* 1 Of or pertaining to St Ignatius Loyola (1491–1556) or the Society of Jesus, of which he was a founder. E17. 2 Of or pertaining to St Ignatius, bishop of Antioch, martyred at Rome *c* 107, or the letters attributed to him. M19. B *n.* A follower of St Ignatius Loyola; a Jesuit. E17.

Ignatius's bean /ɪgˈneɪʃəsɪz biːn/ *n. phr.* Also **Ignatius' bean** /ɪgˈneɪʃəs/. M18. [St *Ignatius* Loyola (see prec.).] The highly poisonous seed of a climbing tropical shrub, *Strychnos ignatii* (family Loganiaceae). Also more fully *St Ignatius'(s) bean.*

igneous /ˈɪgnɪəs/ *a.* M17. [f. L *igneus* f. *ignis* fire, + -OUS: see -EOUS.] 1 Pertaining to or of the nature of fire; fiery; produced by the action of fire. M17. 2 *Geol.* Produced by volcanic or magmatic agency; (of rock) that has solidified from lava or magma. L18.

ignes fatui *n. phr.* pl. of IGNIS FATUUS.

ignicolist /ɪgˈnɪkəlɪst/ *n.* E19. [f. L *ignis* fire + *-cola* (f. *colere* to worship) + -IST.] A fire-worshipper.

igniferous /ɪgˈnɪf(ə)rəs/ *a.* E17. [f. L *ignifer* fire-bearing, f. *ignis* fire: see -FEROUS.] Producing fire.

ignify /ˈɪgnɪfʌɪ/ *v.t. rare.* L16. [f. L *ignis* fire + -FY.] Cause to burn; set on fire.

ignimbrite /ˈɪgnɪmbrʌɪt/ *n.* M20. [f. L *ignis* fire + *imbris, imber* shower of rain, storm cloud + -ITE[1].] *Geol.* Any pyroclastic rock, typically a welded tuff, deposited from or formed by the settling of a *nuée ardente*.

ignipotent /ɪgˈnɪpət(ə)nt/ *a.* M17. [f. L *ignipotent-* (Virgilian epithet of Vulcan), f. *ignis* fire + *potent-* POTENT *a.*[2]] Ruling or having power over fire.

ignis fatuus /ˌɪgnɪs ˈfatjʊəs/ *n. phr.* Pl. **ignes fatui** /ˌɪgniːz ˈfatjʊʌɪ, ˌɪgneɪz ˈfatjʊiː/. M16. [mod.L = foolish fire, so called from its erratic flitting from place to place.] 1 A phosphorescent light seen hovering or floating over marshy ground, perh. due to the combustion of methane; a will-o'-the-wisp. M16. 2 *fig.* A delusive guiding principle, hope, or aim. L16.

2 Y. MENUHIN I don't fear indolence, confident . . that the gift is not an ignis fatuus, there one minute and gone the next.

†**ignite** *a.* LME–E18. [L *ignitus* pa. pple of *ignire*: see next.] Glowing with heat, white- or red-hot; *fig.* hot, ardent.

ignite /ɪgˈnʌɪt/ *v.* M17. [L *ignit-* pa. ppl stem of *ignire* set on fire, f. *ignis* fire.] 1 *v.t.* Make intensely hot; *spec.* (*Chem.*) heat to the point of combustion or chemical change. M17. 2 *v.t.* Set fire to, kindle. E19. 3 *v.i.* Catch fire, begin to burn. E19. 4 *v.t.* Bring (an electric arc) into being. E20.

2 D. M. THOMAS The stokers set the fire going by igniting the people's hair. *fig.*: *Company* She felt no-one could match Alan or ignite the special feelings she'd had with him. 3 L. DEIGHTON Bombcases stuffed full of benzol, rubber and phosphorus that ignited on impact.

ignitaˈbility *n.* ignitibility E19. **ignitable** *a.* ignitible M19. **ignitiˈbility** *n.* ability to be ignited E20. **ignitible** *a.* able to be ignited M17.

igniter /ɪgˈnʌɪtə/ *n.* In sense 2 also **-tor.** L19. [f. IGNITE *v.* + -ER[1].] 1 A device which or a person who ignites something; *esp.* a device to set fire to an explosive or combustible. L19. 2 *Electronics.* In an ignitron, a small auxiliary anode that serves to restrike the arc in each cycle. M20.

ignition /ɪgˈnɪʃ(ə)n/ *n.* E17. [(Fr. f.) med.L *ignitio(n-)*, f. as IGNITE *v.*: see -ION.] 1 The action of subjecting something to the full action of fire; *spec.* (*Chem.*) heating to the point of combustion or chemical change. E17. 2 The action of setting fire to something; the process of catching fire or beginning to burn. E19. 3 The action of starting the combustion of the mixture in the cylinder of an internal-combustion engine; the mechanism for starting this process. E20. 4 The striking of an electric arc. E20.

Comb.: **ignition key**: to operate the ignition mechanism of a motor vehicle engine; **ignition tube** *Chem.* a small test-tube of heat-resistant glass.

ignitor *n.* see IGNITER.

ignitron /ɪgˈnʌɪtrɒn/ *n.* M20. [f. IGNITE *v.*, IGNITION + -TRON.] *Electronics.* A mercury-arc rectifier of a kind having a pool cathode, a single anode, and an igniter, the timing of the igniter being used to control the rectifier output. Cf. EXCITRON.

ignivomous /ɪgˈnɪvəməs/ *a.* E17. [f. late L *ignivomus* (f. *ignis* fire + *-vomus* -vomiting) + -OUS.] Vomiting or discharging fire.

ignoble /ɪgˈnəʊb(ə)l/ *a.*, *v.*, & *n.* LME. [(Fr. f.) L *ignobilis*, f. as I-[2] + (*g*)*nobilis* NOBLE *a.*] A *adj.* 1 Not noble in birth or rank; of humble origin or social status. LME. 2 Not noble in character or quality; dishonourable, mean-spirited. L16.

1 E. A. FREEMAN A West-Saxon house which, two generations back, had been undistinguished, perhaps ignoble. **ignoble hawk** *Falconry* any of the short-winged hawks (e.g. the goshawk and sparrowhawk) which chase or rake after their prey instead of swooping down on it. 2 MILTON Counsel'd ignoble ease, and peaceful sloath.

B *v.t.* Make ignoble; give a bad reputation to. *rare.* L16.

C *n.* A person of ignoble rank or character. Usu. in *pl.* Now *rare.* E17.

ignoˈbility *n.* ignoble quality LME. **ignobleness** *n.* LME. **ignobly** *adv.* L16.

ignominious /ɪgnəˈmɪnɪəs/ *a.* LME. [((O)Fr. *ignominieux* f.) L *ignominiosus*, f. *ignominia*: see next, -OUS.] 1 Causing ignominy or (public) disgrace; humiliating. LME. 2 Of a person: covered with or deserving ignominy; infamous. L16.

1 A. MASON The lamentable gulf between the prophesied glory and the ignominious fact. 2 D. H. LAWRENCE Hermione appeared . . to ridicule him and make him look ignominious in the eyes of everybody.

ignominiously *adv.* E17. **ignominiousness** *n.* E18.

ignominy /ˈɪgnəmɪni/ *n.* M16. [(Fr. *ignominie* f.) L *ignominia*, f. as I-[2] + (var. of) *nomen* name, reputation: see -Y[3].] 1 Public disgrace or dishonour; infamy. M16. 2 Infamous quality or conduct. *arch.* M16.

1 *Gentleman (Bombay)* He had to suffer the ignominy of being dropped from the team. 2 LD MACAULAY He then repays by ingratitude the benefits which he has purchased by ignominy.

ignomy /ˈɪgnəmi/ *n.* Now *arch. rare.* M16. [Contr.] = IGNOMINY.

ignoramus /ɪgnəˈreɪməs/ *n.* L16. [L = we do not know, (in legal use) we take no notice of (it). In sense 2 perh. f. *Ignoramus*, a comedy by George Ruggle (1615) satirizing lawyers.] 1 The endorsement formerly made by a grand jury on an indictment which they rejected as not being backed by sufficient evidence to bring before a petty jury. Chiefly in *find, return,* or *bring (in) an ignoramus. obs.* exc. *Hist.* L16. 2 An ignorant person. E17.

ignorance /ˈɪgn(ə)r(ə)ns/ *n.* ME. [(O)Fr. f. L *ignorantia*, f. *ignorant-*: see next, -ANCE.] 1 The fact or condition of being ignorant; lack of knowledge (general or particular). ME. b In full *time of ignorance.* The period of Arab history prior to the teaching of Muhammad. L18. †2 An offence or sin caused by lack of knowledge. LME–E17.

1 W. SOYINKA Every care was taken to ensure that he was kept in ignorance of what had occurred. P. BARKER She didn't know what an ovary was but she wasn't going to admit ignorance. *invincible ignorance*: see INVINCIBLE 1b.

Also **ignorancy** *n.* (long *rare*) E16.

ignorant /ˈɪgn(ə)r(ə)nt/ *a.* & *n.* In sense A.3 also (*non-standard* & *joc.*) **iggerant** /ˈɪg(ə)r(ə)nt/. LME. [(O)Fr. f. L *ignorant-* pres. ppl stem of *ignorare*: see IGNORE, -ANT[1].] A *adj.* 1 Lacking knowledge (general or particular); not versed *in* a subject, unaware *of* a fact, *that.* LME. b Marked by or resulting from ignorance. Also *poet.*, that keeps one in ignorance. LME. †2 Of a thing: unknown. LME–M17. 3 Ill-mannered, uncouth. *dial.* & *colloq.* L19.

1 A. RADCLIFFE I am ignorant that till now I ever made you this offer. G. STEIN Melanctha with all her . . wisdom was really very ignorant of evil. I. MURDOCH But I'm so stupid and ignorant. . . I know nothing. A. FRASER The trooper who was supposed to know the district proved alarmingly ignorant. b SHAKES. *Wint. T.* If you know aught which does behove my knowledge . . imprison't not In ignorant concealment.

B *n.* An ignorant person. Now *rare.* LME.

ignorantly *adv.* LME.

ignoratio elenchi /ɪgnəˌreɪʃɪəʊ ɪˈlɛŋkʌɪ/ *n. phr.* Pl. ***ignorationes elenchi*** /ˌɪgnəreɪʃɪˈəʊniːz/. L16. [med.L, tr. Gk *hē tou elegkou agnoia* ignorance of the conditions of valid proof.] A logical fallacy which consists in apparently refuting an opponent while actually disproving something not asserted; *gen.* any argument which is irrelevant to its professed purpose.

ignoration /ɪgnəˈreɪʃ(ə)n/ *n.* E17. [L *ignoratio(n-)*, f. *ignorat-* pa. ppl stem of *ignorare*: see IGNORE, -ATION.] 1 The fact or condition of being ignorant. *rare.* E17. 2 The action of ignoring or disregarding someone or something; the fact of being ignored. M19.

ignore /ɪgˈnɔː/ *v.t.* L15. [((O)Fr. *ignorer* f.) L *ignorare*, f. as I-^{2} + base *gno-* know.] 1 Be ignorant of. Now *arch. rare.* L15. 2 Refuse to recognize or take notice of; disregard intentionally. E19. 3 Of a grand jury: reject (an indictment) on the grounds of insufficient evidence (cf. IGNORAMUS I). *obs.* exc. *Hist.* M19.

1 R. BOYLE Others . . desirous to be taught by me, the little that I know, and they ignore. 2 D. H. LAWRENCE Was he going to ignore her, was he going to take no further notice of her? R. K. NARAYAN She ignored her surroundings . . , her attention being concentrated upon her movements. L. GORDON She followed natural paths which ignored artificial boundaries.

ignorable *a.* M19.

ignotum per ignotius /ɪgˌnəʊtəm pər ɪgˈnəʊtɪəs/ *n. phr.* LME. [Late L, lit. 'the unknown by means of the more unknown'.] An explanation which is harder to understand than what it is meant to explain.

iguana /ɪˈgwɑːnə/ *n.* M16. [Sp. f. Arawak *iwana.*] 1 A large arboreal lizard, *Iguana iguana*, of Central and S. America. Also, any of various similar or related lizards of the same family, Iguanidae. M16. 2 In Africa: a large monitor lizard of the genus *Varanus*; *esp.* the Nile monitor, *V. niloticus*. Cf. GOANNA. M18.

1 *marine iguana*: see MARINE *a.*

iguanian *n.* & *a.* (*a*) *n.* an iguanid or related lizard; *spec.* an iguanid, agamid, or chameleon; (*b*) *adj.* of, pertaining to, or designating such lizards: M19. **iguanid** *n.* & *a.* (*a*) *n.* any lizard of the family Iguanidae, typified by the genus *Iguana* and largely confined to the New World; (*b*) of, pertaining to, or characteristic of this family: L19. **iguanoid** *n.* & *a.* = IGUANID M19.

iguanodon /ɪˈgwɑːnədɒn/ *n.* E19. [f. prec. + -ODON, from its teeth being similar to an iguana's.] Any of various large extinct ornithischian dinosaurs of the genus *Iguanodon*, of late Jurassic and early Cretaceous times, with well-developed hind limbs and a long thick tail.

ihram /ɪxˈrɑːm, ɪˈrɑːm/ *n.* E18. [Arab. *'iḥrām*, ult. f. *ḥarama* forbid. Cf. HAREM.] 1 The sacred state into which a Muslim must enter before performing a pilgrimage, during which sexual intercourse, shaving, cutting one's nails, and several other actions are forbidden. E18. 2 The costume worn by a Muslim in this state, consisting of two lengths of seamless usu. white fabric, one worn about the hips, the other over the shoulders or sometimes only over the left shoulder. E18.

iimbongi *n.pl.* see IMBONGI.

iiwi /iˈiːwi/ *n.* L18. [Haw.] A Hawaiian honey-creeper, *Vestiaria coccinea*, whose red feathers were formerly used to make the cloaks of Hawaiian chiefs.

Ijo /ˈiːdʒəʊ/ *n.* & *a.* Also **Ijaw** /ˈiːdʒɔː/. M19. [Ijo *ịjọ.*] A *n.* Pl. same. A member of a people inhabiting the Niger delta; the Niger-Congo language of this people. M19. B *attrib.* or as *adj.* Of or pertaining to the Ijo or their language. M20.

ijolite /ˈiːə(ʊ)lʌɪt/ *n.* L19. [f. Sw. *Ijo* (= Finn. *Ii*) a village and district on the Finnish coast + -LITE.] *Petrogr.* A plutonic rock consisting essentially of nepheline and pyroxene, without feldspar.

ijoˈlitic *a.* M20.

ikat /ˈiːkɑːt/ *n.* M20. [Malay, lit. 'tie, fasten'.] (A fabric made using) an Indonesian technique of textile decoration in which warp or weft threads, or both, are tied at intervals and dyed before weaving.

attrib.: *New Yorker* Heavy woven cotton rugs in ikat patterns, forty-two by seventy-two inches.

ikbal /ˈɪkbɑːl/ *n.* E20. [Turk., lit. 'good fortune', f. Arab. *'iḳbāl.*] *Hist.* A favoured member of the harem of an Ottoman Sultan.

ike *n.* see IKEY.

ikebana /ɪkɪˈbɑːnə/ *n.* E20. [Jap.] The art of Japanese flower arrangement, with formal display according to strict rules.

ikey /ˈʌɪki/ *n.* & *a. slang. derog.* (usu. considered *racially offensive*). As n. also **ike** /ʌɪk/. M19. [Colloq. abbrev. of Jewish male forename *Isaac.*] A *n.* (A person resembling) a Jew; a moneylender. M19. B *adj.* Artful, knowing; having a good opinion of oneself. L19.

ikon *n.* var. of ICON.

il- /ɪl/ *pref.*^{1} Var. of L IN-^{2} bef. *l.* Cf. IM-^{2}, IR-^{2}.

il- /ɪl/ *pref.*^{2} Var. of L IN-^{3} bef. *l.* Cf. I-^{2}, IM-^{2}, IR-^{2}.

-il /əl, ɪl/ *suff.* [Repr. L *-ilis.*] Forming adjs. and occas. ns., some adopted through Fr., as *civil*, *fossil*, *utensil*. Cf. -ILE.

Ila /ˈiːlə/ *n.* & *a.* Pl. **Ba-ila** /bəˈiːlə/, (of n.) same. E20. [Bantu.] A *n.* 1 A member of a Bantu-speaking people inhabiting Zambia. E20. 2 The language of this people. E20. B *attrib.* or as *adj.* Of or pertaining to the Ila or their language. E20.

Ilamba *n.* & *a.* var. of LAMBA *n.*^{2}

ilang-ilang *n.* var. of YLANG-YLANG.

Ilanun *n.* var. of ILLANUN.

Ilchester /ˈɪltʃɪstə/ *n.* & *a.* M20. [A town in Somerset, SW England.] (Designating) a variety of cheese made from Cheddar, beer, garlic, and spices.

†ile *n.* var. of AISLE.

-ile /ʌɪl/ *suff.* Var. of -IL, esp. in adoptions through Fr., as *agile*, *erectile*, *fragile*; *spec.* in *Statistics* (on the model of L ordinal numerals of the type *sextilis* etc.), forming ns. denoting those values of a variate that divide a population into the indicated number of equal groups, or the groups themselves (*decile*, *percentile*).

ileal /ˈɪlɪəl/ *a.* L19. [f. ILEUM + -AL^1.] *Anat.* & *Zool.* Of, within, or supplying the ileum.

ileectomy /ɪlɪˈɛktəmi/ *n.* L19. [f. ILEO- + -ECTOMY.] Surgical removal of all or part of the ileum; an instance of this.

ileitis /ɪlɪˈʌɪtɪs/ *n.* M19. [f. ILEUM + -ITIS.] *Med.* Inflammation of the ileum.

ileo- /ˈɪlɪəʊ/ *comb. form.* Bef. a vowel also **ile-**. [f. ILEUM + -O-.] Chiefly *Med.* Of, pertaining to, or involving the ileum.

ileoˈcaecal *a.* related to or (esp.) connecting the ileum and the caecum L19. **ileocoˈlitis** *n.* inflammation of the ileum and the colon L19. **ileocoˈlostomy** *n.* (an instance of) surgical connection of the ileum with the colon; the passage so formed: L19. **ileˈostomy** *n.* [Gk *stoma* mouth] (an instance of) surgical attachment of the ileum to the abdominal wall to form an artificial anus; the opening so formed: L19.

†ileon *n.* LME–M18. [med.L (in Gk form). Cf. (O)Fr. *iléon.*] = ILEUM.

ileum /ˈɪlɪəm/ *n.* L17. [med.L, var. of ILIUM app. by confusion with *ileus* (see next).] *Anat.* & *Zool.* The third portion of the small intestine, between the jejunum and the caecum. Also, the homologous or analogous part in lower vertebrates, insects, etc.

ileus /ˈɪlɪəs/ *n.* L17. [L *ileus*, *ileos* f. Gk *ileos*, *eileos* colic, app. f. *eilein* to roll.] *Med.* (Painful) obstruction of the intestine, esp. the ileum, due to mechanical obstruction or (more fully *paralytic ileus*) failure of peristalsis.

ilex /ˈʌɪlɛks/ *n.* LME. [L = holm-oak.] 1 = HOLM *n.*^{2} 2. LME. 2 Any of various trees of the genus *Ilex* (family Aquifoliaceae); = HOLLY *n.* I. M16.

ilia *n.pl.* see ILIUM.

iliac /ˈɪlɪak/ *a.* & *n.* E16. [Late L *iliacus*, f. *ilia*: see ILEUM, ILIUM, -AC.] A *adj.* 1 Of the nature of or pertaining to ileus; pertaining to or affecting the ileum. Chiefly in *iliac passion* below. Now *rare* or *obs.* E16. 2 Of or pertaining to the flank, or to the ilium or hip-bone. M16.

Special collocations: **iliac artery**: branching from the abdominal aorta and supplying the legs and pelvis. **iliac passion** (now *rare* or *obs.*) = ILEUS. **iliac vein** any of several major veins draining blood from the lower body to the inferior vena cava.

B *n.* †1 = ILEUS. Only in M16. 2 An iliac artery, vein, etc. L18.

iliacus /ɪˈlʌɪəkəs/ *n.* E17. [Late L: see prec.] *Anat.* A muscle in the groin region which, with the psoas, flexes the hip. Also †*iliacus internus*, *iliacus muscle*.

Iliad /ˈɪlɪad/ *n.* E17. [Title of an epic poem attributed to Homer, describing the climax of the siege of Troy, f. L *Iliad-*, *Ilias* f. Gk *Iliados*, *Ilias*, (*poiēsis*) (poem) of Troy, f. *Ilion* Troy (whence L *Ilium*): see -AD^1.] 1 A long story or Homeric epic, *esp.* one dealing with martial feats. E17. 2 A long series or account of events, esp. disasters. E17.

Iliadic /ɪlɪˈadɪk/ *a.* of, pertaining to, or of the nature of an Iliad L19. **Iliadist** *n.* a writer of Iliads E18.

Ilian /ˈɪlɪən/ *a.* & *n.* L16. [f. L *Ilium*: see prec., -AN.] A *adj.* Of or pertaining to any of the successive towns of Ilium in the Trojan plain. L16. B *n.* A native or inhabitant of Ilium. M19.

Iliat /ˈɪlɪɑːt/ *n.* E19. [Turk. *ilāt* pl. of *il* country, wandering pastoral tribe.] Any of several nomadic tribes scattered throughout Iran (Persia).

iligant /ˈɪlɪg(ə)nt/ *a.* Chiefly *Anglo-Ir.* Also **ill-**. E19. [Repr. a pronunc.] Elegant.

ilio- /ˈɪlɪəʊ/ *comb. form*^{1}. E19. [f. ILIUM 3: see -O-.] Chiefly *Anat.* Relating to or involving the ilium, as *iliofemoral*, *iliolumbar*, *iliosacral*. Also, involving or including the iliacus, as *iliopsoas*.

†ilio- *comb. form*^{2}. Only in M19. [f. ILIUM I: see -O-.] = ILEO-.

†ilion *n.* see ILIUM.

-ility /ˈɪlɪti/ *suff.* [Fr. *-ilité* or its source L *-ilitas*: see -ITY.] In or forming ns. f. adjs. ending in *-il*, *-ile*, or *-le*, with senses as -ITY, as *civility*, *servility*, *ability*.

ilium /ˈɪlɪəm/ *n.* Also (earlier) in Gk form **†ilion**. Pl. **ilia** /ˈɪlɪə/, **†ilions**. LME. [L: in cl.L only in pl. *ilia* flanks, sides, (also) entrails. See also ILEUM.] †1 = ILEUM. LME–E19. 2 The anterior or superior bone of the pelvis, the hip-bone, usu. (as in humans) articulating with the sacrum, and fused with the ischium and pubis to form the innominate bone. L16. †3 In *pl.* The flanks. L16–E18.

ilk /ɪlk/ *a.*^{1}, *pron.*^{1}, & *n.* [OE *ilca* masc., *ilce* fem. & neut., f. Gmc pron. stem repr. also in Goth. *is*, OHG *ir*, (also mod.) *er* he, L *is* that, *idem* same, + base of ALIKE *a.*: cf. SUCH *a.* & *pron.*, WHICH. See also THILK.] A *adj.* Same, very same. *obs.* exc. *Sc. arch.* OE.

B *pron.* & *n.* 1 *The* or *that* same person or thing. *obs.* exc. *Sc. arch.* OE. 2 spec. *The* or *that* same place, estate, or name. Only in *of that ilk*. *Sc.* L15. 3 A family, a class, a sort, a kind. L18.

2 SIR W. SCOTT Knockwinnocks of that Ilk. 3 M. LOWRY Were not Bolowski and his ilk the enemies of their own race. *London Review of Books* Pronouncements of this ilk seem mainly designed to leave one's readers breathless and spluttering.

ilk /ɪlk/ *a.*^{2} & *pron.*^{2} *Sc.* & †*north.* Now *rare.* ME. [f. as EACH.] Each.

ilka /ˈɪlkə/ *a.* (in mod. usage also classed as a *determiner*). Now only *Sc.* ME. [f. prec. + A *a.*] Each, every.

ill /ɪl/ *n.* ME. [f. the adj.] 1 Evil; the opposite of good. ME. b Wickedness, depravity. Formerly also, an instance or act of this. *arch.* ME. 2 Hostility, malevolence, unfriendly feeling. Now only, something unfriendly, unfavourable, or injurious. ME. 3 (A) misfortune, disaster, trouble. ME. 4 Harm, injury. LME. 5 A disease, a sickness. Now chiefly *dial.* LME.

1 TENNYSON Oh yet we trust that somehow good Will be the final goal of ill. 2 W. TREVOR Mrs Maylam . . . would hear no ill of Studdy and was clearly on his

side. *speak ill of*: see SPEAK *v.* 3 T. GRAY No sense have they of ills to come. 5 *louping-ill, tail-ill*, etc.

ill /ɪl/ *a.* & *adv.* Compar. WORSE *a.*, superl. WORST *a.* ME. [ON *illr* adj., *illa* adv., *ilt* use as n. of neut. of adj.: ult. origin unkn.] A *adj.* 1 Of a person (*obs.* exc. *dial.*), conduct, or actions: morally evil, wicked, depraved, immoral. *arch.* ME. b Of opinion, reputation, etc.: attributing or implying wickedness or immorality. L15. 2 Malevolent; hostile, unkind; harsh. ME. b Of an animal: savage, vicious. Now *dial.* L15. 3 Doing or tending to do harm; hurtful, injurious; prejudicial; disagreeable, objectionable. ME. b Of an omen, conditions, etc.: unlucky, unpropitious, disastrous; miserable, wretched. ME. †c Of food: unwholesome, injurious to health. L15–E18. 4 Difficult, hard, (*to do*). *arch.* ME. 5 Inferior in quality or condition; not good; defective; unsatisfactory; unskilful; inefficient. ME. b Of manners or conduct: impolite, unseemly, rude. L16. 6 Not in good health, sick, (chiefly *pred.*); (of health) unsound. (The predominant mod. sense.) LME.

1 T. HARDY The roads were dotted with roving characters of possibly ill intent. 2 SHELLEY Ill tongues shall wound me. 3 J. BUCHAN 'Ill weather,' said Jaikie. 'Hellish,' was the answer. b POPE Ill fortune led Ulysses to our isle. *Proverb*: It's an ill wind that blows nobody good. 4 E. NESBIT And if a lad is ill to bind, Or some young maid is hard to lead. 5 J. RUSKIN The first shoots of it enfeebled by ill gardening. 6 J. AUSTEN Lady Bertram, in consequence of a little ill-health, . . gave up the house in town. V. BRITTAIN Soon after we returned from Italy I became ill with jaundice. J. GATHORNE-HARDY Children . . . can look very well one moment, and an hour . . later be extremely ill.

B *adv.* 1 Wickedly, evilly, immorally. *obs.* exc. as passing into other senses. ME. 2 Malevolently, unkindly; with hostility; unfavourably. ME. 3 Painfully, injuriously; unpleasantly. *obs.* exc. *dial.* ME. 4 Unpropitiously; unhappily. ME. 5 Not well, badly, defectively, faultily; improperly; unskilfully, inefficiently; with difficulty. ME.

2 G. GREENE Even Burnet found it hard to speak ill of her at that time. 4 B. JONES This urge to be away / . . bodes ill both for your life and art. 5 E. WAUGH Some books I have sent to be bound in Bristol came back very ill done. N. FREELING Well, my dear, it would ill become me to complain. P. LIVELY There were demobbed soldiers everywhere, conspicuous in their ill-fitting new suits.

Special collocations, comb., & *phrases*: *be taken ill*: see TAKE *v.* **do an ill turn to** harm (a person or his or her interests). *ill-advised*: see ADVISED 3. **ill-affected** *a.* (*a*) not well-disposed, unfriendly; †(*b*) affected with illness. **ill-assorted** *a.* not well matched. **ill at ease** embarrassed, uneasy. **ill-behaved** *a.* badly brought up, rude. **ill-beloved** *a.* (*arch.*) not loved, disliked. *ill blood*: see BLOOD *n.* **ill-boding** *a.* boding evil, of ill omen. **ill-bred** *a.* badly brought up, rude. **ill breeding** bad manners, rudeness. **ill-concealed** *a.* that one does not feel the need to conceal. **ill-conditioned** *a.* (*a*) of evil disposition; (*b*) in bad condition. **ill-deedy** *a.* (now *arch. Sc.*) given to evil deeds, mischievous. **ill-defined** *a.* not clearly defined. **ill-disposed** *a.* (*a*) disposed to evil; malevolent; (*b*) unfavourably disposed, disinclined. **ill effect** a harmful effect, an unpleasant consequence, (freq. in *pl.*). **ill-equipped** *a.* not adequately equipped or qualified. **ill fame** or **repute** disrepute (*house of ill fame, repute*: see HOUSE *n.*[1]). **ill-fated** *a.* (*a*) having or destined to an evil or unhappy fate; (*b*) bringing bad fortune. *ill feeling*: see FEELING *n.* **ill-formed** *a.* badly formed; *spec.* in *Ling.*, incorrectly formed or derived from stated grammatical rules, grammatically incorrect. **ill-formedness** *n.* the state or condition of being ill-formed. **ill-founded** *a.* (of an idea etc.) not well founded, groundless. **ill-got** *a.* (*arch.*), **ill-gotten** *a.* gained by wicked or unlawful means. **ill-judged** *a.* unwise; badly considered. **ill-looking** *a.* unattractive, ugly. **ill luck** bad luck, misfortune. **ill-mannered** *a.* having bad manners, rude. **ill-matched** *a.* unsuited; not fit to be a pair, be adversaries, etc. **ill-omened** *a.* having a bad omen, inauspicious. **ill-placed** *a.* badly placed; inopportune. *ill repute*: see *ill fame* above. **ill-starred** *a.* born under an evil star; ill-fated, unlucky, destined to failure. **ill success** partial or complete failure. **ill temper** bad temper. *ill* THIEF. **ill-timed** *a.* done or occurring at an inappropriate time. **ill-treat** *v.t.* treat badly or cruelly, abuse. **ill treatment, ill usage, use** [USE *n.*] bad or cruel treatment, abuse. **ill-use** *v.t.* [USE *v.*] = *ill-treat* above. **ill will** = *ill feeling* above. **ill-willer** a person who harbours ill will towards another. **ill-willing** *a.* harbouring ill will, malevolent. **ill-wisher** = *ill-willer* above. *in ill part*: see PART *n.* *take a thing ill*: see TAKE *v.* *with an ill grace*: see GRACE *n.*

illachrymable /ɪˈlakrɪməb(ə)l/ *a. rare.* E17. [L *illacrimabilis*, f. as IL-[2] + *lacrimare* weep: see -ABLE. Cf. LACHRYMAL.] Incapable of weeping.

Illanun /ɪˈljɑːnən/ *n.* & *a.* Also **Ila-** /ɪˈlɑː-/. Pl. of n. same. L19. [Illanun, lit. 'lake people'.] A member of, of or pertaining to, a Moro people in the Philippines; (of) the language of this people.

Earlier **Illano** /ɪˈljɑːnəʊ/ *n.* (now *rare*), pl. **-os** L18.

illapse /ɪˈlaps/ *n.* Now *rare.* E17. [L *illapsus*, f. as next.] The action of slipping or falling in or of gently permeating something.

illapse /ɪˈlaps/ *v.i.* Now *rare.* M17. [L *illaps-* pa. ppl stem of *illabi* slip or fall in: see IL-[1], LAPSE *v.*] Slip or fall in, gently permeate.

illaqueate /ɪˈlakwɪeɪt/ *v.t.* Now *rare.* M16. [L *illaqueat-* pa. ppl stem of *illaqueare*, f. as IL-[1] + *laqueare* to snare, f. *laqueus* noose, snare: see -ATE[3].] Catch (as) in a noose; ensnare, entrap.

illaqueable *a.* (*rare*) able to be ensnared L17.

illatinate /ɪˈlatɪnət/ *a. rare.* E20. [f. IL-[2] + LATIN *a.* & *n.* + -ATE[2], after ILLITERATE *a.*] Having no knowledge of Latin.

illation /ɪˈleɪʃ(ə)n/ *n.* M16. [L *illatio(n-)*, f. *illat-*: see next, -ATION.] The action of inferring or drawing a conclusion from premisses; an inference, a conclusion.

illative /ɪˈleɪtɪv/ *n.* & *a.* L16. [L *illativus*, f. *illat-* ppl stem of *inferre* INFER.] A *n.* 1 A word or phrase introducing or stating an inference, as English *so, therefore*, etc. L16. 2 *Gram.* The illative case; a word, form, etc., in the illative case. M20. B *adj.* 1 Of a word or phrase: introducing or stating an inference. E17. 2 Inferential. M17. 3 *Gram.* Designating, being in, or pertaining to a case in some inflected languages expressing motion into. L19.

illatively *adv.* M17.

illaudable /ɪˈlɔːdəb(ə)l/ *a.* L16. [L *illaudabilis*, f. as IL-[2] + LAUDABLE.] Not laudable, unworthy of praise.

illaudably *adv.* (*rare*) M18.

Illawarra /ɪləˈwɒrə/ *n.* L19. [See below.] 1 Used *attrib.* to designate trees native to Illawarra, a district in New South Wales, Australia. L19. 2 In full *Illawarra (dairy) shorthorn*. (An animal of) a breed of usu. red or roan dairy cattle. E20.

1 **Illawarra (mountain) pine** an Australian cypress pine, *Callitris rhomboidea*.

illegal /ɪˈliːg(ə)l/ *a.* & *n.* E17. [(O)Fr. *illégal* or med.L *illegalis*, f. L IL-[2] + *legalis* LEGAL *a.*] A *adj.* Not legal; contrary to or forbidden by law. E17.

C. HILL All taxation without consent of Parliament was declared illegal. W. WHARTON The car wasn't registered. . . It was strictly illegal. *Sunday (Calcutta)* The party has also asked the government to . . evict all illegal migrants from tribal . . lands. **illegal operation** *spec.* an abortion performed illegally.

B *n.* 1 An illegal immigrant. M20. 2 A Soviet secret agent working in a foreign country. M20.

1 *Times* The 'illegals' . . will be deported back to the homelands. P. THEROUX Half the people who worked there were illegals.

illegalize *v.t.* make illegal E19. **illegally** *adv.* E17.

illegality /ɪliːˈgalɪti, ɪlɪ-/ *n.* M17. [(O)Fr. *illégalité* or med.L *illegalitas*, f. as prec.: see -ITY.] 1 The quality or condition of being illegal. M17. 2 An illegal act. L19.

illegible /ɪˈlɛdʒɪb(ə)l/ *a.* M17. [f. IL-[2] + LEGIBLE.] 1 Not legible. M17. †2 Incomprehensible to read. M18–E19.

1 D. LEAVITT Her illegible messages zigzagging off the page in a pencil-breaking scrawl.

illegiˈbility *n.* the quality of being illegible E19. **illegibly** *adv.* E19.

illegit /ɪlɪˈdʒɪt/ *n. colloq.* E20. [Abbrev.] = ILLEGITIMATE *n.* 1.

illegitimacy /ɪlɪˈdʒɪtɪməsi/ *n.* M17. [f. next: see -ACY.] The quality or state of being illegitimate.

illegitimate /ɪlɪˈdʒɪtɪmət/ *a.* & *n.* M16. [f. late L *illegitimus* after LEGITIMATE *a.*: see IL-[2], -ATE[2].] A *adj.* 1 Born to parents who are not lawfully married, not entitled in law to full filial rights. M16. 2 *gen.* Not legitimate; not in accordance with or authorized by law; not in accordance with a rule; irregular, abnormal. L16. 3 Of drama: concerned with spectacle rather than literary quality. E19.

1 A. FRASER He was an illegitimate son, born before her marriage. 2 A. J. AYER Physical symbols . . fail to satisfy this condition, and some positivists . . regard . . them as illegitimate.

B *n.* 1 An illegitimate person; a person who does something illegitimate or irregular. L17. 2 A free settler in Australia. *obs.* exc. *Hist.* E19.

¶By the civil and canon laws, and since 1926 by the law of England, a child born out of wedlock is legitimated by the subsequent marriage of the parents.

illegitimately *adv.* M17. **illegitimatize** *v.t.* = ILLEGITIMATE *v.* E19.

illegitimate /ɪlɪˈdʒɪtɪmeɪt/ *v.t.* E17. [f. the adj.: see -ATE[3]. Cf. LEGITIMATE *v.*] Declare illegitimate.

illegitimation /ˌɪlɪdʒɪtɪˈmeɪʃ(ə)n/ *n.* L15. [med.L *illegitimatio(n-)*, f. as ILLEGITIMATE *a.*: see -ATION.] 1 The action of declaring someone or something to be illegitimate; a declaration of illegitimacy. L15. †2 Illegitimacy. L16–E18.

illfare /ˈɪlfɛː/ *n.* Now chiefly *joc.* ME. [f. ILL *a.* + FARE *n.*[1]] The condition of faring badly, mishap, unsatisfactoriness.

ill-favoured /ɪlˈfeɪvəd/ *a.* Also ***-favored**. M16. [f. ILL *a.* + FAVOUR *n.* + -ED[2].] Having a displeasing appearance, unattractive; disagreeable, objectionable.

ill-favouredly *adv.* M16. **ill-favouredness** *n.* M16.

ill humour /ɪl ˈhjuːmə/ *n. phr.* Also ***-or.** M16. [f. ILL *a.* + HUMOUR *n.*] †1 A disordered or diseased bodily humour. M16–M17. 2 A bad mood; bad temper, irritability; sullenness, moroseness. L17.

ill-humoured *a.* bad-tempered, sullen L17. **ill-humouredly** *adv.* L18.

illiberal /ɪˈlɪb(ə)r(ə)l/ *a.* M16. [(O)Fr. *illibéral* f. L *illiberalis* mean, sordid, f. as IL-[2] + *liberalis* LIBERAL *a.*] 1 Not suitable to or characteristic of a free person; not relating to or acquainted with the liberal arts; ill-bred, unrefined; mean, vulgar, rude. M16. 2 Not generous; mean, stingy. E17. 3 Narrow-minded, bigoted; opposed to liberal principles. M17.

1 R. HAKLUYT Mechanicall & illiberall crafts. 3 G. S. FRASER His illiberal prejudice against the Germans no doubt helped.

illiberalism *n.* illiberality, absence of liberal principles M19. **illiberalize** *v.t.* make illiberal E19. **illiberally** *adv.* E17.

illiberality /ɪˌlɪbəˈralɪti/ *n.* L16. [Fr. *illibéralité*, f. as prec.: see -ITY.] The quality of being illiberal.

illicit /ɪˈlɪsɪt/ *a.* E16. [(O)Fr. *illicite* or L *illicitus*, f. as IL-[2] + LICIT.] Not allowed; improper, irregular; unlawful; *esp.* not sanctioned by law, rule, or custom.

D. L. SAYERS My unhappy son had formed an illicit connection with a young woman. E. WAUGH The . . trout . . were taken by . . illicit means without respect for season or ownership. **illicit process** *Logic* a syllogistic fallacy in which a term not distributed in the premisses is distributed in the conclusion.

illicitly *adv.* E19. **illicitness** *n.* E19. †**illicitous** *a.* illicit: only in 17.

illigant *a.* var. of ILIGANT.

illimitable /ɪˈlɪmɪtəb(ə)l/ *a.* L16. [f. IL-[2] + LIMITABLE.] Unable to be limited or bounded; limitless, boundless.

D. H. LAWRENCE The great dark, illimitable kingdom of death, there humanity was put to scorn.

illimitaˈbility *n.* M19. **illimitableness** *n.* M19. **illimitably** *adv.* M18.

illimitation /ɪˌlɪmɪˈteɪʃ(ə)n/ *n. rare.* E17. [f. IL-[2] + LIMITATION.] Freedom from or lack of limitation.

illimited /ɪˈlɪmɪtɪd/ *a.* E17. [f. IL-[2] + LIMITED.] Unlimited, unrestricted, unrestrained.

illimitedly *adv.* E17. **illimitedness** *n.* M17.

illinition /ɪlɪˈnɪʃ(ə)n/ *n.* Now *rare* or *obs.* L17. [Late L *illinitio(n-)* f. *illinit-* pa. ppl stem of *illinire* var. of L *illinere*, f. as IL-[1] + *linere* smear: see -ION.] 1 The smearing on or rubbing in of ointment etc. L17. †2a A process for calcining metals by rubbing with salt solutions. Only in L17. b A thin crust or coating on a metal, cloth, etc. L18–E19.

illinium /ɪˈlɪnɪəm/ *n.* E20. [f. *Illinois* University, USA, where the element was mistakenly reported to have been identified: see -IUM.] *Hist. Sci.* The element of atomic no. 61, later named *promethium*.

Illinoian /ɪlɪˈnɔɪ(j)ən/ *n.* & *a.* M19. [f. *Illinois* (see next) + -AN.] A *n.* 1 = ILLINOISAN. M19. 2 *Geol.* A Pleistocene glaciation in N. America, preceding the Wisconsin and approximating to the Saale of northern Europe, or its deposits. L19. B *adj. Geol.* Designating or pertaining to the Illinoian. L19.

Illinois /ɪlɪˈnɔɪ(z)/ *n.* & *a.* E18. [Fr. f. Algonquian, in some uses repr. the name of the State.] A *n.* Pl. same. 1 A member of a confederation of Algonquian Indian peoples formerly inhabiting an area in and around the present Midwestern State of Illinois in the US. E18. 2 The Algonquian language of the Illinois. E18. B *adj.* Of or pertaining to the Illinois or the State of Illinois. E18.

Illinoisan /ɪlɪˈnɔɪ(j)ən, -ɔɪz(ə)n/ *n.* M19. [f. *Illinois* (see prec.) + -AN.] A native or inhabitant of the Midwestern State of Illinois, USA. Cf. ILLINOIAN *n.*

illipe /ˈɪlɪpi/ *n.* Also **illupi** /ˈɪlʊpi/ & other vars. M19. [Tamil *iluppai*, *ir-*, Malayalam *iruppa*.] An evergreen tree of southern India, *Madhuca longifolia* (family Sapotaceae), the seeds of which yield a fat used for candles and soap, and as a substitute for butter.

illiquid /ɪˈlɪkwɪd/ *a.* L17. [f. (as) IL-[2] + LIQUID *a.*] 1 *Law* (now only *Sc.*). Of a right, debt, or claim: not clear or manifest; not ascertained and constituted by a written obligation or a decree of a court. L17. 2 Of an asset, investment, etc.: not easily or readily realizable. E20.

illiˈquidity *n.* the character of being illiquid E20.

illish /ˈɪlɪʃ/ *a. rare.* M17. [f. ILL *a.* + -ISH[1].] Somewhat unwell.

D. WELCH She had been half asleep and was still illish from 'flu.

illite /ˈɪlʌɪt/ *n.* M20. [f. ILLINOIS a State of the US + -ITE[1].] *Min.* Any of a group of clay minerals resembling micas whose lattice does not expand on absorption of water.

illitic /ɪˈlɪtɪk/ *a.* composed of or containing illite M20.

illiteracy /ɪˈlɪt(ə)rəsi/ *n.* M17. [f. ILLITERATE *a.* + -ACY.] 1 The quality or state of being illiterate; lack of education; *esp.* inability to read and write. Also *gen.*, ignorance, lack of understanding (of any activity etc.). M17. 2 A manifestation of illiteracy, an error due to illiteracy. E18.

1 R. DAVIES Money illiteracy is as restrictive as any other illiteracy. A. BURGESS She . . had left school at ten, and this explained her illiteracy. 2 J. K. TOOLE The illiteracies and misconceptions burbling from the dark minds of these students.

illiterate /ɪˈlɪt(ə)rət/ *a.* & *n.* LME. [L *illitteratus*, f. as IL-[2] + LITERATE *a.*] A *adj.* 1 Of a person: uneducated, *esp.* unable to read and write; (of a thing) characterized by or showing ignorance of reading or writing; uneducated, unlearned, unpolished. LME. b *gen.* Characterized by ignorance or lack of education or subtlety (in any activity etc.). M20. 2 Unwritten; inarticulate. *rare.* M17.

1 CONAN DOYLE Certain letters . . . were in an illiterate handwriting. R. GITTINGS He married an illiterate girl—she could not write her own name. A. BURGESS My grandmother was illiterate and had to have the evening newspaper read out to her. b A. J. P. TAYLOR I am musically illiterate I cannot follow sonata form, let alone a fugue.

B *n.* An illiterate person; *esp.* a person unable to read and write. E17.

A. TATE Impressionistic education . . is . . making us a nation of illiterates: a nation of people without letters. G. BORDMAN Berlin, a musical illiterate, undoubtedly understood that composing an opera . . required more.

illiterately *adv.* L17. **illiterateness** *n.* M17. **illiterati** /ɪˈlɪtərɑːtiː/ *n.pl.* [L pl. of *illitteratus*] illiterate, unlearned, or uneducated people L18. **illiterature** *n.* [after LITERATURE] (*a*) illiteracy, lack of education; (*b*) literature of poor quality: L16.

ill nature /ɪl ˈneɪtʃə/ *n. phr.* M17. [f. ILL *a.* + NATURE *n.*] Malevolent or unkind character; spitefulness, churlishness.

¶Earlier in ILL-NATURED.

ill-natured /ɪlˈneɪtʃəd/ *a.* E17. [f. (as) prec. + -ED[2].] Having an ill nature; spiteful, churlish.

ill-naturedly *adv.* L17.

illness /ˈɪlnɪs/ *n.* E16. [f. ILL *a.* + -NESS.] †1 Wickedness, depravity, immorality. E16–E18. †2 Unpleasantness, disagreeableness; hurtfulness; difficulty. L16–E18. 3 Ill health; the state of being ill; (a) disease, (a) sickness, (an) ailment. L17.

3 J. GATHORNE-HARDY Personal conflicts, stress and problems are a common cause of physical illness. N. MAILER I was like a man who is told he has a mortal illness. P. ROTH Not until she'd phoned . . had he . . been aware of his brother's illness.

illocal /ɪˈləʊk(ə)l/ *a.* Now *rare.* E17. [Late L *illocalis*, f. as IL-[2] + *localis* LOCAL *a.*] Not local; having no location in space.

illoˈcality *n.* the quality or condition of being illocal L17.

illocution /ɪləˈkjuːʃ(ə)n/ *n.* M20. [f. IL-[1] + LOCUTION.] *Philos.* & *Ling.* An action performed by saying or writing something, e.g. ordering, warning, promising. Cf. PERLOCUTION 2.

illocutionary *a.* of, pertaining to, or of the nature of an illocution (cf. LOCUTIONARY, PERLOCUTIONARY) M20.

illogic /ɪˈlɒdʒɪk/ *n.* M19. [f. IL-[2] + LOGIC, after next.] Illogicality; lack of or opposition to logic.

Nature With the same illogic with which the Englishman will eat cow but not dog.

illogical /ɪˈlɒdʒɪk(ə)l/ *a.* L16. [f. IL-[2] + LOGICAL *a.*] Not logical; devoid of or contrary to logic; lacking the principles of sound reasoning.

illogiˈcality *n.* illogical quality or character; lack of logic; unreasonableness: M19. **illogically** *adv.* M17. **illogicalness** *n.* M17.

illoyal /ɪˈlɔɪəl/ *a. rare.* E17. [f. IL-[2] + LOYAL *a.*] Not loyal; disloyal.

ill-tempered /ɪlˈtɛmpəd/ *a.* E17. [Partly f. ILL *adv.* + TEMPERED; partly f. ILL *a.* + TEMPER *n.* + -ED[2].] †1 In an unhealthy or disordered condition. Only in 17. 2 Having a bad temper; irritable. E17.

ill-temperedly *adv.* L19.

illth /ɪlθ/ *n. rare.* M19. [f. ILL *a.* + -TH[1].] Being ill; the opposite of health or wealth.

illucidate /ɪˈluːsɪdeɪt, ɪˈljuː-/ *v.t. rare.* M16. [Late L *illucidat-* pa. ppl stem of *illucidare* after L *elucidare* ELUCIDATE with substitution of IL-[1].] Shed light on; explain, make clear, elucidate.

illude /ɪˈluːd, ɪˈljuːd/ *v.t.* Now *literary.* LME. [L *illudere*: see ILLUSION.] †1 Make fun of; deride. LME–E17. 2 Trick, impose upon, deceive with false hopes, delude. LME.

2 MORTIMER COLLINS They had allowed their imaginations to illude them.

illuk /ˈɪlʊk/ *n.* M19. [Sinhalese *iluk.*] The lalang grass.

illume /ɪˈluːm, ɪˈljuːm/ *v.* & *n.* Chiefly *poet.* LME. [Contr. of ILLUMINE.] A *v.t.* 1 Light up; make bright or shining; illumine; illuminate (*lit.* & *fig.*). LME. †2 Set alight, kindle. *rare.* E–M18. B *n.* Illumination. M19.

illuminance /ɪˈluːmɪn(ə)ns, ɪˈljuː-/ *n.* M20. [f. ILLUMINATE *v.* + -ANCE.] *Physics.* The amount of luminous flux per unit area; = ILLUMINATION 2c.

illuminant /ɪˈluːmɪnənt, ɪˈljuː-/ *n.* & *a.* Now *rare.* M17. [L *illuminant-* pres. ppl stem of *illuminare*: see ILLUMINATE *v.*, -ANT[1].] A *n.* A thing which illumines or illuminates; a source of illumination. M17. B *adj.* Illuminating, enlightening. L17.

illuminate /ɪˈluːmɪnət, ɪˈljuː-/ *n. arch.* E17. [f. as next: see -ATE[1].] A spiritually or intellectually enlightened person; a person claiming special enlightenment or knowledge.

illuminate /ɪˈluːmɪneɪt, ɪˈljuː-/ *v.* Pa. pple & ppl a. (*arch.*, earlier) **-ate** /-ət/, **-ated.** LME. [Earliest as pa. pple, f. L *illuminatus*, f. *illuminat-* pa. ppl stem of *illuminare*, f. as IL-[1] + *lumin-*, *lumen* light: see -ATE[2], -ATE[3]. Cf. ILLUMINE *v.*] I *v.t.* 1 Light up, give light to, make bright by light; decorate with lights, esp. in celebration. LME. b Direct a beam of microwaves or other radiation at (an object, area, etc.). M20. 2 Shed spiritual light on; enlighten spiritually. Now only as *fig.* use of sense 1 above. L15. 3 Enlighten intellectually; give knowledge or understanding to. M16. 4 Throw light on (a subject); explain, make clear; elucidate. L16. 5 Decorate (an initial letter etc. in a manuscript, a manuscript) with elaborate tracery or designs in gold, silver, and colours. L16. 6 Make splendid or illustrious; shed a lustre on. E17. 7 Set alight, kindle. *rare.* M17.

1 CONAN DOYLE Striking a match, he illuminated the melancholy place. J. C. POWYS Philip produced an electric flashlight . . to illuminate their way. E. BOWEN The Waterloo victory, for which Dublin illuminated herself. *fig.*: G. VIDAL For an instant a look of pure delight illuminated that lean, sombre face. 2 DEFOE That He . . would further illuminate them with a beam of his heavenly grace. 3 M. RULE They have confused rather than illuminated scholars. 4 L. DURRELL I . . do not feel that they explain Justine, but . . they do illuminate her actions. 6 DISRAELI Hampden was to have illuminated with his genius this new order of government.

II *v.i.* 8 Light up; be decorated with lights, esp. in celebration. E18.

illuminated *a.* (*a*) that has been or is being illuminated; (*b*) *spec.* of or pertaining to illuminati: E17. **illuminatingly** *adv.* in an illuminating manner L19.

illuminati *n.pl.* see ILLUMINATO.

illumination /ɪˌluːmɪˈneɪʃ(ə)n, ɪˌljuː-/ *n.* ME. [(O)Fr. f. late L *illuminatio(n-)*, f. *illuminat-*: see ILLUMINATE *v.*, -ATION.] 1a An instance of spiritual enlightenment; an inspiration, a revelation. Freq. in *pl.* ME. b Spiritual enlightenment, divine inspiration. LME. 2 The action of illuminating with light; the fact or condition of being illuminated with light; a lighting up, a supplying of light; light. M16. b The lighting up of a building, street, town, etc., esp. with coloured lights arranged in designs, as part of a celebration or as an attraction, an instance of this; in *pl.*, lights used in such a decoration. L17. c *Physics.* = ILLUMINANCE. M19. 3 Intellectual enlightenment; information, learning. Formerly also in *pl.*, intellectual gifts. M17. 4 The decoration of (an initial letter etc. in) a manuscript with elaborate tracery or designs in gold, silver, and colours; a design or illustration used in such decoration, an illuminated page. Formerly also, the colouring of maps or prints. L17.

1 *Ashmolean* Buddha . . reached what is known as the illumination, i.e. grasped the fundamental of his . . doctrine. 2 P. SCOTT A naked electric bulb provided illumination. J. HIGGINS It was a place of shadows, the only illumination coming from the candles. 3 R. S. BALL The illumination which mathematics alone can afford. 4 K. CLARK Many of them were printed on vellum and had illuminations, like manuscripts.

illuminatism /ɪˈluːmɪnətɪz(ə)m, ɪˈljuː-/ *n.* Now *rare.* L18. [f. ILLUMINATO or G *Illuminaten* + -ISM.] = ILLUMINISM.

illuminatist *n.* = ILLUMINIST M19.

illuminative /ɪˈluːmɪnətɪv, ɪˈljuː-/ *a.* M17. [Fr. *illuminatif*, *-ive* or med.L *illuminativus*, f. L *illuminat-*: see ILLUMINATE *v.*, -ATIVE.] 1 Capable of illuminating, lighting up, or giving light. M17. 2 Capable of enlightening spiritually or intellectually. M17.

1 K. DIGBY The illuminative action of fire. 2 SOUTHEY The purgative, illuminative, and unitive stages of devotion.

illuminato /ɪˌluːmɪˈnɑːtəʊ, ɪˌljuː-/ *n.* Also **I-.** Usu. in pl. **-ti** /-ti/. L16. [It. = enlightened; pl. partly f. L *illuminati* pl. of *illuminatus*: see ILLUMINATE *v.* In German context tr. G *Illuminaten.*] A member of any of various sects or societies claiming special enlightenment, *spec.* (*a*) a sect of 16th-cent. Spanish heretics, (*b*) a secret society founded by Adam Weishaupt in Bavaria in 1776, holding deistic and republican principles and organized like the Freemasons.

Also *gen.*, a person claiming special knowledge on any subject.

illuminator /ɪˈluːmɪneɪtə, ɪˈljuː-/ *n.* L15. [eccl.L, f. L *illuminat-*: see ILLUMINATE *v.*, -OR.] **1** A shedder of spiritual light, a spiritual enlightener. Now only as *fig.* use of sense 2 below. L15. **2** A person who or thing which lights up something; an illuminating agent. L16. **3** A person who illuminates manuscripts. L17. **4** An intellectual enlightener; a giver of knowledge or understanding. L18.

3 J. BACKHOUSE The great nunneries must have supported their own scribes and illuminators. 4 J. WAIN The greatness of Coghill as an illuminator of Shakespeare.

illuminatory *a.* (*rare*) illuminative, explanatory M18.

illumine /ɪˈluːmɪn, ɪˈljuː-/ *v.* Chiefly *literary*. ME. [(O)Fr. *illuminer* f. L *illuminare* ILLUMINATE *v.*] **I** *v.t.* **1** = ILLUMINATE *v.* 2. ME. **2** = ILLUMINATE *v.* 1. LME. **b** Brighten as with light, make radiant. E16. **3** = ILLUMINATE *v.* 3. E16. **4** = ILLUMINATE *v.* 5. E16.

2 J. STEINBECK Then he lighted another cigarette, and the match illumined his dark face. E. BOWEN Gas-lighting came to Dublin in 1825, in time to illumine the new premises. b SHAKS. *Ven. & Ad.* And as the bright sun glorifies the sky, So is her face illumined with her eye. R. DAVIES Sort of tribute from play-goers whose life he had illumined. 3 LYTTON This benighted mind, only illumined by a kind of miserable astuteness.

II *v.i.* **5** = ILLUMINATE *v.* 8. E16.

illuminable *a.* M18. **illuminer** *n.* LME.

illuminé /ilymine (*pl. same*); ɪˈluːmɪneɪ, ɪˈljuː-/ *n.* Also ***I-***. L18. [Fr. = enlightened.] = ILLUMINATO.

illuminise *v.* var. of ILLUMINIZE.

illuminism /ɪˈluːmɪnɪz(ə)m, ɪˈljuː-/ *n.* Also **I-**. L18. [Fr. *illuminisme*, f. as ILLUMINE *v.*: see -ISM.] The doctrine or principles of any illuminati; (a doctrine involving) belief in or a claim to intellectual or spiritual enlightenment.

illuminist *n.* an adherent of illuminism, a person who claims spiritual or intellectual enlightenment E19. **illumiˈnistic** *a.* pertaining to or of the nature of illuminism M19.

illuminize /ɪˈluːmɪnʌɪz, ɪˈljuː-/ *v. rare.* Also **-ise**. E19. [f. ILLUMINE *v.* + -IZE.] **1** *v.i.* Be an illuminist. E19. **2** *v.t.* Initiate into illuminism or a body of illuminati. E19.

illuminometer /ɪˌluːmɪˈnɒmɪtə, ɪˌljuː-/ *n.* L19. [f. ILLUMINATION + -OMETER.] A photometer, *esp.* one for measuring illuminance.

†illuminous *a.*[1] L15–M18. [f. IL-[1] + LUMINOUS.] Bright, illuminatory.

illuminous /ɪˈluːmɪnəs, ɪˈljuː-/ *a.*[2] *rare.* M17. [f. IL-[2] + LUMINOUS.] Not luminous, dark, opaque.

illupi *n.* var. of ILLIPE.

illusion /ɪˈluːʒ(ə)n, ɪˈljuː-/ *n.* ME. [(O)Fr. f. L *illusio(n-)*, f. *illus-* pa. ppl stem of *illudere* mock, jest at, f. as IL-[1] + *ludere* play: see -ION.] **I†1** The action of deceiving, esp. by appearances; an act of deception. ME–L17. **2** A thing that deceives or deludes by giving a false impression. In early use sometimes *spec.* an apparition. LME. **3** The fact or condition of being deceived or deluded by appearances; a deception, a delusion; (an instance of) misapprehension of the true state of affairs. L16. **4** (An instance of) the sense-perception of an external object suggesting a false belief as to its nature. L18. **5** A thin and transparent kind of tulle. M19.

2 *New York Times* The current notion that token integration will satisfy his people . . is an illusion. Y. MENUHIN Each of us had married an illusion, she as well as I. 3 E. FROMM Most people are . . unaware that most of what they hold to be true . . is illusion. J. BRODSKY A communal apartment . . strips off any illusions about human nature. **be under the illusion** believe wrongly (*that*). 4 G. ORWELL When you said it to yourself you had the illusion of actually hearing bells. **argument from illusion** *Philos.* the argument that the objects of sense-experience, usu. called ideas, appearances, or sense-data, cannot be objects in a physical world independent of the perceiver since they vary with his or her condition and environment. *optical illusion*: see OPTICAL *a.*

†II 6 (An instance of) derision or mockery. LME–M17.

illusional *a.* pertaining to, characterized by, or subject to illusions E20. **illusionary** *a.* characterized by illusions; resembling an illusion; illusory: L19.

illusionism /ɪˈluːʒ(ə)nɪz(ə)m, ɪˈljuː-/ *n.* M19. [f. prec. + -ISM.] **1** The theory that the material world is an illusion; disbelief in objective existence; theory dealing with illusions. M19. **2** The use of illusionary effects, esp. in art. M20.

illusionist /ɪˈluːʒ(ə)nɪst, ɪˈljuː-/ *n.* M19. [f. as prec. + -IST.] **1** An adherent of illusionism. M19. **2** A person who produces illusions; *spec.* a conjuror, a magician. M19.

illusioˈnistic *a.* of or pertaining to illusionism or illusionists E20.

illusive /ɪˈluːsɪv, ɪˈljuː-/ *a.* Now *rare.* E17. [med.L *illusivus*, f. *illus-*: see ILLUSION, -IVE.] Tending to illude or deceive by false appearances; deceptive, illusory.

illusively *adv.* E19. **illusiveness** *n.* E18.

illusor /ɪˈluːsə, ɪˈljuː-/ *n. rare.* LME. [eccl.L, f. *illus-*: see ILLUSION, -OR.] A deceiver, a deluder.

illusory /ɪˈluːs(ə)ri, ɪˈljuː-/ *a.* L16. [eccl.L *illusorius*, f. as prec.: see -ORY[2].] Tending to deceive or delude by false appearances; having the character of an illusion; deceptive.

B. UNSWORTH He was haunted by small sounds and movements, most of them illusory. J. MCDOUGALL His illusory paradise was brutally destroyed by the arrival of his first little brother. A. ARONSON The Elizabethan preoccupation with faulty visual perception and with the illusory nature of eyesight.

illusorily *adv.* M17. **illusoriness** *n.* E18.

illustratable /ɪləˈstreɪtəb(ə)l, ˈɪləstreɪt-/ *a.* M19. [f. ILLUSTRATE *v.* + -ABLE.] Able to be illustrated; suitable for illustration.

†illustrate *a.* M16–E18. [L *illustratus* pa. pple, f. as next: see -ATE[2].] Illuminated, resplendent, clear.

illustrate /ˈɪləstreɪt/ *v.t.* Pa. pple **†-ate** (earlier), **-ated**. E16. [L *illustrat-* pa. ppl stem of *illustrare*, f. as IL-[1] + *lustrare* illuminate: see -ATE[3].] **I†1** Shed light on, light up, illumine. E16–L19. **2** Shed lustre on; make illustrious or famous; confer distinction on. Now *rare.* M16. **†3** Make lustrous or bright; adorn. L16–M18. **4** Set in a good light; display to advantage. Now *rare* or *obs.* E17.

1 C. COTTON The Windows . . Illustrating the noble Room. *fig.*: R. BOYLE The Mind of Man . . Illustrated by the Beams of Heavenly Light, and Joy. 2 GIBBON Mr. Wedderburne . . who now illustrates the title of Lord Loughborough. 3 S. RICHARDSON Her head-dress was a Brussels-lace mob . . A sky blue ribband illustrated that. 4 H. CROSSE The deformitie of the one doth much illustrate and beautifie the other.

II 5 Make clear, elucidate, explain; *esp.* clarify or support using examples, give an example or illustration of, exemplify. M16. **6** Support or clarify (a description, account, etc.) using drawings, photographs, or other pictures; *esp.* provide (a book, magazine article, etc.) with pictorial illustrations. M17.

5 T. BEDDOES Many experiments . . tending to illustrate this important subject. R. KIPLING Kim illustrated the motion and stood like a stork. C. CONNOLLY He chose his quotations to illustrate how . . the present can always be illuminated by the past. 6 R. MACAULAY Painting water-colour sketches to illustrate travel books. *Soldier* The route is not without its hazards as the picture . . illustrates.

illustrated /ˈɪləstreɪtɪd/ *a.* & *n.* M19. [f. ILLUSTRATE *v.* + -ED[2].] **A** *adj.* Having illustrations. M19.

J. BRODSKY This was a copiously illustrated encyclopedia.

B *n.* An illustrated newspaper or magazine. L19.

illustration /ɪləˈstreɪʃ(ə)n/ *n.* LME. [(O)Fr. f. L *illustratio(n-)*, f. as ILLUSTRATE *v.*: see -ATION.] **I†1** Lighting up, illumination; spiritual or intellectual enlightenment. LME–M18. **2** The action of making someone or something illustrious or famous; the fact of being made illustrious or famous; distinction; an instance of this. Now *rare.* E17.

1 DONNE Such an illustration, such an irradiation, . . that by that light . . he could have read in the night. E. VAUX A divine illustration cleared his understanding. 2 THACKERAY My maxim is, that genius is an illustration, and merit is better than any pedigree.

II 3 The action or fact of making something clear or evident; setting out clearly or with supporting examples; elucidation; explanation; exemplification. M16. **b** A thing which makes something clear or evident; an explanation, a clarification; an example, an instance. L16. **4** The illustrating of a subject pictorially; the provision of a book, magazine article, etc., with drawings, photographs, or other pictures. E19. **b** A picture illustrating a description, account, reference, etc.; a drawing, photograph, or other picture in a book, magazine article, etc. E19.

3b P. BROOK *Sergeant Musgrave's Dance* can be taken . . as an illustration of how true theatre comes into being. 4b R. JARRELL Have you ever thought of doing illustrations for *The Jungle Book*?

illustrational *a.* of or pertaining to illustration; illustrative: L19.

illustrative /ˈɪləstrətɪv, ɪˈlʌst-/ *a.* M17. [f. ILLUSTRATE *v.* + -IVE.] Serving or tending to illustrate or make clear; providing an illustration or example (*of*); explanatory.

J. TYNDALL Taking, as an illustrative case, the passage from air into water. *Southern Rag* Essential information . . of which the films would be illustrative.

illustratively *adv.* M17.

illustrator /ˈɪləstreɪtə/ *n.* L16. [eccl.L, f. as ILLUSTRATE *v.*: see -OR. Later directly f. ILLUSTRATE *v.*] A person who or thing which illustrates something; *esp.* a person who illustrates a book etc.

illustratory /ˈɪləstreɪt(ə)ri, ɪˈlʌstrə-/ *a.* Now *rare.* M18. [f. ILLUSTRATE *v.* + -ORY[2].] Illustrative.

†illustricity *n.* M17. [Irreg. f. L *illustris* + -ITY: see next, -ICITY.] **1** An illustrious person. Only in M17. **2** Illustriousness. M–L18.

illustrious /ɪˈlʌstrɪəs/ *a.* M16. [f. L *illustris* clear, bright, evident, distinguished, famous + -OUS.] **1** Having the lustre of high rank, fame, or eminence; distinguished, renowned. M16. **†2** Lit up; lustrous, bright, shining. E17–L19. **b** Not lustrous, dull. *rare* (Shakes.). Only in E17. **†3** Clearly evident, obvious. M17–L18.

1 C. LAMB She traced her descent . . to the illustrious, but unfortunate, house of Derwentwater. CONAN DOYLE When . . a client is sufficiently illustrious, even the rigid British law becomes human and elastic.

illustriously *adv.* M17. **illustriousness** *n.* M17.

illustrissimo /ɪlʌˈstrɪsɪməʊ/ *n.* & *a.* Now *rare.* Pl. of n. **-mos**, **-mi** /-mi/. E17. [It. f. L *illustrissimus* superl. of *illustris* ILLUSTRIOUS.] (A person who is) most illustrious, esp. as belonging to the Italian aristocracy.

illuvial /ɪˈluːvɪəl, ɪˈljuː-/ *a.* E20. [f. IL-[1] + *-luvial*, after ALLUVIAL, ELUVIAL.] *Soil Sci.* Pertaining to or resulting from illuviation; illuviated.

illuviation /ɪˌluːvɪˈeɪʃ(ə)n, ɪˌljuː-/ *n.* E20. [f. as prec. + -ATION.] *Soil Sci.* The introduction of salts or colloids into one soil horizon from another by percolating water.

iˈlluviated *ppl a.* having received material by illuviation E20.

illy /ˈɪlli/ *adv.* Now chiefly *US.* LME. [f. ILL *a.* + -LY[2].] Badly, ill.

Illyrian /ɪˈlɪrɪən/ *a.* & *n.* M16. [f. L *Illyrius* (= Gk *Illurios*), f. *Illyria* (see below) + -AN.] **A** *adj.* **1** Of or pertaining to a region of varying extent primarily on the east coast of the Adriatic known as Illyria, in ancient times a country extending northwards to the Danube, conquered by the Romans in the 3rd and 2nd cents. BC, for much of the 19th cent. and until 1918 a division of the Austro-Hungarian empire, and now part of Slovenia and Croatia. M16. **2** Designating or pertaining to the group of ancient dialects represented by modern Albanian. Formerly also, designating or pertaining to a division of the South Slavonic languages. E17. **B** *n.* **1** A native or inhabitant of Illyria; *esp.* a member of an Indo-European people inhabiting ancient Illyria. L16. **2** The language of Illyria; the group of ancient dialects represented by modern Albanian. Formerly also, a division of the South Slavonic languages. L19.

Illyrism /ˈɪlɪrɪz(ə)m/ *n.* M19. [f. as prec. +

-ISM.] Advocacy of Slovene, Croatian, and Serb nationalism.

Illyrist *a.* & *n.* (*a*) *adj.* of or pertaining to Illyrism, supporting Illyrism; (*b*) *n.* a supporter of Illyrism: E20.

illywhacker /ˈɪlɪwakə/ *n.* *Austral. slang.* Also **-wacker** /-w-/. M20. [Origin unkn.] A confidence trickster.

ilmenite /ˈɪlmənʌɪt/ *n.* E19. [f. the *Ilmen* Mountains (in the southern Urals) + -ITE[1].] *Min.* A common trigonal oxide of ferrous iron and titanium, occurring in massive form or as opaque black crystals, often as an accessory mineral in basic igneous rocks, and a source of titanium.

ilmenorutile /ɪlmənəʊˈruːtʌɪl/ *n.* M19. [f. ILMENITE + -O- + RUTILE.] *Min.* A black variety of rutile containing iron, niobium, and tantalum.

Ilocano /ɪləˈkɑːnəʊ/ *n.* & *a.* L19. [Philippine Sp., f. *Ilocos*, name of two provinces in the Philippines.] A *n.* Pl. **-os**. A member of a people inhabiting the north-western part of Luzon in the Philippines; the Austronesian language of this people. L19. B *adj.* Of or pertaining to the Ilocanos or their language. E20.

Also **Iloco** *n.* & *a.* M19.

ilot *n.* var. of ISLOT.

ilsemannite /ˈɪlsəmənʌɪt/ *n.* L19. [f. J. C. *Ilsemann* (1727–1822), Ger. chemist, + -ITE[1].] *Min.* A blue molybdenum-containing mineral, probably a hydrated oxide, which forms as a soluble crust or earthy deposit.

ilvaite /ˈɪlvəʌɪt/ *n.* E19. [f. L *Ilva* Elba + -ITE[1].] *Min.* A basic silicate of calcium and iron, crystallizing in either the monoclinic or the orthorhombic system.

im- /ɪm/ *pref.*[1] Var. of L IN-[2] bef. *b*, *m*, *p*. Cf. IL-[1], IR-[1].

im- /ɪm/ *pref.*[2] Var. of L IN-[3] bef. *b*, *m*, *p*. Cf. I-[2], IL-[2], IR-[2].

image /ˈɪmɪdʒ/ *n.* ME. [(O)Fr., f. L *imago*, *imagin-* rel. to *imitari* IMITATE.] 1 A representation of the external form of a person or thing in sculpture, painting, etc.; *esp.* a statue or figurine of a saint etc. as an object of veneration. ME. †b A constellation considered as the figure or delineation of a person etc. LME–L17. c A person who in manner, look, etc., resembles an artificial representation of the human form; *colloq.* someone as an object of amusement or contempt. M16. 2 An optical appearance or counterpart produced by light or other radiation from an object reflected in a mirror, refracted in a lens, etc. ME. 3 Aspect, appearance, form; semblance, likeness. (Now chiefly in ref. to *Gen.* 1:26, 27.) ME. b A visible appearance; a figure; an apparition. Long *arch. rare.* M16. 4 A person or thing in which the appearance etc. of another is reproduced; a counterpart, a copy. ME. b A symbol, an emblem. M16. c An embodiment (esp. *of* a particular quality); a type; a typical example. M16. 5 A mental representation of something; an idea, a conception. LME. b The character of a person, organization, product, etc., as perceived by the public; *esp.* a cultivated favourable reputation. E20. 6 A spoken or written description, *esp.* a vivid or graphic one. E16. 7 A simile, a metaphor, a figure of speech. M16. 8 *Math.* The element or set into which a given element or set is mapped by a particular function or transformation. (Foll. by *of* the given thing; *by* or *under* the function etc.) L19. 9 *Radio.* An undesired signal whose frequency is as much above that of the local oscillator of a superheterodyne receiver as the signal sought is below it, and which therefore may cause interference. M20.

1 AV *Matt.* 22.20 And he sayth unto them, Whose is this image and superscription? S. SPENDER The floor of the vault was covered with images removed from buildings. *graven image*, *waxen image*. c S. RICHARDSON Can the pretty image speak, Mrs Jervis? I vow she has speaking eyes! J. CONRAD How goes it, you old image? 2 K. CLARK The *camera obscura* which projects an image onto a white sheet. *after-image*: see AFTER-. *double image*: see DOUBLE *a.* & *adv.* *latent image*: see LATENT *a.* & *n.* *mirror image*: see MIRROR *n.* *multiple image*: see MULTIPLE *a.* 3 E. H. SEARS We grow into the image of what we love. M. L. KING We fail to think of them as fellow human beings .. moulded in the same divine image. b TENNYSON An image seem'd to pass the door, To look at her. 4 T. GRANGER Sleepe is the image of death. OED He is the very image of his father. **living image of** a person with a striking resemblance to (another). *spit* (*and*) *image*: see SPIT *n.*[2] *spitting image*: see SPIT *v.*[2] b W. TENNANT This noisome dungeon .. affords .. an image of the gate of Tartarus, rather than the porch of Paradise. c M. E. BRADDON Mr. Sampson dropped his cigar, and sat transfixed, an image of half amused astonishment. 5 A. RADCLIFFE She endeavoured to dismiss his image from her mind. W. JAMES We .. saw no need of optical and auditory images to interpret optical and auditory sensations by. L. HUDSON Snakes are a remarkably common image in .. dreams. b K. AMIS It was time to improve the paper's image, give it a touch of quality. *brand image*, *corporate image*, etc. 6 M. W. MONTAGU Theocritus .. has only given a plain image of the way of life amongst the peasants. 7 R. C. TRENCH To speak of death as a sleep, is an image common to all languages.

Comb.: **image-breaker** a breaker of images, an iconoclast; **image converter** an electronic device for converting an invisible image (formed by infrared radiation, X-rays, etc.) into a visible image; an image tube; **image dissector** a form of television camera in which the current emitted by the photoemissive surface is directly amplified to form the video signal; **image intensifier** an image tube or similar device used to produce a brighter version of an image incident on a photoelectric screen; **image-maker** (*a*) a carver, sculptor, etc., of images; (*b*) a person concerned with creating a public image of a politician, product, etc.; *image* ORTHICON; **image tube** an electron tube in which an image, formed by light or other radiation on a photoemissive surface, produces a flow of electrons which can be used to reproduce the image in a different form; **image-worship** the worship of images; idolatry.

imageless *a.* E19.

image /ˈɪmɪdʒ/ *v.t.* LME. [Partly f. (O)Fr. *imager*, partly f. the n.] 1 a Form a mental image of (something to be executed); devise, plan. Now *rare* or *obs.* exc. as in sense b. LME. b Imagine, picture (*to oneself*). E18. 2 Describe, esp. vividly or graphically. E17. 3 Copy, imitate; resemble. *rare.* E17. 4 Reflect, mirror. L18. 5 Make a representation of the external form of (someone or something) in sculpture, painting, etc.; represent by an image (*lit.* & *fig.*); obtain a representation of by television, radar, or other technique. E19. 6 Symbolize, typify. E19.

1b J. MOORE We image to ourselves the Tarpeian Rock as a tremendous precipice. 2 ADDISON Satan's Approach to the Confines of the Creation, is finely imaged in the beginning of the Speech. 3 G. CHAPMAN They his clear virtues emulate, In truth and justice imaging his state. POPE None imag'd e'er like thee my master lost. 4 S. ROGERS Hail, noblest structures imaged in the wave. 5 J. A. FROUDE Traces of the fair beauty of the monastic spirit we may yet see imaged in the sculptured figures. A. C. CLARKE The familiar rocky terrain was imaged on TV and sonar screen. *magnetic resonance imaging*: see MAGNETIC *a.* *thermal imaging*: see THERMAL *a.* 6 SHELLEY O stream! .. Thou imagest my life.

imageable *a.* L17.

imaged /ˈɪmɪdʒd/ *a.* L16. [f. IMAGE *n.*, *v.*: see -ED[2], -ED[1].] 1 Represented by an image (*lit.* & *fig.*). L16. 2 Decorated with an image or images. *rare.* L18.

imager /ˈɪmɪdʒə/ *n.* LME. [OFr. *image*(*u*)*r* (mod. *imagier*), f. as IMAGE *n.*: see -ER[2].] 1 a *Hist.* A maker of images; a sculptor, a carver. LME. b A device which reproduces an image of something. L20. 2 A person who describes something vividly or graphically. L19. 3 A person who forms a mental image or images. M20.

imagery /ˈɪmɪdʒ(ə)ri/ *n.* ME. [OFr. *imagerie*, f. *image*(*u*)*r*: see prec., -ERY.] 1 Images collectively; statuary, carving. Formerly also, an image. ME. †b Figured work on a textile fabric; embroidery. LME–L18. †2 The use of images as objects of veneration; idolatry. LME–E17. †3 The art of painting; the art of carving or statuary. M16–E17. †4 Workmanship, make; fashion. L16–M17. †5 The embodiment of a quality etc. L16–M17. 6 The use of rhetorical images; such images collectively. Also, ornate figurative illustration, esp. as used for a particular effect. L16. 7 Orig., the formation of mental images; imagination, groundless belief. Later, mental images collectively. E17.

1 W. HALLIFAX A Statue, which the Turks, zealous enemies of all Imagery, have thrown down. *transf.*: WORDSWORTH The visible scene .. With all its solemn imagery, its rocks, Its woods. 4 JER. TAYLOR Dress your people unto the imagery of Christ. 6 J. H. NEWMAN The glowing imagery of prophets. M. FORSTER We were told, in that quaint hospital imagery, that Em had 'turned the corner'. 7 J. SPEED Nor is she to be condemned vpon the imagerie of his suspicious head. SHELLEY Like a dream's dim imagery.

imagic /ˈɪmɪdʒɪk/ *a.* M20. [f. IMAGE *n.* + -IC.] Like an image.

imaginable /ɪˈmadʒɪnəb(ə)l/ *a.* LME. [Late L *imaginabilis*, f. *imaginare*: see IMAGINE, -ABLE.] That can be imagined; conceivable.

F. HOWERD I managed to stammer that it was the most exciting prospect imaginable.

imaginaˈbility *n.* (*rare*) M19. **imaginableness** *n.* E18. **imaginably** *adv.* M17.

imaginal /ɪˈmadʒɪn(ə)l/ *a.*[1] M17. [App. f. IMAGINE + -AL[1].] Of or pertaining to the imagination; *rare* imaginary. Also, of or pertaining to a mental image or images.

imaginally *adv.* (*rare*) E20.

imaginal /ɪˈmadʒɪn(ə)l/ *a.*[2] L19. [f. L *imagin-* (see IMAGE *n.*) + -AL[1].] *Entomol.* Of or pertaining to an insect imago; of the nature of an imago.

imaginal disk any of a number of thickenings of the epidermis in the larvae of holometabolous insects, which on pupation develop into organs of the imago.

imaginary /ɪˈmadʒɪn(ə)ri/ *a.* & *n.* LME. [L *imaginarius*, f. *imagin-*, *imago*: see IMAGE *n.*, -ARY[1].] A *adj.* 1 Existing only in the imagination; not real or actual. LME. b Of a line etc.: thought of as being drawn through or between specified points. E17. c *Math.* That is, that relates to or involves, the square root of a negative quantity. E18. †2 Relating to the imagination; imaginative. LME–L17. †3 Of the nature of an image or representation. L16–M17. †4 Supposed; putative. *rare.* Only in M17. †5 Imaginable. M–L17.

1 J. M. MURRY I do not believe it is imaginary; I have based my narrative squarely on the facts. 2 SHAKES. *Sonn.* My soul's imaginary sight Presents thy shadow to my sightless view. 3 SHAKES. *Lucr.* Much imaginary work was there .. A hand, a foot, a face, .. Stood for the whole to be imagined. 4 DONNE His Imaginary father Joseph. 5 A. LOVELL All imaginary enquiry was made after them, but .. there was no news to be had.

B *n.* †1 The standard-bearer in a Roman legion who carried the image of the emperor. Only in LME. †2 An imagination; a fancy. E–M18. 3 *Math.* An imaginary quantity or expression. M19.

imaginarily *adv.* L16. **imaginariness** *n.* (*rare*) E18.

imagination /ɪˌmadʒɪˈneɪʃ(ə)n/ *n.* ME. [(O)Fr. f. L *imaginatio*(*n*-), f. *imaginat-* pa. ppl stem of *imaginari* IMAGINE: see -ATION.] 1 The action of imagining or forming mental images or concepts of external objects not present to the senses; the result of this process. ME. 2 The mental faculty which forms images or concepts of external objects not present to the senses, and of their relations (to each other or to the subject). ME. †3a Scheming or devising; a device, a plan, a plot; a fanciful project. LME–M18. b Expectation, anticipation. E–M17. 4a The faculty of fanciful thought; fancy. LME. b The creative faculty of the mind; the ability to frame new and striking concepts. E16. 5 The mind; thinking; thought, opinion. Long *rare* or *obs.* LME.

1 J. FORTESCUE We nede in this case to vse coniecture and ymaginacion. C. S. LEWIS I never mistook imagination for reality. 2 SHAKES. *All's Well* I have forgot him; my imagination Carries no favour in't but Bertram's. K. GERSHON Like every living Jew I have in imagination seen the gas-chamber the mass-grave. 3a AV *Lam.* 3:60 Thou hast seene all their vengeance; and all their imaginations against me. b MARVELL To tell you truly mine owne imagination, I thought he would not open it while I was there. 4a C. JACKSON It's that over-active imagination of yours .. that sees things that aren't there. b SHAKES. *Mids. N. D.* And as imagination bodies forth The forms of things unknown. 5 J. DAVIES Upon the first sight

thereof, it run into our imagination, that they were the Cosaques.

imaginative /ɪˈmadʒɪnətɪv/ *a.* LME. [(O)Fr. *imaginatif*, *-ative* f. med.L *imaginativus*, f. L *imaginat-*: see prec., -ATIVE.] **1** Given to using, or having, the faculty of imagination. LME. **2** Of or pertaining to the faculty of imagination or its use. LME. **3** Existing only in the imagination; unreal, imaginary. Long *rare* or *obs.* L15. **4** Characterized by, resulting from, or showing in a high degree, the faculty of imagination. E19.

1 DAY LEWIS Had I been an imaginative child, I should have looked for the Sleeping Beauty there. L. BLUE All the best cooks tell you to be imaginative with offal. 2 M. TIPPETT Schönberg's imaginative life was unusually rich and powerful. 3 T. CARTWRIGHT His righteousnesse imputed unto us, is not an imaginative, but a true righteousnesse. 4 J. F. LEHMANN It seemed to me to have a quite extraordinary imaginative power.

imaginatively *adv.* LME. **imaginativeness** *n.* M17.

imagine /ɪˈmadʒɪn/ *v.* ME. [(O)Fr. *imaginer* f. L *imaginare* form an image of, represent, *imaginari* picture to oneself, fancy, f. *imagin-*, *imago*: see IMAGE *n.*] **I** *v.t.* **1** Form a mental image or concept of, picture to oneself (something non-existent or not present to the senses). ME. **2** Create as a mental conception, conceive; assume. LME. **3** Devise, plot, plan. *arch.* LME. †**4** Consider, ponder. LME–L16. **5** Conjecture, guess, suspect, suppose; *colloq.* suppose, be of the opinion (*that*). LME. **6** Form an idea with regard to (something not known with certainty); form the idea (*that*). M16.

1 W. WHARTON These are really show birds. We can't imagine where they come from. J. LE CARRÉ In his mind's eye, Smiley now imagined the scene that was playing inside the bank. 2 R. GRAFTON Imagine you see before your eyes your wyves, and daughters in daunger. 3 T. KEIGHTLEY Fisher . . also was arraigned for imagining to deprive the King of his title and dignity. 4 LD BERNERS Euer he imagined, how to do plesure to the peple. 5 W. ROBERTS You might imagine him in the full prime and mettle of his years. E. BOWEN I imagine she meant it kindly. 6 M. EDGEWORTH He did not imagine that he could reform every abuse.

II *v.i.* †**7** Consider, meditate; plan. LME–L16. **8** Form mental images or ideas (†*of*); exercise the faculty of imagination. L16.

7 T. COGAN Divines that imagine and study upon high and subtile matters. 8 SYD. SMITH If it can be shown that women may be trained to reason and imagine as well as men.

imaginator *n.* (*rare*) = IMAGINER LME. **imaginer** *n.* a person who imagines L15. **imagining** *n.* the action of the vb; (freq. in *pl.*) something imagined, a fantasy: ME. **imaginist** *n.* (*rare*) an imaginative person E19.

imagines *n.pl.* see IMAGO.

imagist /ˈɪmɪdʒɪst/ *n.* & *a.* Also **I-**. E20. [f. IMAGE *n.* + -IST.] **A** *n.* **1** A member of a group of early 20th-cent. poets who, in revolt against romanticism, sought clarity of expression through the use of precise images. E20. **2** *Philos.* A conceptualist who believes that universals exist as mental images as opp. to mental concepts. M20. **B** *attrib.* or as *adj.* Of or pertaining to imagists or imagism. E20.

imagism *n.* the doctrine or practice of imagists E20. **imaˈgistic** *a.* of or pertaining to imagism E20. **imaˈgistically** *adv.* M20.

imago /ɪˈmeɪɡəʊ/ *n.* Pl. **imagines** /ɪˈmeɪdʒɪniːz/, **imagos**. L18. [L: see IMAGE *n.*] **1** *Entomol.* The final, fully developed form of an insect after passing through all stages of metamorphosis. L18. **2** *Psychoanalysis.* An unconscious image of an archetype or of someone (esp. a parent) which influences a person's behaviour etc. E20.

imam /ɪˈmɑːm/ *n.* E17. [Arab. *ʾimām* leader, f. *ʾamma* lead the way.] **1** The leader of prayers in a mosque. E17. **2** (**I-**.) (A title of) any of various Muslim leaders, esp. one succeeding Muhammad as the leader of Shiite Islam. M17.

imamate *n.* the office or dignity of an imam E18.

imambara /ɪmɑːmˈbɑːrə/ *n.* M19. [Urdu, f. as prec. + Hind. *bāṛā* enclosure.] In the Indian subcontinent: (the gardens, courtyards, etc., surrounding) a building in which Shiite Muslims assemble at the time of Muharram; *transf.* a large tomb.

Imam Bayildi /ɪˌmɑːm ˈbɑːjɪldi/ *n. phr.* M20. [Turk. *imam bayıldı*, lit. 'the imam fainted' (from pleasure at, or because of the cost of, the dish).] A dish, originating in Turkey, consisting of aubergines stuffed with a garlic-flavoured onion-and-tomato mixture and cooked in oil.

imaret /ɪˈmɑːrɛt, ˈɪmərɛt/ *n.* E17. [Turk. *imaret* f. Arab. *ʿimāra* building, edifice.] In Turkey: a hospice for pilgrims and travellers; now usu., a soup-kitchen.

Imari /ɪˈmɑːri/ *n.* L19. [A town in NW Kyushu, Japan.] Used *attrib.* to designate (articles of) a type of Hizen porcelain.

imbalance /ɪmˈbaləns/ *n.* L19. [f. IM-[2] + BALANCE *n.*] An unbalanced condition; a lack of proportion or relation between corresponding things.

†**imbalm** *v.* var. of EMBALM.

imbalsamation /ɪmˌbɔːlsəˈmeɪʃ(ə)n/ *n. rare.* E19. [f. IM-[1] + BALSAM *n.* + -ATION.] Embalming. Chiefly *fig.*

†**imbank** *v.*, †**imbar** *v.* vars. of EMBANK, EMBAR.

†**imbarcation** *n.* var. of EMBARKATION.

†**imbarge** *n.* & *v.*, †**imbargo** *n.* & *v.* vars. of EMBARGE, EMBARGO.

imbark /ɪmˈbɑːk/ *v.*[1]*t.* Also †**em-**. M17. [f. IM-[1], EM-[1] + BARK *n.*[2]] Enclose in or cover with bark.

†**imbark** *v.*[2], †**imbarkation** *n.* vars. of EMBARK *v.*[1], EMBARKATION.

†**imbarn** *v.t.* Also **em-**. E17–L18. [f. IM-[1], EM-[1] + BARN *n.*[1]] Gather into a barn or barns.

†**imbarque** *v.* var. of EMBARK *v.*[1]

†**imbase** *v.* var. of EMBASE.

†**imbathe** *v.*, †**imbattle** *v.* vars. of EMBATHE, EMBATTLE *v.*[1]

imbauba /ɪmˈbɔːbə, ɪmbəˈuːbə/ *n.* M19. [Port. *imbaúba*, *imbaiba* f. Tupi *ãbaiʹib* hollow tree.] (The timber of) any of several tropical American trees of the genus *Cecropia*, of the mulberry family, *esp.* the trumpet-tree, *C. peltata*.

imbecile /ˈɪmbɪsiːl/ *a.* & *n.* M16. [Fr. †*imbécille* (now *-ile*) f. L *imbecillus*, *-is* lit. 'without support', f. *in-* IM-[2] + var. of *baculum* stick, staff.] **A** *adj.* **1** Weak, feeble; *esp.* physically weak, impotent. Now *rare* or *obs.* M16. **2** Mentally weak; stupid, idiotic. E19. **B** *n.* A person of abnormally weak intellect; *esp.* an adult with intelligence equal to that of a child of five; *colloq.* a stupid person, a fool. E19.

imbecilely *adv.* M19.

imbecilic /ɪmbɪˈsɪlɪk/ *a.* E20. [f. prec. + -IC.] Characteristic of an imbecile; idiotic.

imbecilitate /ɪmbɪˈsɪlɪteɪt/ *v.t.* Now *rare* or *obs.* M17. [f. next after *debilitate*, *facilitate*, etc.: see -ATE[3].] Make imbecile, weak, or feeble; enfeeble.

imbecility /ɪmbɪˈsɪlɪti/ *n.* LME. [(O)Fr. *imbécillité* f. L *imbecillitat-* f. *imbecillus*: see IMBECILE, -ITY.] **1** Weakness, debility, feebleness, impotence; incapacity (*to do*). Now *rare* or *obs.* LME. **2** Abnormal intellectual weakness, esp. as manifested by an adult with the intelligence of a child of five; *colloq.* stupidity, foolishness. Also, an imbecilic act. E17.

imbed *v.* var. of EMBED.

†**imbellish** *v.*, †**imbellishment** *n.* vars. of EMBELLISH, EMBELLISHMENT.

†**imbetter** *v.* var. of EMBETTER.

imbibe /ɪmˈbʌɪb/ *v.t.* LME. [L *imbibere*, f. *in-* IM-[1] + *bibere* drink.] †**1** Cause to absorb moisture or liquid; soak, imbue, or saturate with moisture; steep. LME–E19. **2** Of a thing: suck up, drink in, absorb (moisture). LME. **3** Take up, absorb, assimilate (gas, rays, heat, etc.). Also, take into solution or suspension. LME. **4** *fig.* Drink in, absorb, assimilate (knowledge, ideas, etc.); take into one's mind or moral system. M16. †**b** Instil *into*. M18–E19. **5** Drink (a liquid, esp. alcoholic liquor). Also, inhale. M17. †**b** *transf.* & *fig.* Swallow up. M17–E18.

2 W. COWPER So barren sands imbibe the shower. 4 E. WAUGH The poor fellow had come . . from the United States to imbibe European culture. 5 P. ROTH They dizzily imbibed sweet chocolate drinks.

imbiber *n.* M18.

imbibition /ɪmbɪˈbɪʃ(ə)n/ *n.* L15. [med.L *imbibitio(n-)* absorption, infusion, f. *imbibit-* pa. ppl stem of *imbibere*: see prec., -ITION.] †**1** Soaking or saturation with liquid; steeping, solution; an instance of this. L15–L17. **2** The taking up of liquid etc.; absorption; *fig.* assimilation of ideas etc. E17. **3** Drinking. M19.

imbibitional *a.* of, pertaining to, or resulting from imbibition E20.

†**imbind** *v.*, †**imbitter** *v.*, †**imblaze** *v.* vars. of EMBIND, EMBITTER, EMBLAZE *v.*[1]

imblossom *v.* var. of EMBLOSSOM.

imbodiment *n.*, **imbody** *v.* see EMBODIMENT, EMBODY.

†**imbog** *v.*, †**imbold** *v.*, vars. of EMBOG, EMBOLD.

imbolden *v.* var. of EMBOLDEN.

imbongi /ɪmˈbɒŋɡi/ *n. S. Afr.* Pl. **izimbongi** /ɪz-/, **iimbongi** /iː-/. M19. [Xhosa, Zulu.] A (composer and) reciter of praise poems.

†**imborder** *v.* var. of EMBORDER.

imbosom *v.* var. of EMBOSOM.

†**imboss** *v.*[1], *v.*[2], †**imbossed** *a.*, †**imbossment** *n.* vars. of EMBOSS *v.*[1], *v.*[2], EMBOSSED, EMBOSSMENT.

†**imbosture** *n.* var. of EMBOSTURE

imbound *v.* var. of EMBOUND.

†**imbow** *v.*, **imbowed** *a.* vars. of EMBOW, EMBOWED.

†**imbowel** *v.* var. of EMBOWEL.

imbower *v.* see EMBOWER.

†**imbrace** *v.* & *n.*, †**imbracement** *n.*, †**imbracer** *n.* vars. of EMBRACE *v.*[1] & *n.*, EMBRACEMENT, EMBRACER *n.*[1]

imbrangle *v.* var. of EMBRANGLE.

imbreathe /ɪmˈbriːð/ *v.t.* Also **em-** /ɪm-, ɛm-/. LME. [f. IM-[1], EM-[1] + BREATHE *v.* Cf. INBREATHE.] **1** Breathe in, inhale. LME. **2** Inspire (*with*); instil. LME.

†**imbred** *a.*, **imbreed** *v.* vars. of INBRED, INBREED.

imbreviate /ɪmˈbriːvɪeɪt/ *v.t.* E17. [med.L *imbreviat-* pa. ppl stem of *imbreviare*, f. *in-* IM-[1] + late L *brevis*, *breve* summary, (med.L) writ, letter: see -ATE[3].] Put into the form of a brief; enrol, register.

imbrex /ˈɪmbrɛks/ *n.* Pl. **imbrices**. /ˈɪmbrɪsiːz/. M19. [L, f. *imber* rain-shower.] *Archaeol.* A curved roof-tile used to cover joints in a Roman tiled roof. Cf. TEGULA 2.

imbricate /ˈɪmbrɪkət, -keɪt/ *a.* E17. [L *imbricatus* pa. pple of *imbricare* cover with rain-tiles, f. *imbrex*, *imbric-* roof-tile: see prec., -ATE[2].] †**1** Formed like a gutter-tile or pantile. E–M17. **2** Chiefly *Bot.* & *Zool.* Covered with or composed of scales or scalelike parts overlapping like roof-tiles. M17. **b** Overlapping like tiles. L18. **3** = IMBRICATED 4. L19.

imbricate /ˈɪmbrɪkeɪt/ *v.* L18. [L *imbricat-* pa. ppl stem of *imbricare*: see prec., -ATE[3].] **1** *v.t.* Place so as to overlap like roof-tiles. L18. **2** *v.t.* & *i.* Overlap like roof-tiles. E19.

imbricative *a.* = IMBRICATE *a.* 2.

imbricated /ˈɪmbrɪkeɪtɪd/ *a.* E18. [f. as prec. + -ED[1].] †**1** Of a leaf: curved like a gutter-tile. Only in E18. **2** Composed of parts which overlap like roof-tiles; covered by overlapping leaves, scales, tiles, etc. M18. **3** Of leaves, scales, etc.: arranged so as to overlap each other like roof-tiles. M18. **4** Resembling in pattern a surface of overlapping roof-tiles. L19.

imbrication /ɪmbrɪˈkeɪʃ(ə)n/ *n.* M17. [f. IMBRICATE *v.* or *a.* + -ION.] †**1** Covering with tiles. Only in M17. **2** An overlapping as of roof-tiles; a decorative pattern or arrangement of scales etc. resembling overlapping tiles. E18.

imbrices *n.* pl. of IMBREX.

imbroccata /ɪmbrəˈkɑːtə/ *n.* Also †**em-**, †**-ocado**. L16. [It. f. *imbroccare* give a thrust over the opponent's weapon in fencing, f. *brocco*, †*brocca* stud, nail.] *Hist.* A downward pass or thrust in fencing.

imbroglio /ɪmˈbrəʊlɪəʊ/ *n.* Also †**em-**. Pl. **-os.** M18. [It., f. *imbrogliare* confuse, corresp. to Fr. *embrouiller* EMBROIL *v.*[1]] 1 A confused heap. *arch.* M18. 2 A state of great confusion; a complicated or difficult (esp. political or dramatic) situation; a confused misunderstanding. E19.
2 J. CAREY A misty imbroglio of past loves and losses. S. KNIGHT This imbroglio of corruption, blackmail and murder brought down the coalition government.

†**imbroil** *v.* & *n.*, **imbrown** *v.* vars. of EMBROIL *v.*[1] & *n.*, EMBROWN.

imbrue /ɪmˈbruː/ *v.t.* Also **em-** /ɪm-, ɛm-/. LME. [OFr. *embruer*, *embrouer* bedaub, bedabble, f. *en-* IM-[1] + OFr. *breu*, *bro* (ult. f. Gmc base of BROTH).] **I**†1 Stain, dirty, defile. LME–L16. 2 Stain (one's hands, sword, etc.) *in* or *with* (blood etc.). E16. **b** Cover with blood from bleeding wounds. L16. †3 Soak; steep *in*; saturate *with*. M16–M17. †4 *fig.* Steep *in*, imbue *with* (ideas, opinions etc.); infect. M16–L17. †5 Make bloody; wound; pierce, cut. L16–M19. †**II** 6 Pour (liquid). *rare* (Spenser). Only in L16.
imbruement *n.* (*rare*) tincture, infusion, imbuing L16.

imbrute /ɪmˈbruːt/ *v.* Also **em-** /ɪm-, ɛm-/. M17. [f. IM-[1], EM-[1] + BRUTE *n.*] 1 *v.t.* Degrade to the level of a brute; make bestial; brutalize. M17. 2 *v.i.* Sink or lapse to the level of a brute; become bestial or degraded. M17.
imbrutement *n.* E19.

imbue /ɪmˈbjuː/ *v.t.* LME. [Fr. *imbu*, †*imbu(i)t* pa. pple f. L *imbutus* pa. pple of *imbuere* moisten, stain, imbue.] 1 Saturate, wet through; dye, tinge, impregnate (*with*). LME. **b** = IMBRUE *v.* 2. M19. 2 Permeate, pervade, inspire (*with* an opinion, habit, feeling, etc.). M16.
1 WORDSWORTH Beamy radiance, that imbues Whate'er it strikes with gem-like hues. 2 D. CARNEGIE This experience imbued him with a confidence that was invaluable.
imbuement *n.* (*rare*) L17.

imburse /ɪmˈbɜːs/ *v.t.* Now *rare* or *obs.* M16. [med.L *imbursare* put in one's purse, appropriate, f. *in-* IM-[1] + late L *bursa* purse.] 1 Put into a purse; stow away, store up. M16. 2 Pay, reimburse. Formerly also, enrich. M17.
imbursement *n.* (*rare*) M17.

imbuya /ɪmˈbwiːə/ *n.* E20. [Port. *imbuia* f. Guarani.] (The timber of) a Brazilian tree, *Phoebe porosa*, of the laurel family.

-imeter /ɪmɪtə/ *suff.* Form of -METER with *-i-* provided by first element or merely connective (*calorimeter*, *evaporimeter*). Cf. -OMETER.

imfe *n.* var. of IMPHEE.

imidazole /ɪmɪˈdeɪzəʊl, ɪˈmɪdəzəʊl/ *n.* L19. [f. next + AZO- + -OLE[2].] *Chem.* A colourless crystalline azole, $C_3H_4N_2$. Also called *glyoxaline*.

imide /ˈɪmʌɪd/ *n.* M19. [Fr., arbitrary alt. of AMIDE.] *Chem.* Any of a class of compounds containing the divalent group ·NH· or ·NR· (R = alkyl), esp. where this is bonded to acid groups (i.e. occurs as ·CONHCO·). Cf. IMINE.
imidic *a.* pertaining to or of the nature of an imide; (of an acid) having the formula R·C(NH)OH: L19.

imido- /ɪˈmʌɪdəʊ/ *comb. form.* [f. prec. + -O-.] *Chem.* Forming ns. w. the senses 'of an imide', 'that is an imide'.

imine /ˈɪmiːn/ *n.* L19. [f. AMINE on the analogy of *imide*, *amide*.] *Chem.* Any of a class of organic compounds containing the divalent group ·NH· or ·NR· (R = alkyl) bonded to one or two non-acidic carbon atoms. Cf. IMIDE.

imino- /ɪˈmiːnəʊ/ *comb. form.* Also as attrib. adj. **imino**. [f. prec. + -O-.] *Chem.* Designating or containing the group characteristic of imines.
imino acid *n.* an organic acid containing both an imino and a carboxyl group E20.

imipramine /ɪˈmɪprəmiːn/ *n.* M20. [f. IMI(NE + PR(OPYL + AMINE.] *Pharm.* A tricyclic tertiary amine, $C_{19}H_{24}N_2$, used to treat depression.
¶A proprietary name for this drug is TOFRANIL.

imitable /ˈɪmɪtəb(ə)l/ *a.* M16. [Fr., or late L *imitabilis*, f. *imitari* IMITATE: see -ABLE. Cf. earlier INIMITABLE.] †1 Deserving of imitation. M16–L18. 2 Able to be imitated. L16.
imitaˈbility *n.* L17. **imitableness** *n.* M17.

imitate /ˈɪmɪteɪt/ *v.t.* M16. [L *imitat-* pa. ppl stem of *imitari* copy, rel. to *imago* image: see -ATE[3].] 1 Do or try to do after the manner of; follow the example of; copy in action. M16. **b** Mimic, counterfeit. E17. †**c** Endeavour *to do* something. E17–E19. 2 Make or produce a copy or representation of. L16. **b** Use (a literary composition etc.) as a model. E18. 3 Be, become, or make oneself like, simulate (intentionally or unintentionally). L16.
1 GIBBON In the form and disposition of his . . epistles, he imitated the younger Pliny. E. M. FORSTER Isn't it intolerable that a person whom we're told to imitate should go round spreading slander. **b** J. C. POWYS Sam answered the owl's cry, imitating it exactly. **2b** DRYDEN The adventures of Ulysses . . are imitated in the first six books of Virgil's Æneis. 3 OED A lath painted to imitate iron.

imitation /ɪmɪˈteɪʃ(ə)n/ *n.* & *a.* LME. [(O)Fr. f. L *imitatio(n-)*, f. as prec.: see -ATION.] **A** *n.* 1 The action or practice of imitating or copying. LME. 2 The result or product of imitating; a copy, an artificial likeness; a thing made to look like something else; a counterfeit. E17. 3 A method of translation looser than paraphrase in which modern examples and illustrations are used for old, and domestic for foreign; a composition of this nature. M17. 4 *Mus.* The repetition of a phrase or melody, usually at a different pitch, in another part or voice, with or without other modifications. E18. **B** *adj.* Made in imitation of a real or genuine article or substance. M19.
imitational *a.* M19.

imitative /ˈɪmɪtətɪv/ *a.* L16. [Late L *imitativus*, f. as IMITATE: see -ATIVE.] 1 Characterized by or consisting in imitation. L16. 2 Given to imitation; prone to imitate, copy, or mimic. M18. 3 That imitates the appearance of something else; simulative, fictitious, counterfeit. M19.
1 : *imitative arts*: see ART *n.*[1] **imitative word** a word that reproduces a natural sound (e.g. *fizz*) or whose sound is felt to correspond to the appearance etc. of the object or action described (e.g. *blob*, *jag*, *jam*, *jerk*).
imitatively *adv.* L19. **imitativeness** *n.* M19.

imitator /ˈɪmɪteɪtə/ *n.* E16. [L (orig. partly through Fr. *imitateur*), f. as IMITATE: see -OR.] A person who or thing which imitates, copies, or follows another; a person who produces an imitation of something.
imitatress *n.* = IMITATRIX M19.

imitatrix /ɪmɪˈteɪtrɪks/ *n.* Pl. **-trices** /-trɪsiːz/, **-trixes.** E17. [L, fem. of IMITATOR: see -TRIX.] A female imitator.

immaculacy /ɪˈmakjʊləsi/ *n.* L18. [f. IMMACULATE + -ACY.] Immaculate condition or quality.

immaculate /ɪˈmakjʊlət/ *a.* LME. [L *immaculatus*, f. as IM-[2] + MACULATE *a.*] 1 Free from moral stain; pure, spotless, unblemished. LME. 2 Spotlessly clean or neat; perfectly tidy, in perfect condition. L16. **b** Chiefly *Bot.* & *Zool.* Without spots. E19. 3 Free from fault or error. M19.
1 A. B. JAMESON Convinced of his wife's immaculate purity. **Immaculate Conception** *Theol.* the doctrine that the Virgin Mary was from the moment of her conception free from original sin. **Immaculate Lamb** Jesus Christ (after *1 Pet.* 1:19). 2 C. MCCULLERS He was always immaculate and . . soberly dressed. *Times* An immaculate mill house beautifully situated in the country. **b** T. BEWICK He describes the male bird to be of an immaculate white. 3 G. GORDON Adding his wild squiggle to her immaculate typing. M. RULE The Deanes took pains to record the guns with immaculate watercolour sketches.
immaculately *adv.* E18. **immaculateness** *n.* M17.

immalleable /ɪˈmalɪəb(ə)l/ *a. rare.* L17. [f. IM-[2] + MALLEABLE.] Not malleable.

immanacle /ɪˈmanək(ə)l/ *v.t. rare.* M17. [f. IM-[1] + MANACLE *n.*] Bind with manacles; fetter.

immane /ɪˈmeɪn/ *a. arch.* E17. [L *immanis* monstrous, huge, savage, (earlier) wicked, cruel, f. as IM-[2] + *manis*, *manus* good.] 1 Monstrous in size or strength. E17. 2 Monstrous in character; inhumanly cruel. E17.
immanely *adv.* E17. †**immanity** *n.* (*a*) monstrous cruelty; (*b*) hugeness: M16–L17.

immanence /ˈɪmənəns/ *n.* E19. [f. next + -ENCE.] The fact or condition of being immanent.
Comb.: **immanence philosophy** a theory developed in Germany in the late 19th cent. that reality exists only through being immanent in conscious minds.
immanency *n.* the quality of being immanent M17.

immanent /ˈɪmənənt/ *a.* M16. [Late L *immanent-* pres. ppl stem of *immanere*, f. as IM-[1] + L *manere* remain, dwell: see -ENT.] 1 Indwelling, inherent (*in*); (of God) permanently pervading and sustaining the universe. Cf. TRANSCENDENT. M16. 2 *Philos.* Of an action: that is performed entirely within the mind of the subject, and produces no external effect. Opp. *transient* or *transitive*. Now *rare*. E17.
1 W. J. BATE This sense of process is immanent throughout all of Johnson's writing.
immaˈnental *a.* of or pertaining to immanence L19. **immanently** *adv.* E18.

immanentism /ˈɪmənəntɪz(ə)m/ *n.* E20. [f. prec. + -ISM.] Belief in immanence, esp. the immanence of God.
immanentist *a.* & *n.* (*a*) *adj.* holding or characterized by the doctrine of immanentism; (*b*) *n.* a believer in the immanence of God: E20.

immanifest /ɪˈmanɪfɛst/ *a. rare.* M17. [Late L *immanifestus* obscure, f. as IM-[2] + L *manifestus* MANIFEST *a.*] Not manifest or evident.

immantation /ɪmanˈteɪʃ(ə)n/ *n.* L19. [med.L *immantatio(n-)*, f. *immantat-* pa. ppl stem of *immantare* clothe with a mantle, f. *mantum* MANTLE *n.*: see -ATION.] The investiture of a newly elected pope with the ceremonial mantle.

immantle /ɪˈmant(ə)l/ *v.t.* E17. [f. IM-[1] + MANTLE *n.*] Cover with, or as with, a mantle.

immarble /ɪˈmɑːb(ə)l/ *v.t. rare.* M17. [f. IM-[1] + MARBLE *n.* Cf. ENMARBLE.] Make into marble; make as cold, hard, or immovable, as marble.

immarcescible /ɪmɑːˈsɛsɪb(ə)l/ *a.* Now *rare*. Also **-essible.** LME. [Late L *immarcescibilis*, f. as IM-[2] + *marcescere*, *marcere* fade: see -IBLE.] Unfading; imperishable.

immarginate /ɪˈmɑːdʒɪnət/ *a.* E19. [f. IM-[2] + MARGINATE *a.*] *Bot.* & *Entomol.* Having no distinct margin.

†**immask** *v.t. rare* (Shakes.). Only in L16. [f. IM-[1] + MASK *n.*[2] or *v.*[2]] Disguise.

immaterial /ɪməˈtɪərɪəl/ *a.* & *n.* LME. [Late L *immaterialis*, f. as IM-[2] + *materialis* MATERIAL.] **A** *adj.* 1 Not material; not consisting of matter; spiritual. LME. **b** Having little substance, flimsy. *rare*. E17. †2 Not pertinent to the matter in hand. L16–M17. 3 Of an abstract thing: of no consequence, unimportant. L17.
1 J. BRODSKY We sensed a strange intensity in the air, something immaterial. 3 CONAN DOYLE You will be given a perfectly free hand. Surely the actual name of your client is immaterial. P. G. WODEHOUSE Whether Wilfred Slingsby was crushed or defiant was immaterial.
B *n.* In *pl.* Non-material things. M17.
immateriˈality *n.* (*a*) the quality or character of being immaterial; (*b*) *rare* an immaterial thing: L16. **immaterialize** *v.t.* make immaterial or incorporeal M17. **immaterially** *adv.* M17.

immaterialism /ɪməˈtɪərɪəlɪz(ə)m/ *n.* E18. [f. prec. + -ISM, after *materialism*.] The doctrine that all things exist only as the ideas or perceptions of a mind.
immaterialist *n.* E18.

immatriculate /ɪməˈtrɪkjʊleɪt/ *v.t. rare.* E18. [f. IM-[1] + MATRICULATE *v.* Cf. Fr. *immatriculer*.] Matriculate.
immatricuˈlation *n.* L19.

immature /ɪməˈtjʊə/ *a.* M16. [L *immaturus* untimely, unripe, f. as IM-[2] + *maturus* MATURE *a.*] †1 Of death: premature. M16–M19. 2 Not mature; not yet fully developed; unripe; lacking emotional or intellectual development. L16.
2 ANTHONY HUXLEY A 'June drop' of immature fruits. V. WOOLF She was extremely immature, like a child still, attached to dolls, to old slippers. **immature cataract** *Ophthalm.*: markedly but not yet fully opaque, with the lens usu. swollen and its superficial layers largely transparent. **immature soil** *Soil Sci.*: not having a fully developed profile.
immaturely *adv.* M17.

immaturity /ɪmə'tjʊərɪti/ *n.* M16. [f. prec. + -ITY.] †**1** Prematureness, untimeliness. M16–L17. **2** Immature condition or state; unripeness; lack of maturity of character etc. E17. **3** An immature thing; an action etc. which shows the person who does it to be immature. M17.

immeasurable /ɪ'mɛʒ(ə)rəb(ə)l/ *a.* LME. [f. IM-^{2} + MEASURABLE.] Not measurable; immense.
immeasura'bility *n.* E19. **immeasurableness** *n.* M16. **immeasurably** *adv.* LME.

immeasured /ɪ'mɛʒəd/ *a.* L16. [f. UNMEASURED, with prefix-substitution. Cf. Fr. †*immesuré*.] Unmeasured; immense.

†**immechanical** *a.* E18. [f. UNMECHANICAL, with prefix-substitution.] **1** Not of a physical or material nature or origin. Only in 18. **2** Of a person: not practical. Only in M18.

immediacy /ɪ'miːdɪəsi/ *n.* E17. [f. next + -ACY.] The quality or condition of being immediate; direct relation; directness.
H. JAMES Questions . . bearing with varying degrees of immediacy on the subject. K. VONNEGUT The bone-rattling immediacy of front-line journalism.

immediate /ɪ'miːdɪət/ *a.* & *adv.* LME. [(O)Fr. *immédiat* or late L *immediatus*, f. as IM-^{2} + *mediatus* MEDIATE *a.*] **A** *adj.* **1** Of a person or thing in relation to another: not separated by any intervening agent or medium. LME. **b** *spec.* (*Hist.*) Designating the feudal relation between two people, one of whom derives the right of possession from the other directly. M16. **2** Nearest, next, or close, in space or order. LME. **3** Of relation or action between two things: direct, without any intervening medium or agency. M16. **4** Present or nearest in time; most urgent, occurring or taking effect without delay; done at once, instant. M16. **5** That directly concerns a person etc.; having a direct bearing. E18.
1 R. HOOKER The true immediate cause why baptisme . . is necessary. L. DEIGHTON My immediate boss is working on one of those interminable reports. **2** P. LEVI We did at least get to know our immediate district. **3** J. ROSENBERG The painting has all the freshness of an immediate study from life. **4** A. TREW We must ask him to take immediate steps to keep sightseers away. R. WEST The immediate preludes . . were not auspicious. J. MORTIMER She forgot about the past, and thought of her immediate future. J. A. MICHENER The exiled dictator faced immediate death if he returned to Mexico. **5** P. DRISCOLL I had one immediate concern: the British consulate. Bosw. SMITH She allowed her colonies to trade only so far as suited her own immediate interests.
Special collocations: **immediate access store** *Computing* a store whose access time is negligible. **immediate constituent** *Ling.* any of the main grammatical or morphological subdivisions of a sentence, phrase, or word. **immediate inference**: drawn from a single premiss, without the intervention of a middle term. **immediate knowledge**: gained without reasoning.
B *adv.* [Partly f. med.L *immediate.*] Immediately. Long *obs.* exc. *rare non-standard.* LME.
W. OWEN If it were not so,—I should hop it, immejit.
immediateness *n.* M17.

immediately /ɪ'miːdɪətli/ *adv.* & *conj.* LME. [f. prec. + -LY^{2}, rendering med.L *immediate.*] **A** *adv.* **1** Without intermediary agency; in direct connection or relation; so as to affect directly. LME. **2** With no person, thing, or distance intervening; next (before or after); closely. LME. **3** Without delay, at once, instantly. LME.
B *conj.* At the moment that, as soon as. M19.

immediatism /ɪ'miːdɪətɪz(ə)m/ *n.* E19. [f. IMMEDIATE *a.* + -ISM.] **1** Immediacy. *rare.* E19. **2** The principle or practice of immediate action; *US Hist.* the policy of the immediate abolition of slavery. M19.
immediatist *n.* M19.

immedicable /ɪ'mɛdɪkəb(ə)l/ *a.* M16. [L *immedicabilis*, f. as IM-^{2} + *medicabilis* curable, MEDICABLE.] Incurable; irremediable.
immedicableness *n.* (*rare*) E18. **immedicably** *adv.* M19.

Immelmann /'ɪm(ə)lmən/ *n.* Also **-man.** E20. [Max *Immelmann* (1890–1916), Ger. fighter pilot.] In full *Immelmann turn.* An aerobatic manoeuvre consisting of a half loop followed by a half roll, resulting in reversal of direction and increased height.

immelodious /ɪmɪ'ləʊdɪəs/ *a.* E17. [f. IM-^{2} + MELODIOUS.] Unmelodious.

immember /ɪ'mɛmbə/ *v.t. rare.* M17. [f. IM-^{1} + MEMBER *n.*] Incorporate as a member.

immemorable /ɪ'mɛm(ə)rəb(ə)l/ *a.* M16. [L *immemorabilis*, f. as IM-^{2} + *memorabilis* MEMORABLE.] **1** Not memorable; not worth remembering. M16. †**2** = next. M17–L18.

immemorial /ɪmɪ'mɔːrɪəl/ *a.* E17. [med.L *immemorialis*, f. as IM-^{2} + L *memorialis* MEMORIAL *a.*] Ancient beyond memory or record; very old; long established. Freq. *postpositive* in *time immemorial* s.v. TIME *n.*
TENNYSON The moan of doves in immemorial elms.
immemorially *adv.* E17. **immemorialness** *n.* E18.

immense /ɪ'mɛns/ *a.* & *n.* LME. [(O)Fr. f. L *immensus* immeasurable, f. as IM-^{2} + *mensus* pa. pple of *metiri* measure (after Gk *ametros*).] **A** *adj.* **1** Extraordinarily or immeasurably large or great; vast, boundless. LME. **2** Extremely good, splendid. *slang.* M18.
1 W. BOYD The immense mock-Tudor Government House. G. GREENE She felt an immense relief because nothing . . had been required.
B *n.* Immense extent; immensity. L18.
immensely *adv.* in an immense degree; *colloq.* very much: M17. **immenseness** *n.* E17.

immensikoff /ɪ'mɛnsɪkɒf/ *n. slang.* Now *rare* or *obs.*. L19. [Fanciful elaboration of *immense* to rhyme with *toff*, in a music hall song (*c*1868) by Arthur Lloyd, who wore a fur-trimmed overcoat.] A heavy overcoat.

immensity /ɪ'mɛnsɪti/ *n.* LME. [(O)Fr. *immensité* or L *immensitas*, f. *immensus* IMMENSE: see -ITY.] **1** Immeasurableness, boundlessness; vastness; vast magnitude. LME. **2** Infinite being; infinity; infinite space. M17. **3** An immense quantity or extent (*of*); a thing, being, etc., of immense scale. L18.

immensurable /ɪ'mɛnʃ(ə)rəb(ə)l, -sjə-/ *a.* L15. [Fr., or late L *immensurabilis*, f. as IM-^{2} + *mensurabilis* MENSURABLE.] Immeasurable.

†**immensurate** *a.* M17–M18. [Late L *immensuratus*, f. as IM-^{2} + L *mensuratus* pa. pple of *mensurare* MEASURE *v.*: see -ATE^{2}.] Immense, unmeasured.

immer *n.* var. of EMBER *n.*^{2}

immerd /ɪ'məːd/ *v.t. rare.* M17. [f. med.L (whence (O)Fr. *emmerder*), f. as IM-^{1} + L *merda* dung, ordure.] Bury in or cover with dung.

immerge /ɪ'məːdʒ/ *v.* Now *rare.* Also (now *rare*) **emerge.** E17. [L *immergere*: see IMMERSE.] **1** *v.t.* Dip or plunge in a liquid; immerse. E17. **2** *v.t. fig.* = IMMERSE 2. E17. **3** *v.i.* Plunge or dip oneself in a liquid; sink. E18. †**b** Of a celestial object: enter into the shadow of another in an eclipse; disappear in an occultation; sink below the horizon. Cf. IMMERSION 2. Only in 18.
immergence *n.* M19.

†**immerit** *n.* E17–M18. [f. IM-^{2} + MERIT *n.*] Lack of merit; demerit.

†**immerited** *a.* E17–L18. [f. IM-^{2} + *merited* pa. pple of MERIT *v.*] Undeserved.

†**immeritorious** *a.* M17–L18. [f. IM-^{2} + MERITORIOUS.] Undeserving.

immerse /ɪ'məːs/ *v.* E17. [L *immers-* pa. ppl stem of *immergere*, f. as IM-^{1} + *mergere* dip, MERGE.] **1** *v.t.* Dip, plunge, or submerge in a liquid; *spec.* baptize by immersion. E17. †**b** *fig.* Include; merge. E17–M18. **2** *v.t. fig.* Involve deeply, absorb in a particular activity or condition. Usu. in *pass.* or *refl.* M17. **3** *v.i.* Plunge oneself, become absorbed. Now *rare* or *obs.* M17.
1 R. P. JHABVALA Some buffaloes were bathing, immersed so deeply that only their heads were visible above water. *transf.*: J. TYNDALL A traveller immersed to the waist in the jaws of a fissure. **b** I. WATTS We ought . . to immerse our private in the public safety. **2** J. KRANTZ Fauve immersed herself in the world of modeling. B. EMECHETA You're immersed in your work.
immersible *a.* M19.

immersed /ɪ'məːst/ *a.* LME. [f. prec. + -ED^{1}.] **1** That has been immersed; submerged. LME. †**2** *Astron.* In darkness, eclipsed. M17–M19. **3** *Bot.* & *Zool.* Embedded, sunken. E19.

immersion /ɪ'məːʃ(ə)n/ *n.* Also (now *rare*) **emersion.** L15. [Late L *immersio(n-)*, f. L *immers-*: see IMMERSE, -ION.] **1** Immersing or being immersed; *fig.* absorption in an activity or condition. L15. **b** The administration of Christian baptism by plunging the whole person in water. M17. **2** *Astron.* The disappearance of a celestial object behind another or into its shadow, as in an eclipse or occultation. L17. **3** A method of teaching a foreign language by the exclusive use of that language, usu. at a special school. Chiefly *N. Amer.* M20.
1 ADDISON The Doctor . . gives her Two or Three total Emersions in the Cold Bath. M. IGNATIEFF Our dull and patient immersion in the records of the past. **3** *attrib.*: *Time* I've been taking immersion courses in French.
Comb.: **immersion foot** *Med.* trench foot; **immersion heater** an electric heater designed for direct immersion in a liquid to be heated, esp. as a fixture in a hot-water tank; **immersion suit**: designed to give the wearer buoyancy and insulation when in the water.
immersionism *n.* the doctrine or practice of immersion in baptism M19. **immersionist** *n.* an adherent of immersionism M19.

immesh /ɪ'mɛʃ/ *v.t.* L18. [f. IM-^{1} + MESH *n.*] = ENMESH.

immethodical /ɪmɪ'θɒdɪk(ə)l/ *a.* L16. [f. IM-^{2} + METHODICAL.] Having no method; unmethodical.
immethodically *adv.* E17.

immetrical /ɪ'mɛtrɪk(ə)l/ *a.* L16. [f. IM-^{2} + METRICAL *a.*^{1}] Not metrical; unmetrical.
immetrically *adv.* L19. **immetricalness** *n.* M19.

immie *n.* var. of IMMY.

immigrant /'ɪmɪgr(ə)nt/ *n.* & *a.* L18. [L *immigrant-* pres. ppl stem of *immigrare*, after EMIGRANT: see next.] **A** *n.* **1** A person who settles as a permanent resident in a different country. Also (esp. in Britain), a descendant of such a person. L18. **2** *Biol.* etc. An animal or plant living or growing in a region to which it has migrated; a cell growing in tissue into which it has moved. L19.
1 E. WILSON The immigrants from feudalism and famine in Europe were finding in the crowded American cities new misery. LANDED *immigrant.*
B *attrib.* or as *adj.* Of or pertaining to immigrants; that is an immigrant. E19.
Times There was some criticism . . at this high proportion of immigrant children. P. ROTH My immigrant grandparents . . . coming, at the turn of the century, to America.

immigrate /'ɪmɪgreɪt/ *v.* E17. [L *immigrat-* pa. ppl stem of *immigrare*, f. as IM-^{1} + *migrare* MIGRATE: see -ATE^{3}.] **1** *v.i.* Come to settle as a permanent resident in a different country. Foll. by *into.* E17. **b** *Biol.* etc. (Of a cell) move into different tissue; (of an animal or plant) migrate to a different geographical region. L19. **2** *v.t.* Bring (a person) into a country as a settler. L19.

immigration /ɪmɪ'greɪʃ(ə)n/ *n.* M17. [f. prec. + -ATION.] **1** The action of immigrating; the process of authorizing this (freq. *attrib.*). M17. **b** A department at a frontier, airport, etc., where the documentation of (potential) immigrants is scrutinized on their arrival. *colloq.* M20. **2** A group of immigrants. *US.* M19.
1 T. WARTON The Saracens . . at their immigration into Spain. *attrib.*: C. PHILLIPS Bertram concentrated on the signs . . behind the desk of the immigration officer. **b** F. HOYLE Quickly we were into the reception hall and through immigration [at London Airport]. **2** *Saturday Review* A far vaster immigration . . began pouring through the city portals.

imminence /'ɪmɪnəns/ *n.* E17. [L *imminentia*, f. as next: see -ENCE.] **1** A thing that is imminent; *esp.* impending evil. Now *rare.* E17. **2** The quality or fact of being imminent. M17.
1 SHAKES. *Tr. & Cr.* I . . dare all imminence that gods and men Address their dangers in. **2** R. COBB She appeared to carry the imminence of death in every part of her. L. WHISTLER Report came of the imminence of war over Czechoslovakia.
imminency *n.* = IMMINENCE 2 M17.

imminent /ˈɪmɪnənt/ *a.* LME. [L *imminent-* pres. ppl stem of *imminere* project, be impending, f. as IM-¹ + *minere* project: see -ENT.] 1 Of an event, esp. danger or disaster: impending, soon to happen. LME. †2 Immanent. E17–M19. 3 Projecting, overhanging. *arch.* E18.

1 E. WAUGH The prospect of action, for a few days imminent, now postponed. B. BAINBRIDGE He wondered what Meyer had meant by danger. Was it imminent or to come later? C. PHILLIPS He displayed no signs of imminent departure.

imminently *adv.* M16.

immingle /ɪˈmɪŋg(ə)l/ *v.t.* E17. [f. IM-¹ + MINGLE *v.*] Mingle, blend.

†**imminution** *n.* L16–L18. [L *imminutio(n-)*, f. *imminut-* pa. ppl stem of *imminuere* lessen, f. as IM-¹ + *minuere* lessen: see -ION.] Lessening, decrease.

immiscible /ɪˈmɪsɪb(ə)l/ *a.* L17. [Late L *immiscibilis*, f. as IM-² + MISCIBLE.] Unable to be mixed; *spec.* (of a liquid) incapable of forming a true solution *with* or *in* another liquid.

T. CHALMERS Like water and oil, they are immiscible.

immisciˈbility *n.* M18.

immiseration /ɪˌmɪzəˈreɪʃ(ə)n/ *n.* M20. [f. IM-¹ + MISER(ABLE + -ATION, tr. G *Verelendung.*] Impoverishment.

J. K. GALBRAITH The prospect of the progressive immiseration of the masses, worsening economic crises and . . bloody revolution.

iˈmmiserate *v.t.* [back-form.] impoverish L20. **immiseriˈzation** *n.* = IMMISERATION M20.

immission /ɪˈmɪʃ(ə)n/ *n.* Now *rare.* E16. [L *immissio(n-)*, f. *immiss-* pa. ppl stem of *immittere*: see next, -ION.] 1 A thing that is immitted. E16. 2 The action of immitting; insertion, injection. L16.

immit /ɪˈmɪt/ *v.t.* Now *rare.* Infl. **-tt-**. LME. [L *immittere* send in, introduce, f. as IM-¹ + *mittere* send.] Put in, insert, introduce.

immitigable /ɪˈmɪtɪgəb(ə)l/ *a.* L16. [Late L *immitigabilis*, f. as IM-² + MITIGABLE.] Unable to be mitigated.

immitigably *adv.* E19.

immittance /ɪˈmɪt(ə)ns/ *n.* M20. [Blend of IMPEDANCE and ADMITTANCE.] *Electr.* Admittance and impedance (as a combined concept).

immix /ɪˈmɪks/ *v.t.* Now *rare.* Orig. & chiefly as pa. pple †**immixt**, **immixed** /ɪˈmɪkst/. LME. [Orig. pa. pple, f. L *immixtus* pa. pple of *immiscere*, f. as IM-¹ + *miscere* mix; vb (E16) as back-form. or f. IM-¹ + MIX *v.*] Mix in, mix up; involve (*in*).

immixture /ɪˈmɪkstʃə/ *n.* M19. [f. IM-¹ + MIXTURE.] The action of mixing up or mingling; the fact of being involved (*in*).

immobile /ɪˈməʊbʌɪl/ *a.* ME. [(O)Fr. f. L *immobilis*, f. as IM-² + *mobilis* MOBILE *a.*] Incapable of moving or being moved, immovable; motionless, stationary.

P. G. WODEHOUSE There was something . . immobile about the boy's attitude . . to suggest that nothing could shift him. A. S. BYATT The man watched him, expecting him to move again, but he sat, immobile.

immobilise *v.* var. of IMMOBILIZE.

immobilism /ɪˈməʊbɪlɪz(ə)m/ *n.* M20. [Fr. *immobilisme*, f. as IMMOBILE: see -ISM.] A policy or attitude of extreme conservatism or opposition to change.

immobility /ɪmə(ʊ)ˈbɪlɪti/ *n.* LME. [(O)Fr. *immobilité* or late L *immobilitas*, f. *immobilis*: see IMMOBILE, -ITY.] The quality or condition of being immobile.

immobilize /ɪˈməʊbɪlʌɪz/ *v.t.* Also **-ise**. L19. [Fr. *immobiliser*, f. as IMMOBILE: see -IZE. Cf. MOBILIZE.] 1 Make or keep immobile; restrict the free movement of; *spec.* keep (a limb, a patient) restricted in movement for healing purposes. L19. b Withdraw (coin) from circulation to support banknotes. L19. 2 *Biol.* Esp. of an organism: convert (a plant nutrient or other substance) into a form in which it is unavailable to (other) organisms. M20.

1 R. MACAULAY She stood still, immobilized by shock. M. RULE The English carracks were immobilised with scarcely a breath of wind. *Times* Use wheel clamps to immobilize offending vehicles.

immobiliˈzation *n.* L19. **immobilizer** *n.* a device for immobilizing a motor vehicle L20.

immoderacy /ɪˈmɒd(ə)rəsi/ *n. rare.* L17. [f. next + -ACY.] Immoderateness.

immoderate /ɪˈmɒd(ə)rət/ *a.* LME. [L *immoderatus*, f. as IM-² + *moderatus* MODERATE *a.*] Not moderate; lacking in moderation; unrestrained, excessive; extreme. Formerly also (*rare*), boundless.

LD MACAULAY His immoderate zeal against the unfortunate clan. E. JOHNSON A rather short, plump . . youngster, jolly-looking and given to immoderate laughter.

immoderately *adv.* LME. **immoderateness** *n.* L16.

immoderation /ɪˌmɒdəˈreɪʃ(ə)n/ *n.* LME. [Fr. *immodération* or L *immoderatio(n-)*, f. as IM-² + *moderatio(n-)* MODERATION.] Immoderateness, excess. Formerly also, an extreme; an immoderate act.

immodest /ɪˈmɒdɪst/ *a.* L16. [Fr. *immodeste* or L *immodestus*, f. as IM-² + MODEST.] Lacking modesty or decency; forward, impudent, boastful; indelicate, improper.

R. MACAULAY Female bathing was thought extremely immodest. P. LIVELY I was by far the best looking . . and the most immodest.

immodestly *adv.* L16.

immodesty /ɪˈmɒdɪsti/ *n.* L16. [Fr. *immodestie* or L *immodestia*, f. as IM-² + MODESTY.] Lack of modesty or decency; forwardness, impudence; indelicacy, impropriety.

immodulated /ɪˈmɒdjʊleɪtɪd/ *a. rare.* M18. [f. IM-² + *modulated* pa. pple of MODULATE.] Without (vocal) modulation.

immolate /ˈɪmə(ʊ)lət/ *a. arch.* M16. [L *immolatus* pa. pple, f. as next: see -ATE².] Immolated.

immolate /ˈɪmə(ʊ)leɪt/ *v.t.* M16. [L *immolat-* pa. ppl stem of *immolare* (orig.) sprinkle with sacrificial meal, f. as IM-¹ + *mola* meal: see -ATE³.] 1 Offer in sacrifice; kill (a victim) in sacrifice. M16. 2 Give up to destruction, loss, etc., for the sake of something else; sacrifice (*to*). M17.

1 D. WILSON Human victims were immolated to the Thunderer. M. M. KAYE The old Rani, immolating herself in the flames that consumed the body of her husband. 2 E. BOWEN Railings . . had been immolated to a forgotten war. CLIVE JAMES In him there is no element of the self-immolating drudge.

immolation /ɪmə(ʊ)ˈleɪʃ(ə)n/ *n.* LME. [L *immolatio(n-)*, f. as prec.: see -ATION.] 1 Sacrificial slaughter of a victim. LME. b A sacrificial victim. Long *rare.* L16. 2 Deliberate destruction or loss for the sake of something else. L17.

immolator /ˈɪmə(ʊ)leɪtə/ *n.* M17. [L, f. as IMMOLATE *v.*: see -OR.] A person who kills a victim in sacrifice.

†**immoment** *a. rare* (Shakes.). Only in E17. [f. IM-² + MOMENT *n.*] Of no moment; trifling.

immomentous /ɪmə(ʊ)ˈmɛntəs/ *a. rare.* E18. [f. IM-² + MOMENTOUS.] Not momentous; unimportant.

immoral /ɪˈmɒr(ə)l/ *a.* M17. [f. IM-² + MORAL *a.*] Not consistent with or not conforming to accepted moral principles; *esp.* dissolute, depraved.

G. GREENE They form the immoral background to that extraordinary period of haphazard violence. *immoral earnings*: see EARNING *n.*¹ 3.

immoralism *n.* [after G *Immoralismus*] a system of thought or behaviour which rejects accepted moral principles E20. **immoralist** *n.* an advocate of immorality L17. **immoralize** *v.t.* make immoral M18. **immorally** *adv.* E18.

immorality /ɪməˈralɪti/ *n.* M16. [med.L *immoralitas*, f. as IM-² + late L *moralitas* MORALITY.] 1 Disregard for moral principles; immoral character or conduct; dissoluteness, depravity. M16. 2 An immoral act or practice; a vice. M17.

†**immorigerous** *a.* E17–M18. [f. IM-² + MORIGEROUS.] Obstinate; disobedient, rebellious.

immortal /ɪˈmɔːt(ə)l/ *a.* & *n.* LME. [L *immortalis* undying (also as n.pl., the gods), f. as IM-² + *mortalis* MORTAL *a.*] A *adj.* 1 Not mortal; undying, living for ever. LME. b Of or pertaining to immortal beings or immortality; divine. M16. 2 Everlasting, eternal, unfading, imperishable; *spec.* (of fame or someone or something famous) remembered or celebrated forever. L15.

1 F. HOYLE Such 'primitive' cells are potentially immortal, dying only in adverse conditions. 2 E. BOWEN Everything, . . would stay sealed up, immortal, in an inner room in his consciousness. *the Immortal Memory*: see MEMORY.

B *n.* 1 An immortal being; *esp.* in *pl.*, the gods of classical antiquity. M17. 2 (**I-**.) In *pl.* The royal bodyguard of ancient Persia. E19. 3 A person of enduring fame; *spec.* (**I-**) a member of the Académie Française. L19.

immortalism *n.* (*rare*) belief in immortality L18. **immortalist** *n.* a person who believes in immortality M17. **immortally** *adv.* L15.

immortalise *v.* var. of IMMORTALIZE.

immortality /ɪmɔːˈtalɪti/ *n.* ME. [L *immortalitas*, f. as IMMORTAL: see -ITY.] 1 Endless life or existence; exemption from death; perpetuity. ME. 2 Enduring fame or remembrance. M16.

immortalize /ɪˈmɔːt(ə)lʌɪz/ *v.t.* Also **-ise**. M16. [f. IMMORTAL *a.* + -IZE.] 1 Make everlasting; perpetuate; confer enduring fame upon. M16. 2 Endow with eternal life. M17.

1 H. T. COCKBURN A genius . . who has immortalized Edinburgh,—Walter Scott.

immortaliˈzation *n.* E17. **immortalizer** *n.* E18.

immortelle /ɪmɔːˈtɛl/ *n.* M19. [Fr. f. *fleur immortelle* everlasting flower.] = EVERLASTING *n.* 4; esp. *Xeranthemum annuum* (see XERANTHEMUM).

immortification /ɪˌmɔːtɪfɪˈkeɪʃ(ə)n/ *n.* E17. [med.L *immortificatio(n-)*, f. as IM-² + eccl.L *mortificatio(n-)* MORTIFICATION.] Lack of mortification of the soul or passions.

immortified *a.* [repr. med.L *immortificatus*] not mortified M19.

immote /ɪˈməʊt/ *a.* Long *rare.* E17. [L *immotus*, f. as IM-² + *motus* pa. pple of *movere* MOVE *v.*] Unmoved.

immotile /ɪˈməʊtʌɪl/ *a.* L19. [f. IM-² + MOTILE.] Not motile; incapable of movement.

immotive /ɪˈməʊtɪv/ *a.* E17. [f. IM-² + MOTIVE *a.*] Unmoving; incapable of movement.

immovable /ɪˈmuːvəb(ə)l/ *a.* & *n.* Also (now the usual form in *Law*) **-veable**. LME. [f. IM-² + MOVABLE.] A *adj.* 1 Unable to be moved; incapable of movement; motionless, stationary. LME. 2 *fig.* Unalterable, fixed; (of a person) steadfast, unyielding; emotionless, impassive. LME. 3 *Law.* Of property: not liable to be removed, permanent (as land, buildings, etc.). LME.

1 D. BREWSTER The sun stood immovable in the centre of the universe. 2 H. BELLOC The young man . . lives in a static world. For him things are immovable. J. BUCHAN There was a mild and immovable fanaticism in his pale eyes. *immovable feast*: see FEAST *n.*

B *n. Law.* Immovable property. Usu. in *pl.* L16.

immovaˈbility *n.* LME. **immovableness** *n.* E17. **immovably** *adv.* LME.

immram /ˈɪmrɑːm/ *n.* Also *imram*. Pl. **-a** /-ə/. L19. [OIr. *imram* (mod. *iomramh*), f. *imm-rá* row around.] Any of various stories of fabulous sea voyages written in Ireland between the late 8th and 11th cents.

immund /ɪˈmʌnd/ *a. rare.* E17. [L *immundus*, f. as IM-² + *mundus* clean, pure.] Dirty; impure.

immundity *n.* dirtiness; impurity: M18.

immune /ɪˈmjuːn/ *a.* & *n.* LME. [L *immunis* exempt from a service or charge, f. as IM-² + *munis* ready for service.] A *adj.* 1 Exempt; free (*from* some liability). Now only in *Law.* LME. 2 *Biol.* (Partially or wholly) invulnerable to (an) infection, poison, etc., esp. owing to the inherited or (naturally or artificially) induced presence of antibodies specific to the agent. Foll. by *against*, *from*, *to*. L19. b Of, pertaining to, or producing immunity. E20. 3 *fig.* Wholly protected (*from* something injurious or distasteful); not susceptible (*to*). L19. **b** Of a computer system: protected against damage by hackers and viruses. L20.

1 W. S. CHURCHILL The officials pleaded that they were immune because they were acting under Government orders. **2b** K. LANDSTEINER The immune antibodies . . react . . with the antigens that were used for immunizing. *Times* A deficiency disease of the body's immune defence system. **3** *New York Times* Golden ages when these who governed . . have been immune from acts of rage and insanity. B. CHATWIN She failed to charm him: he was immune to her kind of charm.

Special collocations: †**immune body** an antibody. **immune globulin** (*a*) a preparation containing antibodies, suitable for use as an antiserum; (*b*) = IMMUNOGLOBULIN. **immune response** the reaction of the body to the introduction of an antigen. **immune system** those structures and functions of an organism responsible for maintaining immunity.

B *n.* An immune person or thing. L19.

immune /ɪˈmjuːn/ *v.t. rare.* M19. [f. the adj.] Make immune.

immunise *v.* var. of IMMUNIZE.

immunity /ɪˈmjuːnɪti/ *n.* LME. [L *immunitas*, f. as IMMUNE *a.* & *n.*: see -ITY.] **1** *Law.* Exemption *from* taxation, jurisdiction, an obligation or duty, etc.; *gen.* privilege. LME. **b** An exemption or privilege; *spec.* (*Eccl.*) (an) exemption from a secular or civil liability, duty, etc. LME. †**2** Undue freedom, licence. L16–L17. **3** Freedom or protection from or *from* anything injurious or distasteful; lack of susceptibility (*to*). L16. **4** *Biol.* The ability to resist a specific infection, poison, etc., esp. owing to lymphocytes and phagocytes and (in vertebrates) antibodies. Cf. IMMUNE *a.* 2. L19.

1 *diplomatic immunity*: see DIPLOMATIC *a.* **3** P. ACKROYD He was offered immunity from prosecution if he would testify. **4** BETTY SMITH Vaccination was a giving of the harmless form of smallpox to work up immunity.

immunize /ˈɪmjʊnʌɪz/ *v.* Also **-ise**. L19. [f. IMMUNE *a.* + -IZE.] **1** *v.t.* Make immune, esp. by inoculation. L19. **2** *v.i.* Of an antigen: produce immunity *against* an agent. M20.

immuniˈzation *n.* L19. **immunizer** *n.* E20.

immuno- /ˈɪmjʊnəʊ, ɪˈmjuːnəʊ/ *comb. form* of IMMUNE *a.*, IMMUNITY, IMMUNOLOGY: see -O-.

immunoˈassay *n.* (a) determination of the presence or quantity of a substance, esp. a protein, through its properties as an antigen M20. **immunoˈcompetent** *a.* having a normal immune response M20. **immunoˈcompromised** *a.* having an impaired immune system L20. **immunocytoˈchemistry** *n.* the cytochemistry of the immune system M20. **immunodeˈficiency** *n.* a reduction in the normal immune defences of the body M20. **immunodeˈficient** *a.* (partly) lacking in immunity L20. **immunodeˈpressant** *a.* & *n.* = IMMUNOSUPPRESSANT M20. **immunodeˈpressed** *a.* = IMMUNOSUPPRESSED L20. **immunodeˈpression** *n.* = IMMUNOSUPPRESSION M20. **immunodeˈpressive** *a.* = IMMUNOSUPPRESSIVE *a.* M20. **immunodiˈffusion** *n.* a technique for detecting or measuring antibodies and antigens by their precipitation when diffused together through a gel or other medium M20. **immunofluoˈrescence** *n.* a technique for determining the location of an antigen (or antibody) in tissues by reaction with an antibody (or antigen) labelled with a fluorescent dye M20. **immunofluoˈrescent** *a.* of, pertaining to, or involving immunofluorescence M20. **iˈmmunogen** *n.* any substance that elicits an immune response or produces immunity in the recipient E20. **immunoˈgenic** *a.* of, pertaining to, or possessing the ability to elicit an immune response M20. **immunosuˈppressant** *a.* & *n.* = IMMUNOSUPPRESSIVE M20. **immunosuˈppressed** *a.* (of an individual) rendered incapable of an effective immune response M20. **immunosuˈppression** *n.* suppression of the immune response in an individual, esp. to prevent rejection of transplanted tissue M20. **immunosuˈppressive** *a.* & *n.* (*a*) *adj.* suppressing the function of the immune system; (*b*) *n.* a drug which promotes immunosuppression: M20. **immunoˈtherapy** *n.* the prevention or treatment of disease by modification of the immune response E20.

immunochemistry /ˌɪmjʊnəʊˈkɛmɪstri, ɪˌmjuːnəʊ-/ *n.* E20. [f. IMMUNO- + CHEMISTRY.] The chemical study of immunity; biochemical study or investigation of or using immunoglobulins.

immunochemical *a.* E20. **immunochemically** *adv.* M20. **immunochemist** *n.* an expert in or student of immunochemistry M20.

immunoelectrophoresis /ˌɪmjʊnəʊɪˌlɛktrəfəˈriːsɪs, ɪˌmjuːnəʊ-/ *n.* M20. [f. IMMUNO- + ELECTROPHORESIS.] A technique for identification of proteins in a mixture (as serum) by electrophoresis and subsequent immunodiffusion.

immunoelectrophoretic *a.* M20. **immunoelectrophoretically** *adv.* M20.

immunogenetics /ˌɪmjʊnəʊdʒɪˈnɛtɪks, ɪˌmjuːnəʊ-/ *n.* M20. [f. IMMUNO- + GENETICS.] Genetics studied by means of immunological techniques; the branch of medicine that deals with the genetic aspects of immunity.

immunogenetic *a.* of or pertaining to immunogenetics M20. **immunogenetically** *adv.* L20.

immunoglobulin /ˌɪmjʊnəʊˈglɒbjʊlɪn, ɪˌmjuːnəʊ-/ *n.* M20. [f. IMMUNO- + GLOBULIN.] *Biochem.* & *Med.* Any of a group of proteins present in vertebrates in the serum and cells of the immune system, which have a characteristic arrangement of subunits in their molecular structure, and function as antibodies.

immunology /ɪmjʊˈnɒlədʒi/ *n.* E20. [f. IMMUN(ITY + -OLOGY.] The branch of science which studies resistance to infection in humans and animals.

immunoˈlogic, **-ˈlogical** *adjs.* of or pertaining to immunology or immunity E20. **immunoˈlogically** *adv.* E20. **immunologist** *n.* E20.

immure /ɪˈmjʊə/ *v.* & *n.* L16. [Fr. *emmurer* or med.L *immurare*, f. as IM-[1] + *murus* wall.] **A** *v.t.* †**1** Surround with a wall or walls; fortify. L16–M18. **2** Enclose within walls; confine (as) in a prison; *fig.* enclose, surround, confine. L16. **3** Build into or entomb in a wall. L17.

2 I. MURDOCH Otto was still immured in the summer-house. K. LINES You shall be immured in a vault . . until you are released by death. JO GRIMOND The increasing volume of legislation which keeps Members . . immured together and isolated from the world. **3** G. G. SCOTT The end of the tomb has been immured in the lower part of the chapel.

†**B** *n.* A wall. *rare* (Shakes.). Only in E17.

immuˈration *n.* imprisonment, confinement L19. **immurement** *n.* = IMMURATION M18.

immusical /ɪˈmjuːzɪk(ə)l/ *a.* Now *rare.* E17. [f. IM-[2] + MUSICAL *a.*] Unmusical.

immutable /ɪˈmjuːtəb(ə)l/ *a.* LME. [L *immutabilis*, f. as IM-[2] + *mutabilis* MUTABLE.] **1** Not mutable; not subject or liable to change; unalterable. LME. **2** Not varying in different cases; invariable. E17.

1 P. USTINOV Those for whom the . . law is immutable, instead of being as changeable as the seasons.

immutaˈbility *n.* L15. **immutably** *adv.* E17.

immy /ˈɪmi/ *n.* Also **immie**. M20. [Prob. f. IMITATION: see -Y[6].] A kind of glass marble made to imitate one of another material.

imp /ɪmp/ *n.* OE. [Rel. to next.] **1** A young shoot of a plant; a sapling; a sucker, a scion. *obs.* exc. *Sc.* OE. †**b** A young person. LME–L16. †**2** A shoot or slip used in grafting; a graft. LME–E18. **3** A scion or descendant, esp. of a noble family; an offspring, a child. *arch.* LME. **b** A follower, an adherent, esp. of glory, chivalry, etc. *arch.* LME. **4** A (person regarded as a) child of the Devil; a little devil. E16. †**5** A young man, a youth; a lad, a boy. L16–L19. **6** A piece added on to eke out or enlarge something. *obs.* exc. *dial.* L16. **7** A mischievous child; a scamp, an urchin. M17.

4 LINCOLN *imp.*

imp /ɪmp/ *v.t.* [OE *impian* corresp. to OHG *impfōn* (G *impfen*), shortened analogues of *impitōn* (MHG *impfeten*), f. Proto-Romance, f. med.L *impotus* graft, f. Gk *emphutos* implanted, engrafted, vbl adj. of *emphuein*, f. *en-* IM-[1] + *phuein* plant.] †**1** Graft, engraft. OE–M18. **2** *fig.* Implant, set or fix in. *arch.* ME. **3** *Falconry.* †**a** Add (feathers) to the wing of a bird to improve the power of flight. Also foll. by *in.* L15–E18. **b** Add feathers to (the wing of a bird) to improve the power of flight. Also foll. by *with.* L16. **4** Enlarge, add to, (as) by grafting. *arch.* L16.

3b imp the wings of strengthen or improve the flight or power of.

impack /ɪmˈpak/ *v.t. rare.* L16. [AL *impaccare* pack, f. as IM-[1] + *paccare* pack wool etc.: see PACK *v.*[1]] Pack (up); press together into a mass.

impact /ˈɪmpakt/ *n.* L18. [f. L *impact-* pa. ppl stem of *impingere* IMPINGE.] **1** The striking of one body on or against another; a collision. L18. **2** The (strong) effect of one thing, person, action, etc., on another; an influence; an impression. E19.

1 A. TREW The impact was softened by the sand. *Manchester Evening News* The car . . careered . . into the path of the wagon. She was killed on impact. **2** L. WOOLF To describe the impact of illness or insanity upon such a remarkable mind. **make an impact** have an effect (*on*).

Comb.: **impact crater** a crater or hollow supposedly produced by the impact of a meteorite; **impact printer**: that depends on mechanical pressure to transfer ink from a ribbon to the paper; **impact strength** the ability of a material to resist breaking when struck; **impact test** any of various tests which measure an object's resistance to breaking under sudden stress, usu. by applying a blow; **impact wrench** an electric or pneumatic power wrench used for inserting and removing nuts, bolts, screws, etc.

impact /ɪmˈpakt/ *v.* E17. [Partly f. L *impactus* pa. pple of *impingere* IMPINGE, partly back-form. f. IMPACTED.] Chiefly as *impacted* pa. pple. **1** *v.t.* Press closely or fix firmly (*in*, *into*). E17. **2** *v.t.* Stamp or impress *on*. *rare.* L17. **3** *v.i.* Come forcibly into contact with a (larger) body or surface. (Foll. by *against*, *on*, etc.) E20. **b** Have a pronounced effect *on*. E20. **4** *v.t.* Cause to impinge *on*, *against*, etc. M20.

1 *fig.*: A. CARTER Both intent on impacting a thousand stories into the single night.

impacted /ɪmˈpaktɪd/ *a.* E17. [f. L *impactus* (see prec.) + -ED[1].] **1** Pressed closely in, firmly fixed. E17. **b** *Med.* Of faeces: wedged in the intestine. Of the intestine: blocked by hardened faeces. M19. **c** *Med.* Of a bone fracture: having the broken parts driven firmly together. M19. **d** Of a tooth: prevented from erupting by bone or another tooth. L19. **2** That has been struck by an impacting body; (of an impacting body) that has struck something. E20. **3** *fig.* Of an area: overcrowded, esp. so as to put severe pressure on public services etc. *US.* M20.

1d *Practical Health* The shock of having impacted wisdom teeth removed.

impaction /ɪmˈpakʃ(ə)n/ *n.* M18. [f. IMPACT *v.* + -ION.] **1** The action of becoming or condition of being impacted. M18. **2** *spec.* in *Med.* The lodging of a mass of (usu. hardened) faeces in the intestine so that defecation is prevented or impeded; the obstruction so caused. M19. **b** An impacted mass of faeces. E20. **3** The action or process of causing a body to impact on a surface etc. M20.

impactite /ɪmˈpaktʌɪt/ *n.* M20. [f. IMPACT *n.* + -ITE[1], after TEKTITE.] *Geol.* Any piece of glassy material formed in or around a meteorite crater by the heat of impact.

impactive /ɪmˈpaktɪv/ *a.* M20. [f. IMPACT *n.* + -IVE.] Of, pertaining to, or characterized by impact; having an impact.

impactor /ɪmˈpaktə/ *n.* E20. [f. IMPACT *v.* + -OR.] **1** A device etc. that delivers impacts or blows. E20. **2** An impinger, *esp.* one in which particles are deposited on a dry surface rather than in a liquid. M20.

impaint /ɪmˈpeɪnt/ *v.t.* Long *rare.* L16. [f. IM-[1] + PAINT *v.*] Depict by painting on something.

impair /ɪmˈpɛː/ *n.*[1] *arch.* M16. [f. IMPAIR *v.*] An act of impairing; the fact of being impaired; impairment.

impair /ˈɪmpɛː; *in senses A.3, B.1 foreign* ɛ̃pɛr (*pl. same*)/ *a.* & *n.*[2] E17. [Fr. = unequal, f. as IM-[2] + PAIR *n.*[2] & *a.*] **A** *adj.* †**1** Unfit, inferior. *rare* (Shakes.). Only in E17. **2** Not paired; not forming one of a pair. M19. **3** *Roulette.* Of or pertaining to an odd number or the odd numbers collectively. M20. **B** *n.* **1** *Roulette.* An odd number; the odd numbers collectively. M19.

2 An unpaired individual thing; an odd one. *rare*. L19.

impair /ɪmˈpɛː/ *v.* Orig. †**app-**; also †**em-**. ME. [OFr. *empeirier* f. Proto-Romance, f. as IM-[1] + late L *pejorare*, f. L *pejor* worse.] 1 *v.t.* Make less effective or weaker; devalue; damage, injure. ME. 2 *v.i.* Become less effective or weaker; deteriorate; suffer injury or loss. Now *rare* or *obs.* ME.

1 A. BURGESS Being toothless did not impair one's capacity to eat army food. *Which?* Corneal ulcers . . can permanently impair vision. 2 SOUTHEY His own health and faculties impairing day by day.

impairer *n.* L16. **impairment** *n.* the action of impairing, the fact of being impaired ME.

impaired /ɪmˈpɛːd/ *ppl a.* E17. [f. IMPAIR *v.* + -ED[1].] 1 *gen.* That has been impaired. E17. 2 Of the driver of a vehicle, or driving: adversely affected by alcohol or narcotics. *Canad.* M20.

1 F. SPALDING An attack of rheumatic fever . . left his health permanently impaired. J. GATHORNE-HARDY They become anxious, their performance impaired. 2 *Toronto Daily Star* Ange Gardien . . was charged with impaired driving.

impala /ɪmˈpɑːlə, -ˈpalə/ *n.* Also **-lla**. L19. [Zulu *i-mpala*: cf. PALLAH.] A medium-sized reddish-brown grazing antelope, *Aepyceros melampus*, of southern and eastern African savannah, the male of which has lyre-shaped horns.

impalace /ɪmˈpalɪs/ *v.t. arch.* L18. [f. IM-[1] + PALACE.] Place or install in a palace. Usu. in *pass.*

impale /ɪmˈpeɪl/ *v.t.* Also **em-** /ɪm-, ɛm-/. M16. [Fr. *empaler* or med.L *impalare*, f. as IM-[1] + *palus* stake, PALE *n.*[1]] 1 Enclose with pales, stakes, etc.; surround (as) with a palisade; fence in (*lit.* & *fig.*). Now *rare*. M16. †b *Mil.* Enclose or surround (troops) for defence. M16–M17. 2 Surround for adornment; encircle as with a crown or garland; border, edge. *arch.* M16. 3 *Her.* Combine (two coats of arms, or one coat *with* another) by placing them side by side on one shield, separated by a vertical line down the middle. E17. 4 Transfix (a body etc. *on* or *with* a stake etc.), esp. (*Hist.*) as a form of torture or capital punishment. E17.

1 T. HOOD So he might impale a strip of soil. 2 LYTTON All the laurels that ever with praise Impaled human brows. 3 T. H. WHITE It was charged with the impaled arms of her husband and of her father. 4 R. GRAVES He would hang or impale any man found guilty of rape. B. COTTLE The cruel shrike . . impales his little victims on thorns. *fig.*: P. ACKROYD Impaled upon his own lacerating self-consciousness he has fantasies of suicide.

impaler *n.* L17. **impaling** *n.* (*a*) the action of the vb; (*b*) = IMPALEMENT 2: L16.

impalement /ɪmˈpeɪlm(ə)nt/ *n.* Also **em-** /ɪm-, ɛm-/. L16. [Fr. *empalement*, f. *empaler*: see prec., -MENT. Later f. the vb.] 1 The action or an act of enclosing with pales, stakes, etc.; an enclosing fence or palisade. L16. 2 *Her.* The combining of two coats of arms placed side by side on one shield and separated by a vertical line down the middle; the arms so combined. E17. 3 The action or an act of transfixing a body etc. on, *on*, or *with* a stake etc., esp. (*Hist.*) as a form of torture or capital punishment; the fact of being so impaled. M17. †4 *Bot.* The calyx of a flower; (in a plant of the composite family) the involucre. L17–L18.

impall /ɪmˈpɔːl/ *v.t. rare.* M17. [f. IM-[1] + PALL *n.*[1]] Enfold or wrap (as) in a pall.

impalla *n.* var. of IMPALA.

impalpable /ɪmˈpalpəb(ə)l/ *a.* E16. [Fr., or late L *impalpabilis*, f. as IM-[2] + PALPABLE.] 1 Imperceptible to the touch; intangible; *esp.* (of powder) very fine, not containing grains that can be felt. E16. 2 Not easily grasped or understood by the mind; producing no definite mental impression. L18.

2 H. STURGIS Sainty was aware of the slightest, most impalpable change in his friend's manner.

impalpaˈbility *n.* E17. **impalpably** *adv.* L18.

impalsy /ɪmˈpɔːlzi, -ˈpɒl-/ *v.t. rare.* L16. [f. IM-[1] + PALSY *n.*[1]] Affect (as) with palsy; paralyse.

impanate /ɪmˈpeɪnət/ *a.* M16. [med.L *impanatus* pa. pple of *impanare*, f. as IM-[1] + *panis* bread: see -ATE[2].] *Chr. Ch.* Of the body and blood of Christ: present in the bread (and wine) after consecration.

impanated /ɪmˈpeɪnətɪd/ *a.* Long *rare*. L16. [f. med.L *impanat-* (see next) + -ED[1].] = IMPANATE.

impanation /ɪmpəˈneɪʃ(ə)n/ *n.* M16. [med.L *impanatio(n-)*, f. *impanat-* pa. ppl stem of *impanare*: see IMPANATE, -ATION.] *Chr. Ch.* In Eucharistic doctrine: the presence of the body and blood of Christ in the bread (and wine) after consecration.

impanator /ˈɪmpəneɪtə/ *n.* M19. [med.L, f. as prec.: see -OR, -ATOR.] *Chr. Ch.* A person who holds the doctrine of impanation.

impanel /ɪmˈpan(ə)l/ *v.*[1]*t. rare.* Infl. **-ll-**, ***-l-**. L16. [f. IM-[1] + PANEL *n.*[1]] 1 Fit (as) with a panel or panels. L16. 2 Insert as a panel or panels. M19.

impanel *v.*[2] & *n.* var. of EMPANEL.

imparadise /ɪmˈparədʌɪs/ *v.t.* Also **em-** /ɪm-, ɛm-/. L16. [f. IM-[1], EM-[1] + PARADISE. Cf. Fr. *emparadiser*, It. *imparadisare*.] 1 Place (as) in paradise; bring into a state of supreme happiness; enrapture. L16. 2 Make a paradise of (a state or place). M17.

†**impardonable** *a.* E16–L18. [f. IM-[2] + PARDONABLE.] Not to be pardoned, unpardonable.

imparipinnate /ɪmˌparɪˈpɪnət/ *a.* M19. [f. L *impar* uneven after PARIPINNATE.] *Bot.* Pinnate with a terminal leaflet and an odd number of leaflets in all.

imparisyllabic /ɪmˌparɪsɪˈlabɪk/ *a.* & *n.* M18. [f. L *impar* unequal after PARISYLLABIC.] *Gram.* A *adj.* Of a Greek or Latin noun: not having the same number of syllables in all cases of the singular. M18. B *n.* An imparisyllabic noun. L19.

imparity /ɪmˈparɪti/ *n.* Now *rare* or *obs.* M16. [Late L *imparitas*, f. L *impar* unequal, uneven, f. as IM-[2] + *par* equal. Cf. PARITY *n.*[1]] 1 The quality or condition of being unequal: inequality. M16. †2 The quality of being unlike; dissimilarity in nature or character. Only in 17. †3 The quality, in a whole number, of not being divisible into two equal integral parts; an odd number. Only in M17.

impark /ɪmˈpɑːk/ *v.t.* LME. [AN *enparker*, OFr. *emparquer* (AL *imparcare*), f. as EM-[1], IM-[1] + *parc* PARK *n.*] 1 Enclose (animals) in a park. LME. 2 Enclose (land) for a park; fence in. LME.

imparl /ɪmˈpɑːl/ *v. obs.* exc. *Hist.* Also †**em-**. LME. [AN *enparler*, OFr. *emparler* speak, plead, f. as EM-[1], IM-[1] + *parler* speak: see PARLE.] 1 *v.i. Law.* (Obtain time to) confer in order to settle a dispute amicably. LME. †2 *v.i.* Consult *together* or *with* another on a matter; confer. LME–E17. †3 *v.t.* Talk over; discuss. *rare.* E17–E19.

imparlance /ɪmˈpɑːləns/ *n. obs.* exc. *Hist.* Also †**em-**. L16. [OFr. *emparlance*, f. *emparler*: see prec., -ANCE.] †1 The action of consulting together on a matter, esp. before taking action; conference, discussion. L16–E19. 2 *Law.* An extension of the time allowed for a response in pleading a case, so that the two parties can confer and negotiate an amicable settlement; a petition for, or the granting of, this time. E17.

imparsonee /ɪmˌpɑːsəˈniː/ *a.* E17. [Repr. med.L (*persona*) *impersonata*, f. L *im-* IN-[2] + AL *personata* fem. pa. pple of *personare* indict, institute, f. L *persona*: see PARSON, PERSON *n.*, -EE[1].] *Eccl. Hist.* Presented, instituted, and inducted into a parsonage or rectory. Only in *parson imparsonee.*

impart /ɪmˈpɑːt/ *v.* LME. [OFr. *impartir* f. L *impartire*, f. as IM-[1] + *part-*, *pars* PART *n.*] 1 *v.t.* Give a part or share of (a thing *to* a person etc.); bestow, give. LME. †2 *v.i.* Share, partake *in*. L15–E17. b *v.t.* Have or get a share of; share, partake. (Foll. by *of*.) M16–M17. 3 *v.t.* Communicate (information, news, etc., *to*); tell, relate, (a story, an account, etc.). M16. †4 *v.t.* Give a share of (something) to each of a number of people; distribute. M16–E17.

1 J. GALSWORTHY The moustache . . imparted a somewhat military look to his face. R. C. HUTCHINSON A particular countryside imparts a special character to the men it breeds. 3 J. AGATE The first object in writing is to impart information.

impartable *a.* (long *rare*) LME. **imparˈtation** *n.* the action of imparting, impartment, communication E19. **imparter** *n.* L16. **impartment** *n.* the action or fact of imparting; something imparted, *esp.* a communication: E17.

impartial /ɪmˈpɑːʃ(ə)l/ *a.* L16. [f. IM-[2] + PARTIAL *a.*] 1 Not partial; not favouring one party or side more than another; unprejudiced, unbiased; fair. L16. †2 Partial. L16–E17. †3 Not partial or fragmentary; entire, complete. *rare.* Only in E18.

1 J. G. FARRELL An impartial and objective justice was abandoned. P. NORMAN Mrs Durham made no distinction, treating Anthony and him with impartial severity.

impartialist *n.* a person who is or professes to be impartial M17. **impartially** *adv.* E17.

impartiality /ɪmˌpɑːʃɪˈalɪti/ *n.* E17. [f. IMPARTIAL + -ITY.] 1 The quality or character of being impartial; freedom from prejudice or bias; fairness. E17. †2 Completeness. *rare.* Only in E18.

impartible /ɪmˈpɑːtɪb(ə)l/ *a.* & *n.* L16. [Late L *impartibilis*, f. as IM-[2] + *partibilis* PARTIBLE.] A *adj.* Incapable of being divided or parted; indivisible L16. B *n.* A thing that is indivisible. L18.

impartiˈbility *n.* M17. **impartibly** *adv.* M17.

imparticipable /ɪmpɑːˈtɪsɪpəb(ə)l/ *a.* & *n.* L18. [f. IM-[2] + PARTICIPABLE.] (A thing that is) unable to be shared or participated in.

impartite /ɪmˈpɑːtʌɪt/ *a. rare.* M19. [f. IM-[2] + PARTITE.] Not divided into parts, undivided.

impassable /ɪmˈpɑːsəb(ə)l/ *a.* M16. [f. IM-[2] + PASSABLE, perh. through Fr. *impassable*.] 1 Impossible to traverse or travel through. M16. †2 That cannot pass (away or through). L18–M19. 3 Unable to be passed or made to pass. *rare.* M19.

1 M. KEANE Now, most of the paths were choked and impassable. 2 *Examiner* As impassable through Heaven's gates, as is a camel through the needle's eye. 3 *Pall Mall Gazette* When half a million gilt sixpences in circulation make half-sovereigns practically impassable.

impassaˈbility *n.* L18. **impassableness** *n.* E18. **impassably** *adv.* E19.

impasse /amˈpɑːs, ˈampɑːs, *foreign* ɛ̃pɑːs/ *n.* M19. [Fr., f. as IM-[2] + stem of *passer* PASS *v.*] 1 A position from which there is no escape, a deadlock. M19. 2 *lit.* A road etc. without an outlet, a blind alley. L19.

1 F. ASTAIRE I find myself blocked by a sort of mental impasse. E. M. BRENT-DYER Margot . . scribbled in the details . . thankful to be out of the impasse so easily.

impassible /ɪmˈpasɪb(ə)l/ *a.* ME. [(O)Fr. f. eccl.L *impassibilis*, f. as IM-[2] + PASSIBLE.] 1 Chiefly *Theol.* Incapable of suffering or feeling pain. ME. 2 Incapable of suffering injury or damage. L15. †3 Not to be endured; insufferable. E16–M17. 4 Incapable of feeling or emotion. L16.

impassiˈbility *n.* ME. **impassibleness** *n.* M17. **impassibly** *adv.* L17.

impassion /ɪmˈpaʃ(ə)n/ *v.t.* Also †**em-**. L16. [It. †*impassionare* (now *-nn-*), f. as IM-[1] + *passione* PASSION *n.*] Fill with passion; arouse the feelings of; excite.

impassionment *n.* (*rare*) the action of impassioning; the state of being impassioned: L16.

impassionate /ɪmˈpaʃ(ə)nət/ *a.*[1] Now *rare*. L16. [It. †*impassionato* pa. pple of †*impassionare*: see prec., -ATE[2].] = IMPASSIONED.

impassionately *adv.* E19.

impassionate /ɪmˈpaʃ(ə)nət/ *a.*[2] Now *rare*. E17. [f. IM-[2] + PASSIONATE *a.*] Free from passion; calm, dispassionate.

impassionate /ɪmˈpaʃ(ə)neɪt/ *v.* Now *rare* or *obs.* L16. [f. IMPASSIONATE *a.*[1]: see -ATE[3].] 1 *v.t.* = IMPASSION. L16. †2 *v.i.* Be or become impassioned. Only in M17.

impassioned /ɪmˈpaʃ(ə)nd/ *a.* Also †**em-**. E17. [f. IMPASSION + -ED[1].] Filled with passion; deeply moved or excited; passionate, ardent.

M. BARING An ardent naturalist and an impassioned bird's egg collector. P. GAY Erikson's book . . generated some impassioned debates.

impassionedly *adv.* M19. **impassionedness** *n.* L19.

impassive /ɪmˈpasɪv/ *a.* E17. [f. IM-[2] + PASSIVE *a.*] **1** Not subject or liable to suffering. E17. **2** Without sensation; impervious to injury; invulnerable. L17. **b** Deprived of sensation; unconscious. M19. **3** Unmoved by or not displaying emotion; calm. L17.

1 J. WESLEY He was impassive, incapable of suffering. 2 POPE On the impassive Ice the light'nings play. b DICKENS The two medical students seemed to look on the impassive form with . . so little hope. 3 F. POHL Knefhausen kept his face impassive, although his heart was filled with glee. S. HAZZARD Nicholas Cartledge was impassive, neither patient nor impatient.

impassively *adv.* E19. **impassiveness** *n.* M17. **impaˈssivity** *n.* L18.

impaste /ɪmˈpeɪst/ *v.t.* M16. [It. *impastare*, f. *im*- IM-[1] + *pasta* PASTE *n.*] **1** Enclose in or encrust (as) with a paste. M16. **2** Make or form into a paste or crust. L16. **3** Paint by laying colour on thickly. E18.

impasto /ɪmˈpastəʊ/ *n.* L18. [It., f. as prec.] **1** The action of painting by laying colour on thickly; this manner of painting. L18. **2** *Ceramics.* Enamel etc. colours standing out in relief on a surface. E20.

impatience /ɪmˈpeɪʃ(ə)ns/ *n.* LME. [(O)Fr. f. L *impatientia*, f. as IM-[2] + PATIENCE *n.*] **1** Failure to bear suffering, annoyance, etc., with equanimity; irascibility; intolerance *of*. Also foll. by *at*, *with*. LME. **2** Intolerance of delay; restless longing or eagerness (*for*, *to do*). L16.

2 M. KEANE His good manners hardly hid his impatience to be alone.

impatiency /ɪmˈpeɪʃ(ə)nsi/ *n.* Now *rare* or *obs.* M16. [L *impatientia*: see prec., -ENCY.] The quality or condition of being impatient; impatience; an instance of this.

impatiens /ɪmˈpatɪɛnz/ *n.* Pl. same. L18. [mod.L (see below) f. L = IMPATIENT, w. ref. to the readiness of the capsules to burst open when touched.] Any plant of the genus *Impatiens* (family Balsaminaceae), the members of which bear irregular spurred usu. showy flowers and include the garden balsam, *I. balsamina*, and the busy Lizzie, *I. walleriana*. Also called *balsam*, *touch-me-not*.

impatient /ɪmˈpeɪʃ(ə)nt/ *a.* & *n.* LME. [(O)Fr. f. L *impatient-*, *-ens*, f. as IM-[2] + PATIENT *a.*] **A** *adj.* †**1** Intolerable, unbearable. LME–M17. **2** Lacking patience; irritable, intolerant, easily provoked. LME. **b** Unable or unwilling to endure or put up with something; intolerant *of*. Also foll. by *at*, *with*. L15. **3** Unwilling to endure delay; in a hurry *for*, *to do*. L16. **4** Characterized by or expressive of impatience. E18.

2 SHAKES. *Mids. N. D.* Will you tear Impatient answers from my gentle tongue? C. G. WOLFF She certainly perceived her mother as remote, disapproving, impatient and unloving. b U. S. GRANT They were growing impatient at lying idle so long. L. GORDON He was impatient of the kind of research that seemed incapable of fruitful conclusions. 3 JANET MORGAN He was impatient for more authority. 4 M. SHADBOLT There was an impatient knock on the glass . . : someone else was waiting.

B *n.* An impatient person. E16.

impatiently *adv.* LME. **impatientness** *n.* (long *rare* or *obs.*) M16.

†**impatronize** *v.* Also **-ise**. L16. [Fr. *impatroniser* alt. of OFr. *empatroner*, *-ir*, f. or after It. *impatronire*, *impadronire*, f. as IM-[1] + (O)Fr. *patron*, It. *padrone* PATRON *n.*: see -IZE.] **1** *v.t.* Put (oneself, another) in possession *of*. L16–L17. **2** *v.t.* Take possession of. E17–L18.

†**impatronization** *n.* the action or an act of putting in possession *of* or taking possession of; mastery, possession: E17–M19.

impave /ɪmˈpeɪv/ *v.t. rare.* M17. [f. IM-[1] + PAVE *v.*] Set in a pavement, pave.

impavid /ɪmˈpavɪd/ *a. rare.* M19. [L *impavidus*, f. as IM-[2], PAVID.] Unafraid, undaunted.

impawn /ɪmˈpɔːn/ *v.t.* L16. [f. IM-[1] + PAWN *n.*[3] & *v.*] **1** Put in pawn, pledge as security; pawn. L16. **2** Pledge (*lit.* & *fig.*). E17.

1 SHAKES. *1 Hen. IV* Let there be impawn'd Some surety for a safe return again. J. WEST She offered to impawn the family jewels.

impayable /ɪmˈpeɪəb(ə)l; *in sense 3 foreign* ɛ̃pɛjabl/ *a.* ME. [Fr., f. as IM-[2] + *payer* PAY *v.*[1]: see -ABLE.] †**1** Implacable, unappeasable. Only in ME. **2** Impossible to pay or discharge. L18. **3** Priceless, invaluable; extraordinary, absurd. E19.

3 G. ALLEN I shrieked with laughter, 'Elsie,' I cried . . . 'you are *impayable*'.

impeach /ɪmˈpiːtʃ/ *n.* Also †**em-**. M16. [f. the vb.] †**1** Hindrance, impediment, prevention. M16–E17. †**2** Injury, damage, detriment. L16–E17. **3** Calling in question; (an) accusation. L16.

impeach /ɪmˈpiːtʃ/ *v.* Also †**em-**. LME. [OFr. *empe(s)cher* (mod. *empêcher* prevent) f. late L *impedicare* catch, entangle, f. as IM-[1] + *pedica* FETTER *n.*] †**1** *v.t.* Impede, hinder, prevent. LME–L17. **b** Prevent access to, blockade. LME–L16. **c** Embarrass or trouble *oneself*. L15–M16. †**2** *v.t.* Affect detrimentally; hurt, damage, impair. LME–L17. **3** *v.t.* Challenge, call in question; disparage. LME. **4** *v.t.* Make an accusation against (a person); accuse *of*, charge *with*. LME. **b** Give evidence against (esp. an accomplice); inform against. E17. **c** Find fault with (a thing). E19. **5** *v.t.* Accuse of treason or other high crime (esp. against the State) before a competent tribunal. LME.

3 A. K. GREEN My daughter's happiness is threatened and her character impeached. 4 W. GODWIN Go to the next justice of the peace and impeach us. b W. WYCHERLEY Because you know your self most guilty, you impeach your Fellow Criminals first. 5 H. COX Latimer was impeached and accused by the voice of the Commons. P. F. BOLLER The only President ever to be impeached, he behaved with dignity . . during the . . trial.

impeachable *a.* able to be impeached; liable to accusation or charge: LME. **impeacher** *n.* M16.

impeachment /ɪmˈpiːtʃm(ə)nt/ *n.* Also †**em-**. LME. [OFr. *empe(s)chement* (mod. *empêchement*), f. as prec. + -MENT.] †**1** Hindrance, prevention, obstruction. LME–L17. **2** Challenge, calling in question; disparagement, deprecation. LME. **3a** An accusation, a charge. Now *obs.* exc. (w. ref. to Sheridan's *The Rivals*) in *the soft impeachment*. LME. **b** Law. *impeachment of waste*, the liability of a tenant to make compensation for any damage to the rented property. LME. **c** The accusation and prosecution of a person for treason or other high crime (esp. against the State) before a competent tribunal. M17. †**4** Detriment, impairment, injury, damage. M16–M17.

impearl /ɪmˈpəːl/ *v.t. poet.* Also **em-** /ɪm-, ɛm-/. L16. [Fr. *emperler* or It. *impelare*, f. as EM-[1], IM-[1] + PEARL *n.*[1]] **1** Deck with pearls or pearl-like drops. L16. **2** Form into pearl-like drops. L16. **3** Make pearly or pearl-like. M17.

2 MILTON Dew-drops, which the Sun Impearls on every leaf and every flouer.

impeccable /ɪmˈpɛkəb(ə)l/ *a.* & *n.* M16. [L *impeccabilis*, f. as IM-[2] + *peccare* to sin: see -ABLE.] **A** *adj.* **1** Incapable of sin or error. M16. **2** Faultless, unblemished; unerring. E17.

1 H. LATIMER Though she never sinned, yet she was not so impeccable, but she might have sinned. A. SILLITOE It wouldn't do for the old folks to see him less than impeccable. 2 I. MURDOCH She had observed an impeccable discretion . . , so that hardly anyone knew her for a sympathizer. A. J. P. TAYLOR Thompson, a man of impeccable orthodoxy, had been appointed Dean of Divinity.

B *n.* An impeccable person. M18.

impeccaˈbility *n.* E17. **impeccableness** *n.* L17. **impeccably** *adv.* L19.

impeccancy /ɪmˈpɛk(ə)nsi/ *n.* E17. [eccl.L *impeccantia*, f. as IM-[2] + *peccantia* PECCANCY.] The quality of being without sin or error.

impeccant /ɪmˈpɛk(ə)nt/ *a.* M18. [f. IM-[2] + L *peccare* to sin + -ANT[1], or f. earlier PECCANT.] Without sin or error; blameless.

impecuniary /ɪmpɪˈkjuːnɪəri/ *a.* E19. [f. IM-[2] + PECUNIARY.] **1** = IMPECUNIOUS. E19. **2** Not having to do with money. M19.

impecunious /ɪmpɪˈkjuːnɪəs/ *a.* L16. [f. IM-[2] + PECUNIOUS.] In need of money; poor, penniless.

E. JOHNSON An impecunious youth making a precarious living.

impecuniˈosity *n.* lack of money, poverty E19. **impecuniousness** *n.* L20.

impedance /ɪmˈpiːd(ə)ns/ *n.* L19. [f. IMPEDE *v.* + -ANCE.] **1** *Electr.* The combined opposition to the passage of an (alternating) electric current exerted by the resistance (*R*) and the reactance (*X*), measured as the ratio of the electromotive force to the resulting current, and representable as $Z = \sqrt{(R^2 + X^2)}$ or as a complex number $R + jX$. L19. **2** *Mech.* & *Acoustics.* Any of several analogous properties of oscillatory mechanical systems that represent the force, pressure, etc., necessary to produce a given speed, rate of flow, etc. E20.

2 **acoustic impedance** the ratio of the pressure over an imaginary surface in a sound wave to the rate of flow across it. **mechanical impedance** the ratio of the force in the direction of motion to the velocity of the vibration. **specific acoustic impedance** the ratio of the pressure at any point in a sound wave to the resulting particle velocity.

impede /ɪmˈpiːd/ *v.t.* L16. [L *impedire*, lit. 'shackle the feet', f. as IM-[1] + *ped-*, *pes* foot.] Stand in the way of; obstruct, hinder.

W. GERHARDIE Our progress had been impeded by a car that blocked the road. A. S. NEILL He is holding back the work, and they may throw him out for impeding progress.

impedient /ɪmˈpiːdɪənt/ *a.* LME. [f. IMPEDE *v.* + -ENT, after EXPEDIENT *a.*] That impedes or hinders; obstructive.

impediment /ɪmˈpɛdɪm(ə)nt/ *n.* LME. [L *impedimentum* hindrance, pl. *-menta* baggage, f. *impedire* IMPEDE: see -I-, -MENT.] **1** The fact of impeding someone or something, the condition of being impeded; a hindrance, an obstruction. LME. **2** A physical defect, now esp. in one's speech, as a stammer, a stutter. L15. **3** *sing.* & (usu.) in *pl.* Travelling equipment, esp. of an army etc.; impedimenta. M16.

1 SHAKES. *Rich. III* Thus far . . Have we march'd on without impediment. P. LIVELY My gender was never an impediment. 2 A. FRASER His stiff manner, to which a speech impediment contributed. M. DRABBLE He had stammered atrociously . . . but he had learned to turn his impediment to advantage.

impediˈmental *a.* constituting an impediment; obstructive: L16.

impedimenta /ɪmˌpɛdɪˈmɛntə/ *n.pl.* E17. [L: see prec.] Travelling equipment, esp. of an army etc.; encumbrances.

G. GISSING Having stowed away certain impedimenta . . , he took his travelling-bag in his hand. HARPER LEE There was no sign of piano, organ, hymn-books, church programmes—the familiar ecclesiastical impedimenta.

impedite /ˈɪmpɪdʌɪt/ *v.t.* Now *rare* or *obs.* Pa. pple & ppl a. **-ited**, †**-ite**. M16. [L *impedit-* pa. ppl stem of *impedire* IMPEDE: see -ITE[2].] †**1** = IMPEDE. M16–L17. **2** *Astrol.* In *pass.* Of a planet: have its influence hindered by the position of another. M17.

impeditive /ɪmˈpɛdɪtɪv/ *a.* M17. [f. IMPEDITE *v.* + -IVE.] Tending to impede or obstruct; obstructive.

impel /ɪmˈpɛl/ *v.t.* Infl. **-ll-**. LME. [L *impellere*, f. as IM-[1] + *pellere* drive.] **1** Drive or cause to move onward; propel. LME. **2** Drive, force, or constrain (a person) *to* or *into* an action, *to do* something; urge, incite. L15.

1 J. IMISON A ship impelled by the wind and tide. 2 M. IGNATIEFF Man's . . . needs impel him forward on the path to their satisfaction.

impellent *a.* & *n.* (*a*) *adj.* driving or urging on, impelling; (*b*) *n.* an impelling force or agent: E17. **impeller** *n.* (*a*) *gen.* a person who or thing which impels; (*b*) *esp.* (the rotating part of) a machine designed to move a fluid by rotation, as a centrifugal pump or a compressor: L17. **impellor** *n.* = IMPELLER (b) E20.

impend /ɪmˈpɛnd/ *v.* L16. [L *impendere*, f. as IM-[1] + *pendere* hang.] **1** *v.i.* Of evil or danger: hang threateningly (*over*); loom. Also *gen.*, be about to happen; be imminent. L16. **2** *v.t.* Hover or loom over; be imminent or near to. *rare.* M17. **3** *v.i.* Hang or be suspended *over*; overhang. L18.

1 E. BOWEN A trough of low pressure, a negative feeling of bother, impended over her. G. PATTEN The strange thrill . . that invariably came upon him when danger threatened or battle impended. 2 W. PENN

The dreadful Judgments that now impend the Nation. 3 K. WHITE Mournful larches o'er the wave impend.

impendent /ɪm'pɛnd(ə)nt/ *a.* Now *rare.* L16. [L *impendent-* pres. ppl stem of *impendere*, or f. IMPEND: see prec., -ENT.] 1 = IMPENDING I. L16. 2 = IMPENDING 2. E17.

impendence *n.* imminence M17. **impendency** *n.* imminent or threatening character; an impending circumstance: M17.

impending /ɪm'pɛndɪŋ/ *a.* L17. [f. IMPEND + -ING².] 1 Of evil, danger, etc.: threatening, imminent. L17. 2 Overhanging. Now *rare.* M18.

1 R. COBB She had an annoying habit of being able to spot impending disaster well ahead. R. V. JONES It was brought about by the impending collapse of France—now only five days away. 2 W. COWPER Terribly arch'd and aquiline his nose, And overbuilt with most impending brows.

impenetrability /ɪm,pɛnɪtrə'bɪlɪti/ *n.* M17. [f. next: see -ABILITY.] 1 That property of matter in virtue of which two bodies cannot occupy the same space at the same time. M17. 2 The quality or condition of being impenetrable; imperviousness, inscrutability. E18.

impenetrable /ɪm'pɛnɪtrəb(ə)l/ *a.* LME. [(O)Fr. *impénétrable* f. L *impenetrabilis*, f. as IM-² + *penetrabilis* PENETRABLE.] 1 Impossible to penetrate, pierce, or enter. LME. 2 Impossible to understand; inscrutable, unfathomable. M16. 3 Impervious to intellectual or moral influences, impressions, or ideas. L16. 4 Of matter: having impenetrability. M17.

1 TOLKIEN Coats of mail gilded and silvered and impenetrable. J. JOHNSTON Impenetrable banks of rhododendrons bordered the avenue. 2 A. POWELL Features at once expressive and impenetrable, concealing as much as they revealed. *Times* Passages of rhapsodic flimflam recalling Marie Corelli at her most impenetrable. 3 E. WHARTON Minds impenetrable to reason have generally some crack through which suspicion filters.

impenetrableness *n.* L17. **impenetrably** *adv.* M17.

impenetrate /ɪm'pɛnɪtreɪt/ *v.t.* M19. [f. IM-¹ + PENETRATE.] Penetrate deeply, permeate.

impene'tration *n.* M19.

impenetrative /ɪm'pɛnɪtrətɪv/ *a. rare.* L17. [f. IM-² + PENETRATIVE.] Not penetrating or incisive.

impenitence /ɪm'pɛnɪt(ə)ns/ *n.* E17. [Late (eccl.) L *impaenitentia*, f. as IM-² + *paenitentia* PENITENCE. Cf. Fr. *impénitence.*] The fact or condition of being impenitent; hardness of heart, obduracy.

impenitency *n.* the quality or state of being impenitent M16.

impenitent /ɪm'pɛnɪt(ə)nt/ *a.* & *n.* LME. [eccl.L *impaenitent-*, f. as IM-² + *paenitent-*: see PENITENT *a.* Cf. Fr. *impénitent.*] A *adj.* Not penitent; having no contrition for sin; obdurate, unrepentant. LME.

J. CAIRD To forgive an impenitent man and to continue to punish a penitent are equally impossible.

B *n.* An impenitent person. M16.

impenitently *adv.* M17.

†impeople *v.* var. of EMPEOPLE.

†imperate *v.t.* Pa. pple & ppl a. **-ate** (earlier), **-ated.** LME-E18. [Orig. pa. pple, f. L *imperatus* pa. pple of *imperare* command, rule: see -ATE², -ATE³.] Command, rule.

†imperation *n.* (*rare*) the action of commanding: only in L18.

imperatival /ɪm,pɛrə'tʌɪv(ə)l/ *a.* L19. [f. next + -AL¹.] *Gram.* Of or pertaining to the imperative mood.

imperative /ɪm'pɛrətɪv/ *a.* & *n.* LME. [Late L *imperativus* lit. 'specially ordered' tr. Gk *prostaktikē* (*egklisis* mood), f. L *imperat-* pa. ppl stem of *imperare* command, rule: see EMPEROR, -ATIVE.] A *adj.* 1 *Gram.* Designating or pertaining to a grammatical mood expressing a command, request, or exhortation. LME. 2 Having the quality or property of commanding; characterized by or expressing a command; peremptory. L16. 3 Demanding obedience, action, etc.; that must be done or performed; urgent; obligatory. E19.

1 **imperative logic** *Philos.* a system of formal logic based on the commands and obligations contained in the imperative mood. 2 M. KEANE She gave these orders in an imperative, hot rush of words. 3 T. COLLINS It was absolutely imperative that I should go thirty miles.

B *n.* 1 *Gram.* The imperative mood; a word, form, etc., in the imperative mood. M16. 2 An imperative action, speech, condition, etc.; an action etc. involving or expressing a command. E17.

2 C. G. WOLFF Edith Wharton.. had rejected the social imperative of feminine passivity. CATEGORICAL *imperative. territorial imperative*: see TERRITORIAL *a.*

imperatively *adv.* E17. **imperativeness** *n.* M19. **imperativism** *n.* (*Philos.*) a form of reasoning based on the concept of obligation contained in the imperative mood E20. **imperativist** *n.* & *a.* (*Philos.*) (*a*) *n.* a person who bases his or her reasoning on a concept of obligation; (*b*) *adj.* of or pertaining to reasoning based on a concept of obligation: M20.

imperator /ɪmpə'rɑːtɔː/ *n.* Also (as a title) **I-.** M16. [L, f. *imperat-*: see IMPERATIVE, -OR. Cf. PRINCEPS.] 1 *Rom. Hist.* Orig., commander (a title conferred by the salutation of soldiers on a victorious general under the Republic). Later, head of the State (in whose name all victories were won), emperor. Cf. PRINCEPS. M16. 2 *gen.* An absolute ruler, an emperor; a commander. Long *rare* or *obs.* L16.

imperatorship *n.* the rank or position of imperator M19.

imperatorial /ɪm,pɛrə'tɔːrɪəl/ *a.* M17. [f. L *imperatorius*, f. as prec., + -AL¹.] Of or pertaining to an imperator, emperor, or commander; imperial.

impera'torially *adv.* (*rare*) M19.

imperatrix /ɪmpə'rɑːtrɪks/ *n.* Also (as a title) **I-.** Pl. **-trices** /-trɪsiːz/. E17. [L, fem. of IMPERATOR: see -TRIX.] An empress.

imperceivable /ɪmpə'siːvəb(ə)l/ *a. rare.* E17. [f. IM-² + PERCEIVABLE.] Imperceptible.

imperceivableness *n.* E18. **imperceivably** *adv.* E17.

†imperceiverant *a. rare* (Shakes.). Only in E17. [f. IM-² + alt. (w. insertion of *-er-*) of Fr. *percevant* pres. pple of *percevoir* PERCEIVE: see -ANT¹.] Not perceiving; undiscerning.

imperceptibility /,ɪmpəsɛptɪ'bɪlɪti/ *n.* E17. [f. next + -ILITY.] The quality or condition of being imperceptible; inability to be perceived.

imperceptible /ɪmpə'sɛptɪb(ə)l/ *a.* & *n.* LME. [Fr., or f. med.L *imperceptibilis*, f. as IM-² + late L *perceptibilis* PERCEPTIBLE.] A *adj.* 1 Unable by its nature to be perceived. LME. 2 So slight, gradual, or subtle, as to be hardly perceptible. M17.

1 A. TUCKER Some diseases.. proceeding from an imperceptible vermin within us. 2 P. CAREY A series of moves as imperceptible as the hands of a clock.

B *n.* An imperceptible thing. E18.

imperceptibleness *n.* L17. **imperceptibly** *adv.* E17.

imperception /ɪmpə'sɛpʃ(ə)n/ *n.* M17. [f. IM-² + PERCEPTION.] Absence or lack of perception.

imperceptive /ɪmpə'sɛptɪv/ *a.* M17. [f. IM-² + PERCEPTIVE *a.*] Not perceptive or perceiving; lacking perception.

impercipient /ɪmpə'sɪpɪənt/ *a.* & *n.* E19. [f. IM-² + PERCIPIENT *a.*] A *adj.* Not perceiving; lacking perception. E19. B *n.* A person who lacks perception. L19.

impercipience *n.* L19.

imperfect /ɪm'pəːfɪkt/ *a.* & *n.* ME. [(O)Fr. *imparfait* f. L *imperfectus*, f. as IM-² + *perfectus* PERFECT *a.*] A *adj.* I 1 Lacking some quality or attribute necessary for full efficiency or normality; substandard; faulty. ME. 2 Lacking some usual or necessary part; not fully formed or done; incomplete. LME. †3 Committing a fault, vicious, evil. LME-M17. 4 Of a person: not fully accomplished or instructed *in.* L16. II 5 *Gram.* Designating, being in, or pertaining to a verbal aspect or a tense denoting a (usu. past) action going on but not completed. LME. 6 *Mus.* Orig. (of a note), that is twice rather than three times the length of a note of the next lower denomination. Later (of an interval), that is other than a fourth, fifth, or octave. LME. †7 *Math.* (Of a number) not equal to the sum of its factors; (of a square, cube, etc.) having an irrational root. M16-E18. 8 *Bot.* Of a flower: lacking some normal part; now *esp.* lacking functional stamens or pistils. E18. b *Mycol.* (Of a state or stage in the fungal life cycle) characterized by asexual spores, or by absence of spores; (of a fungus) in the asexual state, *esp.* having no (known) sexual state. L19. 9 *Law.* Not binding. M19.

Special collocations: **imperfect cadence** *Mus.* a cadence ending on a chord other than the direct chord of the tonic. **imperfect competition** *Econ.* a commercial situation in which elements of monopoly allow individual producers or consumers to exercise some control over a market price. **imperfect induction** *Philos.* induction from an incomplete set of instances. **imperfect rhyme** a rhyme that only partly satisfies the usual criteria (e.g. English *love* and *move*).

B *n.* 1 *Gram.* The imperfect aspect or tense; a word, form, etc., in an imperfect aspect or tense. L19. 2 In *pl.* Goods of imperfect quality that must be sold at a reduced price. M20.

imperfectly *adv.* LME. **imperfectness** *n.* LME.

imperfect /ɪm'pəːfɪkt, ɪmpə'fɛkt/ *v.t.* M16. [f. IMPERFECT *a.* or f. IM-² + PERFECT *v.*] 1 Make imperfect; destroy the perfection of. Long *rare.* M16. 2 Not make perfect; not complete. Chiefly as *imperfected* ppl a. M16.

imperfectible /ɪmpə'fɛktɪb(ə)l/ *a. rare.* M19. [f. IM-² + PERFECTIBLE.] Unable to be made perfect.

imperfecti'bility *n.* M19.

imperfection /ɪmpə'fɛkʃ(ə)n/ *n.* LME. [(O)Fr. f. late L *imperfectio(n-)*, f. *imperfectus* IMPERFECT *a.*: see -ION.] 1 The condition or quality of being imperfect; incompleteness; faultiness. Also, an instance of this; a fault, a blemish. LME. 2 *Mus.* The action of causing a note to be twice rather than three times the length of a note of the next lower denomination. Also, the condition of such a note. Now *rare* or *obs.* L16. 3a *Printing.* In *pl.* Letters that are lacking in a font; types cast or supplied to make up a deficiency in a font. *obs.* exc. *Hist.* L17. b *Bookbinding.* A surplus or missing sheet. L17.

1 A. MASON He must be free from any imperfection of body, any frailty of mind. J. VIORST With all its imperfections, the psychoanalytic perspective offers the most profound insights.

imperfective /ɪmpə'fɛktɪv/ *n.* & *a.* E17. [f. IMPERFECT *a.* + -IVE.] A *n.* †1 An imperfection. *rare.* Only in E17. 2 *Gram.* An imperfective aspect or form of a verb. M20. B *adj.* †1 Characterized by imperfection; imperfect. Only in L17. 2 *Gram.* Designating, being in, or pertaining to a verbal aspect expressing action without reference to its completion. M19.

imperforable /ɪm'pəːf(ə)rəb(ə)l/ *a.* M17. [med.L *imperforabilis*, f. as IM-² + *perforare* PERFORATE *v.* + -ABLE.] Unable to be perforated.

imperforate /ɪm'pəːfərət/ *a.* L17. [f. IM-² + PERFORATE *a.*] 1 Chiefly *Anat.* & *Zool.* Not perforated; having no perforation, opening, or foramen; (of the anus etc.) not having the opening normally present. L17. 2 Of a sheet of postage stamps or a single stamp: not provided with rows of perforations. L19.

imperforated /ɪm'pəːfəreɪtɪd/ *a.* M17. [f. IM-² + PERFORATED.] Not perforated, imperforate.

imperforation /,ɪmpəːfə'reɪʃ(ə)n/ *n.* M17. [f. IM-² + PERFORATION.] The condition of being imperforate; an instance of this.

imperformable /ɪmpə'fɔːməb(ə)l/ *a. rare.* L17. [f. IM-² + PERFORMABLE.] Unable to be performed.

imperial /ɪm'pɪərɪəl/ *a.* & *n.* Also **†em-.** LME. [(O)Fr. *impérial* f. L *imperialis*, f. *imperium* rule, EMPIRE: see -AL¹, -IAL.] A *adj.* I 1 Of or pertaining to an empire or a sovereign State ranking with an empire; *spec.* (*Hist.*) of or pertaining to the British Empire. LME. 2 Of or pertaining to an emperor (also in honorific titles). LME. 3 Of the nature or rank of an emperor or supreme ruler; supreme in authority. LME. 4 Having a commanding quality or aspect; majestic; august. LME. b Assuming or affecting a commanding manner; domineering; imperious. L16. 5 Appropriate to an emperor or supreme ruler; magnificent. M18.

1 A. GHOSH A drive by the imperial government to recruit Indians for an expeditionary force. 2 J. BRODSKY Tsarskoe Selo . . was the summer residence of the imperial family. *Her* etc. *Imperial Highness*, *Your* etc. *Imperial Majesty*.

II 6 Designating any of various products or commodities of a certain (esp. a great) size or quality. M17. **b** *spec.* Chiefly *Hist.* Designating a size of paper, 30 × 22 inches (762 × 559 mm) or (*US*) 31 × 23 inches (787 × 584 mm). M17. **7** Of non-metric weights and measures: used or formerly used by statute in Britain. M19.

Special collocations: **imperial eagle** a large eagle, *Aquila heliaca*, of southern Europe and central Asia, having dark plumage with white on the head and neck. **imperial elephant, mammoth**: of the extinct species *Mammuthus imperator*, of the Pleistocene of N. America. *imperial* GALLON. *imperial mammoth*: see *imperial elephant* above. *imperial pint*: see PINT *n.*[1] I. **imperial preference** a system of tariff concessions granted by members of the British Empire or Commonwealth to one another.

B *n.* †**1** A kind of silk cloth. L15–L19. **2** A follower or adherent of an emperor; a member of a body of imperial troops. E16. **b** An emperor; an imperial personage. L16. **3** A kind of card-game combining features of écarté and piquet. Now *rare* or *obs.* L16. **4 a** A former Flemish coin. *obs.* exc. *Hist.* L17. **b** A gold coin formerly in use in Russia. *obs.* exc. *Hist.* M19. **5** A former size of paper, 30 × 22 inches (762 × 559 mm) or (*US*) 787 × 584 mm. E18. **6** Chiefly *Hist.* A trunk for luggage fitted on to or adapted for the roof of a coach. L18. **7** [Chiefly associated with the Emperor Napoleon III of France.] A small part of a beard left growing beneath the lower lip. M19.

imperially *adv.* M16. **imperialness** *n.* E18.

imperialise *v.* var. of IMPERIALIZE.

imperialism /ɪmˈpɪərɪəlɪz(ə)m/ *n.* M19. [f. IMPERIAL + -ISM.] **1** An imperial system of government; the (esp. despotic or arbitrary) rule of an emperor. M19. **2** The principle or spirit of empire; *spec.* (*Hist.*) the extending of the British Empire where trade required the protection given by imperial rule, the union of different parts of the British Empire for purposes of warlike defence, internal commerce, etc. L19. **3** (The belief in the desirability of) the acquisition of colonies and dependencies, or the extension of a country's influence through trade, diplomacy, etc. Usu. *derog.* E20.

1 *fig.*: D. H. LAWRENCE Let us have done with the ugly imperialism of any absolute. 3 N. GORDIMER South Africa is an advanced capitalist state in the last stage of imperialism.

imperialist /ɪmˈpɪərɪəlɪst/ *n.* & *a.* E17. [f. IMPERIAL + -IST, after Fr. *impérialiste*.] **A** *n.* **1** A follower or adherent of an emperor, esp. (1600–1800) of the Holy Roman Emperor. E17. **2** An advocate of imperial rule or of an imperial form of government. E19. **3** An advocate or agent of (esp. British or American) imperialism. L19. **B** *attrib.* or as *adj.* Adhering, pertaining to, or characteristic of imperialism. M19.

imperiaˈlistic *a.* of, pertaining to, or characteristic of an imperialist or imperialism L19. **imperiaˈlistically** *adv.* L19.

imperiality /ˌɪmpɪərɪˈalɪti/ *n.* LME. [f. IMPERIAL + -ITY.] †**1** Imperial rank, power, or authority. LME–E17. **2** An emperor; an imperial personage, such personages collectively. *joc.* L19.

imperialize /ɪmˈpɪərɪəlʌɪz/ *v.* Also **-ise**. M17. [f. as prec. + -IZE.] †**1** *v.i.* Behave as an emperor or absolute ruler. *rare.* Only in M17. **2** *v.t.* †**a** Attach to the cause of an emperor. *rare.* Only in M17. **b** Cause to be or adhere to an empire or imperial policy. E19.

imperil /ɪmˈpɛrɪl, -r(ə)l/ *v.t.* Also †**em-**. Infl. **-ll-**, ***-l-**. LME. [f. IM-[1], EM-[1] + PERIL, prob. after *endanger*.] Bring or put into danger, risk.

J. BERMAN The mother's life was also imperilled.

imperious /ɪmˈpɪərɪəs/ *a.* M16. [L *imperiosus*, f. *imperium* rule, EMPIRE + -OUS.] **1** Overbearing, domineering, dictatorial. M16. †**2** Having imperial rank; belonging or appropriate to an emperor or supreme ruler. L16–E18. †**3** Exercising a commanding influence; ruling, sovereign; having a commanding position, demeanour, etc.; majestic. L16–E19. **4** That conveys an absolute command or demand; urgent, imperative. (Earlier in IMPERIOUSLY 2.) E17.

1 L. STRACHEY There were signs of an imperious, a peremptory temper, an egotism that was strong and hard. 4 O. MANNING Gibbon held up an imperious hand and Beaker's apology limped to a halt.

imperiously /ɪmˈpɪərɪəsli/ *adv.* M16. [f. prec. + -LY[2].] **1** In a domineering manner; overbearingly, dictatorially. M16. **2** In the manner of an absolute command or demand; urgently, imperatively. M16. †**3** In the manner of supreme or absolute rule, imperially, majestically. L16–M17.

imperiousness /ɪmˈpɪərɪəsnɪs/ *n.* L16. [f. as prec. + -NESS.] †**1** Imperial character or dignity; absolute rule or sovereignty; empire. L16–L17. **2** Overbearing character, disposition, or manner. E17. **3** Overmastering or imperative quality; urgency. M17.

imperishable /ɪmˈpɛrɪʃəb(ə)l/ *a.* & *n.* M17. [f. IM-[2] + PERISHABLE *a.*] **A** *adj.* That cannot perish; not subject to decay; indestructible, immortal, enduring. M17. **B** *n.* An imperishable person or thing. E20.

imperishaˈbility *n.* E19. **imperishableness** *n.* E19. **imperishably** *adv.* E19.

†**imperite** *a.* E17–E18. [L *imperitus* inexperienced, unskilled, f. as IM-[2] + *peritus* experienced.] Unskilled, ignorant.

imperium /ɪmˈpɪərɪəm/ *n.* M17. [L.] Command; absolute power; supreme or imperial power; empire.

imperium in imperio /ɪn ɪmˈpɪərɪəʊ/ a supreme authority within the jurisdiction of another authority.

impermanent /ɪmˈpəːmənənt/ *a.* M17. [f. IM-[2] + PERMANENT *a.*] Not permanent or lasting; unenduring; transient.

impermanence *n.* the fact or condition of being impermanent; lack of permanence: L18. **impermanency** *n.* the quality or state of being impermanent, impermanence M17.

impermeable /ɪmˈpəːmɪəb(ə)l/ *a.* L17. [Fr. *imperméable* f. late L *impermeabilis*, f. as IM-[2] + *permeabilis* PERMEABLE.] **1** Unable to be penetrated through. L17. **2** *spec.* Not permitting the passage of water, or of other liquids or gases. M18.

impermeaˈbility *n.* M18.

impermeated /ɪmˈpəːmɪeɪtɪd/ *a.* E19. [f. IM-[2] + PERMEATE *v.* + -ED[1].] Not permeated, not penetrated.

impermissible /ɪmpəˈmɪsɪb(ə)l/ *a.* M19. [f. IM-[2] + PERMISSIBLE.] Not permissible; not to be allowed.

impermissiˈbility *n.* M20.

imperscriptible /ɪmpəˈskrɪptɪb(ə)l/ *a. rare.* M19. [f. IM-[2] + L *perscript-* pa. ppl stem of *perscribere* write at length, register, f. as PER-[1] + *scribere* write, + -IBLE.] Not backed by a written authority.

impersistent /ɪmpəˈsɪst(ə)nt/ *a.* M19. [f. IM-[2] + PERSISTENT *a.*] Not persistent or enduring.

impersonal /ɪmˈpəːs(ə)n(ə)l/ *a.* & *n.* LME. [Late L *impersonalis*, f. as IM-[2] + *personalis* PERSONAL *a.*] **A** *adj.* **1** *Gram.* Of a verb: used only in the 3rd person sing. without a definite subject, as English *it snows*, *methinks*. Of a pronoun: used to designate an unspecified referent, as English *any*, *some*, *anyone*, *something*. LME. **2** Having no personal feeling, reference, or tone. M17. **3** Having no personality; not existing as a person. M19.

2 E. GLASGOW An economic disaster was as impersonal as an earthquake. J. BRODSKY Even the most ardent anti-Semitic remarks bore an air of impersonal inertia.

B *n. Gram.* An impersonal verb. E17.

impersoˈnality *n.* (*a*) impersonal quality; (*b*) an impersonal being or creation: M18. **impersonally** *adv.* L16. **impersonalness** *n.* L19.

impersonate /ɪmˈpəːs(ə)nət/ *a. arch.* E19. [f. as next: see -ATE[2].] Embodied in a person; invested with personality; impersonated.

impersonate /ɪmˈpəːs(ə)neɪt/ *v.t.* E17. [f. IM-[1] + L *persona* PERSON *n.* + -ATE[3], after *incorporate*.] **1** Represent in a personal or bodily form; personify. E17. **b** Manifest in one's own person; typify. M19. **2** Pretend to be (another person) for the purpose of entertainment or fraud; act (a character). E18.

1 W. WARBURTON The Jews and Christians, as well as the Heathens, impersonated Chance under the name of Fortune. H. H. MILMAN His age acknowledged Benedict as the perfect type of . . religion, and Benedict impersonated his age. 2 CONAN DOYLE He would have to dispose of the body . . and . . find a substitute who would impersonate her. K. TYNAN The plot requires all three of its women to impersonate beardless boys.

impersonation /ɪmˌpəːsəˈneɪʃ(ə)n/ *n.* E19. [f. prec.: see -ATION.] **1** The action of impersonating someone; the fact of being impersonated; personification. E19. **b** An instance of this; a person or thing representing a principle, idea, etc. M19. **2** The dramatic or comic representation of a character; an instance of this. E19.

1 R. TRAVERS Had McHattie spoken to . . 'Lee Weller' . . Frank Butler would have been arrested . . for impersonation. **b** C. MERIVALE He proclaimed himself . . the supreme impersonation of the laws. 2 W. H. AUDEN Started to joke about their time at St Edmund's and . . do impersonations of the staff.

impersonator /ɪmˈpəːs(ə)neɪtə/ *n.* M19. [f. IMPERSONATE *v.* + -OR.] A person who impersonates others.

FEMALE *impersonator*. *male impersonator*: see MALE *a.* & *n.*

impersonify /ɪmpəˈsɒnɪfʌɪ/ *v.t. arch.* E19. [f. IM-[1] + PERSONIFY, after *impersonate*.] Personify.

impersonifiˈcation *n.* L18.

imperspirable /ɪmpəˈspʌɪərəb(ə)l/ *a.* Now *rare.* L17. [f. IM-[2] + PERSPIRABLE.] Not capable of perspiring.

impersuadable /ɪmpəˈsweɪdəb(ə)l/ *a.* E18. [f. IM-[2] + PERSUADABLE.] Not persuadable.

impertinence /ɪmˈpəːtɪnəns/ *n.* E17. [(O)Fr., or f. IMPERTINENT *a.*: see -ENCE. Cf. next.] **1** Lack of pertinence; irrelevance. Also, an instance of this; an irrelevance. E17. **2** The fact or character of being out of place; inappropriateness; absurdity. Also, an instance of this; an incongruity; an absurdity. E17. **3** Impertinent interference; presumption; insolence in speech or behaviour, esp. to a superior; lack of proper respect. Also, an instance of this. E18.

1 MILTON Of like impertinence is that Example of Jacob, . . who . . vow'd the Tenth of all that God should give him. 2 R. SOUTH A Petition, fraught with Nonsense and Incoherence, Confusion and Impertinence. 3 HAZLITT We resent wholesome counsel as an impertinence. C. S. FORESTER Your impertinence in presenting yourself . . in your present state of ignorance.

impertinency /ɪmˈpəːtɪnənsi/ *n.* Now *rare.* L16. [f. as prec.: see -ENCY.] **1** = IMPERTINENCE 2. L16. **2** = IMPERTINENCE 1. E17. **3** = IMPERTINENCE 3. E17.

impertinent /ɪmˈpəːtɪnənt/ *a.* & *n.* LME. [(O)Fr., or late L *impertinent-*, *-ens* not pertinent: see IM-[2], PERTINENT *a.*] **A** *adj.* **1** Not belonging (*to*); unconnected, unrelated. Long *rare* or *obs.* LME. **2** Not pertaining to the matter in hand; irrelevant. Now *rare* exc. *Law.* LME. **3** Out of place; inappropriate, incongruous; absurd. L16. †**b** Of a person: absurd, silly. M17–E18. **4** Interfering in what does not concern one; presumptuous; insolent in speech or behaviour, esp. to a superior; lacking in proper respect. E17.

1 COLERIDGE The more distant, disjointed and impertinent to . . any common purpose, will they appear. 2 J. S. WHARTON The costs occasioned by any impertinent matter . . to be paid by the party introducing it. 3 P. BARROUGH Many ignorant practitioners . . have endeavoured to cure this infirmity with many impertinent medicines. 4 I. MURDOCH People will ask questions, including impertinent ones about your sex life. A. MUNRO He would think it impertinent, for anybody to assume he is sad.

B *n.* †**1** An impertinent or irrelevant matter. Only in E17. **2** An impertinent person. *arch.* M17.

2 W. P. SCARGILL Henry St. John . . rebuked the young impertinents.

impertinently *adv.* LME. **impertinentness** *n.* (long *rare* or *obs.*) L17.

imperturbable /ɪmpəˈtəːbəb(ə)l/ *a.* LME. [Late L *imperturbabilis*, f. as IM-² + *perturbare* PERTURB: see -ABLE.] Not perturbable or excitable; (habitually) calm.

A. LEWIS Weston looked at her, surprised at the emotion . . this normally imperturbable woman was showing.

imperturbaˈbility *n.* M19. **imperturbableness** *n.* M19. **imperturbably** *adv.* M19.

imperturbation /ˌɪmpəːtəˈbeɪʃ(ə)n/ *n.* M17. [Late (eccl.) L *imperturbatio(n-)*, f. as IM-² + PERTURBATION.] Freedom from perturbation; calmness.

imperturbed /ɪmpəˈtəːbd/ *a.* E18. [f. IM-² + PERTURBED.] Not perturbed; undisturbed, unmoved.

imperviable /ɪmˈpəːvɪəb(ə)l/ *a.* E19. [Alt. of IMPERVIOUS: see -ABLE.] Impervious; impermeable.

impervious /ɪmˈpəːvɪəs/ *a.* M17. [f. L *impervius*, f. as IM-² + PERVIOUS: see -OUS.] **1** Not affording passage (*to* water etc.); impenetrable. M17. **2** *fig.* Not responsive (*to* argument, feeling, etc.). M17.

1 N. CALDER The overlying rocks must be impervious, otherwise the oil simply escapes. **2** H. GUNTRIP There is something wrong . . if our theoretical ideas remain . . impervious to change for too long. M. DRABBLE They were impervious both to his charm and to his aggression.

imperviously *adv.* L18. **imperviousness** *n.* E18.

impest /ɪmˈpɛst/ *v.t.* Also **em-** /ɛm-, ɪm-/. L16. [Fr. *empester*, f. as EM-¹, IM-¹ + PEST.] Infect with a plague or pestilence.

impetigo /ɪmpɪˈtʌɪɡəʊ/ *n.* Pl. **-tigos**, **-tigines** /-ˈtɪdʒɪniːz/. LME. [L, f. *impetere* assail, attack: see IMPETUS.] *Med.* Any of various pustular skin diseases. Now *esp.* a contagious acute superficial skin infection (esp. of children) usu. caused by staphylococci and producing vesicles and crusted inflammation.

impetiginous /ɪmpɪˈtɪdʒɪnəs/ *a.* pertaining to, resembling, or of the nature of impetigo E17.

impetrate /ˈɪmpətrət/ *a.* Long *obs.* exc. *Sc.* L15. [L *impetratus* pa. pple, f. as next: see -ATE².] Obtained by request; impetrated.

impetrate /ˈɪmpətreɪt/ *v.t.* Pa. t. & pple **-ated**, (long *obs.* exc. *Sc.*) **-ate** /-ət/. L15. [L *impetrat-* pa. ppl stem of *impetrare*, f. as IM-¹ + *patrare* bring to pass: see -ATE³. Cf. PERPETRATE.] **1** Chiefly *Theol.* Obtain by request or entreaty; procure. L15. **2** Entreat, beseech; ask for. Now *rare.* M16.

impetrative *a.* (*rare*) impetratory E17. **impetratory** *a.* (chiefly *Theol.*) having the quality of obtaining something (as) by request E17.

impetration /ɪmpəˈtreɪʃ(ə)n/ *n.* L15. [AN *impetracioun* or L *impetratio(n-)*, f. as prec.: see -ATION.] **1** Chiefly *Theol.* The action or an act of obtaining something by request. L15. **b** *Eccl. Hist.* The obtaining from the court of Rome of English church benefices in the gift of the king etc. L15. **c** *Law* (now *Hist.*). The obtaining of a writ. M17. **2** Entreaty, request. E17.

impetuosity /ɪmˌpɛtjʊˈɒsɪti/ *n.* LME. [(O)Fr. *impétuosité* f. late L *impetuositas*, f. *impetuosus*: see next, -ITY.] The quality or character of being impetuous; vehemence; an instance of this.

J. PINKERTON Flames . . issued forth with great impetuosity. S. T. WARNER I have always regretted the impetuosity with which I have given books and letters away.

impetuous /ɪmˈpɛtjʊəs/ *a.* LME. [f. (O)Fr. *impétueux* f. late L *impetuosus*, f. as IMPETUS: see -OUS, -UOUS.] **1** Moving violently or rapidly. LME. **2** Acting with or done with rash or sudden energy; vehement; ardent. LME.

1 S. WILLIAMS Strength to resist the most impetuous winds. **2** S. HAZZARD After the impetuous beginning, he would puzzle them by turning out staid and cautious. J. BARNES An ardent, impetuous nature which fretted at any wanton infliction of disappointment or boredom.

impetuously *adv.* L15. **impetuousness** *n.* LME.

impetus /ˈɪmpɪtəs/ *n.* M17. [L = assault, force, f. *impetere* assail, f. as IM-¹ + *petere* seek.] **1** The force or energy with which a body moves; impulsion. M17. **2** *fig.* Moving force, (an) impulse, a stimulus. M17.

1 A. THWAITE The current . . takes its impetus and gathers speed Only beyond the sluice-gate. **2** H. ARENDT Only in Austria did the revolutionary impetus find its natural outlet. M. MUGGERIDGE A visit . . by Gandhi . . gave a great impetus to Swarajist sentiment among the students.

Impeyan /ˈɪmpɪən/ *a.* & *n.* Also **i-**. L19. [f. Sir Elijah *Impey* (1732–1809), Eng. jurist, and his wife Mary (d. 1818) + -AN.] **A** *adj. Impeyan pheasant*, a stocky pheasant, *Lophophorus impeyanus*, of the Himalayas, the male of which has brilliant iridescent plumage. L19. **B** *n.* An Impeyan pheasant. L19.

¶Also called (*Himalayan*) *monal.*

imphee /ˈɪmfi/ *n.* Also **imfe**. M19. [Zulu *imfe* sweet cane.] Any of several southern African varieties of sorghum.

impi /ˈɪmpi/ *n.* M19. [Zulu.] Chiefly *Hist.* A body of Zulu warriors or armed tribesmen.

impicture /ɪmˈpɪktʃə/ *v.t.* Also **em-** /ɪm-, ɛm-/. E16. [f. IM-¹, EM-¹ + PICTURE *n.*] Represent (as) in a picture; portray.

impierce *v.* var. of EMPIERCE.

†impierceable *a.* LME–L17. [f. IM-² + PIERCEABLE.] Not pierceable; unable to be pierced.

impiety /ɪmˈpʌɪɪti/ *n.* ME. [(O)Fr. *impiété* or L *impietas*, f. *impius*: see IMPIOUS, -TY¹.] **1** Lack of reverence for God or a god; ungodliness; an instance of this. ME. **2** Lack of respect or dutifulness; an instance of this. M16.

1 AV *2 Esd.* 3:29 When I came thither, and had seen impieties without number. H. WILLIAMSON Phidias eventually was accused of impiety . . what in a later age would be called blasphemy. **2** W. LAW Can you think it a less impiety to contemn and vilify a brother? R. SCRUTON To neglect my parents in old age is . . an act of impiety.

†impight *v.* var. of EMPIGHT.

impignorate /ɪmˈpɪɡnəreɪt/ *v.t.* Chiefly *Sc.* Pa. pple **-ate** (earlier), **-ated**. M16. [Orig. pa. pple, f. med.L *impignoratus* pa. pple of *impignorare* pledge, mortgage, f. as IM-¹ + *pignor-*, *-nus* a pledge: see -ATE², -ATE³.] Pledge, pawn, mortgage.

impignoˈration *n.* L15.

impinge /ɪmˈpɪn(d)ʒ/ *v.* M16. [L *impingere*, f. as IM-¹ + *pangere* drive in.] **1** *v.t.* Fasten or fix on forcibly (*lit.* & *fig.*). M16. **2** *v.i.* Strike; come into forcible contact; collide. (Foll. by *on*, *upon*.) E17. **3** *v.t.* Strike or throw (a thing) forcibly on or *on* something else. *rare.* M17. **4** *v.i.* Encroach, have an effect, *on* or *upon*. M18. **5** *v.t.* Strike; come into forcible contact with; collide with. L18.

1 SYD. SMITH Appealing to the absurdities of a past age, and impinging them upon the present. **2** JOYCE Through one of the broken panes I heard the rain impinge upon the earth. **3** T. L. PEACOCK He impinged his foot with a force that overbalanced himself. **4** *Illustrated London News* I should be impinging on the province of the reviewers. R. DAHL Still the same habit of thrusting his face forward at you, impinging on you. **5** *Practitioner* The striker's thumb . . impinges the skull of his opponent.

impingement *n.* L17. **impinger** *n.* any of various instruments used for collecting samples of particles suspended in air etc. E20.

impious /ˈɪmpɪəs, ɪmˈpʌɪəs/ *a.* M16. [f. L *impius*, f. as IM-² + PIOUS: see -OUS.] **1** Not pious; lacking in reverence for God or a god; wicked, profane. M16. **2** Lacking in respect or dutifulness. *rare.* E17.

impiously *adv.* L16. **impiousness** *n.* (long *rare*) L16.

impish /ˈɪmpɪʃ/ *a.* E17. [f. IMP *n.* + -ISH¹.] Of or like an imp; mischievous.

E. FEINSTEIN A series of practical jokes that recall her impish treatment of Nina. I. MCEWAN She was pretty, impish and freckled, with a pointed chin.

impishly *adv.* M19. **impishness** *n.* L19.

impiteous /ɪmˈpɪtɪəs/ *a. rare.* L15. [f. IM-² + PITEOUS.] Ruthless, pitiless.

implacable /ɪmˈplakəb(ə)l/ *a.* LME. [L *implacabilis*, f. as IM-² + *placabilis* PLACABLE.] **1** Unable to be appeased; irreconcilable; inexorable. LME. **2** Unable to be assuaged or mitigated. Now *rare* or *obs.* L15.

1 C. G. WOLFF A . . lonely child, convinced of the world's implacable hostility. J. CHEEVER The . . Duke was an implacable anti-Fascist. **2** SPENSER O how I burne with implacable fire.

implacaˈbility *n.* M16. **implacableness** *n.* M17. **implacably** *adv.* M17.

implacental /ɪmpləˈsɛnt(ə)l/ *a.* & *n.* M19. [f. IM-² + PLACENTAL.] *Zool.* (A mammal) that develops no placenta, as a monotreme marsupial.

implant /ˈɪmplɑːnt/ *n.* L19. [f. the vb.] **1** A thing that has been implanted, esp. in the body, as a piece of tissue, a capsule containing radioactive material, etc. L19. **2** The action or an act of implanting a thing, esp. in the body. M20.

1 *New Scientist* In recent years surgeons have been fitting an increasing number of implants. **2** *Times* French doctors today made the world's first implant of an atomic powered heart simulator.

implant /ɪmˈplɑːnt/ *v.* LME. [Late L *implantare* engraft, f. as IM-¹ + *plantare* PLANT *v.*] **1** *v.t.* Embed, insert, or fix *in* something. Usu. in *pass.* LME. **b** *Surg.* Place or insert (tissue, or some artificial object) in the body. L19. **c** Chiefly *Med.* Provide *with* by implantation. E20. **d** *Physics.* Introduce (atoms, ions, etc.) into a substance by bombardment. M20. **2** *v.t.* Instil, establish, (a principle, idea, etc., *in* a mind etc.). Freq. in *pass.* M16. **3** *v.t.* Set in the ground, plant. Also, plant (ground etc.) *with*. E17. **4** *v.i. Embryol.* Of an ovum: undergo implantation. M20.

1 J. PINKERTON Patrinite sometimes occurs in globular masses, implanted in other rocks. **2** E. HEMINGWAY We are making a huge conscript army without the time to implant the discipline. E. AMADI Tam Jaja . . stared at her intensely as if trying to implant his . . view in her mind. **3** H. J. STEPHEN Trees, while still implanted in the ground, are parcel of the freehold.

implantable *a.* M20. **implanter** *n.* M17.

implantation /ɪmplɑːnˈteɪʃ(ə)n, -plan-/ *n.* L16. [Fr., f. *implanter*, f. as IMPLANT *v.*: see -ATION.] **1** *Anat.* The (manner or place of) insertion of a tooth, a muscle, etc. L16. **2** The action or an act of planting something in the ground. E17. **3** The instilling or establishing of a principle, idea, etc., in the mind etc. M17. **4** *Surg.* The process or an act of implanting something in the body. L19. **5** *Embryol.* The attachment of a fertilized ovum (blastocyst) to the wall of the uterus. E20. **6** *Physics.* The introduction of atoms or other particles into a substance by bombardment. M20.

implausible /ɪmˈplɔːzɪb(ə)l/ *a.* E17. [f. IM-² + PLAUSIBLE *a.*] **†1** Not worthy or desirous of applause. Only in E17. **2** Not having the appearance of truth, probability, or acceptability; not plausible. L17.

2 R. SCRUTON It is most implausible that the Church should retain political while losing its spiritual authority. H. JACOBSON She had invented a number of transparently implausible domestic tasks for herself.

implausiˈbility *n.* L16. **implausibly** *adv.* E19.

impleach /ɪmˈpliːtʃ/ *v.t. poet.* Also **†em-**. L16. [f. IM-¹, EM-¹ + PLEACH *v.*] Entwine, interweave. Usu. in *pass.*

implead /ɪmˈpliːd/ *v.t.* Also **†em-**. LME. [AN *empleder* = OFr. *empleidier*, *emplaidier*, f. as IM-¹, EM-¹ + *plaidier* PLEAD.] **1** Prosecute or take proceedings against (a person, organization, etc.); involve in a lawsuit. LME. **†2** Arraign, accuse, impeach. L16–M19. **3** Plead (*with*). *rare.* M17.

†impleadable *a.* (*a*) (of a person) that may be sued, (of a suit) that may be prosecuted; (*b*) able to be pleaded or made a plea: L16–E19. **†impleader** *n.* L16–L18.

impledge /ɪmˈplɛdʒ/ *v.t.* Now chiefly *literary.* Also **†em-**. M16. [f. IM-¹, EM-¹ + PLEDGE *n.*] Pledge, give as security; pawn.

implement /ˈɪmplɪm(ə)nt/ *n.* LME. [Partly f. med.L *implementa* pl., f. *implere* employ, spend, extended use (by assoc. w. *implicare* EMPLOY *v.*) of L *implere*; partly f. late L *implementum* filling up, f. L *implere* fill up, fulfil, f. as IM-¹ + *plere* fill: see -MENT.] **1** A piece of equipment; an article of furniture, dress, etc. Now only in *pl.* LME. **†b** *gen.* In *pl.* Requisites. E17–M18. **2** A tool, instrument, or utensil, employed in a particular trade, activity, etc.; *Archaeol.* a weapon or tool, usu. deliberately shaped (freq. w. specifying wd denoting association with a particular period or culture). M16. 3 *Sc. Law.* Fulfilment, full performance. M17.

1 A. B. JAMESON They wear the stole and alba.. and bear the implements of the mass. 2 W. TREVOR Spades we need.. and forks and secateurs and all garden implements.

imple'mental *a.* L17.

implement /'ɪmplɪmɛnt, -m(ə)nt/ *v.t.* E18. [f. the n.] 1 Complete or execute (a contract etc.); fulfil (an undertaking); put (a decision or plan) into effect. E18. b Satisfy or fulfil (a condition). *rare.* M19. 2 Fill up, supplement. M19. 3 Provide or fit with an implement or implements. *rare.* L19.

1 E. CRANKSHAW It was left to Arakcheyev to implement the system. ANTHONY SMITH A regulation.. was issued.. but was never implemented. R. HOLE The NHS reforms, uncosted and untried anywhere and implemented at speed against much opposition.

implemen'tation *n.* E20.

implementiferous /,ɪmplɪmɛn'tɪf(ə)rəs/ *a.* L19. [f. as prec. + -I- + -FEROUS.] *Geol.* Of a deposit: containing (stone) implements of human origin.

impletion /ɪm'pliːʃ(ə)n/ *n. arch.* L15. [Late L *impletio(n-)*, f. L *implet-* pa. ppl stem of *implere* (see IMPLEMENT *n.*) + -ION.] The action of filling; the condition of being filled; fullness. Formerly also, fulfilment.

†implex *a.* Only in 18. [L *implexus* pa. pple, f. as next.] Involved, complicated.

†implex *v.t.* E17–M19. [L *implex-* pa. ppl stem of *implectere* entwine, f. as IM-[1] + *plectere* twist, plait.] Entwine; complicate. Chiefly as *implexed* ppl a.

impliable /ɪm'plʌɪəb(ə)l/ *a. rare.* E17. [f. IM-[2] + PLIABLE.] Not pliable; inflexible.

implicans /'ɪmplɪkanz/ *n.* Pl. **-cants** /-kants/. E20. [L, pres. pple of *implicare*: see IMPLICATE *v.*] *Logic.* In implication, the proposition that implies another.

implicate /'ɪmplɪkət/ *a.* & *n.* LME. [L *implicatus* pa. pple, f. as next: see -ATE[2], -ATE[1].] A *adj.* 1 Intertwined, twisted together; wrapped up *with*, involved or entangled *in*. Now *rare.* LME. †2 Involved, intricate. M16–M17.

B *n.* †1 Entanglement, confusion. Only in M17. 2 That which is implied or involved. L19.

2 A. M. FAIRBAIRN The doctrine and its implicates must simply be stated.

implicate /'ɪmplɪkeɪt/ *v.t.* LME. [L *implicat-* pa. ppl stem of *implicare*, f. as IM-[1] + *plicare* fold: see -ATE[3].] I 1 Intertwine; entwine, entangle. Now *rare.* LME.

1 *fig.*: H. ROGERS Christianity was not designed to be.. implicated with the fortunes of any earthly polity.

II 2 Involve in its nature or meaning; lead to as a consequence or inference; imply. E17. 3 Show or purport to show (a person) to be concerned or involved (*in* a crime, charge, etc.). L18. 4 In *pass.* Be affected or involved in the operation of something. Freq. foll. by *in*. L18.

2 E. PARSONS So much reserve and mystery.. assuredly implicated something wrong. P. ACKROYD The demands of 'social utility' are implicated in the idea of the poet as dramatist. 3 W. SOYINKA He has implicated you in his statement. 4 *Scientific American* Strings were originally implicated in the formation of galaxies.

implication /ɪmplɪ'keɪʃ(ə)n/ *n.* LME. [L *implicatio(n-)*, f. as prec.: see -ATION.] 1 The action or an act of intertwining, entwining, or entangling; the condition of being intertwined, entwined, or entangled. Now *rare.* LME. 2 The action of implying; the fact of being implied or involved, without being plainly expressed; a thing implied or involved in something else. M16. b *Logic.* A relationship between propositions such that the one implies the other. Also, a proposition asserting such a relationship. E20.

1 J. MARTINEAU The mystic implication of his nature with ours. 2 B. BETTELHEIM To different persons the same symbol could have entirely different implications. M. GORDON She hadn't known exactly what he'd meant, but the implications hadn't pleased her. **by implication** by what is implied; as a natural inference. b *logical implication*: see LOGICAL *a.* *material implication*: see MATERIAL *a.* STRICT *implication*.

implicational /ɪmplɪ'keɪʃ(ə)n(ə)l/ *a.* L19. [f. prec. + -AL[1].] *Logic.* Of, concerned with, or using implication.

implicationally *adv.* E20.

implicative /ɪm'plɪkətɪv/ *a.* E17. [f. IMPLICATE *v.* + -IVE.] 1 Having the quality of implying; tending to imply or implicate. E17. 2 *Logic.* Designating or pertaining to a relationship between propositions such that the one implies the other. Also, designating or pertaining to a proposition asserting such a relationship. E20.

implicatively *adv.* L16. **implicativeness** *n.* M20.

implicit /ɪm'plɪsɪt/ *a.* L16. [Fr. *implicite* or L *implicitus* entangled, entwined, later form of *implicatus*: see IMPLICATE *a.* & *n.*] 1 Implied though not plainly expressed; necessarily or naturally involved (*in*); able to be inferred. L16. b Of an idea or feeling: not clearly formulated, vague, indefinite. Now *rare.* M17. c Virtually or potentially contained *in*. M17. 2 Of faith, obedience, etc., not independently reached by the individual but resting on the authority of the Church etc.; absolute, unquestioning. E17. b Of a person: characterized by implicit faith, obedience, etc. Now *rare* or *obs.* L17. †3 Entangled, entwined, twisted together; involved. E17–E19.

1 M. BRADBURY I was offering a paraphrase of its implicit as opposed to its surface meaning. C. PRIEST It was nothing she said, it was just implicit in her every glance. b D. HUME Views and sentiments.. so implicit and obscure that they often escape our strictest attention. c J. M. MURRY The reference to Shakespeare is implicit in every page. 2 E. ROOSEVELT I had implicit confidence in his ability to help the country in a crisis. 3 J. BEATTIE No hand had wove the implicit maze.

implicitly *adv.* E17. **implicitness** *n.* the quality of being implicit; implicit belief or obedience: L17. **implicity** *n.* (long *rare* or *obs.*) implicitness E17.

impling /'ɪmplɪŋ/ *n. rare.* L18. [f. IMP *n.* + -LING[1].] A little imp.

implode /ɪm'pləʊd/ *v.i.* & *t.* L19. [f. IM-[1] + L *plodere*, *plaudere* clap, after *explode*.] (Cause to) burst or collapse inwards.

imploration /ɪmplə'reɪʃ(ə)n/ *n.* Now *rare.* L16. [Fr. †*imploration* or L *imploratio(n-)*, f. *implorat-* pa. ppl stem of *implorare*: see IMPLORE *v.*, -ATION.] The action or an act of imploring; supplication, beseeching.

G. CATLIN Their earnest implorations for divine forgiveness and mercy.

†implorator *n. rare* (Shakes.). Only in E17. [med.L, f. L *implorat-*: see prec., -OR.] A person who implores.

†implore *n. rare.* L16–E17. [f. the vb.] An act of imploring; imploration.

implore /ɪm'plɔː/ *v.* E16. [Fr. *implorer* or L *implorare* invoke with tears, f. as IM-[1] + *plorare* weep.] 1 *v.t.* Beg earnestly for (help, forgiveness, etc.); entreat (a person *to do*). E16. b Utter as a supplication or entreaty. M19. 2 *v.i.* Utter entreaties, supplicate. E16.

1 A. RADCLIFFE He threw himself at her feet to implore forgiveness. W. STYRON 'Nathan, don't go!' she implored him desperately. b G. GREENE He simply implored, 'Stop it, please stop it.' 2 W. LITHGOW Holding up my hand, and imploring for our lives.

imploringly *adv.* in an imploring manner E19. **imploringness** *n.* (an) imploring quality M19.

implosion /ɪm'pləʊʒ(ə)n/ *n.* L19. [f. IMPLODE after *explosion*.] 1 A bursting or collapsing inward. L19. 2 *Phonet.* The sharp intake of air in the pronunciation of some consonants. L19.

1 J. NARLIKAR When the core of a star collapses.. the inner part.. undergoes an implosion, while the outer part undergoes an explosion. *fig.*: *Listener* There was an implosion, as firms rushed together from great financial conglomerates.

implosive /ɪm'pləʊsɪv/ *a.* & *n.* L19. [f. as prec. after *explosive*.] A *adj.* Formed by implosion; tending to implode. L19. B *n.* *Phonet.* A sound formed by implosion. L19.

implosively *adv.* L19. **implosiveness** *n.* M20.

†imploy *n.*, *v.*, †**-er** *n.*, †**-ment** *n.* vars. of EMPLOY *n.*, *v.*, etc.

implume *v.* var. of EMPLUME.

implunge /ɪm'plʌn(d)ʒ/ *v.t.* Now *rare.* Also †**em-**. L16. [f. IM-[1], EM-[1] + PLUNGE *v.*] Plunge *in* or *into*.

impluvium /ɪm'pluːvɪəm/ *n.* Pl. **-ia** /-ɪə/. E19. [L, f. *impluere* rain into.] *Rom. Antiq.* The square basin in the centre of the atrium of a Roman house, which received rainwater from an opening in the roof.

imply /ɪm'plʌɪ/ *v.t.* Also †**em-**. LME. [OFr. *emplier* f. L *implicare*: see IMPLICATE *v.* Cf. EMPLOY *v.*] †1 Enfold, entangle, (*lit* & *fig.*). LME–E19. 2 Involve as a necessary consequence; involve the truth or existence of (a thing not expressly asserted). E16. b Of a word etc.: mean, signify. E17. †3 Employ. M16–M17. 4 Express indirectly; insinuate, suggest, hint (at). L16.

1 C. LAMB If it be egotism to imply and twine with his.. identity the griefs.. of another. 2 I. WALTON In Job.. mention is made of fish-hooks, which must imply Anglers in those times. J. MCDOUGALL The wish for nirvana.. does not necessarily imply a wish to die. 4 D. H. LAWRENCE Her voice seemed to imply that she was glad to get back to Shortlands. B. BETTELHEIM Translators need to be very sensitive not only to what is written but also to what is implied.

impocket /ɪm'pɒkɪt/ *v.t.* Also **em-** /ɪm-, ɛm-/. E18. [f. IM-[1], EM-[1] + POCKET *n.*] Pocket; put into one's pocket.

†impoison *v.* var. of EMPOISON.

impolder /ɪm'pəʊldə/ *v.t.* Also **em-** /ɪm-, ɛm-/. L19. [Du. *impolderen*, f. as IM-[1] + POLDER.] Reclaim from the sea; make a polder of.

impolicy /ɪm'pɒlɪsi/ *n.* M18. [f. IM-[2] + POLICY *n.*[1], after IMPOLITIC.] Bad policy; inexpediency.

impolite /ɪmpə'lʌɪt/ *a.* E17. [L *impolitus*, f. as IM-[2] + *politus* POLITE.] †1 Not polished; *fig.* unrefined. Only in 17. 2 Not courteous; uncivil, ill-mannered, rude. M18.

2 K. VONNEGUT She imagined that I used certain impolite words.. to cause a sensation. A. S. BYATT Celia felt it would be impolite to ask how old he was.

impolitely *adv.* M18. **impoliteness** *n.* L18.

impolitic /ɪm'pɒlɪtɪk/ *a.* L16. [f. IM-[2] + POLITIC *a.*] Not politic; not according to good policy; inexpedient.

impolitical *a.* (now *rare*) = IMPOLITIC M18. **impolitically** *adv.* M18. **impoliticly** *adv.* E17. **impoliticness** *n.* (now *rare*) L18.

imponderabilia /ɪm,pɒnd(ə)rə'bɪlɪə/ *n.pl.* E20. [mod.L, neut. pl. of *imponderabilis* that cannot be weighed: see -IA[2].] Imponderables, imponderable factors.

imponderable /ɪm'pɒnd(ə)rəb(ə)l/ *a.* & *n.* L18. [f. IM-[2] + PONDERABLE.] A *adj.* 1 Chiefly *Physics.* Having no weight. L18. b Of extremely small weight or amount. M19. 2 *fig.* Unable to be assessed or calculated. E19.

2 *Guardian* It is not so much the calculable cost but the possible, imponderable one.

B *n.* An imponderable thing; *esp.* a thing that cannot be assessed or calculated. M19.

A. BURGESS A faith of blood and instinct and somatic consciousness and other imponderables.

imponderableness *n.* M19. **imponderably** *adv.* L19.

imponderous /ɪm'pɒnd(ə)rəs/ *a. rare.* M17. [f. IM-[2] + PONDEROUS.] Imponderable.

†impone *v.t.* E16. [L *imponere*, f. as IM-[1] + *ponere* to place.] 1 Place upon something; impose. E16–E18. 2 Stake, wager. *rare* (Shakes.). Only in E17.

imponent /ɪm'pəʊnənt/ *n.* M19. [Alt. of IMPOSER after OPPONENT, OPPOSER.] A person who imposes something.

imporous /ɪm'pɔːrəs/ *a.* Long *rare.* M17. [f. IM-[2] + POROUS *a.*] Not porous.

import /'ɪmpɔːt/ *n.* L16. [f. the vb.] 1 Something implied or signified by a word, document, etc; meaning; great significance, importance. L16. 2 Something imported or brought in, the amount or value of what is imported; an imported article or commodity. Usu. in *pl.* L17. 3 The action of importing, importation. L18.

1 H. KELLER She grasps the import of whole sentences, catching.. the meaning of words she

doesn't know. V. SACKVILLE-WEST His visit had not been without import to him. B. BETTELHEIM A word that, because of its ancient religious associations, suggests something of deepest import. *existential import*: see EXISTENTIAL *a.* 2. 2 *Sunday* (*Calcutta*) Not much progress has been made in reducing imports of . . , fertilisers, and iron and steel. *attrib.*: *Soldier* There are strict import regulations about bringing such animals into the United Kingdom. *invisible imports*: see INVISIBLE *a.* & *n.* 3 G. J. GOSCHEN It is an error . . to look on the balance of trade as a mere question of import and export.

import /ɪmˈpɔːt, ˈɪmpɔːt/ *v.* LME. [L *importare* carry or bring in, (in med.L) imply, mean, be of consequence, f. as IM-[1] + *portare* carry.] I Convey; signify; matter; cause. 1 *v.t.* Signify, denote, mean; involve, imply, indicate. LME. b Convey as information; express, state. LME. c Portend. Cf. IMPORTUNE *v.* 4. Long *rare.* L15. 2 *v.t.* Be of consequence or importance to; relate to, concern; be incumbent on. Only in 3rd person (freq. impers.). *arch.* M16. b *v.i.* Be of consequence or significance; be important, matter. Only in 3rd person. *arch.* M16. †3 *v.t.* Bring about, cause; involve as a consequence. M16–E18.

1 R. SOUTH Having thus seen, what is imported in a Man's trusting his Heart. b LD MACAULAY They . . passed a resolution importing that they relied . . on His Majesty's gracious promise. 2 SIR W. SCOTT Let me say . . what it imports thee to know. JAS. MILL There is nothing which more vitally imports the American people.

II Bring in, introduce; communicate. 4 *v.t.* Bring or introduce from an external source or from one use etc. to another; *spec.* bring in (goods etc.) from another country. E16. 5 *v.t.* Bring or communicate (information etc.). *obs.* exc. as passing into senses 1b,4. M16.

4 F. L. WRIGHT America has always assumed that culture . . had to come from European sources—be imported. W. WHARTON Most canaries in the United States are imported from Germany and Japan.

importable *a.* able to be imported or introduced M16.

importance /ɪmˈpɔːt(ə)ns/ *n.* E16. [Fr. f. med.L *importantia* significance, consequence, f. *important-*: see next, -ANCE.] I 1 The fact or quality of being important; significance, consequence. E16. b An important person or thing. L16. c Personal consequence, dignity. L17. †2 Urgency; importunity. L16–L18.

1 D. H. LAWRENCE It's of no importance . . . it doesn't matter in the least. N. MAILER The importance of the journey must be estimated by my dread of doing it. b R. GRAVES Old importances came swimming back—Wine, meat, log-fires, a roof over the head. c R. INGALLS His only importance comes through her. M. DRABBLE He thinks he is enjoying his work, his new importance, his power, his eminence.

†II 3 Meaning, import. M16–E18.

importancy *n.* (*a*) = IMPORTANCE 1; †(*b*) = IMPORTANCE 2: M16.

important /ɪmˈpɔːt(ə)nt/ *a.* LME. [med.L *important-*, *-ans* pres. pple of *importare* be of consequence: see IMPORT *v.*, -ANT[1].] 1 Having great significance; carrying with it great or serious consequences; weighty, momentous. LME. b Of a person: having high rank; consequential; pompous, pretentious. E18. c Of an antique etc.: very valuable. E20. d Preceded by an adv. of degree and modifying a sentence or complete phrase (passing into *adv.*): what is *more, most,* etc., important; *more, most,* etc., significantly. Cf. IMPORTANTLY 2. M20. †2 Urgent, importunate. L16–M17.

1 A. J. CRONIN His work was the important thing, beside it all else was trivial. N. MOSLEY It becomes so important to me that I see a whole stretch of days ruined if I do not get it. b R. P. WARREN People from Washington . . began to come, . . important people whose names were in the papers. A. SCHLEE Charlotte, important with the burden of her guilt, was not to be restrained. d R. H. W. BROWN One must wait until the soil is damp enough and, more important, warm enough. *Physics Bulletin* Most important of all, the foreign guests must be assured that the hosts will ease all problems of entry into their country.

importantly /ɪmˈpɔːt(ə)ntli/ *adv.* E17. [f. prec. + -LY[2].] 1 In an important manner; to an important degree. E17. 2 Modifying a sentence or complete phrase, usu. preceded by an adv. of degree: what is (*more, most,* etc.) important; (*more, most,* etc.) significantly. (Considered *erron.* by some.) Cf. IMPORTANT 1d. M20.

1 D. WELCH He glided in and out of Mr Butler's room, carrying papers importantly. M. SPARK Ruth assumed Barbara to be someone importantly on her side. 2 C. WILLIAMS The first outrage against *pietas*, and (more importantly) the first imagined proclamation of *pietas* from the heavens. *Daily Telegraph* But, importantly in this case, there is a well-built girl attendant who is chased about the stage.

importation /ɪmpɔːˈteɪʃ(ə)n/ *n.* E17. [f. IMPORT *v.* + -ATION.] 1 The action of importing or bringing in something, *spec.* goods from another country. E17. 2 A thing which is imported. M17. 3 *Logic.* The inference that if a proposition implies that a second proposition implies a third, then the first and second together imply the third. E20.

importee /ɪmpɔːˈtiː/ *n.* M19. [f. IMPORT *v.* + -EE[1].] A person imported from another country.

importer /ɪmˈpɔːtə/ *n.* E18. [f. IMPORT *v.* + -ER[1].] A person who or thing which imports something, *esp.* a merchant who imports goods from other countries.

†**importless** *a. rare* (Shakes.). Only in E17. [f. IMPORT *n.* + -LESS.] Without import; trivial.

importunacy /ɪmˈpɔːtjʊnəsi/ *n.* M16. [f. next + -ACY.] = IMPORTUNITY 3.

importunate /ɪmˈpɔːtjʊnət/ *a.* E16. [f. L *importunus* (see IMPORTUNE *a.*) + -ATE[2], perh. after OBSTINATE *a.*] 1 Persistently demanding, pressing. E16. b Urgent; busy. *arch.* M16. †2 Inopportune, untimely. E16–M17. †3 Grievous; troublesome. M16–E19.

1 V. SACKVILLE-WEST They were accosted by importunate women. K. HULME I apologise for being importunate. b W. C. BRYANT This maze of dusty streets, Forever shaken by the importunate jar Of commerce.

importunately *adv.* L15. **importunateness** *n.* M16.

importunate /ɪmˈpɔːtjʊneɪt/ *v.t.* Long *rare.* L16. [f. prec.: see -ATE[3].] = IMPORTUNE *v.* 1.

importunator *n.* E17.

importune /ɪmpɔːˈtjuːn/ *a.* & *n.* LME. [Fr. *importun, -une* or L *importunus* inconvenient, unsuitable, unseasonable, f. as IM-[2] + *Portunus* the protecting god of harbours (opp. *opportunus* OPPORTUNE).] A *adj.* 1 = IMPORTUNATE *a.* 1. LME. †2 = IMPORTUNATE *a.* 3. LME–M19. †3 = IMPORTUNATE *a.* 1b. LME–M17. †4 = IMPORTUNATE *a.* 2. LME–E18. †B *n.* An importunate person. L16–M18.

importunely *adv.* (now *rare*) LME.

importune /ɪmpɔːˈtjuːn/ *v.* M16. [Fr. *importuner* or med.L *importunari*, f. L *importunus*: see prec.] 1 *v.t.* & *i.* Ask or request of (a person) persistently or pressingly. M16. †b Urge or impel (a person or thing). Only in E17. c Solicit for purposes of prostitution. M19. 2 *v.t.* Ask or beg for (a thing) persistently and pressingly. L16. †3 *v.t.* Burden, trouble, pester. L16–L18. †4 *v.t.* Portend. Cf. IMPORT *v.* 1c. Only in L16.

1 P. S. BUCK His uncle . . came importuning to his door. B. CHATWIN She importuned them for money. 2 SHAKES. *L.L.L.* The daughter of the King of France . . Importunes personal conference with his Grace.

importuner *n.* M17.

importunity /ɪmpɔːˈtjuːnɪti/ *n.* LME. [(O)Fr. *importunité* f. L *importunitas*, f. *importunus*: see IMPORTUNE *a.*, -ITY.] 1 Persistency or insistency in requesting or demanding. LME. †2 Trouble, grievousness. LME–M18. †3 Inopportunity; untimeliness. L15–L16.

1 D. WELCH I began to hate his wheedling importunity.

†**impose** *n. rare.* L16–E17. [f. the vb.] Imposition.

impose /ɪmˈpəʊz/ *v.* Also †**em-**. L15. [(O)Fr. *imposer*, †*em-*, based on L *imponere* place on or into, inflict, deceive (see IM-[1]), but re-formed on L pa. pple *impositus* and (O)Fr. *poser*: see POSE *v.*[1]] I *v.t.* †1 Lay (a crime etc.) to the account of; impute to. Foll. by *on, upon.* L15–M17. 2 Put, apply, or bestow authoritatively. *obs.* exc. as passing into sense 4. E16. 3 Subject *to.* Long *rare.* M16. 4 Lay or inflict (a tax, duty, charge, obligation, etc.) (*on* or *upon*), esp. forcibly; compel compliance with; force (oneself) *on* or *upon* the attention etc. of. L16. 5 Lay, place, or put, on (*arch.*); *spec.* in *Printing*, arrange (pages of type) in order so as to form the correct sequence after printing and folding. L16. b Place in command or office; appoint. *obs.* exc. as passing into sense 4. E17. 6 Palm or pass off (a thing) *upon* (a person). E17.

1 SHAKES. *Hen. V* The imputation of his wickedness . . should be imposed upon his father that sent him. 2 J. BRYANT The name was imposed antecedent to his birth. 4 R. GRAVES A new tax was imposed . . to provide money for the German wars. N. BLAKE He was more accustomed to imposing discipline than to being disciplined. A. FRASER Not one single condition was suggested, let alone imposed on the king. K. MOORE The present imposed itself once more upon her consciousness.

II *v.i.* †7 Levy a tax (*upon* persons or goods). E17–L19. 8 Exert influence (*on* or *upon*) by impressive character or appearance; presume *on* or *upon*, force oneself *on* or *upon*, take advantage. E17. 9 Practise deception *on* or *upon*. M17.

8 J. LUBBOCK Mechanism that imposes through its extreme simplicity. C. ISHERWOOD Most rich people, . . can be imposed upon to almost any extent. T. HEGGEN The crew members imposed on him outrageously with their demands for . . his time.

imposable *a.* (*rare*) M17. **imposement** *n.* (*rare*) the action of imposing, an imposition M17. **imposer** *n.* L16.

imposing /ɪmˈpəʊzɪŋ/ *a.* M17. [f. IMPOSE *v.* + -ING[2].] 1 Dictatorial; exacting. Now *rare.* M17. 2 Deceptive. Now *rare.* M18. 3 Impressive or daunting in appearance or manner. L18.

3 A. DAVIS There was something imposing about him which evoked total silence and attention. R. DAHL An imposing country mansion . . . a mighty house with turrets on its roof.

imposingly *adv.* E19. **imposingness** *n.* E19.

imposition /ɪmpəˈzɪʃ(ə)n/ *n.* LME. [(O)Fr., or L *impositio(n-)*, f. as IM-[1] + *positio(n-)* POSITION *n.*] 1 The action of putting or laying something on; *spec.* (*a*) *Eccl.* the laying on of hands in blessing, ordination, etc.; (*b*) *Printing* the imposing of pages. LME. 2 The action of applying, bestowing, or ascribing. LME. †b Imputation, accusation. *rare* (Shakes.). Only in E17. 3 The action of imposing a charge, obligation, duty, etc; the action of imposing oneself. Formerly also, taxation. LME. 4 A thing imposed or inflicted; an unfair or inconvenient demand or burden. Formerly also, a command or charge laid on a person. LME. b A piece of work imposed as punishment at school. M18. 5 The action or an act of deceiving or being deceived; deception. M17.

3 C. HAMPTON The imposition of blanket censorship and the silencing of all opposition newspapers. 4 E. WAUGH There is a woeful imposition called 'a week on duty'. D. DELILLO Is this an imposition, James? Just say so.

impossibilism /ɪmˈpɒsɪbɪlɪz(ə)m/ *n.* L19. [f. IMPOSSIBLE *a.* + -ISM.] Belief in ideas or policy, esp. on social reform, that are held to be unrealizable or impractical.

impossibilist *n.* M19.

impossibilitate /ɪmˌpɒsɪˈbɪlɪteɪt/ *v.t. rare.* E17. [med.L *impossibilitat-* pa. ppl stem of *impossibilitare*, f. L *impossibilitas*: see next, -ATE[3]. Cf. Sp. *imposibilitar*, It. *impossibilitare.*] Make impossible.

impossibility /ɪmˌpɒsɪˈbɪlɪti/ *n.* LME. [(O)Fr. *impossibilité* or L *impossibilitas*, f. *impossibilis*: see next, -ITY.] 1 The quality of being impossible; an impossible thing. LME. †2 Inability, impotence. LME–L18.

1 R. CAMPBELL It was a sheer impossibility for any doctor, . . to make rain. E. H. JONES The impossibility of reconciling the Church with modern civilization.

impossible /ɪmˈpɒsɪb(ə)l/ *a.* & *n.* ME. [(O)Fr., or L *impossibilis*, f. as IM-[2] + *possibilis* POSSIBLE *a.*] A *adj.* 1 Not possible; unable to be done or exist; extremely difficult, inconvenient, or implausible. ME. b *Math.* = IMAGINARY *a.* 1c. Opp. POSSIBLE *a.* 5. Now *rare.* L17. 2 Outrageous, unsuitable, intolerable. Opp. POSSIBLE *a.* 4. *colloq.* E19.

1 B. EMECHETA He had made it impossible for Ezekiel to know the whereabouts of his son. I. MCEWAN It's . . difficult for me to walk down stairs, and completely impossible to walk up them. N. SAHGAL The voyage was a quest, . . and Cythera a paradise, an impossible dream. A. MUNRO She deals easily with . . impossible questions. 2 H. JAMES Grace is impossible—I don't know what's the matter with her. A. BURGESS Without a car life in Malaya was impossible Life in Malaya was impossible anyway.

B *n.* **1** An impossible thing, an impossibility. Usu. in *pl.* ME. **2** With *the*: that which is or seems impossible. L18.

2 F. NANSEN The difficult . . takes a little time; the impossible . . takes a little longer.

impossibleness *n.* (*rare*) LME. **impossibly** *adv.* L16.

impost /ˈɪmpəʊst/ *n.*[1] L15. [It. *imposta* use as n. of fem. pa. pple of *imporre*, f. L *imponere* IMPOSE *v.*] **1** The upper course of a pillar, often in the form of a projecting ornamental moulding, on which the foot of an arch rests. L15. **2** A horizontal block supported by upright stones, as in a dolmen. M18.

impost /ˈɪmpəʊst/ *n.*[2] M16. [Fr. (now *impôt*) f. med.L *impostus*, *-um* use as n. of masc. or neut. of L *impostus*, *impositus* pa. pple of *imponere* IMPOSE *v.*] **1** A tribute, a tax, a duty; *spec.* a customs duty. M16. **2** The weight carried by a horse in a handicap race. *slang.* L19.

1 G. GORER Very high imposts on alcoholic drinks have had a greater influence on national sobriety.

imposter *n.* var. of IMPOSTOR.

†imposthumate *v.*, **imposthumation** *n.*, **imposthume** *n.* vars. of IMPOSTUMATE, IMPOSTUMATION, IMPOSTUME.

impostor /ɪmˈpɒstə/ *n.* Also **-er**, (earliest) **†-ure**. L16. [Fr. *imposteur* f. late L contr. of *impositor*, f. L *imposit-* pa. ppl stem of *imponere* IMPOSE *v.*: see -OR. In earliest use confused w. IMPOSTURE.] A deceiver, a cheat; *esp.* a person who assumes a false identity in order to deceive others.

E. H. GOMBRICH An artist was little better than an impostor who demanded ridiculous prices for something that could hardly be called honest work. J. BARNES Her parrot was clearly authentic, and . . the Hôtel-Dieu bird was definitely an impostor.

impostorship *n.* E17. **impostress** *n.* (now *rare*) a female impostor E17.

impostorous /ɪmˈpɒst(ə)rəs/ *a.* M16. [In sense 1 f. IMPOSTURE; in sense 2 f. IMPOSTOR: see -OUS. Cf. next.] **†1** Of the nature of an imposture. M16–M17. **2** Having the character of an impostor, practising as an impostor. E17.

impostrous /ɪmˈpɒstrəs/ *a.* E17. [Contr.] 1 = IMPOSTOROUS 2. E17. 2 = IMPOSTOROUS 1. M17.

†impostumate *v.t.* & *i.* Also **-sthum-**. Pa. pple & ppl a. **-ate**, **-ated**. L16–L18. [Alt. of APOSTUMATE after IMPOSTUME.] Form an abscess (in).

impostumation /ɪmˌpɒstjʊˈmeɪʃ(ə)n/ *n.* Now *rare*. Also **-sthum-**. E16. [Alt. of APOSTUMATION after IMPOSTUME.] **1** An abscess, a cyst. E16. **2** The formation of an abscess; suppuration. M16.

impostume /ɪmˈpɒstjuːm/ *n.* Now *rare*. Also **-sthume**. LME. [OFr. *empostume* alt. of *apostume*: see APOSTUME.] An abscess, a cyst.

fig.: BROWNING The imposthume I prick to relieve thee of,—Vanity.

imposture /ɪmˈpɒstʃə/ *n.* M16. [Fr. f. late L *impostura*, f. L *impost-* pa. ppl stem of *imponere* IMPOSE *v.*: see -URE.] **1** (An act of) wilful and fraudulent deception. M16. **†2** Var. of IMPOSTOR. L16–M17.

imposturous *a.* (now *rare*) †(*a*) given to practising imposture; (*b*) deceptive, fraudulent: E17.

imposure /ɪmˈpəʊʒə/ *n. rare*. L17. [f. IMPOSE *v.* + -URE.] An imposition.

impotable /ɪmˈpəʊtəb(ə)l/ *a.* E17. [f. IM-[2] + POTABLE *a.*] Undrinkable.

impotence /ˈɪmpət(ə)ns/ *n.* LME. [(O)Fr. f. L *impotentia*, f. as IM-[2] + *potentia*: see POTENCE *n.*[1]] **1** Lack of strength or power; helplessness; weakness; feebleness. LME. **2** Inability to achieve erection of the penis; (esp. of a male) inability to have sexual intercourse or to reach orgasm or *pop.* to procreate. L15. **†3** Lack of self-restraint. E16–E18.

1 F. W. H. MYERS A feeling of terrible impotence burdens me—I am so powerless. 2 P. GAY Don Juan is afraid of impotence, perhaps of being a repressed homosexual.

impotency /ˈɪmpət(ə)nsi/ *n.* LME. [L *impotentia*: see prec., -ENCY.] 1 = IMPOTENCE 1. LME. †2 = IMPOTENCE 3. M16–E18. 3 = IMPOTENCE 2. L16.

impotent /ˈɪmpət(ə)nt/ *a.* & *n.* LME. [(O)Fr. f. L *impotent-*, *-ens*, f. as IM-[2] + POTENT *a.*[2]] **A** *adj.* **1** Powerless, helpless, ineffective; physically weak, decrepit. LME. **2** Unable to achieve erection of the penis; (esp. of a male) unable to have sexual intercourse or to reach orgasm or *pop.* to procreate. L15. **†3** Unrestrained, passionate. L16–E18.

1 ISAIAH BERLIN Individual wills may not be all-powerful, but neither are they totally impotent. 2 W. WHARTON An . . artificial-insemination business for wives of sterile or impotent men.

B *n.* **1** An impotent person. L15. **2** *collect. pl. The* class of impotent people. M18.

2 R. H. TAWNEY The Council . . insists on regular reports as to the . . relief of the impotent.

impotently *adv.* (*a*) powerlessly, feebly; †(*b*) unrestrainedly: E17. **†impotentness** *n.* (*rare*) M16–E18.

impound /ɪmˈpaʊnd/ *v.t.* Also **†em-**. LME. [f. IM-[1], EM-[1] + POUND *n.*[2]] **1** Shut up (esp. seized cattle) in a pound. LME. **2** Shut in or enclose (a person or thing) as in a pound. M16. **b** *spec.* Confine and store (water) in a reservoir; confine water so as to form (a reservoir). M19. **3** Take legal possession of, confiscate. M17.

impoundable *a.* L17. **impoundage** *n.* = IMPOUNDMENT E17. **impounder** *n.* E19. **impoundment** *n.* (*a*) the action of impounding, the condition of being impounded; (*b*) a body of water confined to form a reservoir: M17.

impoverish /ɪmˈpɒv(ə)rɪʃ/ *v.t.* Also **†em-**. LME. [OFr. *empoveriss-* lengthened stem of *empov(e)rir* (mod. *empauvrir*), f. as EM-[1], IM-[1] + *povre* POOR *a.*: see -ISH[2].] **1** Make poor, reduce to poverty. LME. **†b** Strip *of* some form of wealth. E17–E18. **2** *fig.* Weaken or reduce the quality of; deprive of some quality; affect adversely. M17.

1 J. GATHORNE-HARDY I found no evidence of over-high rents—why should councils wish to impoverish their local practices? M. PIERCY She would end up homeless and impoverished. 2 E. WAUGH Endowed with the most splendid language . . young writers seem intent to debase and impoverish it.

impoverisher *n.* E17.

impoverishment /ɪmˈpɒv(ə)rɪʃm(ə)nt/ *n.* Also **†em-**. LME. [AN *empoverissement*, f. OFr. *empov(e)rir*: see prec., -MENT.] The action of impoverishing someone or something; the condition of being impoverished; an instance of this.

†impower *v.* var. of EMPOWER.

impracticable /ɪmˈpraktɪkəb(ə)l/ *a.* & *n.* M17. [f. IM-[2] + PRACTICABLE.] **A** *adj.* **1** Not practicable; unable to be carried out or done; impossible in practice. M17. **2a** Of a road etc.: impassable. M17. **b** Of a person or thing: unmanageable, intractable. E18.

1 J. F. LEHMANN In the end the scheme was abandoned as impracticable. 2a G. GROTE The pass appeared impracticable. b B. H. MALKIN One of those impracticable beings, on whom good example, good advice . . are equally thrown away.

B *n.* An impracticable person. *rare*. E19.

impractica'bility *n.* (*a*) the quality or condition of being impracticable; (*b*) an impracticable thing: M18. **impracticableness** *n.* M17. **impracticably** *adv.* L18.

impractical /ɪmˈpraktɪk(ə)l/ *a.* M19. [f. IM-[2] + PRACTICAL *a.*] Not practical. Also, impracticable.

M. RULE The idea had to be abandoned as impractical on our site. M. SCAMMELL She was . . naive and impractical and unsuited to the tough, scheming world of the young Soviet republic.

impracti'cality *n.* E20. **impractically** *adv.* M20. **impracticalness** *n.* (*rare*) E20.

imprecate /ˈɪmprɪkeɪt/ *v.* E17. [L *imprecat-* pa. ppl stem of *imprecari*, f. as IM-[1] + *precari* PRAY *v.*: see -ATE[3].] **1** *v.t.* **a** Invoke or call down (evil *on* a person etc.). E17. **b** Beg for; entreat (something good). *rare*. M17. **2** *v.t.* Invoke evil on (a person); curse. Now *rare* or *obs.* E17. **3** *v.t.* Pray to, call on, (a god etc.). Long *rare* or *obs.* M17. **†4** *v.i.* Pray; invoke evil. M–L17.

1a SMOLLETT She . . imprecated a thousand curses upon his head. 2 W. MINTO His co-religionists were imprecating him as the man who had brought this persecution upon them. 3 W. PRYNNE Which I shall dayly imprecate the God of Peace speedily to accomplish.

imprecation /ɪmprɪˈkeɪʃ(ə)n/ *n.* LME. [L *imprecatio(n-)*, f. as prec.: see -ATION.] **1** The action or an act of imprecating, *spec.* of invoking or calling down evil on a person etc.; cursing. LME. **2** A prayer, an entreaty. Now *rare*. L16. **3** An invocation of evil; *esp.* a spoken curse or other expression of hostility. E17.

3 T. MO An immense crowd of Chinese, howling imprecations and with offensive weapons in their hands.

imprecatory /ˈɪmprɪkeɪt(ə)ri, ɪmˈprɛkət(ə)ri/ *a.* L16. [med.L *imprecatorius*, f. as IMPRECATE *v.*: see -ORY[2].] Expressing or involving imprecation; maledictory.

imprecatorily *adv.* L19.

imprecise /ɪmprɪˈsʌɪs/ *a.* E19. [f. IM-[2] + PRECISE *a.*] Not precise; lacking precision.

imprecisely *adv.* M20. **impreciseness** *n.* E20.

imprecision /ɪmprɪˈsɪʒ(ə)n/ *n.* E19. [f. IM-[2] + PRECISION *n.*] Lack of precision.

impredicable /ɪmˈprɛdɪkəb(ə)l/ *a.* E17. [f. IM-[2] + PREDICABLE.] Unable to be predicated.

impredica'bility *n.* E20.

impredicative /ɪmˈprɛdɪkətɪv/ *a.* M20. [f. IM-[2] + PREDICATIVE *a.*] *Logic.* Of a proposition, thing, etc.: not definable except in terms of a totality of which it is itself a part.

impregn /ɪmˈpriːn/ *v.t.* Now only *poet.* LME. [Late L *impregnare*: see IMPREGNATE *v.*] **1** Make (a female) pregnant; fertilize (*lit.* & *fig.*). LME. **2** Fill *with*; imbue, permeate, (*with*). M17.

impregnable /ɪmˈprɛgnəb(ə)l/ *a.*[1] LME. [OFr. *imprenable*, f. as IM-[2] + *prenable* takeable, f. *pren-* stem of *prendre* take f. L *prehendere*: see -ABLE; *-g-* perh. after *reign*, and OFr. vars.] (Of a fortress etc.) unable to be taken by force; *fig.* proof against attack, unassailable.

A. MACLEAN The Schloss Adler is inaccessible and impregnable It would require a battalion of paratroops to take it. A. STORR She carries within an impregnable conviction of being lovable.

impregna'bility *n.* M19. **impregnableness** *n.* (long *rare*) E17. **impregnably** *adv.* E17.

impregnable /ɪmˈprɛgnəb(ə)l/ *a.*[2] L19. [f. IMPREGNATE *v.* + -ABLE.] Able to be impregnated.

impregnant /ɪmˈprɛgnənt/ *a.* & *n.* L15. [Partly f. IM-[1] + PREGNANT *a.*[1], partly f. late L *impregnant-* pres. ppl stem of *impregnare*: see IMPREGNATE *v.*, -ANT[1].] **A** *adj.* **†1** Impregnated, pregnant. L15–E18. **2** That impregnates, impregnating. *arch. rare.* E19. **B** *n.* A thing which impregnates; *spec.* a substance used for the impregnation of something else. M17.

impregnate /ɪmˈprɛgnət/ *a.* L15. [Late L *impregnatus* pa. pple, f. as next: see -ATE[2].] **1** Pregnant, fruitful, (*lit.* & *fig.*). L15. **2** Imbued, permeated, *with*. M17.

impregnate /ˈɪmprɛgneɪt, ɪmˈprɛgneɪt/ *v.* E17. [Late L *impregnat-* pa. ppl stem of *impregnare*, f. as IM-[1] + *pregnare* be pregnant: see -ATE[3].] **1** *v.t.* Orig., fill. Later, fill (something) *with* a substance etc. diffused through it; imbue, saturate. Usu. in *pass.* E17. **b** *fig.* Imbue or fill (*with* feelings, moral qualities, etc.). M17. **2** *v.t.* Be diffused through (something); permeate, fill, saturate. M17. **3** *v.t.* Make (a female) pregnant; *Biol.* fertilize (a female reproductive cell or ovum). M17. **b** *v.i.* Become pregnant, conceive. *rare*. E18. **4** *v.t.* *fig.* Make fruitful or productive. M17.

1 J. ARBUTHNOT Water impregnated with some penetrating Salt. b LYTTON He had sought to impregnate his colleagues with the same loftiness of principle. L. DURRELL Seek an atmosphere less impregnated with the sense of deracination and failure.

impregnatable *a.* E20. **impregnator** *n.* a person who or thing which impregnates E18.

impregnation /ɪmprɛɡˈneɪʃ(ə)n/ *n.* LME. [(O)Fr., or f. as prec.: see -ATION.] **1** The action or process of making a female pregnant; fertilization. LME. **2** The action of imbuing or the fact of being imbued with something; diffusion through a substance; saturation. M17. **b** *spec.* The saturation of wood with a preservative. L19. **3** That with which something is impregnated; an impregnating element etc. E18.

impreparation /ɪm,prɛpəˈreɪʃ(ə)n/ *n.* Long *rare.* L16. [f. IM-^{2} + PREPARATION.] Lack of preparation; unpreparedness.

impresa /ɪmˈpreɪzə/ *n.* L16. [It. = undertaking, device, f. Proto-Romance vb, whence also EMPRISE. Cf. IMPRESE.] **1** An emblem, a device; *esp.* one accompanied by a motto. L16. **2** A sentence accompanying an emblem; a motto, a maxim, a proverb. Long *rare.* E17.

impresario /ɪmprɪˈsɑːrɪəʊ/ *n.* Pl. **-os.** M18. [It., f. as prec. + *-ario* -ARY^{1}.] An organizer or sponsor of public entertainments; a manager of an operatic or a concert company.

imprescriptible /ɪmprɪˈskrɪptɪb(ə)l/ *a.* L16. [med.L *imprescriptibilis*, f. as IM-^{2} + PRESCRIPTIBLE.] Not subject to prescription; unable to be legally taken away or abandoned.

T. PAINE The natural and imprescriptible rights of man . . are liberty, property, security, and resistance of oppression.

imprese /ɪmˈpreɪz/ *n.* Long *rare.* L16. [Obs. Fr. f. It. IMPRESA. See also IMPRESS *n.*^{3}] **1** = IMPRESA 1. L16. †**2** = IMPRESA 2. E17–E19.

impress /ˈɪmprɛs/ *n.*^{1} L16. [f. IMPRESS *v.*^{1}] **1** The act of impressing or stamping; a mark made by pressure of a seal, stamp, etc. (Foll. by *of.*) L16. **2** *fig.* A characteristic or distinctive mark or quality; a lasting effect or influence. L16. **b** An impression on the mind or senses. Now *rare.* L16.

1 T. MEDWIN Bluish marks . . as if made by the impress of the fingers. H. N. HUMPHREYS The reverse is incused with the impress of an amphora. **2** E. A. POE His obscurity . . bore the impress of his genius. H. JAMES She would . . have left a deeper impress upon her time. **b** E. K. KANE Some painful impress of solitary danger . . kept them closing up continually.

impress /ˈɪmprɛs/ *n.*^{2} *obs.* exc. *Hist.* Now *rare.* E17. [f. IMPRESS *v.*^{2}] Impressment; enforced service in the army or navy.

impress /ˈɪmprɛs/ *n.*^{3} *obs.* exc. *Hist.* E17. [Var. of IMPRESE, assoc. w. IMPRESS *n.*^{1}] **1** = IMPRESA 1. E17. †**2** = IMPRESA 2. Only in 17.

†**impress** *n.*^{4} E17. [Var. of IMPREST *n.*] **1** = IMPREST *n.* 1. E17–E18. **2** A charge made on the pay of a naval officer who had not accounted satisfactorily for public money advanced to him. Only in E19.

impress /ɪmˈprɛs/ *v.*^{1} Pa. t. & pple **impressed,** †**imprest.** LME. [(O)Fr. *empresser*, f. as EM-^{1}, IM-^{1} + PRESS *v.*^{1} after L *imprimere* (see IMPRESSION).] **I** *v.t.* **1** Apply with pressure; press (a thing) *on* another so as to leave a mark; imprint or stamp (a character or quality) *on*, as if by pressure. LME. **b** Produce or communicate (motion), exert (force), by pressure. (Foll. by *on.*) E18. **c** *Electr.* Apply (a voltage) to a device or circuit. L19. **2** *fig.* Cause to have a lasting effect or influence or to make an impression *on* or *upon* a person, the mind, etc., (foll. by simple obj., *that*, *what*, etc.); enforce or urge (a rule of conduct etc.) *on* or *upon.* LME. †**3** Print; make a typographical impression of. E16–L18. **4** Exert pressure on; mark (something) *with* the pressure of a stamp, seal, etc. L16. **b** *fig.* Stamp or imprint *with* a particular character, quality, etc. E19. **5** Produce a lasting effect or influence on the mind or feelings of; affect or influence deeply; make a favourable impression on; strike. (Foll. by *with.*) M18.

1 SHELLEY He did impress On the green moss his tremulous step. **b** C. LYELL Movements . . impressed on a wide expanse of ocean. **2** R. G. COLLINGWOOD My work in archeology . . impressed upon me the importance of the 'questioning activity'. S. UNWIN He . . impressed upon me that I must walk there. **4** A. RADCLIFFE The Marquis seizing her hand, impressed it with kisses. L. STEPHEN The ring . . was impressed with the seal of the Prophet. **b** LYTTON The words were impressed with a wild and melancholy depth of feeling. **5** J. GALSWORTHY The fellow had impressed him—great range, real genius! J. BUCHAN How did he impress you, Dick, when you knew him? D. PLANTE I wondered if she was trying to impress me with what she knew.

II *v.i.* †**6** Press in; press or throng *about.* LME–L15. **7** Appear impressive; make a favourable impression. M20.

impressed *a.* (*a*) *gen.* that has been impressed (*lit.* & *fig.*); deeply and favourably affected or influenced; (*b*) *Zool.* & *Bot.* sunk in, depressed, marked by surface depressions: LME.

impress /ɪmˈprɛs/ *v.*^{2}*t.* Pa. t & pple **impressed,** †**imprest.** L16. [f. IM-^{1} + PRESS *v.*^{2}] **1** Chiefly *Hist.* Levy or provide (a force) for military or naval service, enlist; *spec.* compel (men) to serve in the army or esp. the navy. Also, seize (goods etc.) for royal or public service. L16. **2** Enlist or make use of in an argument etc. *arch.* M17.

1 A. DUGGAN A travel-warrant . . authorising them to impress transport and requisition billets. C. RYAN A number of Poles, impressed into the German Army. **2** F. W. FARRAR Hypotheses into the service of which Philology was impressed.

†**impress** *v.*^{3}*t.* *rare.* Pa. t. & pple **impressed, imprest.** M17. [Var. of IMPREST *v.*^{1} Cf. IMPRESS *n.*^{4}] **1** = IMPREST *v.*^{1} 1. M17–E19. **2** Levy a charge on (the pay of a naval officer) because of unsatisfactory accounting for public money advanced. Only in E19.

impressible /ɪmˈprɛsɪb(ə)l/ *a.* Also (earlier) †**-able.** LME. [f. IMPRESS *v.*^{1} + -ABLE, -IBLE.] Able to be impressed (*lit.* & *fig.*); susceptible, impressionable.

impressiˈbility *n.* M18.

impression /ɪmˈprɛʃ(ə)n/ *n.* & *v.* LME. [(O)Fr. f. L *impressio(n-)*, f. *impress-* pa. ppl stem of *imprimere*, f. as IM-^{1} + *premere* PRESS *v.*^{1}: see -ION.] **A** *n.* **1a** Pressure applied by one thing on or into the surface of another; an instance or effect of such pressure; the stamping of a character or quality *on.* LME. †**b** A charge, an attack, an assault. LME–L18. †**c** *Pros.* & *Rhet.* A stress, an emphasis. M17–E19. **d** An impact or shock of an atmospheric or physical force. Now *rare* or *obs.* L17. **2** A mark produced on a surface by pressure, esp. by the application of a stamp, seal, etc. Also, a cast, a copy. LME. **b** *Dentistry.* A mould (from which a positive cast may be made) formed by the imprint of the teeth, gums, etc., in a soft material. M19. **3** The effective action of one thing on another; influence; a change produced in a passive subject by the operation of an external cause. LME. †**b** *spec.* An atmospheric influence, condition, or phenomenon. LME–L17. **4a** An effect produced on the mind, conscience, or feelings. LME. **b** An effect produced on the senses; a sensation. E17. **c** A (vague or mistaken) notion or belief impressed on the mind. E17. **5a** The process of printing. Now *rare.* E16. **b** The result of printing; a print taken from type or other surfaces. M16. **c** (The printing of) the number of copies of a book, newspaper, etc., issued at one time. L16. **d** An essentially unaltered reprint of a book etc. from standing type, plates, film, etc., as opp. to a new edition. E20. **6** A representation of a person or thing by an artist, a mimic, etc.; a brief impersonation of a well-known personality. M20.

1a B. JOWETT The creation of the world is the impression of order on a previously existing chaos. **b** S. JOHNSON Elephants . . by the violence of their impression . . often threw the enemy into disorder. **2** G. BERKELEY As . . a seal [is said] to make an impression upon wax. D. L. DINELEY Moulds or impressions are left in any soft mud or sand. *fig.*: W. COWPER If it bear The stamp and clear impression of good sense. **3** J. IMISON One of the hardest metals; a file can scarcely make any impression on it. W. S. CHURCHILL Rupert's cavalry . . could make no impression on the London pikemen and musketeers. **4a** E. A. FREEMAN A deep impression had been made on the minds of Englishmen. P. ROTH Strong first impressions had of course been formed. **b** B. JOWETT Our impressions of hearing may be affected by those of sight. **c** OED It is a mere impression, and I may easily be mistaken. R. TRAVERS Burgess . . dug his own grave under the impression he was opening a mining shaft. **5a** GIBBON The impression of the fourth volume had consumed three months. **b** M. M. HEATON Very early impressions of Dürer's engravings are seldom now to be met with. **c** J. COLLINGES 6000 of his books being sold, if 1500 be allowed to an Impression. **d** J. GROSS The book . . quickly ran through half-a-dozen impressions, and Birrell . . found himself a minor celebrity. **6** D. NATHAN Peter would come in and do a few impressions of Kenneth Horne and others.

B *v. rare.* †**1** *v.i.* Stamp; make an impression. Only in E17. **2** *v.t.* Make an impression on, affect. M19.

Comb.: **impression compound** an impression material manufactured from a number of different ingredients, *esp.* one that is a non-elastic thermoplastic solid; **impression material** a substance used in taking dental impressions.

impressional *a.* (*a*) impressionable; (*b*) of or pertaining to an impression or impressions: M19. **impressionless** *a.* (*rare*) M19.

impressionable /ɪmˈprɛʃ(ə)nəb(ə)l/ *a.* M19. [Fr., f. *impressionner*, f. as prec.: see -ABLE.] **1** Susceptible to impressions; easily influenced. M19. **2** Able to be impressed. *rare.* L19.

1 J. MORTIMER How impressionable he was—he had been speaking French when they came out of *Hiroshima Mon Amour.* **2** *Life* Tinfoil thin enough to be impressionable by the metal style.

impressionaˈbility *n.* M19. **impressionableness** *n.* M19.

impressionary /ɪmˈprɛʃ(ə)n(ə)ri/ *a.* L19. [f. IMPRESSION *n.* + -ARY^{1}.] Impressionistic.

impressionism /ɪmˈprɛʃ(ə)nɪz(ə)m/ *n.* In branch II also **I-.** M19. [In branch I directly f. IMPRESSION *n.*, in branch II f. Fr. *impressionnisme*, f. as next: see -ISM.] †**I 1** The philosophy of David Hume (1711–76) regarding sensations. *rare.* Only in M19. **II 2** A school or style of painting, originating in France in the late 19th cent., aiming at representation of the visual impression or overall effect of a subject, scene, etc., rather than of its detail; *transf.* an analogous literary style. L19. **3** A style of musical composition in which clarity of structure and theme is subordinate to harmonic effects, characteristically using the whole-tone scale. L19.

impressionist /ɪmˈprɛʃ(ə)nɪst/ *n.* & *a.* Also **I-.** L19. [Fr. *impressionniste* (orig. applied unfavourably in 1874 w. ref. to Claude Monet's painting *Impression: soleil levant*), f. as IMPRESSION *n.*: see -IST.] **A** *n.* **1** An adherent or practitioner of impressionism in painting, literature, or music. Also, a painting by an impressionist. L19. **2** An entertainer whose act consists of imitations or impersonations of well-known personalities etc. M20. **B** *attrib.* or as *adj.* Of or pertaining to impressionists or impressionism. L19.

impressionistic /ɪm,prɛʃəˈnɪstɪk/ *a.* L19. [Partly f. prec., partly f. IMPRESSION *n.*: see -ISTIC.] Of, pertaining to, or characteristic of impressionism or impressionists; subjective, unsystematic.

impressionistically *adv.* E20.

impressive /ɪmˈprɛsɪv/ *a.* L16. [f. IMPRESS *v.*^{1} + -IVE.] †**1** Able to be easily impressed; susceptible (*to*); impressible. L16–M17. **2** Making a deep impression on the mind or senses, esp. so as to cause approval or admiration; (of language, a scene, etc.) capable of exciting deep feeling. L16.

1 J. SPENCER The multitude . . cannot but be greatly impressive to any great and religious Perswasions concerning Prodigies. **2** D. W. GOODWIN There is now impressive evidence that drinking and pregnancy do not mix. B. LOPEZ What was so impressive about the bear we saw . . was how robust he seemed.

impressively *adv.* E19. **impressiveness** *n.* M17.

impressment /ɪmˈprɛsm(ə)nt/ *n.*^{1} L18. [f. IMPRESS *v.*^{2} + -MENT.] The action or practice of impressing someone or something for public service; enlistment or use in an argument etc.

impressment /ɪmˈprɛsm(ə)nt/ *n.*^{2} *rare.* M19. [Fr. *empressement*, f. as IMPRESS *v.*^{1} + -MENT.] Earnestness, ardour.

impressure /ɪmˈprɛʃə/ *n.* Now *rare.* L15. [f. IMPRESS *v.*[1] + -URE, after *pressure.*] **1** The action of impressing or exerting pressure. L15. **2** A mark made by pressure; an impression; an indentation. E17. **3** An impression on the mind or senses. E17.

imprest /ˈɪmprɛst/ *n.* & *a.* M16. [f. IM-[1] + PREST *n.*[1], prob. partly after *in prest* (see PREST *n.*[1]), though *im-* appears in med.L cognates (cf. next). See also IMPRESS *n.*[4]] **A** *n.* **1** Money advanced to a person for use in State business. Formerly also, advance pay for those in military and naval service. M16. **2** *gen.* An advance, a loan. L17.

2 J. LE CARRÉ He.. lavished a sizable part of our secret imprest on encouraging more breeds of trout.

Comb.: **imprest system** *Comm.* a system under which a person is advanced a fixed sum of money to meet expenses and at the end of a definite period is advanced a further sum equal to the amount spent, so as to restore the float to the original amount.

†**B** *adj.* Of money: lent or paid in advance, esp. to those in military, naval, or public service. L16–M18.

†**imprest** *v.*[1]*t.* M16. [f. It. and med.L *imprestare* lend, advance as an imprest, f. as IM-[1] + L *praestare* furnish, (in med.L) lend, rel. to *praesto* at hand, within reach.] **1** Advance or lend (money). M16–E19. **2** Draw (a bill etc.) *upon* an account or a person. E–M17.

†**imprest** *v.*[2]*t.* M17–E18. [f. pa. pple of IMPRESS *v.*[2], perh. also confused w. IMPREST *v.*[1]] Impress for the army or navy.

†**imprest** *v.*[3], *v.*[4], *v.*[5] pa. t. & pple: see IMPRESS *v.*[1], *v.*[2], *v.*[3]

imprevisible /ɪmprɪˈvɪzɪb(ə)l/ *a. rare.* L19. [f. IM-[2] + PREVISE + -IBLE.] Unable to be foreseen.

imprévu /ɛ̃prevy/ *n.* M19. [Fr., f. as IM-[2] + *prévu* pa. pple of *prévoir* foresee.] *The* unexpected, *the* unforeseen.

imprimatur /ɪmprɪˈmeɪtə, -ˈmɑːtə, -ˈmɑːtʊə/ *n.* M17. [L = let it be printed, 3rd person sing. pres. subjunct. pass. of *imprimere* IMPRINT *v.*] In the Roman Catholic Church, an official licence authorizing the printing of an ecclesiastical or religious work etc.; *gen.* official approval, an official sanction.

J. BRONOWSKI Galileo collected.. four imprimaturs, and early in 1632 the book was published. P. GAY The psychological function of this partially unconscious fiction is to give the imprimatur to the child's aggressive impulses.

imprimatura /ˌɪmpriːməˈtʊərə, *foreign* ˌimpri maˈtuːra/ *n.* M20. [It. *imprimitura.*] A usu. coloured transparent primer or glaze applied to an artist's canvas or panel.

†**imprime** *v.* & *n.* Also **em-**. L16. [f. IM-[1], EM-[1] + PRIME *a.* or *n.*[1] or L *primus* first.] *Hunting.* **A** *v.t.* Separate (a deer) from the rest of the herd. L16–L18. **B** *n.* An act of separating a deer from the rest of the herd. L16–M18.

imprimis /ɪmˈprʌɪmɪs/ *adv. arch.* LME. [L, assim. form of *in primis* among the first things, f. *in* IN *prep.* + *primis* abl. pl. of *primus* first.] In the first place.

imprimitive /ɪmˈprɪmɪtɪv/ *a.* E18. [f. IM-[2] + PRIMITIVE *a.*] †**1** Not following primitive usage or tradition. *rare.* Only in E18. **2** *Math.* Of a group: not primitive. L19.

imprint /ˈɪmprɪnt/ *n.* Also (earlier) †**em-**. LME. [(O)Fr. *empreinte* use as n. of fem. pa. pple of *empreindre*: see next, PRINT *n.*] **1** A mark produced by pressure on a surface; an impression, a stamp. LME. **b** *fig.* A lasting impression or sign of some emotion, experience, action, etc.; an influence; an effect. E17. **2** A publisher's or printer's name, often with an address, date, and other details of publication, printed in a book etc., usu. on the title-page, or at the foot of a single sheet; any of various names used as imprints by a publishing house; *loosely* a publishing house. L18. **3** Something printed; *spec.* a postage stamp printed on the paper to be used. L19. **4** (**I-**.) A typeface derived from Caslon [named after the periodical for which it was designed]. E20.

1 H. MOORE Clay is wonderful stuff to punch and feel that the imprint of your fist is left in it. J. T. STORY He put coal dust on the blotter and read the imprint of my letter. b C. G. WOLFF Edith Wharton had to contend with the part of herself that carried Mother's imprint. P. D. JAMES His face, his clothes, the confident gaze, all bore the unmistakable imprint of success. 2 P. ACKROYD The Woolfs had agreed to print Eliot's.. work under the imprint of the Hogarth Press. A. BLOND The New English Library (.. an imprint of Hodder and Stoughton). 3 *Library* The Library now has an almost complete collection of Norwegian imprints.

imprint /ɪmˈprɪnt/ *v.t.* Also (earlier) †**em-**. LME. [OFr. *empreinter*, f. *empreint* pa. pple of *empreindre*, ult. f. L *imprimere*, f. as IM-[1] + *premere* PRESS *v.*[1] Cf. PRINT *v.*] **1** Mark by pressure; make an imprint or impression of (a figure etc.) *on*; impress *with* a figure etc. LME. †**b** Print (a book etc.) by means of a press and type. L15–E19. **2** *fig.* Impress *on* or fix *in* the mind, memory, etc.; impart, impress (a quality, character, etc.) *on* or *in* a person or thing. LME. **3** *Psychol.* Cause (esp. a young animal) to accept or recognize a person, animal, or thing as the proper object of an innate response, esp. as a parent; cause (an animal etc.) to be so accepted or recognized. Foll. by *on, to.* Freq. in *pass.* and as *imprinting* vbl n. M20.

1 M. SHELLEY A land never before imprinted by the foot of man. DICKENS Each sometimes stops and slowly imprints a deeper footstep in the fallen leaves. 2 C. BLACKWOOD She had remained for ever imprinted on his memory. C. PHILLIPS He would pick out a spot, .. and try and imprint it on his mind. 3 B. THORPE The parent.. fish may become imprinted to the young as well as the young to the parent.

imprinter *n.* M16.

imprison /ɪmˈprɪz(ə)n/ *v.t.* Also (earlier) †**em-**. ME. [OFr. *emprisoner* (mod. *-onner*), f. as EM-[1], IM-[1] + PRISON *n.*] Put or keep in a prison or other place of confinement; confine, shut up, (*lit.* & *fig.*).

G. K. CHESTERTON A desperate thing imprisoned in this box of thin wood. V. GLENDINNING She was imprisoned for her political activities and for her advocacy of birth control. KARL MILLER The inscrutable child who appears.. both excluded and imprisoned, locked out and locked in. P. LIVELY I.. am as imprisoned by my time as you were by yours.

imprisonable *a.* able to be imprisoned, liable to imprisonment; (of an offence) for which a person can be imprisoned: E17. **imprisoner** *n.* M17.

imprisonment /ɪmˈprɪz(ə)nm(ə)nt/ *n.* LME. [AN *emprisounement*, OFr. *-one-*, f. as prec.: see -MENT.] The action or an act of imprisoning someone or (*transf.* & *fig.*) something; the fact or condition of being imprisoned.

E. CRANKSHAW Imprisonment was not enough. They must receive six thousand lashes. *false imprisonment*: see FALSE *a.*

impro /ˈɪmprəʊ/ *n. slang.* L20. [Abbrev.: cf. IMPROV.] Improvisation in performance.

improbability /ɪmˌprɒbəˈbɪlɪti/ *n.* L16. [f. next: see -ITY.] **1** The quality of being improbable. L16. **2** An improbable circumstance or thing. E17.

improbable /ɪmˈprɒbəb(ə)l/ *a.* L16. [Fr., or L *improbabilis* hard to prove, f. as IM-[2] + *probabilis* PROBABLE *a.*] Not probable; not likely to be true or to happen; unlikely; difficult to believe, though true or existent.

ISAIAH BERLIN These alternatives may be improbable; but they must at least be conceivable. E. J. HOWARD Listing.. a number of improbable things which could not possibly have happened to it. J. S. HUXLEY The improbable plumage and glorious brightness of some exotic birds. N. MAILER It seemed not improbable that Pangborn could be the maniac who did it.

improbableness *n.* E18. **improbably** *adv.* M17.

improbation /ɪmprəˈbeɪʃ(ə)n/ *n.* M16. [L *improbatio(n-)* disproof, refutation, f. *improbat-* pa. ppl stem of *improbare* disapprove, reject, f. as IM-[2] + *probare* PROVE *v.*: see -ATION. In sense 2 f. Fr.] **1** Disproof. Long only *spec.* (*Sc. Law*), disproof of a writ as invalid or forged; *esp.* an action brought to disprove a writ on these grounds. M16. †**2** Disapproval. M17–L18.

improbative /ɪmˈprəʊbətɪv/ *a.* M18. [AL *improbativus* tending to refute, f. L *improbat-*: see prec., -ATIVE. Cf PROBATIVE.] Liable to disproof; not proved to be genuine.

improbity /ɪmˈprəʊbɪti, -ˈprɒb-/ *n.* LME. [L *improbitas*, f. as IM-[2] + *probitas* PROBITY.] †**1** Audacity. Only in LME. **2** Wickedness, lack of moral integrity; dishonesty. L16.

improficiency /ɪmprəˈfɪʃ(ə)nsi/ *n.* Now *rare.* M17. [f. IM-[2] + PROFICIENCY.] Lack of proficiency.

†**improfitable** *a.* ME–E18. [f. IM-[2] + PROFITABLE.] Unprofitable.

improgressive /ɪmprəˈgrɛsɪv/ *a.* Now *rare.* E19. [f. IM-[2] + PROGRESSIVE *a.*] Not progressive.

improgressively *adv.* M19. **improgressiveness** *n.* E19.

improlific /ɪmprəˈlɪfɪk/ *a. rare.* M17. [f. IM-[2] + PROLIFIC.] Not prolific.

†**imprompt** *a.* L16–M18. [f. IM-[2] + PROMPT *a.*] Unready.

impromptu /ɪmˈprɒm(p)tjuː/ *adv.*, *n.*, *a.*, & *v.* M17. [Fr. f. L *in promptu* at hand, in readiness, f. *promptus* readiness: see PROMPT *n.*] **A** *adv.* Without preparation; on the spur of the moment; extempore. M17.

G. GREENE The actor had been ready to play impromptu the part of Chavel.

B *n.* Something composed, uttered, or done impromptu; an improvisation; *spec.* a musical composition having the character of an improvisation. L17.

B. EARNSHAW The music that he played, Furious and subtle with an impromptu that might be art. G. GREENE 'I still don't know how you came here.' 'Just an impromptu. I was in an inn about sixty miles from here.'

C *adj.* Composed, uttered, or done impromptu; improvised; makeshift. M18.

J. CAREY He threw away brilliant impromptu things in conversation. N. MAILER Dennis had an impromptu press conference right on the steps of the prison. D. M. THOMAS Some were making impromptu labels out of bits of string and torn-off paper.

D *v.t.* & *i.* Improvise; extemporize. E19.

improper /ɪmˈprɒpə/ *a.* LME. [(O)Fr. *impropre* or L *improprius*, f. as IM-[2] + *proprius* PROPER *a.*] **1** Incorrect, inaccurate, irregular, wrong. LME. **2** Unsuitable, inappropriate. L16. **3** Unbecoming, unseemly, indecorous. E17.

1 I. MURDOCH These would make terrible wounds, and Pat felt.. it would be improper to use them. H. WILSON To provide.. contact with the party machine, which it would be unprocedural, if not improper, to attempt through the Civil Service. **improper fraction** *Math.* a fraction whose value is greater than one, with the numerator greater than the denominator. 2 R. BOYLE A Plain being a very improper place for such a purpose. 3 G. SANTAYANA This deportment, undignified.. on weekdays, was positively improper on Sundays. A. CARTER Melanie felt improper, like a chorus girl taking Holy Communion in fishnet tights.

improperly *adv.* LME. **improperness** *n.* (*rare*) E17.

†**improper** *v.t.* LME–M17. [AL *impropriare*: see IMPROPRIATE.] = IMPROPRIATE.

improperium /ɪmprəˈpɪərɪəm/ *n.* Pl. **-ria** /-rɪə/. L19. [Late L = reproach.] *RC Ch.* Each of a series of antiphons with responses forming part of the liturgical service for Good Friday, purported to echo Christ's reproach of the Jewish people (as representing all humanity). Usu. in *pl.*

†**improportional** *a.* E17–L18. [f. IM-[2] + PROPORTIONAL *a.*] Disproportionate.

impropriate /ɪmˈprəʊprɪeɪt/ *v.t.* Pa. pple & ppl a. **-ate** /-ət/, **-ated**. E16. [AL *impropriat-* pa. ppl stem of *impropriare*, f. L IM-[1] + *proprius* PROPER *a.*: see -ATE[3]. Cf. earlier IMPROPER *v.*] Appropriate. Now only *spec.*, annex (an ecclesiastical benefice) to a corporation or person as corporate or private property; *esp.* place (tithes or ecclesiastical property) in lay hands.

impropriation /ɪmˌprəʊprɪˈeɪʃ(ə)n/ *n.* M16. [AL *impropriatio(n-)*, f. as prec.: see -ATION.] **1** The action of impropriating a benefice etc.; the proprietorship conveyed by this action. M16. **2** An impropriated benefice; property, tithes, etc., held by an ecclesiastical or lay organization.

M16. †3 *gen.* Appropriation; a thing appropriated. E17–E18.

impropriator /ɪmˈprəʊprɪeɪtə/ *n.* E17. [f. IMPROPRIATE + -OR.] A person to whom a benefice is impropriated.

impropriˈatrix *n.* a female impropriator L18.

impropriety /ɪmprəˈprʌɪəti/ *n.* E17. [Fr. *impropriété* or L *improprietas*, f. *improprius* IMPROPER *a.*: see -ITY.] 1 Incorrectness; inaccuracy. E17. 2 Unbecomingness, unseemliness, indecency; improper conduct. E17. 3 Unsuitableness, inappropriateness. L17. 4 An instance of improper conduct, language, etc. L17.

1 J. S. MILL We may therefore say, without impropriety, that the quality forms part of its signification. 2 G. S. HAIGHT There was undeniable impropriety in a young girl's going about alone. 4 A. N. WILSON His name could not be mentioned; it was on a level with the coarsest impropriety or profanity.

†improsperity *n.* E16–E18. [f. IM-[2] + PROSPERITY.] The state or condition of being unprosperous, absence of prosperity.

improsperous /ɪmˈprɒsp(ə)rəs/ *a.* Now *rare* or *obs.* L16. [f. IM-[2] + PROSPEROUS.] †1 Of luck etc: unpropitious. L16–M17. 2 Unprosperous; unlucky. E17.

†improsperously *adv.* L16–L17.

improv /ˈɪmprɒv/ *n. slang.* L20. [Abbrev.: cf. IMPRO.] An improvisation in performance.

†improvable *a.*[1] *rare.* Also **improve-**. E17–E18. [f. IMPROVE *v.*[1] + -ABLE.] Able to be disproved or condemned.

improvable /ɪmˈpruːvəb(ə)l/ *a.*[2] Also **improve-**. M17. [f. IMPROVE *v.*[2] + -ABLE.] 1 That may be taken advantage of or used profitably; serviceable. Now *rare* or *obs.* M17. 2 Orig. (of land), able to be profitably cultivated; able to be made more productive by cultivation. Now chiefly *gen.*, able to be made better. M17.

2 *New Yorker* Bill saw the world as . . quite bad; Gina saw it as improvable.

improvaˈbility *n.* L18. **improvableness** *n.* M17. **improvably** *adv.* M18.

improve /ɪmˈpruːv/ *n. Austral. slang.* M20. [f. IMPROVE *v.*[2]] A course of improvement. Only in *on the improve*, improving, getting better in health etc.

†improve *v.*[1]*t.* LME. [OFr. *improver* (mod. *improuver*) f. L *improbare* condemn, disapprove, f. as IM-[2] + *probare* approve.] 1 Disprove, refute. LME–E17. 2 Disapprove, disallow; censure, condemn. E16–M18.

improve /ɪmˈpruːv/ *v.*[2] Also (earlier) **†em-**, **†improw**. E16. [AN *emprower*, *emprouer* (in AL *appro(w)are, appruare*), f. OFr. *em-* EM-[1], IM-[1] + *prou* profit (f. late L *prode*, evolved from L *prodest* is of advantage), later infl. by PROVE *v.* Cf. APPROVE *v.*[1]] I *v.t.* 1 †a *refl.* Make a profit for (oneself), avail (oneself) *of* profitably. E16–M17. †b Increase the price or value of (esp. land). M16–M18. c Turn (land) to profit; cultivate or make more productive or valuable by cultivation. *obs.* exc. as passing into sense 4. M17. †d Invest or lay out (money) profitably. M17–M19. 2a Avail oneself of, utilize, (a person or thing). Now only *US*, make use of or occupy (a place). E16. b Make good use of, take advantage of, (an occasion, event, etc.); *arch.* make use of for spiritual edification. M16. 3 Make greater in amount or degree; increase, develop, intensify. *obs.* exc. as passing into sense 4. E16. 4 Increase the quality or value of; bring into a better or more desirable condition or state; make better; *arch.* make better or more advantageous by converting *into*. E17. 5 Lose or cause to disappear in the process of making better or more profitable. Foll. by *away, off*, etc. L18.

2b BOSW. SMITH The Roman army improved the victory of their fleet by . . marching to Egesta. E. P. THOMPSON He . . had been improving the time in prison by collecting examples . . of other parodists. *improve the* SHINING *hour.* 4 H. JAMES The purpose of improving one's mind by foreign travel. S. J. PERELMAN Flowers . . studied the *Harvard Classics*, with which he was improving himself. R. DAVIES Ismay was abroad, staying with a French family to improve her accent. *Dumfries Courier* Union Members . . in search of an improved pay offer.

II *v.i.* 6 Increase, advance, develop. Now *dial.* exc. as passing into sense 8. M17. 7 Foll. by *on*, *upon*: make or produce something better than. L17. 8 Increase in value or excellence; become better. E18.

7 J. B. PRIESTLEY We all know this England, which at its best cannot be improved upon. G. GREENE Ford's apprenticeship with Conrad had borne its fruit, but he had improved on the Master. 8 E. WAUGH Some of the characters improve with age, they grow wiser and kinder. B. PYM She began to plan a visit, after the New Year, when the weather improved.

improveable *a.*[1], *a.*[2] vars. of IMPROVABLE *a.*[1], *a.*[2]

improvement /ɪmˈpruːvm(ə)nt/ *n.* Also (earlier) **†em-**, **†improwement**. LME. [AN *emprowement*, f. as IMPROVE *v.*[2]: see -MENT.] †1 Profitable management or use; the realization of the profits of something; profit. LME–E16. b Profitable investment of money. M17–E18. 2 The turning of land to profit; the cultivation of land, or now *esp.* the erection of buildings, fences, etc., on land, to improve the condition and value. Also, a piece of land improved by cultivation, building, etc.; now *esp.* buildings, fences, etc., by which a piece of land is improved. Now *N. Amer.* & *NZ* and passing into senses 5 and 6. L15. †3 The action or process of making or becoming greater; (an) increase, (a) growth, development, intensification. M16–L18. 4 The utilization of a person or thing. Now only, the making good use or taking advantage of an occasion, event, etc.; *arch.* the profitable use of something for spiritual edification. E17. 5 The action or process of making or becoming better or more valuable; the state of being better. M17. 6 An act of making or becoming better; an addition or alteration which increases the quality or value of something. L17. 7 The production of something better than something else; a result of this. Foll. by *on, upon*. E18.

5 H. BLAIR Exercise is the chief source of improvement in all our faculties. D. W. GOODWIN The goal is not so much a . . cure . . as it is to bring about improvement. 6 H. JAMES It's a great advantage to have a new house; you get all the latest improvements. GEORGE MOORE Better to retain his . . mistakes than to accept any suggestions, even if they were improvements. 7 A. EDEN The appearance and manner of the boys . . seemed to be an improvement on my generation. R. ELLMANN 'I suffer, therefore I may be,' was his improvement upon Descartes.

improver /ɪmˈpruːvə/ *n.* M17. [f. IMPROVE *v.*[2] + -ER[1].] 1 A person who improves something; *esp.* a person who makes improvements to increase the quality or value of a thing. M17. b A person who works for a low wage or none to improve his or her skill. M19. 2 Something that improves; *spec.* (*a*) = *dress-improver* s.v. DRESS *n.*; (*b*) a chemical substance added to a foodstuff by a manufacturer to improve it in some way. M17.

1b J. FOWLES His apprentices, improvers and the rest were atrociously lodged. 2 *Scotsman* Recent . . proposals recommended banning the use of all flour 'improvers' which included preservatives.

improvership *n.* the position of an improver (IMPROVER 1b) L19.

improvidence /ɪmˈprɒvɪd(ə)ns/ *n.* LME. [Late L *improvidentia*, f. as IM-[2] + *providentia* PROVIDENCE.] The fact or quality of being improvident.

R. NIEBUHR The poverty of the workers was due to their laziness and their improvidence.

improvident /ɪmˈprɒvɪd(ə)nt/ *a.* L15. [f. IM-[2] + PROVIDENT *a.*, or f. late L *improvident-*, f. as IM-[2] + *provident-* pres. ppl stem of *providere* PROVIDE *v.*: see -ENT.] 1 Unforeseeing. L15. 2 Incautious, unwary; heedless. L16. 3 Lacking foresight; spendthrift; failing to provide for the future. E17.

1 W. S. CHURCHILL Parliament . . was eager for war, improvident in preparation, and resentful in paying for it. 2 J. C. OATES She was to be accused of reckless, improvident thinking. 3 H. KELLER I am improvident enough to prefer present joy to hoarding riches against a rainy day.

improvidently *adv.* LME. **improvidentness** *n.* (*rare*) E18.

improving /ɪmˈpruːvɪŋ/ *ppl a.* M17. [f. IMPROVE *v.*[2] + -ING[2].] That makes or becomes better; *spec.* that improves the mind, understanding, or character.

A. J. P. TAYLOR No Sexton Blake, no comics, nothing but improving works.

improvingly *adv.* M19.

improvisation /ˌɪmprəvʌɪˈzeɪʃ(ə)n, -prɒvɪ-/ *n.* L18. [f. IMPROVISATOR or IMPROVISATORE: see -ATION.] The action of improvising; something done or produced on the spur of the moment; *spec.* a piece of improvised music or verse.

Q. CRISP Matters would . . have been even worse if my entire programme had been an improvisation. *Photographer* Equipment was 'very basic' so he discovered a lot about improvisation.

improvisational *a.* of or pertaining to improvisation, of the nature of an improvisation E20. **improvisationally** *adv.* M20.

improvisator /ɪmˈprɒvɪzeɪtə/ *n.* L18. [Anglicized f. next.] An improviser.

improvisatore /improvizaˈtoːre; ˌɪmprəviːzəˈtɔːri/ *n.* Also **-vv-** /-vv-/. Pl. ***-ri*** /-ri/, ***-res*** /-rɪz/. M18. [It. *improvvisatore*, f. *improvvisare* IMPROVISE. See also prec.] An (Italian) improviser; an improviser in an Italian manner.

improvisatorial /ˌɪmprəvʌɪzəˈtɔːrɪəl, -prɒvɪz-/ *a.* E19. [f. IMPROVISATOR + -IAL.] Of, pertaining to, or of the nature of an improviser; improvisatory.

improvisatory /ɪmprəvʌɪˈzeɪt(ə)ri, -prɒvɪ-, -ˈvʌɪzə-/ *a.* E19. [f. as prec.: see -ORY[2].] Of or pertaining to improvisation; of the nature of (an) improvisation.

Times Lit. Suppl. His way of writing, his pouncing, wiredrawn, improvisatory eloquence, amounts to a classic style.

improvisatrice /improvizaˈtriːtʃe, ˌɪmprəviːzəˈtriːtʃi/ *n.* Also **-vv-**. Pl. ***-ci*** /-tʃi/. E19. [It., fem. of *improvvisatore*: see IMPROVISATORE, -TRICE.] A female *improvisatore*.

improvise /ˈɪmprəvʌɪz/ *v.t.* & *i.* E19. [Fr. *improviser* or its source It. *improvvisare*, f. *improvviso* extempore f. L *improvisus* unforeseen, f. as IM-[2] + *provisus* pa. pple of *providere* PROVIDE.] 1 Compose (music or verse) or utter or do (anything) on the spur of the moment. E19. 2 Provide or construct (something) as a makeshift. M19.

1 J. B. PRIESTLEY He was able to improvise the most amusing little tunes. R. G. COLLINGWOOD No rule can tell you how to act . . . you must improvise as best you can. 2 K. GRAHAME Knotting the sheets . . together and tying . . the improvised rope round the central mullion. P. ROTH Each appeared to have improvised a uniform from a heap of old clothes.

improviser /ˈɪmprəvʌɪzə/ *n.* E19. [f. prec. + -ER[1].] A person who improvises or composes extempore.

improvvisatore, ***-trice*** *ns.* vars. of IMPROVISATORE, -TRICE.

†improw *v.*, **†improwement** *n.* see IMPROVE *v.*[2], IMPROVEMENT.

imprudence /ɪmˈpruːd(ə)ns/ *n.* LME. [(O)Fr., or L *imprudentia*, f. as next: see -ENCE.] 1 The quality or fact of being imprudent; lack of prudence; indiscretion; rashness. LME. 2 An instance of this; an imprudent act. LME.

Also **†imprudency** *n.* L16–E19.

imprudent /ɪmˈpruːd(ə)nt/ *a.* LME. [L *imprudent-*, f. as IM-[2] + *prudent-* PRUDENT.] Not prudent, lacking in discretion; rash, incautious.

imprudently *adv.* M16. **imprudentness** *n.* (*rare*) E18.

impsonite /ˈɪmps(ə)nʌɪt/ *n.* E20. [f. *Impson* Valley in Oklahoma, USA + -ITE[1].] An asphaltic mineral similar to albertite.

impudence /ˈɪmpjʊd(ə)ns/ *n.* LME. [L *impudentia*, f. as IMPUDENT: see -ENCE.] 1 Shamelessness; immodesty, indelicacy. *obs.* exc. *dial.* LME. 2 Shameless effrontery; insolent disrespect; insolence, presumption. E17. 3 Freedom from diffidence, cool confidence. E17.

impudency /ˈɪmpjʊd(ə)nsi/ *n.* Now *rare.* E16. [f. as prec.: see -ENCY.] 1 = IMPUDENCE 2. E16. 2 = IMPUDENCE 1. M16. †3 = IMPUDENCE 3. Only in E17.

impudent /ˈɪmpjʊd(ə)nt/ *a.* & *n.* LME. [L *impudent-*, *-ens*, f. as IM-[2] + *pudent-*, *-ens* ashamed, modest, orig. pres. pple of *pudere* feel ashamed: see -ENT.] A *adj.* †1 Lacking in shame or modesty; indelicate. LME–M18. 2 Presumptuous, shamelessly forward; insolently disrespectful. M16.

2 N. MONSARRAT The remark had been injudicious and . . undeniably impudent.

B *n.* An impudent person. Now *rare* or *obs.* L16.

impudently *adv.* M16. **impudentness** *n.* (*rare*) L16.

impudicity /ɪmpjʊˈdɪsɪti/ *n.* E16. [Fr. *impudicité* f. L *impudicitia*, f. *impudicus* shameless, f. as IM-[2] + *pudicus*, f. *pudere* feel ashamed: see -ICITY.] Shamelessness, immodesty.

impugn /ɪmˈpjuːn/ *v.t.* LME. [L *impugnare*, f. as IM-[1] + *pugnare* to fight.] †1 Fight against; attack, assail, assault (a person, city, etc.). LME–E17. b Fight in resistance against; withstand, oppose. L16–M17. 2 Assail (an opinion, action, etc.) by argument; call into question; dispute the truth or validity of; oppose as erroneous. LME. b Assail the actions of, question the statements etc. of; find fault with; accuse. Now *rare*. LME.

impugnable *a.* liable to be impugned LME. **impugner** *n.* LME. **impugnment** *n.* the action or fact of impugning something or (now *rare*) someone M19.

impugnation /ɪmpʌgˈneɪʃ(ə)n/ *n.* Now *rare* or *obs.* LME. [L *impugnatio(n-)*, f. *impugnat-* pa. ppl stem of *impugnare* IMPUGN: see -ATION.] †1 The action of attacking or assaulting a person; spiritual assault, temptation. LME–M17. 2 The action of impugning something or someone; calling into question, disputing. LME.

impuissance /ɪmˈpjuːɪs(ə)ns, -ˈpwɪs-/ *n.* L15. [(O)Fr., f. as IM-[2] + PUISSANCE.] Impotence, powerlessness, weakness.

impuissant /ɪmˈpjuːɪs(ə)nt, -ˈpwɪs-/ *a.* E17. [Fr., f. as IM-[2] + PUISSANT.] Impotent, powerless, weak.

impulse /ˈɪmpʌls/ *n.* M17. [f. L *impulsus* n., f. *impuls-* pa. ppl stem of *impellere* IMPEL.] I 1 A physical act of impelling; an application of (sudden) force causing motion; a thrust, a push. M17. 2 The effect of impulsion; motion caused by (sudden) application of force; momentum, impetus. M17. 3 *Physics.* An indefinitely large force of brief duration, producing a finite momentum. L18. b The average value of a force multiplied by its time of action, equal to the change of momentum of a body acted on by the force. L19. 4 *Physics.* Each of the oscillations making up a wave; a sudden momentary change in amplitude, a pulse. E19. 5 *Physiol.* The wave of electrical excitation that passes along a nerve during conduction of a signal. M19. 6 *Med.* The pulse; *esp.* the beat of the heart felt on the wall of the chest. Now *rare*. M19.

3b **specific impulse** the ratio of the thrust produced in a rocket engine to the rate of consumption of propellant.

II 7 Incitement or stimulus to action arising from a state of mind or feeling; an instance of this. M17. 8 Force or influence exerted on the mind by an external stimulus; an instance of this; (a) suggestion, incitement, instigation. M17. 9 Sudden or involuntary inclination to act, without premeditation; an instance of this. M18.

7 B. WEBB Haldane has one overpowering impulse: he likes to be . . behind the scenes at the seat of power. 8 WORDSWORTH One impulse from a vernal wood May teach you more . . Than all the sages can. 9 A. DAVIS I had a sudden impulse to turn around. M. M. KAYE He had . . acted on impulse and without giving due thought to the possible consequences of the action. T. MALLON What made him purchase the boon was more impulse than focused intention.

Attrib. & *comb.*: In the sense 'done, made, or acting on impulse', as *impulse buy, buyer, buying*. Special combs., as **impulse clock** a secondary clock operated by regular electrical impulses transmitted from a master clock; **impulse turbine**: in which the rotor is driven by the change of momentum of the working fluid without a drop in pressure.

impulse /ˈɪmpʌls/ *v.t.* E17. [f. the n., or f. L *impuls-*: see prec.] Give an impulse to; impel; instigate.

impulsion /ɪmˈpʌlʃ(ə)n/ *n.* LME. [(O)Fr., or L *impulsio(n-)*, f. *impuls-*: see IMPULSE *n.*, -ION.] 1 The action or an act of impelling or imparting motion; thrusting, pushing, pressing against something; the condition of being pushed or thrust. LME. 2 An external influence exerted on the mind or conduct; instigation. M16. 3 Determination to action resulting from natural tendency or excitement; an impulse. M16. 4 A tendency to onward movement imparted by a force or influence; impetus. L18.

impulsive /ɪmˈpʌlsɪv/ *a.* & *n.* LME. [(O)Fr. *impulsif*, *-ive* or late L *impulsivus*, f. *impuls-*: see IMPULSE *n.*, -IVE.] A *adj.* 1 Having the property of impelling or imparting motion; characterized by onward movement or impetus. LME. b *Physics.* Of a force, current, etc.: consisting of, or of the nature of, an impulse or impulses. E19. 2 Impelling or determining to action. M16. 3 Actuated or characterized by impulse; apt to be moved by sudden impulse or emotion; prompted by sudden impulse. M18.

3 D. H. LAWRENCE A quick, careless, impulsive boy. S. MORLEY I wish David would think rather more carefully before he does these impulsive things.

†B *n.* An impelling agent or cause. E–M17.

impulsively *adv.* M18. **impulsiveness** *n.* M17. **impulˈsivity** *n.* impulsiveness L19.

†**impulsor** *n.* M17–E18. [L, f. *impuls-*: see IMPULSE *n.*, -OR.] A person who or thing which impels something.

impulsory /ɪmˈpʌls(ə)ri/ *a.* *rare.* M17. [f. L *impuls-* (see IMPULSE *n.*) + -ORY[2].] Tending to impel or force forward.

impunctate /ɪmˈpʌŋkteɪt/ *a.* E19. [f. IM-[2] + PUNCTATE *a.*] *Biol.* & *Med.* Not punctate; not marked or studded with points, dots, or spots.

†**impune** *a.* E17–M18. [L *impunis*: see IMPUNITY.] Having impunity, unpunished.

†**impunely** *adv.* with impunity, without punishment E17–M18.

impunible /ɪmˈpjuːnɪb(ə)l/ *a.* *rare.* M17. [f. IM-[2] + med.L *punibilis*, f. *punire* punish: see -IBLE.] Not punishable.

impunibly *adv.* without punishment; with impunity: M18.

impunitive /ɪmˈpjuːnɪtɪv/ *a.* M20. [f. IM-[2] + PUNITIVE *a.*] *Psychol.* Adopting or characterized by an attitude of acceptance of frustration without anger or any attempt to blame someone.

impunitively *adv.* M20.

impunity /ɪmˈpjuːnɪti/ *n.* M16. [L *impunitas*, f. *impunis* unpunished, f. as IM-[2] + *poena* penalty, punishment, *punire* punish: see -ITY.] Exemption from punishment; exemption from injury or loss as a consequence of action, security. Freq. in *with impunity*, in such a way as to be exempt(ed) from punishment or from injury or loss.

impure /ɪmˈpjʊə/ *a.* & *n.* LME. [L *impurus*, f. as IM-[2] + *purus* pure.] A *adj.* 1 Containing some offensive matter; dirty. LME. b Not ceremonially pure; unhallowed. E17. 2 Not morally pure; defiled by sin; lewd; unchaste. M16. 3 Mixed with or containing some foreign matter, esp. of an inferior kind; contaminated, adulterated. E17. b Mixed in style; (of a language etc.) containing foreign idioms, grammatical blemishes, or imprecise terminology. E17. c Of a colour: containing a mixture of another colour. M19. B *n.* An unchaste or lewd person. Now *rare*. L18.

impurely *adv.* E17. **impureness** *n.* M16.

impurify /ɪmˈpjʊərɪfʌɪ/ *v.t.* L17. [f. IMPURE *a.* after *purify*.] Make impure.

impurist /ɪmˈpjʊərɪst/ *n.* M20. [f. IMPURE *a.* after *purist*.] A person who is not a purist; an opponent of purism.

impuritan /ɪmˈpjʊərɪt(ə)n/ *n.* E17. [f. IMPURE *a.* after *puritan*.] A person who is impure; a person who is not a puritan; *Hist.* an opponent of puritanism (also **I-**) a person who is not a Puritan, an opponent of Puritanism.

impuritanism *n.* E19.

impurity /ɪmˈpjʊərɪti/ *n.* LME. [Fr. †*impurité* (now *impureté*) or L *impuritas*, f. as IMPURE *a.*: see -ITY.] 1 The quality or condition of being morally impure; moral corruption; lewdness, unchastity; a morally impure thing. LME. 2 The quality or condition of containing some offensive matter; dirtiness; foul matter, dirt. L16. 3 The quality or condition of containing foreign matter, esp. of an inferior kind, or of being impure in style; contamination, adulteration; a constituent or element which detracts from purity. E17. b An impurity atom; *esp.* an atom of dopant in the lattice of a semiconductor. M20.

Comb.: **impurity atom**: of an element different from the bulk of the substance in which it is present; **impurity level** an energy level in a semiconductor due to an impurity atom; **impurity semiconductor**: in which most of the carriers of electric current are electrons and holes from impurity atoms.

†**impurple** *v.* var. of EMPURPLE.

imputable /ɪmˈpjuːtəb(ə)l/ *a.* E17. [med.L *imputabilis*, f. L *imputare*: see IMPUTE, -ABLE.] 1 That may be imputed *to*; chargeable, attributable, *to*. E17. †2 Liable to imputation; culpable. M17–L18.

imputaˈbility *n.* L18.

imputation /ɪmpjʊˈteɪʃ(ə)n/ *n.* M16. [Fr., or late L *imputatio(n-)*, f. L *imputat-* pa. ppl stem of *imputare* IMPUTE: see -ATION.] 1 The action of imputing or attributing something, esp. a fault or crime, to a person; the fact of being charged with a fault, crime, etc.; *spec.* (*a*) *Chr. Theol.* attribution to believers of the righteousness of Christ and to Christ of human sin; (*b*) *Econ.* attribution of value to resources in accordance with the value of the products to which they contribute. M16. 2 An instance of imputing a fault, crime, etc., to a person; an accusation, a charge. L16.

2 A. JOHN I was absolved from all blame: all charges, all imputations were withdrawn.

Comb.: **imputation tax**: levied according to the total profits of a company.

imputative /ɪmˈpjuːtətɪv/ *a.* L16. [Late L *imputativus*, f. *imputat-*: see prec., -ATIVE.] Characterized by being imputed; existing or arising by imputation.

imputatively *adv.* by imputation L16.

impute /ɪmˈpjuːt/ *v.t.* LME. [(O)Fr. *imputer* f. L *imputare* bring into the reckoning or charge, f. as IM-[1] + *putare* reckon.] 1 Foll. by *to*: regard (esp. a fault or crime) as being done or caused or possessed by; attribute or ascribe to the discredit (less commonly, the credit) of; *spec.* (*a*) *Chr. Theol.* attribute (righteousness or guilt) to by vicarious substitution; (*b*) *Econ.* attribute or assign (value) to a product or process by inference from the value of the products or processes to which it contributes. LME. †2 Reckon, take into account; consider. M16–L18. 3 Charge or arraign *with* a fault, etc.; accuse. Long *rare*. L16. †4 Impart. L16–L17.

1 R. WELLEK I do not believe there . . was a single reputable 'New' critic who has taken the position imputed to him. E. WAUGH We must not impute damnation to a human soul. C. G. WOLFF Lily is . . not guilty of the transgression he imputes to her.

imputer *n.* (*rare*) E17.

imputrescence /ɪmpjuːˈtrɛs(ə)ns/ *n.* M17. [f. IM-[2] + PUTRESCENCE.] Absence of putrescence or decomposition.

imputrescible /ɪmpjuːˈtrɛsɪb(ə)l/ *a.* M17. [f. IM-[2] + PUTRESCIBLE.] Not subject to putrefaction or decomposition; incorruptible.

imputresciˈbility *n.* E18.

imram, ***imrama*** *ns.* see IMMRAM.

imshi /ˈɪmʃi/ *v.i.* (*imper.*) *Mil. slang.* Also **-shee**. E20. [f. colloq. Arab. *'mšī* imper. of *mišī* go.] Go away!

in /ɪn/ *n.* M17. [f. IN *adv.*] 1 *ins and outs*, (less commonly) *outs and ins*: a All the details or ramifications of a matter; devious turns to and fro in a course of action, a road, etc. M17. b *Hist.* People who were constantly being admitted to and discharged from the workhouse. L19. 2 *Polit.* A member of the party that is in office. Usu. in *pl.*, contrasted w. *outs*. M18. 3 In some games: a member of the side whose turn it is to play. E19. 4 An entrance; permission to enter. *Sc.* L19. 5 An introduction to, or influence with, a person of power or authority or a famous person. (Foll. by *with*.) *colloq.* E20.

in /ɪn/ *attrib. a.* L16. [IN *adv.* used attrib., or as positive of *inner*, *inmost*.] 1 That is in; internal; that lies, remains, lives, is situated, or is used in or within. L16. 2 Fashionable; confined to or common to a particular group. M20.

2 A. Hailey The bar of Jim's Garage . . was currently an 'in' place in downtown Detroit.

in /ɪn/ *v.* Also †**inn**. [OE (*ge*)*innian* (cf. OHG (*ge*)*innōn* take up), partly f. Gmc base of IN *adv.*, partly f. INN *n.*] I *v.t.* 1 Take in, include; enclose (esp. waste land). Formerly also, give or put in. Now *dial.* OE. 2 Gather into a barn or stockyard; harvest; get in, collect. LME. II *v.i.* †3 Go in; make a beginning. OE–M17.

in /ɪn/ *adv.* [OE (i) *in*(*n*), used w. vbs of motion (= OFris., OS, Du. *in*, OHG *in* (with secondary lengthening), G *ein*, ON, Goth. *inn*); (ii) *inne*, used w. vbs of position (= OFris., OS *inna*, OHG *inna*, *-i*, *-e*, ON *inni*, Goth. *inna*), orig. locative.] I Of motion. 1a Expr. motion from a point outside a space to a point inside it; so as to pass into a place or medium, esp. a building or a room. OE. b Expr. motion in the direction of some point, specified or implied; to a position attained by coming from outside; near to some point or limit. E18. 2 In addition to the due amount or number; into the bargain. M17.

1a J. Conrad I went in and sat down. G. Household He must have a boat to take him . . to the rock face where he plunged in. b W. Black The swans were sailing close in by the reeds. *join in*, *muck in*, *pitch in*, etc. 2 *throw in*: see THROW *v.*

II Of position. 3 Within a certain space or medium, esp. a building or a room; inside one's usual place of abode or work; so as to be enclosed or confined. ME. 4 On the inside. ME.

3 Hor. Walpole A dame over the way, that has just locked in her boarders. J. N. McIlwraith A number of soldiers were in swimming at the foot of the bluff. J. P. Donleavy 'May I please speak to Mr. MacDoon.' 'I'll see if he's in.' 4 H. B. Tristram A sheepskin coat with the woolly side in.

III *spec.* 5 In prison. L16. 6 Engaged or implicated in a matter, esp. an unlawful one; included among those chosen, published, etc. L16. 7 Of a politician or party: in or into office, in or into power. E17. 8 Of a fire or flame: burning, continuing to burn. M17. 9 Of the tide: with the water higher and nearer. L17. 10 In fashion; in season. L17. 11 In some games: having the turn to play, esp. (*Cricket*) to bat. M18. 12 Of a school: in session, in progress. *Sc.* & *NZ.* E19. 13 Of a train, ship, etc.: at the platform, dock, etc. Of a harvest, order, etc.: having arrived or been received. L19. 14 Of a person's fortune or luck: exerting favourable action or influence. E20.

10 *Time* Mass communication is out, personal communication is in. 11 C. Causley He might have been last man in for England. 13 *New Yorker* Verdicts on our attempts to ransom hostages with arms sales . . are not in yet.

Phrases: *be in at the finish*: see FINISH *n.* **day in, day out** throughout a long succession of days. **in at** present at; contributing to. **in between** = BETWEEN *adv.* **in for** (*a*) about to undergo (esp. something unpleasant) (*have it in for*, seek revenge on); (*b*) competing in or for; (*c*) involved in; committed to. **in on** sharing in; privy to (a secret etc.). **in with** on friendly or good terms with; *Naut.* close in to, near, (land). **week in, week out, year in, year out** throughout a long succession of weeks (years).

in /ɪn/ *prep.* Bef. a consonant (now *arch.* & *dial.*) also **i'**. [OE *in* = OFris., OS, OHG (Du., G), Goth. *in*, ON *í* rel. to L *in* (older *en*), Gk *en*, *eni*, OIr. *i n-*, Welsh *yn*, Lith. *į*, OPruss. *en*, Old Ch. Slav. *vŭ*(*n-*), Russ. *v* (*vo*, *vn-*), f. IE.] I Of position and location. 1 Within the limits or bounds of; within. OE. b With names of towns having public or private importance. Cf. AT 1b. OE. 2 Referring to non-physical things treated as having extension or content. OE. 3 In relation to; in the context of; as a member of. OE. 4 Expr. relation to a garment, covering, etc., which envelops or is worn. OE. 5 On (with ref. to position). Long *rare* exc. *Sc.* OE. †6 Among. OE–M16. 7 Defining the part of something affected. ME. 8 With numbers, ns. of quantity, etc.: as a proportionate part of. L16.

1 M. Keane Jane was sitting up in bed drinking . . tea. I. Murdoch Sarah was in Australia with her husband. L. Bruce He talked exactly like the balloons in comic strips. b Southey A day in London is more wearying to me than a walk up Scawfell. 2 J. Austen To see such an undersized . . man, set up for a fine actor, is very ridiculous in my opinion. K. Gershon Like every living Jew I have in imagination seen the gas-chamber. 3 Ld Macaulay The place of the clergyman in society. B. Webb In opinion, Snowden is now a collectivist liberal. *Belfast Telegraph* It is up to us in local government to press ahead with our plans. 4 Longfellow A huge tome, bound In brass and wild-boar's hide. G. Greene A little old man in a black cassock. 5 T. Hardy No other boy in the heath has had such a bonfire. 7 G. B. Shaw The prima donna was deaf in the left ear. 8 *Law Times* A debtor . . offered 6*s.* 8*d.* in the pound. E. Course From Redhill to Tonbridge the maximum gradient was 1 in 250.

II Of situation, manner, etc. 9a Expr. situation as determined by location, environment, or a material thing. OE. b Expr. situation within the range of one of the senses or within a sphere of action. LME. 10 Expr. manner, degree, or means. OE. b Expr. the material of construction or execution. M17. c Following a phr. specifying a superl.: within the category of things mentioned. M19. 11 Having the condition of; in a state of. OE. b With ref. to animals: pregnant with. L16. 12 Expr. occupation in an activity: in the process of, in the act of. Chiefly w. ns. of action & vbl ns. ME. †b Used bef. a vbl n. expr. either occupation or an action to which a thing or person is subjected, = A *prep.*[1] 8, and now omitted, the vbl n. functioning as pres. pple. LME–M19. 13 Expr. aim or purpose: with abstract ns. ME.

9a J. A. Froude Brought in chains to Rome. J. Tyndall His guides had lost their way in the fog. M. Roberts They sit in silence for the rest of the journey. *New Yorker* Walking in the dark . . we felt . . vulnerable. b Milton Spirits that stand In sight of God's high Throne. A. Trollope The living of Framley was in the gift of the Lufton family. 10 H. Fielding He was drinking her ladyship's health . . in a cup of her ale. M. Pattison Bede is writing in a dead language. F. Hall Drift-wood was lying about in large quantities. G. B. Shaw His success with Mozart's symphony in E flat. *Television Today* Half the first night audience were seated in two arcs behind the stage. D. Abse He spoke in his special booming voice. *in confidence*, *in fun*, *in jest*, *in part*, *in the same way*, etc. b Dickens Half-length portraits, in crayons. c *Radio Times* The most dazzling cruises in holiday history. 11 Ld Macaulay Leaving their castles in ruins. I. Murdoch He woke in horror to the sound of a howling dog. *in cash*, *in flower*, *in love*, *in print*, *in tears*, etc. b *in calf*, *in foal*, etc. 12 H. James A young lady seated on a bench in deep and lonely meditation. R. Hardy The Warden lifted his stick in salute. b W. Whiston He went on in worshipping them. W. Hone This carriage . . had been three years in building. 13 Milton She thus in answer spake. J. F. Cooper He went in quest of his new applicant. J. Conrad In memory of her eldest brother.

III Of time. 14 In contexts where another prep. or no prep. is now usual. OE. 15 Within the limits of (a specified period of time); during (a process occupying time); in the course of. OE. b Preceding a n. denoting a period of time during which something has not happened, must not happen, etc., or has not been exceeded; for. L15. 16 Before or at the end of (a specified length of time). ME.

14 Swift This engine . . set out in four hours after my landing. G. Crabbe No Sunday shower Kept him at home in that important hour. J. Beresford In a chilling evening . . after you have carefully stirred a very ticklish fire. 15 G. Berkeley I never saw a first-rate picture in my life. T. Jefferson I think our acquaintance commenced in 1764. J. White All the gentlemen's houses you see in a railway excursion. *New Yorker* Elevators were in their infancy. b R. A. Heinlein The place smelled like a vault that has not been opened in years. *Scientific American* The greatest dust storm in more than a century. 16 G. B. Shaw You'll be fast asleep in ten minutes.

IV Of motion and direction. 17 Into. Now only w. vbs implying motion or change. OE. †18 Against, towards; to. ME–M16. 19 On, upon; along. Long *obs.* exc. *Sc.* ME.

17 R. Hardy I'm going to put all this in my next bulletin. W. Golding He . . looked in the window of the bookshop. B. Bainbridge Tell them to jump in the lake.

V Pregnant & ellipt. uses. 20 With refl. pron.: apart from any relation to others; in a person's or thing's own essence or nature. ME. 21 In spiritual union with. ME. 22 Inherent in; within the capacity of. ME. 23 In the person of, with the identity of; in the case of. LME. 24 In the hands of; legally vested in. LME. 25 Partaking or sharing in; implicated in; engaged in. E18. b Engaged in dealing with, as a trade or business. M20.

20 J. S. Mill Of things absolutely or in themselves. *in* ITSELF. 21 AV *1 Cor.* 15:22 As in Adam all die, euen so in Christ shall all be made aliue. 22 *Nature* Anyone who has it in him to do heroic deeds. 23 E. A. Freeman How great a captain England possessed in her future King. 25 E. Wright He and Brady might have been in this from the start. b E. Bowen Her father is rich, he is in tea.

VI Constructional uses. 26 Expr. the relation which a vb has to an indirect obj. OE. 27 Expr. the relation of an adj. or n. to a certain sphere to which its qualification, attribute, etc., is limited. OE. 28 Expr. the relation of a quantitative statement or measurement to the thing measured. ME. 29 In advb. & prep. phrs. where *in* precedes a n. (or an adj.). ME.

26 S. Austin A regular war with France was not to be engaged in without negotiations. B. Jowett The wise and mighty one who is to be held in honour. F. M. Peard She spent a fortune in shoes and gloves. J. Conrad The inhabitants delight in describing it as the 'Pearl of the Ocean'. 27 Boswell We talked of belief in ghosts. W. C. Smith Let nothing shake your trust in her. T. H. Huxley The river-water . . is usually rich in organic impurities. I. Murdoch Ann was reading for a degree in English. *New Yorker* He . . took deep pleasure in his friendship with the . . peasants. 28 Milton Equal in number to that Godless crew. W. Sharp A man six feet two inches in height. *Daily Telegraph* £380 million in grants and loans. 29 *in common*, *in conclusion*, *in fact*, *in general*, *in truth*, etc.; *in case of*, *in common with*, *in favour of*, *in honour of*, *in regard to*, etc.

Phrases: *have it in one*: see HAVE *v.* **in it** (*a*) in a matter and of an advantageous or beneficial nature (chiefly in *what is in it for* (a specified person etc.)? & similar phrs.); (*b*) in a matter and of significance. **in so far as** to the extent or degree that. **in that** in the fact that; seeing that; because. **not be in it** *colloq.* be nothing in comparison; not count for anything. **nothing** (**not much**, **little**) **in it** no or little difference between things being compared; no or little advantage to be seen in one possibility rather than another.

in- /ɪn/ *pref.*[1] (*comb. form*). [f. IN *adv.*, IN *prep.* & (later) IN *a.*] 1 In OE IN *adv.* was freely used in collocation w. vbs of motion or change of state; in the inf. it usu. preceded the vb, in derived vbl ns. & adjs. it always did. In this position it came at length to be written in comb. w. the vb: so *income*, *incomer*, *incoming*, beside *come in*. Also in other (OE & later) formations w. the sense 'in, within, internal', as *inborn*, *inland*; *in-patient*; w. the sense of IN *a.* 2, as *in-group*, *in-joke*. 2 Prep. phrs. composed of IN *prep.* + n. give rise to (usu. hyphenated) attrib. adjs., as *in-calf*, *in-car*. 3 *Geom.* Repr. *inscribed*, as *incentre*, *in-circle*.

in-basket *n.* (a basket used as) an in-tray M20. **in-car** *a.* occurring, situated, or carried in a car M20. **in-'college** *a.* living in a college; designating or pertaining to teaching, administration, etc., carried out within college precincts: L19. **in-ground** *a.* (of a swimming pool) embedded in the ground L20. **in-hand** *a.* held in the hand; immediately available; (of a horse) led by hand, not ridden: M20. **in-joke** *n.* a joke which can be appreciated by only a limited group of people M20. **in-'milk** *a.* (of a cow etc.) producing milk M20. **in-'service** *a.* (esp. of training) given or received while the person concerned is in an occupation; (of reliability etc.) during the period of use of an object: M20. **in-side** *n.* (*Cricket*) the side which is batting M19. **in-spawn** *a.* that is about to spawn E20. **in-thing** *n.* a fashionable thing (*to do*) M20. **in-transit** *a.* that is being transported or in transit E20. **in-tray** *n.* a tray for incoming documents in an office M20.

in- /ɪn/ *pref.*[2] Bef. *l* **il-** /ɪl/; bef. *b*, *m*, or *p* **im-** /ɪm/; bef. *r* **ir-** /ɪr/. Repr. L *in-* f. *in* prep., used esp. w. vbs & their derivs. w. the senses 'into, in, within', 'on, upon', 'towards, against', sometimes expr. onward motion or continuance, sometimes intensive, sometimes trans., & in other cases with no appreciable force. Often w. parallel forms in EN-[1] (EM-[1]).

in- /ɪn/ *pref.*[3] Bef. *l* **il-** /ɪl/; bef. *b, m* or *p* **im-** /ɪm/; bef. *r* **ir-** /ɪr/; bef. *gn* **i-** /ɪ/ (not productive). Repr. L *in-* = Gk *a-, an-*, Gmc *un-*, prefixed chiefly to adjs. & their derivs. to express negation or privation. The mod. tendency is to restrict *in-* to wds answering to L types and to use *un-* in other cases.

-in /ɪn/ *suff.*[1] See also -EIN. [Alt. of -INE[5].] *Chem.* 1 Forming ns. denoting (*a*) neutral organic compounds, esp. proteins, glycerides, and glycosides, as *albumin, alizarin, haematin, insulin, pepsin*; (*b*) some pharmaceutical products, as *niacin, penicillin.* 2 Forming ns. denoting heterocyclic compounds with a single unsaturated ring of six atoms, none of which is nitrogen, as *dioxin.*

-in /ɪn/ *suff.*[2] [f. IN *adv.*] Appended to vbs & derived agent-ns. (occas. to adjs.) to form ns. denoting an event at which many people publicly and collectively perform some action together, usu. as a form of protest, as *sing-in, sit-in, sleep-in, teach-in.*

-ina /ˈiːnə/ *suff.*[1] [Repr. L fem. suff. found in *regina* queen, extended in It. or Sp., and thence in Eng.] Forming feminine titles, as *tsarina*, and female forenames, as *Christina.* Also forming names of musical instruments, as *concertina.*

-ina /ˈʌɪnə/ *suff.*[2] [Repr. L neut. pl. of adjs. in *-inus*: see -INE[1].] Forming names of some plant and animal groups, as *globigerina.*

inability /ɪnəˈbɪlɪti/ *n.* L15. [f. IN-[3] + ABILITY. Cf. (O)Fr. *inhabilité*, med.L *inhabilitas.*] 1 The condition of being unable; lack of ability, power, or means. (Foll. by *to do*; (arch.) *for, of doing.*) L15. †2 *spec.* Physical infirmity. M17–M19.

1 R. SOUTH Their Inability for, and frequent contrariety to the bringing about such designs. A. MASON He could not even—the inability distressed him out of all proportion—read people's minds. N. SYMINGTON A central difficulty in her life was an inability to say directly . . what she felt.

†**inable** *v.* var. of ENABLE *v.*

in absentia /ɪn abˈsɛntɪə, -ʃɪə/ *adv. phr.* L19. [L.] In his, her, or their absence.

inabstinence /ɪnˈabstɪnəns/ *n.* M17. [f. IN-[3] + ABSTINENCE.] Lack of abstinence; failure to abstain.

in abstracto /ɪn abˈstraktəʊ/ *adv. phr.* E17. [L = in the abstract.] As an abstract thing.

inaccentuation /ˌɪnaksɛntjʊˈeɪʃ(ə)n/ *n.* M19. [f. IN-[3] + ACCENTUATION.] The condition of being unaccented.

inacceptable /ɪnəkˈsɛptəb(ə)l/ *a.* L19. [f. IN-[3] + ACCEPTABLE.] Unacceptable.

ˌ**inaccepta'bility** *n.* E20.

inaccessible /ɪnəkˈsɛsɪb(ə)l/ *a.* LME. [(O)Fr., or late L *inaccessibilis*, f. as IN-[3] + ACCESSIBLE.] Not accessible; that cannot be reached or entered; (of a person) not open to friendly approaches or influence.

GIBBON This savage hero was not inaccessible to pity. D. DELILLO A few rocky beaches, the best of them inaccessible except by boat. P. GAY The inaccessible regions of the mind are more sizable, and doubtless more important.

ˌ**inaccessi'bility** *n.* M17. **inaccessibleness** *n.* E17. **inaccessibly** *adv.* E18.

inaccordant /ɪnəˈkɔːd(ə)nt/ *a.* E19. [f. IN-[3] + ACCORDANT.] Not in agreement or harmony; inharmonious.

inaccuracy /ɪnˈakjʊrəsi/ *n.* M18. [f. next: see -ACY.] The quality or condition of being inaccurate; imprecision; an instance of this.

inaccurate /ɪnˈakjʊrət/ *a.* M18. [f. IN-[3] + ACCURATE.] Not accurate; inexact, imprecise, incorrect.

inaccurately *adv.* M17. **inaccurateness** *n.* L17.

inacquaintance /ɪnəˈkweɪnt(ə)ns/ *n.* E17. [f. IN-[3] + ACQUAINTANCE.] The state of being unacquainted; lack of acquaintance.

inact /ɪnˈakt/ *v.* M17. [f. IN-[2] + ACT *v.*] †1 *v.t.* Actuate. Only in M17. 2 *v.i.* Act *in, within. rare.* M19.

inaction /ɪnˈakʃ(ə)n/ *n.* M17. [f. IN-[3] + ACTION *n.*] Absence of action; inertness, sluggishness.

inactivate /ɪnˈaktɪveɪt/ *v.t.* E20. [f. INACTIVE + -ATE[3].] Make inactive.

inacti'vation *n.* E20.

inactivator /ɪnˈaktɪveɪtə/ *n.* M20. [f. prec. + -OR.] A person who or thing which inactivates something; *spec.* in *Pharm.* & *Physiol.*, a person considered in respect of his or her speed of metabolizing and hence inactivating a drug.

inactive /ɪnˈaktɪv/ *a.* E18. [f. IN-[3] + ACTIVE *a.*] 1 Not active; disinclined to act; indolent; passive. E18. 2 *Chem.* Not rotating the plane of polarization of polarized light. Freq. qualified by *optically.* M19.

inactively *adv.* M18.

inactivity /ɪnakˈtɪvɪti/ *n.* M17. [f. IN-[3] + ACTIVITY.] The quality or condition of being inactive; lack of activity; sluggishness; passiveness.

J. C. CALHOUN The highest wisdom of a state is a wise and masterly inactivity. C. G. WOLFF She did not write. . . They were not, however, months of total inactivity.

inactuate /ɪnˈaktjʊeɪt, -tʃʊ-/ *v.t. arch.* M17. [f. IN-[2] + ACTUATE.] Make active; stir into activity.

inadaptability /ˌɪnədaptəˈbɪlɪti/ *n.* M19. [f. IN-[3] + ADAPTABILITY.] Lack of adaptability; inability to be adapted.

inadaptable /ɪnəˈdaptəb(ə)l/ *a.* E20. [f. IN-[3] + ADAPTABLE.] Unable to be adapted.

inadaptive /ɪnəˈdaptɪv/ *a.* L19. [f. IN-[3] + ADAPTIVE.] Not adaptive.

inadept /ɪnəˈdɛpt, ɪnˈadɛpt/ *a. rare.* L19. [f. IN-[3] + ADEPT *a.*] Not adept.

inadequacy /ɪnˈadɪkwəsi/ *n.* L18. [f. next: see -ACY.] The condition or quality of being inadequate; an instance of this.

V. BRITTAIN Lives were being thrown away through the inadequacy of the medical services in the Mediterranean. R. BUSH A perpetual feeling of unworthiness—a sense of inadequacy attendant on a life of self-examination. *Maledicta* People . . who confess their inadequacies or even villainies.

inadequate /ɪnˈadɪkwət/ *a.* & *n.* L17. [f. IN-[3] + ADEQUATE *a.*] A *adj.* Not adequate; insufficient; (of a person) incompetent, unable to deal with a situation. (Foll. by *to, for, to do.*) L17.

J. R. GREEN The ordinary resources of the Crown . . were inadequate to meet the expenses of war. C. PHILLIPS Leslie Carter's shop stood alone, its wooden walls thin with age, its roof inadequate.

B *n.* A person whose character or abilities are insufficient to meet the expectations of society. M20.

inadequately *adv.* L17. **inadequateness** *n.* L17.

inadequation /ˌɪnadɪˈkweɪʃ(ə)n, -ʒ(ə)n/ *n.* M17. [f. IN-[3] + ADEQUATION.] Lack of equivalence or exact correspondence.

inadhesive /ɪnədˈhiːsɪv, -zɪv/ *a.* E19. [f. IN-[3] + ADHESIVE *a.*] Not adhesive.

inadmissible /ɪnədˈmɪsɪb(ə)l/ *a.* L18. [f. IN-[3] + ADMISSIBLE.] Unable to be admitted or allowed.

ˌ**inadmissi'bility** *n.* E19. **inadmissibly** *adv.* M19.

in-a-door /ˈɪnədɔː/ *adv. arch.* E17. [f. IN *adv.* + A *a.* + DOOR.] Indoors; at home.

inadventurous /ɪnədˈvɛntʃ(ə)rəs/ *a. rare.* M19. [f. IN-[3] + ADVENTUROUS.] = UNADVENTUROUS.

inadventurousness *n.* M19.

inadvertence /ɪnədˈvəːt(ə)ns/ *n.* LME. [med.L *inadvertentia*, f. as IN-[3] + ADVERTENCE.] The quality or character of being inadvertent; inattention; carelessness; an instance of this.

O. WILDE Whether by inadvertence or direction . . the Duchess left out some essential words.

Also **inadvertency** *n.* L16.

inadvertent /ɪnədˈvəːt(ə)nt/ *a.* M17. [f. IN-[3] + L *advertent-* pres. ppl stem of *advertere* ADVERT *v.*: see -ENT.] 1 Of a person: not properly attentive or observant. M17. 2 Of an action: unintentional. E18.

2 V. GLENDINNING The pregnancy was inadvertent and unwanted by Rebecca.

inadvertently *adv.* L17.

inadvisable /ɪnədˈvʌɪzəb(ə)l/ *a.* L19. [f. IN-[3] + ADVISABLE.] Not expedient; imprudent.

ˌ**inadvisa'bility** *n.* M19.

For other words beginning with *in-* see the entry for **in-**[1]

inadvisedly /ɪnədˈvʌɪzɪdli/ *adv. rare.* M17. [f. IN-[3] + ADVISEDLY.] Without proper consideration; imprudently, rashly.

inaesthetic /ɪniːsˈθɛtɪk, -ɛs-/ *a.* Also ***ines-**. M19. [f. IN-[3] + AESTHETIC *a.*] Unaesthetic.

inagglutinable /ɪnəˈgluːtɪnəb(ə)l/ *a.* E20. [f. IN-[3] + AGGLUTINABLE.] *Biol.* & *Med.* Unable to be agglutinated.

ˌ**inagglutina'bility** *n.* E20.

†**inaidable** *a. rare* (Shakes.). Only in E17. [f. IN-[3] + AIDABLE.] Unable to be aided.

inajá /ɪnəˈdʒɑː/ *n.* M19. [Port. f. Tupi *inaiá.*] A palm tree of the Amazon region and Trinidad, *Maximiliana maripa*, with very long leaves.

inaka *n.* var. of INANGA.

inalienable /ɪnˈeɪlɪənəb(ə)l/ *a.* M17. [f. IN-[3] + ALIENABLE.] Not alienable; that cannot be transferred from its present ownership or relation.

R. NIEBUHR Defeating the experiment in feudalism . . and giving each family inalienable rights in the soil.

inaliena'bility *n.* L18. **inalienably** *adv.* M18.

inalterable /ɪnˈɔːlt(ə)rəb(ə)l, -ˈɒl-/ *a.* M16. [f. IN-[3] + ALTERABLE.] Unalterable; not subject to change.

inaltera'bility *n.* E18. **inalterably** *adv.* M17.

inambitious /ɪnamˈbɪʃəs/ *a. rare.* E17. [f. IN-[3] + AMBITIOUS *a.*] Not ambitious.

†**inamel** *n., v.* vars. of ENAMEL *n., v.*

†**inamelled** *a.* var. of ENAMELLED.

inamissible /ɪnəˈmɪsɪb(ə)l/ *a.* Now *rare.* M17. [Fr., or med.L *inamissibilis*, f. as IN-[3] + AMISSIBLE.] Not liable to be lost.

ˌ**inamissi'bility** *n.* M18. **inamissibleness** *n.* E18.

inamorata /ɪˌnaməˈrɑːtə/ *n.* Also †**en-**. M17. [It. (now *innam-*), fem. of INAMORATO.] A female lover.

inamorate /ɪˈnam(ə)rət/ *a.* & *n.* L16. [Anglicized f. It. †*inamorato, -ta* (now *innam-*) pa. pple of *inamorare*: see next, -ATE[2].] A *adj.* Enamoured, in love. L16. †B *n.* A lover. Only in E17.

†**inamorate** *v.t.* Also (earlier) **en-**. L16–E18. [It. *inamorare* (now *innam-*) fall in love, f. *in-* IN-[2] + *amore* love: see -ATE[3].] Inspire with love, enamour.

inamoration /ɪˌnaməˈreɪʃ(ə)n/ *n. rare.* M17. [f. prec. + -ATION.] Enamourment.

inamorato /ɪˌnaməˈrɑːtəʊ/ *n.* Also †**en-**. Pl. **-os.** L16. [It. (now *innam-*), pa. pple of *inamorare*: see INAMORATE *v.*] A male lover.

†**inamour** *v.* var. of ENAMOUR.

in and in /ɪn (ə)nd ˈɪn/ *adv., n., & a. phr.* Also (the usual form as adj.) **in-and-in.** M17. [f. IN *adv.* + AND *conj.*[1] + IN *adv.*] A *adv. phr.* Further and further in; continually inwards. M17.

1 *breed in and in*: see BREED *v.*

B *n. phr.* †1 A throw with four dice, falling all alike or as two doublets; a gambling game based on this. M–L17. 2 A space which opens up and reveals continually something yet further in. L19. 3 The stage in a swindle at which the swindler risks his or her own money with that of the dupe. *slang.* M20.

C *adj.* (*phr.*). Designating breeding within a limited stock; *fig.* intimate and exclusive. M19.

in and out /ɪn (ə)nd ˈaʊt/ *adv. & a. phr.* Also (the usual form as adj.) **in-and-out.** ME. [f. IN *adv.* + AND *conj.*[1] + OUT *adv.*] A *adv. phr.* 1 Alternately in and out; now in, now out. ME. 2 Inside and outside. L19.

B *adj.* (*phr.*). Designating a person who or thing which is alternately in and out of something. M17.

in-and-out boy or **man** *slang* a man who is in and out of prison; a burglar. **in-and-out work** discontinuous work; irregular or illegal practice.

in-and-outer *n.* a person who is only moderately skilled, or erratic in performance; a person who holds office intermittently: E20.

inane /ɪˈneɪn/ *a.* & *n.* M16. [L *inanis* empty, vain.] A *adj.* Empty, void; silly, senseless, pointless. M16.

C. KINGSLEY Dilating into vast inane infinities. A. HIGGINS They had stared at her before making inane

suggestions. Hopeless, she thought, they know nothing.
B *n.* A void or empty thing; empty space; emptiness. *arch.* L17.
inanely *adv.* L19. **inaneness** *n.* L20.

inanga /ˈiːnaŋə/ *n. NZ.* Also **inaka** /ˈiːnakə/. M19. [Maori.] 1 A small migratory Australasian fish, *Galaxias maculatus*, the young of which are eaten as whitebait. Also called *jolly-tail.* M19. 2 An evergreen shrub or small tree, *Dracophyllum longifolium*, of the family Epacridaceae, native to New Zealand. L19.

inanimate /ɪnˈanɪmət/ *a.* & *n.* LME. [Late L *inanimatus* lifeless, f. as IN-^{3} + ANIMATE *a.*] A *adj.* 1 Destitute of life, lifeless; *spec.* not endowed with animal life. LME. 2 Without the activity of life; spiritless, dull. E18.
1 N. Symington As human beings we share certain essential features with the inanimate world as a whole. **inanimate nature** all of nature other than the animal world. 2 D. Pae His arms grasped the girl's inanimate form.
B *n.* An inanimate thing; inanimate nature. M17.
†**inanimated** *a.* = INANIMATE *a.* M17–E19. **inanimately** *adv.* L19. **inanimateness** *n.* M17.

inanimate /ɪnˈanɪmeɪt/ *v.t.* Now *rare.* L16. [Late L *inanimat-* pa. ppl stem of *inanimare* inspire, fire, f. as IN-^{2} + ANIMATE *v.*] Animate, infuse life into; encourage, enliven.

inanimation /ˌɪnanɪˈmeɪʃ(ə)n/ *n.* L18. [f. IN-^{3} + ANIMATION.] Absence of life or liveliness.

inanition /ɪnəˈnɪʃ(ə)n/ *n.* LME. [Late L *inanitio(n-)*, f. L *inanit-* pa. ppl stem of *inanire* make empty, f. as INANE: see -ITION.] The action or process of emptying; the condition of being empty; a condition of exhaustion resulting from lack of nourishment.

inanity /ɪˈnanɪti/ *n.* E16. [L *inanitas*, f. as INANE: see -ITY.] 1 Lack of substance or solidity; unsatisfactoriness; lack of ideas; senselessness, silliness; the quality of being devoid of interest. E16. b An inane remark or practice. M17. c Lack of active interest in life; idleness. L18. 2 The quality or condition of being void or empty; emptiness. E17.
1 P. Carey I return my eyes to the inanity of the television. b P. Lively I corrected the inanities encouraged by her grandmothers.

in antis /ɪn ˈantɪs/ *a. phr.* M19. [L.] *Class. Archit.* (Of columns) positioned between two antas; (of a building) having walls prolonged beyond the front, with terminating pilasters in line with columns of a façade.

inapparent /ɪnəˈpar(ə)nt/ *a.* E17. [f. IN-^{3} + APPARENT.] Not apparent or manifest.

inappeasable /ɪnəˈpiːzəb(ə)l/ *a.* M19. [f. IN-^{3} + APPEASABLE.] Unable to be appeased.

inappellable /ɪnəˈpɛləb(ə)l/ *a.* E19. [Fr. †*inappelable*, f. *appeler* APPEAL *v.*: see IN-^{3}, -ABLE.] Unable to be appealed against.

inappetence /ɪnˈapɪt(ə)ns/ *n.* L17. [f. IN-^{3} + APPETENCE.] Lack of appetite, desire, or longing. Also **inappetency** *n.* E17.

inappetent /ɪnˈapɪt(ə)nt/ *a.* L18. [f. IN-^{3} + APPETENT.] Without appetite, desire, or longing.

inapplicable /ɪnˈaplɪkəb(ə)l, ɪnəˈplɪk-/ *a.* M17. [f. IN-^{3} + APPLICABLE.] Not applicable; unsuitable.
inapplicaˈbility *n.* the quality or condition of being inapplicable; an instance of this: L17. **inapplicably** *adv.* M19.

inapplication /ˌɪnaplɪˈkeɪʃ(ə)n/ *n.* E18. [f. IN-^{3} + APPLICATION.] 1 Lack of application; failure to apply oneself to duties, negligence. E18. 2 Inapplicability. L18.

inapposite /ɪnˈapəzɪt/ *a.* M17. [f. IN-^{3} + APPOSITE *a.*] Not apposite.
inappositely *adv.* M17. **inappositeness** *n.* L19.

inappreciable /ɪnəˈpriːʃəb(ə)l, -ʃɪə-/ *a.* L18. [f. IN-^{3} + APPRECIABLE.] †1 Unable to be sufficiently appreciated; priceless. L18–M19. 2 Imperceptible; insignificant. E19. 3 Unable to be appreciated. M19.
inappreciably *adv.* M19.

inappreciation /ˌɪnəpriːʃɪˈeɪʃ(ə)n, -sɪ-/ *n.* M19. [f. IN-^{3} + APPRECIATION.] Lack of appreciation; failure to appreciate someone or something sufficiently.

inappreciative /ɪnəˈpriːʃ(ɪ)ətɪv/ *a.* M19. [f. IN-^{3} + APPRECIATIVE.] Not appreciative.
inappreciatively *adv.* L19. **inappreciativeness** *n.* M19.

inapprehensible /ˌɪnaprɪˈhɛnsɪb(ə)l/ *a.* M17. [Late L *inapprehensibilis*, f. as IN-^{3} + APPREHENSIBLE.] Not apprehensible; unable to be grasped by the senses or intellect.

inapprehension /ˌɪnaprɪˈhɛnʃ(ə)n/ *n.* M18. [f. IN-^{3} + APPREHENSION.] Lack of apprehension; failure to grasp by the senses or intellect.

inapprehensive /ˌɪnaprɪˈhɛnsɪv/ *a.* M17. [f. IN-^{3} + APPREHENSIVE.] Not grasping with the senses or intellect; not anxious.
inapprehensiveness *n.* M17.

inapproachable /ɪnəˈprəʊtʃəb(ə)l/ *a.* E19. [f. IN-^{3} + APPROACHABLE.] Not approachable; inaccessible.

inappropriate /ɪnəˈprəʊprɪət/ *a.* E19. [f. IN-^{3} + APPROPRIATE *a.*] Not appropriate; unsuitable.
R. D. Laing Responsiveness adequate to the infant will be inappropriate to an older child.
inappropriately *adv.* M19. **inappropriateness** *n.* M19.

inapt /ɪnˈapt/ *a.* L17. [f. IN-^{3} + APT. Cf. INEPT.] 1 Not suitable; inappropriate. L17. 2 Unskilful, awkward. E19.
inaptly *adv.* M19. **inaptness** *n.* E19.

inaptitude /ɪnˈaptɪtjuːd/ *n.* E17. [f. IN-^{3} + APTITUDE. Cf. INEPTITUDE.] Unsuitableness; unskilfulness.

inarable /ɪnˈarəb(ə)l/ *a.* M17. [med.L *inarabilis*; later f. IN-^{3} + ARABLE *a.*] Not arable; impossible to plough.

inarch /ɪnˈɑːtʃ/ *v.*^{1}*t.* Also †**en-**. E17. [f. IN-^{2}, EN-^{1} + ARCH *v.*^{1}] *Hort.* Graft by connecting a growing branch without separation from the parent stock.

inarch *v.*^{2} var. of ENARCH *v.*^{1}

inarguable /ɪnˈɑːgjʊəb(ə)l/ *a.* L19. [f. IN-^{3} + ARGUABLE.] Not open to argument; irrefutable.
Washington Post Generally, they said there was no inarguable reasoning to support either course of action.
inarguably *adv.* M20.

inarm /ɪnˈɑːm/ *v.t. poet.* Also **en-** /ɪn-, ɛn-/. E17. [f. IN-^{1} or IN-^{2}, EN-^{1} + ARM *n.*^{1} Cf. Fr. *embrasser.*] Clasp within or as with the arms; embrace.
Browning Gallant and lady . . Enarming each the other. F. W. H. Myers Norway's inarming melancholy sea.

inarticulacy /ɪnɑːˈtɪkjʊləsi/ *n.* E20. [f. next: see -ACY.] The quality or condition of being inarticulate; lack of clarity or fluency in expressing oneself.
Daily Telegraph 'Y' know' and 'I mean' and other apologies for inarticulacy.

inarticulate /ɪnɑːˈtɪkjʊlət/ *a.* E17. [f. IN-^{3} + ARTICULATE *a.*; in sense 2 corresp. to late L *inarticulatus.*] 1 Not jointed or hinged; *spec.* in *Zool.* & *Bot.*, not having joints or articulations. E17. b *Zool.* Designating or pertaining to (an animal of) the division Inarticulata of brachiopods having valves not joined by a hinge. L19. 2 Of sound or speech: not articulate. Also, indistinctly pronounced. E17. 3 Unable to speak distinctly, dumb; unable to express oneself clearly and fluently. M18. b Not expressed, unspoken. E20. 4 Having no distinct meaning; unintelligible. M19.
2 J. Beattie Inarticulate sounds may be divided into musical sound and noise. G. Swift Inarticulate sounds—coughs, grunts, clearings of the throat. 3 R. Church He was . . gentle and inarticulate He never spoke. A. S. Byatt He could give an inarticulate woman the right hints about . . her clumsy sentences. b P. H. Gibbs Nobody cheered as the President passed, but there was the deep silence of inarticulate emotion. 4 G. Brimley Inarticulate gibberish.
inarticulated *a.* = INARTICULATE 1,2 E19. **inarticulately** *adv.* M17. **inarticulateness** *n.* M18.

inarticulation /ˌɪnɑːtɪkjʊˈleɪʃ(ə)n/ *n. rare.* M18. [f. IN-^{3} + ARTICULATION.] Absence of distinct articulation; inarticulate utterance.
Chesterfield It was by the ambiguity of the expression . . not by the inarticulation of the words.

in articulo mortis /ɪn ɑːˌtɪkjʊləʊ ˈmɔːtɪs/ *adv. phr.* L16. [L = in the article of death.] At the point or moment of death.

inartificial /ˌɪnɑːtɪˈfɪʃ(ə)l/ *a. arch.* L16. [f. IN-^{3} + ARTIFICIAL *a.*; in sense 1 f. L *inartificialis* (tr. Gk *atekhnos*) not according to the rules of logic (lit. 'art').] †1 Of an argument: not deduced by logic from accepted premisses but derived from authority or testimony. L16–E18. 2 Not in accordance with artistic principles; rude, clumsy, inartistic. *arch.* E17. †3 Not produced by artifice or constructive skill; natural. M–L17. 4 Not pretending or pretended; artless, unaffected, natural. M17. 5 Without complexity or elaboration; plain, simple, straightforward. E19.
inartificially *adv.* E17.

inartistic /ɪnɑːˈtɪstɪk/ *a.* M19. [f. IN-^{3} + ARTISTIC.] 1 Not in accordance with artistic principles. M19. 2 Without artistic skill, talent, or appreciation. L19.
1 Geo. Eliot Inartistic figures crowding the canvass of life without adequate effect. 2 E. C. Stedman An inartistic nature and a dull or commonplace mind.
inartistically *adv.* M19.

inasmuch /ɪnəzˈmʌtʃ/ *adv.* ME. [Orig. 3 wds, f. IN *prep.* + AS *adv.* + MUCH *a.* or *n.*, tr. OFr. *en tant (que)*, L *in tantum (ut).*] 1 Foll. by *as*: in so far as, to such a degree as. ME. 2 Foll. by *as*: in that; seeing or considering that; since, because. LME.
1 C. Blackwood Inasmuch as she could be pleased, the idea of this marriage pleased her. 2 B. Guest Inasmuch as Gray was Perdita's father, he was to be treated with . . respect.

inattention /ɪnəˈtɛnʃ(ə)n/ *n.* L17. [f. IN-^{3} + ATTENTION.] 1 Failure to pay attention or take notice; heedlessness, negligence. L17. 2 Lack of courteous personal attention. L18.

inattentive /ɪnəˈtɛntɪv/ *a.* L17. [f. IN-^{3} + ATTENTIVE.] 1 Not paying attention; heedless, negligent. L17. 2 Neglecting to show courtesy. L18.
inattentively *adv.* M18. **inattentiveness** *n.* M18.

inaudible /ɪnˈɔːdɪb(ə)l/ *a.* LME. [Late L *inaudibilis*, f. (as) IN-^{3} + AUDIBLE.] Not audible; imperceptible to the ear.
Shakes. *All's Well* Th' inaudible and noiseless foot of Time. V. Brittain He was so shy that his few remarks were almost inaudible.
inaudiˈbility *n.* E19. **inaudibly** *adv.* L18.

inaugur /ɪˈnɔːgə/ *v.t.* Now *rare* or *obs.* M16. [(O)Fr. *inaugurer* or L *inaugurare*: see INAUGURATE.] †1 = INAUGURATE 1. M16–E18. 2 = INAUGURATE 4. L19.

inaugural /ɪˈnɔːgjʊr(ə)l/ *a.* & *n.* L17. [Fr., f. *inaugurer* inaugurate f. L *inaugurare* INAUGURATE: see -AL^1.] A *adj.* Of or pertaining to inauguration; forming part of an inauguration ceremony. Of a lecture, meeting, etc.: first in a series or course. L17. B *n.* An inaugural speech, address, or lecture. M19.

inaugurate /ɪˈnɔːgjʊreɪt/ *v.t.* L16. [L *inaugurat-* pa. ppl stem of *inaugurare* take omens from the flight of birds, f. as IN-^{1} + *augurari* AUGUR *v.*: see -ATE^3.] 1 Admit to office (*US* esp. the presidency) by a formal ceremony. L16. 2 Make auspicious; confer solemnity or sanctity upon. *rare.* E17. 3 Enter into (an undertaking or course of action, a significant period of time) formally or ceremoniously; initiate, introduce, begin. M18. 4 Open or dedicate to public use by a formal ceremony. M19.
3 E. F. Benson She said that we . . must inaugurate an intellectual regeneration in London. P. Ackroyd His return to Harvard also inaugurated a period in which he was beset by worries.
inauguratory *a.* pertaining to inauguration; inaugural: L18. **inaugurative** *a.* having the function of inaugurating; inaugural: M19.

inauguration /ɪˌnɔːgjʊˈreɪʃ(ə)n/ *n.* M16. [(O)Fr., or late L *inauguratio(n-)*, f. as prec.: see -ATION.] 1 Formal or ceremonial admission to an office (*US* esp. the presidency); an inaugural occasion or ceremony. M16. 2 The formal or definite beginning of or introduction to a course of action, a significant period of time, etc. M19.

3 The formal or ceremonious introduction of something into public use. M19.

1 J. S. MILL I . . always dated from these conversations my own . . inauguration as an original and independent thinker. **Inauguration Day** *US* the day (currently 20 January following the presidential election) on which the president is inaugurated. 2 J. A. FROUDE To the one . . the advent of Antichrist, to the other the inauguration of the millennium.

†inaunter *conj.* var. of ENAUNTER.

inauspicious /ɪnɔːˈspɪʃəs/ *a.* L16. [f. IN-[3] + AUSPICIOUS.] Portending evil; ill-omened, unlucky.

A. COWLEY On that Trees Top an inauspicious Crow Foretold some ill to happen. SHAFTESBURY I begin this inauspicious Work, which my ill Stars and you have assign'd me.

inauspiciously *adv.* L17. **inauspiciousness** *n.* M17.

inauthentic /ɪnɔːˈθɛntɪk/ *a.* L16. [f. IN-[3] + AUTHENTIC *a.*] Not authentic; not genuine; unreliable, unreal.

,inauthen'ticity *n.* L19.

inauthoritative /ɪnɔːˈθɒrɪtətɪv, -teɪtɪv/ *a.* M17. [f. IN-[3] + AUTHORITATIVE.] Not authoritative; having no authority.

in banco /ɪn ˈbaŋkəʊ/ *adv. phr.* M19. [L = on the bench.] *Hist.* Of a lawcourt: sitting as a full bench of judges.

in-being /ˈɪnbiːɪŋ/ *n.* L16. [f. IN *adv.* + BEING *n.*] †1 *Theol.* Each of the constituents of the Trinity. L16–M17. 2 The fact of being within; existence in something else. E17. 3 Inward or essential nature. M17.

1 A. GOLDING In the same most single essence are three Persons or In-beings. 2 T. WARREN 'Tis such an union and in-being in Christ. J. NEILL Believing . . gives them a real subsistence and in-being in the Soul. 3 J. RUSKIN Men get to know . . their inbeing—to know themselves . . what is in them.

inbent /ˈɪnbɛnt/ *a.* Long *rare.* L16. [f. IN *adv.* + BENT *a.*] Bent or curved inwards; directed inwards.

in-between /ɪnbɪˈtwiːn/ *n.* & *a.* E19. [f. *in between* s.v. IN *adv.*] **A** *n.* 1 An interval. E19. 2 A person who intervenes. E19. **B** *adj.* Intermediate, placed between. L19.

in-betweener /ɪnbɪˈtwiːnə/ *n.* E20. [f. as prec. + -ER[1].] A person who occupies or takes up an intermediate (esp. mental) position or attitude.

inbind /ɪnˈbʌɪnd/ *v.t.* Pa. t. & pple **inbound** /ɪnˈbaʊnd/. L18. [f. IN-[1] + BIND *v.*] Bind within; *spec.* bind within a book or manuscript. Usu. in *pass.*

Ampleforth Journal A transcription of the fragment inbound in the Sarum Missal in the monastery library. *fig.*: D. H. LAWRENCE He had never been very closely inbound into the family.

inboard /ˈɪnbɔːd/ *adv., prep., a.,* & *n.* Orig. *Naut.* M19. [f. IN *prep.* + BOARD *n.*] **A** *adv.* Within the sides or towards the centre of a boat, aircraft, vehicle, etc. M19.

E. K. KANE It passes inboard through a block. *Times* Inboard-mounted disc brakes.

B *prep.* Within (a boat etc.), inside. M19.

C *adj.* Situated within or towards the centre of a boat, aircraft, vehicle, etc.; interior. M19.

Rudder Even in large sailing boats the use of an inboard engine is sometimes not advisable.

D *n.* (A boat equipped with) a motor mounted within the hull. *N. Amer.* E20.

inborn /ˈɪnbɔːn, ɪnˈbɔːn/ *a.* OE. [f. IN-[1] + BORN *a.*, after late L *innatus* INNATE.] †1 Born in the place or country specified or in question; native. OE–L19. 2 (Of a quality etc.) existing in a person from birth, innate; *Med.* (esp. of a metabolic disorder) congenital and hereditary. E16. 3 Of a person: born such, such by nature. E19.

1 MILTON Those old and inborn names of successive Kings. 2 L. DURRELL A native and inborn scepticism kept me free from the toils of any denominational religion. 3 *Westminster Gazette* Every in-born artist has a natural method, like the song-birds of the air.

inbound /ˈɪnbaʊnd/ *a.* L19. [f. IN *adv.* + BOUND *a.*[1]] Bound or headed inward, homeward-bound.

inbound *v.* pa. t. & pple of INBIND.

inbread /ˈɪnbrɛd/ *n.* Now *rare.* M17. [f. IN *adv.* + BREAD *n.*[1]] The extra loaf in a baker's dozen.

inbreak /ˈɪnbreɪk/ *n. rare.* L17. [f. IN *adv.* + BREAK *n.*[1], after *outbreak.*] An invasion, a forcible entry.

Also **inbreaking** *n.* M17.

inbreath /ˈɪnbrɛθ/ *n.* E20. [f. IN *adv.* + BREATH.] A drawing in of the breath, an inhalation.

inbreathe /ɪnˈbriːð/ *v.t.* LME. [f. IN-[1] + BREATHE *v.*, after L *inspirare.* Cf. IMBREATHE.] 1 Introduce or instil by breathing. (Foll. by *into.*) LME. 2 Give inspiration to. E19. 3 Draw in as breath; inhale. L19.

1 *fig.*: T. GATAKER They cannot inbreath into us such knowledg that shal quiet and allay our . . hearts. J. A. SYMONDS So true and delicate a spirit is inbreathed into the old forms. 3 J. R. ILLINGWORTH He felt himself inbreathing power from on high.

inbred /ɪnˈbrɛd, ˈɪnbrɛd/ *a.* Also **†im-**. L16. [f. IN *adv.* + BRED *a.*] 1 Inborn, innate, inherent. L16. †2 Bred in the place specified or in question; native. E–M17. 3 Characterized or produced by inbreeding. L19.

1 R. BOYLE Your inbred Curiosity, and love of Experimental Learning. 3 R. L. STEVENSON Sore-eyed, short-lived, inbred fishermen.

inbreed /ɪnˈbriːd/ *v.* Also **im-** /ɪm-/. Pa. t. & pple **-bred** /-ˈbrɛd/. M16. [f. IN-[1] + BREED *v.* In sense 3, prob. back-form. f. INBREEDING.] †1 *v.i.* Come into being, originate. Only in M16. 2 *v.t.* Breed, engender, or produce internally. L16. 3 *v.t.* & *i.* Breed from closely-related members of a species, esp. over several generations. Cf. earlier INBREEDING. M20. **b** *v.i.* (Marry and) produce offspring from within a family or small social group, for successive generations. M20.

2 M. SULLIVAN Stressing positive attributes creates or inbreeds these values, which become the . . guiding beliefs of employees.

inbreeding /ˈɪnbriːdɪŋ/ *vbl n.* M19. [f. IN *adv.* + BREEDING.] Breeding from closely-related members of a species (as siblings, parent and offspring, etc.). Also, (marriage and) the production of offspring from within a closed community.

inbring /ɪnˈbrɪŋ/ *v.t.* Long *obs.* exc. *Sc.* Infl. as BRING. OE. [f. IN-[1] + BRING, tr. L *offerre.*] Bring in, introduce; *esp.* in *Sc. Law*, bring in by legal authority, produce in court, confiscate.

inbringer *n.* a person who introduces or imports something E16.

in-build /ɪnˈbɪld/ *v.t.* Pa. t. & pple **-built** /-ˈbɪlt/. E20. [f. IN-[1] + BUILD *v.* Cf. next.] Build in; incorporate as part of a structure.

Press & Journal (Aberdeen) Timber-frame has to be well supervised to make sure that you don't in-build problems.

inbuilt /ˈɪnbɪlt/ *ppl a.* E20. [f. IN *adv.* + *built* pa. pple of BUILD *v.*] Incorporated in a structure; already part of or (naturally) present in something.

Catholic Herald Any nation has an in-built resistance to immigrants. *Daily Telegraph* They . . contain an in-built device to ensure that no dazzle occurs.

†inburning *ppl a. rare* (Spenser). Only in L16. [f. IN *adv.* + BURNING *a.*] Burning inwardly.

inburst /ˈɪnbəːst/ *n. rare.* M19. [f. IN *adv.* + BURST *n.*: cf. *outburst.*] An irruption; a sudden entry or incursion.

inburst /ɪnˈbəːst/ *v.i. rare.* M16. [f. IN-[1] + BURST *v.*] Burst in; come in suddenly or violently.

in-bye /ɪnˈbʌɪ/ *adv.* & *a.* Chiefly *Sc.* & *north.* Also **in-by**. E18. [f. IN *adv.* + BY *adv.*] **A** *adv.* In an inward direction; closer or further towards the centre or interior. E18. **B** *adj.* Inner, in the interior; *spec.* designating or pertaining to a farm's land lying nearest to the farm buildings. E19.

Inc. /ɪŋk/ *ppl a. N. Amer.* E20. [Abbrev.] In names of companies: incorporated, constituted as a legal corporation.

H. L. MENCKEN An Englishman writes *Ltd.* after the name of a limited liability bank . . as we write *Inc.*

Inca /ˈɪŋkə/ *n.* & *a.* Also (earlier) **†Ing(u)a.** L16. [Quechua = lord, king, royal person. Earlier form is Sp. corruption.] **A** *n.* Pl. **-s**, same. 1 A member of a S. American Indian people of the central Andes before the Spanish conquest in the early 16th cent.; *spec.* their king or emperor, a member of the royal family. L16. 2 (Usu. **i-**.) Any of several hummingbirds of the genus *Coeligena.* M20.

1 J. BRONOWSKI From 1438 onwards, the Incas had conquered three thousand miles of coastline.

B *attrib.* or as *adj.* Of or pertaining to the Incas. E17.

Inca dove a small dove of Central America and the south-western US, *Scardafella inca.* **Inca tern** a dark grey tern, *Larosterna inca*, of Peru and Chile.

†incage *v.* var. of ENCAGE.

Incaic /ɪŋˈkeɪɪk/ *a.* E20. [f. INCA + -IC.] = INCAN.

incalculable /ɪnˈkalkjʊləb(ə)l/ *a.* L18. [f. IN-[3] + CALCULABLE.] 1 Of an amount or number too great for calculation. L18. 2 Unable to be estimated or forecast. L18. 3 Of a person, disposition, etc.: unpredictable. L19.

1 LYTTON They say his wealth is incalculable. S. MORLEY His influence on David was incalculable. 2 G. F. CHAMBERS The incalculable number of meteor-streams that must exist in the solar system. *Pall Mall Gazette* The incalculable dangers of the 'narcotic' remedies. 3 GEO. ELIOT Anxiety about the beloved but incalculable son.

incalcula'bility *n.* L19. **incalculableness** *n.* M19. **incalculably** *adv.* E19.

incalescent /ɪnkəˈlɛs(ə)nt/ *a.* Now *rare* or *obs.* L17. [L *incalescent-* pres. ppl stem of *incalescere*, f. as IN-[2] + *calescere* grow warm: see -ENT.] Becoming hot or warm; increasing in warmth.

incalescence *n.* the action or process of becoming hot or warm; a rise in temperature: M17.

in-calf /ɪnˈkɑːf, ˈɪnkɑːf/ *a.* M16. [f. IN-[1] + CALF *n.*[1]] Of a cow: that is in calf, pregnant.

in'calver *n.* an in-calf cow M19.

incall /ɪnˈkɔːl/ *v.* Long *obs.* exc. *Sc.* ME. [f. IN-[1] + CALL *v.*, after L *invocare* INVOKE.] 1 *v.t.* Call in, call upon, invoke. ME. 2 *v.i.* Call *on* or *upon*; pray *for, that.* L16.

in camera /ɪn ˈkam(ə)rə/ *adv. phr.* E19. [Late L = in the chamber: see CAMERA.] In a judge's private chambers, not in open court; *gen.* in secret or private session, not in public.

†incameration *n.* L17–E18. [Fr. *incamération*, f. *incamérer*, f. It. *incamerare*, f. *in-* IN-[2] + *camera* chamber, the papal treasury.] Annexation to the papal domain.

†incamp *v.*, **†incampment**, vars. of ENCAMP, ENCAMPMENT.

Incan /ˈɪŋk(ə)n/ *a.* L19. [f. INCA + -AN.] Of or pertaining to the Incas.

incandesce /ɪnkanˈdɛs/ *v.* L19. [Back-form. f. INCANDESCENT.] 1 *v.i.* Be or become incandescent; glow with heat. L19. 2 *v.t.* Make incandescent; cause to glow. *rare.* L19.

incandescence /ɪnkanˈdɛs(ə)ns/ *n.* M17. [f. as next: see -ENCE.] 1 The state of being inflamed with anger, passion, etc.; ardency, fervour. M17. 2 The state of being incandescent; the emission of light by a heated object or body. L18. **b** Glowing or intense heat. *rare.* M19. **c** Glowing or incandescent matter. M19.

1 D. LESSING Now she sounded listless, flat, all the incandescence of fury gone. 2 J. TYNDALL Meteorites . . brought to incandescence by friction against the earth's atmosphere. W. SPOTTISWOODE The light is due to the incandescence of a fine thread of carbon.

incandescent /ɪnkanˈdɛs(ə)nt/ *a.* & *n.* L18. [Fr. f. L *incandescent-* pres. ppl stem of *incandescere* glow, f. as IN-[2] + *candescere* become white, f. *candidus* white: see CANDID, -ESCENT.] **A** *adj.* 1 Glowing with heat. L18. **b** Of a lamp etc.: producing light by means of a white-hot glowing filament. L19. 2 Glowing, brightly shining, luminous. M19. 3 (Becoming) warm or intense in feeling, expression, etc.; ardent, fiery. M19.

1 J. IMISON If the heated body is not luminous or incandescent, as hot water, for instance. J. TYNDALL The spectrum of incandescent sodium-vapour consists of a brilliant band. 2 W. GOLDING It was incandescent daylight . . an atmosphere with a luminescence in it. 3 P. LIVELY She feels incandescent, aflame with private triumphs.

B *n.* An incandescent lamp or burner. E20.

incandescently *adv.* E19.

incant /ɪnˈkant/ *v.* M16. [L *incantare* chant, charm, f. as IN-[2] + *cantare* sing.] 1 **†a** *v.t.* & *i.* Use incantation or enchantment (on). M16–M17.

For other words beginning with *in-* see the entry for **in-**[1]

b *v.t.* Raise (a spirit) by a charm or incantation. *rare.* E20. **2** *v.t.* Chant, intone. M20.

2 M. SPARK They sat in the twilight .. incanting witches' spells.

incantation /ɪnkan'teɪʃ(ə)n/ *n.* LME. [(O)Fr. f. late L *incantatio(n-)*, f. L *incantat-* pa. ppl stem of *incantare*: see prec., -ATION.] A magical formula chanted or spoken; an utterance of such a formula, the use of such a formula in magic; *gen.* (the use of) any magical act or ceremony.

J. JONES He is using words as incantation, magically.

incantational *a.* incantatory M20. **'incantator** *n.* (*rare*) a person who uses incantations, an enchanter LME. **in'cantatory** *a.* using or of the nature of (an) incantation M17.

incapable /ɪn'keɪpəb(ə)l/ *a.* & *n.* L16. [Fr., or late L *incapabilis*, f. as IN-[3] + *capabilis* CAPABLE.] **A** *adj.* **1** Lacking or deficient in ordinary powers or natural ability; incompetent; not capable of rational conduct. L16. †**2** Foll. by *of*: unable to receive, contain, or keep something. E17–M19. **b** Impatient or intolerant *of.* M17–E18. **3** Foll. by *of*: unable to be affected or influenced by; insensible to. Now *rare* or *obs.* E17. **4** Not having the capacity or fitness for a specified purpose, action, etc.; unable. Foll. by *of*, †*to do.* E17. **b** *spec.* Too honest etc. to be capable *of.* M18. **5** Not (esp. legally) qualified or entitled; disqualified. Foll. by *of*, †*to do.* M17. **6** Of a nature or in a condition not allowing or admitting of a specified thing; not susceptible *of* (improvement etc.). Foll. by *of*, †*to do.* L17.

1 LD MACAULAY That the finances might not be ruined by incapable and inexperienced Papists. C. MACKENZIE He's utterly drunk and incapable. 2 LEIGH HUNT This dandy would be incapable of his own wealth. b STEELE Your Temper is Wanton, and incapable of the least Pain. 3 SHAKES. *Haml.* As one incapable of her own distress. 4 A. T. ELLIS Something in me .. was arid and incapable of desire. L. GORDON The madman, living in mental isolation, is incapable of judging the quality of his ideas. b E. YOUNG The world .. was incapable of so great a guilt. SIR W. SCOTT My foes .. have laid things to my charge whereof I am incapable. 5 ADDISON The Jews .. are in most, if not all, Places incapable of either Lands or Offices. 6 B. STEWART Unavoidable loss of heat which is incapable of accurate measurement.

B *n.* An incompetent or incapable person. E19.

incapa'bility *n.* M17. **incapableness** *n.* M17. **incapably** *adv.* M19.

incapacious /ɪnkə'peɪʃəs/ *a.* Now *rare.* E17. [f. late L *incapac-*, *-ax*, f. as IN-[3] + CAPACIOUS.] **1** Lacking mental ability or capacity for something; unable to comprehend or apprehend; incapable. E17. †**2** Not sufficiently capacious; not spacious; *fig.* narrow, limited. M17–E18.

incapacitant /ɪnkə'pasɪt(ə)nt/ *n.* M20. [f. INCAPACIT(ATE + -ANT[1].] A substance capable of temporarily incapacitating a person etc. without wounding or killing.

incapacitate /ɪnkə'pasɪteɪt/ *v.t.* M17. [f. INCAPACIT(Y + -ATE[3].] Make incapable or unfit; disqualify, *spec.* in law.

M. MEYER The fear that he might find himself incapacitated by illness. S. HAZZARD By undertaking to raise them, Dora had incapacitated herself for earning a livelihood.

incapaci'tation *n.* L18.

incapacity /ɪnkə'pasɪti/ *n.* E17. [Fr. *incapacité* or late L *incapacitas*, f. as IN-[3] + *capacitas* CAPACITY.] **1** Lack of capacity; inability, powerlessness; an instance of this. (Foll. by *for*, *of*, *to do.*) E17. **b** Inability to take, receive, or deal with something in some way. Foll. by *for*, *of.* M17. **2** Legal disqualification; an instance of this. M17.

1 G. A. BIRMINGHAM A man who might make a wreck of a boat through incapacity to manage her. E. CRANKSHAW Inhibited by .. ignorance and intellectual incapacity, he failed to think of anything effective to do. 2 C. MERIVALE The laws .. inflicted upon him civil incapacity to the fullest extent.

Incaparina /ɪŋkəpə'riːnə/ *n.* M20. [f. *I*nstitute of *N*utrition of *C*entral *A*merica and *P*anama + Amer. Sp. *f*)*ariña* powdered manioc (f. L *farina* flour, meal).] A preparation of vegetable protein, used as a dietary supplement.

in capite /ɪn 'kapɪteɪ/ *adv. phr.* M16. [L.] = *in chief* (a) s.v. CHIEF *n.*

incapsulate *v.* var. of ENCAPSULATE.

†**incaptivate** *v.* var. of ENCAPTIVATE.

incarcerate /ɪn'kɑːs(ə)rət/ *ppl a. arch.* E16. [med.L *incarceratus* pa. pple, f. as next: see -ATE[2].] Imprisoned; confined, shut in.

incarcerate /ɪn'kɑːsəreɪt/ *v.t.* M16. [med.L *incarcerat-* pa. ppl stem of *incarcerare*, f. as IN-[2] + *carcer* prison: see -ATE[3].] Imprison, confine, shut in.

E. CRANKSHAW They were incarcerated in the damp and gloomy cells of the Peter and Paul Fortress.

incarcerated *ppl a.* (*a*) *Med.* (esp. of a hernia) confined or constricted so as to be immovable or irreducible; (*b*) *gen.* that has been incarcerated: L18. **incarcerator** *n.* E19.

incarceration /ɪnˌkɑːsə'reɪʃ(ə)n/ *n.* LME. [(O)Fr. f. med.L *incarceratio(n-)* imprisonment, f. as prec.: see -ATION.] **1** *Med.* †**a** Retention of pus in a wound. Only in LME. **b** Obstruction or strangulation of a hernia. E19. **2** *gen.* The action of incarcerating; the fact of being incarcerated. M16.

incardinate /ɪn'kɑːdɪneɪt/ *v.t.* E17. [Late L *incardinat-* pa. ppl stem of *incardinare* ordain to the first rank in a church, f. as IN-[2] + *cardin-*, *cardo* hinge, *cardinalis* chief presbyter: see CARDINAL *n.*, -ATE[3].] *Chr. Ch.* Institute as principal priest, deacon, etc., at a particular church or place; institute to a cardinalship; place under the jurisdiction of an ordinary.

incarn /ɪn'kɑːn/ *v. arch.* LME. [Late L *incarnare*: see INCARNATE *v.*] **1** *v.t.* Cover with flesh, heal over (a wound etc.). LME. **b** *v.i.* Cause flesh to grow, induce healing. M16. **c** *v.i.* Become covered with flesh; heal. L17. **2** *v.t.* Embody in flesh; incarnate. *rare.* M16.

incarnadine /ɪn'kɑːnədʌɪn/ *a.*, *v.*, & *n.* Now *arch.* & *poet.* As vb also **en-** /ɪn-, ɛn-/. L16. [Fr. *incarnadin(e)* f. It. *incarnadino* var. of *incarnatino* carnation, flesh-colour, f. *incarnato* f. as INCARNATE *a.*: see -INE[1].] **A** *adj.* Flesh-coloured, crimson; occas. (in allus. to Shakes.: see sense B. below), bloodstained. L16.

B *v.t.* Dye flesh-coloured or crimson; (in allus. to Shakes. *Macb.*) stain with blood. E17.

SHAKES. *Macb.* This my hand will rather The multitudinous seas incarnadine, Making the green one red.

C *n.* Flesh-colour, crimson; blood-red. M17.

BYRON No Barbaric blood can reconcile us now Unto that horrible incarnadine.

incarnalize *v.* var. of ENCARNALIZE.

incarnate /ɪn'kɑːneɪt, -ət/ *a.* LME. [eccl.L *incarnatus* pa. pple of *incarnari* be made flesh, f. as IN-[2] + *carn-*, *caro* flesh; in sense 2 f. Fr. *incarnat* or mod.L *incarnatus*: see -ATE[2].] **1** Of a person, spirit, quality, etc.: embodied in flesh, in human form; embodied in a recognizable or the most perfect form. Freq. *postpositive.* LME. **2** Flesh-coloured; light rosy pink or crimson. *obs.* exc. *Bot.* M16.

1 SIR W. SCOTT Whether there be a devil incarnate in you or no. E. O'BRIEN Phrases such as 'how are you' .. or 'dear one' were mockery incarnate. 2 C. DARWIN The common red and incarnate clovers.

incarnate /'ɪnkɑːneɪt, ɪn'kɑː-/ *v.* M16. [eccl.L *incarnat-* pa. ppl stem of *incarnare*, *-ari* make, be made, flesh: see prec., -ATE[3].] †**I 1** *v.t.* = INCARN I. M16–E18. **b** *v.i.* = INCARN IC. L17–M18. **2** *v.t.* Make carnal, degrade from spiritual nature. M–L17.

II 3 *v.t.* Embody in flesh or (esp.) in a human form. M16. **4** *v.t.* **a** Put (an idea etc.) into concrete form; realize. L16. **b** Be the living embodiment or type of; embody (a quality etc.). E19.

4 E. CLODD The ennobling qualities incarnated in some hero .. meet with admiring response. b D. CECIL Chosen less for herself than because she seemed momentarily to incarnate a boyish ideal.

incarnation /ɪnkɑː'neɪʃ(ə)n/ *n.* & *a.* ME. [(O)Fr. f. eccl.L *incarnatio(n-)*, f. as prec.: see -ATION.] **A** *n.* **I 1 a** *Chr. Theol.* (Freq. **I-**.) The embodiment of God in human form as Jesus. ME. **b** *gen.* The action of incarnating or fact of being incarnated in flesh or (esp.) in human form. E17. **2 a** A body etc. in which a soul or spirit is incarnated; an incarnate form (of something); the form or appearance assumed by a thing at a particular time; the period of time spent in such an incarnation. M18. **b** A living type or embodiment (*of* a quality etc.). E19.

1 G. PRIESTLAND He picked the form of a young Galilean Jew. Christians call it 'The Incarnation' b R. W. EMERSON The thoughts he delights to utter are the reason of his incarnation. 2a E. YOUNG When shall my soul her incarnation quit? L. MACNEICE There are few bodies which I should prefer for my next incarnation. L. ALTHER In its current incarnation, the town hosted tourists and skiers. A. BROOKNER In some future incarnation they would reap the reward promised in the Bible. b W. GERHARDIE I leaned forward, the incarnation of attention.

II 3 (A dye or pigment of) flesh-colour, light rosy pink, or crimson. *arch.* LME. **4** The growth of new flesh on or in a wound etc.; healing up. Also, a growth of new flesh. Now *rare.* LME. †**5** Conception (in the womb). *rare.* M16–L17.

B *attrib.* or as *adj.* Flesh-coloured; of a light rosy pink or crimson. ME.

incarnational *a.* of or pertaining to the theological doctrine of the incarnation E20. **incarnationist** *n.* a believer in an incarnation M19.

†**incarnative** *a.* & *n.* LME–E18. [Fr. *incarnatif*, *-ive* or med.L *incarnativus*, f. as INCARN: see -ATIVE.] (A medicine or application intended for) promoting healing and causing flesh to grow on or in a wound etc.

†**incase** *v.* var. of ENCASE.

incasement *n.* see ENCASEMENT.

incatenation /ˌɪnkatɪ'neɪʃ(ə)n/ *n. arch.* M18. [med.L *incatenatio(n-)*, f. *incatenat-* pa. ppl stem of *incatenare* enchain, f. as IN-[2] + *catenare* bind with chains: see CATENATE, -ATION.] Putting or fastening in chains; harnessing; linking, being linked.

†**incautelous** *a.* E17–M18. [f. IN-[3] + CAUTELOUS.] Incautious.

incaution /ɪn'kɔːʃ(ə)n/ *n.* E18. [f. IN-[3] + CAUTION *n.*] Lack of caution; heedlessness, rashness.

incautious /ɪn'kɔːʃəs/ *a.* M17. [f. IN-[3] + CAUTIOUS, after L *incautus*.] Not cautious; heedless, rash.

A. BURGESS His rage and nausea made Lawrence incautious in talking against the war. R. ELLMANN He was incautious enough to form a friendship with Lord Ronald Gower.

incautiously *adv.* E18. **incautiousness** *n.* L18.

incavation /ɪnkə'veɪʃ(ə)n/ *n.* L18. [Alt. of EXCAVATION: see IN-[2].] The action of hollowing or bending inwards. Also, a hollow depression, a hollowed place.

†**incave** *v.* var. of ENCAVE.

incede /ɪn'siːd/ *v.i. rare.* LME. [L *incedere*, f. as IN-[2] + *cedere* go.] Move on, advance, esp. with a measured or stately pace.

incend /ɪn'sɛnd/ *v.t.* Long *rare.* E16. [L *incendere*: see INCENSE *n.*, *v.*[2]] †**1** Inflame (the mind, feelings, etc.); incite to action. E16–L17. †**2** Engender (bodily heat); heat (the body or a part of the body). M16–E17. **3** Set on fire, kindle. L16.

incendiary /ɪn'sɛndjəri/ *a.* & *n.* LME. [L *incendiarius*, f. *incendium* conflagration, f. *incendere* set fire to: see INCENSE *n.*, -ARY[1].] **A** *adj.* **1 a** Combustible; *spec.* (*Mil.*) adapted or used for setting on fire an enemy's buildings, ships, etc. LME. **b** Of or pertaining to the malicious setting on fire of property. E17. **2** *fig.* Tending to stir up strife; inflammatory. E17.

1a **incendiary bomb**: filled with a substance for causing a fire at the point of impact. b D. M. MULOCK The glare of some incendiary fire. 2 J. REED Their newspapers .. publish incendiary and crime-inciting appeals to mob violence.

B *n.* **1** A person who maliciously sets property on fire; an arsonist. LME. **b** = *incendiary bomb* above. M20. **2** *fig.* A person who stirs up strife; an inflammatory agitator. L16. †**b** A thing which stirs up passion, strife, etc.; an incentive to evil. E17–E18.

incendiarism *n.* (*a*) inflammatory agitation; (*b*) the practice or commission of arson: L17.

incendiate /ɪnˈsɛndɪeɪt/ *v.t. rare.* E18. [f. as next + -ATE[3].] Set on fire.
†incendiator *n.*: only in M17.

†incendium *n.* M17–M18. [L: see INCENDIARY.] A conflagration; a volcanic eruption.

incendivity /ɪnsɛnˈdɪvɪti/ *n.* E20. [f. L *incendere* (see INCENSE *n.*) + -IVITY.] The ability to effect ignition or set something on fire.
inˈcendive *a.* of or pertaining to incendivity; capable of effecting ignition: M20.

incensation /ɪnsɛnˈseɪʃ(ə)n/ *n.* M19. [f. INCENSE *v.*[1] + -ATION.] The action or an act of censing.

incense /ˈɪnsɛns/ *n.* Also (earlier) **†en-**. ME. [(O)Fr. *encens* f. eccl.L *incensum* use as n. of neut. of *incensus* pa. pple of *incendere* set fire to, f. as IN-[2] + root of *candere* to glow.] **1a** An aromatic gum or spice used for producing a sweet smell when burned. ME. **b** The smoke or perfume of this, esp. when burned as part of religious ceremonial. LME. **2** Orig., the smoke or odour of a burnt sacrifice. Later, a pleasant perfume or fragrance. ME. **3** *fig.* Something offered in homage; prayer, praise, flattery. LME.
1a P. S. BUCK He burned a little incense before them. b M. COX Palm Sunday found Monty . . in Milan Cathedral—all banners and incense. *male incense*: see MALE *a.* & *n.* 2 SHELLEY The matin winds from the expanded flowers Scatter their hoarded incense. 3 H. REED The incense of flattery which his satellites were forever burning beneath his nostrils.
Comb.: **incense-cedar** a cedar of western N. America, *Calocedrus decurrens*, whose leaves smell of turpentine when bruised; **incense tree** any of various tropical trees yielding fragrant gum; esp. *Protium heptaphyllum*, of the torchwood family, of S. America; **incense-wood** the wood of *Protium heptaphyllum* (see *incense tree* above).

incense /ˈɪnsɛns/ *v.*[1] Also (earlier) **†en-**. ME. [(O)Fr. *encenser*, f. *encens*, or eccl.L *incensare*, f. *incensum*: see prec.] **1** *v.t.* Waft incense towards, esp. as part of religious ceremonial; burn incense to (a god etc.); cense. ME. **2** *v.i.* Burn or offer incense. Long *rare.* LME. **3** *v.t.* Suffuse with fragrance, scent. Formerly, drive *out* by diffusing fragrance. E16. **4** *v.t.* Burn or offer as incense (*lit.* & *fig.*). E17. **5** *v.t.* Offer homage or adulation to, flatter. Now *rare* or *obs.* M18.
1 *Toronto Life* At the end of Mass Father Walsh incenses the casket. 3 L. L. NOBLE Wild roses incensed the fresh air.

incense /ɪnˈsɛns/ *v.*[2]*t.* Also (earlier) **†en-**. LME. [OFr. *incenser*, f. L *incens-* pa. ppl stem of *incendere*: see INCENSE *n.*] **†1a** Inflame, excite, (a person *with* ardent feeling etc.). LME–M17. **b** Inflame, excite, (ardent feeling). L16–E19. **2** *spec.* Make angry, enrage; exasperate. L15. **†3** Set on fire, kindle; consume with fire, burn. L15–E18. **†4** Incite to some action; urge, instigate. (Foll. by *to*, *to do*.) M16–M17.
2 P. ROTH It put our Portnoy into a rage, incensed The Temper Tantrum Kid. 4 T. FULLER By which speech he incensed the English to go on with him.
incensement *n.* (now *rare*) the fact of being incensed; anger, exasperation: L16.

incensed /ɪnˈsɛnst/ *a.* M16. [f. INCENSE *v.*[2] + -ED[1].] **†1** Set on fire, kindled; *fig.* aroused, excited. M16–L17. **2** Angry, enraged; exasperated. L16. **3** *Her.* Of an animal: having flames coming out of its mouth and ears. L16.

incenser /ˈɪnsɛnsə/ *n.* M16. [Fr. *encenseur*, f. as INCENSE *v.*[1]: see -ER[2].] A person who burns or offers incense.

†incension *n.* LME. [L *incensio(n-)* burning, f. *incens-* pa. ppl stem of *incendere*: see INCENSE *n.*, -ION.] **1** Burning; conflagration. LME–M17. **2** Bodily heating or inflammation. L16–M18.

†incensive *a.* & *n. rare.* L16. [Fr. †*incensif*, *-ive* or med.L *incensivus*, f. L *incens-*: see prec., -IVE.] **A** *adj.* **1** Angry. Only in L16. **2** Tending to excite angry feelings. M–L17. **B** *n.* = INCENTIVE *n.* I. Only in E17.

incensory /ˈɪnsɛns(ə)ri/ *n.* E17. [med.L *incensorium*, f. *incensum* INCENSE *n.*: see -ORY[1].] **†1** (An altar of) a burnt offering. *rare.* Only in E17. **2** A censer, a thurible. M17.

incenter *n.* see INCENTRE.

incentive /ɪnˈsɛntɪv/ *n.* LME. [L *incentivum* use as n. of neut. of *incentivus*: see next.] **1** Something that arouses feeling or incites to action; an incitement *to*; a provocation; a motive. LME. **2** A payment, concession, etc., made to stimulate greater productivity by workers. M20.
1 H. ARENDT Behind these obvious . . incentives to anti-Jewish attitudes there was a deeper cause. I. MURDOCH Her visit was an incentive to tidy the flat.
incentivize *v.t.* give an incentive to M20.

incentive /ɪnˈsɛntɪv/ *a.* E17. [In branch I f. L *incentivus* setting the tune, inciting, f. *incent-* var. of *incant-* (see INCANTATION): see -IVE. In branch II also infl. by INCENSIVE.] **I 1** Tending to arouse feeling or incite to action; provocative. E17. **2** Serving as an incentive to productivity; involving such incentives. M20.
1 R. NORTH The Lord Shaftesbury . . made an incentive speech in the House of Lords. 2 J. UPDIKE It shows up in the books and affects everybody's end-of-the-month incentive bonus. *Sydney Morning Herald* We offer our top performers overseas incentive travel.
†II 3 Having the property of setting on fire or kindling. M17–E18.

incentor /ɪnˈsɛntə/ *n.* Now *rare.* L16. [Late L = setter of a tune, inciter, f. L *incent-*: see prec., -OR.] A person who stirs up strife etc.; a person who incites *to* action.

incentre /ˈɪnsɛntə/ *n.* Also ***-ter**. E20. [f. IN-[1] + CENTRE *n.*] *Geom.* The centre of the inscribed circle of a figure, esp. of a triangle.

incept /ɪnˈsɛpt/ *v.* M16. [L *incept-*: see next.] **1** *v.t.* Undertake, begin, enter upon. Now *rare* or *obs.* M16. **2** *Hist.* *v.i.* = COMMENCE *v.* 3. M19. **3** *v.t. Biol.* Take in (food etc.), ingest. M19.

inception /ɪnˈsɛpʃ(ə)n/ *n.* LME. [((O)Fr. f.) L *inceptio(n-)*, f. *incept-* pa. ppl stem of *incipere* begin: see INCIPIENT.] **1** The action of entering upon some undertaking, process, or stage of existence; beginning, commencement. LME. **2** The action of incepting, esp. (*Hist.*) commencement at a university. L17.
1 R. G. COLLINGWOOD He feels it not only after his work is completed, but from its inception.

Inceptisol /ɪnˈsɛptɪsɒl/ *n.* M20. [f. L *inceptum* a beginning, f. *incipere* begin (see INCIPIENT), + -I- + -SOL.] *Soil Sci.* A soil of an order in which the formation of distinct horizons is not far advanced, and which shows little severe weathering.

inceptive /ɪnˈsɛptɪv/ *n.* & *a.* E17. [Late L *inceptivus*, f. as INCEPT: see -IVE.] **A** *n.* *Gram.* An inceptive verb. E17. **B** *adj.* **1** Commencing, incipient; marking the beginning of something, initial. M17. **2** *Gram.* & *Logic.* Expressing the beginning of (an) action; esp. in *inceptive verb*. M17.

inceptor /ɪnˈsɛptə/ *n.* L15. [med.L (in cl.L = beginner), f. as INCEPT: see -OR.] *Hist.* A person who incepts or is about to incept at a university.

†incertain *a.* LME–M18. [(O)Fr., f. as IN-[3], CERTAIN.] Uncertain.
†incertainly *adv.* M16–E18.

†incertainty *n.* L15–L18. [OFr. *incertaineté*, f. as prec. after *certaineté* CERTAINTY.] Uncertainty.

incertitude /ɪnˈsəːtɪtjuːd/ *n.* LME. [((O)Fr. f.) late L *incertitudo*, f. as IN-[3], CERTITUDE.] **1** Subjective uncertainty; doubt, hesitation. LME. **2** (An) objective uncertainty; unpredictability. E17.
1 A. ALISON The King was distracted by the most cruel incertitude. 2 A. G. GARDINER He knows nothing . . of the incertitudes of life.

incessable /ɪnˈsɛsəb(ə)l/ *a. arch. rare.* LME. [(Fr. †*incessable* f.) late L *incessabilis*, f. *cessare* CEASE *v.*: see IN-[3], -ABLE.] Incessant.
incessably *adv.* E16.

incessant /ɪnˈsɛs(ə)nt/ *a.* & *adv.* LME. [((O)Fr. f.) late L *incessant-*, f. as IN-[3] + L *cessant-* pres. ppl stem of *cessare* CEASE *v.*: see -ANT[1].] **A** *adj.* **1** Ceaseless, continual, unremitting. LME. **†2** Never-ending, perpetual. M16–M17.
1 D. LESSING The noise of the wind was an incessant metallic whispering. W. SOYINKA Daodu was an incessant conversationalist.
B *adv.* Without pause, unceasingly. *poet.* M16.
incessancy *n.* the quality of being incessant E17. **incessantly** *adv.* (*a*) unceasingly; †(*b*) without pause, immediately: LME. **incessantness** *n.* E18.

†incession *n. rare.* M16–M19. [Late L *incessio(n-)*, f. *incess-* pa. ppl stem of *incedere*: see INCEDE, -ION.] Onward motion, progression (*lit.* & *fig.*).

incest /ˈɪnsɛst/ *n.* ME. [L *incestus* n. (or *incestum* use as n. of neut. of *incestus* adj., unchaste), f. as IN-[3] + *castus* chaste.] Sexual intercourse between close relatives; *spec.* (*Law*) the crime of sexual intercourse between parent and child or grandchild, or between siblings or half-siblings; formerly, under ecclesiastical law, sexual intercourse between any persons related within the prohibited degrees as regards marriage.

incestuous /ɪnˈsɛstjʊəs/ *a.* E16. [Late L *incestuosus*, f. L *incestus*: see prec., -OUS.] **1** Of the nature of, involving, or guilty of incest. E16. **†b** Adulterous. M–L17. **†2** Begotten by incest. L16–E17. **3** *fig.* Of a relationship etc.: unwholesomely close; operating within an excessively restricted circle. M20.
1 N. SYMINGTON He was beginning to become aware of his incestuous wishes towards his mother. 3 *Washington Post* The incestuous old-boy network.
incestuously *adv.* E16. **incestuousness** *n.* M17.

inch /ɪn(t)ʃ/ *n.*[1] [Late OE *ynće*, corresp. to OHG *unza*, Goth. *unkja*, f. L *uncia* twelfth part: see OUNCE *n.*[1]] **1** As a measure of length: the twelfth part of a foot; 2.54 cm. Also, an area or volume equal to that of a square or cube whose edges are one inch long. LOE. **b** As a unit of rainfall: the quantity sufficient to cover a horizontal surface to the depth of one inch, equivalent to 3630 cubic feet on an acre (approx. 253.7 cu. metres on a hectare). M19. **c** As a unit of measurement of the flow of water (more fully *miner's inch*, *inch of water*): the amount of water that will pass in 24 hours through an opening of 1 square inch under a constant head of 6 inches (about 14,000 gallons, 64,000 litres). M19. **d** As a unit of atmospheric or hydrostatic pressure: a pressure equal to that exerted by a column of mercury 1 inch high; 33.86 mb. L19. **2** *transf.* & *fig.* A very small distance, measure, amount, or degree; the least amount or part (of space, time, etc.). ME. **3** In *pl.* (Considerable) height, stature. E17.
1 G. CRABBE Jonas Kindred . . Was six feet high, and look'd six inches higher. L. D. STAMP A useful map . . on the scale of 25 miles to one inch. 2 W. COWPER That I may avail myself of every inch of time. H. NISBET He could not see an inch before him. A. J. CRONIN There isn't an inch of space. 3 *Graphic* To make the most of her inches she had . . the habit of holding her head thrown back.
Phrases: **by inches** = *inch by inch* below. *every inch*: see EVERY *a.* I. **inch by inch** by small or imperceptible degrees, little by little. **within an inch of** *fig.* very close to. **within an inch of one's life** almost to death; *hyperbol.* extremely severely.
Attrib. & *comb.*: With a numeral etc. prefixed, = INCHED, as *six-inch*. **inchworm** = GEOMETER *n.* 3.

inch /ɪn(t)ʃ/ *n.*[2] ME. [Gael. *innis* /ˈɪnɪʃ/ island = (O)Ir. *inis*, Welsh *ynys*, prob. rel. (obscurely) to L *insula* island.] **1** A small island. Freq. in Sc. place-names. *Sc.* & *Ir.* ME. **2** *transf.* A meadow on the bank of a river. Also, a piece of rising ground in the middle of a plain. *Sc.* E16.

inch /ɪn(t)ʃ/ *v.* L16. [f. INCH *n.*[1]] **1** *v.i.* & *t.* Make (one's way) by inches or by small degrees. L16. **2** *v.t.* Eke *out* by inches or small amounts. Now *rare.* L16. **3** *v.t.* Drive or push by inches or small degrees. M17. **4** *v.t.* Measure the number of inches in. Now *rare* or *obs.* L17.
1 W. GOLDING He inched along the path, with shuffling steps. M. SHADBOLT The man inched his way across the face of the building. 3 E. BOWEN Inching open the door, he took a dekko into the outer office.

†inchangeable *a. rare.* L16–L18. [f. IN-[3] + CHANGEABLE.] Unchangeable.

†inchant *v.*, **†inchanter**, **†inchantment** *ns.* vars. of ENCHANT etc.

†incharitable *a.* L15–L17. [f. IN-[3] + CHARITABLE *a.*] Not charitable.

inchastity /ɪnˈtʃastɪti/ *n.* Now *rare.* L16. [f. IN-[3] + CHASTITY.] Lack of chastity.

inched /ɪn(t)ʃt/ *a.* E17. [f. INCH *n.*[1], *v.*: see -ED[2], -ED[1].] With a numeral etc. prefixed: that is (so many) inches in length, diameter, etc.

†**incheer** *v.* var. of ENCHEER.

incher /ˈɪn(t)ʃə/ *n.* L19. [f. INCH *n.*[1] + -ER[1].] With a numeral prefixed: a thing having a length, diameter, etc., of the number of inches specified.

inchmeal /ˈɪn(t)ʃmiːl/ *adv.* & *n.* M16. [f. INCH *n.*[1] + -MEAL.] A *adv.* By inches; little by little. M16. B *n. by inchmeal* = sense A. above. M16.

inchoate /ɪnˈkəʊeɪt, ˈɪnk-, -ət/ *a.* M16. [L *inchoatus* pa. pple of *inchoare* var. of *incohare* begin: see -ATE[2].] 1 Just begun, incipient, rudimentary; not yet fully formed or developed. M16. 2 Chaotic, confused; (of thought or language) incoherent. E20.

1 R. HUNTFORD All three were now troubled by inchoate doubts about survival. SYD. SMITH Many inchoate acts are innocent, the consummation of which is a capital offence. 2 G. GREENE I have seldom listened to more inchoate rubbish. *Times Lit. Suppl.* The inchoate welter of recent published poetry.

inchoately *adv.* E17. **inchoateness** *n.* M19.

inchoate /ˈɪnkəʊeɪt/ *v.* Now *rare.* E17. [L *inchoat-* pa. ppl stem of *inchoare*: see prec., -ATE[3].] 1 *v.t.* Produce the first stages of, commence. Also, cause to begin, bring about. E17. 2 *v.i.* Make a beginning, commence. E17.

inchoation /ɪnkəʊˈeɪʃ(ə)n/ *n.* LME. [Late L *inchoatio(n-)*, f. as prec.: see -ATION.] †1 Elementary knowledge, first principles. Only in LME. 2 Beginning, commencement; an initial stage. M16.

inchoative /ɪnˈkəʊətɪv, ˈɪnkəʊ-/ *n.* & *a.* M16. [Late L *inchoativus*, f. as prec.: see -IVE.] A *n.* An inchoative or inceptive verb. M16. B *adj.* 1 That is in an initial stage; rudimentary, inchoate. M17. 2 Of a verb: denoting the beginning of an action; inceptive. M17.

†**incicurable** *a. rare.* M17–L18. [f. IN-[3] + L *cicurare* CICURATE + -ABLE.] Of a plant: that cannot be naturalized.

incide /ɪnˈsʌɪd/ *v.* Now *rare* or *obs.* L16. [L *incidere* INCISE.] 1 *v.t.* & *i.* In surgery: make an incision (in). L16. 2 *v.t.* Of an internal remedy: loosen, disperse, (phlegm etc.). E17.

incidence /ˈɪnsɪd(ə)ns/ *n.* LME. [(O)Fr., f. *incident*, or med.L *incidentia*, f. *incident-*: see INCIDENT *a.*, -ENCE.] †1 A casual or subordinate occurrence or matter. LME–M17. 2a *Physics.* The falling of a line, or of something (esp. light) moving in a line, upon a surface. E17. b *gen.* The fact or action of falling upon or affecting something. M17. 3 The range or scope of a thing; the extent of a thing's influence; *esp.* the rate or frequency of occurrence *of* a phenomenon among a group of people. E19.

2a R. W. DITCHBURN The direction of reflection is on the side of the normal opposite to the direction of incidence. F. HOYLE The normal rate of incidence of cosmic rays on the Earth. **angle of incidence** the angle between a ray etc. incident on a surface and the normal to the surface at the point of incidence. 3 D. W. GOODWIN Studies have shown a high incidence of alcoholism in a parent of women alcoholics. N. SYMINGTON He..noted the frequent incidence of religious imagery in their utterances. A. BRIGGS Battles in Parliament about the incidence of taxation on different sections of the community.

†**incidency** *n.* E17. [f. as prec. + -ENCY.] 1 A casual or subordinate occurrence or circumstance. E17–E18. 2 The quality of being liable to fall or happen (*to* a person); a thing liable to befall (someone). Only in 17. 3 *Physics.* = INCIDENCE *n.* 2a. M17–E18.

1 SHAKES. *Wint. T.* Declare What incidency thou dost guess of harm Is creeping toward me.

incident /ˈɪnsɪd(ə)nt/ *n.* LME. [(O)Fr., use as n. of adj.: see next.] 1 Something that occurs casually in connection with something of which it forms no essential part; a subordinate or accessory event. LME. 2 *gen.* A distinct occurrence or event, *esp.* one that attracts general attention or is noteworthy in some way. LME. †b A matter, an affair. *rare.* L15–M18. c An event which increases international tension or may precipitate open warfare; a particular episode in a war; a fracas; a public disturbance. E20. 3 A natural or characteristic accompaniment. Now chiefly (*Law*), a privilege, burden, custom, etc., commonly attaching to an office, an estate, etc. E17. 4a A distinct piece of action in a play or poem, orig. one subordinate to the main plot. L17. b A single feature in a picture, *esp.* one that does not form part of the main design. *rare.* E18. 5 An incidental charge or expense. Usu. in *pl.* Now chiefly *Sc.* M18.

2 E. H. JONES Apart from one or two incidents, she ..recalled hardly anything of these years. c M. SPARK It would be..unfair..to involve the British Consulate in an incident of that kind. *Clitheroe Advertiser & Times* Young vandals were probably responsible for two incidents in the town. 3 R. H. TAWNEY They entrusted to bureaucracies work which ..had formerly been done as an incident of tenure.

Comb.: **incident room** a centre set up by the police (freq. near the scene of the occurrence) to coordinate operations connected with a particular crime, accident, etc.

incident /ˈɪnsɪd(ə)nt/ *a.* LME. [((O)Fr. f.) L *incident-* pres. ppl stem of *incidere* fall upon, happen to, f. as IN-[2] + *cadere* to fall: see -ENT.] I †1 = INCIDENTAL *a.* 2, 2b. LME–M18. †2a Relevant or pertinent *to.* LME–E17. b *Law.* Attaching itself as a privilege, burden, etc., *to* an office, estate, etc. L15. 3 Apt or liable to happen (*to*); naturally attaching (*to*) or consequent (*on*, *upon*). L15. †4 Liable or subject *to.* E17–M18.

3 T. REID The fallacies incident to categorical syllogisms. J. LANG The noise..incident on..the breaking up of the little camp.

II 5 Esp. of light or other radiation: falling on or striking against a surface. M17.

5 F. HOYLE Clean ice absorbs about two-thirds of the sunlight incident upon it.

incidently *adv.* (now *rare*) incidentally E16.

incidental /ɪnsɪˈdɛnt(ə)l/ *a.* & *n.* E17. [Orig. f. med.L *incidentalis* (cf. *angulus incidentalis* angle of incidence), f. L *incident-*: see prec., -AL[1]. In mod. use f. INCIDENT *n.* + -AL[1].] A *adj.* 1 Liable to happen *to*; naturally attaching *to.* E17. 2 Occurring as something casual or of secondary importance; not directly relevant *to*; following (*up*)*on* as a subordinate circumstance. M17. b Of an expense or charge: incurred apart from the main sum disbursed. M18. c Casually met with. *rare.* M19.

1 J. INGLIS The dangers incidental to pigsticking. 2 H. SPENCER With the..moral man, correct conduct.. is merely incidental upon the fulfilment of his own nature. O. W. HOLMES Writing verse should be an incidental occupation only, not interfering with the hoe..or the ledger. **incidental music**: used as a background to the action of a play, film, broadcast, etc.

B *n.* An incidental circumstance, event, etc.; in *pl.*, incidental expenses. E18.

incidentalist *n.* a person who describes or insists on what is merely incidental E20. **incidentally** *adv.* in an incidental manner, as a casual or subordinate circumstance; (introducing a remark not strictly relevant) as a further thought: M17.

†**incider** *n.* L16–M18. [f. INCIDE + -ER[1].] A medicine that loosened or dispersed phlegm etc.; an instrument for making surgical incisions.

incinerate /ɪnˈsɪnəreɪt/ *v.* Pa. pple **-ated,** †**-ate.** L15. [med.L *incinerat-* pa. ppl stem of *incinerare*, f. as IN-[2] + *ciner-*, *cinis* ashes: see -ATE[3].] 1 *v.t.* Burn to ashes; *spec.* (esp. *US*) cremate (a body). L15. 2 *v.i.* Be burnt to ashes. E19.

incineˈration *n.* E16. **incinerator** *n.* an apparatus for incinerating refuse etc. L19.

†**incipher** *v.* see ENCIPHER.

incipient /ɪnˈsɪpɪənt/ *n.* & *a.* L16. [L *incipient-* pres. ppl stem of *incipere* undertake, begin, f. as IN-[2] + *capere* take: see -ENT.] A *n.* †1 A beginner. Only in L16. 2 *Heb. Gram.* The verbal form denoting an uncompleted action. Now usu. called *imperfect.* M19.

B *adj.* In an initial or early stage; beginning to develop. M17.

A. S. BYATT She examined herself hopefully for signs of incipient nervous breakdown. **incipient species** a group of plants or animals in the process of evolving and not yet sufficiently distinct to be described as a full species.

incipience *n.* beginning, commencement; an initial or early stage: M19. **incipiency** *n.* incipience E19. **incipiently** *adv.* M19.

incipit /ˈɪnsɪpɪt/ *n.* L19. [L, 3 sing. pres. indic. of *incipere* (see prec.), used by medieval scribes to indicate the beginning of a new treatise, poem, division, etc.] The opening words of a manuscript, a printed book (usu. an early one), a chanted liturgical text, etc. Cf. EXPLICIT *n.*

†**incircle** *v.* var. of ENCIRCLE.

in-circle /ˈɪnsəːk(ə)l/ *n.* L19. [f. IN-[1] + CIRCLE *n.*] *Geom.* A circle inscribed in a figure so as to touch its sides.

incircumscription /ɪnˌsəːkəmˈskrɪpʃ(ə)n/ *n.* Now *rare.* M17. [Late L *incircumscriptio(n-)*, f. as IN-[3], CIRCUMSCRIPTION.] The condition of not being limited; boundlessness; infinitude.

incircumspect /ɪnˈsəːkəmspɛkt/ *a.* Now *rare.* M16. [f. IN-[3] + CIRCUMSPECT.] Not circumspect.

incisal /ɪnˈsʌɪz(ə)l/ *a.* E20. [f. INCIS(OR + -AL[1].] *Dentistry.* Designating or pertaining to the cutting edge of an incisor or a canine tooth.

incise /ɪnˈsʌɪz/ *v.* M16. [Fr. *inciser*, f. L *incis-* pa. ppl stem of *incidere*, f. as IN-[2] + *caedere* to cut.] 1 *v.t.* Cut into, make a cut in; cut marks upon; engrave *with* figures. M16. 2 *v.t.* Produce, form, or trace by cutting; carve or engrave (a figure, inscription, etc.). M17. b *v.t.* & *i. Geol.* Of a river: cut (a channel or valley) in a landform. L19.

incised *a.* (*a*) that has been incised; (*b*) *Bot.* & *Zool.* having notches in the edge: LME.

incisiform /ɪnˈsʌɪzɪfɔːm/ *a.* L19. [f. INCIS(OR + -I- + -FORM.] *Zool.* Having the form of an incisor, esp. a mouse's incisor.

incision /ɪnˈsɪʒ(ə)n/ *n.* LME. [(O)Fr., or late L *incisio(n-)*, f. L *incis-*: see INCISE, -ION.] 1 A division made by cutting, as one made in soft tissue during surgery; *esp.* (*Surg.*) the initial opening through the surface of the body. LME. b *Bot.* & *Zool.* A sharp and deep indentation, as in a leaf or an insect's wing. L16. 2 The action or an act of cutting into something, esp. in the course of a surgical operation. LME. b *fig.* Incisiveness, keenness of action or apprehension. M19. †3 = INSITION. Only in 17. 4 The cutting and deepening of its channel by a river; the channel so formed. E20.

2b Y. MENUHIN The incision and drive of a Toscanini performance were unmistakeable.

incisional *a.* of, pertaining to, or resulting from a surgical incision E20.

incisive /ɪnˈsʌɪsɪv/ *a.* & *n.* LME. [med.L *incisivus*, f. L *incis-*: see INCISE, -IVE.] A *adj.* 1 Having the quality of cutting into something; cutting, penetrating. LME. †2 Sharp or keen in physical qualities or activities; piercing; (of medicine) that loosens phlegm etc. LME–L17. 3 *Dentistry.* Designating or pertaining to an incisor. E19. 4 Mentally sharp; producing a very clear and impressive mental effect; trenchant. M19.

4 CONAN DOYLE A faint but incisive scent was apparent. P. GROSSKURTH Joan Riviere had one of the most brilliant and incisive minds.

†B *n.* A drug for loosening phlegm etc. LME–E18.

incisively *adv.* L19. **incisiveness** *n.* M19.

inciso- /ɪnˈsʌɪzəʊ/ *comb. form.* M19. [f. L *incisus* pa. pple of *incidere*: see INCISE, -O-.] *Bot.* & *Zool.* Forming chiefly adjs. describing shapes of leaves etc., w. the sense 'incised and —', as *inciso-dentate*, *inciso-serrate*, etc.

incisor /ɪnˈsʌɪzə/ *n.* L17. [med.L, in *dens incisor* incisor tooth, f. L, lit. 'cutter', f. *incis-*: see INCISE, -OR.] A narrow-edged tooth adapted for cutting; in humans, any of the front four teeth in each jaw. Also *incisor tooth.*

incisure /ɪnˈsɪʒə/ *n.* Also in L form **incisura** /ɪnsɪˈʒʊərə/. L16. [L *incisura*, f. *incis-*: see INCISE, -URE.] A deep indentation in an edge or surface; a notch.

incitation /ɪnsʌɪˈteɪʃ(ə)n, -sɪ-/ *n.* LME. [(O)Fr., or L *incitatio(n-)*, f. *incitat-* pa. ppl stem of *incitare*: see INCITE, -ATION.] 1 The action of inciting; incitement, stimulation. LME. †2 = INCITEMENT 2. M16–E18. †3 Power of inciting. M–L17.

incite /ɪnˈsʌɪt/ *v.t.* L15. [(O)Fr. *inciter* f. L *incitare*, f. as IN-[2] + *citare* set in rapid motion, raise: see CITE.] 1 Urge, spur on, (a person); stir up, animate; stimulate *to do* something. Also foll. by *to, against.* L15. 2 Provoke, prompt, (an action). E17.

1 R. G. COLLINGWOOD Young people . . read these stories, and . . are thereby incited to a career of crime. J. BERGER The anarchist leaders are inciting the workers to attack the centre. 2 N. GORDIMER He went on trial . . for inciting the strike.

inciteful *a.* offering incitement; provocative: L20. **inciter** *n.* L16.

incitement /ɪnˈsʌɪtm(ə)nt/ *n.* L15. [f. prec. + -MENT.] 1 The action or an act of inciting to action. L15. 2 A thing which incites a person or provokes an action; a stimulus, an incentive. L16.

1 A. J. AYER He and his wife were arrested and charged with incitement to civil disobedience.

incitive /ɪnˈsʌɪtɪv/ *n.* & *a. rare.* M18. [f. INCITE + -IVE.] A *n.* An incitement, an incentive. M18. B *adj.* Having the quality of inciting. L19.

incitory /ɪnˈsʌɪtəri/ *a. rare.* M20. [f. INCITE + -ORY[2].] = INCITIVE *a.*

†**incivil** *a.* M16. [(O)Fr., or L *incivilis*, f. as IN-[3] + *civilis* CIVIL *a.*] 1 Not of the rank of a free citizen. Only in M16. 2 Savage, barbarous. Only in L16. 3 Not according to civil law. Only in E17. 4 Unmannerly, uncivil. Only in 17.

incivility /ɪnsɪˈvɪlɪti/ *n.* M16. [Fr. *incivilité* or late L *incivilitas*, f. L *incivilis*: see prec., -ITY.] 1 a Uncivil or impolite behaviour; discourtesy, rudeness. M16. †b Lack of good manners or good breeding. L16–L17. †2 Lack of civilization; uncivilized condition, barbarism. L16–E19. 3 An act of rudeness. M17.

incivilization /ɪnˌsɪvɪlʌɪˈzeɪʃ(ə)n/ *n.* Also **-isa-**. E19. [f. IN-[3] + CIVILIZATION.] Uncivilized condition; lack of civilization.

incivism /ˈɪnsɪvɪz(ə)m/ *n.* Also in Fr. form ***incivisme*** /ɛ̃sivism/. L18. [Fr. *incivisme*, f. *in*- IN-[3] + *civisme* CIVISM.] Lack of loyalty to the State, esp. (*Hist.*) to the French Republic after the Revolution.

†**inclasp** *v.* var. of ENCLASP.

inclave *a.* see ENCLAVÉ.

inclemency /ɪnˈklɛm(ə)nsi/ *n.* M16. [L *inclementia*, f. *inclement*-: see next, -ENCY.] 1 Severity of weather or climate; (an instance of) severe, esp. cold or stormy, weather. M16. †2 Lack of clemency of disposition; pitilessness. L16–M17.

inclement /ɪnˈklɛm(ə)nt/ *a.* E17. [Fr. *inclément* or L *inclement*-, f. as IN-[3], CLEMENT.] 1 Of climate or weather: not mild or temperate; severe, *esp.* cold or stormy. E17. †2 Not merciful or kind; pitiless, severe, cruel. E17–M19.

inclemently *adv.* L18.

inclinable /ɪnˈklʌɪnəb(ə)l/ *a.* Also †**en-**. LME. [OFr. *enclinable*, f. as INCLINE *v.*: see -ABLE.] 1 Favourably disposed; willing to assent or submit *to*; amenable. LME. 2 Mentally inclined or disposed *to do* something. Formerly also *absol.* & foll. by *to, for, that.* LME. 3 Having an inclination or tendency *to* some physical quality, condition, or action. E17. 4 Able to be inclined or sloped. *rare.* L18.

3 B. LOPEZ The kind of wind nineteenth-century sailors called 'inclinable to calm'.

†**inclinableness** *n.* E17–E18.

inclination /ɪnklɪˈneɪʃ(ə)n/ *n.* LME. [(O)Fr., or L *inclinatio(n-)*, f. *inclinat-* pa. ppl stem of *inclinare*: see INCLINE *v.*, -ATION.] I 1 The condition of being mentally inclined *to do* something; an instance of this; a tendency of the mind, will, or desires towards a particular thing; a propensity *for*. Also foll. by *to, toward,* †*of*. LME. †b A person's natural disposition or character. LME–E18. c Liking, affection. M17. †2 The action of inclining or directing the mind to something. E16–E17. 3 An action or practice to which a person is inclined. E16. †b A person for whom one has a (special) liking. L17–E18. 4 A tendency or propensity in a thing to a physical condition or quality. Formerly, the general character of a thing. L16.

1 C. G. WOLFF Although Edith was clearly intellectual by inclination she never attended school. E. AMADI She had neither the strength nor the inclination to do so. H. JACOBSON He had never . . shown the slightest inclination towards music or the theatre.

II 5 The action or an act of bending towards something; *spec.* a bending of the body or head in a bow. L15. †b The action of tilting a container in order to pour out liquid without disturbing the sediment. M17–M18. 6 The fact or condition of sloping; deviation from the normal horizontal or vertical position; slope, slant. Also, the amount of this. L15. b *Physics.* The (amount of) dip or deviation from the horizontal of a magnetic needle or a magnetic field, esp. the earth's. L17. 7 The angle between the orbital plane of a planet, comet, etc., and the plane of the ecliptic, or (for a satellite) that of the equator of the primary (*Astron.*); *gen.* (the amount of) the deviation of one line or plane relative to another, usu. measured by the angle between them. M16.

inclinational *a.* (*rare*) E19.

inclinatory /ɪnˈklʌɪnət(ə)ri/ *a.* E17. [f. L *inclinat-* INCLINATION + -ORY[2].] Pertaining to or characterized by inclination or dip. Chiefly in *inclinatory needle*, a dipping needle.

incline /ˈɪnklʌɪn/ *n.* E17. [f. the vb.] †1 Mental tendency; disposition. Only in E17. 2 An inclined plane or surface; a slope, esp. on a road or railway. M19.

incline /ɪnˈklʌɪn/ *v.* Also †**en-**. ME. [OFr. *encliner* f. L *inclinare*, f. as IN-[2] + *clinare* bend.] I *v.t.* 1 Bend or bow (the head, the body, oneself) towards a thing, or forward and downward. ME. †2 *fig.* Cause to obey or be subject *to* a person or thing; subject. LME–L15. 3 Bend (the mind, the will, etc.) towards a course of action; make willing or favourably disposed (*to do, to* a thing). LME. b Desire. M18. †4 Direct (something immaterial) towards a particular object; apply, bestow. M16–E17. 5 Cause to depart from a given direction, esp. the vertical or horizontal; bend, slope, tilt. L16.

1 P. LIVELY The young man inclines his head graciously. **incline one's ear** listen favourably (*to*). 3 J. WESLEY To hear them speak . . might incline one to think they were not far from the kingdom of God. BURKE I hope . . your good-nature will incline you to some degree of indulgence towards human frailty. JANET MORGAN It is easy to understand why she started to write; character, skills and circumstance all inclined her in that direction. 5 A. R. AMMONS The wind inclines the cedars.

II *v.i.* 6 Bend the head or body forward, esp. in a bow. Now *rare.* ME. b *fig.* Submit, yield, (*to*); accede (*to*). LME. 7 Have a mental leaning *towards*; be predisposed or have an inclination *to* or *to do*; turn in mind or feeling in a given direction; take sides with a particular party, cause, etc. ME. 8 Have or take a direction or position which departs from a given direction, esp. from the vertical or horizontal; slope, slant; have or take an oblique position; deviate. E16. b *Mil.* Move in a direction at angles with the front of the formation in order to gain ground to the flank whilst advancing. L18. 9 Tend, esp. towards a specified quality or condition; have an attribute in an incipient degree. Foll. by *to, towards.* M16.

7 D. H. LAWRENCE If she inclined towards self-indulgence in any direction, it was in the direction of food. J. HILTON When it comes to believing things without actual evidence, we all incline to what we find most attractive. V. WOOLF She would not push her way. She inclined to be passive. H. J. LASKI The upper house of Convocation . . naturally inclined to his side. 8 T. HARDY The clock slowly inclined forward and fell. M. LOWRY His steps teetered to the left, he could not make them incline to the right. 9 GIBBON Victory inclined to the side of the allies. T. BEWICK The top of the head . . dark brown, inclining to black. C. BEATON She was . . short . ., inclining towards the petite and the plump.

inclining *n.* (*a*) the action of the vb; the state of being inclined; (*b*) *arch.* a following, a party: LME.

inclined /ɪnˈklʌɪnd/ *ppl a.* Also (earlier) †**en-**. LME. [f. INCLINE *v.* + -ED[1].] 1 Having a mental tendency or propensity towards a particular thing; favourably disposed (*to do*; *to, for*). LME. 2 Having a physical tendency *to* or *to do* something. LME. 3 Having a direction or position that departs from the vertical or horizontal, or makes an angle with something else; sloping. M16.

1 J. MARQUAND I was inclined to agree with him. E. WAUGH Do come with her whenever you feel inclined. B. MALAMUD My father was criminally inclined. B. T. BRADFORD He was inclined to shyness. P. GROSSKURTH Arthur . . had plenty of opportunities for illicit amours if so inclined. 3 **inclined plane** a sloping plane, esp. as a means of reducing the force needed to raise a load.

incliner /ɪnˈklʌɪnə/ *n.* E17. [f. INCLINE *v.* + -ER[1].] A person who or thing which inclines; *spec.* a chair in which a person can lie back with legs supported.

inclinometer /ɪnklɪˈnɒmɪtə/ *n.* M19. [f. L *inclinare* (as etymon of *inclination*) + -OMETER.] 1 An instrument for measuring the angle between the earth's magnetic field and the horizontal. M19. 2 An instrument for measuring the inclination of a slope. M19. 3 An instrument for measuring the inclination of a ship or aircraft to the horizontal. E20.

inclip /ɪnˈklɪp/ *v.t. arch. rare.* Infl. **-pp-**. E17. [f IN-[1] + CLIP *v.*[1]] Clasp, enclose, embrace.

†**incloistered** *a.* see ENCLOISTERED.

inclose *v.*, **inclosure** *n.*, vars. of ENCLOSE, ENCLOSURE.

†**incloud** *v.* var. of ENCLOUD.

include /ɪnˈkluːd/ *v.t.* LME. [L *includere*, f. as IN-[2] + *claudere* to shut.] 1 Shut in; enclose. *obs.* exc. in *pass.* LME. 2 Contain as part of a whole or as a subordinate element; contain by implication, involve. LME. 3 Place in a class or category; treat or regard as part of a whole; allow to share in a right, privilege, or activity. M16. †4 Bring to a close, conclude. *rare* (Shakes.). Only in L16.

2 W. CRUISE A power of appointment . . includes a right to appoint . . absolutely. V. WOOLF Nor is it true that bananas include moisture as well as sustenance. G. ORWELL An underground organization which had included almost every human being he had ever known. 3 D. WELCH She . . did not seem to mind when Li . . did not include her in the invitation. A. BRIGGS Harrington included the gentry in his 'nobility', but historians . . distinguished between the two. **include in** *joc.* & *colloq.* specifically include. **include out** *joc.* & *colloq.* specifically exclude.

includable *a.* L18. **includible** *a.* E19.

included /ɪnˈkluːdɪd/ *a.* M16. [f. prec. + -ED[1].] 1 That is included. M16. 2 *spec.* a *Bot.* Of a stamen or style: not protruding beyond the corolla. M19. b *Bot.* (Of phloem) embedded in secondary xylem; (of sapwood) embedded in heartwood. M20. c *Ling.* Forming part of a sentence; not constituting a sentence. M20.

including /ɪnˈkluːdɪŋ/ *prep.* M19. [Use of pres. pple of INCLUDE *v.*: see -ING[2].] If one takes into account; inclusive of.

J. RUSKIN A large body of . . landscapists comes into this class, including most clever sketchers from nature. *Times* There were five females among the passengers, including the stewardess.

includingly /ɪnˈkluːdɪŋli/ *adv. rare.* LME. [f. *including* pres. pple of INCLUDE: see -ING[2], -LY[2].] In a manner that includes.

incluse /ɪnˈkluːs/ *a.* & *n. obs.* exc. *Hist.* Also †**en-**. LME. [L *inclusus* pa. pple of *includere* INCLUDE.] †A *adj.* Confined, shut in. Only in LME. B *n.* A hermit, a recluse. LME.

inclusion /ɪnˈkluːʒ(ə)n/ *n.* E17. [L *inclusio(n-)*, f. *inclus-* pa. ppl stem of *includere* INCLUDE: see -ION.] 1 The action or an act of including; the fact or condition of being included; an instance of this. E17. 2 A thing which is included; *spec.* (*Geol.*), a solid fragment or a globule of liquid or gas enclosed within a rock or mineral; (*Metall.*, *Cytol.*, etc.) a discrete body or particle recognizably distinct from the substance in which it is embedded. M19. 3 *Math.* In full *inclusion function, map(ping)*. A mapping of a set A into a set B containing A which maps each element of A on to itself. M20.

1 A. BROOKNER The idea of being Heather's best friend seemed to guarantee my inclusion in any future festivities.

Comb.: **inclusion body** a protein capsule enclosing infective particles in a virus.

inclusive /ɪnˈkluːsɪv/ *a.* L16. [med.L *inclusivus*, f. L *inclus-*: see prec., -IVE.] **1** That includes, encloses, or contains; *esp.* that includes rather than excludes (also foll. by *of*); including much or all, esp. all incidental or accessory items; comprehensive. L16. **†2** That is included. L16–M18.

1 WORDSWORTH Altar and image, and the inclusive walls. G. GORER The categories . . were . . too inclusive, lumping together answers which could usefully have been analysed separately. H. BASCOM The police patrol launch . . , registered to carry fifty policemen inclusive of her small crew. *Times* Inclusive holidays offered by various tour operators. **inclusive language**: that includes people of both sexes on a literal interpretation and avoids words like *he* and *man* when the reference is to females as well as males. *inclusive OR*: see OR *n.*^{2}

inclusiveness *n.* M18. **inclusivism** *n.* the principle or practice of being inclusive L20. **inclusivist** *n.* L20. **incluˈsivity** *n.* (*rare*) inclusiveness M20.

inclusive /ɪnˈkluːsɪv/ *adv.* LME. [med.L, f. *inclusivus* (see prec.) + advb. ending *-e*.] So as to include the stated limits or extremes in a series. Opp. *exclusive*.

P. G. HAMERTON From Monday till Saturday inclusive.

inclusively /ɪnˈkluːsɪvli/ *adv.* LME. [In sense 1 f. prec.; in sense 2 f. as INCLUSIVE *a.*: see -LY^2.] **1** = prec. LME. **2** So as to include; by including a part or parts of a whole. L15.

inclusory /ɪnˈkluːs(ə)ri/ *a. rare.* L18. [f. L *inclus-* (see INCLUSION) + -ORY^2.] Inclusive.

incoagulable /ɪnkəʊˈagjʊləb(ə)l/ *a.* M17. [med.L *incoagulabilis*, f. as IN-^{3} + *coagulabilis* COAGULABLE.] Not coagulable.

incoagulaˈbility *n.* E20.

incoctible /ɪnˈkɒktɪb(ə)l/ *a. rare.* L17. [f. L *incoctus* uncooked, f. as IN-^{3} + *coctus*, f. *coct-* pa. ppl stem of *coquere* to cook, + -IBLE.] Indigestible.

incoercible /ɪnkəʊˈəːsɪb(ə)l/ *a.* E18. [f. IN-^{3} + COERCIBLE.] **1** Of a substance: volatile; incapable of being liquefied. Now *rare* or *obs.* E18. **2** That cannot be coerced or restrained; irrepressible. M18.

†incoffin *v.* var. of ENCOFFIN.

incog /ɪnˈkɒg/ *n.*, *a.*, & *adv. colloq.* L17. [Abbrev.] = INCOGNITO.

incogitable /ɪnˈkɒdʒɪtəb(ə)l/ *a.* E16. [L *incogitabilis*, f. as IN-^{3} + COGITABLE.] Unthinkable, inconceivable.

†incogitancy *n.* E17. [L *incogitantia*, f. *incogitant-*: see next, -ANCY.] **1** Thoughtlessness, negligence. E17–M18. **2** Lack of the faculty of thought. M–L17.

incogitant /ɪnˈkɒdʒɪt(ə)nt/ *a.* E17. [L *incogitant-*, f. as IN-^{3} + *cogitant-* pres. ppl stem of *cogitare* think: see -ANT^1.] **1** Thoughtless; inconsiderate. E17. **2** Lacking the faculty of thought. E18.

incogitantly *adv.* M17.

incogitative /ɪnˈkɒdʒɪtətɪv/ *a. rare.* L17. [f. IN-^{3} + COGITATIVE.] = prec.

incognisable *a.* var. of INCOGNIZABLE.

incognita /ɪnˈkɒgnɪtə/ *n.*^{1}*pl.* M19. [L, neut. pl. of *incognitus* unknown: see INCOGNITO.] Unknown things or places.

incognita /ɪnkɒgˈniːtə, *foreign* inˈkoːɲita/ *a.* & *n.*^{2} L17. [It., fem. of *incognito* unknown: see next.] **A** *adj.* Of a woman: disguised; unknown. L17. **B** *n.* Pl. **-tas**, *-te* /-te/. A disguised or unknown woman, esp. one's lover. E18.

incognito /ɪnkɒgˈniːtəʊ, ɪnˈkɒgnɪtəʊ/ *a.*, *adv.*, & *n.* M17. [It. f. L *incognitus* unknown, f. as IN-^{3} + *cognitus* pa. pple of *cognoscere* know.] **A** *adj.* Of a person: concealed under a disguised or assumed identity; unknown. M17.

K. TYNAN The disguise . . renders him about as effectively incognito as a walrus in a ballet-skirt.

B *adv.* Under a disguised or assumed identity. M17.

A. FRASER Brother and sister travelled incognito.

C *n.* Pl. **-os.** **1** A person who conceals his or her identity; an anonymous or unknown person. M17. **2** The condition of being unknown, anonymity; assumed or pretended identity. E19.

2 S. LEACOCK He had appeared . . in the costume of a Unitarian Clergyman, under the incognito of the Bishop of Bongee.

incognizable /ɪnˈkɒ(g)nɪzəb(ə)l/ *a.* Also **-isable**. M18. [f. IN-^{3} + COGNIZABLE.] Not cognizable; unable to be known, recognized, or understood.

incognizaˈbility *n.* M19.

incognizance /ɪnˈkɒ(g)nɪz(ə)ns/ *n.* M19. [f. IN-^{3} + COGNIZANCE.] The quality or condition of being incognizant.

incognizant /ɪnˈkɒ(g)nɪz(ə)nt/ *a.* M19. [f. IN-^{3} + COGNIZANT.] Not cognizant; without knowledge or understanding *of*; unconscious, unaware, *of*.

incognoscible /ɪnkɒgˈnɒsɪb(ə)l/ *a.* L17. [Late L *incognoscibilis*, f. as IN-^{3}, COGNOSCIBLE.] Unknowable; unable to be learned.

incognosciˈbility *n.* E19.

incoherence /ɪnkə(ʊ)ˈhɪər(ə)ns/ *n.* E17. [f. IN-^{3} + COHERENCE.] **1** Lack of coherence or connection, esp. in thought or language; incongruity, inconsistency; an instance of this, an incoherent or disconnected statement. E17. **2** Lack of cohesion. L17. **3** *Physics.* The property (of waves or wave phenomena) of being incoherent; lack of a definite or stable phase relationship between waves at different points (in space or in time). M20.

incoherency *n.* = INCOHERENCE 1 L17.

incoherent /ɪnkə(ʊ)ˈhɪər(ə)nt/ *a.* E17. [f. IN-^{3} + COHERENT.] **1** Consisting of or forming a group of incongruous parts; not unified in any way; uncoordinated. E17. **2** (Of thought, language, etc.) without logical connection; disconnected, disjointed; inconsistent; (of a person etc.) characterized or marked by such thought or language. M17. **3** Without physical coherence or cohesion; unconnected, loose; incongruous, incompatible. M17. **4** *Physics.* Producing, involving, or consisting of waves that lack any definite or stable phase relationship with each other. E20.

1 G. BERKELEY An incoherent fortuitous system, governed by chance. 2 ALDOUS HUXLEY Abject and agitated, he moved among the guests, stammering incoherent apologies. 4 *Nature* If light from two incoherent sources . . enters the holes, each source will produce its own fringes.

incoherently *adv.* M17.

incohesion /ɪnkə(ʊ)ˈhiːʒ(ə)n/ *n.* L19. [f. IN-^{3} + COHESION.] Lack of cohesion.

incohesive /ɪnkə(ʊ)ˈhiːsɪv/ *a.* E19. [f. IN-^{3} + COHESIVE.] Not cohesive.

incoincidence /ɪnkəʊˈɪnsɪd(ə)ns/ *n.* L18. [f. IN-^{3} + COINCIDENCE.] Lack of coincidence or agreement.

incoincident /ɪnkəʊˈɪnsɪd(ə)nt/ *a.* M17. [f. IN-^{3} + COINCIDENT.] Not coincident; not identical.

incombustible /ɪnkəmˈbʌstɪb(ə)l/ *a.* & *n.* L15. [med.L *incombustibilis*, f. as IN-^{3} + *combustibilis* COMBUSTIBLE.] **A** *adj.* Not combustible. L15. **B** *n.* An incombustible substance or constituent. E19.

incombustiˈbility *n.* L17. **incombustibleness** *n.* E18.

income /ˈɪnkʌm/ *n.*^{1} ME. [In early use f. ON *innkoma* arrival; later f. IN *adv.* + COME *v.*] **1** Entrance, arrival; beginning. Now *rare* exc. *Sc.* ME. **b** *spec.* The coming of divine influence into the soul. Now *rare* or *obs.* M17. **†2** A fee paid on entering, an entrance fee. M16–E18. **3** A newcomer, a new arrival. Now chiefly *Sc.* M16. **4** The (amount of) money or other assets received or due to be received from employment, business, investments, etc., esp. periodically or in the course of a year. Formerly also in *pl.*, receipts, emoluments. L16.

4 J. K. GALBRAITH Men who are without work *do* miss the income they no longer earn. G. ORWELL His total income was fifteen shillings a week. C. G. WOLFF The couple managed to live very well on the income from their combined inheritances.

Comb. & *phrases*: FIXED *income*; **income group** a section of the population graded by income; **incomes policy** a Government policy aimed at controlling inflation by restricting increases in wages, dividends, etc.; **income support** a system by which people on low incomes can, according to their circumstances, claim a payment from the State; **income tax**: levied on personal income; *negative income tax* (a scheme entailing) a State payment to an individual based on the extent to which his or her income is below a prescribed level; *national income*: see NATIONAL *a.*; *psychic income*: see PSYCHIC *a.*; *unearned income*: see UNEARNED *a.*

incomeless *a.* E19.

income /ˈɪnkʌm, ˈɪŋkʌm/ *n.*^{2} *Sc.* & *north.* E19. [f. IN *adv.* + COME *v.* Cf. ANCOME, ONCOME, UNCOME.] A swelling such as a boil, abscess, or tumour.

income /ɪnˈkʌm/ *v.i.* Long *obs.* exc. *Sc.* Infl. as COME *v.* OE. [f. IN-^{1} + COME *v.* Now chiefly repl. by *come in*.] Come in, enter. Now chiefly as *income* ppl a.

incomer /ˈɪnkʌmə/ *n.*^{1} LME. [f. IN-^{1} + COMER.] A person who enters or comes in; a visitor; a newcomer; an immigrant; a successor to a position vacated by another; *Shooting* a bird which flies towards the gun.

incomer /ˈɪnkʌmə/ *n.*^{2} L20. [f. INCOME *n.*^{1} + -ER^1.] A person who earns a specified kind or level of income. Usu. w. specifying wd.

high incomer, *low incomer*, etc.

incoming /ˈɪnkʌmɪŋ/ *n.* ME. [f. IN-^{1} + COMING *n.*] **1** The action or fact of coming in; arrival, entrance. ME. **†2** A place of entrance. LME–E16. **3** = INCOME *n.*^{1} 4. Usu. in *pl.* L16.

incoming /ˈɪnkʌmɪŋ/ *a.* M18. [f. IN-^{1} + COMING *a.*] That comes in, enters, or arrives; (of a person) succeeding another; (of profit) accruing.

S. BELLOW I was about to board a plane and he was on the incoming flight. E. FEINSTEIN The flat . . was soon to be occupied by incoming tenants.

in commendam /ɪn kɒˈmɛndam/ *adv. phr.* M17. [L *dare in commendam* give (a benefice) in charge or trust, f. *commendare* COMMEND *v.*] *Eccl. Hist.* With the revenues of a benefice accruing to the holder (orig., temporarily, pending the arrival of a new incumbent, later, for life, esp. when a former incumbent was allowed to retain his benefice and its revenues following preferment).

incommensurable /ɪnkəˈmɛnʃ(ə)rəb(ə)l, -sjə-/ *a.* & *n.* M16. [Late L *incommensurabilis*, f. as IN-^{3} + COMMENSURABLE.] **A** *adj.* **1** *Math.* Having no common measure, integral or fractional (*with* another quantity); irrational. M16. **2** Having no common standard of measurement; not comparable in respect of magnitude or value. M17. **3** Foll. by *with*: not worthy to be compared with; utterly disproportionate to; falling short of. M19.

2 D. H. LAWRENCE The vision on the canvas is for ever incommensurable with the canvas, or the paint. 3 S. TURNER The forces of either were so incommensurable with the numbers and bravery of the people they attacked.

B *n.* An incommensurable quantity. Usu. in *pl.* M18.

ˌincommensuraˈbility *n.* L16. **incommensurableness** *n.* (*rare*) L17. **incommensurably** *adv.* incomparably M17.

incommensurate /ɪnkəˈmɛnʃ(ə)rət, -sjə-/ *a.* M17. [f. IN-^{3} + COMMENSURATE *a.*] **†1** Having parts out of proportion; disproportioned. Only in M17. **2** Not of equal or corresponding measure or degree; out of proportion; inadequate. Foll. by *with*, *to*. L17. **3** = INCOMMENSURABLE *a.* 2. L17.

2 D. MELTZER They find the responsibilities incommensurate with the powers to implement their judgements.

incommensurately *adv.* E19. **incommensurateness** *n.* E18.

incommiscible /ɪnkəˈmɪsɪb(ə)l/ *a. rare.* E17. [Late L *incommiscibilis*, f. as IN-^{3} + *commiscibilis*, f. *commiscere* mix together, f. as COM- + *miscere* MIX *v.*: see -IBLE.] Unable to be mixed together.

incommodate /ɪnˈkɒmədeɪt/ *v.t.* Long *rare.* Pa. pple **†-ate, -ated.** E17. [f. as next: see -ATE^3.] Inconvenience, incommode.

incommodation /ˌɪnkɒməˈdeɪʃ(ə)n/ *n.* Now *rare* or *obs.* M17. [f. L *incommodat-* pa. ppl stem of *incommodare* INCOMMODE *v.* + -ATION.] The action of incommoding; the fact of being incommoded, (an) inconvenience.

†incommode *n.* & *a.* E16. [Fr. f. L *incommodus*: see INCOMMODITY.] A *n.* An inconvenience. Only in E16. B *adj.* = INCOMMODIOUS 1, 4. L17–M18.

incommode /ɪnkəˈməʊd/ *v.t.* L16. [Fr. *incommoder* or L *incommodare*, f. as IN-³ + *commodus* convenient: see COMMODIOUS.] 1 Subject to inconvenience or discomfort; put to trouble; annoy. L16. 2 Hinder, impede, obstruct, (an action etc.). E18.

1 E. BOWEN In order that they might not incommode the patients, the pupils came and went by a basement door. Y. MENUHIN We were not the only travelers to be incommoded by the flood.

incommodious /ɪnkəˈməʊdɪəs/ *a.* M16. [f. IN-³ + COMMODIOUS.] 1 Causing inconvenience or discomfort; troublesome, annoying. M16. †b Of a person, a person's character: troublesome, difficult to get on with. L16–L18. †2 Unprofitable; unsuitable; inappropriate. M16–E18. †3 Injurious, harmful. L16–M17. 4 Of a place, room, etc.: not convenient for the purpose; not affording good accommodation. E17.

incommodiously *adv.* M16. **incommodiousness** *n.* the quality of being incommodious; (an) inconvenience: E17.

incommodity /ɪnkəˈmɒdɪti/ *n.* LME. [(O)Fr. *incommodité* f. L *incommoditas*, f. *incommodus*, f. as IN-³ + *commodus* convenient: see IN-³, COMMODIOUS, -ITY.] An incommodious quality, condition, or state; (an) inconvenience, (a) disadvantage, (a) discomfort.

incommunicable /ɪnkəˈmjuːnɪkəb(ə)l/ *a.* M16. [Late L *incommunicabilis* not to be imparted, f. as IN-³ + *communicabilis*: see COMMUNICABLE.] 1 = INCOMMUNICATIVE. M16. 2 Unable to be imparted or shared. L16. 3 Unable to be communicated by speech; unspeakable, unutterable; ineffable. M17. 4 Not in communication; lacking communication. M17.

2 C. JOHNSTON To wrest from the sovereign an essential part of the incommunicable power of the crown. 3 J. F. FERRIER Its true meaning is utterly incommunicable by one being to another.

ˌincommunicaˈbility *n.* M17. **incommunicableness** *n.* E17. **incommunicably** *adv.* E17.

incommunicado /ˌɪnkəmjuːnɪˈkɑːdəʊ/ *a.* & *adv.* Also in Sp. form **incomunicado** /*also foreign* inkomuniˈkaðo/. M19. [Sp. *incomunicado* pa. pple of *incomunicar* deprive of communication.] A *adj.* Having no means of communication with others; *esp.* (of a prisoner) held in solitary confinement. M19.

R. HUNTFORD He would be incommunicado for a year at least.

B *adv.* Without means of communication with others. M20.

Independent He was held incommunicado for 48 hours clad only in underpants.

incommunicating /ɪnkəˈmjuːnɪkeɪtɪŋ/ *a.* L17. [f. IN-³ + COMMUNICATE *v.* + -ING².] Not communicating; lacking communication.

incommunicative /ɪnkəˈmjuːnɪkətɪv/ *a.* L17. [f. IN-³ + COMMUNICATIVE.] Uncommunicative.

incommunicatively *adv.* M19. **incommunicativeness** *n.* L18.

incommutable /ɪnkəˈmjuːtəb(ə)l/ *a.* LME. [Sense 1 f. L *incommutabilis*, f. as IN-³, COMMUTABLE; sense 2 f. IN-³ + COMMUTABLE.] 1 Not changeable; not liable to alteration; immutable. LME. 2 Unable to be commuted or exchanged. L18.

incommutaˈbility *n.* L17.

incompact /ɪnkəmˈpakt, ɪnˈkɒmpakt/ *a.* E17. [f. IN-³ + COMPACT *a.*] Not compact; lacking cohesion (*lit.* & *fig.*).

incompactly *adv.* E18. **incompactness** *n.* E18.

in-company /ɪnˈkʌmp(ə)ni/ *a.* M20. [f. IN-¹ + COMPANY *n.*] Occurring or existing within a company; *esp.* designating training received by a person while employed by a company.

incomparable /ɪnˈkɒmp(ə)rəb(ə)l/ *a.*, *adv.*, & *n.* LME. [(O)Fr. f. L *incomparabilis*, f. as IN-³ + *comparabilis* COMPARABLE.] A *adj.* 1 With which there is no comparison, esp. for excellence; unequalled in manner, kind, or degree; matchless, peerless. LME. 2 Unable to be compared (*with*, *to*). E17.

1 H. G. WELLS Almost every man . . finds it necessary to believe that he is . . incomparable as a lover. 2 *Scientific American* Two rectangles are called incomparable if neither one can be placed inside the other and aligned.

†B *adv.* Incomparably. L15–M17.

C *n.* An incomparable person or thing. E18.

incomparaˈbility *n.* L15. **incomparableness** *n.* M17. **incomparably** *adv.* in an incomparable manner or degree; in a way that does not admit of comparison: LME.

†incompass *v.* var. of ENCOMPASS.

incompatibility /ˌɪnkəmpatɪˈbɪlɪti/ *n.* E17. [Fr. *incompatibilité*, f. *incompatible*, f. as next: see -ITY.] 1 The property or condition of being incompatible. E17. b *Biol.* & *Med.* The incapacity of cells or tissues of one individual to tolerate those of another when a union between them is attempted, esp. in grafting and transplantation, in blood transfusion, and in parasitism. E20. c *Biol.* Inability to produce viable offspring despite the bringing together of fertile gametes; now *esp.* such inability occurring among conspecific individuals (as in many fungi and angiosperms). E20. 2 An incompatible thing or quality; an instance of being incompatible. L17.

1b *Woman's Own* The Rhesus incompatibility which can affect their babies. 2 *New Yorker* Divorce for trivial incompatibilities continues to offend.

incompatible /ɪnkəmˈpatɪb(ə)l/ *a.* & *n.* LME. [med.L *incompatibilis*, f. as IN-³ + *compatibilis* COMPATIBLE.] A *adj.* 1 Incapable of existing together in the same person; opposed in character; discordant. (Foll. by *with*, †*to*.) LME. †b Of a person: intolerant *of*. E–M17. c Of an item of equipment: unable to be used in conjunction with some other item. M20. 2 Unable to agree or be in harmony together; at variance. M16. 3 *Eccl.* Of benefices etc.: unable to be held together. L16. †4 Irreconcilable. *rare.* E–M17. 5 Of a drug or drugs: reacting (*with* another substance) in such a way that the two should not be administered together. E19. 6 *Biol.* & *Med.* Exhibiting or causing immunological or reproductive incompatibility. E20.

1 I. MURDOCH Taman's state of mind . . became a dark battlefield of incompatible emotions. M. T. TSUANG Complete recovery was not incompatible with a diagnosis of dementia praecox. 2 M. HOLROYD They were fond of each other, but incompatible.

B *n.* An incompatible person or thing. E18.

incompatibleness *n.* E17. **incompatibly** *adv.* E18.

incompetence /ɪnˈkɒmpɪt(ə)ns/ *n.* M17. [Fr. *incompétence* after *incompétent* INCOMPETENT: see -ENCE.] The property, quality, or fact of being incompetent.

R. HUNTFORD Allowing *Discovery* to be frozen in so that she could not escape was considered professional incompetence.

incompetency *n.* (an instance of) incompetence E17.

incompetent /ɪnˈkɒmpɪt(ə)nt/ *a.* & *n.* L16. [(Fr. *incompétent* f.) late L *incompetent-*, f. as IN-³ + *competent-* COMPETENT *a.*] A *adj.* 1 Not legally competent. L16. 2†a Insufficient, inadequate. E17–E19. b *Med.* Esp. of a valve or sphincter: unable to function properly, thus causing reflux or incontinence. M19. 3 Chiefly of a person: of inadequate ability or fitness; lacking the requisite capacity or qualification; incapable. M17. 4 Logically inadmissible or illegitimate. M19. 5 *Geol.* Of a rock or stratum: apt to undergo plastic deformation when compressed. Of a structure or process: largely involving incompetent rocks. L19.

2b G. BOURNE An incompetent cervix will cause miscarriage at about the 20th week of pregnancy.

B *n.* An incompetent person. M19.

incompetently *adv.* M17.

incompletable /ɪnkəmˈpliːtəb(ə)l/ *a.* E20. [f. IN-³ + COMPLETABLE.] Unable to be completed.

incompletableness *n.* L19. **incompletaˈbility** *n.* E19.

incomplete /ɪnkəmˈpliːt/ *a.* LME. [Late L *incompletus*, f. as IN-³ + L *completus* COMPLETE *a.*] 1 Not complete; not fully formed; unfinished; not whole or thorough; lacking something, imperfect. LME. 2 *Logic* & *Math.* Of a formal system: containing true propositions for which no proof of validity is possible using only the formal rules of the system. M20.

1 incomplete symbol *Philos.* a symbol that does not designate something having independent reality. *verb of incomplete predication*: see PREDICATION 2.

incompletely *adv.* LME. **incompleteness** *n.* M17.

incompleted /ɪnkəmˈpliːtɪd/ *a.* M19. [f. IN-³ + *completed* pa. pple of COMPLETE *v.*] = UNCOMPLETED.

incompletion /ɪnkəmˈpliːʃ(ə)n/ *n.* E19. [f. IN-³ + COMPLETION.] The property of not having been completed or of not having completed something.

incompletive /ɪnkəmˈpliːtɪv/ *a.* & *n.* M20. [f. INCOMPLETE + -IVE.] *Gram.* (Designating) an aspect of verbs in some languages that indicates the incompletion of an action or process.

incomplex /ɪnˈkɒmplɛks/ *a.* M17. [Late L *incomplexus*, f. as IN-³ + L *complexus* COMPLEX *a.*] Not complex; simple, not complicated.

incompliance /ɪnkəmˈplʌɪəns/ *n.* Now *rare.* M17. [f. IN-³ + COMPLIANCE.] †1 Lack of conformity. Only in M17. †2 Unaccommodating disposition; lack of complaisance. L17–E19. 3 Failure to comply, non-compliance. E18.

incompliancy *n.* (*rare*) M17. **incompliant** *a.* (now *rare*) M17.

†incomplicate *a.* *rare.* L17–E19. [f. IN-³ + COMPLICATE *a.*] Not complicated; simple.

†incomplying *a.* *rare.* M17–M18. [f. IN-³ + COMPLY + -ING².] Unaccommodating; not compliant.

†incomposed *a.* E17. [f. IN-³ + COMPOSED.] 1 Discomposed, agitated; disordered. E17–M18. 2 Not composite or compound. M–L17.

†incomposedly *adv.* E–M17. **†incomposedness** *n.* M17–E18.

incomposite /ɪnˈkɒmpəzɪt/ *a.* L17. [L *incompositus*, f. as IN-³ + *compositus* COMPOSITE *a.*] Not composite.

incompossible /ɪnkəmˈpɒsɪb(ə)l/ *a.* E17. [med.L *incompossibilis*, f. as IN-³ + *compossibilis* COMPOSSIBLE.] Not possible together; incompatible.

ˌincompossiˈbility *n.* E17.

†incompounded *a.* E17–M18. [f. IN-³ + COMPOUNDED.] Not compounded, not compound.

incomprehended /ˌɪnkɒmprɪˈhɛndɪd/ *a.* *rare.* M17. [f. IN-³ + *comprehended* pa. pple of COMPREHEND.] Not comprehended; beyond understanding.

incomprehending *a.* (*rare*) lacking understanding L19.

incomprehensible /ˌɪnkɒmprɪˈhɛnsɪb(ə)l/ *a.* & *n.* LME. [L *incomprehensibilis*, f. as IN-³ + *comprehensibilis* COMPREHENSIBLE.] A *adj.* 1 Chiefly *Theol.* Unable to be contained or circumscribed within limits; boundless. *arch.* LME. 2 Unable to be understood, unintelligible; *arch.* beyond the reach of intellect or research, unfathomable. LME. †3 Unable to be physically grasped or taken hold of; impalpable. *rare.* E17–M18.

2 D. ACHESON The papers were long, tremendously complex, and totally incomprehensible.

B *n.* An incomprehensible thing or being. M16.

inˌcomprehensiˈbility *n.* the property or attribute of being incomprehensible; an inconceivable or unintelligible thing: L16. **incomprehensibleness** *n.* E17. **incomprehensibly** *adv.* LME.

incomprehension /ˌɪnkɒmprɪˈhɛnʃ(ə)n/ *n.* E17. [f. IN-³ + COMPREHENSION.] The fact of not understanding; failure to understand.

incomprehensive /ˌɪnkɒmprɪˈhɛnsɪv/ *a.* M17. [f. IN-³ + COMPREHENSIVE.] 1 Deficient in understanding. M17. 2 Incomprehensible. Now *rare.* M17. 3 Not inclusive. L18.

incompressible /ɪnkəmˈprɛsɪb(ə)l/ *a.* M18. [f. IN-³ + COMPRESSIBLE.] Unable to be compressed into a smaller volume.

ˌ**incompressi'bility** *n.* M18.

incomputable /ɪnkəm'pjuːtəb(ə)l/ *a.* E17. [f. IN-^{3} + L *computabilis* COMPUTABLE.] Unable to be computed; incalculable.

incomunicado *a.* & *adv.* see INCOMMUNICADO.

inconceivable /ɪnkən'siːvəb(ə)l/ *a.* & *n.* E17. [f. IN-^{3} + CONCEIVABLE.] **A** *adj.* Unable to be mentally conceived of; unthinkable, unimaginable; *colloq.* very remarkable, extraordinary. E17.

B. JOWETT Even these inconceivable qualities of space . . may be made the subject of reasoning. H. JAMES A domain of immeasurable extent and almost inconceivable splendour. R. RENDELL It was inconceivable to him that anyone would give three hundred pounds for such a thing.

B *n.* An inconceivable thing. E18.

ˌ**inconceiva'bility** *n.* M19. **inconceivableness** *n.* M17. **inconceivably** *adv.* in an inconceivable manner; to an inconceivable degree, unimaginably; *colloq.* remarkably, exceedingly: M17.

inconcinnity /ɪnkən'sɪnɪti/ *n.* *arch.* E17. [L *inconcinnitas*, f. as IN-^{3} + CONCINNITY, or f. IN-^{3} + CONCINNITY.] Lack of proportion; awkwardness, inelegance; impropriety, unsuitableness.

†**inconcinnous** *a.* M17. [L *inconcinnus*, f. as IN-^{3} + CONCINNOUS, or f. IN-^{3} + CONCINNOUS.] **1** Incongruous. Only in M17. **2** *Mus.* Inharmonious, contrary to the principles of harmony. E18–E19.

inconcludent /ɪnkən'kluːd(ə)nt/ *a.* *rare.* L17. [f. IN-^{3} + CONCLUDENT.] Inconclusive.

inconclusible /ɪnkən'kluːsɪb(ə)l/ *a.* *rare.* M17. [f. IN-^{3} + CONCLUSIBLE.] Unable to be concluded.

inconclusion /ɪnkən'kluːʒ(ə)n/ *n.* M19. [f. IN-^{3} + CONCLUSION.] Inconclusiveness; an inconclusive result.

inconclusive /ɪnkən'kluːsɪv/ *a.* L17. [f. IN-^{3} + CONCLUSIVE.] **1** Not conclusive in argument or evidence; not convincing or decisive. L17. **2** Not conclusive in action; reaching no final result, producing no conclusive effect. M19.

inconclusively *adv.* M18. **inconclusiveness** *n.* L17.

inconcrete /ɪn'kɒnkriːt/ *a.* Now *rare.* E17. [Late L *inconcretus* incorporeal, f. as IN-^{3} + L *concretus* CONCRETE *a.*] Not concrete; abstract; immaterial.

in concreto /ɪn kɒn'kriːtəʊ/ *adv. phr.* E17. [L.] As a concrete thing.

†**inconcussible** *a.* Also **-able**. L16–E18. [Fr. †*inconcussible*, f. as IN-^{3} + L *concuss-* (see CONCUSS *v.*): see -IBLE.] Unable to be shaken; firmly fixed; stable.

incondensable /ɪnkən'dɛnsəb(ə)l/ *a.* E19. [f. IN-^{3} + CONDENSABLE.] Unable to be condensed; *esp.* unable to be reduced from gas or vapour to a liquid condition.

Also **incondensible** *a.* M18.

incondite /ɪn'kɒndɪt/ *a.* M16. [L *inconditus*, f. as IN-^{3} + *conditus* pa. pple of *condere* put together.] Crude, unpolished, unrefined; (esp. of literary or artistic works) badly constructed or composed.

inconditely *adv.* E19.

inconditionate /ɪnkən'dɪʃ(ə)nət/ *a.* & *n.* M17. [f. IN-^{3} + CONDITIONATE *a.* & *n.*] **A** *adj.* Not subject to or limited by conditions; unconditioned. Now *rare.* M17. **B** *n.* *Philos.* An unconditioned entity; a form under which the unconditioned is conceived. E19.

Inconel /'ɪnkənɛl/ *n.* M20. [App. f. *I*nternational *N*ickel *Co*mpany + (*n*)*el* (after *nickel*).] (Proprietary name for) any of various alloys of nickel containing chromium and iron, and resistant to corrosion at high temperatures.

inconfidence /ɪn'kɒnfɪd(ə)ns/ *n.* *rare.* E17. [f. IN-^{3} + CONFIDENCE *n.*] Lack of confidence, distrust.

inconfident /ɪn'kɒnfɪd(ə)nt/ *a.* *rare.* E17. [f. IN-^{3} + CONFIDENT *a.*] **1** Breaking a trust or confidence; untrustworthy, indiscreet. E17. †**2** Not confident, distrustful. Only in M17.

1 *Church Times* It would be commercially inconfident and improper to go into details.

inconformable /ɪnkən'fɔːməb(ə)l/ *a.* E17. [f. IN-^{3} + CONFORMABLE *a.*] **1** Inconsistent *with*, not according in form or character *to*. E17. **2** Of a person: refusing or omitting to conform; *esp.* (*Eng. Hist.*) not conforming to the practices of the Established Church. M17.

inconformity /ɪnkən'fɔːmɪti/ *n.* *arch.* L16. [f. IN-^{3} + CONFORMITY.] **1** Refusal or omission to conform (*to, with*); nonconformity. L16. **2** Dissimilarity, incongruity; lack of conformity (*to, with*). E17.

incongenial /ɪnkən'dʒiːnɪəl/ *a.* Now *rare* or *obs.* L18. [f. IN-^{3} + CONGENIAL.] Not congenial, uncongenial.

incongruence /ɪn'kɒŋgrʊəns/ *n.* E17. [L *incongruentia*, f. as next: see -ENCE.] Lack of congruence; disagreement, incongruity.

incongruent /ɪn'kɒŋgrʊənt/ *a.* LME. [L *incongruent-*, f. as IN-^{3} + CONGRUENT.] Not congruent; incompatible, unsuitable, incongruous.

incongruent melting point *Chem.* the dissociation temperature of a solid compound which is not stable as a liquid.

incongruently *adv.* in an incongruent manner; incongruously; *Chem.* as independent components (w. ref. to phase changes, as melting of alloys, etc.): M16.

incongruity /ɪnkən'gruːɪti/ *n.* M16. [Late L *incongruitas*, f. as IN-^{3} + *congruitas* CONGRUITY.] **1** Lack of harmony or consistency of parts or elements; incoherence; an instance of this. M16. †**2** *Gram.* Violation of rules of concord; solecism. M16–E17. **3** Lack of appropriateness or suitability; absurdity; an instance of this. L16. **4** Disagreement in character or qualities; discrepancy, inconsistency; an instance of this. E17.

1 J. BUTLER Hence arises that amazing incongruity, and seeming inconsistency of character. SIR W. SCOTT He must have smiled at the incongruity of the clerk's apparel. 3 B. JOWETT He felt no incongruity in the veteran . . correcting the youthful Socrates. 4 J. F. W. HERSCHEL There we find no contradictions, no incongruities, but all is harmony. C. KINGSLEY The quaint incongruity of the priestly and the lay elements in his speech.

incongruous /ɪn'kɒŋgrʊəs/ *a.* E17. [f. L *incongruus*, f. as IN-^{3} + CONGRUOUS: see -OUS.] †**1** *Gram.* Violating the rules of concord; incorrect. Only in 17. **2** Not appropriate; unsuitable, out of place, absurd. E17. **3** Disagreeing in character or qualities; out of keeping, discordant, inconsistent. (Foll. by *with*, †*to*.) (Passing into sense 2.) E17. **4** Having disparate or inharmonious parts or elements; incoherent. M17.

2 R. WARNER To be thinking of . . love while dressing for a funeral may seem an incongruous thing. D. ATHILL His hands—broad peasant hands . . look incongruous because the rest of him is finely made. 3 W. HOLTBY The cats were the only incongruous occupants of that precise impersonal room. D. CECIL A . . mixture of incongruous characteristics as to bewilder anyone who came into contact with him. 4 BURKE We are not at all embarrassed . . by any incongruous mixture of coercion and restraint.

incongruously *adv.* M17. **incongruousness** *n.* E18.

inconjunct /ɪnkən'dʒʌŋkt/ *a.* E17. [f. IN-^{3} + CONJUNCT *a.*] Not in conjunction; *spec.* in *Astrol.* (of two planets or their positions) so placed that neither affects the other.

inconnected /ɪnkə'nɛktɪd/ *a.* *rare.* M18. [f. IN-^{3} + CONNECTED.] Not connected, disconnected.

inconnectedness *n.* L19.

†**inconnection** *n.* Also **-exion**. E17–E19. [f. IN-^{3} + CONNECTION.] Lack of connection; unconnectedness.

inconnu /'ɪŋkənuː; *foreign* ɛ̃kɔny (*pl. same*)/ *n.* In sense 1 fem. **-ue**. Pl. (in sense 1) **-u(e)s**, (in sense 2) same. E19. [Fr. = unknown.] **1** An unknown person, a stranger. E19. **2** A predatory freshwater salmonid game-fish, *Stenodus leucichthys*, of the Eurasian and N. American Arctic. Orig. *Canad.* E19.

inconquerable /ɪn'kɒŋk(ə)rəb(ə)l/ *a.* M17. [f. IN-^{3} + CONQUERABLE.] Unconquerable.

inconscience /ɪn'kɒnʃ(ə)ns/ *n.* L19. [f. IN-^{3} + CONSCIENCE.] Lack of conscience or consciousness.

inconscient /ɪn'kɒnʃɪənt/ *a.* L19. [f. IN-^{3} + CONSCIENT.] Unconscious, unwitting.

inconsciently *adv.* E20.

inconscious /ɪn'kɒnʃəs/ *a.* Now *rare.* L17. [f. late L *inconscius* unaware, ignorant + -OUS; later f. IN-^{3} + CONSCIOUS *a.*] Unconscious; unaware (*of*).

inconsciously *adv.* M19.

inconsecutive /ɪnkən'sɛkjʊtɪv/ *a.* M19. [f. IN-^{3} + CONSECUTIVE.] Not consecutive, not in order or sequence; inconsequent.

Times They follow one another in an absolutely inconsecutive and irrelevant manner. V. WOOLF Odd little gusts of inconsecutive conversations reached her.

inconsecutively *adv.* M19. **inconsecutiveness** *n.* M19.

inconsequence /ɪn'kɒnsɪkw(ə)ns/ *n.* L16. [L *inconsequentia*, f. as next: see -ENCE.] **I 1** Lack of logical sequence; illogicality, inconclusiveness. Also, an instance of this; an illogical conclusion or argument. L16. **2** The practice or habit of thinking, speaking, or acting disconnectedly or illogically. E19. **3** Lack of natural connection of ideas, action, or events; irrelevance, disconnection. Also, an instance of this; an irrelevant action or circumstance. M19.

1 T. GATAKER Mr. S. himself could not but see the inconsequence of his own argument. 2 W. J. LOCKE Her inconsequence and flapperish immaturity. 3 E. A. POE The whole of this paragraph must now appear a tissue of inconsequence and incoherence.

II 4 The condition or fact of being of no consequence or importance. M18.

inconsequent /ɪn'kɒnsɪkw(ə)nt/ *a.* L16. [L *inconsequent-*, not logically consequent, f. as IN-^{3} + *consequent-* CONSEQUENT *a.*] **I 1** Involving illogical reasoning or fallacious argument. L16. **b** Not following naturally, having no rational connection, irrelevant. L19. **2** Not following logically, erroneously inferred. E17. **b** Of ideas or subjects: disconnected, haphazard. M19. **3** Of a person: characterized by inconsequence in thought, speech, or action. L18. †**II 4** Of no consequence, unimportant, trivial. *rare.* Only in M18.

inconsequently *adv.* E17. **inconsequentness** *n.* (*rare*) E18.

inconsequential /ˌɪnkɒnsɪ'kwɛnʃ(ə)l/ *a.* & *n.* E17. [f. IN-^{3} + CONSEQUENTIAL.] **A** *adj.* **1** Characterized by inconsequence of reasoning, thought, or speech; inconsequent. E17. **2** Of no consequence, unimportant, trivial. L18.

1 O. CROMWELL I cannot let such gross mistakes and inconsequential reasonings pass. J. NORRIS The loose and inconsequential Reasoner . . in his wild ramble may happen to light upon Truth.

B *n.* A thing of little importance; a triviality. E20.

Economist News never buried under frothy inconsequentials.

inconsequenti'ality *n.* M19. **inconsequentially** *adv.* M18. **inconsequentialness** *n.* M20.

inconsiderable /ɪnkən'sɪd(ə)rəb(ə)l/ *a.* L16. [Fr. †*inconsidérable* or late L *inconsiderabilis*, f. as IN-^{3} + CONSIDERABLE *a.*] †**1** Impossible to reckon or imagine; incalculable. L16–M17. **2** Not worth considering; unimportant, insignificant, trifling. M17. **b** Of very small value, amount, or size. M17. †**3** Inconsiderate, thoughtless. M17–E18.

2 STEELE A trifling inconsiderable Circumstance. b A. GHOSH It was a large head, with a not inconsiderable cranial capacity.

inconsiderableness *n.* M17. **inconsiderably** *adv.* M17.

†**inconsideracy** *n.* *rare.* M18–M19. [f. INCONSIDERATE: see -ACY.] Inconsiderateness.

inconsiderate /ɪnkən'sɪd(ə)rət/ *a.* & *n.* LME. [L *inconsideratus*, f. as IN-^{3} + CONSIDERATE *a.*] **A** *adj.* **I 1** Done, made, or acting thoughtlessly; unadvised, precipitate, rash. LME. †**2** Careless or regardless *of*. Only in 17. **3** Lacking or showing lack of consideration or regard for the feelings of others. M19.

1 POPE Inconsiderate authors wou'd rather be admir'd than understood. ISAAC TAYLOR An inconsiderate application of genuine principles to

particular instances. 3 P. ANGADI He is too lazy and inconsiderate to put himself out for anybody. B. T. BRADFORD How inconsiderate of me, I haven't even asked you about your health.

†II4 Of no importance; inconsiderable, trifling. M17–E18.

B *n.* An inconsiderate or thoughtless person. L16.

inconsiderately *adv.* LME. **inconsiderateness** *n.* L16.

inconsideration /ˌɪnkənsɪdəˈreɪʃ(ə)n/ *n.* E16. [Fr. *inconsidération* or late L *inconsideratio(n-)*, f. as IN-[3] + L *consideratio(n-)* CONSIDERATION.] 1 Failure or refusal to consider; thoughtlessness, rashness. E16. †b An instance of this; a thoughtless act. L16–M17. 2 Lack of consideration or regard for the feelings of others. L19.

inconsidered /ɪnkənˈsɪdəd/ *a. rare.* L16. [f. IN-[3] + CONSIDERED, after L *inconsideratus*, Fr. *inconsidéré*.] Not thought about or considered.

DONNE God will scarce hearken to sudden inconsidered irreverent Prayers.

inconsistence /ɪnkənˈsɪst(ə)ns/ *n.* Now *rare* or *obs.* M17. [f. INCONSISTENT after *consistence*: see -ENCE.] 1 = INCONSISTENCY 1. M17. 2 = INCONSISTENCY 2. M17.

inconsistency /ɪnkənˈsɪst(ə)nsi/ *n.* M17. [f. INCONSISTENT after *consistency*: see -ENCY.] 1 Lack of consistency; incompatibility, discrepancy. (Foll. by *between, with*.) M17. 2 An inconsistent thing or act; a discrepancy. M17.

1 ADDISON An eminent instance of the inconsistency of our Religion with Magic. B. JOWETT Nor is there any inconsistency in wise and good fathers having foolish and worthless sons. C. THUBRON In nothing is the inconsistency of Soviet Communism greater than in the emperors it reveres or forgets. 2 S. JOHNSON The many inconsistencies which folly produces, or infirmity suffers in the human mind. N. CHOMSKY It is a simple matter . . to discover inconsistencies and even absurdities in their answers.

inconsistent /ɪnkənˈsɪst(ə)nt/ *a.* & *n.* M17. [f. IN-[3] + CONSISTENT *a.*] A *adj.* I 1 Not in keeping, discordant, at variance. Foll. by *with*, †*to*. M17. b Of two or more things: incompatible, incongruous. M17. 2 Lacking harmony between different parts or elements; self-contradictory. M17. 3 Of a person: not consistent in thought or action; acting at variance with principles or former conduct. E18.

1 H. A. L. FISHER Privileges are freely granted . ., which are inconsistent with the exercise of state authority. b P. F. BOLLER I always thought that the sword and the gospel were utterly inconsistent. 2 J. GALSWORTHY His feelings were too mixed, too inconsistent for expression. 3 E. YOUNG Ah! how unjust to nature, and himself, Is thoughtless, thankless, inconsistent man!

†II4 Of a substance: not solid or firm, fluid. L17–M19.

B *n.* In *pl.* Inconsistent things, acts, or statements. M17.

F. BOWEN Two Inconsistents . . cannot both be true.

inconsistently *adv.* M17.

inconsolable /ɪnkənˈsəʊləb(ə)l/ *a.* L16. [Fr., or L *inconsolabilis*, f. as IN-[3] + *consolabilis*, f. *consolari* CONSOLE *v.*: see -ABLE.] 1 Of grief, trouble, etc.: unable to be alleviated or assuaged. L16. 2 Of a person: unable to be consoled or comforted; disconsolate. L17.

1 T. BLACKLOCK Impell'd by deep inconsolable grief, She breathes her soft, her melancholy strain. 2 M. BARING Lady Hengrave promised Marjorie a new doll, but Marjorie was inconsolable.

ˌinconsolaˈbility *n.* M19. **inconsolableness** *n.* E18. **inconsolably** *adv.* E18.

inconsonance /ɪnˈkɒns(ə)nəns/ *n.* E19. [f. INCONSONANT after *consonance*: see -ANCE.] Lack of agreement or harmony.

inconsonancy *n.* (*rare*) M17.

inconsonant /ɪnˈkɒns(ə)nənt/ *a.* M17. [f. IN-[3] + CONSONANT *a.*] Not consonant or agreeable *to*; not agreeing or harmonizing *with*.

inconsonantly *adv.* M19.

inconspicuous /ɪnkənˈspɪkjʊəs/ *a.* E17. [f. L *inconspicuus* (f. as IN-[3] + CONSPICUOUS) + -OUS.] †1 Unable to be seen or perceived; invisible, indiscernible. E17–L18. 2 Not easily seen or noticed; not prominent or striking; *spec.* in *Bot.* (of flowers) small, and green or pale. E19.

2 H. W. BATES The majority of forest-trees in equatorial Brazil have small and inconspicuous flowers. M. AMSTERDAM He started looking around for a place to throw it, that would be inconspicuous.

inconspicuously *adv.* M17. **inconspicuousness** *n.* E17.

†**inconstance** *n.* LME. [(O)Fr. f. as next: see -ANCE.] 1a = INCONSTANCY 1a. LME–E18. b = INCONSTANCY 1b. E16–E17. 2 = INCONSTANCY 2. Only in E16.

inconstancy /ɪnˈkɒnst(ə)nsi/ *n.* E16. [L *inconstantia*, f. *inconstant-*: see INCONSTANT, -ANCY. Cf. prec.] 1a Lack of stability or steadfastness of character or purpose; fickleness. E16. b Of things or events: lack of uniformity, variability, irregularity. E17. †2 Inconsistency (of statements etc.); an instance of this. M16–E17. †3 [Alt. of INCONTINENCY.] Incontinence. L16–E17.

1a H. JAMES You are contrasting my inconstancy with your own fidelity. b J. COWELL The inconstancy of mans estate, and the mutability of time.

inconstant /ɪnˈkɒnst(ə)nt/ *a.* & *n.* LME. [OFr., or L *inconstant-*, f. as IN-[3] + *constant-* CONSTANT *a.*] A *adj.* 1 Not steadfast or faithful; fickle, changeable. LME. 2 Of things: variable, irregular. E16. †3 Inconsistent *with*. Only in M17.

1 H. P. BROUGHAM The fickle, inconstant, volatile temper of the people. M. SEYMOUR-SMITH Woman as deceiver and inconstant lover. 2 SHAKES. *Rom. & Jul.* O, swear not by . . th' inconstant moon, That monthly changes in her circled orb. E. POSTE The orthography of the Veronese MS. is extremely inconstant.

B *n.* An inconstant person or thing. M17.

inconstantly *adv.* M16.

inconstruable /ɪnkənˈstruːəb(ə)l/ *a.* L19. [f. IN-[3] + CONSTRUABLE.] Unable to be construed.

inconsumable /ɪnkənˈsjuːməb(ə)l/ *a.* M17. [f. IN-[3] + CONSUMABLE *a.*] 1 Unable to be consumed (by fire etc.). M17. 2 *Econ.* Intended for repeated use and not for consumption. L18.

1 SHELLEY Ever still Burning, yet ever inconsumable. 2 L. GRONLUND The inconsumable things, like machinery, leather, coin.

†**inconsumptible** *a.* L16–E18. [Fr. †*inconsomptible*, *-sumpt-*, or late L *inconsumptibilis*, f. as IN-[3] + *consumptibilis*, f. *consumpt-* pa. ppl stem of *consumere* CONSUME *v.*: see -IBLE.] = INCONSUMABLE 1.

incontaminate /ɪnkənˈtamɪnət/ *a.* Long *rare.* LME. [L *incontaminatus*, f. as IN-[3] + *contaminatus* pa. pple of *contaminare*: see CONTAMINATE *v.*] Uncontaminated, undefiled.

incontestable /ɪnkənˈtɛstəb(ə)l/ *a.* Also **-ible**. L17. [Fr., or med.L *incontestabilis*, f. as IN-[3] + *contestabilis*, f. *contestari* CONTEST *v.*: see -ABLE, -IBLE.] Not open to question or argument; unquestionable, indisputable.

B. WEBB He is disliked and distrusted . ., but his cleverness . . as an after-dinner speaker is incontestable.

incontestaˈbility *n.* (*rare*) M19. **incontestableness** *n.* (*rare*) E18. **incontestably** *adv.* E18.

†**incontested** *a.* Only in 18. [f. IN-[3] + CONTEST *v.* + -ED[1].] Uncontested, undisputed.

incontestible *a.* var. of INCONTESTABLE.

incontinence /ɪnˈkɒntɪnəns/ *n.* LME. [(O)Fr., or L *incontinentia*, f. as IN-[3] + *continentia* CONTINENCE. Cf. next.] 1 Lack of self-restraint with regard to sexual desire; promiscuity. LME. 2 *Med.* Lack of voluntary control over the passing of urine or faeces. (Foll. by *of*.) M18. 3 *gen.* Lack of constraint; inability to contain or restrain. (Foll. by *of*.) M19.

1 J. A. SYMONDS Handsome youths are admonished by Pindar to beware of lawlessness and shun incontinence. 2 P. PARISH This makes the patient empty his bladder more frequently, and . . this often leads to incontinence. 3 CARLYLE [They] do not waste themselves by incontinence of tongue.

incontinency /ɪnˈkɒntɪnənsi/ *n.* Now *rare.* LME. [f. as prec.: see -ENCY.] 1 = INCONTINENCE 1. LME. 2 = INCONTINENCE 3. E18. 3 = INCONTINENCE 2. L18.

incontinent /ɪnˈkɒntɪnənt/ *a.* LME. [(O)Fr., or L *incontinent-*, f. as IN-[3] + CONTINENT *a.*] 1 Lacking self-restraint, esp. with regard to sexual desire; promiscuous. LME. 2 *gen.* Unable to contain or restrain. Usu. foll. by *of*. M17. 3 *Med.* Lacking voluntary control over the passing of urine or faeces. E19.

3 *doubly incontinent*: see DOUBLY 1.

incontinent /ɪnˈkɒntɪnənt/ *adv.* Now *arch. rare.* LME. [OFr. *incontenant*, *en-* = Sp., It. *incontinente*, f. late L *in continenti* (sc. *tempore*) 'in continuous time', without an interval. Cf. CONTINENT *a.*] = next.

incontinently /ɪnˈkɒntɪnəntli/ *adv.*[1] *arch.* LME. [f. prec. + -LY[2].] At once, immediately, without delay.

incontinently /ɪnˈkɒntɪnəntli/ *adv.*[2] M16. [f. INCONTINENT *a.* + -LY[2].] In an incontinent manner; with lack of (esp. sexual) self-restraint.

incontinuity /ˌɪnkɒntɪˈnjuːɪti/ *n. rare.* M19. [f. IN-[3] + CONTINUITY.] Lack of continuity, discontinuity.

incontinuous /ɪnkənˈtɪnjʊəs/ *a. rare.* M19. [f. IN-[3] + CONTINUOUS.] Not continuous, discontinuous.

incontrollable /ɪnkənˈtrəʊləb(ə)l/ *a.* Now *rare.* L16. [f. IN-[3] + CONTROLLABLE.] 1 Impossible to restrain or regulate; uncontrollable. L16. †2 Fixed, unalterable, unchangeable. E–M17. †3 Incontrovertible, unquestionable. Only in M17.

incontrollably *adv.* M17.

incontrovertible /ˌɪnkɒntrəˈvəːtɪb(ə)l/ *a.* M17. [f. IN-[3] + CONTROVERTIBLE.] Indisputable, indubitable.

M. RENAULT Laurie . . had had this explained to him many times and accepted it as incontrovertible fact.

ˌincontrovertiˈbility *n.* L18. **incontrovertibly** *adv.* M17.

in contumaciam /ɪn kɒntjʊˈmeɪsɪəm/ *adv. phr.* L19. [L.] While in contempt of court.

inconvenience /ɪnkənˈviːnɪəns/ *n.* & *v.* LME. [OFr. (mod. *inconvenance*) f. L *inconvenientia* incongruity, inconsistency, f. as IN-[3] + CONVENIENCE *n.* Cf. next.] A *n.* †1 (An) incongruity, (an) inconsistency, (an) absurdity. LME–E18. †2 Unsuitableness, unfitness. LME–L17. †3 Unbecoming or unseemly behaviour, (an) impropriety. LME–M16. 4 (A) mischief, (an) injury, (a) misfortune. *obs.* exc. as passing into sense 5. LME. 5 Lack of adaptation to personal requirements or ease; (a) disadvantage, (a) discomfort. L15.

5 E. M. FORSTER I really came . . to thank you for so kindly giving us your rooms last night. I hope that you have not been put to any great inconvenience. J. GATHORNE-HARDY As we get older we begin to suffer from an increasing amount of major and minor illnesses, diseases and inconveniences.

B *v.t.* Put to inconvenience, cause inconvenience to. E17.

E. WAUGH An umbrella under his left arm further inconvenienced him. A. T. ELLIS I believe in God . . but on the whole this belief inconveniences rather than supports me.

inconveniency /ɪnkənˈviːnɪənsi/ *n.* Now *rare.* LME. [L *inconvenientia*: see prec., -ENCY.] †1 = INCONVENIENCE *n.* 4. LME–E18. †2 = INCONVENIENCE 1. M16–L17. 3 = INCONVENIENCE *n.* 5. M16. †4 = INCONVENIENCE *n.* 3. E17–M18.

inconvenient /ɪnkənˈviːnɪənt/ *a.* & *n.* LME. [OFr. f. L *inconvenient-*, f. as IN-[3] + CONVENIENT *a.*] A *adj.* †1 Incongruous, inconsistent, absurd. LME–L17. †2 Unsuitable, unfitting, (*for*, *to*). LME–M19. †3 Unbecoming, unseemly improper. L15–L17. 4 Unfavourable to ease or comfort; awkward, troublesome, disadvantageous. M17. †B *n.* 1 An incongruity, an inconsistency, an absurdity. Only in LME. 2 An unbecoming act, an impropriety. LME–M16. 3 An inconvenience. LME–M19.

inconveniently *adv.* E16.

†**inconversable** *a.* Also **-ible**. L16–E18. [f. IN-[3] + CONVERSABLE.] Not conversable; unsociable; uncommunicative.

inconvertible /ɪnkənˈvəːtɪb(ə)l/ *a.* M17. [Fr., or late L *inconvertibilis*, f. as IN-[3] + L *convertibilis* CONVERTIBLE *a.*; later f. IN-[3] + CONVERTIBLE *a.*] 1 Unable to be changed into something else. M17. 2 Not interchangeable; not equivalent or synonymous. E18. 3 Unable to be exchanged for something else; *spec.* (of currency) that cannot be converted into another form on demand. M19.

inconverti'bility *n.* E19. **inconvertibleness** *n.* E18. **inconvertibly** *adv.* L19.

inconvincible /ɪnkən'vɪnsɪb(ə)l/ *a.* M17. [f. IN-^{3} + CONVINCIBLE.] Not convincible; not open to conviction.

†incony *a. slang.* L16–M17. [Origin unkn.] Rare, fine, delicate.

incoordination /ˌɪnkəʊɔːdɪ'neɪʃ(ə)n/ *n.* Also **inco-or-**, ***incoör-**. L19. [f. IN-^{3} + COORDINATION.] Lack of coordination, esp. of muscular action.

incoronate /ɪn'kɒrənət/ *a.* M19. [It. *incoronato* or med.L *incoronatus* pa. pple of *incoronare* to crown, f. as IN-^{2} + L *corona* CROWN *n.*: see -ATE^{2}.] Wearing or having a crown; crowned.

incoronation /ˌɪnkɒrə'neɪʃ(ə)n/ *n.* Now *rare.* L15. [f. med.L *incoronat-* pa. ppl stem of *incoronare* (see prec.), + -ATION. Partly f. It. *incoronazione.*] A coronation, a crowning.

incorporable /ɪn'kɔːp(ə)rəb(ə)l/ *a. rare.* E17. [f. INCORPORATE *v.* + -ABLE.] Able to be incorporated.

†incorporal *a.* M16–M18. [L *incorporalis*, f. as IN-^{3} + *corporalis* CORPORAL *a.*] Immaterial, incorporeal.

†incorporality *n.* E17–L18. [Late L *incorporalitas*, f. as prec.: see -ITY.] The state or quality of being incorporeal.

incorporate /ɪn'kɔːp(ə)rət/ *a.*^{1} *rare.* LME. [Late L *incorporatus* not embodied, f. *in-* IN-^{3} + *corporatus* CORPORATE *a.*] Without body or material substance; incorporeal.

incorporate /ɪn'kɔːp(ə)rət/ *a.*^{2} LME. [Late L *incorporatus* pa. pple of *incorporare*: see next, -ATE^{2}.] 1 United in or *in, into* one body; combined (*with* another thing). Now *rare.* LME. 2a Of a company etc.: formally constituted as a corporation. LME. †b Of a person: admitted to fellowship with others, as a member of the same corporation. L16–L17. †c That constitutes a close connection. L16–M18. 3 Having a bodily form; embodied. LME.

incorporate /ɪn'kɔːpəreɪt/ *v.* LME. [Late L *incorporat-* pa. ppl stem of *incorporare*, f. as IN-^{2} + *corporare* CORPORATE *v.*: see -ATE^{3}.] I *v.t.* 1 Combine or unite into one body or uniform substance; mix together. LME. 2 Put (one thing) *in* or *into* another to form one whole; include, absorb. LME. 3a Combine or form into an organization; *esp.* constitute as a legal corporation. Usu. in *pass.* LME. b Admit, enrol (a person) *into, in* an organization; *spec.* admit as a graduate of another university *ad eundem.* M16. 4 Provide with a body; embody. *rare.* E17.

1 CAPT. COOK Stirring up the several ingredients, till they were perfectly incorporated. 2 ALDOUS HUXLEY The amoeba, when it finds a prey, flows round it, incorporates it, and oozes on. M. GIROUARD Often an orchard, or a vegetable garden . ., was incorporated into the layout. 3a T. LUNDBERG When a company is incorporated, the initial subscribing shareholders . . enter into a form of contract.

II *v.i.* 5 Of one thing: combine *with* to form one body. L16. 6 Of two or more things: unite so as to form one body; form a close union. Now *rare* or *obs.* E17. 7 Become constituted as a legal corporation. M20.

5 D. BREWSTER The Water will gradually incorporate with the Syrup.

incorporating *a.* (*a*) that incorporates; (*b*) *Ling.* employing or formed by incorporation; polysynthetic: E17.

incorporation /ɪnˌkɔːpə'reɪʃ(ə)n/ *n.* LME. [Late L *incorporatio(n-)*, f. as prec.: see -ATION.] 1 The action of incorporating two or more things, or one thing with another; the process or condition of being incorporated. LME. b *Ling.* The combination of two or more different parts of speech in one word, as when the object of a verb is inserted between its stem and termination. L19. 2a The action or process of forming into a community or corporation. LME. †b A document which gives legal status to a corporation. L15–E17. c The action of incorporating a graduate of one university into another. M20. 3 An incorporated society or company; a corporation. M16. 4 (An) embodiment. *rare.* M17.

incorporative /ɪn'kɔːp(ə)rətɪv/ *a.* L16. [f. INCORPORATE *v.* + -IVE.] Characterized by or tending to incorporation.

incorporator /ɪn'kɔːpəreɪtə/ *n.* E19. [f. INCORPORATE *v.* + -OR.] 1 A person who incorporates or combines things into one body or substance. E19. 2 A person who takes part in the formation of an incorporated company. L19. 3 A member of one university who is incorporated into another. L19.

in corpore /ɪn 'kɔːpəreɪ/ *a.* & *adv. phr.* E20. [L, lit. 'in the body'.] *Biol.* = IN VIVO.

incorporeal /ɪnkɔː'pɔːrɪəl/ *a.* & *n.* LME. [f. L *incorporeus* (f. as IN-^{3} + *corporeus*, f. *corpor-*, *corpus* body) + -AL^{1}.] A *adj.* 1 Not composed of matter; of or pertaining to immaterial beings. LME. 2 *Law.* Having no material existence in itself, but connected as a right to some actual thing. E17.

2 *incorporeal hereditament.*

B *n.* In *pl.* Incorporeal things. E17.

ˌincorpore'ality *n.* M19. **incorporeally** *adv.* E17.

incorporeity /ˌɪnkɔːpə'riːɪti, -'reɪɪti/ *n.* E17. [med.L *incorporeitas*, f. as prec.: see -ITY.] The quality or state of being incorporeal; an incorporeal attribute.

incorpsed /ɪn'kɔːpst/ *a. rare.* E17. [f. IN-^{2} + CORPSE *n.* + -ED^{2}.] Made into one body (*with*).

incorrect /ɪnkə'rɛkt/ *a.* LME. [Fr., or L *incorrectus*, f. as IN-^{3} + CORRECT *a.*] †1 *gen.* Uncorrected. LME–E17. 2 Of a book: not corrected for the press; containing many errors. L15. 3 Of style, behaviour, etc.: improper, faulty. L17. 4 Of a statement, description, etc.: erroneous, inaccurate. E19.

3 T. MEDWIN According to . . Brummel, it is highly incorrect to be helped a second time to soup. 4 J. H. SHORTHOUSE That lazy facility which always gives a meaning, though often an incorrect one. N. SYMINGTON It is incorrect to think that Freud was the first to challenge the notion.

incorrectitude *n.* (*rare*) the state of being incorrect; incorrectness: L19. **incorrectly** *adv.* E17. **incorrectness** *n.* the quality of being incorrect; an instance of this, an error: L17.

incorrespondence /ˌɪnkɒrɪ'spɒnd(ə)ns/ *n. rare.* M17. [f. IN-^{3} + CORRESPONDENCE.] Lack of correspondence or harmony.

Also **incorrespondency** *n.* E19.

incorrigible /ɪn'kɒrɪdʒɪb(ə)l/ *a.* & *n.* ME. [(O)Fr., or L *incorrigibilis*, f. as IN-^{3} + *corrigibilis* CORRIGIBLE.] A *adj.* 1 Of a person, a habit, etc.: incurably bad or depraved. ME. †2 Of something defective: that cannot be set right. Of disease: incurable. M16–E19. 3†a So good that it cannot be improved. *rare.* Only in E17. b That cannot be verified or proved false. *rare.* M20.

1 L. STRACHEY Within a few weeks the incorrigible reprobate was at his tricks again.

B *n.* 1 An incorrigible person. M18. 2 A thing not open to verification. *rare.* M20.

incorrigi'bility *n.* L15. **incorrigibleness** *n.* M17. **incorrigibly** *adv.* E17.

incorrodible /ɪnkə'rəʊdɪb(ə)l/ *a.* M19. [f. IN-^{3} + CORRODIBLE.] Unable to be corroded.

incorrupt /ɪnkə'rʌpt/ *a.* LME. [L *incorruptus*, f. as IN-^{3} + *corruptus* CORRUPT *a.*] 1 Of a dead human body, or other organic matter: free from decomposition. LME. 2 Morally uncorrupted; honourable. Now *rare.* LME. 3 Not debased or perverted; *spec.* (of a text etc.) not affected by error or corruption. Now *rare.* M16.

†incorrupted *a.* = INCORRUPT E16–M18. **incorruptly** *adv.* (now *rare*) L16. **incorruptness** *n.* L17.

incorruptible /ɪnkə'rʌptɪb(ə)l/ *a.* & *n.* ME. [(O)Fr., or eccl.L *incorruptibilis*, f. as IN-^{3} + CORRUPTIBLE.] A *adj.* 1 Unable to decay or decompose; everlasting. ME. 2 Unable to be morally corrupted, *esp.* unable to be bribed. M17.

1 AV *1 Cor.* 15:52 The trumpet shall sound, and the dead shall be raised incorruptible. 2 DICKENS A man of incorruptible integrity.

B *n.* 1 *Eccl. Hist.* A member of an early Christian sect who maintained the incorruptibility of the body of Jesus. Usu. in *pl.* E18. 2 An incorruptible person, a person of rigid honesty or uncompromising idealism. Only in *sea-green incorruptible* (after Carlyle's *French Revolution*, where applied to Robespierre). M19.

incorrupti'bility *n.* L15. **incorruptibleness** *n.* (now *rare* or *obs.*) LME. **incorruptibly** *adv.* L16.

incorruption /ɪnkə'rʌpʃ(ə)n/ *n.* LME. [(O)Fr., or eccl.L *incorruptio(n-)*, f. as IN-^{3} + *corruptio(n-)* CORRUPTION.] 1 Freedom from physical decomposition. Freq. in biblical allusions. LME. 2 Freedom from corrupt conduct. E17.

1 AV *1 Cor.* 15:42 It is sowen in corruption, it is raised in incorruption.

†incounter *n.*, *v.* vars. of ENCOUNTER *n.*, *v.*

in-country /'ɪnkʌntri/ *n.* & *a.* M16. [f. IN-^{1} + COUNTRY *n.*] A *n.* The inland or central part of a country; the mainland. *Sc.* Now *rare.* M16.

B *adj.* In the country; in a country understood contextually. M20.

Daily Telegraph 2,500 American Marines are to leave South Vietnam. . . This will reduce America's 'in-country' military strength to 484,000 troops.

†incourage *v.*, **†incouragement** vars. of ENCOURAGE, ENCOURAGEMENT.

incourse /'ɪnkɔːs/ *n. arch. rare.* LME. [L *incursus*, f. *incurs-* (see INCURSION), assim. to *concourse* etc.] An inflow, an inrush, an incursion.

incover *v.* var. of ENCOVER.

incrassate /ɪn'krasət/ *a.* L15. [Late L *incrassatus* pa. pple, f. as next: see -ATE^{2}.] †1 Thickened in consistency. L15–L17. 2 *Bot.* & *Zool.* Of thick or swollen form. M18.

incrassate /ɪn'kraseɪt/ *v.t.* & *i.* Now *rare.* E17. [Late L *incrassat-* pa. ppl stem of *incrassare*, f. as IN-^{2} + *crassare* make thick, f. *crassus* thick: see -ATE^{3}.] Thicken in consistency or form.

incrassated *a.* thickened; *esp.* (*Bot.* & *Zool.*) = INCRASSATE *a.* 2: M17. **incra'ssation** *n.* M17.

increase /'ɪŋkriːs, ɪn'kriːs/ *n.* Also **†en-**. LME. [f. the vb.] 1 The action, process, or fact of making or becoming greater; growth, enlargement, extension. LME. †b *spec.* The rising of the tide; the waxing of the moon. M16–M17. c The action or a method of increasing in knitting. L19. 2 Growth in number or frequency; multiplication; *spec.* the multiplication of humans, animals, or plants; reproduction. LME. †3 Growth in some specified quality or respect, esp. wealth or power. LME–E19. 4 The result of increasing; the amount by which something is increased, an addition. LME. 5 Offspring (of humans or animals); *arch.* crops; *fig.* the product or result of any action. M16.

2 SHAKES. *Lear* Dry up in her the organs of increase. 4 W. S. JEVONS When their wages are raised, the increase comes out of the pockets of their employers. 5 AV *1 Sam.* 2:33 And all the increase of thine house shall die in the floure of their age.

Phrases: **on the increase** increasing, becoming greater or more frequent.

†increaseful *a.* (*rare*) productive, fruitful: only in L16.

increase /ɪn'kriːs, 'ɪŋkriːs/ *v.* Also **†en-**. ME. [AN *encres-* = OFr. *encreis-* stem of *encreistre* f. L *increscere*, f. as IN-^{2} + *crescere* grow.] 1 *v.t.* & *i.* Make or become greater in size, amount, duration, or degree; enlarge, extend, intensify. ME. b *spec.* in *Knitting.* Add (a specified number of stitches) to the number of stitches in a row so as to widen the piece. M19. 2 *v.i.* & *t.* Become or make more numerous, multiply, esp. by propagation. ME. 3 *v.i.* & (now *rare* or *obs.*) *t.* Become or make greater or more advanced in some specified quality or respect. LME. 4 *v.i.* & *t.* Become or make richer or more powerful; (cause to) thrive. *arch.* LME. 5 *v.i. Latin Gram.* Of a noun or adjective: have one syllable more in the genitive than in the nominative. *arch.* E17.

1 S. PLATH I could sense the boy's interest dwindle as the pull of his mother increased. *Economist* Wage rates have increased by 10 per cent. D. W. GOODWIN

Whether increasing the price of alcohol results in a decrease of alcoholism is not known. 2 TENNYSON And watch her harvest ripen, her herd increase. 3 SLOAN WILSON Diamonds had increased in value a great deal since the war.

increasable *a.* capable of or liable to increase M16. **increasableness** *n.* L17. **increaser** *n.* (*a*) a person who or thing which makes something greater; (*b*) *arch.* a person who promotes or advances something; (*c*) an animal or plant which multiplies to a specified extent: LME. **increasingly** *adv.* to an increasing degree, at an increasing rate; more and more: L16.

increasement /ɪnˈkriːsm(ə)nt/ *n.* Now *rare.* Also †**en-**. LME. [f. prec. + -MENT.] 1 The action or process of increasing; growth, extension, multiplication. LME. 2 The result of increasing; progeny, produce; an addition. LME.

increate /ɪnkriːˈeɪt/ *a.* LME. [eccl.L *increatus*, f. as IN-[3] + L *creatus* pa. pple of *creare* CREATE *v.*: see -ATE[2].] Of a divine being or attribute: not created.

Also †**increated** *a.* M16–E18.

incredibility /ɪnˌkrɛdɪˈbɪlɪti/ *n.* E17. [L *incredibilitas*, f. as next: see -ITY.] The quality or fact of being incredible; an incredible thing.

incredible /ɪnˈkrɛdɪb(ə)l/ *a.* LME. [L *incredibilis*, f. as IN-[3] + CREDIBLE.] 1 Not credible; that cannot be believed. LME. b Hard to believe; of exceedingly great quantity, quality, etc.; surprising. Now *colloq.* L15. †2 Unbelieving. LME–M18.

1 F. FERGUSSON Wishes to reveal this figment of the Greek imagination as, literally, incredible. b T. MORRISON The fury she created in the women of the town was incredible. R. INGALLS He was possessed of incredible strength.

incredibleness *n.* E17. **incredibly** *adv.* L15.

increditable /ɪnˈkrɛdɪtəb(ə)l/ *a. rare.* L17. [f. IN-[3] + CREDITABLE.] Not creditable.

incredulity /ɪnkrɪˈdjuːlɪti/ *n.* LME. [(O)Fr. *incrédulité* f. L *incredulitas*, f. as next: see -ITY.] 1 Unwillingness to believe; disbelief. LME. †2 *spec.* Religious disbelief. M16–M17.

1 A. T. ELLIS She believed him, her native incredulity powerless against the force of her affection. A. MASON These were so bizarre that Simon listened at first out of sheer incredulity.

incredulous /ɪnˈkrɛdjʊləs/ *a.* L16. [f. L *incredulus* (f. as IN-[3] + CREDULOUS) + -OUS: see -ULOUS.] 1 Unwilling to believe; sceptical; (of an action) marked or prompted by incredulity. Formerly also *spec.*, lacking religious belief. L16. †2 Not to be believed; incredible. E17–M18.

1 P. G. WODEHOUSE At first he was blankly incredulous It could not be Judson. A. MACLEAN Earth's first visitor from outer space . . couldn't . . have been the object of more incredulous consternation.

incredulously *adv.* E19. **incredulousness** *n.* E18.

incremation /ɪŋkrɪˈmeɪʃ(ə)n/ *n.* Now *rare* or *obs.* E19. [f. IN-[2] + CREMATION.] = CREMATION.

increment /ˈɪŋkrɪm(ə)nt/ *n.* & *v.* LME. [L *incrementum*, f. stem of *increscere* INCREASE *v.*: see -MENT.] A *n.* 1 The action or process of (esp. gradually) increasing or becoming greater; an increase, a growth, *esp.* a uniform or regular one. LME. b *Her.* The waxing of the moon. Now only in *in* (*her*) *increment*, increscent. E17. c *Rhet.* = AUXESIS I. M18. 2 The amount of increase; an addition; an amount gained, a profit, *esp.* a uniform or regular one. LME. b *Math.* & *Physics.* A small (or infinitesimal) positive or negative change in a variable quantity or function. E18. c *Forestry.* (The value of) the increase in the quantity of wood produced by a tree or group of trees during a limited period. L19. †3 Something that promotes growth in a plant. *rare.* LME–E18.

2 J. GATHORNE-HARDY £650 a year. And that went on, you got miniscule increments I think. UNEARNED *increment.*

B *v.t.* & *i.* Increase by an increment or increments. M19.

incremental /ɪŋkrɪˈmɛnt(ə)l/ *a.* E18. [f. INCREMENT *n.* + -AL[1].] Of or pertaining to an increment or increments; advancing by increments.

Times The increases for the district nurses amount to £40 a year at the lower end of the incremental scale and £60 at the upper end. M. IGNATIEFF The slow, incremental liberalization of restrictions on Jews.

incrementalism *n.* belief in change by degrees, gradualism M20. **incrementalist** *n.* & *a.* (*a*) *n.* an adherent of incrementalism; (*b*) *adj.* of or pertaining to incrementalism or incrementalists: L20. **incrementally** *adv.* in an incremental manner, by increments M20.

increpation /ɪŋkrɪˈpeɪʃ(ə)n/ *n. arch.* E16. [L *increpatio(n-)*, f. *increpat-* pa. ppl stem of *increpare* scold, chide, f. as IN-[2] + *crepare* make a noise, creak: see -ATION.] (A) reproof, (a) rebuke.

increscent /ɪnˈkrɛs(ə)nt/ *n.* & *a.* L16. [L *increscent-* pres. ppl stem of *increscere* INCREASE *v.*: see -ENT.] A *n.* Chiefly *Her.* The waxing moon. B *adj.* Increasing; *esp.* (of the moon) waxing (in *Her.* depicted with the horns directed to the dexter side). Cf. DECRESCENT *a.* M17.

incriminate /ɪnˈkrɪmɪneɪt/ *v.t.* M18. [Late L *incriminat-* pa. ppl stem of *incriminare* accuse, f. as IN-[2] + *criminare* CRIMINATE: see -ATE[3].] Charge with a crime; involve in an accusation or charge; tend to prove the guilt of.

E. WILSON An incriminating manifesto, which would have cost . . Michelet his head, was lying . . on the table. D. MAY She managed to say nothing that would incriminate herself or the organisation.

incriminating *ppl a.* incriminatory M19. **incrimiˈnation** *n.* M17. **incriminator** *n.* (*rare*) M19. **incriminatory** *a.* tending to incriminate someone M19.

incrimson *v.* var. of ENCRIMSON.

incrispated /ɪnˈkrɪspeɪtɪd/ *a. rare.* M18. [f. late L *incrispat-* pa. ppl stem of *incrispare* curl, f. as IN-[2] + *crispare* curl, wrinkle: see -ED[1].] Stiffly curled.

†**incroach** *v.* & *n.* var. of ENCROACH.

incroyable /ɛ̃krwajabl/ *n.* Pl. pronounced same. L18. [Fr. = incredible.] *Hist.* A French fop or dandy of the period 1795–9.

incrust *v.* see ENCRUST.

incrustate /ɪnˈkrʌsteɪt/ *a.* E17. [L *incrustatus* pa. pple of *incrustare*, f. as IN-[2] + *crustare* form a crust (f. *crusta* crust): see -ATE[2].] †1 Formed or hardened into a crust. E17–M18. 2 Enveloped (as) with a crust. *obs.* exc. *Bot.* L17.

incrustate /ˈɪnkrʌsteɪt/ *v.t.* Now *rare.* Also **en-** /ɪn-, ɛn-/. L16. [L *incrustat-* pa. ppl stem of *incrustare*: see prec., -ATE[3].] Cover with a crust or hardened coating or layer.

incrustation /ɪnkrʌˈsteɪʃ(ə)n/ *n.* Also **en-** /ɪn-, ɛn-/. E17. [Fr., or late L *incrustatio(n-)*, f. as prec.: see -ATION.] 1 An outer layer or crust of fine material or ornamentation covering a rough substance; *esp.* a facing of marble etc. on a building. Formerly also *fig.*, an adventitious ornament or affectation. E17. 2 A crust formed naturally on the surface of an object; a scab; *esp.* a calcareous or crystalline deposit. M17. b *fig.* An impenetrable layer of accumulated habits, vices, etc. E19. 3 The formation of a crust; the fact or condition of being encrusted. M17.

1 M. GIROUARD The extra diversion of a rich incrustation of sunflowers—in stone or wrought iron. 2 P. H. JOHNSON Their salty incrustations sparkled in the gilding of the street lamps. b P. ZIEGLER Under an encrustation of traditional dogma a truth that . . seemed heretical but was soon accepted.

incubate /ˈɪŋkjʊbeɪt/ *n.* M20. [f. next after *filtrate*, *precipitate* etc.: see -ATE[1].] A preparation or material that has been incubated.

incubate /ˈɪŋkjʊbeɪt/ *v.* M17. [L *incubat-* pa. ppl stem of *incubare* lie on, f. as IN-[2] + *cubare* lie: see -ATE[3].] 1 *v.t.* Hatch or aid the development of (eggs) by maintaining warmth, either (as with most birds) by sitting upon, or by other natural or artificial means. M17. b *v.t. gen.* Maintain (esp. cells or micro-organisms) in a controlled environment suitable for growth and development; maintain at a constant temperature. E20. c *v.i.* Undergo incubation; develop, grow. E20. 2 *v.i.* (Chiefly of a bird) sit on eggs; *fig.* brood. M17.

1 J. A. MICHENER In time the other eggs, incubated solely by action of the sun, hatched. R. DAWKINS Gannets and guillemots incubate one egg at a time. b *Science Journal* The inoculated samples were incubated for up to 27 days at various temperatures. c J. BRONOWSKI The full moon . . gives the time needed for the eggs to incubate undisturbed. *fig.*: N. ANNAN His grouches incubate in the heat of his devotion.

incubation /ɪŋkjʊˈbeɪʃ(ə)n/ *n.* E17. [L *incubatio(n-)* brooding, f. as prec.: see -ATION.] 1 The action of incubating eggs; the embryonic development of an animal within an egg. E17. b The process or an instance of incubating something in a controlled environment. E20. 2 *Med.* (The process occurring during) the period elapsing between exposure to an infection or disease and the appearance of the first symptoms. M19. 3 *Gk Hist.* The practice of sleeping in a temple in the hope of experiencing a vision etc. L19.

incubational *a.* M19.

incubative /ˈɪŋkjʊbeɪtɪv/ *a.* M19. [f. INCUBATE *v.* + -IVE.] Of, pertaining to, or characterized by incubation, esp. of a disease.

incubator /ˈɪŋkjʊbeɪtə/ *n.* M19. [f. INCUBATE *v.* + -OR.] 1 An animal, esp. a bird, which incubates its eggs. M19. 2 An apparatus for hatching eggs under artificial conditions. M19. b An apparatus in which a constant temperature is maintained, esp. for rearing premature babies or for culturing micro-organisms. L19.

Comb.: **incubator bird** = MEGAPODE.

incubatory /ɪŋkjʊˈbeɪt(ə)ri/ *a.* L19. [f. INCUBATE *v.* + -ORY[2].] = INCUBATIVE.

incubi *n.pl.* see INCUBUS.

†**incubiture** *n.* M17–M18. [f. L *incubit-* pa. ppl stem of *incubare* lie on, INCUBATE *v.* + -URE.] = INCUBATION I.

incubous /ˈɪŋkjʊbəs/ *a.* M19. [f. L *incubare* lie on, INCUBATE *v.* + -OUS.] *Bot.* (Of a leaf, esp. in a foliose liverwort) pointing forward so that its upper edge overlaps the lower edge of the leaf above; (of a plant) having its leaves so arranged. Opp. SUCCUBOUS.

incubus /ˈɪŋkjʊbəs/ *n.* Pl. **-buses, -bi** /-bʌɪ/. ME. [Late L = L *incubo* nightmare, f. *incubare*: see INCUBATE *v.*] 1 An evil spirit supposed to descend upon sleeping people and esp. to have sexual intercourse with sleeping women. ME. 2 An oppressive nightmare; a person who or thing which oppresses or troubles like a nightmare. M16.

2 M. L. KING The incubus of racial injustice. P. ACKROYD What an incubus my aesthetic personality might become if I were . . trapped within it.

incud- *comb. form* see INCUDO-.

incudes *n.* pl. of INCUS.

incudo- /ɪnˈkjuːdəʊ/ *comb. form.* Bef. a vowel **incud-**. L19. [f. L *incud-* INCUS: see -O-.] *Anat.* Forming adjs. & ns. w. the sense 'of the incus of the ear and —', as *incudo-stapedial.*

†**in cuerpo** *adv. phr.* E17–E20. [f. IN *prep.* + Sp. *cuerpo* body f. L *corpus.*] Without a cloak or upper garment to conceal the shape of the body; in unsuitable dress; undressed.

inculcate /ˈɪnkʌlkeɪt/ *v.t.* M16. [L *inculcat-* pa. ppl stem of *inculcare* stamp in with the heel, press in, f. as IN-[2] + *calcare* tread, f. *calc-*, *calx* heel: see -ATE[3].] Instil (an idea, habit, etc.) into a person or a person's mind by forceful admonition or persistent repetition. (Foll. by *in*, *on*, etc.)

M. MITCHELL Mammy . . laboured to inculcate in her the qualities that would make her . . desirable as a wife. A. STORR Military training is designed to inculcate the notion that men are by no means equal. ISAIAH BERLIN They would at least inculcate into the barbarous Scythians the Latin language.

inculcator *n.* L17. **inculcatory** *a.* (*rare*) L19.

inculcation /ɪnkʌlˈkeɪʃ(ə)n/ *n.* M16. [Late L *inculcatio(n-)*, f. as prec.: see -ATION.] The action of inculcating something.

A. J. TOYNBEE Indoctrination . . counteracted by the inculcation of some less narrow loyalty.

inculpable /ɪnˈkʌlpəb(ə)l/ *a.* Now *rare.* L15. [Late L *inculpabilis*, f. as IN-[3] + L *culpabilis* CULPABLE.] Not culpable; blameless.

inculpaˈbility *n.* M18. **inculpableness** *n.* M16. **inculpably** *adv.* M16.

†**inculpate** *a. rare.* E–M17. [Late L *inculpatus*

pa. pple, f. as next: see -ATE[2].] Unblamed, blameless.

inculpate /ˈɪnkʌlpeɪt/ *v.t.* L18. [Late L *inculpat-* pa. ppl stem of *inculpare*, f. as IN-[2] + L *culpare* to blame, f. *culpa* fault: see -ATE[3]. Cf. prec.] 1 Accuse; blame. L18. 2 Involve in a charge, incriminate. M19.

1 E. JONES He blamed himself, but also inculpated his fiancée. 2 CONAN DOYLE Someone came into your room and placed the pistol there in order to inculpate you.

incul'pation *n.* L18. **in'culpative** *a.* = INCULPATORY E19. **in'culpatory** *a.* attributing fault or blame M19.

incult /ɪnˈkʌlt/ *a.* Now *rare.* L16. [L *incultus*, f. as IN-[3] + *cultus* pa. pple of *colere* cultivate.] 1 Of a person, manners, style, etc.: unpolished, unrefined; inelegant. L16. 2 Of land etc.: uncultivated. M17.

†**incultivate** *a.* M17–E19. [f. IN-[3] + L *cultivatus* pa. pple of *cultivare* CULTIVATE: see -ATE[2].] = next.

†**incultivated** *a.* M17–E18. [f. IN-[3] + CULTIVATE + -ED[1].] Uncultivated, unpolished.

†**inculture** *n. rare.* M17–M19. [f. IN-[3] + CULTURE *n.*] Absence of culture or cultivation.

incumbence /ɪnˈkʌmbəns/ *n.* Now *rare.* E17. [f. as next: see -ENCE.] A matter that is incumbent; a duty, an obligation. Also, the fact of being incumbent.

incumbency /ɪnˈkʌmb(ə)nsi/ *n.* E17. [f. INCUMBENT *n.*: see -ENCY. Cf. AL *incumbentia*.] 1 The quality of being incumbent as a duty; an incumbent duty or obligation. Now *rare.* E17. 2 The condition of lying or pressing on something; brooding (*lit.* & *fig.*). Also, an incumbent weight or mass. Now *rare* or *obs.* M17. 3 The position, tenure, or sphere of an incumbent. M17.

1 DONNE The duties of a man, of a friend . . and all the incumbencies of a family. BROWNING Speaks or keeps silence . . Without the least incumbency to lie. 2 WORDSWORTH Felt Incumbencies more awful, visitings Of the Upholder of the tranquil soul. *Cornhill Magazine* The stream is choked with its compact incumbency of snow. 3 R. MACAULAY The living of St. Anne's, . . one of those incumbencies with what is known as scope.

incumbent /ɪnˈkʌmbənt/ *n.* LME. [AL *incumbent-*, *-ens* use as n. of pres. pple of L *incumbere*: see next, -ENT.] 1 The holder of an ecclesiastical benefice. LME. 2 *gen.* The holder of any post or position. L17.

1 K. AMIS The post of private chaplain . . had had half a dozen incumbents. 2 J. C. RANSOM The principal resistance . . will come from the present incumbents of the professorial chairs.

incumbent /ɪnˈkʌmbənt/ *a.* L15. [L *incumbent-* pres. ppl stem of *incumbere* lie on, lean on, apply oneself to, f. as IN-[2] + *-cumbere*: see CUMBENT.] †1a Impending, imminent, threatening. L15–L18. b Weighing on the mind or feelings. M–L17. †2 Bending or applying one's energies to some work; closely occupied with something. (Foll. by *on, over, to.*) M16–E19. 3 Resting or falling on a person as a duty or obligation. Freq. foll. by *on, upon.* M16. †b Falling as a charge or pecuniary liability. L17–L18. 4†a In occupation of an ecclesiastical benefice. (Foll. by *on.*) E–M17. b *gen.* In occupation or having the tenure of any post or position. M20. 5 That lies or presses with its weight *on* something else. Also (*poet.*), overhanging, leaning *over*; *Geol.* (of a stratum etc.) overlying. E17. b *Bot.* & *Zool.* Lying close along a surface, as an anther along a filament, or an insect's wing laid flat. M18.

1a G. MORRIS The proselytes will return to their original sentiments as soon as the incumbent terror is removed. b HOBBES Ambition, and Covetousnesse are Passions . . that are perpetually incumbent, and pressing. 2 CLARENDON The multiplicity of business the king was incumbent to at that time. 3 E. CRANKSHAW Responsibility towards his own people which it was incumbent upon a Russian autocrat to shoulder. J. I. M. STEWART It was incumbent on me to follow where he led. 4a T. FULLER He was never incumbent on any living with cure of souls. b E. ROOSEVELT I never fooled myself about the difficulties of defeating the incumbent administration.

incumber *n.*, *v.*, **incumberment** *n.*, **incumbrance** *n.* vars. of ENCUMBER *n.*, *v.*, ENCUMBERMENT, ENCUMBRANCE.

incunable /ɪnˈkjuːnəb(ə)l/ *n.* L19. [Fr., f. as next.] = INCUNABULUM 2.

incunabulum /ɪnkjʊˈnabjʊləm/ *n.* Pl. (earlier) **-la** /-lə/. E19. [L *incunabula* neut. pl. swaddling-clothes, cradle, f. as IN-[2] + *cunae* cradle.] 1 In *pl.* The early stages of development of a thing. E19. 2 A book printed at an early date; *spec.* one printed before 1501. M19.

incunabular *a.* of or pertaining to an incunabulum or incunabula L19. **incunabulist** *n.* a person who collects or is interested in incunabula E20.

incur /ɪnˈkəː/ *v.* Infl. **-rr-**. LME. [L *incurrere*, f. as IN-[2] + *currere* run.] I *v.t.* 1 Find, or make, oneself subject to (danger, displeasure, etc.); bring on oneself (expense, obligation, etc.). LME. †2 Run into; come upon, meet with. L16–L17. †3 Cause to be incurred; bring (something) *on* someone; entail. E17–L18.

1 H. JAMES The responsibility Olive had incurred in undertaking to form this generous young mind. R. G. COLLINGWOOD I did not even neglect my work to the extent of incurring punishment for idleness. G. CLARE The medical fees incurred during his illness. 3 G. HAKEWILL Not naming it expressely, lest . . he should incurre hatred against the Christian . . Religion.

II *v.i.* 4†a Fall or come *to* or *into*; fall, occur, (within a given period of time etc.). M16–L17. †b Become apparent to the eye etc.; occur. Only in 17. c Devolve, accrue; supervene. Long *rare* or *obs.* L18. †5 Run *into* (danger etc.); make oneself liable *to*. M16–E17.

4a M. HALE Kircherus . . supposeth the first 15 Dynasties to have incurred before the Flood. c T. JEFFERSON The principal, with the interest incurring.

incurrable *a.* (*rare*) E19.

incurable /ɪnˈkjʊərəb(ə)l/ *a.* & *n.* ME. [(O)Fr., or late L *incurabilis*, f. as IN-[3] + *curabilis* CURABLE.] A *adj.* Unable to be cured (*lit.* & *fig.*). ME.

LD MACAULAY The faults of James's head and heart were incurable. R. LOWELL He was dying of the incurable Hodgkin's disease.

B *n.* A person who cannot be cured. M17.

R. KIPLING Heatherlegh, the Doctor, kept . . a hospital . . for Incurables.

incura'bility *n.* M17. **incurableness** *n.* E17. **incurably** *adv.* E16.

incuriosity /ɪnˌkjʊərɪˈɒsɪti/ *n.* E17. [f. next after CURIOSITY.] The quality of being (subjectively) incurious; lack of curiosity about things.

incurious /ɪnˈkjʊərɪəs/ *a.* L16. [Partly f. L *incuriosus* careless, f. as IN-[3] + *curiosus* careful (see CURIOUS), + -OUS; partly f. IN-[3] + CURIOUS *a.*] I Subjectively. 1 Careless, heedless; untroubled. (Foll. by *of.*) *arch.* L16. 2 Uninquiring; devoid of curiosity. E17. †3 Not precise or particular; uncritical; undiscriminating. M17–M18. 4 Not careful in observation; inattentive. L17.

1 CLARENDON In his Cloaths . . , he was not only incurious, but too negligent. 2 DAY LEWIS Too lazy now to conduct . . research, and too incurious. 3 R. HERRICK Base in action as in clothes; Yet . . they will please The incurious villages. 4 J. HENRY Resembles the latter, in the bark and leaf so much, that an incurious eye might be deceived.

II Objectively. †5 Not carefully or exquisitely prepared, made, or done; plain, coarse. E17–E19. †6 Not elaborate or abstruse; simple. *rare.* E–M17. 7 Not remarkable; deficient in interest, not arousing curiosity. M18.

incuriously *adv.* E17. **incuriousness** *n.* E17.

incurrence /ɪnˈkʌr(ə)ns/ *n.* M17. [f. as next: see -ENCE.] The action or fact of incurring liabilities etc.

incurrent /ɪnˈkʌr(ə)nt/ *a.* L16. [L *incurrent-* pres. ppl stem of *incurrere* INCUR: see -ENT.] 1 Orig., falling within (a period). Later, running in; penetrating into the interior. L16. 2 Serving as or providing an entrance. M19.

incursion /ɪnˈkəːʃ(ə)n/ *n.* Also †**en-**. LME. [L *incursio(n-)*, f. *incurs-* pa. ppl stem of *incurrere* INCUR: see -ION.] 1 A hostile invasion; a sudden attack; a raid. LME. 2 The action of running in or running against. E17.

1 N. CHOMSKY Thailand blockaded the Cambodian coast and carried out border incursions. *fig.*: W. PALEY The sudden and critical incursion of the disease. 2 S. JOHNSON The inevitable incursion of new images.

incursive /ɪnˈkəːsɪv/ *a.* L16. [med.L *incursivus*, f. L *incurs-*: see prec. -IVE.] Given to making incursions; aggressive; invasive.

incurvate /ɪnˈkəːvət/ *a.* LME. [L *incurvatus* pa. pple, f. as next: see -ATE[2].] Incurved.

incurvate /ˈɪnkəːveɪt/ *v.* L16. [L *incurvat-* pa. ppl stem of *incurvare* INCURVE *v.*: see -ATE[3]. Cf. prec.] 1 *v.t.* Bring into a curved shape; bend; crook; *spec.* bend or curve inwards. L16. †2 *v.i.* Curve; bend, bow. M–L17.

incurvation /ɪnkəːˈveɪʃ(ə)n/ *n.* E17. [L *incurvatio(n-)*, f. as prec.: see -ATION.] 1 The action or process of bending or curving; an instance of this. E17. †b Bowing in reverence or worship. E17–E18. 2 The condition of being bent; curved formation, curvature; an instance of this. M17. 3 A curving inwards; the condition of being curved inwards. E19.

incurvature /ɪnˈkəːvətʃə/ *n. rare.* E19. [f. as INCURVATE *v.*: see -URE.] A curving inwards; an inward curvature or bend.

incurve /ˈɪnkəːv/ *n.* L19. [f. the vb.] An inward curve; *spec.* in *Baseball* & *Softball*, the curving of a pitched ball inwards (towards the batter), (the course of) a ball pitched so as to curve in this way.

incurve /ɪnˈkəːv/ *v.* LME. [L *incurvare*, f. as IN-[2] + *curvare* CURVE *v.*] 1 *v.t.* Bend into a curve; bend (something) inwards. Freq. as *incurved* ppl a. LME. 2 *v.i.* Curve or bend (inwards). E18.

incus /ˈɪŋkəs/ *n.* Pl. **incudes** /ˈɪŋkjʊdiːz, ɪnˈkjuːdiːz/. M17. [L *incus*, *incud-* anvil (from its shape).] 1 *Anat.* & *Zool.* The middle of the three small bones which conduct sound through the mammalian ear, homologous with the quadrate of reptiles. Cf. MALLEUS, STAPES. M17. 2 *Zool.* In rotifers, a part of the chitinous mouth-apparatus, upon which the mallei work. M19.

incuse /ɪnˈkjuːz/ *a.* & *n.* E19. [L *incusus* pa. pple of *incudere*: see next.] (A figure or an impression on a coin etc.) that has been hammered or stamped in.

incuse /ɪnˈkjuːz/ *v.t.* M19. [L *incus-* pa. ppl stem of *incudere* forge.] Impress (a figure etc.) by stamping; mark (a coin etc.) with an impressed figure.

incut /ˈɪnkʌt/ *a.* L19. [f. IN-[1] + CUT *ppl a.*] Set in (as if) by cutting.

incyst *v.* var. of ENCYST.

indaba /ɪnˈdɑːbə/ *n.* E19. [Zulu *indaɓa* discussion.] 1 A conference between or with members of southern African Black peoples. E19. 2 A person's business, problem, or concern. *S. Afr. colloq.* L20.

indagate /ˈɪndəgeɪt/ *v.t.* Now *rare* or *obs.* E17. [L *indagat-* pa. ppl stem of *indagare* investigate: see -ATE[3].] Search into; investigate.

inda'gation *n.* L16. **indagator** *n.* an investigator E17.

indamine /ˈɪndəmiːn/ *n.* L19. [f. INDO-[2] + AMINE.] *Chem.* A blue dye, $NH_2C_6H_4N{:}C_6H_4{:}NH$; any of various blue and green derivatives of this, used to make safranines.

†**indanger** *v.* var. of ENDANGER.

Indanthrene /ˈɪndanθriːn/ *n.* Also **-en** /-ɛn/, **i-**. L19. [f. INDO-[2] + ANTHR(ACENE + -ENE.] *Chem.* (Proprietary name for) any of a large class of vat dyes derived from or containing indanthrone or other anthraquinone compounds. Also (**i-**), indanthrone.

indanthrone /ˈɪndanθrəʊn/ *n.* E20. [f. prec. + -ONE.] *Chem.* (Any of numerous dyes derived from) a blue aromatic compound, $C_{28}H_{14}N_2O_4$, the molecule of which consists of two anthraquinone nuclei linked by imino groups.

indart /ɪnˈdɑːt/ *v.t.* Also †**endart**. L16. [f. IN-[1], EN-[1] + DART *v.*] Cause to dart in.

indazole /ˈɪndəzəʊl/ *n.* L19. [f. INDO-[2] + AZ(O- + -OLE[2].] *Chem.* (Any derivative of) a crystalline compound, $C_7H_6N_2$, in which a benzene ring is fused to a pyrazole ring.

†indear *v.*, **†indearment** *n.* vars. of ENDEAR, ENDEARMENT.

†indeavour *v.* & *n.* var. of ENDEAVOUR.

Indebele *n.pl.* see NDEBELE.

indebt /ɪnˈdɛt/ *v.t.* L16. [Back-form. f. next, perh. after Fr. *endetter*.] 1 Involve in debt. Chiefly *refl.* L16. 2 Bring under an obligation. E17.

indebted /ɪnˈdɛtɪd/ *a.* Also **†en-**. ME. [f. OFr. *endetté* pa. pple of *endetter* involve in debt, refash. after L (med.L *indebitare*): see IN-[2], DEBT *n.*, -ED[1].] 1 Under obligation to another on account of some liability incurred or claim unsatisfied; liable for some omission of duty etc.; bound. Long *arch. rare.* ME. 2 Under obligation on account of money borrowed; owing money, in debt (*to*). LME. 3 Under obligation for favours etc. received; owing gratitude *to* (someone or something) *for* a benefit. LME.

1 JOSEPH HALL When I have promised, I am indebted; and debts may be claimed, must be paid. 2 **†be indebted** owe (a specified sum). 3 F. MARRYAT They were indebted to him for the situation they hold now in the forest.

indebtedness *n.* (*a*) the condition of being under obligation for services etc. rendered; (*b*) the condition of being in debt; the sum owed: M17. **indebtment** *n.* (*rare*) indebtedness M17.

†indecence *n. rare.* Only in 18. [f. INDECENT (perh. after Fr. *indécence*): see -ENCE.] = INDECENCY 1.

indecency /ɪnˈdiːs(ə)nsi/ *n.* L16. [L *indecentia*, f. *indecent-*: see next, -ENCY.] 1 Unseemliness; unbecoming or outrageous conduct; an instance of this. L16. †2 Unseemliness of form; an instance of this. L16–M17. 3 A quality or condition which offends against recognized standards of decency. Also, an indecent act, an offence against decency. L17.

1 H. SPENCER The indecency of excluding . . the English at the same time that other strangers are received. 2 J. SYLVESTER Th'unpleasing blemish of deformed marks; As lips too great, . . Or sinking nose, or such indecencies. 3 C. DARWIN The hatred of indecency . . is a modern virtue.

indecent /ɪnˈdiːs(ə)nt/ *a.* L16. [(O)Fr. *indécent* or L *indecent-*, f. as IN-[3] + DECENT.] 1 Unbecoming; in extremely bad taste; highly unsuitable. L16. †2 Uncomely, inelegant. L16–M18. 3 Offending against recognized standards of decency; immodest; suggesting or tending to obscenity. E17.

1 J. A. FROUDE It is indecent to owe money to a political antagonist. *Sunday* (*Calcutta*) Most such foundation stones were laid in indecent haste. 2 J. BLAGRAVE His thighs lean, his feet and knees indecent. 3 E. TEMPLETON The nightgown was not made of transparent stuff; this would have been indecent. R. ELLMANN Yeats circulated a testimonial of support for Wilde at the time of the prosecution for indecent behaviour. **indecent assault** a sexual attack not involving rape. *indecent* EXPOSURE.

indecently *adv.* L16. **indecentness** *n.* (*rare*) E18.

indeciduous /ɪndɪˈsɪdjʊəs/ *a.* M17. [f. IN-[3] + DECIDUOUS.] †1 Not liable to be shed; permanently attached. Only in M17. 2 *Bot.* Not deciduous; evergreen. M18.

indecipherable /ɪndɪˈsʌɪf(ə)rəb(ə)l/ *a.* E19. [f. IN-[3] + DECIPHERABLE.] Unable to be deciphered.

indeciphera'bility *n.* L19. **indecipherableness** *n.* E19.

indecision /ɪndɪˈsɪʒ(ə)n/ *n.* M18. [Fr. *indécision*, f. as IN-[3] + DECISION.] Lack of decision; inability to make up one's mind; hesitation. Also (*rare*), an instance of this.

indecisive /ɪndɪˈsʌɪsɪv/ *a.* E18. [f. IN-[3] + DECISIVE. Cf. UNDECISIVE.] 1 Not such as to decide a matter; inconclusive. E18. 2 Characterized by indecision; undecided; hesitating. L18. 3 Uncertain; not definite, indistinct. E19.

1 LD MACAULAY On the Upper Rhine . . an indecisive predatory war was carried on. E. DOWDEN In place of truth he found only a conflict of indecisive reasonings. 2 C. BLACKWOOD Always an indecisive man, he was incapable of either rejecting or accepting their advice. 3 T. HARDY A contrasting prospect eastward, in the shape of indecisive and palpitating stars.

indecisively *adv.* E19. **indecisiveness** *n.* L18.

indeclinable /ɪndɪˈklʌɪnəb(ə)l/ *a.* & *n.* LME. [Fr. *indéclinable* f. L *indeclinabilis*, f. as IN-[3] + *declinare* DECLINE *v.*: see -ABLE.] A *adj.* †1 Undeviating, unchangeable, constant. LME–M17. 2 *Gram.* Unable to be declined; having no inflections. LME. B *n. Gram.* An indeclinable word. M16.

indeclinableness *n.* M17. **indeclinably** *adv.* E17.

indecomposable /ˌɪndiːkəmˈpəʊzəb(ə)l/ *a.* E19. [f. IN-[3] + DECOMPOSABLE.] Unable to be decomposed.

indecomposa'bility *n.* M20.

indecorous /ɪnˈdɛk(ə)rəs/ *a.* L17. [f. L *indecorus*, f. as IN-[3] + DECOROUS, + -OUS.] †1 Unbecoming, inappropriate. Only in L17. 2 Lacking decorum or propriety; improper; in bad taste. Also (*rare*), immodest, indecent. L17.

2 M. SINCLAIR Quietly, and with no indecorous haste, she went . . into the drawing-room to receive Rawcliffe. W. S. CHURCHILL Stories of keyholes, of indecorous costumes and gestures, regaled the public ear.

indecorously *adv.* E19. **indecorousness** *n.* L17.

indecorum /ɪndɪˈkɔːrəm/ *n.* L16. [L, use as n. of neut. sing. of *indecorus* adj.: see prec.] 1 An indecorous action or proceeding; an offence against recognized standards of behaviour. L16. 2 The quality of being indecorous; lack of decorum; improper behaviour. M17.

1 G. GROTE This was a flagrant indecorum, and known violation of the order of the festival. 2 A. BELL A general improvement in public behaviour helped to prevent any further general indecorum.

indeed /ɪnˈdiːd/ *adv.* Orig. two wds. ME. [f. IN *prep.* + DEED *n.* See also *in deed* s.v. DEED *n.*] I 1 In truth, really; *postpositive* definitely, without doubt. ME. 2 In reality; in real nature etc. as opp. to what is merely apparent. LME. 3 In point of fact, as a matter of fact. M16. 4 Admittedly. M16. 5 In speech, expr. an emphasized (affirmative or negative) reply or response. L16. b With approving or ironic echo. M18. 6 (*interrog.*) Really? Is it so? L16.

1 L. MORRIS Amid the crowd of youths He showed a Prince indeed. D. H. LAWRENCE He was indeed a brave man. S. BEDFORD Melanie's sister was very ill indeed. **indeed and indeed** *arch. colloq.* really and truly. 2 L. MORRIS The Muses' Eyes, who were indeed Women, though god-like. 3 D. DU MAURIER John . . might leave the cups till morning to be washed, as indeed he had. 4 J. T. FOWLER Latin, not classical indeed, but good of its kind. 5 R. LEHMANN 'Poor fellow. You give him my greetings.' . . 'I will indeed'. b DISRAELI 'Who is this Mr. Grey?' 'Who, indeed!' 6 DICKENS 'That's Jarsper's.' 'Indeed?' said Mr Datchery.

II 7 As *int.* Expr. irony, contempt, incredulity, etc. M19.

7 J. RUSKIN Damask curtains indeed! That's all very fine. B. JOWETT 'O, indeed,' I said, 'what a wonderful thing, and what a great blessing!'

indeedy *adv.* (*colloq.*, chiefly *N. Amer.*) = INDEED *adv.* 5 M19.

indefatigable /ɪndɪˈfatɪɡəb(ə)l/ *a.* E17. [Fr. †*indéfatigable* (now *infatigable*) or L *indefatigabilis*, f. as IN-[3] + DE- + *fatigare* exhaust: see -ABLE.] Unable to be wearied or tired out; untiring; unremitting in effort.

C. CHAPLIN The American is . . an indefatigable tryer. P. GAY His indefatigable efforts to secure the guardianship.

indefatiga'bility *n.* M17. **indefatigableness** *n.* M17. **indefatigably** *adv.* L16.

indefeasible /ɪndɪˈfiːzɪb(ə)l/ *a.* M16. [f. IN-[3] + DEFEASIBLE.] (Esp. of a claim, right, etc.) not liable to be made void; unable to be forfeited or annulled.

indefeasi'bility *n.* E19. **indefeasibleness** *n.* (*rare*) M18. **indefeasibly** *adv.* M16.

indefectible /ɪndɪˈfɛktɪb(ə)l/ *a.* M17. [f. IN-[3] + DEFECTIBLE.] 1 Not liable to failure or decay; that cannot fall short or be destroyed. M17. 2 Not subject to defect; faultless. M19.

indefecti'bility *n.* E17. **indefectibly** *adv.* (*rare*) M19.

†indefective *a.* M17–E18. [med.L *indefectivus*, f. as IN-[3] + late L *defectivus* DEFECTIVE.] Free from defect; faultless, flawless.

indefensible /ɪndɪˈfɛnsɪb(ə)l/ *a.* E16. [f. IN-[3] + DEFENSIBLE.] 1 Unable to be defended or maintained in argument; unjustifiable. E16. 2 Incapable of being defended by armed force. M16.

1 A. LURIE To do that would be both morally and practically indefensible. 2 J. A. MICHENER Barbarians were free to come storming across their indefensible eastern frontier.

indefensi'bility *n.* E19. **indefensibleness** *n.* L17. **indefensibly** *adv.* L18.

†indeficient *a.* L15–M19. [Fr. †*indéficient* or late L *indeficient-*, f. as IN-[3] + DEFICIENT.] Unfailing, unceasing.

†indeficiency *n.* E17–M18. **†indeficiently** *adv.* LME–E17.

indefinable /ɪndɪˈfʌɪnəb(ə)l/ *a.* & *n.* L17. [f. IN-[3] + DEFINABLE.] A *adj.* Unable to be defined or exactly described; not susceptible of definition. L17.

H. STURGIS There was that indefinable sense of spring in the air.

B *n.* An indefinable person or thing. E19.

indefina'bility *n.* E20. **indefinableness** *n.* L19. **indefinably** *adv.* M19.

indefinite /ɪnˈdɛfɪnɪt/ *a.* & *n.* M16. [L *indefinitus*, f. as IN-[3] + DEFINITE *a.*] A *adj.* I 1 Having no clearly determined being or character; indeterminate, vague, undefined. M16. 2 Of undetermined extent, amount, or number; unlimited. L16. †b Boundless, infinite. M17–M18.

1 O. MANNING The smudge, pale and indefinite at first, deepened in colour. B. EMECHETA He had to be satisfied with that indefinite answer. 2 U. BENTLEY She had been taken into a nursing home for an indefinite period.

II *spec.* 3 *Gram.* Of a word or tense: not defining or determining the thing, place, time, or manner to which it refers. M16. 4 *Logic.* Of a proposition: having no mark of quantity, not distinguishing between some and all. M16. 5 *Bot.* a Of stamens or other floral parts: too numerous to be easily counted. M19. b Of an inflorescence etc.: racemose and capable of continued (axial) growth. M19.

Special collocations: **indefinite article** the individualizing adjective *a*, *an*, or its equivalents in other languages. **indefinite integral** *Math.* an integral expressed without limits and hence containing an indeterminate additive constant.

B *n.* An indefinite thing, word, statement, etc.; a thing of indefinite nature or meaning, or which cannot be classed, specified, or defined. L16.

indefinitely *adv.* (*a*) to an indefinite extent, for an indefinite period; (*b*) in an indefinite manner, without specification, vaguely: LME. **indefiniteness** *n.* L16.

indefinition /ˌɪndɛfɪˈnɪʃ(ə)n/ *n.* L19. [f. IN-[3] + DEFINITION.] A condition of being indefinite.

indefinitive /ɪndɪˈfɪnɪtɪv/ *a. rare.* L16. [f. IN-[3] + DEFINITIVE *a.*] Not definitive; indeterminate.

indefinitude /ɪndɪˈfɪnɪtjuːd/ *n.* L17. [f. INDEFINITE after *infinite*, *infinitude*.] †1 The condition of having no known limit; indefinable number or amount. Only in L17. 2 Lack of definiteness or precision; undefined state. E19.

indefinity /ɪndɪˈfɪnɪti/ *n. rare.* E17. [f. INDEFINITE after *infinite*, *infinity*.] †1 = INDEFINITUDE 1. Only in 17. 2 = INDEFINITUDE 2. M18.

indeformable /ɪndɪˈfɔːməb(ə)l/ *a.* L19. [f. IN-[3] + DEFORMABLE.] Not deformable; unable to be put out of shape.

indehiscent /ɪndɪˈhɪs(ə)nt/ *a.* E19. [f. IN-[3] + DEHISCENT.] *Bot.* Of a fruit: not dehiscent, not splitting open to release the seed.

indehiscence *n.* M19.

indelectable /ɪndɪˈlɛktəb(ə)l/ *a. rare.* M18. [f. IN-[3] + DELECTABLE.] Unpleasant, disagreeable.

indeliberate /ɪndɪˈlɪb(ə)rət/ *a.* Now *rare.* E17. [f. IN-[3] + DELIBERATE *a.*] †1 Of a person, quality, etc.: lacking in deliberation; rash. Only in 17. 2 Of an action: done without deliberation or forethought; hasty; spontaneous. M17.

indeliberately *adv.* L17. **indelibe'ration** *n.* E17.

indelible /ɪnˈdɛlɪb(ə)l/ *a.* L15. [Fr. *indélébile* or L *indelebilis*, f. as IN-[3] + DELIBLE.] Unable to be deleted, blotted out, or effaced (*lit.* & *fig.*); permanent; (of ink, a pencil, etc.) that makes permanent marks.

C. DARWIN Man still bears in his bodily frame the indelible stamp of his lowly origin. J. C. POWYS The striking originality . . of the young servant had made an indelible impression upon the peer's mind. W. S. CHURCHILL The King . . bears the indelible shame of the deed. G. PRIESTLAND A priest has private and indelible powers to celebrate the Mass.

indeli'bility *n.* (*rare*) E19. **indelibly** *adv.* E17.

indelicate /ɪn'dɛlɪkət/ *a.* M18. [f. IN-³ + DELICATE.] 1 Lacking in or offensive to a sense of delicacy or propriety; coarse; indecent. M18. †2 Of food: coarse. M–L18. 3 Lacking in tact or regard for the feelings of others. E19.

indelicacy *n.* E18. **indelicately** *adv.* E19.

indemnify /ɪn'dɛmnɪfʌɪ/ *v.t.* E17. [f. L *indemnis* unhurt + -FY. Cf. med.L *indemnificare*.] 1 Preserve, protect, or keep free *from*, secure *against* (harm or loss); secure against legal responsibility for events; give an indemnity to. E17. 2 Compensate *for* loss suffered, expenses incurred, disadvantages, annoyances, hardships, etc. L17. †3 Make up for. Only in M18.

1 W. BLACKSTONE The fact indemnified the peace officers . . if they killed any of the mob in endeavouring to suppress such riot. 2 BURKE One way of indemnifying one's self for the plainness of one's habit. H. L. MENCKEN The man who has been injured should be indemnified for all his expenses.

indemnifi'cation *n.* (*a*) the action or fact of being indemnified; (*b*) a payment or other recompense so made: M17. **indemnifier** *n.* L19.

indemnity /ɪn'dɛmnɪti/ *n.* LME. [(O)Fr. *indemnité* f. late L *indemnitas*, f. *indemnis* free from loss or hurt, f. as IN-³ + *damnum*: see DAMAGE *n.*, -ITY.] 1 (An undertaking to provide) security or protection against hurt, damage, or loss. LME. 2 Compensation for loss or damage incurred; indemnification. LME. b A sum paid as compensation, orig. & formerly *spec.* to a bishop or archdeacon for losses incurred when a church was impropriated to an abbey etc. Now *esp.*, a payment exacted by a victorious belligerent as a condition of peace. M16. 3 A legal exemption from the penalties or liabilities incurred by a course of action. L17.

Phrases: **act of indemnity** a parliamentary etc. act granting exemption from the penalties attached to any unconstitutional or illegal proceeding. *double indemnity*: see DOUBLE *a.* & *adv.*

indemonstrable /ɪndɪ'mɒnstrəb(ə)l, ɪn'dɛmən-/ *a.* L16. [f. IN-³ + DEMONSTRABLE.] Unable to be demonstrated or proved; *esp.* primary, axiomatic.

indemonstra'bility *n.* L18. **indemonstrably** *adv.* M17.

indene /'ɪndiːn/ *n.* L19. [f. IND(OLE + -ENE.] *Chem.* A colourless liquid bicyclic aromatic hydrocarbon, C_9H_8, which is obtained from coal tar and is an intermediate in the manufacture of synthetic resins etc.; any derivative of this.

indent /ɪn'dɛnt, 'ɪndɛnt/ *n.*¹ L15. [f. INDENT *v.*¹] 1 = INDENTURE *n.* 2. L15. b A certificate of a money claim; *spec.* an indented certificate issued by a government for the principal or interest due on the public debt. *obs.* exc. *Hist.* L18. 2 An incision in the edge of a thing; a deep angular recess. L16. 3 An official requisition for stores. L18. 4 An order for goods, *esp.* (*Hist.*) one sent to Britain from abroad. E19. 5 An indention in printing or writing; an indented line. L19.

indent /'ɪndɛnt/ *n.*² L17. [f. INDENT *v.*²] A dent or depression in a surface.

indent /ɪn'dɛnt/ *v.*¹ LME. [AN *endenter*, med.L *indentare*, f. as IN-² + L *dent-*, *dens* tooth.] I 1 a *v.t.* Make a toothlike incision or incisions in the edge of; notch; give a zigzag outline to. LME. b *v.t.* Form a deep recess or recesses in (a coastline etc.); penetrate deeply. M16. c *v.i.* Recede, form a recess. L18. †2 *v.i.* Move in a zigzag or serrated line; turn from side to side in one's course. M16–M17. 3 *v.t.* Set inward from the margin of the column the beginning of (one or more lines of writing or type); begin (a line etc.) with a blank space. L17. 4 *v.t.* Make an incision in (a board, etc.) for the purpose of mortising or dovetailing; join together by this method. M18.

1 R. TATE Five longitudinal ribs which indent the edges of the plate. b A. TREW The southern side was heavily indented by the bay at Uklarvik, and by Kolfjord. c G. GROTE At the spot here mentioned, the gulf indents eastward. 2 SHAKES. *Ven. & Ad.* See the dew-bedabbled wretch Turn, and return, indenting with the way. 3 J. MOXON You must indent your Line four Spaces at least. S. CURRAN Outline tabs let you indent the first line of paragraphs automatically.

II 5 *v.t.* Cut (a document drawn up in duplicate) with a zigzag, wavy, or other line, so that the two parts exactly tally; draw up (a document) in two or more corresponding copies. LME. †6 *v.i.* Enter into an engagement by indentures; make a formal agreement; covenant (*with* a person *for* a thing). L15–L18. †7 *v.t.* Contract for, bind oneself to, or promise (as) by making indentures; stipulate, promise. M16–L18. †b Engage (a person) as a servant etc. (as) by indentures. L18–E19. 8 *v.i.* Make out a written order with a duplicate or counterfoil; make a requisition (*up*)*on* a person *for* a thing. E19. 9 *v.t.* Order by an indent; order a supply of (a commodity). L19.

6 GOLDSMITH I fire with indignation when I see persons wholly destitute of . . genius indent to the press, and thus turn book-makers. 7 P. HOLLAND He would not indent ought for his owne securitie. 8 A. BURGESS You will indent for further supplies . . through Dr. Hazard.

†**indentment** *n.* L16–E18.

indent /ɪn'dɛnt/ *v.*² LME. [f. IN-² + DENT *v.*] †1 *v.t.* Inlay, set, emboss. LME–M18. 2 *v.t.* Form as a dent or depression; strike or force inwards so as to form a dent or hollow; imprint by pressure. LME. 3 *v.t.* Make a dent in the surface of (a thing); mark with a surface hollow. L16. 4 *v.i.* Receive or take an indentation; become indented. M17.

2 DRYDEN Deep Scars were seen indented on his Breast. POPE Deep in the neck his fangs indent their hold. 3 DICKENS Mr. Pickwick . . indenting his pillow with a tremendous blow. E. BOWEN His nose poked slyly out between two of the rails and the same two rails indented his forehead.

indentation /ɪndɛn'teɪʃ(ə)n/ *n.* E18. [f. INDENT *v.*¹, *v.*² + -ATION.] I f. INDENT *v.*¹ 1 A cut, notch, or angular incision in an edge; a deep recess in a coastline; a series of incisions. E18. 2 The action of indenting; the condition of being indented. M19. 3 = INDENTION 2. M19.

1 H. T. BUCKLE The Greek coast is full of indentations. H. JACOBSON A faint fetching indentation in her left nostril which intrigued me. 2 F. HEATH The indentation assuming various shapes, often being deeply incised. 3 *hanging indentation*: see HANGING *a.*

II f. INDENT *v.*² 4 The action of impressing so as to form a dent; a depression thus formed; a deep depression in a surface. M19.

4 *Times* Injurious compression of . . soil, by the indentation of its wheels. E. O'BRIEN The . . goblets . . have beautiful indentations to fit exactly the print of a thumb or a finger.

Comb.: **indentation hardness**: as determined by an indentation test; **indentation test**: for determining the hardness of a solid by making an indentation in a sample under standard conditions and measuring its size or the distance moved by the indenter.

indented /ɪn'dɛntɪd/ *ppl a.* LME. [f. INDENT *v.*¹, *v.*² + -ED¹.] I f. INDENT *v.*¹ 1 Having the edge or margin cut with angular incisions; deeply or strongly serrated. LME. b Having a serrated or zigzag figure, direction, or course; constructed with salient and re-entrant angles. L16. 2 *Her.* Of an ordinary etc.: having a series of toothlike indentations or notches. LME. 3 Of a legal document: cut zigzag or wavy at the top or edge; cut into counterparts by a zigzag line. LME. 4 Bound or engaged by an indenture or formal covenant. M18. 5 (Of type or writing) set inward so as to break the line of the margin. M19. II f. INDENT *v.*² 6 Impressed, forced in so as to make a hollow in a surface. Also, marked with depressions or dents. M17.

indenter /ɪn'dɛntə/ *n.* Also **-or**. M17. [f. INDENT *v.*¹, *v.*² + -ER¹, -OR.] I f. INDENT *v.*¹ 1 A person who orders something by indent. M17. II f. INDENT *v.*² 2 A thing which produces indentations; *spec.* a small hard object used for producing an indentation in a solid (as in an indentation test). E20.

indenting /ɪn'dɛntɪŋ/ *n.* LME. [f. INDENT *v.*¹, *v.*² + -ING ¹.] I f. INDENT *v.*¹ 1 = INDENTATION 1, 2. LME. 2 The making of an indenture or indent. LME. II f. INDENT *v.*² 3 = INDENTATION 4. L16. †4 Inlaying or embossing; inlaid work. Only in M18.

indention /ɪn'dɛnʃ(ə)n/ *n.* M18. [Irreg. f. INDENT *v.*¹, *v.*² + -ION.] I f. INDENT *v.*¹ 1 = INDENTATION 1, 2. M18. 2 The indenting of a line etc. in printing or writing; the leaving of a blank space at the beginning of a line at the commencement of a new paragraph. E19.

2 *hanging indention*: see HANGING *a.*

II f. INDENT *v.*² 3 = INDENTATION 4. *rare*. M19.

indentor *n.* var. of INDENTER.

indenture /ɪn'dɛntʃə/ *n.* LME. [Branch I f. AN *endenture* f. med.L *indentura*, f. *indentatus* pa. pple of *indentare*: see INDENT *v.*¹, -URE; branch II f. INDENT *v.*²] I 1 †a Jointing by means of notches or indentations. Only in LME. b The action of indenting or notching an edge; an incision, indentation, or notch on the edge of a thing. L17. 2 A deed between two or more parties with mutual covenants executed in copies which all have their edges indented for identification; a sealed agreement or contract. LME. b A contract by which an apprentice is bound to a master. Formerly also, a contract by which a person was bound to service in the British colonies. LME. c An official or formal list, inventory, certificate, voucher, etc., orig. one prepared in duplicate. LME. d *fig.* A contract; (a) mutual agreement. M16. †3 A zigzag line or course; a doubling back. L16–L18.

2b **take up one's indentures** receive one's indentures back on completion of apprenticeship.

II †4 An inlaying or embossing. Only in M17. 5 A hollow or depression in a surface. L18.

indentureship *n.* the position of being indentured as an apprentice, servant, etc. L19.

indenture /ɪn'dɛntʃə/ *v.* M17. [f. the n.] †1 *v.i.* Move in a zigzag line. Only in M17. †2 *v.i.* Enter into an indenture; covenant. Only in M17. 3 *v.t.* Bind by indentures, esp. as an apprentice. Freq. as *indentured* ppl a. M17. 4 *v.t.* Make an indentation in; indent. L18.

independable /ɪndɪ'pɛndəb(ə)l/ *a.* E19. [f. IN-³ + DEPENDABLE.] Not dependable; untrustworthy.

independence /ɪndɪ'pɛnd(ə)ns/ *n.* M17. [f. INDEPENDENT *a.*, partly after Fr. *indépendance*: see -ENCE.] 1 The condition or quality of being independent. M17. 2 An income sufficient to relieve one from the need to earn one's living. E19.

1 W. STUBBS The proud independence of the Percies was becoming . . a source of danger. C. IVES Americans . . still have enough independence of thought . . to work out their own way of progress. LYNDON B. JOHNSON The new West African republic of Senegal was celebrating its independence. *Declaration of Independence*: see DECLARATION 4. 2 THACKERAY You are heir to a little independence.

Comb.: **Independence Day** a day celebrating the anniversary of national independence; *esp.* 4 July in the US, commemorating the making of the Declaration of Independence in 1776.

independency /ɪndɪ'pɛnd(ə)nsi/ *n.* E17. [f. as prec. + -ENCY.] 1 = INDEPENDENCE 1. Now *rare*. E17. 2 *Chr. Ch.* (**I-**.) The principle that each local congregation is autonomous and responsible to God alone; *spec.* Congregationalism. Now *Hist.* M17. 3 = INDEPENDENCE 2. M18. 4 An autonomous State. E19.

independent /ɪndɪ'pɛnd(ə)nt/ *a.*, *n.*, & *adv.* E17. [f. IN-³ + DEPENDENT *n.*, *a.*, partly after Fr. *indépendant*.] A *adj.* 1 Not subject to the authority or control of any person, country, etc.; free to act as one pleases, autonomous. (Foll. by *of*.) E17. 2 a Not dependent or contingent on something else for its existence, validity, effectiveness, etc. Foll. by *of*, †*on*. E17. b Not influenced or affected by others; (of an inquiry, audit, investigator, observer, etc.) (carried out by people) outside the organization concerned. L18. 3 *Chr. Ch.* (**I-**.) Believing in or practising Independency; *spec.* Congregational. Now *Hist.* M17. 4 Not dependent on another for financial support; *spec.* rich enough not to need to earn one's living. L17. b Of income: sufficient to make one financially independent. Esp. in *independent means*. L18. 5 Not influenced by others in one's opinions or conduct; thinking or acting for oneself. M18. b That is an independent in politics; not attached to any particular party. L19. c Refusing to become indebted to others for help. L19. 6 *Math.* a (Of one of a set of axioms, equations, or quantities) incapable of being expressed in terms of, or derived or deduced from, the others; (of a set) consisting of such axioms etc. M18. b Not depending on another quantity for its value. M19.

1 ADAM SMITH An independent workman, such as a weaver or shoe-maker. E. R. PITMAN In 1829, Greece was acknowledged as an independent state, having its own king. H. J. LASKI The Church is independent of all civil institution. 2a STEELE Beauty and Merit are Things real, and independent on Taste and Opinion. H. MOORE It has a life of its own, independent of the object it represents. b J. A. H. MURRAY Here four independent witnesses . . confirm each other. 4 G. GISSING What I inherited . . makes me independent; there is no need of any arrangements about money. 5 R. COBDEN An independent and energetic man who will vote as he pleases. c OED The widow . . is very independent, and refuses all pecuniary aid.

Special collocations: **Independent Broadcasting Authority** a UK corporation which superseded the Independent Television Authority in 1972 and also took responsibility for commercial sound broadcasting. **independent float** in critical path analysis, the amount of leeway which can occur in any one activity without affecting the overall timing. **Independent Labour Party**: founded by Keir Hardie in 1893, orig. to coordinate efforts to secure parliamentary representation for labour unions, independent of Liberal support. **independent school**: that receives no grant from the Government and is not subject to the control of a local authority. **independent suspension** (in motor vehicles etc.) a form of suspension in which each wheel is supported independently of the others. **independent television** the television service controlled by the Independent Television (or Broadcasting) Authority; *Independent Television (Authority)*, a corporation, free of direct government control and not financed by licence fees, which until 1972 supervised commercial television broadcasting in Britain. **independent variable** *Math.*: whose variation does not depend on that of another.

B *n.* 1 *Chr. Ch.* (**I-**.) A member of an Independent church; *spec.* a Congregationalist. Now *Hist.* M17. 2 A person who or thing which is independent; *esp.* a retailer whose shop is not part of a chain. L17. b A politician etc. who is not attached to any particular party. Also in names of newspapers. E19.

C *adv.* Independently or irrespective *of.* Formerly also, apart *from.* L17.

G. GROTE Quite independent of regard to the feelings of others.

independentism *n.* the principles of a person independent in politics or religion; *spec.* (**I-**) = INDEPENDENCY 2: M17. **independently** *adv.* M17.

indeprivable /ɪndɪˈpraɪvəb(ə)l/ *a.* Now *rare.* M18. [f. IN-[3] + DEPRIVABLE.] Of which one cannot be deprived; that cannot be taken away.

indescribable /ɪndɪˈskraɪbəb(ə)l/ *a.* & *n.* L18. [f. IN-[3] + DESCRIBABLE.] A *adj.* 1 That cannot be described; indefinite, vague. L18. 2 That is beyond description; too beautiful, terrible, etc., to be adequately described. L18.

1 QUILLER-COUCH A bald-headed man with hairy hands . . and the indescribable air of a matrimonial agent. 2 A. J. P. TAYLOR It gave me a decade of intense, almost indescribable misery.

B *n.* Something that cannot be described; *spec.* in *pl.* (*obs. slang*), trousers. L18.

indescribaˈbility *n.* (*a*) the quality of being indescribable; (*b*) an indescribable thing: E19. **indescribableness** *n.* (*rare*) L19. **indescribably** *adv.* L18.

indesert /ɪndɪˈzəːt/ *n.* Now *rare.* E17. [f. IN-[3] + DESERT *n.*[1]] 1 In *pl.* Faults. E17. 2 Lack of merit. M17.

indesignate /ɪnˈdɛzɪgnət/ *a.* *arch.* M19. [f. IN-[3] + DESIGNATE *a.*] *Logic.* Not quantified; indefinite.

†**indesinent** *a.* E17–L18. [f. IN-[3] + L *desinent-* pres. ppl stem of *desinere* leave off: see -ENT.] Unceasing, perpetual.

†**indesinently** *adv.* L16–M18.

indestructible /ɪndɪˈstrʌktɪb(ə)l/ *a.* & *n.* L17. [f. IN-[3] + DESTRUCTIBLE.] A *adj.* Impossible to destroy. L17. B *n.* An indestructible thing. M19.

indestructiˈbility *n.* L17. **indestructibleness** *n.* M19. **indestructibly** *adv.* M19.

indetectable /ɪndɪˈtɛktəb(ə)l/ *a.* M19. [f. IN-[3] + DETECTABLE.] Impossible to detect; too slight to be detected.

Also **indetectible** *a.* M19.

indeterminable /ɪndɪˈtəːmɪnəb(ə)l/ *a.* L15. [Late L *indeterminabilis*, f. as IN-[3] + *determinabilis* finite: see DETERMINABLE.] †1 Unable to be limited in respect of range, number, etc. *rare.* L15–L17. 2 Of a dispute, difficulty, etc.: unable to be decided. E17. 3 Unable to be established or ascertained definitely. M17. b *Biol.* Of which the species etc. cannot be determined. M19.

indeterminableness *n.* (*rare*) L19. **indeterminably** *adv.* in an indeterminable or (formerly) indefinite manner L15.

indeterminacy /ɪndɪˈtəːmɪnəsi/ *n.* M17. [f. next + -ACY.] The quality of being indeterminate; lack of definiteness.

indeterminacy principle, **principle of indeterminacy** *Physics* = UNCERTAINTY *principle.*

indeterminate /ɪndɪˈtəːmɪnət/ *a.* LME. [Late L *indeterminatus*, f. as IN-[3] + DETERMINATE *a.*] †1 Not marked or specified. Only in LME. 2 Not fixed in extent, amount, character, etc.; of uncertain size etc.; indefinite. E17. b *Math.* Of an equation: having an unlimited number of solutions. Of a quantity: having no definite value; having no definable value (as 0/0, ∞ – ∞, etc.). E18. c Of a statement, word, etc.: vague, lacking in precision. L18. d *Engin.* = HYPERSTATIC. Usu. w. *statically*. E20. 3 Not fixed or established; uncertain. E17. 4 Not settled or decided. M17. 5 Not determined by motives; acting freely. M19.

2 V. WOOLF All were dressed in indeterminate shades of grey and brown. A. BROOKNER A lady of indeterminate age, her hair radiantly ash blonde, her nails scarlet. c H. WILSON The evidence is scrappy and indeterminate, partly because of the informal nature of Cabinet proceedings. 3 W. H. PRESCOTT The place of its sittings, before indeterminate . . was fixed at Valladolid.

Special collocations: **indeterminate sentence**: that leaves the date of a prisoner's release dependent on his or her conduct and progress. **indeterminate vowel** the obscure vowel /ə/ heard in '*a* moment *ago*'; = SCHWA.

indeterminately *adv.* (*a*) vaguely, indefinitely; †(*b*) without distinction, indifferently: L16. **indeterminateness** *n.* M17.

indetermination /ɪndɪtəːmɪˈneɪʃ(ə)n/ *n.* E17. [f. prec. + -ATION.] †1 An indeterminate number or quantity. Only in E17. 2 Undetermined or unsettled quality or condition; uncertainty. M17.

indetermined /ɪndɪˈtəːmɪnd/ *a.* Now *rare.* E17. [f. IN-[3] + DETERMINED *a.*] Not determined, fixed, or decided; indeterminate.

indeterminism /ɪndɪˈtəːmɪnɪz(ə)m/ *n.* L19. [f. IN-[3] + DETERMINISM.] 1 The theory that human action is not wholly determined by motives. L19. 2 = INDETERMINACY. E20.

indeterminist *n.* & *a.* (*a*) *n.* a holder of the doctrine of indeterminism; (*b*) *adj.* of, pertaining to, or holding the doctrine of indeterminism: L19. **indetermiˈnistic** *a.* E20.

†**indevirginate** *a.* *rare.* E17–E19. [f. IN-[3] + obs. pa. pple of DEVIRGINATE.] Virgin; unsullied.

†**indevoted** *a.* M17–M18. [f. IN-[3] + DEVOTED *a.*] Disloyal (*to*), disaffected.

indevotion /ɪndɪˈvəʊʃ(ə)n/ *n.* E16. [f. IN-[3] + DEVOTION.] Lack of (religious) devotion; indevout feeling or conduct.

indevout /ɪndɪˈvaʊt/ *a.* LME. [f. IN-[3] + DEVOUT: orig. tr. late L *indevotus*, f. as IN-[3] + L *devotus*: see DEVOUT.] Lacking in religious spirit; not devout.

indevoutly *adv.* L17. **indevoutness** *n.* M19.

index /ˈɪndɛks/ *n.* Pl. **indexes**, (esp. *techn.*) **indices** /ˈɪndɪsiːz/. LME. [L *index*, *indic-* forefinger, informer, etc., f. as IN-[2] + *-dex*, *-dic-*, f. base repr. by *dicere* say, Gk *deiknunai* show.] 1 The finger used in pointing, the forefinger. Now usu. *index finger*. LME. b *Ornith.* The second (occas. the first) digit of the manus in a bird's wing. L19. 2 A piece of wood, metal, etc., which serves as a pointer; *spec.* (in a scientific instrument) a pointer which moves along a graduated scale so as to show movements or amounts. L16. b The arm of a surveying instrument; an alidade. L16. c A hand of a clock or watch; the gnomon of a sundial. Now *rare.* L16. 3 A thing which serves to point *to* a fact or conclusion; a sign or indication *of.* L16. 4 A list of things in (usu. alphabetical) order; *esp.* a list, usu. at the end of a book, giving the names, topics, etc., mentioned in the book and the places where they occur. Formerly also, a table of contents. L16. 5†a *Mus.* = DIRECT *n.* 2. L16–M19. b *Typogr.* A hand-shaped symbol with a pointing finger used to draw attention to a note etc. Also called *fist.* E18. 6 *Math.* a A subscript or superscript symbol denoting some characteristic of a quantity or function, as the exponent in x^2, etc. L17. †b The integral part of a logarithm. L17–E19. c *Computing.* A quantity which is fixed in relation to the operations laid down by a program, but which takes a prescribed sequence of values as the program is run. M20. d *Computing.* Any of a sequence of numbers, each specifying one of an ordered set of items. M20. 7 A number or formula expressing a specific property, esp. a ratio; *esp.* in *Anat.*, a formula expressing the ratio between two dimensions (esp. of the skull). E19. 8 *Econ.* (A number in) a scale relating (usu. in the form of a percentage) the level of prices, wages, etc., at a particular time to those at a date taken as a base. L19. 9 *Engin.* Each of the predetermined movements during indexing. M20.

3 M. HOLROYD Her letters . . are a good index to her state of mind. CLIVE JAMES A town where the index of all achievement is to have your name in lights. *card index*: see CARD *n.*[2] **Expurgatory Index** = *Index Expurgatorius* below. **Index Expurgatorius** /ˌɛkspəːgəˈtɔːrɪəs/ [L = expurgatory] *RC Ch.* (now *Hist.*) a list of passages to be deleted from a book before it was considered fit for reading; a list of authors considered fit to read only after the removal of objectionable matter from their works, later included in the *Index Librorum Prohibitorum*. **Index Librorum Prohibitorum** /lɪˈbrɔːrəm ˌprəʊhɪbɪˈtɔːrəm/ [L = of forbidden books] *RC Ch.* (now *Hist.*) an official list of heretical or otherwise undesirable books forbidden to the faithful or sanctioned only after the removal of objectionable passages. **the Index** = *Index Librorum Prohibitorum* above. 7 *cephalic index*: see CEPHALIC *a.* *refractive index*: see REFRACTIVE 4. *wind-chill index*: see WIND *n.*[1] 8 *cost-of-living index*, *retail price index*, etc.

Comb.: *index finger*: see sense 1 above; **index fossil** a fossil that is useful for dating and correlating the strata in which it is found; also called *guide fossil*; **index-link** *v.t.* adjust the value of (a pension etc.) to the level of the cost-of-living index; **index-linked** *a.* (of a pension, bond, etc.) of which the value is adjusted in line with the cost-of-living index, to offset the effects of inflation; **index number** (*a*) = sense 8 above; (*b*) a number in an index; *esp.* a vehicle registration number; **index register** *Computing* a register whose contents may be added to or subtracted from the address portion of an instruction before execution, which is thus increased or decreased by a prescribed amount, enabling the instruction to be used repeatedly on different operands.

indexless *a.* (of a book etc.) lacking an index M19.

index /ˈɪndɛks/ *v.* E18. [f. the n.] 1 *v.t.* Provide (a book etc.) with an index; enter (an item) in an index. E18. 2 *v.t.* Serve as an index to; indicate. L18. 3 *v.t.* *RC Ch.* (now *Hist.*). Place (a book) on the *Index Librorum Prohibitorum*. E19. 4 *v.t.* & *i.* *Engin.* Move (esp. by partial rotation) from one predetermined position to another, in order that an operation may be repeated at different locations, or different operations performed; obtain (a desired number of divisions or operations) thus. E20. 5 *v.t.* *Computing.* Modify (an instruction or its address) by causing the addition of the contents of an index register to the address before execution; carry out (a series of operations) by this means. M20.

indexable *a.* M20. **indeˈxation** *n.* adjustment in rates of payment etc. to reflect variations in the cost-of-living index or other economic indicator M20. **indexer** *n.* a person who compiles an index to a book etc. M19. **indexible** *a.* M20.

indexical /ɪnˈdɛksɪk(ə)l/ *a.* E19. [Irreg. f. INDEX *n.* + -ICAL.] Arranged like or relating to the index of a book etc.

indexically *adv.* in the manner of an index, alphabetically E18.

indi- /ˈɪndi/ *comb. form.* [f. INDIGO.] *Chem.* Derived from or related to indigo.

indiˈrubin *n.* a red crystalline substance, $C_{16}H_{10}O_2N_2$, resembling indigotin but with oxidized indolyl rather than indoxyl nuclei M19.

India /ˈɪndɪə/ *n.* M17. [A subcontinent, and a country occupying much of that subcontinent, in southern Asia.] **1** Used *attrib.* to designate things made in, associated with, or imported from the subcontinent of India, or the present Republic of India, or (*Hist.*) pertaining to the East India Company or the government of India under British rule (1858–1947). Cf. INDIAN *a.* 1. M17. **2** *ellipt.* India paper, India silk, etc. E18.

1 India House *Hist.* the office of the East India Company in London. **India ink** (now *N. Amer.*) = *Indian ink* s.v. INDIAN *a.* **India Office** *Hist.* the department of the British Government dealing with Indian affairs. **India paper** (*a*) a thin paper orig. imported from China, used for high quality prints and illustrations; (*b*) a thin tough opaque printing-paper, used esp. for bibles. **India proof** an artist's or engraver's proof specially printed on India paper. See also INDIARUBBER.

indialite /ˈɪndɪəlʌɪt/ *n.* M20. [f. prec. + -LITE.] *Min.* The hexagonal dimorphous form of cordierite.

Indiaman /ˈɪndɪəmən/ *n.* Pl. **-men**. E18. [f. INDIA + MAN *n.* as in *man of war*, etc.] *Hist.* A ship engaged in trade with the Indian subcontinent; *spec.* (also *East Indiaman*) a ship of large tonnage belonging to the East India Company.

Indian /ˈɪndɪən/ *n.* & *a.* ME. [f. INDIA + -AN. See also INJUN.] **A** *n.* **1** A native or inhabitant of the subcontinent of India or (in recent use) the Republic of India, in southern Asia. ME. **b** *Hist.* A European, esp. a Briton, (formerly) resident in the Indian subcontinent. Chiefly in *old* or *returned Indian*. M18. **2** A member of any of the aboriginal peoples of America. Also more fully *American Indian*. Cf. INJUN. M16. **b** Any of the hunted players in the children's game of cowboys and Indians. L19. **3** The language spoken by any American Indian people or (*rare*) any of the Indian peoples of Asia. M16. **4** *ellipt.* Indian corn, tea, etc. M17. **5a** An indigenous inhabitant of the Philippines, *esp.* one who has converted to Christianity. L17. **†b** An indigenous inhabitant of Australia or New Zealand. M18–M19. **6** *The* southern constellation Indus. L17.

2 *Apache Indian, Sioux Indian*, etc. *North American Indian, South American Indian*, etc. *Red Indian*: see RED *a.*

B *adj.* **1** Belonging to, made in, or originating from the subcontinent of India or the present Republic of India. Formerly also, oriental, Asian. LME. **2** Of, belonging to, or characteristic of the aboriginal peoples of America. L16.

1 MILTON Toward the Springs Of Ganges or Hydaspes, Indian streams. W. ROBERTS Of China . . the Emperor and other Indian monarchs. **2** WORDSWORTH The shrouded Body . . Answering with more than Indian fortitude.

Special collocations: **Indian almond** (the edible kernel of) a Malayan terminalia, *Terminalia catappa*, widely planted in the tropics. *Indian cedar*: see CEDAR 1. **Indian clubs** (a pair of) bottle-shaped clubs swung to exercise the arms in gymnastics. *Indian corn*: see CORN *n.*[1] 3b. **Indian cress** the nasturtium, *Tropaeolum majus*, formerly used as a salad plant. **Indian cup** the pitcher-plant, *Sarracenia purpurea*. **Indian currant** = *coral-berry* s.v. CORAL *n.* **Indian defence** *Chess* any of various defences in which Black opens by moving the king's knight, usu. following with a fianchetto. *Indian devil*: see DEVIL *n.* 5. *Indian* ELEPHANT. **Indian English**: spoken by an inhabitant of the Indian subcontinent whose native language is not English. **Indian fig** = *prickly pear* s.v. PRICKLY *a.* **Indian fig tree** = *banyan tree* s.v. BANYAN 4. **Indian file** (in) single file, the order usu. adopted by N. American Indians in moving through woods. **Indian giver** *N. Amer.* a person who asks back a present he or she has given or expects an exact equivalent in return. **Indian grass** *N. Amer.* a tall perennial prairie grass, *Sorghastrum nutans*, often grown as fodder. **Indian hemp** (*a*) a tropical race of hemp, *Cannabis sativa* subsp. *indica*, the source of marijuana; (*b*) a N. American plant, *Apocynum cannabinum* (family Apocynaceae), the bark of which yields a fibre formerly used to make ropes etc. **Indian ink** (*a*) a black pigment made orig. in China and Japan; (*b*) a dark ink made from this, used esp. in drawing and technical graphics. **Indian lake** a crimson pigment made from stick-lac treated with alum and alkali. **Indian liquorice** (the root of) the jequirity, *Abrus precatorius*. *Indian madder*: see MADDER *n.* 1. **Indian mallow** a yellow-flowered mallow, *Abutilon theophrasti*, of warmer parts of Eurasia, which yields a fibre like jute and is widely naturalized; also called *American* or *Chinese jute, velvet-leaf*. **Indian meal**: ground from maize. **Indian millet** (*a*) = BULRUSH *millet*; (*b*) = DURRA. *Indian Mutiny*: see MUTINY *n.* 2. **Indian Ocean** the ocean south of India, extending from the east coast of Africa to Malaya. **Indian paint** a N. American boraginaceous plant, *Lithospermum canescens*, whose root yields a red dye. *Indian paintbrush*: see *paintbrush* (b) s.v. PAINT *n.* **Indian path** *N. Amer.* a narrow path through the woods, such as is made by Indians moving in single file. *Indian* PEAFOWL. **Indian pear** = *Juneberry* s.v. JUNE. **Indian physic** any of several N. American plants with medicinal properties, esp. *Gillenia trifoliata*, of the rose family. **Indian pink** = CAROLINA *pink*. **Indian pipe** a N. American saprophytic plant, *Monotropa uniflora* (family Pyrolaceae), with a solitary drooping flower. **Indian plantain** any of several N. American plants of the genus *Arnoglossum*, of the composite family. *Indian poke*: see POKE *n.*[2] 2b. **Indian potato** any of several plants with tubers eaten by American Indians, *esp.* the potato-bean, *Apios americana*. **Indian problem** *Chess*: based on the theme of combining two pieces to allow an opponent to escape from stalemate, while using them to prepare a trap in the form of discovered checkmate. **Indian pudding** a New England dish made of maize, molasses, and suet. **Indian red** orig., a yellow-red earth containing ferric oxide; now chiefly, (the colour of) any of various red pigments prepared by oxidation of ferrous salts. **Indian restaurant**: operated by people from the Indian subcontinent, serving Indian food. *Indian rice*: see RICE *n.*[2] 2. **Indian rope-trick** the supposed feat, by natives of the Indian subcontinent, of climbing an upright unsupported length of rope. *Indian* ROSEWOOD. **†Indian rubber** = INDIARUBBER. *Indian runner*: see RUNNER 5d. *Indian saffron*: see SAFFRON *n.* *Indian* SARSAPARILLA. *Indian shot*: see SHOT *n.*[1] 14. **Indian sign** *N. Amer.* (*a*) a track revealing the presence of Indians; (*b*) *colloq.* a magic spell; a curse, a jinx. *Indian silk-cotton tree*: see SILK *n.* & *a.* **Indian summer** a period of calm dry warm weather in late autumn in the northern US or elsewhere; *fig.* a tranquil late period of life etc. **Indian tea** (*a*) tea grown in India or Sri Lanka (Ceylon), considered stronger than China tea; (*b*) any of several N. American plants whose leaves are used to make an infusion. *Indian teak*: see TEAK *n.* 1. **Indian tobacco** a N. American medicinal plant, *Lobelia inflata* (family Lobeliaceae), which tastes like tobacco when chewed. *Indian* TRAGACANTH.**Indian turnip** (the edible corm of) a N. American aroid plant, *Arisaema triphyllum*. **Indian weed** *arch.* (*US*) tobacco. **Indian yellow** an orange-yellow pigment orig. obtained from the urine of cows fed on mango-leaves.

¶See also EAST INDIAN, WEST INDIAN.

Indianan /ɪndɪˈɑːnən/ *n.* M20. [f. *Indiana* (see INDIANIAN) + -AN.] = INDIANIAN.

Indianesque /ɪndɪəˈnɛsk/ *a.* M19. [f. INDIAN + -ESQUE.] Of N. American Indian type.

Indianian /ɪndɪˈanɪən/ *n.* L18. [f. *Indiana* (see below) + -IAN.] A native or inhabitant of Indiana, a north central State of the US.

Indianise *v.* var. of INDIANIZE.

Indianism /ˈɪndɪənɪz(ə)m/ *n.* M17. [f. INDIAN + -ISM.] **1** (Devotion to) the customs and culture of N. American Indians. M17. **2** A word or idiom characteristic of Indian English or N. American Indians. M19.

Indianist *n.* a student of or expert in the languages, customs, etc., of the Indian subcontinent M19.

Indianize /ˈɪndɪənʌɪz/ *v.* Also **-ise**. L17. [f. INDIAN + -IZE.] **†1** *v.i.* Live like a N. American Indian. *rare.* L17–E18. **2** *v.t.* Make Indian or N. American Indian in character, form, habits, etc. E18.

Indianiˈzation *n.* E20.

Indianness /ˈɪndɪənnɪs/ *n.* M20. [f. INDIAN + -NESS.] The quality of being Indian or displaying Indian characteristics.

Indianologist /ɪndɪəˈnɒlədʒɪst/ *n.* L19. [f. INDIAN + -OLOGIST.] An expert on American Indians.

indiarubber /ˈɪndɪəˌrʌbə, ˌɪndɪəˈrʌbə/ *n.* & *a.* Also **I-**, and (earlier) as two wds. L18. [f. INDIA + RUBBER *n.*[1]] **A** *n.* **1** Rubber, caoutchouc. L18. **2** An eraser made of rubber. L18. **3** In *pl.* Rubber overshoes. *US.* M19.

Comb.: **indiarubber plant** = *rubber plant* s.v. RUBBER *n.*[1]

B *adj.* Made of indiarubber; flexible or elastic like indiarubber. M19.

Indic /ˈɪndɪk/ *a.* M19. [L *Indicus* f. Gk *Indikos*, f. INDIA: see -IC.] Of or pertaining to India; *esp.* designating or pertaining to the Indian branch of the Indo-Iranian languages (cf. INDO-ARYAN).

indican /ˈɪndɪkan/ *n.* M19. [f. L *indicum* INDIGO + -AN.] *Chem.* **1** An indoxyl glucoside occurring in the leaves of woad and indigo plants and yielding indigo on hydrolysis and oxidation. M19. **2** A substance (orig. thought similar to the above) found in urine, in which it occurs as a product of amino-acid metabolism: (the potassium salt of) indoxylsulphuric acid, $C_8H_6NOSO_2OH$. M19.

indicaˈnuria *n.* (*Med.*) the presence of excessive amounts of indican in the urine L19.

indicant /ˈɪndɪk(ə)nt/ *a.* & *n.* E17. [L *indicant-* pres. ppl stem of *indicare* INDICATE: see -ANT[1].] **A** *adj.* That indicates; indicative. *rare.* E17. **B** *n.* A thing which indicates. E17.

indicate /ˈɪndɪkeɪt/ *v.t.* Pa. pple **-ated**, (earlier) **†-ate**. E17. [L *indicat-* pa. ppl stem of *indicare*, f. as IN-[2] + *dicare* proclaim: see -ATE[3].] **1** Point out or to, make known, show; (of a meter etc.) register a reading of; (esp. *Med.*) suggest as a desirable or necessary course of action (usu. in *pass.*). E17. **b** Of a person: direct attention to (by speech or writing, occas. by gesture). E19. **2** Point to the presence, existence, or reality of; be a sign or symptom of; imply. E18. **3** State or express briefly; give an indication of. M18.

1 *British Medical Journal* Recourse to this method is . . indicated when the teeth to be replaced are front teeth. P. G. WODEHOUSE Strategy, rather than force, seemed to the curate to be indicated. J. MARQUAND The rather battered silver travelling clock . . indicated that the hour was a quarter past six. N. MAILER I mention this as a way of indicating how hard it was to locate his place. **b** C. HAMPTON He indicates a pile of books on a table by the bed. **2** N. SYMINGTON Then she said something which indicated a powerful resentment of me. D. W. GOODWIN Studies indicate that most of the drinking drivers are . . serious problem drinkers. **3** A. BAIN My last argument . . can only be indicated here; the full illustration belongs to a more advanced stage of the exposition. O. MANNING Quintin indicated he could find his own way up to the drawing-room.

indication /ɪndɪˈkeɪʃ(ə)n/ *n.* LME. [L *indicatio(n-)*, f. as prec.: see -ATION.] **1** The action or an instance of indicating; something that indicates or suggests; a sign, a symptom, a hint; *Med.* a symptom which suggests a particular disease, syndrome, or remedial course of action. LME. **b** A reading registered by a meter or other instrument. M18. **c** *Mining.* Something that indicates the presence of ore, oil, etc. *US.* M19. **2** Something indicated or suggested; *Med.* a remedy or treatment which is indicated by the symptoms as desirable. LME.

1 J. B. PRIESTLEY There was every indication now that the fine autumn weather . . had at last come to an end. K. CLARK A great artist whose early work gives no indication of the character of his genius. G. HUNTINGTON He would have liked to hear whether she was going. She gave no indication either way. W. GOLDING Day after day a complex of tiny indications had added up and now presented me with a picture.

indicative /ɪnˈdɪkətɪv/ *a.* & *n.* LME. [(O)Fr. *indicatif*, *-ive* f. late L *indicativus* (tr. Gk *horistikē* (sc. *egklisis* mood), f. as INDICATE: see -ATIVE.] **A** *adj.* **1** *Gram.* Designating the mood of a verb of which the essential function is to state an objective fact (as opp. to something wished, thought of, etc., by the speaker). LME. **b** Of a statement etc.: having the verb in the indicative mood. M17. 2 That indicates or points out; that hints or suggests. LME. 3 Giving indications *of*; suggestive *of*. M17.

1b A. J. AYER Every indicative sentence, whether it is literally meaningful or not, shall be regarded as expressing a statement. 2 R. SAUNDERS The next is called Index, the indicative or demonstrative finger. 3 P. G. WODEHOUSE Percy gave a languid gesture indicative of the man of affairs whose time was not his own.

B *n. Gram.* (An instance of) the indicative mood; a verb in the indicative mood. M16.

indicatively *adv.* E17.

indicator /ˈɪndɪkeɪtə/ *n.* M17. [f. INDICATE + -OR. In branch II tr. L *indicator*, (sense 7) Fr. *indicateur*.] **I** 1 A thing that serves to give an indication or suggestion (*of* something else); an indication. M17. b A geological clue to the presence of gold. L19. c *Ecol.* A group or species of plants or animals whose presence acts as a sign of particular environmental conditions. E20. 2 A person who or thing which points out or indicates. E19. b *Philos.* A word which is the only one usable as a means of reference to something. M20. 3 A device which indicates the condition of a machine etc.; a recording instrument attached to a piece of apparatus; a pointer, light, etc., which draws attention or gives warning. M19. b A display board giving current information, e.g. for train or aircraft departures. E20. c A device (now usu. a flashing light) on a motor vehicle for indicating an intended change of direction. M20. 4 Something used in a scientific experiment to indicate some quality, change, etc.; *esp.* in *Chem.*, a substance which may be used to indicate whether the concentration of some ion (esp. hydrogen) is above or below a particular value, usu. by a characteristic colour. M19. b An isotope used as a (radioactive) tracer. E20.

1 J. A. FROUDE They [clothes] were the outward indicators of the inward and spiritual nature. A. LURIE The sack suit is a middle-class indicator. 2 J. A. FROUDE Birds . . were celestial indicators of the gods' commands. b *attrib.*: W. V. QUINE The indicator words: 'this', 'that', 'I', 'you', 'he', 'now', 'here', 'then', 'there', 'today', 'tomorrow'. 3 *attrib.*: *Which?* For most cookers, . . the indicator light going out gave a satisfactory indication that the oven was nearly at its steady temperature.

II †5 *Anat.* The muscle which extends the index finger. *rare.* L17–E20. 6 = *honeyguide* (a) s.v. HONEY *n.* L18. 7 *Math.* = TOTIENT. E20.

Comb.: **indicator diagram**: of the variation of pressure and volume within the cylinder of a reciprocating engine; **indicator lamp**: which lights up to show that a machine etc. is in a certain condition.

indicatory /ɪnˈdɪkət(ə)ri, ˈɪndɪkeɪt(ə)ri/ *a.* L16. [f. INDICATE + -ORY[2].] †1 *Med.* Indicating the nature or tendency of a disease; symptomatic. L16–E17. 2 Serving to indicate; indicative *of* something. M18.

2 C. W. THOMSON The box which covers the coil and indicatory part of the thermometer. W. BELSHAM Great preparations . . indicatory of an approaching siege.

indicatrix /ɪndɪˈkeɪtrɪks, ɪnˈdɪkətrɪks/ *n.* Pl. **-trices** /-trɪsiːz/. M19. [mod.L, fem. of L INDICATOR: see -TRIX.] 1 *Geom.* The curve in which a surface is cut by a plane close and parallel to the tangent plane at a point, indicating the nature of the curvature at that point. *rare.* M19. 2 *Cryst.* An imaginary ellipsoidal surface whose axes represent the refractive indices of a crystal. Also *optical indicatrix.* L19.

indicavit /ɪndɪˈkeɪvɪt/ *n. obs.* exc. *Hist.* L16. [L = he has pointed out, 3 sing. perf. indic. used as n.] *Law.* A writ of prohibition by which a suit raised by one ecclesiastic against another for tithes amounting to at least a fourth part of the profits of an advowson might be removed from the ecclesiastical court to the king's court.

indices *n.pl.* see INDEX *n.*

indicia *n.* pl. of INDICIUM.

indicial /ɪnˈdɪʃ(ə)l/ *a.* M19. [f. INDICIUM + -AL[1].] Of, pertaining to, or of the nature of an index or indicium; indicative.

indicible /ɪnˈdɪsɪb(ə)l/ *a.* Long *rare.* L15. [Fr., or late L *indicibilis* f. as IN-[3] + L *dicere* say + *-ibilis* -IBLE.] Unspeakable, inexpressible.

indicium /ɪnˈdɪsɪəm/ *n.* Pl. **-cia** /-sɪə/. E17. [L f. as INDEX *n.*] An indication, a sign; a distinguishing mark. Usu. in *pl.*

SIR W. SCOTT The corpse afforded no other *indicia* respecting the fate of Kennedy.

†**indico** *n.* & *a.* var. of INDIGO.

indicolite /ɪnˈdɪkəlʌɪt/ *n.* Also **-g-** /-g-/. E19. [f. L *indicum* INDIGO + -O- + -LITE.] An indigo-blue variety of tourmaline, used as a gemstone.

indict /ɪnˈdʌɪt/ *v.*[1]*t.* Also (earlier) †**endite**, †**indite**. ME. [Legal AN *enditer* corresp. in form but not in sense to OFr. *enditier* (= INDITE *v.*[2]), f. Proto-Romance, f. L *indict-* pa. ppl stem of *indicere* proclaim, appoint, impose, f. as IN-[2] + *dicere* pronounce, utter.] 1 Bring a charge against; accuse (a person) of a crime or *as* a culprit by legal process. ME. 2 Make a subject of indictment *against*. *rare.* M17.

1 L. STEFFENS The son of a former mayor was indicted for misconduct in office. *Orlando* (*Florida*) *Sentinel* Brown was indicted . . on a charge of giving a gun to a felon. *fig.*: J. I. M. STEWART No learned man cares to be indicted of inaccuracy. 2 SIR W. SCOTT It is indited against Simon Glover . . that he hath spoken irreverent discourses.

indic'tee *n.* a person indicted for a crime L16. **indicter** *n.* LME.

†**indict** *v.*[2]*t.* M16–E18. [L *indict-*: see prec.] Declare authoritatively, announce, proclaim.

indictable /ɪnˈdʌɪtəb(ə)l/ *a.* LME. [f. INDICT *v.*[1] + -ABLE.] 1 Liable to be indicted for an offence. LME. 2 Of an offence: that makes a person liable to indictment, with trial by jury. Opp. *summary.* E18.

indictably *adv.* E19.

indiction /ɪnˈdɪkʃ(ə)n/ *n.* LME. [L *indictio(n-)*, f. *indict-*: see INDICT *v.*[1], -ION.] 1 *Hist.* The fiscal period of fifteen years, instituted by the Emperor Constantine in AD 313, which became a means of dating ordinary events and transactions. LME. b A specified year in the indiction, indicated by number. LME. c The decree of the Roman Emperors fixing the valuation on which the property tax was assessed at the beginning of each indiction; the tax paid on the basis of this assessment. L16. 2 The action of ordaining or announcing authoritatively and publicly; an appointment, a declaration, a proclamation. *arch.* M16.

2 H. L'ESTRANGE According to the Kings indiction, the Assembly met . . at Edenburgh.

indictional *a.* (*rare*) E18.

in dictione /ˌɪn dɪktɪˈəʊni/ *a. phr.* E19. [L, tr. Gk *para tēn lexin* in relation to the wording (Aristotle).] Of a logical fallacy: arising from the wording used to express it. Cf. EXTRA DICTIONEM.

†**indictive** *a.* M17. [Sense 1 f. L *indictivus*, f. *indict-*; sense 2 f. INDICT *v.*[1]: see -IVE.] 1 Proclaimed or appointed by authority. M17–E18. 2 Containing an indictment, accusatory. *rare.* Only in L19.

indictment /ɪnˈdʌɪtm(ə)nt/ *n.* Also (earlier) †**endite-**, †**indite-**. ME. [AN *enditement*, f. as INDICT *v.*[1]: see -MENT.] 1 The action of indicting or accusing, a formal accusation; the legal process (in Eng. Law *Hist.*) in which a formal accusation is preferred to and presented by a grand jury. ME. b The legal document containing a written accusation of a serious crime to be tried by jury or (in Eng. Law *Hist.*) grand jury. E16. 2 *Sc. Law.* A form of process by which a person is brought to trial at the instance of the Lord Advocate; the corresponding formal written charge. M18. 3 *transf.* & *fig.* Censure, condemnation; a writing, a circumstance, etc., that serves to censure or condemn. L19.

1 BUNYAN How sayest thou? Art thou guilty of this indictment or not? **bill of indictment** (*a*) (in Eng. Law *Hist.*) a written accusation as preferred to a grand jury. (*b*) = sense 1b above. 3 M. IGNATIEFF A speech whose indictment of the Cabinet rang at the end of every paragraph. M. MEYER He composed this poem . . as an indictment of his countrymen for their lassitude.

indie /ˈɪndi/ *n.* & *a. colloq.* Also **indy**. E20. [Abbrev. of INDEPENDENT *n.* & *a.*: see -IE.] **A** *n.* 1 An independent producer of films, broadcast programmes, records, etc. E20. 2 A musician or band whose music is recorded by an independent company. L20. 3 Deliberately spontaneous and independent music as produced by such bands. L20. b A person fond of such music. L20. **B** *adj.* Independent; *spec.* of or pertaining to an indie or indies. M20.

Indies /ˈɪndɪz/ *n.pl.* M16. [Pl. of *Indy* obs. & dial. var. of INDIA.] 1 (Usu. w. *the.*) India and adjacent regions of SE Asia. Also (now *rare*), the West Indies. *arch.* M16. †2 A region of great wealth, esp. one to which profitable voyages may be made. L16–M18.

¶See also *East Indies* s.v. EAST *a.*, *West Indies* s.v. WEST *a.*

indifference /ɪnˈdɪf(ə)r(ə)ns/ *n.* LME. [f. as next: see -ENCE.] 1 The quality of being indifferent or neutral, neither good nor bad. Now only, mediocrity. *rare.* LME. †2 Absence of bias or favour for one side or another; impartiality. L15–M18. 3 Absence of active feeling for or against; *esp.* absence of care or concern for, or interest in, a person or thing; unconcern, apathy. (Foll. by *to.*) M17. 4 Lack of difference or distinction between things. Now *rare.* M17. 5 The fact of not mattering, or making no difference; unimportance; an instance or thing of unimportance. M17. 6 Freedom of thought or choice; equal power to take either of two courses. Now *rare.* E18.

2 H. FIELDING Gentlemen . . to be seated with . . seeming indifference . . unless there be any . . whose degrees claim . . precedence. 3 W. C. WILLIAMS She . . fascinated me, not for her beauty . ., but for a provocative indifference to rule and order. E. O'BRIEN 'I really don't care'. It was a thing he said often . . to assure himself of his indifference. 5 C. FREEMAN That brief meeting was of complete indifference to him; she was only one of the many people who had inquired about the apartments. 6 W. CUNNINGHAM The indifference of the human will, its perfect ability to choose this or that.

Comb.: **indifference curve** *Econ.* a curve on a graph (the axes of which represent quantities of two commodities), which links those combinations of quantities which the consumer regards as of equal value; **indifference map** *Econ.* a graph displaying a family of indifference curves; **indifference point** (*a*) the midpoint of a magnet where the attractions of both poles are equal; (*b*) *Psychol.* a position on a scale at which there is apparent subjective equality of two contrasted sensations (as warmth and coolness) or tendencies (as under- or overestimation of magnitude).

indifferency /ɪnˈdɪf(ə)r(ə)nsi/ *n.* Now *rare* or *obs.* LME. [L *indifferentia*, f. *indifferent-*: see next, -ENCY.] 1 = INDIFFERENCE 2. LME. †2 = INDIFFERENCE 6. M16–L17. 3 Lack of difference in nature or character; substantial equivalence. M16. 4 = INDIFFERENCE 5. M16. 5 Ambiguity, equivocality. L16. 6 = INDIFFERENCE 3. E17.

indifferent /ɪnˈdɪf(ə)r(ə)nt/ *a.*, *n.*, & *adv.* LME. [(O)Fr. *indifférent* or L *indifferent-* f. as IN-[3] + DIFFERENT *a.*] **A** *adj.* 1 Not inclined to prefer one person or thing to another; unbiased, impartial, disinterested; fair, just, even-handed. Now *rare.* LME. 2 Having no inclination or feeling for or against a person or thing; lacking interest in or feeling for something; unconcerned, unmoved, uninterested. (Foll. by *to.*) LME. †3 Not different; equal, even; identical. LME–E18. 4 Regarded as not mattering either way; unimportant, immaterial; non-essential. *arch.* E16. †5 Having a neutral relation *to* (two or more things); impartially applicable; (of a word) equivocal, ambiguous. E16–L17. †6 Not extreme; moderate; of medium quality, character, size, etc. E16–E18. †7 Having freedom of thought or choice; having equal power to take either of two courses. M16–L17. †8 Not more advantageous to one person or party than to another. M16–M17. 9 Not definitely possessing either of two opposite qualities; *esp.* neither good nor bad. M16. b Not very good; poor, inferior, quite bad. M16. c In poor health, ailing. *obs.* exc. *dial.* M18. **10**

Neutral in some physical property, as chemically, magnetically, or electrically. Also *Biol.* (*arch.*) (of tissue etc.) undifferentiated. M19.

1 H. P. BROUGHAM They dare not go before an impartial judge and indifferent jury. 2 E. BOWEN Max seemed indifferent to the rain; though he certainly would not seek it. J. AGEE Richard tried to be sure whether this was said in affection or dislike, . . it was neither, just an indifferent statement of fact. E. JOHNSON Dickens liked and disliked people; he was never merely indifferent. 3 R. SCOT It is indifferent to saie in the English toong; She is a witch; or, She is a wise woman. 4 DRYDEN Whigs, 'Tis indifferent to your humble servant, whatever your party says or thinks of him. 6 G. MARKHAM Make not your career too long . . or too short . . but competent and indifferent. 7 J. LOCKE A man is at Liberty to lift up his Hand . . or to let it rest quiet: He is perfectly indifferent to either. 8 T. FULLER An indifferent Place, for mutual Ease, in mid-way betwixt both. 9 P. F. STRAWSON The finding of reasons, good, bad or indifferent, for what we believe on instinct. b A. S. NEILL Indifferent scholars who, under discipline, scrape through college . . and become . . mediocre doctors, and incompetent lawyers. I. COLEGATE He was an indifferent shot, though not a positively bad one. c H. NELSON I have been but very indifferent, but I am much recovered.

B *n.* **1** A person who is neutral or not partisan; an apathetic person. M16. **2** In *pl.* Immaterial or unimportant things; non-essentials. Now *rare* or *obs.* E17.

1 THACKERAY The indifferents might be counted on to cry King George or King James, according as either should prevail.

C *adv.* = INDIFFERENTLY 4. *arch.* L16.

SIR W. SCOTT You have seen me act my part indifferent well.

indifferentism /ɪnˈdɪf(ə)r(ə)ntɪz(ə)m/ *n.* L18. [f. prec. + -ISM.] A spirit of indifference professed and practised; *esp.* the principle that differences of religious belief are of no importance; absence of interest in religious matters.

R. A. VAUGHAN The signs of a growing toleration or indifferentism meet him on every side. R. BOLDREWOOD These people either did not know . . or, with the absurd indifferentism of Englishmen, did not care.

indifferentist *n.* & *a.* (*a*) *n.* an adherent or advocate of indifferentism; (*b*) *adj.* of or pertaining to indifferentism or indifferentists: L18.

indifferently /ɪnˈdɪf(ə)r(ə)ntli/ *adv.* LME. [f. as prec. + -LY[2].] **1** Equally, alike, indiscriminately. LME. †**2** Impartially. LME–M19. **3** Unconcernedly. LME. **4** To some extent, moderately, fairly (*well* etc.). Now *rare.* M16. †**5** Neutrally. E17–E18. **6** Not very well; poorly, badly. L17.

indigena /ɪnˈdɪdʒɪnə/ *n. arch.* Pl. **-nae** /-niː/. L16. [L: see INDIGENOUS.] A native, an aboriginal.

indigenal *a.* & *n.* E18.

indigence /ˈɪndɪdʒ(ə)ns/ *n.* LME. [(O)Fr., or L *indigentia*, f. *indigent-*: see INDIGENT, -ENCE.] †**1** The fact or condition of needing; lack or need *of* a thing; lack, deficiency; requirement. LME–L18. **2** Lack of the means of subsistence; poverty, destitution. LME. †**3** An instance of want; a need. LME–L17.

Also **indigency** *n.* E17.

indigene /ˈɪndɪdʒiːn/ *a.* & *n.* L16. [Fr. *indigène* f. L INDIGENA.] †**A** *adj.* Native, indigenous. L16–L17. **B** *n.* A native, an aboriginal; *Austral.* a native of Papua or New Guinea. M17.

indigenisation *n.* var. of INDIGENIZATION.

indigenity /ɪndɪˈdʒɛnɪti/ *n.* L19. [f. INDIGENOUS + -ITY.] The quality of being indigenous.

indigenization /ɪnˌdɪdʒɪnʌɪˈzeɪʃ(ə)n/ *n.* Also **-isation**. M20. [f. next + -IZATION.] The act or process of making predominantly indigenous; adaptation or subjection to indigenous influence or dominance; *spec.* the increased use of indigenous people in government, employment, etc.

inˈdigenist *n.* & *a.* (*a*) *n.* a supporter of indigenization; (*b*) *adj.* pertaining to or favouring indigenization: M20. **inˈdigenize** *v.t.* M20.

indigenous /ɪnˈdɪdʒɪnəs/ *a.* M17. [f. L *indigena* (*a*) native f. *indi-* strengthened form of *in-* IN-[2] + *-gena* f. base of *gignere* beget: see -OUS.] **1** Born or produced in a particular land or region; (esp. of flora and fauna) native or belonging naturally *to* (a region, a soil, etc.), not introduced. M17. **b** *transf.* & *fig.* Inborn, innate. M19. **2** Of, pertaining to, or concerned with the native inhabitants of a region. M19.

1 RIDER HAGGARD The indigenous flora and fauna of Kukuanaland. C. STEAD He could tell the indigenous Malays from the new imports from India. C. FRANCIS My . . garden turned out to have only four plants which are indigenous to Britain. b L. TRILLING Poetry is indigenous to the very constitution of the mind. 2 H. READ Objects made by uncultured peoples in accordance with a native and indigenous tradition. N. CHOMSKY What is remarkable about the Indochina war is the inability of the American invaders to establish indigenous governments that can rule effectively.

indigenously *adv.* M19. **indigenousness** *n.* L19.

indigent /ˈɪndɪdʒ(ə)nt/ *a.* & *n.* LME. [(O)Fr. f. L *indigent-*, pres. ppl stem of *indigere* lack, f. *indi-* (see prec.) + *egere* be in want, need: see -ENT.] **A** *adj.* **1** Lacking in what is necessary; falling short of the proper standard; deficient. LME. **b** Destitute *of*, void *of. arch.* L15. †**c** In need *of*; requiring the aid of. L16–E18. **2** Lacking the necessities of life; characterized by poverty; poor, needy. LME. **B** *n.* An indigent or poor person. LME.

†**indigest** *a.* & *n.* LME. [L *indigestus* unarranged, f. as IN-[3] + *digestus* pa. pple of *digerere* DIGEST *v.*] **A** *adj.* Undigested; crude, immature, confused; unarranged. LME–E19. **B** *n.* A shapeless mass. *rare* (Shakes.). Only in L16.

indigest /ɪndɪˈdʒɛst, -dʌɪ-/ *v.* Chiefly *joc.* E19. [f. IN-[3] + DIGEST *v.*, after INDIGESTION.] **1** *v.t.* Fail to digest. E19. **2** *v.i.* Fail to be digested; cause or suffer indigestion. M19.

indigested /ɪndɪˈdʒɛstɪd, -dʌɪ-/ *a.* L16. [f. IN-[3] + *digested* pa. pple of DIGEST *v.*] **1** Not ordered or arranged; shapeless, unformed, chaotic. L16. **b** Not ordered in the mind; not thought out; ill-considered. L16. **2** That has not undergone digestion in the stomach. E17.

indigestible /ɪndɪˈdʒɛstɪb(ə)l, -dʌɪ-/ *a.* L15. [Fr., or late L *indigestibilis*, f. as IN-[3] + *digestibilis* DIGESTIBLE.] Incapable of being digested, difficult to digest; not easily assimilated as food.

F. KING She felt heavy and sick, as though sated from an indigestible meal. *fig.*: T. SHARPE The contents of Sir Godber's speech were wholly indigestible.

indigestiˈbility *n.* E19. **indigestibleness** *n.* (*rare*) E17. **indigestibly** *adv.* M19.

indigestion /ɪndɪˈdʒɛstʃ(ə)n, -dʌɪ-/ *n.* LME. [(O)Fr., or late L *indigestio(n-)*, f. as IN-[3] + DIGESTION.] **1** Difficulty in digesting; pain or discomfort in the abdomen after eating, often (mistakenly) thought due to a failure to digest food. LME. **b** A case or attack of indigestion. E18. **2** Undigested condition; (an instance of) disorder, imperfection. *rare.* M17.

indigestive /ɪndɪˈdʒɛstɪv, -dʌɪ-/ *a.* M17. [f. IN-[3] + DIGESTIVE.] Characterized by, suffering from, or liable to indigestion.

indigitate /ɪnˈdɪdʒɪteɪt/ *v.* E17. [L *indigitat-* pa. ppl stem of *indigitare* call upon, invoke. Erron. assoc. w. L *digitus* finger.] †**1** *v.t.* Call; indicate by name; proclaim; declare. Only in 17. †**2** *v.t.* Point out (as) with a finger; show, indicate. E17–E18. **3** *v.i. Anat.* = INTERDIGITATE I. M19.

indigitation /ɪnˌdɪdʒɪˈteɪʃ(ə)n/ *n.* M17. [f. as prec. + -ATION.] †**1** The action of pointing out or indicating; an indication; a declaration. M17–E18. **2** Computing or conversing by means of the fingers. E19. **3** *Anat.* Interdigitation (esp. of muscle and tendon). Now *rare.* M19.

indign /ɪnˈdʌɪn/ *a.* Now only *poet.* ME. [(O)Fr. *indigne* or L *indignus*, f. as IN-[3] + *dignus* worthy.] **1** Unworthy, undeserving. (Foll. by *of*, *to*.) ME. **2** Unworthy of a person or circumstance; unbecoming; shameful, disgraceful. M16. **b** Of punishment or suffering: undeserved. M18.

indignant /ɪnˈdɪɡnənt/ *a.* L16. [L *indignant-* pres. ppl stem of *indignari* regard as unworthy, f. *indignus*: see prec., -ANT[1].] Affected with indignation; provoked to anger by something regarded as unworthy or unjust; moved by a mixture of anger, scorn, and contempt. (Foll. by *at*, *with*, *that*.)

DICKENS He feels indignant that Helena's brother should dispose of him so coolly. C. R. MARKHAM He published an indignant pamphlet on the subject of his wrongs.

indignance *n.* (*rare*) L16. **indignancy** *n.* (*rare*) L18. **indignantly** *adv.* †(*a*) *rare* with indignity; (*b*) in an indignant manner: E17.

indignation /ɪndɪɡˈneɪʃ(ə)n/ *n.* LME. [(O)Fr., or L *indignatio(n-)*, f. *indignat-* pa. ppl stem of *indignari*: see prec., -ATION.] †**1 a** The action of treating as unworthy of notice; disdain, contempt; contemptuous behaviour. LME–M16. **b** Treating with indignity; an indignity. Long *rare.* E16. **2** Anger excited by a sense of wrong, or by injustice, wickedness, or misconduct; righteous anger. Foll. by *against*, *at*, *with*, †*of*, †*upon*. LME. †**3** Discomfort of the stomach; nauseated condition. *rare.* LME–M17.

Comb.: **indignation meeting**: a meeting to express collective indignation.

indignatory /ɪnˈdɪɡnət(ə)ri/ *a. rare.* E17. [f. L *indignat-* (see prec.) + -ORY[2].] Expressive of indignation.

†**indignify** *v.t.* L16–M18. [f. IN-[3] + DIGNIFY.] Treat with indignity; dishonour; represent as unworthy.

indignity /ɪnˈdɪɡnɪti/ *n.* L16. [Fr. *indignité* or L *indignitas*, f. *indignus* INDIGN: see -ITY.] †**1** The quality or condition of being unworthy; unworthiness; in *pl.*, undeserving traits. L16–L17. **2** Unbecoming or dishonourable condition; loss or lack of dignity; humiliating quality. Also, a shameful or undignified action. L16. **3** Scornful, contemptuous, or humiliating treatment; injury accompanied by insult; an act which causes humiliation, a slight, an affront. L16. †**4** Anger excited by a wrong; indignation. L16–L18.

2 GOLDSMITH A mind too proud to stoop to such indignities. A. T. ELLIS The indignity of peering into other people's intimacies had appalled me. 3 SHAKES. *Temp.* The poor monster's my subject, and he shall not suffer indignity. A. S. BYATT She was afraid . . . of peripheral indignities inflicted by hospitals.

indigo /ˈɪndɪɡəʊ/ *n.* & *a.* Also †**-ico**. M16. [Sp. *indico* f. L *indicum* f. Gk *indikon*, f. *indikos*: see INDIC.] **A** *n.* Pl. **-os**. **1** A dark blue powder used as a vat dye, orig. obtained from certain plants but now mainly made synthetically. Also, the chief chemical constituent of this, indigotin. M16. **b** A kind or sample of this dye. E17. **2** Any of various plants, esp. of the tropical leguminous genus *Indigofera*, from which indigo or a similar dye is obtainable. E17. **3** A deep violet-blue, located in the spectrum between blue and violet. E17.

2 **bastard indigo** *US* a leguminous plant of the genus *Amorpha*, esp. *A. fruticosa*. **false indigo** (*a*) a leguminous plant of the genus *Baptisia*, esp. *B. tinctoria*; (*b*) = *bastard indigo* above.

Comb.: **indigo-bird** (*a*) a N. American bunting, *Passerina cyanea*, the male of which has bright blue plumage; (*b*) any of several parasitic African weaver-birds of the genus *Vidua* and the subfamily Viduinae, the males of which have glossy plumage of a blue- or purplish-black colour; **indigo bunting** = *indigo-bird* (a) above; **indigo finch** = *indigo-bird* above; **indigo plant** = sense 2 above; **indigo snake** a large blue-black, brown, or particoloured colubrid snake, *Drymarchon corais*, found in the south-eastern US and tropical America; also called *cribo*, *gopher snake*; **indigo white** a white soluble crystalline compound, $C_{16}H_{12}N_2O_2$, obtained by reduction of indigotin.

B *attrib.* or as *adj.* Of a deep violet-blue colour. M19.

indigo blue /ˌɪndɪɡəʊ ˈbluː/ *n.* & *a. phr.* E18. [f. prec. + BLUE *n.*, *a.*] **A** *n. phr.* **1** The violet-blue colour of indigo. E18. **2** = INDIGOTIN. M19. **B** *adj. phr.* Of the blue colour of indigo. M19.

indigoferous /ɪndɪˈɡɒf(ə)rəs/ *a.* E19. [f. INDIGO + -FEROUS.] Bearing or producing indigo.

indigoid /ˈɪndɪɡɔɪd/ *a.* & *n.* E20. [f. INDIGO + -OID.] *Chem.* **A** *adj.* Related to indigotin in molecular structure. E20. **B** *n.* An indigoid compound, esp. a dye. M20.

indigolite *n.* var. of INDICOLITE.

indigotic /ɪndɪˈɡɒtɪk/ *a.* M19. [f. as next + -IC.] Of, pertaining to, or produced from indigo.

indigotin /ɪnˈdɪɡətɪn, ɪndɪˈɡəʊtɪn/ *n.* M19. [f. INDIGO + euphonic *-t-* + -IN[1].] *Chem.* A dark-blue crystalline compound, $C_{16}H_{10}N_2O_2$, which is the essential constituent of indigo and has a molecule consisting of two linked indoxyl molecules.

†indiligent *a.* M16–M18. [L *indiligent-*, f. as IN-[3] + *diligent-* attentive, careful: see DILIGENT.] Inattentive, heedless, careless; idle, slothful.
†indiligence *n.* L15–M17. **†indiligently** *adv.* M17–L18.

†indiminishable *a. rare.* M17–L18. [f. IN-[3] + DIMINISH + -ABLE.] That cannot be diminished.

Indio /ˈɪndɪəʊ/ *n.* Pl. **-os.** M19. [Sp. *indio*, Port. *índio* Indian.] A member of any of the indigenous peoples of America or eastern Asia in areas formerly subject to Spain or Portugal.

indirect /ɪndɪˈrɛkt, ɪndʌɪ-/ *a.* LME. [(O)Fr., or med.L *indirectus*, f. as IN-[3] + DIRECT *a.*] **1** *Gram.* **†a** Not in full grammatical concord. Only in LME. **b** Of speech or narration: put in a reported form, not in the speaker's own words; oblique. M19. **2** Of a route, path, etc.: not straight, crooked, devious. Also, of a movement: oblique. L15. **b** Of an action or feeling: not straightforward and honest; not open; deceitful, corrupt. Now *rare* or *obs.* M16. **c** Of a succession, title, etc.: not derived by direct descent. L16. **3** Not taking the shortest course to the desired objective; not going straight to the point; not acting or exercised with direct force; roundabout. L16. **b** *Logic.* Of a proof, method, etc.: proceeding by consideration of the proposition contradictory to that in question. M17. **c** Of taxation: levied on goods and services (and hence paid by the consumer in the form of increased prices) rather than on income or profits. E19. **d** Of a scientific technique, process, etc.: involving intermediate stages, not effecting a simple conversion. M19. **4** Not directly aimed at or attained; not immediately resulting from an action or cause. E19. **5** Of or pertaining to work and expenses which cannot be apportioned to any particular job or undertaking; pertaining to overhead charges or subsidiary work. E20.
4 B. JOWETT Happiness is not the direct aim, but the indirect consequence of the good government.
Special collocations: **indirect address** *Computing*: specifying the location of information about the address of the operand, rather than the location of the operand itself. **indirect aggression** aggression against another nation by other than military means. **indirect evidence** = CIRCUMSTANTIAL *evidence*. **indirect fire** gunfire aimed at a target which cannot be seen. **indirect lighting**: that makes use of light diffused by reflection from the ceiling, walls, or other surface(s). **indirect object** *Gram.*: denoting a person or thing affected by a verbal action but not primarily acted on (e.g. *him* in *give him the book*). **indirect passive** *Gram.*: having for its subject the indirect or prepositional object of the active (e.g. *he* in *he was given the book, he was laughed at*). **indirect question** *Gram.* a question in indirect speech (e.g. *they asked who I was*). **indirect rule** a system of government in which the governed people retain certain administrative and legal etc. powers.
indirectness *n.* E17.

†indirected *a. rare.* E17–E19. [f. IN-[3] + *directed* pa. pple of DIRECT *v.*] Not directed or guided.

indirection /ɪndɪˈrɛkʃ(ə)n, ɪndʌɪ-/ *n.* L16. [f. INDIRECT after *direction*.] **1** Lack of straightforwardness in action; an act or practice which is not straightforward and honest; deceit, malpractice. L16. **2** Indirect movement or action; a devious or circuitous course; roundabout means or method. E17.

indirectly /ɪndɪˈrɛktli, ɪndʌɪ-/ *adv.* LME. [f. INDIRECT + -LY[2].] **1** By indirect action, means, or connection; through an intervening person or thing. LME. **b** Not in express terms; by suggestion or implication. L16. **2** Not in a straight line or with a straight course; circuitously, obliquely. L15. **†b** By crooked methods; wrongfully, unfairly. L16–E17. **†c** Not to the point; evasively. L16–E18. **3** *Gram.* In or by indirect speech. L19.

indiscernible /ɪndɪˈsəːnɪb(ə)l/ *a.* & *n.* M17. [f. IN-[3] + DISCERNIBLE.] **A** *adj.* **1** Unable to be discerned; imperceptible, undiscoverable. M17. **2** Unable to be distinguished (*from* something else); indistinguishable. M17. **B** *n.* A thing that cannot be discerned; a thing that cannot be distinguished from some other thing. E18.
indiscerniˈbility *n.* L19. **indiscernibleness** *n.* M17. **indiscernibly** *adv.* M17.

†indiscerpible *a.* M17–M19. [f. IN-[3] + DISCERPIBLE.] = next.

indiscerptible /ɪndɪˈsəːptɪb(ə)l/ *a.* M18. [f. IN-[3] + DISCERPTIBLE.] Unable to be divided into parts; not destructible by dissolution of parts.
indiscerptibility *n.* M18.

indisciplinable /ɪnˈdɪsɪplɪnəb(ə)l, ˌɪndɪsɪˈplɪn-/ *a.* Now *rare.* E17. [f. IN-[3] + DISCIPLINABLE.] Unable to be disciplined; not amenable to discipline; intractable.

indiscipline /ɪnˈdɪsɪplɪn/ *n.* L18. [f. IN-[3] + DISCIPLINE *n.*] Absence or lack of discipline; lack of order or control by authority.

indiscoverable /ɪndɪˈskʌv(ə)rəb(ə)l/ *a.* E17. [f. IN-[3] + DISCOVERABLE.] Not discoverable, undiscoverable.

indiscreet /ɪndɪˈskriːt/ *a.*[1] Also (earlier) **†-crete.** LME. [L *indiscretus* (see INDISCRETE *a.*[1]) in med.L sense 'careless, indiscreet'.] **†1** Lacking discernment or sound judgement. LME–L17. **2** Injudicious or imprudent in speech or action; unwary, unthinking; not discreet, esp. about other people's secrets. L16.
indiscreetly *adv.* LME. **indiscreetness** *n.* M17.

†indiscreet *a.*[2] see next.

indiscrete /ɪndɪˈskriːt/ *a.*[1] Also (earlier) **†-creet.** E17. [L *indiscretus* unseparated, undistinguished, f. as IN-[3] + DISCRETE *a.*] **†1** Not separate or distinguishable from contiguous objects or parts. E–M17. **2** Not divided or divisible into distinct parts. L18.
2 M. MONIER-WILLIAMS Next all was water, all a chaos indiscrete.

†indiscrete *a.*[2] see INDISCREET *a.*[1]

indiscretion /ɪndɪˈskrɛʃ(ə)n/ *n.* ME. [(O)Fr. *indiscrétion* or late L *indiscretio(n-)*, f. as IN-[3] + *discretio(n-)*: see DISCRETION.] **1** Lack of discretion, the fact or quality of being indiscreet. Orig. chiefly, lack of discernment or discrimination. Now, lack of sound judgement in speech or action; injudicious or unwary conduct; imprudence; *euphem.* a transgression of social morality. ME. **2** An indiscreet or imprudent act; *euphem.* a transgression of social morality. E17.
1 S. CHITTY That his mistress should sleep naked.. he regarded as the height of indiscretion. 2 Q. CRISP His indiscretion in telling so many people of what.. was a private matter between them.

indiscriminate /ɪndɪˈskrɪmɪnət/ *a.* L16. [f. as IN-[3] + L *discriminatus* DISCRIMINATE *a.*] **1** Not distinguished by discernment or discrimination; done without making distinctions; haphazard; not selective. L16. **2** Of a person: not using or exercising discrimination; making no distinctions. L18.
1 *Birds Magazine* Hedges, too many of which are being destroyed by indiscriminate stubble burning. 2 M. R. MITFORD Without being one of his indiscriminate admirers, I like parts of his books.
indiscriminately *adv.* M17. **indiscriminateness** *n.* L19.

indiscriminating /ɪndɪˈskrɪmɪneɪtɪŋ/ *a.* M18. [f. IN-[3] + DISCRIMINATING.] Not discriminating; that does not make or recognize distinctions.
indiscriminatingly *adv.* E19.

indiscrimination /ˌɪndɪskrɪmɪˈneɪʃ(ə)n/ *n.* M17. [f. IN-[3] + DISCRIMINATION.] The fact of not discriminating; lack of distinction; lack of discrimination or discernment.

indiscriminative /ɪndɪˈskrɪmɪnətɪv/ *a.* M19. [f. IN-[3] + DISCRIMINATIVE.] Not discriminative; not characterized by or inclined to discrimination.
†indiscriminatively *adv.* L17–E18.

indispensable /ɪndɪˈspɛnsəb(ə)l/ *a.* & *n.* Also (now *rare*) **-ible.** M16. [med.L *indispensabilis*, *-ibilis* f. as IN-[3] + DISPENSABLE.] **A** *adj.* **†1** Unable to be allowed or provided for by ecclesiastical dispensation. M16–M17. **2** Of an obligation, duty, etc.: unable to be dispensed with, disregarded, or neglected. Now *rare.* M17. **3** Unable to be dispensed with or done without; absolutely necessary or vital. L17.
2 GIBBON The citizens.. had purchased an exemption from the indispensable duty of defending their country. 3 E. JOHNSON A knowledge of shorthand was almost indispensable for a career in journalism. H. BAILEY Winifred was indispensable to Vera, who could not go.. unless she left a responsible adult in the house.
B *n.* An indispensable person or thing; in *pl.* (*arch. colloq.*), trousers. L17.
indispensaˈbility *n.* M17. **indispensableness** *n.* M17. **indispensably** *adv.* E17.

indispose /ɪndɪˈspəʊz/ *v.t.* M17. [f. IN-[3] + DISPOSE *v.*] **1** Make unfit or incapable (*to do*, *for*). Now *spec.* affect with illness or injury, incapacitate. Cf. INDISPOSED 4. M17. **2** Make averse or unwilling; disincline. L17. **3** Cause to be unfavourably disposed; make unfriendly. Now *rare.* M18. **4** Remove or avoid a physical tendency or inclination *to*; make not liable or subject *to*. E19.
1 J. WILKINS That prejudice.. did indispose them for an equal judgment of things. DEFOE He was a little indisposed by a Fall that he had received. 2 J. SCOTT The miseries of the revolution.. had totally indisposed the people towards any interference with politics. 3 J. H. HARRIS She has long indisposed the whole kingdom against her. 4 COLERIDGE Inoculation.. has so entered into the constitution, as to indispose it to infection.

indisposed /ɪndɪˈspəʊzd/ *a.* LME. [Partly f. Fr. *indisposé* or L *indispositus*; partly f. IN-[3] + DISPOSED.] **†1** Not properly arranged or organized; disordered, disorganized, unprepared. LME–L17. **†2** Not properly fitted, unqualified. *rare.* LME–M17. **†3** Of evil disposition or inclination. LME–L16. **4** Suffering from a (usu. slight) physical disorder; unwell. LME. **5** Disinclined, unwilling, averse (*to* or *to do* something). LME. **6** Not favourably disposed or inclined (*towards*); unfriendly, unfavourable. Now *rare.* M17. **7** Not having a physical inclination or tendency; not liable or subject (*to*). M17.
4 H. FIELDING Mr. Allworthy had been for some days indisposed with a cold. 5 G. CRABBE Unfit to rule and indisposed to please. 6 CLARENDON The king.. was sufficiently indisposed towards the persons or the principles of Mr. Calvin's disciples. 7 J. WEDGWOOD The saturated marine solution is indisposed to crystallize.

indisposition /ˌɪndɪspəˈzɪʃ(ə)n/ *n.* LME. [Fr., or f. IN-[3] + DISPOSITION, after prec.] **†1** Lack of adaptation to some purpose or circumstances; unfitness, incapacity. LME–M18. **2** Physical disorder; ill health, (esp. slight) illness. LME. **3** The state of not being mentally disposed (*to* or *to do* something); disinclination, unwillingness. LME. **4** The state of being unfavourably disposed *to* or *towards*; aversion. Now *rare.* LME. **†5** Lack of arrangement or order; disorder. L16–L17. **6** Lack of physical inclination or tendency; the condition of not being liable or subject *to* something. E20.
1 R. BOYLE We examine other plants.. and observe.. their disposedness or indisposition to yield spirits or oyls. 2 G. GISSING A trifling indisposition kept her to her room. 3 CASTLEREAGH He declined the proposal evidently from indisposition to receive a British force within his dominions. 4 CLARENDON This Indisposition of the King towards the Duke was exceedingly encreased and aggravated.

indisputable /ɪndɪˈspjuːtəb(ə)l, ɪnˈdɪspjʊtəb(ə)l/ *a.* M16. [Late L *indisputabilis*, f. as IN-[3] + *disputabilis* DISPUTABLE.] Unable to be disputed; unquestionable.
P. G. WODEHOUSE They.. did not deny his great talents, which were.. indisputable. A. THWAITE An indisputable fact, which didn't seem to offer any matter for discussion.
indisputaˈbility *n.* L19. **indisputableness** *n.* E18. **indisputably** *adv.* M17.

indisputed /ɪndɪˈspjuːtɪd/ *a.* Now *rare* or *obs.* M17. [f. IN-[3] + *disputed* pa. pple of DISPUTE *v.*] Not disputed, unquestioned.

indisseverable /ɪndɪ(s)ˈsɛv(ə)rəb(ə)l/ *a. rare.* M17. [f. IN-³ + DISSEVER + -ABLE.] Indivisible; unable to be dissevered.

indisseverably *adv.* L16.

indissociable /ɪndɪˈsəʊʃ(ɪ)əb(ə)l, -sɪə-/ *a.* M17. [IN-³ + DISSOCIABLE.] Unable to be dissociated.

H. WOTTON Your tender and generous heart (for these attributes are indissociable).

indissoluble /ɪndɪˈsɒljʊb(ə)l/ *a.* L15. [L *indissolubilis*, f. as IN-³ + *dissolubilis* DISSOLUBLE.] 1 Of a bond or connection: unable to be dissolved, undone, or broken; perpetually binding, firm. Chiefly *fig.* L15. 2 Unable to be dissolved into its elements; unable to be decomposed, disintegrated, or destroyed; indestructible. M16. †3 *Chem.* = INSOLUBLE 3. Also, infusible. M17–E19.

1 L. GORDON The indissoluble link that made Virginia closer to her father . . was his profession as man of letters. R. STRANGE A pledge which binds them in an indissoluble union for the rest of their lives.

indissolub(i)list *n.* & *adj.* (*a*) *n.* a person who believes that marriage is indissoluble and that divorced people should not remarry in church; (*b*) *adj.* of or holding this belief: M20. **indissoluˈbility** *n.* L17. **indissolubleness** *n.* M17. **indissolubly** *adv.* M16.

†indissolvable *a.* M16–L18. [f. IN-³ + DISSOLVABLE.] = prec.

indissuadable /ɪndɪˈsweɪdəb(ə)l/ *a. rare.* E20. [f. IN-³ + DISSUADE + -ABLE.] That cannot be dissuaded; inexorable.

indissuadably *adv.* L19.

†indistant *a.* M17–L18. [med.L *indistant-*, f. as IN-³ + *distant-* DISTANT.] Not distant, not separated by a gap; without gap or interval, continuous.

indistinct /ɪndɪˈstɪŋkt/ *a.* M16. [L *indistinctus*, f. as IN-³ + DISTINCT.] 1 Not apprehended by the senses or mental faculties so as to be clearly distinguished or discerned, or to present a clear distinction of parts; confused, blurred; faint, dim, obscure. M16. 2 Not distinct or distinguished from each other or from something else; not clearly defined or delimited. Now *rare.* E17. 3 Not distinguishing between different things; undiscriminating. Now *rare.* M17.

1 B. EMECHETA Any warning voices she might hear in herself were too indistinct to be effective. A. MACLEAN Captain Bower's words were blurred and indistinct. C. GEBLER Night began to fall. The elm tree became a dark indistinct shape. B. T. BRADFORD He had died in 1909, . . and her memories of him were smudged and indistinct. 2 T. WRIGHT Three sacred persons in Trinitie, distinguished really, and yet indistinct essentially.

indistinctly *adv.* LME. **indistinctness** *n.* E18.

indistinction /ɪndɪˈstɪŋkʃ(ə)n/ *n.* Now *rare.* E17. [f. IN-³ + DISTINCTION, after *indistinct.*] 1 The fact of not distinguishing or making distinctions; failure to perceive or make a difference. E17. 2 The condition or fact of not being distinct or different; lack of distinguishing characteristics. M17. †3 Indistinctness, obscurity, dimness. M17–L18. 4 Lack of distinction or eminence. *joc. rare.* M19.

4 *Athenaeum* Persons of distinction or in-distinction.

indistinctive /ɪndɪˈstɪŋktɪv/ *a.* Now *rare.* M19. [f. IN-³ + DISTINCTIVE.] Without distinctive character or features; not markedly different.

indistinctively *adv.* without distinction; without discriminating: L17. **indistinctiveness** *n.* M19.

indistinguishable /ɪndɪˈstɪŋgwɪʃəb(ə)l/ *a.* E17. [f. IN-³ + DISTINGUISHABLE.] 1 Unable to be distinguished as different *from* something else, or from each other; of which the parts are not distinguishable. E17. 2 Unable to be clearly perceived (by the senses or the mind); imperceptible. M17.

1 R. W. CLARK In the unconscious, fact was indistinguishable from emotionally charged fiction. J. WINTERSON The woman forced wire and flower into an indistinguishable whole. 2 D. L. SAYERS The symptoms of arsenical poisoning and of acute gastritis are really indistinguishable.

indistinguishaˈbility *n.* L19. **indistinguishableness** *n.* M18. **indistinguishably** *adv.* L17.

indistinguished /ɪndɪˈstɪŋgwɪʃt/ *a.* Now *rare.* E17. [f. IN-³ + DISTINGUISHED.] Not distinguished; undistinguished.

indistributable /ɪndɪˈstrɪbjʊtəb(ə)l, ˌɪndɪstrɪˈbjuːtəb(ə)l/ *a. rare.* M19. [f. IN-³ + DISTRIBUTABLE.] Unable to be distributed.

indisturbable /ɪndɪˈstəːbəb(ə)l/ *a. rare.* M17. [f. IN-³ + DISTURB *v.* + -ABLE.] Unable to be disturbed.

indisturbance /ɪndɪˈstəːb(ə)ns/ *n.* Now *rare.* M17. [f. IN-³ + DISTURBANCE.] Absence of disturbance; undisturbed condition; quietness, peace.

indite /ɪnˈdʌɪt/ *v.*¹*t.* Now *rare.* Also (earlier) †**en-**. ME. [OFr. *enditier*: see INDICT *v.*¹] 1 Put into words, compose (a poem, story, speech, etc.); give a literary form to; express or describe in a literary composition. ME. b Put into writing; write (a letter etc.). LME. †2 Speak, suggest, or inspire (a form of words to be repeated or written down); = DICTATE *v.* 1. LME–E19. †3 Enjoin as a law or precept; = DICTATE *v.* 2. Also, dictate to (a person). LME–E18.

1 AV *Ps.* 45:1 My heart is inditing a good matter. DISRAELI Men far too well acquainted with their subject to indite such tales. b P. G. WODEHOUSE A writer should surely find . . golden sentences bubbling up . . when he is inditing a letter to the girl he loves.

inditer *n.* LME. **inditing** *n.* the action of the vb; something indited, a letter, speech, etc.: LME.

†indite *v.*² see INDICT *v.*¹

inditement /ɪnˈdʌɪtm(ə)nt/ *n.*¹ Now *rare.* M16. [f. INDITE *v.*¹ + -MENT.] The action of composing in prose or verse; composition.

†inditement *n.*² see INDICTMENT *n.*

indium /ˈɪndɪəm/ *n.* M19. [f. INDI(GO + -IUM, f. two characteristic indigo lines in its spectrum.] A soft silvery-white metallic chemical element, atomic no. 49, occurring esp. in zinc ores. (Symbol In.)

indivertible /ɪndʌɪˈvəːtɪb(ə)l, ɪndɪ-/ *a. rare.* E19. [f. IN-³ + DIVERTIBLE.] Unable to be diverted or turned aside.

†individable *a.* E–M17. [f. IN-³ + DIVIDABLE.] Unable to be divided; indivisible.

individua *n.pl.* see INDIVIDUUM.

individual /ɪndɪˈvɪdjʊ(ə)l/ *a.* & *n.* LME. [med.L *individualis*, f. L *individuus*, f. *in-* IN-³ + *dividuus* divisible (f. as DIVIDE *v.*): see -UAL.] A *adj.* †1 One in substance or essence; indivisible. LME–L17. †2 That cannot be separated; inseparable. L16–M17. 3 Existing as a separate indivisible identity; numerically one; single, as distinct from others of the same kind; particular. E17. †b Identical, self-same. M17–E19. 4 Of, pertaining or peculiar to a single person or thing, rather than a group; characteristic of an individual. E17. b Intended to serve one person; designed to contain one portion. L19. 5 Distinguished from others by qualities of its own; marked by a peculiar or striking character. M17.

3 BURKE All powers delegated from the board to any individual servant of the company. T. HARDY So familiar with the spot that he knew . . individual cows by their names. 4 M. MITCHELL No public protest could be raised . . , and individual protests were silenced with jail sentences. R. INGALLS He had died after an ordinary anaesthetic . . all anyone could say in explanation was 'individual reaction'. B. BETTELHEIM All rules are based on generalizations, they disregard what is individual. **individual variable** *Logic* a variable that denotes various individuals. b *Listener* We then took six individual dariole moulds, the kind used for baking little castle cakes. 5 G. GREENE The writing seemed to him, after the copper-plate of the office, very individual.

B *n.* 1 A single thing or a group of things regarded as a unit; a single member of a class or group. E17. b A thing which is determined by properties peculiar to itself and cannot be subdivided into others of the same kind. E17. c *Biol.* An organism regarded as having a separate existence; a single member of a species, or of a colonial or compound organism. L18. 2 A single human being, as opp. to a group. E17. b A human being, a person. M18. †3 *ellipt.* One's individual person, self. M17–E19.

2 A. S. NEILL Individuals composing the crowd may be unanimous in hating the rules. b F. HUME He appeared to be an exceedingly unpleasant individual. C. HOPE Individuals arrived there in their private cars.

individualise *v.* var. of INDIVIDUALIZE.

individualism /ɪndɪˈvɪdjʊ(ə)lɪz(ə)m/ *n.* E19. [f. INDIVIDUAL + -ISM, after Fr. *individualisme.*] 1 Self-centred feeling or conduct as a principle; a way of life in which an individual pursues his or her own ends or ideas; free and independent individual action or thought; egoism. E19. 2 The social theory which advocates the free and independent action of the individual; laissez-faire. M19. 3 = INDIVIDUALITY 2,3. M19. 4 *Philos.* The doctrine that reality is constituted of individual entities. Also, the doctrine that the self is the only knowable existence. *rare.* L19. 5 A characteristic or peculiarity of one person or thing. L19. 6 *Biol.* Symbiosis in which the product of the association appears to be a distinct organism, as in lichen. L19.

1 W. HOLTBY Sarah could hardly forbear to cheer this triumph of co-operation over individualism. *Sunday Times* It is as though our youth do not have any individualism—they just follow the mob. 3 *Blackwood's Magazine* Their ideas of God did not possess that individualism and personality. P. GAY He is bound to be committed to individualism, to seek out what is unique.

individualist *n.* & *a.* (*a*) *n.* a person who takes an independent or egoistic course in thought or action; an adherent of individualism; (*b*) *adj.* = INDIVIDUALISTIC: M19. **individuaˈlistic** *a.* of or pertaining to individualism or individualists; characterized by individualism: L19. **individuaˈlistically** *adv.* L19.

individuality /ˌɪndɪvɪdjʊˈalɪti/ *n.* E17. [f. INDIVIDUAL + -ITY. In early use f. med.L *individualitas.*] 1 The sum of the attributes which distinguish one person or thing from others of the same kind; strongly marked individual character; in *pl.*, individual characteristics. E17. 2 Indivisibility, inseparability; an indivisible or inseparable thing. Now *rare* or *obs.* M17. 3 The fact or condition of existing as an individual; separate and continuous existence; the action or position of individual members of a society. M17. 4 An individual thing or personality. L18.

1 J. MCDOUGALL It is parents who give their children a sense of self, enjoyment in their individuality. 3 BURKE Individuality is left out of their scheme of government. The state is all in all. W. PALEY Consciousness carries identity and individuality along with it.

individualize /ɪndɪˈvɪdjʊ(ə)lʌɪz/ *v.t.* Also **-ise**. M17. [f. INDIVIDUAL + -IZE.] 1 Make individual or give an individual character to; characterize, distinguish by distinctive qualities, esp. from other persons or things. M17. 2 Point out or notice individually; specify, particularize. Now *rare.* M17.

individualizer *n.* M19. **individualiˈzation** *n.* the action of individualizing; the fact or condition of being individualized: M18.

individually /ɪndɪˈvɪdjʊ(ə)li/ *adv.* L16. [f. INDIVIDUAL + -LY².] †1 Indivisibly; inseparably. L16–E17. 2 Personally; in an individual capacity. M17. 3 In an individual or distinctive manner; as individuals; singly, one by one. M17.

2 M. R. MITFORD To me individually it would be a great release to be quit . . of the garden. 3 D. ROWE Individually we are very weak, but as part of a group we can be . . strong.

Phrases: †**individually the same** identically the same. **individually different** different as individuals though perhaps identical in species.

†individuate *a.* E17. [med.L *individuatus* pa. pple, f. as next: see -ATE².] 1 Undivided, indivisible, inseparable. E17–M18. 2 = INDIVIDUATED 2. Only in 17.

individuate /ɪndɪˈvɪdjʊeɪt/ *v.t.* E17. [med.L *individuat-* pa. ppl stem of *individuare*, f. L *individuus*: see INDIVIDUAL, -ATE³.] 1 Give an individual character to; distinguish from others of the same kind; individualize; single out. E17. 2 Form into an individual or distinct entity; give individual organization or form to. M17.

1 P. L. COURTIER The heart, that loves its object to select, To individuate. 2 J. SCOTT That which individuates any Society, or makes it a distinct Body . . , is the Charter or Law.

individuative *a.* (*rare*) individualizing M19.

individuated /ɪndɪˈvɪdjʊeɪtɪd/ *ppl a.* M17. [f. prec. + -ED¹.] †1 Undivided, indivisible, inseparable. M–L17. 2 Made individual; individualized. L17. b *Psychol.* Of a person: that has been through the process of individuation. M20.

individuation /ˌɪndɪvɪdjʊˈeɪʃ(ə)n/ *n.* E17. [med.L *individuatio(n-)*, f. as INDIVIDUATE *v.*: see -ATION.] 1 The action or process of individuating, or of distinguishing as individual; *Scholastic Philos.* the means to individual existence, as distinct from that of the species. E17. b *Psychol.* In Jungian psychology, the process of establishing the wholeness and autonomy of the individual self by the integration of consciousness and the collective unconscious. E20. 2 The condition of being an individual; individuality, personal identity. M17. 3 *Biol.* The development or maintenance of a functional organic unity; in colonial organisms, the development of separate but interdependent units. M19.

†**individuity** *n.* E17–E19. [med.L *individuitas*, f. L *individuus*: see INDIVIDUAL, -ITY.] Individuality.

individuum /ɪndɪˈvɪdjʊəm/ *n.* Now *rare.* Pl. **-dua** (chiefly in senses 1, 2), **-duums** (chiefly in sense 3). M16. [L = indivisible particle, atom, (in late L) an individual, use as n. of neut. of *individuus*: see INDIVIDUAL.] 1 Esp. in *Scholastic Logic.* A member of a species; = INDIVIDUAL *n.* 1b. M16. 2 Something which cannot be divided; an indivisible entity. L16. 3 An individual person or thing. L16.

indivisible /ɪndɪˈvɪzɪb(ə)l/ *a.* & *n.* LME. [Late L *indivisibilis*, f. as IN-³ + *divisibilis* DIVISIBLE.] A *adj.* Not divisible; that cannot be divided; incapable of being distributed among a number. LME.

C. THUBRON So flat and brown were both land and water they seemed indivisible.

B *n.* Something which cannot be divided; an indivisible entity. M17.

indivisiˈbility *n.* M17. **indivisibleness** *n.* (now *rare*) M17. **indivisibly** *adv.* M16.

indivision /ɪndɪˈvɪʒ(ə)n/ *n.* Now *rare.* E17. [Late L *indivisio(n-)*, f. L IN-³ + *divisio(n-)* DIVISION.] Lack of division; undivided condition.

Indo- /ˈɪndəʊ/ *comb. form*¹. [f. L *Indus*, Gk *Indos* Indian: see -O-.] Forming ns. and adjs. w. the sense 'Indian and —', chiefly denoting the combination of Indian with some other (ethnological or linguistic) characteristic.

Indo-Abyˈssinian *a.* of or pertaining to both the Dravidians of India and the Hamites of NE Africa L19. **Indo-ˈAfrican** *a.* (*a*) of or pertaining to both India and Africa; (*b*) pertaining to Indians and Africans in South Africa: M19. **Indo-ˈAnglian** *a.* & *n.* (*a*) *adj.* of or pertaining to literature in English written by Indian authors; (*b*) *n.* a writer of such literature: L19. **Indo-ˈBritish** *a.* of or pertaining to both India and Great Britain, or Indo-Britons, or British rule in India; Anglo-Indian: E20. **Indo-ˈBriton** *n.* = ANGLO-INDIAN *n.* M19. **Indo-Chiˈnese** *a.* & *n.* (*a*) *adj.* of or pertaining to Indo-China, the SE Asian peninsula containing Myanmar (Burma), Thailand, Malaya, Laos, Cambodia (Kampuchea), and Vietnam, or (*Hist.*) French Indo-China, the French colonies of Laos, Cambodia (Kampuchea), and Vietnam; (*b*) *n.* (pl. same) a native or inhabitant of (French) Indo-China: E19. **Indo-Gerˈmanic** *n.* & *a.* = INDO-EUROPEAN *n.* 1 & *a.* E19. **Indo-ˈGermanist** *n.* = INDO-EUROPEANIST L19. **Indo-ˈHittite** *n.* a hypothetical language believed to be the common ancestor of Indo-European and Hittite E20. **Indo-Maˈlayan** *a.* of or pertaining to both India and Malaya; *spec.* designating an ethnological region comprising Sri Lanka (Ceylon), the Malay peninsula, and the Malayan islands: M19. **Indo-Paˈcific** *a.* & *n.* (*a*) *adj.* of or pertaining to the Indian Ocean and the adjacent parts of the Pacific; of or pertaining to the group of languages (usu. called *Austronesian*) spoken in the islands of this region; (*b*) *n.* the Indo-Pacific seas or ocean: L19. **Indo-Pak** *a.* (*colloq.*) = INDO-PAKISTANI *a.* M20. **Indo-Pakiˈstan, -Pakiˈstani** *adjs.* pertaining to both India and Pakistan, or their inhabitants M20. **Indo-Portuˈguese** *n.* & *a.* (of or pertaining to) modified Portuguese as used in parts of India L19. **Indo-Saraˈcenic** *a.* designating or pertaining to an architectural style combining Indian and Muslim features L19. **Indo-ˈScythian** *n.* & *a.* (*a*) *n.* a member of an ancient central Asian people of Scythian origin, dominant in northern India and Bactria *c*128 BC–*c*AD 450; (*b*) *adj.* of or pertaining to the Indo-Scythians: L18.

indo- /ˈɪndəʊ/ *comb. form*². [f. IND(IGO + -O-.] *Chem.* Used in names of compounds related to or derived from indigo, esp. derivatives of indole.

indoˈaniline *n.* a violet aniline dye, O:C_6H_4:N·$C_6H_4NH_2$; any derivative of this: L19.

Indo- /ˈɪndəʊ/ *comb. form*³. [f. *Indus* (see below) + -O-.] Of or pertaining to the River Indus in the northern part of the Indian subcontinent.

Indo-Ganˈgetic *a.* of the Rivers Indus and Ganges; *spec.* designating the plain through which they flow, occupying much of the northern part of the Indian subcontinent: L19.

Indo-Aryan /ɪndəʊˈɛːrɪən/ *a.* & *n.* M19. [f. INDO-¹ + ARYAN.] (Designating or pertaining to) the Indian branch of the Indo-Iranian language family, including Sanskrit, Prakrit, and Pali, and the modern languages Hindi, Bengali, Marathi, Nepalese, Sinhalese, etc., and often also including the Dard languages (in this wider sense also called *Indic*).

indochinite /ɪndəʊˈtʃʌɪnʌɪt/ *n.* M20. [f. *Indo-China* (see INDO-CHINESE + -ITE¹.] *Geol.* A tektite from the strewn field of Indo-China.

†**indocible** *a.* M16–L18. [Fr., or late L *indocibilis* f. *docibilis* DOCIBLE, or f. IN-³ + DOCIBLE.] Incapable of being taught or instructed; unteachable.

†**indocibility** *n.* E17–M19.

indocile /ɪnˈdəʊsʌɪl/ *a.* E17. [Fr., or L *indocilis* f. *docilis* DOCILE, or f. IN-³ + DOCILE.] Not docile; not teachable or submissive, intractable.

indoˈcility *n.* M17.

indoctrinate /ɪnˈdɒktrɪneɪt/ *v.t.* Also (*rare*) †**en-**. E17. [f. next + -ATE³, or f. IN-², EN-¹ + DOCTRINATE.] 1 Teach (a person); instruct *in* a subject, bring *into* the knowledge of something. E17. b Teach (a subject etc.) *rare.* E19. 2 Imbue with an idea or doctrine; *spec.* teach systematically to accept (esp. partisan or tendentious) ideas uncritically; brainwash. M19.

1 D. LIVINGSTONE No pains whatever are taken to indoctrinate the adults of the tribe. C. GEIKIE He rather trained their spiritual character than indoctrinated them in systematic theology. 2 W. LIPPMANN With the instruments of the terror, censorship and propaganda, the fascist leaders indoctrinated the mass. D. LODGE They had been indoctrinated since adolescence with the idea . . that contraception was a grave sin.

indoctriˈnation *n.* the action or process of indoctrinating; formal instruction; brainwashing: M17. **indoctrinator** *n.* L19. **indoctrinatory** *a.* that indoctrinates; relating or pertaining to indoctrination: M20.

†**indoctrine** *v.t.* Also (earlier) **en-**. LME–E19. [OFr. *endoctriner*, f. as EN-¹, IN-² + DOCTRINE.] Teach, instruct.

Indo-European /ˌɪndəʊjʊərəˈpiːən/ *n.* & *a.* E19. [f. INDO-¹ + EUROPEAN.] A *n.* 1 a The group of cognate languages which includes most European and many Asian ones; the hypothetical parent language of this group (also called *primitive Indo-European* or *Proto-Indo-European*). E19. b A speaker of an Indo-European language; *spec.* a speaker of Proto-Indo-European. M19. 2 †a An Indianized European. *rare.* Only in E19. b A native or inhabitant of SE Asia who is wholly or partly of European descent. M20. B *adj.* Of, pertaining to, or characteristic of Indo-European or Indo-Europeans. E19.

Indo-Europeanist *n.* an expert in or student of the Indo-European languages E20.

Indo-Iranian /ˌɪndəʊɪˈreɪnɪən, -ˈrɑː-/ *a.* & *n.* L19. [f. INDO-¹ + IRANIAN.] A *adj.* Of or pertaining to both India and Iran; *spec.* designating a branch of Indo-European comprising the Indo-Aryan (Indic) and Iranian languages. L19. B *n.* The Indo-Iranian languages collectively; a speaker of (any of) these. L19.

indole /ˈɪndəʊl/ *n.* Also (now *rare*) **-ol** /-ɒl/. M19. [f. INDO-² + -OLE².] *Chem.* A crystalline heteroaromatic compound, C_8H_7N, which has a molecule consisting of fused benzene and pyrrole rings, has an unpleasant odour, and occurs in coal tar, in faeces, and (as derivatives) in plants.

Comb.: **indoleacetic** *a.*: *indoleacetic acid*, each of seven isomeric acetic acid derivatives of indole; *esp.* one of these (*indole-3-acetic acid*), which is an important plant growth hormone.

inˈdolic *a.* containing, derived from, characteristic of, or characterized by indole E20. **ˈindolyl** *n.* the radical ·C_8H_6N, of which seven isomers exist, derived from indole (*indolylacetic acid* = *indoleacetic acid* above) E20.

indolence /ˈɪnd(ə)l(ə)ns/ *n.* E17. [Fr., or L *indolentia* freedom from pain, f. as IN-³ + *dolent-* pres. ppl stem of *dolere* suffer or give pain: see -ENCE.] †1 Insensibility or indifference to pain. E17–E18. †2 Freedom from pain; a neutral state in which neither pain nor pleasure is felt. M17–M18. 3 The inclination to avoid exertion or trouble; love of ease, laziness; idleness. E18.

3 A. MUNRO Tahiti to her means palm trees . . and the sort of . . indolence that has never interested her. C. PETERS Her indolence—she habitually stayed in bed all morning.

Also †**indolency** *n.* E17–M18.

indolent /ˈɪnd(ə)l(ə)nt/ *a.* M17. [Late L *indolent-*, *-ens*, f. as IN-³ + *dolent-*: see prec., -ENT.] 1 *Med.* Of an ulcer, tumour, etc.: causing no pain, painless. Also, slow to heal, (of a disease or condition) slow to develop. M17. 2 Averse to work or exertion; self-indulgent, lazy, idle. E18.

2 HOR. WALPOLE I am naturally indolent and without application to any kind of business. R. P. WARREN An appearance of swiftness and great competence despite the indolent posture. E. TEMPLETON She wandered from one dusky room into the other, too indolent to put the light on.

indolently *adv.* E18.

indoles /ˈɪndɒliːz/ *n. rare.* L17. [L, f. *indu-* in, within, + root of *alescere* grow up: see ADOLESCENT.] Innate quality or character.

Indology /ɪnˈdɒlədʒi/ *n.* L19. [f. INDO-¹ + -LOGY.] The branch of knowledge that deals with the history, literature, philosophy, etc., of India.

Indoˈlogical *a.* M20. **Indologist** *n.* E20.

†**indomable** *a.* L15–E18. [Fr., or L *indomabilis*, f. as IN-³ + *domabilis* tameable, f. *domare* to tame: see -ABLE.] Untameable.

indomitable /ɪnˈdɒmɪtəb(ə)l/ *a.* M17. [Late L *indomitabilis*, f. as IN-³ + *domitare*: see DAUNT *v.*, -ABLE.] †1 Intractable, untameable. Only in M17. 2 Difficult or impossible to subdue; resolute against adversity or opposition; stubbornly persistent. E19.

2 J. COLVILLE Reynaud is as indomitable as Pétain is defeatist. A. BROOKNER The will was there, the indomitable will, the refusal to give up.

indomitaˈbility *n.* M19. **indomitableness** *n.* M19. **indomitably** *adv.* M19.

Indonesian /ɪndəˈniːzjən, -ʒ(ə)n/ *n.* & *a.* M19. [f. *Indonesia* (see below), f. INDO-¹ + Gk *nēsos* island + -IA¹: see -AN.] A *n.* 1 A native or inhabitant of Indonesia, a large island group in SE Asia, and now esp. of the federal republic of Indonesia, comprising Java, Sumatra, southern Borneo, western New Guinea, the Moluccas, Sulawesi, and many other smaller islands. M19. b A member of the chief pre-Malay population of the island group Indonesia. L19. 2 The western branch of the Austronesian language family; *spec.* the national language of the republic of Indonesia (= BAHASA *Indonesia*). M20. B *adj.* 1 Of or pertaining to Indonesia or Indonesians. M19. 2 Of, pertaining to, or designating the language(s) of Indonesia. M19.

indoor /ˈɪndɔː/ *a.* E18. [f. IN *prep.* + DOOR *n.*, replacing earlier *within-door*.] 1 Situated, done, carried on, or used within a building or under cover; designed or adapted to be so used etc. E18. 2 *Hist.* Within the workhouse or poorhouse. M19.

For other words beginning with *in-* see the entry for **in-**¹

1 THACKERAY I don't care for indoor games . . but I . . long to see a good English hunting-field. L. GORDON Mrs Dalloway paid for the luxury of an indoor lavatory. S. MORLEY Promoters whose plan it was to start . . an indoor pony-racing track in Atlantic City. *indoor cricket*: see CRICKET *n.*[2] 2 H. FAWCETT The indoor relief given in London is a charge upon the whole metropolis.

indoors /ɪnˈdɔːz/ *adv.* L18. [f. as prec. + -S[1], replacing earlier *within doors*.] Within or into a house or other building; under cover.

J. BUCHAN If I spoke to a child its mother would snatch it . . and race indoors with it. G. ORWELL The light indoors was too dull to read by. *her indoors*: see HER *pers. pron.*[1] 1.

Indophile /ˈɪndəʊfʌɪl/ *n.* M19. [f. INDO-[1] + -PHILE.] A lover or admirer of India or Indian things.

indorsation /ɪndɔːˈseɪʃ(ə)n/ *n.* Chiefly *Sc.* Also (earlier) **en-** /ɪn-, ɛn-/. L15. [f. *indorse* var. of ENDORSE *v.* + -ATION.] = ENDORSEMENT.

indorse *v.*, **indorsement** *n.* vars. of ENDORSE *v.*, ENDORSEMENT.

†**indow** *v.* see ENDOW.

†**indowment** *n.* var. of ENDOWMENT.

indoxyl /ɪnˈdɒksʌɪl, -sɪl/ *n.* L19. [f. INDO-[2] + OXY- + -YL.] *Chem.* A bright yellow soluble crystalline compound, C_8H_7NO, 3-hydroxyindole, which oxidizes in air to give indigotin; a radical derived from this by loss of the hydroxyl proton.

indraft *n.* see INDRAUGHT.

†**indrape** *v.t.* E17–M19. [f. IN-[2] + DRAPE *v.*] Make into cloth; weave.

indraught /ˈɪndrɑːft/ *n.* Also ***indraft**. L16. [f. IN-[1] + DRAUGHT *n.*] 1 An inward flow or stream, as of air or water. L16. 2 An opening into land from the sea; an inlet, an inward passage. *obs.* exc. *dial.* L16. 3 The act of drawing in; inward attraction. L17.

1 G. ADAMS The larger the fire, the sharper is the indraught of the air. 3 *Daily News* The indraft of the towns is irresistible, . . the capable young men abandon country labour.

indraw /ɪnˈdrɔː/ *v.t.* Pa. t. **indrew** /ɪnˈdruː/; pa. pple **indrawn** /ɪnˈdrɔːn/. LME. [f. IN-[1] + DRAW *v.*] Draw in. Chiefly as *indrawing* ppl a. & vbl n., *indrawn* ppl a.

indrawal *n.* (*rare*) the action of drawing in; an indraught: M19.

†**indrench** *v.t.* Also (earlier) **en-**. L16–E17. [f. IN-[2], EN-[1] + DRENCH *v.*] Immerse, soak, drown.

indrew *v.* pa. t. of INDRAW.

indri /ˈɪndri/ *n.* Also **indris** /ˈɪndrɪs/. M19. [f. Malagasy *indry!* lo! behold!, or *indry izy!* there he is!, mistaken for the name of the animal, which in Malagasy is *babakoto* (see BABACOOTE).] A large woolly black and white lemur of Madagascar, *Indri indri*, having long hind legs and a short tail and progressing by long leaps between trees. Also, any lemur of the family Indriidae, as the sifaka.

woolly indri: see WOOLLY *a.*

†**indubious** *a.* E17–M19. [f. L *indubius* + -OUS, or f. IN-[3] + DUBIOUS.] Not open to doubt or question; certain, indubitable.

indubitable /ɪnˈdjuːbɪtəb(ə)l/ *a.* LME. [L *indubitabilis* f. *dubitabilis* DUBITABLE, or f. IN-[3] + DUBITABLE.] Impossible to doubt; certain, evident.

indubitaˈbility *n.* M20. **indubitableness** *n.* E18. **indubitably** *adv.* unquestionably, without doubt L15.

indubitatively /ɪnˈdjuːbɪtətɪvli/ *adv. rare.* M19. [f. IN-[3] + DUBITATIVELY.] = INDUBITABLY.

induce /ɪnˈdjuːs/ *v.t.* Also †**en-**. LME. [L *inducere*, f. as IN-[2] + *ducere* lead, or f. Fr. *enduire* (cf. ENDUE).] 1 Lead, persuade, influence (a person). Foll. by *to do* something, (now *rare*) *to* an action, condition, etc. LME. †2 Introduce (a practice, law, condition, etc.). Foll. by *into*. LME–M19. b Introduce by way of argument or illustration; adduce, quote. LME–M17. c Introduce or present (a person); bring in as a character in a literary work. L15–M18. 3 Bring about, produce, give rise to. LME. b *Physics.* Produce (an electric current, a magnetic state) by induction. L18. c *Med.* Initiate (labour) artificially; bring on labour in (a mother), accelerate the birth of (a child). M19. d *Microbiol.* Cause (a bacterium containing a prophage) to begin the lytic cycle. M20. †4 Introduce (a person) *to* a subject; initiate (*into*), accustom *to*; instruct, teach. L15–M16. †5 Lead to as a conclusion; suggest, imply. L15–M17. 6 Infer; derive by reasoning from particular facts. M16. †7 Put (*up*)*on* or *over* as a covering. M16–L18.

1 BURKE To induce us to this, Mr. Fox laboured hard. G. GREENE The twist in Dr Downman's character which induced him to put into blank verse his advice. K. M. E. MURRAY I am tired and am trying to induce someone to carry me. **nothing will induce me to** — I will never be persuaded to —. 3 *Nature* ^{224}Ra with a short . . half life induces in man chiefly osteosarcomas. D. DU MAURIER Endeavoured to induce in me his passion for the planting of rare shrubs. J. HALIFAX Shamanistic trance, frequently induced by powerful hallucinogens. c *absol.*: S. KITZINGER Some hospitals induce if the baby is as much as a week 'overdue'. 6 *Science* From a sufficient number of results a proposition or law is induced.

inducer *n.* a person who or thing which induces; *esp.* an agent that brings about induction: M16.

induced /ɪnˈdjuːst/ *ppl a.* E17. [f. prec. + -ED[1].] Brought on, caused, produced, by attraction, persuasion, etc.; caused or brought into being artificially, or by some external agent or process; not spontaneous; having been produced or affected by induction.

induced drag *Aeronaut.* that part of the drag on an aerofoil due to trailing vortices; also called *vortex drag*. **induced radioactivity**: produced in normally non-radioactive material by irradiation. **induced reaction** *Chem.* a reaction that is accelerated by the presence of an inductor.

inducement /ɪnˈdjuːsm(ə)nt/ *n.* L16. [f. INDUCE + -MENT.] 1 A thing which induces someone *to do* something; an attraction, an incentive. L16. †b A ground or reason which inclines one to a belief or course of action. L16–L17. †2 The action of inducing; persuasion, influence. E–M17. 3†a A preamble or introduction to a book or subject. Only in E17. b *Law.* Introduction; introductory matter. Chiefly in *matters of inducement*, introductory statements in a pleading explaining the matter in dispute. L18.

1 J. A. FROUDE He resisted the inducements which . . were urged upon him to come forward in the world. A. FRASER He had no personal inducement to linger in a country which had treated him so ill.

inducible /ɪnˈdjuːsɪb(ə)l/ *a.* M17. [f. INDUCE + -IBLE.] †1 Able to be inferred. Only in M17. 2 Able to be brought on, brought about, or caused. L17. b *Biochem.* Of an enzyme system: activated in the presence of an appropriate inducer. M20.

induciˈbility *n.* (esp. *Biochem.*) the property or state of being inducible M20.

inducive /ɪnˈdjuːsɪv/ *a. rare.* E17. [f. INDUCE + -IVE.] Tending to induce or give rise to something. (Foll. by *of*, *to*.)

induct /ɪnˈdʌkt/ *v.t.* LME. [L *induct-* pa. ppl stem of *inducere* INDUCE.] 1 a *Eccl.* Introduce formally into possession of a benefice or living. LME. b Introduce formally into office; install. M16. c Place or install in a seat, a room, etc. E18. 2 Lead, conduct *into*. *rare.* E17. 3 Introduce *to*; initiate *into*. E17. 4 Enrol or conscript for military service. *US.* M20.

1 N. HAWTHORNE Lately he has taken orders, and been inducted to a small country living. c DICKENS Received with signal marks of approbation, and inducted into the most honourable seats. 3 THACKERAY The pleasures to which the footman inducted him. J. S. HUXLEY I was inducted into the mysteries of Eton football.

inducˈtee *n.* (*US*) a person inducted into military service M20.

inductance /ɪnˈdʌkt(ə)ns/ *n.* L19. [f. INDUCTION + -ANCE.] *Electr.* 1 That property of a circuit or device by virtue of which any variation in the current flowing through it induces an electromotive force in the circuit itself or in another conductor; the magnitude of this. L19. 2 = INDUCTOR 3c. E20.

1 *mutual inductance*: see MUTUAL *a.* SELF-INDUCTANCE.

inductile /ɪnˈdʌktʌɪl/ *a.* M18. [f. IN-[3] + DUCTILE.] Not ductile or pliable; unyielding, stubborn.

induction /ɪnˈdʌkʃ(ə)n/ *n.* LME. [(O)Fr., or L *inductio(n-)*, f. as INDUCT: see -ION.] 1 a *Logic.* The process of inferring or verifying a general law or principle from the observation of particular instances; an instance of this; a conclusion thus reached. Cf. DEDUCTION 3. LME. b The citing or enumerating *of* a number of separate facts etc. esp. in order to prove a general statement. M16. c *Math.* The process of proving the truth of a theorem by showing that if it is true of any one case in a series then it is true of the next case, and that it is true in a particular case. Freq. more fully *mathematical induction*. M19. 2 *Eccl.* The action or ceremony of formally placing an incumbent in possession of a church and its revenues. LME. b In Presbyterian Churches: the placing of a minister already ordained into a new pastoral charge. L19. 3 Formal introduction to an office or position; installation. LME. b Enlistment into military service. *US.* M20. †4 The action of inducing by persuasion; inducement. L15–L16. 5 Introduction to or initiation into the knowledge of something. Freq. *attrib.* E16. 6 That which leads on or in *to* something; an introduction. Now *rare.* M16. b An introductory statement; a preface (to a book etc.). *arch.* M16. †c The initial step in an undertaking. *rare* (Shakes.). Only in L16. 7 The action of introducing or bringing in (a person, a custom, etc.). *rare.* E17. 8 The action of bringing on, producing, or causing something. M17. b *Med.* The artificial initiation of labour. M19. c *Embryol.* The determination of the pattern of development or differentiation of a region or group of cells by the influence of another. E20. d *Biochem.* Initiation or acceleration of synthesis of an enzyme as a result of the introduction of a specific substance (the inducer). M20. e *Microbiol.* The initiation of the lytic cycle in a bacterium containing a prophage. M20. 9 *Physics.* The action or process of producing an electrical or magnetic state in a body by proximity to an electrified or magnetized body, without physical contact. E19. b Magnetic or electric flux or flux density. Usu. w. specifying wd. M19.

1a T. FOWLER Induction . . is the inference from the particular to the general, from the known to the unknown. R. FRY I . . put forward my system as . . a provisional induction from my own aesthetic experiences. *imperfect induction* see IMPERFECT *a.* b H. ROGERS Rather as a most extensive induction of facts, than as an instance of their successful application. 3b *attrib.*: *Times Lit. Suppl.* One summer the dreaded Induction Notice comes and he goes to war. 5 B. MASON Oh, I knew it was The Test, our puberty rite, our induction into manly ways. 6 G. BUCK An induction to those succeeding evils which pursued that inconsiderate marriage. 8d SEQUENTIAL *induction*. 9 UNIPOLAR *induction*.

Comb.: **induction coil**: in which an electric current is induced; *esp.* a transformer in which a current in a primary coil induces a current (esp. as high-voltage pulses) in a (concentric) secondary coil; **induction furnace**: for melting metals by induction heating; **induction hardening**: of steel surfaces by induction heating followed by quenching; **induction heating**: of a material by inducing an electric current within it; **induction motor** an a.c. electric motor in which the force results from the interaction of a magnetic field in the stationary windings with the currents induced in the rotor.

inductional *a.* E19.

inductive /ɪnˈdʌktɪv/ *a.* LME. [OFr. *inductif*, *-ive*, or late L *inductivus* hypothetical, (in med.L) inducing, leading to, f. as INDUCT: see -IVE.] 1 Leading on (*to* an action etc.); inducing. LME. †2 Productive *of*, giving rise *to*. E17–L18. 3 *Logic.* Of, based on, or characterized by induction; using a method of induction. Cf. DEDUCTIVE. M18. 4 *Physics.* Of the nature of, pertaining to, or due to electric or magnetic induction; possessing inductance. M19. 5 Introductory. M19. 6 *Embryol.* Of, pertaining to, or producing induction of development or differentiation. M20.

inductively *adv.* E18. **inductiveness** *n.* M19. **induc'tivity** *n.* (*rare*) power of or capacity for (esp. magnetic) induction L19.

inductivism /ɪnˈdʌktɪvɪz(ə)m/ *n.* M19. [f. prec. + -ISM.] The use of or preference for inductive methods; the belief that scientific laws can be inferred from observational evidence. Opp. DEDUCTIVISM.

inductivist *n.* & *a.* (*a*) *n.* a person who advocates inductivism or inductive methods; (*b*) *adj.* of, pertaining to, or employing inductivism or inductive methods: M20.

inductomeric /ɪnˌdʌktə(ʊ)ˈmɛrɪk/ *a.* M20. [f. INDUCTION after ELECTROMERIC.] *Chem.* Of, pertaining to, or designating the polarizing effect exerted along a saturated chemical bond by an external electric field.

inductor /ɪnˈdʌktə/ *n.* M17. [Late L, or f. INDUCT + -OR.] 1 A person who inducts or initiates. *rare.* M17. 2 A person who inducts a member of the clergy to a benefice. E18. 3 A part of an electrical apparatus which acts inductively on another, esp. to produce an electromotive force or a current. M19. b A conductor or device in which an electromotive force or current is induced. M19. c A device (usu. a coil) possessing inductance or used on account of its inductance. E20. 4 *Chem.* A substance which accelerates a reaction by reacting with one of the substances involved, so differing from a catalyst by being consumed. E20. 5 *Embryol.* (A substance produced by) a region of an embryo capable of causing induction of development or differentiation. E20.

inductory /ɪnˈdʌkt(ə)ri/ *a. rare.* M17. [f. INDUCTIVE by suffix-substitution, or f. INDUCT: see -ORY[2].] Introductory.

indue *v.* var. of ENDUE.

indulge /ɪnˈdʌldʒ/ *v.* E17. [L *indulgere* allow space or time for, give rein to.] I *v.t.* 1 Treat (a person) with excessive kindness; gratify by compliance or absence of restraint; humour by yielding to the wishes of. (Foll. by *in*.) E17. b *refl.* Give free course to one's inclination or liking; gratify oneself. (Foll. by *in*.) M17. c Favour or gratify (a person) *with* something given or granted. L18. 2 Grant an indulgence, privilege, or dispensation to. M17. 3 Gratify (a desire or inclination); give free course to, yield to, give oneself up to; cherish, foster. M17. 4 Bestow, grant as a favour; allow or concede as an indulgence. Now *rare.* M17. 5 *Comm.* Grant an indulgence on (a bill), or to (a person) on a bill. M18.

1 HARPER LEE She's never let them get away with anything, she never indulged them. b L. BRUCE I would indulge myself in bizarre melodramatic fantasies. 3 E. F. BENSON She was quite willing to indulge any foolish prejudices of her husband. L. NAMIER He . . retires to his closet . . . to indulge the melancholy enjoyment of his own ill humour. 4 S. HALLIFAX A Valuable privilege is likewise indulged to Graduates in this faculty.

II *v.i.* †6 Grant indulgence *to* (a propensity etc., *rarely* a person); give free course *to*, give way *to*. M17–L18. 7 Foll. by *in*: give rein to one's inclination for; gratify one's desire or appetite for; take one's pleasure in. E18. 8 Gratify a desire, appetite, etc.; take one's pleasure; *spec.* (*colloq.*) partake (freely) of intoxicants. E18.

7 H. T. LANE We believe that children develop bad habits by indulging in them. T. SHARPE Observing his fellow travellers and indulging in British Rail's high tea. 8 P. O'DONNELL Tarrant . . took out his cigar case. He had not indulged all night.

indulged *ppl a.* (*a*) that has received and accepted an indulgence; *esp.* (*Sc. Hist.*) (of a Presbyterian minister) licensed to hold services; (*b*) gratified or favoured by compliance; humoured: L17. **indulger** *n.* M17. **indulging** *ppl a.* that indulges; indulgent: M18. **indulgingly** *adv.* L18.

indulgence /ɪnˈdʌldʒ(ə)ns/ *n.* LME. [(O)Fr., f. L *indulgentia*, f. *indulgent-*: see INDULGENT, -ENCE.] I 1 The act of indulging a person; the fact of being indulgent; gratification of another's desire or humour; overly lenient treatment. LME. b An instance of this; a favour or privilege granted. L16. 2 The action of indulging an inclination etc.; yielding to or gratification of a propensity (foll. by *of*, *to*); the action of indulging *in* a practice. M17. b The practice of indulging one's own inclinations; self-gratification, self-indulgence. Also, an indulgent habit, a luxury. M17.

1 H. MARTINEAU Indulgence is given her as a substitute for justice. H. JAMES I had not been properly introduced and could only throw myself upon her indulgence. b LD MACAULAY He ordered them to be . . supplied with every indulgence. 2 J. MORTIMER Overcome with . . the indulgence of grief, he sank to his knees. P. GAY The indulgence in heedless pleasure entails later pain. b M. SHELLEY The time . . arrives, when grief is rather an indulgence than a necessity. R. W. EMERSON Human nature is prone to indulgence.

II 3 *RC Ch.* A grant of remission of the temporal punishment still due to sin after sacramental absolution. LME. †b Remission of sin. Only in LME. 4 *Hist.* A grant of religious liberties, as special favours rather than legal rights, to Nonconformists. M17. b A licence offered during the reigns of Charles II and James II (VII) to Presbyterian ministers in Scotland to hold services on various conditions. L17. 5 *Comm.* An extension, made as a favour, of the time within which a bill of exchange or a debt is to be paid. E19.

3 D. LODGE An indulgence was a kind of spiritual voucher obtained by performing some devotional exercise. 4 **Declaration of Indulgence** a proclamation of religious liberties; *esp.* either of those made in Scotland under Charles II in 1672 and James II (VII) in 1687. *plenary indulgence*: see PLENARY *a.*

indulgence /ɪnˈdʌldʒ(ə)ns/ *v.t.* L16. [f. the n.] †1 Grant or permit as an indulgence or favour. Only in L16. 2 *RC Ch.* Attach an indulgence to (a particular act or object). Freq. as *indulgenced* ppl a., conveying an indulgence. M19.

indulgency /ɪnˈdʌldʒ(ə)nsi/ *n.* Now *rare.* M16. [L *indulgentia*: see INDULGENCE *n.*, -ENCY.] 1 The quality or practice of being indulgent; indulgent disposition or action. M16. b An indulgence; a favour. M18. 2 = INDULGENCE *n.* 2. L17. †3 = INDULGENCE *n.* 3. L17–M19.

indulgent /ɪnˈdʌldʒ(ə)nt/ *a.* E16. [Fr., or L *indulgent-* pres. ppl stem of *indulgere*: see INDULGE, -ENT.] 1 That indulges; disposed to gratify by compliance or humour, or to overlook failings; ready to show favour or leniency; (overly) lenient, not exercising (due) restraint. (Foll. by *to*.) E16. 2 Indulging or disposed to indulge oneself; self-indulgent. L17.

1 E. CALDWELL He came along in a generation that was fed so much sugar and cream by indulgent parents. D. H. LAWRENCE He followed her look, and laughed quietly, with indulgent resignation. 2 E. O'BRIEN Soon she would be indulgent and order a champagne cocktail.

indulgently *adv.* L16.

induline /ˈɪndjʊliːn/ *n.* Also **-in** /-ɪn/. L19. [f. INDO-[2] + -ULE + -INE[5], -IN[1].] *Chem.* Any of a group of insoluble blue azine dyes.

indult /ɪnˈdʌlt/ *n.* L15. [Fr. f. late L *indultum* grant, concession, use as n. of neut. of L *indultus* pa. pple of *indulgere* INDULGE.] 1 *RC Ch.* A licence granted by the Pope authorizing an act that the common law of the Church does not sanction. L15. †2 A special privilege granted by authority; a licence or permission. M16–E17.

indulto /ɪnˈdʌltəʊ, *foreign* inˈdulto/ *n.* Pl. **-os** /-əʊz, *foreign* -ɔs/. M17. [Sp. & Port. = exemption, privilege, licence, f. late L *indultum*: see prec.] †1 = prec. M17–E19. 2 *Hist.* A duty paid to the King of Spain or Portugal, *spec.* on imported goods. L17.

indument /ˈɪndjʊm(ə)nt/ *n.* Now *rare.* L15. [L *indumentum* garment, f. *induere* put on: see -MENT.] †1 Clothing, apparel; a garment, a vesture. L15–L17. b *fig.* A material body. L16–L17. 2 A covering of hairs, feathers, etc.; an integument; an indumentum. L16.

indumentum /ɪndjʊˈmɛntəm/ *n.* Pl. **-ta** /-tə/. M19. [f. as prec.] *Bot.* The covering of hairs, scales, etc., on (part of) a plant, esp. when dense.

induna /ɪnˈduːnə/ *n. S. Afr.* M19. [Zulu, f. nominal pref. *in-* + *duna* councillor, headman, overseer, captain.] 1 A tribal councillor or headman. M19. 2 *transf.* A person, esp. a Black person, in authority; a foreman. M20.

induplicate /ɪnˈdjuːplɪkət/ *a.* E19. [f. IN-[2] + DUPLICATE *a.*] *Bot.* Of leaves, petals (when in the bud): folded or rolled in at the edges without overlapping.

indupli'cation *n.* (*Bot.* & *Zool.*) (an instance of) folding or doubling in L19.

indurable /ɪnˈdjʊərəb(ə)l/ *a. rare.* LME. [med.L *indurabilis*, f. as IN-[3] + *durabilis* DURABLE.] Not durable; not lasting.

†indurance *n.* var. of ENDURANCE.

indurate /ˈɪndjʊrət/ *ppl a.* Now *rare.* LME. [L *induratus* pa. pple, f. as next: see -ATE[2].] 1 Made hard, hardened. LME. 2 Morally hardened, made callous; obstinate. LME.

indurate /ˈɪndjʊreɪt/ *v.* M16. [L *indurat-* pa. ppl stem of *indurare* make hard, f. as IN-[2] + *durus* hard: see -ATE[3].] 1 *v.t.* Harden (the heart); make callous or unfeeling; make obstinate. M16. 2 *v.t.* Make (a substance) hard; harden, solidify. L16. 3 *v.t.* Make hardy; inure. L16. 4 *v.i.* Become or grow hard. M17. b Of a custom: become fixed or established. M19.

1 H. M. WILLIAMS It is the curse of revolutionary calamities to indurate the heart. 2 R. KIRWAN Two beds of indurated clay. O. SACKS The superficial temporal artery may become exquisitely tender . . and visibly indurated. 4 J. BARNES Soft cheeses collapse; firm cheeses indurate.

¶Freq. as *indurated* ppl a.

induration /ɪndjʊˈreɪʃ(ə)n/ *n.* LME. [(O)Fr., or late L *induratio(n-)*, f. as prec.: see -ATION.] 1 The action of hardening; the process of being hardened or becoming hard; hardened condition; *esp.* (*a*) consolidation or hardening of a rock or soil by heat, pressure, chemical action, etc.; (*b*) *Med.* abnormal hardening of an organ or tissue. LME. 2 A hardening of character or feeling; obstinacy, stubbornness; callousness. L15.

indurative /ˈɪndjʊərətɪv/ *a.* L16. [f. as INDURATE *v.*: see -ATIVE.] Having a hardening tendency or quality.

†indure *v.* var. of ENDURE.

Indus /ˈɪndəs/ *n.* E18. [L = an Indian.] (The name of) a constellation of the southern hemisphere between Capricorn and Pavo; the Indian.

indusium /ɪnˈdjuːzɪəm/ *n.* Pl. **-ia** /-ɪə/. E18. [L = tunic, f. *induere* put on (a garment).] *Biol.* & *Anat.* Any of various thin membranous coverings, as (*a*) (now *rare*) the amnion; (*b*) the larval case of some insects; (*c*) a collection of hairs enclosing the stigma of some flowers; (*d*) a flap of tissue covering a sorus on a fern leaf; (*e*) the thin layer of grey matter on the upper surface of the corpus callosum.

indusial *a.* E19. **indusiate** *a.* having an indusium M19.

industrial /ɪnˈdʌstrɪəl/ *a.* & *n.* L15. [f. (as) INDUSTRY + -AL[1]; later after Fr. *industriel.*] A *adj.* 1 Pertaining to or of the nature of industry or productive labour; resulting from industry; engaged in or connected with industry, esp. with manufacturing. L15. 2 Of a substance or material: of a quality suitable for industrial use. E20. 3 Characterized by highly developed industries. E20.

1 J. L. MOTLEY Such of the industrial classes as could leave . . had wandered away to Holland and England. U. BENTLEY The city's buildings were still charred with two hundred years of industrial soot. 3 J. D. BERNAL Only the industrial countries of Europe . . contributed to modern science.

Special collocations: **industrial action** action such as a strike or working to rule taken by employees. **industrial archaeology** the branch of archaeology that deals with the equipment and workings of industry in former times. **industrial disease** a disease contracted in the course of employment, esp. in a factory. **industrial dispute** a dispute between employers and employees. **industrial espionage** spying directed towards discovering the secrets of a rival manufacturer or other industrial company. **industrial estate** an area of land devoted to industrial use, usu. with an integrated plan. **industrial injury**: sustained in the course of employment, esp. in a factory. *industrial* MELANISM. **industrial park** = *industrial estate* above. **industrial relations**: between employers and employees. **industrial revolution** the rapid development of a nation's industry through the introduction of machines, esp. (freq. w. cap. initials) in Britain in the late 18th and early 19th cents. **industrial school** *Hist.* a school established in Britain in the 19th cent. to enable needy children to learn a trade. *industrial tribunal*: see TRIBUNAL *n.*

B *n.* 1 A person engaged in industrial activities. M19. 2 (A share in) a joint-stock industrial enterprise. L19.

industrialism *n.* a social or economic system arising from the existence of great industries; the organization of industrial occupations: M19. **industrialist** *n.* a person engaged in or connected with (the management or ownership of) industry; a manufacturer: M19. **industrially** *adv.* M19.

industrialize /ɪnˈdʌstrɪəlʌɪz/ *v.* Also **-ise**. L19. [f. prec. + -IZE.] 1 *v.t.* Affect with or devote to industrialism; occupy or organize industrially. Freq. as *industrialized* ppl a. L19. 2 *v.i.* Become industrial. M20.

1 **industrialized building** a form of construction in which industrial methods are used (esp. prefabrication, mechanization, standardization); a building erected by such methods.

industriali'zation *n.* the process of industrializing; the fact of being industrialized; the conversion of an organization into an industry: E20.

industrious /ɪnˈdʌstrɪəs/ *a.* L15. [Fr. *industrieux* or late L *industriosus*, f. *industria*: see INDUSTRY, -OUS.] †1 Showing intelligent or skilful work; skilful, clever, ingenious. L15–L17. 2 Showing application, endeavour, or effort; painstaking, zealous, attentive. (Foll. by *in*, *to do*.) M16. 3 Showing assiduous or steady work; diligent, hard-working. L16. †4 Showing design or purpose; intentional, designed, voluntary. E17–E19. 5 = INDUSTRIAL *a. rare*. E19.

industriously *adv.* L15. **industriousness** *n.* L16.

industry /ˈɪndəstri/ *n.* LME. [(O)Fr. *industrie* or L *industria* diligence: see -Y[3].] 1 Diligence or assiduity in the performance of a task or effort; close and steady application to a task; exertion. LME. 2 Systematic work or labour; habitual employment in useful work. Now *esp.* work in manufacturing and production; trade and manufacture collectively. LME. †3 Intelligent working; skill, ingenuity, cleverness. L15–E17. †4 An application of skill, cleverness, or craft; a device; a crafty expedient. L15–E17. 5 A particular form or branch of productive labour; a trade, a manufacture. M16. 6 *Archaeol.* A collection of prehistoric implements of the same age found at an archaeological site, generally with typical debris from their manufacture, and used as evidence of the original technique of working; the technique so revealed. E20. 7 A particular (profitable) activity; *esp.* diligent work devoted to the study of a particular person or other subject. *colloq.* M20.

1 K. TYNAN A climax towards which she has climbed, with unflourished industry. 2 R. BURNS A man that has been bred up in the trade of begging, will never . . fall to industry. CARLYLE The Leaders of Industry . . are virtually the Captains of the World. R. INGALLS She had started out with the introduction of agriculture, the coming of industry. 5 S. O'FAOLÁIN The founder of an industry—glass-making. *Studio Week* The most . . . productive tool in the music industry today. 7 *Daily Telegraph* The brisk pick-up of business in the abortion industry. C. OSBORNE I did not want to become involved in the Eliot industry.

Phrases.: *basic industry*: see BASIC *a.* I. COTTAGE *industry*. *growth industry*: see GROWTH *a. heavy industry*: see HEAVY *a. light industry*: see LIGHT *a.*[1] *primary industry*: see PRIMARY *a. secondary industry*: see SECONDARY *a. tertiary industry*: see TERTIARY *a.*

Comb.: **industry-wide** *a.* extending or prevalent throughout a particular industry.

indwell /ɪnˈdwɛl/ *v.* Pa. t. & pple **-dwelt** /-dwɛlt/. LME. [f. IN-[1] + DWELL *v.*, orig. rendering L *inhabitare* inhabit.] 1 *v.t.* Dwell in, inhabit, occupy as a dwelling. Now chiefly *fig.*, (esp. of God, the Holy Spirit) be permanently present in, possess (the heart, soul, mind, etc.). LME. 2 *v.i.* Dwell, abide, live (*in*). LME.

'indweller *n.* (*a*) a person who lives in a place, an inhabitant; (*b*) a mere resident, a sojourner: LME. **'indwelling** *a.* (*a*) that dwells within, inhabits, or possesses; (*b*) *Med.* (of a catheter, electrode, etc.) left more or less permanently fixed in the body: LME.

indy *n.* & *a.* var. of INDIE.

-ine /ʌɪn, ɪn, iːn/ *suff.*[1] [Repr. Fr. *-in*, *-ine* or L *-inus*, *-ina*, *-inum*. Cf. -INE[3], -INE[4].] Forming adjs. with the sense 'of, pertaining to, of the nature of'. Orig. & chiefly w. L noun stems, as *Alpine*, *aquiline*, *canine*, *supine*; freq. in *Biol.*, forming adjs. from the names of genera, as *bovine*, *equine*, *feline*, or of subfamilies (in L *-inae*) or tribes (in L *-ini*).

-ine /ʌɪn/ *suff.*[2] [Repr. L *-inus*, f. Gk *-inos*.] Forming adjs. w. the sense 'of the nature of, resembling', esp. f. names of minerals, plants, etc., as *adamantine*, *crystalline*, *hyacinthine*.

¶ Formerly also pronounced /ɪn, iːn/.

-ine /ɪn, iːn/ *suff.*[3] [Repr. or after Fr. *-ine*, L *-ina*, Gk *-inē*: see -INE[1].] Forming fem. ns., as *heroine*, *margravine*, *Trappistine*.

-ine /ɪn, iːn, ʌɪn/ *suff.*[4] [Repr. Fr. *-ine*, L *-ina* in uses as ns. of adjs.: see -INE[1].] Forming (esp. abstract) ns., as *concubine*, *doctrine*, *fascine*, *medicine*, *rapine*. Now freq. forming names of derived substances, similative appellations, diminutives, etc., as *brilliantine*, *dentine*, *figurine*, *nectarine*, *tambourine*.

-ine /iːn, ɪn/ *suff.*[5] See also -EINE. [f. prec.] 1 Used in *Chem.* to form names of substances (orig. & chiefly with stems representing the sources of the substances), esp. alkaloids (*cocaine*, *strychnine*), amino acids (*glycine*, *thymine*), amines (*aniline*, *hydrazine*), and halogens (*chlorine*), and formerly also in *Min.* (*olivine*). 2 *Chem.* Forming ns. denoting compounds with a single ring of six atoms, one at least of which is nitrogen, as *azine*.

inearth /ɪˈnəːθ/ *v.t.* Chiefly *poet.* E19. [f. IN-[1] + EARTH *n.*[1]] Bury, inter.

inebriant /ɪˈniːbrɪənt/ *n.* E19. [f. INEBRIATE *v.* after *intoxicant*: see -ANT[1].] An inebriating substance or agent; an intoxicant.

inebriate /ɪˈniːbrɪət/ *n.* L18. [f. (as) next: see -ATE[1].] An intoxicated person; *esp.* a habitual drunkard.

inebriate /ɪˈniːbrɪeɪt/ *v.t.* Pa. pple & ppl a. **-ated**, (*arch.*) **-ate** /-ət/. LME. [Orig. pa. pple, f. L *inebriatus* pa. pple of *inebriare*, f. as IN-[2] + *ebriare* intoxicate, f. *ebrius* drunk: see -ATE[2], -ATE[3].] 1 Make drunk; intoxicate. LME. †2 Water, moisten; refresh (as) with drink. E–M17.

1 W. COWPER While . . the cups That cheer but not inebriate, wait on each. *fig.*: DISRAELI A sophisticated rhetorician, inebriated with the exuberance of his own verbosity.

inebriation /ɪˌniːbrɪˈeɪʃ(ə)n/ *n.* E16. [Late L *inebriatio(n-)*, f. L *inebriat-* pa. ppl stem of *inebriare*: see prec., -ATION.] The action of inebriating someone; the condition of being inebriated; intoxication.

inebriety /ɪnɪˈbrʌɪəti/ *n.* L18. [f. IN-[2] + EBRIETY.] The state or habit of being inebriated; (habitual) drunkenness.

inebrious /ɪˈniːbrɪəs/ *a. rare.* LME. [f. IN-[2] + L *ebriosus* + -OUS, perh. after OFr. or med.L; later directly f. IN-[2] + EBRIOUS.] †1 Inebriating, intoxicating. LME–E18. 2 Inebriated, (habitually) drunken. M19.

inedible /ɪnˈɛdɪb(ə)l/ *a.* E19. [f. IN-[3] + EDIBLE *a.*] Not edible, unfit to be eaten; *colloq.* unpalatable.

P. BOWLES It would not be amusing . . to sleep in dirty beds, eat inedible meals.

inedi'bility *n.* L19.

inédit /inedi/ *n.* Pl. pronounced same. E20. [Fr.: cf. next.] An unpublished work; *fig.* something secret or unrevealed.

inedita /ɪnˈɛdɪtə/ *n.pl.* L19. [mod.L, use as n. of neut. pl. of L *ineditus*, f. as IN-[3] + *editus* pa. pple of *edere* give out, EDIT *v.*] Unpublished writings.

inedited /ɪnˈɛdɪtɪd/ *a.* M18. [f. IN-[3] + EDIT *v.* + -ED[1].] 1 Not edited, not published; not described in any published work. M18. 2 Published without editorial alterations or additions. M19.

ineducable /ɪnˈɛdjʊkəb(ə)l, -dʒʊ-/ *a.* & *n.* L19. [f. IN-[3] + EDUCABLE.] A *adj.* Unable to be educated, esp. as a result of mental handicap. L19. B *n.* An ineducable person. M20.

ineduca'bility *n.* E20.

ineffable /ɪnˈɛfəb(ə)l/ *a.* & *n.* LME. [(O)Fr., or L *ineffabilis*, f. as IN-[3] + *effabilis*, f. *effari* speak out, f. as EF- + *fari* speak: see -ABLE.] A *adj.* 1 Too great to be expressed in words; unutterable, indefinable, indescribable. LME. 2 Not to be uttered. Formerly also, not to be disclosed. L16. †3 Unpronounceable. *rare.* M–L17.

B *n.* 1 A person or thing not to be mentioned or named; *spec.* (*arch.*) in *pl.*, trousers. E19. 2 A person, thing, or condition which is beyond description or expression. M20.

2 *Library* A flight of spiritual stairs leading the contemplator ever closer to the ineffable.

ineffa'bility *n.* E17. **ineffableness** *n.* L17. **ineffably** *adv.* L15.

ineffaceable /ɪnɪˈfeɪsəb(ə)l/ *a.* E19. [f. IN-[3] + EFFACE + -ABLE.] Impossible to efface or obliterate; indelible.

SOUTHEY The everlasting and ineffaceable infamy of bombarding Copenhagen.

ineffacea'bility *n.* L19. **ineffaceably** *adv.* E19.

ineffective /ɪnɪˈfɛktɪv/ *a.* & *n.* M17. [f. IN-[3] + EFFECTIVE.] A *adj.* 1 Not producing any, or the desired, effect; ineffectual, inoperative, inefficient. M17. 2 Lacking in artistic effect. M19.

1 J. R. ACKERLEY Since her hostile attitude was seen to be as inconvenient as it was ineffective, she relented. W. WHARTON I also feel ineffective, helpless; Vron could do these things ten times better than I can.

B *n.* An ineffective person or thing. M19.

ineffectively *adv.* M17. **ineffectiveness** *n.* M19.

ineffectual /ɪnɪˈfɛktʃʊəl/ *a.* LME. [med.L *ineffectualis*; later f. IN-[3] + EFFECTUAL.] 1 Having no effect; unavailing, unsuccessful, fruitless. LME. 2 Not producing the desired effect; not fulfilling expectations; tame. L18. 3 Failing in one's purpose or role; inadequate. M19.

1 D. BREWSTER When he found his reasoning ineffectual, he appealed to direct experience. 2 E. K. KANE The phosphorescence was not unlike the ineffectual fire of the glow-worm. 3 S. MORLEY We spent a year . . in a science class taken by an absurd and ineffectual master.

ineffectu'ality *n.* L17. **ineffectually** *adv.* E17. **ineffectualness** *n.* M17.

inefficacious /ˌɪnɛfɪˈkeɪʃəs/ *a.* M17. [f. IN-[3] + EFFICACIOUS.] Not efficacious; ineffective.

inefficaciously *adv.* E18. **inefficaciousness** *n.* M17.

inefficacy /ɪnˈɛfɪkəsi/ *n.* E17. [Late L *inefficacia*; later f. IN-[3] + EFFICACY.] Lack of efficacy; inability to produce the desired effect.

R. L. STEVENSON The usual inefficacy of the lamps, which . . shed but a dying glimmer even while they burned.

Also **ineffi'cacity** *n.* (*rare*) E18.

inefficiency /ɪnɪˈfɪʃ(ə)nsi/ *n.* M18. [f. IN-[3] + EFFICIENCY.] Lack of efficiency; ineffectiveness, incompetence.

inefficient /ɪnɪˈfɪʃ(ə)nt/ *a.* & *n.* M18. [f. IN-[3] + EFFICIENT.] A *adj.* Not efficient; unable to work effectively; incompetent; wasteful. M18. B *n.* An inefficient person. L19.

inefficiently *adv.* E19.

inegalitarian /ˌɪnɪgalɪˈtɛːrɪən/ *a.* & *n.* M20. [f. IN-[3] + EGALITARIAN.] A *adj.* Of or pertaining to inequality; favouring or marked by inequality. M20. B *n.* A person who denies or opposes equality between people. M20.

inegalitarianism *n.* M20.

inelaborate /ɪnɪˈlab(ə)rət/ *a.* E17. [f. IN-[3] + ELABORATE *a.*] Not elaborate; simple in design or workmanship; not complicated or ornate.

inelaborately *adv.* E19.

inelastic /ɪnɪˈlastɪk/ *a.* M18. [f. IN-[3] + ELASTIC *a.*] 1 Not elastic or resilient, either rigid or plastic. M18. b *Physics.* Of a collision or scattering (esp. of subatomic particles): involving a reduction in total translational kinetic energy of the bodies or particles colliding. M19. 2 *fig.* Not adaptable; inflexible, unyielding. M19. b *Econ.* Of demand or supply: unresponsive to, or varying less than in proportion to, changes in price. L19.

2 *Spectator* The House of Lords show not firmness . . but inelastic obstinacy and obstructiveness. G. S. FRASER Jonson with his strong . . but inelastic mind would shy away from Donne's agility in paradox. b

Lancet Demand for cigarettes is inelastic... If prices rise by 1% demand falls, but by.. less than 1%.

inelastically *adv.* M20. **inelasticity** /ˌɪnɪlaˈstɪsɪti/ *n.* the quality or condition of being inelastic; an instance of this: E19.

inelegance /ɪnˈɛlɪɡ(ə)ns/ *n.* E18. [f. next: see -ANCE.] The quality or fact of being inelegant; lack of refinement; clumsiness; an instance of this.

Also **inelegancy** *n.* (now *rare*) E18.

inelegant /ɪnˈɛlɪɡ(ə)nt/ *a.* E16. [Fr. *inélégant* f. L *inelegant-*, f. as IN-[3] + *elegant-*: see ELEGANT.] 1 Lacking elegance or refinement; ungraceful, clumsy; coarse, crude; (of language or style) unpolished. E16. 2 Lacking in aesthetic refinement or delicacy. M17.

inelegantly *adv.* L17.

ineligible /ɪnˈɛlɪdʒɪb(ə)l/ *a.* & *n.* L18. [f. IN-[3] + ELIGIBLE.] A *adj.* †1 Of an action: inexpedient, unsuitable, undesirable. Only in L18. 2 Legally or officially disqualified for election to an office or position. L18. 3 Not suitable or desirable, esp. as a partner in marriage. E19.

2 T. JEFFERSON My wish.. was that the President should be elected for seven years, and be ineligible afterwards.

B *n.* An ineligible person; *spec.* an undesirable marriage partner. L19.

Westminster Gazette Eligible men as a class are so much less agreeable than the ineligibles.

ineligiˈbility *n.* L18. **ineligibly** *adv.* M19.

ineliminable /ɪnɪˈlɪmɪnəb(ə)l/ *a.* L19. [f. IN-[3] + ELIMINABLE.] Unable to be eliminated.

ineloquent /ɪnˈɛləkwənt/ *a.* M16. [f. IN-[3] + ELOQUENT.] Not eloquent; lacking eloquence.

ineloquence *n.* M19. **ineloquently** *adv.* E19.

ineluctable /ɪnɪˈlʌktəb(ə)l/ *a.* E17. [L *ineluctabilis*, f. as IN-[3] + *eluctari* struggle out: see -ABLE.] Unable to be resisted or avoided; inescapable.

M. BEERBOHM 'There', he said, 'is the ineluctable hard fact you wake to... The gods have spoken.' I. MURDOCH He felt himself confronted with an ineluctable choice between an evident truth and a fable.

inelucta'bility *n.* M20. **ineluctably** *adv.* M17.

ineludible /ɪnɪˈluːdɪb(ə)l, -ˈljuː-/ *a.* L17. [f. IN-[3] + ELUDE + -IBLE.] Unavoidable, inescapable.

Earlier **ineludable** *a.* (*rare*) M17.

inenarrable /ɪnɪˈnarəb(ə)l/ *a.* LME. [(O)Fr. *inénarrable* f. L *inenarrabilis*, f. as IN-[3] + *enarrare* narrate: see E-, NARRATE, -ABLE.] Unable to be narrated or told; indescribable, unspeakable.

M. DAVIES That sacred.. Mystery of the Holy Trinity is ineffable and inenarrable by any Creature. *Listener* The music has an inenarrable greatness which quite transcends the occasion of its composition.

inenubilable /ɪnɪˈnjuːbɪləb(ə)l/ *a. rare.* E20. [f. IN-[3] + L *enubilare* make clear (see ENUBILATE) + -ABLE.] Unable to be cleared of clouds or mist; *fig.* inexplicable.

M. BEERBOHM There is nothing in England to be matched with.. that mysterious inenubilable spirit, spirit of Oxford.

inept /ɪˈnɛpt/ *a.* M16. [L *ineptus*, f. as IN-[3] + *aptus* APT. Cf. INAPT.] 1 Unsuitable *for* (or †*to*) a purpose, unfit (*arch.*). In *Sc. Law*, invalid, void. M16. 2 Lacking in judgement or skill; foolish, clumsy, incompetent. E17. 3 Not suited to the occasion; out of place, inappropriate. L17.

1 J. RAY The Air.. would contain but few nitrous Particles, and so be inept to maintain the Fire. SIR W. SCOTT Extrajudicial confession.. was totally inept, and void of all strength and effect from the beginning. 2 W. HARDING Alcott, inept as ever, dreamily felled a tree without looking where it was going. A. ALVAREZ The young graduate student, too shy and inept to make conversation. 3 J. MARTINEAU If the doctrine were true, could anything be more inept than an allusion to it?

ineptly *adv.* E16. **ineptness** *n.* E17.

ineptitude /ɪˈnɛptɪtjuːd/ *n.* M16. [L *ineptitudo*, f. *ineptus* INEPT: see -TUDE and cf. INAPTITUDE.] 1 Lack of aptitude or fitness *for* (or †*to*) something; unsuitability, invalidity. M16. 2 Lack of judgement or ability; incompetence, clumsiness; an instance of this, an inept action. M17.

1 STEELE That Ineptitude for Society, which is frequently the Fault of us Scholars. 2 C. BLACKWOOD His farm, which he ran with an amateurish ineptitude that resulted in an.. annual loss. A. POWELL The complaints.. were in connection with some ineptitude committed in regard to the luggage.

inequable /ɪnˈɛkwəb(ə)l/ *a.* E18. [L *inaequabilis*, f. as IN-[3] + EQUABLE.] Not uniform; uneven, unequal.

inequal /ɪnˈiːkw(ə)l/ *a.* Now *rare.* LME. [L *inaequalis*, f. as IN-[3] + EQUAL *a.*] Unequal; (of a surface) uneven.

inequal hours *Hist.*: formed by dividing daytime and night-time each into twelve equal parts, and so varying in length according to the season.

inequalitarian /ˌɪnɪkwɒlɪˈtɛːrɪən/ *n.* & *a.* L19. [f. INEQUALITY after EQUALITARIAN: see -ARIAN.] = INEGALITARIAN.

inequality /ɪnɪˈkwɒlɪti/ *n.* LME. [OFr. *inequalité* (mod. *inégalité*) or L *inaequalitas*, f. as INEQUAL: see -ITY.] 1 Lack of equality between persons or things; disparity in size, number, quality, etc. LME. b Difference of rank or circumstances; social or economic disparity. L15. c Superiority or inferiority in relation to something; *esp.* the condition of being unequal *to* a task, inadequacy. M16. 2 Lack of uniformity; unevenness, irregularity, fluctuation; an instance of this. LME. 3 Inconsistency in treatment of people or distribution of things; unfairness, inequity. M16. 4 *Astron.* A deviation from uniformity in the motion of a planet or satellite. L17. 5 *Math.* An expression of the relation between quantities that are not of equal value or magnitude, employing a sign such as ≠ 'not equal to', > 'greater than', < 'less than'. L19.

1 *New York Review of Books* Inequality of opportunity is no longer a concern of federal government. b M. EDGEWORTH The inequality between the rich and the poor shocked him.

inequilateral /ˌɪniːkwɪˈlat(ə)r(ə)l, ˌɪnɛ-/ *a.* M17. [f. IN-[3] + EQUILATERAL.] Having unequal sides.

inequitable /ɪnˈɛkwɪtəb(ə)l/ *a.* M17. [f. IN-[3] + EQUITABLE.] Not equitable, unfair.

inequitably *adv.* M19.

inequity /ɪnˈɛkwɪti/ *n.* M16. [f. IN-[3] + EQUITY.] Lack of equity or justice; unfairness, bias; an instance of this.

H. KISSINGER Allende.. blamed the capitalist system for social and economic inequities. E. FEINSTEIN The inequity of their mother's demands on them.

inequivalent /ɪnɪˈkwɪv(ə)l(ə)nt/ *a. rare.* M16. [f. IN-[3] + EQUIVALENT *a.*] Chiefly *Math.* Not equivalent, not of equal value.

inequivalence *n.* L19.

inequivalve /ɪnˈiːkwɪvalv/ *a.* L18. [f. IN-[3] + EQUI- + VALVE *n.*] *Conchol.* Having the valves of the shell of different sizes.

Also **inequivalved**, **inequiˈvalvular** *adjs.* E19.

ineradicable /ɪnɪˈradɪkəb(ə)l/ *a.* E19. [f. IN-[3] + ERADICATE + -ABLE.] Unable to be eradicated or rooted out.

inerasable /ɪnɪˈreɪzəb(ə)l/ *a.* E19. [f. IN-[3] + ERASE + -ABLE.] Unable to be erased or effaced.

†inergetical *a. rare.* L17–E18. [f. IN-[3] + EN)ERGETICAL.] Without energy; sluggish, inactive.

Also **†inergetic** *a.* (*rare*) E–M19.

inerrable /ɪnˈɛrəb(ə)l, -ˈəːr-/ *a.* M16. [L *inerrabilis*, f. as IN-[3] + *errare* err, wander: see -ABLE.] Incapable of erring; not liable to err; infallible.

inerraˈbility *n.* E17.

inerrant /ɪnˈɛr(ə)nt/ *a.* M17. [L *inerrant-* fixed, f. as IN-[3] + *errant-*: see ERRANT.] †1 *Astron.* Of a star: fixed. Only in M17. 2 That does not err; unerring. M19.

inerrancy *n.* M19.

inerratic /ɪnɪˈratɪk/ *a.* M17. [f. IN-[3] + ERRATIC *a.*] Not erratic or wandering; fixed; following a fixed course.

inert /ɪˈnəːt/ *a.* & *n.* M17. [L *inert-*, *iners* unskilled, inactive, f. as IN-[3] + *art-*, *ars* skill, ART *n.*[1]] A *adj.* 1 Of matter or a material thing: having no inherent power of action, motion, or resistance; inanimate; having the property of inertia. M17. b Without active chemical or physiological properties; unreactive. E19. 2 Of a person, an animal, etc.: inactive, slow; not inclined for or capable of action or movement; motionless. L18.

1 F. BOWEN If matter is essentially inert, every change in it must be produced by the mind. 2 R. P. WARREN He lay beneath the high carved headboard of his bed, inert as a log. A. BROOKNER With their curiously inert attitude to life, I doubt that they would even notice my absence.

Special collocations: **inert gas** (*a*) a (relatively) unreactive gas; (*b*) *spec.* = *noble gas* s.v. NOBLE *a.* (usu. in *pl.*).

B *n.* An inert or unreactive substance. M20.

inertly *adv.* M18. **inertness** *n.* M17.

inertia /ɪˈnəːʃə/ *n.* E18. [L = inactivity, f. as prec.: see -IA[1].] 1 *Physics.* The property of a body, proportional to its mass, by virtue of which it continues in a state of rest or uniform straight motion in the absence of an external force. E18. b In other physical properties: the tendency to continue in some state, to resist change. L19. 2 *transf.* Inactivity; disinclination to act or exert oneself; sloth; apathy. E19. 3 *Photogr.* The notional exposure for zero density, used to calculate the speed of emulsions and obtained by extrapolation of the straight portion of the characteristic curve. L19.

1 J. F. LAMB Blood has a high inertia and so a prolonged force must be applied to it. *centre of inertia*: see CENTRE *n.* MOMENT *of inertia*. *product of inertia*: see PRODUCT *n.* b *thermal inertia*. 2 L. GORDON Her diary admits to terrible rage followed by inertia and depression. E. MANNIN It was a landscape of total inertia to which only the river gave life.

Comb.: **inertia reel**: allowing the automatic adjustment and esp. locking during rapid deceleration of a safety-belt rolled round it; **inertia selling** the sending of goods not ordered, in the hope that the recipient will not take action to refuse them and will later make payment.

inertialess *a.* having no inertia; responding instantaneously to a change in the action of a force: E20.

inertial /ɪˈnəːʃ(ə)l/ *a.* M19. [f. prec. + -AL[1].] 1 Of, pertaining to, or of the nature of inertia. M19. 2 *Physics.* Designating a frame of reference in which bodies continue at rest or in uniform straight motion unless acted on by a force. M19.

Special collocations: **inertial guidance**: of a vehicle or vessel by an inertial navigation system. **inertial homoiothermy**: achieved by virtue of thermal inertia in a massive animal. **inertial navigation**: in which the course is computed from measurements of acceleration, without external observations. **inertial system** (*a*) *Physics* an inertial frame of reference; (*b*) a system for carrying out inertial guidance.

inertially *adv.* by means of or as a result of inertia or inertial forces M20.

inertion /ɪˈnəːʃ(ə)n/ *n.* M16. [f. INERT after EXERTION: see -ION.] Inert condition; inertness, inactivity, sloth.

inerudite /ɪnˈɛrʊdʌɪt/ *a.* E19. [L *ineruditus*, f. as IN-[3] + ERUDITE.] Unlearned; uninstructed.

inescapable /ɪnɪˈskeɪpəb(ə)l, ɪnɛ-/ *a.* L18. [f. IN-[3] + ESCAPE *v.* + -ABLE.] Unable to be escaped or avoided; inevitable.

inescapaˈbility *n.* M20. **inescapably** *adv.* L19.

inescutcheon /ɪnɪˈskʌtʃ(ə)n, ɪnɛ-/ *n.* E17. [f. IN-[1] + ESCUTCHEON.] *Her.* A small shield or coat of arms placed within a larger shield.

inesite /ˈɪnɪzʌɪt, ˈʌɪnəzʌɪt/ *n.* L19. [f. Gk *ines* fibres + -ITE[1].] *Min.* A triclinic hydrated calcium manganese silicate occurring as pink fibrous masses.

in esse /ɪn ˈɛsi/ *a. phr.* L16. [L.] In actual existence. Opp. IN POSSE.

inessential /ɪnɪˈsɛnʃ(ə)l/ *a.* & *n.* L17. [f. IN-[3] + ESSENTIAL *a.*] A *adj.* 1 Devoid of essence; insubstantial, immaterial. L17. 2 Not necessary to the constitution of a thing; not essential. M19.

1 SHELLEY His inessential figure cast no shade Upon the golden floor. 2 A. STORR A number of what appear inessential details are in fact important.

B *n.* An inessential thing. L18.

D. M. DAVIN I am.. going to cut out inessentials.

inessentiality /-ʃɪˈal-/ *n.* M19.

inessive /ɪnˈɛsɪv/ *a.* & *n.* L19. [f. L *inesse* be in or at, f. as IN-[2] + *esse* be: see -IVE.] *Gram.* A *adj.* Designating, being in, or pertaining to a case (esp. in Finnish) indicating location or position in or within. L19. **B** *n. The* inessive case; a word, form, etc., in the inessive case. L19.

inesthetic *a.* see INAESTHETIC.

inestimable /ɪnˈɛstɪməb(ə)l/ *a.* & *adv.* LME. [(O)Fr. f. L *inaestimabilis*, f. as IN-[3] + *aestimabilis* ESTIMABLE.] **A** *adj.* **1** Unable to be estimated, reckoned, or computed; too great or profound to be assessed or calculated. LME. **2** Too precious to be estimated, of surpassing value; priceless, invaluable. L16. †**B** *adv.* Inestimably. LME–L16.

inestimably *adv.* in an inestimable manner, to an inestimable degree LME.

ineuphonious /ɪnjuːˈfəʊnɪəs/ *a.* L19. [f. IN-[3] + EUPHONIOUS.] Not euphonious.

inevasible /ɪnɪˈveɪsɪb(ə)l/ *a.* M19. [f. IN-[3] + L *evas-* (see EVASION) + -IBLE.] Unable to be evaded.

inevictable /ɪnɪˈvɪktəb(ə)l/ *a. rare.* L19. [f. IN-[3] + EVICT + -ABLE.] Unable to be evicted.

inevidence /ɪnˈɛvɪd(ə)ns/ *n.* Now *rare.* M17. [med.L *inevidentia*, f. as next: see -ENCE.] †**1** Lack of evidence or manifestation (*of* something). M–L17. †**2** Uncertainty. M–L17. **3** The condition of not being evident or clearly discernible; lack of clearness, obscurity. L17.

inevident /ɪnˈɛvɪd(ə)nt/ *a.* Now *rare.* E17. [Late L *inevident-*, f. as IN-[3] + *evident-*: see EVIDENT.] Not evident or manifest; not clear, obscure.

inevitable /ɪnˈɛvɪtəb(ə)l/ *a.* & *n.* LME. [L *inevitabilis*, f. as IN-[3] + *evitabilis* EVITABLE.] **A** *adj.* **1** Unable to be avoided; unavoidable. LME. **2** Bound or sure to occur or appear; *colloq.* tiresomely familiar. L19. **b** Of character-building, plot-development, etc.: so true to nature etc. as to preclude alternative treatment or solution. E20.

1 G. GREENE For the first time he realised the pain inevitable in any human relationship. B. EMECHETA She would delay the hearing of it until it became inevitable. **2** D. JACOBSON A large china vase, containing the inevitable pair of dead flies. L. GORDON She tended to dramatize the inevitable disappointments that attend high aspiration. **b** *Notes & Queries* The 'inevitable' phrase, that gift to the world past all praise.

B *n.* A thing which cannot be escaped or avoided; an inevitable fact, event, truth, etc.; a person who or thing which is bound to be used, employed, etc. M19.

inevitaˈbility *n.* M17. **inevitableness** *n.* E17. **inevitably** *adv.* LME.

inexact /ɪnɪɡˈzakt, ɪnɛɡ-/ *a.* E19. [f. IN-[3] + EXACT *a.*] Not exact; not strictly correct or precise; not strict or rigorous.

inexactly *adv.* M19. **inexactness** *n.* E19.

inexactitude /ɪnɪɡˈzaktɪtjuːd, ɪnɛɡ-/ *n.* L18. [f. IN-[3] + EXACTITUDE.] The quality or character of being inexact; lack of exactitude, accuracy, or precision; an inaccuracy.

TERMINOLOGICAL *inexactitude.*

in excelsis /ɪn ɛkˈsɛlsɪs/ *adv. phr.* LME. [L = in the highest (places): cf. EXCELSIOR.] = *in the highest* s.v. HIGH *a.*, *adv.*, & *n.*

inexcitable /ɪnɪkˈsʌɪtəb(ə)l, ɪnɛk-/ *a. rare.* E17. [L *inexcitabilis*, f. as IN-[3] + *excitare* EXCITE + -ABLE; in sense 2 f. IN-[3] + EXCITABLE.] †**1** From which one cannot be roused. E–M17. **2** Not excitable. E19.

inexcitaˈbility *n.* (*rare*) M19.

inexclusively /ɪnɪkˈskluːsɪvli, ɪnɛk-/ *adv.* L18. [f. IN-[3] + EXCLUSIVELY.] Not exclusively; so as not to exclude others.

inexcusable /ɪnɪkˈskjuːzəb(ə)l, ɪnɛk-/ *a.* LME. [L *inexcusabilis*, f. as IN-[3] + *excusabilis* EXCUSABLE.] Not excusable; unable to be excused or justified.

inexcusableness *n.* E17. **inexcusably** *adv.* L16.

†**inexecrable** *a. rare* (Shakes.). Only in L16. [f. IN-[2] + EXECRABLE.] Most execrable or abhorred.

SHAKES. *Merch. V.* O, be thou damn'd, inexecrable dog!

¶By many editors thought to be an error for *inexorable.*

inexecutable /ɪnˈɛksɪkjuːtəb(ə)l/ *a.* E19. [f. IN-[3] + EXECUTABLE.] Unable to be executed or carried into effect.

inexecution /ˌɪnɛksɪˈkjuːʃ(ə)n/ *n.* L17. [f. IN-[3] + EXECUTION.] Lack or neglect of execution or performance; the fact or condition of not being carried into effect.

inexertion /ɪnɪɡˈzəːʃ(ə)n/ *n.* L18. [f. IN-[3] + EXERTION.] Lack of exertion; failure to exert oneself or exercise a power or faculty.

inexhausted /ɪnɪɡˈzɔːstɪd/ *a.* E17. [f. IN-[3] + EXHAUST *v.* + -ED[1].] Not exhausted.

inexhaustible /ɪnɪɡˈzɔːstɪb(ə)l/ *a.* E17. [f. IN-[3] + EXHAUSTIBLE.] **1** Unable to be exhausted, consumed, or used up; (of a receptacle or vessel) unable to be exhausted or emptied. E17. **2** Of a person or personal attribute: unable to be exhausted or worn out. M18.

1 R. LINDNER From a literally inexhaustible storehouse of material I have chosen a handful of stories. **2** *Times* He was an inexhaustible participant in the International Union of Crystallography.

inexhaustiˈbility *n.* M19. **inexhaustibleness** *n.* E19. **inexhaustibly** *adv.* L17.

inexhaustive /ɪnɪɡˈzɔːstɪv/ *a.* E18. [f. IN-[3] + EXHAUST *v.* + -IVE.] = INEXHAUSTIBLE 1.

inexhaustively *adv.* L19.

inexist /ɪnɪɡˈzɪst, ɪnɛɡ-/ *v.i.* L17. [f. IN-[1] + EXIST. Cf. INEXISTENT *a.*[1]] Exist *in* something; be inherent *in.*

inexistence /ɪnɪɡˈzɪst(ə)ns, ɪnɛɡ-/ *n.*[1] Now *rare.* E17. [f. IN-[3] + EXISTENCE.] The fact or condition of not existing; non-existence.

Also †**inexistency** *n.* L17–M18.

inexistence /ɪnɪɡˈzɪst(ə)ns, ɪnɛɡ-/ *n.*[2] M17. [f. IN-[2] + EXISTENCE.] The fact or condition of existing in something; inherence.

inexistent /ɪnɪɡˈzɪst(ə)nt, ɪnɛɡ-/ *a.*[1] M16. [Late L *inexistent-* pres. ppl stem of *inexistere*, f. as IN-[2] + *existere*: see EXIST, and cf. INEXIST *v.*] Existing in something; inherent.

†**inexistent** *a.*[2] M17–E18. [f. IN-[3] + EXISTENT.] Not existing; non-existent.

inexorable /ɪnˈɛks(ə)rəb(ə)l/ *a.* & *n.* M16. [Fr., or L *inexorabilis*, f. as IN-[3] + EXORABLE.] **A** *adj.* Unable to be moved or persuaded by entreaty or request (esp. for mercy), rigidly severe; immovable, relentless (*lit.* & *fig.*). M16.

H. JAMES He was therefore dismissed with gracious but inexorable firmness. O. MANNING The train, slow and inexorable as time, slid on.

B *n.* A person who is inexorable. M18.

inexoraˈbility *n.* E17. **inexorableness** *n.* E17. **inexorably** *adv.* E17.

inexpectancy /ɪnɪkˈspɛkt(ə)nsi, ɪnɛk-/ *n. rare.* M17. [f. IN-[3] + EXPECTANCY.] Absence of expectancy; the condition of not being expectant.

inexpectant /ɪnɪkˈspɛkt(ə)nt, ɪnɛk-/ *a.* M19. [f. IN-[3] + EXPECTANT *a.*] Not expectant; devoid of expectation.

inexpedience /ɪnɪkˈspiːdɪəns, ɪnɛk-/ *n.* Now *rare.* L16. [f. as next: see -ENCE.] = next.

inexpediency /ɪnɪkˈspiːdɪənsi, ɪnɛk-/ *n.* M17. [f. IN-[3] + EXPEDIENCY, or f. next: see -ENCY.] The quality of being inexpedient; disadvantageousness; unadvisableness.

inexpedient /ɪnɪkˈspiːdɪənt, ɪnɛk-/ *a.* L16. [f. IN-[3] + EXPEDIENT *a.*] Not expedient; not advantageous, useful, or suitable; inadvisable.

inexpensive /ɪnɪkˈspɛnsɪv, ɪnɛk-/ *a.* M19. [f. IN-[3] + EXPENSIVE.] **1** Not expensive or costly; cheap. M19. **2** Not extravagant; not spending a great deal. M19.

inexpensively *adv.* M19. **inexpensiveness** *n.* M19.

inexperience /ɪnɪkˈspɪərɪəns, ɪnɛk-/ *n.* L16. [Fr. *inexpérience* f. late L *inexperientia*, f. as IN-[3] + *experientia* EXPERIENCE *n.*] Lack of experience; the condition of not having practical acquaintance with some work, activity, etc.; the lack of knowledge or skills resulting from this.

C. G. WOLFF She . . begged to be forgiven for her inexperience and ignorance. A. T. ELLIS My mother . . changed the subject out of deference to my youth and inexperience.

inexperienced /ɪnɪkˈspɪərɪənst, ɪnɛk-/ *a.* E17. [f. IN-[3] + EXPERIENCED.] Not experienced (*in*); lacking the knowledge or skill resulting from experience.

T. HARDY Like an inexperienced actress who, having at last . . spoken her speeches, does not know how to move off.

inexpert /ɪnˈɛkspəːt/ *a.* & *n.* LME. [OFr. f. L *inexpertus* untried, inexperienced, f. as IN-[3] + *expertus* EXPERT *a.*] **A** *adj.* †**1** Without experience, inexperienced. Foll. by *in*, *of.* LME–M19. **2** Lacking the readiness, aptitude, or dexterity derived from experience; not expert. L16. **B** *n.* An unskilled person; a person who is not an expert. L19.

inexpertise /ˌɪnɛkspəːˈtiːz/ *n.* E20. [f. IN-[3] + EXPERTISE.] Lack of expertise.

inexpiable /ɪnˈɛkspɪəb(ə)l/ *a.* LME. [L *inexpiabilis*, f. as IN-[3] + *expiabilis* EXPIABLE.] **1** Of an offence: unable to be expiated or atoned for. LME. **2** Of a feeling: unable to be appeased by expiation; irreconcilable. L16.

1 R. MACAULAY They appear conscious of some immense and inexpiable sin. **2** J. WAIN But in Shakespeare guilt is not inexpiable; the self-inflicted wound can heal.

inexpiate /ɪnˈɛkspɪət/ *a.* E17. [L *inexpiatus*, f. as IN-[3] + EXPIATE *a.*] †**1** Unappeased. Only in E17. **2** Not expiated or atoned for. E19.

inexplainable /ɪnɪkˈspleɪnəb(ə)l, ɪnɛk-/ *a. rare.* E17. [f. IN-[3] + EXPLAINABLE.] Unable to be explained; inexplicable.

†**inexpleble** *a.* M16–L18. [L *inexplebilis*, f. as IN-[3] + *explere* fill up: see -BLE.] Unable to be filled or satisfied; insatiable.

inexplicable /ɪnɪkˈsplɪkəb(ə)l, ɪnɛk-, ɪnˈɛksplɪ-/ *a.* & *n.* LME. [Fr., or L *inexplicabilis* that cannot be unfolded or loosened, f. as IN-[3] + *explicabilis* EXPLICABLE.] **A** *adj.* **1** Unable to be explained or accounted for; inscrutable; unintelligible. LME. †**2** Unable to be expressed in words; indescribable. E16–L17. †**3** Unable to be unfolded, untwisted, or disentangled; very intricate or complex. M16–E18. **B** *n.* An inexplicable thing. M18.

inexplicaˈbility *n.* the quality of being inexplicable; an inexplicable thing: L18. **inexplicableness** *n.* M17. **inexplicably** *adv.* M17.

inexplicit /ɪnɪkˈsplɪsɪt, ɪnɛk-/ *a.* E19. [f. IN-[3] + EXPLICIT *a.*] Not explicit; not definitely or clearly expressed.

inexplorable /ɪnɪkˈsplɔːrəb(ə)l, ɪnɛk-/ *a.* M17. [f. IN-[3] + EXPLORE + -ABLE.] Unable to be explored.

inexplosive /ɪnɪkˈspləʊsɪv, ɪnɛk-/ *a.* M19. [f. IN-[3] + EXPLOSIVE *a.*] Not explosive; not liable to or capable of explosion.

inexpressible /ɪnɪkˈsprɛsɪb(ə)l, ɪnɛk-/ *a.* & *n.* E17. [f. IN-[3] + EXPRESSIBLE.] **A** *adj.* Unable to be expressed in words; unutterable, indescribable. E17. **B** *n.* **1** An inexpressible thing. M17. **2** *spec.* In *pl.* Breeches or trousers. *arch. colloq.* L18.

inexpressibly *adv.* M17.

inexpressive /ɪnɪkˈsprɛsɪv, ɪnɛk-/ *a.* M17. [f. IN-[3] + EXPRESSIVE.] **1** = INEXPRESSIBLE *a. arch.* M17. **2** Not expressive; not expressing (a) meaning, feeling, character, etc. M18.

inexpressively *adv.* E19. **inexpressiveness** *n.* E19.

inexpugnable /ɪnɪkˈspʌɡnəb(ə)l, ɪnɛk-/ *a.* LME. [(O)Fr. f. L *inexpugnabilis*, f. as IN-[3] + *expugnabilis* EXPUGNABLE.] (Of a fortress, army, country, etc.) unable to be taken by assault or overthrown by force; impregnable; invincible.

fig.: MRS H. WARD A certain inexpugnable dignity surrounded him.

inexpugnably *adv.* M17. **inexpugnableness** *n.* E18.

inexpungible /ɪnɪkˈspʌndʒɪb(ə)l, ɪnɛk-/ *a.* Also **-geable** /-dʒəb(ə)l/. L19. [f. IN-[3] + EXPUNGE + -IBLE.] Unable to be expunged or obliterated.

inextended /ɪnɪkˈstɛndɪd, ɪnɛk-/ *a. rare.* M18. [f. IN-[3] + EXTENDED.] Unextended; without extension.

inextensible /ɪnɪkˈstɛnsɪb(ə)l, ɪnɛk-/ *a.* M19. [f. IN-[3] + EXTENSIBLE.] Not extensible; unable to be stretched or drawn out in length.

inextensiˈbility *n.* (*rare*) E19.

in extenso /ɪn ɪkˈstɛnsəʊ, ɛk-/ *adv. phr.* E19. [L, f. *in* in + *extenso* abl. of *extensus*: see EXTENSE.] In full, at length.

M. MEYER A wonderfully mature assessment which repays quoting *in extenso.*

For other words beginning with *in-* see the entry for **in-**[1]

inextinct /ɪnɪk'stɪnkt, ɪnɛk-/ *a. rare.* E17. [L *inex(s)tinctus*, or f. IN-[3] + EXTINCT *a.*] Unextinguished. Chiefly *fig.*
J. WILSON He had not supposed such a capacity of love had yet remained inextinct.

inextinguishable /ɪnɪk'stɪŋgwɪʃəb(ə)l, ɪnɛk-/ *a.* L15. [f. IN-[3] + EXTINGUISH + -ABLE.] Unable to be extinguished; unquenchable; indestructible.
inextinguishably *adv.* E19.

inextinguished /ɪnɪk'stɪŋgwɪʃt, ɪnɛk-/ *a.* Now *rare.* M18. [f. IN-[3] + EXTINGUISH + -ED[1].] Not extinguished; still burning.

inextirpable /ɪnɪk'stəːpəb(ə)l, ɪnɛk-/ *a.* E17. [L *inex(s)tirpabilis*, f. as IN-[3] + *ex(s)tirpare* EXTIRPATE: see -ABLE.] Unable to be extirpated or rooted out.

in extremis /ɪn ɛk'striːmɪs, ɪk-/ *adv. phr.* M16. [L, f. *in* in + *extremis* abl. pl. of *extremus*: see EXTREME.] At the point of death; in great difficulty.

inextricable /ɪn'ɛkstrɪkəb(ə)l, ɪnɪk'strɪk-/ *a.* M16. [L *inextricabilis*, f. as IN-[3] + *extricare* EXTRICATE: see -ABLE.] 1 (Of a circumstance) unable to be escaped from; (of a place, esp. a maze) so complicated or confusing that no means of exit can be found (now *rare*). M16. 2 (Of a knot, coil, etc.) unable to be disentangled or untied; (of a problem, difficulty, argument, etc.) unable to be solved or resolved, intricately involved or confused. E17. b Of a grasp: unable to be loosened or detached. M19. 3 Intricate, elaborate, exquisitely wrought. *rare.* L17.
1 E. COOKE That he should run himself into inextricable Danger by going on. 2 S. SPENDER They know inextricable knots which bind each to himself. L. DURRELL For those of us . . who are at all conscious of the inextricable tangle of human thoughts. 3 HANNAH MORE A net of such exquisite art and inextricable workmanship.
inextrica'bility *n.* M19. **inextricably** *adv.* L16.

†ineye *v.t. rare.* LME–E18. [f. IN-[2] + EYE *n.*, after L *inoculare.*] *Hort.* Engraft.

inf /ɪnf/ *n.* M20. [Abbrev.] *Math.* Infimum (of).

inface /'ɪnfeɪs/ *n.* L19. [Contr. of *in*ward *fac*ing escarpment.] *Physical Geogr.* The steep scarp-face of a cuesta.

infall /'ɪnfɔːl/ *n.* M17. [f. IN-[1] + FALL *n.*[2], after Du. *inval.*] 1 An attack, inroad, or incursion *upon* an army, town, etc., or *into* a country. Now *rare.* M17. 2 The place where water enters a reservoir, canal, etc. M17. 3 Chiefly *Astron.* (An instance of) falling into or upon a body (esp. a planet) from an outside source; material which falls or has fallen (e.g. cosmic dust). L19.

infallibility /ɪn,falɪ'bɪlɪti/ *n.* E17. [Fr. *†infaillibilité* or med.L *infallibilitas*, f. as IN-[3] + FALLIBLE: see -ITY.] The quality or fact of being infallible.
N. MOSLEY Goering . . likened what he saw as Hitler's infallibility to that of the Pope.

infallible /ɪn'falɪb(ə)l/ *a.* L15. [Fr. *infaillible* or late L *infallibilis*, f. as IN-[3] + L *fallere* deceive: see -IBLE.] 1 Of a person, judgement, etc.: not liable to err or be deceived; *spec.* (*RC Ch.*) (of the Pope) incapable of erring in pronouncing dogma as doctrinally defined. L15. 2 Of a thing: not liable to prove false or erroneous; not liable to fail in action or operation; *rare* that cannot fail to be or come, certain. L15.
1 P. HOWARD It would be nice to pretend that *The Times* is infallible. 2 W. SOYINKA And it barely managed to be sweet, thus failing the infallible test of a real fruit. P. FERGUSON There's always an infallible way to be popular with nurses.
infallibilism *n.* the principle of the infallibility of a person or thing, esp. of the Pope L19. **infallibilist** *n.* a person who believes in or upholds the infallibility of a person or thing, esp. of the Pope L19. **infallibleness** *n.* (*rare*) infallibility L16. **infallibly** *adv.* L15.

infalling /'ɪnfɔːlɪŋ/ *n.* Now *rare* or *obs.* M16. [f. IN-[1] + FALLING *n.*] A falling in. Formerly also, an invasion.

infalling /'ɪnfɔːlɪŋ/ *a.* M20. [f. IN-[1] + FALLING *ppl a.*] Falling into or towards something.

infamatory /ɪn'famət(ə)ri/ *a. rare.* E17. [med.L *infamatorius*, f. *infamat-* pa. ppl stem of *infamare* INFAME *v.*: see -ORY[2].] Bringing infamy. Formerly also, defamatory.

infame /ɪn'feɪm/ *n.* Long *arch. rare.* LME. [OFr. (also *en-*) f. late L *infamium* for cl.L *infamia* INFAMY.] = INFAMY.

†infame *a.* E16–M18. [Fr. *infâme* f. L *infamis*: see INFAMY.] = INFAMOUS.

infame /ɪn'feɪm/ *v.t.* Now *arch.* or *joc.* LME. [OFr. *enfamer* f. L *infamare*, f. *infamis*: see INFAMY.] 1 Make infamous; hold up to infamy. LME. †2 Defame, speak ill of; accuse of something infamous. L15–L18.
1 W. PENN This inhuman Practice will infame your Government.

infamize /'ɪnfəmʌɪz/ *v.t.* Now *rare* or *obs.* Also **-ise.** L16. [f. L *infamis* (see INFAMY) + -IZE.] = INFAME *v.*

†infamonize *v.t. rare* (Shakes.). Only in L16. [Alt.] = INFAMIZE.

infamous /'ɪnfəməs/ *a.* LME. [med.L *infamosus* for L *infamis*: see INFAMY, -OUS.] 1 Of ill fame or repute; notorious, esp. for wickedness, evil, etc. LME. 2 Deserving of infamy, shamefully wicked or vile; abominable. L15. 3 *Law* (now *Hist.*). (Of a person) deprived of all or certain citizen's rights as a consequence of conviction for a serious crime such as forgery, perjury, etc.; (of a crime or punishment) involving or entailing such loss of rights. M16.
1 C. THIRLWALL He appears to have been more infamous for sacrilege than for bloodshed. C. FRANCIS The vessels packed with Irish emigrants were infamous for overcrowding, disease and frequency of shipwrecks. 2 H. MAUNDRELL Detest the very ground on which was acted such an infamous Treachery.
Special collocations: **infamous crime** *spec.* (*Law*, now *Hist.*) buggery.
infamously *adv.* E17. **infamousness** *n.* (*rare*) M17.

infamy /'ɪnfəmi/ *n.* L15. [(O)Fr. *infamie* f. L *infamia*, f. *infamis*, f. as IN-[3] + *fama* FAME *n.*: see -Y[3].] 1 Bad reputation; scandalous repute; public shame or disgrace; an instance of this. L15. 2 The quality of being shamefully vile; a disgraceful act. L15. 3 *Law* (now *Hist.*). The loss of all or certain citizen's rights resulting from conviction for a serious crime such as forgery, perjury, etc. E17.
1 R. GRENEWEY Now was the time to blot out the infamies of their former conspiracies. E. A. FREEMAN Two caitiffs . . whose names are handed down to infamy. 2 Q. BELL He . . realised the infamy of slavery when he saw how monstrously a Negro might be treated. P. ACKROYD At the time of my greatest success, I was suspected of the greatest infamies.

infancy /'ɪnf(ə)nsi/ *n.* LME. [L *infantia* inability to speak, childhood, f. *infant-*, *infans*: see INFANT *n.*[1], -ANCY.] 1 The condition of being an infant; the earliest period of human life, early childhood, babyhood. Also (chiefly *literary*), infants collectively. LME. 2 The earliest period in the history of a thing capable of development; the initial and rudimentary stage in any process of growth. M16. 3 *Law.* The condition of not yet being of full age. M17.
1 P. THOMPSON When tender infancy evinces needless terror at cow, or dog, or shaggy goat. N. MOSLEY This move from prep school to public school was traditionally held to be a release from infancy. M. SCAMMELL There had been twins, but they had been born prematurely and had died in infancy. 2 R. HUNTFORD The science of nutrition was then in its infancy.

†infand *a.* E17–L19. [L *infandus*, f. as IN-[3] + *fandus* gerundive of *fari* speak: see -AND.] Unspeakable; nefarious.
Also **†infandous** *a.* M17–L19.

†infang *n. Sc. rare.* M16–E19. [Abbrev.] = INFANGTHIEF.

infangthief /'ɪnfaŋθiːf/ *n.* OE. [f. IN *adv.* + pa. pple of FANG *v.*[1] + THIEF.] *Law* (now *Hist.*). The right of the lord of a manor to try and to punish a thief caught within the limits of his demesne.

infant /'ɪnf(ə)nt/ *n.*[1] & *a.* LME. [(O)Fr. *enfant* f. L *infant-*, *infans* use as n. of *infans* unable to speak, f. as IN-[3] + pres. pple of *fari* speak: see -ANT[1].] A *n.* 1 A child during the earliest period of life after birth or (now *rare*) in the womb; a baby, a young child. LME. b A beginner in or newcomer to an activity etc.; something in an early stage of development. E16. 2a *Law.* A person not yet of full age. E16. b A ruler who has not yet attained the age at which he or she is constitutionally capable of exercising sovereignty. L18. †3 A youth of noble birth. *rare.* L16–E17. 4 A thing of exceptional size, strength, etc. *joc.* M19.
1 D. W. GOODWIN If the mother is intoxicated while breast feeding, the infant will be intoxicated. J. CRACE I slept, glad to be free of squalling infants and the attentions of the Professor. TERRIBLE *infant.* b *New Brunswick Daily Mail* As every political infant cannot fail to recognise, the . . question was . . unconnected with party politics.
B *attrib.* or as *adj.* 1 That is or is like an infant; in the earliest stage of development; undeveloped, nascent, incipient. L16. 2 Of, belonging to, or suitable for an infant or infants; childlike; childish, infantile. L16.
1 K. AMIS The sheep clustered by the infant oak-tree looked up suddenly and turned their heads. T. MO A girl of seven carries her infant brother in a gay cloth sling. 2 D. WALCOTT Like the sound Of infant voices from the Mission School.
Special collocations & comb.: **infant mistress** a female infant teacher. **infant mortality** the death of infants, *spec.* of those less than a year old. **infant prodigy** a very precocious or talented child. **infant school** (chiefly *Hist.*) a primary school intended for children between the ages of 5 and 7. **infant teacher** a teacher of young children; *spec.* a teacher in an infant school.
infanthood *n.* infancy M19. **†infantical** *a.* (*rare*) of or pertaining to infants E17–M18. **infantize** *v.t.* (*rare*) †(*a*) give birth to; (*b*) make childlike: E17.

infant /'ɪnf(ə)nt/ *n.*[2] Now *rare* or *obs.* M16. [f. as INFANTE.] = INFANTA, INFANTE.

infanta /ɪn'fantə/ *n.* L16. [Sp., Port. fem. of INFANTE.] *Hist.* A daughter of the King and Queen of Spain or Portugal; *spec.* the eldest daughter who is not heir to the throne. Formerly also *gen.*, a girl, a princess.

infante /ɪn'fantə/ *n.* M16. [Sp. & Port. f. L *infant-*, *infans*: see INFANT *n.*[1]] *Hist.* A son of the King and Queen of Spain or Portugal other than the heir to the throne; *spec.* the second son.

infanteer /ɪnf(ə)n'tɪə/ *n. slang.* M20. [f. INFANT(RY + -EER.] An infantryman.

infanticide /ɪn'fantɪsʌɪd/ *n.* M17. [Fr. f. late L *infanticidium*, *-da*, f. L *infant-*: see INFANT *n.*[1], -CIDE.] 1a The killing of infants; *esp.* (chiefly *Hist.*), the custom of killing newborn infants. M17. b *spec.* in *Law.* The killing of an infant after its birth by one or both of the parents or with parental consent. L18. 2 A person who kills an infant, esp. his or her own child. L17.
¶In the UK, under the Infanticide Act of 1938, the killing of a child under 12 months by his or her mother during postnatal depression etc. is treated as manslaughter.
infanti'cidal *a.* of, pertaining to, or practising infanticide M19.

infanticipate /ɪnf(ə)n'tɪsɪpeɪt/ *v.i.* Chiefly *US* & *joc.* M20. [f. INFANT *n.*[1] + ANT)ICIPATE *v.*] Be expecting the birth of one's child.
infantici'pation *n.* the state of expecting the birth of one's child M20.

infantile /'ɪnf(ə)ntʌɪl/ *a.* LME. [Fr., or L *infantilis*, f. *infant-*: see INFANT *n.*[1], -ILE.] 1 Of, pertaining to, or characteristic of an infant or infancy; being in infancy or the earliest stage of development; childish, immature. LME. 2 *Physical Geogr.* Of, pertaining to, or characteristic of the earliest stages of erosion. L19.
1 H. JOLLY Infantile eczema is commoner in babies fed on cow's milk. M. GORDON It was infantile to cry like this, at thirty-eight, because she wanted her parents. **infantile paralysis** poliomyelitis (esp. in children).

infantilise *v.* var. of INFANTILIZE.

infantilism /ɪn'fantɪlɪz(ə)m/ *n.* L19. [f. INFANTILE + -ISM.] *Med. & Psychol.* Persistence or recurrence, in adult life, of an infantile or childish condition or behaviour pattern; abnormal physical, sexual, or psychological immaturity.
infanti'listic *a.* M20.

infantility /ɪnf(ə)nˈtɪlɪti/ *n.* M17. [f. INFANTILE + -ITY.] The quality or fact of being infantile; an instance of infantile behaviour.

¶ Rare bef. 20.

infantilize /ɪnˈfantɪlʌɪz/ *v.t.* Also **-ise**. M20. [f. INFANTILE + -IZE.] Prolong or inculcate a state of infancy or infantile behaviour in; treat (a person) as infantile.

C. G. WOLFF Take care of your complexion, my dear ... Such injunctions toward women are ultimately infantilizing.

infantiliˈzation *n.* M20.

infantine /ˈɪnf(ə)ntʌɪn/ *a.* Chiefly *literary*. E17. [Fr. †*infantin* var. of (O)Fr. *enfantin*, f. as INFANT *n.*[1]: see -INE[1].] = INFANTILE 1.

infantry /ˈɪnf(ə)ntri/ *n.* L16. [Fr. *infanterie* f. It. *infanteria*, f. *infante* youth, foot-soldier, f. L *infant-*: see INFANT *n.*[1], -ERY.] 1 Soldiers marching or fighting on foot; the body of foot-soldiers. L16. 2 *collect.* Infants. *joc.* E17.

1 C. V. WEDGWOOD Two hundred infantry and forty horsemen crossed from the mainland to the Isle of Wight. *light infantry*: see LIGHT *a.*[1] **mounted infantry** soldiers who are mounted for transit but who fight on foot. 2 M. NEEDHAM The little dirty Infantry, which swarms up and down in Alleys and Lanes.

Comb.: **infantryman** a soldier of an infantry regiment.

infarct /ɪnˈfɑːkt/ *n.* L19. [mod.L *infarctus*, f. *infarct-* pa. ppl stem of *infarcire* stuff into or with, f. as IN-[2] + *farcire* stuff.] *Med.* An area of tissue affected by infarction; a region of dead tissue caused by the blocking of an artery or other vessel. Also, an instance of (esp. myocardial) infarction.

infarcted *a.* affected by infarction E19.

infarction /ɪnˈfɑːkʃ(ə)n/ *n.* L17. [f. as prec. + -ION.] *Med.* Orig., congestion or (vascular) obstruction. Now, the death of tissues due to the blocking of (esp. the arterial) blood supply. Also, an infarct.

infare /ˈɪnfɛː/ *n.* OE. [f. IN-[1] + FARE *n.*[1]] †1 The action of entering; an entrance, a way in. OE–ME. 2 A feast or entertainment given on entering a new house; *esp.* a reception for a bride in her new home. *Sc.*, *north.*, & *US.* LME.

†**infatigable** *a.* E16–E18. [Fr. f. L *infatigabilis*, f. as IN-[3] + *fatigare* FATIGUE *v.* + -ABLE.] = INDEFATIGABLE.

infatuate /ɪnˈfatjʊət, -tʃʊ-/ *a.* & *n.* L15. [L *infatuatus* pa. pple, f. as next: see -ATE[2], -ATE[1].] A *adj.* Infatuated. Now *rare.* L15.

M. BEERBOHM The young man, .. at once thrifty and infatuate, had planned a luncheon *à deux*.

B *n.* An infatuated person. M20.

infatuate /ɪnˈfatjʊeɪt, -tʃʊ-/ *v.t.* M16. [L *infatuat-* pa. ppl stem of *infatuare*, f. as IN-[2] + FATUOUS: see -ATE[3].] †1 Reduce to foolishness, show the foolishness of; frustrate, bring to nothing. M16–E18. 2 Orig., make foolish or fatuous, inspire with folly. Now chiefly, inspire with an intense esp. amorous and usu. transitory passion. M16.

1 R. YOUNGE That I have unmasked their faces, is to infatuate their purpose. 2 R. WARNER He was, it was said, quite ridiculously infatuated with the lady. I. MURDOCH You're just infatuated with Oxford, you think it's all so impressive and grand.

infatuatedly *adv.* in an infatuated manner M19.

infatuation /ɪnˌfatjʊˈeɪʃ(ə)n, -tʃʊ-/ *n.* M17. [f. prec. + -ATION.] The action of infatuating someone; the condition of being infatuated; an instance of this.

J. AUSTEN Your infatuation about that girl blinds you. E. FEINSTEIN To her, love was felt for 'what is akin' and infatuation only for what is alien.

infauna /ˈɪnfɔːnə/ *n.* E20. [f. IN-[1] + FAUNA.] *Zool.* The animal life found within a marine sediment.

infaunal *a.* L20.

infaust /ɪnˈfɔːst/ *a.* Now *rare* or *obs.* E17. [L *infaustus*, perh. through Fr. †*infauste.*] Unlucky, unfortunate.

infeasible /ɪnˈfiːzɪb(ə)l/ *a.* M16. [f. IN-[3] + FEASIBLE.] Not feasible, impracticable; impossible.

Nineteenth Century They pronounced it not only infeasible, but of very doubtful benefit.

infeasiˈbility *n.* M17.

†**infect** *a.* LME. [L *infectus* pa. pple, f. as next.] 1 Affected detrimentally. Only in LME. 2 Tainted *with* disease, infected. LME–M16. 3 Tainted or contaminated *with* a fault, defect, or vice; morally corrupted (*rare* after E17). LME–L19.

infect /ɪnˈfɛkt/ *v.t.* LME. [L *infect-* pa. ppl stem of *inficere* dip in, stain, taint, spoil, f. as IN-[2] + *facere* put, do.] 1 Affect (a person, animal, or organ) with disease; introduce a disease-causing micro-organism into. LME. b Affect (a computer) with a computer virus. L20. 2 Contaminate (air, water, etc.) with harmful organisms or noxious matter; make harmful to health. LME. 3 Taint or contaminate with moral corruption; deprave; exert a bad influence upon. LME. †4 Affect injuriously or unpleasantly; spoil or corrupt with some addition; adulterate. LME–L17. b Infest, beset. M16–E18. 5 Affect or impregnate with a (freq. noxious) substance; taint. Formerly also, dye, colour, stain. L15. 6 Instil a (now only bad or harmful) belief or opinion into. L15. 7 Affect (esp. a person) *with* some quality, esp. a feeling, communicate a feeling to (a person); (of a feeling) take hold of. L16. b *Celtic Philol.* Of a sound: affect and alter the quality of (a sound in a syllable) by proximity. L19. 8 Taint with crime; involve in crime. Now *rare.* L16. b *Law* (now *Hist.*). Involve (a ship or cargo) in the seizure to which contraband etc. is liable. M18.

1 P. THEROUX Every cut became infected and had to be scrubbed with hot water. E. FEINSTEIN The tuberculosis that infected, and finally killed, all of his children. 3 S. JOHNSON Indolence is .. one of the vices from which those whom it infects are seldom reformed. 5 E. K. KANE Our snow-water has been infected .. by a very perceptible flavor and odor of musk. 6 J. WHYTE Books .. full of pestilent doctrines, blasphemy and heresy, to infect the people. 7 N. ALGREN The very heat that enervates men infects women with restlessness.

¶ Senses 3–7 are now usually interpreted as fig. uses of sense 1.

infectible *a.* able to be infected E17. †**infecter** *n.* E16–M18. **infector** *n.* L16.

infection /ɪnˈfɛkʃ(ə)n/ *n.* LME. [(O)Fr., or late L *infectio(n-)*, f. as prec.: see -ION.] I 1a The contamination of air, water, etc., by disease-causing agents. Now *rare* or *obs.* LME. b The agency by which disease is caused or transmitted. LME. c The transmission of disease (formerly esp. without direct contact); the introduction into the body of disease-causing micro-organisms; the process of infecting; the state of being infected. M16. d (An) infectious disease; an epidemic. M16. e The entry of a virus into, or the presence of a virus in, a computer. L20. 2 Moral or spiritual contamination; (a) depravity. LME. †3 The action or process of affecting injuriously; the fact of being spoilt or corrupted. LME–E17. 4 Instillation of bad or harmful beliefs or opinions. E16. 5 The communication of a feeling or quality from one person to another. E17. b *Celtic Philol.* Alteration of a sound under the influence of a sound in a neighbouring syllable. L19. 6 *Law* (now *Hist.*). The communication to the rest of a cargo or to a ship of liability to seizure from association with contraband etc. L19.

1d H. BAILEY She was often very ill with .. streptococcal infections. 5 R. DAVIES It was impossible that he should love Ismay so much without her loving him by infection.

†II 7 Affection, liking. *joc. rare* (Shakes.). Only in L16.

infectious /ɪnˈfɛkʃəs/ *a.* M16. [f. INFECTION + -OUS. Cf. INFECTUOUS.] 1 Able to cause disease, unhealthy, infecting. M16. 2 Of (a) disease: communicable; liable to be transmitted from one person to another by transfer of micro-organisms. Also, (of a person) infected, liable to infect others. M16. †3 Affected with disease. M16–E18. 4 Tending or liable to contaminate character, morals, etc. Now *rare.* M16. 5 Of an action, emotion, etc.: having the quality of spreading from one to another; easily communicable. E17. 6 *Law* (now *Hist.*). Of contraband etc.: rendering the rest of a cargo or the ship liable to seizure. L19.

1 *infectious hepatitis*, *infectious mononucleosis*, *infectious parotitis*, etc. 5 E. PHILLPOTTS Her volubility was infectious They talked one against the other.

infectiously *adv.* E17. **infectiousness** *n.* E17.

infective /ɪnˈfɛktɪv/ *a.* LME. [med.L *infectivus*, f. as INFECT *v.*: see -IVE. In recent medical use f. INFECT *v.* + -IVE.] Capable of infecting (with disease); pathogenic. Also, morally infectious.

infectiveness *n.* L19. **infecˈtivity** *n.* the quality of being infective; the degree of infectiousness or virulence: L19.

infectum /ɪnˈfɛktəm/ *n.* M20. [L use as n. of neut. of *infectus* unfinished f. as IN-[3] + *factus* pa. pple of *facere* make imperfect.] *Latin Gram.* The aspectual category including the present, imperfect, and simple future tenses.

†**infectuous** *a.* L15–M18. [f. late L *infectus* dyeing + -OUS.] = INFECTIOUS.

infecund /ɪnˈfɛk(ə)nd, ɪnˈfiːk-/ *a.* LME. [L *infecundus*, f. as IN-[3] + *fecundus* FECUND.] Not fecund; barren, unproductive.

infecundity /ɪnfɪˈkʌndɪti/ *n.* E17. [L *infecunditas*, f. as prec.: see -ITY.] The quality of being infecund; barrenness, unproductiveness.

infeed /ˈɪnfiːd/ *n.* E20. [f. IN-[1] + FEED *n.*] The action or process of supplying a machine with work; a mechanism which carries out this process.

infeft /ɪnˈfɛft/ *v.t.* Pa. t. & pple **infeft**. LME. [Sc. var. of ENFEOFF.] *Sc. Law* (now *Hist.*). Invest with heritable property; = ENFEOFF 1.

infeftment *n.* LME.

infelicitous /ɪnfɪˈlɪsɪtəs/ *a.* M19. [f. IN-[3] + FELICITOUS.] Not felicitous; unhappy, unfortunate; *esp.* not appropriate.

infelicitously *adv.* M19.

infelicity /ɪnfɪˈlɪsɪti/ *n.* LME. [L *infelicitas*, f. *infelic-*, *-ix* unhappy, f. as IN-[3] + *felix* happy: see -ITY.] 1 The state of being unhappy or unfortunate; unhappiness, misery; bad luck, misfortune. Also, an instance of misfortune; a cause of unhappiness. LME. 2 The quality of not being appropriate to an occasion or circumstance; inappropriateness, inaptness; an inappropriate expression or detail of style. E17.

1 P. HEYLIN By the unhappiness of my Destiny, or the infelicity of the Times, deprived of my Preferments. *Spectator* These infelicities of travel were of frequent occurrence, and endured with cheerfulness. 2 P. LIVELY He used to write back .. correcting what he considered infelicities of style.

†**infeoff** *v.* var. of ENFEOFF.

infer /ɪnˈfəː/ *v.* Infl. **-rr-**. L15. [L *inferre* bear or bring in, inflict, make (war), cause, (in med.L) deduce, f. as IN-[2] + *ferre* BEAR *v.*[1]] †1 *v.t.* Bring about; inflict; wage (war). L15–M18. b Confer, bestow. L15–E17. c Make, cause to be. W. adj. compl. *rare.* Only in M17. †2 *v.t.* Bring in, introduce in conversation or writing; mention, relate; adduce. L15–E18. 3 *v.t.* Deduce or draw as a conclusion from or *from* facts or reasoning. E16. b *v.i.* Draw a conclusion or inference. L16. 4 *v.t.* Involve as a consequence; imply. (This use is widely considered incorrect, esp. with a person as the subject.) M16.

3 D. M. DAVIN You would have been able to infer from the room alone the nature of those who lived in it. H. GREEN She inferred from this last remark that she had his blessing. *New York Review of Books* We cannot penetrate Bach's mind, but we can infer something about how it developed. 4 SIR W. SCOTT They are .. more benign in demeanour than their physiognomy or aspect might infer. B. RUSSELL I do not wish to infer that they should have been allowed to go on hunting heads. *Private Eye* I can't stand fellers who infer things about good clean-living Australian Sheilahs.

inferable /ɪnˈfəːrəb(ə)l/ *a.* Also **-rr-**. L18. [f. INFER + -ABLE.] Able to be inferred; deducible.

inferaˈbility *n.* E20. **inferably** *adv.* by inference E20.

inference /ˈɪnf(ə)r(ə)ns/ *n.* L16. [med.L *inferentia*, f. L *inferent-* pres. ppl stem of *inferre*: see INFER, -ENCE.] 1 The action or process of inferring; *Logic* the drawing of a conclusion from data or premisses; illation. L16. 2 A conclusion drawn from data or premisses; an implication; the conclusion that is intended to be drawn. E17.

1 W. STUBBS This . . is not a matter of inference It is a recorded fact of history. 2 R. MACAULAY You draw no inference from your facts. P. H. KOCHER These four are named 'first', with the inference that they deserve priority.

inferential /ɪnfəˈrɛnʃ(ə)l/ *a.* M17. [f. as prec. + -AL[1].] Of, pertaining to, or depending on inference; of the nature of (an) inference.

inferentially *adv.* in an inferential manner; in the way of or by means of inference: L17.

inferible *a.* var. of INFERRIBLE.

inferior /ɪnˈfɪərɪə/ *a.* & *n.* LME. [L, compar. of *inferus* low: see -IOR.] A *adj.* 1 Lower in position. Now chiefly *techn.* LME. b *Anat.* & *Biol.* Designating a part or organ situated below another (esp. of the same kind), or in a relatively low position. M16. c *Astron.* Of a planet: having its orbit within that of the earth (as Mercury, Venus). M17. d Of a letter, figure, or symbol: written or printed below the line L19. 2 Lower in degree, rank, quality, importance, etc.; subordinate. (Foll. by *to*.) Cf. earlier B.1 below. L15. 3 Low in rank, quality, etc.; comparatively bad. M16. 4 Later. *rare.* M17.

1 J. D. DANA The old Glacial drift . . being observed in several places as an inferior deposit. 2 J. C. POWYS Barter had been so humiliated . . that . . he felt himself to be inferior to every educated man he met. B. BETTELHEIM Not an inferior copy of his parents but a person in his own right. 3 GLADSTONE The country with which he shows so inferior an acquaintance.

Special collocations: *inferior conjunction*: see CONJUNCTION 2. **inferior meridian** the part of the celestial meridian which lies below the pole. **inferior ovary** *Bot.*: positioned below the calyx, enclosed in the receptacle. †**inferior stone** = LUNAR *caustic*.

B *n.* 1 A person inferior to another, esp. in rank; a subordinate. LME. 2 A thing inferior to another, esp. in importance. L16. 3 *Typogr.* An inferior letter, figure, or symbol. L19.

1 H. L. MENCKEN Never let your inferiors do you a favor.

inferiorly *adv.* M16.

inferiority /ɪnˌfɪərɪˈɒrɪti/ *n.* L16. [Prob. f. med.L *inferioritas*, f. as INFERIOR + -ITY.] The quality or condition of being inferior; lower rank, position, or state.

Comb.: **inferiority complex** in Adlerian psychology, an unrealistic feeling of general inadequacy caused by actual or supposed inferiority in one sphere, sometimes with aggressive behaviour in compensation; *colloq.* an exaggerated feeling of personal inadequacy.

infernal /ɪnˈfəːn(ə)l/ *a.* & *n.* LME. [(O)Fr. f. Chr.L *infernalis*, f. *infernus* below, subterranean, later used as n. = hell, after masc. pl. *inferni* the shades, neut. pl. *inferna* the lower regions; parallel to L *inferus* (see INFERIOR) as *supernus* SUPERNAL to *superus* (see SUPERIOR): see -AL[1].] A *adj.* 1 Of, pertaining to, or characteristic of the underworld of ancient mythology, or hell in Jewish and Christian belief. LME. 2 Devilish, fiendish. LME. 3 Detestable, tiresome. *colloq.* M18.

1 MILTON The flocking shadows pale Troop to the infernal jail. C. KINGSLEY The infernal hiss and crackle of the flame. 2 W. K. KELLY An infernal plot . . had been formed; . . miscreants went about, poisoning food. 3 E. WAUGH What's all this infernal nonsense about boots?

Special collocations: **infernal machine** *arch.* an apparatus (usu. disguised) for producing an explosion to destroy life or property.

B *n.* 1 An inhabitant of the underworld or hell; a devil. Usu. in *pl.* L16. b A person or thing of infernal character. Formerly *spec.* an infernal machine. Now *rare.* L16. 2 In *pl.* The infernal regions. Long *rare.* E17.

inferˈnality *n.* †(*a*) *rare* the infernal world and its occupants; (*b*) the quality of being infernal; an instance of this: L16. **infernalize** *v.t.* give a fiendish or infernal character to E19. **infernally** *adv.* M17.

inferno /ɪnˈfəːnəʊ/ *n.* Pl. **-os.** M19. [It. f. Chr.L *infernus*: see prec.] Hell, esp. (*the inferno*) w. ref. to Dante's *Divine Comedy*; a scene of horror or distress; *esp.* a raging fire.

infero- /ˈɪnf(ə)rəʊ/ *comb. form.* M19. [f. L *inferus* low: see -O-.] Chiefly *Zool.* Forming mainly adjs. w. the sense 'in or towards the lower part and —', as *infero-anterior*, *infero-lateral*, *infero-posterior*.

inferrable *a.* var. of INFERABLE.

inferrible /ɪnˈfəːrɪb(ə)l/ *a.* Also **inferible**. M17. [med.L *inferibilis*, f. as INFER + -IBLE.] = INFERABLE.

inferriˈbility *n.* M19. **inferribly** *adv.* (*rare*) E20.

infertile /ɪnˈfəːtʌɪl/ *a.* L16. [Fr., or late L *infertilis*, f. as IN-[3] + *fertilis* FERTILE.] Not fertile; unproductive; incapable of producing offspring.

C. DARWIN Animals and plants, when removed from their natural conditions, are often rendered . . infertile or completely barren. P. THEROUX Littered with rocks and sand, the soil could not have looked more infertile.

infertility /ɪnfəˈtɪlɪti/ *n.* M16. [Late L *infertilitas*, f. *infertilis*: see prec., -ITY.] The quality or condition of being infertile; unproductiveness; incapability of producing offspring.

infest /ɪnˈfɛst/ *v.t.* LME. [(O)Fr. *infester* or L *infestare*, f. *infestus* hostile, unsafe.] 1 Attack or annoy persistently; harass. Now *rare.* LME. 2 Attack, trouble, be present, in large numbers or persistently; overrun. M16.

2 J. C. OATES His mattress was filthy and infested with bedbugs. A. T. ELLIS She wished that Finn's caique might sink in waters infested with small sharks. *fig.*: V. GLENDINNING Her essay . . was infested with 'mere, irresponsible silliness.'

infestation /ɪnfɛˈsteɪʃ(ə)n/ *n.* LME. [(O)Fr., or late L *infestatio(n-)*, f. L *infestat-* pa. ppl stem of *infestare*: see prec., -ATION.] The action of infesting someone or something; an attack of infesting insects etc.; the state or condition of being infested.

†**infestious** *a.* L16–E18. [Irreg. f. L *infestus* or INFEST, after *infectious*: see -OUS.] Hostile; troublesome.

Also †**infestuous** *a.* L16–E18.

†**infestive** *a.*[1] *rare.* L16–E18. [f. INFEST + -IVE.] Tending to infest someone or something; troublesome.

infestive /ɪnˈfɛstɪv/ *a.*[2] *rare.* E17. [L *infestivus*, f. as IN-[3] + FESTIVE.] Not festive; without mirth.

infeˈstivity *n.* absence of festivity; dullness: E18.

infeudation /ɪnfjuːˈdeɪʃ(ə)n/ *n.* L15. [med.L *infeudatio(n-)*, *infeod-*, f. *infeudat-* pa. ppl stem of *infeudare*, *infeodare* enfeoff, f. *feudum*, *feodum*: see FEE *n.*[2], -ATION.] *Law* (now *Hist.*). Enfeoffment; a deed of enfeoffment.

infeudation of tithes the granting of tithes to laymen.

infibulate /ɪnˈfɪbjʊleɪt/ *v.t.* E17. [L *infibulat-* pa. ppl stem of *infibulare*, f. as IN-[2] + FIBULA: see -ATE[3].] Fasten with a clasp or buckle (*rare*). Now *spec.* perform infibulation on (a woman). Chiefly as *infibulated* ppl a.

infibulation /ɪnˌfɪbjʊˈleɪʃ(ə)n/ *n.* M17. [f. prec. + -ATION.] The action of fastening something, esp. the sexual organs with a clasp. Now *spec.* the partial stitching together of the labia, freq. after excision of the clitoris, to prevent copulation.

infidel /ˈɪnfɪd(ə)l/ *n.* & *a.* L15. [Fr. *infidèle* or L *infidelis* unfaithful, unbelieving, f. as IN-[3] + *fidelis* faithful, f. *fides* FAITH.] A *n.* 1 Chiefly *Hist.* An adherent of a religion other than one's own; *spec.* (*a*) (from a Christian point of view) a Muslim; (*b*) (from a Muslim point of view) a Christian; (*c*) (from a Jewish point of view) a Gentile. L15. †2 A person who is unfaithful to a duty. E16–M17. 3 A person who does not believe in religion, or in a particular religion; *esp.* (*Hist.*) a person who does not believe in the traditional (Christian) religion of a country. *derog.* M16. 4 A person who does not believe in a specified (non-religious) thing. Foll. by *in*, †*to*, †*against*. E17.

1 DEFOE Propagating the Christian faith among infidels. A. HALEY Their wares of . . beer were for infidels only, since the Moslem Mandinkas never drank. 3 D. CUPITT Religious doctrines and rituals stress the distinction between believers and infidels.

B *adj.* 1 Chiefly *Hist.* Of a person: unbelieving; adhering to a religion other than one's own; pagan, heathen. L15. †b Incredulous, sceptical. *rare.* E17–E18. 2 Of an action, a view, etc.: of, pertaining to, or characteristic of an infidel or infidels. M18.

1 J. CLAVELL This victory had saved . . Christendom from being ravaged . . by the infidel hordes. 2 *Times Lit. Suppl.* Carlile's dogged commitment to the freedom of the press and to infidel ideas.

infiˈdelic *a.* (*rare*) E17. **infidelism** *n.* (*rare*) M19.

infidelise *v.* var. of INFIDELIZE.

infidelity /ɪnfɪˈdɛlɪti/ *n.* LME. [(O)Fr. *infidélité* or L *infidelitas*, f. *infidelis*: see INFIDEL, -ITY.] 1 Lack of faith; disbelief in religious matters or a particular religion, esp. Christianity. LME. †b An infidel opinion or practice. *rare.* M16–M17. 2 Unfaithfulness or disloyalty to a friend, superior, etc. Now *esp.* lack of sexual faithfulness to a partner. LME. b An unfaithful act. E18. 3 *gen.* Disbelief, incredulity. L16.

infidelize /ˈɪnfɪd(ə)lʌɪz/ *v. rare.* Also **-ise**. M19. [f. INFIDEL + -IZE.] 1 *v.t.* Make infidel or heathen. M19. 2 *v.i.* Profess infidelity. L19.

infield /ˈɪnfiːld/ *n.* & *adv.* L15. [f. IN-[1] + FIELD *n.*] A *n.* 1 The (usu. arable) farm land lying near a farmstead; *transf.* arable land as opp. to pasture; land regularly manured and cropped. L15. 2 *Baseball.* The area enclosed within the base lines, the diamond; each of the four fielders stationed on its boundaries. M19. 3 *Cricket.* The part of the playing area near the wicket; any fielder(s) stationed in this area. L19. 4 The area enclosed by a racetrack. *US.* E20.

1 **infield and outfield** *Hist.* a system of husbandry confining manuring and tillage to the infield land.

B *adv.* In or towards the centre of a playing field. M19.

infielder /ˈɪnfiːldə/ *n.* M19. [f. INFIELD *n.* + -ER[1].] *Cricket* & *Baseball.* A fielder stationed in the infield.

infieldsman /ˈɪnfiːldzmən/ *n.* Pl. **-men**. E20. [f. IN-[1] + FIELDSMAN.] *Cricket.* An infielder.

in fieri /ɪn ˈfʌɪərʌɪ/ *a. phr.* M17. [med.L, f. L IN *prep.* + *fieri* be made, come into being.] In the process of being made or coming into being.

infight /ˈɪnfʌɪt/ *v.* ME. [f. IN-[1] + FIGHT *v.*] †1 *v.t.* Fight or strive against, attack. Only in ME. 2 *v.i.* Fight or box at close quarters. E20.

in-fighting /ˈɪnfʌɪtɪŋ/ *n.* E19. [f. IN-[1] + FIGHTING *n.*] 1 Fighting or boxing at closer quarters than arm's length. E19. 2 *fig.* Hidden conflict or competitiveness within a group or organization. E20.

1 L. WOOLLEY Two [spears] have plain butts and are intended for in-fighting. 2 WILBUR SMITH She would use even the dirtiest in-fighting to see that Rod was not overlooked.

in-fighter *n.* E19.

infigured /ɪnˈfɪgəd/ *a.* E17. [f. IN-[2] + FIGURED.] Marked or adorned with figures.

infill /ˈɪnfɪl/ *n.* M20. [f. the vb.] 1 The filling in of a cavity, space, etc.; *spec.* (*Town Planning*) the filling of vacant gaps between houses. M20. 2 Something used to fill up a hole or cavity. M20.

infill /ɪnˈfɪl/ *v.t.* & *i.* M19. [f. IN-[1] + FILL *v.*] Fill up or in (a cavity, space, etc.).

ˈinfilling *n.* = INFILL *n.* L19.

infilter /ɪnˈfɪltə/ *v.t.* M19. [f. IN-[1] + FILTER *v.*] = INFILTRATE *v.* 1.

infiltrate /ˈɪnfɪltreɪt, ɪnˈfɪl-/ *n.* L19. [f. the vb.] Chiefly *Med.* An infiltrated substance; an infiltration.

infiltrate /ˈɪnfɪltreɪt/ *v.* M18. [f. IN-[2] + FILTRATE *v.*] 1 *v.t.* Introduce (a fluid) by filtration. (Foll. by *into*, *through*.) M18. 2 *v.t.* & *i.* Permeate (*into*, *through*) by filtration. M18. 3 *v.t.* & *i.* Penetrate, gain entrance or access to, (enemy lines, an opposing political organization, etc.) surreptitiously and by degrees. M20. b *v.t.* Introduce (troops, a spy, etc.) into enemy lines, an opposing political organization, etc., in this way. M20.

1 *British Medical Journal* 2% plain lignocaine was infiltrated into the wound. 2 *Scientific American* To collect floodwater that infiltrates the gravel beds of desert streams. 3 I. WALLACE The Reds might infiltrate every free nation of Africa, and control the continent in a year. J. A. MICHENER Six thousand mounted troops . . started cautiously infiltrating toward the western edge. *fig.*: S. NAIPAUL He was . . resentful of her for thus infiltrating his consciousness.

b R. DEACON Any spies who might have been infiltrated into the ranks of prisoners-of-war.
in'filtrative *a.* (*rare*) of the nature of or productive of infiltration M19. **infiltrator** *n.* M20.

infiltration /ɪnfɪl'treɪʃ(ə)n/ *n.* LME. [f. prec. + -ION.] **1** The action or process of infiltrating (something); the process or condition of being infiltrated. LME. **2** An infiltrated deposit. E19.
1 J. L. MYRES The southward infiltration of Albanian and Slav into districts formerly Romanized. *Times* Alleged Communist infiltration into the Oxford branch of the National Union of Railwaymen. A. POWELL The only hint of human infiltration of these pastures came from distant sheep.
Comb.: **infiltration anaesthesia** local anaesthesia; **infiltration capacity** the maximum rate at which soil in a given condition can absorb water.

infiltrometer /ɪnfɪl'trɒmɪtə/ *n.* M20. [f. INFILTR(ATION + -OMETER.] An apparatus for measuring the rate at which soil absorbs water.

infimum /ɪn'fʌɪməm/ *n.* M20. [L = lowest part, use as n. of neut. of *infimus* lowest.] *Math.* The largest number that is less than or equal to each of a given set of real numbers; an analogous quantity for a subset of any other ordered set. Opp. *supremum*.

in fine /ɪn 'fʌɪni, 'fiːni/ *adv. phr.* M16. [L.] Finally, in short, to sum up.

infinitation /ˌɪnfɪnɪ'teɪʃ(ə)n/ *n.* M17. [L *infinitatio(n-)*, f. *infinitat-* pa. ppl stem of *infinitare* make infinite, f. as next: see -ATION.] *Logic.* The action of making infinite; the condition of being made infinite.

infinite /'ɪnfɪnɪt/ *a.*, *adv.*, & *n.* LME. [L *infinitus* unbounded, unlimited, f. as IN-[3] + FINITE *a.* & *n.*] **A** *adj.* **1** Having no limit or end; boundless, endless; immeasurably great in extent, duration, degree, etc. LME. †**b** Occupying an indefinitely long time; tedious, endless. L16–M17. **2** Innumerable, very many. LME. †**3** Indefinite in nature, meaning, etc.; indeterminate. E16–M17. **4** *Gram.* Of a verb part or form: not limited by person or number. M16. **5** *Math.* Having no limit; greater than any assignable number or magnitude; having an uncountable number of elements, digits, terms, etc. L17. **6** *Mus.* Of a musical structure: that can be repeated infinitely. E19.
1 J. BUCHAN For the humble and unfortunate he had infinite charity. B. BETTELHEIM What goes on in the infinite (or possibly finite, but nevertheless unimaginably vast) outer space. **infinite regress** a sequence of reasoning, argument, justification, etc., which can never come to an end.
†**B** *adv.* Infinitely. E16–L17.
C *n.* **1** That which is infinite or has no limit; an infinite being, thing, quantity, etc.; *spec.* (*a*) *the infinite*, infinite space; (*b*) *the Infinite*, God. M16. **2** *An* exceedingly large number or (formerly) amount. Foll. by *of*. *arch.* M16. **3** *Math.* An infinite quantity. M17.
1 J. RUSKIN That Calais tower has an infinite of symbolism in it. P. DAVIES Measuring the infinite must rank as one of the greatest enterprises of the human intellect.
infinitely *adv.* LME. **infiniteness** *n.* LME.

infinitesimal /ˌɪnfɪnɪ'tɛsɪm(ə)l/ *n.* & *a.* M17. [mod.L *infinitesimus*, f. as INFINITE (cf. CENTESIMAL): see -AL[1].] **A** *n.* †**1** *Math.* The member of a series corresponding to infinity. Only in M17. **2** *Math.* An infinitesimal quantity; a fraction which approaches zero. E18. **3** An extremely small or insignificant quantity, amount, etc. M19.
B *adj.* **1** (Of a quantity) infinitely or indefinitely small; relating to or involving quantities which approach zero. E18. **2** *gen.* Extremely minute or insignificant. M18.
1 *infinitesimal calculus*: see CALCULUS 1.
infinitesimally *adv.* E19.

infinitise *v.* var. of INFINITIZE.

infinitist /ɪn'fɪnɪtɪst/ *n.* L19 [f. INFINITE + -IST.] A person who believes that God or the world is infinite.
infinitism *n.* the views or belief of an infinitist E20.

infinitival /ˌɪnfɪnɪ'tʌɪv(ə)l/ *a.* M19. [f. as next + -AL[1].] *Gram.* Of or pertaining to the infinitive.
infinitivally *adv.* L19.

infinitive /ɪn'fɪnɪtɪv/ *a.* & *n.* LME. [L *infinitivus* unlimited, indefinite, infinitive, f. as IN-[3] + *finitivus* definite, f. as FINITE *a.*: see -IVE.] *Gram.* **A** *adj.* Designating or pertaining to a form of a verb expressing the verbal notion without relation to a particular subject (traditionally classed as a mood). LME.
B *n.* The infinitive form of a verb; a verb in this. M16.
split infinitive: see SPLIT *ppl a.*
infinitively *adv.* in the infinitive form E18.

infinitize /ɪn'fɪnɪtʌɪz/ *v.t. rare.* Also **-ise**. E20. [f. INFINITE + -IZE.] Make infinite.

infinitude /ɪn'fɪnɪtjuːd/ *n.* M17. [f. as INFINITE after *magnitude*: see -TUDE.] **1** = INFINITY 1. M17. **2** = INFINITY 2. M17.

infinitum /ɪnfɪ'nʌɪtəm/ *n.* L16. [L, f. as INFINITE.] Infinity; an infinitude, an endless amount or number. Cf. AD INFINITUM.

infinity /ɪn'fɪnɪti/ *n.* LME. [(O)Fr. *infinité* f. L *infinitas*, f. as INFINITE: see -ITY.] **1** The quality or attribute of being infinite or having no limit; boundlessness. LME. **2** An infinite thing; infinite extent, amount, duration, etc.; a boundless expanse; an unlimited time. LME. **3** Immensity, vastness; an indefinitely great amount or number. Foll. by *of*. LME. **4** *Math.* Infinite quantity (denoted by ∞); an infinite number (*of* something). L17. **b** Infinite distance; a point which is (effectively) infinitely distant; *esp.* in *Optics*, any distance from which an image can be focused with a lens set for maximum distance, i.e. from which light rays arrive effectively parallel. M19.
1 M. IGNATIEFF What we have in common with each other beneath the infinity of our differences. 2 T. ROETHKE I learned not to fear infinity, The far field, the windy cliffs of forever. L. NIVEN It seemed to go out forever . . to a point at infinity. 3 ALDOUS HUXLEY Every object and event contains within itself an infinity of depths within depths. **to infinity** endlessly, without limit.

infirm /ɪn'fəːm/ *a.* LME. [L *infirmus*, f. as IN-[3] + *firmus* FIRM *a.*] **1** Weak, unsound; unable to resist pressure or weight, frail, feeble. Now *rare*. LME. **b** *transf.* Of an argument, title, etc.: weak; invalid. Now *rare*. M16. **2** Of the mind, a decision, etc.: not firm or strong in character or purpose; weak, irresolute. E16. **3** Not physically strong or healthy; weak or feeble, esp. through old age. L16.
infirmly *adv.* E17. **infirmness** *n.* L16.

infirm /ɪn'fəːm/ *v.t.* Now *rare*. LME. [L *infirmare* weaken, invalidate, f. as prec.] †**1** Weaken the hold of (belief) over the mind; impair the force of (an argument, reason, etc.); make doubtful or less certain. LME–L17. †**2** Make physically infirm or frail; weaken, impair the strength of. M16–M17. **3** Invalidate (a law, custom, evidence, etc.); declare invalid, call into question. M16.

infirmarer /ɪn'fəːm(ə)rə/ *n.* LME. [OFr. *enfermerier*, f. *enfermerie* infirmary, f. as next: see -ER[2].] *Hist.* A person in charge of (the patients in) an infirmary in a medieval monastery.

infirmary /ɪn'fəːm(ə)ri/ *n.* LME. [med.L *infirmaria*, f. as INFIRM *a.*: see -ARY[1].] (A part of) a building for the treatment of the sick or wounded, orig. in a religious establishment, school, etc.; a hospital.
infir'marian *n.* (*Hist.*) = INFIRMARER M17.

infirmation /ɪnfəː'meɪʃ(ə)n/ *n. rare.* E19. [L *infirmatio(n-)*, f. *infirmat-* pa. ppl stem of *infirmare*: see INFIRM *v.*, -ATION.] The action of weakening or invalidating evidence etc.

infirmative /ɪn'fəːmətɪv/ *a. rare.* E17. [f. INFIRM *v.* + -ATIVE.] Tending to weaken or invalidate.

infirmity /ɪn'fəːmɪti/ *n.* LME. [L *infirmitas*, f. as INFIRM *a.*: see -ITY.] **1** Weakness or lack of strength; lack of power to do something; an instance of this. LME. **b** Lack of validity in an argument or title. E17. **2** Physical weakness, debility, frailty of body, etc., resulting from some defect, disease, or (esp.) old age; a specific physical weakness; *esp.* a failing in one of the faculties. Formerly also, an illness. LME. **3** (A) weakness or defect of character; (a) moral weakness or frailty. LME. †**4** A noxious vegetative growth. *rare*. L16–M18.

infix /'ɪnfɪks/ *n.* E17. [f. (as) next; in sense 2 after *prefix*, *suffix*.] †**1** A fixing in; fixed position. Only in E17. **2** *Gram.* An affix inserted into a word. L19.

infix /ɪn'fɪks/ *v.t.* E16. [Partly f. L *infix-* pa. ppl stem of *infigere* fix in f. as IN-[2] + *figere* fasten; partly f. IN-[1] or IN-[2] + FIX *v.*] **1** Fix or fasten (a thing) in or *in*; implant or insert firmly. E16. **b** Fix or fasten on something. E17. **2** Fix or impress (a fact etc.) *in* the mind or memory. M16. **3** *Gram.* Insert (an affix) into a word. M19.
1 *fig.*: E. WHITE So deeply is this habit of thought infixed in modern readers.
infixation *n.* (*Gram.*) the action of infixing; the state of being infixed: E20. **infixion** *n.* (*rare*) = INFIXATION M17.

in flagrante /ɪn flə'granti/ *adv. phr. colloq.* E17. [Abbrev. of next or similar L phr.] = next.
¶Rare bef. 20.

in flagrante delicto /ɪn fləˌgranti dɪ'lɪktəʊ/ *adv. phr.* L18. [L = in the heat of the crime: cf. prec., FLAGRANT, DELICT.] In the very act of committing an offence; *spec.* in the act of adultery or other sexual misconduct.
E. PAUL His cringing wife and the imaginary lover he had always sworn to catch *in flagrante delicto*.

inflame /ɪn'fleɪm/ *v.* Also (now *rare*) **en-** /ɪn-, ɛn-/. ME. [(O)Fr. *enflammer* f. L *inflammare*, f. as IN-[2] + *flamma* FLAME *n.*] **I** *v.t.* **1** Excite with strong feeling or passion; rouse to anger or animosity. ME. **b** Rouse (a passion). ME. **2** Set on fire, kindle. Now *rare*. LME. **b** Light up as with flame. L15. **3** Heat, make hot; *esp.* raise (the body or blood) to a feverish temperature. LME. **b** Induce inflammation or painful swelling in. M17. **4** Make worse or more intense; aggravate. Formerly also, increase (a price or charge). E17.
1 W. ROBERTSON Stimulants like wine inflame the senses. S. T. WARNER A dance wanton enough to inflame a maypole. P. HOWARD The gruesome horror stories that had inflamed public opinion. 2 W. FALCONER The fuse . . inflames the powder. b SHELLEY The torches Inflame the night to the eastward. 3 R. CHANDLER We had . . lattices to admit the air, while cool; and shutters to exclude it, when inflamed. b M. SPARK Freddy had arrived with an arm swollen and inflamed from a new vaccination. 4 V. GLENDINNING Lettie inflamed Rebecca's raw self-doubt and was never forgiven for it.
II *v.i.* **5** Catch fire. Formerly also, become very hot. LME. **6** Become passionately excited. M16. **7** Become heated by disease or stimulants; be affected by inflammation or painful swelling. L16.
5 J. TYNDALL It first smokes and then violently inflames. 6 CARLYLE I know how soon your noble heart inflames when sympathy and humanity appeal to it.
†**inflameable** *a.* = INFLAMMABLE *a.* E17–E18. **inflamer** *n.* a person who or thing which inflames; *esp.* an instigator: E17.

inflammable /ɪn'flaməb(ə)l/ *a.* & *n.* LME. [med.L *inflammabilis*, f. *inflammare*: see prec., -ABLE.] **A** *adj.* †**1** Of a part of the body: liable to become inflamed. Only in LME. **2** Liable to catch fire; readily ignited. E17. **3** Easily roused or excited; passionate, excitable. E19.
2 †**inflammable air** hydrogen. 3 D. H. LAWRENCE The Englishman was in a strange, inflammable state, the German was excited.
B *n.* An inflammable substance. Usu. in *pl.* L18.
¶With reference to fire freq. repl. in official use by *flammable*, to avoid possible misunderstanding as 'not flammable', with interpretation of the prefix as IN-[3].
inflamma'bility *n.* M17. **inflammableness** *n.* L17. **inflammably** *adv.* M19.

inflammation /ɪnflə'meɪʃ(ə)n/ *n.* LME. [L *inflammatio(n-)*, f. *inflammat-* pa. ppl stem of *inflammare*: see INFLAME, -ATION. Perh. partly f. (O)Fr. *inflammation*.] **1** *Med.* The condition, usu. involving redness, warmth, swelling, and pain, produced locally in the tissues as a reaction to injury, infection, etc.; an instance of this. LME. **2** The action of setting on fire or catching fire; the condition of being in flames. E16. †**b** A blazing object or phenomenon. M16–M18. **3** The

For other words beginning with *in-* see the entry for **in-**[1]

action of exciting or rousing to strong emotion; the condition of being so roused. L16. †4 Increase in cost. *rare*. Only in E19.

inflammatory /ɪnˈflamət(ə)ri/ *n.* & *a.* L17. [f. INFLAMMAT(ION + -ORY[2].] A *n.* A thing that inflames or excites strong feeling or passions. Now *rare* or *obs.* L17.

B *adj.* 1 Tending to excite with strong feeling or passion. Now usu., tending to rouse anger or animosity. E18. 2 Tending to heat the blood or excite the senses; stimulating. Now *rare*. M18. 3 Of the nature of, resulting from, or characterized by inflammation of the tissues. M18. †4 Characterized by or causing a blazing condition. M–L18.

1 D. WIGODER We.. attacked each other, with vicious inflammatory verbal threats.

inflammatorily *adv.* M19.

inflate /ɪnˈfleɪt/ *ppl a.* Now *rare* or *obs.* LME. [L *inflatus* pa. pple, f. as next: see -ATE[2].] = INFLATED.

inflate /ɪnˈfleɪt/ *v.* LME. [L *inflat-* pa. ppl stem of *inflare*, f. as IN-[2] + *flare* to blow: see -ATE[3].] 1 *v.t.* Distend by filling with air or gas; *gen.* swell, distend. LME. 2 *v.t.* Puff up with or *with* pride, vanity, satisfaction, etc.; elate. M16. 3 *v.t.* Increase greatly or beyond accepted limits; *spec.* (*Econ.*) bring about inflation in relation to (a currency, an economy), raise (prices) artificially. M19. b *v.i.* Resort to (monetary) inflation; undergo (excessive) increase or monetary inflation. M20.

1 S. BELLOW A beach ball you inflated with your breath. 2 J. PORTER Character that prosperity could not inflate, nor adversity depress. 3 W. S. JEVONS Prices and credit mutually inflate each other. C. HOPE The enemies of our country like nothing better than to inflate the figures of those killed. b *Daily Telegraph* In these days of rapidly inflating house prices. *Weekend Australian* A permanent population of 25,000 which inflates to 100,000 during holiday periods.

inflatable *a.* & *n.* (*a*) *adj.* able to be blown up or filled with air or gas; (*b*) *n.* an inflatable dinghy, toy, etc.: L19. **inflated** *a.* (*a*) that has been distended or inflated; *esp.* (of language) turgid, bombastic; (*b*) *Zool.* & *Bot.* having a bulging form and hollow interior, as if filled with air: L16. **inflatedness** *n.* M19. **inflater, -or** *ns.* a person who or thing which inflates something; *spec.* an air-pump for inflating tyres etc.: L19.

inflation /ɪnˈfleɪʃ(ə)n/ *n.* ME. [L *inflatio(n-)*, f. *inflat-*, f. as prec.: see -ATION.] 1 The action of inflating with air or gas; the condition of being inflated with air or gas or of being distended as if with air. ME. 2 The condition of being puffed up with pride, vanity, satisfaction, etc. E16. 3 Turgidity of style; bombast. E17. 4 (Unduly) great expansion or increase; *spec.* (*a*) *Econ.* (undue) increase in the quantity of money circulating, in relation to the goods available for purchase; (*b*) *pop.* inordinate general rise in prices leading to a fall in the value of money. Opp. *deflation*. M19.

3 K. ALLOTT She can express an apocalyptic element in feeling without inflation. 4 *Dumfries & Galloway Standard* A major part of our economic policy is to keep inflation as low as possible.

Comb.: **inflation-proof** *v.t.* & *a.* protect(ed) from the effects of economic inflation.

inflationary *a.* of, characterized by, or leading to monetary inflation (*inflationary spiral*, a vicious circle caused by higher wages leading to higher prices, which in turn force up wages) E20. **inflationism** *n.* (*Econ.*) the policy of inflating a currency; the condition of being inflated: E20. **inflationist** *n.* an advocate of inflation, esp. as being beneficial to trade L19.

inflect /ɪnˈflɛkt/ *v.* LME. [L *inflectere*, f. as IN-[2] + *flectere* to bend.] 1 *v.t.* Bend inwards; bend into a curve or angle; *gen.* bend, curve. LME. †2 *v.t. Optics.* Diffract. M17–M19. 3 *Gram.* a *v.t.* Modify the form of (a word) to express a particular grammatical function or attribute: see INFLECTION 2. M17. b *v.i.* Undergo inflection. L19. 4 *v.t.* Vary the intonation of (the voice); *Mus.* flatten or sharpen (a note) by a chromatic semitone. E19.

1 *fig.*: O. SACKS Most of Miss H's hating and blaming was inflected inwards upon herself. 4 A. S. BYATT His voice was.. a southern industrial Yorkshire, less inflected and singing than Winifred's northern one.

inflectable *a.* (*Gram.*) able to be inflected M20. **inflected** *a.* (*a*) that has been inflected; (*b*) *spec.* (of a language) characterized by inflection: M17. **inflectedness** *n.* E19.

inflection /ɪnˈflɛkʃ(ə)n/ *n.* Also **-exion**. LME. [(O)Fr. *inflexion* or L *inflexio(n-)*, f. *inflex-* pa. ppl stem of *inflectere*: see prec., -ION.] 1 The action of bending (inwards). Formerly, ability to bend. LME. b The condition of being inflected or bent; a bend, a curvature. M17. 2 *Gram.* Modification in the form of a word by means of affixation, vowel change, etc., to express a particular grammatical function or attribute, as number, case, gender, tense, mood, etc. L16. b An inflected form of a word. Also, an affix used to inflect a word. M17. 3 Change of intonation of the voice; (in speaking or singing) a change in tone or pitch. L16. †4 *Optics.* Diffraction. E18–M19. 5 *Geom.* Change in the direction of curvature. E18.

1 *fig.*: J. BRYANT The allusion will not be.. obtained by undue inflexions or distortions. b D. STOREY Ellipses.. drawn.. with scarcely an inflection that broke the line. 3 E. CALDWELL She whispered quietly with a cautious inflection of her voice that sounded.. wistful and apprehensive. *fig.*: C. CONNOLLY Sentences which were able to express the subtlest inflections of sensibility and meaning. 5 **point of inflection** a point on a curve at which inflection occurs.

inflectionless *a.* without modulation or grammatical inflection L19.

inflectional /ɪnˈflɛkʃ(ə)n(ə)l/ *a.* Also **-flex-**. M19. [f. prec. + -AL[1].] 1 Of, pertaining to, or characterized by grammatical inflection. M19. 2 *Geom.* Of or pertaining to a point of inflection. M19.

inflectionally *adv.* L19.

inflective /ɪnˈflɛktɪv/ *a.* M17. [f. INFLECT + -IVE.] †1 Of the air: tending to diffract rays of light. M17–E18. 2 Of, pertaining to, or characterized by grammatical inflection. L18.

inflexed /ɪnˈflɛkst/ *a.* M17. [f. L *inflex-* pa. ppl stem of *inflectere* INFLECT + -ED[1].] Bent or curved inwards.

inflexible /ɪnˈflɛksɪb(ə)l/ *a.* LME. [L *inflexibilis*, f. as IN-[3] + *flexibilis* FLEXIBLE.] 1 Unable to be bent; rigid, not pliant. LME. 2 Adhering unswervingly to a purpose or opinion; obstinate, uncompromising. LME. 3 Unalterable, rigidly fixed. L17.

2 D. PRATER He remained inflexible against any form of compromise. 3 G. H. NAPHEYS Nature's laws are more inflexible than iron.

inflexiˈbility *n.* E17. **inflexibly** *adv.* M16.

inflexion *n.*, **inflexional** *a.* vars. of INFLECTION, INFLECTIONAL.

inflict /ɪnˈflɪkt/ *v.t.* M16. [L *inflict-* pa. ppl stem of *infligere*, f. as IN-[2] + *fligere* strike down.] 1 Afflict (a person) *with* something painful or disagreeable. Now *rare* & *joc.* M16. 2 Impose or lay (a wound, blow, penalty, defeat, etc.) on a person or thing as something painful or unpleasant to be endured. (Foll. by *on*, *upon*.) L16. b Force (an unwelcome person or thing) *on*, *upon*. Freq. *joc.* E19.

1 *Macmillan's Magazine* We should be inflicted with less.. twaddle and useless verbosity. 2 E. WAUGH Punitive expeditions suffered more harm than they inflicted. N. ANNAN The oppressive regime which Leslie inflicted on his daughter. b R. BOLT I was commanded into office; it was inflicted on me. *Southern Rag* People who want to *share* the music, not have it inflicted on them.

inflictable *a.* that may be imposed or inflicted E19. **inflicter** *n.* E17. **inflictor** *n.* M18.

infliction /ɪnˈflɪkʃ(ə)n/ *n.* M16. [Late L *inflictio(n-)*, f. as prec.: see -ION.] 1 The action of inflicting pain, punishment, annoyance, etc. Formerly also, the fact of being inflicted. M16. 2 An instance of pain, punishment, etc., inflicted; *colloq.* a nuisance. L16.

1 R. J. SULLIVAN The infliction of such exemplary punishment. 2 R. BOYLE Distress'd by such Persecutions, as seem to be Divine Inflictions. M. BRIDGMAN What an infliction he must be!

inflictive /ɪnˈflɪktɪv/ *a.* E17. [f. as INFLICT + -IVE.] Inflicting or tending to inflict pain or suffering; of or pertaining to infliction.

inflight /ˈɪnflʌɪt/ *a.* M20. [f. IN-[1] + FLIGHT *n.*[1]] Occurring, supplied, etc., during an aircraft's flight.

inflorescence /ɪnflɔːˈrɛs(ə)ns, -flə-/ *n.* M18. [mod.L *inflorescentia*, f. late L *inflorescere* come into flower: see IN-[2], FLORESCENCE.] *Bot.* 1 The mode in which the flowers of a plant are arranged in relation to the axis and to each other. M18. b The flowers of a plant collectively. M19. 2 The process of flowering or coming into flower. E19.

1 DEFINITE *inflorescence*.

inflow /ˈɪnfləʊ/ *n.* M19. [f. IN-[1] + FLOW *n.*[1]] The action of flowing in, influx; that which flows in.

Daily Telegraph The inflow of money from savers had picked up.

inflow /ɪnˈfləʊ/ *v.i.* LME. [f. IN-[1] + FLOW *v.*] 1 Flow in. LME. †2 Esp. of a star: exert influence. LME–M17.

influence /ˈɪnflʊəns/ *n.* LME. [(O)Fr., or med.L *influentia* (whence also Prov., Sp. *influencia*, It. *influenza*), f. L *influent-* pres. ppl stem of *influere* flow in, f. as IN-[2] + *fluere* flow: see -ENCE.] †1 The action of flowing in, influx; flowing matter. LME–E18. 2 *Astrol.* A supposed emanation of ethereal fluid or (in later theories) occult force from the stars affecting human character, destiny, etc. LME. †b Inherent nature or disposition, ascribed to astral influence. LME–M17. †3 The inflow of a divine or secret force or principle; the force etc. flowing in thus. LME–M17. 4 An action exerted, imperceptibly or by indirect means, by one person or thing on another so as to cause changes in conduct, development, conditions, etc. (Foll. by *in*, *on*, *upon*.) L16. b Ascendancy, moral or political power (*over* or *with* a person or group). M17. 5 A person or thing exercising such action or power. M18. 6 *Electr.* Induction. *arch.* L19.

2 SPENSER What euill starre On you hath frown'd, and pourd his influence bad? J. RUSKIN One of the leaden influences on me of the planet Saturn. *transf.*: MILTON Store of ladies, whose bright eyes Rain influence. 3 AV *Wisd.* 7:25 A pure influence flowing from the glory of the Almighty. 4 J. ROSENBERG No traces of this first teacher's influence appear in Rembrandt's work. B. T. BRADFORD In England she might conceivably be able to exercise some influence over him. *sphere of influence*: see SPHERE *n.* 6. **under the influence** *colloq.* drunk. UNDUE *influence*. b M. MOORCOCK My uncle's influence must be considerable. He had pulled strings in every department. 5 P. G. HAMERTON Musical studies, the most powerful of softening influences. C. HOPE Looper would act as a moderating influence on her daughter when she was gone.

Comb.: **influence line** *Engin.* a graph showing how, at a given point in a structure, the stress, moment, etc., varies with the position of the load; **influence pedlar, peddler** *N. Amer.* a person who uses his or her position or political influence in exchange for money or favours.

influence /ˈɪnflʊəns/ *v.* M17. [f. the n.] 1 *v.t.* a Affect (sometimes improperly or corruptly) the mind or actions of. M17. b Affect the condition of, have an effect on. M17. †2 *v.t.* Cause to flow in; infuse, instil. M17–E18. 3 *v.i.* Exert influence. Orig. foll. by †*on*, †*upon*. L17.

1a E. W. BEMIS Expenditures to 'influence' city council. *Femina* Bhindranwale was a magnetic speaker and he influenced a lot of local people. b G. R. PORTER Specific gravity of glass is influenced by the degree of heat to which it has been exposed. D. HALBERSTAM He wanted to influence events, to be a mover.

influenceable *a.* M19. **influencer** *n.* M17. **influencive** *a.* (*rare*) influential E18.

influent /ˈɪnflʊənt/ *a.* & *n.* LME. [L *influent-*: see INFLUENCE *n.*, -ENT.] A *adj.* 1 Flowing in. LME. 2 Exercising astral influence or occult power. Long *arch.* LME. 3 *Ecol.* That is an influent (see B.2 below). LME. B *n.* 1 A stream (esp. a tributary) which flows into another stream or a lake. M19. 2 *Ecol.* An organism having a major effect on the balance of a plant or animal community. *arch.* E20.

influential /ɪnflʊˈɛnʃ(ə)l/ *a.* & *n.* L16. [f. med.L *influentia* INFLUENCE *n.* + -AL[1].] A *adj.* †1 *Astrol.* Pertaining to, of the nature of, or exercising astral influence. L16–M17. b *transf.* Exercising or caused by divine or supernatural influence. M17–M18. 2 Exerting a powerful influence or effect *on*. M17. 3 Having or marked by great power or influence. M18.

2 I. BARROW Hurtful errours, influential on practice. 3 J. BERMAN Her influential books helped to transform the condition of women in early twentieth century America. N. GORDIMER Carole . . became influential in the debating society.

B *n.* An influential person. M19.

influentially *adv.* (*a*) by or in the way of influence; †(*b*) *Electr.* by induction: M17.

influenza /ɪnflʊ'ɛnzə/ *n.* M18. [It., lit. 'influence', f. med.L *influentia* INFLUENCE *n.* Cf. FLU.] A highly contagious viral infection of the lining of the trachea and bronchi, often epidemic, and usu. marked by fever, weakness, muscular aches, coughing, and watery catarrh. Freq. loosely, any acute respiratory infection accompanied by fever.

gastric influenza: see GASTRIC *a.* *Spanish influenza*: see SPANISH *a.*

¶It. *influenza* has, in addition to the various senses of Eng. *influence*, that of 'outbreak of an epidemic', hence *absol.* 'an epidemic'; its specific application to the 1743 influenza epidemic which began in Italy led to its adoption as the standard English term for the disease.

influenzal *a.* E19.

influx /'ɪnflʌks/ *n.* L16. [(Fr. f.) late L *influxus*, f. L *influere* to flow in: see IN-², FLUX *n.*] 1 An inflow of liquid, air, light, etc. L16. b The point at which a stream or river flows into a larger stream, a lake, etc. M17. 2 *transf.* A continuous entry of people (esp. visitors or immigrants) or things into a place. M17. †3 = INFLUENCE *n.* 3, 4, 4b. M17–E18.

2 I. COLEGATE The influx of tourists and foreign residents has made my local villagers richer. A. BROOKNER This sudden influx of money might seem to promise them a different life.

influxion /ɪn'flʌkʃ(ə)n/ *n.* Now *rare.* E17. [Late L *influxio(n-)*, f. *influx-* pa. ppl stem of *influere*: see IN-², FLUXION.] Inflow, influx.

info /'ɪnfəʊ/ *n.* *colloq.* E20. [Abbrev.] Information.

L. CODY Look, what's the info on this kidnapping? *Woman's Realm* Big, colourful pictures and info about today's pop stars.

info'mania *n.* (*colloq.*) excessive enthusiasm for the accumulation and dissemination of information L20.

in-foal /'ɪnfəʊl/ *a.* E20. [f. IN-¹ + FOAL *n.*] Of a mare: that is in foal, pregnant.

infold /'ɪnfəʊld/ *n.* Also (earlier) †**en-**. L16. [f. IN-², EN-¹ + FOLD *n.*²] A convolution; a fold.

infold *v.*¹, *v.*² see ENFOLD *v.*¹, *v.*²

infolded /ɪn'fəʊldɪd/ *ppl a.* L19. [f. IN-¹ + FOLD *v.*¹ + -ED¹.] Turned or folded in.

infolding /'ɪnfəʊldɪŋ/ *n.* L19. [f. IN-¹ + FOLDING *n.*] A folding or turning in; an inward fold.

Scientific American The two vocal folds (which . . are actually elastic infoldings of the mucous membrane lining the larynx).

infolio /ɪn'fəʊlɪəʊ/ *n. rare.* Pl. **-os.** M19. [f. IN-¹ + FOLIO *n.*] A folio volume.

infomercial /ɪnfə'mɜːʃ(ə)l/ *n.* Chiefly *US.* Also **inform-**. L20. [Blend of INFORMATION and COMMERCIAL: cf. INFO.] An advertising film, esp. on television, which promotes a product etc. in an informative and purportedly objective style.

inforce *v.* see ENFORCE *v.*

†**inforcible** *a.* var. of ENFORCIBLE.

inform /ɪn'fɔːm/ *a.* Now *rare* or *obs.* M16. [Fr. *informe* or L *informis*, f. as IN-³ + *forma* FORM *n.*] 1 Having no definite or regular form; shapeless, misshapen, deformed. M16. 2 Without form; having no shaping or actuating principle. M17.

1 C. COTTON Bleak Crags, and naked Hills, And the whole Prospect so inform and rude. 2 R. VILVAIN An inform lump . . without a Soul is neither Man nor Beast. J. NORRIS In the old creation we read of a void and inform mass.

inform /ɪn'fɔːm/ *v.* Also (earlier) †**en-**. ME. [OFr. *enfo(u)rmer* (mod. *informer*) f. L *informare* shape, form an idea of, describe, f. as IN-² + *forma* FORM *n.*] I Give form to; shape. †1 *v.t.* Give form or shape to; arrange, compose, fashion. ME–L17. b *v.i.* Take form or shape; materialize. L16–M17. 2 *v.t.* Give a formative principle or vital quality to; imbue *with* a feeling, principle, or quality. LME. b Be the essential quality or principle of; permeate, inspire. LME. 3 *v.t.* Of a soul or life-giving source: impart life or spirit to; inspire, animate. E17.

2 TENNYSON Her constant beauty doth inform Stillness with love, and day with light. H. BELLOC As a poem is informed by a . . scheme of rhythm. b B. MAGEE The depth of passion which informs this defence of liberty. 3 M. PRIOR Long as Breath informs this fleeting Frame.

II Impart knowledge to; tell, instruct, teach. 4 *v.t.* Form (the mind or character); impart knowledge or instruction to; teach. Now *rare* or *obs.* ME. †b Instruct (a person) in a subject or course of action. Foll. by *how, in, of, to, to do.* ME–M18. †c Give instructions or directions, direct or bid *to do.* LME–M18. †d Direct, guide. M17–M19. †5 *v.t.* Give instruction in (a subject); teach or spread (a faith etc.). ME–E17. 6 *v.t.* Give (a person) knowledge of a particular fact, occurrence, etc. Foll. by *about, of,* (arch.) *on, that.* LME. †7 *v.t.* Make (a fact or occurrence) known; tell (a thing) to (a person). LME–E19. †8a *v.t.* Give (a magistrate etc.) accusatory information *against* a person. Only in E16. b *v.i.* Give accusatory information *on* or *against* a person. L16. 9 *v.refl.* Get instruction or information *on* or *about*; get to know, learn, *of, that.* E17. †10 *v.i.* Give information, report. Only in 17.

4 ROBERT BURTON That leaves his son to a covetous Schoolemaster to be informed. W. GIFFORD So may thy varied verse, from age to age Inform the simple, and delight the sage. 6 T. HARDY When Somerset reached the hotel he was informed that somebody was waiting to see him. B. EMECHETA To make sure that all the arrangements were made before he informed her. P. ACKROYD Neither of them had informed their parents in advance about their intentions. R. ELLMANN 'I was ploughed, of course,' Wilde informed a friend afterwards. 7 W. LAUD The bishop informs that that county is very full of impropriations. SOUTHEY My mother will inform you my town direction as soon as I have one. 8b M. SCAMMELL Someone who knew Taissa's background informed on her, and she was soon dismissed. 9 W. DAMPIER They came purposely to view our Ship, and . . to inform themselves what we were. C. JOHNSTON The motive . . was to inform myself particularly in the laws.

informal /ɪn'fɔːm(ə)l/ *a.* LME. [f. IN-³ + FORMAL *a.*] I 1 Not done or made according to a recognized form; irregular, unofficial, unconventional. LME. 2 Without formality or ceremony; unceremonious. Of language, clothing, etc.: everyday, casual. E19.

1 M. RULE An informal alliance was formed between the Barbers' Company and the Fellowship of Surgeons. *Sunday Express* This garden is . . very informal I don't think you could find a straight edge anywhere! **informal ballot paper, vote** *Austral.* & *NZ* a spoilt or invalid ballot paper. **informal patient**: admitted to a psychiatric hospital on a non-compulsory basis. 2 R. JARRELL He was a nice-looking and informal and unassuming man, a very human one. N. PODHORETZ Everything . . was easy and informal . . and no one seemed to care whether my tie was on or off. A. THWAITE A few . . guests were encouraged to stay on for a cold informal supper.

†II 3 Deranged, insane. *rare* (Shakes.). Only in E17.

infor'mality *n.* absence of formality; an instance of this, an informal act: L16. **informally** *adv.* E19.

informant /ɪn'fɔːm(ə)nt/ *n.* M17. [f. INFORM *v.* + -ANT¹.] †I 1 Something which inspires, animates, or actuates. Only in M17.

II 2 *gen.* A person who gives information. L17. 3 *Law.* A person who informs against another; an informer. L18. 4 A person from whom a linguist, anthropologist, etc., obtains information about language, dialect, or culture. L19.

2 E. F. BENSON I don't care whether your informants are correct or not in what they tell you. 4 *Language* The language must be learnt from the lips of a native informant.

informatics /ɪnfə'matɪks/ *n.* M20. [f. INFORMAT(ION + -ICS, tr. Russ. *informatika.*] Information science and technology.

information /ɪnfə'meɪʃ(ə)n/ *n.* LME. [(O)Fr. f. L *informatio(n-)*, f. *informat-* pa. ppl stem of *informare* INFORM *v.*: see -ATION.] I 1 Formation or moulding of the mind or character; training, instruction, teaching. Now *rare* or *obs.* LME. †b An instruction. LME–M18. †c Divine instruction; inspiration. LME–M16. 2 Communication of the knowledge of some fact or occurrence. LME. 3 Knowledge or facts communicated about a particular subject, event, etc.; intelligence, news. LME. †b An item of news; (in early use) an account (*of* something). E16–M19. c Without necessary relation to a recipient: that which inheres in or is represented by a particular arrangement, sequence, or set, that may be stored in, transferred by, and responded to by inanimate things; *Math.* a statistically defined quantity representing the probability of occurrence of a symbol, sequence, message, etc., as against a number of possible alternatives. E20. 4 *Law.* a A formal (written) statement or accusation presented to a court or magistrate in order to institute criminal proceedings. LME. b A statement of the facts of a civil claim presented by the Attorney-General or other officer on behalf of the Crown. E17. c *Sc. Law* (now *Hist.*). A written argument on a criminal case ordered by the High Court of Justiciary if the case raises difficult points of law or (formerly) by a Lord Ordinary in the Court of Session when reporting to the Inner House. Now *rare.* L17. 5 The action of informing against, charging, or accusing a person. *obs.* exc. as a transf. use of sense 4a. L15.

2 G. BORROW For your information, however, I will tell you that it is not. 3 C. G. WOLFF Edith Wharton began to collect background information for an historical novel. W. WHARTON Can you give me any information about the patient? You were close to him. B. EMECHETA Missy screamed in excitement at this piece of information. *inside information*: see INSIDE *a.* *white information*: see WHITE *a.* c *Nature* The precise sequence of the bases is the code which carries the genetical information.

†II 6 The giving of a form or essential character to something; inspiration (as of the body by the soul). M17–L19.

Comb.: **information booth, bureau, centre, desk**: where information is given and questions answered; **information officer** a person engaged in the provision of specialized information; **information processing** the processing of information so as to yield new or more useful information; **information retrieval** the tracing of information stored in books, computers, etc.; **information revolution** (the economic and industrial impact of) the increase in the availability of information and the changes in its storage and dissemination owing to the use of computers; **information room** a communications centre within a police station where information is collected and disseminated; **information science** (the branch of knowledge that deals with) the storage, retrieval, and dissemination of (esp. scientific or technical) information; **information scientist** a person employed to provide an information service; a person who studies the methods used to do so; an expert in or student of information science; **information technologist** an expert in or student of information technology; **information technology** technology that deals with the storage, processing, and dissemination of information esp. using computers; **information theory** the quantitative theory, based on a precise definition of information and the theory of probability, of the coding and transmission of signals and information.

informational *a.* of or pertaining to information; conveying information: E19. **informationally** *adv.* M20.

informative /ɪn'fɔːmətɪv/ *a.* LME. [med.L *informativus*, f. L *informat-*: see prec., -IVE.] 1 Formative; giving life, shape, or an essential quality. LME. 2 Of the nature of or pertaining to legal information. E17. 3 Giving information; instructive. M17.

3 T. FULLER The most informative Histories to Posterity . . are such as were written by the Eye-witnesses thereof. P. LIVELY One of those busy informative paintings full of detail. **informative double** = INFORMATORY *double.*

informatively *adv.* M16. **informativeness** *n.* E20.

informator /ɪn'fɔːmətə/ *n. obs.* exc. *Hist.* M16. [Late L, f. L *informat-*: see INFORMATION, -OR.] An instructor, a teacher.

informatory /ɪn'fɔːmət(ə)ri/ *a.* LME. [f. L *informat-* (see INFORMATION) + -ORY^{2}.] Instructive, informative.

informatory double *Bridge* a double intended to give information to one's partner rather than to score a penalty.

¶Rare bef. L19.

informatorily *adv.* (*Bridge*) informatively, in order to inform E20.

informed /ɪn'fɔːmd/ *a.* LME. [f. INFORM *v.* + -ED^{1}.] Knowing or acquainted with the facts; educated, knowledgeable. Now freq. in *well-* or *ill-informed*

Daily Express Lights . . to keep the driver informed when anything goes wrong with the lubrication. W. K. HANCOCK Informed opinion was ready to welcome the report. M. SEYMOUR-SMITH It is essential to view his beliefs from an anthropologically informed point of view. R. C. A. WHITE In such cases the consent is illusory because it is not informed.

informedly /-mɪdli/ *adv.* M17. **informedness** /-mɪdnɪs/ *n.* M20.

informer /ɪn'fɔːmə/ *n.* LME. [f. INFORM *v.* + -ER^{1}.] **I** †**1** An instructor, a teacher. LME–M17. **2** A person who gives information or intelligence, an informant. LME. **3** A person who informs against another, *spec.* for reward. E16.

1 R. MATHEWS Experience which is the truest informer, speaks aloud in this matter also. **2** SIR W. SCOTT He talks no Gaelic, nor had his informer much English. **3** R. MACAULAY She's an informer She set the police on us. C. HOPE Their campus spy, usually an overworked informer. *common informer*: see COMMON *a.*

II 4 A person who or thing which gives form, life, or inspiration. *poet.* LME.

4 POPE Nature! informer of the Poet's art, Whose force alone can raise or melt the heart.

informercial *n.* var. of INFOMERCIAL.

informidable /ɪn'fɔːmɪdəb(ə)l, ɪnfɔː'mɪd-/ *a. rare.* L17. [f. IN-^{3} + FORMIDABLE.] Not formidable, not to be feared.

informity /ɪn'fɔːmɪti/ *n.* Long *rare.* L16. [Late L *informitas*, f. L *informis*: see INFORM *a.*, -ITY.] The condition of being unformed, shapeless, or misshapen.

informosome /ɪn'fɔːməsəʊm/ *n.* M20. [f. INFORM(ATION + -O- + -SOME^{3}.] *Cytol.* A type of ribonucleoprotein in which the messenger RNA may be undetectable until later in development, found in the eggs of certain fishes and echinoderms.

†**infortunate** *v.t.* L16–L18. [med.L *infortunat-* pa. ppl stem of *infortunare*, f. as IN-^{3} + FORTUNATE *v.*] Subject to evil or unlucky influence; make unfortunate.

infortune /ɪn'fɔːtʃuːn, -tʃ(ə)n/ *n.* LME. [(O)Fr., f. as IN-^{3} + FORTUNE *n.*] †**1** Lack of good fortune, ill luck; a misfortune, a mishap. LME–M17. **2** *Astrol.* An inauspicious or malevolent planet or aspect, *esp.* Saturn or Mars. LME.

†**infortunity** *n.* LME–E18. [OFr. *infortunité*, f. as prec.: see -ITY.] Unfortunate condition, ill luck, adversity; an instance of this, a misfortune.

infotainment /ɪnfə'teɪnm(ə)nt/ *n.* L20. [f. INFO(RMATION + ENTER)TAINMENT.] Broadcast matter that seeks both to inform and to entertain.

infra /'ɪnfrə/ *adv.* L19. [L.] Later, further on (in a book or article); = BELOW *adv.* 1c.

infra- /'ɪnfrə/ *pref.* [L *infra* below, underneath, beneath, (in med.L also) within.] Forming mainly adjs. w. the senses 'below, beneath' (in situation or position), 'lower, inferior' (in status or quality).

¶Opp. SUPRA-. Freq. also treated as opp. SUPER- (cf. SUB-).

infraclass *n.* (*Taxon.*) a taxonomic grouping ranking next below a subclass M20. **infra'costal** *a.* (*Anat.*) situated beneath the ribs L19. **infra'human** *a.* that is below the human level L19. **infra'littoral** *a.* (*Ecol.*) (*a*) = SUBLITTORAL *a.*; (*b*) designating or pertaining to the region of a lake containing rooted vegetation: M19. **infra'marginal** *a.* & *n.* (a structure, organ, etc.) situated below the margin or border M19. **inframa'xillary** *a.* (*a*) = SUBMANDIBULAR; (*b*) of or pertaining to the lower jawbone: M19. **infra-'orbital** *a.* (*Anat.*) situated below the orbit of the eye E19. **infraorder** *n.* (*Taxon.*) a taxonomic grouping ranking next below a suborder M20. **infra'renal** *a.* (*Anat.*) situated below the kidneys L19. **infraspe'cific** *a.* (*Taxon.*) at a level lower than that of the species M20.

infract /ɪn'frakt/ *a.* Long *rare.* M16. [L *infractus*, f. as IN-^{3} + *fractus* broken.] Unbroken, unimpaired; sound, whole.

infract /ɪn'frakt/ *v.t.* Chiefly *US.* L18. [L *infract-* pa. ppl stem of *infringere* INFRINGE.] Break (a rule, an agreement, etc.); violate, infringe.

infractor *n.* E16.

infraction /ɪn'frakʃ(ə)n/ *n.* LME. [L *infractio(n-)*, f. as prec: see -ION.] **1** The action or an act of breaking an agreement; (a) violation, (an) infringement. LME. **2** The action of breaking or fracturing; a fracture. E17.

1 A. S. NEILL These and other infractions of rules carry automatic fines. A. BROOKNER Any infraction of the liberty of such simple people would be a form of assault.

infradian /ɪn'freɪdɪən/ *a.* M20. [f. INFRA- + *-dian*, after CIRCADIAN.] *Physiol.* Of a rhythm or cycle: having a frequency lower than circadian, i.e. a period longer than a day. Cf. ULTRADIAN.

infra dig /ɪnfrə 'dɪg/ *a. phr. colloq.* E19. [Abbrev. of L *infra dignitatem* beneath (one's) dignity.] Beneath the dignity of one's position; undignified.

Scouting A bit infra dig, . . touting for reader-support like this? S. BELLOW Doing the floors on his knees, didn't bother him. . . It never occurred to him that it was infra dig.

infragrant /ɪn'freɪgr(ə)nt/ *a.* E19. [f. IN-^{3} + FRAGRANT.] Lacking fragrance; malodorous.

SYD. SMITH We shall both be a brown infragrant powder in thirty or forty years. M. WEBB Sparsely in the hedges grew the pale, infragrant flowers of early autumn.

infralapsarian /ɪnfrəlap'sɛːrɪən/ *n.* & *a.* Also **I-**. M18. [f. as INFRA- + L *lapsus* fall, LAPSE *n.* + -ARIAN. Cf. SUPRALAPSARIAN.] *Theol.* **A** *n.* A Calvinist holding the view that God's election of only some to everlasting life was not originally part of the divine plan, but a consequence of the Fall of Man. M18. **B** *adj.* Of or pertaining to the infralapsarians or their doctrine. L18.

infralapsarianism *n.* the doctrine of the infralapsarians M19.

inframe *v.* var. of ENFRAME.

†**infranchise** *v.* var. of ENFRANCHISE.

infrangible /ɪn'frandʒɪb(ə)l/ *a.* L16. [Fr., or med.L *infrangibilis*, f. as IN-^{3} + *frangibilis* FRANGIBLE.] **1** Unbreakable. L16. **2** Unable to be infringed; inviolable. M19.

1 F. W. ROBERTSON No iron bar is absolutely infrangible. *fig.*: J. UPDIKE That heaping measure of maternal love which makes for an infrangible soundness of spirit.

infrangi'bility *n.* E19. **infrangibly** *adv.* E19.

infrared /ɪnfrə'rɛd/ *a.* & *n.* L19. [f. INFRA- + RED *a.*, *n.*] **A** *adj.* **1** Of electromagnetic radiation: lying beyond the red end of the visible spectrum, having a wavelength between that of red light and that of microwaves (about 800 nm to 1 mm). L19. **2** Involving, producing, or pertaining to (the use of) infrared radiation, esp. as emitted by heated bodies; sensitive to infrared radiation. E20.

B *n.* (Usu. w. *the.*) The infrared part of the spectrum. L19.

the far, near infrared the part of the infrared far from, close to, the visible spectrum.

infrasonic /ɪnfrə'sɒnɪk/ *a.* E20. [f. INFRA- + SONIC.] Of, pertaining to, or designating sound waves or vibrations having a frequency below the audible range (i.e. less than 15–30 Hz).

infrasound /'ɪnfrəsaʊnd/ *n.* M20. [f. INFRA- + SOUND *n.*^{2}] (A) sound of infrasonic frequency.

infrastructure /'ɪnfrəstrʌktʃə/ *n.* E20. [Fr., f. as INFRA- + STRUCTURE *n.*] The foundation or basic structure of an undertaking; *spec.* (*a*) the collective permanent installations (airfields, naval bases, etc.) forming a basis for military activity; (*b*) the installations and services (power stations, sewers, roads, housing, etc.) regarded as the economic foundation of a country.

Broadcast The best laid plans . . come to nothing unless there is a sound and properly considered infrastructure. *Guardian* Britain needs to invest an extra £3.5 billion . . in its basic infrastructure of housing, roads, and sewers.

infrastructural *a.* M20.

infrequency /ɪn'friːkw(ə)nsi/ *n.* E17. [L *infrequentia*, f. as next: see -ENCY.] †**1** The fact or condition of being deserted or seldom visited. Also, fewness. Only in 17. **2** The fact or condition of being infrequent or occasional; rarity. L17.

1 P. HOLLAND It was the solitude and infrequency of the place that brought the dragon thither. **2** C. LAMB The relish of such exhibitions must be in proportion to the infrequency of going. A. FLINT The infrequency of gangrene is shown by its having occurred in but one of 133 cases.

Also **infrequence** *n.* (*rare*) M17.

infrequent /ɪn'friːkwənt/ *a.* M16. [L *infrequent-*, f. as IN-^{3} + *frequent-* FREQUENT *a.*] †**1** Little used or practised; unaccustomed, uncommon. Only in M16. **2** Not occurring often; happening rarely; (qualifying an agent-n.) seldom doing the action indicated. E17. **3** Seldom met with, not plentiful, uncommon. L17.

2 W. WOLLASTON A sparing and infrequent worshiper of the Deity. H. JACOBSON Our meetings became more and more infrequent and then stopped altogether.

infrequently *adv.* L17.

infrigidate /ɪn'frɪdʒɪdeɪt/ *v.t.* Long *rare.* M16. [Late L *infrigidat-* pa. ppl stem of *infrigidare*, f. as IN-^{2} + *frigidus* cold, FRIGID: see -ATE^{3}.] Make cold; chill, cool.

infrigidation /ˌɪnfrɪdʒɪ'deɪʃ(ə)n/ *n.* Now *rare.* LME. [Late L *infrigidatio(n-)*, f. as prec.: see -ATION.] The action of cooling; the condition of being cooled.

infringe /ɪn'frɪn(d)ʒ/ *v.* M16. [L *infringere*, f. as IN-^{2} + *frangere* to break.] †**1** *v.t.* Break (down), destroy; foil, defeat, frustrate. M16–E18. **2** *v.t.* Break (a law), violate (an oath, treaty, etc.); contravene. M16. †**3** *v.t.* Refute, contradict, deny. L16–M17. †**4** *v.t.* Break the force of, diminish the strength of; enfeeble, impair. Only in 17. **5** *v.i.* Break in or encroach *on* or *upon.* M18.

2 CLARENDON The undoubted Fundamental priviledge of the Commons in Parliament, . . had never been infringed, or violated. A. TREW By taking his submarine within 15 kilometres of Krakoy, Yenev would be infringing Norwegian territorial rights. **5** B. GUEST Jealousy toward a rival who had infringed upon his former domain.

infringer *n.* M16.

infringement /ɪn'frɪn(d)ʒm(ə)nt/ *n.* L16. [f. prec. + -MENT.] †**1** Refutation, contradiction. L16–M17. **2** (A) breaking or breach of a law, obligation, right, etc. E17. **3** A breaking in, an encroachment, an intrusion. L17.

2 E. CRANKSHAW The least infringement of the rules was savagely punished. A. BRINK Minor infringements like staying out after ten at night. **3** N. SHUTE Designers . . , energetic in fighting the least infringement upon . . their own sphere of action.

infructescence /ɪnfrʌk'tɛs(ə)ns/ *n.* L19. [f. IN-^{2} + L *fructus* fruit, after INFLORESCENCE.] *Bot.* An aggregate fruit.

infructuous /ɪn'frʌktjʊəs/ *a.* E17. [f. L *infructuosus*, f. as IN-^{3} + *fructuosus* FRUCTUOUS: see -OUS.] Not bearing fruit; unfruitful, barren; *fig.* unprofitable, ineffective.

infructuose *a.* = INFRUCTUOUS E18. **infructuously** *adv.* E19.

infrustrable /ɪn'frʌstrəb(ə)l/ *a. rare.* L17. [f. IN-^{3} + FRUSTRABLE.] Unable to be frustrated or foiled.

infrustrably *adv.* M18.

infula /'ɪnfjʊlə/ *n.* Pl. **-lae** /-liː/. E17. [L.] **1** *Eccl.* Either of the two ribbons of a bishop's mitre. E17. **2** *Rom. Antiq.* A woollen headband worn by a priest etc. or placed on a sacrificial victim. E18.

infundibulum /ɪnfʌn'dɪbjʊləm/ *n.* Pl. **-la** /-lə/. M16. [L = funnel, f. *infundere* pour in: see INFUSE.] *Anat.* & *Zool.* Any of various funnel-shaped cavities and structures of the body; *esp.*

the hollow stalk which connects the hypothalamus and the posterior pituitary gland.

infundibular *a.* (*Anat.*) funnel-shaped; of or pertaining to an infundibulum: E18. **infundibuliform** *a.* (*Bot.* & *Zool.*) funnel-shaped M18.

infuriant /ɪnˈfjʊərɪənt/ *n.* M20. [med.L *infuriant-* pres. ppl stem of *infuriare*: see INFURIATE *v.*, -ANT[1].] A fact, condition, etc., which provokes a person to anger.

infuriate /ɪnˈfjʊərɪət/ *a.* Now *literary.* M17. [med.L *infuriatus* pa. pple, f. as next: see -ATE[2].] Provoked to fury; mad with rage, frantic.

infuriately *adv.* L19.

infuriate /ɪnˈfjʊərɪeɪt/ *v.t.* M17. [med.L *infuriat-* pa. ppl stem of *infuriare*, f. as IN-[2] + *furiare* madden, f. *furia* FURY: see -ATE[3].] Provoke to fury; make extremely angry.

B. T. BRADFORD Audra was so infuriated by his attitude . . she could barely contain herself.

infuriating *a.* provoking, maddeningly vexatious L19. **infuriatingly** *adv.* L19. **infuriˈation** *n.* M19.

infuse /ɪnˈfjuːz/ *v.* LME. [L *infus-* pa. ppl stem of *infundere*, f. as IN-[2] + *fundere* pour.] **1** *v.t.* Introduce (a liquid ingredient) by pouring; pour in; *Med.* perform infusion of. (Foll. by *into.*) LME. **b** *transf.* & *fig.* Instil (grace, life, spirit, etc.) into the mind, heart, etc. Formerly also, insinuate. E16. †**2** *v.t.* Pour, shed, *on*, *upon.* LME–L17. **3** *v.t.* Steep (a herb, tea, etc.) in a liquid so as to extract the soluble constituents; macerate. LME. **b** *v.i.* Undergo the process of infusion. E17. **4** *v.t.* Affect, esp. flavour, (a liquid) *with* some substance, as a herb steeped in it; *fig.* imbue or pervade with or *with* a quality etc. Usu. in *pass.* M16.

1 SWIFT By the force of that soporiferous medicine infused into my liquor. *American Journal of Physiology* Saline was infused into a vein. b W. S. CHURCHILL Lanfranc . . rapidly infused new life into the English Church. M. COX An educational institution can infuse ideals and mould . . a personality. 3 C. LUCAS They infuse the ashes of burned vegetables in their water. 4 R. HOGGART Very banal verses [may be] infused with decent emotion. P. V. PRICE Hippocrates . . used wine infused with cinammon. C. THUBRON The intemperance of a Vesuvius infuses his whole frame.

infuser *n.* (*a*) a person who infuses or instils some quality; (*b*) a device for infusing tea leaves in a cup of water: L16. **infusive** *a.* †(*a*) divinely infused, innate; (*b*) having the quality of infusing or instilling something; M17.

infusible /ɪnˈfjuːzɪb(ə)l/ *a.* M16. [f. IN-[3] + FUSIBLE.] Unable to be fused or melted.

infusiˈbility *n.* L18.

infusion /ɪnˈfjuːʒ(ə)n/ *n.* LME. [(O)Fr., or L *infusio(n-)*, f. as INFUSE: see -ION.] **1** The pouring in of a liquid, the fact of being poured in; a liquid that is poured in. LME. **b** *Med.* Continuous injection into a vein or tissue, esp. of large volumes of fluid over a long period. E17. **2a** An extract obtained by steeping a substance in water. Formerly also, (a small body of) water containing dissolved organic matter. LME. **b** The steeping of a substance in a liquid in order to impregnate it with the soluble constituents. L16. **3** The infusing or instilling into the mind, heart, etc., of a principle, quality, etc. LME. †**b** Character infused into a person at birth; innate quality. *rare* (Shakes.). Only in E17. †**c** (An) insidious suggestion. M17–M18. **4** The introduction of a modifying element; an infused element, an admixture. E17. **5** The pouring of water over a person in baptism (opp. *immersion*); = AFFUSION. M18.

2a S. RUSHDIE Infusions of herbs in well-boiled water were constantly administered. 3 P. ROTH Carried along by an exciting infusion of Wild West bravado. 4 A. J. TOYNBEE The present population is mainly native American in race, with a . . small infusion of European . . blood.

infusoriform /ɪnfjʊˈsɔːrɪfɔːm/ *a.* L19. [f. next + -FORM.] *Zool.* Having the form of an infusorium; *spec.* designating a dispersive larva or larval stage in some mesozoan cephalopod parasites.

infusorium /ɪnfjʊˈsɔːrɪəm/ *n.* Also I-. Pl. **-ia** /-ɪə/. L18. [Use as n. of neut. of mod.L *infusorius*, f. as INFUSE.] *Zool.* (now *Hist.*). A member of the former class Infusoria of sessile and free-swimming protozoans first found in infusions of decaying organic matter. Usu. in *pl.*

infusorial *a.* of or pertaining to (a member of) the Infusoria M19. **infusorian** *a.* & *n.* (*a*) *adj.* infusorial; (*b*) *n.* = INFUSORIUM: M19.

infusory /ɪnˈfjuːs(ə)ri, -z-/ *a.* & *n. arch.* E19. [f. INFUSORIUM + -ORY[2].] *Zool.* **A** *adj.* = INFUSORIAL. E19. **B** *n.* = INFUSORIUM. M19.

†**Ing** *n.* & *a.* see YIN *n.*[2] & *a.*[2]

-ing /ɪŋ/ *suff.*[1] [OE *-ung*, *-ing* = OS *-unga* (MLG, MDu. *-inge*, Du. *-ing*), OHG *-unga*, *-ung* (MHG *-unge*, G *-ung*), ON *-ung*, *-ing*.] **1** Forming ns. usu. from vbs, occas. by analogy from ns. or advs., denoting (*a*) vbl action, as *fighting*, *swearing*, *blackberrying*, or an instance of it, an act (w. pl. *-ings*), as *wedding*, *outing*; also, an occupation or skill, as *banking*, *fencing*, *glassblowing*; (*b*) (sometimes usu. in *pl.*) a thing resulting from or produced by an action or process, as *building*, *carving*, *earnings*; also, a thing involved in an action or process, as *covering*; (*c*) the material, substance, or things involved in an action or process, as *bedding*, *clothing*, *flooring*, *washing*; freq. from ns. without any corresp. vb, as *sacking*, *scaffolding*. **2** Forming the gerund of vbs, i.e. a n. which is a distinct part of the vb and retains certain of its functions, esp. those of governing an obj. and being qualified by an adv. instead of by an adj., as *I love reading* (= the reading of) *poetry*; *after having written* (= after the completion of writing) *a letter*; *the habit of speaking loosely* (= loose speaking). Developed from 1, initially perh. partly in imit. of the L gerund, in the late 14th cent.; not found in other Gmc langs.

-ing /ɪŋ/ *suff.*[2] [Alt. of OE *-ende* = L *-ent-*, Gk *-ont-*, Skt *-ant-*.] Forming the pres. pple of vbs; freq. in adjs. of ppl origin or force, as *charming*, *cunning*, *willing* (and occas. in adjs. formed from ns. in imitation of these, as *hulking*); also in preps. and advs. of ppl origin, as *during*, *notwithstanding*.

-ing /ɪŋ/ *suff.*[3] [OE f. Gmc: cf. -LING[1].] Forming derivative masc. ns. w. the sense 'one belonging to or of the kind of', hence as patronymics or diminutives, as *atheling*, *farthing*, *gelding*, *sweeting*.

†**Inga** *n.* & *a.* see INCA.

†**ingage** *n.*, *v.*, †**ingagement** *n.* see ENGAGE *n.*, *v.*, ENGAGEMENT.

ingan /ˈɪŋən/ *n. dial.* (chiefly *Sc.*). E18. [Repr. a pronunc.] = ONION *n.*

ingaol *v.* var. of ENJAIL.

†**ingarrison** *v.* var. of ENGARRISON.

ingate /ˈɪngeɪt/ *n. north.* LME. [f. IN-[1] + GATE *n.*[2]] **1** The action or faculty of entering. Also, entry upon a period of life. LME. **2** A way in, an entrance. L16. **3** *sing.* & (usu.) in *pl.* Goods coming into a town or port; duty on these. Cf. OUTGATE 3. Now only *Hist.* E17.

ingather /ɪnˈgaðə/ *v.t.* M16. [f. IN-[1] + GATHER *v.*] Gather in (esp. a harvest).

ingatherer *n.* L15. **ingathering** *n.* (*a*) the gathering in of crops etc.; *Sc.* the collecting of money due; (*b*) the congregating of Jews in (modern) Israel: E16.

ingem *v.* var. of ENGEM.

ingeminate /ɪnˈdʒɛmɪneɪt/ *v.t.* Also (earlier) †**en-**. L16. [L *ingeminat-* pa. ppl stem of *ingeminare*, f. as IN-[2] + GEMINATE *v.*] **1** Utter two or more times; reiterate. Now chiefly in *ingeminate peace*, call repeatedly for peace. L16. †**2** Double (a thing); repeat (an action). *rare.* Only in 17.

ingemination /ɪnˌdʒɛmɪˈneɪʃ(ə)n/ *n.* Now *rare.* L16. [f. as prec.: see -ATION.] **1** Repeated utterance, reiteration. L16. **2** The action or process of doubling, duplication. M17.

†**ingender** *v.* var. of ENGENDER.

†**ingendrure** *n.* var. of ENGENDRURE.

ingenerable /ɪnˈdʒɛn(ə)rəb(ə)l/ *a.* Now *rare.* LME. [Late L *ingenerabilis*, f. as IN-[3] + GENERABLE.] Unable to be generated. Chiefly in *ingenerable and incorruptible.*

ingeneraˈbility *n.* L16.

ingenerate /ɪnˈdʒɛn(ə)rət/ *a.*[1] Now *rare.* L16. [L *ingeneratus* pa. pple of *ingenerare*: see INGENERATE *v.*] Inborn, innate. Formerly also, congenital.

ingenerate /ɪnˈdʒɛn(ə)rət/ *a.*[2] M17. [eccl.L *ingeneratus*, f. as IN-[3] + GENERATE *ppl a.*] Not generated; self-existent.

ingenerateness *n.* L17.

ingenerate /ɪnˈdʒɛnəreɪt/ *v.t.* Now *rare.* Pa. pple **-ated**, †**-ate**. E16. [L *ingenerat-* pa. ppl stem of *ingenerare*, f. as IN-[2] + GENERATE *v.*] Generate within; engender, produce.

ingeneˈration *n.* M17.

†**ingenia** *n.* pl. of INGENIUM.

ingenio /ɪnˈdʒiːnɪəʊ/ *n. obs.* exc. *Hist.* Pl. **-os.** E17. [Sp. = engine, mill.] In the W. Indies: a sugar-mill, a sugar-works.

ingeniosity /ɪnˌdʒiːnɪˈɒsɪti/ *n.* Now *rare.* LME. [(Fr. *ingéniosité* f.) med.L *ingeniositas*, f. L *ingeniosus*: see next, -ITY.] The quality of being ingenious; ingenuity.

ingenious /ɪnˈdʒiːnɪəs/ *a.* LME. [(Fr. *ingénieux* f.) L *ingeniosus*, f. INGENIUM: see -OUS.] **I 1** Orig., possessing high mental ability, talented, intelligent, discerning. Now *spec.* clever at making, inventing, or contriving things, esp. of a curious or unexpected nature. LME. **2** Exemplifying high mental ability, showing intelligence. Now *spec.* cleverly contrived or made. L15.

1 T. BROWN Wine . . makes the dull ingenious. T. GENT Travels of Cyrus . . worthy the Perusal of every ingenious Person. J. BARZUN To be ingenious about devising activities is the mark of the 'imaginative' teacher. 2 T. HEARNE 'Twas a good ingenious Sermon, about Praise. H. JACOBSON He was a great advocate for electricity and ingenious electrical gadgets.

†**II** Used by confusion for INGENUOUS or L *ingenuus*. **3** Having a noble disposition; *spec.* honourably candid or straightforward. L16–L18. **4** Well-born. Of education etc.: befitting a well-born person. L16–L18.

ingeniously *adv.* LME. **ingeniousness** *n.* M16.

†**ingenit** *a.* Also **-ite**. E17–E18. [L *ingenitus* pa. pple of *ingignere* engender, f. as IN-[2] + *gignere* beget.] Inborn, innate. Also, native.

ingenium /ɪnˈdʒiːnɪəm/ *n.* Pl. **-ia** /-ɪə/. L19. [L = mind, intellect.] Mental ability, talent; a person possessing this. Also, mental inclination, disposition.

†**ingenteel** *a.* M17–L18. [f. IN-[3] + GENTEEL *a.*] Ungenteel.

ingénue /anʒeɪˈnjuː; *foreign* ɛ̃ʒeny (*pl. same*)/ *n.* Also **-gen-**. M19. [Fr., fem. of *ingénu* INGENUOUS.] An artless innocent young woman, esp. as a stage role; an actress playing such a role.

ingenuity /ɪndʒɪˈnjuːɪti/ *n.* L16. [L *ingenuitas*, f. as next: see -ITY.] **I** Senses conn. w. INGENUOUS. †**1** Freeborn status. L16–M17. †**2** Nobility of character; high-mindedness. L16–E18. **3** Candour, ingenuousness. Now *rare.* L16.

3 W. GODWIN An expression of frankness, ingenuity, and unreserve.

II Senses conn. w. INGENIOUS. **4** Orig., high mental ability, talent, intelligence, discernment. Now *spec.* cleverness at making, inventing, or contriving things, esp. of a curious or unexpected nature; skilfulness of contrivance or design. L16. **5** An ingenious device, an artifice. M17.

4 A. S. BYATT She had supposed human ingenuity would find ways round food shortages and overpopulation.

ingenuous /ɪnˈdʒɛnjʊəs/ *a.* L16. [f. L *ingenuus* lit. 'native, inborn', f. as IN-[2] + base of *gignere* beget: see -OUS, -UOUS.] **I 1** Noble in character; generous, high-minded. Now *rare* or *obs.* L16. †**b** Of an animal or thing: of high quality or character. E–M17. †**2** Of education, studies: liberal, befitting a free-born person. E17–M18. **3** Honourably straightforward; frank, candid. E17. **b** Innocently frank or open; artless. L17. **4** Chiefly *Rom. Hist.* Free-born. M17.

3 W. HOGARTH I will be ingenuous enough to confess something of this may be true. b J. CONRAD A young civilian . . with an ingenuous young countenance.

†**II 5** = INGENIOUS I. L16–L18.

ingenuously *adv.* L16. **ingenuousness** *n.* the quality of being ingenuous; *esp.* (innocent) frankness, openness: E17.

ingest /ɪnˈdʒɛst/ *v.t.* E17. [L *ingest-* pa. ppl stem of *ingerere* carry in, bring in, thrust in, f. as IN-[2] + *gerere* bear, carry.] Take (food or drink) into the body by swallowing or absorbing.

P. ROTH The child refuses to ingest any food—takes it and holds it in his mouth for hours, but refuses to swallow. R. F. CHAPMAN In some insects . . digestion may begin before the food is ingested. *fig.*: C. THUBRON The machine ingested our money but gave back no apple juice.

ingesta /ɪnˈdʒɛstə/ *n.pl.* E18. [L, neut. pl. of *ingestus* pa. pple of *ingerere*: see prec.] Substances introduced into the body as nourishment; food and drink.

ingestion /ɪnˈdʒɛstʃ(ə)n/ *n.* E17. [Late L *ingestio(n-)*, f. as INGEST: see -ION.] The taking of food or drink into the body by swallowing or absorption.

ingestive /ɪnˈdʒɛstɪv/ *a.* M19. [f. INGEST + -IVE.] Having the function of taking in nourishment.

Ingin *n.* & *a.* see INJUN.

ingine *n.*, †**ingined** *a.* see ENGINE *n.*, ENGINED.

†**ingineer** *n.* var. of ENGINEER *n.*

ingle /ˈɪŋg(ə)l/ *n.*[1] Orig. *Sc.* E16. [Perh. f. Gael. *aingeal* fire, light, Ir. *aingeal* live ember.] **1** A domestic fire; a fire burning on a hearth. E16. **2** An open fireplace, an inglenook. M19.

Comb.: **ingle-bench** a bench beside a fire; **ingle-cheek** *Sc.* the jamb of a fireplace; **inglenook** a chimney corner; **ingleside** a fireside.

ingle /ˈɪŋg(ə)l/ *n.*[2] & *v.* L16. [Origin unkn.] **A** *n.* **1** A catamite. L16. **2** An intimate friend. *rare.* M17. †**B** *v.t.* Fondle, caress; coax. L16–L19.

ingliding /ˈɪnglaɪdɪŋ/ *ppl a.* M20. [f. IN *adv.* + GLIDE *v.* + -ING[2].] *Phonet.* Having a glide towards a central vowel sound (as /ə/).

American Speech The low-country ingliding diphthongs in *date, boat*.

inglorious /ɪnˈglɔːrɪəs/ *a.* M16. [f. L *inglorius* (f. *gloria* GLORY *n.*) + -OUS, or f. IN-[3] + GLORIOUS.] **1** Bringing no glory or honour (to a person); shameful, ignominious. M16. **2** Not glorious or famous. Now *rare.* L16.

1 LD MACAULAY It involved the country in an inglorious, unprofitable, and interminable war. **2** T. GRAY Some mute inglorious Milton here may rest.

ingloriously *adv.* L16. **ingloriousness** *n.* M17.

†**inglut** *v.* var. of ENGLUT.

ingluvies /ɪnˈgluːviːz/ *n.* Pl. same. E18. [L = crop, maw.] *Zool.* The crop of a bird, insect, etc.

ingluvial *a.* M19.

in-goal /ˈɪngəʊl/ *n.* & *a.* L19. [f. IN-[1] + GOAL *n.*] *Rugby Football.* (Designating) the part of a rugby ground at either end of the field of play, between the goal-line and the dead ball line.

ingoing /ɪnˈgəʊɪŋ/ *n.* Now *rare.* ME. [f. IN-[1] + GOING *n.*] **1** The action or an act of going in or entering. ME. **2** A sum paid by a tenant or purchaser for fixtures etc. on taking over premises. E20.

ingoing /ˈɪngəʊɪŋ/ *a.* E19. [f. IN-[1] + GOING *a.*] **1** That goes in or inwards; that enters. E19. **2** Penetrating, thorough. E20.

ingorge *v.* see ENGORGE.

ingot /ˈɪŋgət/ *n.* LME. [Perh. f. IN-[1] + OE *goten* pa. pple of *ġeotan* pour, cast in metal.] †**1** A mould in which metal is cast. LME–L18. **2** A block (usu. oblong) of cast metal, esp. of gold, silver, or (now) steel. L16.

Comb.: **ingot iron**: containing too little carbon to temper, and nearly pure by industrial standards.

ingoted *a.* wealthy, rich M19.

Ingoush *n.* & *a.* var. of INGUSH.

†**ingrace** *v.* var. of ENGRACE.

†**ingraff** *v.* var. of ENGRAFF.

†**ingraft** *v.* var. of ENGRAFT.

ingrain /ˈɪngreɪn, ɪnˈgreɪn/ *a.* & *n.* M16. [f. *in grain* s.v. GRAIN *n.*[1]] **A** *adj.* **1** Dyed in grain; dyed with fast colours before manufacture; thoroughly dyed. M16. **b** Of a carpet: reversible, with different colours interwoven. M19. **2** Of a quality, disposition, habit, etc.: inborn, inherent, firmly fixed. M19. **B** *n.* **1** (A) material dyed in grain. *rare.* M19. **2** A thing which is ingrained or inherent. L19.

ingrain /ɪnˈgreɪn/ *v.t.* Also (earlier) **en-** /ɛn-, ɪn-/. LME. [f. IN-[1], EN-[1] + GRAIN *v.*[1]] †**1** Dye with cochineal; dye in fast colours, dye in grain. LME–M19. **2** Cause (a dye) to sink deeply into the texture of a fabric; work into a substance's fibre or *fig.* into a person's character etc. M17.

ingrained /ɪnˈgreɪnd/ *a.* E16. [Orig. f. INGRAIN *v.* + -ED[1]; later f. IN *adv.* + GRAINED *a.*[2]] **1** In the inmost texture; deeply rooted, inveterate. E16. **2** Of a person: thorough. M17.

1 G. K. CHESTERTON It was an ingrained simplicity and arrogance. P. ROTH Out of the oldest and most ingrained of habits, I wanted to please them.

ingrainedly /-nɪdli/ *adv.* M19.

ingram /ˈɪŋgrəm/ *a.* & *n.* Long *obs.* exc. *dial.* M16. [Alt. of IGNORANT.] **A** *adj.* Ignorant; stupid. M16. **B** *n.* An ignorant person. M17.

†**ingrandize** *v.* var. of ENGRANDIZE.

ingrate /ˈɪngreɪt, ɪnˈgreɪt/ *a.* & *n.* LME. [L *ingratus* unpleasant, ungrateful, f. as IN-[3] + *gratus* pleasing, grateful.] **A** *adj.* †**1** Not of a pleasant or friendly disposition; unfriendly. LME–M16. **2** Not feeling or showing gratitude; ungrateful. LME. †**3** Not pleasing or acceptable to the mind or senses; disagreeable, unwelcome. E16–E18. **B** *n.* An ungrateful person. E17.

ingrateful /ɪnˈgreɪtfʊl, -f(ə)l/ *a.* Now *rare.* M16. [f. IN-[3] + GRATEFUL.] †**1** = INGRATE *a.* 1. M16–M18. **2** = INGRATE *a.* 2. M16.

†**ingratefully** *adv.* M16–E18. †**ingratefulness** *n.* L16–M17.

ingratiate /ɪnˈgreɪʃɪeɪt/ *v.* E17. [f. L *in gratiam* into favour + -ATE[3], after It. †*ingratiare*, *ingraziare*.] **1** *v.refl.* Get oneself into favour; gain grace or favour (*with*); make oneself agreeable (*to*). E17. †**2** *v.t.* Bring (a person or thing) into favour (*with* someone); make (a person or thing) agreeable (*to*). M17–M18. **3** *v.i.* Gain grace or favour (†*with*). M17.

1 D. H. LAWRENCE He never ingratiated himself anywhere, . . but kept to himself. M. M. KAYE Courtiers who had once flattered and fawned on him hastened to ingratiate themselves with the new power behind the throne. **3** A. STORR 'Good' behaviour designed to placate and to ingratiate.

ingratiating *a.* that ingratiates, intended to gain grace or favour M17. **ingratiatingly** *adv.* L19. **ingratiˈation** *n.* E19. **ingratiatory** *a.* tending to ingratiate, ingratiating M19.

ingratitude /ɪnˈgratɪtjuːd/ *n.* ME. [(O)Fr., or late L *ingratitudo*, f. as INGRATE: see -TUDE.] **1** Lack or absence of gratitude, ungratefulness. ME. †**2** Unpleasant feeling, unfriendliness. L15–M16.

†**ingrave** *v.*[1], *v.*[2] vars. of ENGRAVE *v.*[1], *v.*[2]

†**ingraven** *v.* var. of ENGRAVEN.

†**ingraver** *n.* var. of ENGRAVER.

ingravescent /ɪngrəˈvɛs(ə)nt/ *a.* E19. [f. L *ingravescent-* pres. ppl stem of *ingravescere* grow heavy or worse, f. as IN-[2] + *gravescere*, f. *gravis* heavy, severe: see -ESCENT.] *Med.* (Gradually) increasing in severity.

ingravescence *n.* E19.

ingravidate /ɪnˈgravɪdeɪt/ *v.t.* Now *rare.* M17. [Late L *ingravidat-* pa. ppl stem of *ingravidare* make heavy or pregnant, f. as IN-[2] + *gravidus*: see GRAVID, -ATE[3].] Load, weigh; make heavy; impregnate.

ingraviˈdation *n.* the action of ingravidating; the state of being ingravidated; pregnancy: E17.

ingredience /ɪnˈgriːdɪəns/ *n.* & *v.* Now *rare.* E16. [Orig. a respelling of *ingredients*; sense 2 f. as INGREDIENT (see -ENCE).] **A** *n.* †**1** *pl.* & *sing.* The ingredients in or content of a medicine, potion, etc.; a mixture containing various ingredients. E16–M17. **b** A single ingredient or element. L16–M17. **2** The fact or process of entering in as an ingredient or by physical movement. M16. †**B** *v.t.* Introduce as an ingredient; provide with ingredients. M17–E19.

†**ingrediency** *n.* M17–M19.

ingredient /ɪnˈgriːdɪənt/ *a.* & *n.* LME. [L *ingredient-* pres. ppl stem of *ingredi* enter, f. as IN-[2] + *gradi* proceed, walk: see -ENT.] **A** *adj.* **1** Entering into a thing as a constituent element. *arch.* LME. †**2** Entering into a thing by moving or running in. E–M17.

B *n.* **1** A component part or constituent element in a mixture or combination. LME. †**2** The chief or main constituent. E–M17.

1 J. T. STORY I began to appreciate that Felix was the homicidal ingredient in all this madness. R. INGALLS She had all the salad ingredients out.

Ingres paper /ˈaŋgrə ˌpeɪpə/ *n. phr.* E20. [J. A. D. *Ingres* (1780–1867), Fr. painter.] A French mould-made paper for drawing; thick and mottled paper.

ingress /ˈɪngrɛs/ *n.* LME. [L *ingressus*, f. *ingress-* pa. ppl stem of *ingredi*: see INGREDIENT.] **1 a** A place or means of entrance; an entrance. LME. **b** The action or fact of going in or entering; capacity or right of entrance. L15. **2** The action of beginning a thing; a beginning, an attempt; the commencement of something. *arch.* LME. **3** *Astrol.* & *Astron.* The arrival of the sun or a planet in a certain part of the sky; the beginning of a transit. M17.

1b T. S. ELIOT We have been forced to allow ingress to innumerable dull and tedious books.

ingress /ɪnˈgrɛs/ *v.t.* & *i. rare.* ME. [L *ingress-*: see prec.] Enter, go in(to), invade.

ingression /ɪnˈgrɛʃ(ə)n/ *n.* L15. [Fr. †*ingression* or L *ingressio(n-)*, f. as prec.: see -ION.] The action of going in or entering; entrance; invasion.

ingressive /ɪnˈgrɛsɪv/ *a.* & *n.* M17. [f. L *ingress-* (see INGRESS *n.*) + -IVE.] **A** *adj.* **1** Having the quality or character of entering; *spec.* (*Gram.*) denoting entering upon action, inceptive. M17. **2** *Phonet.* Of a speech sound: made with intake of air. Of an airflow: inward. M20. **B** *n.* An ingressive verb; an ingressive sound. M20.

ingressively *adv.* E20.

Ingrian /ˈɪngrɪən/ *n.* & *a.* E18. [f. *Ingria* (see below) + -AN.] **A** *n.* **1** A native or inhabitant of Ingria, a region at the eastern end of the Gulf of Finland. E18. **2** An almost extinct Finno-Ugric language of Ingria. M20. **B** *adj.* Of or pertaining to Ingria or the Ingrians. L18.

ingroove *v.* var. of ENGROOVE.

†**ingross** *v.* var. of ENGROSS.

in-group /ˈɪngruːp/ *n.* E20. [f. IN-[1] + GROUP *n.*] A small group of people whose common interest tends to exclude others.

ingrowing /ˈɪngrəʊɪŋ/ *a.* M19. [f. IN *adv.* + GROW *v.* + -ING[2].] Growing inwards or within something; *spec.* (of a toenail) growing so as to press into the flesh.

ingrown /ˈɪngrəʊn/ *a.* L17. [f. IN-[1] + GROWN.] **1** That has or is grown within a thing; native, innate. L17. **2** Of a toenail: that has grown into the flesh. L19. **3** *Physical Geogr.* Of a meander: asymmetric due to lateral erosion during formation. E20.

ingrowth /ˈɪngrəʊθ/ *n.* M19. [f. IN-[1] + GROWTH.] **1** The action of growing inwards. M19. **2** A thing which has grown inwards or within something. M19.

†**Ingua** *n.* & *a.* see INCA.

Inguaeonic *n.* & *a.* var. of INGVAEONIC.

ingubu /ɪŋˈguːbuː/ *n. S. Afr.* M19. [Zulu *ingubu*] blanket, cloak.] Orig., a skin blanket or garment. Later, any article of clothing.

inguinal /ˈɪŋgwɪn(ə)l/ *a.* LME. [L *inguinalis*, f. *inguin-*, *inguen* groin: see -AL[1].] *Anat.* Of, belonging to, or situated in the groin.

inguinally *adv.* E20.

ingulf *v.* see ENGULF.

ingurgitate /ɪnˈgəːdʒɪteɪt/ *v.* L16. [L *ingurgitat-* pa. ppl stem of *ingurgitare*, f. as IN-[2] + *gurgit-*, *gurges* whirlpool, gulf: see -ATE[3].] **1** *v.t.* Swallow greedily or immoderately. L16. **b** Cram with food. L16. **2** *v.i.* Eat or drink to excess; gormandize, guzzle. L16. **3** *v.t.* Swallow up as a gulf or whirlpool; engulf. E17.

ingurgiˈtation *n.* M16.

Ingush /ˈɪŋgʊʃ, ɪnˈgʊʃ/ *n.* & *a.* Also **-goush.** E20. [Russ.] **A** *n.* Pl. same, **-es.** **1** A member of a N. Caucasian people living in the Checheno-Ingush Autonomous Republic. E20. **2** The North Caucasian language of this people. M20.

B *attrib.* or as *adj.* Of or pertaining to this people. E20.

ingustable /ɪnˈɡʌstəb(ə)l/ *a.* Now *rare.* E17. [f. IN-³ + GUSTABLE.] Unable to be tasted; not perceptible by the sense of taste.

Ingvaeonic /ɪŋvɪˈɒnɪk/ *n.* & *a.* Also **Inguae-** /ɪŋwɪ-/. M20. [f. L *Ingaevones* a Germanic tribe + -IC.] *Philol.* (Of or pertaining to) the hypothetical language from which the earliest recorded dialects of West Germanic (except Old High German) descended.

†ingyre *v.t.* E16–M18. [Fr. *ingérer* or L *ingerere*: see INGEST. The *y* is unexpl.] Introduce forcibly or violently. Chiefly *refl.*, intrude.

†inhabile *a.* E16–M19. [(O)Fr., or L *inhabilis*, f. as IN-³ + *habilis*: see ABLE *a.*, HABILE *a.*] Unfit, unable; unqualified.

†inhability *n.* LME–M18.

inhabit /ɪnˈhabɪt/ *v.* Also **†en-**. LME. [OFr. *enhabiter* or L *inhabitare*, f. as IN-² + *habitare*: see HABIT *v.*] **1** *v.t.* Dwell in, occupy as an abode; live permanently or habitually in (a region, element, etc.). LME. **2** *v.i.* Dwell, live; have one's abode; lodge. LME. **†3** *v.t.* Settle or people (a place). (Foll. by *with.*) LME–M17. **†4** *v.t.* Establish or settle (a person, etc.) in a place; provide with a habitation; house. L15–E17. **b** *v.i.* Take up one's abode, settle. M–L16.

1 E. BOWEN He and she could inhabit one house in intact solitude. D. ABSE I inhabited a serious suit; black tie, armband. M. SARTON The spirit that inhabited this house was unique.

inhabited *a.* (*a*) that is inhabited, lived-in, having inhabitants; (*b*) storiated: L16. **inhabiter** *n.* (*arch.*) (*a*) an inhabitant; †(*b*) a colonist: LME. **inhabitress** *n.* a female inhabitant E17.

†inhabitable *a.*¹ LME. [(O)Fr. f. L *inhabitabilis*, f. as IN-³ + *habitabilis* HABITABLE.] **1** Not habitable, not adapted to human habitation. LME–M18. **2** Uninhabited. E16–E17.

inhabitable /ɪnˈhabɪtəb(ə)l/ *a.*² L16. [f. INHABIT + -ABLE. Earlier in UNINHABITABLE.] Able to be inhabited, suitable for habitation.

¶Earlier in UNINHABITABLE.

inhabitaˈbility *n.* M19.

inhabitance /ɪnˈhabɪt(ə)ns/ *n.* Now *rare.* L15. [f. as next: see -ANCE.] **†1** A habitation, an abode, a dwelling. L15–E17. **2** Residence, inhabitation. L16.

inhabitancy /ɪnˈhabɪt(ə)nsi/ *n.* L17. [f. as next: see -ANCY.] The fact of inhabiting; residence as an inhabitant, esp. for a specified period so as to become entitled to the rights and privileges of a regular inhabitant.

inhabitant /ɪnˈhabɪt(ə)nt/ *a.* & *n.* LME. [AN, OFr. *enhabitant*, *in-*, f. as INHABIT: see -ANT¹.] **A** *adj.* Inhabiting, dwelling, resident. Now *rare* or *obs.* exc. in *inhabitant householder, occupier.* LME. **B** *n.* **1** A person who or animal which inhabits a place; a permanent resident. (Foll. by *of*, †*in.*) LME. **2** A person who fulfils the residential or legal requirements for being a member of a State or parish. *US.* L18.

†inhabitate *v.t.* E17–L18. [L *inhabitat-* pa. ppl stem of *inhabitare*: see INHABIT, -ATE³.] = INHABIT 1.

inhabitation /ɪnˌhabɪˈteɪʃ(ə)n/ *n.* LME. [Late L *inhabitatio(n-)*, f. as prec.: see -ATION.] **1** The action of inhabiting; the fact or condition of being or becoming inhabited. LME. **b** *fig.* Spiritual indwelling. E17. **†2** An inhabited region or building; a dwelling. LME–M17. **†3** A collection of inhabitants; inhabitants collectively; population. *rare.* L16–E19.

inhabitiveness /ɪnˈhabɪtɪvnɪs/ *n.* E19. [f. INHABIT + -IVE + -NESS.] *Phrenol.* The disposition always to live in the same place; attachment to country and home.

inhalant /ɪnˈheɪl(ə)nt/ *a.* & *n.* Also **-ent**. E19. [f. INHALE *v.* + -ANT¹.] **A** *adj.* Of or pertaining to inhalation; serving for inhalation. E19. **B** *n.* **1** An inhalant opening or pore. *rare.* E19. **2** A device for inhaling; a preparation for inhaling. L19.

inhalation /ɪnhəˈleɪʃ(ə)n/ *n.* E17. [med.L *inhalatio(n-)*, f. *inhalat-* pa. ppl stem of *inhalare*: see INHALE *v.*, -ATION.] **1** The action or an act of inhaling or breathing in; *spec.* the inhaling of medicines or anaesthetics in the form of a gas or vapour. E17. **2** *Med.* A preparation to be inhaled in the form of a vapour or spray. L19.

inhalational *a.* M20.

inhalator /ˈɪnhəleɪtə/ *n.* E20. [f. INHALE *v.* + -ATOR.] A device for inhaling (esp. oxygen); a respirator.

inhalatorium /ɪnˌheɪləˈtɔːrɪəm/ *n.* Pl. **-ria** /-rɪə/, **-riums**. E20. [f. INHALE *v.* after *sanatorium.*] *Med.* (now *Hist.*). A building or room used for the treatment of respiratory complaints with vaporized medicaments.

inhale /ɪnˈheɪl/ *v.* & *n.* E18. [L *inhalare*, f. as IN-² + *halare* breathe.] **A** *v.t.* & *i.* Breathe in; draw in by breathing; take (esp. tobacco smoke) into the lungs. E18.

L. DURRELL I inhaled the warm summer perfume of her dress and skin. J. HELLER I do smoke... I even inhale. A. BRINK He inhaled the smoke, savouring it. B. T. BRADFORD She..took several deep breaths, inhaling and exhaling for a few seconds.

B *n.* An act of inhaling, esp. of inhaling tobacco smoke. M20.

New Yorker I had just finished my inhale and was about to blow out.

inhalent *a.* & *n.* var. of INHALANT.

inhaler /ɪnˈheɪlə/ *n.* L18. [f. INHALE *v.* + -ER¹.] **1** A device for administering a medicinal or anaesthetic gas or vapour, esp. to relieve nasal or bronchial congestion. Formerly also, a respirator. L18. **2** A person who inhales. M19.

†inhance *v.* var. of ENHANCE.

inharmonic /ɪnhɑːˈmɒnɪk/ *a.* L19. [f. IN-³ + HARMONIC *a.*] Chiefly *Mus.* Not harmonic; dissonant.

†inharmonical *a.* L17–L19.

inharmonious /ɪnhɑːˈməʊnɪəs/ *a.* E18. [f. IN-³ + HARMONIOUS.] **1** Of sound: not in harmony; sounding disagreeably; discordant. E18. **2** Not harmonious in relation, action, or sentiment; disagreeing; not in accordance. M18.

inharmoniously *adv.* E19. **inharmoniousness** *n.* M18.

inharmony /ɪnˈhɑːməni/ *n. rare.* L18. [f. IN-³ + HARMONY.] Lack of harmony; discord.

inhaul /ˈɪnhɔːl/ *n.* M19. [f. IN-¹ + HAUL *n.*] *Naut.* An appliance for hauling in; *spec.* a rope used to haul in the clew of a sail.

Also **inhauler** *n.* L18.

inhaust /ɪnˈhɔːst/ *v.t. rare.* M16. [f. IN-² + L *haust-* pa. pple of *haurire* draw.] Draw or suck in; inhale; imbibe.

inhearse /ɪnˈhəːs/ *v.t.* Also **en-** /ɪn-, ɛn-/. L16. [f. IN-¹, EN-¹ + HEARSE *n.*¹] Put into a hearse.

inheaven /ɪnˈhɛv(ə)n/ *v.t.* Also **en-** /ɪn-, ɛn-/. E17. [f. IN-¹, EN-¹ + HEAVEN *n.*] Place in or raise to heaven; delight.

inhell /ɪnˈhɛl/ *v.t. rare.* E17. [f. IN-¹ + HELL *n.*] Put or confine in hell.

inhere /ɪnˈhɪə/ *v.i.* M16. [L *inhaerere*, f. as IN-² + *haerere* to stick.] **†1** Adhere, cling *to. rare.* Only in M16. **2** Exist as an essential, permanent, or characteristic attribute, quality, etc., of a thing; form an element of something; belong to the intrinsic nature of something. Foll. by *in.* L16. **b** Of a right, power, function, etc.: be vested *in.* M19. **†3** Stick *in*, be or remain fixed or lodged *in*, (*lit.* & *fig.*). E17–M19.

2 D. HUME The particular qualities, which form a substance, are commonly refer'd to an unknown something, in which they are supposed to inhere. H. READ From what has already been said of the nature of beauty, it will be evident that this quality inheres in any work of art. R. NIEBUHR The significant social power is the power which inheres in the ownership of the means of production.

inherence /ɪnˈhɪər(ə)ns, -ˈhɛr-/ *n.* L16. [med.L *inherentia*, f. *inherent-* var. of L *inhaerent-*: see next, -ENCE.] The fact or condition of inhering; the state or quality of being inherent; permanent existence *in* something.

Also **inherency** *n.* E17.

inherent /ɪnˈhɪər(ə)nt, -ˈhɛr-/ *a.* L16. [L *inhaerent-* pres. ppl stem of *inhaerere*: see INHERE, -ENT.] **†1** Fixed, situated, or contained in or *in* something (*lit.* & *fig.*). L16–E19. **2** Existing in something as an essential, permanent, or characteristic attribute or quality; forming an element of something; intrinsic, essential. (Foll. by *in.*) L16. **b** Of a right, power, or function: vested *in* or attached to a person, office, etc. E17.

2 J. A. MICHENER The little building has an inherent poetry that could not have sprung entirely from the hands of an architect. A. TOFFLER There is nothing inherent in the evolutionary process to guarantee man's own survival. E. FROMM Change and growth are inherent qualities of the life process.

inherently *adv.* E17.

inherit /ɪnˈhɛrɪt/ *v.* Orig. **†en-**. ME. [OFr. *enheriter* make heir f. late L *inhereditare* appoint as heir, f. as IN-² + *hered-*, *heres* heir.] **1** *v.t.* Come into possession of, as a right; receive or hold as one's portion. Chiefly in biblical translations and allusions. ME. **2** *v.t.* Take or receive (property, a privilege, title, etc.) as an heir at the death of a former possessor; get or come into possession of by legal descent or succession. LME. **b** Derive or possess (a quality or character, physical or mental) by transmission from a progenitor or progenitors. L16. **c** Receive or have from a predecessor or predecessors in office etc. M19. **†3** *v.t.* Make heir, put in possession. LME–L16. **4** *v.t.* Be heir to (a person); succeed as heir. LME. **5** *v.i.* Come into or take possession of an inheritance. M16. **b** Derive being or a quality *from.* L19.

1 AV *Luke* 18:18 Good master, what shall I doe to inherit eternall life? **2b** JO GRIMOND His children.. inherited the exemplary character and looks of their parents. **c** G. K. CHESTERTON It is the rule, inherited from the old régime. *Southern Rag* The musical culture which we inherit in this country is frequently.. sexist. **5** E. H. JONES He has presumably inherited, his parents being dead.

inheritable /ɪnˈhɛrɪtəb(ə)l/ *a.* Also **†en-**. LME. [AN *enheritable* able to be made heir, f. as prec.: see -ABLE.] **1** Capable of inheriting; entitled to succeed (to property etc.) by legal right. LME. **2** Able to be inherited; that may or can descend by law to an heir. L15.

inheritaˈbility *n.* L18. **inheritableness** *n.* L18. **inheritably** *adv.* M16.

inheritage /ɪnˈhɛrɪtɪdʒ/ *n. rare.* M16. [f. INHERIT + -AGE.] That which is inherited; an inheritance, a heritage.

inheritance /ɪnˈhɛrɪt(ə)ns/ *n.* Also **†en-**. LME. [AN *inheritaunce* being admitted as heir, f. as INHERIT: see -ANCE.] **I 1** Hereditary succession to a property, title, office, etc.; a continual right to an estate invested in a person and his or her heirs. LME. **2** The fact or property of inheriting or having inherited something. LME.

1 C. G. SELIGMAN The eldest son is the chief heir; women have no right of inheritance. **2** H. CARE English Liberties, or the free-born Subject's Inheritance. R. DAWKINS Inheritance of many genetic characters such as human height.

II 3 Property, or an estate, which passes by law to an heir or heirs on the death of the possessor. LME. **b** A property, quality, characteristic, etc., inherited from a progenitor or progenitors. E17. **4** A thing that one obtains or comes into possession of by right or divine grant; *esp.* (in biblical use) the blessings received by God's chosen people. M16.

3 R. HOLMES His maternal grandmother died, leaving him a considerable inheritance of.. thirty thousand francs. **b** L. M. MONTGOMERY The merry expression which was her inheritance from her father.

Comb.: **inheritance tax** a tax on inherited property levied on individual beneficiaries, *spec.* one varying according to their degrees of relationship to the testator.

inheritor /ɪnˈhɛrɪtə/ *n.* LME. [f. INHERIT + -OR.] A person who inherits something; an heir. (Foll. by *of.*)

inheritress /ɪnˈhɛrɪtrɪs/ *n.* E16. [f. prec.: see -ESS¹.] = next.

inheritrix /ɪnˈhɛrɪtrɪks/ *n.* Pl. **-trices** /-trɪsiːz/, **-trixes**. M16. [f. as prec.: see -TRIX.] A female inheritor, an heiress.

Also **†inheritrice** *n.* E16–L17.

inhesion /ɪnˈhiːʒ(ə)n/ *n.* M17. [Late L *inhaesio(n-)*, f. L *inhaes-* pa. ppl stem of *inhaerere*: see INHERE, -ION.] The action or fact of inhering, esp. as a quality or attribute; inherence.

inhiate /ˈɪnhʌɪeɪt/ *v.i.* Now *rare.* M16. [L *inhiat-* pa. ppl stem of *inhiare* gape at, f. as IN-[2] + *hiare* gape: see -ATE[3].] Open the mouth wide, gape.

inhibin /ɪnˈhɪbɪn/ *n.*[1] M20. [f. L *inhibere* INHIBIT: see -IN[1].] *Physiol.* A gonadal hormone which inhibits the secretion of follicle-stimulating hormone.

inhibin *n.*[2] var. of next.

inhibine /ˈɪnhɪbiːn/ *n.* Also **-in** /-ɪn/. M20. [f. INHIBIT + -INE[5].] Any of a group of natural antibacterial substances found mainly in honey and saliva.

inhibit /ɪnˈhɪbɪt/ *v.t.* LME. [L *inhibit-* pa. ppl stem of *inhibere* hold in, hinder, f. as IN-[2] + *habere* hold.] 1 Forbid (a person) to do something, prohibit from doing something; *spec.* forbid (an ecclesiastic) to exercise clerical functions. (Foll. by *from doing*, †*from* a thing, †*to do.*) LME. †2 Forbid or prohibit the doing of or engaging in (a thing, action, or practice). L15–E19. 3 Restrain, prevent. M16.

1 LD MACAULAY A clause was.. inserted which inhibited the Bank from advancing money. 2 C. LAMB At school all play-going was inhibited. 3 DAY LEWIS A kind of near-neurotic inertia or negativism which inhibited me from pressing my love upon her. P. GOODMAN Certain aims are forbidden and punishable ..; so we inhibit them and put them out of our mind. B. PYM Her presence inhibited any attempt at that kind of conversation. I. MURDOCH I had the satisfaction of seeing her inhibit her impulse to ask me where I was going. *Flex* The zinc ion has been shown to inhibit viral duplication.

inhibited *a.* (*a*) that has been inhibited; forbidden, restrained; (*b*) subject to inhibition, unable to express feelings or impulses: E17. **inhibitedness** *n.* M20. **inhibiter** *n.* = INHIBITOR 1 E17. **inhibiting** *a.* (*a*) forbidding, prohibitive; (*b*) causing restraint or inhibition: E17. **inhibitingly** *adv.* M20. **inhibitive** *a.* serving or tending to inhibit someone or something M19.

inhibition /ɪn(h)ɪˈbɪʃ(ə)n/ *n.* LME. [(O)Fr., or L *inhibitio(n-)*, f. as prec.: see -ION.] 1 Chiefly *Eccl.* & *Law.* The action or an act of forbidding; a (formal) prohibition. LME. **b** *spec.* In *Eng. Law*, an order prohibiting dealing with a specified piece of land for a given period or until further notice; formerly also, a writ forbidding a court to proceed in a suit on the grounds that it is beyond the cognizance of that court, a prohibition. In *Eccl. Law*, an order suspending the jurisdiction of an inferior court during an episcopal visitation; an order suspending a member of the clergy from ministerial duty. In *Sc. Law*, a writ prohibiting a person from contracting a possible charge on or selling heritable property; formerly also, a writ obtained by a husband to prevent his wife from obtaining credit. M16. 2 The action or an act of preventing, hindering, or checking. E17. **b** *Physiol.* The checking or repression of an organ or function, esp. in the nervous system, by the action of another or of a drug. L19. **c** *Chem.* & *Biochem.* The slowing or prevention of a reaction or process by a specific substance. E20. 3 (A) scrupulous or emotional resistance to thought, action, etc. In *Psychol.*, (a) voluntary or involuntary restraint on the direct expression of a natural impulse; the process whereby a learned response is weakened in the absence of reinforcement. L19.

2 S. JOHNSON It is said that no torture is equal to the inhibition of sleep, long continued. E. P. THOMPSON A 'religion of the heart'.. notorious for the inhibition of all spontaneity. 3 C. HILL Cromwell.. had no inhibitions about using the loyalty and enthusiasm of the lower-class radicals. E. H. JONES She tried out her half-formed ideas in her circle without inhibition. *Hairdo Ideas* Answers all your questions and helps free you of inhibitions. *reactive inhibition*: see REACTIVE *a.* 3. *retroactive inhibition*: see RETROACTIVE 3.

inhibitor /ɪnˈhɪbɪtə/ *n.* M19. [f. INHIBIT + -OR. Cf. earlier INHIBITER.] 1 A person who inhibits something; *spec.* in *Sc. Law*, a person who takes out an inhibition. M19. 2 A thing which inhibits someone or something. E20. **b** *Genetics.* A gene whose presence prevents the expression of some other gene at a different locus. E20. **c** *Chem.* & *Biochem.* A substance which slows down or prevents a particular reaction or process, or diminishes the activity of some reactant or catalyst. E20.

2 W. JAMES Danger is for most men the great inhibitor of action.

inhibitory /ɪnˈhɪbɪt(ə)ri/ *a.* L15. [med.L *inhibitorius*, f. as INHIBIT + -ORY[2].] 1 Prohibitory. L15. 2 That restrains or prevents something; causing inhibition. M19.

1 J. LINGARD An inhibitory breve, forbidding all archbishops.. to give judgment in the.. cause of Henry against Catharine. 2 P. GROSSKURTH Anxiety, if excessive, can be inhibitory to development.

†**inhold** *v.t.* L15. [f. IN-[1] + HOLD *v.*] 1 Keep in, retain, withhold. L15–E18. 2 Contain, enclose. Only in E17.

†**inholder** *n.* (*a*) a tenant; (*b*) a thing which holds or contains something: L16–L17.

inhomogeneity /ɪn,hɒmə(ʊ)dʒɪˈniːɪti, -ˈneɪɪti; ɪn,həʊm-/ *n.* L19. [f. IN-[3] + HOMOGENEITY.] 1 A thing which is not homogeneous with its surroundings; a local irregularity. L19. 2 The property of being inhomogeneous; lack of homogeneity. E20.

inhomogeneous /,ɪnhɒmə(ʊ)ˈdʒiːnɪəs, -ˈdʒɛn-; ,ɪnhəʊm-/ *a.* E20. [f. IN-[3] + HOMOGENEOUS.] 1 Not uniform throughout; composed of diverse constituents; heterogeneous. E20. 2 *Math.* Consisting of terms that are not all of the same degree or dimensions. M20.

inhomogeneously *adv.* E20.

†**inhoop** *v.t. rare* (Shakes.). Only in E17. [f. IN-[1] + HOOP *n.*[1] or *v.*[1]] Place in a hoop; surround by a hoop.

inhospitable /ɪnhɒˈspɪtəb(ə)l, ɪnˈhɒspɪt-/ *a.* L16. [Fr., f. as IN-[3] + HOSPITABLE.] 1 Not welcoming to strangers; not showing hospitality to guests. L16. 2 Of a region: not offering shelter or sustenance; bleak, hostile. E17.

1 G. B. SHAW Hector: I'm sorry to be inhospitable; but will you kindly leave the house? 2 B. LOPEZ The tree line, where one first encounters the inhospitable soils of the tundra.

in,hospita'bility, **inhospitableness** *ns.* M17. **inhospitably** *adv.* M17.

†**inhospital** *a.* L16–E18. [L *inhospitalis*, f. as IN-[3] + *hospitalis* hospitable: see HOSPITAL *a.*] = INHOSPITABLE.

inhospitality /,ɪnhɒspɪˈtalɪti/ *n.* L16. [L *inhospitalitas*, f. as prec.: see -ITY.] The quality or practice of being inhospitable; lack of hospitality.

in-house /*as adj.* ˈɪnhaʊs, *as adv.* ɪnˈhaʊs/ *a.* & *adv.* M20. [f. IN-[1] + HOUSE *n.*[1]] **A** *adj.* Of or pertaining to the internal affairs of an institution or organization; existing within an institution or organization. M20.

Lebende Sprachen Microcircuits.. made by outside suppliers or by.. in-house facilities. S. I. LANDAU Will it be written entirely by an in-house staff of dictionary editors?

B *adv.* Internally; without outside assistance. M20.

Flight International Avoid carrying out tasks in-house which can be executed by subcontractors. *Bookcase* Gary felt it was time to keep a good idea and develop it in-house.

inhuman /ɪnˈhjuːmən/ *a.* & *n.* Also (earlier) †**-ane**. LME. [L *inhumanus*, f. as IN-[3] + *humanus* HUMAN *a.*] **A** *adj.* 1 Of a person: callous, unfeeling, merciless. Of conduct, an action, etc.: brutal, barbarous, cruel. Cf. INHUMANE 2. LME. 2 Not human; not of the normal human type. M16.

1 SHAKES. *Tit. A.* Her spotless chastity, Inhuman traitors, you constrain'd and forc'd. C. G. WOLFF Having been dehumanized, they act with inhuman indifference to the feelings of others. 2 J. B. CABELL Planet-stricken folk, who had spied.. upon an inhuman loveliness, and so, must pine away.

†**B** *n.* A brutal or subhuman person. M17–M18.

inhumanly *adv.* L15. **inhumanness** /-n-n-/ *n.* (*rare*) M17.

inhumane /ɪnhjʊˈmeɪn/ *a.* LME. [Orig. var. of INHUMAN *a.*; later f. IN-[3] + HUMANE.] †1 See INHUMAN *a.* LME. 2 Not humane; without compassion for misery or suffering. Cf. INHUMAN *a.* 1. E19.

inhumanely /ɪnhjʊˈmeɪnli/ *adv.* L16. [f. prec. + -LY[2].] Orig., inhumanly, cruelly. Now, not humanely; without compassion (though not with intentional cruelty).

D. ROWE The 'mentally ill'... are often treated inhumanely and sometimes very cruelly.

inhumanism /ɪnˈhjuːmənɪz(ə)m/ *n.* E20. [f. IN-[3] + HUMANISM.] Lack of humanism; inhumanity.

inhumanitarian /,ɪnhjʊmanɪˈtɛːrɪən/ *n.* & *a.* M20. [f. IN-[3] + HUMANITARIAN.] **A** *n.* A person who does not accept the views and practices of humanitarianism. M20. **B** *adj.* Rejecting or disregarding humanitarian views or practices. M20.

inhumanity /ɪnhjʊˈmanɪti/ *n.* L15. [(O)Fr. *inhumanité*, or L *inhumanitas*, f. *inhumanus* INHUMAN *a.*: see -ITY.] 1 The quality of being inhuman or inhumane; lack of compassion, cruelty. L15. **b** An instance of this; a cruel act. M17. †2 Lack of politeness; incivility. M16–M17.

inhumate /ɪnˈhjuːmeɪt, ˈɪnhjʊmeɪt/ *v.t. rare.* E17. [L *inhumat-* pa. ppl stem of *inhumare* INHUME: see -ATE[3].] Bury, inter; = INHUME 1.

inhumation /ɪnhjʊˈmeɪʃ(ə)n/ *n.* L16. [f. INHUMATE or INHUME: see -ATION.] †1 A method of distillation in which vessels were buried in earth within a circular fire. L16–M17. 2 The action or practice of burying the dead; the fact of being buried; interment. M17. 3 The burying of something in or under the ground. M17.

2 F. SMYTH Any corpse dug up after a period of inhumation in the area.. would contain.. arsenic. *Scientific American* Inhumation of the bones.. was the last stage in the treatment of the deceased.

inhume /ɪnˈhjuːm/ *v.t.* E17. [L *inhumare*, f. as IN-[2] + *humus* ground.] 1 Bury (a corpse); place in the grave, inter. E17. †**b** Of the earth or a tomb: cover (the dead). E17–L18. 2 *gen.* Bury in the ground; cover with soil. Now *rare* or *obs.* E17.

inhumorous /ɪnˈhjuːm(ə)rəs/ *a.* E20. [f. IN-[3] + HUMOROUS.] Not humorous; without humour.

inhumorously *adv.* L19.

iniencephalus /,ɪnɪɛnˈkɛf(ə)ləs, -ˈsɛf-/ *n.* M19. [f. INION + Gk *egkephalos* brain.] *Med.* (A deformed foetus exhibiting) iniencephaly.

inience'phalic *a.* L19. **iniencephaly** *n.* a developmental abnormality of the skull and upper spine, in which the brain and spinal cord protrude through an opening in the occiput and upper spinal canal E20.

inimic /ɪˈnɪmɪk/ *a. arch. rare.* L17. [L *inimicus*: see ENEMY.] Adverse, hostile.

inimicable /ɪˈnɪmɪkəb(ə)l/ *a. rare.* E19. [f. IN-[3] + AMICABLE, after *inimical.*] = INIMICAL.

inimical /ɪˈnɪmɪk(ə)l/ *a.* E16. [Late L *inimicalis*, f. *inimicus*: see ENEMY, -AL[1].] 1 Unfriendly, hostile, (*to*). E16. 2 Adverse, injurious, harmful, (*to*). M17.

1 H. A. L. FISHER The only organized and educated body of men,.. instead of being inimical, was an ally. H. CARPENTER He was firmly convinced.. that the female psychology was.. different from—and largely inimical to—that of the male. 2 P. F. BOLLER A dangerous monopoly inimical to the interests of the majority.

inimi'cality *n.* L18. **inimically** *adv.* M19. **inimicalness** *n.* M17.

†**inimicitious** *a.* M17–M18. [f. L *inimicitia* enmity, f. *inimicus* ENEMY, + -OUS.] = INIMICAL.

†**inimicous** *a.* L16–E18. [f. L *inimicus* ENEMY + -OUS.] = INIMICAL.

inimitable /ɪˈnɪmɪtəb(ə)l/ *a.* & *n.* L15. [Fr., or L *inimitabilis*, f. as IN-[3] + *imitabilis* IMITABLE.] **A** *adj.* Surpassing or defying imitation; without compare, peerless. L15.

Sunday Express In his own inimitable way he tells us what to drink.

B *n.* An inimitable person or thing. M18.

Times A creditable and exuberant expression of one of the great inimitables of jazz.

inimita'bility *n.* E18. **inimitableness** *n.* M17. **inimitably** *adv.* M17.

in infinitum /ɪn ɪnfɪˈnʌɪtəm/ *adv. phr.* M16. [L.] To infinity, without end. Cf. AD INFINITUM.

inion /ˈɪnɪɒn/ *n.* E19. [Gk = nape of the neck.] *Anat.* The projecting part of the occipital bone at the base of the skull.

†inique *a.* E16–M18. [L *iniquus*, f. as IN-³ + *aequus* equal, just.] Unjust, iniquitous.

iniquitous /ɪˈnɪkwɪtəs/ *a.* E18. [f. INIQUITY + -OUS.] Characterized by or full of iniquity; grossly unjust, wicked.
iniquitously *adv.* L18. **iniquitousness** *n.* L19.

iniquity /ɪˈnɪkwɪti/ *n.* ME. [OFr. *iniquité* f. L *iniquitas*, f. *iniquus*: see INIQUE, -ITY.] **I 1** Immoral, unrighteous, or harmful action or conduct; gross injustice, wickedness, sin. Also, the quality of being wicked or sinful. ME. **b** In *pl.* Wrongful acts; sins, injuries, injustices. L15. **2** (**I-**.) A (comic) character in morality plays, representing a particular vice or vice in general. L16. **3** Inequality, inequity, unfairness. *obs.* exc. as passing into sense I. L16.
1 R. WATSON The iniquity and unrelenting cruelty exercised. A. J. P. TAYLOR My father regarded Oxford as a sink of iniquity. **b** A. BRINK To.. expose the iniquities of the Security Police. M. SCAMMELL A feudal system whose iniquities were to provide much of the fuel for the Revolution.
†II 4 Unfavourable or adverse influence or operation. M16–E17.

†iniquous *a.* M17–L18. [f. L *iniquus* (see INIQUE) + -OUS.] Unjust, wicked, iniquitous.

inirritable /ɪnˈɪrɪtəb(ə)l/ *a.* Now *rare* or *obs.* L18. [f. IN-³ + IRRITABLE.] Chiefly *Physiol.* Not irritable, unresponsive to stimulus.
inirritaˈbility *n.* L18.

inisle *v.* var. of ENISLE.

initial /ɪˈnɪʃ(ə)l/ *n.* E17. [f. the adj.] **1** An initial letter; *esp.* (in *pl.*) the initial letters of two or more names of a person, or of words forming any name or phrase. E17. **2** An initial stage or element *of* something; a beginning. Now *rare*. M17. **3** *Mus.* More fully *absolute initial*. Each of the prescribed notes on which a plainsong melody may begin in any given mode. L19. **4** *Bot.* An initial cell. E20.
1 A. UTTLEY A big blue handkerchief with his initials embroidered in the corner. J. HUTCHINSON The earliest books left spaces for initials.. which were completed by illuminators. *New Scientist* The commands are based on initials such as CV for 'centre vertically'.

initial /ɪˈnɪʃ(ə)l/ *a.* E16. [L *initialis*, f. *initium* beginning: see -AL¹.] **1** Of or pertaining to the beginning; existing at, constituting, or occurring at the beginning; first, primary. E16. **b** *Bot.* Of a plant-cell: dividing into two daughter cells, one of which develops into the tissues and organs of the plant while the other remains within the meristem. L19. **2** Standing at the beginning of a word, of a division in a book or piece of writing, or of the alphabet. E17.
1 J. GALSWORTHY From this initial mistake of hers all the subsequent trouble, sorrow and tragedy have come. *Gentleman* (*Bombay*) The trade protocol.. was valid for an initial period of five years. C. PETERS After a while the initial euphoria of having a place of his own wore off. **initial line** *Math.* (in a system of polar coordinates) the line from which an angle is measured. **initial teaching alphabet** a 44-letter phonetic alphabet used to help those beginning to read and write English. 2 G. BURNET The initial letters of his name.., as W. E... for Will. Exon.
initially *adv.* E17.

initial /ɪˈnɪʃ(ə)l/ *v.t.* Infl. **-ll-**, ***-l-**. M19. [f. the n.] Mark or sign with initials; put one's initials to or on; *spec.* signify thus the intention of later formal ratification.
Time The signing of a Panama Canal treaty that was initialed last month.

initialese /ɪˌnɪʃəˈliːz/ *n.* M20. [f. INITIAL *n.* + -ESE.] The use of abbreviations formed by using the initial letters of the words to be shortened.

initialise *v.* var. of INITIALIZE.

initialism /ɪˈnɪʃ(ə)lɪz(ə)m/ *n.* L19. [f. INITIAL *n.* + -ISM.] A group of initial letters used as an abbreviation, *esp.* one in which each letter is pronounced separately (cf. ACRONYM); the use of such initials.

initialize /ɪˈnɪʃ(ə)lʌɪz/ *v.t.* & *i.* Also **-ise**. M19. [f. INITIAL *n.* + -IZE.] **1** Designate by or use an initial or initials instead of the full name. *rare*. M19. **2** *Computing.* Set or become set to a value or in a state suitable for the start of an operation. M20.
2 *Personal Software* There is a substantial amount of code to be entered to initialise the program. *Television* The ROM and the CPU were.. faulty, but the machine still wouldn't initialise when these had been replaced.
initialiˈzation *n.* (*Computing*) the action or process of initializing; the computer operations involved in this: M20.

initiand /ɪˈnɪʃɪand/ *n.* M20. [L *initiandus* gerundive of *initiare* INITIATE *v.*: see -AND.] A person about to be initiated.

initiate /ɪˈnɪʃɪət/ *a.* & *n.* E17. [L *initiatus* pa. pple, f. as next: see -ATE².] **A** *adj.* **1** Admitted into some society or position; instructed in some (secret) knowledge. E17. **†b** Of or belonging to a newly initiated person. *rare* (Shakes.). Only in E17. **2** Begun, commenced, introduced. M18.
1 M. AYRTON Lycus was deeply religious and initiate in the mysteries of the Mother.. Demeter.
B *n.* **†1** Something initiated or newly introduced. *rare*. Only in E17. **2** A person who has been initiated; a beginner, a novice. E19.
2 J. BAYLEY It is hinted that only initiates, those really in the know, can understand. W. STYRON For the initiate ours is a cruel language.

initiate /ɪˈnɪʃɪeɪt/ *v.* M16. [L *initiat-* pa. ppl stem of *initiare* begin, f. *initium* beginning: see -ATE³.] **1** *v.t.* Introduce (a person) with due ceremonies or rites into a society or position, or into the knowledge of some (esp. secret or occult) principle or practice; *gen.* acquaint with or instruct in the elements of anything. (Foll. by *in*, *into*.) M16. **b** *v.i.* Perform or undergo an initiation. E18. **2** *v.t.* Begin, introduce, set going, originate. E17. **b** *v.i.* Have its beginning; commence. E17.
1 I. MCEWAN It was Raymond who initiated me into the secrets of adult life. 2 E. F. BENSON Whether it was customary for unmarried ladies to initiate a call on an unmarried man. J. K. TOOLE I have succeeded in initiating several work-saving methods. **b** S. TOLANSKY If pure deuterium gas can be raised to a temperature.. of 500 million degrees C., then a thermo-nuclear reaction should initiate.

initiated /ɪˈnɪʃɪeɪtɪd/ *ppl a.* & *n.* L16. [f. prec. + -ED¹.] **A** *ppl a.* That has been initiated. L16.
B *n.* **1** An initiate. M18. **2** *collect. pl. The* people who have been initiated. M19.
2 A. EDEN A catch was concealed which the initiated could press to open a door.

initiation /ɪˌnɪʃɪˈeɪʃ(ə)n/ *n.* L16. [L *initiatio(n-)* (in sense 2 in med.L), f. as INITIATE *v.*: see -ATION.] **1** Formal introduction with due ceremonies or rites into a society, position, or (secret) knowledge; instruction in the elements of a subject or practice; an instance of this. L16. **2** The action or an act of beginning or originating something; the fact of being begun; commencement, origination. M17.
1 L. VAN DER POST The long night of the initiation of the Esquire into Knighthood. J. VIORST The recognition that others have.. claims upon her love is our initiation into jealousy. *initiation ceremony, rite*, etc.

initiative /ɪˈnɪʃɪətɪv, -ʃə-/ *n.* L18. [Fr., f. as INITIATE *v.* + -IVE.] **1** The action of initiating something or of taking the first step or the lead; an act setting a process or chain of events in motion; an independent or enterprising act. L18. **b** *spec.* A proposal made by one nation or group of nations to another, with a view to improving relations between them. M20. **2** The power or right to begin something. L18. **b** *spec.* The right of (a specified number of) citizens outside the legislature to propose legislation (as in Switzerland and parts of the US). L19. **3** Mental power to initiate things; enterprise, self-motivation to action. E20.
1 W. SOYINKA Did he contact you or did the initiative come from you? H. KISSINGER The most important diplomatic initiative.. was toward Hanoi. *Dance Theatre Journal* These companies were set up as purely regional initiatives. **b** *Strategic Defense Initiative*: see STRATEGIC *a.* 2 C. G. WOLFF The outside world and all that went with it: autonomy and initiative. 3 S. LEACOCK The peculiar quality that is called initiative—the ability to act promptly on one's own judgment.
Phrases: **have the initiative** have the first choice of action; *esp.* (*Mil.*) be able to influence or control the enemy's movements. **on one's own initiative** without being prompted by others. **take the initiative** be the first to take action.

initiative /ɪˈnɪʃɪətɪv, -ʃə-/ *a.* M17. [f. INITIATE *v.* + -IVE.] Characterized by initiating something; of or pertaining to initiation.
Times Bowater.. will take the first initiative step.. next week.
initiatively *adv.* M17.

initiator /ɪˈnɪʃɪeɪtə/ *n.* L17. [f. INITIATE *v.* + -OR.] **1** A person who or thing which initiates someone or something. L17. **2** An explosive or device used to detonate the main charge. E20. **3** *Chem.* Any substance which starts a chain reaction. M20.
initiatress *n.* (*rare*) a female initiator M19. **initiˈatrix** *n.*, pl. **-trices** /-trɪsiːz/, **-trixes**, a female initiator M19.

initiatory /ɪˈnɪʃɪət(ə)ri, ɪˌnɪʃɪˈeɪt(ə)ri/ *a.* E17. [f. INITIATE *v.* + -ORY².] **1** Pertaining to or constituting a beginning; initial, introductory, preliminary. E17. **2** Pertaining to initiation; serving to initiate into some society, position, or special knowledge. M17.
1 T. HARDY Those automatic initiatory acts and touches which represent among housewives the installation of another day. 2 W. WARBURTON Which he did by the initiatory Rite of water-baptism.

inition /ɪˈnɪʃ(ə)n/ *n. rare.* LME. [(O)Fr. f. med.L *initio(n-)*, f. L *init-* pa. ppl stem of *inire* go into, enter: see -ION.] Entrance, beginning, initiation.

injail *v.* var. of ENJAIL.

†injealous *v.* see ENJEALOUS.

inject /ɪnˈdʒɛkt/ *v.t.* L16. [L *inject-* pa. ppl stem of *inicere* throw in, f. as IN-² + *jacere* throw.] **†1** Throw or cast *on* a thing. L16–E18. **2** Drive or force (esp. a fluid, medicine, etc.) into a passage, cavity, or solid material under pressure; introduce by injection. E17. **b** Introduce or feed (a current, beam of particles, charge carriers, etc.) into a substance or device. M20. **c** *Astronaut.* Put *into* (*an*) *orbit*. M20. **3** *fig.* Introduce suddenly or with force or by way of interruption; insert; suggest, interject. M17. **4** Fill or charge (a cavity etc.) by injection; administer a medicine etc. to (a person or animal) by injection. (Foll. by *with*.) M18.
2 A. DAVIS They had begun to inject the drug into the veins in their necks. J. S. FOSTER Cavity fills may be blown or injected into the cavity wall after construction. 3 J. BARZUN A delivers an opinion while B thinks of the one he will inject as soon as he decently can. M. RULE Full of new ideas and injecting new enthusiasm into the project. 4 C. LYELL Such rents must be injected with melted matter. R. INGALLS They injected me a lot.. so I fell asleep.
injected *a.* that has been injected; *spec.* (*a*) *Med.* bloodshot, congested; (*b*) (more fully *fuel-injected*) having fuel injection: M18.

injectable /ɪnˈdʒɛktəb(ə)l/ *a.* & *n.* M19. [f. prec. + -ABLE.] **A** *adj.* Able to be injected, esp. into the body; suitable for injection. M19. **B** *n.* A substance suitable for injection; *esp.* a drug or medicine suitable for injection directly into the bloodstream. M20.

injection /ɪnˈdʒɛkʃ(ə)n/ *n.* LME. [Fr., or L *injectio(n-)*, f. as INJECT: see -ION.] **1** The action of or an act of driving or forcing (a fluid) into a passage, cavity, or solid material under pressure; *esp.* in *Med.*, introduction of a medicine, preservative, etc., by means of a (hypodermic) syringe. LME. **b** In full *fuel injection*. The direct introduction of fuel under pressure into the combustion unit of an internal-combustion engine. E20. **c** The act of introducing a current, beam of particles, etc., into a substance or device. M20. **d** *Astronaut.* The (time of) entry or placing (of a spacecraft, satellite, etc.) into an orbit or trajectory. M20. **2** A substance which is injected. LME. **3** *fig.* The sudden or forceful introduction of a thing from outside; the suggestion of an idea into the mind; the interjection of a statement into an argument etc.; a suggestion, a hint. E17. **4** *Med.*

Congestion with blood; bloodshot condition. E19. 5 *Math.* A one-to-one mapping. M20.

1 A. BROOKNER I . . summoned the doctor, demanded vitamin injections. b *solid injection*: see SOLID *a.* & *adv.* 3 A. BEVAN The injection of several million pounds here would refresh the Service.

Comb.: **injection moulding** the making of moulded articles from rubber or plastic by injecting heat-softened material into a mould; **injection well**: into which gas, air, or water is forced so as to increase the yield from interconnected wells.

injective /ɪnˈdʒɛktɪv/ *a.* M20. [f. INJECT + -IVE.] *Math.* Of the nature of or pertaining to an injection or one-to-one mapping.

injector /ɪnˈdʒɛktə/ *n.* M18. [f. INJECT + -OR.] A thing which or (occas.) person who injects something; *esp.* (*a*) a device for injecting water into a steam engine; (*b*) (more fully *fuel injector*) the nozzle and valve through which fuel is sprayed into a combustion chamber.

†injewel *v.* var. of ENJEWEL.

†injoin *v.* var. of ENJOIN.

†injoint *v.i. rare.* (Shakes.). Only in E17. [f. IN-^{1} + JOINT *v.*] Unite, join.

injucundity /ɪndʒʊˈkʌndɪti/ *n. rare.* E17. [L *injucunditas*, f. *injucundus* unpleasant, f. as IN-^{3} + *jucundus* JOCUND + -ITY. Partly f. IN-^{3} + JUCUNDITY.] Unpleasantness, disagreeableness.

injudicial /ɪndʒʊˈdɪʃ(ə)l/ *a. rare.* E17. [f. IN-^{3} + JUDICIAL *a.*] Not judicial. Formerly also, injudicious.

injudicially *adv.* M17.

injudicious /ɪndʒʊˈdɪʃəs/ *a.* E17. [f. IN-^{3} + JUDICIOUS.] 1 Not displaying judgement or discretion; showing lack of judgement; unwise, ill-judged. E17. †2 Of a person: lacking sound judgement. M17–M18.

injudiciously *adv.* E17. **injudiciousness** *n.* M17.

Injun /ˈɪndʒ(ə)n/ *n.* & *a. colloq.* (chiefly *N. Amer.*). Also (earlier, now *rare*) **Ingin**. L17. [Repr. colloq. & dial. pronunc. of INDIAN.] A *n.* A N. American Indian. L17.

honest Injun honestly, really, genuinely.

B *adj.* Of or pertaining to N. American Indians. M19.

injunct /ɪnˈdʒʌŋ(k)t/ *v.t.* L19. [L *injunct-* pa. ppl stem of *injungere* ENJOIN, after next.] Prohibit or restrain by injunction.

injunction /ɪnˈdʒʌŋ(k)ʃ(ə)n/ *n.* LME. [Late L *injunctio(n-)*, f. as prec.: see -ION.] I 1 The action of enjoining or authoritatively directing someone; an authoritative or emphatic admonition or order. LME. 2 *Law.* A judicial process whereby a person is restrained from beginning or continuing an action threatening or invading the legal right of another, or is compelled to carry out a certain act, e.g. to make restitution to an injured party. M16.

1 E. JONES He sent her a sum of money with strict injunctions that she was to spend it . . on a holiday. 2 H. EVANS I had taken the decision to publish in great secrecy, fearing an injunction to stop us.

†II 3 Conjunction; union. L15–M17.

injunctive /ɪnˈdʒʌŋ(k)tɪv/ *a.* & *n.* E17. [f. as INJUNCT + -IVE.] A *adj.* 1 Having the character or quality of directing or ordering. E17. 2 *Gram.* Designating or pertaining to a form of a verb in some Indo-European languages that has secondary personal endings and expresses injunction. E20. B *n. Gram.* An injunctive verb. E20.

injunctively *adv.* E17.

injure /ˈɪndʒə/ *v.* LME. [Back-form. f. INJURY *n.*] 1 *v.t.* Do injustice or wrong to (a person); wrong. LME. 2 *v.t.* Do harm to; inflict damage on, esp. on the body of; hurt, harm, impair. LME. b *v.i.* Become injured, receive injury. M19. †3 *v.t.* Insult, abuse, slander. M16–M17.

2 W. S. CHURCHILL Peel fell from his horse . . and was fatally injured. R. MACAULAY Anything was right that might injure the authorities. M. SCAMMELL Kopelev . . . was aware of the colonel's ire when his pride was injured.

injurer *n.* L16.

injured /ˈɪndʒəd/ *a.* M17. [f. prec. + -ED^{1}.] That has been injured; wronged; offended; hurt. Also, expressing a feeling of offendedness.

J. K. TOOLE 'Where do you think up excuses like that?' 'Well, it's true,' Darlene answered in an injured voice. R. INGALLS His parents . . were in the hospital, were badly injured. *absol.*: A. TREW 'How are the injured?' . . 'There are seven receiving treatment. Three for burns.' **injured innocence** (freq. *iron.*) the offended attitude of a person who is undeservedly accused of something.

injuria /ɪnˈdʒʊərɪə/ *n.* Pl. **-iae** /-ɪiː/. L19. [L: see INJURY.] *Law.* An invasion of another's rights; an actionable wrong.

injurious /ɪnˈdʒʊərɪəs/ *a.* LME. [f. Fr. *injurieux* or L *injuriosus*, f. *injuria* INJURY: see -OUS.] Hurtful, harmful, wrongful; (of language or, formerly, a person) insulting, calumnious.

SHAKES. *Coriol.* Call me their traitor! Thou injurious tribune! SIR W. SCOTT He holds a late royal master of mine in deep hate for some injurious treatment . . which he received at his hand. O. MANNING Only his diplomat's charm had remained untouched by this injurious climate. B. BETTELHEIM We worry that his actions are harmful at the moment or may be injurious to his future. **injurious affection** *Law* a situation in which part of a person's land is acquired compulsorily under statutory powers and the remaining part is consequently reduced in value. **injurious falsehood** *Law* the tort consisting of a maliciously false statement intended to cause damage to another person as regards property.

injuriously *adv.* L15. **injuriousness** *n.* M17.

injury /ˈɪn(d)ʒ(ə)ri/ *n.* LME. [AN *injurie* (mod.Fr. *injure* insult) f. L *injuria* use as n. of fem. of *injurius* unjust, wrongful, f. as IN-^{3} + *jur-*, *jus* right: see -Y^{3}.] 1 Wrongful action or treatment; violation or infringement of another's rights; suffering wilfully inflicted; a wrongful act, a wrong inflicted or suffered. LME. †2 Intentionally hurtful or offensive speech or words; an insult, an affront, a taunt. LME–E18. 3 Hurt or loss caused to or sustained by a person or thing; harm, detriment; damage, esp. to the body; an instance of this. LME.

3 J. BARNES William the Conqueror fell from his horse and received the injury from which he later died. *Which?* A good shoe will lessen the risk of injury. **do oneself an injury** hurt oneself. *personal injury*: see PERSONAL *a.*

Comb.: **injury time** *Football* extra playing-time allowed by a referee to compensate for time lost in dealing with injuries.

†injust *a.* LME–E18. [(O)Fr. *injuste* f. L *injustus*, f. as IN-^{3} + *justus* JUST *a.*] Not just; opposed to justice.

†injustly *adv.* LME–E18.

injustice /ɪnˈdʒʌstɪs/ *n.* LME. [(O)Fr. f. L *injustitia*, f. *injustus*: see prec., -ICE^{1}.] Unjust action; wrong; unfairness; an unjust act.

do a person an injustice judge a person unfairly.

†injustifiable *a. rare.* M17–E18. [f. IN-^{3} + JUSTIFIABLE.] Unjustifiable.

ink /ɪŋk/ *n.*^{1} ME. [OFr. *enque* (mod. *encre*) f. late L *encau(s)tum* f. Gk *egkauston* purple ink, f. *egkaiein* burn in.] 1 Coloured fluid used in writing with a pen on paper etc.; coloured viscous paste used to mark paper etc. in printing, duplicating, writing with a ball-pen, etc.; an example of this. ME. 2 The black liquid ejected by cuttlefish and other cephalopods to assist in escaping predators, etc., and from which sepia is obtainable. L16. 3 Cheap wine, esp. red wine. Cf. INKED 2. *slang* (chiefly *US* & *Austral.*). E20.

1 M. MILNER I . . made a fairly accurate drawing of them in ink and oil chalks. J. CRACE He sits with clean parchment, newly mixed inks. *black ink*, *blue ink*, *invisible ink*, etc. *marking-ink*, *printer's ink*, *printing ink*, *sympathetic ink*, *writing-ink*, etc. *Indian ink*: see INDIAN *a. Japan ink*: see JAPAN *n. red ink*: see RED *a.* 2 G. DURRELL Fishermen . . with . . dark stains of octopus ink on their shirts.

Comb.: **ink ball** *Printing Hist.* a hand-held rounded pad used for inking type; **inkberry** a low-growing N. American holly, *Ilex glabra*, with black berries and nearly thornless leaves; **ink block** *Printing Hist.* a block or table on which ink was spread before being taken up by rollers or ink balls; **ink-blot test** (an example of) the Rorschach test; **ink-cap** any of several fungi of the genus *Coprinus*, of which the gills dissolve into a black liquid after maturation; SHAGGY *ink-cap*; **ink-fish** a cuttlefish or squid; **ink-jet printer** a printer in which characters and other marks are formed by a jet of ink projected on to the paper etc.; **ink-pad** an ink-soaked pad, usu. in a box, used for inking a rubber stamp; **inkpot** a small pot for holding writing-ink; **inkshed** *joc.* [after *bloodshed*] the shedding or spilling of ink; consumption or waste of ink in writing; **ink-slinger** *derog.* a professional writer; **inkstand** a stand for one or more bottles to hold ink, often with a pen-tray etc.; **inkweed** *Austral.* & *NZ* a tropical American pokeweed, *Phytolacca octandra*, naturalized in Australasia, so called from its small black berries, which contain a reddish juice; **ink-well** a pot for ink fitted into a hole in a desk.

inkless *a.* E19.

ink /ɪŋk/ *n.*^{2} L16. [Origin unkn.] †1 A mill-rind. L16–E18. 2 A socket in which a vertical shaft or spindle rests. *rare.* L19.

ink /ɪŋk/ *v.t.* M16. [f. INK *n.*^{1}] 1 Mark, stain, or smear with or as with ink. M16. b Cover (types etc.) with ink in order to print from them. E18. 2 Go or cover *over* with ink; trace *in* with ink (lines previously drawn in pencil); blot *out* with ink; cover *up* with ink. E19. 3 Sign, put one's signature to, (a contract etc.); engage by contract. *colloq.* (chiefly *N. Amer.*). M20.

3 G. VIDAL He promptly inked a multiple nonexclusive contract with Universal.

inked /ɪŋ(k)t/ *a.* L18. [f. INK *v.*, *n.*^{1}: see -ED^{1}, -ED^{2}.] 1 Covered or smeared with ink; coloured with ink. Also *inked-in* etc. L18. 2 Intoxicated, drunk. *Austral. slang.* L19.

inken /ˈɪŋk(ə)n/ *a.* Now *rare.* E17. [f. INK *n.*^{1} + -EN^{4}.] Of ink; written in ink.

inker /ˈɪŋkə/ *n.* L19. [f. INK *v.* + -ER^{1}.] A person who or thing which uses or applies ink; *spec.* (*a*) *Hist.* a telegraph instrument which recorded messages in ink; (*b*) *Printing* any of a set of rollers which coat a printing surface with ink.

inkhorn /ˈɪŋkhɔːn/ *n.* & *a.* LME. [f. INK *n.*^{1} + HORN *n.*] A *n. Hist.* A small portable vessel for holding writing-ink. LME. B *attrib.* or as *adj.* Of a term, word, language, etc.: literary, bookish, learned. M16.

inkhornism *n.* (*rare*) use of inkhorn terms, pedantry L16.

†inkindle *v.* var. of ENKINDLE.

inkish /ˈɪŋkɪʃ/ *a. rare.* L17. [f. INK *n.*^{1} + -ISH^{1}.] Inky, black.

inkle /ˈɪŋk(ə)l/ *n.* M16. [Origin unkn.] *Hist.* 1 A kind of linen tape formerly much used, as to make laces; a piece of this tape. M16. 2 The linen thread or yarn from which this tape was manufactured. M16.

inkle /ˈɪŋk(ə)l/ *v. rare.* LME. [Origin unkn. In later use back-form. f. next.] 1 *v.t.* Give a hint of, communicate in an undertone or whisper. LME. 2 *v.t.* & *i.* Get an inkling or a notion of or *of*. M19.

inkling /ˈɪŋklɪŋ/ *n.* LME. [f. INKLE *v.* + -ING^{1}.] 1 The action of mentioning in an undertone; a faint or slight mention or rumour. *obs.* exc. *dial.* LME. 2 A hint or slight intimation given or received; a suggestion; a vague knowledge or notion; a suspicion. (Foll. by *of.*) E16. †b A suspicion *of* or *against* a person. E17–E18. 3 An inclination, a slight desire. *dial.* L18.

2 E. ROOSEVELT The admiral refused to give me the slightest inkling of what he had decided to do. P. FERGUSON She had had no inkling of his identity. V. SETH If Jan's surprised, she shows no inkling Of it at all.

in-kneed /ˈɪn-niːd, ɪnˈniːd/ *a.* Now *rare.* E18. [f. IN *adv.* + KNEE *n.* + -ED^{2}.] Having the legs bent inwards at the knees.

inknot /ɪnˈnɒt/ *v.t. rare.* Also **en-** /ɪn-, ɛn-/. Infl. **-tt-**. E17. [f. IN-^{1}, EN-^{1} + KNOT *v.*] Include in or with a knot; tie in.

inkosi /ɪŋˈkəʊsi/ *n. S. Afr.* M19. [Nguni.] (The title of) a Zulu ruler, chief, or high official.

inkosikazi /ɪŋkəʊsɪˈkɑːzi/ *n.* [Nguni *-kazi* wife of] (*a*) the wife of a Zulu chief; (*b*) (a respectful name for) a married woman: M19.

inky /ˈɪŋki/ *a.* L16. [f. INK *n.*^{1} + -Y^{1}.] 1 Of or pertaining to ink; written in ink; using ink; literary. L16. 2 Full of ink. L16. 3 Black, dark. L16. 4 Stained with ink. E17.

1 *Listener* It had started off as a music magazine to rival the weekly inky press. 3 W. GERHARDIE The inky

blackness of the night. J. BUCHAN Long pools of inky water filled the ruts. **inky cap** = *ink-cap* s.v. INK *n.*[1]

inkiness *n.* (*rare*) E17.

inlaid *v.* pa. t. & pple of INLAY *v.*

in-lamb /ɪnˈlam, ˈɪnlam/ *a.* M16. [f. IN-[1] + LAMB *n.*] Of a ewe: pregnant.

inland /ˈɪnlənd, -land; *as adv. also* ɪnˈland/ *n.*, *a.*, & *adv.* OE. [f. IN-[1] + LAND *n.*[1]] A *n.* 1 *Hist.* The inner part of an estate, feudal manor, or farm cultivated by the owner. Opp. OUTLAND *n.* 1. OE. 2 *sing.* & (now *rare*) in *pl.* The interior part of a country or region, remote from the sea or frontiers. Formerly also, the part of a country near to the capital and centres of population. M16.

2 A. GARVE Our inland is still very empty country, and a lot of it isn't easily accessible.

B *adj.* 1 Of or pertaining to the interior part of the country or region; remote from the sea or frontiers. M16. †b Having the sophistication characteristic of the capital or population centres of a country. Only in E17. 2 Carried on or operating within the limits of a country. M16.

1 P. HEYLIN All the In-land Towns in this large Estate. 2 SWIFT A pamphlet printed in England for a general excise or inland duty.

Special collocations: **inland duty** a tax payable on inland trade. **inland ice** (**sheet**) an extensive thick sheet of ice underlain by rock; *spec.* the ice-cap over the interior of Greenland. *inland* NAVIGATION. *inland port*: see PORT *n.*[1] 2. **inland revenue** in the UK, the revenue consisting of taxes and inland duties; (w. cap. initials) the government department responsible for assessing and collecting these. **inland sea** an entirely land-locked large body of salt or fresh water.

C *adv.* In or towards the interior part of a country; away from the sea or frontiers. L16.

T. MO Where the river rises thousands of miles inland. V. S. NAIPAUL On the coast there would have been . . descendants of the slave mahogany log-cutters. Inland, there was a Mayan population.

inlander *n.* a native or inhabitant of the inland of a country E17. **inlandish** *a.* of or pertaining to the interior of a country or region L16.

†**inlarge** *v.*, †**inlargement** *n.* vars. of ENLARGE, ENLARGEMENT.

inlaut /ˈɪnlaʊt/ *n.* L19. [G, f. *in* in + *Laut* sound.] *Philol.* A medial or internal sound; a sound which occurs in the middle of a word.

inlaw /ˈɪnlɔː/ *v.* & *n. obs.* exc. *Hist.* LOE. [f. IN *adv.* + LAW *n.*[1], after *outlaw*.] A *v.t.* Bring within the authority and protection of the law; reverse the outlawry of (a person). LOE. B *n.* A person who is within the domain and protection of the law. ME.

in-law /ˈɪnlɔː/ *n.* & *a. colloq.* L19. [f. next.] A *n.* A relative by marriage. Usu. in *pl.* L19. B *attrib.* or as *adj.* Of or pertaining to relatives by marriage. L19.

-in-law /ɪnˈlɔː/ *suff.* [f. IN *prep.* + LAW *n.*[1], after AN *en ley*, OFr. *en loi* (*de mariage*) in law (of marriage).] Appended to ns. of personal relationship w. the sense 'by marriage, in the eye of canon law', as *father-in-law*, *sister-in-law*.

inlay /ˈɪnleɪ, ɪnˈleɪ/ *n.* E17. [f. the vb.] 1 The process or art of inlaying. *rare.* E17. 2 A piece of material inlaid or prepared for inlaying; inlaid work. L17. b *Dentistry.* A filling of gold, porcelain, etc., which is preformed in the required shape before being cemented into a cavity. L19.

inlay /ɪnˈleɪ/ *v.t.* Pa. t. & pple **inlaid**. M16. [f. IN-[1] + LAY *v.*[1]] †1 Lay (as) in a place of concealment or preservation M16–M17. 2 Lay (a thing) in the substance of something else so that their surfaces are flush. L16. b Insert (a page of a book, an illustration, etc.) in a space cut in a page that is larger and thicker. E19. 3 Fit (a thing) with a substance of a different kind embedded in its surface; diversify by the insertion of another material in a decorative design. L16.

inlayer *n.* M17.

inleague *v.* see ENLEAGUE.

inleak /ˈɪnliːk/ *n.* E20. [f. IN-[1] + LEAK *n.*] Leakage into the inside of a thing.

in-leakage /ˈɪnliːkɪdʒ/ *n.* E20. [f. IN-[1] + LEAKAGE.] = prec.

inlet /ˈɪnlɛt, -lɪt/ *n.* ME. [f. IN-[1] + LET *v.*[1]] 1 Letting in; admission. Now *rare.* ME. 2 A small arm of the sea, a narrow indentation of a sea-coast or the bank of a lake or river. L16. 3 A way of admission; an entrance. E17. 4 A piece inserted or inlaid. L18. 5 *Anat.* An aperture giving entrance to a cavity; the upper opening into the pelvic, thoracic, etc., cavities. Cf. OUTLET *n.* 1c. E19.

3 *attrib.*: *inlet pipe, valve*, etc. *inlet manifold*: see MANIFOLD *n.* 5.

inlet /ˈɪnlɛt/ *v.t.* Infl. **-tt-**. Pa. t. & pple **inlet**. ME. [f. IN-[1] + LET *v.*[1]] †1 Allow to enter; admit. ME–L17. 2 Insert, inlay. M19.

inlier /ˈɪnlʌɪə/ *n.* M19. [f. IN-[1] after OUTLIER.] An area or outcrop of rock surrounded by rocks younger in age. Cf. OUTLIER.

†**inlight** *v.*, †**inlighten** *v.* vars. of ENLIGHT, ENLIGHTEN.

in limine /ɪn ˈlɪmɪni/ *adv. phr.* E19. [L.] On the threshold; at the outset.

in-line /ˈɪnlʌɪn/ *n.* & *a.* E20. [f. IN-[1] + LINE *n.*[2]] A *n.* 1 *Typogr.* A typeface with a white line running through the thick strokes of the letters. E20. 2 An in-line engine. M20. B *adj.* 1 (Composed of parts) arranged or situated in a line; *esp.* (of an internal-combustion engine) having (usu. vertical) cylinders arranged in one or more rows. E20. 2 Chiefly *Engin.* Involving, employing, or forming part of a continuous, usu. linear, sequence of operations or machines (as in an assembly line). M20. 3 *Computing.* a Designating data processing which does not require input data to be sorted into batches. M20. b = ONLINE *a.* 1. M20. 4 *Typogr.* Designating or pertaining to a typeface with a white line running through the thick strokes of the letters. M20.

†**inlink** *v.*, †**inlist** *v.*, †**inlive** *v.*, vars. of ENLINK etc.

†**inliven** *v.* var. of ENLIVEN.

†**inlock** *v.* var. of ENLOCK.

in loco /ɪn ˈləʊkəʊ/ *adv.* & *prep. phr.* L17. [L.] A *adv. phr.* In a place; in the place, locally. *rare.* L17. B *prep. phr.* In place of. Chiefly in *in loco parentis* /pəˈrɛntɪs/, in place of a parent. E18.

inlook /ˈɪnlʊk/ *n.* M19. [f. IN-[1] + LOOK *n.*] Looking within; introspection.

inlooker /ˈɪnlʊkə/ *n. rare.* L16. [f. IN-[1] + LOOKER.] A person who looks into a thing, an inspector.

in-lot /ˈɪnlɒt/ *n.* Long only *N. Amer.* M17. [f. IN-[1] + LOT *n.*] 1 A plot of land or allotment that is part of a larger plot. M17. 2 *N. Amer. Hist.* A plot of land for settlement, large enough for a house, garden, and outbuildings. L18.

†**inly** *a.* OE–E17. [f. IN *adv.* + -LY[1]; later prob. f. INLY *adv.*] Inward, internal; heartfelt.

inly /ˈɪnli/ *adv.* Now *literary.* OE. [f. IN *adv.* + -LY[2].] Inwardly; within, internally, in the inner nature; in a way that goes to the heart; intimately, closely; thoroughly.

inlying /ˈɪnlʌɪɪŋ/ *a.* M19. [f. IN-[1] + LYING *a.*[1]] Lying inside; placed or situated in the interior.

in-maintenance /ˈɪnmeɪnt(ə)nəns, -tɪn-/ *n.* M19. [f. IN-[1] + MAINTENANCE.] Chiefly *Hist.* Maintenance for a person living in a workhouse etc.

inmate /ˈɪnmeɪt/ *n.* & *a.* L16. [Prob. orig. f. INN *n.* (later assoc. with IN *adv.*) + MATE *n.*[2]] A *n.* 1 A person who shares a house with another or others. In early use *spec.* a lodger, a subtenant. Now *rare.* L16. 2 An inhabitant or occupier *of* a house, esp. along with others. Now chiefly, an inhabitant *of* an institution, as an asylum or a prison. L16. 3 A person not native to the place where he or she lives; a stranger, a foreigner. Now *rare* or *obs.* L16.

1 H. JAMES We have never had a lodger or any kind of inmate. 2 M. AMSTERDAM The warden, . . at the asylum, noticed one of the inmates sitting on a small stool.

†B *attrib.* or as *adj.* That is an inmate. E17–E19.

For other words beginning with *in-* see the entry for **in-**[1]

inmeat /ˈɪnmiːt/ *n. obs.* exc. *dial.* LME. [f. IN-[1] + MEAT *n.*] *sing.* & (usu.) in *pl.* The edible viscera of an animal; entrails.

in medias res /ɪn ˌmɛdɪɑːs ˈreɪz, ˌmiːdɪɑːs ˈriːz/ *adv. phr.* L18. [L.] Into the midst of things; *esp.* into the middle of a narrative, without preamble.

in medio /ɪn ˈmiːdɪəʊ/ *adv. phr.* E17. [L.] In the middle; in an undecided state.

in memoriam /ɪn mɪˈmɔːrɪam/ *prep.* & *n. phr.* M19. [L.] A *prep. phr.* To the memory of, in memory of. M19. B *n. phr.* A poem, notice, etc., in memory of a dead person. L19.

in-migrant /ˈɪnmʌɪɡr(ə)nt/ *n.* & *a.* Orig. *US.* M20. [f. IN-[1] + MIGRANT.] (Designating) a person who has migrated from one place to another in the same country.

in-migration /ˈɪnmʌɪɡreɪʃ(ə)n/ *n.* Orig. *US.* M20. [f. IN-[1] + MIGRATION.] The action of migrating from one place to another within the same country, as from one State to another in the US.

inmix /ɪnˈmɪks/ *v.t.* & *i.* L19. [f. IN-[1] + MIX *v.*] Mix in, blend.

inmost /ˈɪnməʊst/ *a.*, *n.*, & *adv.* OE. [f. IN *adv.* + -MOST.] A *adj.* Situated furthest within, most inward; *spec.* (of thoughts, feelings etc.) most intimate, deepest, closest. OE.

SHELLEY From the inmost depths of its green glen. O. SACKS To know about a man, we ask 'What is his story—his real, inmost story?' W. RAEPER It was to Helen that he confided many of his inmost thoughts.

B *n.* The inmost part. OE.

J. FORD Be sure To lodge it in the inmost of thy bosom.

C *adv.* Most inwardly. *rare.* OE.

inmostly *adv.* (*rare*) M19.

inn /ɪn/ *n.* [OE *inn* (corresp. to ON *inni*) f. Gmc, f. base of IN *adv.*] 1 *sing.* & in *pl.* A dwelling-place, an abode, a lodging; a house. Long *obs.* exc. *Sc.* OE. 2 [tr. L *hospitium.*] A house of residence for students. *obs.* exc. as preserved in names of buildings (orig.) so used, esp. *Inns of Chancery*, *Inn of Court* below. ME. 3 A public house providing accommodation, refreshments, etc., for payment, esp. for travellers. Now also, a public house serving alcoholic liquor for consumption on the premises, whether providing accommodation or not. LME.

1 *fig.*: COVERDALE *Isa.* 32:18 The soule is the Inne of God. 3 E. H. JONES The inns where the family stayed on . . the journey. *fig.*: SIR W. SCOTT That dark inn, the grave!

Phrases: **Inns of Chancery** *Hist.* buildings in London formerly used as hostels for law students. **Inn of Court** (*a*) any of the sets of buildings in London belonging to the four legal societies having the exclusive right of admitting people to the English bar; any of these societies; (*b*) a similar society in Ireland. *motor inn*: see MOTOR *n.* & *a.*

Comb.: **innholder** (now *rare* or *obs.*), **innkeeper** a person who manages or owns an inn. **innkeeping** *n.* & *a.* (*a*) *n.* the owning or managing of an inn; (*b*) *adj.* that owns or manages an inn.

inn /ɪn/ *v.*[1] Now *rare.* OE. [f. the n.] 1 *v.t.* Lodge, house, find accommodation for. OE. 2 *v.i.* Lodge, find accommodation, stay. LME. b Of a coach etc.: stop at an inn. M18.

†**inn** *v.*[2] var. of IN *v.*

innards /ˈɪnədz/ *n.pl. colloq.* E19. [Repr. a pronunc. of *inwards* pl. of INWARD *n.*] Entrails; bowels; *fig.* the inside or internal parts.

R. KIPLING 'E feels 'is innards 'eavin', 'is bowels givin' way. R. H. MORRIESON I saw her . . curious and scornful expression that wrung out my innards. E. BLISHEN He . . stared into the piano, as if making an inventory of its innards.

innascibility /ɪ(n)ˌnasɪˈbɪlɪti/ *n.* Now *rare.* E17. [eccl.L *innascibilitas*, f. *innascibilis* incapable of being born, f. as IN-[3] + *nascibilis* who can be born, f. *nasci* be born: see -IBLE, -ITY.] *Chr. Theol.* The attribute of being independent of birth.

R. CUDWORTH God is the only . . Unmade Being . . his very essence is Ingenerability or Innascibility.

innate /ɪˈneɪt, ˈɪneɪt/ *a.* LME. [L *innatus* pa. pple of *innasci*, f. as IN-[2] + *nasci* be born.] 1 Inborn, natural, inherent. LME. 2 *Bot.* Of a part or organ: attached at the apex of another, not adnate. M19.

1 T. COLLINS The horse has not half the innate sagacity of the ox. J. F. KENNEDY As believers in a democratic system, we have always had faith in its innate powers of resistance. A. STORR The disagreement between biologists as to what is learned and what is innate.

innately *adv.* M17. **innateness** *n.* E18. **innatism** *n.* (belief in) the innateness of a quality, aptitude, etc. E20. †**innative** *a.* [after NATIVE *a.*] innate; native: E16–M19.

innavigable /ɪ'navɪgəb(ə)l, ɪn'na-/ *a.* E16. [Fr., or L *innavigabilis*, f. as IN-^{3} + NAVIGABLE.] Not navigable; impassable by boat or ship.

inner /ɪnə/ *a.* & *n.* [OE *inner(r)a*, *in(n)ra* (compar. of IN *adv.*) = OFris. *inra*, OHG *innaro*, *-ero* (G *innere*), ON *innri*, *iðri*: see -ER^{3}.] A *adj.* 1 Situated (more) within or inside; (more or further) inward; internal; *fig.* more secret, central, or essential. Opp. *outer.* OE. 2 Designating the mind or soul; mental; spiritual. Cf. OUTER *a.* 2. OE.

1 U. BENTLEY From the entrance hall.., glassy corridors led away into the inner reaches of the school. M. PIERCY He was a widely social man with inner and outer circles of pals. 2 A. STORR Dreams are dramatizations of situations existing in the patient's inner world. C. G. WOLFF The difficulties..of her life—the sense of inner desolation and loneliness.

Special collocations & comb.: **inner bar** *Law* King's or Queen's Counsel collectively. **inner Cabinet** a group of decision-makers within a ministerial Cabinet etc. **inner circle** an exclusive group of friends or associates within a larger group. **inner city** the central area of a city, esp. if dilapidated or characterized by overcrowding, poverty, etc. **inner-directed** *a.* (*Psychol.*) governed by one's own standards formed in childhood and not by external pressures. *inner ear*: see EAR *n.*^{1} **inner forme** *Printing* the printing surface (orig. type) containing the pages from which the inner side of a sheet is printed, including matter for the second page of the printed sheet. **inner light** in the Society of Friends, direct spiritual contact with God. **inner man** or **woman** (*a*) the soul or mind (of a man or woman); (*b*) *joc.* the stomach (of a man or woman). **inner reserve** *Finance* a secret reserve not disclosed in a balance sheet and due to an understatement of certain capital assets. **inner space** (*a*) the region between the earth and outer space, or below the surface of the sea; (*b*) the part of the mind not normally accessible to consciousness. **inner speech** the mental or internal system or structure which lies behind language. **inner-spring** *a.* & *n.* (*N. Amer.*) (*a*) *adj.* = INTERIOR-*sprung*; (*b*) *n.* an interior-sprung mattress. *Inner Temple*: see TEMPLE *n.*^{1} 6. **inner tube** a separate inflatable tube inside the cover of a pneumatic tyre. *inner woman*: see *inner man* above.

B *n.* The inner part of something; an inner position; *spec.* (a shot which hits) the division of a target next outside the bull's-eye. L19.

Stardust (Bombay) Eagle Casseroles come in a variety of shapes..with..stainless steel inners.

innermore *adv.* & *a.* (*obs.* exc. *dial.*) †(*a*) more inward or within; (*b*) situated more within, inner: ME. **innerness** *n.* L19.

innerly /'ɪnəli/ *a.* Long *obs.* exc. *Sc.* LME. [f. INNER *a.* + -LY^{1}.] 1 Inner, interior. LME. 2 Kindly, affectionate. *Sc.* E19.

innerly /'ɪnəli/ *adv.* Now *literary.* ME. [f. INNER *a.* + -LY^{2}.] Inwardly, internally. Formerly also, more within.

innermost /'ɪnəməʊst/ *a.* & *n.* LME. [f. INNER *a.* + -MOST.] A *adj.* Most or furthest within; inmost, deepest, most secret. LME.

B. BETTELHEIM Asking a child to reveal his.. innermost thoughts to us is a questionable procedure.

B *n.* The or an innermost part. Now *rare.* L17.

innervate /'ɪnəveɪt, ɪ'nəːveɪt/ *v.t.* L19. [f. IN-^{2} + NERVE *n.* + -ATE^{3}.] *Anat.* & *Physiol.* Supply (an organ or part) with nerves, or with nervous stimulation. Chiefly as *innervated* ppl a.

innervation /ɪnə'veɪʃ(ə)n, ɪnəː-/ *n.* M19. [f. as prec. + -ATION.] 1 *Anat.* & *Physiol.* The action or process of innervating; nervous stimulation. Also, the condition of being innervated; the supply of nerve fibres to, or disposition of nerve fibres within, an organ or part. M19. 2 *Psychol.* = KINAESTHESIS. L19.

innerve /ɪ'nəːv/ *v.t.* E19. [f. IN-^{2} + NERVE *v.* or *n.*] Animate, invigorate.

inness /'ɪn-nɪs/ *n.* M19. [f. IN *adv.* or *attrib. a.* + -NESS.] The quality or state of being in.

†**innew** *v.* var. of ENNEW.

inning /'ɪnɪŋ/ *n.*^{1} OE. [f. IN *v.* + -ING^{1}. See also INNINGS.] †1 A putting or getting in; contents; income. Only in OE. 2 The action of getting in, esp. of crops; harvesting. Now *rare* or *obs.* LME. 3 The action of taking in, inclosing, etc.; *esp.* the reclaiming of marsh or flooded land. M16. b In *pl.* Land taken in or reclaimed (from the sea etc.). E18. 4 = INNINGS (earlier). *N. Amer.* M19.

inning /'ɪnɪŋ/ *n.*^{2} Now *rare* or *obs.* OE. [f. INN *v.*^{1} + -ING^{1}.] The action of INN *v.*^{1}; lodging, housing; a lodging.

innings /'ɪnɪŋz/ *n.* Pl. same, (*colloq.*) -es. M18. [f. INNING *n.*^{1} + -S^{1}.] 1 In cricket and similar games: a portion of a game during which a side or a player is in, e.g. batting, hitting, etc.; the play or score of one player during one spell of being in. M18. 2 The time during which a person, party, principle, etc., is in power or possession; a term of or opportunity for an activity; a turn. M19.

1 M. COX Mr. White-Thomson's side owed their victory to the splendid innings of A. C. Benson, Esq. 2 W. R. GREG The new ideas..got their innings, and.. have ruled the national policy from 1830 till 1875. **a good** or **long innings** *colloq.* a long life.

Inniskilling /ɪnɪ'skɪlɪŋ/ *n.* E18. [The county town of Fermanagh, N. Ireland (now *Enniskillen*).] *Hist.* A soldier of a regiment originally raised for the defence of Enniskillen in 1689, later the 5th Royal Inniskilling Dragoon Guards (cf. *the Skins* s.v. SKIN *n.*).

Inniskilliner *n.* L18.

innit /'ɪnɪt/ *int. colloq.* M20. [Repr. a pronunc.] Isn't it. Cf. ENNIT.

†**innoble** *v.* var. of ENNOBLE.

innocence /'ɪnəs(ə)ns/ *n.* ME. [(O)Fr. f. L *innocentia*, f. *innocent-*: see INNOCENT, -ENCE. Cf. next.] 1a Freedom from sin or guilt in general; the state of being untouched by evil; moral purity. ME. b Freedom from specific guilt; the fact of not being guilty of a charge; guiltlessness. M16. 2 Freedom from cunning or artifice; guilelessness, artlessness, simplicity, lack of suspicion; lack of knowledge or sense, naivety. LME. 3 An innocent person or thing. Now *rare.* LME. 4 Harmlessness, innocuousness. *rare.* E19. 5 *Bot.* = BLUET (b). *US.* E19.

1a R. SOUTH How came our first Parents to sin, and to lose their Primitive Innocence? 2 ADDISON My little Daughter..asked me with a great deal of innocence, why I never told them. B. EMECHETA None of them wished to display their innocence..by asking any more questions.

Phrases: INJURED *innocence*.

innocency /'ɪnəs(ə)nsi/ *n.* LME. [L *innocentia*: see prec., -ENCY.] 1a = INNOCENCE 1a. LME. b = INNOCENCE 1b. E16. 2 = INNOCENCE 2. L15. 3 = INNOCENCE 4. M17. 4 = INNOCENCE 3. E18.

innocent /'ɪnəs(ə)nt/ *a.* & *n.* ME. [(O)Fr., or L *innocent-*, f. as IN-^{3} + *nocent-* pres. ppl stem of *nocere* hurt, injure: see -ENT.] A *adj.* 1 Free from sin or guilt in general; morally pure; untouched by evil. ME. 2 Free from specific guilt; that has not committed the offence in question; not deserving the punishment etc. inflicted; not guilty. (Foll. by *of.*) LME. b Foll. by *of*: Free or devoid of; without. *colloq.* E18. c Entirely free of responsibility for or involvement in an event, while suffering circumstantially from it. E19. 3 Devoid of cunning or artifice; guileless, artless, simple; unsuspecting; naive, inexperienced, ingenuous; (now *dial.*) lacking intelligence or sense, halfwitted, imbecile. LME. 4 Not arising from or involving evil intent or motive; producing no ill effect or result; harmless, innocuous; *Med.* not malignant, benign. E16. b That does not break the law; lawful, permitted. E19.

1 M. LEITCH Changing from the innocent slip of a young thing..to the ugly old whore. 2 H. ARENDT Trying to save an innocent man they employed the.. methods..adopted in the case of a guilty one. P. H. JOHNSON He was innocent of the particular badness with which F. had charged him. Z. MEDVEDEV Grishin was possibly not entirely innocent of corruption.

innocent party *Law* (*spec.*, now *Hist.*, in matrimonial proceedings) the party adjudged or agreed to be innocent. b J. COLBORNE The windows are small apertures..innocent of glass. G. DURRELL His skull-cap was innocent of decoration. c *innocent bystander* etc. 3 G. GREENE Milly felt inexperienced and stupidly innocent in front of Kay. K. A. PORTER I *was* innocent ..as a calf;..a simple soul without a care. 4 W. DAMPIER Calabash..is of a sharp and pleasing Taste, and is very innocent. B. FRANKLIN I think no pleasure innocent, that is to man hurtful. **innocent conveyance** *Law* a conveyance which does not have any tortious operation, and does not create a discontinuance or result in forfeiture.

B *n.* 1 A person free from sin, not disposed to do harm, or unacquainted with evil, *esp.* a young child; the class of innocent people. ME. 2 A person innocent of a charge or undeserving of punishment; a guiltless person. Now *rare* or *obs.* ME. 3 A guileless, simple, naive, or unsuspecting person; a person lacking knowledge or intelligence, a simpleton, an idiot. LME. 4 *Bot.* Usu. in *pl.* (treated as *sing.*). = INNOCENCE 5. *US.* M19.

1 ADDISON The pretty Innocent walks blindfold among burning Plough-shares, without being scorched ..by them. **(Holy) Innocents** *the* young children murdered by Herod after the birth of Jesus (*Matt.* 2:16); (*Holy*) *Innocents' Day*, 28 December, on which the massacre of the Holy Innocents is commemorated. 2 J. CHAMBERLAYNE Those who shall conspire to indict an Innocent falsely and maliciously of Felony.

innocently *adv.* LME. †**innocentness** *n.* (*rare*) L15–E18.

innocuity /ɪnɒ'kjuːɪti/ *n.* M19. [f. as next + -ITY.] Innocuousness.

innocuous /ɪ'nɒkjʊəs/ *a.* L16. [f. L *innocuus*, f. as IN-^{3} + *nocuus*, f. *nocere* hurt, + -OUS.] Not harmful or injurious; harmless; inoffensive.

R. L. STEVENSON A tumblerful of the playful, innocuous American cocktail. I. MURDOCH These 'relationships' which Millie cultivated remained at a level of innocuous flirtation.

innocuously *adv.* M17. **innocuousness** *n.* M17.

innominable /ɪ'nɒmɪnəb(ə)l/ *a. arch.* LME. [L *innominabilis*, f. as IN-^{3} + *nominabilis* NOMINABLE.] Impossible to name; not fit to be named.

Fraser's Magazine Those innominable garments, the mere allusion to which is sufficient to shock ears polite.

innominate /ɪ'nɒmɪnət/ *a.* M17. [Late L *innominatus*, f. as IN-^{3} + NOMINATE *a.*] 1 Not named; anonymous. Now *rare* exc. *Anat.* (see below). M17. 2 *Law.* Of a contract: not belonging to any of the recognized categories. L18.

1 **innominate artery** *Anat.* a large artery which branches from the aortic arch and divides into the right common carotid and right subclavian arteries. **innominate bone** *Anat.* either of the two hip-bones formed by the fusion of the ilium, ischium, and pubis. **innominate vein** *Anat.* either of two large veins of the neck formed by the junction of the external jugular and subclavian veins.

in nomine /ɪn 'nəʊmɪneɪ, 'nɒm-/ *n. phr.* M17. [L = in the name (of).] An instrumental composition in fugal style (prob. orig. one set to a Latin text including the words *in nomine*); a free fugue in which the answer does not exactly correspond with the subject.

innovate /'ɪnəveɪt/ *v.* M16. [L *innovat-* pa. ppl stem of *innovare* renew, alter, f. as IN-^{2} + *novare* make new, f. *novus* new: see -ATE^{3}.] †1 *v.t.* Change (a thing) into something new; alter; renew. M16–E19. 2 *v.t.* Introduce (something) for the first time; introduce as new; *Comm.* introduce on to the market. M16. 3 *v.i.* Bring in or introduce something new; make a change or changes in something established. L16.

1 SIR W. SCOTT The dictates of my father were..not to be altered, innovated, or even discussed. 2 *Times Review of Industry* Nylon..was first invented in 1928, but not innovated until 1939. 3 BURKE To innovate is not to reform. *Physics Bulletin* The very large firms,.. do not truly innovate and..may hinder innovation because they are so inflexible.

innovation /ɪnə'veɪʃ(ə)n/ *n.* LME. [L *innovatio(n-)*, f. as prec.: see -ATION.] 1 The action of innovating; the introduction of a new thing; the alteration of something established;

For other words beginning with *in-* see the entry for **in-**^{1}

spec. †(*a*) (political) revolution; (*b*) *Sc. Law* = NOVATION 2; (*c*) *Comm.* the introduction of a new product on to the market. LME. **2** A result or product of innovating; a thing newly introduced; a change made in something; a new practice, method, etc.; *spec.* †(*a*) a (political) revolution; (*b*) *Comm.* a product newly introduced on to the market. LME. **3** *Bot.* A newly formed shoot which has not completed its growth; *spec.* (in a moss) a shoot formed at or near the apex of the thallus, the older parts dying off behind. M19.

1 *Dumfries & Galloway Standard* The Government place considerable emphasis on promoting innovation and enterprise. **2** RBT JOHNSON Neither doth he willingly arme them for feare of sedition and innovations. L. M. MONTGOMERY They've never had a female teacher . . before and she thinks it is a dangerous innovation. E. M. ROGERS It matters little whether or not an innovation has . . advantage over the idea it is replacing.

innovational *a.* E19. **innovationist** *n.* (*rare*) a person who favours innovations E19.

innovative /ˈɪnəveɪtɪv, -vət-/ *a.* E17. [f. INNOVATE + -IVE.] Having the character or quality of innovating; characterized by innovation.

innovatively *adv.* L20. **innovativeness** *n.* M20.

innovator /ˈɪnəveɪtə/ *n.* L16. [Late L, f. as INNOVATE: see -OR.] A person who innovates, an introducer of innovations. Formerly also *spec.*, a revolutionary.

innovatory /ɪnəˈveɪt(ə)ri, ˈɪnəvət-/ *a.* M19. [f. INNOVATE + -ORY[2].] Of innovating character or tendency.

innoxious /ɪˈnɒkʃəs/ *a.* Now *rare.* E17. [f. L *innoxius*, f. as IN-[3] + NOXIOUS, + -OUS.] †**1** Innocent, guiltless, blameless. *rare.* E17–L18. **2** Not noxious; harmless, innocuous. M17.

innoxiously *adv.* M17. **innoxiousness** *n.* M17.

in nubibus /ɪn ˈnjuːbɪbəs/ *adv.* & *a. phr.* L16. [L.] In the clouds; as yet unsettled; undecided; incapable of being carried out.

in nuce /ɪn ˈnuːkeɪ/ *adv. phr.* M19. [L.] In a nutshell; in a condensed form.

innuendo /ɪnjʊˈɛndəʊ/ *v.* E18. [f. the n.] **1** *v.i.* Make innuendoes. E18. **2** *v.t.* Imply or convey by innuendo; attack (a person) by making an innuendo. M18. **3** *v.t.* Chiefly *Law.* Interpret or construe by attaching an innuendo. M19.

innuendo /ɪnjʊˈɛndəʊ/ *adv.* & *n.* M16. [L = by nodding at, pointing to, intimating, abl. gerund of *innuere* nod to, signify, f. as IN-[2] + *nuere* nod.] **A** *adv.* Meaning, that is to say, to wit, (esp. in legal documents, introducing a parenthetical explanation of the precise reference of a preceding noun or pronoun). M16.

B *n.* Pl. **-o(e)s.** **1** A parenthetical explanation of, or construction put upon, a word or expression; *esp.* in an action for libel or slander, the injurious meaning alleged to be conveyed by a word or expression not in itself actionable. L17. **b** A word or expression parenthetically explained; a blank to be filled with the name of the person to whom it is alleged to refer. *arch.* M18. **2** An allusive or oblique remark, hint, or suggestion, usu. disparaging; a remark with a (usu. suggestive) double meaning; allusion, hinting, suggestion. L17.

2 A. WILSON Innuendo, direct attack, or friendly teasing, she had had enough . . criticism for today. L. DEIGHTON Her ears were attuned to chance remarks and she never missed an innuendo. Y. MENUHIN The Kreisler sound was all subtle emphasis, innuendo, dropped hints.

Innuit *n.* & *a.* var. of INUIT.

†**innumberable** *a.* LME–E18. [(O)Fr. *innombrable* f. as next, assim. to *number.*] = next.

innumerable /ɪˈnjuːm(ə)rəb(ə)l/ *a.* & *n.* ME. [L *innumerabilis*, f. as IN-[3] + NUMERABLE.] **A** *adj.* Too many to be counted; numberless, countless. Freq. *postpositive.* ME.

I. WATTS Behold the innumerable host Of Angels cloth'd in light! J. A. MICHENER The Saracens . . would borrow from them concepts innumerable. A. GHOSH The light was filtered through the innumerable . . coconut palms which grew around the house.

B *absol.* as *n.* Countless numbers, many, (†*of*). M16.

innumeraˈbility *n.* E17. **innumerableness** *n.* L16. **innumerably** *adv.* L16.

innumeracy /ɪˈnjuːm(ə)rəsi/ *n.* M20. [f. IN-[3] + NUMERACY.] The quality or state of being innumerate.

innumerate /ɪˈnjuːm(ə)rət/ *a.* & *n.* M20. [f. IN-[3] + NUMERATE *a.*] **A** *adj.* Unacquainted with the basic principles of mathematics and science; not numerate. M20. **B** *n.* An innumerate person. L20.

innumerous /ɪˈnjuːm(ə)rəs/ *a.* Now *literary.* M16. [Late L *innumerosus*, f. as IN-[3] + NUMEROUS.] Innumerable.

innutrition /ɪnjʊˈtrɪʃ(ə)n/ *n.* L18. [f. IN-[3] + NUTRITION.] Lack of nutrition or nourishment.

innutritious /ɪnjʊˈtrɪʃəs/ *a.* L18. [f. IN-[3] + NUTRITIOUS.] Not nutritious; providing no nourishment.

innutritive /ɪˈnjuːtrɪtɪv/ *a.* M19. [f. IN-[3] + NUTRITIVE.] = prec.

ino- /ˈɪnəʊ/ *comb. form* of Gk *is* (genit. *inos*) fibre, muscle: see -O-. Forming mostly ns. in *Physiol.* & *Biochem.*

inogen *n.* (*obs.* exc. *Hist.*) the supposed energy-yielding substance of muscle L19. **inolith** *n.* (*Med.*) a fibrous concretion L19.

-ino /ˈiːnəʊ/ *suff.* Pl. **-inos.** [Extracted from NEUTRINO.] *Particle Physics.* Forming names of particles and quanta from the names of bosons of which they are supersymmetric counterparts, as *gravitino.*

†**inobedience** *n.* ME–L19. [OFr. *inobediance* f. late L *inoboedientia*, f. as IN-[3] + L *obedientia* OBEDIENCE.] = DISOBEDIENCE.

†**inobedient** *a.* ME–E19. [OFr. *inobedient* or late L *inobedient-*, f. as IN-[3] + L *oboedient-* OBEDIENT.] = DISOBEDIENT.

inobnoxious /ɪnəbˈnɒkʃəs/ *a. rare.* M17. [f. IN-[3] + OBNOXIOUS.] Not obnoxious; not exposed *to.*

inobservable /ɪnəbˈzəːvəb(ə)l/ *a.* Long *rare.* E17. [L *inobservabilis*, f. as IN-[3] + *observabilis* OBSERVABLE *a.*] Unable to be observed, not noticeable.

inobservance /ɪnəbˈzəːv(ə)ns/ *n.* E17. [Fr., or L *inobservantia*, f. as IN-[3] + *observantia* OBSERVANCE.] **1** Failure to observe or notice; inattention. E17. **2** Failure to keep or observe a law, custom, promise, etc. E17.

Also **inobservancy** *n.* (*rare*) L17.

inobservant /ɪnəbˈzəːv(ə)nt/ *a.* M17. [Late L *inobservant-*, f. as IN-[3] + OBSERVE + -ANT[1].] That does not observe or notice; unobserving.

inobservation /ˌɪnɒbzəˈveɪʃ(ə)n/ *n. rare.* L16. [f. IN-[3] + OBSERVATION.] †**1** = INOBSERVANCE 2. L16–E18. **2** = INOBSERVANCE I. E18.

inobtrusive /ɪnəbˈtruːsɪv/ *a. rare.* L18. [f. IN-[3] + OBTRUSIVE.] Unobtrusive; modest, retiring.

inoccupation /ˌɪnɒkjʊˈpeɪʃ(ə)n/ *n.* L18. [f. IN-[3] + OCCUPATION.] Lack of occupation; unoccupied condition.

inocula *n.* pl. of INOCULUM.

inoculable /ɪˈnɒkjʊləb(ə)l/ *a.* M19. [f. INOCULATE + -ABLE.] Able to be infected or transmitted by inoculation.

inoculaˈbility *n.* M19.

inoculant /ɪˈnɒkjʊl(ə)nt/ *n.* E20. [f. INOCULATE + -ANT[1].] A substance suitable for inoculating, esp. (*Metall.*) into molten metal.

inoculate /ɪˈnɒkjʊleɪt/ *v.* LME. [L *inoculat-* pa. ppl stem of *inoculare* engraft, implant, f. as IN-[2] + *oculus* eye, bud: see -ATE[3].] **1** *v.t. Hort.* Graft (a bud, a shoot) into a plant of a different type; subject (a plant) to budding. Now *rare* or *obs.* LME. **2** *Med.* & *Biol.* **a** *v.t.* Introduce (an infective agent) into an organism. Also, introduce (cells or organisms) into a culture medium. E18. **b** *v.t.* Introduce an infective agent into (an organism), esp. so as to immunize against a disease; vaccinate. Also, introduce cells or organisms into (a culture medium). E18. **c** *v.i.* Perform inoculation. M18. **d** *v.t. fig.* Imbue (a person, community, etc.) *with* a feeling, habit, etc. E19. **3** *v.t. Metall.* Add a substance to (a molten metal) in order to modify the microstructure of the cast metal. M20.

1 *fig.*: SHAKES. *Haml.* Virtue cannot so inoculate our old stock but we shall relish of it.

inoculative *a.* characterized by or pertaining to inoculation E18. **inoculator** *n.* E17.

inoculation /ɪˌnɒkjʊˈleɪʃ(ə)n/ *n.* LME. [L *inoculatio(n-)* grafting, f. as prec.: see -ATION.] †**1** *Hort.* Grafting, esp. of a bud into a plant of a different type. LME–L18. **2a** *Med.* & *Vet. Med.* The deliberate introduction into the body of a micro-organism (orig. *spec.*, of smallpox virus), esp. in order to induce immunity to a disease; vaccination. Also occas., accidental infection through a wound. E18. **b** *Microbiol.* The (usu. deliberate) introduction of a micro-organism into a plant, or into a culture medium. L19. **3** *Metall.* The addition of an inoculant to molten metal. M20.

inoculist /ɪˈnɒkjʊlɪst/ *n. rare.* L18. [f. INOCULATION + -IST. Cf. Fr. *inoculiste.*] A person who practises or advocates inoculation.

inoculum /ɪˈnɒkjʊləm/ *n.* Pl. **-la** /-lə/. E20. [f. L *inoculare* INOCULATE after *coagulum.*] (A quantity of) infective material used for or capable of inoculating an organism or culture medium.

†**inodiate** *v.t.* M17–E18. [Late L *inodiat-* pa. ppl stem of *inodiare*, ult. f. L *in odio*: see ANNOY *n.*, -ATE[3].] Make odious.

inodorous /ɪnˈəʊd(ə)rəs/ *a.* M17. [f. L *inodorus* (f. as IN-[3] + *odorus* ODOROUS) + -OUS, or f. IN-[3] + ODOROUS.] **1** Without odour, smell, or scent. M17. **2** Having an unpleasant smell; malodorous. E19.

inodorously *adv.* M19.

in-off /ɪnˈɒf/ *n.* M20. [f. IN *adv.* + OFF *prep.*] *Billiards & Snooker.* = *losing hazard* s.v. HAZARD *n.*

inoffensive /ɪnəˈfɛnsɪv/ *a.* E17. [f. IN-[3] + OFFENSIVE *a.*] **1** Not objectionable or offensive; not causing offence. E17. **2** Doing or causing no harm; innocuous, unoffending. M17.

1 J. HELLER He laughed in the friendliest, most inoffensive fashion. **2** R. DAVIES Sherry is not the inoffensive drink innocent people suppose.

inoffensively *adv.* L16. **inoffensiveness** *n.* M17.

inofficial /ɪnəˈfɪʃ(ə)l/ *a. rare.* M17. [f. IN-[3] + OFFICIAL *a.*] Not official, unofficial.

inofficious /ɪnəˈfɪʃəs/ *a.* E17. [L *inofficiosus*, f. as IN-[3] + *officiosus* OFFICIOUS, or f. IN-[3] + OFFICIOUS.] †**1** Not ready to do one's duty; not inclined to oblige. E17–M19. **2** *Law.* Not in accordance with moral duty. M17. **3** Without purpose, function, or operation. L19.

2 inofficious testament: making no legacy to relatives or others who have a moral claim on the testator.

inoperable /ɪnˈɒp(ə)rəb(ə)l/ *a.* L19. [f. IN-[3] + OPERABLE.] **1** Unable to be operated on successfully, unsuitable for a surgical operation. L19. **2** Unable to be operated or used; unfit for use; unworkable, impractical. M20.

1 I. MURDOCH She developed a quick inoperable tumour and passed away. **2** *Daily Telegraph* Eight of the fire extinguishers were inoperable. V. S. NAIPAUL That gift of fantasy became inoperable as soon as I came to England.

inoperaˈbility *n.* M20. **inoperably** *adv.* L20.

inoperative /ɪnˈɒp(ə)rətɪv/ *a.* M17. [f. IN-[3] + OPERATIVE *a.*] Not operative; not working; *Law* without practical force, invalid.

inoperativeness *n.* L19.

inoperculate /ɪnəˈpəːkjʊlət/ *a.* & *n.* M19. [f. IN-[3] + OPERCULATE *a.*] *Bot.* & *Zool.* **A** *adj.* Lacking an operculum (as certain snails, fungal asci, etc.). M19. **B** *n.* An inoperculate organism (esp. a fungus). M20.

†**inopinate** *a.* L16–E19. [L *inopinatus*, f. as IN-[3] + *opinatus* pa. pple of *opinari* suppose, believe, think: see -ATE[2].] Not thought of; unexpected.

inopportune /ɪnˈɒpətjuːn, ˌɪnɒpəˈtjuːn/ *a.* E16. [Late L *inopportunus* unfitting, f. as IN-[3] + *opportunus* OPPORTUNE.] Not opportune; inappropriate, inconvenient; unsuited to the moment or occasion; untimely.

inopportunely *adv.* M16. **inopportuneness** *n.* M19.

For other words beginning with *in-* see the entry for **in-**[1]

inopportunism *n.* the habit of acting inopportunely; the state or fact of being inopportune: L19.

inopportunist /ˌɪnɒpəˈtjuːnɪst/ *n.* & *a.* L19. [f. prec. + -IST, after *opportunist*.] A *n.* A person who believes a policy or action to be inopportune; *esp.* (*Hist.*) a person who in 1870 opposed the doctrine of papal infallibility as inopportune. L19. B *adj.* Of or belonging to inopportunists. L19.

inopportunity /ˌɪnɒpəˈtjuːnɪti/ *n.* E16. [Late L *inopportunitas*, f. as INOPPORTUNE, or f. INOPPORTUNE: see -ITY.] The quality or fact of being inopportune.

inoppressive /ɪnəˈprɛsɪv/ *a. rare.* M17. [f. IN-[3] + OPPRESSIVE *a.*] Not oppressive.

inoppugnable /ɪnəˈpʌgnəb(ə)l/ *a. rare.* L19. [f. IN-[3] + OPPUGN + -ABLE.] Unassailable.

inorb /ɪˈnɔːb/ *v.t.* M19. [f. IN-[2] + ORB *n.*[1]] Place in an orb; enclose or surround with an orb; encircle.

inorderly /ɪnˈɔːdəli/ *adv.* & *a.* Chiefly *Sc.* Now *rare.* L15. [f. IN-[3] + ORDERLY *adv.*, *a.*] A *adv.* In a disorderly manner, irregularly. L15. B *adj.* Disorderly, irregular. L16.

inordinacy /ɪˈnɔːdɪnəsi/ *n.* E17. [f. INORDINATE: see -ACY.] The quality or condition of being inordinate; immoderation.

†**inordinance** *n.* LME–L18. [f. IN-[3] + ORDINANCE, assoc. w. INORDINATE.] An inordinate action or practice; an excess.

inordinancy /ɪˈnɔːdɪnənsi/ *n.* Now *rare.* E17. [f. as prec.: see -ANCY.] = INORDINACY.

inordinate /ɪˈnɔːdɪnət/ *a.* LME. [L *inordinatus*, f. as IN-[3] + *ordinatus* pa. pple of *ordinare* ORDAIN: see -ATE[2].] 1 Devoid of order; deviating from the rule; irregular; not controlled or restrained. LME. 2 Not kept within orderly limits; immoderate, excessive. LME. 3 Of a person: not conforming or subject to law or order; disorderly, unrestrained in feelings or conduct. LME. †4 *Math.* Irregular; not in regular order; not equilateral. L16–E19.

1 J. R. ILLINGWORTH To restore this inordinate state of humanity to order. 2 A. S. BYATT There are faces in history that have attracted an inordinate share of devotion. 3 K. TYNAN Shakespeare is dealing with the problem of inordinate men.

inordinately *adv.* LME. **inordinateness** *n.* L16.

inordination /ɪˌnɔːdɪˈneɪʃ(ə)n/ *n.* Now *rare.* E17. [L *inordinatio(n-)* disorder, f. as IN-[3] + *ordinatio(n-)* ORDINATION.] Inordinacy.

inorganic /ɪnɔːˈganɪk/ *a.* & *n.* L18. [f. IN-[3] + ORGANIC.] A *adj.* 1a Not having the characteristics of living organisms; inanimate; not composed of or derived from living matter. L18. b *Chem.* Orig., of, pertaining to, or designating substances not derived from or found in living organisms. Now, of, pertaining to, or designating substances which do not contain carbon (except in some simple cases: see note below). Cf. ORGANIC *a.* 4b. M19. 2 Not provided with or acting by bodily organs. E19. 3 Not arising or growing naturally from an organization or structure; artificial; extraneous. M19. 4 Without organization or systematic arrangement. M19.

1b **inorganic chemistry** the branch of chemistry that deals with the properties and reactions of inorganic substances. 2 SHELLEY Speak Spirit! from thine inorganic voice I only know that thou art moving near.

B *n. Chem.* An inorganic chemical. M20.

¶Simple compounds of carbon, as oxides, carbonates, carbides, and forms of the pure element, as diamond and graphite, are classed as inorganic.

†**inorganical** *a.* (*a*) = INORGANIC *a.* 2; (*b*) = INORGANIC *a.* 1: only in 17. **inorganically** *adv.* (*a*) without (reference to) organization; (*b*) not by the action of living organisms: L17.

inorganization /ˌɪnɔːg(ə)nʌɪˈzeɪʃ(ə)n/ *n.* Also **-isation**. M19. [f. IN-[3] + ORGANIZATION.] Absence of organization; unorganized condition.

inorganized /ɪnˈɔːg(ə)nʌɪzd/ *a.* Also **-ised**. M17. [f. IN-[3] + ORGANIZE *v.* + -ED[1].] Not organized; lacking organization.

inornate /ɪnˈɔːnɪt, ɪnɔːˈneɪt/ *a.* E16. [L *inornatus*, f. as IN-[3] + *ornatus* ORNATE, or f. IN-[3] + ORNATE *a.*] Not ornate; unadorned, plain; simple.

inosculate /ɪˈnɒskjʊleɪt/ *v.i.* & *t.* L17. [f. IN-[2] + L *osculare* furnish with a mouth or outlet, f. *osculum* dim. of *os* mouth, after Gk *anastomoun* (see ANASTOMOSIS): see -ATE[3].] 1 Chiefly *Anat.* (Cause to) be united by interpenetrating or fitting closely together; intertwine. (Foll. by *with.*) *arch.* L17. 2 *Anat.* Connect or be connected by anastomosis; anastomose. *arch.* L17. 3 *transf.* & *fig.* (Cause to) grow together, pass into, or unite closely. E19.

inoscuˈlation *n.* L17.

inosic /ɪˈnəʊsɪk/ *a.* M19. [f. INO- + -OSE[2] + -IC.] = INOSINIC.

inosate *n.* = INOSINATE M19.

inosine /ˈɪnə(ʊ)siːn/ *n.* Also †**-in**. E20. [f. as prec. + -INE[5], -IN[1].] *Biochem.* A naturally occurring nucleoside composed of hypoxanthine linked to ribose, which is an important intermediate in the metabolism of purine and is used in kidney transplantation to provide a temporary source of sugar.

inosinic /ɪnə(ʊ)ˈsɪnɪk/ *a.* M19. [f. as prec. + -IC.] Biochem. *inosinic acid*, a colourless crystalline organic acid, the phosphate of inosine, which is important in nucleic acid synthesis.

inosinate /ɪˈnəʊsɪneɪt/ *n.* a salt or ester of inosinic acid M19.

†**inosite** *n.* M–L19. [f. as INOSIC + -ITE[1].] *Chem.* = next.

inositol /ʌɪˈnəʊsɪtɒl/ *n.* L19. [f. prec. + -OL.] *Biochem.* Each of the nine stereoisomers of hexahydroxycyclohexane, $(\cdot CHOH\cdot)_6$; *spec.* = MYO-INOSITOL.

inostensible /ɪnɒˈstɛnsɪb(ə)l/ *a.* L18. [f. IN-[3] + OSTENSIBLE.] Not ostensible; unavowed.

inostensibly *adv.* L18.

inotropism /ɪnə(ʊ)ˈtrəʊpɪz(ə)m/ *n.* E20. [f. INO- + TROPISM.] *Physiol.* Modification of the force or speed of contraction of muscle.

inotropic /-ˈtrəʊpɪk, -ˈtrɒpɪk/ *a.* E20.

in ovo /ɪn ˈəʊvəʊ/ *adv. phr.* M19. [L.] In the egg; in embryo (*lit.* & *fig.*).

inower /ɪnˈaʊə, ɪnˈəʊə/ *adv. Sc.* M16. [f. IN *adv.* + Sc. form of OVER *adv.*] In towards some point; *esp.* nearer a fire.

inoxidable /ɪnˈɒksɪdəb(ə)l/ *a. rare.* M19. [f. IN-[3] + OXIDABLE.] = INOXIDIZABLE.

inoxidizable /ɪnˈɒksɪdʌɪzəb(ə)l/ *a.* Also **-isable**. M19. [f. IN-[3] + OXIDIZABLE.] Not (readily) oxidizable; not susceptible to rusting.

in pari materia /ɪn ˌpɑːri məˈtɛːrɪə, ɪn ˌpɛːri məˈtɪərɪə/ *adv. phr.* M19. [L.] In an equivalent case or position.

in partibus /ɪn ˈpɑːtɪbəs/ *adv. phr.* L17. [L *in partibus* (*infidelium*) in the regions (of the infidels).] *RC Ch.* In full *in partibus infidelium* /ɪnfɪˈdeɪlɪəm, -ˈdiːl-/. In heretical territory (w. ref. to a titular bishop etc., esp. in a Muslim country).

in parvo /ɪn ˈpɑːvəʊ, -wəʊ/ *adv. phr.* E20. [L.] In little, in miniature, on a small scale.

in-patient /ˈɪnpeɪʃ(ə)nt/ *n.* M18. [f. IN-[1] + PATIENT *n.*] A patient who stays overnight in a hospital where he or she receives medical attention. Opp. *out-patient*.

in pectore /ɪn ˈpɛktəri/ *adv. phr.* M19. [L = in one's breast.] = IN PETTO 1.

in perpetuum /ɪn pəˈpɛtjʊəm/ *adv. phr.* M17. [L.] For all time, in perpetuity.

in personam /ɪn pəˈsəʊnam/ *a. phr.* L18. [L = against a person.] *Law.* Made or availing against or affecting a specific person only; imposing a personal liability. Freq. *postpositive*. Cf. IN REM.

in petto /ɪn ˈpɛtəʊ/ *adv. phr.* L17. [It. = in the breast.] 1 In contemplation; undisclosed, secretly, (esp. of the appointment of cardinals not named as such). L17. 2 [By confusion w. PETTY *a.*] In miniature, on a small scale; in short. M19.

in-phase /ˈɪnfeɪz, ɪnˈfeɪz/ *a.* E20. [f. IN-[1] + PHASE *n.*] Of, pertaining to, or designating electrical signals that are in phase.

in-pig /ɪnˈpɪg, ˈɪnpɪg/ *a.* M20. [f. IN-[1] + PIG *n.*[1]] Of a sow: that is in pig; pregnant.

in pontificalibus /ɪn ˌpɒntɪfɪˈkeɪlɪbəs, -ˈkɑːl-/ *adv. phr.* LME. [L: see also PONTIFICALIBUS.] In the full vestments of a cardinal, archbishop, etc.; in pontificals.

in posse /ɪn ˈpɒsi/ *a. phr.* L16. [L.] In the condition of being possible. Opp. IN ESSE.

in potentia /ɪn pəˈtɛnʃɪə/ *adv. phr.* E17. [L.] In potentiality.

inpouring /ˈɪnpɔːrɪŋ/ *n.* E18. [f. IN-[1] + POURING *n.*] The action or an act of pouring something in; (an) infusion. Also, (an) inflow, (an) inrush.

in propria persona /ɪn ˌprəʊprɪə pəˈsəʊnə, pɔː-/ *adv. phr.* M17. [L.] In one's own person.

in puris naturalibus /ɪn ˌpjʊərɪs natjʊˈrɑːlɪbəs, -ˈreɪl-/ *adv. phr.* E17. [L. Cf. PURIS NATURALIBUS.] In one's natural state; stark naked.

input /ˈɪnpʊt/ *n.* E16. [f. IN-[1] + PUT *n.*[1]] †1 An insertion. *Sc.* Only in E16. 2 A sum put in; a contribution. *Sc.* M17. 3 What is put into or utilized by any process or system; something contributed to a whole. L19. b The energy supplied to a machine; *spec.* an electrical signal entering an electronic device. E20. c *Econ.* The total resources (including raw materials, manpower, etc.) necessary to production, which are deducted from output in calculating profits. E20. d Data or program instructions fed into or processed by a computer. M20. 4 A place where or a device through which an input (esp. an electrical signal) may enter a system. E20. 5 The process of putting in or feeding in; *esp.* the feeding of data etc. into a computer. M20.

3 C. HOPE We weren't connected to the structures of Government power, we had no input there. c *Ecologist* The poor.. never will be able to pay for.. the inputs required for technological agriculture. 4 *Hi-Fi Sound* This recorder has inputs for microphone, radio and magnetic and/or ceramic pickup cartridges. 5 H. M. ROSENBERG A counter.. enables the data to be recorded automatically in digital form for computer input.

input /ˈɪnpʊt/ *v.t.* Infl. **-tt-**. Pa. t. & pple **-put**, (sense 3 also) **-putted**. LME. [f. IN-[1] + PUT *v.*[1]: in earliest use after L *imponere*, in mod. use after the n.] †1 Put on, impose. Only in LME. †2 Install as a tenant; appoint to an office. *Sc.* L15–M18. 3 Feed (data, a program) into a computer. (Foll. by *to*, *into*.) M20.

inquartation /ɪnkwɔːˈteɪʃ(ə)n/ *n.* L19. [Fr., or f. IN-[2] + QUARTATION.] The addition of silver to gold so as to make the proportions at least three to one prior to purification of the gold using nitric acid.

inquest /ˈɪnkwɛst/ *n.* Also †**en-**. ME. [OFr. *enqueste* (mod. *enquête*) f. Proto-Romance & med.L *inquesta* use as n. of fem. pa. pple of Proto-Romance var. of L *inquirere* INQUIRE.] 1 A judicial inquiry by means of a jury to decide a matter of fact; *spec.* an inquiry by a coroner's court into the cause of a sudden, unexplained, or suspicious death. Formerly, any official inquiry into a matter of public interest. ME. 2 A jury appointed to decide a matter of fact; *spec.* a coroner's jury. ME. 3 *gen.* & *transf.* †a A question, a query. LME–M19. †b A search for something; orig. *esp.* a knight's quest for adventure. L15–L17. c An investigation into a matter. Now chiefly (*colloq.*) a discussion, after the event, of a (poor) performance in a game, an examination, etc. E17.

1 W. STUBBS The great inquest of all, the Domesday survey. S. COX The searching inquest of the Judge eternal. **inquest of office** an inquiry held by a jury and an officer of the Crown to decide cases of escheat, forfeiture, etc., that would entitle the Crown to the possession of land. 2 **grand** or **great inquest** *Hist.* a grand jury (*grand* or *great inquest of the nation*, the House of Commons).

inquiet /ɪnˈkwʌɪət/ *a.* Now *rare.* LME. [L *inquietus*, f. as IN-[3] + QUIET *a.*] †1 Restless, turbulent. LME–M16. 2 Anxious, uneasy in mind. E16.

inquietly *adv.* (*rare*) LME.

inquiet /ɪnˈkwʌɪət/ *v.t.* Now *rare.* LME. [(O)Fr. *inquiéter* f. L *inquietare*, f. as prec.] 1 Disturb the peace or repose of (a person); harass, molest. LME. 2 Make uneasy, disquiet. L15.

inquieˈtation *n.* the action of disturbing or molesting; the condition of being disturbed: LME.

inquietude /ɪnˈkwʌɪətjuːd/ *n.* LME. [(O)Fr. *inquiétude* or late L *inquietudo*, f. as INQUIET *a.*: see -TUDE.] †1 Disturbance of one's peace or repose; molestation. LME–L18. 2 *Med.* Restlessness of the body caused by pain, discomfort, etc. Now *rare.* L16. 3 Uneasiness of mind, disquietude; in *pl.*, disquieting thoughts. M17.

inquiline /ˈɪnkwɪlʌɪn/ *n.* M17. [L *inquilinus* sojourner, f. *incolere* inhabit, f. as IN-[2] + *colere* dwell: see -INE[1].] 1 A person who sojourns or lodges in a place. *rare.* M17. 2 An animal which lives in the abode of another which tolerates its presence; *spec.* in *Entomol.*, an insect which lodges in a gall produced by another species. L19.

inquilinism /ˈɪnkwɪlɪnɪz(ə)m/ *n.* the habit or condition of being an inquiline L20. **inquiˈlinous** *a.* living in the nest or gall of another animal L19.

inquinate /ˈɪnkwɪneɪt/ *v.t.* Now *rare.* M16. [L *inquinat-* pa. ppl stem of *inquinare* pollute: see -ATE[3].] Pollute, taint, corrupt.

inquiˈnation *n.* (*a*) the action of polluting; polluted condition; (*b*) a defilement, a polluting agent: LME.

inquirable /ɪnˈkwʌɪərəb(ə)l/ *a.* Now *rare* or *obs.* Also **en-** /ɪn-, ɛn-/. L15. [f. INQUIRE + -ABLE.] Chiefly *Law.* That admits or calls for inquiry.

inquiration /ɪnkwʌɪˈreɪʃ(ə)n/ *n. dial.* & *colloq.* Also **en-** /ɪn-, ɛn-/. L18. [Irreg. f. next + -ATION.] Enquiry; an enquiry.

inquire /ɪnˈkwʌɪə/ *v.* Also **en-** /ɪn-, ɛn-/ (see note below). ME. [OFr. *enquerre* (mod. new formation *enquérir*) f. Proto-Romance var. of L *inquirere*, f. as IN-[2] + *quaerere* ask.] 1 †**a** *v.t.* Examine, investigate. ME–L18. **b** *v.i.* Make investigation (*into*). ME. 2 *v.t.* Seek knowledge of (a thing) by asking a question; ask to be told. (Foll. by subord. cl. (& direct speech) or (now less usu.) simple obj., *of* or (*Sc.*) *at* the person asked.) ME. 3 *v.i.* Put a question or questions; ask. (Foll. by *about* or *after* a matter, *of* or (*Sc.*) *at* the person asked.) ME. **b** Foll. by *for*, (arch.) *after*: make request for (a thing); ask to see (a person). E16. †4 *v.t.* Question, interrogate, (a person). ME–L17. †5 *v.t.* Search for, try to find; *esp.* search *out.* ME–L18. †6 *v.t.* Call for, require. *rare.* E16–M17. †7 *v.t.* Name, call. *rare* (Spenser). Only in L16.

1a J. WOODALL The use of a Probe . . sometimes to enquire the depth of a wound. **b** B. BETTELHEIM He felt no need to inquire into my motives. 2 R. BURNS The wily mother . . inquires his name. S. LEWIS Club members . . stopped him to inquire, 'How's your good lady getting on?' W. TREVOR She enquired of me if I knew . . Lady Lord-Blood. 3 H. JAMES She enquired scrupulously about her husband's health. M. COX He had been encouraged to inquire freely of his parents on religious matters. **inquire after** *spec.* make inquiries about the health etc. of. **b** AV *Acts* 9:11 Inquire in the house of Judas, for one called Saul of Tarsus. *Harper's Magazine* I enquired at house after house for board.

¶Recent UK usage tends to distinguish *enquire* = ask, *inquire* = make investigation; the distinction is not made in North America.

inquirer *n.* L16. **inquiring** *ppl a.* that inquires; seeking or disposed to seek information, answers, etc.: L16. **inquiringly** *adv.* M17.

inquirendo /ɪnkwʌɪˈrɛndəʊ/ *n.* Pl. **-os.** E17. [L (= by inquiring), abl. gerund of *inquirere* INQUIRE.] 1 *Law* (now *Hist.*). An authorization to an official to make investigation on behalf of the Crown or government. E17. 2 *gen.* An investigation. M19.

inquiry /ɪnˈkwʌɪri/ *n.* Also **en-** /ɪn-, ɛn-/ (see note below). LME. [f. INQUIRE + -Y[3].] I 1 Investigation, examination. LME. 2 An investigation, an examination, *esp.* an official one; *spec.* (in full *public inquiry*) a judicial investigation, held under the auspices of a Government department, into a matter of public concern. E16.

2 J. BARTH A special . . inquiry into the circumstances surrounding his death.

II 3 The putting of a question, asking, interrogation; *Comm.* demand for a commodity. LME. 4 A question, a query. M16.

3 A. GOLDING We coulde learne nothinge therof by enquiry. *Stock & Land* (*Melbourne*) Inquiry for good cattle from northern N.S.W. had strengthened considerably since the rain. 4 N. MAILER Leonard . . had already made his inquiries about who owned the estate.

Phrases: *court of inquiry*: see COURT *n.*[1] *directory enquiries*: see DIRECTORY *n.* *help the police in* (or *with*) *their enquiries*: see HELP *v.* 5c. *jury of inquiry*: see JURY *n.* *public inquiry*: see sense 2 above. *tribunal of inquiry*: see TRIBUNAL *n.* 3. *writ of inquiry*: see WRIT *n.* 2.

Comb.: **inquiry agent** a private detective; **inquiry office** an office answering questions from callers etc.

¶In Britain now freq. spelt *in-* in branch I, *en-* in branch II: cf. INQUIRE *v.*

†**inquisite** *v.t.* M17–M18. [f. L *inquisit-* (see next) or back-form. f. INQUISITION *n.*] 1 Proceed against (a person) by the methods of the Inquisition. M17–M18. 2 Make inquiry into, investigate. M17–M18.

inquisition /ɪŋkwɪˈzɪʃ(ə)n/ *n.* In sense 3 usu. **I-**. LME. [(O)Fr. f. L *inquisitio(n-)*, f. *inquisit-* pa. ppl stem of *inquirere* INQUIRE: see -ION.] 1 (An instance of) the action or process of inquiring deeply into a matter in order to discover the facts; (a) searching examination or investigation. LME. 2 A judicial inquiry, an inquest. Also, a document recording the results of such an inquiry. LME. 3 *Hist.* *The* judicial institution set up by the papacy in 1232 for the persecution of heresy by special ecclesiastical courts. Also (in full *Spanish Inquisition*), *the* organization with similar functions established under the Spanish crown in 1479, which became notorious for its severity. E16. 4 A relentless questioning of a person. M19.

4 K. WILLIAMS An interview which she described as 'a 1½ hour inquisition'.

inquisitional *a.* pertaining to the Inquisition or to (esp. harsh or relentless) inquiry M17.

inquisition /ɪŋkwɪˈzɪʃ(ə)n/ *v.t.* M17. [f. the n.] *Hist.* Proceed against by the Inquisition.

inquisitive /ɪnˈkwɪzɪtɪv/ *a.* LME. [OFr. *inquisitif*, *-tive* f. late L *inquisitivus*, f. L *inquisit-*: see INQUISITION *n.*, -IVE.] Given to or desirous of inquiring; of an inquiring turn of mind; intellectually curious; *spec.* unduly curious about the affairs of others, prying.

CONAN DOYLE The garbage papers which cater for an inquisitive public. A. F. DOUGLAS-HOME Man is incurably inquisitive, and always trying to discover the origin of things. J. MORTIMER A pale man with inquisitive, almost colourless eyes. A. BROOKNER They were not inquisitive about my habits or relationships.

inquisitively *adv.* L16. **inquisitiveness** *n.* L16.

inquisitor /ɪnˈkwɪzɪtə/ *n.* In sense 2 also **I-**. LME. [Fr. *inquisiteur* (AN *-tour*) f. L *inquisitor*, f. *inquisit-*: see INQUISITION *n.*, -OR.] 1 A person whose official duty is to inquire or examine (in matters of crime, taxation, etc.); *gen.* a curious inquirer, an investigator. LME. †**b** An informer, a spy. L16–L18. 2 *Hist.* An officer of the Inquisition, esp. the Spanish Inquisition. M16.

2 **Grand Inquisitor** the director of the court of the Inquisition in some countries. **Inquisitor-General** the head of the Spanish Inquisition.

inquisitorship *n.* M19. **inquisitress** *n.* a female inquisitor E18.

inquisitorial /ɪnˌkwɪzɪˈtɔːrɪəl/ *a.* M18. [f. as next + -AL[1].] 1 Of, relating to, or functioning as an (official) inquisitor. M18. **b** Offensively or impertinently curious; prying. L18. 2 Of a system of criminal procedure: in which the judge rather than a prosecutor investigates the facts. Opp. *accusatorial.* M19.

inquisitorially *adv.* M19. **inquisitorialness** *n.* M19.

inquisitory /ɪnˈkwɪzɪt(ə)ri/ *a.* Now *rare* or *obs.* M17. [med.L *inquisitorius*, f. L INQUISITOR: see -ORY[2].] = INQUISITORIAL 1.

inquorate /ɪnˈkwɔːrət, -eɪt/ *a.* L20. [f. IN-[3] + QUORATE.] Of a meeting: not quorate, not having a quorum.

†**inrage** *v.* var. of ENRAGE.

†**inrail** *v.t.* Also (earlier) **en-**. E16–E18. [f. IN-[1], EN-[1] + RAIL *v.*[2]] Enclose (as) with rails; rail in.

†**inrapture** *v.* var. of ENRAPTURE.

in re /ɪn ˈreɪ, ɪn ˈriː/ *adv.*, *a.*, & *prep. phr.* E17. [L.] **A** *adv. phr.* In reality. E17. **B** *adj. phr.* 1 *Logic.* = EXTRA DICTIONEM. M19. 2 *Philos.* Of a universal: existing only in the particulars that instantiate it. Cf. ANTE REM, POST REM. L19. **C** *prep. phr.* In the (legal) case of; with regard to. Cf. RE *prep.* L19.

†**inregister** *v.* see ENREGISTER.

in rem /ɪn ˈrɛm/ *a. phr.* M18. [L = against a thing.] *Law.* Made or availing against or affecting a thing, and therefore other people generally; imposing a general liability. Freq. *postpositive.* Cf. IN PERSONAM.

in rerum natura /ɪn ˌreɪrəm nəˈtjʊərə, ˌrɪərəm/ *adv. phr.* L16. [L.] In nature, in the physical world.

†**inrich** *v.* var. of ENRICH.

inro /ˈɪnrəʊ/ *n.* Pl. **-os**, same. E17. [Jap. *inrō*, f. *in* seal + *rō* basket.] An ornamental box with compartments for seals, medicines, etc., formerly worn by Japanese on a girdle.

inroad /ˈɪnrəʊd/ *n.* M16. [f. IN *adv.* + ROAD *n.*, in sense 'riding'.] 1 A hostile incursion; a raid, a foray. M16. 2 *transf.* & *fig.* A serious or significant encroachment (*on*, *upon*) or intrusion (*into*). Now usu. in *pl.* M17.

2 J. R. GREEN They protested against . . Papal inroads on the liberties of the Church. B. T. BRADFORD The Ninth Earl . . had . . made considerable inroads into their immense wealth. *Atlantic Monthly* Democrats have made substantial inroads among affluent upper-middle-class voters.

inroad /ˈɪnrəʊd/ *v.* E17. [f. the n.] †1 *v.t.* Make an inroad into, invade. E–M17. 2 *v.i.* Make inroads. *rare.* M19.

†**inrol** *v.* var. of ENROL.

inrolled /ˈɪnrəʊld, ɪnˈrəʊld/ *a.* L19. [f. IN-[1] + ROLL *v.* + -ED[1].] *Bot.* Having the margins rolled inwards; involute.

inrolling /ˈɪnrəʊlɪŋ/ *ppl a.* L19. [f. IN-[1] + ROLLING *a.*] Of a wave etc.: that rolls in.

inroot *v.* var. of ENROOT.

inrun /ˈɪnrʌn/ *n.* L19. [f. IN-[1] + RUN *n.* In sense 2 tr. G *Anlauf.*] 1 An act of running in; an inrush. L19. 2 In ski-jumping: an approach run. M20.

inrunning /ˈɪnrʌnɪŋ/ *ppl a.* M19. [f. IN-[1] + RUNNING *ppl a.*] Of a bay etc.: extending far inland. Of a stream: flowing into a larger stream, the sea, etc.

inruption /ɪnˈrʌpʃ(ə)n/ *n.* E19. [Refash. of IRRUPTION, emphasizing *in-*.] A violent bursting in.

inrush /ˈɪnrʌʃ/ *n.* E19. [f. IN-[1] + RUSH *n.*[2]] A rushing in, an influx.

inrush /ɪnˈrʌʃ/ *v.i.* Now *rare.* E17. [f. IN-[1] + RUSH *v.*[2]] Enter with force or speed; rush in.

inrushing /ˈɪnrʌʃɪŋ/ *ppl a.* M19. [f. IN-[1] + RUSH *v.*[2] + -ING[2].] Entering with speed or force; rushing in.

†**insabbatist** *n. rare.* M17–E19. [f. Fr. *insabbaté* or med.L *insabbatus*, *-sab(b)atatus*, + -IST.] A member of the sect of the Waldenses.

in saecula saeculorum /ɪn ˈsʌɪkjʊlə sʌɪkjʊˈlɔːrəm/ *adv. phr.* L16. [Late L = to the ages of ages.] To all eternity; for ever.

insalivate /ɪnˈsalɪveɪt/ *v.t.* M19. [f. IN-[2] + SALIVATE.] 1 Mix or impregnate (food) with saliva. M19. 2 Moisten with saliva. L19.

insaliˈvation *n.* M19.

insalubrious /ɪnsəˈl(j)uːbrɪəs/ *a.* M17. [f. L *insalubris*, f. as IN-[3] + *salubris* SALUBRIOUS: see -OUS.] Esp. of a climate or locality: not salubrious, unhealthy.

insalubrity /ɪnsəˈl(j)uːbrɪti/ *n.* M17. [Fr. *insalubrité* or f. IN-[3] + SALUBRITY.] Unhealthy character (esp. of a climate or locality); unwholesomeness.

insalutary /ɪnˈsaljʊt(ə)ri/ *a.* L17. [f. IN-[3] + SALUTARY *a.*] 1 Harmful to health; insalubrious. L17. 2 Not having a healthy mental or social influence. *rare.* M19.

For other words beginning with *in-* see the entry for **in-**[1]

insane /ɪnˈseɪn/ *a.* & *n.* M16. [L *insanus*, f. as IN-^{3} + SANE.] A *adj.* 1 In a state of mind that precludes normal perception and behaviour, and ordinary social interaction; mad; psychotic. M16. b Reserved or intended for the use of mentally ill people. E19. †2 Causing insanity. Only in E17. 3 Of an action: extremely foolish, irrational. M19.

1 P. THEROUX She lost her mind and died insane. b D. WIGODER I didn't need to be locked up in an insane asylum. 2 SHAKES. *Macb.* Have we eaten on the insane root That takes the reason prisoner? 3 D. DELILLO 'When are you off?' 'A seven o'clock flight. . Isn't it insane?'

B *n.* 1 An insane person. *arch.* L18. 2 *collect. pl. The* class of insane people. E19.

2 *general paralysis of the insane*: see PARALYSIS 1.

insanely *adv.* M19. **insaneness** *n.* L19.

†**insanguine** *v.* see ENSANGUINE.

†**insanie** *n.* Only in L16. [Fr. †*insanie* f. L *insania*, f. as INSANE.] Insanity, madness.

insanify /ɪnˈsanɪfʌɪ/ *v. rare.* E19. [f. INSANE *a.* + -I- + -FY.] 1 *v.t.* Make insane. E19. 2 *v.i.* Cause insanity. L19.

insanitary /ɪnˈsanɪt(ə)ri/ *a.* L19. [f. IN-^{3} + SANITARY.] Not sanitary; harmful to health.

insanitariness *n.* L19.

insanitation /ɪnˌsanɪˈteɪʃ(ə)n/ *n.* L19. [f. IN-^{3} + SANITATION.] Lack of sanitation; insanitary condition.

insanity /ɪnˈsanɪti/ *n.* L16. [L *insanitas*, f. as INSANE: see -ITY.] 1 The state or condition of being insane; mental derangement. L16. 2 Extreme folly or irrationality; an instance of this. M19.

1 A. G. GARDINER The mother . . whom she slew in one of her fits of insanity. A. CLARE He was . . found not guilty by reason of insanity.

insatiable /ɪnˈseɪʃəb(ə)l/ *a.* LME. [OFr. *insaciable* or L *insatiabilis*, f. as IN-^{3} + SATIATE *v.*: see -ABLE.] Not satiable; unable to be satisfied; inordinately greedy.

R. LINDNER You call me insatiable; you're the one who's never satisfied. J. CAREY A man with an insatiable appetite for shellfish.

insatiaˈbility *n.* M17. **insatiableness** *n.* M16. **insatiably** *adv.* L16.

insatiate /ɪnˈseɪʃɪət/ *a.* LME. [L *insatiatus*, f. as IN-^{3} + *satiatus* pa. pple of *satiare* SATIATE *v.*] That is not satiated; never satisfied. (Foll. by *of*, *for*.)

O. WILDE He has already had an enormous sum . . but is insatiate for money.

insatiated /ɪnˈseɪʃɪeɪtɪd/ *a. rare.* E18. [f. IN-^{3} + SATIATE *v.* + -ED^1.] Not satiated.

insatiety /ɪnsəˈtʌɪɪti/ *n.* Now *rare.* L16. [OFr. *insacieté* f. L *insatietas*, f. as IN-^{3} + *satietas* SATIETY.] The condition of being insatiate; unsatisfied desire or demand.

insaturable /ɪnˈsatʃʊrəb(ə)l, -tjʊr-/ *a.* LME. [L *insaturabilis*, f. as IN-^{3} + *saturare* SATURATE *v.*: see -ABLE.] †1 Insatiable. LME–M17. 2 Unable to be saturated. M19.

inscape /ˈɪnskeɪp/ *n.* M19. [Perh. f. IN *adv.* + SCAPE *n.*^{3} Cf. SCAPE *n.*^{4}] The inward essential unique quality of an observed object as embodied in literary, artistic, etc., expression. Cf. INSTRESS.

¶Orig. in the poetic theory of the English poet Gerard Manley Hopkins (1844–89).

inscenation /ɪnsɪˈneɪʃ(ə)n/ *n.* L19. [f. IN-^{2} + SCENE *n.* + -ATION, prob. after G *Inszenierung.*] Theatrical representation.

inscience /ˈɪnsɪəns/ *n.* Now *rare.* L16. [L *inscientia* ignorance, f. as IN-^{3} + *scientia* knowledge: see SCIENCE.] The condition of not knowing; ignorance.

inscient /ˈɪnsɪənt/ *a.* Now *rare.* L16. [L *inscient-*, *-ens* ignorant, f. as IN-^{3} + *scient-* having knowledge: see SCIENCE.] Not knowing; ignorant.

†**insconce** *v.* var. of ENSCONCE.

inscribe /ɪnˈskrʌɪb/ *v.t.* LME. [L *inscribere*, f. as IN-^{2} + *scribere* write.] 1 Write (a letter, word, sentence, etc., *in* or *on* stone, metal, paper, etc.), esp. so as to be conspicuous or durable. LME. b Enter the name of (a person) on an official document or list; enrol. E17. c Issue (stock etc.) in the form of shares with registered holders. Chiefly as *inscribed* ppl a. L19. 2 *Geom.* Draw (a figure) within another so that their boundaries touch but do not intersect. L16. 3 Mark (a sheet, tablet, etc.) with characters etc., esp. so as to be conspicuous or durable. M17. b Place an informal dedication (*to* a person) in or on (a book etc.). M17.

1 SAKI Francesca . . inscribed the figure 4 on the margin of her theatre programme. V. MEYNELL The names inscribed on the small brass tablet . . were Skeat and Wylie. 2 C. HUTTON To inscribe a circle in a regular polygon. 3 V. WOOLF A disc inscribed with a name. b P. ROTH It was the night I received the little dictionary inscribed 'From me to you'.

inscribable *a.* (chiefly *Geom.*) able to be inscribed M19. **inscriber** *n.* L18.

inscript /ˈɪnskrɪpt/ *n.* E17. [L *inscriptum* use as n. of neut. of *inscriptus* pa. pple, f. as next.] Something inscribed; an inscription.

inscriptible /ɪnˈskrɪptɪb(ə)l/ *a. rare.* L17. [f. L *inscript-* pa. ppl stem of *inscribere* INSCRIBE + -IBLE.] *Geom.* Inscribable.

inscription /ɪnˈskrɪpʃ(ə)n/ *n.* LME. [L *inscriptio(n-)*, f. *inscript-*: see prec., -ION.] 1 Orig., a short descriptive or dedicatory passage placed at the beginning of a book; a title, a heading. Later, an informal dedication of a book etc. LME. †2 *Civil & Sc. Law.* An accusation or challenge made with the condition that proof of its falsity would render the accuser liable to penalty for calumny. L15–E18. 3 A letter, word, sentence, etc., that is inscribed on stone, metal, paper, etc., esp. so as to be conspicuous or durable. M16. 4 *Anat.* A marking on some organ produced by contact with another, esp. where a tendon crosses a muscle. L16. 5 *Geom.* The action of inscribing one figure within another. L16. 6 *gen.* The action of inscribing. Chiefly *fig.* M17. 7 The action of issuing stock etc. in the form of shares with registered holders; inscribed stock. L18.

3 W. TREVOR An inscription on a brass plaque that read: *To Charles Edward Burrows.* M. COX Monty composed a memorial inscription.

inscriptional *a.* L18. **inscriptionless** *a.* M17.

inscriptive /ɪnˈskrɪptɪv/ *a.* M18. [f. L *inscript-* (see INSCRIPTIBLE) + -IVE.] Of the nature of an inscription; belonging to or used in inscriptions.

inscroll /ɪnˈskrəʊl/ *v.t. arch.* L17. [f. IN-^{1}, IN-^{2} + SCROLL *n.*] Inscribe or enter on a scroll.

inscrutable /ɪnˈskruːtəb(ə)l/ *a.* & *n.* LME. [eccl.L *inscrutabilis*, f. as IN-^{3} + *scrutari* to search: see SCRUTINY, -ABLE.] A *adj.* 1 That cannot be understood by investigation; wholly mysterious. LME. 2 Impenetrable, unfathomable. *rare.* E19.

1 R. CHRISTIANSEN A supreme being of infinite power, inscrutable to human reason. 2 N. HAWTHORNE The guide . . held his torch down into an inscrutable pit beneath our feet.

B *n.* An inscrutable thing. M17.

inscrutaˈbility *n.* M17. **inscrutableness** *n.* E18. **inscrutably** *adv.* L16.

insculp /ɪnˈskʌlp/ *v.t.* Now *rare* or *obs.* Pa. pple **-sculpt, -sculped.** LME. [L *insculpere*, f. as IN-^{2} + *sculpere* carve.] 1 Carve or sculpture (a figure, inscription, etc.). LME. 2 Shape by cutting; ornament with carved figures or inscriptions. L16.

insculptor /ɪnˈskʌlptə/ *n. rare.* L16. [f. L *insculpt-* pa. ppl stem of *insculpere*: see prec., -OR.] A person who carves or sculptures a figure, inscription, etc.; a sculptor.

†**insculpture** *n.* E–M17. [Fr., f. as IN-^{2} + SCULPTURE *n.*] A carved or sculptured figure, inscription, etc.

insculpture /ɪnˈskʌlptʃə/ *v.t. arch.* L18. [f. IN-^{2} + SCULPTURE *v.*] Carve or sculpture (a figure, inscription, etc.).

in se /ɪn ˈsiː, ˈseɪ/ *adv. phr.* M19. [L.] *Philos.* In itself.

†**insearch** *v.* var. of ENSEARCH.

insecable /ɪnˈsɛkəb(ə)l/ *a. rare.* E17. [L *insecabilis*, f. as IN-^{3} + *secabilis*, f. *secare* cut: see -ABLE.] Unable to be cut.

insect /ˈɪnsɛkt/ *n.* Pl. **insects, insecta** /ɪnˈsɛktə/ (now only as mod.L taxonomic name). E17. [L (sc. *animal*) *insectum*, pl. *insecta*, f. *insect-* pa. ppl stem of *insecare* cut up or into, f. *in-* IN-^{2} + *secare* cut; tr. Gk (sc. *zōion*) *entomon*: see ENTOMO-.] 1 Orig., any small invertebrate or (occas.) other cold-blooded animal, esp. with a segmented body and several pairs of legs. Now only as a loose extension of sense 2, any terrestrial arthropod. E17. 2 Any member of the class Insecta of small arthropods which have the body divided into head, thorax, and abdomen, the thorax bearing three pairs of legs and usu. one or two pairs of wings. E17. 3 *fig.* An insignificant, contemptible, or annoying person. L17.

1 R. LOVELL Of Insects, few are used as meat, except snailes. MILTON At once came forth whatever creeps the ground, Insect or Worme. 3 T. HEARNE He, the little Insect, was recommended to King William. *New Society* 'Insects' are occasional railway enthusiasts; they swarm all over the place at certain times of year.

Comb.: **insect-powder**: for killing or driving away insects.

¶The modern scientific sense 2 was only gradually distinguished from the classical and popular sense 1.

inˈsectan *a.* of, belonging to, or characterizing an insect, or the class Insecta L19. **insecˈtarium** *n.*, pl. **-ia, -iums,** a place for keeping and breeding insects L19. **insectary** *n.* = INSECTARIUM L19. **insecˈtiferous** *a.* producing or containing insects E19. **insect-like** *a.* like an insect L18. **inˈsectual** *a.* resembling an insect or insects; insignificant: E20. **insecty** *a.* full of or containing many insects M19.

insect /ɪnˈsɛkt/ *v.t.* M17. [L *insect-*: see prec.] Cut into. Chiefly as *insected* ppl a.

insecta *n.pl.* see INSECT *n.*

insecticide /ɪnˈsɛktɪsʌɪd/ *n.* & *a.* M19. [f. INSECT *n.* + -CIDE.] A *n.* 1 A person who or thing which kills insects; *spec.* a substance used to kill insects. M19. 2 The killing of insects. *rare.* M19. B *adj.* Insecticidal. M19.

insectiˈcidal *a.* of, pertaining to, or of the nature of an insecticide; tending to kill insects: M19.

insectile /ɪnˈsɛktʌɪl/ *a.* E17. [f. INSECT *n.* + -ILE.] Resembling, characteristic of, or of the nature of an insect or insects; insectan; insecty.

insection /ɪnˈsɛkʃ(ə)n/ *n.* M17. [Late L *insectio(n-)*, f. *insect-*: see INSECT *n.*, -ION.] The action of cutting into something; incision; division into sections; an incision, a division.

insectivore /ɪnˈsɛktɪvɔː/ *n.* M19. [f. mod.L *Insectivora* pl. (see below), f. *insectivorus*: see next.] An insectivorous animal or plant; *spec.* any animal of the order Insectivora of small, short-legged, mostly nocturnal mammals, having simple teeth and often a mobile sensitive snout, including moles, hedgehogs, shrews, etc.

insectivorous /ɪnsɛkˈtɪv(ə)rəs/ *a.* M17. [f. mod.L *insectivorus* (after L *carnivorus* CARNIVOROUS) + -OUS: see INSECT *n.*, -VOROUS.] Feeding on insects; (of a plant) able to capture and digest insects (as the sundew, the Venus fly-trap, etc.).

insectivory *n.* the habit of feeding on insects L20.

insectology /ɪnsɛkˈtɒlədʒi/ *n.* Now *rare.* M18. [f. INSECT *n.* + -OLOGY.] Entomology, esp. as it deals with insects in relation to human economics.

insecure /ɪnsɪˈkjʊə/ *a.* M17. [med.L *insecurus* unsafe, or f. IN-^{3} + SECURE *a.*] 1 Lacking assurance or confidence, uncertain. M17. 2 Unsafe; not firm; (of ice, ground, etc.) liable to give way. M17.

1 B. BETTELHEIM How anxious and insecure we were behind our show of defiance. C. THUBRON Like an insecure child, I began to crave for any kind of contact, even abuse. 2 J. TYNDALL The ice on the edge . . was loose and insecure. T. TANNER There *was* social order and stability, but it was always precarious and insecure.

insecurely *adv.* E18. **insecureness** *n.* (*rare*) E18.

insecurity /ɪnsɪˈkjʊərɪti/ *n.* M17. [med.L *insecuritas* or f. IN-^{3} + SECURITY.] 1 The quality or state of lacking assurance or confidence, uncertainty. M17. 2 The quality or condition of being unsafe; lack of firmness; liability of ice, ground, etc., to give way. Also, an insecure or dangerous state of affairs. M17. **b** An instance or case of insecurity; an insecure thing. M17.

1 D. DELILLO There was a deep restlessness in him, an insecurity. L. VAN DER POST He found at the core of their neurosis a sense of insecurity. 2 J. H. NEWMAN The insecurity of great prosperity has been the theme of poets and philosophers.

inseeing /ˈɪnsiːɪŋ/ *a. rare.* L16. [f. IN-[1] + SEEING *ppl a.*] Seeing into something; having insight.

inseity /ɪnˈsiːɪti, -ˈseɪɪti/ *n.* L19. [f. IN SE + -ITY.] *Philos.* The quality or state of being in itself.

inselberg /ˈɪns(ə)lbəːɡ, -z-/ *n.* Pl. **-s**, **-e** /-ə/. E20. [G, f. *Insel* island + *Berg* mountain.] *Physical Geogr.* An isolated hill or mountain which rises abruptly from the surrounding landscape, esp. from an arid plain.

inseminate /ɪnˈsɛmɪneɪt/ *v.t.* E17. [L *inseminat-* pa. ppl stem of *inseminare*, f. as IN-[2] + *seminare* sow: see -ATE[3].] **1** Sow (*lit.* & *fig.*). (Foll. by *in.*) E17. **2** *spec.* Introduce semen into (a female) by natural or (esp.) by artificial means. E20.

inseminator *n.* M20.

insemination /ɪnˌsɛmɪˈneɪʃ(ə)n/ *n.* M17. [f. prec.: see -ATION.] **1** The action or an act of inseminating, the fact of being inseminated. M17. **2** *spec.* The introduction of semen into a female by nátural or (esp.) by artificial means. M19.

2 *artificial insemination*: see ARTIFICIAL *a.* 1.

insensate /ɪnˈsɛnseɪt, -sət/ *a.* L15. [eccl.L *insensatus*, f. as IN-[3] + *sensatus* SENSATE *a.*] **1** Without sense or understanding; stupid, foolish. L15. **2** Without physical sensation or feeling; inanimate. E16. **3** Without sensibility, unfeeling. M16.

1 N. MOSLEY His insensate silly . . chaff . . makes Viv rude and on the defensive. 2 J. R. MACDUFF Dull, pulseless, unresponsive as the insensate stone. *fig.*: I. MURDOCH Conrad Lomas appeared . ., making his way across the dance floor, thrusting the insensate couples aside. 3 N. MONSARRAT The worst characteristics of a Norman baron: insensate cruelty, consuming greed.

insensately *adv.* M19. **insensateness** *n.* (*rare*) M17.

insense /ɪnˈsɛns/ *v.t. obs.* exc. *dial.* Also (earlier) †**en-**. LME. [OFr. *ensenser*, f. as EN-[1] + SENSE *n.*: see IN-[2]] Cause (a person) to understand or know something; inform, enlighten.

insensibility /ɪnˌsɛnsɪˈbɪlɪti/ *n.* LME. [Partly f. (O)Fr. *insensibilité* or late L *insensibilitas*, partly f. IN-[3] + SENSIBILITY.] **1** Incapability or deprivation of physical feeling or sensation; unconsciousness. LME. **b** Physical insensitiveness (*to* something). E19. **2** The quality of being imperceptible. *rare.* M17. **3** Lack of or incapacity for mental feeling or emotion; indifference. L17.

1 E. W. LANE I fell from my horse in a state of insensibility. b W. IRVING Perfect hardihood and insensibility to the changes of the seasons. 3 R. SOUTH An utter insensibility of any good or kindness done him by others. L. HELLMAN The insensibility that forced Arthur to make fun of what had harmed me.

insensible /ɪnˈsɛnsɪb(ə)l/ *a.* LME. [Partly f. (O)Fr., or L *insensibilis*, partly f. IN-[3] + SENSIBLE *a.*] **1** Unable to be perceived by the senses; non-material. Now *rare.* LME. **b** Too small or gradual to be perceived; inappreciable. L16. **2a** Incapable of physical sensation. Now *rare.* LME. **b** Deprived of physical sensation; unconscious. LME. **c** Incapable of physically feeling or perceiving (something specified). Foll. by *of*, *to*. E16. **3** Chiefly *Law.* Unable to be understood; unintelligible. M16. **4** Lacking sense or intelligence. Now *rare* or *obs.* M16. **5** Incapable of mentally feeling or perceiving (something specified); unaware; indifferent. (Foll. by *of*, *to*, or subord. cl.) E17. **b** Incapable of feeling or emotion; callous, apathetic. E17.

1b OED Passing by insensible gradations into the next sense. 2a M. FOTHERBY Fire, Haile, and Snow, meere insensible things. b C. THUBRON Two or three more vodkas . . and I'd be insensible. c GEO. ELIOT The martial fury by which men became insensible to wounds. 3 T. HUTCHINSON Several inaccuracies and insensible expressions in the New England Bill. 4 G. ADAMS People stupid and insensible, illiterate and incapable of learning. 5 C. MERIVALE Not insensible how much he owed to their faithful services. J. CONRAD I had to appear insensible to her distress. b A. G. GARDINER It would be an insensible heart that did not feel the surge of this strong music.

†**insensibleness** *n.* M16–E18. **insensibly** *adv.* LME.

insensitive /ɪnˈsɛnsɪtɪv/ *a.* L16. [f. IN-[3] + SENSITIVE *a.*] **1** Lacking mental or moral sensitivity; not susceptible; indifferent; unsympathetic. L16. †**2** Lacking physical feeling or consciousness; inanimate. E17–E18. **3** Of an organ, limb, etc.: lacking in feeling or sensation. M19. **b** Of a substance, device, etc.: not susceptible or responsive to some physical influence, as that of light. L19. **c** *Math.* & *Physics.* Of a quantity: (relatively) unaffected by variation in some related quantity. M20.

insensitively *adv.* M20. **insensitiveness** *n.* M19. **insensiˈtivity** *n.* lack of sensitivity M20.

insentient /ɪnˈsɛnʃ(ə)nt/ *a.* M18. [f. IN-[3] + SENTIENT *a.*] Not sentient; lacking physical feeling or consciousness; inanimate.

insentience *n.* the fact or condition of being insentient M19.

inseparable /ɪnˈsɛp(ə)rəb(ə)l/ *a.* & *n.* LME. [L *inseparabilis*, f. as IN-[3] + SEPARABLE.] **A** *adj.* Not separable; unable to be separated or disjoined (*from*); *Gram.* (of a prefix, or a verb in respect of a prefix) that cannot be used as a separate word. LME.

T. CAPOTE For seven years the two friends had been inseparable, each . . irreplaceable to the other. *Femina* Pain is . . an inseparable part of my life.

B *n.* An inseparable person, esp. a friend, or thing. Usu. in *pl.* E16.

R. DAVIES Off the stage they were inseparables.

inseparaˈbility *n.* E17. **inseparableness** *n.* L16. **inseparably** *adv.* LME.

inseparate /ɪnˈsɛp(ə)rət/ *a.* Now *rare.* L16. [f. IN-[3] + SEPARATE *a.*] Not separate (*from*); united, undivided; inseparable.

inseparately *adv.* M16.

insequent /ˈɪnsɪkwənt, ɪnˈsiːk-/ *a.* L19. [f. IN-[3] + *-sequent* as in CONSEQUENT *a.*, SUBSEQUENT.] *Physical Geogr.* Of a stream, valley, or drainage pattern: apparently haphazard in form, not determined by underlying structures.

insert /ˈɪnsəːt/ *n.* L19. [f. next, or abbrev. of INSERTION.] A thing (to be) inserted, as a loose page of advertisements etc. in a magazine, a piece of material in a garment, a shot in a cinema film, etc.

Gramophone I did not read the insert before playing the cassette. *Broadcast* The . . magazine will . . carry a couple of pages of advertising and some inserts.

insert /ɪnˈsəːt/ *v.t.* Pa. pple **-serted**, †**-sert**. L15. [L *insert-* pa. ppl stem of *inserere*, f. as IN-[2] + *serere* plant, join, put into.] **1** Introduce (a word, paragraph, etc.) into a piece of text; interpolate; put as an advertisement, article, etc., into a newspaper or magazine; include. L15. **2** Put or place in or between; fit or thrust in. (Foll. by *in*, *into*, *between*.) E16. **3** *Anat.*, *Zool.*, & *Bot.* Attach (an organ, esp. a muscle) at a specified point. Chiefly as *inserted* ppl a. E19.

1 P. G. WODEHOUSE Insert that advertisement in the *Daily Mail.* 2 A. NIN I inserted the key in the lock. M. DRABBLE She raised a small forkful to her mouth, inserted it, chewed.

insertable *a.* L19. **inserting** *n.* (*a*) the action of the vb; (*b*) something inserted: E17. **inserter** *n.* E17. **insertor** *n.* L16.

insertion /ɪnˈsəːʃ(ə)n/ *n.* M16. [Late L *insertio(n-)*, f. as prec.: see -ION.] **1** Something which is inserted; a word, paragraph, etc., inserted in a piece of text; each appearance of an advertisement etc. in different issues of a newspaper or magazine. M16. **b** A piece of embroidery or needlework made to be inserted in plain material as a decoration. M19. **2** The action of inserting; introduction into or between something. L16. **b** *Astronaut.* = INJECTION 1d. M20. **3** *Anat.*, *Zool.*, & *Bot.* The (place or manner of) attachment of an organ, esp. a muscle. L16.

1 E. W. LANE When I find trifling insertions of this kind . . in my translation. *great insertion*: see GREAT *a.* 2 OED Trade notices are charged at the rate of 1/6 per insertion. A. MASON The gap between the shutters was wide enough for the insertion of a knife blade.

Comb.: **insertion gain**, **loss** *Electr.* the increase, decrease, in power, voltage, or current resulting from insertion of a device or network between a load and the power source.

insertional *a.* M19. **insertioned** *a.* (*Needlework*) decorated with an insertion L19.

insertive /ɪnˈsəːtɪv/ *a.* M17. [L *insertivus*, f. as INSERT *v.* + -IVE.] Characterized by insertion.

†**insertment** *n. rare.* L17–E19. [f. INSERT *v.* + -MENT.] *Bot. sing.* & in *pl.* The medullary rays.

†**inservient** *a.* M17–E19. [L *inservient-* pres. ppl stem of *inservire* be serviceable, f. as IN-[2] + *servire* SERVE *v.*[1]: see -ENT.] Serving or subservient *to* some purpose; serviceable, useful.

insessorial /ɪnsɛˈsɔːrɪəl/ *a.* M19. [f. mod.L *Insessores* perchers pl. of late L *insessor*, agent-n. of *insidere* sit upon, f. as IN-[2] + *sedere* sit: see -IAL.] *Ornith.* Adapted for perching.

inset /ˈɪnsɛt/ *n.* M16. [f. IN-[1] + SET *n.*[1]] **1** Orig., a place where water flows in, a channel. Later, an inflow of water. M16. **2** Something set in or inserted; *esp.* an extra page or pages inserted in a book etc.; a small map, photograph, etc., inserted within the border of a larger one; a piece of cloth etc. let into a garment. L16.

1 C. LYELL There are tidal influences combined with the general insets from the Atlantic. 2 J. S. FOSTER Simple plan shapes with the minimum of insets and projections. I. MCEWAN A boxed inset at the foot of the page.

inset /ɪnˈsɛt/ *v.t.* Infl. **-tt-**. Pa. pple **-set**, **-setted**. OE. [f. IN-[1] + SET *v.*[1]] †**1** Institute, initiate. Only in OE. †**2** Set (a person) in office; appoint. ME–L16. **3** Set (a jewel) in or *in* precious metal or jewellery. *rare.* M17. **4** Set in, insert, make flush; *spec.* insert as an inset, decorate with an inset. L19.

4 *Times* The map . . now includes inset maps. *Which?* If you want to mow close to walls, . . choose a model with inset wheels.

insetter *n.* a person who or thing which insets pages etc. L19. **insetting** *n.* (*a*) *Typogr.* indention; (*b*) insertion, fixing: E16.

inseverable /ɪnˈsɛv(ə)rəb(ə)l/ *a.* M16. [f. IN-[3] + SEVERABLE.] Unable to be severed or divided; inseparable.

G. CATLIN The offence is lost in the inseverable iniquity in which all join.

inseverably *adv.* M17.

inshallah /ɪnˈʃalə/ *int.* M19. [Arab. *in šā' Allāh.*] If God wills it; *Deo volente.*

inshell /ɪnˈʃɛl/ *v.t.* Also **en-** /ɪn-, ɛn-/. *rare.* E17. [f. IN-[1], EN-[1] + SHELL *n.*] Withdraw within a shell.

inshining /ˈɪnʃʌɪnɪŋ/ *n.* E18. [f. IN *adv.* + SHINE *v.* + -ING[1].] A shining in; illumination.

inshining /ˈɪnʃʌɪnɪŋ/ *a.* M19. [f. IN *adv.* + SHINING *a.*] That shines in.

†**inship** *v.t.* Infl. **-pp-**. L16–E17. [f. IN-[1] + SHIP *n.*] Put into a ship; embark.

inshoot /ˈɪnʃuːt/ *n.* L19. [f. IN-[1] + SHOOT *n.*[1]] *Baseball.* The act of causing the ball to move rapidly by pitching with a curve; a ball which moves in this way.

inshore /ɪnˈʃɔː, ˈɪnʃɔː/ *a.* & *adv.* E18. [f. IN-[1] + SHORE *n.*[1]] **A** *adj.* Situated or carried on close to a shore. E18.

B *adv.* Towards a shore; close(r) to a shore. M18.

inshore of nearer to the shore than.

†**inshrine** *v.* var. of ENSHRINE.

inside /ɪnˈsʌɪd, *as adj.* ˈɪnsʌɪd/ *n.*, *adv.*, *a.*, & *prep.* LME. [f. IN-[1] + SIDE *n.*] **A** *n.* **1a** *sing.* & in *pl.* The interior of the body; the stomach and bowels. Chiefly *colloq.* LME. **b** *gen.* The inner part of something; the interior. M16. **c** Inward nature, thought, or meaning. L16. **d** *The* middle part *of* a week etc. L19. **e** Private information on a specified topic; a position affording such information. E20. **2** The inner side or surface; the side of a path etc. that is next to a wall or away from a road. E16. **b** *Fencing.* The right-hand side of a sword. Now *rare.* L17. **3** Chiefly *Hist.* (The place of) a passenger travelling inside a coach etc. L18. **4** *Football*, *Hockey*, etc. A position towards the centre of the field; a player in that position. L19.

For other words beginning with *in-* see the entry for **in-**[1]

1a R. LINDNER Her insides contracted in a spasm of disgust. b M. ATWOOD She's been sick of the taste of the inside of her own mouth. C. ISHERWOOD He sucked the insides out of the eggs. *patent insides*: see PATENT *a.* d C. ISHERWOOD I can't even keep a man faithful to me for the inside of a month. 2 M. FORSTER There was ice on the inside of the window. **inside out** with the inner surface turned out; *know inside out*, know thoroughly; *turn inside out*, turn the inner side outwards; *colloq.* cause confusion or a mess in. 3 R. BOLDREWOOD I picked myself up and went to help out the insides. 4 J. POTTER George and Boozy moved up on the German insides like a pair of avenging demons.

B *adv.* 1 Into or in the inner part; within; internally. LME. b In a position affording private information on a specified topic. *rare.* L19. c In prison. *slang.* L19. 2 On the inner side. E19. 3 Foll. by *of*: within the space of, less than, a specified period. M19.

1 G. GREENE He mistook the house . . for a quiet inn and walked inside. C. GEBLER The little mustard dish that had blue glass inside. H. BASCOM He . . is strangely calm inside Over-confident? c C. HOPE During his years inside there had circulated copies of his speech from the dock.

C *adj.* 1 Situated on, or in, the inside; interior; internal. E17. b Derived from the inside, involving private information on a specified topic. L19. 2 Of a person: travelling inside a coach etc. (chiefly *Hist.*); employed within a house etc., working indoors. E19. 3 *Football*, *Hockey*, etc. Designating (a player in) a position towards the centre of the field. L19.

1 A. MUNRO He reaches quickly into his inside pocket. b A. BULLOCK Bevin's position in the Government gave them . . inside knowledge of what was happening. 3 *inside forward*, *inside left*, *inside right*, etc.

D *prep.* Inside of; on or to the inner side of, in or into the inner part of; within. L18.

M. B. KEATINGE All must hurry inside the gates. D. DELILLO A mule was standing just inside the olive grove. *Running* Who would be the first man inside the magic 12 hours?

Special collocations & comb.: **inside country** *Austral.* settled areas near the coast. **inside information**: not accessible to outsiders. **inside job** *colloq.* a crime etc. involving a person living or working on the premises burgled etc. *inside straight*: see STRAIGHT *n.*[1] **inside track** the track of a racecourse etc. which is shorter because of a curve; *fig.* a position of advantage.

insider /ɪnˈsʌɪdə/ *n.* E19. [f. prec. + -ER[1].] 1 Chiefly *Hist.* An inside passenger in a coach etc. E19. 2 A person who is within some society, organization, etc.; a person who is party to a secret, esp. so as to gain an unfair advantage. M19. 3 A pocket, a pocketbook. *US slang.* M19.

2 *Independent* Insiders cashed in on their knowledge. I. MCEWAN Charles . . brought back an insider's tales of drunkenness . . in the House of Commons. **insider dealing** *Stock Exch.* trading to one's own advantage through having inside knowledge.

insidious /ɪnˈsɪdɪəs/ *a.* M16. [f. L *insidiosus* cunning, deceitful, f. *insidiae* ambush, trick: see -OUS.] Full of wiles or plots; proceeding or progressing secretly or subtly; treacherous; crafty.

R. L. STEVENSON They assailed me with artful questions and insidious offers of correspondence in the future. M. T. TSUANG The insidious course of the disease.

insidiously *adv.* M16. **insidiousness** *n.* L17.

insight /ˈɪnsʌɪt/ *n.*[1] ME. [Prob. of Scand. & LG origin: cf. Sw. *insikt*, Da. *insigt*, Du. *inzicht*, G *Einsicht*. See IN-[1], SIGHT *n.*] †1 Internal sight, mental vision. Also, understanding, wisdom. ME–M17. b Knowledge *of* or skill *in* (a particular subject or area). ME–M17. †2 A mental looking *to* or *upon* something; consideration; respect. ME–L15. †3 Physical sight; inspection; a look. LME–M17. 4 Penetration (into character, circumstances, etc.) with the understanding; an instance of this. L16. b *Psychol.* (A) sudden perception of the solution to a problem or difficulty (in animals, indicative of ideation and reasoning); *esp.* in *Psychoanalysis*, perception of one's repressed drives and their origin. E20.

4 A. BULLOCK With greater historical insight . . he compared Attlee to Campbell-Bannerman. C. PHILLIPS His thoughts did contain astute insights into the current state of the island.

insighted *a.* having insight, insightful L16. **insightful** *a.* full of insight E20. **insightfully** *adv.* M20. **insightfulness** *n.* L20.

†**insight** *n.*[2] *Sc.* & *north.* LME–L19. [Perh. same wd as prec.] Goods; *esp.* household furniture. Opp. OUTSIGHT *n.*[1]

insigne /ɪnˈsɪgni/ *n.sing.* Pl. (earlier) INSIGNIA. L18. [L: see INSIGNIA.] A badge, an ensign, an emblem.

†**insigne** *a.* LME–E18. [Fr. f. L *insignis*: see next.] Distinguished; eminent; remarkable.

insignia /ɪnˈsɪgnɪə/ *n.* M17. [L, pl. of *insigne* mark, sign, badge of office, use as n. of neut. of *insignis* distinguished (as by a mark), f. as IN-[2] + *signum* sign: see -IA[2]. Cf. ENSIGN *n.*] 1 *pl.* Badges or distinguishing marks (*of* office, honour, etc.); emblems (*of* a nation, person, etc.). M17. 2 *sing.* (Pl. **-ias**.) A badge or distinguishing mark (*of* office, honour, etc.); an emblem (*of* a nation, person, etc.). L18. 3 Usu. as *pl.* Marks or tokens indicative of something. L18.

1 J. G. BALLARD The squadron insignia were still legible. 2 *Times* I saw not a single racer . . bearing an insignia that seemed out of place. 3 P. ROTH His deeply furrowed face bore all the insignia of his lifelong exertion.

insignificance /ɪnsɪgˈnɪfɪk(ə)ns/ *n.* L17. [f. INSIGNIFICANT *a.* (see -ANCE), or f. IN-[3] + SIGNIFICANCE.] 1 The state or quality of being insignificant; lack of significance or force; unimportance; triviality. L17. 2 Lack of meaning. *rare.* M18.

1 B. BETTELHEIM Her own wounded feelings receded into insignificance. *pale into insignificance*: see PALE *v.*[2]

insignificancy /ɪnsɪgˈnɪfɪk(ə)nsi/ *n.* M17. [f. as prec. (see -ANCY), or f. IN-[3] + SIGNIFICANCY.] †1 Lack of meaning; an instance of this. M–L17. 2 Lack of significance or force; unimportance, triviality. Also, an instance of this; an insignificant thing or person. M17.

insignificant /ɪnsɪgˈnɪfɪk(ə)nt/ *a.* & *n.* M17. [f. IN-[3] + SIGNIFICANT.] A *adj.* 1 Lacking signification; meaningless. M17. †2 Devoid of weight or force; ineffective, ineffectual. M17–M18. 3 Of no importance; trivial, trifling; contemptible. M17. 4 Small in size; petty, mean. M18.

3 R. LYND He would never be anything more than an insignificant doctrinaire with a gift for saying bitter things. L. GORDON A document which her male descendants assumed to be insignificant.

B *n.* A meaningless thing; an unimportant or contemptible person. E18.

insignificantly *adv.* M17.

†**insignificative** *a.* M17–M18. [f. IN-[3] + SIGNIFICATIVE.] Not significative.

insignis /ɪnˈsɪgnɪs/ *n.* M19. [mod.L (f. former taxonomic name *Pinus insignis*) f. L = remarkable.] The Monterey pine, *Pinus radiata*.

insimplicity /ɪnsɪmˈplɪsɪti/ *n. rare.* L19. [f. IN-[3] + SIMPLICITY.] Lack of simplicity.

insincere /ɪnsɪnˈsɪə/ *a.* M17. [L *insincerus*, f. as IN-[3] + *sincerus* SINCERE.] Not sincere; disingenuous; not candid.

M. SCAMMELL A reaction against excessive and often insincere adulation.

insincerely *adv.* E17.

insincerity /ɪnsɪnˈsɛrɪti/ *n.* M16. [Late L *insinceritas*, f. as IN-[3] + *sinceritas* SINCERITY.] †1 Lack of purity; corruption. Only in M16. 2 The quality of being insincere; an instance of this. L17.

†**insinew** *v.t.* Also **en-**. L16–E17. [f. IN-[2], EN-[1] + SINEW.] Provide with sinews; *fig.* inspire with strength.

insinking /ˈɪnsɪŋkɪŋ/ *n.* L19. [f. IN-[1] + SINKING *n.*] A sinking in; a depression.

insinuant /ɪnˈsɪnjʊənt/ *a. rare.* M17. [f. INSINUATE *v.* + -ANT[1].] Insinuating, wheedling, ingratiating.

insinuate /ɪnˈsɪnjʊeɪt/ *v.* E16. [L *insinuat-* pa. ppl stem of *insinuare*, f. as IN-[2] + *sinuare* to curve: see -ATE[3].] 1 *v.t. Law.* Enter (a deed or document) on the official register; lodge (a deed or document) for registration. Now *rare* or *obs.* exc. in the Commissions issued by the Bishop of Winchester to the Deans of Jersey and Guernsey as his Commissaries. E16. 2 *v.t.* Introduce or impart to the mind indirectly or covertly; instil subtly and imperceptibly. E16. 3 *v.t.* Convey (a statement etc.) indirectly or obliquely, hint (*that*). M16. 4 *v.t.* Express indirectly; suggest, imply. *arch.* M16. 5 *v.t.* Introduce (oneself, another, etc.) into favour, office, etc., by subtle manipulation. Freq. foll. by *into*. M16. †b *v.i.* Work or wheedle oneself *into*, ingratiate oneself *with*. L16–M18. 6 *v.t.* Introduce (a thing, oneself) subtly and deviously into a place; cause (a thing) to enter gradually. L16. †b *v.i.* Be introduced subtly and deviously into a place; penetrate gradually. E17–L18. †7 *v.t.* Draw, attract, (a person etc.) subtly or covertly *to* something. L16–L17.

2 F. D. MAURICE In which wisdom was to be insinuated not enforced. 3 A. ARONSON Iago . . poisons Othello's mind by insinuating what Desdemona must have 'seen'. M. SCAMMELL She insinuated that he had neglected his mother. 4 SIR W. SCOTT Our metropolis . . whereby I insinuate Glasgow. 5 T. MORRISON An idea insinuated itself. P. D. JAMES Insinuating himself into the family. 6 M. BEERBOHM Into the lobe of her left ear he insinuated the hook of the black pearl. P. G. WODEHOUSE A head insinuated itself into the room furtively. E. LINKLATER Juan was able to squeeze and insinuate himself among the other sight-seers.

insinuatingly *adv.* in an insinuating manner E19. **insinuatingness** *n.* (*rare*) the state of being insinuating E18. **insinuator** *n.* L16. **insinuatory** *a.* insinuative L19.

insinuation /ɪn,sɪnjʊˈeɪʃ(ə)n/ *n.* L15. [L *insinuatio(n-)*, f. as INSINUATE: see -ATION.] †1 Notification, publication. *Sc.* Only in L15. †2 *Law.* The production or delivery of a will for official registration. E16–E18. 3 The action or an act of introducing something to the mind indirectly or covertly. M16. 4 The action or an act of conveying a statement etc. indirectly or obliquely; an oblique hint. M16. †b *Rhet.* A speech designed to win over its hearers. M16–E17. 5 The action of introducing oneself, another, etc., into favour, office, etc., by subtle manipulation; an instance of this. M16. 6 The action or an act of introducing a thing, oneself, subtly and deviously into a place; covert entrance. E17. 7 A winding, a twisting. *rare.* E17.

insinuative /ɪnˈsɪnjʊətɪv/ *a.* E17. [f. as INSINUATE + -IVE.] 1 Tending to insinuate; having the property of insinuating. E17. 2 Characterized by or involving insinuation; given to making insinuations. M17.

insinuatively *adv.* E17. **insinuativeness** *n.* (*rare*) E18.

insinuendo /ɪn,sɪnjʊˈɛndəʊ/ *n.* Pl. **-os**. L19. [Blend of INSINUATION and INNUENDO *n.*] (An) insinuation.

insipid /ɪnˈsɪpɪd/ *a.* & *n.* E17. [Fr. *insipide* or late L *insipidus*, f. as IN-[3] + *sapidus* SAPID.] A *adj.* 1 Tasteless; having only a slight taste; lacking flavour. E17. 2 *fig.* Lacking liveliness; dull, uninteresting. E17. †3 Devoid of intelligence or judgement; stupid, foolish. E17–L18.

1 C. GEBLER Horn-shaped pastries filled with insipid-tasting custard. 2 W. SOYINKA His assistants . . appeared insipid, starved parodies of himself.

B *n.* An insipid person or thing; a person who is deficient in sense, spirit, etc. E18.

insipidly *adv.* M17. **insipidness** *n.* E17.

insipidity /ɪnsɪˈpɪdɪti/ *n.* E17. [f. prec. + -ITY.] 1 Lack of taste or flavour. E17. †2 Lack of intelligence or judgement; stupidity, folly. E17–M18. 3 Lack of life or interest, dullness. E18. 4 An insipid remark, person, etc. E19.

insipience /ɪnˈsɪpɪəns/ *n.* Now *rare* or *obs.* LME. [f. as next: see -ENCE.] The quality of being insipient.

insipient /ɪnˈsɪpɪənt/ *a.* & *n.* Now *rare* or *obs.* LME. [L *insipient-*, *-ens*, f. as IN-[3] + *sapient-*: see SAPIENT *a.*] A *adj.* Lacking in wisdom; foolish. LME. †B *n.* An unwise or foolish person. L15–M17.

insist /ɪnˈsɪst/ *v.* LME. [L *insistere*, f. as IN-[2] + *sistere* stand.] 1 *v.i.* Dwell at length or emphatically *on*, †*in*, †*to* a matter; (foll. by *on*) maintain positively. LME. b *v.t.* Maintain positively *that*. E18. 2 *v.i.* Stand or rest *on*. Now *rare* or *obs.*

L16. 3 *v.i.* Persist *in* a course of action; follow steadfastly *in* a person's steps; persevere. *arch.* L16. 4 *v.i.* Make a persistent demand for something. (Foll. by *on.*) E17. b *v.t.* Demand persistently *that.* L17. 5 *v.t.* Utter insistently. L19.

1 B. JOWETT Socrates is not prepared to insist on the literal accuracy of this description. b J. P. HENNESSY Henry Trollope insisted that he was well enough to join his parents. 4 C. HILL The Short Parliament.. insisted on peace with the Scots. D. CUSACK You are not to upset yourself, I insist. R. HUNTFORD Scott nonetheless insisted on pushing blindly on. b J. HELLER I.. insisted they let her go. J. C. OATES Della insisted.. that the wedding party be held at her house. 5 D. H. LAWRENCE 'But which village do the bandits come from?' she insisted.

insister *n.* E17. **insistingly** *adv.* with insistence, insistently M19. **insistive** *a.* having the character or quality of insisting M17.

insistence /ɪn'sɪst(ə)ns/ *n.* LME. [f. prec.: see -ENCE.] The action of insisting; the fact or quality of being insistent.

A. W. KINGLAKE A.. tone of insistence bordering at times on intimidation. J. RATHBONE On the insistence of the girls we.. joined them.

insistency /ɪn'sɪst(ə)nsi/ *n.* M19. [f. next: see -ENCY.] Insistence; an instance of this.

insistent /ɪn'sɪst(ə)nt/ *a.* & *n.* E17. [f. INSIST + -ENT.] A *adj.* 1 Standing or resting on something. *rare.* E17. 2 That dwells emphatically on something maintained or demanded; persistent; obtruding itself on one's attention. M19.

2 J. AGATE John Gielgud was anxious, even insistent, that I should not write about.. last night's performance. P. BOWLES An insistent electric bell shrilled without respite.

B *n.* An insistent person. *rare.* M19.

insistently *adv.* L19.

†insisture *n. rare* (Shakes.). Only in E17. [f. INSIST *v.* + -URE.] Constancy, persistency, continuance.

†insition *n.* LME–M19. [L *insitio(n-)*, f. *insit-* pa. ppl stem of *inserere* engraft, f. as IN-² + *serere* sow, plant: see -ITION.] The action of engrafting, engraftment, a graft, (*lit.* & *fig.*).

insititious /ɪnsɪ'tɪʃəs/ *a.* M17. [L *insiticius*, f. *insit-*: see prec., -ITIOUS¹.] Of engrafted or inserted nature, introduced from outside, (*lit.* & *fig.*).

in situ /ɪn 'sɪtjuː/ *adv. phr.* M18. [L.] In its (original) place; in position.

†inslave *v.*, **†insnare** *v.* vars. of ENSLAVE, ENSNARE.

†insnarl *v.* see ENSNARL.

insobriety /ɪnsə'brʌɪəti/ *n.* E17. [f. IN-³ + SOBRIETY.] Lack of sobriety; intemperance, esp. in drinking.

insociable /ɪn'səʊʃəb(ə)l/ *a.* Now *rare.* L16. [L *insociabilis*, f. as IN-³ + *sociabilis* SOCIABLE.] †1 That cannot be associated; incompatible. L16–L17. 2 Not disposed to mix with others; unsociable. L16.

insocia'bility *n.* unsociableness M18.

insolate /'ɪnsəleɪt/ *v.t.* E17. [L *insolat-* pa. ppl stem of *insolare*, f. as IN-² + *sol* sun: see -ATE³.] Expose to the sun's rays, esp. in order to dry.

insolation /ɪnsə'leɪʃ(ə)n/ *n.* E17. [L *insolatio(n-)*, f. as prec. + -ATION.] Exposure to the sun's rays, esp. for drying or bleaching or as medical treatment; injurious exposure to the sun's rays; *spec.* sunstroke.

insole /'ɪnsəʊl/ *n.* M19. [f. IN *a.* + SOLE *n.*²] The inner sole of a shoe or boot. Also, a detachable piece of material worn inside a shoe or boot for warmth etc.

insolence /'ɪns(ə)l(ə)ns/ *n.* LME. [L *insolentia*, f. as INSOLENT: see -ENCE.] 1 Orig., arrogant or overbearing conduct or disposition. Later, impertinently insulting behaviour. Also (now *rare*), an instance of this, an insolent act. LME. †2 The condition of being unused to a thing. Also, unusualness. LME–M17.

1 MILTON The Sons of Belial, flown with insolence and wine. E. M. FORSTER 'May me and Lucy get down from our chairs?' he asked, with scarcely veiled insolence.

insolency /'ɪns(ə)l(ə)nsi/ *n.* Now *arch. rare.* L15. [f. as prec.: see -ENCY.] 1 = INSOLENCE 1. L15. †2 Unusualness; an unusual act or occurrence. E–M17.

insolent /'ɪns(ə)l(ə)nt/ *a.* & *n.* LME. [L *insolent-*, f. as IN-³ + *solent-* pres. ppl stem of *solere* be accustomed: see -ENT.] A *adj.* I 1 Orig., arrogant or overbearing in conduct or behaviour. Later, offensively contemptuous; impertinently insulting. LME. †2 Going beyond the bounds of propriety; extravagant, immoderate. LME–E18.

1 J. GAY 'What arrogance!' the snail replied; 'How insolent is upstart pride!' R. WEST Cook's face was bland, but her tone was unmistakably insolent. 2 STEELE All the Extremities of Household Expence, Furniture and insolent Equipage.

†II 3 Unaccustomed to a thing; inexperienced. L15–L16. 4 Unusual, strange. L16–M17.

4 J. BRINSLEY Words which are insolent, hard and out of use, are to be as warily avoided.

B *n.* An insolent person. L16.

insolently *adv.* LME.

insolidity /ɪnsə'lɪdɪti/ *n.* Now *rare* or *obs.* L16. [f. IN-³ + SOLIDITY.] Lack of firmness or substantialness; flimsiness.

insolubilize /ɪn'sɒljʊbɪlʌɪz/ *v.t.* Also **-ise.** L19. [f. L *insolubilis* INSOLUBLE *a.* + -IZE.] Make incapable of dissolving.

insolubili'zation *n.* E20.

insoluble /ɪn'sɒljʊb(ə)l/ *a.* & *n.* LME. [(O)Fr., or L *insolubilis*, f. as IN-³ + *solubilis* SOLUBLE *a.*] A *adj.* 1 Impossible to loosen or untie; indissoluble. Now *rare.* LME. †b Of an argument: irrefutable. M16–L17. 2 Of a difficulty, problem, etc.: impossible to solve. LME. 3 Unable to be dissolved in a liquid. E18. 4 Of a debt: impossible to discharge. M19.

2 P. FERGUSON They were a problem, annoying but not insoluble. M. RULE The difficulties appeared to be insoluble. 3 F. SMYTH Arsenious oxide is practically insoluble in cold water.

B *n.* An insoluble difficulty or problem. LME.

insolu'bility *n.* E17. **insolubleness** *n.* L17. **insolubly** *adv.* L19.

insolvable /ɪn'sɒlvəb(ə)l/ *a.* M17. [f. IN-³ + SOLVABLE.] †1 = INSOLUBLE *a.* 1. M17–E18. 2 = INSOLUBLE *a.* 2. L17. 3 = INSOLUBLE *a.* 3. E19. 4 Unable to be cashed. *rare.* M19.

insolva'bility *n.* M19. **insolvably** *adv.* L18.

insolvent /ɪn'sɒlv(ə)nt/ *a.* & *n.* L16. [f. IN-³ + SOLVENT *a.*] A *adj.* 1 Unable to pay one's debts or meet one's liabilities; bankrupt. L16. b Of a law etc.: relating to insolvents or insolvency. M19. †2 Unable to be cashed. M17–E18.

1 E. FERBER Gifts.. from insolvent patients who proffered them in lieu of cash.

B *n.* An insolvent person. E18.

insolvency *n.* M17.

insomnia /ɪn'sɒmnɪə/ *n.* Also (earlier) **†-nie, -nium** /-nɪəm/. E17. [L, f. *insomnis* sleepless (f. as IN-³ + *somnus* sleep) + -IA¹.] Chronic inability to sleep; sleeplessness.

insomniac *n.* & *a.* (*a*) *n.* a person who suffers from insomnia; (*b*) *adj.* affected with or exhibiting insomnia: E20.

insomnolent /ɪn'sɒmnələnt/ *a.* & *n. rare.* M19. [f. IN-³ + SOMNOLENT.] (A person) affected with insomnia.

insomnolence *n.* E19. **insomnolency** *n.* E19.

insomuch /ɪnsə(ʊ)'mʌtʃ/ *adv.* LME. [Orig. 3 wds, f. IN *prep.* + SO *adv.* + MUCH *a.* or *n.*, tr. OFr. *en tant (que)*: at first alternative to INASMUCH, later differentiated.] 1 To such an extent; so much. *rare.* LME. 2 Foll. by *as*: a Inasmuch as, seeing that. LME. †b To such an extent that, so that. L16–M17. c To such an extent as, so as. M17. 3 Foll. by *that*: to such an extent that, so that. LME. †4 Inasmuch as, in that. LME–E17.

1 J. BADCOCK If one fact.. has lost a particle of its interest.. insomuch is the Editor's design frustrated. 2a *Westminster Review* The present law is inoperative; insomuch as the Universities.. contain teachers who have never subscribed this.. confession. 3 A. ALISON The rain fell in torrents, insomuch that.. the soldiers were often ankle-deep in water.

insouciance /ɪn'suːsɪəns, *foreign* ɛ̃susjɑ̃ːs/ *n.* L18. [Fr., f. as next: see -ANCE.] Carefreeness, lack of concern.

N. PEVSNER His landscapes have.. the happiest insouciance of handling. *Observer* 'Size is no problem, I promise you,' he says with refreshing insouciance.

insouciant /ɪn'suːsɪənt, *foreign* ɛ̃susjɑ̃/ *a.* E19. [Fr., f. as IN-³ + *souciant* pres. pple of *soucier* to care, f. L *sollicitare* disturb: see -ANT¹.] Carefree, undisturbed.

J. UPDIKE Norma.. he had last seen wandering in insouciant nudity.

insouciantly *adv.* L19.

insoul *v.* see ENSOUL.

inspan /ɪn'span/ *v.t.* *S. Afr.* Infl. **-nn-**. E19. [Afk. f. Du. *inspannen*, f. *in-* IN-¹ + *spannen* SPAN *v.*²] 1 Yoke (oxen, horses, etc.) in a team to a vehicle; harness (a wagon). E19. 2 *fig.* Persuade (a person) to give assistance or service; use as a makeshift. E20.

2 *Rand Daily Mail* Mrs Barton often gets on the telephone and inspans private householders to help out.

inspeak /ɪn'spiːk/ *v.t.* Infl. as SPEAK *v.* L17. [f. IN-¹ + SPEAK *v.*: cf. G *einsprechen.*] In devotional language: produce in the soul by speech.

†inspect *n.* L15–M18. [App. f. L *inspectus*, f. as next.] Inspection, examination.

inspect /ɪn'spɛkt/ *v.* E17. [L *inspect-* pa. ppl stem of *inspicere*, f. as IN-² + *specere* look, or L *inspectare* frequent. of *inspicere.*] 1 *v.t.* View or examine closely and critically, esp. in order to assess quality or to check for shortcomings; *spec.* examine officially (documents, military personnel, etc.). E17. †2 *v.i.* Make an examination *into, among.* Only in 18.

1 J. STEINBECK He leaned over and inspected the sacking closely. M. SCAMMELL Prisoners were obliged to stand by their beds while they were inspected by two officers. *Which?* Planning applications.. are kept by the council, and you have the right to inspect them.

inspection /ɪn'spɛkʃ(ə)n/ *n.* LME. [(O)Fr. f. L *inspectio(n-)*, f. as prec.: see -ION.] 1 Careful examination or scrutiny; *spec.* official examination; an instance of this. (Foll. by *of*, †*into*, †*over*, †*upon.*) LME. 2 Insight, perception. Now *rare* or *obs.* E16. †3 A plan of a piece of ground etc. which has been inspected; a survey. L17–L18.

1 V. BRITTAIN Our Matron came round.. on a tour of inspection of our cubicles. J. A. MICHENER An inspection of the man's work forced him to recognize it as a superior job.

Comb.: **inspection-car** (chiefly *US*): used in inspecting a railway-track; **inspection chamber** a manhole; **inspection cover** a manhole cover.

inspectional *a.* of or relating to inspection; *spec.* able to be understood at sight: E18.

inspective /ɪn'spɛktɪv/ *a.* E17. [Late L *inspectivus*, f. as INSPECT *v.*: see -IVE.] †1 Concerned with investigation; theoretical. E–M17. 2 Watchful, attentive. L17.

inspector /ɪn'spɛktə/ *n.* Also (as a title) **I-**. E17. [L, f. as INSPECT *v.*: see -OR.] 1 A person who examines or looks carefully at something; *spec.* an official appointed to report on the workings of a service etc., esp. with regard to the observance of regulations or standards, or to conduct a public inquiry. E17. b A person who looks *into* a thing from curiosity, for information, etc. Now *rare.* M17. 2 A police officer ranking below a superintendent and above a sergeant. M19.

1 *inspector of factories, of mines and quarries, of nuclear installations, of schools*, etc. **inspector-general** the head of an inspectorate. **inspector of taxes** an official who assesses income tax payable. SANITARY *inspector.*

inspectoral *a.* = INSPECTORIAL M19.

inspectorate /ɪn'spɛkt(ə)rət/ *n.* M18. [f. prec. + -ATE¹.] 1 The office or function of an inspector; a body of official inspectors. M18. 2 A district under official inspection. M19.

inspectorial /ɪnspɛk'tɔːrɪəl/ *a.* M18. [f. as prec. + -IAL.] Of or relating to an inspector; having the rank of an inspector.

inspectorship /ɪn'spɛktəʃɪp/ *n.* M18. [f. as prec. + -SHIP.] The rank or position of an inspector.

inspectress /ɪn'spɛktrɪs/ *n.* Now *rare.* L18. [f. as prec. + -ESS¹.] A female inspector.

†inspersion *n.* M16–M18. [L *inspersio(n-)*, f. *inspers-* pa. ppl stem of *inspergere*, f. as IN-² + *spargere* scatter, sprinkle: see -ION.] The action or an act of sprinkling something on.

inspeximus /ɪnˈspɛksɪməs/ *n.* E17. [L, lit. 'we have inspected': the first wd in recital of the inspection of charters etc.] *Hist.* A charter in which the grantor vouched for having inspected an earlier charter which was recited and confirmed.

insphere *v.* var. of ENSPHERE.

in-sphere /ˈɪnsfɪə/ *n.* L19. [f. IN-¹ + SPHERE *n.*] *Math.* A sphere which touches all the faces of a given polyhedron.

inspirate /ˈɪnspɪreɪt/ *v.t.* E17. [L *inspirat-* pa. ppl stem of *inspirare*: see INSPIRE, -ATE³.] Orig., = INSPIRE. Now only (*Phonet.*), utter during inhalation.

inspiration /ɪnspəˈreɪʃ(ə)n/ *n.* ME. [(O)Fr. f. late L *inspiratio(n-)*, f. as prec: see -ATION.] **I 1 a** *spec.* Divine prompting or guidance; *esp.* that under which the books of Scripture are believed by some to have been written. ME. **b** *gen.* The prompting of the mind to exalted thoughts, to creative activity, etc. Also, a quality of a thing that shows creative activity. M17. **c** Undisclosed prompting from an influential source to express a particular viewpoint. L19. **2** A thought, utterance, etc., that is inspired; a sudden brilliant or timely idea. L16. **3** An inspiring influence; a source of inspiration. M19.

1a B. F. WESTCOTT The early Fathers teach us that Inspiration is an operation of the Holy Spirit acting through men. **moral inspiration**: according to which the inspiration of Scripture is confined to moral and religious teaching. **plenary inspiration**: according to which the inspiration of Scripture extends to all subjects treated. **verbal inspiration**: according to which every word of Scripture is dictated by God. **b** M. GIROUARD The swags in the deep plasterwork frieze were of late eighteenth-century inspiration. A. MUNRO The importance of Prince Henry the Navigator was in the inspiration . . of other explorers. **2** *Time* Downey had an inspiration to do something on behalf of . . 'our senior citizens'. M. SCAMMELL Among his many inspirations was a device for deflecting radar beams. **3** *Church Times* The 'elders' or spiritual fathers, whose counsel and prayer is an inspiration to many.

II 4 The action or an act of drawing in breath. LME. **†5** The action of blowing on or into something. E16–E18.

inspirational /ɪnspəˈreɪʃ(ə)n(ə)l/ *a.* M19. [f. prec. + -AL¹.] **1** Deriving character or substance from inspiration, that is under the influence of inspiration. M19. **2** Of or relating to inspiration. L19. **3** Inspiring. L19.

inspirationally *adv.* under the influence of inspiration; as regards inspiration: L19.

inspirationist /ɪnspəˈreɪʃ(ə)nɪst/ *n.* M19. [f. as prec. + -IST.] A believer in inspiration. Usu. w. specifying wd, as *plenary inspirationist*, a believer in plenary inspiration.

inspirator /ˈɪnspəreɪtə/ *n.* E17. [Late L, f. as INSPIRATE: see -OR. In sense 2, f. INSPIRE + -ATOR: cf. *respirator*.] **1** A person who or thing which provides inspiration. Now *rare*. E17. **2** An apparatus for drawing in air or vapour. L19.

inspiratory /ɪnˈspʌɪrət(ə)ri/ *a.* L18. [f. INSPIRATE + -ORY².] Serving to draw in the air in respiration.

inspire /ɪnˈspʌɪə/ *v.* Also (earlier) **†en-**. ME. [(O)Fr. *inspirer* f. L *inspirare*, f. as IN-² + *spirare* breathe.] **I 1 a** *v.t.* Of a divine or supernatural agency: impart a truth, impulse, idea, etc., to. ME. **b** *v.t. gen.* Animate *with* a (noble or exalted) feeling, *to do* something (noble or exalted). LME. **c** *v.i.* Provide inspiration; elevate or exalt the mind. LME. **2** *v.t.* **a** Of a divine or supernatural agency: impart, suggest, (a revelation, idea, etc.). LME. **b** *gen.* Arouse in the mind, instil, (a feeling, impulse, etc.). L16. **3** *v.t.* Of an influential source: secretly prompt (a person etc.); suggest the expression of (a viewpoint). L19.

1a L. STRACHEY He mused, and was inspired: the Great Exhibition came into his head. C. HOPE Church and Regime believed themselves divinely inspired. **b** OED Romanus was inspired to compose these hymns. W. S. CHURCHILL The American republic had . . inspired the mass of Frenchmen with a new taste for liberty. Z. MEDVEDEV A leader who is capable of inspiring people to work harder. **2b** R. NIEBUHR The symbols . . which inspire awe and reverence in the citizen. R. WARNER There was much in him that inspired confidence. D. ACHESON The General's retirement inspired sincere regret.

II 4 a *v.t.* Breathe upon or into. Now *rare* or *obs.* LME. **†b** *v.i.* Breathe, blow. Only in 16. **5** *v.t.* **a** Breathe (life, a soul, etc.) *in*, *into*. Now chiefly *fig.* LME. **†b** Blow, breathe (a vapour etc.) into or on something. M16–L17. **6** *v.t.* & *i.* Take (air) into the lungs in breathing; inhale. Opp. *expire*. LME.

4a POPE Descend, ye Nine! . . The breathing instruments inspire. **5b** J. SYLVESTER The wily Snake A poysoned air inspired . . In Eve's frail breast.

inspired *a.* that is inspired; *esp.* (*a*) as though prompted by divine inspiration; (of a guess) intuitive but correct; (*b*) secretly prompted by an influential source: LME. **inspiredly** /-rɪdli/ *adv.* L16. **inspirer** *n.* a person who or thing which inspires LME. **inspiring** *ppl a.* that inspires; *esp.* that elevates or exalts the mind: M17. **inspiringly** *adv.* E19.

inspirit /ɪnˈspɪrɪt/ *v.t.* E17. [f. IN-¹ + SPIRIT *n.*] Put life or spirit into; encourage, incite (*to* action, *to do*).

H. T. BUCKLE Those great men, who, by their writings, inspirited the people to resistance.

inspiritingly *adv.* in a manner that inspirits someone E19.

inspissate /ɪnˈspɪsət/ *ppl a.* Now *rare*. E17. [Late L *inspissatus* pa. pple, f. as next: see -ATE².] Made thick or dense.

inspissate /ɪnˈspɪseɪt/ *v.* E17. [Late L *inspissat-* pa. ppl stem of *inspissare*, f. as IN-² + *spissus* thick, dense: see -ATE³.] **1** *v.t.* Make thick or dense; *esp.* reduce (a liquid) to a semi-solid consistency. E17. **2** *v.i.* Become thick or dense. M18.

1 G. BERKELEY Pitch is tar inspissated.

inspiˈssation *n.* E17. **ˈinspissator** *n.* an apparatus for thickening serum etc. by heat L19.

inst. /ɪnst/ *a.* L18. [Abbrev.] *Comm.* = INSTANT *a.* 2b. Now usu. w. 'day' understood, following an ordinal numeral.

instability /ɪnstəˈbɪlɪti/ *n.* LME. [Fr. *instabilité* f. L *instabilitas*, f. *instabilis*: see next, -ITY.] The quality of being unstable; lack of stability. Also, an instance of this.

L. NKOSI The constant . . flights of fancy . . create an impression of emotional instability.

instable /ɪnˈsteɪb(ə)l/ *a.* Now *rare*. LME. [(O)Fr., or f. L *instabilis*, f. as IN-³ + *stabilis* STABLE *a.*, or f. IN-³ + STABLE *a.*] Not stable; characterized by instability; unstable.

install /ɪnˈstɔːl/ *v.t.* Also **-stal**, infl. **-ll-**. LME. [med.L *installare*, f. as IN-² + *stallum* STALL *n.*¹] **1** Invest (a person) with an office or rank by seating in a stall or official seat, or by some other ceremonial procedure. Freq. foll. by *in*. LME. **b** Establish (a person etc.) in a place, condition, etc. Freq. foll. by *in*. L16. **2** Place (an apparatus, system, etc.) in position for service or use. M19.

1 G. PEELE Amurath's soldiers have by this install'd Good Abdelmelec in his royal seat. D. HUME Cromwell was declared protector; and with great solemnity installed in that high office. **b** J. KRANTZ Two other permanent house guests were immediately installed in the house. R. HUNTFORD To cope with workaday detail, Shackleton installed a business manager. **2** S. BELLOW I arranged to have the garbage-disposal unit installed in the sink. I. MURDOCH The new art nouveau lantern which Pat had installed illuminated the steps.

installer *n.* E17.

installation /ɪnstəˈleɪʃ(ə)n/ *n.* LME. [med.L *installatio(n-)*, f. *installat-* pa. ppl stem of *installare*: see prec., -ATION.] **1** The action or an act of installing something or someone; the fact of being installed. LME. **2** An apparatus, system, etc., that has been installed for service or use. L19. **3** An art exhibit constructed within a gallery as part of an exhibition. M20.

1 J. LINGARD The cardinal had invited the nobility . . to assist at his installation. H. BAILEY With the . . installation of Winifred's old nanny as housekeeper. R. LARDNER The thirty-four-dollar synthetic radio had done nothing but croak since . . its installation. *attrib.*: *Which?* British Telecom can supply home pay-phones . . but . . there are installation costs to consider. **2** F. FITZGERALD A thousand Vietnamese Marines . . seized the radio station, the corps headquarters, and other key installations.

installment *n.*¹, *n.*² see INSTALMENT *n.*¹, *n.*²

instalment /ɪnˈstɔːlm(ə)nt/ *n.*¹ Now *rare*. Also **-ll-**. L16. [f. INSTALL + -MENT.] **1** The action of installing something or someone; the fact of being installed; installation. L16. **†2** A place or seat in which a person is installed. *rare*. L16–E17.

instalment /ɪnˈstɔːlm(ə)nt/ *n.*² Also ***-ll-**. M18. [Alt. (prob. by assoc. w. prec.) of ESTALMENT.] **†1** The arrangement of the payment of a sum of money in fixed portions at fixed times. M–L18. **2** Each of the several parts, successively falling due, of a sum payable. L18. **3** Any of several parts (esp. of a serial story etc.) supplied, published, etc., at different times. E19.

2 R. DAHL What about the monthly installments on the television set? E. FROMM Buying all that he can afford to buy either for cash or on instalments. **3** C. RYCROFT Freud's *The Psychopathology of Everyday Life* first appeared in two instalments . . as articles. B. WEBB Five instalments of news at 10, 1, 4, 7 and 9.30 break up the day.

Comb.: **instalment plan** *N. Amer.* hire purchase.

Instamatic /ɪnstəˈmatɪk/ *n.* Also **i-**. M20. [f. INSTA(NT *a.* + AUTO)MATIC.] (Proprietary name for) a type of small fixed-focus camera for taking snapshots.

†instamp *v.* see ENSTAMP.

instance /ˈɪnst(ə)ns/ *n.* ME. [(O)Fr. f. L *instantia*, in med.L objection, example to the contrary (tr. Gk *enstasis* objection), f. *instant-*: see INSTANT *a.*, -ANCE.] **I 1** Urgency in speech or action; urgent entreaty; earnestness, persistence. Now chiefly in *at the instance of* below. ME. **†b** In *pl.* Urgent or repeated entreaties. M17–M19. **†2** An impelling motive or cause. L16–M17.

1 H. JAMES He had asked her, with much instance, to come out and take charge of their friend.

†II 3 Presence; the present time. LME–L16. **4** An instant, a moment. M–L17.

III †5 *Scholastic Logic.* A case adduced in objection to or disproof of a universal assertion. L16–L17. **6** A fact or example illustrating a general truth; a person or thing for which an assertion is valid; a particular case. L16. **†b** A particular or point characteristic of or included in something general or abstract; a detail. M17–M18. **†7** A thing which proves or indicates something; a sign, a token; evidence. L16–L18.

6 J. THURBER There are dozens of . . instances of the dwindling of the male in the animal kingdom. H. J. LASKI The signs of change are in each instance slight, though collectively they acquire significance. **7** H. FIELDING I beg you to accept a guinea as a small instance of my gratitude.

IV 8 *Sc. Law.* An indictment which must be pursued at the appointed time, failing which no further action can be taken. E17. **9** A process in a court of justice; a suit. M17.

Phrases: **at the instance of** at the request or suggestion of. **court of first instance** *Law* a court of primary jurisdiction. **for instance** (*a*) as an example; (*b*) *colloq.* an example. **in the first** (or **second** etc.) **instance** in the first (or second etc.) place; at the first (or second etc.) stage of a proceeding. **in this instance** in this case, on this occasion.

Comb.: **Instance Court** *Hist.* a branch of the Admiralty Court dealing with private maritime matters.

instance /ˈɪnst(ə)ns/ *v.* LME. [f. the n.] **†I 1** *v.t.* Urge, entreat earnestly, importune. LME–M18.

II 2 *v.i.* Cite an instance; adduce an example in illustration or proof. (Foll. by *in*.) Now *rare*. E17. **3** *v.t.* Illustrate or prove by means of an example etc.; exemplify. E17. **4** *v.t.* Cite (a fact, a case) as an example or instance. E17.

2 G. WHITE It would be needless to instance in sheep, which frequently flock together. **3** F. SPALDING Bloomsbury's interest in the affairs of buggers . . instanced their radicalism. **4** POPE He proceeds to instance several others who . . have no farther notice taken of them. P. GAY I instance only the amazing papers on technique dating from before World War I.

instancy /ˈɪnst(ə)nsi/ *n.* E16. [L *instantia*: see INSTANCE *n.*, -ANCY.] **1** The quality of being pressing; urgency; solicitation; pressing nature. E16. 2 Closeness, imminence. *rare*. M17. 3 Immediacy, instantaneity. *rare*. M19.

instant /ˈɪnst(ə)nt/ *n*. LME. [f. next after med.L *instans* (sc. *tempus*) present moment of time.] 1 An extremely short space of time; a moment. LME. 2 A precise (esp. the present) point of time; a particular moment; *Comm*. the current month. E16. 3 An instant beverage, *spec*. instant coffee. M20.

1 G. ORWELL He did see them, for a fleeting instant. 2 P. BROOK These were only fragmentary impressions that . . came into being at the instant they were required. 3 *Punch* One of those dispensers which trickle hot water onto a tiny measure of dusty instant.

Phrases: **in an instant, on the instant** immediately. **the instant** *advb*. as soon as, the very moment that. **this instant!** now, at once!

instant /ˈɪnst(ə)nt/ *a*. & *adv*. LME. [(O)Fr. f. L *instant-* pres. ppl stem of *instare* be present or at hand, apply oneself to, f. as IN-[2] + *stare* stand: see -ANT[1].] A *adj*. 1a Pressing, urgent. LME. b Of a person, an action: urgent, importunate. *arch*. L15. 2a Present now or at the time in question; current. *arch*. LME. b *Comm*. Of the current month. Now usu. w. 'day' understood, following an ordinal numeral. Freq. abbrev. INST. LME. 3 Close at hand, impending, imminent. Now *rare*. E16. 4 Occurring immediately or without delay. L16. 5 Of food: that can be prepared easily for immediate use. E20. b *fig*. Hurriedly produced. M20.

1a J. H. NEWMAN He has instant need of you. b J. TYRRELL The Bishops were instant with the King to make Peace. 3 STEELE The evil which . . may seem distant, to him is instant and ever before his eyes. 4 A. THWAITE Gosse took an instant dislike to him. A. BROOKNER She . . had obtained instant relief from acupuncture. **instant replay** *Television* the immediate repetition of a sequence in a filmed (sports) event, often in slow motion. 5 *News Chronicle* Instant bread comes as small frozen pebble shapes which fluff up to fresh crisp rolls. b A. TOFFLER No product is more swiftly fabricated or more ruthlessly destroyed than the instant celebrity.

B *adv*. Immediately, at once. *poet*. E16.

instantaneous /ɪnst(ə)nˈteɪnɪəs/ *a*. M17. [f. med.L *instantaneus*, f. L *instant-* (see prec.) after med.L *momentaneus*: see -ANEOUS.] 1 Occurring or done within an instant or instantly. M17. b *Photogr*. (now chiefly *Hist*.). Of, pertaining to, or designating an exposure of brief duration controlled by a rapid shutter mechanism (in contrast to a time exposure). M19. 2 *Math*. & *Physics*. Of a variable value, axis of rotation, etc.: existing at or pertaining to a particular instant. E19.

1 W. GOLDING The applause was instantaneous and overwhelming.

instantaˈneity *n*. the quality of being instantaneous M18. **instantaneously** *adv*. M17. **instantaneousness** *n*. E18.

instanter /ɪnˈstantə/ *adv*. Now *arch*. or *joc*. L17. [L.] Immediately, at once.

instantial /ɪnˈstanʃ(ə)l/ *a*. M17. [f. L *instantia* INSTANCE *n*. + -AL[1].] Of or pertaining to an instance or instances; providing an instance.

instantial premiss *Logic* a premiss concerned with or arising from a particular case.

instantiate /ɪnˈstanʃɪeɪt/ *v.t*. M20. [f. as prec. + -ATE[3].] Represent by an instance.

J. HOLLOWAY Two apples . . both instantiate the single universal redness. D. R. HOFSTADTER Our intelligence is not disembodied, but is instantiated in physical objects: our brains.

instantiˈation *n*. M20.

instantize /ˈɪnstəntʌɪz/ *v.t*. Also **-ise**. M20. [f. INSTANT *a*. + -IZE.] Make (food) available in an instant form. Chiefly as *instantized* ppl a.

New Scientist The formulated, instantised, convenience foods will no longer look like meat, milk, cereal or vegetable.

instantly /ˈɪnst(ə)ntli/ *adv*. & *conj*. LME. [f. INSTANT *a*. + -LY[2].] A *adv*. 1 Urgently, persistently, with importunity. *arch*. LME. †2 Just at this or that moment; just, now. L15–M17. 3 Immediately, at once. E16.

3 F. CHICHESTER Though I closed the throttle instantly, it seemed an age before the engine stopped.

B *conj*. The moment that, as soon as. L18.

THACKERAY He ran across the grass instantly he perceived his mother.

instar /ˈɪnstɑː/ *n*. L19. [L = form, figure, likeness.] *Zool*. (An individual animal at) any of the stages in the life of an insect or other arthropod, between successive ecdyses.

instar /ɪnˈstɑː/ *v.t*. *poet*. Infl. **-rr-**. L16. [f. IN-[1] + STAR *n*.[1]] 1 Set among the stars; make a star of. L16. 2 Adorn (as) with a star or stars. M17.

1 J. FORD Our heart is high instarr'd in brighter spheres. 2 POPE The shining circles of his golden hair . . Instarr'd with gems and gold.

instate /ɪnˈsteɪt/ *v.t*. Also †**en-**. E17. [f. IN-[2], EN-[1] + STATE *n*. Cf. earlier REINSTATE.] 1 Put (a person etc.) into a certain position or condition; install, establish, (*in* office etc.). E17. †2 Endow or invest (a person) *with*. E–M17.

1 E. BOWEN What seemed a provisional measure worked so well as to instate yet another tradition.

instatement *n*. (now *rare*) L17.

in statu nascendi /ɪn ˌstatjuː naˈsɛndiː/ *a. phr*. L19. [L.] In the process of creation, formation, or construction.

in statu pupillari /ɪn ˌstatjuː pjuːpɪˈlɑːriː/ *a. phr*. M19. [L.] Under guardianship; of junior status at a university; not having a master's degree.

in statu quo /ɪn ˌstatjuː ˈkwəʊ/ *a. phr*. E17. [L.] More fully *in statu quo ante* /ˈantiː/, (rare) *prius* /ˈprʌɪəs/. In the same state as formerly.

instauration /ɪnstɔːˈreɪʃ(ə)n/ *n*. E17. [L *instauratio(n-)*, f. *instaurat-* pa. ppl stem of *instaurare* restore, f. as IN-[2] + stem also of *restaurare* RESTORE *v*.: see -ATION.] 1 The action of restoring or repairing something; renovation, renewal. E17. 2 Institution, founding, establishment. Now *rare*. E17.

instaurator /ˈɪnstɔːreɪtə/ *n*. E17. [Late L, f. *instaurat-*: see prec., -OR.] A person who repairs or renews something. Also, a person who establishes something, a founder.

instead /ɪnˈstɛd/ *adv*. ME. [Orig. two wds, f. IN *prep*. + STEAD *n*. Cf. *in a person's stead* s.v. STEAD *n*.] 1 *instead of*, in place of, in lieu of, for; rather than. ME. 2 As a substitute or alternative. M17.

1 OED I found it on the floor instead of in the drawer. D. ABSE He had whisky instead of blood running through his body. J. KRANTZ Instead of taking you to the station, I should have driven you straight home. 2 *Newsweek* Not to put their petro-billions into U.S. Treasury bonds, but to invest in American industry instead. *Soldier* He failed to find a single 'tough old bird' but instead returned with pictures of three charming young ladies.

†**insteep** *v.t*. Also **en-**. L16–L18. [f. IN-[1], EN-[1] + STEEP *v*.[1]] Immerse; steep or soak *in*.

instep /ˈɪnstɛp/ *n*. LME. [Origin unkn.: cf. WFris. *ynstap* opening in a shoe for insertion of the foot.] 1 The portion of the human foot comprising the arch between the toes and the ankle. LME. 2 The part of a shoe, stocking, etc., fitting over or under the instep. E17. 3 A thing resembling an instep in shape. L17. 4 *Zool*. A part of an animal's foot corresponding to the human instep. *rare*. E18.

instigate /ˈɪnstɪgeɪt/ *v.t*. M16. [L *instigat-* pa. ppl stem of *instigare*, f. as IN-[2] + *stigare* prick, incite: see -ATE[3].] 1 Urge on, incite, (a person *to* an action, *to do* esp. something evil). M16. 2 Bring about, initiate, provoke. M19.

1 B. JOWETT You must not instigate your elders to a breach of faith. 2 E. FEINSTEIN He instigated the relationship himself by calling upon Marina at home.

instigative *a*. (*rare*) tending to instigate; stimulative, provoking: M17. **instigator** *n*. a person who instigates something; an inciter: L16. **instiˈgatrix** *n*. (*rare*), pl. **-trices** /-trɪsiːz/, a female instigator E17.

instigation /ɪnstɪˈgeɪʃ(ə)n/ *n*. LME. [(O)Fr., or L *instigatio(n-)*, f. as prec.: see -ATION.] 1 The action or an act of instigating someone or something; urging, incitement. LME. 2 An incentive, a stimulus, a spur. E16.

1 S. UNWIN At my instigation work was started on a Guide to Royalty.

instil /ɪnˈstɪl/ *v.t*. Also ***-ll**. Infl. **-ll-**. LME. [L *instillare*, f. as IN-[2] + *stillare*, f. *stilla* a drop.] 1 Put (liquid) *into* a thing by drops or in small quantities. LME. 2 Introduce (a feeling, idea, or principle) *in* or *into*, esp. gradually or covertly. M16. 3 Imbue *with*. M17.

2 C. HAMPTON We have to instil in them a work ethic tied to a reward system. M. MOORCOCK I . . could easily instil my own confidence into those seeking my help. 3 *Sunday Express* I went to Norfolk, and there I was instilled with a love of the countryside.

instiˈllation *n*. the action of instilling; that which is instilled: M16. **instiller** *n*. E17.

instinct /ˈɪnstɪŋ(k)t/ *n*. LME. [L *instinctus* instigation, impulse, f. *instinct-* pa. ppl stem of *instinguere* incite, impel, f. as IN-[2] + *stinguere* prick.] †1 Instigation, impulse, prompting. LME–M18. 2 Orig., intuitive power. Later, innate impulsion; a natural propensity to act without conscious intention; *spec*. an innate usu. fixed pattern of behaviour in most animals in response to certain stimuli. LME. b Unconscious skill; intuition; an instance of this. L16.

2 OED The instinct to suck as possessed by the young of all mammals. A. P. HERBERT By instinct she ran first towards the wharf gate. D. NOBBS His first wild instinct was to accelerate. *the herd instinct*: see HERD *n*.[1] b C. CHAPLIN Her instinct was unfailing in recognising those that had genuine talent. K. CORNELL As an actress, what I've had has been an instinct for being somebody else.

instinctless *a*. L19.

instinct /ɪnˈstɪŋ(k)t/ *a*. M16. [L *instinctus* pa. pple of *instinguere*: see prec.] †1 Naturally present; innate. M16–E17. †2 Impelled, excited, animated. (Foll. by *with*.) M16–E18. 3 Imbued or inspired *with*. L18.

3 B. CORNWALL Through all the palace . . Instinct with light, a living splendour ran. M. BRADBURY He looks at these people, instinct with the times.

†**instinct** *v.t*. M16. [L *instinct-*: see INSTINCT *n*.] 1 Instigate, prompt. M16–L17. 2 Implant naturally or as an instinct. M16–M18.

†**instinction** *n*. LME. [Fr., or late L *instinctio(n-)*, f. as prec.: see -ION.] 1 Instigation, prompting, inspiration. LME–L17. 2 Natural impulse, instinct. M16–M18.

instinctive /ɪnˈstɪŋ(k)tɪv/ *a*. & *adv*. L15. [f. INSTINCT *n*. + -IVE.] A *adj*. Of or pertaining to instinct; (as if) resulting from instinct. L15.

J. DEWEY The human being is born with a greater number of instinctive tendencies than other animals. N. MOSLEY Women's knowledge was instinctive while men's had to be learned. J. LEHANE The break is usually automatic and . . becomes instinctive, but . . a verbal signal may be given.

B *adv*. Instinctively. *poet*. *rare*. E18.

instinctively *adv*. in an instinctive manner, by instinct E17.

instinctual /ɪnˈstɪŋ(k)tjʊ(ə)l/ *a*. E20. [f. INSTINCT *n*. + -UAL.] Of or pertaining to instinct; involving or dependent on instinct.

instinctually *adv*. M20.

institor /ˈɪnstɪtə/ *n*. M17. [L, f. *instit-* pa. ppl stem of *insistere* step on, follow, pursue, begin work on: see INSIST, -OR.] Chiefly *Rom*. & *Sc*. *Law* (now *Hist*.). A factor, an agent; a broker, a retailer.

instiˈtorial *a*. of or pertaining to an institor M19. **institorian** *a*. institorial M19.

institute /ˈɪnstɪtjuːt/ *n*.[1] L15. [L *institutum* design, precept, use as n. of neut. pa. pple of *instituere*: see INSTITUTE *v*.] †1 Purpose, design. L15–L17. 2 Something instituted; an established law, custom, etc.; an institution. L15. 3 A principle or element of instruction; in *pl*., a digest of the elements of a subject, esp. of jurisprudence. M16. 4 A society or organization for the promotion of a scientific, educational, etc., object; the building used by such a society or organization. E19.

2 MILTON Teaching and promoting . . the institutes and customs of civil life. 3 R. H. TAWNEY The edition of the *Institutes* [*of Justinian*] which appeared in 1559. 4 J. MASTERS When we got to the Institute, Victoria went off to play whist. *Medway Extra* Participation is open to all . . research institutes and universities within the community. *Rural Institute*: see RURAL *a*. *Women's Institute*: see WOMAN *n*.

institute /ˈɪnstɪtjuːt/ *n*.[2] L17. [L *institutus* pa. pple, f. as next.] *Rom*., *Civil*, & *Sc*. *Law*. The person to whom an estate is first given in a testament or destination.

institute /ˈɪnstɪtjuːt/ *v.t.* Pa. pple & ppl a. †**-tute** (earlier), **-tuted**. ME. [L *institut-* pa. ppl stem of *instituere* establish, arrange, teach, f. as IN-² + *statuere* set up.] 1 Establish (a person) in a position; appoint (a person *to* or *into* a position) now only to a cure of souls. ME. b *Rom.* & *Civil Law.* Appoint as heir. L16. 2 Set up, establish, found; bring into use or practice. LME. †b Ordain *that.* L15–M17. †c Order, arrange. M16–M18. d Set in operation; initiate, start. L18. †3 Ground or establish in principles; train, instruct. M16–M19.

1 D. MASSON Young.. was instituted to the united vicarages of St. Peter and St. Mary. b S. HALLIFAX All children.. were to be instituted or disinherited by name. 2 ISAIAH BERLIN Adequate safeguards were instituted against too reckless a trampling upon the.. past. d A. BRINK Ben.. instituted inquiries. I. MURDOCH Do you imagine that you can institute a revolution by propounding theory?

instituter *n.* M16. **institutive** *a.* having the character or quality of instituting something; tending to the institution of something: E17.

institution /ɪnstɪˈtjuːʃ(ə)n/ *n.* & *a.* LME. [(O)Fr. f. L *institutio(n-)*, f. *institut-*: see prec., -ION.] A *n.* 1 The action or an act of instituting something; the fact of being instituted. LME. b *Chr. Ch.* The establishment of a sacrament, esp. the Eucharist, by Christ. Also, a passage (e.g. *this is my body, this is my blood*) of the prayer used in consecrating the Eucharist. M16. 2a *Chr. Ch.* The appointment of a person to a cure of souls. LME. b *Rom.* & *Civil Law.* The appointment of an heir. M17. 3 An established law, custom, or practice. LME. b A well-established or familiar practice or object. *colloq.* M19. †4 The giving of form or order to a thing; orderly arrangement; the established order by which a thing is regulated. E16–E19. †5 Training, instruction, education. M16–L18. †6 = INSTITUTE *n.*[1] 3. M16–E19. 7 A society or organization, *esp.* one founded for charitable or social purposes and freq. providing residential care; the building used by such a society or organization. E18.

1 ADAM SMITH Before the Institution of coined money.. people must always have been liable to the grossest frauds. 3 W. S. CHURCHILL The institution of Negro slavery had long reigned almost unquestioned. *peculiar institution*: see PECULIAR *a.* b R. MACAULAY The British Sunday was an institution. 7 D. WIGODER I would not be here, in a mental institution.

B *attrib.* or as *adj.* In, of, or pertaining to an institution. E19.

institutional /ɪnstɪˈtjuːʃ(ə)n(ə)l/ *a.* E17. [f. prec. + -AL¹.] 1 Of, pertaining to, or originated by institution; organized. E17. b Of a religion: expressed or organized through institutions. E20. c *Ling.* Institutionalized. M20. 2 Of, pertaining to, or concerned with (a digest of) the elements of a subject, esp. of jurisprudence. M18. 3 Of or pertaining to a society or organization for the promotion of a purpose, esp. a charitable or social one. Also, supposedly characteristic of such an institution; lacking individuality; routine, uniform. L19. b Of advertising: that lays stress on a firm rather than on its product. E20.

1 R. C. A. WHITE Necessary institutional and procedural background is given. b A. E. J. RAWLINSON The Christianity of history is a sacramental and institutional religion. 3 J. MORTIMER The only institutional buildings left unchanged are the church.. and the Rectory. G. SWIFT He pours into pale blue institutional teacups.

institutionally *adv.* M19.

institutionalise *v.* var. of INSTITUTIONALIZE.

institutionalism /ɪnstɪˈtjuːʃ(ə)n(ə)lɪz(ə)m/ *n.* M19. [f. INSTITUTIONAL + -ISM.] The system of institutions; belief in such a system. Also *spec.*, the principles of institutional religion; the characteristics of institutional life.

institutionalist /ɪnstɪˈtuːʃ(ə)n(ə)lɪst/ *n.* E19. [f. as prec. + -IST.] A person who writes on the elements of a subject. Also, an adherent of institutionalism.

institutionalize /ɪnstɪˈtjuːʃ(ə)n(ə)lʌɪz/ *v.t.* Also **-ise**. M19. [f. INSTITUTIONAL + -IZE.] 1 Make institutional; convert into or treat as an institution. Freq. as *institutionalized* ppl a. M19. b *Ling.* Of a speech community: recognize or accept (a word, phrase, etc.). Usu. in *pass.* M20. 2 Place or keep (a person needing care) in an institution; subject to institutional life, esp. for a period of time resulting in unfitness for life outside an institution. Freq. as *institutionalized* ppl a. E20.

1 C. FRANCIS The Spaniards.. had institutionalised torture under the guise of the Inquisition. M. SEYMOUR-SMITH A marvellous satirist.. who had sold out to institutionalized religion. 2 *Daily Telegraph* Because he was hopelessly institutionalised he was unable to look after himself when free. G. PALEY You're a handicapped person mentally... You should have been institutionalized years ago.

institutionali'zation *n.* M20.

institutionary /ɪnstɪˈtjuːʃ(ə)n(ə)ri/ *a.* M17. [f. INSTITUTION + -ARY¹.] †1 Of or pertaining to (elements of) instruction; educational. M17–M18. 2 Of or pertaining to institution or an institution or institutions. E19.

institutor /ˈɪnstɪtjuːtə/ *n.* M16. [L, f. as INSTITUTE *v.* + -OR.] 1 A person who institutes or establishes something; a founder, an organizer. M16. †2 A person who teaches. E17–E19. 3 In the American Episcopal Church: a bishop or presbyter who institutes a minister into a parish or church. E19.

institutress *n.* a female institutor L18. **insti'tutrix** *n.*, pl. **-trices** /-trɪsiːz/, an institutress E18.

†**instore** *v.t.* LME. [L *instaurare*: see INSTAURATION.] 1 Restore, repair, renew. LME–M16. 2 Erect, establish, commence. Only in LME. 3 Provide, supply; store *with.* LME–M19.

in-store /ˈɪnstɔː/ *a.* M20. [f. IN-¹ + STORE *n.*] Of or relating to goods etc. held in store; situated or taking place in a store.

instreaming /ˈɪnstriːmɪŋ/ *n.* M19. [f. IN-¹ + STREAMING *n.*] The action or an act of streaming in; inflow.

instreaming /ˈɪnstriːmɪŋ/ *ppl a.* M19. [f. IN-¹ + STREAMING *ppl a.*] That streams in; inflowing.

instress /ˈɪnstrɛs/ *n.* M19. [f. IN-¹ + STRESS *n.*] The force of the individual or essential quality of an observed object on the mind of the observer. Cf. INSCAPE.

¶In the poetic theory of the English poet Gerard Manley Hopkins (1844–89).

in-stroke /ˈɪnstrəʊk/ *n. rare.* L19. [f. IN-¹ + STROKE *n.*¹] A stroke directed inwards; a striking inwards; *esp.* the action which carries a piston further into the cylinder of an engine.

instruct /ɪnˈstrʌkt/ *v.t.* Pa. pple & ppl a. †**instruct** (earlier), **-ed**. LME. [L *instruct-* pa. ppl stem of *instruere* set up, furnish, fit out, teach, f. as IN-² + *struere* pile up, build.] I 1 Provide with knowledge or information; teach, educate. (Foll. by *in* a subject, a religious belief, etc., †*to*, †*to do.*) LME. 2 Give information to (a person) about a particular fact etc.; inform *that.* L15. b *Law.* Give information as a client to (a solicitor) or as a solicitor to (a counsel); authorize (a solicitor, a counsel) to act for one. M19. 3 Provide with authoritative directions as to action; direct, command, (a person *to do*). E16.

1 SHAKES. *Tit. A.* I was their Tutor to instruct them. J. C. OATES Vernon instructed them.. in composition, literature, and 'elocution'. 2 T. KENEALLY The journal was at pains to instruct citizens on their rights. b DICKENS Having been instructed by Mrs. Martha Bardell, to commence an action against you. M. GILBERT Our client.. instructs us most emphatically that she dispatched three undervests. 3 G. BOYCOTT We were instructed not to leave the hotel.

II †4 Provide *with*; put in order; prepare, equip. Chiefly *poet.* L15–L18. 5 *Sc. Law.* Provide (a statement) with evidence or proof; confirm by evidence; prove. L16.

5 P. WALKER It was also a day of very astonishing apparitions.. which I can instruct the truth of.

instructer *n.* (now *rare*) an instructor M16. **instructible** *a.* (*rare*) E17.

instruction /ɪnˈstrʌkʃ(ə)n/ *n.* LME. [(O)Fr. f. L *instructio(n-)*, f. as prec.: see -ION.] 1 The action or an act of instructing; teaching, education. Freq. foll. by *in.* LME. 2 (An item of) the knowledge etc. taught; an instructive rule; a precept. LME. †3 (An item of) information given to a person about a particular fact etc. LME–M17. 4 A direction, an order, (*to* a person). Freq. in *pl.* LME. b *Law.* In *pl.* Directions given to a solicitor or a counsel. M18. c *Computing.* A direction in a computer program defining and effecting an operation. M20.

1 J. C. OATES Hiram gave instructions.. in arithmetic, classical mythology, and world geography. 4 R. INGALLS Suzanne had given them four different sets of detailed instructions. J. WAIN I gave very careful instructions that they were to be kept away from you. b M. GILBERT My instructions are quite clear... He is prepared to plead guilty to the offence as charged.

instructional *a.* E19.

instructive /ɪnˈstrʌktɪv/ *a.* & *n.* E17. [f. INSTRUCT *v.* + -IVE.] A *adj.* 1 Having the character or quality of instructing; conveying instruction; enlightening. E17. 2 *Gram.* Designating, being in, or pertaining to the case used in the Finno-Ugric and other language groups to express means. M19. B *n. Gram.* *The* instructive case; a word, form, etc., in the instructive case. L19.

instructively *adv.* M17. **instructiveness** *n.* M17.

instructor /ɪnˈstrʌktə/ *n.* LME. [L, f. as INSTRUCT *v.* + -OR.] 1 A person who instructs; a teacher, a demonstrator. LME. 2 A teacher in higher education ranking below a professor. *N. Amer.* E18.

1 A. BURGESS I was a map-reading instructor in the army. 2 *Partisan Review* The academic hierarchy, from instructor up to full professor.

instructorship *n.* the rank or position of an instructor L19. **instructress** *n.* a female instructor M17.

instrument /ˈɪnstrʊm(ə)nt/ *n.* ME. [(O)Fr. f. L *instrumentum*, f. *instruere*: see INSTRUCT *v.*, -MENT.] 1 A thing used in or for performing an action; a means. ME. b *transf.* A person so made use of. ME. 2 More fully *musical instrument.* A contrivance or device for producing musical sounds by vibration, wind, percussion, etc. ME. 3 *Law.* A formal legal document. LME. b *Sc. Law.* A formal and duly authenticated record, drawn up by a notary public, of any transaction. M16. †4 A part of the body having a special function; an organ. LME–E18. 5 A tool, an implement, *esp.* one used for delicate or scientific work. LME. b A device whose function is to register and measure; *spec.* a measuring-device in an aeroplane etc. serving to determine the position or speed. L17. †c Apparatus. Only in L17.

1 H. J. LASKI The Cabinet.. had already become the fundamental administrative instrument. D. M. FRAME For self-study the material is experience, the instrument judgment. b *New York Times* The accused assassin must be an instrument of the radical right. 2 B. EMECHETA They heard stringed instruments like guitars. *original instrument*: see ORIGINAL *a.* 3 I. MURDOCH A sort of informal document, not.. a legal instrument, was drawn up. G. F. KENNAN It would be wrong to attribute excessive importance to the instruments signed at Brest-Litovsk. 5 P. GALLICO The chattering sound of printing machines, stock tickers and telegraph instruments. P. O'BRIAN The surgeons were putting a final razor edge on their instruments. b C. A. LINDBERGH It was often necessary to fly through them, navigating by instruments only. D. BAGLEY All instruments would be working, recording air pressure, humidity, temperature.

Comb.: **instrument board, panel** a surface, esp. in a car or aeroplane, containing the dials etc. of measuring instruments.

instrument /ˈɪnstrʊm(ə)nt/ *v.* E18. [f. the n.] 1 *Law.* a *v.i.* Draw up an instrument. E18. b *v.t.* Address an instrument to, petition by means of an instrument. M18. 2 *v.t. Mus.* Make an instrumental arrangement or score of (a piece of music). E19. 3 *v.t.* Equip or provide with instruments (for measuring, recording, etc.). M20.

instrumental /ɪnstrʊˈmɛnt(ə)l/ *a.* & *n.* LME. [(O)Fr. f. med.L *instrumentalis*, f. as INSTRUMENT *n.*: see -AL¹.] A *adj.* 1 Serving as an instrument or means to achieve a particular end or purpose. (Foll. by *to, in.*) LME. b Serving well for a particular purpose; useful, efficient. Now *rare* or *obs.* E17. 2 Of music: performed on or composed for an instrument or instruments, *spec.* not accompanying a vocal part. E16. **b** Of the nature of or belonging to a musical instrument. *rare.* L17. 3 Of, pertaining to, or arising from an instrument. M16. †4 (Of a part of the body) having a special function; organic. M16–E17. 5 *Gram.* Expressing the means used; *spec.* designating, being in, or pertaining to a case (in Russian etc.) indicating a means or instrument. E19. 6 *Psychol.* Of or designating a form of conditioning in which the reinforcing stimulus is applied only after a particular response of the organism. M20.

1 P. GAY The passion for power may be instrumental in the acquisition of money. R. ELLMANN She . . was instrumental in arranging for a series of English productions of his plays. b SWIFT It would be very instrumental to have a law made. 2 M. TIPPETT When the music is to be instrumental only, more is left to our imagination. 3 J. F. W. HERSCHEL We are obliged to have recourse to instrumental aids.

B *n.* †1 A part of the body having a special function; an organ. Only in M16. †2 A thing which serves as an instrument or means to achieve a particular end or purpose. L16–M17. 3 *Gram. The* instrumental case; a word, form, etc., in the instrumental case. E19. 4 A piece of music (to be) performed by an instrument or instruments, not by the voice. M20.

instrumentally *adv.* L16. **instrumentalness** *n.* M17.

instrumentalism /ɪnstrʊˈmɛnt(ə)lɪz(ə)m/ *n.* E20. [f. prec. + -ISM.] The pragmatic philosophy of the American philosopher John Dewey (1859–1952), holding that thought is an instrument designed to solve practical problems over a wide range and that truth is not final and static but changes as these problems change.

instrumentalist /ɪnstrʊˈmɛnt(ə)lɪst/ *n.* E19. [f. INSTRUMENTAL *a.* + -IST.] 1 A person who plays a musical instrument; a performer of instrumental music. E19. 2 An adherent of instrumentalism. E20.

instrumentality /ˌɪnstrʊmɛnˈtalɪti/ *n.* M17. [f. INSTRUMENTAL *a.* + -ITY.] 1 The quality or condition of being instrumental; the fact or function of serving as an instrument or means to achieve a particular end or purpose. M17. 2 A thing which is employed for a purpose or end; a means. L17.

instrumentary /ɪnstrʊˈmɛnt(ə)ri/ *a.* M16. [f. INSTRUMENT *n.* + -ARY[1].] †1 Serving for a particular vital function; organic. M16–M17. †2 Of the nature of or serving as an instrument or means. E–M17. 3 *Sc. Law.* Of or relating to a deed or legal instrument. E18.

instrumentation /ˌɪnstrʊmɛnˈteɪʃ(ə)n/ *n.* M19. [Fr., f. as INSTRUMENT *v.* + -ATION.] 1 The arrangement or composition of music for particular musical instruments; the instruments used in any one piece of music. Also (*rare*), playing on musical instruments. M19. 2 Operation or provision of means; instrumental agency. M19. 3 The use of an instrument, esp. for delicate or scientific work; operation with an instrument. L19. 4 The design and provision of instruments for measurement, control, etc.; such instruments collectively. M20.

instyle /ɪnˈstʌɪl/ *v.t.* Also **en-** /ɪn-, ɛn-/. L16. [f. IN-[2], EN-[1] + STYLE *n.* or *v.*] Call by the style or name of.

insuavity /ɪnˈswɑːvɪti/ *n.* Now *rare* or *obs.* E17. [L *insuavitas*, f. as IN-[3] + SUAVITY.] Lack of suavity; unpleasantness.

insubjection /ɪnsəbˈdʒɛkʃ(ə)n/ *n. rare.* E19. [f. IN-[3] + SUBJECTION.] Lack of subjection; the state of not being subject to authority or control.

insubmergible /ɪnsəbˈməːdʒɪb(ə)l/ *a.* Now *rare.* E19. [f. IN-[3] + SUBMERGIBLE *a.*] Unable to be submerged, = next.

insubmersible /ɪnsəbˈməːsɪb(ə)l/ *a. rare.* M19. [f. IN-[3] + SUBMERSIBLE *a.*] Unable to be submerged, = prec.

insubmissive /ɪnsəbˈmɪsɪv/ *a. rare.* M19. [f. IN-[3] + SUBMISSIVE.] Not submissive; not disposed to submit.

insubordinate /ɪnsəˈbɔːdɪnət/ *a.* & *n.* M19. [f. IN-[3] + SUBORDINATE *a.*] **A** *adj.* Not obedient to orders; defiant of authority; rebellious, disobedient. M19. **B** *n.* An insubordinate person. L19.

insubordinately *adv.* L19.

insubordination /ˌɪnsəbɔːdɪˈneɪʃ(ə)n/ *n.* L18. [f. (as) prec. + -ATION.] The fact or condition of being insubordinate; disobedience to orders; defiance of authority; rebelliousness.

insubstantial /ɪnsəbˈstanʃ(ə)l/ *a.* E17. [Late L *insubstantialis*, f. as IN-[3] + *substantialis* SUBSTANTIAL.] 1 Not existing in substance or reality; not real, imaginary, illusory. E17. 2 Lacking solidity or substance; not substantial. E17.

1 J. R. SEELEY It was no insubstantial city, such as we fancy in the clouds. 2 E. B. BROWNING A common cough striking on an insubstantial frame began my bodily troubles. F. DONALDSON A novel of a purely popular kind, with an insubstantial plot.

insubstantiˈality *n.* M19. **insubstantially** *adv.* L20.

insuccess /ɪnsəkˈsɛs/ *n.* M17. [f. IN-[3] + SUCCESS.] Lack of success.

insudation /ɪnsʊˈdeɪʃ(ə)n/ *n.* M17. [f. L *insudat-* pa. ppl stem of *insudare*, f. as IN-[2] + *sudare* sweat: see -ATION. Cf. EXUDATION.] †1 Sweating; *fig.* heavy labour. *rare.* Only in M17. 2 *Med.* Seepage of plasma or other constituents of blood into or through the walls of a blood-vessel. M20.

†**insue** *v.* var. of ENSUE.

insufferable /ɪnˈsʌf(ə)rəb(ə)l/ *a.* LME. [f. IN-[3] + SUFFERABLE, perh. through Fr. *insouffrable* (now dial.).] Unable to be borne or endured; intolerable, unbearable. Now *esp.* unbearably arrogant or conceited.

P. G. WODEHOUSE There was an insufferable suggestion of . . fatherliness in his attitude which she found irritating. N. COWARD You're quite insufferable; I expect it's because you're drunk.

insufferableness *n.* L16. **insufferably** *adv.* E17.

insuffice /ɪnsəˈfʌɪs/ *v.i. rare.* M19. [f. IN-[3] + SUFFICE *v.*] Be insufficient.

insufficience /ɪnsəˈfɪʃ(ə)ns/ *n.* Now *rare* or *obs.* LME. [OFr., f. as next: see -ENCE.] 1 = INSUFFICIENCY 1. LME. 2 = INSUFFICIENCY 2. L15.

insufficiency /ɪnsəˈfɪʃ(ə)nsi/ *n.* E16. [Late L *insufficientia*, f. *insufficient-*: see next, -ENCY.] 1 Inability of a person to fulfil requirements; unfitness, incompetence; an instance of this. *arch.* E16. 2 Deficiency in the force, quality, or amount of something; inadequacy. M16. 3 *Med.* Physical incapacity or impotence; impaired ability of an organ or system to do its natural work. E18.

2 C. G. WOLFF She is limited . . by the insufficiency of her experience in the actual world. J. BRODSKY I am far from accusing the English language of insufficiency. 3 *Lancet* Limbs with chronic venous insufficiency.

insufficient /ɪnsəˈfɪʃ(ə)nt/ *a.* LME. [OFr. f. late L *insufficient-* f. as IN-[3] + *sufficient-* SUFFICIENT.] †1 Of a person: not capable of fulfilling requirements; unfit; incompetent. LME–L17. **b** Not having enough of a thing; inadequately provided with money etc. LME–E17. 2 Of a thing: deficient in force, quality, or amount; inadequate. LME.

1 SPENSER Soe as the bishop . . may justly rejecte them as incapable and insufficient. 2 R. ELLMANN The staples were weak gruel, suet and water. . . Such food was revolting and insufficient.

insufficiently *adv.* LME. **insufficientness** *n.* (long *rare* or *obs.*) LME.

insufflate /ˈɪnsəfleɪt/ *v.t.* L17. [Late L *insufflat-* pa. ppl stem of *insufflare*, f. as IN-[2] + L *sufflare* SUFFLATE.] 1 *Theol.* †**a** Blow or breathe (a spirit etc.) into a person. Only in L17. **b** Blow or breathe on (a person) to symbolize spiritual influence. E20. 2 *Med.* Blow (air, gas, powder, etc.) into an opening or cavity of the body. L17.

insufflator *n.* (chiefly *Med.*) an instrument for insufflating air, powder, etc., esp. into the lungs L19.

insufflation /ɪnsəˈfleɪʃ(ə)n/ *n.* LME. [Late L *insufflatio(n-)*, f. as prec.: see -ATION.] 1 *Theol.* **a** The action or an act of blowing on a person to symbolize spiritual influence. LME. **b** The action or an act of blowing or breathing a spirit etc. into a person. E17. 2 Chiefly *Med.* The blowing or breathing (of a gas, powder, etc.) into an opening or cavity (of the body). E19. 3 *Med.* Distension with air. L19.

insula /ˈɪnsjʊlə/ *n.* Pl. **-lae** /-liː/. M19. [L = island.] 1 *Rom. Hist.* A block of buildings; a square or space mapped out or divided off. M19. 2 *Anat.* A region of the brain deep in the cerebral cortex. Also called *island of Reil.* L19.

insular /ˈɪnsjʊlə/ *n.* & *a.* M16. [Late L *insularis*, f. as prec.: see -AR[1].] **A** *n.* A native or inhabitant of an island; an islander. Now *rare.* M16.

B *adj.* 1 Of or pertaining to an island; inhabiting or situated on an island. E17. **b** *Physical Geogr.* Of climate: equable because of the influence of the sea (as that of islands and sheltered coasts). M19. 2 Of the nature of an island; forming an island. M17. 3 Of, pertaining to, or characteristic of islanders; ignorant of or indifferent to cultures, peoples, etc., outside one's own experience; narrow-minded. L18. **b** *Palaeogr.* Designating or pertaining to a development of Latin script current in the British Isles in the early Middle Ages. E20. 4 Detached, separated, isolated; *Med.* of or pertaining to the insula, or the islets of Langerhans; *spec.* (of sclerosis) disseminated. L19.

2 A. R. WALLACE A description of the great insular land—Australia. 3 G. SANTAYANA He felt how incredibly insular it was to suppose that England meant home for everybody. B. GUEST The magazine would not be insular, but international in intent.

insularism *n.* the quality of being insular; narrow-mindedness: L19. **insularize** *v.t.* (*rare*) make insular; represent as an island: L19. **insularly** *adv.* M19. **insulary** *a.* & *n.* (now *rare* or *obs.*) (*a*) *adj.* insular; (*b*) *n.* an inhabitant of an island; an islander: L16.

insularity /ɪnsjʊˈlarɪti/ *n.* M18. [f. as prec. + -ITY.] 1 The state or condition of being an islander; ignorance of or indifference to cultures, peoples, etc., outside one's own experience; narrow-mindedness. M18. 2 The state or condition of being an island. L18.

1 BARONESS ORCZY When our prejudiced insularity was at its height, when to an Englishman . . the whole of . . Europe was a den of immorality. 2 J. PINKERTON The insularity of Britain was first shown by Agricola, who sent his fleet round it.

insulate /ˈɪnsjʊlət/ *a.* Now *rare.* E18. [L *insulatus*, f. as INSULA: see -ATE[2].] Detached, isolated; insulated.

insulate /ˈɪnsjʊleɪt/ *v.t.* M16. [f. L INSULA or as prec.: see -ATE[3].] 1 Make (land) into an island. *arch.* M16. 2 Cause (a thing etc.) to stand detached from its surroundings; isolate. E18. 3 Isolate by the interposition of non-conductive materials, to prevent the passage of electricity, heat, or sound. M18.

1 D. WILSON Ere Britain had been insulated from the continent. 2 M. M. KAYE Insulated by distance and the slower pace of life . . Ash had soon lost interest in . . political wrangling. 3 *Pall Mall Gazette* Two coils of insulated copper wire. *Home Plumbing* Insulating jackets are available to lag hot water cylinders. **insulating tape**: impregnated with an insulating compound and used to cover exposed electrical wires etc.

insulative *a.* of or pertaining to insulation; providing insulation: M20.

insulation /ɪnsjʊˈleɪʃ(ə)n/ *n.* M18. [f. INSULATE *v.* + -ATION.] 1 The action of insulating or the condition of being insulated against the passage of electricity, heat, or sound; the degree to which something is insulated. M18. **b** Insulating or non-conductive material. L19. 2 The action or an act of detaching or separating a thing etc. from its surroundings; the state or condition of being isolated. L18. 3 The action of making land into an island; the fact of being made into an island; an island. M19.

1 *Electrical Review* Higher Voltage demands better insulation. **b** J. S. FOSTER Practical ways of incorporating insulation in wall construction. 2 G.

For other words beginning with *in-* see the entry for **in-**[1]

WAKEFIELD An absolute insulation . . from the reasonable benefits of society.

insulator /ˈɪnsjʊleɪtə/ *n.* E19. [f. as prec. + -OR.] A substance or device which resists or prevents the passage of electricity, heat, or sound.

insulin /ˈɪnsjʊlɪn/ *n.* Also †**-ine**. E20. [f. L INSULA (w. ref. to the islets of Langerhans: see below) + -IN^{1}, -INE^{5}.] A polypeptide hormone (whose composition varies slightly between species) which is produced by the islets of Langerhans and is involved in carbohydrate metabolism in humans and some other vertebrates, and whose deficiency causes diabetes mellitus.

Comb.: **insulin coma**: caused by insulin shock; **insulin shock** (*a*) hypoglycaemia, with weakness and sweating, resulting from excess blood insulin; (*b*) = *insulin treatment* below; **insulin treatment** treatment of mental illness by inducing insulin coma.

insulse /ɪnˈsʌls/ *a.* Now *rare* or *obs.* E17. [L *insulsus*, f. as IN-^{3} + *salsus* witty, lit. 'salted', pa. pple of *salere* to salt, f. *sal* salt.] 1 Lacking wit or sense; dull, stupid; senseless. E17. 2 Tasteless, insipid. L17.

insulsity *n.* E17.

insult /ˈɪnsʌlt/ *n.* E17. [Fr. *insulte* or eccl.L *insultus*, f. as IN-^{2} + L *saltus* leap, after *insultare*: see next.] 1 An act or the action of attacking; (an) attack, (an) assault. Formerly *spec.* (*Mil.*), an open and sudden attack without formal preparations. *arch.* E17. b *Med.* An action or process causing injury to the body or disturbance of its normal functions; the injury or disturbance so caused; trauma. E20. 2 The action or an act of insulting a person etc.; an instance of this; an insulting remark or action. Also (*colloq.*), a thing so worthless or contemptible as to be offensive. L17.

1 H. H. WILSON The . . pirate . . by whom the trade of the Company was subjected to repeated insult. b D. W. GOODWIN The body adapts rapidly to chemical insults. 2 W. S. CHURCHILL Many are the insults and slanders which we have allowed to pass . . unanswered. W. WHARTON Vegas, plumb smack in the middle of a desert, is an insult to nature. **add insult to injury** behave offensively as well as harmfully.

insult /ɪnˈsʌlt/ *v.* M16. [L *insultare*, f. as IN-^{2} + *saltare* iterative-intensive of *salire* leap, jump.] 1 *v.i.* Show arrogance or scorn; boast, exult, esp. insolently or contemptuously. Also foll. by *over*, *on*, the person or thing scorned; *in*, *of*, the cause of boasting. *arch.* M16. 2 *v.t.* Treat with scornful abuse; subject to indignity; (of a person or thing) offend the modesty or self-respect of. E17. †3 *v.i.* Make an attack or assault. M–L17. 4 *v.t.* Attack, assault, (now only *fig.*). Formerly *spec.* (*Mil.*), attack openly and suddenly without formal preparations. L17.

1 S. DANIEL They know how, The Lyon being dead euen Hares insult. S. PEPYS The Dutch do mightily insult of their victory, and they have great reason. DE QUINCEY We all know that it was not in his nature to insult over the fallen. 2 J. UPDIKE This stranger should be told that insulting local people was not the way to win friends. I. MURDOCH You insult us by implying that we don't care. 4 G. P. R. JAMES A group of night-ramblers walked along insulting the ear of night with cries.

insultable *a.* (*rare*) able to be insulted M19. **insultant** *a.* (*rare*) insulting E17. **insulter** *n.* L16. **insultingly** *adv.* in an insulting manner E17. †**insultment** *n.* (*rare*, Shakes.) the action of insulting, insult: only in E17.

insultation /ɪnsʌlˈteɪʃ(ə)n/ *n.* Now *rare* or *obs.* E16. [OFr., or L *insultatio(n-)*, f. *insultat-* pa. ppl stem of *insultare*: see prec., -ATION.] 1 The action or an act of insulting; contemptuous speech or behaviour; insult. E16. †2 Attack, assault. L16–M17.

†**insume** *v.t.* L16–M17. [Alt. by substitution of IN-^{2} of ASSUME *v.*] Take in, absorb.

insuperable /ɪnˈsuːp(ə)rəb(ə)l, -ˈsjuː-/ *a.* ME. [OFr., or L *insuperabilis*, f. as IN-^{3} + SUPERABLE.] 1 Unable to be overcome or vanquished; unconquerable, invincible. Now *rare* or *obs.* exc. as passing into sense 3. ME. 2 Of a barrier, gulf, etc.: unable to be surmounted or passed over. Now chiefly as passing into sense 3. M17. 3 *fig.* Of a difficulty, problem, etc.: unable to be surmounted or overcome. M17. 4 Unable to be surpassed. *rare.* M19.

1 P. HOLLAND Three hundred thousand fighting men . . all invincible soldiers, and appointed with armes insuperable. 2 HENRY MORE Whether we . . admire the height of some insuperable and inaccessible Rock or Mountain. 3 E. WAUGH At first the difficulties of imitation appeared to be insuperable. I. MURDOCH The absence of any insuperable barrier to their advance to higher levels of income. D. ADAMS He had finally won through against what had seemed to be insuperable odds. 4 A. BURGESS A crystal set, a miracle . . for music and speech of insuperable clarity.

insuperaˈbility *n.* E18. **insuperably** *adv.* L17.

insupportable /ɪnsəˈpɔːtəb(ə)l/ *a.* M16. [(O)Fr., f. as IN-^{3} + SUPPORT *v.*: see -ABLE.] 1 Unable to be endured or borne; insufferable; unbearable. M16. †2 Unable to be resisted; irresistible. L16–L17. 3 Unable to be supported or sustained by reasons; unjustifiable, indefensible. M17.

1 G. K. CHESTERTON He . . became that elegant and rather insupportable person whom Gregory had first encountered. M. MEYER The combination of overwork, poverty and literary failure became almost insupportable. 3 M. GORDON He was always making large insupportable statements like, 'London was nothing after the eighteenth century.'

insupportableness *n.* L16. **insupportably** *adv.* L17.

insupposable /ɪnsəˈpəʊzəb(ə)l/ *a. rare.* M17. [f. IN-^{3} + SUPPOSABLE.] Unable to be supposed.

insuppressible /ɪnsəˈprɛsɪb(ə)l/ *a.* E17. [f. IN-^{3} + SUPPRESS + -IBLE.] Unable to be suppressed; irrepressible.

SMOLLETT Seized with insuppressible sorrow at the prospect of my misery he burst into tears.

insuppressive /ɪnsəˈprɛsɪv/ *a. rare.* E17. [f. IN-^{3} + SUPPRESSIVE.] Insuppressible.

insurance /ɪnˈʃʊər(ə)ns/ *n.* Also (earlier) †**en-**. LME. [OFr. *enseürance*, f. as ENSURE, INSURE: see -ANCE.] 1 The action or a means of ensuring or making certain; assurance, guarantee. Now chiefly as passing into sense 2. LME. 2 The act or process of insuring property, life, etc.; a contract by which one party undertakes on receipt of a premium to secure another against financial loss by a payment in the event of loss, damage, injury, etc. Cf. ASSURANCE 6. M17. b The sum paid for insuring something; a premium. M17. c A sum (to be) paid out as compensation; the amount for which property or life is insured. M19. d In full *National Insurance*. A system of compulsory contribution from employed adults below pension age and from employers to provide State assistance in sickness, unemployment, retirement, etc. L19. 3 Something which provides safety (*against*). E20.

1 W. J. MICKLE An offering grateful to their gods, as the most acceptable insurance of the divine protection. E. CRANKSHAW The British were . . thinking . . , only of insurance against possible German aggression. 2 *Dumfries & Galloway Standard* The insurance cannot stop the motor car going wrong but it can take care of the expense. *Society* (*Bombay*) Here we have good health insurance and that takes care of many of our problems. *social insurance*: see SOCIAL *a.* b *London Gazette* The Insurance upon our Convoy to the Levant is very high. OED His Insurance falls due this month.

Comb.: **insurance agent**: employed to collect premiums from door to door; **insurance company**: engaged in insuring lives, property, etc.; **insurance policy** (*a*) a contract of insurance; (*b*) a document detailing such a policy and constituting a contract; (*c*) *fig.* a measure taken as a precaution; **insurance premium** = sense 2c above; **insurance stamp** a stamp certifying the payment of a sum, usu. paid weekly, for National Insurance.

†**insurancer** *n.* a person who provides insurance or assurance M17–E19.

insurant /ɪnˈʃʊər(ə)nt/ *n.* M19. [f. next + -ANT^{1}.] The person to whom an insurance policy is issued.

insure /ɪnˈʃʊə/ *v.* LME. [Alt. by substitution of IN-^{2} of ENSURE.] †1 *v.t.* Make (a person) sure (*of* a thing); assure. LME–L17. 2 *v.t.* Secure the payment of a sum of money in the event of loss of, damage to, or injury to (property, life, a limb, etc.) by the payment of a premium; secure the payment of (a sum of money) in the event of or *against* such a loss etc. by the payment of a premium. M17. b *v.i.* Issue an insurance policy; take out insurance. M17. 3 *v.t.* Make certain, guarantee (a thing, event, etc.). L17. 4 *v.t.* Make safe, secure (*against*, *from*). E18.

1 T. PRESTON I insure you he is a king most vile and pernicious. J. SCOTT The most effectual Care . . to insure us of God's performing his Part. 2 **the insured** the person in respect of whom an insurance payment is secured, or on whose death, illness, or injury insurance becomes due. 3 J. RUSKIN Want of care in the points which insure the building's endurance. 4 J. D. BURNS The evidence of trials past does not insure them against trials that may come.

insuraˈbility *n.* the quality of being insurable L19. **insurable** *a.* able to be insured, suitable for insuring; sufficient to make a ground for insurance: E19. **insurer** *n.* M16.

insurge /ɪnˈsəːdʒ/ *v.* Now *rare* or *obs.* E16. [L *insurgere*: see INSURGENT.] †1 *v.i.* Arise, spring up. Only in 16. †2 *v.i.* Rise in opposition or rebellion *against*; revolt. M16–E17. 3 *v.t.* Stir up; raise in rebellion. L18.

insurgence /ɪnˈsəːdʒ(ə)ns/ *n.* M19. [f. as INSURGENT: see -ENCE.] Insurgency.

insurgency /ɪnˈsəːdʒ(ə)nsi/ *n.* E19. [f. as prec.: see -ENCY.] The quality or state of being insurgent; the tendency to be insurgent; a rising, a revolt.

F. FITZGERALD Fortified villages such as the British had used against the Communist insurgency in Malaya.

insurgent /ɪnˈsəːdʒ(ə)nt/ *n.* & *a.* M18. [Fr. †*insurgent* f. L *insurgent-* pres. ppl stem of *insurgere*, f. as IN-^{2} + *surgere* rise: see -ENT.] A *n.* A person who rebels or rises in active revolt against authority; a rebel, a revolutionary. M18.

DAY LEWIS The unexpectedness of an ultimatum delivered by insurgents who have achieved a revolution.

B *adj.* 1 Of the sea etc.: surging up, rushing in. L18. 2 Rising in active revolt, rebelling; rebellious. E19.

1 *fig.*: D. H. LAWRENCE Her voice was full of insurgent tenderness. 2 R. WHELAN Insurgent planes swooped down over the road to machine-gun the helpless refugees.

insurmountable /ɪnsəˈmaʊntəb(ə)l, -səː-/ *a.* L17. [f. IN-^{3} + SURMOUNTABLE.] Unable to be surmounted or overcome.

C. HOPE The problem seemed insurmountable.

insurmountably *adv.* M18.

insurpassable /ɪnsəˈpɑːsəb(ə)l, -səː-/ *a. rare.* M19. [f. IN-^{3} + SURPASSABLE.] Unable to be surpassed.

insurrect /ɪnsəˈrɛkt/ *v.i.* Now *rare* or *obs.* M17. [L *insurrect-* pa. ppl stem of *insurgere*: see INSURGENT.] †1 Arise. Only in M17. 2 Rise in insurrection or revolt. E19.

insurrection /ɪnsəˈrɛkʃ(ə)n/ *n.* LME. [(O)Fr. f. late L *insurrectio(n-)*, f. as prec.: see -ION.] The action or an act of rising against authority or government; a rebellion, a revolt, an uprising.

E. WILSON Driven underground, they now plotted an insurrection. *fig.*: P. ROTH Your escapade, your risk, your daily insurrection against all your overwhelming virtues.

insurrectional *a.* (now *rare*) E19. **insurrectionary** *a.* & *n.* (*a*) *adj.* of, pertaining to, or resembling insurrection; given to insurrection; (*b*) *n.* a person who takes part in or encourages insurrection: L18. **insurrectionist** *n.* an insurrectionary M19.

insurrecto /ɪnsəˈrɛktəʊ/ *n.* Pl. **-os**. E20. [Sp., f. L *insurrectus* pa. pple of *insurgere*: see INSURGENT.] Esp. in Spain and Spanish-speaking countries: an insurgent, a rebel; an insurrectionist.

insusceptible /ɪnsəˈsɛptɪb(ə)l/ *a.* E17. [f. IN-^{3} + SUSCEPTIBLE *a.*] Not susceptible; not able to receive impressions; not liable to be affected or influenced.

R. H. CHARLES Souls in Sheol were conceived as insusceptible of ethical progress. L. P. BROCKETT Insusceptible to all those influences . . which so powerfully affect most peoples.

insusceptiˈbility *n.* E19.

inswinger /ˈɪnswɪŋə/ *n.* E20. [f. IN-^{1} + SWINGER *n.*^{1}] 1 *Cricket.* A ball bowled with a swerve or swing from off to leg; a bowler who bowls such balls. E20. 2 *Football.* A pass or kick that sends the ball curving towards the goal. L20.

For other words beginning with *in-* see the entry for **in-**^{1}

inswing *n.* [back-form.] *Cricket* the swerve or swing imparted to an inswinger E20.

i'nt *v.* see BE.

†intablature *n.* var. of ENTABLATURE.

intabulate /ɪn'tabjʊleɪt/ *v.t.* M17. [med.L *intabulat-* pa. ppl stem of *intabulare*, f. L IN-[2] + *tabula* table: see -ATE[3]. In sense 2 back-form. f. next.] 1 Enter or inscribe in a table or list. *rare.* M17. 2 *Mus.* Make an intabulation of. L20.

intabulation /ɪn,tabjʊ'leɪʃ(ə)n/ *n.* M17. [f. as prec.: see -ATION. In sense 2 tr. It. *intavolatura* writing in tablature, f. as IN-[2] + *tavolatura* TABLATURE.] †1 The laying down of boards or planks. *rare.* Only in M17. 2 *Mus.* An arrangement for lute or keyboard. M20.

intact /ɪn'takt/ *a.* LME. [L *intactus*, f. as IN-[3] + *tactus* pa. pple of *tangere* to touch.] Untouched; not affected by anything that causes injury, damage, or loss; unblemished; unimpaired.

M. RULE A wooden warship had been recovered almost intact. B. T. BRADFORD Her love for Vincent remained intact and unchanged.

intactness *n.* L19.

intacta /ɪn'taktə/ *a.* M20. [L, fem. of *intactus* (see prec.), extracted f. VIRGO INTACTA.] Inviolate, unaffected; not spoiled or sullied.

†intaglia *n.* var. of INTAGLIO *n.*

intagliated /ɪn'talɪeɪtɪd/ *a.* L18. [f. It. *intagliato* pa. pple of *intagliare*: see next, -ED[1].] Carved on the surface; engraved in or as in intaglio; incised.

intaglio /ɪn'talɪəʊ, -'tɑːl-/ *n.* & *v.* Also **†-ia.** M17. [It., f. *intagliare* engrave, f. as IN-[2] + *tagliare* to cut.] A *n.* Pl. **-os.** 1 A figure or design incised or engraved; a cutting or engraving in a hard material. M17. 2 A thing ornamented with incised work; *esp.* a precious stone having a figure or design cut on its surface. M17. b A mould of something to be cast or struck in relief. E19. 3 The process or art of engraving or carving in a hard material; printing in which the image is engraved or etched into a metal plate or cylinder so that it lies below the non-printing areas. Also, the condition of being incised. M18.

3 *Ashmolean* Men of the Renaissance shared . . a passion for precious . . stones carved in relief or intaglio. *attrib.*: H. ALLEN He began to indent rapidly a deft little intaglio design of vines and flowers.

B *v.t.* Engrave with a sunken pattern; execute in intaglio. M19.

†intail *n.*, *v.* vars. of ENTAIL *n.*[2], *v.*[2]

intake /'ɪnteɪk/ *n.* & *a.* Orig. *Sc.* & *north.* ME. [f. phr. *take in*: see IN *adv.*, TAKE *v.*] A *n.* 1 A piece of land taken in from a moorland, common, etc.; an enclosure. Chiefly *north.* ME. 2 The place where water is channelled from a body of water to drive a mill, supply a canal, etc. LME. 3 A narrowing or abrupt contraction made in the width of a tube, stocking, etc.; the point at which this is made. M18. 4 The act of taking in or receiving from outside; a thing which is taken in, a quantity received. E19. b (A member of) a group of entrants to the army, a school, a trade, etc. M20. 5 An imposition; a cheat. *Sc.* E19. 6 *Mining.* A passage by which a current of air is introduced into a mine. M19. 7 A duct or passage by which air etc. is introduced into a machine. M20.

B *attrib.* or as *adj.* That takes in; of the nature of or pertaining to an intake. E20.

intake manifold: see MANIFOLD *n.* 5.

intaking /ɪn'teɪkɪŋ/ *n.* L16. [f. IN-[1] + TAKING *n.*] 1 The action of capturing or taking by force. *Sc.* Long *arch.* L16. 2 The taking of moorland into cultivation. *Sc.* E19. 3 A taking in from the outside. E20.

intangible /ɪn'tandʒɪb(ə)l/ *a.* & *n.* E17. [Fr., or med.L *intangibilis*, or f. IN-[3] + TANGIBLE.] A *adj.* 1 Not tangible; unable to be touched; impalpable. E17. 2 *fig.* Unable to be mentally grasped. L19.

1 J. TYNDALL The assumption of this wonderful intangible aether. P. GAY It was that intangible thing, morale, . . that gave Britain her victories.

B *n.* An intangible thing; an asset which cannot be precisely measured. E20.

Economist Net tangible assets may be defined as total assets less 'intangibles' (goodwill, patents, etc.), current liabilities, and funded debt. H. ROBBINS That was the intangible in the back of Johnny's mind.

intangi'bility *n.* (*a*) inviolability; (*b*) intangible quality: L18. **intangibleness** *n.* (*rare*) E19. **intangibly** *adv.* L17.

†intangle *v.*, **†intanglement** *n.* vars. of ENTANGLE, ENTANGLEMENT.

intarissable /ɪn'tarɪsəb(ə)l/ *a. rare.* M17. [Fr., f. as IN-[3] + *tarissable*, f. *tariss-*, *tarir* dry up: see -ABLE.] Unable to be dried up; inexhaustible.

intarsia /ɪn'tɑːsɪə/ *n.* In sense 1, 2 also **-io** /-ɪəʊ/, pl. **-os.** M19. [It. *intarsio*.] 1 (A piece of) mosaic woodwork, esp. made in 15th-cent. Italy; the art of making this. Also called *tarsia*. M19. 2 (A piece of) similar inlaid work in stone, metal, or glass. M19. 3 A method of knitting with a number of colours in which a separate length or ball of yarn is used for each area of colour (as opp. to the different yarns being carried at the back of the work). Freq. *attrib.* M20.

1 *attrib.*: H. F. JONES The seats of the stalls . . ornamented with intarsia work. *fig.*: *Listener* Poems, with their tesselated intarsia of natural scenery, natural passion and liturgical imagery.

integer /'ɪntɪdʒə/ *a.* & *n.* E16. [L = intact, f. as IN-[3] + *tag-*, *teg-* base of *tangere* to touch.] A *adj.* †1 Having no part lacking; entire. Only in E16. †2 Marked by moral integrity; honest. Only in M17. 3 *Math.* That is a whole number; integral. *obs.* exc. as attrib. use of the n. M17. B *n.* 1 *Math.* A whole number. L16. †2 A unit of measurement or reckoning. E-M19. 3 A whole or entire thing or entity; a thing complete in itself. M19.

integrable /'ɪntɪgrəb(ə)l/ *a.* E18. [f. INTEGRATE *v.* + -ABLE.] Chiefly *Math.* Able to be integrated.

integra'bility *n.* E19.

integral /'ɪntɪgr(ə)l, *as adj. also* ɪn'tɛgr(ə)l/ *a.* & *n.* M16. [Late L *integralis*, f. as INTEGER: see -AL[1].] A *adj.* 1 Belonging to or making up a whole; constituent, component; necessary to the completeness or integrity of the whole, not merely attached. M16. 2 Made up of component parts which together constitute a unity; *esp.* in *Logic*, consisting of or divisible into parts external to each other. L16. 3 Having no part or element separated or lacking; whole, complete. E17. 4 *Math.* a That is, or is denoted by, a whole number; involving only whole numbers, not fractional. M17. b Relating to or involving integrals (see sense B.4 below) or integration. E18.

1 E. M. GOULBURN Recreation must form an integral part of human life. R. T. GLAZEBROOK This cylinder has an open-ended steel barrel with integral fins. *Motor Trend* Its front air dam has integral foglights. 2 *Which?* An integral washer/drier which washes and tumble dries in one drum. 3 A. STORR Their novels are attempts to make some kind of coherent, integral whole. 4b *integral calculus*: see CALCULUS 1. **integral sign** the sign ∫ placed before the integrand, denoting an integral.

B *n.* 1 An entire or undivided thing; a whole. Now only as a *fig.* use of sense 4, a total sum. E17. †2 An integral part or element; a constituent, a component. M-L17. †3 *Gram.* A word or part of speech that expresses a distinct notion rather than a relation between notions. L17-M19. 4 *Math.* An expression of which a given function is a derivative, and which expresses the area under the curve of the graph of the given function. Also, a function which satisfies a given differential equation. E18.

1 *Nature* What is seen in a sun-spot is the integral . . of all that is taking place . . in many thousand miles of solar atmosphere. 4 *definite integral*: see DEFINITE *a.* *indefinite integral*: see INDEFINITE *a.* *particular integral*: see PARTICULAR *a.*

inte'grality *n.* E17. **integrally** *adv.* L15.

integralism /ɪn'tɛgr(ə)lɪz(ə)m/ *n.* L19. [f. prec. + -ISM.] A doctrine or theory that involves the concept of an integral whole.

integralist *n.* & *a.* (*a*) *n.* an adherent of integralism; (*b*) *adj.* of or pertaining to integralism or integralists: E20.

integrand /'ɪntɪgrand/ *n.* L19. [L *integrandus* gerundive of *integrare* INTEGRATE *v.*: see -AND.] *Math.* A function that is to be integrated.

integrant /'ɪntɪgr(ə)nt/ *a.* & *n.* M17. [Fr. *intégrant*, f. *intégrer* f. L *integrare*: see INTEGRATE *v.*, -ANT[1].] A *adj.* Of parts: making up or contributing to a whole; constituent; essential to the completeness of the whole. M17. B *n.* A thing which integrates; a component. E19.

integraph /'ɪntɪgrɑːf/ *n.* L19. [Fr. *intégraphe*, f. *intégral* (f. as INTEGRAL) or *intégrer* (see prec.) + *-graphe* -GRAPH.] A device which automatically plots a curve expressing the variation in the integral of a given function as a parameter is varied.

integrate /'ɪntɪgrət/ *a.* LME. [L *integratus* pa. pple of *integrare*: see next, -ATE[2].] 1 Made up of separate parts, composite; belonging to a whole; complete, perfect. LME. 2 *Psychol.* In E.R. Jaensch's theory: of, pertaining to, or designating people with strong eidetic imagery. M20.

integrate /'ɪntɪgreɪt/ *v.* M17. [L *integrat-* pa. ppl stem of *integrare*, f. as INTEGER: see -ATE[3].] 1 *v.t.* Make entire or complete; make up, compose, constitute (a whole). M17. b Complete or perfect by the addition of the necessary parts. L17. 2 *v.t.* *Math.* Obtain the integral of. E18. b *gen.* Indicate or register the mean value or total sum of (a physical quantity, as area, temperature, etc.). Freq. as *integrating* ppl a. (of instruments). M19. 3 *v.t.* Put or bring together (parts) to form a whole; combine into a whole. E19. 4 *v.t.* Bring (racially or culturally differentiated peoples) into equal membership of a society or system. Also, desegregate. Cf. SEGREGATE *v.* 1b. M20. b *v.i.* Become (racially or culturally) integrated. M20.

1 W. CHILLINGWORTH The particular doctrines which integrate Christianity. 3 J. UPDIKE Bech's books still waited to be integrated with the books already there. 4 C. HOPE Father Lynch . . insisted on integrating the two dozen black servants . . into the white congregation. b V. GLENDINNING Johnny integrated happily enough in the coarse goldrush life.

integrator *n.* an instrument for performing integration, esp. for indicating or registering the total amount or mean value of some physical quantity L19.

integrated /'ɪntɪgreɪtɪd/ *ppl a.* L16. [f. prec. + -ED[1].] 1 Combined into a whole; united; undivided. L16. b Designating or characterized by a personality in which the component elements combine harmoniously. M20. c Uniting several components previously regarded as separate. M20. 2 Of an institution, group, etc.: not divided by considerations of race or culture; not segregated. M20.

1b *Lancet* The plaintiff was well integrated and had learned to live with the problem. c *Business Education Today* An integrated course is one in which separate aspects of the curriculum . . are subordinate to an overall unifying factor. **integrated circuit** *Electronics* a single chip etc. of material replacing a conventional electric circuit.

integration /ɪntɪ'greɪʃ(ə)n/ *n.* E17. [L *integratio(n-)*, f. *integrat-*: see INTEGRATE *v.*, -ATION.] 1 The making up or composition of a whole by adding together or combining separate parts; combination into a whole. E17. b The harmonious combination of the different elements in a personality. M20. 2 *Math.* The process or an instance of obtaining the integral of a function (the reverse of *differentiation*). E18. 3 The process of bringing about or achieving equal membership of a population or social group; removal or absence of discrimination against groups or people on racial or cultural grounds; desegregation. Cf. SEGREGATION 1(f). M20.

2 **constant of integration** the indeterminate additive constant which arises when any function is integrated (the derivative of any constant being zero). *integration by parts*: see PART *n.*

integrational *a.* M20. **integrationist** *n.* & *a.* (*a*) *n.* an advocate of (racial or cultural) integration; (*b*) *adj.* of or pertaining to people or policies favouring integration: M20.

integrative /'ɪntɪgrətɪv/ *a.* M19. [f. INTEGRATE *v.* + -IVE.] Having the quality of integrating; tending to integrate.

integrism /'ɪntɪgrɪz(ə)m/ *n.* M20. [Fr. *intégrisme*, f. *intégrer*: see INTEGRANT, -ISM.] = INTEGRALISM.

integrist *n.* & *a.* = INTEGRALIST *n.* & *a.* E20.

integrity /ɪnˈtɛgrɪti/ *n.* LME. [Fr. *intégrité* or L *integritas*, f. as INTEGER: see -ITY.] **1** The condition of having no part or element taken away or lacking; undivided state; completeness. LME. **2** The condition of not being marred or violated; unimpaired or uncorrupted condition; original state; soundness. LME. **3** †**a** Freedom from moral corruption; innocence, sinlessness. M16–L17. **b** Soundness of moral principle; the character of uncorrupted virtue; uprightness, honesty, sincerity. M16.

1 C. LYELL The integrity of the cones . . shows that the country has not been agitated by violent earthquakes. H. MACMILLAN To preserve the integrity and independence of Jordan. 2 S. JOHNSON This prayer, that I might try the integrity of my faculties, I made in Latin verse. 3b W. SOYINKA Old comrades . . divest themselves of reason and integrity and plunge greedily into . . exploitation. C. HOPE Their aim was personal sanctity combined with financial integrity.

integro-differential /ˌɪntɪgrəʊdɪfəˈrɛnʃ(ə)l/ *a.* E20. [f. INTEGRAL *a.* + -O- + DIFFERENTIAL *a.*] *Math.* Involving both integral and differential quantities.

integument /ɪnˈtɛgjʊm(ə)nt/ *n.* E17. [L *integumentum*, f. *integere* cover in, f. as IN-[2] + *tegere* to cover: see -MENT.] **1** Something with which an object is covered, enclosed, or clothed; a covering, a coating. E17. **2** A natural outside covering of (part of) an animal or plant body, as a skin, husk, rind, shell, etc. M17.

integuˈmental *a.* M19. **integuˈmentary** *a.* M19.

intellect /ˈɪntɪlɛkt/ *n.* LME. [(O)Fr., or L *intellectus* perception, discernment, meaning, sense, f. *intellect-* pa. ppl stem of *intellegere*: see INTELLIGENT.] **1** The faculty of knowing and reasoning; power of thought; understanding; analytic intelligence. LME. †**2** The meaning or purport (of a word or passage). Only in 16. **3** A person of (usu. great) intelligence, an intellectual; *collect.* intellectual people. Formerly also, a rational being. E17. **4** In *pl.* Intellectual powers, mental faculties; wits, senses. *arch. colloq.* L17.

1 M. L. KING The mind's faith, wherein the intellect assents to a belief that God exists. 3 CARLYLE Where . . nearly all the Intellect of the place assembled of an evening. A. J. P. TAYLOR A cleverer man than his son, . . one of the most formidable intellects I have encountered. 4 S. JOHNSON My judgment embarrassed, and my intellects distorted.

intellected *a.* (*rare*) endowed with intellect (of specified kind or quality) L18.

intellectible /ɪntɪˈlɛktɪb(ə)l/ *a.* M16. [Late L *intellectibilis*, f. L *intellect-*: see prec., -IBLE.] *Philos.* †**1** Capable of understanding. -L16. **2** Able to be apprehended by the intellect alone. M19.

intellection /ɪntɪˈlɛkʃ(ə)n/ *n.* LME. [Late L *intellectio(n-)* sense, understanding, f. L *intellect-*: see INTELLECT, -ION.] †**1** The faculty of understanding; intellect. LME–L18. **b** The immediate knowledge or intelligence ascribed to divine beings. E17–M18. **2** (The result of) a particular act of understanding; a notion, an idea. Freq. in *pl.* Now *rare.* L16. **3** The action or process of understanding; the exercise or activity of the intellect; *spec.* understanding, as distinct from imagination. E17.

2 B. H. SMART An intellection having once occurred, remains with us as a notion or something known. 3 J. NORRIS They . . seem to leave no room for any distinction between intellection and imagination.

intellective /ɪntɪˈlɛktɪv/ *a.* LME. [Late L *intellectivus*, f. L *intellect-*: see INTELLECT, -IVE.] **1** Having the faculty of understanding; having intellect. LME. **2** Of or pertaining to (the) understanding or intellect. LME. **3** Characterized by a high degree of understanding; intelligent. E16. †**4** = INTELLECTIBLE 2; *Gram.* abstract. M17–E19.

intellectively *adv.* †(*a*) intelligibly; (*b*) in relation to the intellect: L16.

intellectual /ɪntɪˈlɛktjʊəl/ *a.* & *n.* LME. [L *intellectualis*, f. *intellectus* INTELLECT: see -UAL.] A *adj.* **1** Of or pertaining to the intellect or understanding; that is describable as such in relation to the intellect. LME. **b** That appeals to, engages, or requires the exercise of the intellect. M19. †**2** (Able to be) apprehended only by the intellect; non-material, spiritual. LME–E18. **3a** Characterized by or possessing understanding or intelligence. *obs.* exc. as in sense b. L15. **b** Possessing a high degree of understanding or (esp. analytic) intelligence; given to the exercise of the intellect. Also, of, pertaining to, or characteristic of an intellectual or intellectuals. E19.

1 L. MACNEICE Spiritually bankrupt Intellectual snobs. A. J. AYER The moment of his greatest intellectual awakening was his discovery of the geometry of Euclid. F. WELDON They applied their intellectual energies . . to the practical details of domestic life. **intellectual property** *Law* property that is the product of creativity and does not exist in tangible form (as patents, copyright, etc.). b E. A. FREEMAN Skill in the more intellectual branches of warfare. 2 BACON To descend from spirits and intellectual forms to sensible and material forms. 3a MILTON Who would loose . . this intellectual being? b J. TYNDALL The interest which the intellectual public of England take in the question. E. F. BENSON I thought you would have spectacles . . . large kind hands . . . an intellectual expression.

B *n.* †**1** The intellect, the mind. L16–M17. **2** In *pl.* **a** Intellectual powers, mental faculties; wits. *arch. colloq.* E17. **b** Things pertaining to the intellect. Now *rare* or *obs.* M17. **3** A person of superior (or supposedly superior) intellect, *esp.* one having an analytic mind; an enlightened person. M17.

3 C. HILL Cromwell was no intellectual: the cast of his mind was practical, pragmatic, never doctrinaire. P. HOWARD Delane was not an intellectual He had little taste for literature or learning.

intellectuˈality *n.* [late L *intellectualitas*] the quality or state of being intellectual; intellectual power or ability: LME. **intellectually** *adv.* LME. **intellectualness** *n.* (*rare*) M19.

intellectualise *v.* var. of INTELLECTUALIZE.

intellectualism /ɪntɪˈlɛktjʊəlɪz(ə)m/ *n.* E19. [f. INTELLECTUAL + -ISM, after G *Intellektualismus.*] **1** *Philos.* The doctrine that knowledge is derived from the action of the intellect or pure reason. E19. **2** Devotion to intellectual pursuits; (excessive) exercise of the intellect rather than the emotions. M19.

intellectualist /ɪntɪˈlɛktjʊəlɪst/ *n.* & *a.* E17. [f. as prec. + -IST.] A *n.* A devotee of the intellect; *Philos.* an adherent of intellectualism. E17. **B** *adj.* Of or pertaining to intellectualism or intellectualists; of the nature of an intellectualist. M19.

intellectuaˈlistic *a.* pertaining to or characteristic of intellectualists or intellectualism L19. **intellectuaˈlistically** *adv.* E20.

intellectualize /ɪntɪˈlɛktjʊəlʌɪz/ *v.* Also **-ise**. E19. [f. as prec. + -IZE.] **1** *v.t.* Make intellectual; give an intellectual character to. E19. **2** *v.i.* Exercise the intellect; talk or write intellectually. E19.

1 A. LORDE Black women writers . . don't seem to need to intellectualize this capacity to feel. 2 *Blackwood's Magazine* Yet could I sit and moralize, and intellectualize, for hours.

intellectualiˈzation *n.* E19.

intelligence /ɪnˈtɛlɪdʒ(ə)ns/ *n.* & *v.* LME. [(O)Fr. f. L *intelligentia*, f. as INTELLIGENT: see -ENCE.] A *n.* **1** The faculty of understanding; intellect. LME. **2** Quickness or superiority of understanding, sagacity. LME. **3** The action or fact of understanding something; knowledge, comprehension (*of* something). Now *rare* or *obs.* LME. **4** An intelligent or rational being, esp. a spiritual one; a spirit. LME. **5** Knowledge communicated by or obtained from another; news; information, *spec.* of military value. Formerly also in *pl.*, items of information. LME. **b** Exchange of knowledge, information, opinion, etc.; communication, esp. of secret information. Now *rare* or *obs.* M16. †**c** A relation or basis of communication between people or parties; an understanding *between* or *with.* L16–E19. **6** (People employed in) the obtaining of information, esp. of military or political value; the secret service, espionage. E17.

1 S. SASSOON Was it a mistake . . to try and keep intelligence alive when I could no longer call my life my own? *artificial intelligence*: see ARTIFICIAL *a.* 2. 2 C. G. WOLFF He was a man of considerable intelligence and intellectual promise. *Atlantic Monthly* Nothing so gives the illusion of intelligence as personal association with large sums of money. 3 JOHN HAMILTON It helpis us to the trew intelligence of the scripture. 4 B. MAGEE History is being directed by some outside intelligence (usually God) in accordance with its own purposes. C. SAGAN There may be a time . . when contact will be made with another intelligence on a planet of some far-distant star. 5 R. V. JONES I had the ultimate responsibility for providing Intelligence, . . pictures of what the Germans were doing. R. DAHL We were enthralled by this piece of intelligence. b G. ORWELL They had confessed to intelligence with the enemy. c BACON That ill intelligence that we many times see between great personages.

Attrib. & *comb.*: In the sense 'of or concerned with the gathering of information', as *intelligence agency, department, officer, service*, etc. Special combs., as **intelligence quotient** a number arrived at by intelligence tests and intended to denote the ratio of a person's intelligence to the normal or average; **intelligence test**: designed to measure intelligence rather than acquired knowledge.

†**B** *v.* **1** *v.t.* Bring news of; bring news to, inform. L16–M17. **2** *v.i.* Convey intelligence; tell tales; act as a spy. Freq. as *intelligencing* ppl a. E17–E18.

intelligenced *a.* (*rare*) having intelligence (of a specified kind or quality) E17.

intelligencer /ɪnˈtɛlɪdʒ(ə)nsə/ *n.* M16. [f. prec. + -ER[1], perh. after Fr. †*intelligencier.*] **1** A person who conveys intelligence or information; *spec.* an informer, a spy, a secret agent. *arch.* M16. **2** A bringer of news, a messenger, an informant. *arch.* exc. (**I-**) in titles of newspapers. L16.

intelligency /ɪnˈtɛlɪdʒ(ə)nsi/ *n.* Now *rare.* L16. [L *intelligentia*: see INTELLIGENCE, -ENCY.] †**1** = INTELLIGENCE *n.* 5b. L16–E18. **2** = INTELLIGENCE *n.* 4. M17. †**3** = INTELLIGENCE *n.* 5. L17–M18. **4** = INTELLIGENCE *n.* 1. L19.

intelligent /ɪnˈtɛlɪdʒ(ə)nt/ *a.* & *n.* E16. [f. L *intelligent-*, earlier *intellegent-* pres. ppl stem of *intellegere* lit. 'choose among', f. as INTER- + *legere* pick up, gather, choose, read: see -ENT.] A *adj.* **1** Having the faculty of understanding, possessing intelligence; *spec.* having or showing a high degree of understanding, quick to comprehend, sagacious. E16. **2** Cognizant *of*, acquainted *with*, well-versed *in*. M16. †**3** Giving information, communicative. *rare* (Shakes.). Only in E17. **4** Of a device, system, or machine: able to vary its behaviour in response to varying situations, requirements, and past experience; *spec.* (esp. of a computer terminal) having its own data-processing capability, incorporating a microprocessor. M20.

1 C. SAGAN Those planets in which intelligent forms have arisen. A. BURGESS Unit officers were considered intelligent enough to be able to take in the facts.

B *n.* †**1** A recipient of information. *rare.* Only in E16. **2** An intelligent or rational being. Now *rare.* E17. †**3** A person who conveys intelligence or information; an informant, a spy. E17–M18.

intelligently *adv.* L17.

intelligential /ɪnˌtɛlɪˈdʒɛnʃ(ə)l/ *a.* E17. [f. L *intelligentia* INTELLIGENCE + -AL[1].] **1** = INTELLECTUAL *a.* 1. E17. **2** = INTELLECTUAL *a.* 3. M17.

intelligentsia /ɪnˌtɛlɪˈdʒɛntsɪə/ *n.* E20. [Russ. *intelligentsiya* f. Pol. *inteligencja* f. L *intelligentia* INTELLIGENCE.] The part of a nation (orig. in pre-revolutionary Russia) having aspirations to intellectual activity, a section of society regarded as possessing culture and political initiative; *pl.* the members of this section of a nation or society, intellectuals.

G. STEINER As Stalinism turned to nationalism and technocracy . . the revolutionary intelligentsia went to the wall.

intelligible /ɪnˈtɛlɪdʒɪb(ə)l/ *a.* & *n.* LME. [L *intellegibilis, intelli-*, f. *intellegere*: see INTELLIGENT, -IBLE.] A *adj.* †**1** Capable of understanding; intelligent. LME–L18. **2** *Philos.* Able to be apprehended only by the understanding, not by the senses. Opp. SENSIBLE *a.* 1. LME. **3** Able to be understood; comprehensible. E16.

1 T. GALE Plato supposeth the Universe . . a living intelligible creature. 2 J. NORRIS The Intelligible

world, . . of a nature purely spiritual and intellectual, . . not sensible, but intelligible only. 3 H. JAMES I can give no intelligible account of how I fought out the interval. I. A. RICHARDS Most of the difficult and obscure points about the structures of the arts . . become easily intelligible.

B *n.* That which is intelligible; an object of understanding. E17.

intelligi'bility *n.* L17. **intelligibleness** *n.* E17. **intelligibly** *adv.* E17.

intelligize /ɪn'tɛlɪdʒʌɪz/ *v.* Also **-ise**. E19. [Irreg. f. L *intellegere* (see INTELLIGENT) + -IZE.] **1** *v.i.* Exercise the intelligence. *rare.* E19. **2** *v.t.* Make intelligent or intellectual; take into the intellect. L19.

Intelpost /'ɪntɛlpəʊst/ *n.* L20. [f. *Int*ernational *El*ectronic *Post*.] The electronic transmission of messages and graphics internationally by fax, telex, or microcomputer.

Intelsat /'ɪntɛlsat/ *n.* Also **INTELSAT**. M20. [f. *Int*ernational *Tel*ecommunications *Sat*ellite (Consortium).] An international organization operating a system of commercial communication satellites; a satellite owned by this organization.

intemerate /ɪn'tɛm(ə)rət/ *a.* Now *rare.* LME. [L *intemeratus*, f. as IN-[3] + *temeratus* pa. pple of *temerare* violate: see -ATE[2].] Inviolate; unblemished.

intemperance /ɪn'tɛmp(ə)r(ə)ns/ *n.* LME. [(O)Fr. *intempérance* or L *intemperantia*, f. as IN-[3] + *temperantia* TEMPERANCE.] †**1** Intemperateness, inclemency, severity of weather or climate. LME–E18. **2** Lack of moderation or restraint; excess, immoderation; (an act of) overindulgence. LME. **3** Overindulgence in or addiction to alcohol. E17.

Also †**intemperancy** *n.* M16–L17.

intemperate /ɪn'tɛmp(ə)rət/ *a.* LME. [L *intemperatus*, f. as IN-[3] + TEMPERATE *a.*] **1** Not temperate; (esp. of climate or weather) inclement, severe. Now *rare.* LME. **2** Characterized by or given to overindulgence in a passion or appetite. LME. **b** *spec.* Immoderate in the use of alcoholic drink; addicted to alcohol. L17. **3** Lacking temperance or moderation in conduct, action, etc.; exceeding normal restrictions; immoderate; violent. E16.

1 W. LEYBOURN The Zones are either Temperate or Intemperate, and the Intemperate are either Cold or Hot. 2 SHAKES. *Meas. for M.* His concupiscible intemperate lust. b H. WILLIAMSON Was it the rum in the trenches that had started him off on his intemperate habits? 3 R. WATSON The intemperate zeal of the reformers.

intemperately *adv.* LME. **intemperateness** *n.* M16.

†**intemperature** *n.* M16. [f. IN-[3] + TEMPERATURE.] **1** An abnormal or distempered condition of the body. M16–L18. **2** Inclemency, severity of weather or climate. L16–E19.

intempestive /ɪntɛm'pɛstɪv/ *a.* E17. [L *intempestivus*, f. as IN-[3] + TEMPESTIVE.] Untimely, unseasonable, inopportune.

intempestively *adv.* (*rare*) M16.

intemporal /ɪn'tɛmp(ə)r(ə)l/ *a.* M17. [f. IN-[3] + TEMPORAL *a.*[1]] Not temporal; eternal, everlasting.

intend /ɪn'tɛnd/ *v.* Also (earlier) †**en-**. ME. [(O)Fr. *entendre*, †*intendre* f. L *intendere* extend, direct, intend, promote, f. as IN-[2] + *tendere* to stretch.] †**I** Direct the attention to. **1a** *v.i.* Direct the mind, pay heed, *to*, *unto*. ME–E17. **b** *v.refl.* Devote oneself; in *pass.*, be devoted. E16–E17. **2** *v.i.* Endeavour, strive, *to do*. LME–L17. **3** *v.i.* & *t.* Listen, give ear (to). LME–M16. **4** *v.i.* & *t.* Give personal service or attendance (to). LME–M17. **5** *v.t.* Occupy oneself with, look after. LME–L18. **b** Superintend, direct. Cf. INTENDANT *n.* L18–M19.

5 J. COLLIER The Priest is supposed only to intend the Affairs of Religion.

†**II** Apprehend mentally. **6** *v.t.* Understand. ME–E17. **7** *v.i.* Have or come to an understanding; agree together. LME–E16. **8** *v.i.* Have an opinion; think, judge. L16–M17. **9** *v.t.* Understand as being, in law; interpret legally. Cf. INTENDMENT *n.* 3b. E17–L18.

III Direct the mind to something to be done. †**10** *v.i.* Be minded or resolved. Chiefly with *adv.* LME–M17. **11** *v.t.* Have as one's purpose (an action etc.); plan *to do*, contemplate *doing*. LME. **12** *v.t.* Design or destine for or *for* a purpose or use, *as* a thing; have the desire for (a person or thing) *to be*, *to do*. Foll. by *for* a person: have the desire that (a person) shall have or enjoy, or be depicted by. L16. **13** *v.t.* Mean or refer to by one's words. Also (now *rare*), of a word, phrase, etc.: signify, denote. L16. †**b** Designate as something; call. *rare.* L16–E17.

10 M. GROVE Let me heare from you, how that you doe entend. 11 G. GREENE Mr Smith asked me to stop the car . . and I thought he intended to take a photograph. T. MO Atkins is the last man to take umbrage where offence was not intended. B. T. BRADFORD He brought his fist down on the table much harder than he had intended. *Soldier* I . . intend staying to the end of my time. 12 R. MONTAGU The regales that are intended for him not being yet at an end. DICKENS A degree of familiarity which he . . intended for a . . compliment. E. O'NEILL In a welcoming . . grimace, intended as a smile. J. BUCHAN I was not intended by Providence for a philologist. I. MURDOCH He had . . informed her that he intended their liaison to be lasting. K. AMIS I think we were intended to meet. 13 H. FIELDING This word . . intends persons without virtue or sense. N. MOSLEY They rewrote some of his books to say the opposite of what he had intended. b SPENSER Vesper, whom we the Euening-starre intend.

IV Fix in a course, direct. **14** *v.t.* Direct (the eyes, thoughts, etc.) *to* or *towards* an object. Now *rare.* LME. **15** *v.i.* & *t.* Direct (one's course), make (one's way). *arch.* LME. †**b** *v.i.* Set out for or *for* a destination. Sometimes as ellipt. use of sense 11, plan to go or start. M17–E19. †**16** *v.i.* Incline or tend in a given direction. LME–M17. †**17** *v.t.* Institute (legal proceedings). *Sc.* L16–M18. †**18** *v.t.* Assert, claim; pretend. (Foll. by *that*.) L16–M17.

14 C. PATMORE Intend thine eye Into the dim and undiscovered sky. 15 JAS. HARRIS As if . . a company of travellers, in some wide forest, were all intending for one city. G. CRABBE Guide him to Fairy-land, who now intends That way his flight. b J. WESLEY Pray let us know when you or your brother intend for this Kingdom. 16 A. GOLDING The wil intendeth rather to commaund than to obey, and vnto freedom rather than bondage. 18 SHAKES. *Rich. III* Tremble and start at wagging of a straw, Intending deep suspicion.

†**V** Stretch, extend. **19** *v.t.* Stretch (out), esp. to the maximum limit; strain, make tense. L16–M19. **20** *v.t.* Increase the intensity of. L16–E18.

19 T. MOORE One of the wings of the Swan has been . . intended . . to cover . . Leda. W. HAMILTON When we intend the vital powers above the suitable degree we occasion a hindrance, a pain. 20 C. PURSHALL A small quantity of *Aqua Vitae* sprinkled upon the Freezing Mixture, wonderfully intends its Force.

intended *ppl a.* & *n.* (*a*) *ppl a.* that has been intended; *esp.* designed to be what is denoted by the n.; formerly also, (of a person) resolved *to do*; (*b*) *n.* (*colloq.*) one's intended husband or wife: L15. **intendedly** *adv.* by design, on purpose M17.

intendance /ɪn'tɛnd(ə)ns/ *n.* M18. [Fr., f. as INTENDANT: see -ANCE.] **1** The function of an intendant; superintendence, direction. Also *spec.*, a department of the French public service, e.g. the war commissariat; the officials conducting it. M18. **2** The official quarters of an intendant. L19.

intendancy /ɪn'tɛnd(ə)nsi/ *n.* Also **-ency**. L16. [f. INTENDANT: see -ANCY. In sense 2 f. Sp. *intendencia*.] **1** The position, function, or period of office of an intendant; a body of intendants. L16. **2** In S. America: a district under the control of an intendant. E19.

intendant /ɪn'tɛnd(ə)nt/ *n.* Also †**-ent**. M17. [Fr., f. L *intendent-* pres. ppl stem of *intendere*: see INTEND, -ANT[1].] **1** Chiefly as the title of certain officials: a superintendent, a director; *esp.* (in 17th- and 18th-cent. France) any of certain agents of the King appointed to supervise the administration of justice, finance, etc., in the provinces on behalf of central government. M17. **2** The administrator of an opera-house or theatre. Also, a musical director, a conductor. L19.

1 EVELYN Sir Christopher Wren, his Majesties Surveyor and Intendent of his Buildings. **intendant-general** a chief intendant.

intendence /ɪn'tɛnd(ə)ns/ *n.* LME. [f. INTEND *v.* + -ENCE.] The paying of attention; attendance. Now only (*Hist.*) in *writ of intendence and respondence*, a writ issued under the Great Seal in the 13th to 15th cents. in favour of a person who had received an appointment from the King, ordering all concerned to attend him and respond to his requests.

intendency *n.* var. of INTENDANCY.

†**intendent** *n.* var. of INTENDANT.

intender /ɪn'tɛndə/ *n.* E16. [f. INTEND + -ER[1].] A person who intends or purposes.

†**intender** *v.* var. of ENTENDER.

†**intendiment** *n.* E16. [med.L *intendimentum*: cf. INTENDMENT.] **1** Knowledge, understanding. Only in 16. **2** Purpose, intention. L16–E17. **3** Attentive consideration. *rare* (Spenser). Only in L16.

intending /ɪn'tɛndɪŋ/ *ppl a.* M17. [f. INTEND + -ING[2].] That intends; *esp.* (with agent-n.) who intends to be.

Times I have to warn intending visitors that they will find the exhibition plunged in . . gloom.

intendment /ɪn'tɛndm(ə)nt/ *n.* Also (earlier) †**en-**. LME. [(O)Fr. *entendement*, f. *entendre*: see INTEND, -MENT. Cf. INTENDIMENT.] †**1** The faculty or action of understanding. LME–E17. †**2** Way of understanding something; interpretation. LME–M17. **3a** Meaning intended; signification, import. Now *rare.* LME. **b** *Law.* The sense in which the law understands a thing. L16. †**4** What a person aims at; purpose, intention. Also, the purpose of a thing. LME–E19. †**5** Tendency, inclination. E16–E17.

3a *Notes & Queries* A phrase of sinister and odious intendment. b *Times* Doubts whether the use of such powers . . was within the intendment of the legislation.

intenerate /ɪn'tɛnəreɪt/ *v.t.* Now *rare.* L16. [mod.L *intenerat-* pa. ppl stem of *intenerare*, f. as IN-[2] + L *tener* tender: see -ATE[3].] Make soft or tender.

intene'ration *n.* E17.

†**intenible** *a.* *rare* (Shakes.). Only in E17. [Perh. f. IN-[3] + var. of TENABLE *a.*, with active force as in INCAPABLE *a.* 2 unable to contain.] Incapable of holding or containing something.

SHAKES. *All's Well* This captious and intenible sieve.

intensate /ɪn'tɛnseɪt/ *v.t.* *rare.* M19. [f. INTENSE + -ATE[3].] Make intense, intensify.

inten'sation *n.* E19.

intensative /ɪn'tɛnsətɪv/ *n.* & *a.* M19. [Extension of INTENSIVE.] = INTENSITIVE.

intense /ɪn'tɛns/ *a.* LME. [(O)Fr. *intens(e)* or L *intensus* stretched tight, strained, pa. pple of *intendere* INTEND.] **1** Of a condition, quality, feeling, etc.: existing in a very high degree; extremely strong, keen, or pronounced. Of a colour: very deep. LME. **b** Of a thing: having a quality in a very high degree; intensely bright, hot, etc.; *Photogr.* dense. M17. **2** Of personal, esp. mental, action: strenuously directed to an end; highly concentrated. M17. **3** Possessing, exhibiting, or marked by intensity of feeling. Formerly, intent *upon* or *about*. M17.

1 E. BOWEN She felt an intense morbid solicitude. R. SILVERBERG Though it was not yet noon, the heat was intense. *Atlantic Monthly* The pressure of human crowding is most intense in the cities. b P. BOWLES The intense sky, too blue to be real. 2 A. SILLITOE The afternoon visit was preceded by a few hours of intense preparation. C. HOPE Feeling uncomfortable beneath her cool, intense scrutiny. 3 T. MORRISON Their friendship was as intense as it was sudden. M. PIERCY Tracy was intense Enthusiastic. All the way on or all the way off. *Wisden Cricket Monthly* David does have a tendency to get intense about the game. *transf.*: R. LEHMANN A short but very intense song.

intensely *adv.* †(*a*) with concentrated effort or attention; (*b*) in a very high degree, very strongly or greatly; (*c*) with intensity of feeling: E17. **intenseness** *n.* E17.

intensification /ɪn,tɛnsɪfɪ'keɪʃ(ə)n/ *n.* M19. [f. INTENSIFY + -FICATION.] **1** The action of intensifying; intensified condition. M19. **2**

Photogr. The process of increasing the opacity of a negative. L19.
1 RITE *of intensification.*

intensify /ɪnˈtɛnsɪfʌɪ/ *v.* E19. [f. INTENSE + -I- + -FY: app. coined by Coleridge.] 1 *v.t.* Make intense; augment, strengthen, heighten, deepen. E19. b *Photogr.* Increase the opacity of (a negative), so as to produce a stronger contrast of light and shade. M19. 2 *v.i.* Grow in intensity. M19.
1 J. RABAN The oil boom has simply intensified Dubai's traditional buzz of water traffic. N. SYMINGTON In psychosis all the emotions are enormously intensified. 2 I. MCEWAN As the morning heat had intensified, the crowds had diminished.
intensifier *n.* a thing which intensifies; *spec.* (*a*) *Photogr.* a chemical used to intensify a negative; (*b*) = *hydraulic intensifier* s.v. HYDRAULIC *a.*; (*c*) *Gram.* a word or prefix giving force or emphasis; (*d*) = *image intensifier* s.v. IMAGE *n.*: M19.

intension /ɪnˈtɛnʃ(ə)n/ *n.* E17. [L *intensio(n-)*, f. *intens-* pa. ppl stem of *intendere*: see INTEND, -ION. A doublet of INTENTION.] 1 The action of stretching or straining. Now *rare* or *obs.* E17. 2 Strenuous exertion of the mind or will; earnest attention, intentness. E17. 3 Increase in degree or force; intensification. E17. 4 (Notable) degree of a quality; strength, force, intensity. Freq. opp. EXTENSION 3. E17. 5 *Logic.* The internal content of a concept; the sum of the attributes contained in it. Opp. EXTENSION 4b. M19.
1 T. HOGG His voice . . was intolerably shrill, harsh . . of the most cruel intension. 2 *Cornhill Magazine* Suddenly I found myself springing to my feet, and listening with an agony of intension. 3 W. SANDERSON Brightness is the Intension of Light. 4 *Nineteenth Century* The essence of farming on virgin soils is extension; on old land it is intension.
intensional *a.* (*Philos.*) relating to the attributes contained in a concept L19. **intensionalist** *n.* & *a.* (*Philos.*) (*a*) *n.* a person who considers a concept from the standpoint of its inner attributes; (*b*) *adj.* relating to the attributes contained in a concept: M20. **intensioˈnality** *n.* (*Philos.*) the state or fact of being intensional M20. **intensionally** *adv.* (*Philos.*) by way of intension L19.

intensitive /ɪnˈtɛnsɪtɪv/ *a.* & *n.* E19. [Irreg. f. INTENSITY + -IVE.] (A word, prefix, etc.) that serves to intensify or emphasize.

intensity /ɪnˈtɛnsɪti/ *n.* M17. [f. INTENSE + -ITY.] 1 The quality of being intense; extreme degree of or *of* a quality, condition, etc. M17. b Concentrated quality of an action, emotion, etc. M19. 2 *Physics* etc. A (measurable) amount of energy, brightness, magnetic field, etc. L18.
1 H. E. BATES Momentarily the intensity of his anger blinded him. J. RULE The sun . . seemed robbed of its intensity by a cool wind. B. EMECHETA The intensity of the knocks progressed from the first mild knock to a final thunderous one. b J. WAIN She . . stared into his face with an intensity that scorched him. R. HOLMES Shelley was writing with a creative intensity he had never before achieved. 2 E. RUTHERFORD A magnetic field of only moderate intensity. N. TINBERGEN Powers of adaptation to low light intensities.

intensive /ɪnˈtɛnsɪv/ *a.* & *n.* LME. [(O)Fr. *intensif*, *-ive* or med.L *intensivus*, f. as INTENSE: see -IVE.] A *adj.* †1 Of a very high degree; vehement, intense. LME–L17. 2 Of an activity: assiduously directed towards an object; highly concentrated. E17. 3 Of or relating to intensity or logical intension as opp. to extent; having the quality of intensity. E17. 4 Having the property of intensifying; *esp.* (*Gram.*) giving force or emphasis. E17. 5 *Econ.* Of a method of farming etc.: designed to increase productiveness within a limited area (rather than enlarging the area of production). M19. 6 As 2nd elem. of comb.; making much use of the thing specified. Esp. in *capital-intensive*, *labour-intensive*. M20.
2 L. VAN DER POST His intensive reading of philosophy . . had provided him with a knowledge in depth. R. INGALLS The creature . . appears from intensive analysis to be a giant lizard-like animal. **intensive care** special medical treatment, with constant monitoring, of a dangerously ill patient; *intensive care unit*, the part of a hospital where this is performed. 3 *Educational Review* In visiting the schools . . one comes to learn that the knowledge acquired is more intensive than extensive.

B *n.* A thing which intensifies; *spec.* (*Gram.*) an intensifier. E19.
intensively *adv.* L15. **intensiveness** *n.* M17.

intent /ɪnˈtɛnt/ *n.* Also (earlier) †**en-**. ME. [OFr. *entent* f. L *intentus* vbl n. f. *intendere* INTEND, and (O)Fr. *entente* f. Proto-Romance, also f. L *intendere*.] 1 Chiefly *Law*: the act or fact of intending; intention, purpose. Formerly also, inclination, will; what is willed, one's desire. ME. †b A design, a project. ME–M19. †2 Attention, heed; intent observation. ME–E18. †3 Assiduous effort. ME–L15. †4 Mind, understanding; opinion, judgement. ME–E17. †5 Meaning, import; *Law* intendment. ME–M18. 6 The object of an action etc.; an aim, a purpose. Now *rare* exc. in *to* (or *for*) *all intents and purposes*, *to all intents*, for all practical purposes, in effect. ME. †7 The subject of a discourse etc. LME–L17.
1 T. KENEALLY The intent of the . . prisoners from Brinnlitz was to deliver the Schindlers . . across the Swiss border. *letter of intent*: see LETTER *n.*[1] **with intent** with the intention of committing a crime. b G. P. R. JAMES The nobles joining in his intent, showered their largess upon their retainers. 5 W. BLACKSTONE Merchandize, within the intent of the statute, by which a profit may be fairly made. 6 N. SYMINGTON When a story is used to convey a conscious intent the result is poor literature. †**to the intent** (**that**) in order that.

intent /ɪnˈtɛnt/ *a.* LME. [L *intentus* pa. pple of *intendere*: see prec.] 1 Having the mind concentrated on something; engrossed in an activity etc., firmly resolved on a purpose. (Foll. by *on*, †*to do*, *upon*.) LME. 2 Of the faculties, a look, etc.: directed with strained attention; intense. LME.
1 J. LONDON It would have been easier to go on the train, but . . he was intent on saving money. E. BLISHEN A fleet of planes, murderously intent. G. SWIFT Your head was lowered and you were intent on your reading. 2 K. AMIS His face . . wore a small intent frown, as if he were hard of hearing.
intently *adv.* LME. **intentness** *n.* M17.

†**intent** *v.* Also **en-**. ME. [OFr. *ententer*, (in sense 3) Fr. *intenter*, both f. L *intentare* frequent. of *intendere* INTEND.] 1 *v.t.* Purpose, intend (an action, *to do*). ME–L16. 2 *v.i.* & *t.* Direct the mind (to a thing). LME–E17. 3 *v.t.* Institute (legal proceedings). *Sc.* E16–E19.

intention /ɪnˈtɛnʃ(ə)n/ *n.* Also †**en-**. LME. [OFr. *entencion* (mod. *intention*) f. L *intentio(n-)*, f. *intent-* pa. ppl stem of *intendere*: see INTEND, -ION. A doublet of INTENSION.] I *gen.* 1a (Intense or concentrated) direction of or *of* the mind, attention, eyes, etc., to an object. *arch.* LME. †b The action of stretching or making something tense. L16–M17. †2 The mind, the understanding; one's judgement or opinion. LME–E16. 3 Meaning, import. *arch.* LME. 4 The action or fact of intending to do a thing; what one intends to do, one's aim or design. Also, the purpose of an action etc. LME. b In *pl.* Intended mode of behaviour, esp. (*colloq.*) towards a woman in respect of marriage. L18. c An author's aim or intended meaning in a literary work. M20. †5 Intensification. E17–M18.
1a JONSON My soule . . Is hurt with mere intention on their follies. M. HALE When thou prayest do it considerately, advisedly, with the whole Intention of thy Soul. 4 M. KEANE None of them showed the smallest intention of getting out of the car. A. SCHLEE Absently or with some intention, he had let his hand fall on the back of it. *Which?* Overall, the intention is to leave pensioners' benefit entitlement broadly unchanged. b T. CAPOTE Mr. Bell, entirely unaware of his guests' intentions, which included throttling him with a belt . . , was glad to have company. A. BROOKNER So delicate a suitor is Lautner that Mimi has no idea of his intentions. *honourable intentions*: see HONOURABLE *a.*
II *spec.* 6 *Med.* An aim in a healing process; a method of treatment. *arch.* exc. in *first intention* (a), *second intention* (a) below. LME. 7 *Scholastic Logic.* A concept formed by directing the mind towards an object. Usually in *first intention* (b), *second intention* (b) below. M16. 8 *RC Ch.* a The special object for which a mass is celebrated, an intercession offered, etc. L16. b The serious purpose, on the part of the celebrant, to perform the rites prescribed by the Church (regarded as essential to the validity of the sacrament). M19.
Phrases: **first intention** (*a*) *Med.* the healing of a wound by natural union of the parts without granulation; (*b*) *Scholastic Logic* a primary concept, formed by the direct application of the mind to the thing itself, e.g. the concepts of *a tree*, *an oak*. **particular intention** *RC Ch.* = sense 8a above. **second intention** (*a*) *Med.* the healing of a wound by granulation after suppuration; (*b*) *Scholastic Logic* a secondary concept, formed by the application of the mind to first intentions in their relations to each other, e.g. the concepts of *genus*, *species*, *difference*, *identity*. **special intention** *RC Ch.* = sense 8a above.
Comb.: **intention movement** a movement by an animal serving simply to signal that a further movement will follow; **intention tremor**: manifested whenever a movement is attempted, freq. a consequence of brain damage.

intentional /ɪnˈtɛnʃ(ə)n(ə)l/ *a.* M16. [Fr. *intentionnel* or med.L *intentionalis*, f. L *intentio(n-)*: see prec., -AL[1].] 1 Of or pertaining to intention; existing (only) in intention. M16. 2 In scholastic logic and (later) phenomenology: of or pertaining to the operations of the mind; existing in or for the mind. M16. 3 Done on purpose; deliberate. E18.
1 W. CRUISE The second will never operated, it was only intentional. **intentional fallacy**: that consists in confusing an author's intended meaning in a work with its actual meaning. 2 **intentional concept**: denoting a mental state whose object may or may not exist. **intentional object** (in phenomenology) the object (real or imaginary) to which each act of consciousness is directed. 3 SYD. SMITH We accuse nobody of intentional misrepresentation.
intentioˈnality *n.* the quality or fact of being intentional; *esp.* (in phenomenology) the fact of being directed at an object (as a supposed quality of every act of consciousness): E17. **intentionally** *adv.* in an intentional manner or relation; *esp.* deliberately, on purpose: E17.

intentionalism /ɪnˈtɛnʃ(ə)n(ə)lɪz(ə)m/ *n.* L19. [f. prec. + -ISM.] 1 The theory that the world is the result of conscious design. *rare.* L19. 2 The theory that a literary work should be judged in terms of the author's intentions: see *intentional fallacy* s.v. INTENTIONAL *a.* 1. L19.
intentionalist *n.* & *a.* (*a*) *n.* a person who advocates intentionalism; (*b*) *adj.* of or pertaining to intentionalism: M20.

intentioned /ɪnˈtɛnʃ(ə)nd/ *a.* M17. [f. INTENTION + -ED[2].] Having intentions (of a specified kind). Usu. w. qualifying adv., esp. *well.*

intentive /ɪnˈtɛntɪv/ *a.* Now *rare* or *obs.* Also (earlier) †**en-**. LME. [OFr. *ententif*, *intentif*, *-ive*, f. *entent*: see INTENT *n.*, -IVE.] 1 Of a person: attentive, assiduous. LME. 2 Of the faculties or thoughts, an action, a look, etc.: intently directed. LME.
2 ALBERT SMITH Many . . were at breakfast . . with such intentive appetites, that they took no notice of the courteous salute.
intentively *adv.* ME. **intentiveness** *n.* M16.

inter /ˈɪntə/ *a.* & *n. colloq.* Also **inter.** (point). L19. [Abbrev. of INTERMEDIATE *a.* & *n.*] A *adj.* Intermediate. L19. B *n.* An intermediate examination in a degree course etc. M20.

inter /ɪnˈtəː/ *v.t.* Infl. **-rr-**. ME. [(O)Fr. *enterrer* f. Proto-Romance, f. as IN-[2] + L *terra* earth.] 1 Deposit (a corpse) in the earth, or in a grave or tomb; bury. ME. b *fig.* Cover, hide, or imprison (esp. oneself) in something. E17. †2 Place in the ground; cover with soil. E17–E18.

inter- /ˈɪntə/ *comb. form.* [Repr. (O)Fr. *inter-*, *entre-* (cf. ENTER-[1]) or its source L *inter-*, f. *inter* (prep. & adv.) between, among, amid, in between, in the midst.] 1 In advb. relation to vbs (or their derivs.) or adjs., or in adj. relation to ns., w. sense 'situated, occurring, etc.) between or among persons or things', often expr. mutual or reciprocal action or relation, as *inter-agent*, *interbreed*, *interchange*, *interlace*, *interlocution*. In wds adopted f. Fr. and L and in Eng. wds modelled on these, and as a freely productive pref. 2 In prepositional relation to ns. expressed or implied, w. the sense 'situated, occurring, etc. between (things of the kind indicated)', often in contrast to wds in INTRA-, as *intercity, intercontinental, intermolecular*.

inter-'allied *a.* existing or constituted between allies or allied forces E20. **interal'veolar** *a.* (*Anat.* & *Zool.*) situated or existing between alveoli M19. **inter-A'merican** *a.* existing between the countries of N. and S. America; of or pertaining to relationships between such countries: M20. **inter'animate** *v.t.* (*rare*) animate mutually M17. **interani'mation** *n.* mutual animation E20. **inter'annual** *a.* existing between (that of) different years L20. **interar'terial** *a.* existing between or connecting arteries E20. **interar'ticular** *a.* situated or occurring between contiguous surfaces of a joint E19. **intera'tomic** *a.* situated, existing, or occurring between atoms M19. **interavaila'bility** *n.* the fact of being interavailable E20. **intera'vailable** *a.* (of train tickets etc.) equally available from and valid on different transport undertakings L20. **interbank** *a.* agreed, arranged, or operating between banks M20. **interbrain** *n.* (*Anat.*) the diencephalon L19. **interca'pillary** *a.* (*Anat.*) existing or occurring between the capillaries M19. **inter'cellular** *a.* occurring between the cells of one or more organisms M19. **inter'cellularly** *adv.* between cells M20. **inter'censal** *a.* occurring between two censuses; of or pertaining to a period between censuses: L19. **interchapter** *n.* a passage of text placed between chapters M19. **inter'church** *a.* concerning (members of) several Christian denominations E20. **inter'city** *a.* & *n.* (*a*) *adj.* occurring or travelling between cities; *spec.* designating a fast train or train service between main towns; (*b*) *n.* an intercity train: E20. **inter-class** *a.* occurring or carried on between social classes E20. **inter'clavicle** *n.* (*Zool.*) a membrane-bone between the two clavicles in many amphibians and reptiles and in monotremes L19. **intercla'vicular** *a.* & *n.* (*Zool.* & *Anat.*) (a bone) situated between the clavicles M19. **inter'coastal** *a.* existing, carried on between, or connecting different coasts E20. **intercollege** *a.* intercollegiate E20. **interco'llegiate** *a.* occurring or conducted between colleges; involving (members of) different colleges: L19. **interco'lonial** *a.* connecting, occurring between, or concerning different colonies M19. **intercombi'nation** *n.* mutual combination; *spec.* (*Physics*) an electronic transition between atomic states of different multiplicities; (in full *intercombination line*) a spectral line produced by such a transition: M19. **interco'mmunal** *a.* existing or occurring between communities or races E20. **interco'mmunity** *n.* the quality of being common to various things; the condition of having things in common or taking part in the same things: L16. **inter'company** *a.* made or occurring between different companies E20. **intercom'parison** *n.* (a) comparison of each of a number of things with one another M19. **intercon'version** *n.* the process of converting each of two or more things into the other(s) M19. **intercon'vert** *v.t.* convert into one another M20. **interconverti'bility** *n.* the quality of being interconvertible M19. **intercon'vertible** *a.* mutually convertible E19. **inter'correlate** *v.t.* & *i.* correlate with one another E20. **intercorre'lation** *n.* statistical correlation that relates each of a number of variates with the others E20. **inter-county** *a.* occurring or carried on between counties L19. **inter'cranial** *a.* situated or occurring within the skull E20. **inter'crural** *a.* situated or occurring between the legs L17. **inter'crystalline** *a.* situated or occurring between crystals, esp. those which form a metal E20. **inter'cultural** *a.* (*a*) (of tillage) carried out while a crop is still growing; (*b*) taking place or forming a communication between cultures, belonging to or derived from different cultures: L19. **interdefina'bility** *n.* (*Logic*) the quality of being interdefinable M20. **interde'finable** *a.* (*Logic*) able to be defined by each other M20. **interdenomi'national** *a.* pertaining to different Christian denominations; involving or composed of members of different denominations: L19. **interdenomi'nationally** *adv.* between or as regards different Christian denominations L20. **interdepart'mental** *a.* occurring between or pertaining to different departments L19. **interdepart'mentally** *adv.* between departments E20. **interdia'lectal** *a.* taking place or existing between dialects; belonging in common to or derived from different dialects: M20. **interdi'ffuse** *v.t.* & *i.* diffuse among other things or in another substance, esp. a gas L19. **interdi'ffusion** *n.* mutual diffusion M19. **inter'dine** *v.i.* (of members of different castes or tribal groups) eat a meal together E20. **inter-do'minion** *a.* (*Austral.* & *NZ*) occurring or carried on between dominions of the British Commonwealth M20. **inter-e'lectrode** *a.* (of the interval) that exists between two or more electrodes E20. **inter-'ethnic** *a.* occurring or existing between ethnic groups; belonging to or used by different ethnic groups: E20. **interfaith** *a.* pertaining to different religions; involving or composed of members of different religions: M20. **interfa'milial, inter'family** *adjs.* existing or occurring between (members of) different families M20. **interfa'scicular** *a.* (*Anat.* & *Bot.*) situated between fascicles M19. **inter'femoral** *a.* (chiefly *Zool.*) situated between the thighs E19. **interfenes'tration** *n.* the spacing of the windows of a building E19. **inter'fertile** *a.* capable of producing seed or offspring when crossed with an individual of another variety, race, etc. E20. **interfer'tility** *n.* the property of being interfertile E20. **inter'fibrillar** *a.* existing or occurring between fibrils L19. **inter'file** *v.t.* file among each other or among other items M20. **inter'finger** *v.i.* (*Geol.*) = INTERDIGITATE I E20. **inter-firm** *a.* carried on between two or more business firms M20. **interfoli'aceous** *a.* (*Bot.*) situated between two opposite leaves M18. **inter'foliar** *a.* (*Bot.*) interfoliaceous M19. **interga'lactic** *a.* of, pertaining to, or occurring in the regions between galaxies; involving more than one galaxy: E20. **interga'lactically** *adv.* by means of or as regards intergalactic travel L20. **intergene'rational** *a.* existing or occurring between different generations of people; involving more than one generation: M20. **intergene'rationally** *adv.* between generations; from one generation to another: L20. **interge'neric** *a.* (*Biol.*) formed or obtained from (individuals of) different genera E20. **intergenic** /-'dʒɛn-/ *a.* occurring or existing between neighbouring genes M20. **inter'glandular** *a.* (*Anat.*) situated or occurring between glands L19. **intergovern'mental** *a.* involving (representatives of) more than one government E20. **intergovern'mentally** *adv.* by (representatives of) more than one government L20. **inter'granular** *a.* situated or occurring between granules or grains L19. **intergroup** *a.* existing or occurring between (members of) different groups, esp. different social or political groups M20. **inter'halogen** *a.* (of a chemical compound) composed of two different halogens M20. **interhemi'spheric** *a.* situated or existing between the two hemispheres of the brain E20. **inter'ictal** *a.* (*Med.*) occurring during or characteristic of a period between one ictus and another M20. **interindi'vidual** *a.* existing or occurring between individuals L19. **interindustry** *a.* (*Econ.*) existing or occurring between industries; based on more than one industry: M20. **inter'influence** *n.* influence of a number of things on each other M20. **inter'influencing** *n.* the fact of influencing each other E20. **inter'insular** *a.* existing or occurring between islands M19. **interi'onic** *a.* existing or occurring between ions E20. **inter-island** *a.* existing or occurring between islands; pertaining to travel or communication between islands; involving (representatives of) more than one island: M19. **†interjoin** *v.t.* (*rare*, Shakes.) join reciprocally: only in E17. **inter'knit** *v.t.* & *i.* intertwine, interweave L16. **inter'knot** *v.t.* knot together E17. **interla'boratory** *a.* occurring between or involving different laboratories: M20. **interla'custrine** *a.* situated between lakes E20. **interla'mellar** *a.* (*Zool.*) situated between or among lamellae (esp. of the gills) M19. **interlevel** *n.* a level of language serving to relate other linguistic levels M20. **inter'library** *a.* (esp. of book lending) between libraries L19. **inter'lobate** *a.* (*Physical Geogr.*) situated or deposited between the lobes of a glacier L19. **inter'lobular** *a.* (*Anat.* & *Med.*) situated or occurring between lobes or lobules M19. **interlo'cation** *n.* (*rare*) (*a*) an interposition; something interposed; (*b*) an intermediate location: E17. **inter'lucent** *a.* (*rare*) shining between things E18. **interme'tallic** *a.* & *n.* (designating) a compound formed from two or more metallic elements E20. **intermi'gration** *n.* interchange of abode or habitat L17. **inter'mine** *v.t.* (*rare*) intersect with mines or veins E17. **intermi'totic** *n.* & *a.* (*Cytol.*) (a cell) capable of further division; existing or occurring between mitoses: M20. **intermodu'lation** *n.* (*Electronics*) mutual distortion of two sinusoidal signals M20. **intermo'lecular** *a.* situated, existing, or occurring between molecules M19. **intermo'lecularly** *adv.* between molecules M20. **intermont** *a.* intermontane E20. **inter'montane** *a.* situated between mountains E19. **inter'mountain** *a.* intermontane E20. **inter'neural** *a.* & *n.* (*Zool.*) (a spine, ray, etc.) situated between neural spines or arches M19. **inter'nuclear** *a.* situated, occurring, or existing between nuclei L19. **inter'nuptial** *a.* (*a*) of or pertaining to intermarriage; (*b*) occurring between two marriages: M19. **inter'orbital** *a.* (*Anat.*) situated between the eye sockets M19. **inter'osculate** *v.i.* inosculate, interpenetrate; (esp. of biological species) intergrade, overlap in characteristics: L19. **interoscu'lation** *n.* the action or fact of interosculating L19. **inter'osseous** *a.* (*Anat.*) situated between bones M18. **inter'page** *v.t.* print or insert on intermediate pages M19. **inter'palpebral** *a.* situated between the eyelids L19. **interpa'rietal** *a.* & *n.* (*Anat.*) (the bone) situated at the back of the skull, between the parietal bones M19. **interpha'langeal** *a.* (*Anat.*) situated between two adjacent phalanges L19. **inter'plait** *v.t.* & *i.* plait together E19. **inter'planar** *a.* (*Cryst.*) existing between the planes of a crystal lattice M20. **interplane** *a.* (*Aeronaut.*) situated between or connecting the upper and lower wings of a biplane E20. **inter'planetary** *a.* situated or existing between planets; of or pertaining to travel between planets: L17. **in'terplicate** *v.t.* (*rare*) fold between or together E17. **inter'pluvial** *a.* & *n.* (of, pertaining to, or designating) any period of relatively dry conditions in equatorial regions during the geological past, esp. in the Pleistocene (cf. INTERGLACIAL) E20. **inter'point** *v.t.* & *i.* insert a point or points in (a thing) or between (things) L16. **inter'polar** *a.* situated between the poles (of a battery, etc.) L19. **interpole** *n.* an auxiliary pole placed between the main poles to increase the efficiency of a commutator E20. **interpro'vincial** *a.* situated or carried on between provinces M19. **inter'proximal** *a.* (*Dentistry*) of, situated in, or relating to the region between adjacent teeth L19. **inter'pubic** *a.* situated between the right and left pubic bones M19. **interpulse** *a.* & *n.* (*a*) *adj.* existing or occurring between one pulse and the next; (*b*) *n.* (*Astron.*) a weaker pulse occurring between the main pulses of radiation from some pulsars: M20. **inter'pupillary** *a.* existing between the pupils of the eyes E20. **inter'quartile** *a.* (*Statistics*) situated between the first and third quartiles of a distribution L19. **inter'radial** *a.* & *n.* (*Zool.*) (a part or structure) situated between rays or radii, as of an echinoderm L19. **inter'radius** *n.* (*Zool.*) an interradial part or axis L19. **inter'renal** *a.* situated between the kidneys; *spec.* (*Zool.*) designating the steroid-producing tissue of fish: L19. **inter'scapular** *a.* (*Anat.* & *Zool.*) situated between the scapulae E18. **interscho'lastic** *a.* occurring between schools E20. **inter'segment** *n.* †(*a*) *Math.* an intercept; (*b*) *Zool.* in certain segmented animals, the part of the body between two segments: L17. **inter'sensory** *a.* registered by two or more senses M20. **intersen'tential** *a.* (*Ling.*) existing, or pertaining to the relationship, between sentences M20. **inter'septal** *a.* (*Anat.* & *Zool.*) situated between septa M19. **inter-'service** *a.* existing between, formed from, or common to the armed services M20. **inter'shoot** *v.t.* & *i.* (*arch.*) shoot or dart between or among (things) M19. **intersi'dereal** *a.* situated or occurring between the stars M17. **inter'social** *a.* existing between associates M19. **inter'sow** *v.t.* (now *rare*) intersperse E17. **interspe'cific** *a.* formed or obtained from (individuals of) different species; occurring among individuals of different species: L19. **inter'sphere** *v.t.* (*arch.*) bring within another's sphere L19. **inter'spinal, inter'spinous** *adjs.* (*Anat.*) situated between the spines or spinous processes of the vertebrae M19. **inter'stadial** *a.* & *n.* (*Geol.*) (pertaining to, characteristic of, or designating) a minor period of ice retreat during a glacial period E20. **interstage** *a.* situated or occurring between successive stages of an apparatus E20. **inter-'station** *a.* occurring between two stations or tuning positions on a radio M20. **inter'stellar** *a.* situated between stars; of or relating to the regions of space between the stars: E17. **inter-strain** *a.* (*Biol.*) existing or occurring between (genetic) strains; formed by crossing two strains: M20. **intersy'llabic** *a.* occurring between syllables M20. **intersystem** *a.* existing or occurring between systems; *intersystem crossing* (Physics), radiationless transition of an excited molecule to a state of different multiplicity: E20. **interterri'torial** *a.* existing between or involving different territories L19. **intertesta'mental** *a.* designating or pertaining to Jewish writings composed approximately between 200 BC and AD 100 (after the latest Old Testament book and before the beginning (or the end) of the New Testament period), and regarded as non-canonical M20. **intertextu'ality** *n.* (a) relationship between texts; the fact of relating or alluding to other texts: M20. **inter'tidal** *a.* occurring or living between the limits of low and high tides L19. **inter'tillage** *n.* (*US*) intercropping E20. **inter'tilled** *a.* (*US*) that has been intercropped E20. **inter'tonic** *a.* (*Ling.*) occurring between tones or stresses E20. **intertranslata'bility** *n.* the property of being intertranslatable M20. **intertrans'latable** *a.* able to be translated from one language to another and vice versa M19. **intertrans'verse** *a.* (*Anat.*) situated between the transverse processes of the vertebrae M19. **inter'trochlear** *a.* (*Anat.*) situated in the trochlear surface of a joint L19. **intertu'bercular** *a.* (*Anat.*) situated or existing between tubercles L19. **inter'tubular** *a.* situated between tubes or tubules M19. **inter'union** *n.* & *a.* (*a*) *n.* mutual or reciprocal union; interblending; (*b*) *adj.* occurring between trade unions: E19. **inter-uni'versity** *a.* existing or occurring

For other words beginning with *inter-* see the main alphabetic sequence of entries between universities; involving (members of) different universities: L19. **interva'rietal** *a.* formed from or occurring between (members of) different plant varieties E20. **inter'veinal** *a.* situated or occurring between the veins of a leaf M20. **inter'vertebral** *a.* situated or existing between vertebrae L18. **interven'tricular** *a.* (*Anat.*) situated between the ventricles (of the heart or brain) M19. **inter'vital** *a.* (*rare*) existing between two lives or two stages of existence M19. **inter'war** *a.* existing in the period between two wars, *spec.* the period 1919–39 M20. **interweft** *n.* (*rare*) interweaving; interwoven work: E20. **inter'xylary** *a.* (*Bot.*) (of phloem) situated within the secondary xylem L19. **inter'zonal** *a.* existing or carried on between zones L19.

interact /ˈɪntərakt/ *n.* M18. [f. INTER- 2 + ACT *n.*, after Fr. ENTR'ACTE.] = ENTR'ACTE.

interact /ɪntərˈakt/ *v.i.* M19. [f. INTER- 1 + ACT *v.*] Act reciprocally, act on each other; behave in a way that influences and responds to another. (Foll. by *with*.)

D. ATTENBOROUGH The molecules began to interact with one another to form even more complex compounds. R. BUSH Two streams of modernism grew, interacted and diverged in Eliot's poetry.

interactant *n.* a person who or thing which interacts M20. **interactor** *n.* a person who interacts with others M20.

interaction /ɪntərˈakʃ(ə)n/ *n.* M19. [f. INTERACT *v.* + -ION.] **1** Reciprocal action; action or influence of persons or things on each other. M19. **2** *Physics.* A particular way in which matter, particles, and fields affect one another, e.g. through gravitation or electromagnetism. M20.

2 *strong interaction, weak interaction*, etc.

interactional *a.* L19. **interactionally** *adv.* M20.

interactionism /ɪntərˈakʃ(ə)nɪz(ə)m/ *n.* E20. [f. prec. + -ISM.] *Philos.* The theory that there are two entities, mind and body, each of which can have an effect on the other.

¶ See also SYMBOLIC *interactionism*.

interactionist /ɪntərˈakʃ(ə)nɪst/ *n.* & *a.* E20. [f. as prec. + -IST.] **A** *n.* A person who advocates interactionism or interaction, esp. as an explanation of something. E20.

B *adj.* Of or pertaining to interactionism or interactionists. E20.

Nature Piaget rejects both extremes of the heredity-environment controversy without lapsing into an interactionist stance.

interactive /ɪntərˈaktɪv/ *a.* M19. [f. INTERACT *v.* + -IVE.] **1** Reciprocally active; acting upon or influencing each other. M19. **2** Designating or pertaining to a computer terminal or system that allows a two-way flow of information between it and a user; responding to input from a user. M20.

interactively *adv.* L20. **interac'tivity** *n.* (*a*) an activity that involves interaction; (*b*) the property of being interactive: M20.

inter-agency /ɪntərˈeɪdʒ(ə)nsi/ *n.* & *a.* M18. [f. INTER- 1,2 + AGENCY.] **A** *n.* The fact of being an inter-agent. M18. **B** *adj.* Occurring between different agencies; constituted from more than one agency. M20.

inter-agent /ɪntərˈeɪdʒ(ə)nt/ *n.* M18. [f. INTER- 1 + AGENT.] An intermediate agent; an intermediary.

inter alia /ɪntər ˈeɪlɪə, ˈal-/ *adv. phr.* M17. [L, f. *inter* among + *alia* accus. neut. pl. of *alius* another.] Among other things.

inter alios /ɪntər ˈeɪlɪəʊs, ˈal-/ *adv. phr.* M17. [L, f. *inter* among + *alios* accus. masc. pl. of *alius* another.] Among other people.

interamnian /ɪntərˈamnɪən/ *a.* L18. [f. L *interamnus*, f. as INTER- + *amnis* river, + -IAN.] Lying between two rivers; enclosed by rivers.

interbed /ɪntəˈbɛd/ *v.t.* Infl. **-dd-**. E19. [f. INTER- 1 + BED *v.*] *Geol.* Embed (esp. a stratum) among others; interstratify. Chiefly as *interbedded ppl a.*

interblend /ɪntəˈblɛnd/ *v.* L16. [f. INTER- 1 + BLEND *v.*[2]] †**1** *v.t.* Interpose. *rare.* Only in L16. **2** *v.t.* & *i.* Blend intimately; intermingle. L16.

interbreed /ɪntəˈbriːd/ *v.* Pa. t. & pple **-bred** /-ˈbrɛd/. M19. [f. INTER- 1 + BREED *v.*] **1** *v.i.* Of animals of different races or stocks, or of a single population: breed with each other. M19. **2** *v.i.* Cause animals to interbreed; practise breeding between the members of two stocks. M19. **3** *v.t.* Breed (offspring) from individuals of different races or species; produce by crossbreeding. M19.

intercalarium /ɪntəkəˈlɛːrɪəm/ *n.* Pl. **-ia** /-ɪə/. L19. [mod.L *intercalarium* neut. sing. of *intercalarius* INTERCALARY *a.*] *Zool.* **1** An element between adjacent neural arches in the vertebral column of elasmobranchs and some other fishes. L19. **2** In cyprinoid fishes, an ossicle forming part of the Weberian apparatus linking the inner ear with the swim-bladder. L19.

intercalary /ɪnˈtəːkəl(ə)ri, ɪntəˈkal(ə)ri/ *a.* & *n.* E17. [L *intercalari(u)s*, f. *intercalare*: see INTERCALATE, -Y[3].] **A** *adj.* **1** Of a day or month: inserted at intervals in a calendar in order to harmonize with the solar year. E17. **2** Of a year: having an intercalated day or month. M17. †**3** Of a line or stanza: inserted at intervals in a composition; of the nature of a refrain. M17–E19. **4** Of the nature of an insertion between the members of a series or the parts of a whole; intervening. M18. **B** *n.* = INTERCALARIUM 1. E20.

intercalate /ɪnˈtəːkəleɪt; *as n. also* ɪntəˈkaleɪt/ *v.* & *n.* E17. [L *intercalat-* pa. ppl stem of *intercalare* proclaim the insertion of a day etc. in the calendar, f. as INTER- + *calare* proclaim solemnly: see -ATE[3].] **A** *v.* **1** *v.t.* Insert into the calendar as an intercalary day or month. E17. **2** *v.t.* Insert or interpose as an additional or extraneous item; *Geol.* interbed; *Chem.* introduce an extraneous atom, molecule, etc., between the layers of a crystal lattice. Chiefly as *intercalated* ppl a. E19. **3** *v.i.* Become part of a sequence etc. as an extraneous item; become intercalated *in* or inserted *into*. M20. **B** *n. Chem.* An atom, molecule, etc., that enters between the layers of a crystal lattice; a compound formed in this way. M20.

intercalative *a.* characterized by intercalation L19. **intercalator** *n.* a molecule which is inserted into another, larger molecule, esp. of a nucleic acid L20. **intercalatory** *a.* (*rare*) = INTERCALARY E17.

intercalation /ɪntəkəˈleɪʃ(ə)n/ *n.* L16. [Fr., or L *intercalatio(n-)*, f. as prec.: see -ATION.] **1** The insertion of an additional day or month into the calendar in a particular year; an intercalated day or space of time. L16. **2** *gen.* The action of intercalating something; (an) interpolation. M17.

†**intercale** *v.t.* E17–E19. [Fr. *intercaler* or its source L *intercalare*: see INTERCALATE.] = INTERCALATE *v.* 1, 2.

intercameral /ɪntəˈkam(ə)r(ə)l/ *a.* E20. [f. INTER- 2 + L CAMERA chamber + -AL[1].] Involving or occurring between the two chambers of a legislature; situated between or separating two chambers of an organism.

intercede /ɪntəˈsiːd/ *v.* L16. [(O)Fr. *intercéder* or L *intercedere*, f. as INTER- + *cedere* go.] **1** *v.i. Rom. Hist.* Interpose a veto. L16. **2** *v.i.* Interpose on behalf of another; plead (*with* a person, *for*, *on behalf of* another). L16. †**3** *v.t.* & *i.* Come between or *between*; intervene (between). L16–L18. †**4** *v.i.* Intervene by obstruction or prevention. Only in M17.

2 N. MONSARRAT He prayed to the saint to intercede on his behalf.

interceder *n.* M17.

intercept /ˈɪntəsɛpt/ *n.* E19. [f. the vb.] **1** An interception, esp. of a ball passed or thrown towards an opponent. E19. **2** *Math.* The part of a coordinate axis between the origin and the point where a line etc. cuts the axis. M19. **3** A message, signal, etc., intended for someone else and obtained by covert means, esp. in espionage or warfare. E20. **4** The difference between the observed altitude of a celestial object and the calculated one. E20.

intercept /ɪntəˈsɛpt/ *v.* LME. [L *intercept-* pa. ppl stem of *intercipere*, f. as INTER- + *capere* take, seize.] **1** *v.t.* Mark off or include (a certain length or line) between two points or lines; contain between limits. LME. **2** *v.t.* Put an end to, check, (an action, effect, etc.). LME. †**b** Prevent, hinder, (a person or thing). L16–L18. **3** *v.t.* Obstruct so as to prevent from continuing to a destination; stop in the course of a journey; obtain covertly (a message etc. meant for another); obstruct the passage of (light, heat, etc.). M16. **b** Stop (passage, motion through space). L16. †**4** *v.t.* Interrupt, break in on, (esp. a narrative or a person speaking). L16–M18. †**5** *v.i.* Intervene. Only in 17. **6** *v.t.* Cut off (a thing) *from* another thing; cut off from sight, access, etc. M17.

3 M. MEYER A shortage of letters led him to suspect .. that his mail was being intercepted. R. V. JONES They were detected by our radar, and intercepted by two Spitfires. M. DRABBLE Hilda intercepted her gaze. F. NOLAN Are you suggesting .. that the Russian messages intercepted at Bletchley are not genuine?

interceptable *a.* L20. †**intercepter** *n.* (*rare*) E17–L19. **interceptible** *a.* L20.

interception /ɪntəˈsɛpʃ(ə)n/ *n.* LME. [L *interceptio(n-)*, f. as prec.: see -ION.] †**1** *Med.* The interruption of the motion or passage of bodily humours. LME–M17. **2** The action or an act of intercepting; the fact of being intercepted. L16. **b** *spec.* The action of closing in on and trying to destroy an enemy aircraft or missile. M20. **3** The fact of containing or enclosing between points, lines, or boundaries. *rare.* M17.

interceptive /ɪntəˈsɛptɪv/ *a.* LME. [f. L *intercept-* (see INTERCEPT *v.*) + -IVE.] Having the quality of intercepting.

¶ Rare bef. E19.

interceptor /ɪntəˈsɛptə/ *n.* L16. [L, f. as INTERCEPT *v.*: see -OR.] **1** A person who or thing which intercepts. L16. **2** *spec.* A fast aircraft designed for intercepting hostile aircraft. Also more fully *interceptor fighter, interceptor plane*. M20.

intercession /ɪntəˈsɛʃ(ə)n/ *n.* LME. [(O)Fr., or L *intercessio(n-)*, f. *intercess-* pa. ppl stem of *intercedere*: see INTERCEDE, -ION.] **1** The action of interceding or pleading on behalf of another, esp. by prayer; a prayer on behalf of another; in *pl.*, the part of a church service at which such prayers are said. LME. †**b** A petition or pleading on one's own behalf. L15–M18. **2** *Rom. Hist.* The action of interposing a veto. L16. †**3** Cessation, intermission. L16–L17. †**4** Interposition, intervention. E–M17.

1 *Times* A service of thanksgiving and intercession at 2.45 pm on Wednesday.

intercessional *a.* M19. **intercessionary** *a.* employed in intercession; intercessional: M19.

intercessive /ɪntəˈsɛsɪv/ *a.* E17. [Late L *intercessivus*, f. *intercess-*: see prec., -IVE.] Characterized by intercession; intercessory.

intercessor /ɪntəˈsɛsə/ *n.* L15. [OFr. or L, f. *intercess-*: see INTERCESSION, -OR.] **1** A person who intercedes on behalf of another, esp. by prayer. L15. †**2** An intermediary, a go-between. M16–E17.

interce'ssorial *a.* L18.

intercessory /ɪntəˈsɛs(ə)ri/ *a.* L16. [med.L *intercessorius*, f. L *intercessor*: see prec., -ORY[2].] Having the function or purpose of intercession; that intercedes for others.

interchain /ˈɪntətʃeɪn/ *a.* L20. [f. INTER- 2 + CHAIN *n.*] *Chem.* Existing between different polymer chains.

interchain /ɪntəˈtʃeɪn/ *v.t. rare.* L16. [f. INTER- 1 + CHAIN *v.*] Chain or link to one another.

interchange /ˈɪntətʃeɪndʒ/ *n.* Also †**enter-**. LME. [Partly f. the vb, partly f. OFr. *entrechange*, f. as ENTER-[1], INTER- + CHANGE *n.*] **1 a** The action or an act of giving and receiving reciprocally; reciprocal exchange between two parties; *spec.* an exchange of words. LME. **b** The change of either of two things for the other, or of one thing for another; the taking by each of the place or nature of the other. L16. **2** Alternate or varied succession; alternation. M16. **3 a** In full *interchange station*. A station where passengers can change from one railway line, bus service, etc., to another. L19. **b** A junction of two or more roads designed on several levels to allow vehicles to go from one road to another without crossing a flow of traffic. M20.

1a J. MCDOUGALL His daily interchange with colleagues. b E. CLODD Lower races still ascribe power of interchange to man and brute. 2 A. STORR Sometimes our will prevails, and sometimes that of the other . . and we accept this interchange as a normal part of life.

interchange /ɪntəˈtʃeɪndʒ/ *v.* Also †**enter-**. LME. [OFr. *entrechangier*, f. as ENTER-[1], INTER- + *chang(i)er* CHANGE *v.*] **1** *v.t.* **a** Of two parties: exchange with each other; give and receive reciprocally. LME. **b** Of one party: exchange *with* another. M16. **2** *v.t.* Put each of (two things) in the place of the other; transpose. Formerly also, to exchange (one thing) *for* another. LME. **3** *v.t.* Cause (things) to follow each other alternately or in succession. LME. **b** *v.i.* Alternate *with*. L15. **4** *v.i.* (Of two parties or things) take one another's place; (of one) change places (*with*). E20.

1 W. IRVING There were repeated cheerings and salutations interchanged between the shore and the ship. **b** H. MACMILLAN I interchanged some useful messages with Menzies. 2 T. WRIGHT *L* and *r* were constantly interchanged in the languages of the middle ages. 4 *Journal of Genetics* One-half of chromosome IX had interchanged . . with an end-piece of the long chromosome. A. CAMPBELL An important principle of Old English word-formation is that etymologically related suffixes can interchange.

interchanger *n.* (*a*) a person who interchanges something; (*b*) a heat exchanger: M19.

interchangeable /ɪntəˈtʃeɪndʒəb(ə)l/ *a.* & *adv.* LME. [OFr. *entrechangeable*, f. as prec.: see -ABLE.] **A** *adj.* †**1** Mutual, reciprocal. LME–M17. **2** Of two things: able to be interchanged; allowing an exchange of place or function. Of one thing: able to be exchanged *with* another. L15. †**3** Alternating. M16–L18. †**4** Subject to change, changeable. L16–M18.

2 J. S. FOSTER Progress in the manufacture of interchangeable components . . is still slow. C. THUBRON The peasant women looked interchangeable with their men, unsexed by the same shapeless trousers and jackets.

†**B** *adv.* Mutually. LME–M17.

interchangeaˈbility *n.* E19. **interchangeableness** *n.* M16. **interchangeably** *adv.* (*a*) (now *rare*) mutually, respectively; †(*b*) alternately; (*c*) by way of interchange; (of the use of words) synonymously, with equal meaning or force: LME.

†**interchangement** *n. rare.* E17–L18. [OFr. *entrechangement*, f. as INTERCHANGE *v.*: see -MENT.] = INTERCHANGE *n.* 1a.

†**intercision** *n.* L16. [Fr. †*intercision* or L *intercisio(n-)*, f. *intercis-* pa. ppl stem of *intercidere* cut through, f. as INTER- + *caedere* to cut: see -ION.] **1** The action or an act of cutting through something; a cross-section. L16–E18. **2** The action or an act of stopping or interrupting something, esp. temporarily. E17–E19.

†**interclose** *n.* var. of ENTERCLOSE.

†**intercl ude** *v.t.* E16. [L *intercludere* f. as INTER- + *claudere* shut.] **1** Close or block (a passage); prevent the passage of. E16–L17. **2** Shut up, confine. E16–E19. **3** Shut off or cut off *from*. M16–E17.

†**interclusion** *n.* L16–L18.

intercolumn /ˈɪntəkɒləm/ *n.* M17. [L *intercolumnium*, f. as INTER- + *columna* pillar.] *Archit.* = INTERCOLUMNIATION 1.

intercolumnar /ɪntəkəˈlʌmnə/ *a.* M19. [f. INTER- 2 + COLUMNAR.] Situated or placed between two columns.

intercolumniation /ˌɪntəkəlʌmnɪˈeɪʃ(ə)n/ *n.* Also **-columnation** /-kɒləmˈneɪʃ(ə)n/. E17. [f. as INTERCOLUMN + -ATION.] *Archit.* **1** The space between two adjacent columns. E17. **2** The spacing of the columns of a building. M19.

intercoˈlumniary *a.* (*rare*) = INTERCOLUMNAR M17.

intercom /ˈɪntəkɒm/ *n. colloq.* M20. [Abbrev. of INTERCOMMUNICATION.] A system of internal communication by telephone, radio, etc., between or within units of an organization, e.g. aircraft, security patrols.

D. LODGE The captain came on the intercom to inform the passengers that the plane had burst a . . tyre.

intercommon /ɪntəˈkɒmən/ *v.* & *n.* Also (earlier) †**enter-**. LME. [AN *entrecomuner*, f. as ENTER-[1], INTER- + *comuner*: see COMMUNE *v.*] **A** *v.i.* †**1** Have communication or dealings with each other or with another; associate. (Foll. by *with*.) LME–L17. †**2** Share or participate *with* others, or mutually. L16–M17. **3** Share in the use of the same common land. M17.

1 W. PENN The Brittains and Saxons began to grow tame to each other, and intercommon amicably.

B *n.* The action, practice, or right of intercommoning. Now *rare*. LME.

intercommonage *n.* the practice of sharing something, esp. common pasture E17. **intercommoner** *n.* M16.

intercommune /ɪntəkəˈmjuːn, ɪntəˈkɒmjuːn/ *v.* Also (earlier) †**enter-**. LME. [f. as prec.: cf. COMMUNE *v.*] **1** *v.i.* Have communication or conversation with each other or with another. Now *rare* or *obs.* LME. **2** *v.i.* Have dealings or relations, esp. with rebels or denounced people. *obs.* exc. *Sc. Law* (now *Hist.*). LME. **3** *v.t. Sc. Law* (now *Hist.*). Denounce by writ of intercommuning; prohibit communication with. L17.

2 **letter** or **writ of intercommuning**: issued by the Privy Council and prohibiting communication with person(s) named.

intercommuner *n.* (*Sc. Law*, now *Hist.*) a person who has dealings with a person denounced by law E17.

intercommunicate /ɪntəkəˈmjuːnɪkeɪt/ *v.* Also (earlier) †**enter-**. L16. [AL *intercommunicat-* pa. ppl stem of *intercommunicare*, f. as INTER-, COMMUNICATE *v.*] **1** *v.i.* Communicate with each other; (of rooms etc.) have access from each into the other. L16. **2** *v.t.* Communicate, impart, or transmit to and from each other. Long *rare* or *obs.* E17.

intercommunicaˈbility *n.* the quality of being intercommunicable L19. **intercommunicable** *a.* capable of or suitable for intercommunication E19. **intercommunicative** *a.* (*rare*) characterized by or designed for intercommunication M17.

intercommunication /ˌɪntəkəmjuːnɪˈkeɪʃ(ə)n/ *n.* Also (earlier) †**enter-**. LME. [AL *intercommunicatio(n-)*, f. as prec.: see -ATION.] **1** The action or fact of intercommunicating; *esp.* the mutual exchange of ideas, information, etc. LME. **2** (A means of) passage to and fro by connecting routes or lines of communication. M19.

intercommunion /ɪntəkəˈmjuːnjən/ *n.* M18. [f. INTER- 1 + COMMUNION.] **1** Mutual fellowship, esp. between members of different religions or denominations. M18. **b** Participation in each others' Eucharists, to the extent of receiving Communion, by members of different Christian denominations. E20. **2** Mutual action or relation between things with regard to their functions. E19.

2 B. JOWETT When all these studies reach the point of intercommunion and connection with one another.

interconnect /ɪntəkəˈnɛkt/ *v.t.* & *i.* M19. [f. INTER- 1 + CONNECT.] Connect with each other.

Scientific American The human brain is composed of . . nerve cells, each of which projects . . fibres that . . interconnect. T. MO A maze of interconnected waterways.

interconnectedness *n.* the property or state of being interconnected E20. **interconnection**, **-connexion** *n.* mutual connection M19. **interconnector** *n.* something that interconnects things, esp. electrically M20.

intercontinental /ˌɪntəkɒntɪˈnɛnt(ə)l/ *a.* M19. [f. INTER- 2 + CONTINENTAL.] Situated or existing between, or connecting, different continents; (capable of) travelling from one continent to another.

intercontinental ballistic missile a ballistic missile able to be sent from one continent to another.

intercontinentally *adv.* between continents M20.

intercooler /ˈɪntəkuːlə/ *n.* E20. [f. INTER- 1 + COOLER.] An apparatus for cooling gas heated by compression, esp. before it is compressed a second time (e.g. in a supercharged engine).

intercool *v.t.* equip or provide with an intercooler E20.

intercostal /ɪntəˈkɒst(ə)l/ *a.* & *n.* L16. [f. INTER- 2 + L *costa* rib + -AL[1].] **A** *adj.* Situated or occurring between the ribs (of the body or of a ship). L16. **B** *n.* In *pl.* Intercostal muscles, nerves, arteries, etc. L17.

intercostally *adv.* between the ribs L19.

intercourse /ˈɪntəkɔːs/ *n.* & *v.* Also (earlier) †**enter-**. LME. [(O)Fr. *entrecours* exchange, commerce, f. L *intercursus*, f. *intercurs-* pa. ppl stem of *intercurrere* intervene, f. as INTER- + *currere* to run.] **A** *n.* **I 1** Communication or dealings (orig. *spec.* of a mercantile kind) between countries, localities, etc. LME. **2a** *sing.* & (now *rare* or *obs.*) in *pl.* Social communication between individuals; habitual contact in conversation, correspondence, or action. M16. **b** = SEXUAL *intercourse*. L18. **3** Communion between a human being and God or other spiritual being. M16. †**4** Exchange of ideas; discussion. L16–L17. †**5** Intercommunication between things or parts; a means of intercommunication; an entrance. L16–L18. **6** Continuous interchange *of* letters, looks, etc. Now *rare* or *obs.* L16. †**7** Interchange of one thing with another, alternation. L16–M17.

1 W. LIPPMANN An increasing freedom of trade and intercourse within a state makes for an increasing participation in the common life of mankind. 2a H. JAMES The intercourse between these two ladies had been neither frequent nor intimate. R. HUGHES Mrs Thornton thought it good for them to have some intercourse with other children outside their own family. **b** JOYCE He . . did not scruple . . to attempt illicit intercourse with a female domestic. *Boston Globe* The ailment can be transmitted by male homosexual intercourse. 6 I. D'ISRAELI These letters were afterwards followed by an intercourse of civilities.

†**II 8** Intervention; an intervening course or space, an interval. M16–M18.

†**B** *v.* **1** *v.t.* & *i.* Run (through or across). *rare.* L16–E17. **2** *v.i.* Have social intercourse (*with*). *rare.* L16–L18.

intercrop /*as vb* ɪntəˈkrɒp, *as n.* ˈɪntəkrɒp/ *v.* & *n.* L19. [f. INTER- 1 + CROP *v.*] **A** *v.i.* & *t.* Infl. **-pp-**. Raise (a crop) among plants of a different kind, usu. in the space between rows; cultivate (land) in this way. L19. **B** *n.* A crop raised by intercropping. M20.

intercross /*as vb* ɪntəˈkrɒs, *as n.* ˈɪntəkrɒs/ *v.* & *n.* E18. [f. INTER- 1 + CROSS *v.*, *n.*] **A** *v.t.* & *i.* **1** Cross (each other); place across each other. E18. **2** Of animals or plants of different breeds, varieties, etc.: (cause to) breed or propagate with each other. M19. **B** *n.* An instance or result of intercrossing animals or plants. M19.

intercurrent /ɪntəˈkʌr(ə)nt/ *a.* E17. [L *intercurrent-* pres. ppl stem of *intercurrere*: see INTERCOURSE, -ENT.] **1a** Of time or events: intervening. E17. †**b** Of objects: intervening; situated between others. M–L17. **2** Of a disease, esp. an infection: occurring by chance during the course of another more chronic disease; recurring. Formerly also (of a fever), apt to occur at any time of year. L17. **3** Of the pulse: having an extra beat. E18.

intercurrence *n.* the fact or state of being intercurrent E17.

intercut /ɪntəˈkʌt/ *v.* Infl. **-tt-**. Pa. t. & pple **intercut**. E17. [f. INTER- 1 + CUT *v.*] †**1** *v.t.* Cut into; divide (as) by cutting; intersect. *rare.* E17–E18. **2** *Cinemat.* Insert a scene or shot into (an existing scene); alternate (shots from different scenes). (Foll. by *with*.) M20.

2 I. C. JARVIE Resnais . . intercuts scenes from the heroine's memories . . with her present *affaire*. T. BARR He will be intercutting from you standing, to you sitting, and back to you standing.

interdeal /ɪntəˈdiːl/ *v.i.* Pa. t. & pple **-dealt** /-dɛlt/. L16. [f. INTER- 1 + DEAL *v.*] Deal or negotiate mutually.

interdealer /ɪntəˈdiːlə/ *a.* M20. [f. INTER- 2 + DEALER.] *Stock Exch.* Made or occurring between dealers; (of a broker) trading chiefly with dealers or market-makers.

interdental /ɪntəˈdɛnt(ə)l/ *a.* & *n.* L19. [f. INTER- 2 + DENTAL.] **A** *adj.* **1** Situated or placed between teeth or the teeth. L19. **2** *Phonet.* Pronounced by placing the tip of the tongue between the teeth. L19. **B** *n. Phonet.* An interdental sound. M20.

interdentally *adv.* E20.

interdepend /ɪntədɪˈpɛnd/ *v.i.* M19. [f. INTER- 1 + DEPEND.] Depend on each other.

interdependent /ɪntədɪˈpɛnd(ə)nt/ *a.* M18. [f. INTER- 1 + DEPENDENT *a.*] Dependent on each other.

interdependence *n.* E19. **interdependency** *n.* M19. **interdependently** *adv.* L19.

†**interdice** *n.* E17–E18. [Origin unkn. Cf. INTERTIE.] = INTERTIE.

interdict /ˈɪntədɪkt/ *n.* Also (earlier) †**entredit(e)**. ME. [OFr. *entredit* f. L *interdictum* (to which the Eng. wd was later assim.), use as n. of neut. pa. pple of *interdicere* interpose by speech, forbid by decree, f. as INTER- + *dicere* say.] **1** *RC Ch.* An authoritative sentence debarring a designated person, group, or place from ecclesiastical functions and privileges. ME. **2a** *Rom. Law.* A decree of the magistrate, commanding or forbidding something. E17. **b** *Sc.* & *Civil Law.* A court order forbidding an act or proceedings complained of as illegal or wrongful; an injunction. M18. **3** *gen.* An authoritative or peremptory prohibition. E17.

1 M. ELPHINSTONE He . . suspended all the ceremonies of religion, as if the country were under an interdict. **2b** *Oban Times* Mr. Muir went to the Court of Session. . . An interdict was granted.

interdict /ɪntəˈdɪkt/ *v.t.* Also (earlier) †**entredite**. Pa. t. & pple **-dicted**, (now *literary*) **-dict**. ME. [f. prec. after OFr. *entredire* f. L *interdicere*: see prec.] **1** *RC Ch.* Cut off authoritatively from ecclesiastical functions and privileges; lay under an interdict. ME. **2** Forbid, prohibit, esp. (*Law*) by interdiction; debar or preclude (as) by a command; restrain (oneself) *from* an action. (Foll. by *from*; with double obj.) LME. **3** Impede (an enemy, supplies) by aerial bombing. M20.

2 G. SANDYS Who . . will . . interdict thee his tabernacle. H. COGAN They interdicted that great Court from proceeding any further against them.

interdictive *a.* interdictory E17. **interdictory** *a.* having the effect of interdicting something or someone; conveying interdiction, prohibitory: M18.

interdiction /ɪntəˈdɪkʃ(ə)n/ *n.* Also (earlier) †**enter-**. LME. [L *interdictio(n-)*, f. *interdict-*: see next, -ION.] **1** The issuing of an interdict; the action of interdicting a person etc.; the condition of being interdicted. LME. **2** *Sc. Law* (now *Hist.*). A restraint imposed on a person judged incapable of managing his or her own affairs owing to mental weakness or instability. L16. **3** The interruption of supply operations by aerial bombing. M20.

interdictor /ɪntəˈdɪktə/ *n.* M17. [Late (eccl.) L, f. *interdict-* pa. ppl stem of *interdicere*: see INTERDICT *n.*, -OR.] **1** A person who issues an interdict; *Sc. Law* (now *Hist.*) a person responsible for consent to heritable transactions by someone under an interdiction. M17. **2** An aircraft designed for interdiction. M20.

interdigital /ɪntəˈdɪdʒɪt(ə)l/ *a.* M20. [f. INTER- 2 + DIGIT + -AL[1].] **1** Situated between or connecting fingers or toes. M20. **2** *Electronics.* Esp. of a transducer: having the form of two interdigitating series of parallel strips. M20.

interdigitally *adv.* L20.

interdigitate /ɪntəˈdɪdʒɪteɪt/ *v.* M19. [f. INTER- 1 + DIGIT + -ATE[3].] **1** *v.i.* Interlock like the fingers of two clasped hands; project or be inserted alternately. (Foll. by *with*.) M19. **2** *v.t.* Cause to interdigitate. Chiefly as *interdigitated* ppl a. M19.

2 J. OSBORNE Normal interdigitated relationship of the upper and lower posterior teeth.

interdigiˈtation *n.* the action or condition of interdigitating; an interdigitating process etc.: M19.

interdisciplinary /ɪntəˈdɪsɪplɪn(ə)ri, ˌɪntədɪsɪˈplɪn(ə)ri/ *a.* E20. [f. INTER- 2 + DISCIPLINE *n.* + -ARY[1].] Of or pertaining to two or more branches of learning; contributing to or derived from two or more disciplines.

ˌ**interdiscipliˈnarity** *n.* interdisciplinary quality L20. ˈ**interdiscipline** *n.* an interdisciplinary subject L20. **interˈdiscipline** *a.* = INTERDISCIPLINARY M20.

†**interess** *n.* LME. [AN *interesse* f. med.L *interesse*, use as n. of L inf.: see INTEREST *n.*] **1** = INTEREST *n.* I. LME–M17. **2** = INTEREST *n.* 2, 3. LME–E18. **3** = INTEREST *n.* II. LME–L15. **4** = INTEREST *n.* 10. E16–E18.

†**interess** *v.t.* Pa. pple **-ed**, **-rest**. L16. [Fr. *intéresser* concern, (formerly) damage, f. L *interesse*: see INTEREST *n.*] **1** = INTEREST *v.* I. L16–L17. **2** = INTEREST *v.* 2. Usu. in *pass.* L16–M17. **3** Injure; damage. L16–M17. **4** Cause to take an active part (*in*); = INTEREST *v.* 4. E17–E18. **5** = INTEREST *v.* 5. M–L17.

†**interessee** *n.* (*rare*) an interested party E17–E19.

interesse termini /ɪntərˌɛsi ˈtəːmɪnʌɪ/ *n. phr.* M17. [med.L, lit. 'interest of term or end'.] *Law* (now *Hist.*). A right of entry on a leasehold estate, acquired through a demise.

interest /ˈɪnt(ə)rɪst/ *n.* LME. [f. INTERESS *n.*, partly by addition of parasitic *t*, partly by assoc. with OFr. *interest* damage, loss (mod. *intérêt*), app. use as n. of L *interest* it makes a difference, it concerns, it matters, 3rd person sing. pres. indic. of *interesse* differ, be of importance, f. as INTER- + *esse* be.] **I 1** The fact or relation of having a share or concern in, or a right to, something, esp. by law; a right or title, esp. to (a share in) property or a use or benefit relating to property; (a) share *in* something. LME. †**b** Participation in doing or causing something. M17–M18. **c** A financial share or stake in something; the relation of being one of the owners or beneficiaries of an asset, company, etc. L17. **2** A thing which is to the advantage of someone; (a) benefit, (an) advantage. Freq. in *pl.* LME. **3** The relation of being involved or concerned as regards potential detriment or (esp.) advantage. M16. **4** = SELF-INTEREST. E17. **5** Personal influence (*with* a person etc.). E17. **6** A thing that is of some importance to a person, company, state, etc. Freq. in *pl.* E17. **7** A business, cause, or principle that is of some importance to a number of people; a party or group having such a thing in common, esp. in matters of politics or business. L17. **8** A state of feeling in which one wishes to pay particular attention to a thing or person; (a feeling of) curiosity or concern. L18. **9** The quality or power of arousing such a feeling; the quality of being interesting. E19.

1c J. MORTIMER Has someone else got an interest in the film rights? **2** R. HUNTFORD He always had the interests of his protégés at heart. **6** J. MORTIMER Simeon pursued his political interests more doggedly. M. PIERCY He would suggest she take up some new interest or hobby. **7** J. GALSWORTHY Mrs. Smeech, . . an aged person, connected with the charring interest. C. V. WEDGWOOD Cooke . . was now wholly in the King's interest. P. GAY Institutions can be captured by special interests. **8** J. RUSKIN He who can take no interest in what is small. K. AMIS I seem to have failed to hold your interest. E. H. JONES They had no interest in field-sports. **9** C. G. WOLFF It is not . . a novel whose interest lies in plot.

II Senses rel. to med.L *interesse* compensation for a debtor's defaulting. **10** Money charged for the use of money lent or for not having to repay a debt, according to a specified ratio. M16. †**11** Injury, detriment; compensation for injury. L16–E17.

10 E. NESBIT You shall pay me back the pound, and sixty per cent interest.

Phrases: **at interest** (of money borrowed or lent) on the condition that interest is to be charged. **compound interest**: reckoned on the principal together with the accumulated unpaid interest. *controlling interest*: see CONTROL *v.* **declare an** or **one's interest** make known one's financial etc. interest in an undertaking before the discussion of it. *human interest*: see HUMAN *a.* **in the best interest(s) of** to the greatest advantage or benefit of. **in the interest(s) of** (*a*) *arch.* on the side of; (*b*) out of consideration for, to the advantage or benefit of. LANDED *interest*. **lose interest (in)** (of a person) become bored (with); (of a thing) become boring. *open interest*: see OPEN *a.* *outside interest*: see OUTSIDE *a.* *public interest*: see PUBLIC *a.* **simple interest**: reckoned on the principal only and paid at fixed intervals. *Site of Special Scientific Interest*: see SITE *n.* *special interest*: see SPECIAL *a.* *vested interest*: see VESTED *ppl a.*[1] 2. **with interest** with interest charged or paid; *fig.* with increase or augmentation.

Comb.: **interest group** a group of people sharing a common identifying interest.

interest /ˈɪnt(ə)rɪst/ *v.t.* E17. [Alt. of INTERESS *v.* after prec.] **1** Invest (a person) with a share in or title to something, esp. a spiritual privilege. E17. **2** Cause (a person) to have an interest or concern *in* (a matter); involve. Usu. in *pass.* E17. **3** Of a thing: concern, affect, relate to. Now *rare* or *obs.* M17. **4** Cause (a person) to take a personal interest or share *in* a scheme, business, etc.; cause to become interested (*in*); *refl.* take an active part *in*. M17. **5** Affect with a feeling of interest; arouse the curiosity or concern of. E18.

4 M. ATWOOD He'd tried to interest Alma in chess and mathematics. **5** B. WEBB Human nature and its problems interest me.

interested /ˈɪnt(ə)rɪstɪd/ *a.* E17. [f. prec. + -ED[1].] **1** Characterized by a feeling of interest (*in*). Also foll. by *to learn*, *see*, etc. E17. **2** Influenced by considerations of personal advantage or self-interest. E18. **3** Having an interest, share, or concern, in something; affected, involved. E19.

1 *Lady's Pictorial* I shall be interested to know how the wedding goes off. J. HELLER They don't seem interested in doing much more. **2** LD MACAULAY He was generally thought interested and grasping. **3** *New York Law Journal* The witness . . was an interested witness. P. HOWARD The Times is steered by all these and other interested parties.

interestedly *adv.* M18. **interestedness** *n.* E18.

interesterification /ˌɪntərɪstɛrɪfɪˈkeɪʃ(ə)n, -rɛs-/ *n.* M20. [f. INTER- 1 + ESTERIFICATION.] *Chem.* The exchange of alkoxy or acyl groups between an ester and another compound.

interesˈterify *v.t.* & *i.* subject to or undergo this process M20.

interesting /ˈɪnt(ə)rɪstɪŋ/ *a.* E18. [f. INTEREST *v.* + -ING[2].] †**1** That concerns or is relevant (*to*); important. E18–E19. **2** That affects a person with a feeling of interest; having qualities which arouse interest. E18.

2 *in an interesting condition*: see CONDITION *n.* 8.

interestingly *adv.* in an interesting manner, so as to arouse interest; (modifying a sentence) it is interesting that; (earlier in UNINTERESTINGLY *adv.*): E19. **interestingness** *n.* M18.

interface /ˈɪntəfeɪs/ *n.* & *v.* L19. [f. INTER- 1 + FACE *n.*] **A** *n.* **1** A surface at which two portions of matter or space meet. L19. **2** A means or place of interaction between two systems, organizations, etc.; a meeting point or common ground between two parties, disciplines, etc. M20. **3** An apparatus for connecting two electrical or electronic devices or systems so that they can be operated jointly or communicate with each other; an apparatus enabling a user to communicate with a computer. M20.

1 *Science Journal* Ways of reducing drag at the interface between ski and snow. A. C. CLARKE The sharply defined plane which marked the water-air interface on the sonar screen. **2** *New Scientist* Estuaries occupy an interface which is administrative as well as topographical. *Globe & Mail (Toronto)* The successful candidate will . . function as a prime interface to development and manufacturing. **3** S. CURRAN A few modern typewriters . . are specifically designed with an optional computer communications interface.

B *v.* **1** *v.t.* Connect (scientific equipment) *with* or *to* so as to make joint operation possible. M20. **2** *v.i.* Be operated jointly (*with*). M20. **3** *v.i.* Of a person, organization, etc.: come into interaction, interact, *with*. M20.

1 *Which Micro?* It can be interfaced with virtually any micro on the market. **2** *Offshore Engineer* The responder . . can interface with most existing vehicle tether systems. **3** *New York Times* Business has to interface with government increasingly.

interfacial /ɪntəˈfeɪʃ(ə)l/ *a.*[1] M19. [f. INTER- 2 + L *facies* face + -AL[1].] Included between two faces of a crystal.

interfacial /ˈɪntəfeɪʃ(ə)l/ *a.*[2] E20. [f. INTERFACE *n.* + -IAL.] Existing or occurring at an interface.

interfacially *adv.* M20.

interfacing /ˈɪntəfeɪsɪŋ/ *n.* M20. [f. INTER- 1 + FACING.] (A piece of) stiffish material, esp. buckram, between two layers of fabric in collars etc.

interfere /ɪntəˈfɪə/ *v.* Also †**enter-**. LME. [Branch I f. OFr. *entreferir*; branch II f. OFr. *s'entreferir* strike each other; both f. as ENTER-[1], INTER- + *ferir* (mod. *férir*) f. L *ferire* to strike.] †**I** *v.t.* **1** Intermingle; intersperse *with*; interpose. LME–L15.

II *v.i.* **2** Of a person or persons: enter into something without right or invitation, or intending to hinder or obstruct (foll. by *with*). Of a thing: come into conflict or collision (*with*). Of things: strike against each other (now *rare*).

LME. b Foll. by *with*: molest or assault sexually. M20. 3 Of a horse: = CUT *v.* 30. Of a hoof or foot: strike the inside of the fetlock of another leg. M16. †4 *v.i.* Clash in opinions, tendencies, etc.; conflict. M17–M19. †5 Intersect, cross each other. M17–E18. 6 Intervene so as to affect an action. (Foll. by *in*, *between*.) M18. 7 Of light or other waves: mutually act upon each other and produce interference. (Foll. by *with*.) E19. 8 *Chess*. Of a piece: obstruct the line of action of another piece. (Foll. by *with*.) E20. 9 *Broadcasting*. Transmit a signal which is received simultaneously *with* the signal sought by the receiver; cause or emit interference. E20. 10 *Baseball* & *Amer. Football*. Interpose so as to obstruct an opposing player. E20.

2 B. T. BRADFORD I wouldn't want her to think he was interfering, queering her pitch. A. STORR The primary instinct was being blocked or interfered with. J. JOHNSTON Her nails . . were . . short, so as not to interfere with her piano playing. 6 P. G. WODEHOUSE It is better for a third party to quarrel with a buzz-saw than to interfere between husband and wife. N. COWARD I'm not going to interfere Let them fight if they want to. *Times* Nato should not seek to interfere in Italy's internal affairs.

interferer *n.* E19. **interfering** *ppl a.* that interferes; *esp.* (of a person) having a propensity to interfere in other people's affairs: L16. **interferingly** *adv.* M19. **interferingness** *n.* L19.

interference /ɪntəˈfɪər(ə)ns/ *n.* M18. [f. prec. + -ENCE, after *difference* etc.] 1 The action or fact of interfering or meddling (*with* a person, *in* a thing, etc.). M18. 2 *Sci.* The mutual action of two waves of similar wavelength when they combine and form a resultant wave in which the amplitude is increased or reduced. M19. 3 Disturbance of the transmission or reception of radio waves by extraneous signals or phenomena; signals etc. causing such disturbance; unwanted effects arising from such disturbance. L19. 4 *Mech.* a The collision of the tips of the teeth of a gearwheel with the flanks of those of the mating wheel. E20. b The amount by which the external dimension of a part exceeds the internal dimension of the part into which it has to fit. M20. 5 *Ling.* The influence of the pronunciation or other features of a person's native language on a later acquired language. M20.

1 M. IGNATIEFF He sought to defend the autonomy of the universities from government interference. 3 A. MCCOWEN When his car came down the drive, electrical interference could be seen on our new television set.

Comb.: **interference fit** *Mech.* a fit between two mating parts for which, within the tolerances, there is always an interference between them; **interference fringe** each of a series of light and dark bands, or bands of different colours, produced by the interference of light (e.g. from two point sources); usu. in *pl.*; **interference pattern**: of interference fringes.

interferential /ɪntəfəˈrɛnʃ(ə)l/ *a.* L19. [f. prec. + -IAL, after *differential* etc.] Involving or employing interference, esp. of light.

interferogram /ɪntəˈfɪərəgram/ *n.* E20. [f. as next + -O- + -GRAM.] A pattern formed by wave interference, *esp.* one represented in a photograph or diagram.

interferometer /ɪntəfəˈrɒmɪtə/ *n.* L19. [f. INTERFERE + -OMETER.] An instrument in which wave interference is employed to make precise measurements of length or displacement in terms of the wavelength.

ˌ**interferoˈmetric** *a.* of or pertaining to interferometry; employing or of the nature of an interferometer: M20. ˌ**interferoˈmetrically** *adv.* by means of interferometry M20. **interferometry** *n.* the action or art of measuring interference phenomena; (the branch of science that deals with) the use of interferometers: E20.

interferon /ɪntəˈfɪərɒn/ *n.* M20. [f. as prec. + *-on*.] Any of several proteins which are produced by and released from animal cells in response to the entry of a virus, and inhibit virus replication in other cells.

interflow /ˈɪntəfləʊ/ *n.* E17. [f. INTER- 1 + FLOW *n.*[1]] †1 A flow between things; a channel, a strait. Only in E17. 2 An instance of interflowing, an intermingling. M19.

interflow /ɪntəˈfləʊ/ *v.* L16. [f. INTER- 1 + FLOW *v.*] 1 *v.i.* & †*t.* Flow between (things). L16. 2 *v.i.* Flow into each other, intermingle. M19.

interfluent /ɪntəˈfluːənt/ *a.* M17. [f. L *interfluent-* pres. ppl stem of *interfluere*: see next, -ENT.] 1 Flowing between things, interflowing. Now *rare*. M17. 2 Flowing into each other, intermingling. L19.

interfluence *n.* (*rare*) E19.

interfluous /ɪnˈtəːfluəs/ *a.* M17. [f. L *interfluus* (f. *interfluere* interflow f. as INTER- + *fluere* to flow) + -OUS.] = prec.

interfluve /ˈɪntəfluːv/ *n.* E20. [f. next.] *Geol.* An interfluvial region, *esp.* one between the valleys of a dissected upland.

interfluvial /ɪntəˈfluːvɪəl/ *a.* M19. [f. INTER- 2 + FLUVIAL.] Situated between (the valleys of) adjacent watercourses.

interfold /ɪntəˈfəʊld/ *v.t.* Also †**enter-**. L16. [f. INTER- 1, ENTER-[1] + FOLD *v.*[1]] Fold together or within each other.

interfulgent /ɪntəˈfʌldʒ(ə)nt/ *a.* *rare*. E18. [f. INTER- 1 + FULGENT.] Shining among or between things.

interfuse /ɪntəˈfjuːz/ *v.* L16. [L *interfus-* pa. ppl stem of *interfundere*, f. as INTER- + *fundere* pour.] 1 *v.t.* Permeate (a thing) *with* an infusion or mixture of something else. Usu. in *pass.* L16. 2 *v.t.* Pour in among something. Usu. in *pass.* M17. 3 *v.t.* In *pass.* Be fused or blended together. M19. 4 *v.i.* Of two things: fuse or blend with each other. M19. 5 *v.t.* Of one thing: permeate and blend with. L19.

1 W. BLACK The wonderful light greens of the Spring foliage seemed to be interfused with a lambent sunshine. 2 WORDSWORTH A sense sublime Of something far more deeply interfused, Whose dwelling is the light. 3 J. R. LOWELL The character and its intellectual product are inextricably interfused. 4 R. FIRBANK Moon-lit lawns and . . trees stretched away, interfusing far off into soft deeps of velvet.

interfusion *n.* the action of interfusing; the fact of being interfused: E19.

interglacial /ɪntəˈgleɪsɪəl, -ʃ(ə)l/ *a.* & *n.* M19. [f. INTER- 2 + GLACIAL.] *Geol.* A *adj.* Occurring or formed between glacial periods. M19. B *n.* An interglacial period. E20.

interglaciation /ˌɪntəgleɪsɪˈeɪʃ(ə)n/ *n.* M20. [f. INTER- 2 + GLACIATION.] *Geol.* = INTERGLACIAL *n.*

intergrade /ˈɪntəgreɪd/ *n.* L19. [f. INTER- 2 + GRADE *n.*] Chiefly *Biol.* An intermediate form.

intergrade /ɪntəˈgreɪd/ *v.i.* L19. [f. INTER- 1 + GRADE *v.*] Chiefly *Biol.* Pass into another form by a series of intervening forms.

intergraˈdation *n.* the action or fact of intergrading L19.

intergrow /ɪntəˈgrəʊ/ *v.* Infl. as GROW *v.* L19. [f. INTER- 1 + GROW *v.*] 1 *v.i.* Esp. (*Min.*) of crystals: grow into each other. L19. 2 *v.t.* Intersperse with something growing. Only as *intergrown* ppl a. *rare*. L19.

intergrowth /ˈɪntəgrəʊθ/ *n.* M19. [f. INTER- 1 + GROWTH.] The growing (of things) into each other; a thing produced by intergrowing.

interim /ˈɪnt(ə)rɪm/ *n.*, *adv.*, & *a.* M16. [L (adv.), f. *inter* between + advb. ending *-im*.] A *n.* 1 *Eccl. Hist.* (Usu. **I-**.) A provisional arrangement for the adjustment of religious differences between the German Protestants and the Roman Catholic Church in the mid 16th cent. M16. b *gen.* A temporary or provisional arrangement. M16. †2 A thing done in an interval; an interlude. L16–M17. 3 An intervening time; *the* meantime. E17. 4 An interim dividend. M20.

3 SIR W. SCOTT How we shall prevent the guilty person from escaping in the interim.

B *adv.* In the meantime; meanwhile. Now *rare*. L16.

C *adj.* Done, made, provided, etc., in or for the meantime; provisional, temporary. Formerly (of time), intervening. E17.

interim dividend: announced on the basis of a company's financial results for a period less than a full financial year (usu. six months).

interiˈmistic *a.* = INTERIM *a.* M19. †**interimistical** *a.* = INTERIM *a.*: only in M17.

Interimsethik /ˈɪnterɪmsˌeːtɪk/ *n.* Also Anglicized as ***interim-ethic*** /ˈɪntərɪmˌɛθɪk/. E20. [G, f. as INTERIM + *Ethik* ethics.] *Theol.* The moral principles of Jesus interpreted as meant for people expecting the imminent end of the world; *transf.* a code of behaviour for use in a specific temporary situation.

interior /ɪnˈtɪərɪə/ *a.* & *n.* L15. [L = inner, compar. adj. f. *inter* between: see -IOR.] A *adj.* 1 Situated (more) within or inside; belonging to or concerned with the inside. Opp. *exterior*. L15. 2 Mental; spiritual; pious, devout. E16. 3 Concerned with or pertaining to the domestic (as opp. to foreign) affairs of a State. M18. 4 Situated within a country or region and at a distance from the coast or frontier, inland; belonging to interior regions. L18.

1 **interior to** on the inner side or inside of. 2 M. SCHAPIRO Little or no interior life, at most a charming appearance.

Special collocations: **interior angle** *Geom.*: between adjacent sides of a rectilinear figure. *interior* BALLISTICS. **interior decoration** the planned coordination for artistic effect of colours and furniture, etc., in a room or building. **interior design** the design of the interior of a building according to artistic and architectural criteria. **interior monologue** a form of writing in which the inner thoughts of a person are presented. **interior spring mattress**: having coiled springs inside it. **interior-sprung** *a.* (of a mattress) having coiled springs inside.

B *n.* 1 The interior part of something; the inside. L16. b The interior part of a country or region. L18. c (A picture or representation of) the inside of a room or building. E19. d The internal organs of the body, *esp.* the digestive system. *colloq.* M19. 2 Inner nature or being; inward mind; soul, character. Now usu. w. *of*. L16. 3 The internal affairs of a State; the department of Government concerned with these. M19.

1c *Dutch interior*: see DUTCH *a.*

interiorly *adv.* (*a*) in or on the inside, internally; (*b*) inwardly, intimately; (*c*) mentally, spiritually: E17.

interiorise *v.* var. of INTERIORIZE.

interiority /ɪnˌtɪərɪˈɒrɪti/ *n.* E18. [med.L *interioritas*, f. as INTERIOR: see -ITY.] The quality of being interior or inward; inner character or nature; depth of feeling, subjectivity.

interiorize /ɪnˈtɪərɪərʌɪz/ *v.t.* Also **-ise**. E20. [f. INTERIOR + -IZE.] = INTERNALIZE 1, 2; connect with the soul.

interioriˈzation *n.* M20.

interjacent /ɪntəˈdʒeɪs(ə)nt/ *a.* M16. [L *interjacent-* pres. ppl stem of *interjacere*, f. as INTER- + *jacere* to lie: see -ENT.] Situated or existing between things; intervening.

interjacency *n.* M17.

interject /ɪntəˈdʒɛkt/ *v.* L16. [L *interject-* pa. ppl stem of *interjicere* interpose, f. as INTER- + *jacere* to throw, cast.] 1 *v.t.* Introduce abruptly, esp. into a conversation; remark parenthetically or as an interruption. L16. b In *pass.* Lie or be situated *between*. Long *rare*. L16. †2 *v.i.* Intersect; intervene. *rare*. L16–L17.

1 B. T. BRADFORD 'We'll get to that later,' Estelle interjected . . brusquely. B. UNSWORTH He was reading from a script but interjecting his own remarks from time to time.

interjector *n.* a person who makes an interjection L19. **interjectory** *a.* characterized by interjections; of the nature of an interjection: M19.

interjection /ɪntəˈdʒɛkʃ(ə)n/ *n.* LME. [(O)Fr. f. L *interjectio(n-)*, f. as prec.: see -ION.] 1 The utterance of an exclamation expressing emotion; an exclamation; an interjected remark. LME. 2 An exclamation regarded as a part of speech. LME. 3 The action of interjecting or interposing something. L16.

1 R. GITTINGS His excited interjections of 'By God!' when anything moved him. 2 SHAKES. *Much Ado* How now! interjections? Why then, some be of laughing, as ha, ha, he.

interjectionary *a.* interjectory L19.

interjectional /ɪntəˈdʒɛkʃ(ə)n(ə)l/ *a.* M18. [f. prec. + -AL[1].] Of, pertaining to, or of the nature of an interjection.

interjectionally *adv.* M19.

For other words beginning with *inter-* see the entry for **inter-**

interjectural /ɪntəˈdʒɛktʃ(ə)r(ə)l/ *a.* L18. [Alt. of INTERJECTIONAL after *conjectural*.] = INTERJECTIONAL.

interkinesis /ɪntəkɪˈniːsɪs, -kʌɪ-/ *n.* E20. [f. INTER- 1 + KINESIS.] *Cytol.* A stage in cell division sometimes occurring between the first and second divisions of meiosis.

interlace /ˈɪntəleɪs/ *n.* E20. [f. the vb.] **1** The action or result of interlacing. E20. **2** *Television.* The system, process, or result of scanning with interlaced lines or dots. M20.

1 *Daily Mail* The upturned brim has fancy straw interlace, giving a ribbon effect. *attrib.*: E. H. GOMBRICH He was obviously trained in the intricate interlace work of eleventh-century ornament.

interlace /ɪntəˈleɪs/ *v.* Also (earlier) †**enter-**. LME. [OFr. *entrelacier*, f. *entre-* ENTER-[1], INTER- + *lacier* LACE *v.*] **I** *v.t.* **1** Unite (two or more things) by interweaving strands. Chiefly *fig.*, bind together intricately, entangle, involve. LME. **2** Cross alternately over and under each other; *fig.* mix by alternation. E16. †**3** Weave (a thing) into another; insert, interpolate. M16–L17. **4** Intersperse, vary, mix *with*. L16. **5** *Television.* Scan so that alternate lines or other sets of picture elements form one sequence which is followed by the other lines etc. in a second sequence; build up (a picture) in this way. E20.

1 W. COWPER Close interlaced with purple cordage strong. 2 F. W. FARRAR The two are inextricably interlaced. A righteous life is the result of faith, and faith is deepened by a righteous life. I. MCEWAN He was holding Stephen's hand, their fingers were interlaced. 4 *fig.*: W. BLACK Beautiful green meadows interlaced with streams.

II *v.i.* †**6** Become entangled or involved. LME–E17. **7** Cross and recross as if woven together; lie in alternate directions as the fingers of clasped hands. L16.

interlacedly *adv.* in an interlaced manner M17. **interlacement** *n.* interweaving, intermingling; an interlaced arrangement or structure: E17.

interlaid *v.* pa. t. & pple of INTERLAY *v.*

interlaminar /ɪntəˈlamɪnə/ *a.* M19. [f. INTER- 2 + LAMINA + -AR[1].] **1** *Anat.* Situated between laminae or plates. M19. **2** Situated or occurring between the layers of a laminate or composite. M20.

interlaminate /ɪntəˈlamɪneɪt/ *v.t.* E19. [f. INTER- 1 + LAMINATE *v.*] Insert in or between alternate laminae or plates.

interlamiˈnation *n.* the action of interlaminating; an interlaminated formation: M19.

interlanguage /ˈɪntəlaŋgwɪdʒ/ *n.* E20. [f. INTER- 1 + LANGUAGE *n.*[1]] An auxiliary language; a blend of languages, as (*a*) a pidgin; (*b*) a language student's idiom deriving from his or her native language and the language being learned.

interlanguage /ɪntəˈlaŋgwɪdʒ/ *a.* M20. [f. INTER- 2 + LANGUAGE *n.*[1]] Occurring between or pertaining to two or more languages.

interlard /ɪntəˈlɑːd/ *v.t.* Also (earlier) †**enter-**. LME. [(O)Fr. *entrelarder*, f. *entre-* ENTER-[1], INTER- + *larder* LARD *v.*] †**1** Mix with alternate layers of fat; thread (lean meat) with strips of fat before cooking. LME–L18. **2** Interpolate, interpose. Now *rare.* M16. **3** *fig.* = LARD *v.* 4. L16. **b** Become intermingled with; run through. M17.

1 *transf.*: W. LITHGOW Grey Marble, interlarded with white Alabaster. 2 T. CARTE Boyish speeches in which he often interlarded the words O tempora, O mores. 3 C. CONNOLLY My jokes, a combination of puns and personal remarks interlarded with . . wisecracks. D. PRATER He also began to write a history . . interlarding his prose text with verse. b W. CONGREVE Lying is a figure of speech that interlards the greatest part of my conversation.

interlardment *n.* the action of interlarding; something interlarded: M18.

interlay /ˈɪntəleɪ/ *n.* E20. [f. the vb.] An inserted layer; *spec.* in *Printing* (now *Hist.*), a sheet of (cut out) paper placed between a letterpress printing plate and its base to give increased pressure on certain areas.

interlay /ɪntəˈleɪ/ *v.t.* Pa. t. & pple **-laid** /-ˈleɪd/. E17. [f. INTER- 1 + LAY *v.*[1]] Lay between or among, interpose; provide with inserted material.

interlayer /ˈɪntəleɪə/ *n.* & *a.* M20. [f. INTER- 1, 2 + LAYER *n.*] **A** *n.* A layer sandwiched between two others. M20. **B** *adj.* Situated or occurring between two layers. M20.

interleaf /ˈɪntəliːf/ *n.* Pl. **-leaves** /-liːvz/. M18. [f. INTER- 2 + LEAF *n.*[1]] An extra leaf to prevent set-off or for additional notes etc., inserted between the ordinary leaves of a book.

interleave /ˈɪntəliːv/ *n.* M20. [f. the vb.] *Computing.* The action or process of interleaving digits etc.

interleave /ɪntəˈliːv/ *v.t.* M17. [f. INTER- 2 + LEAF *n.*[1] (pl. *leaves*).] **1** Insert (blank) leaves between the ordinary leaves of (a book). M17. **2** *transf.* & *fig.* Foll. by *with*: insert something at regular intervals between (the parts of). M19. **3** *Computing.* Combine (sequences of digits, addresses, etc.) by successively taking one item from each of a number of groups. M20.

1 J. G. LOCKHART He is going to interleave his copy and annotate largely. 2 DE QUINCEY Any feasible plan for interleaving days of hardship with days of ease. A. BROOKNER She would start . . laying cups and plates, interleaved with tiny napkins of écru linen.

interleukin /ɪntəˈluːkɪn/ *n.* L20. [f. INTER- 2 + LEUK(OCYTE + -IN[1].] *Physiol.* Any of several glycoproteins which are produced by leucocytes and are involved in lymphocyte formation and the immune response.

interline /ˈɪntəlʌɪn/ *a.* M20. [f. INTER- 2 + LINE *n.*[2]] Designating or pertaining to transport using more than one route, service, etc.

Aviation News The motorway link between the airports is sufficient for interline traffic.

interline /ɪntəˈlʌɪn/ *v.*[1] Also (earlier) †**enter-**. LME. [med.L *interlineare*, f. as INTER- + L *linea* LINE *n.*[2]] **1** *v.t.* Insert additional words between the lines of (a document). Usu. in *pass.* (Foll. by *with.*) LME. **2** *v.t.* Insert (a word or words) between the lines of a document. L16. **3** *v.i.* Make interlinear insertions. L16. †**4** *v.t.* Mark with lines, esp. of various colours. L16–M17. †**5** *v.t.* Intersperse with lines of something else; insert as lines in something. E17–M18.

1 G. SHELVOCKE Written by several hands, and interlin'd in a great many places. 2 W. STUBBS These words were found interlined in Richard's grant. 3 SWIFT Blot out, correct, insert, refine, Enlarge, diminish, interline. 5 T. WATSON Mercy interlined with judgment. DEFOE I saw the foot . . interlined among the horse.

interline /ɪntəˈlʌɪn/ *v.*[2]*t.* L15. [f. INTER- 1 + LINE *v.*[1]] Put an extra layer of (stiffened) material between the lining and the outer material of (the whole or part of a garment).

interline /ɪntəˈlʌɪn/ *v.*[3] L20. [f. INTER- 2 + LINE *n.*[2]] **1** *v.i.* **a** Use transport by more than one route, service, etc. L20. **b** Provide interconnections with another service. L20. **2** *v.t.* Provide interconnecting transport for. L20.

interlineal /ɪntəˈlɪnɪəl/ *a.* E16. [Fr. *interlinéal* or med.L *interlinealis*, f. as INTER- + late L *linealis* LINEAL.] = INTERLINEAR 1.

interlinear /ɪntəˈlɪnɪə/ *a.* LME. [med.L *interlinearis*, f. as INTER- + L *linearis* LINEAR.] **1** Written or printed between the lines of a text. LME. **2** Of a book: having the same text in different languages printed on alternate lines. E17.

1 **Interlinear Gloss** *spec.* Anselm's gloss on the Vulgate, written in manuscripts between the lines of the Latin text.

interlinearly *adv.* M19. **interlineary** *a.* interlinear E17.

interlineate /ɪntəˈlɪnɪeɪt/ *v.t.* & *i.* L17. [med.L *interlineat-* pa. ppl stem of *interlineare*: see INTERLINE *v.*[1], -ATE[3]. In mod. use perh. back-form. f. next.] = INTERLINE *v.*[1] Chiefly as *interlineated* ppl a.

interlineation /ˌɪntəlɪnɪˈeɪʃ(ə)n/ *n.* E16. [med.L *interlineatio(n-)*, f. as prec.: see -ATION.] The insertion of a word or words between the lines of a document or text; a word, phrase, etc., so inserted.

Notes & Queries This manuscript shows late additions in the form of interlineations and marginal balloons.

interlingua /ɪntəˈlɪŋgwə/ *n.* E20. [f. INTER- 1 + L *lingua* tongue.] An artificially devised international language; *spec.* (**I-**) that promoted by the International Auxiliary Language Association of New York, formed of elements common to the Romance languages, and also called *Latino sine flexione*.

interlingual /ɪntəˈlɪŋgw(ə)l/ *a.* M19. [f. INTER- 1, 2 + LINGUAL *a.*] Between or relating to two languages; of or relating to an artificial interlanguage.

interlinguist /ɪntəˈlɪŋgwɪst/ *n.* E20. [f. INTER- 1 + LINGUIST.] A scholar or an advocate of an interlanguage or interlanguages.

interlinguistic /ɪntəlɪŋˈgwɪstɪk/ *a.* L19. [f. INTER- 1 + LINGUISTIC.] †**1** Intermingling in speech. *rare.* Only in L19. **2** Of or relating to an interlanguage; between or relating to two languages. M20.

interlinguistics /ɪntəlɪŋˈgwɪstɪks/ *n.* M20. [f. INTER- 1 + LINGUISTICS.] The branch of knowledge that deals with the relationships between languages; the study of interlingual relationships in order to devise an interlanguage.

interlining /ɪntəˈlʌɪnɪŋ/ *n.*[1] LME. [f. INTERLINE *v.*[1] + -ING[1].] = INTERLINEATION.

interlining /ˈɪntəlʌɪnɪŋ/ *n.*[2] L19. [f. INTER- 1 + LINING *n.*[1] Cf. INTERLINE *v.*[2]] An extra layer placed between the outer material and the lining of a garment or quilt for added stiffness or warmth; the material for this.

interlink /ɪntəˈlɪŋk/ *v.t.* & *i.* L16. [f. INTER- 1 + LINK *v.*[1]] Link or be linked together (*with*).

interlinkage *n.* the action of interlinking, the state of being interlinked; an interlinked system: E20.

interlock /ˈɪntəlɒk/ *n.* & *a.* L19. [f. the vb.] **A** *n.* **1** The fact or condition of being interlocked. *rare.* L19. **2a** *Cinemat.* Synchronism between two or more electric motors in separate pieces of equipment; the mechanism by which this is effected. E20. **b** A mechanism for preventing a set of operations being performed other than in the prescribed sequence. M20. **B** *adj.* Designating a fabric knitted with closely interlocking stitches. E20.

interlock /ɪntəˈlɒk/ *v.* M17. [f. INTER- 1 + LOCK *v.*[1]] **1** *v.i.* Engage with each other or fit together by partial overlapping or interpenetration of parts. M17. **b** Of head-waters of different rivers: lie in an alternating sequence, although flowing in different directions. *US.* M18. **2** *v.t.* Lock or clasp within each other. Usu. in *pass.* E19. **3** *v.t.* Chiefly *Railways.* Connect (switches, controls, etc.) so that they cannot be operated independently or unsafely. L19. **4** *v.t.* *Cinemat.* Connect (the electric motors in separate pieces of equipment) so as to ensure synchronous operation. E20.

1 R. S. R. FITTER There were still large patches of green country interlocking with the tongues of buildings. J. A. MICHENER Powerful thorns that interlocked with those of other plants to make the globe impenetrable. 2 R. WARNER The ailerons of the two planes were almost interlocked as they climbed together. S. BRETT In a state of high nervous tension, constantly interlocking and unwinding his fingers.

interlocker *n.* a device for interlocking switches etc. L19.

interlocution /ɪntələˈkjuːʃ(ə)n/ *n.* M16. [L *interlocutio(n-)*, f. *interlocut-* pa. ppl stem of *interloqui*, f. as INTER- + *loqui* speak: see -ION.] **1** The action of persons speaking and replying; dialogue, discourse, conversation. M16. †**b** Alternate reading or speaking, as in making responses or reading alternate verses. L16–M17. †**2** The action of replying; a reply, a response. L16–L18. †**3** The action of interrupting (one's own or another's) speech; an interruption, an interpolation. L16–L17. †**4** *Law.* A judgement deciding a point within a case, but not the whole case. Cf. INTERLOCUTOR *n.*[2] Only in E18.

interlocutor /ɪntəˈlɒkjʊtə/ *n.*[1] E16. [mod.L, f. L *interlocut-*: see prec., -OR.] **1** A person who takes part in a conversation, dialogue, or discussion. E16. **b** With possess.: the person with whom one is in conversation. M19. 2 The middleman of a minstrel troupe, who questions the endmen and acts as compère. *US*. L19.

1 R. BENTLEY The Interlocutors in this Dialogue, are Socrates and one Minos an Athenian. b H. JAMES He looked at his interlocutor as if the question might have a double meaning.

interlocutress, **-trice**, **-trix** *ns*. a female interlocutor M19.

interlocutor /ɪntəˈlɒkjʊtə/ *n*.[2] E16. [f. med.L *interlocutorius*, f. L *interlocut-* pa. ppl stem of *interloqui* (in late L = pronounce an interlocutory sentence): see INTERLOCUTION, -OR.] *Sc. Law*. A judgement deciding a point within a case, but not necessarily the whole case; any order of a civil court.

interlocutory /ɪntəˈlɒkjʊt(ə)ri/ *a*. & *n*. L15. [med.L *interlocutorius*, f. L *interlocut-*: see prec., -ORY[2].] A *adj*. 1 *Law*. Of a decree or judgement: given in the course of an action or as a preliminary to coming to trial; preliminary, provisional, interim. L15. 2 Of, pertaining to, or occurring in dialogue or conversation. L16. 3 Interpolated into a conversation or narrative. E19. †B *n*. *Law*. An interlocutory decree. E17–L18.

interlope /ɪntəˈləʊp/ *v*. E17. [Back-form. f. next.] 1 *v.i*. Orig. (*obs*. exc. *Hist*.), trade without authorization, interfere with another's trade or privileges. Now, intrude, meddle in another's affairs. E17. †2 *v.t*. a Introduce without authorization. Only in M17. b Intrude on. *rare*. Only in E18.

interloˈpation *n*. (*rare*) an act of interloping, an intrusion E19.

interloper /ˈɪntələʊpə/ *n*. L16. [f. INTER- 1 + *-loper* as in LAND-LOPER.] 1 An unauthorized trader; one who trespasses on the rights of a trade monopoly. Also, a vessel engaged in unauthorized trading. *obs*. exc. *Hist*. L16. 2 A person who meddles in another's business (esp. for profit); an intruder. M17.

interlucation /ɪntəluːˈkeɪʃ(ə)n/ *n*. *rare*. M17. [L *interlucatio(n-)*, f. *interlucat-* pa. ppl stem of *interlucare* lop or thin a tree, f. as INTER- + *luc-*, *lux* light: see -ATION.] The action or an instance of thinning a tree or wood.

interlude /ˈɪntəluːd, -ljuːd/ *n*. & *v*. Also (earlier) †**enter-**. ME. [med.L *interludium*, f. as INTER- + *ludus* play.] A *n*. 1 A short, usu. light, dramatic piece, orig. one performed between acts of the miracle plays, later one performed separately. ME. †b Any performance or action considered as drama. LME–M17. 2 An interval, as between acts of a play or between broadcast programmes; something performed or done during this. M17. b *Mus*. An instrumental piece played between verses of a psalm or hymn, or in the interval of a church service. M19. 3 An intervening time, space, or event which contrasts with what goes before or after; *spec*. a temporary amusement; an entertaining episode. M18.

2 G. BERKELEY We went to see a play, with interludes of music. 3 H. A. L. FISHER The reign of Canute was but an interlude, more important for Scandinavian than for British history. A. C. BOULT On our way to Munich we had an amusing interlude. P. ABRAHAMS Harriet was a beautiful and painful interlude in his young life.

B *v*. †1 *v.i*. Write or perform a dramatic interlude. L16–E17. 2 *v.t*. & *i*. Interrupt or come between as an interlude. *rare*. M19.

interˈludial *a*. L19.

interlunar /ɪntəˈluːnə/ *a*. L16. [App. f. Fr. †*interlunaire* f. L *interlunium* after *lunaire* (f. as LUNAR): see INTER-.] Designating or pertaining to the period between the disappearance of the old and the appearance of the new moon.

interluˈnation *n*. (now *rare*) an interlunar period; *fig*. a dark interval: E19. **ˈinterlune** *n*. (*rare*) an interlunar period M19.

intermarriage /ɪntəˈmarɪdʒ/ *n*. Also †**enter-**. L16. [f. INTER- 1, ENTER-[1] + MARRIAGE.] 1 The action or an act of marrying; marriage. *obs*. in *gen*. sense. L16. 2 Marriage between people of different ethnic groups, castes, religions, etc. E17. 3 Marriage between near relations. L19.

intermarriageable *a*. capable of intermarrying L19.

intermarry /ɪntəˈmari/ *v.i*. Also †**enter-**. L16. [f. INTER- 1, ENTER-[1] + MARRY *v*.] 1 Enter into marriage, marry. *obs*. in *gen*. sense. L16. 2 Of the members of an ethnic group, caste, religion, etc.: become connected by marriage to one another or to members of a different ethnic group, caste, religion, etc. (Foll. by *with*.) E17. 3 Of near relations: marry each other. M19.

2 J. RABAN They intermarried. They mixed Persian and Indian culture with their own Arabian stock.

intermaxillary /ɪntəmakˈsɪləri/ *a*. & *n*. Now *rare*. E19. [f. INTER- 2 + MAXILLA + -ARY[2].] *Anat*. & *Zool*. A *adj*. Situated between the maxillae (of the vertebrate upper jaw). Also, premaxillary. E19. B *n*. An intermaxillary bone. M19.

intermeddle /ɪntəˈmɛd(ə)l/ *v*. *arch*. Also †**enter-**. LME. [AN *entremedler* = OFr. *entremesler*, f. as ENTER-[1], INTER- + *mesler* MEDDLE.] †1 *v.t*. Mix together, intermingle, *with*. LME–M18. 2 *v.i*. & †*refl*. Concern or occupy oneself *with* or *in*; *esp*. interfere. L15.

intermeddler *n*. †(*a*) a person who is concerned or occupied with something; (*b*) a person who interferes, a meddler: L16.

intermède /ɛ̃tɛrmɛd/ *n*. Pl. pronounced same. L18. [Fr. f. as INTERMEDIO.] †1 = INTERMEDIUM 3. Only in L18. 2 *Mus. Hist*. = INTERMEDIO. E19.

¶Formerly fully naturalized.

intermedi *n.pl*. see INTERMEDIO.

intermedia *n.pl*. see INTERMEDIUM.

intermediacy /ɪntəˈmiːdɪəsi/ *n*. E18. [f. INTERMEDIATE *a*.: see -ACY.] The state or fact of being intermediate.

intermedial /ɪntəˈmiːdɪəl/ *a*. & *n*. L16. [f. INTER- 1 + MEDIAL.] A *adj*. 1 Intermediate. L16. †2 = INTERMEDIARY *a*. 2. M17–M19. B *n*. An intermediate. Long *rare*. E17.

intermediary /ɪntəˈmiːdjəri/ *a*. & *n*. L18. [Fr. *intermédiaire* f. It. *intermediario*, f. L *intermedius*: see next, -ARY[2].] A *adj*. 1 Situated or occurring between two things; intermediate. L18. 2 Mediatory; serving as a means of mediation or interaction. E19.

1 J. HAWTHORNE During this intermediary stage of her life.

B *n*. 1 A person who acts between others, a mediator, a go-between. L18. 2 Something acting between persons or things; a medium, a means. M19. 3 An intermediate form or stage. M19.

1 H. KISSINGER We approached the North Vietnamese directly without a foreign intermediary.

intermediate /ɪntəˈmiːdɪət/ *a*. & *n*. LME. [med.L *intermediatus*, f. L *intermedius*, f. as INTER- + *medius* middle: see -ATE[2].] A *adj*. 1 Coming or occurring between two things in time, place, order, character, etc. LME. b *spec*. Designating (a nuclear missile of) a range less than intercontinental. M20. 2 *Petrogr*. Of a rock: having a silicate content between that of acidic and that of basic rocks. L19. 3 *Nuclear Physics*. (Of a neutron) having less energy than a fast neutron but more than a thermal neutron; (of a reactor) utilizing such neutrons. M20.

1 A. S. BYATT Facing them . . were several rows of little girls, intermediate girls, larger girls. R. SCRUTON *Tristan* seems to mark . . an intermediate step between Mozart and Schoenberg. b *Sunday Post (Glasgow)* An agreement on longer range intermediate missiles.

Special collocations: **intermediate host** *Zool*. an organism infected by a juvenile or asexual stage of a parasitic animal. **intermediate frequency**: to which a radio signal is converted during heterodyne reception. **intermediate school** *NZ* a school for children aged between about eleven and thirteen.

B *n*. 1 An intermediate person or thing. M17. b *Chem*. & *Biochem*. A compound which after being produced in one reaction participates in another; *spec*. a substance manufactured from naturally occurring materials for use in the synthesis of dyes, plastics, etc. E20. 2 An intermediary, a go-between. L19.

1 A. S. NEILL The youngest range from five to seven, the intermediates from eight to ten, and the oldest from eleven to fifteen.

intermediately *adv*. M18. **intermediateness** *n*. M19.

intermediate /ɪntəˈmiːdɪeɪt/ *v.i*. E17. [f. INTER- 1 + MEDIATE *v*. Cf. next.] 1 Act as an intermediary, mediate. E17. †2 Interfere. E17–E18.

intermediˈation *n*. E17.

intermediator /ɪntəˈmiːdɪeɪtə/ *n*. E16. [med.L, f. as INTERMEDIATE *a*. & *n*.: see -OR.] A person who or thing which intermediates; a mediator.

intermedii *n.pl*. see INTERMEDIO.

intermedin /ɪntəˈmiːdɪn/ *n*. M20. [f. mod.L (*pars*) *intermedia* intermediate part (of the pituitary) + -IN[1].] *Physiol*. = MELANOCYTE-*stimulating hormone*.

intermedio /interˈmɛːdjo, ɪntəˈmɛdɪəʊ/ *n*. Pl. **-d(i)i** /-d(j)i/. L19. [It. f. as INTERMEDIUM. Cf. INTERMÈDE.] A musical interlude between the acts of a play or an opera. Cf. INTERMEZZO.

intermedium /ɪntəˈmiːdɪəm/ *n*. Pl. **-ia** /-ɪə/, **-iums**. L16. [Late L, use as n. of neut. sing. of L *intermedius*: see INTERMEDIATE *a*. & *n*.] 1 An intervening action or performance. Now only *spec*. (*Mus*.), = INTERMEDIO. L16. 2 An interval of time or space. Now *rare* or *obs*. E17. 3 An intermediate agent, an intermediary. M17. b *Physics*. A medium through which energy is transmitted. Now *rare* or *obs*. E19. 4 *Zool*. [mod.L *os intermedium*] In tetrapods: a carpal in the centre of the wrist joint; a tarsal in the centre of the ankle joint. L19.

†**intermell** *v*. LME. [OFr. *entremeller*, *-mesler* (mod. *-mêler*), f. as ENTER-[1], INTER- + MELL *v*.] 1 *v.t*. Mix together, intermingle. LME–M19. 2 *v.i*. Meddle, interfere *with*. L15–L16.

interment /ɪnˈtəːm(ə)nt/ *n*. ME. [f. INTER *v*. + -MENT.] The action or an act of interring or burying; (a) burial, esp. with ceremony.

J. CRACE Nowadays, one selects either cremation or interment.

intermesh /ɪntəˈmɛʃ/ *v.i*. E20. [f. INTER- 1 + MESH *v*.] Mesh or interlock with one another.

R. D. LAING To see how interpersonal and neurological recovery intermeshed to generate . . a new personality.

†**intermess** *n*. var. of ENTREMESS.

intermewed /ɪntəˈmjuːd/ *a*. Now *rare*. L16. [f. OFr. *entremué* half-moulted + -ED[2].] Of a hawk: that has moulted in captivity but not reached full adult plumage.

intermezzo /ɪntəˈmɛtsəʊ/ *n*. Pl. **-zzi** /-tsi/, **-zzos**. L18. [It. f. as INTERMEDIUM. Cf. MEZZO *adv*.] 1 A short light dramatic, musical, or other performance inserted between the acts of a play or (formerly) an opera. L18. 2 A short connecting instrumental movement in an opera or other musical work; a similar piece performed independently; a short piece for a solo instrument. M19.

interminable /ɪnˈtəːmɪnəb(ə)l/ *a*. LME. [(O)Fr., or late L *interminabilis*, f. as IN-[3] + *terminare*: see TERMINATE *v*., -ABLE.] 1 Endless. LME. 2 With no prospect of an end; tediously long or habitual. M19.

1 J. CONRAD The sea-reach . . stretched before us like the beginning of an interminable waterway. 2 B. TARKINGTON He went back to the library, waited an interminable half hour, then returned. A. J. P. TAYLOR Mrs Jones . . was already studying the interminable committees. P. LIVELY Malcolm . . turned a rich coffee brown during that interminable languid Dorset summer.

interminaˈbility *n*. L17. **interminableness** *n*. L17. **interminably** *adv*. LME.

interminate /ɪnˈtəːmɪnət/ *a*. Now *rare*. L15. [L *interminatus*, f. as IN-[3] + TERMINATE *a*.: see -ATE[2].] Endless; infinite.

interminate decimal *Math*.: recurring or infinite.

intermingle /ɪntəˈmɪŋg(ə)l/ *v*. L15. [f. INTER- 1 + MINGLE *v*.] 1 *v.t*. & *i*. Mix or mingle together. Freq. foll. by *with*. L15. 2 *v.t*. Intersperse (a thing) *with* some other thing. M16.

1 R. STRANGE These three themes emerge and intermingle constantly in what follows. 2 H. A. L. FISHER The intermingling of manual labour with study and devotional exercises.

interminglement *n*. (*rare*) L19.

interministerial /ˌɪntəmɪnɪˈstɪərɪəl/ *a*. M19. [f. INTER- 2 + MINISTERIAL. Cf. next.] 1 Of or pertaining to a period between two ministries. M19. 2 Involving or constituted from the ministers, representatives, or members of different departments of state. M20.

interministerium /ˌɪntəmɪnɪˈstɪərɪəm/ *n. rare.* M18. [f. INTER- 2 + L *ministerium* MINISTRY.] The period between two ministries.

†**intermise** *n.* var. of ENTERMISE.

intermission /ɪntəˈmɪʃ(ə)n/ *n.* LME. [(O)Fr., or L *intermissio(n-)*, f. *intermiss-* pa. ppl stem of *intermittere*: see INTERMIT, -ION.] **1** The fact of ceasing for a time; a temporary pause or cessation. LME. **b** Temporary rest or respite (*from*). Now *rare* or *obs.* L16. **2** A space of time between events or periods of action; *spec.* the interval between the parts of a play, film, concert, etc. M16.

1 JOHN PHILLIPS This eruption lasted two nights and two days without intermission. 2 N. GORDIMER She was struggling back through the crowded foyer at intermission.

intermissive /ɪntəˈmɪsɪv/ *a.* L15. [f. INTERMISSION + -IVE.] Of the nature of or pertaining to (an) intermission; intermittent.

intermit /ɪntəˈmɪt/ *v.* Infl. **-tt-**. M16. [L *intermittere*, f. as INTER- + *mittere* let go.] **1** *v.t.* Cease, suspend, (an action, practice, etc.) for a time. Formerly also, interrupt (a person, an action, etc.). M16. **b** Omit, leave out. L16. **2** *v.i.* Esp. *Med.* Cease or stop for a time. L16.

1b A. S. BYATT Marcus should intermit a year of his education, in order to recuperate.

intermittedly *adv.* in an intermitted manner E19. **intermittingly** *adv.* in an intermitting manner, intermittently M17.

intermittence /ɪntəˈmɪt(ə)ns/ *n.* L18. [Fr., f. *intermittent*, f. as INTERMITTENT: see -ENCE.] The quality or fact of being intermittent; (a) cessation or suspension for a time.

J. UPDIKE Intermittences of peace . . . afford glimpses of what might be a better world.

intermittency /ɪntəˈmɪt(ə)nsi/ *n.* M17. [f. next: see -ENCY.] = prec.

Comb.: **intermittency effect** *Photogr.* the difference in the density of an emulsion when exposed to a given amount of light in short bursts, and as a continuous exposure.

intermittent /ɪntəˈmɪt(ə)nt/ *a.* & *n.* M16. [L *intermittent-* pres. ppl stem of *intermittere*: see INTERMIT, -ENT.] **A** *adj.* That ceases for a time; occurring at intervals; not continuous. M16.

D. DELILLO As the terrain rises and drops, you get intermittent views of those rock masses. D. WIGODER I must have relapsed into intermittent sleep and restlessness. *intermittent* CLAUDICATION. **intermittent sterilization** *Microbiol.*: by alternately allowing heat-resistant spores to germinate and raising the temperature to kill the resulting vegetative cells.

B *n.* An intermittent fever. L17.

intermittently *adv.* M19.

intermix /ɪntəˈmɪks/ *v.t.* & *i.* M16. [Orig. pa. pple, f. L *intermixtus* pa. pple of *intermiscere*, f. as INTER- + *miscere* mix.] Mix or blend together.

intermixable *a.* M20. **intermixedly** *adv.* (long *rare*) with intermixture L16.

intermixture /ɪntəˈmɪkstʃə/ *n.* L16. [f. L *intermixt-* pa. ppl stem of *intermiscere* (see prec.) + -URE, after MIXTURE.] **1** The action of intermixing; the fact of being intermixed. L16. **2** (A quantity of) something intermixed with or added to something else. L16.

intermodal /ɪntəˈməʊd(ə)l/ *a.* M20. [f. INTER- 2 + MODE *n.* + -AL[1].] Designating the conveyance of goods by more than one method of transport.

intermodalism *n.* the use of more than one method of transport in conveying goods L20.

intern /ɪnˈtəːn; *as n. also* ˈɪntəːn/ *a.* & *n.* As n. also **interne**. E16. [(O)Fr. *interne* f. L *internus* inward, internal, f. *in* adv. + *-ternus* suff.] **A** *adj.* **1** = INTERNAL *a.* 2. E16. **2** = INTERNAL *a.* 1, 3. E17. **B** *n.* **1** A recent medical graduate, resident and working under supervision in a hospital as part of his or her training. Chiefly *N. Amer.* L19. **2** A person in any profession gaining practical experience under supervision. Chiefly *N. Amer.* E20.

internship *n.* (chiefly *N. Amer.*) the position of an intern; the period of such a position: E20.

intern /ɪnˈtəːn; *in sense 3 usu.* ˈɪntəːn/ *v.* E17. [Fr. *interner*, f. as prec.] †**1** *v.i.* Become incorporated or united with another being. Only in E17. **2** *v.t.* Confine as a prisoner; oblige to reside within prescribed limits of a country etc. without permission to leave them. M19. **3** *v.i.* Act as an intern. Chiefly *N. Amer.* M20.

2 S. SPENDER At the outbreak of war, they were in France where Franz was interned as an enemy alien. B. MALAMUD When they caught me peddling I was interned for six months in a work camp. 3 M. FRENCH Norm finished med school . . but then he was interning.

interˈnee *n.* a person who is interned E20.

internal /ɪnˈtəːn(ə)l/ *a.* & *n.* E16. [mod.L *internalis*, f. L *internus*: see INTERN *n.* & *a.*, -AL[1].] **A** *adj.* **1** Of or pertaining to the mind or soul, mental or spiritual; of or pertaining to the inner nature of a thing, intrinsic. E16. **2** Of or pertaining to the inside or interior of something; within the limits of something; *spec.* of or affecting the inside of a body. L17. **b** *Anat.* Situated further from the surface of the body, or nearer the median line. Opp. *external.* M19. **3** Of or pertaining to the domestic affairs of a nation. L18. **4** Designating a student or examiner who is in residence at a university as well as taking or marking its examinations. L19. **5** Used or applying within an organization. M20.

1 P. BARKER Those who were compelled to talk to themselves, thrashing out some unending internal feud. 2 B. BAINBRIDGE The Connolly woman has internal bleeding from a boot in her belly. M. RULE The whole of the internal structure was unstable and inherently dangerous. 3 R. NIEBUHR Social inequality leads not only to internal strife but to conflict between various national communities. 5 M. FRAYN He put down the outside phone and picked up the internal one.

Special collocations: **internal clock** a person's innate sense of time; *Biol.* = BIOLOGICAL *clock*. **internal-combustion engine**: with its motive power generated by the explosion of gases or vapour with air in a cylinder. **internal conversion** *Physics* (*a*) transfer of the whole energy of a gamma-ray photon emitted by a nucleus to an orbital electron; (*b*) radiationless transition of an excited molecule from one electronic energy state to another of the same multiplicity. **internal ear** = *inner ear* s.v. EAR *n.*[1] **internal energy** *Physics* the energy possessed by a system in consequence of the positions, relative motions, and interactions of its components. **internal evidence**: derived from the content of the thing discussed. **internal exile** penal banishment from a part of one's own country. **internal friction** resistance to the deformation or flow of a substance, arising from the interaction of component molecules etc. **internal medicine** the branch of medicine that deals with the diagnosis and treatment of disease by medical as opp. to surgical means. **internal object** *Psychoanalysis* a fantasized subjective image of an object as the target of emotions otherwise directed at the object itself. **internal pressure**: arising in a liquid from intermolecular attraction. **internal property** *Philos.* a property belonging essentially to an object or proposition. *internal* RELATION. **internal rhyme**: involving a word in the middle of a line and another at the end of the line or in the middle of the next. **internal revenue** *US* inland revenue. **internal secretion** *Physiol.* the secretion of substances into the blood; a substance secreted into the blood, *esp.* a hormone. **internal stress**: arising within a substance (e.g. through differential heating), not imposed from without.

B *n.* **1** An intrinsic or essential attribute, quality, etc. Now only in *pl.* M17. †**2** The inner nature or soul. M17–L18. †**3** A medicine or remedy to be taken internally. L17–E18.

interˈnality *n.* the quality or fact of being internal E19. **internally** *adv.* L16.

internalize /ɪnˈtəːn(ə)lʌɪz/ *v.t.* Also **-ise**. L19. [f. INTERNAL *a.* + -IZE.] **1** Make internal; give an internal or subjective character to. L19. **2** Adopt or incorporate as one's own (the attitudes, values, etc., of another person or social group). M20. **b** Transfer emotions felt for an object to (a fantasized subjective image of that object); redirect (an emotion) away from its target towards oneself. M20. **3** *Ling.* Acquire knowledge of and the ability to apply (a set of rules) as part of native-speaker competence. M20.

2 M. FRENCH It would never have occurred to *me* to have an affair. . . God, how I'd internalized sexual morality.

internaliˈzation *n.* L19.

international /ɪntəˈnaʃ(ə)n(ə)l/ *a.* & *n.* L18. [f. INTER- 2 + NATIONAL.] **A** *adj.* **1** Existing, occurring, or carried on between nations; pertaining to relations, communications, travel, etc., between nations. L18. **2** Agreed on by many nations; used by, or able to be used by, (the people of) many nations. L19. **3** Of or pertaining to the First International (see sense B.3 below). L19.

1 A. BULLOCK From this in turn followed the rejection of force in settling international disputes. *Sunday Express* The two rushed off to an international phone box in Leicester Square. 2 R. P. JHABVALA It was an international hotel and was largely filled with foreign travellers.

Special collocations: *International Baccalaureate*: see BACCALAUREATE 3. **International Brigade** *Hist.* a body of volunteers raised internationally by foreign Communist Parties, which fought for the Republic in the Spanish Civil War of 1936–9. *international candle*: see CANDLE *n.* 3. **international code** a code of signals by which sailors of all nations can hold communication at sea. *international comity*: see COMITY 2a. **International Court of Justice** a judicial court of the United Nations. **international date-line** = *date-line* (a) s.v. DATE *n.*[2] **international driving licence, permit**: allowing the holder to drive a specified class of vehicle in various countries. **international Gothic** a style in painting, sculpture, and the decorative arts that spread across western Europe in the late 14th and early 15th cents., characterized by secular themes and delicate naturalistic detail. **international law** a body of rules established by custom or treaty and agreed as binding in the relations between one nation and another. **International Monetary Fund** an organization with a monetary pool on which member nations can draw, established in 1945 to promote international trade and stabilization of currencies. **international orange** *a.* & *n.* (of) a bright orange colour, visible from a great distance. **International Phonetic Alphabet** a set of phonetic symbols for international use, based on the Roman and Greek alphabets with the addition of some special symbols and diacritical marks. **international standard book number** an identification number allocated internationally to each (edition or format of a) book published; abbrev. *ISBN*; (cf. *standard book number* s.v. STANDARD *a.*). **international style** (*a*) a naturalistic functional style of 20th-cent. architecture; (*b*) = *international Gothic* above. **International System of Units** a system of physical units (with a set of scaling prefixes) derived without multiplying factors from the basic independent units of the metre, kilogram, second, ampere, kelvin, candela, and mole. **international unit** *Biol.* & *Med.* any of various units of activity or potency defined for vitamins, sera, hormones, etc.

B *n.* **1** A person having relations with two different nations, esp. as native of one and resident in another. L19. **2** A contest, usu. in sports, between representatives or teams from different nations; a person taking part in such a contest. L19. **3** (**I-**.) Any of various socialist organizations founded for the worldwide promotion of socialism or Communism; *spec.* = *First, Second, Third, Fourth, International* below. Also, a member of any of these organizations. L19. **4** *the International*, = INTERNATIONALE 2. E20.

1 S. MORLEY They were internationals who just happened to live in California and came from England. 2 *Gentleman (Bombay)* He is the best Indian bat for Tests as well as one-day internationals. 3 **First International** an international workers' association founded in 1864 by Karl Marx to promote the joint political action of the working classes in all countries and dissolved in 1876. **Second International** a socialist organization founded in Paris in 1889 to celebrate the 100th anniversary of the French Revolution, now a loose association of social democrats. **Third International** an organization founded in Moscow in 1919 by delegates from twelve countries to promote Communism and support the Russian Revolution and dissolved in 1943; also called *Comintern*. **Fourth International** a body of Trotskyist organizations formed in 1938 in opposition to the Stalin-dominated Third International.

internatioˈnality *n.* international quality, condition, or character M19. **internationally** *adv.* M19.

Internationale /ˌɪntənaʃjəˈnɑːl/ *n.* L19. [Fr., use as n. (in sense 2 sc. *chanson* song) of fem. of *international* international.] **1** = INTERNATIONAL *n.* 3. L19. **2** *the Internationale*, a revolutionary song composed by Eugène Pottier in 1871 and adopted by (orig. French) socialists. E20.

internationalise *v.* var. of INTERNATIONALIZE.

internationalism /ɪntəˈnaʃ(ə)n(ə)lɪz(ə)m/ *n.* M19. [f. INTERNATIONAL + -ISM.] **1** International character or spirit; the advocacy of a community of interests among nations. M19. **2** (**I-**.) The principles of or support for any of the Internationals. L19.
internationalist *n.* M19.

internationalize /ɪntəˈnaʃ(ə)n(ə)lʌɪz/ *v.t.* Also **-ise**. M19. [f. as prec. + -IZE.] Make international in character or use; *spec.* bring a country, territory, etc. under the protection or control of two or more nations.
internationaliˈzation *n.* L19.

interne *n.* see INTERN *a.* & *n.*

internecinal /ɪntəˈnɛsɪn(ə)l/ *a. rare.* M19. [f. as next + -AL[1].] Destructive, deadly.

internecine /ɪntəˈniːsʌɪn/ *a.* M17. [L *internecinus*, f. *internecio(n-)* general slaughter, extermination, f. *internecare* slaughter, exterminate, f. as INTER- + *necare* kill: see -INE[1].] **1** Deadly; characterized by great slaughter. M17. **2** Mutually destructive. Now also, of or pertaining to internal conflict in an organization etc. M18.

internecive /ɪntəˈniːsɪv/ *a. rare.* E19. [L *internecivus* var. of *internecinus* INTERNECINE: see -IVE.] Mutually destructive.

interneuron *n.* var. of INTERNEURONE.

interneuronal /ɪntənjʊˈrəʊn(ə)l/ *a.* M20. [Partly f. next + -AL[1], partly f. INTER- 2 + NEURONAL.] *Physiol.* Occurring or existing between neurones; of, pertaining to, or affecting an interneurone.

interneurone /ɪntəˈnjʊərəʊn/ *n.* Also **-ron** /-rɒn/. M20. [f. INTER(NUNCIAL + NEURONE.] *Physiol.* Any neurone which transmits impulses between other neurones, esp. as part of a reflex arc.

internist /ɪnˈtəːnɪst/ *n. N. Amer.* E20. [f. INTERN(AL + -IST.] A general physician. Also, a specialist in internal medicine.

internment /ɪnˈtəːnm(ə)nt/ *n.* L19. [f. INTERN *v.* + -MENT.] The action of interning someone; confinement within the limits of a country etc.
Comb.: **internment camp** a detention camp for prisoners of war and aliens.

internode /ˈɪntənəʊd/ *n.* Also (now *rare*) in L form **-nodium** /-ˈnəʊdɪəm/, pl. **-dia** /-dɪə/. M17. [L *internodium*, f. as INTER- 2 + NODE.] **1** *Bot.* The part of a plant stem between adjacent nodes. M17. **2** *Anat.* & *Zool.* A slender part between two nodes or joints, as a finger-bone; *spec.* a myelinated length of nerve fibre between two nodes of Ranvier. E18.
interˈnodal *a.* M19.

†**internunce** *n.* Also **-nonce**. M17–M19. [Fr. f. as next.] = INTERNUNCIO.

internuncial /ɪntəˈnʌnʃ(ə)l/ *a.* M19. [f. L *internuntius* (see next) + -AL[1].] **1** *Physiol.* Conveying signals between parts of the (nervous) system; of the nature of an interneurone. M19. **2** Of or pertaining to an internuncio; having the function of conveying messages between parties etc. L19.

internuncio /ɪntəˈnʌnsɪəʊ/ *n.* Pl. **-os**. M17. [It. *internunzio* f. L *internuntius*, f. as INTER- + *nuntius* messenger.] **1** A messenger between two parties; a go-between. M17. **2** An official papal representative or ambassador at a foreign court, ranking below a nuncio. L17. **3** *Hist.* A minister representing a government (esp. of Austria) at Constantinople (Istanbul). E18.

internuncius /ɪntəˈnʌnsɪəs/ *n.* L17. [med.L var. of L *internuntius*: see prec.] = INTERNUNCIO 1.

interocean /ɪntərˈəʊʃ(ə)n/ *a.* E20. [f. INTER- 2 + OCEAN.] = next.

interoceanic /ˌɪntərəʊʃɪˈanɪk, -sɪ-/ *a.* M19. [f. INTER- 2 + OCEANIC.] Situated between oceans; connecting two oceans.

interoceptor /ɪntərəʊˈsɛptə/ *n.* E20. [f. INTER(IOR + -O- + RE)CEPTOR: cf. EXTEROCEPTOR.] *Physiol.* A sensory receptor which receives stimuli from within the body, esp. from the gut.
interoˈceptive *a.* E20.

interoperable /ɪntərˈɒp(ə)rəb(ə)l/ *a.* M20. [f. INTER- 1 + OPERABLE.] Able to operate in conjunction.
interoperaˈbility *n.* L20.

inter partes /ɪntə ˈpɑːtiːz/ *a. phr.* E19. [L.] *Law.* (Of an action) relevant only to the two parties in a particular case; (of a deed etc.) made between two parties.

†**interpel** *v.t.* Infl. **-ll-**. LME. [L *interpellare* interrupt by speaking, f. as INTER- + *-pellare* thrust or direct oneself.] **1** Appeal to, petition. LME–L16. **2** Interrupt (a person) in speaking. M16–M17. **3** *Sc. Law.* Prohibit, prevent. E18–M19.

interpellant /ɪntəˈpɛl(ə)nt/ *n.* M19. [Fr., pres. pple of *interpeller* f. L *interpellare*: see prec., -ANT[1].] A person who addresses an interpellation in a foreign parliament.

interpellate /ɪnˈtəːpɪleɪt/ *v.t.* L16. [L *interpellat-* pa. ppl stem of *interpellare*: see INTERPEL, -ATE[3].] †**1** Interrupt. Only in L16. **2** In a parliament: interrupt the order of the day by questioning (a minister) on a point of government policy. L19.
interpellator *n.* E17.

interpellation /ɪnˌtəːpɪˈleɪʃ(ə)n/ *n.* E16. [L *interpellatio(n-)*, f. as prec.: see -ATION.] †**1** The action of appealing to or entreating someone; intercession. E16–M17. †**2** A summons. L16–E18. †**3** Interruption. E17–M19. **4** The action of interpellating a minister in a parliament. M19.

interpenetrate /ɪntəˈpɛnɪtreɪt/ *v.* E19. [f. INTER- 1 + PENETRATE *v.*] **1** *v.t.* Penetrate thoroughly; permeate, pervade. E19. **2** *v.i.* & *t.* Of two or more things: penetrate (each other). E19. **3** *v.t.* & *i.* (w. *with*). *Archit.* Appear to penetrate (a moulding etc.). M19.
interpeneˈtration *n.* (*a*) the action of interpenetrating; (*b*) *Archit.* the intersection and (*spec.*) the continuation beyond the intersection of two or more mouldings etc.: E19. **interpenetrative** *a.* M19.

interpersonal /ɪntəˈpəːs(ə)n(ə)l/ *a.* M19. [f. INTER- 2 + PERSONAL.] (Of a relationship, behaviour, etc.) that is between people; pertaining to or involving a relationship between people.
C. LASCH Reforms designed to improve the quality of communication .. and promote interpersonal skills. *New Internationalist* Greater scope for individual initiative and better interpersonal relationships.
interpersoˈnality *n.* M20. **interpersonally** *adv.* M20.

interphase /ˈɪntəfeɪz/ *n.* & *a.* E20. [f. INTER- 2 + PHASE *n.*] **A** *n.* **1** *Cytol.* In cell division, the stage between successive mitoses, or between the first and second divisions of meiosis. E20. **2** *Physical Chem.* The region between two phases in which properties differ from the bulk properties of either phase. M20. **B** *adj.* Occurring or existing between two phases or states of matter; of or pertaining to (an) interphase. M20.

interplant /ɪntəˈplɑːnt/ *v.t.* E20. [f. INTER- 1 + PLANT *v.*] Plant (a specified crop or plant) together *with* another crop or plant; plant (land) with a mixture of crops or plants.
G. WRIGLEY On the fertile soils of East Africa bananas are interplanted with coffee. *Anthropology Today* Most of the plots are small and interplanted.

interplay /ˈɪntəpleɪ/ *n.* M19. [f. INTER- 1 + PLAY *n.*] Reciprocal or free interaction; the operation or influence of two or more things on each other.
E. CRANKSHAW The state of Russia .. is the outcome of the interplay between the subject people .. and the autocracy.

interplay /ˈɪntəpleɪ/ *v.i.* L19. [f. INTER- 1 + PLAY *v.*] Exert mutual influence.

interplead /ɪntəˈpliːd/ *v.* Also †**enterplede**. M16. [AN *enterpleder*, f. as INTER- + PLEAD.] **1** *v.i. Law.* Of people: litigate with each other to determine a matter for the assistance of a third party. M16. †**2** *v.t.* Plead in excuse or defence. L16–E18.

interpleader /ɪntəˈpliːdə/ *n.* M16. [AN *enterpleder* use as n. of infinitive: see prec., -ER[4].] *Law.* A suit pleaded between two parties to determine a matter of claim or right to property held by a third party and esp. to determine to which claimant delivery or payment should be made.

Interpol /ˈɪntəpɒl/ *n.* M20. [Abbrev. of *International police*.] The International Criminal Police Commission founded in 1923 and based in Paris.

interpolable /ɪnˈtəːpələb(ə)l/ *a.* L19. [f. INTERPOLATE *v.* + -ABLE.] Able to be interpolated.
interpolaˈbility *n.* M20.

interpolate /ɪnˈtəːpələt/ *n.* E20. [f. as next + -ATE[1].] *Math.* A value arrived at by interpolation.

†**interpolate** *a.* LME–M17. [L *interpolatus* pa. pple, f. as next: see -ATE[2].] Esp. of a fever: intermittent, interrupted. Cf. INTERPOLATE *v.* 6.

interpolate /ɪnˈtəːpəleɪt/ *v.* E17. [L *interpolat-* pa. ppl stem of *interpolare* refurbish, alter, f. as INTER- + *-polare* rel. to *polire* POLISH *v.*] **I**†**1** *v.t.* Polish; refurbish. *rare.* E17–E18. **2** *v.t.* Alter (a book) by the insertion of new material, esp. in order to mislead as to date of composition etc. E17. **b** Modify by new additions. M19. **3** *v.t.* Insert (esp. misleading words or passages) in a book etc. M17. **b** *transf.* Insert as something additional or different; *esp.* interject (a remark etc.) in conversation. E19. **4** *v.i.* Make insertions or interpolations. E18. **5** *v.t. Math.* Insert (a term, a value) into a series by interpolation. L18. **b** *v.i.* Perform or use interpolation. L19.
2 T. WRIGHT The poem of Beowulf .. has been much interpolated by Christian transcribers. 3 R. GITTINGS He interpolated an extra stanza into his own poem. b E. F. BENSON 'You don't really mean that?' interpolated the other.
†**II 6** *v.t.* Interrupt with a pause. Cf. INTERPOLATE *a.* Only in L17.
interpolant *n.* (*Math.*) a value or expression used in finding another by interpolation E20. **interpolative** *a.* having the effect of interpolation E19. **interpolatory** *a.* serving to interpolate M20.

interpolation /ɪnˌtəːpəˈleɪʃ(ə)n/ *n.* E17. [Fr., or L *interpolatio(n-)*, f. as prec.: see -ATION.] †**1** The action of polishing or refurbishing. Only in 17. **2** The action of inserting words into or altering a book etc., esp. in order to mislead; an interpolated word or passage. E17. **3** (An) insertion of something additional or different; *spec.* (*Math.*) insertion of an intermediate term or value into a series by estimation or calculation from the known values. M18.
2 N. FREELING There are heaps of interpolations and irrelevancies in different coloured inks.

interpolator /ɪnˈtəːpəleɪtə/ *n.* M17. [f. INTERPOLATE *v.* + -OR.] **1** A person who interpolates something. M17. **2** *Engin.* A device or apparatus which guides a tool through a smooth curve when provided with a set of points defining the curve. M20.

interpolymer /ˈɪntəpɒlɪmə/ *n.* M20. [f. INTER- 1 + POLYMER.] *Chem.* A copolymer, *esp.* one having the units in completely random order.
interpolymeriˈzation *n.* the process of interpolymerizing M20. **interpoˈlymerize** *v.t.* & *i.* combine to form an interpolymer M20.

†**interpone** *v.t.* E16–L19. [L *interponere* place between, f. as INTER- + *ponere* to place.] Chiefly *Sc. Law.* Interpose. Freq. in *interpone one's authority*, intervene to prevent something.

interposal /ɪntəˈpəʊz(ə)l/ *n.* E17. [f. next + -AL[1].] = INTERPOSITION.

interpose /ɪntəˈpəʊz/ *v.* L16. [(O)Fr. *interposer*, based on L *interponere* (see INTERPONE) but re-formed on L pa. pple *interpositus* and (O)Fr. *poser*: see POSE *v.*[1]] **1** *v.t.* Place *between* (in space or time), put in an intermediate position, esp. to obstruct or delay. L16. **b** *v.i.* Come between in position, stand in the way. E17. †**c** *v.t.* Place in alternation, cause to alternate. Only in 17. **d** *v.t.* & *i. Chess.* Move (a piece) so as to obstruct another piece, esp. when this is giving check. M18. †**2** *v.t.* Obstruct, intercept, (a person or thing). Only in 17. **3** *v.t.* Exercise or advance (a veto or objection) by way of interference. E17. 4 *v.i.* & †*refl.* Interfere in a matter, intervene between parties or on a person's behalf. (Foll. by *between.*) E17. 5 *v.t.* & *i.* Introduce (an opinion, an aside, etc.) as a digression; *esp.* say (words) as an interruption. E17.

1 G. SANTAYANA His champagne glass had been filled .. before he could interpose a deprecating hand. A. BURGESS Growing impatient with art, he seems to .. interpose nothing between the reader and the vision. b H. H. WILSON Three columns .. moved to the right, as if intending to interpose between the lines and the town. 4 W. COWPER None interposed To avert his woeful doom. J. R. GREEN The Archbishop interposed between the rival claimants to the crown. 5 S. BRETT 'I don't think you've met my wife, Frances,' Charles interposed hastily.

interposer *n.* L16. †**interposure** *n.* interposition E17–M18.

interposition /ɪntəpəˈzɪʃ(ə)n/ *n.* LME. [(O)Fr., or L *interpositio(n-)*, f. *interposit-* pa. ppl stem of *interponere*: see INTERPONE, -ION.] 1 The action or an act of placing oneself or something between; the fact or condition of being placed between. LME. 2 The action or an act of interfering in a matter; (an) intervention. LME.

interpret /ɪnˈtəːprɪt/ *v.* LME. [(O)Fr. *interpréter* or L *interpretari* explain, translate, f. *interpret-*, *-pres* agent, broker, translator, interpreter, f. as INTER- + base corresp. to Skt *prath-* spread about.] 1 *v.t.* Explain the meaning of (something mysterious or abstruse, foreign words, a dream, etc.). Formerly also, translate. LME. b Explain to oneself, understand. L18. c Obtain significant information from (a photograph), esp. for military purposes. M20. 2 *v.t.* Give a particular explanation of; explain or construe (an action etc.) in a specified manner. LME. †b Explain or translate by a specified term. M16–L17. 3 *v.i.* Give the meaning or explanation of something; *spec.* act as an interpreter, esp. of a foreign language. LME. 4 *v.t.* Bring out or represent stylistically the meaning of (a creative work, a dramatic role, etc.) according to one's understanding of the creator's ideas. M19. 5 *v.t. Computing.* Execute (a source language statement or program) as an interpreter. M20.

1 C. HOPE Father Lynch would interpret this .. saying that by that 'place' Kruger undoubtedly meant a physical location. b GEO. ELIOT Her knowledge of the youth of nineteen might help .. in interpreting the man of thirty-four. 2 I. MURDOCH He gave a jerky gesture which was interpreted by Donald as a gesture of dismissal. K. CLARK The medieval mind, which was adept at interpreting everything symbolically. D. DELILLO I wanted a sign, something to interpret as favorable.

interpretable /ɪnˈtəːprɪtəb(ə)l/ *a.* E17. [Late L *interpretabilis*, f. *interpretari*: see prec., -ABLE.] Able to be interpreted or explained.

interpretaˈbility *n.* M19.

interpretant /ɪnˈtəːprɪt(ə)nt/ *n.* E20. [f. INTERPRET + -ANT¹.] *Philos.* The effect of a proposition or sign-series on the person who interprets it.

interpretate /ɪnˈtəːprɪteɪt/ *v.t.* & *i.* Now *rare* or *obs.* E17. [L *interpretat-* pa. ppl stem of *interpretari*: see INTERPRET, -ATE³.] Interpret.

interpretation /ɪn,təːprɪˈteɪʃ(ə)n/ *n.* LME. [(O)Fr. *interprétation* or L *interpretatio(n-)*, f. as prec.: see -ATION.] 1 The action of explaining the meaning of something; *spec.* the proper explanation or signification of something. Formerly also, (a) translation of a book etc. LME. b The technique of obtaining significant information from a photograph. M20. 2 An explanation given; a way of explaining; (a) construction put upon an action etc. Formerly also, a commentary on a book etc. LME. 3 (A) stylistic representation of a creative work, dramatic role, etc., according to one's understanding of the creator's ideas. L19.

interpretational *a.* M19.

interpretative /ɪnˈtəːprɪtətɪv/ *a.* M16. [med.L *interpretativus*, f. as INTERPRETATE: see -IVE.] 1 Having the quality or function of interpreting; explanatory. M16. 2 Deduced or deducible by interpretation; inferential. Now *rare* or *obs.* E17.

interpretatively *adv.* E17. **interpretativeness** *n.* M20.

interpreter /ɪnˈtəːprɪtə/ *n.* LME. [AN *enterpretour*, *inter-* = OFr. *interprete(e)ur*, *entre-* f. late L *interpretator*, f. as INTERPRETATE: see -ER².] 1 †a A person who interprets laws, texts, etc., in an official capacity; a commentator. LME–L17. b A person who interprets a (particular) thing (in a particular way); a person who construes an action etc. in a specified manner. M16. 2 A person, esp. an official, who translates orally the words of people speaking different languages. Formerly also, a translator of books etc. LME. †3 A messenger of the gods; *spec.* Mercury. L15–L17. 4 *Computing.* a A machine which prints on to a punched card the characters equivalent to the pattern of holes. M20. b A program which executes a source program one statement at a time. M20.

1b *Times* Beecham's gifts tend to typecast him as an interpreter of even-numbered Beethoven.

interpretership *n.* the position of an (esp. official) interpreter M19.

†**interpretess** *n.* E18–L19. [f. INTERPRET(ER + -ESS¹.] = INTERPRETRESS.

interpretive /ɪnˈtəːprɪtɪv/ *a.* M17. [f. INTERPRET + -IVE.] 1 = INTERPRETATIVE. M17. 2 *Computing.* Of a routine or program: functioning as an interpreter. M20.

interpretress /ɪnˈtəːprɪtrɪs/ *n.* Now *rare.* L18. [f. INTERPRETER + -ESS¹.] A female interpreter.

interpunction /ɪntəˈpʌŋ(k)ʃ(ə)n/ *n.* Now *rare* or *obs.* E17. [L *interpunctio(n-)*, f. *interpunct-* pa. ppl stem of *interpungere*, f. as INTER- + *pungere* to prick: see -ION.] Punctuation.

interpunctuation /,ɪntəpʌŋ(k)tʃʊˈeɪʃ(ə)n, -tjʊ-/ *n.* Now *rare.* E18. [f. INTER- 1 + PUNCTUATION.] Punctuation.

interˈpunctuate *v.t.* & *i.* punctuate; use punctuation: M19.

interracial /ɪntəˈreɪʃ(ə)l/ *a.* L19. [f. INTER- 2 + RACIAL *a.*] Of, involving, or existing between different races.

interracially *adv.* M20.

interreges *n.* pl. of INTERREX.

interregnum /ɪntəˈrɛgnəm/ *n.* Pl. **-nums, -na** /-nə/. L16. [L, f. as INTER- 2 + *regnum* REIGN *n.* Cf. next.] †1 Temporary authority or rule exercised during a vacancy of the throne or a suspension of the normal government. L16–L18. 2 An interval during which the normal government is suspended, esp. during the period between the end of a monarch's rule and the accession of his or her successor; any period of cessation or suspension of rule, authority, etc. L16. 3 An interval, a pause, a break. M17.

2 *fig.*: J. R. ACKERLEY His courtship .. persisted through all her marriages, becoming articulate again in the interregnums.

interregnal *a.* pertaining to or of the nature of an interregnum M17.

interreign /ˈɪntəreɪn/ *n.* Now *rare.* M16. [f. INTER- 2 + REIGN *n.*, after prec. Cf. (O)Fr. *interrègne.*] †1 = INTERREGNUM 1. M16–E17. 2 = INTERREGNUM 2. L16.

interrelate /ɪntərɪˈleɪt/ *v.t.* & *i.* E19. [f. INTER- 1 + RELATE *v.*] Relate mutually or one to another.

interrelatedness *n.* the quality or condition of being interrelated M19.

interrelation /ɪntərɪˈleɪʃ(ə)n/ *n.* M19. [f. INTER- 1 + RELATION.] Mutual or reciprocal relation.

interrelationship *n.* M19.

interrer /ɪnˈtəːrə/ *n.* E17. [f. INTER *v.* + -ER¹.] A person who inters or buries someone or something.

interrex /ˈɪntərɛks/ *n.* Pl. **interreges** /ɪntəˈriːdʒiːz/. L16. [L, f. as INTER- + *rex* king.] A person holding the supreme authority in a State during an interregnum.

interrogant /ɪnˈtɛrəg(ə)nt/ *n. arch.* M17. [L *interrogant-* pres. ppl stem of *interrogare*: see next, -ANT¹.] = INTERROGATOR.

interrogate /ɪnˈtɛrəgeɪt/ *v.* Also †**enter-**. L15. [L *interrogat-* pa. ppl stem of *interrogare*, f. as INTER- + *rogare* ask: see -ATE³.] 1 *v.t.* Question (a person), esp. closely, thoroughly, or formally. Also, ask or utter as a question. L15. †b Ask about (something). Only in 17. 2 *v.i.* Chiefly *Law.* Ask questions. E17. 3 *v.t.* Transmit a signal to (a transponder, or a vehicle etc. fitted with one) to elicit a response, usu. as a coded signal giving information about identity, condition, etc. M20. b Elicit information from (a computer file etc.) by electronic means. M20.

1 H. SPURLING I sat between the two ladies and was amiably interrogated by both. E. FEINSTEIN The French police interrogated him extensively and released him for lack of evidence.

interrogaˈtee *n.* a person who is interrogated E19. **interrogatingly** *adv.* in an interrogating manner L19.

interrogation /ɪn,tɛrəˈgeɪʃ(ə)n/ *n.* LME. [(O)Fr., or L *interrogatio(n-)*, f. as prec.: see -ATION.] 1 The action or process of interrogating someone or asking questions; an instance of this, a questioning. LME. 2 A question, an enquiry. LME. 3 *Rhet.* Questioning, or a question, as a form of speech. M16. 4 (A) transmission of a signal to a transponder etc. to elicit a response, usu. as a coded signal; a signal so transmitted. M20.

1 A. BRIEN Being held without interrogation or charge .. is definitely a breach of the law. I. MURDOCH Jean .. sat staring at Rose, waiting for the next question, as in an interrogation.

Comb.: **interrogation mark, interrogation point** a question mark.

interrogational *a.* interrogative L19.

interrogative /ɪntəˈrɒgətɪv/ *a.* & *n.* E16. [Late L *interrogativus*, f. as INTERROGATE: see -IVE.] A *adj.* 1 Pertaining to or of the nature of questioning; having the form or force of a question; (of a word, particle, etc.) used in formulating questions. E16. 2 Given to asking questions, inquisitive. *rare.* E18.

1 *interrogative pronoun* etc.

B *n.* 1 A word or form used in formulating questions; *esp.* an interrogative pronoun. E16. 2 A question. *rare.* L16.

interrogatively *adv.* L16.

interrogator /ɪnˈtɛrəgeɪtə/ *n.* M18. [Late L, f. as INTERROGATE: see -OR.] 1 A person who interrogates someone. M18. 2 A radio or radar transmitter designed to interrogate a transponder etc. M20.

interrogatory /ɪntəˈrɒgət(ə)ri/ *n.* & *a.* M16. [As n. f. med.L *interrogatoria* pl. of *interrogatorium*; as adj. f. late L *interrogatorius*, f. as INTERROGATE: see -ORY¹, -ORY².] A *n.* 1 A question; *spec.* (*Law*) a formal, esp. written, question put to a party or witness and required to be answered on oath. M16. 2 *Law.* Questioning of an accused person. *rare.* E19. B *adj.* = INTERROGATIVE *a.* L16.

interrogee /ɪn,tɛrəˈgiː/ *n.* M20. [f. INTERROG(ATE + -EE¹.] A person who is interrogated.

in terrorem /ɪn tɛˈrɔːrɛm/ *adv.* & *a. phr.* E17. [L = into a state of terror.] (Done) as a warning or to deter.

interrupt /ɪntəˈrʌpt/ *n.* M20. [f. the vb.] *Computing.* (A signal causing) an interruption of the execution of a program, e.g. to allow immediate execution of another program.

†**interrupt** *a.* LME–M17. [OFr. f. L *interruptus* pa. pple, f. as next.] Interrupted; *rare* forming a breach or gap.

MILTON Our adversarie, whom no bounds Prescrib'd .. nor yet the main abyss Wide interrupt, can hold.

interrupt /ɪntəˈrʌpt/ *v.* LME. [L *interrupt-* pa. ppl stem of *interrumpere*, f. as INTER- + *rumpere* to break.] †1 *v.t.* Stop or prevent (an action); thwart (a person) in some action (foll. by *of*, *to do*). LME–M17. b Put an end to, destroy. L16–E17. 2 *v.t.* & *i.* Act so as to break (usu. temporarily) the continuous progress of (an action, condition, etc.); break in on the activity, esp. speech, of (a person). LME. †b *v.t.* Suspend (a law). LME–L16. c *v.t.* Say in interruption. E19. 3 *v.t.* Break the continuity of, make a gap or space in; obstruct (a view etc.). M17.

2 R. GRAVES This condition would interrupt his right over her as a permanent chattel. G. VIDAL 'I was not aware ... ' I began, but she interrupted me with an airy wave of her hand. P. HOWARD The First World War

interrupted these pioneering experiments. c C. HOPE 'The trouble was ...'. Blashford interrupted angrily, 'The trouble was Lynch was mad.' 3 K. ISHIGURO An expanse of paved concrete interrupted occasionally by thin young trees.

interruptable *a.* = INTERRUPTIBLE M20. **interrupter** *n.* (*a*) a person who interrupts; (*b*) a device for interrupting an electric current: L16. **interruptible** *a.* able to be interrupted E17. **interruptingly** *adv.* in the way of interruption M17. **interruptive** *a.* having the quality of interrupting M17. **interruptor** *n.* [L] = INTERRUPTER E16. **interruptory** *a.* = INTERRUPTIVE M19.

interrupted /ɪntəˈrʌptɪd/ *a.* M16. [f. prec. + -ED[1].] **1** That has been interrupted. M16. **2** *Bot.* Of an inflorescence etc.: divided by intervals of bare axis; discontinuous. Of a pinnate leaf: having smaller leaflets interposed between the main leaflets. M19.

Special collocations: **interrupted cadence** *Mus.*: where the penultimate dominant chord is followed not by the expected chord of the tonic but by another, usu. that of the submediant. **interrupted screw**: with part of its thread cut away.

interruptedly *adv.* M17.

interruption /ɪntəˈrʌpʃ(ə)n/ *n.* LME. [(O)Fr., or L *interruptio(n-)*, f. as INTERRUPT *v.*: see -ION.] †**1** The action or an act of preventing something or thwarting someone; obstruction. LME–L16. **2** A break (usu. temporary) in the continuous progress of an action, condition, etc., esp. speech; (a) hindrance of the course or continuance of something. LME. **b** Temporary cessation, suspension. E17. **3** A breach of continuity in space or order; the formation or existence of a gap or space. LME. **4** *Law.* (A) legal action to prevent the exercise of a right or privilege. Long only *spec.* (*Sc.*) (a) legal action taken to lengthen the period of time during which a prescriptive right is established. LME.

inter se /ɪntə ˈseɪ/ *adv. phr.* M19. [L.] Between or among themselves.

interseam /ɪntəˈsiːm/ *v.t.* Long *rare.* L16. [Fr. *entresemer* sow among, f. as ENTER-[1], INTER- + *semer* f. L *seminare* sow. Freq. assoc. w. SEAM *v.*] Adorn *with* something sprinkled or scattered between. Usu. in *pass.*

intersect /ˈɪntəsɛkt/ *n.* M17. [f. (as) next.] †**1** = INSECT *n.* Only in M17. **2** *Geom.* A point of intersection. L19.

intersect /ɪntəˈsɛkt/ *v.* E17. [L *intersect-* pa. ppl stem of *intersecare* cut asunder, intersect, f. as INTER- + *secare* cut.] **1** *v.t.* Divide by passing through or lying across; cross. Freq. in *pass.* (foll. by *by*, *with*). E17. **b** *Geom.* Of a line, surface, etc.: cross (a line or surface) so as to have at least one point in common. M17. **c** Of a person: come across (a person, a path); intercept. *rare.* M19. **2** *v.i.* Of lines, surfaces, roads, etc.: cross or cut each other or *with* another. M19.

1 P. CAREY That perfect green landscape of his imagination, intersected with streams and redolent of orange blossom. A. MUNRO The street crossed the railway tracks. At the foot of the hill, it intersected the main street. 2 B. TARKINGTON He set up fountains . . where the streets intersected. *fig.*: M. L. KING The crisis of Negro aspirations intersects with the urban crisis.

intersectant *a.* (*rare*) intersecting M19.

intersection /ɪntəˈsɛkʃ(ə)n/ *n.* M16. [L *intersectio(n-)*, f. as prec.: see -ION.] **1** The action or fact of intersecting. M16. **2** The place where two or more things intersect; *spec.* (*Geom.*) the point at which a line intersects a line or surface, or the line common to two intersecting surfaces. M16. **b** A place where two or more roads intersect or form a junction. Chiefly *N. Amer.* M19. **3** *Math.* & *Logic.* The relation of two classes each of which includes part of the other; the resulting set of elements common to both. E20.

intersectional /ɪntəˈsɛkʃ(ə)n(ə)l/ *a.*[1] M19. [f. prec. + -AL[1].] Of, pertaining to, or characterized by intersection.

intersectional /ɪntəˈsɛkʃ(ə)n(ə)l/ *a.*[2] M19. [f. INTER- 2 + SECTION *n.* + -AL[1].] Existing or prevailing between sections.

intersegmental /ɪntəsɛgˈmɛnt(ə)l/ *a.* L19. [f. INTER- 2 + SEGMENT *n.* + -AL[1].] Esp. *Zool.* & *Ling.* Situated or occurring between segments.

intersegmentally *adv.* between segments E20.

†**intersert** *v.t.* Also **enter-**. L16–M18. [L *intersert-* pa. ppl stem of *interserere* f. as INTER- + *serere* put, place, insert.] Insert between other things; *rare* supply with insertions.

†**intersertion** *n.* (*a*) the action of inserting; (*b*) something which is inserted: E17–L18.

intersertal /ɪntəˈsəːt(ə)l/ *a.* L19. [f. as prec. + -AL[1].] *Petrogr.* Of or designating the texture of igneous rocks consisting largely of feldspar laths, with granular augite or other minerals occupying the spaces between them.

intersex /ˈɪntəsɛks/ *n.* E20. [f. INTER- 1 + SEX *n.*] *Biol.* (The condition of being) an abnormal form or individual of a dioecious species, having characteristics of both sexes.

intersexual /ɪntəˈsɛksjʊəl, -ʃʊəl/ *a.* & *n.* M19. [f. INTER- 1, 2 + SEXUAL.] **A** *adj.* **1** Existing between the sexes. M19. **2** *Biol.* Having characteristics of both sexes. E20. **B** *n. Biol.* An intersexual individual. E20.

intersexuˈality *n.* E20.

intershock /ɪntəˈʃɒk/ *v. rare.* E17. [In sense 1 f. Fr. *s'entrechoquer.* In sense 2 f. INTER- 1 + SHOCK *v.*[2]] †**1** *v.t.* Strike or attack mutually. Only in E17. **2** *v.i.* Strike together, collide. M17.

intersole *n.* var. of ENTRESOL.

interspace /ˈɪntəspeɪs/ *n.* LME. [f. INTER- 1 + SPACE *n.*] **1** A space between two things. LME. **2** A space of time between two events etc. E17.

interspace /ɪntəˈspeɪs/ *v.t.* L17. [f. INTER- 1 + SPACE *v.*] Put or occupy a space between.

intersperse /ɪntəˈspəːs/ *v.t.* Also †**entersparse**. M16. [L *interspers-* pa. ppl stem of *interspergere*, f. as INTER- + *spargere* scatter, sprinkle.] **1** Diversify, adorn, or provide (a thing) *with* things scattered or placed at intervals. M16. **2** Scatter among or between other things; place here and there in the course of something. M17.

1 R. P. JHABVALA He interspersed his recitation with commentaries and sometimes broke into song. I. MURDOCH Waltzes, tangos and slow foxtrots, interspersed with eightsome reels. 2 C. LYELL Large heaps of oysters . . with interspersed stone implements.

interspersal *n.* (*rare*) interspersion L19. **interspersedly** *adv.* in an interspersed manner M17.

interstate /ˈɪntəsteɪt/ *a.*, *adv.*, & *n.* Chiefly *US* & *Austral.* M19. [f. INTER- 2 + STATE *n.*] **A** *adj.* Existing or carried on between States, esp. of the US or Australia. M19. **B** *adv.* To, in, or into another State. *Austral.* E20. **C** *n.* A road, esp. a motorway, between States. L20.

interstice /ɪnˈtəːstɪs/ *n.* LME. [L *interstitium*, f. *intersistere* stand between, f. as INTER- + *sistere* stand.] **1** An intervening (usu. empty) space; *esp.* a relatively small or narrow space, a chink, a crevice. LME. **b** *Physics.* The space between adjacent atoms or ions in a crystal lattice. M20. **2** An intervening space of time. Now chiefly *Chr. Ch.* in *pl.*, the intervals required between the reception of the various degrees of holy orders. M17.

1 N. GORDIMER She oiled herself, spreading her toes to get at the interstices.

interstitia *n.pl.* see INTERSTITIUM.

interstitial /ɪntəˈstɪʃ(ə)l/ *a.* & *n.* M17. [f. (as) prec. + -AL[1].] **A** *adj.* **1** Pertaining to, forming, or occupying interstices. M17. **b** *Anat.* & *Med.* (Of tissue) situated between the cells of other tissue; (of a condition or process) occurring in the interstices of an organ, or in interstitial tissue. E19. **c** *Physics.* Situated between the normally occupied points of a crystal lattice. M20. **d** *Cryst.* Containing ions or atoms in interstitial positions (see sense 1C above). M20. **2** Occupying an interval in time or order. M19.

Special collocations: **interstitial cell** *Anat.* a Leydig cell in the testis.

B *n. Physics.* An interstitial atom or ion. M20.

interstitialcy *n.* (*Cryst.*) an imperfection in a crystal lattice, associated with the displacement of lattice atoms by interstitial atoms M20. **interstitially** *adv.* in or through interstices L18.

interstitium /ɪntəˈstɪʃɪəm/ *n.* Pl. **-iums**, **-ia** /-ɪə/. L16. [f. as INTERSTICE.] †**1** = INTERSTICE 1. L16–E18. **b** = INTERSTICE 2. L16–E18. **2** *Anat.* & *Zool.* The tissue or region lying between the principal cells, tissues, etc., of a part of the body. M20.

interstratify /ɪntəˈstratɪfʌɪ/ *v.t.* E19. [f. INTER- 1 + STRATIFY.] *Geol.* In *pass.*: (of strata) be alternated or interspersed *with* other strata.

interstratifiˈcation *n.* the condition of being interstratified; an interstratified layer or deposit: M19.

intersubjective /ɪntəsəbˈdʒɛktɪv/ *a.* L19. [f. INTER- 1 + SUBJECTIVE *a.*] *Philos.* Existing between conscious minds; shared by more than one conscious mind.

intersubjectively *adv.* M20. **ˌintersubjecˈtivity** *n.* M20.

intertangle /ɪntəˈtaŋg(ə)l/ *v.t.* Also †**enter-**. L16. [f. INTER- 1, ENTER-[1] + TANGLE *v.*] Tangle together; intertwine confusedly and inextricably.

intertanglement *n.* intertangled state or condition; something intertangled: E19.

intertex /ɪntəˈtɛks/ *v.t.* Long *rare* or *obs.* L16. [L *intertexere*, f. as INTER- 1 + *texere* weave.] Weave together, intertwine.

intertexture /ɪntəˈtɛkstʃə/ *n.* M17. [f. L *intertext-* pa. ppl stem of *intertexere* (see prec.) + -URE.] **1** The action of interweaving; the fact or condition of being interwoven. M17. **2** An intertwined or interwoven structure. M17.

intertie /ˈɪntətʌɪ/ *n.* E18. [Orig., alt. of INTERDICE interpreted as pl. Later, f. INTER- 1 + TIE *n.*[1]] A horizontal piece of timber etc. connecting two vertical pieces.

intertissued /ɪntəˈtɪʃuːd, -sjuːd/ *a.* Also †**enter-**. L16. [f. OFr. *entretissu*, f. as ENTER-[1], INTER- + TISSUE *n.*, + -ED[1].] Interwoven.

intertribal /ɪntəˈtrʌɪb(ə)l/ *a.* M19. [f. INTER- 2 + TRIBAL *a.*] Existing or carried on between different tribes.

intertrigo /ɪntəˈtrʌɪgəʊ/ *n.* E18. [L = a sore place caused by chafing.] *Med.* Inflammation caused by the rubbing of one skin surface against another.

intertropical /ɪntəˈtrɒpɪk(ə)l/ *a.* L18. [f. INTER- 2 + TROPICAL *a.*] Of or pertaining to regions between the tropics; tropical.

intertwine /ˈɪntətwʌɪn/ *n. rare.* E19. [f. the vb.] Intertwinement; something intertwined.

intertwine /ɪntəˈtwʌɪn/ *v.* M17. [f. INTER- 1 + TWINE *v.*[1]] **1** *v.t.* Twine (things) together; entwine (one thing *with* another). M17. **2** *v.t.* Twine round. *rare.* E18. **3** *v.i.* Become entwined. L18.

1 M. SCAMMELL The history of the Church was inextricably intertwined with the history of the nation.

intertwinement *n.* the fact of intertwining; intertwined state or condition; an intertwined formation: M19. **intertwiningly** *adv.* so as to intertwine E19.

intertwist /ɪntəˈtwɪst/ *v.t.* M17. [f. INTER- 1 + TWIST *v.*] Twist together; intertwine; intertangle.

Intertype /ˈɪntətʌɪp/ *n.* E20. [f. *Inter*national *Type*setting Machine Company, which manufactured machines of this type.] *Printing.* (Proprietary name for) a composing-machine which produces type in whole lines rather than individual letters.

interurban /ɪntərˈəːb(ə)n/ *a.* & *n.* L19. [f. INTER- 2 + URBAN *a.*] **A** *adj.* Carried on between, or connecting, different cities or towns. L19. **B** *ellipt.* as *n.* An interurban railway or train. *US.* E20.

interval /ˈɪntəv(ə)l/ *n.* Also (in sense 5) * **-vale** /-veɪl/. ME. [OFr. *entreval(e)*, *-valle* (mod. *intervalle*) ult. f. L *intervallum* orig. = space between ramparts, f. as INTER- 2 + *vallum* rampart. Var. in sense 5 by assoc. w. VALE *n.*[2]] **1** The period of time between two events, actions, parts of an action, etc.; a pause; *spec.* a break in a theatre etc. performance. ME. **b** *spec.* The period between recurrences of a disease or condition, esp. an intermittent fever. Now *rare* or *obs.* M17. **2** An open space between two things or two parts of the same thing; a gap, an opening. LME. **3** The space of time intervening between two points of time; an intervening time.

For other words beginning with *inter-* see the entry for **inter-**

Orig. in *by intervals* below. L16. **b** *Physics*. A quantity, invariant under the Lorentz transformation, that represents the separation of two events in space-time. E20. **4** *Mus.* The difference of pitch between two sounds, in melody or harmony. E17. **5** A low level tract of land, esp. along a river. M17. **6** The distance between persons or things in respect of position, qualities, etc. M19. **7** *Math.* A range between one numerical value and another; *spec.* a set composed of all the numbers between two given numbers, or an analogously defined subset of any partially ordered set. M19.

1 R. ELLMANN He was bored at times, during intervals between visits of friends. 3 W. S. CHURCHILL The interval of twelve years had been filled by events without name or sanction. 4 A. KOESTLER Attunement of the strings to the intervals in the scale. 6 A. BAIN From turtle to stale oat-cakes, or a piece of black bread, what a mighty interval!

Phrases: **at intervals** (*a*) now and again, not continuously; (*b*) here and there. *at short intervals*: see SHORT *a.* †**by intervals** (*a*) = *at intervals* (a) above; (*b*) alternately. **closed, open interval** *Math.*: including, excluding the terminal numbers. *compound interval*: see COMPOUND *a. open interval*: see *closed interval* above. *simple interval*: see SIMPLE *a.*

Comb.: **interval signal**: indicating continuity of transmission during a short break in a broadcast programme; **interval training** *Athletics*: in which a runner alternately runs and jogs over set distances (cf. REPETITION *training*).

inter'vallary *a.* (*rare*) = INTERVALLIC M19. **inter'vallic** *a.* of or pertaining to an interval or intervals M19.

interval /ˈɪntəv(ə)l/ *v. rare.* Infl. **-ll-**, ***-l-**. M17. [f. the n.] †**1** *v.i.* Come between or in an interval; form an interval. Only in M17. **2** *v.t.* Orig., separate by an interval; administer at intervals. Later, break or interrupt at intervals. M17.

intervale *n.* see INTERVAL *n.*

†**intervallum** *n.* Pl. **-lla, -llums**. L16–M17. [L: see INTERVAL *n.*] = INTERVAL *n.* 1, 3.

intervalometer /ɪntəvəˈlɒmɪtə/ *n.* M20. [f. INTERVAL *n.* + -OMETER.] *Photogr.* An attachment for a camera that enables photographs to be taken regularly at set intervals.

intervein /ɪntəˈveɪn/ *v.t.* E17. [f. INTER- 1 + VEIN *n.* or *v.*] **1** Intersect (as) with veins. E17. **2** Place in alternate veins. Usu. in *pass.* E19.

intervene /ɪntəˈviːn/ *v.* L16. [L *intervenire*, f. as INTER- + *venire* come.] †**1** *v.t.* Come between, interfere with; prevent, hinder. L16–M19. **2** *v.i.* Come in as something extraneous. L16. **3** *v.i.* Happen or take place between other events; occur in the meantime. E17. **4** *v.i.* (Of space or time) extend or lie *between* places or events; (of a thing) lie, be situated, *between*. E17. **5** *v.i.* Come between, esp. so as to modify or prevent a result etc.; interfere; *Law* (formerly esp. of the King's or Queen's Proctor in a divorce case) interpose in a lawsuit to which one was not an original party. M17.

1 DE QUINCEY Woodlands of birch . . intervening the different estates with natural sylvan marches. 2 WORDSWORTH In his worst pursuits . . sometimes there did intervene Pure hopes of high intent. 3 CARLYLE If some cleaning of the Augis stable have not intervened for a long while. 4 J. BUCHAN The long ridge which intervenes between the Chilterns and Cotswold. T. PYNCHON In the years intervening Oedipa had remembered Jesus. 5 W. S. CHURCHILL Britain . . had refused to intervene in the internal affairs of Italy. R. CHURCH Before Mother could intervene, Jack accepted the situation.

intervener /ɪntəˈviːnə/ *n.*[1] E17. [f. prec. + -ER[1].] A person who intervenes; *Law* a person who intervenes in a lawsuit to which he or she was not an original party.

Also **intervenor** *n.* M19.

intervener /ɪntəˈviːnə/ *n.*[2] M19. [f. as prec. after *interpleader* etc.: see -ER[4].] *Law.* The intervention of a person in a lawsuit.

intervenient /ɪntəˈviːnɪənt/ *a.* & *n.* L16. [L *intervenient-* pres. ppl stem of *intervenire*: see INTERVENE, -ENT.] **A** *adj.* **1** That comes in between; that comes in as something extraneous. L16. **2** That lies or is situated between other things or points in space. E17. **3** Occurring between certain points of time or events. E17. **4** Intervening in action; intermediary. M17. **B** *n.* A person who intervenes, an intervener. E17.

†**intervenience** *n.* the fact of intervening; (an) intervention: E17–E19.

intervent /ɪntəˈvɛnt/ *v.t.* Long *rare.* L16. [L *intervent-*: see next.] Come between, obstruct, thwart.

intervention /ɪntəˈvɛnʃ(ə)n/ *n.* LME. [Fr., or L *interventio(n-)*, f. *intervent-* pa. ppl stem of *intervenire*: see INTERVENE, -ION.] **1** The action or an act of coming between or interfering, esp. so as to modify or prevent a result etc.; *Law* the action or an act of one, not originally a party to a suit, who intervenes. LME. **2** Intermediate agency; the fact of coming in or being employed as an intermediary. M17. **3** The fact of coming or being situated between in place, time, or order. M17. **b** An intervening thing, event, or period of time. L17.

1 N. CHOMSKY A massive American intervention in the internal affairs of Laos in an effort to defeat the . . insurgents. G. WINOKUR Depression is a clinical state often requiring intervention. 2 A. BROOKNER A world from which Oscar had been miraculously freed by the intervention of chance. 3 ADAM SMITH Notwithstanding the intervention of one or two dear years.

interventional *a.* of or pertaining to intervention E19. **interventionism** *n.* the principle or practice of intervention E20. **interventionist** *n.* a person who favours intervention M19.

interventor /ɪntəˈvɛntə/ *n.* E18. [L, in late L = mediator, f. as prec.: see -OR.] A person who intervenes.

interversion /ɪntəˈvəːʃ(ə)n/ *n.* M18. [Late L *interversio(n-)*, f. L *intervers-* pa. ppl stem of *intervertere*: see next, -ION.] †**1** Embezzlement. Only in M18. **2** The action or an act of giving a different turn to; changing, inverting. M20.

intervert /ɪntəˈvəːt/ *v.t.* Now *rare.* L16. [L *intervertere*, f. as INTER- + *vertere* to turn.] †**1** Put to a use other than that intended; misapply, misuse. L16–M17. **b** Divert to one's own use, embezzle. E17–M19. **2** Give a different turn to; change, invert. M17.

interview /ˈɪntəvjuː/ *n.* Also †**enter-**. E16. [Fr. †*entreveue, -vue*, f. *entrevoir* have a glimpse of, *s'entrevoir* see each other (f. as ENTER-[1], INTER- + *voir* see), after *vue* VIEW *n.*] **1** A meeting of people face to face, esp. for the purpose of consultation. E16. **b** A meeting or conversation between a journalist or radio or television presenter and a person whose views are sought for publication or broadcasting; the published or broadcast result of this. M19. **c** An oral examination of a candidate for employment, a place in higher education, etc. Also, an interrogation of a person by the police etc. about a specific event. E20. †**2a** Looking into, inspection. M–L16. **b** A view, a glance, a glimpse, (*of* a thing). E17–E18. †**3** Mutual view (*of* each other). *rare.* E–M17.

1 M. M. KAYE The interview had been a short one . . both had confined themselves to a few words. b C. ACHEBE I read an interview he gave to a popular magazine. W. SOYINKA My picture appeared in the New York Times as the result of a press interview. c T. CAPOTE Young Rupp . . had already undergone one extensive interrogation, and . . was scheduled for a second interview. R. INGALLS She looked through the want ads and wrote for interviews.

interview /ˈɪntəvjuː/ *v.* Also †**enter-**. M16. [Partly f. Fr. *entrevu* pa. pple of (*s'*)*entrevoir* (see prec.) on the analogy of INTERVIEW *n.*, partly f. INTERVIEW *n.*] †**1** *v.i.* & *t.* Have a personal meeting (with). Only in M16. †**2** *v.t.* Catch a glimpse of, glance at, view. L16–E17. **3** *v.t.* Conduct an interview with (a person), esp. (of a journalist or radio or television presenter) with someone whose views are sought for publication or broadcasting. Also, conduct an oral examination of (a candidate for employment, a place in higher education, etc.); (of the police etc.) interrogate (a person) about a specific event. M19. **b** *v.i.* Conduct an interview or interviews. M20. **4** *v.i.* Of a candidate for employment, a place in higher education, etc.: undergo an interview; perform *well, badly*, etc., when being interviewed. L20.

3 B. MOORE The reporters tried to interview him. *Sunday Post (Glasgow)* The police chief issued a description of a man they want to interview.

interview'ee *n.* a person who is interviewed L19. **interviewer** *n.* M19.

intervisit /ɪntəˈvɪzɪt/ *v.i.* E17. [Fr. *entrevisiter*, f. as ENTER-[1], INTER- + *visiter* to visit.] Exchange visits.

inter vivos /ɪntə ˈviːvəʊs/ *adv.* & *a. phr.* M19. [L.] (Made) between living people (esp. of a gift as opp. to a legacy).

intervocal /ɪntəˈvəʊk(ə)l/ *a. rare.* L19. [f. INTER- 2 + L *vocalis* vocal, a vowel.] Intervocalic.

intervocalic /ˌɪntəvə(ʊ)ˈkalɪk/ *a.* L19. [f. as prec. + -IC.] Occurring between vowels.

intervocalically *adv.* M20.

intervolution /ɪntəvəˈluːʃ(ə)n/ *n.* M19. [f. next after *involve, involution*.] Intervolved condition; a winding.

intervolve /ɪntəˈvɒlv/ *v.* M17. [f. INTER- 1 + L *volvere* to roll, after *involve* etc.] **1** *v.t.* Wind or roll up (things) within each other; wind or involve (a thing) within the coils of something else. M17. **2** *v.i.* Wind within each other. *rare.* L19.

interweave /ɪntəˈwiːv/ *v.* Also †**enter-**. Pa. t. **-wove** /-ˈwəʊv/; pa. pple **-woven** /-ˈwəʊv(ə)n/, **-wove**. L16. [f. INTER- 1 + WEAVE *v.*[1]] **1** *v.t.* Weave together, interlace, (things, one thing *with* another). L16. **2** *v.t.* Blend (things) intimately. L16. **3** *v.i.* Be or become interwoven. E19.

1 *Scotsman* The interweaving of delicately-coloured silk threads on a grey ground. 2 D. W. GOODWIN Drinking became interwoven with everything pleasurable.

interwind /ɪntəˈwʌɪnd/ *v.* Pa. t. & pple **-wound** /-ˈwaʊnd/. L17. [f. INTER- 1 + WIND *v.*[1]] **1** *v.t.* Wind together (things, one thing *with* another); intertwine. L17. **2** *v.i.* Be or become interwound. L19.

interwork /ɪntəˈwəːk/ *v.* Pa. t. & pple **interworked**, (earlier, now *arch.* & *literary*) **interwrought** /ɪntəˈrɔːt/. E17. [f. INTER- 1 + WORK *v.*] **1** *v.t.* Work (a thing) into and through another; combine (things) by interpenetration. E17. **2** *v.i.* Work upon each other; interact. M19.

interwound *v.* pa. t. & pple of INTERWIND.

interwove *v.* pa. t. & pple: see INTERWEAVE.

interwoven /ɪntəˈwəʊv(ə)n/ *a.* M17. [pa. pple of INTERWEAVE.] Woven together, interlaced; intimately blended together.

interwovenly *adv.* (*rare*) L17.

interwoven *v.* pa. pple: see INTERWEAVE.

interwreathe /ɪntəˈriːð/ *v.t.* M17. [f. INTER- 1 + WREATHE *v.*] Wreathe together; intertwine (as) in a wreath.

interwrought *v.* see INTERWORK.

†**intestable** *a.* L16. [Late L *intestabilis*, f. as IN-[3] + *testabilis*, f. *testari*: see INTESTATE.] **1** Legally incapable of making, or of benefiting by, a will. L16–M18. **2** Disqualified from being a witness or giving evidence. Only in M17.

intestacy /ɪnˈtɛstəsi/ *n.* M18. [f. INTESTATE *a.* + -ACY.] *Law.* The condition or fact of dying without having made a will.

intestate /ɪnˈtɛsteɪt/ *a.* & *n.* LME. [L *intestatus*, f. as IN-[3] + TESTATE *a.*[1]: see -ATE[2].] **A** *adj.* **1** Not having made a will. LME. **2** Not disposed of by will; belonging to the estate of an intestate; of or pertaining to an intestate. M16.

1 R. GITTINGS Her husband had died intestate, and she . . took a year to obtain administration of his estate. 2 S. HALLIFAX The Roman Law concerning Intestate Succession.

B *n.* A person who dies without making a will. M17.

intestation /ɪntɛˈsteɪʃ(ə)n/ *n. rare.* M19. [f. IN-[3] + TESTATION, after *intestate*.] Deprivation of the right of making a will.

intestinal /ɪnˈtɛstɪn(ə)l/ *a.* LME. [f. next + -AL[1].] Of or pertaining to the intestines; found in or affecting the intestines.

intestinal flora symbiotic bacteria normally present in the gut. VASOACTIVE *intestinal (poly)peptide*.

intestine /ɪnˈtɛstɪn/ *n.* LME. [L *intestinum*, use as n. of neut. of *intestinus*: see next.] *sing.* & (usu.) in *pl.* The lower part of the alimentary canal, from the pyloric end of the stomach to the anus. In *sing.* also the whole alimentary canal from the mouth downward, esp. in invertebrate animals. Cf. BOWEL *n.*, GUT *n.*

large intestine the caecum, colon, and rectum collectively. **small intestine** the duodenum, jejunum, and ileum collectively.

intestine /ɪnˈtɛstɪn/ *a.* LME. [L *intestinus*, f. *intus* within: see -INE[1].] 1 Taking place within a nation; internal, domestic, civil. LME. †2 Inborn, inward, innate. L16–L17. †3 Taking place within the body; seated in the bowels; intestinal. E17–E18. 4 Taking place within any thing or place; internal, interior. Now *rare*. E17.

†**inthral**, -**ll** *vs.* vars. of ENTHRAL.

†**inthrone** *v.* var. of ENTHRONE.

inthronize *v.* var. of ENTHRONIZE.

inthrust /ˈɪnθrʌst/ *a. rare.* M17. [f. IN-[1] + pa. pple of THRUST *v.*] That is or has been thrust in.

inti /ˈɪnti/ *n.* Pl. same. L20. [Sp. f. Quechua *ynti* sun, the Inca sun god.] A former monetary unit of Peru, equal to 100 centimos.

†**intice** *v.*, †**inticement** *n.*, vars. of ENTICE, ENTICEMENT.

intichiuma /ˌɪntɪtʃɪˈuːmə/ *n.pl.* L19. [Aranda.] Sacred ceremonies performed by some Central Australian Aborigines with the purpose of increasing the totemic plants or animals, and thus ensuring a good food supply.

intifada /ɪntɪˈfɑːdə/ *n.* L20. [Arab. *intifāḍa* shaking off.] An uprising by Arabs; *spec.* that begun by Palestinians in 1987 against Israelis.

intill /ɪnˈtɪl/ *prep.* Also **intil**. ME. [f. IN *adv.* + TILL *prep.*] 1 Of motion, direction, change of condition: into. *Sc.* & *north.* ME. 2 Of place, position, condition, state, time: = in. *Sc.* LME.

intilted /ˈɪntɪltɪd/ *ppl a.* M20. [f. IN-[1] + TILT *v.*[1] + -ED[1].] Tilted inwards.

intima /ˈɪntɪmə/ *n.* Pl. **-mae** /-miː/. L19. [Abbrev. of TUNICA *intima*.] *Anat.* & *Zool.* The innermost coating or membrane of a part or organ, esp. of a vein or artery.

intimacy /ˈɪntɪməsi/ *n.* M17. [f. INTIMATE *a.* + -ACY.] 1 Intimate friendship or acquaintance; close familiarity; an instance of this. M17. b *euphem.* Sexual intercourse. L17. †2 Inner or inmost nature; an inward quality or feature. M17–L18. 3 Intimate or close connection or union. *rare.* E18. 4 Closeness of observation or knowledge. E18.

1 A. FRASER So great was their intimacy that rumours of a stronger tie—amorous, even marital—persisted. b *Westminster Gazette* She stayed the night . . at his father's house. . . Intimacy took place on that occasion.

†**intimado** *n.* Pl. **-os**. L17–E19. [Alt. of INTIMATE *n.* after Sp. wds in -ADO.] = INTIMATE *n.* 2.

intimal /ˈɪntɪm(ə)l/ *a.* E20. [f. INTIMA + -AL[1].] *Anat.* & *Zool.* Of the intima.

intimate /ˈɪntɪmət/ *n.* & *a.* E17. [Late L *intimatus* pa. pple of *intimare*, f. *intimus* (n.) a close friend, (adj.) innermost: see -ATE[2].] A *n.* †1 A characteristic example of a human type. Only in E17. 2 A very close friend or associate. E17.

B *adj.* 1 Of or pertaining to the inmost nature or fundamental character of a thing; essential; intrinsic. Now chiefly in scientific use. M17. b Entering deeply or closely into a matter. E19. 2 Proceeding from, concerning, or relating to one's deepest thoughts or feelings; closely personal, private. M17. 3 Involving very close connection or union; thoroughly mixed, united. M17. 4 Of knowledge: resulting from close familiarity; deep, extensive. M17. 5 United by friendship or other personal relationship; familiar, close. Also, pertaining to or dealing with close personal relations. M17. b Familiarly associated; closely personal. L19. c Having or seeking to create an informal, warm, friendly atmosphere. E20. 6 *euphem.* Having sexual intercourse (*with, together*). L19. b Pertaining to or involving the sexual organs or bodily orifices. E20.

3 R. W. EMERSON There is an intimate interdependence of intellect and morals. 5 L. M. MONTGOMERY An intimate friend, . . a really kindred spirit to whom I can confide my inmost soul. A. N. WILSON Having children in common . . they had something more . . intimate than could ever be shared by friends and lovers. J. KRANTZ Waking up with someone seemed more intimate than making love in some ways. b H. JAMES These diminutive intimate things bring one near to the Old Roman life. c W. BOYD The armchairs had been arranged in intimate groups. 6 R. MACAULAY Some of them were . . what newspapers call intimate together, without having undergone marriage. b K. AMIS There was a long, fairly passionate embrace with a certain amount of intimate caressing. *Times* Intimate searches (of body orifices) will be conducted by police officers.

intimately *adv.* M17.

intimate /ˈɪntɪmeɪt/ *v.t.* E16. [Late L *intimat-* pa. ppl stem of *intimare* announce: see prec., -ATE[3].] 1 Make known formally; announce, state. E16. 2 *gen.* Make known; indicate; imply, hint at. M16. b Mention indirectly or in passing. M17. †3 Make intimate, familiarize. E–M17.

1 *Manchester Examiner* A notice . . intimating a reduction of ten per cent in the wages of miners. 2 B. T. BRADFORD He had gently intimated that he thought the committee members were panicking unnecessarily. A. ARONSON Those areas of human conflict that the stage could only intimate but not portray.

intimation /ɪntɪˈmeɪʃ(ə)n/ *n.* LME. [(O)Fr., or late L *intimatio(n-)*, f. as prec.: see -ATION.] 1 The action or an act of making known or announcing something; (a) formal notification or announcement. LME. b *Law.* Notification of a requirement made by law, coupled with an announcement of the penalty that will be incurred in case of default. Now *rare* or *obs.* M17. 2 The action or an act of making known informally or indirectly; an indication; a suggestion, a hint. M16.

intime /ɛ̃tim/ *a.* E17. [Fr., f. L *intimus* innermost.] Intimate. Now only *spec.* friendly, familiar, cosy.

¶ Formerly fully naturalized.

intimidate /ɪnˈtɪmɪdeɪt/ *v.t.* M17. [med.L *intimidat-* pa. ppl stem of *intimidare*, f. L IN-[2] + *timidus* TIMID: see -ATE[3].] Terrify, overawe, cow. Now *esp.* force to or deter from some action by threats or violence.

M. MEAD They permit themselves to be . . bullied and intimidated and bribed by their more aggressive neighbours. L. GORDON She was intimidated by the achievements of Austen, Meredith, and Hardy.

intimiˈdation *n.* the action of intimidating someone, now *esp.* in order to interfere with the free exercise of political or social rights; the fact or condition of being intimidated: M17. **intimidator** *n.* a person who intimidates someone or employs intimidation M19. **intimiˈdatory** *a.* tending, or intended, to intimidate M19.

intimism /ˈɪntɪmɪz(ə)m/ *n.* Also ***intimisme*** /ɛ̃timism/. E20. [Fr. *intimisme*, f. as INTIME, -ISM.] A style of intimate domestic genre painting using impressionist techniques.

intimist /ˈɪntɪmɪst/ *n.* & *a.* Also ***intimiste*** /ɛ̃timist (*pl. same*)/ E20. [f. (as) prec.: see -IST.] A *n.* A painter following the principles of intimism. E20. B *adj.* Of or pertaining to intimism. M20.

intimity /ɪnˈtɪmɪti/ *n.* E17. [f. INTIME + -ITY. In sense 2 app. f. Fr. *intimité*.] 1 Close friendship, intimacy. *rare.* E17. 2 Intimate quality or nature; inwardness; privacy. L19.

1 W. OWEN I . . suffer a hunger for Intimity . . I ought to be in love and am not. 2 *Saturday Review* One of the very best pictures of . . a Court 'in intimity' that exists.

intinction /ɪnˈtɪŋ(k)ʃ(ə)n/ *n.* M16. [Late L *intinctio(n-)*, f. L *intinct-* pa. ppl stem of *intingere* dip in: see -ION.] †1 *gen.* The action of dipping in, esp. in something coloured; the liquid in which something has been dipped. M16–M17. 2 *Eccl.* The action or practice of dipping the bread of the Eucharist in the wine so that the communicant may receive both together. L19.

intine /ˈɪntɪn, -aɪn/ *n.* M19. [f. L *intimus* innermost, after EXTINE.] *Bot.* The inner wall of a pollen grain. Opp. EXINE.

†**intire** *a.*, *adv.*, & *n.* var. of ENTIRE *a.*, *adv.*, & *n.*

†**intitle** *v.* var. of ENTITLE.

intitulation /ɪnˌtɪtjʊˈleɪʃ(ə)n/ *n.* LME. [OFr., or med.L *intitulatio(n-)* f. late L *intitulat-* pa. ppl stem of *intitulare*: see next, -ATION.] 1 The action of entitling or furnishing something with a title or superscription; a superscription, a title. LME. 2 The action of bestowing a title; a designation. L16.

intitule /ɪnˈtɪtjuːl/ *v.t.* Also †**en-**. L15. [(O)Fr. *intituler* ENTITLE.] 1 Provide (a book or document) with a heading or superscription; entitle (a book etc.). L15. †b Ascribe (a book) *to* a person as its author. M–L16. †c Prefix *to* a book the name of a person to whom it is dedicated. M–L17. †2 Dedicate *to* by name or title; name after someone. L15–E18. 3 Give a (specified) title or designation to. *arch.* M16. †4 Provide (a person) with a title *to* an estate; *gen.* give (a person or thing) a rightful claim *to* a possession, privilege, designation, etc., or *to be*, *have*, or *do* something. L16–L18. †b Invest with a rank, function, etc. L16–E17. †5 Represent (something) as the cause of a particular action or effect. (Foll. by *to*.) M17–E18.

into /ˈɪntʊ, ˈɪntə/ *prep.* & *a.* [OE *in(n)tō* f. IN *adv.* + TO *prep.*, where the adv. expresses general direction, and the prep. refers to a particular point or place.] A *prep.* I Of motion or direction: ordinary uses. 1 After words expr. or implying motion: to a position within a space or thing having material extension; to the interior of; so as to enter. OE. b With the verb understood by ellipsis, or expressed in a verbal n. or other word. L15. 2 Pregnant uses. a So as to be possessed by. OE. b Before a collective n.: expr. admission to membership or participation. M16. 3 Introducing a new condition, state, or activity entered upon or begun. OE. 4a Introducing the substance or form which anything becomes or takes up. ME. b Introducing the condition or result brought about by some action. M16. 5 Introducing the parts produced by division, breaking, folding, etc. LME. 6 In reference to a non-physical thing, esp. a realm of thought or department of the mind, treated as having extension or content. E16. 7 *Math.* a Expr. the relationship of a multiplier to a multiplicand. *arch.* M16. b Expr. the relationship of a divisor to a dividend. M20. c Expr. the relationship of a set to its image under a mapping when not every element of the image set has an inverse image in the first set. Cf. sense B. below and ONTO. M20. 8 To a (freq. far advanced) point in (a period of time). L16. 9 Expr. direction without actual motion of the agent after such verbs as *turn, look, search*. E17. 10 As an addition to. Now only in *into the bargain* s.v. BARGAIN *n.* 2. M17. 11 So as to collide with or come in forcible contact with. E19.

1 J. BUCHAN I got into the train at Victoria. J. STEINBECK He slipped his feet into his sandals. A. CARTER A cold misery was seeping into her bones. V. S. PRITCHETT Sheep . . loaded into lorries. b R. KIPLING At dusk he harries the Abazai—at dawn he is into Bonair. 2a *Law Times* Alternative modes of getting the legal estate into the same person. b J. BARNES She had been born into the Norman nobility. P. BOOTH She had been . . the first to buy into the Polo Club. 3 V. WOOLF What awful fix had they got themselves into? G. GREENE We would launch into literary criticism. I. MURDOCH She went into . . infectious fits of laughter. 4a T. HARDY A yew bush cut into a quaint . . shape. R. HARDY The sound seemed . . first sibilant, then deepening into menace. W. BRONK To . . translate what someone said / in one language into another. b *Argosy* Only too glad . . to drink themselves into a stupor. W. GOLDING Plato's Golden Children are bred and trained into fitness. 5 THOMAS HUGHES Tearing up old newspapers . . into small pieces. R. MACAULAY Jane went . . , her world

tumbling into bits about her. 6 R. MACAULAY Things Katherine . . just took into consideration. I. MURDOCH Sidney . . offered to initiate me into the pleasures of . . wine. 7a J. PLAYFAIR The weight multiplied into the height to which it is raised. 8 A. S. BYATT After parties, he worked into the small hours. R. COBB My mother . . could walk quite fast well on into her seventies. 9 D. ABSE Then he stared into the fire. R. HARDY He . . removed his shirt, facing into the faint wind. 11 *Cape Times* The delivery van ran into a flock of sheep, killing 25. G. HOUSEHOLD I nearly walked slap into a sentry. *tear into*: see TEAR *v.*[1]

II 12 Of position: = IN *prep.* Long chiefly *Sc.* OE. 13 Interested or involved in; knowledgeable about. *colloq.* M20.

12 J. KNOX Devouring woulves into sheip skynnes. 13 *Listener* Margaret is 'into' astrology and consults the *I-Ching*. M. ATWOOD They could be violent, into whips.

†III 14 Even to (a place or point); to the very —. ME–M16. 15 Towards, in the direction of. Cf. sense 9 above. ME–M17. 16 Until, on to, up to (a time or date). LME–M16. 17 Unto, to (a thing or person). LME–E17. 18 Unto (a purpose or result); in order to, with a view to. LME–E16. 19 Defining the particular part of anything in which it is penetrated, pierced, etc. E16–L18.

17 SHAKES. *Cymb.* That he enchants societies into him. 19 DEFOE I . . fired again, and shot him into the head.

B *adj. Math.* Designating a mapping of one set on a subset of another. M20.

in-toed /ˈɪntəʊd/ *a.* L18. [f. IN *adv.* + TOED.] Having the toes turned inwards.

intolerable /ɪnˈtɒl(ə)rəb(ə)l/ *a.* & *adv.* LME. [(O)Fr. *intolérable* or L *intolerabilis*, f. IN-[3] + *tolerabilis* TOLERABLE.] A *adj.* 1 That cannot be tolerated or put up with; unbearable, insupportable. LME. †b Excessive, extreme, exceedingly great. Cf. AWFUL *a.* 4. M16–E18. 2 That cannot be withstood, irresistible. *rare.* LME.

1 A. MACLEAN The strain on the . . arm was intolerable, . . as if the shoulder sinews were being torn apart. J. KRANTZ He was intolerable, she loathed the very sound of his voice. b SHAKES. *1 Hen. IV* O monstrous but one halfpenny-worth of bread to this intolerable deal of sack! 2 *Harper's Magazine* To . . scourge away . . Hassan's men with intolerable musketry.

†B *adv.* Intolerably, insufferably; exceedingly, extremely. L16–E18.

M. COWPER Dr. Dunster preached an intolerable dull Sermon.

intoleraˈbility *n.* the quality of being intolerable; intolerableness: L16. **intolerableness** *n.* L16. **intolerably** *adv.* (*a*) in an intolerable manner or degree; unbearably; †(*b*) excessively, extremely: LME.

intolerant /ɪnˈtɒl(ə)r(ə)nt/ *a.* & *n.* M18. [L *intolerant-*, f. IN-[3] + *tolerant-* pres. ppl stem of *tolerare* TOLERATE: see -ANT[1].] A *adj.* 1a Not having the capacity to tolerate or endure a specified thing. Foll. by *of.* M18. b *Ecol.* Unable to flourish under certain conditions; *spec.* (of trees or other plants) unable to flourish in deep shade. L19. 2 *spec.* Not tolerating opinions or practices different from one's own, esp. in religious matters; denying or refusing to others the right to dissent. M18.

1a D. W. GOODWIN More women than men are physiologically intolerant of alcohol. 2 H. MORLEY One or other of the rival creeds in its most . . intolerant form.

B *n.* An intolerant person. M18.

intolerance *n.* (*a*) the fact or quality of being intolerant *of* something; (*b*) *spec.* absence of tolerance for difference of opinion or practice, esp. in religious matters; narrow-minded or bigoted opposition to dissent: M18. †**intolerancy** *n.* (*rare*) = INTOLERANCE E17–L18. **intolerantly** *adv.* M18.

†**intolerating** *a.* E18–M19. [f. IN-[3] + *tolerating* pres. pple of TOLERATE.] = INTOLERANT.

intoleration /ˌɪntɒləˈreɪʃ(ə)n/ *n. rare.* M16. [f. IN-[3] + TOLERATION.] Lack of toleration; intolerance. Formerly also, impatience.

†**intomb** *v.* var. of ENTOMB.

intombi /ɪnˈtɒmbi/ *n.* E19. [Xhosa, Zulu.] In southern Africa: a young Black woman who has been ritually prepared for marriage.

intonable /ɪnˈtəʊnəb(ə)l/ *a.* M19. [f. INTONE *v.* + -ABLE.] Able to be intoned.

intonaco /ɪnˈtəʊnəkəʊ/ *n.* Also **-ico** /-ɪkəʊ/. Pl. **-os**. E19. [It. *intonico*, †*-aco*, f. *intonicare* cover with plaster, ult. f. L *tunica* coat, TUNIC.] The final coating of plaster spread upon a wall or other surface, esp. for fresco painting.

intonate /ˈɪntəneɪt/ *v.*[1]*t.* Now *rare.* E17. [L *intonat-* pa. ppl stem of *intonare*, f. IN-[2] + *tonare* to thunder: see -ATE[3].] Utter with a loud voice like thunder.

intonate /ˈɪntəneɪt/ *v.*[2]*t.* L18. [med.L *intonat-* pa. ppl stem of *intonare* INTONE *v.*: see -ATE[3].] 1 Recite in a singing voice; intone. L18. 2 Utter or pronounce with a particular tone; give a specified intonation to. E19. 3 *Phonet.* Voice (a consonant). *rare.* M19.

intonation /ɪntəˈneɪʃ(ə)n/ *n.* E17. [med.L *intonatio(n-)*, f. as prec.: see -ATION.] 1 *Ch. Mus.* The opening phrase of a plainsong melody, preceding the reciting-note, and usu. sung either by the priest alone, or by one or a few of the choristers; the recitation of this. E17. 2 The action of intoning, or reciting in a singing voice; *esp.* the musical recitation of psalms, prayers, etc., in a liturgy, usu. in monotone. L18. 3 The utterance or production (by the voice, an instrument, etc.) of musical tones, w. ref. to manner or style, esp. to exactitude of pitch or relation to the key or harmony. L18. 4 Manner of utterance of the tones of the voice in speaking; modulation of the voice; accent. L18.

3 J. A. SYMONDS A . . soprano . . true to the least shade in intonation. 4 J. WAIN The . . voice went on, in a . . sub-Cockney intonation.

Comb.: **intonation contour** a succession of levels of pitch extending over an utterance; **intonation curve** the rising and falling of pitch within an utterance; **intonation pattern** a pattern of variations in pitch; **intonation phoneme** = INTONEME.

intonational *a.* of or pertaining to intonation L19. **intonationally** *adv.* M20.

intonator /ˈɪntə(ʊ)neɪtə/ *n.* M18. [f. INTONE *v.* + -ATOR.] 1 A monochord for the study of musical intervals, furnished with a diagram indicating the divisions of the string necessary for the production of the notes of the scale in exact intonation. Formerly, a tuning-fork. M18. 2 A person who intones. *rare.* M19.

intone /ɪnˈtəʊn/ *n.* M16. [f. the vb.] †1 Something intoned; a song or chant. Only in M16. 2 The action of intoning; the tone of voice used in intoning. L19.

intone /ɪnˈtəʊn/ *v.* Also (earlier, now *rare*) **en-**. L15. [med.L *intonare*, f. as IN-[2] + *tonus* TONE *n.*; *en-* f. OFr. *entoner* (mod. *entonner*).] 1 *v.t.* & *i.* Utter in musical tones, chant; *spec.* recite in a singing voice (esp. a psalm, prayer, etc. in a liturgy), usu. in a monotone. L15. 2 *v.t.* Utter with a particular tone or intonation. M19.

1 A. BURGESS An age-old Hindu prayer was intoned. B. EMECHETA The priest . . kept mumbling and intoning. 2 G. P. MARSH A clear . . and properly intoned . . pronunciation.

intonement *n.* (*rare*) the action of intoning or chanting M19. **intoner** *n.* M19.

intoneme /ɪnˈtəʊniːm/ *n.* M20. [Contr. of INTONATION *phoneme*: see -EME.] An intonation pattern that contributes to the meaning of an utterance.

intonico *n.* var. of INTONACO.

intorsion /ɪnˈtɔːʃ(ə)n/ *n.* M18. [Fr. f. late L *intorsio(n-)*, *intortio(n-)*, f. IN-[2] + *torsio(n-)* TORSION.] The action of twisting; *spec.* (*a*) *Bot.* the spiral twisting of the stem of a plant; (*b*) *Ophthalm.* rotation of the eyeballs in which the tops approach each other and the bottoms move away from each other.

intorted /ɪnˈtɔːtɪd/ *a.* Now *rare.* E17. [f. L *intort-* pa. ppl stem of *intorquere*, f. IN-[2] + *torquere* to twist: see -ED[1].] Twisted or curled inwards; twisted, wreathed, involved (*lit.* & *fig.*).

in toto /ɪn ˈtəʊtəʊ/ *adv. phr.* L18. [L.] Completely, without exception; altogether, in all.

Intourist /ˈɪntʊərɪst/ *n.* M20. [Russ. *Inturist* abbrev. of *inostrannyĭ turist* foreign tourist.] (The name of) the State Travel Bureau of the former USSR, dealing with tourists from abroad.

in-town /ˈɪntaʊn; *as adv.* ɪnˈtaʊn/ *n.*, *a.*, & *adv.* M16. [f. IN *adv.* + TOWN *n.*] A *n.* = INFIELD *n.* 1. *Sc.* M16. B *adj.* Situated or taking place within the centre of a town. E19. C *adv.* Into the centre of a town. M20.

intoxicant /ɪnˈtɒksɪk(ə)nt/ *a.* & *n.* M19. [f. INTOXICATE *v.*: see -ANT[1]. See also TOXICANT.] A *n.* An intoxicating substance or liquor. M19. B *adj.* Intoxicating. L19.

intoxicate /ɪnˈtɒksɪkət/ *ppl a.* Now *rare.* LME. [med.L *intoxicatus* pa. pple, f. as next: see -ATE[2].] †1a Impregnated in or smeared with poison; rendered poisonous. LME–M17. b Killed by poison. L15–E17. 2 Inebriated, intoxicated (*lit.* & *fig.*). L15.

2 J. TODHUNTER Such sun and air make me intoxicate With a strange passion.

intoxicate /ɪnˈtɒksɪkeɪt/ *v.* LME. [med.L *intoxicat-* pa. ppl stem of *intoxicare*, f. IN-[2] + L *toxicum* poison: see TOXIC *a.*, -ATE[3].] †1 *v.t.* Poison; *fig.* corrupt morally or spiritually. LME–M19. 2 *v.t.* Stupefy, madden or deprive of the ordinary use of the senses or reason with a drug or alcoholic liquor; inebriate, make drunk. L16. b *fig.* Make unsteady or delirious in mind or feelings; excite or exhilarate beyond self-control. L16. 3 *v.i.* Cause intoxication. L17.

2 P. PARISH The double scotch . . makes a novice drinker feel unpleasantly intoxicated. b J. BUCHAN After . . confinement in London the . . countryside intoxicated me. V. WOOLF Round they whirled, intoxicated by the music. 3 G. BERKELEY Cordials, which heat and intoxicate.

intoxicatedly *adv.* like a person who is intoxicated L19. **intoxicating** *ppl a.* causing intoxication (freq. *fig.*) M17. **intoxicatingly** *adv.* L19. **intoxicative** *a.* (*rare*) (*a*) tending to intoxicate; †(*b*) poisonous; (*c*) pertaining to or characteristic of intoxication: M17. **intoxicator** *n.* (*rare*) a person who intoxicates; formerly, a poisoner: M18.

intoxication /ɪnˌtɒksɪˈkeɪʃ(ə)n/ *n.* LME. [Fr., or med.L *intoxicatio(n-)*, f. as prec.: see -ATION. See also TOXICATION.] 1 The action of poisoning; (an instance of) the state of being poisoned. *obs.* exc. *Med.* (now *rare*). LME. †b *fig.* The corruption of the moral or mental faculties; a cause or occasion of this. L15–E18. 2 The action of inebriating or making someone stupid, insensible, or disordered in intellect, with a drug or alcoholic liquor; the condition of being so stupefied or disordered. M17. b *fig.* The action or power of exhilarating or highly exciting the mind; elation or excitement beyond the bounds of sobriety. E18.

1 P. MANSON A class of intoxication diseases which depend on toxins generated by germs. 2b ALDOUS HUXLEY The intoxication of success had evaporated.

intoximeter /ɪnˈtɒksɪmiːtə/ *n.* Orig. *US.* Also **I-**. M20. [f. INTOXI(CATION + -METER.] A device for measuring the alcohol content of a person's breath, esp. in cases of suspected drunken driving.

¶ Orig. a proprietary name in the US.

intra- /ˈɪntrə/ *comb. form.* [(Chiefly mod.) L *intra* on the inside, within. This use of *intra-* does not occur in cl.L, and is rare in late L.] Forming adjs. (usu. f. adjs.) w. the sense 'situated, occurring, or carried on within'. Opp. EXTRA-.

¶ Sometimes confused with INTER-.

intra-abˈdominal *a.* situated or occurring within the abdomen L19. **intra-arˈterial** *a.* occurring within or administered into an artery L19. **intra-aˈtomic** *a.* occurring or existing within an, or the, atom E20. **intraˈcapsular** *a.* (*Anat.*) situated or occurring within a capsule L19. **intraˈcardiac, -ˈcardial** *adjs.* situated or occurring within the heart L19. **intraˈcardially** *adv.* into the heart E20. **intraˈcellular** *a.* (*Biol.*) situated or occurring within a, or the, cell or cells L19. **intraˈcellularly** *adv.* (*Biol.*) within a cell or cells L19. **intraˈcerebral** *a.* situated or occurring within the cerebrum of the brain L19. **intraˈcerebrally** *adv.* in or into the cerebrum E20. **intraciˈsternal** *a.* (*Med.*) occurring within or administered into a cistern of the body, esp. of the brain M20. **intraciˈsternally** *adv.* (by injection) into a cistern M20. **intraˈcoastal** *a.* situated close to the coast E20. **intracontiˈnental** *a.* situated or occurring entirely within a continent E20.

intra'cranial *a.* situated or occurring within the cranium or skull M19. **intra'cranially** *adv.* within or into the cranium E20. **intra'cultural** *a.* occurring within a culture M20. **intra'culturally** *adv.* within a culture M20. **intracu'taneous** *a.* = INTRADERMAL L19. **intracu'taneously** *adv.* = INTRADERMALLY E20. **intra-day** *a.* occurring within one day L20. **intra'dermal** *a.* situated or applied within the skin E20. **intra'dermally** *adv.* in or into the skin E20. **intra'dermic** *a.* = INTRADERMAL L19. **intra-epi'thelial** *a.* situated within the epithelium L19. **intra-Euro'pean** *a.* occurring or carried on within Europe M20. **intrafa'llopian** *a.* (*Med.*) situated or occurring within a Fallopian tube; ZYGOTE *intrafallopian transfer.* L20. **intrafa'scicular** *a.* (*Bot.*) situated within a vascular bundle. **intrafoli'aceous** *a.* (*Bot.*) situated on the inner side of a leaf M18. **intrafor'mational** *a.* (*Geol.*) formed or occurring within a geological formation L19. **intra'gastric** *a.* applied or situated within the stomach E20. **intra'gastrically** *adv.* into the stomach M20. **intra'genic** *a.* (*Biol.*) situated or occurring within a gene L20. **intragroup** *a.* existing or occurring within a group or between members of a group E20. **intrahe'patic** *a.* situated or occurring within the liver E20. **intra'lingual** *a.* (*a*) *Med.* situated or occurring within the tongue; (*b*) = INTRA-LINGUISTIC: L19. **intra-lin'guistic** *a.* within a given language; within the bounds of language M20. **intra'lobular** *a.* (*Anat.*) (esp. of vessels) situated or occurring within the lobules of an organ or structure M19. **intrame'dullary** *a.* situated or performed within the medulla of an organ or structure, as of the spinal cord, a bone, etc. L19. **intra'membranous** *a.* (*Biol.*) situated within or between the layers of a membrane, esp. a cell membrane L19. **intramer'curial** *a.* (*Astron.*) situated within the orbit of Mercury L19. **intra'montane** *a.* situated in a mountainous area M19. **intramun'dane** *a.* situated or existing within the (material) world M19. **intra'muscular** *a.* situated or taking place within, or administered into a muscle L19. **intra'muscularly** *adv.* (by injection) into a muscle E20. **intra'national** *a.* occurring or carried on within a nation-state E20. **intra'nuclear** *a.* situated within a nucleus (esp. of a cell) L19. **intra-'ocular** *a.* situated or occurring within the eyeball E19. **intra-'oral** *a.* situated within the mouth L19. **intraperi'cardial** *a.* situated within or administered into the pericardium L19. **intraperito'neal** *a.* situated or taking place within (the cavity of) the peritoneum M19. **intraperito'neally** *adv.* within or (esp. by injection) into (the cavity of) the peritoneum L19. **intra'petiolar** *a.* (*Bot.*) (*a*) (of an axillary bud) formed immediately under the base of the petiole and surrounded by it so as not to appear until the leaf has fallen; (*b*) (of a stipule or pair of confluent stipules) situated between the petiole and the axis: M19. **intra'psychic, -ical** *adjs.* (*Psychol.*) occurring or existing within the psyche or self E20. **intra'pulmonary** *a.* occurring or administered within the lungs L19. **intra'racial** *a.* within, or occurring within, a biological race E20. **intra'regional** *a.* occurring or carried on within a region M20. **intra'spinal** *a.* occurring within or administered into the spinal cord M19. **intra-sub'jective** *a.* (*Psychol.*) (of a reaction, response, etc.) occurring within a person E20. **intratho'racic** *a.* situated or occurring within the thorax M19. **intra'tropical** *a.* situated or occurring within the tropics E19. **intra-'urban** *a.* carried on within an urban area L19. **intrava'ginal** *a.* (*a*) *Anat.* situated within the vagina; (*b*) *Bot.* within the sheath of a leaf: M19. **intrava'rietal** *a.* (*Biol.*) occurring or existing between individuals of the same variety E20. **intraven'tricular** *a.* (*Anat.*) situated or contained within a ventricle of the brain or heart L19. **intraven'tricularly** *adv.* (*Anat.*) into or within a ventricle M20. **intra'verbal** *a.* within a word M20.

intractable /ɪn'traktəb(ə)l/ *a.* L15. [L *intractabilis*, f. as IN-³ + TRACTABLE.] 1 Of a thing: difficult to shape or work; not easily treated or dealt with. L15. 2 Of a person or animal: not manageable or docile; uncontrollable; refractory, stubborn. M16.

1 J. KRANTZ His hair still jumped up in that intractable cowlick. *Scientific American* Cancer and such intractable viral diseases as AIDS. 2 H. READ The young schoolmaster who had struggled for two years with an intractable group of . . boys.

intracta'bility *n.* L16. **intractableness** *n.* M17. **intractably** *adv.* E19.

intractile /ɪn'traktɪl, -ʌɪl/ *a. rare.* E17. [f. IN-³ + TRACTILE.] †1 Incapable of being drawn out in length; not ductile. Only in E17. 2 = INTRACTABLE *a.* 1. L19.

intrada /ɪn'trɑːdə/ *n.* M18. [It. *intrata*, older form of *entrata* entry, prelude.] *Mus.* An introduction, a prelude.

intrados /ɪn'treɪdɒs/ *n.* L18. [Fr., f. as INTRA- + *dos* back.] *Archit.* The lower or inner curve of an arch; *esp.* the lower curve of the voussoirs which form the arch. Cf. EXTRADOS.

intraglacial /ɪntrə'gleɪʃ(ə)l, -sɪəl/ *a.* L19. [f. INTRA- + GLACIAL.] *Geol.* 1 Embedded within a glacier; = ENGLACIAL *a.* L19. 2 Designating or pertaining to the terrain formerly occupied by a glacier or ice sheet. L19.

†**intrail** *n.* var. of ENTRAIL *n.*[1]

intramolecular /ɪntrəmə'lɛkjʊlə/ *a.* L19. [f. INTRA- + MOLECULAR.] Situated, existing, or occurring within a molecule or the molecules of a body or substance.

intramolecularly *adv.* within a molecule M20.

intramural /ɪntrə'mjʊər(ə)l/ *a.* M19. [f. INTRA- + L *murus* wall + -AL¹.] 1 Situated, existing, or performed within the walls of a city or building or within a community, institution, etc. M19. b Forming part of normal university or college studies. E20. c Taking place within one educational establishment only. Chiefly *N. Amer.* M20. 2 *Anat.* & *Biol.* Situated within the wall of a hollow organ, or of a cell. L19.

intramurally *adv.* E20.

†**intrance** *v.* var. of ENTRANCE *v.*

intraneous /ɪn'treɪnɪəs/ *a. rare.* LME. [f. late L *intraneus* inner + -OUS.] Inner, internal; domestic.

intransferable /ɪntrans'fəːrəb(ə)l, ɪn'transf(ə)r-; -trɑː-, -nz-/ *a.* L18. [f. IN-³ + TRANSFERABLE.] Not transferable; unable to be transferred.

intransgressible /ɪntranz'grɛsɪb(ə)l, -trɑː-, -ns-/ *a.* E17. [f. IN-³ + TRANSGRESS *v.* + -IBLE] That cannot or may not be transgressed.

intransient /ɪn'transɪənt, -'trɑː-, -nz-/ *a.* Now *rare.* M17. [f. IN-³ + TRANSIENT *a.*] Permanent, unchanging: not passing away or to another.

intransigeance *n.*, **-geant** *a.* & *n.* vars. of INTRANSIGENCE, -ENT.

intransigence /ɪn'transɪdʒ(ə)ns, -'trɑː-, -nz-/ *n.* Also **-geance**. L19. [f. next + -ENCE.] The quality of being intransigent; uncompromising hostility; irreconcilability.

Also **intransigency** *n.* L19.

intransigent /ɪn'transɪdʒ(ə)nt, -'trɑː-, -nz-/ *a.* & *n.* Also **-geant**. L19. [Fr., f. Sp. *los intransigentes* the party of the extreme left in the Spanish Cortes (1873–4); ult. f. as IN-³ + pres. pple of L *transigere* come to an understanding: see TRANSACT, -ENT.] A *adj.* Unwilling to negotiate or make any concession; obdurate, uncompromising. L19.

A. MACLEAN The Lieutenant . . is uncooperative, intransigent and downright disobedient. C. PETERS The Duke of Wellington's intransigent stand against reform might block the passage of the bill.

B *n.* An uncompromising holder of (orig. republican) principles. L19.

intransigentism *n.* the republican principles of the early intransigents L19. **intransigently** *adv.* E20.

intransitable /ɪn'transɪtəb(ə)l, -'trɑː-, -nz-/ *a. rare.* M19. [f. IN-³ + TRANSITABLE.] Intraversable; not offering any means of transit.

intransitive /ɪn'transɪtɪv, -'trɑː-, -nz-/ *a.* & *n.* E17. [Late L *intransitivus* not passing over, f. as IN-³ + TRANSITIVE.] A *adj.* 1 *Gram.* Of a verb, the construction of a verb: expressing action which is limited to the subject; not taking a direct object. Cf. TRANSITIVE *a.* 2, NEUTER *a.* 1b. E17. 2 That does not pass on to another person, or beyond certain limits (specified or implied). *rare.* M17. 3 *Logic* & *Math.* Of a relation: of a kind which can exist between a first thing or person and a second, and between the second and a third, but need not exist between the first and the third. Of a group: containing elements in intransitive relation. L19.

3 B. RUSSELL *Spouse* is symmetrical but intransitive; . . *father* is both asymmetrical and intransitive.

B *n.* An intransitive verb. E19.

intransitively *adv.* M17. **intransi'tivity** *n.* the property or quality of being intransitive L19.

intransitivize *v.t.* (*Gram.*) make intransitive; chiefly as *intransitivizing* ppl *a.*: M20.

intransparency /ɪntran'spar(ə)nsi, -trɑː-; -'spɛː-/ *n.* E20. [f. IN-³ + TRANSPARENCY.] The quality of being opaque; an instance of this.

intransparent /ɪntran'spar(ə)nt, -trɑː-; -'spɛː-/ *a.* M19. [f. IN-³ + TRANSPARENT.] Not transparent; unable to be seen through.

intrant /'ɪntr(ə)nt/ *n.* & *a.* Chiefly *Sc.* E16. [L *intrant-* pres. ppl stem of *intrare* enter, in med.L senses: see -ANT ¹.] A *n.* 1 A person who takes legal possession of land etc. Now *rare.* E16. 2 A person who enters a college, institution, association, etc. M16. 3 A person who enters a room, building, etc. *rare.* M17. 4 A person who enters into holy orders. M17. B *adj.* Entering (an office, profession, etc.); newly appointed. L16.

†**intrap** *v.* var. of ENTRAP.

intrapluvial /ɪntrə'pluːvɪəl/ *a.* & *n.* M20. [f. INTRA- + PLUVIAL *a.*] *Geol.* A *adj.* Of, pertaining to, or designating relatively short, drier periods (less marked than interpluvials) that may have occurred during pluvials. M20. B *n.* An intrapluvial period. M20.

intrapolation /ɪn,trapə'leɪʃ(ə)n/ *n.* E20. [f. INTRA- + INTER)POLATION.] = INTERPOLATION 3. Also more widely, (an) inference within the scope or framework of what is known.

in'trapolate *v.t.* & *i.* = INTERPOLATE *v.* 5, 5b M20.

intraspecies /'ɪntrəspiːʃiːz/ *a.* E20. [f. INTRA- + SPECIES.] = next.

intraspecific /ɪntrəspə'sɪfɪk/ *a.* E20. [f. INTRA- + SPECIFIC.] Produced, occurring, or existing within a (taxonomic) species or between individuals of a single species.

intratelluric /ɪntrətɛ'ljʊərɪk/ *a.* L19. [f. INTRA- + TELLURIC *a.*²] *Geol.* Situated, occurring, or originating in the interior of the earth.

intrathecal /ɪntrə'θiːk(ə)l/ *a.* L19. [f. INTRA- + THECAL.] 1 *Zool.* Contained or enclosed within the theca (e.g. of a polyp). L19. 2 *Med.* Occurring within or administered into the spinal theca. E20.

intrathecally *adv.* E20.

intrauterine /ɪntrə'juːtərʌɪn, -rɪn/ *a.* M19. [f. INTRA- + UTERINE.] Situated, occurring, or passed within the uterus.

intrauterine device a contraceptive device to be placed in the uterus.

intravasation /ɪn,travə'seɪʃ(ə)n/ *n.* L17. [f. INTRA- after EXTRAVASATION.] *Med.* The entrance into a vessel of matter (e.g. pus) formed in the surrounding tissues.

intravascular /ɪntrə'vaskjʊlə/ *a.* L19. [f. INTRA- + VASCULAR.] Chiefly *Anat.* Situated or occurring within a vessel of an animal or plant, esp. within a blood-vessel.

intravascularly *adv.* within the vascular system E20.

intravenous /ɪntrə'viːnəs/ *a.* & *n.* M19. [f. INTRA- + VENOUS.] A *adj.* Existing or taking place within a vein or the veins. M19. B *n.* An intravenous injection or feeding. M20.

intravenously *adv.* L19.

intraversable /ɪntrə'vəːsəb(ə)l/ *a.* E19. [f. IN-³ + TRAVERSABLE.] That cannot be traversed or crossed.

intra vires /ɪntrə 'vʌɪriːz/ *adv. phr.* L19. [L = within the powers.] Chiefly *Law.* Within the powers or legal authority (*of* a corporation or person). Opp. ULTRA VIRES.

intravital /ɪntrə'vʌɪt(ə)l/ *a.* L19. [f. INTRA- + VITAL *a.*, perh. infl. by next.] *Biol.* Performed on, applied to, or occurring in something alive; in vivo.

intravitally *adv.* during life, in a living organism M20.

intra vitam /ɪntrə 'viːtam/ *a. phr.* L19. [L.] *Biol.* Taking place during life; while still living. Cf. IN VIVO.

intrazonal /ɪntrə'zəʊn(ə)l/ *a.* E20. [f. INTRA- + ZONAL.] *Soil Sci.* Designating any soil which differs from the soil characteristic of its climatic and vegetational zone owing to the overriding influence of relief, parent material, or other local factor.

intreat *v.* see ENTREAT.

†**intreaty** *n.* var. of ENTREATY.

intrench /ɪnˈtrɛn(t)ʃ/ *v.* M16. [f. IN-² + TRENCH *n.* & *v.* See also ENTRENCH.] 1 *v.t.* & *i.* Var. of ENTRENCH. M16. 2 *v.t.* Make a trench in; furrow. M18.

†**intrenchant** *a. rare.* Only in E17. [f. IN-³ + TRENCHANT *a.*] Unable to be cut.

intrenched *ppl a.*, **intrenchment** *n.* vars. of ENTRENCHED, ENTRENCHMENT.

intrepid /ɪnˈtrɛpɪd/ *a.* L17. [Fr. *intrépide* or L *intrepidus*, f. as IN-³ + *trepidus* agitated, alarmed.] Fearless; undaunted; daring; brave.

H. MARTINEAU Is there to be no pride in intrepid patriotism? E. H. JONES Others remembered her as an intrepid slider on frozen ponds.

intreˈpidity *n.* the quality of being intrepid; fearlessness, courage, boldness: E18. **intrepidly** *adv.* E18. **intrepidness** *n.* intrepidity E17.

intricacy /ˈɪntrɪkəsi/ *n.* E17. [f. next + -ACY.] 1 The quality or state of being intricate; complexity; complicated or involved condition. E17. 2 A complication; an entangled or involved state of affairs; a perplexing difficulty. In *pl.*, the fine detail and complexities of a subject or practice. E17.

1 DRYDEN It often puzzles the reader with the Intricacy of its Notions. J. E. T. ROGERS The lock must have varied in value, according to . . the intricacy of its workmanship. 2 D. WELCH It isn't easy, even for a doctor, to understand all the intricacies of nursing.

intricate /ˈɪntrɪkət/ *a.* LME. [L *intricatus* pa. pple of *intricare* entangle, perplex f. as IN-² + *tricae* trifles, tricks, perplexities, f. *tricari* make difficulties: see -ATE².] 1 Perplexingly entangled or involved; interwinding in a complicated manner. LME. 2 Of ideas, statements, etc.: perplexingly involved or complicated in meaning; entangled; obscure. LME.

1 D. DELILLO Along the intricate and twisting paths. J. CRACE Every beast is woven an intricate necklace of straw. 2 L. EDEL Winston was impatient, irritable; he could not wait for the end of such long and intricate sentences.

intricately *adv.* M16. **intricateness** *n.* intricacy L16.

intricate /ˈɪntrɪkeɪt/ *v.t.* Now *rare.* M16. [L *intricat-* pa. ppl stem of *intricare*: see prec., -ATE³.] 1 Make (a thing) involved or obscure; complicate. M16. 2 Entangle or ensnare (an animal or person); involve, embarrass, perplex. M16.

†**intrication** *n.* the action of intricating; the condition of being intricated; complication, entanglement: LME-L18.

intrigant *n.* & *a.* var. of INTRIGUANT.

intrigante *n.* var. of INTRIGUANTE.

intriguant /ˈɪntrɪɡ(ə)nt; *foreign* ɛ̃triɡɑ̃ (*pl. same*)/ *n.* & *a.* Also **-gant.** L18. [Fr., pres. pple of *intriguer*: see INTRIGUE *v.*, -ANT¹.] A *n.* An intriguer. L18. B *adj.* Intriguing; scheming. E19.

intriguante /ɛ̃triɡɑ̃ːt/ *n.* Also ***-gante.*** Pl. pronounced same. E19. [Fr., fem. of *intriguant*: see prec.] A woman who intrigues.

intrigue /ɪnˈtriːɡ, ˈɪntriːɡ/ *n.* M17. [Fr. f. It. *intrigo*, *-ico*, f. *intrigare* entangle, f. L *intricare*: see INTRICATE *a.*] †1 Intricacy, complexity; a complicated contrivance, state of affairs, or mode of action. M-L17. 2 Underhand plotting or scheming; an instance of this, a plot. M17. †3 The plot of a play, poem, or romance. M17-E18. 4 A clandestine love affair. M17. b *transf.* The combination of queen and jack in certain card-games. M19.

2 B. BAINBRIDGE Unknowingly enmeshed in a tangle of shady dealings and secret intrigues. *Country Quest* Power and political intrigue were very much the matters of the day in thirteenth century Britain. 4 STEELE Taken in an Intrigue with another Man's wife.

intrigue /ɪnˈtriːɡ/ *v.* E17. [Fr. *intriguer* f. It. *intrigare*: see prec.] 1 *v.t.* Trick, deceive, cheat; embarrass, puzzle, perplex. Now *rare* or *obs.* E17. 2 *v.i.* Carry on a secret or illicit love affair. M17. 3 *v.i.* Use influence secretly to achieve one's ends; plot *with* a person; scheme. L17. b *v.t.* Accomplish by underhand scheming. Now *rare.* L17. 4 *v.t.* Entangle, involve; complicate. Now *rare* or *obs.* L17. 5 *v.t.* Arouse the curiosity or interest of; puzzle, fascinate. Usu. in *pass.* L19.

1 S. WILLIAMS To intrigue and baffle a brave and meritorious people out of their rights and liberties. 2 S. PEPYS The people . . make no scruple of saying that the king do intrigue with Mrs. Stewart. 3 L. MACNEICE Donald, Lord of the Isles, intrigued with Henry of England and crossed the Minch as a rebel. 4 J. CHILD The way . . is not . . hidden from us in the dark, or intrigued with difficulties. 5 C. SAGAN Something puzzles him, intrigues him, has implications that excite him.

intriguer *n.* a person who carries on an intrigue M17. **intriguess** *n.* (*rare*) a female intriguer M18. **intriguing** *a.* (*a*) forming secret plots or schemes; (*b*) arousing interest, or curiosity, curious, fascinating: L17. **intriguingly** *adv.* M18.

intrinse /ɪnˈtrɪns/ *a. rare.* E17. [Perh. abbrev. of INTRINSICATE.] Intricate, entangled, involved.

intrinsic /ɪnˈtrɪnsɪk/ *a.* & *n.* L15. [(O)Fr. *intrinsèque* f. late L *intrinsecus*, f. L *intrinsecus* adv. inwardly, inwards: see -IC.] A *adj.* 1a Situated within; interior, inner. *obs.* in *gen.* sense. L15. b *Anat.* Of a muscle: contained wholly within the organ on which it acts. Also, (of a tumour) arising in the part or tissue in which it is found. M19. †2 Inward, secret, private. L15-L17. b Intimate. E-M17. 3 Belonging to a thing in itself, or by its very nature; inherent, essential, natural (*to*). Of worth: real, not illusory or superficial. M17. b *Math.* Not involving reference to external coordinates. M19. c *Physics.* Of a semiconductor: owing its electrical conductivity to thermally excited electrons from the principal substance present, rather than to electrons from impurity atoms. Also, designating or pertaining to such conduction. M20.

3 M. SEYMOUR-SMITH These, whatever their intrinsic interest, are the letters of a famous poet. D. CAUTE Measuring the intrinsic value of a course by the size of its audience. A. ARONSON Their compassionate realisation of the existence of evil as an intrinsic part of the human condition. **intrinsic factor** *Biochem.* a glycoprotein secreted by the stomach which enables the body to absorb vitamin B_{12}. b W. WHEWELL The intrinsic equation to the circle is $s = a\theta$, a being the radius.

B *n.* An intrinsic part or quality. Long *rare.* M17.

intrinsical /ɪnˈtrɪnsɪk(ə)l/ *a.* Now *rare.* M16. [f. late L *intrinsecus* (see prec.) + -ICAL.] †1 = INTRINSIC *a.* 2. M16-M17. b = INTRINSIC *a.* 2b. E17-L19. 2 = INTRINSIC *a.* 3. M16. †3 = INTRINSIC *a.* 1. L16-L17.

intrinsiˈcality *n.* (an instance of) intrinsicalness M19. **intrinsicalness** *n.* the state or quality of being intrinsic L17.

intrinsically /ɪnˈtrɪnsɪk(ə)li/ *adv.* L16. [f. INTRINSIC *a.* or prec.: see -ICALLY.] †1 Internally, inwardly, within (*lit.* & *fig.*). L16-M17. 2 By, or in relation to, the inner nature of the thing: in itself; inherently, essentially. E17.

†**intrinsicate** *a.* M16-E17. [App. f. It. *intrinsecato*, *-sicato* familiar, confused in meaning with *intricato* intricate.] Intricate, involved, entangled.

intro /ˈɪntrəʊ/ *n. colloq.* Also **intro.** (point). Pl. **-os.** E19. [Abbrev.] = INTRODUCTION.

intro- /ˈɪntrəʊ/ *pref.* [L *intro* adv. 'to the inside'.] In wds adopted f. L and in Eng. formations modelled on these, and as a freely productive pref., with the senses 'within', 'inwards'.

intro-ˈactive *a.* having the property of acting within; mutually active: M19. **introˈessive** *a.* & *n.* (*Gram.*) (designating, being in, or pertaining to) the case which expresses 'motion into' E20. **introˈflexed** *ppl a.* bent or curved inwards M19. **introˈflexion** *n.* an inward bending or curvature M19. **intromoˈlecular** *a.* (*rare*) intramolecular L19. **introˈpulsive** *a.* having the quality of driving inwards E19. **introˈsuction** *n.* (long *rare*) the action of sucking inwards M17.

introduce /ɪntrəˈdjuːs/ *v.t.* LME. [L *introducere*, f. as INTRO- + *ducere* lead, bring.] 1a Bring (a person) into a place, society, or group. LME. b Bring, put, or lead into or in; insert. LME. †2 Bring about, induce. LME-L17. †3 Bring (a person) into the knowledge of something; initiate; instruct. Cf. INTRODUCTION 3. L15-E16. 4 Add or incorporate, esp. as a new feature or element. (Foll. by *into.*) L15. 5 Bring into use or practice; institute (a law, custom, etc.). E17. 6 Usher in, bring forward with preliminary or preparatory matter; announce; begin, come immediately before the start of. M17. 7 Bring into personal acquaintance; make known to or *to* a person or group. Orig. *introduce into the acquaintance of.* M17. b Present formally, as at court, in an assembly such as the House of Lords or Commons, to society, etc. L17. c Acquaint (a person) with an idea or thing. Foll. by *to.* M18. 8 Bring to the notice or cognisance of a person or group; bring a bill or proposal before Parliament etc. M18.

1a G. GREENE The fourth member was . . Liz, . . introduced for reasons of utility. b I. MURDOCH He took a piece of . . paper and . . introduced it carefully underneath the little curled up thing. R. DAWKINS They introduced a baby swallow into a magpie's nest. 4 A. BRIGGS Spenser introduced many allegorical devices into his . . *Epithalamion.* 5 J. A. MICHENER Thus chewing gum was introduced to the States. *Clitheroe Advertiser & Times* A suggestion to relieve traffic congestion . . by introducing a parking restriction. 6 A. HAMILTON Rain introduced with much Thunder and Lightning. SIR W. SCOTT This discussion served to introduce the young soldier's experiences. T. MORRISON Unless Eva . . introduced the subject, no one ever spoke of her disability. 7 T. S. ELIOT Let me introduce you to my wife. P. ACKROYD Eliot and Verdenal were introduced and did not simply meet by chance. b *Law Times* A new . . Peer of Ireland . . is not introduced, but simply takes and subscribes the oath. F. HUME Curtis introduced her to society. c L. GORDON Janet Case . . introduced her to the feminist cause. 8 LYNDON B. JOHNSON Mills . . introduced the new bill to the House.

introduceable *a.* L17. **introduced** *ppl a.* (*a*) brought in, inserted, made known; (*b*) *Bot.* & *Zool.* (of a species) not native to the area in which it occurs: M17. †**introducement** *n.* the action of introducing; an introduction: M16-L18. **introducer** *n.* E17. **introducible** *a.* able to be introduced or brought in L17.

introduction /ɪntrəˈdʌkʃ(ə)n/ *n.* LME. [(O)Fr., or L *introductio(n-)*, f. *introduct-* pa. ppl stem of *introducere*: see prec., -ION.] †1 The action or process of leading to or preparing for something; a preliminary or initiatory step or stage. LME-M17. 2a The action or an act of introducing a person or thing. LME. b A practice or thing newly introduced; a plant or animal species brought into a region in which it is not native. E17. c The issuing of new shares by a company through the medium of a stock exchange. E20. †3 Initiation in the knowledge of a subject; instruction in rudiments; a first lesson; in *pl.*, rudiments, elements. Cf. INTRODUCE 3. LME-E18. 4a A preliminary explanation of an author's or speaker's design or purpose; the part of a book, lecture, speech, etc., which leads up to the subject treated. E16. b A text explaining the elementary principles of a subject. M16. c A preliminary course of study; matter introductory to the special study of a subject. L19. 5a The action of personally introducing a person; *esp.* the formal presentation of one person to another. E18. b The process of becoming acquainted with a thing; a means of this. E19. c A letter of introduction. E19. 6 *Mus.* The preliminary passage or movement of a piece of music, often thematically different from the main section. L19.

2a *Times* The divisions . . in Protestant . . circles, since the introduction of direct rule. 4b A. J. BALFOUR By an Introduction to a subject is meant a brief survey. c J. FERGUSSON The study of Etruscan art is a necessary introduction to that of Roman. 5a W. IRVING Boswell was made happy by an introduction to Johnson. D. PARKER No introductions, . . for each guest wore a card with his . . name . . on it. *letter of introduction*: see LETTER *n.*¹ c *Radio Times* The BBC's New York office has given me introductions to the broadcasting people in Montreal.

introductive /ɪntrəˈdʌktɪv/ *a.* L15. [med.L *introductivus*, f. L *introduct-*: see prec., -IVE.] 1 Causing or promoting the introduction *of* something. L15. 2 Leading on to something that follows. M17.

introductor /ɪntrəˈdʌktə/ *n. arch.* M17. [Late L, f. L *introduct-*: see INTRODUCTION, -OR.] An introducer; *spec.* an official who introduces people at a royal court.

introductory /ɪntrəˈdʌkt(ə)ri/ *a.* & *n.* LME. [Late L *introductorius*, f. L *introduct-*: see INTRODUCTION, -ORY².] A *n.* †1 An introductory text. LME–M16. 2 A preliminary step. M17. B *adj.* †1 Serving to introduce something. Foll. by *of.* E17–E19. 2 Leading up or on to something; preliminary. M17. 3 Serving to introduce someone personally. L18.

2 R. INGALLS There were even introductory drum-rolls. *NATFHE Journal* The book is intended as an introductory textbook.

introductorily *adv.* in an introductory manner; by way of introduction: M19.

introductress /ɪntrəˈdʌktrɪs/ *n.* M17. [f. INTRODUCTOR + -ESS¹.] A female introducer.

introgression /ɪntrəˈɡrɛʃ(ə)n/ *n.* M17. [f. L *introgredi* step in, f. as INTRO- + *gradi* proceed, walk, after *egress, egression, ingress, ingression*: see -ION.] 1 A going or coming in. M17. 2 *Biol.* The transfer of genetic information from one (usu. plant) species to another as a result of hybridization between them and repeated back crossing. M20.

introgress *v.i.* (*Biol.*) (of a species, or of a gene) undergo introgression M20. **introgressed** *ppl a.* transferred by or resulting from introgression M20.

introgressive /ɪntrəˈɡrɛsɪv/ *a.* M20. [f. prec. + -IVE.] *Biol.* Characterized by, bringing about, or resulting from introgression.

introgressive hybridization = INTROGRESSION 2.

introit /ˈɪntrɔɪt, ɪnˈtrəʊɪt/ *n.* LME. [(O)Fr. *introït* f. L *introitus* entrance, f. *introire* enter, f. as INTRO- + *ire* go.] 1 The action or an act of going in; (an) entrance. Long *rare.* LME. 2 *Eccl.* An antiphon or psalm sung while the priest approaches the altar to celebrate the Eucharist. Also, the first two or three words of the office of a particular day. L15.

introjection /ɪntrə(ʊ)ˈdʒɛkʃ(ə)n/ *n.* M19. [f. INTRO- after *projection.*] 1 The action of throwing oneself into, or eagerly beginning, some course or pursuit. M19. 2 *Philos.* A theory according to which external objects are images of elements within the consciousness of the individual. L19. 3a *Psychoanalysis.* The transfer of emotional energy from an object to a subjective image of it; internalization. E20. b *Psychol.* The inward adoption of the attitudes, values, and expectations of one's parents or others by whom one is anxious to be accepted; identification. M20.

introject *v.t.* (*Psychol.*) incorporate an inward image of (an external object, or the values and attitudes of others) into oneself E20. **introjectionism** *n.* belief in a theory of introjection E20. **introjectionist** *a.* pertaining to introjection E20. **introjective** *a.* (*Psychol.*) that is introjected; characterized by introjection: M20.

intromission /ɪntrə(ʊ)ˈmɪʃ(ə)n/ *n.* M16. [Fr., or L *intromissio(n-)*, f. as INTRO- + *missio(n-)* MISSION *n.*] 1 Interference; *esp.* (chiefly *Sc. Law*) the action of assuming the possession and management of another's property, either with or without legal authority. Also, the transactions of an agent or subordinate with the money of his or her employer or principal. M16. 2 The action of sending, letting, or putting something in; *spec.* the insertion of the penis into the vagina in sexual intercourse. E17.

1 **vicious intromission** intromission without legal authority.

intromit /ɪntrə(ʊ)ˈmɪt/ *v.* Infl. **-tt-**. LME. [L *intromittere* introduce, f. as INTRO- + *mittere* send.] 1 *v.i.* Interfere, meddle. Also foll. by *with.* Now *Sc.* LME. b *Sc. Law.* Have monetary dealings; *esp.* deal with property or effects, either as administrator, agent, etc., or without legal right. Usu. foll. by *with.* E16. 2 *v.refl.* Interfere (*with* or *in* something). Now *rare.* L15. 3 *v.t.* Cause or allow to enter; put, send, or let in. Now *rare.* L16.

intromitter *n.* a person who intromits, *spec.* (*Sc. Law*) with the property of another L15.

intromittent /ɪntrə(ʊ)ˈmɪt(ə)nt/ *a.* M19. [L *intromittent-* pres. ppl stem of *intromittere*: see prec., -ENT.] Chiefly *Zool.* Having the function of intromission; usu. designating the male copulatory organ.

intron /ˈɪntrɒn/ *n.* L20. [f. INTR(AGENIC + -ON.] *Genetics.* A segment of an RNA molecule which does not code for proteins, is excised during or soon after transcription, and takes no part in forming the eventual gene product; a section of DNA which codes for this. Cf. EXON *n.*²

in'tronic *a.* L20.

intropunitive /ɪntrə(ʊ)ˈpjuːnɪtɪv/ *a.* M20. [f. INTRO- + PUNITIVE *a.*] *Psychol.* Blaming oneself rather than other people or events; of or pertaining to an unreasonable feeling of responsibility or guilt.

intropunitiveness *n.* M20.

introrse /ɪnˈtrɔːs/ *a.* M19. [L *introrsus*, f. *introversus* (turned) inwards, f. INTRO- + *versus* pa. pple of *vertere* turn.] *Bot.* & *Entomol.* (Of a part) turned or directed inwards; *spec.* (of an anther) releasing its pollen towards the centre of the flower.

introscope /ˈɪntrəskəʊp/ *n.* M20. [f. INTRO- + -SCOPE.] *Engin.* A long narrow instrument incorporating a light source and designed to permit visual examination of the interior of tubes, narrow-mouthed vessels, etc.

introspect /ɪntrə(ʊ)ˈspɛkt/ *v.* L17. [L *introspect-* pa. ppl stem of *introspicere* look into, or f. *introspectare* frequent. of this, f. INTRO- + *specere* look.] 1 *v.t.* Look into, esp. intellectually; examine in detail. Now *rare.* L17. 2 *v.i.* Examine one's own thoughts or feelings. L19.

introspectable *a.* = INTROSPECTIBLE M20. **introspectible** *a.* able to be examined by introspection E20.

introspection /ɪntrə(ʊ)ˈspɛkʃ(ə)n/ *n.* L17. [f. prec. + -ION.] Close inspection, intellectual examination, esp. of one's own mind; observation of one's own thoughts, feelings, or mental state.

G. S. HAIGHT The habit of introspection, which led to .. psychological analysis.

introspectionism *n.* (*Psychol.*) (*a*) = INTROSPECTIVE *psychology*; (*b*) = INTROSPECTION: E20. **introspectionist** *n.* a person who practises introspection, esp. as a method in psychological inquiry L19.

introspective /ɪntrə(ʊ)ˈspɛktɪv/ *a.* E19. [f. INTROSPECT or INTROSPECTION + -IVE.] Of, pertaining to, or characterized by introspection; given to introspection.

W. C. WILLIAMS A silent, introspective sort of chap. S. NAIPAUL Education .. will be .. introspective, .. coming to terms with the inner motions of mind body and soul. **introspective psychology** psychology based on the direct observation of one's own mental states.

introspectively *adv.* M19. **introspectiveness** *n.* L19.

†**introsume** *v.t.* M17–E18. [f. INTRO- + L *suere* take, as a var. of INSUME, after *assume, consume.*] Take (medicine) internally; absorb (nutriment).

introsusception /ɪntrə(ʊ)səˈsɛpʃ(ə)n/ *n.* Now *rare* or *obs.* L18. [f. INTRO- after *intussusception.*] = INTUSSUSCEPTION.

introsuscepted *a.* = INTUSSUSCEPTED M19.

introuvable /ɛ̃truvabl/ *a.* E19. [Fr., f. as IN-³ + *trouver* find + -ABLE.] Unfindable, undiscoverable.

introversible /ɪntrə(ʊ)ˈvəːsɪb(ə)l/ *a.* L19. [f. INTRO- as the opposite of EVERSIBLE.] Able to be introverted or drawn within, as the finger of a glove.

introversion /ɪntrə(ʊ)ˈvəːʃ(ə)n/ *n.* M17. [f. INTROVERT *v.* after *evert, eversion*, etc.: see -ION.] 1 a The action or an act of turning the thoughts inwards to the contemplation of one's own thoughts or feelings or of inward or spiritual things. M17. b The fact or tendency of having one's thoughts and interests directed chiefly inwards and withdrawing from the external world. Opp. EXTROVERSION 3. E20. 2 The action of physically turning inwards, esp. of drawing an outer part into the interior; the condition of being turned inwards. L18.

1a J. WESLEY The attending to the voice of Christ within you is .. Introversion. b V. BROME Jung characterized introversion as 'a hesitant, reflective, retiring nature'.

introversive *a.* characterized by or having the quality or effect of introversion E19.

introvert /ˈɪntrəvəːt/ *n.* & *a.* L19. [f. prec. Cf. CONVERT *n.*] A *n.* †1 *Zool.* A part or organ that is or can be introverted. Only in L19. 2 A person characterized by introversion; a withdrawn or reserved person. Opp. EXTROVERT *n.* E20.

2 A. S. NEILL The introvert sits in a corner and dreams of what should be.

B *adj.* Given to or characterized by introversion; introverted. Opp. EXTROVERT *a.* E20.

introvert /ɪntrə(ʊ)ˈvəːt/ *v.t.* M17. [mod.L *introvertere*, f. as INTRO- + *vertere* to turn.] 1 Turn (the mind, one's thinking, etc.) inwards upon itself; direct (one's interest or effort) to that which is internal or spiritual. M17. 2 Turn or bend inwards (physically); *esp.* in *Zool.* turn (a part or organ) inside out within its own tube or base (cf. EVERT). L18.

introvertive *a.* introversive M19.

intrude /ɪnˈtruːd/ *v.* Also (earlier) †**en-**. M16. [L *intrudere*, f. *in-* IN-² + *trudere* to thrust.] 1 *v.i.* & *refl.* †a Usurp an office, a right, etc., without legitimate title or claim. Also foll. by *on, upon.* Cf. INTRUSION I. M16–L17. b Enter forcibly or encroach, without consent, invitation, or welcome. Foll. by *into*, †*in* (a place, company, etc.), *on, upon* (a person or group, a person's privacy, etc.). L16. 2 *v.t.* Introduce (a thing) forcibly or without consent (foll. by *between, into*, †*in*). Also, force (something unwelcome) *on* or *upon* a person. M16. 3 *v.t.* †a Enter forcibly. *rare.* Only in L16. b *Geol.* Be forced or thrust into. E20.

1b Q. CRISP The telephone .. enables people to barge into our homes .. and .. they intrude upon us. I. MURDOCH If you intrude on someone's grief, you're like a spectator. M. MILNER Into such reflections intruded the image of the .. stone. 2 J. BRYCE The tendency which intruded earthly Madonnas .. between the worshipper and the .. Deity. R. BUCHANAN Prepared to intrude ministers .. at the point of the bayonet.

intruder *n.* (*a*) a person who or thing which intrudes; (*b*) *spec.* a housebreaker, a trespasser: M16. **intrudingly** *adv.* in an intruding manner E18.

intruded /ɪnˈtruːdɪd/ *a.* M16. [f. prec. + -ED¹.] 1 Brought, crowded, or thrust in, esp. forcibly or without consent. M16. 2 *Geol.* = INTRUSIVE *a.* 2b. M19.

intruse /ɪnˈtruːs/ *v.t.* & *i. obs.* exc. *Sc.* LME. [L *intrus-* pa. ppl stem of *intrudere* INTRUDE.] = INTRUDE.

intrusion /ɪnˈtruːʒ(ə)n/ *n.* LME. [(O)Fr., or med.L *intrusio(n-)*, f. L *intrus-* pa. ppl stem of *intrudere*: see INTRUDE, -ION.] 1 Orig., invasion; usurpation. Now, the action or an act of usurping a vacant estate or office without legitimate title or claim; *spec.* (*Law*) the entry of a stranger after the determination of a particular estate of freehold (as a life tenancy) before the remainder man or reversioner; also, a trespass on the lands of the crown. LME. b The settlement of a minister of the Church of Scotland without the consent of the congregation. E18. 2 The action or an act of entering forcibly or without invitation or welcome, or of introducing something inappropriately; uninvited or unwelcome entrance or appearance; encroachment on a person's property or rights. L16. 3 The action or an act of introducing or forcing a thing in; the fact of being so introduced. Also, something thrust in, a forcible or unwelcome addition. M17. b *spec.* in *Geol.* The influx of (molten) rock into fissures or between strata; a portion of intruded rock. M19.

2 N. GORDIMER There was an intrusion The telephone rang. D. PRATER The intrusion of visitors who arrived with letters of introduction. D. WIGODER I resented the intrusion into my private world. 3 A. G. GARDINER Word-magic belongs to poetry. In prose it is an intrusion. E. O'BRIEN Whether his presence was welcome or an intrusion. b F. HOYLE Ailsa Craig, a small intrusion of granite in the Firth of Clyde.

intrusive /ɪnˈtruːsɪv/ *a.* & *n.* M17. [f. L *intrus-* (see prec.) + -IVE.] A *adj.* 1 Characterized by intruding; done or carried out with intrusion. M17. 2 That has been introduced or thrust in. M19. b *Geol.* Of an igneous rock: forced, while molten, into fissures or between strata of other rocks. M19.

1 R. ELLMANN The biographer is necessarily intrusive, a trespasser. V. GLENDINNING There had been some upsettingly intrusive interviews. **intrusive growth** the growth of some plant cells by intrusion between others (opp. *symplastic growth*). 2 **intrusive r** an *r* pronounced in hiatus, as in the phr. *the idea(r) of*. b *Naturalist* Intrusive igneous rocks in sills and dykes.

B *n. Geol.* An intrusive rock or rock mass. L19.

intrusively *adv.* M19. **intrusiveness** *n.* M19.

intrust *v.* var. of ENTRUST.

intubate /ˈɪntjʊbeɪt/ *v.t.* E17. [f. IN-[2] + L *tuba* tube + -ATE[3].] †1 Form into tubes. Only in E17. 2 *Med.* Insert a tube into an aperture of the body of (a patient), subject to intubation. L19.

intubation /ɪntjʊˈbeɪʃ(ə)n/ *n.* L19. [f. prec. + -ATION.] Chiefly *Med.* The insertion of a tube into (a part of) the body, esp. the trachea or oesophagus, for the purpose of diagnosis, treatment, force-feeding, etc.

intue /ɪnˈtjuː/ *v.t. rare.* M19. [L *intueri*: see INTUITION.] Know or perceive by intuition; intuit.

intuent /ˈɪntjʊənt/ *a. rare.* M19. [L *intuent-* pres. ppl stem of *intueri*: see INTUITION, -ENT.] That knows by intuition.

intuit /ɪnˈtjuːɪt/ *v.* L18. [L *intuit-*: see next.] †1 *v.t.* Tutor, instruct. *rare.* Only in L18. 2a *v.i.* Receive or assimilate knowledge by direct perception. M19. b *v.t.* Know immediately without reasoning; know by intuition. M19.

2b *Notes & Queries* Objects can be intuited as existing without us. D. MELTZER We intuit rather than observe the emotional atmosphere in the consulting room.

intuitable *a.* L19. **intuiter** *n.* L19.

intuition /ɪntjʊˈɪʃ(ə)n/ *n.* LME. [Late L *intuitio(n-)*, f. L *intuit-* pa. ppl stem of *intueri* look upon, consider, contemplate, f. as IN-[2] + *tueri* look: see -ION. Cf. Fr. *intuition.*] 1 *Scholastic Philos.* Spiritual insight or perception; instantaneous spiritual communication. LME. †2 The action of looking at or into; an inspection, a look. L15–M17. 3 Immediate apprehension by the mind without the intervention of reasoning, direct or immediate insight; an instance of this. Also, the faculty of apprehending in this way. L16. b *Philos.* Immediate apprehension by the intellect alone; an instance of this. M17. c *Kantian Philos.* Immediate apprehension by a sense or senses; an instance of this. L18. †4 The action of mentally examining; contemplation, consideration; perception, recognition. E17–M18. †5 Purpose, intention; reference, respect. E17–E18.

1 ADDISON Our Superiors are guided by Intuition, and our Inferiors by Instinct. 3 P. BOWLES Her intuition generally let her know when Port was up to something. D. BAGLEY Wyatt didn't have any real facts—merely vague intuitions. A. GRAY A flash of intuition separate from logic or evidence made him sure this man was the thief. b J. S. MILL The truths known by intuition are the original premises from which all others are inferred.

intuitional /ɪntjʊˈɪʃ(ə)n(ə)l/ *a.* M19. [f. prec. + -AL[1].] 1 Of, pertaining to, or derived from intuition; of the nature of intuition. M19. 2 Of or pertaining to a theory or philosophical school which holds that certain elements of knowledge are perceived directly by the intellect alone. M19. 3 Having intuition. L19.

intuitionally *adv.* by intuition, intuitively L19.

intuitionalism /ɪntjʊˈɪʃ(ə)n(ə)lɪz(ə)m/ *n. rare.* M19. [f. prec. + -ISM.] *Philos.* The doctrine or theory of the intuitional school; = INTUITIONISM 1, 2.

intuitionalist *n.* = INTUITIONIST M19.

intuitionism /ɪntjʊˈɪʃ(ə)nɪz(ə)m/ *n.* M19. [f. INTUITION + -ISM.] 1 *Philos.* The doctrine that in perception external objects are known immediately by intuition. M19. 2 *Philos.* The doctrine that certain basic truths are perceived directly by intuition. Now also, any ethical theory that is founded in intuition. L19. 3 *Math.* The theory that mathematics is founded on extralinguistic constructs based on pure intuition, and in particular that the law of the excluded middle might not be valid for infinite classes. E20.

intuitionist /ɪntjʊˈɪʃ(ə)nɪst/ *n.* & *a.* M19. [f. as prec. + -IST.] *Philos.* A *n.* A person who holds a theory of intuitionism. M19. B *adj.* Of or pertaining to a theory or school of intuitionism. L19.

intuitioˈnistic *a.* holding a theory of intuitionism L19. **intuitioˈnistically** *adv.* M20.

intuitive /ɪnˈtjuːɪtɪv/ *a.* & *n.* L15. [med.L *intuitivus*, f. *intuit-*: see INTUITION, -IVE. Cf. Fr. *intuitif, -ive.*] A *adj.* †1 (Of sight or vision) clear, accurate, unerring; (of spiritual perception) instant, all-encompassing. L15–M17. 2a Of a faculty or gift: innate, not acquired by learning. E17. b Of knowledge or mental perception: known or apprehended immediately and fully without reasoning. M17. 3 Of the mind or a mental process: acting or comprehending immediately and without reasoning, operating through intuition. Opp. *discursive.* M17. 4 Of a person: possessing intuition. M17. 5 *Philos.* Of or pertaining to the theory or school which holds that certain basic truths are apprehended by intuition; intuitionist. M19.

2b J. GATHORNE-HARDY Diagnosis is intuitive sometimes. You simply know. 3 J. ROSENBERG A contrast between the intellectual approach of the great French artist and Rembrandt's more intuitive one. *Atlantic Monthly* People perceive themselves to be immune and . . possessed of an intuitive power . . to choose safe partners. 5 B. RUSSELL Our immediate knowledge of truths may be called intuitive knowledge.

B *n.* A person who works by intuition. E20.

intuitively *adv.* L16. **intuitiveness** *n.* M19.

intuitivism /ɪnˈtjuːɪtɪvɪz(ə)m/ *n.* M19. [f. prec. + -ISM.] 1 The doctrine that certain basic truths can be established by intuition. M19. 2 The faculty of intuition; insight. L19.

intuitivist /ɪnˈtjuːɪtɪvɪst/ *a.* M19. [f. as prec. + -IST.] Of or pertaining to the theory or school of intuitivism.

intumesce /ɪntjʊˈmɛs/ *v.i.* L18. [f. L *intumescere* swell up, f. as IN-[2] + *tumescere* inceptive of *tumere* be swollen: see -ESCE.] Swell up, bubble up.

intumescence /ɪntjʊˈmɛs(ə)ns/ *n.* M17. [Fr., f. L *intumescere*: see prec., -ENCE.] 1 The process of swelling up. M17. 2 The bubbling up of a fluid or molten mass. M17. 3 *Med.* & *Bot.* A swelling of any part of the body or of a plant. E19.

intumescent /ɪntjʊˈmɛs(ə)nt/ *a.* L19. [f. INTUMESCE, INTUMESCENCE + -ENT.] Swelling up; bubbling, foaming.

†**interbidate** *v.t. rare.* L17–M19. [f. IN-[2] + TURBID + -ATE[3].] Make turbid, cloud; disturb, confuse.

inturn /ˈɪntəːn/ *n.* L16. [f. IN *adv.* + TURN *n.*] 1 An inward turn or curve; *spec.* a turning in of the toes. L16. †2 *Wrestling.* The act of putting a leg between the thighs of an opponent and lifting him up. Only in 17. 3 *Curling.* An inward turn of the elbow and an outward turn of the hand made in delivering a stone. L19.

inturned *ppl a.* turned inward M19. **inturning** *vbl n.* a turning in LME.

†**intuse** *n. rare* (Spenser). Only in L16. [L *intusum* use as n. of neut. pa. pple of *intundere* bruise.] A bruise.

intussusception /ɪntəsəˈsɛpʃ(ə)n/ *n.* E18. [Fr., or mod.L *intussusceptio(n-)*, f. L *intus* within + *susceptio(n-)* SUSCEPTION. In sense 1 formed on SUSCEPTION.] 1 Absorption, taking in. E18. 2 *Biol.* Growth by the intercalation or insertion of new material into an existing structure. M18. 3a *Med.* The inversion or telescoping of one portion of intestine within the next; an instance of this. Also, the mass of intestine involved in this. E19. b An insertion in the manner of intestinal intussusception. E19.

intussuscepted *a.* having undergone intussusception E19. **intussusceptum** /ɪntəsəˈsɛptəm/ *n.* [mod.L, neut. pa. pple of *intussuscipere* take within] *Med.* the inner, enveloped portion of intestine in an intussusception M19. **intussuscipiens** /ɪntəsəˈsɪpɪɛnz/ *n.* [mod.L, pres. pple of *intussuscipere* take within] *Med.* the outermost portion of intestine in an intussusception M19.

†**intwine** *v.* var. of ENTWINE *v.*

intwist *v.* var. of ENTWIST.

Inuit /ˈɪnjʊɪt, ˈɪnʊɪt/ *n.* & *a.* Also **Innuit**. M18. [Eskimo (Inuit), pl. of *inuk* person. Cf. next.] A *n.* Pl. same, -s. A Canadian Eskimo. Also, the language of the Canadian Eskimos. M18. B *adj.* Of or pertaining to the Canadian Eskimos or their language. M19.

Inuk /ˈɪnʊk/ *n.* & *a.* E19. [Eskimo (Inuit), lit. 'person'. Cf. prec.] A *n.* Pl. same, -s. An Eskimo of Canada or Greenland. Also, the language of such Eskimos. E19. B *adj.* Of or pertaining to the Inuk or their language. M20.

Inuktitut /ɪˈnʊktɪtʊt/ *n.* & *a.* Also **-tituk** /-tɪtʊk/. L20. [Eskimo (Inuit), lit. 'the Eskimo way', title of a periodical.] In Canada: (of) the language of the Inuit.

inula /ˈɪnjʊlə/ *n.* E19. [L: see ELECAMPANE.] Any of various showy yellow-rayed composite plants of the genus *Inula*; *esp.* elecampane, *I. helenium*.

inulase /ˈɪnjʊleɪz/ *n.* L19. [f. INUL(IN + -ASE.] *Biochem.* An enzyme which hydrolyses inulin to fructose, found esp. in some fungi.

inulin /ˈɪnjʊlɪn/ *n.* E19. [f. as INULA + -IN[1].] *Chem.* A fructan present in the roots of various composite plants.

†**inumbrate** *v.t.* LME–E19. [L *inumbrat-* pa. ppl stem of *inumbrare*, f. as IN-[2] + *umbra* shade, shadow: see -ATE[3].] Cast a shadow on; shade; overshadow.

inunct /ɪˈnʌŋkt/ *v.t. rare.* E16. [L *inunct-* pa. ppl stem of *inunguere*, f. as IN-[2] + *unguere* smear, anoint.] Apply ointment to, smear.

inunction /ɪˈnʌŋ(k)ʃ(ə)n/ *n.* L15. [L *inunctio(n-)*, f. as prec.: see -ION.] †1 The anointing with oil in consecration and other religious rites. Cf. UNCTION. L15–L17. 2 The action or an act of anointing or rubbing in oil or ointment. E17.

inundant /ɪˈnʌnd(ə)nt/ *a.* E17. [L *inundant-* pres. ppl stem of *inundare*: see INUNDATE, -ANT[1].] Overflowing, inundating, flooding.

inundatal /ˈɪnʌndeɪt(ə)l/ *a.* Now *rare.* M19. [Irreg. f. next + -AL[1].] *Ecol.* Of a plant: growing in areas subject to flooding.

inundate /ˈɪnʌndeɪt/ *v.t.* L16. [L *inundat-* pa. ppl stem of *inundare*, f. as IN-[2] + *undare* flow: see -ATE[3].] 1 Flood, submerge, cover with water etc. L16. 2 *transf.* & *fig.* Overwhelm, cover, provide *with* in abundance. E17.

1 J. BARNES Rain fell heavily; the plain they were crossing became inundated. 2 G. WASHINGTON I was inundated with letters.

inundation /ɪnʌnˈdeɪʃ(ə)n/ *n.* LME. [OFr. *inondacion* (mod. *-tion*) or L *inundatio(n-)*, f. as prec.: see -ATION.] 1 The action of inundating; the fact of being inundated; a flood. LME. 2 *transf.* & *fig.* Overwhelming abundance; an overflowing, a superabundance, an invasion. M16.

1 S. HAUGHTON Rich plains . . fertilized by their periodic inundations. 2 A. TOFFLER In every conceivable field . . we face an inundation of innovation.

Inupiaq /ɪˈnuːpɪak/ *n.* & *a.* Also **Inupik** /ɪˈnuːpɪk/. M20. [Eskimo (Inuit), f. *inuk* person + *piaq* genuine.] (Of) the Eskimo-Aleut language spoken in Alaska, Canada, and Greenland. Cf. YUPIK.

Inupiat /ɪˈnuːpɪat/ *n.* & *a.* L20. [Eskimo (Inuit) pl., f. as prec.] A *n.* Pl. same, -s. A member of an Eskimo people of Alaska. L20. B *adj.* Of or pertaining to the Inupiat. L20.

Inupik *n.* & *a.* see INUPIAQ.

inurbane /ɪnəːˈbeɪn/ *a.* E17. [L *inurbanus*, f. as IN-[3] + *urbanus* URBANE.] Uncouth, unpolished; *esp.* uncivil, rude.
inurbanely *adv.* E17.

inurbanity /ɪnəːˈbanɪti/ *n.* L16. [Fr. *inurbanité* or med.L *inurbanitas*, f. IN-[3] + L *urbanitas* URBANITY.] Lack of urbanity; uncouthness; *esp.* rudeness, impoliteness.

inure /ɪˈnjʊə/ *v.*[1] Also **enure** /ɛˈnjʊə, ɪˈnjʊə/. LME. [AN, f. phr. meaning 'in use, in practice'; cf. IN-[2], EN-[1], URE *n.*[1]] 1 *v.t.* Accustom or habituate *to*, harden or render impervious *to*. LME. †2 *v.t.* Put into effect or operation, practise, perform. L15–L16. 3 *v.i.* Chiefly *Law*. Take effect, come into operation; accrue. L16.
1 R. MAY We have become .. inured to living in a state of quasi-anxiety. R. MCALMON We .. must inure ourselves to the sight of grim reality. M. FORSTER The hospital staff were sad, inured though they were to such tragedies. 3 GLADSTONE A relation .. that might virtually inure by usage only. *National Observer (US)* Showing that the public at large derives benefits approaching those that inure directly to mail users.
inurement *n.* the action of inuring; the state of being inured: L16.

†**inure** *v.*[2]*t.* L16. [L *inurere* burn in, f. as IN-[2] + *urere* burn.] 1 Brand in, impress by burning. L16–L17. 2 Burn in a flame. Only in E18.

inurn /ɪˈnəːn/ *v.t.* Also **enurn** /ɪˈnəːn, ɛˈnəːn/. E17. [f. IN-[2], EN-[1] + URN *n.* & *v.*[1]] Put (ashes) in an urn after cremation; bury, inter.
inurnment *n.* M20.

inusitate /ɪˈnjuːzɪteɪt/ *a.* Now *rare*. M16. [L *inusitatus*, f. as IN-[3] + *usitatus* pa. pple of *usitari* use often: see -ATE[2].] Unusual, little-used, out of use.
inusitateness *n.* (*rare*) L19. **inusiˈtation** *n.* (*rare*) E19.

†**inustion** *n.* E17. [Late L *inustio(n-)* branding, f. *inust-* pa. ppl stem of *inurere* INURE *v.*[2]: see -ION.] 1 Burning. Only in E17. 2 Burning in, branding. Only in M17. 3 Cauterization. L17–E19.

in utero /ɪn ˈjuːtərəʊ/ *adv.* & *a. phr.* E18. [L.] In the womb; before birth.

inutile /ɪnˈjuːtɪl/ *a.* LME. [(O)Fr., f. L *inutilis*, f. as IN-[3] + *utilis* useful. Cf. UTILE *a.*] Useless, pointless, unprofitable.

inutility /ɪnjuːˈtɪlɪti/ *n.* L16. [Fr. *inutilité* f. L *inutilitas*, f. as IN-[3] + *utilitas*: see prec., -ITY.] 1 Uselessness, pointlessness, unprofitableness. L16. 2 An instance of uselessness; a useless thing or person. E19.

inutterable /ɪnˈʌt(ə)rəb(ə)l/ *a.* Now *rare*. E17. [f. IN-[3] + UTTERABLE.] That cannot be uttered; unutterable.

invaccinate /ɪnˈvaksɪneɪt/ *v.t. rare*. L19. [f. IN-[2] + VACCINATE.] Introduce into the system by vaccination.
invacciˈnation *n.* L19.

in vacuo /ɪn ˈvakjʊəʊ/ *adv. phr.* M17. [L.] In a vacuum.

invade /ɪnˈveɪd/ *v.* LME. [L *invadere*, f. *in-* IN-[2] + *vadere* go.] 1 *v.t.* Attack, assault (a person, a group, etc.). *obs.* exc. *dial.* LME. 2 *v.t.* & *i.* Enter or make an incursion into (a place, a country, etc.), esp. in a hostile manner, in large numbers, or with armed force; attack; *Med.* & *Ecol.* spread into. Also foll. by *into*, *on*, *upon*. L15. 3 *v.t.* Intrude on, infringe, or violate (property, rights, liberties, etc.). E16. †b Usurp, take possession of. E17–E18.
2 S. CHITTY On 23 August 1914 the Germans invaded. *British Medical Journal* These tumours .. may directly invade into the mandible. *transf.*: C. PHILLIPS It disturbed him that these memories should invade his mind. 3 W. TREVOR She had invaded his greatest privacy.
invadable *a.* M18. **invader** *n.* E16.

invaginate /ɪnˈvadʒɪneɪt/ *v.* M17. [f. INVAGINATION: see -ATE[3].] 1 *v.t.* Put in a sheath. Long *rare*. M17. 2 *v.t. Anat.* & *Med.* Turn or double (a tubular sheath) back within itself. M19. 3 *v.i.* Become invaginated. L19.

invaginated /ɪnˈvadʒɪneɪtɪd/ *ppl a.* M19. [f. prec. + -ED[1].] Orig., inserted or received into a sheath or opening; *esp.* intussuscepted. Now usu., having undergone invagination, folded or pushed inwards to form a hollow.

invagination /ɪnˌvadʒɪˈneɪʃ(ə)n/ *n.* M17. [mod.L *invaginatio(n-)*, f. as IN-[2] + VAGINA: see -ATION.] Orig., the action of sheathing something; *esp.* intussusception. Now usu., the folding in of a surface or membrane to form a hollow cavity or pouch; the cavity so formed.

invalid /ɪnˈvalɪd/ *a.*[1] M16. [L *invalidus*, f. IN-[3] + *validus* VALID. See also next.] 1 Having no force, efficacy, or cogency, esp. in law; void. M16. †2 Without power or strength; weak, feeble. M17–E19.
1 R. GRAVES He declared the wills technically invalid because of some legal flaw.
invalidly *adv.* so as to be invalid, without validity *adv.* E18. **invalidness** *n.* M17.

invalid /ˈɪnvəliːd, -ɪd/ *a.*[2] & *n.* M17. [Use of prec.] A *adj.* Infirm or disabled from sickness, disease, or injury. M17.
J. BARNES His invalid son, who had just suffered his first attack of epilepsy.
B *n.* 1 An infirm or sickly person. E18. 2 A person, esp. a member of the armed forces, disabled by illness or injury. E18.
1 J. WAIN My wife's a hopeless invalid, completely bedridden. *invalid car, chair, diet, table*, etc.
invalidish *a.* E19. **invalidism** *n.* the state or condition of being an invalid; chronic infirmity or ill health that prevents activity: L18. **invalidy** *a.* (*colloq.*, *rare*) L19.

invalid /ɪnˈvalɪd/ *v.*[1]*t.* Now *rare*. M17. [f. INVALID *a.*[1]: cf. INVALIDATE.] Make invalid; invalidate.

invalid /ˈɪnvəliːd, -ɪd/ *v.*[2] L18. [f. INVALID *a.*[2]] 1 *v.t.* Treat as an invalid; remove or discharge from employment or active service on account of illness or injury. L18. 2 *v.t.* Make an invalid; disable by illness or injury. Usu. in *pass.* E19. 3 *v.i.* Become an invalid, become unfit for active work through illness. E19.
1 M. SCAMMELL Wounded in the lung and .. invalided out of the army with TB. 2 H. CARPENTER His mother, invalided for many years with tuberculosis, died when he was eight.

invalidate /ɪnˈvalɪdeɪt/ *v.t.* M17. [med.L *invalidat-* pa. ppl stem of *invalidare* invalidate, annul, f. as INVALID *a.*[1]: see -ATE[3]. Perh. partly after Fr. *invalider*.] Make (an argument, contract, etc.) invalid; *esp.* deprive of legal efficacy.
J. BERMAN Freud's neurotic symptoms do not invalidate his psychological theories.
invaliˈdation *n.* L18.

invalidity /ɪnvəˈlɪdɪti/ *n.* M16. [Fr. *invalidité* or med.L *invaliditas*, f. as INVALID *a.*[1]: see -ITY. In sense 3 partly f. INVALID *a.*[2]] 1 The quality of being (esp. legally) invalid. M16. †2 Weakness, incapacity. L16–L17. 3 The condition of being an invalid; bodily infirmity. L17.
1 F. MYERS Suspicion of the invalidity of the evidence. 3 *invalidity allowance, benefit, pension*, etc.

invaluable /ɪnˈvaljʊ(ə)b(ə)l/ *a.* L16. [f. IN-[3] + VALUABLE.] 1 Above and beyond valuation; of surpassing or transcendent worth or merit, priceless; inestimable. L16. 2 Without value. M17.
1 A. TREW As Vrakoy's only .. teleprinter operator, she was .. an invaluable source of information.
invaluableness *n.* M17. **invaluably** *adv.* E17.

†**invalued** *a. rare. poet.* E17–E19. [f. IN-[3] + VALUED.] Of which the value has not been reckoned; invaluable.

Invar /ˈɪnvɑː/ *n.* E20. [Abbrev. of INVARIABLE.] (Proprietary name for) an alloy of iron or steel (*c*64 per cent) and nickel (*c*36 per cent), which has a very small coefficient of expansion.

invariable /ɪnˈvɛːrɪəb(ə)l/ *a.* & *n.* LME. [(O)Fr., or late L *invariabilis*, f. IN-[3] + *variabilis* VARIABLE *a.*] A *adj.* 1 Unchangeable, unalterable; unchanging, constant; unvarying. LME. 2 *Math.* (Of a quantity) constant; (of a point, line, etc.) fixed. E18.
1 J. GALSWORTHY She had asked Phil to dinner many times; his invariable answer had been 'Too busy'.
B *n. Math.* An invariable quantity, a constant. M19.
invariaˈbility *n.* M17. **invariableness** *n.* M17. **invariably** *adv.* without change; without exception: M17.

invariance /ɪnˈvɛːrɪəns/ *n.* L19. [f. next: see -ANCE.] 1 *Math.* The character of remaining unaltered after an operation or (esp. linear) transformation. (Foll. by *under*.) L19. 2 *gen.* The property of remaining unaltered or of being the same in different circumstances; an instance of this, an invariant. M20.
Also **invariancy** *n.* L19.

invariant /ɪnˈvɛːrɪənt/ *n.* & *a.* M19. [f. IN-[3] + VARIANT.] A *n.* 1 *Math.* a A function of the coefficients in an expression such that, if that expression is linearly transformed, the same function of the new coefficients is equal to the first function multiplied by some power of a constant pertaining to the transformation. M19. b Any quantity or expression which is invariant under a specified transformation or operation. E20. 2 *gen.* An invariant property or feature. M20. B *attrib.* or as *adj.* 1 Unvarying, invariable. L19. 2 *Physical Chem.* Having no degrees of freedom. L19. 3 *Math.* & *Physics*. Unchanged by a specified transformation or operation. (Foll. by *under*.) E20.

invaried /ɪnˈvɛːrɪd/ *a. rare*. L17. [f. IN-[3] + VARIED.] Not varied; unvaried.

invasion /ɪnˈveɪʒ(ə)n/ *n.* LME. [(O)Fr., or late L *invasio(n-)*, f. L *invas-* pa. ppl stem of *invadere*: see INVADE, -ION.] 1 a The action of invading a country or territory, esp. with armed force; a hostile incursion. LME. b *fig.* A harmful incursion of any kind, e.g. of the sea, disease, moral evil, etc. E16. c *Med.* The spreading of pathogenic micro-organisms or malignant cells that are already in the body to new sites. L19. †2 An assault or attack on a person, a building, etc. LME–M18. 3 Intrusion; encroachment upon a person's property, rights, privacy, etc. LME. 4 *Ecol.* The spread of a plant or animal population into an area formerly free of that species. E20.
1a J. M. ROBERTS A whole world .. going under in a chaos of barbarian invasions. 3 D. C. PEATTIE Being spanked by a parent never struck me as an invasion of the soul's dignity.
invasionist *n.* a person who advocates or believes in an invasion M19.

invasive /ɪnˈveɪsɪv/ *a.* LME. [Fr. †*invasif*, -*ive* or med.L *invasivus*, f. L *invas-*: see prec., -IVE.] 1 Of, pertaining to, or of the nature of invasion or attack; offensive. LME. 2 Characterized by invasion; invading. L16. b *Med.* Of, exhibiting, or characterized by invasiveness. E20. c *Med.* Of a diagnostic procedure: involving the entry of an instrument into the body. L20. 3 Tending to intrude upon the domain or rights of another. L17.
1 A. FORBES What course of invasive action did it behove Lord Chelmsford to pursue? 2 C. TOMALIN She sensed the evident hostility many .. felt for the invasive white people. 3 H. J. S. MAINE A proceeding invasive of tribal rights and calculated to enfeeble them.
invasiveness *n.* (*Med.*) the ability of pathogenic micro-organisms or malignant cells that are already in the body to spread to new sites M20.

invecked /ɪnˈvɛkt/ *a.* Now *rare*. L15. [Anglicized f. L *invect-*: see INVECTIVE.] Chiefly *Her.* Bordered by or (of an edge) consisting of a series of small convex lobes; scalloped.

†**invect** *v.* M16. [f. L *invect-*: see INVECTIVE.] 1 *v.t.* Bring in, import, introduce. Only in M16. 2 *v.i.* Inveigh, utter invectives. Only in E17.

invected /ɪnˈvɛktɪd/ *a.* M17. [f. as prec. + -ED[1].] †1 Brought in, introduced. Only in M17. 2 *Her.* = INVECKED. M17.

invective /ɪnˈvɛktɪv/ *a.* & *n.* LME. [(O)Fr. *invectif*, -*ive* adj., *invective* n., f. late L *invectivus*, as n. *invectiva (oratio)*, f. *invect-* pa. ppl stem of *invehere*: see next, -IVE.] A *adj.* Using or characterized by denunciatory language; vituperative, abusive. Now *rare*. LME.
Weekend Magazine (Montreal) He became invective, insisted he be served a coffee.
B *n.* 1 A violent verbal attack or denunciation. E16. 2 Denunciatory or opprobrious language; vehement denunciation; vituperation. L16.

1 C. HOPE The .. tirade of Father Lynch's invective as he briskly cursed the scrambling altar boys. 2 V. BROME His invective against his enemies included phrases like 'slimy bastard'.

invectively *adv.* (now *rare*) M16. **invectiveness** *n.* (*rare*) M17.

inveigh /ɪnˈveɪ/ *v.* Also †**en-**. L15. [L *invehere* carry in, mediopassive *invehi* be borne into, attack, assail with words, f. *in-* IN-[2] + *vehere* carry.] †**1** *v.t.* Orig., carry in, introduce (*rare*). Later, entice, inveigle. L15–L17. **2** *v.i.* Speak in order to denounce, reproach, or censure; speak vehemently. Foll. by *against*, †*upon*. E16.

2 R. OWEN In language which recalled Stalinist socialist realism he inveighed against 'alien' Western influences.

inveigher *n.* (*rare*) L16.

inveigle /ɪnˈviːg(ə)l, ɪnˈveɪg(ə)l/ *v.t.* Also †**en-**. L15. [AN *envegler* alt. (cf. ENSAMPLE *n.*) of (O)Fr. *aveugler* to blind, f. *aveugle* blind, prob. f. Proto-Romance Cf. VEIGLE.] †**1** Beguile, deceive. L15–E18. **2a** Win over or captivate by deceitful allurement; entice, seduce. M16. †**b** Entrap, ensnare, entangle. M16–E18. **c** Guilefully draw (a person), *into, to, from*, etc., an action, conduct, a place, etc. M16.

2a J. L. MOTLEY An organized system of harlotry, by which the soldiers and politicians of France were inveigled. 2 R. HAYMAN He blamed his son for inveigling him into the investment.

inveiglement *n.* M16. **inveigler** *n.* M16.

†**inveil** *v.* var. of ENVEIL.

invein /ɪnˈveɪn/ *v.t. rare.* Also (earlier) †**en-**. E16. [f. IN-[2] (EN-[1]) + VEIN *v.*] Streak or diversify with or as with veins.

†**invelop** *v.* var. of ENVELOP.

†**invenom** *v.* var. of ENVENOM.

invent /ɪnˈvɛnt/ *v.t.* L15. [L *invent-* pa. ppl stem of *invenire* come upon, discover, f. *in-* IN-[2] + *venire* come.] **1** Find out, discover, esp. by search or endeavour. Now *rare* or *obs.* L15. **2**†**a** Devise, contrive; plan, plot. Also w. inf. M16–E19. **b** Devise as an untruth (a statement or story, or an element of one). M16. †**c** Devise (a subject, idea, or method of treatment for a work of art or literature) by means of the intellect or imagination. L16–L17. **3** Create, produce, or construct by original thought or ingenuity; devise or originate (a new art, instrument, process, etc.). Formerly also w. inf. M16. †**4** Found, establish, institute, appoint. M16–L17.

2b J. VAN DRUTEN She's an imaginary character I invented. 3 H. L. MENCKEN There was no .. progress in the cure of disease until man began inventing remedies.

inventable, **inventible** *adjs.* M17. **inventor** *n.* E16. **inventress** *n.* E16. **inventrix** *n.* (long *rare*) E17.

inventar /ˈɪnvɪntə/ *n.* & *v. obs.* exc. *Sc.* As n. also **-er**. LME. [OFr. *inventaire* f. late L *inventarium*: see INVENTORY.] **A** *n.* = INVENTORY *n.* LME. **B** *v.t.* Make an inventory of, catalogue. M17.

†**inventary** *n.* & *v.* var. of INVENTORY.

†**inventer** *n.*[1] M16–E19. [f. INVENT + -ER[1].] An inventor.

inventer *n.*[2] var. of INVENTAR *n.*

invention /ɪnˈvɛnʃ(ə)n/ *n.* ME. [L *inventio(n-)*, f. as INVENT: see -ION.] **I 1** An act or the action of finding out; discovery. *arch.* ME. **b** *Rhet.* The selecting of topics to be treated, or of arguments to be used. LME. †**c** The solving of a problem. L15–M17. **2** The faculty of inventing or devising; creativity, inventiveness. L15. **3** An act or the action of devising, contriving, or fabricating something. L15. **b** The devising of a subject, idea, or method of treatment for a work of art or literature, by means of the intellect or imagination. L15. †**4** The manner in which a thing is devised or constructed; design. E16–E18. **5** The contrivance or production of a new art, instrument, process, etc.; origination, introduction. M16.

2 W. H. PRESCOTT His invention was ever busy devising intrigues. 3 R. W. SOUTHERN Inventions of new words are important historical events. b J. BRODSKY Neither in invention nor in .. world view does .. Russian prose of today offer anything .. new. 5 P. GOODMAN The essence of invention is to be hitherto-unthought-of.

II 6 Something devised; a contrivance, a design, a plan. Formerly also, a discovery. LME. **b** A fictitious statement or story; a fabrication. E16. †**7** A work of art or literature as produced by means of the intellect or imagination. L15–E17. **8** A new art, instrument, process, etc., originated by the ingenuity of some person. L15.

6b T. S. ELIOT The aunt was a pure invention On the spur of the moment. 8 M. MEAD It is no longer possible .. to keep inventions like gunpowder to use in firecrackers.

Phrases: **Invention of the Cross** (a festival held on 3 May commemorating) the reputed finding of the Cross by Helena, mother of the Emperor Constantine, in AD 326.

inventive /ɪnˈvɛntɪv/ *a.* LME. [Fr. *inventif*, *-ive* or med.L *inventivus*, f. as INVENT: see -IVE.] **1** Having the faculty of invention; original, apt, or quick in contriving or devising. Also foll. by *of*. LME. **2** Characterized by invention; produced by or showing original contrivance. E17.

1 G. GREENE He had been too inventive; he had to draw the line .. between what was real .. and unreal. 2 J. RUSKIN Great art .. must be inventive, that is, be produced by the imagination.

inventively *adv.* M19. **inventiveness** *n.* M17.

inventory /ˈɪnv(ə)nt(ə)ri/ *n.* & *v.* Also †**-ary**, (*rare*) †**invitory**. LME. [med.L *inventorium* alt. of late L *inventarium* lit. 'a list of what is found', f. as INVENT: see -ORY[1]. Cf. INVENTAR.] **A** *n.* **1** A detailed list of items such as goods in stock, a person's property, the contents of a storage box, room, building, etc., occas. with a statement giving the nature and value of each item. LME. **2** *gen.* A list, a catalogue; a detailed account. E16. **b** *spec.* (*Ling.*) A list of a specified type of linguistic features in a language. M20. **3** *transf.* The quantity or stock of goods etc. which are or may be made the subject of an inventory. L17.

1 S. BELLOW She .. made an inventory of all the objects on the desk. E. HARDWICK Alex was making an inventory of Sarah's Philadelphia house. 2 J. G. BALLARD Scanning the timber store, making an inventory of its possibilities. 3 *High Times* Buying out local inventories endlessly, because the shelves could .. be restocked by smugglers.

B *v.t.* & (*rare*) *i.* Make an inventory or descriptive list of goods, a person's characteristics, etc.; enter in an inventory, catalogue; amount (to) in an inventory. E16.

G. H. LORIMER She inventoried about $10,000 as she stood. D. L. SAYERS He had the air of inventorying its contents with a view to assessing their value.

invenˈtorial *a.* L20. **invenˈtorially** *adv.* (*rare*, Shakes.): only in 17. **inˈventorize** *v.t.* & *i.* make an inventory (of) E17.

inveracious /ɪnvəˈreɪʃəs/ *a.* L19. [f. IN-[3] + VERACIOUS.] Untruthful, untrue.

inveracity /ɪnvəˈrasɪti/ *n.* M19. [f. IN-[3] + VERACITY.] Untruthfulness; an untruth, a false statement.

inverecund /ɪnˈvɛrɪkʌnd/ *a. rare.* M17. [L *inverecundus* shameless, f. as IN-[3] + *verecundus* reverent, modest, f. *vereri* revere.] Unabashed, shameless.

inverisimilitude /ɪn,vɛrɪsɪˈmɪlɪtjuːd/ *n.* E19. [f. IN-[3] + VERISIMILITUDE.] Lack of verisimilitude; unlikelihood; improbability.

invermination /ɪn,vəːmɪˈneɪʃ(ə)n/ *n.* E19. [f. IN-[2] + VERMINATION.] The condition of being infested with (intestinal) worms or other vermin.

Inverness /ɪnvəˈnɛs/ *n.* M19. [A town in the Highland region of Scotland.] **1** *Inverness cape*, the cape from an Inverness cloak. M19. **2** *Inverness cloak*, *(over)coat*, a man's sleeveless cloak with a removable cape. L19.

inverse /ˈɪnvəːs, ɪnˈvəːs/ *a.* & *n.* LME. [f. L *inversus* pa. pple of *invertere* INVERT *v.*] **A** *adj.* **1** Turned upside down; inverted. LME. **2** *Math.* **a** Of two operations, relations, etc.: such that the starting-point or antecedent of the one is the result or conclusion of the other, and vice versa; (of one such operation, relation, etc.) opposite in nature or effect (to the other). Opp. *direct*. M17. **b** *Geom.* Of a point, line, curve, etc.: related to another point, line, curve, etc. by a geometrical inversion. L19. **3** Inverted in position, order, or relations; proceeding in the opposite or reverse direction or order. M19. **4** *Cryst.* Having the reverse of some usual relation. Now only *spec.* (of a spinel structure) having half the trivalent cations in the tetrahedral holes normally occupied by the divalent cations. L19.

1 T. HOOD A tower builded on a lake, Mock'd by its inverse shadow. 3 B. MAGEE Such fascinated detestation is a kind of inverse love.

Special collocations: **inverse proportion** = *inverse ratio* (b) below. **inverse ratio** (*a*) a ratio in which the terms are reversed with respect to a given ratio; (*b*) the relationship of two quantities, one of which increases (esp. in exact proportion) as the other decreases, and vice versa. **inverse spelling** an unetymological spelling based on the spelling of another word containing an element that is no longer pronounced, as *limb* from OE *lim* after *lamb* (from OE *lamb*). **inverse square** the relation of two quantities one of which varies inversely as the square of the other; *inverse square law*, by which the intensity of an effect, as gravitational attraction, illumination, etc., decreases in inverse proportion to the square of the distance from the source of the effect.

B *n.* **1** An inverted state or condition. Also, a thing which is in reverse order to something else. L17. **2** *Math.* & *Logic.* A ratio, process, curve, proposition, etc., which is the result of inversion; an inverse ratio; an inverse function. L17. **b** *spec.* in *Math.* An element which, when combined with a given element by a given operation, produces the identity element for that operation. E20. **3** In rouge-et-noir, the section of the table in which are placed bets that the colour of the first card dealt will not be the same as that of the winning row. Also, the game of rouge-et-noir. M19.

2b OED The inverse of any number with respect to multiplication is the reciprocal.

inverse /ɪnˈvəːs/ *v.t.* Now *rare.* E17. [f. prec.] Turn upside down; invert; reverse in order or direction.

inversed *ppl a.* (long *rare*) reversed; turned upside down; turned inward: LME.

inversely /ɪnˈvəːsli/ *adv.* M17. [f. INVERSE *a.* + -LY[2].] **1** In an inverse manner or order; by inversion; in inverse proportion. M17. **2** Invertedly; upside down. L18.

2 **inversely conical**, **pyramidal**: with the vertex downward.

inversion /ɪnˈvəːʃ(ə)n/ *n.* M16. [L *inversio(n-)*, f. *invers-* pa. ppl stem of *invertere*: see INVERT *v.*, -ION.] **I** Reversal, transposition. †**1** *Rhet.* The turning of an argument against the person who advances it. M16–M17. **2** A reversal of position, order, sequence, or relation. L16. **3** *Rhet.* = ANASTROPHE. L16. **4** *Mil.* A drill movement by which the relative positions of the troops are changed; *spec.* one by which a rank becomes a file. M17. **5** *Math.* **a** The reversal of a ratio by interchanging the antecedent and consequent. M17. **b** *Geom.* A transformation in which each point of a given figure is replaced by another point on the same straight line from a fixed point, esp. in such a way that the product of the distances of the two points from the centre of inversion is constant. Also, any similar transformation involving a more complex relation of corresponding points or lines. L19. **c** *Math.* The process of finding a function $g(y)$ which either yields a variable x when its argument is a given function $y = f(x)$ of that variable, or else yields a given function under a given transformation. L19. **6** *Mus.* The action of inverting an interval, chord, phrase, or subject. Also, the interval, chord, etc., so produced (in relation to the original one). E19. **7** *Chem.* **a** Decomposition of an optically active carbohydrate (esp. sucrose) by which the direction of the optical rotatory power is reversed. M19 **b** Orig., the reversal of the direction of optical rotation observed in certain substitution reactions. Now, the change of configuration which occurs when a reactant enters along the axis of the bond between a central atom and the leaving group, causing the other substituents on the central atom to pass through a plane perpendicular to this axis (regardless of any effect on optical activity). Also more fully WALDEN *inversion* [P. von *Walden* (1863–1957), Latvian chemist]. L19. **8** *Logic*. A form of immediate inference in which a new proposition is formed whose subject is the negative of that of the original proposition. L19. **9** In full *sexual inversion*. Homosexuality. Also, the adoption of dress, behaviour, or a role, typical of the opposite sex. L19. **10** *Meteorol.* In full *temperature inversion*. An increase of air temperature with height (the reverse of the usual decrease); a layer of air having such a reversed gradient. Also, an increase of temperature with depth of water. E20. **11** *Biol.* A (chromosome segment exhibiting) reversal of the order of the genes as compared with the normal order on the chromosome. E20. **12** *Electr.* The conversion of direct current into alternating current. Opp. *rectification*. E20. **13** *Physical Chem.* A transformation of a substance, esp. an enantiotropic one, from one solid form to another. E20. **14** *Telecommunications*. Reversal of the order of the component frequencies of a signal. M20. **15** *Computing*. The conversion of either of the two binary digits or signals into the other; negation. M20. **16** *Physics*. In full *population inversion*. A transposition of the relative numbers of atoms or molecules occupying certain energy levels. M20. **II** Alteration in use. †**17** = METAPHOR I. M–L16. †**18** Diversion to an improper use; perversion. E–M18. **III** The action of turning, or state of being turned, vertically. **19** A turning upside down. L16. **20** *Geol.* The folding back of stratified rocks upon each other, so that older strata overlie newer. M19. **IV** The action of turning, or state of being turned, in or inwards. **21** Chiefly *Med.* Introversion; a turning inside out (esp. of the uterus). L16. **22** *Med.* A twisting of the foot so that the sole faces inwards. M19.

Comb.: **inversion compound** a place-name in which the second element is a name, title, etc., in the genitive case or otherwise showing ownership of the first element; **inversion temperature** (*a*) *Physics* the temperature (for any particular gas) at which the Joule–Thomson effect changes sign, so that the gas is neither heated nor cooled when allowed to expand without doing any work; (*b*) *Physical Chem.* the temperature at which two solid forms of a substance can coexist in equilibrium.

inversive /ɪnˈvəːsɪv/ *a.* L19. [f. L *invers-* (see INVERSION) + -IVE.] Characterized by inversion.

†**inversor** *n. rare*. Only in M19. [f. INVERSE *v.* + -OR.] = INVERTOR I.

invert /ˈɪnvəːt/ *n.* & *a.* M19. [f. the vb.] A *n.* **1** An inverted arch, as at the bottom of a canal or sewer. M19. **2** *Psychol.* A person who exhibits instincts or behaviour characteristic of the opposite sex. L19. **3** Sugar formed by the breaking up of sucrose into dextrose and laevulose. E20.

B *attrib.* or as *adj.* Inverted. L19.

invert soap: whose surface-active ion is a cation (rather than the more usual anion); a cationic detergent. **invert sugar** = sense A.3 above.

invert /ɪnˈvəːt/ *v.* M16. [L *invertere*, f. as IN-[2] + *vertere* turn (lit. 'turn inside-out').] **I** Reverse, transpose. **1** *v.t.* Turn back to front, reverse; change the relations of so as to produce the opposite. M16. **b** *v.i.* Change to the opposite. Now *rare* or *obs.* E17. †**2** *v.t. Rhet.* Turn an argument against the person who advances it. M17–L18. **3** *v.t. Mus.* Change the relative position of the notes of (an interval or chord) by raising the lowest note (usu. by an octave). Also, modify (a phrase or subject) by reversing the direction of its movement in pitch. M19. **4a** *v.i. Geom.* Be transformed by inversion *into*. Now *rare* or *obs.* M19. **b** *v.t. Math.* Transform by inversion; find the inverse of. M20. **5** *v.t. Chem.* Subject (a compound) to inversion; *esp.* break up (sucrose) into dextrose and laevulose. M19. **6** *v.i. Chem.* Of a substance: undergo inversion. L19. **7** *v.t. Logic*. Obtain the inverse of (a proposition). L19. **8** *v.t. Telecommunications*. Subject (a signal) to a heterodyne process that reverses the order of the component frequencies. M20. **II** Change the use of. †**9** *v.t.* Use (a word) metaphorically rather than literally. Only in L16. †**10** *v.t.* Divert from its proper purpose; pervert to another use. L16–L17. **III** Turn upside down. **11** *v.t.* Turn upside down. Formerly also *fig.*, overthrow, upset. L16. **IV 12** *v.t.* Chiefly *Med.* Turn inside out. E17. †**13** *v.t.* Turn in or inward. Only in M17.

invertant /ɪnˈvəːt(ə)nt/ *a. rare*. E19. [f. INVERT *v.* + -ANT[1].] *Her.* = INVERTED 2.

invertase /ˈɪnvəːteɪz, ɪnˈvəːt-/ *n.* L19. [f. INVERT *v.* + -ASE.] *Biochem.* An enzyme, extractable from yeast, which catalyses the inversion of sucrose. Also called *saccharase*, *sucrase*.

invertebracy /ɪnˈvəːtɪbrəsi/ *n. joc.* L19. [f. INVERTEBRATE *a.* 2: see -ACY.] Spinelessness; lack of firmness or conviction.

invertebral /ɪnˈvəːtɪbr(ə)l/ *a. rare*. E19. [f. IN-[3] + VERTEBRAL.] = INVERTEBRATE *a.*

Invertebrata /ɪnˌvəːtɪˈbrɑːtə/ *n.pl.* E19. [mod.L, f. Fr. *invertébrés*, f. *in-* IN-[3] + VERTEBRA.] *Zool.* (Members of) a group which includes all animals except vertebrates.

¶No longer in use in formal taxonomy.

invertebrate /ɪnˈvəːtɪbrət/ *a.* & *n.* E19. [f. prec.: see -ATE[1], -ATE[2].] A *n.* **1** An animal without a backbone or spinal column; an animal not belonging to the subphylum Vertebrata. E19. **2** *fig.* A person without strength of character or principles. M19. B *adj.* **1** (Of an animal) not having a backbone or spinal column; of or pertaining to invertebrates. M19. **2** *fig.* Without moral courage, firmness, or consistency. L19.

inverted /ɪnˈvəːtɪd/ *a.* L16. [f. INVERT *v.* + -ED[1].] **1** Reversed in position, relation, or order; turned upside down or back to front; turned inwards or inside out. L16. **2** *Her.* Of a charge: used upside down. Of a bird's wings: with the tips pointed downwards. Of two animals: facing each other across the middle of the field. E17. **3** *Mus.* Of a chord or interval: having the lowest note raised (usu. by an octave). E19. **4** *Phonet.* Produced with the tip of the tongue turned upwards towards the hard palate. L19. **5** *Psychol.* Of the sex instincts: turned towards one's own sex; homosexual. L19.

Special collocations: *inverted comma*: see COMMA 4. *inverted pendulum*: see PENDULUM *n.* **inverted pleat**: with two parallel contrary pleats forming a recessed band. **inverted snob** a person who likes or takes pride in what a snob normally disapproves of. **inverted snobbery** the practices or attitudes of an inverted snob. **inverted spelling** = *inverse spelling* s.v. INVERSE *a.*

invertedly *adv.* in an inverted manner; upside down; with inversion of order: L17.

invertend /ˈɪnvətend/ *n.* L19. [L *invertendus*, f. *invertere* INVERT *v.*: see -END.] *Logic*. The proposition from which another proposition is obtained by inversion.

inverter /ɪnˈvəːtə/ *n.* E17. [f. INVERT *v.* + -ER[1].] **1** *gen.* A person or thing which inverts or produces inversion. *rare*. E17. **2** *Electr.* An apparatus which converts direct current into alternating current. Cf. INVERTOR I. E20. **b** *Telecommunications*. A device that inverts a signal. M20. **c** *Computing*. A device that converts either of the two binary digits or signals into the other. M20.

invertible /ɪnˈvəːtɪb(ə)l/ *a.* L19. [f. INVERT *v.* + -IBLE.] **1** Able to be inverted. L19. **b** That tends to invert the usual order. *rare*. L19. **2** *Math.* Of an element of a set: having an inverse (*spec.* an inverse for multiplication) in the set. M20.

invertiˈbility *n.* M20.

invertor /ɪnˈvəːtə/ *n.* E20. [f. INVERT *v.* + -OR.] **1** *Electr.* An instrument for reversing an electric current; a commutator. Also occas., = INVERTER 2. E20. **2** *Anat.* A muscle which turns a part (as the foot) inwards. E20.

invest /ɪnˈvɛst/ *v.* M16. [(O)Fr. *investir* or L *investire* clothe, surround, f. as IN-[2] + *vestis* clothing. In branch II after It. *investire*.] **I 1** *v.t.* Clothe; envelop, or surround *in*, *with*, or as with, a garment. Of a garment etc: clothe, cover, adorn. M16. **b** Put on as clothes or ornaments; don. L16. **c** Embed in or surround *with* hardened refractory material. L19. **2** *v.t.* Clothe *with* or *in* the insignia of a position or rank; install *in* a position or rank with the customary rites or ceremonies. M16. **3** *v.t.* Establish (a person) *in* any rank, position, property, etc.; endow *with* power, authority, or privilege. M16. **b** Settle (a right or power) *in* (a person). L16. **4** *v.t.* Provide or endow with attributes, qualities, or a character. Foll. by *with*, †*in*. E17. **5** *v.t. Mil.* Surround with a hostile force; besiege, beleaguer. E17.

3 J. GILBERT The innocent being is by law invested with the right to enjoy security. b R. D. LAING I was frightened by the power invested in me as a psychiatrist. 4 P. BOWLES Her superstitious fancy had invested them with magical importance. M. PIERCY She tried to invest her tone with some of the bitter irony she felt.

II 6 *v.t.* Expend (money, effort) in something from which a return or profit is expected, now esp. in the purchase of property, shares, etc., for the sake of the interest, dividends, or profits accruing from them. E17. **b** *v.i.* Make an investment, invest capital; *colloq.* lay out money *in* a (useful) purchase. M19. **c** *v.t.* & *i.* Lay out (money) in betting on a horse-race, or in football pools, etc. M20.

6 P. H. JOHNSON She had inherited money from an aunt — enough, invested, to bring in five hundred a year. J. A. MICHENER A new life where we can invest our money and our energy and build our own paradise. b OED To invest in a .. time-table. c H. CECIL He went to the £5 tote windows and invested .. £100 on Maiden Aunt.

inˈvestable, **-ible** *a.* able to be invested L19. †**investient** *a.* coating, enveloping, enfolding L17–M18. **investor** *n.* a person who invests or makes an investment L16.

†**investigable** *a.*[1] LME–E18. [eccl.L *investigabilis*, f. as IN-[3] + *vestigare* track, trace: see -ABLE.] Incapable of being traced; undiscoverable, unsearchable.

investigable /ɪnˈvɛstɪgəb(ə)l/ *a.*[2] L16. [Late L *investigabilis*, f. *investigare*: see INVESTIGATE, -ABLE.] Able to be investigated, traced out, or searched into; open to investigation, inquiry, or research.

investigate /ɪnˈvɛstɪgeɪt/ *v.* E16. [L *investigat-* pa. ppl stem of *investigare*, f. as IN-[2] + *vestigare* track, trace out: see -ATE[3].] **1** *v.t.* Search or inquire into; examine (a matter) systematically or in detail; make an (official) inquiry into. E16. **2** *v.i.* Make a search or systematic inquiry. E16.

1 *Dumfries Courier* Police and fire brigade officials are investigating the cause of the fire. R. ELLMANN R. B. Haldane .. as a member of the Home Office committee investigating prisons had access to any prison. 2 R. BRADBURY They'll never come and investigate to see what happened to us.

investigator *n.* a person who investigates; a researcher, a detective: M16. **investigaˈtorial** *a.* pertaining to or characteristic of an investigator or investigation E19. **investigatory** *a.* of an investigating nature or character M19.

investigation /ɪnˌvɛstɪˈgeɪʃ(ə)n/ *n.* LME. [(O)Fr., or L *investigatio(n-)*, f. as prec.: see -ATION.] **1** The action or process of investigating; systematic examination; careful research. LME. **2** An instance of this; a systematic inquiry; a careful study of a particular subject. L18.

1 G. CHEYNE There is scarce a Geometer, but has his own Method of Investigation. 2 J. THURBER A recent investigation of the worries and concerns of five thousand selected Americans. N. SYMINGTON The central area of Freud's investigations was the unconscious.

investiˈgational *a.* E20.

investigative /ɪnˈvɛstɪgətɪv, -geɪtɪv/ *a.* E19. [f. L *investigat-* (see INVESTIGATE) + -IVE.] **1** Characterized by or inclined to investigation. E19. **2** Of journalism or broadcasting: investigating and seeking to expose malpractice, miscarriage of justice, etc. Of a journalist etc: engaged in this. Orig. *US*. M20.

1 *Time* The laws .. put heavy restraints on the investigative and prosecutorial powers of the state. 2 *Daily Telegraph* Mr Lewis's classic piece of investigative reporting into the plight of the Indians in the Brazilian rainforest.

investitive /ɪnˈvɛstɪtɪv/ *a.* L18. [f. L *investit-* (see next) + -IVE.] Having the property or function of investing.

investiture /ɪnˈvɛstɪtjə, -tʃə/ *n.* LME. [med.L *investitura*, f. L *investit-* pa. ppl stem of *investire* INVEST: see -URE.] 1 The action or ceremony of clothing someone in the insignia of a position or rank; the ceremonial or formal investing of a person with a position, rank, or benefice. LME. 2 Endowment with an attribute or quality; establishment in any state of privilege or honour. E17. 3 The action of clothing or robing; a thing which clothes or covers. Chiefly *fig.* M17. 4 = INVESTMENT 4. Now *rare.* M17. †5 = INVESTMENT 5. M18–M19.

investment /ɪnˈvɛs(t)m(ə)nt/ *n.* L16. [f. INVEST + -MENT.] I 1 The act of putting on clothes or vestments; clothing; robes, vestments. Now *rare* or *obs.* L16. 2a An outer covering of any kind; an envelope; a coating. M17. b Refractory material used to embed or surround an object and allowed to harden, to allow soldering (in *Dentistry*), or to form a mould for investment casting. L19. 3 The action of investing or fact of being invested with a position, rank, right, or attribute; endowment. M17. 4 *Mil.* The surrounding or blockading *of* a place by a hostile force. E19. II 5 The investing of money (now also time or effort); an instance of this. E17. 6 An amount of money invested. Also, anything in which money etc. is or may be invested. M19.

Comb.: **investment bond** a single-premium investment in a life-insurance policy; **investment casting** a lost-wax technique for making small, accurate castings in refractory alloys using a mould formed around a pattern of wax or similar material which is then removed by melting; **investment currency** the currency used in the buying and selling of foreign securities through a market separate from a controlled market in foreign exchange; **investment material** = sense 2b above; **investment trust** a limited company whose business is the investment of shareholders' funds, the shares being traded like those of any other public company.

investure /ɪnˈvɛstʃə, -tjə/ *n.* L16. [f. INVEST + -URE.] Investiture into a position, rank, or benefice. Also, the military investment of a city etc.

inveteracy /ɪnˈvɛt(ə)rəsi/ *n.* L17. [f. next: see -ACY.] The quality of being inveterate; the state of being entrenched or of long standing. Also, an instance of this; deep-rooted or long-lasting prejudice or hostility.

inveterate /ɪnˈvɛt(ə)rət/ *a.* & *n.* LME. [L *inveteratus* pa. pple of *inveterare* make old, f. as IN-[2] + *veter-*, *vetus* old: see -ATE[2].] A *adj.* 1 Of disease: of long standing, chronic; resisting treatment. LME. b Long established, ancient, old. Now chiefly of a (bad) habit, prejudice, etc.: deep-rooted, obstinate, ingrained E16. c Persistent, lasting. L18. 2 Settled or confirmed in a habit or practice; habitual, hardened, obstinate. L15. 3 Full of obstinate prejudice or hatred; embittered, malignant; virulent. Now *rare* or *obs.* E16.

1 H. LYTE Medicines against an old inueterate cough. b EVELYN Rotten wood, . . especially that which is taken out of an Inveterate willow tree. J. A. FROUDE His relations with Francis . . were those of inveterate hostility. c E. MANNIN A big part of Ahmad's charm was his inveterate desire to please. 2 H. T. LANE She had been made a hard liar by hard treatment, and was . . an inveterate mischief-maker. D. M. THOMAS She . . enjoyed writing—she was, for example, an inveterate letter-writer.

B *n.* A person who is confirmed in some (bad) habit; a confirmed or hardened offender. E18.

inveterately *adv.* M17. **inveterateness** *n.* M17.

†**inveterate** *v.t.* L16–M19. [f. prec. or f. L *inveterat-* pa. ppl stem of *inveterare*: see prec., -ATE[3].] Make inveterate; establish by long usage or custom; harden, confirm.

†**inveteration** *n.* (*rare*) the action of making something inveterate; the process of becoming inveterate: M17–E18.

inviable /ɪnˈvʌɪəb(ə)l/ *a.* E20. [f. IN-[3] + VIABLE *a.*[1]] *Biol.* Unable to survive; unable to germinate, grow, or develop; unable to perform its proper biological role.

invia'bility *n.* the state or condition of being inviable E20.

invidious /ɪnˈvɪdɪəs/ *a.* E17. [L *invidiosus*, f. *invidia* ill will: see ENVY *n.*, -IOUS.] 1 Giving or likely to give offence or arouse ill feeling. E17. †b Viewed with ill will or dislike; odious *to* a person. *rare.* Only in E18. 2 Of a thing: likely to arouse ill feeling or envy against the possessor. M17. 3 Envious, grudging, jealous. Now *rare* or *obs.* M17. 4 Of a comparison or distinction: unjust, unfairly discriminating. E18.

1 DRYDEN He rose, and took th'advantage of the times, To load young Turnus with invidious crimes. D. ADAMS It's none of my business and it puts me in an invidious position. 2 LD MACAULAY Catharine saw all the peril of such a step, and declined the invidious honor. 4 E. JOHNSON Amid the . . plenty of Dickens's creation it is almost invidious to single out individual novels.

invidiously *adv.* M17. **invidiousness** *n.* L17.

†**invigilancy** *n. rare.* E17–E18. [f. IN-[3] + VIGILANCY.] Absence of vigilance or watchfulness.

invigilate /ɪnˈvɪdʒɪleɪt/ *v.* M16. [L *invigilat-* pa. ppl stem of *invigilare*, f. as IN-[2] + *vigilare* watch, f. *vigil* watchful: see -ATE[3].] 1 *v.i.* & *t.* Keep watch; watch carefully. Now *spec.* watch over students at (an examination). M16. †2 *v.t.* Arouse; make watchful. *rare.* Only in E17.

invigi'lation *n.* L19. **invigilator** *n.* a person who watches over students at an examination L19.

invigor *v.* see INVIGOUR.

invigorate /ɪnˈvɪg(ə)rət/ *ppl a. rare.* E18. [f. as next.] Filled with vigour; invigorated.

invigorate /ɪnˈvɪgəreɪt/ *v.t.* M17. [med.L *invigorat-* pa. ppl stem, f. as IN-[2] + L *vigorare* make strong, f. *vigor*: see VIGOUR *n.*, -ATE[3].] Make vigorous; fill with life and energy; strengthen, animate. Freq. as *invigorating* ppl a.

B. T. BRADFORD The quick walk from the evening performance had been invigorating. D. ADAMS I find your scepticism rewarding and invigorating.

invigorant *n.* something that invigorates; an invigorating drink or medicine, a tonic: E19. **invigoratingly** *adv.* so as to invigorate someone or something L19. **invigo'ration** *n.* M17. **invigorative** *a.* (*rare*) that tends to invigorate; invigorating: M19. **invigorator** *n.* M19.

invigour /ɪnˈvɪgə/ *v.t.* Also ***-or**; (earlier) †**en-**. E17. [(O)Fr. *envigo(u)rer* f. as EN-[1], IN-[2] + L *vigorare* (see prec.); later f. IN-[2] + VIGOUR.] Fill with vigour; invigorate.

†**invinate** *ppl a. rare.* M16. [med.L *invinatus* pa. pple of *invinare*: see next.] Embodied or included in wine.

invination /ɪnvɪˈneɪʃ(ə)n/ *n.* M18. [f. L *invinare*, f. as IN-[2] + *vinum* wine: see -ATION.] *Chr. Ch.* In Eucharistic doctrine: the presence of the blood (and, according to most holders of the doctrine, also the body) of Christ in the wine after consecration.

invincible /ɪnˈvɪnsɪb(ə)l/ *a.* & *n.* LME. [(O)Fr. f. L *invincibilis*, f. as IN-[3] + *vincibilis*, f. *vincere* conquer: see -IBLE.] A *adj.* 1 Unable to be vanquished, overcome, or subdued; unconquerable. LME. b Insurmountable, insuperable. LME. †2 Unable to be excelled; unsurpassable. E16–E17.

1 *Sunday Express* Honeyghan . . surprised everyone by ripping the . . title off the previously invincible Don Curry. b **invincible ignorance**: which the ignorant person does not have the means to overcome.

B *n.* A person who is invincible. M17. **the Invincibles** an Irish political assassination society, developed from the Fenians about 1881–2.

invinci'bility *n.* invincibleness L17. **invincibleness** *n.* E17. **invincibly** *adv.* M16.

inviolable /ɪnˈvʌɪələb(ə)l/ *a.* LME. [(O)Fr., or L *inviolabilis*, f. as IN-[3] + VIOLABLE.] 1 To be kept sacred or free from attack; not to be infringed or dishonoured. LME. †2 Not yielding to force or violence; unable to be broken, forced, or injured. L15–E18.

inviola'bility *n.* the quality or fact of being inviolable L18. **inviolableness** *n.* (now *rare*) inviolability E17. **inviolably** *adv.* L15.

inviolate /ɪnˈvʌɪələt/ *a.* LME. [L *inviolatus*, f. as IN-[3] + *violat-* pa. ppl stem of *violare* VIOLATE *v.*: see -ATE[2].] Free or exempt from violation; uninjured, unimpaired, unbroken; not profaned or debased.

JOHN BROOKE He took with him assurances of the King's inviolate attachment. B. MAGEE The truth is to be kept inviolate, and handed on unsullied.

inviolacy *n.* inviolateness M19. **inviolately** *adv.* L15. **inviolateness** *n.* the quality of being inviolate M19.

inviolated /ɪnˈvʌɪəleɪtɪd/ *a.* M16. [f. IN-[3] + *violated* pa. pple of VIOLATE *v.*] Not violated, inviolate.

†**invious** *a.* E17–E18. [f. L *invius*, f. as IN-[3] + *via* way, road: see -OUS.] Having no roads or ways; pathless, trackless.

†**inviron** *v.* var. of ENVIRON.

invirtuate /ɪnˈvəːtjʊeɪt/ *v.t. rare.* M17. [f. IN-[2] + VIRTUE + -ATE[3].] Make virtuous; endow with virtue or power.

inviscate /ɪnˈvɪskeɪt/ *v.t.* LME. [Late L *inviscat-* pa. ppl stem of *inviscare* smear with or snare with birdlime, f. as IN-[2] + *viscum* birdlime: see -ATE[3].] 1 Make viscid or sticky; mix or cover with a sticky substance. LME. 2 Catch in some sticky substance. *rare.* M17.

invi'scation *n.* LME.

inviscid /ɪnˈvɪsɪd/ *a.* E20. [f. IN-[3] + VISCID *a.*] 1 Not viscid or sticky. E20. 2 *Physics.* Having no or negligible viscosity. E20.

†**invised** *a. rare* (Shakes.). Only in L16. [f. L *invisus* unseen + -ED[1].] Unseen, invisible.

invisible /ɪnˈvɪzɪb(ə)l/ *a.* & *n.* ME. [(O)Fr., or L *invisibilis* f. as IN-[3] + *visibilis* VISIBLE.] A *adj.* 1 Unable to be seen; that by its nature is not perceivable by the eye. ME. b Of an association: covert, not having a visible, open organization. M17. 2 Not in sight; hidden, obscured. Also, kept hidden, secret. M16. 3 Too small or inconspicuous to be easily discerned; imperceptible. M17.

1 N. TINBERGEN Ultraviolet light, which is entirely invisible to us. R. WEST She moved past me . . , holding her hands in front of her as though she bore invisible gifts. *transf.*: *Observer* Its . . absorbent surfaces and special metals are designed to make it almost invisible to radar. *the Church Invisible*: see CHURCH *n.* 3. 2 F. FORSYTH The president's palace was invisible, hidden behind the warehouse. J. HELLER He remains invisible and anonymous. 3 J. BALDWIN He sank far down in his seat, as though crouching might make him invisible. J. CAIRD Mabel . . had worn her . . hair in a bun, over which she put a fine 'invisible' net.

Special collocations: **invisible earnings**: from invisible exports. **invisible export**, **import** any of the items such as shipping services, insurance, profits on foreign investment, money spent by foreign visitors, etc., which are not tangible commodities but which involve payment between countries (usu. in *pl.*). **invisible green** a very dark shade of green, almost black. *invisible import*: see *invisible export* above. **invisible ink**: for writing words etc. which cannot be seen until the paper is heated or otherwise treated. **invisible man** (*a*) (with direct or implied allusion to H. G. Wells's novel *The Invisible Man*) a man who cannot be seen; (*b*) a man who is (deliberately) inconspicuous. **invisible mending** repair of material, clothing, etc., so carefully done as to be undetectable. **invisible mender** a person who or business which undertakes invisible mending.

B *n.* 1 An invisible thing, person, or being. M17. 2 In *pl.* Invisible exports and imports. M20.

1 **the invisible** the unseen world; God. 2 *Daily Mirror* America . . is now beginning to record deficits on the invisibles, which add to its basic trade deficit.

invisi'bility *n.* (*a*) the quality or condition of being invisible; (*b*) an invisible entity: M16. **invisibleness** *n.* M16. **invisibly** *adv.* LME.

invita Minerva /ɪnˌvʌɪtɑː mɪˈnəːvɑː/ *adv. phr.* L16. [L = Minerva (the goddess of wisdom) unwilling.] When one is not in the mood; without inspiration.

invitation /ɪnvɪˈteɪʃ(ə)n/ *n.* LME. [Fr., or L *invitatio(n-)* , f. *invitat-* pa. ppl stem of *invitare* invite.] A *n.* 1 The action of inviting someone to come, attend, or take part. LME. b The spoken or written form in which a person is invited. E17. 2 The action or an act of enticing or attracting; attraction, inducement, allurement. L16. b *Bridge.* A bid which encourages, but does not compel, the bidder's partner to continue to game or slam. E20.

B *attrib.* or as *adj.* 1 Containing or constituting an invitation. E19. 2 Of an event, contest, etc.:

open only to those who have received an invitation. E19.

1 *invitation card, invitation letter, invitation list.* 2 *Press & Journal (Aberdeen)* The top sprinters . . have all enjoyed a diet of invitation races on the . . circuits.

invitational /ɪnvɪˈteɪʃ(ə)n(ə)l/ *a.* & *n.*[1] Chiefly *N. Amer.* E20. [f. prec. + -AL[1].] A *adj.* Characterized by invitation. Of a contest etc.: open only to those invited. E20.

Chambers's Journal Philip walked the room's length with invitational pauses.

B *absol.* as *n.* An invitational contest etc. E20.

Evening Telegram (Newfoundland) John Hamilton won the June Invitational on his first try Monday.

invitatory /ɪnˈvʌɪtət(ə)ri/ *a.* & *n.* ME. [Late L *invitatorius*, f. L *invitare* invite: see -ORY[2].] A *adj.* 1 Eccl. *invitatory psalm*, the *Venite*, Psalm 95 (94 in the Vulgate), with its antiphon, which begins the first office of the day. ME. 2 That invites or tends to invite; containing or conveying an invitation. M17. B *n.* 1 Any of various forms of invitation used in religious worship; *spec.* the invitatory psalm. LME. b *RC Ch.* (now *Hist.*). The introit. LME. 2 An invitation. M17.

invite /ˈɪnvʌɪt/ *n. colloq.* E17. [f. next.] †1 An attraction, a bait. Only in E17. 2 The act of inviting; an invitation. M17.

2 F. BURNEY Everybody bowed and accepted the invite but me. W. H. AUDEN An invite with gilded edges.

invite /ɪnˈvʌɪt/ *v.t.* M16. [Fr. *inviter* or L *invitare*.] 1 Ask (a person) to come with one's permission *to* or *into* a place or *to* an event. Foll. by *in*: ask (a person) to come into one's house. M16. b *refl.* Announce one's intention or desire to come; impose oneself. M16. 2 Ask (a person) *to do* something assumed to be agreeable or advantageous. M16. b Politely request (something) from a person. M19. 3 Entice or encourage (a person) *to do* something or *to go* somewhere. Now only of a thing. M16. 4 Tend to bring on; encourage unintentionally. L16. †5 Attract physically, draw. L17–E19.

1 T. HARDY He . . invited Margery and her father to his house. R. LARDNER Ada was invited to a party. b P. FERGUSON He'll have to take us as he finds us, inviting himself round here. 2 T. HARDY They were also invited to dine. DAY LEWIS A small girl called Violet who . . invited me to kiss her. b A. S. NEILL After the lecture, I invited questions. 3 D. M. THOMAS The dining room was . . so large . . that it invited people to eat in silence. 4 F. MORYSON One looke invites another. C. S. FORESTER In war as in the jungle, to fly is to invite pursuit and attack.

invitant /ˈɪnvɪt(ə)nt/ *n.* (*a*) a person who gives an invitation; (*b*) a person who is invited: L16. **invited** *a.* that has received an invitation M17. **inviˈtee** *n.* a person who is invited; *spec.* (*Law*) a person who is invited on to the premises by the owner or occupier for some business or material object: M19. **invitement** *n.* (now *rare* or *obs.*) (*a*) invitation; (*b*) inducement; allurement; encouragement to come: L16. **inviter** *n.* L16. **inviting** *a.* (*a*) that invites or gives an invitation; (*b*) attractive; alluring; tempting: L16. **invitingly** *adv.* M17. **invitingness** *n.* the quality of being alluring; attractiveness: M17. **invitress** *n.* a female inviter E17.

†invitory *n.* & *v.* see INVENTORY.

in vitro /ɪn ˈviːtrəʊ/ *a.* & *adv. phr.* L19. [L, lit. 'in glass'.] *Biol.* (Performed, obtained, or occurring) in a test-tube or elsewhere outside a living organism.

in vivo /ɪn ˈviːvəʊ/ *a.* & *adv. phr.* E20. [L.] *Biol.* (Performed, obtained, or occurring) within a living organism. Cf. INTRA VITAM.

invocable /ˈɪnvəkəb(ə)l/ *a.* M19. [f. INVOKE + -ABLE.] Able to be invoked or called upon.

invocant /ˈɪnvək(ə)nt, ɪnˈvəʊk(ə)nt/ *n.* M18. [f. INVOKE + -ANT[1].] A person who invokes someone or something.

invocate /ˈɪnvəkeɪt/ *v.* Now *rare.* M16. [L *invocat-* pa. ppl stem of *invocare* INVOKE: see -ATE[3].] 1 *v.t.* Invoke, call upon, appeal to. M16. †2 *v.i.* Make an invocation; call in prayer (*on* or *upon*). L16–E19.

invocation /ɪnvə(ʊ)ˈkeɪʃ(ə)n/ *n.* LME. [(O)Fr., f. L *invocatio(n-)* f. as prec.: see -ATION.] 1 The action or an act of invoking or calling upon God, a deity, etc., in prayer (an act or form of supplication). LME. b *Eccl.* A form of invocatory prayer as part of a public religious service; a petition. Also, the name or appellation used in invoking a divinity, etc. E19. 2 The action or an act of summoning a devil, spirit, etc., by incantation; an incantation used for this; a charm, a spell. LME. 3 *Law.* The calling in of papers or evidence from another case. E19.

invocative /ɪnˈvɒkətɪv/ *a.* E19. [f. prec.: see -IVE.] Characterized by invocation.

invocatory /ɪnˈvɒkət(ə)ri, ˈɪnvəkeɪt(ə)ri/ *a.* L17. [f. INVOCATION: see -ORY[2].] Of the nature of, characterized by, or used in, invocation.

invoice /ˈɪnvɔɪs/ *n.* & *v.* M16. [Orig. pl. of †*invoy*, f. Fr. †*envoy*, ENVOI.] A *n.* 1 A list of items of goods sent or services performed, with a statement of the sum due. M16. 2 A consignment of invoiced goods. *rare.* L19. B *v.t.* Send an invoice to (a person, a company). Also, list (goods etc.) on an invoice. L17.

invoke /ɪnˈvəʊk/ *v.t.* L15. [(O)Fr. *invoquer* f. L *invocare*, f. as IN-[2] + *vocare* call.] 1 Call on (God, a deity, etc.) in prayer or as a witness. L15. 2 Summon (a spirit) by charms or incantation; conjure; *fig.* give rise to, evoke. E17. b Utter (a sacred *name*) in invocation. L17. 3 Call for earnestly; beg for, implore. E17. 4 Appeal to or call upon to come or to do something. L17. 5 *Law.* Call in papers or evidence from another case. E19. 6 Appeal to in support or confirmation; cite as authority; postulate as an explanation. M19. 7 Put into operation or into effect; call for the observance or performance of. M19.

1 A. ALVAREZ A broken necklace or a cold in the nose, and they'd be weeping and invoking heaven. 2 LYTTON Thou shalt stand by my side while I invoke the phantom. R. BUSH He wrote a dramatic lyric that invokes the romance of Italy. b T. BROWN Wrinkled witches, when they truck with hell, Invoke thy name, and use it for a spell. 3 E. MANNIN Linton invoked God's blessing on his house. V. WOOLF She invoked his help against this attack upon the jolly human heart. 4 J. MICHIE A criminal invokes conscience to his aid To support an individual withdrawal from a communal crusade. 6 A. DAVIS The argument he had invoked when he rejected our bail motion. J. BERMAN Eliot invokes a clinical authority to confirm his intuition. 7 K. M. E. MURRAY There was a dismissal clause to be invoked if the Editor should not proceed as fast as the Delegates considered reasonable. *Which Computer?* The GD command invokes the graphics drawing language.

invoker *n.* M17.

involatile /ɪnˈvɒlətʌɪl/ *a.* M17. [f. IN-[3] + VOLATILE.] †1 Not flying, wingless. *rare.* Only in M17. 2 Not volatile; unable to be vaporized. M19.

involucel /ɪnˈvɒljʊsɛl/ *n.* Also (earlier) in L form **involucellum** /ɪnˌvɒljʊˈsɛləm/. M18. [mod.L *involucellum* dim. of INVOLUCRUM: cf. Fr. *involucelle*.] *Bot.* A whorl of bracts surrounding one of the divisions in an inflorescence, a partial or secondary involucre; *spec.* the epicalyx of one of the flowers in the capitulum of a scabious or allied plant.

involuˈcellate *a.* having an involucel or involucels E19.

involucra *n.* pl. of INVOLUCRUM.

involucre /ˈɪnvəl(j)uːkə/ *n.* L16. [Fr., or f. L INVOLUCRUM.] 1 Something which envelops or enwraps; a case, a covering, an envelope; *esp.* formerly in *Anat.*, an envelope of (membranous) tissue. L16. 2 *Bot.* A whorl or rosette of bracts surrounding an inflorescence (esp. a capitulum), or at the base of an umbel. L18. b A sheath of tissue surrounding the male or female sexual organs of some liverworts. L19.

2 *partial involucre*: see PARTIAL *a.*

invoˈlucral *a.* (*Bot.*) of or pertaining to an involucre E19. **invoˈlucrate** *a.* (*Bot.*) having an involucre M19.

involucrum /ɪnvəˈl(j)uːkrəm/ *n.* Pl. **-cra** /-krə/. L17. [L, f. *involvere* INVOLVE.] 1 An outer covering, an envelope; a covering membrane; = INVOLUCRE 1. L17. 2 *Bot.* = INVOLUCRE 2. M18.

involuntary /ɪnˈvɒlənt(ə)ri/ *a.* M16. [f. IN-[3] + VOLUNTARY *a.*] 1 Not done willingly or by choice; independent of volition, unintentional. M16. b *Physiol.* Of a nerve, muscle, etc.: concerned in bodily actions or processes which are independent of the will. M19. †2 Unwilling; not exercising the will. L16–M18.

1 D. LESSING Our experiences, some chosen, some involuntary, mature us differently. M. SCAMMELL He experienced that involuntary sense of guilt we all seem to feel when a loved one dies.

involuntarily *adv.* in an involuntary manner; without exercise or cooperation of the will: M16. **involuntariness** *n.* M17.

involute /ˈɪnvəl(j)uːt/ *a.* & *n.* M17. [L *involutus* pa. pple of *involvere* INVOLVE.] A *adj.* 1 Involved; entangled; intricate. Formerly also, hidden, obscure. M17. 2 Chiefly *Zool.* Rolled up in a spiral; *esp.* (of a shell) having the whorls wound closely round the axis. M17. 3 *Math.* In the form of an involute. E18. 4 *Bot.* Of a leaf etc.: rolled inwards at the edges. M18. B *n. Math.* A curve such as is traced out by a point on a taut string unwound from a given curve in the plane of that curve. Cf. EVOLUTE *n.* & *a.* L18.

involute /ˈɪnvəl(j)uːt/ *v.i.* E20. [Back-form. f. next.] Chiefly *Physiol.* Shrink, fold in upon itself; undergo involution.

involuted /ˈɪnvəl(j)uːtɪd/ *a.* E19. [f. INVOLUTE *a.* & *n.* + -ED[1].] 1 Chiefly *Biol.* Folded in upon itself; involute; convoluted. E19. 2 *fig.* Convoluted; involved. E20.

invoˈlutedly *adv.* L19.

involution /ɪnvəˈluːʃ(ə)n/ *n.* LME. [L *involutio(n-)*, f. *involut-* pa. ppl stem of *involvere* INVOLVE: see -ION.] 1 *Anat.* A folding, curling, or turning inwards; (a part of) a structure so formed. LME. 2a A thing that enfolds; an envelope, a covering. L16. b The action of involving or fact of being involved; implicit inclusion; implication. E17. 3 Entanglement, complication; intricacy of (literary) construction or style. Also, something complicated; an intricate movement, a tangle. E17. 4 *Math.* a The raising of a quantity to any (orig., a positive) power. *arch.* E18. b *Geom.* A projective correspondence between pairs of points on a line, such that the product of the distances of each pair from a certain fixed point on the line is constant. M19. c A function or transformation that is equal to its inverse. E20. 5 *Physiol.* Shrinkage, regression, or atrophy of a part or organ (esp. the uterus) when inactive, or in old age. M19.

involutional *a.* (chiefly *Psychol.*) of or pertaining to physiological involution or mental disturbances associated with this change; *involutional depression* or *melancholia*, prolonged depression beginning late in life: E20. **involutionary** *a.* characterized by involution; retrograde E20. **involutory** *a.* (*Math.*) that is an involution M20.

involve /ɪnˈvɒlv/ *v.t.* Also **†en-**. LME. [L *involvere*, f. as IN-[2] + *volvere* roll.] 1 Wrap, surround, enfold, envelop. Foll. by *in*, †*with*. LME. 2 Make obscure or difficult to understand; complicate, entangle. LME. 3 Bring (a person) into a matter; embroil (a person) *in* trouble, difficulties, perplexity, etc. Freq. in *pass.* LME. b Commit emotionally; concern closely *with* another, *in* a matter. Freq. in *pass.* M20. 4 Wind spirally; wreathe, coil. M16. b *fig.* Join as by winding together; intertwine *with.* M17. 5†a Include covertly *in* or *under* something; wrap up. E17–E18. b Include, contain, comprehend. M17. c Contain implicitly; include as essential; imply, call for, entail. M17. d Affect, concern directly. M19. 6 Absorb completely; envelop, overwhelm. E17. b Engross; occupy (a person) fully. M20. 7 Implicate in a charge or crime; cause or prove (a person) to be concerned. M17. 8 *Math.* Raise (a quantity) to a power. Now *rare* or *obs.* L17.

1 E. B. BROWNING I saw Fog only, the great tawny weltering fog, Involve the passive city. 2 E. PAGITT This doctrine . . is involved with absurdities, and inexplicable contradictions. OED We must not further involve the statement; it is intricate enough already. 3 A. MILLER If you want to commit suicide do it alone, don't involve others. J. HELLER I dislike getting involved in long conversations. b M. PIERCY I thought you'd be involved with some guy. J. GATHORNE-HARDY I don't think you can help people unless you're prepared to be involved. 4 MILTON Some of the Serpent kinde, . . involv'd Thir Snakie foulds. b L. STERNE Our misfortunes were involved together. 5c P. ROTH I didn't realise that there was so much

psychology involved in dentistry. G. PRIESTLAND Being a Christian involves constant growth. **d** U. S. GRANT The safety of the nation was involved. I. COMPTON-BURNETT You, .. are virtually of the family and involved in its changes. H. WILSON There have been twenty-one changes of prime minister this century, involving fifteen men. **6** TENNYSON My love involves the love before; My love is vaster passion now. **b** R. P. JHABVALA He was completely involved in the work of the movement.

involver *n.* M19.

involved /ɪnˈvɒlvd/ *a.* E17. [f. prec. + -ED[1].] **1** Curved spirally; entwined, enwrapped, entangled. E17. †**2** Not straightforward and open; underhand, covert. E17–E18. **3** Intricate, complicated. M17. **b** Contained by implication, implicit. *rare.* M19. **4** Concerned, caring, committed. L20.

3 G. GREENE The involved beautiful unintelligible handwriting. 4 *Observer* The involved and caring father .. eases up on his career just as his wife does when their baby is born.

involvedly /-vɪdli/ *adv.* in a way that is involved implicitly E17. **involvedness** /-vɪdnɪs/ *n.* M17.

involvement /ɪnˈvɒlvm(ə)nt/ *n.* M17. [f. INVOLVE + -MENT.] †**1** An enveloping structure; a wrapping; an envelope, a case, a covering. Only in M17. **2** The action or process of involving something or someone; the fact or condition of being involved. E18. **b** An involved condition, manner, or style; an entanglement, a confused or complicated state of affairs. E19. **3** What is involved or implied in something; a necessary consequence or condition. L19.

2 P. BOWLES He hoped to avoid involvement in the affair. J. BERMAN The dangers of emotional involvement with his patient. *Sunday* (*Calcutta*) A sense of belonging and involvement. **b** *Fraser's Magazine* The plot .. depended .. on the 'involvement' consequent on the fact that every one .. is in love with .. Celeste. V. GLENDINNING A brief and trivial involvement with the Austrian girl.

invulnerable /ɪnˈvʌln(ə)rəb(ə)l/ *a.* L16. [L *invulnerabilis*, f. IN-[3] + *vulnerare* wound: see -ABLE.] Not liable to damage or harm, esp. from attack; unassailable. Of a person: unable to be physically or emotionally hurt.

I. BANKS Invulnerable, uncaring, the silver planes fly on through the furious hail of exploding shells. R. ELLMANN His role of invulnerable and detached profligate is challenged by love.

invulneraˈbility *n.* the quality or state of being invulnerable L18. **invulnerableness** *n.* M17. **invulnerably** *adv.* so as to be invulnerable M19.

invultuation /ɪnˌvʌltjʊˈeɪʃ(ə)n/ *n. rare.* Also **invultation** /ɪnvʌlˈteɪʃ(ə)n/. M19. [med.L *invultuatio(n-)* f. *invultuare* make a likeness, f. as IN-[2] + *vultus* visage, likeness: see -ATION.] The making of a likeness, esp. a waxen effigy of a person for purposes of witchcraft.

in-wale /ˈɪnweɪl/ *n.* L19. [f. IN *adv.* + WALE *n.*[1]] A horizontal timber on the inside of a boat.

inwall /ˈɪnwɔːl/ *n.* E17. [f. IN *adv.* + WALL *n.*[1]] An inner or inside wall.

inwall *v.* var. of ENWALL.

inward /ˈɪnwəd/ *a.* & *n.* [OE *innanweard*, *inneweard*, *inweard*, f. inflected forms or base of IN *adv.*, *prep.* + *-weard* -WARD.] **A** *adj.* **1** Situated within; that is the inner or innermost part; that is on the inside. OE. **b** Situated in or belonging to the interior of a country or region; inland. Now *rare.* M17. **c** Of speech etc.: not clearly enunciated; muffled, indistinct. L18. **2** Within or of the mind, soul, or spirit; mental, spiritual. ME. †**b** Deeply felt, earnest, heartfelt. LME–E17. **c** Spiritually minded, pious; contemplative; introverted, reserved. LME. **3** Close, intimate; familiar, well acquainted. Now *rare.* L15. †**4** Existing in or pertaining to a country or place; domestic, civil. E16–E19. †**5** Secret, private; confidential. M16–E17. **6** Directed or proceeding towards the inside; coming in from outside. M19.

2 J. M. MURRY The most intimate motion of Keats' inward life. J. STEINBECK What he said .. made her give a small inward start. 3 F. QUARLES Friendly to all men, inward but with few. 6 *Independent* In order to help China modernise .. the Government has encouraged foreign inward investment.

B *n.* **1** In *pl.* & (now *rare*) *sing.* The inner part, the inside. Usu. *spec.* the internal parts or organs of the body, the entrails. OE. **2** The inner nature or essence of a thing or person; thoughts, mental processes. *rare.* OE. †**3** An intimate or familiar acquaintance. *rare.* Only in E17. **4** In *pl.* Articles coming in or imported, dues on such articles. M18.

inward /ˈɪnwəd/ *adv.* [OE *innanweard* etc.: see prec.] **1** Towards the inside or interior; into a country or place. OE. †**b** On the inside, within, internally. LME–L17. **2** *fig.* †**a** Within the mind or soul, mentally, inwardly. OE–M17. **b** Into the mind or soul; into one's own thoughts. ME.

2b C. WILSON Yeats's reaction .. was to turn inward, into a world of fantasy.

Comb.: **inward-looking** *a.* introverted, self-absorbed; parochial, insular.

inwardly /ˈɪnwədli/ *adv.* OE. [f. INWARD *a.* & *n.* + -LY[2].] **1** †**a** In or from the inmost heart; with deep emotion or feeling; heartily, fervently, earnestly. OE–M17. **b** In mind or thought, mentally; at heart; in reality; secretly. ME. †**2** Intimately, thoroughly; closely. ME–E18. **3** On the inside, in the inner part; within, internally. L15. **b** In words to oneself, not aloud. M16. **4** Towards the inside or inner part; towards that which is within, into the mind or soul. Now *rare* or *obs.* M17.

1b J. UPDIKE Harry calculates inwardly that he has made a thousand a month on his gold. L. WHISTLER He was inwardly apprehensive as well as outwardly adventurous. *groan inwardly*: see GROAN *v.*

inwardness /ˈɪnwədnɪs/ *n.* LME. [f. INWARD *a.* + -NESS.] †**1** The inner part or region; in *pl.*, inner parts, entrails. Only in LME. **2** Intimacy, familiarity; close friendship. Now *rare.* L16. **3** Intrinsic character; inner nature, essence, or meaning. E17. **4** The quality or condition of being inward or inside something else. *lit.* & *fig.* E17. **5a** Depth or intensity of feeling or thought. M19. **b** Preoccupation with one's inner self, self-absorption; concern with spiritual or philosophical matters rather than externalities; spirituality. M19.

5a *Gramophone* Arrau plays with sublime inwardness and a flow of rhythm and tone which is uniquely fine. **b** D. PRATER One whose gift was to be the expression of inwardness and the visionary. A. BROOKNER The sight of those whom he loved .. lifted the veil of inwardness from Oscar's face.

inwards /ˈɪnwədz/ *adv.* & *a.* ME. [f. INWARD *adv.* + -S[3].] **A** *adv.* = INWARD *adv.* ME. **B** *adj.* = INWARD *a.* 6. *rare.* M16.

inwarp /ɪnˈwɔːp/ *v.t. rare.* E19. [f. IN-[1] + WARP *v.*] Weave in, interweave.

inweave /ɪnˈwiːv/ *v.t.* Also **en-**. Pa. t. **-wove** /-ˈwəʊv/; pa. pple **-woven** /-ˈwəʊv(ə)n/, **-wove**. LME. [f. IN-[1], or IN-[2], EN-[1] + WEAVE *v.*[1]] **1** Combine or decorate *with* something inserted or entwined. LME. **2** Weave in; weave (things) together; interweave. L16. **3** Insert or depict by weaving in or entwining. Foll. by *in*, *into*, *on*. L16. **4** Form by weaving or plaiting. *rare.* M17.

2 *fig.*: J. RUSKIN Our moral feelings are .. inwoven with our intellectual powers. 3 D. ROCK A vast number of figures and animals inwoven into its fabric. *fig.*: COLERIDGE To inweave in a poem of the loftiest style .. such minute matters of fact.

inwick /ˈɪnwɪk/ *n.* & *v.* E19. [f. IN *adv.* + WICK *v.*[1]] *Curling.* **A** *n.* A shot made so as to strike the inside of another stone and glance off it to the tee. E19. **B** *v.i.* Make an inwick. E19.

inwind *v.* var. of ENWIND.

inwinter /ˈɪnwɪntə/ *v.t.* M20. [f. IN-[1] + WINTER *v.*] Protect (animals, esp. severe sheep) by providing food and shelter during severe weather.

inwit /ˈɪnwɪt/ *n. arch.* ME. [f. IN *adv.* + WIT *n.*] **1** Conscience; inward sense of right and wrong. ME. **2** Reason, understanding; wisdom. ME. †**3** Courage; heart, soul, mind. *rare.* Only in LME.

inwith /ɪnˈwɪð/ *prep.* & *adv. obs.* exc. *Sc.* ME. [f. IN *adv.* + WITH *prep.* Cf. WITHIN.] †**A** *prep.* **1** Of place: within, inside of. ME–E16. **2** Of time: within the period of. Only in ME. **B** *adv.* †**1** Of position: within, inside. ME–M16. **2** Of direction: inwards. M18.

†**inwomb** *v.* var. of ENWOMB.

For other words beginning with *in-* see the entry for **in-**[1]

inwork /ɪnˈwəːk/ *v. rare.* Infl. as WORK *v.* L16. [f. IN-[1] or IN *adv.* + WORK *v.* See also INWROUGHT.] **1** *v.i.* Work within or inside. L16. **2** *v.t.* Work, embroider, or weave (something) *in* or *on.* L17. **3** *v.t.* Work or produce (some effect) *in.* M19.

ˈ**inworker** *n.* a person who works within; now *esp.* a person who works on the employer's premises: L16. ˈ**inworking** *n.* †(*a*) action, energy; (*b*) internal operation, working within: L16.

inwove, **inwoven** *vs.* see INWEAVE.

inwrap *v.* var. of ENWRAP.

inwreathe *v.* var. of ENWREATHE.

inwrought /ɪnˈrɔːt, *attrib.* ˈɪnrɔːt/ *ppl a.* Also **en-** /ɪn-, ɛn-/. M17. [f. IN *adv.* + *wrought* pa. pple of WORK *v.*] **1** Of a fabric etc.: decorated *with*, having something worked in. *lit.* & *fig.* M17. **2** Of a pattern, figure, etc.: worked into or embroidered on a fabric. M18. **3a** Worked into something as a constituent. M18. **b** Worked together or blended *with* something; combined, intermingled, entangled. E19.

1 G. BIRDWOOD Sumptuously inwrought apparel. 2 WORDSWORTH Flowers enwrought On silken tissue.

inyala *n.* see NYALA.

inyanga /ɪnˈjɑːŋə/ *n. S. Afr.* M19. [Zulu.] A traditional herbalist and medicine man, sometimes acting as diviner or magician.

inyoke /ɪnˈjəʊk/ *v.t. rare.* L16. [f. IN-[1] + YOKE *v.*] Yoke or join (*to*, *unto*, etc.).

Io /ˈʌɪəʊ/ *n.*[1] & *int. arch.* L16. [L *io*, Gk *iō*.] (An exclamation) expr. joy or triumph.

Comb.: *Io paean*: see PAEAN I.

io /ˈʌɪəʊ/ *n.*[2] Pl. **ios**. L19. [mod.L, f. Gk *Iō*, the daughter of the river-god Inachus.] In full *io moth*. A large, mainly yellow N. American moth, *Automeris io*, having prominent eyespots on the hindwings.

iod- *pref.* see IODO-.

iodargyrite /ʌɪəˈdɑːdʒɪrʌɪt/ *n.* M19. [f. IODO- + CER)ARGYRITE.] Native silver iodide, AgI, a yellow or greenish mineral crystallizing in the hexagonal system.

iodate /ˈʌɪədeɪt/ *n.* E19. [f. IODIC + -ATE[1].] *Chem.* A salt of iodic acid; *spec.* a salt of iodic(v) acid. Cf. PERIODATE.

iodated /ˈʌɪə(ʊ)deɪtɪd/ *a.* M19. [f. IOD(INE *n.* + -ATE[3] + -ED[1].] Impregnated or treated with iodine; iodinated.

iodic /ʌɪˈɒdɪk/ *a.* E19. [f. IODO- + -IC. Cf. Fr. *iodique.*] **1** *Chem.* Of or pertaining to iodine. Chiefly in *iodic acid*, any of several oxo acids of iodine, *esp.* that of its pentavalent oxidation state (HIO_3). Cf. PERIODIC *a.*[2] E19. **2** *Med.* Caused by administration of iodine. *arch. rare.* L19.

iodide /ˈʌɪədʌɪd/ *n.* E19. [f. IODINE *n.* + -IDE.] *Chem.* A compound of iodine with a less electronegative element or radical; a salt or ester of hydriodic acid.

iodimetry /ʌɪəˈdɪmɪtri/ *n.* L19. [f. IODI(NE *n.* + -METRY.] *Chem.* Redox titration using iodine; *spec.* the quantitative analysis of a solution of a reducing agent by titration with a standard solution of iodine. Cf. IODOMETRY.

iodiˈmetric *a.* of or pertaining to iodimetry L19. **iodiˈmetrically** *adv.* by means of iodimetry L19.

iodinate /ˈʌɪədɪneɪt, ʌɪˈɒdɪneɪt/ *v.t.* E20. [f. IODINE *n.* + -ATE[3].] Treat with iodine; *Chem.* introduce one or more iodine atoms into (a compound or molecule), usu. in place of hydrogen. Freq. as *iodinated* ppl a.

iodinatable *a.* (chiefly of a protein) able to be iodinated L20. **iodiˈnation** *n.* L19.

iodine /ˈʌɪədiːn, -ʌɪn, -ɪn/ *n.* & *v.* E19. [f. Fr. *iode* f. Gk *iōdēs* violet-coloured, f. *ion* violet + *-eidēs* like: see -OID, -INE[5].] **A** *n.* A chemical element of the halogen group, atomic no. 53, which is a greyish-black solid that forms a dense violet vapour. (Symbol I.) E19. **B** *v.t.* Treat with iodine. M19.

Comb.: **iodine number** the degree of unsaturation of a hydrocarbon chain, etc., as measured by the number of grams of iodine absorbed by 100 grams of the substance; **iodine scarlet** mercuric iodide, HgI_2, a brilliant red toxic powder; **iodine value** = *iodine number* above.

i'odinized *a.* (of a material) treated or impregnated with iodine E20.

iodise *v.* var. of IODIZE.

iodism /ˈʌɪədɪz(ə)m/ *n.* M19. [f. IODO- + -ISM.] *Med.* Chronic poisoning by iodine (or its compounds).

iodize /ˈʌɪədʌɪz/ *v.t.* Also **-ise**. M19. [f. IODO- + -IZE.] Orig. (in *Photogr.*), treat or impregnate with silver iodide. Now usu., add iodine or an iodide to (a substance, e.g. table salt). Chiefly as *iodized* ppl a.

iodi'zation *n.* the process or practice of iodizing something; the addition of iodine or an iodine compound to a substance: E20.

iodo- /ˈʌɪədəʊ, ʌɪˈəʊdəʊ/ *comb. form.* Bef. a vowel also **iod-**. E20. [f. mod.L *iodum* IODINE: see -O-.] **1** *Chem.* Denoting compounds formed by replacement of one or more hydrogen atoms by iodine, as *iodobenzene*, *iodoform*, *iodophenol*, or other compounds or mixture containing iodine. **2** Of or pertaining to iodine.

iodomethane *n.* a sweet-smelling liquid, CH_3I (methyl iodide), used as a methylating agent L19. **i'odophil(e** *a.* (esp. of bacteria which contain compounds similar to starch) readily stained by iodine E20. **iodo'philic** *a.* = IODOPHIL M20. **iodo'protein** *n.* any protein containing iodine E20.

iodoform /ʌɪˈəʊdə(ʊ)fɔːm, ˈʌɪədə(ʊ)fɔːm/ *n.* M19. [f. IODO- + FORM(YL, after *chloroform*.] A yellow crystalline compound of iodine, CHI_3, analogous to chloroform, having a strong sweetish odour and used in tests for alcohols, and as an external antiseptic; triiodomethane.

iodometry /ʌɪəˈdɒmɪtri/ *n.* L19. [f. IODO- + -METRY.] *Chem.* Redox titration using iodine; *spec.* the quantitative analysis of a solution of an oxidizing agent by addition of excess iodide to liberate iodine which is then titrated, usu. with thiosulphate using starch as indicator. Cf. IODIMETRY.

iodo'metric *a.* of or pertaining to iodometry M19. **iodo'metrically** *adv.* by means of iodometry E20.

iodophor /ʌɪˈəʊdə(ʊ)fɔː, ˈʌɪəd-/ *n.* M20. [f. IODO- + -PHOR(E.] *Chem.* Any compound which complexes with iodine; *spec.* any substance in which iodine is stabilized and solubilized by combination with a surfactant for use as a disinfectant.

†ioduret *n.* E-M19. [f. IODO- + -URET.] *Chem.* = IODIDE.

†iodduretted *a.* = IODATED M-L19.

iodyrite /ʌɪˈɒdɪrʌɪt/ *n.* M19. [f. IODO- after CERARGYRITE.] *Min.* = IODARGYRITE.

iolite /ˈʌɪə(ʊ)lʌɪt/ *n.* E19. [G *Iolit(h)*, f. Gk *ion* violet + *lithos* stone: see -LITE.] *Min.* = CORDIERITE.

ion /ˈʌɪən/ *n.* M19. [Gk, neut. pres. pple of *ienai* go.] *Physics* & *Chem.* Orig., either of the constituents which pass to the electrodes during electrolysis. Now *gen.*, any individual atom, molecule, or group having a net electric charge (either positive or negative) due to loss or gain of one or more electrons. Cf. ANION, CATION.

Comb.: **ion burn** the damaging of the phosphor of a cathode-ray tube by negative ions focused on the screen; an ion spot so produced; **ion chamber** an ionization chamber; **ion drive** (*a*) = *ion propulsion* below; (*b*) = *ion engine* below; **ion engine**: that employs ion propulsion; **ion etching** the controlled removal of extremely thin layers of material from a surface with a beam of ions; **ion exchange**: of ions of like charge between an insoluble solid and a solution in contact with it; *ion-exchange resin*, any synthetic polymer suitable for use as an ion exchanger, usu. having a porous cross-linked molecular network with ionized or ionizable groups weakly attached; **ion exchanger** a solid involved or used in ion exchange; an apparatus for effecting ion exchange; **ion gun** a device which produces a beam of ions; **ion implantation**: of ions in a substance to make a semiconductor; **ion pair** (*a*) a pair of oppositely charged ions held together in a solution by electrostatic attraction; (*b*) a negative ion (or an electron) and a positive ion formed from a neutral atom or molecule by the action of radiation; **ion propulsion** rocket propulsion in which thrust is produced by the electrically accelerated ejection of ions formed inside the engine; **ion rocket** a rocket (engine) that employs ion propulsion; **ion source** a device for producing ions, *spec.* an ion gun; **ion spot** (*a*) a dark spot on a screen caused by ion burn; (*b*) a white spot in a television picture produced by ionized gas molecules striking the target of the camera; **ion trap** a device designed to catch ions to prevent them from causing an ion spot on a screen.

-ion /(ə)n, ɪən, jən/ *suff.* [Repr. Fr. *-ion*, L *-ion-*, *-io*.] Forming ns. denoting (*a*) vbl action, as *excision*, *damnation*, *pollution*; (*b*) an instance of this, as *a suggestion*, *a notion*, *an action*; (*c*) a resulting state or product, as *vexation*, *concoction*, *completion*. Usu. appears in *-tion*, *-sion*, *-xion*, esp. -ATION.

Ionian /ʌɪˈəʊnɪən/ *n.* & *a.* M16. [f. L *Ionius* f. Gk *Iōnios* (f. *Iōnia* Ionia) + -AN.] **A** *n.* A member of the Hellenic people who occupied Attica and colonized western Asia Minor (part of which was named Ionia after them), the islands of the Aegean and those off the west coast of Greece, etc.; a native or inhabitant of Ionia. M16.

B *adj.* Of or pertaining to Ionia or the Ionians; Ionic. M16.

Ionian mode *Mus.* (*a*) an ancient Greek mode, characterized as soft and light; (*b*) the last of the church modes (with C as final and G as dominant), corresponding to the modern major key of C.

Ionic /ʌɪˈɒnɪk/ *a.*[1] & *n.* L16. [L *Ionicus* f. Gk *Iōnikos*, f. *Iōnia* Ionia: see -IC.] **A** *adj.* **1** *Archit.* Designating one of the three Greek orders, characterized by a column with scroll-shapes on either side of the capital. L16. **†2** *Mus.* In the ancient Ionian mode. L16-E19. **3** Of or pertaining to Ionia or the Ionians; Ionian. L16. **4** *Class. Pros.* Designating a foot consisting of two long syllables followed by two short or two short followed by two long; pertaining to or consisting of such feet. M17.

3 Ionic dialect the most important of the three main branches of ancient Greek. **Ionic school, sect of philosophy**: founded by Thales of Miletus in Asiatic Ionia.

B *n.* **†1** An Ionian; a member of the Ionic school of philosophy. L16-E17. **2** *Class. Pros.* An Ionic foot or verse; Ionic metre. E17. **3** The Ionic dialect of ancient Greek. M17. **4** *Typogr.* A typeface distinguished by prominent serifs and a high degree of legibility. M19.

Ionicism /-sɪz(ə)m/ *n.* something characteristic of Ionians or the Ionic dialect; Ionic character: E19. **Ionicize** /-sʌɪz/ *v.* (*a*) *v.i.* use the Ionic dialect; (*b*) *v.t.* make Ionic: M19. **Ionism** /ˈʌɪənɪz(ə)m/ *n.* = IONICISM L18.

ionic /ʌɪˈɒnɪk/ *a.*[2] L19. [f. ION + -IC.] *Physics* & *Chem.* **1** Of or pertaining to ions; composed of or containing ions; that is an ion. L19. **2** Involving or employing ions; *spec.* (of a bond) electrovalent. E20.

ionically *adv.* by means of ions or an ionic bond; as regards or in terms of ions: E20.

ionicity /ʌɪəˈnɪsɪti/ *n.* M20. [f. IONIC *a.*[2]: see -ICITY.] *Chem.* Ionic character (in a chemical bond or a crystal).

ionisation *n.*, **Ionise** *v.*[1], **ionise** *v.*[2] vars. of IONIZATION etc.

ionium /ʌɪˈəʊnɪəm/ *n.* E20. [f. ION + -IUM.] *Chem.* A radioactive isotope of thorium with atomic mass 230, produced by the α -decay of uranium-234. (Symbol ^{230}Th.)

ionization /ʌɪənʌɪˈzeɪʃ(ə)n/ *n.* Also **-isation**. L19. [f. ION + -IZATION.] **1** The state of being ionized; the process of ionizing. L19. **2** *Med.* = CATAPHORESIS 1. E20.

1 *specific ionization*: see SPECIFIC *a.*

Comb.: **ionization chamber** an instrument for measuring radiation intensity by measuring the charge on the ions produced by the radiation in a volume of gas; **ionization constant** *Physical Chem.* = DISSOCIATION *constant*; **ionization current**: arising out of the movement in an electric field of the ions and electrons in an ionized gas; **ionization energy** = *ionization potential* below; **ionization gauge** an instrument for measuring the degree of vacuum in a vessel from the ionization current produced in the residual gas; **ionization potential** the energy required to remove an electron in its lowest energy state from an atom.

Ionize /ˈʌɪənʌɪz/ *v.*[1]*i.* & *t.* Also **-ise**. E19. [Gk *iōnizein*, f. *Iōnia* Ionia: see -IZE.] Ionicize.

ionize /ˈʌɪənʌɪz/ *v.*[2] Also **-ise**. L19. [f. ION + -IZE.] **1** *v.t.* & *i. Physics.* Convert (an atom) into an ion by loss or gain of one or more electrons; produce ions in (a substance). L19. **2** *v.i. Physics.* Dissociate into ions; become converted into an ion or ions. E20. **3** *v.t. Med.* **a** Introduce (a substance) into tissue by means of cataphoresis. (Foll. by *into*.) E20. **b** Treat by cataphoresis. E20.

ionizable *a.* E20. **ionizer** *n.* an agent which produces ionization, *spec.* with the purpose of improving the quality of air in a room E20. **ionizing** *ppl a.* that ionizes; chiefly in *ionizing radiation*, radiation of sufficient energy to cause ionization in matter through which it passes: L19.

ionogen /ˈʌɪənədʒ(ə)n, ʌɪˈɒnədʒ(ə)n/ *n.* Now *rare*. E20. [f. ION + -O- + -GEN.] *Physical Chem.* Any compound which exists as ions when dissolved in a solvent.

ionogenic /ʌɪˌɒnə(ʊ)ˈdʒɛnɪk/ *a.* E20. [f. as prec. + -IC.] *Chem.* **†1** Of an atom or radical: promoting ionization elsewhere in the molecule of which it forms part. Only in E20. **2** Able to be ionized chemically. E20.

ionogram /ʌɪˈɒnə(ʊ)gram/ *n.* M20. [f. ION (in sense 1 extracted f. IONOSPHERE) + -O- + -GRAM.] **1** A record of reflected radio pulses produced by an ionosonde. M20. **2** *Chem.* The result of an ionographic separation, usu. a series of spots or bands on the support medium. M20.

ionography /ʌɪəˈnɒgrəfi/ *n.* M20. [f. ION + -OGRAPHY.] *Chem.* The migration in an electric field of ions or charged colloidal particles in a buffer solution held on a support (usu. filter paper), esp. as used to separate components of a mixture.

iono'graphic *a.* of or pertaining to ionography M20.

ionomer /ʌɪˈɒnəmə/ *n.* M20. [f. ION + -O- + -MER.] Any of a class of thermoplastic resins in which there is ionic bonding between the polymer chains.

ionone /ˈʌɪənəʊn/ *n.* L19. [Gk *ion* violet + -ONE.] *Chem.* (Proprietary name in the US for) either of two isomeric liquid aromatic ketones (*α-ionone* and *β-ionone*), $(CH_3)_3C_6H_6CH{:}CH{\cdot}CO{\cdot}CH_3$, used esp. in perfumery for their strong odour of violets.

ionophore /ʌɪˈɒnə(ʊ)fɔː/ *n.* M20. [f. ION + -O- + -PHORE.] *Biol.* An agent which is able to transport ions across a lipid membrane in a cell.

ionophorous /ʌɪəˈnɒf(ə)rəs/ *a.* M20.

ionophoresis /ʌɪˌɒnə(ʊ)fəˈriːsɪs/ *n.* M20. [f. ION after *electrophoresis*.] *Biochem.* The migration in an electric field of ions in solution, esp. as used to separate the components of a mixture.

ionophoretic /-ˈrɛtɪk/ *a.* M20.

ionosonde /ʌɪˈɒnə(ʊ)sɒnd/ *n.* M20. [f. IONO(SPHERE + SONDE.] An instrument sent aloft to investigate the ionosphere by transmitting radio pulses into it and recording their echoes.

ionosphere /ʌɪˈɒnəsfɪə/ *n.* E20. [f. ION + -O- + -SPHERE.] A region of the outer atmosphere, upwards of 50–80 km (30–50 miles), which contains many ions and free electrons and is able to reflect radio waves, allowing long-range transmission; also, a corresponding region above the surfaces of other planets.

ionospheric /ʌɪˌɒnə(ʊ)ˈsfɛrɪk/ *a.* of, pertaining to, or involving the ionosphere M20. **iono'spherically** *adv.* by the ionosphere M20. **iono'spher(ic)ist** *n.* (*rare*) a person who studies the ionosphere M20.

ionotropy /ʌɪəˈnɒtrəpi/ *n.* E20. [f. ION + -O- + Gk *tropia* turning (f. *trepein* turn) + -Y[3].] *Chem.* **1** Tautomerism occurring through the migration of part of the molecule as an ion. E20. **2** The ordering of particles in a gel that results when an electrolyte is added to a colloidal suspension. M20.

ionotropic /-ˈtrəʊpɪk, -ˈtrɒpɪk/ *a.* pertaining to or exhibiting ionotropy M20.

iontophoresis /ʌɪˌɒntə(ʊ)fəˈriːsɪs/ *n.* E20. [f. Gk *iont-*, ION pres. pple of *ienai* go + -O- + -PHORESIS.] *Med.* = CATAPHORESIS 1, *spec.* for the passage of ions into the body.

iontophoretic /-ˈrɛtɪk/ *a.* of, pertaining to, or employing iontophoresis M20. **iontophoretically** *adv.* by means of iontophoresis M20.

-ior /ɪə, jə/ *suff.* [L.] Forming adjs. of comparison, as *inferior, superior, ulterior, junior, senior.*

iota /ʌɪˈəʊtə/ *n.* LME. [Gk *iōta*, of Phoenician origin: cf. YOD.] **1** The ninth (and smallest) letter (*I*, ι) of the Greek alphabet). LME. **2** *fig.* The smallest or a very small part or quantity. Cf. JOD, JOT *n.*[1] M17.

1 **iota subscript** a small iota written beneath a long vowel, forming the second element of a diphthong but not pronounced. 2 E. LEWIS You have not changed one iota since you left me at college. N. SYMINGTON I could not remember an iota more than that.

iotacism /ʌɪˈəʊtəsɪz(ə)m/ *n.* M16. [Late L *iotacismus* f. late Gk *iōtakismos*, f. as prec. + -ISM w. hiatus-filling *k*.] Excessive use or repetition of the letter iota or I; *spec.* the pronunciation of other Greek vowels like iota. Cf. ITACISM.

IOU /ʌɪəʊˈjuː/ *n.* L18. [Repr. pronunc. of 'I owe you'.] A document constituting a formal acknowledgement of a debt, usu. bearing the three letters 'IOU', a specified sum, and a signature.

¶Repr. the statement 'I owe you' the letters *IOU* occur E17.

-ious /ɪəs, əs/ *suff.* [f. *-i* (cf. -I-) + -OUS, repr. L *-iosus*, Fr. *-ieux*.] Forming adjs. w. the sense 'characterized by, full of', as *cautious, curious, spacious.* Often corresp. to ns. in *-ion*, esp. those in *-tion, -cion, -sion*, as *rebellion, rebellious, infection, infectious.* See -ITIOUS[2], -OUS.

Iowan /ˈʌɪəwən/ *n.* & *a.* M19. [f. *Iowa* (see below) + -AN.] **A** *n.* A native or inhabitant of Iowa, a State of the US. M19. **B** *adj.* Of or pertaining to Iowa; *spec.* in *Geol.* of, pertaining to or designating one of the glacial episodes in the Pleistocene of N. America. L19.

ipecac /ˈɪpɪkak/ *n. colloq.* L18. [Abbrev.] = next.

ipecacuanha /ˌɪpɪkakjʊˈanə/ *n.* E17. [Port. f. Tupi-Guarani *ipekaaguéne* f. *ipe* small + *kaa* leaves + *guéne* vomit.] **1** The root of *Cephaelis ipecacuanha*, a Brazilian plant of the madder family; an extract or preparation of this, formerly much used as an emetic and expectorant. Also, the plant itself. E17. **2** Any of various other plants with emetic roots; a preparation of such a root. E18.

2 **American ipecacuanha** a plant of the rose family, *Gillenia trifoliata*, of the US. **bastard ipecacuanha** a S. American plant, *Asclepias curassavica* (family Asclepiadaceae). **black ipecacuanha, Peruvian ipecacuanha** a S. American plant of the madder family, *Psychotria emetica*, used as an inferior substitute for ipecacuanha. **white ipecacuanha** a S. American plant of the violet family, *Hybanthus calceolaria*.

Comb.: **ipecacuanha wine** the filtered infusion of ipecacuanha root in wine.

ipiti /ɪˈpiːti/ *n. S. Afr.* M19. [Zulu *i-phithi*.] The blue duiker, *Cephalophus monticola*, a very small antelope of southern and central African forests.

ipoh /ˈiːpəʊ/ *n.* L18. [Malay.] The upas-tree, *Antiaris toxicaria*, of the mulberry family, or a creeping shrub, *Strychnos ignatii* (family Loganiaceae), both native to SE Asia and having a poisonous sap. Also, the poison itself.

ipomoea /ɪpəˈmiːə/ *n.* L18. [mod.L (see below), f. Gk *ip-* *ips* woodworm + *homoios* like.] *Bot.* Any of various mostly tropical twining or creeping plants of the genus *Ipomoea*, of the bindweed family, which includes the morning glory, *I. purpurea*, and many other ornamentals, and the sweet potato, *I. batatas*.

ippon /ˈɪpɒn/ *n.* M20. [Jap.] A score of one full point in judo, karate, etc.

iproniazid /ʌɪprə(ʊ)ˈnʌɪəzɪd/ *n.* M20. [f. *isopropyl* (see ISO-) + ISO)NIAZID.] *Pharm.* A derivative of isoniazid, $(CH_3)_2CH{\cdot}NH{\cdot}NH{\cdot}CO{\cdot}C_5H_4N$, used, usu. as the crystalline phosphate, in the treatment of depression and (formerly) tuberculosis.

ipse dixit /ɪpsiː ˈdɪksɪt, ɪpseɪ/ *n.* Pl. ***ipse dixits***. L16. [L, lit. 'he himself said (it)', tr. Gk *autos epha*, phr. used of Pythagoras by his followers.] An unproved assertion resting only on the authority of a speaker; a dogmatic statement; a dictum.

ipseity /ɪpˈseɪɪti, ɪpˈsiːɪti/ *n.* M17. [f. L *ipse* self + -ITY, after EGOITY.] Personal identity; selfhood; self-centredness.

ipsilateral /ɪpsɪˈlat(ə)r(ə)l/ *a.* E20. [f. L *ipse* self + LATERAL *a.*] *Med.* Belonging to or occurring on the same or on one side of the body; connecting two parts on the same side. Opp. *contralateral*.

ipsilaterally *adv.* on the same or on one side of the body M20.

ipsissima verba /ɪpˌsɪsɪmə ˈvəːbə/ *n. phr.* E19. [L.] The precise words used by a writer or speaker.

ipso facto /ɪpsəʊ ˈfaktəʊ/ *adv. phr.* M16. [L.] By that very fact or act; by the fact itself; thereby. Cf. EO IPSO.

ipso jure /ɪpsəʊ ˈdʒʊəreɪ, ˈdʒʊəri/ *adv. phr.* L16. [L.] By the operation of the law itself.

Ipswichian /ɪpˈswɪtʃɪən/ *a.* & *n.* M20. [f. *Ipswich*, a town in Suffolk, East Anglia + -IAN.] *Geol.* **A** *adj.* Designating or pertaining to the most recent interglacial of the Pleistocene in Britain, and the corresponding stratigraphic stage. M20. **B** *n.* The Ipswichian interglacial or stage. M20.

†-ique *suff.* var. of -IC.

ir- /ɪ/ *pref.*[1] Var. of L IN-[2] bef. *r.* Cf. IL-[1], IM-[1].

ir- /ɪ/ *pref.*[2] Var. of L IN-[3] bef. *r.* Cf. I-[2], IL-[2], IM-[2].

iracund /ˈʌɪrəkʌnd/ *a. rare.* E19. [L *iracundus*, f. *ira* anger + *-cundus* inclining to.] Inclined to anger; choleric, irascible.

ira'cundity *n.* M19.

irade /ɪˈrɑːdi/ *n.* L19. [Turk. *irade* f. Arab. *'irāda* will, decree, f. *'arāda* intend.] *Hist.* A written decree issued in the name of a Sultan of Turkey during the Ottoman period.

†Iraki *n.* & *a.* see IRAQI.

Iranian /ɪˈreɪnɪən, ɪˈrɑː-/ *n.* & *a.* L18. [f. *Iran* (see below) + -IAN.] **A** *n.* **1** A native or inhabitant of Iran (formerly Persia), a country in the Middle East; a speaker of an Iranian language. L18. **2** *Ling.* One of the two groups of languages in the Indo-Iranian branch of Indo-European, comprising Old Persian and Avestan and their modern descendants or cognates; the language of the Iranians. E19. **B** *adj.* Of or pertaining to Iran (formerly Persia) or Iranian. M19.

Iranianist *n.* a student of Iran or Iranian L20. **Iranic** /ɪˈranɪk/ *a.* M19. **Iranize** /ɪˈranʌɪz/ *v.t.* make Iranian in character etc. L19.

Iraqi /ɪˈrɑːki/ *n.* & *a.* Also **-qui**, (earlier) **†-ki**. E19. [f. *Iraq* (see below) + -I[2].] **A** *n.* A native or inhabitant of Iraq, a country in the Middle East. E19. **B** *adj.* Of or pertaining to Iraq or its inhabitants. E20.

Iraqi'zation *n.* making Iraqi in character etc. M20. **Iraqize** *v.t.* make Iraqi in character etc. M20.

irascible /ɪˈrasɪb(ə)l/ *a.* LME. [(O)Fr. f. late L *irascibilis*, f. L *irasci* grow angry, f. *ira* anger: see -IBLE.] **1** Easily provoked to anger or resentment; prone to anger; irritable, hot-tempered. LME. **2** Of an emotion, action, etc.: characterized by, arising from, or exhibiting anger. M17.

1 C. BLACKWOOD These irascible old figures started to make their habitual peevish fuss. **irascible principle** (in Platonic philosophy) one of the two parts of irrational human nature (the other being the *concupiscible*), the seat of courage, anger, etc. 2 P. GROSSKURTH A domestic tyrant, Jakob oppressed his family with his irascible temper.

irasci'bility *n.* LME.

irate /ʌɪˈreɪt/ *a.* M19. [L *iratus*, f. *ira* anger: see -ATE[2].] Angry, incensed, enraged.

irately *adv.* L19. **irateness** *n.* L20.

ire /ˈʌɪə/ *n.* Now chiefly *rhet.* ME. [(O)Fr. f. L *ira* anger.] Anger; wrath.

ireful *a.* (*a*) angry; (*b*) irascible: ME. **irefully** *adv.* angrily L15. **irefulness** *n.* (*rare*) wrathfulness LME. **ireless** *a.* E19.

irenarch /ˈʌɪrɪnɑːk/ *n. rare.* E18. [Late L *irenarcha* f. Gk *eirēnarkhēs*, f. *eirēnē* peace + *-arkhēs* -ARCH.] *Hist.* An Eastern provincial governor or keeper of the peace, under the Roman and Byzantine Empires.

irenic /ʌɪˈrɛnɪk, -ˈriː-/ *a.* Also **ei-**. M19. [Gk *eirēnikos*, f. *eirēnē* peace: see -IC. Cf. Fr. *irénique*.] Pacific; conciliatory, non-polemical; irenical.

irenical /ʌɪˈrɛnɪk(ə)l, -ˈriː-/ *a.* Also **ei-**. M17. [f. as prec. + -AL[1].] Peaceful; conciliatory, tending to promote peace, esp. in theological or ecclesiastical disputes.

irenically *adv.* L19.

irenicon *n.* see EIRENICON.

irenics /ʌɪˈrɛnɪks, -ˈriː-/ *n.* L19. [f. IRENIC: see -ICS.] Irenical theology. Opp. *polemics*.

Irgun /ɪəˈgʊn/ *n.* M20. [mod.Heb. *'irgūn* (*sĕbā'ī lĕ'ummī*) (national military) organization.] A militant right-wing Zionist organization founded in 1931 and disbanded after the creation of Israel in 1948.

Irgunist *n.* a member of this organization M20.

Irianese /ɪrɪəˈniːz/ *n.* & *a.* M20. [f. *Irian* Jaya (see below) + -ESE.] **A** *n.* Pl. same. A native or inhabitant of Irian Jaya (formerly Dutch New Guinea or Netherlands New Guinea), since 1963 a province of Indonesia. M20. **B** *adj.* Of or pertaining to Irian Jaya. L20.

Iricism /ˈʌɪrɪsɪz(ə)m/ *n.* M18. [Irreg. f. IRISH after *Scotticism*.] An Irish expression, characteristic, etc.

irid /ˈʌɪrɪd/ *n.* E19. [Gk *irid-* IRIS: see -ID[2].] **1** The iris of the eye. *rare.* E19. **2** *Bot.* Any plant of the iris family. M19.

irid- *comb. form* see IRIDO-.

iridaceous /ʌɪrɪˈdeɪʃəs, ɪr-/ *a.* M19. [f. mod.L *iridaceus*, f. L *irid-*, IRIS: see -ACEOUS.] *Bot.* Of or pertaining to the family Iridaceae, which includes the genus *Iris*.

iridal /ˈʌɪrɪd(ə)l/ *a.* M19. [f. L *irid-*, IRIS + -AL[1].] **1** Of or pertaining to the rainbow. *rare.* M19. **2** *Anat.* & *Med.* Of or pertaining to the iris of the eye; = IRIDIC *a.*[2] M19.

iridectomy /ʌɪrɪˈdɛktəmi, ɪr-/ *n.* Also (earlier) **†-omia**. E19. [f. as prec. + -ECTOMY.] Surgical removal of a part of the iris; an instance of this.

iridectomize *v.t.* perform iridectomy on L19.

iridencleisis /ˌʌɪrɪdɛnˈklʌɪsɪs, ˌɪr-/ *n.* M19. [f. IRID- + Gk *egkleiein* shut up, after Gk ns. of action in *-isis*.] *Med.* Surgical trapping of a portion of the iris in an incision of the cornea, usu. to relieve glaucoma; an instance of this.

irideremia /ˌʌɪrɪdəˈriːmɪə, ˌɪr-/ *n.* M19. [f. as prec. + Gk *erēmia* lack, absence.] *Med.* Congenital absence of the iris.

irides *n.pl.* see IRIS *n.*

iridescent /ɪrɪˈdɛs(ə)nt/ *a.* L18. [f. L *irid-*, IRIS + -ESCENT.] Displaying colours like those of the rainbow, or those reflected from soap-bubbles etc.; glittering or flashing with an array of colours which changes as the observer moves.

E. WAUGH The brook.. broke into innumerable iridescent cascades as it fell. *fig.*: J. S. BLACKIE The best fictions, without a deep moral significance beneath, are only iridescent froth.

iridesce *v.i.* (*rare*) shine in an iridescent manner L19. **iridescence** *n.* the quality of being iridescent; a glittering play of changing colours: E19. **iridescently** *adv.* L18.

iridial /ʌɪˈrɪdɪəl/ *a.* E20. [Irreg. f. as next + -IAL.] *Anat.* & *Med.* = IRIDAL *a.* 2, IRIDIC *a.*[2]

iridian /ʌɪˈrɪdɪən/ *a. rare.* M19. [f. L *irid-*, IRIS + -IAN.] **1** = IRIDAL *a.* 2, IRIDIC *a.*[2] M19. **2** Rainbow-like; brilliantly coloured. L19.

iridic /ɪˈrɪdɪk, ʌɪ-/ *a.*[1] *rare.* M19. [f. IRIDIUM + -IC.] *Chem.* Of or containing iridium; *esp.* of iridium in the tetravalent state (cf. IRIDIOUS).

iridic /ʌɪˈrɪdɪk/ *a.*[2] L19. [f. L *irid-*, IRIS + -IC.] *Anat.* & *Med.* Of or pertaining to the iris of the eye.

iridious /ɪˈrɪdɪəs, ʌɪ-/ *a. rare.* M19. [f. next + -OUS.] *Chem.* Containing iridium; *esp.* of iridium in the trivalent state (cf. IRIDIC *a.*[1]).

iridium /ɪˈrɪdɪəm, ʌɪ-/ *n.* E19. [f. L *irid-*, *iris* rainbow (on account of its forming compounds of various colours) + -IUM.] A white metallic chemical element, atomic no. 77, belonging to the platinum group and used in certain hard alloys. (Symbol Ir.)

irido- /ˈʌɪrɪdəʊ, ˈɪr-/ *comb. form* of Gk *irid-*, IRIS: see -O-. Bef. a vowel also **irid-**. Chiefly *Med.*, in the sense 'of the iris of the eye'; occas. in other senses of *iris*.

iridocy'clitis *n.* inflammation of the iris and the ciliary body L19. **iridocyte** *n.* (*Zool.*) a refractive cell which causes iridescence in the skin of certain fishes, cephalopods, etc. L19. **iridodi'alysis** *n.* (surgical or traumatic) separation of the iris from the ciliary ring L19. **iri'dodesis** *n.* [Gk *desis* binding] a surgical operation in which the iris is secured in a certain position by a ligature M19. **iridodonesis** /-dəʊ'niːsɪs/ *n.* [Gk *doneein* shake] tremulousness of the iris L19. **irido'plegia** *n.* paralysis of the iris L19. **iri'dotomy** *n.* (an instance of) surgical incision of the iris M19.

iridology /ʌɪrɪ'dɒlədʒi, ɪr-/ *n.* E20. [f. prec. + -LOGY.] The study of the iris of the eye, esp. as a diagnostic method in alternative medicine.

iridologist *n.* L20.

iridosmine /ɪrɪ'dɒsmʌɪn, ʌɪr-/ *n.* E19. [f. IRIDIUM + OSMIUM + -INE[5].] A native alloy of iridium and osmium, *spec.* with about two-thirds iridium, crystallizing in the hexagonal system. Cf. OSMIRIDIUM.

iris /'ʌɪrɪs/ *n.* & *v.* LME. [L f. Gk *iris*, *irid-* rainbow, iris.] A *n.* Pl. **irises**, (esp. sense 4a) **irides** /'ʌɪrɪdiːz/. 1 A variety of quartz (formerly, any mineral) producing iridescent reflections. LME. 2 Any plant of the large genus *Iris* (family Iridaceae), widespread in the northern hemisphere, members of which are characteristically tuberous or bulbous with sword-shaped equitant leaves and showy blooms; a plant of any of several related genera. Also, a flower of such a plant. LME. 3 A rainbow, esp. (freq. **I-**) personified; a many-coloured refraction of light from drops of water; a rainbow-like or iridescent appearance; a coloured halo; a combination of brilliant colours. *poet.* L15. b (**I-**) *Gk Mythol.* The goddess of the rainbow, who acted as the messenger of the gods; *fig.* a messenger. L16. 4a *Anat.* & *Zool.* A flat circular coloured membrane suspended vertically in the aqueous humour of the eye, and separating the anterior from the posterior chamber, having within its centre an opening (the pupil) which varies so as to control the amount of light reaching the retina. E16. b *Photogr.* & *Cinemat.* In full *iris diaphragm*. An adjustable diaphragm of thin overlapping plates for regulating the size of a control hole, esp. for admitting light to a lens or lens system. Also, the action or an act of irising. M19.

2 *bearded iris, Florentine iris, Japanese iris, mourning iris, peacock iris, snake's head iris, stinking iris*, etc. 3 SHAKES. *Tr. & Cr.* His crest, that prouder than blue Iris bends. *fig.*: SHELLEY If Liberty Lent not life its soul of light, Hope its iris of delight. 4b K. REISZ An iris may . . introduce . . a shot in a more telling way than a fade. *Scientific American* The lens was too fast . . , and so he stopped it down to *f9* with a cardboard iris.

B *v.i. Photogr.* & *Cinemat.* Operate or act (in the manner of) an iris diaphragm. Chiefly foll. by *in* (or *out*): fade in a picture from the centre of the frame outwards (or from the edges inwards). M20.

irisate *v.t.* (*rare*) make iridescent E19. **iri'sation** *n.* the process of making iridescent; iridescence: M19.

irised /'ʌɪrɪst/ *a.* E19. [f. IRIS *n.* + -ED[2].] 1 Coloured like a rainbow; iridescent. E19. 2 With qualifying adj.: having an iris (of the eye) of a specified kind. L19.

Irish /'ʌɪrɪʃ/ *a.* & *n.* ME. [f. OE *Īr(as* inhabitants of *Īrland* Ireland (obscurely based on OIr. *Ériu*: see HIBERNIAN) + -ISH[1]. Cf. ON *Írskr*. See also ERSE.] A *adj.* 1 Of, pertaining to, or native to Ireland, an island lying west of Great Britain, now divided into the Republic of Ireland and Northern Ireland. ME. †b Of or belonging to (the Gaelic inhabitants of) the Scottish Highlands. M16–M18. 2 In, of, or pertaining to the language Irish. M16. 3 Having a nature or quality (regarded as) characteristic of Ireland or its people; (of an expression or statement) paradoxical, (apparently) illogical, self-contradictory. L16.

1 *Northern Irish*: see NORTHERN *a. Southern Irish*: see SOUTHERN *a.* 3 R. HILL 'Marcus wouldn't dare to tell a lie . . unless it was true!' 'Irish,' said Pascoe.

Special collocations & comb.: **Irish American** an American of Irish origin. **Irish-American** *a.* of or pertaining to an Irish American or the Irish community in the US. **Irish apricot** *joc.* a potato. **Irish Australian** an Australian of Irish origin. **Irish-Australian** *a.* of or pertaining to an Australian of Irish origin or the Irish community in Australia. *Irish blackguard*: see BLACKGUARD *n.* 6. **Irish bridge** an open stone drain carrying water across a road. *Irish bull*: see BULL *n.*[4] 1. *Irish coffee*: see COFFEE *n.* **Irish deer, elk** a large extinct deer, *Megaceros giganteus*, remains of which have been found in Ireland and other parts of Europe. **Irish Gaelic** = sense B.2 below. **Irish green** = CONNEMARA *marble*. **Irish harp** = CLAIRSCHACH. **Irish horse** *Naut. slang* (now *Hist.*) tough salt beef. **Irish hurricane** = *Irishman's hurricane* s.v. IRISHMAN. **Irish lace** any of a variety of laces made in Ireland, esp. crochet. *Irish mantle*: see MANTLE *n.* **Irish martingale** (in riding) a short leather strap connecting two rings through which the reins of a horse are passed. **Irish moss** = CARRAGEEN. **Irish pennant** *Naut. slang* an untidy end of rope flying loose in the wind. **Irish point** a kind of needlepoint lace made in Ireland. *Irish potato*: see POTATO *n.* 2. *Irish pound*: see POUND *n.*[1] **Irish promotion, rise** = *Irishman's promotion, rise* s.v. IRISHMAN. **Irish Sea** the sea separating Ireland from England and Wales. **Irish setter** (an animal of) a breed of setter with a long silky dark red coat and a long feathered tail. **Irish stew**: of mutton, potato and onion. **Irish Sweep, Sweepstake**: organized by Irish hospitals on the results of English horse-races, esp. the Derby and the Grand National. **Irish terrier** (an animal of) a breed of large wire-haired terrier, with a sandy or reddish-coloured coat. **Irish whiskey**: distilled in Ireland, esp. from malted barley. **Irish wolfhound** (an animal of) a breed of large, rough-coated hound, often grey in colour. **Irish yew** a fastigiate variety of yew, *Taxus baccata*, freq. cultivated.

B *n.* Pl. same, (in sense 1b) †**Irishes**. 1 *collect. pl. The* people of Ireland, or their immediate descendants in other countries, *esp.* those of Celtic origin. ME. †b An Irishman. Chiefly *Sc.* L16–E19. 2 The form of Gaelic used in Ireland. LME. †b Scottish Gaelic. E16–E18. 3 *ellipt.* Irish linen, whiskey, etc. L18. 4 Temper; passion. *colloq.* M19.

1 *black Irish*: see BLACK *a. the luck of the Irish*: see LUCK *n.* **wild Irish** *Hist.* those people of Ireland not subject to English rule. 2 *Old Irish*: see OLD *a.* 3 J. K. JEROME He had found a place . . where you could really get a drop of Irish worth drinking. 4 *Islander* (*Victoria, BC*) I'm afraid she'd really get her 'Irish' up.

Irisher *n.* (*colloq.*) a person of Irish origin E19. **I'rishian** *n.* a person familiar with the Celtic language or antiquities of Ireland E19. **Irishism** *n.* an Irish expression, statement, etc. (see IRISH *a.* 3) E18. **Irishize** *v.t.* make Irish in character M19. **Irishly** *adv.* L16. **Irishness** *n.* E19. **Irishy** *a.* like the Irish, somewhat Irish L19.

Irishman /'ʌɪrɪʃmən/ *n.* Pl. **-men**. ME. [f. IRISH *a.* + MAN *n.*] 1 A man of Irish birth or descent. ME. 2 In full *wild Irishman* = MATAGOURI. *NZ.* M19.

Phrases: **Irishman's hurricane** *Naut. slang* a dead calm. **Irishman's promotion, rise** *colloq.* a reduction in wages. **wild Irishman** (*a*) *Hist.* any of the wild Irish; (*b*) see sense 2 above.

Irishry /'ʌɪrɪʃri/ *n.* LME. [f. IRISH *a.* + -RY.] 1 *collect.* (*Hist.*) The native Irish, as opp. to English settlers in Ireland. LME. 2 Irish character or nationality; an Irish trait. M19.

Irishwoman /'ʌɪrɪʃwʊmən/ *n.* Pl **-women** /-wɪmɪn/. LME. [f. IRISH *a.* + WOMAN *n.*] A woman of Irish birth or descent.

iritis /ʌɪ'rʌɪtɪs/ *n.* E19. [Irreg. f. L IRIS + -ITIS.] *Med.* Inflammation of the iris.

iritic /ʌɪ'rɪtɪk/ *a.* pertaining to or affected with iritis; affecting the iris: M19.

irk *n.*[1] var. of ERK.

irk /əːk/ *v.* & *n.*[2] ME. [Perh. f. ON *yrkja* WORK *v.*, Sw. *yrka* claim, demand, insist.] A *v.* 1 *v.i.* Grow weary (*of*); feel vexed, annoyed, or disgusted (*with, at*); be reluctant, find it tiresome, *to do*. Now *rare*. ME. †2 *v.t.* Be weary of or disgusted with; loathe. LME–E17. 3 *v.t.* Make weary, bore; irritate, annoy; disgust. LME. B *n.* Irksomeness, annoyance. *rare*. L16.

irksome /'əːks(ə)m/ *a.* LME. [f. IRK *v.* + -SOME[1].] †1 Weary; disgusted; bored. Foll. by *of*. LME–M19. 2 Tedious, tiresome; troublesome, annoying. Formerly also, painful, disgusting, loathsome. LME.

2 ISAIAH BERLIN Laws . . will only seem irksome to those whose reason is dormant.

irksomely *adv.* †(*a*) painfully; (*b*) in a tiring, annoying, or troublesome way: M16. **irksomeness** *n.* LME.

†**irnen** *a.* var. of IRONEN.

iroha /i'roha, ɪ'rəʊhɑː/ *n. arch.* Also †***-fa***. M19. [Jap., f. the opening syllables *i, ro, ha* or (formerly) *fa* in one method of listing.] The Japanese kana or syllabary.

iroko /ɪ'rəʊkəʊ, iː-/ *n.* Pl. **-os**. L19. [Yoruba.] Any of various African trees of the genus *Chlorophora*, of the mulberry family, esp. *C. excelsa* and *C. regia* (in full *iroko tree*). Also, the timber of such a tree. Also called *West African* or *Nigerian teak, yellow-wood*.

iron /'ʌɪən/ *n.* & *a.* [OE *īren*, perh. alt. of *īse(r)n* = OS, OHG *īsarn* (Du. *ijzen*, G *Eisen*), ON *ísarn*, Goth. *eisarn*, f. Gmc, prob. f. Celt. and rel. to L *aes, ais* bronze, OE *ār* ORE *n.*[1], Skt *ayas*.] A *n.* I 1 A malleable, magnetic, readily oxidizable metal which is a chemical element of the transition series (atomic no. 26), occurs abundantly in certain ores and in meteorites, and is widely used, chiefly in alloys such as steel, for tools, implements, structures, machinery, etc. (Symbol Fe.) OE. b A variety or sort of iron or ferrous alloy. Freq. w. specifying wd. M17. 2 *Med.* A preparation of a compound of iron, used chiefly to treat anaemia. E19. 3 *Geol.* A meteorite which contains a high proportion of iron. E19.

1b *bog iron, cast iron, ingot iron, pig-iron, red iron, white (cast) iron, wrought iron*, etc.

II A thing made of iron. 4 Any of various instruments, appliances, tools, or utensils, now or formerly made of the metal. Freq. preceded by specifying wd. OE. 5 An iron weapon; a sword. Also, iron weapons collectively. *obs.* exc. *dial.* OE. 6 An iron shackle or fetter. Usu. in *pl. arch.* OE. 7 An instrument heated and used for branding or cauterizing. LME. 8 *Hist.* In *pl.* Dies used in striking coins. L15. 9 Any of various devices used when heated to press fabrics. In mod. use *spec.* an (electrical) appliance with a heavy flat base which uses dry heat or steam. E17. 10 *Whaling* etc. A harpoon (= HARPING-IRON). L17. 11 Money. Cf. IRON MAN 2, BRASS *n.* 3. *slang.* L18. 12 *Golf.* A club having an iron or steel head which is angled in order to loft the ball. Now freq. with a number prefixed indicating the degree of angle. E19. 13 A gun; *spec.* a pistol. Also, firearms collectively. *slang.* M19. 14 In *pl.* Leg-supports to correct malformations. M19. 15 *Horsemanship.* A stirrup (usu. in *pl.*); *esp.* a stirrup iron. L19. 16 In *pl.* More fully *eating irons*. Eating utensils. *dial.* & *slang.* E20. 17 = *corrugated iron* s.v. CORRUGATE. Chiefly *Austral.* & *NZ.* E20. 18 An old motor vehicle. *slang.* M20. 19 A jemmy, a crowbar. *Criminals' slang.* M20. 20 = *iron hoof* below. *slang.* M20. 21 *Theatr. slang.* = *fire-curtain* s.v. FIRE *n.* (see *iron curtain* below). M20.

4 *climbing-iron, curling-iron, fire-iron, grappling iron, pinking-iron, soldering iron*, etc. 5 SHAKES. *Twel. N.* Meddle you must, that's certain, or forswear to wear iron about you. 6 LD MACAULAY When the Earl reached the Castle his legs were put in irons. 7 J. A. MICHENER I'll get the smithy to make us some irons. 9 E. HARDWICK The scent of a hot iron on a shirt collar. *flat-iron, goffering iron, steam iron*, etc. 12 *Golf World* Better to practise . . with the same club—something like a 6-iron. 13 R. BOLDREWOOD Put down your irons . . or . . we'll drop ye where ye stand. J. CARROLL I never carry iron This ain't Chicago. *shooting-iron*. 14 V. CANNING A few children . . legs in irons, armpits moist with crutch-pad sweat. 15 E. BAIRD The toe is well into the iron. *Horse & Hound* Cold Blood's rider lost both irons. 16 JOCELYN BROOKE I thought some tea would be nice, only I hadn't any eating-irons.

III *transf.* & *fig.* 22 As an allusion to warfare or slaughter. OE. 23 As a type of extreme hardness or strength. E17.

22 *Daily News* Great questions . . are decided, not by speeches and majorities, but by iron and blood. 23 P. GALLICO She was no longer a woman of ice, iron and whalebone.

Phrases: **Clerk of the Irons** (*obs.* exc. *Hist.*) an officer of the Royal Mint who had charge of the manufacture and use of the dies. *corrugated iron*: see CORRUGATE 1. **fresh** (or **new**) **off the irons** fresh from school or studies; newly made or prepared; brand-new. *have nerves of iron*: see NERVE *n.* **have (too) many irons in the fire** (*a*) be engaged in (too) many occupations or undertakings; (*b*) use several expedients or alternatives to attain a purpose. **in irons** (*a*) having the feet or hands fettered, *fig.* in bondage, in captivity; (*b*) (of a sailing vessel) head to wind and unable to come about or tack either way. **iron hand in a velvet glove** firmness or inflexibility masked by a gentle or urbane manner. *new off the irons*: see *fresh off the irons* above. *standing iron*: see STANDING *a.* **strike while the iron is hot** act promptly; seize an opportunity. **the iron entered into his soul** [*Ps.* 105:18, f. L mistr. Heb. for 'his person entered into the iron', i.e. fetters] he became deeply and permanently affected by captivity or ill treatment.

B *adj.* I Of iron. 1 Consisting or made of iron. OE.

1 I. MURDOCH The iron side-pieces had long ago rusted into the head and foot boards. G. GREENE The window was guarded by iron bars.

II Resembling or held to resemble iron. 2 Physically hard or strong; robust, tough, enduring. LME. 3 Cruel, merciless, implacable, stern, severe. L16. b Firm, inflexible; stubborn, obstinate, unyielding. E17. 4 Base, debased; wicked. L16. 5 Resembling iron in appearance; iron-coloured. Also (*rare*), resembling iron oxide; rust-coloured. E17. 6 Of metallic tone, harsh, dull, unmusical. L19.

2 BYRON Though aged, he was so iron of limb, Few of our youth could cope with him. J. STEINBECK She tapped his arm with an iron finger. 3 BURKE The first Republick in the world . . is under her iron yoke. b J. STEINBECK He . . held back in his impatience with an iron control. C. G. WOLFF The daughter developed into a woman of iron determination. 4 HENRY SMITH Look not for a golden life in an iron world.

Comb. & *special collocations*: **iron age** (*a*) the last and worst age of the world according to Greek and Roman mythology; a time of wickedness or oppression; (*b*) (with cap. initials) *Archaeol.* a period when weapons and implements were first made of iron; *iron* ALUM; **iron bacterium** any of various chiefly freshwater bacteria which are capable of oxidizing ferrous salts (some obtaining energy thereby) and storing the resulting ferric hydroxide; **ironbark** *Austral.* (the wood of) any of several eucalypts with very hard bark; esp. *Eucalyptus paniculata* (more fully *grey ironbark*), and *E. sideroxylon* (more fully *red ironbark*); **iron-binding** *a.* & *n.* (*Chem.*) (*a*) *adj.* able to combine with iron atoms; (*b*) *n.* combination with iron; **iron blue** (*a*) (of) a blue colour like some kinds of iron or steel; (*b*) the pigment Prussian blue; **iron-blue (dun, fly, spinner)** *Angling* (an artificial fly imitating) a mayfly of the genus *Baetis*; **iron-bound** *a.* bound with or as with iron; (of a coast) rock-bound; rigorous, hard and fast; **Iron Chancellor** Bismarck (see BISMARCKIAN); **iron chink** a machine for cleaning and gutting fish; **iron-clay** *n.* & *a.* (*a*) *n.* = *clay ironstone* s.v. CLAY *n.*; (*b*) *adj.* of mixed iron and clay; **Iron Cross** a German (orig. Prussian) decoration awarded for distinguished services in war; **iron curtain** an impenetrable barrier (orig. a fire-curtain in a theatre); *spec. Hist.* (w. cap. initials) a notional barrier to the passage of people and information between the Soviet bloc and the West; **Iron Duke** the first Duke of Wellington (1769–1852); **iron gang** *Austral.* a gang of prisoners working in irons; **iron-glance** specular haematite; **Iron Guard** an anti-Semitic, Fascist, terrorist Romanian political party; **iron-handed** *a.* inflexible; severe, rigorous; despotic; **iron-hard** *a.* as hard as iron; extremely hard; **iron-headed** *a.* capped or tipped with iron; *fig.* hard-headed, determined; **iron-hearted** *a.* extremely hard-hearted; cruel, pitiless; **iron hoof** *slang* [rhyming slang for *poof*] a homosexual man; **iron horse** (*a*) a steam locomotive; (*b*) a bicycle or motorcycle; **iron jubilee** the seventieth anniversary of an event; **iron lace** *Austral.* decorative cast ironwork; **iron lady** a brave, tough, or intransigent woman; **iron law** *Econ.*: stating that wages tend to sink to mere subsistence level; **iron loss** *Electr.* = *core loss* s.v. CORE *n.*[1]; **iron lung** a rigid airtight metal case fitted over a patient's body, used for giving prolonged artificial respiration by means of mechanical pumps; **iron maiden** an instrument of torture consisting of a box lined with iron spikes, into which the victim is shut; **iron mask** a mask, supposedly made of iron, worn by a political prisoner who died in the Bastille in 1703 and whose identity is disputed; the prisoner himself; **ironmaster** the proprietor of an iron-foundry or ironworks; **iron mike** *slang* an automatic steering device on a ship; **iron mountain** a mountain rich in iron ore; **iron ore** any rock or mineral from which iron is or may be extracted; **iron pan** *Soil Sci.* a hardpan in which iron oxides are the chief cementing agents; **iron paper** extremely thin sheet iron; *iron pyrites*: see PYRITES 2; **iron rations** (esp. a soldier's) emergency rations of preserved food, biscuits, etc.; **iron-sand** *Geol.*: containing particles of iron ore; **iron-shot** *a.* (*Min.*) containing streaks or markings of iron; **ironsmith** (now *rare* or *obs.*) a person who works iron, a blacksmith; **iron-sponge** iron, or iron oxide, in a spongy form having a large surface area; **iron tree** any of various trees and shrubs with very hard wood; *esp.* the Malaysian *Metrosideros vera*, of the myrtle family; **ironware** small ware or goods made of iron; **ironweed** (*a*) *dial.* hard-head, *Centaurea nigra*; (*b*) *N. Amer.* any of various plants of the genus *Vernonia*, of the composite family, related to hemp agrimony; **ironwood** the extremely hard wood of various trees of many different families and countries; any of the trees producing such wood.

ironless *a.* without iron; not containing iron: LME. **iron-like** *a.* resembling (that of) iron (*lit.* & *fig.*) L16.

iron /ˈʌɪən/ *v.* LME. [f. the n.] 1 *v.t.* Fit, cover, or arm with iron. Chiefly as pa. pple: see IRONED *a.* 2. LME. 2 *v.t.* Shackle; put in irons. M17. 3 *v.t.* & *i.* Smooth or press (cloth etc.) with a heated iron. Also *transf.* & *fig.*, (foll. by *out*) smooth, flatten; resolve (a problem). L17. b *v.i.* Of a garment, material, etc.: become smooth by being pressed with an iron. M20. 4 [back-form. f. IRONY *n.*] a *v.t.* Treat with irony, speak ironically to. Chiefly *joc.* M18. b *v.i.* Use irony, speak ironically. Chiefly *joc.* E19.

1 R. W. EMERSON What if Trade . . thatch with towns the prairie broad With railways ironed o'er. *Lancashire Life* We had to take our clogs to be 'ironed'. 2 P. F. TYTLER Wallace was cast into a dungeon and heavily ironed. 3 P. ROTH Dressed in a light, freshly laundered shirt whose lapels were ironed flat. *Headlight* The car is independently sprung and irons out the road very well. *Ring* He connected with the jab . . , followed with a right. That . . ironed Mike to the canvas. b *Modern Language Notes* The 'potential intransitive', . . as . . 'this dress *washes* and *irons* . . easily'.

Comb.: **iron-on** *a.* that can be attached to a fabric by ironing.

ironer *n.* a person who irons; *spec.* a person whose occupation is ironing clothes etc.: L18.

ironclad /ˈʌɪənklad/ *a.* & *n.* M19. [f. IRON *n.* & *a.* + *clad* pa. pple of CLOTHE.] A *adj.* 1 Protected or covered with iron; *esp.* (of a naval vessel) armour-plated. M19. 2 *fig.* Strict, rigorous, hard and fast. M19. 3 Of a plant: able to withstand cold and frost. *US.* L19.

2 M. PUZO You know you got an ironclad contract . . and I can't fire you.

B *n.* 1 An ironclad ship. M19. 2 *transf.* & *fig.* Something resembling an armoured ship; something tough or impregnable. M19.

ironed /ˈʌɪənd/ *a.* ME. [f. IRON *n.*, *v.*: see -ED[2], -ED[1].] †1 Made of iron. Only in ME. 2 That has been ironed; *spec.* (*a*) fitted, furnished, covered, armed, or strengthened with iron; (*b*) put in irons; fettered. LME.

ironen /ˈʌɪənən/ *a. obs.* exc. *dial.* Also †**irnen**. ME. [f. IRON *n.* + -EN[4].] Made (solely) of iron.

iron-grey /ʌɪənˈgreɪ/ *a.* & *n.* Also **-gray**. OE. [f. IRON *n.* + GREY *a.*] A *adj.* Of the dark grey colour of freshly broken iron, or of dark hair when turning grey. OE. B *n.* 1 An iron-grey horse or dog; a person whose dark hair is grizzled. E16. 2 A dark grey colour resembling that of freshly broken iron. M16.

ironic /ʌɪˈrɒnɪk/ *a.* M17. [Fr. *ironique* or late L *ironicus* f. Gk *eirōnikos* dissembling, feigning ignorance, f. as IRONY *n.*: see -IC.] Pertaining to irony; uttering or given to irony; of the nature of or containing irony; = IRONICAL 1, 2.

ironical /ʌɪˈrɒnɪk(ə)l/ *a.* L16. [f. as prec.: see -ICAL.] 1 Of the nature of irony; wry, sarcastic; meaning the opposite of what is expressed. In mod. use also incongruous, paradoxical. L16. 2 That (habitually) uses irony. L16. †3 Dissembling; feigned, pretended. *rare.* M17–E18.

ironically *adv.* L16. **ironicalness** *n.* L18.

ironing /ˈʌɪənɪŋ/ *n.* E18. [f. IRON *v.* + -ING[1].] The pressing and smoothing of clothes, household linen, etc., with a heated iron; the clothes etc. which are to be or have been ironed.

Comb.: **ironing blanket** a thick blanket folded and used to protect a surface on which clothes etc. are ironed; **ironing-board** a long narrow padded board, on adjustable legs, on which clothes etc. are ironed; **ironing cloth**: (dampened and) put between an iron and fabric being ironed.

ironise *v.* var. of IRONIZE.

ironist /ˈʌɪr(ə)nɪst/ *n.* E18. [f. Gk *eirōn* dissembler, user of irony + -IST.] A person who uses irony; an ironical speaker or writer.

ironize /ˈʌɪr(ə)nʌɪz/ *v.* Also **-ise**. E17. [f. as prec.: see -IZE.] 1 *v.t.* Make ironical, use ironically. E17. 2 *v.i.* Use irony, speak ironically. M17.

iron man /ˈʌɪən man/ *n. phr.* Pl. **iron men**. E17. [f. IRON *n.* & *a.* + MAN *n.*] 1 A man of iron; a brave, tough, or intransigent man; *esp.* a robust sportsman. E17. b A multi-event sporting contest demanding stamina; *spec.* a triathlon involving consecutively a 2.4 mile (3.9 km) swim, a 112 mile (180 km) cycle ride, and a 26.2 mile (42.2 km) run. L20. 2 A dollar; *Austral.* formerly also, a pound. Cf. IRON *n.* 11. *slang* (chiefly *US*). E20.

iron-mold, †**-mole** *ns.* see IRON-MOULD.

ironmonger /ˈʌɪənmʌŋgə/ *n.* ME. [f. IRON *n.* + MONGER.] A dealer in metal utensils, tools, etc.; a hardware merchant.

ironmongery /ˈʌɪənmʌŋg(ə)ri/ *n.* E18. [f. prec.: see -ERY.] 1 The goods dealt in by an ironmonger; hardware. E18. b *transf.* Paraphernalia; machinery, tackle. L19. c Firearms. *slang.* E20. 2 An ironmonger's shop or place of business. M19. 3 The craft or business of the ironmonger; smith's work. L19.

iron-mould /ˈʌɪənməʊld/ *n.* & *v.* Also **-mold**, (earlier) †**-mole**. E17. [f. IRON *n.* + MOLE *n.*[1], MOULD *n.*[5], perh. by assoc. w. MOULD *n.*[4]] A *n.* A spot or discoloration on cloth etc. caused by rust or an ink-stain. E17. B *v.t.* & *i.* Stain or become stained with iron-mould. E18.

Ironside /ˈʌɪənsʌɪd/ *n.* ME. [f. IRON *a.* + SIDE *n.*] 1 (A name for) a man of great bravery; *spec.* (*a*) Edmund II, king of England (1016); (*b*) (also *Ironsides*) Oliver Cromwell. ME. 2 In *pl.* Cromwell's troopers in the English Civil War. Also occas. in *sing.* a Puritan soldier; a devout warrior. M17.

ironstone /ˈʌɪənstəʊn/ *n.* E16. [f. IRON *n.* + STONE *n.*] Any of various freq. hard rocks which contain a high proportion of iron minerals; iron ore; *esp.* any iron-rich, coarsely banded or unbanded sedimentary rock.

clay ironstone: see CLAY *n. red ironstone*: see RED *a.*

Comb.: **ironstone china** a hard, white, opaque type of stone-china.

ironwork /ˈʌɪənwəːk/ *n.* LME. [f. IRON *n.* + WORK *n.*] 1 Work in iron; that part of anything which is made of iron, iron goods collectively. LME. 2 In *pl.*, freq. treated as *sing.* An establishment where iron is smelted, or where heavy iron goods are made. L16.

ironworker *n.* a person who works in iron; a person employed in an ironworks: LME.

irony /ˈʌɪrəni/ *n.* E16. [L *ironia*, Gk *eirōneia* simulated ignorance, f. *eirōn* dissembler: see -Y[3].] 1 Dissimulation, pretence; *esp.* the pretence of ignorance practised by Socrates as a step towards confuting an adversary. E16. 2 The expression of meaning using language that normally expresses the opposite; *esp.* the humorous or sarcastic use of praise to imply condemnation or contempt. E16. b An instance of this; an ironical utterance or expression. M16. 3 *fig.* Discrepancy between the expected and the actual state of affairs; a contradictory or ill-timed outcome of events as if in mockery of the fitness of things. M17. 4 The use of language with one meaning for a privileged audience and another for those addressed or concerned. E20.

1 *Socratic irony*: see SOCRATIC *a.* 4 *tragic irony*: see TRAGIC *a.*

irony /ˈʌɪəni/ *a.* LME. [f. IRON *n.* + -Y[1].] Consisting of or containing iron; of the nature of or resembling iron.

Iroquoian /ɪrəˈkwɔɪən, -ˈkɔɪ-/ *a.* & *n.* L17. [f. IROQUOIS + -AN.] A *adj.* Of or pertaining to the Iroquois Indians or the language family Iroquoian (see B.1 below). L17. B *n.* 1 A language family which includes Iroquois, Huron, Cherokee, and several other American Indian languages. L19. 2 An Iroquois Indian. M20.

Iroquois /ˈɪrəkwɔɪ, -kɔɪ/ *a.* & *n.* M17. [Fr., f. Algonquian.] A *adj.* Of or pertaining to a group of N. American Indian peoples comprising the Mohawks, Oneidas, Senecas, Onondagas, Tuscaroras, and Cayugas, or the languages of this group. M17. B *n.* Pl. same. 1 A member of this group. L17. 2 The language of (any of) this group. M18.

irradiance /ɪˈreɪdɪəns/ *n.* M17. [f. next + -ANCE.] 1 The fact of irradiating; the emission of rays of light, emitted radiance. Also (*fig.*), the shedding of spiritual or intellectual radiance. M17. 2 The flux of radiant energy per unit area (normal to the direction of flow of radiant energy through a medium). M20.

irradiancy *n.* = IRRADIANCE 1 M17.

irradiant /ɪˈreɪdɪənt/ *a.* E16. [L *irradiant-* pres. ppl stem of *irradiare* IRRADIATE *v.*: see -ANT[1].] Emitting rays of light; shining brightly. Also (*fig.*), shedding spiritual or intellectual radiance.

irradiate /ɪˈreɪdɪət/ *a.* L15. [L *irradiatus* pa. pple, f. as next: see -ATE[2].] Illuminated, made bright or brilliant. (Foll. by *with.*)

POPE The Theban Bard, depriv'd of sight, Within, irradiate with prophetic light.

irradiate /ɪˈreɪdɪeɪt/ *v.* L16. [L *irradiat-* pa. ppl stem of *irradiare*, f. as IR-[1] + *radiare* shine, f. *radius* ray: see -ATE[3].] 1 *v.i.* Emit rays, shine (*on, upon*). L16. 2 *v.t.* Direct rays of light on; make bright by causing light to fall on, illuminate. L16. b *Astrol.* Cast influence on. E17. c Expose to the action of some kind of radiation other than visible light, as X-rays, ultraviolet radiation, or neutrons. E20. 3 *v.t. fig.* & *transf.* a Illuminate with spiritual, intellectual, etc., light; *esp.* throw light on (something intellectually obscure). E17. b Brighten as with light; light up (the face) with beauty, gladness, animation, etc. M17. c Adorn with splendour. *poet.* E18. 4 *v.t.* Radiate, send out (as) in rays. E17. †5 *v.i.* Radiate, diverge in the form of rays. L17–L18. 6 *v.i.* Become radiant; light up. Now *rare* or *obs.* E19.

1 G. HORNE Day was the state of the hemisphere, on which light irradiated. 2 W. GOLDING The candles of the saloon irradiated her face. c *Technology* Food can be preserved for long periods if irradiated. 3a P. V. PRICE The great wine will irradiate all the others .. chosen to accompany it. b H. ALLEN A smile of vivid brightness irradiated the face of the stranger. 4 G. ADAMS Their powers decay according to their distances from the centres from which they irradiated. 6 W. IRVING The eye is taught to brighten, the lip to smile, and the whole countenance to irradiate.

irradiated *a.* (*a*) that has been irradiated; (*b*) *Her.* represented as surrounded by rays: L18.

irradiation /ɪˌreɪdɪˈeɪʃ(ə)n/ *n.* L16. [(O)Fr., or late L *irradiatio(n-)*, f. as prec.: see -ATION.] 1 The action of irradiating; subjection to or emission of rays of light. L16. b A ray of light, a beam. M17. 2 *fig.* a Intellectual enlightenment; illumination of the mind. L16. b A diffusion of spiritual light. M17. 3 The (real or supposed) emission or emanation of a fluid, influence, principle, or virtue, from an active centre. Orig. chiefly *Physiol.* E17. 4a *Optics.* The apparent extension of the edges of a strongly illuminated object when seen against a dark ground. M19. b *Photogr.* The scattering of light by silver halide crystals in the emulsion, causing diffuseness of the image. E20. 5 Exposure to the action of some kind of radiation other than visible light (esp. ionizing radiation); (an instance of) the action or process of irradiating something in this way. E20.

3 BACON There seemeth .. in the Act of Enuy, an Eiaculation, or Irradiation of the Eye. G. DANIEL Metallurgy and megalith building in Europe before any irradiation from the Aegean or the ancient East. 5 *Nature* Human diploid cells can be transformed *in vitro* into tumorogenic cells by x-ray irradiation. *Super Marketing* Many microbiologists favoured irradiation because it was practically the only .. safeguard against food poisoning bacteria.

irradiative /ɪˈreɪdɪətɪv/ *a.* M19. [f. IRRADIATE *v.* + -IVE.] Tending to irradiate; illuminative.

irradiator /ɪˈreɪdɪeɪtə/ *n.* M18. [f. IRRADIATE *v.* + -OR.] A person who or thing which irradiates (now usu. with invisible radiation).

irradicable /ɪˈradɪkəb(ə)l/ *a. rare.* E18. [f. IR-[2] + L *radicare* take root (taken as if = uproot) + -ABLE.] Unable to be rooted out; = INERADICABLE.

†irrased *ppl a.* L15–L19. [f. IR-[1] + *rased* pa. pple of RASE *v.*[1] Cf. med.L *irrasus* scraped in.] *Her.* = INDENTED 2. Cf. ERASE *v.* 1.

irrationable /ɪˈraʃ(ə)nəb(ə)l/ *a.* Now *rare* or *obs.* L16. [L *irrationabilis*, f. IR-[2] *rationabilis*, f. as RATIO *n.* + -ABLE.] 1 Not endowed with reason; = IRRATIONAL *a.* 2. L16. 2 Not in accordance with reason; unreasonable; = IRRATIONAL *a.* 3. M17.

irrationa'bility *n.* unreasonableness, irrationality M17.

irrational /ɪˈraʃ(ə)n(ə)l/ *a.* & *n.* LME. [L *irrationalis*, f. as IR-[2] + *rationalis* RATIONAL *a.*, *n.*[1]] A *adj.* 1 *Math.* Of a number, quantity, or magnitude: not rational, not commensurable with the natural numbers, not expressible by an ordinary (finite) fraction but only by an infinite continued fraction or an infinite series (e.g. a non-terminating decimal). LME. 2 Not endowed with reason. L15. 3 Contrary to or not in accordance with reason; unreasonable, utterly illogical, absurd. M17. 4 *Gk Pros.* (Of a syllable) having a metrical value not corresponding to its actual time-value; (of a metrical foot) containing such a syllable. M19.

1 P. DAVIES All irrational numbers, such as π, need infinite decimals. 2 C. G. WOLFF The irrational component of man's nature—the element that he shares with all other animals. 3 M. PIERCY Maybe all husbands acted in irrational rage sometimes.

B *n.* 1 A being not endowed with or guided by reason. M17. 2 *Math.* An irrational number or quantity; a surd. L17.

irrationalize *v.t.* make irrational L19. **irrationally** *adv.* M17.

irrationalism /ɪˈraʃ(ə)n(ə)lɪz(ə)m/ *n.* E19. [f. prec. + -ISM.] A system of belief or action that disregards or contradicts rational principles.

irrationalist *n.* & *a.* (*a*) *n.* a person who practises or advocates irrationalism; (*b*) *adj.* marked by or advocating irrationalism: M19. **irrationa'listic** *a.* characterized by irrationalism; contrary to reason, illogical: E20.

irrationality /ɪˌraʃəˈnalɪti/ *n.* L16. [f. IRRATIONAL *a.* + -ITY.] 1 *Math.* The quality of being irrational. L16. 2 The quality of not being guided by, or not being in accordance with, reason; absurdity of thought or action. M17. b An irrational thing, action, or thought; an absurdity. L17. 3 *Optics.* The inequality of the ratios of the dispersion of the various colours in spectra produced by refraction through different substances. L18. 4 The quality of being devoid of reason. E19. 5 *Gk Pros.* The quality of being an irrational syllable or foot. M19.

irrealisable *a.* var. of IRREALIZABLE.

irreality /ɪrɪˈalɪti/ *n. rare.* E19. [f. IR-[2] + REALITY.] Unreality.

irrealizable /ɪˈrɪəlʌɪzəb(ə)l/ *a.* Also **-isable**. M19. [f. IR-[2] + REALIZABLE.] Unable to be realized; unrealizable.

irrebuttable /ɪrɪˈbʌtəb(ə)l/ *a.* M19. [f. IR-[2] + REBUTTABLE.] Unable to be rebutted.

irreceptive /ɪrɪˈsɛptɪv/ *a.* M19. [f. IR-[2] + RECEPTIVE.] Not capable of receiving; unreceptive.

irreciprocal /ɪrɪˈsɪprək(ə)l/ *a.* L19. [f. IR-[2] + RECIPROCAL *a.*] Not reciprocal.

irreciprocity /ɪˌrɛsɪˈprɒsɪti/ *n.* L19. [f. IR-[2] + RECIPROCITY.] Absence of reciprocity.

irreclaimable /ɪrɪˈkleɪməb(ə)l/ *a.* E17. [f. IR-[2] + RECLAIMABLE.] †1 Uncontrollable, implacable. *rare.* Only in E17. 2 Unable to be reformed or redeemed. M17. 3 Of land: unable to be brought under cultivation. L18. 4 Unable to be called back or revoked; irrevocable. M19.

ˌirreclaima'bility *n.* L19. **irreclaimableness** *n.* L18. **irreclaimably** *adv.* without the possibility of being reclaimed M17.

irreclaimed /ɪrɪˈkleɪmd/ *a. rare.* E19. [f. IR-[2] + RECLAIM *v.* + -ED[1].] Not brought under civilization or cultivation; unreclaimed.

irrecognisable *a.* var. of IRRECOGNIZABLE.

irrecognition /ɪˌrɛkəgˈnɪʃ(ə)n/ *n.* E19. [f. IR-[2] + RECOGNITION.] Absence of recognition; non-recognition.

irrecognizable /ɪˈrɛkəgnʌɪzəb(ə)l/ *a.* Also **-isable**. M19. [f. IR-[2] + RECOGNIZABLE.] Unable to be recognized; unrecognizable.

irrecogniza'bility *n.* M19. **irrecognizably** *adv.* M19.

irrecollection /ɪˌrɛkəˈlɛkʃ(ə)n/ *n.* Now *rare.* M18. [f. IR-[2] + RECOLLECTION.] Absence of recollection; forgetfulness.

irreconcilable /ɪˌrɛk(ə)nˈsʌɪləb(ə)l, ɪˈrɛk(ə)nsʌɪləb(ə)l/ *a.* & *n.* Also **-ileable**. L16. [f. IR-[2] + RECONCILABLE.] A *adj.* 1 Of people, their feelings, etc.: unable to be reconciled or brought into friendly relations; implacably hostile. (Foll. by *to.*) L16. 2 Of statements, ideas, etc.: unable to be brought into harmony or made consistent; incompatible. (Foll. by *to, with.*) E17.

1 H. JAMES They belonged by temperament to irreconcilable camps. 2 N. SYMINGTON How characteristics, seemingly irreconcilable, can exist in the same person.

B *n.* 1 A person who refuses to be reconciled; *esp.* a politician who refuses to compromise. M18. 2 In *pl.* Principles, ideas, etc., that cannot be harmonized with each other. L19.

irreconcila'bility *n.* M19. **irreconcilableness** *n.* E17. **irreconcilably** *adv.* E17.

†irreconciled *a.* L16–M18. [f. IR-[2] + RECONCILE + -ED[1].] Not reconciled; *spec.* in a state at variance with God.

irreconcilement /ɪˈrɛk(ə)nsʌɪlm(ə)nt/ *n.* M18. [f. IR-[2] + RECONCILEMENT.] The state or fact of being unreconciled.

irreconciliable /ɪˌrɛk(ə)nˈsɪlɪəb(ə)l/ *a.* Now *rare.* E17. [Fr. *irréconciliable* f. late L *irreconciliabilis*, f. IR-[2] + *reconciliare* RECONCILE: see -ABLE.] = IRRECONCILABLE *a.*

irreconcilia'bility *n.* M19. **irreconciliableness** *n.* M17. **irreconciliably** *adv.* E17.

irreconciliation /ɪˌrɛk(ə)nsɪlɪˈeɪʃ(ə)n/ *n.* M17. [f. IR-[2] + RECONCILIATION.] The fact or condition of being unreconciled.

irrecoverable /ɪrɪˈkʌv(ə)rəb(ə)l/ *a.* LME. [f. IR-[2] + RECOVERABLE. Cf. Fr. *irrécouvrable.*] 1 Chiefly of something lost: that cannot be recovered or retrieved. LME. 2a *fig.* Unable to be remedied or rectified; irretrievable. LME. b Unable to be restored to health; incurable; that cannot be restored to life, as after drowning, suffocation, etc. *arch.* L16. †3 Unable to be recalled or revoked; irrevocable. M16–E19. †4 Unable to be recovered from. Only in 17.

1 L. GORDON The childhood summers at St Ives were marked in memory as the irrecoverable paradise. 2a C. NESS A final and irrecoverable fall. 3 A. TUCKER Persons lying under an irrecoverable sentence of death.

irrecoverableness *n.* E17. **irrecoverably** *adv.* L16.

irrecuperable /ɪrɪˈkuːp(ə)rəb(ə)l/ *a.* Long *arch.* LME. [OFr. f. late L *irrecuperabilis*, f. as IR-[2] + L *recuperare* RECUPERATE: see -ABLE.] Unable to be recovered from, incurable. Formerly also, that cannot be regained.

irrecusable /ɪrɪˈkjuːzəb(ə)l/ *a. arch.* L18. [Fr. *irrécusable* or late L *irrecusabilis*, f. as IR-[2] + *recusabilis*, f. *recusare* to refuse: see RECUSANT, -ABLE.] Of a statement etc.: unable to be refused acceptance.

HOR. WALPOLE I will give him an irrecusable proof.

irrecusably *adv.* M19.

irredeemable /ɪrɪˈdiːməb(ə)l/ *a.* & *n.* E17. [f. IR-[2] + REDEEMABLE.] A *adj.* 1 Unable to be redeemed or bought back. Of a Government annuity: not terminable by repayment of the sum originally paid by the annuitant. E17. b Of paper currency: not convertible into cash. M19. 2 *fig.* That admits of no release or change of state; absolute, fixed, hopeless; beyond redemption; thoroughly depraved. M19.

1 **irredeemable debenture**: which contains no provision for repayment of the principal money. 2 E. A. POE An air of stern, deep, and irredeemable gloom

hung over and pervaded all. W. SOYINKA The smell of irredeemable corruption that travels with you.

B *n.* Something irredeemable; *spec.* †(*a*) an irredeemable annuity; (*b*) an irredeemable debenture. E18.

ˌirredeemaˈbility *n.* (*rare*) L18. **irredeemably** *adv.* in an irredeemable manner; *esp.* so as to be past redemption, hopelessly, utterly: L16.

irredenta /irreˈdenta, ɪrɪˈdɛntə/ *n.* Pl. ***-te*** /-te/, ***-tas*** /-təz/. E20. [It.: see next.] A region containing people ethnically related to the inhabitants of one State but politically subject to another.

ALDOUS HUXLEY British Honduras still is regarded by the Guatemalans as an *irredenta*.

irredentist /ɪrɪˈdɛntɪst/ *n.* & *a.* Also **I-**. L19. [It. *irredentista*, f. (*Italia*) *irredenta* unredeemed or unrecovered (Italy) + *-ista* -IST.] **A** *n.* In Italian politics (after 1878): an advocate of the return to Italy of all Italian-speaking districts subject to other countries. Also, an advocate of a policy of reuniting to one country a territory for the moment subject to another country. L19.

B *adj.* Of or pertaining to irredentists or irredentism; advocating irredentism. L19.

Belfast Telegraph The Irish Government is.. frightened of being seen to betray its irredentist claim to Northern Ireland.

irredentism *n.* the policy or programme of irredentists, in Italy or elsewhere L19.

irreducible /ɪrɪˈdjuːsɪb(ə)l/ *a.* M17. [f. IR-² + REDUCIBLE.] **1** Unable to be brought to or *to* a desired form, state, condition, etc. M17. **b** *spec.* Unable to be reduced to a simpler or more intelligible form; unable to be resolved into elements or brought under any recognized principle. M19. **2** *Med.* Esp. of a hernia: whose contents cannot be returned to the normal position by other than surgical treatment. M19. **3** Unable to be reduced to a smaller number or amount; the fewest or smallest possible. M19. **4** Unable to be reduced to submission; invincible, insuperable. M19.

1 H. HALLAM The fashions of dress and amusements are generally capricious and irreducible to rule. 3 R. D. LAING The irreducible elements of psychotherapy are a therapist, a patient, and a regular.. time and place.

ˌirreduciˈbility *n.* L18. **irreducibleness** *n.* E19. **irreducibly** *adv.* M19.

irreductible /ɪrɪˈdʌktɪb(ə)l/ *a. rare.* M18. [Fr. *irréductible*, f. IR-² + *réductible*, f. L *reduct-* pa. ppl stem of *reducere* REDUCE: see -IBLE.] = IRREDUCIBLE.

ˌirreductiˈbility *n.* M19.

irredundant /ɪrɪˈdʌnd(ə)nt/ *a.* E20. [f. IR-² + REDUNDANT.] *Math.* Containing no redundant elements.

irredundance *n.* E20. **irredundancy** *n.* M20.

irreferable /ɪˈrɛf(ə)rəb(ə)l, ɪrɪˈfəː-/ *a. rare.* E19. [f. IR-² + REFERABLE.] Not referable; unable to be referred *to* something.

irreflection /ɪrɪˈflɛkʃ(ə)n/ *n.* Also **-flexion**. M19. [f. IR-² + REFLECTION, perh. after Fr. *irréflexion*.] Lack of reflection in action or conduct.

irreflective /ɪrɪˈflɛktɪv/ *a.* M19. [f. IR-² + REFLECTIVE, perh. after Fr. *irréfléchi*.] Unreflecting, unthinking.

irreflectively *adv.* M19. **irreflectiveness** *n.* M19.

irreflexion *n.* var. of IRREFLECTION.

irreflexive /ɪrɪˈflɛksɪv/ *a.* L19. [f. IR-² + REFLEXIVE.] Not reflexive. Chiefly *Logic* & *Math.*, (of a relation) which never holds between a term and itself. Cf. REFLEXIVE *a.*

irreflexiveness *n.* M20. **irreflexˈivity** *n.* M20.

irreformable /ɪrɪˈfɔːməb(ə)l/ *a.* E17. [f. IR-² + REFORMABLE. Sense 2 prob. after Fr. *irréformable*.] **1** Unable to be reformed. E17. **2** Chiefly of papal dogma: incapable or revision or alteration. E19.

ˌirreformaˈbility *n.* L19.

irrefragable /ɪˈrɛfrəgəb(ə)l/ *a.* M16. [Late L *irrefragabilis*, f. as IR-² + *refragari* oppose, contest, opp. *suffragari* (cf. SUFFRAGE): see -ABLE.] **1** Unable to be refuted or disproved; incontrovertible, incontestable, undeniable. M16. **2** Unable or not allowed to be broken; indestructible; inviolable; irresistible. Now *rare.* M16.

1 J. C. OATES In deference to.. the irrefragable nature of her decision, they were absolutely silent.

irrefragaˈbility *n.* the quality of being irrefragable; *rare* an irrefragable statement: E17. **irrefragably** *adv.* L16.

irrefrangible /ɪrɪˈfrandʒɪb(ə)l/ *a.* E18. [f. IR-² + REFRANGIBLE.] **1** Unable to or not allowed to be broken or violated; inviolable. E18. **2** *Optics.* Not refrangible; unable to be refracted. E20.

irrefrangibly *adv.* L19.

irrefutable /ɪˈrɛfjʊtəb(ə)l, ɪrɪˈfjuː-/ *a.* E17. [Late L *irrefutabilis*, f. IR-² + *refutabilis*, f. *refutare* REFUTE: see -ABLE.] Unable to be refuted or disproved; incontrovertible.

ˌirrefutaˈbility *n.* M19. **irrefutably** *adv.* L17.

irregardless /ɪrɪˈgɑːdlɪs/ *a.* & *adv.* Chiefly *N. Amer.* (*non-standard* or *joc.*). E20. [Prob. blend of IRRESPECTIVE and REGARDLESS.] = REGARDLESS.

irregenerate /ɪrɪˈdʒɛn(ə)rət/ *a. rare.* M17. [f. IR-² + REGENERATE *a.*] Not regenerate; unregenerate.

irregular /ɪˈrɛgjʊlə/ *a.* & *n.* LME. [OFr. *irreguler* (later and mod. *irrégulier*) f. late and (esp.) med.L *irregularis*: see IR-², REGULAR.] **A** *adj.* **I** *gen.* **1** Not conforming to rule, law, or moral principle; lawless, disorderly. LME. **2** Of a thing: not in conformity with rule, principle, accepted convention, customary procedure, etc.; not in accordance with what is usual, normal, or prescribed; anomalous, abnormal. L15. **3** Not of regular or symmetrical form or arrangement; (of a surface) uneven. L16. **4** Not uniform in continuance, occurrence, or succession; occurring at unequal rates or intervals. Also, of an agent: doing something at irregular intervals. E17.

2 LD MACAULAY The Declaration of Right, an instrument which was indeed revolutionary and irregular. E. BOWEN His frequent presence about a house where young girls were could have been thought irregular. V. GLENDINNING There had been complaints.. about her irregular private life. 3 E. WAUGH They could see the irregular roofs of the palace buildings. A. GHOSH His only irregular features are his eyebrows, which are slightly out of alignment. 4 E. TEMPLETON Taking a deep breath to steady the irregular beating of her heart. C. CHAPLIN His theatrical engagements became irregular.

II *spec.* **5** *Eccl.* (chiefly *RC Ch.*). Not in conformity with the rule of the Church or of some ecclesiastical order; disqualified for ordination or exercise of clerical functions. LME. **6** *Gram.* Of a part of speech, esp. a verb: not following the usual or normal mode of inflection or conjugation. Of an inflection: formed in this way. L16. **7** *Bot.* Of a flower: having the parts of one of its whorls (esp. the petals) differing in form, size, etc.; *esp.* = ZYGOMORPHIC. L18. **8** *Astron.* **a** Of a galaxy: having an irregular shape, lacking any apparent axis of symmetry or central nucleus. E19. **b** Of a variable star: fluctuating in brightness with no regular cycle. E20. **9** *Mil.* Of forces, troops: not belonging to the regular or established army organization; not forming an organized military body. M19.

9 E. A. FREEMAN The Danes.. put the irregular English levies to flight.

B *n.* **1** A person not belonging to the regular body or doing something irregularly; an irregular or occasional practitioner, attendant, member of the clergy, etc. LME. **b** *Mil.* A soldier not of the regular army. Usu. in *pl.*, irregular troops. M18. **2** An imperfect piece of merchandise, esp. cloth, sold at a reduced price. Usu. in *pl. N. Amer.* M20.

1b M. MOORCOCK They had no identifiable uniforms at all. I guessed they were irregulars.

irregularly *adv.* L16.

irregularity /ɪˌrɛgjʊˈlarɪti/ *n.* ME. [(O)Fr. *irrégularité* f. late L *irregularitas*, f. *irregularis*: see prec., -ITY.] **1** *Eccl.* (chiefly *RC Ch.*). Infraction of the rules as to entrance into or exercise of holy orders; an impediment or disqualification by which a person is debarred from normal clerical functions or advancement. ME. **2** *gen.* A breach of rule or principle; an irregular, lawless, or disorderly act. L15. **b** Lack of conformity to rule, law, or principle; deviation from what is usual or normal; abnormality, anomalousness. L16. **3** Lack of regularity, symmetry, evenness, or uniformity, in shape, arrangement, succession, etc.; inequality of form, position, rate, etc.; *spec.* in *Bot.*, unlikeness of the petals etc. of a flower (see IRREGULAR *a.* 7). M17. **b** An instance of this; *esp.* a part not uniform or symmetrical with the rest, as an unevenness of a surface etc. M17.

2a W. TENNANT In a rude age.. crimes and irregularities are more frequent. *Sunday (Calcutta)* There were a lot of irregularities like non-payment to teachers. 3b V. S. NAIPAUL They intended to turn all the irregularities of nature into straight lines or graded curves.

irregulate /ɪˈrɛgjʊleɪt/ *v.t.* Now *rare.* E17. [Prob. f. IR-² + REGULATE *v.*, after *irregular.*] Make irregular; disorder.

irregulated /ɪˈrɛgjʊleɪtɪd/ *a. rare.* M17. [f. IR-² + REGULATE *v.* + -ED¹: cf. med.L *irregulatus.*] Unregulated.

†irregulous *a. rare* (Shakes.). Only in E17. [f. IRREGULAR, by substitution of -OUS (cf. -ULOUS).] Unruly, disorderly, lawless.

irrelate /ɪrɪˈleɪt/ *a. rare.* M19. [f. IR-² + L *relatus* pa. pple: see RELATE *v.*, -ATE².] Not related, unrelated.

irrelation /ɪrɪˈleɪʃ(ə)n/ *n.* M19. [f. IR-² + RELATION.] Absence of relation, lack of connection.

irrelative /ɪˈrɛlətɪv/ *a.* M17. [f. IR-² + RELATIVE *a.*] **1** Not having relations to each other, or *to* something else; unrelated, unconnected. Also *spec.* (*Metaphysics*), having no relations, absolute. M17. **2** Having no bearing on the matter in hand; irrelevant. M17.

irrelatively *adv.* M17. **irrelativeness** *n.* M17.

irrelevance /ɪˈrɛlɪv(ə)ns/ *n.* Orig. *Sc.* M16. [f. next: see -ANCE.] The fact or quality of being irrelevant, lack of pertinence; an irrelevant remark, circumstance, etc.

Also **irrelevancy** *n.* L16.

irrelevant /ɪˈrɛlɪv(ə)nt/ *a.* Orig. *Sc.* M16. [f. IR-² + RELEVANT. Cf. Fr. †*irrelevant.*] Not relevant or pertinent to the case; that does not apply. (Foll. by *to.*)

D. WELCH He would treat my remark as an irrelevant interruption. D. W. GOODWIN Why alcoholics drink is irrelevant to the diagnosis of alcoholism.

irrelevantly *adv.* E19.

irrelievable /ɪrɪˈliːvəb(ə)l/ *a.* L17. [f. IR-² + RELIEVABLE.] Not relievable, unable to be relieved.

irreligion /ɪrɪˈlɪdʒ(ə)n/ *n.* L16. [Fr. *irréligion* or late L *irreligio(n-)*, f. as IR-² + L *religio(n-)*: see RELIGION.] **1** Lack of religion; hostility to or disregard of religious principles; irreligious conduct. L16. **†2** A false or perverted religion. L16–M17.

irreligionism *n.* a system of irreligion; irreligious theory: M19. **irreligionist** *n.* a person who supports or practises irreligion; a professed opponent of religion: L18.

irreligious /ɪrɪˈlɪdʒəs/ *a.* LME. [L *irreligiosus*, f. as IR-² + *religiosus*: see RELIGIOUS. Cf. Fr. *irréligieux.*] **1** Not religious; hostile to or showing disregard for religion; ungodly; godless. LME. **†2** Believing in, practising, or pertaining to a false religion. L16–M17.

1 H. ROGERS The irreligious monarch.. slept during the greater part of the sermon.

irreligiously *adv.* L16. **irreligiousness** *n.* L16.

irreluctant /ɪrɪˈlʌkt(ə)nt/ *a. rare.* L17. [f. IR-² + RELUCTANT.] Not reluctant; willing.

irremeable /ɪˈrɛmɪəb(ə)l, ɪˈriːmɪəb(ə)l/ *a.* Now chiefly *poet.* M16. [L *irremeabilis*, f. IR-² + *remeare* go back, f. RE- + *meare* go, pass: see -ABLE.] Admitting of no return; from, by, or through which there is no return.

J. HAWKESWORTH The irremeable waters of Styx.

irremeably *adv.* E19.

irremediable /ɪrɪˈmiːdɪəb(ə)l/ *a.* LME. [L *irremediabilis*, f. as IR-² + *remediabilis*: see REMEDIABLE. Cf. Fr. *irrémédiable.*] Not remediable; that does not admit of remedy, cure, or correction; incurable, irreparable.

irremediableness *n.* E17. **irremediably** *adv.* LME.

irrememberable /ɪrɪˈmɛmb(ə)rəb(ə)l/ *a. rare.* M19. [f. IR-[2] + REMEMBERABLE.] Unable to be remembered.

irremissible /ɪrɪˈmɪsɪb(ə)l/ *a.* LME. [(O)Fr. *irrémissible* or eccl.L *irremissibilis*, f. as IR-[2] + L *remissibilis*: see REMISSIBLE.] 1 Unable to be forgiven; unpardonable. LME. 2 Unable to be remitted as an obligation or duty; unalterably binding. M17.

irremissibly *adv.* L15.

irremissive /ɪrɪˈmɪsɪv/ *a. rare.* L16. [f. IR-[2] + REMISSIVE.] Continuous, unremitting.

irremovable /ɪrɪˈmuːvəb(ə)l/ *a.* & *n.* L16. [f. IR-[2] + REMOVABLE.] A *adj.* 1 Not removable; unable to be removed or displaced; not subject to removal. L16. b Unable to be displaced from office or position; permanent. M17. †2 Unable to be moved; immovable, inflexible (*lit.* & *fig.*). L16–E19. B *n.* A person who cannot be removed, a person whose position is permanent. M19.

ˌirremovaˈbility *n.* E19. **irremovableness** *n.* E17. **irremovably** *adv.* M17.

irremunerable /ɪrɪˈmjuːn(ə)rəb(ə)l/ *a. rare.* E17. [f. IR-[2] + REMUNERABLE. Cf. med.L *irremunerabilis*.] Unable to be remunerated, rewarded, or repaid.

†irrenowned *a. rare* (Spenser). Only in L16. [f. IR-[2] + RENOWNED.] Without renown or fame; unrenowned.

irrepairable /ɪrɪˈpɛːrəb(ə)l/ *a.* Now *rare.* L16. [f. IR-[2] + REPAIRABLE.] 1 = IRREPARABLE I. L16. 2 Too far decayed or damaged to be repaired. E18.

1 *Car Mechanics* Irrepairable damage to you might be a . . welding job to someone else.

irreparable /ɪˈrɛp(ə)rəb(ə)l/ *a.* LME. [(O)Fr. *irréparable* f. L *irreparabilis*, f. IR-[2] + *reparabilis* REPARABLE.] 1 Not reparable; unable to be rectified, remedied, or made good. LME. 2 Unable to be repaired; = IRREPAIRABLE 2. *rare.* L18.

1 *New York Times* These inhuman crimes do irreparable damage to the good name of Ireland. J. C. OATES She wept with the pain of it: the sense of irreparable loss.

irreparaˈbility *n.* M18. **irreparableness** *n.* E18. **irreparably** *adv.* in an irreparable manner; so as to be beyond reparation or remedy: LME.

irrepassable /ɪrɪˈpɑːsəb(ə)l/ *a. rare.* L16. [f. IR-[2] + RE- + PASSABLE.] Unable to be passed again.

irrepealable /ɪrɪˈpiːləb(ə)l/ *a.* M17. [f. IR-[2] + REPEALABLE.] Unable to be repealed or annulled; irrevocable.

ˌirrepealaˈbility *n.* E19. **irrepealably** *adv.* M17.

irrepentance /ɪrɪˈpɛnt(ə)ns/ *n. rare.* E17. [f. IR-[2] + REPENTANCE.] Absence of repentance.

irreplaceable /ɪrɪˈpleɪsəb(ə)l/ *a.* E19. [f. IR-[2] + REPLACEABLE.] Not liable to be restored or repaid, irredeemable; of which the loss cannot be made good or the place filled by an equivalent.

B. T. BRADFORD She was fully convinced that no one was irreplaceable. M. FLANAGAN They're mortal—irreplaceable as a life.

irreplaceably *adv.* M20.

irrepleviable /ɪrɪˈplɛvɪəb(ə)l/ *a.* Now *rare.* M16. [med.L *irrepleviabilis*, f. IR-[2] + *repliviabilis*, f. *repleviare* f. as REPLEVY *v.*: see -ABLE.] *Law.* = next.

irreplevisable /ɪrɪˈplɛvɪsəb(ə)l/ *a.* Now *rare.* E17. [f. IR-[2] + REPLEVISABLE.] *Law.* Unable to be replevied or delivered on sureties.

irreprehensible /ˌɪrɛprɪˈhɛnsɪb(ə)l/ *a.* Now *rare.* LME. [Late L *irreprehensibilis*, f. IR-[2] + *reprehensibilis* REPREHENSIBLE.] Not reprehensible or blameworthy; irreproachable.

irrepresentable /ˌɪrɛprɪˈzɛntəb(ə)l/ *a.* L17. [f. IR-[2] + REPRESENTABLE.] Not representable.

irrepressible /ɪrɪˈprɛsɪb(ə)l/ *a.* E19. [f. IR-[2] + REPRESS + -IBLE.] Unable to be repressed, restrained, or put down.

J. P. HENNESSY She was by nature gay and vivacious, with an irrepressible sense of humour.

ˌirrepressiˈbility *n.* M19. **irrepressibly** *adv.* M19.

irreproachable /ɪrɪˈprəʊtʃəb(ə)l/ *a.* M17. [Fr. *irréprochable*, f. IR-[2] + *réprochable* REPROACHABLE.] Not reproachable; free from blame, faultless.

H. JAMES Harold's irreproachable—hasn't a vice.

ˌirreproachaˈbility *n.* M19. **irreproachableness** *n.* E19. **irreproachably** *adv.* E18.

irreproducible /ˌɪriːprəˈdjuːsɪb(ə)l/ *a.* M19. [f. IR-[2] + REPRODUCIBLE.] Not reproducible.

irreproduciˈbility *n.* L20.

irreprovable /ɪrɪˈpruːvəb(ə)l/ *a.* Now *rare.* LME. [f. IR-[2] + REPROVABLE.] 1 Undeserving of reproof; blameless, irreproachable. LME. †2 Unable to be disproved or confuted; irrefutable. L16–M17.

irreption /ɪˈrɛpʃ(ə)n/ *n.* L16. [Late L *irreptio(n-)*, f. *irrept-* pa. ppl stem of *irrepere* creep in, f. IR-[1] + *repere* creep: see -ION.] Creeping in, stealthy entrance; a thing which has crept in, esp. into a text.

Encounter Protection against casual and deplorable irreptions creeping into the language. G. W. S. FRIEDRICHSEN There had been casual but continued irreptions from the old Latin.

irreptitious /ɪrɛpˈtɪʃəs/ *a.* characterized by (an) irreption L17.

†irreputable *a.* E–M18. [f. IR-[2] + REPUTABLE.] Not reputable, not of good repute; disreputable.

irresistable /ɪrɪˈzɪstəb(ə)l/ *a.* Now *rare.* E17. [f. IR-[2] + RESIST *v.* + -ABLE.] = IRRESISTIBLE.

P. GREENHALGH They were by no means irresistable by Pompey's army. R. DAVIES Ismay had a coarse streak . . part of her irresistable allurement.

ˌirresistaˈbility *n.* M17. **irresistableness** *n.* L17. **irresistably** *adv.* M17.

irresistance /ɪrɪˈzɪst(ə)ns/ *n.* M17. [f. IR-[2] + RESISTANCE.] Absence of resistance; non-resistance.

irresistible /ɪrɪˈzɪstɪb(ə)l/ *a.* L16. [med.L *irresistibilis* or f. IR-[2] + RESISTIBLE.] Unable to be withstood; too strong, weighty, or fascinating to be resisted.

ˌirresistiˈbility *n.* E17. **irresistibleness** *n.* E17. **irresistibly** *adv.* in a irresistible manner; so as to be irresistible: M17.

†irresistless *a.* M17–L18. [Blend of IRRESISTIBLE and RESISTLESS.] Resistless, irresistible.

irresoluble /ɪˈrɛzɒljʊb(ə)l/ *a.* M17. [L *irresolubilis* indissoluble, f. as IR-[2] + RE- + SOLUBLE.] 1 Unable to be decomposed, dissolved, or liquefied M17. 2 Unable to be solved or explained. M17.

2 *Times* Mr Foot's irresoluble leadership dilemma is obvious.

irresolute /ɪˈrɛzəluːt/ *a.* L16. [L *irresolutus* not loosened, or f. IR-[2] + RESOLUTE *a.*] †1 Unexplained; left ambiguous or obscure. L16–E17. 2 Uncertain or undecided as to a course of action. L16. 3 Lacking in resolution or decisiveness. E17.

2 I. D'ISRAELI Buckingham was irresolute, and scarcely knew what to decide on. 3 J. H. NEWMAN Cicero . . was irresolute, timid and inconsistent.

irresolutely *adv.* E17. **irresoluteness** *n.* L17. **irresoˈlution** *n.* L16.

irresolvable /ɪrɪˈzɒlvəb(ə)l/ *a.* M17. [f. IR-[2] + RESOLVABLE.] 1 Of a problem, dilemma, etc.: unable to be resolved or solved. M17. 2 Unable to be resolved into elements or parts; that cannot be analysed. L18.

irresolved /ɪrɪˈzɒlvd/ *a.* Long *rare.* L16. [f. IR-[2] + RESOLVED.] Not resolved; undecided, uncertain; irresolute.

irrespectful /ɪrɪˈspɛktfʊl, -f(ə)l/ *a. rare.* L17. [f. IR-[2] + RESPECTFUL.] Disrespectful.

irrespective /ɪrɪˈspɛktɪv/ *a.* & *adv.* M17. [f. IR-[2] + RESPECTIVE *a.*] A *adj.* †1 Disrespectful. Only in M17. 2 Characterized by disregard of particular persons, circumstances, or conditions. Now *rare.* M17. 3 Existing or considered without respect or regard to something else. Also foll. by *of.* L17.

B *adv.* Without regard to or consideration of something else; independently. Foll. by *of.* M17.

A. J. AYER People sometimes judge actions to be right irrespective of their consequences.

irrespectively /ɪrɪˈspɛktɪvli/ *adv.* E17. [f. prec. + -LY[2].] †1 In a manner showing disregard of particular persons or circumstances. Also, disrespectfully. E17–E18. 2 = IRRESPECTIVE *adv.* Also foll. by *of*, †*to.* M17.

irrespirable /ɪˈrɛsp(ə)rəb(ə)l, ɪrɪˈspʌɪ-/ *a.* E19. [f. IR-[2] + RESPIRABLE or f. Fr. *irrespirable.*] Not breathable; unfit for respiration.

irresponsible /ɪrɪˈspɒnsɪb(ə)l/ *a.* & *n.* M17. [f. IR-[2] + RESPONSIBLE.] A *adj.* Not answerable for conduct or actions; exempt from or incapable of legal responsibility. Also lacking, or done without, a sense of responsibility. M17.

T. DE W. TALMAGE The prisoner was idiotic and irresponsible. D. H. LAWRENCE I'm irresponsible as a puff of wind. *Listener* We are not dealing . . with an irresponsible, politically-motivated organization in trade unions.

B *n.* An irresponsible person. L19.

L. MUMFORD His adolescent years found him one of the . . irresponsibles of his little town.

ˌirresponsiˈbility *n.* E19. **irresponsibleness** *n.* M17. **irresponsibly** *adv.* M19.

irresponsive /ɪrɪˈspɒnsɪv/ *a.* M19. [f. IR-[2] + RESPONSIVE.] Not responding to a force or stimulus; giving no answer to a question or inquiry.

irresponsively *adv.* L20. **irresponsiveness** *n.* M19.

irrestrainable /ɪrɪˈstreɪnəb(ə)l/ *a.* M17. [f. IR-[2] + RESTRAINABLE.] Not restrainable.

irrestrainably *adv.* L17.

irrestrictive /ɪrɪˈstrɪktɪv/ *a.* E18. [f. IR-[2] + RESTRICTIVE.] Not restrictive; without restriction.

irretention /ɪrɪˈtɛnʃ(ə)n/ *n.* E19. [f. IR-[2] + RETENTION.] Lack of retention; failure to retain something.

irretentive /ɪrɪˈtɛntɪv/ *a.* M18. [f. IR-[2] + RETENTIVE *a.*] Not retentive.

irretentiveness *n.* M19.

irreticence /ɪˈrɛtɪs(ə)ns/ *n.* E20. [f. IR-[2] + RETICENCE.] The condition of being irreticent; an instance of this.

irreticent /ɪˈrɛtɪs(ə)nt/ *a.* M19. [f. IR-[2] + RETICENT.] Not reticent.

irretraceable /ɪrɪˈtreɪsəb(ə)l/ *a.* M19. [f. IR-[2] + RETRACE + -ABLE.] Unable to be retraced.

irretractable /ɪrɪˈtraktəb(ə)l/ *a. rare.* L16. [f. IR-[2] + RETRACTABLE.] Unable to be retracted or taken back.

irretrievable /ɪrɪˈtriːvəb(ə)l/ *a.* L17. [f. IR-[2] + RETRIEVABLE.] Unable to be retrieved; irrecoverable; irreparable.

A. BROOKNER All wrongs were righted; nothing was irretrievable.

ˌirretrievaˈbility *n.* M19. **irretrievably** *adv.* in an irretrievable manner; so as to be irretrievable: L17.

irreverence /ɪˈrɛv(ə)r(ə)ns/ *n.* ME. [L *irreverentia*, f. *irreverent-*: see IRREVERENT, -ENCE.] 1 The fact or quality of being irreverent; absence or violation of reverence. ME. 2 An irreverent act or utterance. M18.

irreveˈrential *a.* irreverent M17. **ˌirreveˈrentially** *adv.* L17.

irreverend /ɪˈrɛv(ə)r(ə)nd/ *a.* L16. [f. IR-[2] + REVEREND *a.*] 1 = IRREVERENT I. L16. 2 Not reverend; unworthy of veneration. M18.

irreverent /ɪˈrɛv(ə)r(ə)nt/ *a.* LME. [L *irreverent-*, f. IR-[2] + *reverent-* pres. ppl stem of *revereri* REVERE: see -ENT.] 1 Not reverent; showing disrespect to a sacred or venerable person or thing. LME. †2 = IRREVEREND 2. Only in L15.

1 H. JAMES She . . became . . in impatience and the expression of contempt, very free and absolutely irreverent. I. MURDOCH I don't like seeing the gods portrayed on the stage. It's irreverent.

irreverently *adv.* LME.

irreversible /ɪrɪˈvəːsɪb(ə)l/ *a.* M17. [f. IR-[2] + REVERSIBLE.] 1 Unable to be undone, repealed, or annulled; unalterable, irrevocable; unable to be turned in the opposite direction or overturned. M17. 2 *Physical Chem.* Of a colloid or colloidal system: unable to be changed from a gelatinous state into a sol by a reversal of the treatment which turns the sol into a gel or gelatinous precipitate. E20.

1 E. SHOWALTER Lobotomy is the most extreme and irreversible form of medical intervention in

schizophrenia. J. HELLER I began to perceive the first signs of irreversible physical decay.

ˌirreversiˈbility *n.* E19. **irreversibleness** *n.* (now *rare* or *obs.*) E17. **irreversibly** *adv.* in an irreversible manner; so as not to be reversed: E17.

irrevocable /ɪˈrɛvəkəb(ə)l/ *a.* LME. [((O)Fr. *irrévocable* f.) L *irrevocabilis*, f. IR-² + *revocabilis* REVOCABLE.] 1 Unable to be recalled or recovered. LME. 2 Unable to be annulled or undone; unalterable, irreversible. LME.

1 I. MURDOCH It's gone, . . the past, it is irrevocable. 2 D. ADAMS There is nothing you can do. . . It was done. It was irrevocable.

irrevocaˈbility *n.* E17. **irrevocableness** *n.* M17. **irrevocably** *adv.* beyond recall or recovery; unalterably, irreversibly: L15.

irrevoluble /ɪˈrɛvəljʊb(ə)l/ *a. rare.* M17. [f. IR-² + REVOLUBLE.] Having no finite period of revolution, whose revolution is never completed.

irrigable /ˈɪrɪgəb(ə)l/ *a.* M19. [f. next + -ABLE.] Able to be irrigated.

irrigate /ˈɪrɪgeɪt/ *v.* E17. [L *irrigat-* pa. ppl stem of *irrigare*, f. IR-¹ + *rigare* wet, water: see -ATE³.] 1 *v.t.* Supply with moisture; moisten, wet. Now *rare.* E17. 2a *v.t.* & *i.* Water (land) by means of channels or streams passing through, or with a sprinkler system; (of a stream etc.) supply (land) with water. E17. b *v.t. Med.* Supply (a part, a wound, etc.) with a constant flow of liquid, for the purpose of cooling, cleansing, disinfection, etc. L19. 3 *v.t. fig.* Refresh or make fruitful as with water. L17. 4 *v.i.* Drink; take a drink. *slang* (chiefly *US*). M19.

2a J. YEATS The country was . . artificially irrigated by a network of canals. *New Yorker* If you want anything growing besides native things, you have to irrigate. G. S. FRASER The green Nile irrigates a barren region.

irrigative *a.* serving to irrigate; of or pertaining to irrigation: M19. **irrigator** *n.* E19. **irrigatory** *a.* of or pertaining to irrigation L19.

irrigation /ɪrɪˈgeɪʃ(ə)n/ *n.* E17. [L *irrigatio(n-)*, f. as prec.: see -ATION.] 1 The action or fact of supplying or being supplied with moisture; a moistening or wetting. Now *rare.* E17. 2a The action of supplying land with water by means of channels or streams, or by sprinkling water over the surface of the ground. E17. b *Med.* The application of a constant stream or shower of liquid to a part of the body, in order to cool, cleanse, disinfect, etc. E17. 3 *fig.* Refreshment; fertilization. M17.

2a E. HEATH The occasional green square where crops were being grown under irrigation. *attrib.*: *irrigation canal, ditch*, etc.

irrigational *a.* L19. **irrigationist** *n.* a person interested in irrigation L19.

irriguous /ɪˈrɪgjʊəs/ *a.* Now *rare.* L15. [f. L *irriguus* supplied with water, f. IR-¹ + *riguus* watered, f. *rigare*: see IRRIGATE, -OUS.] 1 Supplying water or moisture. L15. 2 Irrigated; moistened, wet; (esp. of land) well-watered, watery. M17.

irrision /ɪˈrɪʒ(ə)n/ *n. arch.* E16. [L *irrisio(n-)*, f. *irris-* pa. ppl stem of *irridere* laugh at, f. IR-¹ + *ridere* laugh: see -ION.] Derision, mockery.

irritable /ˈɪrɪtəb(ə)l/ *a.* M17. [L *irritabilis*, f. *irritare*: see IRRITATE *v.*¹, -ABLE.] 1 Readily excited to anger or impatience; easily annoyed. M17. 2 (Of a thing) readily excited to action; highly responsive to stimulus; (of a bodily organ or part) excessively or abnormally sensitive. L18. 3 *Biol.* Capable of actively responding to physical stimulus of some kind. L18.

1 P. H. GIBBS He was not always in a good humour. Sometimes he was irritable and nervy. 2 **irritable bowel (syndrome)** a stress-related condition with recurrent abdominal pain and bowel dysfunction.

irritaˈbility *n.* the quality or state of being irritable M18. **irritably** *adv.* M19.

irritament /ˈɪrɪtəm(ə)nt/ *n.* Now *rare* or *obs.* M17. [L *irritamentum*, f. *irritare* IRRITATE *v.*¹: see -MENT.] A thing that excites or provokes an action, feeling, or state; an irritant.

irritant /ˈɪrɪt(ə)nt/ *a.*¹ & *n.* E17. [f. IRRITATE *v.*¹ + -ANT¹.] A *adj.* †1 Exciting, provocative, rousing. E–M17. 2 Causing physical (or occas. mental) irritation; irritating. E19.

2 R. ADAMS Buckthorn had been bitten . . and the wound . . was irritant and painful. P. PARISH Potassium salts are irritant when taken by mouth; they may cause ulceration of the stomach.

B *n.* An irritant substance, body, or agency; a poison etc. which produces irritation; *fig.* something which is (mentally) irritating. E19.

J. MILLER Any irritant which succeeds in entering the windpipe . . excites the . . cough reflex.

irritancy *n.*¹ irritating quality or character; irritation, annoyance: M19.

irritant /ˈɪrɪt(ə)nt/ *a.*² E16. [Late L *irritant-* pres. ppl stem of *irritare*: see IRRITATE *v.*², -ANT¹.] *Rom., Civil, & Sc. Law.* Making null and void.

irritancy *n.*² the fact of making, or condition of being made, null and void L17.

irritate /ˈɪrɪteɪt/ *v.*¹*t.* M16. [L *irritat-* pa. ppl stem of *irritare*: see -ATE³.] †1 Excite, provoke, rouse (a person etc.). Foll. by *to, into, to do.* M16–M19. b Aggravate, excite, provoke (an action, emotion, etc.). E17–E19. 2 Excite to impatient or angry feeling; annoy, exasperate, provoke. L16. 3 *Med.* Excite (a bodily organ or part) to abnormal action or an abnormal condition; produce an uneasy sensation in, inflame mildly. L17. 4 *Biol.* Produce an active response in (an organ etc.) by the application of a stimulus; stimulate to vital action. E19.

2 J. C. POWYS These things irritated her so much that she could have boxed his ears. V. GLENDINNING These domestic crises bored and irritated Wells. R. INGALLS So boring, and actually sometimes irritating. 3 G. NAYLOR Too much coffee would irritate his ulcer. 4 C. DARWIN The central glands of a leaf were irritated with a small . . brush.

irritatedly *adv.* in an irritated manner L19. **irritatingly** *adv.* in a irritating manner M19. **irritative** *a.* causing irritation M17. **irritator** *n.* (*rare*) M19.

irritate /ˈɪrɪteɪt/ *v.*²*t.* E17. [Late L *irritat-* pa. ppl stem of *irritare* make void, f. L *irritus* invalid: see -ATE³.] *Rom., Civil, & Sc. Law.* Make null and void; annul.

irritation /ɪrɪˈteɪʃ(ə)n/ *n.* LME. [L *irritatio(n-)*, f. as IRRITATE *v.*¹: see -ATION.] 1 The action of provoking to activity; incitement. Now *rare.* LME. 2 *Med.* Production of abnormal sensitiveness or action in a bodily part or organ; production of mild inflammation. L17. 3 Anger, impatience, provocation; a cause of this. E18. 4 *Biol.* The production of some active response (as motion, contraction, nervous impulse) in an organ, tissue, etc., by the application of a stimulus. L18.

1 DE QUINCEY Arts and sciences . . vast machinery for the irritation and development of the human intellect. 3 J. GARDNER It was not frightening . . but acutely annoying, one more irritation among a thousand. D. WIGODER 'Can't you get here on time?' he asked, covering his irritation with . . casualness.

†irrite *a.* LME–M18. [AN, OFr. *irrit* or L *irritus*, f. IR-² + *ratus* established, valid.] Void, of no effect.

irrorate /ˈɪrərət/ *a. rare.* E19. [L *irroratus* pa. pple, f. as next: see -ATE².] *Entomol.* Irrorated.

irrorate /ˈɪrəreɪt/ *v.t.* E17. [L *irrorat-* pa. ppl stem of *irrorare* bedew, f. IR-¹ + *rorare* drop dew, f. *ror-, ros* dew: see -ATE³.] †1 Wet or sprinkle as with dew; moisten. Only in 17. 2 *Entomol.* As *irrorated* pa. pple: sprinkled minutely (*with* dots). M19.

irroration /ɪrəˈreɪʃ(ə)n/ *n.* E17. [Late L *irroratio(n-)*, f. as prec.: see -ATION.] †1 (A) sprinkling or wetting as with dew; (a) moistening. E17–L18. 2 *Entomol.* A sprinkling of minute dots or spots of colour. M19.

irrotational /ɪrəʊˈteɪʃ(ə)n(ə)l/ *a.* L19. [f. IR-² + ROTATIONAL.] *Physics.* Esp. of fluid motion: not rotational, having no rotation.

ˌirrotatioˈnality *n.* M20. **irrotationally** *adv.* L19.

irruent /ˈɪrʊənt/ *a. rare.* M17. [L *irruent-* pres. ppl stem of *irruere* rush in or upon: see -ENT.] Rushing (in); running rapidly.

irrumate /ˈɪrʊmeɪt/ *v.t.* M17. [L *irrumat-* pa. ppl stem of *irrumare* give suck, f. IR-¹ + *ruma* teat: see -ATE³.] †1 Suck in. Only in M17. 2 Perform irrumation on (a person). L19.

irrumator *n.* L19.

irrumation /ɪrʊˈmeɪʃ(ə)n/ *n.* L19. [L *irrumatio(n-)*, f. as prec.: see -ATION.] Insertion of the penis into a sexual partner's mouth.

irrupt /ɪˈrʌpt/ *v. rare.* M19. [L *irrupt-* pa. ppl stem of *irrumpere* break in, f. IR-¹ + *rumpere* break.] 1 *v.t.* Break into. M19. 2 *v.i.* Burst or break in, enter forcibly. L19.

2 S. NAIPAUL Its roots were . . threatening to irrupt through the floor.

irruptive *a.* having the quality or character of bursting in; making, or tending to, irruption: L16.

irruption /ɪˈrʌpʃ(ə)n/ *n.* M16. [L *irruptio(n-)*, f. as prec.: see -ION.] I 1 The action of bursting or breaking in; a violent entry or invasion, esp. of a hostile force or people. M16. 2 *spec.* An abrupt local increase in the numbers of a migrant bird or other animal. E20.

1 M. IGNATIEFF This sudden irruption of riot into the little frame of Natasha's existence. 2 *Bird Watching* Immigrations or irruptions of Continental birds looking for 'open ground'.

II 3 [By confusion.] = ERUPTION. E17.

Irvingite /ˈəːvɪŋʌɪt/ *n.* & *a.* M19. [f. *Irving* (see below) + -ITE¹.] A *n.* A member of the Catholic Apostolic Church, which followed the teachings of Edward Irving (1792–1834), orig. a minister of the Church of Scotland. M19. B *attrib.* or as *adj.* Of or pertaining to the Irvingites. L19.

Irvingism *n.* the doctrines and principles of the Irvingites M19.

is /ɪz/ *n. rare.* L19. [f. the vb.] That which exists, that which is; the fact or quality of existence.

is *v.* see BE *v.*

is- *comb. form* see ISO-.

Isabel /ˈɪzəbɛl/ *n.* E19. [Fr. *Isabelle* = ISABELLA.] 1 = ISABELLA 1. E19. 2 A kind of fancy pigeon, a small variety of the pouter so called from its colour. M19. 3 A variety of N. American grape; = ISABELLA 2b. M19.

Isabella /ɪzəˈbɛlə/ *n.* E17. [A female forename, Fr. *Isabelle*, but the immediate ref. is unkn.] 1 In full *Isabella colour.* (A) greyish yellow; a light buff. E17. 2a A kind of peach. M17. b In full *Isabella grape.* A N. American vine *Vitis labrusca*, with large fruit, sometimes purple, often green and red; the fruit of this vine. M17.

isabelline /ɪzəˈbɛlɪn, -ʌɪn/ *a.* M19. [f. prec. + -INE¹.] Of an Isabella colour, greyish-yellow.

isadelphous /ʌɪsəˈdɛlfəs/ *a.* M19. [f. *is-* var. of ISO- + Gk *adelphos* brother + -OUS.] *Bot.* Of a flower: having diadelphous stamens with the same number in each bundle.

isagoge /ʌɪsəˈgəʊdʒiː, -giː/ *n.* M16. [L f. Gk *eisagōgē*, f. *eis* into + *agein* to lead.] An introduction.

isagogic /ʌɪsəˈgɒdʒɪk/ *a.* & *n.* E19. [L *isagogicus* f. Gk *eisagōgikos*, f. *eisagōgē*: see prec., -IC.] A *adj.* Of or pertaining to an isagoge; introductory to any branch of study. E19. B *n.* Usu. in *pl.* (treated as *sing.*). Introductory studies; *esp.* the branch of theology which is introductory to exegesis and deals with the literary and external history of the books of the Bible. M19.

Isaian /ʌɪˈzʌɪən, ʌɪˈzeɪən/ *a.* L19. [f. *Isaiah* (see below) + -AN.] Of or belonging to the prophet Isaiah or the book of the Old Testament and Hebrew Scriptures that bears his name.

Also **Isaiˈanic** *a.* E19.

isallobar /ʌɪsˈaləbɑː/ *n.* E20. [f. IS(O)- + ALLO- + BAR *n.*⁴] *Meteorol.* A line (imaginary or on a map) connecting points at which the barometric pressure has changed by an equal amount during a specified time.

isalloˈbaric *a.* E20.

isangoma *n.* var. of SANGOMA.

isapostolic /ˌʌɪsapəˈstɒlɪk/ *a.* M19. [f. eccl.Gk *isapostolos* equal to an apostle: see IS-, APOSTLE, -IC.] Equal to, or contemporary with, the apostles: an epithet given in the Orthodox Church to a notable associate of the apostles, or to the evangelist of a non-Christian people.

isatin /ˈʌɪsətɪn/ *n.* M19. [f. L *isatis* woad f. Gk: see -IN¹.] *Chem.* A reddish-orange crystalline heterocyclic compound, $C_8H_5NO_2$, related to indole and indigo.

isatoˈgenic *a.*: *isatogenic acid*, an unstable crystalline acid, $C_8H_4NO_2{\cdot}COOH$, related to isatin L19.

-isation *suff.* var. of -IZATION.

isatoic /ʌɪsəˈtəʊɪk/ *a.* L19. [f. ISATIN + -OIC.] *Chem.* 1 *isatoic acid*, *N*-carboxyanthranilic acid, $C_6H_4(COOH)(NHCOOH)$, known only as its derivatives; formerly also, isatoic anhydride. L19. 2 *isatoic anhydride*, the bicyclic anhydride, $C_8H_5NO_3$, of isatoic acid, obtained by oxidation of isatin. L19.

Isaurian /ʌɪˈsɔːrɪən/ *n.* & *a.* L18. [f. *Isauria* (see below) + -AN.] A *n.* A native or inhabitant of Isauria, an ancient country in Asia Minor, between Cilicia and Phrygia; *spec.* any of a line of emperors of the Eastern Roman Empire. L18. B *adj.* Of or pertaining to Isauria or the emperors called after it. M19.

isba /izˈba/ *n.* Also ***izba***. L18. [Russ. *izba* (rel. to STOVE *n.*).] A Russian hut or log-house.

isblink /ˈiːsblɪŋk/ *n.* L18. [Sw., or f. corresp. wds in Da., G, Du.] = *iceblink* s.v. BLINK *n.* 5a.

Iscariot /ɪˈskarɪət/ *n.* M17. [L *Iscariota* f. Gk *Iskariōtēs*, surname of Judas, the disciple who betrayed Jesus; perh. f. Heb. *ʾīš qĕriyyōt* man of Qerioth (a place in ancient Palestine).] A traitor or betrayer of the worst kind; = JUDAS I.

Iscariotic /ɪˌskarɪˈɒtɪk/ *a.* of or pertaining to Judas Iscariot L19. **Iscariˈotical** *a.* characteristic of or resembling Judas Iscariot; wickedly treacherous: E17. **Iscariotism** *n.* a practice characteristic of Judas Iscariot, *esp.* parsimonious employment of church funds (cf. *John* 12:5) L19.

ischaemia /ɪˈskiːmɪə/ *n.* Also ***ischemia**. L19. [mod.L, f. Gk *iskhaimos* stopping blood, f. *iskhein* hold + *haima* blood: see -IA[1].] *Med.* Orig., the stanching of bleeding. Now only, local anaemia; deficiency of blood supply to (part of) an organ.

ischaemic *a.* pertaining to or characterized by ischaemia L19. **ischaemically** *adv.* by, or as a result of, ischaemia M20.

ischia *n.* pl. of ISCHIUM.

ischiadic /ɪskɪˈadɪk/ *a.* Now *rare.* E18. [L *ischiadicus* f. Gk *iskhiadikos*, f. *iskhiad-*, *iskhias* pain in the hip, f. *iskhion* hip-joint: see -IC.] Of or pertaining to the ischium; ischiatic.

ischial /ˈɪskɪəl/ *a.* M19. [f. ISCHIUM + -AL[1].] Of or pertaining to the ischium; ischiadic.

ischial tuberosity the projection of the ischium into the middle of the buttock, which takes the weight when sitting.

ischiatic /ɪskɪˈatɪk/ *a.* M17. [med.L *ischiaticus* (after adjs. in *-aticus*), for L *ischiadicus*: see ISCHIADIC.] 1 Troubled or affected with sciatica. Now *rare* or *obs.* M17. 2 *Anat.* Of or near the ischium or hip. M18.

2 **ischiatic notch** = *sciatic notch* s.v. SCIATIC *a.* I.

ischio- /ˈɪskɪəʊ/ *comb. form.* [f. ISCHIUM: see -O-.] Chiefly *Anat.* Relating to or involving the ischium and —, as *ischioanal*, *ischioiliac*, *ischiorectal*.

ischiorrhogic /ˌɪskɪə(ʊ)ˈrɒdʒɪk/ *a.* M19. [Gk *iskhiorrhōgikos*, orig. = having broken hips, limping, f. *iskhion* hip-joint + *rhōg-* *rhōx* broken.] *Class. Pros.* Of an iambic line: having a spondee in the second, fourth, or sixth place.

ischium /ˈɪskɪəm/ *n.* Pl. **-ia** /-ɪə/. E17. [L f. Gk *iskhion* hip-joint, (later) ischium.] The posterior or inferior bone of the pelvis, on which the body rests when sitting, fused with the ilium and the pubis to form the innominate bone.

ischuria /ɪˈskjʊərɪə/ *n.* Now *rare* or *obs.* Also Anglicized as **ischury** /ˈɪskjʊri/. E17. [Late L f. Gk *iskhouria*, f. *iskhein* hold + *ouron* urine: see -IA[1].] Difficulty in passing urine, due either to suppression or to retention.

-ise /ʌɪz, iːz/ *suff.*[1] Forming (usu. abstract) ns. and repr. (O)Fr. *-ise*, OFr. *-ice*, either f. L *-itia*, *-itium* or of independent formation; as *exercise*, *franchise*, *merchandise*, *expertise*. Cf. -ICE[1].

-ise *suff.*[2] var. of -IZE.

isel /ˈʌɪz(ə)l/ *n.* Now *dial.* Also **izle**. [OE *ysel*, *ysle*, cogn. w. MHG *usele*, *usel*, mod.G dial. *Üsel*, *Ussel*, *Issel* spark, ON *usli* fire, f. same base as L *ust-*, *urere* burn.] A spark; an ember; usu. in *pl.*, sparks, embers; ashes. Also, floating sparks from a conflagration; extinct sparks, particles of soot, smuts.

isentropic /ʌɪsɛnˈtrɒpɪk/ *a.* & *n.* L19. [f. ISO- + ENTROPIC.] *Physics.* A *adj.* Of equal entropy; (of a line in a diagram) joining points representing successive states of a system in which the entropy remains constant; (of a process) involving no change in entropy. L19. B *n.* An isentropic line. L19.

isentropically *adv.* without change in entropy M20.

-iser *suff.* var. of -IZER.

isethionic /ʌɪˌsiːθɪˈɒnɪk/ *a.* M19. [f. *is-* var. of ISO- + ETHIONIC.] Chem. *isethionic acid*, a monobasic acid, $HO{\cdot}CH_2{\cdot}CH_2{\cdot}SO_3H$, used as a detergent and surfactant; 2-hydroxyethanesulphonic acid.

iseˈthionate *n.* a salt of isethionic acid M19.

Isfahan /ɪsfəˈhɑːn, ˈɪsfəhɑːn/ *a.* & *n.* Also **Isp-** /ɪsp-/. M20. [A province and town in west central Iran (Persia).] A *adj.* Designating a type of hand-woven rug, the most distinguished examples of which were produced in Isfahan in the 16th cent. M20. B *n.* An Isfahan rug. M20.

-ish /ɪʃ/ *suff.*[1] [OE *-isc* corresp. to Goth. *-isks*, ON *-iskr*, OHG, OS, OFris. *-isc*, G, Du. *-isch*, f. Gmc: cogn. with Gk *-iskos* dim. suff. of ns.] Forming adjs.: (*a*) from national or other class names, as *English*, *Jewish*, *Scottish*, *Turkish*; (*b*) from other ns., w. the sense 'of the nature or character of (a person, animal, etc.)', now chiefly *derog.*, 'having the (bad or objectionable) qualities of', as *boorish*, *boyish*, *foolish*, *sluggish*, *waspish*, *womanish*; also from names of things, w. the sense 'of the nature of, tending to', as *bookish*, *feverish*; or from other parts of speech, as *snappish*, *uppish*; (*c*) from adjs., w. the sense 'approaching the quality of, somewhat', app. first with words of colour, as *bluish*, *reddish*, etc.; later also with other adjs., and now, in colloq. use, possible with nearly all monosyllabic adjs., and some others, e.g. *brightish*, *coldish*, *narrowish*, *oldish*; (*d*) *colloq.* from names of hours of the day or numbers of years, w. the sense 'round about, somewhere near (the time or period of)', as *elevenish*, *fortyish*.

-ish /ɪʃ/ *suff.*[2] Forming vbs repr. Fr. *-iss-* lengthened stem of verbs in *-ir* f. L *-isc-* inceptive suff. as *abolish*, *establish*, *finish*, *punish*; sometimes repr. other Fr. endings, as *astonish*, *distinguish*.

ishan /ˈiːʃɑːn/ *n.* E20. [Perh. f. Arab. dial. *īšān* f. Pers. *nīšān* mark.] A prehistoric mound in Iraq.

Ishihara /ɪʃɪˈhɑːrə/ *n.* E20. [Shinobu *Ishihara* (1879–1963), Japanese ophthalmologist.] *Ophthalm.* Used *attrib.* with ref. to a test for colour-blindness (the *Ishihara test*) devised by Ishihara, in which the subject is asked to distinguish numbers or pathways printed in coloured spots on a background of spots of a different colour or colours.

Ishmael /ˈɪʃmeɪl/ *n.* M17. [The son of Abraham and Hagar: see *Gen.* 16 and 25.] A person resembling Ishmael, *esp.* an outcast, a person at war with society.

Ishmaelite *n.* (*a*) a descendant of Ishmael, as some Arabs claim to be; (*b*) = ISHMAEL: L16. **Ishmaelitish** *a.* of, pertaining to, of the nature of an Ishmaelite L17. **Ishmaelitism** *n.* the character and action of an Ishmaelite L19.

Isiac /ˈʌɪsɪak, ˈɪs-/ *n.* & *a.* E18. [L *Isiacus* f. Gk *Isiakos*, f. *Isis* (see below): see -AC.] A *n.* A priest or worshipper of Isis. E18. B *adj.* Of or relating to Isis, the principal goddess of ancient Egyptian mythology. M18.

Iˈsiacal *a.* = ISIAC *a.* E17.

isidium /ʌɪˈsɪdɪəm/ *n.* Pl. **-dia** /-dɪə/. M19. [mod.L genus name formerly used to include all genera bearing isidia, f. *Isis Isidis* the goddess Isis (w. ref. to her disc and horns).] *Bot.* A coral-like or wartlike excrescence of the thallus in certain lichens, having the function of vegetative propagation after detachment.

isidial *a.* of or pertaining to an isidium E20. **isidiate** *a.* bearing isidia M20. **isiˈdiferous** *a.* = ISIDIATE L19. **isidioid** *a.* resembling or of the nature of an isidium; bearing isidia: M19.

Isidorian /ɪzɪˈdɔːrɪən/ *a.* L19. [f. *Isidorus* (see below) + -IAN.] Of or pertaining to Isidorus or Isidore, esp. St Isidore, archbishop of Seville 600–636, author of several historical and ecclesiastical works, and of twenty books of *Origines* (Etymologies), of value for the history of Latin.

Isindebele *n.* & *a.* var. of SINDEBELE.

isinglass /ˈʌɪzɪŋglɑːs/ *n.* M16. [Alt. (w. assim. to *glass*) of early Du. †*huysenblas*, f. †*huysen*, †*huys* sturgeon + †*blas* (now *blaas*) bladder (cf. G *Hausenblase*).] 1 A firm whitish semitransparent substance, a comparatively pure form of gelatin, obtained from the swim-bladders of some freshwater fishes, esp. the sturgeon, and used in cookery for making jellies etc., for clarifying liquors, in the manufacture of glue, and for other purposes. Also, any of several similar substances made from hides, hoofs, etc. M16. 2 Mica (from its resembling in appearance some kinds of isinglass). M17.

Islam /ˈɪzlɑːm, ˈɪs-; ɪsˈlɑːm, ɪz-/ *n.* E17. [Arab. *ʾislām*, f. *ʾaslama* submit, surrender (spec. to God). Cf. MUSLIM.] 1 The religious system established through the prophet Muhammad; the Muslim religion; the body of Muslims, the Muslim world. E17. †2 An orthodox Muslim. E17–E19.

Islamiˈzation *n.* = ISLAMICIZATION M20. **Islamize** *v.t.* & *i.* convert to or practise Islam M19.

Islamic /ɪzˈlamɪk, ɪzˈlɑːmɪk, ɪs-/ *a.* L18. [f. prec. + -IC.] Of or pertaining to Islam; Muslim.

Islamicization /-ɪsʌɪˈzeɪʃ(ə)n/ *n.* the process of Islamicizing L20. **Islamicize** /-ɪsʌɪz/ *v.t.* convert (a country, institution, etc.) to Islamic principles L20.

Islamism /ˈɪzləmɪz(ə)m, ˈɪs-/ *n.* M18. [f. as prec. + -ISM.] = ISLAM I.

Islamist *n.* (*a*) an orthodox Muslim; (*b*) an expert on Islam: M19.

Islamite /ˈɪzləmʌɪt, ɪs-/ *n.* & *a. arch.* L18. [f. ISLAM + -ITE[1].] A *n.* A Muslim. L18. B *adj.* Islamic, Muslim. M19.

Islaˈmitic *a.* Muslim L18.

island /ˈʌɪlənd/ *n.*[1] [OE (Anglian) *ēgland*, (WS) *īegland*, *īgland*, later *īland* (= OFris. *eiland*, MDu., MLG *eilant*, ON *eyland*), f. *īeg*, *īg* island, (in compounds) water, sea + LAND *n.*[1]] 1 A piece of land completely surrounded by water. Formerly also (and still in certain place-names, as *Thorney Island*), a peninsula; a place cut off at high water or during floods. OE. b In *pl.* In biblical translations: the lands beyond the sea, the coasts of the Mediterranean. Cf. ISLE *n.*[1] 2. M16. c *spec.* (*ellipt.*) Any of certain specific islands (the Isle of Wight, the Hebrides, certain Pacific islands, etc.). Also, a specific prison on an island. E19. 2 *transf.* An elevated piece of land surrounded by marsh or river plain; a piece of woodland surrounded by prairie or flat open country; a detached block of buildings. Also, an individual or a people, detached or standing out alone. E17. b More fully *traffic island*, (US) *safety island*. A raised or marked area in the road to direct traffic and provide a refuge for pedestrians. M19. c *Anat.* = ISLET 2b. L19. d A small isolated ridge or structure between the lines in fingerprints. L19. e More fully *speech island*. A small area inhabited by speakers of a language or dialect other than that spoken in the surrounding areas. L19. f A piece of furniture in a private house or in a museum, library, etc., surrounded by unoccupied floor space. Freq. *attrib.* M20. g The superstructure of a ship, esp. of an aircraft-carrier. M20.

1 R. INGALLS Dense pinewoods . . covered all the islands of the archipelago. 2 J. LEONI This House . . stands in an Island, being surrounded by four streets. J. CHEEVER Sheep surrounded the bus, isolated this little island of elderly Americans.

Phrases: †**island of ice** an iceberg; a large mass of floating ice. *island of* REIL. THOUSAND *island*. *Vulcanian Islands*: see VULCANIAN *a.*

Comb.: **island arc** *Geogr.* any curved chain of (freq. volcanic) islands typically located at a tectonic plate margin and having a deep trench on the convex side; **Island Carib** (*a*) the Carib people of the Lesser Antilles; (*b*) the language of this people; **island-hill** a hill or mountain rising directly out of a plain; **island-hop** *v.i.* move from one island to another; *spec.* (of the US army in the Pacific during the war of 1941–45) recapture Japanese-occupied islands one after another; **islandman** (now *dial.*) an islander; **island-mountain**

= *island-hill* above; **island platform** a platform at a railway station, with through lines on each side of it; *island universe*: see UNIVERSE 2C.

islandless *a.* devoid of islands M19.

†Island *n.*[2] var. of ICELAND.

island /ˈʌɪlənd/ *v.t.* M17. [f. ISLAND *n.*[1]] **1** Make into or like an island; place or enclose (as) on an island; insulate, isolate. M17. **2** Set or dot with or as with islands. E19.

1 M. LOWRY The narrow sloping lawn, islanded by rose beds.

islander /ˈʌɪləndə/ *n.* M16. [f. ISLAND *n.*[1] + -ER[1].] A native or inhabitant of an island.

Andaman Islander, Channel Islander, Falkland Islander, South Islander, South Sea Islander, Virgin Islander, etc.

isle /ʌɪl/ *n.*[1] Now chiefly *literary* & in place-names. ME. [OFr. *ile* (mod. *île*), (Latinized) †*isle* f. L *insula*.] **1** = ISLAND *n.*[1] 1. Now usu., a small island. ME. **2** In biblical translations: a land beyond the sea (esp. in *the isles of the Gentiles*). Cf. ISLAND *n.*[1] 1b. LME.

1 *Ecologist* The early Phoenician traders .. called Britain the Isle of Honey. *British Isles, Isle of Purbeck, Isle of Man, Isle of Wight, Western Isles*, etc.

Comb.: **isleman** *rare* = ISLESMAN.

isleless /-l-l-/ *a.* devoid of islands L16.

†isle *n.*[2] var. of AISLE.

isle /ʌɪl/ *v.t.* L16. [f. ISLE *n.*[1]] Make an isle of; place or set as or in an isle; insulate; = ISLAND *v.* 1.

Isle of Wight disease /ʌɪl əv ˈwʌɪt dɪ,ziːz/ *n. phr.* E20. [*Isle of Wight*, an island off the coast of Hampshire, England.] A disease of bees first found in the Isle of Wight in 1904, caused by the parasitic mite *Acarapis woodi*.

islesman /ˈʌɪlzmən/ *n.* Pl. **-men**. E19. [f. ISLE *n.*[1] + -'S[1] + MAN *n.*] A native or inhabitant of any group of islands, esp. of the Hebrides, Orkneys, or Shetland.

islet /ˈʌɪlɪt/ *n.* M16. [OFr. *islet*, *-ete* (mod. *îlette*) dim. of ISLE *n.*[1]: see -ET[1].] **1** A little island, an ait. M16. **2** *transf.* **a** Something resembling a small island; a small piece of land markedly differing in character from its surroundings; an isolated tract or spot. Cf. ISLAND *n.*[1] 2. M17. **b** *Anat.* An isolated portion of tissue or group of cells, surrounded by parts of a different structure; *esp.* = *islet of Langerhans* s.v. LANGERHANS 1. M19.

isleted *a.* placed like an islet; studded with islets: L19.

islomania /ʌɪlə(ʊ)ˈmeɪnɪə/ *n.* M20. [f. ISLE *n.*[1] + -O- + -MANIA.] A passion or craze for islands.

islot /ˈʌɪlət/ *n.* Now *rare*. Also **ilot**. L18. [OFr. (later *îlot*) dim. of ISLE *n.*[1]: see -OT[1].] An islet.

ism /ˈɪz(ə)m/ *n.* Chiefly *derog.* L17. [-ISM used generically. Cf. WASM.] A form of doctrine, theory, or practice having, or claiming to have, a distinctive character or relationship.

Kendal Mercury Irrespective of isms and creeds. G. B. SHAW The proletarian Isms are very much alike.

-ism /ɪz(ə)m/ *suff.* [Fr. *-isme*, chiefly f. L *-ismus* f. Gk *-ismos* forming ns. of action f. vbs in *-izein*, in part also f. L *-isma* f. Gk, forming ns. expr. something done.] Forming usu. abstract ns. expr. (*a*) a process or practice or its result, as *baptism, criticism, organism*, freq. with corresp. vbs in -IZE; (*b*) the conduct characteristic of a class of people, as *heroism, patriotism*; a (sometimes abnormal) condition of a person or thing, as *alcoholism, barbarism, dwarfism, parallelism*; (*c*) (adherence to) a system of theory, belief, or practice (religious, philosophical, political, scientific, etc.), as *atheism, Buddhism, Darwinism, feminism, hedonism, Marxism, socialism, Wesleyism*; also, a system of discrimination based on a particular criterion, as *racism, sexism*: usu. with corresp. personal ns. in -IST and freq. with adjs. in -ISTIC; (*d*) a peculiarity or characteristic of a nation, individual, etc., esp. in language, as *Americanism, colloquialism, Spoonerism*.

Ismaeli *n.* & *a.* var. of ISMAILI.

Ismaelite /ˈɪzmeɪəlʌɪt, ˈɪs-/ *n.* Now *rare*. In sense 2 also **Ismailite**. LME. [f. Fr., L, & Gk *Ismael* Ishmael (see ISHMAEL) or (in sense 2) f. as next + -ITE[1].] **1** A descendant of Ishmael. Formerly also, an Arab regarded as a descendant of Ishmael; *gen.* a Muslim. LME. **2** An Ismaili. M19.

Ismaelism *n.* (*a*) the doctrinal system of the Ismailis; †(*b*) Islam: L18. **Ismaelitic** *a.* of or belonging to the Ismailis L19.

Ismaili /ɪsmeɪˈiːli, -ˈɪli/ *n.* & *a.* Also **Ismaeli**. M19. [f. Arab. *ʾIsmāʿīl* (see below) + -I[2].] (A person) belonging to the branch of Shiite Islam which holds that at the death in 765 of the sixth Shiite imam the imamate ought to have descended to the posterity of his deceased eldest son ʾIsmāʿīl.

Ismailian *n.* & *a.* M19.

Ismailite *n.* see ISMAELITE.

Isnik /ɪzˈnɪk/ *a.* M20. [A town in Asian Turkey, the classical Nicaea. Cf. NICENE *a.*] Designating a type of pottery or tiles made at Isnik, or imitations of it, from the 15th to the 17th cents., characterized by the use of brilliant pigments.

iso- /ˈʌɪsəʊ/ *comb. form.* Also occas. bef. a vowel **is-**. Also (*Chem.*) as attrib. adj. **iso**. [Gk *isos* equal.] **1** Used in wds adopted f. Gk and in Eng. wds modelled on these, and as a freely productive pref., mainly in scientific and technical use, w. the sense 'equal'. **2** [Extracted f. ISOMER.] *Chem.* Forming names of compounds and radicals which are isomers of those whose names follow, as *isoborneol, isomaltose, isophthalate*, etc.; *spec.* designating hydrocarbons containing a $(CH_3)_2CH\cdot$ group at the end of a chain, as *isobutyl, isopentane*, etc. (Formerly regarded as a separable prefix and printed in italics (often with a hyphen). The IUPAC recommendation is that it should always be directly attached to the remainder of the parent name (and be printed in ordinary type).)

isenˈthalpic *a.* of or relating to equal enthalpy E20. **isoˈallele** *n.* (*Genetics*) an allele indistinguishable from another allele in its effect on the phenotype except when special techniques are employed M20. **isoaˈllelic** *a.* of (the nature of) an isoallele M20. **isoˈantibody** *n.* (*Immunol.*) an antibody elicited by an isoantigen E20. **isoˈantigen** *n.* (*Immunol.*) a natural antigen in one individual which is capable of eliciting antibody formation only in other, genetically different, individuals of the same species M20. **isoantiˈgenic** *a.* of, pertaining to, or being an isoantigen M20. **isobath** /-baθ/ *n.* [Gk *bathos* depth] a line (imaginary or on a map) joining places where water has equal depth; an underwater contour: L19. **isoˈbathic** *a.* of the nature of an isobath; depicting isobaths: L19. **isoˈbathytherm** *n.* = ISOTHERMOBATH L19. **isobiˈlateral** *a.* having the same structure on both sides; *esp.* (of leaves) having no evident distinction of upper and under surface: L19. **isoˈcaloric** *a.* of equal calorific value E20. **isocaˈlorically** *adv.* in a way that leaves the calorific value unchanged M20. **isoˈcephaly** *n.* the convention, in Greek reliefs, of representing the heads of all the figures at nearly the same level E20. **isoˈcercal** *a.* [Gk *kerkos* tail] *Ichthyol.* having equal lobes in the tail, with the vertebral column straight, not bent up (cf. HOMOCERCAL) L19. **isochore** /-kɔː/ *n.* [Gk *khōra* space] a curve on a diagram that represents a physical system at constant volume E20. **isochroous** /ʌɪˈsɒkrəʊəs/ *a.* [Gk *khroa* colour] of a uniform colour M19. **isoˈcitrate** *n.* an ester or salt of isocitric acid E20. **isoˈcitric** *a.*: *isocitric acid*, a tribasic carboxylic acid, $C_6H_8O_7$, isomeric with citric acid, which is an intermediate in the Krebs cycle M19. **isoˈcrymal** *a.* & *n.* [Gk *krumos* cold] (a line, imaginary or on a map) connecting places at which the temperature is the same during a specified coldest part of the year M19. **isocryme** *n.* = ISOCRYMAL *n.* M19. **isoˈdiaphere** *n.* [Gk *diapherein* differ] each of two or more nuclides in which the difference between the numbers of protons and neutrons is the same, as a nucleus and its α-decay product L20. **isodiˈmorphism** *n.* (*Cryst.*) isomorphism between two dimorphous substances in both of their forms M19. **isodiˈmorphous** *a.* (*Cryst.*) exhibiting isodimorphism M19. **isoˈeugenol** *n.* an aromatic liquid phenol that occurs in essential oils, esp. ylang-ylang; 2-methoxy-4-propenylphenol: L19. **isogeˈneic** *a.* (*Immunol.*) = SYNGENEIC *a.* M20. **isograft** *n.* & *v.t.* (a) graft between individuals of the same species (cf. HOMOTRANSPLANT), esp. between genetically identical individuals E20. **ˌisohaemaggluˈtiˈnation** *n.* (*Immunol.*) isoagglutination of red blood cells E20. **ˌisohaemaˈgglutinin** *n.* (*Immunol.*) an isoagglutinin which is an antibody to a blood group antigen E20. **isoˈhalsine** *n.* [irreg. f. Gk *hals* salt] = ISOHALINE *n.* E20. **isohel** *n.* [Gk *hēlios* sun] a line (imaginary or on a map) connecting points having the same amount or duration of sunshine E20. **isohelic** /-ˈhiːlɪk/ *a.* of the nature of an isohel L19. **isohyet** /-hʌɪɪt/ *n.* [Gk *huetos* rain] = ISOHYETAL *n.* L19. **isohyetal** /-ˈhʌɪɪt(ə)l/ *a.* & *n.* (a line on a map etc.) connecting places having equal annual or seasonal rainfall L19. **isoiˈmmune** *a.* of, producing, or exhibiting isoimmunization M20. **isoimmuniˈzation** *n.* (an instance of) the development of an isoantibody in an individual against an antigen derived from another individual of the same species M20. **isokiˈnetic** *a.* characterized by a constant or equal speed; *esp.* (*a*) (of sampling methods for moving fluids) not disturbing the flow; (*b*) (of a machine) producing a constant speed irrespective of power input; (*c*) *Physiol.* of or pertaining to muscular action with a constant rate of movement: M20. **isokiˈnetically** *adv.* at a constant or equal speed M20. **isoˈlecithal** *a.* [Gk *lekithos* yolk] = HOMOLECITHAL E20. **isoˈlectic** *a.* (*Ling.*) = ISOLEXIC E20. **isolex** *n.* (*Ling.*) a line (imaginary or on a map) bounding an area in which some item of vocabulary occurs; a lexical isogloss: E20. **isoˈlexic** *a.* (*Ling.*) pertaining to or of the nature of an isolex E20. **isoline** = ISOPLETH 1 M20. **isolux** *a.* = ISOPHOTAL *a.* E20. **isomagˈnetic** *n.* & *a.* (*a*) *n.* a line (imaginary or on a map) connecting places which have the same value of a particular parameter of the earth's magnetic field; (*b*) *adj.* designating or (of a chart) depicting such lines: L19. **isomeˈtropia** *n.* [after *isometric, hypermetropia*] equal refractive power in both eyes (opp. ANISOMETROPIA) E20. **isoˈnitrile** *n.* = ISOCYANIDE L19. **iso-osˈmotic** *a.* (*Physiol.*) = ISOSMOTIC E20. **isopheˈnomenal** *a.* (of a line on a map etc.) connecting places at which phenomena of any kind are equal M19. **isopiestic** /-pʌɪˈestɪk/ *a.* & *n.* [Gk *piestos* compressible] (*a*) *adj.* = ISOBARIC *a.* 1; (*b*) *n.* = ISOBAR *n.* 1: L19. **isoˈplastic** *a.* = HOMOPLASTIC 2 E20. **isoˈplasty** *n.* = HOMOPLASTY E20. **isoˈpropanol** *n.* a liquid secondary alcohol, $CH_3CHOH\cdot CH_3$, used as a solvent and in the production of acetone; propan-2-ol: M20. **isoˈpropyl** *n.* the radical $(CH_3)_2CH$— (*isopropyl alcohol* = ISOPROPANOL) M19. **isosmotic** /ʌɪsɒzˈmɒtɪk/ *a.* (*Physiol.*) of or having the same osmotic pressure (foll. by *with*) L19. **isospore** *n.* (*Bot.*) an undifferentiated spore L19. **isosporous** /ʌɪˈsɒsp(ə)rəs/ *a.* (*Bot.*) = HOMOSPOROUS L19. **isoˈstructural** *a.* (*Min.*) having the same or similar crystal structure (foll. by *with*) E20. **isoˈthermobath** *n.* a line (imaginary or on a map) connecting points of equal temperature at various depths in a vertical section of the sea L19. **isotone** *n.* [f. ISOTOPE, with *n* for *neutron* replacing *p* for *proton*] *Physics* each of two or more different nuclides having the same number of neutrons M20. **isoˈzooid** *n.* (*Biol.*) a zooid, or individual of a colonial animal, not differentiated from the rest M19.

isoagglutination /ˌʌɪsəʊəgluːtɪˈneɪʃ(ə)n/ *n.* E20. [f. ISO- + AGGLUTINATION.] *Immunol.* Agglutination of cells (esp. sperms or erythrocytes) of an individual by a substance from a (genetically different) conspecific individual.

isoaˈgglutinate *v.t.* & *i.* cause isoagglutination (of) E20. **isoaˈgglutinative** *a.* pertaining to or causing isoagglutination E20. **isoaˈgglutinin** *n.* an agglutinin from an individual that agglutinates cells of (genetically different) conspecific individuals; *esp.* an isohaemagglutinin: E20. **isoaggluˈtinogen** *n.* (*Immunol.*) a substance (esp. a blood group antigen) that elicits or reacts with an isoagglutinin E20.

isobar /ˈʌɪsə(ʊ)bɑː/ *n.* In sense 2 orig. **†isobare**. M19. [f. Gk *isobaros* of equal weight, f. *iso-* ISO- + *bare-*, *baros* weight, *barus* heavy.] **1** *Physical Geogr.* & *Meteorol.* A line (on a map or chart, or imaginary) connecting places at which the atmospheric pressure is the same (at a given time, or on average). M19. **2** *Physics.* A line or formula that represents a physical system at constant pressure. L19. **3** *Physics.* Each of two or more nuclides which have the same mass number but different atomic numbers (and so belong to different elements). E20.

isobaric /ʌɪsə(ʊ)ˈbarɪk/ *a.* & *n.* L19. [f. prec. + -IC.] **A** *adj.* **1a** Indicating equal atmospheric pressure; containing or relating to isobars. L19. **b** Occurring at or pertaining to a constant pressure. E20. **2** *Physics.* Of, pertaining to, or being nuclides that are isobars. (Foll. by *with*.) E20. **3** *Med.* Of, pertaining to, or designating a solution for spinal anaesthesia having the same density as the cerebrospinal fluid. M20.

2 isobaric spin = ISOSPIN.

B *n.* = ISOBAR 2. E20.

isobarically *adv.* at constant pressure, without a change in pressure M20. **isobaro'metric** *a.* (*rare*) = ISOBARIC *a.* 1a M19.

isocarboxazid /ˌʌɪsə(ʊ)kɑːˈbɒksəzɪd/ *n.* M20. [f. ISO- + CARB(ONYL + OX- + HYDR)AZID(E, elems. of the chemical name.] *Pharm.* A hydrazine derivative used in the form of a white powder as an antidepressant.

¶A proprietary name for this drug is MARPLAN.

isocheim /ˈʌɪsə(ʊ)kʌɪm/ *n.* M19. [f. ISO- + Gk *kheima* winter weather.] *Physical Geogr.* A line (imaginary or on a map) connecting places having the same mean winter temperature; an isotherm of mean winter temperature.

iso'cheimal *a.* & *n.* (of or pertaining to) an isocheim M19.

isochimenal /ʌɪsə(ʊ)ˈkʌɪmɪn(ə)l/ *a.* & *n.* M19. [f. Fr. *isochimène*, f. as ISO- + Gk *kheimainein* be stormy, be wintry, f. *kheima* winter weather, + -AL[1].] A *adj.* = ISOCHEIMAL *a.* M19. B *n.* = ISOCHEIM. M19.

isochromatic /ˌʌɪsə(ʊ)krə(ʊ)ˈmatɪk/ *a.* & *n.* E19. [f. ISO- + CHROMATIC *a.*] A *adj.* 1 *Optics.* Of a single colour or tint; *spec.* designating a fringe in an interference pattern obtained with birefringent material (as a biaxial crystal) which in photoelastic testing indicates points where the difference between the principal stresses is the same. Also, representing or depicting such fringes. E19. 2 *Photogr.* = ORTHOCHROMATIC. *obs.* exc. *Hist.* L19. B *n.* An isochromatic fringe or line. E20.

isochron /ˈʌɪsə(ʊ)krɒn/ *a.* & *n.* Also (earlier, & in senses A, B.1 always) **-chrone** /-krəʊn/. L17. [Gk *isokhronos* (see ISOCHRONAL).] A *adj.* = ISOCHRONOUS *a.* 1. L17. B *n.* †1 A curve in which a body descends through equal spaces in equal times. Only in L18. 2 A line (imaginary or on a map) connecting points at which a particular event occurs or occurred at the same time. L19. 3 A line (imaginary or on a map or diagram) connecting points at which some chosen time interval has the same value. M20. 4 *Geol.* In the isotopic dating of rock, a straight line whose gradient represents the time since the isotopic content of a sample was fixed (e.g. by crystallization), obtained by plotting against each other the ratios of the amounts of two radioisotopes to that of a single stable isotope, in two or more samples having the same history but different ratios. M20. 5 *Geol.* A line (imaginary or on a map) connecting points on the sea floor formed at the same time. M20.

isochronal /ʌɪˈsɒkrən(ə)l/ *a.* & *n.* L17. [f. mod.L *isochronus*, f. Gk *isokhronos* (f. as ISO- + *khronos* time): see -AL[1].] A *adj.* 1 = ISOCHRONOUS *a.* 1. L17. 2 Of a line: connecting points at which a particular event occurs or occurred at the same time. Of a diagram: depicting such lines. E20. B *n.* = ISOCHRON *n.* 2. M20.

isochronally *adv.* = ISOCHRONOUSLY L19.

isochronic /ʌɪsə(ʊ)ˈkrɒnɪk/ *a.* L18. [f. as prec. + -IC.] 1 = ISOCHRONOUS *a.* 1. L18. 2 = ISOCHRONAL *a.* 2; *spec.* in *Geogr.* (of a line on a map etc.) connecting points which can be reached in a specified time from a given starting-point. L19.

isochronical *a.* (*rare*) = ISOCHRONIC L18.

isochronism /ʌɪˈsɒkrənɪz(ə)m/ *n.* L18. [f. as prec. + -ISM.] 1 The character or property of being isochronous, or of oscillating or taking place in equal spaces of time. L18. 2 *Pros.* The character or property of being isochronous. M20.

isochronous /ʌɪˈsɒkrənəs/ *a.* E18. [f. as ISOCHRONAL + -OUS.] 1a Equal in duration, or in frequency, as the motions of a pendulum; characterized by or relating to (repetitive) motions of equal duration; *spec.* in *Pros.*, equal in metrical length. E18. b Equal in duration, frequency, etc., *to* or *with* something. L18. 2 *Palaeont.* Originating or formed at the same period. L19.

isochronously *adv.* M18.

isochrony /ʌɪˈsɒkrəni/ *n.* M20. [f. as ISOCHRONISM after *synchrony* etc.] = ISOCHRONISM.

isoclinal /ʌɪsə(ʊ)ˈklʌɪn(ə)l/ *a.* & *n.* M19. [f. ISO- + Gk *klinein* to lean, slope + -AL[1].] A *adj.* 1 Of lines: having equal slope; *spec.* in *Physical Geogr.*, indicating or connecting points on the earth's surface at which the magnetic inclination is the same. M19. 2 *Geol.* Designating a fold so acute that the two limbs are parallel, or strata so folded. L19. B *n.* Chiefly *Physical Geogr.* An isoclinal line. L19.

isoclinally *adv.* M20.

isocline /ˈʌɪsə(ʊ)klʌɪn/ *n.* L19. [f. Gk *isoklinēs* equally balanced, f. as prec.] 1 An isoclinal line or fold. L19. 2a *Surveying.* A line (imaginary or on a map) connecting points of equal gradient. M20. b *gen.* A line connecting points where the rate of change of some quantity is the same. M20.

isoclinic /ʌɪsə(ʊ)ˈklɪnɪk/ *a.* & *n.* M19. [f. as ISOCLINAL + -IC.] A *adj.* 1 = ISOCLINAL *a.* 1. M19. 2 Corresponding to or depicting the locus of points in a body where each of the principal stresses is in some fixed direction. E20. B *n.* 1 Each of two or more lines of equal slope. Freq. in *pl.* L19. 2 An isoclinic line or curve. E20.

isocolon /ʌɪsə(ʊ)ˈkəʊlən/ *n. rare.* M16. [f. as ISO- + COLON *n.*[2]] *Gk Rhet.* & *Pros.* (The use of) a succession of phrases of equal (syllabic) length or structure.

isocracy /ʌɪˈsɒkrəsi/ *n.* M17. [Gk *isokratia* equality of power or political rights, f. as ISO- + *kratos*, *krate-* strength, power: see -CRACY.] Equality of power or rule; a system of government in which all the people possess equal political power.

isocratic /ʌɪsə(ʊ)ˈkratɪk/ *a.* E19. [f. as prec.: see -IC.] 1 Of, pertaining to, or advocating isocracy. E19. 2 *Chem.* Of or involving a mobile chromatographic phase whose composition is kept constant and uniform. L20.

'isocrat *n.* an advocate of isocracy L19.

isocyanate /ʌɪsə(ʊ)ˈsʌɪəneɪt/ *n.* L19. [f. ISO- + CYANATE.] *Chem.* The radical ·N=C=O; any of the class of compounds containing this, some of which are used in making polyurethane.

isocy'anic *a.*: *isocyanic acid*, an isomeric form of cyanic acid, HN=C=O L19.

isocyanide /ʌɪsə(ʊ)ˈsʌɪənʌɪd/ *n.* L19. [f. as ISO- + CYANIDE.] *Chem.* Any of the class of toxic, malodorous, usu. liquid compounds having the formula RNC (where R is an alkyl, aryl, etc., radical). Also called *carbylamine*, *isonitrile*.

isodiabatic /ˌʌɪsə(ʊ)dʌɪəˈbatɪk/ *a.* M19. [f. ISO- + Gk *diabatikos* able to pass through. Cf. ADIABATIC.] *Physics.* Relating to or indicating the transmission of equal amounts of heat to and from a body or substance.

isodiametric /ˌʌɪsə(ʊ)dʌɪəˈmɛtrɪk/ *a.* L19. [f. ISO- + DIAMETRIC.] Having equal diameters; *spec.* (*a*) *Bot.* (of a cell) roughly spherical or polyhedral; (*b*) *Cryst.* (of a crystal) having three equal axes.

isodose /ˈʌɪsə(ʊ)dəʊs/ *n.* E20. [f. ISO- + DOSE *n.*] An imaginary line or surface, or a graphical representation of one, connecting points (esp., in the human body) that receive equal doses of radiation. Now usu. *attrib.*, as *isodose chart*, *isodose contour*, *isodose surface*, etc.

isodynamic /ˌʌɪsə(ʊ)dʌɪˈnamɪk/ *a.* M19. [f. Gk *isodunamos* equal in power, f. as ISO- + *dunamis* power, + -IC.] 1 Of equal force, value, or efficacy. *rare.* M19. 2 Chiefly *Physical Geogr.* Indicating or connecting points (on the earth's surface, etc.) at which the intensity of the magnetic force is the same. Cf. ISOGAM 2. M19.

isodynamical *a.* M19.

isoelectric /ˌʌɪsəʊɪˈlɛktrɪk/ *a.* L19. [f. ISO- + ELECTRIC.] 1 Equal in electrical potential; containing or indicating no potential difference. L19. 2 (Composed of particles) having no net electric charge; equal as regards electric charge. Chiefly in *isoelectric point*, the point (usually pH value) at which an amphoteric molecule or a colloidal particle is electrically neutral in a solution. E20. b Carried out or occurring at the isoelectric point. Esp. in *isoelectric focusing*, electrophoresis in which the resolution is improved by maintaining a pH gradient between the electrodes. M20.

isoelectrically *adv.* (*Biochem.*) by making use of the different isoelectric points of the components of a mixture (in order to separate them) M20.

isoelectronic /ˌʌɪsəʊɪlɛkˈtrɒnɪk, -ɛl-/ *a.* E20. [f. ISO- + ELECTRON *n.*[2] + -IC.] *Chem.* & *Physics.* (Composed of atoms or molecules) having the same number of (valence) electrons. (Foll. by *with*.)

isoenzyme /ˈʌɪsəʊˌɛnzʌɪm/ *n.* M20. [f. ISO- + ENZYME.] *Biochem.* Each of two or more chemically different forms of an enzyme.

isoen'zymic *a.* M20.

isoflor /ˈʌɪsə(ʊ)flɔː/ *n.* M20. [f. ISO- + FLOR(A.] A line (imaginary or on a map) linking areas containing equal numbers of plant species.

isogam /ˈʌɪsə(ʊ)gam/ *n.* E20. [App. f. ISO- + GAMMA *n.*] 1 A line (imaginary or on a map) connecting points where the acceleration due to gravity has the same value. Freq. *attrib.* E20. 2 An isodynamic line. M20.

isogamy /ʌɪˈsɒgəmi/ *n.* L19. [f. ISO- + -GAMY.] *Biol.* The reproductive union of two equal and similar gametes or cells. Opp. ANISOGAMY, HETEROGAMY.

isogamete /ʌɪsə(ʊ)ˈgamiːt/ *n.* either of two similar uniting cells L19. **isogamous** *a.* characterized by isogamy L19.

isogenic /ʌɪsə(ʊ)ˈdʒɛnɪk, -ˈdʒiːnɪk/ *a.* M20. [f. ISO- + GENE + -IC.] *Biol.* Having the same or a closely similar genotype.

isogenous /ʌɪˈsɒdʒɪnəs/ *a.* L19. [f. ISO- + -GENOUS. Cf. eccl.Gk *isogenēs* equal in kind or nature.] *Biol.* Chiefly of organs or parts: having the same or a similar (esp. embryological) origin.

isogeny *n.* the condition of being isogenous L19.

isogeotherm /ʌɪsə(ʊ)ˈdʒiːə(ʊ)θəːm/ *n.* M19. [f. ISO- + GEO- + Gk *thermē* heat, *thermos* hot.] *Geol.* A line or surface (imaginary or on a diagram) connecting points in the interior of the earth having the same temperature.

isogeo'thermal *a.* of the nature of an isogeotherm M19.

isogloss /ˈʌɪsə(ʊ)glɒs/ *n.* E20. [f. ISO- + Gk *glōssa* tongue, word.] *Ling.* (A line on a map indicating) the boundary of an area of occurrence of a significant linguistic feature (as of vocabulary or pronunciation).

iso'glossic *a.* E20.

isoglottal /ʌɪsə(ʊ)ˈglɒt(ə)l/ *a.* M20. [f. ISO- + Gk *glōtta*, *glōssa* tongue + -AL[1].] = ISOGLOSSIC. Also **isoglottic** *a.* M20.

isogon /ˈʌɪsəg(ə)n, -gɒn/ *n.* L17. [f. Gk *isogōnios* equiangular: see ISO-, -GON.] 1 *Geom.* An isogonal figure. Now *rare* or *obs.* L17. 2 An isogonic line. E20.

isogonal /ʌɪˈsɒg(ə)n(ə)l/ *a.* M19. [f. prec. + -AL[1].] 1 = ISOGONIC *a.*[1] M19. 2 Having equal angles, equiangular. L19.

isogonic /ʌɪsə(ʊ)ˈgɒnɪk/ *a.*[1] & *n.* M19. [f. as prec. + -IC.] A *adj.* Indicating equal angles; *spec.* in *Physical Geogr.* (chiefly of lines on a map etc.) indicating or connecting points of the earth's surface at which the magnetic declination, wind direction, etc., is the same. M19. B *n.* An isogonic line. L19.

isogonic /ʌɪsə(ʊ)ˈgɒnɪk/ *a.*[2] E20. [Fr. *isogonique*, perh. f. as prec.] *Biol.* Of an organ: growing in proportion (with its parent body).

isogony /ʌɪˈsɒgəni/ *n.* = ISOMETRY 2 M20.

isogram /ˈʌɪsə(ʊ)gram/ *n.* L19. [f. ISO- + -GRAM.] = ISOPLETH 1.

isograph /ˈʌɪsə(ʊ)grɑːf/ *n.* M19. [f. ISO- + -GRAPH.] 1 A drawing instrument consisting of two (or more) short rulers joined in parallel or by a hinge. M19. 2 *Ling.* = ISOGLOSS. M20.

isohaline /ʌɪsə(ʊ)ˈheɪlʌɪn/ *a.* & *n.* E20. [f. ISO- + Gk *hal-*, *hals* salt + -INE[1].] *Oceanogr.* A *adj.* Of a constant salinity throughout; (of a line or surface) connecting points which have the same salinity. E20. B *n.* An isohaline line or surface. M20.

isohydric /ʌɪsə(ʊ)ˈhʌɪdrɪk/ *a.* L19. [f. ISO- + HYDRIC *a.*[1]] 1 *Physical Chem.* Of solutions:

having the same (hydrogen) ion concentration; that mix without change of ionization. L19. 2 *Physiol.* Occurring without causing any change in pH, as the removal of carbon dioxide from the tissues by the blood. E20.

isoionic /ʌɪsəʊʌɪˈɒnɪk/ *a.* E20. [f. ISO- + IONIC *a.*[2]] *Chem.* Of a solute or solution: giving rise to or containing no non-colloidal ions other than those formed by dissociation of the solvent.

isoionic point the point (usu. pH value) at which the average number of protons attached to the basic groups of solute molecules is equal to the average number dissociated from the acidic groups.

isolable /ˈʌɪs(ə)ləb(ə)l/ *a.* M19. [f. ISOLATE *v.* + -ABLE.] Able to be isolated.

isolaˈbility *n.* L20.

isolatable /ˈʌɪsəleɪtəb(ə)l, ʌɪsə(ʊ)ˈleɪ-/ *a.* M20. [f. as prec.] = prec.

isolataˈbility *n.* M20.

isolate /ˈʌɪs(ə)lət/ *a.* & *n.* E19. [f. (as) ISOLATED.] A *adj.* = ISOLATED. E19. B *n.* 1 An isolated thing; *esp.* a thing abstracted from its normal context for study. L19. 2 *Perfumery.* A compound purified from a natural oil. E20. 3 *Microbiol.* A group, esp. a pure culture, of similar micro-organisms isolated for study. M20. 4 *Sociol.* & *Psychol.* A person, community, group, or (occas.) an animal isolated from normal social interaction, from choice or through separation or rejection. M20. 5 *Biol.* A population which has become distinct from the parent species through the operation of an isolating mechanism. M20.

isolate /ˈʌɪsəleɪt/ *v.t.* E19. [Back-form. f. ISOLATED (now regarded as the pa. pple of the vb); partly after Fr. *isoler*: see -ATE[3].] 1 Place or set apart or alone; cause to stand alone or detached, separated from or unconnected with other things or persons. Also, distinguish, identify. E19. 2 *Chem.* Obtain or extract (a substance) in a pure form. M19. 3 *Electr.* Insulate, esp. by a physical gap; disconnect. M19. 4 Subject (an infected person or place) to strict quarantine. L19.

1 W. S. CHURCHILL Until agrarian problems could be isolated from other political issues, there was little hope. M. MEYER Strindberg withdrew into himself and isolated himself . . from his colleagues. A. MUNRO Blizzards still isolate the towns and villages. J. M. COETZEE I isolated over four hundred different characters in the script. 2 M. PYKE A few milligrams of vitamin B12 had been isolated and the nature of its complex molecule established.

isolated /ˈʌɪsəleɪtɪd/ *a.* M18. [f. Fr. *isolé* f. It. *isolato* f. late L *insulatus* made an island, f. L *insula* island: see -ATE[2], -ED[1]. Cf. prec.] Placed or standing apart or alone; detached or separate from other things or persons; unconnected with anything else; solitary.

J. REED There were still isolated cases of defiance towards the new Government, but they were rare. B. EMECHETA An isolated place, hidden . . by the surrounding desert and hills. L. NKOSI A bitter man, secretive and isolated. **isolated pawn** *Chess*: without other pawns of the same colour in adjacent files.

isolati *n.pl.* see ISOLATO.

isolating /ˈʌɪsəleɪtɪŋ/ *ppl a.* M19. [f. ISOLATE *v.* + -ING[2].] That isolates; *Ling.* (of a language) in which words tend not to vary in form (by either agglutination or inflection) according to grammatical function; = ANALYTIC *a.* 3.

isolating barrier, isolating mechanism a geographical, ecological, seasonal, physiological, or other factor which limits or prevents interbreeding between groups of plants or animals.

isolation /ʌɪsəˈleɪʃ(ə)n/ *n.* & *a.* M19. [f. ISOLATE *v.* + -ATION, partly after Fr. *isolation.*] A *n.* 1 The action of isolating something or someone; the fact or condition of being or having been isolated; separation from other things or persons; solitariness. M19. 2 The separation of a chemical substance in a pure state. M19. 3 *spec.* The complete separation of patients with a contagious or infectious disease from contact with other people; the prevention of access to a place so infected. L19. 4 a *Psychol.* & *Sociol.* The separation of a person or thing from the normal (social) environment or context, either deliberately for study, or as a result of some inherent tendency. L19. b *Psychoanalysis.* A defence mechanism whereby a particular wish or thought loses emotional significance by being isolated from its normal context. E20. 5 *Biol.* The limitation or prevention of interbreeding between groups of plants or animals by some isolating mechanism, leading to the development of new species or varieties. E20.

1 **in isolation** considered singly and not relative to something else. SPLENDID *isolation.*

B *attrib.* or as *adj.* Designating a procedure, place of confinement, etc., by which isolation is effected. M19.

isolation camp, hospital, ward, etc.

isolationism /ʌɪsəˈleɪʃ(ə)nɪz(ə)m/ *n.* E20. [f. prec. + -ISM.] The policy of seeking (political or national) isolation.

isolationist /ʌɪsəˈleɪʃ(ə)nɪst/ *n.* & *a.* L19. [f. as prec. + -IST.] A *n.* A person who favours or advocates (political or national) isolationism. L19. B *adj.* Characteristic of or being an isolationist. L19.

isolative /ˈʌɪsəleɪtɪv/ *a.* L19. [f. ISOLATE *v.* + -ATIVE.] 1 *Philol.* Of a sound-change: taking place independently of adjacent sounds. Opp. COMBINATIVE 2. L19. 2 *gen.* Tending to isolate something or someone. M20.

isolato /iːsəˈlɑːtəʊ/ *n.* Pl. **-ti** /-ti/, **-tos**. M19. [It.] An isolated person, an outcast.

isolator /ˈʌɪsəleɪtə/ *n.* M19. [f. ISOLATE *v.* + -OR.] A person who or thing which isolates something or someone; a contrivance for isolating something; an insulator.

isoleucine /ʌɪsə(ʊ)ˈluːsiːn/ *n.* E20. [f. ISO- + LEUCINE.] *Biochem.* A hydrophobic amino acid, $CH_3CH_2CH(CH_3)CH(NH_2)COOH$, which occurs in proteins and is essential in the human diet; 2-amino-3-methylpentanoic acid.

isolog *n.* see ISOLOGUE.

isologous /ʌɪˈsɒləgəs/ *a.* M19. [f. ISO- + Gk *logos* relation, ratio (see LOGOS) + -OUS, after *homologous.*] 1 *Chem.* Of two or more (series of) compounds: having comparable or related molecular structures; now usu. *spec.*, (of compounds) having identical molecular structure but different atoms of the same valency at some position(s) in the molecule. Cf. HOMOLOGOUS *a.* 4. M19. 2 *Med.* & *Biol.* Genetically identical, esp. as regards immunological factors; involving such individuals. M20.

isologue /ˈʌɪsə(ʊ)lɒg/ *n.* Also ***-log**. L19. [f. ISO- + -LOGUE.] *Chem.* Each of two or more isologous compounds.

isomer /ˈʌɪsəmə/ *n.* M19. [f. Gk *isomerēs* sharing equally, f. as ISO- + *meros* part, share.] 1 *Chem.* A substance isomeric with another; any of a number of isomeric compounds or forms of a compound. M19. 2 *Physics.* Each of two or more nuclei having the same atomic number and mass number but different radioactive properties, as a result of being in different energy states; *esp.* a nucleus in a metastable excited state rather than the ground state. Also *nuclear isomer.* M20.

1 *geometrical isomer, optical isomer, structural isomer*, etc.

isomerase /ʌɪˈsɒməreɪz/ *n.* M20. [f. prec. + -ASE.] *Biochem.* Any of various enzymes which bring about an isomerization reaction.

isomeric /ʌɪsə(ʊ)ˈmɛrɪk/ *a.* M19. [f. as ISOMER + -IC.] 1 *Chem.* Of two or more compounds, or of one compound in relation to another: composed of the same elements in the same proportions, and having the same molecular weight, but forming substances with different properties owing to the different grouping or arrangement of the constituent atoms. (Foll. by *with.*) M19. 2 *Physics.* Of, pertaining to, or designating nuclear isomers. M20.

¶In sense 1, formerly extended to include compounds in which the number of atoms in one is a multiple of those in the other, or restricted to those with similar functional groups and hence similar properties.

isomerically *adv.* as regards isomers; by isomerization: L19.

isomeride /ʌɪˈsɒmərʌɪd/ *n. rare.* M19. [f. as ISOMER + -IDE.] *Chem.* = ISOMER 1.

isomerise *v.* var. of ISOMERIZE.

isomerism /ʌɪˈsɒmərɪz(ə)m/ *n.* M19. [f. ISOMER + -ISM.] 1 *Chem.* The fact or condition of being isomeric; identity of percentage composition in compounds differing in properties. M19. 2 *Physics.* The fact or condition of being nuclear isomers. M20.

1 **geometrical isomerism**: in which compounds differ in the spatial arrangement of atoms relative to a (rigid) double bond. **optical isomerism**: in which compounds differ in the spatial arrangement of atoms around one or more asymmetric carbon atoms, and hence usu. in optical activity. STEREOISOMERISM. **structural isomerism**: in which molecules having the same constituent atoms have different structures, the atoms being joined in different sequences.

isomerize /ʌɪˈsɒmərʌɪz/ *v.t.* & *i.* Also **-ise**. L19. [f. ISOMER + -IZE.] *Chem.* Change into an isomer (of the original substance). Usu. foll. by *into, to.*

isomeriˈzation *n.* (*Chem.*) the conversion of a compound into an isomer of itself L19.

isomerous /ʌɪˈsɒm(ə)rəs/ *a.* M19. [f. Gk. *isomerēs* (see ISOMER) + -OUS.] *Biol.* Having the same number of (similar) parts; *spec.* in *Bot.* (of a flower) having the same number of parts in each whorl (opp. HETEROMEROUS 2b).

isometric /ʌɪsə(ʊ)ˈmɛtrɪk/ *a.* & *n.* M19. [f. Gk *isometria* equality of measure, f. as ISO- + -METRY: see -IC.] A *adj.* 1 Of equal measure or dimensions. M19. 2 *Drawing.* Designating a method of projection or perspective in which the three principal dimensions are represented by three axes 120° apart, with all measurements on the same scale, used in technical and architectural drawing. M19. 3 *Cryst.* = CUBIC *a.* 2b. M19. 4 *Physiol.* Of, pertaining to, or designating muscular action in which tension is developed without contraction of the muscle. L19. 5 *Physics.* Relating to, or taking place under, conditions of constant volume. L19. 6 *Biol.* Of growth: maintaining constant proportions with increase in size. M20. 7 *Math.* That is an isometry; related by an isometry. Foll. by *to.* M20. B *n.* 1 *Physics.* A line in a diagram that corresponds to or represents states of equal volume. L19. 2 In *pl.* A system of stationary physical exercises in which muscles are caused to act isometrically against one another or against an unyielding object. M20.

isometrical /ʌɪsə(ʊ)ˈmɛtrɪk(ə)l/ *a.* M19. [f. as prec. + -AL[1].] = ISOMETRIC *a.* 2, 3.

isometrically /ʌɪsə(ʊ)ˈmɛtrɪk(ə)li/ *adv.* M19. [f. ISOMETRIC *a.* or prec.: see -ICALLY.] 1 *Drawing.* In the manner of isometric projection. M19. 2 *Physiol.* Under isometric conditions. E20. 3 *Math.* By means of or in the manner of an isometry. M20.

isometry /ʌɪˈsɒmɪtri/ *n.* M20. [f. as ISOMETRIC: see -Y[3].] 1 *Math.* A one-to-one transformation of one metric space into another that preserves the distances or metrics between each pair of points. M20. 2 *Biol.* (Growth exhibiting) constancy of proportion with increase in size. Cf. ALLOMETRY. M20.

isomorph /ˈʌɪsə(ʊ)mɔːf/ *n.* M19. [f. ISO- + -MORPH.] 1 A substance or organism isomorphic with another. M19. 2 *Ling.* A line (imaginary or on a map) bounding an area in which a particular morphological form occurs; a morphological isogloss. *rare.* E20.

isomorphic /ʌɪsə(ʊ)ˈmɔːfɪk/ *a.* M19. [f. as prec. + -IC.] 1 *Chem.* & *Min.* Isomorphous; pertaining to or involving isomorphism. M19. 2 *Math.* & *Philos.* Of groups or other sets: corresponding to each other in form, and in the nature and product of their operations; related by or being an isomorphism. Foll. by *to, with.* L19. 3 *Biol.* Of closely similar form but independent origin. *rare.* L19. 4 *Bot.* In algae and certain fungi: designating a type of alternation of generations in which the two forms are morphologically similar. M20. 5 *Ling.* Similar in morphological structure, having similar morphological forms. M20.

isomorphically *adv.* (*a*) *Math.* & *Philos.* by an isomorphism; (*b*) in an isomorphic manner: M20.

isomorphism /ʌɪsə(ʊ)'mɔːfɪz(ə)m/ *n.* E19. [f. as prec. + -ISM.] 1 *Chem.* & *Min.* The property of crystallizing in the same or closely related forms, esp. as exhibited by substances of analogous composition. E19. 2 *Math.* & *Philos.* Identity of form and operations between two or more groups or other sets; an exact correspondence as regards the number of constituent elements and the relations between them; *spec.* a one-to-one homomorphism. L19. 3 *Biol.* A similarity of appearance displayed by organisms having different genotypes. E20. 4 *Psychol.* A correspondence assumed to exist between the structure of mental events and that of the underlying neural events. M20.

isomorphous /ʌɪsə(ʊ)'mɔːfəs/ *a.* E19. [f. as prec. + -OUS.] 1 *Chem.* & *Min.* Having the property of crystallizing in the same or closely related geometric forms, esp. owing to analogous composition. Cf. HOMOEOMORPHOUS. E19. 2 *Math.* = ISOMORPHIC 2. *rare.* L19.

isomorphously *adv.* (*Min.*) in such a way as to produce isomorphous substances E20.

-ison /ɪs(ə)n/ *suff.* Repr. OFr. *-aison*, *-eison*, *-eson*, *-ison*, L *-atio(n-)* (later adopted in the learned form -ATION), *-etio(n-)*, *-itio(n-)*, in ns., as *comparison*, *jettison*, *orison*, *venison*.

isoniazid /ʌɪsə(ʊ)'nʌɪəzɪd/ *n.* M20. [f. ISO- + NI(COTINIC + HYDR)AZID(E.] *Pharm.* A soluble colourless crystalline compound, $C_5H_5N{\cdot}CO{\cdot}NH{\cdot}NH_2$, which is used as a bacteriostatic drug esp. in the treatment of tuberculosis.

isonomy /ʌɪ'sɒnəmi/ *n.* E17. [It. *isonomia* f. Gk, ult. f. as ISO- + *nomos* law: see -Y³.] Equality of people before the law; equality of political rights among the citizens of a State.

isonomic /ʌɪsə(ʊ)'nɒmɪk/ *a.* (*a*) characterized by isonomy; (*b*) *rare* having equal laws or rights: M19.

isooctane /ʌɪsəʊ'ɒkteɪn/ *n.* E20. [f. ISO- + OCTANE.] †1 A liquid hydrocarbon, $CH_3{\cdot}(CH_2)_4{\cdot}CH(CH_3){\cdot}CH_3$, that occurs in petroleum; 2-methylheptane. Only in E20. 2 A colourless liquid hydrocarbon, $(CH_3)_3C{\cdot}CH_2{\cdot}CH(CH_3){\cdot}CH_3$, used in aviation fuels, as a solvent and antiknock, and as a standard in the determination of octane numbers; 2,2,4-trimethylpentane. M20.

isopach /'ʌɪsə(ʊ)pak/ *n.* E20. [f. ISO- + Gk *pakhus* thick.] 1 *Geol.* = ISOPACHYTE. E20. 2 = ISOPACHIC *n.* M20.

isopachic /ʌɪsə(ʊ)'pakɪk/ *a.* & *n.* M20. [f. as prec. + -IC.] A *adj.* Corresponding to or depicting the locus of points in a body where the sum of the principal stresses has the same value. M20. B *n.* An isopachic line or curve. M20.

isopachous /ʌɪsə(ʊ)'pakəs, ʌɪ'sɒpəkəs/ *a.* E20. [f. as prec. + -OUS.] *Geol.* Depicting or pertaining to isopachytes; of the nature of an isopachyte.

isopachyte /ʌɪsə(ʊ)'pakʌɪt/ *n.* E20. [f. ISO- + Gk *pakhutēs* thickness.] *Geol.* A line (on a map or diagram) joining points below which a particular stratum or group of strata has the same thickness.

isoperimeter /ˌʌɪsəʊpə'rɪmɪtə/ *n.* M16. [Gk *isoperimetros*, f. as ISO- + PERIMETER.] *Geom.* Each of two or more figures having equal perimeters. Usu. in *pl.*

isoperimetrical /ˌʌɪsə(ʊ)pɛrɪ'mɛtrɪk(ə)l/ *a.* of or pertaining to isoperimeters, having equal perimeters E18. **isoperimetry** *n.* (*rare*) the branch of mathematics that deals with (problems concerning) isoperimetrical figures E19.

isophane *n.*¹ var. of ISOPHENE.

isophane /'ʌɪsə(ʊ)feɪn/ *a.* & *n.*² M20. [f. ISO- + Gk *-phanēs* showing, appearing, f. *phainein* show.] *Pharm.* A *adj.* Designating the ratio of the amounts of protamine and insulin which are respectively necessary to precipitate all the insulin and all the protamine in solutions of these, such that the resulting mixed solutions have equal turbidity. M20.

isophane insulin = sense B. below.

B *n.* A crystalline mixture of insulin and protamine in the isophane ratio with zinc, which has longer lasting effects than pure insulin. M20.

isophene /'ʌɪsə(ʊ)fiːn/ *n.* Also **-phane** /-feɪn/. E20. [f. as prec.: cf. PHENO- 2.] A line (imaginary or on a map) linking places in which seasonal biological phenomena (the flowering of plants etc.) occur at the same time.

iso'phenal *a.* E20.

isophone /'ʌɪsə(ʊ)fəʊn/ *n. rare.* E20. [f. ISO- + PHONE *n.*¹] *Ling.* A line (imaginary or on a map) bounding an area in which some feature of pronunciation occurs; a phonetic isogloss.

iso'phonic *a.* E20.

isophote /'ʌɪsə(ʊ)fəʊt/ *n.* Also **-phot** /-fɒt/. E20. [f. ISO- + Gk *phōt-*, *phōs* light.] A line (imaginary or in a diagram) connecting points where the intensity of light or other radiation is the same.

iso'photal *a.* & *n.* (depicting or of the nature of) an isophote E20. **iso'photic** *a.* = ISOPHOTAL *a.* M20.

isopleth /'ʌɪsə(ʊ)plɛθ/ *n.* E20. [f. Gk *isoplēthēs* equal in quantity, f. as ISO- + *plēthos* multitude, quantity.] 1 A line (imaginary or on a map or diagram) connecting points for which some chosen quantity has the same value. E20. 2 *Physical Chem.* A line or surface (in a diagram) joining points that represent mixtures having the same composition. E20.

isoplethal /-'pliːθ(ə)l/ *a.* carried out or occurring at constant composition E20.

isopod /'ʌɪsəpɒd/ *n.* M19. [f. mod.L *Isopoda* (see below), f. Gk *iso-* ISO- + *pod-*, *pous* foot.] *Zool.* Any crustacean of the order Isopoda, characterized by a dorsoventrally flattened body, and seven similar pairs of thoracic legs equal in length, and comprising the terrestrial woodlice and allied marine and freshwater species, some being parasitic. Cf. AMPHIPOD.

isopodan /ʌɪ'sɒpəd(ə)n/ *a.* & *n.* (*a*) *adj.* = ISOPODOUS; (*b*) *n.* = ISOPOD: M19.

isopodous /ʌɪ'sɒpədəs/ *a.* E19. [f. as prec. + -OUS.] *Zool.* Belonging to or having the characteristics of the order Isopoda (see prec.).

isopolity /ʌɪsə(ʊ)'pɒlɪti/ *n.* M19. [Gk *isopoliteia*, f. as ISO- + POLITY.] Chiefly *Hist.* Equality of rights of citizenship between different communities or States; mutual recognition of civic rights.

isoprenaline /ʌɪsə(ʊ)'prɛnəliːn/ *n.* M20. [f. elems. of the systematic name N-*iso*propyl-nor*adren*aline.] *Pharm.* A sympathomimetic amine, $C_6H_3(OH)_2CH(OH)CH_2NHCH(CH_3)_2$, a derivative of adrenalin used, freq. in aerosol form, for the relief of bronchial asthma and pulmonary emphysema. Also called (in US) *isoproterenol*.

isoprene /'ʌɪsə(ʊ)priːn/ *n.* M19. [App. f. ISO- + PR(OPYL)ENE.] A volatile, flammable, colourless liquid, $CH_2{:}C(CH_3)CH{:}CH_2$, obtainable from petroleum and forming the structural unit of natural and synthetic rubbers; 2-methyl-1,3-butadiene.

Comb.: **isoprene rule**: that the carbon skeleton of a terpene is made up of linked isoprene units; **isoprene unit** the arrangement of five carbon atoms found in (polymers of) the isoprene molecule (the single or double nature of the bonds being disregarded).

isoprenoid /'ʌɪsə(ʊ)prɪnɔɪd, ʌɪsə(ʊ)'priːnɔɪd/ *a.* & *n.* (*a*) *adj.* containing or designating the isoprene unit; composed of such units; (*b*) *n.* an isoprenoid compound: M20.

isoproterenol /ˌʌɪsə(ʊ)prəʊtə'riːnɒl/ *n. US.* M20. [f. elems. of the semi-systematic name N-*iso*propylarterenol.] *Pharm.* = ISOPRENALINE.

isopycnal /ʌɪsə(ʊ)'pɪkn(ə)l/ *n.* & *a.* E20. [f. ISO- + Gk *puknos* dense + -AL¹.] *Oceanogr.* A *n.* A line (imaginary or on a map or chart) or an imaginary surface connecting points which have the same density. E20. B *adj.* That is an isopycnal. M20.

isopycnic /ʌɪsə(ʊ)'pɪknɪk/ *a.* & *n.* L19. [f. as prec. + -IC.] A *adj.* (Connecting points) of the same density or of constant density. Also (*Biochem.*), pertaining to or designating ultracentrifugal separative techniques which rely on differences in density between the components of a mixture. L19. B *n. Meteorol.* A line (imaginary or on a map or chart) or an imaginary surface connecting points at which the density (esp. of the atmosphere) is the same. Cf. ISOSTERE 1a. L19.

isorhythm /'ʌɪsə(ʊ)rɪð(ə)m/ *n.* Also **-rrh-**. M20. [f. ISO- + RHYTHM.] The rhythmic structure of isorhythmic music.

isorhythmic /ʌɪsə(ʊ)'rɪðmɪk/ *a.* Also **-rrh-**. L19. [f. ISO- + RHYTHMIC.] 1 Of a poem etc.: constructed in the same rhythm or metre (as another). L19. 2 *Mus.* Of, characterized by, or designating a line or part, esp. a canto fermo, in which the rhythm is often repeated but the pitch of the notes is varied each time. M20.

isorrhythm *n.*, **isorrhythmic** *a.* vars. of ISORHYTHM, ISORHYTHMIC.

isosbestic /ʌɪsə(ʊ)s'bɛstɪk/ *a.* E20. [f. ISO- + Gk *sbestos* extinguished (f. *sbennunai* quench) + -IC.] Physical Chem. *isosbestic point*, a wavelength at which absorption of light by a liquid remains constant as the equilibrium between its component substances is shifted.

isosceles /ʌɪ'sɒsɪliːz/ *a.* & *n.* M16. [Late L f. Gk *isoskelēs*, f. as ISO- + *skelos* leg.] *Geom.* A *adj.* Of a triangle: having two of its sides equal. Of a trapezoid: having the two non-parallel sides equal. M16. B *n.* An isosceles triangle. *rare.* L16.

isoseismal /ʌɪsə(ʊ)'sʌɪzm(ə)l/ *a.* & *n.* M19. [f. ISO- + SEISMAL.] A *adj.* Of a line (imaginary or on a map): connecting points at which the intensity of an earthquake shock is the same. M19. B *n.* An isoseismal line. M19.

isoseismic *a.* = ISOSEISMAL *a.* M19.

isospin /'ʌɪsə(ʊ)spɪn/ *n.* M20. [Contr. of *isotopic spin*, *isobaric spin*.] *Physics.* A vector quantity associated with subatomic particles and atomic nuclei, expressing that the strong interaction does not depend on the electric charge, its quantum number (symbol *T* or *I*) being so assigned that similar particles differing only in charge-related properties can be treated as different states of a single particle.

isostasy /ʌɪ'sɒstəsi/ *n.* L19. [f. ISO- + Gk *stasis* station + -Y³.] Chiefly *Geol.* Equilibrium or stability due to equality of (hydrostatic) pressure; *spec.* the general state of equilibrium thought to exist within the earth's crust, portions of the lithosphere beneath the oceans and continents being supported by underlying denser material that yields or flows under their weight.

isostatic /ʌɪsə(ʊ)'statɪk/ *a.* L19. [f. prec.: see -STATIC.] 1 *Geol.* Pertaining to, produced by, or characterized by isostasy. L19. 2 Performed under or involving conditions in which equal pressure is applied from all directions. M20.

1 B. W. SPARKS Large ice sheets caused an isostatic depression of the areas they occupied.

isostatically *adv.* (*a*) *Geol.* as regards isostasy; by, or as a result of, isostatic forces; (*b*) by pressure applied equally from all directions: E20.

isostere /'ʌɪsə(ʊ)stɪə/ *n.* In sense 2 also **-ster**. E20. [f. ISO- + Gk *stereos* solid.] 1 a Chiefly *Meteorol.* & *Limnol.* A line (imaginary or on a map or diagram) or an imaginary surface connecting points where something (e.g. a body of water, the atmosphere) has equal specific volumes. Cf. ISOPYCNIC *n.* E20. b *Physical Chem.* A line on a graph showing the pressure of a gas required to produce a given amount of adsorption at different temperatures. E20. 2 *Chem.* Each of two or more isosteric molecules or ions (see ISOSTERIC 4). E20.

isosteric /ʌɪsə(ʊ)'stɛrɪk/ *a.* M19. [f. as prec. + -IC.] †1 Having equal atomic volumes. M–L19. 2 Relating to equal specific volume. E20. 3 *Physical Chem.* Of a heat of adsorption: corresponding to a constant amount of adsorbed material as the pressure and temperature vary (equilibrium being maintained). E20. 4 *Chem.* Having the same number of valence electrons arranged in a similar manner. E20.

isosterism /-'stɪər-/ *n.* (*Chem.*) the condition of being isosteric M19.

isotactic /ʌɪsə(ʊ)'taktɪk/ *a.* M20. [f. ISO- + Gk *taktos* arranged, ordered + -IC.] *Chem.* Having or designating a polymeric structure in which all the repeating units have the same stereochemical configuration.

isotac'ticity *n.* M20.

isoteles /ʌɪ'sɒtɪliːz/ *n.* Pl. same. M19. [f. Gk *isotelēs* adj. = paying equal taxes, f. as ISO- + *telos* tax.] *Gk Hist.* Any of a favoured class of resident aliens at Athens, who were given civic though not political rights.

isotely *n.* the condition of an isoteles M19.

isotheral /ʌɪ'sɒθ(ə)r(ə)l, ˌʌɪsə(ʊ)θɪər(ə)l/ *a.* & *n.* M19. [f. as next + -AL[1].] *Physical Geogr.* A *adj.* Of a line (imaginary or on a map): connecting places having the same mean summer temperature. M19. B *n.* = next. M19.

isothere /'ʌɪsə(ʊ)θɪə/ *n.* M19. [Fr. *isothère*, f. as ISO- + Gk *there-*, *theros* summer.] *Physical Geogr.* An isotheral line; an isotherm of mean summer temperature.

isotherm /'ʌɪsə(ʊ)θəːm/ *n.* M19. [Fr. *isotherme*, f. as ISO- + Gk *thermē* heat, *thermos* hot.] 1 *Physical Geogr.* A line (imaginary or on a map) passing through points (esp. on the earth's surface) having the same mean temperature; an isothermal line. M19. 2 An isothermal line in a diagram. L19.

2 LANGMUIR (*adsorption*) *isotherm*.

iso'thermic *a.* = ISOTHERMAL *a.* L19.

isothermal /ˌʌɪsə(ʊ)'θəːm(ə)l/ *a.* & *n.* E19. [f. as prec. + -AL[1].] A *adj.* 1 a *Physical Geogr.* Of a line (imaginary or on a map or chart): connecting places on the earth's surface at which the temperature for a particular period, or the mean annual temperature, is the same. E19. b *Physics.* Designating (imaginary) lines or surfaces of equal temperature in a heated body, as a crystal. M19. c *Physics.* Of a line in a diagram: joining points representing states or conditions of equal temperature. L19. 2 Occurring at a constant temperature; pertaining to or involving constancy of temperature with time. L19. 3 Having the same temperature throughout. E20. B *n.* An isothermal line, *spec.* in a diagram; an isothermal surface. M19.

isothermally *adv.* at a constant temperature, without change in temperature L19.

isotonic /ˌʌɪsə(ʊ)'tɒnɪk/ *a.* E19. [f. Gk *isotonos* of equal tension or tone, f. as ISO- + *tonos* TONE *n.*: see -IC.] 1 *Mus.* Of a system of tuning: characterized by equal intervals, as equal temperament (see TEMPERAMENT *n.* 9). E19. 2 *Physiol.* Designating or pertaining to a solution having the same osmotic pressure as some particular solution (esp. that in a cell, or a body fluid). (Foll. by *with*.) L19. 3 *Physiol.* Of, pertaining to, or designating muscular action in which the muscle contracts more or less freely. L19.

isotonically *adv.* (*Physiol.*) under isotonic conditions M20. **isotonicity** /-'nɪsɪti/ *n.* (*a*) the property or state of being equal in osmotic pressure; (*b*) the osmotic pressure (of the blood): L19.

isotope /'ʌɪsətəʊp/ *n.* E20. [f. ISO- + Gk *topos* place (w. ref. to occupying the same place in the periodic table).] 1 Each of two or more varieties of a particular chemical element which have different numbers of neutrons in the nucleus, and therefore different relative atomic masses and different nuclear (but the same chemical) properties. Also freq., any distinct kind of atom or nucleus (= NUCLIDE). E20. 2 *spec. Biol.* & *Biochem.* A less common, usu. radioactive, isotope of an element as used in tracer or other studies. M20.

2 *Science* Mice were labeled .. by injection with 10 μc of isotope.

Comb.: **isotope dilution** diminution of the concentration of one isotope (or isotopically labelled compound) by the addition of another isotope of the same element (or of the unlabelled compound), esp. as a technique for measuring the amount of an element or compound in a system by introducing a known amount of a different isotope (or a labelled compound) and then measuring its concentration in a sample of the mixture; **isotope effect** a variation in some physical or chemical characteristic between one isotope of an element and another; **isotope shift** a small difference in the wavelength of corresponding spectral lines of different isotopes of an element owing to the different masses and charge distributions of their nuclei.

isotopism *n.* = ISOTOPY E20.

isotopic /ˌʌɪsə'tɒpɪk/ *a.* E20. [f. prec. + -IC.] 1 Of, pertaining to, or being an isotope or isotopes of an element. E20. 2 Of or pertaining to isospin. Orig. & chiefly in *isotopic spin* = ISOSPIN. M20. 3 Containing or being a less common or special isotope, e.g. as a label. Cf. ISOTOPE 2. M20. 4 (Of a method) employing or depending on isotopes; obtained by such a method. M20.

1 **isotopic number** the number of neutrons in a nucleus minus the number of protons.

isotopically *adv.* as regards isotopes or isotopic constitution; by means of isotopes or isotopic methods: M20.

isotopy /ʌɪ'sɒtəpi/ *n.* E20. [f. ISOTOPIC + -Y[3].] The fact or condition of being isotopic, or of having isotopes.

isotransplantation /ˌʌɪsə(ʊ)transplɑːn'teɪʃ(ə)n, -trɑː-/ *n.* E20. [f. ISO- + TRANSPLANTATION.] *Med.* & *Biol.* †1 = HOMOTRANSPLANTATION. Only in E20. 2 The operation of transplanting tissue from one individual to another of the same inbred strain. M20.

iso'transplant *n.* a piece of tissue transplanted from one individual to another of the same inbred strain (cf. ISOGRAFT) M20. **isotrans'planted** *a.* that is an isotransplant M20.

isotron /'ʌɪsə(ʊ)trɒn/ *n.* M20. [f. ISO(TOPE + -TRON.] *Physics.* A machine for separating isotopes in the form of ions, by differential deflection in an electric field.

isotropic /ˌʌɪsə(ʊ)'trɒpɪk/ *a.* M19. [f. ISO- + Gk *tropos* turn + -IC.] Of a material or a body: having the same physical properties in all directions. Of a property: not varying with direction. Opp. ANISOTROPIC.

isotropically *adv.* equally in all directions L19. **isotropous** /ˌʌɪsə(ʊ)'trəʊpəs/ *a.* = ISOTROPIC L19. **isotropy** /ʌɪ'sɒtrəpi/ *n.* the condition or quality of being isotropic L19.

isotype /'ʌɪsə(ʊ)tʌɪp/ *n.*[1] L19. [f. ISO- + Gk *tupos* TYPE *n.* (cf. Gk *isotupos* shaped alike).] †1 *Biol.* A type or form of animal or plant common to different countries or regions. L19–E20. 2 *Min.* A mineral which is isotypic with another; an assemblage of isotypic minerals. E20. 3 *Bot.* A duplicate of the holotype. E20.

isotype /'ʌɪsə(ʊ)tʌɪp/ *n.*[2] Also **I-**. M20. [Acronym, f. *I*nternational *s*ystem *o*f *typ*ographic picture *e*ducation.] An international picture language devised by the Austrian sociologist Otto Neurath (1882–1945), used esp. to display statistical information in a visual form. Also, an individual pictographic symbol.

isotypic /ˌʌɪsə(ʊ)'tɪpɪk/ *a.* E20. [f. ISOTYPE *n.*[1] + -IC.] *Min.* Having analogous crystal structure and (usu.) chemical composition; exhibiting such similarity. Foll. by *with*.

isotypism /ˌʌɪsə(ʊ)'tʌɪpɪz(ə)m/, **isotypy** /'ʌɪsə(ʊ)tʌɪpi/ *ns.* the character or state of being isotypic; isotypic relationship: M20.

isoxazole /ʌɪ'sɒksəzəʊl/ *n.* L19. [f. ISO- + OXAZOLE.] *Chem.* An isomer of oxazole, with similar properties; any substituted derivative of this.

isozyme /'ʌɪsə(ʊ)zʌɪm/ *n.* M20. [f. ISO- + EN)ZYME.] *Biochem.* = ISOENZYME.

iso'zymic *a.* M20.

ispaghul /'ɪspəguːl/ *n.* E19. [Pers., Urdu *ispaġol* f. *asp* horse + Urdu *ġol* ear, w. allus. to the shape of the leaves.] A plantain, esp. *Plantago ovata*, native to southern Asia, the dried seeds of which are used medicinally.

Ispahan *a.* & *n.* var. of ISFAHAN.

ispravnik /is'pravnik, ɪs'prɑːvnɪk/ *n.* Pl. ***-i*** /-i/, ***-s***. M19. [Russ., lit. 'executor'.] *Hist.* A chief of police in a rural district in tsarist Russia.

I-spy /ʌɪ'spʌɪ/ *n.* Also (now *rare*) **hi-**, **Hy-** /hʌɪ-/. L18. [f. I *pron.* + SPY *v.*] Any of various children's games involving looking or seeing: orig., a form of hide-and-seek in which the hiders, when discovered (with a cry of 'I spy'), chased the seekers back to a den; now usu., a verbal guessing game in which one participant gives the initial letter of a visible object which the others have to identify.

Israel /'ɪzreɪl/ *n.* OE. [L f. Gk f. Heb. *Yiśrā'ēl* lit. 'he that strives with God', name conferred on Jacob (*Gen.* 32:29).] 1 The Hebrew nation or people whose descent is traditionally traced from the patriarch Jacob (also called Israel), each of whose twelve sons became the founder of a tribe. Cf. *children of Israel* s.v. CHILD *n.* OE. 2 *Chr. Ch.* The Christian Church, or true Christians collectively, regarded as the chosen people of God. LME.

Israeli /ɪz'reɪli/ *a.* & *n.* M20. [f. *Israel* (see below, also the northern kingdom of the ancient Hebrew nation) + -I[2].] A *adj.* Of or pertaining to Israel, a country in SW Asia with the River Jordan forming part of its eastern border and with a coastline on the Mediterranean Sea. M20. B *n.* A native or inhabitant of Israel. M20.

Israelite /'ɪzrəlʌɪt/ *n.* & *a.* LME. [Late L (Vulgate) *Israelita* f. Gk *Israēlitēs*, Heb. *yiśrĕ'ēlī*, f. *Yiśrā'ēl*: see prec., -ITE[1].] A *n.* 1 A member of the people of ancient Israel; a member of the Hebrew people; a Jew. LME. 2 *Chr. Ch.* A Christian regarded as one of the chosen people of God; a true Christian. *arch.* LME. B *adj.* Of or pertaining to ancient Israel; Jewish. M19.

Israelitic *a.* (*rare*) = ISRAELITISH E17. **Israelitish** *a.* of or pertaining to the Israelites or ancient Israel; Jewish: M16.

issuable /'ɪʃ(j)ʊəb(ə)l, 'ɪsjʊ-/ *a.* M16. [f. ISSUE *n.*, *v.* + -ABLE.] 1 *Law.* That admits of an issue being taken; with regard to which or during which issue may be joined. M16. 2 Of a writ, summons, etc.: that may be issued; liable or authorized to be issued. M17. 3 Liable to issue as the proceeds of any property, investment, or source of revenue. L17.

issuably *adv.* in an issuable manner; so as to raise an issue: L18.

issuance /'ɪʃ(j)ʊəns, 'ɪsjʊ-/ *n.* *US.* M19. [f. next: see -ANCE.] The action of issuing, putting out, or giving out.

issuant /'ɪʃ(j)ʊənt, 'ɪsjʊ-/ *a.* E17. [f. ISSUE *v.* + -ANT[1], after Fr. pres. pples in *-ant*.] 1 *Her.* Esp. of an animal of which the upper half alone is visible: rising from the base of a chief, or (less usually) from another bearing or from the base of an escutcheon. E17. 2 Issuing or proceeding from a place or source. Now *rare*. M17.

issue /'ɪʃuː, 'ɪsjuː/ *n.* ME. [(O)Fr. *issue*, †*eissue* f. Proto-Romance, ult. f. L EXITUS. In branch VI f. the vb.] I 1 The action of going, passing, or flowing out; (power of) egress or exit; outgoing, outflow. ME. †b A sally, a sortie. L15–L17. 2 *Med.* A discharge of blood or other matter from the body, either due to disease or produced surgically by counterirritation; an incision or artificial ulcer made for the purpose of causing such a discharge. Now *rare* or *obs.* LME. 3 The termination or close of an action or proceeding or (formerly) a period of time. Now *rare*. L15.

1 J. TYNDALL The whole volume .. escaped from beneath the ice .. forming a fine arch at its place of issue. 3 W. ROBERTSON Before the negotiations at Crespy were brought to an issue.

II 4 A place or means of egress; a way out, an outlet. ME. b The point where a body of water flows out; the mouth of a river, the outlet of an inland sea, etc. Also, an outflowing stream. LME.

4 THACKERAY As my Lady .. passed through one door .. my Lord .. departed by another issue.

III 5 Produce, proceeds; the profits arising from lands or tenements, amercements, or fines. *obs.* exc. in *Law.* ME. †b A fine; an order for levying this. LME–M18. 6 a Offspring, progeny; a child, children; a descendant, descendants. Now chiefly in *Law* exc. w. ref. to legal succession. LME †b A race, a stock, a breed. Only in 17. c A young animal. *rare*. L18. 7 The outcome or product *of* a practice or condition. E17. †b An action, a deed (in relation to the doer). *rare* (Shakes.). Only in E17.

6a E. LINKLATER He married a Miss Harriet Dormer, by whom he had issue Hildebrand, .. Cuthbert, and Anne. 7 W. SANDERSON From an Artizan's excellencies, proceed those extravagant varieties . . which are not the issues of an idle brain. b SHAKES. *Jul. Caes.* There shall I try, In my oration, how the people take The cruel issue of these bloody men.

IV 8 The way an action or course of proceedings turns out; the event, a result, a consequence. LME. †**b** The event or fortune happening to a person; luck in an undertaking. LME–M17. †**c** The result of a discussion or examination of a question; a decision, a conclusion. LME–E18. **d** The outcome of an argument, evidence, etc. E17.

8 R. GRAVES Pharas . . doubted the issue of the day and wished to be in a neutral position. **b** SHAKES. *Ant. & Cl.* Jointing their force 'gainst Caesar, Whose better issue in the war from Italy Upon the first encounter drave them.

V 9 *Law.* The point in question, at the conclusion of the pleadings between contending parties in an action, when one side affirms and the other denies. LME. **b** *transf.* A point on the decision of which something depends or is made to rest; a point or matter in contention between two parties. LME. **c** A matter the decision of which involves important consequences. M19. **d** A choice between alternatives, a dilemma. M19.

9b G. F. KENNAN In Britain, the question of relations with Russia was a hotly contested issue. M. SCAMMELL The main issue between them was still whether or not to have children. **c** M. FOOT Their pusillanimity in tackling the great issue of mass unemployment. *Studio Week* On an issue as vital as this there is no room for complacency.

VI 10 The action of issuing or giving or sending out officially or publicly banknotes, bonds, shares, postage stamps, certificates, etc. M19. **b** The set number or amount of coins, notes, stamps, shares, copies of a newspaper, book, or periodical, etc., issued at one time, or distinguished in pattern, design, colour, content, or numbers, from those issued at another time. M19. **c** An item or amount of something given out or distributed, esp. in the army. M19. **11** *Bibliogr.* A subdivision of an edition or of an impression constituting a distinct form of the edition (or impression) sheets, normally indicated by the provision of a new title-page, with or without other changes. E20. **12** A book issued in a library. Usu. in *pl.*, as an item in statistics of books issued to borrowers. M20.

10 *Leeds Mercury* Larger powers of control should be given to the local authorities over the issue of the licenses. **b** P. HOWARD *The Times* maintained publication and never lost an issue. *What Investment* The City Letter will tell you how . . to invest, which issues to apply for. **c** C. MCCULLOUGH They were dressed in a new issue of jungle green. *attrib.*: *Royal Air Force Journal* I put on a pair of R.A.F. issue shoes. *Guns & Weapons* Whatever they bought had to fire issue ammunition.

Phrases: **at issue** (*a*) *Law* in the position of parties of which one affirms and the other denies a point; *gen.* (of people or parties) taking opposite sides of a case or contrary views of a matter; (*b*) (of a matter or question) in dispute. *bank of issue* see BANK *n.*[3] 3. *collateral issue*: see COLLATERAL *a.* *false issue*: see FALSE *a.* *force the issue*: see FORCE *v.*[1] **in the issue** as things turn or turned out; in the event. **issue of fact** *Law* an issue raised by denying something alleged as a fact. **issue of law** *Law* an issue raised by conceding a fact alleged but denying the application of the law. **join issue** (*a*) *Law* (of the parties) submit an issue jointly for decision; (of one party) accept the issue tendered by the opposite party; (*b*) *transf.* accept or adopt a disputed point as the basis of argument in a controversy; proceed to argument *with* a person *on* a particular point, offered or selected; (*c*) take up a contrary view on or *on* a question. **make an issue of** make a fuss about, turn into a subject of contention. *rights issue*: see RIGHT *n.*[1] *side issue*: see SIDE *n.* **take issue** = *join issue* (b), (c) above. **the (whole) issue** *slang* everything, the lot.

issueless *a.* without issue; *esp.* having no offspring: LME.

issue /ˈɪʃuː, ˈɪsjuː/ *v.* ME. [f. the n.] **I** *v.i.* **1 a** Go or come out; flow out. Freq. w. *out, forth, from.* ME. **b** *transf.* & *fig.* Go or come out of a state or condition; emerge. L15. **c** Come out as a branch, branch out. Formerly also, stand or stick out, protrude. M16. **2** Proceed as offspring; be born or descended. *obs.* exc. in *Law.* ME. **3** Come as proceeds or revenue; accrue. Chiefly in *issuing out of* (lands etc.). ME. **4** Proceed as from a source; take one's or its origin, be derived, spring. L15. **b** Proceed or arise as a result or consequence; result. L16. **5** Come to a result (in a specified way); end or result *in.* M17. **6** Be sent out officially or publicly; be published. M17.

1 G. SANTAYANA Mr. Alden might be seen at church time issuing from his mansion. P. BROOK Words issuing as sounds from people's mouths. C. PETERS An English family nervously issuing forth to see the show. **b** T. BRUGIS He had had many quarrels, and had issued out of them advantagiously. **c** T. HERBERT From his head issue foure great hornes. **2** AV *2 Kings* 20:18 Thy sonnes that shall issue from thee, which thou shalt beget. **4** T. S. ELIOT The kind of faith that issues from despair. **b** G. ORWELL All wisdom, all happiness, all virtue, are held to issue directly from his leadership and inspiration. **5** DEFOE We have had a hard day's work, but I hope it will issue well. J. A. FROUDE A philosophy which issues in such conclusions. **6** A. CRUMP The number of coins issuing from the mint each year varies considerably.

II *v.t.* **7** Of a containing thing or (formerly) a means of exit or operative force: allow to pass out; let out, emit, discharge. LME. †**8** Give birth to; bear (offspring). Usu. in *pass.*, be born, spring. LME–L17. **9** Give or send out authoritatively or officially; publish, emit, put into circulation (coins, banknotes, etc.). Formerly freq. foll. by *out, forth.* E17. **10** †**a** Bring to an issue or settlement; settle (a dispute etc.); terminate. Chiefly *US.* M17–E18. **b** Give a certain issue or result to; cause to end *in* something. Now *rare.* L17. **11** Give (something) out officially to (a person); supply (a person) officially *with.* E20.

7 W. TOOKE A mountain . . is continually issuing smoke. R. S. BALL Agents which stored up heat in summer and issued it in winter. *absol.*: SHAKES. *Hen. V* I must perforce compound With mistful eyes, or they will issue too. **9** G. VIDAL After the directors' meeting he'll issue a statement. R. L. FOX He issued orders that his army should not plunder the native land. P. ACKROYD A reader's ticket was issued to him. *when-issued*: see WHEN *adv.* & *conj.* **10b** H. BUSHNELL The child is sure to be issued finally in a feeling of confirmed disrespect. **11** J. LE CARRÉ A machine took his money and issued him with a ticket. A. BURGESS We were issued with pint mugs.

issuer *n.* L15. **issuing** *n.* (*a*) the action of the vb; †(*b*) a place of issue, an outlet: LME.

ist /ɪst/ *n.* Chiefly *derog.* & *joc.* E19. [-IST used generically.] A follower of an ism; a holder of some special doctrine or system of belief; an expert in a particular science, art, or pursuit. Chiefly used in a context suggesting some group of words in *-ist.*

L. MANN He himself wasn't a Socialist or any other ist.

-ist /ɪst/ *suff.* [Fr. *-iste*, L *-ista*, Gk *-istēs* forming agent-ns. from vbs in *-izein*: see -IZE.] Forming personal ns., sometimes agent-ns. corresp. to vbs in -IZE, as *antagonist*; more freq. denoting (*a*) a person who makes a systematic study of a particular art or science or who is occupied with something professionally or on a large scale: orig. corresp. to Gk abstract ns. in *-ia, -mat-*, etc., as *chemist, dramatist, economist, geologist*; later formed f. ns. of other origins, as *dentist, pianist, tobacconist*; (*b*) an adherent of a particular system of beliefs, principles, discrimination, etc., corresp. to ns. in -ISM, and often used also as adjs., as *Buddhist, Darwinist, idealist, Marxist, positivist, racist.*

istana /ɪˈstɑːnə/ *n.* M19. [Malay f. Skt *āsthāna* place of audience.] In Malay kingdoms: a ruler's palace.

isthmi *n.pl.* see ISTHMUS.

isthmian /ˈɪsθmɪən, ˈɪstm-, ˈɪsm-/ *a.* E17. [f. L *isthmius* f. Gk *isthmios*, + -AN.] Of or pertaining to an isthmus, *spec.* (**I-**) the isthmus of Corinth in southern Greece.

isthmic *a.* = ISTHMIAN L16.

isthmus /ˈɪsθməs, ˈɪstməs, ˈɪsməs/ *n.* Pl. **-muses**, (*rare*) **-mi** /-maɪ/. M16. [L f. Gk *isthmos.*] **1** *Geogr.* A narrow portion of land, enclosed on each side by water and connecting two larger bodies of land; a neck of land. M16. **2** *Anat.* & *Zool.* A narrow part or organ connecting two larger parts, as the fauces between the mouth and the pharynx, or the band of tissue between the two lobes of the thyroid gland. E18.

-istic /ɪstɪk/ *suff.* [Fr. *-istique* orig. f. L *-isticus*, Gk *-istikos*, f. *-ikos* -IC added to n. stems in *-istēs* -IST.] Forming adjs. f. ns. in -IST or -ISM, as *antagonistic, realistic*, or occas. corresp. to vbs in -IZE in the absence of a n. in -IST, as *characteristic.*

istle /ˈɪstli, ˈɪst(ə)l/ *n.* M19. [Amer. Sp. *ixtle* f. Nahuatl *ixtli.*] A fibre obtained (in Mexico and Central America) from *Bromelia sylvestris* and species of *Agave*, esp. *A. funkiana* and *A. lecheguilla*, and used for cordage, nets, carpets, etc.

Istrian /ˈɪstrɪən/ *a.* & *n.* E17. [f. *Istria* (see below) + -AN.] **A** *adj.* Of or pertaining to Istria, a peninsula near the head of the Adriatic Sea. E17.

Istrian marble or **stone** a fine limestone resembling marble.

B *n.* A native or inhabitant of Istria. E17.

it /ɪt/ *n. colloq.* Also **It.** M20. [Abbrev. of ITALIAN *a.*] Italian vermouth. Only in *gin and it.*

it /ɪt/ *pers. pron.*, *3 sing. neut. subjective* (*nom.*) & *objective* (*dat.* & *accus.*), & *possess. a.* Orig. †**hit.** Also (before or after certain wds, *arch.*) **'t.** [OE *hit* neut. nom. & accus. of Gmc demonstr. stem repr. also in HE *pron.*] **A** *pron.* **I** Subjective uses. **1** The inanimate or abstract thing or (where sex is not particularized) the animal or young child or (*contempt.*) the person previously mentioned, implied, or easily identified. OE. **2** The subject of thought, attention, enquiry, etc.; the person or thing in question. (As subj. of BE *v.*, with a n. or pers. pron. as pred., freq. followed by a rel. cl. (often used to emphasize the pred.: cf. sense 4c below) or with such a cl. implied, in statements or questions regarding identity.) OE. †**b** There *is* etc. ME–E17. **c** Introducing a ballad etc.: the subject of the song or tale. *arch.* E17. **3** As subj. of an impers. vb or impers. statement, without ref. to any agent, in statements of weather, the time of day, the season of the year, a state of affairs, a physical or mental sensation, etc. OE. **b** In statements as to amount of space, distance, or length of time. L16. **4** Placed before the vb as anticipatory subj., when the logical subj. of the vb is an inf. phr., a cl. (esp. after a vb in *pass.*), or a sentence. OE. **b** As anticipatory subj., repr. the topic of a sentence, when the logical subj. is a n., esp. with attributes. Now *poet., rhet.*, & *colloq.* OE. **c** In a periphrastic introductory cl. w. *be*, bringing into prominence an adverbial adjunct or the subj. of a cl. ME.

1 B. NILSON Heat the milk until it is just lukewarm. D. LESSING Rosemary began sobbing, as a child does when it finds a refuge. I. MCEWAN When people shake their heads, . . it can mean all sorts of things. C. DALE I take each day as it comes. **2** SCOTT FITZGERALD Some one was walking in the kitchen, and he knew by the light footfall that it was not his wife. T. ALLBEURY What is it you want? **b** C. MARLOWE Cousin, it is no dealing with him now. **c** COLERIDGE It is an ancient mariner. **3** T. HARDY It being summer time the miller was much occupied with business. OED It is all over with poor Jack. E. TAYLOR It's not yet ten o'clock. J. HIGGINS It was suddenly very quiet in the preparation room. *it blows hard, it rains, it thunders*, etc. **b** *News Chronicle* It is a long way from 1937. **4** TENNYSON We die—does it matter when? SCOTT FITZGERALD It disturbed him that her smile could have no root in mirth. D. LESSING It's the landlord's business to fix the rent. I. MURDOCH Mrs. Witcher, it was said, had once been a shorthand typist. R. P. JHABVALA It may be due to the ghostly light that she looks like a ghost. J. SIMMS It is not easy to live with a genius. **b** J. L. HERLIHY It was a disturbing spectacle, this crazy-eyed searcher flailing his arms. **c** OED It is not everybody who can afford to take a holiday. *Proverb*: It's an ill wind that blows nobody any good.

II Objective uses. **5** As obj. (direct, indirect, or after preps.): the thing etc. (see sense 1 above) previously mentioned, implied, or easily identified. OE. **b** Used as anticipatory obj. when the logical obj. is an inf. phr. or a cl. Cf. sense 4 above. L16. **c** Itself: direct & indirect objective. *arch.* exc. after preps. L16. **6** As a vague or indefinite obj. of a trans. vb, after a prep., etc. Also as obj. of a vb which is predominantly intrans., giving the same meaning as the intrans.

use, and as obj. of many vbs formed (freq. as nonce-wds) f. ns. meaning 'act the character, use the thing, indicated'. M16.

5 D. H. LAWRENCE He folded his rain-coat and laid it along the . . ledge. J. STEINBECK He bought a gallon of red wine and drank most of it himself. D. WELCH He kissed the puppy's nose and cuddled it in his arms. J. D. SALINGER I can't always pray when I feel like it. C. LASSALLE Now come on . . give it a go! C. DALE He called her 'love' as if he meant it. b T. HARDY She thought it best to secure a protector of some kind. M. DICKENS I take it your mother has gone to America. c SHAKES. *John* My heart hath one poor string to stay it by. OED The tree draws to it all the moisture from the adjacent ground. 6 MILTON Trip it as ye go On the light fantastick toe. J. K. JEROME We decided that we would . . inn it, and pub it when it was wet. J. MASTERS We . . lord it over the country entirely by the good will of the average native. J. I. M. STEWART Make it snappy. Taxi's waiting. M. GEE Watch it, Mum. You'll knock off all the needles. *In imprecations*: *damn it*, *hang it*, etc.

III 7 As antecedent to a relative expressed or understood: that (which), the one (that). *rare*. ME.

7 AV *Isa.* 51:9 Art thou not it that hath cut Rahab?

IV 8 Sexual intercourse. Cf. *do it* (a) s.v. DO *v.* Now *colloq.* E17. **9** In emphatic *pred.* use: the actual thing required or expected; the acme. M19. **10** In *pred.* use: in children's games, the player who has to catch others. M19. **11** Sex appeal. *colloq.* E20.

9 H. M. SMITH I have some new plus-fours which are 'it'. 11 *Bystander* A film star who has proved to producers . . that she is blessed with that undefinable quality called 'It'.

Phrases etc.: (A selection of cross-refs. only is included.) *at it*: see AT *prep.* *be for it*: see FOR *prep.* *get it*: see GET *v.* *go for it*: see GO *v.* *have it in for*: see HAVE *v.* *hit it off*: see HIT *v.* *in it*: see IN *prep.* **it says, tells**, etc., it is said, told, etc. (in a book, article, etc.). **'taint** *non-standard* it ain't, it isn't. **that's it** *colloq.* (*a*) there is no more to it than that; (*b*) = *this is it* below. **this is it** *colloq.* (*a*) the event previously spoken about or feared is about to happen; (*b*) that is the difficulty. **'tis** it is. **'twas** it was. **'twere** it were. **'twill** it will. **'twould** it would. *watch it*: see WATCH *v.* *with it*: see WITH *prep.* *worth it*: see WORTH *a.*

B *possess. adj.* = ITS *possess. a.* Now *dial.* LME.

A. GOLDING It hath no forme of it owne.

ita /ˈiːtə/ *n.* Also **eta** /ˈiːtə/. M19. [Arawak *ite*.] (More fully *ita palm*) a tropical American fan palm, *Mauritia flexuosa*; a drink made from its fermented sap.

itabirite /iˈtabɪrʌɪt/ *n.* M19. [f. *Itabira*, a town in Minas Gerais, Brazil + -ITE[1].] *Petrogr.* An iron-rich slate consisting chiefly of layers of quartz and iron oxides.

itacism /ˈiːtəsɪz(ə)m/ *n.* M19. [mod.L *itacismus*, f. Gk *ēta* ETA *n.*[1], prob. after L *iotacismus*: see IOTACISM.] *Ling.* In Greek, the pronunciation of the vowel eta as, or the reduction of various vowels and diphthongs to, the sound /iː/ (represented in classical Greek by the letter iota); (an instance of) the erroneous substitution in Greek manuscripts of iota for another vowel or diphthong. Cf. IOTACISM.

itacist /-sɪst/ *n.* a person who practises or favours itacism M19. **itacistic** /-ˈsɪstɪk/ *a.* characterized by itacism L19.

itacolumite /ɪtəˈkɒljʊmʌɪt/ *n.* M19. [f. *Itacolumi*, a mountain in Minas Gerais, Brazil + -ITE[1].] *Petrogr.* A schistose quartzite, usu. containing mica, chlorite, and talc, sometimes forming flexible slabs.

itaconic /ɪtəˈkɒnɪk/ *a.* M19. [f. partial anagram of ACONITINE (involved in its orig. preparation) + -IC.] Chem. *itaconic acid*, a crystalline acid, CH_2:C(COOH)·CH_2COOH, obtained in fermentation of sugar by the mould *Aspergillus terreus*; methylenesuccinic acid.

itaconate /ɪˈta-/ *n.* a salt or ester of itaconic acid M19.

Italian /ɪˈtaljən/ *n.* & *a.* LME. [It. *italiano*, f. *Italia* Italy: see -AN.] **A** *n.* **1** A native or inhabitant of Italy, a country in southern Europe comprising a peninsula jutting into, and offshore islands in, the Mediterranean Sea. LME. **2** The Romance language of Italy. L15. **3** *ellipt.* A thing or (kind of) article originating in Italy; *spec.* (*a*) Italian cloth; (*b*) Italian vermouth. L19.

B *adj.* Of or pertaining to Italy, its people, or its modern Romance language; native to or originating or produced in Italy. E16.

Italian cypress: see CYPRESS *n.*[1]1. **Italian earth** the colour sienna. **Italian garden**: characterized by clipped trees, box-edged beds of flowers, paved paths, statues, fountains, etc., and often arranged in terraces. **Italian hand, handwriting** *arch.* the kind of handwriting first developed in Italy and now current in almost all countries using the Roman alphabet. **Italian iron** (*obs.* exc. *Hist.*) a cylindrical iron used for fluting or crimping lace, frills, etc. **Italian millet** foxtail millet. **Italian opening** *Chess*: in which each player moves successively the king's pawn, the knight on a dark square, and the king's bishop to the fourth rank; also called *Giuoco Piano*. **Italian paste** the dough from which macaroni and vermicelli are made. **Italian pink** = *Dutch pink* s.v. DUTCH *a.* **Italian quilting**: manufactured in a design composed of parallel lines of stitching. **Italian roof** a hip-roof. *Italian* RYEGRASS. **Italian stitch** a form of cross-stitch. **Italian vermouth** a sweet kind of vermouth. **Italian warehouse** a shop etc. supplying Italian groceries, fruits, olive oil, etc.

Italia'nesque *a.* Italian in style or character M19. **Italianity** /ɪtalɪˈanɪti/ *n.* Italian quality or character L19. **Italianly** *adv.* (*rare*) L16.

Italianate /ɪˈtaljəneɪt, -nət/ *a.* L16. [It. *italianato*, f. as prec.: see -ATE[2].] Made Italian; (that has become or been made) Italian in character or appearance.

Italianate /ɪˈtaljəneɪt/ *v.t.* Long *rare*. M16. [f. as prec.: see -ATE[3].] Make Italian; Italianize. Orig. & chiefly as *Italianated* ppl a.

Italianise *v.* var. of ITALIANIZE.

Italianism /ɪˈtaljənɪz(ə)m/ *n.* L16. [f. ITALIAN + -ISM.] **1** An Italian practice or characteristic; an Italian expression or idiom. L16. **2** Italian spirit or taste; attachment to Italian ideas; sympathy with Italy. E19.

Italianist /ɪˈtaljənɪst/ *n.* & *a.* L16. [f. ITALIAN + -IST.] **A** *n.* **1** An Italianate person. *rare*. L16. **2** An expert in or student of Italian language, literature, and culture. M20. **B** *adj.* Of, pertaining to, or characterized by Italianism. L19.

Italianize /ɪˈtaljənʌɪz/ *v.* Also **-ise**. L16. [Fr. *italianiser*, f. as ITALIAN: see -IZE.] **1** *v.t.* Make Italian in character or style. L16. **2** *v.i.* Practise Italian styles or habits; become Italian in character, tastes, etc. M17.

Italiani'zation *n.* M19. **Italianizer** *n.* M19.

Italic /ɪˈtalɪk/ *a.* & *n.* LME. [L *Italicus* f. Gk *Italikos*, f. *Italia* Italy f. L: see -IC.] **A** *adj.* †**1** = ITALIAN *a.* LME–M18. **2a** *Archit.* = COMPOSITE *a.* 2. M16. **b** *Class. Hist.* Of or pertaining to the Greek colonies in southern Italy, *esp.* of or pertaining to the Pythagorean and Eleatic schools of philosophy founded there in the 6th cent. BC. M17. **c** *Hist.* Of or pertaining to ancient Italy or its peoples; *spec.* of or pertaining to parts of ancient Italy other than Rome. L17. **3** (Usu. **i-**.) Of printed or handwritten characters: generally cursive and sloping to the right. Also, of type, printing, or handwriting: composed of such characters. E17. **b** Of handwriting: modelled on the style used by professional scribes in 16th-cent. Italy. M20. **4** *Ling.* Of, pertaining to, or characteristic of Italic (see sense B.3 below). M19. **B** *n.* **1** A member of an Italic school of philosophy (see sense A.2b above). L16. **2** (Usu. **i-**.) In *pl.* & *sing.* Italic characters (in printing now usu. employed for emphasis, in titles of works, or to distinguish a word or phrase, esp. a foreign one). L17. **3** A branch of the Indo-European language family including Osco-Umbrian, Latin, and the Romance languages; *spec.* (*a*) the ancient languages of this group; (*b*) Osco-Umbrian. L19.

Italicism /-sɪz(ə)m/ *n.* (*rare*) an Italian expression or idiom L18.

italicize /ɪˈtalɪsʌɪz/ *v.t.* Also **-ise**. L18. [f. ITALIC + -IZE.] Print in italics; (in writing) underscore with a single line, to indicate characters to be printed in italic. Now also *fig.*, pronounce with emphasis.

COLERIDGE Now for the italicized words *if I can*. C. BEATON Ordinarily unpretentious men and women . . started to italicize certain phrases by their inflections.

italici'zation *n.* L19.

Italiot /ɪˈtalɪət/ *n.* & *a.* M17. [Gk *Italiōtēs*, f. *Italia* Italy: see -OT[2].] **A** *n.* A person of Greek descent living in ancient Italy. M17. **B** *adj.* Of or pertaining to the Greek colonies in ancient southern Italy. M17.

Italo- /ˈɪtələʊ, ɪˈtaləʊ/ *comb. form.* [f. ITAL(IAN + -O-.] Forming adj. and n. combs. with the meaning 'Italian (and)' as *Italo-Byzantine*, *Italo-Grecian*.

Italo-'Celtic *a.* & *n.* (of or pertaining to) a postulated common parent language of Italian and Celtic L19. **Italophil(e)** *a.* & *n.* (a person who is) friendly to Italy or fond of Italy and Italian things E20. **Italo'phobia** *n.* dread or dislike of Italy and Italian things E20.

itatartaric /ɪtətɑːˈtarɪk/ *a.* L19. [f. ITA(CONIC + TARTARIC.] Chem. *itatartaric acid*, a crystalline acid, dihydroxyitaconic acid, CH_2OH·C(OH)·(COOH)·CH_2COOH, obtained as a by-product in the production of itaconic acid by fermentation.

ita'tartrate *n.* a salt or ester of itatartaric acid L19.

itch /ɪtʃ/ *n.* OE. [f. the vb.] **1** A sensation of irritation in the skin, causing a desire to scratch or rub it; *spec.* (now *rare*) the skin disease scabies. Also (w. specifying wds), any of various skin diseases of which itching is a symptom. OE. **2** *fig.* A restless or urgent desire (*for*, *to do*); a hankering (*after*). M16.

1 M. PIERCY I feel a cumulative dissatisfaction like an itch between my shoulder blades. *barber's itch*, *dhobi itch*, *grocer's itch*, *ground itch*, *swimmer's itch*, etc. 2 G. M. TREVELYAN Leaders of the Eighteenth Century were not harassed by the perpetual itch to make money. SEVEN YEAR *itch*.

Comb.: **itch-mite** a parasitic acarid mite, *Sarcoptes scabiei*, which burrows in the human skin, causing scabies; **itchweed** *N. Amer.* false hellebore, *Veratrum viride*.

itch /ɪtʃ/ *v.* [OE *ġiććan*, *ġyććan*, corresp. to OS *jukkian*, (M)Du. *jeuken*, OHG *jucchen* (G *jucken*), f. WGmc.] **1** *v.i.* Experience an itch of the skin; (of a part of the body) be the site of an itch, cause a desire to scratch or rub. OE. **2** *v.i.* Have a restless or urgent desire (*to do*, *for*). ME. **3** *v.t.* Cause to itch. L16.

1 H. G. WELLS You scratch the tip of your nose because it itches. 2 E. NESBIT Young wives come in, a-smiling, grave, With secrets that they itch to tell. **itching ears** (people with) a restless desire to hear something new. **itching palm** avarice. 3 R. CAMPBELL The thick super-salty water of the Mediterranean, which tires and itches the naked eye.

itching /ˈɪtʃɪŋ/ *n.* ME. [f. ITCH *v.* + -ING[1].] **1** A feeling of irritation in the skin, causing a desire to scratch or rub. ME. **2** *fig.* A restless desire or hankering, = ITCH *n.* 2. ME.

itchy /ˈɪtʃi/ *a.* Now *colloq.* M16. [f. ITCH *n.* + -Y[1].] Affected by itching or an itch; *fig.* restless.

itchiness *n.* L19.

ite /ʌɪt/ *n.* M19. [Use as independent wd of -ITE[1]. Cf. ISM.] A person or thing that is or may be designated by a noun in *-ite*.

-ite /ʌɪt/ *suff.*[1] [Corresp. to Fr. *-ite*, L *-ita* (*-ites*), f. Gk *-itēs*.] **1** Forming ns. and adjs. denoting (*a*) a native of a place, a member of a people, etc., as *Gibeonite*, *Levite*, *Stagirite*, etc.; (*b*) (freq. *derog.*) a follower of a person, doctrine, or school, as *Irvingite*, *Luddite*, *Pre-Raphaelite*, *Trotskyite*, etc. **2a** *Palaeont.* Forming names of fossil organisms, as *ammonite*, *belemnite*, *echinite*, etc. **b** Forming names of minerals and rocks, comprising names of ancient origin, as *anthracite*, *chlorite*, *haematite*, etc., and many mod. formations, as *andesite*, *brewsterite*, *cobaltite*, *carbonatite*, *labradorite*, etc. (often superseding names in *-ine* etc.). **c** Forming names of tektites from different regions, as *australite*, *indochinite*, etc. **3** *Anat.* & *Zool.* Forming names of constituent parts, segments, or joints of a body or organ, as *coxopodite*, *somite*, etc. **4** *Chem.* **a** Forming names of substances, esp. explosives and other commercial products, as *cordite*, *dynamite*, *ebonite*, *vulcanite*, etc., and (formerly) sugars and other polyhydric compounds, as *dulcite*, *inosite*, *mannite*, etc. (often superseded by names in *-itol*). **b** Forming names of salts or esters of acids ending in *-ous*, as *nitrite*, *sulphite*, etc.

-ite /ʌɪt/ *suff.*[2] [f. L *-itus*, pa. ppl ending of vbs in *-ire*, *-ere*, or f. corresp. Proto-Romance *-ito*.] In adjs., ns., and vbs derived f. L or Romance, as *erudite*, *composite*, *favourite*; *appetite*; *expedite*, *unite*.

item /ˈʌɪtəm/ *adv.*, *n.*, & *v.* LME. [L = just so, similarly, moreover, f. *ita* thus, so.] **A** *adv.* Likewise, also. Chiefly used to introduce and draw attention to a new statement, particular, or entry, esp. in a list or formal document. LME.

A. PRICE Item, one emerald-and-diamond necklace, . . item one diamond tiara.

B *n.* **1** Formerly, a statement, maxim, or warning, orig. such as was introduced by the word 'item' (see sense A above). Now (*US dial.*), an intimation, a hint. M16. **2** An individual thing, article, or unit included in a set, list, computation, or total, as (*a*) an entry or thing entered in an account or register; (*b*) a detail or category of expenditure; (*c*) a news story; (*d*) a member of a set of linguistic units. L16. **b** *Computing*. Any quantity of data treated as a unit, e.g. a field, a group of fields, or a record. M20.

2 R. INGALLS On a news programme . . that item had not been heard by other people. M. SCAMMELL A few items of warm clothing could make all the difference. M. MEYER He missed Swedish food, asking friends to send him such items as split peas and dill. D. ADAMS I think you will find an item in the bill to that effect.

C *v.t.* Itemize. Now *rare*. E17.

itemize /ˈʌɪtəmʌɪz/ *v.t.* Also **-ise**. M19. [f. ITEM *n.* + -IZE.] Set down by items; enter as an item; specify the items of (a bill etc.).

J. KRANTZ She knew there were other expenses . . but couldn't itemize them off-hand. B. BETTELHEIM The idea that if you . . adhere to certain itemized instructions, certain results will automatically follow.

itemiˈzation *n.* the action of itemizing something; an instance of this: L19. **itemizer** *n.* L19.

iter /ˈɪtə, ˈʌɪtə/ *n.* Pl. **iters**, **itinera** /ʌɪˈtɪn(ə)rə/. L16. [L = journey, way, road.] **1** *Hist.* A circuit of an itinerant judge, esp. a justice in eyre. Formerly also, a record of proceedings during a circuit. L16. **2** A Roman road or line of travel. M18. **3** *Anat.* A narrow passage; *spec.* the cerebral aqueduct. *arch.* L19.

iterant /ˈɪtər(ə)nt/ *a.* E17. [L *iterant-* pres. ppl stem of *iterare*: see ITERATE *v.*, -ANT[1].] That iterates or repeats something; repeating, echoing.

iterance *n.* iteration, repetition E17. **iterancy** *n.* the condition of being iterant; iterance: L19.

iterate /ˈɪtərət/ *n.* E20. [f. the vb, or f. L *iteratus* pa. pple of *iterare*: see next, -ATE[1].] *Math.* A quantity arrived at by iteration.

iterate /ˈɪtəreɪt/ *v.* M16. [L *iterat-* pa. ppl stem of *iterare* repeat, f. *iterum* again: see -ATE[3].] **1** *v.t.* Do (something) over again; repeat (an action). Now *rare*. M16. **2** *v.t.* Say again, state repeatedly. M16. **3** *v.i. Math.* Employ iteration; make repeated use of a formula by substituting in it each time the result of the previous application. M20.

iteration /ɪtəˈreɪʃ(ə)n/ *n.* LME. [L *iteratio(n-)*, f. as prec.: see -ATION.] **1 a** (A) repetition of an action, process, or performance. LME. **b** *Math.* The repetition of an operation on its product; *esp.* the repeated use of a formula which provides a closer approximation to the solution of a given equation when an approximate solution is substituted in the formula, so that a series of successively closer approximations is obtained; (a single application of) such a formula. E20. **2** The repetition of something said. M16.

iterative /ˈɪtərətɪv/ *a.* & *n.* L15. [Fr. *itératif*, *-ive* (in sense 1) and late L *iterativus* (in sense 2), f. as prec.: see -IVE.] **A** *adj.* **1 a** Characterized by repeating or being repeated. L15. **b** *Math.* Of the nature of, employing, or resulting from iteration. E20. **2** *Gram.* Denoting repetition of action; frequentative. E19. **B** *n. Ling.* **1** An iterative verb or aspect. M19. **2** A word expressing repetition of an action, sound, etc. M20.

iteratively *adv.* M19. **iterativeness** *n.* M19.

iteroparous /ˈɪtərə(ʊ)parəs/ *a.* M20. [f. L *iterum* again + -O- + -PAROUS.] *Biol.* Of or designating a species or organism which reproduces more than once during its lifetime. Cf. SEMELPAROUS.

iteroparity /-ˈparɪti/ *n.* the state or condition of being iteroparous M20.

I-Thou /ʌɪˈðaʊ/ *a.* M20. [G *ich-du*, f. *ich* I + *du* you (sing.).] Of a personal relationship (esp. with God): formed by direct encounter.

ithyphallic /ɪθɪˈfalɪk/ *n.* & *a.* E17. [Late L *ithyphallicus* f. Gk *ithuphallikos*, f. *ithuphallos*, f. *ithus* straight + *phallos* PHALLUS: see -IC.] **A** *n.* A poem in ithyphallic metre. Also, an obscene or sexually explicit poem. E17. **B** *adj.* **1** Of a cult, ceremony, carved figure, etc.: associated with or characterized by (the symbol of) a phallus, esp. in the context of Bacchic festivals in ancient Greece; *spec.* composed in the metre of the Bacchic hymns (the trochaic dimeter brachycatalectic). L18. **2** Grossly indecent, obscene. M19.

ithyphallus /ɪθɪˈfaləs/ *n.* L19. [Gk *ithuphallos*: see prec.] A phallus.

Iti /ˈʌɪtʌɪ/ *n.* & *a. derog. slang.* Also **Itie**, **Ity**. M20. [Dim. of ITALIAN or alt. of EYETIE.] (An) Italian. Cf. EYETIE.

-itic /ɪtɪk/ *suff.* [Corresp. to Fr. *-itique*, L *-iticus*, Gk *-itikos*: see -IC.] **1** Forming adjs. from ns. in -ITE[1], as *Capernaitic*, *dendritic*, *Semitic*. **2** Forming adjs. and ns. from ns. esp. in -ITIS, or from other bases, as *arthritic*, *diphtheritic*, *gabbroitic*, *Nigritic*.

Itie *n.* & *a.* var. of ITI.

itinera *n.pl.* see ITER.

itineracy /ɪˈtɪn(ə)rəsi, ʌɪ-/ *n.* E19. [f. ITINER(ATE *a.* + -ACY.] = next.

itinerancy /ɪˈtɪn(ə)r(ə)nsi, ʌɪ-/ *n.* L18. [f. next: see -ANCY.] **1** Itinerant preaching or ministry, esp. as practised on Methodist circuits. L18. **2** The state or condition of being itinerant; a journey from place to place. E19.

itinerant /ɪˈtɪn(ə)r(ə)nt, ʌɪ-/ *a.* & *n.* L16. [Late L *itinerant-* pres. ppl stem of *itinerari*, f. L *itiner-*, *iter*: see ITINERARY *a.*, -ANT[1].] **A** *adj.* **1** Of a judge: travelling from place to place on circuit. L16. **2** Journeying; travelling or pertaining to travel, esp. in the course of selling or other work; (of a Methodist etc. minister) preaching in a circuit. M17. **3** Movable from place to place. L17.

2 A. THWAITE He decided to make his living as an itinerant painter . . and travelled England on foot.

B *n.* A person who travels from place to place, esp. as a preacher, actor, etc. M17.

itinerarium /ɪˌtɪnəˈrɛːrɪəm/ *n.* Pl. **-ria** /-rɪə/. E18. [Late L: see next.] **1** *Surg.* A rod used in lithotomy. *rare* (Dicts.). E18. **2** = ITINERARY *n.* 2, 3. M18.

itinerary /ʌɪˈtɪn(ə)rəri, ɪ-/ *n.* LME. [Late L *itinerarium* use as n. of neut. of *itinerarius*: see next, -ARY[1].] **1** A line or course of travel; a route. LME. **2** A record or account of a journey. L15. **3 a** A book describing a route or routes and providing detailed information for travellers; a guide-book. M16. **b** A sketch of a proposed route; a travel plan. M19. **4** An itinerant. *rare.* E18.

1 B. LOPEZ They moved nomadically . . according to the itineraries of the animals they pursued. 3b *Sunday Express* If you've plenty of time and a flexible itinerary, do as the locals do, risk standby.

itinerary /ʌɪˈtɪn(ə)rəri, ɪ-/ *a.* M16. [Late L *itinerarius*, f. L *itiner-*, *iter* journey, way, road: see -ARY[1].] **1** Of or pertaining to a journey, travelling, or (the description) of roads. M16. **2** = ITINERANT *a.* E17.

†**itinerate** *a.* E17–M18. [f. as next: see -ATE[2].] = ITINERANT *a.*

itinerate /ɪˈtɪn(ə)reɪt, ʌɪ-/ *v.* E17. [Late L *itinerat-* pa. ppl stem of *itinerari*: see ITINERANT, -ATE[3].] **1** *v.i.* Travel from place to place. E17. **b** Travel from place to place preaching, esp. on a Methodist circuit. L18. **2** *v.t.* Journey through. *rare.* M19.

itineration /ɪˌtɪnəˈreɪʃ(ə)n, ʌɪ-/ *n.* E17. [f. prec. + -ATION.] The action of itinerating; a preaching or lecturing tour.

-ition /ˈɪʃ(ə)n/ *suff.* [Repr. Fr. *-ition*, L *-itio(n-)* suff. forming ns. f. vbs with pa. ppl stem in *-it-*: cf. -ION.] Forming ns., chiefly w. the senses of -ATION, as *audition*, *disposition*, *rendition*, *volition*, etc.

-itious /ˈɪʃəs/ *suff.*[1] [Late L *-itius* alt. of L *-icius*: cf. -OUS.] Forming adjs., as *adventitious*, *factitious*, *fictitious*, *supposititious*, etc.

-itious /ˈɪʃəs/ *suff.*[2] [Repr. L *-itiosus*, f. *-itio(n-)* -ITION + *-osus* -OUS: cf. -IOUS.] Forming adjs. corresp. chiefly to ns. in *-ition*, as *ambitious*, *nutritious*, *superstitious*, etc.

itis /ˈʌɪtɪs/ *n.* E20. [Use as independent wd of -ITIS.] A condition or disease (that may be) designated by a word ending in *-itis*.

Canadian Magazine He was home in six months with . . 'every kind of "itis" you could think of.'

-itis /ˈʌɪtɪs/ *suff.* [Gk suff. forming the fem. of adjs. ending in *-itēs*, combined with (expressed or implied) *nosos* disease, to form names of diseases affecting a specified part of the body.] Forming ns. denoting diseased states or symptoms, esp. involving inflammation, affecting particular parts of the body, as *appendicitis*, *bronchitis*, *peritonitis*, *tonsillitis*, etc. Now also occas. (*colloq.*) forming ns. denoting a state of mind or tendency that is compared to a disease, as *telephonitis*.

-itol /ɪtɒl/ *suff.* [f. -ITE[1] + -OL.] *Chem.* Forming the names of polyhydric alcohols, as *hexitol*.

-itous /ɪtəs/ *suff.* [f. -IT(Y + -OUS, f. or after Fr. *-iteux*, L *-itosus*.] Forming adjs. corresp. to ns. ending in *-ity*, as *calamitous*, *felicitous*, *gratuitous*, *iniquitous*, etc.

its /ɪts/ *possess. pron. rare.* E17. [Absol. use of next.] Its one(s), that or those belonging or pertaining to it.

its /ɪts/ *possess. a.* (in mod. usage also classed as a *determiner*), *3 sing. neut.* Also **it's** (now considered *erron.*). L16. [f. IT *pron.* + -'S[1].] Of it; of itself; which belongs or pertains to it(self).

V. WOOLF She came in like a swan swimming its way. G. M. TREVELYAN Country house life, with its hunting and shooting, and its political and literary 'house-parties'. I. MURDOCH The question had arisen of its being sold. G. VIDAL Henry appeared with the telephone on its extension cord.

itself /ɪtˈsɛlf/ *pron.* OE. [f. IT *pron.* + SELF *a.* (but long interpreted as SELF *n.*).] **I** *refl.* **1** Refl. form (indirect, direct, & after preps.) of IT *pron.*: (to, for, etc.) the thing in question. OE.

1 I. MURDOCH A sturdy foot, which had begun to insert itself in the crack of the door. J. C. POWYS His family had completely ruined itself in its service of the king. E. H. GOMBRICH If something is only designed to fit its purpose we can let beauty look after itself. **by itself** apart from its surroundings; automatically, spontaneously. **in itself** considered separately from other things. *speak for itself*: see SPEAK *v.* *thing in itself*: see THING *n.*[1]

II *emphatic.* **2** In apposition to a n. (subjective or objective): that particular thing, the very thing, that thing alone. OE. **3** (Not appositional.) It; not something else. L16.

2 I. MURDOCH The Abbey itself is quite hidden in trees. C. RAYNER The big table upon which was spread a white cloth, itself covered with an array of instruments. H. JAMES She was kindness itself to me. 3 OED The dear old place looked just itself.

itsy-bitsy /ɪtsɪˈbɪtsi/ *a. colloq.* M20. [f. childish form of LITTLE *a.* + BITSY *a.*: see -SY.] Small, (charmingly) insubstantial, tiny. Also (*derog.*) fiddly, arty-crafty, twee. Cf. ITTY-BITTY *a.*

Observer The rather sentimental and itsy-bitsy patterns . . for wear by the young. H. HOWARD If Frankie was here he'd break you into itsy-bitsy pieces.

itsy-bitsiness *n.* M20.

itty /ˈɪti/ *a. colloq.* L18. [f. childish form of LITTLE *a.* + -Y[6].] Little (chiefly of or in speaking to babies or small domestic animals).

D. RUNYON He . . starts whispering, 'There, there, there, my itty oddleums'.

itty-bitty /ɪtɪˈbɪti/ *a. colloq.* M20. [f. prec. + BITTY *a.*] = ITSY-BITSY *a.*

-itude *suff.* see -TUDE.

Ity *n.* & *a.* var. of ITI.

-ity /ɪti/ *suff.* After *i* **-ety**. [f. or after (O)Fr. *-ité* f. L *-itas*, *-itatis*. Cf. -TY[1].] Forming ns. expressing state or condition, as *purity*, *authority*, *dubiety*, *majority*, *superiority*, etc., an instance of this as *a profanity*, *a monstrosity*, etc., or a quantity measuring the degree of a condition as *porosity*, *humidity*, etc.

itzebu /ɪtsɪˈbuː/ *n.* Also **-boo**. E17. [f. Jap. *ichi*, †*itze* one + *bu* division, quarter.] A gold or silver coin worth a quarter of a ryo, formerly used in Japan. In later use, a quarter of a dollar or yen.

iulidan /ʌɪˈjuːlɪd(ə)n/ *n.* L19. [f. mod.L *Iulidae* (see below), f. as next: see -AN.] *Zool.* A millipede of the family Iulidae.

iulus /ʌɪˈjuːləs/ *n.* Now *rare*. Also **julus** /ˈjuːləs, ˈdʒuː-/. Pl. **-li** /-lʌɪ, -liː/. M17. [L f. Gk *ioulos* down, catkin, millipede.] †**1** A catkin. M17–M18. **2** A millipede; *spec.* one of the genus *Julus*. M17.

-ium /ɪəm/ *suff.* [mod.L f. L, repr. Gk *-ion*.] **1** *gen.* In various ns. derived from or modelled on L or Gk wds, as *alluvium*, *auditorium*, *euphonium*, *geranium*, *proscenium*, etc. **2** *Chem.* **a** Forming the names of most metallic elements, as *cadmium*, *iridium*, *lithium*, *magnesium*, *osmium*, *palladium*, *potassium*, *rhodium*, *sodium*, *titanium*, *uranium*, etc., and occas. other cationic species, as *ammonium*. **b** Used (after *ammonium*) to form the names of various protonated, mostly organic, bases, as *ethidium*, *hydrazinium*, etc. Cf. -ONIUM. **3** *Anat.* & *Bot.* Forming the names of anatomical structures, esp. receptacles, as *archegonium*, *epithelium*, *gametangium*, *mycelium*, *pericardium*, etc. Cf. -IDIUM.

Ivan /ˈʌɪv(ə)n, iːˈvan/ *n. slang.* L19. [Russian male forename, corresp. to *John*.] A Russian, *esp.* a Russian soldier. Orig. *Ivan Ivanovitch* /ʌɪˈvanəvɪtʃ/ [w. added patronymic = son of Ivan], a typical Russian, a personification of the Russian people.

-ive /ɪv/ *suff.* [(O)Fr. *-if*, *-ive* (= It., Sp. *-ivo*), f. L *-ivus*.] Forming adjs. w. the sense 'tending to, having the nature or quality of', as *active*, *descriptive*. Also forming derived ns., as *adjective*, *locomotive*. Cf. -ATIVE.

†**Ivena** *n.* & *a.* see YUAN *n.*[1] & *a.*

ivi /ˈiːviː/ *n.* M19. [Fijian *ivi*, Samoan *ifi*.] The Tahiti chestnut, *Inocarpus fagifer*, a leguminous evergreen tree bearing spikes of white or yellow flowers and dark edible fruit.

Ivicene /ˈɪvɪsiːn/ *n.* & *a.* E20. [f. Fr. *Iviça* Ibiza (see below) + Sp. *-eño* -ENE.] (An animal of) a breed of hound from the Balearic Island of Ibiza, characterized by large, pointed, pricked ears and white, fawn, or reddish-brown colouring. Also called *Ibicencan hound*, *Ibizan hound*.

ivied /ˈʌɪvɪd/ *a.* Also **ivyed**. L18. [f. IVY *n.* + -ED[2].] Overgrown or covered with ivy. Also *fig.* (*US*), (academically) distinguished, prestigious, (cf. *Ivy League* s.v. IVY *n.*).

H. JACOBSON I loved the ivied cloisters. *New Yorker* An ivied golf club might set a new member back . . ten thousand dollars.

-ivity /ˈɪvɪti/ *suff.* [f. -IVE + -ITY.] Forming ns. f. adjs. in *-ive* expressing a state or condition, as *captivity*, *sensivity*, etc., an instance of this, as *activity*, *festivity*, etc., or a quantity measuring the degree of a condition, as *conductivity* etc.

-ivore *suff.* see -VORE.

Ivorian /ʌɪˈvɔːrɪən/ *a.* & *n.* M20. [f. IVORY + -IAN, after Fr. *ivoirien*.] **A** *adj.* Of or pertaining to the Ivory Coast, a republic (formerly a French protectorate) on the Gulf of Guinea in W. Africa. M20. **B** *n.* A native or inhabitant of the Ivory Coast; *spec.* a member of any of the indigenous peoples, as opp. to one of French descent. L20.

ivoride /ˈʌɪvərʌɪd/ *n.* & *a.* L19. [f. IVORY + -IDE.] (Made of) a kind of artificial ivory.

OED Table-knives with ivoride handles.

ivoried /ˈʌɪvərɪd/ *a.* ME. [f. IVORY + -ED[2].] Made of ivory; made like ivory; provided or adorned with ivory.

Nineteenth Century On thy bare and ivoried shoulder. W. DE LA MARE Tipped arrow, ivoried bow, and rain-soaked quiver.

ivorine /ˈʌɪvəriːn, -ʌɪn/ *n.* L19. [f. IVORY + -INE[4].] (Proprietary name for) any of various products, either imitating ivory or (as cosmetics, dentifrices, etc.) producing a colour or smoothness resembling that of ivory.

ivorine /ˈʌɪvəriːn, -ʌɪn/ *a. rare.* LME. [f. IVORY + -INE[1].] †**1** Consisting or made of ivory. Only in LME. **2** White and smooth like ivory. L19.

-ivorous *suff.* see -VOROUS.

ivory /ˈʌɪv(ə)ri/ *n.* & *a.* ME. [OFr. *yvoire* f. Proto-Romance, f. L *ebor-*, *ebur* ivory, rel. to Egyptian *āb*, *ābu*, Coptic *ebou*, *ebu* elephant.] **A** *n.* **1 a** The very hard, white, elastic, fine-grained dentine composing the main part of the tusks of the elephant, mammoth, hippopotamus, walrus, and narwhal, highly valued as a material for articles of use or ornament. ME. **b** A tusk or tooth made of this. L19. **2** The colour of ivory; ivory white. L16. **3** A substance resembling ivory, or made in imitation of it. M18. **4** *collect. sing.* & in *pl.* The teeth. *slang.* L18. **5** *collect. sing.* & in *pl.* The keys of a piano or similar instrument. *colloq.* E19. **6** Any of various objects formerly made of ivory, as †(*a*) a season ticket; (*b*) (*collect. sing.* & in *pl.*) dice; (*c*) in *pl.*, billiard-balls. *colloq.* or *slang.* M19. **7** An ornament, carving, etc., made of ivory. L19.

2 *Daily News* Nearly all recent brides have worn ivory. 4 *Guardian* I gets his head in a leg scissors and he sinks his ivories into my thigh. 5 THACKERAY It's a wonder how any fingers can move over the jingling ivory so quickly as Miss Cann's. B. MASON A piano with peeling ivories. 7 W. MASKELL The famous Assyrian ivories . . preserved in the British Museum.

Phrases: †**black ivory** *slang* Black African slaves as a commodity. **fossil ivory**: obtained from the tusks of mammoths. **tickle** or **tinkle the ivories** *colloq.* play the piano. **vegetable ivory** the hard albumen of the nut or seed of certain palms, esp. the tropical American *Phytelephas macrocarpa*, which resembles ivory in hardness, colour, and texture, and is used for ornamental work, buttons, etc.

B *adj.* **1** Made or consisting of ivory. LME. **2** Resembling ivory; of the colour or texture of ivory. L16.

1 A. S. BYATT Little butter knives with blunt ends and ivory handles. 2 OUIDA She turned her ivory shoulder on him. A. MUNRO Beryl was dressed up in a satiny ivory dress.

Comb. & *special collocations*: **ivory-bill** a rare N. American woodpecker, *Campephilus principalis*; **ivory-billed** *a.* having a bill resembling ivory; *ivory-billed woodpecker* = *ivory-bill* above; **ivory black** a black pigment from calcined ivory; **ivory board** a kind of pasteboard with both surfaces smooth; **ivory gull** an all-white circumpolar gull, *Pagophila eburnea*; **ivory-nut** the seed of *Phytelephas macrocarpa*, the albumen of which hardens into vegetable ivory; **ivory(-nut) palm** any of various tropical American palms of the genus *Phytelephas*, or Micronesian ones of the genus *Metroxylon*, which bear nuts yielding vegetable ivory; **ivory-paper** art paper or thin card with a polished surface; **ivory plum** *US* (the fruit of) the checkerberry, *Gaultheria procumbens*, or its ally the creeping snowberry, *G. hispidula*; **ivory tower** a state of seclusion from the ordinary world and protection from the harsh realities of life; **ivorytype** *Photogr.* a hand-coloured print produced by various processes, intended to resemble a painting on ivory; **ivory-white** *n.* & *a.* (of) the colour of ivory; **ivorywood** the Australian tree *Siphonodon australe* (family Siphonodontaceae), or its timber, which is used for drawing instruments etc.

ivory-like *a.* resembling (that of) ivory M19.

ivy /ˈʌɪvi/ *n.* [OE *īfiġ*, rel. to OHG *ebah* (G dial. *Efa(i)*, *Ewich*) and the first elem. of MLG *iflōf*, *iwlōf*, LG, Du. *eilof* (with LEAF *n.*[1]), MHG *ebehöu*, *ephöu*, G *Efeu* (with HAY *n.*[1]).] **1** An evergreen woody climber, *Hedera helix* (family Araliaceae), covering old walls, tree-trunks, shady banks, etc., of which the western European form has dark green shining leaves, palmately lobed on the non-flowering shoots, and umbels of greenish-yellow flowers, succeeded by dark berries. Also (usu. w. specifying wd), any plant of the genus *Hedera*. OE. †**b** [With ref. to the ivy's having formerly been sacred to Bacchus.] Ivy used outside a building as a sign that wine was sold inside. Cf. *ivy-bush*, *ivy-garland* below. LME–E17. **c** = *poison ivy* s.v. POISON *n.*, *a.*, & *adv. US.* L18. **2** With specifying wd. Any of various (usu. climbing or creeping) plants of other genera. LME.

2 *Boston ivy*: see BOSTON *n.* 5. *German ivy*: see GERMAN *n.*[1] & *a.*[1] *ground ivy*: see GROUND *n.* KENILWORTH IVY. SWEDISH *ivy*.

Comb.: **ivy-berry** *US* the wintergreen, *Gaultheria procumbens*; **ivy-bush** a bushy branch of ivy; formerly, (a representation of) such a branch displayed outside an inn as a sign that wine was sold there; **ivy-garland** a garland of ivy, formerly the sign of a house where wine was sold; **ivy geranium** a pelargonium with five-angled leaves, *Pelargonium peltatum*; **ivy-leaf** (*a*) a leaf of ivy; †(*b*) *fig.* a thing of little value, a trifle; **Ivy League** a group of long-established eastern US universities of high academic and social prestige; **Ivy Leaguer** a (former) member of one of the universities of the Ivy League; **ivy-leaved** *a.* having palmately lobed leaves like those of the ivy; *ivy-leaved bellflower*, a creeping plant of the bellflower family, *Wahlenbergia hederacea*, bearing nodding blue flowers and found in boggy places in western Europe; *ivy-leaved speedwell*, a Eurasian speedwell of cultivated ground, *Veronica hederifolia*; *ivy-leaved toadflax*, a trailing plant of the figwort family, *Cymbalaria muralis*, with mauve and yellow flowers, native on rocky ground in southern Europe and widely naturalized on old walls; **ivy-tod** *arch.* an ivy-bush; **ivy tree** (*a*) *NZ* any of several evergreen trees of the genus *Neopanax*, related to the ivy; (*b*) *N. Amer.* mountain laurel, *Kalmia latifolia*.

ivy /ˈʌɪvi/ *v.t.* M19. [f. the n., or back-form. f. IVIED.] Cover with or as with ivy.

ivyed *a.* var. of IVIED.

iwis /ɪˈwɪs/ *a.*, *n.*, & *adv.* Long *arch.* Also **ywis**. [OE *ġewis* = OHG *giwiss* (G *gewiss*) f. Gmc, f. base also of WISE *a.*, WIT *v.* Cf. WIS *v.*[1], *v.*[2]] †**A** *adj.* Certain. Only in OE. †**B** *n.* Certainty: in *mid iwis*, [MID *prep.*[1]] with certainty, certainly. OE–ME. **C** *adv.* Certainly, assuredly, indeed, truly. ME.

¶In later use freq. written *I wis* and taken erron. as = *I wot* (I know), as if from WIT *v.*: see also WIS *v.*[2]

ixia /ˈɪksɪə/ *n.* M16. [L f. Gk.] †**1** = CHAMELEON 2. M16–E17. **2** *Bot.* Any of various southern African plants of the genus *Ixia*, of the iris family, with large showy flowers of various colours. Also called *corn lily*. L18.

Ixionian /ɪksɪˈəʊnɪən/ *a.* L17. [f. *Ixion* (see below) + -IAN.] Of or pertaining to Ixion, in Greek mythology a king of Thessaly punished by being bound to an eternally revolving wheel in Hades.

Ixionian wheel endless torment.

ixodid /ɪkˈsəʊdɪd/ *n.* & *a.* E20. [mod.L *Ixodidae* (see below), f. *Ixodes* genus name, f. Gk *ixōdēs* sticky.] **A** *n.* Pl. **-ids**, **-ides** /-ɪdiːz/. A tick of the family Ixodidae. E20. **B** *attrib.* or as *adj.* Designating or pertaining to a tick of the family Ixodidae. E20.

ixora /ɪkˈsɔːrə/ *n.* E19. [mod.L (see below), f. Port. *Iswara* f. Skt *īśvara* lord, master, epithet of Hindu deities, the flowers of certain species being used as votive offerings.] Any of various evergreen shrubs or small trees of the genus *Ixora*, of the madder family, mostly native to tropical Africa and Asia, which bear compact corymbs of white or brightly coloured flowers.

Iyyar /ˈiːjɑː/ *n.* M18. [Heb. *ʾiyyār*.] In the Jewish calendar, the eighth month of the civil and second of the religious year, usu. coinciding with parts of April and May. Formerly called *Ziv*.

izar /ɪˈzɑː/ *n.* M19. [Arab. *ʾizār*.] An enveloping outer garment worn by Muslim women (and, in some countries, Muslim men). Also, the lower garment of the *ihram*.

izard /ˈɪzəd/ *n.* L18. [Fr. *isard*, Gascon *isart*, perh. of Iberian origin.] The Pyrenean variety of the chamois.

Izarra /iːˈzɑːrə/ *n.* Also **Izzara**. E20. [Basque, lit. 'star'.] A brandy-based liqueur from the Pyrenees, flavoured with herbs.

-ization /ʌɪˈzeɪʃ(ə)n/ *suff.* Also **-isation**. [f. or after Fr. *-isation* (It. *-izzazione*, Sp. *-ización*): see -IZE, -ATION.] Forming nouns of action from vbs in -IZE, or by analogy where no vb exists, as *metrization*.

izba *n.* var. of ISBA.

-ize /ʌɪz/ *suff.* Also **-ise**. [f. or after Fr. *-iser* (It. *-izzare*, Sp. *-izar*) f. late L *-izare*, f. Gk *-izein*.] **1** Forming trans. vbs w. the sense 'make or treat in a specified way', as *anatomize*, *characterize*, *idolize*, *tantalize*, etc. **2** Forming intrans. vbs w. the sense 'do in a specified way, follow a specified practice', as *agonize*, *apologize*, *botanize*, *sympathize*, *theorize*, etc. **3** Forming trans. and intrans. vbs w. the sense 'bring or come into some specified state', as *authorize*, *extemporize*, *fertilize*, *fossilize*, *jeopardize*, *moralize*, *pedestrianize*, *temporize*, etc. **4** Forming trans. and intrans. vbs from ethnic adjs. w. the sense 'make or become like the country, people, language, etc. in character, naturalize as', as *Americanize*, *Anglicize*, *Gallicize*, *Latinize*, *Russianize*, etc. **5** Forming trans. and intrans. vbs from personal names, w. the sense 'treat or act like or according to the method of', as *bowdlerize*, *galvanize*, *mesmerize*, etc. **6** Forming trans. vbs from names of substances, w. the sense 'impregnate, treat, combine, affect, or influence with', as *alkalize*, *carbonize*, *oxidize*, etc.

-izer /ˈʌɪzə/ *suff.* Also **-iser**. [f. as -IZE + -ER[1].] Forming agent-ns. from vbs in -IZE.

izimbongi *n.pl.* see IMBONGI.

izle *n.* var. of ISEL.

Izod /ˈʌɪzɒd/ *n.* Also **i-**. E20. [E. G. *Izod* (fl. 1903), Brit. engineer, who devised the test.] Used *attrib.* with ref. to an impact test (*Izod test*) in which a notched specimen is broken by a blow from a pendulum, the energy absorbed (*Izod value*) being determined from the decrease in the swing of the pendulum.

Izzara *n.* var. of IZARRA.

izzard /ˈɪzəd/ *n. arch.* & *dial.* M18. [Alt. of ZED.] The letter Z.

izzat /ˈɪzʌt/ *n.* Also **izzut**. M19. [Pers., Urdu *ʿizzat*, f. Arab. *ʿizza* glory.] Honour, reputation, credit, prestige.

E. M. FORSTER Trying to increase his izzat—in plain Anglo-Saxon, to score.

J

J, j /dʒeɪ/, the tenth letter of the modern Eng. alphabet, orig. a modification of the letter I. From the 11th to the 17th cent. the letter I, i represented both the vowel sound of *i*, and the sound /dʒ/. To keep the inconspicuous small ı distinct various scribal expedients were used: an initial ı was often prolonged above or below the line, or both; a final ı was generally prolonged below the line; and in both cases the tail in cursive writing at length became a curve. The 'dot' was also used with the tailed form, giving rise to the mod. letter j. This was at first merely a final form of i, used in Latin in such forms as 'filij', and in roman numerals, as j, ij, iij, vj, viij, xij. In the 17th cent. the two forms of the letter came to be differentiated, i remaining for the vowel and j being used for the consonant, with the capital form of the latter, J, being introduced. The sound normally represented by the letter in Eng. is the palato-alveolar affricate /dʒ/. In certain words, esp. in proper names or alien terms from Ger. and other languages, j retains the Roman value /j/. In a few Fr. words, distinctly recognized as alien, j retains the Fr. sound /ʒ/. In the transliteration of oriental names j is used with its Eng. value. Pl. **J's, Js.**

I 1 The letter and its sound. 2 The shape of the letter.

2 **J-curve** *Statistics* a J-shaped graph or distribution. **J-shaped** *a.* having a shape or a cross-section like the capital letter J (without a right-angled crosspiece).

II Symbolical uses. 3 Used to denote serial order; applied e.g. to the tenth group or section, sheet of a book, etc. Formerly *rare* (the old order of the Roman alphabet, H, I, K, being retained). 4 Used to replace the roman numeral i in final position, as in j, ij, vj, etc. Now *rare.* 5 *Physics.* a [Abbrev. of JOULE.] The mechanical equivalent of heat. b Quantized angular momentum, *esp.* the total angular momentum of an electron (*j*) or assemblage of electrons (*J*). 6 *Electr.* (Italic *j.*) a Electric current. b The imaginary quantity $\sqrt{-1}$, the square root of minus one. Cf. I, I 7.

3 **J acid** *Chem.* 2-amino-5-naphthol-7-sulphonic acid, $C_{10}H_9NO_4S$, an intermediate in the production of azo dyes by coupling reactions. **JK flip-flop** *Electronics* a flip-flop with two inputs and two outputs which changes to the complementary state when both triggering pulses are one.

III 7 Abbrevs.: (A small selection only is given here. Those all in caps. or small caps. also occur with full stops after each letter; some of those all in caps. also occur (i) with initial cap. only, (ii) in small caps.) **J** = joule(s). **JA** = Judge Advocate; Justice of Appeal. **Jam.** = Jamaica; James (New Testament). **Jan.** = January. **Jas.** = James (also in New Testament). **JATO** /ˈdʒeɪtəʊ/ = jet-assisted take-off. **JCL** (*Computing*) = job-control language. **JCR** = Junior Common (or Combination) Room. **Jer.** = Jeremiah (Old Testament). **JFET** (*Electronics*) = junction field-effect transistor. **JG** = junior grade (esp. of naval rank). **JICTAR** /ˈdʒɪktɑː/ = Joint Industry Committee for Television Advertising Research. **j.n.d.** (*Sci.*) = just noticeable difference. **Jnr.** = junior. **Jon.** = Jonah (in the Bible). **Jos.** = Joseph. **Josh.** = Joshua (in the Bible). **JP** = Justice of the Peace. **Jr.** = Junior. **jt.** = joint. **Jud.** = Judith (Apocrypha). **Judg.** = Judges (in the Bible). **Jul.** = July. **Jun.** = June; Junior. **Junr.** = Junior. **Jy** (*Astron.*) = jansky.

jab /dʒab/ *v.* & *n.* *colloq.* E19. [Var., orig. Sc., of JOB *v.*[1]] A *v.* Infl. **-bb-**. 1 *v.t.* Pierce or poke with the end or point of something; stab. E19. b Give (a person) a quick short blow with the fist, hit with a straight punch. E20. 2 *v.t.* Thrust (something) with a quick sharp blow (*in, into*). E19. 3 *v.i.* Stab a person or thing; throw quick short punches. E19. 4 *v.t.* & *i.* Inject or inoculate (a person, a vein) with a hypodermic needle. M20.

1 B. BAINBRIDGE A broken bough . . jabbed Adolf in the ribs. 2 I. MCEWAN He kept talking, jabbing his forefinger in the air. 3 H. BASCOM The combatants circle each other, feinting and jabbing.

B *n.* 1 An act of jabbing; a quick short blow with something pointed, or with the fist; a straight punch. L19. 2 A hypodermic injection, *esp.* a vaccination. *colloq.* E20. 3 A radio signal of momentary duration. M20.

1 *fig.*: E. AMADI He winced with . . a particularly searing jab of pain. 2 *Holiday Which?* Typhoid and polio jabs are recommended by the DHSS for all the islands.

jabber /ˈdʒabə/ *v.* & *n.* L15. [Imit.: cf. GABBER *v.*, JABBLE *v.*[1], JAVVER.] A *v.* 1 *v.i.* Talk rapidly and indistinctly; speak fluently but with little sense; chatter, gabble, prattle; *contempt.* talk in a language the hearer does not understand. L15. b Utter inarticulate sounds rapidly and volubly; chatter like a monkey, bird, etc. E19. 2 *v.t.* Utter or say rapidly and indistinctly; express by jabbering; *contempt.* speak (a language) without being understood. M16.

1 H. ALLEN She jabbered at him in a dialect he could not understand. W. STYRON I began jabbering at Sophie with brainless unrestraint. *New Yorker* Friends would come over . . to jabber and gossip about all the excitement. 2 HUGH MILLER Poor idiot, . . come every day to the churchyard, to . . jabber in broken expressions his grief.

B *n.* The action of jabbering; rapid and indistinct or unintelligible talk; gabble, chatter; gibberish. E18.

jabberer *n.* L17.

jabbers /ˈdʒabəz/ *n.* Also **jabers** /ˈdʒeɪbəz/. E19. [Alt. of *Jesus*: cf. BEJABERS.] Jesus: chiefly as int., expr. amazement or emphasis.

jabberwocky /ˈdʒabəwɒki/ *a.* & *n.* E20. [Title of a poem in Lewis Carroll's *Through the Looking-Glass.*] A *adj.* Nonsensical, meaningless; reversed in order. E20. B *n.* Invented or meaningless language; nonsensical behaviour. Also, a piece of nonsensical writing or speech, esp. for comic effect. E20.

jabble /ˈdʒab(ə)l/ *n.* Chiefly *Sc.* L18. [f. JABBLE *v.*[2]] A slight agitated movement of water etc.; a splashing in small waves or ripples.

jabble /ˈdʒab(ə)l/ *v.*[1]*t.* & *i.* L16. [Imit.: cf. GABBLE *v.*, JABBER *v.*] = JABBER *v.*

jabble /ˈdʒab(ə)l/ *v.*[2] *Sc.* M18. [App. imit.: see -LE[3].] 1 *v.t.* Shake up or agitate (esp. a liquid); cause to splash. M18. 2 *v.i.* Splash in small waves or ripples. E19.

jabers *n.* var. of JABBERS.

jabiru /ˈdʒabɪruː/ *n.* L18. [Tupi-Guarani *jabirú*, f. *j* (demonstr.) that which has + *abirú* swollen (w. ref. to the large neck of the jabiru (sense 1)): cf. Port. *jaburu.*] 1 A large white stork, *Ephippiorhynchus mycteria*, of tropical and subtropical America. Also *jabiru stork.* L18. 2 Either of two other storks of the genus *Ephippiorhynchus*, (*a*) the black-necked stork, *E. asiaticus*, of SE Asia and Australia, and (*b*) the saddlebill stork, *E. senegalensis*, of Africa. L18.

jaborandi /dʒabəˈrandi/ *n.* Also (earlier) †**jaburandiba.** E17. [Port. f. Tupi-Guarani *jaburandi* lit. 'a person who makes saliva, one who spits'; also *jaburandiba* (*iba* plant, tree).] A drug made from the dried leaves of any of several S. American plants of the genus *Pilocarpus*, of the rue family, which contain the alkaloid pilocarpine and promote salivation when chewed. Also, any of these plants or other S. American plants with similar properties.

jabot /ˈʒabəʊ/ *n.* Pl. pronounced same. E19. [Fr. = bird's crop, shirt-frill, prob. f. a Proto-Romance base meaning 'crop, maw, gullet'.] 1 A frill on the front of a man's shirt, edging the opening. Now chiefly *Hist.* E19. 2 An ornamental frill on a woman's bodice. L19.

jaboticaba /ˌdʒabɒtɪˈkɑːbə/ *n.* Also **-but-.** E17. [Port. f. Tupi *iauotiʔkaua.*] A Brazilian evergreen tree, *Myrciaria cauliflora*, of the myrtle family, which bears clusters of white flowers and purple fruits directly on the trunk and branches. Also, the fruit of this tree.

†**jaburandiba** *n.* see JABORANDI.

jacal /həˈkɑːl/ *n.* M19. [Mex. Sp. f. Nahuatl *xacalli* contr. of *xamitl calli* adobe house.] A hut built of erect stakes filled in with wattle and mud, common in Mexico and the south-western US; an adobe house. Also, the material or method used in building such a hut.

jacamar /ˈdʒakəmɑː/ *n.* E19. [Fr., app. f. Tupi.] Any of various small insectivorous birds of tropical S. America of the family Galbulidae, with partly iridescent plumage.

jacana /ˈdʒakənə/ *n.* Also **jaçana** /dʒasəˈnɑː/. M18. [Port. *jaçanã* f. Tupi-Guarani *jasanã.*] Any of various small tropical wading birds of the family Jacanidae, which have greatly elongated toes and claws, enabling them to walk on floating vegetation.

wattled jacana: see WATTLED 2.

jacaranda /dʒakəˈrandə/ *n.* M18. [Port. f. Tupi-Guarani *jakaraʼna.*] 1 Any of various tropical American trees with fragrant and ornamental wood. Now chiefly, any tree of the genus *Jacaranda* (family Bignoniaceae), with showy tubular blue or purple flowers and usu. pinnate leaves; esp. *J. mimosifolia*, native to Brazil, much grown as a street tree in warm climates. M18. 2 The wood of any of these trees. M19.

jacent /ˈdʒeɪs(ə)nt/ *a.* Long *rare.* M16. [L *jacent-* pres. ppl stem of *jacere* lie: see -ENT.] Lying, recumbent; *fig.* sluggish.

jacinth /ˈdʒasɪnθ, ˈdʒeɪ-/ *n.* & *a.* ME. [OFr. *iacinte* (mod. *jacinthe*) or med.L *iacintus*, alt. of L *hyacinthus* HYACINTH.] A *n.* 1 A kind of precious stone; = HYACINTH 1. ME. b The colour of jacinth, blue or occas. reddish orange; *Her.* the colour tenné, reddish orange, in blazoning by precious stones. LME. †2 A dyed fabric of a blue or violet colour. Only in LME. 3 = HYACINTH 2, 3. Now *rare.* M16. 4 = HYACINTH 4. M19. B *attrib.* or as *adj.* Of the colour of jacinth. E16.

jacitara /dʒasɪˈtɑːrə/ *n.* M19. [Port. f. Tupi *yasitara.*] In full *jacitara palm.* Any of various tropical American prickly climbing palms of the genus *Desmoncus*, esp. *D. orthacanthos*, native to the Amazon region.

Jack /dʒak/ *n.*[1] Also **j-.** Pl. **-s**, (in sense 22, also) same. LME. [Pet-form of male forename *John*, perh. through dim. *Jankin*; the resemblance to Fr. *Jacques* (f. Proto-Romance f. L *Jacobus* JACOB) is unexpl.] I (A figure of) a man. 1a (A name for) a (male) representative of the common people, (a name for) an ordinary man. LME. b A lad, a chap; *esp.* an ill-mannered man, a knave. *obs.* exc. *dial.* M16. c Used as a form of address to an unknown person. *colloq.* (orig. *US*). L19. 2 A figure of a man which strikes the bell on the outside of a clock. Also *jack of the clock.* Cf. branch II below. L15. 3a A sailor. Now more fully *Jack tar.* M17. b A serving-man; a labourer; an odd-job man. E18. c A lumberjack. *N. Amer. colloq.* L19. d A (military) policeman; a detective. Cf. JOHN 3. *slang.* L19. 4 *Cards.* Orig., the knave of trumps in the game of all fours. Later (formerly considered *slang*), any of the lowest court-cards bearing the representation of a male youth, a knave. L17.

1a J. WAINWRIGHT He had that world-weary look of the working jack who'd seen everything. 2 *quarter-jack*. 4 *Field* His partner had an equally important card—the jack of diamonds.

II A thing which saves human labour; a device, a tool. **5** A machine for turning the spit when roasting meat, either wound up like a clock or operated by the current of heated air up a chimney. Also *roasting-jack*. LME. **6** Any of various contrivances consisting (solely or essentially) of a roller or winch. LME. **7** A frame on which to saw wood. L16. **8** A part of the mechanism in a spinet, harpsichord, etc., connecting a key to its corresponding string, and causing the string to be plucked when the key is pressed down; a key of a spinet etc. L16. **9** A bootjack. Now *rare* or *obs.* L17. **10** A device, usually portable, for lifting or moving heavy objects by a force acting from below; *spec.* one placed under a vehicle to raise it off the ground so that a wheel can be changed or the underneath examined. E18. **11 a** An oscillating lever, such as those in a stocking-frame or knitting-machine. M18. **b** *Spinning & Weaving.* = HECK *n.*[1] 6. M19. **12 a** *Hist.* A counter made to resemble a sovereign. M19. **b** Money. *slang* (orig. *US*). L19. **c** *sing.* & (occas.) in *pl.* Five pounds; a five-pound note. Also *Jack's alive*. *slang.* M20. **13** *Electr.* More fully *jack-socket*. A socket with two or more pairs of terminals, for the rapid introduction of a device into a circuit by means of a suitable plug. L19.

10 *Rally Sport* They then had to change two punctures, during which the car fell off the jack. 12b J. DOS PASSOS I thought I better come up here and see the folks before I spent all my jack.

III A thing of smaller than normal size. †**14** A very small amount; the least bit; a whit. Only in M16. **15 a** *Bowls.* A smaller bowl placed as a mark for the players to aim at. Also (now *rare*) *jack-bowl*. E17. **b** In *pl.* & (occas.) *sing.*, a game played by tossing and catching small round pebbles or star-shaped pieces of metal; *sing.* a pebble or piece of metal used for this. Also more fully *jackstone(s)*. Cf. DIBS *n.*[1] E19. **16** *Building.* A small brick used as a closer at the end of a course. Long *rare* or *obs.* E18. **17** A quarter of a pint; an imperial gill. *dial.* M18. **18** *Naut.* Either of a pair of iron bars at the head of the topgallant mast, supporting the royal and sky-sail masts. Also *jack cross-tree*. M19. **19** A portable cresset or fire-basket used in hunting or fishing at night. *US.* M19. **20** A small schooner-rigged vessel used in the Newfoundland fisheries. Also *jack boat*. M19. **21** A tablet of heroin. *slang.* M20.

IV In names of animals. **22 a** Orig., a pike, *Esox lucius*, esp. when young or small. Now also, any of various similar fishes, as the pike-perch. Also *jack-fish*. L16. **b** Any of numerous marine fishes of the family Carangidae, many of which are used as food. Also *jack-fish*. Cf. SCAD *n.*[2] Orig. *W. Indies*. L17. **23** The male of various animals; *spec.* (*a*) a male hawk, *esp.* a male merlin (in full †*jack-merlin*; (*b*) *US* a male ass, *esp.* one kept for breeding mules (= JACKASS 1). E17. **24 a** = *jacksnipe* below. L19. **b** A laughing jackass, a kookaburra. Cf. JACKO, JACKY 4. *Austral.* L19. **c** = JACKRABBIT. L19.

Phrases & comb.: *a roll Jack Rice couldn't jump over*: see ROLL *n.*[1] **before one can say Jack Robinson** very quickly or suddenly. **California jack** a card-game resembling all fours. *Cousin Jack*: see COUSIN *n.* **every man jack** colloq. each and every person. *goggle-eye Jack*: see GOGGLE-EYE 2(b). **I'm all right, Jack** *colloq.*: expr. selfish complacency. **Jack-a-Lent** *arch.* (*a*) *rare* a character in a mummers' play; (*b*) a figure of a man, set up to be pelted, in a game played during Lent; (*c*) a contemptible or insignificant person or thing; (*d*) a puppet. **Jack and Jill** boy and girl, man and woman. **Jack ashore** *n.* & *a. phr.* (*slang*) (the condition or state of being) excited, elated, etc. **jack bean** a subtropical climbing leguminous plant of the genus *Canavalia*, esp. *C. ensiformis*. **jack-block** *Naut.* a large wooden block used to raise and lower a topgallant mast. *jack boat*: see sense 20 above. *jack-bowl*: see sense 15a above. †**jack-boy** a boy employed in menial work; *spec.* a stable-boy, a groom, a postillion. **jack-by-the-hedge** garlic-mustard, *Alliaria petiolata*. *jack cross-tree*: see sense 18 above. **jack curlew** a whimbrel, *Numenius phaeopus*. *jack-fish*: see sense 22 above. **jack-fishing** (*a*) fishing for jack; (*b*) *US* fishing at night by means of a jack or cresset. *Jack Frost*: see FROST *n.* **Jack-go-to-bed-at-noon** the yellow goat's-beard, *Tragopogon pratensis*, whose flowers close about midday. **jackhammer** a portable rock-drill worked by compressed air. **jack-hunting** *US* hunting by means of a jack-light. **jack-in-a-bottle** *dial.* a long-tailed tit (from the shape of its nest). **Jack-in-office** a self-important minor official. **Jack in the basket** *Naut.* a kind of warning beacon. **Jack-in-the-bush** (*a*) *local* = GARLIC-*mustard*; (*b*) = *Jack-in-the-green* (a) below. **Jack-in-the-green** (*a*) a man or boy enclosed in a pyramid of wood or wicker and leaves as part of May-Day celebrations; (*b*) a variety of the primrose in which the calyx is transformed into leaves. **jack-in-the-hedge** = *jack-by-the-hedge* above. **Jack-in-the-pulpit** any of various plants of the arum family with an erect spadix overarched by the enfolding spathe, *esp.* (*a*) *dial.* cuckoo-pint, *Arum maculatum*; (*b*) *N. Amer.* any of several woodland plants of the genus *Arisaema*. **Jack-jump-about** *dial.* any of several spreading plants, *esp.* ground elder, *Aegopodium podagraria*. **Jack Ketch** [an executioner, 1663–86] *Hist.* an executioner, a hangman. **jack-ladder** *Naut.* (*a*) = JACOB'S LADDER 2; (*b*) = JACK-CHAIN 2. **jack-light** *US* a light carried in a jack or cresset for hunting or fishing at night. **jack mackerel** a carangid game-fish, *Trachurus symmetricus*, of the eastern Pacific. *jack-merlin*: see sense 23(a) above. **Jack Mormon** *US* (*a*) a non-Mormon on friendly terms with Mormons; (*b*) a nominal or backsliding Mormon. *Jack Napes*: see JACKANAPES. **jack oak** = *black jack*, *blackjack* (d) s.v. BLACK *a.* **jack of all trades** a person who can do many different kinds of work. **Jack of both sides** (now *rare*) a person who shifts his or her support. *jack of the clock*: see sense 2 above. †**jack out of office** a person who has been dismissed from office, or whose official role has gone. **jack-pin** *Naut.* a belaying-pin. **jack-pine** a small N. American pine, *Pinus banksiana*, with short needles. **jack plane** a long heavy plane used for rough work. **jack plug** *Electr.*: for use with a jack(-socket). **jack-pudding** a buffoon, a clown. **jack-roll** *n.* & *v.* (*a*) *n.* a winch or windlass turned directly by handles; (*b*) *v.t.* steal from (a drunken person). *Jack's alive*: see sense 12c above. **jack salmon** *US* the pike-perch, *Stizostedion vitreum*. †**Jack-sauce** a saucy or impudent fellow. **jack-screw** a jack (see sense 10 above) having a rack and a pinion wheel or screw and a handle turned by hand, used esp. to move heavy cargo in a ship's hold. **jack shaft** *Engin.* any of various kinds of auxiliary or intermediate shaft driven by another shaft or by a set of gears. **jack-sharp** *north.* a stickleback. †**jacksmith** a maker of roasting-jacks. **jacksnipe** a small dark snipe, *Lymnocryptes minimus*; any of various similar birds, *esp.* (*US*) the pectoral sandpiper. *jack-socket*: see sense 13 above. **jack-spaniard** a large Caribbean wasp of the genus *Polistes*. **jackstay** *Naut.* (*a*) a rope, metal bar, or batten placed along a yard to bend the head of a square sail to; (*b*) a line secured at both ends to serve as a support for an awning etc. *jackstone*: see sense 15b above. *Jack tar*: see sense 3a above. **Jack-the-Lad** [nickname of Jack Sheppard, an 18th-cent. thief] (*a*) a young troublemaker; (*b*) a working-class hero; (*c*) a wanted criminal. *Jack the Ripper*: see RIPPER 1b. **jack-towel** a roller towel. †**jack-weight**: forming part of the mechanism in an early form of the roasting-jack. *lazy-jack*: see LAZY *a.* **on one's Jack (Jones)** *slang* alone. **play the jack** play the knave, do a mean trick. THREE-*cornered jack*. *yellow jack*: see YELLOW *a.* See also JACK-A-DANDY, JACK-O'-LANTERN, JACKRABBIT, etc.

jack /dʒak/ *n.*[2] *arch.* LME. [(O)Fr. *jaque*, perh. immed. f. Sp., Port. *jaco*, perh. f. Arab.] **1** A sleeveless tunic or jacket, usu. of quilted leather and later freq. plated with iron for protection in battle; a coat of mail. In early use also, any jacket. LME. **2** A vessel for holding liquor or for drinking from, usu. of waxed leather coated outside with tar or pitch (cf. *black jack* s.v. BLACK *a.*); a (leather) jug or tankard. L16.

jack /dʒak/ *n.*[3] Also **jak**. L16. [Port. *jaca* f. Malayalam *chakka*.] A tree of tropical Asia, *Artocarpus heterophyllus*, related to the breadfruit, but with a larger and coarser fruit; the fruit of this tree.

jack /dʒak/ *n.*[4] M17. [Prob. a use of JACK *n.*[1], as if short for 'jack flag', i.e. a small flag (as distinguished from the ensign).] A small version of a national flag flown at the bow of a vessel in harbour to indicate its nationality. See also *Union Jack* s.v. UNION *n.*[2]

Comb.: **jackstaff** (*a*) a short staff, usu. set at the bow of a ship, on which a jack is hoisted; (*b*) a staff carrying the flag that is to show above the masthead.

†**Jack** *n.*[5] *colloq.* L17–M18. [Abbrev.] = JACOBITE *n.*[2]

jack /dʒak/ *a.* *Austral. slang.* E20. [f. JACK *v.*] Tired *of* something or someone; bored.

jack /dʒak/ *v.* M19. [f. JACK *n.*[1]] **1** *v.i.* Hunt or fish at night with a jack (JACK *n.*[1] 19). *US.* M19. **2** *v.t.* Foll. by *up*: a Lift up with a jack (JACK *n.*[1] 10). M19. **b** Increase; force or bolster up. *colloq.* E20. **c** Arrange, organize. *NZ slang.* M20. **3 a** *v.t.* Ruin; abandon. Usu. foll. by *up*. M19. **b** *v.i.* Give *up* suddenly or promptly. *colloq.* M19. **4** *v.t.* Foll. by *in*: abandon, leave; give up, stop. M20. **5** *v.i.* Foll. by *off*: a Go away, depart. M20. **b** Masturbate. *slang.* M20.

2a *Practical Motorist* In order to lift the car high enough . . we had to jack up the body. b A. TYLER Her son's an old skinflint. Always wanting to jack up the price. c D. M. DAVIN There'll be some cold meat in the safe. . . I'll jack up a feed. 4 B. TRAPIDO She jacked in Oxford after knowing Jacob . . and went to live with him instead.

jacker *n.* L19.

jack-a-dandy /dʒakəˈdandi/ *n.* M17. [f. JACK *n.*[1] + *dandy*: see DANDY *n.*[2]] A pert or conceited man; a dandy.

jackal /ˈdʒakɔːl, -k(ə)l/ *n.* & *v.* E17. [f. (w. assim. to JACK *n.*[1]) Turk. *çakal* f. Pers. *šagāl* rel. to Skt *śrgāla*.] **A** *n.* **1** Any of several wild omnivorous doglike mammals of the genus *Canis*, of Africa and S. Eurasia, which have erect ears and a bushy tail and hunt in packs as foragers; *spec.* (more fully *golden* or *common jackal*) *C. aureus*. E17. **2** *fig.* A person who acts like a jackal, *esp.* one who serves or does subordinate preparatory work or drudgery for another. L17.

1 *saddleback jackal*: see SADDLEBACK *n.* 2. 2 M. C. CLARKE [Richard's] . . ingratitude towards his jackal, Buckingham, who wrought hard to help him to his bad eminence.

B *v.i.* Do subordinate work or drudgery. E20.

Jack-a-lantern *n.* var. of JACK-O'-LANTERN.

jackanapes /ˈdʒakəneɪps/ *n.* Orig. †**Jack Napes**. Pl. same, **-napeses**. E16. [Perh. f. a playful name for a tame ape, with *n-* as in *newt*, *nickname*, etc., and *-s* as in *Hobbs* and other surnames.] **1** A tame ape or monkey. *arch.* E16. **2** A person displaying qualities or behaviour associated with apes; a ridiculous upstart; an impertinent person; *joc.* a pert, forward child. M16.

2 C. KINGSLEY A whiskered Jackanapes, . . set to command grey-headed men before he can command his own temper. T. MO Nor will I be judged by a pair of young jackanapes with . . time on their hands.

jackaroo /dʒakəˈruː/ *n.* & *v.* *Austral. colloq.* Also **-er-**. L19. [f. JACK *n.*[1] + KANG)AROO *n.*] **A** *n.* Orig., a new colonist working to gain experience in the bush. Now, a novice on a sheep-station or cattle-station. L19. **B** *v.i.* Lead the life of a jackaroo; gain experience of bush-farming. L19.

jackass /ˈdʒakas/ *n.* E18. [f. JACK *n.*[1] + ASS *n.*[1]] **1** A male ass or donkey. E18. **2** The kookaburra, *Dacelo novaeguineae*, so called from its loud discordant cry. Also more fully *laughing jackass*. L18. **b** In Tasmania: the grey butcher-bird, *Cracticus torquatus*. L19. **3** A stupid or foolish person; = ASS *n.*[1] 2. *derog.* E19. **4** *Naut.* a A kind of heavy rough boat used in Newfoundland, *esp.* a two-masted vessel with square sails on the mainmast, formerly used in seal hunting. E19. **b** A tapering canvas bag stuffed with oakum etc., used to block the hawse-holes of a seagoing vessel. *US.* L19.

3 I. ASIMOV He's an undiplomatic young jackass.

Comb.: **jackass barque** a ship with the same sails as a barquentine but rigged differently; **jackass brig**: having a square topsail and topgallant-sail instead of a gaff-topsail; **jackass-fish** an Australian marine food fish, *Nemadactylus macropterus*, with an elongated pectoral fin ray; also called *morwong*; **jackass frigate** a small frigate; **jackass penguin** a penguin, *Spheniscus demersus*, with a harsh braying cry; †**jackass-rabbit** = JACKRABBIT; **jackass-rigged** *a.* (of a schooner) having three masts with square sails set on the foremast and having no maintopmast; **jackass schooner** a jackass-rigged schooner.

ja'ckassery *n.* stupidity; a piece of folly: M19.

jackboot /ˈdʒakbuːt/ *n.* Also **jack-boot**. L17. [f. JACK *n.*[1] or JACK *n.*[2] + BOOT *n.*[2]] **1** A large strong leather boot, the top of which covers the knee, worn esp. by cavalry soldiers in the 17th and 18th cents. and by German soldiers under the Nazi regime. L17. **2** *fig.* Military oppression; rough bullying tactics. M18.

1 *Sun* (*Baltimore*) The . . master race types are still swaggering through the streets in their polished jackboots. 2 *Listener* A county about to be obliterated under the casual jack-boot of a boundaries commission.

jackbooted *a.* wearing jackboots M19.

jack-chain /ˈdʒaktʃeɪn/ *n.* M17. [f. JACK *n.*[1] + CHAIN *n.*] **1** A chain of unwelded links each consisting of a double loop of wire resembling a figure of 8, but with the loops in planes at right angles to each other. M17. **2** *Forestry.* A continuous spiked chain used to move logs as if on a conveyor belt. E20.

jackdaw /ˈdʒakdɔː/ *n.* M16. [f. JACK *n.*[1] + DAW *n.*] **1** A small, gregarious, grey and black Eurasian crow, *Corvus monedula*, which often nests in old buildings, and may hoard small objects or food. M16. **2** = *boat-tail* s.v. BOAT *n. US.* E18.

jacked /dʒakt/ *a.* LME. [f. JACK *n.*[2] + -ED[2].] †**1** Wearing a jack (JACK *n.*[2] 1). Only in LME. **2** Hardened and thickened as leather for jackboots. E18.

jackeen /dʒaˈkiːn/ *n. Anglo-Ir.* M19. [Dim. of JACK *n.*[1]: see -EEN[2].] A self-assertive worthless person; *spec.* a city-dweller.

jackeroo *n.* & *v.* var. of JACKAROO.

jacket /ˈdʒakɪt/ *n.* LME. [OFr. *ja(c)quet* dim. of *jaque*: see JACK *n.*[2], -ET[1].] **I 1** An outer garment for the upper part of the body, now usu. with sleeves. Also, a short coat without tails worn in shooting, riding, cycling, etc. LME. **b** A waistcoat. *US.* E18. **c** A jockey's loose-fitting blouse of silk or satin (orig. a jacket) in a racehorse-owner's distinctive colours. M19. **d** A thing worn or fastened round the torso for protection, support, etc. E20. **2** *transf.* With qualifying colour adj.: a person wearing a jacket of the specified colour, esp. as a uniform. E19.

1 C. GEBLER Soldiers in their shirt sleeves, their jackets thrown over their shoulders. *bedjacket, bomber jacket, dinner jacket, Eton jacket, Nehru jacket, reefer jacket, smoking jacket, tuxedo jacket, waxed jacket, Zouave jacket*, etc. *dust a person's jacket*: see DUST *v.* **d** *flak-jacket, life-jacket, strait-jacket*, etc. **2** *bluejacket* etc.

II 3a The natural (usu. hairy) covering or coat of various animals; the skin of a seal, fish, etc. E17. **b** The skin of a cooked potato. M19. **4a** An outer covering or casing, *esp.* one placed round a pipe, a steam-cylinder, a boiler, etc., to insulate or protect it. E19. **b** More fully *dust-jacket*. A protective (and usu. decorative) paper cover placed round a bound book, usu. with the title and author's name printed on it. L19. **c** A folder or envelope containing an official document, and displaying a list of its contents, instructions for its disposition, etc. *US.* L19. **d** *Mil.* A coil or cylinder of wrought iron or steel placed round the barrel of a gun to strengthen or protect it. L19.

3a *Stock & Land* (*Melbourne*) Breeding first cross ewes . . carrying a good jacket of fine wool is the aim. 4a M. FARADAY A jacket of sheet caoutchouc was put over the saddle.

Comb.: **jacket crown** *Dentistry* an artificial crown fitted over a natural crown, which is usually ground down to receive it; **jacket potato** a potato cooked in its skin.

jacketless *a.* M19.

jacket /ˈdʒakɪt/ *v.t.* E19. [f. the n.] **1** Eject (a person) from a rightful place. *slang.* E19. **2** Cover with or enclose in a jacket, esp. a strait-jacket. M19. **3** Beat, thrash. *dial.* & *colloq.* L19.

Jackey *n.* var. of JACKY.

Jack-in-the-box /ˈdʒakɪnðəbɒks/ *n.* Also **Jack-in-a-box** /-ɪnəbɒks/. M16. [f. JACK *n.*[1] + IN *prep.* + THE + BOX *n.*[2]] †**1** *Chr. Ch.* The consecrated host (alluding to its reservation in a pyx). *derog.* Only in M16. †**2** A cheat; *spec.* a thief giving tradesmen empty boxes instead of ones containing payment. L16–E18. **3** A kind of firework; *spec.* one that glows for a period before suddenly erupting with a loud bang into a shower of sparks. M17. **4** A toy consisting of a box containing a figure on a spring, which leaps up when the lid is raised. E18. **5** Any of various mechanical devices consisting essentially of a screw and a box or frame. E18. **6a** A West Indian tree, *Hernandia sonora* (family Hernandiaceae), bearing large nuts that rattle in their pericarps when shaken. M18. **b** Wild arum, *Arum maculatum. dial.* L19.

jackknife /ˈdʒaknʌɪf/ *n.* & *v.* Pl. **-knives** /-nʌɪvz/. E18. [f. *jack* (perh. JACK *n.*[1]) + KNIFE *n.*] **A** *n.* **1** A large clasp-knife carried in the pocket. E18. **2** *Swimming.* A kind of dive executed by first doubling up and then straightening the body before entering the water. More fully *jackknife dive*. E20. **3** A case of jackknifing by an articulated lorry (see sense B.2 below). M20. **4** *Statistics.* A method of assessing the variability of data by repeating a calculation on the sets of data obtained by removing one value from the complete set. M20. **B** *v.* **1** *v.t.* Cut with a jackknife. E19. **2** *v.i.* Double up like a jackknife; *spec.* of (the sections of) an articulated lorry: fold against (themselves or) itself, e.g. when skidding or reversing. L19. **3** *v.i.* Do a jackknife dive. E20.

jackleg /ˈdʒaklɛg/ *n.*[1] & *a. US colloq.* & *dial.* M19. [f. JACK *n.*[1] + LEG *n.*] (A person who is) incompetent, unskilled, unscrupulous, or dishonest.

jacklegged *a.* incompetent, unskilled, unscrupulous, dishonest M19.

jackleg *n.*[2] var. of JOCKTELEG.

jack-line /ˈdʒaklʌɪn/ *n.* E17. [f. JACK *n.*[1] + LINE *n.*[2]] A kind of thin three-stranded rope or line used esp. in sailing.

jackman /ˈdʒakmən/ *n. Sc. obs.* exc. *Hist.* Pl. **-men**. M16. [App. f. JACK *n.*[1] 3b + MAN *n.* Referred by Sir W. Scott to JACK *n.*[2]] An attendant or retainer of a nobleman or landowner.

Jacko /ˈdʒakəʊ/ *n. Austral. slang.* Pl. **-os**. E20. [f. JACK(ASS + -O.] A kookaburra. Cf. JACK *n.*[1] 24b, JACKY 4.

Jack-o'-lantern /ˈdʒakəlantən/ *n.* Also **Jack-a-lantern**, (in sense 1 and 2, earlier) **Jack-with-the-lantern**. M17. [f. JACK *n.*[1] + O' *prep.*[2] + LANTERN *n.*] †**1** A man with a lantern; a night-watchman. M17–E18. **2** An ignis fatuus, a will-o'-the-wisp; *fig.* something misleading or elusive. Also (chiefly *Naut.*), corposant, St Elmo's fire. L17. **3** A lantern made of the rind of a large turnip or a pumpkin, in which holes are cut to represent eyes, nose, and mouth. *north., Sc., & N. Amer.* M19.

jackpot /ˈdʒakpɒt/ *n.* L19. [f. JACK *n.*[1] + POT *n.*[1]] **1** *Cards.* In draw-poker, a pot or pool that accumulates until one of the players can open the betting with a pair of jacks or better; *fig.* any large prize, as from a lottery or gambling machine, *esp.* one that accumulates until it is won. L19. **2** A dilemma; trouble, esp. with the law; an arrest. *slang.* E20.

1 J. DIDION I won two twenty-five-dollar jackpots. F. DONALDSON Others get the jackpots and the girls. *hit the jackpot*: see HIT *v.*

jackrabbit /ˈdʒakrabɪt/ *n. N. Amer.* M19. [Abbrev. of JACKASS-*rabbit* (so called from its long ears).] Any of several large N. American hares of the genus *Lepus*, with very long ears and legs.

Jack Russell /dʒak ˈrʌs(ə)l/ *n.* E20. [f. Revd John (*Jack*) *Russell* (1795–1883), Eng. clergyman and dog-breeder.] A small working terrier with short legs and a rough or smooth coat, usu. white with dark black or brown markings. Also *Jack Russell terrier*.

¶Not a recognized breed, but cf. *Parson* (*Jack*) *Russell* (*terrier*) s.v. PARSON.

jackshay /ˈdʒakʃeɪ/ *n. Austral.* Also **-shea**. L19. [Origin unkn.] A tin quart-pot.

jacksie /ˈdʒaksi/ *n. slang.* Also **-sy**. L19. [f. JACK *n.*[1] + -SY.] The buttocks.

Jacksonian /dʒakˈsəʊnɪən/ *a.*[1] & *n.* E19. [f. *Jackson* (see below) + -IAN.] **A** *adj.* Pertaining to or characteristic of Andrew Jackson (1767–1845), seventh president of the United States of America, a prominent Democrat. E19. **B** *n.* A follower of Jackson. E19.

Jacksonianism *n.* the political convictions of Jacksonians E20.

Jacksonian /dʒakˈsəʊnɪən/ *a.*[2] L19. [f. John Hughlings *Jackson* (1835–1911), Eng. physician and neurologist + -IAN.] *Med.* Designating or characteristic of a form of epilepsy in which seizures begin at one site (usu. a digit or the angle of the mouth); designating a seizure of this kind.

jackstraw /ˈdʒakstrɔː/ *n.* Also **jack-straw**. L16. [f. JACK *n.*[1] + STRAW *n.* Partly f. *Jack Straw*, a leader in the rising of the Commons in 1381.] **1** A person of no substance, worth, or consideration. L16. **2** In *pl.* A set of straws or other thin strips, used in a game in which they are thrown in a heap, and each must be picked up singly without disturbing any other; (treated as *sing.*) this game. E19. **3** A jot, a whit. E19.

jacksy *n.* var. of JACKSIE.

jack-up /ˈdʒakʌp/ *n.* M20. [f. JACK *v.* + UP *adv.*[1]] A type of offshore oil-drilling rig, the legs of which are lowered to the seabed from the operating platform. Also *jack-up rig*.

Jack-with-the-lantern *n.* see JACK-O'-LANTERN.

Jacky /ˈdʒaki/ *n.* Also **-ey**, **j-**. L18. [Dim. of JACK *n.*[1]: see -Y[6].] **1** Gin. *slang.* L18. **2** In full *Jacky-Jacky*. An Aborigine. *Austral. slang* (freq. considered *racially offensive*). M19. **3** A sailor. *slang.* L19. **4** A kookaburra. Cf. JACK *n.*[1] 24b, JACKO. *Austral. colloq.* L19.

Comb.: **Jacky Winter** *Austral.* the brown flycatcher, *Microeca leucophaea* (family Eopsaltridae); also called *post-boy, spinks*.

jackyard /ˈdʒakjɑːd/ *n.* L19. [f. JACK *n.*[1] + YARD *n.*[2]] *Naut.* A spar used in fore-and-aft rigged craft, chiefly yachts, to spread the foot of a large gaff topsail out beyond the peak of the mainsail.

jackyarder *n.* a jackyard topsail L19.

Jacob /ˈdʒeɪkəb/ *n.* M17. [Male forename, f. eccl.L *Jacobus*, Gk *Iakōbos*, f. Heb. *Yaʿăqōḇ*: sense 4 w. ref. to *Gen.* 30:39–42. Cf. JAMES.] †**1** = JACOBUS. Only in M17. **2** A ladder. *slang.* Now *rare* or *obs.*. E18. †**3** A foolish person. *slang.* Only in E19. **4** (An animal of) a piebald breed of sheep, usu. two- or four-horned, kept since the 18th cent. as an ornamental park breed and, esp. in the Hebrides, for wool. Also *Jacob('s) sheep*. E20.

Jacobaea /dʒakəˈbiːə/ *n.* M18. [mod.L, perh. f. G *S. Jacobs Kraut*.] **1** *Jacobaea lily*, = *Jacobean lily* s.v. JACOBEAN *a.* M18. **2** Orig., ragwort, *Senecio jacobaea* (formerly called *St James's wort*). Now, a related purple-flowered southern African plant, *S. elegans*, grown for ornament. L18.

Jacobean /dʒakəˈbiːən/ *a.* & *n.* L18. [f. mod.L *Jacobaeus* f. eccl.L *Jacobus* James: see JACOB, -EAN.] **A** *adj.* **1** Of or pertaining to the apostle St James or the Epistle of St James. L18. **2** Of, pertaining to, or characteristic of the reign or times of James I, king of England 1603–25 (the later part of his reign as James VI of Scotland, 1567–1625). M19. **b** *spec.* Designating the architectural style prevalent in England around this time, consisting of very late Gothic combined with many classical features. L19. **c** Of furniture: made in the style of the Jacobean period; of the colour of dark oak. E20. **3** Of or pertaining to the American novelist and critic Henry James (1843–1916), = JAMESIAN *a.* 2. E20.

Special collocations: **Jacobean lily** a Mexican ornamental bulbous plant, *Sprekelia formosissima* (family Amaryllidaceae), with crimson funnel-shaped flowers.

B *n.* **1** A person, esp. a statesman or writer, of the time of James I. L19. **2** = JACOBITE *n.*[2] 2. E20.

Jacobethan /dʒakəˈbiːθ(ə)n/ *a.* M20. [Blend of JACOBEAN and ELIZABETHAN.] Of design:

displaying a combination of the Elizabethan and Jacobean styles.

Jacob Evertsen /dʒeɪkəb 'ɛvəts(ə)n, *foreign* jakɒp 'ɪəvəts(ə)n/ *n. S. Afr.* E18. [Said to be a 17th-cent. Du. sea-captain.] = JACOPEVER.

Jacobi /'dzakəbi/ *n.* L19. [See next.] *Math.* **1** *Jacobi('s) equation*, *Jacobi identity*, an identity of the form $a(bc) + b(ca) + c(ab) = 0$, where a, b, c are operators or functions. L19. **2** *Jacobi('s) polynomial*, any of a set of polynomial functions of three variables, $J_n(p, q; x)$, equivalent to the hypergeometric functions $F(-n, p+n; q; x)$. L19.

Jacobian /dʒə'kəʊbɪən/ *a.* & *n.* M19. [f. *Jacobi* (see below) + -AN.] *Math.* **A** *adj.* Designating or pertaining to any of various concepts discovered, introduced, or investigated by the German mathematician K. G. J. Jacobi (1804–51). M19.

Jacobian function = *theta function* (a) s.v. THETA.

B *n.* A determinant whose constituents are the derivatives of a number of functions (u, v, w, ...) with respect to each of the same number of variables (x, y, z, ...). L19.

Jacobin /'dʒakəbɪn/ *n.*[1] & *a.*[1] ME. [(O)Fr. f. med.L *Jacobinus* f. eccl.L *Jacobus*: see JACOB, -IN[2]. Sense 1 f. assoc. w. the church of S. Jacques in Paris.] **A** *n.* **1** A friar of the order of St Dominic; a Dominican. ME. **2** *Hist.* A member of a French political society established in 1789 at the old Dominican convent in Paris to maintain and propagate the principles of democracy and equality. L18. **3** A sympathizer with the principles of the Jacobins of the French Revolution; a radical or revolutionary in politics or social organization. L18.

3 M. J. LASKY The Black Jacobins of Africa.

B *adj.* **1** Of or pertaining to the Dominican friars. M16. **2** Of or pertaining to the Jacobins of the French Revolution (*Hist.*); radical, revolutionary. L18.

2 E. P. THOMPSON The Jacobin tradition .. of self-education and of rational criticism of political and religious institutions.

Jaco'binic, **Jaco'binical** *adjs.* of, pertaining to, or characteristic of the Jacobins of the French Revolution; radical: L18. **Jacobinize** *v.t.* imbue with radical or revolutionary ideas L18.

†Jacobin *n.*[2] & *a.*[2] E16–M18. [OFr. f. med.L *Jacobinus* alt. of *Jacobita* JACOBITE *n.*[1] & *a.*[1]] = JACOBITE *n.*[1] & *a.*[1]

jacobin /'dʒakəbɪn/ *n.*[3] L17. [Fr. *jacobine* fem. of JACOBIN *n.*[1]] **1** A breed of fancy pigeon with reversed feathers on the back of the neck like a cowl or hood; a pigeon of this breed. L17. **2** Either of two hummingbirds with neck-feathers resembling a hood, *Florisuga mellivora* and *Melanotrochilus fuscus*. M19.

Jacobinism /'dʒakəbɪnɪz(ə)m/ *n.* L18. [Fr. *Jacobinisme*, f. as JACOBIN *n.*[1] & *a.*[1]: see -ISM.] The doctrine or practice of the Jacobins of the French Revolution; radical or revolutionary principles.

Jacobite /'dʒakəbʌɪt/ *n.*[1] & *a.*[1] LME. [med.L *Jacobita*, f. *Jacobus*: see JACOB, -ITE[1].] **A** *n.* **1** *Eccl. Hist.* A member of a Monophysite Christian Church taking its name from Jacobus Baradaeus of Edessa, a Syrian monk who revived the Eutychian doctrine in the 6th cent. LME. **†2** = JACOBIN *n.*[1] 1. M16–E19. **B** *adj. Eccl. Hist.* Of or pertaining to the Jacobites. M17.

Jacobite /'dʒakəbʌɪt/ *n.*[2] & *a.*[2] E17. [f. eccl.L *Jacobus* (see JACOB) + -ITE[1].] **A** *adj.* **†1** Of or pertaining to James I, king of England; Jacobean. Only in E17. **2** *Hist.* Designating, of, or pertaining to a Jacobite or the Jacobites. L17. **b** Of glass or pottery: bearing inscriptions and emblems which indicate Jacobite sympathies. M20. **B** *n.* **1** *Hist.* A supporter of James II, King of England (reigned 1685–8), after his removal from the throne in 1688, or of his descendants or the Stuarts. Cf. WILLIAMITE *n.* 2. L17. **2** An admirer of Henry James (see JACOBEAN *a.* 3). E20.

Jacobitical /-'bɪt-/ *a.* of or pertaining to the Jacobites, holding Jacobite principles L18. **Jacobitish** *a.* (*rare*) = Jacobitical E18. **Jacobitishly** *adv.* (*rare*) L19. **Jacobitism** *n.* (*Hist.*) the principles of the Jacobites; adherence to or sympathy with the Stuart cause: E18.

Jacob's ladder /dʒeɪkəbz 'ladə/ *n. phr.* M18. [W. allus. to Jacob's dream of a ladder reaching to heaven, as described in *Gen.* 28:12.] **1** A common garden plant and rare British native of limestone scree, *Polemonium caeruleum* (family Polemoniaceae), with corymbs of blue (or white) flowers, so called from its long pinnate leaves with closely spaced leaflets. M18. **2** *Naut.* A rope or chain ladder. M19. **3** An elevator consisting of a series of bucket-shaped receptacles attached to an endless chain. M19.

Jacob's membrane /'dʒeɪkəbz 'mɛmbreɪn/ *n. phr.* M19. [Arthur *Jacob* (d. 1874), Ir. ophthalmic surgeon.] *Anat.* The layer of rods and cones in the retina of the eye.

Jacobson /'dʒeɪkəbs(ə)n/ *n.* M19. [Ludwig Levin *Jacobson* (1783–1843), Da. anatomist and physician.] **1** Anat. *Jacobson's nerve*, the tympanic nerve, a branch of the glosso-pharyngeal (ninth cranial) nerve. M19. **2** Zool. *Jacobson's organ*, an olfactory organ well-developed in many vertebrates, notably snakes and lizards, occurring as (one of) a pair of sacs or tubes usu. in the roof of the mouth. L19.

Jacob's staff /dʒeɪkəbz 'stɑːf/ *n. phr.* M16. [W. allus. to St James (eccl.L *Jacobus*), whose symbols are a pilgrim's staff and a scallop shell, or *Gen.* 30:37–43, 32:10.] **†1** A pilgrim's staff. M16–M17. **2a** *Hist.* An instrument for taking the altitude of a celestial object. M16. **b** An instrument for measuring distances and heights, consisting of a rod fitted with a cursor. L18.

Jacobus /dʒə'kəʊbəs/ *n.* E17. [eccl.L: see JACOB.] *Hist.* (An unofficial name for) an English gold coin, the sovereign or unite, struck in the reign of James I and equivalent to 20, 22, or 24 shillings.

jaconet /'dʒakənɪt/ *n.* M18. [Hind. *Jagannāth(purī)* (now Puri) in India, its place of origin: see JUGGERNAUT.] A cotton cloth resembling cambric, *esp.* a dyed waterproof variety used for poulticing etc.

jacopever /'jakəpiːvə/ *n.* Chiefly *S. Afr.* Pl. same. E20. [f. JACOB EVER(TSEN.] Any of several edible marine fishes distinguished by reddish skin and large eyes; *esp.* the S. Atlantic scorpaenid *Sebastichthys capensis*.

jacquard /'dʒakɑːd, -kəd/ *a.* & *n.* Also **J-**. M19. [J. M. *Jacquard*, Fr. inventor (1752–1834).] **A** *adj.* **1** Designating an attachment to a loom which enables the pattern in the cloth to be produced automatically by means of punched cards; designating a loom fitted with this. M19. **2** Designating a fabric, article, or pattern made with the aid of this; of an intricate variegated design. M19.

2 A. LURIE A lavender jacquard sweater.

B *n.* **1** A jacquard fabric, pattern, or article. M19. **2** A jacquard attachment or loom. L19.

1 *Radio Times* Many other quality fabrics .. including plains, florals and jacquards.

Jacqueminot /'ʒakmɪnəʊ, *foreign* ʒakmino (*pl. same*)/ *n.* Earlier as GÉNÉRAL JACQUEMINOT. L19. [Vicomte J. F. *Jacqueminot* (1787–1865), Fr. general.] A hybrid perpetual rose with deep crimson flowers. Also *Jacqueminot rose*.

jacquerie /'dʒeɪk(ə)ri, *foreign* ʒakri (*pl. same*)/ *n.* E16. [(O)Fr., f. male forename *Jacques*. Cf. JACK *n.*[1] 1.] The revolt of the peasants of northern France against the nobles in 1357–8; any popular rising of the peasantry.

jactance /'dʒakt(ə)ns/ *n. rare.* LME. [(O)Fr., or L *jactantia* boasting, f. *jactant-* pres. ppl stem of *jactare*: see next, -ANCE.] Boasting, bragging.

jactancy *n.* boastfulness, boasting LME.

jactation /dʒak'teɪʃ(ə)n/ *n.* L16. [L *jactatio(n-)*, f. *jactat-* pa. ppl stem of *jactare*, frequent. of *jacere* to throw: see -ATION.] **1** Boasting, bragging, ostentatious display. L16. **2** (A) restless tossing and turning of the body. L17.

jactitation /dʒaktɪ'teɪʃ(ə)n/ *n.* M17. [med.L *jactitatio(n-)* false declaration tending to someone's detriment, f. L *jactitare* bring forward in public, utter, (later) boast, frequent. of *jactare*: see prec., -ATION. In sense 2 app. an expressive extension of JACTATION 2.] **1** Public display or declaration, esp. of a boastful nature; boasting, bragging. Now *rare* or *obs.* exc. in *jactitation of marriage* below. M17. **2** *Med.* Orig., = JACTATION 2. Now, convulsive movement of a limb, muscle, or muscle group. M17.

1 **jactitation of marriage** *Law* false declaration that one is married to a specified person.

jacu /dʒə'kuː/ *n.* E19. [Port. f. Tupi *jacú*.] Any of various guans of the genus *Penelope*, esp. *P. marail* or *P. jacquacu*.

jaculate /'dʒakjʊleɪt/ *v. rare.* E17. [L *jaculat-* pa. ppl stem of *jaculari* dart, hurl, f. *jaculum* a dart, f. *jacere* to throw: see -ATE[3].] **1** *v.t.* Dart, hurl. E17. **2** *v.i.* Dart forward. E17.

jacu'lation *n.* the action of hurling or throwing; a throw: E17. **jaculator** *n.* (*a*) a person who hurls or throws; †(*b*) (in full *jaculator fish*) = ARCHER 4 : M18.

jacutinga /dʒakjʊ'tɪŋgə/ *n.* M19. [Port. f. Tupi = a guan (whose plumage the ore is said to resemble), f. *jacú* JACU + *tinga* white.] Any of various kinds of soft gold-bearing iron ore found in Brazil.

Jacuzzi /dʒə'kuːzi/ *n.* Also **j-**. M20. [Candido *Jacuzzi* (*c* 1903–86), US inventor.] (Proprietary name for) a kind of large bath which uses underwater jets of warm water to massage the body.

jadam /'dʒadam/ *n.* E20. [Malay.] A type of silver or brass niello ware from the Malay peninsula and Sumatra, used esp. for decorating belt buckles.

jade /dʒeɪd/ *n.*[1] LME. [Origin unkn.] **1** An inferior or worn-out horse, a nag. Now *rare*. LME. **2** A woman, *esp.* a headstrong or disreputable one; a tart, a hussy. *arch.* or *joc.* M16.

2 *fig.*: CLIVE JAMES Grand Central Station was saved by public outcry but public outcry is a fickle jade.

jadish *a.* (now *rare*) L16. **jady** *a.* (*rare*) L19.

jade /dʒeɪd/ *n.*[2] & *a.* L16. [Fr. (*le jade* for earlier *l'ejade*) f. Sp. *ijada* (in *piedra de ijada* lit. 'colic stone') f. Proto-Romance, f. L *ilia* flanks.] **A** *n.* **1** Either of two hard minerals used for implements and ornaments, *esp.* a pale green variety of gem quality, (*a*) = NEPHRITE; (*b*) = JADEITE. Also, any of various other ornamental green minerals. L16. **2** A colour resembling that of jade; a light bluish-green. E20.

1 *serpentine jade*: see SERPENTINE *n.*

Comb.: **jade-green** = sense A.2 above; **jade-stone** = sense A.1 above.

B *adj.* Made of or resembling jade; of the colour of jade. M19.

jade /dʒeɪd/ *v.* E17. [f. JADE *n.*[1]] **1** *v.t.* Exhaust, wear out; fatigue, tire; sate, dull. E17. **2** *v.i.* Become tired or worn out; flag. E17. **†3** *v.t.* Fool, trick. Only in 17.

jaded /'dʒeɪdɪd/ *a.* L16. [f. JADE *n.*[1], *v.*: see -ED[2], -ED[1].] **†1** Disreputable. Only in L16. **2** Dulled or sated by continual experience or indulgence. M17. **3** Tired, worn out. L17.

2 *Sunday Express* I'm not cynical though—just a little jaded perhaps. *Sunday Times* Jaded fashion editors and blasé buyers. 3 T. HARDY A little rest for the jaded animal being desirable, he did not hasten. M. S. POWER He was too jaded, too drunk to do anything about it.

jadedly *adv.* L19. **jadedness** *n.* L19.

jadeite /'dʒeɪdʌɪt/ *n.* M19. [f. JADE *n.*[2] + -ITE[1].] *Min.* A monoclinic silicate of sodium, aluminium, and ferric iron, of the pyroxene group, resembling nephrite and prized as jade.

jadeitic /dʒeɪ'dɪtɪk/ *a.* approximating to jadeite in composition M20.

j'adoube /ʒadub/ *int.* E19. [Fr., f. *je*, *j'* I + 1st person sing. of *adouber*: see DUB *v.*[1]] *Chess.* Indicating that a player wishes to touch a piece without making a move.

Jaeger /'jeɪgə/ *n.*[1] M19. [E. R. *Jaeger* von Jastthal (1818–84), Austrian ophthalmologist.] Used in *possess.* and *attrib.* to designate a series of short passages printed in typefaces of different sizes and used for testing sharpness of vision.

jaeger /'dʒeɪgə/ *n.*[2] Also (earlier) **jager**, **†jäger**. M19. [Anglicized f. JÄGER.] **I 1** Formerly, any predatory sea bird. Now *spec.* each of three Arctic-breeding skuas, *Stercorarius pomarinus*, *S. parasiticus*, and *S. longicaudus*. M19.

1 **long-tailed jaeger** the long-tailed skua, *Stercorarius longicaudus*. **parasitic jaeger** = *Arctic* SKUA. POMARINE *jaeger*.

II 2 See JÄGER.

Jaffa /'dʒafə/ *n.* L19. [A port in Israel (biblical *Joppa*).] In full *Jaffa orange*. A large, oval, thick-skinned, seedless variety of orange first cultivated near Joppa.

jag /dʒag/ *n.*[1] LME. [f. JAG *v.*] 1 *Hist.* An ornamental point or projection made by cutting the edge of a garment; a slash or cut made in the surface of a garment to show a different colour underneath. LME. 2 A projecting tendril, branch, bristle, or thread; *Sc.* a prickle, a thorn. LME. 3 A shred of cloth, a scrap, a fragment; in *pl.*, rags, tatters. *obs.* exc. *dial.* M16. 4 A sharp projection or point; a pointed division of a wing or leaf; a sharp or rugged point of rock etc. L16. 5 A prick with something sharp; *spec.* an injection. Chiefly *Sc.* L17. 6 A jagged piece of metal fitted to the end of a ramrod, fastened to a rag and used to clean a rifle barrel. M19.

4 H. N. HUTCHINSON Clutching an outstanding jag of the rock. *fig.*: *Time* Tinkering with numbers . . could cause a sharp downward jag in an earnings report.

jaggy *a.* jagged; *Sc.* prickly: E18.

jag /dʒag/ *n.*[2] L16. [Origin unkn.] 1 A small load of hay, wood, etc. *dial.* & *US.* L16. b A bag, a bundle. *dial.* & *US.* L18. c A portion, a quantity. *US.* M19. 2a As much alcoholic drink as a person can take. Also, a drinking-bout; the state or a period of being drunk. *dial.* & *colloq.* L17. b An intense period of indulgence in a particular activity, emotion, interest, etc. *colloq.* (orig. *US*). E20.

2a J. T. FARRELL But it wasn't like a jag, for that could be slept off. b M. BINCHY Starting a crying jag that was going to last two hours. *New York Times* An amphetamine-powered talking jag.

jag /dʒag/ *v.t.* LME. [Rel. to JOG *v.*: cf. RAG *v.*[1], TAG *n.*[1]] 1 Stab, pierce. Now only (*Sc.*, *north.*, & *US dial.*) prick (as) with a thorn, needle, etc. LME. 2 *Hist.* Slash or pink (a garment etc.) for ornamentation. LME. 3 Make indentations in the edge or surface of; cut or tear unevenly. M16.

†Jagannath *n.* see JUGGERNAUT.

Jagatai *n.* & *a.* see CHAGATAI.

jagati /'dʒʌgəti:/ *n.* M19. [Skt.] A Vedic metre of four twelve-syllable lines.

jäger /'jeɪgə/ *n.* Also **jaeger**. See also JAEGER. L18. [G, f. *jagen* hunt, pursue. See also YAGER *n.*[1]] I 1 Orig., a marksman in the German or Austrian infantry. Later, a member of a battalion of riflemen in these armies. Now, a member of a regiment using the name as an official title. L18. 2 A (German or Swiss) huntsman or hunter. E19. 3 An attendant wearing a huntsman's costume. Cf. CHASSEUR 2a. E19. II See JAEGER *n.*[2]

jagged /'dʒagɪd, *in sense 2 also* dʒagd/ *a.*[1] LME. [f. JAG *n.*[1], *v.*: see -ED[2], -ED[1].] 1 Edged with sharp projections and deep indentations; having a ragged or uneven edge; irregularly and sharply pointed. LME. 2 *Hist.* Of a garment etc.: cut into jags for ornamentation; pinked, slashed. LME. 3 Of a leaf, petal, etc.: having sharp projections and deeply and irregularly indented edges. Of a plant: having jagged leaves or flowers. LME.

1 A. J. CRONIN The jagged edge of broken glass. C. FRANCIS The jagged teeth of the Scilly rocks. C. HOPE Jagged dark blue stripes. 3 : **jagged chickweed** a small weed of the pink family, *Holosteum umbellatum*, with toothed or jagged white petals.

jaggedly *adv.* L17. **jaggedness** *n.* E16.

jagged /dʒagd/ *a.*[2] *colloq.* (chiefly *US*). M18. [f. JAG *n.*[2] + -ED[2].] 1 Drunk, intoxicated by alcohol. M18. 2 Intoxicated by or under the influence of drugs. M20.

jagger /'dʒagə/ *n.*[1] *dial.* E16. [f. JAG *n.*[2], *v.* + -ER[1].] 1 A pedlar, a hawker. Also, a carrier, a carter. E16. 2 *Mining* (now *Hist.*). A driver of packhorses, a person in charge of trains of trucks. M18.

jagger /'dʒagə/ *n.*[2] *obs.* exc. *Hist.* Also **yager**, **yagger**, /'jag-/. E17. [Du. *jager*, abbrev. of *haringjager*, f. *haring* herring + *jager* hunter (cf. JÄGER), f. *jagen* hunt, pursue.] A vessel taking supplies to deep-sea fishing boats and bringing back their catches.

jagger /'dʒagə/ *n.*[3] E19. [f. JAG *v.* + -ER[1].] A person who or thing which jags something.

jaggery /'dʒag(ə)ri/ *n.* L16. [Port. *xagara*, *jag(a)ra*, *jagre* f. Malayalam *cakkarā* f. Skt *śarkarā* sugar.] A coarse dark brown sugar made in India by evaporation of the sap of various palms.

Comb.: **jaggery palm** any of several palms that yield jaggery, esp. *Caryota urens*.

jagir /'dʒɑ:gɪə/ *n.* Also **jaghir**. E17. [Pers. & Urdu *jāgīr*, f. Pers. *jā* place + *gīr* holding.] In parts of the Indian subcontinent: a grant of the public revenues or produce of a district to an individual or group, for either private use or public benefit; a district subject to such a grant; the income derived from such a grant.

jagirdar /'dʒɑ:gɪədɑ:/ *n.* a holder of a jagir L18.

jagt /jakt/ *n.* M19. [Da. = YACHT *n.*: cf. Norw., Sw. *jakt*.] In Scandinavia, a small single-masted coastal vessel, rigged either with square sails or as a cutter or sloop.

jaguar /'dʒagjʊə/ *n.* E17. [Port. f. Tupi-Guarani *yaguára* carnivorous animal, jaguar (cf. next).] A large carnivorous feline, *Panthera onca*, of Central and S. America, mainly yellowish-brown with dark spots grouped in rosettes.

jaguarete /dʒagjʊə'rɛteɪ/ *n.* M18. [Tupi-Guarani *yaguareté* jaguar, f. as prec. + *-eté* true.] A supposed variety of the jaguar.

¶The Guarani name for the jaguar (as opp. to carnivores in general), mistaken by European writers for a distinct variety.

jaguarundi /dʒagwə'rʌndi, jagwɑ:-/ *n.* Also **-rondi** /-'rɒndi/. M19. [Port. f. Tupi-Guarani, f. as JAGUAR + *undi* dark.] An American wild cat, *Felis yagouaroundi*, larger than the domestic cat, with a long body and tail and inhabiting forest and scrub from Arizona to Argentina.

Jah /dʒɑ:, jɑ:/ *n.* M16. [Repr. (orig. in the Bible) Heb. *Yāh*, abbrev. of *Yahweh* JEHOVAH.] God.

¶Rare bef. M20 when it was popularized by the Rastafarian movement.

Jahveh *n.* var. of YAHWEH.

Jahvism *n.* var. of YAHWISM.

jai alai /hʌɪ ə'lʌɪ/ *n. phr.* E20. [Sp., f. Basque *jai* festival + *alai* merry.] = PELOTA I.

Jai Hind /dʒʌɪ 'hɪnd/ *int.* M20. [Hind., f. *jai* long live! + *Hind* India.] In India: a salutation used in exchange of greetings, at a public meeting, etc.

jail /dʒeɪl/ *n.* & *v.* Also **gaol**. ME. [ONFr. *gaiole*, *gayolle*, *gaole* or OFr. *jaiole*, *geole*, etc. (mod. *geôle*) prison, f. Proto-Romance and pop.L dim. of L *cavea* CAGE *n.*] A *n.* 1 A place or building for the confinement of people accused or convicted of a crime or offence. Now *spec.* a public prison for the detention of people committed by process of law. ME. 2 Imprisonment. LME. 3 *transf.* & *fig.* A place of confinement. LME.

1 JOSEPH HALL He was committed to the gayle of Newgate. *deliver a jail*: see DELIVER *v.* 2. 2 *Radio Times* Campaigning to free her husband and other Jewish refusniks from jail in the USSR. 3 SPENSER His happie soule to heaven went Out of this fleshlie gaole.

Comb.: **jail-bait** *slang* a girl under the age of consent; **jailbird** a prisoner, *esp.* a long-term prisoner; a habitual criminal, a rogue; **jailbreak** an escape from a jail; *jail-delivery*: see DELIVERY *n.* I; **jail fever** typhus, formerly endemic in jails and other crowded places; **jailhouse** (chiefly *US*) a prison.

B *v.t.* Imprison; put in or as in jail. E17.

¶In Britain *gaol* is the spelling in official use, but both *gaol* and *jail* are in literary use. In the US and elsewhere *jail* is the usual spelling.

jailer /'dʒeɪlə/ *n.* Also **gaoler**, **jailor**. ME. [f. (as) prec. + -ER[2].] A person in charge of a jail or the prisoners in a jail.

jaileress *n.* a female jailer M18. **jailership** *n.* the position or office of a jailer L15.

Jain /dʒʌɪn, dʒeɪn/ *n.* & *a.* Also **Jaina** /'dʒʌɪnə, 'dʒeɪnə/. L18. [Hind. f. Skt *jaina* of or pertaining to a Jina, f. *jina* (see JINA), lit. 'victor, overcomer', f. *ji-* conquer or *jyā-* overcome.] A *n.* An adherent of a non-brahminical religion established about the 6th cent. BC, characterized by its stress on non-violence and strict asceticism as means to liberation. L18. B *adj.* Of or pertaining to the Jains or their religion. E19.

Jainism *n.* the Jain religion M19. **Jainist** *n.* & *a.* (now *rare*) = JAIN E19.

Jaipur /dʒʌɪ'pʊə/ *a.* L19. [See below.] Of, pertaining to, or made in Jaipur, capital of the Indian State of Rajasthan, or the former Indian State of Jaipur.

Jaipuri /dʒʌɪ'pʊəri/ *n.* the Rajasthani dialect of the Jaipur area E20.

jak *n.* var. of JACK *n.*[3]

jake /dʒeɪk/ *n.*[1] *US colloq.* M19. [Prob. the male forename *Jake*, abbrev. of *Jacob*.] In full *country jake*. A rustic lout or simpleton.

jake /dʒeɪk/ *n.*[2] *slang* (orig. *US*). E20. [Abbrev. of *Jamaica*.] An alcoholic drink made from Jamaica ginger. Also, methylated spirits used as an alcoholic drink.

jake /dʒeɪk/ *a. slang* (chiefly *Austral.* & *NZ*). E20. [Origin unkn.] Excellent, admirable, fine.

Also **jakea'loo**, **jaker'loo** *a.* E20.

jakes /dʒeɪks/ *n.* M16. [Perh. f. male forename *Jacques* or the genit. of *Jack*: see JACK *n.*[1]] 1 A privy, a lavatory. M16. 2 Excrement; filth. L16.

jakkalsbessie /'jak(ə)ls,bɛsi, *foreign* 'jakals-/ *n.* *S. Afr.* M19. [Afk., f. *jakkals* jackal + *bessie* berry.] (The fruit of) either of two tropical African trees, an ebony, *Diospyros mespiliformis*, and *Sideroxylon inerme* (family Sapotaceae).

Jakun /dʒɑ:'ku:n/ *n.* & *a.* M19. [Jakun.] A *n.* Pl. **-s**, same. A member of an aboriginal people of the southern part of the Malay peninsula; the language of this people. M19. B *attrib.* or as *adj.* Of or pertaining to the Jakuns or their language. M20.

jalap /'dʒaləp, 'dʒɒləp/ *n.* & *v.* M17. [Fr. f. Sp. *jalapa*, in full *purga de Jalapa*, f. *Jalapa*, *Xalapa* a Mexican city. Cf. JOLLOP *n.*[2]] A *n.* 1 A purgative drug obtained from the tuberous roots of a Mexican climbing plant, *Ipomoea purga*, and from certain other plants of the bindweed family. M17. 2 The plant yielding this drug; (with specifying wd) any of certain other plants yielding a similar drug. L17.

2 **false jalap** = *marvel of Peru* s.v. MARVEL *n.*[1]

B *v.t.* Dose or purge with jalap. *rare.* M18.

jalapeño /halə'peɪnjəʊ, -'pi:nəʊ/ *n.* Pl. **-os**. M20. [Mex. Sp.] A very hot green chilli pepper. Also *jalapeño pepper*.

jalebi /dʒə'leɪbi:/ *n.* M19. [Hind. *jalebī*.] An Indian sweet made by frying a coil of batter and then soaking it in syrup.

jaleo /xa'leo/ *n.* M19. [Sp., lit. 'halloo'.] Clapping to accompany Andalusian dancing; a lively Andalusian dance.

jalopy /dʒə'lɒpi/ *n. colloq.* E20. [Origin unkn.] A battered old motor vehicle or aeroplane.

jalouse /dʒə'lu:z/ *v.t.* L17. [Fr. *jalouser* regard with jealousy, f. *jaloux*, *-ouse* JEALOUS.] 1 Have a suspicion of; surmise, guess. *Sc.* L17. 2 Suspect; be suspicious about. *Sc.* E18. 3 Regard with jealousy. Also, begrudge jealously. L19.

jalousie /'dʒaluzi:/ *n.* M18. [Fr., lit. 'jealousy'; also, a type of blind or shutter.] A blind or shutter made from a row of angled slats to exclude sun and rain and control the entry of air and light.

jaloused *a.* provided with a jalousie M19.

Jam /dʒɑ:m/ *n.*[1] E18. [Origin unkn.] *Hist.* (A hereditary title of) any of certain princes and noblemen in Sind, Kutch, and Saurashtra in the Indian subcontinent.

jam /dʒam/ *n.*[2] M18. [Perh. f. JAM *v.*[1]] 1 A conserve of fruit and sugar boiled to a thick consistency. M18. 2 Something easy, good, or pleasant. L19. 3 Affected manners; self-importance. *Austral. slang.* L19.

1 E. ACTON To preserve . . the true flavour and the colour of fruit in jams . . boil them rapidly. 2 T. A. GUTHRIE Ah! . . I thought you wouldn't find it all jam.

Phrases: **jam on it** some additional pleasure, ease, advantage, etc. (in *have*, *like*, *want*, etc., *jam on it*). **jam tomorrow** a pleasant thing continually promised but usu. never produced. *money for jam*: see MONEY *n.*

Comb.: **jam-jar** (*a*) a jar designed for holding jam; (*b*) *rhyming slang* a motor car.

jam /dʒɑːm/ *n.*[3] *obs.* exc. *Hist.* L18. [f. JAMA *n.*[1]] A kind of dress for a child.

jam /dʒam/ *n.*[4] E19. [f. JAM *v.*[1]] 1 The action of jamming; the fact or condition of being jammed; a crush, a squeeze; a mass of things or persons crowded together or interlocked so as to prevent individual movement; *spec.* such an accumulation of logs in a river or traffic in a street. E19. b *fig.* An awkward or difficult situation. E20. 2 The action or an act of jamming radio, radar, etc., signals. E20. 3 Jazz or popular music simultaneously improvised by a number of performers; a period of playing such music, an informal gathering of musicians improvising together, (also *jam session*). *colloq.* E20.

1 *log jam*, *traffic jam*, etc. b P. H. GIBBS 'I'm in the devil of a jam,' said Robin gloomily. 3 *Southern Rag* Meadowcroft fetched his instrument and joined in an impromptu jam session.

Comb.: **jam-proof** *a.* protected against jamming; *jam session*: see sense 3 above; **jam-up** *colloq.* = sense 1 above.

jam /dʒam/ *v.*[1] Infl. **-mm-**. E18. [Prob. symbolic.] 1 *v.t.* Press or squeeze (an object) tightly between two converging bodies or surfaces; wedge or fix immovably in a space. E18. b Bruise or crush by pressure. M19. c Block (a passage etc.) by crowding in. M19. 2 *v.i.* Become fixed, wedged, or held immovably; stick fast. E18. 3 *v.t.* Press, squeeze, crowd, or force (a number of objects) together in a compact mass. M18. 4 *v.t.* Thrust, drive, or force, esp. violently. Usu. foll. by *against*, *in*, *into*, *on*, etc. L18. 5 *v.t.* Cause (a component of a machine) to become wedged or immovable; make (a machine, gun, etc.) unworkable in this way. M19. b *v.i.* Of a machine, gun, etc.: become wedged or immovable and so unworkable. L19. c *v.t.* Interfere, esp. deliberately, with (radio or radar signals) so as to make them unintelligible or useless; prevent reception of (a signal) by doing this. E20. 6a *v.i.* Play in a jam or jam session (see JAM *n.*[4] 3). *colloq.* M20. b *v.t.* Improvise (a tune etc.). M20.

1 M. PIERCY Our three chairs are jammed between chimney and basement door. b E. AMADI Adults jammed their doorways to watch. 2 C. RYCROFT She had to use a public telephone but the coins jammed and she had to loosen them. 3 J. G. BALLARD They . . floated in the canals, jammed together around the pillars of the bridges. 4 W. WHARTON I jam the brakes but they don't grab straight and we almost flip. P. FERGUSON Gareth wordlessly jammed his scraper . . into the cupboard's edge. 5 J. DIDION A Garuda 727 that had jammed its landing gear. b C. HOPE A comparatively new weapon . . inclined to jam when fired in haste. c *Daily Telegraph* The Post Office is jamming broadcasts by the pirate radio ship.

jam /dʒam/ *v.*[2]*t. colloq.* Infl. **-mm-**. M19. [f. JAM *n.*[2]] 1 Spread with jam. M19. 2 Make into jam. M19.

jam /dʒam/ *adv.* & *a.* Orig. *US.* E19. [f. JAM *v.*[1]] A *adv.* Closely; in close contact, with firm pressure. Foll. by *against*, *up*. E19.

Comb.: **jam-full** *a.* packed full, completely filled; **jam-pack** *v.t.* pack tightly, fill; **jam-packed** *a.* tightly packed, closely crowded or squeezed together.

B *adj.* Excellent, perfect; thorough. Usu. foll. by *up*. *colloq.* M19.

jama /ˈdʒɑːmə/ *n.*[1] Also **jamah**. L18. [Urdu f. Pers. *jāma* clothing. Cf. PYJAMAS.] A long cotton gown worn in the Indian subcontinent.

jama /ˈdʒʌmə/ *n.*[2] Also **jumma**. L18. [Urdu *jam(a)ʻ* collection, amount, account f. Arab. *jamaʻ* addition, total, aggregate.] During British rule in India, the assessment for land revenue from an estate or division of country.

jamabundi /-bʌndi/ [Pers. & Urdu *-bandī* a tie, a band, f. Skt *bandh* settlement] (a document recording) the settlement of revenues.

jama /ˈdʒɑːmə/ *n.*[3] *colloq.* M20. [Abbrev.] Pyjama. Usu. in *pl.*

jamadar /ˈdʒʌmədɑː/ *n.* Also **jem-** /ˈdʒɛm-/. M18. [Urdu *jam(a)ʻdār* f. Pers., f. Arab. *jamaʻ*, *jamāʻa(t)* muster + Pers. *-dār* holding, holder.] In the Indian subcontinent: a junior army or police officer; a minor official; the head of a body of servants; *Hist.* an Indian officer in a sepoy regiment.

jamah *n.* var. of JAMA *n.*[1]

Jamaica /dʒəˈmeɪkə/ *n.* M18. [A large W. Indian island.] 1 Used *attrib.* to designate things native to or imported from Jamaica. M18. 2 *ellipt.* Jamaica coffee, rum, etc. L18.

1 **Jamaica ebony** = COCUS; the tree yielding cocus. **Jamaica ginger** = *white ginger* s.v. GINGER *n.* *Jamaica satinwood*: see SATIN *n.* **Jamaica pepper** allspice. *Jamaica sorrel*: see SORREL *n.*[1] 2.

Jamaican /dʒəˈmeɪk(ə)n/ *n.* & *a.* L17. [f. prec. + -AN.] A *n.* 1 A native or inhabitant of the W. Indian island of Jamaica. L17. 2 The variety of English spoken in Jamaica. M20. B *adj.* Of or pertaining to Jamaica or the Jamaicans. L19.

Jamaicanism *n.* a Jamaican word or idiom M20.

jaman /ˈdʒɑːmən/ *n.* Also **jamoon** /ˈdʒɑːmuːn/. E19. [Hind. *jāmun*, *jāman*, Panjabi *jammūṇ*, f. Skt *jambula*, *jambūla*.] = JAMBOLAN.

jamb /dʒam/ *n.* Also **jambe**. ME. [(O)Fr. *jambe* leg, vertical support, f. Proto-Romance (whence late L *gamba* hoof) f. Gk *kampē* flexure, joint.] 1 *Archit.* Either of the side posts of a doorway, window, or mantelpiece, on which the lintel rests; in *pl.*, the stone sides of a fireplace. Cf. CHEEK *n.* 5. ME. 2 Either of any two side-pieces. *rare.* LME. 3a A piece of leg armour made of metal or hardened leather. Cf. JAMBEAU, JAMBER. LME. b *Her.* = GAMB. L15. 4 A projecting wing of a building. *Sc.* M16. 5 A column; a columnar mass or pillar in a quarry or mine. L17. 6 *Mining.* A bed of clay or stone running across a mineral vein or seam. E18.

1 M. PIERCY She slid a dinner knife between jamb and frame and popped the bolt of the lock.

jambalaya /dʒambəˈlaɪə/ *n.* Orig. *US.* L19. [Louisiana Fr. f. Prov. *jambalaia*.] A dish composed of rice mixed with shrimps, ham, chicken, turkey, etc.; *fig.* a mixture, a jumble.

jambe *n.* var. of JAMB.

†**jambeau** *n.* Pl. **-s**, **-x**. LME–E18. [App. AN deriv. of Fr. *jambe*: see JAMB *n.*] A piece of leg-armour; a leg. Cf. JAMB 3a, next.

†**jamber** *n.* Also **-bier**. ME–E18. [AN *jamber*, (O)Fr. *jambière* leg armour, f. *jambe* leg.] A piece of leg armour, *esp.* a greave. Cf. JAMB 3a, prec.

jambo /ˈdʒambəʊ/ *n.* Pl. **-os**. Also **-bu** /-buː/. L16. [Skt *jambu*, *-bū*, and its derivs., as *jambula*, *jambūla*: cf. next.] In the Indian subcontinent: any of various trees of the genera *Syzygium* and *Eugenia* (family Myrtaceae), or their fruit; *esp.* (*a*) the rose-apple, *S. jambos*; (*b*) the jambolan, *S. cumini*; (*c*) the Malay apple, *S. malaccense*.

jambolan /ˈdʒambəlan/ *n.* E17. [Skt *jambula*, *jambūla*, f. as prec.] An Indian and SE Asian tree, *Syzygium cumini* (family Myrtaceae); the fruit of this tree, an edible purplish-red berry. Also called *jaman*.

jamboree /dʒambəˈriː/ *n.* Orig. *US slang.* M19. [Origin unkn.] A noisy revel; a spree; an occasion when a lot of people meet for a common purpose regarded as pleasurable or frivolous.

Observer The Institute of Directors' annual jamboree.

jambu *n.* var. of JAMBO.

jamdani /dʒɑːmˈdɑːni/ *n.* M19. [Pers. & Urdu *jāmdānī*.] In the Indian subcontinent: a kind of brocaded muslin, usu. with a floral pattern.

James /dʒeɪmz/ *n.* M16. [Male forename, f. OFr. = Prov., Catal. *Jaume*, *Jacme*, Sp. *Jaime*, It. *Giacomo*, f. Proto-Romance alt. of L *Jacobus* JACOB.] 1 †a *James Royal*, a silver coin of James VI of Scotland. Only in M16. b A sovereign (the coin). Cf. JACOBUS. *arch. slang.* M19. 2 = JEMMY 3. E19. 3 = JEMMY 4. E19.

1b **half-James** a half sovereign.

Jamesian /ˈdʒeɪmzɪən/ *a.* & *n.* L19. [f. the surname *James* (see below) + -IAN.] A *adj.* 1 Of or pertaining to the American philosopher and psychologist William James (1842–1910) or his work. L19. 2 Of or pertaining to his brother, the American (later naturalized British) novelist and critic Henry James (1843–1916) or his work. Cf. JACOBEAN *a.* 3. E20. B *n.* A follower or admirer of William James or Henry James or their work. M20.

jamesonite /ˈdʒeɪms(ə)nʌɪt/ *n.* E19. [f. Robert *Jameson* (1774–1854), Sc. mineralogist + -ITE[1].] *Min.* A grey monoclinic sulphide of lead, antimony, and iron, usu. occurring as fibrous masses. Also called *feather-ore*.

James's powder /ˈdʒeɪmzɪz ˈpaʊdə/ *n. phr. obs.* exc. *Hist.* M18. [f. Robert *James* (1703–76), Eng. physician.] An antimonial preparation formerly much used as a febrifuge.

†**Jamestown weed** *n. phr.* see JIMSON.

Jamie Green /dʒeɪmɪ ˈgriːn/ *n.* M19. [Pers. name, of unkn. origin.] *Naut.* A type of sail found on tea-clippers. Cf. *Jimmy Green* s.v. JIMMY *n.*[2]

jamma *n.* var. of JUMMA.

jammer /ˈdʒamə/ *n.* M20. [f. JAM *v.*[1] + -ER[1].] A person who or thing which jams; *spec.* a transmitter used for jamming.

jammy /ˈdʒami/ *a.* M19. [f. JAM *n.*[2] + -Y[2].] Covered with jam, sticky; *fig.* (*colloq.*), excellent, very lucky, easy.

jamoon *n.* var. of JAMAN.

jampan /ˈdʒɑːmpɑːn/ *n.* M19. [Bengali *jhā̃mpān*, Hind. *jhappān*.] A kind of sedan chair carried by four people, used in hill country in the Indian subcontinent.

jams /dʒamz/ *n.pl.* M20. [Abbrev. of PYJAMAS.] Loose knee-length shorts or swimming-trunks.

†**jane** *n.*[1] LME–L17. [OFr. *Janne*(*s*: see JEAN.] A small silver Genoan coin introduced into England towards the end of the 14th cent.

Jane /dʒeɪn/ *n.*[2] Also **j-**. E20. [Female forename.] 1 *plain Jane*, a plain or unattractive girl or woman. E20. 2 A woman, a girl; a girlfriend. *slang* (orig. *US*). E20.

Janeite /ˈdʒeɪnʌɪt/ *n.* L19. [f. *Jane* (see below) + -ITE[1].] An admirer of the writings of the English novelist Jane Austen (1775–1817).

jangada /dʒaŋˈgɑːdə/ *n.* L16. [Port. f. Malayalam *caṅṅādam* f. Skt *saṃghāṭa* joining together.] A log raft with a seat and lateen sail, used as a fishing boat in the north of Brazil and Peru. Formerly also, a type of catamaran used in southern India.

jangle /ˈdʒaŋg(ə)l/ *n.* ME. [Orig. f. AN or OFr. *jangler* (see next); later f. next.] 1 Idle talk, chatter, jabber; an idle word. Long *obs.* exc. *dial.* ME. 2 Contention, altercation, bickering. Now *rare.* ME. 3 A discordant sound, ring, or clang. L18. 4 Confused and noisy talk; the mingled din of voices. M19.

3 C. MCCULLERS The sharp jangle of the doorbell.

jangle /ˈdʒaŋg(ə)l/ *v.* ME. [OFr. *jangler*, *gengler* = Prov. *janglar*, prob. f. Gmc form repr. by (M)Du. *jangelen*.] I *v.i.* 1 Talk excessively or noisily; chatter, babble. *obs.* exc. *dial.* ME. 2 Speak angrily, harshly, or discordantly; grumble; dispute, squabble. *arch.* ME. 3 Make a discordant or unmusical noise. L15.

3 N. SHUTE Morris dancing . . with flying ribbons and little bells that jangled at the knee.

II *v.t.* 4 Say or utter in a noisy, babbling, discordant, or contentious manner; produce (a sound that is harsh and discordant). LME. 5 Cause (a bell etc.) to make a harsh discordant sound; *transf.* irritate (the nerves etc.). E17.

5 F. KING A gust of wind jangled a metal shop sign. B. CASTLE Getting up in a rush always jangles my nerves.

jangler *n.* †(*a*) a chatterer; a storyteller, a jester; (*b*) a noisy disputant: ME. **jangly** *a.* harsh-sounding, discordant; irritating; irritable: L19.

Janglish /ˈdʒaŋglɪʃ/ *n. colloq.* L20. [Blend of JAPANESE and ENGLISH *n.*] = JAPLISH.

janissary *n.* var. of JANIZARY.

janitor /ˈdʒanɪtə/ *n.* M16. [L, f. *janua* door, entrance: see -OR.] 1 A doorkeeper, a porter; *Hist.* an ostler. M16. 2 A caretaker of a building, esp. a school, responsible for its cleaning, heating, etc. E18.

jani'torial *a.* L19. **janitress** *n.* a female janitor E19. **janitrix** *n.* (*rare*) = JANITRESS M19.

janizary /ˈdʒanɪz(ə)ri/ *n.* Also **-iss-** /-ɪs-/. E16. [Fr. *janissaire*, ult. f. Turk. *yeniçeri*, f. *yeni* new +

çeri troops.] 1 *Hist.* A member of a body of Turkish infantry, orig. composed mainly of tributary children of Christians, forming the Sultan's guard and the main part of the standing army from the 14th to the 18th cents. E16. 2 A devoted follower, supporter, or guard. M16. 3 *Hist.* A member of a Turkish armed escort for travellers in the East. E17.

Comb.: **janizary music** = *Turkish music* s.v. TURKISH *a.*

janken /ˈdʒaŋk(ə)n/ *n.* M20. [Jap.] A children's game played by using the hands to represent one of three things, paper, scissors, or stone.

janker /ˈdʒaŋkə/ *n. Sc.* See also JINKER *n.*[2] E19. [Origin unkn.] A long pole on wheels for carrying logs, casks, etc.

jankers /ˈdʒaŋkəz/ *n. Mil. slang.* E20. [Origin unkn.] Punishment for a defaulter; the cells used for this.

jann /dʒɑːn/ *n.* L18. [Arab. *jānn* jinnee.] = JINNEE.

jannock /ˈdʒanək/ *n. north.* L15. [Origin unkn.] A loaf of leavened oaten bread.

jannock /ˈdʒanək/ *a.* & *adv. dial.* See also JONICK. E19. [Origin uncertain: perh. f. prec.] A *adj.* Fair, straightforward; genuine. E19. B *adv.* In a fair, genuine, or straightforward manner. M19.

Jansenist /ˈdʒans(ə)nɪst/ *n.* M17. [f. Cornelis *Jansen* (1585–1638), Bishop of Ypres, Flanders + -IST.] *Eccl. Hist.* An adherent of the Roman Catholic school of thought holding the doctrines of Jansen, who maintained (claiming the support of St Augustine) the perverseness and inability for good of the natural human will.

Jansenism *n.* M17. **Jansеˈnistic** *a.* of, pertaining to, or holding the doctrines of Jansenism or the Jansenists M18. **Janseˈnistical** *a.* = JANSENISTIC M18.

jansky /ˈdʒanski/ *n.* M20. [Karl C. *Jansky* (1905–50), US radio engineer.] A unit used in radio astronomy to express the strength of radio sources, equal to 10^{-26} watt per sq. metre per hertz. (Symbol Jy.)

janty *a.* see JAUNTY *a.*

January /ˈdʒanjʊ(ə)ri/ *n.* OE. [L *Januarius* use as n. (sc. *mensis* month) of adj. f. *Janus*: see next.] The first month of the year in the Gregorian calendar.

May and January: see MAY *n.*[2]

Janus /ˈdʒeɪnəs/ *attrib. a.* M17. [L, name of a god who in Roman mythology was the guardian of doors and gates and presided over beginnings, being represented with two faces, one on the front and another on the back of his head.] 1 Having a dual function, purpose, attitude, etc. Also *Janus-faced.* M17. 2 (Of a material) having a double facing; (of a device) having a two-way action. M19. 3 *Chem.* Designating any of a group of basic azo dyes containing a quaternary ammonium group, often with safranine as the diazo component. L19.

1 A. STORR Aggression seems . . both necessary and undesirable . . —a Janus aspect. 3 **Janus green** either of two basic azo dyes derived from safranine, used as biological stains.

Jap /dʒap/ *n.* & *a. colloq.* (freq. *derog.* & usu. considered *offensive*). L19. [Abbrev.] = JAPANESE.

Jap silk *arch.* = *Japanese silk* s.v. JAPANESE *a.*

Japan /dʒəˈpan/ *n.* Also †**-on.** L16. [See below.] **I** 1 Used *attrib.* to designate things native to or brought from Japan, a country in the Far East off the east coast of the Asian land mass. (Now largely superseded by JAPANESE *a.*) L16.

1 **Japan cedar** = CRYPTOMERIA. **Japan clover** = LESPEDEZA. **Japan current** *the* Kuroshio. **Japan earth** = CATECHU. **Japan ink** a high-quality black ink, glossy when dry. *Japan lacquer*: see LACQUER *n.* 3. **Japan laurel** = AUCUBA. **Japan paper** = *Japanese paper* s.v. JAPANESE *a. Japan pepper*: see PEPPER *n. Japan quince*: see QUINCE 2. **Japan rose** (*a*) = *Japanese rose* (a) s.v. JAPANESE *a.*; †(*b*) the camellia. **Japan varnish** = *Japanese lacquer* s.v. LACQUER *n.* 3. **Japan wax** = *Japanese wax* s.v. JAPANESE *a.*

II †2 A native of Japan; a Japanese. Only in E17. 3 (Usu. **j-**.). A varnish of exceptional hardness which originally came from Japan. Also, any of several similar varnishes, *esp.* (*a*) a black varnish obtained by cooking asphalt with linseed oil, used for producing a black gloss on metal and other materials; (*b*) a varnish-like liquid made from shellac, linseed oil, and turpentine, used as a medium in which to grind colours and for drying pigments. L17. b *fig.* Deceptive outward appearance, veneer. M19. 4 (Also **j-**.) a Japanese porcelain. E18. †b Japanese silk. E18–E19. 5 (Also **j-**.) Japanese work, work in the Japanese style; *esp.* work that is varnished and adorned with painted or raised figures. E18.

japan /dʒəˈpan/ *v.t.* Also **J-**. Infl. **-nn-**. L17. [f. the n.] 1 Lacquer with japan; varnish with a material that gives a hard black gloss. L17. 2 Make black and glossy. E18. 3 [With ref. to the black clerical coat.] = ORDAIN *v.* 9. *slang.* M18.

Japanese /dʒapəˈniːz/ *n.* & *a.* E17. [f. JAPAN *n.* + -ESE.] A *n.* Pl. same, †**-eses**. 1 A native of Japan; a person of Japanese descent. E17. 2 The Japanese language. E19.

B *adj.* Of or pertaining to Japan, its people, or its language. E18.

Special collocations: **Japanese anemone** any of several autumn-flowering cultivated varieties or hybrids of *Anemone hupehensis*, bearing large pink or white flowers. *Japanese anise*: see ANISE 2. **Japanese ape** = *Japanese macaque* below. *Japanese artichoke*: see ARTICHOKE 3. **Japanese beetle** a scarabaeid beetle, *Popillia japonica*, which has become a pest of foliage and grasses in eastern N. America. **Japanese cedar** = CRYPTOMERIA. **Japanese cherry** any of several ornamental flowering cherries, the Japanese *Prunus serrulata* and hybrids of it. **Japanese current** = KUROSHIO. **Japanese deer** = SIKA *n.*[1] **Japanese flower** a piece of coloured paper which unfolds like a flower when placed in water. **Japanese garden**: in which clipped shrubs, water, bridges, rocks, gravel, stone lanterns, etc., are used in a formal design, without masses of bright colour. **Japanese iris** a variety of the irises *Iris kaempferi* or *I. laevigata.* **Japanese knotweed** a tall rhizomatous Japanese plant, *Fallopia japonica* (family Polygonaceae), grown for ornament and now widely naturalized, with broad cuspidate leaves and axillary panicles of small white flowers. *Japanese lacquer*: see LACQUER *n.* 3. **Japanese lantern** = *Chinese lantern* (a) s.v. CHINESE *a.* **Japanese laurel** a Far Eastern aucuba, *Aucuba japonica*, much grown for ornament in the west. **Japanese macaque** a pink-faced macaque of Japan, *Macaca fuscata.* **Japanese maple** any of several maples native to Japan, esp. *Acer palmatum* and *A. japonicum*, cultivated for their decorative foliage. **Japanese medlar** = LOQUAT. **Japanese monkey** = *Japanese macaque* above. *Japanese oyster*: see OYSTER *n.* 1. **Japanese paper**: made by hand, originally and chiefly in Japan, from the bark of the mulberry tree. *Japanese privet*: see PRIVET 1. *Japanese quince*: see QUINCE 2. *Japanese* RAISIN *tree.* **Japanese rose** (*a*) any of several roses native to Japan; esp. = RUGOSA; (*b*) = KERRIA. **Japanese screen** an embroidered screen made in Japan. **Japanese silk** fine soft silk of a type orig. made in Japan, = HABUTAI. **Japanese spaniel** (an animal of) a breed of small, black and white or brown and white, long-coated dog. **Japanese tissue (paper)** a type of strong thin transparent paper. **Japanese vellum** a costly paper handmade in Japan from the inner bark of the mulberry tree. **Japanese waltzing mouse, Japanese waltzer** a mutant of *Mus musculus bactrianus*, a house mouse native to central and eastern Asia (cf. WALTZER 2). **Japanese wax** a yellow wax obtained from the berries of certain sumacs (*Japanese wax-tree*: see WAX *n.*[1]). *Japanese wineberry*: see *wineberry* s.v. WINE *n. Japanese wisteria*: see WISTERIA 1.

Japanesery /dʒapəˈniːz(ə)ri/ *n.* L19. [f. JAPANESE, after Fr. JAPONAISERIE.] Japanese characteristics or fashion; in *pl.*, Japanese ornaments, knick-knacks, etc.

Japanesey /dʒapəˈniːzi/ *a. colloq.* Also **-sy.** L19. [f. JAPANESE *a.* + -Y[1].] Having or inclining to a Japanese character.

Japanesque /dʒapəˈnɛsk/ *a.* & *n.* L19. [f. JAPAN *n.* + -ESQUE.] A *adj.* Japanese in style or manner. L19. B *n.* A design or ornament in Japanese style. L19.

Japanesy *a.* var. of JAPANESEY.

Japanise *v.* var. of JAPANIZE.

Japanism /dʒəˈpanɪz(ə)m/ *n.* L19. [f. JAPAN *n.* + -ISM.] The branch of knowledge that deals with Japanese things; devotion to Japanese things; a thing characteristic of Japan.

Japanize /ˈdʒapənʌɪz/ *v.t.* Also **-ise.** L19. [f. as prec. + -IZE.] Make Japanese.

Japaniˈzation *n.* L19.

japanned /dʒəˈpand/ *a.* L17. [f. JAPAN *v.*, JAPAN *n.*: see -ED[1], -ED[2].] 1 That has been japanned. L17. 2 (**J-**.) Made or become Japanese. *rare.* M19.

1 **japanned leather**: treated with Japan lacquer and dried by heat.

Japanner /dʒəˈpanə/ *n.* E17. [f. JAPAN *n.*, JAPAN *v.* + -ER[1].] †1 A Japanese. E17–M18. 2 (**j-**.) A person who japans things. L17. †b A shoe-black. *joc.* E–M18.

japanning /dʒəˈpanɪŋ/ *n.* L17. [f. JAPAN *v.* + -ING[1].] The action of japanning things; material used in japanning.

Japano- /ˈdʒapənəʊ/ *comb. form.* [f. JAPAN *n.* + -O-.] Forming adjs. w. the sense 'of Japan or the Japanese (and)', as *Japano-Chinese, Japano-Korean.*

Japaˈnolatry *n.* excessive devotion to Japanese art and customs L19. **Japaˈnologist** *n.* an expert on Japanese matters L19. **Japanophile** *n.* a lover of Japan or the Japanese E20.

jape /dʒeɪp/ *n.* ME. [Rel. to next.] †1 A trick, a device to deceive or cheat; a deception, a fraud. ME–E19. 2 A device to amuse; a merry or idle tale; a jest, a joke, a gibe. ME. †3 A trifle, a toy, a trinket, a plaything. LME–L16.

2 *Sunday Express* For Nik Kershaw . . the hardships of army life are a jolly jape.

¶Obs. generally by E17, but revived in literary use in 19.

jape /dʒeɪp/ *v.* LME. [App. combining the form of OFr. *japer* (mod. *japper*) to yelp, yap, w. the sense of OFr. *gaber* mock, deride.] †1 *v.t.* Trick, beguile, deceive. Only in LME. †2 *v.t.* & *i.* Seduce or have sexual intercourse with (a woman). LME–L16. †3 *v.t.* Mock, deride, insult. LME–E19. 4 *v.i.* Say or do something in jest or mockery; jest, joke, jeer. LME.

¶Obs. generally by E17, but revived in literary use in 19.

japer /ˈdʒeɪpə/ *n.* LME. [f. prec. + -ER[1].] †1 A trickster, an impostor; a seducer. LME–L15. 2 A person who jests or plays jokes; *esp.* a professional jester. LME.

¶In sense 2 obs. by L16, but revived in 19.

japery /ˈdʒeɪp(ə)ri/ *n.* Long *rare.* ME. [f. JAPE *n.*, *v.* + -ERY.] Jesting speech, ribaldry; a joke, a jest.

Japhetic /dʒəˈfɛtɪk/ *a.* E19. [f. *Japheth* (L *Japhetus*) (see below) + -IC.] Of or (supposedly) descended from Japheth, one of the sons of Noah; *arch.* Indo-European.

Japhethite /ˈdʒeɪfəθʌɪt/, **-tite** /-tʌɪt/ *n.* a (supposed) descendant of Japheth M19.

japish /ˈdʒeɪpɪʃ/ *a.* E20. [f. JAPE *n.* + -ISH[1].] Of the nature of a jape; inclined to jest.

japishly *adv.* L19. **japishness** *n.* L19.

Japlish /ˈdʒaplɪʃ/ *n. colloq.* M20. [Blend of JAPANESE and ENGLISH *n.*] A blend of Japanese and English spoken by Japanese, either the Japanese language freely interlarded with English expressions or English used unidiomatically by a Japanese. Cf. JANGLISH.

†**Japon** *n.* var. of JAPAN.

japonaiserie /ʒapɔnɛzri/ *n.* L19. [Fr.: cf. CHINOISERIE.] = JAPANESERY.

†**Japonian** *n.* & *a.* L16. [f. JAPON + -IAN.] A *n.* A Japanese. L16–L17. B *adj.* Japanese. E17–L18.

japonic /dʒəˈpɒnɪk/ *a.* Also †**J-**. L17. [f. as prec. + -IC.] Japanese. *obs.* exc. in *japonic acid*, an acid said to occur in catechu.

japonica /dʒəˈpɒnɪkə/ *n.* E19. [mod.L, fem. of *Japonicus* pertaining to Japan.] Any of several plants originally native to Japan; esp. *Chaenomeles speciosa*, the Japanese quince, a spring-flowering pink flowered ornamental shrub of the rose family; the round white, green, or yellow edible fruit of this. Formerly also, the camellia, *Camellia japonica.*

jar /dʒɑː/ *n.*[1] L15. [Rel. to JAR *v.*[1]] 1 Disagreement; (a) divergence or conflict of opinions; dissension, quarrelling; a dispute, a quarrel, *esp.* one of a petty or domestic nature. Now *rare.* L15. 2 A harsh inharmonious or grating sound or combination of sounds; a quivering or tremulous sound. Formerly *spec.* in *Mus.*, a discord. L15. †**3** A vibration or tick of the clock. *rare* (Shakes.). Only in E17. **4** A vibration or tremulous movement resulting from concussion, *esp.* one felt in the body; a thrill of the nerves, mind, or feelings caused by, or resembling the effect of, a physical shock. E19. **5** *Oil Industry. sing.* & in *pl.* A tool used to produce a heavy upward blow in a drill hole, e.g. on a bit that has become stuck. M19.

1 W. COWPER Thy senate is a scene of civil jar. A. JESSOPP Once .. a family jar put two households at war. **at (a) jar** at discord, in a state of dissension or variance. **2** SIR W. SCOTT Bolt and bar Resumed their place with sullen jar. I. D'ISRAELI The critic's fastidious ear listens to .. the jar of rude rhymes. **3** SHAKES. *Wint. T.* I love thee not a jar o' th' clock behind What lady she her lord. **4** K. AMIS The train .. stopped without the slightest jar.

Comb.: **jar ramming** *Founding* = *jolt ramming* s.v. JOLT *n.*

jar /dʒɑː/ *n.*[2] L16. [Fr. *jarre* f. Arab. *jarra.*] **1** A usu. cylindrical container of glass, earthenware, or stoneware with no spout or handle (or with two handles). Orig., a large earthenware vessel for holding water, oil, wine, etc. L16. **2** Such a container and its contents; as much as a jar will hold (formerly a measure of capacity varying according to the commodity). L16. **b** A glass of beer or other alcoholic drink. *colloq.* E20. †**3** *Electr.* A unit of capacity equal to 1111 picofarads. E–M20.

1 LEYDEN *jar.* **2** A. MUNRO I've made about five million jars of jam. **b** *Air Gunner* We called into the pub for a quick jar.

jar /dʒɑː/ *n.*[3] *arch.* L17. [Later form of CHAR *n.*[1]: see AJAR *adv.*[1] & *pred. a.*[1]] *on the jar*, †*at jar*, †*on (a) jar*, (of a door) partly open, ajar.

jar /dʒɑː/ *v.*[1] Infl. **-rr-**. E16. [Prob. imit.] **I 1** *v.i.* Make a harsh grating sound or a musical discord; sound in discord with other sounds. E16. **2** *v.i.* Fall harshly *on*, or (formerly) sound harshly *in*, the ear. Freq. *fig.*, strike with a discordant or painful effect *on* the nerves, feelings, mind, conscience, etc. M16. **3** *v.t.* Shake into vibration; trill. Formerly, grind (one's teeth). M16. **b** Give a jar or shock to (the nerves, mind, or feelings). L18. †**4a** *v.i.* (Of a clock) tick; (of minutes) tick by. L16–E17. **b** *v.t.* Cause to tick. *rare* (Shakes.). Only in L16. **5** *v.i.* Strike against something (or each other) with a grating sound or so as to cause vibration; clash. Foll. by *(up)on*, *with*, *against*. M17. **6** *v.t.* Cause to sound discordantly. M17. **7** *v.i.* Vibrate audibly, esp. with a grating or grinding sound; vibrate or shake from an impact or shock. M18. **8** *v.t.* Drive into a position or condition by a jarring sound or vibration. E19. **9** *v.t.* Injure by concussion or impact. L19.

1 BYRON My heart and harp have lost a string, And both may jar. **2** THACKERAY His laugh jars on one's ear. R. CROMPTON Her voice .. began to jar upon his nerves. G. S. FRASER The rhymes that jar on me. **3** O. W. HOLMES A sudden gust .. jars all the windows. **b** G. GREENE She was jarred .. by the heave of the train. J. BAYLEY It is a comment which jars me in the reading. **5** M. O. W. OLIPHANT His boat of life had .. jarred upon the .. shores of the eternal land. **6** DE QUINCEY Every impulse of bad health jars .. some string in the .. harp of human volition. **7** J. WESLEY The ship shook and jarred with so .. grating a motion. D. WELCH The truck was jarring to a standstill. **8** J. HERSEY The siren jarred her awake. P. DE VRIES Words seemed to have been jarred out of him by a bump in the road.

II 10 *v.i.* Of opinions, statements, systems, etc., or (formerly) persons: be at discord in character or effect; be at variance, disagree, conflict. M16. **b** Come into conflict, clash. E17. **11** *v.i.* Be at strife; dispute, bicker, wrangle. M16.

10 P. BROOK Blending .. so that contradictory styles do not jar. M. GIROUARD Unity of colour prevented one room .. jarring with the next. **b** G. BRIMLEY Clashing sympathies jarred .. harshly within him. **11** C. BURY We were .. jarring and saying disagreeable things.

jar /dʒɑː/ *v.*[2]*t.* Infl. **-rr-**. M18. [f. JAR *n.*[2]] Preserve (fruit) in a jar; bottle.

jarabe /xaˈrabe/ *n.* Also **-ve**. M19. [Amer. Sp. f. Sp. = syrup.] A Mexican pair dance in which the man dances the zapateado steps, performed esp. as an exhibition dance in national costume.

jararaca /dʒɑːrəˈrɑːkə/ *n.* E17. [Port. f. Tupi-Guarani *yararáka.*] Any of several S. American pit vipers of the genus *Bothrops*, esp. *B. jararaca* of Brazil.

jarave *n.* var. of JARABE.

jardinière /ʒɑːdɪˈnjɛː/ *n.* M19. [Fr., lit. 'female gardener'.] **1** An ornamental receptacle, pot, or stand for the display of growing or cut flowers. M19. **2** *Cookery.* A garnish made with cooked vegetables. M19.

jarful /ˈdʒɑːfʊl, -f(ə)l/ *n.* M19. [f. JAR *n.*[2] + -FUL.] As much or a many as a jar will hold.

jargle /ˈdʒɑːg(ə)l/ *v.i.* Long *obs.* exc. *dial.* M16. [OFr. *jargoillier*, *garg-* warble as a bird, murmur as a brook, prob. f. an imit. base: cf. JARGON *n.*[1]] Utter a harsh or shrill sound; chatter, jar.

jargon /ˈdʒɑːg(ə)n/ *n.*[1] LME. [OFr. *jargoun*, *gergon*, *gargon*: ult. origin unkn.] **1** (A vocal sound resembling) the inarticulate utterance of birds, twittering, chattering. *arch.* LME. **2** Unintelligible or meaningless talk or writing; nonsense, gibberish. LME. **3** A jingle or assonance of rhymes. *rare.* L16. †**4** A conventional method of writing or conversing by means of otherwise meaningless symbols; a cipher, a code. L16–E18. **5** A barbarous or debased language or variety of speech; *esp.* a hybrid speech arising from a mixture of languages. Also (*contempt.*), a language one does not understand. M17. **6** (A form of) speech or writing having many unfamiliar terms or restricted to a particular category of people or occupation. M17. **7** A medley or babel of sounds. E18.

5 H. C. BAILEY Proclaimed her wrongs in a jargon of several languages. *Chinook Jargon*: see CHINOOK *n.* 2. **6** L. DEIGHTON He .. avoided jargon, as much as one can .. when dealing with .. new techniques. E. AMADI The coup .. was bloodless, in the jargon of journalists. **7** R. FIRBANK There uprose a jargon of voices.

jargonaut *n.* [after ARGONAUT] a person who uses jargon M20. **jargo'neer** *n.* a person who uses jargon E20. **jargo'nesque** *a.* characterized by the use of jargon, composed in jargon L19. **jar'gonic** *a.* (*rare*) pertaining to or of the nature of jargon E19. **jargonish** *a.* resembling or characteristic of jargon M19. **jargonist** *n.* a person who uses jargon M19.

jargon /ˈdʒɑːg(ə)n/ *n.*[2] Also **-goon** /-ˈguːn/. M18. [Fr. f. It. *giargone*, usu. identified (ult.) with ZIRCON.] A colourless, yellowish, or smoky variety of the mineral zircon found in Sri Lanka (Ceylon). Also called *Matura diamond.*

jargon /ˈdʒɑːg(ə)n/ *v.* LME. [OFr. *jargonner*, f. as JARGON *n.*[1]] **1** *v.i.* Warble, twitter, chatter. *arch.* LME. **2** *v.i.* Utter jargon; talk unintelligibly. L16.

jargoner *n.* a person who uses jargon L19.

jargonelle /dʒɑːgəˈnɛl/ *n.* Also **-el**. L17. [Fr., dim. of JARGON *n.*[2]: see -EL[2].] An early-ripening (orig. inferior) variety of pear.

jargonize /ˈdʒɑːg(ə)nʌɪz/ *v.* Also **-ise**. E19. [f. JARGON *n.*[1] + -IZE.] **1** *v.i.* Talk or use jargon. E19. **2** *v.t.* Bring into or *into* a condition by means of jargon; translate into jargon. E19.

jargoni'zation *n.* E19.

jargoon *n.* var. of JARGON *n.*[2]

†**jark** *n. Criminals' slang.* M16–E19. [Origin unkn.] A seal, a certificate.

Comb.: **jarkman** an educated beggar who fabricated counterfeit passes, licences, and certificates for others.

jarl /jɑːl/ *n.* E19. [ON: see EARL.] *Hist.* A Norse or Danish chieftain or under-king.

jarldom *n.* the territory governed by a jarl E19. **jarlship** *n.* the function or office of a jarl M19.

jarless /ˈdʒɑːlɪs/ *a.* L19. [f. JAR *n.*[1] + -LESS.] Free from jars or jolts; causing no jar.

jarool /dʒəˈruːl/ *n.* Also **jarul**. M19. [Hind. *jāral*, Bengali *jārul*, f. Skt *jāṭali.*] A deciduous tree, *Lagerstroemia speciosa*, of the purple loosestrife family, native to tropical Asia and bearing large panicles of purple or white flowers; the wood of this tree. Also called *pride of India*, *queen's flower.*

jarosite /ˈdʒarəsʌɪt/ *n.* M19. [f. the *Jaroso* ravine in Almeria, S. Spain + -ITE[1].] *Min.* A hexagonal basic sulphate of potassium and iron that is a secondary mineral occurring as yellow or brown crusts on ferruginous ores.

jarovization /jarəvʌɪˈzeɪʃ(ə)n/ *n.* Also **-isation**. M20. [f. Russ. *yarovizatsiya*, f. *yarovoĭ* spring-sown: see -IZATION.] = VERNALIZATION.

jarrah /ˈdʒarə/ *n.* M19. [Aborig. *djarryl*, *jerrhyl.*] The mahogany gum tree, *Eucalyptus marginata*, of western Australia; its reddish-brown timber, noted for durability.

jarring /ˈdʒɑːrɪŋ/ *a.* M16. [f. JAR *v.*[1] + -ING[2].] That jars; *esp.* grating on the ear or on the feelings or nerves; discordant, conflicting, clashing.

F. DONALDSON Life continued, with not a jarring incident to mar the serenity.

jarringly *adv.* L16. **jarringness** *n.* M19.

jarul *n.* var. of JAROOL.

jarvey /ˈdʒɑːvi/ *n. colloq.* Now *rare.* E19. [By-form of *Jarvis*, *Jervis*, male forename.] **1** A hackney-coachman; *Anglo-Ir.*, the driver of a jaunting car. E19. **2** A hackney-coach. E19.

Comb.: **jarvey-car** *Anglo-Ir.* a jaunting car.

jasey /ˈdʒeɪzi/ *n. arch. joc.* & *colloq.* L18. [Perh. alt. of JERSEY *n.*[2], so called because made of Jersey yarn.] A wig, *esp.* one made of worsted.

jasmine /ˈdʒazmɪn, ˈdʒaz-/ *n.* Also **-in**, (*arch.*) **jessamin(e)** /ˈdʒɛsəmɪn/. M16. [Fr. *jasmin*, †*jessemin* f. Arab. *yāsamīn* (Hispano- & N. Afr. Arab. *yasmīn*, whence Sp. *jazmín*, Port. *jasmin*) f. Pers. *yāsaman.* See also JESSAMY.).] **1** Any of various ornamental and climbing shrubs of the genus *Jasminum* of the olive family, cultivated for their fragrant white or yellow salver-shaped flowers; *esp.* one of the common species *J. officinale*, with white flowers, and the yellow-flowered *J. humile* and *J. mesnyi.* Also (w. specifying wd), any of various fragrant plants of other genera and families. M16. **2** A perfume derived from the flowers of the jasmine. L17.

1 Arabian jasmine an evergreen climbing jasmine, *Jasminum sambac*, with fragrant clusters of white flowers that are used to flavour tea; also called *mogra.* *Cape jasmine*: see CAPE *n.*[1] **Carolina jasmine** = GELSEMIUM. **Chilean jasmine** a S. American woody liana, *Mandevilla laxa* (family Apocynaceae), with fragrant white flowers. MADAGASCAR *jasmine.* **night jasmine** a shrub or small tree of southern Asia, *Nyctanthes arbor-tristis*, allied to the jasmine, with fragrant night-blooming flowers. **red jasmine** = FRANGIPANI 2. **winter jasmine** a winter-flowering jasmine, *Jasminum nudiflorum*, bearing yellow flowers on leafless branches.

Comb.: **jasmine-tea**: perfumed with jasmine.

jasmined *a.* adorned with jasmine E19.

jasp /dʒɑːsp, dʒasp/ *n.* Now *rare* or *obs.* ME. [(O)Fr. *jaspe*: see JASPER *n.*[1]] = JASPER *n.*[1] 1.

jaspé /ˈdʒaspeɪ, *foreign* ʒaspe/ *a.* M19. [Fr., pa. pple of *jasper* to marble.] Marbled, mottled, variegated.

jasper /ˈdʒaspə/ *n.*[1] & *a.* ME. [OFr. *jaspre* var. of *jaspe* (also mod.) f. L *iaspis* f. Gk, of oriental origin.] **A** *n.* **1** Formerly, any bright-coloured chalcedony other than cornelian, the most valued being of a green colour. Now, an opaque cryptocrystalline variety of quartz, usu. red, yellow, or brown, owing to the presence of haematite. ME. **2** A kind of hard fine porcelain invented by Josiah Wedgwood and used for Wedgewood cameos and other delicate work. Also *jasper-ware.* E19.

Comb.: **jasper-opal** an impure opal containing haematite and having the colour of yellow jasper; *jasper-ware*: see sense 2 above.

B *adj.* Made or consisting of jasper. E18.

jaspered *a.* = JASPER *a.* E17. **jasperize** *v.t.* convert by petrifaction into jasper or a form of silica resembling jasper M19. **jaspery** *a.* of the nature of, resembling, or containing jasper L18.

jasper /ˈdʒaspə/ *n.*[2] *US colloq.* (usu. *derog.*). L19. [*Jasper*, male forename.] A person, a fellow; *spec.* a rustic simpleton.

jasperoid /ˈdʒaspərɔɪd/ *a.* & *n.* L19. [f. JASPER *n.*[1] + -OID.] **A** *adj.* Like jasper in appearance or structure. L19. **B** *n. Geol.* A rock in which silica, in the form of fine-grained quartz or chalcedony, has replaced some of the original constituents (usually the carbonate of limestone). L19.

jaspis /ˈdʒaspɪs/ *n.* Long *rare* or *obs.* LME. [L *iaspis*: see JASPER *n.*[1]] = JASPER *n.*[1] 1.

jasponyx /dʒasˈpɒnɪks/ *n.* Long *rare* or *obs.* E17. [L *iasponyx* f. Gk *iasponux*, f. *iaspis* JASPER *n.*[1] + *onux* ONYX.] (An) onyx partaking of the character of jasper or containing bands of jasper.

jassid /ˈdʒasɪd/ *a.* & *n.* L19. [mod.L *Jassidae* (see below), f. *Iassus* genus name f. L name of a former town in Asia Minor: see -ID[3].] *Zool.* **A** *adj.* Of, pertaining to, or designating the homopteran family Cicadellidae of leafhoppers, which includes several pests of cereals, fodder crops, etc. L19. **B** *n.* A leafhopper of this family. L19.

Jat /dʒɑːt/ *n.*[1] & *a.* E17. [Hind. *Jāṭ*] **A** *n.* A member of a population group settled in the north-west of the Indian subcontinent, present also by immigration in Afghanistan and Iran, and identified with the Gypsies of Syria. E17. **B** *attrib.* or as *adj.* Of or pertaining to the Jats. M19.

jat /dʒɑːt/ *n.*[2] Also **jati** /ˈdʒɑːti/. L19. [Hind. *jāt*, *jāti* f. Skt *jāti* birth.] In the Indian subcontinent: a caste, a tribe, a class.

jat́ /jatj/ *n.* Also (earlier) †**yat** & other vars. M18. [Old Ch. Slav. *jatĭ.*] The Slavonic character written ⱑ in the Glagolitic alphabet and ѣ in the Cyrillic alphabet, generally transliterated from both alphabets as *ě*; the sound represented by these characters; the Common Slavonic sound from which it developed.

Jataka /ˈdʒɑːtəkə/ *n.* E19. [Pali *jātaka* birth, nativity (story) f. Skt, f. *jan-* be born.] In Buddhist literature, a story of one or other of the former incarnations of the Buddha; a collection of such stories.

jatha /dʒəˈtɑː/ *n.* E20. [Panjabi, Hind. *jāthā*] In the Indian subcontinent: an armed or organized band of Sikhs.

jati *n.* var. of JAT *n.*[2]

jauk /dʒɔːk/ *v.i. Sc.* L15. [Origin unkn.] Trifle, delay, dawdle.

jaunce /dʒɔːns/ *v.* & *n.* L16. [Perh. f. OFr.: cf. JAUNT *v.*] **A** *v.t.* & *i.* (Cause to) prance; traipse. *arch.* L16. **B** *n.* A tiring journey. Long *obs.* exc. *dial.* L16.

jaundice /ˈdʒɔːndɪs/ *n.* ME. [OFr. *jaunice* (mod. *-isse*) yellowness, f. *jaune* yellow: see -ICE[1]. For the intrusive *d* cf. *sound.*] **1** *Med.* A condition characterized by yellowness of the skin, conjunctiva, and tissues, and occas. disordered vision, often due to obstruction of the bile duct or disease of the liver. ME. **2** *fig.* A jaundiced condition or viewpoint; envy, jealousy, resentment. L16. †**3** = ICTERUS 2. E–M17.

1 *obstructive jaundice*: see OBSTRUCTIVE *a.* 2. 2 DRYDEN Jealousie, the jaundice of the soul. D. FRANCIS 'It sounds dry,' I said with jaundice.

jaundice /ˈdʒɔːndɪs/ *v.t.* L18. [App. back-form. f. next.] **1** Affect with jaundice. Chiefly *fig.*, tinge with envy, jealousy, or resentment. L18. **2** Tinge with yellow, make yellow. L19.

jaundiced /ˈdʒɔːndɪst/ *a.* M17. [f. JAUNDICE *n.* + -ED[2].] **1** Affected with jaundice. Of the complexion: unnaturally yellow. M17. **2** *gen.* Yellow-coloured. Now *rare.* M17. **3** Affected or tinged with envy, jealousy, or resentment. L17.

2 LYTTON A comely matron . . in a jaundiced satinet gown. 3 W. WHEWELL He was naturally querulous and jaundiced in his views. M. EDWARDES The 'tea break strike' . . reinforced the jaundiced view of Britain from overseas.

jaune /ʒoːn/ *a.* LME. [Fr. f. L *galbinum* greenish-yellow.] Yellow. *obs.* exc. in names of pigments.

jaune brilliant cadmium yellow.

¶Formerly fully naturalized.

jaunt /dʒɔːnt/ *n.* L16. [Rel. to the vb.] **1** A tiring or troublesome journey. Now only as an *iron.* use of sense 2. L16. **2** An excursion, a journey; *esp.* a pleasure trip. L17. **3** Jaunty manner or bearing. *rare.* E18.

2 P. THEROUX A tourist on a ten-day jaunt through ruins and cathedrals. C. WILLIAMS My jaunts to the Law Courts . . had ceased. 3 K. LAING A second-division clerk with an outrageous jaunt in his walk.

jaunt /dʒɔːnt/ *v.* L16. [Origin unkn.: cf. JAUNCE.] †**1** *v.t.* Exercise or tire (a horse) by riding it up and down. L16–E17. †**2** *v.t.* Carry about on a prancing horse or in a vehicle. *rare.* L16–E19. **3** *v.i.* Traipse about; run to and fro. L16. **4** *v.i.* Make a short journey, trip, or excursion, esp. for pleasure; take a jaunt. M17. **5** *v.i.* Move jauntily. *rare.* L19.

4 D. LESSING I've rushed around London, . . jaunted off to Somerset and Dorset.

Comb.: **jaunting car** in Ireland, a light, two-wheeled horse-drawn vehicle for carrying four passengers seated either back to back or facing inwards, with a seat in front for the driver.

jaunty /ˈdʒɔːnti/ *n. Naut. slang.* Also **jonty** /ˈdʒɒnti/. E20. [Perh. alt. of GENDARME.] The master-at-arms on a ship.

jaunty /ˈdʒɔːnti/ *a.* Also (earlier) †**janty**. M17. [Fr. *gentil*: see GENTLE *a.*, GENTEEL.] †**1** (Of a person, manner, etc.) well-bred, gentlemanly, genteel; (of a thing) elegant, stylish, smart. M17–M19. **2** Having or expressing a sprightly confident manner; perky, carefree, debonair. L17. **b** Lively, brisk. E18.

2 S. RUSHDIE He leaned round corners on his bicycle, taking them at a jaunty angle. P. FERGUSON Downstairs the doorbell gave out its jaunty chimes. I. MURDOCH His jaunty roguish teasing air of a spoilt boy. b K. MANSFIELD He couldn't . . stride off, jaunty as a young man.

jauntily *adv.* E19. **jauntiness** *n.* E18.

jaup /dʒɔːp/ *n.* & *v. Sc.* & *north.* Also **jawp**. E16. [Prob. imit.] **A** *n.* **1** The splash of liquid against a surface; a spot of water, mud, etc., resulting from splashing. E16. **2** The sound made by liquid sloshing around in a container. E19. **B** *v.* **1** *v.i.* Splash, slosh around; make a splashing sound. E16. **2** *v.t.* Cause (liquid) to splash or slosh around; splash with water, mud, etc. E16.

Java /ˈdʒɑːvə/ *n.* M19. [A large island in the Malay archipelago, now part of Indonesia.] **1** Used *attrib.* to designate things from or associated with Java. M19. **2** Coffee from Java; *gen.* (*slang*) coffee. M19.

1 **Java almond** a SE Asian tree, *Canarium luzonicum* (cf. KANARI). **Java canvas** open-weave canvas for embroidery etc. **Java man** a fossil hominid, *Homo* (formerly *Pithecanthropus*) *erectus*, remains of which were first found in Java in 1891. *Java pepper*: see PEPPER *n.* **Java plum** = JAMBOLAN. **Java sparrow** a bird of the waxbill family, *Padda oryzivora*, native to Java and Bali and often kept as an aviary bird.

javaite /ˈdʒɑːvəʌɪt/ *n.* M20. [f. prec. + -ITE[1].] *Geol.* A tektite from the strewn field of Java.

Javan /ˈdʒɑːv(ə)n/ *a.* & *n.* E17. [f. as prec. + -AN.] **A** *adj.* Of or pertaining to Java or its people. E17. **B** *n.* A native or inhabitant of Java. E17.

Javanese /dʒɑːvəˈniːz/ *n.* & *a.* E18. [f. prec. + -*n*- + -ESE.] **A** *n.* Pl. same, †**-eses**. **1** A native or inhabitant of Java. E18. **2** The Austronesian language of central Java. M19. **B** *adj.* Of or pertaining to Java, its people, or their language; Javan. E18.

javanite /ˈdʒɑːv(ə)nʌɪt/ *n.* M20. [f. as prec. + -ITE[1].] *Geol.* = JAVAITE.

javel /ˈdʒav(ə)l/ *n.* Long *rare.* LME. [Origin unkn.] A rogue, a wretch, a rascal.

javelin /ˈdʒav(ə)lɪn/ *n.* & *v.* LME. [(O)Fr. *javeline* alt. of JAVELOT.] **A** *n.* **1** A light throwing-spear used as a weapon or in field athletics; the sporting event in which this is thrown. LME. †**2** A pike; a lance. E16–M19. **3** *Her.* A charge consisting of a short spear with a barbed head. L19.

1 *Dumfries Courier* Ian had to settle for 3rd place in the javelin. *fig.*: J. G. WHITTIER Piercing the waves . . With the slant javelins of rain.

Comb.: **javelin fish** an Indo-Pacific food fish, *Pomadasys hasta*, of the grunt family; **javelin man** *Hist.* (*a*) a member of a sheriff's retinue armed with a pike who escorted the judges at assizes; (*b*) a javelineer; **javelin-snake** a dart-snake, *esp.* a snakelike lizard of the genus *Acontias*.

B *v.t.* Strike or pierce with or as with a javelin. M19.

javeliˈneer *n.* a soldier armed with a javelin E17.

Javelle water /ʒaˈvɛl ˌwɔːtə/ *n. phr.* Also **Javel water**, †**Javel(le)'s water**. E19. [*Javel*, a village, now a suburb of Paris, where the solution was first used.] A solution of sodium or potassium hypochlorite, used as a bleach or disinfectant. Also called *eau de Javelle*.

†**javelot** *n.* ME–E18. [(O)Fr. f. Proto-Gallo-Romance *gabalottus.*] A small spear or javelin thrown with the hand or from a catapult.

Javel water *n. phr.* var. of JAVELLE WATER.

javver /ˈdʒavə/ *v.i.* Long *obs.* exc. *dial.* LME. [Imit.: cf. JABBER.] = JABBER *v.* 1.

jaw /dʒɔː/ *n.*[1] LME. [OFr. *joe* cheek, jaw, AN *jowe* cheek, jaw, of uncertain origin.] **1** Either of the bony structures forming the framework of the mouth, and the seizing, biting, or masticating apparatus of vertebrates; *sing.* usu. the mandible (the *lower jaw*), less commonly the maxilla (the *upper jaw*); the part of the head containing these. LME. **b** Any of various parts or organs associated with the mouth in certain invertebrates and used for grasping, piercing, or grinding during feeding etc. L19. **2** In *pl.* The bones and associated structures of the mouth including the teeth, regarded as instruments of biting, gripping, crushing, and devouring; the cavity formed by these parts; the mouth, the throat. LME. **3** A side of a narrow pass or channel (usu. in *pl.*); in *pl.*, the narrow entrance into something. LME. **4** *fig.* In *pl.* The grip of any devouring agency, as death, time, etc. M16. **5** Talkativeness; idle or impudent talk; a (long) talk, a speech; a chat, incessant chatter. Cf. JAW-JAW *n. colloq.* M18. **6** In *pl.* The seizing or holding parts of a machine etc., arranged in pairs and usu. able to open and close; *spec.* (*Naut.*) the end of a boom or gaff which clasps the mast with its projecting ends. L18.

1 M. MOORCOCK He had a clean-shaven jaw. J. A. MICHENER He did see some jaws drop in fear. *locked jaw*: see LOCKED *a.*[2] LUMPY *jaw*. b T. H. HUXLEY In the Arthropoda, what are usually termed jaws are modified limbs. 2 SPENSER The hungry Spaniells . . With greedy iawes her ready foe to teare. M. MILNER A girl acrobat hanging onto the rope with only her jaws. *jaws wag*: see WAG *v.* 3 J. A. SYMONDS The torrent, foaming down between black jaws of rain-stained granite. *Snooker Scene* The cue-ball striking the jaw of the middle pocket. 4 TENNYSON Into the jaws of Death, Into the mouth of Hell Rode the six hundred. *Guardian* Watch for the moment that snatches defeat from the jaws of victory. 5 G. B. SHAW Lets have a jaw over some supper. *Times Lit. Suppl.* Committee work is just endless jaw. 6 *DIY Success!* Grip the upright piece in a vice or the jaws of a portable work-bench.

Comb.: **jaw-breaker** *colloq.* (*a*) a word with many syllables or difficult to pronounce; (*b*) a large, hard, or sticky sweet; **jaw-breaking** *a.* (*colloq.*) difficult to pronounce; **jaw clutch** a dog-clutch or other form of clutch in which one part engages in the jaws of the other; **jaw-crusher** a machine with jaws for crushing ore etc.; **jaw-fallen** *a.* having the lower jaw fallen or hanging loose; dejected; **jaw-rope** *Naut.* the rope which fastens the jaws of a boom or gaff round a mast; **jawsmith** *US slang* a talkative person; *esp.* a loud-mouthed demagogue; **jaw-tooth** a molar tooth.

jawed *a.* having jaws (of a specified kind) E16. **jawless** *a.* lacking jaws; *Zool.* (of a fish) agnathan: E18. **jawy** *a.* (*rare*) (*a*) of or pertaining to the jaw; (*b*) forceful in language: M17.

jaw /dʒɔː/ *n.*[2] *Sc.* & *north.* E16. [Origin unkn. Cf. next.] **1** The rush of a wave; a surging wave, a billow. E16. **2** A quantity of water or other liquid dashed, splashed, or poured out. E19.

jaw /dʒɔː/ *v.*[1] *Sc.* E16. [Origin unkn. Cf. prec.] **1** *v.i.* Rush in waves; dash, pour, splash; surge. E16. **2** *v.t.* Pour or dash (water) in waves; throw (liquid) in quantity. L17.

jaw /dʒɔː/ *v.*[2] E17. [f. JAW *n.*[1]] †**1** *v.t.* Seize or devour with the jaws; use the jaws on. Only in E17. **2** *v.i.* Speak, talk, esp. at length; chatter. Cf. JAW-JAW *v. colloq.* M18. **3** *v.t.* Admonish, lecture, scold. *colloq.* E19.

2 G. BENFORD They've been jawing about the new hydro plant for ten hours. 3 F. NORRIS She jawed him for making an exhibition of himself.

jawan /dʒəˈwɑːn/ *n.* Also **ji-** /dʒɪ-/. M19. [Urdu *jawān* f. Pers. = young man: ult. rel. to YOUNG *a.*] In the Indian subcontinent, a private soldier.

jawar, -ari *ns.* vars. of JOWAR, -ARI.

jawbone /ˈdʒɔːbəʊn/ *n.* & *v.* L15. [f. JAW *n.*[1] + BONE *n.*] **A** *n.* **1** A bone of the jaws; *spec.* the bone of the lower jaw, the mandible; either (left or right) half of this. L15. **2** An animal's jawbone used as a musical instrument; also (in *pl.*), castanets. M19. **3** = CREDIT *n.* 6. *N. Amer. slang.* M19. **B** *v.t.* & *i.* Seek to restrain (a trade union or other body in a dispute) by persuasion. Chiefly as *jawboning* vbl n. *US slang.* M20.

jaw-hole /ˈdʒɔːhəʊl/ *n.* M18. [Partly f. JAW *n.*[1], partly f. JAW *n.*[2], *v.*[1], + HOLE *n.*[1]] **1** A hole into which dirty water etc. is thrown, a drain. *Sc.* & *north.* M18. **2** An opening, an abyss. M19.

Jawi /ˈdʒɑːwi/ *n.* & *a.* E19. [Malay.] **A** *n.* Orig., the Malay vernacular. Now, the Malay language written in Arabic script. E19. **B** *attrib.* or as *adj.* Of or pertaining to Jawi. E20.

jaw-jaw /ˈdʒɔːdʒɔː/ *v.* & *n.* M19. [Redupl. of JAW *v.*[2], *n.*[1]] **A** *v.i.* Talk, esp. at length or to no purpose. M19. **B** *n.* Talking; *esp.* lengthy and pointless discussion. M20.

¶Rare bef. M20.

jawp *n.* & *v.* var. of JAUP.

jaws harp /dʒɔːz ˈhɑːp/ *n. phr.* Also **jaw's harp.** L19. [Alt.] = *Jew's harp* s.v. JEW *n.*

jay /dʒeɪ/ *n.* & *a.* L15. [OFr. (mod. *geai*) f. late L *gaius, gaia*, perh. f. male praenomen *Gaius*.] **A** *n.* **1** Any of various medium-sized birds of the crow family, with varied, often colourful, plumage; *spec.* the Eurasian *Garrulus glandarius*, a raucous, woodland bird with pinkish-brown plumage marked with black, white, and blue. L15. **2** Any of various other birds; *esp.* a jackdaw; a chough. *obs.* exc. *dial.* L15. **3** An impertinent chatterer. Also, a flashy or absurdly dressed person; a stupid or silly person. *colloq.* E16.

1 *blue jay*: see BLUE *a.* CANADA *jay. Siberian jay*: see SIBERIAN *a.* STELLER('*s*) *jay.*

Comb.: **jay-bird** *colloq.* = sense A.1 above (*naked as a jay-bird*: see NAKED *a.*); **jay-hawker** (chiefly *US*), a raiding guerrilla or irregular soldier (orig. in and around eastern Kansas).

B *attrib.* or as *adj.* Dull, unsophisticated, inferior, poor. *US colloq.* L19.

Jaycee /dʒeɪˈsiː/ *n. colloq.* M20. [f. initial letters of *Junior Chamber.*] A member of a Junior Chamber of Commerce.

Jaycette /dʒeɪsiːˈɛt/ *n.* a female Jaycee M20.

jaywalker /ˈdʒeɪwɔːkə/ *n.* Orig. *US.* E20. [f. JAY + WALKER *n.*[2]] A pedestrian who crosses or walks in a street without regard for traffic.

jaywalk *v.i.* behave as a jaywalker (chiefly as *jaywalking* vbl n) E20.

jazerant /ˈdʒaz(ə)r(ə)nt/ *n. obs.* exc. *Hist.* Also (earlier) †**jesserant.** LME. [OFr. *jaseran(t), -enc* orig. an adj., in *osberc* (*hauberc*) *jazerant*, = Sp. *cota jacerina*, of unkn. origin.] A light coat of armour made of small metal plates riveted to each other or attached to a tunic of leather or stout cloth.

jazz /dʒaz/ *n.* & *a.* E20. [Origin unkn.] **A** *n.* **1** A type of music of US Black origin, characterized by its use of improvisation, syncopated phrasing, and a regular or forceful rhythm; *loosely* syncopated dance-music. E20. **2** Energy, excitement, excitability. *colloq.* E20. **3** Meaningless or empty talk, nonsense; pretentious behaviour; unnecessary ornamentation; nonsensical stuff. *colloq.* E20. **4** Sexual intercourse. *slang.* E20.

1 D. BRUBECK When there is not complete freedom of the soloist, it ceases to be jazz. MODERN *jazz. symphonic jazz*: see SYMPHONIC 3. **2** J. GALSWORTHY With all the jazz there is about, she'd appreciate somebody restful. **3** E. MCBAIN 'How was school today, darling?' 'Oh, the same old jazz'. **and all that jazz** and all that sort of thing, et cetera.

B *attrib.* or as *adj.* **1** Of or pertaining to jazz; involved in, featuring, or based on jazz. E20. **2** Of fantastic design; gaudy, vivid; jazzy. E20.

1 B. SCHULBERG How true jazz music was, how it echoed everything . . churning inside me. J. RULE They were all part of a huge, exuberant jazz symphony. **2** *Daily Mail* Jazz patterns in dress.

Special collocations & comb.: **jazz age** the era of jazz; *spec.* the early nineteen twenties; **jazzman** a (male) jazz musician; **jazz-rock** music that has the characteristics of both jazz and rock.

jazz /dʒaz/ *v. colloq.* E20. [f. the n.] **1** *v.t.* Play (music) in the style of jazz; give a jazz style to; enliven, brighten up; make more colourful or exciting; excite. Freq. foll. by *up.* E20. **2** *v.i.* Play jazz; dance to jazz music; move in a bizarre or fantastic manner. E20. **3** *v.t.* & *i.* Have sexual intercourse (with). *slang.* E20.

1 L. OLIVIER A hideously jazzed-up version of 'God Save the Queen'. *Sunday Express* Jazz it up with fruity olive oil, paprika and fresh parsley. **2** P. SCOTT Water reflections are jazzing on the undersurface of the shade. **3** J. T. FARRELL She was a woman now, who got regular jazzing and knew what it was all about.

jazzer *n.* (*colloq.*) a person who plays or dances to jazz; a jazz enthusiast: E20.

jazzbo /ˈdʒazbəʊ/ *n. arch. US slang.* Pl **-os.** E20. [Origin unkn.: perh. rel. to JAZZ *n.*] **1** Poor variety theatre, vulgar comedy. E20. **2** A person, *esp.* a Black; *spec.* (*a*) a (Black) performer in variety theatre; (*b*) an old or dissolute (Black) person. E20.

Jazzercise /ˈdʒazəsʌɪz/ *n.* Also **j-.** L20. [f. JAZZ *n.* + EXERCISE *n.* Cf. DANCERCISE.] Physical exercise in the form of dancing to the accompaniment of jazz music.

¶Proprietary name in the US.

jazzify /ˈdʒazɪfʌɪ/ *v.t.* E20. [f. JAZZ *n.* + -I- + -FY.] Make jazzy; jazz up.

jazzifiˈcation *n.* M20.

jazzy /ˈdʒazi/ *a.* E20. [f. JAZZ *n.* + -Y[1].] Pertaining to or resembling jazz; characterized by jazz; spirited, lively, exciting; vivid, gaudy; *derog.* pretentiously showy, unrestrained.

Chambers's Journal To sing some jazzy stuff called 'Alexander's Rag Time Band'. B. BROADFOOT He bought a new car, the jazziest in Calgary. W. ALLEN A couple dressed like American tourists, wearing jazzy Hawaiian shirts.

jazzily *adv.* E20. **jazziness** *n.* E20.

jealous /ˈdʒɛləs/ *a.* ME. [OFr. *gelos* (mod. *jaloux*) f. med.L *zelosus*, f. Chr.L *zelus* f. Gk *zēlos* ZEAL: see -OUS.] **1 a** Troubled by the fear, suspicion, or belief that one is being or might be displaced in someone's affections; (disposed to be) distrustful of the fidelity of a spouse or lover; overly possessive of a friend, lover, or spouse. (Foll. by *of*.) ME. **b** Of God: demanding absolute faithfulness and exclusive worship. ME. **c** *gen.* Resentful or envious of another person or of his or her possible or actual success, advantage, or superiority; disposed to rivalry. LME. †**2** Devoted, zealous; *rare* angry. LME–M17. †**3** Amorous; fond; lustful. LME–E17. **4** Foll. by *of*: protective of; careful in guarding; watchful over. LME. **5** Suspicious; apprehensive, worried, fearful. (Foll. by *of* or subord. cl.) *obs.* exc. *dial.* LME. †**b** Doubtful, mistrustful. Only in 17. **6** Vigilant, watchful, careful. L18.

1a H. E. BATES A person of possessive and jealous desire. J. BARTH Some guys would get jealous if their wife played tennis with another man. N. MAILER He was so insanely jealous Couldn't stand the thought of her meeting another man. **c** R. K. NARAYAN He is very jealous, won't tolerate a pinch of original work. M. WEST I was jealous because she was getting something I never had. M. SEYMOUR-SMITH The poet . . was jealous of Riding's poetic accomplishments. **4** SIR W. SCOTT The chief is young, and jealous of his rank. **6** H. KELLER I guarded both doll and cradle with the most jealous care.

jealously *adv.* LME. **jealousness** *n.* (now *rare*) LME.

jealousy /ˈdʒɛləsi/ *n.* ME. [OFr. *gelosie* (mod. *jalousie*), f. *gelos*: see prec., -Y[3].] **1 a** The consuming fear, suspicion, or belief that one is being or might be displaced in someone's affections; distrust of the fidelity of a spouse or lover. ME. **b** Of God: intolerance of the worship of other gods. ME. **c** Resentment or envy of another person or of his or her possible or actual success, advantage, or superiority; rivalry. LME. †**2 a** Anger, wrath. LME–M17. **b** Devotion, eagerness. LME–M16. **3** Concern or anxiety for the preservation or well-being of something or someone; vigilance or care in guarding something or someone. LME. **4** Suspicion; apprehension of evil; mistrust. *obs.* exc. *dial.* LME. **5** = JALOUSIE. Chiefly *Jamaican.* L18.

1a AV *S. of S.* 8:6 Iealousie is cruel as the graue: the coales thereof are coales of fire. A. S. NEILL Jealousy arises from the combination of love with possessiveness about the loved object. **c** L. GORDON Malice . . arose from her jealousy of her sister-in-law, who managed to publish stories. R. INGALLS Their quarrels, misunderstandings and jealousies were . . like those of other families.

jean /dʒiːn/ *a.* & *n.* L15. [OFr. *Janne* (mod. *Gênes*) f. med.L *Janua* Genoa, city in Italy.] **A** *adj.* †**1** Originating from Genoa, Genoese. L15–E17. **2** Designating a heavy twilled cotton fabric, now usu. denim; made of this. L18.

2 *City Limits* Paul's in his late 20's, wears a jean jacket.

B *n.* **1** Orig. †*jean fustian.* A heavy twilled cotton fabric, now usu. denim. L16. **2** In *pl.* Garments of this material. Now usu. hard-wearing trousers of this (or other) material, worn esp. for leisure or for physical work (also *pair of jeans*). M19.

2 N. GORDIMER He was barefoot and in white canvas jeans and a checked shirt. P. BOOTH The faded blue jeans were immaculately pressed. *attrib.*: M. ATWOOD He wears crumbling jeans suits.

jeaned *a.* wearing jeans M20.

jeannette /dʒəˈnɛt/ *n.* Also **jeanette.** L18. [f. prec. + -ETTE.] Any of various types of material resembling jean.

jebel /ˈdʒɛbəl/ *n.* M19. [Arab. *jabal*, (colloq.) *jebel*, pl. *jibāl*, mountain.] In the Middle East and N. Africa: a mountain, a range of hills. Freq. in specific names.

jee /dʒiː/ *v.*, *int.*, & *n.* Chiefly *Sc.* Pa. t. & pple **jeed.** E18. [Origin unkn. Cf. GEE *v.*[2], *int.*[1]] **A** *v.* **1** *v.i.* Move, stir; move to one side. E18. **2** *v.t.* Cause to move; move aside, shift. E18. **B** *int.* = GEE *int.*[1]; instructing a horse pulling a plough etc. to move or turn. E19. **C** *n.* A move, a motion, a sideways turn. Also, an instruction to a horse pulling a plough etc. to move or turn. E19.

jeep /dʒiːp/ *n.* & *v.* Orig. *US.* Also **J-.** M20. [f. GP general *p*urpose, prob. infl. by 'Eugene the Jeep', a shape-changing character of great resourcefulness and power introduced into the cartoon strip 'Popeye' in 1936.] **A** *n.* (Proprietary name for) a small sturdy motor vehicle having emergency four-wheel drive, orig. and esp. one used for military purposes. M20. **B** *v.i.* & *t.* (Usu. **j-.**) Travel by Jeep. M20.

jeepable *a.* negotiable by Jeep M20.

jeepers /ˈdʒiːpəz/ *int. slang* (orig. *US*). Also **jeepers creepers** /ˈdʒiːpəz ˈkriːpəz/. E20. [Alt. of JESUS.] = JEEZ *int.*

DENNIS POTTER Jeepers, Joanie. What lovely, lovely little rosebuds!

jeepney /ˈdʒiːpni/ *n.* M20. [f. JEEP + JIT)NEY.] In the Philippines: a jitney bus converted from a Jeep; a small bus, a minibus.

jeer /dʒɪə/ *n.*[1] L15. [Perh. var. of GEAR.] *Naut. sing.* & (usu.) in *pl.* Tackle for hoisting and lowering the lower yards.

jeer /dʒɪə/ *v.* & *n.*[2] M16. [Origin unkn.] **A** *v.* **1** *v.i.* Speak or call out in derision or mockery; scoff derisively. (Foll. by *at.*) M16. **b** *v.t.* Say or call out in derision or mockery. E20. **2** *v.t.* Address or treat with scornful derision; mock, taunt. L16. **3** *v.t.* Drive or force (*into*, *out of*, etc.) by jeering. M17.

1 D. M. THOMAS Some looked sorry for them, but others laughed and jeered. P. ANGADI I jeer at her uneducated, brainless approach to life and laugh openly at her. **b** A. MCCOWEN When passing a waiting bus queue, he would often jeer, 'Look at the poor!' **2** C. M. YONGE The mob pelted him and jeered him by his assumed name of King Arthur. **3** H. MARTINEAU They would jeer me off the stand.

B *n.* †**1** A huff, a bad temper. *rare.* Only in L16. **2** An act of jeering; a scoff, a gibe, a taunt. E17. †**3** The action of jeering; mockery, scoffing, derision. M17–M18.

2 C. H. SPURGEON A blow is much sooner forgotten than a jeer.

jeerer *n.* M16. **jeeringly** *adv.* in a jeering manner M17.

jeerga *n.* see JIRGA.

Jeeves /dʒiːvz/ *n.* M20. [A character in the novels of P. G. Wodehouse.] A valet, a personal attendant, *esp.* one who is resourceful and omniscient.

Jeez /dʒiːz/ *int. slang.* Also **G-**, **-ze**. E20. [Abbrev. of JESUS.] Expr. asseveration, discovery, enthusiasm, or surprise; = GEE *int.*[2]

†jeezy *n.* see GIZZ.

jeff /dʒɛf/ *n. US slang. derog.* L19. [f. *Jefferson Davis* (1808–89), president of the Confederate States 1861–5.] A tedious man, a bore; a rustic, a hick, *esp.* a Southerner; (among Blacks) a White man. Also *Jeff Davis* /ˈdeɪvɪs/.

Mutt and Jeff: see MUTT.

jeff /dʒɛf/ *v.i. Printers' slang* (now *Hist.*). M19. [Origin unkn.] Throw or gamble with quadrats used as dice.

Jeffersonian /dʒɛfəˈsəʊnɪən/ *n.* & *a.* L18. [f. *Jefferson* (see below) + -IAN.] *US Hist.* **A** *n.* A supporter or follower of Thomas Jefferson, president of the US 1801–9; an adherent of the political doctrines held by or attributed to Jefferson; a Democrat. L18. **B** *adj.* Of or pertaining to President Jefferson; supporting the doctrines of Jefferson or his followers; Democratic. L18.

Jeffersonianism *n.* L19.

Jeffrey /ˈdʒɛfri/ *n.* M19. [John *Jeffrey*, Sc. plant-collector.] *Jeffrey('s) pine*, a large pine of California and Oregon, *Pinus jeffreyi*, with a spreading head of drooping branches.

jehad *n.* var. of JIHAD.

Jehoshaphat /dʒɪˈhɒʃəfat/ *int.* Orig. *US.* Also **-sa-** /-sə-/. M19. [A king of Judah (*2 Sam.* 8:16 etc.).] Expr. surprise, asseveration, alarm, etc. Freq. in *jumping Jehoshaphat*.

Jehovah /dʒɪˈhəʊvə/ *n.* M16. [med.L *Iehoua(h)* f. Heb. *YHWH*, *JHVH* repr. the Tetragrammaton or divine name (too sacred for utterance), with insertion of the vowels of *ʼădōnāy* my lord. Cf. ADONAI, YAHWEH.] (The principal and personal name of) God in the Old Testament; the Lord.

Jehovah's Witness, **Jehovah Witness** a member of a fundamentalist millenary sect, the Watchtower Bible and Tract Society, which rejects institutional religion and gives precedence to the claims of the sect when these conflict with those of the State.

¶Popularized in Christian usage at the Renaissance and occurring in Tindale's translation of the Bible.

Jehovist /dʒɪˈhəʊvɪst/ *n.* M18. [f. prec. + -IST.] †1 An adherent of the view that the Hebrew word YHWH or JHVH in the Old Testament and Hebrew Scriptures was originally pronounced 'Jehovah'. Only in M18. 2 *The* author(s) of those parts of the Pentateuch in which the name for God is Jehovah. Cf. ELOHIST, YAHWIST. M19.

Jehoˈvistic *a.* of or pertaining to the Jehovist or Jehovists; characterized by the use of the name Jehovah: M19.

Jehu /ˈdʒiːhjuː/ *n.* & *v. joc.* E17. [A king of Israel, who drove his chariot furiously (*2 Kings* 9:20).] **A** *n.* A coach or cab driver, *esp.* one who drives fast or recklessly. E17. **B** *v.i.* & *t.* Drive. *rare.* E19.

jejunal /dʒɪˈdʒuːn(ə)l/ *a.* L19. [f. JEJUNUM + -AL[1].] Of or pertaining to the jejunum.

jejune /dʒɪˈdʒuːn/ *a.* E17. [L *jejunus* fasting, barren, unproductive, meagre. Sense 2b perh. f. idea that wd is f. L *juvenis* young (compar. *junior*) or Fr. *jeune* young.] †1 Without food, fasting; undernourished, hungry. E17–M18. 2 Intellectually unsatisfying, lacking substance, shallow, simplistic; dull, dry, insipid, vapid. E17. **b** Puerile, childish; naive. L19. 3 Not nourishing or substantial; scanty; meagre, frugal; (of land) poor, barren. M17.

2 A. TROLLOPE Jejune words and useless empty phrases. C. I. GLICKSBERG Such methods were jejune and spurious, unproductive of genuine critical insight. **b** G. B. SHAW His jejune credulity as to the absolute value of his concepts. 3 W. SALMON The Cider is impoverished and made thin, Jejune, hard and ill-tasted.

jejunely *adv.* E17. **jejuneness**, **jejunity** *ns.* E17.

jejuno- /dʒɪˈdʒuːnəʊ/ *comb. form* of next: see -O-.

jejuno-duoˈdenal *a.* related to or (esp.) connecting the jejunum and duodenum L19. **jejunoˈileum** *n.* the small intestine excluding the duodenum; the jejunum and ileum considered together: L19. **jeˌjunojejuˈnostomy** *n.* (the making of) a connection between two parts of the jejunum, bypassing the intervening part E20. **jejunostomy** /dʒɛdʒʊˈnɒstəmi/ *n.* (an instance of) surgical opening of the jejunum through the abdominal wall, usu. for the purpose of introducing food L19.

jejunum /dʒɪˈdʒuːnəm/ *n.* M16. [med.L, f. L adj. (sc. *intestinum*) neut. of *jejunus* fasting: so called because usu. found to be empty after death.] *Anat.* The second part of the small intestine, connecting the duodenum and ileum.

Jekyll /ˈdʒɛkɪl, ˈdʒiː-/ *n.* L19. [The hero of R. L. Stevenson's story 'Strange Case of Dr Jekyll and Mr Hyde' (1886).] The good side to a person's or thing's character; an apparently good and respectable person or thing. Cf. HYDE.

I. HAY We encountered surprisingly few Hydes. Nearly all were Jekylls . . of the most competent and courteous type. **Jekyll and Hyde** (a person or thing) having two opposed aspects.

jelab *n.* var. of JELLABA.

Jelalaean *a.* var. of GELALAEAN.

jelick /ˈdʒɛlɪk, ˈjɛlɪk/ *n.* Also **yelek**. E19. [Turk. *yelek*.] A waistcoat or bodice worn by Turkish women.

jell /dʒɛl/ *v.* & *n. colloq.* M18. [Back-form. f. JELLY *n.*[1] & *v.*] **A** *v.* 1 *v.i.* Become a jelly; congeal, jelly. M18. **b** *fig.* Take or hold a definite or satisfactory shape, cohere, crystallize. Cf. GEL *v.* E20. 2 *v.t.* Turn into jelly, jellify. Also (*fig.*), give shape to, make clear and definite. E20.

1 L. M. ALCOTT The jelly won't jell. **b** K. TYNAN The three plots simply do not jell. *Times* The present Parliament . . will jell in time.

B *n.* A jelly, a gel. L19.

jellaba /ˈdʒɛləbə/ *n.* Also **dj-**, **-bah**, **jelab** /ˈdʒɛləb/, & other vars. E19. [Moroccan Arab. *jellāb(a)*, *jellābiyya*: cf. GALABIYA.] A loose hooded long-sleeved usu. woollen cloak of a kind worn orig. by Arab men in N. Africa.

jellied /ˈdʒɛlɪd/ *a.* LME. [f. JELLY *n.*[1] & *v.*: see -ED[1], -ED[2].] 1 Coated with jelly; set in jelly. LME. 2 Turned into jelly; brought to or having the consistency of jelly; congealed, coagulated. L16.

1 *jellied eels*: see EEL *n.* 1.

jellify /ˈdʒɛlɪfʌɪ/ *v.* E19. [f. JELLY *n.*[1] + -FY.] 1 *v.t.* Convert into jelly; reduce to the consistency of jelly. E19. 2 *v.i.* Become or turn into a jelly. L19.

jellifiˈcation *n.* L19.

jello /ˈdʒɛləʊ/ *n.* Chiefly *N. Amer.* Also **J-**, (proprietary) **Jell-O**. E20. [f. JELLY *n.*[1] + -O.] (The powder used to make) a fruit-flavoured gelatin dessert; jelly.

Black Scholar Her firm young breasts quivering like a dish of molded jello.

jelloped /ˈdʒɛləpt/ *a.* Also **joll-** /ˈdʒɒl-/, **jowl-** /ˈdʒaʊl-/, **-pp-**. E17. [f. alt. of JOLLOP *n.*[1] + -ED[2].] *Her.* Having wattles of a specified tincture distinct from that of the body, wattled.

jelly /ˈdʒɛli/ *n.*[1] & *v.* LME. [(O)Fr. *gelée* frost, jelly, f. use as n. of L *gelata* fem. pa. pple of *gelare* freeze, f. *gelu* frost.] **A** *n.* 1 An item of food having the form of a soft, firm, somewhat elastic, usu. semi-transparent material made by cooling (in a mould or dish) a liquid preparation containing gelatin etc. and (orig.) meat or fish stock, (now more commonly) sweetened fruit juice, etc.; a flavoured and coloured product from which a similar substance can be made; a dessert made of this. Also, a conserve of fruit boiled with sugar and strained. LME. †**b** Gelatin. E–M19. 2 Matter with the consistency of a jelly; a gelatinous substance or object of any kind. E17. **b** A gelatinous mass formed by the alga *Nostoc* on soil, formerly supposed to be the remains of a fallen meteor. M17. **c** With specifying wd (esp. *sea*): a jellyfish or similar animal. L17.

1 *Punch* He shook all over like a badly-set jelly. T. STERLING The lamb was tender. . . She ate the mint jelly separately. R. GODDEN My favourite, a pink fruit jelly . . I ate it all. *blackcurrant jelly*, *redcurrant jelly*, etc. *table jelly*: see TABLE *n.* 2 V. NABOKOV A brain of a different brand than that of the synthetic jellies preserved in the skulls around him. *Guardian* Her doctor . . prescribed a diaphragm and a contraceptive jelly. B. BYARS Normally this would have turned his knees to jelly. *mineral jelly*: see MINERAL *a.* PETROLEUM *jelly.* **royal jelly** the secretion produced by honey bees to feed the larvae of the colony, esp. those that will become queens. WHARTON'*s jelly.* **c** *comb-jelly*: see COMB *n.*[1]

Comb.: **jelly baby** a soft gelatinous sweet in the shape of a baby; **jelly bag**: through which fruit pulp is strained in the making of jelly; **jelly bean** (orig. *US*) (*a*) a bean-shaped sweet with a gelatinous centre and a hard sugar coating; (*b*) *slang* an unpleasant, weak, or dishonest person; *spec.* a pimp; **jelly-bellied** *a.* (*slang*) fat; **jelly-belly** *slang* a fat person; **jelly paint** a non-drip paint with the consistency of jelly; **jelly-plant** any of various Australian seaweeds from which commercial gelling agents are extracted; **jelly powder** a crystalline powder used in the preparation of jellies; **jelly roll** *N. Amer.* (*a*) a cylindrical cake containing jelly or jam; (*b*) *slang* a lover; sexual intercourse; the vagina.

B *v.* Cf. earlier JELLIED *a.* 1 *v.i.* Come to the consistency of jelly; set as a jelly; congeal, solidify, coagulate. E17. 2 *v.t.* Convert into jelly; cause to set or coagulate; reduce to the consistency of jelly. E17.

jellygraph *n.* & *v.* (*obs.* exc. *Hist.*) (*a*) *n.* an appliance used for copying documents etc., of which the essential part is a sheet of jelly; (*b*) *v.t.* copy with a jellygraph: E20. **jelly-like** *a.* resembling (that of) jelly, *esp.* having the consistency of jelly L18.

jelly *n.*[2] var. of GELLY.

jellyfish /ˈdʒɛlɪfɪʃ/ *n.* Pl. **-es** /-ɪz/, (usu.) same. E18. [f. JELLY *n.*[1] + FISH *n.*[1]] †1 A kind of oceanic fish (perh. = *lancet-fish* (b) s.v. LANCET *n.*). *rare.* Only in E18. 2 Any marine coelenterate invertebrate of medusoid form, having a dome-shaped gelatinous body with hanging tentacles; *esp.* a member of the class Scyphozoa in which this form is dominant. Cf. earlier JELLY *n.*[1] 2c. M19. **b** *fig.* A feeble, irresolute, spineless, or sluggish person. *colloq.* L19.

jelutong /dʒɛˈluːtɒŋ/ *n.* M19. [Malay.] Any of several Malaysian trees of the genus *Dyera* (family Apocynaceae), esp. *D. costulata*, which produces a latex when tapped; this latex; the light-coloured wood of such a tree.

jemadar *n.* var. of JAMADAR.

Jemima /dʒɪˈmʌɪmə/ *n. colloq.* Also **j-**. L19. [Female forename.] 1 A made-up tie. L19. 2 In *pl.* Elastic-sided ankle boots. E20.

jemmy /ˈdʒɛmi/ *n.* & *v.* M18. [Pet-form of male forename *James*: see -Y[6].] **A** *n.* †1 A dandy, a fop. Also *Jemmy Jessamy* adj., dandified, foppish. *slang.* M18–E19. †2 A kind of riding-boot. Also *jemmy boot. slang.* M–L18. 3 A short crowbar used by burglars to force open windows and doors, freq. one made in sections that screw together. Cf. JAMES 2, JIMMY *n.*[1] E19. 4 A sheep's head as a culinary dish. Cf. JAMES 3. *arch. slang.* M19. **B** *v.t.* Force open (a lock, window, etc.) with a jemmy or similar implement. *colloq.* M20.

je ne sais quoi /ʒənsɛkwa, dʒə nə seɪ ˈkwɑː/ *n. phr.* M17. [Fr., lit. 'I do not know what'.] An indefinable quality, something indescribable or inexpressible.

Smash Hits She positively oozes style. She has that certain *je ne sais quoi*.

Jennerian /dʒɛˈnɪərɪən/ *a.* E19. [f. *Jenner* (see below) + -IAN.] Of, pertaining to, or commemorating the English physician Edward Jenner (1749–1823), who pioneered the principles of vaccination; made by or following the methods of Jenner.

jennet /ˈdʒɛnɪt/ *n.* Also **gen(n)et**. LME. [Fr. *genet* f. Sp. †*ginete* (now *jinete*) light horseman f. Sp. Arab. *Genētī* (Arab. *Zanātī*) f. *Zanāta* Berber tribe famed for horsemanship.] A small Spanish horse, esp. a pacer.

jenneting /ˈdʒɛnɪtɪŋ/ *n.* E17. [f. Fr. *Jeannet* pet-form of *Jean* JOHN, as in Norman Fr. *pomme* (apple) *de Jeannet* (it is ripe by St John's Day, 24 June): see -ING[3].] An early-ripening variety of apple.

jenny /ˈdʒɛni/ *n.* E17. [Pet-form of female forenames *Janet*, *Jennifer*, or *Jane*, serving as a fem. of *Jack*.] 1 Used *attrib.* to designate a female animal, esp. a bird, or a small one. E17. b A female ass or donkey. L18. 2 *Hist.* = *spinning-jenny* s.v. SPINNING *n.* L18. 3 A large locomotive crane. M19. 4 *Billiards*. A losing hazard made with the object-ball close to a cushion. M19.

Comb. & phrases: CREEPING *Jenny*; **jenny-long-legs** *Sc.* a crane-fly; **jenny spinner** (*a*) *Sc.* & *north.* a crane-fly; (*b*) *Angling* (an artificial fly imitating) a male mayfly of the genus *Baetis*; **jenny-wren** (*a*) (pop. and nursery name for) the wren; (*b*) *US* = HERB *Robert*.

jeofail /ˈdʒɛfeɪl/ *n.* M16. [AN *jeo fail* I am at fault, i.e. *jeo* (Fr. *je*) I, *fail* 1st person sing. pres. indic. of *faillir* FAIL *v.*] 1 *Law*. A mistake or oversight in pleading or other legal proceeding: an acknowledgement of such error. *obs.* exc. *Hist.* M16. †2 A mistake, an error. M16–E19.

jeon *n.* see JUN.

jeopard /ˈdʒɛpəd/ *v. arch.* LME. [Back-form. f. JEOPARDY.] 1 *v.t.* Jeopardize, endanger, put at risk. LME. †b *v.i.* Risk oneself, run a risk; venture, adventure. LME–L16. †2 *v.t.* Stake, bet. LME–L16.

¶Obs. by M17, but revived in E19.

jeopardize /ˈdʒɛpədʌɪz/ *v.t.* Also **-ise**. M17. [f. prec. or next + -IZE.] Put into jeopardy, endanger, put at risk.

K. VONNEGUT The drunk and vicious people, who jeopardize all life on earth. M. COX This . . behaviour could jeopardize Monty's chance of gaining a scholarship.

jeopardy /ˈdʒɛpədi/ *n.* ME. [OFr. *iu parti*, later *ieu* (*geu*) *parti* divided play, even game, uncertain chance: in med.L *jocus partitus*. For the change of *t* to *d* cf. CARD *n.*², DIAMOND *n.* & *a.*; for the spelling *-eo-* cf. PEOPLE *n.*] †1 *Chess* etc. A puzzle, a problem. ME–L15. †b A device, a trick, a stratagem. ME–M16. †2 A deed involving peril; a daring exploit. ME–E19. 3 Risk of loss, harm, or death; peril, danger; *Law* danger arising from being on trial for a criminal offence. Freq. in *in jeopardy*. ME. †4 A state of uncertainty as to the outcome of a game, undertaking, etc. ME–L16.

3 *Times* The chances of an important . . match at Twickenham are put in jeopardy by the weather. E. KUZWAYO This would place me in jeopardy with the authorities, who already saw me as a troublemaker. *double jeopardy*: see DOUBLE *a.* & *adv.*

jequirity /dʒɪˈkwɪrɪti/ *n.* Also **-quer-**. L19. [Fr. *jéquirity* f. Tupi-Guarani *jekiriti*.] A leguminous vine, *Abrus precatorius*, native to the Indian subcontinent and widely naturalized in the tropics, whose roots are used as a substitute for liquorice; its red-and-black seeds, used in India etc. as beads or weights. Also called *Indian liquorice*, *crab's eyes*, etc.

jer /jɛː/ *n.* M18. [Old Ch. Slav. *jerŭ*, *jerĭ*, Russ. *er* (pl. *ery*), *er'*.] Either of the pairs of Slavonic characters written Ⱏ, Ⱐ in the Glagolitic alphabet and ъ, ь in the Cyrillic alphabet; (an example of) any of the forms of these characters; either or both of the sounds represented by these characters or the Common Slavonic sounds from which they developed.

jerbil *n.* var. of GERBIL.

jerboa /dʒəːˈbəʊə, ˈdʒəːbəʊə/ *n.* M17. [mod.L *jerboa*, *gerboa* f. Arab. *yarbūʿ*(*a*), dial. *jarbūʿ*.] Any of various small chiefly nocturnal rodents of the family Dipodidae, of arid regions in Africa and Eurasia, which have very long hind legs and short forelegs, a long tufted tail, and great powers of jumping.

Comb.: **jerboa kangaroo** = BETTONG; **jerboa-mouse** an American kangaroo-rat; **jerboa-rat** *Austral.* any of various jumping rodents of the Australian genera *Notomys* and *Conilurus*.

jereed *n.* var. of JERID.

jeremejevite /jɛrɪˈmeɪəvʌɪt/ *n.* Also **ere-**. L19. [f. P. V. *Eremeev* (1830–99), Russ. mineralogist + -ITE¹.] *Min.* A hexagonal aluminium borate mineral, usu. occurring as colourless prisms.

jeremiad /dʒɛrɪˈmʌɪad/ *n.* L18. [Fr. *jérémiade*, f. *Jérémie* f. eccl.L *Jeremias* Jeremiah (see next), w. allus. to the Lamentations of Jeremiah in the Bible: see -AD².] A lamentation; a list of woes or complaints; a doleful tirade.

D. J. ENRIGHT Jeremiads about poor sick England. J. BERMAN The author . . is ready to denounce his own colleagues in a single jeremiad.

Jeremiah /dʒɛrɪˈmʌɪə/ *n.* L18. [A Hebrew prophet (see prec.), Heb. *Yirmĕyāhū* app. lit. 'Yahweh loosens (the womb)'.] A person given to lamentation or woeful complaining, a denouncer of the times, a dismal prophet.

E. H. GOMBRICH The Jeremiahs of his time who decried contemporary styles.

Jeremianic /ˌdʒɛrɪmʌɪˈanɪk/ *a.* L19. [f. prec. after *Messianic*.] Of or pertaining to the prophet Jeremiah or the book of the Old Testament and Hebrew Scriptures which bears his name.

jerepigo /dʒɛrɪˈpiːɡəʊ/ *n. S. Afr.* Also **-pico**. M19. [Alt. of GEROPIGA.] A sweet fortified wine.

†**jerfalcon** *n.* var. of GYRFALCON.

Jericho /ˈdʒɛrɪkəʊ/ *n. colloq.* E16. [A town in the Jordan Valley, where King David told his servants to stay until their beards were grown (*2 Sam.* 10:5).] (The name of) a place of retreat or concealment; a remote place.

THACKERAY She may go to Bath, or she may go to Jericho for me.

¶See also *rose of Jericho* s.v. ROSE *n.*

jerid /dʒəˈriːd/ *n.* Also **jereed**. M17. [Arab. *jarīd* palm branch stripped of its leaves, lance, javelin.] *Hist.* A wooden javelin used in equestrian games in Muslim countries, esp. in the Ottoman Empire; a game in which this was used.

jerk /dʒəːk/ *n.*¹ M16. [Prob. imit.: cf. JERT *n.* & *v.*, YERK *v.* & *n.*] †1 A stroke with a whip, a lash; *fig.* a lash of sarcasm, a cutting remark. M16–L18. 2 A quick suddenly arrested movement; a sharp sudden pull, throw, push, thrust, or twist. L16. b In *pl.* (usu. w. *the*). Involuntary spasms of the limbs or features, esp. due to religious excitement. E19. c *Physiol.* An involuntary muscular contraction caused by, and used to test, a spinal motor reflex; an involuntary contraction of a group of muscles, myoclonus. L19. d (The name of) a dance characterized by jerking movements. M20. e *Weightlifting*. The rapid lifting of a weight from shoulder-level to above the head by straightening the arms (and legs). M20. 3 *fig.* A short sharp witty speech; a sally. Now *rare* or *obs.* L16. 4 An insignificant or contemptible person; a fool, a stupid person; an unpleasant person. Cf. JERKWATER. *slang* (orig. *US*). M20. 5 *Physics*. Rate of change of acceleration (with respect to time). M20.

2 B. TARKINGTON The contrivance stopped with a heart-shaking jerk before Isabel's house. R. K. NARAYAN This lady surprised me by throwing me off her back with a jerk. P. BARKER The minute hand moved, not smoothly, but in a series of jerks. e *clean and jerk*. 4 *Melody Maker* I think he's a jerk . . I hate all loud, ignorant people of whatever political persuasion. M. FORSTER He was just a dull, boring, harmless jerk.

Phrases: **physical jerks** *colloq.* physical or gymnastic exercises. **put a jerk in it** *colloq.* act vigorously, smartly, or quickly.

jerk /dʒəːk/ *n.*² L18. [f. JERK *v.*²: see also JERKY *n.*¹] Jerked meat, charqui.

jerk /dʒəːk/ *v.*¹ M16. [f. (as) JERK *n.*¹] †1 *v.t.* Strike with or as with a whip, lash; *fig.* lash with satire or ridicule. M16–E18. 2 *v.t.* Move by a sharp suddenly arrested motion; give a sudden thrust, push, pull, or twist to. L16. b Throw or toss with a quick sharp motion. L18. 3 *v.i.* Give a jerk; bow or nod with a jerk; move with a jerk. L16. 4 *v.t.* Utter (words or sounds) abruptly or sharply. Usu. foll. by *out*. E17. †5 *v.i.* Aim satire, sneer, carp, (*at*). M17–E18. 6 *v.t.* Serve up (soda, beer, etc.) at a soda fountain, bar, etc. Cf. SODA *jerk*. *US colloq.* L19. 7 *v.i.* & *t.* Foll. by *off*: masturbate. *coarse slang*. E20. 8 *v.t. Weightlifting*. Raise (a weight) from shoulder-level to above the head by straightening the arms (and legs). M20.

2 J. R. LOWELL We poor puppets, jerked by unseen wires. J. STEINBECK The little man jerked down the brim of his hat. A. TREW 'Resume normal scanning,' echoed Krasnov, jerking his chin outwards. b *fig.*: J. LONDON The alarm clock went off, jerking Martin out of sleep. 3 D. ABSE The trams . . jerked to a halt. F. TUOHY She did not answer but jerked away. A. HIGGINS The rabbit jerked once or twice, involuntary muscular spasms, then was still. 8 *clean and jerk*.

Comb.: **jerk-line** *N. Amer.* a rope used instead of reins to guide a team of mules etc.; **jerk-off** *a.* & *n.* (*coarse slang*, orig. *US*) (*a*) *adj.* pornographic; contemptible, pathetic; (*b*) *n.* = JERK *n.*¹ 4.

jerker *n.* a person who or thing which jerks (*tear-jerker*: see TEAR *n.*¹) L16. **jerkingly** *adv.* jerkily L19.

jerk /dʒəːk/ *v.*²*t.* E18. [Amer. Sp. *charquear*, f. *charqui* f. Quechua *echarqui* dried flesh in long strips, *echarquini* prepare dried meat: cf. CHARQUI.] Cure (meat, esp. beef) by cutting it into pieces and drying it, orig. in the sun.

jerk *v.*³ var. of JERQUE.

jerkin /ˈdʒəːkɪn/ *n.* E16. [Origin unkn.] Orig. (now *Hist.*), a man's close-fitting jacket or doublet, often of leather, with or without sleeves and having a short skirt. Now, a sleeveless jacket, a long waistcoat.

jerkin-head /ˈdʒəːkɪnhɛd/ *n.* M19. [Perh. f. alt. of *jerking* pres. ppl a. of JERK *v.*¹ + HEAD *n.*, but cf. earlier KIRKIN-HEAD.] *Archit.* The end of a roof that is hipped for only part of its height, leaving a truncated gable.

jerkwater /ˈdʒəːkwɔːtə/ *a. US colloq.* M19. [f. JERK *v.*¹ + WATER *n.*: f. the need of early railway engines in remote locations to be supplied with water from streams using a bucket on a rope.] (Of a train) serving small and remote settlements, running on a branch line; *gen.* small and remote, insignificant, inferior, hick.

J. DOS PASSOS A little jerkwater town back in South Dakota.

jerky /ˈdʒəːki/ *n.*¹ *N. Amer.* M19. [Amer. Sp. *charqui*, *charque*: see CHARQUI. Cf. JERK *n.*², *v.*²] Jerked meat, esp. beef.

jerky /ˈdʒəːki/ *a.* & *n.*² M19. [f. JERK *n.*¹ + -Y¹.] A *adj.* Characterized by jerks or sudden abrupt or twitching movements; *fig.* spasmodic. M19.

G. GREENE The rather jerky succession of short stage scenes is given smoothness and continuity in the cinema. R. DAHL He kept making quick jerky little movements with his head.

B *n.* A springless wagon; a shaky, jolting vehicle. *US*. M19.

jerkily *adv.* in a jerky manner; by fits and starts: L19. **jerkiness** *n.* M19.

jeroboam /dʒɛrəˈbəʊəm/ *n.* E19. [A king of Israel (*1 Kings* 11:28, 14:16).] Orig., a large measure, bowl, or cup of wine etc. Now, a large wine bottle, equivalent to four ordinary bottles.

jerque /dʒəːk/ *v.t.* Now *rare*. Also **jerk**. E19. [Perh. f. It. *cercare* to search.] Search or check (a vessel) to make sure that all the cargo has been duly delivered and declared.

jerquer *n.* an official who searches or checks a vessel in this way E18.

jerrican *n.* var. of JERRYCAN.

jerry /ˈdʒɛri/ *n.*¹ *arch. colloq.* E18. [Pet-form of male forenames *Jeremy*, *Jeremiah*, *Gerald*, or *Gerard*.] †1 *jerry-(cum-)mumble*, (*a*) *v.t.* shake or tumble (someone) about; (*b*) a person who tumbles or shakes. E18–L19. 2 In full *jerry-shop*. A tavern, a rough public house. See also TOM-AND-JERRY *n.* 2. M19. 3 More fully *jerry hat*. A round felt hat. M19. 4 A machine for shearing cloth. L19.

jerry /ˈdʒɛri/ *n.*² *slang*. M19. [Prob. dim. of JEROBOAM: see -Y⁶.] A chamber-pot.

Jerry /ˈdʒɛri/ *n.*³ *colloq.* (orig. *Mil. slang*). E20. [Alt. of GERMAN *n.*¹ & *a.*¹, perh. infl. by JERRY *n.*¹: see -Y⁶.] (A name for) a German, *spec.* a German soldier; a German aircraft. Also, the Germans or German soldiers collectively. Cf. FRITZ *n.*¹

jerry /ˈdʒɛri/ *n.*⁴ *Austral.* & *NZ slang*. E20. [Origin unkn.: cf. JERRY *a.*², *v.*] *take a jerry* (*to*), investigate and understand (something or someone).

jerry /ˈdʒɛri/ *a.*¹ *colloq.* L19. [Abbrev.] Jerry-built; constructed insubstantially and hurriedly from inferior materials.

jerryism *n.* jerry-building L19.

jerry /'dʒɛri/ *a.*² *US slang*. E20. [Origin unkn.: cf. JERRY *v.*, *n.*⁴] *be jerry (on, on to, to)*, be aware (of), understand.

Jerry /'dʒɛri/ *a.*³ *colloq.* M20. [f. JERRY *n.*³] German.

jerry /'dʒɛri/ *v.i. slang* (chiefly *Austral.* & *NZ*). E20. [Origin unkn.: cf. JERRY *a.*², *n.*⁴] Foll. by *to*: understand, realize, get wise to.

jerry-build /'dʒɛrɪbɪld/ *v.t. colloq.* Pa. t. & pple **-built** /-bɪlt/. M19. [Origin unkn.] Build insubstantially from inferior materials; build to sell but not to last. Chiefly as *jerry-built* ppl a.

F. KING The flat's so tiny and so jerry-built that every sound can be heard from one room to another.

jerry-builder *n.* a person who builds houses etc. hurriedly and insubstantially from inferior materials L19.

jerrycan /'dʒɛrɪkan/ *n.* Also **jerrican**. M20. [f. JERRY *a.*³ + CAN *n.*] A container for petrol, water, etc., orig. five-gallon and metal, of a type first used in Germany and later adopted by the Allied forces in the war of 1939–45.

Jersey /'dʒəːzi/ *n.*¹ E18. [New *Jersey*, a State of the US: see NEW JERSEY.] Used *attrib.* to designate people or things coming from or associated with New Jersey.

Jersey blue (*a*) *Hist.* a colonial New Jersey soldier (so called from the blue uniform); (*b*) a native or inhabitant of New Jersey; (*c*) a breed of chicken. **Jersey justice** strict or severe justice. **Jersey lightning** *colloq.* a strong kind of applejack, peach brandy, or whisky. **Jersey pine** the scrub pine, *Pinus virginiana*. **Jersey tea** a small US shrub, *Ceanothus americanus*, of the buckthorn family, the leaves of which have been used as a substitute for tea; also called *New Jersey tea*. **Jersey wagon** a light carriage formerly used in New Jersey.

jersey /'dʒəːzi/ *a.* & *n.*² In senses A.2, B.3 also **J-**. L16. [*Jersey*, the largest of the Channel Islands.] **A** *adj.* **1** Of or from Jersey; *spec.* designating or made of the fabric jersey (see sense B.1 below). L16. **2** Designating, of, or pertaining to a breed of usu. fawn dairy cattle orig. bred in Jersey and producing milk of high fat content. M19.

1 N. FREELING A nearly new jersey cocktail dress.

B *n.* **1** Orig., a fine woollen worsted fabric made in Jersey. Now, any machine-knitted slightly elastic plain fabric. L16. **†b** Combed wool ready for spinning. M17–L19. **2** A knitted usu. woollen pullover or similar garment. Also, a distinguishing upper garment or shirt worn by a football etc. team. M19. **3** (An animal of) the Jersey breed of cattle. M19.

1 *Observer* Short evening dresses . . in silk jersey. 2 P. BOWLES Do you mind bringing me my jersey? . . With this rain and wind I feel cold. D. STOREY Occasionally they changed sides, swapping jerseys. *yellow jersey*: see YELLOW *a.*

jerseyed *a.* wearing a jersey M19.

Jerseyman /'dʒəːzɪmən/ *n.* Pl. **-men**. L17. [f. *Jersey* (see below) + MAN *n.*] **1** A (male) native or inhabitant of the State of New Jersey, USA. Now *rare*. L17. **2** A (male) native or inhabitant of Jersey in the Channel Islands. E19.

jert /dʒəːt/ *n.* & *v. obs.* exc. *dial.* M16. [Prob. imit.: cf. JERK *n.*¹, *v.*¹] **A** *n.* = JERK *n.*¹ M16. **B** *v.t.* & *i.* = JERK *v.*¹ M16.

jerupiga *n.* var. of GEROPIGA.

Jerusalem /dʒə'ruːs(ə)ləm/ *n.* & *int.* LME. [A city in Israel, sacred to Jews, Christians, and Muslims.] **A** *n.* **1** Used *attrib.* and after *of* in names of things from or associated with Jerusalem. LME. **2** *fig.* An ideal or heavenly city, place, or situation. Freq. in *the new Jerusalem*. LME.

1 *Jerusalem artichoke*: see ARTICHOKE. **Jerusalem cherry** a kind of nightshade, *Solanum pseudocapsicum*, grown for its decorative red berries in winter. **Jerusalem cross** *Her.*: having a bar across the end of each limb and a cross potent. **Jerusalem letters** letters or symbols tattooed on the arm or body, such as pilgrims or visitors to Jerusalem sometimes bore in testimony or memory of their visit. **Jerusalem pony** a donkey (so called in reference to Jesus' riding into Jerusalem on an ass). **Jerusalem sage** a Mediterranean labiate plant, *Phlomis fruticosa*, with large yellow flowers, grown for ornament. **Jerusalem thorn** a thorny leguminous tree, *Parkinsonia aculeata*, native to tropical America and grown for ornament. *oak of Jerusalem*: see OAK *n.* 2 W. BLAKE I will not cease from Mental Fight . . till we have built Jerusalem In England's green & pleasant Land. *Listener* Both . . looked forward to the same new Jerusalem . . in which . . bureaucracy would be no more.

B *int.* Expr. mild alarm or surprise. M19.

jes /dʒɛs/ *adv. colloq.* & *dial.* (chiefly *US*, esp. *Black English*). Also **jes'**. M19. [Repr. a pronunc. Cf. JEST *adv.*] = JUST *adv.*

jess /dʒɛs/ *n.* & *v.* ME. [OFr. *ges* nom. sing. & accus. pl. of *get* (mod. *jet* cast) f. Proto-Romance var. of L *jactus* a throw, f. *jacere* to throw.] **A** *n.* A short strap of leather, silk, or other material fastened round each of the legs of a hawk used in falconry, usu. having a small ring to which a leash may be attached. Usu. in *pl.* ME. **B** *v.t.* Put jesses on (a hawk). M19.

jessed /dʒɛst/ *a.* (of a hawk) furnished with or wearing jesses; *Her.* having jesses of a specified tincture: E17.

jessamin(e) *n.* see JASMINE.

jessamy /'dʒɛsəmi/ *n. obs.* exc. *dial.* & *W. Indies* M17. [Alt. of JESSAMINE.] **1** = JASMINE 1. M17. **†2** A man who scents himself with perfume or who wears a sprig of jessamine; a dandy, a fop. Cf. *Jemmy Jessamy* s.v. JEMMY *n.* 1. M18–M19.

jessant /'dʒɛs(ə)nt/ *a.* L16. [In sense 2 f. OFr. *gesant* (later *gisant*) lying, pres. pple of *gésir* f. L *jacere* to lie: see -ANT¹. In sense 1 perh. a different wd.] *Her.* **1** Of a charge (as a branch or flower): represented as held in or issuing from the mouth of an animal etc. L16. **2** Of a charge: represented as lying over and partly covering another. *rare*. E17.

Jesse /'dʒɛsi/ *n.*¹ *obs.* exc. *Hist.* LME. [The father of David and ancestor of Jesus (*1 Sam.* 16:12, *Isa.* 11:1).] More fully *tree of Jesse*. A genealogical tree representing the lineage of Jesus, used in medieval churches as a decoration for a wall, window, vestment, etc., or in the form of a large branched candlestick.

Jessean /dʒɛ'siːən/ *a.* (long *rare* or *obs.*) belonging to Jesse or to his son King David E17.

Jesse /'dʒɛsi/ *n.*² *US slang* (now *rare*). Also **Jessy**. M19. [Perh. f. as prec., f. a joc. interpretation of 'There shall come a rod out of the stem of Jesse' (*Isa.* 11:1).] Severe treatment or handling.

†jesserant *n.* var. of JAZERANT.

Jessie /'dʒɛsi/ *n. slang*. Also **Jessy**, **j-**. E20. [Female forename.] A cowardly or effeminate man; a male homosexual.

Jessy *n.*¹ var. of JESSE *n.*²

Jessy *n.*² var. of JESSIE.

jest /dʒɛst/ *n.* Also **†g-**. See also GEST *n.*¹ LME. [Later spelling of GEST *n.*¹] **I 1** See GEST *n.*¹ I. LME.

II †2 A satirical utterance, a lampoon; an idle tale. LME–E17. **3** A mocking or jeering speech; a taunt, a jeer. Also, a piece of raillery or banter. M16. **4** A saying intended to excite laughter; a witticism, a joke. M16. **b** Something funny to relate; a ludicrous event or circumstance. L16. **5a** The opposite of earnest or seriousness; trifling sport, fun. Chiefly in *in jest*, not seriously, in fun. M16. **b** Jesting, joking, merriment; ridicule. L16. **c** A thing that is not serious or earnest; a jocular affair. M18. **6** A prank, a frolic; a trick played in sport, a practical joke. Now *rare*. L16. **7** An object of or matter for jesting or derision; a laughing-stock. L16.

2 T. WASHINGTON Alexander taking it for a iest would not beleeve it. 3 W. COWPER Might he but set the rabble in a roar, He cared not with what jest. 4 I. MURDOCH Edward giggled feebly at this jest. **b** POPE To complete the Jest, Old Edward's Armour beams on Cibber's breast. **5b** SHAKES. *Haml.* Alas, poor Yorick! . . : a fellow of infinite jest. **c** R. S. THOMAS Life's bitter jest is hollow. 6 W. IRVING Students famous for their love of a jest—set the college on fire. 7 B. TAYLOR Lowly virtue is the jest of fools.

Comb.: **jest-book** a book of jests or amusing stories.

jestful *a.* full of jesting, jocular M19.

jest /dʒɛst/ *v.* Also **†g-**. E16. [Var. of GEST *v.*] **1** *v.i.* Utter gibes or taunts; jeer, mock. Usu. foll. by *at*. E16. **b** *v.t.* Jeer at; ridicule. E18. **2** *v.i.* Speak or act in a trifling manner or not seriously; trifle. M16. **3** *v.i.* Say something amusing or facetious; make witty or humorous remarks; joke. M16. **b** *v.t.* Usu. with adv. or phr. expr. result: bring into a given condition by jesting. M16. **†c** *v.i.* Disport or amuse oneself; make merry. L16–M17.

1 F. BROOKE He . . made an oath he would never jest at spirits again. **b** G. P. R. JAMES He jested his companion upon his gravity. 2 LYTTON Jest not, Pausanius; you will find me in earnest. 3 R. C. HUTCHINSON Grown-ups jesting to hide their troubles from children. *Sunday Express* He has jested that divorce lawyers will soon be extinct. **b** C. LAMB That freak . . jested me out of a good three hundred pounds a year. **c** SHAKES. *Rich. II* As gentle and as jocund as to jest Go I to fight.

jestingly *adv.* in the manner of a person who jests; by way of a joke: M16.

jest /dʒɛst/ *adv. colloq.* & *dial.* E19. [Repr. a pronunc.: cf. JES.] = JUST *adv.*

jester /'dʒɛstə/ *n.* Also **†g-**. ME. [f. JEST *v.*, GEST *v.* + -ER¹.] **1** A professional reciter of romances. *arch.* ME. **2** A mimic, a buffoon; a person whose profession is to amuse; *esp.* a professional joker or clown maintained in a medieval court etc., a fool. E16. **3** A person who jests, or speaks or acts in jest; a person given to uttering jests or witticisms, a joker. E16.

jestership *n.* the position of a jester M19.

Jesu *n.* see JESUS.

Jesuist /'dʒɛzjʊɪst/ *n.* & *a.* Long *rare*. L16. [Fr. †*Jesuiste*, f. as next + -IST.] = next.

Jesuit /'dʒɛzjʊɪt/ *n.* & *a.* M16. [Fr. *jésuite* or mod.L *Jesuita*, f. JESUS + -*ita* -ITE¹.] **A** *n.* **1** A member of the Society of Jesus, a Roman Catholic order which was founded by Ignatius Loyola and others in 1534 to propagate the faith among unbelievers, and was prominent in the Church's struggle against the Reformation. M16. **2** *transf.* A dissembling person; a prevaricator. *derog.* M17. **3** A kind of lady's dress buttoning up to the neck. Long *obs.* exc. *Hist.* M18.

1 **Jesuits' bark** the medicinal bark of species of *Cinchona*, introduced into Europe from the Jesuit Missions in S. America as a source of quinine; **Jesuits' nut** the seed of the water chestnut *Trapa natans*; **Jesuits' tea** an infusion of the leaves of *Psoralea glandulosa*, a S. American leguminous shrub. 2 D. L. SAYERS We are not Jesuits, we are straightforward Englishmen. D. SHUB Lenin is a political Jesuit who . . has molded Marxism to his aims of the moment.

B *attrib.* or as *adj.* That is a Jesuit; of or belonging to the Society of Jesus; Jesuitical. M16.

¶By their enemies the Jesuits were accused of teaching that the end justifies the means, and the lax principles of casuistry put forward by a few of their moralists were ascribed to the order as a whole, thus giving rise to sense A.2 and the corresponding opprobrious uses of *Jesuitical*, *Jesuitry*, and other derivs. These uses give offence to some Roman Catholics.

†Jesuited *a.* made or become a Jesuit; imbued with the principles or character of the Jesuits: E17–M19. **Jesuitess** *n.* (*Hist.*) a nun of an order established on the principles of the Jesuits, but not recognized by papal authority and suppressed by Pope Urban VIII in 1631 E17.

Jesuitical /dʒɛzjʊ'ɪtɪk(ə)l/ *a.* In sense 2 also **j-**. E17. [f. prec. + -ICAL.] **1** Of or pertaining to the Jesuits. E17. **2** Having the character once ascribed to the Jesuits; deceitful, dissembling; practising equivocation or mental reservation. Also, hair-splitting, oversubtle. E17.

2 M. HASTINGS People only call a man jesuitical when they are beaten in an argument.

¶See note s.v. JESUIT.

Jesuitic *a.* (now *rare*) = JESUITICAL M17. **Jesuitically** *adv.* E17.

Jesuitise *v.* var. of JESUITIZE.

Jesuitism /'dʒɛzjʊɪtɪz(ə)m/ *n.* E17. [f. JESUIT *n.* + -ISM.] **1** The system, doctrine, principles, or practice of the Jesuits. E17. **2** Principles or practice such as those once ascribed to the Jesuits; Jesuitry. E17. **3** A Jesuitical quibble or equivocation. *rare*. M18.

Jesuitize /'dʒɛzjʊɪtʌɪz/ *v.* Also **-ise**. E17. [f. JESUIT *n.* + -IZE.] **1** *v.t.* Imbue with Jesuit principles; make Jesuitical. E17. **2** *v.i.* Behave like a Jesuit; propound Jesuitical doctrines. E17.

Jesuitry /'dʒɛzjʊɪtri/ *n.* M19. [f. JESUIT *n.* + -RY.] The principles, doctrine, or practices of

J

the Jesuits. Chiefly *derog.*, subtle casuistry or prevarication; the doctrine that the end justifies the means.

¶ See note s.v. JESUIT.

Jesus /ˈdʒiːzəs/ *n.* & *int.* Also (*arch.*) **Jesu** /ˈdʒiːzjuː/ (now chiefly *voc.*). ME. [Chr.L *Iesus* (in obl. cases *Iesu*) f. Gk *Iēsous* (in obl. cases *Iēsou*) f. late Heb. or Aramaic *Yēšūăʿ* var. of earlier *Yĕhōšūăʿ* Joshua.] A *n.* **1** (The name of) the central figure of the Christian faith, a Jewish preacher (*c*5 BC–*c*AD 30) regarded by his followers as the Son of God and God incarnate. More fully *Jesus Christ* (see CHRIST *n.* 2). ME. **2** A figure or representation of Jesus. L15.

1 CREEPING *Jesus. find Jesus*: see FIND *v.* **Jesus wept!** *int.* expr. strong exasperation. **Society of Jesus** the Jesuit order. *sweet Jesus*: see SWEET *a.* & *adv.*

Comb.: **Jesus freak** a (usu. young) person combining a lifestyle like that of a hippy with fervent evangelical Christianity; *Jesus* PSALTER.

B *int.* Expr. surprise, dismay, disbelief, relief, etc. Also *Jesus Christ.* L16.

P. BOWLES 'Jesus!' he cried. 'I'm glad to be here!'

jet /dʒɛt/ *n.*[1] & *a.* ME. [AN *geet*, OFr. *jaiet*, *jayet* (mod. *jais*) f. L *gagates* GAGATE.] **A** *n.* **1** A hard compact black form of lignite, capable of receiving a brilliant polish, which has the property of attracting light bodies when electrified by rubbing and was formerly much used in making ornaments. Formerly also, a black colouring matter. ME. **2** The colour of jet; a deep glossy black. LME. †**3** Black marble. LME–M17.

Comb.: **jet-black** *a.* black like jet; glossy black.

B *attrib.* or as *adj.* **1** Made or consisting of jet. LME. **2** Of the colour of jet, jet-black. E17.

jet /dʒɛt/ *n.*[2] E17. [Partly f. JET *v.*[2] (and *v.*[1]), partly f. senses of Fr. *jet*, f. *jeter* to throw. See also JUT *n.*[2]] †**1** A projecting part of a building; a pier, a jetty. *rare.* E17–L18. †**2** An affected movement or jerk of the body; a swagger. L17–E18. **3** A stream of liquid, gas, or (more rarely) solid particles shot forward or thrown upwards (either in a spurt or continuously), esp. by pressure from a small opening. L17. **b** *Astron.* A thin elongated structure extending from or emitted by a cometary or galactic nucleus, the solar chromosphere, or other body. M19. **c** In full *jet stream.* A fast narrow current in the atmosphere or ocean; *spec.* one in the upper troposphere at middle latitudes that blows horizontally from west to east. M20. **4** A large ladle. E18. **5** A spout or nozzle for emitting water, gas, etc. E19. **6** A projection at the end of a type in casting, and subsequently broken off. L19. **7** A jet plane; a jet engine. *colloq.* M20.

3 S. SPENDER I directed the jet of water from the nozzle of the hose. A. WEST My father blew out a thin jet of cobalt-blue cigar smoke. 7 J. WYNDHAM More planes went over . . travelling very fast, with their jets shrieking. *jumbo jet*: see JUMBO *a.*

Attrib. & *comb.*: In the sense 'of, pertaining to, or powered by a jet engine', as *jet aircraft, fighter, plane*, etc. Special combs., as **jet age** the era of travel by jet aircraft; **jet engine** an engine in which jet propulsion is used to provide forward thrust; *esp.* an aircraft engine that takes in air and ejects hot compressed air and exhaust gases; **Jetfoil** (US proprietary name for) a type of passenger-carrying hydrofoil with a stabilization and control system based on that of an aircraft; **jet lag** tiredness, temporal disorientation, and other effects suffered by a person after a flight involving marked differences in local time; **jet-lagged** *a.* suffering from jet lag; **jet-propelled** *a.* having or employing a means of jet propulsion; *fig.* very fast, frenzied; **jet propulsion** the ejection of a usu. high-speed jet of gas (or liquid) as a source of propulsive power, esp. for aircraft; **jet set** *colloq.* a (or *the*) set of wealthy and fashionable people who frequently travel by air; **jet-setter** *colloq.* a member of the jet set; *jet stream*: see sense 3c above; **jet turbine** a turbojet engine; **Jetway** (proprietary name for) an air-bridge.

jet /dʒɛt/ *n.*[3] *arch.* M18. [By-form of GIST *n.*[3]] = GIST *n.*[3]

†**jet** *n.*[4] see GET *n.*[2]

†**jet** *v.*[1] Infl. **-tt-**. LME. [App. f. AN *gettre*, OFr. *getter*, *jetter*, mod. *jeter* to throw, cast, etc., but the senses are those of L *jactare se*, *jactari* vaunt oneself, boast.] **I** Of gait and motion. **1** *v.i.* & *t.* (w. *it*). **a** Assume a pompous gait in walking; strut, swagger. Also (of an animal), prance. LME–L17. **b** Move along jauntily, caper, trip. M16–L17. **2** *v.i.* Stroll; walk, go. M16–L18. **3** *v.t.* Traverse ostentatiously, parade (the streets). M–L16. **II** Of behaviour. **4** *v.i.* Act or behave boastfully, brag. E16–M17. **5** *v.i.* Revel, run riot; indulge in riotous living. E16–M17.

jet /dʒɛt/ *v.*[2] Infl. **-tt-**. L16. [(O)Fr. *jeter* throw, cast, f. Proto-Romance var. of L *jactare*: cf. JUT *v.*[2]] †**1** *v.i.* **a** Project, protrude, jut. Freq. foll. by *out.* L16–M18. **b** *transf.* Encroach *on, upon.* L16–M17. †**2** *v.t.* Build *out* (part of a house, etc.); cause to project, furnish with projections. M17–E18. **3** *v.t.* Throw, cast, toss. *obs.* exc. *dial.* M17. †**4** *v.i.* Spring, hop, bound, dart. M17–E19. †**5** *v.i.* Move or be moved with a jerk or jerks; jolt, jog. M–L17. **6** *v.i.* Of a bird: move the tail up and down jerkily. Now *rare.* M17. **7** *v.i.* Spout or spurt forth; issue in a (curved) jet or jets. L17. **8** *v.t.* Emit in a jet or jets. E18. **9** *v.t. Building.* Loosen and remove (sand, gravel, etc.) by directing jets of water or compressed air on to it, esp. so as to make a hole for pile-driving; sink (a pile) by this means. Chiefly as *jetting* vbl n. E20.

1 L. EVANS Little Ridges jetting out from the principal Chains of Mountains. **b** SHAKES. *Tit. A.* Think you not how dangerous It is to jet upon a prince's right? 4 J. MONTGOMERY He hoped to see . . The wingless squirrel jet from tree to tree. 7 V. WOOLF Fountains jet; drops descend. *Trucking International* He opened the tank's main hatches so the petrol jetted out. 8 P. BARKER A tram rattled past and jetted sparks.

jet /dʒɛt/ *v.*[3]*i.* & *t.* *colloq.* Infl. **-tt-**. M20. [f. JET *n.*[2] 7.] Travel or convey by jet plane.

P. FULLER Art bureaucrats are jetting around the capitals of the world.

jetavator /ˈdʒɛtəveɪtə/ *n.* M20. [f. JET *n.*[2] + ELEVATOR.] A ring-shaped deflector surrounding the exit nozzle of a rocket engine which can be swivelled into the exhaust gases to alter the direction of thrust.

jet d'eau /ʒedo/ *n.* Pl. ***jets d'eau*** (pronounced same). L17. [Fr. = jet of water.] An ornamental jet of water rising from a fountain or pipe; a fountain or pipe from which such a jet rises.

jeté /ʒəˈteɪ, *foreign* ʒəte (*pl. same*)/ *n.* M19. [Fr., pa. pple (sc. *pas* step) of *jeter* throw.] *Ballet.* A step in which a spring is made from one foot to land on the other, esp. with one leg extended forwards and the other backwards.

grand jeté /grɑ̃/: achieving a high elevation. **jeté en tournant** /ɒn ˈtʊənɒ̃:, *foreign* ɑ̃ turnɑ̃/: executed with a turning movement; also called *tour jeté.* **split jeté**: in which both legs are raised in a horizontal line.

jeton /ˈdʒɛtən, *in sense 2 foreign* ʒətɔ̃ (*pl. same*)/ *n.* M20. [(O)Fr., f. *jeter* cast up (accounts), calculate: see JET *v.*[2]] **1** = JETTON. M20. **2** A metal disc used instead of a coin for insertion in a public telephone box, esp. in France. M20.

jetsam /ˈdʒɛts(ə)m/ *n.* Also (*arch.*) **jetson** /ˈdʒɛts(ə)n/. L16. [Contr. of JETTISON *n.*] *Law.* **1** Goods discarded from a ship and washed ashore; *spec.* such material thrown overboard in order to lighten a vessel (also called *waveson*). Usu. assoc. w. FLOTSAM; cf. also LAGAN. L16. †**2** The throwing of goods overboard; = JETTISON *n.* M17–L19.

jets d'eau *n.* pl. of JET D'EAU.

†**jetteau** *n.* E–M18. [Confusion of It. *getto* (*d'acqua*) & Fr. JET D'EAU.] = JET D'EAU.

jetted /ˈdʒɛtɪd/ *a.*[1] L19. [f. JET *n.*[1] + -ED[2].] Ornamented with jet; trimmed with jet beads.

jetted /ˈdʒɛtɪd/ *a.*[2] E20. [App. f. JET *v.*[2] + -ED[1].] *Tailoring.* Of a pocket: having no flap, but an outside seam on either edge.

†**jettee** *n.* var. of JETTY *n.*

jettison /ˈdʒɛtɪs(ə)n, -z(ə)n/ *n.* LME. [AN *getteson*, OFr. *getaison* f. L *jactatio(n-)*, f. *jactare*: see -ISON.] **1** The action of throwing goods overboard, esp. in order to lighten a ship in distress. LME. **2** *fig.* Abandonment, disregard. L19.

jettison /ˈdʒɛtɪs(ə)n, -z(ə)n/ *v.t.* M19. [f. the n.] **1** Throw overboard (cargo, articles of merchandise, etc.), esp. in order to lighten a ship in distress. M19. **b** Release or drop from an aircraft or spacecraft in flight; *spec.* drop (a bomb) intentionally from an aircraft elsewhere than over an assigned target. M20. **2** *fig.* Discard, abandon, get rid of, (something no longer wanted). L19.

2 *Daedalus* He jettisoned much of what we think of as Victorianism.

jettisonable *a.* able to be jettisoned; *esp.* designed to be readily detachable from an aircraft etc. in flight: M20.

jetton /ˈdʒɛt(ə)n/ *n.* M18. [Fr. JETON.] A counter or token used to operate slot-machines, as a gambling chip, and (formerly) in accounting.

jetty /ˈdʒɛti/ *n.* Also †**jettee**. LME. [OFr. *jetee*, *getee*, use as n. of fem. pa. pple of *jeter* throw: see JET *n.*[2], -Y[5]. Cf. JUTTY *n.*] **1** A mole, pier, breakwater, etc., constructed at a harbour entrance or running out into the sea, a lake, a river, etc., esp. for protective or defensive purposes. Also, an outwork protecting a pier. LME. **b** A projecting part of a wharf; a landing-pier. LME. **2** A projecting part of a building; *esp.* an overhanging upper storey. *obs.* exc. *Hist.* LME. **3** A bulwark, a bastion. *obs.* exc. *Hist.* M16.

jetty /ˈdʒɛti/ *a.* L15. [f. JET *n.*[1] + -Y[1].] **1** Of the colour of jet; jet-black. Also *jetty-black.* L15. **2** Of the nature or composition of jet. L19.

jetty /ˈdʒɛti/ *v.t.* LME. [f. the n.] **1** Chiefly *Hist.* Cause (the upper storey of a building) to project; provide (a building) with a projecting upper storey. Usu. in *pass.* LME. **2** Provide with a jetty or pier. *rare.* L19.

¶ Rare bef. M20.

jeu /ʒø/ *n.* Pl. ***jeux*** /ʒøː/. [Fr. f. L *jocus* JOKE *n.*] The Fr. for 'play', 'game', occurring in various phrases used in Eng.

jeu de mots /də mo/ [lit. 'of words'] a play on words, a pun M18. ***jeu de paume*** /də pom/ [lit. 'of the palm (of the hand)'] real tennis; a court where this is played: L18. ***jeu de société*** /də sɔsjete/ [lit. 'of society'] a party game or amusement (esp. in *pl.*) E19. ***jeu d'esprit*** /dɛspri/ [lit. 'of wit'] a playful action in which some cleverness is displayed; (now usu.) a humorous literary trifle: E18.

jeune fille /ʒœn fij/ *n.* & *a. phr.* M19. [Fr.] **A** *n. phr.* Pl. **-s -s** (pronounced same). A young girl, an ingénue. M19. **B** *attrib.* or as *adj. phr.* Characteristic of an ingénue. L19.

jeune premier /ʒœn prəmje/ *n. phr.* Also (fem.) ***jeune première*** /prəmjɛːr/. Pl. **-s -s** (pronounced same). M19. [Fr., lit. 'first young man (woman)'.] An actor who plays the part of a principal lover or young hero (or heroine).

jeunes filles, premiers *n. phrs.* pls. of JEUNE FILLE, PREMIER.

jeunesse /ʒœnɛs/ *n.* L18. [Fr.] Young people; the young.

jeunesse dorée /ʒœnɛs dɔre/ *n. phr.* M19. [Fr., lit. 'gilded youth'.] Orig., in France, a group of fashionable counter-revolutionaries formed after the fall of Robespierre. Now (*gen.*), young people of wealth and fashion.

jeux *n.* pl. of JEU *n.*

Jew /dʒuː/ *n.* ME. [OFr. *giu*, earlier *juiu* (mod. *juif*) f. L *Judaeus* f. Gk *Ioudaios* f. Aram. *yĕhūdāy*, Heb. *yĕhūdī*, f. *yĕhūdāh* Judah, a son of the Hebrew patriarch Jacob, the tribe descended from Judah.] **1** A person of Hebrew descent; a person whose religion is Judaism; *Hist.* an Israelite. ME. **2** A person who behaves in a manner attributed to Jews; *spec.* a grasping or extortionate person, one who drives hard bargains. *derog.* & usu. considered *offensive.* E16. **3** A pedlar. *colloq.* E19. **4** A ship's tailor. *Naut. slang.* E20.

1 *Ashkenazic Jew, German Jew, Oriental Jew, Portuguese Jew, Russian Jew, Sephardic Jew*, etc. *Conservative Jew*: see CONSERVATIVE *a.* **Black Jew** (*a*) an Indian or Black of Jewish descent; (*b*) = FALASHA. (*the*) *Wandering Jew*: see WANDERING *ppl a.*

Attrib. & *comb.*: In the sense 'Jewish', as *Jew boy, girl, man* (now usu. *derog.* & considered *offensive*). Special combs., as **Jew-baiter** a person who practises Jew-baiting; **Jew-baiting** systematic harrying or persecution of Jews; **Jew-lizard** a large Australian lizard, *Amphibolurus barbatus*, with spiny scales round the throat; **Jew plum** = OTAHEITE *apple*; **Jew's apple** (the fruit of) the eggplant, *Solanum melongena*; **Jew's-ear** [mistr. med.L *auricula Judae* Judas's ear: so called from its shape and its frequent occurrence on the elder, the tree from which Judas Iscariot reputedly hanged himself] an edible cup-shaped fungus, *Auricularia auricula-Judae*, growing on the roots and trunks of trees; **Jew's eye** (a proverbial expression for) something valued highly; **Jew's harp** a musical instrument consisting of an elastic steel tongue, usu. of metal, fixed at one end to a small lyre-shaped frame, and bent at the other end at right angles, which is played by holding the frame between the teeth and striking the free end of the tongue with the finger; **Jew's mallow** (*a*) a jute-yielding plant, *Corchorus olitorius*, of the linden family, used as a pot-herb in Egypt, Syria, etc.; (*b*) a double-flowered ornamental shrub, *Kerria japonica*, of the rose family; **Jews' stone, Jewstone** [tr. med.L *lapis Judaicus*] (*a*) (now *rare* or *obs.*) marcasite; (*b*) (now *rare* or *obs.*) fossil sea urchin spines found in Syria, formerly used in medicine; (*c*) *local* a hard rock of uneven or difficult fracture; **Jew's trump** (now *rare*) = *Jew's harp* above.

¶In medieval England Jews, though engaged in many pursuits, were particularly familiar as moneylenders, a profession debarred to Christians at this time by canon law. Thus the name 'Jew' came to be associated in the popular mind with the usury and extortionate practices associated with the medieval system of moneylending, and gave rise to the opprobrious sense 2 above.

Jewism *n.* †(*a*) Judaism; (*b*) *rare* an idiom or characteristic of Jews: L16. **Jewy** *a.* (*derog.*) resembling or typical of a Jew or Jews; having characteristics attributed to Jewish people: E20.

Jew /dʒuː/ *v.t. colloq.* Usu. considered *offensive.* Also **j-**. E19. [f. the n.] Drive a hard bargain with, get a financial advantage over, cheat; beat *down* in price.

W. G. HAMMOND We were unmercifully jewed for all the refreshments.

jewel /ˈdʒuːəl/ *n.* ME. [AN *juel, jeuel*, OFr. *joel* (nom. sing. *joyaus*, mod. *joyau*), ult. based on L *jocus* jest.] **1** An article of value used for (personal) adornment, *esp.* one made of gold, silver, or precious stones. Now usu., a small ornament containing a precious stone or stones, worn for personal adornment. ME. **b** An ornament worn as the badge of an order of honour, or as a mark of distinction. L17. **2** *fig.* A thing or person highly prized; something of great beauty or worth. ME. **3** A precious stone, a gem; *esp.* one worn as an ornament. L16. **b** A precious stone, usu. a ruby, used for a pivot-hole in a watch (on account of its hardness and resistance to wear). E19. **c** An imitation of a real gem, esp. as a piece of costume jewellery. L19.

2 J. CARLYLE She is quite a jewel of a servant. **jewel in the crown** the best in a particular class of assets.

Comb.: **jewel-block** *Naut.* either of two small blocks suspended at the ends of main and fore- topsail yards, through which the halyards of studding-sails are passed; **jewel-fish** a scarlet and green cichlid fish, *Hemichromis bimaculatus*, kept in aquaria; **jewel-weed** either of two N. American balsams, the orange-flowered *Impatiens capensis* (naturalized in Britain) and the yellow-flowered *I. pallida*.

jewel /ˈdʒuːəl/ *v.t.* Infl. **-ll-**, ***-l-**. L16. [f. the n.] Chiefly as *jewelled* ppl a. **1** Provide, adorn, or set with jewels. L16. **b** Fit (a watch) with jewels for the pivot-holes. E19. **2** *fig.* Bedeck or adorn as with jewels. E19.

2 P. LIVELY The Nile, at night, is jewelled. The bridges wear necklaces of coloured lights.

jewelling *n.* (*a*) the action of the vb; (*b*) jewels used for pivot-holes in a watch; (*c*) a trimming on a dress consisting of (imitation) jewels: E17.

jeweller /ˈdʒuːələ/ *n.* Also ***-eler**. ME. [AN *jueler*, OFr. *juelier* (mod. *joaillier*), f. as JEWEL *n.*: see -ER[2].] A person who works with precious stones etc.; a dealer in jewellery.

jeweller's putty: see PUTTY *n.* 1. *jeweller's rouge*: see ROUGE *n.*[1] 5.

jewellery /ˈdʒuːəlri/ *n.* Also **jewelry**. LME. [OFr. *juelerie* (mod. *joaillerie*) f. *juelier*: see prec. In mod. use a new formation f. JEWEL *n.*, JEWELLER: see -ERY.] Gems or ornaments made or sold by jewellers, *esp.* precious stones in mountings; jewels collectively or as a form of adornment.

jewelly /ˈdʒuːəli/ *a.* M18. [f. JEWEL *n.* + -Y[1].] **1** Having many jewels; adorned with or wearing jewels. M18. **2** Resembling a jewel; having the brilliancy of a jewel. M19.

jewelry *n.* var. of JEWELLERY.

Jewess /ˈdʒuːɛs, -ɪs/ *n.* ME. [f. JEW *n.* + -ESS[1].] A female Jew; a Jewish woman.

jewfish /ˈdʒuːfɪʃ/ *n.* Pl. **-es** /-ɪz/, (usu.) same. L17. [App. f. JEW *n.* + FISH *n.*[1]] Any of various fishes, esp. of the percoid families Serranidae and Sciaenidae; *spec.* (*a*) a grouper, *Epinephelus itajara*, that is a sporting and food fish of the Atlantic and Pacific coasts of N. America; (*b*) = MULLOWAY; (*c*) a drum, *Otolithes ruber*, of the tropical Pacific and Indian Oceans.

Jewish /ˈdʒuːɪʃ/ *a.* M16. [f. JEW *n.* + -ISH[1].] **1** Of, belonging to, or characteristic of, the Jews; of or relating to Judaism; Israelitish, Hebrew. M16. **2** Marked by the extortion or sharp practices attributed to Jewish moneylenders. *derog.* & usu. considered *offensive.* E17.

Jewishly *adv.* M16. **Jewishness** *n.* †(*a*) Judaism; (*b*) Jewish character or quality: L16.

Jewry /ˈdʒʊəri/ *n.* ME. [AN *juerie*, OFr. *juierie* (mod. *juiferie*), f. as JEW *n.*: see -ERY.] **1** The ancient land of the Jews, Judea; biblical Palestine. *arch.* ME. **2** *Hist.* The district inhabited by Jews in a town or city; a Jews' quarter, a ghetto. ME. †**3** Judaism. ME–M16. **4** The Jewish people, nation, or community; Jews collectively. ME.

jezail /dʒəˈzʌɪl, -ˈzeɪl/ *n.* M19. [Urdu *jazā'il.*] A long heavy Afghan musket.

Jezebel /ˈdʒɛzəbɛl/ *n.* M16. [The wife of Ahab king of Israel (*1 Kings* 21:5–15, *2 Kings* 9:30–37).] A wicked or shameless woman. Also, a woman who wears heavy make-up.

jezia *n.* var. of JIZYA.

jheel /dʒiːl/ *n.* Also **jhil**. E19. [Hindi *jhīl.*] In the Indian subcontinent: a (large) pool or lake left after a flood.

jhula /ˈdʒuːlə/ *n.* M19. [Hind. *jhūlā* swing, swing-rope.] A simple rope suspension bridge in the Himalayas.

jhum /dʒuːm/ *n.* Also †***joom***. M19. [Local name in SE Bangladesh.] A system of shifting cultivation practised in the hill forests of the Indian subcontinent and SE Asia; a tract of land cultivated using this system.

jhuming *n.* cultivation using this system L19.

jiao /dʒaʊ/ *n.* Pl. same. M20. [Chin. *jiǎo.*] A monetary unit of China, equal to one-tenth of a yuan.

jib /dʒɪb/ *n.*[1] M17. [Origin unkn.] **1** On a sailing vessel, a triangular staysail stretching from the outer end of the jib-boom to the fore-topmast head or from the bowsprit to the masthead. M17. **2** The lower lip. Also, the mouth; the face; the nose. *dial.* & *colloq.* E19.

1 *flying jib, slave jib, Yankee jib* , etc. 2 **the cut of a person's jib** *colloq.* the appearance or look of a person.

Comb.: **jib-boom** a spar run out from the end of the bowsprit; **jib-guy** a stout rope supporting a jib-boom; **jib-headed** *a.* (of a topsail) shaped like a jib; **jib-header** a topsail shaped like a jib; **jib-sheet** any of the ropes by which a jib is trimmed; **jib topsail** a light triangular sail set above a gaff mainsail.

jib /dʒɪb/ *n.*[2] M18. [Perh. abbrev. of GIBBET *n.*[1]] The projecting arm of a crane; the boom of a derrick.

jib /dʒɪb/ *n.*[3] M19. [f. JIB *v.*[2]] A horse that jibs.

jib /dʒɪb/ *v.*[1]*t.* & *i.* Infl. **-bb-**. L17. [Origin unkn.] *Naut.* = GYBE *v.* 1.

jib /dʒɪb/ *v.*[2]*i.* Also **gib**. Infl. **-bb-**. E19. [Perhaps f. as GIBE *v.*[1]] **1** Of a horse or other animal in harness: stop and refuse to go on; move restively backwards or sideways instead of going on. E19. **2** Of a person: refuse to proceed or advance; draw back, turn aside; (foll. by *at*) show aversion to or distaste for. L19.

1 A. POWELL Jerking aside his head like a horse jibbing at a proffered apple. 2 J. CAREY Orwell . . jibbed at Auden's mention of 'necessary murder' in his poem 'Spain'.

jibba /ˈdʒɪbə/ *n.* Also **-ah, dj-**. M19. [Repr. a pronunc.] = JUBBA.

jibber /ˈdʒɪbə/ *n.* M19. [f. JIB *v.*[2] + -ER[1].] **1** An animal that jibs. M19. **2** A person who jibs. M20.

jibber /ˈdʒɪbə/ *v.i.* E19. [Imit.: cf. GIBBER *v.*] = GIBBER *v.*

Comb.: **jibber-jabber** *vi.* & *n.* (indulge in) senseless talk.

jib-door /ˈdʒɪbdɔː/ *n.* E19. [f. unexpl. 1st elem. + DOOR.] A door set flush in a wall and decorated so as to be indistinguishable.

jibe *n.*[1] var. of GIBE *n.*

jibe *n.*[2] see GYBE *n.*[2]

jibe /dʒʌɪb/ *v.*[1]*i.* Chiefly *N. Amer.* Also **g-**. E19. [Origin unkn.] Agree; be in harmony or accord. Usu. foll. by *with*.

jibe *v.*[2] var. of GIBE *v.*[1]

jibe *v.*[3] see GYBE *v.*

jicama /ˈhiːkəmə/ *n.* E17. [Mex. Sp. *jícama* f. Nahuatl *xicama.*] The tuberous root of the yam bean, *Pachyrhizus erosus*, as a vegetable eaten cooked or raw, esp. in salads; the plant itself, a leguminous vine cutivated esp. in Central America.

¶Rare bef. M20.

jicara /ˈhikara/ *n.* Also **-ro** /-rо/, pl. **-os** /-ɔs/. M19. [Amer. Sp. *jícara* (the fruit), *jícaro* (the tree) f. Nahuatl *xicalli* container made from the fruit.] In Central America: (the fruit of) the calabash tree, *Crescentia cujete*.

Jicarilla /hɪkəˈriːljə/ *n.* & *a.* M19. [Mex. Sp., dim. of prec.] **A** *n.* Pl. **-s**, same. A member of an Apache Indian people in New Mexico and nearby States; the language of this people. M19. **B** *attrib.* or as *adj.* Of or pertaining to the Jicarilla or their language. L19.

jicaro *n.* var. of JICARA.

jiff /dʒɪf/ *n. colloq.* L18. [Abbrev.] = JIFFY 1.

jiffle /ˈdʒɪf(ə)l/ *v.i.* L17. [Origin unkn.] Shuffle, fidget.

jiffy /ˈdʒɪfi/ *n. colloq.* L18. [Origin unkn.] **1** A very short space of time. Freq. in *in a jiffy*. L18. **2** (**J-**.) In full *Jiffy bag*. (Proprietary name for) a type of padded envelope. M20.

1 W. S. MAUGHAM I can explain that to you in half a jiffy. DENNIS POTTER It won't take a jiffy.

Comb.: *Jiffy bag*: see sense 2 above; **Jiffy pot** (proprietary name for) a type of plant-pot made from wood pulp and peat, used for growing plants from seed, cuttings, etc.

jig /dʒɪg/ *n.*[1] M16. [Origin unkn.] **1** A lively folk-dance usu. in triple time, with jumping movements. M16. **b** A piece of music for such a dance; *spec.* a gigue. L16. †**2** A lively, comic, often scurrilous song; *derog.* a metrical version of a psalm. L16–L17. **3** A comic sketch put on at the end or in an interval of a play. *obs.* exc. *Hist.* L16. **4** A trick, a practical joke; a jest, an object of amusement. Now only in *the jig is up*, the game is up, it is all over. *slang.* L16. **5** Any of various devices or machines for performing operations which involve movements up and down or to and fro; *esp.* (*a*) for catching fish (cf. GIG *n.*[2] 2); (*b*) for dressing ore; (*c*) for holding a piece of work in position and guiding the drills or other tools that operate on it; (*d*) = JIGGER *n.*[1] 7f. M18.

Phrases: **in jig time** *colloq.* (chiefly *US*) extremely quickly, in a very short time.

Comb.: **jig-bore** *v.t.* drill (a hole) with a jig borer; **jig borer** (a person who operates) a machine for drilling holes in or machining the surfaces of a component, usu. having a vertical spindle mounted above an adjustable table; **jig button** a steel bush for positioning a jig plate accurately on a lathe; **jigman** a man who works an ore-dressing jigger; **jig plate** (a part of) a jig consisting of a steel plate which carries bushes which guide the drill.

jig /dʒɪg/ *n.*[2] *US slang. derog.* & usu. considered *racially offensive.* E20. [Origin unkn.] A Black person.

jig /dʒɪg/ *v.* Infl. **-gg-**. L16. [f. JIG *n.*[1]; partly also back-form. f. JIGGER *n.*[1]] **1 a** *v.t.* Sing or play as a jig or in the style of a jig. L16. **b** *v.t.* & *i.* Dance (a jig or similar lively dance). Also *jig it*. L17. **2** *v.t.* & *i.* (Cause to) move up and down or to and fro with a rapid jerky motion. Cf. JIGGER *v.* E17. **3** *v.t.* & *i.* Fish (for) or catch with a jig. M18. **4** *v.t.* Separate coarser and finer portions of (ore) using a jigger. L18. **5** *v.t.* & *i.* Provide or equip (a factory etc.) with jigs. Cf. REJIG *v.* E20.

jigaboo /ˈdʒɪɡəbuː/ *n. US slang. derog.* & usu. considered *racially offensive.* E20. [Rel. to JIG *n.*[2] Cf. *bug, bugaboo.*] A Black person.

jig-a-jig /dʒɪɡəˈdʒɪɡ, ˈdʒɪɡədʒɪɡ/ *adv., a., n.,* & *v.* Also **jig-jig** /dʒɪɡˈdʒɪɡ, ˈdʒɪɡdʒɪɡ/, **-jog** /-dʒɒɡ/. E17. [Imit.: cf. JIG *v.,* JOG *v.*] **A** *adv.* & *adj.* With or having a jigging or jogging motion. E17.
B *n.* **1** A jigging or jogging motion. E17. **2** Sexual intercourse. *slang* (esp. *Pidgin*). M20.
2 G. GREENE Captain want jig jig, my sister pretty girl school-teacher.
C *v.i.* Infl. **-gg-**. **1** Move with a jigging or jogging motion. M17. **2** Have sexual intercourse. *slang* (esp. *Pidgin*). L19.

jigamaree /dʒɪɡəməˈriː/ *n. dial.* & *colloq.* E19. [Arbitrary expansion of JIG *n.*[1]] A trick, a manoeuvre; (usu. *derog.*) fanciful contrivance; a thingummy.

jigger /ˈdʒɪɡə/ *n.*[1] M16. [Chiefly f. (as) JIG *v.* + -ER[1]; the relationship of some senses is obscure.] **I 1 a** A door. *slang.* M16. **b** A passage between or at the back of houses; a back entry or alley. *local.* E20. **2 a** An illicit distillery. *slang.* E19. **b** A drink of spirits, a dram. Also, a measure used in mixing cocktails etc.; a small glass holding this quantity. *N. Amer. slang.* M19. **II 3** A person who dances a jig. L17. **4** In full *jigger coat.* A woman's short loosely fitting jacket. M20. **5** *Forestry.* A short plank, set into a tree-trunk, on which a feller stands to work. *NZ.* M20. **III 6** *Naut.* **a** A small tackle consisting of a double and a single block with a rope. E18. **b** A small sail at the stern; a fishing-vessel with such a sail. M19. **7 a** A contrivance for catching fish which is operated by jerking up and down. M18. **b** *Mining.* A kind of sieve for dressing ore by shaking with water; a person who uses this. L18. **c** = JOLLEY. E19. **d** *Billiards* & *Snooker.* A rest for a cue. Chiefly *Sc.* M19. **e** *Golf.* A short iron with a narrow face, used for approach shots. L19. **f** A device for dyeing by passing pieces of fabric back and forth through a dye-bath over a set of rollers. L19. **8** Any small mechanical device; a gadget. *colloq.* (orig. *US*). L19. **9** A light vehicle; a hand-car; a bicycle. *colloq.* L19.
Comb.: *jigger coat*: see sense 4 above; **jigger-mast** *Naut.* (*a*) a small mast at the stern, on which a jigger is hoisted; (*b*) the aftermost mast of a four-masted sailing vessel; **jigger-tackle** *Naut.* = sense 6a above.
jiggerer *n.* a person who uses or works with a jigger L19.

jigger /ˈdʒɪɡə/ *n.*[2] Also **ch-** /tʃ-/. M18. [Alt. of CHIGOE.] **1** A tropical flea, *Tunga penetrans,* native to the Americas and introduced elsewhere, the female of which burrows beneath human skin causing painful sores; also called *chigoe, pique, red bug, sand flea.* Also *jigger flea.* M18. **2** A harvest-mite. *US.* E20.

jigger /ˈdʒɪɡə/ *v.* M19. [f. JIG *v.,* JIGGER *n.*[1]: in senses 2, 3 prob. euphem. for BUGGER *v.*] **1** *v.i.* Of a fish: jerk or tug repeatedly at a fishing-line. M19. **2** *v.t.* Confound, damn, curse. Freq. in imprecations. *slang.* M19. **3** *v.t.* Tire out, exhaust; damage, spoil, break. Also foll. by *up.* Freq. in *pass. slang.* M19. **4** *v.t. Bookbinding.* Rub (a tool) to and fro along an impressed line etc. in a binding, in order to impart a polish. L19. **5** *v.t. Pottery.* Shape with a jigger or jolley. M20. **6** *v.t.* Manipulate or rearrange (figures etc.), esp. so as to mislead; tamper with. *colloq.* (chiefly *US*). M20.
2 DICKENS 'Well then', said he, 'I'm jiggered if I don't see you home'. X. HERBERT 'The law demands co-operation.' 'Jigger the law.' 3 *Telegraph* (*Brisbane*) The firing pin's jiggered and the sights are sloppy. B. T. BRADFORD I'm looking forward to a nice cup of tea. I suddenly feel jiggered.

jiggery-pokery /ˌdʒɪɡ(ə)rɪˈpəʊk(ə)ri/ *n. colloq.* L19. [Prob. alt. of earlier (Sc.) *joukery-pawkery* s.v. JOUKERY *n.*] Deceitful or dishonest dealing; trickery.

jigget /ˈdʒɪɡɪt/ *v.i. colloq.* L17. [f. JIG *v.*] Jig; hop or jerk about; shake up and down.
jiggety *a.* characterized by jiggeting, inclined to jigget L19.

jiggish /ˈdʒɪɡɪʃ/ *a.* M17. [f. JIG *n.*[1] + -ISH[1].] **1** Inclined to jigging or dancing; frivolous. M17. **2** Resembling a jig; suitable for a jig. E18.

jiggle /ˈdʒɪɡ(ə)l/ *v.* & *n.* M19. [Partly f. JIG *v.* + -LE[3]; partly alt. of JOGGLE *v.*[1] to express smaller movements.] **A** *v.t.* & *i.* Move up and down or to and fro jerkily, rock or shake lightly. M19. **B** *n.* A jiggling movement; a light rapid rocking. L19.

jig-jig, jig-jog *adv., a., n.,* & *v.* vars. of JIG-A-JIG.

jigotai /dʒɪɡəˈtʌɪ/ *n.* M20. [Jap., f. *ji* self + *go* defence + *tai* posture.] A defensive posture in judo.

jigsaw /ˈdʒɪɡsɔː/ *n., a.,* & *v.* L19. [f. JIG *v.* + SAW *n.*[1]] **A** *n.* **1** A saw with a narrow vertically reciprocating blade, used for cutting curved lines or patterns. L19. **2** In full *jigsaw puzzle.* A puzzle consisting of a picture mounted on wood, board, etc., and cut into irregular interlocking pieces to be reassembled. E20.
2 *fig.*: *Oxford Times* As the excavation proceeds more . . pieces of the archaeological jigsaw puzzle will be discovered.
B *attrib.* or as *adj. Archit.* Characterized by the use of fretwork patterns. L19.
C *v.t.* **1** Cut or shape with a jigsaw. L19. **2** (Re)assemble in the manner of a jigsaw puzzle. M20.

jihad /dʒɪˈhɑːd, -ˈhad/ *n.* Also **jehad**. M19. [Arab. *jihād* lit. 'effort'.] Religious warfare or a war for the propagation or defence of Islam; *transf.* a campaign or crusade in some cause.

jildi /ˈdʒɪldi/ *n., adv.,* & *v. Mil. slang* (orig. *Anglo-Ind.*). Also **juldy** /ˈdʒʊldi/ & other vars. L19. [Hind. *jaldī* quickness.] **A** *n.* Haste; *on the jildi,* in a hurry. L19. **B** *adv.* Quickly. E20. **C** *v.t.* & *i.* Hurry. E20.

jill *n.*[1], *n.*[2] vars. of GILL *n.*[4], *n.*[5]

jill /dʒɪl/ *v.i. colloq.* M20. [Origin unkn.] Of a boat: move idly (*about, around*).

jillaroo /dʒɪləˈruː/ *n. Austral. colloq.* Also **jilleroo**. M20. [f. female forename *Jill* after JACKAROO.] A female novice on a sheep-station or cattle-station.

jillet /ˈdʒɪlɪt/ *n. Sc.* M18. [Dim. of female forename *Jill,* or f. GILL *n.*[4]: see -ET[1].] A frivolous or irresponsible young woman; a wench.

jill-flirt *n.* var. of GILL-FLIRT.

jillion /ˈdʒɪljən/ *n. colloq.* (chiefly *N. Amer.*). M20. [Fanciful formation after BILLION, MILLION.] A great many, an extremely large quantity.

jilt /dʒɪlt/ *n.* L17. [Origin uncertain: sense 2 prob. f. the vb.] †**1** An unchaste woman; a kept mistress. Also (*Sc.*), = JILLET. L17–E19. **2** A person (orig. and esp. a woman) who jilts a lover. L17.
jiltish *a.* L17.

jilt /dʒɪlt/ *v.t.* M17. [Origin unkn.] **1** Deceive, cheat, trick, break faith with. Long *rare* (as transf. use of 2). M17. **2** Abruptly reject or abandon (a lover, fiancé, etc.); be faithless to. L17.
1 THACKERAY But Fortune shook her swift wings and jilted him too. 2 J. C. POWYS The youthful Vicar . . had jilted her to marry a maid-servant.

jimber-jawed /ˈdʒɪmbədʒɔːd/ *a. US colloq.* M19. [Prob. f. alt. of GIMBAL + JAWED.] Having a protruding lower jaw.

Jim Crow /dʒɪm ˈkrəʊ/ *n., a.* & *v.* Chiefly *US.* M19. [See below.] **A** *n.* **1 a** The eponymous Black character in the early 19th-cent. plantation song 'Jim Crow'; a performer of this song; the dance involved in its performance. M19. **b** A Black. *slang* (*derog.* & usu. considered *racially offensive*). M19. **c** Racial discrimination, esp. against Blacks in the US. M20. **2** An implement for bending or straightening iron rails by the pressure of a screw. L19.
1a jump Jim Crow (*a*) perform the dance involved in the performance of 'Jim Crow'; (*b*) *fig.* change one's political principles or party. c R. OTTLEY Negro soldiers had suffered all forms of Jim Crow.
B *attrib.* or as *adj.* Characteristic of or set apart for Blacks; racially segregated. M19.
Time Southern newspapers . . relegated announcements of black births, deaths and marriages to special Jim Crow pages. K. BOYLE It was the Jim Crow gallery. Colored people goes upstairs, other people goes down.
C *v.t.* Segregate racially; discriminate against (Blacks or other non-Whites). E20.
Jim Crowism *n.* (*a*) a system or the practice of racial discrimination or segregation; (*b*) the action of changing one's political party: M19.

jim-dandy /dʒɪmˈdandi/ *n.* & *a. N. Amer. colloq.* L19. [f. *Jim* pet-form of male forename *James* + DANDY *n.*[2], *a.*] **A** *n.* An excellent person or thing. L19. **B** *adj.* Remarkably fine, outstanding. L19.

Jiminy /ˈdʒɪmɪni/ *int.* Also **-mm-**. E19. [Alt. of GEMINI *int.*: euphem. for *Jesus* (*Christ*).] Expr. surprise or asseveration. Chiefly in *by Jiminy, Jiminy Christmas, Jiminy cricket.*

jimjam /ˈdʒɪmdʒam/ *n. colloq.* M16. [Fanciful redupl. with vowel variation: cf. FLIMFLAM, WHIM-WHAM.] **1** A fanciful or trivial article, a knick-knack. Long *rare.* M16. **2** *the jimjams,* a state of nervous agitation or apprehension, the jitters; (*spec.*) *slang* delirium tremens. L19.

Jimminy *int.* var. of JIMINY.

jimmy /ˈdʒɪmi/ *n.*[1] & *v. colloq.* (chiefly *N. Amer.*). M19. [Alt. of JEMMY *n.*] **A** *n.* A crowbar used by a burgler; = JEMMY *n.* 3. M19. **B** *v.t.* Force (*open*) with a jemmy. L19.

Jimmy /ˈdʒɪmi/ *n.*[2] Also **Jimmie**. M19. [Pet-form of male forename *James*: see -Y[6].] **1** In full *Jimmy Grant.* An immigrant; an emigrant. *Austral.* & *NZ slang.* M19. **2** In full *Jimmy O'Goblin.* A sovereign; = GOBLIN *n.*[2] *rhyming slang. obs.* exc. *Hist.* L19. **3** In full *Jimmy the One.* First Lieutenant. *Naut. slang.* E20. **4** *the Jimmies,* = JIMJAM 2. *slang.* E20. **5** In full *Jimmy Riddle.* = PIDDLE *n. rhyming slang.* M20. **6** Used as a form of address to a male stranger. *colloq.* (chiefly *Sc.*). L20.
Phrases: *dismal Jimmy*: see DISMAL *a.* 4. **Jimmy Ducks** *Naut. slang* (*obs.* exc. *Hist.*) a sailor in charge of the livestock carried to serve as food on long voyages. *Jimmy Grant*: see sense 1 above. **Jimmy Green** = JAMIE GREEN. *Jimmy O'Goblin*: see sense 2 above. **Jimmy Skinner** *rhyming slang* dinner. *Jimmy the One*: see sense 3 above. **Jimmy Woodser** *Austral.* & *NZ slang* (a drink taken by) a solitary drinker.

jimp /dʒɪmp/ *a.* & *adv. Sc.* & *north.* Also **g-**. E16. [Origin unkn.: cf. GIM.] **A** *adj.* **1** Slender, graceful, neat. E16. **2** Of measure or quantity: barely sufficient, scanty. E17. **B** *adv.* Barely, scarcely. E19.
jimply *adv.* slenderly, scantily L18.

jimson /ˈdʒɪms(ə)n/ *n. US.* Orig. †**Jamestown weed**. Also **jimpson** /dʒɪmps(ə)n/. L17. [Alt. of *Jamestown,* a town in Virginia, USA.] In full *jimson weed.* Thorn-apple, *Datura stramonium.*

jimswinger /ˈdʒɪmswɪŋə/ *n. Southern US.* L19. [Origin unkn.] A swallow-tailed coat, *esp.* a frock coat. Also *jimswinger coat.*

Jina /ˈdʒɪnə/ *n.* E19. [Skt *jina*: see JAIN.] *Jainism.* A great Jain teacher who has attained liberation from karma; a sculptured representation of such a teacher.

Jindyworobak /dʒɪndɪˈwɒrəbak/ *n.* & *a. Austral.* M20. [Aborig.] **A** *n.* A member or supporter of a group founded in Australia in 1938 to promote Australianness in literature, art, etc. M20. **B** *attrib.* or as *adj.* Of or pertaining to this group. M20.

jing /dʒɪŋ/ *n.* & *int.* Also **jings** /-z/. Orig. *Sc.* L18. [Alt.] More fully *by jing(s).* = JINGO *int.* & *n.* 2.

jingall *n.* var. of GINGALL.

jingbang /dʒɪŋˈbaŋ/ *n. slang.* M19. [Origin unkn.] *the whole jingbang,* the lot, everyone, the whole company or affair.

jingle /ˈdʒɪŋɡ(ə)l/ *v.* & *n.* Also †**g-**. LME. [Imit.: cf. JANGLE *v., n.*] **A** *v.* **1** *v.i.* Make a mixed noise as of coins, keys, or other small metallic objects being shaken together; make a light ringing sound more prolonged and continuous than clinking. LME. **b** Proceed or move with such a sound. M18. **2** *v.t.* Cause to make such a sound. LME. **3** *v.i.* **a** Play with (the sounds of) words; *derog.* versify. M17. **b** Of prose or verse: be characterized by a alliteration or other features suggesting a jingle. L17. **B** *n.* **1** A jingling noise; a sound intermediate between clinking and ringing. L16. **2** A thing that jingles, esp. a small bell. E17. **3 a** The affected repetition of the same sound or similar sounds, as in alliteration, rhyme, or assonance; (usu. *derog.*) any arrangement of words achieving its effect by sound rather than by sense. M17. **b** A short tune, verse, slogan, etc., played or sung (as) in a radio or television commercial. M20. **4** Chiefly *Hist.* A two-wheeled one-horse cart with seats, used esp. in the south of Ireland and Australia; a governess cart. E19. **5** (The shell of) a bivalve mollusc of the family Anomidae, having an asymmetric shell with a hole or notch for the siphon; a saddle-oyster. Also *jingle shell*. Orig. *US*. L19.

Phrases & comb.: **jingle-boy** *slang* (*a*) a coin; (*b*) a man with plenty of money in his pockets. *jingle shell*: see sense B.5 above. **jingling Johnny** (*a*) *slang* a Turkish crescent or *pavillon chinois* (percussion instruments with jingling bells); (*b*) *Austral.* & *NZ slang* a person who shears sheep by hand; in *pl.*, hand shears. **jingling match** a game in which one player keeps ringing a bell while the others, all blindfolded, try to catch him or her.

jingly *a.* characterized by jingling, resembling a jingle E19.

jingle-jangle /ˈdʒɪŋg(ə)l,dʒaŋg(ə)l/ *n.* & *v.* L16. [Redupl. of prec. with vowel variation: see JANGLE *n.*, *v.* Cf. TWINGLE-TWANGLE.] **A** *n.* An alternating jingle of sounds; a thing that makes, or an utterance marked by, such a sound. L16. **B** *v.i.* Make or move with an alternating jingle of sounds. L19.

jingler /ˈdʒɪŋglə/ *n.* Also †**g-**. L16. [f. JINGLE *v.* + -ER[1].] **1** A person who or thing which jingles. L16. †**2** A dealer, esp. in horses, at a country fair. *slang. rare.* L17–M19.

jingo /ˈdʒɪŋgəʊ/ *int.*, *n.*, & *a.* Also **J-**. L17. [Origin unkn. Sense A.3 orig. f. a use of *by jingo* in a popular song.] **A** *int.* & *n.* †**1** In full *hey* or *high jingo!* A conjuror's call for, or an exclamation of surprise at, the appearance of something. L17–E18. **2** *by jingo!*, (rare) *by the living jingo!*, expr. asseveration or surprise. *colloq.* L17. **3** Pl. **-oes**. An advocate of a bellicose foreign policy; a loud and blustering patriot, a chauvinist, a jingoist. Orig., one who supported the sending of a British fleet into Turkish waters to resist Russia in 1878. L19. **B** *attrib.* or as *adj.* Of or pertaining to jingoists; characterized by jingoism. L19.

jingoish *a.* = JINGO *a.* L19.

jingoism /ˈdʒɪŋgəʊɪz(ə)m/ *n.* L19. [f. prec. + -ISM.] The advocacy or practice of a bellicose foreign policy; loud and blustering patriotism.

jingoist *n.* & *a.* (*a*) *n.* a supporter of jingoism; (*b*) *adj.* jingoistic: L19. **jingoˈistic** *a.* characterized by jingoism L19.

jings *n.* & *int.* var. of JING.

jink /dʒɪŋk/ *n.* Orig. *Sc.* L17. [Rel. to JINK *v.*[1]] **1** †**a** *high jinks*, antics indulged in at drinking parties, usu. involving the throwing of dice to decide who should perform some frivolous act. L17–L19. **b** In *pl.* Usu. more fully *high jinks*. Boisterous or exuberant play; unrestrained merrymaking. M19. **2** An act of eluding someone or something; a quick turn, *esp.* one made so as to elude a pursuer, a tackler, etc. L18.

jink /dʒɪŋk/ *v.*[1] Orig. *Sc.* E18. [Origin uncertain: perh. imit.] **1** *v.i.* **a** Wheel about in dancing; dance. *Sc.* E18. **b** Move with quick sudden action or turns; change direction nimbly; dart; dodge, move elusively. L18. **2** *v.t.* Elude by dodging, evade. L18. **3** *v.t.* Trick, cheat, swindle. L18.

1b R. JEFFERIES A rabbit . . jinked away under a rhododendron bush. I. FLEMING Jinking occasionally to spoil the men's aim.

jink /dʒɪŋk/ *v.*[2]*t.* & *i.* E19. [Imit.: cf. CHINK *v.*[1]] (Cause to) make a short metallic sound.

jinker /ˈdʒɪŋkə/ *n.*[1] Chiefly *Sc.* E18. [f. JINK *v.*[1] + -ER[1].] A person, animal, or thing that jinks or dodges.

jinker /ˈdʒɪŋkə/ *n.*[2] *Austral.* Also **jun-** /ˈdʒʌŋ-/. L19. [Var. of JANKER.] A contrivance consisting of two pairs of wheels joined by chains, for carrying tree-trunks etc. Also, a two-wheeled vehicle resembling a gig, sometimes with a single seat, used in trotting.

jinker /ˈdʒɪnkə/ *n.*[3] M20. [f. alt. of JINX *v.* + -ER[1].] A person who brings bad luck or who puts a jinx on someone or something.

jinnee /ˈdʒɪniː/ *n.* Pl. **jinn**. Also **jinn, dj-**, /dʒɪn/, pl. **-s**, same. E19. [Arab. *jinnī* masc. sing., pl. *jinn*. Cf. GENIE.] In Arabian stories and Muslim mythology: a spirit of an order lower than the angels, able to appear in human or animal form and to exercise supernatural influence.

jinny /ˈdʒɪni/ *n.* L19. [Pet-form of female forename *Jane*.] *Mining.* A stationary engine used to draw trucks up or down an inclined plane. Also (in full *jinny-road*), an underground inclined plane worked by gravity.

jinricksha /dʒɪnˈrɪkʃə/ *n.* Also **-rikisha** /-ˈrɪkiʃə/. L19. [Jap. *jin-riki-sha*, f. *jin* man + *riki* strength, power + *sha* vehicle.] A rickshaw.

jinx /dʒɪŋks/ *n.* & *v.* Orig. *US*. E20. [Prob. f. JYNX.] **A** *n.* A person who or thing which seems to bring bad luck or exercise evil influence; a hoodoo. E20. **B** *v.t.* Cast a spell on, bring bad luck on. Freq. in *pass.* E20.

jipijapa /hiːpɪˈhɑːpə/ *n.* M19. [*Jipijapa*, a town in Ecuador.] **1** An almost stemless palmlike plant, *Carludovica palmata* (family Cyclanthaceae), native to tropical America; the fibre produced from its leaves. Also called *Panama hat palm* or *plant*. M19. **2** In full *jipijapa hat*. A Panama hat. L19.

jipper /ˈdʒɪpə/ *v.* & *n.* *dial.* & *slang.* E19. [Origin unkn.] **A** *v.t.* = BASTE *v.*[2] 1. E19. **B** *n.* Gravy; dripping; stew. L19.

jippo /ˈdʒɪpəʊ/ *n.* *dial.* & *slang.* E20. [f. prec. + -O.] = JIPPER *n.*

jirene *n.* var. of GYRENE.

jirga /ˈdʒɪəgə/ *n.* Also †**jeerga**. E19. [Pashto.] An assembly or council of Pathan or Baluchi headmen.

jirine *n.* var. of GYRENE.

jism /ˈdʒɪz(ə)m/ *n.* *slang* (orig. *US*). Also **gism** & other vars. M19. [Origin unkn.] Energy, strength; semen, sperm.

jist /dʒɪst/ *adv.* *colloq.* & *dial.* E19. [Repr. a pronunc.] = JUST *adv.*

jit /dʒɪt/ *n.* *arch.* *US slang.* E20. [Abbrev.] = JITNEY 1.

jitney /ˈdʒɪtni/ *n.* & *a.* *N. Amer.* E20. [Origin unkn.] **A** *n.* **1** A five-cent piece, a nickel. *arch. slang.* E20. **2** A bus or other vehicle carrying passengers for a low fare (orig. five cents). E20. **B** *attrib.* or as *adj.* Cheap, improvised, ramshackle. *arch. slang.* E20.

jitter /ˈdʒɪtə/ *n.* & *v.* *colloq.* E20. [Origin unkn.] **A** *n.* **1** In *pl.* Extreme nervousness; a state of emotional (and physical) tension; agitation. Usu. w. *the*. E20. **2** Chiefly *Electronics*. Slight random or irregular variation, esp. in the shape or timing of a regular pulse; unsteadiness of an image etc. due to this. M20.

1 F. M. FORD The publishers here have the jitters so badly . . they won't look at anything new. *Economist* Recession jitters now afflicting . . economists.

B *v.* **1** *v.i.* Move or act nervously; exhibit nervousness. E20. **2** *v.t.* Chiefly *Electronics*. Subject to slight random or irregular variation. M20.

jitterbug /ˈdʒɪtəbʌg/ *n.* & *v.* Orig. *US*. M20. [f. JITTER *v.* + BUG *n.*[2]] **A** *n.* **1** A jittery or nervous person; an alarmist. Also, an attack of the jitters. M20. **2** A jazz musician; a devotee of swing; a person who dances the jitterbug. M20. **3** An energetic dance, popular in the 1940s, performed chiefly to swing music. M20. **B** *v.i.* Infl. **-gg-**. Dance the jitterbug. M20.

jittery /ˈdʒɪtəri/ *a.* *colloq.* M20. [f. JITTER + -Y[1].] Nervy, jumpy, on edge.

jitteriness *n.* M20.

jiu-jitsu, -jutsu *n.* & *v.* see JU-JITSU.

jiva /ˈdʒiːvə/ *n.* E19. [Skt *jīva*.] *Hindu* & *Jain Philos.* The soul; the embodied self; the vital principle.

Jivaro /ˈhiːvərəʊ/ *n.* & *a.* M19. [Sp. *jibaro* prob. f. Jivaro *Shuara*, *Shiwora* (their name for themselves).] **A** *n.* Pl. **-os**, same. A member of an Indian people of Ecuador and Peru; the language of this people. M19. **B** *attrib.* or as *adj.* Of or pertaining to the Jivaro or their language. M19.

jive /dʒʌɪv/ *n.*, *v.*, & *a.* Orig. *US*. E20. [Origin unkn.] **A** *n.* **1** Talk, conversation; *spec.* misleading, empty, or pretentious talk. Now also, something worthless, phoney, or unpleasant; = JAZZ *n.* 3. *slang.* E20. **2 a** Jazz, *esp.* swing. E20. **b** Lively and uninhibited dancing to jazz or other popular music. M20. **3** A variety of American Black English associated esp. with jazz musicians and enthusiasts. Also *jive talk*. M20. **4** Marijuana. *slang.* M20. **B** *v.* **1** *slang.* **a** *v.t.* Mislead, fool; taunt, sneer at. E20. **b** *v.i.* Talk nonsense, jest; fool around. M20. **2** *v.i.* Make sense; fit in. *N. Amer. colloq.* M20. **3** *v.i.* **a** Play jive music. M20. **b** Dance energetically to jive or other popular music. M20. **C** *adj.* Acting wrongly; pretentious, phoney, deceitful. *US slang.* L20.

Comb.: **jive-ass** *US slang* a person who loves fun or excitement; a deceitful or pretentious person.

jiver *n.* a person who jives M20. **jivey** *a.* (*slang*, chiefly *US*) of, pertaining to, or characterized by jive; misleading, phoney, pretentious: M20.

jiwan *n.* var. of JAWAN.

jizya /ˈdʒɪzjə/ *n.* *obs.* exc. *Hist.* Also **jezia** /ˈdʒɛzɪə/. L17. [Pers. *jezya(t)* f. Arab. *jizya*.] A poll tax imposed by Islamic law on non-Muslim subjects in Muslim countries; *spec.* that exacted by the Mughal emperors in India.

jizz /dʒɪz/ *n.*[1] *colloq.* E20. [Origin unkn.] The indefinable combination of characters by which a given bird, plant, etc., can be quickly recognized in the field.

jizz /dʒɪz/ *n.*[2] *slang.* M20. [Abbrev.] = JISM.

jnana /dʒ(ə)ˈnɑːnə, -ˈɲɑːnə/ *n.* E19. [Skt *jñāna*, f. *jñā-* know.] *Hinduism.* Spiritual knowledge, as a means of salvation.

Comb.: **jnana-marga** /-mɑːgə/ [*mārga* path] the way to salvation through spiritual knowledge or asceticism.

jnani /-niː/ *n.* a worshipper or devotee of *jnana-marga* L19.

jo /dʒəʊ/ *n.* *Sc.* Also **joe**. Pl. **joes**. E16. [Sc. form of JOY *n.*] A sweetheart, one's beloved. Freq. as a form of address.

Joachimite /ˈdʒəʊəkɪmʌɪt/ *n.* L18. [f. *Joachim* (see below) + -ITE[1].] *Eccl. Hist.* A heretical follower of Joachim of Fiore (*c*1132–1202), abbot of Fiore in Calabria and Italian mystic.

Joachimism *n.* the doctrines of Joachim of Fiore E20. **Joachimist** *n.* = JOACHIMITE E20. **Joachism** *n.* = JOACHIMISM E20. **Joachist, Joachite** *ns.* = JOACHIMITE E20.

Joan /dʒəʊn/ *n.* L16. [Female forename, orig. (L) *Jo(h)anna* fem. of *Jo(h)annes*: see JOHN.] **1** (A name for) a female rustic. L16. **2** *Hist.* A close-fitting cap worn by women in the latter half of the 18th cent. M18.

joanna /dʒəʊˈanə/ *n.* *rhyming slang.* M19. [*Joanna*, female forename: see prec.] = PIANO *n.*[2] 1.

Joannes *n.* var. of JOHANNES.

job /dʒɒb/ *n.*[1] M16. [Origin unkn.] **1** A piece of work, *esp.* one done for hire or profit; *spec.* a small distinct piece of work done as part of one's occupation or profession or as a separate operation. Also *job of work*. M16. **b** A theft, robbery, or other criminal act, *esp.* one arranged beforehand. *Criminals' slang.* E18. **c** *Printing.* A small piece of miscellaneous work, as the printing of posters, cards, or anything on a single sheet. L18. **2** A public service or position of trust turned to private or party advantage; a transaction in which duty or public interest is sacrificed for private or party advantage. M17. †**b** Personal profit; private interest. M17–L18. **3** Something that has to be done, a transaction, a task; *colloq.* a difficult task. L17. **b** A paid position of employment; *transf.* a person's particular task or responsibility. M19. **c** = *job lot* below. M19. **d** A commission to back a racehorse; a horse on which such bets are placed. L19. **e** Of a manufactured item, esp. a motor vehicle or aircraft, or (*joc.*) a person, esp. a pretty girl: an (excellent) example of its type. *slang.* E20. **4** A state of affairs, an occurrence, a business. Chiefly in *bad job, good job* below. *colloq.* L17. **5** An operation involving plastic surgery. Usu. w. specifying wd. *colloq.* M20.

1 M. ATWOOD I did this grudgingly, as I did most jobs around the house. **b** *Public Opinion* Stolen property sufficient to connect the thief with several 'jobs'. 2 POPE Who makes a Trust or Charity a Job. 3 BROWNING 'Tis an ugly job: but soldiers obey commands. R. BADEN-POWELL My wounds sewn up and dressed, a job which took nearly four hours. *Ulverston* (*Cumbria*) *News* A complete re-roofing and paint job on South Lakeland district council's offices. *Sunday* (*Calcutta*) The Bombay Hospital did a commendable job in saving Dada's life. **b** D. LESSING Young women who had left £7 a week typing jobs in London. *Evening Telegraph* (*Grimsby*) It is not our job to call off the Test. **e** S. BELLOW He drove a dairy truck, one of those electric jobs. *Glasgow Herald* She hung towels over the . . mirrors when she took a bath, convinced they were two-way jobs. 5 *breast job, face job, nose job*, etc.

Phrases etc.: **bad job** (*a*) an unfavourable circumstance (*make the best of a bad job*: see BEST *a.*); (*b*) a thing on which labour is spent in vain (esp. in *give a thing up as a bad job*). *bob a job*: see BOB *n.*[6] *brown job*: see BROWN *a.* **get on with the job** proceed with one's work, continue with one's affairs. **good job** a fortunate fact or circumstance (*that*). **have a job** be hard put to it (*to do*). *inside job*: see INSIDE *a.* *jobs for the boys*: see BOY *n.* **just the job** *colloq.* exactly what is wanted, the very thing. *make a clean job of*: see CLEAN *a.* **make a (good) job of** transact or manage successfully. *odd job*: see ODD *a.* **on the job** (*a*) hard at work, busy; committing a crime; *euphem.* engaged in sexual intercourse; (*b*) (of a racehorse) out to win and well backed. **on-the-job** *a.* done or occurring while a person is at work. *outside job*: see OUTSIDE *a.* *straight job*: see STRAIGHT *a.*[1] & *adv.*[1] **the devil's (own) job** something extremely difficult.

Attrib. & comb.: In the sense 'hired by the job or for a limited time', as *job-coach, -gardener, horse*, etc. Special combs., as **job analysis** analysis of the essential factors of a particular task or piece of work and the necessary qualifications of the person who is to perform it; **job analyst** a person who practises job analysis; **jobcentre** an employment exchange displaying information about available jobs; **job-control** *a.* (*Computing*) designating a language which enables a user to determine the tasks to be undertaken by the operating system; **job creation** the provision of new opportunities for paid employment, esp. as part of a policy to provide work for the unemployed; **jobholder** a person who holds a particular job; **job-hopper** a person who practises job-hopping; **job-hopping** the act or practice of changing from one job to another in quick succession; **job horse** *Hist.* a horse hired out by a jobmaster; **job house** a printing-house specializing in jobwork; **job-hunt** *v.i.* (*colloq.*) seek employment; **job-hunter** *colloq.* a person who seeks employment; **job lot** a miscellaneous group of articles bought together; *derog.* any miscellaneous group of things, persons, etc.; **jobmaster** *Hist.* a person who keeps a livery stable and hires out horses, harnesses, and carriages for any job; **job-office** = *job-house* above; **job press** a small press designed for job-printing; **job-print, -printing** the printing of jobwork; **job-share** *v.* & *n.* (*a*) *v.i.* be employed or work under a job-sharing arrangement; (*b*) *n.* (an instance of) job-sharing; **job-sharer** a person who job-shares; **job sharing** a working arrangement by which a full-time job is done jointly by several part-time employees, who share the remuneration etc.; **jobsheet** a sheet on which are recorded details of a job that has been done; **job shop** (*a*) a workshop where small pieces of work are done; (*b*) = *job-house* above; **job-type** (special or ornamental) type used in jobwork; **jobwork** (*a*) work done and paid for by the job; piece-work; (*b*) the printing of posters, cards, or other miscellaneous items.

jobbish *a.* of the nature of a job; characterized by jobbery: L18. **jobster** *n.* = JOBBER L19.

job /dʒɒb/ *n.*[2] M16. [f. JOB *v.*[1]] An act of jobbing; an abrupt stab with the point or sharp end of something; a peck, a thrust; a jerk or wrench of the bit in a horse's mouth.

Job /dʒəʊb/ *n.*[3] L16. [A biblical patriarch, whose story forms a book in the Old Testament and Hebrew Scriptures.] **1** *Job's tears*, a grass of eastern Asia, *Coix lacryma-jobi*, having round shining grains resembling tears, which are used as beads. L16. **2** *Job's comforter*, a person who aggravates distress under the guise of administering comfort. M18.

job /dʒɒb/ *v.*[1] Infl. **-bb-**. LME. [Imit., app. expr. the sound of a brief forcible action: cf. BOB *v.*[2], DAB *v.*, STAB *v.* See also JAB *v.*] **1** *v.t.* Pierce to a small depth with a forcible but abruptly arrested action; peck, stab, prod, punch; jerk (a horse's mouth) with the bit; strike with a sharp or cutting stroke. LME. **2** *v.i.* Thrust *at* so as to stab or pierce; (of a bird) peck *at*; penetrate *into*. LME. **3** *v.t.* Thrust (a pointed thing) abruptly into something else. L16.

1 S. BARING-GOULD Let the horse go, but don't job his mouth in that way.

job /dʒɒb/ *v.*[2] Infl. **-bb-**. L17. [f. JOB *n.*[1]] **1** *v.i.* Do jobs or odd pieces of work; do piece-work. L17. **2a** *v.t.* Buy and sell (stock or goods) as a middleman or broker. L17. **b** *v.i.* Buy and sell stock; deal or speculate in stocks. E18. **3** *v.t.* Let or deal with for profit. Now usu. foll. by *out*. E18. **4** *v.t.* Give *away* by jobbery; get (a person) *into* some position by jobbery. E18. **5a** *v.i.* Turn a public service or a position of trust to private or party advantage; practise jobbery. M18. **b** *v.t.* Deal with corruptly for or turn to private or party advantage. E19. **6** *v.t.* & *i.* Hire or (*rare*) hire out (a horse, carriage, etc.) for a particular job or period of time. L18. **7** *v.t.* Complete (a task). Chiefly in *that job's jobbed*. *colloq.* M19. **8** *v.t.* Put *off* by artifice. Cf. *fob off* (FOB *v.*[1] 2). L19. **9** *v.t.* Cheat; betray. Cf. FRAME *v.* 10. *slang* (orig. *US*). E20.

2a *Observer* His game plan is to . . buy in, . . then . . job the shares on at a profit. 3 G. KEILLOR Why the state jobbed out the survey to drunks is a puzzle. 5b H. H. ASQUITH The duties of the trierarchy, . . are habitually evaded or jobbed. 6 H. MAYHEW Very few noblemen . . bring their carriage-horses to town; . . they nearly all job.

With advs. in specialized senses: **job backwards** make calculations retrospectively, esp. on Stock Exchange transactions, with the knowledge of subsequent events; *fig.* use hindsight. **job off** sell (goods) at very low prices.

†job *v.*[3] var. of JOBE.

jobation /dʒəʊˈbeɪʃ(ə)n/ *n.* *colloq.* L17. [f. JOBE *v.* + -ATION.] The action of JOBE *v.*; a reproof, esp. of a lengthy and tedious character; a talking to. Also, a long discussion.

jobber /ˈdʒɒbə/ *n.* L17. [f. JOB *v.*[2] + -ER[1].] **1** A person who buys goods etc. in bulk from a producer or importer, and sells them to a retailer or consumer; a broker, a middleman. L17. **2** A person who does odd jobs; a person employed by the job, as opp. to one in continuous employment; a piece-worker. E18. **3** A member of a stock exchange who deals in stocks or shares on his or her own account; a stockjobber, a dealer. Also, a middleman who acts between holders of stocks or shares and brokers, a broker-dealer. (Not now in official use on the British Stock Exchange.) E18. **4** A person who uses a public office or position of trust for private or party advantage. M18. **5** A person who hires out horses etc. for a particular job or period of time; a jobmaster. M19.

jobbery *n.* the turning of a public office, position of trust, etc., to private gain or advantage: M19.

jobbernowl /ˈdʒɒbənəʊl/ *n.* *colloq.* L16. [f. Fr. *jobard*, f. OFr. *jobe* stupid, silly + NOLL.] **1** The head, esp. of a stupid person. L16. **2** A stupid person, a blockhead. L16.

jobbing /ˈdʒɒbɪŋ/ *vbl n.* M18. [f. JOB *v.*[2] + -ING[1].] The action of JOB *v.*[2]; *esp.* the printing of small miscellaneous items.

jobbing /ˈdʒɒbɪŋ/ *ppl a.* E18. [f. JOB *v.*[2] + -ING[2].] That jobs; *spec.* (*a*) employed in odd or occasional pieces of work; (*b*) using a public office etc. for private or party advantage, given to jobbery.

jobbing builder, gardener, printer, etc.

jobble /ˈdʒɒb(ə)l/ *n.* M19. [Imit.: cf JABBLE *n.*] = JABBLE *n.*

†jobe *v.t.* *colloq.* Also **job**. L17–L18. [f. JOB *n.*[3], w. allus. to the lengthy reproofs administered to Job.] Rebuke in a long and tedious harangue.

jobless /ˈdʒɒblɪs/ *a.* & *n.* E19. [f. JOB *n.*[1] + -LESS.] **A** *adj.* **1** Free from jobbery. *rare.* E19. **2** Out of work, unemployed. E20. **B** *n.* *collect.* Unemployed people. L20.

joblessness *n.* the state of being out of work E20.

Jo block /ˈdʒəʊ blɒk/ *n. phr.* *colloq.* M20. [Abbrev. of JOHANSSON.] A Johansson block.

Jocism /ˈdʒəʊsɪz(ə)m/ *n.* M20. [Fr. *Jocisme* acronym, f. *Jeunesse Ouvrière Chrétienne* 'Christian working youth': see -ISM.] An organization aimed at spreading Christianity amongst working people, set up by Joseph Cardijn in Belgium in 1924 and later extended to other parts of Europe.

Jocist *n.* M20.

Jock /dʒɒk/ *n.*[1] E16. [Sc. form of JACK *n.*[1]] **1a** (A name for) a representative male of the common people. *Sc.* E16. **b** A Scottish or (formerly) northern English sailor; a Scottish soldier; a member of a Scottish regiment. More widely, (a form of address to) a Scotsman. Freq. as a nickname. *slang.* L18. **2** A countryman, a rustic, a clown. *Sc.* M16.

1a *Daily News* The proverb says . . 'there is a silly Jock for every silly Jenny'. **b** *Scottish Field* Kilts, trews, bonnets, pipe bands . . have helped enormously to make the Jock the man he is.

jock /dʒɒk/ *n.*[2] *colloq.* L18. [Abbrev.] 1 = JOCKEY *n.* 5. L18. 2 = JOCKEY *n.* 5c. L20.

jock /dʒɒk/ *n.*[3] *coarse slang.* L18. [Origin unkn.] The genitals of a man or (formerly) a woman.

jock /dʒɒk/ *n.*[4] *dial.* & *slang.* L19. [Origin unkn.] Food.

jock /dʒɒk/ *n.*[5] *N. Amer. slang.* E20. [f. JOCK(STRAP.] 1 = JOCKSTRAP 1. E20. 2 = JOCKSTRAP 2. Chiefly *derog.* M20.

2 R. JAFFE I was a big jock at prep school. Football and all that.

jocker /ˈdʒɒkə/ *n.* *N. Amer. slang.* L19. [Perh. f. JOCK *n.*[3] + -ER[1].] **1** A tramp who is accompanied by a youth who begs for him and may act as his catamite. Cf. PRUSHUN. L19. **2** An active male homosexual. E20.

jockette /dʒɒˈkɛt/ *n.* *rare.* M20. [f. JOCK *n.*[2] + -ETTE.] A female jockey.

jockey /ˈdʒɒki/ *n.* L16. [Dim. or pet-form of JOCK *n.*[1]: see -Y[6].] **1** (Also **J-**.) = JOCK *n.*[1] 1a (chiefly *Sc.*). Also, a lad; an underling. L16. **2** A horse-dealer. *obs.* exc. *dial.* M17. **b** A person having the supposed character of a horse-dealer; a fraudulent bargainer, a cheat. *rare.* L17. **†3** A person who rides or drives a horse; a postillion, a courier. M17–M19. **4** A strolling minstrel or beggar; a vagabond. *Sc. obs.* exc. *Hist.* L17. **5** A rider in horse-races, *esp.* a professional one. L17. **b** *transf.* A driver of a motor vehicle. Chiefly *N. Amer.* E20. **c** = *disc jockey* s.v. DISC *n.* M20. **6** *Fashion.* A flat trimming on the shoulder of a close-fitting sleeve. L19. **7** More fully *jockey spider*. A venomous black Australian spider, *Latrodectus hasseltii*, the female of which has a red stripe on the upper side of its abdomen. Also = KATIPO. *Austral.* M20. **8** (Also **J-**.) (Proprietary name for) a man's briefs or shorts. M20.

5 *jump jockey*: see JUMP *v.* 8 J. UPDIKE He takes clean Jockey pants, T-shirts, . . and a sports shirt from the closet.

Comb.: **jockey-boot** a top-boot of a type formerly worn by jockeys; **jockey-box** (*a*) *Hist.* a box in a wagon, under the driver's seat, for carrying small articles; (*b*) *US* a glove compartment; **jockey-cap** a peaked cap of the style worn by jockeys; **jockey club** (*a*) a club or association for the promotion and regulation of horse-racing; *spec.* (w. cap. initials) that established at Newmarket, the supreme UK authority on all matters connected with horse-racing; (*b*) a toilet-water with a scent esp. of rose and jasmine; **jockey-coat** (chiefly *Sc.*) a kind of greatcoat, *esp.* one made of broadcloth with wide sleeves; **jockey pulley** a small wheel which rides either on top of a larger one, esp. to obtain a higher speed of rotation, or on top of a belt or chain between two working pulleys or gears to keep the belt or chain taut; **jockey-sleeve** a wide sleeve like that of a jockey-coat; *jockey spider*: see sense 7 above; **jockey-wheel** (*a*) = *jockey-pulley* above; (*b*) a small adjustable wheel at the nose of a caravan or trailer.

jockey /ˈdʒɒki/ *v.* E18. [f. the n.] **1** *v.t.* Behave towards in the manner attributed to horse-dealers; gain the advantage of or manipulate by trickery; outwit, overreach. E18. **b** Get (a person or thing) *out, into, away*, etc., by trickery; cheat or do *out of*. E18. **2** *v.i.* & *t.* Ride (a horse) as a jockey. M18. **3** *v.i.* Struggle to secure an advantage, esp. by skilful manoeuvres or artifice. Usu. foll. by *for*. E19.

1b F. L. ALLEN He adroitly jockeyed .. Dougherty out of the Cabinet. 3 W. IRVING To get a good seat .. a vast deal of jockeying and unfair play was shown. M. PIERCY Everybody was jockeying for telephone time.

jockeyship /ˈdʒɒkɪʃɪp/ *n.* M18. [f. JOCKEY *n., v.* + -SHIP.] The art of a jockey; skill in horse-racing. Also, the practice of jockeying; trickery, artifice.

Jocko /ˈdʒɒkəʊ/ *n.* Pl. **-os**. L18. [Bantu: cf. *còkó* kind of monkey.] (A personal name for) a chimpanzee or other ape.

jockstrap /ˈdʒɒkstrap/ *n.* L19. [f. JOCK *n.*[3] + STRAP *n.*] **1** A support or protector for a man's genitals, worn esp. by sportsmen. Also (*rare*), a cache-sexe. L19. **2** An athletic (as opp. to an aesthetic or intellectual) man, esp. at a university. *N. Amer. slang.* M20.

jockteleg /ˈdʒɒktəlɛg/ *n.* *Sc.* & *north.* Also **jackleg** /ˈdʒaklɛg/, **†joctaleg**, & other vars. Orig. **†Jock the leg**. M17. [Perh. f. JOCK *n.*[1] + *the* + LEG *n.*, w. ref. to the leg-shape of some early knives.] A (large) clasp knife.

jocose /dʒəˈkəʊs/ *a.* L17. [L *jocosus*, f. *jocus* JOKE *n.*: see -OSE[1].] **1** Of a person, a person's disposition, etc.: fond of joking; playful, waggish, jocular. L17. **2** Of speech, writing, or action: of the nature of or containing a joke; said or done jokingly; playful, jocular. L17.

jocosely *adv.* E18. **jocoseness** *n.* E18.

jocoserious /dʒəʊkəʊˈsɪərɪəs, dʒɒk-/ *a.* M17. [f. L *joco-* comb. form of *jocus* JOKE *n.* (see -O-) + SERIOUS.] Half jocular, half serious; blending jokes and serious matters.

jocosity /dʒəˈkɒsɪti/ *n.* E16. [f. as JOCOSE + -ITY.] **1** Jocose quality or disposition, esp. in speech or action; mirth, merriment. E16. **2** A jocose saying or act; a piece of jesting. M19.

joctaleg *n.* var. of JOCKTELEG.

†jocular *n.* LME–E19. [OFr. *joculer* alt. (after L) of *jougler(e)*, *-leur*: see JUGGLER.] A professional jester or minstrel.

jocular /ˈdʒɒkjʊlə/ *a.* E17. [L *jocularis*, f. *joculus* dim. of *jocus* JOKE *n.*: see -AR[1].] **1** Of a person or a person's disposition: fond of joking; speaking or acting in jest or merriment. E17. **2** Of speech or action: of the nature of or containing a joke; said or done jokingly. L17.

1 B. T. BRADFORD Trying to be jocular and making a bad joke about tragic heroines. 2 S. MORLEY Letters couched .. in jocular self-deprecation.

jocuˈlarity *n.* the quality or an instance of being jocular; mirthfulness, jocundity: M17. **jocularly** *adv.* M17.

joculator /ˈdʒɒkjʊleɪtə/ *n.* *obs.* exc. *Hist.* LME. [L, f. *joculat-* pa. ppl stem of *joculari* to jest: see -ATOR. Cf. JONGLEUR, JUGGLER.] A professional jester, minstrel, or jongleur.

jocund /ˈdʒɒk(ə)nd, ˈdʒəʊk-/ *a.* Now only *literary*. LME. [OFr. *jocond*, *jocund* f. L *jocundus* late var. of *jucundus* pleasant, agreeable (f. *juvare* to help, to delight) by assoc. w. *jocus* JOKE *n.*] Feeling or expressing cheerfulness; mirthful, merry, light-hearted; pleasant, cheering, delightful.

H. WOUK A jocund crowd poured into the canopied entrance for the wedding brunch.

jocundly *adv.* LME.

jocundity /dʒɒˈkʌndɪti/ *n.* LME. [Late L *jucunditas*, f. *jucundus*: see prec., -ITY.] **1** Jocund quality or condition; mirth, gaiety. LME. **†2** Spiritual joy or delight. LME–E17.

jod /dʒɒd, jəʊd/ *n.* Long *rare*. L16. [med.L f. as YOD: cf. IOTA, JOT *n.*[1]] A jot, an iota.

jodel *v.* & *n.* see YODEL.

jodhpurs /ˈdʒɒdpəz/ *n.pl.* Also **J-**, **-pors** /-pɔːz/. In attrib. use & in comb. usu. in sing. **jodhpur**. L19. [*Jodhpur*, a town and district in Rajasthan, NW India.] **1** Long riding-breeches, wide around the hips but close-fitting from knee to ankle. Also *jodhpur riding-breeches*. L19. **2** Indian trousers cut loosely at the top but close-fitting below the knee. E20.

Comb.: **jodhpur boot** an ankle-high boot, orig. worn with jodhpurs.

jodhpured *a.* wearing jodhpurs M20.

Jodo /ˈdʒəʊdəʊ/ *n.* & *a.* Also **Jo-do**. E18. [Jap. *jōdo* lit. 'pure land'.] (Designating or pertaining to) a Japanese Buddhist sect which teaches salvation through absolute faith in their Buddha, the Buddha Amida, and constant repetition of a prayer invoking his name.

jods /dʒɒdz/ *n.* *colloq.* M20. [Abbrev.] Jodhpurs.

joe /dʒəʊ/ *n.*[1] M18. [Abbrev.] *Hist.* = JOHANNES.

Joe /dʒəʊ/ *n.*[2] & *v.* *slang.* L18. [Familiar abbrev. of the male forename *Joseph*.] **A** *n.* **1** = In full *Joe Miller* [Eng. comedian (1684–1738), whose name was attached to a popular joke-book after his death]. A book of jokes. Also, a joke, *esp.* a stale joke. L18. **2** A fellow, a chap; an average man. Also, an American. M19. **3** *Hist.* [f. Charles *Joseph* La Trobe (1801–75), Lieutenant-Governor of Victoria.] A taunt to, or warning of the approach of, a policeman. Also as *int.* *Austral.* M19. **4** A French Canadian. *Canad.* M20.

2 J. OSBORNE While everyone else is sitting on their hands you're the Joe at the back cheering.

Comb. & phrases: GI *Joe*; *Holy Joe*: see HOLY *a.*; **Joe Blake** *Austral. rhyming slang* a snake; **Joe Bloggs** (a nickname for) a hypothetical average man; **Joe Blow** (chiefly *N. Amer.*) = *Joe Bloggs* above; *Joe* MANTON; *Joe Miller*: see sense 1 above; **Joe Public** (a member of) an audience; (a nickname for) an average member of the public; **Joe Soap** (a nickname for) a slow-witted or ordinary person; *little Joe*: see LITTLE *a.*; SLOPPY *joe*.

B *v.t.* Taunt (esp. a policeman) with a cry of 'Joe': see sense A.3 above. *Austral.* M19.

joe /dʒəʊ/ *n.*[3] *N. Amer. slang.* M20. [Origin unkn.] Coffee.

joe *n.*[4] var. of JO.

joe-pye weed /ˈdʒəʊpʌɪ wiːd/ *n. phr. N. Amer.* E19. [Origin unkn.] Either of two tall perennial plants, *Eupatorium purpureum* and *E. maculatum*, of the composite family, bearing clusters of tubular purplish flowers.

joes /dʒəʊz/ *n.pl.* *Austral. slang.* E20. [Origin unkn.] Depression, the blues.

Joey /ˈdʒəʊi/ *n.*[1] M19. [Familiar abbrev. of male forename *Joseph* (see JOE *n.*[2], -Y[6]), in branch I f. Joseph Hume (1777–1855), politician and financial expert, in branch II f. the clown Joseph Grimaldi (1779–1837).] **I** **†1** A fourpenny piece. *slang.* M–L19. **2** A threepenny bit. *slang. obs.* exc. *Hist.* M20. **II** **3** A clown. *colloq.* L19.

joey /ˈdʒəʊi/ *n.*[2] *Austral.* & *NZ.* M19. [Aborig. *joè*.] A young kangaroo; a young animal or child.

jog /dʒɒg/ *n.*[1] E17. [f. JOG *v.*] **1a** An act of jogging or moving mechanically up and down. E17. **b** An act of jogging along; a slow measured walk or trot. M17. **c** A gentle run taken as a form of exercise. M20. **2** An act of jogging a thing or person; a shake; a slight push, a nudge. M17.

1b R. BOLDREWOOD The slow, hopeless, leg-weary jog to which .. the horses .. had long been reduced. c *Sun* Your bedroom curtains were still drawn when I passed on my morning jog. 2 *fig.*: B. REID I have no memory of things past until I'm given a little jog.

jog /dʒɒg/ *n.*[2] E18. [In sense 1 var. of JAG *n.*[1] With senses 2 and 3 cf. JOGGLE *n.*[2]] **†1** A projecting point on an edge or surface (cf. JAG *n.*[1] 4); a protuberance, a swelling. *rare.* E–M18. **2** A right-angled notch or step in a surface or straight line; the space cut out by such a notch. *US.* M19. **3** *Cryst.* A step in a dislocation where it passes from one atomic plane to another. M20.

2 *Scientific American* Following a road northward, there are abrupt jogs to the east or west.

jogged *a.* having a jog or jogs M18.

jog /dʒɒg/ *v.* Infl. **-gg-**. LME. [Var. of JAG *v.*: cf. SHOG *v.*] **†1** *v.t.* = JAG *v.* 1. Only in LME. **2** *v.t.* Shake, move, or throw *up* (esp. a heavy body) with a push or jerk; shake *up*. M16. **3** *v.i.* Walk or ride with a jolting pace; move on at a heavy pace; trudge (*on, along*). Also, move on, be off. M16. **b** Run at a gentle pace, esp. for physical exercise. M20. **4** *v.t.* **a** Give a slight push to, so as to shake; nudge, esp. so as to arouse to attention. L16. **b** *fig.* Give a gentle reminder to (esp. one's memory). E17. **5** *v.i.* Move up and down or to and fro with a heavy unsteady motion; move about as if shaken. L16.

2 W. C. RUSSELL Masses of this froth .. were jogged clean off the water, and struck the deck. 3 R. CHURCH Once an hour a horse-bus jogged along. *fig.*: E. M. FORSTER We live and let live, and assume that things are jogging on fairly well elsewhere. b *Free Post* (*Detroit*) Jog with some-one so you won't look foolish running all by yourself. 4 G. SWIFT He looked into his .. glass and jogged the sliver of lemon at the bottom. 5 B. BAINBRIDGE He was jogging up and down .. on the tips of his toes.

¶Rare bef. 16.

joget /ˈdʒɒgət/ *n.* L19. [Malay.] A popular Malay dance in which the dancers improvise to music; a place where such dancing occurs.

jogger /ˈdʒɒgə/ *n.* L17. [f. JOG *v.* + -ER[1].] A person who or thing which jogs; *spec.* (*a*) a person who runs at a gentle pace for physical exercise; (*b*) a device for giving a slight push to some part of a mechanism.

joggle /ˈdʒɒg(ə)l/ *n.*[1] E18. [f. JOGGLE *v.*[1]] An act or the action of joggling; a jog, a jolt; a shaking loosely from side to side.

joggle /ˈdʒɒg(ə)l/ *n.*[2] E18. [Perh. f. JOG *n.*[2] + -LE[1].] A joint between two pieces of stone, concrete, etc., in which a projection on one fits into a recess in the other, or both have a recess holding a piece of stone or other masonry, so as to prevent their being pulled apart; a piece of stone etc. in such a joint.

joggle /ˈdʒɒg(ə)l/ *v.*[1]*t.* & *i.* E16. [Dim. or frequent. of JOG *v.*: see -LE[3].] (Cause to) move to and fro with a succession of short jerky movements; shake or rock about, as if loose or unsteady.

H. B. STOWE My grandmother's broad shoulders joggling with a secret laugh. A. MUNRO Both parents busy themselves .. with the children .. joggling them, singing to them.

joggly *a.* (*dial.* & *colloq.*) shaky, unsteady E19.

joggle /ˈdʒɒg(ə)l/ *v.*[2]*t.* E19. [f. JOGGLE *n.*[2]] Join (stone etc.) by means of a joggle; fasten with a joggle.

jog-jog /ˈdʒɒgdʒɒg/ *adv.* & *a.* L18. [Redupl. of JOG *v.*] **A** *adv.* With a jogging motion or pace. L18. **B** *adj.* Characterized by jogging; = JOG-TROT *a.* L18.

jog-trot /ˈdʒɒgtrɒt/ *a., n., adv.,* & *v.* M17. [f. JOG *v., n.*[1] + TROT *n.*[1]] **A** *adj.* **1a** Of action: steady unhurried; routine; monotonous, humdrum. M17. **b** Of a person: acting in a steady, unhurried way; easy-going; keeping up a monotonous routine. M18. **2** Of the nature of or suitable for a jog-trot. L18.

1b GOLDSMITH Honest jog-trot men, who go on smoothly and dully.

B *n.* A jogging trot; a slow, dull, or easy-going pace; *fig.* a steady, unhurried, but persistent way of doing something. M18.

C. J. LEVER There was nothing to break the monotonous jog-trot of daily life.

C *adv.* At a jog-trot pace. M19.

D *v.i.* & *t.* (with *it*). Go or move at a jog-trot. M19.

Johannean /dʒə(ʊ)ˈhanɪən/ *a.* M19. [f. med.L *Johannes* (see JOHN) + -AN.] = JOHANNINE.

Johannes /dʒə(ʊ)ˈhaniːz/ *n.* Also **Joannes**. M18. [Late L *Joannes*, med.L *Johannes* (see JOHN) in the legend of the coin: see below.] *Hist.* A Portuguese gold coin minted by Joannes or João V (1703–50), current in New England and later also Ireland.

Johannine /dʒə(ʊ)ˈhanʌɪn/ *a.* M19. [f. as prec. + -INE[1].] *Chr. Ch.* Of, belonging to, or characteristic of, the apostle John or his gospel.

Johannisberger /dʒə(ʊ)ˈhanɪsbəːgə/ *n.* E19. [G, f. *Johannisberg*: see below.] A fine white wine produced at Johannisberg in the Rheingau, Germany.

Johannite /dʒə(ʊ)ˈhanʌɪt/ *n.* M16. [med.L *Jo(h)annitae* pl. f. Gk *Iōannitai*, *Iōannēs* JOHN: see -ITE[1].] **†1** A knight of an order called the Knights of St John. M16–E18. **2** A follower or adherent of John Chrysostom (*c*347–407), bishop of Constantinople, after his deposition from the patriarchate in 404. *obs.* exc. *Hist.* L17.

Johansson /jə(ʊ)'hans(ə)n/ *a.* E20. [Carl E. *Johansson*, 20th-cent. Swed. armaments inspector.] Designating a steel block made with flat parallel faces to a highly accurate prescribed length, used with others of different sizes to make up standard lengths.

johar /'dʒəʊhə/ *n.* E19. [Hind. *jauhar*, *johar* f. Skt *jatu-gṛha* a house built of combustible materials.] *Hist.* The sacrificial burning of Rajput women to avoid their being captured by an enemy.

John /dʒɒn/ *n.* LME. [Male forename f. late L *Joannes*, med.L *Johannes* f. Gk *Iōannēs* f. Heb. *Yōḥānān* for *Yĕhōḥānān* lit. 'God (Yahweh) is gracious'.] 1 (A form of address to) a man, esp. a male servant. *colloq.* LME. †2 A priest. Chiefly in *Sir John derog.* LME–M17. 3 (Also **j-**.) A policeman. Also [after Fr. *gendarme*] *Johndarm*. Cf. JACK *n.*[1] 3d. *slang.* M17. 4 (Also **j-**.) The client of a prostitute. *slang* (orig. *US*). E20. 5 In full *John Thomas*. The penis. *slang.* M20. 6 (**j-**.) A lavatory. *colloq.* (chiefly *N. Amer.*). M20.

1 THACKERAY Crimson footmen, .. came in. It was pitiable to see the other poor Johns slink off. 3 V. PALMER The police came ... and it was me that was nabbed. But the Johns let me off. 4 *Atlantic Monthly* The old stereotypes of johns—husbands seeking relief .. traveling businessmen .. are still valid. 6 L. DUNCAN I'm going to .. cut up Griffin's credit cards and flush them down the john. M. SARTON She must try to get to the bathroom, brush her teeth, go to the john.

Comb. & phrases: *Dear John* (*letter*): see DEAR *a.*[1]; **John-a-dreams** a dreamy or idle fellow; †**John-a-nokes** [*John* (who dwells) *at the oak*] an anonymous party, usu. the plaintiff, in a legal action; an ordinary person; **John-apple** = APPLE-*john*; †**John-a-stiles** an anonymous party, usu. the defendant, in a legal action; *John Barleycorn*: see BARLEY-CORN 1b; **John boat** *US* a small, flat-bottomed boat chiefly for use on inland waterways; **John Citizen** an ordinary man, esp. as a member of the community; *John Collins*: see COLLINS *n.*[1]; **John Company** *joc.* (*Hist.*) the East India Company; *Johndarm*: see sense 3 above; **John Doe** (*a*) *US Law* an anonymous party, usu. the plaintiff, in a legal action, formerly *spec.* (*Eng. Law*) in the now obsolete action of ejectment (cf. RICHARD *Roe*); (*b*) *N. Amer. colloq.* an ordinary or typical citizen; (*c*) *US colloq.* a signature; **John-go-to-bed-at-noon** *dial.* any of several plants with flowers which close about midday; *esp.* yellow goat's-beard, *Tragopogon pratensis*; **John Hancock**, (*local*) **John Henry** *US colloq.* a signature; **John hop** *Austral.* & *NZ slang* = sense 3 above; **John Innes (compost)** any of a group of composts prepared according to formulae developed at the John Innes Horticultural Institution in the late 1930s; **John Q. Public** *N. Amer. colloq.* (a member of) the general public; *John Roscoe*: see ROSCOE; *John Thomas*: see sense 5 above; *long john*: see LONG *a.*[1]; *Sir John*: see sense 2 above; *square John*: see SQUARE *a.*; *sweet John*: see SWEET *a.* & *adv.*

¶See also *St John's bread, wort* s.v. SAINT *n.* & *a.*

John Bull /dʒɒn 'bʊl/ *n.* L18. [A character repr. the English nation in J. Arbuthnot's satire *Law is a Bottomless Pit* (1712).] 1 The English nation personified; the English collectively. L18. 2 An individual Englishman exemplifying the supposedly typical national character. L18.

John-'Bullish *a.* typically English L18. **John-'Bullishness** *n.* L19. **John-'Bullism** *n.* the typical English character; a typically English act, utterance, or characteristic: L18.

John Canoe /dʒɒn kə'nuː/ *n.* *W. Indies.* Also **Jonkanoo.** L18. [Prob. f. Ewe.] An elaborately masked dancer in a celebration held at Christmas; this celebration.

John Crow /dʒɒn 'krəʊ/ *n.* *W. Indies.* E19. [Alt. of *carrion crow* s.v. CROW *n.*[1] 1.] 1 The turkey-buzzard, *Cathartes aura*. E19. 2 *John Crow('s) nose*, a bright red plant, *Scybalium jamaicense* (family Balanophoraceae), resembling a fungus and parasitic on trees. M19.

John Dory /dʒɒn 'dɔːri/ *n.* M18. [f. JOHN + DORY *n.*[1]] A dory, *Zeus faber*, found in inshore waters of the eastern Atlantic and the Mediterranean.

American John Dory a dory, *Zenopsis ocellata*, of the Atlantic coast of N. America.

Johne /'jəʊnə/ *n.* E20. [H. A. *Johne* (1839–1910), Ger. veterinary surgeon.] Vet. Med. *Johne's disease*, an infectious enteritis of cattle and sheep, characterized by diarrhoea and progressive emaciation. Hence *Johne's bacillus*, the bacterium that causes it, *Mycobacterium johnei*.

Johnny /'dʒɒni/ *n.* Also **Johnnie.** L17. [Dim. of JOHN: see -Y[6], -IE.] 1 A fellow, a chap. Freq. as a derog. form of address to a man regarded as inferior, *esp.* a soldier of a colonized country in the army of the colonizing power. *colloq.* L17. **b** = JOHN 3. *slang.* M19. 2 = A gentoo penguin. Also *Johnny penguin.* M19. 3 (**j-**.) = JOHN 6. *colloq.* (chiefly *US*). M20. 4 (**j-**.) A condom. Also *rubber johnny. slang.* M20.

1 G. A. BIRMINGHAM That's the sort of way those scientific Johnnies talk. L. DEIGHTON This is the johnny who interrogated Bernard.

Phrases: *jingling johnny*: see JINGLE. *rubber johnny*: see sense 4 above.

Comb.: **Johnny-come-lately** (*a*) a newcomer; (*b*) = *Johnny Raw* below; **Johnny Crapaud, Crapeau** *arch. colloq.* (*a*) a Frenchman, a French Canadian; †(*b*) the French nation personified; **Johnny Head-in(-the)-Air** *colloq.* a dreamy fellow; **Johnny-jump-up** *N. Amer.* any of several kinds of wild or cultivated pansy or violet; **Johnny Newcome** (*a*) = *Johnny Raw* below; (*b*) a newcomer of any kind; *Johnny penguin*: see sense 2 above; **Johnny Raw** an inexperienced youngster; a novice. **Johnny Reb** *US* (a northern name for) a Confederate soldier during the American Civil War.

johnny-cake /'dʒɒnɪkeɪk/ *n.* M18. [f. unkn. 1st elem. + CAKE *n.*] A maize-meal cake usu. baked or toasted (*US*); a wheatmeal cake usu. baked or fried (*Austral.*); a type of scone (*W. Indies*).

Johnson /'dʒɒns(ə)n/ *n.* M19. [A surname.] 1 The penis. *slang.* M19. 2 *Johnson bar*, a long heavy lever used to reverse the motion of a steam locomotive. *US.* M20.

1 M. AMIS You're naked and shielding your Johnson in a cataract of breaking glass.

Johnsonese /dʒɒnsə'niːz/ *n.* M19. [f. as next + -ESE.] (Language imitative of) the style of Dr Johnson (see next).

Johnsonian /dʒɒn'səʊnɪən/ *a.* L18. [f. Dr Samuel *Johnson* (see below) + -IAN.] Of or pertaining to Dr Samuel Johnson (1709–84), a celebrated English man of letters and lexicographer; *esp.* characteristic, typical, or reminiscent of Johnson's style of English, having many words derived or formed from Latin.

Johnsoni'ana *n.* sayings, writings, etc., of or about Dr Johnson, or matters connected with him L18. **Johnsonianism** *n.* Johnsonian style; a Johnsonian phrase: E19. **'Johnsonism** *n.* = JOHNSONIANISM M19.

Johnson noise /'dʒɒns(ə)n nɔɪz/ *n. phr.* M20. [J. B. *Johnson* (b. 1887), naturalized US physicist.] *Electronics.* Electrical noise caused by the random thermal motion of conduction electrons.

Johnswort /'dʒɒnzwəːt/ *n.* *US.* M18. [Abbrev.] = *St John's wort* s.v. SAINT *n.* & *a.*

joie de vivre /ʒwadəvivr, ʒwɑː də 'viːvrə/ *n. phr.* L19. [Fr. = joy of living.] A feeling of healthy enjoyment of life; exuberance, high spirits.

join /dʒɔɪn/ *n.* E17. [f. the vb.] 1 An act of joining; the fact of being joined; a point, line, or surface at which two or more things are joined. E17. 2 *Math.* = UNION *n.*[2] 12. M20.

1 P. LIVELY The paving was worn smooth by feet, the joins between the stones almost obliterated.

join /dʒɔɪn/ *v.* ME. [(O)Fr. *joign-* pres. stem of *joindre* f. L *jungere*, f. IE base repr. also by YOKE *n.*[1]] I Put together. 1 *v.t.* Put together, so as to unite or make continuous; fasten, attach, connect, unite, (one thing to another, or several together); (freq. foll. by *to, together*). Formerly also, combine in a mixture. ME. †**b** *spec.* Harness; yoke. LME–E18. **c** *Geom.* Connect (points) by a straight line. M17. 2 *v.t.* Construct or form (a whole, wooden furniture, etc.) by putting parts together. *obs.* exc. in *join company*. ME. 3 *v.t.* Bring or combine (troops etc.) into one body or company. Formerly also *refl.*, attach (oneself) to a company etc. ME. 4 *v.t.* Link or unite (people etc. together, or one *with* or *to* another) in marriage, friendship, or any kind of alliance; unite, ally. ME. 5 *v.t.* Put (a female animal, as a cow) to mate with a male. Now only *NZ* & *Austral.* LME. 6 *v.t.* Put or bring into close contact, cause to touch each other. Chiefly *arch.* LME. †7 *v.t.* Add so as to increase the amount or number. LME–E18.

1 I. MURDOCH Donald seemed to attach himself directly to Tim as if invisible threads joined their bodies. B. EMECHETA A bridge joining the village to the mainland. J. MCDOUGALL The threads of discourse, broken off in .. childhood, can now be joined once more. 4 *Book of Common Prayer* We are gathered together .. to joyn together this man and this woman in holy matrimony. E. YOUNG Life is the .. solitude; Death joins us to the great majority. *joined patent*: see PATENT *a.* 2. 5 *Stock & Land* (*Melbourne*) Mr Wyllie joined several heifers last year and one of them is barren. 6 POPE O'er the pale marble shall they join their heads. I. MURDOCH Join his two hands palm to palm.

II Come or be put together. 8 *v.i.* Come or be brought into contact; become connected or fastened together; be in contact; be adjacent, adjoin (foll. by †*to*, †*with*). ME. 9 *v.i.* **a** Combine in action or purpose, enter into association, *with*. LME. **b** Take part *in* an action etc. (specified or *absol.* understood). M16. 10 *v.i.* Come together or meet in conflict. Now *rare* or *obs.* LME. 11 *v.i.* Of qualities etc.: come or exist together in operation. LME. †12 *v.i.* *Astron.* & *Astrol.* Come into conjunction; be in conjunction. LME–L17.

8 I. D'ISRAELI Parallel lines can no more join together in politics than in geometry. OED On the side where the two gardens join. 9a W. CRUISE His co-trustees .. refused to join with him in the execution of the trust. R. HUGHES Sickening giddiness joined with the shock and pain to give .. poignancy to her crying. **b** N. MOSLEY I tried to get these two to join in some of the activities. J. K. TOOLE On the second chorus the entire ensemble joined in the song. P. BOWLES He laughed good-naturedly and she joined in. 11 TENNYSON Tho' truths in manhood darkly join.

III Come into contact, contiguity, company, or union with. 13 *v.t.* Come or go into the company of (a person); accompany; take part with (a person or persons) *in* an action etc.; take one's place with or in (a group, procession, etc.). E18. 14 *v.t.* & *i.* Become a member of (a society, organization, etc.). E18. 15 *v.t.* Be or become connected or continuous with; be adjacent to, adjoin. Also, go to and follow (a path, a road, etc.) esp. at a specified point; get on (a train, bus, etc.) at a specific point or time. E18.

13 R. K. NARAYAN You joined Gandhi and lost all sense of caste. P. ROTH He should join the revolution. J. MORTIMER He .. had joined an old doctor on his rounds. C. PHILLIPS They .. joined the thin line of traffic streaming away from the capital. I. MURDOCH Duncan .. waved to her, beckoning her to join him. 14 OED Is he a member of our society? When did he join? M. S. POWER He .. joined the police force. *Dumfries Courier* He stayed on .. for an extra year then joined the Worthing firm. 15 G. GREENE He joined the Orient Express at Ostend. E. H. JONES A little stream ran down through the plot to join the .. river.

Phrases: **join action** enter into a debate or dispute. *join battle*: see BATTLE *n.* *join forces*: see FORCE *n.*[1] *join hands*: see HAND *n.* *join issue*: see ISSUE *n.* *join the majority*: see MAJORITY.

With advs. in specialized senses: **join up** (*a*) enlist in one of the armed forces; (*b*) unite, connect, (*with*).

joinable *a.* (*rare*) LME. **joining** *n.* (*a*) the action or an act of the vb; the fact of being joined; (*b*) a place where things join or are joined; a thing which joins or connects: LME.

joinant /'dʒɔɪnənt/ *a.* Now *rare* or *obs.* LME. [(O)Fr. *joignant* pres. pple of *joindre*: see prec., -ANT[1].] Adjoining, adjacent. Long only in *Her.*, conjoined.

joinder /'dʒɔɪndə/ *n.* LME. [AN, use as n. of (O)Fr. *joindre*: see JOIN *v.*, -ER[4].] Chiefly *Law.* The act of joining; union.

†**joined-stool** *n.* see JOINT-STOOL.

joiner /'dʒɔɪnə/ *n.* & *v.* ME. [AN *joignour*, OFr. *joigneor*, f. *joindre*: see JOIN *v.*, -ER[2].] **A** *n.* 1 A person who (as a profession) does light woodwork and esp. constructs furniture, fittings, etc., by joining pieces of wood. ME. 2 *gen.* A person who joins, connects, or unites people or things. Now *rare* or *obs.* L15. 3 A person who readily joins societies etc. *colloq.* L19.

1 J. YEATS The workshops . . of joiners and cabinet-makers. 3 S. NAIPAUL Steve was . . a joiner of societies.

Comb.: **joiner('s)-work** woodwork made by a joiner.

B *v.i.* Do the work of a joiner. Chiefly as *joinering* vbl n. M19.

joinery /ˈdʒɔɪnəri/ *n.* L17. [f. JOINER *n.* + -Y^{3}: see -ERY.] The art of a joiner; the construction of wooden furniture etc.; *collect.* articles made by a joiner.

Do-It-Yourself Their sheds have . . cedar as exterior cladding, while joinery, such as windows, is in softwood.

joint /dʒɔɪnt/ *n.* ME. [(O)Fr. (also †*jointe*) use as n. of *joint(e)* pa. pple of *joindre*: see JOIN *v.*] **I** The place at which things or parts join. **1** An anatomical structure or mechanism by which two bones are fitted and held together, usu. so that relative movement is possible; the place of connection of two movable parts in an invertebrate, esp. an arthropod. ME. **2** A point at which, or a contrivance by which, two parts of an artificial structure are joined, either rigidly (as with bricks, timbers, etc.), or so as to allow movement (as in a hinge etc.). LME. **b** *Bookbinding.* A piece of flexible material forming the hinge of a book-cover. M19. **3** The part of a plant stem from which a leaf or branch grows; a node. E16. **4** *Geol.* A crack or fissure intersecting a mass of rock, usually occurring in sets of parallel planes. E17.

1 P. ROTH The tissue of my muscles and the joints between my bones. W. SOYINKA The fingers have become . . stiff at the joints. K. WILLIAMS Every bone and joint ached. 2 *dovetail joint, mitre-joint, scarf joint,* etc.

II Any of the parts or sections whose connection makes up a body or structure. †**5** *gen.* A portion, an item. *rare.* Only in ME. **6** A part of an animal, plant, or other structure connected by a joint or joints to an adjacent part or parts; *esp.* such a part of a digit or limb; a phalanx; *Bot.* an internode. LME. **7** *spec.* Any of the parts into which an animal carcass is divided for food. L16.

6 SHAKES. *Tr. & Cr.* I have with exact view perus'd thee, Hector, And quoted joint by joint. J. WILCOX The pipe has twelve separate joints. *Garden News* This will keep the leaf joints short and . . increase the number of flowers. 7 R. CROMPTON They ate . . a joint of cold beef. *Courier (N. Kent)* The fresh meat department . . giving shoppers a wider choice of joints for any occasion.

III †**8** = JOINTURE 2. Only in E16. **9** A place of meeting for drinking or (formerly) *spec.*, for illicit drinking, opium-smoking, etc.; *gen.* a place, a house. *colloq.* (chiefly *N. Amer.*). E19. **b** A stall or tent at a circus or fair. *slang* (orig. *US*). E20. **c** Prison. *US slang.* M20. **10** A marijuana cigarette. *colloq.* M20.

9 D. HEWETT No one's got any manners in this joint. E. TROOP A beachside hamburger joint used by the college surfing trade. F. DONALDSON The above address . . is a joint belonging to a friend of mine. *juke-joint*: see JUKE *n.*

Phrases: **out of joint** (*a*) (of a bone or bodily part) dislocated; *put a person's nose out of joint*: see NOSE *n.*; (*b*) *fig.* disordered, out of order. SYNOVIAL *joint. universal joint*: see UNIVERSAL *a.*

Comb.: **joint bolt**: threaded at both ends for holding together the two parts of a joint; **joint box** a junction-box; **joint-grass** *US* a creeping grass, *Paspalum distichum*, which roots at the nodes; **joint mouse** a loose fragment of cartilage, bone, etc., floating in the cavity of a joint (usu. in *pl.*); **joint-plane** *Geol.* a plane in rock in which a joint exists or is liable to form; an exposed surface that was once such a plane; **joint-rule** a folding rule made of jointed or hinged pieces; **joint-saw**: with a curved working face for making compass joints etc.; **joint-snake** = *glass snake* s.v. GLASS *n.* & *a.*; **jointweed** *US* a small jointed plant, *Polygonella articulata*, related to and resembling knotgrass.

joint /dʒɔɪnt/ *a.* (orig. *pa. pple*). ME. [(O)Fr. *joint(e)* pa. pple of *joindre*: see JOIN *v.*] **1** Joined, combined, united; *spec.* (of the lives of two or more people) contemporaneous, concurrent. Now only *attrib.* ME. †**b** Made up of parts joined or fastened together. LME–E18. **2** Of a person or persons: sharing *with* another or others in some possession, action, state, etc.; *esp.* being or doing (what is expressed by the n.) together or in common. LME. **3** Of a single thing, action, etc.: held, done, made, etc., by two or more people etc. in conjunction; of or belonging to more than one at once. LME.

1 J. H. NEWMAN Civilized by the joint influences of religion and of chivalry. E. E. KAY During the joint lives of the trustees. 2 SHAKES. *Coriol.* I . . Made him joint-servant with me. C. G. WOLFF Aunt Eliza and Evelina are the joint proprietors of a little notions shop. M. IGNATIEFF Paul was named joint heir of the Maltser industrial empire. 3 J. RULE All of their joint property. A. THWAITE He wrote a . . letter to Gosse, encouraging him in their joint aim. *Which?* If built after 1937, the drain is the joint responsibility of all the householders. **joint and several** (of an obligation etc.) undertaken and signed by two or more people, of whom each is liable for the whole obligation etc.

Special collocations & comb.: *joint account*: see ACCOUNT *n.* 2. **joint adventure** *Sc. Law* a partnership entered into only for a particular enterprise and not constituting a firm for continuing business. **joint committee**: composed of members nominated by two or more distinct bodies. **joint denial** *Logic* the negation of each of two or more propositions. **joint family** an extended family in which married children share the family home, living under the authority of the head of the family. *joint patent*: see PATENT *a.* 2. †**joint-ring** a finger-ring made of two separable halves. **joint stock** capital held jointly; a common fund. **joint-stock bank, company**: formed on the basis of a joint stock. **joint-tenancy** the holding of an estate by two or more joint-tenants. **joint-tenant** a person holding an undivided estate jointly with another or others and whose interest, on death, passes to the survivor or survivors. **joint venture** a commercial enterprise undertaken jointly by two or more parties otherwise retaining their separate identities.

joint /dʒɔɪnt/ *v.* M16. [f. JOINT *n.*] **1** *v.t.* Connect or fasten together by a joint or joints. M16. **b** Fill up the joints of (masonry) with mortar etc., point. E18. **c** Prepare (a board etc.) for being joined to another by planing the edge. E19. **2** *v.t.* Divide (a body or member) at a joint or into joints. M16. **3** *v.i.* Fit exactly *into* as a joint. Long *rare.* L17. **4** *v.i.* Of a growing plant: form joints. L18.

1 *Practical Woodworking* Those old chairmakers knew exactly how to joint these components to one another. 2 R. GRAVES He himself skinned and jointed the hare.

jointed /ˈdʒɔɪntɪd/ *a.* LME. [f. JOINT *n.* + -ED^{2}.] **1** Provided with, constructed with, or having joints. LME. **b** *spec.* (*Bot.*) Having or appearing to have joints; separating readily at the joints. L16. **2** Having joints of a specified kind. L16.

jointedly *adv.* M19. **jointedness** *n.* L19.

†**jointer** *n.*^{1} M–L16. [f. JOINT *a.* or *joint-* in JOINTURE: see -ER^{1}. Cf. JOINTRESS.] A joint possessor; a person who holds a jointure.

jointer /ˈdʒɔɪntə/ *n.*^{2} M17. [f. JOINT *v.* + -ER^{1}.] **1** *Carpentry.* A long plane used in jointing. Also *jointer plane.* M17. **2** A tool for jointing masonry. E18. **3** *W. Indies.* Any of several shrubs of the genus *Piper* having prominent nodes on the stem. M19. **4** A person employed in jointing wires, pipes, etc. M19.

jointing /ˈdʒɔɪntɪŋ/ *n.* LME. [f. JOINT *v.* + -ING^{1}.] **1** A joint; a junction. LME. **2** The action of JOINT *v.* L16. **3** The formation of joints or fissures in rock etc.; the nature or arrangement of these. L17.

jointless /ˈdʒɔɪntlɪs/ *a.* M16. [f. JOINT *n.* + -LESS.] Without a joint or joints; stiff, rigid. Also, in one piece.

jointly /ˈdʒɔɪntli/ *adv.* ME. [f. JOINT *a.* + -LY^{2}.] **1** In conjunction, in combination; unitedly; not severally or separately. ME. †**2** So as to be spatially joined; in contact; adjacently. LME–E18. †**b** Continuously in space or time. LME–M16. †**3** At the same time, simultaneously. LME–L17.

jointress /ˈdʒɔɪntrɪs/ *n.* E17. [f. JOINTER *n.*^{1} + -ESS^{1}.] A widow who holds a jointure; a dowager.

joint-stool /ˈdʒɔɪntstuːl/ *n. obs.* exc. *Hist.* Earlier †**joined-stool**. LME. [Orig. f. pa. pple of JOIN *v.* + STOOL *n.*; later alt. after JOINT *n.*] A stool made of parts skilfully joined or fitted together by a joiner.

¶Freq. mentioned between the 16th and 18th cents. as an article of furniture; also (the reason for which is unkn.) in allusive or proverbial phrs. expr. disparagement or ridicule.

jointure /ˈdʒɔɪntjʊə/ *n.* & *v.* ME. [(O)Fr. f. L *junctura* JUNCTURE.] **A** *n.* **1** A joining, a junction, a joint. Formerly also, the action of joining, union. Now *rare.* ME. **2** Orig., the joint holding of property by a husband and wife for life, or in tail as a provision for the latter in the event of her widowhood. Now, an estate settled on a wife for the period during which she survives her husband. LME. †**b** A dowry. L15–E17. †**3** A joint-tenancy. L16–M18. **B** *v.t.* Settle a jointure on; provide with a jointure. M17.

jointured *a.* provided with a jointure M18.

jointuress /ˈdʒɔɪntjʊərɪs/ *n.* L17. [Alt. of JOINTRESS after prec.] = JOINTRESS.

jointworm /ˈdʒɔɪntwəːm/ *n.* E18. [f. JOINT *n.* + WORM *n.*] †**1** A tapeworm. Only in E18. **2** (The larval form of) any of several chalcid flies of the genus *Harmolita* (or *Tetramesa*) which form galls near joints on grain stems, causing them to bend. *US.* M19.

jointy /ˈdʒɔɪnti/ *a.* L16. [f. JOINT *n.* + -Y^{1}.] Having numerous joints.

joist /dʒɔɪst/ *n.* & *v.* Earlier †**gist**. LME. [OFr. *giste* beam supporting a bridge (mod. *gîte*), f. use as n. of Proto-Romance neut. pa. pple of L *jacere* lie down.] **A** *n.* Each of a series of parallel supporting beams of timber, steel, etc., to which floorboards, ceiling laths, etc., are attached. LME. **B** *v.t.* Provide with or fix on joists. M16.

joisting *n.* the structure or arrangement of joists; joists collectively: L16. **joistless** *a.* M19.

jojoba /həˈhəʊbə, həʊ-/ *n.* E20. [Mex. Sp.] A desert shrub, *Simmondsia chinensis* (family Simmondsiaceae), of Mexico and the south-western US, whose seeds yield an oil used as a lubricant and in cosmetics.

Jokari /dʒəˈkɑːri/ *n.* M20. [Origin unkn.] (Proprietary name for) any of various games played with bat and ball.

joke /dʒəʊk/ *n.* L17. [Orig. slang, perh. f. L *jocus* jest, wordplay: cf. G *Jucks, Jux* joke, spree, Du. *jok* jest.] **1** A thing said or done to excite laughter or amusement, freq. in the form of a short anecdote or a question and answer; a witticism, a jest. Also, a ridiculous person, thing, or circumstance. L17. **b** A laughing-stock. L18. **2** Something not serious or true; a matter to be dismissed lightly. E18.

1 K. MANSFIELD He looked like a little comic picture waiting for the joke to be written underneath. J. MORTIMER Fred had made a joke and Henry hadn't laughed. *attrib.*: C. PHILLIPS The taxi was . . popular when he first arrived . . but had rapidly become a joke car. **b** J. F. COOPER I shall be the standing joke of the mess-table. J. CAREY He was . . a flop at gaining support. As a Labour MP he was a joke. 2 J. WAIN Bad luck, superstition, fear, they aren't jokes.

Phrases: *beyond a joke*: see BEYOND *prep.* 6. **no joke** *colloq.* a serious matter. **practical joke** a trick played on a person to have a laugh at his or her expense. *standing joke*: see STANDING *a. take a joke*: see TAKE *v.*

Comb.: **jokesmith** a maker or inventor of jokes.

jokeless *a.* devoid of jokes, lacking humour or wit M19. **jokelet** *n.* a little joke M19. **jokesome** *a.* characterized by jokes, facetious E19.

joke /dʒəʊk/ *v.* L17. [f. the n. or f. L *jocari* to jest.] **1** *v.i.* Make a joke or jokes, jest. L17. **b** *v.t.* Utter as a joke. E20. **2** *v.t.* Make the object of a joke or jokes; poke fun at. M18. **3** *v.t.* Obtain by joking. Foll. by *out.* M19.

1 M. STEWART You've got to be joking. *Star & Style (Bombay)* Even from his sick bed he laughed and joked with everyone. P. ROTH It's too awful even to joke about. **joking relationship** *Anthropol.*: in which one individual or group is permitted or obliged to make fun of another. **b** M. GEE 'Things of beauty should be kept together,' he had joked, . . though Less hadn't noticed the humour. 2 SMOLLETT Miss Snapper . . pretended to joke me upon my passion for Narcissa. 3 C. CLARKE A fellow who will joke and laugh the money out of your pocket.

jo'kee *n.* (*colloq.*) a person on whom a joke is played M19. **jokingly** *adv.* in a joking manner E18.

joker /ˈdʒəʊkə/ *n.* E18. [f. JOKE *v.* + -ER^{1}.] **1** A person who jokes. E18. **2** A man, a fellow. *slang* (esp. *Austral.* & *NZ*). E19. **3** A playing-card usu.

ornamented with the figure of a jester, used orig. as the top trump in euchre and later in poker as a wild card, now esp. in rummy games. Also, a device used in playing a trick. L19. 4 A clause unobtrusively inserted in a bill or document which affects its operation in a way not immediately apparent, esp. by frustrating its intention or disadvantaging one of the concerned parties; *fig.* a drawback, a snag. *US*. E20.

1 T. S. ELIOT Are you a devil Or merely a lunatic practical joker? W. WHARTON In our family my role is the joker, the comedian. **practical joker** a person who plays practical jokes. 2 M. SHADBOLT I like the looks of you. You look a clean living young joker. 3 **joker in the pack** *fig.* an unpredictable factor or participant.

jokery *n.* jesting, raillery M18.

jokester /ˈdʒəʊkstə/ *n.* L19. [f. JOKE *v.* + -STER.] A person who makes (esp. petty) jokes.

jokey *a.* var. of JOKY.

jokist /ˈdʒəʊkɪst/ *n.* E19. [f. JOKE *n.* + -IST.] A professed or habitual joker.

jokul /ˈjœkʊl/ *n.* L18. [Icel. *jökull* icicle, ice, glacier, f. ON *jǫkull*: see ICKLE *n.* Cf. ICICLE.] In Iceland, a mountain permanently covered with snow and ice; (in proper names) a glacier.

joky /ˈdʒəʊki/ *a.* Also **jokey**. E19. [f. JOKE *n.* + -Y[1].] Inclined to joke; having the quality of a joke; subject to jokes, ridiculous.

R. DAVIES Dr Jerome . . the jokey chattering man. N. GORDIMER She wrapped both serious and jokey presents elaborately. I. MCEWAN The conversation was joky and mock-cynical, but embodied some truth.

jokily *adv.* L20. **jokiness** *n.* M19.

jole *n.*[1], *n.*[2], *n.*[3] vars. of JOWL *n.*[1], *n.*[2], *n.*[3]

jolie laide /ʒɔli lɛd/ *n. phr.* Pl. ***-s -s*** (pronounced same). L19. [Fr., f. *jolie* pretty + *laide* ugly (fem. adjs.).] An attractively or fascinatingly ugly woman.

jolley /ˈdʒɒli/ *n.* Also **jolly**. L19. [Origin unkn.] A horizontal lathe used in pottery-making; a jigger.

jolleying *n.* the practice of using a jolley E20.

jollier /ˈdʒɒlɪə/ *n.*[1] Also **jollyer**. L19. [f. prec. + -ER[1].] A person who makes pottery using a jolley.

jollier /ˈdʒɒlɪə/ *n.*[2] *US*. L19. [f. JOLLY *v.* + -ER[1].] A jovial or sociable person.

jollification /ˌdʒɒlɪfɪˈkeɪʃ(ə)n/ *n. colloq.* E19. [f. JOLLY *a.* + -FICATION.] Jollity; (a) merrymaking; *spec.* a party.

H. GREEN I'm too old for that sort of idiot jollification. K. WATERHOUSE Various functions, . . leaving parties and other jollifications.

jollify /ˈdʒɒlɪfʌɪ/ *v. colloq.* E19. [f. as prec. + -FY.] 1 *v.t.* Make jolly or merry; *esp.* make slightly tipsy. E19. 2 *v.i.* Make merry; *esp.* indulge in alcoholic drink. M19.

jollily /ˈdʒɒlɪli/ *adv.* ME. [f. JOLLY *a.* + -LY[2].] In a jolly manner.

jolliment /ˈdʒɒlɪm(ə)nt/ *n.* Long *obs.* exc. *dial.*. L16. [f. JOLLY *a.* + -MENT.] Mirth, merriment.

jolliness /ˈdʒɒlɪnɪs/ *n.* LME. [f. JOLLY *a.* + -NESS.] The state or quality of being jolly.

†jollitry *n.* L17–M18. [f. next after *gallantry*, *pleasantry*, etc.] = JOLLITY I, 2.

jollity /ˈdʒɒlɪti/ *n.* ME. [OFr. *jolité*, f. *joli*: see JOLLY *a.* & *adv.*, -TY[1].] 1 The quality or condition of being jolly, cheerful, or festive; exuberant mirth or cheerfulness. ME. †b A joke, a jest. L16–E17. 2 Merrymaking, revelry; in *pl.*, festivities. ME. †b Splendour, magnificence. M16–L17. †3 Pleasure; *esp.* sexual pleasure, lust. ME–E17. †4 Insolence, presumption. ME–E17.

1 R. CROMPTON He dreamed of . . a life of untrammelled joy and jollity. P. FERGUSON She sang . . music-hall songs . . defused of all jollity. 2 J. CAREY Children weren't encouraged in Happy Valley, since they interfered with the jollity. P. THEROUX Years ago, when we ran around painted with woad, those jollities turned into orgies.

jollo /ˈdʒɒləʊ/ *n. Austral. slang.* Pl. **-os**. E20. [f. JOLL(ITY + -O.] A party, a merrymaking; a spree.

Jollof /ˈdʒɒlɒf/ *n.* & *a.* Orig. **†-oif**. Also **Jolof** /ˈdʒəʊlɒf/. M18. [Wolof.] = WOLOF.

Jollof rice a W. African stew made with fish, meat, rice, chilli peppers, etc.

jollop /ˈdʒɒləp/ *n.*[1] M17. [Prob. alt. of JOWL *n.*[2] + LAP *n.*[1] Cf. DEWLAP.] The wattle of a cock or turkey.

¶Earlier in *jolloped* JELLOPED.

jollop /ˈdʒɒləp/ *n.*[2] *slang.* E20. [Alt. of JALAP.] 1 (A drink of) strong liquor. E20. 2 A purgative, a medicine. M20.

jollop(p)ed *a.* var. of JELLOPED.

jolly /ˈdʒɒli/ *n.*[1] *slang.* E19. [Absol. use of JOLLY *a.*] 1 A Royal Marine. E19. 2 A cheer, a shout. M19.

jolly /ˈdʒɒli/ *n.*[2] E19. [Abbrev.] = JOLLY-BOAT.

Jolly /ˈdʒɒli, ˈjɒli/ *n.*[3] L19. [P. von *Jolly* (1809–84), Ger. physicist.] *Jolly* (or *†Jolly's*) *balance*, a balance in which the elongation of a helical spring indicates the weight of the body hanging on it, used esp. in determining the specific gravities of minerals.

jolly /ˈdʒɒli/ *n.*[4] *colloq.* L19. [Abbrev.] = JOLLIFICATION. Also *jolly-up*.

W. HAGGARD A splendid wedding, the sort of big jolly Charles Russell enjoyed.

jolly *n.*[5] var. of JOLLEY.

jolly /ˈdʒɒli/ *a.* & *adv.* ME. [OFr. *jolif* (later and mod. *joli*) †merry, †pleasant, pretty, perh. f. ON *jól* midwinter festival, feast, YULE: see -Y[7].] A *adj.* I 1 Of cheerful disposition or character; good-humoured; merry, bright, lively. ME. †b *spec.* Lively on account of youth or good health. ME–L16. 2 In high spirits; exhilarated. Chiefly *pred.* ME. b *spec.* Exhilarated with drink, tipsy. M17. 3 Characterized by conviviality and merriment; festive. LME.

1 D. H. LAWRENCE A big jolly fellow, with a touch of the bounder about him. E. FEINSTEIN The jolly peasant nannies who looked after her. 2 J. NAGENDA Monkey, as befitted a guest, . . was endeavouring to look jolly. b Z. TOMIN The locals . . were in various—mostly jolly—stages of inebriation. 3 THACKERAY He became a viveur and jolly dog about town. B. PYM To make our Christmas a particularly jolly one.

II †4 Of cheerful courage, gallant, brave; *derog.* excessively self-confident, defiantly bold. ME–M17.

III †5 Bright or colourful in appearance; showy, splendid; finely dressed; *fig.* (of words etc.) specious. LME–L17. 6 Good-looking; handsome; pretty. Now *dial.* LME. 7 Well-built, plump. Now chiefly w. connotations of cheerfulness. *colloq.* M17.

IV 8 †a Amorous; wanton, lustful. LME–M17. b Of an animal: in heat. *obs.* exc. *dial.* E16.

V 9 *gen.* Splendid, excellent. *arch.* M16. 10 Very pleasant or agreeable. Now *colloq.* M16. 11 Used w. intensive force: great, fine. Now *colloq.* M16.

9 DRYDEN Graze not too near the Banks, my jolly Sheep. F. W. FARRAR For he's a jolly good fe-el-low, Which nobody can deny. 10 J. UPDIKE Getting old could be jolly if you stayed strong. 11 C. DARWIN Are not these a jolly lot of assumptions?

Special collocations & comb.: **Jolly Roger** a pirates' flag, usu. black with a white skull and crossbones. **jolly-tail** *Austral.* any small freshwater fish of the genus *Galaxias*, *esp.* the inanga, *G. maculatus*.

B *adv.* 1 Extremely, very. Now *colloq.* M16. 2 In a jolly manner; merrily; pleasantly. E17.

1 J. GRENFELL Jolly well played! Absolutely smashing! H. SECOMBE It's all jolly exciting, isn't it?

jolly /ˈdʒɒli/ *v.* E17. [f. JOLLY *a.*] 1 *v.i.* Make merry, enjoy oneself. *rare.* E17. 2 *v.t.* Keep or make jolly or cheerful by friendly behaviour etc. Foll. by *along*, *up*, etc. *colloq.* M19. 3 *v.t.* Ridicule, poke fun at, tease. L19.

2 J. B. PRIESTLEY Arranging . . entertainments . . and generally jollying everybody along. J. T. STORY Trying to jolly each other up with anecdotes. 3 R. ELLMANN Wilde . . jollies us for being so much harsher that he is.

jolly-boat /ˈdʒɒlɪbəʊt/ *n.* L17. [Origin of 1st elem. uncertain: perh. rel. to YAWL *n.*[1]] A clinker-built ship's boat, smaller than a cutter, with a bluff bow and very wide transom.

jollyer *n.* var. of JOLLIER *n.*[1]

†jollyhead *n. rare* (Spenser). Only in L16. [f. JOLLY *a.* + -HEAD.] Jollity.

jolt /dʒəʊlt, dʒɒlt/ *n.* L16. [Rel. to next.] †1 A knock of the head etc. against something. *rare.* L16–E17. 2 An abrupt movement or jerk (esp. in a moving vehicle) causing a person or thing to alter position briefly and violently. M17. b *fig.* A mental shock, a surprise. L19. c A blow in boxing. E20. 3 A drink or small quantity of spirits. *slang* (chiefly *US*). E20. b A prison sentence. *slang* (orig. *US*). E20. c A quantity of a drug, esp. as an injection. *slang* (chiefly *US*). E20.

2 P. BOWLES A cigarette which, after awakening with a jolt, he accepted automatically. D. A. DYE The solid jolt of the weapon against his shoulder was reassuring. T. O. ECHEWA He . . braked suddenly, . . giving everyone an uncomfortable jolt. b *Scotsman* Labour is only just recovering from the jolt in the . . by-election. 3 R. THOMAS She took two . . glasses. . . I poured a generous jolt into both of them.

Comb.: **jolt ramming** *Founding* repeated lifting and dropping of a moulding box, containing a pattern and sand, so as to pack the sand around the pattern (freq. *attrib.*); **jolt-squeeze** *Founding* simultaneous or successive jolting and squeezing of a box containing a pattern and sand so as to pack the sand around the pattern (usu. *attrib.*).

joltless *a.* free from jolts E19.

jolt /dʒəʊlt, dʒɒlt/ *v.* L16. [Perh. rel. to JOT *v.*[1]: cf. prec., JOLT-HEAD.] 1 *v.t.* Shake or disturb from one's seat or position (esp. in a moving vehicle) with a jolt or succession of jolts; transport or convey with a jolt or jolts. L16. b *fig.* Startle, shock. L19. †2 *v.t.* Butt or push with the head, elbow, etc.; knock; nudge. E17–L18. 3 *v.i.* Move with a jolt; (of a vehicle etc.) move along with a succession of jolts, as on a rough uneven road; (of a passenger) be transported in this way. E18.

1 T. HOOD My scanty breath was jolted out with many a sudden groan. W. BLACK We were once more jolted over the unmade roads. b J. S. HUXLEY The dropping of the first atomic bomb on Hiroshima . . deeply jolted our moral conscience. M. AMIS Obstacles intended to jolt and scare me awake with sudden noise. D. PRATER He was to be jolted into a harsher reality. 3 A. G. GARDINER A carriage . . jolting noisily through the night. D. H. LAWRENCE A blinding flash went over his brain, his body jolted. I. MURDOCH She jolted against the side of the passenger seat.

jolter *n.* E17. **jolter** *v.t.* & *i.* (*rare*) [-ER[5]] jolt continuously E19. **joltingly** *adv.* in a jolting manner M19.

jolter-head /ˈdʒəʊltəhɛd/ *n.* Now *rare.* E17. [Extension of JOLT-HEAD.] = JOLT-HEAD 2.

jolter-headed *a.* thick-headed M18. **jolter'headedness** *n.* M19.

jolt-head /ˈdʒəʊlthɛd/ *n.* Now *rare* or *obs.* M16. [Rel. to JOLT *v.*] †1 A large clumsy head; a stupid head. M16–E18. 2 A thick-headed person; a blockhead. L16.

jolt-headed *a.* (now *rare* or *obs.*) thick-headed M16.

jolty /ˈdʒəʊlti, ˈdʒɒlti/ *a.* M19. [f. JOLT *n.* + -Y[1].] Characterized by jolting; having or causing jolts.

joltiness *n.* L19.

Joly /ˈdʒɒli/ *n.* L19. [John *Joly* (1857–1933), Ir. physicist.] *Joly's steam calorimeter*, a device for determining the specific heat of a substance by measuring the weight of steam that condenses on a known mass of the substance in raising its temperature to that of the steam.

Jomon /ˈdʒəʊmɒn/ *a.* M20. [Jap. *jōmon* cord mark.] Designating an early handmade earthenware pottery found in Japan and freq. decorated with impressed rope patterns. Also, designating the early neolithic or pre-neolithic culture characterized by this pottery.

Jonah /ˈdʒəʊnə/ *n.* & *v.* As n. also **†Jonas**. L16. [A Hebrew prophet (Heb. *yōnāh* lit. 'dove'), the subject of a book in the Old Testament and Hebrew Scriptures.] A *n.* 1 A person who seems to bring bad luck. L16. 2 *Jonah crab*, a large deep-water crab, *Cancer borealis*, of the east coast of N. America. L19. B *v.t.* Bring bad luck to. L19.

Jonathan /ˈdʒɒnəθ(ə)n/ *n.* L18. [Male forename.] 1 The United States of America personified; the people of the US collectively; a supposedly typical US citizen. Also *Brother Jonathan*. L18. 2 A variety of red-skinned autumn eating apple, first introduced in the US. M19.

Jonathani'zation *n.* Americanization M19.

Jones /dʒəʊnz/ *n.* L19. [A common British surname.] **1** In *pl.* A person's neighbours or social equals. Chiefly in *keep up with the Joneses*, try to emulate or not to be outdone by one's neighbours. L19. **2** A drug addict's habit. *slang.* M20.

jong /jɒŋ/ *n.*[1] *S. Afr. colloq.* E17. [Afk.] Orig. (*Hist.*), a Coloured male slave or servant. Later, a form of address to a young man or woman, used esp. among young people.

jong /dʒɒŋ/ *n.*[2] Also **dzong**. E20. [Tib. *rdzoṅ* fortress.] In Tibet: a building constituting a prefecture, freq. also used as a fortress or monastery; also, a territorial and administrative division.

jonga /'dʒɒŋgə/ *n.* L19. [Bantu (NW) *njaŋga*.] In Jamaica, a small freshwater prawn, *Macrobrachium jamaicensis*.

jonglery /'dʒɒŋgləri/ *n.* E17. [Fr. *jonglerie*, f. as next: see -ERY.] The performance of a *jongleur*.

jongleur /ʒɔ̃glœːr/ *n.* Pl. pronounced same. L18. [Fr., alt. of *jougleur* (OFr. *jogleor* accus. of *joglere*) f. L *joculator* jester: see JUGGLER.] *Hist.* An itinerant minstrel.

jonick /'dʒɒnɪk/ *a.* & *adv. Austral. colloq.* Also **-nn-**. L19. [Var. of JANNOCK *a.* & *adv.*] Fair(ly); genuine(ly); right.

Jonkanoo *n.* var. of JOHN CANOE.

jonnick *a.* & *adv.* var. of JONICK.

jonnop /'dʒɒnəp/ *n. Austral. slang.* M20. [Contr. of JOHN *hop*.] A policeman.

jonquil /'dʒʌŋkwɪl, 'dʒɒn-/ *n.* & *a.* E17. [mod.L *jonquilla* or Fr. *jonquille* f. Sp. *junquillo* dim. of *junco* f. L *juncus* rush, reed.] **A** *n.* **1** A kind of narcissus, *Narcissus jonquilla*, with rushlike leaves and fragrant yellow flowers, used in perfumery. E17. **2** The colour of a jonquil; a pale yellow. L18.

1 *Queen Anne's jonquil*: see QUEEN ANNE.

B *adj.* Of the colour of a jonquil; pale yellow. E19.

Jonsonian /dʒɒn'səʊnɪən/ *a.* L19. [f. *Jonson* (see below) + -IAN.] Of, pertaining to, or characteristic of the English dramatist Ben Jonson (*c*1573–1637) or his works.

jonty *n.* var. of JAUNTY *n.*

jook *v.*, **jookery** *n.* vars. of JOUK *v.*[2], JOUKERY.

†joom *n.* & *v.* var. of JHUM.

jordan /'dʒɔːd(ə)n/ *n.*[1] LME. [med.L *jurdanus*, of unkn. origin.] **†1** A bulbous pot or vessel formerly used by physicians and alchemists. Only in LME. **2** A chamber-pot; *fig.* a stupid person. Now *dial.* LME.

Jordan /'dʒɔːd(ə)n/ *n.*[2] E20. [M. E. C. *Jordan* (1838–1922), Fr. mathematician.] *Math.* **1** *Jordan curve*, any curve that is topologically equivalent to a circle, i.e. is closed and does not cross itself. E20. **2** *Jordan('s) (curve) theorem*, the theorem that any Jordan curve in a plane divides the plane into just two distinct regions having the curve as their common boundary. E20.

jordan almond /'dʒɔːd(ə)n 'ɑːmənd/ *n. phr.* LME. [App. f. Fr. or Sp. *jardin* garden + ALMOND: in later times assoc. w. the River Jordan.] A fine variety of almond, now coming chiefly from Malaga. Also, a sugar-coated almond.

Jordanian /dʒɔː'deɪnɪən/ *a.* & *n.* M20. [f. *Jordan* (see below), also a river running into the Dead Sea -IAN.] **A** *adj.* Of or pertaining to the kingdom of Jordan in the Middle East. M20. **B** *n.* A native or inhabitant of Jordan. M20.

Jordanite /'dʒɔːd(ə)nʌɪt/ *n.* M20. [f. *Jordan* (see below) + -ITE[1].] A believer in the doctrines of Jordan, a 20th-cent. Jamaican preacher with followers in Guyana.

joree /dʒə'riː/ *n. US.* L19. [Imit. of the bird's call.] = CHEWINK.

jornada /xɔr'naða, hɔː'nɑːdə/ *n.* Pl. ***-as*** /-as, -əz/. M17. [Sp. = It. *giornata*, Fr. *journée* JOURNEY.] **†1** An act of a play; a book or canto of a poem. M17–M19. **2** In Mexico etc.: a day's journey; *spec.* one across a waterless desert tract with no place to halt. E19.

joro /'dʒɔːrəʊ/ *n.* Pl. **-os**. L19. [Jap. *jorō*.] In Japan, a prostitute.

jorram /'jʊərəm/ *n. Sc.* L18. [Gael. *iorram*, *iurram*.] A Gaelic boat-song; *loosely* any Scottish song.

jorum /'dʒɔːrəm/ *n.* M18. [Perh. f. *Joram* (2 *Sam.* 8:10).] A large drinking-bowl; the contents of this; *esp.* a bowl of punch.

joruri /'dʒoːruri/ *n.* L19. [Jap. *jōruri*, f. the name of a character in a popular recitation.] **1** A dramatic recitation to music, accompanying a Japanese puppet performance. L19. **2** Japanese puppet drama. M20.

Joseph /'dʒəʊzɪf/ *n.* L16. [Male forename (Heb. *yōsēp* lit. 'may he (God) increase'), esp. of various biblical characters, spec. one of the twelve sons of Jacob and of the husband of Mary the mother of Jesus.] **1** In plant-names: (*a*) *Joseph's flower* (now *dial.*), yellow goat's-beard, *Tragopogon pratensis*, so called in allus. to the bearded figure of St Joseph in art; (*b*) *Joseph and Mary* (dial.), lungwort, either native, *Pulmonaria longifolia*, or of gardens, *P. officinalis*, so called from the flowers being pink and blue at different stages. L16. **2** *Hist.* A long cloak with a small cape and buttons down the front, worn chiefly by women when riding. M17. **3** A violin made by Joseph Guarnieri del Gesù (1698–1744), Italian violin-maker. Cf. GUARNERIUS. L19.

Josephism *n.* = JOSEPHINISM M19.

Josephine /'dʒəʊzɪfiːn, -ʌɪn/ *a.* M19. [f. *Joseph* (see below) + -INE[1].] Of or pertaining to Emperor Joseph II of Austria (1741–90) or the ecclesiastical measures introduced by him.

Josephinism *n.* the ecclesiastical policy of the Emperor Joseph II L19.

josephinite /'dʒəʊzɪfɪnʌɪt, dʒəʊzɪ'fiːnʌɪt/ *n.* L19. [f. *Josephine* county in Oregon, USA + -ITE[1].] *Min.* The terrestrial (as opp. to meteoric) alloy of nickel and iron, having about 67 to 77 per cent of nickel.

Josephite /'dʒəʊzɪfʌɪt/ *n.*[1] M16. [f. St *Joseph* (1439–1515), Abbot of Volokolamsk, Russ. reformer + -ITE[1].] *Hist.* A member of a party formed among Russian Orthodox monks in the 16th cent., who defended the holding of property by monastic communities.

Josephite /'dʒəʊzɪfʌɪt/ *n.*[2] & *a.* M19. [f. *Joseph* (see below) + -ITE[1].] **A** *n.* A member of any of various religious societies of St Joseph. M19. **B** *adj.* Designating or pertaining to the Josephites. L20.

Josephson /'dʒəʊzɪfs(ə)n/ *n.* L20. [Brian David *Josephson* (b. 1940), Brit. physicist.] *Physics.* Used *attrib.* with ref. to an effect whereby an electric current can flow from one superconducting metal to another with no potential difference between them if they are separated by a sufficiently thin layer of an insulator, the application of a potential difference causing the current to oscillate with a frequency proportional to the voltage.

Scientific American The Josephson junction is the fastest switch known. *Observer* Other computer companies are much less active in Josephson technology.

josh /dʒɒʃ/ *v.* & *n. slang.* M19. [Origin unkn.] **A** *v.* **1** *v.t.* Make fun of, tease. M19. **2** *v.i.* Indulge in banter. M19.

1 B. T. BRADFORD They joshed him unmercifully about being late. **2** E. FERBER This is very pleasant, sitting here gabbing and joshing in the hot of the day. A. HAILEY Brett dropped into the kitchen where he joshed with the cooks.

B *n.* A good-natured or teasing joke; banter. L19.

Saturday Review We found him tired-eyed and peaked, . . not a man for josh and chatter.

josher *n.* L19. **joshingly** *adv.* in a joshing manner M20.

Joshua /'dʒɒʃjʊə/ *n. US.* M19. [Prob. f. *Joshua*, leader of the ancient Israelites, whose story forms a book in the Old Testament and Hebrew Scriptures, w. allus. to the branching shape of the tree resembling that of Joshua brandishing a spear: see *Josh.* 8:18.] More fully *Joshua palm*, *tree*, *yucca*. A small evergreen tree, *Yucca brevifolia*, of the agave family, bearing clustered white flowers and found in western desert regions.

joskin /'dʒɒskɪn/ *n. slang.* L18. [Origin unkn.: cf. BUMPKIN *n.*[1]] A country bumpkin; a foolish person.

joss /dʒɒs/ *n.*[1] E18. [Perh. ult. f. Port. †*deos*, *deus* f. L *deus* god, through Jav. *dejos*: cf. Du. *joosje*, *josie*.] A Chinese figure of a god, an idol.

Comb.: **joss-house** a Chinese temple; **joss-man** a Chinese priest or holy man; a missionary; **joss-stick** a thin stick of fragrant tinder mixed with clay, burnt as incense.

joss /dʒɒs/ *n.*[2] *dial.* or *Austral.* & *NZ slang.* M19. [Origin unkn.] = BOSS *n.*[4] 1.

josser /'dʒɒsə/ *n. slang.* L19. [f. JOSS *n.*[1] + -ER[1].] **1** A clergyman. *Austral.* L19. **2** A fool; a fellow. L19.

jostle /'dʒɒs(ə)l/ *n.* Also **justle** /'dʒʌs(ə)l/. E17. [f. next.] **†1** A struggle, a tussle. Only in E17. **2** The action or an act of jostling; a collision; a rough push or thrust. E17.

jostle /'dʒɒs(ə)l/ *v.* Also (earlier) **justle** /'dʒʌs(ə)l/. LME. [f. JUST *v.*[2] + -LE[3].] **†1** *v.i.* Have sexual intercourse *with*. *rare.* Only in LME. **2** *v.i.* Knock or push *against*, come into collision *with*; push and shove, esp. in a crowd; make one's way by pushing or shoving. M16. **b** Vie or struggle *for* something. (Foll. by *with* another.) E17. **†3** *v.i.* Come into collision in a tournament; joust. L16–M18. **4** *v.t.* Come into rough collision with, knock or push against, elbow. L16. **b** *v.t.* & *i. spec.* Push against (another competitor) during a horse-race so as to obstruct or delay. E18. **5** *v.t.* Push, drive, or force, roughly or unceremoniously, *from*, *into*, *out of*, etc. L16. **6** *v.t.* Bring (things) into collision. M17.

2 M. DE LA ROCHE Piers jostled against him in the doorway. A. WEST They would jostle round him covering him with wet kisses. R. DAHL People were pushing and jostling and trying to get . . closer to the famous girl. D. WIGODER I . . jostled with tens of thousands of young people crammed into Trafalgar Square. **b** A. TREW The . . locals had now to jostle with each other for tables, food and drink. M. RULE In Europe two major powers, France and Spain, jostled for control. **4** V. WOOLF The pavement was crowded with people; jostling each other. *fig.*: F. RAPHAEL All the practical questions . . jostled pettier and grander ones. **5** G. SWIFT The guard jostled me back towards the double doors. **6** J. G. BALLARD The vendors . . jostled their carts against each other.

jostlement *n.* the action of jostling M19.

jot /dʒɒt/ *n.*[1] L15. [L *iota* f. Gk *iōta* IOTA. Cf. JOD.] The smallest letter or written part of any writing; *gen.* (usu. in neg. contexts) the very least or a very little part or amount, a whit.

H. JACOBSON She was not a jot more lucid than I was. B. NEIL Goodness me, you haven't changed one jot.

jot /dʒɒt/ *n.*[2] Long *dial.* M17. [f. JOT *v.*[1]] A jolt, a bump.

jot /dʒɒt/ *v.*[1]*t.* & *i. obs.* exc. *dial.* Infl. **-tt-**. M16. [Cf. JOLT *v.*] Jolt, bump.

jot /dʒɒt/ *v.*[2]*t.* Infl. **-tt-**. E18. [f. JOT *n.*[1]] Write down briefly or hastily; make a short note of. Usu. foll. by *down*.

G. VIDAL I tend to mislay the notes I jot down as reminders. K. WATERHOUSE I brandished the envelope . . on which Douglas had jotted the address.

jotting *n.* (*a*) the action of the vb; (*b*) a brief hasty note: E19. **jotty** *a.* of the nature of fragmentary notes M19.

jota /'xota/ *n.* M19. [Sp.] A northern Spanish folk-dance performed by one or more couples in rapid triple time; a piece of music for this dance.

jotter /'dʒɒtə/ *n.* E19. [f. JOT *v.*[2] + -ER[1].] **1** A person who jots down something. E19. **2** A small pad or exercise book used for making notes etc. L19.

jotun /'jəʊt(ə)n/ *n.* M19. [ON *jǫtunn* = OE *eoten*, f. Gmc.] A member of a supernatural race of giants in Scandinavian mythology.

joual /ʒwɑl, ʒuːˈɑːl/ *n.* M20. [Dial. Canad. Fr. f. Fr. *cheval* horse.] Demotic Canadian French characterized by non-standard pronunciations and grammar, and influenced by English vocabulary and syntax.

joub *n.* var. of JUBE *n.*[2]

jougs /dʒuːgz/ *n.pl.* L16. [Fr. *joug* or L *jugum* yoke. The pl. form refers to the device's hinged halves.] *Sc. Hist.* An instrument of punishment consisting of a hinged iron collar locked round an offender's neck and attached by a chain to a wall or post.

jouissance /ʒwisɑ̃ːs/ *n.* Also †***-isance***. L15. [Fr., f. *jouir* enjoy: see -ANCE.] †**1** The possession and use *of* something advantageous or pleasing. L15–E17. **2** Pleasure, delight; mirth, festivity. L16.

2 R. SCRUTON His eyes were alight with sudden jouissance 'I am not often happy,' .. 'but now I am.'

¶Formerly fully naturalized.

jouk /dʒuːk/ *v.*[1]*i. obs.* exc. *dial.* LME. [ONFr. *joquier, jochier* (mod. *jucher*) be at rest.] †**1** Lie asleep or at rest; lie close. Also, remain. Only in LME. **2** Of a bird: perch, roost, sit (on a branch, perch, etc.). LME.

jouk /dʒuːk/ *v.*[2] *Sc.* & *north.* Also **jook**. LME. [Origin uncertain: perh. rel to DUCK *v.*] **1** *v.i.* †**a** Bend oneself supply like a tumbler or acrobat. Only in LME. **b** Bow, esp. quickly or jerkily, in salutation or obeisance. M16. **2** *v.i.* Bend or turn the body quickly and neatly downwards or sideways to avoid a missile, blow, etc.; dodge; duck. E16. **b** Dart or spring neatly out of the way or out of sight; hide, skulk. E16. **3** *v.t.* Evade or dodge by ducking, bending, or springing aside. L18.

2b R. L. STEVENSON Jouk in here among the trees.

joukery /ˈdʒuːkəri/ *n. Sc.* & *north.* Also **jookery**. LME. [f. prec. + -ERY.] Dodging; trickery, deceit.

Comb.: **joukery-pawkery** [cf. PAWK *n.*] clever trickery, legerdemain.

joule /dʒuːl/ *n.* Also **J-**. Pl. **-s**, same. L19. [James Prescott *Joule* (1818–89), Eng. physicist.] *Physics.* **1** Orig., a unit of electrical energy equal to the amount of work done (or heat generated) by a current of one ampere acting for one second against a resistance of one ohm. Now (equivalently), the SI unit of energy and work equal to the work done by a force of one newton when its point of application moves one metre in the direction of the force; 10^7 ergs. (Symbol J.) L19. **2** (Usu. **J-**.) Used *attrib.* and in *possess.* to designate principles, phenomena, etc., discovered by Joule or arising out of his work. L19.

2 **Joule effect** (*a*) = *Joule heating* below; (*b*) a change in the linear dimensions of a body in a magnetic field. **Joule heating**: that occurs when an electric current flows through a resistance. **Joule's equivalent** = *mechanical equivalent of heat* s.v. EQUIVALENT *n.* **Joule's law**: (*a*) that the heat produced by an electric current i flowing through a resistance R for a time t is proportional to i^2Rt; (*b*) that the internal energy of a given mass of an ideal gas depends only on its temperature.

joulean /ˈdʒuːlɪən/ *a.* (chiefly *US*) of or pertaining to Joule heating L19.

Joule–Thomson /dʒuːlˈtɒms(ə)n/ *n.* L19. [f. J. P. *Joule* (see JOULE) + Sir William *Thomson*, Lord Kelvin (see KELVIN).] Used *attrib.* with ref. to an effect whereby a change of temperature occurs in a gas when it expands through a porous plug or throttle without doing external work, the gas being cooled if initially below its inversion temperature, or heated if above it.

Also **Joule–Kelvin** *n.* E20.

jounce /dʒaʊns/ *v.* & *n.* LME. [Prob. imit.: cf. FLOUNCE *v.*[1]] **A** *v.* **1** *v.i.* Move violently up and down; bump, bounce, jolt *along*. LME. **2** *v.t.* Jolt, bump; shake up and down; give (a person) a shaking. L16.

1 A. TYLER Every time the car jounced, something rattled on the back seat.

B *n.* A bump, a jolt; a jolting pace. L18.

joundy *v.* & *n.* see JUNDY.

jour /ʒuːr/ *n.*[1] Pl. pronounced same. LME. [(O)Fr. f. L *diurnum* neut. sing. (used as n. in pop.L) of *diurnus* DIURNAL.] †**1** A day. LME–M16. **2** A kind of open stitch used in lace-making. Usu. in *pl.* M19.

¶See also BONHEUR DU JOUR, *plat du jour* s.v. PLAT *n.*[4]

jour /dʒəː/ *n.*[2] *US colloq.* E19. [Abbrev.] = JOURNEYMAN.

journal /ˈdʒəːn(ə)l/ *n.* & *a.* LME. [OFr. *jurnal, jornal* (mod. *journal*), use as n. of *journal* adj., for earlier *jornel* f. late L *diurnalis* DIURNAL.] **A** *n.* **I** **A** book, a record. †**1** *Eccl.* = DIURNAL *n.* I. LME–M16. †**2 a** A book containing information for travellers, esp. concerning the daily stages of a route; an itinerary. LME–E17. **b** A record of travel. Long *obs.* exc. as in senses 6, 7 below. E17. **3** *Bookkeeping.* A daily record of commercial transactions entered as they occur, esp. with statements of the accounts to which each is to be debited and credited. L15. †**4** A record of public events or public transactions noted down as they occur. M16–L17. **5** *the Journals*, a record of the daily proceedings in the Houses of Parliament, kept by the Clerk of the House. M16. **6** A personal record of events or matters of interest, written up every day or as events occur, usu. in more detail than a diary. E17. **7** *Naut.* A log, a logbook. L17. **8** A daily newspaper; any daily publication. Also, a periodical. E18.

6 R. P. JHABVALA During my first few months here, I kept a journal so I have some record of my early impressions. C. ACHEBE 'Do you keep a detailed diary of what is happening day to day?' 'I do keep a journal'. 8 B. PYM An article Rupert had .. just written for a journal of which he was editor. E. FEINSTEIN Marina's poetry .. was published in a literary journal.

II †**9** A day's travel; a journey. E–M17. **10** *Hist.* As much land as can be ploughed in a day. M17.

III 11 *techn.* The part of a shaft or axle which rests on the bearings. Also, the bearing itself. E19.

Comb.: **journal-bearing** *techn.* the support at each end of a horizontal shaft or axle; **journal-book** a diary; a daybook; **journal-box** *techn.* the metal housing of a journal and its bearings; **journal-letter** a letter written as a diary.

†**B** *adj.* **1** Performed, happening, or recurring every day; daily. L16–M17. **2** Of or belonging to a single day; ephemeral. *rare.* Only in L17.

journalet *n.* (*rare*) a little journal L18.

journal /ˈdʒəːn(ə)l/ *v.t.* E19. [f. prec.] **1** Record in a journal. E19. **2** *techn.* Provide with or fix as a journal (JOURNAL *n.* 11). L19.

¶Usu. in *pass.*

journalese /dʒəːnəˈliːz/ *n. colloq.* L19. [f. JOURNAL *n.* + -ESE.] The hackneyed style of language supposedly characteristic of some newspaper writing.

Sunday Express You don't write your essays in journalese—your teachers will correct you.

journalier /ʒurnalje (*pl. same*), dʒəːnəˈlɪə/ *a.* & *n.* As fem. adj. also ***-ière*** /-jɛːr/. E18. [Fr., f. JOURNAL *n.* & *a.*] **A** *adj.* †**1** Of a newspaper: published daily. Only in E18. **2** Changeable, variable. M18.

2 A. BROOKNER 'She looks very pretty when .. animated and rather plain when she is not.' '*Journalière*, that used to be called.'

B *n.* A newspaper writer, a journalist. E18.

journalise *v.* var. of JOURNALIZE.

journalism /ˈdʒəːn(ə)lɪz(ə)m/ *n.* M19. [Fr. *journalisme*, f. as JOURNAL *n.* & *a.*: see -ISM.] The occupation or profession of a journalist; journalistic writing; newspapers and periodicals collectively. See also PHOTOJOURNALISM.

Listener For newspapermen throughout the world Washington has always been the Mecca of journalism. *New Journalism*: see NEW *a.*

journalist /ˈdʒəːn(ə)lɪst/ *n.* L17. [f. as prec.: see -IST.] **1** A person who earns a living by writing for or editing a newspaper or periodical. Also, a reporter for radio or television. Cf. also PHOTOJOURNALIST. L17. **2** A person who keeps a journal. Now *rare.* E18.

journaˈlistic *a.* of, pertaining to, or characteristic of journalists or journalism E19. **journaˈlistically** *adv.* in a journalistic manner; by means or through the medium of newspapers or periodicals: L19.

journalize /ˈdʒəːn(ə)lʌɪz/ *v.* Also **-ise**. M18. [f. JOURNAL *n.* + -IZE.] **1** *v.t.* Enter in a journal or book for daily accounts; *spec.* in *Bookkeeping*, make a journal entry for (a transaction, an account) in which the debit and credit accounts are specified. M18. **2** *v.t.* & *i.* Enter, record, or describe (a thing or an event) in or as in a personal journal. L18.

2 N. HAWTHORNE I would gladly journalize some of my proceedings, and describe things and people. G. GISSING A man who can't journalize .. nowadays inevitably turns to fiction.

journalizer *n.* M19.

journey /ˈdʒəːni/ *n.* & *v.* ME. [OFr. *jornee* (mod. *journée* day, day's work or travel) f. Proto-Romance var. of L *diurnum* daily portion, (in late L) day, use as n. of neut. of *diurnus* DIURNAL.] **A** *n.* **I** †**1** A day. ME–M17.

II 2 †**a** The distance that can be travelled in a day (as a specific measure usu. estimated at 20 miles, approx. 32 km). ME–M16. **b** The portion of a march or expedition actually done in a day. Now *rare* or *obs.* L15. **3** An act of going from one place to another or of travelling for a specified distance or period of time; a march, a ride, a drive, etc., or a combination of these; an excursion or expedition, esp. to some distance. (Not usu. applied to sea-travel: cf. *voyage*). ME. **b** *fig.* The passage through life. ME. **c** The travelling of a vehicle along a certain route between two fixed points at a stated time. M19. †**4** A military expedition, a campaign; occas., any military enterprise, as a siege. LME–E17.

3 O. HENRY Ninety miles it was; a six days' journey. E. R. BURROUGHS Within a short journey of the stamping-ground of his tribe. A. BULLOCK His first journey out of the United Kingdom. *Nature* Four journeys to the moon. M. MILNER The journey would be too expensive and I thought I had done enough travelling. b DICKENS A quicker journey to the old man, and a swift inheritance to the young one.

III A day's work. **5** A day's labour; a certain fixed amount of daily labour; a daily spell of work. *obs.* exc. *dial.* ME. †**6** A day's fighting; (the day of) a battle. Cf. DAY *n.* 10. ME–E17. †**7** A day's activity or business; *gen.* activity, business. LME–L17. **8** *techn.* An amount of work done at one time, as in a day. LME. **b** The coinage of a certain weight of gold or silver, orig. the amount which could be coined in a day (180.0321 troy ounces of gold or 720 oz. of silver). L16. **c** *Glass-making.* A spell of work in which a certain quantity of raw material is converted into glass. L19. **9** A set of trams in a colliery. L19.

Comb.: **journey-pride** *dial.* excitement or alarm at the prospect of travelling; **journey-proud** *a.* (*dial.*) excited or alarmed at the prospect of travelling; **Journeys accounts** *Law* (now *Hist.*) the number of days (usu. fifteen) after the abatement of a writ within which a new writ might be obtained; **journey-weight** = sense 8b above.

B *v.* **I 1** *v.i.* Go on or make a journey; travel. ME. **2** *v.t.* Travel over, traverse. Now *rare.* M16.

1 J. SYMONS Stanley journeyed up and down between London and Brighton every day. TOLKIEN I have journeyed in this land.

II †**3** *v.t. Sc. Law.* Remand (a person); postpone (a matter in litigation); adjourn. L15–E17.

journeyer *n.* a person who journeys, a traveller LME.

journeyman /ˈdʒəːnɪmən/ *n.* Pl. **-men**. LME. [f. JOURNEY *n.* + MAN *n.*] **1** A person who, having served an apprenticeship, is qualified to work in an art, craft, or trade, for daily wages or as the assistant or employee of another; a qualified artisan or mechanic who works for another. LME. **2** A person who is not a master of his or her trade or business; a person hired to work for another. Usu. *derog.* M16. **3** *Astron.* More fully *journeyman clock*. A secondary clock in an observatory, used in the comparison of primary or standard clocks. M18. **b** = *impulse clock* s.v. IMPULSE *n.* E20.

1 *Times* A number of sugar barges are idle .. because of a strike of 100 journeymen. 2 HOR. WALPOLE The colouring was worse .. than that of the most errant journeymen to the profession.

journeywoman /ˈdʒəːnɪwʊmən/ *n.* Pl. **-women** /-wɪmɪn/. M18. [f. as prec. + WOMAN *n.*] A woman working at a trade for daily wages.

journey-work /ˈdʒəːnɪwəːk/ *n.* E17. [f. as prec. + WORK *n.*] **1** Work done for daily wages or for hire; the work of a journeyman. E17. **2** Work delegated to a subordinate or done for hire; servile, inferior, or inefficient work. Usu. *derog.* E17.

2 A. C. SWINBURNE The swift impatient journey-work of a rough and ready hand.

journo /ˈdʒəːnəʊ/ *n. slang* (orig. *Austral.*). Pl. **-os**. M20. [Abbrev. of JOURN(ALIST + -O.] = JOURNALIST 1.

joust /dʒaʊst/ *n.* Also **just** /dʒʌst/, †**giust**. ME. [OFr. *juste, jouste* (mod. *joute*), f. *juster*: see next.] *Hist.* A combat between two knights or men-at-arms on horseback with lances; *spec.* such a combat for exercise or sport; a tilt. Also (in *pl.*), a series of such encounters, a tournament.

joust /dʒaʊst/ *v.i.* Also **just** /dʒʌst/. ME. [OFr. *juster, jouster* (mod. *jouter*) bring together, unite, engage on horseback f. Proto-Romance vb meaning 'approach, come together, meet', f. L *juxta* near together.] †**1** Join battle, encounter, engage; *esp.* fight on horseback as a knight or man-at-arms. ME-M17. **2** *Hist.* Engage in a joust or tournament; run at tilt with lances on horseback. ME.

jouster *n.* ME. **jousting** *n.* fighting or tilting on horseback with a lance; *spec.* a tournament: ME.

Jove /ˈdʒəʊv/ *n. poet.* LME. [L *Jovis, Jovem*, etc., obl. cases of OL *Jovis*. Cf. JUPITER.] **1** The chief of the gods of the ancient Romans. LME. **2** The planet Jupiter. LME.

1 *bird of Jove*: see BIRD *n.* **by Jove** *colloq.* expr. surprise or approval. *flower of Jove*: see FLOWER *n.*

jovial /ˈdʒəʊvɪəl, -vj(ə)l/ *a.* L16. [Fr., f. late L *jovialis*, f. as prec.: see -AL¹.] †**1** *Astrol.* Under the influence of Jupiter, said as a natal planet to impart joy and happiness. L16-M19. **2** Characterized by mirth, humour, or festivity; convivial. L16. **3** Of or pertaining to the planet Jupiter. Now *rare.* M17.

2 C. MACKENZIE Dr. Maclaren's usually jovial florid face was lined with bad temper. H. WOUK Something infectiously jovial about him, a spark of devilish amusement in his lively blue eyes.

joviˈality *n.* the quality of being jovial; mirth, festivity, conviviality: E17. **jovialize** *v.t.* make jovial; cause to be jolly: E17. **jovially** *adv.* in a jovial manner; with jollity or mirth: E17. **jovialness** *n.* M17. **jovialty** *n.* (now *rare*) = JOVIALITY E17.

Jovian /ˈdʒəʊvɪən/ *a.* & *n.* M16. [f. as JOVE + -IAN.] **A** *adj.* **1** Of, pertaining to, or resembling (that of) Jove. M16. **2** *Astron.* Of or pertaining to the planet Jupiter; (of a planet) resembling Jupiter, esp. in mass and density; *spec.* designating the four planets Jupiter, Saturn, Uranus, and Neptune in the solar system. L18.

1 V. SACKVILLE-WEST She hated him for his Jovian detachment and superiority. Y. MENUHIN A Jovian figure, . . so immense that a viola in his arms . . seemed no bigger than a violin.

B *n.* **1** A person who resembles or imitates Jove. Long *rare.* L16. **2** An (imagined) inhabitant of the planet Jupiter. E20.

2 R. BRADBURY The blue-skinned Jovian . . said nothing.

jovicentric /dʒəʊvɪˈsɛntrɪk/ *a.* M19. [f. JOVE + -I- + -CENTRIC.] *Astron.* Having Jupiter as the centre. Cf. GEOCENTRIC *a.* 2.

Jovinianist /dʒəʊˈvɪnɪənɪst/ *n.* M19. [f. med.L *Jovinianus* Jovinian (see below) + -IST.] *Eccl. Hist.* A follower or adherent of Jovinian, a 4th-cent. Milanese monk who denied the superiority of virginity over marriage and the particular merit of abstinence, holding that all forms of Christian living are equally rewarded in heaven.

jow /dʒaʊ/ *n. Sc.* & *north.* E16. [Perh. a form of JOWL *n.*⁴] **1** A single stroke or pull in the ringing of a bell; the ringing, tolling, or sound of a bell. *Sc.* E16. **2** A knock, push. L18.

jow /dʒaʊ/ *v. Sc.* & *north.* E16. [Perh. a form of JOWL *v.*] **1** *v.t.* Ring or toll (a bell), esp. without giving a full swing. *Sc.* E16. **b** *v.i.* Of a bell: toll, ring. L18. **2** *v.t.* Knock, strike, (esp. the head). E19.

jowar /dʒaʊˈɑː/ *n.* Also **jawar**. E19. [Hind. *jawār, joār.*] In the Indian subcontinent: a kind of sorghum, = DURRA.

jowari /dʒaʊˈɑːriː/ *n.* Also **jawari**. E19. [Hind. *jawārī, joārī.*] = prec.

jowel /ˈdʒaʊəl/ *n.* Chiefly *dial.* E16. [Origin uncertain: perh. rel. to Fr. *joualle* yoke, arch, space.] Orig., a pier of a wooden bridge. Now, the arch or space between adjacent piers of a bridge.

jower /ˈdʒaʊə/ *v.i. dial.* & *local US.* E17. [Imit.] Growl; scold; mutter or grumble quietly or unintelligibly.

jowl /dʒaʊl/ *n.*¹ Also (now *rare*) **jole** /dʒəʊl/, (earlier) †**chavel** & other vars. [OE *ċeafl* corresp. to OS *kaflun* (dat. pl.), Flem. *kavel* gum, rel. to MHG *kivel*, Du. *kevel.*] **1** A jawbone; a jaw; *esp.* the lower jaw; in *pl.*, the jaws. OE. †**2** Idle or malicious talk; = JAW *n.*¹ 5. ME-L16. **3** Either of the cheeks of the face. M17.

3 *cheek by jowl*: see CHEEK *n.*

¶Forms w. *j*- recorded from 16th cent., perh. after JOWL *n.*³ Cf. next.

jowl /dʒaʊl/ *n.*² Also (now *rare*) **jole** /dʒəʊl/ (earlier) †**cholle** & other vars. [OE *ċeole, -u* = OS, OHG *kela* (G *Kehle*), throat, gullet.] The external throat or neck of a person when pendulous or fleshy; the dewlap of a bovine animal; the crop or the wattle of a bird etc.

F. NORRIS His cheek and . . thick neck ran together to form a great, tremulous jowl.

¶Forms w. *j*- recorded from 16th cent., perh. after next. Cf. prec.

jowl /dʒaʊl/ *n.*³ Also (now *rare*) **jole** /dʒəʊl/, †**cholle** & other vars. LME. [Origin unkn.] **1** The head of a person or an animal. *obs.* exc. *dial.* LME. **2** *spec.* The head of a fish; the head and shoulders of certain fishes, as the salmon, sturgeon, and ling, as food. LME.

jowl /dʒaʊl/ *n.*⁴ Now *dial.* E16. [f. JOWL *v.*] **1** A bump; a blow, esp. on the head; a knock. E16. **2** A single stroke of a bell; the tolling, ringing, or clang of a bell. Cf. JOW *n.* E19.

jowl /dʒəʊl/ *v.* Now *dial.* LME. [Perh. f. JOWL *n.*³] **1** *v.t.* Bump, strike, knock; push. LME. **b** Strike (a ball) with a stick. LME. **2** *v.t.* & *i.* (Cause to) toll, knell, or ring slowly. Cf. JOW *v.* 1. L19.

jowled /dʒaʊld/ *a.* M19. [f. JOWL *n.*¹ + -ED².] Having jowls or jaws, esp. of a specified kind. Chiefly as 2nd elem. of comb.

fat.-jowled, grey-jowled, heavy-jowled, etc.

jowler /ˈdʒaʊlə/ *n. obs.* exc. *dial.* L17. [f. JOWL *n.*¹ + -ER¹.] A heavy-jawed dog, *esp.* a beagle.

jowlop(p)ed *a.* var. of JELLOPED.

jowly /ˈdʒaʊli/ *a.* L19. [f. JOWL *n.*¹ + -Y¹.] Having large or prominent jowls.

P. LIVELY A fattish, jowly face, pointed nose, sharp eyes, grey wig.

joy /dʒɔɪ/ *n.* ME. [OFr. *joie, joye* (mod. *joie*), f. Proto-Romance fem. f. L *gaudia* pl. of *gaudium* joy, f. *gaudere* rejoice.] **1** Vivid pleasure arising from a sense of well-being or satisfaction; exultation; gladness, delight; an instance of this. Also as *int.*, expr. pleasure, delight, etc. ME. **b** The expression of glad feeling; outward rejoicing; mirth. ME. **c** Result, satisfaction, success. Usu. in neg. contexts and freq. *iron. colloq.* M20. **2** A pleasurable, happy, or felicitous state or condition; *esp.* the bliss or blessedness of heaven. Also, paradise, heaven. Long *arch. rare.* ME. **3a** A source, object, or cause of happiness; a delight. ME. **b** A sweetheart, a loved child; darling, beloved. Cf. JO. Chiefly *dial.* E16. †**4** Joyful adoring praise and thanksgiving; = GLORY *n.* 2. ME-L15. †**5** A jewel. L16-E19.

1 DAY LEWIS I was . . flooded with incredulous joy like a prisoner . . released after years of solitary confinement. MERLE COLLINS She felt all the joy of the season of spring. **b** WORDSWORTH The valley rings with mirth and joy. **c** P. D. JAMES The lab will get the . . tissue under the microscope, but I don't think you'll get any joy. **3a** *Daily Telegraph* A joy to look at and a great pleasure to use. B. T. BRADFORD Her darling little baby, . . who was the joy of her life.

Phrases: *give a person (the) joy of*: see *wish a person (the) joy of* below. **joy of a planet** *Astrol.* the fact or condition of a planet being in the house where it is most powerful. *jump for joy*: see JUMP *v. pride and joy*: see PRIDE *n.*¹ STRENGTH *through joy.* TRAVELLER'*s joy.* **wish or** (*arch.*) **give a person** (†**the**) **joy** (**of**) (freq. *iron.*) express one's good wishes to a person (on a happy occasion); congratulate (on).

Comb.: **joy-bells**: rung on a festive occasion; **joy-flight** an aerial joyride; **joy-house** *slang* a brothel; **joy juice** *N. Amer. slang* alcoholic drink; **joy-pop** *slang* (an inhalation or injection of) an illegal drug; **joy-pop** *v.i.* (*slang*) inhale or inject an illegal drug; **joy-popper** *slang* an occasional taker of illegal drugs; **joyride** *n.* & *v.i.* (*colloq.*) (go for) a pleasure trip in a motor car, aeroplane, etc., esp. without the owner's permission; **joyrider** a person who goes on a joyride; **joy-stick** (*a*) *slang* the control-lever of an aeroplane; the controls of a vehicle; (*b*) a small lever that can be moved in either of two dimensions to control a moving image on a television or VDU screen; **joy-wheel** a Ferris wheel.

joyless *a.* without joy, cheerless; having or causing no joy: LME. **joylessly** *adv.* M18. **joylessness** *n.* E17. **joysome** *a.* (*rare*) joyous E17.

joy /dʒɔɪ/ *v.* ME. [OFr. *joïr* (mod. *jouir*) f. Proto-Romance var. of L *gaudere* rejoice.] †**1** *v.refl.* Experience joy; enjoy oneself; rejoice. ME-E18. **2** *v.i.* Feel or show joy; be glad; delight, exult. Also foll. by *in, to do.* ME. **b** *Astrol.* Of a planet: be in the house where it is most powerful. Cf. *joy of a planet* s.v. JOY *n.* M17. **3** *v.t.* Fill with joy; gladden, give delight to. *arch.* ME. †**b** In *pass.* Be delighted; be made joyous. LME-E18. **4** *v.t.* Derive enjoyment from; possess or use with enjoyment; enjoy. Formerly also, have the use or benefit of. *arch.* ME. †**5** *v.t.* Salute or greet with expressions of joy, welcome, or honour. Formerly also, glorify, extol. LME-E18. **b** Give or wish (a person) joy of something; congratulate. (Foll. by *in, of*). L15-E18.

joyance /ˈdʒɔɪəns/ *n.* Chiefly *poet.* L16. [f. JOY *v.* + -ANCE.] **1** The feeling or showing of joy; rejoicing; delight; enjoyment. L16. **2** Enjoying oneself; festivity, merrymaking. L16. **3** Joyous character or quality; delight, charm. M19.

joyancy *n.* the quality or state of being joyous; joyousness: M19. **joyant** *a.* (*rare*) feeling or showing joy; joyous: M19.

Joycean /ˈdʒɔɪsɪən/ *a.* & *n.* E20. [f. *Joyce* (see below) + -AN.] **A** *adj.* Of, pertaining to, or characteristic of the Irish writer James Joyce (1882–1941) or his works. E20. **B** *n.* An admirer or student of Joyce or his work. M20.

joyful /ˈdʒɔɪfʊl, -f(ə)l/ *a.* ME. [f. JOY *n.* + -FUL.] **1** Full of joy; having, showing, or expressing joy; elated, glad, delighted. ME. **2** Causing joy; delightful. ME.

1 A. ARONSON A medley of emotions, joyful anticipation, fear that the lover may fail to come. D. PRATER She admired . . his uncomplicated manliness and joyful acceptance of all that life had to offer. **O** (or **oh**) **be joyful** *slang* alcoholic drink. 2 J. HUXLEY The words I heard inspired by the joyful gift of divine love.

joyfully *adv.* in a joyful manner; so as to cause joy: ME. **joyfulness** *n.* L15.

joyous /ˈdʒɔɪəs/ *a.* ME. [AN, or OFr. *joios* (mod. *joyeux*), f. *joie* JOY *n.*: see -OUS.] **1** Having a joyful nature or mood; full of glad feeling; expressive of joy. ME. **2** Causing joy; gladdening. LME.

1 B. T. BRADFORD She had a joyous, carefree disposition, and laughter sprang readily to her lips.

†**joyousity** *n.* the quality or state of being joyous; joyous or mirthful behaviour: LME-E19. **joyously** *adv.* L15. **joyousness** *n.* M16.

Ju /dʒuː/ *a.* E20. [Wade-Giles *Ju Chou* Ruzhou: see below.] Designating a type of Chinese pottery with buff body and blue-green glaze produced in Ruzhou, in Henan province, in the 12th cent.

juba /ˈdʒuːbə/ *n. US.* M19. [Origin unkn.] A kind of dance originating among plantation slaves of the southern US, accompanied by clapping of the hands, patting of the knees and thighs, striking of the feet on the floor, and a refrain in which the word *juba* is frequently repeated.

jubba /ˈdʒʌbə, ˈdʒʊbə/ *n.* Also **-ah**. M16. [Arab., whence also Fr. JUPE: see also JIBBA.] A type of long open cloth coat with wide sleeves, worn esp. by Muslims.

jube /ˈdʒuːbi/ *n.*¹ E18. [Fr. *jubé* f. L. *jube* imper. of *jubere* bid, order, first wd of the formula *Jube,* *domine, benedicere* Sir, bid a blessing, addressed by a deacon to a celebrant before the reading of the Gospel, which in some places was done from a church's rood-loft.] *Eccl.* †**1** A chair in a church for the preacher. Only in E18. **2** A rood-loft or screen and gallery dividing the choir of a church from the nave. M18.

jube /dʒuːb/ *n.*[2] Also **joub**. E18. [Pers. *jūb*.] In Iranian cities, an open watercourse.

jube /dʒuːb/ *n.*[3] *colloq.* (esp. *Austral* & *NZ*). M20. [Abbrev.] = JUJUBE 2.

jubilance /ˈjuːbɪl(ə)ns/ *n.* M19. [f. next + -ANCE.] Great joy, exulting gladness.

jubilancy *n.* L19.

jubilant /ˈdʒuːbɪl(ə)nt/ *a.* M17. [L *jubilant-* pres. ppl stem of *jubilare* JUBILATE *v.*: see -ANT[1].] Making a joyful noise, rejoicing with songs and acclamations. Now usu., making demonstrations of joy, exultingly glad; expressing or manifesting joy.

E. JONES He.. wrote a jubilant letter as if all the difficulties in his career had now been overcome. J. G. FARRELL Mrs. Rice.. was still flushed and jubilant over her victory.

jubilantly *adv.* M19.

jubilarian /dʒuːbɪˈlɛːrɪən/ *n.* L18. [f. med.L *jubilarius* pertaining to a jubilee + -AN.] A person who celebrates his or her jubilee; *spec.* (*RC Ch.*), a priest, monk, or nun who has been such for fifty years.

jubilate /dʒuːbɪˈleɪti, juːbɪˈlɑːteɪ/ *n.* ME. [f. L = shout for joy!, imper. of *jubilare*: see next.] **1** More fully *jubilate deo* /ˈdiːəʊ, ˈdeɪəʊ/. Psalm 100 (99 in the Vulgate), used as a canticle in the Anglican service of matins; a musical setting of this. ME. **2** A call to rejoice; an outburst of joyous triumph. M18. **3** *RC Ch.* The third Sunday after Easter, so called because Psalm 66 (65 in the Vulgate), which in Latin begins with *Jubilate*, was formerly used as the introit on that day. E20.

jubilate /ˈdʒuːbɪleɪt/ *v.* E17. [L *jubilat-* pa. ppl stem of *jubilare* (rustic word) call, halloo, (in Chr. writers) shout for joy: see -ATE[3].] †**1** *v.t.* Make glad. Only in E17. **2** *v.i.* Utter sounds of joy or exultation; make demonstrations of joy; rejoice, exult. M17.

2 M. MEAD We jubilate over birth and dance at weddings.

jubilation /dʒuːbɪˈleɪʃ(ə)n/ *n.* LME. [L *jubilatio(n-)*, f. as prec.: see -ATION.] Loud utterance of joy, exultation, (public) rejoicing; an expression of exultant joy.

C. R. LOW The jubilations of the garrison were short-lived. R. K. NARAYAN At the Harvest Festival the usual jubilation was absent.

jubilean /dʒuːbɪˈliːən/ *a.* E17. [f. next. + -AN.] Of or pertaining to a jubilee.

jubilee /ˈdʒuːbɪliː/ *n.* LME. [(O)Fr. *jubilé* f. eccl.L *jubilaeus* (sc. *annus* year) (with assim. to *jubilare* JUBILATE *v.*) f. eccl.Gk *iōbēlaios*, f. *iōbēlos* f. Heb. *yōbēl* jubilee, orig. ram, (hence) ram's horn, with which the jubilee year was proclaimed.] **1** More fully *year of jubilee*. A year of emancipation and restoration, according to Mosaic law (*Lev.* 25) to be kept every 50 years, during which Hebrew slaves were to be set free, and lands and houses were to revert to their former owners. LME. **b** *transf.* & *fig.* A time of restitution, remission, or release. L16. **2** *RC Ch.* A period of remission from the penal consequences of sin, granted under certain conditions for a year, usu. at intervals of 25 years. LME. **3** Orig., the fiftieth anniversary of an event; the celebration of the completion of 50 years of reign, activity, or continuance in a particular condition etc.; = *golden jubilee* s.v. GOLDEN *a.* Now (freq. w. specifying wd), a similar anniversary of any round number of years (*rare* bef. 19). LME. †**b** A period of 50 years. M17–E18. **4** A season or occasion of joyful celebration or general rejoicing. LME. **5** Exultant joy, general or public rejoicing, jubilation. E16. **b** Shouting; joyful shouting; sound of jubilation. M16. **c** A folk-song of American Blacks of an optimistic and joyful kind, often having a religious basis. L19.

3 *diamond jubilee*: see DIAMOND *n.* & *a. iron jubilee*: see IRON *n.* & *a. silver jubilee*: see SILVER *n.* & *a.*

jubilize /ˈdʒuːbɪlaɪz/ *v.i.* Now *rare*. Also **-ise**. M17. [f. L *jubilare* JUBILATE *v.* + -IZE.] = JUBILATE *v.* 2.

juck /dʒʌk/ *v.i.* Also **juke** /dʒuːk/. E17. [Imit. (cf. CHUCK *v.*[1]), but perh. orig. transf. use of JUG *v.*[3]] Of a partridge: make its characteristic sound or call.

jucundity /dʒʊˈkʌndɪti/ *n.* Now *rare* or *obs.* M16. [L *jucunditat-*, f. *jucundus* JOCUND: see -ITY.] = JOCUNDITY.

Judaean /dʒuːˈdiːən/ *n.* & *a.* Also ***Judean**. M17. [f. L *Judaeus* f. Gk *Ioudaios*, f. *Ioudaia* Judaea (see below): see -AN.] **A** *n.* A native or inhabitant of Judaea, the southernmost district of ancient Palestine. M17. **B** *adj.* Of or pertaining to Judaea. M19.

Judaeo- /dʒuːˈdiːəʊ/ *comb. form.* Also ***Judeo-**. [f. L *Judaeus* Judaean, Jewish: see JEW *n.*, -O-.] Forming adj. & n. combs. w. the senses 'pertaining to the Jews or Judaism', 'Jewish and', as *Judaeo-Arabic*, *Judaeo-Christian*.

Judaeo-German *n.* & *a.* Yiddish M19. **Judaeophobe** *n.* a person who has a dread or strong dislike of Jews L19. **Judaeo'phobia** *n.* dread or strong dislike of Jews L19. **Judaeo-Spanish** *n.* & *a.* Ladino M19.

Judahite /ˈdʒuːdəaɪt/ *a.* & *n.* L19. [f. *Judah* (see below) + -ITE[1].] *Hist.* **A** *adj.* Of or pertaining to Judah, an ancient Hebrew tribe and kingdom. L19. **B** *n.* A member of the tribe, or an inhabitant of the kingdom, of Judah. E20.

Judaic /dʒuːˈdeɪɪk/ *a.* E17. [L *Judaicus* f. Gk *Ioudaïkos*, f. *Ioudaios* JEW *n.*] Of or pertaining to the Jews, Jewish; of a Jewish character, characteristic of the Jews.

Judaical *a.* = JUDAIC L15. **Judaically** *adv.* L16.

Judaise *v.* var. of JUDAIZE.

Judaism /ˈdʒuːdeɪɪz(ə)m/ *n.* LME. [Chr.L *Judaismus* f. Gk *Ioudaïsmos*, f. *Ioudaios* JEW *n.*: see -ISM.] **1** The profession or practice of the Jewish religion; the religion of the Jews, with a belief in one God and a basis in Mosaic and rabbinical teachings. LME. **2** Adoption of Jewish practices on the part of Christians; a practice or cast of thought associated with Jews. M17. **3** *Hist.* = JEWRY 2. Also, in official documents, the revenue derived by the Crown from Jews; the treasury which received this money. M19.

1 *Conservative Judaism*: see CONSERVATIVE *a. Liberal Judaism*: see LIBERAL *a.*

Judaist *n.* a person who follows Jewish practice or ritual; *esp.* (in *Eccl. Hist.*) a Jewish Christian of the apostolic age: M19. **Juda'istic** *a.* of, pertaining to, or characteristic of Judaists M19.

Judaize /ˈdʒuːdeɪaɪz/ *v.* Also **-ise**. L16. [Chr.L *judaizare* f. Gk *ioudaizein*, f. *Ioudaios* JEW *n.*: see -IZE.] **1** *v.i.* Behave like a Jew; follow Jewish customs or religious rites. L16. **2** *v.t.* Make Jewish; imbue with Jewish doctrines or principles. M17.

Judai'zation *n.* E19. **Judaizer** *n.* a person who Judaizes; *spec.* an early Christian who observed the Mosaic law: M17.

Judas /ˈdʒuːdəs/ *n.* In sense 3 now usu. **j-**. LME. [*Judas* Iscariot, the disciple who betrayed Jesus: see JESUS *n.*] **1** A person who treacherously betrays another under the semblance of friendship; a traitor or betrayer of the worst kind. Cf. ISCARIOT. LME. **2** More fully *Judas of the paschal*. A tall piece of wood, painted like a candle, which rose from the central branch of the seven-branched paschal candlestick and at Easter was surmounted by the paschal candle of wax. *obs.* exc. *Hist.* LME. **3** More fully *judas-hole*, *judas window*. A small aperture in a door (in some old houses, or in prison cells), through which a person can look without being noticed from the other side; a peep-hole. M19.

Comb.: **Judas-colour**, **Judas-coloured** *a.* (of the hair or beard) red (from the medieval belief that Judas Iscariot had red hair and beard); **Judas goat** an animal used to lead others to destruction; *judas-hole*: see sense 3 above; **Judas kiss** an act of betrayal (*Matt.* 26:48); **Judas priest** *int.* alt. of *Jesus Christ* in an oath; **Judas-tree** a leguminous tree of southern Europe, *Cercis siliquastrum*, with abundant purple flowers which appear in spring before the leaves; any of several other trees of this genus; *judas window*: see sense 3 above.

judcock /ˈdʒʌdkɒk/ *n.* E17. [App. f. *judge-cock*, w. allus. to its black crown.] = *jacksnipe* s.v. JACK *n.*[1]

judder /ˈdʒʌdə/ *v.* & *n.* M20. [Imit.: cf. SHUDDER *v.*] **A** *v.i.* (Esp. of a mechanism) shake or vibrate violently; (of the voice in singing) oscillate between greater and less intensity. M20.

G. JOSIPOVICI When one turns the hot water off the whole house jars and judders.

B *n.* An instance of juddering; the condition of juddering. M20.

Judean *n.* & *a.* see JUDAEAN.

Judenrat /ˈjuːd(ə)nraːt/ *n.* Pl. **-e** /-ə/. M20. [G = Jewish council.] A council representing a Jewish community in a locality controlled by the Germans during the war of 1939–45.

judenrein /ˈjuːd(ə)nraɪn/ *a.* M20. [G = free from Jews.] Of a society, organization, etc., *spec.* in Nazi Germany: without Jewish members, out of which Jews have been expelled.

C. ROTH The survivors.. were.. sent to the death camps, Warsaw being now *judenrein*.

Judeo- *comb. form* see JUDAEO-.

judge /dʒʌdʒ/ *n.* ME. [(O)Fr. *juge* f. L *judic-*, *judex*, f. *jus* right, law + *-dicus* saying, speaking.] **1** A public officer appointed to administer the law; a person (now only a qualified lawyer) who has authority to hear and try cases in a court of justice. ME. **2** God or Christ regarded as the supreme arbiter at the Last Judgement. ME. **3** *Hist.* In ancient Israel in the period between Joshua and the kings: an officer (usu. a leader in war) invested with temporary authority. In *pl.* (treated as *sing.*) (**J-**), the Book of Judges, a book of the Old Testament and Hebrew Scriptures, containing the history of the period of the judges. LME. **4** A person appointed to decide in any contest, competition, or dispute; an arbiter, an umpire. LME. **5** A person who or thing which judges of or decides anything in question. Freq. in *be judge*, form an opinion, give a decision. LME. **6** A person qualified to form or pronounce an opinion; one capable of judging or estimating. M16. **7** *Angling.* A kind of artificial fly. M19.

1 C. ISHERWOOD It is the voice of a judge, summing up and charging the jury. **4** J. PARKER No blind man will be appointed as a judge of pictures in the Academy. **5** C. MACKENZIE He must be the judge of the best moment to make his announcement. **6** J. A. MICHENER My daughter was a better judge of men than I was.

Phrases: **as God is my judge**: emphasizing the truth of one's assertion. *circuit judge*: see CIRCUIT *n.* **judge advocate** a barrister who advises a court martial on points of law and sums up the case. **Judge Advocate General** a civil officer in supreme control of courts martial in the army or air force. *judge and warrant*: see WARRANT *n.*[1] *Judge Ordinary*: see ORDINARY *a.* *Judges' lodgings*: see LODGING 4c. *judge's marshal*: see MARSHAL *n.*[1] 4b. **Judges' Rules** rules drawn up by the High Court regarding the admissibility of the accused's statements as evidence. *red judge*: see RED *a.* *salute the judge*: see SALUTE *v.* *sober as a judge*: see SOBER *a.*

Comb.: **judge-made** *a.* (of law) constituted by judicial decisions.

judgelike *a.* & *adv.* (*a*) *adj.* resembling a judge, appropriate to a judge; (*b*) *adv.* in the manner of a judge: M17.

judge /dʒʌdʒ/ *v.* ME. [OFr. *jugier*, later & mod. *juger*, f. L *judicare*, f. *judex*: see prec.] **I** *v.t.* **1** Try, or pronounce sentence on (a person) in a court of justice; sit in judgement on. ME. †**2** *spec.* Pronounce sentence against (a person); sentence, condemn. Foll. by *to* a penalty, *to do*, *to suffer*. ME–L17. **3** Decide judicially or authoritatively *that*, *who*, etc.; order judicially (a person) *to do*. ME. **4** Form an opinion about (a thing) so as to arrive at a correct notion of it; estimate, appraise. ME. **5 a** Foll. by obj. cl.: form the opinion, hold as an opinion; come to a conclusion, infer; think, consider, suppose. ME. **b** Infer, conclude, or suppose (a person or thing) to be or *to be*. ME. **6** Govern or rule (a country), esp. (*Hist.*) as a judge in ancient Israel. LME. **7** Assign or award by judgement; adjudge. Now *rare* or *obs.* LME. **8** Declare or pronounce authoritatively (a person) to be or *to be*. Also foll. by *for*. Now *rare*. LME. **9** Pronounce an opinion on, criticize; *esp.* pronounce an adverse opinion on, condemn, censure. LME. **10** Give sentence concerning (a matter); try (a case); determine, decide, (a question). E16.

1 M. WEST Christ will come a second time, in glory, to judge the living and the dead. **2** BACON Some whose offences are pilfring.. they judge to be whipped. **3** *Grimsby Gazette* The referee judged that Palace goalkeeper George Wood had carried the ball beyond the line. **4** E. WELTY Bowman, who.. judged a woman's age on sight, set her age at fifty. E. AMADI You can only judge people by what they say and do. **5a** P. BOWLES Madame.. judged that the right moment for intervention had arrived. G. GREENE I played the scene.. over again in my mind trying to judge whether any irrevocable words had been spoken. **b** B. MARTIN They judge the Moon to be a Globe like our Earth. J. KRANTZ Vito judged the time ripe to break the silence. **8** *Stock & Land (Melbourne)* A two-year-old red bull.. was judged champion. **9** J. M. ROBERTS He judged it in terms very like those of a Jewish prophet.

II *v.i.* **11** *Hist.* In ancient Israel: exercise the functions of a judge. ME. **12** Act as judge; try a case and pronounce a sentence in a court of justice. Also, pronounce a critical opinion. LME. **13** Give a decision or opinion on any matter, esp. between contending parties; arbitrate. LME. **14** Form an (esp. correct) opinion of or *of* a thing (*from* or *by* data); make up one's mind as to the truth of a matter. Also (*Logic*), make a mental assertion or statement. LME.

12 A. MUNRO People are dead now... It isn't up to us to judge. **13** BROWNING God must judge 'twixt man and me. **14** J. TYNDALL From its form and colour he could.. judge of its condition. L. DURRELL The others are already asleep to judge by the heavy snoring. M. COX Judging from his letters home, Monty was in good spirits.

judgematic /dʒʌdʒˈmatɪk/ *a. colloq.* Now *rare*. Also **judgmatic**. M19. [f. as next.] = JUDGEMATICAL.

judgematical /dʒʌdʒˈmatɪk(ə)l/ *a. colloq.* Now *rare*. Also **judgmat-**. L18. [Irreg. f. JUDGE *n.*, *v.* + *-matic* after *dogmatic*: see -ICAL, -AL[1].] Characterized by good practical judgement; judicious, discerning. Also, behaving like a judge, judicial.

judgematically *adv.* E19.

judgement /ˈdʒʌdʒm(ə)nt/ *n.* Also (the usual form in legal use) **-dgm-**. ME. [(O)Fr. *jugement*, f. *juger*: see JUDGE *v.*, -MENT.] **1** The action of trying a cause in a court of justice; trial. Now *rare*. ME. **2** In full *Last Judgement*. In some faiths: the judgement of humankind by God expected to take place at the end of the world, when each is rewarded or punished according to his or her merits. ME. **3** The sentence of a court of justice; a judicial decision or order in court. ME. **b** *Law*. An assignment of chattels or chattel interests made by judgement or decree of court; the certificate of such judgement as a security or form of property. Cf. *judgement-debt* below. L17. **4** A divine sentence or decision; *spec.* (now freq. *joc.*) a misfortune or calamity regarded as a divine punishment or as a token of divine displeasure. ME. **5** Any formal or authoritative pronouncement, as of an umpire or arbiter. Now *rare*. ME. **6** The pronouncing of a deliberate (esp. adverse or critical) opinion on a person or thing; an opinion so pronounced. ME. **7** In biblical translations: (*a*) justice, righteousness (= DOOM *n.*[1] 4); (*b*) a divine decree or ordinance; (*c*) a sentence or decision in a person's favour; (one's) right. LME. **8** The formation of an opinion or notion concerning something by exercising the mind on it; an opinion, an estimate. LME. **9** The function of the mind by which it arrives at a notion of a thing; the critical faculty. M16. **b** Good judgement; discernment. L16. **†c** A person having (good) judgement. Only in 17. **d** Reason, senses, wits. *Sc.* E19. **10** *Logic*. The action of predicating or mentally apprehending the relation between two objects of thought; a proposition, as formed in the mind. E18.

1 B. GELDOF Adult men making stern accusations stood in judgement of a frightened 11-year-old boy. **2** G. GORER The soul survives after the death of the body and comes to Judgment. **3** *Holiday Which?* This judgment will be used as a guideline in future claims for holiday compensation. **4** J. WAIN The 'plane crash had been a judgement on the parents for wickedness. **5** J. RULE David accepted the teacher's judgement that being left-handed was babyish! **6** A. J. CRONIN Her sense of justice.. detected in the review.. a note of prejudice, a judgment of the man rather than the artist. **7** COVERDALE *Ps.* 119:30 I have chosen the way of treuth, thy iudgmentes haue I layed before me. AV *Isa.* 61:8 For I the Lord loue Iudgement, I hate robbery for burnt offering. AV *Deut.* 10:18 He doeth execute the iudgement of the fatherlesse, and widow. **8** *Times* In his judgment they.. had no occasion to bow down to any one. *Southern Rag* This is a much more difficult judgement to make. **9** D. FRANCIS Take the horses.. and use your own judgement about whether to canter. J. HELLER He shows poor judgment in colors and styles. R. DAVIES He was a man whose enthusiasms sometimes outran his judgement. **b** *Sunday Times* The biographer's gifts—balance, judgement, accuracy—are just the ones Wilde.. ridiculed. **c** SIR T. BROWNE To undervalue a solid Judgment, because he knows not the genealogy of Hector.

Phrases: **against one's better judgement** contrary to what one knows to be wiser or more desirable. *arrest of judgement*: see ARREST *n.* **Day of Judgement** the day on which the Last Judgement is believed to take place, doomsday. *judgement by default*: see DEFAULT *n.* *Last Judgement*: see sense 2 above. **private judgement** the formation of personal or individual opinion (esp. in religious matters), as opp. to the acceptance of a statement or doctrine on authority. **sit in judgement** preside as a judge at a trial; pass judgement (*up*)*on* a person (with an assumption of superiority).

Comb.: **judgement creditor** a creditor in whose favour a judgement has been given ordering the payment of the debt due; **Judgement Day** = *Day of Judgement* above; **judgement debt** a debt for the payment of which a judgement has been given; **judgement debtor**: against whom a judgement ordering payment has been given; **judgement-hall** (chiefly *Hist.*) a public building in which trials at law are held; **judgement note** *US* a promissory note containing a power of attorney to enter judgement and take out execution ex parte if the debtor defaults; **judgement-seat** a seat on which a judge sits when trying a cause or pronouncing judgement; a tribunal; **judgement summons**: issued in a County Court against a person who has failed to pay a judgement debt.

judgemented *a.* (as 2nd elem. of comb. or w. preceding adv.) having judgement or discernment of a specified kind M16.

judgemental /dʒʌdʒˈmɛnt(ə)l/ *a.* Also **judgmental**. E20. [f. prec. + -AL[1].] Involving the exercise of judgement; inclined to make moral judgements.

judgementally *adv.* L20.

judger /ˈdʒʌdʒə/ *n.* LME. [f. JUDGE *v.* + -ER[1].] A person who or thing which judges, a judge; *esp.*. a person who forms, or who is (well or ill) qualified to form, an opinion.

judgeship /ˈdʒʌdʒʃɪp/ *n.* L17. [f. JUDGE *n.* + -SHIP.] The office of judge, the function of a judge.

judgess /ˈdʒʌdʒɪs/ *n.* Now *rare*. M16. [f. JUDGE *n.* + -ESS[1].] A female judge; a woman who judges.

judging /ˈdʒʌdʒɪŋ/ *ppl a.* L16. [f. JUDGE *v.* + -ING[2].] That has the function of judging, judicial; *spec.* able to judge, judicious, discerning. Also, censorious.

judgingly *adv.* M17.

judgmatic, **-ical** *adjs.* vars. of JUDGEMATIC, -ICAL.

judgment *n.* see JUDGEMENT.

judgmental *a.* var. of JUDGEMENTAL.

judication /dʒuːdɪˈkeɪʃ(ə)n/ *n.* E17. [L *judicatio(n-)*, f. *judicat-* pa. ppl stem of *judicare* JUDGE *v.*: see -ATION.] The action of judging; judgement.

judicative /ˈdʒuːdɪkətɪv/ *a.* LME. [med.L *judicativus*, f. L *judicat-*: see prec., -ATIVE.] Having the function of trying causes or passing sentences; judicial, juridical.

judicator /ˈdʒuːdɪkeɪtə/ *n.* M18. [Late L, f. L *judicat-*: see JUDICATION, -ATOR.] A person who judges, a person who acts as a judge.

judicatory /ˈdʒuːdɪkət(ə)ri, dʒʊˈdɪkət(ə)ri/ *n.* L16. [Late L *judicatorium* (glossing Gk *dikasterion*), f. as prec.: see -ORY[1]. In sense 2 f. med.L *judicatorium* in same sense (cf. Fr. †*judicatoire* n.).] **1** A court of judicature; a body having judicial authority; a tribunal. Now chiefly *Sc.* (esp. in *Eccl. Law*). L16. **2** Judicature; a system of judicature. L16.

judicatory /ˈdʒuːdɪkət(ə)ri, dʒʊˈdɪkət(ə)ri/ *a.* Now *rare* or *obs.* E17. [Late (eccl.)L *judicatorius*, f. as JUDICATOR: see -ORY[2].] Having the function of judging or passing sentence; of or pertaining to judgement.

judicature /ˈdʒuːdɪkətʃə, dʒʊˈdɪk-/ *n.* M16. [med.L *judicatura*, f. L *judicat-*: see JUDICATION, -URE.] **1** The action of judging; administration of justice by duly constituted courts; judicial process. Freq. in *court of judicature*. M16. **2** The office, function, or authority of a judge. M16. **3** = JUDICIARY *n.* 2. L16. **†4** *fig.* Mental judgement; formation or authoritative expression of opinion; criticism. M17–M18.

1 Supreme Court of Judicature (in England) the court constituted by Acts of Parliament in 1873 and 1875, which united the former separate Courts of Chancery, King's or Queen's Bench, Common Pleas, Exchequer, Admiralty, etc. **3** RICHARD WATSON If the witnesses of the resurrection had been examined before any judicature.

Comb.: **Judicature Acts** the statutes establishing the Supreme Court of Judicature, and regulating its practice.

judicial /dʒʊˈdɪʃ(ə)l/ *a.* & *n.* LME. [L *judicialis*, f. *judicium* legal proceedings, tribunal, judgement, f. *judic-*, *judex* JUDGE *n.*: see -IAL.] **A** *adj.* **1** Of or pertaining to proceedings in a court of law; of or pertaining to the administration of justice; resulting from or fixed by a judgement in court. LME. **b** Of law: enforced by secular judges and tribunals. Opp. *ceremonial*, *moral*. M16. **c** *Theol.* Inflicted by God as a judgement or punishment; of the nature of a divine judgement. E17. **2a** Pertaining to the judgement of the reputed influence of the celestial objects on human affairs. Chiefly in *judicial astrology* s.v. ASTROLOGY 2. LME. **†b** *Med.* = CRITICAL 1. M16–M17. **c** Giving judgement or a decision on a matter; disposed to pass judgement, critical. L16. **3** That has or shows sound judgement; judicious. Now *rare*. L15. **4** Having the function of judgement; invested with authority to judge causes. M16. **5** Of a judge; proper to a judge. E19.

1 G. M. TREVELYAN Administrative and judicial authority still rested with the gentlemen Justices of the Peace. **c** LD MACAULAY An infatuation such as, in a more simple age, would have been called judicial. **2c** R. W. EMERSON The intercourse of society.. is one wide, judicial investigation of character. **3** C. C. TRENCH Many a country gentleman restored his depleted fortunes by a judicial alliance. **4** H. COX Parliaments were originally judicial as well as legislative assemblies.

Phrases & special collocations: **judicial combat** *Hist.* a combat engaged in to decide a controversy. **Judicial Committee of the Privy Council**: established in 1832 for the disposal of appeals made to the King or Queen in Council, chiefly from courts in dependent countries. **judicial duel** *Hist.* a duel engaged in to decide a controversy. **judicial factor** *Sc. Law* a factor appointed by the Court of Session or the sheriff court to administer the estate of another. **judicial murder** an unjust, though legal, death sentence or execution. **judicial review** a procedure by which a judicial body may pronounce on the validity of an act of legislature (in the US) or a decision of an inferior court or public authority (in the UK). *judicial separation*: see SEPARATION 5. *judicial torture*: see TORTURE *n.*

†B *n.* **1** A judicial law or ordinance. LME–E18. **2** A determination, a decision, a judgement. LME–M17. **b** *Astrol.* A determination as to a future event from the positions of celestial objects; the system of such determinations. L15–M17. **3** A legal judgement. M16–M17.

judici'ality *n.* the quality or character of being judicial M19. **judicialize** *v.t.* make judicial; treat judicially, arrive at a judgement or decision on: L19. **judicially** *adv.* LME.

judiciary /dʒʊˈdɪʃ(ə)ri/ *a.* & *n.* LME. [L *judiciarius*, f. *judicium*: see prec., -ARY[1].] **A** *adj.* **1** = JUDICIAL *a.* 1. Now *rare*. LME. **†2** = JUDICIAL *a.* 2a. Also, pertaining to the giving of judgements or decisions by any kind of divination, as physiognomy. L16–M18. †3 = JUDICIAL *a.* 4. L17–E19.

3 judiciary combat *Hist.* = *judicial combat* s.v. JUDICIAL *a.*

B *n.* †1 Divination as an art; judicial astrology. Also, a judicial astrologer. L16–M17. 2 A body of judges or people having judicial power; a court of justice; a legal tribunal; judges or legal tribunals collectively. E19.

2 *Daily Telegraph* Separation of powers between the legislature, the executive and the judiciary.

judicious /dʒʊˈdɪʃəs/ *a.* L16. [f. Fr. *judicieux*, f. L *judicium* (whence Fr. †*judice*): see JUDICIAL, -OUS.] 1 Of a person, the faculties etc.: having or exercising sound judgement; discreet, wise, sensible. Now *esp.* (*a*) sensible in relation to practical matters; wise in adapting means to ends; capable and careful in action, prudent; (*b*) sensible in intellectual matters; sound in discernment. L16. 2 Of action, thought, etc.: proceeding from or showing sound judgement (esp. in practical matters); marked by discretion, wisdom, or good sense. L16. †3 = JUDICIAL *a.* 1. E–M17.

1 A. COLLINS One of the most Judicious of Interpreters, the great Grotius. J. A. MICHENER A judicious administrator who found personal pleasure when his fields produced more wheat. 2 M. DRABBLE Popularity had been cheaply purchased by the judicious distribution of . . jelly cubes. A. GHOSH A judicious mixture of practical and theoretical knowledge.

judiciously *adv.* E17. **judiciousness** *n.* M17.

judo /ˈdʒuːdəʊ/ *n.* L19. [Jap., f. *jū* gentle + *dō* way.] A refined form of ju-jitsu using principles of movement and balance, practised as a sport or a form of physical exercise.

judoist *n.* a person who practises or is expert in judo M20. **judoka** /ˈdʒuːdəʊkə/ *n.*, pl. **-s**, same, = JUDOIST M20.

Judy /ˈdʒuːdi/ *n. slang.* E19. [Pet-form of female forename *Judith*, orig. w. ref. to the wife of Punch in Punch-and-Judy shows.] A woman, a girl. Formerly also *spec.*, a woman of ridiculous appearance.

Punch-and-Judy show: see PUNCH *n.*[4] 3.

†**juffer** *n.* L17–E19. [Du., lit. 'young woman': see YUFFROUW.] A piece of timber about 12 cm (4¾ inches) square.

jug /dʒʌg/ *n.*[1] Now *rare.* M16. [Pet-form of female forenames *Joan*, *Joanna*, *Jenny*.] 1 A plain woman; a maid-servant; a sweetheart; a mistress; a prostitute. M16. 2 In local names of small birds: *bank-jug*, the chiffchaff; *hedge-jug*, the long-tailed tit. L19.

jug /dʒʌg/ *n.*[2] M16. [Prob. spec. use of prec.] 1 A deep vessel for holding liquids, usu. with a cylindrical, tapering, or swelling body, having a handle and often a spout or lip for pouring. Also *US*, a large jar with a narrow mouth. M16. b A jug used as a wind or rhythm instrument in a jazz or folk group. M20. 2 A jug with its contents; the liquid in a jug. M17. 3 (A) prison, (a) jail. Also more fully *stone-jug. slang.* L18. 4 A bank. *slang.* M19. 5 In *pl.* A woman's breasts. *slang* (chiefly *N. Amer.*). M20.

1 L. MACNEICE Poured water from the jug into the cup. *beer-jug*, *milk-jug*, *toby jug*, etc. 2 H. ALLEN Debrülle now opened small brown jugs of Asti Spumante. 3 D. FRANCIS Just out of jug, he is.

Comb.: **jug-and-bottle** *a.* (*arch.*) designating a bar of a public house at which alcoholic liquors are sold for consumption off the premises; **jug band** a jazz or folk band in which jugs are used as instruments; **jug-handle** (*a*) the handle of a jug; (*b*) a secure hold for climbing, cut into rock; **jug-handle** *a.* shaped like a jug handle; **jug-handled** *a.* (*a*) placed on one side, as the handle of a jug; (*b*) *fig.* (*US*) one-sided, unbalanced. **jughead** *derog. slang* (chiefly *US*) a foolish or stupid person or animal (esp. a horse, a mule, etc.); **jug kettle** a tall kettle resembling a jug with a lid.

juglet *n.* a small jug-shaped vessel M20.

jug /dʒʌg/ *n.*[3] *slang.* E20. [Abbrev.] = JUGGINS.

jug /dʒʌg/ *n.*[4] Also **jug-jug**. M20. [Origin unkn.] A savoury Barbadian dish made with pork and beef, served esp. at Christmas.

Jug /juːg/ *a.* & *n.*[5] *colloq.* (freq. *derog.*). M20. [Abbrev. of JUGOSLAV, JUGOSLAVIAN.] = YUGOSLAVIAN.

jug /dʒʌg/ *v.*[1] Infl. **-gg-**. L16. [f. JUG *n.*[2]] †1 *v.i.* Use a jug; drink. L16–L17. 2 *v.t.* Stew or boil (esp. a hare or rabbit), orig. in a jug or jar. M18. 3 *v.t.* Shut up in jail; imprison; *transf.* confine. *slang.* M19. 4 *v.i.* Fish with a bait attached to a floating jug. *US.* L19.

2 *jugged hare.* 3 S. BELLOW The hotel could jug him for trespassin'.

jug /dʒʌg/ *v.*[2]*i.* Infl. **-gg-**. L16. [Imit.: cf. JUG *int.* & *n.*[6]] Of a nightingale or (less commonly) other bird: make its characteristic sound or note (resembling 'jug').

jug /dʒʌg/ *v.*[3]*i.* Infl. **-gg-**. L16. [App. a by-form of JOUK *v.*[1] w. specialized application. Cf. JUCK *v.*] Of partridges etc.: crowd or nestle together on the ground; collect in a covey.

Shooting They fly . . to where they are going to jug for the night.

jug /dʒʌg/ *int.* & *n.*[6] Freq. redupl. **jug-jug**. E16. [Imit.] (Repr.) the sound or note made by the nightingale or (less commonly) some other bird.

juga *n.* pl. of JUGUM.

jugal /ˈdʒuːg(ə)l/ *a.* & *n.* Now *rare* or *obs.* L16. [L *jugalis*, f. *jugum* YOKE *n.*[1]: see -AL[1].] **A** *adj.* 1 *Anat.* Of or pertaining to the zygoma or bony arch of the cheek; malar, zygomatic. L16. 2 *Zool.* (chiefly *Entomol.*). Of or pertaining to a jugum. M20. **B** *n. Anat.* The zygomatic bone. M19.

jugate /ˈdʒuːgət/ *a.* L19. [L *jugatus* pa. pple of *jugare* join together: see -ATE[2].] 1 *Numism.* Placed side by side. L19. 2 *Entomol.* Pertaining to or possessing wings linked by a jugum. L19.

juge d'instruction /ʒyʒ dɛ̃stryksjɔ̃/ *n. phr.* Pl. ***juges d'instruction*** (pronounced same). L19. [Fr.] In France: an examining magistrate, a police magistrate.

Jugendstil /ˈjuːgənt-ʃtiːl/ *n.* & *a.* E20. [G, f. *Jugend* youth (the name of a German magazine started in 1896) + *Stil* style.] (Of, pertaining to, or designating) German art nouveau.

juger /ˈdʒuːdʒə/ *n.* Also (earlier) in L form †**-erum**, pl. †**-era**. LME. [L *jugerum*.] An ancient Roman measure of land containing 28,800 (Roman) square feet, equivalent to about a quarter of a hectare (three-fifths of an acre).

juges d'instruction *n. phr.* pl. of JUGE D'INSTRUCTION.

jugful /ˈdʒʌgfʊl, -f(ə)l/ *n.* M19. [f. JUG *n.*[2] + -FUL.] As much as a jug will hold.

by a jugful *US slang* by a great deal, by a long way (usu. in neg. contexts).

Juggernaut /ˈdʒʌgənɔːt/ *n.* In sense 1 also **Jagannath** /ˈjagənɑːθ, ˈjʌ-/. M17. [Skt *Jagannātha*, f. *jagat* world + *nātha* lord, protector.] 1 *Hindu Mythol.* A title of Krishna, a preeminent avatar of Vishnu; *spec.* the image of this god at Puri in Orissa, annually carried in procession on an enormous cart, under the wheels of which many devotees are said to have formerly thrown themselves to be crushed. M17. 2 *fig.* An institution, practice, or idea to which a person is blindly devoted or ruthlessly sacrificed. M19. 3 (**j-**.) A large heavy vehicle; *spec.* a large heavy lorry. M19.

2 *Ecologist* One of the most disastrous aspects of the nuclear juggernaut. *Sailplane & Gliding* Misplaced conceptions of national pride, and the whole Olympic bureaucratic juggernaut. 3 D. LODGE Huge concrete highways, vibrating with the thunder of passing juggernauts.

Juggernautish *a.* E19.

juggins /ˈdʒʌgɪnz/ *n. slang.* L19. [Perh. a use of the surname *Juggins*, f. JUG *n.*[1] Cf. MUGGINS.] A simpleton, a person easily taken in or imposed upon.

juggle /ˈdʒʌg(ə)l/ *v.* & *n.* LME. [Back-form. f. JUGGLER, or f. OFr. *jogler*, *jug-* f. L *joculari* to jest, f. *joculus* dim. of *jocus* JOKE *n.*] **A** *v.* †1 *v.i.* Amuse or entertain with jesting, buffoonery, tricks, etc. LME–E17. 2 *v.t.* Deceive, trick, cheat, beguile (*out of*). LME. b Bring, convey, or change by magic, conjuring, trickery, or deceit. L16. 3 *v.i.* Practise magic or legerdemain; conjure. LME. b *v.i.* & *t.* Perform feats of dexterity (with); *esp.* continuously toss and catch (several objects) so as to keep at least one in the air while handling the others; *fig.* adroitly balance, handle, or manipulate (a thing or several things simultaneously). (Foll. by *with*). L19. 4 *v.i. transf.* & *fig.* Play tricks *with* so as to cheat or deceive. E16.

2 J. S. BLACKIE The Spirit of Error . . juggles the plain understandings of men that they become the sport of every quibble. J. BRIGHT They have no system of compounding which would juggle men out of their franchise. b T. JEFFERSON Our debt was juggled from forty-three up to eighty millions. 3 R. DAVIES He can't juggle and he can't walk rope. J. UPDIKE Van Horne juggled . . five tangerines, his hands a frantic blur. b T. C. WOLFE Pearl juggled carefully with the proposals of several young men. A. TYLER She'd been so preoccupied with paying the rent and juggling the budget. 4 *Lancashire Evening Telegraph* Whatever way Mr. Trippier wants to juggle with figures, he is now a member for 869 more people.

B *n.* A conjuror's trick, *esp.* one claimed to be done by magic or occult influence; an act of deception, an imposture, a fraud. M17.

jugglement *n.* (*rare*) the process or a piece of juggling; a juggler's trick: LME.

juggler /ˈdʒʌglə/ *n.* LOE. [OFr. *joglere*, *jug-*, *joug-* (cf. JONGLEUR) f. L *joculator*, f. *joculari*: see prec., -ER[1], and cf. OFr. *jogler* f. med.L *jocularis* buffoon, use as n. of the adj. (see JOCULAR *a.*).] 1 Orig., a person who practises magic or witchcraft, a magician, a wizard, a sorcerer. Now, a conjuror, a performer of feats of dexterity, a person who juggles with several objects. LOE. †2 A jester, a buffoon. Freq. *derog.* ME–L16. 3 *transf.* & *fig.* A deceiver, a trickster. ME.

1 R. DAHL It said there would be jugglers and conjurers and acrobats.

juggleress *n.* (now *rare*) a female juggler LME.

jugglery /ˈdʒʌgləri/ *n.* ME. [OFr. *joglerie*, *jug-*, f. *jogler*, *jug-*: see JUGGLE *v.*, -ERY.] 1 Pretended magic or witchcraft; conjuring, legerdemain. Formerly also, minstrelsy, buffoonery. ME. 2 *transf.* Trickery, deception. L17.

jug-jug *n.*[1] var. of JUG *n.*[4]

jug-jug *int.* & *n.*[2] see JUG *int.* & *n.*[6]

juglone /ˈdʒuːgləʊn, ˈdʒʌg-/ *n.* L19. [f. L *juglans* walnut + -ONE.] *Chem.* A compound obtained from walnuts and acting as a mild herbicide and fungicide; 5-hydroxy-1,4-naphthoquinone, $C_{10}H_6O_3$.

Jugoslav, -ian *ns.* & *adjs.* vars. of YUGOSLAV, YUGOSLAVIAN.

jugular /ˈdʒʌgjʊlə, ˈdʒuːg-/ *a.* & *n.* L16. [Late L *jugularis*, f. L JUGULUM: see -AR[1].] **A** *adj.* 1 *Anat.* Of or pertaining to the neck or throat; *spec.* designating or pertaining to any of several large veins of the neck, as the paired *external jugular vein*, which conveys blood from the face and scalp, and the paired (*internal*) *jugular vein*, which conveys blood from the face, neck, and brain. L16. 2 *Ichthyol.* (Of a fish) having the ventral fins anterior to the pectoral, in the throat region; (of a ventral fin) so situated. M18.

B *n. Anat.* A jugular vein, *esp.* the internal jugular vein. E17.

go for the (or **a person's**) **jugular** attack violently; subject to a strong attack, usu. in speech or writing.

jugulate /ˈdʒʌgjʊleɪt, ˈdʒuːg-/ *v.t.* E17. [L *jugulat-* pa. ppl stem of *jugulare* cut the throat of, slay, f. as JUGULUM: see -ATE[3].] 1 Kill, esp. by cutting the throat. E17. 2 *fig.* Stop (a thing or process, esp. a disease) by powerful restrictive action. L19.

juguˈlation *n.* E17.

jugulo- /ˈdʒuːgjʊləʊ, ˈdʒʌg-/ *comb. form* of JUGULAR *a.* & *n.*, or of JUGULUM: see -O-.

jugulum /ˈdʒuːgjʊləm/ *n.* E18. [L = collar-bone, throat, dim. of *jugum* YOKE *n.*[1]] *Anat.* & *Zool.* Orig., the collar-bone. Now, the throat, or (esp. in birds) the lower front part of the neck; *Entomol.* any of various corresponding parts in insects.

jugum /ˈdʒuːgəm/ *n.* Pl. **-ga** /-gə/. M19. [L = YOKE *n.*[1]] 1 *Bot.* a A pair of leaflets in a pinnate leaf. M19. b Each of the ridges on the carpels of an umbelliferous plant. L19. **2a** *Zool.* A process of the dorsal valve of some articulate brachiopods. L19. **b** *Entomol.* A lobe on the forewing or some moths, serving to interlock with the hindwing in flight. L19. **3** *Anat.* A connecting ridge of bone. Freq. w. mod.L adjs. L19.

juice /dʒuːs/ *n.* ME. [(O)Fr. *jus* f. L *jus* broth, sauce, vegetable juice.] **1** The extractable liquid part of a vegetable or fruit, commonly containing its characteristic flavour and other properties. ME. **b** *spec.* The juice of the grape, made into wine. Now also *gen.* (*N. Amer. slang*), alcoholic drink. LME. **c** The liquor from the sugar cane, esp. made ready for evaporation. L17. **d** Electricity, electric current. *slang.* L19. **e** Petrol. *slang.* E20. **f** A drug; drugs. *slang.* M20. **2** The fluid part of animal or human tissue; *arch.* a body fluid or humour (usu. in *pl.*); *spec.* (w. specifying wd) a digestive secretion. LME. **3** *gen.* The fluid naturally contained in or coming from anything. LME **4** *fig.* The essence of a thing, in which its characteristic (esp. positive) qualities are found. Now also (in *pl.*), a person's vitality or creative, expressive, etc., faculties. LME. †**b** The emoluments or profits of a profession or office. *colloq.* E16–E17. **c** Influence or money obtained by or used in corrupt or criminal activities. Also, money lent at a usurious rate of interest, or the interest extorted usuriously. *US slang.* M20.

1 J. JOHNSTON Juice from the berries stained her fingers purple. A. CARTER The maid squeezed the aromatic juice from an orange into a chilled goblet. b *torpedo juice*: see TORPEDO *n.* e *Road Racer* He ran out of juice on the last lap. 2 C. CONRAN Baste the roast with the juices which have already collected in the tin. J. H. BURN Juices capable of digesting food enter the small intestine from the pancreas. 4 QUILLER-COUCH So stimulating to the creative juices of our . . writers.

Comb.: **juice harp** *slang* [alt.] = *Jew's harp* s.v. JEW *n.*; **juice-joint** *N. Amer. slang* a bar, club, or stall serving either alcoholic or non-alcoholic liquor.

juiceless *a.* E17.

juice /dʒuːs/ *v.t.* E17. [f. the n.] **1** Moisten or suffuse with juice or some other liquid. *rare.* E17. **2** Extract the juice from (a fruit, vegetable, etc.). E17. **3** Inspire; animate, liven *up. slang.* M20.

¶Rare bef. 20.

juiced /dʒuːst/ *a.* L16. [f. JUICE *n.*, *v.*: see -ED[2], -ED[1].] **1** Having juice, esp. of a specified kind or quality. Usu. as 2nd elem. of comb. L16. **2** That has been juiced, having had the juice extracted. M20. **3** Intoxicated. Also foll. by *up. slang.* M20.

juicer /ˈdʒuːsə/ *n.* E20. [f. as prec. + -ER[1].] **1** An electrician. *slang.* E20. **2** An appliance used to extract juice from fruit and vegetables. M20. **3** An alcoholic. *US slang.* M20.

juicy /ˈdʒuːsi/ *a.* LME. [f. JUICE *n.* + -Y[1].] **1** Full of or having much juice; succulent. LME. **2** Of weather: rainy, wet. *colloq.* M19. **3** Interesting, intellectually stimulating. *colloq.* M19. **4** Suggestive, esp. sexually; piquant, sensational. *colloq.* L19. **5** *gen.* Excellent, first-rate. E20.

1 R. CROMPTON The oranges . . were very yellow and juicy and rather overripe. 5 *Melody Maker* We anticipate a juicy new contract.

juicily *adv.* (*slang*) (*a*) excellently, well; (*b*) suggestively, scandalously: E20. **juiciness** *n.* E17.

ju-jitsu /dʒuːˈdʒɪtsuː/ *n.* & *v.* Also **jiu-** /dʒuː-/, **-jutsu** /-ˈdʒʌtsuː/. L19. [Jap. *jūjutsu*, f. *jū* gentle + *jutsu* skill.] **A** *n.* A Japanese system of unarmed combat using an opponent's strength and weight to his or her disadvantage, now also practised as physical training. Cf. JUDO. L19. **B** *v.t.* Overcome by means of ju-jitsu. E20.

juju /ˈdʒuːdʒuː/ *n.* Also **ju-ju**. E17. [W. Afr., prob. f. Fr. *joujou* plaything, redupl. formation f. *jouer* to play f. L *jocare.*] A charm, amulet, fetish, or idol of some W. African peoples; the supernatural or magical power believed to be associated with such an object; a ban or interdiction effected by this (cf. TABOO *n.*). Also, the system of observances connected with such objects.

W. SOYINKA He arrested somebody for using bad juju against another man. That man nearly died. R. WEST She was a ju-ju, she controlled the natural forces which permit us to live.

jujuism *n.* the system of beliefs and observances connected with jujus L19.

ju-ju /ˈdʒuːdʒuː/ *n.*[1] *slang.* M20. [Redupl. of *-ju-* in MARIJUANA.] A marijuana cigarette.

ju-ju *n.*[2] var. of JUJU *n.*

jujube /ˈdʒuːdʒuːb/ *n.* LME. [Fr., or med.L *jujuba* ult. f. L *zizyphum* f. Gk *zizuphos*, *-on.* Cf. ZIZYPHUS.] **1** An edible berry-like drupe, the fruit of various trees of the genus *Ziziphus*, of the buckthorn family. LME. **b** Any of the trees which produce this fruit, esp. *Ziziphus jujuba*, extending from the Mediterranean to China, and *Z. lotus* of N. Africa. Also *jujube tree.* M16. **2** A sweet or confection made of gum arabic, gelatin, etc., orig. one flavoured with or tasting like this fruit. M19.

2 R. DAHL Mint jujubes for the boy next door—they'll give him green teeth for a month.

juke /dʒuːk/ *n.* & *v.*[1] *slang* (orig. *US*). M20. [Prob. f. Gullah *juke*, *joog* disorderly, wicked, of W. Afr. origin: cf. Mande *dyougou* wicked.] **A** *n.* More fully *juke-house*, *juke-joint*. A roadhouse, a brothel; *spec.* one providing food, drinks, and music for dancing. M20. **B** *v.i.* Dance, esp. at a juke-joint or to the music of a jukebox. M20.

juke *v.*[2] var. of JUCK.

jukebox /ˈdʒuːkbɒks/ *n.* Also **juke-box**. M20. [f. JUKE *n.* + BOX *n.*[2]] **1** A machine that automatically plays selected gramophone records or compact discs on insertion of a coin or coins. M20. **2** *Computing.* A device for holding a number of CD-ROMs in such a way that any of them can be played or accessed. L20.

jukskei /ˈjœkskeɪ/ *n. S. Afr.* E19. [Afk., f. *juk* YOKE *n.*[1] + *skei* pin, SKEY *n.*] **1** = SKEY *n.* E19. **2** A game resembling quoits, orig. played with yoke-pins; the bottle-shaped peg used in this game. M20.

juldy *n.*, *adv.*, & *v.* var. of JILDI.

julep /ˈdʒuːlɛp/ *n.* LME. [OFr., or med.L *julapium* f. Arab. *julāb* f. Pers. *gulāb* rose-water, f. *gul* rose + *āb* water.] **1** A sweet drink, esp. as a vehicle for medicine; a medicated drink used as a demulcent or mild stimulant. LME. **2** A mixture of brandy, whisky, or other spirit with sugar, ice, and some flavouring, usu. mint. Chiefly *US.* L18.

Julian /ˈdʒuːlɪən/ *a.* L16. [L *Julianus*, f. *Julius* (see below): see -AN.] Of or pertaining to the Roman statesman Gaius Julius Caesar (d. 44 BC); *spec.* of or pertaining to the reform of the calendar instituted by him in 46 BC.

Julian Alps the Alps in NE Italy and Slovenia, SE Europe. **Julian calendar** the calendar based on a solar year of 365¼ days and with an intercalary day every fourth year, including every centenary year (cf. *Gregorian calendar* s.v. GREGORIAN *a.* 1). **Julian year** (the average length of) a year of the Julian calendar.

Julianist /ˈdʒuːlɪənɪst/ *n.* L17. [f. *Julian* (see below) + -IST.] *Eccl. Hist.* A member of a sect of Monophysites led by Julian, bishop of Halicarnassus early in the 6th cent.

Julia set /ˈdʒjuːlɪə sɛt/ *n. phr.* L20. [G. M. *Julia* (b. 1893), Algerian-born Fr. mathematician.] *Math.* The set of complex numbers which do not converge to any limit when a given mapping, esp. one of the form $z \rightarrow z^2 + c$ (where c is a constant complex number), is repeatedly applied to them.

julienne /dʒuːlɪˈɛn, *foreign* ʒyljɛn (*pl. same*)/ *a.* & *n.* E18. [Fr., f. male forename *Jules* or *Julien.*] **A** *adj.* **1** Designating soup made of various vegetables (esp. carrots), chopped and cooked in meat stock. E18. **2** Designating a small thin strip of a vegetable etc.; (of a vegetable etc.) cut into such strips; (of a dish or garnish) consisting of or containing such strips. L19.

B *n.* **1** Julienne soup. M19. **2** A julienne strip; a dish of julienne vegetables etc. E20.

2 C. CONRAN Sprinkle the salad with the juliennes of mushroom and lemon peel.

julienned *a.* cut into julienne strips M20.

Juliet cap /ˈdʒuːlɪət ˈkap/ *n. phr.* E20. [The heroine of Shakespeare's *Rom. & Jul.* (as worn as part of the usual costume).] A small network ornamental cap worn by brides etc.

julio /ˈdʒuːlɪəʊ/ *n.* Pl. **-os**. Also (earlier) †**july**. M16. [It. *giulio* f. L *Julius* (see below).] *Hist.* An Italian silver coin of small denomination, struck by Pope Julius II (1503–13).

julus *n.* var. of IULUS.

July /dʒʊˈlʌɪ/ *n.*[1] Pl. **-ies**, **-ys**. ME. [AN *julie* f. L *Julius* (sc. *mensis* month): see JULIAN *a.*] The seventh month of the year in the Gregorian calendar.

Fourth of July: see FOURTH *n.* 1.

Comb.: **July highflyer** a day-flying Palaearctic geometrid moth, *Hydriomena furcata*, of variable grey-brown colour.

†**july** *n.*[2] see JULIO.

jumar /ˈdʒuːmə/ *n.* & *v.* M20. [Origin unkn.: orig. Swiss.] *Mountaineering.* **A** *n.* A clamp which when attached to a fixed rope automatically tightens when weight is applied and relaxes when it is removed, thus facilitating the climbing of the rope; a climb using such clips. M20. **B** *v.i.* Climb with the aid of jumars. M20.

jumart /ˈdʒuːmɑːt/ *n.* Also †**gimar**. L17. [Fr., formerly *jumare* f. Prov. *gemerre*, *gemarre.*] A fictitious hybrid animal, said to be born of a mating between a bull and a mare or she-ass, or between a horse or ass and a cow.

jumbal /ˈdʒʌmb(ə)l/ *n.* Also **jumble**. E17. [Perh. var. of GIMBAL.] Orig. a kind of fine sweet cake or biscuit, freq. made in the form of a ring or roll. Now also (*US*), a thin crisp sweet cake, flavoured with lemon peel or almonds.

jumbie *n.* var. of JUMBY.

jumble /ˈdʒʌmb(ə)l/ *n.*[1] M17. [f. JUMBLE *v.*] **I 1** A confused or disorderly mixture or collection, a medley. Also, disorder, muddle. M17. **2** *collect.* Miscellaneous cheap or second-hand articles to be sold at a charitable sale etc. L19. **b** *ellipt.* A jumble sale. M20.

1 R. K. NARAYAN All the dolls and toys were . . all in a jumble. D. WIGODER What a crazy jumble of agitated chaos! **2b** DYLAN THOMAS A pair of postman's trousers from Bethesda Jumble.

II 3 A shock, a shaking, a jolting; *colloq.* a ride in a carriage. *arch.* L17.

Comb.: **jumble sale** a sale of jumble to raise money for charity etc.

jumbly *a.* confused, chaotic, in a jumble M19.

Jumble /ˈdʒʌmb(ə)l/ *n.*[2] *slang.* M20. [Alt. of *John Bull.*] A white person.

jumble *n.*[3] var. of JUMBAL.

jumble /ˈdʒʌmb(ə)l/ *v.* E16. [App. f. imit. base + -LE[3].] **1** *v.i.* Move about in mingled disorder; flounder about in confusion. E16. **b** *fig.* Be or become mixed up *with*; come *together*. *rare.* M16. **2** *v.t.* **a** Mingle in disorder; muddle up, confuse. Usu. foll. by *together*, *up.* M16 . **b** Make (*up*) in a confused or random manner. L16. **c** Confuse mentally, bewilder. M17. **d** Put, bring, or cast in confusion or disorder. Foll. by *in*, *out*, *down*, etc. Now *rare* or *obs.* L17. **3** *v.t.* Stir up or mix the ingredients of (a liquid etc.); shake up or jolt (esp. a person). Now *rare.* M16. **b** *v.i.* Bounce, shake, or jolt about, esp. in travel. Now *rare.* M18. **4** *v.i.* Make a noise, esp. a rumbling or thumping one; play discordantly or noisily on an instrument, strum. Now *rare.* M16. †**5** *v.t.* & *i.* Copulate (with). L16–L17.

2a R. INGALLS She was repeating a lot of misinformation, jumbling thoughts. 3 M. UNDERWOOD As though infants must . . be jumbled in a cradle like travellers in a mail-coach. b J. WINTERSON Our coach jumbles over the Alps.

jumblement *n.* (*a*) the action or an act of jumbling; (*b*) a confused mixture: L17.

jumble-bead /ˈdʒʌmb(ə)lbiːd/ *n.* M19. [Alt. of JUMBY-*bead*, prob. after *mumble.*] A jequirity seed, esp. as used in charms etc.

jumbo /ˈdʒʌmbəʊ/ *n.* & *a.* E19. [Prob. the 2nd elem. of MUMBO-JUMBO. Popularized as the name of an elephant, famous for its size, orig. at London Zoo and in 1882 sold to a circus.] **A** *n.* Pl. **-os**. **1** A big (occas. big and clumsy) person, animal, or thing, esp. an elephant; a thing which is very large of its kind. Also, a very skilful or successful person or thing. E19. **2** *Engin.* Any of various large types of equipment used in drilling, lifting, dumping, etc. E20. **3** *Naut.* The fore staysail in a fore-and-aft rigged vessel; the largest foresail, corresponding to the Genoa jib of the modern yatch rig. E20. 4 = *jumbo jet* below. M20.

1 J. MAY There were bracket fungi . . stiff jumbos . . capable of bearing a man's weight. A. BLOND He published *The Thorn Birds*, a classic jumbo.

B *attrib.* or as *adj.* Very large of its kind; unusually large. L19.

Miami Herald Jumbo bluefish, some up to 15 pounds.

Special collocations & *comb.*: **jumbo jet** a large jet aeroplane with a seating capacity of several hundred passengers. **jumbo-size(d)** *a.* of a very large size.

jumboism *n.* preference for largeness E20. **jumbo'mania** *n.* idolization of largeness L19.

jumboize /ˈdʒʌmbəʊʌɪz/ *v.t.* Also **-ise**. M20. [f. prec. + -IZE.] Enlarge (a ship, esp. a tanker) by inserting a new middle section between the bow and stern.

jumboizer *n.* M20.

jumbuck /ˈdʒʌmbʌk/ *n. Austral.* & *NZ colloq.* E19. [Origin unkn.] A sheep.

jumby /ˈdʒʌmbi/ *n.* Chiefly *W. Indies*. Also **jumbie**. E19. [Kikongo *zumbi* fetish. Cf. ZOMBIE.] A ghost, an evil spirit.

Comb.: **jumby-bead** the hard seed of any of several W. Indian leguminous trees and shrubs; a jumble-bead; **jumby-bean** (*a*) = *jumby-bead* above; (*b*) = *jumby-tree* below; **jumby-bird** a bird of ill omen, *esp.* an ani or an owl; **jumby-tree** any of several W. Indian leguminous trees, *esp.* the lead tree, *Leucaena latisiliqua*.

jume /dʒuːm/ *n.* L19. [S. Amer. name.] A glasswort, *Salicornia bergii*, of southern S. America, which yields much soda when burnt.

jumelle /ʒuːˈmɛl/ *a.* L15. [Fr., fem. (masc. *jumeau*), f. L *gemellus* dim. of *geminus* twin.] Twinned, paired; made or shaped in couples or pairs, double.

jument /ˈdʒuːm(ə)nt/ *n.* Now *rare* or *obs.* LME. [L *jumentum* (contr. of *jugimentum*) yoke-beast, f. *jug-* base of *jungere* join, *jugum* YOKE *n.*[1]] A beast of burden; any beast.

ju'mentous *a.* (*Med.*) (of urine) like that of a horse; highly coloured, rank, and turbid: M19.

jumma *n.* var. of JAMA *n.*[2]

jump /dʒʌmp/ *n.*[1] M16. [f. JUMP *v.*] **1** An act of jumping; a spring from the ground or other base; a leap, a bound; *spec.* an act or type of jumping, as an athletic performance. M16. **b** A distance jumped. Also, a place to be jumped across or (in ski-jumping etc.) from; an obstacle to be cleared by jumping, in hurdle-racing, hunting, etc. M19. **c** A descent on a parachute. E20. **d** A journey, a trip. *slang.* E20. **e** An act of copulation. *slang.* M20. †**2** *fig.* The moment of deciding to act, esp. without knowing the result; a dangerous or critical moment, a crisis. L16–M17. **b** A venture, a hazard, a risk. Only in E17. **3** A movement in which a thing is abruptly thrown up or forward; *spec.* (the angle which measures) the vertical movement of the muzzle of a gun at the moment of discharge. E17. **4** *fig.* A sudden and abrupt rise in position, amount, price, value, etc.; an abrupt change of level either upward or downward; an abrupt rise of level in building; a fault in geological stratification. M17. **5** *fig.* A sudden and abrupt transition from one thing, idea, stage, etc. to another, omitting intermediate stages; an interval or gap involving such sudden transition, in argument, technological development, etc. L17. **b** *Contract Bridge.* A bid higher than is necessary in the suit concerned. E20. **6** A robbery, orig. one involving a jump from a window etc. *arch. slang.* L18. **7** A sudden involuntary movement caused by a shock or excitement; a start. In *pl.*, nervous starts; an affliction characterized by this, *spec.* (*a*) chorea; (*b*) *slang* delirium tremens. L19. **8** Jazz music with a strong rhythm. M20.

1 G. B. L. WILSON The dancer holds a particular pose, . . and progresses in a series of hops or small jumps. *loop jump*, *salchow jump*, *ski-jump*, etc. **b** *Daily Telegraph* Riding . . jumps. *ski-jump*. **c** I. MCEWAN He made a parachute jump for charity and cracked his shin. **2b** SHAKES. *Ant. & Cl.* Our fortune lies Upon this jump. **4** *Daily News* Canary seed exhibits a sudden upward jump of several shillings. G. BORDMAN This encouraging jump in numbers coincided with a . . slump in quality. **5** C. WESTON From paperhanging to murder—that's a pretty big jump. **7** H. JAMES You came up and touched Gordon on the shoulder, and he gave a little jump. T. O'BRIEN At first you get the jumps . . . You feel like J. Edgar Hoover's on your tail. **8** *Melody Maker* A 1940's jump band.

Phrases: *broad-jump*: see BROAD *a.* **for the jump** = *for the high-jump* s.v. HIGH *a., adv.,* & *n.* **get** or **have the jump on** gain or have a lead over, have an advantage over by prompt action. *high-jump*: see HIGH *a., adv.,* & *n. hop, skip,* (or *step*) *and jump*: see HOP *n.*[2] 1. *long-jump*: see LONG *a.*[1] **one jump ahead** one step or stage ahead (of or *of* a rival etc.); just avoiding a pursuer etc. (*lit.* & *fig.*). **on the jump** *colloq.* (chiefly *N. Amer.*) (*a*) moving quickly; (*b*) abruptly; swiftly. *running jump*: see RUNNING *a. split jump*: see SPLIT *ppl a. triple jump*: see TRIPLE *a.* & *adv.* **two etc. jumps ahead** two etc. steps or stages ahead (of or *of* a rival, pursuer, etc.).

Comb.: **jump bid** = sense 5b above; **jump blues** a style of Black popular music which combined elements of swing and blues; **jump boot** a parachutist's boot; **jump-master** a person in charge of parachutists; **jump suit** a one-piece garment covering the whole body, of a kind originally worn by parachutists. (See also combs. of JUMP *v.*)

jump /dʒʌmp/ *n.*[2] *obs.* exc. *Hist.* M17. [Alt. of JUPE.] **1** A man's short coat of the 17th and 18th cents., fitted to the upper torso, and having long sleeves, buttons down the front, and a vented skirt extending to the thighs. Also *jump-coat*. M17. **2** *sing.* & (usu.) in *pl.* A kind of woman's underbodice, usu. fitted to the bust, and worn instead of stays, esp. in the 18th cent. M17.

jump /dʒʌmp/ *v.* E16. [Prob. imit. of the sound of feet coming to the ground: cf. BUMP *v.*[1], THUMP *v.*] **1** *v.i.* Of an inanimate object: be moved or thrown up with a sudden jerk. E16. **2** *v.i.* **a** Spring from the ground or other base by flexion and sudden muscular extension of the legs or (in some animals) some other part of the body; throw oneself upward, forward, backward, or downward, from a base; leap, bound; *spec.* leap with both feet, as opp. to hopping. M16. **b** Move suddenly and quickly, as with a leap, bound, spring, etc. E18. **c** Move with an involuntary jerk as the result of excitement, shock, etc.; start. E18. **d** (Of jazz or similar music) have a strong or exciting rhythm; (of a place, esp. a place of entertainment) be full of activity, excitement, or enjoyment. *colloq.* (orig. *US*). M20. **3** *v.i.* Agree completely, coincide, tally. (Foll. by *together, with.*) M16. **4** *v.i.* **a** Pass abruptly from one thing, idea, state, etc., to another, omitting intermediate stages; rise suddenly in position, amount, price, value, etc. L16. **b** Come *to* or arrive *at* (a conclusion etc.) precipitately, without examining the premisses. E18. **5a** *v.t.* Leap or spring over or across (an obstacle etc.). L16. **b** Get on (a ship, a train, etc.), esp. dangerously or illegally by jumping (*US*). Also, leave (a place or thing) suddenly. L19. **c** Of a thing: spring off, leave (the course, track, rail, etc.). L19. **d** *v.i.* & *t. Contract Bridge.* Raise (a bid) higher than necessary in the suit concerned. E20. †**6** *v.t.* Hastily agree upon or effect (a marriage). L16–E17. **7** *v.t.* Effect or do as with a jump. Now *rare*. E17. †**8** *v.t.* Hazard, risk. *rare* (Shakes.). Only in E17. **9** *v.t.* Skip over, ignore, pass by, evade. M18. **b** Fail to stop at (a red traffic light); *gen.* anticipate permission or a signal to act. M20. **10** *v.t.* **a** Pounce on or attack (a person) unexpectedly; rob, cheat. L18. **b** Take summary possession of (a piece of land) after alleged abandonment or forfeiture by the former occupant. Chiefly *N. Amer.* M19. **11** *v.t.* **a** Cause to jump; drive suddenly forward; startle. E19. **b** Cause (game) to start from cover; spring. M19. **c** Sauté. Chiefly as *jumped* ppl a. L19. **12** *v.t.* Flatten, or shorten and thicken the end of (an iron rail or bar) by endwise blows. M19. **b** Join (rails etc.) end on end, *spec.* by welding the flattened ends together. M19. **13** *v.t. Quarrying.* Drill by means of a jumper. M19.

1 H. CAINE The sea was beginning to jump. C. PHILLIPS The car jumped forward, the man obviously having some trouble with the clutch. **2a** R. K. NARAYAN Perhaps I can jump into the sea. SLOAN WILSON They had jumped from the planes . . at nightfall . . dropped behind the German lines. W. WHARTON I jump up and down, keep the heart muscles pumping. MERLE COLLINS She jumped across the drain. **b** E. WELTY He jumped nimbly to his feet and ran out of the garden. JAN MORRIS Hastily Yasar . . jumped out of the car to open the back door. R. INGALLS Joe jumped up from his seat. **c** J. MCDOUGALL He often jumped with fright when his wife came up behind him. **3** *Guardian* One passage in Mr. Morley's speech jumps with a letter we print today. **4a** TOLKIEN Treebeard often went back to some earlier point, or jumped forward asking questions about later events. *London Daily News* Profits jumped from £737,000 to £1 million in 1986. *Medway Extra* The waiting list . . has jumped . . from 2,187 to 3,202. **b** P. KAVANAGH He was inclined to jump to conclusions sometimes, to act on impulse. **5a** J. DICKEY Lewis went forward from me and jumped the gully. M. CHABON An enormous BMW Motorcycle . . jumped the curb. **b** *Video for You* Desperate escaped prisoners jump passing train. M. MOORCOCK Patsy jumped the first bus he saw going East. *City Limits* Sylvan planned to jump camp and slope off into New York. **9** G. BORDMAN Sam and Steve jump their . . bill. **b** J. PORTER She jumped a red light . . it was a damned silly place to have traffic lights. *Motor Cycle News* I was left at the beginning because they jumped the start but I went well. **10a** J. W. SCHULTZ I was always expecting the war party to jump us. M. PIERCY 'Whose dog was it?' 'I was just minding my own business and the damn thing jumped me.' **11a** J. KELMAN He messed a shot badly . . actually jumped the cueball off the table.

Phrases, & with advs. & preps. in specialized senses: **go (and) jump in the lake** *colloq.* = *jump in the lake* below. **jump at** *colloq.* spring as a predator; *fig.* eagerly accept or take advantage of. *jump bail*: see BAIL *n.*[1] **jump down a person's throat** *colloq.* berate, reprimand, or contradict a person fiercely. **jump for joy** *fig.* be joyfully excited. **jump in the lake** *colloq.* (usu. in *imper.*) go away and stop being a nuisance. *jump Jim Crow*: see JIM CROW *n.* 1a. **jump on** *colloq.* attack or criticize severely and without warning. *jump on the bandwagon*: see *bandwagon* s.v. BAND *n.*[3] **jump out of one's skin** be extremely startled. **jump rope** *N. Amer.* skip with a skipping-rope. *jump salty*: see SALTY *a.*[1] 5. **jump ship** (of a seaman) leave his ship before the expiry of his contract; *gen.* desert. *jump the gun*: see GUN *n.* **jump the queue** move ahead of one's place in a queue of people; *fig.* take unfair precedence over others. *jump through the hoops*: see HOOP *n.*[1] **jump to** *colloq.* accept or obey readily. **jump to it** take prompt and energetic action. **jump to the eyes** be noticed or noticeable. **jump up** (*a*) rise quickly to a standing position; (*b*) dance the jump-up.

Comb.: **jump-about** = *Jack-jump-about* s.v. JACK *n.*[1]; **jump ball** *Basketball* a ball thrown vertically between two opposing players by the referee; **jump-cut** *Cinemat.* & *Television* (*a*) the excision of part of a shot in order to break its continuity of action and time; (*b*) the abrupt transition from one scene to another which is discontinuous in time; **jumped-up** *a.* (*colloq.*) newly or suddenly risen in status or importance, upstart; conceited, presumptuously arrogant; **jump-jet** a jet aircraft which can take off and land vertically; **jump jockey** a jockey who rides in steeplechases; **jump-lead** either of a pair of leads for conveying electric charge from one car battery to another during a jump-start; **jump-off** (*a*) *US colloq.* a place from which a person must jump; (*b*) *US slang* the start of a military operation; (*c*) *Showjumping* an additional round to resolve a tie; **jump-rock** any of several freshwater sucker fishes of the genus *Moxostoma*, of the southern US; **jump-rope** (chiefly *N. Amer.*) a skipping-rope; **jump-seat** (*a*) (a carriage equipped with) a movable carriage-seat; (*b*) a folding seat in a motor car; **jump shot** (*a*) (*Billiards, Snooker*, etc.) a shot which causes the cue-ball to jump over another ball; (*b*) *Basketball* a throw at the net taken with both feet off the ground; **jump spark** a spark produced by a potential difference applied to two electrical conductors separated by a narrow gap; usu. *attrib.*, designating devices or methods employing this; **jump-start** *v.* & *n.* (*a*) *v.t.* start (a vehicle) using the charge from another vehicle's battery by means of jump-leads; (*b*) *n.* an act of jump-starting a vehicle; **jump take-off** *Aeronaut.* a vertical take-off; **jump turn** *Skiing* a turn made while jumping; **jump-up** (*a*) a jump in an upward direction; (*b*) *Austral.* an escarpment; (*c*) an informal West Indian dance; **jump-weld** a weld effected by hammering together the heated ends of two pieces of metal.

jumpable *a.* E19.

jump /dʒʌmp/ *adv.* & *a.* Now *rare* or *obs.* M16. [Rel. to JUMP *v.*] †**A** *adv.* With exact coincidence or agreement; exactly, precisely.

M16–M17. **B** *adj.* Coinciding, exactly agreeing; even; exact, precise. L16.

jumped /dʒʌmpt/ *ppl a.* M19. [f. JUMP *v.* + -ED[1].] That has jumped; *spec.* (*a*) (foll. by *up*) newly or suddenly risen in status or importance; conceited, presumptuously arrogant. (*b*) sautéed.

a A. BURGESS He was wealthy but in the manner of the jumped-up working class, unhealthily frugal. M. FLANAGAN He was clearly pleased with himself and very jumped-up about the show.

jumper /ˈdʒʌmpə/ *n.*[1] E17. [f. JUMP *v.* + -ER[1].] **1** A person who or animal, fish, etc., which jumps or leaps. E17. **b** A ticket-inspector, a ticket-collector. *slang.* E20. **c** *Basketball.* (A player of) a jump ball or jump-shot. M20. **2a** *Quarrying.* A heavy drill worked either by hand or by means of a hammer, used to make blasting-holes in rock etc. M18. **b** A mechanism controlling the starwheel of a repeating clock. M18. **c** *Electr.* A wire used to cut out an instrument or part of a circuit, or to temporarily close a gap in a circuit. M18. **3** *Hist.* (**J-**.) A member of a Methodist sect found in Wales in the 18th cent. whose religious worship was characterized by jumping and dancing. L18. **4** An adult or larval insect characterized by jumping. L18. **b** In full *jumper ant.* An Australian stinging ant of the genus *Myrmecia.* E20. **5** A rough sledge for use on broken or difficult ground. *N. Amer.* E19. **6** A person who summarily takes possession of a piece of land (see JUMP *v.* 10b). Chiefly *N. Amer.* M19. **7** *Naut.* A chain or wire stay from the outer end of the jib-boom to the dolphin-striker in a square-rigged ship. L19.

1 *high-jumper, long-jumper,* etc.

Comb.: *jumper ant*: see sense 4b above; **jumper cable** a jump-lead; **jumper stay** *Naut.* a truss stay from the root of the lower cross-stress to the fore side of the masthead; **jumper strut** a short metal or wooden strut canted forward to add support to the long mast of a Bermuda-rigged yacht; **jumper-wire** = *jumping-wire* s.v. JUMPING *vbl n.*

jumperism *n.* (*Hist.*) the principles of the Methodist Jumpers E19.

jumper /ˈdʒʌmpə/ *n.*[2] M19. [Prob. f. JUMP *n.*[2] + -ER[1].] **1** *Hist.* A loose outer jacket or shirt reaching to the hips, made of canvas, serge, coarse linen, etc., and worn esp. by sailors etc. M19. **2** A knitted pullover, a jersey. Also, a loose-fitting blouse worn over a skirt. E20. **3** In *pl.* A one-piece garment, worn esp. by children; rompers. E20. **4** A pinafore dress. Also *jumper dress. N. Amer.* M20.

Comb.: *jumper dress*: see sense 4 above. **jumper suit** (*a*) a pinafore dress; (*b*) a woman's suit consisting of a jumper and skirt made of the same material, usu. wool.

jumper /ˈdʒʌmpə/ *v.t.* E19. [f. JUMPER *n.*[1]] **1** *Quarrying.* Blast or bore (a hole) with a jumper. E19. **2** *Electr.* Connect by means of a jumper. E20.

jumping /ˈdʒʌmpɪŋ/ *vbl n.* M16. [f. JUMP *v.* + -ING[1].] The action of JUMP *v.*

high-jumping, long-jumping, etc.

Comb. & *phrases*: **jumping-board**, **jumping-off board** a springboard; **jumping-off ground**, **jumping-off place** (*a*) *colloq.* a place at which a person alights at the end of a journey, *spec.* (*N. Amer.*) a place regarded as being the furthest limit of civilization or settlement; (*b*) a place from which a person moves into a region beyond; **jumping-pole** a pole used in jumping long distances or in pole-vaulting; **jumping-wire** a serrated wire running from the stemhead of a submarine to the forward edge of the bridge casing and from the after edge to the stern, for cutting a way through defensive nets when submerged.

jumping /ˈdʒʌmpɪŋ/ *ppl a.* M16. [f. as prec. + -ING[2].] That jumps.

jumping bean (*a*) a tropical American plant seed (esp. of *Sebastiania pavoniana*, family Euphorbiaceae) containing a moth larva whose movements cause the seed to jump about; (*b*) a toy consisting of a small bean-shaped capsule containing a weight which causes it to move unaided down a sloping surface. **jumping deer** *N. Amer.* (*a*) a pronghorn; (*b*) a mule deer. **jumping hare** = *spring hare* s.v. SPRING *n.*[1] **jumping jack** (*a*) a toy figure of a man, esp. with movable limbs attached to strings; (*b*) a small firework producing repeated explosions. **jumping louse** = *flea-louse* s.v. FLEA *n.* **jumping mouse** (*a*) any of several mouselike rodents of the Palaearctic family Zapodidae, having long hind feet; (*b*) = *jumping rat* below. **jumping rat** any rodent of the jerboa family Dipodidae. **jumping seed** = *jumping bean* (a) above. **jumping shrew** = ELEPHANT *shrew.* **jumping spider** any of various small hairy spiders (*spec.* of the family Salticidae) which do not spin webs but catch their prey by leaping on it.

jumpingly *adv.* M16.

jumpy /ˈdʒʌmpi/ *a.* M19. [f. JUMP *n.*[1] + -Y[1].] **1** Characterized by sudden movements from one thing or state to another. M19. **2** Characterized by sudden involuntary movements caused by nervous excitement; nervous, easily startled. L19.

1 J. O'FAOLAIN She wanted to see what happened next but the image had gone jumpy. J. C. OATES His mind is too jumpy for sleep. 2 R. P. JHABVALA She got more nervous, positively jumpy and crazy. M. ANGELOU We left for the elevators . . jumpy with excitement.

jumpily *adv.* L20. **jumpiness** *n.* L19.

jun /dʒʌn/ *n.* Also **jeon** (see below), (*Hist.*) **chon** /tʃɒn/. Pl. same. M20. [Korean.] A monetary unit of Korea (now the jun in North Korea, the jeon in South Korea), equal to one-hundredth of a won.

junco /ˈdʒʌŋkəʊ/ *n.* Pl. **-o(e)s.** E18. [Sp. f. L *juncus* rush.] †**1** The reed bunting, *Emberiza schoeniclus.* Only in E18. **2** Any of several buntings of N. and Central America of the genus *Junco*; a snow sparrow. L19.

junction /ˈdʒʌŋ(k)ʃ(ə)n/ *n.* & *v.* E18. [L *junctio(n-)*, f. *junct-* pa. ppl stem of *jungere* JOIN *v.*: see -ION.] **A** *n.* **1** The action of joining (physically or immaterially); the fact of being joined; union, combination. E18. **2** In full *junction canal, line, railway.* A canal or railway forming a connection between two other lines or with a centre of commerce. Chiefly in proper names. Now *rare.* L18. **3** The point or place at which two things join or are joined, a meeting-place; *spec.* the place or station on a railway where lines meet and unite (freq. in proper names). M19. **b** *Electronics.* A transition zone in a semiconductor between two regions of different conductivity type (usually *n*-type and *p*-type). M20.

1 T. JEFFERSON The latter effected a junction . . with another part of their fleet. M. ARNOLD The junction of a talent for abstruse reasoning with much literary inexperience. 2 *Grand Junction Canal, Lancaster and Preston Junction,* etc. 3 SLOAN WILSON He took a wrong turn at a junction of corridors. D. ATTENBOROUGH The builders . . move these living tubes of glue . . across the leaf junction until the two edges are joined. P. THEROUX At . . a convenient railway junction . . I changed for the Bournemouth train. *Clapham Junction, Willesden Junction,* etc. *T-junction* etc.

Comb.: **junction-box** a closed rigid box or casing used to enclose and protect junctions of electric wires or cables; **junction diode**, **junction rectifier** *Electronics* a diode consisting essentially of a piece of semiconductor containing a rectifying junction between differently doped regions; **junction transistor** *Electronics* a transistor consisting essentially of a piece of semiconductor containing two (or more) junctions that divide it into three (or more) differently doped regions.

B *v.i.* Form a junction, join. Foll. by *with, on to.* Chiefly *Austral.* & *NZ.* E20.

junctional *a.* L19.

juncture /ˈdʒʌŋ(k)tʃə/ *n.* LME. [L *junctura* joint, f. *junct-*: see prec., -URE.] **1** The place at which, or structure by which, two things are joined; a joint, a junction. LME. †**b** A joint of the body. LME–E18. **c** *Ling.* The transition between two speech segments or between an utterance and (potential) preceding or following silence; the phonetic feature that marks such a transition. M20. **2** The action of joining together; the condition of being joined together; joining, junction. LME. **3** A convergence or concurrence of events or circumstances; a particular (esp. critical) posture of affairs or point in time. M17. **4** Something that connects two things; a connecting link; a means of connection or union. *rare.* L17.

1 B. T. BRADFORD The Blackamoor Inn, which was the juncture of several roads. c *open juncture*: see OPEN *a. terminal juncture*: see TERMINAL *a.* 2 F. W. L. ADAMS This . . Khalif . . anticipated the Suez Canal by his juncture of the Nile and the Red Sea. 3 H. GREEN How idiotic to start an illness at this juncture when she would get small help. F. FITZGERALD The United States came to Vietnam at a critical juncture of Vietnamese history.

junctural *a.* (chiefly *Ling.*) M20. **juncturally** *adv.* (chiefly *Ling.*) M20.

jundy /ˈdʒʌndi/ *v.* & *n. Sc.* Also (earlier) †**joundy.** L17. [Origin unkn.] **A** *v.t.* & *i.* Push with the elbow or shoulder; jog, jostle. L17. **B** *n.* **1** A push with the elbow; a jog, a shove. M18. **2** *fig.* A steady course, a jog-trot. L19.

June /dʒuːn/ *n.* ME. [(O)Fr. *juin* f. L *Junius* (sc. *mensis* month) var. of *Junonius* sacred to the goddess Juno.] The sixth month of the year in the Gregorian calendar, in which the summer solstice occurs in the northern hemisphere.

Comb.: **Juneberry** (the fruit of) any of several N. American shrubs of the genus *Amelanchier*, of the rose family, with showy white flowers; **June bug** any of various beetles which appear in June, as (*a*) a scarab of the genus *Phyllophaga*, of the northern US, (*b*) (more fully *green June bug*) a scarab, *Cotinus nitida*, of the southern US; **June grass** *N. Amer.* common meadow-grass, *Poa pratensis.*

june /dʒuːn/ *v.i. US colloq.* & *dial.* M19. [App. f. the n.] Move in a lively fashion, hurry; be restless or aimless; wander *around.*

Junggrammatiker /ˈjʊŋgramatɪkə/ *n.pl.* E20. [G = young grammarians.] *Ling.* The members of a late 19th-cent. school of historical linguists who held that phonetic changes (sound laws) operate without exceptions.

Jungian /ˈjʊŋɪən/ *a.* & *n.* M20. [f. *Jung* (see below) + -IAN.] **A** *adj.* Of or pertaining to Carl Gustav Jung (1875–1961), the Swiss leader of the school of analytic psychology, or his beliefs, as in the collective unconscious. M20. **B** *n.* A follower or adherent of Jung. M20.

Jungianism *n.* the beliefs or psychological system of Jung M20.

jungle /ˈdʒʌŋg(ə)l/ *n.* L18. [Hind. *jaṅgal*, f. Skt *jāṅgala* rough and arid (of terrain).] **1** Orig. in the Indian subcontinent, later in other (esp. tropical) regions: (an area of) uncultivated land overgrown with underwood, long grass, or tangled vegetation, esp. as the home of wild animals; the luxuriant and often almost impenetrable vegetation covering such a tract. L18. **2** *transf.* & *fig.* A wild tangled mass; a place of bewildering complexity or confusion. Now freq., a place where the 'law of the jungle' prevails, a scene of ruthless competition, struggle, or exploitation, (freq. w. specifying wd). M19. **b** A camp for hoboes etc. *N. Amer. slang.* E20.

1 W. BRONK They slashed / the jungle and burned it and planted . . corn. *law of the jungle*: see LAW *n.*[1] 2 S. LEACOCK Our potatoes are buried in a jungle of autumn burdocks. *Sunday Times* Namier . . fitted especially ill in the academic jungle.

Comb.: **jungle-bashing** *slang* movement through a jungle, esp. by soldiers; **jungle bunny** *slang* (*derog.* & usu. considered *racially offensive*) a Black person; **jungle cat** a small wild cat, *Felis chaus*, of forest and scrubland in Indochina and Sri Lanka (Ceylon); **jungle cock** a male jungle fowl; **jungle-fever** malaria; **jungle fowl** (*a*) any of several birds of the Far Eastern genus *Gallus*, closely related to pheasants (*red jungle fowl*: see RED *a.*); (*b*) *Austral.* a megapode; **jungle green** (of) a dark green colour; **jungle gym** a climbing frame for a children's playground; **jungle hen** a female jungle fowl; **jungle juice** *slang* alcoholic liquor, esp. when very powerful or prepared illicitly or under primitive conditions; **jungle law** = *law of the jungle* s.v. LAW *n.*[1]; **jungle-rice** a kind of millet, *Echinochloa colona*, found as a weed of rice-fields in tropical countries; **jungle rot** *slang* any skin disorder acquired in humid tropical regions.

jungle /ˈdʒʌŋg(ə)l/ *v.* M19. [f. the n.] **1** *v.t.* Drive *out* by the influence of the jungle. *rare.* M19. **2** *v.i.* Prepare a meal at or live together in a hoboes' camp. Usu. foll. by *up. US slang.* E20.

jungled /ˈdʒʌŋg(ə)ld/ *a.* M19. [f. JUNGLE *n.* + -ED[2].] Covered with jungle or wild undergrowth.

jungly /ˈdʒʌŋgli/ *a.* In sense 2 also **jungli.** E19. [f. JUNGLE *n.* + -Y[1]. Var. after -I[2]: cf. also Hind. *jaṅglī*, f. as JUNGLE *n.*] **1** Of the nature of, characterized by, or resembling jungle; having much jungle. E19. 2 Inhabiting a jungle. Now *rare*. L19.

Junian /ˈdʒuːnɪən/ *a.* E19. [f. *Junius* (see below) + -AN.] 1 Of or pertaining to the philologist and antiquary Francis Junius (1589–1677). E19. 2 Of or pertaining to the 'Letters of Junius', a series of vituperative letters which appeared in the *Public Advertiser*, 1768–72, attacking various prominent Tory politicians. L19.

junior /ˈdʒuːnɪə/ *a.* & *n.* ME. [L (for *juvenior*) compar. of *juvenis* young: see -IOR. Cf. SENIOR.] A *adj.* 1 After a person's name: that is the younger of two bearing the same name in a family, esp. a son of the same name as his father. Also (now *rare*) = MINOR *a.* 1b. ME. 2 Of a thing or (now *rare*) a person: of later rise or appearance in history, of later date; more modern. (Foll. by *to*). L16. 3†a Belonging to youth or earlier life; youthful, juvenile. E17–L18. b Intended for children or young people. Also, smaller than the normal size. M19. 4 Of lesser age or standing or more recent appointment, of lower position on a scale, (foll. by *to*). In N. American colleges and schools and Scottish universities: belonging to the second last year of a course (in Scotland *spec.* of an honours degree course). M18.

1 DICKENS Snawley junior.. I'll warm you with a severe thrashing. 2 R. BENTLEY The Cretan civilization was apparently junior to that of the Nile valley. 3b *Practical Motorist* A 'junior' frame saw is a useful back-up. 4 G. GREENE I had published a first novel, and I found myself a junior guest.. at a great publisher's do. *Sunday Express* The most junior boy in the house had to do a solo spot.

Special collocations: **junior barrister** = sense B.2 below. **junior college** *US*: offering a two-year course, esp. in preparation for completion at a senior college. **junior combination room** a junior common-room at Cambridge University. **junior common-room** (at certain universities) a common-room for undergraduates, the undergraduates entitled to use a common-room. **junior high school** *N. Amer.*: intermediate between elementary school and high school. *junior* LIGHTWEIGHT. *junior* MIDDLEWEIGHT. **junior miss** (orig. *US*) a young teenage girl. *junior* OPTIME. **junior school** the lower forms in some fee-paying schools; *Hist.* a State school for children in the younger age-range, roughly between 7 and 11. *junior* WELTERWEIGHT.

B *n.* 1 A person who is younger than or junior to another (freq. after possess.). More generally (chiefly *US*), a child, *esp.* a young boy (freq. as a form of address). M16. 2 A barrister who has not taken silk. M19.

1 B. NEIL His mother had run off with a man nine years her junior. *Which?* Be prepared to pay more for .. the top stylist than .. for the less experienced junior.

juniorate *n.* in the Society of Jesus, a two-year course for junior members preparatory to entering the priesthood, a seminary for those taking this course M19. **juniorship** *n.* the condition of a junior, juniority L18.

juniority /dʒuːnɪˈɒrɪti/ *n.* L16. [f. JUNIOR *a.* + -ITY, after earlier *seniority*.] The state or condition of being junior (in age, appointment, rank, etc.).

juniper /ˈdʒuːnɪpə/ *n.* LME. [L *juniperus*.] 1 Any of various coniferous evergreen shrubs and trees of the genus *Juniperus*, *esp.* one of the common European species *J. communis*, a hardy spreading shrub or low tree, which has bluish-black or purple pungent-tasting berries and yields juniper oil. Also *juniper tree*. LME. b Any of various coniferous trees of other genera, *esp.* the American larch or hackmatack, *Larix laricina*, and the white cedar, *Chamaecyparis thyoides*, of the southern US. M18. 2 In biblical translations: a desert plant, *Retama raetam*, a leguminous shrub with rushlike branches. LME.

Comb. & *phrases*: **juniper oil, oil of juniper** a volatile carminative oil from juniper cones, used medicinally and in flavouring gin.

junk /dʒʌŋk/ *n.*[1] LME. [OFr. *junc*, (also mod.) *jonc*, f. L *juncus*.] †1 A rush (plant). LME–E16. 2 *Surg.* An old form of splint consisting of rigid material (orig. rushes or reeds) inside a cloth wrapping. E17.

junk /dʒʌŋk/ *n.*[2] LME. [Origin unkn.] 1 Chiefly *Naut.* †a An old or inferior cable or rope. Usu. *old junk*. LME–M18. b Old cable or rope, cut up into short lengths and used for making oakum etc. M17. c Salt meat (formerly used as food on long voyages), compared to pieces of old rope. Also *salt junk*. M18. 2 A piece or lump of something, a chunk. E18. 3 The mass of thick oily cellular tissue beneath the case and nostrils of a sperm whale, containing spermaceti. M19. 4 Any discarded or waste material that can be put to some use. Now usu., second-hand or discarded articles of little or no use or value; rubbish. M19. 5 A narcotic drug, *esp.* heroin; narcotic drugs collectively. *slang* (orig. *US*). E20. 6 = *junk food* below. L20.

1c BETTY SMITH She and her brother, .. like other Brooklyn kids, collected rags, paper, metal, rubber, and other junk. D. FRANCIS The junk I sold to secondhand shops and the best bits to dealers. 6 P. THEROUX Eating junk, Guppy Cola and jelly sandwiches. 2 H. LAWSON The remains—a meal of junk of badly-hacked bread, a basin of dripping.

Comb.: **junk art** three-dimensional art made from discarded material; **junk bond** *Finance* a high-yielding high-risk security, *esp.* one issued to finance a takeover; **junk-bottle** *US* a thick strong bottle of green or black glass; **junk-dealer** *US* a marine-store dealer; **junk food** food that appeals to popular (esp. juvenile) taste but has little nutritional value; **junk jewellery** = COSTUME *jewellery*; **junk mail** circulars, advertisements, etc., sent by post to a large number of addresses; **junkman** *n.*[1] a dealer in marine stores or second-hand goods; **junk playground** an adventure playground using waste materials; **junk sculpture** = *junk art* above; **junk shop** (*a*) a marine store; (*b*) a shop dealing in miscellaneous cheap second-hand goods or (*derog.*) antiques.

junk /dʒʌŋk/ *n.*[3] M16. [Port. *junco* or Fr. †*juncque* (now *jonque*), f. Malay *jong*, partly also f. Du. *jonk*.] A flat-bottomed type of sailing vessel used in the China seas, with a square prow, prominent stem, full stern, suspended rudder, and lugsails.

Comb.: **junkman** *n.*[2] a member of the crew of a junk.

junk /dʒʌŋk/ *v.t.* L18. [f. JUNK *n.*[2]] 1 Cut into chunks; cut *off* in a lump. L18. 2 Treat as junk or rubbish; discard, abandon. E20.

2 F. FORSYTH He .. junked the can in the trash basket. R. COOVER It's time we junked the whole beastly business. *Combat Handguns* It .. had enough shortcomings to warrant junking the whole idea.

junker /ˈjʊŋkə/ *n.*[1] *obs.* exc. *Hist.* M16. [G, earlier *Junkher(r*, f. MHG *junc* YOUNG *a.* + *herre* (mod. *Herr*) lord, HERR: cf. YOUNKER.] A young German noble; *spec.* a member of the reactionary party of the Prussian aristocracy who aimed to maintain the exclusive privileges of their class; a narrow-minded, overbearing (younger) member of the German aristocracy.

junkerdom *n.* the body or world of junkers; the condition or character of a junker: L19.

junker /ˈdʒʌŋkə/ *n.*[2] *US slang.* E20. [f. JUNK *n.*[2] + -ER[1].] A drug addict; a drug-peddler.

junker *n.*[3] var. of JINKER *n.*[2]

junket /ˈdʒʌŋkɪt/ *n.* & *v.* LME. [(O)Fr. *jonquette*, f. *jonc* rush f. L *juncus*.] A *n.* 1 A basket (orig. made of rushes); *esp.* one for fish. Long *obs.* exc. *dial.* LME. 2 A cream cheese or other preparation of cream (orig. made in a rush basket or served on a rush mat). Now *spec.* a dish consisting of curds sweetened and flavoured, freq. served with fruit or cream. LME. 3 Any dainty sweet, cake, or confection. *obs.* exc. *dial.* M16. 4 A feast, a banquet; a festive gathering. Now also, a picnic-party, a pleasure excursion with eating and drinking; *spec.* (*N. Amer.*) an official's tour at public expense. M16.

4 T. ROETHKE I .. was there last month, as part of a lecture-reading junket.

B *v.i.* Hold or take part in a banquet, feast, or other festive gathering; (chiefly *N. Amer.*) join in a picnic, go on a pleasure excursion. M16.

junke'teer *n.* (orig. *US*) = JUNKETER M20. **junketer** *n.* a person who feasts or takes part in a junketing E19. **junketing** *n.* (*a*) the action of the vb; (*b*) a feast, a banquet, a festive gathering; a picnic: M16.

junkie /ˈdʒʌŋki/ *n.* & *a.* *slang* (orig. *US*). Also (esp. as adj.) **junky**. E20. [f. JUNK *n.*[2] + -IE, -Y[6].] A *n.* A drug addict; *occas.* a drug-peddler. E20.

B *attrib.* or as *adj.* That is a drug addict; of a drug addict. M20.

W. S. BURROUGHS He spoke in his dead, junkie whisper.

junky *n.* & *a.*[1] see JUNKIE.

junky /ˈdʒʌŋki/ *a.*[2] M20. [f. JUNK *n.*[2] + -Y[1].] Worthless, valueless, rubbishy.

Juno /ˈdʒuːnəʊ/ *n.* E17. [L *Juno(n-)*, a Roman god, wife of Jupiter and goddess of marriage and childbirth.] 1 A woman of stately beauty. E17. 2 A jealous wife. Now *rare*. E17.

¶ See also *bird of Juno* s.v. BIRD *n.*

Ju'nonian *a.* of or pertaining to Juno; Junoesque: L18.

Junoesque /dʒuːnəʊˈɛsk/ *a.* M19. [f. as prec. + -ESQUE.] Of a woman: beautiful and stately.

junta /ˈdʒʌntə, ˈhʊ-/ *n.* E17. [Sp., Port. *junta* (whence Fr. *junte*) f. It. *giunta* f. Proto-Romance use as n. of L *juncta* fem. pa. pple of *jungere* JOIN *v.*] 1 A Spanish or Italian deliberative or administrative council or committee. E17. 2 *gen.* A body of people combined for a common (esp. political) purpose; a self-elected committee or council, a cabal. Now freq. *spec.*, a political or military clique or faction taking power after a revolution or *coup d'état*. E18.

junto /ˈdʒʌntəʊ/ *n.* Pl. **-os**. E17. [Alt. of JUNTA after Sp. ns. in *-o*.] 1 = JUNTA 2. E17. †2 = JUNTA 1. E–M18.

jupati /ˈdʒuːpəti/ *n.* M19. [Port. f. Tupi *yupáti*.] A Brazilian palm, *Raphia taedigera*, with large leaves whose long stalks are used locally as a building material.

jupe /dʒuːp; *foreign* ʒyp (*pl. same*)/ *n.* ME. [(O)Fr. f. Arab. JUBBA.] 1 A man's loose jacket, tunic, or jerkin. Now only *Sc.* ME. †2 A woman's jacket, gown, or bodice. In *pl.* also, a kind of bodice or stays. *Sc.* E18–E20. 3 A woman's skirt. E19.

Jupiter /ˈdʒuːpɪtə/ *n.* ME. [L *Juppiter, Jupiter*, f. *Jovis-pater* lit. 'Jove Father', corresp. to Skt *dyaus pitr* lit. 'heaven father': see JOVE.] 1 The chief of the gods of the ancient Romans, corresponding to the Greek Zeus, orig. a sky-god, associated with lightning and the thunderbolt. ME. 2 The fifth planet in order of distance from the sun, and the largest planet in the solar system, whose orbit lies between those of Mars and Saturn. ME. †3 *Alch.* The metal tin. LME–M18. 4 *Her.* The tincture azure in the fanciful blazon of arms of sovereign princes. *obs.* exc. *Hist.* L16.

1 **by Jupiter** *literary*: used as an asseveration, or expr. surprise or approval. **Jupiter's beard** (*a*) a southern European evergreen leguminous shrub, *Anthyllis barba-Jovis*; (*b*) the houseleek, *Sempervivum tectorum*. **Jupiter's distaff** a yellow-flowered sage, *Salvia glutinosa*.

jupon /ˈdʒuːpɒn, dʒuːˈpɒn/ *n.* LME. [OFr. *juppon*, (also mod.) *jupon*, f. JUPE: see -OON. Cf. GIPON.] *Hist.* A close-fitting tunic or doublet; *esp.* one worn under a hauberk, sometimes of thick material and padded Also, a sleeveless surcoat worn outside armour, of rich material and emblazoned with arms.

Jura /ˈdʒʊərə/ *n.* & *a.* E19. [A range of mountains on the border between France and Switzerland.] *Geol.* A *n.* Jurassic rocks or strata; the Jurassic system. E19. B *attrib.* or as *adj.* = JURASSIC *a.* M19.

jural /ˈdʒʊər(ə)l/ *a.* M17. [f. L *jur-*, *jus* right, law + -AL[1].] 1 Of or relating to law or its administration; legal. M17. 2 *Philos.* Of or pertaining to rights and obligations. M19.

jurally *adv.* with reference to law, or to rights and obligations L19.

jurament /ˈdʒʊərəm(ə)nt/ *n.* L15. [Late L *juramentum*, f. *jurare* swear: see -MENT.] 1 An oath. Long *rare*. L15. 2 At Oxford University, a logical disputation. Chiefly in *do juraments*, attend one logical disputation a term, as part of the prescribed BA course. *obs.* exc. *Hist.* L15.

jurant /ˈdʒʊər(ə)nt/ *n.* & *a.* L16. [L. *jurant-* pres. ppl stem of *jurare* swear: see -ANT[1].] A *n.* A person who takes an oath; *spec.* (*Sc. Hist.*) a person who took the oath of allegiance to William and Mary or their successors (opp. NONJURANT *n.*). L16. B *adj.* Taking an oath; *spec.* (*Sc. Hist.*) taking the oath of allegiance to

William and Mary or their successors (opp. NONJURANT *a.*). E18.

Jurassic /dʒʊˈrasɪk/ *a.* & *n.* M19. [Fr. *Jurassique*, f. JURA: see -IC. Cf. *Liassic, Triassic.*] *Geol.* A *adj.* Designating or pertaining to the second period of the Mesozoic era, following the Triassic and preceding the Cretaceous, characterized by the prevalence of oolitic limestone, the predominance of reptiles, and evidence of the first birds. M19. B *n.* The Jurassic period; the system of rocks dating from this time. M19.

jurat /ˈdʒʊərat/ *n.*[1] LME. [med.L *juratus* lit. 'sworn man', use as n. of masc. pa. pple of L *jurare* swear: see -AT[1].] 1 A person who has taken an oath or who performs some duty on oath; *spec.* one sworn to give information and in other ways assist the administration of justice. *obs.* exc. *Hist.* LME. 2 A municipal officer (esp. of the Cinque Ports) holding a position similar to that of an alderman. LME. 3 A municipal magistrate in certain French towns. LME. 4 In the Channel Islands: each of a body of magistrates, elected for life, who in conjunction with the Bailiff form the Royal Court for administration of justice. M16.

jurat /ˈdʒʊərat/ *n.*[2] L18. [L *juratum* use as n. of neut. pa. pple of *jurare* swear: see -AT[1].] *Law.* A memorandum as to where, when, and before whom an affidavit is sworn.

jurator /dʒʊˈreɪtə/ *n. rare.* E17. [L *jurator*, f. *jurat-*: see next, -ATOR.] = JURAT *n.*[1] 1.

juratory /ˈdʒʊərət(ə)ri/ *a.* Now *rare.* M16. [Late L *juratorius* confirmed by oath, f. *jurat-* pa. ppl stem of *jurare* swear: see -ORY[2].] Of or pertaining to an oath or oaths; expressed or contained in an oath.

†**jure** *v.t. rare* (Shakes.). Only in L16. [Back-form. f. JUROR.] Make a juror of (a person).

†**juredictiON** *n.* see JURISDICTION.

jure divino /ˌdʒʊəri dɪˈviːnəʊ/ *adv. phr.* L16. [L.] By divine right or authority.

juriballi /jʊərɪˈbali/ *n.* Also **euri-**, **-bali**. M19. [Arawak.] Any of several S. American trees belonging to the family Meliaceae, esp. *Trichilia moschata*; the bark of this tree, formerly used as a febrifuge.

juridic /dʒʊˈrɪdɪk/ *a.* E16. [L *juridicus*, f. *jur-*, *jus* right, law + *-dicus* saying, speaking, f. *dicere* say: see -IC.] 1 Of or pertaining to law, legal. E16. 2 = JURIDICAL 2. L19.

juridical /dʒʊˈrɪdɪk(ə)l/ *a.* E16. [f. as prec. + -AL[1].] 1 Of, pertaining to, or connected with the administration of law or judicial proceedings; legal. E16. 2 Assumed by law to exist. M19.

juridically *adv.* E17.

jurimetrics /dʒʊərɪˈmɛtrɪks/ *n.* M20. [f. L *jur-*, *jus* right, law + -I- + *-metrics*, after *biometrics*, *econometrics*.] The use of scientific methods in the study of legal matters.

jurimetrician /-ˈtrɪʃ(ə)n/, **jurimetricist** *ns.* an expert in or student of jurimetrics M20.

juring /ˈdʒʊərɪŋ/ *a. rare.* E18. [f. JUR(OR + -ING[2].] *Hist.* Taking the oath of allegiance to William and Mary or their successors. Opp. NONJURING.

jurisconsult /ˌdʒʊərɪskənˈsʌlt/ *n.* E17. [L *jurisconsultus*, f. *juris* genit. of *jus* right, law + *consultus* skilled, f. *consult-*: see CONSULT *v.*] A person learned in law, esp. in civil or international law; an expert in jurisprudence.

jurisdiction /dʒʊərɪsˈdɪkʃ(ə)n/ *n.* Also (earlier) †**juredictiON**. ME. [OFr. *juredictiON*, (also mod.), *jurid-* f. L *jurisdictio(n-)*, f. *juris* genit. of *jus* right, law + *dictio(n-)*: see DICTION. Later assim. to L.] 1 Exercise of judicial authority, or of the functions of a judge or legal tribunal; power of administering law or justice. Also, power or authority in general; administration, control. ME. 2 The extent or range of judicial or administrative power; the territory over which such power extends. LME. 3 A judicature; a court, or series of courts, of justice. L17.

1 M. IGNATIEFF The Cabinet had no jurisdiction over military matters. *contentious jurisdiction*: see CONTENTIOUS 2. *summary jurisdiction*: see SUMMARY *a.* 1C. 2 H. MARTINEAU Whether he should not send on this procession, and keep the next . . within his jurisdiction. *peculiar jurisdiction*: see PECULIAR *a.* 3 J. Q. ADAMS The jurisdictions to which resort must be had . . are those of municipal police.

jurisdictional *a.* M17. **jurisdictionally** *adv.* in the way of a judicial decision; with regard to jurisdiction: L17.

jurisdictive /dʒʊərɪsˈdɪktɪv/ *a. rare.* M17. [f. prec., on the analogy of *administration*, *administrative*, etc.] Of or pertaining to jurisdiction.

jurisprude /ˈdʒʊərɪspruːd/ *n.* M20. [Back-form f. next, after PRUDE *n.*] A jurisprudent, *spec.* one who makes a display of learning or who is overly serious.

jurisprudence /dʒʊərɪsˈpruːd(ə)ns/ *n.* E17. [Late L *jurisprudentia*, f. *juris* genit. of *jus* right, law + *prudentia* skill, proficiency.] 1a Knowledge of or skill in law. Now *rare.* E17. b The science which treats of human laws (written or unwritten) in general; the philosophy of law. M18. 2 A system or body of law; a legal system. Also, the decision of a court. M17.

Phrases: MEDICAL *jurisprudence*.

jurisprudent /dʒʊərɪsˈpruːd(ə)nt/ *n.* & *a.* E17. [Fr. †*jurisprudent*, f. *jurisprudence*, f. as prec.: see -ENT.] A *n.* An expert in or student of jurisprudence; a person learned in law; a jurist. E17. B *adj.* Skilled in jurisprudence; having knowledge of the principles of law. M18.

jurisprudential /ˌdʒʊərɪsprʊˈdɛnʃ(ə)l/ *a.* L18. [f. JURISPRUDENCE after *prudence*, *prudential*.] Of or pertaining to jurisprudence.

jurisprudentialist *n.* a writer on or expert in jurisprudence E19. **jurisprudentially** *adv.* with regard to jurisprudence E19.

jurist /ˈdʒʊərɪst/ *n.* L15. [Fr. *juriste* or med.L *jurista*, f. L *jur-*, *jus* right, law: see -IST.] 1 A person who practises in law; a lawyer; a judge. Now *US.* L15. 2 An expert in law; a legal writer. E17. 3 In the ancient British universities: a person studying or taking a degree in law. L17.

ju'ristic(al) *adjs.* of or belonging to a jurist; pertaining to the study of law: M19. **ju'ristically** *adv.* L19.

juror /ˈdʒʊərə/ *n.* LME. [AN *jurour*, OFr. *jureor* (mod. *jureur*) f. L *jurator*, f. *jurat-* pa. ppl stem of *jurare* swear, f. *jur-*, *jus* right, law: see -OR.] 1 A member of a jury in a court of justice or at a coroner's inquest. LME. †2 [From the corrupt conduct formerly attributed to jurors.] A person who makes a false statement about an accused person; a slanderer, an oppressor; a covetous man. LME–M16. 3 Chiefly *Hist.* A person who takes or has taken an oath; a person who swears allegiance to some body or cause. Cf. NONJUROR. L16. 4 Each of a body of people appointed to judge and award prizes in a competition. M19.

1 *common juror, grand juror, special juror*, etc.

jury /ˈdʒʊəri/ *n.* LME. [AN *juree* jury f. OFr. *juree* oath, juridical inquiry f. AL *jurata* use as n. of fem. pa. pple of L *jurare* swear, f. *jur-*, *jus* right, law.] 1 A group of people (orig. all men), usu. twelve in number, sworn to give a verdict on some question or questions submitted to them in a court of justice or at a coroner's inquest, usu. on evidence presented to them, but orig. from their own knowledge. LME. †2 *transf.* A group of twelve; a dozen. L16–M17. 3 *Hist.* Any of several bodies whose functions corresponded in part to those of a British jury. M19. 4 A body of people appointed to judge and award prizes in a competition. M19.

1 S. BUTLER The barrister who is trying to persuade a jury to acquit a prisoner. J. BUCHAN The jury found it a case of suicide while of unsound mind. *common jury*: see COMMON *a.* *coroner's jury*: see CORONER 1. *grand jury*: see GRAND *a.*[1] *hang a jury*: see HANG *v.* **jury de medietate linguae** /diː mɛdɪəˌteɪti ˈlɪŋgwiː, deɪ mɛdɪəˌtɑːti ˈlɪŋgwʌɪ/ [med.L = of a moiety of language] *Hist.* a jury composed half of Englishmen and half of foreigners, for the trial of some aliens. **jury of matrons** *Hist.* a jury of women empanelled to inquire into a case of alleged pregnancy, *esp.* one involving a woman sentenced to death. *petit jury*: see PETIT *a.*[1] *petty jury*: see PETTY *a.* *special jury*: see SPECIAL *a.* *traverse jury*: see TRAVERSE *n.* *trial jury*: see TRIAL *n.* 2 T. FULLER All the Jurie of the Apostles.

Comb.: **jury-box** an enclosed space in which the jury sits in court; **jury-fixer** *US* a person who bribes or otherwise illegally influences a jury or juror; **jury-fixing** *US* bribery of a jury or jurors; **jury-list**: of people liable to be summoned to act as jurors; **juryman** a man serving on a jury, a male juror; **jurywoman** a woman serving on a jury, a female juror.

jury- /ˈdʒʊəri/ *comb. form.* Also as adj. **jury.** E17. [Perh. ult. f. OFr. *ajurie* aid, f. *aju-* pres. stem of *aidier* AID *v.* + *-rie* -RY.] *Naut.* (Serving) as a temporary expedient, makeshift.

jury-leg *joc.* a wooden leg. **jury-mast** a mast put up in place of one that has been broken or carried away. **jury-rig** *v.t.* supply with temporary rigging. **jury-rudder** a contrivance taking the place of a damaged rudder.

jus /dʒʌs/ *adv. colloq.* & *dial.* Also **jus'**. E19. [Repr. a pronunc.] = JUST *adv.*

jus cogens /dʒʌs ˈkəʊdʒɛnz/ *n. phr.* L19. [L = compelling law.] A principle of international law which cannot be set aside by agreement or acquiescence; a peremptory norm of general international law.

jus gentium /dʒʌs ˈdʒɛnʃɪəm/ *n.* M16. [L = law of nations.] = *international law* s.v. INTERNATIONAL *a.*

jus primae noctis /dʒʌs ˌprʌɪmiː ˈnɒktɪs/ *n.* L19. [L = right of the first night.] = *droit du seigneur* s.v. DROIT *n.*[1]

jusqu'au bout /ʒysko bu/ *adv. phr.* E20. [Fr. = up to the end.] To the bitter end; until a conclusive victory has been gained.

†**jussel** *n.* LME–E19. [OFr. = juice, broth, f. L *juscellum* dim. of *jusculum* dim. of *jus* broth, soup: see -EL[2].] *Cookery.* (A) mixed meat stew or mince.

Jussiaean /dʒʌsɪˈiːən/ *a.* Also **Jussieu(e)an** /dʒʌsɪˈjuːən/. E19. [f. Latinized form of *Jussiaeus*, *Jussieu* (see below) + -AN.] *Bot.* (now *Hist.*) Designating or pertaining to the natural system of plant classification devised by the French botanists Bernard de Jussieu (1699–1777) and his nephew Antoine Laurent de Jussieu (1748–1836).

jussion /ˈdʒʌʃ(ə)n/ *n. rare.* L18. [Fr. f. L *jussio(n-)* order, command, f. as next: see -ION.] Order, command.

jussive /ˈdʒʌsɪv/ *a.* & *n.* M19. [f. L *juss-* pa. ppl stem of *jubere* to command + -IVE.] A *adj.* Esp. of a form of a verb: expressing a command or order. M19. B *n.* A verbal form expressing a command. E20.

†**just** *n.* var. of JOUST *n.*

just /dʒʌst/ *a.* LME. [(O)Fr. *juste* f. L *justus*, f. *jus* right, law.] 1 That does what is morally right, righteous; *Theol.* considered or made righteous, esp. by God. *arch.* LME. 2 Impartial in one's dealings; giving every one his or her due; fair, unbiased. LME. †b Faithful or honourable in one's social relations. Foll. by *of*, *to.* E17–E19. 3a In accordance with the principles of moral right or of equity; equitable, fair; (of a reward, punishment, etc.) deserved, merited. LME. b In accordance with the law, lawful, rightful. LME. 4 Having reasonable or adequate grounds; well-founded. LME. 5 Conforming to a particular standard; proper; correct, appropriate. LME. b *Mus.* Set or tuned according to the exact vibration intervals of the notes; non-tempered, natural. Esp. in *just intonation.* M19. †6 Of a measurement, amount, number, etc.: exact, precise; (of an instrument or action) uniform in operation, regular, even. LME–E19. 7 Of an idea, opinion, etc.: right, true, correct. LME. †b Of a copy, description, etc.: exact, accurate. M16–L18. †8 Corresponding exactly, equal; even, level. M16–E19. †9 Full, proper, complete. L16–L18.

1 *the sleep of the just*: see SLEEP *n.* 2 D. FRANCIS He had decided, as he was a just and logical person, that her sex was immaterial. J. C. OATES Twelve jurors who had seemed . . to be just and upright and unprejudiced men. 3a P. B. HINCHLIFF The just cause must be made to succeed. R. DAVIES The destruction of the existing order was the inevitable preamble to any

beginning of the just society. R. C. A. WHITE The criminal process . . will bring them their just deserts. *Sunday Times* A lower starting rate would be socially just (by cutting the tax burden of the poor). b *Liverpool Mercury* Any wrongful act, done intentionally, without just cause or excuse, was a malicious act. 4 E. HAMILTON Alas! My fears were just.

just /dʒʌst/ *v.*[1]*t. rare.* M16. [Aphet. f. ADJUST.] Adjust.

†**just** *v.*[2] var. of JOUST *v.*

just /dʒʌst/ *adv.* LME. [f. the adj.: cf. advb. use of Fr. *juste*. See also JES, JEST *adv.*, JIST, JUS.] 1 Exactly, precisely; actually; closely, close. LME. †2a So as to fit exactly, in a close-fitting way. L15–L17. b With precision, accurately; punctually; correctly. M16–M18. 3a Exactly at the moment spoken of; precisely now or then. L15. b A very little before; with little preceding interval; within a brief preceding period; very recently. M17. c A very little after, very soon. L17. †4 In expressions of assent: exactly so, just so, right, quite. M16–L17. 5 No more than; only, merely; barely. M17. 6a Neither more nor less than, simply; absolutely; actually, really. E18. b Truly, indeed. *colloq.* M19.

1 T. HARDY They had been standing just by the drawing-room door. T. S. ELIOT It is impossible to say just what I mean! C. P. SNOW Someone dropped a ruler just then. R. K. NARAYAN You are just the person I was looking for. G. GREENE He remembered now: it was just three years ago. J. SIMMS He looked just like an ordinary boy. 3a E. NESBIT Alice was just asking Noel how he would deal with the robber . . when we heard a noise downstairs. b I. MURDOCH Gosh, I believe I've just swallowed a furry caterpillar! c DEFOE Tell his excellency I am just a coming. 5 B. PYM I'm just getting the place ready. J. B. MORTON Using my telescope, I could just make out the name on her bows. *Observer* It is ridiculous to think you can spend your entire life with just one person. M. KEANE Expensive ideas which he felt just young enough to develop. W. WHARTON I get scared just going around Paris. 6a E. BOWEN After all these years, Diana just walking in! A. S. BYATT I just can't settle to any work. b J. B. PRIESTLEY She let herself go all right, didn't she just!

Phrases: †**even just** = senses 1, 3 above. **just about** almost (exactly); almost completely. *just a minute*: see MINUTE *n.* **just as** precisely in the way that, to the same degree as. *just as well*: see WELL *adv.* *just in case*: see CASE *n.*[1] **just in time** narrowly avoiding lateness, at the last possible moment; *Comm.* (relating to or designating) a factory system whereby materials are delivered immediately before they are required. **just it** precisely the thing or point in question. *just my, his, our*, etc., *luck*: see LUCK *n.* **just now** (*a*) only a very short time ago; (*b*) at this exact moment; (*c*) (chiefly *S. Afr.*) very soon, in a little while. *just* QUIETLY. **just so** (*a*) exactly as has been said; (*b*) in the required or appropriate manner; (*c*) very close or friendly; (*d*) very neatly and carefully; (*e*) neat and tidy, fastidious. **just-so story** a story which purports to explain the origin of something, a myth. *just the job*: see JOB *n.*[1] *just the same*: see SAME *adv.* **just too bad** unfortunate but inevitable. *not just a pretty face*: see PRETTY *a.* 3a. **only just** by a very narrow margin, barely.

justaucorps /ʒystokɔːr/ *n.* Pl. same. M17. [Fr., f. *juste* close-fitting + *au corps* to the body.] *Hist.* A close-fitting outer garment; *spec.* (*a*) a man's coat, usu. worn over a waistcoat, with a skirt flaring out to the knees; (*b*) a woman's riding-jacket resembling a frock-coat.

juste milieu /ʒystə miljø/ *n. phr.* M19. [Fr., lit. 'the right mean'.] A happy medium, the golden mean; judicious moderation, esp. in politics.

A. J. P. TAYLOR One looks in vain in their history for a *juste milieu*, for common sense.

justice /ˈdʒʌstɪs/ *n.* LOE. [(O)Fr. f. L *justitia*, f. *justus* JUST *a.*: see -ICE[1].] I Judicial administration of law or equity. 1 Maintenance of legal, social, or moral principles by the exercise of authority or power; assignment of deserved reward or punishment; giving of due deserts. LOE. b Justice personified, *spec.* as a goddess holding balanced scales and a sword. L16. 2 The administration of law or of legal processes; judicial proceedings. ME. †b The people administering the law; a judicial assembly, a court of justice. ME–M17. †3 Infliction of punishment on an offender, *esp.* capital punishment; execution. LME–E17.

1 *Observer* I am glad that justice was done. P. ROTH They should have cut my head off. That would have been justice. *Which?* Who could possibly defend the idea of someone being deprived of legal support to get justice. b A. F. DOUGLAS-HOME A picture . . showing . . Justice holding the scales with her foot on the Duke of Hamilton's neck. 2 *New York Times* We will do everything possible to see that those responsible are brought to justice.

II The quality of being just. 4 The quality or fact of being just; (the principle of) just dealing or conduct; integrity, impartiality, fairness. ME. †5 *Theol.* The state of being righteous, righteousness. M16–E17. 6 Conformity (of an action or thing) to moral right or to reason, truth, or fact; = JUSTNESS 2, 3. L16.

4 T. O. ECHEWA The elders . . in spite of their long-winded orations about justice were prone to deviousness and chicanery. 6 J. UPDIKE Bech . . was enraptured by what seemed the beautiful justice of the remark. P. HOWARD The paper that had thundered for reform . . could see the justice of the case for women's suffrage.

III An administrator of justice. 7 *gen.* A judicial officer, a judge, a magistrate. ME. 8a A judge presiding over or belonging to one of the superior courts; *spec.* in England, a member of the Supreme Court of Judicature. ME. b A justice of the peace (see below); (occas.) any inferior magistrate. Chiefly in *the Justices*. L16.

Phrases: *bed of justice*: see BED *n.* **Chief Justice** (*a*) *Hist.* (the title of) the judge presiding over the court of King's or Queen's Bench or of Common Pleas; (*b*) *US* (the title of) the presiding judge in the Supreme Court or in the supreme court of a State. *College of Justice*: see COLLEGE 1. COMMUTATIVE *justice*. **Department of Justice** *US* a government department headed by the Attorney-General. DISTRIBUTIVE *justice*. **do justice to** (*a*) give (a person) his or her due, treat fairly by acknowledging the merits etc. of (someone); (*b*) treat (a subject or thing) in a manner showing due appreciation, deal with as is right or fitting; †(*c*) pledge with a drink. **do oneself justice** perform something one has to do in a manner worthy of one's abilities. **in justice to** in fairness to. *Jersey justice*: see JERSEY *n.*[1] *Justice Clerk*: see *Lord Justice Clerk* below. *Justice General*: see *Lord Justice General* below. *justice in eyre*: see EYRE 1. **justice of the peace** a lay magistrate appointed to preserve the peace in a county, town, etc., and discharge other local magisterial functions, as hearing minor cases and granting licences; a subordinate magistrate in a specific district; abbrev. *JP*. **justice-seat** a court of justice, a place where justice is dispensed; a sitting of a court. **Lord Chief Justice** (*a*) *Hist.* = *Chief Justice* (a) above; (*b*) (the title of) the judge presiding over the King's or Queen's Bench Division of the High Court. **(Lord) Justice Clerk** *Sc.* (the title of) the vice-president of the High Court of Justiciary. **(Lord) Justice General** *Sc.* (the title of) the president of the High Court of Justiciary. **Lord Justice** (**of Appeal**) (pl. **Lords Justices**) a judge in the Court of Appeal. **Mr** or **Mrs Justice —**: a form of address or mode of reference to a High Court judge. *miscarriage of justice*: see MISCARRIAGE 2. *myrmidon of justice*: see MYRMIDON 3. **poetic**(**al**) **justice** the ideal justice in distribution of rewards and punishments supposed to befit a poem or other work of imagination; well-deserved unforeseen retribution or reward. *rough justice*: see ROUGH *a.* **with justice** with justification, reasonably.

justiceship *n.* the office or position of a justice or judge M16.

justice /ˈdʒʌstɪs/ *v.* Now *rare*. ME. [AN *justicer* = OFr. *justicier* f. med.L *justitiare* exercise justice over, f. L *justitia*: see prec.] †1 *v.t.* Administer justice to; rule, govern. ME–L15. †2 *v.t.* Try in a court of law; bring to trial; punish judicially. ME–M18. 3 *v.i.* Administer justice. Chiefly as *justicing* vbl n. E17.

justicer /ˈdʒʌstɪsə/ *n. arch.* ME. [AN, OFr. *justicier* f. as JUSTICIARY *n.*[1]: see -ER[2].] 1 A person who maintains or carries out justice; a supporter or defender of right. ME. 2 Orig., a ruler or governor invested with judicial authority. Later, a judge, a magistrate. LME. 3 *spec.* = JUSTICE *n.* 8a. M16.

justiciable /dʒʌˈstɪʃəb(ə)l/ *a.* & *n.* LME. [AN & (O)Fr. = (a person) amenable to a jurisdiction, f. as JUSTICE *v.*: see -ABLE.] A *adj.* Liable to be tried in a court of justice; subject to jurisdiction. LME. B *n.* A person subject to the jurisdiction of another. *rare*. L19.

justicia'bility *n.* E19.

justicial /dʒʌˈstɪʃ(ə)l/ *a. rare*. LME. [med.L *justitialis*, f. *justitia* JUSTICE *n.*: see -AL[1].] Of or pertaining to justice or the administration of justice.

Justicialism /dʒʌˈstɪʃ(ə)lɪz(ə)m/ *n.* Also in Sp. form **Justicialismo** /dʒʌˌstɪʃəˈlɪzməʊ/; **j-**. M20. [Sp. *justicialismo*, f. *justicia* justice + *-al* -AL[1] + *-ismo* -ISM.] The political doctrine claimed by Juan Domingo Perón (1895–1974), president of Argentina (1946–55 and 1973–4), a combination of Fascism and socialism. Cf. PERONISM.

Justicialist *a.* M20.

justiciar /dʒʌˈstɪʃə/ *n.* L15. [med.L *justitiarius*: see next, -AR[2].] 1 *Hist.* a = JUSTICE *n.* 8a. L15. b Either of two supreme judges under early Scottish kings. E17. 2 *Hist.* More fully *Chief Justiciar*. The regent and deputy of the Norman and early Plantagenet kings, who presided over the king's court; = JUSTICIARY *n.*[1] 3. L16. 3 *gen.* An administrator of justice; a person who maintains or carries out justice. *arch.* E17. 4 Chiefly *Hist.* Any of various Continental officials or functionaries. M19.

justiciarship *n.* the office of justiciar L17.

justiciary /dʒʌˈstɪʃ(ə)ri/ *n.*[1] M16. [med.L *justitiarius*, *-ciarius* judge, f. L *justitia* JUSTICE *n.*: see -ARY[1].] 1 A person who maintains or carries out justice; an administrator of justice. M16. †2 *Chr. Theol.* A believer in the ability to attain righteousness by one's own efforts. M16–E18. 3 *Hist.* More fully *Chief Justiciary* = JUSTICIAR 2. E18. 4 *Hist.* = JUSTICE *n.* 8a. M18. 5 Any of various Continental officials or functionaries. M18.

justiciaryship *n.* the office of justiciary E18.

justiciary /dʒʌˈstɪʃ(ə)ri/ *n.*[2] *Sc.* LME. [med.L *justitiaria* office of a judge or justiciar, f. as prec. + -ARY[1].] The jurisdiction or office of a justiciar or justiciary.

High Court of Justiciary the supreme criminal court of Scotland.

justiciary /dʒʌˈstɪʃ(ə)ri/ *a.* L16. [med.L *justitiarius* judicial, f. L *justitia* JUSTICE *n.* + *-arius* -ARY[1].] Pertaining to or connected with the administration of justice or the office of a justice.

justicies /dʒʌˈstɪʃiːz/ *n.* M16. [AL, first wd of the writ, 2nd person sing. pres. subjunct. of med.L *justiciare* JUSTICE *v.*] *Law* (now *Hist.*). A writ directed to a sheriff, allowing him to hold plea of debt in his county court for sums exceeding the usual limit of forty shillings.

justifiable /ˈdʒʌstɪfʌɪəb(ə)l/ *a.* E16. [(O)Fr., f. *justifier* JUSTIFY: see -ABLE.] †1 = JUSTICIABLE *a.* E16–M17. 2 Able to be legally or morally justified; able to be shown to be just, reasonable, or correct; defensible. M16. †b Of an assertion etc.: able to be maintained or defended. E–M17.

2 R. CROMPTON In a moment of justifiable exasperation, he threw a beer bottle at her head. J. GATHORNE-HARDY It's quite justifiable to give a massive dose of drugs to sedate them. *justifiable* HOMICIDE.

justifia'bility *n.* L19. **justifiableness** *n.* M17. **justifiably** *adv.* LME.

justification /ˌdʒʌstɪfɪˈkeɪʃ(ə)n/ *n.* LME. [(O)Fr., or Chr.L *justificatio(n-)*, f. *justificat-* pa. ppl stem of *justificare*: see JUSTIFY, -FICATION.] †1 Administration of justice or the law; execution of sentence; capital punishment. Long *Sc. rare*. LME–L19. 2 *Theol.* The action whereby humankind is justified or made righteous by God; the fact or condition of being so justified. LME. †3 An ordinance; an ordained form. LME–E17. 4a The action of justifying or of showing something to be just, right, or proper. L15. b That which justifies; a defence; a good reason or cause. L15. 5 *Law.* a The showing or maintaining in court that one had sufficient reason for doing the thing with which one is charged; a circumstance giving grounds for such a plea. E16. b The justifying of bail. L18. 6 The action of adjusting or arranging something exactly. Now *spec.* the action, process, or result of justifying print or lines of text. L17.

4a J. BUTLER Nothing can with reason be urged in justification of revenge. b M. L. KING The curse of poverty has no justification in our age. R. INGALLS Reading Xenophon's explanation and justification of his conduct.

justificative /ˈdʒʌstɪfɪkeɪtɪv/ *a. rare.* E17. [Fr. *justificatif, -ive*, f. Chr.L *justificat-*: see prec., -IVE.] Serving to justify; justificatory.

justificatory /ˈdʒʌstɪfɪkeɪt(ə)ri, ˌdʒʌstɪfɪˈkeɪt(ə)ri/ *a.* L16. [med.L *justificatorius*, f. Chr.L *justificat-*: see JUSTIFICATION, -ORY².] Tending to justify something; serving or intended to support a statement.

justified /ˈdʒʌstɪfʌɪd/ *a.* M16. [f. next + -ED¹.] Just, right, righteous; warranted; having good cause or reason, correct; supported by evidence; (in printing etc.) that has been justified.

M. BARING What Burstall told him cheered him, and he felt justified in continuing. A. J. CRONIN He would repay it, he would show her.. that her faith in him was justified. B. GELDOF I thought we were justified and therefore any risk was acceptable.

¶ Earlier in UNJUSTIFIED.

justify /ˈdʒʌstɪfʌɪ/ *v.* ME. [(O)Fr. *justifier* f. Chr.L *justificare* do justice to, vindicate, f. L *justus* JUST *a.*: see -FY.] †1 *v.t.* Administer justice to, rule; keep or bring under the rule of law; treat justly. ME–E17. †2 *v.t.* Inflict a judicial penalty on, punish; sentence, condemn; *esp.* (*Sc.*) punish with death, execute. ME–L19. 3 *v.t.* Prove or maintain the rightness, worth, or innocence of; vindicate. LME. 4 *v.t.* Absolve, acquit; *spec.* in *Theol.*, declare righteous on the grounds of Christ's merit, or make inherently righteous by the infusion of grace. LME. 5 *v.t.* Support or back up (an assertion, opinion, etc.) by evidence or testimony; confirm, prove, verify. LME. †b Maintain as true, affirm, assert. L16–L18. †c Acknowledge as true or genuine. Only in E17. 6 *v.i.* & *t. Law.* Show adequate grounds for (doing the thing with which one is charged). E16. 7 *v.t.* a Show or maintain the justice or reasonableness of (an action, claim, etc.); defend as right or proper. M16. b Make right, proper, or reasonable; give adequate grounds for, warrant. M17. 8 *v.t.* Orig., make exact, adjust to exact shape, size, or position. Now *spec.* in *Typogr.* etc., adjust spacing along (a line of text) to a prescribed measure so that adjacent lines are of equal length; arrange (a body of text) into lines of equal length. M16.

3 M. PATTISON The difficult task of justifying science in the eyes of the nation. M. WEST History.. is always written to justify the survivors. M. PIERCY I don't have to justify myself to you. 5 GIBBON The narratives of antiquity are justified by the experience of modern times. 6 **justify bail** show by oath when furnishing bail that one has sufficient funds to do so. 7a MILTON I may assert th' eternal Providence, And justifie the wayes of God to men. J. A. MICHENER We've gathered here.. to hear a great man try to justify his mistakes. M. FOOT No socialist.. would ever have justified the resort to these perverted means to secure his ends. b M. PRIOR The end must justifie the means; He only sins who ill intends. A. MILLER Life is God's most precious gift; no principle.. may justify the taking of it. G. GREENE To justify these payments he had to compose a regular supply of reports.

justifier *n.* a person or thing which justifies someone or something E16. **justifyingly** *adv.* in a justifying manner E18.

justing *vbl n.* var. of JOUSTING.

Justinianian /dʒʌˌstɪnɪˈeɪnɪən/ *a.* E19. [f. *Justinian* (see below) + -IAN.] Of or pertaining to Justinian I, emperor of the Eastern Roman or Byzantine Empire 527-65.

Justinianian code a compilation of Roman law made by order of Justinian I.

Juˈstinianist *n.* a person learned in the Justinianian code, a student of civil law M17.

justle *n.*, *v.* vars. of JOSTLE *n.*, *v.*

justly /ˈdʒʌs(t)li/ *adv.* ME. [f. JUST *a.* + -LY².] 1 Exactly, precisely, accurately, closely. *obs.* exc. *dial.* ME. 2 Uprightly, righteously. *arch.* LME. 3 In accordance with justice or equity, deservedly; with good reason; rightly, properly. LME.

3 J. BUCHAN Your family was unpopular—I understand, justly unpopular. R. LEHMANN He was a beautiful swimmer, and justly proud of his torso.

justness /ˈdʒʌs(t)nɪs/ *n.* LME. [f. JUST *a.* + -NESS.] †1 The quality of being righteous or upright, righteousness. LME–E18. 2 The quality or fact of being morally right or equitable or of having reasonable grounds; rightfulness; fairness; validity. LME. 3 Conformity to truth or to a standard; correctness; propriety. M17.

jut /dʒʌt/ *n.*¹ *obs.* exc. *dial.* M16. [f. (as) JUT *v.*¹] A push, thrust, or knock against a resisting body; the shock of collision.

jut /dʒʌt/ *n.*² E18. [Var. of JET *n.*²: cf. JUT *v.*²] †1 = JET *n.*² 2. Only in E18. 2 A jutting out; a projection, a protruding point. Cf. JET *n.*² 1. L18.

2 M. GRAY The jut of the porch sheltered this window.

Comb.: **jut-jawed** *a.* having a jutting jaw.

jut /dʒʌt/ *v.*¹ *obs.* exc. *dial.* Infl. **-tt-**. M16. [App. imit.] 1 *v.i.* Strike, knock, or push *against*. M16. 2 *v.t.* Push, shove, jolt; knock against. M16.

jut /dʒʌt/ *v.*² Infl. **-tt-**. M16. [Var. of JET *v.*², by assim. to JUTTY *v.*, *n.*] 1 *v.i.* Project, protrude; stick *out*. M16. 2 *v.t.* Cause to jut (*out*). M20.

1 K. MANSFIELD Into the middle of the room a black stove jutted. J. C. POWYS A small landing-stage which jutted out into the river. 2 A. S. BYATT She put up her head and jutted out her chin with.. determination.

juttingly *adv.* in a jutting manner M19.

Jute /dʒuːt/ *n.*¹ [OE *Eotas, Iotas* pl. (cf. Icel. *Jótar* people of Jutland (ON *Jótland*) in Denmark), alt. in LME after med.L *Jutae, Juti.*] A member of a Low German tribe which invaded and settled in parts of southern Britain in the 5th and 6th cents.

Jutish *a.* of or pertaining to the Jutes M19.

jute /dʒuːt/ *n.*² & *a.* M18. [Bengali *jhuṭo* f. Prakrit (of central Asia) *j(h)uṣṭi.*] A *n.* A fibre obtained from the phloem of the plants *Corchorus capsularis* and *C. olitorius*, of the linden family, which is imported chiefly from Bangladesh and West Bengal, and used in the manufacture of coarse sacking, canvas, twine, rope, etc.; either of the plants which furnish this fibre. M18.

American jute, Chinese jute Indian mallow, *Abutilon theophrasti*, used as a substitute for jute.

B *adj.* Made of jute. M18.

jutka /ˈdʒʌtkə/ *n.* L19. [Hind. *jhaṭkā* a jerk, jolt, lurch.] In southern India, a light two-wheeled vehicle drawn by a horse.

†jutty *n.* L15. [Var. of JETTY *n.*: cf. JUT *v.*²] 1 A pier, a breakwater, an embankment; = JETTY *n.* 1. L15–E19. 2 A projecting part of a wall or building; = JETTY *n.* 2. E16–E18.

jutty /ˈdʒʌti/ *a.* E19. [f. JUT *n.*² + -Y¹.] Characterized by jutting out; projecting.

†jutty *v.* LME. [Rel. to JUTTY *n.*: cf. also JETTY *v.*] 1 *v.i.* Project, jut. LME–M19. 2 *v.t.* Project beyond, overhang. Only in L16.

juve /dʒuːv/ *n. slang.* M20. [Abbrev. Cf. JUVIE.] A juvenile, a young person; *spec.* (*a*) a juvenile lead; (*b*) a juvenile delinquent.

juvenal /ˈdʒuːvən(ə)l/ *n.*¹ & *a.* L16. [L *juvenalis* (= *juvenilis*), f. *juvenis* young person: see -AL¹.] †A *n.* A youth; a juvenile. L16–M19. B *adj.* Juvenile. Now *Ornith.* (chiefly *US*). M17.

Juvenal /ˈdʒuːvən(ə)l/ *n.*² L16. [Decimus Junius *Juvenalis* (see below).] A writer whose work can be likened to that of the Roman satirist Juvenal (AD *c* 60–*c* 130); a satirist.

Juveˈnalian *a.* resembling or characteristic of Juvenal M19.

juvenescence /dʒuːvəˈnɛs(ə)ns/ *n.* E19. [f. as next: see -ESCENT.] Youth, youthfulness; the process of becoming young or youthful; the transition from infancy to youth.

juvenescent /dʒuːvəˈnɛs(ə)nt/ *a.* E19. [L *juvenescent-* pres. ppl stem of *juvenescere* reach the age of youth: see -ESCENT.] Becoming young or youthful; in the process of ageing from infancy to youth.

juvenile /ˈdʒuːvənʌɪl/ *a.* & *n.* E17. [L *juvenilis*, f. *juvenis* (a) young (person): see -ILE.] A *adj.* 1 Young, youthful. E17. 2 Belonging to, characteristic of, suited to, or intended for youth or young people; (freq. *derog.*) immature, childish. M17. 3 *Geol.* Of water, gases, etc.: originating from magma and newly brought to the surface; not meteoric. E20.

1 H. B. STOWE The order was.. carried to Aunt Chloe by.. half a dozen juvenile messengers. V. NABOKOV She seemed to have grown less juvenile, more of a woman overnight. 2 R. CROMPTON A book of ghost stories from the juvenile library at school. M. FITZHERBERT Aubrey's views were often juvenile and always muddled.

Special collocations: **juvenile court** a court of law for the trial of young offenders. **juvenile delinquency** the (habitual) committing of offences against the law by a minor or minors. **juvenile delinquent** a person engaged in juvenile delinquency. **juvenile hormone** *Entomol.* each of a number of hormones that control larval development in insects and inhibit metamorphosis. **juvenile lead** = sense B.1b below; *spec.* an actor who plays the leading youthful part in a play etc.; the role so played. **juvenile leaf** a distinct kind of leaf characteristic of the immature stages of certain trees, shrubs, or woody climbers.

B *n.* 1 A young person, a youth; a young creature, *esp.* a bird in its first full plumage. M18. b *Theatr.* An actor who plays a youthful part. L19. 2 A book written for children. M19.

1 M. COX His new book was 'for juveniles'. *Bird Watching* Juveniles look similar to winter adults and can lack the yellow tip to the bill.

juvenilely *adv.* E18. **juvenileness** *n.* E18. **juvenilize** *v.t.* make or keep young or youthful; *Entomol.* arrest the normal development of: M19.

juvenilia /dʒuːvəˈnɪlɪə/ *n.pl.* E17. [L, neut. pl. of *juvenilis* JUVENILE *a.*] Literary or artistic works produced in an author's or artist's youth.

juvenility /dʒuːvəˈnɪlɪti/ *n.* E17. [L *juvenilitas*, f. as JUVENILE *a.*: see -ITY.] 1 Youthfulness; juvenile manner, quality, or character. E17. 2 In *pl.* Juvenile characteristics, acts, or ideas. M17. 3 Young people collectively, youth. E19.

juventude /ˈdʒuːv(ə)ntjuːd/ *n. rare.* LME. [f. L *juventut-*, *juventus*, f. *juvenis*: see JUVENILE, -TUDE Cf. med.L *juventitudo.*] Youth.

juvescence /dʒuːˈvɛs(ə)ns/ *n. rare.* E20. [Irreg. contr. of JUVENESCENCE.] The process of becoming young, juvenescence.

juvia /ˈdʒuːvɪə, ˈhuː-/ *n.* M19. [Amer. Sp. f. Arawak.] The Brazil-nut; (also *juvia tree*) the tree, *Bertholletia excelsa*, bearing Brazil-nuts.

juvie /ˈdʒuːvi/ *n. US slang.* M20. [Abbrev. Cf. JUVE.] A juvenile, a juvenile delinquent. Also, a detention centre or a court for juvenile delinquents.

juxta- /ˈdʒʌkstə/ *pref.* [Repr. L *juxta* adv. & prep.] Near to, by the side of, according to.

juxta-arˈticular *a.* (*Anat.*) situated near a joint E20. **juxta-maˈrine** *a.* situated by the sea L19. **juxta-ˈspinal** *a.* situated by the side of the (or a) spine L19.

juxtaglomerular /ˌdʒʌkstəglɒˈmɛrʊlə/ *a.* M20. [f. JUXTA- + GLOMERULAR.] *Anat.* Situated next to a glomerulus of the kidney; *spec.* designating a body or complex of bodies associated with the afferent arteriole of a glomerulus and containing secretory cells with a regulatory function.

juxtapose /dʒʌkstəˈpəʊz/ *v.t.* M19. [Fr. *juxtaposer*, f. as JUXTA- + POSE *v.*¹] Place (two or more things) side by side or close to one another; place (one thing) beside another.

R. ELLMANN The self only comes to exist when juxtaposed with other people. E. WILSON Juxtaposing .. hues in a rainbow. J. BRODSKY By juxtaposing one faith with another we.. take them out of their context.

juxtaposit /dʒʌkstəˈpɒzɪt/ *v.t. rare.* L17. [f. JUXTA- + L *posit-* pa. ppl stem of *pōnere* put, place.] = prec.

juxtaposition /dʒʌkstəpəˈzɪʃ(ə)n/ *n.* M17. [Fr., f. as JUXTAPOSE: see POSITION *n.*] The action of juxtaposing two or more things; the fact or condition of being juxtaposed.

juxtapositional *a.* relating to or characterized by juxtaposition M19.

juxtapositive /dʒʌkstəˈpɒzɪtɪv/ *a.* L19. [f. prec. + -IVE.] *Gram.* Designating, being in, or pertaining to a case expressing juxtaposition.

jynx /dʒɪŋks/ *n.* Now *rare.* Pl. **jynxes**, **†jynges**. M17. [mod.L f. L *iynx* f. Gk *iugx*, pl. *iugges.*] The wryneck, *Jynx torquilla.*

jyrene, **-ine** *ns.* vars. of GYRENE.

K

K, k /keɪ/, the eleventh letter of the modern Eng. alphabet and the tenth of the ancient Roman one, corresp. to Gk *kappa*, Phoenician and general Semitic *kaph*. The sound denoted by the letter in English, as in Greek and Latin, is the voiceless velar plosive consonant /k/. At an early period of Latin orthography, the letter C (orig. repr. Gk *gamma*) was used for the k sound, and the letter K itself fell into disuse, except in a few archaic spellings. In Old English, K was merely a supplemental symbol occasionally used instead of C for the velar sound. After the Norman Conquest, in accordance with Norman usage, C was retained for the velar only before *a, o, u, l,* and *r*, and K was substituted for the same sound before *e, i, y,* and (later) *n*. Hence, in native words, initial K now appears only before *e, i, y,* and before *n* (= OE *cn-*), where it is no longer pronounced in standard English. Medially and finally, K is used after a consonant (*ask, twinkle*), or long vowel (*make, like, week*); after a short vowel, *ck* is used instead of *cc* or *kk*, but the unstressed suffix, formerly *-ick* (*musick*), is now *-ic*, though, when a suffix in *e* or *i* follows, K reappears (*traffic, trafficker, trafficking*). Beside native K words, largely confined to *ke-, ki-,* and *kn-*, there are now many foreign words of recent adoption, in which K may also precede *a, o, u, l, r,* and *h*. In words from Gk K is also usu. retained rather than Latinized to C, and in some cases, notably words in *kilo-*, K represents Gk *chi*. Pl. **K's, Ks.**

I 1 The letter and its sound.

II Symbolical uses. 2 Used to denote serial order; applied e.g. to the eleventh (also freq. the tenth, either I or J being omitted) group or section, sheet of a book, etc. 3 *Physics* etc. a (Italic *k*.) Thermal conductivity. b (Italic *k*.) Boltzmann's constant. c (Cap. K.) Used to designate a series of short-wavelength X-ray emission lines of an excited atom, arising from electron transitions to the innermost, lowest-energy atomic orbit, of principal quantum number 1; hence *K-shell*, this orbit; *K-electrons*, electrons in this shell; *K-capture*, the capture by an atomic nucleus of one of the K-electrons. Cf. L, L 5b, M, M 6a. d *K-meson, K-particle*, = KAON; *K-mesic*, kaonic. 4 [f. abbrev. of KILO-: cf. branch III below] (Usu. *k*.) In *Computing*, 1,000 (bytes) or, strictly, 1,024 (2^{10}); in *Biochem.*, 1,000 (in expr. molecular weights of proteins); *gen.* (esp. in specifying salaries in job advertisements) a thousand (pounds etc.).

III 5 Abbrevs.: (A small selection only is given here. Those all in caps. or small caps. also occur with a full stop after each letter; some of those all in caps. also occur (i) with initial cap. only, (ii) in small caps.) **K** = (*Chem.*) [L] *kalium* potassium; kelvin; King; King's; Knight; (*Naut.*) knot(s); Köchel (preceding the number of a composition by Mozart in the catalogue made by Ludwig von Köchel). **k** = (as pref.) kilo-. **Kan(s).** = Kansas. **KANU** /ˈkɑːnuː/ Kenya African National Union. **KB** = King's Bench. **KBE** = Knight Commander (of the Order) of the British Empire. **KC** = King's College; King's Counsel. **kc** = kilocycle(s); kilocycles per second. **KCB** = Knight Commander (of the Order) of the Bath. **KCIE** = Knight Commander (of the Order) of the Indian Empire. **KCMG** = Knight Commander (of the Order) of St Michael and St George. **kc/s** = kilocycles per second. **KCSI** = Knight Commander (of the Order) of the Star of India. **KCVO** = Knight Commander of the Royal Victorian Order. **KD** = knocked down. **KE** = kinetic energy. **keV** = kilo-electronvolt. **KG** = Knight (of the Order) of the Garter. **kg** = kilogram(s). **KGB** = [Russ.] *Komitet Gosudarstvennoĭ Bezopasnosti* Committee of State Security, the State security police of the former USSR from 1954. **Kgs.** = Kings (in the Bible). **kHz** = kilohertz. **kJ** = kilojoule(s). **KKK** = Ku Klux Klan. **kl** = kilolitre(s). **km** = kilometre(s). **kn.** (*Naut.*) = knot(s). **Knt.** = Knight. **KO** = kick-off; knocked out; knockout. **KO'd** /keɪˈəʊd/ = knocked out. **KP** (*US*) = kitchen police(man). **KP** = Knight (of the Order) of St Patrick. **k.p.h** = kilometres per hour. **Kr** (*Chem.*) = krypton. **KS** = Kansas; King's Scholar. **K. St J.** = Knight (of the Order) of St John. **KT** = Knight (of the Order) of the Thistle; Knight Templar. **Kt.** = Knight. **kt.** (*Naut.*) = knot(s). **K/T** (*Geol.*) = Cretaceous/Tertiary. **Ku** (*Chem.*) = kurchatovium. **kV** = kilovolt(s). **kVa** = kilovolt-ampere(s). **kW** = kilowatt(s). **KWAC** /kwak/ = keyword and context. **kWh** = kilowatt-hour(s). **KWIC** /kwɪk/ = keyword in context. **KWOC** /kwɒk/ = keyword out of context. **KY, Ky.** = Kentucky.

ka /kɑː/ *n.* L19. [Ancient Egyptian.] The spiritual part of a human being or a god which, according to the ancient Egyptians, survived after death and could reside in a statue of the dead person.

Kaaba /ˈkɑːəbə/ *n.* Also (earlier) **Al-kaaba** /al-/, **C-**. E17. [Arab. (*al-*)*ka'ba* lit. '(the) square house'.] *The* square-shaped building in the centre of the Great Mosque in Mecca, Saudi Arabia, in the direction of which Muslims must face in doing the obligatory prayer.

kaama /ˈkɑːmə/ *n.* Also **k(h)ama**. E19. [Nama.] = HARTEBEEST.

Kaapenaar /ˈkɑːpənɑː/ *n. S. Afr.* Also **Kap-**, (in sense 2) **k-**. M19. [Afk., f. *kaap* Cape + *-enaar* pers. suff.] 1 A native or inhabitant of Cape Town, South Africa, or of the Cape peninsula and its environs. M19. 2 An edible silver sea bream, *Argyrozona argyrozona*. E20.

kab /kab/ *n.* Also **†c-**. M16. [Heb. *qab* hollow or concave vessel. Cf. *2 Kings* 6:25.] An ancient Hebrew unit of capacity equal to approx. 2 litres, or 3½ pints.

Kababish /kəˈbɑːbɪʃ/ *n.pl.* & *a.* L18. [Arab. *kabābīš* pl.] A *n.pl.* A nomadic Arab people of the northern Kordofan and Dongola areas of Sudan. L18. B *attrib.* or as *adj.* Of or pertaining to the Kababish. M19.

kabaddi /kəˈbadi/ *n.* Also **kabadi**. M20. [Origin uncertain: cf. Kurukh *kavaḍa* mouthful, Kannada *kabalisu* to gulp. Skt *kavaḍa*, Hind. *kabaḍḍī* cry at kabaddi.] A team pursuit game popular in the north of the Indian subcontinent in which the two teams alternately send a player into the opposing team's court to try to touch one of the opponents while repeating the word 'kabaddi' (to show that the breath is being held as the rules require).

Kabaka /kəˈbɑːkə/ *n.* L19. [Bantu.] (The title of) the ruler of the former province of Buganda in Uganda, or of the Baganda.

kabane /kəˈbɑːneɪ/ *n.* L19. [Jap.] In ancient Japan, a series or system of titles of rank.

kabaragoya /kəbɑːrəˈgəʊjə/ *n.* L17. [Origin unkn.] A large monitor lizard, *Varanus salvator*, of SE Asia.

Kabardian /kəˈbɑːdɪən/ *a.* & *n.* L19. [f. *Kabarda* (Russ. place-name) + -IAN.] A *adj.* Of or pertaining to a people of the Kabardino-Balkarian Republic of Russia, in the northern Caucasus. L19. B *n.* 1 A member of this people. M20. 2 The NW Caucasian language of this people. M20.

Kabardine *n.* (*rare*) = KABARDIAN *n.* 1 E19. **Kabar'dinian** *a.* & *n.* = KABARDIAN L19.

kabassou /kəˈbasuː/ *n.* L18. [Fr. f. Galibi *capaçou*.] Any of several naked-tailed armadillos of the genus *Cabassous*.

kabbala *n.* var. of CABBALA.

kabeljou /ˈkɑːb(ə)ljəʊ, kɑːb(ə)lˈjəʊ/ *n. S. Afr.* Also **-jauw, -jouw**, & other vars. Pl. same. M18. [Afk. f. Du. *kabeljauw*, cogn. w. Fr. *cabillaud* cod.] = MEAGRE *n.*[1] Also called *kob, salmon bass*.

Kabinett /kabɪˈnɛt, *foreign* -bi-/ *n.* E20. [G *Kabinettwein* lit. 'cabinet or chamber wine', from its orig. being kept in a special cellar.] Wine, esp. German wine, of exceptional quality; *spec.* one made in Germany from grapes that can ferment without added sugar. Also *Kabinett wine*.

Kabistan /kabɪˈstɑːn/ *n.* & *a.* Also **C-**. E20. [For *Kubistan* (see below): cf. KUBA.] (Designating) a finely woven, short-napped rug or carpet with intricate geometric design made in Kubistan, a district in NE Azerbaijan.

kabloona /kəˈbluːnə/ *n. Canad.* L18. [Eskimo (Inuit) *kabluna* big eyebrow.] Among Canadian Eskimos: a person who is not an Eskimo; a White person.

kaboura /kəˈbʊərə/ *n.* Also **-ri** /-ri/. L19. [Origin unkn.] In Guyana: a bloodsucking fly of the genus *Simulium*.

kabuki /kəˈbuːki/ *n.* & *a.* L19. [Jap., orig. (as vb) act dissolutely; later interpreted as f. *ka* song + *bu* dance + *ki* art, skill.] (Of, pertaining to, or characteristic of) a traditional and popular form of Japanese drama with highly stylized song, mime, and dance, performed by male actors only.

Kabuli /kəˈbuːli/ *a.* & *n.* Also **†C-**. L19. [f. *Kabul* (see below) + -I[2].] A *adj.* Of or pertaining to the city or province of Kabul in Afghanistan. L19. B *n.* 1 A native or inhabitant of Kabul; a Kabuli horse. L19. 2 The dialect of Tajik used in Kabul. M20.

Kabyle /kəˈbʌɪl/ *n.* & *a.* M18. [Prob. f. Arab. *ḳabā'il* pl. of *ḳabīla* tribe.] A *n.* 1 An individual or people belonging to a group of Berber peoples inhabiting northern Algeria. M18. 2 The Berber dialect of these peoples. L19. B *attrib.* or as *adj.* Of or pertaining to the Kabyles or their language. M19.

kacha *a.* & *n.* var. of KUTCHA.

Kachin /kəˈtʃɪn/ *n.* & *a.* L19. [Burm.] A *n.* Pl. **-s**, same. A member of a group of Tibeto-Burman peoples inhabiting the mountainous regions in the north-east of Myanmar (Burma); the language of these peoples, having various dialects. L19. B *attrib.* or as *adj.* Of or pertaining to the Kachins or their language. L19.

kachina /kəˈtʃiːnə/ *n.* L19. [Hopi *kacina* supernatural f. Keresan.] A deified ancestral spirit in N. American Pueblo Indian mythology.

Comb.: **kachina dance** a ceremonial dance performed by men in masks and elaborate costumes impersonating the kachinas whom they seek to invoke; **kachina doll** a wooden doll representing a kachina.

kadaitcha *n.* var. of KURDAITCHA.

Kaddish /ˈkadɪʃ/ *n.* E17. [Aram. *qaddīš* holy.] An ancient Jewish doxology regularly recited in the synagogue, including brief prayers for the welfare of Israel and concluding with a prayer for universal peace.

kade *n.* var. of KED *n.*[1]

Kadet *n.* var. of CADET *n.*[2]

Kadhakali *n.* var. of KATHAKALI.

kadi *n.* var. of CADI.

kadin /ˈkɑːdɪn/ *n.* M19. [Turk. *kadın* f. as KHATUN.] *Hist.* A woman of the Sultan of Turkey's harem.

kadish /ˈkɑːdɪʃ/ *n.* E19. [Syrian Arab. *kadīš* f. OTurk. *igdiş* a crossbreed, f. *igid-* feed, rear; cf. Turk. *idiş* gelding.] A part-bred Arabian horse; a nag; a gelding.

kadkhoda /kadˈkoːda, kadˈkəʊdə/ *n.* M20. [Pers. *kadkudā*, f. *kad* house + *kudā* master.] The headman of an Iranian village.

kae /keɪ/ *n. Sc.* & *north.* ME. [Corresp. to MDu. *ca*, *ka(e)* (Du. *ka*), OHG *chaha*, *chā* (MHG *kā*), Da. *kaa*, Norw. *kaae.*] A jackdaw.

kae /keɪ, kɑː/ *v.t.* Long *obs.* exc. *dial.* M16. [Origin uncertain: perh. var. of CLAW *v.* or CA' *v.*] Only in *kae me*, *kae thee* and *kae me and I'll kae thee*: used as a suggestion or proposal of mutual help, service, flattery, etc.

kaemmererite *n.* var. of KÄMMERERITE.

kaempferol /ˈkampfərɒl, ˈkɛ-/ *n.* L19. [f. mod.L *Kaempferia* genus name of the plant from which it was first obtained, f. Engelbert *Kaempfer* (1651–1716), Ger. traveller: see -OL.] *Chem.* A yellow flavonoid, $C_{15}H_{10}O_6$, which occurs in various plants.

kaersutite /kɛːˈsuːtʌɪt/ *n.* L19. [f. *Kaersut* locality in Greenland where it was first found + -ITE[1].] *Min.* A dark variety of hornblende containing titanium, occurring in many volcanic rocks.

kafenion /kafəˈniːən/ *n.* M20. [Gk *kafeneio(n).*] A Greek coffee-house.

Kaffeeklatsch /ˈkafeklatʃ/ *n.* Also ***kaffee-klatch*** /ˈkafɪklatʃ/. L19. [G, f. *Kaffee* coffee + *Klatsch* gossip. Cf. KLATCH.] Gossip over coffee cups; a coffee party.

kafferboom *n.* var. of KAFFIRBOOM.

Kaffir /ˈkafə/ *n.* & *a.* Chiefly *S. Afr.* Also (*arch.*) **Caffre**; **Kafir**. See also KAFIR. M16. [Arab. *kāfir* unbeliever, f. act. pple of *kafara* be unbelieving.] **A** *n.* **1** A non-Muslim; an infidel. *derog.* Now *rare.* M16. **2a** A member of a Bantu-speaking people, esp. the Xhosa, in South Africa. Now *rare* or *obs.* L16. **b** A Black African. *derog.* & usu. considered *racially offensive*, and legally actionable in South Africa. Now *rare.* M19. **c** *White Kaffir*, a White who has adopted a Black African way of life. *derog.* E20. **3** Bantu; *spec.* Xhosa. E19. **4** In *pl.* South African mining shares. *Stock Exch. slang.* L19.

B *attrib.* or as *adj.* Black African (now *rare* & usu. considered *racially offensive* exc. in some collocations below); Bantu, *esp.* Xhosa (now *rare* or *obs.*). L18.

Kaffir beer an alcoholic drink brewed from malted Kaffir corn. **Kaffirboetie** /ˈkafəbʊtiː/ (*derog.* & usu. considered *offensive*) a White South African who shows concern for the welfare of Blacks. **Kaffir bread** any of several southern African cycads with edible pith. **Kaffir corn** a variety of sorghum, *Sorghum bicolor* var. *caffrorum*, grown in southern Africa, esp. for making beer; = MABELE. **Kaffir crane** = CROWNED *crane*. **Kaffir finch** a S. African bishop-bird or widow-bird, *esp.* the red bishop, *Euplectes orix*, and the sakabula, *E. progne*. **Kaffir lily** (*a*) an ornamental plant of the iris family, *Schizostylis coccinea*, bearing spikes of flowers resembling gladioli; (*b*) = CLIVIA. **Kaffir melon** an indigenous southern African melon, *Citrullus caffer*. **Kaffir orange** any of several small trees of the genus *Strychnos* (family Loganiaceae), esp. *S. pungens*; the globose fruit of such a tree, with an edible pulp but poisonous seeds. **Kaffir piano** (now *rare*, usu. considered *racially offensive*) a southern African marimba or xylophone. **Kaffir plum** (the red edible fruit of) an ornamental southern African tree, *Harpephyllum caffrum* (family Anacardiaceae). **Kaffir pot** an iron cooking-pot, usu. on three short metal legs. **Kaffir tea** (*a*) any of various South African plants used to make medicinal teas, esp. *Helichrysum nudifolium*, of the composite family; (*b*) an infusion of the leaves of such a plant; *spec.* = ROOIBOS *tea*. **Kaffir work** (*derog.* & usu. considered *racially offensive*) manual work despised by White South Africans.

kaffirboom /ˈkafəbʊəm/ *n. S. Afr.* Also **kaffer-**. E19. [f. prec. + Afk. *boom* tree.] Any of several southern African kinds of coral tree, esp. *Erythrina caffra* and *E. lysistemon*, the red seeds of which are used as beads.

kaffiyeh *n.* var. of KEFFIYEH.

Kaffrarian /kəˈfrɛːrɪən/ *a.* Also (*arch.*) **C-**. E19. [f. *Kaffraria* (see below) f. as KAFFIR (prob. orig. named by Arab seafarers): see -AN.] Of, pertaining to, or characteristic of Kaffraria, a region along the south-east coast of South Africa, now part of Cape Province.

Kafir /ˈkafə/ *n.* M19. [f. as KAFFIR.] A member of a people inhabiting the Hindu Kush mountains of NE Afghanistan.

Comb.: **Kafir harp** a simple harp with four or five strings used by the Kafirs.

Kafkaesque /kafkəˈɛsk/ *a.* M20. [f. *Kafka* (see below) + -ESQUE.] Of or pertaining to the Austrian writer Franz Kafka (1883–1924) or his writings; similar to or suggestive of the nightmarish atmosphere or situations portrayed in his stories.

kaftan *n.* var. of CAFTAN.

kago /ˈkɑːgo, ˈkɑːgəʊ/ *n.* E18. [Jap.] A kind of Japanese litter, orig. consisting of basketwork slung on a pole and carried on the shoulders of bearers, later made of wood.

kagoule *n.* var. of CAGOULE.

kagu /ˈkɑːguː/ *n.* M19. [Melanesian.] A very rare nocturnal crested gruiform bird, *Rhynochetus jubatus* of New Caledonia, drab grey with display patterns beneath the wings and a red bill.

kagura /ˈkɑːgʊrə/ *n.* L19. [Jap.] A form of traditional sacred music and dance performed at Shinto festivals.

Kahal /ˈkaːhal/ *n.* E20. [Heb. *qāhāl* assembly, community.] (The governing body of) any of the former localized Jewish communities in Europe.

kahawai /ˈkɑːwʌɪ/ *n.* Chiefly *NZ.* M19. [Maori.] = *Australian salmon* s.v. AUSTRALIAN *a.*

kahikatea /kʌɪkəˈtiːə/ *n.* E19. [Maori.] A New Zealand coniferous tree, *Podocarpus dacrydioides* (family Podocarpaceae). Also called *white pine*.

kahili /kəˈhiːli/ *n.* M19. [Haw. *kāhili.*] A feather standard, mounted on a tall pole, symbolic of royalty in Hawaii and used on ceremonial occasions.

Kahn /kɑːn/ *n.* E20. [Reuben Leon *Kahn* (b. 1887), Lithuanian-born US bacteriologist.] Med. *Kahn test*, *reaction*, a diagnostic test for syphilis devised by Kahn in which serum or spinal fluid is mixed with antigen from beef heart and examined for flocculation.

kahuna /kəˈhuːnə/ *n.* L19. [Haw.] In Hawaii: a priest, a wise man; a minister; a sorcerer.

kai /kʌɪ/ *n. NZ colloq.* M19. [Maori.] Food.

kaikai /ˈkʌɪkʌɪ/ *n.* food; feasting; a feast: M19.

kaid /kɑːˈiːd/ *n.* Also (*arch.*) **c-**. E19. [f. Arab. *ḳā'id* leader: see ALCAIDE.] = ALCAIDE.

kaikomako /kʌɪkəʊˈmɑːkəʊ/ *n.* Pl. **-os**. M19. [Maori.] A New Zealand tree, *Pennantia corymbosa* (family Icacinaceae), which bears panicles of fragrant white flowers and black berries.

kail *n.* var. of KALE.

kailyard *n.* var. of KALEYARD.

kaim *n.* var. of KAME.

kaimakam /kʌɪməˈkɑːm/ *n.* Also **†caimacam**, **qaimaqam**. E17. [Turk. *kaymakam*, f. Arab. *ḳā'im maḳām* one standing in the place of another.] In the Ottoman Empire: a lieutenant, a deputy, esp. in the army or the government; *spec.* an official deputizing for the grand vizier. In modern Turkey: the governor of a kaza.

kain /ˈkʌɪn/ *n.*[1] Pl. **-s**, same. L18. [Malay.] In Malaysia and Indonesia: (a piece of) cloth, esp. for use as clothing; a sarong. Freq. w. postpositive adj.

J. KIRKUP Round their waists they wore . . kain songket which is a silver or gold-threaded sarong.

kain *n.*[2] var. of CAIN *n.*[1]

kainga /kɑːˈɪŋgə, *foreign* kɑːˈiŋa/ *n. NZ.* E19. [Maori.] A Maori place of residence, settlement, or village.

kainic /ˈkʌɪnɪk/ *a.* M20. [f. Jap. *kainin*, f. *kainin-sō*, name of the source alga: see -IC.] *kainic acid*, a neurotoxic organic acid extracted from the red alga *Digenea simplex* and used as an anthelmintic.

kainite /ˈkʌɪnʌɪt, ˈkeɪ-/ *n.* Also **-it** /-ɪt/. M19. [G *Kainit*, f. Gk *kainos* new, recent (as being of recent formation): see -ITE[1].] A white monoclinic mineral which is a double salt consisting of hydrated magnesium sulphate and potassium chloride, and is used as a fertilizer.

kainogenesis *n.* var. of CAENOGENESIS.

kairomone /ˈkʌɪrəməʊn/ *n.* L20. [f. Gk *kairos* opportunity, advantage, after PHEROMONE.] *Biol.* A chemical secreted and released by an organism which acts as a signal to the advantage of an organism of a different species.

kairos /ˈkʌɪrɒs/ *n.* M20. [Gk = right or proper time.] Fullness of time; the propitious moment, esp. for decision or action.

Kaiser /ˈkʌɪzə/ *n.*. [OE *cāsere* = OFris. *keisar*, OS *kēsur*, *-ar*, ON *keisari*, Goth. *kaisar*, f. Gmc f. Gk *kaisar* f. L CAESAR; in ME partly f. ON; in mod. use f. G *Kaiser* (cf. Du. *keizer*, †*keiser*, †*keser*).] (The title of) an emperor, *spec.* †(*a*) a Roman Emperor, (*b*) *Hist.* a Holy Roman Emperor, (*c*) an Austrian or German Emperor.

Phrases & comb.: **Kaiser (Bill) moustache** *colloq.* a moustache with the ends turned up, as worn by Wilhelm II, Kaiser of Germany (1888–1918). **kaiser roll** *N. Amer.* a type of bread roll. **Kaiser's war** *the* war of 1914–18. **king or kaiser** *arch.* any powerful earthly ruler.

Kaiserism *n.* (*Hist.*) political absolutism, esp. w. ref. to the German Empire E20. **Kaiserist** *n.* (*Hist.*) an adherent of Kaiserism E20. **Kaisership** *n.* the position or reign of a Kaiser M19.

k'ai shu /kʌɪ ʃuː/ *n. phr.* L19. [Chin. *kǎishu*, f. *kǎi* model + *shū* write.] The usual script used for the Chinese language, suitable for everyday purposes.

kaitaka /kʌɪˈtɑːkə/ *n. NZ.* L19. [Maori.] A flaxen cloak worn by Maoris.

kaizen /kʌɪˈzɛn/ *n.* L20. [Jap. = improvement.] Continuous improvement of working practices, personal efficiency, etc., as a business philosophy.

kajang /ˈkɑːdʒaŋ/ *n.* & *a.* Also (earlier) **cajang**, **†cadjan**. L17. [Malay & Jav.] **A** *n.* Matting or roofing made from the dried leaves of palms or pandanus; a mat, piece of roofing, awning, etc., made from this. L17. **B** *attrib.* or as *adj.* Made from the dried leaves of palms or pandanus; made from kajang(s). E18.

Kajar *n.* var. of QAJAR.

kajaten *n.* see KIAAT.

kajawah /kəˈdʒɑːwə, ˈkadʒəwə/ *n.* M17. [Urdu *kajāwah*, *kaja-*, Pers. *kajāwa.*] In some Eastern countries: a kind of litter for women consisting of a large pannier or wooden frame, a pair of which are carried by a camel.

kaka /ˈkɑːkɑː/ *n.* L18. [Maori.] A New Zealand parrot, *Nestor meridionalis*, which has a long beak and is olive-brown, varied with red or yellow.

Comb.: **kaka-beak**, **-bill** a climbing leguminous New Zealand plant, *Clianthus puniceus*, with vivid red flowers; also called *glory pea*.

kakaki /kəˈkɑːki/ *n.* M20. [Hausa.] A kind of W. African trumpet.

kakapo /ˈkɑːkəpəʊ/ *n.* Pl. **-os**. M19. [Maori.] A large yellow and brownish-green nocturnal flightless parrot, *Strigops habroptilus*, of New Zealand. Also called *ground parrot*, *owl-parrot*.

kakar /ˈkɑːkə/ *n.* Also **-ur**. L19. [Prob. imit.] = MUNTJAC.

kakariki /kɑːkəˈriːki/ *n. NZ.* M19. [Maori.] Either of two New Zealand parakeets, the red-fronted parakeet, *Cyanoramphus novaezelandiae*, and the yellow-fronted parakeet, *C. auriceps*.

kakemono /kɑːkɪˈməʊnəʊ/ *n.* Pl. **-os**. L19. [Jap., f. *kake-* hang + *mono* thing.] A Japanese unframed wall-picture, usu. painted or inscribed on silk or paper.

kaki /ˈkɑːki/ *n.* E18. [Jap.] The Japanese persimmon, *Diospyros kaki*, native to China and Japan and the kind most often cultivated.

Kakiemon /kɑˈkiːɛɪmɒn/ *a.* L19. [See below.] Designating, characteristic of, or in the style of a kind of porcelain first made by the Japanese potter Sakaida Kakiemon (1596–1666) at Arita, characterized by sparse asymmetrical designs painted over a glazed white ground.

kakistocracy /kakɪˈstɒkrəsi/ *n.* E19. [f. Gk *kakistos* worst + -CRACY, after ARISTOCRACY.] The government of a State by the worst citizens.

kakke /ˈkake/ *n.* L19. [Jap.] Beriberi.

kakkerlak /ˈkakəlak/ *n.* Now *rare* or *obs.* L17. [Du. f. G *kakerlak* f. Sp. *cucaracha* COCKROACH.] **1** In SE Asia, esp. Java: an albino. L17. **2** A cockroach. E19.

kakotopia /kakəˈtəʊpɪə/ *n.* E20. [f. Gk *kakos* bad, evil (cf. CACO-) + U)TOPIA.] = DYSTOPIA.

kakur *n.* var. of KAKAR.

kala-azar /kɑːləˈəˈzɑː/ *n.* L19. [Assamese, f. *kālā* black + *āzār* disease.] *Med.* A disease of tropical and subtropical regions caused by a protozoan of the genus *Leishmania* and transmitted by sandflies of the genus *Phlebotomus*, usu. involving emaciation, enlargement of the spleen and liver, anaemia, and fever; visceral leishmaniasis.

kalanchoe /kalənˈkəʊɪ/ *n.* M19. [mod.L (see below) f. Fr., ult. f. Chin. *gāláncài*.] Any of various chiefly African succulent shrubs and herbs of the genus *Kalanchoe* (family Crassulaceae), often grown as house or greenhouse plants, bearing usu. red, pink, or white flowers in terminal panicles and sometimes producing miniature plants from the edge of the leaves.

Kalashnikov /kəˈlaʃnɪkɒf, -ˈlɑːʃ-/ *n.* & *a.* L20. [M. T. *Kalashnikov* (b. 1919) its Russ. developer.] (Designating) a type of rifle or sub-machine-gun made in Russia.

kalashy, **-si**, **-ssi** *ns.* vars. of KHALASSI.

kale /keɪl/ *n.* Also **kail**. ME. [North. form of COLE *n.*[1]] **1** Any of various edible cruciferous plants of the genus *Brassica*; *spec.* a hardy cabbage-like vegetable, consisting of cultivars of *B. oleracea* and *B. napus*, with leaves which do not form a compact head (also called *borecole*). ME. **2** Broth in which Scotch kale or cabbage forms a principal ingredient; *Sc.* soup made with various kinds of vegetables. LME. **3** Money. *N. Amer. slang.* E20.

1 curled, **curly**, or **Scotch kale** a variety of kale in which the leaves are curled and crimped like parsley. *seakale*: see SEA *n.*

Comb.: **kale-bell** (*Sc.*) *the* dinner-bell; **kale-runt**, **-stock** the stem of a kale plant (cf. CASTOCK); **kale-time** *Sc.* dinner-time; **kale-worm** *Sc.* & *north.* a caterpillar, *esp.* that of the cabbage white butterfly.

kaleej *n.* var. of KALIJ.

kaleidoscope /kəˈlʌɪdəskəʊp/ *n.* & *v.* E19. [f. Gk *kalos* beautiful + *eidos* form + -SCOPE.] **A** *n.* **1** An optical toy consisting of a tube containing an arrangement of mirrors and pieces of coloured glass or paper which produce a constantly changing pattern of coloured reflections as the observer looks into the tube and rotates it. E19. **2** A constantly changing group of bright colours or coloured objects; a thing which constantly shifts and changes. E19.

2 K. WATERHOUSE The word *challenging* drops into the kaleidoscope of phrases he's tumbling around. J. WAIN He was no longer the centre of a flashing kaleidoscope of the clever, the beautiful, the worldly.

B *v.t.* & *i.* See or appear as in a kaleidoscope; move into or in a kaleidoscopic pattern. L19.

E. PIZZEY A painting . . over the dining-room mantelpiece whirled round her head, and kaleidoscoped into oblivion.

kaleidoˈscopic *a.* M19. **kaleidoˈscopically** *adv.* M19.

kalendar *n.* var. of CALENDAR *n.*

kalends *n.pl.* var. of CALENDS.

kaleyard /ˈkeɪljɑːd/ *n.* & *a.* *Sc.* Also **kail-**. M16. [f. KALE + YARD *n.*[1]] **A** *n.* A cabbage-garden, a kitchen garden, *esp.* one attached to a small cottage. M16. **B** *attrib.* or as *adj.* (Usu. **K-**.) Designating or pertaining to a group of late 19th-cent. fiction-writers, including J. M. Barrie (1860–1937), who portrayed local town life in Scotland and made much use of the vernacular. L19.

kaleyarder *n.* a writer of the Kaleyard School L19.

kalgan /ˈkɑːlgɑːn/ *n.* & *a.* M20. [*Kalgan* (see below).] (Designating) a fur obtained from a lamb from the area of Kalgan (now called Zhangjiakou), a city in Hebei province, China.

kali /ˈkeɪlʌɪ, ˈkali/ *n.* L16. [Colloq. Arab. *kalī* calcined ashes of Salsola etc.: cf. ALKALI.] **1** Any of several plants of the genus *Salsola*, of the goosefoot family; *esp.* the prickly saltwort, *S. kali*. L16. †**2** Soda ash; = ALKALI 1; vegetable alkali, potash. L18–E19.

kalian /kaˈljɑːn/ *n.* M19. [Pers. *kalyān* f. Arab. *ġalayān*: cf. CALEAN.] An Iranian type of hookah.

kalicine /ˈkalɪsiːn/ *n.* L19. [Irreg. f. mod.L *kalium* potassium + *-c-* + -INE[5].] *Min.* Native potassium bicarbonate, $KHCO_3$, a monoclinic mineral occurring as white crystals.

Also **kaˈlicinite** *n.* E20.

kalij /kɑːˈlɪdʒ/ *n.* Also **kaleej** /kəˈliːdʒ/. M19. [Pahari.] More fully *kalij pheasant*. A pheasant, *Lophura leucomelana*, of SE Asia and the Himalayan region.

kalimba /kəˈlɪmbə/ *n.* M20. [Bantu.] A musical instrument played with the thumbs, consisting of metal strips along a small hollow piece of wood.

kalkoentjie /kalˈkʊɪŋki, -tʃi/ *n.* *S. Afr.* Also **-tje**. M19. [Afk., f. *kalkoen* turkey + *-tjie* dim. suff.] **1** A pipit of the open veld, *Macronyx capensis*. M19. **2** Any of several plants of the iris family with scarlet flowers like a turkey's wattles, esp. *Gladiolus alatus*. E20.

kallidin /ˈkalɪdɪn/ *n.* M20. [f. next + PEPT)ID(E + -IN[1].] *Biochem.* A naturally occurring decapeptide, orig. confused with bradykinin (of which it is a lysyl derivative), which causes contraction of smooth muscle and vasodilation.

kallikrein /ˈkalɪkriːɪn, -kriːn/ *n.* M20. [f. Gk *kallikreas* PANCREAS + -IN[1].] *Biochem.* Any of various enzymes which release a kinin from a plasma protein precursor, so promoting vasodilation; orig. and *esp.* that found in the human pancreas and body fluids.

kallitype /ˈkalɪtʌɪp/ *n.* *obs.* exc. *Hist.* L19. [f. Gk *kalli-* comb. form (see -I-) of *kallos* beauty + -TYPE.] A type of photographic process using a ferric salt developed with silver nitrate.

kalmia /ˈkalmɪə/ *n.* M18. [mod.L (see below), f. Pehr *Kalm* (1716–79), Swed. botanist + -IA[1].] Any of several N. American shrubs of the genus *Kalmia*, of the heath family, with evergreen leaves and clusters of pink or white flowers; *esp.* mountain laurel, *K. latifolia*, and sheep laurel, *K. angustifolia*.

Kalmuck. /ˈkalmʌk/ *n.* & *a.* Also **Kalmyk** /ˈkalmɪk/. E17. [Russ. *Kalmyk*.] **A** *n.* Pl. **-s**, same. **1 a** A member of a Mongolian people living on the north-western shores of the Caspian Sea. E17. **b** The language of this people, a western form of Mongolian. E19. **2** (**k-**.) A kind of shaggy cloth, resembling bearskin. M19. **B** *attrib.* or as *adj.* Of or pertaining to the Kalmucks or their language. L18.

Kalˈmuckian *a.* (*rare*) E18.

kalon /ˈkalən/ *n.* *literary.* Now *rare.* M18. [Gk.] *The* ideal good; the *summum bonum*.

H. FIELDING Good fame is a species of the Kalon and it is by no means fitting to neglect it.

kalong /ˈkɑːlɒŋ/ *n.* E19. [Jav.] Any of several fruit-bats of SE Asia and Indonesia; *esp.* the large common flying fox, *Pteropus vampyrus*.

kalpa /ˈkalpə/ *n.* L18. [Skt.] In Indian cosmology: an aeon, a great age of the world, a cycle of *yugas*; *spec.* in *Hinduism*, a period of 4,320 million years.

kalpack, **-pak** *ns.* vars. of CALPAC.

kalsilite /ˈkalsɪlʌɪt/ *n.* M20. [f. *K, Al, Si* chem. symbols for potassium, aluminium, silicon + -LITE.] *Min.* A rare hexagonal silicate of potassium and aluminium, similar to nepheline, found in some lavas.

kalsomine /ˈkalsəmʌɪn/ *n.* & *v.* M19. [Origin unkn.] **A** *n.* A kind of white or coloured wash for walls; = CALCIMINE. M19. **B** *v.t.* & *i.* Whitewash with kalsomine. M19.

kama *n.* var. of KAAMA.

kamachili /kɑːməˈtʃiːli/ *n.* M19. [Tagalog *kamatsilé* f. Mex. Sp.] A tropical American leguminous tree, *Pithecellobium dulce*, with edible pods and bark that yields a yellow dye.

kamacite /ˈkaməsʌɪt/ *n.* L19. [f. Gk *kamak-*, *kamax* vine-pole + -ITE[1].] *Min.* An alloy of iron and nickel occurring in meteorites as bar-shaped masses.

kamagraphy /kəˈmagrəfi/ *n.* M20. [Fr. *kamagraphie*: see -GRAPHY.] A process for making copies of original paintings, using a special press and treated canvas, which reproduces the colour and texture of the brushstrokes.

kamagraph /ˈkaməgrɑːf/ *n.* [back-form.] (a) printing-press for producing) a reproduction painting copied by kamagraphy M20.

kamahi /ˈkɑːməhi/ *n.* *NZ.* M19. [Maori.] A tall forest tree, *Weinmannia racemosa* (family Cunoniaceae), with racemes of small cream-coloured flowers and dark wood.

Kamakura /ˈkɑːməkʊərə/ *a.* E20. [See below.] Designating or pertaining to the era of Japanese history (1192–1333) during which the seat of government was at Kamakura (a city on S. Honshu) esp. as a period or artistic production.

kamala /ˈkamələ/ *n.* E19. [Skt, prob. of Dravidian origin.] **1** A tree of the spurge family, *Mallotus philippensis*, of India and SE Asia. Also *kamala tree* E19. **2** A fine reddish-orange powder made from the fruit-capsules of this, used locally as an orange dye and an anthelmintic. M19.

Kamares /kəˈmɑːriːz/ *a.* & *n.* L19. [f. Gk *Kamarais* a Minoan cave-sanctuary on Mount Ida in Crete, where the pottery was found.] (Designating or pertaining to) a type of Minoan pottery from the middle Bronze Age, characterized by the use of red, white, and yellow ornaments on a black ground, depicting abstract or stylized plant designs.

kamash *n.* var. of QUAMASH.

kamassi /kəˈmasi/ *n.* L18. [Afk. *kammassie*, prob. f. Nama.] (The hard yellow wood of) a southern African evergreen tree, *Gonioma kamassi* (family Apocynaceae).

Kama Sutra /kɑːmə ˈsuːtrə/ *n.* & *a.* *phr.* L19. [Skt, f. *kāma* love, desire + *sūtra* SUTRA.] **A** *n.* *phr.* (The title of) an ancient Sanskrit treatise on the art of love and sexual technique; a sex manual. L19. **B** *adj. phr.* Sexually explicit; sensual. M20.

Kamba /ˈkambə/ *n.* & *a.* L19. [Bantu. See also WAKAMBA.] **A** *n.* Pl. same, **-s**. **1** A member of a Bantu-speaking people of central Kenya, related ethnically to the Kikuyu. L19. **2** The language of this people. L19. **B** *attrib.* or as *adj.* Of or pertaining to the Kamba or their language. E20.

Kamchadal /ˈkamtʃədal/ *n.* & *a.* M18. [Russ.] **A** *n.* Pl. **-s**, same. **1** A member of a non-Russian people inhabiting the Kamchatka peninsula on the Pacific coast of Siberia. M18. **2** The language of this people, now virtually extinct. M20. **B** *attrib.* or as *adj.* Of or pertaining to the Kamchadals or their language. E20.

Kamchatkan /kamˈtʃatk(ə)n/ *n.* & *a.* L18. [f. *Kamchatka* (see below) + -AN.] **A** *n.* A native or inhabitant of the Kamchatka peninsula on the Pacific coast of Siberia; a Kamchadal. L18. **B** *adj.* Of or pertaining to Kamchatka or its inhabitants. M19.

kame /keɪm/ *n.* Also **kaim**. LME. [Var. of COMB *n.*[1]] **1** = COMB *n.*[1] *Sc.* & *north.* LME. **2** A steep and sharp hill ridge; *spec.* in *Geol.*, a ridge or mound of sand and gravel deposited on or near a glacier. L18.

kameeldoorn /kəˈmɪəldʊən/ *n.* *S. Afr.* Also **-doring** /-dʊərɪŋ/. E19. [Afk. *kameeldoring*, f. Du. *kameel* camel + *doorn* thorn.] = CAMEL-*thorn* (b).

kameez /kəˈmiːz/ *n.* Also **-ze**, (earlier) **camise** /-s, -z/. E19. [Arab. *kamīṣ*, perh. f. late L *camisia*: see CHEMISE.] A loose long-sleeved shirt or tunic worn, esp. by Muslims, in the Indian subcontinent, and by some Muslims elsewhere. SHALWAR-*kameez*.

kamerad /ˈkamərɑːd, *foreign* kaməˈraːt/ *int.* E20. [G, lit. 'comrade', f. Fr. *camerade*, *camarade*: see COMRADE.] Used by a German-speaking soldier notifying to an enemy a wish to surrender.

kami /ˈkɑːmi/ *n.* Pl. same. E17. [Jap.] A Shinto god or deity. Also, the Japanese Emperor, a Japanese lord.

kamik /ˈkamɪk/ *n.* L19. [Eskimo (Inuit).] A long sealskin boot worn by Eskimos.

kamikaze /kamɪˈkɑːzi/ *n.* & *a.* L19. [Jap. = divine wind, f. as KAMI + *kaze* wind.] **A** *n.* **1** In Japanese tradition, the gale that destroyed the fleet of the invading Mongols in 1281. L19. **2** In the war of 1939–45, (a crewman of) a Japanese aircraft, usu. loaded with explosives, making a deliberate suicidal crash on an enemy target; a suicide pilot or plane. M20. **3** *Surfing.* A deliberately taken wipe-out. M20.

B *adj.* Of, pertaining to, or characteristic of a kamikaze; reckless, dangerous, potentially self-destructive. M20.

Spectator The suicidal self confidence of kamikaze pilots ramming an aircraft-carrier. *Evening Standard* The kamikaze liberals who prefer glorious defeat. *Daily Mail* A kamikaze roller-skater who weaves his way through the traffic.

Kamilaroi /kəˈmɪlərɔɪ/ *n.* & *a.* Pl. of n. same. M19. [Aborig.] A member of, of or pertaining to, a group of Australian Aboriginal peoples living between the Gwydir and Lachlan rivers in New South Wales, Australia; (of) the language of these peoples.

kämmererite /ˈkɛmərərʌɪt, ˈkam-/ *n.* Also **kaem-**. M19. [f. A. A. *Kämmerer* (1789–1858), Prussian surveyor of mines + -ITE[1].] *Min.* A reddish or lavender-coloured variety of chlorite, containing chromium.

kampong /kamˈpɒŋ/ *n.* Also (earlier) **c-**; **kampung** /-ˈpʌŋ/. L18. [Malay: see COMPOUND *n.*[2]] In Malaysia: a village, an enclosure.

Kampuchean /kampʊˈtʃiːən/ *a.* & *n.* L20. [f. *Kampuchea* Khmer name of Cambodia (used officially between 1975 and 1989) + -AN.] (A native or inhabitant) of Cambodia (Kampuchea). Cf. CAMBODIAN.

kampung *n.* var. of KAMPONG.

Kan *n.* var. of GAN.

kana /ˈkɑːnə/ *n.* Pl. same. E18. [Jap.] (A character or syllabary in) Japanese syllabic writing. Cf. HIRAGANA, KATAKANA.

kanaka /kəˈnakə, -ˈnɑːkə/ *n.* M19. [Haw. = person, human being.] A South Sea Islander, *esp.* (*Hist.*) one shipped to Queensland, Australia, for forced labour on the sugar plantations.

kanamycin /kanəˈmʌɪsɪn/ *n.* M20. [f. mod.L *kanamyceticus* (see below) + -IN[1]: cf. -MYCIN.] Any of several broad-spectrum antibiotics related to neomycin which are produced by the bacterium *Streptomyces kanamyceticus*.

Kanarese /kanəˈriːz/ *n.* & *a.* Also **C-**. M19. [f. *Kanara* (see below) + -ESE.] **A** *n.* Pl. same. **1** = KANNADA *n.* M19. **2** A member of a Kannada-speaking people of Kanara in western India. L19. **B** *adj.* Of or pertaining to Kanara or its people; *spec.* = KANNADA *a.* M19.

kanari /kəˈnɑːri/ *n.* L18. [Malay *kenari.*] Any of several SE Asian trees of the genus *Canarium* (family Burseraceae), producing edible nuts from which oil is extracted; *esp.* the Java almond, *C. luzonicum*.

kanat *n.* var. of QANAT.

kanban /ˈkanban/ *n.* L20. [Jap. = billboard, sign.] **1** A card used for ordering parts etc. in a Japanese just-in-time manufacturing system. L20. **2** In full *kanban-system*. A Japanese just-in-time manufacturing system in which parts etc. are ordered on cards. L20.

kanchil /ˈkɑːntʃɪl, ˈkan-/ *n.* E19. [Malay *kancil.*] The smallest chevrotain, *Tragulus javanicus*, native to forests in Borneo, Java, and Indochina.

Kandyan /ˈkandɪən/ *a.* & *n.* M19. [f. *Kandy* (see below) + -AN.] **A** *adj.* Of, pertaining to, or characteristic of the town or former kingdom of Kandy in Ceylon (Sri Lanka), or its inhabitants. M19. **B** *n.* A native or inhabitant of Kandy. M19.

Kanesian /kəˈniːʒ(ə)n/ *n.* & *a.* E20. [f. *Kanesh* an ancient city of Asia Minor + -IAN.] (Of) the principal dialect of Hittite. Also called *Nesite*.

kang /kaŋ/ *n.* L18. [Chin. *kàng*.] In China: a kind of stove for warming rooms; also, a brick or wooden structure for sleeping on, warmed from below by a fire.

kanga /ˈkaŋgə/ *n.*[1] *Austral. colloq.* E20. [Abbrev.] A kangaroo.

kanga *n.*[2] var. of KHANGA.

kangany /kanˈgɑːni/ *n.* Also **-ni**. E19. [Tamil *kaṇkāṇi*, f. *kaṇ* eye + *kāṇ-* see.] *Hist.* An overseer or headman of a gang of local labourers in Ceylon (Sri Lanka), southern India, or Malaysia.

kangaroo /kaŋgəˈruː/ *n.* Pl. **-s**, (in sense 1) same. L18. [Aborig.] **1** Any of various herbivorous marsupial mammals of the family Macropodidae, of Australia, New Guinea, and adjacent islands, which have small forelimbs, powerful hind limbs and long feet enabling a leaping bipedal gait, and a long tail for balance; *esp.* any of the larger kinds of the genus *Macropus*. Cf. WALLABY. L18. **2** A member of the Australian international rugby league or (formerly) rugby union team. *colloq.* E20. **3** In Britain, a parliamentary closure by which some amendments are selected for discussion and others excluded. Also *kangaroo closure*. E20.

1 *grey kangaroo*, *rat-kangaroo*, *red kangaroo*, *tree kangaroo*, etc.

Comb.: **kangaroo apple** (the edible fruit of) any of several Australian shrubs of the genus *Solanum*, esp. *S. laciniatum* and *S. vescum*; **kangaroo-beetle** a bright, metallic, jumping leaf-beetle of the genus *Sagra*, with enlarged hind legs; *kangaroo closure*: see sense 2 above; **kangaroo court** (orig. *US*) an improperly constituted court with no legal standing held by strikers, mutineers, etc.; **kangaroo-dog** a large dog trained to hunt kangaroos; **kangaroo-fly** *Austral.* a small irritating fly; **kangaroo-grass** a tall fodder grass, *Themeda australis*, found in Australasia, southern Asia, and Africa; **kangaroo justice** the procedure or product of a decision of a kangaroo court; **kangaroo mouse** (*a*) a marsupial mouse; (*b*) any small N. American desert rodent of the genus *Microdipodops*; **kangaroo paw** any of several Australian plants of the genus *Anigozanthos* (family Haemodoraceae), with showy woolly red or green flowers; **kangaroo-rat** (*a*) a rat-kangaroo; (*b*) any of various small burrowing rodents of the genus *Dipodomys*, of the southern US and Mexico, with elongated hind feet; **kangaroo thorn** a spiny Australian leguminous shrub, *Acacia armata*, used for hedges; **kangaroo vine** an Australian evergreen vine, *Cissus antarcticus*, with dark green heart-shaped leaves, grown as a house-plant.

kangaroo /kaŋgəˈruː/ *v.i.* M19. [f. the n.] **1** Hunt kangaroos. Chiefly as *kangarooing* vbl n. & ppl a. M19. **2** Make a great jump (*lit.* & *fig.*). L19.

kangarooer *n.* a person who hunts kangaroos E20.

K'ang-Hsi /kaŋˈʃiː/ *a.* E20. [Royal name of Hsüan-Yeh (see below).] Designating or pertaining to Chinese pottery and porcelain of the reign of Hsüan-Yeh, emperor of China (1661–1722), notable for very fine blue and white wares and the development of *famille verte* and *famille noire*.

kango /ˈkaŋgəʊ/ *n.* Pl. **-os**. M20. [Origin unkn.] A kind of mechanical hammer. Also *kango hammer*.

kangri /ˈkɑːŋgri/ *n.* E20. [Hind. *kā̃grī*: cf. Kashmiri *kā̃gürü*.] A small wicker-covered clay-lined pot filled with glowing charcoal, carried next to the skin, esp. by Kashmiris, to keep warm.

Kanjar /ˈkandʒə/ *n.* L19. [Origin unkn.] A member of any of various small Gypsy communities in the Indian subcontinent.

kanji /ˈkandʒi, ˈkɑːn-/ *n.* Pl. same. E20. [Jap., f. *kan* Chinese + *ji* letter, character.] (Any of) the set of borrowed and adapted Chinese ideographs used in the Japanese writing system. Cf. KANA.

kankar *n.* var. of KUNKUR.

kankerbos /ˈkaŋkəbɒs/ *n. S. Afr.* Also **-bossie** /-bɒsi/. E20. [Afk.] = *cancer bush* s.v. CANCER *n.*

kankie /ˈkaŋki/ *n.* M18. [Akan.] In W. Africa: a kind of bread made from maize flour.

Kannada /ˈkanədə/ *n.* & *a.* M19. [Kannada *Kannaḍa*.] **A** *n.* The Dravidian language of Kanara and Karnataka in western India, closely allied to Telugu. M19. **B** *attrib.* or as *adj.* Of or pertaining to Kannada. M19.

kanoon /kəˈnuːn/ *n.* E19. [Pers. *ḳānūn* f. Arab., ult. f. Gk *kanōn*.] A plucked musical instrument of the dulcimer or psaltery type, in the classic form with seventy-two strings, now with fifty to sixty.

kan-pei *int.* var. of GANBEI.

kanpu *n.* var. of GANBU.

kans /kɑːns/ *n.* L19. [Hindi *kāṃs* f. Skt *kāśa*.] In the Indian subcontinent: a coarse grass, *Saccharum spontaneum*, used for thatching.

Kansa /ˈkanzə/ *n.* & *a.* Also **Kansas** /ˈkanzəs/. E18. [Illinois f. Kansa *kką́ze*.] **A** *n.* Pl. **Kansa**, **Kansas** /ˈkanzəz, -zəs/. A member of a Sioux Indian people formerly of Kansas and now of Oklahoma; the language of this people. E18. **B** *attrib.* or as *adj.* Of or pertaining to the Kansa or their language. E19.

¶ Also called *Kaw*.

Kansan /ˈkanz(ə)n/ *n.* & *a.* M19. [f. *Kansas* (see below) + -AN. Cf. prec.] **A** *n.* **1** A native or inhabitant of the State of Kansas in the Middle West of the US. M19. **2** *Geol.* One of the Pleistocene glaciations in N. America. M20. **B** *adj.* Of or pertaining to Kansas; *spec.* (*Geol.*) designating or pertaining to the Kansan. L19.

†**Kansian** *n.* a Kansan M–L19.

Kansas *n.* & *a.* see KANSA.

kantar /kanˈtɑː/ *n.* Also **c-**. M16. [Arab. *ḳinṭār*, pl. *ḳanāṭīr*, f. (prob. through Syriac *qanṭēr*) L *centenarius* CENTENARY. Cf. QUINTAL, OFr. *quantar*, *canter*, med.L *cantar(i)um*, It. *cantaro*.] An Arab unit of weight having wide local variations, but in Egypt equal to about 45 kg.

kantele /ˈkantɪli/ *n.* E20. [Finn.] A form of zither used in Finland and the adjoining part of Russia.

Kantian /ˈkantɪən/ *a.* & *n.* L18. [f. *Kant* (see below) + -IAN.] **A** *adj.* Of or pertaining to the German philosopher Immanuel Kant (1724–1804) or his philosophical principles or views, esp. the view that the phenomenal world derives its structure from the nature of the mind that perceives it. L18. **B** *n.* An adherent or student the of philosophical principles or views of Kant. L18.

Kantianism *n.* (adherence to) Kantian principles or views L18. **Kantism** *n.* (now *rare*) Kantianism E19.

kantikoy /ˈkantɪkɔɪ/ *n.* Also **c-** & other vars. L17. [Delaware *kə́ntke:w*, lit. 'he dances'.] Among Algonquian Indians: a ceremonial dance; a party with dancing.

kanuka /ˈkɑːnʊkə/ *n. NZ.* E20. [Maori.] A small white-flowered evergreen tree, *Leptospermum ericoides*, of the myrtle family. Also called *white tea-tree*.

Kanuri /kəˈnuːri/ *n.* Pl. same. L19. [Kanuri.] A member of a group of peoples living in the region of Lake Chad, in Niger and NE Nigeria; the language of these peoples.

kanzu /ˈkanzuː/ *n.* E20. [Kiswahili.] A long white cotton or linen robe worn by E. African men.

kaoliang /keɪəʊljaŋ/ *n.* E20. [Chin. *gāoliang*, f. *gāo* (Wade-Giles *kao*) high + *liáng* fine grain.] A variety of sorghum, *Sorghum bicolor* var. *nervosum*, grown for grain in China and Manchuria.

kaolin /ˈkeɪəlɪn/ *n.* E18. [Fr. f. Chin. *gāolǐng* lit. 'high hill', a place in Jiangxi province where it is found.] A fine white clay resulting from the decomposition of feldspar, used to make porcelain and china, as a filler in paper and textiles, and in medicinal adsorbents and poultices. Also (*Min.*), any of a group of clay minerals which typically occur in such clay, *esp.* kaolinite.

kaoˈlinic *a.* L19.

kaolinise *v.* var. of KAOLINIZE.

kaolinite /ˈkeɪəlɪnʌɪt/ *n.* M19. [f. prec. + -ITE[1].] *Min.* A white or grey clay mineral which is the chief constituent of kaolin.
kaolinitic /keɪəlɪˈnɪtɪk/ *a.* of the nature of or containing kaolinite or other clay minerals of the kaolin group L19.

kaolinize /ˈkeɪəlɪnʌɪz/ *v.t.* Also **-ise**. L19. [f. as KAOLIN + -IZE.] *Geol.* Convert into kaolin. Chiefly as *kaolinized* ppl a.
kaolini'zation *n.* L19.

kaon /ˈkeɪɒn/ *n.* M20. [f. *ka* (repr. pronunc. of the letter K, κ) + -ON.] *Particle Physics.* Any of a group of mesons which have masses several times those of the pions and non-zero hypercharge, and on decaying usu. produce two or three pions, or a muon and a neutrino. Also called *K-meson, -particle*.
ka'onic *a.* of or pertaining to a kaon; (of an atom) having a kaon orbiting the nucleus: M20.

kapa *n.* see TAPA *n.*[1]

kapai /ˈkɑːpʌɪ/ *a.* & *adv.* *NZ.* M19. [Maori *ka pai*.] Good; well, fine. Also as *int.*, expr. pleasure or approval.

kaparring /kəˈparɪŋ/ *n.* *S. Afr.* M19. [Afk. f. Jav. *gamparon*.] A traditional form of wooden sandal worn by Cape Malays.

kapellmeister /kəˈpɛlmʌɪstə/ *n.* M19. [G, f. *Kapelle* court orchestra f. med.L *capella* CHAPEL + *Meister* master.] Chiefly *Hist.* The leader or conductor of a court orchestra, an opera, a choir, etc.

Kapenaar *n.* var. of KAAPENAAR.

kapok /ˈkeɪpɒk/ *n.* M18. [Malay *kapuk*.] A large tropical tree, *Ceiba pentandra* (family Bombacaceae) (also *kapok tree*); the silky fibre surrounding the seeds of this tree, used to stuff mattresses, cushions, etc.
¶ Formerly pronounced /ˈkɑːpək/.

Kaposi /kəˈpəʊsi/ *n.* L19. [M. K. *Kaposi* (1837–1902), Hungarian dermatologist.] Used in *possess.* (now chiefly in *Kaposi's sarcoma*) & *attrib.* to designate a disease involving multiple malignant tumours usu. of the lymph nodes or the skin, often associated with defective immunity.

kappa /ˈkapə/ *n.* LME. [Gk.] **1** The tenth letter (*K*, *κ*) of the Greek alphabet. LME. **2** *Biol.* An infective and independently reproducing particle (now usu. regarded as a commensal bacterium) which occurs within cells of some strains of the ciliate *Paramecium aurelia*, and produces a substance toxic to *Paramecium* cells lacking such particles. Also, such particles collectively. M20.

kappie /ˈkapi/ *n.* *S. Afr.* M19. [Afk. f. Du. *kapje* dim. of *kap* hood.] A sun-bonnet with a large brim to protect the face.

kapu /ˈkapu/ *a.* & *n.* M20. [Haw.] = TABOO *a.* & *n.*

kapur /ˈkapə/ *n.* M20. [Malay.] Any of various large dipterocarp timber trees of the genus *Dryobalanops*, esp. *D. aromatica*, native to Malaya, Sumatra, and Borneo; the wood of such a tree.

kaput /kəˈpʊt/ *a.* *slang.* L19. [G *kaputt* f. Fr. (*être*) *capot* (be) without tricks in piquet etc.: cf. CAPOT *n.*[1] & *v.*] Finished, worn out; dead, destroyed; rendered useless or unable to function; broken.

Karabagh /ˈkarəbɑː/ *n.* & *a.* E20. [A region now forming part of Nagorno-Karabakh in Azerbaijan, SW Asia.] (Designating) a thick knotted carpet or rug of the type originally made in Karabakh, usu. with a floral pattern but occas. with an animal one.

†karabe *n.* M16–L18. [Ult. f. Arab. *kahrabā* f. Pers. *kahrubā* amber (lit. 'attracting straw').] = AMBER *n.* 2.

karabiner /karəˈbiːnə/ *n.* M20. [Abbrev. of G *Karabiner-haken* spring-hook. Cf. KRAB.] A metal oval or D-shaped coupling link with a closure protected against accidental opening, used in mountaineering.

karaburan /karabʊˈran, karəˈbjʊər(ə)n/ *n.* E20. [Turk., f. *kara* black + *buran* whirlwind.] A hot dusty wind which blows in central Asia.

Karaite /ˈkɛːrəʌɪt/ *n.* & *a.* Also (earlier) **†C-**. E18. [f. Heb. *Qārā'īm* scripturalists, f. *qārā'* read: see -ITE[1].] **A** *n.* A member of a Jewish sect founded in the 8th cent. and located chiefly in the Crimea and neighbouring areas, and in Israel, which rejects rabbinical tradition in favour of literal interpretation of the Scriptures. E18. **B** *adj.* Of or pertaining to this sect. E20.
Karaism *n.* the religious system of the Karaites L19.

karaka /kəˈrakə/ *n.* M19. [Maori.] A New Zealand tree, *Corynocarpus laevigata* (family Corynocarpaceae), with orange berries and poisonous seeds which are edible after roasting.

Kara-Kalpak /ˈkarəkal,pak/ *n.* & *a.* Also **Karakalpak**. E18. [Kirghiz, f. *kara* black + *kalpak* cap.] **A** *n.* Pl. **-s**, same. **1** A member of a Turkic people inhabiting a region south of the Aral Sea in Uzbekistan. E18. **2** The Kazakh dialect of this people. L19. **B** *attrib.* or as *adj.* Of or pertaining to the Kara-Kalpaks or their dialect. M19.

karakia /karəˈkiːə/ *n.* & *v.* *NZ.* Pl. same, **-s**. M19. [Maori.] **A** *n.* A Maori incantation. M19. **B** *v.t.* Put a spell on (a person or object) by a karakia. M19.

Kara-Kirghiz /ˈkarəkɪə,gɪz, -ˌkəːgɪz/ *n.* & *a.* Pl. same. L19. [Kirghiz, f. *kara* black + as KIRGHIZ.] = KIRGHIZ.

karakul /ˈkarəkʊl/ *n.* & *a.* Also **caracul**. M19. [Russ. *karakul'*, f. the name of an oasis in Uzbekistan and of two lakes in Tadzhikistan, app. ult. f. Turkic.] **A** *n.* **1** (An animal of) a breed of sheep with a coarse wiry fleece. M19. **2** (Cloth or fur resembling) the glossy curled fleece of a young lamb of this breed. Also called *Persian lamb*. L19. **B** *attrib.* or as *adj.* Of or pertaining to the karakul or karakul. L19.

karamat *n.* & *a.* var. of KRAMAT.

Karamojong /karəˈməʊdʒɒŋ/ *n.* & *a.* Also **Kari** /karɪ-/, (earlier) **-jo** /-dʒəʊ/. E20. [Nilotic.] **A** *n.* Pl. same, **-s**. A member of a Nilotic people of Karamoja in NE Uganda; the language of this people. E20. **B** *attrib.* or as *adj.* Of or pertaining to the Karamojong or their language. E20.

karamu /ˈkarəmuː/ *n.* M19. [Maori.] Any of various Australasian trees and shrubs of the genus *Coprosma*, of the madder family, some of which produce edible fruits.

karana /ˈkʌrənə/ *n.* M20. [Skt *karaṇa* action, posture.] Any of the 108 basic postures in Indian dance.

karanga /ˈkarəŋə/ *n.* *NZ.* E20. [Maori.] A (Maori) ritual chant of welcome.

Karankawa /kəˈraŋkəwə/ *n.* & *a.* Also **Carancahua** /-hwə/. E19. [Amer. Sp. *Carancahuases* (pl.) prob. f. Karankawa.] **A** *n.* Pl. same, **-s**. A member of an American Indian people of the Gulf coast of Texas; the language of this people. E19. **B** *attrib.* or as *adj.* Of or pertaining to the Karankawa or their language. E19.
Karankawan *a.* & *n.* L19.

karanteen /kar(ə)nˈtiːn/ *n.* *S. Afr.* E20. [Origin unkn.] Either of two small marine fishes of the family Sparidae, *Crenidens crenidens* (more fully *white karanteen*), and the bamboo-fish, *Sarpa salpa* (more fully *striped karanteen*).

karaoke /karəˈəʊki, karɪ-/ *n.* L20. [Jap., f. *kara* empty + *oke* abbrev. of *ōkesutora* orchestra.] A form of entertainment (originating in Japan) in which one or more people sing popular songs as soloists against pre-recorded backing music; (in full *karaoke music*) such pre-recorded backing music.
Comb.: **karaoke bar**, **club**: providing karaoke facilities for customers (esp. in Japan); **karaoke machine**: for reproducing the music and at the same time giving a display of the words; *karaoke music*: see above.

karat *n.* see CARAT.

karate /kəˈrɑːti/ *n.* M20. [Jap., f. *kara* empty + *te* hand.] A Japanese system of unarmed combat using the hands and feet as weapons.
Comb.: **karate-chop** *n.* & *v.* (strike with) a sharp slanting blow of the hand.
karateka /kəˈrɑːtɪkɑː/ *n.* an exponent of or expert in karate M20.

karaya /kəˈrʌɪə/ *n.* L19. [Hind. *karāyal* resin.] In full *karaya gum*, *gum karaya*. A gum exuded by the Indian tree *Sterculia urens* (family Sterculiaceae), with uses similar to tragacanth.

karee *n.* var. of KARREE.

karela /kəˈreɪlə/ *n.* M19. [Hind. *karelā* f. Skt *kāravella*.] In the Indian subcontinent: (the fruit of) the balsam pear, *Momordica charantia*.

Karelian /kəˈriːlɪən/ *n.* & *a.* Also **C-**. M19. [f. *Karelia* (see below) + -AN.] **A** *n.* **1** A native or inhabitant of Karelia, a region in eastern Finland and the adjoining part of Russia. M19. **2** The Finno-Ugric language of this people. L19. **B** *adj.* Of or pertaining to Karelia, its people, or their language. M19.

Karen /kəˈrɛn/ *n.* & *a.* In sense A.1 also (earlier) **†Carian(er)**. M18. [Burm. *ka-reng* wild unclean man.] **A** *n.* **1** A member of a non-Burmese Mongoloid people scattered throughout Myanmar (Burma), esp. in the east. M18. **2** The language of this people. M19. **B** *attrib.* or as *adj.* Of or pertaining to the Karens or their language. M19.

karez /ˈkɑːrɛz/ *n.* Also **-ze**. L19. [Pashto f. Pers.] = QANAT.

karezza /kəˈrɛtsə/ *n.* Also **c-**. L19. [It. *carezza* caress.] Sexual intercourse in which ejaculation is avoided.

Karimojong *n.* & *a.* var. of KARAMOJONG.

Karitane /karɪˈtɑːni/ *a.* *NZ.* E20. [A township in the South Island of New Zealand.] Designating, pertaining to, or involving the system of ante- and post-natal care for mothers and babies initiated by the Royal New Zealand Society for the Health of Women and Children. Cf. PLUNKET *a.*[2]
Karitane baby, Karitane hospital, Karitane nurse, etc.

karkun *n.* var. of CARCOON.

karma /ˈkɑːmə, ˈkəːmə/ *n.* E19. [Skt *karman* action, effect, fate.] In *Buddhism* & *Hinduism*, the sum of a person's actions, esp. intentional actions, regarded as determining that person's future states of existence; in *Jainism*, subtle physical matter which binds the soul as a result of bad actions. Now also *gen.*, fate or destiny following as effect from cause.
Yoga & Health The good *Karmas* from your past have helped you. J. DIDION Whatever happens its in her karma.
Comb.: **karma-marga** /-ˈmɑːgə/ [*mārga* path] a strict adherence to Hindu precepts in order to attain a better life in one's next incarnation; ***karma-yoga*** /-ˈjəʊgə/ the attainment of perfection through disinterested action; **karma-yogi** /-ˈjəʊgi/ an exponent of *karma-yoga*.
karmic *a.* of or pertaining to karma L19.

karmadharaya /kɑːməˈdɑːrəjə, kəː-/ *n.* M19. [Skt, f. as prec. + *dhāraya* holding, bearing.] *Ling.* A compound in which the first element describes the second, as *highway*, *steamboat*, etc.

Karman /ˈkɑːmən/ *n.* E20. [Theodore von *Kármán* (1881–1963), Hungarian-born physicist and aeronautical engineer.] *Physics.* Used *attrib.* to designate a vortex street in which the vortices of one line are situated opposite points midway between those of the other line.

Karmathian /kɑːˈmeɪθɪən/ *n.* & *a.* Also **C-**. E19. [f. Ḥamdān Ḳarmaṭ its founder + -IAN.] **A** *n.* A member of a Muslim sect founded in the 9th cent. E19. **B** *adj.* Of or pertaining to this sect. E20.

Karnata /kəˈnɑːtə/ *a.* & *n.* Also (now *rare*) **C-**. L18. [Alternative name for *Karnataka*: see next.] **A** *n.* = KANNADA *n.* Now *rare*. L18. **B** *adj.* = next. E19.

Karnataka /kəˈnɑːtəkə/ *a.* E19. [See below. Cf. CARNATIC, prec.] Of or pertaining to the State of Karnataka (formerly Mysore) in SW India, its language (Kannada), or its music.

Karnaugh /ˈkɑːnɔː/ *n.* M20. [Maurice *Karnaugh* (b. 1924), US physicist.] Math. & Logic. *Karnaugh map, diagram*, a diagram that consists of a rectangular array of squares each representing a different combination of the variables of a Boolean function.

karo /ˈkɑːrəʊ/ *n.* Pl. **-os.** M19. [Maori.] An evergreen shrub or small tree native to New Zealand, *Pittosporum crassifolium* (family Pittosporaceae), with leathery leaves and clusters of small crimson flowers.

Karok /kəˈrɒk/ *n.* & *a.* M19. [f. Karok *karuk* upstream.] A *n.* Pl. **-s**, same. A member of an American Indian people of the Klamath river valley in NW California; the language of this people. M19. B *attrib.* or as *adj.* Of or pertaining to the Karoks or their language. L19.

Karoo /kəˈruː/ *n.* & *a.* Also **-rr-, k-.** L18. [Nama.] A *n.* Any of certain elevated semi-desert plateaux in southern Africa; terrain of this kind. L18. B *attrib.* or as *adj. Geol.* Designating or pertaining to a series of Triassic rocks in southern Africa, chiefly fossiliferous sandstone mixed with volcanic matter. L19.

kaross /kəˈrɒs/ *n. S. Afr.* Also †**kross.** M18. [Afk. *karos*, perh. f. Nama.] A cloak or sleeveless jacket like a blanket made of hairy animal skins, worn by the indigenous peoples of southern Africa. Also, a rug of sewn skins used on a bed or on the floor.

karree /kəˈriː/ *n.* Also **karee.** E19. [Afk. f. Nama *karib.*] Either of two willow-like southern African trees of the genus *Rhus*, *R. lancea* and *R. viminalis* (family Anacardiaceae). Also *karree-boom* /-bʊəm/ [Afk. *boom* = tree].

Karren /ˈkar(ə)n/ *n.pl.* L19. [G.] *Physical Geogr.* The furrows or fissures of a Karrenfeld; terrain characterized by these. Cf. LAPIÉS.

Karrenfeld /ˈkar(ə)nfɛlt, -fɛld/ *n.* Pl. **-felder** /-fɛldə/, **-felds** /-fɛldz/. L19. [G, f. prec. + *Feld* field.] *Physical Geogr.* An area or landscape, usu. of limestone bare of soil, which has been eroded by solution so as to have an extremely dissected surface with conspicuous furrows and fissures, often separated by knifelike ridges. Cf. LAPIÉS.

karri /ˈkari/ *n.* L19. [Aborig.] A tall eucalyptus, *Eucalyptus diversicolor*, of western Australia; the hard red timber of this tree.

Karroo *n.* var. of KAROO.

karrozzin /kəˈrɒtsɪn/ *n.* Also **car(r)ozzi.** E20. [Maltese f. It. *carrozza.*] A horse-drawn cab used in Malta.

karsey *n.* var. of KARZY.

Karshuni *n.* var. of GARSHUNI.

karst /kɑːst/ *n.* L19. [G *der Karst* (perh. rel. to Slovene *Krâs*) a limestone plateau region in Slovenia, SE Europe.] *Physical Geogr.* A kind of topography characteristic of areas of relatively soluble rock (usu. limestone) and mainly underground drainage, marked by numerous abrupt ridges, gorges, fissures, swallow-holes, and caverns; a region dominated by such topography.

tower karst: see TOWER *n.*[1]

Attrib. & *comb.*: In the sense 'characteristic of or of the nature of karst', as *karst land, scenery, topography*, etc. Special combs., as **karst tower** a steep-sided often flat-topped conical hill characteristic of tropical and subtropical karst.

¶ Earliest in attrib. use.

karstic *a.* of the nature of karst; pertaining to or characteristic of karst: E20. **karstifiˈcation** *n.* development of karst or karstic features; alteration into karst: M20. **karstify** *v.t.* subject to karstification (chiefly as *karstified, karstifying* ppl adjs.) M20. **karsting** *n.* = KARSTIFICATION E20.

karsy *n.* var. of KARZY.

kart /kɑːt/ *n.* M20. [Abbrev.] = GO-KART.

karting *n.* = GO-KARTING M20.

kartel *n.* var. of KATEL.

karuna /ˈkʌrʊnə/ *n.* M19. [Skt *karuṇā.*] *Buddhism.* Loving compassion.

karyo- /ˈkarɪəʊ/ *comb. form.* [f. Gk *karuon* nut: see -O-.] *Biol.* Of or pertaining to the nucleus of an animal or plant cell.

karyˈogamy *n.* fusion of cell nuclei L19. **karyogram** *n.* an idiogram; a karyotype: M20. **karyokiˈnesis** *n.* division of a cell nucleus during mitosis L19. **karyokiˈnetic** *a.* of or pertaining to karyokinesis L19. **karyˈolysis** *n.* dissolution of a cell nucleus L19. **karyoˈlytic** *a.* of or pertaining to karyolysis L19. **karyomere** *n.* a vesicle containing a single chromosome, formed in some cells at division E20. **karyomiˈtosis** *n.* karyokinesis L19. **karyomiˈtotic** *a.* karyokinetic L19. **karyoplasm** *n.* nucleoplasm L19. **karyoplasˈplasmic** *a.* of or pertaining to karyoplasm E20. **karyoˈrrhexis** *n.* [Gk *rhēxis* bursting] fragmentation of a cell nucleus L19. **karyosome** *n.* a densely-staining chromatin body within a cell nucleus, *esp.* one distinct from a nucleolus: L19.

karyology /karɪˈɒlədʒi/ *n.* L19. [f. prec. + -LOGY.] *Biol.* 1 The characteristic features of the nuclei *of* a particular cell type, species, strain, etc. L19. 2 The branch of biology that deals with cell nuclei and (esp.) chromosomes. M20.

karyoˈlogic *a.* (chiefly *US*) M20. **karyoˈlogical** *a.* E20. **karyoˈlogically** *adv.* as regards or in relation to karyology E20.

karyotin /ˈkarɪətɪn/ *n.* E20. [f. KARYO- + *-tin*, after *chromatin.*] *Biol.* = CHROMATIN.

karyotype /ˈkarɪətʌɪp/ *n.* & *v.* E20. [f. KARYO- + -TYPE.] *Biol.* A *n.* 1 The chromosomal constitution of a cell (and hence of an individual, species, etc.) represented by the number, size, shape, etc., of the chromosomes (usu. as at metaphase). E20. 2 A systematized (esp. photographic) representation of the chromosomes of a cell or cells. M20. B *v.t.* Determine or investigate the karyotype of (a cell, species, etc.). M20.

karyoˈtypic, **-ˈtypical** *adjs.* of or pertaining to a karyotype M20. **karyoˈtypically** *adv.* as regards karyotypes M20.

karzy /ˈkɑːzi/ *n. slang.* Also **-ey, -s-, c-.** M20. [Alt. of It. *casa* house.] A lavatory.

kasbah /ˈkazbɑː/ *n.* Also **c-.** M18. [Fr. *casbah* f. Maghribi pronunc. of Arab *kaṣaba* fortress.] (The Arab quarter surrounding) a N. African castle or fortress-citadel.

kasha /ˈkaʃə/ *n.*[1] Also (earlier) †*c-*. E19. [Russ.] 1 A porridge made from cooked buckwheat or other grains. E19. 2 A beige colour resembling that of buckwheat groats. M20.

Kasha /ˈkaʃə/ *n.*[2] E20. [Origin unkn.] (Proprietary name for) a soft napped fabric made from wool and hair. Also, a cotton lining material.

Kashan /kəˈʃɑːn/ *n.* & *a.* E20. [A province and town in central Iran.] (Designating) a finely woven rug, usu. of wool or silk, made in Kashan.

Kashgai /ˈkaʃgʌɪ/ *n.* & *a.* Also **Qashgai** & other vars. L19. [Turkic.] A *n.* Pl. **-s**, same. A member of a Turkic people living around Shiraz in Iran. L19. B *adj.* Of or pertaining to the Kashgais. E20.

Kashgar /ˈkaʃgɑː/ *a.* L19. [See below.] Of or pertaining to Kashgar, a city and district of Sinkiang-Uighur (formerly East Turkestan) in China; *spec.* (*a*) designating the Turkic language of Kashgar; (*b*) designating a type of Turkish carpet associated with Kashgar.

Kashmir /ˈkaʃmɪə, kaʃˈmɪə/ *n.* & *a.* L19. [See next. Cf. CASHMERE.] A *n.* 1 = CASHMERE I. *rare.* L19. 2 = KASHMIRI *n.* 2. *rare.* L19.

B *attrib.* or as *adj.* 1 = KASHMIRI *a.* L19. 2 Designating a Caucasian rug or carpet with a flat napless surface and loose ends of yarn on the back. Also called *Soumak.* E20.

1 **Kashmir goat** a goat of a Himalayan breed yielding fine soft wool (used to make cashmere).

Kashmirian *a.* & *n.* (now *rare* or *obs.*) (*a*) *adj.* = KASHMIRI *a.*; (*b*) *n.* = KASHMIRI *n.* 2: L18.

Kashmiri /kaʃˈmɪəri/ *a.* & *n.* L19. [f. prec. + -I[2].] A *adj.* Of or pertaining to Kashmir, a disputed territory in the western Himalayas, formerly a separate State but now divided between India and Pakistan. L19. B *n.* 1 The Dard language of Kashmir. L19. 2 A native or inhabitant of Kashmir. M20.

Kashrut /kaʃˈruːt/ *n.* Also **-ruth** /-ˈruːθ/. E20. [Heb. = legitimacy (in religion), f. as KOSHER *a.*] The body of Jewish religious laws relating to the suitability of food, ritual objects, etc.; the observance of these laws.

Kashube /kəˈʃuːb/ *n.* Also **Kaszube.** L19. [f. *Kashubia* (Pol. *Kaszuby*): see below.] 1 A member of the Slavonic people inhabiting Kashubia, a region of Poland west and north-west of Gdańsk. L19. 2 The dialect of this people, Kashubian. M20.

Kashubian /kəˈʃuːbɪən/ *n.* & *a.* Also (earlier) **Cassub-** /kəˈsuːb-/; **Kaszub-.** M19. [f. as prec. + -AN.] A *n.* 1 The Lechitic dialect of Kashubia. M19. 2 = KASHUBE *n.* 1. M20. B *adj.* Of or pertaining to Kashubia, its people, or their dialect. E20.

Kassite /ˈkasʌɪt/ *n.* & *a.* L19. [f. Assyr. *kaššu* + -ITE[1].] A *n.* 1 A member of an Elamite people from the Zagros mountains in Iran, who ruled Babylon from the 18th to the 12th cent. BC. L19. 2 The language of this people. M20. B *adj.* Of or pertaining to the Kassites or their language. L19.

kasturi /kaˈstuːri/ *n.* Also **-ra** /-rə/. M19. [Skt *kastūrī.*] A Himalayan musk deer.

Kaszube *n.*, **-bian** *n.* & *a.* vars. of KASHUBE, -BIAN.

kat *n.* var. of KHAT.

kat- *pref.* see CATA-.

kata /ˈkɑːtɑː/ *n.* M20. [Jap.] A system of basic exercises or postures and movements used to teach and improve the execution of techniques in judo and other martial arts.

kata- *pref.* see CATA-.

katabasis /kəˈtabəsɪs/ *n. literary.* Pl. **-ases** /-əsiːz/. M19. [Gk, f. *kata* down + *basis* going. Cf. ANABASIS.] A military retreat, *esp.* that of the Greeks under Xenophon, related in his *Anabasis*.

katabatic /katəˈbatɪk/ *a.* In sense 1 **c-.** L19. [Gk *katabatikos*, f. *katabainein* go down: see -IC. Cf. ANABATIC.] †1 *Med.* Gradually declining in severity. *rare.* Only in L19. 2 *Meteorol.* Of a wind: caused by local downward motion of (esp. cool dense) air. Opp. ANABATIC. L19.

katabolic *a.*, **-ism** *n.* vars. of CATABOLIC, -ISM.

katabothron *n.* etc., see KATAVOTHRON.

katakana /katəˈkɑːnə/ *n.* Also **-gana.** E18. [Jap., f. *kata* side + KANA.] An angular form of kana, used in modern Japanese mainly for writing words of foreign origin and for emphasis. Cf. HIRAGANA.

katana /kəˈtɑːnə/ *n.* Also (earlier) †*cattan.* E17. [Jap.] A long single-edged sword used by Japanese samurai.

¶ Recorded in the Anglicized form in E17, then not again until L19 in the form *katana*.

Katangese /kataŋˈgiːz/ *n.* & *a.* M20. [f. *Katanga* (see below) + -ESE.] A *n.* Pl. same. A native or inhabitant of Katanga, now the province of Shaba in SE Zaire. M20. B *adj.* Of or pertaining to Katanga or the Katangese. M20.

katathermometer /katəθəˈmɒmɪtə/ *n.* E20. [f. *kata-* var. of CATA- + THERMOMETER.] A thermometer with an enlarged bulb used to determine the cooling power of ambient air or the rate of airflow by measuring the time taken for the indicated temperature to fall by a specified amount.

†**katatonia** *n.* var. of CATATONIA.

katavothron /katəˈvɒθrən/ *n. arch.* Also **c-, -both-** /-ˈbɒθ-/, **-thra** /-θrə/. Pl. **-thra** /-θrə/, **-thrai** /-θrʌɪ/, **-throns.** E19. [mod.Gk *katabothra*, pl. *-thrai*, *-thres*, f. Gk *kata* down + *bothros* hole (*-v-* repr. mod.Gk pronunc., *-on* f. misunderstanding sing. as neut pl.).] A subterranean channel or deep hole formed by the action of water; a swallow-hole.

Kate Greenaway /keɪt ˈgriːnəweɪ/ *a. phr.* L19. [Kate (Catherine) *Greenaway* (1846–1901), Eng. artist and illustrator of children's books.] Designating (a garment in) a style of children's clothing modelled on Kate Greenaway's drawings.

katel /ˈkɑːt(ə)l/ *n. S. Afr.* Also (*arch.*) **cartle; kartel.** M19. [Afk., app. f. Port. *catel*, *catle* little bed f. Malay *katil* f. Tamil *kaṭṭil* bedstead. Cf. KATIL.] A lightweight portable bed or hammock, used in an ox-wagon.

kat' exochen /kat ˈɛksəʊʃɛn/ *adv. phr.* Now *rare.* L16. [Gk *kat' exokhēn.*] Pre-eminently.

¶ Usu. found in untransliterated Gk characters.

Kathak /ˈkʌtək/ *n.* & *a.* Also (esp. in sense A.2) **k-**. M20. [Skt *kathaka* professional storyteller, f. *kathā* story.] A *n.* Pl. **-s**, (in sense 1) same. **1** A member of a northern Indian caste of storytellers and musicians. M20. **2** A type of northern Indian classical dance alternating passages of mime with passages of dance; an example of this. M20. B *attrib.* or as *adj.* Of or pertaining to the Kathak or Kathak. M20.

Kathakali /kɑːtəˈkɑːli/ *n.* Also (*rare*) **Kadh-**. E20. [Malayalam *kathakaḷi*, f. Skt *kathā* story + Malayalam *kaḷi* play.] A southern Indian dance-drama based on Hindu literature, characterized by stylized costume and make-up, and frequent use of mime.

katharevousa /kaθərəˈvuːsə, kaθəˈrɛvʊsə/ *n.* E20. [mod.Gk *kathareuousa* fem. of *kathareuōn* pres. pple of Gk *kathareuein* be pure, f. *katharos* pure.] The purist form of modern Greek (at one time, but since 1976 no longer, the language officially used by the State).

Katharine *n.* see CATHERINE.

katharometer /kaθəˈrɒmɪtə/ *n.* E20. [f. Gk *katharos* pure + -OMETER.] An instrument for detecting a gas or measuring its concentration in a mixture by measuring changes in thermal conductivity.

katharsis *n.*, **kathartic** *a.* & *n.* see CATHARSIS, CATHARTIC.

kathenotheism /kəˈθɛnəʊ,θiːɪz(ə)m/ *n.* M19. [f. Gk *kath ena* one by one + *theos* god + -ISM.] Vedic polytheism, in which each god in turn for a period of time is considered single and supreme.

Katherine *n.* see CATHERINE.

katheter *n.*, **kathetometer** *n.* vars. of CATHETER, CATHETOMETER.

kathi /ˈkɑːði/ *n.* M20. [Malay *kadi* f. Arab. *ḳāḍī* CADI.] A judge in Islamic law, who also functions as a registrar of Muslim marriages, divorces, etc.

Kathleen Mavourneen /ˌkaθliːn məˈvɔːniːn/ *n.* & *a.* *Austral. slang.* E20. [Title of a song one line of which is 'it may be for years, and it may be forever.'] A *n.* An open-ended jail sentence. Also, a habitual criminal. E20. B *adj.* Open-ended, of indeterminate duration. E20.

†kathode *n.*, **†kathodic** *a.*, **†kathodo-** *comb. form* vars. of CATHODE, CATHODIC, CATHODO-.

kati /ˈkati/ *n.* Also **katti**. E18. [Malay.] In Malaysia: = CATTY *n.*

katil /ˈkɑːt(ə)l/ *n.* *S. Afr.* M20. [Malay: see KATEL.] A bier used by Cape Malays in funeral ceremonies.

katipo /ˈkatɪpəʊ/ *n.* Pl. **-os**. M19. [Maori.] A venomous black New Zealand spider, *Latrodectus katipo*, with a red spot on its back.

katjiepiering /ˈkatjɪˈpɪərɪŋ, ˈkʌɪkɪ-/ *n.* L18. [Afk. f. Malay *kacapiring*.] Any of various southern African gardenias, esp. *Gardenia thunbergia* and *G. jasminoides*.

katonkel /kəˈtɒŋk(ə)l/ *n.* *S. Afr.* M19. [Afk. f. Malay *ketangkai*.] Either of two marine game-fishes of the family Scombridae, the seir, *Scomberomorus commerson*, and the bonito, *Sarda sarda*.

Kat stitch /ˈkat stɪtʃ/ *n. phr.* E20. [f. *Kat* pet-form of female forename *Katharine*, *C-*, after Catherine of Aragon, said to have invented the stitch: see STITCH *n.*[1]] *Lace-making.* A stitch which forms a star-shaped ground net.

katsuo /ˈkatswo/ *n.*E18. [Jap.] A bonito, *Katsuwonus pelamis*, important as a food fish in Japan, fresh or dried.

katsuobushi /katswoˈbuʃi/ *n.* a dried quarter of this fish L19.

katsura /katˈsʊərə/ *n.* E20. [Jap.] **1** A type of Japanese wig worn mainly by women. E20. **2** In full *katsuramono* /kat,sʊərəˈməʊnəʊ/ [*mono* piece, play]. A type of romantic Noh play with a woman as the central character. E20.

Kattern /ˈkatəːn/ *n.* & *v.i.* Also **C-**. M18. [Alt. of St *Catherine* of Alexandria, the patron saint of spinners, martyred in AD 307.] *Hist.* (Celebrate) the feast day of St Catherine, 25 November.

katti *n.* var. of KATI.

katun /ˈkɑːtuːn/ *n.* E20. [Maya.] A period of twenty years, each of 360 days, in the calendar of the Mayan Indians.

katydid /ˈkeɪtɪdɪd/ *n.* Also **c-**. L18. [Imit.] Any of various large usu. green N. American bush-crickets, the males of which make a characteristic sound.

Katyusha /kəˈtjuːʃə/ *n.* M20. [Russ.] A type of Russian rocket mortar.

Comb.: **Katyusha rocket** launched from a Katyusha.

katzenjammer /ˈkats(ə)ndʒamə/ *n.* *US colloq.* M19. [G, f. *Katzen* (comb. form of *Katze* cat) + *Jammer* distress, wailing.] **1** A hangover; a severe headache. M19. **2** *transf.* & *fig.* Confusion, disorder; clamour, uproar. L19.

kauch /kɑːx/ *n.* *Sc.* Also **kiaugh** /kjɑːx/ & other vars. L18. [Origin unkn.] Trouble, worry.

kau-kau /ˈkaʊkaʊ/ *n.* Pl. same. M20. [f. Melanesian pidgin, perh. ult. f. Chin.] In New Guinea: the sweet potato.

kauri /ˈkaʊriː/ *n.* E19. [Maori.] A tall coniferous New Zealand tree, *Agathis australis*; the hard timber of this tree.

Comb.: **kauri gum** the fossil resin of the kauri, used as a varnish.

kausia /ˈkɔːsɪə, ˈkaʊsɪə/ *n.* M19. [Gk.] *Gk Antiq.* A low broad-brimmed felt hat worn in ancient Macedonia.

kava /ˈkɑːvə/ *n.* L18. [Tongan.] A shrub, *Piper methysticum* (family Piperaceae), of the West Pacific islands; a narcotic fermented drink made esp. in Fiji from its macerated roots. Cf. YANGGONA.

kavadi /ˈkɑːvədi/ *n.* M20. [Tamil *kāvaṭi*.] A decorated arch carried on the shoulders as an act of penance in Malaysian Hindu religious practice.

kavass /kəˈvɑːs, kəˈvas/ *n.* Also (*arch.*) **c-**, **-w-**. E19. [Turk. *kavas* guard f. Arab. *ḳawwās* bowman, f. *ḳaws* bow.] In Turkey: orig., an armed officer, servant, or courier; now usu., a uniformed guard or messenger at an embassy, consulate, etc.

kavir /kəˈvɪə/ *n.* Also **kev-**. L19. [Pers.] A salt-desert or (occas.) saline swamp in Iran; terrain characterized by such a feature.

the Kavir the great central salt-desert of Iran.

Kavirondo /kɑːvɪˈrɒndəʊ/ *n.* & *a.* L19. [An area of Kenya, of unkn. origin.] A *n.* Pl. same, **-os**. **1** A member of any of the Nilotic and Bantu-speaking peoples inhabiting the Kavirondo area of Kenya. L19. **2** The Nilotic or Bantu language of any of these peoples. L19.
B *attrib.* or as *adj.* Of or pertaining to the Kavirondo, its people, or (any of) their languages. L19.

Kavirondo crane = CROWNED *crane*.

Kaw /kɔː/ *n.* & *a.* *US.* E19. [f. traders' N. Amer. Fr. abbrev. of KANSA.] = KANSA.

kawakawa /ˈkɑːwəkɑːwə/ *n.*[1] M19. [Maori.] **1** A shrub or small tree, *Macropiper excelsum*, of the pepper family, native to New Zealand and neighbouring islands. Also called *pepper tree*. M19. **2** A variety of nephrite. *NZ.* L19.

kawakawa /kɑːvəˈkɑːvə/ *n.*[2] L19. [Haw.] The little tuna, *Euthynnus affinis*, of the Pacific Ocean.

kawass *n.* var. of KAVASS.

Kawi /ˈkawi/ *n.* E19. [Skt *kavi* poet.] The classic or poetic language of Java and Bali, in which the ancient indigenous language is mixed with many words of Sanskrit origin.

kay /keɪ/ *int.* M20. [Abbrev.] = OK *int.*

kaya /ˈkʌɪə/ *n.* L19. [Jap.] A Japanese coniferous tree, *Torreya nucifera*, related to the yew, with large edible seeds the oil of which is used in cooking. Also, the wood of this tree.

kayak /ˈkʌɪak/ *n.*[1] M18. [Eskimo (Inuit) *qayaq*.] A *n.* **1** An Eskimo canoe, made of a framework of light wood covered with sealskins, and having a small watertight opening in the top to admit a single man. M18. **2** A small covered canoe modelled on this, used for touring or sport. M20.
B *v.i.* Travel by kayak, paddle a kayak. L19.

kayaker *n.* a person who kayaks M19. **kayakist** *n.* a person who paddles a kayak, a kayaker M20.

kayak /ˈkʌɪak/ *n.*[2] *Canad.* Also **kiack**. M19. [Perh. f. (as) prec.] = ALEWIFE 2.

Kayan /ˈkʌɪən/ *n.* & *a.* M19. [Kayan.] A *n.* Pl. **-s**, same. **1** A member of a people of Sarawak and Borneo. M19. **2** The Indonesian language of this people. L19. B *attrib.* or as *adj.* Of or pertaining to the Kayans or their language. M19.

kayles /keɪlz/ *n.pl.* Now *dial.* & *Hist.* Also **kyles** /kʌɪlz/. Sing. form used only in comb. ME. [(M)Du. *kegel*, †*keyl-* (in *keylbane* skittle-alley) = OHG *kegil* (G *Kegel*) tapering stick, cone, skittle.] A variety of ninepins or skittles; the set of wooden or bone pins used in this.

kaylied /ˈkeɪlʌɪd, ˈkeɪlɪd/ *a.* *dial.* & *slang.* M20. [Origin unkn.] Extremely drunk.

kayo /ˈkeɪəʊ/ *a.* & *n.*[1] *slang.* E20. [Reversal of pronunc. of OK under the influence of next.] A *adj.* = OK *a.* E20. B *n.* Pl. **-o(e)s**. = OK *n.* M20.

kayo /ˈkeɪəʊ/ *v.* & *n.*[2] *colloq.* E20. [Repr. pronunc. of *KO* s.v. K, K.] Chiefly *Boxing.* A *v.t.* Knock out; stun or fell, esp. with a blow. E20. B *n.* Pl. **-o(e)s**. A knockout; a knockout blow. M20.

Kayser-Fleischer ring /ˈkʌɪzəflʌɪʃə rɪŋ/ *n. phr.* M20. [f. Bernhard *Kayser* (1869–1954) & Bruno *Fleischer* (b. 1874), Ger. ophthalmologists.] *Med.* A pigmented ring around the cornea, usu. brownish, caused by copper deposition and diagnostic of Wilson's disease.

kaza /ˈkɑːzə/ *n.* Also **c-**. L19. [Turk., f. Arab. *kaza* f. Arab. *ḳaḍā*: see CADI.] In Turkey: formerly, a judicial district; now, an administrative district governed by a kaimakam.

kazachoc /kazəˈtʃɒk/ *n.* Also **kozatchok** & other vars. E20. [Russ., dim. of *kazak* COSSACK.] A Slavonic, chiefly Ukrainian, dance with a fast and usu. quickening tempo, and employing the step *prisiadka*.

Kazak /kəˈzɑːk/ *a.* & *n.* E20. [f. *Kazakh*, a town in Azerbaijan.] (Designating) a type of thick durable Caucasian wool rug, characterized by large geometric designs in striking colours.

Kazakh /kəˈzɑːk/ *n.* & *a.* M19. [Russ., f. as COSSACK.] A *n.* Pl. **-s**, **-i** /-i/. **1** A member of a Turkic people of central Asia, esp. of Kazakhstan. M19. **2** The language of this people. E20. B *attrib.* or as *adj.* Of or pertaining to the Kazakhs or their language. L19.

kazi /ˈkɑːziː/ *n.* E17. [Arab. *ḳāḍī* CADI (repr. a pronunc.).] A cadi in some parts of central and SE India and the Indian subcontinent.

kazoo /kəˈzuː/ *n.* Also **g-** /g-/. L19. [App. imit. of the sound produced.] A toy or (now) jazz musical instrument consisting of a tube with a membrane at each end or over a hole in the side, which produces a buzzing noise when blown into.

kazooer *n.* M20. **kazooist** *n.* L20.

kea /ˈkiːə/ *n.* M19. [Maori.] A large brownish-green parrot of the Southern Alps of New Zealand, *Nestor notabilis*, which has an omnivorous diet including carrion, and was formerly reputed to kill sheep.

Keating's /ˈkiːtɪŋz/ *n.* L19. [f. Thomas *Keating*, 19th-cent. Brit. chemist + -'S[1].] In full *Keating's powder*. (Proprietary name for) a type of insect-powder.

Keatsian /ˈkiːtsɪən/ *a.* & *n.* M19. [f. *Keats* (see below) + -IAN.] A *adj.* Of, pertaining to, or characteristic of the English poet John Keats (1795–1821) or his work. M19. B *n.* An admirer or student of Keats or his work. L19.

Keatsiˈana *n.pl.* [-ANA] publications or other items concerning or associated with Keats E19.

kebab /kɪˈbab, kə-, -ˈbɑːb/ *n.* Also (earlier, now *rare*) **cabob** /kəˈbɒb/. L17. [Arab. *kabāb* (perh. ult. f. Pers.), partly through Urdu, Pers., and Turk.] **1** A dish consisting of pieces of meat (occas. with vegetables) grilled or roasted on a skewer or spit. L17. **2** *Physical Chem.* Each of the platelike crystallites in a shish kebab polymer structure. L20.

1 DONER KEBAB. SHISH KEBAB.

kebaya /kəˈbɑːjə/ *n.* Also (earlier) †***cabaia*** & other vars. L16. [f. Arab. *kabāya* repr. colloq. pronunc. of *kbā'a* fem. of *kbā'* tunic, gown, shirt: in early use through Port. *cabaya* or Pers., in mod. use through Malay *kebaya*.] 1 A light loose tunic of a type worn in SE Asia by women or (formerly) by men. L16. 2 A short tight-fitting long-sleeved jacket, together with a sarong the traditional dress of Malay and Indonesian women. M20.

1 SARONG *kebaya*.

¶After 17 not recorded again until L19.

kebbie /ˈkɛbi/ *n. Sc.* & *north.* E19. [Origin unkn.] A staff or stick with a hooked head.

kebbuck /ˈkɛbək/ *n. Sc.* LME. [Perh. f. Gael. *càbag*.] A whole cheese.

keck /kɛk/ *n. obs.* exc. *dial.* E17. [f. KEX, taken as a pl.] (The dry hollow stem of) a large umbelliferous plant; = KEX.

keck /kɛk/ *v.i.* Now *dial.* E17. [Imit.] 1 Retch; feel an inclination to vomit; (foll. by *at*) reject (food, medicine, etc.) with loathing, express strong dislike or disgust. E17. 2 Of a bird: make an abrupt call, cluck, cackle. M18.

keckle /ˈkɛk(ə)l/ *v.t.* E17. [Origin unkn.] *Naut.* Protect (a hemp cable or hawser) with old rope in order to prevent chafing in the hawse-hole.

kecksie /ˈkɛksi/ *n.* Chiefly *dial.* Also **-y.** L16. [f. *kexes* pl. of KEX, taken as = *kexies*.] = KECK *n.*, KEX.

SHAKES. *Hen. V* Hateful docks, rough thistles, kecksies, burs.

ked /kɛd/ *n.*[1] Also **kade** /keɪd/. L16. [Origin unkn.] Any of various bloodsucking hippoboscid flies parasitic on birds and mammals; *esp.* (more fully *sheep-ked*) a wingless flat-bodied fly, *Melophagus ovinus*, which infests sheep.

Ked /kɛd/ *n.*[2] E20. [Perh. alt. of *ped-* in *pedal* etc.] (Proprietary name, in pl., for) a soft-soled canvas shoe.

keddah *n.* var. of KHEDA.

kedge /kɛdʒ/ *n.* E18. [f. the vb.] In full *kedge anchor*. A small anchor with an iron stock for warping or hauling off after grounding.

kedge /kɛdʒ/ *v.* L15. [Perh. specialized use of CADGE *v.* 1.] *Naut.* 1 *v.i.* & *t.* Warp or tow (a ship) by hauling in a hawser attached to a small anchor dropped at some distance. L15. 2 *v.i.* Of a ship: move by means of kedging. M19.

†**kedger** *n.* = KEDGE *n.* L15–E18.

kedgeree /ˈkɛdʒəriː/ *n.* M17. [Hindi *khicṛī* f. Skt *khiccā* dish of boiled rice and sesame.] 1 An Indian dish of rice boiled with split pulses, onions, eggs, and seasonings. M17. 2 In European cookery, a dish made of boiled rice, eggs, fish, and seasonings. E19. 3 *transf.* & *fig.* A mixture, a jumble. E20.

Comb.: **kedgeree-pot** a large earthenware container for holding water and for cooking.

kedlock /ˈkɛdlɒk/ *n. obs.* exc. *dial.* ME. [App. repr. OE *ċedele* dog's mercury, of unkn. origin.] 1 Any of several yellow-flowered cruciferous weeds, esp. charlock, *Sinapis arvensis*. ME. 2 = KEX. L17.

keech /kiːtʃ/ *n. obs.* exc. *dial.* L16. [Origin unkn.] 1 A lump of congealed fat; the fat of a slaughtered animal rolled up into a lump. L16. 2 A cake, *spec.* a large pastry made with chopped apples and raisins. L17.

keek /kiːk/ *v.* & *n.* Now only *Sc.* & *north.* Also (earlier) †**kike.** LME. [Perh. rel. to MDu. *kīken*, *kieken* (Du. *kijken*), LG *kīken* look, peep. Cf. also PEEK *v.*[1] & *n.*[1]] **A** *v.i.* Peep, esp. surreptitiously as through a narrow opening, or round a corner. Formerly also, glance, gaze. LME.

A. GRAY He keeked between the stems of sorrel . . at the midden.

B *n.* A peep, a surreptitious glance. E17.

Comb.: **keeking-glass** a looking-glass; **keek-keek** *int.* a call used in hide-and-seek.

keeker *n.* (*a*) a person who peeps; *spec.* (*b*) an overseer or inspector in a coal-pit; (*c*) in *pl.*, the eyes: E19.

keel /kiːl/ *n.*[1] ME. [ON *kjǫlr* f. Gmc.] 1 *Naut.* The lengthwise timber or metal structure along the base of a ship or boat, on which the framework of the whole is built up, and which in boats and small vessels forms a prominent central ridge on the undersurface which provides lateral stability. ME. 2a A ship, a vessel. *poet.* M16. b A yacht built with a permanent keel instead of a centreboard. L19. 3 A central ridge along the back or convex surface of an animal or plant organ or structure. L16. b *Ornith.* A prominent ridge along the sternum or breastbone of most birds (carinates), to which the flight muscles are attached; the carina. M18. c *Bot.* The two lower petals of a papilionaceous flower, fused together round the stamens and styles to form a boat-shaped structure. L18. d A prominent sternum in a dog. M20. 4 That part of anything which corresponds in position, form, etc., to a ship's keel; the bottom or undersurface; a keel-like lower part; *spec.* a longitudinal structure running the length of the underside of an aeroplane's fuselage, a seaplane's float, an airship, etc. E18. 5a [Norw. *kjøl*.] *The* spinal ridge of mountains stretching down the centre of Norway. M19. b *Archit.* A ridge or edge on a rounded moulding. L19. 6 (Usu. **K-.**) *The* constellation Carina. E20.

1 *bar-keel, bilge-keel, plate-keel*, etc. **drop-keel** (*a*) a centreboard; (*b*) a projecting keel. *false keel*: see FALSE *a.* **on an even keel** (*a*) with the keel horizontal or level; (*b*) *fig.* balanced, stable. SLIDING *keel*. *vertical keel*: see VERTICAL *a.* **with an even keel** = *on an even keel* above.

Comb.: **keel-bill** the smooth-billed ani, *Crotophaga ani*, of the W. Indies; **keel-block** any of the short pieces of timber etc. supporting the keel of a vessel in a shipyard or dry dock; **keel-plate** any of the plates forming the keel of a metal ship.

keelage *n.* (*rare*) a toll or due payable by a ship on entering or anchoring in a harbour LME. **keelless** /-l-l-/ *a.* L19. **keel-like** /-l-l-/ *a.* resembling (that of) a keel E19.

keel /kiːl/ *n.*[2] ME. [MLG *kēl*, MDu. *kiel* ship, boat (mod. *keel*) = OE *ċēol*, OS, OHG *kiol* (Du. *kiel*, G *Kiel*), ON *kjóll*, f. Gmc.] Chiefly *Hist.* 1 A flat-bottomed boat, esp. of a kind used on the rivers Tyne and Wear in NE England for carrying coal and loading colliers; a lighter. ME. b The quantity of coal carried in a keel, approx. 19.2 tonnes. M18. 2 = CHIULE. E17.

Comb.: **keel-bully** *dial.* a member of the crew of a keel; a Tyneside lighterman; **keelman** *n.*[1] a person who works on a keel or barge.

keel /kiːl/ *n.*[3] Chiefly *Sc.* L15. [Origin unkn.] A variety of red ochreous iron ore used for marking sheep, stone, timber, yarn, etc.; ruddle. Also, a mark made with this.

Comb.: **keelman** *n.*[2] a dealer in ruddle.

keely *a.* (*rare*) containing much keel; of the nature of keel: E18.

keel /kiːl/ *v.*[1] *obs.* exc. *dial.* [OE *cēlan* = OFris. *kēla* (Du. *koelen*), OHG *kuolen* (G *kühlen*), ON *kœla*, f. Gmc, f. base of COOL *a.*] 1 *v.t.* Cool (*lit.* & †*fig.*). OE. b *spec.* Cool (a hot or boiling liquid) by stirring, skimming, or pouring in something cold, in order to prevent it from boiling over. LME. 2 *v.i.* Become or grow cool (*lit.* & *fig.*). ME.

keel /kiːl/ *v.*[2]*t.* Chiefly *Sc.* E16. [f. KEEL *n.*[3]] Mark with ruddle.

keel /kiːl/ *v.*[3] E19. [f. KEEL *n.*[1]] 1 *v.t.* Turn up the keel of, capsize (a boat etc.); overturn, upset (a person, animal, or thing). Freq. foll. by *over*. E19. 2 *v.i.* Turn or be turned over; capsize; fall over or be felled as if by shock. Usu. foll. by *over*. M19. 3 *v.i.* Of a ship: roll on its keel. M19.

2 L. MACNEICE The ship keeled over and sank. A. JUDD He keeled off the table on to his back.

keelboat /ˈkiːlbəʊt/ *n.* L17. [f. KEEL *n.*[1], *n.*[2] + BOAT *n.*] †1 A small keel. L17–M18. 2 A large flat boat used on American rivers. *US.* L18. 3 A yacht built with a permanent keel instead of a centreboard. L19.

Comb.: **keelboatman** *US* a person who works on a keelboat.

keeled /kiːld/ *a.* L18. [f. KEEL *n.*[1] + -ED[2].] Having a keel; *spec.* (*a*) (of a boat) built with a keel; (*b*) *Biol.* (of an organ or structure) having a central ridge, carinate.

keeled scraper [tr. Fr. *grattoir caréné*] *Archaeol.* a prehistoric flint-tool having a central ridge on its upper surface.

keeler /ˈkiːlə/ *n.*[1] *rare.* ME. [f. KEEL *n.*[2] + -ER[1].] A person who works on a keel or barge.

keeler /ˈkiːlə/ *n.*[2] *obs.* exc. *dial.* LME. [f. KEEL *v.*[1] + -ER[1].] A vessel for cooling liquids; a shallow tub used for household purposes.

keelhaul /ˈkiːlhɔːl/ *v.* & *n.* M17. [Du. *kielhalen*, f. *kiel* (see KEEL *n.*[2]) + *halen* HALE *v.*[1]] **A** *v.t.* Haul (a person) through the water under the keel of a ship, as a punishment (*obs.* exc. *Hist.*). Now also *fig.*, rebuke or reprimand severely. M17. **B** *n.* An act of keelhauling. M19.

keelie /ˈkiːli/ *n.* Chiefly *Sc.* & *north.* LME. [Perh. f. as GILLIE *n.*[1] Sense 2 perh. a different wd.] 1 A disreputable person, a rough living in a town or city, now esp. Glasgow. LME. 2 A sparrowhawk, a kestrel. E19.

¶In isolated use bef. 19.

keeling /ˈkiːlɪŋ/ *n.* L19. [f. KEEL *n.*[1] + -ING[1].] The material or make of a ship's keel.

keelivine /ˈkiːlɪvʌɪn/ *n. Sc.* & *north.* Also **keely-.** M17. [Origin unkn.] A pencil, orig. *spec.* a black-lead pencil. Also *keelivine pen*.

keelson /ˈkiːls(ə)n, ˈkɛl-/ *n.* Also **kelson** /ˈkɛl-/, (orig.) †**kelswayn** & other vars. ME. [Rel. to and perh. f. LG *kielswīn*, f. *kiel* KEEL *n.*[1] + (prob.) *swin* SWINE, used, like *cat, dog, horse*, for a timber.] 1 *Naut.* A lengthwise timber or metal structure running internally along the bottom of a ship, parallel with and bolted to the keel, fastening the floor timbers or plating and the keel together. ME. b A structure in the hull of a flying-boat or the float of a seaplane, analogous to the keelson of a ship's hull. E20. 2 = KEEL *n.*[1] 1. *rare.* M19.

keelyvine *n.* var. of KEELIVINE.

Keemun /ˈkiːmuːn/ *n.* L19. [The name of a district in China.] A black tea grown in Keemun, China.

keen /kiːn/ *n.* M19. [Ir. CAOINE, f. as KEEN *v.*[2]] An Irish funeral song accompanied by wailing in lamentation for the dead.

D. M. DAVIN I am contributing my funeral keen, my personal lament.

keen /kiːn/ *a.* & *adv.* [OE *cēne* = MLG *kōne* (Du. *koen*), OHG *kuoni* (G *kühn*) bold, brave, ON *kœnn* skilful, expert, f. Gmc.] **A** *adj.* †1 Wise, learned, clever. Cf. sense 7b below. OE–LME. †2a Brave, valiant, daring. OE–E17. b Mighty, powerful, strong. *poet.* & *rhet.* OE–E16. c (Esp. of a wild animal) fierce, savage; harsh, cruel. OE–E17. d Proud, insolent; heinous. ME–L16. 3 Of a blade etc.: having a very sharp edge or point; able to cut or pierce with ease. Of an edge or point: extremely sharp. ME. b Of a price: competitive. M20. 4a Of cold (or formerly, heat): piercing, intense. Of wind, air, etc.: very sharp, biting. ME. b Of sound: piercing, shrill. Of light: vivid, clear. Of scent: strong. ME. c Of something touched: causing pain, smarting, stinging. Of a taste: acrid, pungent. Now *rare.* LME. d Excellent. *colloq.* (orig. *US*). E20. 5a Of a circumstance, a thought, an emotion, etc.: causing acute pain or deep distress. ME. b Of language: severe, incisive, cutting. ME. 6 Of a person: eager, interested, impassioned, fervent. Of desire, emotion, etc.: intense. Also foll. by *about, for, to do*. Freq. in *keen on* (colloq.), very interested in; much attracted by, in love with. ME. 7a Of the eyes or eyesight: sharp, penetrating. Of the ears or hearing, or the nose or smell, etc.: acute, highly sensitive. Also, of a person or animal: sharp *of* sight, smell, hearing, etc. ME. b Of a person: intellectually acute. Of the mind or a mental process: endowed or conducted with great acumen. ME. c Of the face or appearance: suggestive of perceptiveness or acumen. L18.

3 M. SHADBOLT When the axe was . . keen, he began to chop wood. M. CONEY It was a good knife with a keen blade. 4a O. MANNING Up above . . into the bare rock fields where the cold was keen. *Lancaster Guardian* Early frosts . . assist the colouring of the leaves—a keen frost will hasten their fall. b A. SILLITOE He liked soap that was keen to the smell. 5a

T. GRAY Keen Remorse with blood defil'd. DICKENS Mr. Tremlow . . had betrayed the keenest mental terrors. 5b GIBBON They pointed their keenest satire against a despicable race. 6 R. DAHL The farmers didn't stop for lunch; they were too keen to finish the job. F. HOWERD I wasn't too keen on the way he said 'perhaps'. B. PYM She was a bit keen on me at one time. D. PRATER His wife was . . a keen cyclist. M. DRABBLE They were young and keen and full of ideas. 7a J. MARQUAND My observation had never been so keen. R. CROMPTON William's keen eye had been searching out each detail. I. ASIMOV If our noses were a little keener . . we could probably tell which world we were on with one sniff. b LD MACAULAY Nature had given him a keen understanding.

Phrases: (*as*) *keen as mustard*: see MUSTARD *n.* 1. *keen on*: see sense 6 above.

†B *adv.* Keenly. LME–M17.

keenly *adv.* OE. **keenness** /-n-n-/ *n.* LME.

keen /kiːn/ *v.*[1]*t. rare.* L16. [f. prec.] Make keen; sharpen.

R. DAHL Keens the dog up before a race. G. SEYMOUR The very solitude of the wood . . keened and sharpened his senses.

keen /kiːn/ *v.*[2] M19. [f. Ir. *caoinim* I wail.] 1 *v.i.* Utter or sing a keen; wail or lament bitterly for a dead person. M19. 2 *v.t.* Lament (a death, a loss, etc.) by keening. M19. 3 *v.t.* Utter (a cry etc.) in a shrill wailing tone. L19.

1 F. FORSYTH The body of Johnny was taken by his own people who keened over him. A. ALVAREZ It was his turn to keen and cry.

keener /ˈkiːnə/ *n.*[1] E19. [f. KEEN *v.*[2] + -ER[1].] A person who keens; *spec.* a professional mourner at Irish wakes and funerals.

keener /ˈkiːnə/ *n.*[2] *N. Amer.* M19. [f. KEEN *a.* + -ER[1].] A shrewd person; a person who drives a hard bargain. Also, an eager person.

Keene's cement /kiːnz sɪˈmɛnt/ *n. phr.* M19. [Richard Wynn *Keene*, who patented the plaster in 1838.] A kind of plaster of Paris containing alum or another salt, which sets to a very hard white finish.

keep /kiːp/ *n.* ME. [f. the vb.] †1 Care, heed, notice. Chiefly in *take keep*, (foll. by *of*, *to do*, or *obj. cl.*). ME–L19. 2 Care in tending, watching, or preserving; charge. Orig. in †*take keep. arch.* ME. 3 An article which serves for containing or retaining something; *esp.* (*a*) (now *dial.*) a clasp or similar fastening; (*b*) *rare* a reservoir for fish; a weir or dam for retaining water. LME. b *Coalmining.* Each of a set of movable iron supports on which the cage rests when at the top of the shaft. M19. 4 *Hist.* The innermost and strongest structure or central tower of a medieval castle, serving as a last defence; a stronghold, a donjon. M16. 5 The action of keeping or maintaining a person or thing; the fact of being kept. M18. b The food required to keep a person or animal; provender, pasture; maintenance, support. Now chiefly in *earn one's keep.* E19.

1 A. BARCLAY What God hath done for you ye take no keepe. 2 KEATS If from shepherd's keep a lamb strayed far. 5 M. R. MITFORD Our old spaniel . . and the blue grey-hound . . were sent out to keep for the summer. b J. R. LOWELL You're so darned lazy, I don't think you're hardly worth your keep.

Phrases: **earn one's keep** *fig.* do enough to justify what one receives; provide a sufficient return. **for keeps** *colloq.* (orig. *US*) (*a*) to keep for good; completely, altogether; in deadly earnest; (*b*) *Cricket* defensively, in order to remain at the wicket. **in good keep** well kept, in good condition. **in low keep** in poor condition.

keep /kiːp/ *v.* Pa. t. & pple **kept** /kɛpt/. LOE. [Origin unkn.] †I *v.t.* (with *genit.* in OE, afterwards with *direct obj.*). Early senses: see also KEP. 1 Seize, lay hold of; snatch, take. LOE–L15. 2 Try to catch or get. LOE–ME. 3 Take in, receive, contain, hold. LOE–ME. 4 Take in with the eyes, ears, or mind; take note of, see, observe; watch. LOE–L17. 5 Watch for, await; lie in wait for; intercept. LOE–L15. 6 Meet; encounter; greet, welcome. Only in ME.

II *v.t.* (in early use also *v.i.*). †7 *v.i.* & *t.* Have regard (for), care (for), (foll. by *of* (orig. *genit.*), *to do*, simple *obj.*); take care, attend *to*. LOE–L16. 8 *v.t.* Pay due regard to; observe, abide by, (a law, custom, promise, agreement, set time, etc.). LOE. 9 *v.t.* Observe with due formality and in the prescribed manner (a religious rite, ceremony, etc.); celebrate, solemnize. ME. b Observe by attendance, residence, performance of duty, or in some prescribed or regular way. In later use chiefly in *keep chapels* or *halls* (at college or school), *keep* (prescribed) *terms*, *residence*, etc., and in *keep early*, *late*, *regular*, etc., *hours*. LME. 10 *v.t.* Guard, defend, protect, (*from*). *arch.* exc. in *keep goal*, *keep wicket* below. ME. †11 *v.refl.* & *i.* Take care, beware, *that*. ME–E16. 12 *v.t.* a Take care of, look after, tend, have charge of (a thing, *arch.* & *dial.* a person or animal). ME. b Maintain or preserve (a place etc.) in proper order. LME. 13 *v.t.* Provide with food, clothing, and other requisites of life; maintain, support. Also foll. by *in* a thing regularly provided. ME. b Maintain in return for sexual favours. Earlier as KEEPING *n.* 4b. M16. 14 *v.t.* Preserve in being or operation; continue to have, practise, etc. ME. b Carry on, continue to cause, (a disturbance, etc.). Now usu. *keep up.* LME. 15 *v.t.* With compl.: maintain, or cause to continue in a specified condition, state, place, position, action, or course. ME. 16 *v.t.* Cause or induce to remain in a place; detain; *spec.* (now usu. more fully *keep in jail*, *keep prisoner*, etc.) hold in custody, prevent from escaping. ME. 17 *v.t.* Hold back, restrain, (*from*). ME. 18 *v.t.* Put aside for future use; reserve, store. ME. 19 *v.t.* Retain in one's possession or control; continue to have, hold, or possess. ME. b *v.t.* Have habitually in stock or on sale. L16. 20 *v.t.* Stay in, refrain from leaving, (a place); *esp.* be confined to (one's bed, room) by sickness. ME. b Stay in one's position in or on, against opposition or in spite of circumstances or conditions. LME. 21 *v.t.* Withhold possession or use of (a thing) or the knowledge of (a fact) *from* a person. LME. 22 *v.t.* Continue to follow (a way, path, course, etc.), so as not to lose it or get out of it. LME. 23 *v.t.* Carry on, conduct, as presiding officer or a chief actor (an assembly, court, fair, market, etc.). LME. 24 *v.t.* Carry on and manage, conduct as one's own, (a business, shop, etc.). E16. 25 *v.t.* Maintain continuously (a record, diary, accounts, etc.) by making the requisite entries. M16. 26 *v.t.* Maintain in one's service, or for one's use or enjoyment; own and manage (animals). M16.

8 G. ORWELL If you kept small rules, you could break the big ones. E. O'BRIEN He kept the dinner appointment. 9 V. WOOLF He seldom spoke of the dead, but kept anniversaries with singular pomp. C. V. WEDGWOOD Being Sunday the Commissioners kept it as a fast. b THACKERAY He kept his chapels, and did the college exercises. J. I. M. STEWART They kept long hours in the Bodleian Library. 10 G. M. BROWN They've left a boy To keep the door of the fold, I hope. 12a JOSEPH STRUTT David, who kept his father's sheep. 13 R. DAVIES My father had died, and the shop could keep her. 14 SHAKES. *1 Hen. IV* Two stars keep not their motion in one sphere. P. LARKIN All afternoon . . For miles inland, A slow and stopping curve southwards we kept. *keep company*, *guard*, *a lookout*, *order*, *pace*, *silence*, *the peace*, *time*, *tune*, etc. 15 J. RHYS A little muff to keep your hands warm. E. O'BRIEN Think of anything, so long as the mind keeps itself occupied. *Femina* Be alert. Keep your eyes and ears open. A. BROOKNER People upon whom Blanche could rely to keep the party going. 16 V. WOOLF I'm sorry I'm late . . I got kept. 17 *Black & White* I shall not be able to keep myself from strangling her. ROBERT ANDERSON There's something between fathers and sons that keeps them from being friends. 18 R. H. MOTTRAM Two Canadian majors . . came to claim the table . . and found it kept for them. E. WAUGH If you don't mind . . we will keep our business until after luncheon. 19 E. M. FORSTER England will never keep her trade overseas unless she is prepared to make sacrifices. D. BARNES He . . laid a paper-cutter between the pages to keep his place. B. BETTELHEIM A parent . . should keep his cool in times of trouble. 20 M. KEANE Jane still kept her bed but grew a little stronger every day. W. GOLDING The parson keeps his cabin. We shall see little of him. b W. FAULKNER The streets where no horse could have kept its feet. 21 T. WASHINGTON Where they would not receive his salvation, the same for ever shalbe kept from them. DAY LEWIS If my father . . had worries, they were kept from me. 22 *Field* How the driver kept the track is a marvel. 23 H. FIELDING His wife . . began to keep an assembly, or . . to be 'at home' once a week. 24 G. GREENE Mr. Verloc . . keeps a tiny independent cinema in the East End. 25 J. CONRAD In those books he intended to keep . . a record of his rising fortunes. 26 G. GREENE The doctor kept his own cows. O. MANNING Your father kept a good cellar. R. DAVIES At the top of the class structure were . . families who kept 'maids'.

III *v.i.* (Chiefly w. ellipsis of refl. pron.). 27 Reside, dwell, live, lodge. Now *colloq.* (esp. *Cambridge Univ.* & *US*). LME. 28 Remain for a time in a particular place or spot. LME. b Of a school: be in session. *US.* M19. 29 Remain in good condition, last without spoiling; *fig.* admit of being reserved for another occasion. LME. 30 Continue, go on, in a specified course or action. M16. b Go on *doing.* L18. 31 With compl.: remain or continue in a specified condition, state, place, position, action, or course. M16. 32 *Cricket.* = *keep wicket* below. M19.

27 E. M. W. TILLYARD He kept in the historic set of rooms . . once occupied by the poet Gray. 28 GEO. ELIOT He suggested that she should keep in her own room. 29 F. MARRYAT He brought home more venison than would keep in the hot weather. CONAN DOYLE Your story, however, can keep. 30 W. FAULKNER Just keep right on up the road past the schoolhouse. b B. ENGLAND They were both tired . . but they kept going. *Sunday* (*Calcutta*) The bills . . keep piling up. 31 E. BOWEN I kept out of debt for more than a year. I. MURDOCH I usually keep clear of Soho. A. BULLOCK Bevin kept in constant and close touch with Arthur Deakin.

Phrases: (A selection of cross-refs. only is included: see esp. other ns.) **how are you keeping?** *colloq.* in what state is your health? *keep an eye on*: see EYE *n.* *keep a secret*: see SECRET *n.* **keep goal** act as goalkeeper in football etc. *keep house*: see HOUSE *n.*[1] *keep in touch*: see TOUCH *n.* *keep one's balance*: see BALANCE *n.* *keep one's distance*: see DISTANCE *n.* *keep the wolf from the door*: see WOLF *n.* *keep time* : see TIME *n.* *keep track of*: see TRACK *n.* **keep wicket** act as wicket-keeper in cricket.

With advs. in specialized senses: **keep abreast** (cause to) proceed at an equal pace (*lit.* & *fig.*) (foll. by *with*, *of*). **keep away** (*a*) (cause to) remain absent or at a distance; (*b*) *Naut.* (cause to) sail off the wind or to leeward. **keep back** (*a*) restrain, detain; hold back forcibly; (*b*) withhold; retain or reserve designedly; conceal; (*c*) hold oneself or remain at the back. **keep down** (*a*) cause to remain at a low level (*keep one's head down*: see HEAD *n.*); *fig.* hold in subjection; (*b*) retain (food etc.) in one's stomach without vomiting; (*c*) (cause to) remain low in amount, number, or degree; (*d*) lie low, stay hidden. **keep in** (*a*) confine in a place, esp. in school after hours; not utter or give vent to; *fig.* refrain from giving voice to; (*b*) keep (a fire) burning; (*c*) (now *colloq.*) remain on good terms *with*; (*d*) *keep one's hand in*: see HAND *n.* **keep off** (*a*) hinder from coming near, ward off; avert; (*b*) stay at a distance; **keep on** (*a*) continue to hold, wear, occupy, employ, etc.; (*b*) continue or persist in a course or action; *esp.* go on *doing*; (*c*) *keep on at*, nag or pester (a person) continually (*to do*). **keep out** cause to remain outside; prevent from getting in. **keep over** reserve, hold over. **keep together** (cause to) remain associated or united (*keep body and soul together*: see BODY *n.*). **keep under** hold in subjection or under control. **keep up** (*a*) keep shut up or confined; (*b*) support, prevent from sinking or falling; (*c*) maintain in a worthy or effective condition; support; keep in repair; keep burning; (*d*) maintain, retain, preserve (a quality, state of things, accomplishment, etc.); keep from deteriorating or disappearing; (*keep up appearances*: see APPEARANCE); (*e*) continue, go on with (an action, a course of action); *keep it up*, prolong a party; (*f*) prevent from going to bed; (*g*) *keep up to*, prevent from or insist on not falling below (a level, standard, principle, etc.); keep informed of; (*h*) continue alongside, keep abreast; proceed at an equal pace *with* (*lit.* & *fig.*); *keep up with the Joneses*, strive not to be outdone by one's neighbours; (*i*) continue to maintain a friendship or acquaintance; keep in touch (*with*).

With preps. in specialized senses: **keep at** work persistently at; continue to occupy oneself with; also *keep at it.* **keep from** (*a*) remain absent or away from; (*b*) restrain oneself from. **keep off** avoid, stay away from; *keep off the grass*: see GRASS *n.* **keep to** (*a*) adhere to, abide by (a promise, agreement, etc.); (*b*) confine or restrict oneself to; *keep to oneself*, (colloq.) *keep oneself to oneself*, avoid the society of others. **keep with** remain with, associate with; keep up with.

Comb.: **keep-fit** *a.* & *n.* (*a*) *adj.* designating or pertaining to exercises etc. designed to keep people fit and healthy; (*b*) *n.* keep-fit exercises; keep-fit class; **keep-left** *a.* designating a sign etc. directing traffic to the left of the road; **keep-net** *Angling* a net for keeping fish alive until they are returned to the water; **keep-out** *a.* designating a sign prohibiting entry.

keepable /ˈkiːpəb(ə)l/ *a.* LME. [f. KEEP *v.* + -ABLE.] †1 Of a law: able to be observed. Only in LME. 2 Durable, long-lasting. Now only, (of a foodstuff etc.) able to last without deterioration. L16.

keepaˈbility *n.* L19.

keeper /ˈkiːpə/ *n.* ME. [f. KEEP *v.* + -ER[1].] I f. KEEP *v.* I, II. 1 A person who has charge or oversight of a person or thing; *esp.* (*a*) an attendant in a prison, *arch.* lunatic asylum, etc.; (*b*) the custodian of a museum, art gallery, etc. ME. †b A nurse; a person who has charge of the sick. LME–M17. c An officer who has the charge of a forest, woods, or grounds; now *esp.* = *gamekeeper* s.v. GAME *n.* LME. d *Sport.* A wicket-keeper; a goalkeeper. M18. 2 A person who or thing which keeps or retains something. ME. 3 A person who observes or keeps a command, law, promise, etc. LME. 4 A person who owns or carries on some establishment or business. LME. 5 A mechanical device for keeping something in place; a clasp, catch, etc. Freq., a loop securing the end of a buckled strap. M16. b A bar of soft iron placed across the poles of a horseshoe magnet to prevent loss of power. M19. c A ring that keeps another (esp. a wedding ring) on the finger; a guard ring. M19. d A simple ring worn in the ears to keep a pierced hole open. M20. †6 A man who keeps a mistress. L17–M19.

1 SIR W. SCOTT The herds without a keeper strayed. U. SINCLAIR A keeper came to him with the word that his time was up. R. V. JONES One of the keepers in the botany department of the Natural History Museum. *bookkeeper, door-keeper, gamekeeper, goalkeeper, housekeeper, time-keeper, wicket-keeper,* etc. 2 SHAKES. *Rich. II* He is a flatterer, A parasite, a keeper-back of death. *finders keepers*: see FINDER *n.* 4 *hotel-keeper, shopkeeper,* etc.

II f. KEEP *v.* III. 7 A person who continues or remains *at* a place. *rare.* E17. 8 A fruit, or other product, that keeps (well or badly). M19.

Phrases: **Keeper of the Great Seal** an officer in England and Scotland (in England now the Lord Chancellor) who has the custody of the Great Seal. **Keeper of the Privy Seal** (*a*) *Hist.* in England, the Lord Privy Seal; (*b*) a similar officer in Scotland and the Duchy of Cornwall. **Lord Keeper (of the Great Seal)** = *Keeper of the Great Seal* above.

keepering *n.* the work of a gamekeeper M19. **keepership** *n.* the office or position of a keeper M16.

keeper /ˈkiːpə/ *v.t.* E20. [f. the n. or back-form. f. KEEPERING *n.*] Look after as a gamekeeper.

keeping /ˈkiːpɪŋ/ *n.* ME. [f. KEEP *v.* + -ING[1].] I The action of KEEP *v.* I, II. 1 Observance of a rule, command, ordinance, institution, practice, promise, etc. ME. 2 The action of looking after, guarding, or defending someone or something; custody, charge, guardianship. ME. b Guard, defence. Esp. in *on* (*at, upon*) *one's keeping*, on one's guard. *obs.* exc. *dial.* ME. c Wicket-keeping; goalkeeping. M19. 3 Maintenance of a thing or person in good condition; the condition in which a thing is kept. ME. 4a Maintenance, sustenance with food; food, fodder. ME. b The maintaining of a mistress or lover; the fact or condition of being so maintained. LME. 5 The maintaining of a state or condition. ME. †6 Confinement, imprisonment; prison. ME–E16. 7 The action of retaining as one's own; the owning and managing of animals, a business, etc.; in *pl.*, things kept or retained. ME. 8 Reservation for future use; preservation. LME. 9 *Painting.* The maintenance of proper perspective in a picture; the maintenance of harmony of composition. E18. b *gen.* Agreement, harmony. Esp. *in* or *out of keeping* (*with*). L18.

2 HOBBES The Book of the Law was in their keeping. *goalkeeping, time-keeping, wicket-keeping,* etc. *safe keeping*: see SAFE *a.* 5 *peace-keeping* etc. 7 *bee-keeping* etc. 9b A. BRIGGS His methods were in keeping with the reformation of manners.

II The action of KEEP *v.* III. 10 Staying or remaining in a place or in a certain condition; *spec.* remaining sound. Formerly also, persistence in an activity. LME.

Comb.: **keeping-room** (esp. *Cambridge University* & *US*) a living-room, a parlour.

keeping /ˈkiːpɪŋ/ *ppl a.* LME. [f. KEEP *v.* + -ING[2].] That keeps; *esp.* (of a fruit) that keeps well.

keepsake /ˈkiːpseɪk/ *n.* & *a.* L18. [f. KEEP *v.* + SAKE *n.*[1]: cf. *namesake.*] A *n.* A thing kept or given to be kept for the sake of, or in remembrance of, the giver; *spec.* (*Hist.*) a literary annual consisting of collections of verse, prose, and illustrations, of a type common in the early part of the 19th cent. L18. B *adj.* Constituting or resembling a keepsake; *spec.* (*arch.*) having the inane prettiness of faces in keepsakes or the affected literary style of such books. M19.

keertan *n.* var. of KIRTAN.

keeshond /ˈkeɪshɒnd/ *n.* Pl. **-honden** /-hɒnd(ə)n/, **-honds**. E20. [Du., f. *Kees* pet-form of male forename Cornelius + *hond* dog.] A breed of dog of Dutch origin, which is a variety of the spitz, with long thick grey hair; a dog of this breed.

keester *n.* var. of KEISTER.

keeve /kiːv/ *n.* Also **kive** /kʌɪv/. [OE *cȳf*, perh. f. Gmc but no corresp. forms in the cognate langs.] A tub, a vat; *spec.* a vat for holding liquid in brewing and bleaching; *Mining* a vessel in which tin or copper ore is washed.

kef *n.* see KIEF.

keffiyeh /kəˈfiː(j)ə/ *n.* Also **kaff-, kuf-** & other vars. E19. [Arab. *kūfiyya* (colloq.) *keffiyya.*] A kerchief worn as a head-dress by Bedouin Arabs.

kefir /kəˈfɪə, ˈkɛfə/ *n.* Also **kephir**. L19. [Caucasian name.] An effervescent liquor resembling kumis, prepared from fermented milk and employed as a medicine or food for invalids.

Comb.: **kefir grains** a composite substance used in the Caucasus to ferment milk.

keftedes /kɛfˈtɛðiːz/ *n.pl.* Also **-dhes**. E20. [Gk *kephtes*, pl. *kephtedes* f. Turk. *köfte* f. Pers. KOFTA.] In Greek cookery, small meatballs made with herbs and onions.

Keftian /ˈkɛftɪən/ *n.* & *a.* E20. [f. as next + -AN.] *Ancient Hist.* A *n.* = next. E20. B *adj.* Of or pertaining to the Keftiu. E20.

Keftiu /ˈkɛftjuː/ *n.* Pl. same. E20. [Place-name in Egyptian records, perh. identical w. Caphtor: see CAPHTOR.] *Ancient Hist.* A member of an E. Mediterranean people named in Egyptian records, sometimes identified as the Cretans. Usu. in *pl.*

keg /kɛg/ *n.* E17. [Later form of CAG *n.*] 1 A small barrel or cask, usu. of less than 10 gallons (approx. 45.5 litres) or (*US*) 30 gallons. E17. 2 *spec.* A barrel of beer; beer. *Austral.* & *NZ slang.* M20. 3 In full *keg beer, bitter,* etc. Beer etc. to which carbon dioxide has been added, served from a sealed metal container. M20.

kegler /ˈkɛglə, ˈkeɪglə/ *n. N. Amer.* M20. [G, f. *Kegel* skittle.] A person who plays tenpin bowling, skittles, ninepins, etc.

kehaya /kɛhəˈjɑː/ *n. obs.* exc. *Hist.* L16. [Ottoman Turk. *kehya, kyāhya* corrupt forms of Pers. *kadkhudā*, f. *kad* house + *ḵudā* master.] A Turkish steward, viceroy, deputy, agent, etc.; a local governor; a village chief.

kehilla /kəˈhɪlə, kɛhɪˈlɑː/ *n.* Pl. **-llot(h)** /-ˈlaʊt/. L19. [(Yiddish *kĕhilĕ* f.) Heb. *qĕhillāh* community.] The Jewish community in a town or village.

keif *n.* see KIEF.

keister /ˈkiːstə, ˈkʌɪstə/ *n. N. Amer. slang.* Also **kee-, key-** /ˈkiː-/. L19. [Origin unkn.] 1a A suitcase, a satchel; a handbag; a tool-case; a sample-case. L19. b A strongbox in a safe; a safe. E20. 2 The buttocks. M20.

keitloa /ˈkeɪtləʊə/ *n. rare.* M19. [Setswana *kgetlwa, kh-.*] The black rhinoceros, *Diceros bicornis.*

Kekchi /ˈkɛktʃi/ *n.* & *a.* E19. [Maya.] A *n.* Pl. same, **-s**. A member of an ancient people of the Mayan empire or their modern descendants who now live in Guatemala; the language of these people. E19. B *attrib.* or as *adj.* Of or pertaining to the Kekchi or their language. M20.

Kekulé /ˈkɛkʊleɪ/ *n.* E20. [Friedrich August *Kekulé* (1829–96), Ger. chemist.] *Chem.* Used *attrib.* to designate formulae or structures which represent benzene and related molecules as having a closed ring of six carbon atoms linked by alternate double and single bonds.

kel /kɛl/ *n. slang.* E20. [Abbrev.] = KELLY 2. Earlier as *Darby kel* s.v. DARBY 4.

kelch /kɛltʃ/ *n. slang. derog.* Also **kelt** /kɛlt/, **keltz** /kɛlts/. E20. [Origin unkn.] A White person.

keld /kɛld/ *n. north.* ME. [ON *kelda.*] A well, a spring; a deep, still, smooth part of a river.

¶Frequent in place-names in Cumbria and Yorkshire in N. England.

kelebe /ˈkɛləbi/ *n.* M19. [Gk *kelebē.*] *Gk Antiq.* A wide-mouthed vessel with a broad flat rim and two handles connecting this to the body but not extending above the rim.

kelek /ˈkɛlɪk/ *n.* L17. [Turk.] A raft or float used on rivers in Turkey, Kurdistan, etc., formed of inflated sheepskins, bundles of reeds, etc.

kelewang *n.* var. of KLEYWANG.

Kelim *n.* var. of KILIM.

kell /kɛl/ *n. obs.* exc. *dial.* ME. [Var. of CAUL *n.*[1]] 1 A woman's hairnet, cap, or head-dress. ME. 2 A long cloak or garment; a shroud. LME. 3 Gossamer threads forming a kind of film on grass. E16. 4 An enveloping membrane; a caul. M16.

keller /ˈkɛlə(r)/ *n.* Also **K-**. E20. [G = cellar.] A beer-cellar in Austria or Germany.

Kelly /ˈkɛli/ *n.* Also **k-**. L19. [Prob. f. the common Ir. surname (f. Ir. *Ó Ceallaigh*). See also KEL.] 1 In full *Kelly pool.* A type of pool using fifteen balls. *N. Amer.* L19. 2 = BELLY *n.* 2, 4. Earliest as *Darby kelly* s.v. DARBY 4. *rhyming slang.* E20. 3 A man's hat; *spec.* a derby hat. *slang* (chiefly *US*). E20. 4 *Oil Industry.* (**k-**.) The joint of a drill-string which passes through a hole in the rotary table and has a square cross-section so that it is turned by the table. E20. 5 *Kelly's eye*, number one in the game of bingo. *colloq.* E20. 6 In full *Kelly green.* A light green colour. Orig. *US.* M20.

Phrases: *swing Kelly*: see SWING *v.*

keloid /ˈkiːlɔɪd/ *n.* & *a.* Also **ch-**. M19. [Fr. *chéloïde, kél-*, f. Gk *khēlē* claw of a crab: see -OID.] *Med.* A *n.* (An area of) thickened raised scar tissue that tends to increase in extent. Formerly also, the condition of having this. M19. B *adj.* Designating or consisting of such a scar or tissue. L19.

kelong /ˈkeɪlɒŋ/ *n.* L19. [Malay.] A large fish trap built with stakes, common along the coasts of the Malay peninsula and in other parts of Malaysia and Indonesia. Also, a building erected over such a trap.

kelp /kɛlp/ *n.* LME. [Origin unkn.] 1 Any of various large brown seaweeds, chiefly members of the orders Fucales and Laminariales, which are burnt for the substances found in the ashes; such seaweed collectively; spec. *Macrocystis pyrifera* of the Pacific coast of America, the largest of the seaweeds. LME. 2 The calcined ashes of seaweed used for the salts of sodium, potassium, and iodine which they contain, esp. (formerly) in the manufacture of soap and glass. M17.

Comb.: **kelp crab** a spider crab, *Pugettia producta*, found on the Pacific coast of N. America; **kelp-fish** (*a*) a scaled blenny, *Gibbousia montereyensis*, of tidal pools and kelp beds on the Pacific coast of the US; (*b*) any of several coastal fishes of Australia and New Zealand, esp. of the percoid family Chironemidae.

kelping *n.* the collection or manufacture of kelp E19.

kelper /ˈkɛlpə/ *n.* & *a.* In senses A.2, B. also **K-**. E19. [f. KELP + -ER[1].] A *n.* 1 A kelper or manufacturer of kelp. E19. 2 A native or inhabitant of the Falkland Islands in the S. Atlantic, the shores of which abound in kelp.

M20 **B** *adj.* Of or pertaining to the Falkland Islands or their inhabitants. M20.

kelpie /ˈkɛlpi/ *n.*[1] *Sc.* Also **kelpy**. L17. [Perh. f. Gael. *cailpeach*, *colpach* bullock, colt.] A water-spirit or demon assuming various shapes, usu. that of a horse, reputed to haunt lakes and rivers and to take delight in the drowning of travellers etc. Also *water-kelpie*.

kelpie /ˈkɛlpi/ *n.*[2] *Austral.* E20. [App. f. the name of a particular bitch, *King's Kelpie* (*c*1870).] A smooth-coated, prick-eared, Australian breed of sheepdog derived from imported Scottish collies; a dog of this breed.

kelpy *n.* var. of KELPIE *n.*[1]

kelson, †**kelswayn** *ns.* see KEELSON.

kelt /kɛlt/ *n.*[1] ME. [Origin unkn.] A salmon, sea-trout, or other fish (in bad condition) after spawning, before returning to the sea.

kelt /kɛlt/ *n.*[2] & *a.* *Sc.* & *north. obs.* exc. *Hist.* E16. [Gael., Ir. *cealt* clothes: cf. KELTER *n.*[1]] (Made of) a kind of heavy woollen cloth formerly used for outer garments by country people in Scotland and N. England.

Kelt *n.*[3] var. of CELT *n.*[1]

kelt *n.*[4] var. of KELCH.

kelter /ˈkɛltə/ *n.*[1] & *a.* *Sc.* & *north.* Now *rare.* E16. [Ir. *celtair* (mod. *cealtair*) cloak: cf. KELT *n.*[2]] (Made of) coarse cloth used for outer garments.

kelter /ˈkɛltə/ *n.*[2] *dial.* M19. [Origin unkn.] Rubbish; nonsense.

kelter *n.*[3] var. of KILTER *n.*[1]

Keltic *a.* var. of CELTIC.

keltz *n.* var. of KELCH.

Kelvin /ˈkɛlvɪn/ *n.* Also **k-**. L19. [Sir William Thomson, Ld *Kelvin* (1824–1907), Brit. physicist and inventor.] **1** (**K-**.) Used *attrib.* and in *possess.* to designate instruments and concepts devised by Kelvin. L19. †**2** (**k-**.) A kilowatt-hour. L19–E20. **3** (**k-**.) The SI unit of thermodynamic temperature, one degree of the Kelvin scale (equal in magnitude to the degree Celsius). (Symbol K.) E20.

1 degree Kelvin = sense 1 above. **Kelvin balance** an instrument for measuring the current passing through a set of horizontal coils by balancing the electromagnetic force produced by the current with a sliding weight. **Kelvin (double) bridge** a modification of the Wheatstone bridge used for measuring low resistances. **Kelvin scale** a scale of absolute temperature defined thermodynamically, orig. with the freezing- and boiling points of water 100 degrees apart, but later modified to make the triple point of water exactly 273.16 degrees. **Kelvin's law**: that the most economical cross-sectional area of an electrical conductor used as a transmission line is that for which the cost of the energy dissipated in any period is equal to the charges during the same period on the capital cost of the line. **Kelvin temperature** a temperature on the Kelvin scale.

Kemalism /ˈkɛm(ə)lɪz(ə)m/ *n.* E20. [f. *Kemal* (see below) + -ISM.] The political, social, and economic policies advocated by the Turkish soldier and statesman Kemal Atatürk (*c*1880–1938), which aimed to create a modern republican secular Turkish State out of a part of the Ottoman Empire.

Kemalist *n.* & *a.* (*a*) *n.* an advocate or adherent of Kemalism; (*b*) *adj.* of or pertaining to Kemalism or Kemalists: M20.

kemb /kɛm/ *v.t.* *obs.* exc. *dial.* Pa. t. & pple **kembed, kempt** /kɛm(p)t/. [OE *cemban*, f. Gmc base of COMB *n.*[1] Repl. by COMB *v.*, but survives in KEMPT *a.*, UNKEMPT.] **1** = COMB *v.* 1a. OE. †**2** = COMB *v.* 1b. ME–E18.

kemp /kɛmp/ *n.*[1] *obs.* exc. *dial.* [OE *cempa* = OFris. *kempa*, *kampa*, OS *kempio*, OHG *kempfo*, f. WGmc.] **1** A big, strong, and brave warrior or fighter; a champion; a pugnacious person. OE. **2** A stalk of the ribwort plantain, *Plantago lanceolata*, used in a children's game in which the stalks with their flower-heads are struck against each other. *Sc.* L16.

kemp /kɛmp/ *n.*[2] LME. [ON *kampr* beard, moustache, whisker.] Orig., a coarse or stout hair, as those of the eyebrows. Now, (a) hair of this kind occurring among wool.

kemp /kɛmp/ *v.* & *n.*[3] *Sc.* & *north.* LME. [MDu. *kempen*, *kimpen*, LG *kämpen*, OHG *chemfan*, ON *keppa*, f. Gmc.] **A** *v.i.* Fight or contend *with*; *spec.* compete or strive (*with*) in doing a piece of work, esp. in reaping. LME. **B** *n.* A contest, esp. between reapers. L18.

kemper *n.* (*a*) *Sc.* a person who competes or strives for victory, esp. in reaping; (*b*) *arch.* = KEMP *n.*[1] 1: M17.

kempas /ˈkɛmpəs/ *n.* M19. [Malay.] A leguminous timber tree, *Koompassia malaccensis*, native to Malaya, Sumatra, and Borneo; the wood of this tree.

Kempeitai /ˈkɛmpeɪtʌɪ/ *n.* M20. [Jap. *kenpeitai*.] The Japanese military secret service in the period 1931–45.

kempt /kɛm(p)t/ *a.* OE. [pa. pple of KEMB *v.*] (Of hair or wool) combed, neatly brushed or trimmed; *transf.* neat, tidy. Cf. UNKEMPT.

S. SPENDER Gardens as well kempt as a short haircut. W. SANSOM The kempt yellow gravel of drives. *Sunday Express* Perfectly kempt in a blue cardigan and striped shirt.

kempt *v.* pa. t. & pple: see KEMB *v.*

kempy /ˈkɛmpi/ *n.* *Sc.* & *north.* E16. [f. KEMP *n.*[1] + -Y[6].] = KEMP *n.*[1] 1.

kempy /ˈkɛmpi/ *a.* E19. [f. KEMP *n.*[2] + -Y[1].] (Of wool) having many kemps; resembling kemps.

ken /kɛn/ *n.*[1] M16. [f. the vb.] †**1** The distance that bounds the range of ordinary vision, esp. at sea; a marine measure of about 32 kilometres or 20 miles. M16–E17. **2** Range of knowledge or mental perception. M16. **b** Look, gaze. Now *rare.* M17. **3** Range of sight or vision. Now *rare.* L16. †**4** Sight or view *of* something; possibility or capacity of seeing. L16–M18.

2 P. ARROWSMITH Sex . . was something beyond his ken, which he never consciously thought about. 3 KEATS Then felt I like some watcher of the skies When a new planet swims into his ken. 4 SHAKES. *Lucr.* To drown in ken of shore.

ken /kɛn/ *n.*[2] *slang.* M16. [Origin unkn.] A house, *esp.* one where thieves, beggars, etc., meet or lodge.

ken /kɛn/ *n.*[3] Pl. same. E18. [Jap.] A Japanese unit of length equal to six *shaku*, approximately 2 metres or yards.

ken /kɛn/ *n.*[4] Pl. same. L19. [Jap.] A territorial division of Japan; a prefecture.

ken /kɛn/ *n.*[5] L19. [Jap.] A Japanese game of forfeits played with the hands and with gestures.

ken /kɛn/ *v.* Pa. t. & pple **kenned, kent** /kɛnt/. [OE *cennan* = OFris. *kenna*, *kanna*, OS *kennian*, OHG (Du., G) *kennen*, ON *kenna*, Goth. *kannjan*, f. Gmc, f. IE base also of CAN *v.*[1], KNOW *v.*] **I** Causative. †**1** *v.t.* Make known, declare; impart the knowledge of (something). OE–E17. †**2** *v.t.* Direct, teach, or instruct (a person); teach or show how *to do*. ME–M16. †**3** *v.t.* Direct, guide, or show the way *to* a place or person. ME–L16.

II Non-causative. **4** *v.t.* See; catch sight of; look at, scan. *arch.* ME. **5** *v.t.* Recognize, identify; be able to distinguish (one person or thing *from* another). Now *Sc.* & *north.* ME. †**6** *v.t.* Get to know, ascertain, find out. ME–E17. **7** *v.t.* Know; be acquainted with; understand; be aware *that*. Now chiefly *Sc.* ME. **8** *v.i.* Have knowledge (*of*, *about*); know how (*to do*). Now *Sc.* ME. **9** *v.t.* †**a** Acknowledge, admit to be genuine, valid, etc. ME–L17. **b** *Sc. Law* (now *Hist.*). Recognize as legal heir or successor *to* an estate; *spec.* recognize (a widow) as entitled to a terce of a late husband's estate. LME.

7 G. MACDONALD I dinna ken what ye mean, Alec. T. H. WHITE He kens the difference yet of right and wrong. *Scottish Field* Perhaps the authorities . . didnae ken his faither, for they made his son Professor of . . Astronomy!

Comb.: **ken-mark** a mark by which something can be recognized, *esp.* a brand.

kenaf /kəˈnaf/ *n.* L19. [Pers., var. of *kanab* HEMP.] = AMBARI.

kench /kɛn(t)ʃ/ *n.* *US.* M19. [Origin unkn.] A box or bin used for salting sealskins or fish.

Kendal /ˈkɛnd(ə)l/ *n.* LME. [A town in Cumbria, N. England.] **1** Used *attrib.* to designate things, esp. textiles, originating in or associated with Kendal in England. LME. †**2** A kind of rough green woollen cloth. LME–L17.

1 *Daily Telegraph* They . . included in their packs 'iron rations' of chocolate, raisins and Kendal mint cake. *Kendal cotton*: see COTTON *n.*[2] **Kendal green** *Hist.* (*a*) = sense 2 above; (*b*) the green colour of Kendal cloth.

kendo /ˈkɛndəʊ/ *n.* E20. [Jap., f. *ken* sword + *dō* way.] A Japanese sport of fencing with two-handed bamboo staves.

keneme *n.* var. of CENEME.

Kenilworth ivy /ˈkɛn(ə)lwəːθ ˈʌɪvi/ *n. phr* L19. [*Kenilworth* Castle, Warwickshire, England.] = *ivy-leaved toadflax* s.v. IVY *n.*

Kenite /ˈkiːnʌɪt/ *n.* & *a.* M16. [f. Heb. *qēnī* adj. assoc. w. *qayin* a weapon made of metal, Arab. *ḳayn*, Aram. *qaynāyā* smith, metalworker: see -ITE[1].] **A** *n.* A member of an ancient nomadic people from S. Palestine, freq. mentioned in the Bible. M16. **B** *adj.* Of or pertaining to the Kenites. E20.

kennedya /kɛˈniːdɪə/ *n.* M19. [mod.L (see below), f. Lewis *Kennedy* (d. 1818), Eng. nurseryman.] Any of various climbing leguminous plants of the genus *Kennedya*, with showy esp. crimson flowers, native to Australia and Tasmania.

kennel /ˈkɛn(ə)l/ *n.*[1] & *v.* ME. [f. AN n. = OFr. *chenil* (cf. AL *canillum*, *kenillum*), f. L *canis* dog.] **A** *n.* **1** A small structure for a dog to shelter or live in; a house or range of buildings in which a pack of hounds are kept. Also (usu. in *pl.*, freq. treated as *sing.*), an establishment where dogs are bred or boarded. ME. **b** The hole or lair of a fox or other animal. Now *rare.* M18. **c** A small and mean dwelling or hut, a hovel. M19. **2** A pack of hounds or of other animals. LME. **b** *fig.* A pack, crew, or gang of people. *arch.* L16.

1 W. HOLTBY The . . retriever bitch who drowsed with her head hanging out of the wooden kennel. R. RENDELL I've never left her since she was a puppy. . . I couldn't put her in kennels. She'd fret.

Comb.: **Kennel Club** an organization which establishes dog breeds, records pedigrees, issues the rules for dog shows and trials, etc.; a branch of this organization; **kennelmaid**, **kennelman** a woman, man, who works in a kennel.

B *v.* Infl. **-ll-**, ***-l-**. **1** *v.i.* Shelter or live in a kennel; retire into a kennel or lair. M16. **b** Foll. by *up*: return to one's kennel; *colloq.* keep quiet, shut up. E20. **2** *v.t.* Put into or keep in a kennel or kennels; *colloq.* shut *up*, lodge, hide. L16.

kennelling *n.* (*a*) the action of the vb; (*b*) provision of kennels: E18.

kennel /ˈkɛn(ə)l/ *n.*[2] L16. [Later form of CANNEL *n.*[1] Cf. CANAL *n.*, CHANNEL *n.*[1]] A surface drain in a street; a gutter.

Kennelly layer /ˈkɛn(ə)lɪ ˌleɪə/ *n. phr.* E20. [Arthur Edwin *Kennelly* (1861–1939), US electrical engineer.] = *E-layer* s.v. E, E. Also *Kennelly–Heaviside layer* [see HEAVISIDE LAYER].

kennetic /kɛˈnɛtɪk/ *a.* M20. [f. KEN *v.* after KINETIC *a.*] Of or pertaining to the nature or acquisition of knowledge. Chiefly in *kennetic inquiry*.

kennetjie /ˈkɛnəki, -tʃi/ *n.* *S. Afr.* M20. [Afk.] Tipcat; a tipcat.

kenning /ˈkɛnɪŋ/ *n.*[1] Now *Sc.* & *north.* ME. [f. KEN *v.* + -ING[1].] †**1** Teaching, instruction. ME–M16. †**2** Sign, token; appearance. Only in ME. †**3** = KEN *n.*[1] 4. LME–L17. **4a** Mental cognition; knowledge, understanding; awareness, recognition. LME. **b** A small but perceptible amount, a little. L18. †**5a** = KEN *n.*[1] 1. L15–L17. **b** = KEN *n.*[1] 3. M16–E17.

kenning /ˈkɛnɪŋ/ *n.*[2] L19. [ON, f. *kenna* know, perceive, f. Gmc base of KEN *v.*] A poetic phrase used instead of the simple name of a thing in Old Norse, Old English, and other Germanic poetry, as *oar-steed* for 'ship', *storm of swords* for 'battle'.

keno /ˈkiːnəʊ/ *n.* & *int.* E19. [Origin unkn.] **A** *n.* A game of chance resembling bingo or lotto, based on the drawing of numbers and covering of corresponding numbers on cards. E19. **B** *int.*

Expr. encouragement or approval. *US slang.* M19.

kenogenesis *n.* var. of CAENOGENESIS.

kenosis /kɪ'nəʊsɪs/ *n.* L19. [Gk *kenōsis* an emptying, w. ref. to *Phil.* 2:7 *heauton ekenōse* lit. 'emptied himself'.] *Chr. Theol.* Christ's full or partial renunciation of his divine nature or powers in his incarnation.

kenotic *a.* of or pertaining to kenosis; involving or accepting the doctrine of kenosis: L19. **kenoticism** *n.* the doctrine of or belief in the kenosis of Christ L19. **kenoticist** *n.* a person who believes in the doctrine of kenosis L19.

Kensington /'kɛnzɪŋt(ə)n/ *n.* L19. [A borough of London, now part of the Royal Borough of Kensington and Chelsea.] **1** *Kensington (outline) stitch*, = *split stitch* s.v. SPLIT *a.* L19. **2** Speech supposedly characteristic of Kensington, London. M20.

2 B. MASON The 'both' came out purest Kensington as 'beeouth'.

Kensingtonian /kɛnzɪŋ'təʊnɪən/ *n.* & *a.* (a native or inhabitant) of Kensington L19.

Kensitite /'kɛnzɪtʌɪt/ *n.* & *a.* L19. [f. *Kensit* (see below) + -ITE[1].] *Eccl. Hist.* **A** *n.* A follower of John Kensit (1853-1902), a Low Church extremist who objected to alleged romanizing aspects of the Anglican Church. L19. **B** *attrib.* or as *adj.* Of or pertaining to Kensitites or Kensitism. E20.

Kensitism *n.* M20.

kenspeck /'kɛnspɛk/ *a. dial.* L16. [Of Scand. origin: cf. ON *kennispeki* faculty of recognition, MSw. *kännespaker*, Sw. *känspak*, Norw. *kjennespak* quick at recognizing, f. ON *kenna* KEN *v.* + *spak-*, *spek-* wise, wisdom.] = next.

kenspeckle /'kɛnspɛk(ə)l/ *a. Sc.* & *north.* M16. [f. as prec. + -LE[1].] Easily recognizable, conspicuous.

kent /kɛnt/ *n.*[1] & *v.*[1] *Sc.* & *north.* E17. [Perh. var. of QUANT *n., v.*] **A** *n.* A shepherd's staff; a long pole, *esp.* one used in vaulting ditches etc. or for punting. E17. **B** *v.i.* & *t.* Punt (a boat etc.). E19.

Kent /kɛnt/ *n.*[2] E19. [See KENTISH.] In full *Kent sheep*. (An animal of) a breed of hardy sheep having a long coarse fleece.

kent *v.*[2] pa. t. & pple: see KEN *v.*

kentallenite /kɛn'talnʌɪt/ *n.* E20. [f. *Kentallen*, a village in Strathclyde, Scotland + -ITE[1].] *Geol.* A dark coarse-grained mafic rock consisting of olivine and augite with orthoclase, plagioclase, and biotite.

kente /'kɛntə/ *n.* Also **K-**. M20. [Twi = cloth.] More fully *kente cloth*. In Ghana: a brightly coloured banded material; a long garment made from this material, loosely draped on or worn around the shoulders and waist.

kentia /'kɛntɪə/ *n.* L19. [mod.L (see below), f. William *Kent* (d. 1828), botanical collector + -IA[1].] Any of various pinnate-leaved palms of the former genus *Kentia*, native to Australia and some Pacific islands; esp. *Howeia forsterana* and *H. belmoreana*, freq. grown as house-plants.

Kenticism /'kɛntɪsɪz(ə)m/ *n.* M18. [f. *Kent* (see KENTISH) after *Anglicism* etc.] A word, idiom, or expression peculiar to the Kentish dialect, *spec.* of the Old and Middle English periods.

†**kenting** *n.* M17-L18. [App. f. *Kent* (see KENTISH) + -ING[1].] A kind of fine linen cloth orig. made in Kent.

Kentish /'kɛntɪʃ/ *a.* & *n.* OE. [f. *Cent* Kent (see below) f. L *Cantium* f. Celt. n. meaning either 'border' or 'white': see -ISH[1].] **A** *adj.* Of, pertaining to or characteristic of Kent, a county in SE England, and one of the supposed seven kingdoms of the Angles and Saxons. OE.

Kentish crow *local* a hooded crow. **Kentish fire** rhythmic handclapping, either as applause or as a demonstration of impatience or dissent. **Kentish glory** a large, orange-brown and white patterned moth, *Endromis versicolora*. **Kentish nightingale** a blackcap. **Kentish plover** a small plover, *Charadrius alexandrinus*, resembling a pale ringed plover and of worldwide distribution. **Kentish rag** a hard compact limestone found in Kent, used for paving and building. **Kentish tern** a Sandwich tern.

B *n.* **1** *pl.* The natives or inhabitants of Kent. *rare.* OE. **2** The dialect of Kent *spec.* of the Old and Middle English periods. M19.

†**kentle** *n.* var. of QUINTAL.

kentledge /'kɛntlɪdʒ/ *n.* E17. [OFr. *quintelage* ballast, w. assim. to *kentle* obs. var. of QUINTAL: see -AGE.] *Naut.* Pig-iron or other heavy material used as permanent ballast.

Kentuck /'kɛntʌk/ *a.* & *n. US.* E19. [Abbrev. of KENTUCKY.] = next.

Kentuckian /kɛn'tʌkɪən/ *n.* & *a. US.* L18. [f. KENTUCKY + -IAN.] **A** *n.* A native or inhabitant of Kentucky, a south-eastern State of the US. L18. **B** *adj.* Of or pertaining to Kentucky. E19.

Kentucky /kɛn'tʌki/ *n.* L18. [See below.] Used *attrib.* to designate things from or associated with the State of Kentucky in the south-eastern US.

Kentucky bluegrass the grass *Poa pratensis*, grown for fodder in the central US. **Kentucky coffee tree** a N. American leguminous tree, *Gymnocladus dioicus*, the seeds of which can be used as a substitute for coffee. **Kentucky Derby** a horse-race for three-year-olds run annually at Louisville in Kentucky. **Kentucky rifle** a long-barrelled muzzle-loading flintlock rifle. **Kentucky warbler** an olive-green and yellow warbler, *Geothlypis formosa*, of the eastern US.

kentum *a.* var. of CENTUM *a.*

Kenya /'kɛnjə, 'kiː-/ *n.* M20. [See below.] Used *attrib.* to designate people or things from or associated with Kenya, a country in E. Africa.

Kenya Asian = *Kenyan Asian* s.v. KENYAN *a.* **Kenya coffee** a mild coffee grown in Kenya.

Kenyah /'kɛnjə/ *n.* & *a.* M19. [Kenyah.] **A** *n.* Pl. **-s**, same. A member of one of the aboriginal peoples inhabiting parts of Borneo and Sarawak; the Indonesian language of this people. M19. **B** *attrib.* or as *adj.* Of or pertaining to the Kenyahs or their language. E20.

Kenyan /'kɛnjən, 'kiː-/ *n.* & *a.* M20. [f. KENYA + -AN.] **A** *n.* A native or inhabitant of Kenya. M20.

B *adj.* Of, pertaining to, or characteristic of Kenya or its people. M20.

Kenyan Asian an Asian, esp. one from India or Pakistan, resident or formerly resident in Kenya.

Kenyani'zation *n.* in Kenya, the replacement of settlers and Asians by Kenyan Africans in government posts, the civil service, etc. M20. **Kenyanize** *v.t.* make Kenyan in character, organization, etc. L20.

kep /kɛp/ *v.* & *n. Sc.* & *north.* LME. [Differentiated form of KEEP *v.* (cf. senses 5, 6 & pa. t. *kept*).] **A** *v.t.* **1** Meet, intercept; stop the course of; receive the force of (a blow). LME. **2** Catch so as to prevent from falling; catch (falling liquid) as in a vessel. L15. **B** *n.* **1** = CATCH *n.*[1] 2. E18. **2** A chance, an opportunity. L18. **3** = CATCH *n.*[1] 4. E20.

kephal-, **kephalo-** *comb. forms* see CEPHALO-.

kephir *n.* var. of KEFIR.

kepi /'kɛpi, 'keɪpi/ *n.* M19. [Fr. *képi* f. Swiss G *Käppi* dim. of *Kappe* cap.] A French military cap with a flat circular top which slopes towards the front and a horizontal peak.

Kepler /'kɛplə/ *n.* E18. [Johann *Kepler* (1571-1630), Ger. astronomer.] *Astron.* Used in *possess.* and *attrib.* to designate things discovered or investigated by Kepler.

Kepler's equation the equation $\theta = \phi - e \sin \phi$ relating the mean anomaly θ of a planet to the eccentric anomaly ϕ and the eccentricity e of the orbit. **Kepler's law** each of three propositions: (*a*) that the planets move in ellipses having the sun at one focus; (*b*) that the radius vector of a planet sweeps out equal areas in equal times; (*c*) that the square of a planet's orbital period is directly proportional to the cube of its mean distance from the sun. **Kepler('s) problem** the problem of solving Kepler's equation for the eccentric anomaly of a planet in a known orbit given the mean anomaly, i.e. of finding the position of the planet at any given time.

Keplerian /kɛ'plɪərɪən/ *a.* M19. [f. prec. + -IAN.] Of or pertaining to Kepler or his discoveries and investigations; *spec.* (*a*) designating or pertaining to the free motion of a body in the gravitational field of another more massive body (described by a trajectory that is an ellipse or other conic section); (*b*) designating a refracting telescope with a positive objective and eyepiece, giving an inverted image.

kept /kɛpt/ *ppl a.* L17. [f. KEEP *v.*] That has been or is being kept; *spec.* (esp. of a woman) maintained or supported in return for sexual favours.

¶ Earlier in UNKEPT.

kept *v.* pa. t. & pple of KEEP *v.*

ker- /kə/ *pref. colloq.* (orig. *US*). M19. [Imit.] Forming ns. and ints. imit. of the sound or the effect of the fall of some heavy body, as *kerchunk*, *kerflop*, *kerplunk*, *kerslam*, *kersplash*, *kerthump*, *kerwhop*, etc.

kerasin /'kɛrəsɪn/ *n.* L19. [Irreg. f. Gk *keras* horn + -IN[1].] *Biochem.* A cerebroside normally found in the brain and accumulated in the liver, spleen, and elsewhere in individuals with Gaucher's disease.

keratectasia /kɛrətɛk'teɪzɪə/ *n.* L19. [f. KERATO- + ECTASIA.] *Ophthalm.* Protrusion of part of the cornea.

keratectomy /kɛrə'tɛktəmi/ *n.* L19. [f. KERATO- + -ECTOMY.] *Med.* Surgical excision of part of the cornea; an instance of this.

keratin /'kɛrətɪn/ *n.* M19. [f. Gk *kerat-*, *keras* horn + -IN[1].] *Biochem.* Any of a group of fibrous proteins which have a structure cross-linked by disulphide bonds and form the chief structural constituent of skin, nails, hair, feathers, horn, etc.

keratinisation *n.*, **-ise** *v.* vars. of KERATINIZATION, KERATINIZE.

keratinization /ˌkɛrətɪnʌɪ'zeɪʃ(ə)n, kəˌrat-/ *n.* Also **-isation**. L19. [f. as next + -ATION.] The process of becoming keratinous; *esp.* the hardening of the cells of the skin, hair, etc., by deposition of keratin.

keratinize /'kɛrətɪnʌɪz, kə'rat-/ *v.* Also **-ise**. L19. [f. Gk *keratinos* horny + -IZE.] **1** *v.i.* Become keratinous. L19. **2** *v.t.* Make keratinous, subject to keratinization. Freq. as *keratinized* ppl a. E20.

keratino- /'kɛrətɪnəʊ/ *comb. form* of KERATIN: see -O-.

kera'tinocyte *n.* an epidermal cell which produces keratin M20. **kerati'nolysis** *n.* chemical breakdown of keratin E20. **keratino'lytic** *a.* bringing about keratinolysis M20. **keratino'philic** *a.* (*Bot.*) (chiefly of a fungus) growing on keratinous material, as hair, feathers, etc. M20.

keratinous /kə'ratɪnəs/ *a.* L19. [f. KERATIN + -OUS.] Of the nature of or like horn; consisting of or containing keratin.

keratitis /kɛrə'tʌɪtɪs/ *n.* M19. [f. next + -ITIS.] *Med.* Inflammation of the cornea.

kerato- /'kɛrətəʊ/ *comb. form.* Bef. a vowel **kerat-**. [Gk, f. *kerat-*, *keras* horn: see -O-. Cf. CERATO-.] Chiefly *Med.* **1** Of or relating to keratinous or horny tissues. **2** Of or pertaining to the cornea of the eye.

keratoacan'thoma *n.*, pl. **-mas**, **-mata** /-mətə/, [Gk *akantha* thorn] a nodular growth of the skin which usu. heals spontaneously M20. **kerato-conjunc'tival** *a.* of or pertaining to the cornea and the conjunctiva M20. **keratoconjuncti'vitis** *n.* (a condition involving) inflammation of the cornea and conjunctiva L19. **kerato'conus** *n.* [L *conus* cone] *Ophthalm.* a condition of the eye in which the cornea develops a rounded apex M20. **kerato'derma** *n.* a local or general thickening of the horny layer of the epidermis M20. **kerato'dermia** *n.* keratoderma E20. **kera'togenous** *a.* producing horn or keratin L19. **kerato'hyalin(e)** *n.* (*Biochem.*) an amorphous protein found in association with keratin L19. **kera'toma** *n.*, pl. **-mas**, **-mata** /-mətə/, = KERATOSIS L19. **keratomalacia** /-mə'leɪʃ(ɪ)ə/ *n.* softening of the cornea associated esp. with vitamin A deficiency L19. **kera'tometer** *n.* (*Ophthalm.*) an instrument for measuring the curvature of the cornea by observing images reflected in it (also called *ophthalmometer*) L19. **kerato'metric** *a.* pertaining to or obtained with a keratometer L19. **kera'tometry** *n.* measurement of the curvature of the cornea L19. **keratoplasty** *n.* (an instance of) surgery performed on the cornea, *esp.* corneal transplantation M19. **kera'tosis** *n.*, pl. **-toses** /-'təʊsiːz/, a horny growth, esp. on the skin; a condition marked by such growths: L19. **kera'totic** *a.* of or pertaining to keratosis M20.

keratolysis /kɛrəˈtɒlɪsɪs/ *n.* L19. [f. KERATO- + -LYSIS.] *Med.* Loosening or (partial) destruction of keratinous tissue, esp. that of the skin, through disease or chemical action. Also, destruction of corneal tissue.

keratoˈlytic *a.* & *n.* (*Med.*) (an agent) able to soften or destroy keratinous material L19.

keratophyre /ˈkɛrətəfʌɪə/ *n.* L19. [f. KERATO- + -*phyre* as in *granophyre*.] *Geol.* Any of various fine-grained sodium-rich igneous rocks, typically albitic trachytes.

kerb /kəːb/ *n.* & *v.* Also †**kirb**. M17. [Var. of CURB *n.*] A *n.* I 1 = CURB *n.* 6. M17. 2 = CURB *n.* 9. E18. 3 An edging of stone etc. to a pavement or raised path; = CURB *n.* 8. E19. II 4 = CURB *n.* 1. L17. III 5 = CURB *n.* 5. M19.

Comb.: **kerb-crawl** *v.i.* engage in kerb-crawling; **kerb-crawler** a (usu. male) person who engages in kerb-crawling; **kerb crawling** the practice of driving slowly by the edge of a road, harassing or soliciting esp. female passers-by; **kerb drill** precautionary procedure, esp. looking to right and left, made before crossing a road and often taught to children; **kerb market** (a place for) the sale of securities after hours or of shares not dealt with on a stock exchange; **kerb service** = *curb service* s.v. CURB *n.*; **kerbside** the side of a road or pavement nearer the kerb; a kerb; **kerbstone** any of the stones forming a kerb; a kerb; *kerbstone market* = *kerb market* above; **kerb weight** the weight of a motor car without occupants or baggage.

B *v.t.* Furnish with a kerb. M19.

kerbing *n.* (*a*) the action of the vb; (*b*) the stones collectively forming a kerb: M19.

†**kerch** *n.*[1] LME–L18. [f. as CURCH.] = KERCHIEF 1.

Kerch /kəːtʃ/ *n.*[2] Also **Kertch**. M20. [See below.] Used *attrib.* to designate a type of ancient red-figured Greek pottery found in Kerch, a town in the Crimea, S. Ukraine.

kercher /ˈkəːtʃə/ *n. obs.* exc. *dial.* LME. [Syncopated f. OFr. *couvrechier*, *cuevre-*, erron. ff. *couvrechief* etc.: see next.] = next.

kerchief /ˈkəːtʃɪf/ *n.* ME. [AN *courchef* = OFr. *cuevre-chief*, (also mod.) *couvre-chef*, f. *couvrir* COVER *v.*[2] + *chief* head (see CHIEF *n.*): cf. COVERCHIEF.] 1 A cloth or scarf used to cover the head, esp. by a woman; a covering for the neck or shoulders, a neckerchief, a cravat. ME. 2 A cloth used for any of various other purposes; *spec.* a handkerchief. LME.

kerchiefed *a.* covered with or wearing a kerchief E17.

kêrel /ˈkɛːr(ə)l/ *n. S. Afr. colloq.* Also **kerel**. L19. [Afk. f. Du. = CARL *n.*: cf. CHURL.] A fellow, a chap, a young man; a boyfriend.

kereru /ˈkɛrəruː/ *n.* L19. [Maori.] The New Zealand pigeon, *Hemiphaga novaeseelandiae*. Also called *kuku*.

Keres /ˈkɛrɛs/ *n.* & *a.* Pl. of n. same. E19. [Amer. Sp. *Queres* f. Amer. Indian.] Of or pertaining to, a member of, a Pueblo Indian people inhabiting parts of New Mexico; (of) the language of this people, forming the Keresan group.

Keresan /ˈkɛrəs(ə)n/ *a.* & *n.* L19. [f. prec. + -AN.] A *adj.* Of or pertaining to the Keres of New Mexico; *spec.* designating or pertaining to a linguistic group constituted by Keres. L19. B *n.* The linguistic group constituted by Keres. M20.

kerf /kəːf/ *n.* [OE *cyrf* f. WGmc, f. base of CARVE: cf. ON *kurfr* chip, *kyrfa* cut. See also CARF.] 1 The act of cutting or carving; a cut, a stroke. Now *rare*. OE. 2 The result of cutting; an incision, notch, slit, etc., made by cutting, esp. by a saw. LME. 3 The cut end or surface on a felled or pruned tree. LME. 4 A piece or quantity cut off; a cutting. L17.

kerfed *a.* having incisions or slits L19.

kerfuffle /kəˈfʌf(ə)l/ *n. colloq.* Orig. *Sc.* Also **ca-**, **cu(r)-**. E19. [Perh. f. CURFUFFLE *v.*, but cf. Ir. *cior thuathail* confusion, disorder.] Fuss, commotion, disorder, agitation.

J. FLEMING The kerfuffle over the stolen jewels last week. M. GEE In the kerfuffle, he didn't hear the front door.

Kerguelen /ˈkəːgɪlɪn/ *n.* M19. [A group of islands in the southern Indian Ocean, f. Yves Joseph de *Kerguelen*-Tremarec, 18th-cent. Fr. navigator.] *Kerguelen cabbage*, †*Kerguelen('s) land cabbage*, a cabbage-like cruciferous plant, *Pringlea antiscorbutica*, confined to Kerguelen and neighbouring islands.

keri *n.* var. of QERE.

Kerman *a.* & *n.* var. of KIRMAN.

Kermanji /kəˈmɑːndʒi/ *n.* L19. [Kurdish *kurmānjī*.] = KURDISH *n.*

Kermanshah *n.* & *a.* var. of KIRMANSHAH.

kermes /ˈkəːmɪz/ *n.* L16. [Fr. *kermès* f. Arab. *kirmiz* (= sense 2 below). Cf. CRIMSON, ARMOZEEN.] 1 More fully *kermes oak*. A small evergreen oak, *Quercus coccifera*, of the Mediterranean region. L16. 2 (The dried bodies of) adult females of the scale insect *Kermes ilicis*, which form hard berry-like galls on the kermes oak, used to make dye and (formerly) medicines; the scarlet dye made from these. Cf. ALKERMES. E17. 3 *Chem.* & *Pharm.* A vermilion compound, precipitated antimony trisulphide. Also more fully *kermes mineral*. Now *rare* or *obs.* M18.

kermesse /kəˈmɛs/ *n.* L19. [Fr., f. as next.] 1 = next. L19. 2 *Cycling*. A circuit race. M20.

kermis /ˈkəːmɪs/ *n.* Also **kirmess**. L16. [Du. *kermis*, †*-misse*, f. *kerk* CHURCH *n.* + *misse* MASS *n.*[1]: orig. = mass on annual anniversary of dedication of a church, when a fair was held. Cf. prec.] In the Low Countries, parts of Germany, etc.: an annual fair or carnival. Also (*US*), a similar fair or bazaar, usu. for charitable purposes.

kern /kəːn/ *n.*[1] Also **kerne**. Pl. **-s**, same. LME. [Ir. *ceithearn* f. OIr. *ceithern* band of foot-soldiers. Cf. earlier CATERAN.] 1 *Hist.* A light-armed Irish foot-soldier. Formerly also a band of kerns. LME. 2 A rustic, a peasant. *arch.* L15.

kern /kəːn/ *n.*[2] L16. [Rel. to KERN *v.*[1] & KERNEL *n.*[1]: perh. already in OE: cf. Norw. *kyrne* grain & CURN; in sense 3 extracted f. G *Kernzähler* nucleus counter.] †1 The kernel (of a nut). *rare*. Only in L16. 2 A grain (of wheat, sand, etc.). *rare*. M18. 3 *Meteorol.* A suspended dust particle, *esp.* one which acts as a nucleus for condensation. M20.

Comb.: **kern counter** [G *Kernzähler*] a device in which a sample of air is supersaturated to make kerns visible (by causing condensation) for counting.

kern /kəːn/ *n.*[3] L17. [Perh. f. Fr. *carne* corner, Norman-Picard var. of OFr. *charne* f. L *cardin-*, *cardo* hinge.] *Typogr.* A part of a metal type projecting beyond the body or shank, as parts of some italic letters; a part of a printed character that overlaps its neighbours.

kern /kəːn/ *v.*[1] *obs.* exc. *dial.* ME. [f. Gmc base of CORN *n.*[1]: prob. already in OE.] 1 *v.i.* Of corn: form the hard grains in the ear, seed. ME. †2 *v.t.* Cause to granulate; make (salt) into grains. L16–E18. b Sprinkle or preserve with salt. E17–L19. 3 *v.i.* Of salt etc.: crystallize in grains, become granular. M17.

kern /kəːn/ *v.*[2]*t.* L17. [f. KERN *n.*[3]] *Typogr.* Cast (metal type) with a kern or kerns; make (esp. selected characters) overlap neighbouring characters. Now also, modify the spacing between (characters) as specified by the manufacturer.

kerne *n.* var. of KERN *n.*[1]

kernel /ˈkəːn(ə)l/ *n.*[1] & *v.*[1] [OE *cyrnel* dim. of *corn* seed: see CORN *n.*[1], -EL[1].] A *n.* 1 A seed, *esp.* one in a fruit; a pip, a stone. *obs.* exc. *dial.* OE. 2 The softer (usu. edible) part contained within the hard shell of a nut or of a fruit stone. OE. 3 A rounded swelling in any part of the body; *esp.* an enlarged lymph gland, an inflamed tonsil. Now chiefly *dial.* OE. 4 The seed and hard husk of a grain, esp. wheat. ME. †b A granule, as of sand or salt. LME–E19. 5 A gland or glandular body; a tonsil; a lymphatic gland or ganglion. Now *rare* or *obs.* LME. 6 The nucleus, core, or centre of something. Also (*fig.*), the essential part; the gist of a narrative, the basis of a system, etc. M16. b *Ling.* The stem or common basis of a set of inflectional forms, as *lach-* in the German verb *lachen*. L19. c *Physics*. = CORE *n.*[1] 12. E20. d *Math.* A (given) function of two or more variables from which an integrand is obtained by multiplying by one or more other functions each of just one of the variables. E20. e *Math.* The set of all the elements of a group that are mapped by a given homomorphism into the identity element. M20. f *Ling.* In full *kernel sentence*. In early transformational grammar, a basic or core sentence that results from the application of only a few (obligatory) transformations, and to which other sentences may be related by further transformations; a set of such sentences. M20.

2 *fig.*: J. VIORST Anxiety contains a kernel of hope. 6 J. GALSWORTHY The kernel of life was in . . saving for his children. *Ski Survey* The front of an avalanche . . does not have the same speed as the kernel following behind.

B *v.* Infl. **-ll-**, ***-l-**. †1 *v.i.* Form kernels or seed; (of land) produce grain or corn. LME–E18. 2 *v.t.* Enclose as a kernel in its shell. M17.

kernelled *a.*[1] †(*a*) full of kernels or glands; (*b*) having a kernel: LME. **kernelless** /-l-l-/ *a.* (*rare*) without a kernel L19. **kernelly** *a.* †(*a*) consisting of or full of glands, glandular; (*b*) resembling a kernel: LME.

kernel /ˈkəːn(ə)l/ *n.*[2] & *v.*[2] *obs.* exc. *Hist.* Also †**carnel**. ME. [OFr. *carnel*, *quernel* (mod. *créneau*): see CRENEL *n.*, *v.*] †A *n.* An indentation or embrasure in the battlement of a wall; = CRENEL *n.* Also (usu. in *pl.*), battlements. ME–L17. B *v.t.* Infl. **-ll-**, ***-l-**. Furnish with embrasures or battlements; crenellate. ME.

kernelled *a.*[2] (*rare*) furnished with battlements or embrasures, crenellated E18.

kernicterus /kəːˈnɪkt(ə)rəs/ *n.* Also (earlier) †**-ikt-**. E20. [G *Kernikterus*, f. *Kern* nucleus + *Ikterus* jaundice.] *Med.* The staining and permanent damaging of brain cells with bilirubin, often causing deafness and athetosis, which may occur in haemolytic disease of the newborn.

kernicteric *a.* pertaining to or afflicted with kernicterus M20.

Kernig's sign /ˈkəːnɪgz sʌɪn/ *n. phr.* E20. [V. M. *Kernig* (1840–1917), Russ. physician.] *Med.* Resistance to straightening of the leg at the knee in a patient lying supine with the hips fully flexed, an indication of meningitis.

†**kernikterus** *n.* see KERNICTERUS.

kernite /ˈkəːnʌɪt/ *n.* E20. [f. *Kern* County, California + -ITE[1].] *Min.* A hydrated monoclinic form of sodium borate which occurs as large transparent crystals and is a major source of borax.

kernos /ˈkəːnɒs/ *n.* Pl. **-noi** /-nɔɪ/. E20. [Gk.] *Archaeol.* An ancient Mediterranean and Near Eastern baked clay vessel having small cups around the rim or fixed in a circle to a central stem.

kero /ˈkɛrəʊ/ *n. Austral.* & *NZ colloq.* M20. [Abbrev.] Kerosene.

kerogen /ˈkɛrədʒ(ə)n/ *n.* E20. [f. Gk *kēros* wax + -GEN.] *Geol.* A complex fossilized organic material found in oil shale and other sedimentary rock, which is insoluble in common organic solvents and yields petroleum products on distillation.

kerosene /ˈkɛrəsiːn/ *n.* & *v.* Also **-ine**. M19. [Irreg. f. Gk. *kēros* wax + -ENE, -INE[5].] A *n.* A petroleum distillate containing liquid hydrocarbons which boils in the range 150° to 300°C, and is used as a fuel for tractors and jet engines, and in domestic heaters; paraffin oil. M19. B *v.t.* Saturate with kerosene. L19.

Kerr /kəː/ *n.* E20. [John *Kerr* (1824–1907), Sc. physicist.] *Physics*. Used *attrib.* to designate things studied or devised by Kerr.

Kerr cell a transparent cell containing a liquid across which a voltage may be applied to produce a strong Kerr (electro-optical) effect, used to vary the plane of polarization of light and hence (when placed between crossed polaroids) the intensity of a beam. **Kerr effect** (*a*) the rotation of the plane of polarization of light when reflected from a magnetized surface (more fully *Kerr magneto-optical effect*); (*b*) the production of birefringence in a substance by an electric field (more fully *Kerr electro-optical effect*).

kerria /ˈkɛrɪə/ *n.* E19. [mod.L (see below), f. William *Ker* or *Kerr* (d. 1814), Eng. botanical collector: see -IA[1].] 1 A deciduous yellow-flowered shrub, *Kerria japonica*, of the rose family, native to China and Japan and freq. cultivated esp. in its double-flowered version. E19. 2 *white kerria*, a closely related shrub, *Rhodotypos scandens*, which bears white flowers. E20.

Kerry /ˈkɛri/ *n.*[1] L18. [See sense 1 below.] 1 Used *attrib.* to designate things originating in or associated with Kerry, a county in SW Ireland. L18. 2 A Kerry cow; a Kerry Blue terrier. E19.

1 **Kerry Blue** (**terrier**) (a dog of) a breed of medium-sized terrier with a long silky grey-blue coat. **Kerry cow** (an animal of) a breed of small black dairy cattle.

Kerry /ˈkɛri/ *n.*[2] E20. [A town and neighbouring range of hills in the Welsh county of Powys.] More fully *Kerry Hill* (*sheep*). (An animal of) a breed of sheep having a thick fleece and black markings near the muzzle and feet.

kersey /ˈkəːzi/ *n.* & *a.* Now *rare*. LME. [Prob. f. *Kersey* in Suffolk: cf. AL *pannus cersegus, carsea*, AN *drap de kersy*.] **A** *n.* Pl. **-seys**, **-sies**. **1** A kind of coarse cloth woven from short-stapled wool. LME. 2 A make or variety of kersey (usu. in *pl.*). Formerly also, a piece of kersey of a definite size. LME. 3 In *pl.* Trousers made of kersey. M19.

B *attrib.* or as *adj.* 1 Made of kersey. L16. †2 *fig.* Plain, homely. *rare* (Shakes.). Only in L16.

1 T. KENEALLY He had good kersey breeches on.

kerseymere /ˈkəːzɪmɪə/ *n.* & *a.* L18. [Alt. of CASSIMERE, by assoc. w. prec.] **A** *n.* 1 A medium-weight twilled woollen cloth. L18. 2 In *pl.* & (occas.) *sing.* Trousers made of kerseymere. M19. **B** *attrib.* or as *adj.* Made of kerseymere. E19.

Kertch *n.* var. of KERCH *n.*[2]

keruing /ˈkɛrʊɪŋ/ *n.* E20. [Malay *keruing*.] The light or dark brown hardwood timber of several trees of the genus *Dipterocarpus* (family Dipterocarpaceae), found in western Malaysia, Sabah, and Indonesia.

kerygma /kɪˈrɪgmə/ *n.* Pl. **-mata** /-mətə/. L19. [Gk *kērugma*, f. *kērussein* proclaim.] Chr. Ch. *The* preaching of the Gospels; the element of proclamation as contrasted with didache (teaching) in the communication of the Christian gospel.

keryg'matic *a.* belonging to or of the nature of preaching E20. **keryg'matically** *adv.* M20.

kest /kɛst/ *v.t.* & *i. dial.* Pa. t. & pple **kest**, **kested**. L16. [Var. of CAST *v.*] = CAST *v.*; *esp.* (*a*) cast aside, throw away; (*b*) outdo.

kestrel /ˈkɛstr(ə)l/ *n.* LME. [Perh. f. Fr. *casserelle* dial. var. of *crécerelle*, †*cresserelle* (dial. *cristel*), f. synon. *crécelle* lit. 'rattle', of imit. origin.] Any of several falcons distinguished by the habit of hunting by sustained hovering; esp. *Falco tinnunculus*, widely distributed in the Old World, and (more fully *American kestrel*) the American sparrowhawk, *F. sparverius*.

NANKEEN *kestrel*.

Keswick /ˈkɛzɪk/ *n.* E19. [A town in Cumbria, NW England, where John Sander, who first introduced it, lived.] In full *Keswick codlin*(*g*). A variety of cooking apple which has a greenish skin tinged with red.

ket /kɛt/ *n.*[1] *obs.* exc. *dial.* ME. [ON *kjǫt* flesh (Icel. *ket, kjöt*, Sw. *kött*, Da. *kød, kjød*).] Raw flesh, carrion; *fig.* trash, rubbish.

ket /kɛt/ *n.*[2] M20. [f. BRAC)KET *n.*: cf. BRA *n.*[2]] *Quantum Mech.* A vector in Hilbert space symbolized by |>, *esp.* one representing the state of a quantized system. Freq. *ket vector*. Cf. BRA *n.*[2]

ket- *comb. form* see KETO-.

keta /ˈkiːtə/ *n.* E19. [Russ.] = CHUM *n.*[4]

ketal /ˈkiːtal/ *n.* E20. [f. KETO- + -AL[2].] *Chem.* A compound of the general formula $R^1R^2C(OR^3)OR^4$, where the Rs are alkyl groups. Cf. ACETAL.

ketazine /ˈkiːtəziːn/ *n.* L19. [f. KETO- + AZINE.] *Chem.* A compound of the general formula $R^1R^2C{=}NN{=}CR^3R^4$ (where the Rs are alkyl groups), made esp. by reaction of hydrazine with two ketone molecules.

ketch /kɛtʃ/ *n.* M17. [Later form of CATCH *n.*[2]] *Naut.* A two-masted, fore-and-aft rigged sailing vessel (formerly used esp. for coastal trading) in which the mizen-mast is shorter than the mainmast and stepped forward of the rudder post.

bomb-ketch: see BOMB *n.* 3.

ketch *v.* see CATCH *v.*

ketchup /ˈkɛtʃəp, -ʌp/ *n.* Also **catchup** /ˈkatʃ-/, ***catsup** /ˈkats-/. L17. [Perh. f. Chin. (Cantonese) *k'ē chap* tomato juice.] A spicy sauce, now usu. of a thick consistency, made from tomatoes, or from mushrooms, walnuts, etc., and used as a relish with meat, fish, etc. Freq. w. specification, as *mushroom ketchup*, *tomato ketchup*, etc.

ketene /ˈkiːtiːn/ *n.* Also (earlier) **-en** /-(ə)n/. E20. [f. KETONE + -ENE.] *Chem.* A pungent colourless gas, $CH_2{=}C{=}O$, having wide applications in synthesis owing to its high reactivity; any substituted derivative of this, with the structure $:C{=}C{=}O$.

kethib /kəˈθiːb, -t-/ *n.* Also **-bh**, ***K-***. M17. [Heb. *kěṯīḇ* written.] A traditional reading in the Hebrew text of the Old Testament and Hebrew Scriptures which is unintelligible or unsuitable for public reading and for which a *qere* is substituted.

Kethubim /kɛθuːˈviːm, kɛt-/ *n.pl.* L17. [Heb. *kěṯuḇīm* writings.] = HAGIOGRAPHA.

ketimine /ˈkiːtɪmiːn/ *n.* E20. [f. KETO- + IMINE.] *Chem.* A compound of the general formula $RR'C{=}NH$ (where the Rs are alkyl groups), formed e.g. by the action of ammonia on a ketone.

keto- /ˈkiːtəʊ/ *comb. form.* Bef. a vowel also **ket-**. In sense 2 also as attrib. adj. **keto**. [f. KETONE: see -O-.] 1 Chiefly *Chem.* & *Med.* Of a ketone or ketones. 2 *Chem.* Designating or containing a ketone group, esp. as opp. to an enolic group.

keto-'acid *n.* a compound whose molecule contains both a ketone group and a carboxylic acid group E20. **ketoaci'dosis** *n.* acidosis due to enhanced production of ketone bodies M20. **keto-compound** *n.* a compound containing a ketone group L19. **keto-'enol, -e'nolic** *adjs.* designating tautomerism between keto and enol forms of a compound E20. **keto'genesis** *n.* metabolic production of ketone bodies E20. **keto'genic** *a.* producing ketone bodies; *spec.* (of a diet) rich in fats and low in carbohydrates, sometimes used therapeutically in epilepsy to produce ketosis; (*17-*)*ketogenic steroid*, a steroid which yields a (17-)ketosteroid on oxidation: E20. **α-keto'glutarate** *n.* a salt or ester of α-ketoglutaric acid E20. **α-ketoglu'taric** *a.*: *α-ketoglutaric acid*, a dibasic keto-acid, $HOOC{\cdot}CO{\cdot}CH_2{\cdot}CH_2{\cdot}COOH$, formed by oxidation and decarboxylation of isocitric acid in the Krebs cycle E20. **keto'hexose** *n.* a ketose with six carbon atoms L19. **keto'pentose** *n.* a ketose with five carbon atoms E20. **keto'steroid** *n.* a steroid whose molecule contains a ketone group, *esp.* (in full *17-ketosteroid*) one with this group at the carbon atom designated 17 M20. **ke'toxime** *n.* an oxime of a ketone, a compound of the general formula $RR'C{=}NOH$ (where the Rs are alkyl groups) L19.

ketol /ˈkiːtɒl/ *n.* L19. [f. KETO- + -OL.] *Chem.* A compound having a hydroxyl group attached to a carbon atom adjacent to or near a carbonyl group.

ke'tolic *a.* M20.

ketolysis /kɪˈtɒlɪsɪs/ *n.* M20. [f. KETO- + -LYSIS.] *Biochem.* The metabolic decomposition of ketone bodies.

ketolytic /kiːtə(ʊ)ˈlɪtɪk/ *a.* of, pertaining to, or causing ketolysis E20.

ketonaemia /kiːtə(ʊ)ˈniːmɪə/ *n.* Also ***-nemia**. E20. [f. next + -AEMIA.] *Med.* The presence of an abnormally high concentration of ketone bodies in the blood.

ketone /ˈkiːtəʊn/ *n.* M19. [G *Keton* alt. of *Aketon* ACETONE.] *Chem.* Any of a class of compounds typified by acetone, which have the general structure $RR'{=}O$ (where the Rs are alkyl groups), and are formed esp. by the partial oxidation of secondary alcohols.

Comb.: **ketone body** *Biochem.* each of the three related compounds acetone, acetoacetic acid, and β-hydroxybutyric acid, which are produced in fatty- and amino-acid metabolism; **ketone group** the carbonyl group $:C{=}O$ when attached to two carbon atoms in a molecule.

ketonic /kɪˈtɒnɪk/ *a.* of or pertaining to ketones; of the nature of a ketone: L19. **ketoni'zation** *n.* the process of changing from an enol form into a keto form M20. **ketonize** *v.i.* undergo ketonization M20.

ketonemia *n.* see KETONAEMIA.

ketonuria /kiːtə(ʊ)ˈnjʊərɪə/ *n.* E20. [f. KETONE + -URIA.] *Med.* The excretion of abnormally large amounts of ketone bodies in the urine.

ketosis /kɪˈtəʊsɪs/ *n.* E20. [f. KETO- + -OSIS.] *Med.* The increased metabolic production of ketone bodies, usu. associated with a predominance of fat metabolism as in starvation and in diabetes mellitus.

ketotic /kɪˈtɒtɪk/ *a.* affected or associated with ketosis M20.

kettle /ˈkɛt(ə)l/ *n.* [OE *ċetel*, (WS) *ċietel* = ON *ketill*, OS (Du.) *ketel*, OHG *kezzil* (G *Kessel*), f. Gmc f. L *catillus* dim. of *catinus* deep vessel for serving or cooking food, repl. in ME by forms f. ON.] **I** 1 A vessel, usu. of metal, for boiling water or other liquids; *spec.* (*a*) a covered vessel with a spout and handle, used to boil water for domestic purposes (also *tea-kettle*); (*b*) (in full *fish-kettle*) a long usu. oval pan for cooking fish in liquid. Also, a kettle and its contents; the contents of a kettle; as much as a kettle will hold, a kettleful. OE. 2 A picnic or excursion at which fish is cooked out of doors. *Sc. dial.* L17. 3 A bowl- or saucer-shaped vessel in which operations are carried out on low-melting metals, glass, plastics, etc., in the liquid state. E19. 4 A deep circular hollow scoured out in a rocky river-bed, under a glacier, etc.; a pothole. Also (*Physical Geogr.*) = *kettle hole* below. M19. 5 A watch. *slang* (chiefly *Criminals'*). M19.

1 L. CODY She put the kettle on for tea. *electric kettle, jug kettle, maslin kettle, whistling kettle*, etc. **kettle of fish** (*a*) *Sc. dial.* = sense 2 above; (*b*) a state of affairs: in *a pretty, fine, nice*, etc., *kettle of fish*, a mess, an awkward state of affairs; *a different* or *another kettle of fish*, a different state of affairs or matter altogether.

II †6 = KETTLEDRUM. *rare* (Shakes.). Only in E17.

Comb.: **kettle-bottom** (*a*) a hill with broad flat top and sloping sides; (*b*) *Naut.* a ship with a flat floor; **kettle-holder** a piece of cloth etc. used to protect the hand from the heat of a kettle-handle; **kettle hole** *Physical Geogr.* a deep, often circular depression in the ground formed by the melting of an ice block trapped in glacial deposits; **kettle lake** *Physical Geogr.* a lake in a kettle hole; **kettle moraine** *Physical Geogr.* a moraine in which there are numerous kettle holes.

kettleful *n.* as much as a kettle will hold M19. **kettler** *n.* †(*a*) a person who mends kettles; (*b*) a colour-mixer's assistant who boils dyestuffs: E17.

kettledrum /ˈkɛt(ə)ldrʌm/ *n.* & *v.* M16. [f. KETTLE *n.* + DRUM *n.*[1]] **A** *n.* 1 *Mus.* A percussion instrument, a hollow brass or copper hemisphere over the edge of which parchment or (now) plastic is stretched and tuned to a definite note. Formerly also, a player on this instrument, a kettledrummer. M16. 2 An afternoon tea party, smaller than a drum (DRUM *n.*[1] 4). *colloq.* (now *Hist.*). M19. **B** *v.i.* Infl. **-mm-**. Beat a kettledrum; make a noise like a kettledrum. M19.

kettledrummer *n.* a person who plays the kettledrum M17.

kettle-pins, **kettles** *ns.* var. of KITTLE-PINS, KITTLES.

kettle-stitch /ˈkɛt(ə)lstɪtʃ/ *n.* E19. [G *Kettelstich*, f. *Kettel* small chain + *Stich* stitch.] In bookbinding: a knot made at the head and tail of a book in sewing it, by which the thread holding one sheet is fastened to the thread in the next.

ketubah /kətuːˈbɑː/ *n.* M19. [Heb. *kěṯubbāh* written statement.] A formal Jewish marriage contract which includes financial provisions for the wife in the event of the husband's death or of divorce.

ketyl /ˈkiːtʌɪl, -tɪl/ *n.* E20. [f. KETO- + -YL.] *Chem.* A salt of a metal with a free-radical anion of the formula $RR'CO^-$ (where the Rs are alkyl groups), formed by dissolving a metal in a ketone.

Keuper /ˈkɔɪpə/ *n.* & *a.* M19. [G, orig. a miners' term.] *Geol.* (Designating or pertaining to) a European series of sedimentary rocks of Upper Triassic age, represented in England chiefly by marls and sandstones.

keurboom /ˈkɪəbʊəm/ *n.* M18. [Afk., f. *keur* choice + *boom* tree.] Any of several small southern African leguminous trees of the genus *Virgilia*, esp. *V. capensis*, with pinnate leaves and drooping clusters of usu. mauve scented flowers.

kevel /ˈkɛv(ə)l/ *n.*[1] *obs.* exc. *Sc.* & *north.* Also **kewl** /kjuːl/. ME. [ON *kefli* round stick, small roller, gag, rel. to *kafli* piece.] **1** A bit for a horse's mouth. Also, a gag. ME. **2** A rounded piece of wood; a staff, a cudgel. E19.

kevel /ˈkɛv(ə)l/ *n.*[2] ME. [ONFr. *keville* = (O)Fr. *cheville* pin, peg.] **1** A pin or hasp for fastening something; a tilepin. *obs.* exc. *Hist.* ME. **2** *Naut.* A large cleat fitted to the gunwale of a ship and used in belaying ropes. ME.

kevel /ˈkɛv(ə)l/ *n.*[3] *Sc.* & *north.* ME. [Origin unkn.] A kind of hammer for rough-hewing or breaking stone. Also *kevel-hammer*, *-mell.*

Kevenhuller /ˈkɛv(ə)nhʊlə/ *n. obs.* exc. *Hist.* Also **Khev-**. M18. [A. von *Khevenhüller* (1683–1744), Austrian field-marshal.] **1** In full *Kevenhuller cock.* A high peaked cock given to hats worn by men in the mid-18th cent. M18. **2** In full *Kevenhuller hat.* A hat worn cocked in this fashion. M18.

kevir *n.* var. of KAVIR.

Kevlar /ˈkɛvlɑː/ *n.* L20. [Origin unkn.] (Proprietary name for) a synthetic fibre of high tensile strength used esp. as a reinforcing material for rubber in tyres etc.

kewl *n.* var. of KEVEL *n.*[1]

kewpie /ˈkjuːpi/ *n.* Orig. *US.* Also **K-**, **cupie**. E20. [f. CUP(ID + -IE.] In full *kewpie doll.* (Proprietary name for) a chubby doll with a curl or topknot on its head; *transf.* a person resembling such a doll.

kex /kɛks/ *n.* Now *dial.* ME. [Perh. of Celt. origin: cf. Welsh *cegid*, Corn. *kegaz*, Breton *kegid*. See also KECK *n.*, KECKSIE.] **1** The dry, usu. hollow stalk of a large umbellifer (as cow parsley, hogweed, wild angelica, etc.) or similar plant. ME. **†b** Such stalks collectively or as a material. M16–E18. **2** An umbelliferous plant with a hollow stalk. LME. **†3** The hard case of a chrysalis. Only in 17. **†4** *fig.* A weak spiritless person. E17–E18.

kexy *a.* like a kex; dry and brittle; withered, sapless: E17.

key /kiː/ *n.*[1] & *a.* [OE *cǣg*, *cǣge* = OFris. *kei*, *kay*, of unkn. origin.] **A** *n.* **I 1** An instrument fitting into a lock for locking or unlocking it, usu. made of metal and with more or less elaborate incisions etc. to fit the wards of the lock; a similar instrument for operating a switch in the form of a lock. OE. **2** A key as representing the power of custody, control, admission, etc.; a key as a symbol of office. OE. **3** *Theol.* [With allus. to *Matt.* 16:19] *sing.* & (usu.) in *pl.* The ecclesiastical authority regarded by Roman Catholics as conferred by Christ on St Peter and transmitted to the Popes as his successors; the disciplinary or spiritual power of priests as successors of the Apostles. OE. **4a** A thing that opens up the way to something; *esp.* a sure means to or *to* a desired objective. OE. **b** A place which from the strategic advantages of its position gives control over a territory, sea, etc. LME. **5** A solution or explanation of what is unknown, mysterious, or obscure; *spec.* (*a*) an alphabetical or other system for the interpretation of a cipher, an allegorical statement, etc.; (*b*) a text explaining the abbreviations or symbols used in a book, the figures in a photograph or picture, etc.; (*c*) (a part of) a book containing solutions of mathematical or other problems, translations of exercises in a foreign language, etc. OE. **b** *Chess.* A move in the solution of a problem which determines the style of the whole solution. E19. **c** A scheme for identifying a plant, animal, etc., by selecting one alternative in each of successive pairs or sets of contrasted characters. M19. **d** The device used to key or distinguish an advertisement. Orig. *US.* E20. **6** *Mus.* A system of notes definitely related to each other, based on a particular note and predominating in a piece of music; the sum of melodic and harmonic relations existing between the tones of such a system, tonality. Formerly also = KEYNOTE *n.* 1. LME. **7** *transf.* & *fig.* **a** (High or low) tone (of the voice); pitch. L16. **b** Intensity (of feeling or action); (prevailing) tone or style (of thought or expression). Freq. in *in key*, *out of key* below. L16. **c** Tone or relative intensity of colour. M19.

1 A. S. NEILL I tried the lock with one of my own keys, and managed to open the trunk. W. WHARTON She has a key and lets herself in. J. GORES A.. Mustang with the driver's window open and the key in the ignition. **3** LD MACAULAY Lewis.. was.. accused by the Pope of encroaching on the spiritual power of the keys. **4** R. FORD A supply of cigars, these keys to Spanish hearts. C. GEBLER Self-understanding is the key to any sort of self-improvement. **b** T. MO Those heights are the keys to the city. **5** F. BURNEY I felt his meaning, though I had no key to it. **6** J. PLAYFORD To shew in what Key the Song was set, and how each Musical Key had relation.. to another. A. HOPKINS Certain keys have emotional connotations in composers' minds. *major key*, *minor key*, *natural key*, etc. **7a** W. BLACK Loudly discoursing—in a high shrill and plaintive key—of his troubles. **b** M. B. KEATINGE In a high key of spirits in consequence of the reception he was favoured with. W. STUBBS The writs to the barons are shorter but in the same key. **c** J. RUSKIN Harmonies of amber-colour and purple are full of exquisite beauty in their chosen key.

II A mechanical device resembling the key of a lock. **8a** A thing that holds together or joins the parts of a structure; *esp.* the keystone of an arch. ME. **†b** *fig.* A leading person or thing; *esp.* a cardinal point or principle. M16–L17. **c** The part of a first coat of plaster which passes between the laths and secures the rest; the roughness of a surface which enables plaster etc. to adhere to it. E19. **9** A pin, bolt, or wedge inserted between other pieces, esp. to fasten various parts together; = COTTER *n.*[1] LME. **10a** Each of the levers or buttons pressed down or otherwise moved by the fingers to produce the notes in playing any of various musical instruments, as an organ, piano, flute, concertina, etc. L15. **b** Each of a set of levers or buttons pressed by the fingers to operate a typewriter, word processor, computer terminal, etc. Also, a lever etc. operating a mechanical device for making or breaking an electric circuit, used in telegraphy etc. M19. **11** An instrument for grasping and turning a screw, peg, or nut, esp. (*a*) for winding a clock, watch, or clockwork machine, (*b*) for turning the wrest-pins of a piano, (*c*) for turning a valve or stopcock. E17. **b** An instrument for extracting teeth, esp. molars. *obs.* exc. *Hist.* M19.

10a J. BALDWIN He touched a black key on the piano and it made a dull sound. **b** (*carriage*) *return key*, *shift key*, etc.

III 12 In *pl.* More fully *House of Keys.* A body of twenty-four members which forms the elective branch of the legislature of the Isle of Man. LME.

IV 13 The dry winged fruit of an ash, elm, sycamore, etc., usu. growing in bunches; = SAMARA. E16.

Phrases etc.: **golden key** a bribe to obtain admission. **Greek key** each of the bends of which a Greek fret consists, suggestive of a key. *high-key*: see HIGH *a.* *House of Keys*: see sense 12 above. **in key** in harmony, consonant (*with*). **key of the sea** the pelican's foot shell. *latchings key*: see LATCHING 2. *low-key*: see LOW *a.* *master-key*: see MASTER *n.*[1] & *a.* **out of key** out of harmony, not consonant (*with*). **silver key** = *golden key* above. SKELETON *key.* **St Peter's keys** the cross keys borne in the papal arms. *under lock and key*: see LOCK *n.*[2]

B *attrib.* or as *adj.* Of paramount or crucial importance. Cf. earlier KEYNOTE, KEYSTONE. L19.

Physics Bulletin Two ideas were key in the discovery of the kinoform. S. MIDDLETON He'd assembled a jig-saw only to find that key pieces were missing. S. KITZINGER The sexual tie is a key one in defining who a woman is.

Comb. & *special collocations*: **key-block** a block used in the printing of chiaroscuro and colour pictures to give the outline, and to provide a guide for the accurate registration of the tint or colour blocks; **key-bugle**: fitted with keys to increase the number of its sounds; **key-clog** a piece of wood tied to a key, to prevent its being lost; **key-cold** *a.* (now *rare*) extremely cold (*lit.* & *fig.*), *esp.* cold in death; **key-colour** the leading colour in a picture; **key-drawing** (in lithography and colour printing) an outline drawing which is transferred on to the key-plate and used as a guide to printing the colours; **key grip** *Television* & *Cinemat.* the person in a film crew who is in charge of the camera equipment; **key-holder** a person who keeps the key or keys of a workshop, factory, etc.; **key industry** an industry essential to the carrying on of others; **key man** a person who plays a leading or important role in a group, an industry, etc.; **key map**: in bare outline, to simplify the use of a full map; **key money** a payment required from an incoming tenant for the provision of a key to the premises; **key move** *Chess* = sense A.5b above; **keypad** a miniature keyboard or set of buttons for operating a portable electronic device, a telephone, etc.; **key-plate** (*a*) a plate of metal surrounding a keyhole; (*b*) (in colour-printing from a metal surface) the outline plate answering to a keystone in lithography; **key-ring** a ring on which keys can be hung; **key signature** *Mus.* a group of sharps or flats after the clef at the beginning of each staff, indicating the key in which the piece is to be performed; **key-way** *Mech.* a groove cut in a shaft or in the boss of a wheel to receive a key; **keyword** (*a*) a word serving as a key to a code, cipher, etc.; (*b*) a word or thing of great importance or significance; *spec.* (in an information-retrieval system) any informative word in the title or text of a document etc. chosen as indicating its main content; *keyword-in-context* adj., designating an index or concordance in which keywords are listed alphabetically, preceded and followed by a fixed amount of context.

¶Until *c*1700 pronounced to rhyme with *day*, *way*, etc. The modern pronunc. is app. of northern origin.

key /kiː/ *n.*[2] L17. [Var. of CAY, infl. in spelling and pronunc. by *key* var. of QUAY *n.*] A low island, sandbank, or reef, such as one of those common in the W. Indies or off the coast of Florida.

†key *n.*[3] see QUAY *n.*

key /kiː/ *v.* LME. [f. KEY *n.*[1]] **I** *v.t.* **1** Lock with a key; lock up; fasten securely. *rare.* LME. **2** Fasten by means of a pin, wedge, bolt, etc. L16. **b** Cause (plaster, glued surfaces, pigments, etc.) to adhere; roughen (a surface) to help the adhesion of plaster etc. L19. **3** Regulate the pitch of (the strings of a musical instrument, a stringed instrument); *fig.* give a certain tone or intensity to (a feeling or thoughts). Foll. by *up*: stimulate, raise to a high pitch; cause to be nervous, excited, or tense. Foll. by *down*: lower in pitch or intensity. M17. **b** Fix the strings of a musical instrument on the pegs or keys. L19. **4** Insert the keystone in (an arch). Also foll. by *in.* Now *rare* or *obs.* M18. **5** Distinguish (an advertisement) by some device, as the form of the address given, which will identify the publication generating particular responses. Orig. *US.* E20. **6** *Electronics.* Switch from one state to another (usu. on or off), by means of a key or relay, as in telegraphic transmission; provide with a means for doing this. E20. **7** Set out (kinds of plant, animal, etc.) in a key for the purposes of identification (freq. foll. by *out*). Also, identify by means of a key. E20. **8** Cause to fit *in with* something else or *into* a group, pattern, etc. M20. **9** Transfer or operate on (data), set (copy), or produce (text), by manipulating the keys of a keyboard. Also foll. by *in* etc. M20.

II *v.i.* **10** Fit *into* a group or *in with* something else. M20. **11** Be identified as or *as* a given species if one follows a key. Usu. foll. by *out.* M20.

10 E. BOWEN Lean young skyscrapers.. key in with Rome's general virtuosity.

keyer *n.* a person who or thing which keys something, *spec.* (*Electronics*) a device for switching a signal supply on and off M20.

keyaki /kɪˈɑːki/ *n.* E20. [Jap.] (The pale lustrous wood of) a Japanese tree, *Zelkova serrata*, of the elm family.

keyboard /ˈkiːbɔːd/ *n.* & *v.* E19. [f. KEY *n.*[1] + BOARD *n.*] **A** *n.* **1** *Mus.* A row of keys for producing the notes in an organ, piano, or similar instrument. E19. **b** In *pl.* Keyboard instruments. *colloq.* L20. **2** The set of keys on a typewriter, computer, etc. M19.

1 *shifting keyboard*: see SHIFTING *a.* 1.

Comb.: **keyboard instrument** a musical instrument having a keyboard or keyboards.

B *v.t.* & *i.* Enter (data) by means of a keyboard. M20.

keyboarder *n.* a person who operates a (computer) keyboard, a person who enters data on a keyboard M20. **keyboardist** *n.* a player on a keyboard instrument L20.

keyed /kiːd/ *a.* M16. [f. KEY *n.*[1], *v.*: see -ED[2], -ED[1].] **1** Having a key or keys. M16. **2** Secured, fastened, or strengthened by means of a key; (of an arch) constructed with a keystone. E19. **3** *keyed-up*, nervous, excited, tense. L19.

keyhole /ˈkiːhəʊl/ *n.* & *v.* L16. [f. KEY *n.*[1] + HOLE *n.*[1]] **A** *n.* **1** A hole by which a key is inserted in a lock. L16. **2** In carpentry or engineering: a hole made to receive a peg or key. E18.

1 L. CODY Do come in .. unless you want to stay outside with your ear to the keyhole.

Comb.: **keyhole limpet** a limpet of the family Fissurellidae, having a shell with an aperture at the apex; **keyhole saw** a saw with a long narrow blade for cutting small holes such as keyholes; **keyhole surgery**: performed through a very small hole with the aid of a fibrescope and special instruments.

B *v.i.* Of a bullet: strike the target in such a way as to make a keyhole-shaped hole. L19.

keyless /ˈkiːlɪs/ *a.* E19. [f. KEY *n.*[1] + -LESS.] Having no key or keys.

Pall Mall Gazette We find your work so abstruse, your parables so keyless. JOYCE Gent's .. keyless watch. *Listener* Spain retains small keyless shawms.

Keynesian /ˈkeɪnzɪən/ *a.* & *n.* M20. [f. *Keynes* (see below) + -IAN.] **A** *adj.* Of or pertaining to the English economist John Maynard Keynes (1883–1946) or his economic theories, esp. regarding State control of the economy through money and taxes. M20. **B** *n.* An adherent of Keynes's economic theories. M20.

Keynesianism *n.* M20.

keynote /ˈkiːnəʊt/ *n.* & *v.* M18. [f. KEY *n.*[1] + NOTE *n.*[2]] **A** *n.* **1** *Mus.* The first note of the scale of any key, which forms the basis of, and gives its name to, the key; the tonic. M18. **2** *fig.* The prevailing tone or idea of a speech, piece of writing, course of action, etc. L18.

2 M. SEYMOUR-SMITH The key-note of her character was obstinacy.

Comb.: **keynote address, keynote speech** (orig. *US*) a speech, usu. an opening address, designed to state the main concerns of a conference or (at a political rally) arouse enthusiasm or promote unity.

B *v.t.* Express the prevailing tone or idea of (something); deliver the keynote speech of (a conference etc.). *colloq.* (orig. *US*). M20.

keynoter *n.* (orig. *US colloq.*) a person who delivers a keynote speech E20.

keypunch /ˈkiːpʌn(t)ʃ/ *n.* & *v.* M20. [f. KEY *n.*[1] + PUNCH *n.*[1]] **A** *n.* A keyboard device for transferring data by means of punched holes or notches in cards or paper tape. M20. **B** *v.t.* & *i.* Produce holes or notches in (a card or paper tape) by means of a keypunch; put (text) into the form of punched cards or paper tape by means of a keypunch. M20.

keypunchable *a.* able to be represented on punched cards or paper tape L20. **keypuncher** *n.* (*a*) = KEYPUNCH *n.*; (*b*) a person who operates a keypunch: M20.

keyster *n.* var. of KEISTER.

keystone /ˈkiːstəʊn/ *n.* & *v.* M17. [f. KEY *n.*[1] + STONE *n.*] **A** *n.* **1** The wedge-shaped block or central voussoir at the summit of an arch built of stone. M17. **2** *fig.* The central principle of a system, course of action, etc., on which all the rest depends. E19. **3** *Printing.* In colour lithography, a stone which bears the key-drawing, not normally used in the printing. M19.

2 *Times* The Third Reich .. would have as its keystone the conception of the people and the national idea.

Comb.: **keystone effect** (*Cinemat.* & *Television*) a form of distortion by which a rectangular object produces a trapezial image, resulting from the line of projection (of light or electrons) not being normal to the screen; **Keystone State** *US* the State of Pennsylvania, the seventh of the original thirteen States.

B *v.t. Cinemat.* & *Television.* Distort by a keystone effect. Chiefly as *keystoning* vbl n. M20.

Keystone /ˈkiːstəʊn/ *a.* E20. [The *Keystone* Film Company, formed in 1912.] Pertaining to or characteristic of the slapstick comedy films produced by the Keystone Film Company.

Keystone Kops comically bumbling policemen featured in such films.

keystroke /ˈkiːstrəʊk/ *n.* & *v.* E20. [f. KEY *n.*[1] + STROKE *n.*[1]] **A** *n.* A depression of a key on a keyboard, esp. as a measure of work. E20. **B** *v.t.* = KEY *v.* 9. M20.

keystroker *n.* a person who operates the keys of a keyboard, esp. of a keypunch L20.

kgotla /kəˈgɒtlə/ *n.* Also (earlier) ***kotla*** /ˈkɒtlə/, ***khotla***. M19. [Setswana.] An assembly of tribal elders among certain Bantu-speaking peoples; a place where such assemblies are held. Cf. KUTA.

khabar /ˈkʌbə/ *n.* Also ***khubber***. M19. [Urdu & Pers. *ḵabar* f. Arab.] In the Indian subcontinent: information, news, rumour.

khad *n.* var. of KHUD.

khadar /ˈkɑːdə/ *n.* Also **-ir**. M19. [Hind. *khādar*.] In the Indian subcontinent: a flood-plain; land susceptible to flooding.

khaddar /ˈkadə/ *n.* & *a.* Also **khadi** /ˈkadi/. E20. [Panjabi *khaddar*, Hind. *khādar*, *khādī*.] (Made of) handspun hand-woven cotton (or silk) cloth of the Indian subcontinent.

khadir *n.* var. of KHADAR.

khair /ˈkʌɪə/ *n.* M19. [Hind. *khair*, Skt *khadira*.] An Indian leguminous tree, *Acacia catechu*, from which catechu is obtained.

khaki /ˈkɑːki/ *a.* & *n.* M19. [Urdu *ḵākī* dust-coloured, f. *ḵāk* dust f. Pers.] **A** *adj.* Dust-coloured; dull brownish yellow. Also, made of khaki. M19.

B. GELDOF Now in Africa he donned his casual lightweight khaki tropical gear. T. O. ECHEWA Green khaki shorts with frayed hems.

B *n.* **1** Dust-colour; dull brownish yellow. M19. **2** A dull yellowish-brown fabric, orig. of stout twilled cotton, later also of wool, etc., used esp. for army uniforms. M19. **3** A soldier dressed in khaki; *spec.* (*S. Afr. slang*) a British soldier in the Boer War of 1899–1902. L19. **4** In *pl.* Khaki trousers; khaki clothes. M20.

2 *Sunday Express* Some are in civilian clothes, the rest in army khaki.

Comb.: **khaki bos** /bɒs/, **bush** *S. Afr.* any of several weeds of the composite family supposedly introduced by British troops in the Boer War; esp. *Tagetes minuta*, native to S. America; **khaki election** a general election won by appeal to war spirit or to the military vote; *spec.* (*Hist.*) that won in 1900, during the Boer War, by the Conservatives under Lord Salisbury; **khaki weed** a S. American plant of the amaranth family, *Alternanthera repens*, naturalized in southern Africa and Australia.

khakied *a.* dressed in khaki E20.

khalassi /kəˈlasi/ *n.* Also **-ashi, -asi, ka-**; †**clashee**, †**clashy**. L18. [Urdu *ḵalāṣī*, *ḵalāšī*.] A native of the Indian subcontinent of inferior rank, *esp.* one employed as a seaman.

Khaldian /ˈkaldɪən/ *n.* & *a.* L19. [f. *Khaldis*, *Khaldi* the supreme god in Urartu + -AN, -IAN.] **A** *n.* **1** = URARTIAN *n.* 1. L19. **2** = URARTIAN *n.* 2. E20. **B** *adj.* = URARTIAN *a.* E20.

khalif *n.* var. of CALIPH.

khalifa /kəˈliːfə/ *n.* In sense 2 also **ch-**. E18. [Arab. *ḵalīfa*: see CALIPH.] **1** Chiefly *Hist.* = CALIPH. E18. **2** A Malay ceremony in which a dancer pierces his person with swords, orig. as a demonstration of Islamic faith. *S. Afr.* M19.

khalifate *n.* var. of CALIPHATE.

Khalkha /ˈkɑːlkə/ *n.* & *a.* Also **-ka**. L19. [Origin unkn.] **A** *n.* **1** A member of a section of the Mongolian people, constituting the bulk of the population of Outer Mongolia. L19. **2** The language of these people, a demotic form of Mongolian adopted as the official language of the Mongolian People's Republic. E20. **B** *attrib.* or as *adj.* Of or pertaining to the Khalkhas or their language. L19.

khalsa /ˈkɑːlsə/ *n.* Also **-ah**. L18. [Urdu f. Pers. *ḵāl(i)ṣa* crown land, revenue department, f. fem. of Arab. *ḵāliṣ* pure, free (from), belonging (to).] **1** The governmental revenue department in a State in the Indian subcontinent. L18. **2** The fraternity of warriors into which Sikh males are initiated at puberty. L18.

khama *n.* var. of KAAMA.

khamsin /ˈkamsɪn/ *n.* Also **ham-** /ˈham-/. *colloq.* L17. [Arab. *ḵamāsīn*, f. *ḵamsīn*, *-sūn* fifty (see below).] An oppressive hot southerly wind, which blows in Egypt at intervals for about 50 days in March, April, and May, and fills the air with sand from the desert.

khan /kɑːn, kan/ *n.*[1] LME. [OFr. *chan* or med.L *ca(a)nus* f. Turkic (hence Mongolian, Arab., Pers.) *ḵān* lord, prince, identified w. *ḵaʼan* var. of *ḵāḵān* supreme ruler: cf. CHAGAN, CHAM *n.*] Orig., any of the various successors of Genghis Khan, supreme rulers over Turkish, Tartar, and Mongol peoples and emperors of China in the Middle Ages; later, an Ottoman sultan. Also, a principal noble of the Mughal empire; a ruler, official, or man of rank in Afghanistan, Persia, or other Muslim countries of central Asia. Formerly also used as a polite form of address affixed to a Muslim name (and now a common surname among Muslims of the Indian subcontinent).

khanate *n.* (*Hist.*) a district governed by a khan; the position of khan: L18.

khan /kɑːn, kan/ *n.*[2] Also **han** /hɑːn/, †**cane**. LME. [Pers. *ḵān*.] A caravanserai.

khana /ˈkɑːnə/ *n.* E19. [Hind. *khānā*, f. Skt *khād-* eat.] In the Indian subcontinent: food; a meal.

khanda *n.* var. of KHANJAR.

khanga /ˈkaŋgə/ *n.* Also **kanga**. M20. [Kiswahili.] In E. Africa: a fabric printed in various colours and designs with borders, used esp. for women's clothing.

khanjar /ˈkandʒə/ *n.* Also **han-** /ˈhan-/, **khanda** /ˈkandə/. E17. [(Pers., Turk., Urdu) *ḵanjar* f. Arab.] A dagger worn in certain Muslim countries, esp. in southern Arabia.

khanjee /ˈkɑːndʒiː/ *n.* Also **han-** /ˈhɑːn-/. M19. [Turk. *hānji*, f. as KHAN *n.*[2] + *-ji* agent-suff.] The keeper of a caravanserai.

khansama /ˈkɑːnsəmɑː, kɑːnˈsɑːmə/ *n.* Also ***-man*** /-mən/. E17. [Urdu *ḵānsāmā*, Urdu & Pers. *ḵānsāmān*, f. *ḵān* master, KHAN *n.*[1] + *sāmān* household goods.] In the Indian subcontinent: a male servant combining the functions of house-steward and butler.

Khanty /ˈkanti/ *n.* & *a.* Also **-ti**. Pl. of n. same. M20. [Russ. f. Khanty *Xanti*.] A member of, or pertaining to, a people living in the Ob River basin in western Siberia; (of) the Ob-Ugrian language of this people. Earlier called *Ostyak*.

khanum /ˈkɑːnəm/ *n.* M17. [Pers. *ḵānum* f. Turk. *hanım*, f. *hān* KHAN *n.*[1] + *-ım* 1st person sing. possess. suff.] In certain parts of the Middle East and the Indian subcontinent: a lady of high rank, *Hist.* the wife of a khan. Now also used as a polite form of address affixed to a Muslim woman's name.

khapra /ˈkaprə/ *n.* L19. [Hind. *khaprā*, f. Skt *kharpara* thief.] In full *khapra beetle*. A small brownish-black dermestid beetle, *Trogoderma granarium*, native to India and found widely elsewhere as a pest of stored grain.

kharif /kaˈriːf/ *n.* E19. [Pers. & Urdu f. Arab. *ḵarīf* autumn, autumnal rain.] In the Indian subcontinent: the autumn crop, sown at the beginning of the summer rains.

Kharoshti /kəˈrɒʃti/ *n.* L19. [Skt *kharoṣṭī* f. Semitic: cf. Heb. *ḥāraṣ* cut, engrave.] One of the two oldest alphabets in the Indian subcontinent, derived from Aramaic and used for about seven centuries from *c* 300 BC in NW India and central Asia. Cf. BRAHMI.

Kharri *n.*, **Kharrian** *a.* & *n.* vars. of HURRI, HURRIAN.

Khasi /ˈkɑːsi/ *n.* & *a.* Also **Khasia** /ˈkɑːsɪə/, **Khasiya** /ˈkɑːsijə/. L18. [f. the *Khasi* Hills (see below).] A *n.* 1 A member of a Mongolian people inhabiting the Khasi and Jaintia Hills in NE India. L18. 2 The Mon-Khmer language of this people. M19. B *attrib.* or as *adj.* Of or pertaining to the Khasis or their language. E19.

Khaskura /ˈkaskʊrə/ *n.* E20. [Newari *Khas-kurā*, f. Skt *Khasa*, name of a people + Newari *kurā* speech.] The Nepali language.

khassadar /ˈkasədɑː/ *n.* E20. [Afghan Pers. *ḵāṣṣa-dār*, f. *ḵāṣṣa* possessions of the authorities + *-dār* holder: cf. Pers. *ḵāṣṣa-bardār* (f. *bardār* raiser).] An irregular tribal police officer on the North-West Frontier of India.

khat /kɑːt/ *n.* Also **kat, qat.** M19. [Arab. *ḳāt.*] A shrub, *Catha edulis*, of the spindle tree family, cultivated in Arabia for its leaves, which are chewed or infused as a stimulant; the narcotic drug obtained from these leaves.

khatib /kaˈtiːb/ *n.* E17. [Arab. *ḵaṭīb.*] A Muslim preacher, with responsibility for delivering the *khutbah*.

Khatri /ˈkʌtriː, ˈkatri/ *n.* M17. [Hind. *khat(t)rī* f. Skt *kṣatriya* KSHATRIYA.] = KSHATRIYA.

Khatti *n.* var. of HATTI.

khatun /ˈkɑːtuːn/ *n.* M19. [Turkic *ḳatūn*, Pers. *ḵātūn* perh. f. Sogdian *ḵwat'yn* queen.] In certain parts of the Middle East: a lady of high rank; *Hist.* a queen. Also used as an honorific title affixed to a Muslim woman's name.

khaya /ˈkʌɪjə, ˈkeɪjə/ *n.* E20. [mod.L (see below), f. Wolof *xay.*] Any of various tropical African trees of the genus *Khaya* (family Meliaceae); the timber of such a tree (also called *African mahogany*).

Khazar /kəˈzɑː/ *n.* & *a.* Also **Ch-.** M19. [Origin unkn.] A *n.* A member of a Turkish people who occupied a large part of southern Russia from the 8th to the 11th cent. and who converted to Judaism. M19. B *attrib.* or as *adj.* Of or pertaining to the Khazars. L19.

kheda /ˈkeɪdə, ˈkɛdə/ *n.* Also **keddah, kheddah.** L18. [Assamese & Bengali *khedā.*] In the north of the Indian subcontinent: an enclosure for the capture of wild elephants.

Khedive /kɪˈdiːv/ *n.* M19. [Fr. *khédive* f. Ottoman Turk. *ḵediv* f. Pers. *ḵadiw* prince, var. of *ḵudaiw* petty god, f. *ḵudā* god.] *Hist.* (The title of) the viceroy of Egypt under Turkish rule, 1867–1914.

Khedival, -ial *adjs.* of or pertaining to the Khedive L19. **Khedivate, -iate** *ns.* the office or authority of the Khedive L19.

khet /keɪt/ *n.* M19. [Hind. f. Skt *kṣetra.*] In the Indian subcontinent: a tract of cultivated land; a plantation.

Khevenhuller *n.* var. of KEVENHULLER.

khidmutgar /ˈkɪdmʌtgɑː/ *n.* Also **khit-** /ˈkɪt-/. M18. [Urdu f. Pers. *ḵidmatgār*, f. Arab. *ḵidma(t)* service + Pers. *-gār* agent-suff.] In the Indian subcontinent: a male servant who waits at table.

Khilafat /kɪˈlɑːfət/ *n.* & *a.* E20. [Pers., Turk. f. Arab. *ḵilāfa(t)* caliphate.] A *n.* The spiritual and temporal headship of Islam. E20. B *attrib.* or as *adj. Hist.* Designating or pertaining to a Muslim movement set up in India in 1919 orig. to champion the claims of the Sultan of Turkey to the Khilafat. E20.

khilat /ˈkɪlʌt, kəˈlɑːt/ *n.* L17. [Urdu, Pers. *ḵil'at*, f. Arab. *ḵil'a(t)*.] *Hist.* In India etc.: a set of clothes presented by a person of rank as a mark of distinction; *transf.* any handsome present made by an acknowledged superior.

Khirbet Kerak /ˈkɜːbət ˈkɛrək/ *a.* M20. [A Syrian town by Lake Tiberias.] *Archaeol.* Designating a red and black, highly burnished type of early Bronze Age pottery first found at Khirbet Kerak in the 1940s.

khitmutgar *n.* var. of KHIDMUTGAR.

Khlyst /klɪst, xlɪst/ *n.* Also **Khlist.** Pl. **-sti, -sty,** /-sti/. M19. [Russ. (pl. *khlysty*), lit. 'whip'.] A member of a sect of ascetic Russian Christians, formed in the 17th cent., who believed that Christ could be reincarnated in human beings through their suffering.

Khmer /kmɛː/ *n.* & *a.* L19. [Khmer.] A *n.* Pl. **-s,** same. 1 A native or inhabitant of the ancient kingdom of Khmer in SE Asia, which reached the peak of its power in the 11th cent., or the modern country corresponding to it, Cambodia (Kampuchea). L19. 2 The largely monosyllabic language spoken in Cambodia (Kampuchea), belonging to the Mon-Khmer group of the Austro-Asiatic family. E20.

B *attrib.* or as *adj.* Of or pertaining to the Khmers or their language. M20.

Phrases: **Khmer Rouge** /ruːʒ/, pl. **-s -s** (pronounced same), [Fr. = red] (a member of) a Communist guerrilla movement active in Cambodia (Kampuchea) in the late 1960s and the 1970s, holding power there 1975–9.

Khoikhoi /ˈkɔɪkɔɪ/ *n.* & *a.* Also **Khoi-Khoin** /-kɔɪn/. L18. [Nama, lit. 'men of men'.] A *n.* Pl. same. = NAMA *n.* L18. B *adj.* = NAMA *a.* L19.

Khoisan /ˈkɔɪsɑːn/ *n.* & *a.* M20. [f. KHOI(KHOI + SAN *n.*[2] & *a.*] A *n.* A southern African language family including Nama (Khoikhoi) and San. M20. B *adj.* Designating or pertaining to (peoples who speak languages of) this family. M20.

khoja /ˈkəʊdʒə/ *n.* E17. [(Turk. *hoca* f.) Pers. *ḵʷāja.*] 1 A teacher in a Muslim school; a Muslim scribe or clerk. E17. 2 (*K-.*) A member of a Muslim sect found mainly in western India. L19.

Khond *n.* & *a.* var. of KOND.

khor /kɔː/ *n.* L19. [Repr. a pronunc. of Arab. *ḵawr* low land between two stretches of higher ground, (colloq.) wadi.] In Sudan and neighbouring regions: a dry watercourse or ravine.

Khorassan /kɒrəˈsɑːn/ *n.* & *a.* Also **Khurasan** /kʊrəˈsɑːn/. E20. [A province in NE Iran.] (Designating) a Persian carpet or rug with vivid colouring and a fine silky texture, of a type made in NE Iran.

Khotan /kəʊˈtɑːn/ *a.* L19. [See next.] Designating a type of carpet or rug made in Khotan, usu. with Chinese geometrical patterns or stylized natural designs.

Khotanese /kəʊtəˈniːz/ *n.* & *a.* L19. [f. *Khotan* (see below) + -ESE.] A *n.* Pl. same. 1 A native or inhabitant of the city or district of Khotan in Chinese Turkestan. L19. 2 The Iranian language of Khotan. M20. B *adj.* Of or pertaining to the Khotanese or their language. M20.

khotla *n.* var. of KGOTLA.

khoum /kuːm/ *n.* L20. [Arab. *ḵums* one-fifth.] A monetary unit of Mauritania, equal to one-fifth of an ouguiya.

Khrushchevism /ˈkrʊstʃəfɪz(ə)m/ *n.* M20. [f. *Khrushchev* (see below) + -ISM.] The practice or principles of the Russian statesman Nikita Sergeevich Khrushchev (1894–1971), notable for his denunciation of Stalin and his advocacy of peaceful coexistence with the Western powers.

Khrushchevian /ˈkrʊstʃəfɪən, krʊsˈtʃɒfɪən/ *a.* of, pertaining to, or characteristic of Khrushchev or his policies M20.

khubber *n.* var. of KHABAR.

khud /kʌd/ *n.* Also **khad.** M19. [Hind. *ḳad.*] In the Indian subcontinent: a deep ravine or chasm; a precipitous cleft or descent in a hillside.

Khurasan *n.* & *a.* var. of KHORASSAN.

Khurri *n.*, **Khurrian** *a.* & *n.*, vars. of HURRI, HURRIAN.

khus-khus *n.* var. of CUSCUS *n.*[3]

khutbah /ˈkʊtbə/ *n.* E19. [Arab. *ḵuṭba.*] A form of sermon, consisting of homily and supplication, delivered in mosques before the mid-day Friday prayer, at the time of the two main Muslim festivals, and on other exceptional occasions.

khyal /kɪˈɑːl/ *n.* L19. [Hind.] A traditional type of song of the north of the Indian subcontinent with instrumental accompaniment, usu. containing two main themes.

Khyber /ˈkʌɪbə/ *n. rhyming slang.* M20. [*Khyber Pass*, the chief pass in the Hindu Kush mountains between Afghanistan and NW Pakistan.] More fully *Khyber Pass.* = ARSE *n.* 1.

ki /kiː/ *n.* M19. [Haw. = Polynesian TI *n.*[1]] A shrub of the agave family, *Cordyline fruticosa*, found in China and the Pacific islands, the fermented root of which yields an alcoholic drink. Cf. TI *n.*[1]

kiaat /kɪˈɑːt/ *n. S. Afr.* Also (earlier) **kajaten** /kʌɪˈɑːt(ə)n/, & other vars. E19. [Afk. f. Malay *kajaten* wood, teak.] More fully *kiaat hout* /həʊt/ [Afk. = wood]. A leguminous tree, *Pterocarpus angolensis*, of southern Africa; the wood of this tree, resembling teak.

kiack *n.* var. of KAYAK *n.*[2]

kiang /kɪˈaŋ/ *n.* Also **kyang.** M19. [Tib. *kyang*, *rkyang.*] A wild ass, *Equus hemionus*, of a subspecies native to the Tibetan plateau. Also called *dziggetai*. Cf. KULAN, ONAGER.

kia ora /kɪə ˈɔːrə/ *int. NZ.* L19. [Maori.] (A greeting) expr. good will, or wishing good health.

kiap /ˈkiːʌp, ˈkiːap/ *n.* E20. [Pidgin Eng., f. *captain* or G *Kapitän.*] In Papua New Guinea: a White patrol or police officer.

kiaugh *n.* var. of KAUCH.

kiawe /kiːˈɑːveɪ/ *n.* E20. [Haw.] A S. American mesquite, *Prosopis juliflora*, naturalized in Hawaii. Also *kiawe-tree*.

kibble /ˈkɪb(ə)l/ *n.*[1] LME. [MHG, G *Kübel* f. med.L *cupellus*, *-ppa* corn measure, drinking-vessel, f. *cuppa* CUP *n.*] *Mining.* A large wooden or (later) iron or steel bucket, for conveying ore or rubbish to the surface.

kibble /ˈkɪb(ə)l/ *n.*[2] L16. [Origin uncertain: perh. f. the surname *Kibble.*] In full *kibble-hound*. A breed of hound related to the beagle; a dog of this breed.

kibble /ˈkɪb(ə)l/ *n.*[3] L19. [Perh. alt. of COBBLE *n.*, but partly f. KIBBLE *v.*] 1 In *pl.* = COBBLE *n.* 2. L19. 2 *sing.* & in *pl.* Coarsely ground grain, pulses, etc.; (chiefly *N. Amer.*) dry pet-food containing coarsely ground grain. E20.

kibble /ˈkɪb(ə)l/ *v.t.* L18. [Origin unkn.] Grind (esp. grain) coarsely; crush into small pieces.

kibbler *n.* (a person who operates or tends) a machine which kibbles or grinds grain, pulses, etc., coarsely L19.

kibbutz /kɪˈbʊts/ *n.* Pl. **-im** /-ɪm/, (occas.) **-es.** M20. [mod.Heb. *qibbūṣ* gathering.] A collective (esp. farming) settlement in Israel, owned communally by its members, and organized on cooperative principles.

kibbutznik *n.* a member of a kibbutz M20.

kibe /kʌɪb/ *n.* & *v.* LME. [Origin unkn.] A *n.* 1 A chapped or ulcerated blister or chilblain, *esp.* one on the heel. Now *arch.* & *dial.* LME. 2 *transf.* A sore on the foot of a horse, sheep, etc. Now *rare* or *obs.* M17.

1 SHAKES. *Haml.* The toe of the peasant comes so near the heel of the courtier, he galls his kibe. **on the kibes of** following on the heels of.

B *v.t.* Affect with blisters or chilblains. Chiefly as *kibed* ppl a. Now *dial.* L15.

kiby *a.* (now *dial.*) affected with blisters or chilblains E16.

kibitka /kɪˈbɪtkə/ *n.* L18. [Russ., f. Turkic *kebit*, *kibit* (ult. f. Sogdian *kpyd*) + Russ. suff. *-ka.*] 1 A circular tent made of lattice work and covered with thick felt, formerly used by Tatars; *transf.* a Tatar household or family. L18. 2 A Russian wagon or sledge with a rounded cover or hood. L18.

kibitz /ˈkɪbɪts/ *v.i. slang* (chiefly *N. Amer.*). E20. [Yiddish f. G *kiebitzen*, f. *Kiebitz* lapwing, pewit, interfering onlooker at cards.] Look on at cards, or some other activity, esp. offering unwanted advice.

Life Dulles kibitzes briefly at the card game. *National Observer (US)* Crowded places . . full of people who argue and kibitz.

kibitzer *n.* a person who kibitzes; a busybody, a meddler: E20.

kiblah /ˈkɪblə/ *n.* Also **q-, -a.** M17. [Arab. *ḳibla* that which is opposite.] 1 (The direction of) the place to which Muslims must turn for prayer, now the Kaaba at Mecca. M17. 2 = MIHRAB 2. L18.

kiboko /kɪˈbəʊkəʊ/ *n.* Pl. **-os**. E20. [Kiswahili = hippopotamus.] A strong heavy whip made of hippopotamus hide.

kibosh /ˈkʌɪbɒʃ/ *n.* & *v. slang.* Also **ky-**. M19. [Origin unkn.] **A** *n.* **1** *put the kibosh on*, put an end to; dispose of finally. M19. **2** Nonsense. L19.

1 C. SANDBURG Put the kibosh on 'em so they'll never come back.

B *v.t.* Put an end to; finish off. M19.

Kichaga /kɪˈtʃagə/ *n.* & *a.* L19. [Bantu, f. *ki-* pref. + *Chaga* CHAGGA.] (Of) the Bantu language of the Wachagga.

kick /kɪk/ *n.*[1] M16. [f. KICK *v.*[1]] **I 1** An act of kicking; a blow or thrust with the foot; *spec.* an act of striking a ball with the foot. M16. **2** *fig.* A grave or humiliating setback; a severe criticism or punishment. Esp. in *a kick in the pants* or *teeth*. E17. **b** An objection; an expression or display of opposition. M19. **3** A fashion, a fad; the latest style; an (esp. temporary) interest in or enthusiasm for a specified subject, manner of behaving, etc. *slang.* L17. **4** A recoil of a gun when discharged. E19. **5** A jerk, a jolt; jerking motion. Also, a sudden surge of electricity. M19. **6** A sudden strong stimulant effect, esp. caused by alcohol or a drug. Also, a thrill, an excitement, a pleasure; a cause of excitement etc. M19. **7** A person who kicks (well or badly), a (*good* or *bad*) kicker, esp. in rugby and American football. M19. **8** Ability or disposition to kick or rebel. L19. **9** *Athletics.* A sudden burst of speed, esp. towards the end of a middle-distance race. M20.

1 M. GEE A touch on . . his calf, a very slight kick, it felt like a foot. *Evening Telegraph (Grimsby)* Knowles took the kick . . with the ball careering on to the bar. *corner-kick, drop-kick, penalty kick, place-kick*, etc. 2 LYTTON His . . policy was wittily described . . as a 'quick alternation of kicks and kindness'. 3 M. DUFFY They're still all on the health food kick. 4 M. MITCHELL The back kick of the pistol made her reel. 6 J. KEROUAC It's just kicks. . . We're having a good time. H. WOUK I get a kick out of giving the press the slip. B. BOVA They drank something chalky white, thick; it had an alcoholic kick to it. 8 K. WEATHERLY This blow was a better one, and it took some kick out of the roo. 9 G. A. SHEEHAN The runner with the kick will beat his opponent.

II 10 A sixpence. *arch. slang.* L17. **11** In *pl.* a Breeches, trousers, pants, knickers. Cf. KICKSEYS. *slang* & *dial.* L17. **b** Shoes. *slang* (orig. *US*). L19. **12** A pocket. *slang.* M19.

12 F. DONALDSON At any moment I might be in the chips with 40,000 dollars in my kick.

Phrases: **for kicks** purely for (esp. reckless) pleasure or excitement. *free kick*: see FREE *a.* *high kick*: see HIGH *a.* **more kicks than halfpence** more harshness than kindness. *top kick*: see TOP *a.*

Comb.: **kick-boxer** a person who participates in kick-boxing; **kick-boxing** a form of boxing incorporating elements of karate, esp. kicking with bare feet; **kick-pleat** a pleat in a narrow skirt to allow more freedom of movement; **kicksorter** *colloq.* an instrument that registers the number of electrical pulses received in each of a set of amplitude ranges; a pulse-height analyser; **kick-stand** a metal prop, attached to the frame, for holding up a bicycle or motor cycle, when not in use; **kick-start** *n.* & *v.* (*a*) *n.* a device allowing the starting of a motor cycle etc. by a downward thrust on a pedal; a method or an act of starting a motor cycle etc. in this way; (*b*) *v.t.* & *i.* start (an engine) in this way; *fig.* start or restart (a process etc.) by providing some initial impetus; **kick-starter** a device allowing the kick-starting of an engine etc.; **kick-tail** *n.* & *a.* (designating) a sharp upward slope at the rear of a skateboard or a skateboard having this; **kick-turn** a standing turn in skiing; **kick-wheel** a potter's wheel worked by a foot pedal.

kick /kɪk/ *n.*[2] M19. [Origin uncertain: perh. a use of prec. but cf. NICK *n.*[1] 10.] An indentation in the bottom of a glass bottle which diminishes the internal capacity and increases stability. Cf. KICK-UP 5.

kick /kɪk/ *v.*[1] LME. [Origin unkn.] **1** *v.i.* Strike out with the foot. Also, raise the leg vigorously, esp. in dancing. LME. **2** *v.i. fig.* Express anger, defiance, or dislike; rebel; object strongly. Usu. foll. by *against, at*. LME. **3** *v.t.* Strike (something or someone) with the foot. L16. **b** Reproach or be annoyed with (oneself). L19. **4** *v.t.* Impel, drive, or move (as) by kicking. Usu. w. adv. or prep. extension. L16. **b** Dismiss, discharge, reject (esp. a suitor). *US slang.* E19. **5** *v.i.* & *t.* (w. *it*). Die. Formerly foll. by *up*. Cf. *kick the bucket* s.v. BUCKET *n.*[2] *slang.* M17. **6** *v.t. transf.* Strike (something) with a violent impact (chiefly in *kick the beam* s.v. BEAM *n.*). Of a gun: strike in the recoil. M17. **7** *v.i. transf.* **a** Of a gun: recoil when fired. M19. **b** *Cricket.* (Of a ball) rebound almost vertically from the pitch; (of a pitch or a bowler) cause a ball to do this. Also foll. by *up*. M19. **c** *Telegr.* Of a relay: break contact momentarily. E20. **8** *v.t. Football.* Score (a goal) by a kick. M19. **9** *v.t.* & *i.* Give up or overcome (a habit, esp. drug-taking). *colloq.* M20.

1 P. MATTHIESSEN In the vicinity of females, the male 'kicks'—a loose twitch of the leg. R. INGALLS She . . kicked and thrashed while they dragged her along the sidewalk. 2 M. MCLUHAN I find my lecture schedule . . heavier . . but nothing to kick about. E. CRANKSHAW In childhood this great disciplinarian had kicked against all discipline. 3 A. MASON A foot kicked him hard in the ribs. M. MCCONNELL To get a space shuttle off the ground, you can't just . . kick the tires. b L. OLIVIER I . . was beginning to kick myself for my lack of perception. 4 W. WHARTON She kicked her only daughter out of the house at sixteen. A. L. ROWSE Vansittart . . was kicked out of the way for Cadogan, more amenable to Chamberlain. 5 F. DHONDY The confusion only started when he kicked it. Died, I mean. 6 *Guns Review* That little gun tends to kick the user very hard. 9 N. MAILER It's easier to give up the love of your life than to kick cigarettes.

Phrases: *alive and kicking*: see ALIVE *a.* **kick against the pricks** *fig.* rebel, be recalcitrant, esp. to one's own hurt. **kick a person's ass** (*slang*, chiefly *N. Amer.*) dominate, defeat, or punish a person. **kick ass** (*slang*, chiefly *N. Amer.*) act forcefully or in a domineering manner. *kick down the ladder*: see LADDER *n.* 2. *kick one's heels*: see HEEL *n.*[1] **kick over the traces** (of a horse) get a leg over the traces and become out of control; *fig.* (of a person) throw off usual restraints. *kick the beam*: see BEAM *n.* *kick the bucket*: see BUCKET *n.*[2] *kick the habit*: see HABIT *n.* *kick the shit out of*: see SHIT *n.* *kick the tar out of*: see TAR *n.*[1] 1.

With advs. in specialized senses: **kick about, around** (*a*) *colloq.* walk or wander about, esp. aimlessly; (*b*) *be kicking about, around*, (of a thing) lie around, esp. untidily; be available, unused, or unwanted; (*c*) (chiefly *N. Amer.*) kick (a thing) in all directions; *fig.* treat (a person) harshly, unfairly, or contemptuously; (*d*) discuss or examine in an informal or unstructured way, try out (a subject, idea, etc.). **kick back** (*a*) = BACKFIRE *v.* 2; (*b*) *colloq.* give a refund or rebate (to). **kick down** operate a kick-down device (see below). **kick in** (*a*) break down (a door etc.) by kicking against the outer side; *spec.* (*US slang*) break into (a building etc.); (*b*) *slang* (orig. *US*) contribute (money, one's share, etc.). **kick off** (*a*) throw off (a shoe etc.) by kicking; (*b*) *v.i.* (*Football*) begin or resume a match; *fig.* start, begin (*with*); (*c*) *slang* die. **kick on** *Austral. slang* continue to play well; *transf.* make an effort. **kick out** (*a*) expel, eject, esp. with a kick; (*b*) *Surfing* perform a kick-out (see below). **kick up** raise (dust etc.) (as) by kicking; *fig.* make (a disturbance or nuisance) (*kick up a row*: see ROW *n.*[3]; *kick up a shindy*: see SHINDY 2; *kick up a stour*: see STOUR *n.*); (see also sense 7b above). **kick upstairs** *colloq.* remove (a person) from the scene of action by promotion to an ostensibly higher post.

Comb.: **kick-about** an informal form of football; an informal game of football; **kick-and-rush** *a.* designating football played with more vigour than skill; **kick-ball** (*a*) football; **kick-down** *n.* & *a.* (designating) a device operated by the foot, *spec.* (on a motor vehicle with automatic transmission) for changing to a lower gear by fully depressing the accelerator pedal; **kick-in** *Football* a practice at goal-shooting before the start of a match; **kick-off** (*a*) *Football* the start or resumption of a match; (*b*) *fig.* the start, the beginning; an inaugural or opening event; **kick-out** *Surfing* a manoeuvre executed by thrusting down on the rear of one's surfboard and pivoting it on its tail so as to ride up and over the top of a wave; **kick-the-can, kick-the-tin** a children's game in which a tin can is kicked.

kickable *a.* M17. **ki'ckee** *n.* [-EE[1]] a person who is kicked E19. **kickish** *a.* (*obs.* exc. *dial.*) given to kicking; irritable: L16. **kickster** *n.* a person whose behaviour is governed principally or solely by the desire for pleasure or excitement M20. **kicky** *a.* (*a*) *Sc.* inclined or apt to kick or provide kicks; *spec.* clever, lively; provoking, annoying; (*b*) *Cricket* causing the ball to kick; (*c*) *N. Amer. colloq.* exciting: L18.

kick /kɪk/ *v.*[2]*t. slang.* L18. [Perh. a use of prec.] Ask (a person) *for* something; obtain by asking.

Kickapoo /ˈkɪkəpuː/ *n.* & *a.* L17. [Kickapoo *kiikaapoa*.] **A** *n.* Pl. **-s**, same. **1** A member of an Algonquian Indian people now of Kansas, Oklahoma, and Mexico. L17. **2** The language of this people. M20. **B** *attrib.* or as *adj.* Of or pertaining to the Kickapoos or their language. E19.

kickback /ˈkɪkbak/ *n. colloq.* M20. [f. KICK *v.*[1] + BACK *adv.*] **1** A refund, a rebate; the return of (esp. stolen) money, goods, etc.; a payment (usu. illegal) made to a person who has facilitated a transaction, appointment, etc. M20. **2** A strong reaction or repercussion; an undesirable result. M20. **3** *Railways.* A section of track sloping sharply upwards so as to reverse the direction of a wagon etc. by the force of gravity. M20. **4** Surplus preservative released from timber during the preservation process. M20.

1 D. FRANCIS Order extensively from him and in return receive a sizable commission. A kickback. 2 *Listener* One of the kick-backs . . is . . the over-administering of education.

kicker /ˈkɪkə/ *n.* M16. [f. KICK *v.*[1] + -ER[1].] **1 a** A person or thing which kicks; *spec.* a horse etc. given to kicking. M16. **b** *fig.* A person who protests, objects, or rebels. Chiefly *US*. L19. **2** *Mining.* Earth etc. left in place in first cutting a vein, to support its sides. M18. **3** *Cricket.* A ball that rebounds more sharply than usual from the pitch. L19. **4** *Poker.* A high third card retained in the hand with a pair at the draw. L19. **5** (A boat driven by) an outboard motor. *N. Amer. colloq.* E20. **6** *Printing.* A device which, as newspapers come off the press, pushes one out of line at regular intervals so as to create separate batches of a specified number. M20.

†kickie-wickie *n. rare* (Shakes.). Only in E17. [Fanciful.] A wife.

kicking /ˈkɪkɪŋ/ *vbl n.* M16. [f. KICK *v.*[1] + -ING[1].] The action of KICK *v.*[1]

Comb.: **kicking plate** a metal plate fixed to the lower part of a door etc. to prevent damage or wear; **kicking-strap** (*a*) a strap adjusted to prevent a horse from kicking in harness; (*b*) *Naut.* a rope lanyard fixed to the boom to prevent it from rising.

kickseys /ˈkɪksɪz/ *n.pl. arch. slang.* Also **kicksies**. E19. [f. KICK *n.*[1]] Breeches; trousers. Cf. KICK *n.*[1] 11a.

kickshaw /ˈkɪkʃɔː/ *n.* & *a. arch.* Orig. **†quelque chose**. L16. [Fr. *quelque chose* something.] **A** *n.* **1** A fancy dish in cookery, usu. French, as opp. to a familiar, substantial English dish. Usu. *derog.* L16. **2** Something dainty or elegant, but impractical; a toy, a trifle. E17. **3** A frivolous person. *obs.* exc. *dial.* M17. **B** *attrib.* or as *adj.* Frivolous, trifling. M17.

kickshawed *a.* consisting of or treated with kickshaws E17.

kicksies *n.pl.* var. of KICKSEYS.

kick-up /kɪˈkʌp, ˈkɪkʌp/ *n.* L18. [f. KICK *v.*[1] + UP *adv.*[1]] **1** A violent disturbance or row. L18. **2** A dance, a party. *colloq.* (orig. *US*). L18. **3** An act of kicking a leg or the legs in the air. M19. **4** *Mining.* A device for overturning and emptying trams, wagons, etc. L19. **5** = KICK *n.*[2] E20.

kid /kɪd/ *n.*[1] ME. [ON *kið* rel. to OHG *chizzī*, *kizzīn* (G *Kitze*), f. Gmc.] **1** A young goat. ME. **b** A young antelope or similar animal; formerly *spec.*, a roe-deer in its first year. ME. **2** The flesh of a young goat as food. LME. **3** The skin of a kid, lamb, etc., esp. made into a soft pliable leather used chiefly to make gloves and shoes; in *pl.*, gloves or shoes made of this. L15. **4 a** A child, esp. a young child. *colloq.* L16. **b** *N. Amer. Hist.* An indentured servant, esp. on a plantation. Cf. KIDNAP. E18. **c** An expert young criminal, esp. a fighter, a thief, etc. *slang.* Now *rare*. E19. **d** A young person. Also used as a familiar form of address. *colloq.* (orig. *US*). L19. **5** *sing.* & in *pl.* With *the*: two stars in the constellation Auriga, represented as kids held in the hand of the charioteer. Also. *kid-star*. *rare*. E17.

1 M. MILNER A mother goat appearing with her three kids. 3 H. E. BATES A final look at her hands, their coarseness hidden . . by the clean white kid. VICI *kid*. 4 L. DUNCAN What would the kids at school

think? P. ROTH He was a good father to the kids. d J. D. MACDONALD We can't talk here, kid. J. BRODSKY We were young, we were kids. **our kid** *colloq.* one's (only) younger brother or sister.

Comb.: **kid brother** *colloq.* (orig. *US*) a person's younger brother; **kidflick** *slang* a film for children; **kid glove** a glove made of kidskin (*handle with kid-gloves*, handle or treat gently, delicately, discreetly, or gingerly); **kid-glove** *a.* characterized by wearing kid-gloves or (*fig.*) by dainty, delicate, discreet, or gingerly treatment; **kid-gloved** *a.* (*a*) wearing kid gloves; (*b*) = *kid-glove* above; **kid sister** *colloq.* (orig. *US*) a person's younger sister; **kidskin** the skin of a kid, lamb, etc., made into leather; *kid-star*: see sense 5 above; **kids'** or **kid's stuff** *colloq.* (orig. *US*) something suitable for children; a very simple or trivial task etc.; **kidvid** *slang* television or video programmes for children.

kiddish *a.* (*rare*) †(*a*) of, pertaining to, or resembling a kid; (*b*) *slang* childish: M16. **kiddo** *n.* (*colloq.*) a young person or child (freq. as a familiar form of address) L19. **kidlet** *n.* a young child L19. **kidling** *n.* (*a*) a small young goat; (*b*) a small child or baby: L16.

kid /kɪd/ *n.*[2] *obs.* exc. *dial.* ME. [Origin unkn.] A faggot or bundle of twigs, brushwood, gorse, etc., used for burning, or as a prop for loose soil etc.

kid /kɪd/ *n.*[3] M18. [Perh. var. of KIT *n.*[1]] 1 A small wooden tub for domestic use; *esp.* a sailor's mess-tub. M18. 2 A box or wooden pen on the deck of a fishing-vessel to receive fish as they are caught. *US*. L19.

kid /kɪd/ *n.*[4] *colloq.* L19. [f. KID *v.*[3]] Deception, falsehood, pretence. Also (*Austral.* & *NZ slang*), *kid-stakes*.

no kid = *no kidding* s.v. KID *v.*[3] 2.

kid /kɪd/ *a.* Long *arch. rare.* Also **kyd**. ME. [pa. pple of KITHE.] Made known, mentioned; famous, renowned; notorious.

kid /kɪd/ *v.*[1]*i.* Infl. **-dd-**. LME. [f. KID *n.*[1]] Give birth to a kid.

kid /kɪd/ *v.*[2]*t. obs.* exc. *dial.* E16. [f. KID *n.*[2]] Bind up (brushwood etc.) in bundles or faggots. Also, prop up or secure (loose soil etc.) using bundles of twigs etc.

kid /kɪd/ *v.*[3] *colloq.* Infl. **-dd-**. E19. [Perh. f. KID *n.*[1] in sense 'make a kid or goat of' or 'make a child of'.] 1 *v.t.* Deceive or hoax (a person); joke with or tease (a person). Also foll. by *along*, *on*. E19. 2 *v.i.* Deceive, pretend, joke with, tease. Also foll. by *around*. E19.

1 H. MAYHEW He kids them on by promising three times more than the things are worth. F. DONALDSON I don't seem able to kid myself that is real literature. J. UPDIKE My nose looks like a strawberry; Toby kids me about it. 2 J. DIDION You have to kid around with them, be more fun. W. WHARTON I thought she was kidding, but she's serious. **no kidding** that is the truth.

kiddingly *adv.* in a kidding manner, teasingly M20.

†**kid** *v.*[4] pa. pple: see KITHE.

kidang *n.* var. of KIJANG.

kidder /ˈkɪdə/ *n.*[1] *colloq.* L19. [f. KID *v.*[3] + -ER[1].] A person who kids another or others; a hoaxer, a joker, a teaser, a deceiver.

kidder *n.*[2] var. of KIDDIER.

Kidderminster /ˈkɪdəmɪnstə/ *n.* L17. [A town in Worcestershire, England.] 1 Used *attrib.* to designate things originating or produced in Kidderminster, *spec.* a kind of pileless reversible carpet in which the pattern is formed by the intersection of two cloths of different colours. L17. 2 Kidderminster carpeting, a Kidderminster carpet. M18.

kiddie /ˈkɪdi/ *n. colloq.* Also **-y**. L16. [f. KID *n.*[1] + -IE.] 1 A young goat. L16. 2 A young criminal or other person who assumes a flash manner and style of dress. *arch.* L18. 3 A child; a young person. M19.

Comb.: **kiddie brother** = *kid brother* s.v. KID *n.*[1]; **kiddie car** (orig. *US*) (*a*) a small toy car for a child to ride; (*b*) a pram; **kiddie-porn** child pornography; **kiddie sister** = *kid sister* s.v. KID *n.*[1]; **kiddiewink(ie)** (chiefly *joc.*) a small child.

kiddier /ˌkɪdɪə/ *n. obs.* exc. *dial.* Also **kidder** /ˈkɪdə/. M16. [Origin unkn.] A person who buys provisions from the producers and sells them at a market; = BADGER *n.*[1]

kiddle /ˈkɪd(ə)l/ *n.* Now *rare*. ME. [AN *kidel* (whence AL *kidellus*), OFr. *quidel*, *guidel* (mod.Fr. *guideau*).] A dam, weir, or barrier in a river, having an opening fitted with nets etc. for catching fish. Also, a barrier constructed of stakes and nets on a sea-beach for the same purpose.

kiddush /ˈkɪdʊʃ/ *n.* Also **K-**. M18. [Heb. *qiddūš* sanctification.] A ceremony of prayer and blessing over wine, performed by the head of a Jewish household at the meal ushering in the Sabbath (on a Friday night) or a holy day or at the lunch preceding it.

kiddushin /kɪˈduːʃiːn/ *n.* Also **K-**. L19. [Aram. *qiddūshīn*.] *Judaism.* The section of the Mishnah dealing with betrothal and marriage. Also, the Jewish ceremony of betrothal; the gift given by a Jewish groom to effect a betrothal.

kiddy *n.* var. of KIDDIE.

kidnap /ˈkɪdnap/ *v.* & *n.* L17. [Back-form. f. KIDNAPPER.] A *v.t.* Infl. **-pp-**, *__-p-__. Carry off by illegal force or fraud, abduct, (a person, esp. a child) formerly, to provide servants or labourers for the American plantations, now esp. to obtain ransom. L17.

B *n.* An act of kidnapping someone. M20.

R. CROMPTON It's a kidnap . . We'll get a ransom on it. *Eastern Daily Press* (*Norwich*) The kidnap victim . . was taken from his home.

kidnapper /ˈkɪdnapə/ *n.* Also *__-naper__. M17. [f. KID *n.*[1] + NAPPER *n.*[2]] A person who kidnaps someone.

kidney /ˈkɪdni/ *n.* ME. [Origin uncertain: perh. f. elem. rel. to COD *n.*[1] + EY *n.*] 1 Either of a pair of glandular organs of rounded shape with a shallow indentation on one side, situated in humans in the back of the abdominal cavity, which maintain the composition of the blood, removing waste nitrogenous and other matter and excreting it as urine. Also, a similar gland in vertebrates and some invertebrates, those of cattle, sheep, and pigs being used as food. ME. 2 *fig.* Orig., a temperament, a constitution, a disposition. Now also, a kind, sort, or class (of person). ME. 3 Something resembling a kidney, esp. in shape; *spec.* †(*a*) *rare* an ovary; (*b*) an oval variety of potato; also *kidney potato*. L16.

2 W. HOLTBY Here he lacked men of his own kidney.

Comb. & *phrases*: **artificial kidney** = *kidney machine* below; **kidney bean** (*a*) any of several bean plants with kidney-shaped seeds, *esp.* a dwarf French bean, *Phaseolus vulgaris*; (*b*) the seed of such a plant, esp. when of a dark red variety; **kidney dish** a kidney-shaped dish, esp. used as a receptacle in surgery; **kidney fern** a New Zealand fern, *Cardiomanes reniforme*, with kidney-shaped leaves; **kidney graft** the operation of transplanting a kidney from one person to another; **kidney machine** a machine for effecting dialysis of the blood; also called *artificial kidney*, *haemodialyser*; **kidney ore** haematite occurring as kidney-shaped masses; **kidney-piece** a cam on a watch wheel with a kidney-shaped outline; *kidney potato*: see sense 3 above; **kidney punch** *Boxing* an illegal punch to the kidney area; **kidney-shaped** *a.* shaped like a kidney, with one side concave and the other convex; **kidney-stone** (*a*) a kidney-shaped stone, a cobble; (*b*) a renal calculus; **kidney table**: having a kidney-shaped top; **kidney vetch** a leguminous plant, *Anthyllis vulneraria*, of chalk grassland and sea-cliffs, with heads of usu. bright yellow flowers; also called *lady's fingers*; **kidney worm** either of two parasitic nematodes, *Stephanurus dentatus*, which infests pigs, and *Dioctophyma renale*, which infests humans, dogs, and other mammals; *pulpy kidney* (*disease*): see PULPY 1.

kidology /kɪˈdɒlədʒi/ *n. colloq.* M20. [Irreg. f. KID *v.*[3] + -OLOGY.] The art or practice of kidding people; deliberate deception, mockery, or teasing.

kidult /ˈkɪdʌlt/ *a.* & *n. slang* (freq. *derog.*). M20. [Blend of KID *n.*[1] and ADULT.] A *adj.* Designating or pertaining to television programmes, films, etc., intended to appeal to both children and adults. M20. B *n.* 1 A television programme, film, etc., intended to appeal to both children and adults. M20. 2 An immature adult, *spec.* one with childish tastes in television viewing etc. L20.

kief /kiːf/ *n.* In sense 1 also **kef** /kɛf/, **keif** /keɪf/; in sense 2 also **kif**. E19. [Arab. *kayf* (repr. colloq. pronunc.).] 1 A state of drowsiness or dreamy intoxication produced by the use of cannabis etc. Also, the enjoyment of idleness. E19. 2 In Morocco and Algeria: cannabis or some other substance smoked to produce dreamy intoxication. L19.

1b **make** (or **do**) **kief** pass the time in idleness.

Kieffer /ˈkiːfə/ *n.* L19. [Peter *Kieffer* (1812–90), US horticulturist, who developed it.] In full *Kieffer pear*. A disease-resistant variety of pear, a hybrid between the common pear, *Pyrus communis*, and the Chinese pear, *P. pyrifolia*.

kiekie /ˈkiːkiː/ *n.* M19. [Maori.] A New Zealand climbing plant, *Freycinetia banksii* (family Pandanaceae), with edible bracts and leaves used for weaving baskets etc.

kielbasa /kiːlˈbasə, kjel-/ *n.* M20. [Pol. *kiełbasa* sausage.] A type of highly seasoned Polish sausage, usu. containing garlic.

kiepersol /ˈkɪpəs(ə)l, -sɒl/ *n.* Also **kippersol**. L19. [Afk. f. KITTISOL sunshade, umbrella, w. ref. to the shape of its crown.] Any of several small southern African trees of the genus *Cussonia*, of the ivy family, with leaves in tufts at the ends of the branches and with a root which is chewed for its sap.

kier /kɪə/ *n.* L16. [ON *ker* vessel, tub = OHG *kar*, Goth. *kas*.] A vat; *spec.* †(*a*) a brewing-vat; (*b*) a large vat in which cloth is boiled, bleached, etc.

kierful *n.* L19. **kiering** *n.* boiling in a kier or vat E20.

kierie /ˈkɪri/ *n. S. Afr.* Also (earlier) †**kirri**. M18. [Nama.] A short club or knobbed stick used as a weapon by indigenous peoples of South Africa. Cf. KNOBKERRIE.

Kierkegaardian /kɪəkəˈgɑːdɪən, -ˈgɔːd-/ *a.* & *n.* M20. [f. *Kierkegaard* (see below) + -IAN.] A *adj.* Of or pertaining to the Danish philosopher Sören Kierkegaard (1813–55) or his philosophy, esp. as criticizing traditional Christianity and idealism from an existentialist position. M20. B *n.* An adherent or student of Kierkegaard's philosophy. M20.

kieselguhr /ˈkiːz(ə)lgʊə/ *n.* L19. [G, f. *Kiesel* gravel (see CHESIL) + GUHR.] A soft diatomaceous earth used as an absorbent in explosives, a filtering medium, etc.

kieserite /ˈkiːzərʌɪt/ *n.* M19. [f. D. G. *Kieser* (1779–1862), Ger. physician + -ITE[1].] *Min.* Hydrated magnesium sulphate, occurring naturally as a white fine-grained monoclinic mineral, esp. in salt-mines.

Kievan /ˈkiːɛf(ə)n, -v-/ *a.* M20. [f. *Kiev* (see below) + -AN.] Of or pertaining to the Ukrainian city of Kiev, esp. in the historical period (*c*900–*c*1150) when it dominated European Russia.

Also **Kievian** *a.* E20.

kiewiet /ˈkiːvɪt/ *n. S. Afr.* Also **-wit**. L18. [Afk.: imit.] The crowned lapwing, *Vanellus coronatus*, of southern and eastern Africa.

Also **kiewietjie** /ˈkiːvɪki/ *n.* [Afk. *-tjie* dim. suff.] L19.

kif *n.* see KIEF.

†**kiff** *n.* L16–E18. [Alt.] = KITH *n.* 3.

kijang /kɪˈdʒaŋ/ *n.* Also **kidang** /kɪˈdaŋ/. L18. [Malay *kijang*, Jav. *kidang*.] A barking deer or muntjac.

kikar /ˈkɪkə/ *n.* L19. [Hind. *kīkar*.] In the Indian subcontinent: = BABUL.

kike /kʌɪk/ *n.*[1] *slang* (*derog.* & usu. considered *racially offensive*). E20. [Origin unkn.] A Jew.

kike *v.* & *n.*[2] see KEEK.

kikoi /kɪˈkɔɪ/ *n. E. Afr.* M20. [Kiswahili.] A distinctive striped cloth with an end fringe, worn round the waist.

Kikongo /kɪˈkɒŋgəʊ/ *n.* & *a.* L19. [Kikongo, f. *ki-* pref. + KONGO.] (Of) the Bantu language of the Kongo people, used in Congo, Zaire, and adjacent areas.

Kikuchi /kɪˈkuːtʃi/ *n.* M20. [Seishi *Kikuchi* (1902–74), Japanese physicist.] Physics. *Kikuchi lines*, *Kikuchi pattern*, lines in an electron diffraction pattern which are attributed to the elastic scattering of previously inelastically scattered electrons and may be used to determine the orientation of crystals.

Kikuyu /kɪˈkuːjuː/ *n.* & *a.* Pl. of n. same, **-s**. M19. [Bantu.] 1 Of or pertaining to, a member of, a Bantu-speaking people constituting the largest ethno-linguistic group in Kenya. M19. 2 (Of) the Bantu language of this people. E20.

1 **Kikuyu grass** a creeping perennial grass, *Pennisetum clandestinum*, native to the highlands of Kenya and cultivated elsewhere as a lawn and fodder grass.

kilderkin /ˈkɪldəkɪn/ *n.* LME. [f. MDu. *kinderkin*, var. of *kin(n)eken*, *-kijn*, dim. of *kintal*, *quintal* QUINTAL: see -KIN.] 1 A cask for liquids, fish, butter, etc., containing half a barrel, or 16 or 18 gallons. LME. 2 This filled with some commodity; the quantity contained in this, esp. as a measure of capacity. LME.

kilhig /ˈkɪlhɪg/ *n.* *US.* E20. [Origin unkn.] A short stout pole used as a lever or brace to direct the fall of a tree.

kilian /ˈkɪlɪən/ *n.* Also **-ll-**, **K-**. M20. [Origin unkn.] A fast ice-dance executed by a pair of skaters side by side.

Kilim /kɪˈliːm/ *a.* & *n.* Also **Ke-**. L19. [Turk. *Kılım* f. Pers. *gelīm*.] (Designating) a pileless woven carpet, rug, etc., made in Turkey, Kurdistan, and neighbouring areas.

Kilkenny /kɪlˈkɛni/ *n.* E19. [A county and city in Leinster in the Republic of Ireland.] Used *attrib.* to designate things found in or associated with Kilkenny.

Kilkenny cat either of a pair of cats fabled to have fought until only their tails remained; *fig.* either of a pair of combatants who fight until they annihilate each other. **Kilkenny marble** a grey limestone which becomes dark blue or black when polished.

kill /kɪl/ *n.*[1] ME. [f. KILL *v.*[2]] I †1 A stroke, a blow. *rare*. Only in ME.

II 2 An act of killing an animal hunted as prey or game; an animal killed as prey or game. M19. 3 *Tennis* etc. An act of striking a ball so that it cannot be returned. Cf. KILL *v.*[2] 11. E20. 4 *Mil.* An act of destroying or disabling an enemy aircraft, submarine, etc.; an aircraft etc. destroyed in this way. *colloq.* M20. 5 An act of bringing something to an end; a victory; a knockout in boxing etc. *colloq.* M20.

2 R. DAHL Always being right up with the hounds . . for fear that she might miss a kill. R. K. NARAYAN It'd do them good to watch their mother hunt and share a fresh kill. **in at the kill** present at or benefiting from the killing of an animal or (*fig.*) the successful conclusion of an enterprise. 4 *Royal Air Force News* A tally of 27 enemy aircraft 'kills', eight probably destroyed and six damaged. 5 *quick kill*: see QUICK *a.* & *adv.*

Comb.: **kill ratio** *US* the proportion of casualties on each side in a military action; **kill zone** = *killing zone* s.v. KILLING *n.*

kill /kɪl/ *n.*[2] *US local.* M17. [Du. *kil*, MDu. *kille* river-bed, channel.] A stream, a creek, a tributary river.

kill /kɪl/ *n.*[3] E19. [Ir., Gael. *cill* f. OIr. *cell* (f. L *cella* CELL *n.*[1]) cell, church, burial place (esp. as first elem. of place-names).] *Hist.* The cell of a Celtic monk or hermit; an ancient Irish or Scottish church or monastic settlement.

kill *n.*[4] & *v.*[1] see KILN.

kill /kɪl/ *v.*[2] ME. [Prob. f. Gmc wd rel. to QUELL *v.*[1] & already in OE.] I †1 *v.t.* & *i.* Strike, hit, beat. Only in ME. 2 *v.t.* Put to death; cause the death of, deprive of life. ME. b Procure (meat) by killing animals. Now *rare*. M16. 3 *v.t.* Expel, suppress, destroy, (a feeling, desire, thought, reaction, etc.); subdue, neutralize, nullify (an effect, a quality, etc.). ME. 4 *v.t.* Deprive (an organism, a substance, a process, etc.) of vitality, activity, effect, etc. Now also, destroy, break, or ruin (a thing). L15. 5 *v.t.* a Cause severe pain or suffering to; overexert (esp. oneself, *doing*). E16. b Overwhelm (a person) by a strong impression, as of admiration, anger, delight, grief, etc.; impress, thrill; convulse with laughter, *refl.* laugh heartily. M17. 6 *v.t.* Prevent the passing of (a bill) in Parliament. E17. 7 *v.t.* Spend (time) engaged in some activity, esp. while waiting for a specific event. E18. 8 *v.t.* Consume; eat or drink; *spec.* consume the entire contents of (a bottle of liquor). *colloq.* M19. 9 *v.t.* Cancel or delete (text etc.) from a book, journal, etc., before publication, or from a computer file. In *Journalism*, suppress or deny (a story etc.). *colloq.* M19. 10 *v.t.* Extinguish, turn off (a light, an engine etc.), put out (a cigarette etc.). *colloq.* M19. 11 *v.t.* In *Tennis* etc., strike (a ball) so that it cannot be returned. In *Football*, *Hockey*, etc., stop (a ball) dead. L19. 12 *v.t.* *Metall.* Treat (molten steel) so as to prevent the evolution of oxygen on solidification, *spec.* by adding a reducing agent. Freq. as *killed* ppl a. L19.

2 J. C. MORISON Bentley did kill his adversary dead. L. JONES He's dead because I killed him. V. CANNING Nearly killed myself on the tower ladder. 3 O. W. HOLMES Quantities of black tea to kill any extra glass of red claret he may have swallowed. D. W. JERROLD [He] detected his wife painfully endeavouring to kill a laugh. W. BLACK You have killed her faith as well as ruined her life. E. F. BENSON There was something in Edgar that, for her, killed romance. J. C. COX The high blank walls . . kill the grace of the lancet windows. 4 A. YOUNG Potatoes have quite killed the land. 5a A. BROOKNER The girls in the workroom complain. I could kill Christian Dior. B. EMECHETA Twenty five kobo would not kill him, but he worked very hard for his money too. *New Yorker* Her new shoes are killing her. b *Q* He's a genius . . like Chaplin. I've never seen anybody kill an audience like them. *Melody Maker* During the Elton John tour in the States . . man, we killed them night after night. 7 L. STEPHEN Tapestry, in which ladies employed their needles by way of killing time. B. EMECHETA He had killed his waiting time by going daily to the farm with his father. 8 B. SCHULBERG We . . topped off the evening by killing the second bottle of Scotch. 9 B. T. BRADFORD I'll have the story killed and the journalist fired immediately. 10 C. HOPE The coach turned into a large parking lot and the driver killed the engine. *Arena* If we kill the light now . . we might be able to go right back to sleep.

II 13 *v.i.* Cause a death or deaths. M16. 14 *v.i.* Of an animal: yield meat *well* etc. when slaughtered. M19.

13 AV *Exod.* 20:13 Thou shalt not kill. F. HARRIS If looks could kill, he'd have had short shrift.

Phrases: *dressed to kill*: see DRESS *v.* 6a. **kill or cure** (of a remedy etc.) drastic, extreme. *kill the goose that lays* (or *laid*) *the golden eggs*: see GOOSE *n.* *kill two birds with one stone*: see BIRD *n.* **kill with kindness** harm or spoil (a person) by mistaken or excessive kindness or overindulgence. *shoot to kill*: see SHOOT *v.*

With advs. in specialized senses: **kill off** (*a*) remove or get rid of by killing, destroy completely; (*b*) (of an author) represent (a fictional character) as killed or dead, write the death of into a plot. **kill out** (*a*) cull by killing; (*b*) (of an animal) yield a specified amount of meat when slaughtered (foll. by *at* the amount).

Comb.: **killbuck** (*obs.* exc. *dial.*) a fierce-looking fellow; **kill-cow** *n.* & *a.* (*obs.* exc. *dial.*) (*a*) *n.* a bully, a braggart; a terrible, great, or important person; a serious, terrible, or tragic event; †(*b*) *adj.* bragging, bullying; terrifying; **kill-crazy** *a.* (*colloq.*) insanely desiring to kill, murderous; **kill-devil** (*obs.* exc. *Hist.*) (*a*) rum; (*b*) *Angling* an artificial bait made to spin in the water like a wounded fish; **killjoy** a person who or thing which dampens or destroys enjoyment or pleasure; **kill-lamb** *US* sheep laurel or lambkill, *Kalmia angustifolia*; **kill-time** an activity intended to consume spare time; a tactic used in sport etc. to allow time to elapse with no change of score.

killable *a.* (*a*) able to be killed, easy to kill; (*b*) fit to be killed for food etc.: E19.

killadar /ˈkɪlədɑː/ *n.* L18. [Urdu & Pers. *ḳil'adār* f. Arab. *ḳal'a* fort, castle + Pers. *-dār* holder.] *Hist.* In India, the commandant or governor of a fort or castle.

Killamook *n.* & *a.* see TILLAMOOK.

Killarney /kɪˈlɑːni/ *n.* M19. [A town in Co. Kerry, Ireland.] Used *attrib.* to designate things found in or associated with Killarney.

Killarney fern a bristle-fern, *Trichomanes speciosum*, formerly abundant in the neighbourhood of Killarney.

killas /ˈkɪləs/ *n.* L17. [Prob. f. Corn.] A clay slate of Devonian age, found in Cornwall lying over granite.

killcrop /ˈkɪlkrɒp/ *n.* *rare.* M17. [LG *kilkrop*, G *Kielkropf*, 2nd elem. corresp. to CROP *n.*] An insatiable child, supposed in folklore to be a fairy changeling.

killdeer /ˈkɪldɪə/ *n.* Pl. same, **-s**. Also **-dee** /-diː/. M18. [Imit. of the bird's call.] A large brown and white plover, *Charadrius vociferus*, of N. America.

killer /ˈkɪlə/ *n.* & *a.* LME. [f. KILL *v.*[2] + -ER[1].] A *n.* I 1 A person who or thing which kills. LME. 2 *Angling.* An effective bait. L17. 3 = *killer whale* below. E18. 4 An impressive, admirable, or formidable person or thing; a hilarious joke; a decisive blow. *colloq.* E20.

1 I. MURDOCH She wanted to be the victim not the killer. *British Medical Journal* Might this be relevant to Alzheimer's disease, now America's number four killer? *impulse killer*, *revenge killer*, etc. *lady-killer*, *painkiller*, etc. *humane killer*: see HUMANE *a.* SERIAL *killer*. 3 **false killer** a black whale, *Pseudorca crassidens*, mainly of warm oceans, which feeds on cuttlefish. 4 ALAN BENNETT Witty talk. Clever talk. Dirty talk. Parliamentary talk. You're a killer Dad, you really are. *New Yorker* So I gave him a dirty look at one point—a real killer.

II 5 A cow, sheep, etc., reared for slaughter. Usu. in *pl.* *colloq.* (chiefly *Austral.* & *NZ*). L19.

B *attrib.* or as *adj.* 1 That kills, deadly. L19. 2 Impressive, admirable, formidable. *slang.* L20.

1 I. ILLICH Death has paled into a metaphorical figure, and killer diseases have taken his place. *Daily Colonist* Would you stick your arm up to the elbow in a swarm of 'killer bees'? 2 *Arena* Woody Allen can still knock out killer one liners. *City Limits* Sometimes James Brown's albums stank, but there was always one killer track.

Comb. & *special collocations*: **killer-diller** *n.* & *a.* (*slang*) (*a*) *n.* = sense A.4 above; (*b*) *adj.* = sense B.2 above; **killer instinct** (*a*) an innate tendency to kill, a homicidal tendency; (*b*) *fig.* a keenly competitive or ruthless streak; **killer submarine**: designed to hunt and destroy enemy submarines under water; **killer whale** a predatory toothed whale, *Orcinus orca*, with black and white markings and a high narrow dorsal fin.

¶ Recorded ME as a surname.

killian *n.* var. of KILIAN *n.*

killick /ˈkɪlɪk/ *n.* Also **-ock** /-ək/. M17. [Origin unkn.] *Naut.* 1 A heavy stone held in a wooden anchor-shaped frame, used on a small vessel as a substitute for an anchor. Also, a small anchor. M17. 2 A leading seaman's badge, bearing the symbol of an anchor; a leading seaman. *colloq.* E20.

killifish /ˈkɪlɪfɪʃ/ *n.* Pl. **-es** /-ɪz/, (usu.) same. E19. [App. f. KILL *n.*[2] + FISH *n.*[1]] Any of several small, often brightly coloured toothcarps of the families Cyprinodontidae and Poeciliidae; *esp.* any of the genus *Fundulus*, found esp. in sheltered rivers and estuaries of eastern N. America. Also called *topminnow*.

killiki(n)nick *n.* var. of KINNIKINNICK.

killing /ˈkɪlɪŋ/ *n.* LME. [f. KILL *v.*[2] + -ING[1].] 1 The action of KILL *v.*[2]; an instance of this. LME. 2 A large profit; a quick and profitable success in business etc. *slang.* L19.

1 *Christian Aid News* Fr. Josimo . . had been witness to the expulsions, torture . . and killings of peasants for many years. *attrib.*: *Soldier* Flanders is the killing ground in which the fate of the countries of Europe has been decided. 2 J. O'FAOLAIN The old man . . had made a killing in real estate.

Comb.: **killing bottle**: containing poisonous vapour for killing captured insects etc.; **killing-circle** the area within which the shot from a gun is sufficiently compact to kill game; **killing-time** (*a*) the time at which an animal is (ready to be) killed; (*b*) *Sc. Hist.* any of the periods during which many Covenanters were put to death; **killing zone** (*a*) the area of a military engagement with a high concentration of fatalities; (*b*) the area of the human body where entry of a projectile would kill, esp. as indicated on a target for shooting-practice.

killing /ˈkɪlɪŋ/ *a.* & *adv.* LME. [f. KILL *v.*[2] + -ING[2].] A *adj.* 1 That kills; deadly, destructive. LME. 2 *hyperbol.* a Overwhelming; *spec.* (*a*) crushing, oppressive; (*b*) very beautiful or attractive; (*c*) arduous, exhausting. E17. b Excruciatingly funny, hilarious. *colloq.* M19.

1 *Daily Colonist* The wind . . will be followed . . by calm, cold weather with killing frosts. B. EMECHETA Anything is possible to the man with a killing weapon. 2a H. ROBBINS He couldn't keep working at a pace

like that forever. It was killing. P. L. FERMOR Their floppy hats were worn at killing angles.

B *adv.* = KILLINGLY. L17.

R. L. STEVENSON The ocean breeze blew killing chill.

killingly *adv.* in a killing manner L16. **killingness** *n.* M19.

killock *n.* var. of KILLICK.

killogie /kɪˈləʊgi/ *n. Sc.* Now *rare*. Also **-logy**. E16. [f. *kill* var. of KILN *n.* + LOGIE.] The covered space in front of the fireplace of a kiln, providing a draught for the fire and sheltering the person attending it.

Kilmarnock /kɪlˈmɑːnək/ *n.* M17. [A town in Strathclyde, Scotland.] **I** 1 Used *attrib.* to designate things originating or found in Kilmarnock. M17.

1 **Kilmarnock bonnet, cap**, etc., a cap resembling a tam-o'-shanter. **Kilmarnock willow** a pendulous cultivar of the goat willow, *Salix caprea*.

II 2 A Kilmarnock cap or bonnet. E19.

kiln /kɪln/ *n.* & *v.* Also (now *Sc.*) **kill** /kɪl/. OE. [L *culina* kitchen, cooking-stove.] **A** *n.* An industrial furnace, oven, etc., for burning, baking, or drying, *spec.* (*a*) for calcining lime, (*b*) for baking bricks, (*c*) for firing pottery, (*d*) for drying grain, hops, etc. OE.

progressive kiln: see PROGRESSIVE *a.* **set the kiln on fire** cause a serious commotion or turmoil.

Comb.: **kiln-dry** *v.t.* dry in a kiln.

B *v.t.* Burn, bake, or dry in a kiln. E16.

kilnful *n.* the amount a kiln can hold LME.

Kilner jar /ˈkɪlnə dʒɑː/ *n. phr.* M20. [Manufacturers' name.] (Proprietary name for) a type of preserving jar.

kilo /ˈkiːləʊ/ *n.* Pl. **-os**. L19. [Fr., abbrev. of *kilogramme*, *kilomètre*.] 1 = KILOGRAM. L19. 2 = KILOMETRE. L19.

kilo- /ˈkɪləʊ, ˈkiːləʊ/ *comb. form.* [Fr., f. Gk *khilioi* thousand: see -O-.] Used in names of units of measurement to denote a factor of one thousand, as *kilojoule*, *kilolitre*, *kilopascal*, etc., or (in *Computing*) a factor of 1,024 (2^{10}), as *kilobyte* etc. Abbrev. *k*.

kilobase *n.* (*Biochem.*) a unit of size of nucleic acid chains, equal to one thousand base-pairs (also *kilobase-pair*) L20. **kilobit** *n.* (*Computing*) a unit of memory size equal to 1,024 bits M20. **kilobuck** *n.* (*slang*) a thousand dollars M20. **kilocalorie** *n.* = CALORIE (a) L19. **kilocycle** *n.* (*a*) a thousand cycles (of some periodic phenomenon); (*b*) = KILOHERTZ: E20. **kilohertz** *n.* a thousand hertz or cycles per second E20. **kilovolt** *n.* a thousand volts L19. **kilovoltage** *n.* voltage expressed in kilovolts M20. **kilowatt** *n.* a thousand watts (*kilowatt-hour*, a unit of energy equal to that produced in one hour by a power of one kilowatt (= 3.6 million joule)) L19. **kilowattage** *n.* power expressed in kilowatts M20.

kilobyte /ˈkɪləbʌɪt/ *n.* L20. [f. KILO- + BYTE.] *Computing.* A unit of memory size equal to 1,024 (2^{10}) bytes.

kilogram /ˈkɪləgram/ *n.* Also **-gramme**. L18. [Fr. *kilogramme*, f. as KILO- + GRAM *n.*[2]] A fundamental unit of mass or (*loosely*) weight in the metric system (equal to approx. 2.205 lb), orig. defined as the mass of a cubic decimetre of pure water, now as an SI unit defined as equal to the mass of a unique standard cylinder of platinum-iridium alloy kept at Sèvres near Paris. Also, (in full *standard kilogram*) this or a similar object acting as a standard mass. (Symbol kg.)

Comb.: **kilogram calorie** = CALORIE (a); **kilogram-force**, pl. **kilograms-force**, a unit of force or weight equal to the weight of a mass of one kilogram under standard gravity; **kilogram-metre** a unit of energy equal to that required to raise a mass of one kilogram to the height of one metre under standard gravity.

kilometre /ˈkɪləmiːtə, kɪˈlɒmɪtə/ *n.* Also *__*-meter__. L18. [Fr. *kilomètre*, f. as KILO- + METRE *n.*[2]] A unit of length or distance equal to one thousand metres, equivalent to approx. 3280.84 feet or approx. five-eighths of a mile.

kiˈlometrage *n.* the number of kilometres covered or travelled L20. **kiloˈmetric** *a.* pertaining to a kilometre or kilometres; marking a distance of a kilometre: M19.

kiloton /ˈkɪlətʌn/ *n.* M20. [f. KILO- + TON *n.*[1]] One thousand tons; usu. *spec.*, a unit of explosive power, equal to that of one thousand tons of TNT.

kilt /kɪlt/ *n.* M18. [f. the vb.] A kind of skirt reaching to the knee, usu. made of pleated tartan cloth, as traditionally worn by men from the Scottish Highlands. Now also, any similar garment worn elsewhere or by women and children.

kilted *a.* wearing a kilt E19.

kilt /kɪlt/ *v.* ME. [Of Scand. origin: cf. Sw. dial. *kilta* to swathe, Da. *kilte* (*op*) tuck (up), ON *kilting* a skirt, *kjalta* the lap.] 1 *v.t.* Tuck up (skirts) round the body. Also foll. by *up*. ME. 2 *v.t.* Tie or hoist up (a thing); hang (a person). Now *rare* or *obs.* L17. 3 *v.i.* Go quickly, hasten, as if with the skirts kilted up. *Sc.* E19. 4 *v.t.* Gather in vertical pleats. L19.

1 D. H. LAWRENCE She, with her skirts kilted up, flew round at her work, absorbed.

kilting *n.* (*a*) the action of the vb; (*b*) clothing or material tucked up or gathered in pleats: E16.

kilta /ˈkɪltə/ *n.* L19. [Origin unkn.] In the Indian subcontinent, esp. in the Himalayan region: a kind of long conical wicker basket carried on the back.

kilter /ˈkɪltə/ *n.*[1] Also **kelter** /ˈkɛltə/. E17. [Origin unkn.] Good condition or order; good state of health or spirits. Chiefly in *out of kilter*, *in* (*good*) *kilter*.

kilter /ˈkɪltə/ *n.*[2] L19. [Prob. var. of KELTER *n.*[2]] An unorthodox poker hand containing no card higher than nine, nor any ace, pair, flush, or straight.

kiltie /ˈkɪlti/ *n.* & *a. colloq.* M19. [f. KILT *n.* + -IE.] **A** *n.* A person, esp. a Highland soldier, wearing a kilt. M19. **B** *adj.* Kilted. E20.

kimberlite /ˈkɪmbəlʌɪt/ *n.* L19. [f. *Kimberley*, diamond-mining centre in South Africa + -ITE[1].] *Geol.* A rare intrusive blue-green igneous rock, a porphyritic mica-peridotite, which occurs in South Africa and Siberia and is a source of diamonds. Also called *blue ground*.

kimchi /ˈkɪmtʃi/ *n.* L19. [Korean.] A raw strongly-flavoured cabbage pickle, the Korean national dish.

Kimeridge *n.* var. of KIMMERIDGE.

kim-kam /ˈkɪmkam/ *a.* & *adv.* Now chiefly *dial.* L16. [App. redupl. of CAM *a.* & *adv.* w. vowel variation: cf. FLIMFLAM, JIMJAM.] Crooked(ly), awkward(ly), perverse(ly).

kimmer *n.* var. of CUMMER.

Kimmeridge /ˈkɪmərɪdʒ/ *n.* Also (earlier) **Kimer-**. M18. [A village on the Dorset coast of SW England.] *Geol.* Used *attrib.* to designate sedimentary deposits of Jurassic age which are especially well developed near Kimmeridge.

Kimmeridge clay (a bed of) a fossiliferous clay containing bituminous shale which forms deposits extending across much of southern England and parts of Europe. **Kimmeridge coal** bituminous shale from the Kimmeridge clay which can be burnt as fuel.

Kimmeˈridgian *a.* & *n.* (designating or pertaining to) a division of the Upper Jurassic including the Kimmeridge clay M19.

kimnel /ˈkɪmn(ə)l/ *n.* Long *obs.* exc. *dial.* ME. [App. rel. to COOMB *n.*[1]] A tub used for brewing, kneading, salting meat, and other household purposes.

ki-mon /ˈkiːmɒn/ *n.* L19. [Jap., f. *ki* demon, devil + *mon* gate.] In Japanese tradition (taken from Chinese geomancy): the north-east, the traditional source of evil.

kimono /kɪˈməʊnəʊ/ *n.* & *a.* M17. [Jap., f. *ki* wearing + *mono* thing.] **A** *n.* Pl. **-os**. A long Japanese robe with wide sleeves, tied with a sash. Now also, in Western countries, a garment (esp. a dressing-gown) modelled on this. M17. **B** *attrib.* or as *adj.* Resembling or characteristic of a kimono. E20.

kimonoed *a.* wearing a kimono L19.

Kim's game /ˈkɪmz geɪm/ *n. phr.* E20. [f. *Kim* (the eponymous hero of) a book by Rudyard Kipling (1865–1936), in which a similar game is played.] A memory-testing game in which players try to remember as many as possible of a set of objects briefly shown to them.

kin /kɪn/ *n.* & *a.* [OE *cyn*(*n* = OFris. *kin*, *ken*, *kon*, OS, OHG *kunni* (Du. *kunne*), ON *kyn*, Goth. *kuni*, f. Gmc, f. IE base also of Gk *genos*, L *genus* race, GENUS.] **A** *n.* **I** Family, race, blood relations. 1 A group of people descended from a common ancestor; *spec.* a family, a clan. Formerly also, the progeny *of* a specified ancestor. Long *rare*. OE. 2a *collect.* One's family, one's relatives; relatives; *transf.* people or things of a similar kind. OE. b A member of one's family, a relative. *arch.* OE. 3 Ancestral stock; family. Esp. in (*come*) *of good* (or *noble* etc.) *kin*. Long *obs.* exc. *dial.* OE. 4 The quality, condition, or fact of being related by birth or descent; kinship, consanguinity. Now *rare* or *obs.* LME.

2a E. INGERSOLL The martens . . , skunks, otters and their kin of the family Mustelidae. G. STEIN These relatives of hers . . were the only kin she had. A. TOFFLER We expect ties with our immediate family, and to a lesser extent with other kin. A. BURGESS George . . gave a great dinner for his kin at the Midland Hotel. *Sunday Times* The middle-classes and their kin.

II Class, group, division. †5 A natural class, group, or division of people, animals, plants, etc., with shared attributes or ancestry; *spec.* a race, a species. OE–E16. †b A kind of (person or thing). OE–L16.

Phrases: *kissing kin*: see KISSING *ppl a.* *kith and kin*: see KITH *n.* 3. **near of kin** closely related. **next of kin** the living person or persons standing in the nearest degree of relationship to another, and entitled to share in his or her personal estate in case of intestacy. **of kin** (*a*) (long *rare*) by birth or descent; (*b*) related by blood or in character, akin. *store the kin*: see STORE *v.*

Comb.: **kin group** a group of people related by blood or marriage; **kin selection** *Biol.* a form of natural selection in which an apparently disadvantageous characteristic (esp. altruistic behaviour) increases in the population due to increased survival of individuals genetically related to those possessing the characteristic.

B *pred. a.* Related; akin (*to*). L16.

SHAKES. *Tr. & Cr.* One touch of nature makes the whole world kin.

kin /kɪn/ *aux. v.* Chiefly *US* (*Black English* & *dial.*). L19. [Repr. a pronunc. of CAN *v.*[1]] Can; be able to.

-kin /kɪn/ *suff.* [f. or after MDu. *-kijn*, *ken*, G *-chen*, as in MDu. *husekijn*, *huusken*, G *Häuschen* little house.] Forming dim. ns., as *catkin*, *lambkin*, *manikin*.

kina /ˈkiːnə/ *n.*[1] *NZ.* M20. [Maori.] An edible sea urchin, *Evechinus chloroticus*.

kina /ˈkiːnə/ *n.*[2] Pl. **-s**, same. L20. [Tok Pisin.] The basic monetary unit of Papua New Guinea, equal to 100 toea.

kinaesthesia /kɪnɪsˈθiːzɪə, kʌɪn-/ *n.* Also *__*kines-__. L19. [f. Gk *kinein* move + *aisthēsis* sensation: see -IA[1].] The faculty of being aware of the position and movement of parts of the body, by means of sensory nerves (proprioceptors) within the muscles, joints, etc.; the sensation producing such awareness.

kinaesthesiˈometer *n.* an instrument for measuring kinaesthetic sensitivity L19. **kinaesthesis** *n.* = KINAESTHESIA L19. **kinaesthetic** /-ˈθɛtɪk/ *a.* of or pertaining to kinaesthesia; involving or utilizing kinaesthesia: L19. **kinaesthetically** *adv.* by means of kinaesthesia M20.

kinaki /kɪˈnaki/ *n. NZ.* E19. [Maori.] A Maori relish; a tasty or savoury addition to a Maori meal.

kinase /ˈkʌɪneɪz/ *n.* E20. [f. Gk *kinein* move + -ASE.] *Biochem.* 1 A substance which converts an inactive precursor into an active enzyme. Now *rare* or *obs.* E20. 2 Any of various enzymes that catalyse the transfer of a phosphate group from ATP to another molecule. M20.

kinchin /ˈkɪntʃɪn/ *n. slang.* Now *rare* or *obs.* M16. [G *Kindchen* dim. of *Kind* child: cf. -KIN.] A young child. Orig. & usu. in *comb.* (see below).

Comb.: †**kinchin-cove** a young boy; **kinchin-lay** the practice of stealing money from children sent on errands; †**kinchin-mort** [see MOT *n.*[1]] a young girl.

kincob /ˈkɪŋkɒb/ *n.* & *a.* E18. [Urdu & Pers. *kamkāb* gold or silver brocade, alt. of *kamkā* damask silk, f. older Chin. *kįəmχwa* ornate (applied to brocade), f. *kįəm* gold + *χwa* flower, decoration.] (Made of) a rich Indian fabric, embroidered with gold or silver.

kind /kʌɪnd/ *n.* Also †**kynd**. [OE *cynd(e)*, earlier *ġecynd(e)*, f. Gmc, f. bases of Y-, KIN *n.*] I Nature. **1** (The regular course of) nature; the established order of things. Long *arch.* OE. **2** Innate character, native constitution; natural disposition. Long *rare.* OE. †**3** Natural state, form, or condition; a natural property or quality. OE–LME. **4** A manner, a way, a fashion; *spec.* the manner natural or proper to a person or thing. *arch.* OE. **5** Character regarded as determining the class to which a thing belongs; generic or specific nature. E17.

1 W. MORRIS O ye who sought to find Unending life against the law of Kind. 2 H. T. BUCKLE For as to the men themselves, they merely acted after their kind. 4 T. HALE Being in no kind desirous that his Majesty should be under any Obligation. 5 D. LESSING There was a difference in degree but not in kind.

II A class, a sort, a type. **6** A group of animals or plants having a common origin; a race. Now *literary.* OE. **7** A class of individuals or objects distinguished by common essential characteristics; a genus, a species; a sort, a variety. (After *these* or *those* pl. sometimes same.) OE. **b** *collect.* A sex. Long *rare.* M16. **c** A literary genre. M17.

6 T. SMITH Without this society of man and woman the kind of man could not long endure. DEFOE They would sooner starve than eat any Thing that lived on human kind. 7 GOLDSMITH Of the bear, there are three different kinds. J. BUCHAN The shutters . . were the kind that lock with a key. S. BELLOW A bronchial infection of a rare kind. D. JOHNSON The bartender was my kind of person. b R. HUNTFORD Emily took the revenge of her kind by mothering her man. c G. HOUGH The impetus to the theory of kinds was initially given by Aristotle.

III Descent, birth, sex. †**8a** One's native place or position; a natural entitlement; a birthright, a heritage. OE–M17. **b** Birth, descent. OE–M17. †**9a** Gender; sex. OE–L16. **b** The sexual organs. *rare.* OE–ME. **c** Semen. LME–M16. †**10a** Offspring, progeny; descendants. OE–L16. **b** (A generation of) a family; a clan, tribe, etc. ME–L17. **11** Ancestral race or stock; family. *arch.* ME.

11 SHAKES. *Per.* She's such a one that, were I well assur'd Came of gentle kind and noble stock, I'd wish no better choice.

Phrases: **a kind of** a person or thing resembling or roughly equivalent to (another). *all kind(s) of*: see ALL *a.* †**by kind** by nature, naturally. *Communion in one kind, in both kinds*: see COMMUNION 5. **in kind** (*a*) in goods or labour as opp. to money; (*b*) in a similar form, likewise. **kind of** somewhat, to some extent (cf. KINDA). *kissing kind*: see KISSING *ppl a.* **law of kind** *arch.* the natural order of things, nature. **nothing of the kind** not at all like the thing in question; (expr. denial) in no way, not at all. **of a kind** (*a*) *derog.* scarcely worthy of a specified term or description; (*b*) (of two or more persons or things) similar in some important respect. **of its kind** within the limitations of the class to which it belongs. **one's own kind** (the) people with whom one has a great deal in common. **something of the kind** something like the thing in question; (expr. agreement) to some extent, in some ways. *these kind of*: see THESE *a.* 1. *the worst kind*: see WORST *a.*, *adv.*, & *n.* *those kind of*: see THOSE *a.* 2.

Comb.: **kind payment** payment in kind, payment in goods or labour as opp. to money.

kinda, **-er** /ˈkʌɪndə/ *adv.* (*non-standard*) [repr. a pronunc.: see A *prep.*[2]] somewhat, to some extent, = *kind of* above M19.

kind /kʌɪnd/ *a.* & *adv.* [OE *ġe*)*cynd(e)* f. Gmc, f. base of KIND *n.*] **A** *adj.* I Natural, native. †**1** Implanted by or conforming to nature; proper, appropriate. OE–L17. **2**†**a** Of an heir, inheritance, etc.: lawful, rightful. OE–E18. **b** Native, indigenous. Long *obs.* exc. *Sc.* ME. †**c** Of a person: related to oneself; one's own. ME–E16. †**d** Having a specified character or position by nature or birth. LME–L16.

II Good by nature. **3**†**a** Well-born, of gentle birth; well-bred. ME–L19. **b** Of a good kind; having the natural qualities well developed. *obs.* exc. *dial.* ME. **4** Having or displaying a gentle, sympathetic, or benevolent disposition; showing consideration for others. Formerly also, courteous. (Foll. by *to.*) ME. **5** Of a person, action, etc.: affectionate, loving, fond; intimate. Now *rare* exc. *dial.* ME. †**6** Acceptable, agreeable, pleasant. ME–L18. **7** Grateful, thankful. *obs.* exc. *dial.* LME. **8** Soft, tender; easy to work. *dial.* & *techn.* M18.

4 J. RULE The kindest thing Evelyn could do was to ignore her nervousness. A. BURGESS Mother Andrea had a sweet face and was kind and gentle. *fig.*: R. CHURCH The winter . . of damp and sulphurous fogs, had not been kind to her. 5 POPE Do lovers dream, or is my Delia kind.

B *adv.* Kindly. *colloq.* E17.

kindergarten /ˈkɪndəɡɑːt(ə)n/ *n.* M19. [G, lit. 'children's garden'.] **1** Orig., a school teaching young children according to a method devised by Friedrich Fröbel (see FROEBEL) for developing their intelligence by means of interesting objects, exercises with toys, games, singing, etc. Now, any nursery school. M19. **2** *Hist.* The group of young men with imperialist ideals recruited by Lord Milner, High Commissioner of South Africa, to help with reconstruction work after the second Boer War of 1899–1902. E20.

kindergartener *n.* a teacher or pupil at a kindergarten L19.

kinder, kirche, küche /ˈkɪndər ˈkɪrçə ˈkyçə/ *n. phr. pl.* Freq. *iron.* L19. [G, lit. 'children, church, kitchen'.] The domestic and religious concerns traditionally regarded as appropriate for a woman.

kinderspiel /ˈkɪndəʃpiːl/ *n.* E20. [G, lit. 'children's play'.] A dramatic piece performed by children.

kind-hearted /kʌɪndˈhɑːtɪd/ *a.* M16. [f. KIND *a.* + HEARTED.] Having a kind disposition.

kind-heartedly *adv.* E20. **kind-heartedness** *n.* L16.

kindle /ˈkɪnd(ə)l/ *n.* ME. [App. f. KIND *n.* + -LE[1].] **1** A litter of kittens. Formerly also, the young of any animal; a young one. Long *rare.* ME. **2** *in kindle*, (of a hare, rabbit, etc.) pregnant, with young. Chiefly *dial.* L19.

kindle /ˈkɪnd(ə)l/ *v.*[1] ME. [f. ON *kynda* + -LE[3], suggested by ON *kindill* candle, torch.] I *v.t.* **1** Set fire to (combustible material); ignite; light (a flame, a fire). ME. **2** Inflame, arouse, inspire, (an emotion, feeling, etc.); give rise to (trouble etc.). ME. **3** Excite, stir up (a person, the imagination, etc.). Also foll. by *to*, *to do.* ME. **4** Make bright or glowing as with fire. E16.

1 D. M. THOMAS She . . kindled a fire in the stove. 2 D. DELILLO I'm happy to say I've kindled an interest. A. BROOKNER She . . never did anything to kindle the emotions of other drivers.

II *v.i.* **5** Begin to burn; catch fire. ME. **6** (Of an emotion, feeling, etc.) rise, be aroused, be excited; (of a person) become impassioned or excited, respond with animation. ME. **7** Become bright or glowing like fire. L18.

5 *New York Times* To-day, a light kindles in the long night of horror in El Salvador. 6 J. REED They greeted him with an immense crusading acclaim, kindling to the daring of it. G. GREENE His imagination kindled with a more daring project.

kindler *n.* LME.

kindle /ˈkɪnd(ə)l/ *v.*[2]*t.* & *i.* Now chiefly *dial.* ME. [App. f. KIND *n.* + -LE[3], or f. KINDLE *n.*] Of a hare, rabbit, etc.: give birth to (young).

kindless /ˈkʌɪndlɪs/ *a.* Now *rare.* ME. [f. KIND *n.* + -LESS; in sense 2 as if f. KIND *a.*] †**1** Without natural power, feeling, etc.; unnatural. ME–E17. **2** Devoid of kindness. M19.

kindlily /ˈkʌɪndlɪli/ *adv.* E19. [f. KINDLY *a.* + -LY[2].] In a kindly manner.

kindliness /ˈkʌɪndlɪnɪs/ *n.* LME. [f. as prec. + -NESS.] **1** The quality or habit of being kindly. LME. †**2** Mildness of climate etc. that is favourable to vegetation. M17–L18.

kindling /ˈkɪndlɪŋ/ *n.*[1] ME. [f. KINDLE *v.*[1] + -ING[1].] **1** The action of KINDLE *v.*[1]; an instance of this. ME. **2** Material for lighting a fire. E16.

Comb.: **kindling-wood** dry wood suitable for lighting fires.

kindling /ˈkɪndlɪŋ/ *n.*[2] Now chiefly *dial.* ME. [f. KINDLE *v.*[2] + -ING[1].] **1** The action of KINDLE *v.*[2]; an instance of this. ME. **2** (A member of) a brood or litter; progeny, offspring. ME.

kindly /ˈkʌɪndli/ *a.* OE. [f. KIND *n.* + -LY[1].] I Pertaining to nature or birth. **1a** Existing or occurring according to (the laws of) nature; natural (*to*); proper, suitable. Long *obs.* exc. *Sc.* OE. †**b** Implanted by nature; innate. OE–E17. **2** Having a hereditary right to a position, tenancy, etc.; rightful, lawful; (of a child) legitimate. Now *rare.* OE. **b** Native, indigenous. *obs.* exc. *Sc.* E17. †**3** Belonging to one by birth; hereditary. ME–M17.

II Good by nature. **4** Of good natural qualities; excellent of its kind; healthy, thriving. Now *arch.* & *dial.* LME. **5** Acceptable, agreeable, pleasant; *spec.* (of climate, conditions, etc.) benign, favourable to growth. LME. **6** Having or displaying a friendly benevolent disposition; kind, good-natured. E16.

5 A. WEST They . . sat about in deck chairs in kindly weather. 6 DAY LEWIS Aunt Alice I remember as a kindly, comfortable, clucking woman. A. N. WILSON Tibba in the most matter-of-fact and yet kindly way had . . taken control.

kindly /ˈkʌɪndli/ *adv.* OE. [f. KIND *a.* + -LY[2].] **1**†**a** In accordance with nature; characteristically. Later also, thoroughly, exactly. OE–L16. **b** In a manner appropriate to the nature of a thing; properly, fittingly; readily, spontaneously; successfully. Now *rare* exc. *dial.* LME. **2** In a kind manner; sympathetically, considerately, benevolently; affectionately. ME. **3** In a way that pleases or is agreeable to the recipient. Now chiefly in polite requests and (*iron.*) in demands. L16.

3 J. K. TOOLE Will you kindly go away? A. MACLEAN If not, kindly refrain from sending pointless signals.

Phrases: **take kindly** accept as a kindness, be pleased by. **take kindly to** find acceptable, pleasant, or endearing. **thank kindly** thank heartily and appreciatively.

kindness /ˈkʌɪn(d)nɪs/ *n.* ME. [f. KIND *a.* + -NESS.] **1** The quality or habit of being kind; kind nature or disposition; kind behaviour. ME. **2** A kind deed, a considerate act. Formerly also, a benefaction. ME. **3** Kind feeling; fondness, affection; good will. Now *rare* or *obs.* LME. †**4** A natural inclination or aptitude. *rare.* LME–L17. †**5** Kinship; close relationship. LME–L17. †**6** Hereditary right, *spec.* to a tenancy. *Sc.* E16–M17.

1 *kill with kindness*: see KILL *v.*[2] *milk of human kindness*: see MILK *n.*

kindred /ˈkɪndrɪd/ *n.* & *a.* ME. [f. KIN *n.* & *a.* + -RED, w. phonet. devel. of *d* between *n* and *r* as in *thunder.*] **A** *n.* **1a** Relationship between people, esp. by blood or descent; kinship. ME. **b** *fig.* Affinity of character; resemblance. L16. **2** A group of people related by blood; a family, a clan, a tribe. Now *rare.* ME. †**b** The family or descendants *of* a specified ancestor. ME–M17. †**c** A generation. ME–M16. †**d** Descent, pedigree. LME–L16. †**3** Ancestral stock; family. ME–E16. **4a** *collect.* One's family or relatives. ME. †**b** A kinsman, a kinswoman. LME–E18.

B *attrib.* or as *adj.* **1** Allied in nature or properties; possessing similar qualities; cognate. ME. **2a** Related by birth or marriage. M16. **b** Of, pertaining to, or done by relatives. L16.

1 **kindred spirit** a person whose character and outlook have much in common with one's own; in *pl.*, people whose character and outlook have much in common.

kindredness *n.* kindredship M19. **kindredship** *n.* the quality or state of being akin; kinship: M18.

kindy /ˈkɪndi/ *n.* *Austral* & *NZ colloq.* M20. [Abbrev.] A kindergarten.

kine /kʌɪn/ *n.*[1] M20. [Back-form. f. KINESICS.] An isolable element of body movement or gesture made in non-vocal communication.

kine *n.*[2] see COW *n.*[1]

kine *a.*, **kinema** *n.* see CINE *a.*, CINEMA.

kinematic /kɪnɪˈmatɪk, kʌɪn-/ *a.* M19. [f. Gk *kinēmat-*, *kinēma* movement (f. *kinein* move) + -IC.] Of or pertaining to kinematics; relating to pure motion, considered without reference to force or mass; *spec.* (*Mech.*) designating a set of mechanical elements the relative position and motion of any one of which is uniquely determined by the relative position and motion of the other(s).

kinematic viscosity: see VISCOSITY 2.

kinematical *a.* = KINEMATIC M19. **kinematically** *adv.* as regards or by means of kinematics L19.

kinematics /kɪnɪˈmatɪks, kʌɪn-/ *n.pl.* M19. [f. as prec. + -ICS.] **1** The branch of mechanics that deals with pure motion, considered without reference to the objects in motion, or to the forces acting on them. Treated as *sing.* Cf. KINETICS 1. M19. **2** The kinematic features or properties of something. Treated as *sing.* or *pl.* M20.

kinematograph *n.* & *v.*, **-graphic** *a.*, **-graphy** *n.* see CINEMATOGRAPH etc.

kineme /ˈkʌɪniːm/ *n.* M20. [f. Gk *kinē(sis* movement + -EME.] A meaningful unit of body movement or gesture made in non-vocal communication.

kinep *n.* var. of GUINEP.

kinescope /ˈkɪnɪskəʊp/ *n.* & *v.* Chiefly *US.* M20. [f. Gk *kinē(sis* movement + -SCOPE: orig. a proprietary name.] *Television.* **A** *n.* **1** A kind of television picture tube. M20. **2** A film recording of a television broadcast; a telerecording. M20. **B** *v.t.* Make a telerecording of. M20.

kinesic /kɪˈniːsɪk, kʌɪ-/ *a.* M20. [f. Gk *kinēs(is* movement + -IC.] Of or pertaining to communication effected non-vocally through movements or gestures.

kinesically *adv.* M20.

kinesics /kɪˈniːsɪks, kʌɪ-/ *n.pl.* (usu. treated as *sing.*). M20. [f. as prec. + -ICS.] The branch of knowledge that deals with the way body movements and gestures convey meaning non-vocally; such movements and gestures.

kinesiology /kɪˌniːsɪˈɒlədʒi, kʌɪ-/ *n.* L19. [f. Gk *kinēsis* movement + -OLOGY.] The branch of science that deals with the mechanics of (human) bodily movement.

kinesioˈlogic, **kinesioˈlogical** *adjs.* M20. **kinesiologist** *n.* M20.

kinesis /kɪˈniːsɪs, kʌɪ-/ *n.* Pl. **kineses** /-siːz/. E17. [Gk *kinēsis* movement.] **1** *gen.* Motion; a kind of movement. *rare.* E17. **2** *Biol.* An undirected movement of an organism that occurs in response to a particular kind of stimulus. E20. **3** *Zool.* Mobility of the bones of the skull, as in some birds and reptiles. M20.

kinesthesia *n.* see KINAESTHESIA.

kinetheodolite /ˌkɪnɪθɪˈɒdəlʌɪt, ˌkʌɪ-/ *n.* M20. [f. Gk *kinē(sis* movement + THEODOLITE.] A telescope used to follow the path of a projectile, aircraft, etc., and mounted so that its elevation and azimuth angles are indicated.

kinetic /kɪˈnɛtɪk, kʌɪ-/ *a.* M19. [Gk *kinētikos*, f. *kinein* move: see -IC.] **1** Of, pertaining to, or relating to motion; due to or resulting from motion. M19. **b** *Biol.* Of, pertaining to, or of the nature of a kinesis. E20. **c** *fig.* Active, dynamic, full of energy. M20. **2** *Chem.* Of, pertaining to, or governed by the kinetics of a reaction. L19. **3** *Cytol.* Pertaining to or involved in mitotic division; undergoing division. Cf. KINESIS 1. L19. **4** *Phonet.* Of a consonant, vowel, etc.: changing in quality during utterance as opp. to being held constant. M20. **5** (Of art, a work of art) depending on movement for its effect; of, pertaining to, or producing works of this kind. M20.

1c H. G. WELLS They were at least kinetic, they wanted to make things happen.

Special collocations: **kinetic energy** energy which a body possesses by virtue of being in motion (cf. *potential energy* s.v. POTENTIAL *a.*). **kinetic heating** heat generated by the compression and acceleration of air by a fast-moving body. **kinetic theory** a theory which explains physical properties of matter in terms of the motions of constituent particles; *spec.* either of those theories relating respectively to heat and the gaseous state.

kinetically *adv.* in a kinetic manner, as regards kinetics E20.

kineticist /kɪˈnɛtɪsɪst, kʌɪ-/ *n.* M20. [f. next + -IST.] **1** Chiefly *Chem.* An expert in or student of kinetics. M20. **2** A kinetic artist. L20.

kineticism *n.* kinetic art M20.

kinetics /kɪˈnɛtɪks, kʌɪ-/ *n.pl.* Exc. in sense 2b, usu. treated as *sing.* M19. [f. KINETIC + -ICS.] **1** The branch of dynamics that deals with the relations between the motions of bodies and the forces acting on them. Cf. DYNAMICS 1, STATICS 1. M19. **2** *Chem.* The branch of physical chemistry that deals with the mechanisms and rates of chemical processes. Also (*gas kinetics*), the science of the properties of gases as systems of moving particles. L19. **b** Usu. treated as *pl.* Those aspects of a process that relate to its rate; the details of the way a reaction occurs, esp. as regards its rate. E20.

kinetin /ˈkʌɪnɪtɪn/ *n.* M20. [f. next + -IN[1].] *Biochem.* A synthetic compound, 6-furfurylaminopurine, $C_{10}H_9N_5O$, having the properties of a plant growth hormone or kinin.

kineto- /kɪˈniːtəʊ, kʌɪ-/ *comb. form.* [Gk, f. *kinētos* movable: see -O-.] Moving, associated with movement.

kinetochore *n.* [Gk *khōros* place] *Cytol.* = CENTROMERE M20. **kinetoˈdesma** *n.*, pl. **-mas**, **-mata** /-mətə/, *Biol.* (in ciliates and flagellates) a thin fibre consisting of a number of fibrils each terminating in a kinetosome M20. **kinetoˈgenesis** *n.* the (theoretical) origination of animal structures in animal movements L19. **kinetograph** *n.* (*Hist.*) an early form of film camera, the resulting images being viewed through a kinetoscope L19. **kinetoˈnucleus** *n.* (*Biol.*) = KINETOPLAST E20. **kinetoplast** *n.* (*Biol.*) a mass of mitochondrial DNA lying close to a kinetosome in some protozoa, esp. trypanosomes E20. **kinetoscope** *n.* †(*a*) *rare* a sort of moving panorama; (*b*) *Hist.* an early motion-picture device in which the images were viewed through a peephole: M19. **kinetosome** *n.* (*Biol.*) a cytoplasmic structure which forms the base of a cilium or flagellum E20.

kinety /ˈkʌɪnəti/ *n.* M20. [Fr. *cinétie*, f. Gk *kinētikos* KINETIC: see -Y[3].] *Biol.* In ciliates and flagellates, a kinetodesma together with its associated kinetosomes.

kinfolk /ˈkɪnfəʊk/ *n.* Chiefly *N. Amer.* Also **-folks**. L19. [f. KIN *n.* & *a.* + FOLK.] = KINSFOLK.

king /kɪŋ/ *n.* Also (esp. in titles) **K-**. [OE *cyning*, later *cyng*, *cing* = OFris. *kining*, *kon-*, *ken-*, OS, OHG *kuning* (Du. *koning*, G *König*), f. Gmc, prob. f. bases of KIN *n.*, -ING[3].] **1** A male sovereign (esp. hereditary) ruler of an independent State, a male monarch. Also, the head of a region, a tribe, etc., having the status of such a ruler. OE. **b** Any of the kings of Israel and Judah. In *pl.* (treated as *sing.*) (**K-**), each of two (formerly four) books of the Old Testament and Hebrew Scriptures dealing with the history of the kings (also *Book of Kings*). LME. **2** (Usu. **K-**.) God or Christ regarded as omnipotent. Freq. in *King of heaven, of bliss, of glory*, etc. OE. **3** A woman who rules or bears herself like a king, a queen. *rare.* ME. **4** A person pre-eminent in a given sphere or class; *esp.* (preceded by specifying wd) a great merchant, manufacturer, etc., of the thing indicated, a magnate. ME. **5** An animal, plant, fruit, or other thing regarded as supreme or outstandingly excellent in its class. Also (orig. *US*), a thing of outstanding economic importance. LME. **6** †**a** [tr. L *rex*.] A queen bee. LME–E18. **b** A fully developed male termite. L19. **7** In games. **a** *Chess.* The piece which each player must protect against the moves made by the other, so as to prevent it from being finally checkmated. LME. **b** *Cards.* One card in each suit, bearing the representation of a king, ranking immediately above the queen and usu. below the ace (but orig. the highest card in the pack). M16. **c** *Billiards.* An ivory peg formerly placed at one end of the table. *obs.* exc. *Hist.* L17. **d** *Draughts.* A piece with an extra capacity of moving, made by crowning an ordinary piece that has reached the opponent's baseline. E19. **8** Any of certain people holding symbolic or pretended supreme authority; *esp.* the chief player in any of certain children's games (see below). M16. **9** *ellipt.* **a** A toast in which the king's health is drunk. M18. **b** (Usu. **K-**.) The British national anthem in the reign of a male monarch, 'God Save the King'. M20. **10** *techn.* **a** In *pl.* One of the classes into which fullers' teasels are sorted. L18. **b** A kind of salmon-fly for angling. L18.

1 W. S. GILBERT Britain set the world ablaze In good King George's glorious days. W. S. CHURCHILL We have a King and Queen . . at the summit of . . the British nation. 2 H. F. LYTE Praise, my soul, the King of heaven. 4 *Sunday Times* Carlos Lehder Rivas, the reputed Columbian cocaine king. *gold king*, *railway king*, etc. 5 *Times* Cheap coal could still be the energy king.

Phrases & comb.: *Book of Kings*: see sense 1b above. *divine right of kings*: see DIVINE *a.* 2. **King Alfred daffodil** a commonly grown yellow trumpet daffodil. **king and country**: the objects of allegiance for a patriot whose head of State is a king. **King-at-Arms** = *King of Arms* below. **kingbolt** a main or large bolt in a mechanical structure; *esp.* (*a*) an iron rod in a roof, used instead of a king-post; (*b*) a vertical bolt passing through the axle of a horse-drawn carriage or railway coach and forming a pivot on which the axle swings in taking curves. **King Caesar** an old children's game in which two sets of players run between opposite bases and another player tries to catch them. **king-carp** a variety of the common carp, *Cyprinus carpio*, covered with uniform scales. **King Charles** = *King Charles's spaniel* below. **King Charles's head** [the obsession of Mr Dick in Dickens's *David Copperfield*] an obsession, an *idée fixe*. **King Charles's spaniel** a small black-and-tan breed of spaniel; a dog of this breed. **king cobra** a large, venomous, hooded Indian snake, *Ophiophagus hannah*; also called *hamadryad*. **King Country** *NZ* an extensive region in the North Island of New Zealand, formerly allotted to the Maoris under a king. **king crab** (*a*) = HORSESHOE *crab*; (*b*) any of various very large crabs of the family Lithodidae, which resemble the spider crabs and are found in cold waters of the N. Pacific. **kingcup** (*a*) the marsh marigold, *Caltha palustris*; (*b*) *dial.* any of several buttercups found in meadows. **king-devil** *US* a European hawkweed, *Hieracium praealtum*, a troublesome weed in parts of N. America. **King Edward** (**VII potato**) an oval variety of potato with a white skin mottled with red. *king-*EIDER. **king fern** *NZ* a large fern, *Marattia salicina*, with fronds up to 4.5 metres long. **king-hit** *n.* & *v.* (*Austral. slang*) (*a*) *n.* a knockout blow, a hard punch; a hard fighter, a bully, a leader; (*b*) *v.t.* punch hard, knock out. **king-hunter** any of various African and Australian kingfishers which do not feed on fish. **King James Bible** or **Version** the Authorized Version of the Bible (1611). **King Log** [with ref. to the fable of Jupiter and the frogs] a ruler going to an extreme of laissez-faire (cf. *King Stork* below). **king lory** = *king parrot* below. **king mackerel** a game-fish of the American Atlantic coast, *Scomberomorus cavalla*; also called *Spanish mackerel*, *kingfish*. **kingmaker** a person who controls the appointment of kings or (*transf.*) other people of authority through his or her political influence; *spec.* an epithet of Richard Neville, Earl of Warwick, in the reigns of Henry VI and Edward IV. **king-nut** *US* a kind of hickory, *Carya laciniosa*, with a large nut. **King of Arms** (the title of) each of three chief heralds of the College of Arms, viz. Garter, Norroy and Ulster, Clarenceux (see also LYON *King of Arms*). **king of beasts** the lion. **king of birds** the eagle. **king of kings** *rhet.* (*a*) a king who has lesser kings under him (esp. as a title adopted by oriental rulers); (*b*) God. **king of terrors** death personified. **King of the Castle** a children's game involving dislodging a player from a mound. **king of the herrings** any of various fishes popularly supposed to lead shoals of herring, *esp.* the oarfish, *Regalecus glesne*. *King of the Romans*: see ROMAN *n.*[1] *king of the vultures*: see VULTURE *n.* *king or* KAISER. **king parrot** any of various small Australasian parrots of the genus *Alisterus*. **king penguin** a large penguin, *Aptenodytes patagonica*, of the Falklands and other Antarctic islands. **king-post** *Carpentry* an upright post in the centre of a roof-truss, extending from the ridge to the tie-beam. **king prawn** any of several large prawns of the genus *Penaeus*, obtained esp. in Australian waters. **king rail** a large rail, *Rallus elegans*, of freshwater marshes in eastern N. America. *king* ROOIBEKKIE. **king salmon** the Chinook salmon, *Oncorhynchus tshawytscha*. *King's Attorney*: see ATTORNEY *n.* 2. **king's bad bargain** *Naut.* a lazy or incompetent sailor. **King's Bench** (*a*) see BENCH *n.* 3b; (*b*) (in full *King's Bench prison*) a former prison for debtors and criminals jailed by the supreme courts at Westminster etc. **king's bishop, knight, rook** *Chess* the bishop etc. on the king's side of the board at the start of a game. **king's blue** cobalt blue. *king's bounty*: see BOUNTY 4. *King's Champion*: see CHAMPION *n.*[1] *King's Counsel*: see COUNSEL *n.* 7b. **king's cushion** *Sc.* a seat made by the crossed hands of two people. *king's evil*: see EVIL *n.*[1] 5b. **King's Friends** *Hist.* a political party (*c* 1760–80) which sought to increase the power of the Crown in order to maintain political stability. **king's gambit** *Chess*: in which a sacrifice of the king's bishop's pawn is offered. *King's Guide*: see GUIDE *n.* 1c. **king's hard bargain** *Naut.* = *king's bad bargain* above. *King's highway*: see HIGHWAY 1. **king's-hood** *Sc.* the reticulum or second stomach of a ruminant. **king-side** *n.* & *a.* (*Chess*) (*a*) *n.* = *king's side* below; (*b*) *adj.* made or done on the king's side of the board; (of a piece) situated on that side. **king-size** *a.* & *n.* (*a*) *adj.* (esp. of a cigarette) of a size larger than normal; (*b*) *n.* a king-size cigarette. **king-sized** *a.* = *king-size adj.* above. *king's knight*: see *king's bishop* above. *King's messenger*: see MESSENGER *n.* **king-snake** any of various large N. American colubrid snakes of the genus *Lampropeltis*, which prey on other snakes. **king's pawn** *Chess* the pawn immediately in front of the king at the start of a game; *king's pawn opening*: in which White begins by advancing the king's pawn two squares. *king's peace*: see PEACE *n.* **king's peg** a mixture of brandy and champagne. *King's Proctor*: see PROCTOR *n.* 3. *King's quarantain*: see QUARANTAIN 1. **king's ransom** a very large sum of money. *King's Remembrancer*: see REMEMBRANCER 1a. *king's rook*: see *king's bishop* above. **King's Scholar** a scholar in a school founded by royal charter (esp. Eton College). *King's Scout*: see SCOUT *n.*[3] **king's ship** *Hist.* (*a*) a ship of the fleet provided and maintained out of royal revenue, a ship of the royal navy; (*b*) a warship equipped at public expense. **king's side** *Chess* the half of the board on which both kings stand at the start of a game. **king's silver** *Hist.* money paid in the Court of Common Pleas for licence to levy a fine. **king's spear** any of several tall plants of the lily family, esp. *Asphodeline lutea*, with dense racemes of yellow flowers. **King Stork** [see *King Log* above] a ruler going to an extreme of active oppression. *king's truce*: see TRUCE *n.* **king's yellow** orpiment or yellow arsenic used as a pigment. **king vulture** a neotropical vulture, *Sarcorhamphus papa*, having a brightly coloured head. **King William's cravat** a cravat of the kind worn by King William III (1689–1702). **King Willow** the game of cricket personified (cf. WILLOW *n.* 5). **kingwood** any of several tropical woods used in marquetry, esp. those of *Dalbergia cearensis* (family Leguminosae) and *Astronium fraxinifolium* (family Anacardiaceae). LYON *King of Arms*. *Pearly King*: see PEARLY *a.* *silver king*: see SILVER *n.* & *a.* *take the King's* SHILLING. *the king over the water*: see WATER *n.* *the King's colour*: see COLOUR *n.* 7. *the King's English*: see ENGLISH *a.* & *n.* *the kings of Cologne*: see *the three kings* below. *the King's peace*: see PEACE *n.* *the King's Serjeant*: see SERGEANT. *the King's speech*: see SPEECH *n.* *the sport of kings*: see SPORT *n.* **the three kings** three wise men or Magi (*Matt.* 2:1–12); also *the (three) kings of Cologne* [because their bodies were believed to be preserved at that city]. *turn King's evidence*: see EVIDENCE *n.*

kinghood *n.* kingship; the rank, authority, or office of king; kingly spirit or character: LME. **kingless** *a.* ME. **kinglessness** *n.* M19. **kinglike** *a.* & *adv.* (*a*) *adj.* resembling, characteristic of, or befitting a king; kingly, regal; (*b*) *adv.* like a king, in a manner befitting a king: LME. **kingling** *n.* (freq. *derog.*) a petty king L16.

king /kɪŋ/ *v.* LME. [f. the n.] 1 *v.i.* & *t.* (w. *it*). Act the part of a king; rule, govern. LME. 2 *v.t.* Make (a person) into a king. L16. 3 *v.t.* Rule over (a country) as king. *rare*. L16.

1 *Times* Matchan kinged over his 165-acres domain. 3 SHAKES. *Hen. V* She is so idly king'd, Her sceptre so fantastically borne.

kingbird /ˈkɪŋbəːd/ *n.* Also **king bird**. M18. [f. KING *n.* + BIRD *n.*] †1 A darling. *N. Amer. rare*. M–L18. 2 Any of several N. American tyrant flycatchers of the genus *Tyrannus*. L18. 3 A bird of paradise, *Cicinnurus regius*. Now usu. *king bird of paradise*. L18. 4 A royal bird; an eagle. *poet.* M19.

kingcraft /ˈkɪŋkrɑːft/ *n.* M17. [f. KING *n.* + CRAFT *n.*] The art of ruling as a king, esp. in the use of clever or crafty tactics in dealing with subjects.

kingdom /ˈkɪŋdəm/ *n.* & *v.* [OE *cyningdōm* = OS *kuningdōm*, ON *konungdómr*, f. Gmc bases of KING *n.*, -DOM.] **A** *n.* †1 Kingly function, authority, or power; sovereignty, kingship. OE–L17. 2 An organized community having a king as its head; a monarchical State or government. ME. 3 The territory or country subject to a king; the area over which a monarch's rule extends; a realm. ME. **b** *The* Scottish local government area (formerly county) of Fife, which was one of the seven Pictish kingdoms. E18. 4 *transf.* & *fig.* a More fully *the kingdom of God* or *of heaven*. The spiritual sovereignty of God or Christ, or the sphere over which this extends, in heaven or on earth. ME. **b** The spiritual rule or realm of evil or infernal powers. ME. **c** A realm or sphere in which a condition or quality is supreme. LME. **d** Any sphere in which one has dominion like that of a king. Esp. in *come into one's kingdom* [cf. *Luke* 23:42], acquire power, attractiveness, etc. L16. **e** Anything compared to a country ruled by a king; a domain. L16. 5 A province of nature; *esp.* each of the three traditional divisions (animal, vegetable, and mineral) into which natural objects have been classified; *Biol.* the highest category in most systems of taxonomic classification. L17.

1 SHAKES. *Rich. III* Else my kingdom stands on brittle glass. 2 BURKE The opinion that all the kingdoms of Europe were at a remote period elective. *Middle Kingdom*: see MIDDLE *a.* *New Kingdom*: see NEW *a.* *Old Kingdom*: see OLD *a.* *United Kingdom*: see UNITED *a.* 4a *Christadelphian* We . . pray that we may be able to help one another . . towards the Kingdom. **kingdom come** [f. *thy kingdom come* in the Lord's Prayer] (*a*) *colloq.* the next world, eternity; *till kingdom come*, for an indefinitely long period; (*b*) the millennial kingdom of Christ. **c** V. S. PRITCHETT The kingdoms of fantasy and mirth are long-lasting and not of this world. **d** S. T. FELSTEAD Towards the end of the 'eighties, the music-hall had come into its kingdom.

B *v.t.* †1 With *it*: pose as a kingdom. *rare*. Only in E17. 2 Take possession of, as a kingdom. L19.

kingdomed *a.* (*a*) provided with or constituted as a kingdom; (*b*) (as 2nd elem. of comb.) divided into (so many) kingdoms: E17.

kingfish /ˈkɪŋfɪʃ/ *n.* Pl. **-es** /-ɪz/, (usu.) same. M18. [f. KING *n.* + FISH *n.*[1]] 1 Any of various fishes notable for their size, appearance, or value as food; *esp.* (*a*) the opah, *Lampris guttatus*; (*b*) = YELLOWTAIL *kingfish*; (*c*) = *king mackerel* s.v. KING *n.*; (*d*) a barb (*Menticirrhus*); (*e*) the barracouta, *Thyrsites atun*; (*f*) a trevally of the genus *Caranx*. M18. 2 A leader, a boss. Freq. as a nickname. *US slang*. M20.

kingfisher /ˈkɪŋfɪʃə/ *n.* & *a.* Also (earlier) **†king's-fisher**. ME. [f. KING *n.* + FISHER.] **A** *n.* 1 A small European bird, *Alcedo atthis*, with a long beak and brilliant blue and orange plumage, feeding on fish and aquatic animals which it captures by diving; any bird of the family Alcedinidae, most members of which feed in this manner. ME. 2 = *kingfisher blue* below. E20.

1 *malachite kingfisher, pied kingfisher*, etc.

Comb. **kingfisher blue** (of) a brilliant blue colour.

B *adj.* Of kingfisher blue. M20.

Kingite /ˈkɪŋʌɪt/ *n.* & *a.* M19. [f. KING *n.* + -ITE[1].] *NZ Hist.* **A** *n.* A follower of the Maori king, to whom the King Country was allotted. M19. **B** *attrib.* or as *adj.* Of or pertaining to the Kingites. L19.

kingklip /ˈkɪŋklɪp/ *n.* *S. Afr.* E19. [Afk. f. Du. *koningklipvisch*, f. *koning* king + *klipvisch* KLIPFISH.] More fully *kingklipfish*. Any of various edible serranid marine fishes, esp. *Epinephelus andersoni*.

King Kong /kɪŋ ˈkɒŋ/ *n.* M20. [An apelike monster in the film of that name.] (A nickname for) a person of outstanding size or strength.

kinglet /ˈkɪŋlɪt/ *n.* E17. [f. KING *n.* + -LET.] 1 A petty king; a king ruling over a small territory. Usu. *derog.* E17. 2 Any of several tiny birds of the genus *Regulus*; esp. *R. satrapa* and *R. calendula*, of N. America, and (formerly) the goldcrest, *R. regulus*. M19.

¶The birds (sense 2) are usu. included in the warbler family, Sylviidae, but sometimes assigned to a distinct family Regulidae.

kingly /ˈkɪŋli/ *a.* & *adv.* LME. [f. KING *n.* + -LY[1].] **A** *adj.* 1 Of the rank or nature of a king or kings. LME. 2 Of or belonging to a king; held, exercised, or issued by a king. LME. **b** Of government: monarchical. M17. 3 Having the character or quality of a king; kinglike, majestic. LME.

1 E. PEYTON The Divine Catastrophe of the Kingly Family of the House of Stuarts. 2 B. EMECHETA His kingly eyes shone and his was the voice of authority. *New Yorker* President Reagan . . held sway over the American political scene with an almost kingly authority. 3 DRYDEN A generous, laudable, and kingly pride.

B *adv.* In a kingly manner; royally, regally. LME.

J. CLEVELAND This Way he could not but dye Kingly, at least, like a Gentleman.

kingliness *n.* L15.

kingpin /ˈkɪŋpɪn/ *n.* E19. [f. KING *n.* + PIN *n.*] †1 The tallest (central) pin in the game of kayles. Only in E19. 2 = *kingbolt* s.v. KING *n.* Freq. (*fig.*), a thing holding together a complex system or arrangement; the most important person in a party, organization, etc. M19.

2 *Daily Telegraph* The owner of three shops was the kingpin behind a wholesale shoplifting plot.

†king's-fisher *n.* see KINGFISHER.

kingship /ˈkɪŋʃɪp/ *n.* ME. [f. KING *n.* + -SHIP.] 1 The office of king; the fact of being king; reign as a king. ME. 2 The rule of a king; monarchical government. M17. 3 With possess. adj. as *his* etc. *kingship*: his etc. majesty. M17. 4 The territory of a king, a kingdom. M19.

kingsman /ˈkɪŋzmən/ *n.* Pl. **-men**. Also **king's man**, pl. **men** /mɛn/; **K-**. E17. [f. KING *n.* + -'s[1] + MAN *n.*] I *Hist.* 1 *the King's Men*, a company of actors under the patronage of James I. E17. 2 A partisan of the king; a royalist. M17. 3 A person who supported the British cause at the time of the American Revolution. *US*. L18. 4 A customs officer. E19. II 5 A member of King's College, Cambridge. E19.

kingston /ˈkɪŋst(ə)n/ *n.* *obs.* exc. *local*. M17. [Origin unkn.] The monkfish, *Squatina squatina*.

Kingston valve /ˈkɪŋst(ə)n valv/ *n. phr.* M19. [John *Kingston*, 19th-cent. Brit. dockyard foreman, its inventor.] *Naut.* A kind of conical valve for closing an orifice in a ship's side below the water-line, opening outwards with a screwing action.

kingy /ˈkɪŋi/ *n.* M20. [f. KING *n.* + -Y[6].] A children's chasing game played with a ball, the winner being declared 'king'.

†kinic *a.* var. of QUINIC.

kinin /ˈkʌɪnɪn/ *n.* M20. [f. Gk *kinein* set in motion + -IN[1]. In sense 1 after BRADYKININ.] *Biochem.* 1 Any of a group of low molecular-weight peptides formed in body tissue in response to injury, which have local effects including pain and vasodilation. M20. 2 Any of a class of compounds that (with auxins) control plant growth and development. Also called *cytokinin*. M20.

kiˈninogen *n.* a biologically inactive precursor of a kinin (sense 1) M20.

kinjal /kɪnˈdʒɑːl/ *n.* M19. [Caucasian Turkic (= Russ. *kinzhal*) f. as KHANJAR.] In the Caucasus, Kurdistan, etc.: a dagger.

kink /kɪŋk/ *n.*[1] *Sc.* & *north*. Also (earlier) **ch-** /tʃ-/. ME. [f. KINK *v.*[1]] A fit of laughter or coughing that catches the breath. Formerly also, whooping-cough.

kink /kɪŋk/ *n.*[2] L17. [(M)LG *kinke* (Du. *kink*) f. base meaning 'bend': cf. Icel. (ON) *kikna* bend at the knees.] 1 A short twist in a rope, thread, wire, etc., where it is bent back on itself, *esp.* one stiff enough to cause obstruction (orig. *Naut.*); a tight wave in human or animal hair. Also (*transf.*), a crick in the neck. L17. **b** A sudden bend in a line, course, etc., that is otherwise straight or smoothly curved. L19. 2 *fig.* **a** A mental twist or quirk. Now chiefly, a bizarre sexual practice or preference. E19. **b** A clever idea for or method of doing something. Chiefly *US*. E19. 3 A person who has bizarre sexual tastes or is given to bizarre sexual practices; *loosely* an eccentric. Orig. *US*. M20.

1 *Hairdo Ideas* A special planning technique that takes the kink out of curls. 2a T. JEFFERSON Adair . . had his kink He believed . . the Indians of America to be descended from the Jews. R. DAVIES You know that homosexuality is an O.K. kink nowadays. 3 *Independent* He was a bit of a kink He liked to be caned.

kinkless *a.* without a kink; *spec.* (*Electronics*) (of a tetrode) designed so as to have a smooth characteristic curve: M20.

kink /kɪŋk/ *v.*[1]*i. Sc. & north.* Also (earlier) **ch-** /tʃ-/. [OE *cincian*, app. a nasalized var. of Gmc base repr. by MHG *kīchen* to gasp: cf. KINKCOUGH.] Gasp convulsively for breath in a fit of coughing (esp. whooping-cough) or laughing.

kink /kɪŋk/ *v.*[2] L17. [Prob. f. Du. *kinken*, f. as KINK *n.*[2]] **1** *v.i.* Form a kink; (of a rope etc.) twist or curl stiffly, esp. at one point, so as to catch or get entangled; (of something straight) take a sudden backward bend. L17. **2** *v.t.* Cause to kink, twist stiffly; make kinky. Usu. in *pass.* E19.

1 W. GOLDING The river kinks violently in a right angle then gets back on course again. 2 *Punch* The sinister kinked logic governing the behaviour of the characters. A. S. BYATT A middle-aged man with . . long, kinked, greasy fringes of hair.

kinkajou /ˈkɪŋkədʒuː/ *n.* L18. [Fr. *quincajou*, alt. of Fr. CARCAJOU Ojibwa *kwi:nkwaˀa:ke:* wolverine. Cf. QUICKHATCH.] A fruit-eating arboreal Central and S. American mammal, *Potos flavus*, related to the racoon, with a prehensile tail.

kinkcough /ˈkɪŋk-kɒf/ *n. Sc. & north.* Also **ch-** /tʃ-/. LME. [f. KINK *v.*[1] + COUGH *n.*] Whooping-cough.

kinkey *a.* & *n.* var. of KINKY.

kinkhost /ˈkɪŋkhɒst/ *n. obs.* exc. *Sc.* ME. [f. KINK *v.*[1] + HOAST *n.*, perh. through MLG *kinkhōste.*] = KINKCOUGH.

kinkle /ˈkɪŋk(ə)l/ *n.* M19. [f. KINK *n.*[2] + -LE[1].] A slight kink or twist.

kinkled *a.* having kinkles or kinks; (of hair) frizzed: L19.

kinky /ˈkɪŋki/ *a.* & *n.* Also **-ey**. M19. [f. KINK *n.*[2] + -Y[1].] A *adj.* **1** Having kinks or twists; (of hair) tightly curled. M19. **2** *fig.* **a** Strange, eccentric. *colloq.* L19. **b** Of property: dishonestly come by. *Criminals' slang.* E20. **c** Having or marked by bizarre sexual tastes or practices; (of clothing etc.) suggestive of bizarre sexual tastes. *colloq.* M20.

1 M. ANGELOU My real hair . . would take the place of the kinky mass . . Momma wouldn't let me straighten. 2a E. M. FORSTER This jaundiced young philosopher, with his kinky view of life, was too much for him. c *Listener* One of the girls—a buxom specimen in kinky patent leathers. F. WARNER Kinky sex makes them feel inadequate. *Chicago Sun* The impression that these lascivious men are all *child porn, kinky weirdos*.

B *n.* **1** A person with kinky hair. *colloq.* Usu. *derog.* E20. **2** An object dishonestly obtained. *Criminals' slang.* E20. **3** A person with bizarre sexual tastes. *colloq.* M20.

kinkily *adv.* M20. **kinkiness** *n.* E20.

kinless /ˈkɪnlɪs/ *a.* M17. [f. KIN *n.* + -LESS.] Having no relatives or kindred.

kinnikinnick /ˌkɪnɪkɪˈnɪk/ *n.* Also **killi-** /ˌkɪlɪ-/, **-kinik**, & other vars. L18. [Delaware (Unami) *kələk:əni:k:an* admixture.] **1** A mixture used by N. American Indians as a substitute for tobacco or for mixing with it, usu. consisting of dried sumac leaves and the inner bark of dogwood or willow. L18. **2** Any of the various plants used for this, *esp.* bearberry, *Arctostaphylos uva-ursi.* E19.

kino /ˈkiːnəʊ/ *n.* Pl. **-os**. L18. [App. f. a W. Afr. lang.] The astringent gum of certain tropical trees and other plants, used locally in medicine, tanning, etc.; orig. (in full *African kino* or GAMBIA KINO) that of a W. African leguminous tree, *Pterocarpus erinaceus*, now esp. (in full *East Indian* or *Malabar kino*) that of a related tree of India and Sri Lanka (Ceylon), *P. marsupium.* Also, any of the trees or plants which yield this gum.

Bengal kino (the gum of) the dhak tree, *Butea monosperma.* **Jamaican kino** (the gum of) the sea-grape, *Coccoloba uvifera.*

kino- /ˈkʌɪnəʊ/ *comb. form* of Gk *kinein* set in motion: see -O-.

kinoˈcilium *n.*, pl. **-cilia**, *Biol.* a cilium which is capable of moving; *spec.* one borne singly on each hair-cell of the maculae of the inner ear amid many stereocilia: M20. **kinoplasm** *n.* (*Biol.*) a supposed kind of fibrillar cytoplasm formerly held to give rise to the active parts of a cell (e.g. the membrane and mitotic apparatus) L19.

†**kinone** *n.* var. of QUINONE.

†**kinovic** *a.* var. of QUINOVIC.

-kins /kɪnz/ *suff.* [Extension of -KIN.] Forming dim. ns. expr. endearment, as *babykins, boykins.* Formerly also in certain oaths, as *bodikins.*

kinsfolk /ˈkɪnzfəʊk/ *n.pl.* Also (now *rare*) **-folks**. LME. [f. KIN *n.* + -'S[1] + FOLK.] The people to whom one is related by blood (or by marriage); (one's) relatives. Cf. KINFOLK, KINSPEOPLE.

kinship /ˈkɪnʃɪp/ *n.* M19. [f. KIN *n.* + -SHIP.] **1 a** Blood relationship. M19. **b** *Anthropol.* The recognized ties of relationship (by descent, marriage, etc.) forming the basis of social organization in a culture. M19. **2** Similarity of characteristics or origins; (an) affinity. L19.

1a A. J. P. TAYLOR Their father . . claimed kinship with the Thompsons. 2 P. V. WHITE No evidence of intellectual kinship in any of her small circle of acquaintance. M. FITZHERBERT He felt a kinship with the despised Christians.

Comb.: **kinship group** *Anthropol.* a unit of social organization based on kinship.

kinsman /ˈkɪnzmən/ *n.* Pl. **-men**. LOE. [f. KIN *n.* + -'S[1] + MAN *n.*] A man of one's own kin; an adult male relative; in *pl.* also, kinsfolk.

kinsmanly *a.* appropriate to or characteristic of a kinsman M19. **kinsmanship** *n.* M19.

kinspeople /ˈkɪnzpiːp(ə)l/ *n.pl. US.* L18. [f. KIN *n.* + -'S[1] + PEOPLE *n.*] = KINSFOLK.

kinswoman /ˈkɪnzwʊmən/ *n.* Pl. **-women** /-wɪmɪn/. ME. [f. KIN *n.* + -'S[1] + WOMAN *n.*] A woman of one's own kin; an adult female relative.

†**kintal** *n.* var. of QUINTAL.

kinzigite /ˈkɪntsɪgʌɪt/ *n.* L19. [f. *Kinzig*, a valley in Germany + -ITE[1].] *Geol.* A metamorphic schistose rock containing garnet, biotite, and varying amounts of quartz, plagioclase, sillimanite, and cordierite.

Kioko /kɪˈəʊkəʊ/ *n.* & *a.* Pl. of n. same, **-os**. L19. [Bantu.] Of or pertaining to, a member of, an African people inhabiting Zaire and Angola; (of) the Bantu language of this people.

kiore /kɪˈɔːreɪ/ *n.* M19. [Maori.] = POLYNESIAN *rat.* Also *kiore rat.*

kiosk /ˈkiːɒsk/ *n.* E17. [Fr. *kiosque* f. Turk. *köşk* f. Pers. *kušk* pavilion.] **1** An open pavilion or summer-house of light construction, often supported by pillars and having a balustrade, in Turkey, Iran, etc. E17. **2** A similar structure used as a shelter or bandstand in gardens and parks elsewhere. M19. **3** A light, often movable, booth from which newspapers, refreshments, cigarettes, tickets, etc., are sold. Also (*Austral.*), a building in which refreshments are served in a park, zoo, etc. M19. **4** More fully *telephone kiosk.* A booth or box in which a public telephone is installed. E20.

Kiowa /ˈkʌɪəwə/ *n.* & *a.* E19. [Amer. Sp. *Caygua* f. Kiowa *kɔ̀ygú* (pl.).] A *n.* Pl. **-s**, same. **1** A member of an Indian people of the southern plains of the US. E19. **2** The language of this people. M19.

B *attrib.* or as *adj.* Of or pertaining to the Kiowa or their language. E19.

Kiowa Apache (a member of) an Athapaskan people associated with the Kiowa; the language of this people.

kip /kɪp/ *n.*[1] LME. [Origin uncertain: perh. rel to MDu. *kip, kijp* pack or bundle (of hides).] The hide of young or small sheep or cattle as used for leather; a set or bundle of such hides, containing a specific number (usu. 30 or 50).

kip /kɪp/ *n.*[2] L16. [Origin uncertain: cf. LG *Kippe* point, peak, tip.] **1** The sharp point of a hill; a jutting outcrop of rock; something pointed or beaked; *spec.* the hooked tip of the lower jaw of a breeding male salmon (cf. KIPPER *n.*[1] 1, KYPE). *Sc.* L16. **2** *Gymnastics.* A basic movement in which the body is rapidly straightened from an inverted pike position by pushing the hips forward and the legs back. *US.* E20.

kip /kɪp/ *n.*[3] *slang.* M18. [Origin uncertain: cf. Da. *kippe* hovel, tavern, *horekippe* brothel.] **1** A brothel. M18. **2** A cheap lodging-house, a doss-house; a lodging, a bed. L19. **3** A sleep, a nap; the action of sleeping. L19.

Comb.: **kip house** a cheap lodging-house, a doss-house; **kip-shop** a doss-house; a brothel.

kip /kɪp/ *n.*[4] *Austral. & NZ.* L19. [Origin uncertain: cf. KIPPEEN.] A small piece of wood from which coins are spun in the game of two-up.

kip /kɪp/ *n.*[5] Orig. *US.* E20. [Prob. f. KI(LO- + P(OUND *n.*[1]] *Engin.* A unit of force equal to a weight of 1,000 lb (approx. 453.6 kg), used in expressing loads.

kip /kɪp/ *n.*[6] Pl. same, **-s**. M20. [Thai.] The basic monetary unit of Laos, equal to 100 ats.

kip /kɪp/ *v.*[1]*i. slang.* Infl. **-pp-**. L19. [f. KIP *n.*[3]] Go to bed, sleep; lie or settle *down* to sleep.

K. AMIS I . . kipped for a spell in the library. Nobody ever disturbed you there. M. FORSTER He could never live in one place for long, preferring to kip down where he found himself.

kip /kɪp/ *v.*[2]*i. US.* Infl. **-pp-**. E20. [f. KIP *n.*[2]] *Gymnastics.* Perform a kip.

kipa(h) *n.* var. of KIPPA.

Kipchak /kɪpˈtʃɑːk/ *n.* & *a.* Pl. of n. same, **-s**. E19. [Russ. f. Turk. *Kıpçak.*] Of or pertaining to, a member of, a Turkic people (now extinct) of central Asia and the region north of the Caucasus (also called *Cumans, Polovtsy*) or *loosely* any of various nomadic Turkic-speaking peoples of these areas; (of) the language of the original Kipchak (also called *Cuman*); (designating or pertaining to) the north-western group of Turkic languages and dialects.

Kiplingese /kɪplɪŋˈiːz/ *n.* L19. [f. *Kipling* (see below) + -ESE.] The literary style and characteristics of the writer Rudyard Kipling (1865–1936).

Kiplingesque *a.* resembling Kipling in style L19. **Kiplingesquely** *adv.* M20. **ˈKiplingism** *n.* views or style of expression characteristic of Kipling L19. **ˈKiplingite** *n.* & *a.* (*a*) *n.* an admirer or student of Kipling or his work; (*b*) *adj.* characteristic of Kipling: L19. **ˈKiplingize** *v.t.* make like Kipling E20.

kippa /kɪˈpɑː/ *n.* Also ***kipa(h)***, ***kippah***. M20. [mod.Heb. *kippāh.*] A skullcap, usu. of crocheted thread, worn by Orthodox male Jews.

kippage /ˈkɪpɪdʒ/ *n. Sc.* M16. [Aphet. f. Fr. *équipage* EQUIPAGE *n.*] **1** The crew of a ship. Cf. EQUIPAGE *n.* 1. *obs.* exc. *Hist.* M16. **2** Disorder, confusion; a state of excitement or irritation. E19.

kippah *n.* var. of KIPPA.

kippeen /kɪˈpiːn/ *n. Anglo-Ir.* Also **kippin** /ˈkɪpɪn/. M19. [Ir. *cipin*: cf. Gael. *cipean* stump, peg, stick or dibble for planting.] A stick or dibble used for planting; a short thin stick.

kipper /ˈkɪpə/ *n.*[1] & *a.*[1] [OE *cypera*, used once w. *leax* salmon (LAX *n.*[1]) = OS *kupiro*, perh. conn. w. COPPER *n.*[1] & *a.*, f. the colour of the male salmon.] A *n.* **1** A male salmon or sea trout during the breeding season. Cf. KIP *n.*[2] 1, SHEDDER *n.* OE. **2** A kippered fish, now esp. a herring. ME. **3 a** A person, *esp.* a young or small person, a child. *slang.* E20. **b** An English person, *spec.* an immigrant in Australia. *Austral. slang.* M20. **4** A torpedo. Cf. FISH *n.*[1] 1b. *Naut. slang.* M20.

Comb.: **kipper tie** a brightly coloured and very wide necktie.

†B *adj.* Designating or characteristic of a male salmon or sea trout at the breeding season; unhealthy, thin. LME–E19.

kipper /ˈkɪpə/ *n.*[2] *Austral.* M19. [Aborig.] A young Aboriginal male who has been initiated and is admitted to the rights of manhood.

kipper /ˈkɪpə/ *a.*[2] *north.* L17. [Perh. symbolic. See also CHIPPER *a.*] Nimble; lively; cheerful; eager.

kipper /ˈkɪpə/ *v.t.* L18. [f. KIPPER *n.*[1]] Cure (herring etc.) by splitting open, salting, and drying in the open air or in smoke.

fig.: P. LIVELY His white moustache was kippered a delicate tan on the right hand side.

kipperer *n.* E20.

kipper-nut /ˈkɪpənʌt/ *n.* L16. [f. unkn. 1st elem. + NUT *n.*] The pignut, *Conopodium majus.*

kippersol *n.* var. of KIEPERSOL.

kippin *n.* var. of KIPPEEN.

Kipp's apparatus /ˈkɪps apəˈreɪtəs/ *n. phr.* L19. [P. J. *Kipp* (1808–64), Ger. chemist.] *Chem.* An apparatus for the controlled generation of a gas (esp. hydrogen sulphide) by the action of a liquid on a solid at room temperature, consisting of three glass bulbs in which the pressure of evolved gas is balanced against a head of liquid.

kipsie /ˈkɪpsi/ *n. Austral. slang.* Also **-sy**. E20. [f. KIP *n.*[3] + -SY.] A house, a home; a shelter, a lean-to.

Kipsigis /ˈkɪpsɪgɪs/ *n.* & *a.* M20. [Kipsigis.] A *n.* Pl. same. 1 A member of a people inhabiting western Kenya. M20. 2 The Nilotic language of this people. M20. B *attrib.* or as *adj.* Of or pertaining to the Kipsigis or their language. M20.

kipsy *n.* var. of KIPSIE.

Kir /kɪə, kəː/ *n.* Also **k-**. M20. [Canon Félix *Kir* (1876–1968), mayor of Dijon in France, who is said to have invented the recipe.] (Proprietary name for) a drink made from dry white wine and cassis.

†kirb *n.* & *v.* var. of KERB.

Kirby /ˈkəːbi/ *n.* E19. [Charles *Kirby*, 17th-cent. English fish-hook maker.] Used *attrib.* and (formerly) in *possess.* to designate a design of fish-hook originated by Kirby.

kirby-grip /ˈkəːbɪgrɪp/ *n.* Also (proprietary) **Kirbigrip**. E20. [f. *Kirby*, Beard & Co. Ltd., orig. manufacturers + GRIP *n.*[1]] A type of sprung hairgrip.

Kirchhoff's law /ˈkɪətʃɒfs lɔː, *foreign* ˈkɪrxhɔfs/ *n.* M19. [G. R. *Kirchhoff* (1824–87), Ger. physicist.] 1 *Electr.* Either of two laws concerning electric networks in which steady currents are flowing: (*a*) (*Kirchhoff's first law*) that the algebraic sum of the currents in all the conductors that meet in a point is zero; (*b*) (*Kirchhoff's second law*) that the algebraic sum of the products of current and resistance in each part of any closed path in a network is equal to the algebraic sum of the electromotive forces in the path. M19. 2 *Physics.* The law that the absorptivity of a body for radiant energy of any particular wavelength is equal to its emissivity at the same temperature for the same wavelength. E20.

Kirghiz /kɪəˈgiːz, ˈkəːgɪz/ *n.* & *a.* Also **Kirgiz**, **-s**. E17. [Russ. *Kirgiz* f. Turk. *Kırğız*.] A *n.* Pl. same, **-es** /-ɪz/. 1 A member of a widespread people of west central Asia, now chiefly inhabiting Kyrgyzstan. E17. 2 The Turkic language of this people. L19.
B *attrib.* or as *adj.* Of or pertaining to the Kirghiz or their language. M19.
Kirghiz pheasant = MONGOLIAN *pheasant*.
¶ See also KARA-KIRGHIZ.

kiri /ˈkɪəri/ *n.* E18. [Jap.] A Chinese tree, *Paulownia tomentosa* (also *kiri tree*); the wood of this tree, esp. as used for cabinet-work in Japan.

kirin /ˈkɪərɪn/ *n.* Also *K-*. E18. [Jap. f. as KYLIN.] A mythical beast of composite form resembling a unicorn, freq. portrayed in Japanese pottery and art.

Kiriwinian /kɪrɪˈvɪnɪən/ *n.* & *a.* E20. [f. *Kiriwina* (see below) + -IAN.] A *n.* A native or inhabitant of Kiriwina, the largest of the Trobriand Islands. E20. B *adj.* Of or pertaining to Kiriwina. E20.

kirk /kəːk/ *n.* & *v. Sc.* & *north.* In sense 2 also **K-**. ME. [ON *kirkja* f. OE *ċir(i)ċe* CHURCH *n.*] A *n.* 1 = CHURCH *n.* ME. 2 *The* Church of Scotland as opp. to the Church of England or the Episcopal Church in Scotland. M16.
1 M. LEITCH The sound of hymn-singing .. coming from a kirk somewhere in his own country.
Phrases: **Free Kirk** the Free Church of Scotland. **Kirk of Scotland** *Hist.* the Church of Scotland. *the Wee Free Kirk*: see WEE *a.*
Comb.: **kirk-assembly** the assembly of the Church of Scotland; **kirkman** a clergyman; a member of the Church of Scotland; **kirk-master** (now *north.*) a churchwarden; *kirk-session*: see SESSION *n.*; **kirk-town** *Sc.* (*a*) the village, hamlet, or (area of) town in which a parish church is situated; (*b*) = GLEBE 2b; **kirkyard** *Sc.* a churchyard.
B *v.t.* = CHURCH *v.* 1. Now *Sc.* LME.
kirkless *a.* (*Sc.*) = CHURCHLESS E19. **kirkward**(s) *adv.* = CHURCHWARDS LME.

kirkin-head /ˈkəːkɪnhɛd/ *n.* E18. [App. f. arbitrary alt. of prec. + HEAD *n.*] *Archit.* = JERKIN-HEAD.

Kirlian /ˈkəːlɪən/ *n.* L20. [S. D. and V. K. *Kirlian*, 20th-cent. Russ. electricians.] Used *attrib.* to designate (pictures obtained by) a process of recording corona discharges from the surfaces of objects directly on to photographic material.

Kirman /kɪəˈmɑːn, kə-/ *a.* & *n.* Also **Ker-**. L19. [A province and town in SE Iran.] (Designating) a carpet or rug made in Kirman, usu. having soft delicate colouring and naturalistic designs.

Kirmanshah /kəˈmɑːnʃɑː, kəːmənˈʃɑː/ *n.* & *a.* Also **Ker-**. E20. [A city in west Iran.] (Designating) a carpet or rug made in Kirman, usu. one with a white field and flowered medallion and borders.
¶ Erroneously named, by confusion with prec.

kirmess *n.* var. of KERMIS.

kirn /kəːn/ *n.*[1] & *v. Sc.* & *north.* ME. [Var. of CHURN, infl. by ON *kirna*.] A *n.* A churn. ME. B *v.t.* & *i.* = CHURN *v. Sc.* M16.

kirn /kəːn/ *n.*[2] *Sc.* & *north.* Now *rare.* L16. [Origin unkn.] 1 A feast held on the completion of a harvest, a harvest home. L16. 2 The last handful of corn cut on the harvest-field. L18.
2 get, win the kirn gain the distinction of cutting down the last armful of corn; succeed in finishing the harvest.
Comb.: **kirn-baby, dolly** a crude doll made from the last handful of corn, a corn-dolly.

kirpan /kəːˈpɑːn/ *n.* E20. [Panjabi & Hind. *kirpān* f. Skt *kṛpāṇa* sword.] The dagger or sword worn by Sikhs as a religious symbol.

kirri *n.* see KIERIE.

kirsch /kɪəʃ/ *n.* M19. [G, abbrev. of *Kirsch(en)wasser*: see KIRSCHWASSER.] An alcoholic spirit distilled, chiefly in Germany and Switzerland, from the fermented juice of cherries.

kirschenwasser *n.* var. of KIRSCHWASSER.

Kirschner value /ˈkɪəʃnə ˌvaljuː/ *n. phr.* E20. [Aage *Kirschner* (b. 1870), Da. chemist.] A number expressing the proportion of certain fatty acids (esp. butyric acid) in a fat.

kirschwasser /ˈkɪəʃvasə/ *n.* Also (now *rare*) **kirschen-** /ˈkɪəʃ(ə)n-/. E19. [G, f. *Kirsche* cherry + *Wasser* water.] = KIRSCH.

kirsh *n.* var. of QURSH.

Kir-Shehr /ˈkəːʃɪə/ *n.* & *a.* Also **Kirshehir**. E20. [A town in central Turkey.] (Designating) a brightly coloured prayer rug made in Kir-Shehr.

kirtan /ˈkɪətən/ *n.* Also **keer-**. L19. [Skt *kīrtana*.] In the Indian subcontinent: a devotional song or hymn.

kirtle /ˈkəːt(ə)l/ *n.* & *v.* Now *arch.* or *Hist.* [OE *cyrtel* = ON *kyrtill* tunic, f. Gmc, ult. prob. f. L *curtus* short: see CURT, -LE[1].] A *n.* 1 A man's tunic or coat, usu. reaching to the knees or lower. OE. 2 A woman's gown or outer petticoat. OE. B *v.t.* Cover or clothe (as) with a kirtle. L19.
kirtled *a.* wearing a kirtle M17.

kisaeng /ˈkiːsaŋ, -ɛŋ/ *n.* L19. [Korean.] A trained female entertainer, the Korean equivalent of a geisha.

kisan /kɪˈsɑːn/ *n.* M20. [Hind. *kisān* f. Skt *kṛṣāṇa* person who ploughs.] In the Indian subcontinent: a peasant, an agricultural worker.

kish /kɪʃ/ *n.*[1] L18. [Ir. *cis, ceis* basket, hamper.] In Ireland: a large wickerwork basket or cart-body with removable wickerwork sides, used chiefly for carrying turf.

kish /kɪʃ/ *n.*[2] E19. [Origin uncertain: cf. Fr. *chiasse* (dial. *quiasse*) scum on metal.] *Metall.* A floating scale of impure graphite, formed on molten iron during smelting.

kishke /ˈkɪʃkə/ *n.* Also **-ka**, **-keh**. M20. [Yiddish f. Pol. *kiszka* or Ukrainian *kishka*: cf. Russ. *kishka*.] 1 Beef intestine casing stuffed with a savoury filling. M20. 2 *sing.* & in *pl.* The guts. *slang.* M20.

Kisii /ˈkɪsiː/ *n.* & *a.* Pl. of n. same. E20. [Bantu.] Designating or pertaining to, a member of, a people living in Kisii, a district on the east side of Lake Victoria, Kenya; (of) the Bantu language of this people.

kiskadee /kɪskəˈdiː/ *n.* Also **keskidee** /kɛskɪˈdiː/. L19. [Imit. of the bird's call.] Any of various tyrant flycatchers of Central and S. America; *esp.* (more fully *great kiskadee*) the large *Pitangus sulphuratus*, which has a black and white striped head and yellow underparts.

Kislev /ˈkɪslɛf/ *n.* Also **†Casleu**, **Kislew**. LME. [Heb. *Kislēw*.] In the Jewish calendar, the third month of the civil and ninth of the religious year, usu. coinciding with parts of November and December.

kismet /ˈkɪzmɛt, -mɪt, -s-/ *n.* E19. [Turk. *kismet* f. Arab. *ḳisma(t)* division, portion, lot, fate.] Destiny, fate.

kiss /kɪs/ *n.* [OE *coss* f. Gmc. base of KISS *v.*, refash. after KISS *v.*] 1 A touch or caress given with slightly pursed lips as an expression of affection, sexual desire, greeting, etc., or reverence; an act of kissing. OE. 2 *fig.* A light touch or impact. L16. b *Billiards, Snooker*, etc. A light touching of one ball by another. M19. 3 A representation of a kiss in the form of an x, esp. at the close of a letter. M18. 4 A small cake or piece of confectionery; a sweet, a chocolate. E19. 5 A drop of sealing-wax accidentally let fall beside the seal of a letter. *colloq.* Now *rare.* E19.
1 C. S. LEWIS I never could endure the embrace or kiss of my own sex. J. C. OATES He .. pressed upon her anxious lips a warm, passionate, husbandly kiss. 2 DAY LEWIS The .. feeling which the cold kiss of the dew spreads through one's whole body. 3 C. FREMLIN A row of 'x's', hurried kisses, all he had time to scribble.
Phrases: *blow a kiss*: see BLOW *v.*[1] BUTTERFLY *kiss. deep kiss*: see DEEP *a. French kiss*: see FRENCH *a.* **kiss of peace** *Eccl.* a ceremonial kiss, esp. in the Eucharist, as a sign of unity. **the kiss of death** a seemingly kind or well-intentioned action, look, association, etc., which brings disastrous consequences. **the kiss of life** the mouth-to-mouth method of artificial respiration.
Comb.: **kiss-curl** a small flat curl worn on the forehead, in front of the ear, or at the nape of the neck; **kiss impression** *Printing*: by which ink is deposited on to paper by letterpress printing using the lightest possible contact; **kissproof** *a.* (esp. of lipstick) not greatly affected or harmed by kissing.
kissless *a.* E18.

kiss /kɪs/ *v.* Pa. t. & pple **kissed**, (*arch.*) **kist**. [OE *cyssan* = OFris. *kessa*, OS *cussian* (Du. *cussen*), OHG *kussen* (G *küssen*), ON *kyssa*, f. Gmc.] 1 *v.t.* Press or touch (esp. a person's lips or face) with slightly pursed lips to express affection, sexual desire, greeting, etc., or reverence. OE. b *transf.* Of a bird: touch lightly with the bill in a supposed caress. LME. 2 *v.i.* Of two people: exchange a kiss or kisses. ME. 3 *fig.* a *v.i.* Usu. of two things: touch lightly. ME. b *v.t.* Touch or brush against lightly. LME. 4 *Billiards, Snooker*, etc. a *v.t.* Cause a ball to touch (another ball) lightly; (of a ball) touch (another ball) lightly. L16. b *v.i.* Of two balls: knock together lightly. L19. 5 *v.t.* Bring into a certain state or position by kissing; take *away*, remove *from*, by kissing. E17. 6 *v.t.* Express by kissing. Also w. cognate obj., give (a kiss). M19.
1 D. H. LAWRENCE She leaned forward and kissed him, with a slow, luxurious kiss, lingering on the mouth. L. CODY She did not like being kissed. G. VIDAL He kissed her averted cheek and left the room. 2 H. FAST When had they last kissed or embraced? 3b R. GRAVES My arrow kissed his shoulder and glanced off. 6 TENNYSON We will kiss sweet kisses, and speak sweet words. W. MAXWELL Bedtime came and I kissed my mother good night.
Phrases, & with advs. in specialized senses: (**as**) **easy as kiss my** or **your, hand, finger**, & vars., very easy. **kiss and be friends, kiss and make up** become reconciled. **kiss and tell** recount one's sexual exploits. **kiss a person's arse, behind, bum** *coarse slang* behave obsequiously towards (a person). **kiss better**

colloq. comfort (a sick or injured person, esp. a child) by kissing him or her, esp. on the sore or injured part of the body, kiss as a gesture of removing pain. **kiss goodbye (to)** say goodbye (to) with a kiss; (foll. by *to*) resign oneself to the loss of. **kiss hands** kiss the hand(s) of the monarch etc. as a ceremonial duty, esp. on taking up an official appointment. **kiss my arse** *coarse slang* go away!, go to hell! **kiss off** *slang* (chiefly *N. Amer.*) (*a*) dismiss, get rid of, kill; (*b*) go away, die. **kiss the book**: i.e. the Bible, New Testament, or Gospels, in taking an oath (cf. BOOK *n.* 4a). **kiss the cup** take a sip of liquor; drink. **kiss the dirt** or **dust** be overthrown or killed; submit. **kiss the ground** prostrate oneself in homage; *fig.* be overthrown. *kiss the pope's toe*: see TOE *n.* **kiss the rod** accept chastisement or correction submissively.

Comb.: **kiss-in-the-ring** a children's game in which all the players stand in a ring with hands joined except for one who runs round and touches one of the opposite sex, who then pursues and tries to kiss him or her; **kiss-me-quick** (*a*) *Hist.* a small bonnet standing far back on the head; (*b*) *kiss-me-quick hat*, a hat bearing the words 'kiss-me-quick' (or some other, usu. joc., phrase) on the front; **kiss-off** *slang* (chiefly *N. Amer.*) a dismissal; a thing marking the end of a relationship etc.

kissaˈbility *n.* the quality of being kissable, suitability for being kissed L19. **kissable** *a.* able to be kissed, suitable for kissing, such as to invite kissing E19. **kissably** *adv.* in a manner which invites kissing L19. **kissage** *n.* (*literary* or *joc.*) kissing L19. **kissy** *a.* (*colloq.*) characterized by or given to kissing; *play kissy face* (*US*), engage in light amorous kissing: E20.

Kissagram *n.* see KISSOGRAM.

kissar /ˈkɪsə/ *n.* M19. [Repr. colloq. pronunc. of Arab. *ḳītār*, *ḳītār* KITAR.] A kind of lyre used in Ethiopia and other parts of N. Africa.

kissel /ˈkɪs(ə)l, kiˈsjɛl/ *n.* E20. [Russ. *kiselʹ*, f. same base as *kislyĭ* sour.] A dessert dish made from fruit juice or purée boiled with sugar and water and thickened with potato or cornflour.

kisser /ˈkɪsə/ *n.* M16. [f. KISS *v.* + -ER[1].] **1** A person who kisses; the giver of a kiss. M16. **2** The mouth; the face. Orig. *Boxing slang.* M19.

1 J. KRANTZ Lester . . was one terrific kisser.

Kissi /ˈkɪsi/ *n.* & *a.* L19. [Kissi.] **A** *n.* Pl. same, **-s**. A member of an agricultural people inhabiting the regions of Guinea, Sierra Leone, and Liberia near the headwaters of the Niger; the Niger-Congo language of this people. L19. **B** *attrib.* or as *adj.* Of or pertaining to the Kissi or their language. M20.

kissing /ˈkɪsɪŋ/ *vbl n.* ME. [f. KISS *v.* + -ING[1].] The action of KISS *v.*

(when) the kissing has to stop (when) the honeymoon period finishes; (when) one is forced to recognize harsh realities.

Comb.: **kissing-ball**, **-bough**, **-bunch**, **-bush** a Christmas wreath or ball of evergreens hung from the ceiling, under which a person may be kissed; **kissing-comfit** a perfumed comfit for sweetening the breath; **kissing-gate** a small gate swinging in a U- or V-shaped enclosure, so as to allow only one person to pass at a time; **†kissing-strings** *Hist.* a woman's bonnet- or cap-strings tied under the chin with the ends hanging loose; **kissing time** the time to kiss (freq. a joc. reply to children who ask the time).

kissing /ˈkɪsɪŋ/ *ppl a.* L16. [f. KISS *v.* + -ING[2].] That kisses (a person or thing).

kissing bug *US* a bloodsucking reduviid bug, spec. *Melanolestes picipes*, which can inflict a painful bite on humans. **kissing cousin** a relative or friend with whom one is on close enough terms to greet with a kiss. **kissing gourami** [from the fish's habit of touching objects with its lips pursed as if for a kiss] a small SE Asian gourami, *Helostoma temminckii*, often kept in aquaria. **kissing kin**, **kind** = *kissing cousin* above.

kissingly *adv.* M19.

kissogram /ˈkɪsəgram/ *n.* Also (proprietary) **Kissagram**. L20. [f. KISS *n.* or *v.* + -O- + -GRAM.] A novelty greetings message sent through a commercial agency, delivered (usu. by a provocatively dressed young woman) with a kiss.

attrib.: *News on Sunday* Emma . . once worked as a kissogram girl.

kist /kɪst/ *n.*[1] & *v. Sc.* & *north.* ME. [ON *kista*: see CHEST *n.*] **A** *n.* **1** A chest, a trunk, a coffer. ME. **2** A coffin; *esp.* a stone coffin, a sarcophagus. ME. **b** *Archaeol.* = CIST *n.*[1] M19. **3** A chest or place in which money is kept, a treasury; a store of money. *rare.* E17. **4** A basket. *rare.* E18.

1 kist o' whistles (now *rare*) an organ.

B *v.t.* Put into a chest, esp. a coffin. M17.

kistful *n.* (*rare*) as much as a kist will hold M17.

kist /kɪst/ *n.*[2] M18. [Urdu *ḳist* f. Pers. *ḳist* f. Arab. = portion, instalment.] In the Indian subcontinent: an instalment (of a yearly land revenue or other payment).

Comb.: **kistbandi** [Urdu, Pers. *bandī* settlement] an agreement to pay a debt in specified instalments.

kistvaen /ˈkɪstvʌɪn/ *n.* Also **c-**. E18. [Welsh *cistfaen*, f. *cist* chest (CIST *n.*[1]) + *faen* (*maen*) stone.] *Archaeol.* A stone burial-chamber.

Kiswa /ˈkɪswə/ *n.* L16. [Arab. = attire, apparel, curtaining.] The black cloth covering the walls of the Kaaba, made annually in Egypt and brought to Mecca with the pilgrimage caravan, now usu. made of black brocade with the Islamic creed outlined in the weave and a gold-embroidered band bearing Koranic texts.

Kiswahili /kiːswəˈhiːli, kɪswɑː-/ *n.* & *a.* M19. [Bantu, f. *ki-* pref. + SWAHILI.] (Of) a major language of the Bantu family, spoken widely and used as a lingua franca in E. Africa and Zaire.

kit /kɪt/ *n.*[1] ME. [MDu. *kitte* (Du. *kit* tankard), of unkn. origin.] **1 a** A cylindrical wooden tub, barrel, or pail, with or without a lid and usu. having a handle or handles. ME. **b** A basket or box, esp. for holding fish. Also, the contents of a kit, as a measure of weight. M19. **2 a** A collection of articles forming part of the equipment of a soldier; the bag or knapsack containing these with or without its contents. Now also (*gen.*), a set of clothing needed for any specific purpose, esp. for sport; a costume, an outfit, a uniform. L18. **b** A collection of personal effects or necessaries, esp. as packed up for travelling. E19. **c** Orig., the outfit of tools required by a workman, esp. a shoemaker. Now also, a set of articles or equipment needed for any specific purpose. M19. **d** More fully *drum kit*. An outfit of drums, cymbals, and other percussion devices and accessories used by a drummer in a pop, rock, or jazz group etc. E20. **e** A quantity of printed matter on a specified topic for students etc. M20. **3** A number of things or persons viewed as a whole; a set, a lot, a collection. Esp. in *the whole kit*. *N. Amer. slang.* L18. **4** A set of parts or constituents from which a thing may be assembled or made. M19.

2a H. BAILEY Roland's returned kit, including his bullet-holed tunic and blood-stained vest. B. BEHAN Geordie came round with the kits—blue jackets, shorts, shoes, shirts. *football kit* etc. *attrib.*: E. BLUNDEN The first kit inspection proved that we were short of . . rifles, leather equipment, gas masks. **c** *bicycle-repair kit*, *first-aid kit*, *tool kit*, etc. *fig.*: B. EMECHETA Our little secrets make us women; they are part of our survival kit. **4** *model aircraft kit*, *wine-making kit*, etc. *attrib.*: *Sunday Times* Jumpers available in either kit form or ready made.

Comb.: **kitbag** a stout usu. cylindrical bag in which to carry a soldier's, traveller's, or sports player's kit; **kit-car** a motor car sold in parts for assembly by the owner; **kit furniture**: sold in parts for assembly by the owner; **kitset** *NZ* the components and aids for assembling an article or model.

Phrases: HATTED *kit*. **the whole kit and boodle** or **caboodle** *slang* the whole set or lot, everything, everyone (cf. CABOODLE).

kitless *a.* M19.

kit /kɪt/ *n.*[2] Now *rare*. E16. [Origin uncertain: perh. f. first syll. of L *cithara*, Gk *kithara* CITHER.] *Hist.* A small fiddle, esp. as used by a dancing-master.

kit /kɪt/ *n.*[3] M16. [Abbrev. of KITTEN *n.*] A young cat, a kitten; the young of certain other animals as the fox, badger, beaver, and ferret.

kit /kɪt/ *n.*[4] *NZ.* M19. [Maori *kete*.] A basket plaited from flax.

kitful *n.* as much or as many as a kit will hold L19.

kit /kɪt/ *n.*[5] L19. [App. f. G dial. *Kitte*, *Kütte* covey, flight of doves etc.] A school or small flying group of pigeons.

kit /kɪt/ *v.*[1]*t.* Infl. **-tt-**. E18. [f. KIT *n.*[1]] **1** Put or pack (esp. fish) in a kit or kits. E18. **2** Equip (a person or thing) with a uniform, an outfit, equipment, etc.; provide with a kit. Freq. foll. by *out*, *up*. E20.

2 *Sunday Express* Ramblers kitted out with boots and rucksacks. A. MARS-JONES We'll see about getting you kitted up with the documents . . that you'll be needing.

kit /kɪt/ *v.*[2]*i.* & *t. rare.* Infl. **-tt-**. M18. [f. KIT *n.*[3]] Of a cat, ferret, beaver, etc.: bear (young), kitten.

Kitab /kɪˈtɑːb/ *n.* L19. [Arab. *kitāb* piece of writing, record, book.] The Koran. Also, among Muslims, the sacred book of any of certain other revealed religions, as Judaism or Christianity.

kitar /kɪˈtɑː/ *n. rare.* M17. [Arab. *ḳīṭār* f. Gk *kithara* CITHARA: cf. KISSAR.] An Arabian form of guitar or lute.

Kit-cat /ˈkɪtkat/ *n.* & *a.* Also **-Cat**, (sense 3) **k-**. E18. [f. *Kit* (= Christopher) *Cat* or *Catling*, keeper of the pie-house in London where the club orig. met. Sense 3 f. a series of portraits of the club's founders.] **1** (Designating) a club of Whig politicians and men of letters founded in the reign of James II. E18. **2** A member of this club. E18. **3** (Designating or pertaining to) a portrait of less than half length but including the hands (usu. 36 x 28 in.). M18.

kitchen /ˈkɪtʃɪn, -tʃ(ə)n/ *n.*, *a.*, & *v.* [OE *cyćene* (MLG *kökene*, MDu. *cokene*, Du. *keuken*), OHG *chuhhina* (MHG *Küchen*, G *Küche*), f. WGmc f. late L *coquina*, f. *coquere* cook.] **A** *n.* **I 1** The room or part of a house in which food is prepared and cooked; a place fitted with apparatus for cooking. OE. **2** Cookery; a culinary establishment; the cuisine of a particular country etc. L17. **3** A part of a casino at Monte Carlo where gamblers place smaller bets than in the *salles privées*. M20. **4** The percussion section of an orchestra or band. *slang.* M20. **5** A set of matching units for use in storing and preparing food, often with cooker, refrigerator, etc., esp. as sold together. M20.

1 D. PRATER A tiny kitchen where he could prepare his porridge. **2** G. BERKELEY On breaking up of the Duke's kitchen, one of his under-cooks may be got. **5** *Which?* A fitted kitchen built from manufactured units.

II 6 Food, as meat, cheese, butter, etc., eaten with bread or other plain fare as a relish; drink taken with food. Chiefly *Sc.* & *N. Ir.* LME.

Phrases: **hell's kitchen** an area or place regarded as very disreputable or unpleasant; *spec.* a district of New York City once regarded as the haunt of criminals. *Pullman kitchen*: see PULLMAN 5. **thieves' kitchen** a place inhabited or used by thieves or other criminals.

B *attrib.* or as *adj.* Of or pertaining to a kitchen; used or found in a kitchen. LME.

Comb. & *special collocations*: **kitchen cabinet** (orig. *US*) (*a*) a group of unofficial advisers (orig. of the president of the US) popularly believed to have greater influence than elected or appropriate officials; a private or unofficial group of advisers thought to be unduly influential; (*b*) a cabinet for domestic and culinary utensils etc. in a kitchen; **kitchen-diner** a room serving both as a kitchen and as a dining-room; **kitchen Dutch** (now *rare*) [tr. Du. *kombuis-Hollands*] the dialect of Afrikaans spoken by Cape Coloured people in the Western Province of South Africa; *derog.* Afrikaans; **kitchen evening** *Austral.* & *NZ* an evening event at which guests bring gifts of kitchenware to a bride-to-be (cf. *kitchen tea* below); **kitchen-fee** (now *Sc.*) dripping; tallow; **kitchen garden** a garden or a part of a garden in which vegetables and sometimes fruit or herbs are grown esp. for domestic use; **kitchen-gardener** a person who tends a kitchen garden; **kitchen-gardening** the tending of a kitchen garden; **Kitchen Kaffir** (now *rare* & *derog.*) a lingua franca of southern Africa, = FANAGALO; **kitchen-knave** *arch.* a boy employed in a kitchen, a cook's boy; **kitchen-Latin** inferior Latin, dog Latin; **kitchen-maid** a female servant employed in a kitchen, usu. under a cook; **kitchen midden** [tr. Da. *kjökkenmödding*, *kökken-* f. *kökken* kitchen] *Archaeol.* a prehistoric refuse-heap associated with a site of human habitation, consisting chiefly of shells and animal bones, but also sometimes containing stone implements and other relics; **kitchen paper** absorbent paper used for drying and cleaning purposes in a kitchen etc., often sold as a roll; **kitchen-parlour** a room serving both as kitchen and parlour; **†kitchen-physic** *joc.* nourishment for an invalid (as a form of treatment); **kitchen-plot** = *kitchen garden*; **kitchen police** *US Army* enlisted men detailed to help the cook, wash dishes, etc.; the work of such men; **kitchen shower** *N. Amer.* = *kitchen tea* below;

kitchen sink a sink in a kitchen, in which dirty dishes, vegetables, etc., are washed (freq. used as a symbol of women's enslavement to the kitchen or of the drab and mundane); *everything but the kitchen sink*, everything possible or imaginable; **kitchen-sink** *a.* designating or pertaining to art, esp. drama dealing with domestic reality, esp. in its drab or sordid aspects; **kitchen stove** a stove in a kitchen; *everything but the kitchen stove* = *everything but the kitchen sink* above; **kitchen-stuff** refuse or waste from a kitchen, *esp.* dripping; **kitchen tea** *Austral., NZ.,* & *S. Afr.* a party to which guests bring gifts of kitchenware for a bride-to-be (cf. *kitchen evening* above); **kitchenware** utensils for use in a kitchen; **kitchen-wench** *arch.* a girl employed in a kitchen, a kitchen-maid.

C *v.t.* †1 Entertain in the kitchen, supply with food. *rare* (Shakes.). Only in L16. 2 Serve as relish for; make palatable, season. Also, use sparingly as relish with food; make (food) go far. *Sc.* E18.

kitchenable *a.* suitable for cooking and eating E20. **kitcheny** *a.* of, pertaining to, or suggestive of a kitchen L19.

kitchener /ˈkɪtʃɪnə/ *n.*[1] LME. [f. KITCHEN *n.* + -ER[1].] 1 A person employed in a kitchen; *esp.* in a monastery, the person in charge of the kitchen. LME. 2 A cooking-range fitted with various appliances such as ovens, plate-warmers, water-heaters, etc. L19.

Kitchener /ˈkɪtʃɪnə/ *n.*[2] & *a.* E20. [f. *Kitchener* (see below).] A *n.* 1 A man thought to resemble the British soldier Horatio Herbert Kitchener (1850–1916), first Earl Kitchener of Khartoum, esp. in having an imposing and taciturn personality E20. 2 *Hist.* A soldier recruited while Kitchener was Secretary of State for War (1914–16). E20.

B *attrib.* or as *adj.* Of, pertaining to, or characteristic of Kitchener or soldiers recruited when he was Secretary of State for War. E20.

E. BLUNDEN The first Kitchener battalion . . to hold the sector. A. CADE A drooping Kitchener moustache.

Kitchener bun *Austral.* a cream-filled bun coated with cinnamon and sugar.

kitchenette /kɪtʃɪˈnɛt/ *n.* Orig. *US.* E20. [f. KITCHEN *n.* + -ETTE.] A small kitchen; an alcove or a part of a room fitted as a kitchen.

Kitchen rudder /ˈkɪtʃɪn ˈrʌdə, ˈkɪtʃ(ə)n/ *n. phr.* E20. [J. G. A. *Kitchen*, Englishman who patented the device in 1914.] A steering device for small craft consisting of a pair of curved deflectors either side of the propeller whose position is altered to change the course or speed of the vessel.

kite /kʌɪt/ *n.* [OE *cȳta*, f. base also of MHG *Kūze* (G *Kauz*) screech-owl & other wds echoing various cries.] 1 Any of various medium-sized birds of prey of the genus *Milvus* and related genera (family Accipitridae), with long wings, forked tail, and soaring flight; *esp.* (more fully *red kite*) a reddish-brown European kite, *Milvus milvus*. OE. 2 A person who preys on or exploits others, a sharper, a shark; a worthless or contemptible person, a wretch. *arch.* M16. 3 A toy consisting of a light frame covered with a light thin material, usu. in the form of an isosceles triangle with a circular arc as base or a quadrilateral symmetrical about the longer diagonal and having a tail for balance, flown in the wind at the end of a long string. Also, a modification of a toy kite designed to support a person in the air or to form part of an unpowered aircraft. M17. b An aeroplane. *slang* (orig. *Mil.*). E20. 4a A bill of exchange used for raising money on credit; an accommodation bill. *slang.* E19. b A letter, a communication, *esp.* an illicit one; *spec.* a letter or verbal message smuggled into, out of, or within a prison. *slang.* M19. c A cheque, *esp.* a fraudulent one. *slang.* E20. 5 *Naut.* a In *pl.* The highest sails of a ship, set only in a light wind. Also *flying-kites*. M19. b On a minesweeper: a device attached to a sweep-wire submerging it to the requisite depth when it is towed over a minefield. E20. 6 *Geom.* A quadrilateral figure symmetrical about one diagonal. L19.

1 *black kite, brahminy kite, swallow-tailed kite, whistling kite*, etc. 2 SHAKES. *Lear* Detested kite! thou liest. 3 L. DURRELL Children flying their coloured kites in the quick fresh evening wind. *fly a kite*: see FLY *v. go fly a kite*: see FLY *v. high as a kite*: see HIGH *a.*

Comb.: **kite balloon** a balloon anchored to the ground with a long string or wire, used for scientific or other purposes; **kite bar** a bar or stripe of an undesirable colour in the plumage of a fancy pigeon; **kitefish** = *moonfish* (d) s.v. MOON *n.*[1]; **kite-flyer** a person who flies a kite (*lit.* & *fig.*); **kite-flying** (*a*) the flying of a kite on a string; (*b*) the raising of money by writing or passing fraudulent or unbacked cheques; (*c*) the trying out of a proposal etc.; the making of an announcement or taking of a step in order to ascertain public opinion; **kite-man** a person who obtains money against bills of exchange or cheques that will not be honoured; **Kitemark** a kite-shaped mark granted for use on goods approved by the British Standards Institution; **kite-mark** *v.t.* use the Kitemark on; **kite-photograph** a photograph taken by means of a camera attached to a kite or kite balloon; **kite's-foot tobacco** a bright-coloured variety of tobacco.

kite /kʌɪt/ *v.* M19. [f. the n.] 1 a *v.i.* Fly, soar, or move through the air like a kite; *fig.* move quickly, rush, rise quickly, (foll. by *around, off, up*, etc.). M19. b *v.t.* Cause to fly high like a toy kite. M19. 2a *v.t.* & *i.* Write or use (a cheque, bill, or receipt) fraudulently or without cover; raise (money) by dishonest means. *slang.* M19. b *v.t.* & *i.* Send (a communication); *spec.* smuggle (a letter) into, out of, or within a prison. *slang.* E20.

1a T. PYNCHON Birds in the sunlight kiting behind him. 2a A. MILLER Dozens of small businessmen with seven-year sentences for kiting not very large checks. *New Yorker* Even if loans were kited . . what did that imply?

kitenge /kɪˈtɛŋgi/ *n.* Also **vi-** /vɪ-/. M20. [Kiswahili *kitengele*.] In E. Africa: a fabric, usu. of cotton and printed in various colours and designs with distinctive borders, used esp. for women's clothing.

kit-fox /ˈkɪtfɒks/ *n.* E19. [Prob. f. KIT *n.*[3] w. ref. to its small size: see FOX *n.*] The swift fox, *Vulpes velox*; *esp.* the form of this inhabiting the south-western US and northern Mexico (sometimes regarded as a distinct species, *V. macrotis*).

kith /kɪθ/ *n.* [OE *cȳþ(þ*, earlier *cȳþþu* = OHG *chundida* f. Gmc, f. base also of KITHE: cf. COUTH. See also KIFF.] †1a Knowledge; information. OE–LME. †b Knowledge of how to behave; rules of etiquette. LME–E19. †2 One's native land or region, home; *gen.* a country, a region. OE–E16. 3 *collect.* One's friends, acquaintances, neighbours, or fellows; later also, kin. *arch.* exc. in *kith and kin*, (orig.), country and kinsfolk, friends and relatives, (now also) one's relatives, one's family. OE.

4 E. O'BRIEN She . . had neither kith nor kin of her own. G. PRIESTLAND There are the Falkland islanders—our own kith and kin.

kithless *a.* M18.

kithara *n.* var. of CITHARA.

kithe /kʌɪð/ *v.* Now *Sc.* & *north.* Also **kythe**. Pa. pple **kithed, kythed**; †**kid**, †**kyd**. See also KID *a.* [OE *cȳþan* = OFris. *kētha*, OS *kuþian*, OHG *kunden*, ON *kynna*, Goth. *kunþjan*, f. Gmc, f. base also of KITH: cf. COUTH.] 1 *v.t.* †a Proclaim, declare, tell. OE–M16. b Show, reveal, make manifest; prove, demonstrate. ME. †2 *v.t.* Exhibit or display (a feeling, quality, etc.); exercise, practise, perform. OE–E18. †3 *v.t.* Acknowledge, confess; recognize. OE–E17. 4 *v.i.* Show oneself or itself, become manifest, appear. ME.

kithing *n.* (*rare*) (*a*) the action of the vb.; (*b*) an act of showing or telling, a proclamation, a manifestation: ME.

kitling /ˈkɪtlɪŋ/ *n.* Now *dial.* ME. [Perh. f. ON *ket(t)lingr* (Norw. *kjetling*) kitten.] †1 The young of any animal; a cub, a whelp. ME–E17. 2 A young cat, a kitten. LME. 3 A child, a young person, an offspring; a person thought to resemble a kitten, *spec.* a soft effeminate man. L15.

kitsch /kɪtʃ/ *n.* & *a.* Also **K-**. E20. [G.] A *n.* Art or artefacts perceived as being of poor quality, esp. when garish or sentimental; these enjoyed in a perverse or self-conscious way; the qualities associated with such art or artefacts. E20.

JILLY COOPER Flying ducks were only acceptable if they were outside and moving. Now they've become kitsch. *Listener* A galloping fancy for Victoriana, a sophisticated and uncritical taste for Kitsch and the cute.

B *adj.* Of the nature of or pertaining to kitsch; garish, sentimental, tasteless. M20.

Listener Director Jeremy Mortimer does offer irony . . with some brilliantly kitsch use of Country music. J. CAREY They rented a kitsch house in Pacific Palisades, Los Angeles, with luminous dogs as lamps.

kitschily *adv.* in a kitsch manner L20. **kitschiness** *n.* the quality or condition of being kitsch L20. **kitschy** *a.* possessing the characteristics of kitsch M20.

kittel /ˈkɪt(ə)l/ *n.* L19. [Yiddish (G = overall, smock), f. MHG *ki(e)tel* cotton or hempen outer garment.] A white cotton or linen robe worn by orthodox Jews on certain holy days; such a robe used as a shroud.

kitten /ˈkɪt(ə)n/ *n.* & *v.* LME. [f. AN var. of OFr. *chitoun, chet-* (mod. *chaton*) dim. of *chat* CAT *n.*[1]: the ending assim. to -EN[1].] A *n.* 1 A young cat. LME. 2 The young of certain other animals, as the fox, ferret, beaver, and rabbit. L15. 3 More fully *kitten-moth*. Any of certain moths of the genus *Furcula* (family Notodontidae), with furry bodies. E19. 4 A girl or young woman, *esp.* a coy or flirtatious one. L19.

1 M. ANGELOU Frankel turned around like a kitten trying to catch its tail. 3 *alder kitten, poplar kitten, sallow kitten.*

Phrases: **have kittens** (*fig.*) *colloq.* be or become very angry, anxious, or upset.

B *v.i.* Of a cat, ferret, beaver, etc.: give birth to a kitten or kittens. LME.

kittenhood *n.* the state, condition, or period of being a kitten M19. **kittenlike** *a.* resembling a kitten, kittenish M19.

kittenish /ˈkɪt(ə)nɪʃ/ *a.* M18. [f. prec. + -ISH[1].] Like a kitten or that of a kitten; playful, lively; coy, flirtatious.

DICKENS She was all girlishness, and playfulness, and wildness, and kittenish buoyancy.

kittenishly *adv.* L19. **kittenishness** *n.* E20.

†**kittisol** *n.* L16–L19. [Port. & Sp. *quitasol*, f. *quitar* take away + *sol* sun. Cf. PARASOL.] A sunshade, a parasol, an umbrella; *spec.* a Chinese umbrella made of bamboo and oiled paper.

Kittitian /kɪˈtɪʃ(ə)n/ *n.* & *a.* M20. [f. St *Kitts* (see below) + *-itian* as in *Haitian*.] A *n.* A native or inhabitant of the island of St Kitts in the W. Indies. M20. B *adj.* Of or pertaining to St Kitts or its inhabitants. L20.

kittiwake /ˈkɪtɪweɪk/ *n.* Orig. *Sc.* E17. [Imit. of the bird's cry.] A small maritime gull of the genus *Rissa*, spec. *R. tridactyla*, of the N. Atlantic and Arctic Oceans.

kittle /ˈkɪt(ə)l/ *a.* Orig. *Sc.* & *north.* M16. [f. next.] Ticklish (*lit.* & *fig.*) difficult to deal with or manage; risky, precarious; capricious, rash, erratic in behaviour.

kittle cattle (people who or animals which are) capricious, rash, or erratic in behaviour; (things which are) difficult to use or deal with.

kittle /ˈkɪt(ə)l/ *v.*[1]*t.* Now *dial.* (chiefly *Sc.*). [OE (in *kitelung* n.) corresp. to OS *kitilon* (Du. *kittelen*), OHG *kizzilōn* (G *kitzeln*), ON *kitla*, f. Gmc: superseded in ME by forms f. ON.] 1 Tickle, touch as if tickling (a person or thing). OE. 2 Stimulate, excite, rouse, please. ME. 3 Puzzle with a question etc., perplex. E19.

kittly *a.* (*Sc.*) ticklish; causing a tickling sensation; difficult, puzzling: E19.

kittle /ˈkɪt(ə)l/ *v.*[2] Now *Sc.* & *north.* M16. [Perh. back-form. f. KITLING, but cf. Norw. *kjetla* in same sense.] 1 *v.i.* = KITTEN *v.* M16. 2 *v.i.* & *t.* (in *pass.*). Be engendered or produced; come into being. E19.

kittle-pins /ˈkɪt(ə)lpɪnz/ *n. obs.* exc. *dial.* Also **kettle-** /ˈkɛt(ə)l-/. M17. [1st elem. rel. to next.] The game skittles.

kittles /ˈkɪt(ə)lz/ *n.* Now *rare* or *obs.* Also **kettles** /ˈkɛt(ə)lz/. L16. [Origin unkn.: cf. prec.] The game skittles.

kittul /ˈkɪtuːl/ *n.* L17. [Sinhalese *kitul*.] The jaggery palm, *Caryota urens*; a fibre obtained from the leaf-stalks of this, used for making ropes, brushes, etc.

kitty /'kɪti/ *n.*[1] E18. [Abbrev. of KITTEN *n.* + -Y[6].] (A pet name for) a kitten or a cat.

J. C. OATES Followed along after the cat, calling *Here kitty*.

kitty /'kɪti/ *n.*[2] E19. [Origin unkn.] **1** A prison, a jail. *north.* E19. **2** A pool of money in some card-games etc. made up of contributions from each player and used as winnings or for refreshments etc. Also, a sum of money made up of contributions by people involved in a common activity, a reserve fund. L19. **3** *Bowls.* The jack. L19.

2 B. BAINBRIDGE Every Friday the two men put money into a kitty towards its . . purchase. *Scotsman* Even in times of vastly reduced income . . the wives . . were blamed if the kitty ran dry. *scoop the kitty*: see SCOOP *v.* 5a.

kiva /'kiːvə/ *n.* L19. [Hopi *kiva.*] A chamber, built wholly or partly underground, used by male Pueblo Indians for religious rites etc. Cf. ESTUFA.

kive *n.* var. of KEEVE.

kiver /'kɪvə, 'kiː-/ *n. obs.* exc. *dial.* ME. [App. f. *kive* var. of KEEVE.] A shallow wooden vessel or tub.

Kiwanis /kɪ'wɑːnɪs/ *n.* E20. [Origin unkn.] In full *Kiwanis Club*. A N. American society of business and professional men formed for the maintenance of commercial ethics and as a social and charitable organization.

Kiwanian *n.* a member of a Kiwanis Club E20.

kiwi /'kiːwiː, -wi/ *n.* In sense 2 **K-**. M19. [Maori.] **1** Any of several dark brown or grey tailless, flightless, nocturnal ratite birds of the genus *Apteryx*, of New Zealand forest and scrub, having a long bill and hairlike feathers, a national emblem of New Zealand. M19. **2** A New Zealander, esp. a soldier or member of a national sports team. *colloq.* E20. **3** A non-flying member of an air force. *arch. slang.* E20. **4** In full *kiwi fruit*. The oval fruit of an eastern Asian climbing plant, *Actinidia chinensis* (family Actinidiaceae), cultivated in New Zealand and elsewhere, with brown skin, green flesh, and black seeds. Also called *Chinese gooseberry*. M20.

2 *Telegraph* (*Brisbane*) 10-wicket haul leads Kiwis to Test victory. *Times* The Kiwis take all the credit for Antipodean anti-Pom feelings. *attrib.*: M. S. POWER He . . managed to affect the nasal Kiwi twang almost to perfection.

ki-yi /kʌɪ'jʌɪ/ *v.* & *n. US colloq.* M19. [Imit.] **A** *v.i.* Pres. pple **ki-yi-ing**; pa. t. **ki-yi-ed**. (Of a dog) howl, yelp; howl or yelp like a dog. M19. **B** *n.* **1** The howl or yelp of a dog; a whoop or shout resembling this. L19. **2** A dog. L19.

Kizil /kɪ'zɪl/ *n.* & *a.* Pl. of n. **-s**, same. L19. [Turk. *kızıl* red.] Of or pertaining to, a member of, a Turkic people of southern Siberia.

Kizilbash /'kɪzɪlbɑːʃ/ *n.* M17. [Turk. *kızılbaş*, f. as prec. + *baş* head.] **1** A Persianized Turk in Iran or Afghanistan. M17. **2** A member of any of several cultural or religious minorities in Asian Turkey. E20.

Kjeldahl /'kɛldɑːl/ *n.* L19. [Johann *Kjeldahl* (1849–1900), Da. chemist.] *Biochem.* Used *attrib.* and in *possess.* to designate a method of estimation of nitrogen in organic substances by treatment with concentrated sulphuric acid and conversion of the resulting ammonium sulphate to ammonia, which is then titrated.

Kjeldahl flask a glass flask with a round bottom and a long wide neck, used in the Kjeldahl method.

Klaas's cuckoo /'klɑːsɪz 'kʊkuː/ *n. phr.* Also **Klaas' cuckoo**. M19. [*Klaas*, a servant of the Fr. explorer François Le Vaillant (1753–1824).] A bronze and green cuckoo, *Chrysococcyx klaas*, of sub-Saharan Africa. Cf. MIETJIE.

klaberjass /'klabəjas/ *n.* Also **clobiosh** /'klɒbɪjɒʃ/ & other vars. L19. [G f. Du. *klaverjas.*] *Cards.* A two-handed card-game distantly related to bezique, in which points are scored for winning value cards in tricks and for declaring combinations.

Klamath /'klaməθ/ *n.* & *a.* Pl. of n. **-s**, same. E19. [Chinook *łámał* Klamath.] Of or pertaining to, a member of, a Penutian Indian people of the Oregon–California border, USA; (of) the language of this people.

Klamath weed *US* common St John's wort, *Hypericum perforatum*, naturalized as a weed in the US.

Klan /klan/ *n.* & *a.* M19. [Abbrev.] **A** *n.* The Ku Klux Klan. M19.

Comb.: **Klansman** a member of the Ku Klux Klan.

B *attrib.* or as *adj.* Of or pertaining to the Ku Klux Klan. E20.

Klang /klaŋ/ *n.* L19. [G = sound.] *Mus.* A tone composed of fundamental and overtones.

Comb.: ***Klangfarbe*** /-farbə, -fɑːbə/ [G *Farbe* colour] musical quality of a note, timbre; ***Klangfarbenmelodie*** /-farbənmelo,diː, -fɑːbən,melədi/ melody of timbres.

klapmatch *n.* var. of CLAPMATCH.

klapper /'klapə/ *n. S. Afr.* M19. [Perh. f. Afk. f. Malay *kelapa* coconut, or f. Afk. *klapper* rattle.] = *Kaffir orange* s.v. KAFFIR.

klatch /klatʃ/ *n.* Also ***Klatsch***. M20. [G *Klatsch* gossip.] A social gathering, a party, *spec.* a coffee party. Cf. KAFFEEKLATSCH.

Klaxon /'klaks(ə)n/ *n.* & *v.* Orig. *US.* Also **k-**. E20. [Name of the original manufacturers.] **A** *n.* (Proprietary name for) an electric horn or warning hooter, orig. one on a motor vehicle. E20.

J. LE CARRÉ He heard the klaxons, . . moaning out . . like the howl of starving animals.

B *v.i.* Sound a Klaxon. E20.

Kleagle /'kliːg(ə)l/ *n.* Also **k-**. E20. [f. KL(AN + EAGLE *n.*] An officer of the Ku Klux Klan.

klebsiella /klɛbzɪ'ɛlə/ *n.* E20. [mod.L (see below), f. *Klebs* (see next) + -I- + -ELLA.] *Med.* & *Bacteriol.* Any of various Gram-negative coliform bacteria of the genus *Klebsiella*, which includes several associated with respiratory, urinary, and wound infections.

Klebs–Löffler /klɛbz'ləːflə/ *n.* L19. [T. A. E. *Klebs* (1834–1913) and F. A. J. *Löffler* (1852–1915), Ger. bacteriologists.] *Med.* & *Bacteriol.* Used *attrib.* to designate the coryneform bacillus *Corynebacterium diphtheriae*, which causes diphtheria in humans and similar diseases in other animals.

Kleenex /'kliːnɛks/ *n.* Orig. *US.* Also **k-**. Pl. same, **-es** /-ɪz/. E20. [Invented name.] (Proprietary name for) an absorbent disposable paper tissue, used esp. as a handkerchief.

L. CODY She mopped the puddle in her saucer with a piece of Kleenex. P. LIVELY She got out a Kleenex and blew her nose.

kleft *n.* var. of KLEPHT.

Klein bottle /klʌɪn 'bɒt(ə)l/ *n. phr.* M20. [Felix *Klein* (1849–1925), Ger. mathematician.] *Math.* A closed surface both sides of which, at any point, are parts of the same continuous surface, freq. represented in three dimensions as a bottle with the neck passed through the side and joined to a hole in the base.

Kleinian /'klʌɪnɪən/ *a.* & *n.* M20. [f. *Klein* (see below) + -IAN.] **A** *adj.* Of or pertaining to the psychoanalyst Melanie Klein (1882–1960) or her theories, esp. concerning child psychoanalysis, or her school of psychoanalysis which stressed people's need for social relationships. M20. **B** *n.* An advocate of the theories of Melanie Klein; an adherent of the Kleinian school of psychoanalysis. M20.

klendusity /klɛn'djuːsɪti/ *n.* M20. [f. Gk *kleis* bar, bolt + *endusis* entry + -ITY.] *Bot.* Ability of a plant to escape infection through the possession of some inhibiting property.

klendusic *a.* exhibiting klendusity M20.

klep /klɛp/ *n. slang.* L19. [Abbrev.] = KLEPTOMANIAC.

klepht /klɛft/ *n.* Also **kleft**. E19. [mod.Gk *klephtēs* f. Gk *kleptēs* thief.] A Greek brigand or bandit. Also, a Greek fighter for independence, *spec.* against the Turks in the 15th cent. or during the war of independence (1821–8).

klephtic *a.* M19.

klepto /'klɛptəʊ/ *n. slang.* Pl. **-os**. M20. [Abbrev.] = KLEPTOMANIAC.

kleptocracy /klɛp'tɒkrəsi/ *n.* E19. [f. Gk *klepto-* (see KLEPTOMANIA) + -CRACY.] (Government by) a ruling body of thieves; a nation ruled by thieves.

'kleptocrat *n.* a member of a kleptocracy, a thieving ruler M20.

kleptolagnia /klɛptə(ʊ)'lagnɪə/ *n.* E20. [f. as next + Gk *lagneia* lust, after ALGOLAGNIA.] *Psychiatry.* The practice of achieving sexual arousal through stealing; the compulsive urge to steal for this purpose.

kleptomania /klɛptə(ʊ)'meɪnɪə/ *n.* M19. [f. Gk *klepto-* comb. form of *kleptēs* thief, rel. to *kleptein* steal + -MANIA.] The compulsive urge to steal, usu. without regard for need or profit.

kleptomaniac *n.* & *a.* (*a*) *n.* a person affected with kleptomania; (*b*) *adj.* affected with kleptomania, characteristic of a kleptomaniac: M19.

kleptoparasite /klɛptə(ʊ)'parəsʌɪt/ *n.* Also **c-**. L20. [f. as prec. + PARASITE *n.*] *Zool.* A bird, insect, or other animal which habitually robs others (of a different species) of food.

kleptopara'sitic *a.* M20. **kleptoparasitism** *n.* the behaviour of a kleptoparasite M20. **kleptoparasitize** *v.t.* habitually rob (another animal) of food L20.

kleruch *n.* var. of CLERUCH.

kletterschuh /'klɛtəʃuː/ *n.* Pl. **-schuhe** /-ʃuːə/. E20. [G, lit. 'climbing-shoe'.] A cloth- or felt-soled light boot worn esp. for rock-climbing. Usu. in *pl.*

kleywang /'kleɪwaŋ/ *n.* Also **kelewang** /'kɛlɪwaŋ/. L18. [Malay *kelewang*.] A single-edged Indonesian sword.

klezmer /'klɛzmə/ *n.* Pl. same, **klezmorim** /'klɛzmərɪm/. M20. [Yiddish, contr. of Heb. *kᵉlēy zemer* musical instruments.] A member of a group of musicians playing traditional eastern European Jewish music; (in full *klezmer music*) this type of music.

klick /klɪk/ *n. N. Amer. Mil. slang.* Also **klik**. M20. [Origin unkn.] A kilometre.

¶ Originally used in the Vietnam War.

klieg /kliːg/ *n.* E20. [A. T. & J. H. *Kliegl* (1872–1927 & 1869–1959), US inventors.] *Cinemat.* & *Television.* In full *klieg light*. A kind of arc lamp invented for use in film studios; a powerful electric light used in filming.

Comb.: **klieg eye(s)** an eye condition caused by exposure to very bright light, characterized by watering and conjunctivitis.

klik *n.* var. of KLICK.

Klinefelter /'klʌɪnfɛltə/ *n.* M20. [H. F. *Klinefelter* (b. 1912), US physician.] *Med.* Used *attrib.* and in *possess.* to designate a syndrome affecting males in which the cells have an extra X chromosome (in addition to the normal XY), characterized by a tall thin physique, small infertile testes, eunuchoidism, and gynaecomastia.

Kling /klɪŋ/ *n.* Now *rare.* E17. [Malay *Keling* Tamil trader or settler (derog.) f. Skt *Kaliṅga* an old name for a strip of coast along the Bay of Bengal.] An Indian settler in Malaysia. Also †*kling man*.

klino- /'klʌɪnəʊ/ *comb. form* of Gk *klinein* to lean, slope: see -O-. Cf. CLINO-.

klinoki'nesis *n.* (*Biol.*) variation in the rate of turning M20. **klinoki'netic** *a.* (*Biol.*) of or pertaining to klinokinesis M20. **klinostat** *n.* a revolving device on or in which germinating seeds or growing plants can be placed so as to counteract the directional influence of gravity, light, etc., on their growth L19.

klip /klɪp/ *n. S. Afr. colloq.* E19. [Afk. f. Du. = rock, stone.] **1** Hist. *blink klip* [BLINK *a.*] Powdered micaceous iron ore, used as a cosmetic by Africans. E19. **2** A stone, a pebble. M19. **3** A diamond. Also *blink klip*. L19.

klipbok /'klɪpbɒk/ *n.* Also **-buck** /-bʌk/. L19. [Afk., f. Du. *klip* rock + *bok* buck.] = KLIPSPRINGER.

klipdas /'klɪpdas/ *n. S. Afr.* M19. [Afk., f. as Du. *klip* rock + DAS *n.*] = DASSIE 1.

klipfish /'klɪpfɪʃ/ *n.* Pl. **-es** /-ɪz/, (usu.) same. L18. [Partial tr. Du. *klipvisch* (mod. *-vis*) or Da. *klipfisk* rock fish.] **1** Any of various brightly coloured viviparous marine fishes of the family Clinidae, which live in shallow water or rock pools. Cf. KINGKLIP. *S. Afr.* L18. 2 A codfish split open, boned, salted, and dried. M19.

klipkous /ˈklɪpkəʊs/ *n. S. Afr.* M18. [Afk., f. Du. *klip* rock + *kous* stocking.] = ABALONE.

klippe /ˈklɪpə/ *n.* E20. [G = partly submerged or buried rock.] *Geol.* A part of a nappe which has become detached from its parent mass by sliding or by erosion of intervening parts.

klipspringer /ˈklɪpsprɪŋə/ *n.* L18. [Afk., f. Du. *klip* rock + *springer* SPRINGER.] A small antelope, *Oreotragus oreotragus*, inhabiting rocky terrain in sub-Saharan Africa.

klister /ˈklɪstə/ *n.* M20. [Norw. = paste.] *Skiing.* A soft wax for applying to the running surface of skis to facilitate movement, used esp. when the temperature is above freezing.

klompie /ˈklɒmpi/ *n. S. Afr.* Also **-pje**. M19. [Afk. f. Du. *klompje* dim. of *klomp*: see CLUMP *n.*] 1 A group, a cluster, esp. of animals or of shrubs or trees. *colloq.* M19. 2 A type of hard yellow brick, orig. imported from the Netherlands. Also *klompie brick*. E20.

Klondike /ˈklɒndʌɪk/ *n.* & *v.* Also **-dyke**. L19. [A region and river in the Yukon, NW Canada, the scene of a gold-rush in the years following 1896; a name also given to a herring fishery off the west coast of Scotland.] A *n.* 1 A source of valuable material or of wealth. L19. 2 *Cards.* A variety of patience. *N. Amer.* E20. B *v.t.* Also **k-**. Export (fish, esp. mackerel or herring) while fresh, freq. to a foreign factory ship. Chiefly *Sc.* E20.

Klondiker *n.* (*a*) a prospector in the Klondike; (*b*) (chiefly *Sc.*) an exporter of or dealer in fresh fish, esp. mackerel or herring; a ship used for exporting fresh fish: L19.

klong /klɒŋ/ *n.* L19. [Thai.] In Thailand: a canal.

klonkie /ˈklɒŋki/ *n. S. Afr.* M20. [Afk., blend of *klein* small & *jong* boy + dim. suff. *-kie*.] A Black or Coloured boy.

klooch *n.* var. of KLOOTCH.

kloof /kluːf/ *n. S. Afr.* M18. [Du. = cleft: see CLOVE *n.*[4]] A deep valley, a ravine, a gorge.

klootch /kluːtʃ/ *n. N. Amer. dial.* Also **klooch**. M19. [Chinook Jargon *klootchman* f. Nootka *ło·csma* woman, wife.] In full *klootchman*. A N. American Indian woman.

klop *n.* & *v.* see CLOP.

klops /klɒps/ *n.* Pl. same, **-se** /-sə/. M20. [G.] A type of meatball or meat loaf.

kludge /klʌdʒ/ *n.* & *v. slang* (orig. *US*). M20. [Prob. symbolic: cf. BODGE, FUDGE *v.*] A *n.* An ill-matched assortment of parts put together to fulfil a specific purpose; *spec.* in *Computing*, an improvised machine, system, or program, a hastily or awkwardly contrived solution to a fault or bug, a badly structured system in need of re-design. M20. B *v.t.* Improvise or put together (a device, program, etc.) from an ill-matched assortment of parts. L20.

†klumene *n.* M19–E20. [f. mod.L *kalium* potassium (because orig. derived f. potassium carbide) + -ENE.] *Chem.* = ACETYLENE.

klunk /klʌŋk/ *n. US slang.* Also **c-**. M20. [Origin unkn.] = KLUTZ.

klutz /klʌts/ *n.* & *v. N. Amer. slang.* M20. [Yiddish f. G *Klotz* wooden block. Cf. CLOT *n.*] A *n.* A clumsy awkward person, *esp.* one considered socially inept; a fool. M20. B *v.i.* Foll. by *about*, *around*: behave awkwardly or foolishly, move clumsily. L20.

klutziness *n.* awkwardness of manner, foolishness L20. **klutzy** *a.* awkward in manner, foolish M20.

Kluxer /ˈklʌksə/ *n. US slang.* L19. [f. Ku *Klux* Klan + -ER[1].] A member of the Ku Klux Klan.

klydonograph /klʌɪˈdəʊnəgrɑːf/ *n.* E20. [f. Gk *kludōn* wave, billow + -O- + -GRAPH.] *Electr.* An instrument used to determine photographically the voltage and polarity of a surge, by means of a point electrode resting on film behind which is a plate electrode.

klystron /ˈklʌɪstrɒn/ *n.* M20. [f. Gk *klus-* stem of *kluzein* wash or break over + -TRON.] *Electronics.* An electron tube for amplifying or generating microwave signals using the energy of a beam of electrons whose velocities have been modulated by a high-frequency voltage so that they collect into bunches.

klystron oscillator, tube. reflex klystron: see REFLEX *n.* & *a.*

knab *n.* see NOB *n.*[2]

knab /nab/ *v.*[1] *obs.* exc. *dial.* Also **nab**. Infl. **-bb-**. M17. [Imit.: cf. KNAP *v.*[2], KNUB *v.*] 1 *v.t.* Bite lightly, nibble, nip. M17. 2 *v.i.* Bite, nibble, (*on*, *upon*). M17.

knab *v.*[2] see NOB *v.*[1]

†knabby *a.* & *n.* see NOBBY *a.* & *n.*

knack /nak/ *n.*[1] Now *Sc.* LME. [Imit.: cf. Du. *knak*, G *Knack*(*e*).] A sharp sound or blow; a crack, a snap: *fig.* a gibe, a taunt.

knack /nak/ *n.*[2] LME. [Ult. imit., but perh. immed. f. Du., LG *knak*. Cf. prec.] I 1 A trick, *esp.* a clever or (formerly) a deceitful one. LME. 2 An intuitive or acquired talent or skill for doing something cleverly and successfully; the ability to deal with or do something in the best way. L16. 3 A habit of acting or speaking in a particular way, a tendency to do a certain thing. L17.

1 E. O'BRIEN She mastered the knack of walking backward. 2 R. CROMPTON It's jus' a knack It jus' wants practice. *Observer* I only hope I've got my mother's knack of dealing with awkward questions. R. ELLMANN His knack for drawing was shown in some illustrations he made. P. BARKER He's got the knack of talking to your Dad. 3 R. HARLING He always had a knack of falling out with anyone in time. L. VAN DER POST This dreaming process had a knack of following through into my waking imagination.

II 4 An ingenious contrivance; a trinket, a trifle, a knick-knack. *arch.* M16.

knacky *a.* artful, clever, adroit, ingenious E18.

knack /nak/ *v. obs.* exc. *dial.* LME. [Imit.: for senses 3 & 4 cf. Du. *knakken*, MHG *knacken*, *gnacken*, etc.] 1 †a *v.t.* Sing in a lively or ornate way, trill, (a song). Only in LME. b *v.i.* Speak in a lively way, chatter; talk mincingly. E16. 2 *v.t.* Mock, taunt, (a person). Chiefly *Sc.* LME. 3 *v.t.* Strike (things) together so as to produce a sharp abrupt noise; gnash (the teeth); snap (the fingers). L15. b Break or crack (something) with a sharp sound. M16. 4 *v.i.* Make a sharp abrupt noise, as when stones are struck together. E17.

knacker /ˈnakə/ *n.*[1] LME. [f. prec. + -ER[1].] †1 A person who sings in a lively way. Only in LME. 2 A thing that makes a sharp cracking noise; *spec.* a castanet. Usu. in *pl. obs.* exc. *dial.* E17. 3 A testicle. Usu. in *pl. slang.* M19.

knacker /ˈnakə/ *n.*[2] L16. [Origin uncertain: in sense 1 perh. orig. maker of the smaller articles of harness (f. KNACK *n.*[2] + -ER[2]).] 1 A harness-maker; a saddler. *dial.* L16. 2 An old worn-out horse. *dial.* L18. 3 A buyer of old or worn-out horses for slaughter. E19. b A buyer of old houses, ships, etc., for their materials. L19.

3 *fig.*: J. CAREY The knacker's yard of language. This is where clichés come to die.

knackery *n.* a knacker's yard or business M19.

knacker /ˈnakə/ *v.t. slang.* L19. [f. KNACKER *n.*[1] 3 or KNACKER *n.*[2] 3.] Kill; castrate. Now usu., exhaust, wear out; damage severely, ruin.

B. BEAUMONT Roger Uttley had knackered his back bending . . to pick up a piece of apple pie.

knackered *a.* dead; castrated; (now usu.) exhausted, worn out: L19.

knackwurst /ˈnakwəːst, *foreign* ˈknakvʊrst/ *n.* Also **knock-** /ˈnɒk-/. M20. [G, f. *knacken* make a cracking noise + *Wurst* sausage.] A type of short fat highly seasoned German sausage.

knag /nag/ *n.* LME. [G (orig. LG) *Knagge* knot, peg.] 1 A short projection from the trunk or branch of a tree, as a dead branch; a peg, a hook. LME. 2 A knot in wood; the base of a branch. M16. 3 A pointed rock or crag. Now *dial.* M16. †4 Any of the knobs or points of a stag's horn; a tine. L16–M17.

†knagged *a.* knobbed, toothed, jagged LME–E18. **knaggy** *a.* knotty, rough, rugged, jagged M16.

knaidel /ˈkneɪd(ə)l/ *n.* Also **knei-**. Pl. **-dlach** /-dlax/. M20. [Yiddish *kneydel* f. MHG, G KNÖDEL.] A type of dumpling eaten esp. in Jewish households during Passover. Usu. in *pl.*

knallgas /ˈknalgas/ *n.* L19. [G, f. *Knall* bang, detonation + *Gas* gas.] *Chem.* An explosive mixture of gases, esp. one of two volumes of hydrogen with one of oxygen.

knap /nap/ *n.*[1] Chiefly *dial.* [OE *cnæp*(*p*), perh. cogn. w. ON *knappr* knob etc.: cf. KNOP.] The crest or summit of a hill or of rising ground; a small hill or hillock; a stretch of rising ground.

knap /nap/ *n.*[2] Now *dial.* LME. [Imit.: cf. KNAP *v.*[1] See also NAP *n.*[4]] An abrupt stroke or blow, a sharp knock.

knap *n.*[3] see KNAPE.

†knap *n.*[4] var. of NAP *n.*[2]

knap /nap/ *v.*[1] Now *dial.* exc. *Archaeol.* Infl. **-pp-**. LME. [Imit.: cf. Du. & G (orig. LG) *knappen* crack, crackle, KNAP *n.*[2]] 1 *v.t.* & *i.* Strike (a thing or person) with a hard short sound; knock, rap. LME. 2 *v.t.* Break (esp. a stone, *spec.* a flint) with a sharp blow from a hammer etc.; snap, crack, (something). M16. 3 *v.t.* & *i.* Speak or say, esp. affectedly; utter, chatter. *Sc.* & *north.* L16. 4 *v.t.* Break, strike, or knock *off* smartly. E17.

knap /nap/ *v.*[2] *i.* & *t.* Now *dial.* Infl. **-pp-**. L16. [Origin uncertain: cf. KNAB *v.*[1], Du. & G (orig. LG) *knappen* bite.] Bite, nip, snap (at), nibble.

†knap *v.*[3] var. of NAP *v.*[2]

knape /neɪp/ *n.* Long *obs.* exc. *dial.* In sense 3 also **knap** /nap/. [OE *cnapa* = OS *cnapo*, OHG *knappo* (G *Knappe* page, squire). Obscurely rel. to KNAVE.] †1 = KNAVE 1. OE–E17. †2 = KNAVE 2. OE–M16. 3 = KNAVE 3. LME.

knapped /napt/ *a.* M19. [f. KNAP *v.*[1] + -ED[1].] Of flint, a flint: broken by a sharp blow.

B. W. ALDISS A fine church . . refaced with knapped flint in the eighteen-eighties.

knapper /ˈnapə/ *n.* Chiefly *dial.* L18. [f. KNAP *v.*[1] + -ER[1].] A person who or thing which shapes or breaks stones, esp. flints.

knapsack /ˈnapsak/ *n.* E17. [MLG, f. Du. *knapzak* (G *Knapp-sack*), prob. f. G *knappen* bite (cf. KNAP *v.*[2]) + *zak* SACK *n.*[1]] A bag of canvas or other weatherproof material with shoulder-straps, carried on the back esp. by soldiers and hikers.

A. RANSOME The knapsacks on their backs, . . were heavy and uncomfortable.

Comb.: **knapsack pump, sprayer** a sprayer consisting of a hand-held nozzle supplied from a pressurized reservoir that is carried on the back like a knapsack.

knapsacked *a.* equipped with a knapsack or knapsacks E20. **knapsacking** *n.* travelling with a knapsack L19.

knapweed /ˈnapwiːd/ *n.* Orig. **†knopweed**. LME. [f. KNOP *n.* + WEED *n.*[1] For the change of vowel cf. *strop*, *strap*.] Any of several plants of the genus *Centaurea*, , of the composite family, related to the thistles, with heads of usu. purple flowers and hard globular involucres; *esp.* (more fully *lesser knapweed*) hardhead, *C. nigra*, and (more fully *greater knapweed*), *C. scabiosa*, of chalk grassland.

knar /nɑː/ *n.* Also **knaur** /nɔː/, **gn-**. See also KNUR. ME. [MLG, MDu., MHG *knorre* (Du. *knorr*, G *Knorren*) knobbly protuberance.] 1 A rugged rock or stone. Now *dial.* ME. 2 A knot in wood; *spec.* a bark-covered protuberance on the trunk or root of a tree. LME. 3 A burly thickset person. Long *obs.* exc. *Sc.* LME.

knarred *a.* knotted, gnarled M19. **knarry** *a.* (long *arch. rare*) having knars or knots, knotty LME.

knarl /nɑːl/ *n. rare.* L16. [App. deriv. of KNAR: cf. GNARL *n.*, KNURL *n.*] †1 A tangle, a knot. Only in L16. 2 A hunchbacked person, a dwarf. *dial.* E19.

¶The earliest recorded of the set of words in *-l*.

knaur *n.* var. of KNAR.

knave /neɪv/ *n.* [OE *cnafa* = OHG *knabo* (G *Knabe* boy) f. WGmc. Obscurely rel. to KNAPE.] †1 A male child, a boy. Latterly only more fully *knave-bairn*, *knave-child*. OE–E19. 2 A boy employed as a servant; a male servant; a person of low status, a menial. *arch.* OE. 3 An unprincipled or deceitful person, esp. a man; a rogue, a scoundrel. ME. b A fellow, a chap. *joc.* M16. 4 *Cards.* The lowest court-card of each suit, bearing the representation of a male youth; a jack. M16.

3 F. DONALDSON He is far more fool than knave.

Comb.: *knave-bairn*, *-child*: see sense I above; *knave noddy*: see NODDY *n.*[2]

knaveship *n.* †(*a*) *Sc.* a quantity of corn or meal given as a fee to a miller's servant; (*b*) *arch.* (with possess. adj., as *his* etc. *knaveship*) a mock title given to a disreputable person: L15. **knavish** *a.* characteristic of a knave LME. **knavishly** *adv.* L15. **knavishness** *n.* E16.

knavery /ˈneɪv(ə)ri/ *n.* E16. [f. prec. + -ERY.] 1 Unprincipled or deceitful behaviour, trickery; an unprincipled deed or practice. *arch.* E16. †2 A trick, a jest; roguishness, playfulness. L16–M17. b Frippery, finery. *rare* (Shakes.). Only in L16.

knawel /ˈnɔːɪl/ *n.* L16. [G *Knauel*, *Kneuel*.] A low-growing plant of the genus *Scleranthus*, of the pink family, with clusters of small petalless flowers; *esp.* (more fully *annual knawel*), *S. annuus*, a weed frequent in sandy soil.

knead /niːd/ *v.* [OE *cnedan* = OS *knedan* (Du. *kneden*), OHG *knetan* (G *kneten*), f. WGmc.] 1 *v.t.* Work into a homogeneous plastic mass by successively drawing out, folding over, and pressing together; *esp.* work (moistened flour or clay) into dough or paste; make (bread, pottery, etc.) by this process. OE. 2 *v.t.* Blend or weld together; manipulate, mould, form. LME. 3 *v.t.* & *i.* a Massage or squeeze with the hands, as if working dough etc. E17. b Esp. of a cat: paw (a thing or person) repetitively with alternate front paws. M20.

1 S. ORBACH The Italian mama kneading the pasta. 2 H. ROGERS Inconsistencies . . incapable . . of being kneaded into any harmonious system. B. TAYLOR Knead and shape her to your thought. 3a M. AMIS With quivering finger-tips I kneaded my forehead and scalp. b V. CANNING The cat woke me up by kneading determinedly on my chest.

kneadable *a.* E19. **kneader** *n.* ME.

knee /niː/ *n.* [OE *cnēo(w)* = OFris. *kniu*, *knē*, *knī*, OS *knio* (Du. *knie*), OHG *kneo*, *kniu* (G *Knie*), ON *kné*, Goth. *kniu*, f. Gmc f. IE, f. base also of L *genu*, Gk *gonu*.] I A joint. 1 The joint between a person's thigh and lower leg; the region around this joint. Also, the upper surface of the thighs of a sitting person, the lap. OE. b A damaged condition of the knee. (Earliest in *housemaid's knee* s.v. HOUSEMAID.) M19. 2 A joint in an animal limb corresponding or analogous to the human knee; *spec.* (*a*) the carpal articulation of the foreleg of a quadruped; (*b*) the tarsal articulation or heel of a bird. LME. 3 The part of a garment covering the knee. LME.

1 M. DRABBLE He organised himself into a sitting position, his arms around his knees. A. BROOKNER Those rules that girls are supposed to learn at their mother's knee. M. IGNATIEFF In the garden, holding Lionel on her knee. J. FORD Humbly on my knees I kiss your gracious hand. H. BROOKE My knees trembled . . ; a swimming came before my eyes.

II Something resembling the knee. 4 A piece of timber with a natural or artificial angular bend, *spec.* one used as a support in carpentry and shipbuilding; a piece of metal of similar shape and use. LME. 5 A part of a hill, tree, etc., regarded as corresponding to a human knee. Also (*rare*), a natural prominence, as a rock or crag. L16. 6 *Bot.* a The node of a grass. Now *dial.* L17. b A conical protuberance on the roots of the bald cypress and tupelo, rising above the water in which the tree grows. L19. 7 An abrupt obtuse or approximately right-angled bend in a graph between parts where the slope varies smoothly. L19.

Phrases: **across one's knee** (of a person, esp. a child) face-down on or on to the knee to be spanked. **bend** or **bow the knee** kneel, esp. in submission. **bring a person to his** or **her knees** bring a person to a difficult position or to submission. *housemaid's knee*: see HOUSEMAID *n.* **knee by knee** side by side and close together. **knee to knee** (*a*) = *knee by knee* above; (*b*) facing each other with the knees touching. *on bended knee(s)*: see BEND *v. on the knees of the gods*: see GOD *n. the bee's knees*: see BEE *n.*[1] *water on the knee*: see WATER *n.*

Comb.: **knee-action** (*a*) the action or coordination of movement of the knee-joint of a horse; (*b*) exaggerated raising of the knee by an athlete; (*c*) a form of independent front-wheel suspension in a motor vehicle; **knee-bend** *n.* & *v.* (*a*) *n.* an act of bending the (human) knee; *spec.* a physical exercise in which the body is raised and lowered without use of the hands; (*b*) *v.i.* perform a knee-bend or knee-bends; **knee-board** *n.* & *v.* (*a*) *n.* a short surfboard ridden in a kneeling position; (*b*) *v.i.* ride a knee-board; **knee-bone** the patella, the kneecap; **knee-boot**: reaching to the knee; **knee-boss** *Hist.* a piece of armour used to protect the knee, consisting of a cap of leather etc.; **knee-brace** a strut fixed diagonally as reinforcement between two parts of a structure that meet at right angles; **knee-braced** *a.* supported by a knee-brace; **knee-breeched** *a.* wearing knee-breeches; **knee-breeches**: reaching down to or just below the knee; **knee-deep** *a.* (*a*) immersed *in* to the knee, *fig.* deeply involved *in*; (*b*) (covered with water etc.) so deep as to reach to the knee; **knee-halter** *v.t.* (chiefly *S. Afr.*) restrain (an animal, esp. a horse) by fastening a cord or halter from its head to its knees; **knee-high** *a.* immersed in or reaching as high as the knees (*knee-high to a* GRASSHOPPER); **knee-hole** a space for the knees between the drawers of a desk etc.; a desk having a knee-hole; **knee-holly**, **knee-holm** butcher's broom, *Ruscus aculeatus*; **knee-jerk** *n.* & *a.* (*a*) *n.* a sudden involuntary kick caused by a blow on the tendon just below the knee and used as a test of reflexes; (*b*) *adj.* predictable, automatic, stereotyped; **knee-joint** (*a*) the joint between the femur and the tibia in the leg; (*b*) *Mech.* a joint formed of two pieces hinged together endwise, a toggle joint; **knee-length** *a.* reaching to the knee; **knee-pan** = KNEECAP *n.* 2; **knee-piece** (*a*) a bent piece of timber used as a support in carpentry and shipbuilding; (*b*) *Hist.* a flexible piece of armour used to protect the knee; **knee-plate** (*a*) *Hist.* a broad steel plate worn as a protection for the thigh; (*b*) an angled metal plate used as a support in shipbuilding; **knee-rafter** a rafter the lower end of which is bent downwards; a diagonal brace between a rafter and a tie-beam; **knee-roof** = *curb roof* s.v. CURB *n.*; **knee-slapper** *N. Amer.* an uproariously funny joke; **knee-strings**: worn round the knee at the bottom of knee-breeches; **knees-up** *colloq.* [f. 'Knees up, Mother Brown', a popular song by H. Weston, B. Lee., and I. Taylor] a lively party or gathering, a celebration; **knee-timber** timber having a natural angular bend, suitable for use as a support in shipbuilding or carpentry; **knee-trembler** *slang* an act of sexual intercourse between people in a standing position.

kneelike *a.* resembling a knee (in shape or function) L19.

knee /niː/ *v.* Pa. t. & pple **kneed**. LOE. [f. the n.] 1 †a *v.i.* Kneel or bow, esp. in reverence or submission (*to*). LOE–E17. b *v.t.* Show reverence or submission to by kneeling or bending the knee. *arch.* L16. 2 *v.t.* Make (one's way) on one's knees. *rare.* E17. 3 *v.t.* *Carpentry* etc. Fasten (timbers) with a knee or knees. E18. 4a *v.t.* Give a kneelike or angular bend to. *Sc.* E19. b *v.i.* Bend at an angle. *Sc.* E19. 5 *v.t.* Disable (an animal) by making a cut in the knee. *US.* M19. 6 *v.t.* Strike or touch with the knee; *spec.* strike (a person), esp. in the groin, deliberately with the knee. L19.

6 R. B. PARKER I kneed him in the groin.

¶Not recorded between ME and L16 (when re-formed).

kneecap /ˈniːkap/ *n.* & *v.* M17. [f. KNEE *n.* + CAP *n.*[1]] A *n.* 1 A cap or protective covering for the knee; *spec.* a flexible piece of armour covering the knee. M17. 2 The convex bone in front of the knee-joint, the patella. M19. B *v.t.* Infl. **-pp-**. Shoot (a person) in the knee or leg as a punishment, esp. for betraying or defying a terrorist group. L20.

kneed /niːd/ *a.* L16. [f. KNEE *n.*, *v.*: see -ED[2], -ED[1].] 1 a Having an angle like a knee; having or fixed with a knee or knees for support. L16. b *Bot.* Bent at the nodes; geniculate. L16. 2 Furnished with or having knees (of a specified kind). M17. 3 Of trousers: bulging at the knees. L19.

kneel /niːl/ *v.i.* Pa. t. & pple **kneeled**, **knelt** /nɛlt/. [OE *cnēowlian*, corresp. to (M)LG *knēlen*, Du. *knielen*: cf. KNEE *n.*, *v.*] 1 Fall, support oneself, or (less commonly) rise on one's knees or a knee, esp. in reverence or submission (*to* a person, God, etc.). Also w. indirect pass., *be knelt to*. OE. 2 Foll. by *down*: go down on the knees. Foll. by *up*: rise or support oneself on the knees with the body and thighs upright. ME.

1 TENNYSON Good people, you do ill to kneel to me. What is it I . . have done to merit this? M. SCAMMELL He would kneel before the icon and recite his prayers. P. BOWLES The man . . made the complaining animal kneel and receive the extra burden. D. H. LAWRENCE Women were kneeling on the stones, filling red jars. 2 W. WHARTON He kneels down and begins gathering up his tools.

¶The form *knelt* (after *felt*, *dealt*) dates only from 19.

kneeler *n.* (*a*) a person who kneels, esp. in reverence; (*b*) a cushion, hassock, or low bench used for kneeling on, esp. in prayer: LME. **kneeling** *n.* (*a*) the action of the vb; an instance of this; (*b*) a place or space for kneeling in a place of worship: ME.

kneesie /ˈniːzi/ *n.* *colloq.* Also **-sy**. M20. [Joc. dim. of pl. of KNEE *n.*: see -IE.] *sing.* & in *pl.* Amorous play with the knees. Cf. FOOTSIE *n.*[1]

kneidel *n.* var. of KNAIDEL.

Kneipe /ˈknaɪpə/ *n.* Pl. ***-pen*** /-pən/, ***-pes***. M19. [G.] In Germany: a lively social gathering of young people, esp. students, in a bar or restaurant; a public house, a bar.

Kneipp /nʌɪp/ *n.* L19. [Sebastian *Kneipp* (1821–97), Bavarian priest.] Used *attrib.* to designate (a system of) hydropathic treatments advocated by Kneipp, *spec.* walking barefoot through dewy grass.

†**kneiss** *n.* see GNEISS.

knell /nɛl/ *n.* [OE *cnyll* rel. to next. See also KNOLL *n.*[2]] 1 The sound made by a bell when struck or rung, esp. when rung slowly and solemnly (as) for a death or at a funeral. OE. 2 *fig.* A sound, an announcement, or an event regarded as portending death or the end of something. E17.

1 SIR W. SCOTT The heavy knell, the choir's faint swell, Came slowly down the wind. 2 SOUTHEY As if with the Inchcape Bell, The fiends below were ringing his knell. J. GALSWORTHY When . . Dartie had that financial crisis . . the knell of all prosperity seemed to have sounded. DEATH-*knell*.

knell /nɛl/ *v.* *arch.* [OE *cnyllan*: present form (f. LME) perh. by assoc. w. BELL *n.*[1] See also KNOLL *v.*] 1 *v.t.* Strike with a resounding blow, knock. Long *obs.* exc. *Sc.* OE. †2 *v.t.* Ring (a bell), esp. slowly and solemnly (as) for a death or at a funeral; toll (a bell). OE–M17. 3 *v.i.* (Of a bell) ring, esp. for a death or at a funeral, toll; *transf.* & *fig.* sound ominously or dolefully, reverberate. LME. 4 *v.t.* a Summon or call (as) by a knell. LME. b Proclaim (as) by a knell. M19.

knelt *v.* pa. t. & pple: see KNEEL.

Knesset /ˈknɛsɛt/ *n.* M20. [Heb., lit 'gathering'.] The parliament of the State of Israel.

knevel *n.* & *v.* var. of NEVEL.

knew *v.* pa. t. of KNOW *v.*

knez /knɛz/ *n.* Pl. ***knezes*** /ˈknɛzɪz/, same. L16. [Slav. (Serbo-Croat *knêz*, Russ. *knyaz'*, Bulgarian *knez*, etc.) f. Old Ch. Slav. *kŭnęzĭ*, f. Gmc n. meaning 'king'.] *Hist.* In Slavonic countries: a prince, a ruler; a lord, a nobleman.

knick /nɪk/ *n.*[1] & *v.* *Sc.* L16. [Imit.: cf. (w. the n.) MDu *cnic* (Du. *knik*), MLG, G *Knick*, (w. the vb) MDu. *cnicken* (Du. *knikken*), MLG, G *knicken*.] A *n.* A cracking or clicking sound made (as) with the fingers. Long *obs.* exc. *Sc.* L16. B *v.t.* & *i.* Make a cracking or clicking sound with (the fingers etc.). M18.

knick /nɪk/ *n.*[2] Also **nick**. M20. [G = bend, kink, break.] *Physical Geogr.* 1 = KNICKPOINT. M20. 2 The angle formed by a pediment and the adjacent mountain slope. M20.

knicker *n.*[1] see KNICKERS.

knicker *n.*[2] var. of NICKER *n.*[3]

knickerbocker /ˈnɪkəbɒkə/ *n.* M19. [Diedrich *Knickerbocker*, pretended author of W. Irving's *History of New York* (1809).] 1 (**K-**.) A descendant of the original Dutch settlers of the New Netherlands (later divided into New York and New Jersey); a New Yorker. M19. 2 In *pl.* a Short loose-fitting trousers gathered in at the knee or calf. M19. b = KNICKERS 2. L19.

Comb.: **Knickerbocker Glory** a quantity of ice-cream served with fruit, jelly, cream, etc., in a tall glass; **knickerbocker yarn** yarn flecked with different colours.

knickerbockered *a.* wearing knickerbockers M19.

knickers /ˈnɪkəz/ *n.pl.* In attrib. use & in comb. usu. in sing. **knicker** (otherwise *rare*). L19. [Abbrev. of *knickerbockers*: see prec.] 1 Knickerbockers. Also, a boy's short trousers. *colloq.* (now *N. Amer.*). L19. 2 A pair of women's or girls' pants worn as underwear, covering the body from the waist or hips to the tops of the thighs (orig. to the knees). Also *pair of knickers*. L19. b As *int.* Expr. surprise, contempt, disbelief, etc. *colloq.* L20.

1 J. UPDIKE A trio of them were gathered in knickers and Scots caps on a felt putting green. 2 V. GLENDINNING She dressed exotically in a crimson silk shawl over frilled knickers. *Melody Maker* Laugh? That's an easy one. The knickers are still wet. *French knickers*: see FRENCH *a.* **get one's knickers in a twist** *colloq.* become agitated or upset.

Comb.: **knicker yarn** = KNICKERBOCKER *yarn*.

knickered *a.* wearing knickerbockers or knickers L19.

knick-knack /ˈnɪknak/ *n.* Also **nick-nack**. L16. [Redupl. of KNACK *n.*[2] with vowel variation.] †1 A petty trick, an artifice, a subterfuge. L16–L17. 2 A repeated knocking or cracking sound; an instrument producing such a sound. Now *rare*. M17. 3 A small dainty article of furniture, dress, etc.; any trifling frivolous object more for ornament than use; a trinket. L17.

3 I. COLEGATE Tables crowded with knick-knacks and framed photographs. *Sunday Express* Holding her latest knick-knack—a . . full-size replica of the America's Cup.

knick-'knackatory *n.* (now *rare*) [after *conservatory* etc.] a repository of knick-knacks E18. **knick-'knackery** *n.* a knick-knack or trifling ornament; knick-knacks collectively: L18. **knick-knacket** *n.* (*Sc.*) a little knick-knack L18. **knick-knackish** *a.* of the nature of a knick-knack, trifling E19. **knick-knacky** *a.* (*a*) given to acquiring knick-knacks; (*b*) of the nature of a knick-knack, affected, trifling: L18.

knickpoint /ˈnɪkpɔɪnt/ *n.* Also **n-**. E20. [Partial tr. G *Knickpunkt*, f. *Knick* KNICK *n.*[2] + *Punkt* point.] *Physical Geogr.* A break of slope in a river profile, esp. where a new curve of erosion arising from rejuvenation intersects an earlier curve.

knicks /nɪks/ *n.pl. colloq.* L19. [Abbrev.] = KNICKERS.

knife /nʌɪf/ *n.* Pl. **knives** /nʌɪvz/. [Late OE *cnīf* f. ON *knífr* = OFris., MLG *knīf*, MDu. *cnijf* (Du. *knijf*), f. Gmc wd of unkn. origin.] 1 A cutting instrument composed of a blade (usu. of metal with usu. one long edge sharpened) and a handle into which this is fixed either rigidly or with a joint. LOE. b Such an instrument used as a weapon. ME. c Such an instrument used in surgery. Chiefly in *the knife*, surgery, a surgical operation. L19. 2 A sharpened cutting-blade forming part of a machine. M19.

1 ARNOLD BENNETT He ate a little of the lean . . ; then he . . laid down his knife and fork. *fig.*: *Observer* I was skinned by the icy knives of the wind. *bread-knife, butter-knife, carving-knife, fish-knife, flick-knife, palette knife, paper-knife, penknife, sheath knife, steak knife*, etc. b SHAKES. *Tr. & Cr.* Thou lay'st in every gash that love hath given me The knife that made it. c *Listener* No one knows what can happen once the patient is under the knife.

Phrases: **before one can say knife** *colloq.* very quickly or suddenly. **get one's knife into** persecute, be persistently malicious or vindictive towards. *long knife*: see LONG *a.*[1] †**pair of knives** a set of two knives, esp. as carried in a sheath. **that one could cut with a knife** *colloq.* (of an accent) marked, heavily dialectal; (of an atmosphere) oppressive, tense. *the run of one's knife*: see RUN *n.* **twist the knife** *fig.* increase existing suffering, worsen an injury already inflicted.

Comb.: **knife-bar**: holding the knives in a cutting machine; **knife-blade** (*a*) the blade of a knife; (*b*) *Mountaineering* a long thin piton; **knife-board** (*a*) a board on which knives are cleaned; (*b*) *colloq.* (*Hist.*) the double bench on the roof of an early type of bus; **knife-boy**: employed to clean table knives; **knife-edge** (*a*) the edge of a knife; (*b*) a steel wedge on which a pendulum etc. swings; (*c*) a sharp mountain ridge, an arête; (*d*) *fig.* a position of extreme danger or uncertainty; **knife-edged** *a.* having a thin sharp edge like a knife; **knife-fish** any of various narrow-bodied fishes; *spec.* any of various neotropical freshwater fishes of the families Gymnotidae and Rhamphichthyidae, allied to the electric eel, with a long bladelike anal fin; **knife-grinder** (*a*) a person who grinds knives and cutting tools in the process of manufacture; (*b*) a travelling sharpener of knives and cutting tools; (*c*) an instrument for grinding cutting tools; **knife-guard** a small hinged metal arm on the back of a carving-fork to protect the hand against the slipping of the knife; **knife-machine**: for cleaning knives; **knife-man** a person who uses a knife as a tool or weapon; **knife-pleat** a narrow flat pleat on a skirt etc.; **knife-pleated** *a.* having knife-pleats; **knife-point** the pointed end of a knife, esp. as directed at a person as a threat (*at knife-point*, under threat of injury or an ultimatum etc.); **knife-rest** (*a*) a metal or glass rest or support for a carving-knife or -fork at table; (*b*) *Mil. slang* a barrier made of barbed wire and timber; **knife switch** *Electr.*: operated by the movement of a conducting blade or set of blades hinged at one end; **knife-thrower** a person who throws knives at targets as an entertainment, esp. in a circus; **knife-throwing** the throwing of knives at targets, esp. as a circus act; **knife-work** the use of knives as weapons or instruments.

knifeful *n.* as much as a knife will hold or carry M19. **knifeless** *a.* (*rare*) LME. **knifelike** *a.* resembling a knife, having a sharp blade M19.

knife /nʌɪf/ *v.* M19. [f. the n. Cf. KNIVE *v.*] 1 *v.t.* Cut or stab with a knife; *techn.* trim with a knife. M19. 2 (Attempt to) bring about the defeat of (a person) in an underhand way. *slang.* L19. 3 *v.i.* Move as with the action of a knife cutting or passing through. E20.

1 CONAN DOYLE I would have thought no more of knifing him than of smoking this cigar. S. KITZINGER Rape . . is violence, just as much as being knifed. 3 *Coarse Angler* The line knifed up . . through the brown water of the loch.

knifer *n.* (*a*) a person who carries or uses a knife as a weapon; (*b*) a person who trims the soles and heels of shoes and boots: L19.

knifey /ˈnʌɪfi/ *n. colloq.* (chiefly *Sc.*). Also **-fie**. L19. [f. KNIFE *n.* + -Y[6].] = MUMBLE-THE-PEG.

knifey /ˈnʌɪfi/ *a.* M19. [f. KNIFE *n.* + -Y[1].] Resembling the edge of a knife in narrowness or sharpness.

knifie *n.* var. of KNIFEY *n.*

knight /nʌɪt/ *n.* & *v.* [OE *cniht* = OFris. *knecht*, *kniucht*, OS *knecht*, OHG *kneht* (Du. *knecht*, G *Knecht*), f. WGmc wd of unkn. origin.] A *n.* †1 A boy, a youth. Only in OE. †2 A boy or youth employed as an attendant or servant; a male servant or attendant of any age. OE–ME. 3a *Hist.* In the Middle Ages: a male military servant of a person of high rank; a feudal tenant holding land from a superior in exchange for military service; *spec.* a man, usu. a noble, raised to honourable military rank esp. by a monarch after service as a page and squire, and ranking below a baron; such a man serving or attending a woman of rank, esp. as her champion in a war or tournament. OE. b *fig.* A man devoted to the service of a woman, cause, etc. ME. c *Hist.* In full *knight of the shire*. A gentleman representing a shire or county in parliament, orig. either of two of the rank of knight. LME. d A man awarded a title (now non-hereditary) by a sovereign in recognition of personal merit or services rendered, ranking below a baronet, and entitled to be styled *Sir*. M16. 4 Orig. (in ancient history or mythology), a person holding a position or rank similar to that of the medieval knight. Later *spec.* (*a*) *Rom. Hist.* [tr. L *eques* horseman] a member of the class orig. forming the Roman army's cavalry, later of great wealth and political importance; (*b*) *Gk Hist.* [tr. Gk *hippeus* horseman] a citizen of the second class at Athens in the constitution of Solon. ME. †b [tr. L *miles*.] An ordinary soldier. ME–M16. 5 *Chess.* Each of the four pieces (two per player) moving to the next but one square of the opposite colour, and usu. having the upper part shaped like a horse's head. ME. †6 *Naut.* Either of two strong posts or bitts on a deck, having sheaves through which the jeers or halyards were passed. LME–M17.

3a C. S. LEWIS The blood went back to a Norman knight whose bones lie at Battle Abbey. T. H. WHITE 'I shall have to have a lady-love . . ' added the future knight . . 'so that I can . . do deeds in her honour.' *Knight of the Bath, Knight of the Garter, Knight of the Thistle*, etc. b SHAKES. *Rom. & Jul.* O, find him! give this ring to my true knight. TENNYSON In all your quarrels will I be your knight.

Comb. & *phrases*: *knight bachelor*: see BACHELOR 1; *knight banneret*: see BANNERET *n.*[1]; *knight commander*: see COMMANDER 2c; **knight-head** *Naut.* either of two large timbers rising obliquely from the keel behind the stem of a vessel and supporting the bowsprit; *Knight* HOSPITALLER; **knight in shining armour** a chivalrous rescuer or helper, esp. of a woman; *knight marshal*: see MARSHAL *n.*[1]; **Knight of Columbus** *N. Amer.* a member of a society of Roman Catholic men founded at New Haven, Connecticut, in 1882; *Knight of the Holy Sepulchre*: see SEPULCHRE *n.* 1; **knight of the post** *arch.* [w. allus. to a whipping-post] a man making his living by giving false evidence; a notorious perjurer; **knight of the road** (*a*) a highwayman; (*b*) a commercial traveller; (*c*) a tramp; (*d*) a lorry driver; a taxi driver; **knight of the shire** (*a*) see sense 3c above; (*b*) *joc.* a Conservative member for a country constituency who has been knighted for political services; *knight of the spigot*: see SPIGOT *n.* 1; **knight-service** (*a*) *Hist.* the tenure of land on condition of military service; (*b*) (good) service such as was rendered by a knight; *Knight Templar*: see TEMPLAR *n.* 1, 1b; *Teutonic* (*Order of*) *Knights*: see TEUTONIC *a.* 2; *white knight*: see WHITE *a.*

B *v.t.* Confer a knighthood on. ME.

H. BAILEY Her husband, Sir George Catlin, was knighted in 1970.

knightage *n.* (*a*) knights collectively; (*b*) a list and account of knights: M19. **knightess** *n.* (*rare*) (*a*) a woman who fights like a knight; (*b*) a female member of a knightly order: M16. **knightlike** *a.* & *adv.* (*a*) *adj.* resembling or befitting a knight; (*b*) *adv.* = KNIGHTLY *adv.*: LME. **knightling** *n.* (*rare*) a petty or insignificant knight M17. **knightship** *n.* (now *rare*) †(*a*) military service; †(*b*) knightly character; valour; (*c*) the rank or position of a knight: ME.

knight errant /nʌɪt ˈɛr(ə)nt/ *n. phr.* Also **knight-errant**. Pl. **knights errant**, **knight-errants**. LME. [f. KNIGHT *n.* + ERRANT *a.*] 1 A medieval knight wandering in search of chivalrous adventures. LME. 2 *transf.* A man of a chivalrous, adventurous, or quixotic nature. M18.

1 G. BERKELEY From what giants and monsters would these knight-errants undertake to free the world? 2 H. H. ASQUITH The Victorians . . were not a race of knights errant. *fig.*: *Your Business* Design—the knight errant of British business.

knight-errantry *n.* (*a*) the practice or conduct of a knight errant; (*b*) *rare* the body of knights errant: M17. **knight-errantship** *n.* (*rare*) the condition of a knight errant; (with possess. adj., as *your* etc. *knight-errantship*) a mock title of respect given to a knight errant: M17.

knighthood /ˈnʌɪthʊd/ *n.* OE. [f. KNIGHT *n.* + -HOOD.] †1 Boyhood, youth. Only in OE. 2 The rank or dignity of a knight; an award of this. ME. b A man with this rank; a knight. *rare*. L16. 3 The profession or vocation of a medieval knight. ME. †b [tr. L *militia*.] Military service; warfare. ME–M16. 4 The character and qualities befitting a medieval knight. ME. 5 Knights collectively. LME.

2 R. H. SHERARD The middle class contempt for the title of knighthood. E. LINKLATER He had been offered a knighthood for his official War History of the submarines. 3 R. A. VAUGHAN The old virtues of knighthood—its truth and honour, its chastity and courage.

knightly /ˈnʌɪtli/ *a.* OE. [f. KNIGHT *n.* + -LY[1].] †1 Boyish. Only in OE. 2 Having the rank or qualities of a medieval knight. Now *rare*. LME. 3 Of a thing, action, etc.: of, pertaining to, or befitting a medieval knight. LME. 4 Consisting of knights. M19.

3 DRYDEN Preferr'd above the rest, By him with knightly deeds. 4 J. A. MICHENER That was the report circulated through the knightly circles of Europe.

knightlihood *n.* (*rare*) LME. **knightliness** *n.* L16.

knightly /ˈnʌɪtli/ *adv.* LME. [f. KNIGHT *n.* + -LY[2].] After the fashion of or in a manner befitting a medieval knight.

SHAKES. *Rich. II* Say . . why thou comest thus knightly clad in arms.

kniphofia /nɪˈfəʊfɪə, nʌɪ-; nɪpˈhəʊfɪə/ *n.* M19. [mod.L (see below), f. Johann Hieronymus *Kniphof* (1704–63), Ger. botanist + -IA[1].] Any of various tall ornamental plants of the genus *Kniphofia*, of the lily family, native to southern and eastern Africa and bearing long spikes or dense racemes of red, yellow, or orange flowers. Also called *red-hot poker*, *torch lily*. Cf. TRITOMA.

knish /knɪʃ/ *n.* M20. [Yiddish f. Russ. (also *knysh*) kind of bun or dumpling.] A baked or fried dumpling made of flaky dough filled with chopped liver, potato, or cheese.

knit /nɪt/ *n.* L16. [f. the vb.] **1a** The style or stitch in which a thing is knitted; a knitted fabric; knitted work; knitwear. L16. **b** A knitted garment. Freq. in *pl.* M20. **2** A contraction or wrinkle of the brow. L19.

1a *New York Post* Whip up . . day dress in low-cost knit. *Daily Telegraph* Coco Chanel . . seized upon the freedom of knit as early as 1913. **b** *Shetland Times* Warm chunky knits, very welcome in present weather conditions.

knit /nɪt/ *v.* Infl. **-tt-**. Pa. t. & pple **knitted**, (esp. in senses 3–6) **knit**. [OE *cnyttan* = MLG, MDu. *knutten* (G dial. *knütten*), f. WGmc vb, f. base of KNOT *n.*[1]] **I 1** *v.t.* Tie in or with a knot; fasten, bind, attach, or join (as) by knotting. Now *arch.* & *dial.* OE. **†b** Fasten or bundle up; *fig.* reprove, silence. Also foll. by *up*. ME–L16. **†c** Geld (a ram) by tying the scrotum. E17–M18. **2** *v.t.* & *i.* Orig., form (a net) by knotting string in an open mesh pattern. Later, make (a garment, blanket, etc.) by interlocking and entwining a successive series of loops of yarn, esp. wool, using long needles or a machine, *spec.* by bringing the yarn from the back through the next loop in a plain or garter stitch; make (a stitch or a row of stitches) in this way. ME. **3a** *v.t.* Combine or unite closely; bind, join, or connect firmly. Freq. foll. by *together*. Now chiefly *fig.* ME. **b** *v.i.* Join; grow together; unite; *spec.* (of the parts of a broken bone) become joined, heal. L15. **c** *v.i.* Of bees: cluster together in a mass. Now *dial.* L16. **4** *v.t.* Interlace, intertwine; weave or plait together. Now *rare* or *obs.* LME. **5a** *v.t.* Draw (the brows) closely together to form folds or wrinkles. LME. **b** *v.i.* Of the brows: draw closely together. M16. **6** *v.t.* & *i.* Make or become compact or firm by close contraction or combination of parts. LME. **b** *v.i. spec.* Of fruit etc.: form, set. Of a tree or flower: form fruit. LME. **†c** Of a female animal: conceive. E17–L18. **7** *v.t.* Constitute or establish (a covenant, agreement, etc.). LME. **8** *v.t.* Foll. by *up*: **a** Tie or fasten up; make, repair, or finish off (a garment etc.) by knitting. LME. **b** Conclude, finish, end. M16.

2 DYLAN THOMAS Knit one slip one knit two together Pass the slipstitch over. P. MORTIMER You couldn't have knitted a tea-cosy out of that wool. M. WEST Lotte would be waiting . . knitting placidly at the fireside. J. UPDIKE Her russet knit sweater has ridden up from the waist of her slacks. E. O'BRIEN She knit his socks in cable stitch. **3** POPE There, where the juncture knits the channel bone. J. CONRAD The unspoken loyalty that knits together a ship's company. **b** K. KESEY I can't get back in togs till the fracture knits and I get the cast off. *Sunday Times* A very clingy, tightly-knit atmosphere where everybody knows each other's business. **5** SHAKES. *2 Hen. VI* He knits his brow and shows an angry eye. **b** J. HARVEY Whenever Hawkins said something that displeased Riley, his bushy eyebrows knit and met in one. **6** G. SANTAYANA His languid figure grew somewhat better knit. **8a** SHAKES. *Macb.* Sleep that knits up the ravell'd sleeve of care. R. C. TRENCH We see how entirely his own life is knit up with his child's. **b** J. A. FROUDE The tragedy was being knitted up in the deaths of the last actors in it.

II 9 *v.i.* Of beer, wine, etc.: effervesce, form froth. Now *rare* or *obs.* M18.

Comb.: **knitbone** the plant comfrey, *Symphytum officinale*, reputed to mend broken bones; a herbal tea made from this; **knitwork** knitted work; knitting.

knitter *n.* (*a*) a person or thing which ties or unites something; (*b*) a person who knits garments etc.: ME.

knitch /nɪtʃ/ *n.* Long *dial.* Also **nitch**. [OE *ġe)cnyċċe* cogn. w. LG *knuck(e*, G *Knocke* bundle of heckled flax.] **†1** A bond. Only in OE. **2** A bundle of wood, hay, corn, etc.; a sheaf; a faggot. ME.

knitchel *n.* a small bundle E16.

knitch *v.* see NITCH *v.*

knitting /ˈnɪtɪŋ/ *n.* LME. [f. KNIT *v.* + -ING[1].] **1** The action of KNIT *v.* LME. **†b** A tie, a fastening, a knot. LME–L16. **2** The product of knitting; knitted work; *esp.* a garment etc. in the process of being made by knitting. L19.

2 A. CHRISTIE Taking her knitting out of its embroidered . . bag.

Phrases: *double knitting*: see DOUBLE *a.* & *adv.*

Comb.: **knitting-case** (*a*) = *knitting-sheath* below; (*b*) a case for keeping knitting-needles in; **knitting machine**: used for mechanically knitting garments etc.; **knitting-needle**, **knitting-pin** a thin pointed rod of steel, wood, plastic, etc., usu. with a knob at one end, used esp. in pairs in knitting; **knitting sheath** a cylindrical sheath for holding a knitting-needle steady; **knitting-wire** *Sc.* = *knitting-needle* above.

knittle /ˈnɪt(ə)l/ *n.* LME. [f. KNIT *v.*: see -LE[1].] A string or cord for tying or fastening. Long only *spec.* (*a*) *Naut.* a small line made of yarn; (*b*) *dial.* a drawstring.

knitwear /ˈnɪtwɛː/ *n.* E20. [f. *knit* pa. pple of KNIT *v.* + WEAR *n.*] Knitted garments collectively.

knive /nʌɪv/ *v.t.* & *i.* M19. [f. KNIFE *n.* after *strife*, *strive*, etc.] = KNIFE *v.*

knives *n.* pl. of KNIFE *n.*

knob /nɒb/ *n.* & *v.* LME. [MLG *knobbe* knot, knob, bud: cf. Flem. *knobbe(n* lump of bread etc., Du. *knobbel* bump, knot, & KNOP, KNUB *n.*, NOB *n.*[1]] **A** *n.* **1** A rounded lump or protuberance, esp. at the end or on the surface of a thing; *spec.* a handle of a door or drawer shaped like this, a similar attachment for pulling, turning, etc. LME. **b** *Archit.* A carved boss, esp. at the end of a raised moulding or at the intersection of ribs. M18. **c** The penis. *coarse slang.* L20. **2** A prominent isolated rounded mound or hill; any hill. Cf. KNOT *n.*[1] 12. Chiefly *US.* M17. **3** A small usu. round piece *of* butter, sugar, coal, etc. L17. **4** = NOB *n.*[1] 1. *slang.* E18.

1 M. ANGELOU I had my hand on the knob when the door burst open. T. O. ECHEWA Peering into the car's interior . . at the knobs and buttons on its instrument panel. P. ROTH Remember the knobs on the top of the maple bedposts? **with knobs on** *slang* that and more (used in retort to an insult, to express emphatic agreement, etc.).

Comb.: **knob-cone (pine)** a Californian pine, *Pinus attenuata*; **knob-nosed** *a.* having a knob-shaped nose; **knobstick** (*a*) = KNOBKERRIE; (*b*) *arch.* = BLACKLEG *n.* 3; **knobwood** a small southern African tree, *Zanthoxylum capense*, of the rue family, which bears spine-tipped protuberances on its trunk.

B *v.* Infl. **-bb-**. **1** *v.i.* Form a knob or knobs; bulge (*out*). M16. **2** *v.t.* Hit, strike. Cf. NOB *v.*[1] *slang.* E19. **3** *v.t.* Provide with a knob or knobs. L19.

knobbed *a.* provided with or having a knob or knobs; formed into or ending in a knob: LME. **knoblike** *a.* resembling (that of) a knob E19.

knobber /ˈnɒbə/ *n.* L17. [f. KNOB *n.* + -ER[1].] = KNOBBLER.

knobble /ˈnɒb(ə)l/ *n.* LME. [f. KNOB *n.* + -LE[1]. Cf. Du., LG *knobbel* knob, knot. Cf. KNUBBLE *n.*, NUBBLE *n.*] A small knob.

knobbled *a.* L19.

knobble *v.* var. of KNUBBLE *v.*

knobbler /ˈnɒblə/ *n.* L17. [f. KNOBBLE *n.* + -ER[1].] A male deer in its second year; a brocket.

knobbly /ˈnɒbli/ *a.* Also **n-**. M17. [f. KNOBBLE *n.* + -Y[1]. Cf. KNUBBLY, NUBBLY.] Full of or covered with knobbles; of the nature of a knobble.

Listener A knobbly-knees competition at Butlin's.

knobby /ˈnɒbi/ *a.* & *n.* LME. [f. KNOB *n.* + -Y[1].] **A** *adj.* **1** Full of or covered with knobs. LME. **2** Of the nature of a knob, knob-shaped. M18. **B** *n.* An opal. *Austral.* E20.

knobbiness *n.* E17.

knobkerrie /ˈnɒbkɛri/ *n.* Also **-kerry**, **-kierie** /-kɪəri/. M19. [f. KNOB *n.* + KIERIE, after Afk. *knopkierie*.] A short thick stick with a knobbed head, used as a weapon or missile esp. by indigenous peoples of South Africa.

knock /nɒk/ *n.*[1] ME. [f. the vb.] **1** An act of knocking; a blow, a thump; the sound of this; *spec.* a rap or a succession of raps at a door to call attention or gain admittance. ME. **b** A misfortune, a setback, a financial or emotional blow; an adverse criticism. M17. **c** *spec.* A knocking noise in an engine, esp. (in an internal-combustion engine) caused by the detonation of fuel within the cylinder; faulty combustion of this kind; pinking. L19. **2** A clock. *Sc.* LME. **3** *Cricket.* An innings; a spell at batting in a match or at practice; the score achieved by a player during this. *colloq.* L19. **4** An act of copulation. *slang.* M20.

1 M. WEST The knock at the door startled Merdelius. R. INGALLS She . . gave the prearranged knock on the door. *Press & Journal* (*Aberdeen*) He took a bad ankle knock . . and it is very swollen. **knock for knock agreement** an agreement between motor insurance companies by which each pays its own policy-holders irrespective of liability. *postman's knock*: see POSTMAN *n.*[1] 1. **b** T. WILLIAMS Hard knocks my vanity's been given. *Times* The firm . . have had their fair share of knocks. **take a knock** suffer a setback; be criticized adversely. **take the knock** bear or accept responsibility. *the school of hard knocks*: see SCHOOL *n.*[1] **3** *Club Cricketer* He . . averaged 36.75 in four innings . . thanks largely to a knock of 72. *Cricketer International* He scored two first-class hundreds . . and played an especially memorable knock against Nottinghamshire.

Comb.: **knockmeter** an instrument for measuring the intensity of knock in the cylinder of an internal-combustion engine; **knock rating** (the determination of) the insusceptibility of a fuel to knock.

knock /nɒk/ *n.*[2] ME. [In sense 1 f. Gael., Ir. *cnoc* knoll, hillock. With sense 2 cf. Da. dial. *knock* hillock.] **1** A hill; a hillock, a knoll. *Sc.* Now only *poet.* or in place-names. ME. **2** A sandbank. *dial.* L16.

knock /nɒk/ *v.* [OE *cnocian* = MHG *knochen*, ON *knoka*, of imit. origin.] **1** *v.i.* Strike a hard surface with an audible sharp blow; *spec.* strike esp. a door to call attention or gain admittance (foll. by *at*, *on*). Formerly also, deliver a blow or blows. OE. **b** *v.t.* (w. *it* or cognate obj.) give (a knock); convey by knocking. E17. **2** *v.t.* Give a hard blow or blows to; hit, strike, beat, hammer; make (a hole etc.) by beating or hammering. OE. **b** Copulate with (a woman); father (a child) on a woman (foll. by *out of*). *slang.* L16. **c** Rob (esp. a safe or till). *slang.* M18. **d** Make a strong (esp. favourable) impression on. *slang.* L19. **e** Speak ill or slightingly of, criticize, disparage, find fault with. *colloq.* L19. **3** *v.t.* Drive or bring (a thing) violently against or *against* something else. ME. **4** *v.i.* **a** Come into violent collision with something; *colloq.* move energetically, clumsily, noisily, or randomly *about*, *along*, *around*, etc. M16. **b** Of a mechanism etc.: make a rattling or thumping noise, esp. as a result of parts being loose and striking each other. Also *spec.*, (of an internal-combustion engine), suffer from knock caused by faulty combustion, (of fuel) give rise to knock in an engine. M19. **5** *v.t.* Drive or force *away*, *into*, *off*, *out*, etc., by means of a blow or blows or by striking. E17.

1 SHAKES. *Tam. Shr.* What's he that knocks as he would beat down the gate? M. BALDWIN If you knocked at every house You wouldn't find a man who could recognise a louse. D. ADAMS He knocked on the inner door. *fig.*: P. ROTH How tempted I would have been to yield, if opportunity had only knocked. **b** J. H. NEWMAN A visitant Is knocking his dire summons at my door. **2** CONAN DOYLE He knocked a hole . . in the lath and plaster ceiling. K. HULME She leans back . . and knocks the edge of the portrait. B. ZEPHANIAH I used to knock a drum and make a sound. M. MOORCOCK She knocked the lever at the back of the chimney. **d** W. SOYINKA I want to launch it on this tour. Man, it will knock them. **e** V. SETH Don't knock what you haven't tried. *Daily Mirror* Until we . . actually win something . . we will never stop people knocking us. **3** SHAKES. *Hen. V* I'll knock his leek about his pate. **4a** G. ALLEN Knocking up and down all over the country. **b** P. G. WODEHOUSE The engine was not humming so smoothly. It had begun to knock. **5** DEFOE I knocked pieces into the wall of the rock. J. T. STORY Suddenly somebody bounced into me, nearly knocking me flying. P. CAMPBELL I knocked an ashtray off the windowsill. B. PYM People surged forward, nearly knocking them over. R. INGALLS She's knocked the wind out of you. J. MORTIMER She had knocked her kitchen and living room together. *Grimsby Evening Telegraph* Watson . . knocked the ball past two defenders on the line.

Phrases: *knock (a person) all of a heap*: see HEAP *n.* *knock a person off his or her perch*: see PERCH *n.*[2] *knock cold*: see COLD *a.* *knock for six*: see SIX *n.* 4. *knock hell out of*: see HELL *n.* *knock into a cocked hat*: see *cocked hat* s.v. COCK *v.*[1] **knock into the middle of next**

week *colloq.* send (a person) flying, esp. with a blow. *knock one's block off*: see BLOCK *n.* 6b. **knock one's head against** *fig.* come into collision with (unpleasant facts or conditions) (*knock one's head against a brick wall*: see WALL *n.*[1]). **knock on the head** (*a*) stun or kill by a blow on the head; (*b*) *colloq.* put an end to (a scheme etc.). **knock (on) wood** *fig.* (*N. Amer.*) touch wood. *knock* PRISCIAN*'s head*. *knock rotten*: see ROTTEN *adv.* *knock the socks off*: see SOCK *n.*[1] *knock the* STUFFING *out of*. *knock the tar out of*: see TAR *n.*[1] I **knock sideways** *colloq.* disconcert; astonish. *knock silly*: see SILLY *a.* 6. **knock spots off** *colloq.* defeat easily. **knock the bottom out of** *fig.* make invalid or useless, prove to be worthless. *knock the shit out of*: see SHIT *n.* *knock wood*: see *knock on wood* above.

With advs. in specialized senses: **knock about, knock around** (*a*) strike repeatedly; treat roughly; (*b*) *colloq.* wander or roam aimlessly; lead a wandering adventurous life; (*c*) lie around, be available or in the vicinity; (*d*) be a habitual companion of, be associated *with* socially; (*e*) strike (a ball or balls) casually or half-heartedly; (see also sense 4 above). **knock back** (*a*) *colloq.* eat or esp. drink (esp. alcohol) quickly or in large quantities; (*b*) *Austral.* & *NZ colloq.* refuse, rebuff; (*c*) reverse the progress of, check; *fig.* (*colloq.*) disconcert; (*d*) work (risen bread dough) by vigorous kneading and throwing down, to expel air before baking. **knock down** (*a*) hit and knock to the ground; *spec.* (in *pass.*) be hit and knocked to the ground by a vehicle; demolish; (*b*) dispose of (an article) to or *to* a bidder at an auction by a knock with a hammer; (*c*) *colloq.* lower the price of; lower (a price); (*d*) *arch. colloq.* call upon *for* an action etc.; (*e*) take (machinery, furniture, etc.) to pieces for transportation; (*f*) *Austral.* & *NZ slang* spend (a pay cheque etc.) freely; (*g*) *US slang* steal (esp. passengers' fares); (*h*) *US* cause (a ship) to list heavily beyond recovery (usu. in *pass.*); (*i*) *N. Amer.* earn, get paid. **knock off** (*a*) finish or stop work; (*b*) finish or stop (work etc.); (*knock it off!* leave off! stop it!); (*c*) *colloq.* dispatch or dispose of (business); complete or do hastily; *spec.* produce (a literary work, painting, etc.) in a hurried and perfunctory fashion; (*d*) deduct from or *from* an amount or sum; (*e*) *Cricket* score (runs) to ensure victory; (*f*) *slang* steal, rob; (*g*) *slang* kill; (*h*) *slang* arrest (a person); (*i*) *slang* copulate with, seduce, (a woman); (see also sense 5 above). **knock on** *Rugby Football* drive or knock (a ball) with the hand or arm in the direction of the opponent's goal-line (in contravention of the rules); **knock out** (*a*) stun with a blow, knock unconscious; (*b*) *spec.* knock down (a boxing opponent) for a count of 10, so disqualifying him or her; (*c*) defeat, esp. in a competition involving various stages; (*d*) *colloq.* make roughly or hastily; (*e*) *Austral., NZ,* & *US slang* earn; (*f*) get rid of; destroy; (*g*) *colloq.* exhaust (oneself) through effort; (*h*) *slang* please greatly, astonish (freq. in *pass.*); (*i*) empty (a tobacco-pipe) by tapping; (see also sense 5 above). **knock over** *slang* rob, burgle. **knock together** put together or assemble hastily or roughly. **knock under** give in, submit. **knock up** (*a*) drive upwards with a blow; *Bookbinding* & *Printing* even the edges of (a pile of loose sheets) by striking them against a hard surface; (*b*) make, put together, or arrange hastily; (*c*) gain, earn, accumulate; *spec.* (*Cricket*) score (runs) rapidly; (*d*) waken, rouse, by knocking at the door; (*e*) exhaust or make ill (usu. in *pass.*); (*f*) become exhausted or ill; (*g*) *slang* (orig. *US*) make (a woman) pregnant; (*h*) play tennis, squash, etc., for practice, esp. before a match.

Comb.: **knock-back** (chiefly *Austral.* & *NZ colloq.*) a refusal, a rebuff; **knock-kneed** *a.* having knock-knees; **knock-knees** an abnormal condition in which the legs curve inwards at the knee so as to touch when the feet are apart; **knock-me-down** *a.* (*fig.*) overbearing; violent; **knock-off** (*a*) *slang* a robbery; a stolen object, *collect.* stolen objects; (*b*) *slang* a copy or reproduction of a design etc., esp. one made illegally; (*c*) *colloq.* the time when one's work finishes for the day; **knock-stone** a stone or cast-iron plate on which ore is broken; **knock-up** *n.* & *a.* (designating) a practice game in tennis, squash, etc., esp. before a match.

knockabout /ˈnɒkəbaʊt/ *a.* & *n.* Also **knock-about.** M19. [f. *knock about* s.v. KNOCK *v.*] A *adj.* 1 Designating a general labourer or handyman on a station or farm. *Austral.* M19. 2 Wandering vagrant; *spec.* (*Austral.* & *US*) designating a tramp or layabout. L19. 3 Of a garment, clothing, etc.: suitable for rough use. L19. 4 Esp. of comedy: rough, boisterous; slapstick. L19. 5 Designating a sloop-rigged sailing-yacht or a sailing-yacht without a bowsprit; *gen.* designating any small yacht or dinghy. Chiefly *N. Amer.* L19.

2 V. CRONIN This free-and-easy, almost knockabout atmosphere pleased Catherine. *Listener* Mother-in-law jokes, double entendres and slices of knockabout farce.

B *n.* 1 A general labourer or handyman on a station or farm. *Austral.* L19. 2 A tramp, a layabout. *Austral.* & *US*. L19. 3 A knockabout comic performer or performance. L19.

2 T. K. WOLFE Alcoholics, psychopaths, knockabouts . . were arrested in the Bronx.

knock-down /ˈnɒkdaʊn/ *a.* & *n.* Also **knockdown.** L17. [f. *knock down* s.v. KNOCK *v.*] A *adj.* 1 Such as to knock someone or something down or to the ground; *fig.* irresistible, overwhelming. L17. 2 Of furniture etc.: easily dismantled and reassembled; sold in separate parts requiring to be assembled. L18. 3 Of a price; reserve (at an auction); low. Of an article: sold at the reserve price, sold cheaply. L19.

1 T. HOOPER An aerosol fly killer—one containing a pyrethrum knock-down ingredient. 3 *Guardian* BEA will be able to offer seats on scheduled flights . . at knock-down prices. D. EDGAR The Roneo. I got it, knock-down, from the Catholic Association.

B *n.* 1 A thing, *spec.* a blow, that knocks a person down; an act of knocking someone or something down; an instance of being knocked down. Formerly also (*fig.*), strong liquor. L17. b The heeling of a ship by the force of the wind. L19. 2 An introduction (to a person). *US, Austral.,* & *NZ slang.* M19.

1 S. B. FLEXNER Amateur Athletic Club rules . . redefined a *round* by making it not dependent on a knock-down. *fig.*: *Times* Prices slipped. . . Oil shares took the brunt of the knock-down.

Comb.: **knock-down-(and-)drag-out** *a.* & *n.* (designating) a free-for-all fight.

knocker /ˈnɒkə/ *n.* LME. [f. KNOCK *v.* + -ER[1].] 1 A person who or thing which knocks; *esp.* a person who knocks at a door in order to call attention or gain admittance. LME. 2 A hinged metal or wooden usu. ornamental instrument fastened to and used for knocking at a door. Also *door-knocker*. L16. 3 A person of striking appearance. Cf. STUNNER 2. *slang.* Now *rare.* E17. 4 A knock-down blow. *rare.* Long *dial.* L17. 5 A spirit or goblin supposedly living in a mine and indicating the presence of ore by knocking. *dial.* M18. 6 A person who continually finds fault. *colloq.* L19. 7 Either of two leather pads inset near the heel of a pair of hand shears. *Austral.* & *NZ slang.* M20. 8 A person who sells or buys from door to door; the action of selling or buying from door to door. Cf. RAPPER *n.*[1] 6. M20. 9 In *pl.* A woman's breasts. *coarse slang.* M20.

Phrases: *oil the knocker*: see OIL *v.* **on the knocker** (*a*) (engaged in buying or selling) from door to door; (*b*) on credit; (*c*) *Austral.* & *NZ colloq.* promptly. **up to the knocker** *slang* in good condition; to perfection.

Comb.: **knocker-up** *Hist.* a person employed to rouse early workers by knocking at their doors or windows.

knocking /ˈnɒkɪŋ/ *n.* ME. [f. KNOCK *v.* + -ING[1].] 1 The action of KNOCK *v.*; an instance of this. ME. 2 *Mining*, in *pl.* Pieces of ore broken off by hammering or chiselling. M18.

Comb.: **knocking-shop** *slang* a brothel.

knock-on /*as n.* nɒkˈɒn, *as a.* ˈnɒkɒn/ *n.* & *a.* M19. [f. KNOCK *v.* + ON *adv.*] A *n. Rugby Football.* An act of knocking on. M19.

B *adj.* 1 *Physics.* Ejected or produced as a result of the collision of an atomic or subatomic particle with an atom. M20. 2 Of a mechanical part of a vehicle etc.: that may be attached or fastened by knocking or striking. M20.

Comb.: **knock-on effect** a secondary, indirect, or cumulative effect.

knockout /ˈnɒkaʊt/ *a.* & *n.* Also **knock-out.** E19. [f. *knock out* s.v. KNOCK *v.*] 1 (Designating or pertaining to) an auction at which a group of bidders cooperate to keep the bidding low and then sell the purchases amongst themselves. *slang.* E19. 2 (Designating) a blow etc. capable of knocking a person, esp. a boxer, unconscious. L19. 3 (Designating) a competition or the system used in it in which the defeated competitors in each round are eliminated. L19. 4 (A person or thing) of outstanding or superb quality. *colloq.* L19. 5 *Mech.* (Designating or pertaining to) a piece designed to be knocked out to form a hole, or a device for knocking out or ejecting an object from a mould etc. L19.

2 C. ODETS Joe's eyes glitter; his face is hard and flushed. He has won by a knockout. *Health & Strength* The gallant Frenchman . . pounded into a knockout defeat in four rounds. **knockout drops** *colloq.* a liquid drug added to a drink to make the drinker unconscious. *technical knockout*: see TECHNICAL *a.* 4 B. BAINBRIDGE 'Did you enjoy the Hermitage?' . . 'It was a bloody knockout'. E. LEONARD I hear she's a knockout Twenty years old, gorgeous.

knockwurst *n.* var. of KNACKWURST.

knödel /ˈknøːd(ə)l/ *n.* Also ***knoe-***. E19. [G.] In S. Germany and Austria: a type of dumpling.

Knoevenagel /ˈknəːvənɑːɡ(ə)l/ *n.* E20. [Emil *Knoevenagel* (1865–1921), Ger. chemist.] Chem. *Knoevenagel('s) reaction*, *Knoevenagel condensation*, the reaction of an aldehyde or ketone with malonic acid or a related compound to yield an acid with the group ·CHCHCOOH, which occurs in the presence of ammonia or an amine as catalyst.

Knole /nəʊl/ *a.* M20. [*Knole* Park (see below).] Designating a sofa with adjustable sides allowing conversion into a bed, designed after an original (*c* 1605–20) at Knole Park, Kent.

knoll /nəʊl/ *n.*[1] [OE *cnoll* corresp. to MDu. *knolle* clod, ball (Du. *knol* turnip, tuber), MHG *knolle* clod (G *Knolle* clod, lump, tuber), ON *knollr* mountain summit (Norw. *knoll* clod, tuber). See also KNOWE.] 1 The summit or rounded top of a mountain or hill. *obs.* exc. *dial.* OE. 2 A small hill; a hillock, a mound. OE. †3 A turnip. *dial.* L17–L19. 4 A lump, a large piece. *Sc.* E19.

knolly *a.* containing many knolls or hillocks E19.

knoll /nəʊl/ *n.*[2] Now *arch.* & *dial.* LME. [Prob. imit. alt. of KNELL *n.* Cf. next.] †1 A large church-bell. Only in LME. 2 The action or an act of tolling a bell; the toll of a large bell. L15.

knoll /nəʊl/ *v.* ME. [Prob. imit. alt. of KNELL *v.* Cf. prec.] 1 *v.i.* Of a bell or clock: sound, toll, chime. Now chiefly *dial.* ME. b *v.t.* Indicate by ringing, toll out. *rare.* M19. 2 *v.t.* Ring or toll (a bell). Now *arch.* & *dial.* LME. †b Ring a knell for. *rare* (Shakes.). Only in L16. 3 *v.t.* Summon by the sound of a bell. E17.

knoller *n.* a person who rings or tolls a bell E17.

Knoop /nuːp, knuːp/ *n.* M20. [Frederick *Knoop* (1878–1943), US instrument-maker.] Used *attrib.* to designate an indentation test devised by Knoop and the pyramidal diamond indenter used in it.

knop /nɒp/ *n.* ME. [MLG, MDu. *knoppe* (Du. *knop*) = OFris. *knop*, OHG *knoph* (G *Knopf* knob, knot, button). Cf. KNAP *n.*[1]] 1 A small rounded (esp. ornamental) protuberance; a knob, a boss, a stud, a tassel, etc. ME. †b A swelling on the skin; a wart, a pimple, a callus. M16–E19. c An ornamental loop or tuft formed in a strand of yarn. E20. 2 The kneecap; the elbow-joint. *obs.* exc. *dial.* LME. 3 A flower-bud. *arch.* LME.

knopped *a.* (*a*) having knops, knobby; (*b*) formed into a knop or knob: LME.

knopper /ˈnɒpə/ *n.* Pl. **-ern** /-ən/, **-ers.** L19. [G = gall-nut.] More fully *knopper gall*. A kind of oak-gall having the form of a sterile, malformed acorn, caused by the gall-wasp *Andricus quercuscalicis*.

†knopweed *n.* see KNAPWEED.

knorhaan *n.* var. of KORHAAN.

knorr /nɔː/ *n.* L19. [ON *knǫrr* (merchant) ship.] *Hist.* A large wide cargo ship with a single sail, used in medieval northern Europe.

knosp /nɒsp/ *n. rare.* E19. [G *Knospe* bud, boss, knob.] An ornamental knob, boss, or stud, *esp.* one in the form of a bud.

Knossian /ˈknɒsɪən, ˈknəʊ-/ *a.* L19. [f. Gk *Knōssos* Knossos (see below) + -IAN.] Of or pertaining to Knossos, the principal city of Minoan Crete and site of the ruins of a vast labyrinthine palace of the 18th to the 14th cents. BC).

knot /nɒt/ *n.*[1] [OE *cnotta* = Du. *knot*, MLG *knotte*, MHG *knotze* knob, knot, f. WGmc.] **I 1** An intertwining of a rope, string, or other flexible thing, esp. to form a secure fastening or an obstruction when drawn tight; a set method of tying such a fastening; a representation of such an intertwining, esp. a monogram, as a heraldic badge. Also, a tangle in hair, knitting, etc. OE. **b** A ribbon etc. tied as an ornament to be worn on or attached to a garment. LME. †**c** *Astron.* The star α Piscium, which is situated between the two parts of the constellation Pisces. M16–E18. **2** A definite quantity or measure of thread, yarn, etc. *obs.* exc. *Hist.* LME. **3** A design or figure formed of crossing lines. Now *rare* or *obs.* LME. **4** A flower-bed laid out in an intricate design; *gen.* any laid-out garden plot. Now chiefly *Sc.* & *dial.* exc. in *knot-garden* below. L15. **5** *Naut.* Any of a number of divisions marked by knots at fixed intervals on a log-line and used as a measure of speed (orig. from the rate the knots run out while a sand-glass is running). Hence, a unit of measurement equal to one nautical mile per hour (1.15 m.p.h., 1.85 k.p.h.) used esp. to express the speed of ships, aircraft, currents, and winds. M17. **b** A nautical mile. *colloq.* M18. **6** *Hist.* More fully *porter's knot.* A double shoulder-pad and forehead-loop formerly used by London market-porters for carrying loads. E18. **7** *Physical Geogr.* An elevated point or region where several mountain-chains meet. M19. **8** *Math.* A closed unicursal curve in three dimensions; *spec.* one which, on being distorted in any way so as to bring it into a plane without passing one part through another, will always have nodes. L19.

1 R. BOLTON One knot in a thread will stay the Needle's Passage as well as five hundred. R. CROMPTON Can you tie knots what can't come untied? J. L. WATEN Gleaming black hair, gathered in a heavy knot at the back. J. HELLER The knot of his tie is inches down. F. DONALDSON His . . head adorned by a white handkerchief, tied in a knot at each corner. J. CRACE I tied it in a firm knot. K. GIBBONS She would . . comb out the knots for me. Where did you get this pretty hair? *granny('s) knot, love-knot, Matthew Walker knot, reef-knot, slip-knot*, etc. **5** J. A. MICHENER His engine could deliver only six knots forward while the river was flowing four knots in the opposite direction. J. D. MACDONALD Tropical storm Ella . . still holding course and speed, with winds approaching fifty knots. **b** F. MARRYAT We were going twelve knots an hour, and running away from them.

II *fig.* f. sense 1. **9** A difficulty, a complex or confusing problem. OE. **b** *spec.* The main point in a problem; the complication in the plot of a story etc. LME. **10** Something forming or maintaining a union; a tie, a bond, a link; *spec.* a marriage. ME. †**11** An obligation; a binding condition; a restriction. LME–E19.

9 J. C. POWYS What a knot of paradox and contradiction life is. **b** GLADSTONE The very knot of the difficulty not yet overcome.

III *transf.* **12** A hill of moderate height; *esp.* a rocky hill or summit. Chiefly in place-names. Cf. KNOB *n.* 2. ME. **13** A carved knob or embossed ornament; a boss; an ornamental stud or fastening. ME. **14** A hard, esp. rounded, swelling or growth in human or animal tissue; a hard contracted lump, as in a muscle; a mass formed by concretion or coagulation within a substance; *fig.* a contorted mass or lump as felt in the stomach or throat. ME. **15** A thickened part or protuberance in the stem, branch, or root of a plant; a node; a hard mass formed in a tree-trunk at the intersection with a branch; the resulting round cross-grained mark in a board or plank. Also (now only *dial.*), a bud. LME. **16** A small group or cluster (*of* persons or things). LME.

14 J. CLARE Insects of mysterious birth . . Doubtless brought by moisture forth, Hid in knots of spittle white. B. MOORE Her legs were thick and knots of varicose veins stood out under her stockings. W. WHARTON I think they're anxious. I know I am. My stomach's twisted, curled in knots. **15** V. WOOLF He dug the point of it . . into a knot in the table. A. HIGGINS Wooden walls with knots in the planks, some of which had dropped out. **16** E. WHARTON The great hall was empty but for the knot of dogs by the fire. D. DELILLO See that knot of people? He's right in the middle. R. THOMAS A few yards away . . the press had already formed a restless knot.

Phrases: **at a rate of knots** *colloq.* very fast. *encased knot*: see ENCASE *v. French knot*: see FRENCH *a. Gordian knot*: see GORDIAN *a.* 1. *Grecian knot*: see GRECIAN *a. porter's knot*: see sense 6 above. †**seek a knot in a rush** or **bulrush** seek or make difficulties where there are none. SEHNA *knot*. **tie in knots** baffle or confuse completely. *tie the knot*: see TIE *v.*[1] *Windsor knot*: see WINDSOR *a.* 1.

Comb.: **knotberry** *local* the cloudberry, *Rubus chamaemorus*; **knot-garden** an intricately designed formal garden; **knot-head** *n.* & *a.* (*N. Amer.*) (designating) a stupid person or animal; **knot-hole** (*a*) a hole in a board or plank where a knot has fallen out; (*b*) a hollow formed in a tree-trunk by the decay of a branch; (*c*) a hole formed by the excavation of clay; **knot-stitch** a stitch by which ornamental knots are made; **knotweed** (*a*) = KNOTGRASS 1; (*b*) any of various other plants belonging to or formerly included in the genus *Polygonum*, esp. = *Japanese knotweed* s.v. JAPANESE *a.*; **knotwork** ornamental work consisting of or (*spec.* in architecture) representing cords etc. intertwined and knotted together.

knotless *a.* LME.

knot /nɒt/ *n.*[2] LME. [Origin uncertain: perh. imit. of the bird's call. Cf. GNAT *n.*[2]] A short-billed, Arctic-breeding sandpiper, *Calidris canutus*. Also (in full *great knot*), a larger sandpiper, *C. tenuirostris*, which breeds in Siberia.

knot /nɒt/ *v.* Infl. **-tt-**. LME. [f. KNOT *n.*[1]] **1 a** *v.i.* Form lumps, knobs, or knots; become knotty. Formerly of plants: form nodes; bud; begin to develop fruit. Long *obs.* exc. *Sc.* LME. **b** *v.t.* Form lumps, knobs, or knots on or in; make knotty; *esp.* furrow or knit (the brows). E16. **2** *v.t.* Tie in a knot; form a knot or knots in; secure with a knot. M16. **b** *v.i.* Form a knot or knots; be or become twisted into a knot. Chiefly *fig.* E17. **3** *v.t.* & *i.* Unite or gather closely together *spec.* in a knot or group; assemble, congregate. Now *rare.* E17. **4** *v.i.* Make knots for fringing. E18. **b** *v.t.* Make (a fringe) with knots. M18.

1b O. WISTER Perplexity knotted the Virginian's brows. **2** G. ORWELL She . . put her clothes on, knotted the scarlet sash about her waist. J. KOSINSKI Her long hair . . had knotted itself into innumerable thick braids impossible to unravel. E. WILSON It is a good idea to knot the gold thread . . to prevent it from constantly slipping out. J. KRANTZ Even his tie was perfectly knotted. **b** J. POYER His stomach knotted tighter until nausea caught at . . his throat. **3** G. GREENE A small group of middle-aged, bowler-hatted businessmen knotted at the far corner.

knotgrass /ˈnɒtgrɑːs/ *n.* E16. [f. KNOT *n.*[1] + GRASS *n.*] **1** Any of several weeds of the genus *Polygonum* (family Polygonaceae), esp. *Polygonum aviculare*, with wiry jointed creeping stems and small pinkish or whitish flowers in the axils of the leaves. E16. **2** Any of various other plants with jointed stems; *spec.* (*a*) fiorin grass, *Agrostis stolonifera*; (*b*) *US* joint-grass, *Paspalum distichum*; (*c*) a variety of false oat with swollen basal internodes, *Arrhenatherum elatius* subsp. *bulbosum*. L16. **3** Either of two small noctuid moths, *Acronicta rumicis*, and (in full *light knotgrass*) *A. menyanthidis*. Also *knotgrass moth*. E19.

2 whorled knotgrass a small creeping plant of damp sandy places, *Illecebrum verticillatum*, of the pink family.

knotted /ˈnɒtɪd/ *a.* ME. [f. KNOT *n.*[1], *v.*: see -ED[2], -ED[1].] **1** Having a knot or knots tied in it; fastened with a knot. ME. **b** *fig.* Complex, intricate; twisted as in a knot. M17. **2** Characterized by knobs or protuberances; gnarled; (of the brows) furrowed, knitted. LME. **b** Formed into a compact close mass esp. of blossom. Long *dial.* exc. in *knotted* MARJORAM. E17. **c** Decorated with knots or bosses. M19. **3** Of a garden: laid out in an intricate design. L16.

1 A. SILLITOE He wore a knotted tie over a white collar. N. FREELING Every kind of . . junk held together with knotted bits of string. **2** TOLKIEN A huge man with . . great bare arms and legs with knotted muscles. *New Yorker* My father's hands . . are brown and knotted.

Phrases: **get knotted!** *colloq.* go away! stop annoying me! nonsense!

knottedness *n.* the fact or manner of being formed into a knot E20.

knotter /ˈnɒtə/ *n.* E18. [f. KNOT *n.*[1], *v.* + -ER[1].] **1** A person who or machine which ties knots. E18. **2** With prefixed numeral: a boat or ship capable of a speed of a specified number of knots. E20.

knotting /ˈnɒtɪŋ/ *n.* LME. [f. KNOT *v.*, *n.*[1] + -ING[1].] **1** The action of tying a knot or tying something in a knot or knots. LME. **b** The tying of knots in yarn to form a decorative network or pattern; work made in this way. L17. **2** The formation of knots or lumps; the production of buds etc. LME. **3** A preparation applied to knots in boards etc. prior to painting to prevent resin from oozing through; the application of this. E19. **4** The process of removing knots or lumps from cloth, pulp, etc. L19.

knotty /ˈnɒti/ *a.* ME. [f. KNOT *n.*[1] + -Y[1].] **1** Having knots, full of knots; tied or entangled in knots. ME. **2** *fig.* Difficult, complex, hard to explain, puzzling. ME. **3** Having many knots or lumps, covered with knots or lumps; gnarled; (of a board etc.) containing knots. LME. **4** *fig.* Hard and rough in character. Now *rare.* M16.

1 SHAKES. *Haml.* Make . . Thy knotty and combined locks to part, And each particular hair to stand on end. **2** M. PUZO The relief of a conscientious administrator who has solved a knotty personnel problem. **3** F. RAPHAEL Pamela had her warm hands on Fagin's knotty joints. A. LURIE On the wall over the knotty pine sideboard.

Comb.: †**knotty-pated** *a.* (*rare*, Shakes.) stupid.

knottily *adv.* L17. **knottiness** *n.* LME.

knout /naʊt, nuːt/ *n.* & *v.* M17. [Fr. f. Russ. *knut* f. ON *knútr* rel. to KNOT *n.*[1]] *Hist.* **A** *n.* A scourge or whip used in imperial Russia, often causing death. M17. **B** *v.t.* Flog with a knout. M18.

know /nəʊ/ *n.*[1] L16. [f. KNOW *v.*] The fact of knowing; knowledge. Now chiefly in *in the know*, having secret or inside information.

know *n.*[2] var. of KNOWE.

know /nəʊ/ *v.* Pa. t. **knew** /njuː/; pa. pple **known** /nəʊn/. [OE *cnāwan*, earlier *gecnāwan*, corresp. to OHG *-cnāen*, *-cnāhen*, ON pres. indic. *kná*, pl. *knegum*. An orig. reduplicating vb f. IE base repr. also by CAN *v.*[1], KEN *v.*, and L (*g*)*noscere*, *cognoscere*, Gk *gignōskein*.] **I** Recognize, admit. **1** *v.t.* Recognize, perceive; identify; *spec.* perceive (a thing or person) as identical with something or someone already perceived or considered. OE. **b** Distinguish; be able to distinguish (one thing) *from* another. M20. †**2** *v.t.* Acknowledge; admit the claims or authority of. Also, own, confess. ME–M16. **3** *v.t.* In biblical use: take notice of, regard; care for; approve. LME.

1 SCOTT FITZGERALD I knew I had guessed right about those missing hours. J. MORTIMER The Fanners were known as good landlords. *Sunday Times* The art of dressing is to know what you look good in. **b** E. F. BENSON Lady Heron, who did not know a picture from a statue.

II Be acquainted with, have experience of. **4** *v.t.* **a** Be acquainted with (a thing, a place, a person); be familiar with by experience, or through information. Also, become familiar with. ME. **b** *refl.* Understand oneself. ME. **c** Have experience of (an occurrence, an emotion, a circumstance, etc.); have experienced or undergone. Also, be subject to, undergo. ME. **5** *v.t.* Be personally acquainted with (a person); be familiar or friendly with. ME. †**b** *v.t.* In *pass.* Be personally acquainted or familiar *with*. ME–M16. †**c** *v.i.* Of two people: be (mutually) acquainted. Only in E17. **6** *v.t.* Have sexual intercourse with. Now *arch.* or *joc.* ME.

4 MILTON I know each lane, and every alley green . . of this wilde Wood. J. RHYS I am longing to know all your plans and where you are. **b** *Notes & Queries* The folly of that impossible precept 'Know thyself'. **c** THACKERAY I never knew a man die of love. R. BROOKE We, who have known shame. J. BUCHAN The purple gloom which is all the night that Laverlaw knows in early July. **5** E. BOWEN Can't say I ever knew him. c Shakes. *Cymb.* Sir, we have known together in Orleans.

III Come to apprehend, learn. **7** *v.t.* Be aware or apprised of (something), esp. through observation, inquiry, or information. Formerly also, become cognizant of, learn. ME. **b** *v.i.* Be aware of a fact. ME. **8** *v.t.* Be conversant with (a body of facts, principles, a method of action, etc.), esp. through instruction, study, or practice; have learned; be able to recall; be versed or skilled in. Formerly also, learn. ME. **b** Have a good command of (a language, subject, etc.). M19. **9** *v.i.* Have understanding or knowledge. ME. **10** *v.t.* Comprehend as fact or truth; understand with clearness and certainty. Freq. opp. *believe*. ME. †**11** *v.t.* Make (a thing) known or familiar. Also, tell or disclose a thing to (a person). Only in ME.

7 Goldsmith An enemy whom he knew more powerful than himself. N. Shute I don't know that she could manage by herself. W. M. Hailey All languages which are known not to be attached to any of the above Units. E. Welty You'll know when it starts, all right, because of the bang! G. Josipovici You showed no surprise . . it was as if you had known I would be coming. 8 W. Trevor There was more information that he had known but forgotten until now. C. Isherwood We both knew Newbolt's Vitae Lampada by heart, we'd learnt it at school. 9 R. Kipling The boy has devised . . it so that no hint is given except to those who know!

Phrases: **all one knows (how)** everything in one's power, all one can. **and knows it** *colloq.* and is clearly aware of what has been stated. **before one knows where one is** very soon, very quickly, with baffling speed. **be not to know** (*a*) have no way of learning; (*b*) be not to be told. *dear knows*: see DEAR *int.* **don't I know it** *colloq.* I am well aware of it, don't tell me. **don't you know?** *colloq.* (expr. emphasis) wouldn't you say?, isn't it? **(do) you know something?** *colloq.* shall I tell you something?, listen to this. *every schoolboy knows*: see SCHOOLBOY *n.* **for all I, you,** etc., **know** as far as I am, you are, etc., aware or concerned. *for reasons best known to oneself*: see REASON *n.*[1] *get to know*: see GET *v.* *give to know*: see GIVE *v.* **God knows** (*a*) certainly, indeed, it is true; (*b*) I have no idea, no one knows. *(if) you know what I mean*: see MEAN *v.*[1] *if you must know*: see MUST *v.*[1] **I knew it** I was sure this would happen. **I know what** *colloq.* I have an idea, suggestion, etc. **I want to know!** *US colloq.* well, well! **I wouldn't know (about that)** I cannot be expected to know (about that), don't ask me (about that). *know a hawk from a handsaw* or *heronshaw*: see HAWK *n.*[1] *know all the answers*: see ANSWER *n.* **know as** be familiar with under the name of; in *pass.*, be commonly called. **know a thing or two** be experienced or shrewd. *know better (than that, than to do)*: see BETTER *adv.* *know by name*: see NAME *n.* *know enough to come in out of the rain*: see RAIN *n.*[1] *know from nothing*: see *not know from nothing* below. **know how** understand the way, have the expertise or ability (*to do* something). *know how many beans make five*: see BEAN *n.* *know inside out*: see INSIDE *n.* *know like a book*: see BOOK *n.* *know like the back of one's hand*: see BACK *n.*[1] **know little** (or **nothing**) **and care less** be completely unconcerned *about*; be studiously ignorant. *know one's distance*: see DISTANCE *n.* *know one's onions*: see ONION *n.* *know one's own mind*: see MIND *n.*[1] *know one's place*: see PLACE *n.*[1] **know one's stuff** *colloq.* be fully acquainted with or well up in something. *know one's way around* (or *about*): see WAY *n.* *know something backward(s)*: see BACKWARD *adv.* **know the reason why** demand (and get) an explanation. *know the ropes*: see ROPE *n.*[1] **know the score** be aware of what is going on. *know the time of day*: see TIME *n.* **know too much** be in possession of too much important information to be allowed to live or continue as normal. *know to speak to*: see SPEAK *v.* *know what one is talking about*: see TALK *v.* **know what one likes** have fixed or definite tastes in art, poetry, etc., without necessarily having the knowledge or informed opinion to support them. **know what's what** be experienced or shrewd; be aware of what is going on. *know whereof one speaks*: see WHEREOF *rel. adv.* & *conj.* **know where one stands** or **is (with someone)** know how one is regarded (by someone); know the opinions (of someone) on an issue. **know who's who** be aware of the identity, status, etc., of each person. *let a person know*: see LET *v.*[1] 12. **not if I know it** only against my will. *not know from a bar of soap*: see SOAP *n.*[1] *not know from Adam*: see ADAM *n.* *not know from Eve*: see EVE *n.*[1] **(not) know from nothing** *N. Amer. colloq.* be totally ignorant. *not know one's arse from one's elbow*: see ARSE *n.* 1. *not know shit from Shinola*. *not know what hit one*: see HIT *v.* *not know what to do with oneself*: see DO *v.* *not know which way* (or *where*) *to turn*: see TURN *v.* **not want to know** not be interested. *one never knows*: see *you never know* below. **that's all you know (about it)** you are more ignorant than you think. **what do you know (about that)?, wouldn't you (just) know?** expr. mild surprise; well I never!, fancy that! **wouldn't you, he,** etc., **like to know?** I have no intention of telling you, him, etc., in spite of your, his, etc., curiosity. **you know** (*a*) indicating that the person being addressed ought to be aware of something unstated; (*b*) used as a conversation filler: you see. *you know something?*: see *do you know something?* above. **you know what?** I am going to tell you something. *you know what I mean*: see MEAN *v.*[1] *you must know*: see MUST *v.*[1] **you never know, one never knows** something unexpected or surprising may occur, nothing is certain.

With preps. in specialized senses: **know about** have information about. †**know for** (*rare*, Shakes.) be aware of. **know of** † (*a*) be or become assured of; learn of or about; (*b*) be aware of; (*c*) *not that I know of*, not so far as I am aware.

Comb.: **know-little** *rare* a simpleton; *you-know-what, you-know-who*: see YOU *pron.*

knower *n.* a person who knows ME.

knowable /ˈnəʊəb(ə)l/ *a.* & *n.* LME. [f. KNOW *v.* + -ABLE.] **A** *adj.* That may be known; able to be comprehended, ascertained, or recognized. Formerly also, that may know. LME. **B** *absol.* as *n.* That which is knowable; a knowable thing. M17.

knowaˈbility *n.* M19. **knowableness** *n.* M17.

know-all /ˈnəʊɔːl/ *n.* & *a.* Also **know-it-all** /ˈnəʊɪtɔːl/. L19. [f. KNOW *v.* + ALL *n.*] **A** *n.* A person who seems to know everything; a (would-be) smart and clever person. L19.

S. Middleton They were smug Conservative voters, know-alls.

B *adj.* Full of knowledge; smugly or arrogantly knowledgeable. Also, deaf to advice or instruction. L19.

P. G. Wodehouse These know-it-all directors make me tired.

knowe /naʊ/ *n.* Also **know**. E16. [Alt. of KNOLL *n.*[1]] A hillock, a knoll, a piece of rising ground.

know-how /ˈnəʊhaʊ/ *n.* M19. [f. *know how* s.v. KNOW *v.*] Technical expertise; practical ability or invention.

B. Bainbridge They have manpower, resources, know-how. A. Guinness My own lack of know-how and swift rash judgements hampered the allied cause.

knowing /ˈnəʊɪŋ/ *n.* ME. [f. KNOW *v.* + -ING[1].] †**1** Acknowledgement; recognition. Only in ME. †**2** Personal acquaintance. Only in ME. **3** The action of getting to understand, the fact of understanding; knowledge. ME. **4** The state or fact of being aware or informed of something; cognizance. ME. †**b** Something known, an experience. *rare* (Shakes.). Only in E17.

4 there is no knowing no one can tell, one cannot know.

knowing /ˈnəʊɪŋ/ *a.* LME. [f. KNOW *v.* + -ING[2].] **1a** That knows, having knowledge; understanding, intelligent, well-informed; conscious; mentally perceptive. LME. **b** Skilled or versed *in* something. M17. **2** Of a person, an action, a look, etc.: having or showing discernment or cunning; shrewd, cunning. E16. **3** Informed, aware. (Foll. by †*of, to*.) *arch.* M17. **4** Showing awareness of current fashions, style, etc. *colloq. obs.* exc. as passing into sense 2. L18.

1 M. Arnold A matter which does not fall within the scope of our ordinary knowing faculties. B. Jowett He is the most knowing of all living men. 2 N. Coward I've always been sophisticated, far too knowing. D. Welch I saw the nurses exchange superior and knowing smiles.

knowingly *adv.* (*a*) in a knowing manner; (*b*) consciously, intentionally: LME. **knowingness** *n.* E18.

know-it-all *n.* & *a.* see KNOW-ALL.

knowledgable *a.* var. of KNOWLEDGEABLE.

knowledge /ˈnɒlɪdʒ/ *n.* ME. [Prob. f. next.] †**I** Rel. to KNOWLEDGE *v.* and early uses of KNOW *v.* **1** Acknowledgement; confession. ME–M16. **2** Recognition. ME–E17. **3** Legal cognizance; judicial investigation or inquiry. Chiefly *Sc.* LME–M18. **4** *gen.* Cognizance, notice. Only in *take knowledge of*, take cognizance of, notice. Only in E17.

II Rel. to later uses of KNOW *v.* **5** The fact of knowing a thing, state, person, etc.; acquaintance; familiarity gained by experience. ME. †**6** Personal acquaintance, friendship. Also, those with whom one is acquainted. LME–E17. **7** Sexual intercourse. Foll. by *of*, †*with*. *obs.* exc. in *carnal knowledge* s.v. CARNAL *a.* 2. LME. **8** Acquaintance with a fact or facts; a state of being aware or informed; awareness, consciousness. LME. **9** Chiefly *Philos.* Intellectual perception of fact or truth; clear and certain understanding or awareness, esp. as opp. to opinion. Formerly also, intelligence, intellect. (Foll. by *of*.) †**b** *Med.* Diagnosis. M16–M17. **10** Understanding of a branch of learning, a language, etc.; (a) theoretical or practical understanding *of* an art, science, industry, etc. LME. **11** *gen.* The fact or condition of being instructed, or of having information acquired by study or research. Also, a person's range of information; learning, erudition. LME. †**12** Notice, intimation; information. LME–E18. †**13a** A sign or mark by which something is recognized, or distinguished; a token. L15–M16. **b** A perception, intuition, or other cognition. Usu. in *pl.* Now *rare* or *obs.* M16. **c** A branch of learning; a science, an art. Usu. in *pl.* Now *rare*. L16. **14** The sum of what is known. M16.

5 M. Brett These stories can be difficult to understand without some knowledge of the background. 8 L. Gordon The small rain of spring seems to carry some knowledge of human sorrow. B. Moore These things were done without my knowledge. 9 D. Hartley The Infinite Power, Knowledge, and Goodness of God. 10 V. Sackville-West All craftsmen share a knowledge. J. Krantz Billy's knowledge of housekeeping was limited. 11 *Time* Knowledge can be shared; experience cannot.

Phrases: *carnal knowledge (of)*: see CARNAL *a.* 2. **come to a person's knowledge** become known to a person. *common knowledge*: see COMMON *a.* **grow out of (one's) knowledge** (now *rare*) cease to be known, become unfamiliar. *hearsay knowledge*: see HEARSAY *n.* *immediate knowledge*: see IMMEDIATE *a.* 3. *knowledge by* (or *of*) *acquaintance*: see ACQUAINTANCE 3. *knowledge by description*: see DESCRIPTION 1b. *mediate knowledge*: see MEDIATE *a.* 2b. *take knowledge of*: see sense 4 above. **to one's knowledge** (*a*) so far as one is aware; (*b*) as one knows for certain. *to the best of one's knowledge*: see BEST *a.* etc. *tree of knowledge (of good and evil)*: see TREE *n.*

Comb.: **knowledge base** *Computing* the underlying set of facts, assumptions, and inference rules which a computer system has available to solve a problem; a store of information (as in a database) available to draw on; **knowledge-based** *a.* (of an academic discipline) founded on an accumulation of facts, non-empirical; (of a computer system) incorporating a set of facts, assumptions, or inference rules derived from human knowledge; **knowledge box** *joc.* the head; **knowledge factory** *derog.* a university, college, etc., which places emphasis on vocational training or which overemphasizes factual knowledge; **knowledge industry** (*derog.* or *joc.*) the development and use of knowledge, *spec.* in universities, polytechnics, etc.

¶Orig. corresp. to the earliest senses of KNOWLEDGE *v.*, then used as n. of action corresp. to KNOW *v.*, in which role it has partially replaced KNOWING *n.*

knowledged *a.* (*rare*) provided with knowledge M16. **knowledgeless** *a.* (*rare*) M19.

†**knowledge** *v.* [OE *cnāwelǣcing* (for *-ung*) vbl n., f. (*ge*)*cnawan* KNOW *v.* + *-lǣcan*, f. *-lac*: see -LOCK. Simple vb recorded early in ME.] **1** *v.t.* **a** = ACKNOWLEDGE 1. OE–M17. **b** = ACKNOWLEDGE 3. ME–L16. **c** = ACKNOWLEDGE 4. LME–L18. **d** Recognize; *Med.* diagnose (an illness). M16–E17. **2** *v.t.* & *i.* Have sexual intercourse with or *with*. Only in ME. **3** *v.i.* Make confession. LME–E16.

†**knowledging** *n.* (*a*) the action of the vb; (*b*) = KNOWLEDGE *n.*: OE–L16.

knowledgeable /ˈnɒlɪdʒəb(ə)l/ *a.* Also **-dgable**. E17. [In sense 1 f. KNOWLEDGE *v.*, in sense 2 f. KNOWLEDGE *n.*: see -ABLE.] †**1** Able to be perceived or recognized; recognizable; noticeable. Only in E17. **2** Possessing or showing knowledge; well-informed; intelligent. Also, aware *of*. E19.

2 D. Rowe Despite the wise and knowledgeable advice from kindly child-rearing experts, many parents . . still beat . . children.

knowledgea'bility *n.* M20. **knowledgeableness** *n.* L19. **knowledgeably** *adv.* M19.

knowledgement /'nɒlɪdʒm(ə)nt/ *n. arch.* Also **-dgm-**. E17. [f. KNOWLEDGE *v.* + -MENT.] †**1** Formal acknowledgement; legal cognizance. E-M17. **2** Knowledge, cognizance. M17.

known /nəʊn/ *a.* & *n.* ME. [pa. pple of KNOW *v.*] **A** *adj.* **1** Learned, apprehended mentally; familiar, *esp.* familiar to all, generally known or recognized. Also, identified as such. ME. †**2** Possessed of knowledge; acquainted with something; learned *in.* LME-M17.

1 A. CHRISTIE Billy Kellett?.. He's known to the police. F. HOWERD I was leaving surroundings where I had become known and was accepted. I. DRUMMOND His face was not recognised in the rogues' gallery, nor did his description tally with any known criminal. *Sunday Express* There are 700 known species of holly in the world.

B *absol.* as *n.* †**1** An acquaintance. Only in ME. **2** A well-known person. Also, a known criminal. M19. **3** *the known*, that which is known, all known things. M19.

known *v.* pa. pple of KNOW *v.*

know-nothing /'nəʊnʌθɪŋ/ *n.* & *a.* In senses A.2, B.2 also **Know-Nothing**. E19. [f. KNOW *v.* + NOTHING *n.*] **A** *n.* **1a** A person who knows nothing, an ignorant person. E19. **b** A person who holds that nothing can be known; an agnostic. E19. **2** *US Hist.* A member of a political party in the US, prominent from 1853 to 1856, which supported exclusion of immigrants from government, and whose members preserved its original secrecy by denying its existence. M19. **B** *attrib.* or as *adj.* **1a** That knows nothing; grossly ignorant. E19. **b** That holds that nothing can be known; agnostic. E19. **2** *US Hist.* Of or pertaining to the American Know-Nothings. M19.

know-nothingism *n.* (*a*) wilful ignorance; agnosticism; (*b*) the political doctrine of the American Know-Nothings: M19. **know-nothingness** *n.* the state or quality of knowing nothing; complete ignorance: L19.

Knoxian /'nɒksɪən/ *n.* & *a.* E18. [f. *Knox* (see below) + -IAN.] **A** *n.* An adherent of John Knox (*c*1505-72), the Scottish reformer mainly responsible for establishing the Presbyterian Church, or his beliefs. E18. **B** *adj.* Of or pertaining to John Knox or his beliefs. E20.

knub /nʌb/ *n.* Now chiefly *dial.* See also NUB *n.*[1] L16. [MLG *knubbe* var. of *knobbe* KNOB *n.*] **1** A small lump, a protuberance, a knob; *esp.* a small swelling on the body, a boil. L16. **2** The innermost wrapping of a silkworm cocoon. E19.

knub /nʌb/ *v.t. dial.* Now *rare* or *obs.* Also (earlier) †**n-**. Infl. **-bb-**. E17. [Imit.: cf. KNAB *v.*[1] See also KNUBBLE *v.*] **1** = KNUBBLE *v.* E17. †**2** Bite gently, nibble. Only in M17.

knubble /'nʌb(ə)l/ *n. dial.* Now *rare* or *obs.* L17. [f. KNUB *n.* + -LE[1]. Cf. KNOBBLE *n.*, NUBBLE *n.*] A small knob. Formerly also, a knuckle.

knubble /'nʌb(ə)l/ *v.t. dial.* Now *rare* or *obs.* Also (earlier) †**n-**; **knob-**. L17. [f. KNUB *v.* + -LE[3]. See also NOBBLE.] Strike with the knuckles or fist, beat.

knubbly /'nʌbli/ *a. dial.* M19. [f. KNUBBLE *n.* + -Y[1]. Cf. KNOBBLY, NUBBLY.] Full of or covered with knubs or small protuberances.

knuck /nʌk/ *n.* E19. [Abbrev. of KNUCKLE *n.*, KNUCKLER.] **1** A thief, a pickpocket. Cf. KNUCKLE *n.* 2b. *slang.* Now *rare* or *obs.* E19. **2** In *pl.* (treated as *sing.*). A game of marbles in which the winner can shoot a marble at the loser's knuckles. *US.* M19. **3** A knuckleduster. L19.

knuckle /'nʌk(ə)l/ *n.* ME. [MLG *knökel*, corresp. to OFris. *knok(e)le*, MDu. *knokel*, *knökel* (Du. *kneukel*), MHG *knuchel*, *knüchel* (G *Knöchel*), dim. of base of MLG *knoke* (Du. *knok*), MHG *knoche* (G *Knochen*) bone, perh. ult. rel. to KNEE *n.*] **1** The end of a bone at a joint, the more or less rounded protuberance formed when a joint is bent, as in the knee, elbow, and vertebral joints. Formerly also, a fist. Now only *Sc.* & *dial.* exc. as below. ME. **2** *spec.* The hard protuberance formed on the back of the hand by a finger-joint when the fingers are bent or the hand is shut, *esp.* that at the root of a finger. LME. †**b** A pickpocket. Cf. KNUCK 1. L18-M19. **3** Something shaped, angled, or protruding like a knuckle-bone. LME. **4** The projection of the carpal or tarsal joint of a quadruped; a joint of meat consisting of this with the parts above and below it. E17. **5** A knuckleduster. M19.

2 S. BECKETT I stuck in my forefinger up to the knuckle. D. FRANCIS He gripped his binoculars so hard that his knuckles showed white. J. RATHBONE Her hands showed signs of much age, being knotted at the knuckles. 3 S. R. CROCKETT I.. sat on a solid knuckle of rock that shot up from the ribs of the mountain. 5 A. S. NEILL Savage assaults with.. brass knuckles.

Phrases: **go the knuckle** *Austral. slang* fight, punch. **near the knuckle** *colloq.* verging on the indecent. *rap on* or *over the knuckles*: see RAP *v.*[1] 1.

Comb.: **knuckleball** *Baseball* a slow pitch which moves erratically, made by gripping the ball with the fingertips; **knuckle-bow** a guard on a sword-hilt to cover the knuckles; **knuckle-deep** *adv.* (now *rare*) up to the knuckles; *fig.* very deeply; **knuckledust** *v.t.* strike with a knuckleduster; **knuckleduster** a metal guard worn over the knuckles in fist-fighting to protect them and increase the force of a blow; **knuckle-end** the lower or small end of a leg of mutton or pork; **knucklehead** a slow-witted or stupid person; **knuckle-joint** (*a*) a joint at a knuckle (on the hand of a person, or the limb of an animal); (*b*) *Mech.* a joint connecting two parts of a mechanism, in which a projection in one fits into a recess in the other; **knuckle sandwich** *slang* a punch in the mouth; **knuckle timber** *Shipbuilding* a timber having or forming an acute angle; **knuckle-walker** a primate, e.g. the gorilla and chimpanzee, having a quadrupedal gait in which the knuckles (rather than the tips of the fingers or flat of the palm) make contact with the ground; **knuckle-walking** the practice of walking with the gait of a knuckle-walker.

knuckled *a.* having knuckles LME. **knuckler** *n.* (*a*) *slang* a pickpocket; (*b*) *Baseball* a knuckleball: M19. **knucklesome** *a.* (*rare*) knuckly E20. **knuckly** *a.* having large or prominent knuckles M19.

knuckle /'nʌk(ə)l/ *v.* M18. [f. the n.] **I** *v.i.* **1** Place one's knuckles on the ground in playing at marbles. Usu. foll. by *down.* M18. **2** Acknowledge oneself beaten; give way, give in, submit. Usu. foll. by *down* or *under* (*to*). M18. **3** Foll. by *down*: apply oneself earnestly (*to*). M19. **4** Protrude or project like a knuckle. *rare.* M19. **5** *Farriery.* Of the knee or fetlock: project *over* or *forwards* through weakness of the ligaments. L19.

2 R. ELLMANN They had knuckled under to Queensbury's threats.

II *v.t.* **6** Strike, press, or rub with the knuckles. L18. **7** Propel (a marble etc.) from between the knuckle of the thumb and the bent forefinger. E19.

6 P. GALLICO He reached over and knuckled Clary gently under.. the chin. A. CARTER She finished.. crying, knuckling her eyesockets like a child. Z. TOMIN I knuckled a signal.. on a small black door.

knuckle-bone /'nʌk(ə)lbəʊn/ *n.* LME. [f. KNUCKLE *n.* + BONE *n.*] **1** A bone forming a knuckle; *spec.* the rounded end at the joint of a finger-bone. LME. **2a** A limb-bone of an animal with a ball-like knob at the joint-end; the rounded end of such a bone. Also, a knuckle of meat. LME. **b** A metacarpal or metatarsal bone of a sheep; in *pl.*, (such bones used in) a game of jacks. M18.

Knudsen /'knʊds(ə)n/ *n.* M20. [M. H. C. *Knudsen* (1871-1949), Dan. physicist.] *Physics.* Used *attrib.* and in *possess.* to designate apparatus, phenomena, and concepts connected with (*a*) low density fluid flow; (*b*) *Oceanogr.* a method of determining the salinity of seawater by titration with silver nitrate.

Knudsen flow the flow, from an orifice or through a tube, of a rarefied gas with a high Knudsen number, so that resistance to flow arises mainly from collisions of molecules with the walls of the orifice or tube rather than with each other. **Knudsen gas**: having a Knudsen number much greater than one. **Knudsen gauge, manometer** an instrument for measuring the absolute pressure of a rarefied gas. **Knudsen number** the ratio of the mean free path of molecules in a gas to a length derived from the dimensions of the vessel or orifice through which it flows.

knur /nɜː/ *n.* Also **-rr**. LME. [Var. of KNAR.] **1** A hard excrescence or swelling in the flesh. *obs.* exc. *Sc. dial.* LME. **2** A knot or hardened excrescence on the trunk of a tree, a knar; a hard concretion in stone; any swollen formation. M16. **3** = KNURL 2. *north.* L17. **4** A wooden ball used in a game (*knur and spell*) resembling trap-ball; a similar ball used in other games. *north.* M19.

knurl /nɜːl/ *n.* & *v.* Also **n-**. E17. [App. a deriv. of KNUR. Cf. GNARL *n.*, KNARL.] **A** *n.* **1** A small projection or excrescence; a knot, knob, etc.; a small bead or ridge, *esp.* any of a series worked on a metal surface. E17. **2** A thickset stumpy person. *Sc.* & *dial.* L17. **B** *v.t.* Make knurls on the edge of (a coin, a screw-head, etc.); mill, crenate. L19.

knurled *a.* having knurls; crenated, milled: E17. **knurling** *n.* (*a*) the action of the vb; (*b*) knurled work: E17. **knurly** *a.* (*a*) having knurls or knots; (*b*) *Sc.* & *dial.* stumpy, thickset: E17.

knurr *n.* var. of KNUR.

knut /kə'nʌt, nʌt/ *n. arch. slang.* E20. [Alt. of NUT *n.*] A fashionable or showy young man, = NUT *n.* 6.

ko /kəʊ/ *n.*[1] *NZ.* Pl. same, ***kos***. M19. [Maori.] A Maori digging-stick.

Ko /kəʊ/ *n.*[2] L19. [Chin. *gē* (Wade-Giles *ko*) elder brother.] *Ceramics.* In full *Ko ware*, *Ko yao* /jaʊ/ [*yáo* pottery]. A crackled Song ware closely related to Kuan ware. Also, any of various other crackled porcelains.

ko /kəʊ/ *n.*[3] Pl. **-os**. M20. [Chin. *gē* (Wade-Giles *ko*) spear, lance.] *Chin. Antiq.* A dagger, a halberd.

koa /'kəʊə/ *n.* E19. [Haw.] A Hawaiian forest tree, *Acacia koa*; the dark wood of this, used in cabinet-making. Also *koa tree*, *koa-wood*.

koala /kəʊ'ɑːlə/ *n.* L18. [Aborig. *kūl(l)a*.] An Australian arboreal marsupial, *Phascolarctos cinereus*, which resembles a small bear, has thick ash-grey fur, and feeds on eucalyptus leaves. Also *koala bear*: cf. BEAR *n.*[1] 1b.

koan /'kəʊɑːn/ *n.* M20. [Jap. *kōan*, f. Chin. *gōngàn* official business.] *Zen Buddhism.* A riddle without a solution, used to demonstrate the inadequacy of logical reasoning and provoke sudden enlightenment.

kob /kɒb/ *n.*[1] L18. [Wolof *kooba*.] In full *kob antelope*. A grazing antelope, *Kobus kob*, native to African savannah.

UGANDA *kob*.

kob /kɒb/ *n.*[2] *S. Afr.* E20. [Abbrev.] = MEAGRE *n.*[1] Also called *kabeljou*, *salmon bass*.

kobang /'kəʊbaŋ/ *n.* E17. [Jap. *ko-ban*, f. *ko* little + *ban* part, share, division: cf. OBANG.] *Hist.* An oblong gold or silver coin with rounded corners, formerly current in Japan; the sum of money represented by this, one-tenth of an obang.

kobellite /'kəʊb(ə)lʌɪt/ *n.* M19. [f. Franz von *Kobell* (1803-82), Ger. mineralogist + -ITE[1].] *Min.* A monoclinic sulphide of lead, bismuth, and antimony, usu. occurring as lead-grey radiated masses.

kobo /'kəʊbəʊ/ *n.* Pl. same. L20. [Alt. of COPPER *n.*[1]] A monetary unit of Nigeria, equal to one-hundredth of a naira.

kobold /'kəʊbəld/ *n.* M19. [G: cf. COBALT.] *German Folklore.* A familiar spirit, supposed to haunt houses and help the occupants; a brownie. Also, an underground spirit; a goblin, a gnome.

Koch /kɒx, kɒk/ *n.* L19. [Robert *Koch* (1843-1910), Ger. bacteriologist.] *Med.* Used in *possess.* and *attrib.* to designate things discovered or introduced by Koch.

Koch's bacillus (chiefly *Hist.*) the tubercle bacillus, first isolated by Koch. **Koch('s) postulates** a set of four criteria which should be satisfied before a given disease is attributed with certainty to any particular micro-organism. **Koch-Weeks bacillus** [J. E. *Weeks* (1853-1949), US ophthalmologist] the bacterium *Haemophilus aegyptius*, which is a common cause of infectious conjunctivitis.

Kodak /'kəʊdak/ *n.* & *v.* L19. [Arbitrary name invented by the manufacturer.] **A** *n.* **1** (Proprietary name for) a camera of a range produced by Kodak Ltd. Also, any small camera. L19. **2** *transf.* A photograph taken with a Kodak. L19. **B** *v.t.* & *i.* Photograph with a

Kodak; *fig.* describe or capture quickly or vividly. Now *rare.* L19.

Kodaker *n.* (now *rare*) L19.

Kodiak /ˈkəʊdɪak/ *n.* L19. [An island off Alaska.] In full *Kodiak bear.* A brown bear (*Ursus arctos*) of a subspecies endemic to some islands off Alaska, notable for the large size of individuals.

koechlinite /ˈkəːklɪnʌɪt/ *n.* E20. [f. Rudolf *Koechlin* (1862–1939), Austrian museum curator + -ITE[1].] *Min.* An orthorhombic molybdate of bismuth usu. occurring as greenish-yellow plates or soft white to yellow masses.

koeksister /ˈkʊksɪstə/ *n. S. Afr.* Also **koesister** /ˈkʊəsɪstə/. E20. [Afk. *koe(k)sister*, perh. f. *koek* cake + *sissen* sizzle.] A plaited doughnut dipped in syrup, a traditional South African confection.

koel /ˈkəʊəl/ *n.* E19. [Hind. *koēl*, *koīl* f. Skt KOKILA.] Any of certain cuckoos of the genera *Eudynamys* and *Urodynamys*; *spec.* (*a*) *E. scolopacea* of southern and SE Asia; (*b*) *E. cyanocephala* of Australia.

koelreuteria /kəːlrɔɪˈtɪərɪə/ *n.* L18. [mod.L (see below), f. Joseph G. *Koelreuter* (1733–1806), Ger. naturalist: see -IA[1].] A deciduous tree of the eastern Asian genus *Koelreuteria* (family Sapindaceae); esp. *K. paniculata*, from northern China, which has large panicles of yellow flowers and pinnate leaves which turn bright yellow in autumn.

koenenite /ˈkəːnənʌɪt/ *n.* E20. [f. Adolph von *Koenen* (1837–1915), Ger. geologist + -ITE[1].] *Min.* A trigonal hydroxide and chloride of magnesium, aluminium, and sodium, which forms pale yellow scales when pure, but is normally red owing to enclosed haematite.

koesister *n.* var. of KOEKSISTER.

koettigite /ˈkəːtɪgʌɪt/ *n.* M19. [f. Otto *Köttig*, 19th-cent. Ger. chemist + -ITE[1].] *Min.* A monoclinic hydrated arsenate of zinc, containing also cobalt and nickel, usu. forming red or pink prisms.

kofta /ˈkɒftə, ˈkəʊftə/ *n.* L19. [Urdu & Pers. *koftah* pounded meat.] A kind of meat or fish rissole, popular in Eastern cookery.

koftgari /ˈkəʊftgəriː/ *n.* L19. [Urdu & Pers. *kuft-garī* beaten work.] A kind of damascene-work of the Indian subcontinent, in which a pattern traced on steel is inlaid with gold.

kohekohe /ˈkəʊɪˈkəʊɪ/ *n.* M19. [Maori.] A tall forest tree, *Dysoxylum spectabile* (family Meliaceae), native to New Zealand, bearing panicles of fragrant white flowers.

koh-i-noor /ˈkəʊɪnʊə/ *n.* Also (earlier) †**Cohi Noor.** E19. [f. Pers. *kūh* mountain + *i* of + Arab. *nūr* light.] **1** A famous Indian diamond, part of the British Crown jewels since 1849; *transf.* any magnificent large diamond. E19. **2** *fig.* Something that is the most precious or most superb *of* its kind. L19.

kohl /kəʊl/ *n.* & *v.* L18. [Arab. *kuḥl*: see ALCOHOL.] **A** *n.* A powder, usu. consisting of antimony sulphide or lead sulphide, used as eye make-up and as eye ointment, esp. in Eastern countries. L18.

A. S. BYATT She had her father's big black eyes, outlined in Kohl.

B *v.t.* Darken with kohl. M20.

kohlrabi /kəʊlˈrɑːbi/ *n.* E19. [G *Kohlrabi* f. (w. assim. to *Kohl* COLE *n.*[1]) It. *cauli* or *cavoli rape*, pl. of *cavolo rapa* (whence Fr. *chou-rave*), repr. med.L *caulorapa*: see COLE *n.*[1], RAPE *n.*[3]] A variety of cabbage, *Brassica oleracea* var. *gongylodes*, with an edible turnip-shaped base to its stem.

Kohlrausch's law /ˈkəʊlraʊʃɪz lɔː/ *n. phr.* L19. [Friedrich Wilhelm *Kohlrausch* (1840–1910), Ger. physicist.] *Physical Chem.* A law stating that the equivalent electrical conductivity of an electrolyte (strictly, at infinite dilution) is the sum of independent contributions from the cation and the anion present in the electrolyte.

Kohs block /ˈkəʊz blɒk/ *n. phr.* M20. [f. Samuel *Kohs* (b. 1890) US psychologist + BLOCK *n.*] *Psychol.* Any of several coloured cubes making up a set, from which a subject is required to form specified patterns.

kohua /ˈkɔːhʊə/ *n. NZ.* M19. [Maori *kōhua.*] A Maori oven. Also, a three-legged iron pot or kettle.

koi /kɔɪ/ *n.* Pl. same. E18. [Jap.] A carp (in Japan). Now *esp.* a carp of a large ornamental variety bred in Japan. Also *koi carp.*

koi-cha /ˈkɔɪtʃə/ *n.* E18. [Jap., f. *koi* thick + *cha* tea.] In Japan: powdered tea mixed to a thick brew and drunk ceremonially.

koi hai /kɔɪˈhʌɪ/ *n. colloq.* (now chiefly *Hist.*). Also ***qui hi*** /kwʌɪˈhʌɪ/. E19. [f. Hind. *koī hai* is anyone there? (used to call a servant).] A British resident in the Indian subcontinent, esp. in Bengal.

koilonychia /kɔɪləˈnɪkɪə/ *n.* E20. [f. Gk *koilos* hollow + *onukhos*, *onux* nail + -IA[1].] *Med.* A condition of the fingernails in which the outer surfaces are concave instead of convex; spoon-nail.

koine /ˈkɔɪniː/ *n.* L19. [Gk *koinē* fem. sing. of *koinos* common, ordinary.] **1** The common literary language of the Greeks from the close of classical Attic to the Byzantine era. L19. **2** *Ling.* & *Philol.* A language or dialect common to a wide area in which different languages or dialects are, or were, used locally; a lingua franca. L19. **3** A set of cultural or other attributes common to various groups. E20.

2 D. WHITELOCK The general use of the West Saxon literary *koine*.

¶In Gk characters in L19; transliterated from E20.

koinonia /kɔɪˈnəʊnɪə/ *n.* E20. [Gk *koinōnia* communion, fellowship.] *Theol.* Christian fellowship or communion, with God or, more commonly, with fellow Christians.

koji /ˈkəʊdʒi/ *n.* L19. [Jap. *kōji.*] An enzyme preparation derived from various moulds used to cause fermentation in the production of saké, soy sauce, etc.

kojic /ˈkəʊdʒɪk/ *a.* E20. [f. prec. + -IC.] Chem. *kojic acid*, a crystalline pyrone derivative produced from dextrose by some fungi of the genus *Aspergillus*, with mild antibacterial properties.

kokako /ˈkɔːkəkəʊ/ *n.* Pl. **-os.** L19. [Maori.] A New Zealand wattlebird, *Callaeas cinerea*.

kokam *n.* var. of KOKUM.

kokanee /ˈkəʊkani/ *n.* L19. [Shuswap *kəknǽxʷ*.] A sockeye salmon of a non-migratory dwarf subspecies found in lakes in western N. America. Also *kokanee salmon*. Also called *silver trout*.

koker /ˈkəʊkə/ *n.* M19. [Du.] In Guyana: a sluice-gate, a lock-gate; the water between such gates.

kokerboom /ˈkʊəkəbʊəm/ *n. S. Afr.* L18. [Afk., f. Du. *koker* quiver + *boom* tree.] A small aloe tree, *Aloe dichotoma*, the branches of which were formerly used by the Nama to make quivers for arrows.

kokeshi /ˈkəʊkəʃiː/ *n.* Pl. same. M20. [Jap.] A kind of wooden Japanese doll.

kokila /ˈkəʊkɪlə/ *n.* L18. [Skt. Cf. KOEL.] In the Indian subcontinent: the Indian koel, *Eudynamys scolopacea*.

kokko /ˈkəʊkəʊ/ *n.* Also **koko.** M19. [Burm.] **1** A large deciduous leguminous tree, *Albizia lebbeck*, which bears heads of yellowish-white flowers and is native to tropical Asia, though naturalized in Africa and the Caribbean. Also called *East Indian walnut*, *lebbek*, *siris*. M19. **2** The dark brown wood of this tree. M20.

koklass /ˈkəʊkləs, ˈkɒklas/ *n.* Also **-as.** M19. [f. var. of Nepali *phakrās*.] More fully *koklass pheasant*. A pheasant, *Pucrasia macrolopha*, which has a long crest and is native to the Himalayan region and China.

koko *n.* var. of KOKKO.

kokopu /ˈkɔːkəpuː/ *n. NZ.* L19. [Maori.] A small freshwater fish of the genus *Galaxias*.

kokowai /ˈkɔːkɔːwʌɪ/ *n. NZ.* M19. [Maori.] Red ochre, burnt red clay, used to decorate wood etc.

kok-saghyz /kɒksəˈgɪz/ *n.* M20. [Russ. *kok-sagyz*, f. Turkic *kök* root + *sagiz* gum, resin.] A dandelion, *Taraxacum kok-saghyz*, native to Turkestan, the roots of which yield a latex.

koku /ˈkəʊkuː/ *n.* Pl. same. E18. [Jap.] A Japanese unit of capacity equal to ten *to*, used for liquids and solids, esp. rice, and containing approximately 40 gallons (180 litres) or 5 bushels.

kokum /ˈkəʊkəm/ *n.* Also **-am.** M19. [Hind. *kokam.*] In full *kokum butter*, *oil*. An edible semi-solid oil derived from the tropical Asian plant *Garcinia indica* (family Guttiferae).

Kol /kəʊl/ *n.* & *a.* L18. [Origin unkn.] **A** *n.* Pl. **-s**, same. A member of any of various Munda-speaking peoples of the north-east of the Indian subcontinent. L18. **B** *attrib.* or as *adj.* Of or pertaining to the Kols. M19.

kola *n.* var. of COLA *n.*[1]

kolach /ˈkɒlətʃ/ *n.* Pl. **-che** /-tʃiː/, **-ches** /-tʃɪz/. E20. [Czech *koláč*, f. *kolo* wheel, circle.] A small tart or pie popular in the Czech Republic and Slovakia, topped or filled with fruit.

Kolam /ˈkəʊlɑːm/ *n.* & *a.* M19. [Ethnic name.] **A** *n.* Pl. **-s**, same. A member of a Dravidian people of central India. M19. **B** *attrib.* or as *adj.* Of or pertaining to this people. L19.

Kolami *n.* & *a.* (of) the language of this people M19.

Kolarian /kəʊˈlɛːrɪən/ *n.* & *a.* M19. [f. *kolar*, an ancient name for India + -IAN.] = MUNDA.

Kolbe /ˈkɒlbə/ *n.* L19. [A. W. H. *Kolbe* (1818–84), Ger. chemist.] *Chem.* Used *attrib.* and in *possess.* to designate two reactions used in synthesis: (*a*) the electrolysis of a salt of a carboxylic acid, R·COOH, to yield an alkane R_2; (*b*) the reaction of sodium phenoxide with carbon dioxide to yield sodium salicylate.

kolbeckite /ˈkɒlbɛkʌɪt/ *n.* E20. [f. Friedrich *Kolbeck* (1860–1943), Ger. mineralogist + -ITE[1].] *Min.* A rare blue monoclinic hydrated phosphate of scandium, usu. containing calcium, aluminium, and other elements.

Koli /ˈkəʊli/ *n.* & *a.* Also †**Koolee.** E19. [Ethnic name.] **A** *n.* Pl. **-s**, same. A member of an aboriginal people of Gujarat in western India. Earlier as COOLIE *n.* I. E19. **B** *attrib.* or as *adj.* Of or pertaining to the Kolis. M19.

kolinsky /kəˈlɪnski/ *n.* M19. [f. *Kola* a port in NW Russia + pseudo-Russ. ending *-insky.*] (The fur of) a weasel, *Mustela sibirica*, native to northern and eastern Eurasia, Japan, and Taiwan.

kolkhoz /ˈkɒlkɒz, kʌlkˈhɔːz/ *n.* Pl. same, **-zes** /-zɪz/, **-zy** /-zi/. E20. [Russ., f. *kol(lektivnoe khoz(yaĭstvo* collective farm.] In countries of the former USSR: a collective farm.

kollergang /ˈkɒləgaŋ/ *n.* L19. [G = crushing action.] A crushing machine used in milling paper pulp.

kolm /kɒlm/ *n.* M20. [Sw.] *Petrogr.* A form of cannel coal with a relatively high content of metals, found in Swedish shales.

Kol Nidre /kɒl ˈniːdreɪ/ *n.* L19. [Aram. *kol nidrē* all the vows (the opening wds of the prayer).] An Aramaic prayer annulling vows made before God, sung by Jews at the opening of the Day of Atonement service on the eve of Yom Kippur. Also, the service or the melody at or to which this prayer is sung.

kolo /ˈkəʊləʊ/ *n.* Pl. **-os.** L18. [Serbo-Croat = wheel.] A Slavonic dance performed in a circle.

Koma /ˈkəʊmə/ *n.* & *a.* Pl. of n. same. E20. [Local name.] Of or pertaining to, a member of, a people living near the border of Sudan and Ethiopia along the Blue Nile and its tributaries; (of) their language.

Koman *n.* & *a.* (designating) a group of languages of Sudan and Ethiopia that includes Koma M20.

komatiite /kəˈmatɪʌɪt/ *n.* M20. [f. *Komati* river in southern Africa + -ITE[1].] *Geol.* Any of a class of ultramafic extrusive igneous rocks typically displaying a distinctive texture of criss-crossing sheaves of elongated crystals of olivine.

komatiitic /kəmatɪˈɪtɪk/ *a.* L20.

komatik /ˈkɒmətɪk/ *n.* E19. [Eskimo (Inuit) *qamutik.*] A dog-sledge used by the people of Labrador.

†kombaars *n.* see KOMBERS.

kombé /ˈkɒmbeɪ/ *n.* M19. [Nyanja.] The juice obtained from the seeds of a central African climbing plant, *Strophanthus kombe* (family Apocynaceae), which is a source of the drug strophanthin.

kombers /ˈkɒmbəːs/ *n. S. Afr.* Also **†-baars**. E19. [Afk. f. Du. *kombaars* ship's blanket.] A blanket, a rug.

kombu /ˈkɒmbuː/ *n.* L19. [Jap.] A brown seaweed of the genus *Laminaria*, used in Japanese cooking, esp. as a base for stock.

komfoor /kɒmˈfɔː/ *n. S. Afr.* M19. [Du. f. Picard form of OFr. *chaufoire* kettle for hot water.] A small brazier or stove; a chafing-dish.

Komi /ˈkəʊmi/ *n.* & *a.* Pl. of n. same. L19. [Komi.] **1** Of or pertaining to, a member of, a people of northern central Russia, esp. of the Komi Republic. L19. **2** (Of) the Finno-Ugric language of the Komi. M20.

¶Also called *Zyrian*.

komitadji, -aji *ns.* vars. of COMITADJI.

Kommandatura /kəmɑːndəˈtʊərə/ *n.* M20. [Alt. of G *Kommandantur* commandant's headquarters, command post, after Russ. *komendatura.*] The centre of operation of a military government.

Kommers /kɔˈmɛrs/ *n.* Pl. **-e** /-ə/. M19. [G f. L *commercium*: see COMMERCE *n.*] A social gathering of German students.

Komodo /kəˈməʊdəʊ/ *n.* E20. [An Indonesian island.] *Komodo dragon, monitor*, a large monitor lizard, *Varanus komodoensis*, native to Komodo and neighbouring islands.

Komsomol /ˈkɒmsəmɒl/ *n.* M20. [Russ. *komsomol*, short for *Kommunisticheskiĭ Soyuz Molodëzhi* Communist Union of Youth.] *Hist.* (A member of) the Communist youth organization of the USSR.

kona /ˈkəʊnə/ *n.* M19. [Haw., lit. 'leeward', the wind being of opposite direction to the prevailing north-easterlies.] A stormy southerly or south-west wind in the Hawaiian Islands.

konak /kəʊˈnɑːk/ *n.* M19. [Turk. = halting-place, inn.] A large house, palace, or official residence, in Turkey or the former Ottoman Empire.

konaki /ˈkɒnəki/ *n. NZ.* E20. [Maori *kōneke* sledge.] A horse-drawn wooden sledge.

Kond /kɒnd/ *n.* & *a.* Also **Kh-**. M19. [Dravidian *Koṇḍa.*] **A** *n.* **1** A member of a Dravidian people inhabiting Orissa in eastern India. M19. **2** The language of this people. L19. **B** *attrib.* or as *adj.* Of or pertaining to the Konds or their language. M19.

konditorei /ˌkɒnditoˈraɪ/ *n.* Pl. same, **-en** /-ən/. M20. [G, f. *Konditor* confectioner.] Confectionery; a shop selling confectionery or rich pastries.

Kondratieff /kɒnˈdrɑːtjɛf/ *n.* Also **-iev**. M20. [N. D. *Kondratieff* (1892–*c* 1935), Russ. economist.] Econ. *Kondratieff cycle, wave*, each of a series of supposed cycles or waves of economic expansion and contraction lasting from forty to sixty years.

konfyt /kɒnˈfeɪt/ *n. S. Afr.* M19. [Afk. = Du. *konfijt*, prob. f. Fr. CONFITURE.] Fruit preserved in sugar; preserve, jam.

Kongo /ˈkɒŋgəʊ/ *n.* & *a.* Pl. of n. same, **-os**. M19. [Kikongo.] Of or pertaining to, a member of, a Bantu-speaking people of the region of the Zaire (Congo) River in west central Africa; (of) the language of this people, Kikongo.

kongoni /kɒŋˈgəʊni/ *n.* E20. [Kiswahili.] Esp. in E. Africa: the hartebeest, *Alcelaphus buselaphus.*

kongsi /ˈkɒŋsi/ *n.* M19. [Chin. *gōngsī* (Wade-Giles *kungszu*) company, corporation.] In the Malay archipelago: an association, a partnership, *esp.* an association of Chinese people from the same area.

koniaku /kɒnˈjakuː/ *n.* Also (earlier) **konjak** /ˈkɒnjak/. L19. [Jap. *konnyaku, konyaku.*] A Japanese plant, *Amorphophallus rivieri*, (family Araceae); (flour obtained from) the starchy root of this, used in Japanese cooking.

konimeter /kəˈnɪmɪtə/ *n.* E20. [f. Gk *konis* dust + -METER.] A kind of impinger which directs a measured volume of air on to a slide to which any dust particles will adhere.

konini /ˈkɔːniːni/ *n. NZ.* M19. [Maori.] A New Zealand fuchsia, *Fuchsia excorticata*; *collect.* the berries of this shrub.

konjak *n.* see KONIAKU.

Konkani /ˈkəʊŋkəni/ *n.* & *a.* L19. [Marathi & Hind. *kõkṇī*, f. Skt *koṅkaṇa* Konkan (see below).] **A** *n.* Pl. **-s**, same. **1** A native or inhabitant of the Konkan, a coastal region of western India; a member of the Konkani-speaking community of Goa and the Konkan. L19. **2** An Indo-Aryan language that is the main language of Goa. E20. **B** *attrib.* or as *adj.* Of or pertaining to the Konkanis or their language. L19.

kono /ˈkəʊnəʊ/ *n.*[1] L19. [Korean *konu.*] A Korean board game between two players, each having an equal number of pieces and trying to block or capture those of the opponent.

Kono /ˈkəʊnəʊ/ *n.*[2] & *a.* E20. [Mande.] **A** *n.* Pl. **-os**, same. **1** A member of a Mande people of Sierra Leone. E20. **2** The language of the Konos, having affinities with Vai. E20. **B** *attrib.* or as *adj.* Of or pertaining to the Konos or their language. E20.

koodoo *n.* var. of KUDU.

kook /kuːk/ *n.* & *a. slang.* M20. [Prob. abbrev. of CUCKOO *n.* 3 or *a.* 2.] **A** *n.* **1** A crazy or eccentric person. M20. **2** *Surfing.* A bad or inexperienced surfer. M20.

1 *Black World* These marchers were . . a bunch of kooks.

B *attrib.* or as *adj.* Crazy, eccentric. M20.

kooka /ˈkʊkə/ *n. Austral. slang.* M20. [Abbrev.] = next.

kookaburra /ˈkʊkəbʌrə/ *n.* M19. [Aborig.] Any of certain arboreal kingfishers of the genus *Dacelo*, of Australia and New Guinea; *spec.* the large brown *D. novaeguineae*, distinguished by its peculiar laughing cry (also called *laughing jackass*).

kooky /ˈkʊki/ *a. slang.* Also **-ie**. M20. [f. KOOK + -Y[1].] Crazy, eccentric.

E. L. WALLANT I feel like dropping . . this kooky life and marrying a . . tired businessman.

kookily *adv.* M20. **kookiness** *n.* M20.

†Koolee *n.* & *a.* var. of KOLI.

Kootenai *n.* & *a.* var. of KUTENAI.

kootie *n.* var. of COOTIE *n.*

kop /kɒp/ *n.* M19. [Afk. f. Du. *kop* head: cf. COP *n.*[1]] **1** A prominent hill or peak. Freq. in place-names. *S. Afr.* M19. **2** *Soccer.* (**K-**.) A high bank of terracing for standing spectators, usu. supporting the home side, orig. and esp. at the ground of Liverpool Football Club; the spectators massed on such terracing. Also more fully *Spion Kop* /ˈspʌɪən/ [*Spioen Kop*, site of a battle in S. Africa during the Boer War]. E20.

Kop(p)ite *n.* (*Soccer*) a spectator who frequents a Kop M20.

kopa Maori /kɒpə ˈmaʊri/ *n. phr. NZ.* Also **copper Maori**. E19. [f. Maori *kāpura* fire, *kopa* oven + MAORI.] A Maori oven in which food is placed on heated stones and covered with flax or earth.

kopdoek /ˈkɒpdʊk/ *n. S. Afr.* E20. [Afk., f. as KOP + DOEK.] A head-cloth, a headscarf.

kopek /ˈkəʊpɛk, ˈkɒp-/ *n.* Also **-eck, copek**. E17. [Russ. *kopeĭka* dim. of *kop'ë* lance (from figure of a tsar (orig. Ivan IV) bearing a lance instead of sword).] A monetary unit of Russia and some other countries of the former USSR, equal to one-hundredth of a rouble; a coin of this value.

kopi /ˈkəʊpi/ *n. Austral.* L19. [Aborig.] Gypsum- or selenite-bearing rock or mud; powdered gypsum.

kopje *n.* var. of KOPPIE.

Koplik /ˈkɒplɪk/ *n.* L19. [Henry *Koplik* (1858–1927), US paediatrician.] Med. *Koplik('s) spot*, a small greyish-yellow spot, usu. with a red halo, numbers of which occur on the buccal mucosa in the early stages of measles.

koppa /ˈkɒpə/ *n.* LME. [Gk.] A letter (ϙ) between pi and rho of the original Greek alphabet, later displaced by kappa, but retained as a numeral.

¶Rare bef. L19.

koppel /ˈkʌp(ə)l, ˈkɒp-/ *n.* L19. [Yiddish.] A skullcap worn by male Jews.

koppie /ˈkɒpi/ *n. S. Afr.* Also **kopje**. M19. [Afk. f. Du. *kopje* dim. of *kop* head. Cf. KOP.] A small hill, *esp.* any of the flat-topped or pointed hillocks characteristic of the veld.

kora /ˈkɔːrə/ *n.*[1] L18. [f. a W. Afr. lang.] A stringed W. African instrument resembling a harp.

Kora /ˈkɔːrə/ *n.*[2] & *a.* E19. [Origin unkn.] = KORANA.

koradji /ˈkɒrədʒi, kəˈradʒi/ *n. Austral.* Also (earlier) **coradgee** & other vars. L18. [Aborig.] An Aboriginal medicine man.

Koran /kɔːˈrɑːn, kə-/ *n.* Also **Qur'an** /kəˈrɑːn/. E17. [Arab. *ḳur'ān* recitation, reading, f. *ḳara'a* read, recite: cf. Syriac *keryānā* scripture reading (in Christian liturgy). See also earlier ALCORAN.] The sacred book of Islam, believed by Muslims to be the word of God as revealed in Arabic to Muhammad, and arranged after the latter's death.

Koranic /-ˈrɑːnɪk, -ˈranɪk/ *a.* E19.

Korana /kəˈranə/ *n.* & *a.* Also **-nn-**. E19. [Origin unkn.] **A** *n.* Pl. same, **-s**. **1** A member of a group of Nama peoples in southern Africa. E19. **2** The language of these peoples. L19. **B** *attrib.* or as *adj.* Of or pertaining to the Korana or their language. M19.

¶Also called *Kora*.

Koranko /kəˈraŋkəʊ/ *n.* & *a.* Pl. of n. same, **-os**. E19. [Mande.] **1** Of or pertaining to, a member of, a Mande people of Guinea and Sierra Leone. E19. **2** (Of) the language of this people. L19.

Koranna *n.* & *a.* var. of KORANA.

kordax /ˈkɔːdaks/ *n.* Also **c-**. M16. [Gk.] A dissolute dance of ancient Greek comedy.

kore /ˈkɔːreɪ/ *n.* E20. [Gk *korē* = maiden.] A Greek statue of a draped maiden.

Korean /kəˈriːən/ *n.* & *a.* Also (earlier) **†C-**. E17. [f. *Korea* (see below) + -AN.] **A** *n.* **1** A native or inhabitant of Korea in eastern Asia, now divided into the Republic of Korea (or South Korea) and the Korean People's Republic (North Korea). E17. **2** The agglutinative language of Korea, related to Japanese. E19. **3** *ellipt.* A Korean chrysanthemum. M20.

B *adj.* Of or pertaining to Korea or its language. E17.

Korean chrysanthemum a late-flowering hybrid chrysanthemum developed from *Dendranthema zawadskii* and other Far Eastern species. **Korean pine** a slow-growing pine with dark green leaves, *Pinus koraiensis*, native to Korea and Japan.

Koreanize *v.t.* give a Korean character to M20.

Koreish /kəˈrʌɪʃ/ *n.pl.* & *a.* Also (earlier) **†Coreis(h)**; **Quraysh, Qureysh**, & other vars. M17. [Arab. *ḳurayš* Koreish, *ḳurašī* Koreishite.] **A** *n.pl.* The tribe which inhabited Mecca in the time of Muhammad and to which he belonged. M17. **B** *attrib.* or as *adj.* Of or pertaining to the Koreish. L19.

Koreishite *n.* a member of the Koreish E18.

korero /ˈkɔːrərəʊ/ *n. NZ.* Pl. **-os**. E19. [Maori.] Talk, conversation, discussion; a conference.

korfball /ˈkɔːfbɔːl/ *n.* E20. [Du. *korfbal*, f. *korf* basket + *bal* ball.] A game of Dutch origin, resembling basketball but in which players are not permitted to run with the ball, played between teams of mixed sexes (usu. six male and six female on each).

korhaan /kɔːˈhɑːn, kəˈrɑːn/ *n. S. Afr.* Also **kn-** /kn-/. M18. [Afk., f. *kor-, knor-* imit. base (cf. Du. *korren* coo, *knorren* grumble, snarl) + *haan* cock. Cf. Du. *korhaan* woodcock.] A bustard.

kori /ˈkɔːri/ *n.*[1] E19. [Setswana *kgori*.] In full *kori bustard*. A bustard, *Choriotis kori*, of sub-Saharan Africa.

kori /ˈkɔːri/ *n.*[2] Also **K-**. M19. [Sindhi *korī* = Hind. *kolī* f. Skt *kolika* f. Tamil *kōṭikar*.] A member of a low Hindu caste of weavers of northern India.

korimako /kɒrɪˈmɑːkəʊ/ *n. NZ*. Pl. **-os**. M19. [Maori.] A New Zealand honeyeater, *Anthornis melanura*. Also called *bellbird, makomako, moko-moko*.

korin /ˈkɔːrɪn/ *n*. M19. [App. f. a W. Afr. lang.] The red-fronted gazelle, *Gazella rufifrons*, native to Africa from Senegal to Sudan. Also *korin gazelle*.

Kōrin /ˈkɔːrɪn/ *n*. L19. [See below.] *Kōrin school, style*, a school of decorative traditional Japanese painting typified by the work of the Japanese artist Kōrin Ogata (1658–1716).

koringkriek /ˈkɔːrɪŋkrɪk/ *n. S. Afr.* E20. [Afk., f. Du. *koorn* corn + *kriek(en)* chirp.] A long-horned grasshopper.

korkir *n*. var. of CORKIR.

Korku /ˈkɔːkuː/ *n*. & *a*. M19. [Munda.] **A** *n*. Pl. **-s**, same. A member of a Munda people of the central provinces of India; the language of this people. M19. **B** *attrib.* or as *adj*. Of or pertaining to the Korkus or their language. M19.

korma /ˈkɔːmə/ *n*. L19. [Urdu *ḳormā*, *ḳormah* f. Turk. *kavurma*.] A mildly spiced Indian dish of meat or fish marinaded in yoghurt or curds.

chicken korma etc.

kornelite /ˈkɔːnəlʌɪt/ *n*. L19. [f. *Kornel* Hlavacsek, late 19th-cent. Czech engineer + -ITE[1].] *Min*. A violet to pale pink monoclinic hydrated ferric sulphate, usu. occurring as needles or fibrous aggregates.

kornerupine /ˈkɔːnərʊpiːn/ *n*. L19. [f. A. N. *Kornerup* (1857–81), Da. geologist + -INE[5].] *Min*. A green orthorhombic silicate of aluminium and magnesium, usu. occurring in prismatic aggregates.

koro /ˈkɔːrəʊ/ *n*. E19. [Jap. *kōro* incense-pot, censer.] An elaborate Japanese vase, usu. of bronze, jade, or porcelain, in which incense is burned.

koromiko /kɒrəˈmiːkəʊ/ *n*. Pl. **-os**. M19. [Maori.] Any of various New Zealand shrubs of the genus *Hebe*, of the figwort family, esp. *H. salicifolia*.

korowai /ˈkɒrəwʌɪ/ *n. NZ*. E19. [Maori.] A Maori cloak or cape of flax, ornamented with black twisted thrums. Also *korowai mat*.

korrigan /ˈkɒrɪg(ə)n/ *n*. M19. [Breton (Vannes dial.), fem. of *korrig* gnome, dim. of *korr* dwarf.] In Breton folklore, a fairy or witch noted esp. for stealing children.

korrigum /ˈkɒrɪg(ə)m/ *n*. E19. [f. Saharan: cf. Kanuri *kargun*.] A topi (antelope) of the W. African subspecies.

Korsakoff /ˈkɔːsəkɒf/ *n*. E20. [S. S. *Korsakoff* (1854–1900), Russ. psychiatrist.] *Med*. Used in *possess.* to designate a psychotic syndrome, often the result of chronic alcoholism, characterized by disorientation, memory loss for recent events, and consequent confabulation.

koru /ˈkɔːruː/ *n. NZ*. M20. [Maori.] A stylized fern-leaf motif in Maori carving and tattooing.

koruna /ˈkɒrʊnə/ *n*. E20. [Czech = crown.] The basic monetary unit of Bohemia, Moravia, and Slovakia, equal to 100 haléru.

Korwa /ˈkɔːwə/ *n*. & *a*. M19. [Munda.] **A** *n*. Pl. same, **-s**. **1** A member of a Munda people of the Chota Nagpur area of India. M19. **2** The language of the Korwa. L19. **B** *attrib.* or as *adj*. Of or pertaining to the Korwa or their language. M19.

Koryak /ˈkɒrjak/ *n*. & *a*. E18. [Russ. *Koryaki* (pl.).] **A** *n*. Pl. **-s**, same. **1** A member of a people inhabiting the northern part of the Kamchatka peninsula on the Pacific coast of Siberia. E18. **2** The Palaeo-Siberian language of this people. L19. **B** *attrib.* or as *adj*. Of or pertaining to the Koryaks or their language. L18.

kos /kɒs/ *n*. Also **koss, coss, †course**. Pl. same. E17. [Hind. f. Skt *krośa* lit. 'cry, shout'.] In the Indian subcontinent: a measure of length varying in different parts, usu. between 3 and 4 km (2 to 2½ miles).

kosh *n*. & *v*. var. of COSH *n*.[1] & *v*.

Koshare /kə(ʊ)ˈʃɑːriː/ *n*. L19. [Keresan *k' :sari*.] A member of a Pueblo Indian clown society representing ancestral spirits in rain and fertility ceremonies.

kosher /ˈkəʊʃə/ *a., n.,* & *v*. M19. [Heb. *kāšēr* fit, proper.] **A** *adj*. **1** Of food: prepared according to the Jewish law. M19. **2** That sells or prepares such food; where such food is cooked or eaten. L19. **3** Correct, genuine, legitimate. *colloq*. L19.

1 R. HAYMAN Meat cannot be *kosher* unless the animals' throats have been cut by the authorized butcher. 2 *Guardian* The last kosher butcher left for Israel. 3 T. PYNCHON They got the contracts. All drawn up in most kosher fashion. L. CODY Everything seemed fairly kosher until this morning.

B *n*. **1** *ellipt*. Kosher food; a kosher shop. L19. **2** The Jewish law regarding food. Chiefly in *keep kosher*. M20.

C *v.t.* Prepare (food) according to the Jewish law. L19.

kosso *n*. var. of KOUSSO.

kotal /ˈkəʊtal/ *n*. E19. [Pers & Pashto f. Mongolian.] In Afghanistan and adjacent regions: a pass over a mountain; a col; the ridge or summit of a pass.

kotatsu /kəʊˈtatsuː/ *n*. L19. [Jap.] A wooden frame placed over a central hearth or charcoal brazier in Japanese houses and covered with a thick quilt to give an enclosed area for warming the hands and feet. Also, the hearth or brazier and the cover together.

kotla *n*. see KGOTLA.

koto /ˈkəʊtəʊ/ *n*. Pl. **-os**. L18. [Jap.] A long Japanese zither, now usu. having thirteen silk strings, usu. played on the floor.

kotow *n*. & *v*. var. of KOWTOW.

kotuku /ˈkɔːtʊkʊ/ *n. NZ*. M19. [Maori.] The white heron or great egret, *Egretta alba*.

kotwal /kəʊtˈwɑːl/ *n*. Also **c-**. L16. [Hind. *koṭvāl* f. Skt *koṭṭapāla*.] In the Indian subcontinent: a chief officer of police for a city or town; a town magistrate.

kotwali /kəʊtˈwɑːli/ *n*. M19. [Hindi *koṭvālī*, f. as prec.] In the Indian subcontinent: a police-station.

kou /kəʊ/ *n*. E19. [Haw.] A Hawaiian tree, *Cordia subcordata*, of the borage family; the dark brown wood of this tree.

koulan *n*. see KULAN.

koulibiac *n*. var. of COULIBIAC.

koumiss *n*. var. of KUMIS.

kouprey /ˈkuːpreɪ/ *n*. M20. [Khmer.] A rare large grey wild ox, *Bos sauveli*, native to the forests of Indo-China.

koura /ˈkəʊərə/ *n. NZ*. M19. [Maori.] A freshwater crayfish, *Paranephrops planifrons*.

kourbash /ˈkʊəbaʃ/ *n*. & *v*. Also **kur-, c-**. E19. [Arab. *kurbāj*, *kirbāj* f. Turk. *kırbaç* whip.] **A** *n*. A whip of (esp. hippopotamus) hide as an instrument of punishment in Turkey and Egypt. E19. **B** *v.t.* Flog (a person) with a kourbash. M19.

kouros /ˈkuːrɒs/ *n*. Pl. **-roi** /-rɔɪ/. E20. [Gk (Ionic form of *koros* boy).] *Gk Antiq*. A sculptured representation of a youth.

kouskous *n*. var. of COUSCOUS *n*.[1]

kousso /ˈkʊsəʊ/ *n*. Also ***kosso*** /ˈkɒsəʊ/. M19. [Amharic.] The dried flowers of an Ethiopian tree, *Hagenia abyssinica* (family Rosaceae), used as a remedy for tapeworm.

kovsh /kɒvʃ/ *n*. Pl. **-shi** /-ʃi/. L19. [Russ.] In Russia: a ladle or container for drink.

kowhai /ˈkəʊwʌɪ, *NZ* ˈkɔːfʌɪ/ *n*. M19. [Maori.] Any of a number of leguminous shrubs or small trees of the genus *Sophora*; esp. *S. tetraptera*, native to New Zealand and Chile, which bears racemes of golden-yellow flowers (also called *locust tree*).

kowtow /kaʊˈtaʊ/ *n*. & *v*. Also **kotow** /kəʊˈtaʊ/. E19. [Chin. *kētóu* (Wade–Giles *k'ot'ou*), f. *kē* knock, strike + *tóu* head.] **A** *n*. The action or practice, formerly customary in China, of touching the ground with the forehead as a sign of extreme respect, submission, or worship; *fig*. an act of obsequious respect. E19.

B *v.i.* Perform the kowtow; *fig*. act in an obsequious manner. M19.

S. CONRAN She couldn't stand the way that Robert kowtowed to her father.

kowtower *n*. M20.

koyan /kəʊˈjɑːn/ *n*. L18. [Malay.] A unit of weight of the Malay peninsula equal to 40 *piculs* and equivalent to approximately 5,330 lb (2.42 tonnes).

kozatchok *n*. var. of KAZACHOC.

kra /krɑː/ *n*. E19. [Malay *kera*.] The long-tailed or crab-eating macaque, *Macaca fascicularis*, of SE Asia.

kraak porselein /krɑːk ˈpɔːsɪleɪn/ *n. phr.* Also **kraak porcelain** /ˈpɔːs(ə)lɪn/. M20. [Du., f. *kraak* carrack (the type of Portuguese ship from which the porcelain was first captured in 1603) + *porselein* PORCELAIN.] Blue and white Chinese porcelain of the Wan-li period (1573–1619) or later in the 17th cent.; a European imitation of this.

kraal /krɑːl/ *n*. & *v*. M18. [Afk. f. Port. *curral* f. Nama. Cf. CORRAL *n*., CRAWL *n*.[1]] **A** *n*. **1** In southern Africa: a village of huts enclosed by a fence or stockade, and often having a central space for cattle etc.; the community of such a village. M18. **2** In southern Africa: an enclosure for cattle or sheep, a stockade, a pen, a fold. L18. **3** In Sri Lanka (Ceylon): an enclosure into which wild elephants are driven; the process of capturing wild elephants by driving them into an enclosure. L19. **4** = CRAWL *n*.[1] 2. M20. **B** *v.t.* Enclose in a kraal or stockade. E19.

krab /krab/ *n. colloq*. M20. [Abbrev. & contr.] = KARABINER.

kraft /krɑːft/ *n*. E20. [Sw. = strength, in *kraftpapper* kraft paper.] More fully *kraft paper*. A strong smooth brown paper made from unbleached soda pulp.

Krag /krag/ *n. colloq*. L19. [O. H. *Krag*: see KRAG-JØRGENSEN.] = KRAG-JØRGENSEN.

kragdadig /kraxˈdɑːdɪx/ *a. S. Afr.* Also (in attrib. use) **-dige**. M20. [Afk. = Du. *krachtdadig*.] Forceful, vigorous in wielding power, unyielding.

kragdadigheid /-heɪt/ *n*. [-heid -HOOD] forcefulness, vigour in wielding power M20.

Krag–Jørgensen /kragˈjəːg(ə)ns(ə)n/ *n*. E20. [f. O. H. *Krag* (1837–1912) and E. *Jørgensen*, Norwegian firearm designers. Cf. earlier KRAG.] A type of rifle (and carbine) introduced in Denmark and Norway in the late 19th cent. and adopted in the US.

krait /krʌɪt/ *n*. L19. [Hind. *karait*.] Any of several brightly coloured venomous elapid snakes of the genus *Bungarus*, of the Indian subcontinent and SE Asia.

kraken /ˈkrɑːk(ə)n/ *n*. M18. [Norw.] A mythical sea-monster of enormous size, said to appear off the coast of Norway.

krakowiak /krəˈkəʊvɪak/ *n*. L19. [Pol., f. *Kraków* (Cracow) in Poland.] = CRACOVIENNE.

Krama *n*. var. of KROMO.

kramat /kraˈmɑːt, ˈkrɑːmət/ *n*. & *a*. Also **karamat** /kəˈrɑːmət/. L18. [Malay *keramat* (adj.) sacred, holy, (n.) holy place, holy person, f. Arab. *karāma* miracle worked by a saint other than a prophet.] **A** *n*. A Muslim holy place or place of pilgrimage. L18. **B** *adj*. Sacred to Muslims. M20.

krameria /krəˈmɪərɪə/ *n*. M19. [mod.L genus name, f. J. G. H. *Kramer* (d.1742), Austrian botanist + -IA[1].] = RHATANY.

kran /krɑːn/ *n*. L19. [Pers. *ḳrān*.] *Hist*. An Iranian (Persian) coin and monetary unit.

krans /krɑːns/ *n. S. Afr.* Also **krantz** /krants/. L18. [Afk. f. Du. = coronet, chaplet f. OHG, MHG, G *Kranz* coronet, circle, encircling ring of mountains, f. a base meaning 'ring'.] A wall of rock encircling a mountain or summit; a precipitous or overhanging cliff above a river, valley, etc.

krapfen /ˈkrapf(ə)n/ *n.* Pl. same. M19. [G.] In Germany and German-speaking countries: a fritter, a doughnut.

K ration /ˈkeɪ raʃ(ə)n/ *n. phr.* M20. [f. initial letter of surname of Ancel *K*eys (b. 1904), Amer. physiologist + RATION *n.*] An issue of compressed or dehydrated food etc. for use in the absence of regular supplies, esp. as given to soldiers in the war of 1939–45.

kratogen /ˈkratədʒ(ə)n, ˈkreɪt-/ *n.* E20. [f. Gk *kratos* strength + -GEN.] *Geol.* = CRATON.

kratoˈgenic *a.* E20.

kraurosis /krɔːˈrəʊsɪs/ *n.* Pl. **-roses** /-ˈrəʊsiːz/. L19. [f. Gk *krauros* brittle, dry + -OSIS.] *Med.* Atrophy, *spec.* of the skin of the vulva.

kraurotic /-ˈrɒtɪk/ *a.* affected with kraurosis L19.

kraut /kraʊt/ *n.* M19. [G = vegetable, cabbage. Cf. earlier SAUERKRAUT.] **1** Sauerkraut. M19. **2** (Usu. **K-**.) A German, *esp.* a German soldier. *slang. derog.* E20.

kraw-kraw *n.* var. of CRAW-CRAW.

kray /krʌɪ/ *n.* M20. [Russ. *kraĭ*.] In countries of the former USSR: a second-order administrative division, a region, a territory.

Krebs cycle /ˈkrɛbz sʌɪk(ə)l/ *n. phr.* Also **Krebs' cycle**. M20. [Sir Hans Adolf *Krebs* (1900–81), German-born Brit. biochemist.] *Biochem.* A cyclic sequence of enzyme-catalysed metabolic reactions which occur in mitochondria as part of aerobic cell respiration, in which oxaloacetic acid is acetylated, oxidized, and ultimately regenerated by a series of reactions in which ADP is converted to the energy-rich ATP. Also called *tricarboxylic acid cycle*.

kreef /kriːf, krɪəf/ *n. S. Afr.* Pl. same. M19. [Afk. f. Du. *kreeft* lobster.] A southern African crayfish or spiny lobster, *Jasus lalandii*.

kremlin /ˈkrɛmlɪn/ *n.* M17. [Fr. f. Russ. *kreml'* citadel.] A citadel or fortified enclosure within a Russian town or city, *esp.* (**K-**) that of Moscow; (**K-**) *the* government of the former USSR.

Kremliˈnology *n.* the study and analysis of Soviet policies M20. **Kremliˈnologist** *n.* a student or analyst of Soviet policies M20.

Kremnitz white *n. phr.* var. of CREMNITZ WHITE.

Krems white /krɛmz ˈwʌɪt/ *n. phr.* M19. [f. *Krems* a town of N. Austria + WHITE *n.*] A white lead pigment used as a paint base; Cremnitz white.

kreng /krɛŋ/ *n.* Also **crang** /kraŋ/. E19. [Du. *kreng*, MDu. *crenge* carrion, of unkn. origin.] *Whaling*. The carcass of a whale from which the blubber has been removed.

krennerite /ˈkrɛnərʌɪt/ *n.* L19. [f. J. S. *Krenner* (1839–1920), Hungarian mineralogist + -ITE[1].] *Min.* A rare orthorhombic telluride of gold, usu. containing silver, and found in yellow or white prismatic crystals with a metallic lustre.

kreophagous *a.* var. of CREOPHAGOUS.

kreplach /ˈkrɛplɑːx/ *n.pl.* L19. [Yiddish *kreplech* pl. of *krepel* f. dial. G *Kräppel* fritter, cogn. w. KRAPFEN.] Triangular noodles filled with chopped meat or cheese and served with soup.

kretek /ˈkrɛtɛk/ *n.* M20. [Indonesian *keretek*.] An Indonesian (esp. Javanese) cigarette containing cloves.

kreutzer /ˈkrɔɪtsə/ *n.* M16. [G *Kreuzer*, f. *Kreuz* CROSS *n.* after med.L *denarius crucigerus* lit. 'cross-bearing penny': see -ER[1]. Cf. CRAZIA.] A small silver or copper coin, originally stamped with a cross and formerly current in parts of Germany and in Austria.

kriegie /ˈkriːgi/ *n. slang.* M20. [Abbrev. of G *Kriegsgefangener* prisoner of war: see -IE.] A prisoner of war, *esp.* an Allied prisoner of war in Germany during the war of 1939–45.

kriegspiel /ˈkriːgspiːl/ *n.* L19. [G, f. *Krieg* war + *Spiel* game.] **1** A war-game in which blocks representing troops etc. are moved about on maps. L19. **2** A form of chess with an umpire and two players, in which each player plays at a separate board and has only limited information about the other's moves. L19.

krieker /ˈkriːkə/ *n. US.* M19. [G *Kriecher* creeper.] The pectoral sandpiper, *Calidris melanotos*.

Krilium /ˈkrɪlɪəm/ *n.* M20. [f. *kril-* alt. of *a)cryl(onitrile* + -IUM.] (Proprietary name for) any of various mixtures of polyacrylate salts and other carboxylated polymers used to improve the texture of soil and its resistance to erosion.

krill /krɪl/ *n.* Also **kril**. Pl. same. E20. [Norw. *kril* small fish fry.] A small shrimplike planktonic crustacean of the order Euphausiacea, important as food for fish, and for some whales and seals. Chiefly as *collect. pl.*

krimmer /ˈkrɪmə/ *n.* Also **c-**. M19. [G, f. *Krim* (Russ. *Krym*) Crimea (see CRIMEAN): see -ER[1].] The grey or black furry fleece of young lambs from the Crimean area; a cloth resembling this. Cf. ASTRAKHAN, KARAKUL.

Krio /ˈkriːəʊ/ *n.* & *a.* M20. [Prob. alt. of CREOLE.] (Of or pertaining to) an English-based creole language of Sierra Leone.

kris /kriːs/ *n.* Also **crease, creese**. L16. [Malay *keris*, partly through Du. *kris*, G *Kris*, Sp., Port. *cris*, Fr. *criss*, etc.] A Malay or Indonesian dagger with a straight or wavy blade.

Krishnaism /ˈkrɪʃnəɪz(ə)m/ *n.* L19. [f. Skt *Kṛṣṇa* Krishna (see below) + -ISM.] The worship of or belief in the Hindu god Krishna (an incarnation of Vishnu).

Kriss Kringle /krɪs ˈkrɪŋg(ə)l/ *n. US.* Now *rare*. M19. [Prob. alt. of G *Christkindl* Christmas present, (colloq.) Christ-child. Cf. CHRISTINGLE.] Santa Claus.

kriti /ˈkrɪti/ *n.* E20. [Skt *kṛti* a composition.] In the music of the southern part of the Indian subcontinent, a song, often devotional in character, which is deliberately composed and not an improvisation on a set theme.

Kromayer lamp /ˈkrəʊmʌɪə lamp/ *n. phr.* E20. [Ernst *Kromayer* (1862–1933), Ger. dermatologist.] *Med.* A water-cooled mercury-vapour lamp used for local ultraviolet irradiation.

kromesky /krə(ʊ)ˈmɛski, ˈkrɒmɛski/ *n.* M19. [Pol. *kromeczka* small slice.] A croquette made of minced meat or fish rolled in bacon etc. and fried.

Kromo /ˈkrəʊməʊ/ *n.* Also **Krama** /ˈkrɑːmə/. E19. [Jav. *krama*, Indonesian *kromo*.] In Indonesia: the polite form of Javanese, used by those of lower status when addressing social superiors. Cf. NGOKO.

krona /ˈkrəʊnə/ *n.* Pl. **-nor** /-nə/. L19. [Sw. = CROWN *n.* Cf. KRÓNA, KRONE, KROON.] The basic monetary unit of Sweden, equal to 100 öre.

króna /ˈkrəʊnə/ *n.* Pl. **-nur** /-nə/. L19. [Icel. = CROWN *n.* Cf. KRONA, KRONE, KROON.] The basic monetary unit of Iceland, equal to 100 aurer.

krone /ˈkrəʊnə/ *n.* Pl. in branch I **-ner** /-nə/, in branch II **-nen** /-nən/. L19. [Da. & G = CROWN *n.* Cf. KRONA, KRÓNA, KROON.] **I 1** The basic monetary unit of Denmark and Norway, equal to 100 øre. L19. **II** *Hist.* **2** A gold coin of the German Empire worth ten marks. L19. **3** A silver coin of the Austrian Empire worth 100 hellers. L19.

kronen, -ner *ns.pl.* see KRONE.

kronor *n.* pl. of KRONA.

krónur *n.* pl. of KRÓNA.

kroon /kruːn/ *n.* E20. [Estonian = CROWN *n.* Cf. KRONA, KRÓNA, KRONE.] The basic monetary unit of Estonia.

†kross *n.* var. of KAROSS.

Kru /kruː/ *n.* & *a.* Also **Kroo**. Pl. of n. same. M19. [W. Afr.] Of or pertaining to, a member of, a people of the coast of Liberia; (of) the language of this people, or the group of languages including it.

krug /krʊg/ *n.* M19. [G.] In Germany and German-speaking countries: a beer-mug, a tankard.

Krugerism /ˈkruːgərɪz(ə)m/ *n.* L19. [f. *Kruger* (see below) + -ISM.] *Hist.* The policy of Stephanus Johannes Paulus *Kruger* (1825–1904), who led the Afrikaners to victory in the First Boer War and served as President of the Transvaal from 1883 to 1899.

Krugerite *n.* & *a.* (*a*) *n.* an adherent of Kruger or his policy; (*b*) *adj.* of or pertaining to Krugerism or Krugerites: L19.

krugerrand /ˈkruːgərand, -rɑːn, kruːgəˈrɑːnt/ *n.* M20. [f. as prec. + RAND *n.*[2]] A South African gold coin bearing the image of President Kruger, valued as an investment.

Krukenberg tumour /ˈkrʊkənbəːg ˈtjuːmə/ *n. phr.* E20. [Friedrich Ernst *Krukenberg* (1871–1946), Ger. scientist.] *Med.* A secondary ovarian carcinoma usu. associated with a primary growth in the stomach.

krummholz /ˈkrʌmhɒlts/ *n.* E20. [G = elfin-tree, lit. 'crooked wood'.] = *elfin-wood* s.v. ELFIN *a.*

krummhorn /ˈkrʌmhɔːn, ˈkrʊm-/ *n.* Also **crumhorn**. L17. [G, f. *krumm* crooked, curved + *Horn* HORN *n.*] *Mus.* **1** A medieval and Renaissance wind instrument with a double reed and a curved end. L17. **2** An organ reed-stop, usu. of 8-ft pitch, suggestive of a krummhorn or clarinet in tone; = CREMONA *n.*[1], CROMORNE. L19.

Krupp /krʌp/ *n.* L19. [Alfred *Krupp* (1812–87), Ger. metallurgist, founder of a steel and armament works at Essen in Germany.] A gun made at a Krupp factory in Germany.

kryo- *comb. form* see CRYO-.

krypton /ˈkrɪptɒn/ *n.* L19. [Gk *krupton* neut. of *kruptos* hidden, concealed.] A colourless odourless gaseous chemical element, atomic no. 36, which is one of the noble gases, occurring as a trace constituent of the earth's atmosphere and used in lasers and other optical devices. (Symbol Kr.)

krytron /ˈkrʌɪtrɒn/ *n.* L20. [f. obscure 1st elem. + -TRON.] *Electronics*. A high-speed solid-state switching device which is triggered by a pulse of coherent light.

Kshatriya /ˈkʃatrɪə/ *n.* L18. [Skt *kṣatriya*, f. *kṣatra* rule.] A member of the second of the four main Hindu castes. Cf. KHATRI.

Kuan /kwɑːn/ *n.* E19. [Chin. *guān* (Wade–Giles *kuān*) an official.] **1** *Kuan Hua* /hwɑː/ [*huà* speech], = MANDARIN *n.*[1] 2. E19. **2** *Kuan Yin* /jɪn/, a goddess of Chinese Buddhism, to whom intercession for aid or protection is made; a representation of this goddess. M19. **3** In full *Kuan ware*, *Kuan yao* /jaʊ/ [*yáo* pottery]. A type of thickly glazed celadon made in predominantly greyish colours at Hangchow during the Song dynasty; pottery resembling this produced elsewhere in China in later centuries. L19.

Kuba /kuːˈbɑː/ *n.* & *a.* E20. [A town in NE Azerbaijan.] = KABISTAN.

kubong /ˈkuːbɒŋ/ *n.* E19. [Malay.] A flying lemur.

Kuchaean /kʊˈtʃiːən/ *n.* & *a.* Also **Kuchean**. M20. [Fr. *koutchéen*, f. *Kucha* a town in Xinjiang (Sinkiang), China: see -AN, -EAN.] (Of) the western dialect of Tocharian, Tocharian B.

kuchen /ˈkyçən, ˈkuːxən/ *n.* Pl. same, ***küchen*** /ˈkyçən/. M19. [G = cake.] In Germany or among German- or Yiddish-speaking people: a cake; *esp.* a cake taken with coffee.

kudo /ˈkjuːdəʊ/ *n. colloq.* Pl. **-os**. M20. [Back-form. f. next.] An expression of praise or gratitude for an achievement.

kudos /ˈkjuːdɒs/ *n. colloq.* L18. [Gk = praise, renown. Cf. prec.] Glory, fame, renown.

J. COLVILLE The British offensive . . is being called Canadian and British troops are getting hardly any kudos. R. FRAME The kudos of Cambridge and a double first didn't cancel out Surbiton.

kudu /ˈkuːduː, ˈkʊdʊ/ *n.* Also **koodoo**. Pl. **-s**, same. L18. [Afk. *koedoe* f. Xhosa *i-qudu*.] Either of two large white-striped greyish-brown African antelopes with spiral horns, *Tragelaphus strepsiceros* (more fully *greater kudu*), of sub-Saharan savannah and *T. imberbis* (more fully *lesser kudu*), of E. Africa and Arabia.

kudzu /ˈkʊdzuː/ *n.* L19. [Jap. *kuzu*.] In full *kudzu vine*. A climbing leguminous plant, *Pueraria lobata*, of China and Japan, cultivated elsewhere for fodder, as an ornamental, and to prevent soil erosion.

kuei /ˈkuːeɪ/ *n.* M20. [Chin. *gūi* (Wade–Giles *kūei*).] A bronze Chinese food-vessel, usu. with two handles and often surmounted by animal heads.

Kufic /ˈkjuːfɪk/ *a.* Also **C-**. E18. [f. *Kufa* (see below, Arab. *al-Kūfa*) + -IC.] Of or pertaining to the ancient city of Kufa south of Baghdad; *spec.* designating an early form of Arabic script freq. found in inscriptions and attributed to the scholars of Kufa.

kufiyeh *n.* var. of KEFFIYEH.

kuge /ˈkuːɡə/ *n.* Also **-é**. Pl. same. L16. [Jap.] In feudal Japan: the nobility attached to the imperial court at Kyoto; a court noble.

kugel /ˈkuːɡ(ə)l/ *n.* M19. [Yiddish = ball, f. MHG *kugel(e)* ball, globe.] In Jewish cookery: a kind of pudding; *esp.* a savoury pudding, usu. of potatoes or other vegetables, served as a separate course or as a side dish.

kugelhupf *n.* var. of GUGELHUPF.

Kuki /ˈkuːki/ *n.*[1] & *a.* L18. [Prob. f. a Sino-Tibetan lang.] A *n.* Pl. **-s**, same. A member of any of several peoples inhabiting the hills of Manipur and Mizoram, on the border of India and Myanmar (Burma); the language of these peoples. L18. B *attrib.* or as *adj.* Of or pertaining to the Kukis or their language. E19.

kuki /ˈkuːki/ *n.*[2] M19. [Maori f. COOK *n.*] *NZ Hist.* A slave of a Maori chieftain.

Ku Klux /ˈkuːklʌks, ˈkjuː-/ *n.* M19. [Abbrev.] 1 A member of the Ku Klux Klan. M19. 2 The Ku Klux Klan. L19.

Ku Kluxism *n.* L19.

Ku Klux Klan /kuːklʌksˈklan, kjuː-/ *n.* M19. [Perh. f. Gk *kuklos* circle + alt. of CLAN *n.*] 1 An American secret society of White people, founded in the Southern States after the Civil War of 1861–5 to defend the southern way of life, which developed into an organization to intimidate Blacks through terrorism and murder. M19. 2 A group held to resemble the Ku Klux Klan. M20.

Comb.: **Ku Klux Klansman** a member of the Ku Klux Klan.

¶Although the original Ku Klux Klan was outlawed by the American Congress in 1871, a similar organization still exists.

Ku Klux Klanner *n.* a member of the Ku Klux Klan E20.

kukri /ˈkʊkri/ *n.* E19. [Nepali *khukuri*.] A curved knife broadening towards the point and usu. with the sharp edge on the concave side, used by Gurkhas.

kuku /ˈkuːkuː/ *n.* *NZ.* M19. [Maori. Cf. KUKUPA.] = KERERU.

kukui /kʊˈkuːɪ/ *n.* E19. [Haw.] An evergreen tree, *Aleurites moluccana*, of the spurge family, native to the Moluccas and S. Pacific islands, with large seeds which yield an oil used for lighting and other purposes. Also called *candleberry*, *candle-nut*.

kukumakranka /ˌkʊkʊməˈkraŋkə/ *n.* L18. [Nama.] Any of various small bulbous plants of the southern African genus *Gethyllis*, of the daffodil family, bearing fragrant white flowers; the fragrant underground fruit of this, used to scent rooms or to flavour brandy for medicinal use.

kukupa /ˈkuːkuːpə/ *n.* *NZ.* M19. [Maori. Cf. KUKU.] = KERERU.

kula /ˈkuːlə/ *n.* E20. [Melanesian.] In some Pacific communities, esp. in the Trobriand Islands: an inter-island system of ceremonial exchange of items as a prelude to or concomitant of regular trading.

Kulah /ˈkuːlə/ *n.*[1] & *a.* L19. [A town in western Turkey.] (Designating) a type of Turkish rug of a large size with a long loose pile.

kulah /ˈkuːlə/ *n.*[2] E20. [Pers. *kulāh* cap.] A conical cap of felt or lambskin worn by Muslims in the Middle East.

kulak /ˈkuːlak/ *n.* L19. [Russ., lit. 'fist, tight-fisted person' f. Turkic *ḳol* hand.] Orig., a well-to-do Russian farmer or trader. Later, a peasant-proprietor working for his own profit in the Soviet Union.

kulan /ˈkuːlən/ *n.* Also (earlier) **koulan**. L18. [Turkic.] A wild ass, *Equus hemionus*, of a subspecies native to the central Asian steppes. Cf. KIANG, ONAGER.

kulchur /ˈkʌltʃə/ *n.* *joc.* or *derog.* M20. [Repr. pronunc.] = CULTURE *n.* II.

Kulin /kʊˈliːn/ *n.* & *a.* M19. [Skt *kulīna* well-born, f. *kula* family.] In the NE of the Indian subcontinent: (designating) a brahmin of the highest class.

Kulinism *n.* (chiefly *Hist.*) polygamy as practised by Kulins L19.

Kullah /kəˈlɑː/ *n.* E19. [Pegu *Gola* Indian Buddhist immigrant f. Skt *Gauḍa* ancient name of part of the NE of the Indian subcontinent.] In Myanmar (Burma): a foreigner, now *esp.* a European.

kultur /kʊlˈtuːr/ *n.* Also ***K-***. E20. [G f. L *cultura* or Fr. *culture* CULTURE *n.*] German civilization and culture, esp. (*derog.*) seen as racialist, authoritarian, and militaristic.

Comb.: ***kulturgeschichte*** /-ɡəʃɪçtə/ [*Geschichte* history] the history of the cultural development of a country etc.; history of civilization; ***kulturkampf*** /-kampf/ [*Kampf* struggle] the conflict in 19th-cent. Germany between the civil and ecclesiastical authorities for the control of schools and Church appointments; ***kulturkreis*** /-kraɪs/, pl. **-e** /-ə/, [*Kreis* sphere] a cultural group; a cultural complex; ***kulturstaat*** /-ʃtaːt/, pl. **-en** /-ən/, [*Staat* State] a civilized country; ***kulturträger*** /-trɛːɡər/, pl. same, [*Träger* carrier] an agent of cultural transmission.

kulturny /kʊljˈturnɪj, kʊlˈtəːni/ *a.* M20. [Russ. *kul'turnyĭ*, f. *kul'tur* f. L *cultura* or Fr. *culture* CULTURE *n.*] In countries of the former USSR: cultured, civilized; good mannered, well behaved. Cf. NEKULTURNY.

Kuman *n.* & *a.* var. of CUMAN.

kumara /ˈkuːmərə/ *n.* *NZ.* Also **-era**. L18. [Maori.] The sweet potato, *Ipomoea batatas*.

kumbuk /ˈkʌmbʌk, ˈkʊmbʊk/ *n.* M19. [Sinhalese.] An evergreen tree of southern India and Sri Lanka (Ceylon), *Terminalia arjuna* (family Combretaceae); the wood of this tree.

kumera *n.* var. of KUMARA.

kumis /ˈkuːmɪs/ *n.* Also **koumiss**, **kumiss**, **†cosmos**. L16. [Fr. *koumis*, G *Kumiss*, Pol. *kumys*, Russ. *kumys* f. Tartar *kumiz*.] A fermented liquor prepared from mare's or other milk, used as a beverage and medicinally esp. by central Asian nomadic tribes; a spirituous liquor distilled from this.

kumkum /ˈkʊmkʊm/ *n.* M20. [Skt *kuṅkuma* saffron.] A red powder used ceremonially, esp. by Hindu women to make a small distinctive mark on the forehead; the mark so made.

kümmel /ˈkʊm(ə)l/ *n.* M19. [G repr. MHG, OHG *kumil* var. of *kumīn* CUMIN.] A sweet liqueur flavoured with caraway and cumin seeds.

kumpit /ˈkʊmpɪt/ *n.* M20. [Prob. f. Maranao *kompit*.] A trading-vessel of the Philippines.

kumquat /ˈkʌmkwɒt/ *n.* Also **c-**. L17. [Chin. (Cantonese) *kam kwat* lit. 'gold orange'.] 1 A small citrus fruit, like a miniature orange, from any of several Far Eastern trees of the genus *Fortunella*, esp. *F. japonica* and *F. margarita*; the tree producing this, cultivated in China and Japan. L17. 2 More fully *native kumquat*. A citrus tree of NE Australia, *Eremocitrus glauca*; the plum-sized acid fruit of this. *Austral.* L19.

kumri /ˈkʊmri/ *n.* L19. [Kannada *kumari*.] A system of shifting cultivation practised in Karnataka, in SW India. Also called *podu*.

Kumyk /ˈkuːmɪk/ *n.* & *a.* L18. [See below.] A *n.* Pl. same, **-s**. 1 A member of a Turkic people of the Kumyk plateau in the Caucasus. L18. 2 The language of this people. L20. B *attrib.* or as *adj.* Of or pertaining to the Kumyk or their language. M20.

Kuna *n.* & *a.* var. of CUNA.

kunai /ˈkuːnʌɪ/ *n.* *Austral.* M20. [Name in New Guinea.] Lalang grass, *Imperata cylindrica*.

kunbi /ˈkuːnbi/ *n.* L16. [Marathi *kunbī*, *kulambī*, western Hind. *kurmī*, f. Skt *kuṭumbin*.] A member of a Hindu agricultural caste.

kundalini /ˈkʊndəlɪniː/ *n.* L19. [Skt *kuṇḍalinī* lit. 'snake'.] *Yoga.* 1 The latent (female) energy which lies coiled at the base of the spine. L19. 2 In full *Kundalini yoga*. A type of meditation which aims to direct and release this energy. M20.

kung fu /kʊŋˈfuː, kʌŋ-/ *n.* L19. [Chin. *gongfu* (Wade–Giles *kung fu*), f. *gong* (*kung*) merit + *fu* master.] The Chinese form of karate.

kungu /ˈkʌŋɡuː/ *n.* M19. [Nyanja *nkungu*.] In full *kungu fly*. Any of various dipteran flies whose larvae live in E. African lakes, above which the flies can form large swarms.

Comb.: **kungu cake** a kind of cake made from the bodies of large numbers of these gnats compressed together.

kunkur /ˈkʌŋkə/ *n.* Also **-ker**, **kankar**. L18. [Hind. f. *kaṅkar* Skt *karkara*.] In the Indian subcontinent: a coarse, often nodular, limestone used to make lime and in road-building.

Kunstforscher /ˈkʊnstfɔrʃər/ *n.* Pl. same. L19. [G, f. *Kunst* art + *Forscher* researcher.] An art historian.

Kunstgeschichte /ˈkʊnstɡəʃɪçtə/ *n.* L19. [G, f. *Kurst* art + *Geschichte* history.] The history of art, art history.

Kunsthistoriker /ˈkʊnsthɪsˌtoːrikər/ *n.* Pl. same. M20. [G, f. *Kunst* art + *Historiker* historian.] An art historian.

Künstlerroman /ˈkynstlərοˌmaːn/ *n.* Pl. **-e** /-ə/. M20. [G, f. *Künstler* artist + *Roman* novel.] A *Bildungsroman* about an artist.

Kunstprosa /ˈkʊnstproːza/ *n.* M20. [G, f. *Kunst* art + *Prosa* prose.] Literary prose, ornate and stylized prose.

kunzite /ˈkʌntsʌɪt, ˈkʌnzʌɪt/ *n.* E20. [f. George F. *Kunz* (1856–1932), US gemmologist + -ITE[1].] *Min.* A lilac-coloured gem variety of spodumene which fluoresces or changes colour when irradiated.

Kuomintang /kwəʊmɪnˈtaŋ, ɡwəʊ-/ *n.* Also **Guomindang** /ɡwəʊmɪnˈdaŋ/. E20. [Chin. *guómíndǎng* (Wade–Giles *kuo mintang*) national people's party, f. *guó* nation + *mín* people + *dǎng* party.] A Chinese nationalist radical party founded in 1912, holding power from 1928 until succeeded by the Communist Party in 1949, and subsequently forming the central administration of Taiwan.

Kuo-yu /ˈkwəʊjuː/ *n.* M20. [Chin. = national language, f. *guó* (Wade–Giles *kuo*) nation + *yu* language.] A form of Mandarin, the predecessor of modern standard Chinese, adopted for official use.

kupfernickel /ˈkʊpfənɪk(ə)l/ *n.* L18. [G, f. *Kupfer* COPPER *n.*[1] + *Nickel*: see NICKEL *n.*] *Min.* = NICCOLITE.

Kupferschiefer /ˈkʊpfəʃiːfə/ *n.* M19. [G, f. *Kupfer* COPPER *n.*[1] + *Schiefer* shale, slate.] *Geol.* (A stratum of) a bituminous brown or black copper-bearing shale of the Permian series.

Kupffer /ˈkʊpfə/ *n.* E20. [Karl Wilhelm von *Kupffer* (1829–1902), Bavarian anatomist.] Anat. *Kupffer('s) cell*: each of the phagocytic cells which line the sinusoids of the liver and are involved in the breakdown of red blood cells. Usu. in *pl.*

†kuphar *n.* var. of GUFA.

Kur /kuːr/ *n.* Pl. ***-ren*** /-rən/. L19. [G = a cure.] A cure, a medicinal drinking of the waters at a spa in Germany or a German-speaking country; a spa.

kura /ˈkʊrə/ *n.* L19. [Jap.] In Japan: a fireproof storehouse.

kurakkan /ˈkʊrəkɑːn/ *n.* L17. [Sinhalese.] In Sri Lanka (Ceylon): the finger millet or ragi, *Eleusine coracana*, used to make flour which forms a staple food of poorer villagers.

kurbash *n.* & *v.* var. of KOURBASH.

kurchatovium /kəːtʃəˈtəʊvɪəm/ *n.* M20. [f. I. V. *Kurchatov* (1903–60), Russ. nuclear physicist + -IUM.] (A name proposed for) a very unstable radioactive transuranic chemical element, atomic no. 104, produced artificially. (Symbol Ku.) Cf. RUTHERFORDIUM.

Kurd /kəːd/ *n.* E17. [Kurdish.] A member of a mainly pastoral Islamic people living in Kurdistan, a region in contiguous areas of Turkey, Iraq, Iran, and Syria.

kurdaitcha /kəˈdʌɪtʃə/ *n. Austral.* Also **kad-**. L19. [Aborig.] **1** A malignant supernatural being. Also *kurdaitcha man.* L19. **2** A special shoe, worn by an Aborigine on a mission of vengeance. Also *kurdaitcha shoe* etc. L19. **3** A mission on which such shoes are worn. L19. **4** A wearer of such shoes. E20.

Kurdish /ˈkəːdɪʃ/ *n.* & *a.* E19. [f. KURD + -ISH[1].] **A** *n.* The Iranian language of the Kurds. E19. **B** *adj.* Of or pertaining to the Kurds or their language. M19.

Kurdistan /kəːdɪˈstɑːn/ *n.* M20. [See KURD.] More fully *Kurdistan rug.* A rug with a geometric design, handwoven in Kurdistan.

Kuren *n.* pl. of KUR.

kurgan /kʊəˈgɑːn/ *n.* L19. [Russ., of Turkic origin: cf. Turk. *kurgan* castle, fortress.] A prehistoric sepulchral tumulus or barrow such as is found in Siberia and central Asia.

Kurhaus /ˈkuːrhaʊs/ *n.* Pl. ***-häuser*** /-hɔyzər/. M19. [G, f. as KUR + *Haus* HOUSE *n.*[1]] In Germany and German-speaking countries: a building at a health resort where medicinal water is dispensed; a pump room.

kuri /ˈkʊri/ *n. NZ.* M19. [Maori = dog.] = MAORI *dog*. Also, a mongrel; *slang* an unpleasant or disliked person.

Kuril /kʊˈriːl/ *n.* & *a.* Also **-ile**. M18. [Russ.] **A** *n.* An Ainu. Now *rare*. M18. **B** *attrib.* or as *adj.* Of or pertaining to the Ainu. Chiefly *spec.* designating or pertaining to a chain of small islands stretching northwards from Japan to the Kamchatka peninsula. E19.

Kuˈrilian *n.* & *a.* M19.

Kurnai /ˈkʊənʌɪ/ *n.* & *a.* L19. [Aborig.] **A** *n.* Pl. same. A member of an Aboriginal people of SE Australia; the language of this people. L19. **B** *attrib.* or as *adj.* Of or pertaining to the Kurnai or their language. E20.

Kurort /ˈkuːrɔrt/ *n.* Pl. ***-e*** /-ə/. M19. [G, f. as KUR + *Ort* place.] In Germany and German-speaking countries: a health-resort, a spa, a watering-place.

Kuroshio /kʊrə(ʊ)ˈʃiːəʊ/ *n.* Also **-siwo** /-ˈsiːwəʊ/ & other vars. L19. [Jap., f. *kuro* black + *shio* tide.] Usu. w. *the*: (the name of) a warm ocean current flowing north-eastwards past Japan. Also called *Japan current, Japanese current.*

kurper /ˈkəːpə/ *n. S. Afr.* M19. [Afk. f. Du. *karper* carp.] Any of various carplike freshwater fishes, esp. of the genera *Sandelia* and *Tilapia.*

kurrajong /ˈkʌrədʒɒŋ/ *n. Austral.* Also **c-**. E19. [Aborig.] Any of various Australian trees with tough bark which yields a fibre, *esp.* (more fully *black kurrajong*), *Brachychiton populneum.*

Kurrichane thrush /kʌrɪˌtʃaneɪ ˈθrʌʃ/ *n. phr.* E20. [*Kurrichane*, a place in the Transvaal, South Africa.] A thrush, *Turdus libonyanus*, of central and southern Africa.

kursaal /ˈkuːrzaːl, ˈkʊəsɑːl/ *n.* Pl. ***-säle*** /-zɛːlə/, ***-saals***, /-sɑːlz/. M19. [G, f. as KUR + *Saal* hall, room.] Esp. in Germany and German-speaking countries: a public building at a health resort, provided for the use and entertainment of visitors.

kurta /ˈkəːtə/ *n.* E20. [Urdu. & Pers. *kurtah.*] A loose shirt or tunic worn by esp. Hindu men and women.

kurtosis /kəːˈtəʊsɪs/ *n.* E20. [Gk *kurtōsis* a bulging, convexity, f. *kurtos* bulging, convex: see -OSIS.] *Statistics.* The degree of sharpness of the peak of a frequency-distribution curve, *spec.* as measured by the quantity μ_4/μ_2^2 or its excess over 3 (μ_4 and μ_2 being the fourth and the second moments about the mean of the distribution).

kuru /ˈkʊruː/ *n.* M20. [Name in New Guinea.] *Med.* A fatal viral brain disease found among certain peoples of New Guinea.

Kurukh /ˈkʊrʊk/ *n.* & *a.* L19. [Kurukh.] **A** *n.* **1** Pl. same, **-s**. A member of an aboriginal people of the northern Indian subcontinent, now esp. of the State of Bihar. L19. **2** The Dravidian language of this people. E20. **B** *attrib.* or as *adj.* Of or pertaining to the Kurukh or their language. E20.

¶Also called *Oraon.*

kuruma /kʊˈruːmə/ *n.* E18. [Jap.] A Japanese rickshaw.

kurumaya /kʊruːˈmɑːjə/ *n.* a person who pulls a kuruma L19.

Kurume /kʊˈruːmeɪ/ *n.* E20. [A town on the Japanese island of Kyushu.] In full *Kurume azalea.* Any of a group of small evergreen azalea hybrids, chiefly derived from the Japanese *Rhododendron kiusianum* and *R. kaempferi.*

kurus /kəˈruːʃ/ *n.* Also †**grouch**. Pl. same. L19. [Turk. *kuruş* f. G GROSCHEN.] A monetary unit of Turkey, equal to one-hundredth of a Turkish lira.

kurvey /kəːˈveɪ/ *v.i. S. Afr.* L19. [f. Du. *karwei* hard work, big job f. MDu. *corweie* f. Fr. CORVÉE.] Carry goods in an ox-wagon.

kurveyor /kəːˈveɪə/ *n. S. Afr.* L19. [Du. *karweier*, f. as prec.: see -ER[1], -OR.] A travelling trader, a carrier.

Kushan /ˈkʊʃɑːn, kʊˈʃɑːn/ *n.* & *a.* Also **Kushana** /kʊˈʃɑːnə/. L19. [Prakrit *kuṣāṇa* adj. f. Iranian.] **A** *n.* Pl. **-s**, same. A member of an Iranian dynasty who invaded the Indian subcontinent and established a powerful empire in the north-west between the 1st and 3rd cents. AD. L19. **B** *attrib.* or as *adj.* Of or pertaining to this people, esp. their dynasty. L19.

Kushite *n.* & *a.* var. of CUSHITE.

Kushitic *n.* & *a.* var. of CUSHITIC.

kusimanse /kuːsɪˈmansi/ *n.* Also **c-**. M19. [App. f. a W. Afr. lang.] A small dark-brown burrowing long-nosed mongoose, *Crossarchus obscurus*, of W. African forests.

kusti /ˈkʊstiː/ *n.* M19. [Pers. *kustī* girdle, cincture, Gujarati *kusti, kasti.*] A cord worn round the waist by Parsees, consisting of seventy-two threads to represent the chapters of one of the portions of the Zend-Avesta.

kuta /ˈkuːtə/ *n.* M20. [Setswana.] = KGOTLA.

Kutani /kʊˈtɑːni/ *n.* L19. [The village of *Kutanimura* in the former province of Kaga, Japan.] In full *Kutani ware.* A kind of gold and dark red Japanese porcelain.

kutcha /ˈkʌtʃə/ *a.* & *n.* Also **c-**, **kacha**. E19. [Hind. *kaccā* raw, crude, uncooked.] **A** *adj.* In the Indian subcontinent: slight, makeshift, unfinished; built of dried mud. E19. **B** *n.* Dried mud used as a building material in the Indian subcontinent. M19.

kuteera *n.* var. of KUTIRA.

Kutenai /ˈkuːtəneɪ, -ni/ *n.* & *a.* Also **-ay** & other vars. E19. [Blackfoot *Kotonáai-*.] **A** *n.* Pl. **-s**, same. A member of a N. American Indian people of the Rocky Mountains; the language of this people. E19. **B** *attrib.* or as *adj.* Of or pertaining to the Kutenais or their language. L19.

kutira /kəˈtɪərə/ *n.* Also **kuteera**. M19. [Hind. *katīrā.*] In full *kutira gum.* A gum obtained from an Indian shrub, *Cochlospermum religiosum* (family Bixaceae), used as a substitute for tragacanth. Also, a gum from several trees of the genus *Sterculia* (family Sterculiaceae).

kutnahorite /kʊtnəˈhɔːrʌɪt/ *n.* Also **kutno-**. E20. [G *Kutnohorit*, f. *Kutná Hora* a town in Bohemia: see -ITE[1].] *Min.* A rare hexagonal carbonate of calcium and manganese, also containing magnesium and iron, usu. occurring as pink rhombohedra.

kuttar /kʌˈtɑː/ *n.* L17. [Skt *kaṭṭāra.*] In the Indian subcontinent: a short dagger with a handle of two parallel bars, joined by a crosspiece forming the part grasped by the hand.

Kuvasz /ˈkuːvaʃ, -s/ *n.* Pl. **-ok** /-ɒk/, **-es** /-ɪz/. M20. [Hungarian f. Turk. *kavas* guard: see KAVASS.] A breed of large white long-coated dog, orig. from Hungary, used as a guard dog; a dog of this breed.

Kuwaiti /kʊˈweɪti/ *n.* & *a.* E20. [Arab. *kuwaytī*, f. *al-Kuwayt* Kuwait (see below): see -I[2].] **A** *n.* **1** A native or inhabitant of Kuwait, an Arab sheikhdom on the north-west coast of the Persian Gulf. E20. **2** The dialect of Arabic spoken in Kuwait. M20. **B** *adj.* Of or pertaining to Kuwait or the Kuwaitis. M20.

kuzushi /kʊˈzʊʃi/ *n.* M20. [Jap.] *Judo.* The fact or state of being unbalanced by one's opponent; a loss of the initiative.

kvass /kvɑːs/ *n.* Also **kvas, quass**. M16. [Russ. *kvas.*] In Russia and some countries to the west: a fermented beverage, low in alcohol, made from rye flour or bread with malt; rye beer.

kvell /kvɛl/ *v.i. US slang.* M20. [Yiddish *kveln* f. G *quellen* gush, well up.] Boast; feel proud or happy; gloat.

kvetch /kvɛtʃ/ *n.* & *v. N. Amer. slang.* M20. [As n. f. Yiddish *kvetsh*, as vb f. Yiddish *kvetshn*, f. G *Quetsche* crusher, presser, *quetschen*, crush, press.] **A** *n.* An objectionable person; *spec.* someone who complains a great deal, a fault-finder. M20. **B** *v.i.* Complain, whine. Chiefly as *kvetching* vbl n. M20.

kvetcher *n.* M20.

kvutza /ˈkvʊtsɑː, kvʊtˈsɑːn/ *n.* E20. [mod.Heb. *qĕḇhūṣāh* f. Heb. = group.] In Israel: a communal and cooperative settlement, which, with others, may form a kibbutz.

Kwa /kwɑː/ *n.* & *a.* Also (now *rare*) **Qua**. M19. [Kwa.] **A** *n.* Pl. same. The group of related languages, spoken from Ivory Coast to Nigeria, which includes Akan, Ewe, Igbo, and Yoruba. Also (*rare*), a member of a Kwa-speaking people. M19. **B** *attrib.* or as *adj.* Of or pertaining to this group of languages. E20.

kwacha /ˈkwɑːtʃə/ *n.* Pl. same, **-s**. M20. [Bantu = dawn.] **1** The dawn: used as a Zambian nationalist slogan. M20. **2** The basic monetary unit of Zambia and Malawi, equal to 100 ngwee in Zambia, 100 tambala in Malawi. M20.

kwai-lo /ˈkwʌɪləʊ/ *n. derog.* M20. [Chin. (Cantonese) (*faan*) *kwai ló* lit. '(foreign) devil fellow': cf. FOREIGN *devil.*] In China, a foreigner, *esp.* a European.

Kwakiutl /ˈkwɑːkjʊt(ə)l/ *n.* & *a.* M19. [Kwakiutl *Kʷágul.*] **A** *n.* Pl. same, **-s**. **1** A member of an Indian people of the north-west coast of N. America. M19. **2** The language of this people. L19. **B** *attrib.* or as *adj.* Of or pertaining to the Kwakiutl or their language. L19.

kwanga /ˈkwaŋgə/ *n.* E20. [Bantu.] In Zaire: a kind of bread made of manioc.

kwanza /ˈkwanzə/ *n.* Pl. same, **-s**. L20. [Perh. f. Swahili = first.] The basic monetary unit of Angola, equal to 100 lweis.

kwashiorkor /kwɒʃɪˈɔːkɔː, kwa-/ *n.* M20. [Local name in Ghana.] A form of malnutrition caused by severe protein and energy deficiency, chiefly affecting young (esp. newly weaned) children in tropical Africa, and producing apathy, oedema, loss of pigmentation, diarrhoea, and other symptoms.

kwedini /kwiːˈdɪni/ *n. S. Afr.* E20. [Xhosa, voc. of *ikwedini* boy.] A young African (esp. Xhosa) boy.

kweek /kwiːk/ *n. S. Afr.* E20. [Afk. f. Du. = couch grass: cf. QUICK *n.*[2], QUITCH.] In full *kweek grass.* A grass propagating by underground runners, *esp.* dog's tooth grass, *Cynodon dactylon.*

kwela /ˈkweɪlə/ *n.* M20. [Afk., perh. f. Zulu *khwela* climb, mount.] A popular dance, and its accompanying music, resembling jazz, of central and southern Africa.

kya /ˈkʌɪə/ *n.* E20. [Zulu *-khaya* place of abode.] In South Africa, Zimbabwe, etc.: an African's hut; the living accommodation of an African servant.

kyack /ˈkʌɪak/ *n. US.* E20. [Origin unkn.] A kind of packsack consisting of two containers hung on either side of a pack-saddle.

kyang *n.* var. of KIANG.

kyanise *v.* var. of KYANIZE.

kyanite /ˈkʌɪənʌɪt/ *n.* Also **c-** /s-/. L18. [f. Gk *kuan(e)os* dark blue + -ITE[1].] *Min.* A triclinic aluminium silicate mineral usu. occurring as blue, greenish or colourless tabular crystals and used in refractory ceramics.

kyanize /ˈkʌɪənʌɪz/ *v.t.* Also **-ise**. M19. [f. J. H. *Kyan* (1774–1850), Ir. inventor + -IZE.] Impregnate (wood) with a solution of corrosive sublimate as a preservative. Chiefly as *kyanized* ppl a., *kyanizing* vbl n.

kyat /kiːˈɑːt/ *n.* Pl. same, **-s**. M20. [Burm.] The basic monetary unit of Myanmar (Burma) since 1952, equal to 100 pyas.

kybosh *n.* & *v.* var. of KIBOSH.

kyd *a.* var. of KID *a.*

†kyd *v.* pa. pple: see KITHE.

kye /kʌɪ/ *n. Naut. slang.* E20. [Origin unkn.] 1 A mean person. E20. 2 Cocoa, drinking chocolate. E20.

kyle /kʌɪl/ *n.*[1] Long *obs.* exc. *dial.* LME. [ON *kýli.*] A sore, an ulcer, a boil.

kyle /kʌɪl/ *n.*[2] *Sc.* M16. [Gael. *caol*, genit. *caoil* narrow strait or sound, f. *caol* narrow.] A narrow channel between two islands, or between an island and the mainland; a sound, a strait.

kyles *n.pl.* var. of KAYLES.

kylie /ˈkʌɪli/ *n. Austral.* M19. [Aborig.] A boomerang.

kylikes *n.* pl. of KYLIX.

kylin /ˈkiːlɪn/ *n.* M19. [Chin. *qílín*, f. *qí* male + *lín* female.] A mythical animal of composite form figured on Chinese and Japanese pottery, a Chinese unicorn. Cf. KIRIN.

kylix /ˈkʌɪlɪks, ˈkɪl-/ *n.* Pl. **-ikes** /-ɪkiːz/. Also **c-**, pl. **-ices** /-ɪsiːz/. M19. [Gk *kulix.*] *Gk Antiq.* A shallow cup with a tall stem, a tazza.

kyloe /ˈkʌɪləʊ/ *n. Sc.* E19. [Gael. *gaidhealach* Gaelic, Highland.] (An animal of) the breed of Highland cattle.

kymogram /ˈkʌɪmə(ʊ)gram/ *n.* E20. [f. as next: see -GRAM.] A recording made with a kymograph; *esp.* in *Phonet.*, a recording of pressure variations produced during articulation.

kymograph /ˈkʌɪmə(ʊ)grɑːf/ *n.* M19. [f. Gk *kumo-* comb. form of *kuma* wave (see -O-) + -GRAPH.] 1 An instrument for recording variations in pressure e.g. of blood in the blood-vessels, of air during respiration or speech, etc., by the trace of a stylus on a rotating cylinder; a recording manometer. M19. 2 *Med.* An apparatus for recording the movement of the heart or other internal organs on an X-ray plate or film. Also called *roentgenkymograph*. M20.

kymoˈgraphic *a.* pertaining to or made with a kymograph L19. **kymoˈgraphically** *adv.* by means of a kymograph M20. **kymography** /kʌɪˈmɒgrəfi/ *n.* the technique or process of using a kymograph M20.

†kynd *n.* var. of KIND *n.*

†kynded *a. rare* (Spenser). Only in L16. [f. KIND *n.* + -ED[2].] Begotten, sprung.

kynurenic /kʌɪnjʊˈrɛnɪk, kɪ-/ *a.* L19. [f. Gk *kun-*, *kuon* dog + *-uren-* irreg. f. *ouron* urine: see -IC.] Biochem. *kynurenic acid*, an organic acid that results from metabolism of tryptophan and is excreted in the urine of man and various animals; 4-hydroxyquinoline-2-carboxylic acid, $C_{10}H_7NO_3$.

kynurenine /kʌɪˈnjʊərəniːn, kɪ-/ *n.* an amino acid, $H_2N{\cdot}C_6H_4{\cdot}COCH_2CH(NH_2)COOH$, which is a precursor of kynurenic acid in tryptophan metabolism M20.

kyogen /ˈkjəʊgɛn/ *n.* Pl. same. L19. [Jap. *kyōgen.*] A comic interlude presented between performances of Noh plays.

kyoodle /kʌɪˈ(j)uːd(ə)l/ *v.i. US dial.* & *colloq.* E20. [Imit.] Make a loud noise; bark, yap.

kype /kʌɪp/ *n.* M20. [Var. of KIP *n.*[2], perh. infl. by PIKE *n.*[1]] A hook formed on the lower jaw of adult male salmon and trout during the breeding season; a kip.

kyped *a.* possessing a kype M20.

kyphoscoliosis /ˌkʌɪfəskəʊlɪˈəʊsɪs/ *n.* Pl. **-oses** /-ˈəʊsiːz/. L19. [f. as next + SCOLIOSIS.] *Med.* A combination of kyphosis and scoliosis; backward and lateral curvature of the spine.

kyphoscoliotic /-ˈɒtɪk/ *a.* E20.

kyphosis /kʌɪˈfəʊsɪs/ *n.* Pl. **-phoses** /-ˈfəʊsiːz/. Also (earlier) **†c-**. M19. [Gk *kuphōsis* humpbacked condition, f. *kuphos* bent, hunchbacked: see -OSIS.] *Med.* Abnormal outward curvature of the spine causing increased convexity of the back. Cf. LORDOSIS, SCOLIOSIS.

kyphotic /kʌɪˈfɒtɪk/ *a.* pertaining to or affected with kyphosis L19.

Kyrie /ˈkɪrɪeɪ/ *n.* E16. [Abbrev. of KYRIE ELEISON.] 1 = KYRIE ELEISON 1. E16. †2 = KYRIE ELEISON 2. Only in 16.

Kyrie eleison /ˌkɪrɪeɪ ɪˈleɪɪzɒn, -sɒn, -s(ə)n/ *n.* ME. [med.L f. Gk *Kurie eleēson* Lord, have mercy.] 1 The words ('Lord, have mercy') of a short repeated invocation or response used in the Roman Catholic, Greek Orthodox, and Anglican Churches, esp. at the beginning of the Eucharist. Also, a musical setting of these words, esp. as the first movement of a mass. ME. †2 A complaint; a scolding. E16–M17.

kyrielle /kɪrɪˈɛl/ *n.* M17. [Fr. *kyrielle*, OFr. *kyriele* f. med.L *kirieles* (pl.) f. *Kyrie eleison*: see prec.] †1 A long rigmarole. Only in M17. 2 A kind of French verse divided into short equal couplets ending with the same word, which serves for a refrain. L19.

kyte /kʌɪt/ *n. Sc.* & *north.* M16. [Origin unkn.] The belly, the stomach, the paunch.

kythe *v.* var. of KITHE.

kyu /kjuː/ *n.* M20. [Jap. *kyū* class.] Each of the (numbered) grades of the less advanced level of proficiency in judo, karate, and other martial (or orig. martial) arts, (also *kyu grade*); a person who has reached (a specified grade of) this level. Cf. DAN *n.*[4]

L

L, l /ɛl/, the twelfth letter of the modern Eng. alphabet and the eleventh of the ancient Roman one, corresp. to Gk *lambda* and ult. Semitic *lamed*. The sound normally represented by the letter is a lateral consonant, voiced alveolar before a vowel or /j/, voiced velar in final position, before most consonants or syllabically, partially or wholly devoiced following stressed /p, k/. In certain combinations the l has become silent having modified the preceding vowel, as *-alf* /ɑːf/, *-alm* /ɑːm/, *-olk* /əʊk/. See also ELL *n.*[2] Pl. **L's, Ls.**

I 1 The letter and its sound. **2** The shape of the letter; an object shaped like the letter L; *esp.* (*a*) an extension of a building at right angles to the main block; (*b*) a pipe-joint connecting two pipes at right angles, an elbow-joint. Cf. ELL *n.*[2]

2 L-head, -headed *adjs.* designating (a reciprocating internal-combustion engine having) L-shaped combustion chambers, in which the valves are situated in a side arm. **L-shaped** *a.* having a shape or a cross-section like the capital letter L.

II Symbolical uses. **3** Used to denote serial order; applied e.g. to the twelfth (also freq. the eleventh, either I or J being omitted) group or section, sheet of a book, etc. **4** The roman numeral for fifty. **b** *LXX*, the roman numeral for seventy; *spec.* the Septuagint. **5 a** *Chem.* Orig. *l*, now only as a small capital L: as *pref.* denoting (a compound having) a configuration about an asymmetric atom analogous to that of a standard reference molecule (now L-glyceraldehyde for organic compounds). Also, as L(+), L(−), further denoting respectively laevo- or dextrorotation of polarized light by the compound. [Extended use of l- = laevorotatory.] **b** *Physics.* (Cap. L.) Used to designate the series of X-ray emission lines of an excited atom of longer wavelength than the K-series (cf. K, K 3c), arising from electron transitions to the atomic orbit of second lowest energy, with principal quantum number 2; hence *L-shell*, this orbit; *L-electrons*, electrons in this shell; *L-capture*, the capture by an atomic nucleus of one of the L-electrons. **c** *Physics* Denoting the quantum number of the orbital angular momentum of one electron (*l*) or an assemblage of electrons (*L*). **d** *Bacteriol.* (Cap. L.) The designation (now chiefly as *L-form*) of an atypical form of certain bacteria which lacks a cell wall, exhibits a very variable shape, and somewhat resembles a mycoplasma. **e** *L-band*, a frequency band of electromagnetic waves used for radar, extending from 390 to 1550 megahertz.

III 6 Abbrevs.: (A small selection only is given here. Those all in caps. or small caps. also occur with a full stop after each letter; some of those all in caps. also occur (i) with initial cap. only, (ii) in small caps.) **L** = Lake; Lance (in ranks of the British army); large; Latin; learner(-driver), *L-plate*, a learner plate; left; Liberal (in politics); [L] *libra* pound of money (repr. by the conventional sign £, as £100; see also *l.s.d.* below); Licentiate (in academic degrees); (*Taxon.*) Linnaeus; Lire. **l** = left; length; line (in references); litre(s). ***l-*** (*Chem.*) = laevorotatory (cf. sense 5a above). **LA** = Library Association; local authority; Los Angeles; Louisiana. **L-A** = Latin America. **La** (*Chem.*) = lanthanum. **La.** = Louisiana. **LAC** = Leading Aircraftman. **LACW** = Leading Aircraftwoman. **LAFTA** = Latin American Free Trade Association. **Lam.** = Lamentations (in the Bible). **LAN** /lan/ (*Computing*) = local area network. **Lancs.** = Lancashire. **lat.** = latitude. **LATS** (freq. /lats/) (*Med.*) = long-acting thyroid stimulator. **LAUTRO** /ˈlaʊtrəʊ/ = Life Assurance and Unit Trust Regulatory Organization. **LAV** (*Med.*) = lymphadenopathy-associated virus. **lb** = [L] *libra* a pound or pounds (weight). **l.b.** (*Cricket*) = leg bye(s). **LBC** = London Broadcasting Company. **L/Bdr** = Lance-Bombardier. **l.b.w.** (*Cricket*) = leg before wicket. **LC** (*US*) = landing-craft. **l.c.** = letter of credit; [L] *loco citato* in the passage previously cited; (*Typogr.*) lower case. **LCC** (*Hist.*) = London County Council. **LCD** = (*Math.*) least or lowest common denominator; liquid crystal display (freq. *attrib.*, esp. with redundant *display*). **LCJ** = Lord Chief Justice. **LCM** = (*US*) landing-craft, mechanized; (*Math.*) least or lowest common multiple. **L/Cpl** = Lance-Corporal. **LCT** (*US*) = landing-craft, tank. **LD** lethal dose (usu. followed by a numeral indicating that the dose kills that percentage of a sample, as *LD50*). **Ld** = Lord. **Ldg.** = Leading (Seaman etc.). **LDL** (*Biochem.*) = low-density lipoprotein. **LDS** = Licentiate in Dental Surgery. **LE** (*Med.*) = lupus erythematosus. **LEA** = Local Education Authority. **LED** = light-emitting diode. **Leics.** = Leicestershire. **LEM** = lunar excursion module. **Lev.** = Leviticus (in the Bible). **LF** = low frequency. **LGV** = large goods vehicle. **LH** (*Biochem.*) = luteinizing hormone. **l.h.** = left hand. **LI** = Light Infantry; Long Island. **Li** (*Chem.*) = lithium. **LIBOR** /ˈlʌɪbɔː/ = London Inter-Bank Offered Rate. **Lieut.** = Lieutenant. **Liffe** /ˈlɪfi, lʌɪf/ = London International Financial Futures Exchange. **LIFO** /ˈliːfəʊ/ (*Computing*) = last in, first out. **Lincs.** = Lincolnshire. **Linn.** (*Taxon.*) = Linnaeus. **Litt. D.** = [L] *Litterarum doctor* Doctor of Letters. **LJ** = Lord Justice. **L JJ** = Lords Justices. **LL** = [L] *legum* of laws (in academic degrees); Lord Lieutenant. **ll.** = lines (in references). **LL B** = [L] *legum baccalaureus* Bachelor of Laws. **LL D**= [L] *legum doctor* Doctor of Laws. **LL M** = [L] *legum magister* Master of Laws. **LM** = (*Pros.*) long metre; lunar module. **lm** = lumen(s). **LME** = London Metal Exchange. **LMS** = London Mathematical Society; (*Hist.*) London, Midland, and Scottish (Railway); London Missionary Society. **LMT** = local mean time. **ln** = [mod.L] *logarithmus naturalis* natural logarithm. **LNE(R)** (*Hist.*) = London and North-Eastern (Railway). **LNG** = liquefied natural gas. **LOI** = lunar orbit insertion. **long.** = longitude. **LOS** = loss of signal. **LP** = long-playing (gramophone record); (*Meteorol.*) low pressure. **LPG** = liquefied petroleum gas. **Lr** (*Chem.*) = lawrencium. **LS** = letter (not autograph) signed; cf. *ALS* s.v. A, A; Linnean Society. **l.s.** = [L] *locus sigilli* the place of the seal (on a document). **l.s.d.** (*Hist.*) = pounds, shillings, and pence (in former British currency), money, riches. **LSE** = London School of Economics. **LSI** = large-scale integration (of electronic microcircuits). **LT** = low tension. **Lt.** = Lieutenant; light. **LTA** = Lawn Tennis Association. **Ltd.** = limited (of a company). **LTM** = long-term memory. **Lu** (*Chem.*) = lutetium. **LV** = luncheon voucher. **Lw** (*Chem.*, now *Hist.*) = lawrencium (cf. *Lr* above). **lwm** = low-water mark. **lx** = lux. **ly** (*Physics*) = langley(s).

la *n.* see LAH.

La /la/ *a.* (*def. article*). Also **la**. M19. [Fr. or It., fem. def. article, f. L *illa* fem., *ille* that.] Used preceding the name of a prima donna, or (freq. *joc.* or *iron.*) the name of any woman. Cf. THE *a.* 6.

P. G. WODEHOUSE La Brinkmeyer badly needed a toad in her bed. *La* SERENISSIMA.

la /lɑː, la/ *int.* L16. [Natural exclam. Cf. LO *int.*[1], WELLAWAY.] **1** Introducing or accompanying a conventional phrase, or calling attention to an emphatic statement. In later use, a mere expression of surprise. *arch.* L16. **†2** Redupl. **la la.** Expr. derision. L16–E17.

1 W. CONGREVE O la now! I swear and declare, it shan't be so. V. W. MASON La! how you startled me!

laager /ˈlɑːgə/ *n.* M19. [Afk. = G *Lager*, Du. *leger*: see LEAGUER *n.*[1]] A camp, an encampment; *S. Afr. Hist.* a Boer camp marked out and protected by a circle of wagons; *transf.* & *fig.* a defensive position, *esp.* one protected by armoured vehicles; an entrenched policy, viewpoint, etc., under attack from opponents.

Armed Forces Syrian commandos staged a night attack on an Israeli vehicle laager. *attrib.*: *Economist* Sanctions might create a laager mentality.

laager /ˈlɑːgə/ *v.* L19. [f. the n.] **1** *v.t.* Form (wagons) into a laager; encamp (people) in a laager. Also foll. by *up*. L19. **2** *v.i.* Form a laager; make a camp in a laager. Also foll. by *up*. L19.

1 C. FULLER Van Rensburg's wagons were not laagered, but scattered about. *fig.*: *Cape Times* Are we .. going to keep ourselves laagered when other countries in Africa get together? **2** *Tablet* We stopped firing at about seven o'clock, and laagered up for the night.

laagte /ˈlɑːxtə/ *n. S. Afr.* Also **leegte**. M19. [Afk. f. Du. = a valley, f. *laag* LOW *a.*] A valley or shallow dip in the veld.

laari *n.* see LARI.

lab /lab/ *n.*[1] Long *obs.* exc. *dial.* LME. [Prob. imit. Cf. Du. *labben* blab, tell tales, BLAB *n.*[1], *v.*[1]] A blab, a tell-tale.

lab /lab/ *n.*[2] L19. [Abbrev.] A laboratory.

attrib.: *Listener* An honest lab assistant loses his job for refusing to work on a poison gas project.

Lab /lab/ *n.*[3] & *a.* L19. [Abbrev.] (Of or pertaining to) the Labour Party.

¶See also LIB-LAB.

Lab /lab/ *n.*[4] *colloq.* Chiefly *N. Amer.* Also **l-**. M20. [Abbrev.] A Labrador (dog).

Labadist /ˈlabədɪst/ *n.* L17. [Fr. *Labadiste*, f. *Labadie* (see below) + -IST.] *Eccl. Hist.* A follower of the French mystic Jean de Labadie (1610–74), who seceded from the Roman Church and founded a sect holding quietist views.

labakh *n.* var. of LEBBEK.

laban /ˈlaban/ *n.* Also ***leban*** /ˈlɛban/, ***leben*** /ˈlɛbən/. L17. [Arab. = milk.] A drink consisting of coagulated sour milk.

Labanotation /ˈlɑːbənəʊˌteɪʃ(ə)n/ *n.* M20. [f. *Laban* (see below) + NOTATION.] A system of dance notation devised by the Hungarian-born dancer and choreographer Rudolf von Laban (born Rudolf Laban von Varlja) (1879–1958).

labaria /ləˈbɑːrɪə/ *n.* Also (earlier) **labarri** /ləˈbɑːri/. E19. [Amer. Sp., perh. f. Carib.] In Guyana: any of several poisonous coral snakes or pit vipers, *esp.* the fer de lance, *Bothrops atrox*, and the bushmaster, *Lachesis muta*.

Labarraque /labəˈrak/ *n.* Now *rare* or *obs.* E19. [Antoine Germain *Labarraque* (1777–1850), Fr. pharmacist.] *Labarraque's liquid, solution*, Javelle water.

labarri *n.* see LABARIA.

labarum /ˈlabərəm/ *n.* E17. [Late L, whence Byzantine Gk *labaron*.] The imperial standard of Constantine the Great (306–337), with Christian symbols added to Roman military symbols; *gen.* a symbolic banner.

†labdacism *n.* var. of LAMBDACISM.

labdanum /ˈlabdənəm/ *n.* E16. [med.L form of LADANUM.] = LADANUM.

labefaction /labɪˈfakʃ(ə)n/ *n.* E17. [f. L *labefact-* pa. ppl stem of *labefacere* weaken, f. *labi* fall + *facere* make: see -FACTION.] A shaking, weakening; overthrow, downfall.

label /ˈleɪb(ə)l/ *n.* ME. [OFr. = ribbon, fillet (also *lambel*, mod. *lambeau* rag), prob. f. Gmc form rel. to LAP *n.*[1], w. dim. suff.] **I** A strip or band. **1** *Her.* A temporary mark of cadency now distinguishing the eldest son of a family during the lifetime of his father or grandfather, consisting of a band across the upper part of the shield having (usu. three or five) dependent points. Formerly also, each of the dependent points. ME. **2** A narrow strip of cloth etc.; a fillet, a ribbon; the infula of a mitre. ME. †**3** A small strip of paper or parchment attached to a document as a supplementary note; a codicil. LME–M17. †**4** *Astron.* & *Surveying.* In an astrolabe or a circumferentor: a narrow brass rule used chiefly in taking altitudes. LME–L17. †**5** *gen.* A slip or strip of anything. LME–L17. **6** A narrow strip of material attached to a document to carry the seal. L15. **7** *Archit.* A moulding over a door, window, or other opening; a dripstone. E19.

II 8 A slip of paper, cardboard, metal, etc., (intended to be) attached to an object and carrying information, instructions, etc., concerning it; *spec.* a piece of fabric sewn inside a garment bearing the brand name, size, etc. (Now the usual sense.) L17. **b** An adhesive postage-stamp or bill-stamp. M19. **c** A circular piece of paper on the centre of a gramophone record giving details of the record. E20. **9** *fig.* A short classifying phrase or name applied to a person, work of art, idea, etc. L19. **b** In a dictionary entry, a word or phrase indicating the area, content, category, etc., of the word being defined. E20. **10** A brand name; a brand-named product, the manufacturer of a brand-named product; *spec.* (a section of) a recording company producing records under a distinctive name. E20. **11** *Biol.* & *Chem.* A substance (as a distinctive isotope, or a dye) used to label another substance (see LABEL *v.* 2). M20. **12** *Computing.* **a** An arbitrary name for a statement in a program which facilitates reference to it elsewhere in the program. M20. **b** A set of data recorded on a reel of magnetic tape describing its contents and serving for identification by a computer. M20.

8 A. K. GREEN Poison . . bought at a drug-store usually has a label on the bottle. R. HUGHES A number of labels . . which he was pasting onto the various . . packages. b DAVID POTTER Stamps to collect the postage due on underpaid letters are . . described as Postage Due Labels. 9 P. BROOK We rush to give them a label. *Atlantic Monthly* The Democratic governors . . are all progressive pragmatists. That's the label I give myself. 10 *Making Music* We . . decided to put out a single, and started a label.

Comb.: **label-stop** *Archit.* a boss or corbel supporting the end of a label or dripstone.

label /ˈleɪb(ə)l/ *v.t.* Infl. **-ll-**, ***-l-**. E17. [f. the n.] **1** Affix a label to, mark with a label. E17. **b** *fig.* Describe or designate as with a label; categorize. M19. **2** *Biol.* & *Chem.* Make (a substance, a molecule, or a constituent atom) experimentally recognizable but essentially unaltered in behaviour, so that its path may be followed or its distribution ascertained, esp. by replacing a constituent atom by one of a different isotope, identifiable by its radioactivity or its different mass, or by attaching a (usu. fluorescent) dye to the molecule. Cf. LABEL *n.* 11. M20.

1 K. WILLIAMS A cleaning fluid . . which he'd mistakenly labelled 'Cough Syrup'. C. S. FORESTER He was labelled at once as the midshipman who was seasick in Spithead. b *New Republic* The amendment has been labeled a punitive measure.

labeller *n.* L19.

labella *n.* pl. of LABELLUM.

labelled /ˈleɪb(ə)ld/ *a.* Also ***labeled**. L16. [f. LABEL *n.*, *v.*: see -ED[2], -ED[1].] **1** *Her.* Of a mitre: having labels or infulae (of a particular tincture). L16. **2** *Archit.* Having a label or dripstone. M19. **3** Marked with a ticket bearing the name, description of contents, etc., of the article. L19. **4** *Biol.* & *Chem.* Of an atom: of a different isotope (of the element normally present). Of a molecule or substance: made recognizable by labelling (see LABEL *v.* 2). M20.

labellum /ləˈbɛləm/ *n.* Pl. **-lla** /-lə/. E19. [L, dim. of *labrum* lip.] **1** *Entomol.* Either of a pair of lobes terminating the proboscis of certain insects. E19. **2** *Bot.* The lowest segment of the inner whorl of perianth segments of an orchid, usu. larger and different in shape from the remainder. M19.

labia *n.* pl. of LABIUM.

labial /ˈleɪbɪəl/ *a.* & *n.* L16. [med.L *labialis*, f. L *labia* lips: see -AL[1].] **A** *adj.* **1** Of or pertaining to the lips; *spec.* (*Phonet.*) designating those sounds which require complete or partial closure of the lips for their formation, as the consonants /p/, /b/, /m/, /f/, /v/, /w/, and vowels for which the lips are rounded. L16. **2** *Anat.* etc. Pertaining to, of the nature of, associated with, or situated on a lip or labium. M17.

1 labial pipe *Mus.* a flue-pipe in an organ.

B *n.* **1** *Phonet.* A labial sound. M17. **2** A labial part or organ, as any of the scales which border the mouth of a fish or reptile. L19.

labialism *n.* (*Phonet.*) the tendency to labialize sounds; labial pronunciation: L19. **labiˈality** *n.* (*Phonet.*) the quality of being labial L19. **labially** *adv.* (*a*) *Phonet.* with a labial sound or utterance; (*b*) towards the lips: E20.

labialize /ˈleɪbɪəlʌɪz/ *v.t.* Also **-ise**. M19. [f. prec. + -IZE.] *Phonet.* Make (a sound or sounds) labial in character; round (a vowel).

labialiˈzation *n.* the action of labializing, the condition of being labialized; rounding of a vowel: M19.

labiate /ˈleɪbɪət/ *a.* & *n.* E18. [mod.L *labiatus*, f. LABIUM: see -ATE[2].] **A** *adj.* **1** *Bot.* **a** Of a corolla or calyx: = *two-lipped* s.v. TWO *a.* E18. **b** Belonging to the family Labiatae, consisting of herbaceous plants and undershrubs usu. with two-lipped flowers and square stalks (e.g. the mints, ground ivy, the dead-nettles). M19. **2** *Anat.* & *Zool.* Resembling a lip or labium in shape, function, etc. L19. **B** *n. Bot.* A plant of the family Labiatae. M19.

labiated *a.* (now *rare* or *obs.*) = LABIATE *a.* 1a, 2 E18.

labile /ˈleɪbɪl, -ʌɪl/ *a.* LME. [Late L *labilis*, f. *labi* fall: see -ILE.] **1** Liable to lapse. Of a person: apt to err or sin; *Theol.* liable to fall from innocence. LME. **2** Liable to undergo displacement in position or change in nature, form, chemical composition, etc.; unstable; *esp.* in *Chem.* (of an attached ligand or group) readily displaced by another, (of a bond) readily broken. E17. **b** *Psychol.* Emotionally or behaviourally unstable. M20.

1 G. CHEYNE All creatures being . . free, must necessarily, . . be labile, fallible and peccable. *Forum* These funds are no more labile than any other form of trust.

laˈbility *n.* (chiefly *Sci.*) the quality or state of being labile M16.

labilize /ˈleɪbɪlʌɪz/ *v.t.* Also **-ise**. E20. [f. prec. + -IZE.] *Chem.* Make labile (esp. a chemical bond or group).

labiliˈzation *n.* M20. **labilizer** *n.* a labilizing agent M20.

labio- /ˈleɪbɪəʊ/ *comb. form.* [f. L *labium* lip + -O-.] **1** *Phonet.* Forming ns. and adjs. w. the sense '(a sound) formed with the lips and (some other organ)', as *labio-nasal* etc. **2** *Anat.* Forming chiefly adjs. w. the sense 'of or pertaining to the lips and (some other part)', as *labio-alveolar*, *labioglossolaryngeal*, *labioglossopharyngeal*, *labio-lingual*, *labio-mental* [L *mentum* chin], etc.

labioˈdental *a.* & *n.* (a sound) formed with the lips and teeth M17. **labiomancy** *n.* lip-reading L17. **labioˈpalatal** *a.* & *n.* (a sound) formed with the lips and the hard palate L19. **labioˈvelar** *a.* & *n.* (a sound) formed with the lips and the soft palate L19.

labium /ˈleɪbɪəm/ *n.* Pl. **-ia** /-ɪə/. L16. [L = lip: cf. LABRUM.] **1** *Anat.* A liplike structure; *spec.* (chiefly in pl.) the two pairs of folds of skin on either side of the vulva. L16. **2** *Entomol.* The fused mouthpart which forms the floor of the mouth or underlip. E19. **3** *Bot.* The lip, esp. the lower or anterior lip, of a labiate corolla. Cf. GALEA. E19.

1 labia majora /məˈdʒɔːrə/ the larger, outer pair of labia of the vulva. **labia minora** /mɪˈnɔːrə/ the smaller, inner pair of labia of the vulva.

lablab /ˈlablab/ *n.* E19. [Arab. *lablāb.*] A leguminous plant, *Lablab purpureus*, grown as a pulse and animal fodder in India, Egypt, and other tropical countries. Also called *bonavist*, *Egyptian bean*, *hyacinth bean.*

labor *n.* & *a.* see LABOUR *n.* & *a.*

laboratorial /lab(ə)rəˈtɔːrɪəl/ *a.* M19. [f. LABORATORY + -AL[1].] Of or pertaining to a laboratory.

laboratory /ləˈbɒrət(ə)ri, ˈlab(ə)rət(ə)ri/ *n.* E17. [med.L *laboratorium*, f. L *laborat-* pa. ppl stem of *laborare*: see LABOUR *v.*, -ORY[1].] **1** A room or building set aside and equipped for scientific experiments or research (orig. and esp. in chemistry), for teaching science, or for the development or production of chemical or medicinal products. See also *language laboratory* s.v. LANGUAGE *n.*[1] E17. **2** A department of an arsenal where ammunition, explosives, etc., are produced or examined. E18. **3** *Metall.* The hearth of a reverberatory furnace. M19.

Comb.: **laboratory animal** any animal (e.g. rat, monkey, mouse) commonly used for experiments in a laboratory; **laboratory frame (of reference)** *Nuclear Physics*: in which measurements of particle velocity etc. are made with respect to a laboratory regarded as stationary; **laboratory school** *US*: at which student teachers are trained and classroom techniques demonstrated.

labored *a.*, **laborer** *n.*, **laboring** *a.* see LABOURED *a.* etc.

laborious /ləˈbɔːrɪəs/ *a.* LME. [(O)Fr. *laborieux* f. L *laboriosus*, f. *labor*: see LABOUR *n.*, -IOUS.] **1** Industrious, assiduous, hard-working. Now *rare* or *obs.* LME. †**b** = LABOURING *ppl a.* I. M16–L18. **2** Characterized by or involving labour or exertion. LME. **3** Entailing labour in construction or execution. Of literary style etc.: not fluent. M16. **4** *Midwifery.* Giving birth with difficulty. Of labour: difficult. M17.

2 C. DARWIN The laborious breathing necessary in high regions. S. E. FERRIER A most laborious and long-winded letter. 3 J. CRACE Equipped with . . neat, laborious handwriting, and a skill with ledgers.

laboriˈosity *n.* (*rare*) M17. **laboriously** *adv.* L15. **laboriousness** *n.* M17.

Laborism *n.*, **-ist** *n.* & *a.*, etc., see LABOURISM etc.

laborous /ˈleɪb(ə)rəs/ *a.* LME. [f. as prec.: see -OUS.] †**1** = LABORIOUS 1, 2, 3. LME–L18. **2** = LABOURING *ppl a. Sc.* M16.

laborsome *a.* see LABOURSOME.

labour /ˈleɪbə/ *n.* & *a.* Also ***labor**. ME. [OFr. *labo(u)r* (mod. *labeur* ploughing) f. L *labor* toil, trouble, suffering.] **A** *n.* **I 1** Exertion of the faculties of the body or mind, esp. when painful or compulsory; physical or mental toil. ME. †**b** Physical exercise. L16–M17. **2** An instance of bodily or mental exertion; a task (to be) performed. ME. **3** The outcome, product, or result of work. Freq. in *pl. arch.* ME. †**4** Trouble or pains taken; *esp.* the exertion of influence to further a matter or obtain a favour. LME–M17. **5** Childbirth; the period from the onset of regular uterine contractions until the expulsion of the placenta. L16. **6** (Physical) work considered as required for the execution of a task or as supplying the wants of the community; the contribution of the worker to production. L18. **b** *the Labour*, = *Labour Exchange* (b) below. *colloq.* M20. **7** Workers (esp. manual workers) considered as a social class or a political force. Freq. *attrib.* M19. **8** (**L-**.) *ellipt.* The Labour Party. E20.

1 AV *Ps.* 104:23 Man goeth forth unto his worke: and to his labour. D. FRANCIS Physics . . they took to be unacceptably hard mental labour. 2 W. S. CHURCHILL Work with the United Nations in the more fruitful labours of peace. 3 SWIFT My labours, which cost me so much thought and watching. 5 V. CRONIN After a difficult labour, Catherine gave birth to a healthy child. 6 G. M. TREVELYAN Farms worked by a single family without hired labour. b L. HENDERSON I'm going for a job the Labour picked out

for me. 7 *Encycl. Brit.* Organised labour seldom gained . . public sympathy. 8 ALDOUS HUXLEY Tell Brett . . to vote Labour, our only hope. J. BUCHAN The Left Wing of Labour blessed it cordially.

II 9 A group of moles. L15.

Phrases: *direct labour*: see DIRECT *a*. *division of labour*: see DIVISION 2. FORCED *labour*. *free labour*: see FREE *a*. *hard labour*: see HARD *a*. **Herculean labour** = *Labour of Hercules* below. **in labour** (of a woman) giving birth. **labour in vain** fruitless efforts. **Labour of Hercules** a task requiring enormous strength or persistence. **labour of love** a task undertaken for the love of a person or for the work itself. **lost labour** = *labour in vain* above. *organized labour*: see ORGANIZED 3a.

Comb.: **labour brigade** a unit or group of workers, *esp.* one organized by the State or a local authority; **labour camp** a penal settlement where the prisoners must work as labourers; **labour day** (*a*) in China and the former USSR, a unit of labour calculated according to the expected productivity of a worker; (*b*) (*Labour Day*) a day celebrated in honour of workers, often as a public holiday (in many places on 1 May, in N. America on the first Monday of September); *Labour Day Weekend*, in New Zealand, the long weekend preceding and including Labour Day; **Labour Exchange** (*a*) *Hist.* an establishment for the exchange of the products of labour without the use of money; (*b*) (also *labour exchange*) (*Hist. & colloq.*) an employment exchange; **labour force** (*a*) the body of workers employed at a particular place or time; (*b*) the number of people in the population in employment or seeking work; **labour hero, heroine** a title awarded to a male, female, worker who achieves a high output; **labour-intensive** *a.* (of a process or industry) having labour as the largest factor or cost; **labour-market** the supply of labour considered with reference to the demand for it; **labour movement** the effort by organized labour to improve conditions for workers; the organizations and individuals involved in this; **labour-only** *a.* (of a subcontractor, subcontracting) supplying only the labour for a particular piece of work; *labour pains*: see PAIN *n.*[1] 3b; **Labour Party** the political party formed in Britain in 1906 by a federation of trade unions and socialist groups to represent labour in Parliament; any of various similar parties in other countries (*Independent Labour Party*: see INDEPENDENT *a.*); **labour relations** the relations between management and labour; **labour-saving** *a.* designed to reduce or eliminate work; **labour spy** *US* a person employed or enlisted by a company to report on the activities of workers; **labour theory of value** the theory that the value of a commodity should be determined by the amount of labour used in its production; **labour ward** a room in a hospital set aside for childbirth; **Labour Weekend** *NZ* Labour Day Weekend.

B *adj.* Of or pertaining to a Labour Party, *esp.* the British Labour Party. E20.

J. BUCHAN A young Labour member from the Midlands.

labour /ˈleɪbə/ *v.* Also ***labor**. LME. [(O)Fr. *labourer* (now chiefly = plough) f. L *laborare*, f. *labor* LABOUR *n.*] **I** *v.t.* 1 Till, cultivate (the ground); work (a mine). Now *arch.* & *dial.* LME. 2 Work on; produce or execute with labour. *arch.* LME. 3 Elaborate, work out in (excessive) detail. Now usu., treat or insist on (a point, a question, etc.) at (inordinate) length. LME. 4 Work for or with a view to (a result); work hard for (a cause etc.). *arch.* LME. †b Bring into a specified condition or position by strenuous exertion. L15–L17. †5 Endeavour to influence or persuade (a person); advocate (a matter) strenuously. LME–M17. †6 a Make tired, weary; burden, distress. LME–E18. b Work (an animal); use (the body, its parts, occas. the mind) in some work. L15–L19. †7 Work by beating, rubbing, pounding, etc. L15–M17. 8 Belabour, beat, thrash. *obs.* exc. *dial.* L16.

2 DRYDEN They . . labour Honey to sustain their Lives. 3 A. POWELL Perhaps it is tedious to labour the point. 4 BURKE How much I wished for, and how earnestly I laboured, that re-union. b H. MONTAGU To labour the eye to see darkness.

II *v.i.* 9 Exert oneself physically or mentally; toil, esp. hard or against difficulties; do (esp. manual) work to earn one's living. LME. 10 Exert oneself, strive (*for, to do*). LME. †b Exert one's influence in urging a suit or to obtain something desired. Foll. by *to* (a person). L15–L16. 11 Move or travel, esp. with difficulty or against obstacles. LME. b Of a ship: roll or pitch heavily at sea. E17. c Of an engine: work noisily and with difficulty, esp. when under load. M20. 12 Be burdened or troubled, as by disease, shortage of food, etc.; suffer from some disadvantage or defect. Foll. by *under* (also †*of, with, on, in*). LME. †13 Of a woman: be in labour, give birth. LME–L18.

9 M. WEBB I'd laboured . . a long while, and labour brings a thing near the heart's core. Z. MEDVEDEV His . . parents laboured in a steel mill. 10 W. MARCH Rhoda . . laboured so diligently to improve her penmanship. 11 J. STEINBECK A stilted heron laboured up into the air. b BYRON The ship labour'd so, they scarce could hope To weather out much longer. 12 C. KINGSLEY You are labouring under an entire misapprehension.

†**labourable** *a.* (chiefly of land) able to be worked L15–M18.

labourage /ˈleɪb(ə)rɪdʒ/ *n.* ME. [(O)Fr., f. *labourer* LABOUR *v.*: see -AGE. In sense 3 f. LABOUR *n.*] †1 Labouring, labour, work. ME–M17. †2 Ploughing; ploughed or cultivated land. L15–E16. 3 Payment for labour. E19.

laboured /ˈleɪbəd/ *a.* Also ***labored**. LME. [f. LABOUR *v.* + -ED[1].] †1 Learned. Only in LME. †2 a Worn with use. Only in M16. b Used for work; hard worked. L16–E18. †3 Cultivated, tilled, ploughed; (of a mine) worked. L16–M19. 4 Produced or accomplished with labour; performed with great effort. Now freq. *derog.*, overelaborated, lacking spontaneity, heavy. L16.

4 J. FOSTER Other writing of a laboured and tedious kind. M. KINGSLEY The laboured beat of the engines.

labouredly *adv.* L19. **labouredness** *n.* M20.

labourer /ˈleɪb(ə)rə/ *n.* Also ***laborer**. ME. [f. LABOUR *v.* + -ER[1].] 1 A person who performs (esp. unskilled) physical labour as a service or for a livelihood; *spec.* one who assists a skilled worker. ME. 2 *gen.* A person who does work of any kind, a worker. LME. 3 *Entomol.* A worker insect. *rare.* E17.

1 A. BRIEN The labourers who slave in the mills and warehouses. *bricklayer's labourer, dock labourer, farm labourer, mason's labourer*, etc. *casual labourer*: see CASUAL *a.* **labourer-in-trust** *Hist.* an officer ranking next below a clerk of works supervising repairs to royal palaces and other State buildings.

labouring /ˈleɪb(ə)rɪŋ/ *ppl a.* Also ***laboring**. LME. [f. LABOUR *v.* + -ING[2].] 1 That labours; *esp.* (of a person) performing or engaged in unskilled labour. LME. †b Of an animal: used for work. E16–E19. 2 Working hard; striving or struggling against pressure or some obstacle. Of a ship: rolling or pitching heavily. LME. †b Of the moon: eclipsed. E–M17. 3 Of a woman: in labour. M16.

Special collocations: **labouring class(es)** = *working class(es)* s.v. WORKING *a.* **labouring oar**: the hardest to pull; *ply, pull, tug, the labouring oar*, do much of the work.

labouringly *adv.* laboriously M19.

Labourism /ˈleɪbərɪz(ə)m/ *n.* Also ***-bor-, l-**. E20. [f. LABOUR *n.* + -ISM.] (The holding or advocacy of) the principles of a Labour Party or the labour movement.

Labourist /ˈleɪbərɪst/ *n.* & *a.* Also **l-, *-bor-**. E20. [f. LABOUR *n.* + -IST.] A *n.* A supporter of the interests of Labour in politics; an advocate of Labourism. E20. B *adj.* Of or pertaining to the interests of labour or *spec.* the British Labour Party. E20.

Labourite /ˈleɪbərʌɪt/ *n.* & *a.* Also **l-, *-bor-**. L19. [f. LABOUR *n.* + -ITE[1].] = LABOURIST; (esp. of a member of Parliament) of the Labour Party.

labourless /ˈleɪbəlɪs/ *a.* Also ***labor-**. E17. [f. LABOUR *n.* + -LESS.] Without labour; requiring or doing no labour.

laboursome /ˈleɪbəs(ə)m/ *a.* Also ***labor-**. M16. [f. LABOUR *n.* + -SOME[1].] †1 Industrious, hard-working. M16–E17. 2 Requiring, entailing, or accompanied by labour. Now *dial. rare.* L16. 3 Of a ship: apt to pitch and roll violently in a heavy sea. L17.

laboursomely *adv.* M16. **laboursomeness** *n.* M16.

labra *n.* pl. of LABRUM.

Labrador /ˈlabrədɔː/ *n.* M19. [A large peninsula in eastern Canada.] 1 Used *attrib.* to designate things found in or associated with Labrador. M19. 2 *ellipt.* A Labrador retriever. E20.

1 **Labrador current** a surface current running along the northern shore of Baffin Island and continuing southward until it meets the Gulf Stream off the coast of Newfoundland. **Labrador dog** = *Labrador retriever* below. **Labrador duck** a sea-duck of the Labrador coast, *Camptorhynchus labradorius*, extinct since *c* 1875; also called *pied duck*. **Labrador feldspar** = LABRADORITE. **Labrador hornblende** = ENSTATITE. **Labrador retriever** a medium-sized, black or yellow, short-coated retriever of a breed developed in Newfoundland and Labrador. **Labrador spar, stone** = LABRADORITE. **Labrador tea** a low-growing shrub, *Ledum palustre*, of the heath family, which has leathery evergreen leaves used locally in Canada as a tea substitute.

labradorescence /ˌlabrədɔːˈrɛs(ə)ns/ *n.* E20. [f. LABRADORITE + -ESCENCE.] *Min.* The brilliant play of colours exhibited by some specimens of feldspars, esp. labradorite.

Labradorian /labrəˈdɔːrɪən/ *n.* & *a.* M19. [f. LABRADOR + -IAN.] A *n.* A native or inhabitant of Labrador in Eastern Canada. M19. B *adj.* Of or pertaining to Labrador. L19.

labradorite /labrəˈdɔːrʌɪt/ *n.* E19. [f. LABRADOR + -ITE[1].] *Min.* A triclinic silicate of the plagioclase feldspar series which may show a bluish or multicoloured iridescence due to microscopic internal planes of reflection.

labral /ˈleɪbr(ə)l/ *a.* L19. [f. LABRUM + -AL[1].] *Zool.* Of or pertaining to a labrum or liplike part.

labret /ˈleɪbrɪt/ *n.* M19. [f. LABRUM + -ET[1].] A piece of stone, bone, shell, etc., inserted in the lip as an ornament.

labreˈtifery *n.* the practice of wearing labrets L19.

labroid /ˈleɪbrɔɪd/ *a.* & *n.* M19. [f. mod.L *Labrus* genus name + -OID.] *Zool.* A *adj.* Pertaining or belonging to the wrasse family Labridae of perciform fishes of temperate and tropical seas worldwide, or to a closely related family. M19. B *n.* A labroid fish. M19.

labrum /ˈleɪbrəm/ *n.* Pl. **labra** /ˈleɪbrə/. E18. [L = lip, cogn. w. *labium* rel. to Gk *laptein* LAP *v.*[1]] *Zool.* A lip, a liplike part; *esp.* a part forming the upper border or covering of the mouth in insects, crustaceans, etc.

labrys /ˈlabrɪs/ *n.* E20. [Gk *labrus*.] *Class. Antiq.* The sacred double-headed axe of ancient Crete; a representation of this.

laburnum /ləˈbəːnəm/ *n.* M16. [L.] Any of several small leguminous trees of the genus *Laburnum*, esp. *L. anagyroides* and *L. alpinum* and their hybrids, bearing long pendulous racemes of bright yellow flowers followed by pods of poisonous seeds. Also, the dark wood of these trees.

labyrinth /ˈlab(ə)rɪnθ/ *n.* LME. [Fr. *labyrinthe* or L *labyrinthus* f. Gk *laburinthos* of unkn. origin.] 1 A structure consisting of a complex network of tunnels, paths, etc., through which it is difficult to find one's way, a maze; *spec.* (*the Labyrinth*) in *Gk Mythol.*, the maze constructed by Daedalus to contain the Minotaur. LME. b A maze formed by paths bordered by high hedges, usu. as a feature in a garden. E17. 2 *transf.* & *fig.* A complex or confusing situation; an intricate system; a complicated arrangement esp. of streets or buildings. M16. 3 *Anat.* & *Zool.* A complex cavity hollowed out of each temporal bone, containing the organs of hearing and balance; the inner ear. Also, any of various other organs of intricate structure, as the accessory respiratory organs of certain fishes. L17. 4 *Engin.* & *Electr.* Any of various devices containing or consisting of winding passages; *esp.* a series of chambers designed to absorb unwanted vibrations in a loudspeaker. M19.

2 H. ARENDT There are . . few guides . . through the labyrinth of inarticulate facts. R. MACAULAY The real Trebizond . . was in the labyrinth of narrow streets. 3 BONY *labyrinth*. *membranous labyrinth*: see MEMBRANOUS *a.* 1.

Comb.: **labyrinth fish** a fish of the perciform suborder Anabantidae, most members of which (including the gouramis and Siamese fighting fish) have a labyrinth-like accessory breathing organ above the gill chambers.

labyˈrinthal *a.* (*rare*) M17. †**labyrinthial** *a.* M16–E18. **labyˈrinthian** *a.* L16. **labyˈrinthic** *a.* M17. **labyrinthical** *a.* (*rare*) E17.

labyrinth /ˈlab(ə)rɪnθ/ *v.t.* E19. [f. the n.] Enclose in or as in a labyrinth; arrange in the form of a labyrinth.

labyrinthiform /labəˈrɪnθɪfɔːm/ *a.* M19. [f. LABYRINTH *n.* + -I- + FORM *n.*] Having the form of a labyrinth; of a sinuous or intricate structure; *Ichthyol.* having a labyrinth or accessory breathing organ above the gill chamber.

labyrinthine /labəˈrɪnθʌɪn, -ɪn/ *a.* M17. [f. as prec. + -INE[1].] 1 Pertaining to or of the nature of a labyrinth; intricate, complicated, involved. M17. 2 Pertaining to the labyrinth or inner ear. L19.

labyrinthitis /ˌlab(ə)rɪnˈθʌɪtɪs/ *n.* E20. [f. as prec. + -ITIS.] *Med.* Inflammation of the labyrinth or inner ear.

labyrinthodont /labəˈrɪnθədɒnt/ *n.* & *a.* M19. [f. mod.L *Labyrinthodontia* (see below), f. Gk *laburinthos* LABYRINTH *n.* + -ODONT.] *Palaeont.* A *n.* Any of various large fossil amphibians of the Palaeozoic and Triassic order Labyrinthodontia, characterized by teeth of labyrinthine structure having the enamel deeply folded. M19. B *adj.* Of or having labyrinthine teeth; *spec.* of or pertaining to the order Labyrinthodontia. M19.

lac /lak/ *n.*[1] Also †**lack**, (earlier) †**lacca**. See also LAKE *n.*[3] LME. [(med.L *lac*, *lac(c)a* f.) Port. *lac(c)a* f. Hind. *lākh*, Pers. *lāk*. Cf. SHELLAC.] 1 The dark-red resinous incrustation secreted as a protective covering by the females of certain homopteran insects (esp. *Laccifer lacca*) parasitic on SE Asian trees, used (esp. in the Indian subcontinent) to make shellac and dye. LME. †2 The varnish made from lac. Also, any of various resinous wood varnishes. Cf. LACQUER *n.* 2, 3. L16–E18. 3 Ware coated with lac or lacquer. M17. †4 The colour of lac; crimson. Also, a pigment prepared from lac. Cf. LAKE *n.*[3] 1. L17–M18.

1 **seed-lac**: ground in water to remove the dye. **stick-lac** untreated lac encrusted on twigs.

Comb.: **lac-dye** a brilliant scarlet dye prepared from lac; **lac-insect** any lac-producing insect, esp. *Laccifer lacca*.

lac /lak/ *n.*[2] M20. [Abbrev. of LACTOSE.] *Biol.* Used (usu. *attrib.* and printed in italics) orig. to denote the ability (of normal individuals) or inability (of mutants) of the bacterium *Escherichia coli* to metabolize lactose, and now also to designate (the parts of) the genetic system involved in this ability. Also, a *lac*⁺ bacterium; the *lac* operon.

Comb.: **lac operon** a group of adjacent genes in *E. coli* which, in the presence of lactose, cause the synthesis of the enzymes required for lactose metabolism.

lac *n.*[3] var. of LAKH.

†**lacca** *n.* see LAC *n.*[1]

laccase /ˈlakeɪz/ *n.* L19. [f. med.L *lacca* LAC *n.*[1] + -ASE.] *Biochem.* A copper-containing enzyme which oxidizes hydroquinones to quinones, involved in the setting of lac.

laccolite /ˈlakəlʌɪt/ *n.* L19. [f. Gk *lakkos* reservoir + -LITE.] *Geol.* = next.

laccoˈlitic *a.* L19.

laccolith /ˈlakəlɪθ/ *n.* L19. [f. as prec. + -LITH.] *Geol.* A concordant mass of igneous rock thrust up through sedimentary beds, and giving a domed form to the overlying strata.

laccoˈlithic *a.* of, pertaining to, or characteristic of a laccolith L19.

lace /leɪs/ *n.* & *a.* ME. [OFr. *laz*, *las* (mod. *lacs* noose) f. Proto-Romance f. L *laqueus* noose.] A *n.* †1 A net, a noose, a snare. Chiefly *fig.* ME–E17. 2 A cord, a line, a string, a thread, a tie. *obs.* exc. as in sense 3 below. ME. 3 *spec.* a A cord or leather strip used to draw together opposite edges (chiefly of garments or footwear) by being passed in and out through eyelet-holes (or around hooks, studs, etc.) and pulled tight. ME. †b A cord from which a sword, hat, etc., hangs about the body. LME–L16. †4 In building: a tie beam; a brace. ME–E17. 5 Ornamental trimming for dresses, coats, etc. Now only in *gold lace*, *silver lace*, a braid formerly made of gold or silver wire, now of silk or thread with a thin wrapping of gold or silver. ME. 6 A delicate ornamental openwork fabric made by twisting, looping, or knotting threads by hand or machine. M16. 7 A small quantity of spirits etc. mixed with some other drink, esp. coffee. E18.

3 AV *Exod.* 28:28 Bind the brestplate . . unto the rings . . with a lace of blewe. C. GEBLER I slipped my feet into my shoes and began to tie my laces. *boot-lace*, *shoelace*, etc. 6 B. MASON My eyes on the . . petticoat lace below her skirt. *fig.*: L. MACNEICE The brown lace sinking In the empty glass of stout. *blonde lace*, *bobbin-lace*, *Irish lace*, *Medici lace*, *mignonette lace*, *Nottingham lace*, *pillow-lace*, *Valenciennes lace*, etc. *iron lace*: see IRON *n.* & *a.*

B *attrib.* or as *adj.* Made of lace. L19.

Comb. & *special collocations*: **lacebark (tree)** any of several trees and shrubs with lacelike inner bark; *esp.* (*a*) a W. Indian evergreen shrub, *Lagetta lagetto* (family Thymelaeaceae); (*b*) *NZ* = HOUHERE; **lace-border** a geometrid moth, *Scopula ornata*, with a broad lacelike border to the wings; **lacebug** any insect of the family Tingidae of small plant-feeding bugs with lacelike wings; **lacecap** *n.* & *a.* (a hydrangea) having corymbs made up of small fertile flowers or a mixture of these with larger sterile ones, giving the effect of lace; **lace curtain** a window-curtain made of lace which lets in light but makes seeing into the room difficult; **lace-curtain** *a.* having social pretensions, genteel; **lace-fern** any of several finely cut ferns; *esp.* a small N. American fern, *Cheilanthes gracillima*, having the underside of the frond covered with matted wool; **lace-glass** Venetian glass with lacelike designs; **lace-leaf (plant)** = *lattice leaf (plant)* s.v. LATTICE *n.*; **lace-lizard, monitor** any Australian lizard of the genus *Varanus*, esp. the large arboreal *V. varius*; **lace-pillow** a pillow or cushion placed on the lap of a person making lace by hand; †**lace-shade** a lace veil; **lacewing (fly)**, **lace-winged fly** any of various predatory neuropteran insects with delicate lacelike wings, esp. a member of the families Chrysopidae (*green lacewing*) or Hemerobiidae (*brown lacewing*); **lacewood** the wood of the American plane, *Platanus occidentalis*, or a similar wood, suitable for ornamental use.

lacelike *a.* resembling lace L18. **lacery** *n.* (*rare*) lacelike work L19.

lace /leɪs/ *v.* ME. [OFr. *lacier* (mod. *lacer*) f. Proto-Romance base of LACE *n.*] 1 a *v.t.* Fasten or tighten with, or as with, a lace or string, now usu. with a lace or laces passed alternately through two rows of eyelet-holes or around two rows of hooks, studs, etc. (Foll. by *up*, also *down*, *on*, *together*.) ME. b *v.i.* Of a garment etc: be fastened by means of laces. L18. †2 *v.t.* Catch as in a noose or snare; entangle, ensnare. LME–L15. 3 *v.t.* Fasten (a person) *into* a garment etc. by means of a lace or laces; compress the waist of (a person) by drawing corset laces tight. LME. b *v.i.* Tighten or pull *in* corset laces; compress one's waist by so doing. L19. 4 a *v.t.* Thread *with* a lace, string, etc. LME. b *v.t.* Pass (a cord etc.) in and out *through* holes, a fabric, etc. In *Bookbinding*, attach (the boards) to a sewn volume by passing the cords used through perforations in them (foll. by *in*). M17. c *v.t.* Intertwine. L19. d *v.i.* Pass *across* a gap or *about* an object in a manner resembling or suggestive of lacing. L19. e *v.t.* Pass (film or tape) between the guides and other parts of a projector, tape recorder, etc., so that it runs from one spool to the other. Usu. foll. by *up*. M20. 5 *v.t.* Ornament or trim with laces or with lace. L16. 6 *v.t.* a Diversify with streaks of colour. Now freq. *fig.* L16. b Flavour or fortify (a drink) with a dash of spirits, honey, etc.; add an extra ingredient to (a foodstuff), either to enhance or to adulterate it. (Foll. by *with*.) L17. 7 *v.t.* & *i.* w. *into*. Beat, thrash; abuse physically or verbally. *colloq.* L16. †8 *v.t. Cookery.* Make a number of incisions in (the breast of a bird). M17–L18.

1a W. WHARTON I can even lean over to lace my boots. 3 T. HARDY He couldn't have moved from bed, So tightly laced in sheet and quilt . . He lay. E. FEINSTEIN Women were supposed to lace themselves tightly in silk. 4a *fig.*: H. GEORGE We . . lace the air with telegraph wires. c T. O'BRIEN Sarah laced her fingers through mine. d H. G. WELLS A flimsy seeming scaffolding that laced about the . . Council House. 5 SWIFT Have I not . . laced your backs with gold. 6a H. CARPENTER A reputation for lacing his instruction . . with tags of Latin verse. b R. L. STEVENSON A jug of milk, which she had . . laced with whiskey. *Daily Telegraph* She laced his steak and kidney pie with . . weedkiller. 7 E. WALLACE He laced me with a whip. *Time* Reviewers laced into the play.

Comb.: **lace-up** *a.* & *n.* (*a*) *adj.* (of footwear etc.) fastening with a lace or laces; (*b*) *n.* a lace-up shoe or boot (usu. in *pl.*).

laced /leɪst/ *a.* LME. [f. prec. + -ED[1].] †1 Wearing a necklace. Only in LME. 2 Of shoes etc.: made to be fastened or tightened with a lace or laces. E16. †3 Of a plant: entwined with a climbing plant. M16–M17. 4 Ornamented or trimmed with lace or laces. L16. 5 Of a drink: mixed with a small quantity of spirits etc. L17. 6 Marked with streaks of colour. Of a bird: having the edges of the feathers coloured differently from the general surface. M19.

Special collocations: †**laced mutton** *slang* a prostitute. **laced valley** *Building* a valley between the slopes of two adjoining roofs in which the end tile of each row abuts against a tile one and a half times the normal width laid diagonally on the valley board.

Lacedaemonian /ˌlasɪdɪˈməʊnɪən/ *n.* & *a.* Also **-demonian**. LME. [f. L *Lacedaemonius*, Gk *Lakedaimonios* + -AN.] *Gk Hist.* A *n.* A native or inhabitant of Lacedaemon, an area comprising the ancient Greek city of Sparta and its surroundings. LME. B *adj.* Of or pertaining to Lacedaemon or its inhabitants. Of speech etc.: laconic. M16.

lacerate /ˈlasərət/ *a.* M16. [L *laceratus* pa. pple, f. as next: see -ATE[2].] 1 Mangled, torn, lacerated. M16. 2 *Bot.* & *Zool.* Having the edge or point irregularly cut as if torn; jagged. L18.

lacerate /ˈlasəreɪt/ *v.t.* LME. [L *lacerat-* pa. ppl stem of *lacerare*, f. *lacer* mangled, torn: see -ATE[3].] Rip, mangle (esp. flesh or tissues); tear to pieces, tear up; *fig.* afflict, distress, harrow.

B. ENGLAND Jagged edges that lacerated their arms . . leaving slivers of . . cane . . in the flesh. V. NABOKOV He was lacerated with pity.

lacerable *a.* able to be lacerated M17. **laceˈration** *n.* the action or process of lacerating flesh etc.; an instance of this; an open wound in which the skin (and underlying tissue) has been torn rather than cut: L16. **lacerative** *a.* (*rare*) tending to lacerate M17.

Lacerta /ləˈsəːtə/ *n.* L18. [L *lacerta* lizard.] (The name of) an inconspicuous constellation of the northern hemisphere, on the edge of the Milky Way between Cygnus and Andromeda; the Lizard.

lacertian /ləˈsəːtɪən, -ʃ(ə)n/ *a.* & *n.* E19. [f. as prec. + -IAN.] = LACERTILIAN.

lacertid /ləˈsəːtɪd/ *n.* & *a.* L19. [f. as prec. + -ID[3].] *Zool.* A *n.* A lizard of the Old World family Lacertidae, to which most European lizards belong. L19. B *adj.* Of, pertaining to, or designating this family. M20.

lacertilian /lasəˈtɪlɪən/ *a.* & *n.* M19. [f. mod.L *Lacertilia* (see below), f. L *lacerta* lizard + -IL + -IA[2].] A *adj.* Of, pertaining to, or characteristic of the reptilian suborder Lacertilia, which comprises the lizards; lizard-like, saurian. M19. B *n.* A reptile of the suborder Lacertilia; a lizard. M19.

lacertine /ləˈsəːtʌɪn/ *a.* M19. [L *lacerta* lizard + -INE[1].] 1 = LACERTILIAN. M19. 2 Of ornament: consisting of intertwined lizard-like figures. M19.

lacet /ləˈsɛt, leɪ-/ *n.*[1] L19. [f. LACE *n.* + -ET[1].] A braid used to form designs on laces.

lacet /lasɛ/ *n.*[2] Pl. pronounced same. L19. [Fr. = lace, hairpin bend: see -ET[1].] A hairpin bend in a road.

lachenalia /laʃəˈneɪlɪə/ *n.* L18. [mod.L (see below), f. Werner de *la Chenal* (1736–1800), Swiss botanist + -IA[1].] A small bulbous southern African plant of the genus *Lachenalia*, of the lily family, bearing thick, often spotted leaves, and spikes or racemes of tubular or bell-shaped flowers. Also called *Cape cowslip*.

laches /ˈlɑːtʃɪz/ *n.* LME. [AN *laches(se)* = OFr. *laschesse* (mod. *lâchesse* cowardice), f. *lasche* (mod. *lâche*): see LASH *a.*, -ESS[2].] †1 Slackness, remissness, negligence. Also, an act or habit of neglect. LME–L15. 2 *Law.* Delay in asserting a right, claiming a privilege, or making application for redress such as to bar its being granted. Also (now *rare*), negligence in the performance of a legal duty. L16. b *gen.* Culpable negligence. M19.

Lachmann's law /'laxmənz lɔː/ *n. phr.* E20. [Karl *Lachmann* (1793–1851), Ger. philologist.] The rule that in Latin, a short root-vowel in the present-tense stem of a verb is lengthened in the past participle if the present-tense stem ends in a voiced plosive.

lachryma Christi /ˌlakrɪmə 'krɪstʌɪ, -ti/ *n. phr.* L17. [mod.L, lit. 'Christ's tear(s)', in It. *lagrima* (or *-me*) *di Cristo*.] A white, red, or pink Italian wine originally from grapes grown near Mount Vesuvius, now also produced elsewhere in Italy.

lachrymal /'lakrɪm(ə)l/ *a.* & *n.* Also (now the usual form in *Anat.*, *Med.*, etc.) **lacri-**, **lacry-**. LME. [med.L *lachrymalis*, *lacrimalis*, f. L *lacrima* (earlier *lacruma*) tear, rel. to Gk *dakru* tear: see -AL[1].] A *adj.* 1 *Anat.* & *Physiol.* Connected with the secretion of tears; pertaining to or associated with an organ etc. involved in this process. LME. 2 Of or pertaining to tears; occas., characterized by, or indicative of, weeping. Of a vase: (conjectured to be) intended to contain tears. E19.

1 **lacrimal bone** *Anat.* a small bone forming part of the orbit. *lacrimal* CARUNCLE.

B *n.* 1 a A lacrimal organ. Now only in *pl.* Now *rare.* LME. b *Anat.* A lacrimal bone. L19. 2 In *pl.* Fits of weeping. M18. 3 = LACHRYMATORY *n.* 1. M18.

lachrymary /'lakrɪməri/ *a.* & *n.* Also **lacri-**, **lacry-**. E18. [f. L *lacrima* (see LACHRYMAL) + -ARY[1].] = LACHRYMATORY.

lachrymate /'lakrɪmeɪt/ *v.i.* Also **lacri-**, **lacry-**. E17. [L *lacrimat-* pa. ppl stem of *lacrimare* weep, f. *lacrima*: see LACHRYMAL, -ATE[3].] Now chiefly *Med.* & *Physiol.* Weep; produce tears.

lachrymation /lakrɪ'meɪʃ(ə)n/ *n.* Also **lacri-**, **lacry-**. L16. [L *lacrimatio(n-)*, f. as prec.: see -ATION.] The action or an act of weeping; a flow of tears.

lachrymator /'lakrɪmeɪtə/ *n.* Also **lacri-**, **lacry-**. E20. [f. as LACHRYMATE: see -OR.] A substance (usu. as a gas, vapour, or dust) which causes irritation and copious watering on contact with the eyes.

lachrymatory /'lakrɪmət(ə)ri/ *n.* & *a.* Also **lacri-**, **lacry-**. M17. [f. L *lacrima* (see LACHRYMAL), after CHRISMATORY: see -ORY[1].] A *n.* 1 A phial of a kind found in ancient Roman tombs and conjectured to be intended to hold tears. M17. 2 A pocket handkerchief. *joc.* E19. B *adj.* Of or pertaining to tears; tending to cause tears. Of a vase: (conjectured to be) intended to contain tears. M19.

lachrymist /'lakrɪmɪst/ *n.* Also **lacri-**, **lacry-**. E17. [f. as prec. + -IST.] A person who (frequently) weeps.

lachrymogenic /ˌlakrɪmə'dʒenɪk/ *a.* Also **lacri-**, **lacry-**. E20. [f. as prec. + -O- + -GENIC.] Giving rise to tears or weeping; lachrymatory.

lachrymose /'lakrɪməʊs/ *a.* Also **lacri-**, **lacry-**. M17. [L *lacrimosus*, f. *lacrima*: see LACHRYMAL, -OSE[1].] †1 Resembling tears; liable to exude in drops. Only in M17. 2 Tearful, inclined to weep. Of the eyes: full of tears. E18. b Calculated to provoke tears; sad, mournful. E19.

lachrymosely *adv.* M19. **lachry'mosity** *n.* the quality or condition of being lachrymose L19.

lachrymous /'lakrɪməs/ *a. rare.* Also **lacri-**, **lacry-**. L15. [L *lacrima* (see LACHRYMAL) + -OUS.] †1 Of an ulcer: weeping. Only in L15. 2 = LACHRYMOSE 2. M19.

lachsschinken /'laxsʃɪŋkən/ *n.* E20. [G, f. *Lachs* salmon + *Schinken* ham.] Cured and smoked loin of pork.

lacing /'leɪsɪŋ/ *n.* LME. [f. LACE *v.* + -ING[1].] 1 The action of LACE *v.* LME. 2 Something that laces or fastens; a fastening, a tie; a shoestring. LME. b Rope used to attach a sail to a gaff or boom, a bonnet to a sail, etc. M19. 3 Ornamental openwork trimming or braiding. L16. b The coloured border on the petal of a flower. Also, a similar marking on the feathers of a bird. M19. 4 A small quantity of spirits added to another drink. M19.

Comb.: **lacing course** *Building* a special course built into an arch or wall in order to bond different parts together and give added strength.

lacinia /lə'sɪnɪə/ *n.* Pl. **-niae** /-nɪiː/. L17. [L = fringe, hem, rag, strip of cloth.] 1 *Bot.* A slash in a leaf, petal, etc.; a slender lobe between such slashes. L17. 2 *Entomol.* The inner distal lobe of the maxilla. Cf. GALEA. E19.

laciniate /lə'sɪnɪət/ *a.* M18. [f. as prec. + -ATE[2].] *Bot.* & *Zool.* Cut into deep and narrow irregular segments; jagged, slashed.

laciniated *a.* = LACINIATE M17. **lacini'ation** *n.* laciniate condition; a deep or irregular segment: M19.

lacis /'lasi/ *n.* E16. [Fr. = net, network.] 1 A kind of lace made by darning patterns on net. E16. 2 *Anat.* A network of cells surrounding the juxtaglomerular apparatus in a renal corpuscle. Chiefly in *lacis cell.* M20.

lack /lak/ *n.*[1] ME. [Corresp. to (& perh. partly f.) OFris. *lek* blame, MDu., MLG *lak* deficiency, fault, blame (Du. *lak* calumny). Prob. already in OE (cf. AL *lacca*, *laccum*).] †1 A defect; a moral failing, an offence, a crime. ME–L16. 2 A shortage or absence *of* (usu. something desirable or necessary); an instance of this. ME. 3 A fault that brings disgrace; disgrace, shame. (Often coupled with *shame*.) *Sc. arch.* LME. †b Blame, censure for a fault. LME–M16. 4 The state of being in want; indigence, poverty. Also, the condition of lacking food; famine, starvation. M16. †5 The absence of a person or thing. M16–E17. 6 A thing wanted; something of which a need is felt. *rare.* M16.

2 A. BELL It was a lack of security . . which was so worrying. *Punch* The tranquillity, . . convenience and joyfulness, notable lacks at Heathrow. *a painful lack*: see PAINFUL 1. **for**, **from**, **through lack of** for want of. **no lack (of)** enough, plenty (of).

†lack *n.*[2] M17–E19. [Aphet. f. ALACK.] *good lack!*: expr. dissatisfaction, regret, surprise, etc.

†lack *n.*[3] var. of LAC *n.*[1]

†lack *a.* LME. [Perh. f. ON *lakr* defective. Cf. LACK *n.*[1]] 1 Deficient in quality; inferior, poor. *Sc.* LME–M19. 2 Deficient in quantity; short, wanting. L15–M17.

lack /lak/ *v.* ME. [Rel. to LACK *n.*[1] Cf. MDu. *laken* be wanting, blame, ODa. *lakke* deprecate.] I 1 *v.i.* Be wanting or missing; be deficient in quantity or degree. ME. 2 *v.t.* a Be without; have too little of; be destitute of or deficient in, need. ME. †b With *cannot*: do or go without. M–L16. †c Perceive the absence of; miss. *rare* (Shakes.). Only in E17. 3 *v.i.* Want *for* something; be in need (†*of*). E16.

1 AV *Gen.* 18:28 Peraduenture there shall lacke fiue of the fiftie righteous. *BMX Action* Another part that usually lacks on . . bikes is the stem . . that won't hold bars. 2 I. MCEWAN He lacked the concentration for sustained thought. M. PIERCY If they will let me have the two hundred I still lack. 3 AV *Prov.* 28:27 He that giveth vnto the poore, shall not lacke.

II †4 *v.t.* Find fault with, abuse, blame, reproach. In weaker sense: deprecate, disparage. *Sc.* & *north. dial.* ME–M19.

4 to lack to blame, blameworthy.

Comb.: **lackland** *a.* & *n.* (designating) a person owning no land or ruling no territory (orig. w. cap. initial, as a designation of John, King of England 1199–1216); **lack-Latin** *a.* & *n.* (*arch.*) (a person) knowing little or no Latin (chiefly in *Sir John Lack-Latin*, a name for an ignorant priest); **lackwit** a stupid person.

lackadaisical /lakə'deɪzɪk(ə)l/ *a.* M18. [f. next: see -ICAL.] Feebly sentimental, affectedly languishing; dreamily idle, listless, unconcerned, unenthusiastic.

M. BEADLE Homeward bound in a lackadaisical Indian-summer mood.

lackadaisi'cality *n.* the quality of being lackadaisical; an instance of this: E19. **lackadaisically** *adv.* E19. **lackadaisicalness** *n.* E19.

lackadaisy /'lakədeɪzi/ *int.* & *a.* M18. [Extended form of next. Cf. UP-A-DAISY.] A *int.* = LACKADAY. M18. B *adj.* = LACKADAISICAL. L18.

lackaday /'lakədeɪ/ *int. arch.* L17. [Aphet. f. *alack-a-day*: see ALACK.] Expr. surprise, regret, or grief.

D. M. MULOCK Ah! lackaday! it's a troublesome world!

lacker *n.*, *v.* vars. of LACQUER *n.*, *v.*

lackey /'laki/ *n.* & *v.* Also **lacquey**. E16. [Fr. *laquais*, †*alaquais* rel. to Catalan *alacay* (whence also Sp. (*a*)*lacayo*, Port. *lacayo*) = Sp., Port. ALCAIDE.] A *n.* 1 A (liveried) servant; a footman, a valet; a menial. E16. 2 A hanger-on, a camp follower. *arch.* M16. 3 An obsequious person; a toady. Now *spec.* a servile political follower. L16. 4 Any of several lasiocampid moths, esp. *Malacosoma neustria*, having caterpillars with coloured stripes resembling a footman's livery. Also more fully *lackey-moth.* M19.

1 A. N. WILSON Herzen . . had a lackey to carry his books. 3 C. H. SPURGEON It is right to be obliging, but . . not every man's lackey. *American Mercury* American bankers . . have already stepped into the role of lackeys of British Imperialism.

B *v.* 1 *v.i.* Behave or function as a lackey. M16. 2 *v.t.* Serve, esp. in a menial capacity; run errands for, dance attendance on. L16.

1 T. DEKKER The Minutes (that lackey at the heeles of Time). 2 *Quarterly Review* He had lacqueyed and flattered Walpole.

lackeyism *n.* the service or attendance of lackeys, the behaviour of a lackey M19. **lackeyship** *n.* the condition or position of a lackey; lackeys collectively: M19.

lacking /'lakɪŋ/ *a.* L15. [f. LACK *v.* + -ING[2].] 1 Of a thing: not available, missing; in short supply. L15. 2 Deficient (*in* a specified quality), inadequate; *colloq.* deficient in intelligence. Formerly also, crippled. M17. 3 In need; poor, destitute. E19.

1 J. TYNDALL Flour was lacking to make the sacramental bread. 2 R. INGALLS He's thought it wholly lacking in psychological interest.

lacklustre /'laklʌstə/ *a.* Also ***-luster**. L16. [f. LACK *v.* + LUSTRE *n.*[1]] Lacking in lustre or brightness, dull; lacking in vitality, force, or conviction, uninspired.

SHAKES. *A.Y.L.* He drew a dial from his poke, And, looking on it with lack-lustre eye, Says [etc.]. DICKENS A faint lack-lustre shade of grey. T. BERGER Her expression tended towards the lackluster, though her blue eyes were . . bright enough.

Laconian /lə'kəʊnɪən/ *n.* & *a.* L16. [f. L *Laconia* (f. Gk *Lakōn* Laconia: see below) + -AN.] A *n.* 1 A native or inhabitant of Laconia, a territory of ancient Greece and now a department of modern Greece, the capital of which is Sparta. L16. 2 The dialect of ancient Greek spoken in Laconia. M19. B *adj.* Of or pertaining to Laconia, its inhabitants, or its dialect; Lacedaemonian, Spartan. E17.

laconic /lə'kɒnɪk/ *a.* & *n.* In sense A.1 **L-**. M16. [L *Laconicus* f. Gk *Lakōnikos*, f. *Lakōn*: see prec., -IC.] A *adj.* 1 Of or pertaining to Laconia (see prec.) or its inhabitants; Lacedaemonian, Spartan. Now *rare.* M16. 2 Using few words, concise, terse, (the Spartans being known for their terse speech). L16. B *n.* †1 A laconic speaker. Only in 17. 2 Laconic or concise speech; in *pl.*, brief or concise sentences. *rare.* E18.

laconically *adv.* E17. **laconicism** /lə'kɒnɪsɪzəm/ *n.* (*a*) brevity in speech or writing; (*b*) a short pithy sentence: M17.

laconicum /lə'kɒnɪkəm/ *n.* Pl. **-ca** /-kə/. E17. [L neut. of *Laconicus*: see prec.] *Rom. Antiq.* The sweating-room in a Roman bath. (A type of room first used by Spartans.)

Laconise *v.* var. of LACONIZE.

laconism /'lakənɪz(ə)m/ *n.* In sense 2 **L-**. L16. [Gk *lakōnismos*, f. *lakōnizein* LACONIZE: see -ISM.] 1 = LACONICISM. L16. 2 *Gk Hist.* Partiality for the Spartans or the Spartan interest. *rare.* M17.

Laconize /'lakənʌɪz/ *v.* Also **-ise**. E17. [Gk *lakōnizein*, f. *Lakōn*: see LACONIAN, -IZE.] *Gk Hist.* 1 *v.i.* Favour the Spartans; imitate the customs or mode of speech of the Spartans; side with the Spartans in politics. E17. 2 *v.t.* Bring under Spartan dominion or the Spartan form of government. L19.

lacquer /ˈlakə/ *n.* Also **lacker**. L16. [Fr. †*lacre* sealing-wax, f. Port. *la(c)ca* f. as LAC *n.*[1]] †**1** = LAC *n.*[1] I. L16–E18. **2** A varnish consisting of shellac dissolved in alcohol with some (gold) colouring matter, used chiefly as a coating for brass. L17. **3** Any of various resinous wood varnishes capable of taking a hard polish, esp. (more fully *Japan lacquer, Japanese lacquer*) that obtained from the lacquer-tree, *Rhus verniciflua* (see below). L17. **b** Decorative ware made of wood coated with this, often inlaid with ivory, mother-of-pearl, etc. L19. **4** A coating material consisting of polymer dissolved in solvent which dries without chemical change. M19. **5** A kind of fixative for a hairstyle, usu. applied as an aerosol spray. M20. **6** In full *lacquer disc*. A metal or glass disc coated with lacquer on which a groove is cut by a recording stylus, and from which the master disc is made. M20.

Comb.: *lacquer disc*: see sense 6 above; **lacquer-tree** a tree of the cashew family, *Rhus verniciflua*, cultivated in Japan for lacquer and wax; **lacquerware** = sense 3b above; **lacquer-work** (the making of) lacquerware.

lacquer /ˈlakə/ *v.t.* Also **lacker**. L17. [f. the n.] Cover or coat with lacquer; varnish; (of a material) serve as a varnish for. Also foll. by *over*.

lacquerer *n.* a person who lacquers wood etc. M19. **lacquering** *n.* the action or process of coating wood etc. with lacquer; lacquer laid on wood etc.: L17.

lacquey *n.* & *v.* var. of LACKEY.

lacrimae rerum /ˌlakrɪmʌɪ ˈreɪrəm, ˈrɪərəm/ *n.* E20. [L, lit. 'tears for the way things are' (Virgil *Aeneid* I).] The sadness of life; tears for the sorrows of life.

lacrimal *a.* & *n.*, **lacrimary** *a.* & *n.*, etc., see LACHRYMAL etc.

lacrosse /ləˈkrɒs/ *n.* M19. [Fr. (*le jeu de*) *la crosse* (the game of) the hooked stick.] A ball game (orig. played by N. American Indians) in which the ball is thrown, carried, and caught with a long-handled stick with a shallow net at the end, called the crosse.

Comb.: **lacrosse-stick** = CROSSE.

lacrymal *a.* & *n.*, **lacrymary** *a.* & *n.*, etc., vars. of LACHRYMAL etc.

lactalbumin /lakˈtalbjʊmɪn/ *n.* L19. [f. LACTO- + ALBUMIN.] *Biochem.* Orig., the fraction of milk proteins obtained after the removal of casein and soluble in a salt solution. Now usu. α-*lactalbumin*, a protein or mixture of closely similar proteins occurring in this fraction.

lactam /ˈlaktam/ *n.* L19. [f. LACT(ONE + AM(IDE.] *Chem.* A cyclic amide analogous to a lactone, characterized by the group ·NH·CO· as part of a ring.

Comb.: **lactam ring** a ring of the kind characteristic of lactams.

lactamase /ˈlaktəmeɪz/ *n.* M20. [f. prec. + -ASE.] Biochem. *β-lactamase*, any of various bacterial enzymes which cause the breaking of the C—N bond in the lactam ring of penicillins and cephalosporins (so rendering them ineffective as antibiotics).

lactamide /ˈlaktəmʌɪd/ *n.* M19. [f. LACTO- + AMIDE.] *Chem.* The amide of lactic acid.

lactarium /lakˈtɛːrɪəm/ *n.* E19. [mod.L, use as n. of neut. of L *lactarius*: see next.] An establishment for the sale of milk; a dairy.

lactary /ˈlakt(ə)ri/ *a. rare.* M17. [L *lactarius* f. *lac, lact-* milk: see -ARY[1].] Of or pertaining to milk.

lactase /ˈlakteɪz/ *n.* L19. [f. LACTOSE + -ASE.] *Biochem.* An enzyme which catalyses the hydrolysis of lactose to glucose and galactose.

lactate /ˈlakteɪt/ *n.* L18. [f. LACTIC + -ATE[1].] *Chem.* A salt or ester of lactic acid.

lactate /lakˈteɪt/ *v.i.* L19. [Back-form. f. next: see -ATE[3].] Secrete or discharge milk. Earliest & chiefly as *lactating* ppl a.

E. GELLHORN Another function of oxytocin . . : the ejection of milk from the lactating mammillary gland. A. STORR Some primitive societies forbid sexual intercourse with a lactating woman.

lactated *a.* combined with a milk-product L19.

lactation /lakˈteɪʃ(ə)n/ *n.* M17. [Late L *lactatio(n-)*, f. *lactat-* pa. ppl stem of *lactare* suckle, f. *lact-, lac* milk: see -ATION.] **1** The action or process of suckling young; the period of milk secretion normally following childbirth. M17. **2** The process of secreting milk from the mammary glands. M19.

lactational *a.* E20.

lacteal /ˈlaktɪəl/ *a.* & *n.* M17. [f. L *lacteus* (f. *lact-, lac* milk) + -AL[1].] **A** *adj.* **1** Of or pertaining to milk; consisting of or resembling milk. M17. **2** *Anat.* Of a vessel etc.: carrying a milky fluid, esp. chyle. M17. **B** *n. Anat.* Any of the small blind-ended lymph vessels of the small intestines, which convey chyle containing absorbed fats into the lymphatic system. Usu. in *pl.* L17.

lacteous /ˈlaktɪəs/ *a.* M17. [f. as prec. + -OUS.] **1** Of the nature of milk. M17. **2** Resembling milk; of the colour of milk. M17.

lactescent /lakˈtɛs(ə)nt/ *a.* M17. [L *lactescent-* pres. ppl stem of *lactescere*, f. *lactere* be milky, f. *lact-, lac* milk: see -ESCENT.] **1** Becoming milky; having a milky appearance. M17. **2** *Bot.* Yielding a milky juice. L17. **3** Producing or secreting milk. L18.

lactescence *n.* a milky appearance, milkiness L17.

lactic /ˈlaktɪk/ *a.* L18. [f. L *lact-, lac* milk + -IC.] **1** Chiefly *Chem.* & *Biochem.* Of, pertaining to, or derived from milk. L18. **2** Of bacteria: producing lactic acid. Of dairy products, wine, etc.: containing an unusually high proportion of lactic acid. E20.

1 lactic acid a colourless hygroscopic organic acid, $CH_3{\cdot}CH(OH){\cdot}COOH$, present in sour milk and formed metabolically esp. as the end product of glycolysis; 2-hydroxypropanoic acid. **lactic fermentation**: (esp. of milk) due to bacterial conversion of lactose to lactic acid.

lactiferous /lakˈtɪf(ə)rəs/ *a.* L17. [f. as prec. + -I- + -FEROUS.] **1** *Anat., Zool.*, etc. Producing, secreting, or transporting milk. L17. **2** *Bot.* Conveying or yielding a milky juice. L17.

lactifuge /ˈlaktɪfjuːdʒ/ *n.* M19. [f. as prec. + -FUGE.] *Med.* A drug which retards the secretion of milk.

lactim /ˈlaktɪm/ *n.* L19. [f. LACT(ONE + IM(IDE.] *Chem.* Any of the class of cyclic imines which are tautomeric isomers of the lactams and are characterized by the group ·N=C(OH)· as part of a ring.

lacto- /ˈlaktəʊ/ *comb. form.* [f. L *lact-, lac* milk: see -O-.] **1** Of, pertaining to, or derived from milk. **2** Chiefly *Chem.* Relating to or derived from lactic acid or lactose.

lactobaˈcillus *n.* any of various rod-shaped Gram-positive bacteria of the genus *Lactobacillus* which convert carbohydrates to lactic acid in the gut and in fermenting natural (esp. dairy) products E20. **lactoˈbionate** *n.* a salt of lactobionic acid E20. **lactobiˈonic** *a.* [BI- + -ONIC]: *lactobionic acid*, a syrupy organic acid produced by oxidation of lactose L19. **lactocele** *n.* (*Med.*) = GALACTOCELE M19. **lactochrome** *n.* (*Biochem.*) a yellow-orange pigment orig. extracted from milk and now identified with riboflavin L19. **lactoˈferrin** *n.* (*Biochem.*) a bactericidal iron-binding protein found esp. in milk M20. **lactoˈflavin** *n.* (*Biochem.*) = RIBOFLAVIN M20. **lacˈtometer** *n.* an instrument for measuring the relative density of milk E19. **lactoˈnitrile** *n.* a yellow liquid, $CH_3{\cdot}CH(OH){\cdot}CN$, the nitrile of lactic acid, used in the manufacture of acrylonitrile L19. **lacto-ovo-vegeˈtarian** *a.* & *n.* (*a*) *adj.* (of a diet) consisting only of dairy products, eggs, and vegetables; (*b*) *n.* a person who subsists on such a diet: M20. **lactopeˈroxidase** *n.* a peroxidase occurring in milk and saliva M20. **lactoˈphenol** *n.* a solution of phenol and lactic acid in glycerol and distilled water, used for mounting biological specimens L19. **lactoˈprotein** *n.* a protein which occurs normally in milk M19. **lactoscope** *n.* an instrument for measuring the quality of milk from its translucence M19.

lactogenic /laktə(ʊ)ˈdʒɛnɪk/ *a.* M20. [f. LACTO- + -GENIC.] *Physiol.* Pertaining to or initiating the secretion of milk.

ˈlactogen *n.* a lactogenic hormone; *spec.* = PROLACTIN: M20. **lactogenesis** *n.* the initiation of milk secretion M20.

lactoglobulin /laktə(ʊ)ˈglɒbjʊlɪn/ *n.* L19. [f. LACTO- + GLOBULIN.] *Biochem.* Orig., the fraction of milk proteins obtained after the removal of casein and precipitated in a salt solution. Now usu. *β-lactoglobulin*, a protein or mixture of closely similar proteins occurring in the lactalbumin fraction of milk.

lactol /ˈlaktɒl/ *n.* E20. [f. LACTO- + -OL.] *Chem.* Any of the class of cyclic hemiacetals formed by the internal reaction of a hydroxyl and a carbonyl group (esp. in a sugar) and characterized by a ring containing a ·C(OH)·OC· group.

lactone /ˈlaktəʊn/ *n.* M19. [f. LACTO- + -ONE.] *Chem.* †**1** A volatile liquid obtained on heating lactic acid. Only in M19. **2** Any of the class of cyclic esters formed (as) by the elimination of a molecule of water from a carboxylic acid, and characterized by the group ·O·CO· as part of a ring. L19.

lactonic /lakˈtɒnɪk/ *a.* L19. [f. as prec. + -IC.] *Chem.* **1** *lactonic acid*: †**a** = GALACTURONIC *acid*. Only in L19. **b** = LACTOBIONIC *acid*. M20. **2** Containing the characteristic ring structure of a lactone. L19.

lactonize /ˈlaktənʌɪz/ *v.t.* & *i.* Also **-ise**. E20. [f. LACTONE + -IZE.] *Chem.* Change into a lactone.

lactoniˈzation *n.* E20.

lactose /ˈlaktəʊz, -s/ *n.* M19. [f. LACTO- + -OSE[2].] A disaccharide sugar, $C_{12}H_{22}O_{11}$, composed of a glucose and a galactose unit, which is present in milk and is used in food processing and pharmaceutical manufacture. Also called *milk sugar*.

lactosuria /laktə(ʊ)ˈsjʊərɪə/ *n.* M19. [f. prec. + -URIA.] *Med.* The presence of lactose in the urine.

lacto-vegetarian /ˌlaktəʊvɛdʒɪˈtɛːrɪən/ *a.* & *n.* E20. [f. LACTO- I + VEGETARIAN.] **A** *adj.* Consisting of or subsisting on vegetables and milk products (and formerly, eggs) only. E20. **B** *n.* A person who subsists on a lacto-vegetarian diet. E20.

lacto-vegetarianism *n.* M20.

lactulose /ˈlaktjʊləʊz, -s/ *n.* M20. [f. LACTO- + *-ul-* + -OSE[2], perh. after *cellulose*.] *Biochem.* & *Pharm.* A synthetic disaccharide sugar, $C_{12}H_{22}O_{11}$, composed of a fructose and a glucose unit, used as a laxative.

lactyl /ˈlaktʌɪl, -tɪl/ *n.* M19. [f. LACTIC + -YL.] *Chem.* The radical $CH_3CH(OH)CO{\cdot}$ derived from lactic acid. Usu. in *comb.*

lacuna /ləˈkjuːnə/ *n.* Pl. **-nae** /-niː/, **-nas**. M17. [L, f. *lacus* LAKE *n.*[2]] **1** A hiatus, a blank, a missing portion, esp. in a manuscript or text. M17. **2** *techn.* A gap, a depression; a space or cavity, *esp.* within or between the tissues of an organism; *spec.* in *Anat.*, any of the small cavities in bone which contain the osteocytes. E18.

1 D. WILSON The context which fills up the numerous lacunae of the time-worn inscription. M. MEYER These two weeks provide another infuriating lacuna in our knowledge of Ibsen's life.

lacunal *a.* pertaining to or of the nature of a lacuna (in tissue etc.) M19. **lacunate** *a.* (*a*) = LACUNAL; (*b*) having many lacunae: M20.

lacunar /ləˈkjuːnə/ *n.* Pl. **lacunars, lacunaria** /lakjʊˈnaːrɪə, -ˈnɛːrɪə/. L17. [L, f. as prec.: see -AR[1].] *Archit.* A vault or ceiling consisting of recessed panels; any of the panels in such a vault or ceiling.

lacunar /ləˈkjuːnə/ *a.* L19. [f. LACUNA + -AR[1].] = LACUNAL.

Also **lacunary** *a.* M19.

lacune /ləˈkjuːn/ *n.* Now *rare.* E18. [Alt.] = LACUNA.

lacunose /ləˈkjuːnəʊs/ *a.* E19. [L *lacunosus*, f. LACUNA: see -OSE[1].] **1** *Bot.* & *Zool.* Having many lacunae or depressions; furrowed, pitted. E19. **2** Of a manuscript: full of gaps or hiatuses. *rare.* L19.

lacustrian /ləˈkʌstrɪən/ *a. rare.* M19. [f. as next: see -IAN.] Of, pertaining to, or of the nature of a lake-dweller; lake-dwelling.

lacustrine /ləˈkʌstrʌɪn, -rɪn/ *a.* E19. [f. L *lacus* LAKE *n.*[2] after *palustris* marshy.] **1** Of or pertaining to a lake or lakes. E19. **2** Of plants and animals: growing in or inhabiting lakes. M19. **b** Of or pertaining to lake-dwellings or lake-dwellers. M19. 3 *Geol.* Originating by deposition at the bottom of a lake. M19.

lacy /ˈleɪsi/ *a.* E19. [f. LACE *n.* + -Y[1].] Made of or resembling lace.

lacily *adv.* M20. **laciness** *n.* E20.

lad /lad/ *n.* ME. [Origin unkn.] **1** A boy, a youth, a young man; a young son. In extended use: any man (sometimes *iron.*), a fellow; *esp.* (*colloq.*) a workmate, drinking-companion, etc., (usu. in *pl.*). Also used as a familiar form of address (also *my lad*). ME. **2a** A man of humble birth and position; a menial, a labourer. Long *obs.* exc. *dial.* ME. **b** A stable-hand of any age and (in mod. use) either sex, esp. in a racing-stable. M19. **3** A high-spirited or roguish man or boy, a daredevil. Esp. in *a bit of a lad, quite a lad.* M16. **4** A male sweetheart. *Sc.* E18.

1 J. O'HARA A mere strip of a lad, hardly more than a boy. *Beano* Time for your bath, lad! *lad of wax*: see WAX *n.*[1] **the lads** the members of a team or a group of men of any age sharing a common interest on equal terms; *spec.* the rank-and-file members of a trade union. 3 R. DAHL He's . . a genius . . . He's a bit of a lad too . . . Terrific womaniser.

Comb.: **lad-bairn** *Sc.* a male child; **lad's love** the aromatic plant southernwood, *Artemisia abrotanum*.

laddie *n.* (a form of address or endearment to) a lad M16. **laddish** *a.* of or pertaining to a lad or lads; like a lad: M19. **laddo** *n.*, pl. **-os**, (*colloq.*, orig. *Anglo-Ir.*) (a form of address or mode of reference to) a lad L19. **ladhood** *n.* the state of being a lad L19.

Ladakhi /ləˈdɑːki/ *n.* & *a.* M19. [Ladakhi.] **A** *n.* **1** A native or inhabitant of Ladakh, a district of eastern Kashmir. M19. **2** The language of Ladakh, a dialect of Tibetan. L19. **B** *attrib.* or as *adj.* Of or pertaining to Ladakh, the Ladakhis, or their language. L19.

ladang /ləˈdɑːŋ/ *n.* L18. [Malay.] In the Malay archipelago: a piece of land under dry cultivation, often a jungle clearing.

ladanum /ˈladənəm/ *n.* M16. [L *ladanum*, *ledanum* f. Gk *ladanon*, *lēdanon*, f. *lēdon* mastic: cf. LABDANUM.] A gum resin which exudes from plants of the genus *Cistus*, esp. *C. ladanifer* and *C. incanus* subsp. *creticus*, much used in perfumery and for fumigation.

ladder /ˈladə/ *n.* Also (*dial.*) **lether** /ˈlɛðə/. [OE *hlǣd(d)er* = OFris. *hlēdere*, MDu. *lēdere* (Du. leer), OHG *leitara* (G *Leiter*), f. WGmc.] **1** A (fixed or portable) device usu. made of wood, metal, or rope, consisting of a series of bars ('rungs') or steps fixed between two supports, and used as a means of climbing up or down. OE. **b** *spec.* The steps to a gallows. *obs.* exc. *Hist.* M16. **2** A hierarchical structure perceived as resembling a ladder. ME. **3** *gen.* Anything resembling a ladder in appearance or function. ME. **4** In knitted garments or stockings or tights: a vertical strip of unravelled fabric. M19. **5** *Naut.* A series of rangefinding shots up to or back to the target. E20. **6** A league-table or ranking order of contestants. M20. **7** An opportunity or advantageous move in an undertaking (with ref. to the board game of snakes and ladders). M20.

1 R. K. NARAYAN He put up the ladder and climbed to the loft. *extension ladder, rope ladder, scaling-ladder, stepladder*, etc. **see (a hole) through a ladder** see something obvious. *snakes and ladders*: see SNAKE *n.* 1b. **b climb, mount,** or **go up, the ladder** be hanged. **groom of the ladder** the hangman. 2 R. DAHL He bounced up the ladder . . to the top job . ., Archbishop of Canterbury! **kick down the ladder** reject or disown the friends or associations that have helped one to rise in the world. *social ladder*: see SOCIAL *a.* 3 *fish-ladder*: see FISH *n.*[1] 4 J. C. OATES Her silk stockings broke . . in . . runs and ladders. 6 *Star* (*Sheffield*) She . . reached number nine in the junior ladder at the . . Squash Club.

Comb.: **ladder-back** (**chair**): in which the back is formed of horizontal pieces of wood; **ladder-back(ed) woodpecker** a woodpecker of Mexico and adjoining regions with black and white barred markings, *Picoides scalaris*; **ladder competition** (*a*) = *ladder tournament* below; (*b*) *Chess* a competition in which players receive and accumulate points according to the merits of their proposed solutions to a series of problems, until a predetermined number of points is achieved; **ladder fern** any of various chiefly tropical ferns of the genus *Nephrolepis*, which spread by creeping rhizomes, producing new crowns; **ladder point**: (in a competition or tournament) which contributes towards improvement in a competitor's ranking; **ladder polymer**: in which pairs of long straight-chain molecules are joined by recurring cross-links; **ladder-proof** *a.* (of a fabric) not liable to ladder; **ladder shell** a wentletrap, esp. *Epitonium groenlandicum*; **ladder-stitch** a crossbar stitch in embroidery; **ladder-stop** at the top and toe of a stocking, a band of openwork designed to prevent a ladder; **ladder tournament** a tournament in which players are placed in ranking order and move up by successfully challenging the player ranked next above; **ladder-truck** a vehicle for carrying fire-ladders and hooks; **ladder way** a way by which one descends or ascends by means of a ladder in the deck of a ship or the shaft of a mine; **ladder-work**: for which one needs a ladder, as house-painting etc.

ladder /ˈladə/ *v.* LME. [f. the n.] **1** *v.t.* Scale with a ladder or ladders; provide with a ladder or ladders. LME. **2a** *v.i.* Of a garment, esp. of stockings or tights: develop a ladder. E20. **b** *v.t.* Cause a ladder in (a garment). Cf. earlier LADDERED 3. M20. **3** *v.i. Naut.* Fire shots in a ladder. Freq. as *laddering* vbl n. E20.

laddered /ˈladəd/ *a.* E17. [f. LADDER *n.*, *v.*: see -ED[2], -ED[1].] †**1** Of a rope: made into a ladder. Only in E17. **2** Scaled with a ladder or ladders; provided with a ladder or ladders. L19. **3** Of a garment, esp. of stockings or tights: that has developed a ladder, that has been laddered. E20.

lade /leɪd/ *n.*[1] Chiefly *dial.* L17. [Origin uncertain: perh. f. LADE *v.*] A board or rail fixed to the side of a cart or wagon to give greater width.

lade /leɪd/ *n.*[2] E18. [Sense 1 extracted f. Eng. place-names in *-lade* (*Cricklade, Lechlade*, etc.), repr. OE *ġelād* channel, LODE. Sense 2 app. a var. of LEAD *n.*[2], perh. conf. w. a Sc. & north. form of LODE.] **1** A channel, a watercourse, the mouth of a river. E18. **2** A channel for leading water to a mill wheel; a mill-race. Chiefly *Sc.* E18.

lade /leɪd/ *v.* Pa. pple & ppl a. **laden** /ˈleɪd(ə)n/ (the usual form in branch I), **laded** (the only form in branch II). [OE *hladan* = OFris. *hlada*, OS, OHG *hladan* (Du., G *laden*), ON *hlaða*, Goth. *-hlaþan*, f. WGmc base also of LAST *n.*[2]] I Load. **1** *v.t.* Put the cargo on board (a ship). Also, put a load in or on (a vehicle, a beast of burden, a person, etc.) (now only as *laden* ppl a.). OE. **b** Load (a person) *with* gifts etc., (a tree, branch) *with* fruit; fill abundantly. Now only as *laden* ppl a. L15. **c** Burden, weigh down *with*. Now only as *laden* ppl a., burdened (*with* sin, sorrow, etc.). *arch.* M16. **2** *v.t.* Put or place on or in something as a burden, freight, or cargo. Now only, ship (goods) as cargo. OE. **b** *v.i.* Of a ship: take on cargo. LME. †**3** *v.t.* Load or charge (a gun). Also, load (cartridges) in a gun. M–L17. II Draw water. **4** *v.t.* Take up (water or other fluids) from a river, a vessel, etc., with a ladle, scoop, etc.; bale. OE. **b** *v.t.* Empty by baling. *obs.* exc. *dial.* M16. **c** *v.i.* Scoop up liquid, bale. E17. †**5** *v.t.* Of a ship: let in (water). LME–M16.

lader *n.* (now *rare* or *obs.*) M16.

†**lade-bord** *n.* & *a.* see LARBOARD.

laden *pa. pple* & *ppl a.* see LADE *v.*

laden /ˈleɪd(ə)n/ *v.t.* E16. [f. LADE *v.* + -EN[5]. Perh. partly Sc. var. of LOADEN *v.*[1]] Load, burden.

la-di-da /lɑːdɪˈdɑː/ *n.*, *a.*, & *adv. colloq.* Usu. *derog.* Also **lah-de-da**. L19. [Imit. of the style of pronunciation referred to. Cf. LARDY-DARDY.] **A** *n.* (A person given to) pretentious speech, manners, or behaviour. L19. **B** *adj.* Characteristic or imitative of the upper classes; (affectedly) genteel or refined. L19. **C** *adv.* In an affected or excessively refined manner; genteelly. M20.

la-di-da /ˈlɑːdɪdɑː/ *v.i. colloq.* Also **lah-de-da**. E20. [f. the n.] Use affected manners or speech.

la-di-da /ˈlɑːdɪdɑː/ *int. colloq.* E20. [f. the n.] Expr. derision, esp. of a person's pretentious speech or manner. Also (*US*), expr. scorn or lack of concern.

ladify *v.* var. of LADYFY.

Ladik /laˈdiːk/ *n.* & *a.* E20. [A village in Turkey.] (Designating) a type of prayer rug made in the district around Ladik.

Ladin /ləˈdiːn/ *n.* & *a.* M19. [L *Latinus* LATIN *a.* & *n.*] (Designating or pertaining to) the Rhaeto-Romance dialect spoken in N. Italy.

lading /ˈleɪdɪŋ/ *n.* LME. [f. LADE *v.* + -ING[1].] **1** The action of LADE *v.* LME. **2** Freight, cargo. E16.

1 *bill of lading*: see BILL *n.*[3]

ladino /ləˈdiːnəʊ/ *n.*[1] E20. [It.] In full *ladino clover*. A large fast-growing variety of white clover (*Trifolium repens*), native to northern Italy and cultivated elsewhere, esp. in the US, as a fodder crop.

ladino /laˈdiːnəʊ/ *a.* & *n.*[2] In senses A.3, B.3 usu. **L-**. M19. [Sp. f. L *Latinus* LATIN *a.* & *n.*] **A** *adj.* **1** Wild, vicious, cunning. M19. **2** Of or pertaining to a ladino or ladinos. M20. **3** Of or pertaining to Ladino. M20. **B** *n.* Pl. **-os**. **1** A vicious or unmanageable horse, steer, etc.; a stray animal. L19. **2** In Central America: a mestizo or White person. L19. **3** A language based on Old Spanish and written in modified Hebrew characters, used by some Sephardic Jews, esp. in Mediterranean countries. L19.

ladle /ˈleɪd(ə)l/ *n.* [OE *hlædel*, f. *hladan* LADE *v.*: see -EL[1].] **1** A large spoon with a long handle and cup-shaped bowl, used chiefly for serving or pouring liquids; the contents of such a spoon, a ladleful. OE. **b** A vessel for transporting molten metal or glass in a foundry etc. LME. **c** A long-handled instrument for charging a cannon etc. with loose powder. *obs.* exc. *Hist.* L15. **d** In (Scottish) Presbyterian churches: a small wooden box at the end of a long wooden handle used for taking up the collection and Communion tokens. E19. **2** A float-board of a water-wheel. Also *ladle-board*. LME. **3** A tax on grain etc. brought to a burgh market for sale; the amount payable in cash or kind (also *ladle dues*). Also, the vessel used as the measure in assessing this. *Sc. obs.* exc. *Hist.* L16.

ladleful *n.* as much as a ladle will hold LME.

ladle /ˈleɪd(ə)l/ *v.t.* E16. [f. the n.] **1** Equip (a water-mill) with ladle-boards. Long *obs.* exc. *Hist.* E16. **2** Lift out or up with a ladle; transfer to another receptacle using a ladle. Foll. by *out*: distribute, esp. lavishly. M16.

2 H. ROTH His mother . . began ladling out the steaming yellow pea-soup into the bowls. R. BROOKE But it's absurd to ladle out indiscriminate praise, as most people do.

ladler *n.* (*a*) (*Sc.*, *obs.* exc. *Hist.*) a collector of ladle dues; (*b*) a person who ladles something: M17.

la dolce vita *n. phr.* see DOLCE VITA.

ladrone /ləˈdrəʊn/, *in sense 1* ˈladrən/ *n.* In sense 1 also **laidron** /ˈleɪdrən, ˈladrən/. M16. [Sp. *ladrón* f. as LATRON.] **1** A rogue, a rascal, a loafer. *Sc.* M16. **2** A highwayman in Spain or Spanish America. M19.

lady /ˈleɪdi/ *n.* & *a.* [OE *hlǣfdīġe*, f. *hlāf* LOAF *n.*[1] + Gmc base meaning 'knead'. Cf. DEY *n.*[1], DOUGH *n.*] **A** *n.* I As a designation for a woman (or girl). **1** A mistress in relation to servants; the female head of a household. OE. **2** A woman to whom obedience or feudal homage is due: the feminine designation corresponding to *lord*. Now chiefly *poet.* OE. **b** A woman who is the object of chivalrous devotion, one loved and courted by a man. Cf. sense 6 below. LME. **3** *spec.* The Virgin Mary; an image or representation of the Virgin. Now only *Our Lady*. OE. **4** A woman of superior position in society, or to whom such a position is conventionally or by courtesy attributed. Now, the feminine equivalent of *gentleman*, freq. as a more courteous synonym for 'woman'. In extended use: any woman (freq. *iron.* or *derog.*). ME. **b** Used as a form of address to a woman (now *colloq.*). In *pl.*, used as the normal form of address to a number of women. ME. **5a** As an honorific title, used preceding the names of goddesses, allegorical figures, personifications, etc. Now *arch.* exc. in *Lady Luck*, = FORTUNE *n.* 1. ME. **b** Used preceding titles of honour or designations of dignified office, as an added mark of respect. *arch.* exc. in

Lady Mayoress, the wife or consort of a Lord Mayor. LME. **c** Used preceding a name to form part of the customary designation of a woman (or girl) of rank, (*a*) as a less formal substitute for Marchioness (of), Countess (of), Viscountess, Baroness; (*b*) preceding the forename of the daughter of a duke, marquess, or earl; (*c*) preceding the husband's forename of the wife or widow of the holder of a courtesy title in which *Lord* precedes a forename; (*d*) preceding the surname of the wife or widow of a baronet or knight. LME. **d** Used preceding a designation of relationship, by way of respectful address or reference. *arch.* or *joc.* E16. **6** A wife, a consort. Also, a female companion or lover. Cf. sense 2b above. ME. **7** A courteous, refined, or genteel woman. M19.

1 SWIFT When you are sent on a Message, deliver it in your own Words . . not in the Words of your . . Lady. 2 MILTON Here ye shall have greater grace, To serve the Lady of this place. b TENNYSON Never a line from my lady yet. 4 C. STEAD She had been nurtured in the idea that she was to be a great lady. S. PLATH Irwin had a queer, old-world habit of calling women ladies. 5b SIR W. SCOTT They call me Lady Abbess, or Mother. c H. JACOBSON You say her name is Lady Ilchester? 6 C. WATERTON The unfortunate governor and his lady lost their lives. D. DELILLO His current lady.

II *transf.* **8**†**a** A queen at chess. LME–L15. **b** A queen in a pack of playing-cards. *colloq.*, orig. *US*. E20. **9** Any of various butterflies. E17. **10** A calcareous structure in the stomach of a lobster, forming part of the masticatory apparatus and fancifully supposed to resemble the outline of a seated woman. M17. **11** A roofing-slate of a small size. Cf. COUNTESS 2, DUCHESS 4. E19.

B *attrib.* or as *adj.* **1** Female, esp. (*a*) with names of occupations etc., esp. those traditionally associated with men, (*b*) (freq. *joc.*) of an animal. E17. **2** Genteel; (esp. in titles of servants) having or claiming the status of gentlewoman. E19.

1 DICKENS Our observant lady readers. G. R. SIMS The dog . . had five beautiful puppies . . it being a lady-dog. 2 R. M. CRAWSHAY Two lady-helps and . . a strong person . . to do the roughest work.

Phrases, comb., & special collocations: *find the lady*: see FIND *v. fine lady*: see FINE *a.* FIRST *lady. hunt the lady*: see HUNT *v. iron lady*: see IRON *n.* & *a.* **Ladies' Aid (Society)** †(*a*) during the American Civil War, a women's organization devoted to sending garments, bandages, etc., to the soldiers; (*b*) *N. Amer.* an organization of women who support the work of a church by fund-raising, arranging social activities, etc. **ladies and gentlemen**: used as a (formal) form of address to a mixed audience or company. **ladies' cabin, car, carriage** on public transport, a compartment etc. reserved for females. **ladies' chain** a figure in a quadrille etc. **ladies' cloakroom** a cloakroom or lavatory for females. **ladies' fingers** = *lady's finger* below. **Ladies' Gallery** a gallery in the House of Commons reserved for women. **ladies' man** a man who is fond of female company. **ladies' night** a function at a men's club etc. to which women are invited. **ladies' room** = *ladies' cloakroom* above. **Lady altar** an altar in a Lady chapel. **Lady Baltimore (cake)** *US* [the wife of Lord Baltimore, founder of Maryland] a layered white butter cake filled with raisins, nuts, etc. **Lady Bountiful** [orig. a character in Farquhar's play *The Beaux' Stratagem*] a patronizingly generous lady of the manor etc. **lady-chair** a seat formed by the hands of two people standing facing each other, each person grasping one of his or her own wrists and one of the opposite person's. **Lady chapel** a chapel dedicated to the Virgin Mary, in a church or cathedral, often situated east of the high altar. **Lady Chatterley** /'tʃatəli/ [w. allus. to the character in D. H. Lawrence's novel *Lady Chatterley's Lover*] a sexually promiscuous woman, *esp.* one attracted to a man considered socially inferior. **lady-clock, -cow** (*obs.* exc. *dial.*) a ladybird. **Lady Day** a day kept in celebration of some event in the life of the Virgin Mary, now *spec.* 25 March, the feast of the Annunciation. **lady-fern** a delicate fern, *Athyrium filix-femina*, of damp shady places; any fern of the genus *Athyrium*. **ladyfish** any of various marine fishes; *esp.* (*a*) the ten-pounder, *Elops saurus*; (*b*) the bonefish, *Albula vulpes*. **lady-fly** (*obs.* exc. *dial.*) a ladybird. **lady-in-waiting** a lady attending a queen or princess. **lady-killer** a practised and habitual seducer, a dangerously attractive man. **lady-love** a female sweetheart or lover. *Lady Luck*: see sense 5a above. **Lady Macbeth** /mək'bɛθ/ [w. allus. to the character in Shakespeare's *Macbeth*] a remorseless or melodramatic woman, *esp.* one leading or assisting a weak man. *Lady Mayoress*: see sense 5b above. **Lady Muck** *colloq.* (*derog.*) a socially pretentious woman. **lady of easy virtue** a sexually promiscuous woman, a prostitute. *lady of leisure*: see LEISURE *n.* **lady of pleasure** a prostitute, a courtesan. **lady of the bedchamber** = *lady-in-waiting* above. **lady of the lake** in Arthurian legend, Nimue or Vivien. **lady of the manor** the mistress of a manor house. **lady of the night** (*a*) (with hyphens) *Bot.* a W. Indian shrub, *Brunfelsia americana* (family Solanaceae), bearing white flowers which are particularly fragrant at night; (*b*) a prostitute. **lady orchid, orchis** a rare British orchid, *Orchis purpurea*, of woodland on chalk, with dark purple helmet and whitish labellum. *lady's bedstraw*: see BEDSTRAW 2. **lady's companion** a small case or bag arranged to hold implements for needlework etc. **lady's cushion** the mossy saxifrage, *Saxifraga hypnoides*. **lady's delight** *US* the wild pansy, *Viola tricolor*. **lady's ear-drops** *dial.* & *US* any of several garden fuchsias. **lady's finger** (*a*) *sing.* & in *pl.* the kidney-vetch, *Anthyllis vulneraria*; (*b*) a sponge finger; (*c*) *sing.* & (usu.) in *pl.* okra. **lady's horse, hunter**: (*a*) trained to carry a woman riding side-saddle; (*b*) suitably mannered for a lady. **lady's laces** ribbon-grass, *Phalaris arundinadea* var. *picta*; also called *painted grass*. **lady's maid** a lady's personal maidservant. **lady's man** = *ladies' man* above. **lady's mantle** any of various plants of the genus *Alchemilla*, of the rose family, with roundish palmately lobed leaves and cymes of tiny green flowers; *esp.* any plant belonging to the *A. vulgaris* aggregate species. **lady-smock** = *lady's smock* below. **lady's slipper (orchid)** any of several European and N. American orchids of the genus *Cypripedium*, with a large inflated labellum likened to a shoe; *esp.* (in Europe) *C. calceolus*. **lady's-smock** (*a*) the cuckoo-flower, *Cardamine pratensis*; (*b*) *dial.* hedge bindweed, *Calystegia sepium*. **lady's thistle** the milk-thistle, *Silybum marianum*. †**lady's traces** = *lady's tresses* below. **lady's tresses** any of several small orchids of the genus *Spiranthes*, with a spirally twisted row or rows of greenish-white flowers; *esp.* (in full *autumn lady's tresses*) *S. spiralis*; *creeping lady's tresses* = GOODYERA. **Lady Superior** the head of a convent or nunnery in certain orders. **lady's waist** *Austral. colloq.* a small gracefully-shaped glass; a drink served in such a glass. *lady ware*: see WARE *n.*[2] 4b. **lady wife** *colloq.* (used to refer to) a person's wife. *leading lady*: see LEADING *a. lord and lady, lords and ladies*: see LORD *n.* **my lady**: a form of address used chiefly by servants etc. to a holder of the title 'lady'. *naked ladies*: see NAKED *a. old lady*: see OLD *a. Our Lady*: see sense A.3 above. *Our Lady's* PSALTER. PAINTED *lady. pink lady*: see PINK *a.*[2] *scarlet lady*: see SCARLET *a.* **the ladies** the female sex, *spec.* the female members of any group or party. **the Ladies(')** (treated as *sing.*) a public lavatory for females, a ladies' cloakroom. **the lady of the house** the mistress of a household; a housewife. **the lady of** or **with the lamp** (pop. name for) Florence Nightingale (1820–1910), founder of the modern nursing profession; any female nurse. *The Visitation of our Lady*: see VISITATION 4. *walking lady*: see WALKING *ppl a. White Lady*: see WHITE *a. young lady*: see YOUNG *a.*

ladydom *n.* the realm of ladies M19. **ladyhood** *n.* the state or condition of being a lady; the qualities of a lady; ladydom: E19. **ladyish** *a.* resembling a lady; affectedly refined or delicate M19. **ladykin** *n.* a little lady (occas. as a term of endearment) (cf. earlier LAKIN *n.*[2]) M19. **ladyless** *a.* L15.

lady /'leɪdi/ *v.t.* E17. [f. the n.] †**1** Raise to the rank of a lady; address as 'lady'; make ladylike or feminine. E–M17. **2** With *it*: play the lady or mistress. *rare.* E17.

ladybird /'leɪdɪbəːd/ *n.* L16. [f. LADY *n.* + BIRD *n.*] **1** A (female) sweetheart; a darling. Now *rare.* L16. **2**†**a** A kind of butterfly. Only in L16. **b** Any of numerous usu. predatory brightly coloured beetles of the family Coccinellidae, of which the most familiar kinds are brownish red with black spots. L17. **3** The pintail (duck), *Anas acuta. dial.* L19.

ladybug /'leɪdɪbʌg/ *n. dial.* & *N. Amer.* L17. [f. LADY *n.* + BUG *n.*[2]] = LADYBIRD 2b.

ladyfy /'leɪdɪfʌɪ/ *v.t.* Also **ladify**. E17. [f. LADY *n.* + -FY.] Make a lady of; give the title of 'Lady' to.

ladyfied *a.* (*colloq.*) having the airs of a fine lady L19.

ladylike /'leɪdɪlʌɪk/ *a.* M16. [f. LADY *n.* + -LIKE.] **1** Suitable for or appropriate to a lady; *derog.* effeminately delicate or graceful. M16. **2** Having the appearance or manners of a lady; *derog.* (esp. of a man) effeminately delicate or fastidious. E17.

ladylikeness *n.* M19.

ladyship /'leɪdɪʃɪp/ *n.* ME. [f. LADY *n.* + -SHIP.] **1** The condition of being a lady; rank as a lady. ME. **2** With possess. adj. (as *her* etc. *ladyship*): a title of respect given to a lady; *iron.* a mode of reference or address to a woman thought to be giving herself airs. LME.

laen /leɪn/ *n.* [OE *lǣn*: see LOAN *n.*[1]] *Law* (now *Hist.*). In Anglo-Saxon England, an estate held as a benefice.

Comb.: **laen-land** land held as a laen.

Laestrigon *n.*, **-gonian** *n.* & *a.* vars. of LESTRIGON, -GONIAN.

Laetare /liː'tɛːri, lʌɪ'tɑːri/ *n.* L19. [L *laetare* imper. sing. of *laetari* rejoice.] In full *Laetare Sunday*. The fourth Sunday of Lent.

laetic /'liːtɪk/ *a.* M19. [Late L *laeticus*, f. *laetus* joyful, ult. f. Gmc base of LET *v.*[1]: see -IC.] *Hist.* Of, pertaining to, or designating a class of non-Roman cultivators under the later Roman Empire, who occupied lands for which they paid tribute.

Laetrile /'leɪtrʌɪl, -rɪl/ *n.* Also **l-**. M20. [f. LAE(VOROTATORY + NI)TRILE.] (Proprietary name for) a substance that has been used to treat cancer with controversial results and is identical with or related to amygdalin.

laevo- /'liːvəʊ/ *comb. form.* Also ***levo-**. [f. L *laevus* left + -O-.] Turning or turned to the left; *Chem.* laevorotatory. Opp. DEXTRO-.

laevotar'taric *a.*: *laevotartaric acid*, the laevorotatory form of tartaric acid M19. **laevo'tartrate** *n.* a laevorotatory tartrate M19.

laevorotatory /liːvəʊ'rəʊtət(ə)ri/ *a.* Also ***levo-**. L19. [f. prec. + ROTATORY.] *Chem.* Having or relating to the property (possessed by some compounds) of rotating the plane of polarized light to the left, i.e. anticlockwise when viewed in the opposite direction to that of propagation. Opp. DEXTROROTATORY.

laevoro'tation *n.* (the property of) rotating the plane of polarized light in this direction L19.

laevulinic /liːvjʊ'lɪnɪk/ *a.* Also ***lev-**. L19. [f. as next + -IN[1] + -IC.] Chem. *laevulinic acid*, a crystalline keto-acid, $CH_3CO(CH_2)_2COOH$, orig. obtained by heating laevulose.

laevulosan /'liːvjʊləsan/ *n.* Also ***lev-**. M19. [f. next + -AN.] *Chem.* †**1** An anhydride of laevulose. M–L19. **2** A polysaccharide composed chiefly of laevulose residues. E20.

laevulose /'liːvjʊləʊz, -s/ *n.* Also ***lev-**. L19. [f. as LAEVO- + -ULE + -OSE[2].] *Chem.* The laevorotatory (and predominant naturally occurring) form of fructose. Cf. DEXTROSE.

lafayette /lɑːfeɪ'ɛt/ *n. US.* M19. [Marquis de *Lafayette* or *La Fayette* (1757–1834), Fr. soldier & statesman.] A sciaenid fish of N. American Atlantic coasts and rivers, *Leiostomus xanthurus*, now more commonly called *spot*.

Laffer curve /'lafə kəːv/ *n. phr.* L20. [Arthur *Laffer* (b. 1942), US economist.] *Econ.* A supposed relationship between economic activity and the rate of taxation, which suggests that there is an optimum tax rate which maximizes tax revenue.

lag /lag/ *n.*[1] In sense 2 also †**lage**. ME. [Origin unkn. Cf. LAG *v.*[3]] **1** A narrow marshy meadow, usu. beside a stream. Long *obs.* exc. *dial.* ME. **2** Water, urine. *arch. slang.* M16. †**3** *lag of duds*, a wash-load of clothes. *slang.* M16–E18.

lag /lag/ *n.*[2] E16. [Rel. to LAG *a.* Cf. LAG *v.*[2]] **1** The last or hindmost person (in a race, game, sequence of any kind). *slang.* Now *rare.* E16. †**2** In *pl.* What remains in a vessel after the liquor is drawn off; dregs, lees. E16–E18. †**3** The lowest class. (Cf. *lag-end* s.v. LAG *a.*) *rare* (Shakes.). Only in E17. **4** The condition of lagging. M19. **b** A period of time separating any phenomenon or event from an earlier one to which it is related (causally or in some other way) (freq. *time-lag*); (the amount of) a retardation in a current or other movement. See also *jet lag* s.v. JET *n.*[2] M19.

4b *Economist* A . . lag must occur between the dates when . . losses are incurred and compensation is paid. *Nature* A . . lag between the addition of bicarbonate and the . . attainment of the maximum rate. M. GORDON A season . . behind, but that small lag was death. **angle of lag** the fraction of a complete cycle, multiplied by 360° or 2π radians, by which a sinusoidal electric current lags behind the associated sinusoidal voltage. **lag of the tide** the interval by which the tidewave falls behind the mean time in the first and third quarters of the moon (cf. PRIMING *n.*[2]). *leads and lags*: see LEAD *n.*[2]

Comb.: **lag fault** *Geol.* a type of overthrust formed when the uppermost of a series of rocks moves more slowly than the lower ones; **lag phase** *Biol.* the period elapsing between the inoculation of a culture medium etc. with bacteria and the commencement of their exponential growth; **lag time** the period of time elapsing between one event and a later, related, event, esp. between a cause and its effect; (the extent of) a lag.

lag /lag/ *n.*[3] *dial.* E17. [Origin unkn.] **1** A flock of geese. *rare.* E17. **2** A goose. Freq. as *int.*, used in driving farmyard geese. E19.

¶The primary sense is prob. 2, which may be attested earlier in GREYLAG.

lag /lag/ *n.*[4] L17. [Prob. of Scand. origin: cf. Icel. *laggar*, Sw. *lagg* stave, ON *lǫgg* rim of a barrel, f. Gmc base of LAY *v.*[1]] **1** A stave of a barrel. Now *dial.* L17. **2** Each of the staves or laths forming the covering of a band-drum or a steam boiler or cylinder, or the upper casing of a carding-machine; (a piece of) any insulating cover for a boiler etc. Also, each of the wooden crossbars in a loom used to control the weaving of fabric designs. M19.

Comb.: **lag bolt, -screw** a wood-screw with a flat or bolt head used to secure a lag to a cylinder or drum.

lag /lag/ *n.*[5] *slang.* E19. [Origin unkn. Cf. LAG *v.*[4]] **1** A term of imprisonment or (formerly) transportation. E19. **2** A convict. Formerly also, a person sentenced to transportation. E19. **b** A hardened or habitual prisoner, a recidivist. Freq. *old lag.* E20.

lag /lag/ *a. obs.* exc. *dial.* LME. [Perh. a children's & dial. alt. of LAST *a.* Cf. LAG *n.*[2], *v.*[2]] Last, hindmost; belated, lingering behind, lagging, tardy. Also as *int.*, claiming the last turn in a children's game. (Earliest in *lag-man* below.)

Comb.: **lag-end** the hinder or latter part, the fag end. †**lag-man** the last person, the one who brings up the rear.

lag /lag/ *v.*[1]*t.* Long *obs.* exc. *dial.* Infl. **-gg-**. LME. [Origin unkn.] Make wet and muddy; bedraggle.

lag /lag/ *v.*[2] Infl. **-gg-**. M16. [Rel. to LAG *a.* Cf. LAG *n.*[2]] **1** *v.i.* Progress too slowly; fail to keep pace with others; hang back, fall behind, remain in the rear. Freq. foll. by *behind* (adv. or prep.), *after.* M16. **2** *v.t.* Hinder, retard, tire. *obs.* exc. *dial.* L16. **3** *v.t.* Fall behind; be or occur after. M20.

1 K. LINES Very soon they lagged on the steep upward track. K. M. E. MURRAY Britain had lagged behind the Germans in philological study. 3 *Daily Telegraph* Unemployment lags changes in output.

Comb.: **lag-last** a person who lags or lingers to the very last.

laggingly *adv.* in a slow or lingering manner E19.

lag /lag/ *v.*[3] *slang.* Infl. **-gg-**. Also †**lage**. M16. [Origin unkn. Cf. LAG *n.*[1]] †**1** *v.t.* Wash, wash *off.* Only in M16. **2** *v.t.* Adulterate (spirits) with water. E19. **3** *v.i.* Urinate. E19.

lag /lag/ *v.*[4] *arch. slang.* Infl. **-gg-**. L16. [Origin unkn. Cf. LAG *n.*[5]] **1** *v.t.* & *i.* Carry off, steal. L16. **2** *v.t.* Sentence to prison or (formerly) transportation. E19. **3** *v.t.* Catch, apprehend, arrest. M19.

lag /lag/ *v.*[5]*t.* L19. [f. LAG *n.*[4] Cf. earlier LAGGER *n.*[3], LAGGING *n.*[2]] Cover (a boiler, pipe, etc.) with insulating material.

Science News Liquid oxygen tanks . . have to be lagged to reduce the loss of oxygen by boiling.

lagan /ˈlag(ə)n/ *n.* Also **lig-** /ˈlɪg-/. M16. [OFr. (whence med.L *laganum*) perh. f. ON *lagn-*, as in *lagn*, genit. *lagnar* drag-net, f. Gmc base of LAY *v.*[1]] *Law.* Goods or wreckage lying on the bed of the sea. Cf. FLOTSAM, JETSAM.

lagander *n.* (long *obs.* exc. *Hist.*) an official who took charge of lagan or wreckage E16.

lagar /laˈgar, laˈgɑː/ *n.* Pl. ***-res*** /-res, -rɪz/. M19. [Sp. f. L *lacus* vat for freshly pressed wine. Cf. LAKE *n.*[2] 4.] In Spain and Portugal: a large (usu. stone) trough in which grapes are trodden.

lagarto /ləˈgɑːtəʊ/ *n.* Long *rare.* Pl. **-os.** M16. [Sp.: see ALLIGATOR.] An alligator.

Lag b'Omer /lɑːg ˈbəʊmə/ *n.* L19. [Heb. *lāg* pronunc. of the letters LG (*lamed*, *gimel*) symbolizing 33 + *bā* in the + *ʿōmer* OMER.] A Jewish festival held on the 33rd day of the Omer, traditionally regarded as celebrating the end of a plague in the 2nd cent. AD.

†**lage** *n.*, *v.* see LAG *n.*[1], *v.*[3]

lagen /ˈlag(ə)n/ *n. obs.* exc. *Hist.* L16. [L *lagona*, *lagena* flagon f. Gk *lagunos.*] A liquid measure equal to several pints.

lagena /ləˈdʒiːnə/ *n.* Pl. **-nae** /-niː/. L19. [L: see prec.] *Zool.* An extension of the saccule of the ear in some vertebrates, corresponding to the cochlear duct in mammals.

lagenar *a.* M20.

lageniform /ləˈdʒiːnɪfɔːm/ *a.* E19. [f. as prec. + -I- + -FORM.] *Bot.* & *Zool.* Shaped like a bottle or flask.

lager /ˈlɑːgə/ *n.* M19. [G *Lager-Bier* beer brewed for keeping, f. *Lager* storehouse.] A light kind of beer, orig. German or Bohemian, which is stored to mature before use; a drink of this. Also (esp. in early use) *lager beer.*

Comb.: *lager beer*: see above; **lager lout** *colloq.* a young man who behaves badly as a result of excessive drinking.

lager /ˈlɑːgə/ *v.t.* M20. [G *lagern* to store.] Store (beer) to mature.

lagetto /ləˈgɛtəʊ/ *n. W. Indies.* Pl. **-os.** L17. [Amer. Sp. *lageto.*] The lace-bark tree, *Lagetta lagetto.*

laggard /ˈlagəd/ *a.*, *n.*, & *v.* E18. [f. LAG *v.*[2] + -ARD.] **A** *adj.* Lagging behind, hanging back, loitering, slow. E18.

T. WILLIAMS While love made her brilliant, . . it made me laggard and dull.

B *n.* A person who lags behind; a lingerer, a loiterer. E19.

C *v.i.* Hang back, loiter. M19.

laggardly *a.* having the character or spirit of a laggard; hesitant, slow: M20. **laggardly** *adv.* (*rare*) in a slow or hesitant manner M19. **laggardness** *n.* M19.

lagger /ˈlagə/ *n.*[1] E16. [f. LAG *v.*[2] + -ER[1].] A person who lags or hangs back; a lingerer, a loiterer.

lagger /ˈlagə/ *n.*[2] *slang.* Now *rare.* E19. [f. LAG *v.*[4] or *n.*[5] + -ER[1].] A convict or ex-convict.

lagger /ˈlagə/ *n.*[3] E19. [f. (as) LAG *v.*[5] + -ER[1].] A person who installs and maintains insulation for pipes, boilers, etc.

laggin /ˈlagɪn/ *n. Sc.* & *north.* E16. [f. ON *lǫgg*: see LAG *n.*[4]] **1** The projecting part of the staves at the bottom part of a cask or other hooped vessel. E16. **2** The inner angle of a wooden dish, between the sides and the bottom. L18.

lagging /ˈlagɪŋ/ *n.*[1] *slang.* Now *rare.* E19. [f. LAG *v.*[4] + -ING[1].] A sentence or term of imprisonment or penal servitude, *spec.* a term of three years.

lagging /ˈlagɪŋ/ *n.*[2] M19. [f. (as) LAG *v.*[5] + -ING[1].] **1** *sing.* & (now *rare*) in *pl.* Insulation material for boilers, pipes, etc. M19. **2** The action of covering a boiler, pipe, etc., with insulation. L19.

lagniappe /laˈnjap/ *n. US.* M19. [Louisiana Fr. f. Sp. *la ñapa.*] Something given as a bonus or gratuity; extra reward.

S. J. PERELMAN Since the ship was calling there anyway, the trip would be pure lagniappe. *Time* A tasty lagniappe: a special dividend of $2.50 per share on top of the regular . . dividend. **for lagniappe** as a bonus; into the bargain; for good measure.

lagomorph /ˈlagəmɔːf/ *n.* L19. [f. Gk *lagōs* hare + -MORPH.] *Zool.* Any of the herbivorous mammals constituting the order Lagomorpha, which includes the hares, rabbits, and pikas.

lagoon /ləˈguːn/ *n.* & *v.* Also (earlier) †**laguna**, †**lagune**. E17. [It., Sp. *laguna* (partly through Fr. *lagune*), f. L LACUNA: see -OON.] **A** *n.* **1** An area of salt or brackish water separated from the sea by low sandbanks or a similar barrier; *spec.* any of those in the neighbourhood of Venice, Italy. E17. **2** The stretch of water within an atoll or inside a barrier reef. M18. **3** A freshwater (esp. stagnant) lake or pond. *Austral.*, *NZ*, & *US.* M18. **4** A shallow pool constructed for the treatment and concentration of sewage and slurry. E20. **B** *v.t.* Treat and concentrate (sewage and slurry) in lagoons. E20.

lagoonal *a.* of or characteristic of a lagoon or lagoons E20.

lagophthalmos /lagɔfˈθalməs/ *n.* Also (earlier) **-mus.** E17. [(mod.L *lagophthalmus*) f. Gk *lagōphthalmos* adj., f. *lagōs* hare (from the supposed inability of hares to close their eyes) + *ophthalmos* eye.] Inability to close the eyes (as a symptom of disease).

lagophthalmia *n.* = LAGOPHTHALMOS L17. **lagophthalmic** *a.* pertaining to or affected with lagophthalmos L19.

Lagrange /ləˈgrɒ̃ʒ, lɑː-/ *n.* M19. [Joseph Louis *Lagrange* (1736–1813), It.-born mathematician who worked in Prussia and France.] *Math.* Used *attrib.* and in *possess.* to designate various concepts introduced by Lagrange or arising out of his work.

Lagrange('s) equation each of a set of equations of motion in classical dynamics relating the total kinetic energy of a system to a set of generalized coordinates, forces acting, and time.

Lagrangian /ləˈgrɒ̃ʒɪən, lɑː-/ *a.* & *n.* Also **-ean.** M19. [f. prec. + -IAN.] *Math.* & *Astron.* **A** *adj.* Of or pertaining to the work of J. L. Lagrange (see prec.); of the kind introduced by Lagrange or associated with his work. M19.

Lagrangian function the difference between the kinetic energy and the potential energy of a system expressed as a function of generalized coordinates, their time derivatives, and time. **Lagrangian point** each of five points in the orbital plane of two bodies (e.g. a planet and a moon) at which a third body of negligible mass will remain stationary relative to the others.

B *n.* A Lagrangian function. M20.

Lagting /ˈlɑːgtɪŋ/ *n.* M19. [Norw.] A functional division of the Norwegian Parliament, operating primarily for law-making purposes.

†**laguna**, †**lagune** *ns.* vars. of LAGOON.

lah /lɑː/ *n.* Also (earlier) **la.** ME. [f. L *la(bii)*: see UT.] *Mus.* The sixth note of a scale in a movable-doh system; the note A in the fixed-doh system.

lahar /ˈlɑːhɑː/ *n.* E20. [Jav.] *Geol.* A mud-flow of volcanic ash mixed with water.

lah-de-da *n.*, *a.*, & *adv.*, *v.* vars. of LA-DI-DA *n.* etc., *v.*

Lahnda /ˈlɑːndə/ *n.* & *a.* E20. [Panjabi *lahandā*, *lahandī* western, of the west.] (Designating or pertaining to) an Indo-Aryan language of the western Punjab and adjacent areas of Pakistan.

Lahu /lɑːˈhuː/ *n.* & *a.* Pl. of n. same, **-s.** E20. [Lahu.] A member of, of or pertaining to, an aboriginal people of the Lolo group in SW China, esp. Yunnan; (of) the Tibeto-Burman language of this people.

lai /leɪ/ *n.*[1] L18. [OFr.: see LAY *n.*[2]] Any of a number of short narrative poems concerned with love and magic written in England, in either English or French, between the 12th and the 15th cents. Also, a medieval French lyric associated with the *trouvères* of northern France. Also *Breton lai.*

Lai /lʌɪ/ *n.*[2] & *a.* L19. [Lai.] **A** *n.* Pl. **-s**, same. **1** A member of a people living in the Chin hills of Myanmar (Burma). L19. **2** The language of this people. E20. **B** *attrib.* or as *adj.* Of or pertaining to the Lais or their language. L19.

laic /ˈleɪɪk/ *a.* & *n.* M16. [Late L *laicus* f. Gk *laikos*, f. *laos* people: see -IC. Cf. LAY *a.*] **A** *adj.* Of or pertaining to a layman or the laity; non-clerical, secular, temporal. M16. **B** *n.* A member of the laity; a person who is not an ecclesiastic. L16.

laical *a.* L15. **laically** *adv.* L19.

laich /leɪx/ *n.*, *a.*, & *adv. Sc.* Also **laigh**. LME. [Sc. form of LOW *a.*] **A** *n.* A piece of low-lying ground; a hollow. LME. **B** *adj.* On or near the ground, not elevated; inferior in rank or quality; not loud. LME. **C** *adv.* In a low position; to a low point; in a low tone. LME.

laicise *v.* var. of LAICIZE.

laicism /ˈleɪsɪz(ə)m/ *n.* L18. [f. LAIC + -ISM.] The principle of control by members of the laity; secularism.

laicity /leɪˈɪsɪti/ *n.* E20. [f. LAIC + -ITY.] The principles of the laity; the rule or influence of the laity; the fact of being lay.

laicize /ˈleɪɪsʌɪz/ *v.t.* Also **-ise**. L19. [f. LAIC + -IZE.] Withdraw clerical character or status from; secularize; *spec.* place (a school etc.) under lay control; make (an office) tenable by members of the laity.

Pall Mall Gazette To laicize the names of the Paris streets, and banish . . the word 'Sainte'. M. WEST When his priestly vocation no longer satisfied him he had asked to be laicised.

laiciˈzation *n.* L19. **laicizer** *n.* L19.

laid /leɪd/ *ppl a.* M16. [pa. pple of LAY *v.*[1]] **1** That has been laid. Also with advs., as *by, down, off, on, out, up*. M16. **2** Of rope: having strands twisted in a specified manner or style, as *cable-laid, hawser-laid*, etc. M17. **3** Of a scheme: deliberately contrived. *obs.* exc. in *best-laid*. L17. **4** *laid-back*, inclined backwards; *fig.* (orig. *US*), relaxed, casual, nonchalant, detached; (of music) mellow, subdued. E20.

1 H. DE WINDT In the midst of beautifully laid-out gardens, is the . . Palace of the Raja. *Architectural Review* Central heating, lighting, cooking, . . laid-on water and drainage. *Daily Telegraph* Laid-off workers at Coventry are receiving . . £5 unemployment benefit. *Country Life* Reaping a small field of badly laid corn. E. PIZZEY Sitting down to a properly laid table. *Armed Forces* The imperative need to observe laid-down procedures to the letter. **get laid** *slang* have sexual intercourse. **laid paper**: having a ribbed appearance made by parallel wires in the mould or on the dandy roller. **laid work** embroidery consisting of strands of silk etc. laid on the material and held in place by tiny stitches.

laid *v.* pa. t. & pple of LAY *v.*[1]

Laïdes *n.* pl. of LAÏS.

laidly /ˈleɪdli/ *a.* Now *Sc.* & *arch.* Also **†laily**. ME. [North. var. of LOATHLY *a.*] Offensive, hideous, repulsive.

laidron *n.* see LADRONE.

laigh *n.*, *a.*, & *adv.* var. of LAICH.

laik /leɪk/ *v.i. obs.* exc. *dial.* Also **lake**. [OE *lācan* corresp. to ON *leika*, Goth. *laikan* play, repl. in ME by forms f. ON.] **†1** Exert oneself, move quickly, leap, spring; fight. OE–LME. **2** Play, sport; take time off work. Also foll. by *about, away*. ME.

laika /ˈlʌɪkə/ *n.* Pl. **laiki** /ˈlʌɪki/. E20. [Russ. *laĭka*, f. *laĭ* bark.] A dog belonging to a group of Asiatic breeds of the spitz type, characterized by a pointed muzzle, pricked ears, and a stocky body with a tail curling over the back.

†laily *a.* var. of LAIDLY *a.*

lain /leɪn/ *n. obs.* exc. *dial.* L16. [Perh. f. pa. pple of LIE *v.*[1]] A layer, a stratum.

lain *v.* pa. pple of LIE *v.*[1]

lair /lɛː/ *n.*[1] [OE *leger* = OFris. *leger* situation, OS *legar* bed (Du. *leger* bed, camp, LEAGUER *n.*[1]), OHG *leger* bed, camp (G *Lager*, infl. by *Lage* situation), Goth. *ligis*, f. Gmc base of LIE *v.*[1]] **†1** The action or fact of lying or lying down. OE–M18. **2** A grave, a tomb. Now only *Sc.*, a plot in a graveyard. OE. **3** A place where one sleeps; a bed, a couch. OE. **4** A resting-place for domestic animals; *spec.* an enclosure or large shed for cattle on the way to market. LME. **5** A place of rest or concealment for a wild animal; *transf.* a (secret) retreat or base. LME. **6** *Agric.* Nature or kind of soil, with reference to its effect on the quality of crops, or of the animals pastured upon it. LME.

3 CARLYLE Wretchedness . . shivers hunger-stricken into its lair of straw. 5 J. HILTON The tribesmen Kept you in some lair in the mountains. *beard the lion in his lair*: see BEARD *v.* 1.

lair /lɛː/ *n.*[2] *obs.* exc. *dial.* ME. [ON *leir*.] Clay, mire, mud.

lair /lɛː/ *n.*[3] *Austral.* & *NZ slang*. Also **lare**. M20. [Back-form. f. LAIRY *a.*[2]] A flashily dressed man; a show-off.

lair /lɛː/ *v.*[1] ME. [f. LAIR *n.*[1]] **†1** *v.t.* Prostrate, lay on the ground. Only in ME. **2a** *v.i.* Lie, repose (*on* a bed, *in* a lair). L16. **b** *v.t.* Place in a lair; serve as a lair for. L17.

lair /lɛː/ *v.*[2] *obs.* exc. *dial.* M16. [f. LAIR *n.*[2]] **1** *v.t.* Cause or allow to sink in mire or a morass. M16. **2** *v.i.* Stick or sink in mire or bog. L16.

lair /lɛː/ *v.*[3] *Austral.* & *NZ slang*. Also **lare**. M20. [f. LAIR *n.*[3] or *lairy* var. of LEERY *a.*[2]] **1** *v.t.* Dress flashily, dress *up*. Freq. as pa. pple in (*all*) *laired up*. M20. **2** *v.i.* Act in a flashy or knowing manner. M20.

lairage /ˈlɛːrɪdʒ/ *n.* L19. [f. LAIR *n.*[1] or *v.*[1] + -AGE.] The placing of cattle in a lair or lairs; space, or a place, where cattle may be rested or kept on the way to market.

laird /lɛːd/ *n. Sc.* LME. [Sc. var. of LORD *n.*] A landowner, esp. of a large estate; *Hist.* a holder of land directly from the king.

lairdie *n.* a petty laird M18. **lairdly** *a.* having the rank or quality of a laird L19. **lairˈdocracy** *n.* [after *aristocracy*] lairds as forming a ruling class M19. **lairdship** *n.* (*a*) the estate of a laird; (*b*) the condition or dignity of being a laird; (*c*) lairds collectively: M17.

lairy /ˈlɛːri/ *a.*[1] *obs.* exc. *dial.* ME. [f. LAIR *n.*[2] + -Y[1].] Boggy, miry, swampy. Formerly also, earthly, filthy.

lairy *a.*[2] var. of LEERY *a.*[2]

Laïs /ˈlʌɪɪs/ *n.* Now *rare*. Pl. **Laïdes** /ˈlʌɪdiːz/. L16. [Either of two celebrated Greek courtesans of the 5th and 4th cents. BC.] (A name for) a beautiful and accomplished temptress.

laisse /lɛs/ *n.* Pl. pronounced same. L19. [Fr.] In Old French verse: a distinct section of a poem.

laisser-aller, **-faire**, **-passer** *ns.* vars. of LAISSEZ-ALLER etc.

laissez-aller /lɛseɪˈaleɪ, *foreign* lɛseale/ *n.* Also **laisser-**. E19. [Fr., lit. 'allow to go'.] Absence of restraint; unconstrained ease and freedom.

THACKERAY With some justice, though with a good deal too much laissez-aller of tongue. *attrib.*: DICKENS A magnificent high-handed laissez-aller neglect.

laissez-faire /lɛseɪˈfɛː, *foreign* lɛsefɛːr/ *n.* Also **laisser-**. E19. [Fr., lit. 'allow to do'.] Government abstention from interference in the actions of individuals, esp. in commerce; *gen.* non-interference or indifference.

Atlantic Monthly Frequently characterized as an exacting conductor . . Evans has since become alarmingly laissez-faire. *attrib.*: G. M. TREVELYAN The slum-landlords . . according to the prevalent laissez-faire philosophy, were engaged from motives of self-interest.

laissez-faireism /lɛseɪˈfɛːrɪz(ə)m/ *n.* belief in or practice of laissez-faire M19. **laissez-fair(e)ist** /lɛseɪˈfɛːrɪst/ *n.* a believer in laissez-faire, a practitioner of laissez-faire M20.

laissez-passer /lɛseɪˈpɑːseɪ, *foreign* lɛsepɑse/ *n.* (*pl. same*) *n.* Also **laisser-**. E20. [Fr., lit 'allow to pass'.] A permit to travel or to enter a particular place, a pass.

Times He has been granted . . a laissez-passer to the Greek military zone. Y. MENUHIN Music has been my laissez-passer to foreign lands.

lait *n.* var. of LATE *n.*[1]

lait /leɪt/ *v. obs.* exc. *dial.* ME. [ON *leita*.] **1** *v.t.* Look or search for; seek, try to find. ME. **2** *v.i.* Look, search. Also, hesitate in speech. ME.

laitance /ˈleɪt(ə)ns/ *n.* E20. [Fr., f. *lait* milk: see -ANCE.] A milky scum appearing on the surface of freshly laid cement.

laithe *n.* var. of LATHE *n.*[2]

laity /ˈleɪɪti/ *n.* LME. [f. LAY *a.* + -ITY.] **1** The body of people not in ecclesiastical orders as opp. to the clergy; lay people collectively. LME. **2** The condition or state of being a lay person. E17. **3** Those people not following some particular profession or occupation, or not knowledgeable in some particular subject. M19.

1 D. CUPITT Christianity makes a sharper distinction than other faiths between the clergy and the laity. 3 G. B. SHAW All professions are conspiracies against the laity.

lakatoi /ˈlakətɔɪ/ *n.* Pl. same, **-s**. L19. [Papuan.] A vessel made by the Motu of New Guinea by lashing together three or more large dugout canoes and adding a deck and superstructure.

lake /leɪk/ *n.*[1] *obs.* exc. *dial.* [OE *lacu* f. Gmc.] A small stream of running water. Also, a channel for water.

lake /leɪk/ *n.*[2] LOE. [OFr. *lac* f. L *lacus* lake, pool, tank, pit, trough; perh. later assim. to LAKE *n.*[1]] **1** A pond, a pool. Now *US*. LOE. **2** A large body of water entirely surrounded by land; an ornamental stretch of water in a park etc. ME. **b** *transf.* A stored surplus of a liquid commodity. Freq. w. specifying wd, esp. *wine*. Cf. MOUNTAIN 2b. L20. **†3a** A pit; occas., a grave. ME–E16. **b** An underground dungeon; a prison. Only in LME. **†4** [After L *lacus*.] A wine-vat. LME–M17.

2 J. HUXLEY One very severe winter the lake froze right over its eastern end. *fig.*: D. DELILLO A great dark lake of male rage. *go* (*and*) *jump in the lake*: see JUMP *v. Great Lakes*: see GREAT *a. jump in the lake*: see JUMP *v. lady of the lake*: see LADY *n.* & *a.* **the Lakes** = *Lake District* below.

Comb.: **lake-basin** (*a*) a depression which contains, or has contained, a lake; (*b*) the area drained by all the streams entering a lake; **Lake Country** = *Lake District* below; **lake-crater** a crater which contains or has contained a lake; **Lake District** *spec.* the region round the lakes in Cumbria in NW England; **lake-dweller** a prehistoric inhabitant of a lake-dwelling; **lake-dwelling** a prehistoric hut built upon piles driven into the bed or shoe of a lake; *lake* HERRING; **Lake poetry**: written by the Lake poets; **Lake poets** the poets Coleridge, Southey, and Wordsworth, who lived in the Lake District; **lake salmon** = *lake trout* (b) below; **Lake school** the Lake poets; **lake settlement** a prehistoric settlement with lake-dwellings; **lakeside** *attrib. a.* beside a lake; **lake trout** (*a*) a large, pale, partly migrating form of the trout, *Salmo trutta*, occurring in N. European lakes; (*b*) the salmonid *Salvelinus namaycush*, occurring in N. American lakes; **lake village** a prehistoric village made up of lake dwellings; **lake-weed** water-pepper, *Persicaria hydropiper*.

lakeless *a.* having no lakes L19. **lakelet** *n.* a small lake L18.

lake /leɪk/ *n.*[3] E17. [Var. of LAC *n.*[1]] **1** A purplish-red pigment originally obtained from lac, later from cochineal treated with a metallic compound. Also, the colour of this. E17. **2** Any pigment obtained by the combination of an organic colouring matter with a metallic oxide, hydroxide, or salt; *spec.* the insoluble product of a soluble dye and a mordant. L17.

2 *crimson lake, green lake, Indian lake, madder lake, purple lake*, etc.

lake /leɪk/ *v.*[1]*t.* Now *rare* or *obs.* L19. [f. LAKE *n.*[3]] Make (blood or blood cells) lake-coloured, *spec.* by causing haemolysis.

lake *v.*[2] var. of LAIK.

Lakeland /ˈleɪklənd/ *n.* & *a.* Also **l-**. E19. [f. LAKE *n.*[2] + LAND *n.*[1]] **1** (Of or pertaining to) an area of lakes, *spec.* the English Lake District. E19. **2** In full *Lakeland terrier*. A rough-coated, red or black and tan terrier with a stocky body and a broad muzzle, belonging to a breed developed in Lakeland. E20.

1 J. MUNRO A woman . . whose Lakeland accent was difficult for him to understand. 2 T. HORNER A good Lakeland will hang on to his quarry with tremendous grip.

Lakelander *n.* a native or inhabitant of Lakeland L19.

laker /ˈleɪkə/ *n.* In senses 1, 2 also **L-**. L18. [f. LAKE *n.*[2] + -ER[1].] **†1** A visitor to the English Lake District. L18–E19. **2** A Lake poet. *arch. colloq.* E19. **3** A fish living in or taken from a lake; *spec.* = *lake trout* (b) s.v. LAKE *n.*[2] *N. Amer.* E19. **4** A person accustomed to sailing on a lake. M19. **5** A boat constructed for sailing on the Great Lakes of N. America. L19.

lakh /lak/ *n.* Also **lac**. E17. [Hind. *lākh* f. Skt *lakṣa* mark, token, 100,000.] In the Indian subcontinent: one hundred thousand; occas., an indefinite large number.

J. MASTERS Wouldn't it be wonderful if someone gave us a lakh of rupees. *Times of India* The cyclone has left . . a trail of destruction . . leaving lakhs of people in desolation.

lakin /ˈleɪkɪn/ *n.*[1] *obs.* exc. *dial.* LME. [Perh. f. ON *leika* toy: cf. LAIK.] A plaything, a toy. Formerly also, a baby.

†lakin *n.*[2] *colloq.* L15–E17. [Contr. of LADY *n.* + -KIN. Cf. LADYKIN.] *by (our) lakin*, by Our Lady.

lakish /ˈleɪkɪʃ/ *a.* L16. [f. LAKE *n.*[2] + -ISH[1].] **1** †**a** Having many lakes or pools. Only in L16. †**b** Inhabiting a lake. M–L17. **c** Like a lake. L19. **2** Of or pertaining to the Lake poets; resembling the productions of the Lake poets. E19.

Lakist /ˈleɪkɪst/ *n. arch. colloq.* E19. [f. LAKE *n.*[2] + -IST.] A member or adherent of the Lake school of poetry; a Lake poet.

Lakota /ləˈkəʊtə/ *n.* & *a.* Pl. of n. **-s**, same. M19. [Lakota *lakhóta.*] A member of, of or pertaining to, a Sioux Indian people of western South Dakota; (of) the Sioux dialect of this people. Also called *Teton.*

lakoum *n.* var. of LOKUM.

laksamana /laksəˈmɑːnə/ *n.* E17. [Malay f. Skt *lakṣmana* (a mythical hero, Rama's half-brother) lit. 'having fortunate tokens'.] (The title formerly given to) a high dignitary or admiral in the Malay kingdoms.

lakum *n.* var. of LOKUM.

laky /ˈleɪki/ *a.* M19. [f. LAKE *n.*[3] + -Y[1].] Of the colour of lake, purplish-red.

la-la /lɑːˈlɑː, ˈlɑːlɑː/ *a.* Now *rare* or *obs.* L18. [f. *la la* redupl. of LA *int.*] So so, not very good, poor.

la-la /lɑːˈlɑː, ˈlɑːlɑː/ *v.* E20. [f. as prec.] **1** *v.i.* Sing or say the syllable *la* repeatedly, esp. in place of the words or notes of a tune. E20. **2** *v.t.* Sing (a song) in this way. E20.

lalang /ˈlɑːlaŋ/ *n.* Also **-ll-**. L18. [Malay.] A large coarse grass, *Imperata cylindrica*, which overruns pastures and forest clearings in Old World tropics.

lalapaloosa, -za *ns.* vars. of LALLAPALOOSA.

-lalia /ˈleɪlɪə/ *suff.* [Repr. Gk *lalia* speech, chatter.] Used in forming words denoting various disorders or unusual faculties of speech, as in *dyslalia*, *echolalia*, *glossolalia*, *idiolalia*, etc.

Lalique /laˈliːk/ *n.* & *a.* E20. [See below.] (Designating) jewellery or decorative glassware made by or in the style of the French designer René Lalique (1860–1945).

lall /lal/ *v.i. rare.* L19. [Imit., after L *lallare*: see LALLATION.] Speak childishly or unintelligibly, utter meaningless sounds. See also LALLING.

Lallan /ˈlalən/ *a.* & *n. Sc.* As n. now usu. **Lallans** /ˈlalənz/. E18. [Repr. a pronunc. of LOWLAND.] **A** *adj.* Of or pertaining to the Scottish Lowlands. E18. **B** *n.* The Lowland Scots dialect; now *esp.* a revived and modified form of the spoken dialect as a literary language. L18.

lallang *n.* var. of LALANG.

Lallans *n.* see LALLAN.

lallapaloosa /laləpəˈluːsə, -zə/ *n. US slang.* Also **lala-, lolla-** /lɒlə-/, **-za** /-zə/, **-zer** /-zə/, & other vars. L19. [Fanciful.] Something outstandingly good of its kind; an excellent or attractive person or thing.

S. J. PERELMAN All agreed that Luba Pneumatic was a lollapaloosa, the Eighth Wonder of the World. *New Yorker* Palms, marble statues, and indoor fountains galore—a lalapalooza.

lallation /laˈleɪʃ(ə)n/ *n.* M17. [L *lallatio(n-)*, f. *lallat-* pa. ppl stem of *lallare* sing lullaby: see -ATION.] **1** Infantile or imperfect speech, *esp.* the repetition of meaningless sounds by babies; idioglossia. M17. **2** Pronunciation of what should be the phoneme /r/ (*r*) as if /l/ (*l*). Also called *lambdacism.* M19.

lalling /ˈlalɪŋ/ *n. rare.* L19. [f. (as) LALL *v.* + -ING[1].] = LALLATION.

lallygag /ˈlalɪgag/ *n.* & *v. N. Amer. slang.* Also **lolly-** /ˈlɒlɪ-/. M19. [Origin unkn.] **A** *n.* Foolishness, nonsense. M19.

E. L. WHEELER I kin get lots o' jobs if I'd take my pay in friendship an' all sech lollygag.

B *v.i.* Infl. **-gg-**. Fool around; dawdle; kiss and cuddle amorously, canoodle. M19.

lam /lam/ *n. N. Amer. slang.* L19. [f. the vb.] Escape, flight. Chiefly as below.

on the lam on the run. **take it on the** (or **a**) **lam** run away, escape.

lam /lam/ *v.* Infl. **-mm-**. L16. [Perh. of Scand. origin: cf. Norw., Da. *lamme* lame, paralyse.] **1** *v.t.* Beat soundly, thrash, strike. Now *colloq.* L16. **2** *v.i.* Strike, attack with blows etc., (foll. by *into* a person); hit *out. colloq.* L19. **3** *v.i.* Run off, escape. *slang* (chiefly *US*). L19.

1 D. L. SAYERS If you're thinkin' of . . lammin' a millionaire on the head, don't do it. **2** CONAN DOYLE Lam out with your whip as hard as you can lick. R. H. MORRIESON Once Pop really lammed into her, gave her one helluva hiding.

lamming *n.* (*a*) the action of the vb; (*b*) a beating, a thrashing: E17. **lamster** *n.* (*slang*, chiefly *US*) a fugitive, a person on the run E20.

lama /ˈlɑːmə/ *n.* M17. [Tib. *bla-ma* (the *b* is silent).] A Buddhist religious teacher of Tibet or Mongolia.

DALAI LAMA. *grand lama*: see GRAND *a.*[1] PANCHEN *Lama.* TASHI LAMA.

lamaic *a.* pertaining to or characteristic of lamas E19. **lamaism** *n.* the system of doctrine and observances inculcated and maintained by lamas E19. **lamaist** *n.* & *a.* (*a*) *n.* a person who professes lamaism; (*b*) *adj.* of or pertaining to lamaists or lamaism: E19. **lamanism** *n.* = LAMAISM M18. **lamasery** *n.* a monastery of lamas M19.

lamantin /ləˈmantɪn/ *n.* M17. [Fr.] The manatee.

Lamarckian /ləˈmɑːkɪən/ *a.* & *n.* E19. [f. *Lamarck* (see below) + -IAN.] **A** *adj.* Of or pertaining to the French naturalist Jean Baptiste Lamarck (1744–1829) or his theory of organic evolution, which he ascribed to heritable modifications produced in the individual by habit, instinctive propensity, and the direct action of the environment. E19. **B** *n.* A person who holds Lamarckian views. M19.

Lamarckianism *n.* = LAMARCKISM L19. **Lamarckism** *n.* the theory of the origin of species proposed by Lamarck L19.

lamb /lam/ *n.* [OE *lamb* = OFris., OS, OHG *lamb* (Du. *lam*, G *Lamm*), ON, Goth. *lamb* (in Goth. 'sheep'), f. Gmc.] **1** A young sheep. OE. **2** *fig.* **a** A young member of a flock, esp. of the Church. *arch.* OE. **b** A person who is as meek, gentle, innocent, or weak as a lamb. Also used as a term of endearment. OE. **c** A simpleton; a person who is cheated; *esp.* a person who loses money in speculation. LME. **3** Lambskin. LME. **4** The flesh of a lamb used as food. LME.

1 MILTON Ewes and their bleating Lambs. *Proverb*: One might as well be hanged for a sheep as a lamb. **2a** J. WESLEY One who was as hot as any of the lambs at the tabernacle; but she is now a calm, reasonable woman. **b** G. PUTTENHAM It is comely for a man to be a lambe in the house, and a Lyon in the field. P. BOWLES But my dear lamb, whatever are you going to *do* all day? **c** W. GLADDEN The 'lambs' are shorn in this . . stock market alone at eight hundred million dollars a year. **4** J. MASTERS The smell of roasting lamb was all over the place.

Phrases: *as meek as a lamb*: see MEEK *a.* 1b. *beaver lamb*: see BEAVER *n.*[1] **Holy Lamb** Jesus Christ; *Her.* = AGNUS DEI 2. *Immaculate Lamb*: see IMMACULATE *a.* **like a lamb** gently, compliantly. MUTTON *dressed as lamb. paschal lamb*: see PASCHAL *a. Persian lamb*: see PERSIAN *a.* SHORN *lamb.* **the Lamb (of God)** Jesus Christ. *twin lamb disease*: see TWIN *a.* & *n.*

Comb.: **lamb-creep** a hole in a hedge or hurdle just large enough for lambs to get in and out of the fold; **lamb fries** *US* lamb's testicles as food; **lambkill** *N. Amer.* the sheep laurel, *Kalmia angustifolia*; **lamb-pie** (*a*) a pie containing lamb; (*b*) (*obs.* exc. *dial.*) a beating, a thrashing; *eat lamb-pie*, be beaten; **lamb's ears** a labiate garden plant, *Stachys byzantina*, with purple flowers and whitish woolly leaves; **lamb's fry** (*a*) lamb's offal, esp. testicles; (*b*) *Austral.* & *NZ* lamb's liver as food; **lamb's lettuce** the common corn-salad vegetable, *Valerianella locusta*; **lamb's quarter**(s) the weed fat-hen, *Chenopodium album*; **lamb's tails** hazel catkins; **lamb's tongue** the hoary plantain, *Plantago media*, a common plant of chalk grassland; *lamb succory*: see SUCCORY 2; *lamb-suckle*: see SUCKLE *n.*[1] 1.

lambie *n.* a little lamb (used as a term of endearment, esp. for a child) M17. **lambkin** *n.* (*a*) a young or small lamb; (*b*) (a term of endearment for) a young vulnerable person: ME. **lamblike** *a.* resembling a lamb; gentle, meek: L16. **lambling** *n.* a small or young lamb L16.

lamb /lam/ *v.* L16. [f. the n.] **1** *v.i.* Give birth to a lamb. L16. **2** *v.t.* In *pass.* Of a lamb: be born. M17. **3** *v.t.* Of a shepherd: tend (ewes) at lambing-time. Also foll. by *down.* M19. **4** *v.t.* Foll. by *down*: induce or encourage (a person) to spend money recklessly; spend (money), esp. recklessly. *Austral.* M19.

1 *lambing season, time*, etc.

lamba /ˈlambə/ *n.*[1] E18. [Malagasy *làmba.*] A large piece of cloth worn as a cloak by Madagascans.

Lamba /ˈlambə/ *n.*[2] & *a.* Also **Ilamba** /ɪˈlambə/. E20. [Bantu.] **A** *n.* Pl. same, **-s**. A member of a Bantu-speaking people of northern Zambia and Zaire; the language of this people. E20. **B** *attrib.* or as *adj.* Of or pertaining to the Lamba or their language. E20.

lambardar /lambəˈdɑː, lʌm-/ *n.* Also ***lum-*** /lʌm-/. M19. [Urdu *lambardār*, f. *lambar* rank (f. Eng. NUMBER *n.*) + Pers. *-dār* having, holder.] An official headman and tax-gatherer of a village in the Indian subcontinent.

lambaste /lamˈbeɪst/ *v.t.* Also **-bast**. M17. [f. LAM *v.* + BASTE *v.*[3]] **1** Beat, thrash. M17. **2** *fig.* Scold, castigate; criticize severely. L19.

2 A. TOFFLER Intellectuals . . have lambasted television, in particular, for standardizing speech, habits, and tastes. B. NEIL Lambasting me with some choice Italian words.

lambda /ˈlamdə/ *n.* E17. [Gk.] **I 1** The eleventh letter (Λ, λ) of the Greek alphabet. E17. **II 2** *Chem.* A millionth of a litre. Usu. written λ. M20. **3** *Nuclear Physics.* More fully *lambda particle.* A neutral hyperon (or its antiparticle) which has a mass 2183 times that of the electron, a spin of ½, and zero isospin, and on decaying usually produces a nucleon and a pion; orig. also, any of several similar charged hyperons. Freq. written Λ. M20. **4** *Microbiol.* A bacteriophage originally isolated from *Escherichia coli*, used in genetic research. Freq. written λ. M20.

Comb.: **lambda point** *Physics* (*a*) the temperature (approximately 2.18K) below which liquid helium in equilibrium with its vapour is superfluid, and at which there is a sharp maximum in its specific heat; (*b*) any temperature at which the specific heat of a substance exhibits similar behaviour (freq. written as *λ point.*).

lambdacism /ˈlamdəsɪz(ə)m/ *n.* Also **†labd-**. M17. [Late L *la(m)bdacismus* f. Gk *la(m)bdakismos*, f. *la(m)bda* (see prec.) + *-ismos* -ISM w. hiatus-filling *k.*] **1** Too frequent repetition of the phoneme /l/ or letter *l* in speaking or writing. M17. **2** Pronunciation of what should be the phoneme /r/ (*r*) as if /l/ (*l*). Also called *lallation.* M19.

lambdoid /ˈlamdɔɪd/ *a.* L16. [f. LAMBDA + -OID.] **1** *Anat.* = LAMBDOIDAL. L16. **2** *Microbiol.* Relating to or mutated from bacteriophage lambda. M20.

lambdoidal /lamˈdɔɪd(ə)l/ *a.* M17. [f. as prec. + -AL[1].] Resembling the Greek letter lambda (Λ) in form; *spec.* in *Anat.*, designating or pertaining to the suture connecting the two parietal bones with the occipital.

lambeau /lɑ̃bo/ *n.* Pl. ***-eaux*** /-o/. M16. [Fr.: see LABEL *n.*] A strip or fillet hanging from a head-dress or garment. In *Her.*, each of the dependent points of a label; (occas.) a label.

Lambeg /ˈlambɛg/ *n.* M20. [A village near Belfast, N. Ireland.] In full *Lambeg drum.* A large drum of a type traditionally beaten by Orangemen on ceremonial occasions.

Lambegger *n.* a person who beats such a drum M20.

lambent /ˈlambənt/ *a.* M17. [L *lambent-* pres. ppl stem of *lambere* lick: see -ENT.] **1** Of a flame or light: playing lightly upon a surface without burning it; shining with a soft clear light and without fierce heat. M17. **b** Of eyes, the sky, etc.: softly radiant. E18. **c** *fig.* Of wit, style, etc.: lightly brilliant. L19. **2** Licking, that licks. Now *rare.* E18.

1 THACKERAY The lambent lights of the starry host of heaven. B. T. BRADFORD A log spurted and flared . . , the lambent flames illuminating the shadowed face. b E. FIGES The garden was . . lambent with green and gold. M. M. R. KHAN Her mellow soulful lambent gaze masks a determined vengeful hating. c J. MORLEY A humour now and then a little sardonic, but more often genial and lambent.

lambency *n.* the state or quality of being lambent; an instance or occurrence of this: E19. **lambently** *adv.* E19.

†lamber *n.*[1] & *a.* Chiefly *north.* LME–E19. [Fr. *l'ambre* the amber.] (Made of, or of the colour of) amber.

lamber /ˈlamə/ *n.*[2] E19. [f. LAMB *v.* + -ER[1].] A person who looks after ewes when lambing.

Lambert /ˈlambət/ *n.* In sense 3 **l-**. L19. [Johann Heinrich *Lambert* (1728–77), Ger. mathematician.] **1** *Cartography.* Used *attrib.* or in *possess.* to designate certain map projections devised by Lambert, *spec.* a conical conformal projection having two standard parallels along which the scale is true. L19. **2** Physics. *Lambert's law*: (*a*) that the intensity of the light emitted by an element of area of a perfectly diffusing surface is proportional to the cosine of the angle between the direction of emission and the normal to the surface; (*b*) that layers of equal thickness absorb an equal fraction of the light traversing them. L19. **3** (**l-**.) A unit of luminance equal to one lumen per square centimetre (equivalent to approximately 3180 candelas per square metre). E20.

Lambeth /ˈlambəθ/ *n.* & *a.* M19. [A South London borough.] **I 1** Designating events etc. associated with the palace of the Archbishop of Canterbury in Lambeth, the Archbishop of Canterbury himself, or the Church of England generally. M19.

1 **Lambeth Conference** an assembly of the Anglican bishops, usu. held decennially at Lambeth Palace. **Lambeth degree** a degree *honoris causa* conferred by the Archbishop of Canterbury. *Lambeth Quadrilateral*: see QUADRILATERAL 3.

II 2 (Designating) a kind of glazed and painted earthenware manufactured in Lambeth from the 17th to the 19th cent. L19. **3** *Lambeth Walk* [a street in Lambeth], a social dance with a walking step, popular in the late 1930s (following its creation for the revue *Me and my Girl*). M20.

Lambic /lɑ̃bik/ *n.* L19. [Fr.: cf. *alambic* a still.] A strong draught beer brewed in Belgium.

†lambitive *a.* & *n.* M17–E18. [f. L *lambit-* pa. ppl stem of *lambere* lick + -IVE.] (A medicine) taken by licking up with the tongue.

lamboys /ˈlambɔɪz/ *n.* M16. [Perh. f. LAMBEAU.] In Tudor armour: a series of metal plates resembling a skirt or skirts.

lambrequin /ˈlambrɪkɪn/ *n.* E18. [Fr., f. Du. dim. of *lamper* veil: see -KIN.] **1** A piece of material worn over a helmet as a covering, in *Her.* represented with one end (which is cut or jagged) pendent or floating. E18. **2** A cornice with a valance of pendent labels or pointed pieces, placed over a door or window; a short curtain or piece of drapery (with the lower edge either scalloped or straight) suspended for ornament from a mantelshelf. *US.* L19. **3** *Ceramics.* Ornamentation consisting of solid colour with a lower edge of jagged or scalloped outline. L19.

Lamb shift /ˈlam ʃɪft/ *n. phr.* M20. [Willis E. *Lamb* (b. 1913), US physicist.] *Physics.* A displacement of energy levels in hydrogen and hydrogen-like atoms such that those differentiated only by different values of orbital angular momentum are not coincident, as predicted by Dirac's theory, but separated by a very small amount.

lambskin /ˈlamskɪn/ *n.* & *a.* LME. [f. LAMB *n.* + SKIN *n.*] **A** *n.* **1 a** The skin or hide of a lamb with the wool on; this dressed and used for clothing etc. LME. **b** Leather prepared from the skin of a lamb. M18. **†2** A heavy blow. L16–E17.

Comb.: **†lambskinman** *slang* a magistrate, a judge.

B *attrib.* or as *adj.* Made of lambskin. LME.

lambswool /ˈlamzwʊl/ *n.* & *a.* Also **lamb's-wool**. M16. [f. LAMB *n.* + -'S[1] + WOOL *n.*] **A** *n.* **1** Soft fine wool from a lamb used for knitted garments or hosiery; clothing-material made of this. M16. **2** A drink consisting of hot ale mixed with the pulp of roasted apples, sweetened and spiced. L16. **B** *adj.* Made of lambswool. M19.

lamburger /ˈlambəːɡə/ *n.* M20. [f. LAMB *n.* + BURGER.] A hamburger made from minced lamb.

lamdan /ˈlʌmdən/ *n.* E20. [Heb. *lamdān* lit. 'a person who has learned', f. *lāmad* learn.] A person learned in Jewish law; a Talmudic scholar.

lame /leɪm/ *n.*[1] ME. [f. the adj.] **†1** Lameness; infirmity. ME–E16. **2** An outsider; a person unskilled in the behaviour patterns of a particular group. *US slang.* M20.

2 J. WAMBAUGH They're a couple of lames trying to groove with the Kids.

lame /leɪm/ *n.*[2] *obs.* exc. *Hist.* L16. [(O)Fr. f. L *lam(m)ina, lamna.* Cf. LAMIN, LAMINA.] A thin plate, esp. of metal; a thin piece of any substance, a lamina; *spec.* any of the small overlapping steel plates used in old armour.

F. WILKINSON Gauntlets were produced with extra lames, or plates, to give additional flexibility . . to the hand.

lame /leɪm/ *a.* [OE *lama* = OFris. *lam, lom,* OS *lamo* (Du. *lam*), OHG *lam* (G *lahm*), ON *lami,* f. Gmc adj. meaning 'weak in the limbs', rel. to OHG *luomi* dull, slack, gentle.] **1** Crippled, disabled; weak, infirm. Foll. by *on, of* the affected part. *arch.* OE. **b** Imperfect, defective, unsatisfactory, (foll. by *of, in* the defective part). Now chiefly of an excuse, narrative, etc.: weak, unconvincing. LME. **c** Of a person: unskilled in the fashionable behaviour of a particular group; socially inept. *US slang.* M20. **2** *spec.* Crippled through injury to, or defect in, a limb. Now only, disabled in the foot or leg, so as to walk awkwardly and with difficulty. Also foll. by *in, †of, †on, †with* the affected part. OE. **b** Of a limb (now only of the leg or foot): functioning imperfectly or painfully. ME. **c** Of footsteps: halting. Also *fig.* (of metrical feet or verses): metrically defective. LME.

1 E. GRIMSTONE A Germaine . . who was lame of halfe his body, and simple. b SHAKES. *Oth.* Being not deficient, blind, or lame of sense. *TV Guide (Canada)* It suffers from weak jokes, lame characters and—understandably—canned laughter. c *Time* Anyone who does not know that is obviously lame . . . or perhaps just over 25. 2 D. CAUTE Rodney says Thumper is lame in his right foreleg. *absol.*: AV *Job* 29:15 I was eyes to the blind, and feet was I to the lame. b S. JOHNSON Her present qualifications for the niceties of needlework being dim eyes and lame fingers.

Special collocations & comb.: **lame-brain** *colloq.* a dull-witted or stupid person. **lame-brained** *a.* dull-witted, stupid. *lame duck*: see DUCK *n.*[1]

lamely *adv.* L16. **lameness** *n.* M16.

lame /leɪm/ *v.t.* ME. [f. LAME *a.*: earliest as pa. pple after ON *lamiðr.*] Make lame; cripple, disable.

lamé /ˈlɑːmeɪ/ *n.* & *a.* E20. [Fr., f. as LAME *n.*[2]] (Made of) a brocaded fabric consisting of silk or other yarns interwoven with metallic threads.

lamel /ˈlam(ə)l/ *n.* Now *rare* or *obs.* L17. [Anglicized f. next.] = next.

lamella /ləˈmɛlə/ *n.* Pl. **-llae** /-liː/, **-llas**. L17. [L, dim. of *lam(m)ina*: see LAME *n.*[2]] A thin plate, scale, layer, or film; any of the individual layers in a lamellar structure, as in some bones, shells, metals, rocks, etc.; *spec.* (*a*) any of the radiating gills of an agaric; (*b*) *Zool.* any of the sheets of tissue in the gill of an animal; (*c*) *Bot.* any of the photosynthetic membranes in a chloroplast; (*d*) *Ornith.* any of the fine plates in the bill of a lamellirostral bird.

middle lamella: see MIDDLE *a.*

lamellate /ˈlam(ə)lət/ *a.* (*a*) lamellated; (*b*) *Entomol.* (of an antenna) lamellicorn: E19. **lamellated** /ˈlam(ə)leɪtɪd/ *a.* arranged in or having layers or thin sheets E18.

lamellar /ləˈmɛlə/ *a.* L18. [f. prec. + -AR[1].] **1** Consisting of, characterized by, or arranged in lamellae or thin plates or layers. L18. **2** *Physics.* = LAMINAR 2. M20.

lamellibranch /ləˈmɛlɪbraŋk/ *n.* & *a.* M19. [f. mod.L *Lamellibranchia* (see below), f. L LAMELLA + -I- + Gk *bragkhia* gills.] *Zool.* **A** *n.* A bivalve mollusc (class Bivalvia, formerly Lamellibranchia); *spec.* any of those with lamellated gills, which comprise the subclass Lamellibranchia. M19. **B** *adj.* Pertaining to or of the nature of a lamellibranch. M19.

Also **lamelliˈbranchiate** *a.* & *n.* M19.

lamellicorn /ləˈmɛlɪkɔːn/ *a.* & *n.* M19. [f. mod.L *Lamellicornia* former taxonomic name, f. L LAMELLA + -I- + *cornu* horn.] *Entomol.* **A** *adj.* Of, pertaining to, or designating the beetle superfamily Scarabaeoidea whose members typically have antennae with lamelliform segments and include the dung-beetles, chafers, and stag beetles. M19. **B** *n.* A lamellicorn beetle. M19.

lamelliform /ləˈmɛlɪfɔːm/ *a.* E19. [f. LAMELLA + -I- + -FORM.] Having the form or structure of a lamella or thin plate.

lamellipodium /ləmɛlɪˈpəʊdɪəm/ *n.* Pl. **-dia** /-dɪə/. L20. [f. LAMELLA + -I-, after *pseudopodium.*] *Cytol.* A flattened extension of a cell, used in amoeboid locomotion or in adhesion to the substrate.

lamellirostral /ləmɛlɪˈrɒstr(ə)l/ *a.* M19. [f. LAMELLA + -I- + L *rostrum* beak + -AL[1].] *Ornith.* Of a bird, as a duck, flamingo, etc.: having a beak edged with fine plates for filtering food particles from water.

lamellose /ləˈmɛləʊs/ *a.* M18. [f. LAMELLA + -OSE[1].] = LAMELLAR *a.* 1.

lament /ləˈmɛnt/ *n.* M16. [L *lamenta* (pl.) wailing, weeping, groans, laments, or f. the vb.] **1** An (esp. passionate) expression of sorrow or anguish. Also *poet.* lamentation. M16. **2** A poem or song of grief, an elegy; *esp.* a dirge performed at a death or funeral. L17.

1 MILTON A voice of weeping heard, and loud lament. H. SPURLING The book is full of laments for the damage done by 'telephones and newspapers and bicycles'. 2 D. STEWART Solemn and melancholy airs or Laments as they call them.

lament /ləˈmɛnt/ *v.* LME. [Fr. *lamenter* or L *lamentari,* f. *lamenta*: see prec.] **1** *v.t.* Express or (now) feel profound sorrow for or concerning; mourn the loss of; bewail. LME. **b** *refl.* Feel sorry for oneself; bemoan one's fate. *arch.* M18. **2** *v.i.* Express (or feel) profound grief; mourn passionately. Foll. by *for, over,* (rarely) *after.* LME. **†3** *v.t.* Cause grief to, distress. L16–E18.

1 F. RAPHAEL He lamented—and sought to alleviate, . . the fate of his servants. P. FERGUSON 'Cissie had hardly a civil word to say to me,' lamented Jessie. B. GILROY The house was full of people . . lamenting her passing. b A. B. JAMESON He began to lament himself because of the robbery. 2 R. KNOLLES Greatly lamented for by all the Christians in Syria. M. SPARK She was crying and lamenting so much that any form of rational inquiry was useless.

lamenter *n.* L16. **lamentingly** *adv.* in a passionately mournful manner, so as to express profound grief E17.

lamentable /ˈlaməntəb(ə)l/ *a.* LME. [(O)Fr., or L *lamentabilis,* f. *lamentari*: see prec., -ABLE.] **1** Full of or expressing sorrow or grief; mournful, doleful. Now *arch. rare.* LME. **2** That is to be lamented; pitiable, regrettable. LME. **b** Contemptible, deplorable; wretchedly bad. M17.

1 N. HAWTHORNE The lamentable friends, trailing their long black garments. 2 LD MACAULAY Another Macdonald, destined to a lamentable and horrible end. b *Oban Times* A lamentable clutter of buildings . . and brutal modern extensions to pleasant old houses.

lamentableness *n.* L16. **lamentably** *adv.* L15.

lamentation /lamənˈteɪʃ(ə)n/ *n.* LME. [(O)Fr., or L *lamentatio(n-),* f. *lamentat-* pa. ppl stem of *lamentari*: see LAMENT *v.*, -ATION.] **1** The action of lamenting; bewailing, mourning; (in weakened sense) regret. LME. **2** An instance of this; a lament. LME.

1 SHELLEY There shall be lamentation heard in Heaven As o'er an angel fallen. J. MCCOSH Another subject of general lamentation is the evil produced by party spirit. 2 W. IRVING The lamentations of women who had lost some relative in the foray. **Lamentations (of Jeremiah)** (the name of) a book

of the Old Testament and Hebrew Scriptures, traditionally ascribed to the prophet Jeremiah, which laments the destruction of Jerusalem by the Chaldeans.

lamented /lə'mɛntɪd/ *a.* E17. [f. LAMENT *v.* + -ED[1].] Mourned for; bewailed; regretted.

the late lamented (a mode of reference to) a person recently dead.

¶ Earlier in UNLAMENTED.

lamento /la'mento/ *n.* Pl. ***-ti*** /-ti/. M20. [It.] *Mus.* An elegiac or mourning song; in Italian opera, a tragic aria.

lamentoso /lamen'to:zo/ *adv.* & *a.* L19. [It.] *Mus.* (A direction:) in a mournful style.

lametta /la'me:ta/ *n.* M19. [It., dim. of *lama* = LAME *n.*[2]] Brass, silver, or gold foil or wire; *spec.* thin strips of metallic foil used as Christmas decorations.

lamia /'leɪmɪə/ *n.* Pl. **-ias, -iae** /-ii:/. LME. [L f. Gk = mythical monster, carnivorous fish.] A mythical monster supposed to have the body of a woman, and to prey on human beings and suck the blood of children. Also, a witch, a she-demon.

lamin /'lamɪn/ *n.* L15. [f. as next. Cf. also LAME *n.*[2]] A lamina; a thin plate or layer of metal etc.; a plate of metal used as an astrological instrument or as a charm.

lamina /'lamɪnə/ *n.* Pl. **-nae** /-ni:/. M17. [L *la(m)mina*. Cf. LAME *n.*[2], prec.] **1** A thin plate or layer of a metal or other material; *Anat.* & *Biol.* a thin layer of bone, membrane, or other tissue. M17. **b** *Bot.* The flat, expanded portion of a leaf, petal, or thallus. Opp. *unguis*. M18. **2** *Geol.* The thinnest separable layer of a sedimentary rock deposit. M19. **3** *Math.* A plane sheet of negligible thickness. M19.

laminable /'lamɪnəb(ə)l/ *a.* L18. [f. LAMINATE *v.* + -ABLE.] Able to be formed into thin plates or layers.

laminability *n.* M19.

laminagraph /'lamɪnəgrɑ:f/ *n.* Also **lamino-**. M20. [f. LAMINA + -GRAPH.] *Med.* = TOMOGRAPH.

lamina'graphic *a.* M20. **laminagram** *n.* = TOMOGRAM M20. **lami'nagraphy** *n.* M20.

laminal /'lamɪn(ə)l/ *a.* E19. [f. LAMINA + -AL[1].] **1** = LAMINAR I. *rare.* E19. **2** *Phonet.* Produced by the blade of the tongue. M20.

laminar /'lamɪnə/ *a.* E19. [f. LAMINA + -AR[1].] **1** Consisting of or arranged in laminae. E19. **2** *Physics.* Of the flow of a fluid: smooth and regular, not turbulent, the direction of motion at any point remaining constant as if the fluid were moving in a series of layers of different velocity sliding over one another without mixing. L19. **b** Of a body: having a shape that tends to produce laminar flow in the adjacent fluid. M20.

laminaran /'lamɪnəran/ *n.* M20. [f. as next + -AN.] *Biochem.* A polysaccharide which occurs in laminaria and other brown algae.

laminaria /lamɪ'nɛ:rɪə/ *n.* M19. [mod.L (see below), f. L *lam(m)ina* LAMINA + *-aria* -ARY[1].] Any brown seaweed of the genus *Laminaria*, with long thin flat fronds; *collect.* seaweed of this genus. Also called *oarweed, kelp*.

laminarian *a.* of or pertaining to laminaria; *spec.* designating the littoral zone, extending from low-water mark to a depth of about 27.5 m. or 90 ft, in which laminaria grows: M19.

laminarin /'lamɪnərɪn/ *n.* M20. [f. as prec. + -IN[1].] *Biochem.* = LAMINARAN.

laminarize /'lamɪnərʌɪz/ *v.t.* Also **-ise**. M20. [f. LAMINAR + -IZE.] *Aeronaut.* Design so as to maximize the surface area over which the flow in the boundary layer is laminar.

laminari'zation *n.* M20.

laminary /'lamɪn(ə)ri/ *a.* M19. [f. LAMINA + -ARY[1].] = LAMINAR *a.* I.

laminate /'lamɪnət/ *a.* & *n.* M17. [f. LAMINA + -ATE[2].] **A** *adj.* Having the form of or consisting of a lamina; provided with a lamina or laminae. M17.

B *n.* A manufactured laminated structure or material; *esp.* a (rigid or flexible) material made by bonding a number of different layers together, as laminated plastic. M20.

Scientific American Metal laminates . . are constructed . . of . . layers. K. WATERHOUSE He . . makes for the buffet car, already, in his head, tapping coins on laminate.

laminate /'lamɪneɪt/ *v.* M17. [f. LAMINA + -ATE[3].] **1** *v.t.* Beat or roll (metal) into thin plates. M17. **2** *v.t.* & *i.* Separate or split into layers. M17. **3** *v.t.* Cover or coat with laminae or a laminate. L17. **4** *v.t.* Make by bonding layers of material together; unite into a laminate. M19.

laminator *n.* a machine, person, or organization that makes (plastic) laminates M20.

laminated /'lamɪneɪtɪd/ *a.* M17. [f. LAMINATE *v.* + -ED[1].] Consisting of, arranged in, or provided with laminae or a laminate; formed or manufactured in a succession of layers; *spec.* (of a worktop etc.) coated with a protective laminate.

F. RAPHAEL An orange coffee-machine hissed on the laminated work-surface. *Which?* Laminated glass consists of two sheets of . . glass with tough plastic interleaved between them. **laminated plastic** material made by bonding together layers of cloth, paper, etc., that have been impregnated or coated with a synthetic resin.

lamination /lamɪ'neɪʃ(ə)n/ *n.* L17. [f. as prec.: see -ATION.] **1** The action or process of laminating something; the manufacture of laminates. L17. **2** The condition of being laminated or layered; laminated structure. M18. **3** A layer of a laminated material or object. M19.

laminboard /'lamɪnbɔ:d/ *n.* E20. [f. LAMIN(ATED + BOARD *n.*] (A) composite board consisting of numerous thin strips of wood glued face to face between two facing sheets of wood or laminated plastic.

laminectomy /lamɪ'nɛktəmi/ *n.* L19. [f. LAMINA + -ECTOMY.] Surgical removal of one or more of the posterior arches of the vertebrae (each arch being formed by the junction of two laminae), esp. as a method of access to the spinal canal; an instance of this.

lamington /'lamɪŋtən/ *n.* *Austral.* & *NZ.* E20. [App. f. Lord *Lamington*, Governor of Queensland, Australia, 1895–1901.] A square of sponge cake dipped in melted chocolate and grated coconut.

laminitis /lamɪ'nʌɪtɪs/ *n.* M19. [f. LAMINA + -ITIS.] *Vet. Med.* Inflammation of the laminae of a horse's hoof.

lamino- /'lamɪnəʊ/ *comb. form.* M20. [f. LAMIN(AL + -O-.] *Phonet.* Forming adjs. and corresp. ns. denoting sounds produced with the blade of the tongue and some other point of articulation, as *lamino-dental, lamino-palatal*, adjs.

laminose /'lamɪnəʊs/ *a.* E19. [f. LAMINA + -OSE[1].] Consisting of or having the form of laminae.

laminous /'lamɪnəs/ *a.* L17. [f. LAMINA + -OUS.] = prec.

lamish /'leɪmɪʃ/ *a.* L16. [f. LAME *a.* + -ISH[1].] Somewhat lame.

lamium /'leɪmɪəm/ *n.* L17. [mod.L (see below) f. L f. Gk *lamia* gaping mouth (w. ref. to the shape of the flowers).] Any plant of the labiate genus *Lamium*, which includes several kinds of dead-nettle.

Lammas /'laməs/ *n.* [OE *hlāfmæsse*, f. *hlāf* LOAF *n.*[1] + *mæsse* MASS *n.*[1]; later interpreted as f. LAMB *n.* + MASS *n.*[1]] I August, *spec.* as (*a*) celebrated in the early English Church as a harvest festival, at which loaves of bread made from the first ripe corn were consecrated, (*b*) observed in Scotland as one of the quarter days; also *Lammas day*. Also (*arch.*), the part of the year in which Lammas occurs.

latter Lammas: see LATTER *a.*

Comb.: *Lammas day*: see above; **Lammas growth** *Forestry* a shoot produced by a tree in summer, after a pause in growth; **Lammas-land** *Hist.* private land available for common use after Lammas until the following spring; **Lammas shoot** = *Lammas growth* above; **Lammas wheat** winter wheat.

lammergeyer /'laməgʌɪə/ *n.* Also **-geier**. E19. [G *Lämmergeier*, f. *Lämmer* pl. of *Lamm* lamb + *Geier* vulture.] A long-winged, long-tailed vulture, *Gypaetus barbatus*, inhabiting lofty mountains in southern Europe, Asia, and Africa. Also called *bearded vulture*.

lammervanger /'laməvaŋə, -faŋə/ *n.* *S. Afr.* M19. [Afk., f. *lam* lamb + *vanger* catcher.] An eagle, esp. one believed to prey on lambs. Also, = prec.

lammie /'lami/ *n.* Also **lammy**. L19. [Perh. f. LAMB *n.* + -IE, w. allus. to the wool used in making the garment.] A thick quilted woollen overgarment worn by sailors in cold weather. Also more fully *lammie coat, suit*.

Lamout *n.* & *a.* var. of LAMUT.

lamp /lamp/ *n.* ME. [(O)Fr. *lampe* f. late L *lampada* f. accus. of L *lampas* f. Gk *lampas*, *lampad-* torch, rel. to *lampein* to shine.] **1** Orig., a vessel in which oil is burnt at a wick to provide illumination. Now *gen.*, (a device, often consisting of a holder and shade, designed to hold or enclose) a source of artificial illumination, as a candle, a gas-jet, or (usu.) an electric bulb. Also, a device producing infrared, ultraviolet, or other radiation, esp. for therapeutic purposes. ME. **b** A torch. LME. **2** A celestial object producing or reflecting light, *esp.* the sun or the moon. *poet.* LME. **b** In *pl.* The eyes. Formerly *poet.*, now *slang.* L16. **3** A source or centre of spiritual or intellectual light. E16.

1 *Argand lamp, astral lamp, bicycle lamp, desk lamp, flash-lamp, headlamp, indicator lamp, mercury lamp, standard lamp, table lamp*, etc. *the lady with* or *of the lamp*: see LADY *n.* & *a.* *Slave of the Lamp*: see SLAVE *n.*[1] I. *smell of the lamp*: see SMELL *v.* 8a.

Comb.: **lampblack** *n.* & *v.* (*a*) *n.* a pigment consisting of finely divided, almost pure carbon, obtained by collecting the soot produced by burning oil or gas; (*b*) *v.t.* paint, smear, or coat with lampblack; **lampbrush** *attrib. a.* (*Cytol.*) (of a chromosome) having numerous paired lateral loops of DNA, which give the whole chromosome the appearance of a bottle-brush; *lamp-chimney*: see CHIMNEY *n.* 6; **lamp-holder** a device for supporting or securing a lamp, esp. an electric one; **lamp-house** the part of a photographic enlarger or projector which houses the light-source; **lamplit** *a.* lit by a lamp or lamps; **lamp oil** (*a*) oil for burning in a lamp; (*b*) nocturnal study or work; **lamppost** a tall post supporting a street lamp (*between you and me and the lamppost*: see BETWEEN *prep.*); **lamp-shell** a brachiopod; **lamp-socket** = *lamp-holder* above; **lamp standard** a post or other strong support for a lamp; a lamppost.

lampful *a.* (*poet.*) (of the sky) starry L16. **lampist** *n.* a person skilled or employed in making or maintaining lamps M19. **lampless** *a.* E17. **lamplet** *n.* a small lamp E17.

lamp /lamp/ *v.*[1] L16. [f. the n.] **1** *v.t.* Provide with a lamp or lamps. L16. **2** *v.i.* Shine. E17. **3** *v.t.* Light as with a lamp. E19. **4** *v.t.* See, look at, recognize, watch. *slang.* Orig. *US.* L19.

lamp /lamp/ *v.*[2]*i.* *Sc.* E17. [Origin unkn.] Move quickly with long steps.

lampadedromy /lampə'dɛdrəmi/ *n.* M19. [Gk *lampadēdromia*, f. *lampad-*, *lampas* torch + *-dromia* running.] *Gk Hist.* A torch-race.

lampadephoria /,lampədə'fɔ:rɪə/ *n.* Also **-do-**. M19. [Gk *lampadēphoria, -do-*, f. *lampad-*, *lampas* torch + *phor-* stem of *pherein* bear, carry: see -IA[1].] *Gk Hist.* = prec.

lampadite /'lampədʌɪt/ *n.* M19. [f. W. A. *Lampadius* (1772–1842), Ger. chemist + -ITE[1].] *Min.* A cupriferous variety of wad.

lampadomancy /'lampədəmansi/ *n.* M17. [f. Gk *lampad-*, *lampas* torch + -O- + -MANCY.] Divination by the observation of lamps or candles.

lampas /'lampəs/ *n.*[1] LME. [In sense I prob. f. Du. †*lampers* (now *lamfer*); in sense 2 f. Fr. *lampas, -asse*, which may be a different wd.] †**1** A kind of crape. LME–M16. **2** An expensive patterned silk, originally imitating Indian painted and resist-dyed textiles, later imported from China, Iran (Persia), and France. M19.

lampas /'lampəs/ *n.*[2] Also **-ss**; **-ers** /-əz/. E16. [(O)Fr., prob. f. dial. *lāpá* throat, *lāpé* gums, f. nasalized var. of Gmc base of LAP *v.*[1]] *Vet. Med.* A disease of horses, in which there is swelling of the fleshy lining of the roof of the mouth behind the front teeth.

lamper /ˈlampə/ *n.* L19. [f. LAMP *n.* + -ER[1].] **1** A person who trims and maintains household lamps. *rare.* L19. **2** A person who hunts at night, using a bright lamp to dazzle a hunted animal. Cf. LAMPING *n.* L20.

lamper-eel /ˈlampəriːl/ *n.* E16. [Prob. f. var. of LAMPREY + EEL *n.*] A lamprey. Also (*US*), an eelpout. Cf. LAMPREY-*eel*.

lampern /ˈlampən/ *n.* ME. [OFr. *lampreion* etc., dim. of *lampreie* LAMPREY.] A lamprey, *Lampetra fluviatilis*, of rivers and coastal waters of NW Europe. Also called *river lamprey*.

lampers *n.* var. of LAMPAS *n.*[2]

lamping /ˈlampɪŋ/ *n.* L20. [f. LAMP *n.*, *v.*[1] + -ING[1].] A method or the practice of nocturnal hunting, using a bright light to dazzle the hunted animal so as to bewilder it and make it easy to catch or kill.

lamping /ˈlampɪŋ/ *a.* L16. [f. LAMP *v.*[1] + -ING[2].] Flashing, resplendent.

lampion /ˈlampɪən/ *n.* M19. [Fr. f. It. *lampione* augm. of *lampa* (f. Fr. *lampe*) LAMP *n.*] An oil lamp, often of coloured glass, used in illuminations.

lamplight /ˈlamplʌɪt/ *n.* LME. [f. LAMP *n.* + LIGHT *n.*] Light from a lamp or lamps.

lamplighter /ˈlamplʌɪtə/ *n.* M18. [f. LAMP *n.* + LIGHTER *n.*[2]] **1** *Hist.* A person employed to light (gas) street lamps. M18. **2** A device used for lighting a lamp. M19. **3** = CRAPPIE. *N. Amer.* L19.

lampoon /lamˈpuːn/ *n.* & *v.* M17. [Fr. *lampon*, perh. f. *lampons* let us drink (used as a refrain), 1st person pl. imper. of *lamper* gulp down, guzzle, nasalized form of *laper* LAP *v.*[1]: see -OON.] **A** *n.* A virulent or scurrilous satire against a person, a satirical attack. M17. **B** *v.t.* Abuse or satirize virulently or scurrilously, esp. in writing. M17.

lampooner *n.* L17. **lampoonery** *n.* the practice of writing lampoons; the quality of a lampoon, scurrility: E18. **lampoonist** *n.* L19.

lamprey /ˈlampri/ *n.* ME. [OFr. *lampreie* (mod. *lamproie*) f. med.L *lampreda*, whence also OE *lamprede*, OHG *lampreta*, perh. alt. of *lampetra* prob. f. L *lambere* lick + *petra* stone (w. allus. to the lamprey attaching itself to stones). Cf. LIMPET.] Any of various predatory cyclostome fishes of the family Petromyzontidae, which inhabit rivers and coastal waters, and have an eel-like body without scales or paired fins and a jawless mouth like a sucker with horny teeth and rough tongue.

river lamprey, *sea lamprey*.

Comb.: **lamprey-eel** the sea lamprey, *Petromyzon marinus* (cf. LAMPER-EEL).

lampro- /ˈlamprəʊ/ *comb. form* of Gk *lampros*, bright, shining: see -O-.

lamproˈphyllite *n.* [Gk *phullon* leaf] *Min.* a monoclinic silicate of sodium, strontium, and titanium, usu. occurring as golden-brown prisms L19.

lamprophyre /ˈlamprəfʌɪə/ *n.* L19. [f. prec. + Gk *porphureos* purple: cf. PORPHYRY.] *Geol.* Any of a class of porphyritic igneous rocks consisting of a fine-grained feldspathic groundmass with phenocrysts esp. of biotite.

lamproˈphyric *a.* L19.

lampshade /ˈlampʃeɪd/ *n.* & *a.* M19. [f. LAMP *n.* + SHADE *n.*] **A** *n.* A shade placed over a lamp to diffuse or direct the light. M19.

B *attrib.* or as *adj.* Resembling or suggestive of a lampshade. M19.

Daily Chronicle The young ladies of gay Bohemia in . . lamp-shade hats.

lampyrid /ˈlampɪrɪd/ *n.* & *a.* L19. [mod.L *Lampyridae* (see below), f. L *lampyris* glow-worm f. Gk *lampuris*, f. *lampein* shine: see -ID[3].] **A** *n.* Any insect of the coleopteran family Lampyridae, which includes the glow-worms and fireflies. L19. **B** *adj.* Of, pertaining to, or designating this family. E20.

Lamut /ˈlaˈmuːt/ *n.* & *a.* Also **-out**. E18. [Origin unkn.] **A** *n.* **1** A member of a branch of the Tungus people living on the shores of the Sea of Okhotsk. E18. **2** The language of this people, belonging to the Manchu-Tungus family. L18. **B** *attrib.* or as *adj.* Of or pertaining to the Lamuts or their language. L18.

lanai /ləˈnʌɪ/ *n.* Also (earlier) †**ranai**. E19. [Haw.] A porch or veranda, orig. in Hawaii; a roofed structure with open sides near a house.

lanarkite /ˈlanəkʌɪt/ *n.* M19. [f. *Lanarkshire*, former Sc. county + -ITE[1].] *Min.* A monoclinic oxide and sulphate of lead occurring as greenish-white, grey, or yellowish crystals.

lanate /ˈleɪneɪt/ *a.* M18. [L *lanatus*, f. *lana* wool: see -ATE[2].] *Bot.* & *Entomol.* Having a woolly covering or surface.

Lancashire /ˈlaŋkəʃə/ *n.* L16. [A county in NW England.] **1** Used *attrib.* to designate things made in or associated with Lancashire. L16. **b** In full *Lancashire cheese*. A white semi-hard cheese. L19. **2a** A breed of shorthorn cattle from Lancashire; an animal of this breed. M19. **b** A variety of canary developed in Lancashire, with pale yellow plumage. L19.

1 : **Lancashire hotpot** a dish of meat, onion and potato, resembling Irish stew.

Lancaster /ˈlaŋkəstə, -kastə/ *n.* & *a.* M19. [See below.] *Hist.* (Designating) a cannon or rifle with a slightly oval bore designed by the English gunsmith Charles Lancaster (1820–78).

Lancaster cloth /ˈlaŋkəstə klɒθ, ˈlaŋkastə/ *n. phr.* M20. [f. *Lancaster* (see LANCASTRIAN) + CLOTH.] A light washable cloth waterproofed with a linseed oil compound.

Lancasterian /laŋkəˈstɪərɪən/ *a.* E19. [f. *Lancaster* (see below) + -IAN.] *Hist.* Of or pertaining to the English educationalist Joseph Lancaster (1778–1838), or the monitorial form of instruction which he established in schools.

Lancastrian /laŋˈkastrɪən/ *n.* & *a.* M16. [f. *Lancaster* a city in NW England, formerly the county town of Lancashire + -IAN.] **1** *Hist.* (An adherent or supporter) of the family descended from John of Gaunt (1340–99), Duke of Lancaster, fourth son of Edward III, esp. in the Wars of the Roses. Cf. YORKIST. M16. **2** (A native or inhabitant) of Lancaster or Lancashire in NW England. L18.

lance /lɑːns/ *n.* Also (earlier, now only in sense 5) **launce**. ME. [(O)Fr. f. L *lancea*, of alien (prob. Celt.) origin.] **1a** *Hist.* A spear with a long wooden shaft and an iron or steel head, held by a charging horseman. ME. **b** A similar weapon used for spearing fish, harpooning whales, etc. E18. **2a** A mounted soldier armed with a lance; a lancer. LME. **b** *Hist.* A man-at-arms with his attendant archers, foot-soldiers, etc. E19. **c** = *lance-corporal* below. *colloq.* L19. †**3** A branch of a tree, a shoot. LME–M17. **4** *Med.* A lancet. Now *rare.* L15. **5** More fully *sand lance* = *sand eel* s.v. SAND *n.* E17. **6** A small thin case containing a firework. M17. **7a** A thin metal pipe through which oxygen etc. is passed in order to burn away metal, concrete, etc., using heat generated by burning the metal to be cut or the pipe itself. Also *thermic lance*. E20. **b** *Metall.* In full *oxygen lance*. A metal pipe through which oxygen may be injected into molten metal or directed on to its surface. M20. **8** A rigid tube at the end of a hose for pumping or spraying liquid. M20.

1 GIBBON The lance was the . . peculiar weapon of the knight. *fig.*: F. H. BURNETT He liked the big . . trees, with the late afternoon sunlight striking golden lances through them. *break a lance*: see BREAK *v.* **2a** FREELANCE.

Comb.: **lance-bombardier** the rank in the Royal Artillery corresponding to lance-corporal in the infantry; **lance-corporal** (*a*) *Hist.* an acting corporal receiving the pay of a private; (*b*) the lowest rank of non-commissioned army officer; **lance-jack** *Mil. slang* a lance-corporal, a lance-bombardier; **lance-oval** *a.* narrowly oval; **lance-sergeant** a corporal acting as a sergeant; **lance-snake** = FER-DE-LANCE; **lancewood** (the tough elastic wood of) any of various trees, *esp.* (*a*) *Oxandra lanceolata* (family Annonaceae) of the W. Indies; (*b*) *Pseudopanax crassifolius* (family Araliaceae) of New Zealand.

lanced *a.* having a lance; shaped like a lance: L18.

lance /lɑːns/ *v.* ME. [(O)Fr. *lancer*, †*-ier*, f. as prec.: cf. LAUNCH *v.*] **1** *v.t.* Fling, hurl, launch, throw (a dart, fire, a look, etc.); shoot out (the tongue); put forth (blossoms). Also foll. by *forth*, *out*, *up*. Now *poet.* ME. **2** *v.i.* a Bound, move quickly, rush. *obs.* exc. *dial.* ME. †**b** (Of leaves or fire) spring, shoot up; (of pain) shoot. LME–M18. **c** Launch, push *out*. *rare.* E16. **3** *v.t.* Pierce (as) with a lance; cut, gash; slit, slit open. Now *rare* or *obs.* LME. **4** *v.t.* Make an incision in (the gums, an abscess, etc.) with a lancet or other sharp instrument. L15. **5** *v.t.* Cut (a hole) or inject (oxygen) by means of an oxygen lance. M20.

1 M. P. SHIEL The torpedo-boat lances one of her . . needles of steel. **4** B. MALAMUD The surgeon had lanced the sores on his feet. *fig.*: R. BOYLE The Orator . . is more sollicitous to tickle their Ears, than . . to launce their Consciences.

lancegay /ˈlɑːnsgeɪ/ *n. obs.* exc. *Hist.* Also †**launce-**. LME. [OFr. *lancegaye*, perh. alt. of *l'archegaye* javelin, lance, by assoc. w. *lance* LANCE *n.*: cf. ASSEGAI.] A kind of lance.

lance-knight /ˈlɑːnsnʌɪt/ *n.* Also †**-knecht**. E16. [G *Lanzknecht* alt. of *Landsknecht* (see LANSQUENET) after *Lanz* LANCE *n.*] *Hist.* A mercenary foot-soldier, *esp.* one armed with a lance or pike.

lancelet /ˈlɑːnslɪt/ *n.* M16. [f. LANCE *n.* + -LET.] †**1** *Surg.* A lancet. M16–M17. **2** Any of a number of small elongated fishlike chordates of the family Branchiostomidae, that burrow in underwater sand etc. M19.

lanceolate /ˈlɑːnsɪələt/ *a.* M18. [Late L *lanceolatus*, f. L *lanceola* dim. of *lancea* LANCE *n.*: see -ATE[2].] Shaped like a spearhead; narrow and tapering to each end; *Bot.* & *Zool.* tapering from near the base.

Also **lanceolated** *a.* M18.

lancepesade /lɑːnspɪˈzɑːd/ *n.* Also †**lance-prisade**; **lanceprisado** /lɑːnsprɪˈzɑːdəʊ/, pl. **-do(e)s**. M16. [Fr. †*lancepessade* (now *anspessade*) f. It. *lancia spezzata* soldier on a forlorn hope, devoted adherent, lit. 'broken lance', f. *lancia* LANCE *n.* + *spezzata* fem. pa. pple of *spezzare* break; vars. in *-pris-* are due to assoc. w. Sp., It. *presa* seizure, capture.] *Hist.* **1** A member of a class of experienced soldiers separate from ordinary companies. M16. **2** A non-commissioned officer of the lowest grade; a lance-corporal. E17.

lancer /ˈlɑːnsə/ *n.* L16. [Fr. *lancier*, f. *lance* LANCE *n.*: see -ER[2]. Cf. late L *lancearius*.] **1** A (cavalry) soldier armed with a lance (*Hist.*); a soldier belonging to any of several regiments still officially called Lancers. L16. **2** In *pl.* (treated as *sing.*). A kind of quadrille for 8 or 16 pairs; a piece of music for this. M19.

lances *ns.* pls. of LANCE *n.*, LANX.

lancet /ˈlɑːnsɪt/ *n.* LME. [(O)Fr. *lancette*, dim. of *lance* LANCE *n.*: see -ET[1].] †**1** A (small) lance. LME–M18. **2** A surgical knife, usu. broad, two-edged, and with a sharp point, used for bleeding, opening abscesses, etc. LME. **3** *Archit.* **a** More fully *lancet light*, *lancet window*. A high narrow window with a lancet arch. L18. **b** More fully *lancet arch*. An arch with a head resembling the blade of a lancet. E19.

Comb.: *lancet arch*: see sense 3b above; **lancet-fish** (*a*) a surgeon fish; (*b*) any of various long slender spiny-finned predatory marine fishes of the family Alepisauridae; *lancet light*, *lancet window*: see sense 3a above.

lanceted *a.* (of a window) having a lancet arch; (of a church) having lancet windows: M19.

lanciform /ˈlɑːnsɪfɔːm/ *a.* M19. [f. LANCE *n.* + -I- + -FORM.] Shaped like a lance.

lancinate /ˈlɑːnsɪneɪt/ *v.t. rare.* E17. [L *lancinat-* pa. ppl stem of *lancinare* tear, rel. to *lacer*: see LACERATE *v.*, -ATE[3].] Pierce, tear.

lancinating /ˈlɑːnsɪneɪtɪŋ/ *a.* M18. [f. prec. + -ING[2].] Chiefly of pain: acute, piercing.

land /land/ *n.*[1] [OE *land* (= OFris., OS (Du.), ON, Goth. *land*), OHG *lant* (G *Land*), f. Gmc.] **1** The solid part of the earth's surface, as distinguished from the sea or water, or from the air. OE. **2a** Ground or soil, esp. w. ref. to its use or properties. OE. **b** *the land*, the (cultivable) earth regarded as a repository of natural resources and the chief source of human sustenance or livelihood. LME. **c** An area of ground under cultivation; a field. Freq. in *pl. S. Afr.* M18. **3** A part of the earth's surface marked off by natural or political boundaries; a territory, a country, a nation, a State. Also (*fig.*), a realm, a domain. OE. **4** Ground or territory held as public or private property, landed property, (in *Law* usu. together with any buildings etc. above the ground and any minerals, mines, etc., beneath it). In *pl.*, territorial possessions. OE. †**5** The country, as opp. to the town. OE–L18. **6a** A strip of arable land or pasture divided from other similar strips by furrows (formerly freq. taken as a local unit of measure). LME. **b** Chiefly *Engin.* An area or space left between adjacent grooves, holes, etc., in a surface, as (*a*) the top of a tooth on various metal-cutting tools immediately behind the cutting edge; (*b*) the space between the grooves of a rifle bore; (*c*) the space between the furrows of a millstone; (*d*) the space between the grooves of a gramophone record. M19. **7** A tenement building, usu. divided into flats for different households. *Sc.* LME. **8** A stretch of country of undefined extent. Usu. w. specifying wd, as *highland, lowland, mountain-land*, etc. E17. **9** *euphem.* = LORD *n.* 5: in exclamatory phrs. *US.* M19.

2a *arable land, badland(s), flatland, plough-land, stubble land*, etc. **b** G. B. SHAW You must nationalize the land and put a stop to this shameless exploitation. **4a** G. BERKELEY A convenient house with a hundred acres of land adjoining to it. LD MACAULAY Their lands had been divided by Cromwell among his followers. **8** W. WHARTON As I've gone north, the traffic has picked up and the land has flattened out. **9** *the land knows, good land, (for the) land's sake.*

Phrases: **be on the land** *Austral.* be engaged in rural (usu. agricultural) occupations. **by land** by way of the land, on or over the land (as a mode of travel or conveyance), on foot or using a vehicle etc. *common land*: see COMMON *a. fast land*: see FAST *a. firm land*: see FIRM *a. happy land*: see HAPPY *a. height of land*: see HEIGHT *n. Holy Land*: see HOLY *a.* **how the land lies** *fig.* what the situation is. **in the land of the living** alive. **land ahoy!, land ho!** *ints.* (*Naut.*): announcing the sighting of land from the sea. *land of cakes*: see CAKE *n. Land of Little Sticks*: see *Land of the Little Sticks* below. *land of the broad acres*: see BROAD *a.* 2. *land of the Covenant*: see COVENANT *n.* **Land of the Free** *US* the United States of America. **Land of (the) Little Sticks** *Canad.* [Chinook *stik* wood, tree, forest] the subarctic tundra region of northern Canada, characterized by its stunted vegetation. **Land of the Long White Cloud** *NZ* New Zealand. **land of the midnight sun** (that part of) any of the most northerly European countries in which it never gets fully dark during the summer months. **land of the rising sun** Japan. *lands and tenements*: see TENEMENT 2. **land to** *Naut.* just within sight of land, when at sea. *law of the land*: see LAW *n.*[1] *lie of the land*: see LIE *n.*[2] *live off the land*: see LIVE *v. Never Never Land*: see NEVER. *no man's land*: see NO *a. promised land*: see PROMISE *v. red land*: see RED *a. the fat of the land*: see FAT *n.*[2] *the land*: see sense 2b above. *the land of nod*: see NOD *n. ure of land*: see URE *n.*[2] *white land*: see WHITE *a. wide brown land*: see WIDE *a. within land*: see WITHIN *adv., prep., a.,* & *n. yard of land*: see YARD *n.*[2] 4.

Attrib. & *comb.*: In the senses 'belonging, attached to, or characteristic of the land', 'situated or taking place on land (as opp. to on the sea or water or in the air)', 'living on land (as opp. to on or in water)', as *land-battle, -bird, -engine, -journey, -monster, -plant, -prospect, -snail, -soldier*, etc. Special combs., as **land-agency** (*a*) the occupation of a land-agent; (*b*) an agency for the sale etc. of estates; **land-agent** (*a*) a steward or manager of landed property; (*b*) an agent for the sale of land; **land army** (*a*) an army that fights on land; (*b*) (also w. cap. initials) a corps of women established in Britain in 1917 for work on the land esp. in wartime; **land-bred** *a.* (*a*) brought up on land (as opp. to on sea); (*b*) native, indigenous; *land breeze*: see BREEZE *n.*[2] 2; **land-bridge** (*a*) a connection (usu. prehistoric) between two land masses; (*b*) an overland route linking countries more directly than other routes; †**land-carrack** (*a*) a coasting vessel; (*b*) a prostitute; **land-carriage** (the cost of) carriage or transport by land; **land-community** joint or common ownership of land; **land-connection** = *land-bridge* (a) above; **land-crab** any crab of the tropical and subtropical family Gecarcinidae, many members of which spend much time on land; *esp.* (in full *blue land-crab*) a New World crab, *Cardisoma guanhumi*; **land cress** a winter cress, *Barbarea verna*, native to SW Europe and grown as a salad plant (cf. WATERCRESS); **land district** *US* any of the districts into which a State or territory is divided for matters connected with land; **land-drain** a drain made of porous or perforated piping, placed in a gravel-filled trench, and used for subsoil drainage; **land-end** (now *dial.*) a piece of ground at the end of a land in a ploughed field; **land-fast** *a.* firmly attached to the shore; **land fever** *N. Amer.* eager desire for, or excitement about, securing land; **landfill** (*a*) the disposal of refuse by burying it under layers of earth; (*b*) refuse disposed of under layers of earth, an area filled in by this process; †**land-fish** *fig.* an unnatural creature; **land-floe** a sheet of sea-ice extending from the land; **land-flood**; caused by the overflowing of a river or other inland water; **land-folk** the people of a land or country; **land force** an armed force serving on land, as opp. to a naval or air force; in *pl.*, the soldiers composing such a force; **landform** (*a*) a physical feature of the earth's surface; (*b*) (*land-form*) a species (of organism) found on land; **land-fyrd** (*obs.* exc. *Hist.*) a land force; **land-gavel** *Hist.* land-tax; rent for land, ground-rent; **land-girl** a member of the Land Army; **land-grabber** an illegal seizer of land, *esp.* (*Ir. Hist.*) a person who took a farm after the eviction of the previous tenant; **land grant** a grant of public land; *land-grant college* (US), a college set up with federal aid; **landholder** a proprietor, holder, or occupier of land; **land-hunger** keen desire for the acquisition of land; **land-hungry** *a.* eager to acquire land; **land-ice** ice attached to the shore, as distinguished from floe ice; **land-jobber** a person who buys and sells land on speculation; **land law** (*a*) (long *obs.* exc. *Hist.*) the law of a country, the law of the land; (*b*) the law, or a law, relating to landed property; **Land League** *Ir. Hist.* an association of Irish tenant farmers etc. set up in 1879 (and suppressed in 1881), which sought to have rents reduced and ultimately to bring about radical land reform; **Land-leaguer** *Ir. Hist.* a member of or sympathizer with the Land League; **Land-leaguism** *Ir. Hist.* the principles or practice of the Land League; **land-leech** a large terrestrial leech of the tropical genus *Haemodipsa*; **land legs** the ability to walk comfortably on land after being at sea, in a train, etc.; **land line** an overland means of telecommunication; **land-line** *v.t.* transmit over a landline; **land-locked** *a.* (*a*) (almost) enclosed or surrounded by land; (*b*) hemmed in or limited by surrounding land; **land-looker** *US* = CRUISER 2a; **land mass** a large continuous area of land, esp. of continental size; **land-measure** †(*a*) measurement of land; (*b*) a unit of measure or system of such units used in stating the area of land; **land-measurement** the art or process of measuring the area of fields, farms, etc.; **land-measurer** a person whose occupation is land-measurement; **land-measuring** = *land-measurement* above; **land-mine** (*a*) an explosive mine used on land; (*b*) a bomb dropped by parachute from an aircraft; **land-office** *US* (*a*) an office recording dealings in public land; (*b*) *land-office business* (*US colloq.*) enormous trade; **landowner** an owner or proprietor of land; **landowning** *n.* & *a.* owning land, being the proprietor of land; **land-pike** *US* (*a*) = *hellbender* s.v. HELL *n.*; (*b*) a thin, inferior type of pig; **landplane** an aircraft which can only operate from or alight on land (opp. *seaplane*); **land-poor** *a.* (*US*) poor through the burden of taxation resulting from owning much land; **landrail** the corncrake; **land-rat** (*a*) a rat that lives on land; †(*b*) a contemptible person, a thief; **Land Registry** (a building or office housing) a government department with which titles to or charges upon land must be registered; **land-right** (*obs.* exc. *Hist.*) = *land law* (a) above; **Landrover** (proprietary name for) a sturdy four-wheel-drive motor vehicle designed esp. for work in rough or agricultural country; *land scrip*: see SCRIP *n.*[2] 2b; **land-service** service as a soldier on land; **land-shark** *slang* (*a*) a person who makes a living by exploiting seamen when they are ashore; (*b*) = *land-grabber* above; **land ship** (*a*) a vehicle on land (esp. a tank) regarded as resembling in function a ship on the sea; (*b*) a ship erected and kept on land for training purposes; **land-sick** *a.* (*a*) sick through the sight of land; sick of being on land; (*b*) ill from being on land again after a long sea voyage; (*c*) *Naut.* (of a ship) impeded in its movements by being close to land; **land speed** (*a*) speed (of an aircraft) relative to the ground; (*b*) speed on the ground (e.g. in a motor vehicle); **land spring** a spring which comes into action and overflows only intermittently, usu. after heavy rains; **land-steward** a person who manages a landed estate for the owner; **land-stream** a current in the sea due to river waters; **land-surveying** the process, art, or profession of measuring, and making plans of, landed property; **land-surveyor** a person whose profession is land-surveying; **land-swell** the roll of the water near the shore; **land-take** the action of taking land, or an area of land taken, for colonization or development; **land-tax** *Hist.* a tax levied on landed property; **land-thief** a person who robs land or robs on land; **land-tie** a rod, beam, or piece of masonry securing or supporting a wall etc. by connecting it with the ground; **land-value** the economic value of land in all respects, esp. as a basis for rating or taxation; **land-war** (*a*) a war waged on land, as opp. to a naval or air war; (*b*) a dispute or struggle concerning land; **land-wash** (*a*) the wash of the tide near the shore; (*b*) (orig. *N. Amer.*) the part of a beach covered by water at high tide; **land-water** (*a*) water flowing through or over land, as opp. to seawater; (*b*) = *land-flood* above; (*c*) water free from ice along a frozen shore; **land wheel** the wheel of a plough that runs on the unploughed land; **land-wind** a wind blowing seaward from the land; **land wire** = *land line* above; **land yacht** a vehicle with wheels and a sail or sails for recreational use on a beach etc.

Land /lant, land/ *n.*[2] Pl. ***Länder*** /ˈlɛndər/, ***Lands*** /landz/. E20. [G.] A semi-autonomous unit of local government in Germany and Austria.

land /land/ *v.* ME. [f. LAND *n.*[1]] **1** *v.t.* & *i.* Bring or come to land; put or go ashore; disembark. ME. **b** *v.t.* In *pass.* Be given the status of a landed immigrant. *Canad.* E20. **2** *v.t. Angling.* Bring (a fish) to land, esp. with a hook or net. E17. **b** *fig.* Catch (a person); gain or win (money, a prize, etc.); obtain (a job etc.), esp. against strong competition. M19. **3** *v.t.* & *i.* Bring to or arrive at a specified place, point or position; put in or end (*up*) in a specified (esp. unfortunate) position or situation. M17. **b** *v.t.* & *i.* Set down or alight (from a vehicle). Now *rare* or *obs.* L17. **c** *v.t.* Establish (a person) in a safe or favourable situation. *slang.* M19. **d** *v.t.* & *i.* (Cause to) fall to the ground or strike a surface from above. M19. **e** *v.i.* & *t.* Alight on, or bring under control to, earth or some other surface after a flight. L19. **4a** *v.t.* Bring (a horse etc.) first past the winning-post. *colloq.* M19. **b** *v.i.* Win a race. *colloq.* M19. **5a** *v.t.* Encumber or burden (a person) *with.* M19. **b** *v.t.* & *i.* (foll. by *out*). Strike (a blow). L19.

1 MRS H. WARD His hansom landed him at the door of a great mansion. C. ISHERWOOD The Soviet fleet will make an immediate dash for Swinemünde and begin to land troops. E. SAINTSBURY Charles Edward Stuart.. landed on the west coast of Scotland in 1745. **2** K. KESEY George told the doctor he'd have to land his fish or cut it loose. **b** C. P. SNOW Neither he nor Kate could understand how she had finally landed him. S. HASTINGS Back in England he managed to land a job in the City. *Today's Golfer* Putts.. good enough to land the claret jug, the title and the £75,000 first prize. **3** I. MURDOCH Liza's.. lack of common sense constantly landed her in scrapes. N. ANNAN His business failed, he landed in a debtors' gaol. S. MIDDLETON It was past eleven o'clock when he landed upstairs. **land on one's feet** = *fall on one's feet* s.v. FALL *v.* **d** J. B. MORTON He went through the parlour floor and landed in the scullery below. **e** K. W. GATLAND Instead of landing the entire space-ship, a secondary rocket will descend to the surface. F. HERBERT A hawk landed on the sand near his outstretched hand. V. S. NAIPAUL To land at La Guaira airport.. was to come down to a different country. **4a** *Times* Sheikh Muhammad.. landed two winners. **5a** *Punch* Spinks and I were landed with this.. job just as we were about to leave. **b** HARPER LEE It was easy to grab his front hair and land one on his mouth.

With advs. in specialized senses: **land on** (of an aircraft) touch down on the deck of an aircraft carrier. **land up** (*a*) *v.phr.i.* come eventually to a specified state; (*b*) *v.phr.t.* fill or block up (a watercourse, pond, etc.) with earth; silt up.

landammann /ˈlandəmən/ *n.* Also **-man**, **L-**. L17. [Swiss G, f. *Land* LAND *n.*[2] + *Amman(n)* = G *Amtmann*, f. *Amt* office + *Mann* man.] The chief magistrate in certain Swiss cantons. Formerly also, the chief officer in certain smaller administrative districts of Switzerland.

landau /ˈlandɔː, -aʊ/ *n.* M18. [f. *Landau* in Germany, where first made.] Chiefly *Hist.* A four-wheeled horse-drawn carriage, with folding front and rear hoods enabling it to travel open, half-open, or closed. Also *landau carriage*.

landaulet /landɔːˈlɛt, -də-/ *n.* In sense 2 also **-lette**. Chiefly *Hist.* L18. [f. prec. + -LET.] **1** A small landau. L18. **2** A type of motor car with a leather hood above the rear seats. E20.

landbank /ˈlan(d)baŋk/ *v.i.* L20. [f. next.] Accumulate land for future development or investment potential. Chiefly as *landbanking* vbl n.

land-bank /ˈlandbaŋk/ *n.* L17. [f. LAND *n.*[1] + BANK *n.*[3]] 1 A bank which issues currency using land as security. L17. 2 In full *federal land-bank*. Any of a number of banks providing mortgages on farmland, financed by issuing public bonds. *US.* E20. 3 *Comm.* The total amount of land accumulated and held by a private corporation or government body, esp. for future development; a corporation etc. accumulating land for development. M20.

land-boc /ˈlandbəʊk/ *n.* Long *obs.* exc. *Hist.* OE. [f. LAND *n.*[1] + *bóc* BOOK *n.*] A charter or deed by which land was granted.

landdrost /ˈland(d)rɒst/ *n.* M18. [Afk., f. Du. *land* LAND *n.*[1] + *drost* bailiff.] *Hist.* A district magistrate in South Africa.

lande /lɑ̃d/ *n.* Pl. pronounced same. L18. [Fr.: cf. LAUND.] A tract of wild land, a moor, esp. in SW France.

landed /ˈlandɪd/ *a.* OE. [f. LAND *n.*[1], *v.*: see -ED[1], -ED[2].] 1 Possessing (an estate in) land. OE. 2 Consisting of land or in the possession of land; (of revenue) derived from land. E18. 3 That has landed or has been landed. M19. 4 Of an engineering tool etc.: having a land between grooves etc. M20.

Special collocations: **landed immigrant** *Canad.*: admitted to Canada for permanent residence. **landed interest** interest in land as a possession; the owners and holders of land. **landed plunger**: forming an accurate seal when mated with a corresponding mould.

lander /ˈlandə/ *n.*[1] M19. [f. LAND *v.* + -ER[1].] 1a A person who lands or goes ashore. M19. b A spacecraft designed to be landed on the surface of a planet or the moon. M20. 2 *Mining.* The person who receives the kibble at the mouth of a shaft. M19.

lander *n.*[2] see LAUNDER *n.*

Länder *n.pl.* see LAND *n.*[2]

landfall /ˈlan(d)fɔːl/ *n.* E17. [f. LAND *n.*[1] + FALL *n.*[2]] 1 The arrival at or sighting of land from the sea. Now also, (an) arrival at land after a flight over the sea. E17. b A place on land sighted or reached after a journey over the sea. L19. c A place where an undersea pipeline reaches land. L20. 2 An unexpected inheritance of land. M18.

1 C. RYAN Wreathed by flak bursts, the huge armada made landfall over the Dutch coast. **make a good** or **bad landfall** meet with land in accordance with or contrary to one's navigational intentions. b T. BRASSEY The Bahamas will be for ever memorable as the landfall of Columbus. c *Selling Today* Aberdeen, the nearest landfall and port to the Forties field.

landgravate *n.* var. of LANDGRAVIATE.

landgrave /ˈlan(d)greɪv/ *n.* Also (esp. in titles) **L-**. LME. [MLG (= MHG *lantgrāve*, G *Landgraf*), f. *land* LAND *n.*[2] + *grave* GRAVE *n.*[2]] *Hist.* A count with jurisdiction over a German territory.

landgraveship *n.* = LANDGRAVIATE M17. **landgravine** /ˈlan(d)grəviːn/ *n.* the wife of a landgrave; a female ruler of a landgraviate: L17.

landgraviate /landˈgreɪvɪət/ *n.* Also **landgravate** /ˈlan(d)grəveɪt/ E17. [med.L *landgraviatus*, f. LANDGRAVE: see -I-, -ATE[1].] *Hist.* The office, jurisdiction, or territory of a landgrave.

landing /ˈlandɪŋ/ *n.* LME. [f. LAND *v.* + -ING[1].] 1 The action of LAND *v.*; an instance of this. LME. 2 A place for disembarking, loading, or unloading; a landing-place. LME. 3 A platform or resting-place at the top of a staircase or between two flights of stairs; a passage or antechamber at the top of a flight of stairs. L18. b Stone used in or suitable for making staircase landings. M19.

1 *automatic landing*: see AUTOMATIC *a.* 2. *happy landings*: see HAPPY *a.*

Comb.: **landing-beam** *Aeronaut.* a radio beam to guide aircraft when landing; **landing card** a card issued to a passenger on an international flight or voyage, to be surrendered on arrival; **landing-craft** (*a*) *Mil.* a naval vessel designed for putting troops, tanks, etc., ashore; (*b*) *Astronaut.* the section of a spacecraft used for the final descent to the surface of a planet or the moon; **landing-flap** *Aeronaut.* a wing-flap that can be lowered to increase the lift and the drag to make possible lower speeds for take-off and landing; **landing-gear** (*a*) see GEAR *n.* 5c; (*b*) the retractable support at the front of a semi-trailer that supports it when not attached to the tractor; **landing-light** (*a*) a light on a runway to guide an aircraft in a night landing (usu. in *pl.*); (*b*) a light attached to an aircraft to illuminate the ground for a night landing; **landing-net**: for landing a fish that has been hooked; **landing pad** (*a*) a small area of an airfield or heliport, where helicopters land and take off; (*b*) a cushioned or strengthened foot which supports a hovercraft, spacecraft, etc., on the ground; **landing run** (*a*) the distance an aircraft travels in contact with the ground during landing; (*b*) that part of a flight during which a pilot prepares to land; **landing-stage** a (floating) platform, for the landing of passengers and goods; **landing-strip** an airstrip; **landing ticket** = *landing card* above; **landing-wire** *Aeronaut.* a wire on a biplane or light monoplane designed to take the weight of a wing when the aircraft is on the ground.

landing-place /ˈlandɪŋpleɪs/ *n.* E16. [f. prec. + PLACE *n.*[1]] 1a A place for the landing of passengers and goods. E16. b A place where a bird, insect, aircraft, etc., can or does land. L18. 2 = LANDING *n.* 3. Now *rare* or *obs.* E17.

land-junker /ˈlandjʊŋkə/ *n.* Now *rare* or *obs.* M19. [G: see LAND *n.*[1], JUNKER *n.*[1]] A country squire.

landlady /ˈlan(d)leɪdi/ *n.* M16. [f. LAND *n.*[1] + LADY *n.*, after *landlord*.] 1 A woman who lets land or (part of) a building to a tenant. M16. 2 A woman who keeps a public house, lodgings, or a boarding-house. M17.

†land-leaper *n.* LME–E18. [f. LAND *n.*[1] + LEAPER, after MDu. *landlooper*: see LAND-LOPER.] = LAND-LOPER.

ländler /ˈlɛndlə/ *n.* L19. [G.] An Austrian peasant dance, similar to a slow waltz; a piece of music for this dance.

landless /ˈlandlɪs/ *a.* LOE. [f. LAND *n.*[1] + -LESS.] 1 Not possessing land, having no landed property. LOE. 2 Having no land on its surface or within its bounds. *rare.* E17.

landlessness *n.* M19.

land-loper /ˈlandləʊpə/ *n. arch.* Latterly chiefly *Sc.* Also **-louper** /-laʊpə/. L16. [MDu. *landlooper* (Du. *landloper* tramp), f. *land* LAND *n.*[1] + *loopen* run: see LEAP *v.* Cf. LAND-LEAPER, LOAFER.] 1 A vagabond. Formerly also, a renegade. L16. †2 = LANDLUBBER. L16–E18.

landloping *a.* wandering, vagabond L16.

landlord /ˈlan(d)lɔːd/ *n.* OE. [f. LAND *n.*[1] + LORD *n.*] 1 A lord or owner of land, a person who lets land to a tenant. Later also, a person who lets (part of) a building. OE. 2 A person (esp. a man) who keeps a public house, lodgings, or a boarding-house. L17. 3 A private host or entertainer. Chiefly *Sc.* E18.

1 S. HASTINGS He was a good landlord, the tenants' cottages were always kept in repair. 2 *Which?* We visited . . 2,232 pubs and asked the landlords about the drinks they served.

landlordism *n.* (chiefly *Hist.*) the (esp. Irish) system whereby land is owned by landlords to whom tenants pay a fixed rent; the advocacy or practice of this system: M19. **landlordly** *a.* pertaining to or characteristic of a landlord or landlords M19. **landlordry** *n.* (long *rare*) landlords collectively L16. **landlordship** *n.* the position of or a post as a landlord E19.

land-louper *n.* var. of LAND-LOPER.

landlubber /ˈlandlʌbə/ *n.* L17. [f. LAND *n.*[1] + LUBBER.] A person with little or no experience of the sea or sailing; a person who lives on land.

landlubberly *a.* characteristic of a landlubber M19.

landman /ˈlandmən/ *n.* Pl. **-men**. OE. [f. LAND *n.*[1] + MAN *n.*: cf. LANDSMAN *n.*[1]] †1 A native of a particular country. *rare.* OE–M17. 2 A countryman, a peasant. Now *rare* or *obs.* ME. 3 = LANDSMAN *n.*[1] 2. Now *rare* or *obs.* L15. †4 A man possessing landed property. M16–E18. 5 = *leaseman* s.v. LEASE *n.*[3] *US.* E20.

landmark /ˈlandmɑːk/ *n.*, *v.*, & *a.* OE. [f. LAND *n.*[1] + MARK *n.*[1]] A *n.* 1 (An object marking) the boundary of a country, an estate, etc. OE. 2 A conspicuous object in a landscape, serving as a (navigational) guide; any prominent object in a neighbourhood or district. L16. 3 An object, event, etc., which marks a period, (a stage in) a development, or a turning-point. M19.

1 BURKE When . . he returned to . . his estates, . . he found none of the ancient landmarks removed. 2 W. STYRON I gave up pointing out the landmarks of the capital, abandoning the tour-guide approach. I. MURDOCH She could not remember the way and kept looking for landmarks. 3 P. LARKIN This has never been done before. . . I therefore salute a landmark in publishing history. *Woman & Home* Another landmark came in February when Sarah achieved her wings as a qualified pilot.

B *v.t.* Be or act as a landmark to; provide with a landmark. E20.

C *attrib.* or as *adj.* That is or serves as a landmark; signifying an important change, development, etc. M20.

W. FAULKNER There was no territory . . that he did not know—bayou, ridge, landmark trees. R. C. A. WHITE Landmark cases embodying sweeping reforms of the law.

land-marshal /ˈlandmɑːʃ(ə)l/ *n.* Also **L-**. L17. [f. LAND *n.*[1] + MARSHAL *n.*[1], repr. in sense 1 Sw. *landtmarskalk*, in sense 2 G *Landmarschall*.] *Hist.* 1 In Sweden: the speaker or president of the assembly of the first estate. L17. 2 In Austria, Prussia, etc.: the marshal of a province. E18.

Landsborough grass /ˈlandzbərə grɑːs/ *n. phr.* Now *rare* or *obs.* L19. [*f.* William *Landsborough* (1826-86), Austral. explorer.] = *Flinders grass* s.v. FLINDERS *n.*[2] 2.

landmen *n.* pl. of LANDMAN.

landnam /ˈlandnəm/ *n.* M20. [Da. = occupation of land.] *Archaeol.* The clearance of forested land for (usu. short-term) agricultural purposes; evidence of this provided by sudden changes in pollen spectra.

landnám /ˈlandnɑːm/ *n.* M19. [ON *land-nám*, f. *land* land, territory + *nám* f. *nema* to take.] *Hist.* Land-take, esp. w. ref. to the Norse colonization of Iceland.

landocracy /lanˈdɒkrəsi/ *n. joc.* M19. [f. LAND *n.*[1]: see -CRACY.] A class of people with political power based on possession of land.

landrace /ˈlandreɪs/ *n.* M20. [Da. = national breed.] A breed of large white pig, originally developed in Denmark; an animal of this breed.

Landry /ˈlɑːndri/, *foreign* lɑ̃dri/ *n.* L19. [J. B. *Landry* (1826–65), Fr. physician.] Med. *Landry's paralysis* (or *disease*), orig., any acute ascending paralysis, now *spec.* = GUILLAIN-BARRÉ SYNDROME.

landscape /ˈlan(d)skeɪp/ *n.*, *a.*, & *adv.* Also **†landskip**, **†lantskip**. L16. [MDu. *lantscap*, Du. *landschap* landscape, province; *-skip* after Du. pronunc.: see LAND *n.*[1] Cf. -SHIP.] A *n.* 1 A picture of natural (esp. inland) scenery (cf. SEASCAPE). Formerly also, the scenery forming the background of a portrait etc. L16. †b A sketch, an outline; a bird's-eye view, a map. M17–E18. †c *fig.* An epitome *of* some quality. M17–E19. 2 Natural scenery; the pictorial representation of scenery, esp. as an artistic genre. E17. 3a (A view presented by) an expanse of terrain or district which is visible from a particular place or direction; an expanse of (country) scenery. M17. b *Geogr.* A tract or region of land with its characteristic topographical features, esp. as shaped or modified by (usu. natural) processes and agents. L19.

3a B. MOORE The landscape, hilly, empty . . gradually began to change. b N. CALDER The sculpture of landscapes by water, ice and wind. *fig.*: *Scientific American* Trade unions have become a prominent feature of the industrial landscape.

Comb.: **landscape architect** a practitioner of landscape architecture; **landscape architecture** (the art of) planning and designing the open-air environment, esp. with ref. to the harmonious fitting of buildings, roads, etc., into the landscape; **landscape gardener** a practitioner of landscape gardening; **landscape gardening** (the art of) laying out ornamental grounds or grounds imitating natural scenery; **landscape-marble** a variety of marble with markings resembling shrubbery or trees; **landscape-painter** an artist who paints landscapes.

B *adj.* & *adv.* Of a page, book, etc., or the manner in which it is set or printed: having or in a rectangular shape with the width greater than the height. Opp. PORTRAIT *a.* & *adv.* E20.

landscape /ˈlan(d)skeɪp/ *v.* M17. [f. prec.] 1 *v.t.* Represent as a landscape; depict. Now *rare* or *obs.* M17. 2 *v.t.* & *i.* Lay out (a garden etc.) as a landscape; conceal or enhance the appearance of (a building, road, etc.) by means of landscape architecture. E20.

landscaper *n.* a person skilled in landscape architecture or landscape gardening M20. **landscapist** *n.* (*a*) a painter of landscapes; (*b*) a landscaper: E19.

Landseer /ˈlan(d)sɪə/ *n.* L19. [Sir Edwin *Landseer* (1802–73), Eng. painter.] A black and white Newfoundland dog of a type once painted by Landseer. Also more fully *Landseer Newfoundland*.

landside /ˈlan(d)sʌɪd/ *n.*, *a.*, & *adv.* M16. [f. LAND *n.*[1] + SIDE *n.*] A *n.* †1 The shore. Only in M16. 2 The flat side of a plough which is turned towards the unploughed land. M18. 3 The landward side of something. M19. 4 The side or sections of an airport to which the public has admittance. M20. B *adj.* Designating or pertaining to the landside of an airport. L20. C *adv.* To or towards the landside of an airport. L20.

†landskip *n.* var. of LANDSCAPE *n.*

landsknecht *n.* see LANSQUENET.

landsleit *n.* pl. of LANDSMAN *n.*[2]

landslide /ˈlan(d)slʌɪd/ *n.* M19. [f. LAND *n.*[1] + SLIDE *n.*] 1 A landslip, an avalanche. M19. 2 An overwhelming majority of votes for one party or candidate in an election. L19.

landslip /ˈlan(d)slɪp/ *n.* L17. [f. LAND *n.*[1] + SLIP *n.*[3]] The sliding down of a mass of land on a mountain, cliff, etc.; land which has so fallen.

Landsmål /ˈlantsmɔːl/ *n.* Now *rare*. Also ***-maal***. L19. [Norw., f. *land* country + *mål* language.] = NYNORSK. Cf. BOKMÅL, RIKSMÅL.

landsman /ˈlan(d)zmən/ *n.*[1] Pl. **-men**. OE. [f. LAND *n.*[1] + -'S[1] + MAN *n.*] 1†a A native of a particular country. OE–LME. b A fellow-countryman. L16. 2 A person living or working on land as opp. to a seaman; (*obs.* exc. *Hist.*) a sailor on his first sea voyage. M17.

landsman /ˈlɒntsmɒn/ *n.*[2] Pl. ***landsleit*** /ˈlɒntslʌɪt/. M20. [Yiddish, f. MHG *lantsman*, *lantman* a native: cf. LANDMAN.] Among Jews: a fellow Jew; a compatriot.

landsmen *n.* pl. of LANDSMAN *n.*[1]

Landsturm /ˈlantʃtʊrm/ *n.* Pl. ***-stürme*** /-ʃtyrmə/. E19. [G, lit. 'land-storm'.] *Hist.* In Germany and German-speaking countries: a general levy in time of war; an auxiliary militia force.

landswoman /ˈlan(d)swʊmən/ *n.* Pl. **-women** /-wɪmɪn/. M19. [f. LAND *n.*[1] + -'S[1] + WOMAN *n.*, after LANDSMAN *n.*[1]] A woman living on the land or skilled in working on it.

landward /ˈlandwəd/ *n.*, *adv.*, & *a.* LME. [f. LAND *n.*[1] + -WARD.] A *n.* The direction or position of the land. Only in *to (the) landward*, †(*a*) *Sc.* in the country, as opp. to the town; (*b*) (*obs.* exc. *dial.*) towards the land, on the land side (*of*); & in *landward-bred* below. LME.

Comb.: **landward-bred** *a.* (*Sc.*) country-bred.

B *adj.* 1 Belonging to or inhabiting the country; rural, rustic. *Sc.* M16. 2 Facing the land, as opp. to the sea. M19.

C *adv.* Towards the land. E17.

landwards *n.* & *adv.* †(*a*) *n.* = LANDWARD *n.* (only in *to (the) landwards*); (*b*) *adv.* = LANDWARD *adv.*: L16.

Landwehr /ˈlantveːr/ *n.* E19. [G, lit. 'land-defence'.] *Mil.* In Germany and some other countries: that part of the organized land forces of which continuous service is required only in time of war; the army reserve.

lane /leɪn/ *n.*[1] See also LOAN *n.*[2] [OE *lane* = OFris. *lana*, *laen*, MDu. *lāne* (Du. *laan*). Ult. origin unkn.] 1 A narrow path or road between hedges, banks, etc.; a narrow road or street between houses or walls. OE. 2 (A thing resembling) a narrow or comparatively narrow way, channel, or passage, *esp.* a passage between two lines of people or through a crowd. LME. b A channel or path designated for use or regularly used by shipping or aircraft, esp. on busy routes. M19. c *Sport.* A path or channel allocated to an individual (esp. a sprinter or swimmer) in a race, usu. marked out and separated from parallel paths etc. by lines or ropes. E20. d A division along a road, marked out by painted lines and used to segregate traffic according to speed, intended direction, type of vehicle, etc. E20. e In ten-pin bowling etc.: a long narrow strip of floor down which a ball is bowled. M20. 3 A long narrow enclosure from which kangaroos, cattle, etc., are driven into a pen or pound. *Austral.* M19. 4 *Astron.* A narrow band or strip in the sky, in the image of a galaxy, etc., that differs markedly from its immediate surroundings, e.g. in containing no observable stars. L19.

1 R. K. NARAYAN He . . stole along by-ways and lanes. M. LOWRY There was a lane branching to the left . . , no more than a cart-track at first. *Proverb*: It's a long lane that has no turning. 2b P. NORMAN We traverse sea lanes crowded, like a busy street, with . . liners and cargo ships and . . tankers. *Aircraft Illustrated* For flights in British airspace, air traffic control lanes . . are established. c *Marathon & Distance Runner* The gun went, the six athletes in their own lanes were released into the . . bend. *Swimming Times* In the 6-lane . . pool provided for competition. d R. DAHL A policeman on a motor-cycle loomed up alongside us on the inside lane. *attrib.*: *Evening Post (Bristol)* Better lane discipline by all traffic would make roundabouts safer for all. 4 *Nature* A small, irregular, diffuse nebulosity . . with a prominent dark lane.

Phrases: *fast lane*: see FAST *a.* **in lane** in the appropriate or correct lane. *lover's lane*: see LOVER *n.* *memory lane*: see MEMORY *n.* *red lane*: see RED *a.* **the lane** *slang* the throat.

lane *a.*, *adv.*, & *n.*[2] see LONE *a.* etc.

Lane's Prince Albert /leɪnz prɪns ˈalbət/ *n. phr.* L19. [f. John *Lane*, 19th-cent. Eng. horticulturist, who introduced it, and *Prince Albert* (see ALBERT).] A large green variety of cooking apple.

långbanite /ˈlɔːŋbənʌɪt/ *n.* L19. [f. *Långban*, a locality in Sweden + -ITE[1].] *Min.* A trigonal silicate and oxide of antimony, ferric iron, and manganese, black with a metallic lustre.

langbeinite /ˈlaŋbʌɪnʌɪt/ *n.* L19. [f. A. *Langbein*, 19th-cent. Ger. chemist + -ITE[1].] *Min.* A sulphate of potassium and magnesium crystallizing in the cubic system, which occurs in marine salt deposits and is made synthetically, and is used in the production of fertilizers.

langeleik /ˈlaŋəlʌɪk/ *n.* Pl. ***-ken*** /-kən/. Also ***langleik*** /ˈlaŋlʌɪk/. E20. [Norw.] An early Norwegian stringed instrument, resembling the zither.

Langerhans /ˈlaŋəhanz/ *n.* L19. [Paul *Langerhans* (1847–88), Ger. anatomist.] *Anat.* 1 *islet* (or *island*) *of Langerhans*, any of a number of groups of cells in the pancreas which secrete insulin and some other hormones. L19. 2 *Langerhans cell*, *cell of Langerhans*, a kind of dendritic or stellate cell found in the epidermis and characterized by the presence of cytoplasmic granules. L19.

†langfad *n.* see LYMPHAD.

Langhans /ˈlaŋhanz/ *n.* L19. [Theodor *Langhans* (1839–1915), Ger. pathologist.] *Anat.* & *Med.* Used *attrib.*, in *possess.*, and w. *of* to designate (*a*) (a cell of) an inner layer of large cuboidal cells covering chorionic villi beneath the syncytial layer; (*b*) a distinctive kind of polynuclear giant cell observed esp. in tuberculosis and related granulomatous conditions.

Langi *n.* & *a.* var. of LANGO.

langite /ˈlaŋgʌɪt/ *n.* M19. [f. V. von *Lang* (1838–1921), Austrian physicist + -ITE[1].] *Min.* A blue or bluish-green orthorhombic basic sulphate of copper, resembling brochantite.

lang-kale /ˈlaŋkeɪl/ *n.* *Sc.* E18. [f. *lang* var. of LONG *a.*[1] + KALE.] = *Scotch kale* s.v. KALE 1.

langlauf /ˈlaŋlaʊf/ *n.* Also **L-**. E20. [G, lit. 'long run'.] Cross-country skiing; a cross-country skiing race.

langlaufer *n.* a competitor in (a) langlauf. E20.

langleik *n.* var. of LANGELEIK.

langley /ˈlaŋli/ *n.* M20. [Samuel P. *Langley* (1834–1906), US astronomer.] *Meteorol.* A unit of solar energy flux per unit area, equal to one (small) calorie per square centimetre (approx. 41,900 joule per square metre).

Langmuir /ˈlaŋmjʊə/ *n.* M20. [Irving *Langmuir* (1881–1957), US physicist.] Used *attrib.* to designate concepts introduced by Langmuir or arising out of his work.

Langmuir (adsorption) isotherm *Physics* a curve showing the relationship between the extent of adsorption of a gas on a surface and the gas pressure. **Langmuir cell** *Oceanogr.* each of the cells within which water circulates in Langmuir circulation. **Langmuir circulation** *Oceanogr.* the large-scale organized motion, due to convection currents, which takes place near the surface of large bodies of water.

Lango /ˈlaŋɡəʊ/ *n.* & *a.* Also **-ngi** /-ŋi/. E20. [Nilotic.] A *n.* Pl. same. 1 A member of a village-dwelling people of the Nile region of Uganda. E20. 2 The Nilotic language of this people. E20. B *attrib.* or as *adj.* Of or pertaining to the Lango or their language. E20.

Langobard /ˈlaŋɡəbɑːd/ *n.* & *a.* L18. [Late L *Langobardus*: see LOMBARD *n.*[1] Cf. earlier LONGOBARD.] *Hist.* A *n.* = LOMBARD *n.*[1] 1. L18. B *attrib.* or as *adj.* Of or pertaining to the (Germanic) Lombards. M20.

Lango'bardian *a.* E20. **Lango'bardic** *a.* & *n.* (*a*) *adj.* of or pertaining to the Langobards or their language; (*b*) *n.* the West Germanic language of the Langobards: E18.

langooty *n.* see LANGOTI.

langosta /laŋˈɡɒstə/ *n.* Chiefly *US.* L19. [Sp. f. pop.L alt. of L *locusta* LOCUST *n.*] 1 = LOCUST *n.* 1. Now *rare* or *obs.* L19. 2 = LANGOUSTE. E20.

langostino /lango'stino, laŋɡəˈstiːnəʊ/ *n.* Pl. ***-os*** /-ɔs, -əʊz/. E20. [Sp., f. as prec. + *-ino* -INE[1].] = LANGOUSTINE.

langoti /lʌŋˈɡəʊti/ *n.* Also (now *rare*) ***-gooty*** /-ˈɡuːti/. E19. [Hind. *lãgoṭī*.] In the Indian subcontinent: a kind of loincloth.

langouste /ˈlɒŋɡuːst, *foreign* lɑ̃ɡust (*pl. same*)/ *n.* M19. [Fr. f. OProv. *lagosta* f. pop.L alt. of L *locusta* LOCUST *n.*] A lobster; *esp.* the spiny lobster, *Palinurus vulgaris*.

langoustine /ˈlɒŋɡʊstiːn, *foreign* lɑ̃ɡustin (*pl. same*)/ *n.* M20. [Fr., f. as prec.: see -INE[1].] The Norway lobster, esp. as food.

langrage /ˈlaŋɡrɪdʒ/ *n.* M18. [Origin of 1st elem. unkn.: see -AGE.] *Naut.* & *Mil. Hist.* Case-shot loaded with pieces of iron of irregular shape, formerly used to damage the rigging and sails of enemy ships.

Earlier **†langrel** *n.* L16–M19.

langsat /ˈlaŋsat/ *n.* L18. [Malay.] (The edible fruit of) a SE Asian tree, *Lansium domesticum* (family Meliaceae).

langsuir /ˈlaŋsjʊə/ *n.* Also **-suyar**. L19. [Malay.] In Malaysian folklore: a female vampire with a whinnying cry, that preys on newborn children.

lang syne /laŋ ˈsʌɪn/ *adv.* & *n. phr.* *Sc.* E16. [f. *lang* Sc. form of LONG *adv.* + SYNE *adv.*] (The days of) long ago. Now *rare* exc. in AULD *lang syne*.

language /ˈlaŋɡwɪdʒ/ *n.*[1] ME. [(O)Fr. *langage* (AN also *language*, after *langue* tongue, speech) f. Proto-Gallo-Romance, f. L *lingua* tongue, language: see -AGE.] 1a A system of human communication using words, written and spoken, and particular ways of combining them; any such system employed by a community, a nation, etc. ME. b *transf.* A mode of communication by inarticulate sounds used by lower animals, birds, etc. ME. c *transf.* A non-verbal method of human communication, as gesture or facial expression, hand-signing, etc.; a means of artistic expression, as dance, music, or painting. E17. d A way of interpreting or ordering experience shared by a group, a community, etc.; a common code or pattern of behaviour. E20. e *Ling.* = LANGUE 3. E20. f *Computing.* Any of various systems of precisely defined symbols and rules for writing programs or representing instructions and data. M20. 2

The form of words used in communicating something; manner or style of expression. ME. **b** The professional or specialized vocabulary of a discipline, a group of people, etc. E16. **c** The style of a literary composition or of a non-verbal work of art. Also, the wording of a document, statute, etc. E18. **d** More fully *bad language*. Coarse or vulgar expressions. M19. **3a** Power or faculty of speech; ability to speak a foreign language. Now *rare*. LME. **b** Human communication using a system of words and particular ways of combining them. L16. †**4a** The act of speaking or talking; the use of speech. LME–E16. **b** That which is said, talk, report, *esp.* censorious or opprobrious words. LME–M17. **5a** A community of people having the same form of speech, a nation. *arch.* LME. **b** A national division or branch of a religious and military Order. Long *rare* exc. *Hist.* E18.

1a J. MARQUAND I answered him in Chinese, a language which I knew . . Joyce did not understand. c R. G. COLLINGWOOD A dispute between Italian peasants is conducted . . in a highly elaborated language of manual gesture. *Observer* He sends Edith flowers, rather too many . . and speaking not quite the right language. *body language, eye language, sign language*, etc. f *Which Micro?* Most home computers speak the same language . . called BASIC. 2 M. FOOT More than ever before or after, Churchill's language fitted the time. b R. K. NARAYAN I'm picking up the railway language quite successfully. c W. COWPER A tale should be judicious, clear, succinct, The language plain. *Listener* The structural and harmonic tension of Mahler's later musical language. d T. KENEALLY 'I want t'do a fuckin' good job.' 'No language in here!' 3a W. COWPER Oh that those lips had language! b J. UGLOW At the most crucial moments, language may fail. We have to move into silence.

Phrases: *artificial language*: see ARTIFICIAL *a.* 1. *bad language*: see sense 2d above. *command of language*: see COMMAND *n. dead language*: see DEAD *a.* 9. *first language*: see FIRST *a.* **language of flowers** a method of expressing sentiments through a set of symbolic meanings attached to different flowers. MATERNAL *language*. MIXED *language*. MODERN *languages*. *natural language*: see NATURAL *a. plain language*: see PLAIN *a.*[1] & *adv. private language*: see PRIVATE *a. second language*: see SECOND *a.* **speak someone's** or **the same language** have a mutual understanding, get on well, have a similar outlook. **strong language**: indicating violent emotion. **talk someone's** or **the same language** = *speak someone's* or *the same language* above.

Comb.: **language area** (*a*) an area of the cerebral cortex regarded as especially concerned with the use of language; (*b*) a region where a particular language is spoken; **language arts** those subjects (as reading, writing, spelling, etc.) taught in schools to develop oral and written communication skills; **language-game** *Philos.* a complete but limited system of communication, which may form part of the existing use of language; **language lab, laboratory** a classroom equipped with tape recorders etc., where foreign languages are learned by means of repeated oral practice; **language loyalty, language maintenance** *Ling.* the preservation of a native language or dialect by an individual or group in a community where another language is dominant; **language-particular** *a.* = *language-specific* below; **language planning** the preparation of a normative orthography, grammar, and dictionary for a non-homogeneous speech community; official promotion or encouragement of a particular language, vocabulary, etc.; **language shift** *Ling.* a move from one (usu. native) language or dialect to another (usu. culturally dominant) by an individual or speech community; **language-specific** *a.* (*Ling.*) distinctive to a particular language; **language universal** *Ling.* a linguistic feature shared by all languages.

languageless *a.* E17.

language *n.*[2] var. of LANGUID *n.*

language /ˈlaŋgwɪdʒ/ *v.t.* E17. [f. LANGUAGE *n.*[1]] †**1** Express in words. E–M17. **2** *transf.* Express by sign or gesture. E19.

languaged /ˈlaŋgwɪdʒd/ *a.* ME. [f. LANGUAGE *n.*[1], *v.*: see -ED[2], -ED[1].] **1** Skilled *in* a language or languages. Also *well languaged*. ME. **2** Having a language or languages. Freq. w. specifying wd: characterized by or expressed in a specified kind of language or languages. L15. †**3** Expressed in language, worded. M17–L17.

langue /lɑ̃g/ *n.* Pl. pronounced same. ME. [Fr. f. L *lingua* tongue, language.] †**1** A language. *rare*. ME–M17. **2** = LANGUAGE *n.*[1] 5b. Long *rare* exc. *Hist.* L18. **3** *Ling.* A language viewed as an abstract system used by a speech-community, in contrast to the actual linguistic behaviour of individuals. Opp. PAROLE *n.* 4. E20.

langued /laŋgd/ *a.* LME. [f. Fr. *langué* (f. *langue* tongue + *-é* pa. ppl suff.) + -ED[1].] *Her.* Of a charge: having a tongue of a specified tincture.

langue de boeuf /lɑːŋ də ˈbəːf/ *n. phr. obs.* exc. *Hist.* LME. [Fr., lit. 'oxtongue'.] †**1** A rough-leaved plant; *esp.* (*a*) bugloss; (*b*) oxtongue. LME–M18. **2** A type of medieval pike or halberd, with a head shaped like an oxtongue. LME.

langue de chat /lɑ̃g də ʃa, lɑːŋ də ˈʃɑː/ *n. phr.* Pl. ***langues de chat*** (pronounced same). L19. [Fr., lit. 'cat's tongue'.] A long thin piece of chocolate; a long finger-shaped biscuit.

langue d'oc /lɑ̃g dɔːk/ *n. phr.* E18. [(O)Fr., f. as LANGUE + *de* of + *oc* yes (f. L *hoc*).] The language of medieval France south of the Loire, generally characterized by the use of *oc* to mean 'yes', and the basis of modern Provençal. Cf. LANGUE D'OÏL.

Languedocian /laŋgəˈdəʊʃ(ə)n/ *a.* & *n.* M18. [f. *Languedoc* (see below) + -IAN.] **A** *adj.* Of or pertaining to Languedoc, a former province in the south of France. M18. **B** *n.* **1** A native or inhabitant of Languedoc. M18. **2** The language of Languedoc, a dialect of Provençal. E19.

langue d'oïl /lɑ̃g dɔi/ *n. phr.* Also ***langue d'oui*** /lɑ̃g dwi/. E18. [(O)Fr., f. as LANGUE + *de* of + *oïl* (now *oui*) yes (f. L *hoc ille*).] The language of medieval France north of the Loire, generally characterized by the use of *oïl* to mean 'yes', and the basis of standard modern French. Cf. LANGUE D'OC.

langues de chat *n. phr.* pl. of LANGUE DE CHAT.

languet /ˈlaŋgwɪt/ *n.* LME. [OFr. *languete* (mod. *languette*), dim. of *langue* tongue: see -ETTE.] †**1** The tongue of a balance. Only in LME. †**2** A tongue-shaped ornament. LME–M16. †**3** A thong used to tie a shoe. LME–L18. †**4** An instrument for spreading or rolling salve etc. L16–E19. **5** A tongue-shaped part of an implement; *spec.* (*a*) a narrow blade projecting at the edge of a spade; (*b*) a small piece of metal on a sword hilt which overhangs the scabbard. E17. †**6** A narrow projecting piece of land; a tongue. Only in 17. **7** *Zool.* A small tongue-like process, rows of which occur along the dorsal edge of the branchial sac of a tunicate. M19. **8** A flat plate placed in an organ flue-pipe on the top of the foot, opposite the mouth. Cf. LANGUID *n.* 2. M19.

languid /ˈlaŋgwɪd/ *n.* Also **language** /ˈlaŋgwɪdʒ/. L17. [Alt. of prec.] †**1** = LANGUET 3. Only in L17. **2** = LANGUET 8. M19.

languid /ˈlaŋgwɪd/ *a.* L16. [Fr. *languide* or L *languidus*, f. *languere*: see LANGUISH *v.*, -ID[1].] **1** Of a person, an animal, etc.: faint, weak, fatigued; idle, inert. L16. **2** Of energy, motion, etc.: weak, slow-moving. M17. **3a** Of style, language, an idea: wanting force or vividness, uninteresting. L17. **b** Of a person, actions, etc.: spiritless, apathetic, sedentary. E18. **4** Of trade or some other activity: sluggish, inactive. M19.

1 R. THOMAS Suddenly he felt weak, languid and almost comfortable in his exhaustion. 2 LD MACAULAY Two rivers met, the one gentle, languid. 3b R. P. JHABVALA Her manner . . was mostly languid and indifferent.

languidly *adv.* M17. **languidness** *n.* M17.

languish /ˈlaŋgwɪʃ/ *v.* & *n.* ME. [(O)Fr. *languiss-* lengthened stem of *languir* f. Proto-Romance var. of L *languere* languish, rel. to *laxus* LAX *a.*: see -ISH[2].] **A** *v.* **1** *v.i.* Of a living thing: weaken; be or become faint, feeble, or ill; suffer. ME. **b** Exist under conditions which debilitate or depress. Usu. foll. by *in, under*. L15. **2** *v.i.* Droop in spirits; pine with love, grief, etc. Also foll. by *for, to do*. ME. **b** Assume a sentimentally tender or languid look or expression. E18. **3** *v.i.* Of an appetite, activity, interest, etc.: slacken, lose vigour or intensity. Formerly also, (of light, colour, sound, etc.) become dim or indistinct. LME. **4** *v.t.* Pass (a period of time) in languishing. Usu. foll. by *out*. Now *rare*. E17.

1 E. JONES The patient . . is languishing in a semi-conscious state. b *Independent* The grandmother languishes in an old people's home. 2 DE QUINCEY The poor nuns . . were languishing for some amusement. V. SACKVILLE-WEST She trembled for joy in his presence, languished in his absence. 3 P. L. FERMOR Talk would languish and a pensive gloom descend.

B *n.* **1** The action or state of languishing. LME. **2** A tender look or gesture. *rare*. E18.

languisher *n.* L16.

languishing /ˈlaŋgwɪʃɪŋ/ *n.* Now *rare*. LME. [f. prec. + -ING[1].] The action of LANGUISH *v.*; languor. Also, an attack of languor or faintness, esp. proceeding from disease.

languishing /ˈlaŋgwɪʃɪŋ/ *a.* Now *rare*. ME. [f. as prec. + -ING[2].] **1** Declining; suffering; becoming faint, feeble, or ill. ME. **b** Of an illness or death: lingering. E17. **2a** Pining with love or grief. LME. **b** Of behaviour, a look: sentimental. L17. **3** Weary; bored; slow. Also, uninteresting. M17.

languishingly *adv.* L16.

languishment /ˈlaŋgwɪʃm(ə)nt/ *n.* Now *rare*. M16. [f. as prec. + -MENT.] **1** Sorrow, esp. when caused by love or longing; grief, depression; mental pain or distress; a feeling of such sorrow etc. M16. **b** Longing, tenderness; an expression of this. L17. **2** Sickness, weakness, or suffering; a bout or fit of this. L16. **b** Weariness, lassitude; decline, decay; inertness. E17.

1 B. W. PROCTER That inward languishment of mind, which dreams Of some remote and high accomplishment. M. O. W. OLIPHANT Love-agonies and languishments beyond the reach of words.

languor /ˈlaŋgə/ *n.* & *v.* ME. [OFr. (mod. *langueur*) f. L, f. *languere*: see LANGUISH.] **A** *n.* †**1** Disease, illness. ME–E17. †**2** Distressed condition; suffering, sorrow, longing. ME–L16. **3a** Faintness, fatigue; inertia, lassitude. LME. **b** Tenderness of mood, feeling, etc.; lassitude of spirit caused by sorrow, love-sickness, etc. M18. **4a** A heaviness or stillness of the air, sky, etc. M18. **b** Lack of activity or interest, esp. in art, scholarship, trade, etc. M18.

3a A. WILSON Vin had replaced his usual languor by an attempt to sit in an erect, military fashion. b S. ROGERS A softer . . light pervades the whole And steals a pensive languor o'er the soul. 4a R. L. STEVENSON The boom of distant surges disturbed the languor of the afternoon.

B *v.i.* Languish. ME.

languorous *a.* L15. **languorously** *adv.* L19.

langur /ˈlaŋgə, lanˈgʊə/ *n.* E19. [Hind. *langūr*, f. Skt *lāṅgūla* having a tail.] Any of several long-tailed herbivorous cercopithecoid monkeys of India and eastern Asia, of the *Presbytis* and related genera.

douc langur, entellus langur, Hanuman langur, etc.

laniariform /lanɪˈɛːrɪfɔːm/ *a.* M19. [f. next + -I- + -FORM.] Shaped like a laniary tooth.

laniary /ˈlanɪəri/ *a.* & *n.* E19. [L *laniarius* pertaining to a butcher, f. *lanius* butcher, f. *laniare* tear, rend: see -ARY[1].] **A** *adj.* Of a tooth: adapted for tearing, canine. E19. **B** *n.* A canine tooth. M19.

laniate /ˈlanɪeɪt/ *v.t. rare*. E18. [L *laniat-* pa. ppl stem of *laniare*: see prec., -ATE[3].] Tear to pieces.

laniferous /ləˈnɪf(ə)rəs/ *a.* M17. [f. L *lanifer*, f. *lana* wool: see -FEROUS.] Wool-bearing; woolly.

lanigerous /ləˈnɪdʒ(ə)rəs/ *a.* E17. [f. L *laniger*, f. *lana* wool: see -GEROUS.] Wool-bearing; woolly.

lanista /ləˈnɪstə/ *n.* Pl. **-stae** /-stiː/. M19. [L.] *Rom. Hist.* A trainer of gladiators.

lank /laŋk/ *a.*, *n.*, & *v.* [OE *hlanc* f. Gmc base repr. also by (M)HG *lenken* bend, turn, OE (*h*)*lanca* hip, loin, OHG *lancha*. Cf. FLINCH *v.*[1], LINK *n.*[2]] **A** *adj.* **1** Not filled out or plump; shrunken, spare; tall and lean. OE. **2** Of grass: long and flaccid. M17. **3** Chiefly of hair: without curl or wave, straight, flat; dull, lifeless. L17.

1 T. C. WOLFE He was a tall lank boy, and his half-fare age might be called to question. 3 K. VONNEGUT The banners hung lank in the windless day. D. LODGE The girls' hair was lank and greasy from neglect.

B *n.* †1 Leanness, scarcity, thinness. M17–E18. 2 A lanky or lean person. L19.

C *v.t.* & *i.* Make or become lank. E16.

lankly *adv.* E17. **lankness** *n.* E17.

lanky /ˈlaŋki/ *a.* & *n.* L17. [f. LANK *a.* + -Y¹.] A *adj.* Awkwardly or ungracefully lean and long. Formerly also, (of hair) somewhat lank. L17. B *n.* (A nickname for or form of address to) a lanky person. M19.

lankily *adv.* E20. **lankiness** *n.* L19.

lanner /ˈlanə/ *n.* LME. [(O)Fr. *lanier*, perh. use as n. of *lanier* cowardly, f. derog. use of *lanier* weaver f. L *lanarius* wool-merchant, f. *lana* wool: see -ER².] A falcon, *Falco biarmicus*, found in Africa and countries bordering on the Mediterranean; in *Falconry*, the female of this. Also *lanner falcon*.

lanneret /ˈlanərɪt/ *n.* LME. [(O)Fr. *laneret* dim. of prec.: see -ET¹.] *Falconry.* The male of the lanner.

lanolin /ˈlan(ə)lɪn/ *n.* L19. [f. L *lana* wool + *ol(eum* oil + -IN¹.] The fatty matter which permeates sheep's wool, extracted as a yellowish viscous mixture of esters and used as a basis for ointments. Also called *wool-fat*, *wool-oil*, *wool-wax*.

lanose /ˈleɪnəʊs/ *a.* M19. [L *lanosus*, f. *lana* wool: see -OSE¹.] Chiefly *Bot.* & *Zool.* Of the nature of or resembling wool; woolly.

la'nosity *n.* L19.

lanosterol /ləˈnɒstərɒl/ *n.* E20. [f. L *lana* wool + -O- + -STEROL.] *Biochem.* An unsaturated sterol, $C_{30}H_{50}O$, which is an intermediate in the bodily synthesis of cholesterol and in the form of esters is a major component of lanolin.

lansfordite /ˈlansfədʌɪt/ *n.* L19. [f. *Lansford*, a town in Pennsylvania, USA + -ITE¹.] *Min.* A hydrate of magnesium carbonate which crystallizes in the monoclinic system and usu. occurs in colourless stalactitic forms.

lansquenet /ˈlɑːnskənɛt, ˈlans-/ *n.* Also (in sense 1 now the usual form) **landsknecht** /ˈlan(d)sknɛkt/. E17. [(Fr. f.) G *Landsknecht*, f. genit. of *Land* LAND *n.*² + *Knecht* soldier. Cf. LANCE-KNIGHT.] 1 *Hist.* A member of a class of mercenary soldiers in the German and other Continental armies in the 16th and 17th cents. E17. 2 A gambling card-game of German origin. L17.

lant /lant/ *n.* Now *rare.* [OE *hland, hlond.*] Urine, *esp.* stale urine used for various industrial purposes.

lantana /lanˈtɑːnə/ *n.* L18. [mod.L (see below), f. the specific name of the wayfaring-tree, *Viburnum lantana*, to which it bears a superficial resemblance.] Any of various shrubs and perennial herbs of the genus *Lantana*, of the verbena family, chiefly native to subtropical America, bearing axillary heads of red, yellow, white, or varicoloured flowers; esp. *L. camara*, grown in gardens and a weed in some tropical countries.

lanterloo /ˈlantəluː/ *n.* M17. [Fr. *lantur(e)lu*, orig. the meaningless refrain of a popular 16th cent. song.] 1 = LOO *n.*¹ *obs.* exc. *dial.* & *Hist.* M17. 2 Used as a meaningless refrain. *rare.* M20.

lantern /ˈlantən/ *n.* & *v.* Also (*arch.*) **lanthorn** /ˈlantɔːn/. ME. [(O)Fr. *lanterne* f. L *lanterna* f. Gk *lamptēr* torch, lamp (f. *lampein* shine: cf. LAMP *n.*), after *lucerna* lamp.] A *n.* 1 (A lamp consisting of) a transparent case, usu. of glass, horn, paper, etc., containing and protecting a light. ME. 2 *fig.* A thing which or (formerly) person who metaphorically gives light. ME. 3 *Archit.* A square, curved, or polygonal structure on the top of a dome or a room, with the sides glazed or open, so as to admit light; a similar structure used for ventilation or some other purpose. LME. 4 The chamber at the top of a lighthouse, in which the light is placed. Formerly also, a lighthouse. L15. 5 *Mech.* A form of lantern-shaped cog-wheel, a trundle. M17. 6 The megrim, *Lepidorhombus whiffiagonis*. Cf. *lantern-fish* below. *local.* L17. 7a The hollow projection on the head of a lantern-fly. M18. b More fully *Aristotle's lantern*. The framework supporting the masticatory apparatus of certain echinoids. M19.

1 J. HILTON Light was from paper lanterns, motionless in the still air. R. K. NARAYAN There was a dark patch between the light from the shop and the dim lantern. 2 G. BANCROFT The lantern of science has guided us on the track of time.

Phrases: *Chinese lantern*: see CHINESE *a.* *dark lantern*: see DARK *a.* *magic lantern*: see MAGIC *a.* **parish lantern** the moon.

Comb.: **lantern bug** = *lantern-fly* below; **lantern clock** a 17th-cent. wall clock worked by weights and surmounted by a bell in a frame; **lantern-fish** (*a*) *local* = sense 6 above; (*b*) = MYCTOPHID *n.*; **lantern-fly** any of numerous chiefly tropical hemipteran insects of the family Fulgoridae, in many of which the head bears a hollow projecting structure once thought to be luminous; **lantern-jawed** *a.* having lantern jaws; **lantern jaws** long thin jaws, giving a hollow appearance to the cheeks; **lantern-light** (*a*) the light from a lantern; (*b*) *Archit.* a glazed frame in the side of a lantern; (*c*) a skylight; **lantern-man** (*a*) a person who carries a lantern; †(*b*) *spec.* a nightman; **lantern-shell** (the translucent shell of) a bivalve mollusc of the genus *Thracia*; **lantern-slide** a slide for projection by a magic lantern etc.; **lantern-wheel** = sense 5a above.

B *v.t.* 1a Enclose as in a lantern. L18. b Provide or light with a lantern or lanterns. L18. 2 Put to death by hanging on a lamppost. *rare.* E19.

lanternist *n.* a person who uses a magic lantern L19.

lanthanide /ˈlanθənʌɪd/ *n.* E20. [f. next + -IDE.] Any of the series of chemical elements having an atomic number between 57 (lanthanum) and 71 (lutetium) inclusive, which form part of the group of transition metals, have similar chemical properties, and occur together in monazite, gadolinite, and certain other minerals. Cf. *rare earth* s.v. RARE *a.*¹

lanthanum /ˈlanθənəm/ *n.* M19. [f. Gk *lanthanein* lie hidden + -(I)UM.] A metallic chemical element, atomic no. 57, which is the first element of the lanthanide series. (Symbol La.)

lanthana *n.* lanthanum oxide, La_2O_3, a white solid L19. **lanthanite** *n.* (*Min.*) an orthorhombic hydrated carbonate of lanthanum and cerium, usu. occurring as colourless or pale pinkish or yellowish tabular crystals M19. **lanthanoid, lanthanon** *ns.* = LANTHANIDE M20.

lanthorn *n.* & *v.* see LANTERN *n.* & *v.*

†**lantskip** *n.* var. of LANDSCAPE *n.*

lanuginous /ləˈnjuːdʒɪnəs/ *a.* L16. [f. L *lanuginosus*, f. *lanugo* down, f. *lana* wool: see -OUS.] Chiefly *Bot.* & *Zool.* Covered with down or fine soft hair; of the nature of down; downy.

Also **lanuginose** *a.* L17.

lanugo /ləˈnjuːgəʊ/ *n.* LME. [L: see prec.] †1 The fibrous pith of a reed-stem. *rare.* Only in LME. 2 Fine soft hair or down, *spec.* that covering the human foetus; a covering resembling this. L17.

lanx /laŋks/ *n.* Pl. **lances** /ˈlansiːz/. LME. [L.] *Antiq.* A large dish or bowl.

lanyard /ˈlanjəd/ *n.* Also (earlier) †**lanyer**. LME. [(O)Fr. *lanière*, earlier *lasniere*, f. *lasne*, perh. blend of *laz* LACE *n.* and *nasle* f. Gmc (whence also G *Nestel* string, lace): final syll. assoc. w. YARD *n.*²] 1 *Naut.* A short length of rope or line attached to something to secure it; *spec.* one used to secure the shrouds and stays of a sailing ship. LME. †2 A lace, a strap, a thong, a lash. L15–E19. 3 A cord attached to a breech mechanism for firing a gun. Also, a cord used to start an engine etc. E19. 4 A cord passed around the neck, wrist, shoulder, etc., on which a knife, whistle, etc., may be secured. M19.

3 W. BOYD He jerked the lanyard on the motor and with a clatter the engine started up again. 4 *Washington Post* Young staff members with whistles dangling from the lanyards around their necks.

Lao /laʊ/ *n.* & *a.* M18. [Lao. Cf. LAOTIAN.] A *n.* Pl. same, -s. 1 A member of a Tai people of Laos and NE Thailand. M18. 2 The Shan language of this people. M20. B *attrib.* or as *adj.* Of or pertaining to the Lao or their language. E19.

Laocoön /leɪˈɒkəʊɒn/ *n.* E17. [Gk *Laocoōn*, a legendary Trojan priest (Virgil *Aeneid* II).] A statue of the death-struggle of Laocoön and his two sons, who were crushed to death by two sea-serpents. Also (*transf.*), a person resembling such a statue in action or appearance; a (death-)struggle.

DICKENS Scrooge . . making a perfect Laocoön of himself with his stockings. *attrib.*: G. GREENE The desperate contortions of a director caught in the Laocoön coils of an impossible script.

Laodicean /ˌleɪə(ʊ)dɪˈsiːən/ *n.* & *a.* E17. [f. L *Laodicea* (f. Gk *Laodikeia*) (see below) + -AN. See -EAN.] A *n.* A native or inhabitant of the city of Laodicea in Asia Minor. Also (after *Rev.* 3:16), a person who is lukewarm or indifferent, esp. in religion or politics. E17. B *adj.* Of or pertaining to Laodicea. Also, lukewarm or indifferent, esp. in religion or politics. M17.

Laodiceanism *n.* lukewarmness, indifference, esp. in religion or politics L18.

Laotian /ˈlaʊʃ(ə)n, lɑːˈəʊʃ(ə)n/ *a.* & *n.* M19. [f. *Laos* (see below), prob. after *Mars*, *Martian*: see -IAN. Cf. LAO.] A *adj.* Of or pertaining to Laos, a country in SE Asia. M19. B *n.* 1 A native or inhabitant of Laos, *spec.* a Lao. M19. 2 = LAO *n.* 2. M19.

lap /lap/ *n.*¹ [OE *læppa*, corresp. to OFris. *lappa*, OS *lappo*, OHG *lappa*, w. *pp* for *pf* from LG (G *Lappen*): cf. ON *leppr* clout, rag, lock of hair.] 1 A part of a garment etc. which hangs down or projects and can be folded over; a flap, a lappet. OE. 2a A lobe of the ear, liver, lungs, etc. *obs.* exc. in *ear-lap* s.v. EAR *n.*¹ OE. †b A fold of flesh or skin. LME–E17. 3†a The fold of a robe (e.g. a toga) over the breast, which served as a pocket or pouch. Also, the bosom. ME–M17. b The front portion of a skirt when held up to contain or catch something. ME. c A form of loincloth worn by Indians in Guyana. M18. 4a The front portion of the body from the waist to the knees of a person seated, considered with its covering garments as the place *in* or *on* which a child is nursed or an object held. ME. b *transf.* A hollow among hills. M17.

1 JAS. HOGG Wiped his eyes . . with the lap of his plaid. B. HINES One lap of MacDowall's shirt curved out from beneath his sweater . . like half an apron. 4a R. P. JHABVALA He was sitting upright in bed and on his lap lay a large wooden board. A. BROOKNER She lifted the cat off her lap and brushed down her skirt.

Phrases: **drop, throw,** etc., **in** or **into a person's lap** shift or impose (a task, responsibility, etc.) to or on (to) someone. **drop into the lap of** become the responsibility of. **fall into one's lap** come into one's possession, come within one's grasp. **in the lap of luxury** in opulent or luxurious circumstances, surroundings, etc. *in the lap of the gods*: see GOD *n.* *throw in* or *into a person's lap*: see *drop in* or *into a person's lap* above.

Comb.: **lap belt** a safety belt across the lap; **lap-board** a board to lay on the lap, as a substitute for a table; **lap desk** a portable writing-case or surface, *esp.* one for use on the lap; **lap-dog** a pet dog of a kind small enough to sit on the lap; **lap-held** *a.* & *n.* = *laptop* below; **lap-iron** a piece of iron used as a lapstone; **lap portable** a laptop computer; **lap-robe** a rug or cloth to cover the lap of a seated person, esp. in a vehicle; **lapstone** a shoemaker's stone held in the lap to beat leather on; **lap strap** a safety strap across the lap; **lap-table** = *lap-board* above; **laptop** *a.* & *n.* [after DESKTOP] (designating) a computer small and light enough to be used on one's lap.

lapful *n.* as much or as many as will fill a person's lap E17.

lap /lap/ *n.*² LME. [f. LAP *v.*¹] 1 The action or an act of lapping; an amount lapped up; a lick, a smack, a taste. LME. 2 Something that is lapped up; *spec.* (*a*) liquid food for dogs; (*b*) *slang* & *dial.* a weak beverage or thin liquid food (cf. *cat-lap* s.v. CAT *n.*¹); (*c*) *slang* drink, liquor in general. M16. 3 A lapping sound, as that of wavelets on a beach. L19.

lap /lap/ *n.*³ L17. [f. LAP *v.*² Cf. next.] 1 A bundle, esp. of hay or straw. *obs.* exc. *dial.* L17. 2a The amount by which one thing overlaps or covers another; the overlapping part. E19. b In a steam engine, the distance a slide-valve moves beyond what is needed to stop the passage of steam. M19. c *Metall.* A defect consisting of a superficial seam formed when a projecting part is accidentally folded over and pressed against the surface of the metal in rolling etc. E20. 3a A layer or sheet, usu. wound on a roller, into which cotton, wool, or flax is formed during its manufacture. E19. **b** *Warp Knitting.* A loop of yarn on a needle. L19. **4** The act of encircling, or the length of rope, silk, thread, etc., required to encircle, a drum or reel. M19. **5** One circuit of a racetrack etc. M19.

2a Z. M. PIKE Those logs were joined together by a lap of about two feet at each end. 5 *Chicago Tribune* Barney started to burn up the track and opened a big gap, leading the first lap. D. DELILLO I . . swim laps in the college pool.

Phrases: **half lap** a means of joining rails, shafts, etc., by halving the thickness of the ends to be joined and fitting them together; a joint so formed. **lap of honour** a ceremonial circuit of a racetrack, football pitch, etc., by a winner or winners, or by any contestant(s) to receive applause. **last lap** the final section of a journey etc.

Comb.: **lap-dissolve** *v.t.* & *i.* (*Cinemat.* & *Television*) make (a scene) fade as the following scene gradually appears; **lap joint** = *half lap* above; **lap-join** *v.t.* join by means of a lap joint; **lap strake** *n.* & *a.* (*a*) *n.* a clinker-built boat; (*b*) *adj.* clinker-built; **lap weld**: in which the parts to be joined overlap one another; **lap-weld** *v.t.* join with a lap weld; **lap winding** a kind of armature winding in which the two ends of each coil are connected to adjacent commutator segments, so that each coil overlaps the next.

lap /lap/ *n.*[4] E19. [Perh. same wd as prec.] **1** A rotating disk for cutting or polishing gems or metal. E19. **2** A polishing tool of a special shape, coated or impregnated with an abrasive substance. L19.

lap /lap/ *v.*[1] Infl. **-pp-**. [OE *lapian*, corresp. to MLG, MDu. *lapen*, OHG *laffan*, f. Gmc, rel. to L *lambere*, Gk *laptein* lick, lap; partly f. (O)Fr. *laper*.] **1** *v.i.* Take up liquid with the tongue. OE. **2** *v.t.* Of an animal or (*rare*) a person: take up or *up* (liquid etc.) with the tongue; drink up, *up* or *down* greedily. ME. **b** *fig.* Receive or consume avidly. Foll. by *up*. L19. **3** *v.i.* & *t.* Of water: move or wash against (the shore etc.) with a rippling or splashing sound like that made in lapping liquid. Also foll. by *in*, *up*. E19.

2 R. JARRELL A puppy laps water from a can. b *Listener* The Indian Embassy in Bonn will lap up information about Eastern Germany. 3 B. UNSWORTH He watched the gleaming water lap against its containing wall.

lap /lap/ *v.*[2] Infl. **-pp-**. ME. [f. LAP *n.*[1]] **1 a** *v.t.* Coil, fold, wrap (material, a garment, a limb, etc.). (Foll. by *about*, *in*, *round*.) ME. **b** *v.i.* Wrap *about*, *round*. Now chiefly *dial.* M16. **2** *v.t.* Enfold in a wrap or wraps, swathe; bind up, tie round. (Foll. by *in*, *over*, *round*, *up*.) ME. **3** *v.t.* *fig.* †**a** Include; implicate; wrap *up* in a disguise. ME–M17. **b** Of conditions or influences: enfold, surround, esp. with soothing or seductive effect. ME. **4** *v.t.* Fold, fold *up*, *together*; roll *up*. Foll. by *into*. *obs.* exc. *dial.* LME. **5** *v.t.* Enfold caressingly; nurse, fondle; surround with soothing care, protection, etc. Now usu. in *pass.* LME. **6** *v.t.* Cause to overlap; lay (something) *on*, *over* another thing so as partly to cover it. E17. **7** *v.i.* Project; *fig.* extend beyond a limit. Foll. by *over* (adv.). M17. †**8** *v.i.* Lie on something, so as to cover partially or project over it. Foll. by *on to*, *over* (prep.), *upon*. L17–M19. **9 a** *v.t.* Lead (a competitor in a race) by one or more laps; overtake to become one or more laps ahead. M19. **b** *v.t.* & *i.* Of a competitor, a vehicle, etc., in a race: travel over (a distance) as a lap; traverse. E20.

1a SWIFT He would lap a Piece of it about a Sore Toe. A. S. BYATT The anaconda was lapped about herself in one corner of her box. 2 C. READE A good dozen of spices lapped in flax paper. *transf.*: J. BUCHAN The moorlands lap it round as the sea laps a reef. 3b L. MORRIS I who was . . Only a careless boy lapt round with ease. 5 E. M. GOULBURN Moses has been lapped in royal luxury from his infancy. 9a *New Yorker* I could have gone faster . . but it didn't seem nice to lap too many people. *fig.*: *Times* We are constantly being lapped in the wages race. b *Daily Express* There are many machines entered which could lap all day at sixty-five miles an hour. P. EVANS Just lapping the track gently.

lap /lap/ *v.*[3]*t.* Infl. **-pp-**. L19. [f. LAP *n.*[4]] Polish with a lap.

lapageria /lapəˈdʒɪərɪə/ *n.* M19. [mod.L (see below), f. Joséphine Tascher de *la Pagerie* (1763–1814), empress of France: see -IA[1].] A climbing Chilean shrub, *Lapageria rosea* (family Smilacaceae), bearing large bell-shaped pendulous red or white flowers.

laparo- /ˈlapərəʊ/ *comb. form.* [f. Gk *lapara* soft part of the body (between ribs and hip), flank, f. *laparos* slack, loose: see -O-.] *Med.* Of or pertaining to the abdomen, abdominal.

laparoscope *n.* an instrument used for examining the abdomen; *spec.* a tube for insertion into the peritoneal cavity, with a source of light at the inserted end and a means of forming an image of the illuminated region at the other end: M19. **laparoˈscopic** *a.* pertaining to or obtained by laparoscopy M20. **lapaˈroscopist** *n.* a person who uses a laparoscope M20. **lapaˈroscopy** *n.* †(*a*) examination of the loins or abdomen; (*b*) examination of the inside of the peritoneal cavity by means of a laparoscope inserted through a small incision; an operation in which a laparoscope is used: M19. **lapaˈrotomize** *v.t.* perform a laparotomy on E20. **lapaˈrotomy** *n.* (an instance of) a surgical operation in which a substantial opening is made into the peritoneal cavity, esp. for exploratory purposes M19.

lapel /ləˈpɛl/ *n.* M17. [f. LAP *n.*[1] + -EL[2].] That part of the front of a coat etc. which is folded over towards either shoulder.

lapelled *a.* (*a*) provided with a (specified kind of) lapel; (*b*) folded over so as to form a lapel: M18.

†**laperkin** *n.* see LATTERKIN.

lapicide /ˈlapɪsʌɪd/ *n.* M17. [L *lapicida* for *lapidicida*, f. *lapid-*, *lapis* stone: see -CIDE.] A person who cuts stones, or inscriptions on stone.

Also †**lapicidary** *n.*: only in L16.

lapidary /ˈlapɪd(ə)ri/ *n.* & *a.* LME. [L *lapidarius* adj., in late L as n. = stone-cutter, f. *lapid-*, *lapis* stone: see -ARY[1]. For sense A.2 cf. med.L *lapidarium* book of gems.] **A** *n.* **1 a** A cutter, polisher, or engraver of gems or precious stones. LME. †**b** An expert in the nature and kinds of gems; a connoisseur of lapidary work. LME–L18. **2** A treatise on (precious) stones. *obs.* exc. *Hist.* LME.

Comb.: **lapidary('s)-mill**, **-wheel** the grinding and polishing apparatus of a lapidary.

B *adj.* **1 a** Engraved on stone. E18. **b** Of style etc.: characteristic of or suitable for inscriptions; dignified, concise. E18. **2** Concerned with stones. Now *rare*. M19.

1b *Academy* A stanza [which] has a lapidary dignity as of something carved in stone. 2 J. BARNES I . . wrote a lapidary volume issued in a handwritten edition of one.

lapiˈdarian *a.* (*a*) skilled in the knowledge of stones; (*b*) inscribed in stone; characteristic of such an inscription: L17. **lapidarist** *n.* = LAPIDARY *n.* 1 E17.

lapidate /ˈlapɪdeɪt/ *v.t.* *literary.* E17. [L *lapidat-* pa. ppl stem of *lapidare*, f. *lapid-*, *lapis* stone: see -ATE[3].] Throw stones at; stone to death.

lapiˈdation *n.* stoning to death; pelting with stones: E17.

lapideous /ləˈpɪdɪəs/ *a.* Now *rare*. M17. [f. L *lapideus* (f. *lapid-*, *lapis* stone) + -OUS.] Of the nature of stone, stony.

lapidescent /lapɪˈdɛs(ə)nt/ *a.* Now *rare* or *obs.* M17. [L *lapidescent-* pa. ppl stem of *lapidescere* become stony, f. as prec.: see -ESCENT.] That is in the process of becoming stone; (of spring water etc.) tending to turn into stone, petrifying.

†**lapidescence** *n.* M17–L18.

lapidicolous /lapɪˈdɪk(ə)ləs/ *a.* L19. [f. L *lapid-*, *lapis* stone + -I- + -COLOUS.] *Ecol.* Esp. of a beetle: living under stones or similar objects.

laˈpidicole *n.* a lapidicolous animal M20.

lapidific /lapɪˈdɪfɪk/ *a.* Now *rare* or *obs.* M17. [Fr. *lapidifique* or med.L *lapidificare*: see LAPIDIFY, -IC.] Adapted to or concerned with the making of stones.

lapidification /ləˌpɪdɪfɪˈkeɪʃ(ə)n/ *n.* LME. [f. med.L *lapidificat-* pa. ppl stem of *lapidificare*: see next, -FICATION.] The process of hardening or of turning into stone.

lapidify /ləˈpɪdɪfʌɪ/ *v.* M17. [Fr. *lapidifier* or med.L *lapidificare*, f. L *lapid-*, *lapis* stone: see -FY.] †**1** *v.i.* Become stone. Only in M17. **2** *v.t.* Make or turn into stone. L18.

lapidist /ˈlapɪdɪst/ *n.* Long *rare*. M17. [f. L *lapid-*, *lapis* stone + -IST.] = LAPIDARY *n.* 1.

lapiés /ˈlapjɛz, ˈlapɪeɪz/ *n.pl.* Also **lapies**. E20. [Fr. dial. *lapiaz*, *lapiés* (sing. *lapié*) ult. f. L *lapis* stone.] *Physical Geogr.* = KARREN. Also (treated as *sing.*) = KARRENFELD.

lapillus /ləˈpɪləs/ *n.* Pl. **-lli** /-lʌɪ/. M18. [L, dim. of *lapis* stone; in pl. also f. It. *lapilli*, pl. of *lapillo*.] Orig., a small stone or pebble. Now (*Geol.*), a fragment of rock or lava ejected from a volcano, *spec.* one between 2 and 64 mm in size. Usu. in *pl.*

lapis /ˈlapɪs/ *n.* LME. [L.] **1** Stone; *spec.* the philosopher's stone. *rare* exc. in phrs. LME. **2** = LAPIS LAZULI. E19.

Phrases: ***lapis Armenus*** /ɑːˈmiːnəs/ [= Armenian] *Hist.* = AZURITE 2. ***lapis calaminaris*** /kaləmɪˈnɑːrɪs/ [med.L, f. *calamina* CALAMINE] *Hist.* = CALAMINE. ***lapis ollaris*** /ɒˈlɑːrɪs/ [= preserved in jars] *Hist.* = POTSTONE.

lapis lazuli /ˈlapɪs ˈlazjʊlʌɪ, -li/ *n. phr.* LME. [f. L *lapis* stone + med.L *lazuli* genit. of *lazulum*, varying w. *lazur*, *lazurius*, f. Pers. *lāžward* lapis lazuli: cf. AZURE *n.* & *a.*] A blue semiprecious stone composed chiefly of a sulphur-containing silicate of sodium and aluminium; *Hist.* a pigment consisting of crushed grains of this, the original ultramarine; the colour ultramarine. Cf. LAPIS 2.

Lapita /ləˈpiːtə/ *a.* M20. [A site in New Caledonia.] *Archaeol.* Designating a type of decorated pottery found throughout Polynesia and dating from the first millennium BC.

Lapith /ˈlapɪθ/ *n.* Pl. **-ths**, **-thae** /-θiː/. E17. [L *Lapithae* (pl.) f. Gk *Lapithai*.] *Gk Mythol.* A member of a people of Thessaly known for their wars with the centaurs.

Laplace /lɑːˈplɑːs/ *n.* E19. [Pierre Simon, Marquis de *Laplace* (1749–1827), Fr. astronomer and mathematician.] *Math.* Used *attrib.* and in *possess.* to designate concepts and mathematical expressions devised by Laplace or arising out of his work.

Laplace('s) equation the equation $\nabla^2 V = 0$, *esp.* its representation in Cartesian coordinates, $\partial^2 V/\partial x^2 + \partial^2 V/\partial y^2 + \partial^2 V/\partial z^2 = 0$, where V is a function of x, y, and z. **Laplace('s) operator** = LAPLACIAN *n.* **Laplace transform** a function $f(x)$ related to a given function $g(t)$ by the equation $f(x) = \int_0^\infty \exp(-xt)\, g(t)\, dt$. **Laplace transformation** the transformation by which a Laplace transform is obtained from a given function.

Laplacian /lɑːˈplɑːsɪən/ *a.* & *n.* Also **-cean**, **l-**. M19. [f. prec. + -IAN.] **A** *adj.* Of or pertaining to Laplace; originating with Laplace. M19. **B** *n.* The differential operator ∇^2 ('del squared') that occurs in Laplace's equation. M20.

Lapland /ˈlaplənd, -land/ *n.* L16. [Sw. *Lappland*, f. as LAPP + *land* LAND *n.*[1]] Used *attrib.* to designate things found in or associated with Lapland, the region which forms the most northerly portion of the Scandinavian peninsula, divided between Finland, Norway, Sweden, and Russia.

Lapland bunting a bunting, *Calcarius lapponicus*, of northern circumpolar regions. **Lapland longspur** *N. Amer.* = *Lapland bunting*.

Laplander *n.* a native or inhabitant of Lapland, a Lapp E17. **Laplandish** *a.* & *n.* (*a*) *adj.* of or pertaining to Lapland, the Lapps, or Lappish; (*b*) *n.* Lappish: L17.

lap-lap /ˈlaplap/ *v.i.* & *n.* M19. [Imit. redupl. of LAP *v.*[1], *n.*[2]] (Make) a repeated lapping sound.

Laporte rule /ləˈpɔːt ruːl/ *n. phr.* M20. [O. *Laporte* (1902–71), Ger.-born US physicist.] *Physics.* The rule that electron transitions in atoms occur only between states whose l quantum numbers differ by ± 1 or (alternatively) between states of opposite parity (a rule which holds for electric dipole transitions).

Lapp /lap/ *n.* & *a.* L16. [Sw., perh. orig. a term of contempt (cf. MHG *lappe* simpleton), in med.L *Lappo(n-)*.] **A** *n.* **1** A member of the indigenous population of the extreme north of Scandinavia. L16. **2** = LAPPISH *n.* L19. **B** *adj.* Of or pertaining to the Lapps or Lappish. E19.

¶See also SAMI.

lappa /ˈlapə/ *n. W. Afr.* M20. [Hausa, f. Arab. *laffa* wrap up, cover.] A woman's shawl, wrap, or skirt.

lapper /ˈlapə/ *n.*[1] E17. [f. LAP *v.*[1] + -ER[1].] A person who or animal which laps, or takes up liquid with the tongue.

lapper /ˈlapə/ *n.*[2] M18. [f. LAP *v.*[2] + -ER[1].] A person who laps or folds up linen.

lapper /ˈlapə/ *n.*[3] L19. [f. LAP *v.*[3] + -ER[1].] A person who uses a lap or lapidary's wheel.

lappet /ˈlapɪt/ *n.* LME. [f. LAP *n.*[1] + -ET[1].] **1** A lobe of the ear, liver, lung, etc. LME. **b** A fold or pendent piece of flesh, skin, membrane, etc., esp. on some animals. E17. **2** A loose or overlapping part of a garment; a flap, a fold; a lapel. L16. **3** An attached or hanging part of an item of headgear; *spec.* (now *rare*) a streamer attached to a woman's head-dress. Also, in clerical dress, = BAND *n.*[2] 2b. E17. **4** *gen.* A loose hanging part of anything. L17. **5** In full *lappet-moth*. Any of several mostly brown velvety lasiocampid moths whose caterpillars have lappets on their sides; *spec.* a common Eurasian moth, *Gastropacha quercifolia*. E19. **6** *Weaving.* **a** A figure woven on cloth by means of needles placed in a sliding frame; cloth bearing such figures. M19. **b** A mechanism for producing such figures. L19. **7** *Art.* A repeated motif used as a decorative border on Chinese ceramics etc. E20.

2 SWIFT Lifting up the lappet of his coat. **3** E. A. PARKES A sealskin cap with ear lappets. **4** S. T. WARNER A lappet of hair dangles . . over her left eye.

Comb.: *lappet moth*: see sense 5 above; **lappet-weaving** a method of weaving in which figures are produced on the surface of cloth by means of needles placed in a sliding frame.

lappeted *a.* (of a person) wearing lappets; (of a head-dress) provided with lappets: L18.

lappie /ˈlapi/ *n. S. Afr.* L19. [Afk., f. *lap* rag + dim. suff. *-ie*.] A rag, a cloth.

lapping /ˈlapɪŋ/ *n.*[1] LME. [f. LAP *v.*[1] + -ING[1].] The action of LAP *v.*[1]

lapping /ˈlapɪŋ/ *n.*[2] LME. [f. LAP *v.*[2] + -ING[1].] **1** The action of wrapping. Also, a wrapping; trappings, wraps. *obs.* exc. *dial.* LME. **†b** Folding in the arms; embracing, caressing. LME–E17. **2** The action of overlapping or of causing an overlap; a part that overlaps. E17. **3** *Comm.* A method of embezzlement by which (esp. repeated) credits are recorded in accounts as deferred. M20.

lapping /ˈlapɪŋ/ *n.*[3] L19. [f. LAP *v.*[3] + -ING[1].] The action or process of polishing or grinding on a lap.

Lappish /ˈlapɪʃ/ *a.* & *n.* M19. [f. LAPP + -ISH[1].] **A** *adj.* Of or pertaining to the Lapps; *spec.* designating or pertaining to the Finno-Ugric language of the Lapps. M19. **B** *n.* The Lappish language. L19.

Lapponian /laˈpəʊnɪən/ *n.* & *a. arch.* E17. [f. med.L *Lappo(n-)* (see LAPP) + -IAN.] = LAPP.

Lapponic /laˈpɒnɪk/ *a.* E19. [f. as prec. + -IC.] = LAPPISH *a.*

Lapponoid /ˈlapənɔɪd/ *a.* M20. [f. as prec. + -OID.] *Anthropol.* Of physical, esp. cranial, features: characteristic of or associated with early Lapp peoples.

Lapsang /ˈlapsaŋ/ *n.* M20. [Abbrev.] = next.

lapsang souchong /ˈlapsaŋ ˈsuːʃɒŋ/ *n.* L19. [f. invented 1st elem. + SOUCHONG.] A variety of souchong tea with a smoky flavour. Also *lapsang souchong tea*.

lapsarian /lapˈsɛːrɪən/ *n.* & *a.* E20. [f. L *lapsus* fall, LAPSE *n.* + -ARIAN, or back-form. f. *infralapsarian*, *postlapsarian*, *sublapsarian*, etc.] *Theol.* **A** *n.* A believer in the doctrine of the Fall of Man from innocence. E20. **B** *adj.* Of or pertaining to the Fall of Man. E20.

lapse /laps/ *n.* LME. [L *lapsus*, f. *laps-* pa. ppl stem of *labi* glide, slip, fall, rel. to *labare* slip, *labor* LABOUR *n.*] **1** *Law.* The termination of a right or privilege (orig. to ecclesiastical patronage) through disuse or failure to follow appropriate procedures. LME. **2** The gliding or passing away *of* time, one's life, etc.; an interval *of* time elapsed. LME. **b** A gliding or flow of water. Also, a gentle downward motion. *arch.* M17. **3** A slip of the memory, the tongue, the pen, etc.; a mistake, a slight error. L15. **4** A weak or careless deviation or falling from what is right; a moral slip. L15. **b** *Theol.* A falling away *from* the faith or *into* heresy. M17. **5** A decline to a lower state or degree. Formerly also, a fall in temperature. M16. **6** A falling into ruin. *rare.* E17.

2 M. O. W. OLIPHANT A lapse of a hundred years is not much in the story of . . Florence. F. NORRIS The fountain made itself heard, . . marking off the lapse of seconds, the progress of hours. **3** V. BROME Freud now made a long . . attempt to justify his lapse of memory. J. VIORST Expecting to be betrayed, we seize on every flaw and lapse. **4** E. MANNIN His occasional alcoholic lapses shouldn't be held against him. LD MACAULAY The hero sank again into a voluptuary; and the lapse was deep and hopeless. **†the Lapse (of Man)** *Theol.* = *the Fall (of Man)* s.v. FALL *n.*[2]

Comb.: **lapse rate** *Meteorol.* the rate of fall of atmospheric temperature with altitude.

lapse /laps/ *v.* LME. [Partly f. L *lapsare*, f. *laps-* (see prec.); partly f. the n.] **I** *v.i.* **1 a** Of time: pass *away*. LME. **b** *gen.* Glide or pass effortlessly; descend gradually. L18. **c** Of water: flow gently. Also, (of a person or a vessel) float, glide gently over water. M19. **2 †a** Fall into error, heresy, or sin. E–M17. **b** Fall (*away* or *back*) into an inferior or previous state; fail to maintain a position or state, esp. through absence of effort or influence. Foll. by *from*, *into*. M17. **3 a** *Law.* Of a right, privilege, etc.: become void, revert *to* someone, through non-fulfilment of conditions, absence of heirs, etc. E18. **b** *Comm.* Of a contract, agreement, policy, etc.: become void or ineffective, usu. through the withdrawal of one party or the failure to pay a premium. M19.

1c DICKENS Rippling waves that lapsed in silver hush Upon the beach. **2b** V. S. NAIPAUL The system became hard to maintain and he had allowed it to lapse. R. K. NARAYAN He blurted out a couple of questions . . and lapsed into silence. J. M. COETZEE It was only . . work that could keep him from lapsing into gloominess. *Daily Telegraph* Puttnam is a working-class lad made good and he still lapses into Cockney idiom. **3b** A. JOHN I failed to produce the goods . . and our contract lapsed. *Times* Sketchley's $33-a-share offer . . has lapsed.

II *v.t.* **†4** Pounce on as an offender, apprehend. *rare* (Shakes.). Only in E17. **†5** Cause to slip or fall; let slip, let pass. M17–E18. **6** Allow (a right etc.) to lapse; cause or allow (a contract, agreement, policy, etc.) to become void or ineffective, esp. through non-payment; forfeit, lose (esp. a member or one's membership) usu. through breach of rules. M17.

6 *Daily Mail* They were told that they would be lapsed from their union for being in arrears. *Observer* The trouble and expense of lapsing one policy and starting another.

lapsable *a.* (long *rare*) L17. **lapser** *n.* L17.

lapsus /ˈlapsəs/ *n.* Pl. same. E17. [L: see LAPSE *n.*] A lapse, a slip, an error. Chiefly in phrs. below.

lapsus calami /ˈkaləmʌɪ/a slip of the pen. ***lapsus linguae*** /ˈlaŋgwʌɪ/ a slip of the tongue.

Laputan /ləˈpjuːtən/ *a.* M19. [f. *Laputa* (see below) + -AN. Cf. next.] Of or pertaining to Laputa, the flying island in Swift's *Gulliver's Travels*, whose inhabitants were addicted to visionary projects; visionary, fanciful, absurd.

Laputian /ləˈpjuːʃ(ə)n/ *n. rare* (Swift). E18. [f. as prec. + -IAN.] An inhabitant of Laputa (see prec.).

lapwing /ˈlapwɪŋ/ *n.* [OE *hlēapewince*, f. as LEAP *v.* + base (meaning 'move sideways or from side to side') of WINK *v.*[1], assim. to LAP *v.*[2], WING *n.*: named from its manner of flight.] Any of several mostly black and white plovers of the genus *Vanellus*, which have a crested head, wattles, and wing spurs and occur in most temperate and tropical regions except N. America; *spec.* the peewit or green plover, *V. vanellus*, of Europe and Asia.

wattled lapwing: see WATTLED 2.

laquais de place /lakɛ də plas/ *n. phr.* Now *rare.* Pl. same. L18. [Fr., lit. 'place servant': see LACKEY, PLACE *n.*[1]] A manservant temporarily hired during a visit to a foreign city.

laquear /ˈlakwɪɑː/ *n.* Pl. ***-ria*** /-rɪə/. E18. [L *laqueare* panelled ceiling.] *Archit.* A ceiling consisting of panelled recessed compartments, with bands between the panels.

lar /lɑː/ *n.* In sense 1 also **L-**. Pl. **lars, lares** /ˈlɑːriːz/. L16. [L, pl. *lares*.] **1** *Rom. Hist.* A household or ancestral god. Freq. in *pl.*, the protective gods of a house; household gods; also, the home. Cf. PENATES. L16. **2** More fully *lar gibbon*. The common or white-handed gibbon, *Hylobates lar*, of Thailand and Malaysia. E19.

1 lares and penates the home.

lararium /ləˈrɛːrɪəm/ *n.* Pl. ***-ia*** /-ɪə/. E17. [L, f. *lares*: see prec.] *Rom. Hist.* The part of a Roman house where the images of lares or household gods were kept; a private shrine or chapel.

La Raza /laˈrasa/ *n. phr.* M20. [Mex. Sp. f. Sp. = the race.] Mexican-Americans collectively, as a group with a strong sense of racial and cultural identity.

larboard /ˈlɑːbɔːd, -bəd/ *n.* & *a. arch.* Also (earlier) **†lade-bord** & other vars. LME. [Perh. f. LADE *v.* (referring to the side on which cargo was received) + alt. of BOARD *n.*, after STARBOARD.] *Naut.* **A** *n.* = PORT *n.*[5] LME. **B** *attrib.* or as *adj.* Belonging to or situated on the port side of a vessel. L15.

larbolins /ˈlɑːbəlɪnz/ *n.pl.* M18. [Contr. of prec. + -LING[1] + -S[1]. Cf. STARBOLINS.] *Naut.* The crew members of the port watch.

larceny /ˈlɑːs(ə)ni/ *n.* L15. [AN, f. OFr. *larcin* f. L *latrocinium*, f. *latro(n-)* brigand, robber, (earlier) mercenary soldier, f. Gk *latron* pay, *latreus* mercenary, *latreuein* serve.] *gen.* Theft; *Law* theft of personal property (replaced as a statutory crime in English law by *theft*).

grand larceny, petty larceny *Law* (now *Hist.*) theft of personal property to a value greater, less, than a legally specified amount.

larcener *n.* a larcenist M17. **larcenist** *n.* a person who commits larceny E19. **larcenous** *a.* pertaining to or characterized by larceny, thievish M18.

larch /lɑːtʃ/ *n.*[1] M16. [MHG *larche* var. of *lerche* (G *Lärche*) f. OHG f. L *laric-*, *larix*, prob. of alien origin.] **1** Any of various deciduous coniferous trees of the genus *Larix*; spec. *L. decidua*, native to the Alps and cultivated for its tough durable timber. Also *larch tree*. M16. **2** The wood of these trees. M19.

Comb.: **larch blister, canker** a disease caused by the fungus *Trichoscyphella willkommii*, which causes cankers on the bark of larch trees; **larch gum**: similar to gum arabic and extracted from a N. American larch, *Larix occidentalis*; *larch leaf cast*: see LEAF *n.*[1] **larch needle-cast** a disease caused by the fungus *Mycosphaerella laricina*, which attacks and kills the foliage of larch trees; **larch sawfly** a sawfly, *Pristiphora erichsonii*, whose larvae feed on the leaves of larch trees; *larch tree*: see sense 1 above.

larch *n.*[2] see LURCH *n.*[3]

larchen /ˈlɑːtʃ(ə)n/ *a. poet.* E19. [f. LARCH *n.*[1] + -EN[4].] Consisting of larches, that is a larch.

lard /lɑːd/ *n.* ME. [(O)Fr. = bacon f. L *lar(i)dum* rel. to Gk *larinos* fat.] **†1** The fat of a pig; (fat) bacon or pork. ME–E18. **2** The internal fat of the abdomen of a pig, esp. when rendered and clarified for use in cooking and pharmacy. Also, any fatty preparation based on or resembling this. ME. **b** The internal fat of another animal. L15.

Phrases: *bladder of lard*: see BLADDER *n.* 3.

Comb.: **lard-ass** *N. Amer. slang* a person with large buttocks, a fat person; **lard-bladder** *colloq.* a fat person; **lard oil** a clear oil expressed from lard.

lard /lɑːd/ *v.t.* ME. [(O)Fr. *larder*, f. as prec. Cf. INTERLARD.] **1** *Cookery.* Insert strips of bacon or pork in the substance of (meat, poultry, etc.) before cooking. ME. **2** Smear or cover with lard or fat; grease. *rare.* LME. **3** Stick all over *with*; cover, line, or strew *with*. Now *arch. rare.* M16. **4** Intersperse or garnish (speech or writing) with particular words, expressions, ideas, etc.; interlard. M16. **†5** Enrich with or as with fat; fatten. L16–L17. **6** Adulterate with lard. L19.

1 larding needle, pin: for piercing meat so that bacon or pork can be inserted. **2** E. BOWEN Hair that though sternly larded would never stay down. 3 LYTTON Larding himself with sharp knives and bodkins. 4 J. WAIN Larding his essays with phony quotations. *Nature* The organizers have larded their ban with varying expressions of regret.

lardaceous /lɑːˈdeɪʃəs/ *a.* E19. [f. LARD *n.* + -ACEOUS.] *Med.* Resembling lard; = AMYLOID *a.* 2.

larder /ˈlɑːdə/ *n.* ME. [AN *larder*, OFr. *lardier*, med.L *lardarium*, f. as LARD *n.* + -ER[2].] †**1** A supply of meat; meat in storage. ME-L15. **2** A room or cupboard for the storage of food (orig. esp. meat). LME. **3** A store of food hoarded by an animal; *spec.* the collection of prey impaled by a shrike. E20.

Comb.: **larder beetle** a small brown dermestid beetle, *Dermestes lardarius*, whose larvae can be very destructive to stored meat and hides; also called *bacon beetle*.

larderellite /lɑːdəˈrɛlʌɪt/ *n.* M19. [f. Francesco de *Larderel* (1789–1858), It. industrialist + -ITE[1].] *Min.* A monoclinic hydrated ammonium borate, occurring in fumarolic deposits as a white powder.

larderer /ˈlɑːd(ə)rə/ *n.* Now *rare.* L15. [AN (AL *larderarius*), f. as LARDER + -ER[2]. Cf. next.] A person who has charge of a larder.

lardiner /ˈlɑːdɪnə/ *n. obs.* exc. *Hist.* ME. [AN, alt. of prec., or f. AL *lardinarius*, *-erius*.] **1** = LARDER 1. *north.* & *Sc.* ME. **2** An official who has charge of a larder. ME.

lardon /ˈlɑːdən/ *n.* Also **lardoon** /lɑːˈduːn/. LME. [(O)Fr., f. as LARD *n.*: see -OON.] *Cookery.* A strip of bacon or pork used to lard meat.

lardy /ˈlɑːdi/ *a.* L19. [f. LARD *n.* + -Y[1].] Full of or containing lard; like lard.

Comb.: **lardy-cake** a kind of cake made with bread dough, lard, currants, etc.

lardy-dardy /lɑːdɪˈdɑːdi/ *a. colloq.* M19. [Imit. of a style of pronunciation: cf. LA-DI-DA *a.*] = LA-DI-DA *a.*

lare *n.*, *v.* vars. of LAIR *n.*[3], *v.*[3]

laree *n.* var. of LARI.

lares *n.pl.* see LAR.

larf /lɑːf/ *v.i.* & *t.* & *n. non-standard.* M19. [Repr. a pronunc.] Esp. representing Cockney speech: (a) laugh.

Largactil /lɑːˈgaktɪl/ *n.* M20. [Origin unkn.] (Proprietary name for) the drug chlorpromazine.

largamente /lɑːgəˈmɛnti/ *adv.* & *a.* M19. [It. = broadly.] *Mus.* A direction: in a slow dignified style.

large /lɑːdʒ/ *a.*, *adv.*, & *n.* ME. [(O)Fr. (now = broad, wide) f. L *larga* fem. of *largus* abundant, bountiful.] **A** *adj.* **I 1** Liberal in giving; generous; munificent; open-handed. Also, liberal in expenditure, prodigal, lavish. (Foll. by *of*, *in*.) Cf. sense 5b below. Long *obs.* exc. *dial.* ME.

1 SHAKES. *2 Hen. VI* The poor King Reignier, whose large style Agrees not with the leanness of his purse. DRYDEN Large of his treasures.

II Ample, wide, great. †**2** Ample in quantity; copious, abundant. ME-M17. **3** Ample in spatial extent; spacious, roomy, capacious. *obs.* exc. as in sense 8 below. ME. †**4** Extensive in transverse dimension; broad, wide. ME-E18. **5a** Of an immaterial thing: wide in range or capacity; comprehensive, wide-ranging. ME. **b** Of a person: generous or unstinting in an action, possessing or displaying an attribute to the full. Foll. by *in*, †*of*. Cf. sense 1 above. LME. **6a** Of a discourse, narrative, etc.: lengthy. Now *rare* or *obs.* ME. †**b** Of a person: prolix. E17-L18. †**7** Of a measure of space or time: (more than) full, good. Of the time of day: fully come. LME-M18. **8** Of considerable or relatively great size or extent; big, great; extensive; of a kind or variety of greater size than the ordinary. LME. **b** Of a movement, pace, etc.: covering a good extent of ground at a step. LME. **c** Of a meal: heavy, abundant. M18. **d** *Med.* (Of a sound heard in auscultation) full, sonorous (now *rare*); (of the pulse) full. M19. **e** That is engaged in a particular occupation on a large scale. L19. **9** Of speech or manner: pompous, imposing, grandiose. E17.

2 R. HAKLUYT The Kings of France and England gave large money towards the maintenance of the army. 3 COVERDALE *1 Kings* 4:29 God gaue Salomon maruelous greate wyszdome and vnderstondinge, and a large hert. *fig.*: J. S. BLACKIE The brain by knowledge grows, the heart Is larger made by loving. 4 MILTON Southward through Eden went a River large. 5a J. WESLEY How good Thou art, How large thy Grace! LD MACAULAY A good reason for giving large powers to a trustworthy magistrate. W. S. CHURCHILL Neither side in the Crimean War was inspired by large strategic views. b F. M. PEARD He was large in his offers of friendship towards a young nephew of Mr. Pritchard's. 6a J. L. MOTLEY He fell into large and particular discourse with the deputies. 8 D. H. LAWRENCE The stones of the large house were burdened with ivy. G. GREENE The pyjamas she was wearing were too large for her. I. MURDOCH She . . spent a large part of her week-ends in showing them London. U. BENTLEY The houses of most of the boys were small and the families large. *a large order*: see ORDER *n.* *in a large measure*: see MEASURE *n.* *large as life*, *larger than life*: see LIFE *n.* **law of large numbers** a law stating that the result of a series of statistical trials approaches the true probability of the observed outcome more closely as the number of trials increases. b J. KOSINSKI It was difficult to adjust my small steps to the large, measured stride of the soldier. c B. PYM We ate a large tea and ate much. e J. G. PATON Large farmers and small farmers. 9 SHAKES. *Lear* And your large speeches may your deeds approve.

III Not restricted, free. †**10** Indulgent, lax; not strict or rigorous. LME-M18. †**11** Having or observing few or no restrictions or limitations. LME-L18. †**12** Of speech etc.: free, unrestrained; licentious, improper. LME-L16. **13** *Naut.* Of the wind: crossing the line of a sailing ship's course in a favourable direction, esp. on the beam or quarter. L16.

10 J. STRYPE When King Henry was large towards the Protestants, Cranmer was so also. 11 MILTON Leaving my dolorous Prison I enjoy Large liberty to round this Globe of Earth. 12 SHAKES. *Much Ado* The man doth fear God, howsoever it seems not in him by some large jests he will make. 13 J. NARBOROUGH As . . the Wind grew large, we might alter our Course when we would.

Comb. & *special collocations*: *large* CALORIE; **large-eyed** *a.* having a large eye or large eyes; characterized by wide open eyes; **large-handed** *a.* (*a*) having large hands; †(*b*) grasping, rapacious; (*c*) open-handed, generous; **large-hearted** *a.* magnanimous, generous, having wide sympathies; *large intestine*: see INTESTINE *n.*; **large-minded** *a.* having a liberal or generous mind; marked by breadth of ideas; not narrow-minded; **large-mouth(ed) bass** a N. American freshwater bass, *Micropterus salmoides* (family Centrarchidae), introduced elsewhere as a game-fish; **large print** printing in large bold characters designed to be more easily read by partially-sighted people; **large-scale** *a.* drawn to a large scale, on a large scale, extensive, widespread, relating to large numbers; *large ticket item*: see TICKET *n.*; *large* TORTOISESHELL; **large type** = *large print* above.

B *adv.* †**1** Amply; fully, by a great deal; abundantly. Chiefly *north.* & *Sc.* ME-E18. †**2** Liberally, generously. ME-M17. **3** Freely, unrestrainedly, boldly. Now *US.* LME. **4** Of speech and writing: at length, fully. *obs.* exc. in *writ large* (after Milton). LME. **5** Orig., transversely, across. Now *spec.* (*Naut.*) with the wind large, with the wind on the quarter or abaft the beam. LME. †**6** With big steps; with ample gait. M17-E18.

4 MILTON *New Presbyter* is but *Old Priest* writ Large.

Phrases: *by and large*: see BY *adv.* **go** or **lead large** (in a naval or military manoeuvre) break off from a set course and go straight ahead. *writ large*: see WRITE *v.*

C *n.* **1** (Large) size, (large, full) extent. Long *obs.* exc. in phrs. below. LME. **2** Liberty. Long *obs.* exc. in *at large* below. LME. †**3** Liberality, bounty. LME-M16. **4** *Mus.* The longest note recognized in the early notation, equivalent to two or three long notes, according to the rhythm employed; the character denoting this, 𝆶 or 𝆷. L15.

Phrases: **at large** (*a*) at liberty, free; †(*b*) not fixed, unsettled; (*c*) at length, in full; †(*d*) in full size (as opp. to a model or abridged form); (*e*) as a whole, in general, altogether; (*f*) in a general way, without particularizing (AMBASSADOR-*at-large*); †(*g*) over a wide area, abroad; (*h*) without a specific aim. †**at one's large** at liberty. **in large** on a large scale. **in the large** (*a*) = *in large* above; (*b*) in general, as a whole.

largish *a.* somewhat large L18.

large /lɑːdʒ/ *v.* ME. [f. the adj. Cf. OFr. *largir* and (for sense 2) Fr. *larguer.*] †**1** *v.t.* Enlarge, increase, widen. ME-M17. **2** *v.i.* *Naut.* Of the wind: become large (see LARGE *a.* 13). E17.

largely /ˈlɑːdʒli/ *adv.* ME. [f. LARGE *a.* + -LY[2].] **1** Liberally, generously, bountifully. *arch.* ME. **2** To a great extent; extensively, greatly, considerably, abundantly, much. Now usu., principally, on the whole. ME. †**3** At (great) length, in full, fully. LME-M19. **4** With a wide or general application; in a broad sense. *arch.* LME. †**5** Freely, without restraint. LME-M16. **6** In large characters, letters, or outlines. Now *rare.* E17. **7** With lofty demeanour; loftily, pompously. M19.

2 E. M. FORSTER For so young a man he had read largely. E. BOWEN Constructed largely of glass and blistered white paint, Waikiki faced the sea boldly. E. WAUGH In my experience the more responsible posts in the army are largely filled by certifiable lunatics.

largen /ˈlɑːdʒ(ə)n/ *v.t.* & *i. poet.* M19. [f. LARGE *a.* + -EN[5].] Make or grow large or larger.

largeness /ˈlɑːdʒnɪs/ *n.* ME. [f. LARGE *a.* + -NESS.] †**1** Liberality, open-handedness, generosity; prodigality. ME-E17. **2** (Great) size, volume, or bulk; bigness, extensiveness. ME. †**3** Breadth, width. LME-M18. **4** The quality of not being circumscribed or limited in scope, range, or capacity; wide-ranging quality. Opp. *narrowness.* LME. †**5** Lengthiness, prolixity. M16-M17. †**6** Freedom, scope, opportunity. *rare.* Only in M17. **7** Lofty bearing, pomposity. L19.

largesse /lɑːˈʒɛs, -ˈdʒɛs/ *n.* Also **-ess.** ME. [(O)Fr. f. Proto-Romance, f. L *largus*: see LARGE *a.*, -ESS[2].] **1** Liberality, generosity, munificence. Long *obs.* exc. *Hist.* ME. **2** Liberal bestowal of gifts; money or other gifts freely bestowed, esp. by a person in a high position on some special occasion. ME. **b** An act of such giving; a free gift of money etc. M16. †**3** Freedom, liberty. LME-L16.

2 H. WOUK His relish for power and his satisfaction in bestowing largesse. CLIVE JAMES The . . artists who received the largesse of the Whitlam regime seem . . to represent a return to insularity. *fig.*: L. MACNEICE The watch-fires glow and spread their red largesse of flames. (**a**) **largesse!** (*obs.* exc. *Hist.*) a call for a gift of money expressed to an eminent person on some special occasion. **b** T. ARNOLD His triumphs were followed by various largesses of provisions and money to the populace.

¶Formerly more fully naturalized: in 19 usu. spelt *-ess* and with stress on 1st syll.

larghetto /lɑːˈgɛtəʊ/ *adv.*, *a.*, & *n.* E18. [It., dim. of LARGO.] *Mus.* **A** *adv.* & *adj.* (A direction:) in fairly slow time. E18. **B** *n.* Pl. **-os.** A movement or passage played in this way. L19.

largition /lɑːˈdʒɪʃ(ə)n/ *n.* Now *rare.* M16. [OFr. *largicion* or its source L *largitio(n-)*, f. *largit-* pa. ppl stem of *largiri* be bountiful, f. *largus*: see LARGE *a.*, -ITION.] The bestowal of gifts or largesse; bountiful giving; an instance of this.

largo /ˈlɑːgəʊ/ *adv.*, *a.*, & *n.* L17. [It. = broad.] *Mus.* **A** *adv.* & *adj.* (A direction:) in slow time and with a broad dignified treatment. L17. **B** *n.* Pl. **-os.** A movement or passage played in this way. M18.

lari /ˈlɑːriː/ *n.* Also **laree**, (in sense 1) †**larin**, (in sense 2) **laari.** Pl. **-s**, same. L16. [Pers. *lārī*, f. *Lār* a town on the north of the Persian Gulf.] **1** A kind of Persian and Arabic coin consisting of a strip of metal bent over in the form of a hook. *obs.* exc. *Hist.* L16. **2** A monetary unit of the Maldives, equal to one-hundredth of a rufiyaa. L20.

lariat /ˈlarɪət/ *n.* M19. [f. Sp. *la reata*, f. *la* the + *reata*, f. *reatar* tie again, f. *re-* RE- + *atar* f. L *aptare* adjust, f. *aptus*: see APT. Cf. RIATA.] A lasso; a rope for tethering animals, esp. used by cowboys.

larin *n.* see LARI.

larix /ˈlarɪks/ *n.* M16. [L: see LARCH *n.*[1]] †**1** A Middle Eastern plant, *Camphorosma monspeliaca*, of the goosefoot family, used medicinally.

MI6–MI7. 2 A tree of the genus *Larix*; a larch. LI6.

lark /lɑːk/ *n.*[1] Also (chiefly *Sc.* & *north.*) **laverock** /ˈlav(ə)rək/. [OE *lāferce*, older *lǣwerce*, *lāuricæ*, corresp. to MLG, MDu. *lēwer(i)ke* (Du. *leeuwerik*), OHG *lērihha* (G *Lerche*), ON *lævirki* (perh. f. Eng.): ult. origin unkn.] Any of various small brown singing birds of the family Alaudidae, with an elongated hind claw; *spec.* the skylark, *Alauda arvensis*. Also (w. specifying wd), any of various birds resembling but not related to the true larks.

B. W. PROCTER Be constant . . As larks are to the morn or bats to eve. *crested lark, horned lark, meadow lark, shore lark, skylark, titlark, woodlark*, etc. **rise** (or **get up**) **with the lark** get up out of bed very early.

Comb.: **lark bunting** a bunting, *Calamospiza melanocorys*, of the N. American plains; **lark-heel** (*a*) = *lark's heel* below; (*b*) a projecting heel; **lark's heel** (*a*) larkspur; (*b*) nasturtium; **lark sparrow** a N. American ground-nesting sparrow, *Chondestes grammacus*.

larker *n.*[1] (*obs.* exc. *Hist.*) a person whose occupation is catching larks MI7.

lark /lɑːk/ *n.*[2] *colloq.* EI9. [f. LARK *v.*] 1 A frolicsome adventure, a spree; an amusing incident, a (practical) joke. EI9. 2 An affair, a type of activity, a line of business. M20.

1 P. G. WODEHOUSE I hadn't meant to go at first, but I turned up for a lark. J. KRANTZ She had . . thought it might be something of a lark to edit a film in her house. 2 A. SILLITOE This long-distance running lark is the best of all, because it makes me think so good. J. FOWLES If you think you take me in with all this lying in bed lark you're mistaken.

larkish *a.* of the nature of a lark; playful, silly: EI9. **larksome** *a.* given to larking; playful: LI9.

lark /lɑːk/ *v. colloq.* EI9. [Origin uncertain: perh. alt of LAIK, but cf. SKYLARK *v.*] 1 *v.i.* Play tricks, frolic (freq. foll. by *about*). Formerly *esp.* ride in a frolicsome manner, ride across country. EI9. 2 *v.t.* Make fun of, tease (a person); ride (a horse) across country. Now *rare* or *obs.* MI9.

1 THACKERAY Jumping the widest brooks, and larking over the newest gates in the country. W. S. MAUGHAM Stick to your work and don't go larking about with the girls.

larker *n.*[2] a person given to larking about EI9.

larkspur /ˈlɑːkspəː/ *n.* LI6. [f. LARK *n.*[1] + SPUR *n.*[1]] Any of numerous annual plants native to the Mediterranean that constitute the genus *Consolida*, of the buttercup family; esp. *C. ajacis*, grown for its blue, pink, or white flowers. Also (now only w. specifying wd), any plant of the related genus *Delphinium*.

larky /ˈlɑːki/ *a. colloq.* EI9. [f. LARK *n.*[2] + -Y[1].] Inclined or ready for a lark; given to larking about; frolicsome, playful.

larkiness *n.* LI9.

larm /lɑːm/ *n.* Long *rare* or *obs.* MI6. [Aphet.] = ALARM *n.*

Larmor /ˈlɑːmə/ *n.* E20. [Sir Joseph *Larmor* (1857–1942), Irish-born physicist.] *Physics.* Used *attrib.* and in *possess.* to designate concepts arising from Larmor's work.

Larmor frequency: of Larmor precession. **Larmor precession** precession (about the direction of magnetic flux) of the rotational axis of a particle rotating in a magnetic field. **Larmor radius**: of the helical path of a free charged particle spiralling about magnetic field lines.

larmoyant /lɑːˈmɔɪənt/ *a. rare.* EI9. [Fr., pres. pple of *larmoyer* be tearful: see -ANT[1].] Given to tears, lachrymose.

larn *v.* see LEARN *v.*

larnax /ˈlɑːnaks/ *n.* Pl. **larnakes** /ˈlɑːnəkiːz/. LI9. [Gk.] *Gk Antiq.* A chest, ossuary, urn, or coffin, usu. of terracotta and freq. ornamented with designs.

Larnian /ˈlɑːnɪən/ *a.* & *n.* M20. [f. *Larne* a town in Co. Antrim, N. Ireland + -IAN.] *Archaeol.* (Designating or pertaining to) a late mesolithic and neolithic culture of Northern Ireland.

larnite /ˈlɑːnʌɪt/ *n.* E20. [f. as prec. + -ITE[1].] *Min.* A rare monoclinic mineral consisting of a metastable phase of dicalcium silicate.

larrigan /ˈlarɪg(ə)n/ *n. N. Amer.* LI9. [Origin unkn.] A long boot made of undressed leather.

larrikin /ˈlarɪkɪn/ *n.* & *a.* Chiefly *Austral.* MI9. [Origin unkn.] A *n.* A (usu. juvenile) street rowdy, a hooligan. MI9. B *attrib.* or as *adj.* Of the nature of or characteristic of a larrikin. LI9.

larrikinism *n.* rowdy behaviour, hooliganism LI9.

larrup /ˈlarəp/ *v.t. dial.* & *colloq.* EI9. [Origin uncertain: perh. rel. to LATHER *v.*, LEATHER *v.*] Beat, flog, thrash.

larruping *n.* (*a*) the action of the vb; (*b*) a thrashing, a beating: LI9.

larry /ˈlari/ *n.*[1] *dial.* LI9. [Origin unkn.] (A state of) confusion, excitement.

Larry /ˈlari/ *n.*[2] *colloq.* E20. [Origin unkn.: form that of pet-form of male forename *Lawrence*.] *as happy as Larry*, extremely happy.

larum /ˈlɛːrəm, ˈlar(ə)m/ *n.* & *v.* LME. [Aphet. f. ALARUM *n.*] A *n.* 1 A call to arms, a battle-cry; a warning sound. Also, a tumultuous noise; a hubbub, an uproar. Now chiefly *poet.* LME. †b A state of frightened surprise; = ALARM *n.* I. Only in LI6. 2 The alarm of a clock or watch. *obs.* exc. *dial.* LI6. B *v.t.* Sound as an alarm; give the alarm to. *obs.* exc. *dial.* & *poet.* LI6.

larva /ˈlɑːvə/ *n.* Pl. **-vae** /-viː/. MI7. [L = ghost, mask.] 1 A disembodied spirit; a ghost, a spectre. *obs.* exc. *Hist.* MI7. 2 An insect in a state of development (displaying little or no similarity to the adult) lasting from the time of its leaving the egg until its transformation into a pupa; a grub, a caterpillar. Also, an immature form in other animals that undergo some sort of metamorphosis, e.g. amphibians, coelenterates, copepods, tapeworms, etc. MI8.

larval /ˈlɑːv(ə)l/ *a.* MI7. [L *larvalis*, f. as prec. + -AL[1].] †1 Of the nature of or pertaining to a ghost or spirit. Only in MI7. 2 Of, pertaining to, or characteristic of a larva; of the nature of or in the condition of a larva. MI9.

larvated /ˈlɑːveɪtɪd/ *a.* Now *rare* or *obs.* EI7. [f. mod.L *larvatus*, f. L LARVA: see -ATE[2], -ED[1].] Masked, concealed.

†**larve** *n.* EI7. [Fr. f. as LARVA.] 1 = LARVA I. EI7–MI9. 2 A mask. M–LI7. 3 = LARVA 2. MI8–MI9.

larvi- /ˈlɑːvi/ *comb. form* of L LARVA: see -I-.

larviˈcidal *a.* of the nature of a larvicide; that kills larvae: E20. **larvicide** *n.* a preparation adapted to kill larvae; a predator that kills larvae: E20. **larviform** *a.* having the form of a larva MI9. **larˈviparous** *a.* producing young in the condition of larvae EI9. **larvipoˈsition** *n.* the deposition of a larva (rather than an egg) by a female insect E20. **larˈvivorous** *a.* feeding on larvae LI9.

larvikite /ˈlɑːvɪkʌɪt/ *n.* Also (earlier) †**laur-**. LI9. [f. *Larvik* (formerly *Laurvik*), a seaport in Norway + -ITE[1].] *Geol.* An augite-containing syenite, often used as a decorative stone, that has a coarse texture dominated by rhombs of soda or soda-lime feldspar.

lary *a.* var. of LEERY *a.*[2]

laryngal /ləˈrɪŋg(ə)l/ *a.* & *n.* MI9. [f. mod.L *laryng-*, LARYNX + -AL[1].] (A sound) produced in the larynx. Cf. next.

laryngeal /ləˈrɪndʒɪəl/ *a.* & *n.* LI8. [f. mod.L *laryngeus* (f. as prec.) + -AL[1].] A *adj.* 1 *Anat.* & *Med.* Of or pertaining to the larynx; affecting or seated in the larynx; (of an instrument) used to treat or examine the larynx. LI8. 2 (Of a sound) produced in or near the larynx; *Philol.* of or pertaining to laryngeals (see sense B.2 below). E20. B *n.* 1 A laryngeal nerve or artery. LI9. 2 A laryngeal sound; *spec.* (*Philol.*) a reconstructed phonetic element with a laryngeal quality thought to have existed in Proto-Indo-European and to have left traces in extant Indo-European languages. M20.

laryngealist *n.* (*Philol.*) an adherent of the theory that there were laryngeals in Proto-Indo-European M20. **laryngealiˈzation** *n.* the action or fact of being laryngealized M20. **laryngealized** *a.* (of a sound) produced in or affected by the larynx M20.

laryngectomy /larɪnˈdʒɛktəmi/ *n.* LI9. [f. LARYNGO- + -ECTOMY.] Surgical removal of the larynx; an instance of this.

laryngectomee *n.* a person who has undergone laryngectomy M20.

larynges *n.pl.* see LARYNX.

laryngismus /larɪnˈdʒɪzməs/ *n.* EI9. [mod.L, f. as next: see -ISM.] *Med.* Spasmodic closure of the vocal cords, often with noisy indrawing of breath.

laryngitis /larɪnˈdʒʌɪtɪs/ *n.* EI9. [f. mod.L *laryng-*, LARYNX + -ITIS.] Inflammation of the lining membrane of the larynx.

laryngitic /-ˈdʒɪtɪk/ *a.* LI9.

laryngo- /ləˈrɪŋgəʊ/ *comb. form* of mod.L *laryng-*, LARYNX: see -O-. Bef. a vowel **laryng-**.

laryngoˈfissure *n.* surgical incision of the larynx through the midline of the thyroid cartilage LI9. **laryngoˈpharynx** *n.* (the larynx together with) the lower part of the pharynx LI9. **laryngophone** *n.* a throat microphone E20. **laryngospasm** *n.* spasmodic closure of the larynx MI9. **laryngoˈtracheal** *a.* pertaining to both the larynx and the trachea LI9. **laryngotracheobronˈchitis** *n.* inflammation of the larynx, trachea, and bronchi; *spec.* an acute febrile disease (a form of croup) that causes such inflammation and occurs chiefly in young children M20.

laryngology /larɪŋˈgɒlədʒi/ *n.* MI9. [f. prec. + -LOGY.] The branch of medicine that deals with the larynx and its diseases.

laryngoˈlogical *a.* LI9. **laryngologist** *n.* LI9.

laryngoscope /ləˈrɪŋgəskəʊp/ *n.* MI9. [f. as prec. + -SCOPE.] An instrument which enables an observer to inspect a patient's larynx.

laryngoscopic /-ˈskɒpɪk/ *a.* of or pertaining to the laryngoscope or its use MI9. **laryngoˈscopically** *adv.* LI9. **laryngoscopist** /larɪŋˈgɒskəpɪst/ *n.* a person who uses, or is skilled in using, the laryngoscope MI9. **laryngoscopy** /larɪŋˈgɒskəpi/ *n.* inspection of the larynx; the use of a laryngoscope: MI9.

laryngotomy /larɪŋˈgɒtəmi/ *n.* MI7. [Gk *laruggotomia*, f. *larugg-*, *larugx* LARYNX: see -TOMY.] Surgical incision into the larynx from without, esp. (through the cricoid cartilage) in order to provide an aperture for respiration; an instance of this.

larynx /ˈlarɪŋks/ *n.* Pl. **larynges** /ləˈrɪndʒiːz/, **larynxes**. LI6. [mod.L f. Gk *larugx*, *larugg-*.] *Anat.* & *Zool.* A hollow cartilaginous and muscular organ forming the upper part of the trachea or windpipe, and holding the vocal cords in humans and most mammals.

lasagne /ləˈzanjə, -ˈsan-, -ˈsɑːn-/ *n.* Also **-gna**. MI9. [It., pl. of *lasagna*, ult. f. L *lasanum* chamber-pot, perh. also cooking-pot.] Pasta in the form of long wide strips; an Italian dish consisting largely of this and usu. a sauce.

lasagne verdi /ˈvəːdi/ [green] lasagne coloured and flavoured with spinach.

lascar /ˈlaskə/ *n.* EI7. [Pers. & Urdu *laškarī* soldier, f. *laškar* army, camp, (cf. LASHKAR) through Port. *lascari*, *lascarin*, pl. *-res* (repl. *-is*, *-ins*). Cf. next.] 1 Usu. **L-**. A sailor from India or SE Asia. EI7. 2 In the Indian subcontinent: a menial soldier; *spec.* (more fully *gun-lascar*) one employed to do menial work in the artillery. LI8.

1 LONGFELLOW The . . surf, O'er the coral reefs of Madagascar, Washes the feet of the swarthy Lascar. 2 WELLINGTON We can get neither recruits, servants, lascars, coolies, or bullock drivers.

†**lascarine** *n.* Also **L-**. LI6–EI9. [Port. *lascarin*: see prec.] A soldier from India or Ceylon (Sri Lanka). Also, a non-European police officer in India or Ceylon.

†**lasce** *n.* see LASS.

lascivious /ləˈsɪvɪəs/ *a.* LME. [f. late L *lasciviosus*, f. L *lascivia* licentiousness, f. *lascivus* sportive, lustful, wanton: see -OUS.] 1 Inclined to lust, lustful, lecherous, wanton. LME. 2 Conducive to or encouraging lust or lechery. Formerly also, voluptuous, luxurious. LI6.

1 MILTON Hee on Eve Began to cast lascivious Eyes. DENNIS POTTER He did not want any lascivious comments or dirty-minded ogling. 2 J. T. STORY She made . . a lewd movement with her hips as a kind of lascivious promise.

lasciviously *adv.* MI6. **lasciviousness** *n.* MI6.

lascivity /ləˈsɪvɪti/ *n.* Long *rare.* LI5. [Fr. *lascivité* f. L *lascivitat-*, f. *lascivus*: see LASCIVIOUS, -ITY.] Lasciviousness, lust.

lase /leɪz/ *v.i.* M20. [Back-form. f. LASER *n.*[2], as though this were an agent-n. in -ER[1].] Of a substance or device: emit coherent light as (in) a laser; operate as the working substance of a laser.

laser /ˈleɪsə/ *n.*^{1} *obs.* exc. *Hist.* & in *laserwort* below. ME. [L, f. *laserpicium* the plant yielding the resin, also called *silphium* (= Gk *silphion*).] A gum resin obtained from the plant silphium, credited in classical times with great medicinal properties.

Comb.: **laserwort** any of various umbelliferous plants of the genus *Laserpitium*, esp. *L. latifolium*.

laser /ˈleɪzə/ *n.*^{2} M20. [Acronym, f. *l*ight *a*mplification by the *s*timulated *e*mission of *r*adiation, after MASER.] A device that can emit a very intense, narrow, parallel beam of highly monochromatic and coherent light (or other electromagnetic radiation) by using light to stimulate the emission of more light of the same wavelength and phase by excited atoms or molecules. Cf. MASER.

attrib.: *Daily Telegraph* A laser beam .. can weld a detached retina back into place.

Comb.: **laser angioplasty** *Med.*: involving the use of a laser to burn away blocking tissue; **laserdisc**: on which signals or data are recorded to be reproduced by directing a laser beam on to the surface and detecting the reflected or transmitted light; **laser printer** a printer in which a laser is used to form a pattern of dots on a photosensitive drum corresponding to the pattern of print required on a page; **LaserVision** (proprietary name for) a video system in which the signals are on a laserdisc.

lash /laʃ/ *n.*^{1} ME. [f. LASH *v.*^{1} Cf. next.] **1** A stroke with a thong, whip, etc. Formerly also, a sudden or violent blow, a sweeping stroke. ME. **2** The flexible part of a whip. LME. **b** *The* punishment of flogging. M16. **c** A whip, a scourge. Chiefly *poet.* & *rhet.* M17. **3** An eyelash. Usu. in *pl.* L18.

3 DICKENS Long dark lashes .. concealed his downcast eyes.

Phrases: **have a lash (at)** *Austral.* & *NZ* make an attempt (at), have a go (at).

Comb.: **lash rope** *N. Amer.* a rope for lashing a pack or load on a horse or vehicle.

lashed *a.* having eyelashes, usu. of a specified kind L18. **lashless** *a.* having no eyelashes E19.

lash /laʃ/ *n.*^{2} LME. [Perh. LASH *n.*^{1} substituted for other wds of similar sound; or perh. var. of LATCH *n.*^{1}] **1** A string, a cord, a thong. Long *rare.* LME. **2** *Weaving.* = LEASH *n.* 7a. M18.

LASH /laʃ/ *n.*^{3} Also **Lash, lash.** M20. [Acronym, f. *l*ighter *a*board *sh*ip.] Used *attrib.* to designate a ship, or system of shipping, in which loaded barges are placed directly on board the ship.

lash /laʃ/ *a.* Long *obs.* exc. *dial.* LME. [OFr. *lasche* (mod. *lâche*) f. Proto-Romance var. of L *laxus* lax. See also LUSH *a.*] **1** Culpably negligent or remiss, lax. LME. **2** Soft, watery, tender. LME. **3** Slack, relaxed, without energy. E16.

lash /laʃ/ *v.*^{1} ME. [Perh. imit.] **I** Move swiftly or suddenly (now freq. coloured by branch II). **1** *v.i.* Make a sudden movement; dash, dart, spring; (of rain etc.) pour, rush. Usu. foll. by adv. or advb. phr. ME. **2**†**a** *v.t.* Assail, attack. Only in ME. **b** *v.i.* Let fly, rush (*at*); strike or hit *out* violently; (of a horse) kick *out.* LME. **3** *v.t.* Dash, throw, apply liberally. ME. **4** *v.t.* Lavish, squander. Usu. foll. by *out.* E16. †**b** Pour *out* or *forth* impetuously (words etc.). E16–M17. **5** *v.i.* Of a person: rush into excess; break out into violent language; be lavish. Foll. by *out.* M16.

1 J. RUSKIN A lizard .. one expects .. to lash round the shaft and vanish. J. LE CARRÉ A strong sea wind lashed at his city suit. *impers.*: *Woman's Own* It could have lashed down with rain the whole time. **2b** I. MURDOCH We lashed out, hoping that our blows were falling .. upon the unrighteous. I. MCEWAN The other lashed back and .. scratched the first man's eye. **3** *Hair Flair* The lotions we lash on our hair, the potions we put on our face. **5** J. WAIN You're abroad now. Why don't you lash out a bit?

II *spec.* with ref. to LASH *n.*^{1} **6** *v.t.* Beat or strike with a lash etc.; flog, scourge. Also *transf.*, beat on or against. LME. **b** *fig.* Castigate in words, rebuke, satirize. L16. **7** *v.t.* Urge or drive by, or as by, lashes. L16.

6 P. THEROUX The rain lashed Jerry's face. **b** *Time* Bob Bergland .. lashes Earl Butz's laissez-faire policies. **7 lash oneself into a fury** work oneself into a rage.

lashingly *adv.* in a lashing manner; by means of lashing: L16.

lash /laʃ/ *v.*^{2}*t.* LME. [Perh. of LG origin: cf. MDu. *lasche* rag, patch, gusset, Du. *laschen* patch, sew together, scarf (timber).] †**1** Lace (a garment). LME–E17. **2** Chiefly *Naut.* Fasten with cord, rope, twine, etc., (*to* something). Also foll. by *down, on, together.* Formerly also, truss (clothes). E17.

2 *Independent* Ferries often put to sea in calm waters without lashing vehicles down. J. M. COETZEE His mattock was a sharp stone lashed to a stick.

Comb.: **lashed-up** *a.* improvised; **lash-up** (*a*) a makeshift or hastily contrived improvisation; (*b*) a failure, a fiasco.

lasher /ˈlaʃə/ *n.* E17. [f. LASH *v.*^{1}, *v.*^{2} + -ER^{1}.] **1** A person who or (less commonly) a creature or thing which uses a lash. E17. **2** *Naut.* A rope used for fastening, a lashing. M17. **3** On the River Thames in southern England: the body of water that rushes over an opening in a barrier or weir; (the opening in) a weir. L17. **b** The pool into which this water falls. M19.

1 *father-lasher*: see FATHER *n.* **3** J. K. JEROME The pool under Sandford lasher .. is a very good place to drown yourself in.

lashing /ˈlaʃɪŋ/ *n.*^{1} LME. [f. LASH *v.*^{1} + -ING^{1}.] **1** The action of LASH *v.*^{1}; beating, flogging; an instance of this. Foll. by *out*: lavishing, squandering. LME. **2** In *pl.* Large quantities, plenty, abundance, (*of*). Orig. *Anglo-Ir.* E19.

2 J. P. DONLEAVY Porridge with lashings of milk and sugar.

lashing /ˈlaʃɪŋ/ *n.*^{2} M17. [f. LASH *v.*^{2} + -ING^{1}.] Chiefly *Naut.* The action of LASH *v.*^{2}; the action of fastening something with a rope. Also, a rope used for fastening.

soul and body lashing: see SOUL *n.*

lashkar /ˈlaʃkɑː/ *n.* In sense 1 usu. †**leskar.** E17. [Pers. & Urdu *laškar* army, camp: cf. LASCAR.] †**1** A camp of Indian soldiers. E–M17. **2** A body of armed Pathan tribesmen. L19.

lasiocampid /ˌleɪsɪə(ʊ)ˈkampɪd/ *n.* & *a.* L19. [mod.L *Lasiocampidae* (see below), f. *Lasiocampa* genus name, f. Gk *lasios* hairy, shaggy + *kampē* caterpillar: see -ID^{3}.] **A** *n.* Any moth of the large family Lasiocampidae, which includes eggars, lackeys, and lappet-moths, and the larvae of which are called tent-caterpillars. L19. **B** *adj.* Of, pertaining to, or designating this family. E20.

lask /lɑːsk/ *n.*^{1} M16. [AN var. of OFr. *lasche*, f. *lascher*: see LASK *v.*] Looseness of the bowels, diarrhoea; an attack of this; = LAX *n.*^{2} 2. Now only in veterinary use.

lask /lɑːsk/ *n.*^{2} M19. [Perh. f. MDu. *lasche* (mod. *lasch*) piece cut out, flap.] A slice of fish used to bait a fish-hook.

lask /lɑːsk/ *v.* ME. [AN var. of OFr. *lascher* (mod. *lâcher*) loosen, f. Proto-Romance alt. of L *laxare*, f. *laxus* LAX *a.*] †**1** *v.t.* Lower in quality, quantity, or strength, relax; thin (the blood); shorten (life); alleviate (pain). Only in ME. †**2** *v.i.* Suffer from diarrhoea. M16–M17. **3** *v.i.* *Naut.* Sail large with a quartering wind. *arch.* E17.

lasket /ˈlɑːskɪt/ *n.* E18. [Perh. alt. of Fr. *lacet* (see LATCHET *n.*^{1}) in same sense, after GASKET.] *Naut.* Any of the loops or rings of cord by which a bonnet is attached to the foot of a sail.

†**laso** *n.* & *v.* var. of LASSO.

laspring /ˈlasprɪŋ/ *n.* M18. [Perh. f. LAX *n.*^{1} + PINK *n.*^{2}, interpreted as contr. of *last spring.*] A young salmon. Also *gravel laspring.*

lasque /lɑːsk/ *n.* L17. [Perh. f. Pers. *lašk* piece.] A flat, ill-formed, or veiny diamond. Also *lasque diamond.*

lass /las/ *n.* Chiefly *Sc., north.,* & *poet.* Also (earlier) †**lasce.** ME. [Ult. f. ON *laskura* (fem.) unmarried, f. base repr. by OSw. *løsk kona* unmarried woman.] **1** A girl, a young woman. ME. **b** *spec.* A maid-servant. L18. **c** (Used as a playful form of address to) a female animal, e.g. a mare or bitch. M19. **2** A lady-love, a sweetheart. L16. **3** A female member of the Salvation Army. Also *hallelujah lass. colloq.* L19.

1 B. CASTLE I talked to the lass who represents the young Socialists on the N.E.C. **2** W. COWPER There might ye see .. the shepherd and his lass.

Comb.: †**lass-lorn** *a.* forsaken by one's lass or sweetheart.

Lassa /ˈlasə/ *n.* L20. [A village in NE Nigeria (where first reported in 1969).] **1** *Lassa fever*, an acute febrile virus disease that occurs in tropical Africa with a high mortality rate. L20. **2** *Lassa virus*, the virus causing this disease. L20.

'lasses /ˈlasɪz/ *n.* *US colloq.* L18. [Abbrev.] = MOLASSES.

lassi /ˈlʌsi, ˈlasi/ *n.* L19. [Hind. *lassī.*] In the Indian subcontinent: a drink made from a buttermilk or yoghurt base with water.

lassie /ˈlasi/ *n.* Also **lassy.** E18. [f. LASS + -IE.] **1** (A term of endearment for) a girl, a young woman. Chiefly *Sc.* E18. **2** = LASS 3. *colloq.* E20.

lassitude /ˈlasɪtjuːd/ *n.* LME. [Fr. f. L *lassitudo*, f. *lassus* weary: see -TUDE.] Weariness of body or mind; languor; lack of energy resulting from fatigue; disinclination to exert or interest oneself; an instance of this.

B. GELDOF We were .. doing something new in reaction to the lassitude of the more established bands.

lasso /ləˈsuː, ˈlasəʊ/ *n.* & *v.* Also †**laso,** †**lazo.** M18. [Sp. *lazo* (repr. Amer. Sp. pronunc.) = OFr. *laz*: see LACE *n.* & *a.*] **A** *n.* Pl. **-o(e)s. 1** A long rope, esp. of untanned hide, with a noose at one end now used chiefly in the western US for catching cattle and wild horses. M18. **2** *Hist.* A girth placed round a cavalry horse with a lasso or long rope attached, for use in drawing guns etc. Also *lasso-harness.* M19.

Comb.: **lasso-cell** *Zool.* a nematocyst or stinging cell of a coelenterate; a similar cell of a ctenophore, which with others exudes a long sticky thread; *lasso-harness*: see sense 2 above.

B *v.t.* **1** Catch (as) with a lasso. E19. **2** *Mil.* Draw (guns etc.) with lasso-harness. M19.

lassoer *n.* L19.

lassock /ˈlasək/ *n.* *Sc.* E19. [f. LASS + -OCK.] A little girl.

lassy *n.* var. of LASSIE.

lassy me /ˈlasi miː/ *int. slang.* M19. [Perh. contr. of *Lord save me.*] Expr. surprise.

last /lɑːst/ *n.*^{1} [OE *lāst* (masc., sense 1), *lǣst* (fem., sense 2), *lǣste* (sense 3) = MLG *lēst(e*, Du. *leest*, OHG *leist* (G *Leisten*) a last, ON *leistr* foot, sock, Goth. *laists-* footprint, track, f. Gmc base meaning 'follow': cf. LAST *v.*^{1}] †**1** A footstep, a track, a trace. Latterly only in *not a last*, nothing, not at all. OE–L15. †**2** A boot. Only in OE. **3** A shoemaker's model of the foot, for shaping and repairing boots and shoes. OE.

3 stick to one's last refrain from meddling in matters one does not understand.

last /lɑːst/ *n.*^{2} [OE *hlæst* = OFris. *hlest*, (M)LG, (M)Du. *last*, OHG *hlast* (G *Last*), f. WGmc base repr. also by ON *hlass* load, f. Gmc base of LADE *v.*] †**1** A load, a burden, a weight carried. OE–LME. **2** A commercial denomination of weight, capacity, or quantity, varying for different kinds of goods and in different localities, e.g. 12 sacks of wool, 12 barrels of cod, 10 quarters of malt or grain. ME. †**b** *transf.* A huge indefinite number. LME–E18. †**3** A unit in the measurement of a ship's burden equal to 2 tons (occas. 1 ton). M17–L18.

last /lɑːst/ *n.*^{3} *obs.* exc. *Hist.* LOE. [AL *lastum*, *lestum* (Domesday Book *lest*), used for LATHE *n.*^{1}] = LATHE *n.*^{1} Also, an administrative assembly in Kent (more fully *last-court*).

last /lɑːst/ *n.*^{4} ME. [f. LAST *v.*^{1}] **1** Continuance, duration. Now *rare.* ME. **2** Power of holding on or out; staying power. E17.

last /lɑːst/ *v.*^{1} [OE *lǣstan*, corresp. to OFris. *lāsta*, *lēsta* fulfil, OS *lēstian* execute, OHG, G *leisten* afford, yield, Goth. *laistjan* follow, f. Gmc, f. base also of LAST *n.*^{1}] †**1** *v.t.* Orig., follow (a leader); pursue (a course, a practice). Later, carry out (a command, a promise); pay (tribute); maintain (peace). OE–L15. **2** *v.i.* Of a state of things, a process, a period of time: continue, endure, go on. OE. †**b** With compl. prep. phr.: continue in a specified condition, course of action, etc. ME–M17. **3a** *v.i.* Hold out; continue fresh, unbroken, unimpaired, effective, etc. Of a person (also foll. by *out*): manage to continue in a post, a course of action, etc.; remain alive. ME. **b** *v.t.* & *i.* Of provisions, resources, etc.: remain sufficient for the needs of (a person etc.) throughout a period. ME. **c** *v.t.* Continue in vigour as long as or longer than (now usu. foll. by *out*); hold out under or against. ME. †**4** *v.i.* Extend in space; reach, stretch. ME–L16.

2 L. HELLMAN We must have had a lot of wine because our lunch lasted long after everybody left. H. BAILEY A short sharp war, which would last perhaps six months. b MILTON Whence in perpetual fight they needs must last Endless, and no solution will be found. 3 G. GREENE His prose, unlike his poetry, has not lasted well. M. N. COX Is this relief temporary or will it last? W. BOYD If I radically trim my budget I can last for another three weeks. b T. F. POWYS Mr Mayhae garnered and stowed away enough humility to last any man a lifetime. P. BOWLES He finished his cigarette slowly, making it last. J. RHYS I've enough cash to last for two or three months. c *last the pace*: see PACE *n.*[1]

last /lɑːst/ *v.*[2]*t.* E17. [f. LAST *n.*[1]] Put (a boot or shoe) on a last.

last /lɑːst/ *adv.*, *a.*, & *n.*[5] [OE *latost*, (Northumb.) *lætest*, corresp. to OFris. *letast*, *lest*, OS *latst*, *last*, *letist* (Du. *laatst*, *lest*, OHG *lazzōst*, *lezzist* (G *letzt*), ON *latastr*, f. Gmc superl. of base of LATE *a.*, *adv.*: see -EST[1]. (*latest* is a new formation on *late*.)] **A** *adv.* **1** After all others in a series; at the end. OE. **2** On the occasion next before the present; most recently. ME. **3** As the final thing to be mentioned or considered; in the last place, lastly. ME. **4** In the end, finally. M17.

1 E. O'NEILL Paul comes out last carrying an accordion. 2 SHELLEY When did you see him last. W. S. CHURCHILL Nearly ten days have passed since I last addressed you. 3 SHAKES. *2 Hen. IV* First my fear, then my curtsy, last my speech. 4 DRYDEN Pleas'd with his Idol, he . . Adores; and last, the Thing ador'd, desires.

B *adj.* **1** Following all the others in time, order, series, succession, or enumeration; subsequent to all others in occurrence, existence, etc.; *emphatic* last in order of likelihood, suitability, preference, etc. (With a cardinal numeral now placed before the numeral, exc. when in sense 'last-mentioned', formerly usu. after the numeral.) ME. **b** Extreme or remotest in space or position. Formerly also, rearmost. Now *rare*. LME. **2** *spec.* Belonging to the final stages, esp. of a person's life or the world's existence; relating to death or the end of the world. ME. **3** Occurring or presenting itself next before the present or existing one; most recent, latest. LME. **b** Of a period, season, etc.: occurring next before the time of writing or speaking. (With a common n. after *the* or (emphasizing recentness) *this* or *these* or without article or demonstrative; with the name of a month, of a day of the week, etc., placed before or (more formally) after the n.) LME. **4** Remaining or arrived at after others have disappeared or have been removed, exhausted, or spent; the only remaining. LME. **5** Reaching its ultimate limit; attaining a degree beyond which one cannot go; utmost, extreme. Now chiefly in *of the last importance*. LME. **6** After which there is nothing to be done or said; final, conclusive, definitive. Now only in *last word* below. M17.

1 W. H. PRESCOTT She was the last person to be approached with undue familiarity. H. B. STOWE It's the last night we may be together. E. O'NEILL The cockney seems about to challenge this last statement. E. BOWEN The Major was making his last round through the orchards before shutting up the house. DAY LEWIS She was the last of a clan which had been founded some centuries before. A. WILSON The subject of his wife's illness was the last thing that Bernard wished to discuss. R. K. NARAYAN I . . read the Oxford edition from the first page to the last. 2 J. H. NEWMAN Hosius . . with his last breath, abjured the heresy. V. BRITTAIN The last moments of men who had died in hospital. 3 MARVELL Having writ to you last post. b R. GRAVES It was half-past three On Easter Tuesday last. M. BRADBURY Howard had fetched it last time. M. AMIS These last few days I've had no time for reading. *Daily Telegraph* There were conflicting reports last night. 4 M. DICKENS She . . would count the change to the last half-penny. J. KRANTZ Vito waited until the last man had left. 5 LD MACAULAY Their Church was suffering the last excess of injury and insult. J. P. MAHAFFY Rowing . . was of the last importance in their naval warfare. 6 S. JOHNSON Whatever shall be the last decision of the law.

C *absol.* as *n.* **1** After preps., esp. *at*: the last point of time, the end (see phrs. below). ME. **2** The last person or thing of a category, series, etc.; the one coming at the end of a series arranged in order of rank or estimation, the lowest. (Foll. by *of*.) LME. **3** *spec.* The last day or last moments of life; the end of life, death. Chiefly w. possess. LME. **4** *The* concluding, last remaining, or most recent part *of* a thing; *spec.* (now *N. Amer.*) *the* last day *of* a month. M16. **5** With a demonstrative, relative, etc., adj.: the last-mentioned person or thing. M16. **6** With possess. adj.: one's last performance of a certain act (implied by the vb). Esp. in *breathe one's last* (sc. *one's last breath*). L16. **7** With a possess.: a person's most recent letter. Now chiefly in commercial use. L16. **8** *The* last mention or sight of a person or thing. Esp. in *hear the last of*, *see the last of*. *colloq.* M19.

2 POPE Oh may some spark of your celestial fire The last, the meanest of your sons inspire. J. K. JEROME To give the lad time between each lesson to forget what he learned at the last. 3 C. J. LEVER As he drew nigh his last his sufferings gave little intervals of rest. 4 E. O'NEILL Turin comes in . . and overhears the last of her prayer. DYLAN THOMAS She's down to the last of the elderflower wine. 5 W. DAMPIER With a Fireship and 3 Tenders, which last had not a constant crew. 6 ADDISON The swans . . now sung their last, and dy'd. G. PALEY The worms that were the fishes' Sunday dinner had wriggled their last. 7 W. CONGREVE By your last from Dublin I may guess this will find you at Kilkenny.

Special collocations, phrases, & comb. (of adv., adj., & n.): **at last** in the end, finally; after a long time, at length. **at long last** eventually but only after much delay. **at the last** *arch.* = *at last* above. **at the long last** (now *rare* or *obs.*) = *at long last* above. *every last*: see EVERY *a.* 1. *first and last*: see FIRST *adv. first or last*: see FIRST *adv.* **four last things** (*Theol.*) *the* four things (death, judgement, heaven, and hell) studied in eschatology. *from first to last*: see FIRST *n. have the last laugh*: see LAUGH *n.* **if it's the last thing I do** (in emphasizing one's intention or desire to do a thing) even if I die after doing that. †**in the last** *rare* finally, in the end. *in the last analysis*: see ANALYSIS 1. **last across (the road)** a children's game in which the object is to be the last to cross a road (or railway) in the path of an approaching vehicle (or train). *last assize(s)*: see ASSIZE *n.* 3. **last but not least** last in order of mention or occurrence but not of importance. **last but one** immediately preceding the final or most recent. **last but two** next but one before the final or most recent. **last day** (*a*) (now *dial.*) yesterday; (*b*) (*Last Day*) *the* Day of Judgement. **last days** (*a*) *the* concluding period in the life or history *of* a person etc.; (*b*) *the* period including and immediately preceding the Last Judgement. *last ditch*: see DITCH *n.* **last-ditch** *a.* (of opposition, resistance, etc.) maintained to the end; (of an effort etc.) made at the last minute in an attempt to avert distaster. **last end** *arch.* & *dial.* the very end; *esp.* the end of life, death. **last evening** yesterday evening. *last gasp*: see GASP *n.* †**last hand** the finishing touches. **last home** the grave. *last honours*: see HONOUR *n.* **last hurrah** (orig. *US*) the final act in a politician's career; *transf.* any final performance or effort. **last in, first out** (*a*) (of a system of employment) in which those most recently recruited are the first to be made redundant; (*b*) (of a system of accounting) in which the goods most recently acquired by a company are valued as though they are the first to be sold; (*c*) *Computing* (designating or pertaining to) a procedure in which the item removed from a buffer, queue, etc., is always the one most recently added. *Last Judgement*: see JUDGEMENT 2. *last lap*: see LAP *n.*[3] **last man** *Cricket* the batsman who goes in to bat last. **last minute** the time immediately before a critical event. **last-minute** *a.* performed, occurring, bought, etc. at the latest possible time. **last moment** = *last minute* above. **last-moment** *a.* = *last-minute* adj. above. †**last morning** yesterday morning. **last name** a surname. *last office(s)*: see OFFICE *n.* 5. †**last past** (*a*) (with dates) = sense B.3b above; (*b*) (of a period of time) extending to the present, (the) past (year etc.). *last post*: see POST *n.*[6] *last quarter*: see QUARTER *n.* 7b. *last resort*: see RESORT *n.* **last rites, last sacraments** (*RC Ch.*) *the* sacraments (the Eucharist and extreme unction) administered to the dying. *last sleep*: see SLEEP *n. last straw*: see STRAW *n.* **Last Supper**: eaten by Jesus and his disciples on the eve of the Crucifixion. **last thing (at night)** as one's final act before going to bed. **last things** = *four last things* above. **last trump** the trumpet-call that some believe will wake the dead on the Day of Judgement. *last will and testament*: see WILL *n.*[1] **last word** (*a*) *the* final pronouncement on a subject, after which there is nothing more to be said; *have the last word*, speak in such a way as to close an argument; (*b*) (*fig.*) *the* finest, most advanced, etc., example of its kind; *the* latest fashion. **last words** a person's last recorded remark before dying; *famous last words*, (an ironical comment on or rejoinder to) an overconfident or boastful assertion that may well be proved wrong by events. *on its, one's, last legs*: see LEG *n. pay one's last respects*: see RESPECT *n.* **second last** = *last but one* above. *Seven Last Words*: see WORD *n. the last rose*: see ROSE *n.* **third last** = *last but two* above. **to the last** up to the end; *esp.* up to the last moment of life.

lastage /ˈlɑːstɪdʒ/ *n. obs.* exc. *Hist.* LME. [AN, (O)Fr. *lestage* (med.L *lestagium*), f. *lest* LAST *n.*[2]] **1** A toll payable by traders attending fairs and markets. LME. †**2** The ballast of a ship. LME–M18. **3** A payment for liberty to load a ship; a port duty levied at so much per last of cargo. LME.

laster /ˈlɑːstə/ *n.*[1] E18. [f. LAST *v.*[1] + -ER[1].] A person who or thing which lasts; *spec.* (*a*) a fruit that keeps well; (*b*) a person who has staying power.

laster /ˈlɑːstə/ *n.*[2] L19. [f. LAST *n.*[1] or *v.*[2] + -ER[1].] A worker who shapes a boot or shoe by fixing the parts smoothly on a last.

Lastex /ˈlastɛks/ *n.* Also **l-**. M20. [f. E)LAST(IC + *-ex* (arbitrary ending).] (Proprietary name for) an elastic yarn formed from a combination of rubber or man-made elastomeric fibres with silk, cotton, or rayon, used in the manufacture of corsetry etc.

lasting /ˈlɑːstɪŋ/ *n.*[1] ME. [f. LAST *v.*[1] + -ING[1].] The action of LAST *v.*[1]; continuance, duration, permanence.

Comb.: **lasting power** staying power.

lasting /ˈlɑːstɪŋ/ *a.* & *n.*[2] ME. [f. LAST *v.*[1] + -ING[2].] **A** *adj.* **1** Of long continuance, persistent; permanent, enduring. In early use freq. everlasting. ME. **2** Of a material substance: durable. Formerly, of provisions, fruit, etc.: keeping well. ME. **3** Of a horse: possessed of staying power. *Sporting slang.* E19.

1 M. FITZHERBERT Deep & lasting friendships. M. SCAMMELL His decision was to make a lasting impression on Solzhenitsyn. 2 G. BERKELEY Our black cloth is neither so lasting, nor of so good a dye as the Dutch.

B *absol.* as *n.* A durable kind of cloth; = EVERLASTING *n.* 3. M18.

lastingly *adv.* ME. **lastingness** *n.* ME.

lastly /ˈlɑːstli/ *adv.* LME. [f. LAST *a.* + -LY[2].] **1** At the end; finally. Now only, as the last in a series of items, operations, points in a discourse, etc.; in conclusion. LME. †**2** Very lately, recently. L16–M17. †**3** Decisively, once and for all. E–M17.

1 T. HARDY A coat was laid on . . ; then another coat for increased blackness; and lastly a third. 3 MILTON I for his sake will leave Thy bosom . . and for him lastly die.

lasya /ˈlɑːsjə/ *n.* M20. [Skt *lāsya*.] A graceful Indian style of female dancing.

lat /lɑːt/ *n.*[1] E19. [Hind. *lāṭh*, *lāṭ*.] **1** A staff, a pole. *rare.* E19. **2** An obelisk or a columnar monument in the Indian subcontinent; *spec.* any of the ancient Buddhist columns of Eastern India. L19.

lat /lɑːt/ *n.*[2] Pl. **lati** /ˈlati/, **lats**. E20. [f. 1st syll. of *Latvija* Latvia.] A unit of gold currency established by the State of Latvia in August 1922 and discontinued in 1941.

lat /lat/ *n.*[3] *slang.* E20. [Abbrev.] = LATRINE. Usu. in *pl.*

lat /lat/ *n.*[4] *Body-builders' slang.* M20. [Abbrev.] = LATISSIMUS. Usu. in *pl.*

lat *n.*[5] see LATH *n.*

Latakia /latəˈkiːə/ *n.* E19. [See below.] In full *Latakia tobacco*. A fine kind of tobacco produced near and shipped from Latakia, a port in Syria.

latania /ləˈteɪnɪə, ləˈtanɪə/ *n.* L18. [In sense 1 f. Sp. Amer. In sense 2 f. mod.L (see below) f. Fr. LATANIER, the name used in Mauritius.] **1** = LATANIER 1. *US.* L18. **2** Any of several fan palms of the genus *Latania*, native to Mauritius and neighbouring islands. M19.

latanier /ləˈtanɪə/ *n.* E19. [Fr.: cf. prec.] **1** Any of several fan palms found in the southern US and Central America; *esp.* the cabbage palmetto, *Sabal palmetto. US.* E19. **2** (The Mauritian name for) any of several fan palms; *esp.* = LATANIA 2. E20.

latch /latʃ/ *n.*[1] ME. [In sense 1 prob. f. LATCH *v.*[1] In sense 2 prob. f. OFr. *lache* var. of *laz* LACE *n.*: cf. LATCHET *n.*[1]] **1** A fastening for a door or gate, consisting of a small bar which falls or slides into a catch, and is lifted by a lever, string, etc., from outside. Now also (more fully *night-latch*), a small spring-lock for an outer door, which catches when the door is closed and is worked from the outside by a key. ME. **2a** A loop or noose for securing a thing; a snare. Also, a leather thong. *obs.* exc. *dial.* LME. **b** *Electronics.* A logic circuit which retains whatever output state results from a momentary input signal until reset by another signal (also *latch circuit*). Also called *toggle* (*circuit*). M20.

1 B. BEHAN Someone pushed the door but the latch was on, and he had to knock. **off the latch** unlatched, ajar. **on the latch** fastened by a latch only, not locked.

Comb.: **latch bolt** a spring-loaded bolt; *latch circuit*: see sense 2b above; **latchkey** a key to open the spring-lock of an outer door; (*latchkey child*, a child given such a key as a means of entering home after school while his or her parents are still out at work); **latch-string** a string fastened to a latch and passed through a hole in the door, so that the latch may be raised from outside; *esp.* (*US*) such a string left hanging out as a sign of welcome.

†**latch** *n.*[2] see LURCH *n.*[3]

latch /latʃ/ *v.*[1] [OE *læċċan* f. Gmc, f. base rel. to those of Gk *lazesthai*, L *laqueus* noose.] †**1** *v.t.* Take hold of, grasp, seize, esp. with the hand or claws; clasp, embrace; *fig.* grasp with the mind, comprehend. OE–E17. †**b** Put or strike swiftly *off, out, up*; dart *out* (the tongue). ME–M16. †**2** *v.t.* Take with force; capture, seize (a person, goods). OE–M16. **3** *v.t.* Be the recipient of, get, receive. Now only (*dial.*), become infected with, catch (a disease). ME. **4** *v.t.* Intercept the fall of, catch (something falling); catch or receive *in* (a receptacle). *obs.* exc. *dial.* M16. **5** *v.i.* Alight, settle. *dial.* E19. **6** *v.i.* Foll. by *on* (adv.): (*a*) attach oneself *to* a person as a constant companion; give one's adherence *to* an idea etc.; (*b*) get wise (*to* a fact etc.), understand. *colloq.* (orig. *US*). M20.

3 SHAKES. *Macb.* I have words That would be howl'd out in the desert air, Where hearing should not latch them. 6 *New Yorker* Mr. Kelly has latched on to a sound . . idea.

Comb.: **latch-pan** (chiefly *dial.*) a pan placed under a joint to catch the drippings.

latch /latʃ/ *v.*[2] LME. [f. LATCH *n.*[1]] **1** *v.t.* Fasten or secure with a latch. LME. **2** *v.i.* Of a door etc.: shut so that the latch catches. M20.

1 P. THEROUX The shutters of the hut were down and latched. 2 T. S. ELIOT Please *shut the door after you*, so it latches.

latchet /ˈlatʃɪt/ *n.*[1] LME. [OFr. *lachet* var. of *lacet*, f. *laz* LACE *n.*: see -ET[1].] **1** A narrow strip of something; a loop. Now only (*Sc.*), a loop of string used to keep a bricklayer's line horizontal; a tingle. LME. **2** *spec.* A narrow thong or lace for fastening a shoe or sandal. Now *arch.* (esp. in allusion to *Mark* 1:7) & *dial.* LME. †**3** *Naut.* = LASKET. L15–E17.

2 AV *Mark* 1:7 There commeth one mightier than I after me, the latchet of whose shooes I am not worthy to stoupe downe, and vnloose.

latchet /ˈlatʃɪt/ *n.*[2] Also **-ett.** L19. [Origin unkn.] The European red gurnard, *Aspitrigla cuculus.* Also (*Austral.*), a flying gurnard, *Pterygotrigla polyommata.*

latching /ˈlatʃɪŋ/ *n.* LME. [f. LATCH *v.*[1] + -ING[1].] †**1** The action of LATCH *v.*[1] Only in LME. **2** *Naut.* = LASKET. Also *latchings key.* Usu. in *pl.* L18.

late /leɪt/ *n.*[1] Long *obs.* exc. *Sc.* Also **lait.** ME. [Partly f. ON *lát* letting (as in *blóð-lat* blood-letting), (in pl.) manners, sounds, partly f. ON *lǽte* (only in nom. & accus.) manner, sound, both f. Gmc base of LET *v.*[1]] †**1** Appearance, aspect; outward manner or bearing. ME–L15. **2** In *pl.* Manners, behaviour; *esp.* unruly behaviour or actions, goings-on. ME. †**3** Voice, sound. Only in ME.

late /leɪt/ *a.* & *n.*[2] Compar. **later,** LATTER; superl. **latest,** LAST *a.* [OE *læt* = OFris. *let*, OS *lat*, OHG *laz* (G *lass*), ON *latr*, Goth. *lats*, f. Gmc, f. IE base repr. also by L *lassus* weary: rel. to LET *v.*[2]] **A** *adj.* **I 1** Slow, tardy; tedious. Now *dial.* OE. **2** Occurring, coming, or being after the proper, right, or customary time; delayed or deferred in time. Freq. *impers.* in *it is* etc. (*too*) *late* (Foll. by *for, to do.*) OE. **b** Of a plant, fruit, etc.: flowering or ripening at an advanced season of the year. LME. **c** Of a fruit etc.: backward in ripening. Of a season: prolonged or deferred beyond its proper time. M17. **d** Of a woman: whose menstrual period has failed to occur at the expected time. *colloq.* M20. **3** (Occurring) far on in the course of the day, esp. well on into the evening or night (freq. *impers.* in *it is* etc. *late*). Also (*colloq.*), of a person: keeping late hours, going to bed late. OE. **4** Belonging to an advanced stage in a period, the development of a person or thing, the history of a science, language, etc. LME. **b** *attrib.* Of a period, season, etc.: that is at an advanced stage. Also, of a writer, composer, etc.: that is writing, composing, etc., at an advanced stage in his or her artistic development. L18. **5a** Of a person: recently deceased. LME. **b** That was recently (the holder of an office etc.) but is not now. LME. **6** Recent in date; that has recently happened or occurred; recently made, performed, completed; of recent times; belonging to a recent period. Now chiefly in *of late years.* LME.

2 E. WAUGH Trust me . . . It is not too late to escape. J. STALLWORTHY Light woke me early, but the trams were late. A. MACLEAN I was quite ten minutes late for my appointment. b *Stock & Land* (*Melbourne*) There are still some late sunflowers to be harvested. c D. H. LAWRENCE If the season is late . . then mid-September sees the corn still standing in stook. 3 G. GREENE Once the iron roof crumpled as a late vulture settled for the night. J. OSBORNE It is late afternoon, the end of a hot day. M. AYRTON This . . documentary, intended for late showing when children . . are presumed to be in bed. W. WHARTON It's getting late, time for the old man to go home. 4 D. ROCK Late but beautiful Flemish stained glass. H. H. FURNESS *The Tragedie of Coriolanus* is classed among the late plays [of Shakespeare]. b J. M. MURRY The late autumn of 1818. V. S. NAIPAUL He was in his late thirties. *Listener* This prevents him from over-praising early Waugh at the expense of late. D. ROWE Devastating childhood experiences which laid the foundations for anxiety and panic attacks in later life. *the late Bronze Age, late Victorian times*, etc. 5a A. BROOKNER Her late husband was a Wing Commander in the Royal Air Force. b A. J. TOYNBEE Brasilia . . is only about 600 miles from the late capital, Rio de Janeiro. 6 T. HARDY Stables fitted with every late appliance.

II Special uses of superl. *latest.* **7** = LAST *a.* Now *arch.* & *poet.* LME. **8** Most recent; newest, most up to date. L16.

7 SOUTHEY I had her latest look of earthly love, I felt her hands last pressure. 8 A. TOFFLER Doctors . . complain that they cannot keep up with the latest developments. M. MOORCOCK Accordions . . would play the tunes of the moment, as well as the latest songs from France.

Special collocations & comb.: **late blight** a disease of potatoes caused by the fungus *Phytophthora infestans*; = *potato blight* s.v. POTATO *n.* **latecomer** a person who arrives late; a recent arrival, a newcomer. **late cut** *Cricket* a cut, but with the actual stroke delayed until after the usual moment. **late dinner** (esp. in Victorian society) the main evening meal, held later than the children's dinner. **late fee** an increased fee paid in order to secure the dispatch of a letter posted after the advertised time of collection. **late hours**: after most people have gone to bed; esp. in *keep late hours. late Latin*: see LATIN *n.* **late licence** a licence allowing a public house, nightclub, etc., to serve alcohol beyond the usual hours. **late mark**: indicating that a pupil is late for school. **late-model** *a.* (*N. Amer.*), of a car) recently made. **late night** a night when one goes to bed after the usual time. **late-tackling** (*Rugby* & *Soccer* etc.) tackling an opponent illegally, when he or she is no longer in possession of the ball. **late unpleasantness** *the* war that took place recently; *spec.* (*US*) *the* American Civil War. **late wood** a denser section of the annual ring of a tree, formed late in the growing season.

B *n.* The fact of being late or recent. Chiefly & now only in *of late*, lately, recently. ME.

lateness *n.* OE.

late /leɪt/ *adv.* Compar. **later**; superl. **latest,** LAST *adv.* [OE *late* = OHG *laz, lazzo*, f. *lat*-stem of OE *læt* LATE *a.*] †**1** Slowly. OE–LME. **2** At or to an advanced stage in a period, esp. of the day, the year, or a lifetime. Also, after the proper or expected time. OE. **b** In compar.: at a later stage within a period; subsequently. Also *later on.* M16. **c** In *compar.* as *int.* [Ellipt. for (*I'll*) *see you later.*] Farewell for the present. *US slang.* M20. **3** At or to a late hour of day; *esp.* (until) far on in the evening or night. OE. **4a** Recently, of late, not long ago. Now *poet.* ME. **b** Not long since (but not now); recently (but no longer). Cf. LATE *a.* 5b. LME.

2 J. BUCHAN The snow lay late that year. C. P. SNOW I got back from Germany late in September. B. PYM A middle-aged man who had been ordained late in life. L. CODY The show started ten minutes late. *Proverb*: Better late than never. b M. WEST Merdelius promised to call later in the week. R. ELLMANN Neither now nor later would he hesitate to take risks. 3 V. WOOLF His mother had taken him for a burglar when he came home late. N. MITFORD The day after a dance, Nancy was allowed to sleep late. 4a BYRON To Ianthei, Those climes where I have late been straying. b *Daily Telegraph* His father is robustly played by John Paul, late of 'Doomwatch'.

Phrases: *early and late*: see EARLY *adv. late in the day*: see DAY *n. soon or late*: see SOON *adv. sooner or later*: see SOON *adv.*

lated /ˈleɪtɪd/ *a. poet.* L16. [f. LATE *a.* + -ED[1].] = BELATED.

lateen /ləˈtiːn/ *a.* & *n.* Also **latine, latteen.** M16. [Fr. *latine* (in *voile latine* Latin sail, so named as used in the Mediterranean) fem. of *latin* LATIN *a.*] **A** *adj.* Designating a triangular sail suspended by a long yard at an angle of about 45 degrees to the mast, or a vessel, yard, etc., possessing or used with such a sail. M16.

lateen mizzen, rig, etc.

B *n.* A lateener. M19.

lateener *n.* a vessel with a lateen rig L19.

lateish *a.* & *adv.* var. of LATISH.

lately /ˈleɪtli/ *adv.* OE. [f. LATE *a.* + -LY[2].] †**1** Slowly, tardily, sluggishly; reluctantly, sparingly. OE–LME. **2** Within recent times; recently, of late. L15. †**3** After the usual or proper time; at a late hour, late. E16–E17.

2 N. COWARD What have you been doing lately? During these last years? J. KRANTZ Lately he had taken to waking in the night.

latemost /ˈleɪtməʊst/ *a.* Now *arch. rare.* OE. [f. LATE *a.* + -MOST.] Last.

laten /ˈleɪt(ə)n/ *v.i.* & *t.* L19. [f. LATE *a.* + -EN[5].] Become or make late.

latency /ˈleɪt(ə)nsi/ *n.* M17. [f. LATENT *a.*: see -ENCY.] **1** Latent condition, nature, or existence; *spec.* in *Biol.*, that of a disposition or faculty which remains concealed until the necessary conditions for its development are supplied. M17. **b** In psychoanalytic theory: a condition when sexual feelings are held to be sublimated or repressed, lasting from the age of five to puberty. Freq. in *latency period.* E20. **2a** Delay between a stimulus and a response, esp. in muscle; a latent period. L19. **b** *Computing.* More fully *latency time.* The delay before a transfer of data begins following an instruction for its transfer, esp. to or from a rotating storage device. M20.

La Tène /la ˈtɛn/ *a.* L19. [A district at the east end of the Lake of Neuchâtel, Switzerland, where remains of this culture were first discovered.] Designating or pertaining to a culture (lasting from the 5th to the 1st cent. BC) of the second Iron Age of central and western Europe, and the style of art associated with it.

lateness /ˈleɪtnɪs/ *n.* OE. [f. LATE *a.* + -NESS.] The quality or condition of being late, esp. of being advanced in a period or behind the proper time.

latensification /leɪˌtɛnsɪfɪˈkeɪʃ(ə)n/ *n.* M20. [f. LATENT *a.* + INTENSIFICATION.] *Photogr.* Intensification of an existing latent image on a photographic film or plate by treatment with a chemical, prolonged exposure to light, or other means.

latent /ˈleɪt(ə)nt/ *a.* & *n.* LME. [L *latent-* pres. ppl stem of *latere* lie hidden: see -ENT.] A *adj.* 1 Hidden, concealed; present or existing, but not manifest, exhibited, or developed. (Now esp. of a quality, formerly also of a material thing.) Opp. *patent.* LME. b That is really but not overtly what is implied by the noun; disguised. M17. 2 *Med.* Of a disease: in which the usual symptoms are not (yet) manifest. L17. 3 Of a fingerprint: of a kind not normally visible to the naked eye. E20.

1 M. L. KING Often white liberals are unaware of their latent prejudices. A. FRASER Troubles . . had certainly brought out in him virtues which might otherwise have remained latent. b Z. TOMIN I suppose that at best I am a very latent bisexual.

Special collocations: **latent ambiguity** *Law* a doubt as to the meaning of a document, not patent from the document itself, but raised by the evidence of some extrinsic and collateral matter. **latent energy** = *potential energy* s.v. POTENTIAL *a.* **latent heat**: required to convert a solid into a liquid, or a liquid into a vapour, without change of temperature. **latent image** *Photogr.* the invisible image formed in a photographic emulsion by exposure and rendered visible by development. **latent learning** *Psychol.*: that has taken place without any incentive (such as rewards or punishments) and is not manifested until there is a goal to be achieved. **latent partner**: whose name does not appear as a member of a firm or company. **latent period**: between a stimulus and a response, esp. (*a*) *Med.* between infection (or exposure to radiation) and the manifestation of symptoms; (*b*) *Physiol.* between a stimulus (as the arrival of a nerve impulse) and the response. **latent root** *Math.* an eigenvalue of a matrix. **latent virus**: causing no apparent disease in one organism but capable of doing so when transmitted to another.

B *n.* A latent fingerprint. E20.

latently *adv.* M16. **latentness** *n.* M17.

later *a.*, *adv.* see LATE *a.*, *adv.*

-later /lətə/ *suff.* [Gk *-latrēs* worshipper.] Used (usu. preceded by -o-) to form agent-ns. w. the sense '(excessive) worshipper' corresp. to abstract ns. in *-latry*, as *idolater*, *Mariolater*, *bardolater.*

laterad /ˈlatərad/ *adv.* Now *rare.* E19. [f. L *later-*, *latus* side + -AD[3].] *Anat.* Towards the side.

lateral /ˈlat(ə)r(ə)l/ *a.*, *n.*, & *v.* LME. [L *lateralis*, f. *later-*, *latus* side: see -AL[1].] A *adj.* 1 Of or pertaining to the side or sides; situated at or issuing from the side or sides; towards the side, directed sideways. LME. †2 Existing or moving side by side. Of winds: coming from the same half (eastern or western) of the horizon. E–M17. 3a *Anat.* & *Zool.* Situated on one side or other of an organ or organism, esp. in the region furthest from the median plane. (Foll. by *to.*) Opp. *medial.* E18. b *Med.* Of a disease or condition: affecting the side or sides of the body; confined to one side of the body. E18. c *Cryst.* Designating or pertaining to those axes of a crystal (form) which are inclined to the main or vertical axis. E19. d *Physics.* Acting or placed at right angles to the line of motion or of strain. E19. 4 Designating or pertaining to a branch of a family descended from a brother or sister of a person in direct line. L18. 5 *Phonet.* Of (articulation of) a consonant (e.g. English *l*): formed by or involving partial closure of the air passage by the tongue, which is so placed as to allow the breath to flow on one or both sides of the point of contact. M19.

Special collocations & *comb.*: **lateral-cut** *a.* (of a gramophone record) with undulations made by a cutting stylus that moved from side to side (opp. *hill and dale* s.v. HILL *n.*). **lateral line (system)** a system of organs in fish and aquatic amphibians situated on the head and along the sides of the body and sensitive to vibrations and pressure changes. *lateral malleolus*: see MALLEOLUS 2. **lateral moraine**: situated at the side of a glacier. **lateral plate** *Biol.* the unsegmented ventral part of the mesoderm in the early vertebrate embryo. **lateral thinking** a way of thinking which seeks the solution to intractable problems through unorthodox methods, or elements which would normally be ignored by logical thinking.

B *n.* †1 Each of two or more lateral winds. Only in M17. 2 A lateral or side part, branch, tooth, projection, etc. M18. 3 *Phonet.* A lateral consonant. M20. 4 *N. Amer. Football.* A sideways pass. M20.

C *v.i.* Infl. **-ll-**, ***-l-**. *N. Amer. Football.* Make a sideways pass. M20.

lateralise *v.* var. of LATERALIZE.

laterality /latəˈralɪti/ *n.* M17. [f. LATERAL *a.* + -ITY.] 1 The quality of having (distinct) sides, (right- or left-) sidedness; *spec.* the dominance of the right- or the left-hand member of a pair of bodily organs as regards a particular activity or function (such as the hands in writing, or the cerebral hemispheres in controlling speech). M17. 2 *Phonet.* Lateral articulation. M20.

lateralize /ˈlat(ə)rəlʌɪz/ *v.t.* Also **-ise.** M19. [f. LATERAL *a.* + -IZE.] 1 Move to the side; place in a lateral position. Chiefly as *lateralized* ppl a. M19. 2 In *pass.* Be largely under the control of one (usu. specified) side of the brain. M20. 3 *Phonet.* Make (a consonant) lateral. Chiefly as *lateralized* ppl a. M20.

laterali'zation *n.* laterality, esp. of cerebral activity; diagnostic localization of a lesion or pathological process to one or other side of the brain; the property of being lateralized: E20.

laterally /ˈlat(ə)rəli/ *adv.* LME. [f. LATERAL *a.* + -LY[2].] At, to, or from the side; in a lateral or sideways direction.

lateralwards /ˈlat(ə)r(ə)lwədz/ *adv.* E20. [f. LATERAL *a.* + -WARDS.] *Anat.* Laterally; to or from the median plane of the body.

Also **lateralward** *adv.* M20.

Lateran /ˈlat(ə)rən/ *a.* ME. [L *Laterana*, *-um*, f. the ancient Roman family of the Plautii *Laterani.*] Of or pertaining to the district of the Lateran Rome, site of a palace which was formerly the official residence of the popes, and a Basilica or church dedicated to St John; *spec.* designating or pertaining to each of the five general councils of the Western Church held in the Lateran Palace between 1123 and 1512.

latera recta *n. phr.* pl. of LATUS RECTUM.

laterisation *n.* var. of LATERIZATION.

laterite /ˈlatərʌɪt/ *n.* E19. [f. L *later* brick + -ITE[1].] A clayey (usu. red) soil or soil horizon characterized by a high proportion of sesquioxides, esp. of aluminium and iron, and a low proportion of bases and silica, formed by chemical weathering in tropical and subtropical regions; *esp.* one which hardens or has hardened on exposure to air; *loosely* any of various other reddish or iron-rich surface materials in the tropics and sub-tropics.

¶The use and proper application of the word have been the subject of much debate.

lateritic /latəˈrɪtɪk/ *a.* resembling, of the nature of, or approaching the composition of laterite M19.

lateritious /latəˈrɪʃəs/ *a.* Now *rare.* M17. [f. L *lateritius*, *-icius*, f. *later* brick: see -ITIOUS[1].] Chiefly *Med.*, of urinary deposits: of the colour of brick, brick-red.

lateritization /ˌlat(ə)rɪtʌɪˈzeɪʃ(ə)n/ *n.* Also **-isation.** E20. [f. LATERITE + -IZATION.] The formation of laterite and lateritic soils; the weathering or soil-forming process that results in this.

'lateritize *v.t.* convert into laterite (usu. in *pass.*) E20.

laterization /latərʌɪˈzeɪʃ(ə)n/ *n.* Also **-isation.** E20. [f. as prec.] = prec.

'laterize *v.t.* = LATERITIZE E20.

latero- /ˈlatərəʊ/ *comb. form.* [f. L *later-*, *latus* side + -O-.] Forming wds w. the senses 'pertaining to the side (and another part), pertaining to the side of (a specified structure)', as *latero-anterior*, *-cervical*, *-posterior*, adjs., 'on or towards the side', as *lateroflexion*, *lateroversion.*

latero'flexion *n.* (*Anat.*) abnormal bending or curvature to one side M19. **latero'version** *n.* (*Anat.*) abnormal displacement (of an organ, esp. the uterus) to one side M19.

lates /ˈleɪtiːz/ *n.* Pl. same. M20. [mod.L f. Gk *latos* Nile perch.] A fish of the genus *Lates*, comprising large percoid food fishes; *esp.* = NILE *perch.*

latest /ˈleɪtɪst/ *n.* L19. [Absol. use of superl. of LATE *a.*] 1 The most advanced possible hour, the most distant possible date. Only in *at (the) latest.* L19. 2 *The* most recent news, fashion, etc. With possess.: a person's most recent achievement, (esp. reprehensible) action, etc. *colloq.* L19.

2 *latest word*: see WORD *n.*

latest *a.*, *adv.* see LATE *a.*, *adv.*

late-wake /ˈleɪtweɪk/ *n.* E18. [Alt. of LYKE-WAKE after LATE *a.*] = LYKE-WAKE.

†lateward *adv.* & *a.* LME. [f. LATE *a.* + -WARD.] A *adv.* 1 Of late, recently. LME–M17. 2 Late, after the proper time or season. L16–M17. B *adj.* Late, slow; *esp.* (of fruit, a crop, etc.) late in maturing, (of a season) backward. LME–M18.

latex /ˈleɪtɛks/ *n.* & *a.* Pl. **latexes, latices** /ˈleɪtɪsiːz/. M17. [L = liquid, fluid.] A *n.* †1 *Med.* Any of various body fluids; *esp.* the watery part of the blood and other secretions. M17–M18. 2 *Bot.* A milky liquid found in many plants, e.g. of the poppy, spurge, and dogbane families, which exudes when the plant is cut and coagulates on exposure to the air; *spec.* that of *Hevea brasiliensis* or other plants used to produce rubber. M19. 3 A dispersion in water of particles of a polymer that is formed during polymerization and is used to make paints, coatings, etc. M20. B *attrib.* or as *adj.* Consisting of or containing latex; pertaining to latex. L19.

Special collocations: **latex paint**: having a latex as its binding medium.

lath /lɑːθ/ *n.* Pl. **-ths** /-θs, -ðz/. Also (earlier, now *dial.*) **lat** /lat/. [OE *lætt* (corresp. to MDu. *latte*, Du. *lat*, G dial. *Latz*), *lat*; repl. in ME in general use by forms w. *-þþ-* (prob. already in OE, corresp. to OHG *latta* (G *Latte*)).] 1 A thin narrow strip of wood; *spec.* one used to form a groundwork upon which to fasten the slates or tiles of a roof or the plaster of a wall or ceiling, or in the construction of lattice- or trellis-work and Venetian blinds. OE. b Wood in thin narrow strips, used in building (chiefly as a groundwork for a coating of plaster) to form a wall or partition. Freq. in *lath and plaster.* L15. c (A thin narrow piece of wood used for) an imitation weapon. *arch.* L16. 2 The part of an arbalest or cross-bow which bends the bow. *obs.* exc. *Hist.* M16. 3 *transf.* A slender or fragile thing or person. M17. b *Min.* A thin narrow elongated mineral crystal. E20.

1c SHAKES. *Tit. A.* Have your lath glued within your sheath Till you know better how to handle it. 3 F. BURNEY 'Thin as Dr. Lind' says the King. Lind was . . a mere lath.

Comb.: **lath-nail** a nail for fixing laths on battens.

lath /lɑːθ/ *v.t.* LME. [f. the n.] Cover or furnish (a wall or ceiling) with laths for plastering. Also foll. by *over.*

lathe /leɪð/ *n.*[1] *obs.* exc. *Hist.* [OE *læþ*, corresp. to ON *láð* landed possession, land, rel. to Gmc base in Goth. *unlēds* unlanded, poor, OE *unlæd(e* wretched.] Each of the administrative districts (latterly five in number) into which Kent was formerly divided, each comprising several hundreds.

lathe /leɪð/ *n.*[2] *obs.* exc. *north.* Also **laithe.** ME. [ON *hlaða* rel. to *hlaða* LADE *v.*] A barn.

lathe /leɪð/ *n.*[3] ME. [Prob. f. ODa. *lad* stand, supporting framework, as in *drejelad* turning-lathe, *savelad* saw-bench, perh. a special use of *lad* pile, heap f. ON *hlað* rel. to *hlaða* LADE *v.*] 1 A machine for turning wood, metal, ivory, etc., in which the article to be turned is held in a horizontal position by means of adjustable centres and rotated against the tools with which it is cut to the required shape. Also *turning-lathe.* ME. 2 *potter's lathe*, a machine for throwing and turning pottery, the article being placed on a revolving horizontal disc. E18.

1 *capstan lathe*, *pole-lathe*, etc.

Comb.: **lathe-bed** the lower framework of a lathe, having a slot from end to end in which one or both of the heads may be moved backwards or forwards; **lathe-head** the head-stock of a lathe.

lathe /leɪð/ *n.*[4] LME. [Rel. to Sw. *lad*, f. as prec., G *Lade*: see also LAY *n.*[5]] *Weaving*. The movable swing-frame or batten of a loom.

lathe /leɪð/ *v.t. obs.* exc. *dial.* [OE *laþian* = OFris. *lathia, ladia*, OS *laþian*, OHG *ladōn* (G *laden*) ON *laða*, Goth. *laþōn*: cogn. w. Goth. *laþaleikō* willingly.] Invite, call. Chiefly as *lathing* vbl n.

lathee *n.* var. of LATHI.

lathen /ˈlɑːθ(ə)n/ *a. rare.* M19. [f. LATH *n.* + -EN[4].] Made of lath.

lather /ˈlɑːðə, ˈlaðə/ *n.*[1] [OE *lēaþor* = ON *lauðr*, f. Gmc, f. IE base also of Gk *loutron* bath. Later f. LATHER *v.*] †**1** Washing soda; froth from this. Only in OE. **2** A froth or foam made by the agitation of a mixture of soap and water. L16. **b** *transf.* Violent perspiration, *esp.* the frothy sweat of a horse. M17. **c** *fig.* A state of agitation, anxiety, irritation, etc., such as induces sweat. M19. **3** The action of lathering or applying lather to something. E17.

2 E. PIZZEY His hands were gently rubbing the shampoo into a rich lather. **b** M. WEBB There came one riding all in a lather to tell of the great victory. **c** N. SAHGAL Why get into a lather about what you can't undo?

Comb.: **lather-boy** *Hist.* a boy employed in a barber's shop to lather the chins of customers.

lather /ˈlɑːθə/ *n.*[2] ME. [f. LATH *n.*, *v.* + -ER[1].] A person who makes or fixes laths.

lather /ˈlɑːðə, ˈlaðə/ *v.* [OE *lēþran*, *līepran* = ON *leyðra*, f. Gmc, f. base of LATHER *n.*[1] From 16 assim. in form to LATHER *n.*[1]] **1** *v.t.* Cover (as) with a lather; apply lather to; wash in or with a lather; in *pass.* = sense 2 below. OE. **2** *v.i.* Now chiefly of a horse: become covered with foam or frothy sweat. ME. **3** *v.i.* Produce and form a lather or froth. E17. **4** *v.t.* Beat, thrash; *fig.* defeat soundly. *colloq.* L18.

1 M. MITCHELL Uncle Peter . . drove to the hospital, making trip after trip until the old horse was lathered. A. MILLER Roy would snarl . . his jaws lathering.

latherer *n.* a person who applies lather; *esp.* (*Hist.*) = *lather-boy* s.v. LATHER *n.*[1]: L19.

lathery /ˈlɑːð(ə)ri, ˈlað-/ *a.* E19. [f. LATHER *n.*[1] + -Y[1].] Covered with or resembling lather; *fig.* unsubstantial. Of a horse: covered with frothy sweat.

lathi /ˈlɑːtiː/ *n.* Also ***lathee***. M19. [Hind. *lāṭhī*.] In the Indian subcontinent: a long heavy iron-bound stick, usu. of bamboo, used as a weapon.

lathing /ˈlɑːθɪŋ/ *n.* ME. [f. LATH *v.* + -ING[1].] **1** The action of LATH *v.* ME. **2** Lath; work in lath. E16.

lathy /ˈlɑːθi/ *a.* L17. [f. LATH *n.* + -Y[1].] **1** Esp. of a person: resembling a lath; long and very thin. L17. **2** Made of lath (and plaster). E19.

lathyrism /ˈlaθɪrɪz(ə)m/ *n.* L19. [f. LATHYRUS + -ISM.] *Med.* A tropical disease marked by tremors, muscular weakness, and paraplegia, commonly attributed to continued consumption of the seeds of the grass pea, *Lathyrus sativus*.

lathyrus /ˈlaθɪrəs/ *n.* M18. [mod.L (see below) f. Gk *lathuros* a kind of vetch.] Any of various leguminous plants constituting the genus *Lathyrus*, resembling vetches but with hairy styles and usu. winged stems.

lati *n.pl.* see LAT *n.*[2]

Latian /ˈleɪʃ(ə)n/ *a.* & *n.* L16. [f. L *Latium* (see LATIN *a.* & *n.*) + -AN.] **A** *adj.* Of or pertaining to Latium; *literary* Latin. L16. **B** *n.* A native or inhabitant of Latium. L17.

latices *n.pl.* see LATEX.

laticiferous /latɪˈsɪf(ə)rəs/ *a.* M19. [f. L *latici-* comb. form of LATEX -FEROUS.] *Bot.* Conducting or containing latex; (of tissue) containing laticiferous tubes or vessels.

laticlave /ˈlatɪkleɪv/ *n.* M17. [Late L *laticlavium*, *-vus*, f. *latus* broad + *clavus* purple stripe. (In cl.L *latus clavus*.)] *Rom. Antiq.* A badge consisting of two broad purple stripes on the edge of the tunic, worn by senators and other people of high rank.

latifund *n.* see LATIFUNDIUM.

latifundia *n.* pl. of LATIFUNDIUM.

latifundist /latɪˈfʌndɪst/ *n.* Also in Sp. form **latifundista** /ˌlatɪfʌnˈdɪstə/. M20. [Sp. *latifundista*, f. *latifundio*: see next, -IST.] The owner of a latifundium in Spain or Latin America.

latifundium /lɑːtɪˈfʌndɪəm, lat-, leɪt-/ *n.* Pl. **-dia** /-dɪə/. Orig. Anglicized as **-fund**. M17. [L, f. *latus* broad + *fundus* landed estate; partly f. Sp. *latifundio* f. L.] A large landed estate or ranch, freq. worked by slaves or people of semi-servile status; *esp.* one in Spain or Latin America or (*Hist.*) in ancient Rome. Usu. in *pl.*

latigo /ˈlatɪɡəʊ/ *n. US.* Pl. **-o(e)s**. L19. [Sp.] A strap for tightening a cinch.

latimer /ˈlatɪmə/ *n.* Long *obs.* exc. *Hist.* ME. [AN (whence AL *latimerus*, *-rius*, earlier *latimarius*) = OFr. *latimier* alt. of *latinier* (AL *latinarius*, f. *Latin* Latin: see -ER[2]. Cf. LATINER.] An interpreter.

latimeria /latɪˈmɪərɪə/ *n.* M20. [mod.L, f. Marjorie E. D. Courtenay-*Latimer* (b. 1907), S. Afr. museum curator + -IA[1].] *Zool.* Any coelacanth of the extant deep-sea genus *Latimeria*.

Latin /ˈlatɪn/ *a.* & *n.* OE. [L *Latinus*, f. *Latium*: see below, -INE[1]. Cf. LIDDEN.] **A** *adj.* **1** Pertaining to, characteristic of, composed in, or using Latin (see sense B.1 below). OE. **2** Of or pertaining to ancient Latium, the area of central Italy which included Rome, or its inhabitants. ME. **3** *spec.* Designating or pertaining to the branch of the Christian church which once used Latin in all its rites; Roman Catholic. M16. **4** *Hist.* Of or pertaining to the peoples of western Europe, viewed in their relations with the Ottoman Empire and with the Saracens and Turks. *arch.* L18. **5** Pertaining to or characteristic of the European and American peoples speaking languages developed from Latin; *spec.* Latin American. M19.

1 SHAKES. *L.L.L.* Remuneration! O, that's the Latin word for three farthings. 5 R. W. EMERSON The Teutonic tribes have a national singleness of heart, which contrasts with the Latin races. D. ROBINSON He stood . . snapping his fingers to a Latin beat. V. GLENDINNING He was extrovert, physical, unstable, and very Latin.

Special collocations & *comb.*: **Latin America** the countries in Central and S. America in which Spanish or Portuguese is the dominant language. **Latin American** *a.* & *n.* (*a*) *adj.* belonging to or derived from Latin America; *spec.* designating a class of ballroom dancing consisting of dances of Latin American origin or inspiration, such as the rumba, samba, cha-cha-cha, etc.; (*b*) *n.* a native or inhabitant of a Latin American country. **Latin cross** a plain cross with the lowest member longer than the other three. **Latin language** = sense B.1 below. **Latin letter** a letter of the Roman alphabet. **Latin Quarter** [Fr. *Quartier Latin*] the district of Paris on the left or south bank of the Seine, where Latin was spoken in the Middle Ages, and where students and artists live and the principal university buildings are situated. **Latin rights** [L *ius Latii*] *Rom. Hist.* a set of privileges, falling short of full citizenship, enjoyed by inhabitants of Latium and from 89 BC on extended to people outside Italy. **Latin rite** a religious ceremonial using Latin, esp. in the Roman Catholic Church. **Latin square** an arrangement of letters etc. each occurring *n* times, in a square array of n^2 compartments so that no letter appears twice in the same row or column; such an arrangement used as the basis of experimental procedures in which it is desired to control or allow for two sources of variability while investigating a third.

B *n.* **1** The Italic language (orig. the dialect of Latium) spoken in ancient Rome and its empire, which was used internationally in the Middle Ages as a medium of communication among educated people. With specifying wd: a particular form, phase, etc., of Latin. OE. †**b** A translation into Latin, as a school exercise. Usu. in *pl.* L15–L17. **2** A native or inhabitant of Latium; *Rom. Hist.* a person who enjoyed the Latin rights. Formerly also, a speaker of Latin, a Latin author, (usu. in *pl.*). LME. **3** A member or adherent of the Latin Church, *esp.* one living in the Orient. Now *rare.* LME. **4** *Hist.* A person belonging to any of the Western nations of Europe during the Crusades. *arch.* L18. **5** A native or inhabitant of any of the various countries in Europe (France, Italy, Spain, etc.) and America whose language is developed from Latin; *spec.* a Latin American. L19.

1 B. MOORE Mass . . said in Latin because Latin was the language of the Church. *ecclesiastical Latin, popular Latin, vulgar Latin*, etc.

Phrases: **classical Latin**: before about AD 200 *esp.* between about 100 BC and AD 14. *dog Latin*: see DOG *n.* **late Latin**: from about 150 to 600. *law Latin*: see LAW *n.*[1] *Low Latin*: see LOW *a.* & *n.*[4] **medieval Latin**: from about 600 to 1500. **modern Latin**: since 1500, used esp. in scientific classification. **Old Latin**: before about 100 BC. *pig Latin*: see PIG *n.*[1] *silver Latin*: see SILVER *n.* & *a.* **thieves' Latin** the secret language or slang of thieves. *Vulgar Latin*: see VULGAR *a.*

Comb.: **Latin school** *US* a school offering Latin (and sometimes Greek) as part of the syllabus.

Latiˈnesque *a.* resembling Latin, having a Latin character L19. **Latinish** *a.* (*rare*) resembling Latin E17. **Latinless** *a.* without knowledge of Latin M16. **Latinly** *adv.* (now *rare*) (*a*) in (good or pure) Latin; (*b*) in the style of the Latin peoples: LME.

Latin /ˈlatɪn/ *v.t.* Long *arch.* M16. [f. LATIN *a.* & *n.*] Translate into Latin.

Latinate /ˈlatɪneɪt/ *a.* E20. [f. LATIN *a.* & *n.* + -ATE[2].] Of, pertaining to, or derived from Latin; having the character of Latin; (occas.) resembling a native of a Latin country.

latine *a.* var. of LATEEN.

Latiner /ˈlatɪnə/ *n. colloq.* M17. [f. LATIN *n.*, *v.* + -ER[1]. Cf. LATIMER.] A person proficient in Latin; a person who speaks Latin; *Sc.* a pupil studying Latin.

Latinic /ləˈtɪnɪk/ *a.* M19. [f. LATIN *a.* & *n.* + -IC.] Derived from or resembling Latin; Latinate. Also, of or pertaining to the ancient Latians or the modern Latin nations.

Also **Latinical** *a.* L19.

Latinise *v.* var. of LATINIZE.

Latinism /ˈlatɪnɪz(ə)m/ *n.* L16. [med.L *latinismus*, f. as LATIN *a.* & *n.*: see -ISM.] **1** An idiom or form of expression characteristic of Latin, esp. one used by a writer in another language; conformity in style to Latin models. L16. **2** The influence or authority of the Latin Church. E20.

Latinist /ˈlatɪnɪst/ *n.* M16. [med.L *latinista*, f. as LATIN *a.* & *n.*: see -IST. Cf. Fr. *latiniste*.] **1** An expert in or student of Latin. Formerly also, a writer of Latin. M16. **2** A theologian of the Latin Church. M16.

Latiˈnistic *a.* pertaining to or characterized by Latinism; characteristic of a Latinist: E19.

Latinity /ləˈtɪnɪti/ *n.* LME. [L *Latinitas*, *-tat-*, f. as LATIN *a.* & *n.*: see -ITY. Cf. (O)Fr. *latinité*.] **1** Latin speech; the way in which a person speaks or writes Latin; the use of Latin. LME. **2** *Rom. Hist.* The status of enjoying Latin rights. L19. **3** Latin character. E20.

Latinize /ˈlatɪnʌɪz/ *v.* Also **-ise**. L16. [Late L *latinizare*, f. as LATIN *a.* & *n.*: see -IZE. Cf. Fr. *latiniser*.] **1** *v.t.* Give a Latin form to (a word etc. of another language); fill (a language) with words or idioms of Latin origin. L16. **b** *v.i.* Use words or idioms from Latin. M17. **2** *v.t.* Convert (a person, a people) to the ideas, customs, etc., of the Latins, or to the rites etc. of the Latin Church. E17. **3** *v.t.* Transcribe in Roman letters. M19.

Latiniˈzation *n.* M19. **Latinizer** *n.* E17.

Latino /ləˈtiːnəʊ/ *n.* & *a. N. Amer.* Fem. **-na** /-nə/. M20. [Amer. Sp., prob. special use of Sp. *latino* LATIN *a.* & *n.*] **A** *n.* Pl. **-os**, fem. **-as**. A Latin American inhabitant of the United States. M20. **B** *adj.* Of or pertaining to the Latin American inhabitants of the United States. L20.

Latino- /ˈlatɪnəʊ/ *comb. form.* [f. L *Latinus* LATIN *a.* + -O-.] Forming compounds w. the sense 'partly Latin and partly —', as *Latino-Faliscan, -Jazz, -Sabellian*.

Latino sine flexione /ˈlatɪnəʊ ˌsɪnɪ flɛksɪˈəʊni/ *n. phr.* E20. [L (*Latino* abl. of *Latinus* LATIN *a.*) = in Latin without inflection.] The language Interlingua, in which nouns are taken from the ablative case of Latin nouns.

latish /ˈleɪtɪʃ/ *a.* & *adv.* Also **lateish**. E17. [f. LATE *a.*, *adv.* + -ISH[1].] A *adj.* Somewhat late. E17. B *adv.* At a somewhat late hour. E19.

latissimus /lɑːˈtɪsɪməs/ *n.* Pl. **-mi** /-mʌɪ, -miː/. E17. [mod.L, ellipt. for *musculus latissimus dorsi* lit. 'the broadest muscle of the back'.] *Anat.* More fully *latissimus dorsi* /ˈdɔːsʌɪ, -siː/. Either of a pair of large, roughly triangular muscles covering the lower part of the back, from the sacral, lumbar, and lower thoracic vertebrae to the armpits.

latitant /ˈlatɪt(ə)nt/ *a.* & *n.* Now *rare.* M17. [L *latitant-* pres. ppl stem of *latitare* frequent. of *latere* be hidden: see -ANT[1].] A *adj.* That lies concealed; lurking; latent. Formerly *spec.*, hibernating. M17. B *n.* A person who is in hiding, esp. from a legal process. L19.

latitancy *n.* M17.

latitat /ˈlatɪtat/ *n. obs.* exc. *Hist.* M16. [L, 3rd person sing. of pres. indic. of *latitare*: see prec.] *Law.* A writ summoning a defendant assumed to be in hiding to answer in the Court of King's or Queen's Bench.

latitation /latɪˈteɪʃ(ə)n/ *n.* Now *rare.* E17. [L *latitatio(n-)*, f. *latitat-* pa. ppl stem of *latitare*: see LATITANT, -ATION.] The fact of lying concealed; hiding, lurking.

latitude /ˈlatɪtjuːd/ *n.* LME. [L *latitudo*, *-din-*, f. *latus* broad: see -TUDE. Cf. (O)Fr. *latitude.*] I Breadth, width. 1 Transverse dimension; extent as measured from side to side; breadth of a surface, as opp. to length. Also, spaciousness. Now only *joc.* LME. †b A tract or area as defined by its breadth; a wide compass or extent. LME–L18. 2†a The range within which something may vary. LME–L18. b Extent, range, scope. Also, great or full extent. Now *rare.* E17. c *Photogr.* The range of exposures for which an emulsion, printing paper, etc., will give acceptable contrast. L19. 3 Freedom from narrow restrictions; liberality of construction or interpretation; tolerated variety of action or opinion. E17. †b Laxity of conduct or principle. L17–E18.

1 R. L'ESTRANGE 'Tis Field of a Huge Latitude that the Devil has to Dance..in. 2a R. KIRWAN Few stones admit of a greater latitude of composition. b H. L. MANSEL The..passage of Locke..when understood in its proper latitude. 3 L. TRILLING A considerable latitude in our selection of..books.

II *techn.* (opp. LONGITUDE). 4 *Geogr.* a The angular distance on its meridian of any place on the earth's surface from the equator (quantitatively identical with the elevation of the pole above the horizon, and with the declination of the zenith). LME. b Angular distance on a meridian. Only in *degree, minute*, etc., *of latitude.* E17. c A locality as defined by parallels of latitude; a region, a clime. Usu. in *pl.* M17. 5 *Astron.* a Angular distance from the ecliptic, corresp. to terrestrial latitude (also *celestial latitude*) or from a similar line of reference. Cf. DECLINATION 4a. LME. b The angular distance of a point on the surface of a celestial object from the equator. L19.

4a *transf.*: D. FRANCIS The silencer reached the latitude of my heart. c A. HARDY In all latitudes from the polar seas to the tropics.

latitudinal /latɪˈtjuːdɪn(ə)l/ *a.* LME. [f. as prec. + -AL[1].] 1 Relating to breadth or width. Formerly of (esp. abdominal) muscles: transverse. *rare.* LME. 2 Pertaining to or depending on geographical latitude; corresponding to lines of latitude. L18.

latitudinally *adv.* in respect of breadth or latitude M19.

latitudinarian /ˌlatɪtjuːdɪˈnɛːrɪən/ *n.* & *a.* M17. [f. as LATITUDE + -ARIAN, after *trinitarian* etc.] A *n.* A person who practises or favours latitude in opinion or action, esp. in religion; *spec.* (*Eccl. Hist.*) any of a group of 17th-cent. divines who, while attached to episcopal government and liturgical forms of worship, regarded them basically as not of fundamental importance. Also, a person who, though not a sceptic, has no preference among creeds and forms of Church government or worship. M17. B *adj.* Allowing, favouring, or characterized by latitude in opinion or action, esp. in religion; characteristic of a latitudinarian. L17.

latitudinarianism *n.* latitudinarian doctrine, opinions, or practice, esp. in religion L17.

latitudinary /latɪˈtjuːdɪn(ə)ri/ *a. rare.* L17. [f. as prec. + -ARY[1].] = LATITUDINARIAN *a.*

latitudinous /latɪˈtjuːdɪnəs/ *a.* M19. [f. as LATITUDE + -OUS.] 1 Characterized by latitude of interpretation. M19. 2 = LATITUDINAL *a.* 2. E20.

lative /ˈleɪtɪv/ *a.* & *n.* M20. [f. L *lat-* pa. ppl stem of *ferre* bring + -IVE.] *Gram.* A *adj.* Designating, being in, or pertaining to the case used in some languages, e.g. of the Finno-Ugric group, to express motion up to or as far as. Cf. ALLATIVE. M20. B *n. The* lative case; a word, form, etc., in the lative case. M20.

latke /ˈlʌtkə/ *n.* E20. [Yiddish, f. Russ. *latka* earthenware cooking vessel, (dial.) dish cooked in such a vessel.] In Jewish cookery: a pancake, *esp.* one made with grated potato.

latomy /ˈlatəmi/ *n. rare.* Also in Gk form **latomia** /ləˈtəʊmɪə/. M17. [Gk *latomia*, f. *laas*, *las* stone + *-tomia* -TOMY.] *Gk Hist.* A stone quarry; *spec.* (*collect. sing.* & in *pl.*) the quarries at Syracuse, used as a prison.

laton *n.* var. of LATTEN.

Latonian /ləˈtəʊnɪən/ *a.* & *n.* L16. [f. L *Latonius*, f. *Latona* (see below) f. Gk (Aeolic) *Latōn*, (Attic) *Lētō*: see -AN.] A *adj.* Of or pertaining to Latona, in classical mythology the mother of Apollo and Diana. L16. B *n. the Latonian*, Apollo. *poet.* E19.

latosol /ˈlatəsɒl/ *n.* M20. [f. LATERITE + -O- + -SOL.] A lateritic soil.

latoun *n.* see LATTEN.

latrant /ˈleɪtr(ə)nt/ *a. literary.* E18. [L *latrant-* pres. ppl stem of *latrare* to bark: see -ANT[1].] Barking like a dog.

latration /ləˈtreɪʃ(ə)n/ *n. literary.* E17. [med.L *latratio(n-)*, f. L *latrat-* pa. ppl stem of *latrare*: see prec., -ATION.] The barking of a dog; a bark.

latreutic /ləˈtruːtɪk/ *a. rare.* M19. [Gk *latreutikos* pertaining to divine worship, f. *latreuein*: see LATRIA.] Of the nature of latria.

Also **latreutical** *a.* E17.

latria /ləˈtrʌɪə/ *n.* E16. [Late L f. Gk *latreia*, f. *latreuein* wait on, serve with prayer.] *RC Ch.* The highest form of worship, due to God alone; the veneration properly given to God. Cf. DULIA, HYPERDULIA.

latrine /ləˈtriːn/ *n.* ME. [Fr. f. L *latrina* contr. of *lavatrina*, f. *lavare* wash.] A place for urination and defecation, *esp.* a communal one in a camp, barracks, hospital, etc.

Comb.: **latrine rumour** *Mil. slang* a baseless rumour believed to originate in gossip in the latrines.

¶In isolated use bef. 17, rare bef. 19.

latrinogram *n.* (*Mil. slang*) = LATRINE *rumour* M20.

†latrociny *n.* LME. [L *latrocinium*, f. *latro*: see next. Cf. LARCENY.] 1 Highway robbery, freebooting, plundering. LME–M17. 2 A band of robbers. L15–M18.

latron /ˈleɪtrən/ *n.* Long *arch.* L16. [L *latro(n-)*: see LARCENY. Cf. LADRONE.] A robber, a brigand.

-latry /lətri/ *suff.* [Gk *-latreia* worship: cf. LATRIA.] Used (usu. preceded by -o-) in sense '(excessive) worship' in words of Gk origin or formed from Gk elements, as *idolatry*, *demonolatry*, *Mariolatry*; also in jocular formations, as *bardolatry*.

latteen *a.* & *n.* var. of LATEEN.

latten /ˈlat(ə)n/ *n.* & *a.* Also **laton**, (*arch.*) **latoun**. ME. [OFr. *laton*, *leiton* (mod. *laiton*), of unkn. origin.] A *n.* 1 A yellow alloy resembling or identical with brass, hammered into thin sheets and used esp. to make monumental brasses and church ornaments. Now *arch.* or *Hist.* ME. 2 Any metal made in thin sheets; *esp.* tin plate (more fully *white latten*). Now *dial.* E17.

1 **black latten**: rolled and unpolished. **roll latten**: polished on both sides. **shaven latten** a very thin form of latten.

B *attrib.* or as *adj.* Made or consisting of latten. L15.

lattener *n.* a worker in or maker of latten ME.

latter /ˈlatə/ *a.*, *adv.*, & *n.* [OE *lætra* (fem. & neut. *-re*) adj., *lator* adv., compar. of LATE *a.*, *adv. Later* is a new formation on *late.*] A *adj.* †1 Slower. OE–ME. 2 Further on in time or order; nearer the end; *arch.* belonging to a later or more advanced period (now chiefly w. ref. to a period of the year or its produce). ME. 3 Belonging to the final stages, esp. of a person's life or of the world's existence; = LAST *a.* 2. Now chiefly in *latter days*. *arch.* E16. b Recent. Chiefly in *these latter days*, the recent past. E17. 4 The second mentioned of two (opp. *former*); (more loosely) the last mentioned of several. Also, mentioned at or near the end of a preceding clause or sentence. M16.

2 AV *Joel* 2:23 We forbeare to descend to latter Fathers. A. C. SWINBURNE Pale as grass, or latter flowers. *Latter Prophets*: see PROPHET. 3 T. JEFFERSON All the latter years of aged men are overshadowed with its gloom. 4 A. A. MILNE On Wednesday and on Saturday, But mostly on the latter day. *Guardian* The Berlin Wall stands unbreached, passes are needed to get into Bethlehem and Father Christmas has been arrested... It's the latter item that fascinates me.

Special collocations & *comb.*: **latter-day** *a.* belonging to more recent times, modern; *Latter-day Saint*, a member of the Mormon Church (officially called the Church of Jesus Christ of the Latter-day Saints). **latter end** (*a*) the concluding part of a period etc.; the end of life, (one's) death; (*b*) *joc.* the buttocks. **latter Lammas** *joc.* a day that will never come. **†latter-will** *Sc.* a person's last will and testament. See also LATTERMATH.

†B *adv.* 1 More slowly. OE–LME. 2 Later. ME–L16.

C *n. The* second mentioned of two (or, more loosely, *the* last mentioned of several) persons or things. Also, *the* person or thing mentioned at or near the end of the preceding clause or sentence. E17.

F. R. WILSON A nave and chancel, with a small vestry on the north side of the latter. T. CAPOTE Two ..lawyers..replaced Schultz, the latter having resigned from the case. *Oxford Mail* Three accompanied pieces by Bruckner, Brahms and Schubert of which the latter was the most winning.

latterkin /ˈlatəkɪn/ *n.* Orig. **†laperkin**. L17. [Origin unkn.] A glazier's tool, for widening the grooves in the leads of lattice windows.

latterly /ˈlatəli/ *adv.* M18. [f. LATTER *a.* + -LY[2].] In the later stages of a period, esp. a person's life; of late, recently.

HOR. WALPOLE He died..at Hammersmith, though latterly he resided chiefly at Bath. H. GUNTRIP Fairbairn has latterly turned his attention to the problems of psychotherapy.

lattermath /ˈlatəmɑːθ, -maθ/ *n.* Chiefly *dial.* M16. [f. LATTER *a.* + MATH *n.*[1]] The second mowing, the aftermath; the second crop of grass etc.

lattermost /ˈlatəməʊst/ *a.* E19. [f. LATTER *a.* + -MOST.] Last.

lattice /ˈlatɪs/ *n.* & *v.* ME. [Fr. *lattis*, f. *latte* LATH *n.*] A *n.* 1 A structure of laths or strips of metal etc. crossed and fastened together, with open spaces left between, used as a screen, e.g. in window openings; a window, gate, screen, etc., so constructed. ME. b A lattice (usu. painted red) as a mark of a public house or inn; a public house, an inn. Also *red lattice*. *arch.* L16. c Lattices collectively; = *lattice-work* below. L16. 2 *transf.* Something with an open interlaced structure like that of a lattice. M17. b *Her.* = TRELLIS *n.* 1b. *rare.* E19. c In textile manufacture, a lattice-work apron or conveyer used to carry material into or out of a machine. L19. d *Electr.* A network having four impedances and two pairs of terminals, each terminal of one pair being connected by an impedance to each of the other pair. Also more fully *lattice network*. M20. 3a Any regular arrangement of points or pointlike entities that fills a space, area, or line; *spec.* a crystal lattice, a space lattice. L19. b An array of fuel and moderator in the core of a nuclear reactor. M20. 4 *Math.* A partially ordered set in which every pair of elements has an infimum and a supremum. M20.

1 C. ISHERWOOD The iron lattices were drawn down over the bank windows. 3a BRAVAIS LATTICE. *crystal*

lattice: see CRYSTAL *n.* & *a.* *primitive lattice*: see PRIMITIVE *a.* & *n.* *space lattice*: see SPACE *n.*

Comb.: **lattice beam** = *lattice girder* below; **lattice conduction** *Physics* transfer of energy between the vibrating atomic nuclei in a crystal lattice; **lattice conductivity** *Physics* that part of the thermal conductivity of a crystalline substance arising from lattice conduction; **lattice constant** *Cryst.* the length of a side, or the size of an angle, of the unit cell of a lattice; *spec.* the length of each of the sides of the unit cell of a cubic lattice; **lattice energy** *Physics* the energy required to separate the ions of a crystal to an infinite distance from one another; **lattice filter** *Electr.* a filter consisting of components connected so as to form a lattice network; **lattice frame**, **lattice girder** a girder consisting of two horizontal bars connected by diagonal bars, usu. crossed so as to resemble lattice-work; **lattice leaf (plant)** a monocotyledonous aquatic plant of Madagascar, *Aponogeton madagascariensis* (family Aponogetonaceae), in which the submerged leaves are reduced to a network of veins; *lattice network*: see sense 2d above; **lattice plane** *Physics* a plane containing lattice points; a layer of atoms or molecules in a crystal; **lattice point** (*a*) *Math.* a point on a graph or in space having integral coordinates; (*b*) any of the points of which a lattice, esp. a crystal lattice, is composed; **lattice site** a (specified) location in the molecular lattice structure of a metal, crystal, etc.; **lattice vibration** *Physics* (*a*) an oscillation of an atom or molecule about its equilibrium position in a crystal lattice; (*b*) a lattice wave; **lattice wave** *Physics* a displacement of atoms or molecules from their equilibrium position in a crystal which travels as a wave through the crystal; **lattice-window**: furnished with a lattice or composed of small diamond-shaped panes set in lead-work; **lattice-work** interlacing laths or strips of metal etc. forming a lattice.

B *v.t.* **1** Provide (as) with a lattice or lattice-work. Also foll. by *up*, *over*. LME. **2** Form into a lattice, arrange as a lattice. M20.

1 L. BLUE Lattice the top with thin strips of tinned red pimento . . and anchovy fillets.

latticewise *adv.* in the form of a lattice or lattice-work M16.

latticed /ˈlatɪst/ *a.* M16. [f. LATTICE *n.*, *v.*: see -ED², -ED¹.] **1** Provided with a lattice or lattice-work. M16. **2** Shaped or arranged like a lattice; *esp.* (*Bot.* & *Zool.*) having a conformation or marking resembling lattice-work. L16. **b** *Her.* Bearing a charge representing or resembling lattice-work, trellised. *rare.* E18.

latticinio /lattiˈtʃiːnjo, latɪˈtʃiːnjəʊ/ *n.* Also **-no** /-no, -nəʊ/. M19. [It., lit. 'dairy produce', f. med.L *lacticinium*.] An opaque white glass used in threads to decorate clear Venetian glass.

latus /ˈleɪtəs/ *n.* Now *rare* or *obs.* L16. [Late L f. Gk *latos*.] (The classical name of) the Nile perch, *Lates niloticus*. Cf. LATES.

latus rectum /leɪtəs ˈrɛktəm/ *n. phr.* Pl. **latera recta** /lat(ə)rə ˈrɛktə/. E18. [L = right side.] *Geom.* (The length of) a straight line passing through the focus of a conic at right angles to the transverse or major axis.

Latvian /ˈlatvɪən/ *a.* & *n.* E20. [f. *Latvia* (see below), Latvian & Lith. *Latvija* + -AN.] **A** *adj.* Of or pertaining to Latvia, a Baltic State between Estonia and Lithuania, its people, or their language. E20. **B** *n.* **1** A native or inhabitant of Latvia. E20. **2** The Baltic language of Latvia. E20.

¶ Cf. LETTISH.

lau /laʊ/ *n.* E20. [Dinka & Nuer.] A water monster reputed to live in the swamps of the Nile valley.

lauan /ˈlaʊən, laˈwɑːn/ *n.* L19. [Tagalog *lawáʼan*, *láwan*.] The lightweight hardwood timber produced by various Philippine trees of the genus *Shorea* (family Dipterocarpaceae) or closely related genera.

laubmannite /ˈlaʊbmənʌɪt/ *n.* M20. [f. Heinrich *Laubmann* (1865–1951), Ger. mineralogist + -ITE¹.] *Min.* An orthorhombic basic phosphate of ferrous and ferric iron forming yellow- to grey-green crystals.

laud /lɔːd/ *n.*¹ ME. [OFr. *laude*, pl. *laudes* f. L *laudes* pl. of *laus* praise.] **1** *Eccl.* In *pl.* (treated as *sing.* & *pl.*). The first of the daytime canonical hours of prayer, orig. appointed for daybreak; the office, with which may be said the original night office of matins, appointed for this hour. ME. **2** Praise, high commendation. Now *rare* exc. in hymns. LME. **b** A cause or subject for praise. *rare.* M16. **3** A hymn, an ascription of praise. M16.

2 J. M. NEALE All glory, laud, and honour To thee, Redeemer, King.

laud /laˈud/ *n.*² Pl. ***laudes*** /laˈudes/. L19. [Sp. *laúd* f. Arab. *al-ʻūd*: see LUTE *n.*¹] A Spanish lute.

laud /lɔːd/ *v.t.* LME. [L *laudare*, f. *laud-*, *laus* praise.] Praise highly, sing or speak the praises of (orig. as an act of worship); celebrate.

P. GAY He lauded Jung's writings, peppering his enthusiasms with shrewdly placed criticisms.

laudable /ˈlɔːdəb(ə)l/ *a.* Also ***-ible**. LME. [L *laudabilis*, f. as prec.: see -ABLE, -IBLE.] **1** Praiseworthy, commendable. In early use also, of the nature of praise, laudatory. LME. **†2** Satisfactory; healthy, sound, wholesome; *Med.* (of pus) creamy and inoffensive. E16–L19.

1 *Dun's Review* Every new regulation—no matter how laudable its goal—has a price.

laudaˈbility *n.* (*rare*) LME. **laudableness** *n.* L17. **laudably** *adv.* LME.

laudanine /ˈlɔːdəniːn/ *n.* L19. [f. LAUDANUM + -INE⁵.] *Chem.* An alkaloid derived from opium with analgesic properties.

laudanosine /lɔːˈdanəsiːn/ *n.* an alkaloid, laudanine methyl ether, which occurs in opium and is a strong tetanic poison L19.

laudanum /ˈlɔːd(ə)nəm, ˈlɒ-/ *n.* M16. [mod.L, used by Paracelsus as the name of a costly medicament in which opium was early suspected to be the active ingredient, perh. var. of L LADANUM, or suggested by L *laudare* LAUD *v.*] **1** Orig., any of various preparations in which opium was the main ingredient. Later, an alcoholic solution of morphine, formerly commonly used as a painkiller. M16. **†2** = LADANUM. M16–E18.

laudation /lɔːˈdeɪʃ(ə)n/ *n.* LME. [OFr. *laudacion* or L *laudatio(n-)*, f. *laudat-* pa. ppl stem of *laudare* LAUD *v.*: see -ATION.] The giving of praise; an instance of this, a eulogy.

laudative /ˈlɔːdətɪv/ *a.* & *n.* *rare.* LME. [L *laudativus*, f. *laudat-*: see prec., -IVE.] **A** *adj.* Expressive of praise; laudatory. (Foll. by *of*.) LME. **†B** *n.* A laudative expression or discourse; a eulogy. Only in 17.

laudator /lɔːˈdeɪtə/ *n.* Now *rare.* E19. [L, f. *laudat-*: see LAUDATION, -OR.] = LAUDER.

laudator temporis acti /lɔːˌdeɪtə ˌtɛmp(ə)rɪs ˈaktʌɪ/ *n. phr.* Pl. ***laudatores temporis acti*** /lɔːdəˌtɔːriːz/. M18. [L, *laudator temporis acti* (*se puero*) a praiser of past times, (when he himself was a boy) (Horace *Ars Poetica*).] A person who holds up the past as a golden age.

laudatory /ˈlɔːdət(ə)ri/ *a.* M16. [Late L *laudatorius*, f. as LAUDATOR: see -ORY².] Expressive of praise; eulogistic. (Foll. by *of*.)

laudatorily *adv.* M19.

lauder /ˈlɔːdə/ *n.* E17. [f. LAUD *v.* + -ER¹.] A person who praises: a eulogist.

laudes *n.* pl. of LAUD *n.*²

Laudian /ˈlɔːdɪən/ *a.* & *n.* L17. [f. *Laud* (see below) + -IAN.] Chiefly *Hist.* **A** *adj.* Of, pertaining to, or characteristic of William Laud, archbishop of Canterbury 1633–45, noted for his advocacy of pre-Reformation liturgical practices and his opposition to Calvinism; favouring the tenets or practices of Laud; instituted by Laud. L17. **B** *n.* A follower of Laud. E18.

Laudianism *n.* the principles and practice of Laud and his followers L19.

laudible *a.* see LAUDABLE.

Laudism /ˈlɔːdɪz(ə)m/ *n.* M19. [f. William *Laud* (see LAUDIAN) + -ISM.] = LAUDIANISM.

Laudist *n.* = LAUDIAN *n.* M18.

Laue /ˈlaʊə/ *n.* E20. [Max von *Laue* (1879–1960), Ger. physicist.] *Cryst.* Used *attrib.* with ref. to a method of X-ray diffraction in which a narrow beam of X-rays is directed at a thin crystal and the resulting diffraction pattern recorded on a photographic film.

Laue method, *pattern*, etc.

Laufen /ˈlaʊf(ə)n/ *a.* E20. [A town in Germany near Salzburg.] Designating a minor glacial retreat following the last major (Würm) glaciation in the Alps.

laugh /lɑːf/ *n.* L17. [f. the vb.] **1** The action of laughing; inclination to laugh. *rare.* L17. **2** A burst of laughter; a bout of laughing. Also, a person's characteristic manner of laughing. E18. **3a** A laughing-stock. *rare.* E19. **b** An amusing thing, circumstance, or person; (freq. *iron.*) a joke. *colloq.* L19.

1 S. J. DUNCAN Mr. Pratte had very blue eyes with a great deal of laugh in them. 2 J. AUSTEN Elinor could have forgiven everything but her laugh. *barrel of laughs*: see BARREL *n.* **for laughs, for a laugh** merely for one's amusement or as a joke. **good for a laugh** that can be trusted to raise a laugh. **have the last laugh** be vindicated after being initially held up to ridicule. **have** (or **get**) **the laugh on** (or **over**) **a person** be in a position to enjoy the discomfiture of an opponent. **have the laugh on one's side** = *have the laugh on a person* above. *holy laugh*: see HOLY *a.* *play for laughs*: see PLAY *v.* *raise a laugh*: see RAISE *v.* **the laugh is on me** the tables are turned and now I am the person exposed to ridicule.

Comb.: **laugh-line** (*a*) *Theatr.* a comic line received with laughter; (*b*) = *laughter-line* s.v. LAUGHTER *n.*¹; **laugh track** a recording of audience laughter added to a soundtrack.

laugh /lɑːf/ *v.* [OE *hlæhhan*, (WS) *hliehhan* = OFris. *hlakkia*, OHG *hlahhan*, *hlahhēn* (Du., G *lachen*), ON *hlæja*, Goth. *hlahjan*, f. Gmc, ult. f. IE imit. base (cf. Gk *klōssein* to cluck).] **1** *v.i.* Make the spasmodic inarticulate sounds, the movements of the facial muscles, shaking of the sides, etc., which are the instinctive expressions of lively amusement, scorn, exultation, etc., or reactions to certain physical sensations, such as that produced by tickling. Also, have one of the emotions expressed by laughing. OE. **b** Of water, scenery, corn, etc.: be lively with movement or the play of light and colour as if expressing joyous feeling. *poet.* & *rhet.* LME. **†2** *v.t.* Laugh or mock at, deride. OE–M17. **3** *v.t.* Utter (a laugh) as an expression of amusement etc. Also, utter or say laughingly. LME. **4** *v.t.* With obj. & compl. or advb. phr.: bring into a given state or position by laughing; *esp.* persuade (a person) *out of* a belief, a solemn mood, etc., by laughter or mockery. LME.

1 M. WEST Jean Marie laughed—a gusty chuckle of genuine amusement. b S. BARING-GOULD This mountain plateau laughs with verdure. 3 C. E. RIDDELL 'What a flatterer ladies must have found you', laughed Miss Pousnett. 4 J. TRAPP Whose whole life is to eat, and drink . . and laugh themselves fat. A. W. HARE Is there anybody . . who has not . . been laught out of what he ought to have done.

Phrases: **be laughing** *colloq.* be in a position to exult, be fortunate or successful. *enough to make a cat laugh*: see CAT *n.*¹ **†laugh and lay** (or **lie**) **down** an obsolete card-game. **laugh in a person's face** show open contempt for a person. *laugh in one's sleeve*: see SLEEVE *n.* *laugh like a drain*: see DRAIN *n.* **laugh one's head off** laugh heartily or uncontrollably (*at*). **laugh on the other** (or **wrong**) **side of one's face** (or **mouth**) be discomfited after premature exultation. **laugh out of court** dismiss as absurd. **laugh to scorn** *arch.* ridicule, deride. *laugh up one's sleeve*: see SLEEVE *n.*

With advs. & preps. in specialized senses: **laugh at** — (*a*) laugh in response to, see the funny side of; (*b*) deride, make fun of. **laugh away** †(*a*) let go with a laugh; (*b*) = *laugh off* below; (*c*) while away (time) with laughter. **laugh down** subdue or silence with laughter. **laugh off** dismiss (a misfortune, an embarrassment, etc.) with a laugh. **†laugh out** brazen out with laughter. **laugh over** — (prep.) laugh as one thinks about. **†laugh over** (adv.) discuss with laughter or merriment.

laughable /ˈlɑːfəb(ə)l/ *a.* L16. [f. LAUGH *v.* + -ABLE.] Calculated to excite laughter; ludicrous, absurd.

laughableness *n.* M19. **laughably** *adv.* E19.

laugher /ˈlɑːfə/ *n.* LME. [f. LAUGH *v.* + -ER¹.] **1** A person who laughs, a person who likes to laugh. Also, a scoffer. LME. **2** A variety of the domestic pigeon, so called from its peculiar note. M18. **3** A highly amusing or absurd remark, situation, etc.; a (baseball) match so easily won as to be laughable. *US slang.* M20.

laughful /ˈlɑːffʊl, -f(ə)l/ *a.* E19. [f. LAUGH *n.* + -FUL.] Full of laughter or merriment.

laugh-in /ˈlɑːfɪn/ *n.* M20. [f. LAUGH *v.* + -IN[2].] A demonstration, event, or situation marked by or devised for communal laughter or merriment.

laughing /ˈlɑːfɪŋ/ *n.* ME. [f. LAUGH *v.* + -ING[1].] The action of LAUGH *v.*; laughter.

Comb.: **laughing death** = KURU; *laughing-game*: see GAME *n.* 2b; **laughing-gas** nitrous oxide used as an anaesthetic (so called from the exhilarating effect it produces when inhaled); **laughing matter** a fit subject for laughter (*no laughing matter*, a serious matter); **laughing-muscle** the muscle that produces the facial contortions of laughter; **laughing-stock** an object of derisive laughter or general ridicule.

laughing /ˈlɑːfɪŋ/ *a.* ME. [f. LAUGH *v.* + -ING[2].] That laughs. Freq. in names of animals, so called from their cry or appearance.

laughing crow = *laughing-thrush* below. **laughing dove** an African dove, *Stigmatopelia senegalensis*. **laughing goose** the white-fronted goose, *Anser albifrons*. **laughing gull** a N. American gull, *Larus atricilla*; also (*dial.*), the herring gull, the black-headed gull. *laughing hyena*: see HYENA 1a. *laughing jackass*: see JACKASS 2. **laughing owl** a rare owl of New Zealand, *Sceloglaux albifacies*. **laughing thrush** any of various Asian babblers, chiefly of the genus *Garrulax*.

laughingly *adv.* (*a*) in a laughing manner, with laughter; (*b*) *iron.* with laughable inappropriateness: M16.

laughsome /ˈlɑːfs(ə)m/ *a.* E17. [f. LAUGH *n.* + -SOME[1].] Given to laughing; (of a thing) comic, laughable.

laughter /ˈlɑːftə/ *n.*[1] [OE *hleahtor* = OHG *hlahtar* (whence G *Gelächter*), ON *hlátr*, f. Gmc, f. base of LAUGH *v.*] 1 The action of laughing, the sound of laughing. Also, a person's manner of laughing. OE. b An instance of this; a laugh. Now *rare*. OE. 2 A subject for laughter. *poet.* L16.

1 R. P. JHABVALA He made another joke whereupon they dissolved in relieved laughter. HOMERIC *laughter*. *rock with laughter*: see ROCK *v.*[1] b GOLDSMITH They broke out into a laughter for four or five several times successively. 2 SHAKES. *1 Hen. IV* Argument for a week, laughter for a month, and a good jest for ever.

Comb.: **laughter-line** any of the small wrinkles at the corners of the eyes or mouth supposedly formed by years of intermittent laughter.

laughterless *a.* E19.

laughter /ˈlɑːftə/ *n.*[2] Long *obs.* exc. *dial.* LME. [ON *láttr* f. Gmc. f. base of LAY *v.*[1]] The whole number of eggs laid by a fowl before she is ready to sit; a clutch of eggs.

laughworthy /ˈlɑːfwəːði/ *a. rare.* E17. [f. LAUGH *n.* + -WORTHY.] Deserving to be laughed at; ridiculous.

laughy /ˈlɑːfi/ *a. rare.* M19. [f. LAUGH *n.* or *v.* + -Y[1].] Inclined to or full of laughter. Also, comic, laughable.

lauhala /laʊˈhɑːlə/ *n.* E19. [Haw., f. *lau* leaf + *hala* screw pine.] A Polynesian screw pine, *Pandanus tectorius*; (the material plaited from) its dried leaves.

laulau /ˈlaʊlaʊ/ *n.* M20. [Haw., redupl. of *lau* leaf.] A portion of a Hawaiian dish of meat or fish wrapped in leaves and steamed or baked. Also, the wrapping of leaves for this dish.

laumontite /ˈlɔːm(ə)ntʌɪt/ *n.* E19. [f. Gillet de *Laumont* (1747–1834), Fr. mineralogist + -ITE[1].] *Min.* A monoclinic hydrous silicate of aluminium and calcium, occurring as white crystals which lose water and crumble when exposed to the air.

†**launce** *n.*[1] *rare.* Only in L16. [L *lanc-*, *lanx*, It. *lance*.] A scale, a balance.

SPENSER Need teacheth her . . That fortune all in equall launce doth sway.

launce *n.*[2] see LANCE *n.*

†**launcegay** *n.* var. of LANCEGAY.

launch /lɔːn(t)ʃ/ *n.*[1] LME. [f. the vb.] 1 A sudden leap or rapid motion. Now chiefly *dial.*, a long stride. LME. †2 The action or an act of lancing; a prick. M–L16. 3 A ramp or slipway from which a boat is launched. E18. 4 The action or an act of launching a vessel into the sea, esp. for the first time and with appropriate ceremonies; *fig.* the action or an act of launching a person into a business, career, etc. M18. b The starting off of a bird in flight. M19. c The launching of an aircraft or spacecraft. M20. d (An instance of) the launching of a new product on the market. M20.

4 J. CLELAND Making this launch into the wide world, by repairing to London. d *Marketing Week* Two new . . magazine launches are announced this month.

Comb.: **launch pad** = LAUNCHING *pad*; *launch window*: see WINDOW *n.* 3c.

¶ Formerly pronounced /lɑːn(t)ʃ/.

launch /lɔːn(t)ʃ/ *n.*[2] L17. [Sp. *lancha* pinnace, perh. of Malay origin: cf. Port. *lanchara* f. Malay *lancharan*, f. *lanchar* quick, nimble.] 1 *Hist.* A longboat of a man-of-war, more flat-bottomed than that of a merchant ship. L17. 2 More fully *motor-launch*, *steam-launch*, etc. A small motor boat carried on a cruising yacht; a similar boat, usu. partly open, used as a pleasure-boat. M19.

Comb.: **launchman** a man who operates a launch.

¶ Formerly pronounced /lɑːn(t)ʃ/.

launch /lɔːn(t)ʃ/ *v.* ME. [AN *launcher*, ONFr. *lancher*, var. of OFr. *lancier* LANCE *v.*] I *v.t.* †1 Pierce, wound; cut, slit; make (a wound) by piercing; cut with a lancet, lance. ME–L17. 2 Discharge with force, hurl (a missile etc.); *fig.* utter (criticism, threats, etc.) with vehemence. ME. b Dart forward (a weapon, limb, etc.). Now only, dart *out* (something long and flexible). LME. c *refl.* Hurl oneself forward or down, rush, precipitate oneself. L17. 3 Cause (a vessel) to move from land into the water; *esp.* set afloat (a newly built vessel) for the first time, often with ceremonies. LME. b Start (now esp. a rocket, spacecraft, etc.) on its course; release (a balloon or its contents) into the air at the beginning of a flight. E17. 4 *fig.* Start (a person) *in*, *into*, or *on* a business, career, etc. Also foll. by *out*. E17. b Set on foot, initiate (a course of action, scheme, etc.); mount (a campaign, an offensive); bring before the public (a new publication, radio or television programme, etc.); formally introduce (a product etc.) on to the market. L19. 5 *Naut.* Move (heavy goods) by pushing. Formerly, hoist (a yard). E17.

1 DRYDEN Nine Bulls were launch'd by his victorious arm. 2 W. IRVING Much as they thirsted for his blood, they forbore to launch a shaft. W. E. H. LECKY He launched from the pulpit the most scathing invectives. c T. PAINE A spider can launch itself from the top, as playful amusement. 3 DAY LEWIS He launched his coble into a rough sea. 4 C. ISHERWOOD He was going to put up the money to launch Sally upon a stage career. b J. AGATE Barry Neame was giving a luncheon-party to launch Maurice Healy's new book. H. L. MENCKEN I marvel that no one tries to launch a royalist movement in the United States. H. KISSINGER A new assault was launched in the direction of Tehepone. *Kuwait Times* Gavaskar and Krishna Srikkanth launched the Indian innings.

II *v.i.* 6 Make a sudden or rapid motion; rush, plunge. Now only (*dial.*), take long strides, bound. ME. †b *transf.* Shoot, sprout. Also, project. LME–L17. 7 Of people in a vessel: put out to sea. Freq. foll. by *out*, (arch.) *forth*. M16. 8 Enter boldly, eagerly, or without restraint into or *into* a new (freq. ambitious) enterprise, financial outlay, etc.; plunge into or *into* a long recital, a tirade, etc. Freq. foll. by *forth*, *out*. M16. 9a Of a ship: be launched, pass into the water. Now *rare*. M17. b Of a new programme, product, etc.: be launched. L20. 10 Propel a boat with a pole; *spec.* (in wildfowling) punt across mud. E19.

7 C. THIRLWALL Before any Greek navigator ventured . . to launch out beyond Sicily. 8 A. JESSOPP The small man . . is . . slow to launch out into expense. *Observer* Why must a dancer launch out as a choreographer as well? K. WILLIAMS He launched into a long account of his Australian tour. 9b *Daily Telegraph* The first weekly issue of the Sunday Mirror magazine launches this weekend.

¶ Formerly pronounced /lɑːn(t)ʃ/.

launcher /ˈlɔːn(t)ʃə/ *n.* E19. [f. LAUNCH *v.* + -ER[1].] 1 A person who launches. E19. 2 A person who launches something or someone. L19. 3 A device or structure that launches something or is used for launching; *spec.* (*a*) a structure that holds a rocket or missile during launching; (*b*) a rocket from which a satellite is released into orbit. E20.

launching /ˈlɔːn(t)ʃɪŋ/ *vbl n.* LME. [f. LAUNCH *v.* + -ING[1].] The action of LAUNCH *v.*; an instance of this.

Comb.: **launching pad** the area on which a rocket stands for launching; *fig.* a starting-point for a (freq. ambitious) enterprise, career, etc.; **launching-ways** the beds of timber blocks, sloping gradually towards the water, on which the bilge-keels of a ship rest after completion of construction.

laund /lɔːnd/ *n.* Now *arch.* & *dial.* ME. [OFr. *launde* (mod. *lande*) wooded district, heath. See also LAWN *n.*[2]] An open space among woodland, a glade; untilled ground, pasture.

launder /ˈlɔːndə/ *n.* Also (now chiefly in sense 2c) **lander** /ˈlɑːndə/. ME. [Contr. of LAVENDER *n.*[1]] †1 A person who washes linen. ME–E17. 2a A trough for water, either cut in the earth or formed of wood etc.; *esp.* in *Mining*, one for washing ore. M17. b A gutter for rainwater. M17. c *Metall.* A channel for conveying molten metal from a furnace or container to a ladle or mould. E20.

launder /ˈlɔːndə/ *v.* L16. [f. the n.] 1 *v.t.* Wash (clothes, linen, etc.); wash, perhaps starch, and usu. also iron (clothes, linen, etc.). L16. 2 *v.i.* Of a fabric or garment etc: admit of being laundered; bear laundering without damage to the texture, colour, etc. E20. 3 *v.t. fig.* Treat or process (something) to make it appear acceptable. M20. b Transfer (funds or goods) to conceal a dubious or illegal origin, later recovering them from apparently legitimate sources. Also, reduce the tax payable on (profits) by selling assets or transferring funds to a loss-making subsidiary, for later selling back. L20.

2 *Daily Mail* This hard wearing fabric, which launders perfectly. 3 *Toronto Sun* There is nothing we can do to launder the rhetoric of Soviet leaders. b *Police Review* 'Dirty money' which is 'laundered' through Swiss or Caribbean bank accounts, reappearing as apparently legitimate capital.

launderer *n.* LME.

launderette /lɔːndəˈrɛt, lɔːnˈdrɛt/ *n.* Also **laundrette** /lɔːnˈdrɛt/. M20. [f. LAUNDER *v.* + -ETTE.] An establishment with automatic washing machines for the use of customers.

laundermat /ˈlɔːndəmat/ *n.* Chiefly *N. Amer.* M20. [f. LAUNDER *v.* + -MAT. Cf. LAUNDROMAT.] A launderette.

Launder-Ometer /lɔːnˈdrɒmɪtə, -dəˈrɒmɪtə/ *n.* Orig. *US*. Also **launderometer**. E20. [f. LAUNDER *v.* + -OMETER.] (Proprietary name for) a machine for carrying out standardized laundering tests on fabrics, detergents, etc.

laundress /ˈlɔːndrɪs/ *n.* M16. [f. LAUNDER *n.* or LAUNDERER + -ESS[1].] 1 A woman employed to launder clothes etc. M16. 2 *Hist.* A female caretaker of chambers in the Inns of Court. L16.

laundrette *n.* var. of LAUNDERETTE.

Laundromat /ˈlɔːndrəmat/ *n.* Orig. *US*. Also **l-**. M20. [Alt. f. as LAUNDERMAT.] An automatic washing machine. Also, (US proprietary name for) a launderette.

laundry /ˈlɔːndri/ *n.* & *v.* E16. [Contr. of LAVENDRY.] A *n.* 1 The action or process of laundering clothes, linen, etc.; the laundering work presented by a particular quantity of clothes etc. E16. b *fig.* The action of laundering funds etc. L20. 2 An establishment where clothing etc. is laundered. L16. b *fig.* An establishment where funds etc. are laundered. L20. 3 Articles of clothing etc. that need to be, or have been, laundered. E20.

1 J. RULE I'm doing the landlady's laundry and cleaning this week. 2 *Chinese laundry*: see CHINESE *a.* b *New York Times* Bahamian companies provided a convenient 'laundry' for illegitimate mob money looking . . to reach legitimate usage. 3 T. K. WOLFE There was laundry hanging all along the shower curtain rod.

Comb.: **laundryman**, **-woman** (*a*) a launderer of clothes, linen, etc.; (*b*) a person who collects and delivers laundry.

B *v.t.* = LAUNDER *v.* I. L19.

laura /ˈlɔːrə/ *n.* Also ***lavra*** /ˈlavrə/. E18. [Gk = lane, passage, alley.] *Chr. Ch.* A group of huts or cells inhabited by reclusive monks in Egypt and the Middle East. In the Orthodox Church, a monastery consisting of separate cells; a large monastery.

Laura Ashley /lɔːrə ˈaʃli/ *a.* L20. [Brit. fashion and textile designer (1925–85).] Of a garment, fabric, etc.: characteristic of the style of Laura Ashley; *spec.* having a small floral pattern. Also (*fig.*), frilly, feminine, sentimental.

Laura Ashleyish *a.* L20.

Laurasia /lɔːˈreɪʒə/ *n.* M20. [mod.L, f. *Laur*(*entia* the ancient land mass corresp. to N. America (f. as LAURENTIAN *a.*[1]) + *Eur*)*asia* (see EURASIAN *a.* & *n.*).] *Geol.* A supercontinent thought to have existed in the northern hemisphere and to have broken up in Mesozoic or late Palaeozoic times to form N. America, Europe, and most of Asia. Also, these land masses collectively as they exist today.

Laurasian *a.* M20.

laurate /ˈlɔːreɪt/ *n.* L19. [f. LAURIC + -ATE[1].] *Chem.* A salt or ester of lauric acid.

†laureat *a.* & *n.* var. of LAUREATE *a.* & *n.*

laureate /ˈlɒrɪət, ˈlɔː-/ *a.* & *n.* Also **†-at.** LME. [L *laureatus*, f. *laurea* laurel tree, laurel crown, use as n. of fem. of *laureus* adj., f. *laurus* LAUREL *n.*, or f. med.L *laureat-* pa. ppl stem of *laureare* crown with laurels: see -ATE[2].] **A** *adj.* **1 a** Of a crown or wreath: consisting of laurel, imitating a crown or wreath composed of laurel. LME. **b** Crowned with laurel, wearing a laurel crown or wreath as a symbol of distinction or eminence. E17. **2** Distinguished for excellence as a poet. Now chiefly in POET *laureate*. LME. **b** *gen.* Worthy of special distinction or honour, pre-eminent in a certain sphere. E16. **3** Of a thing: worthy of a laurel wreath; deserving to be honoured for eloquence etc. In later use also, of or pertaining to poets. LME.

B *n.* **†1** Glory, honour, distinction. Only in L15. **2 a** (Also **L-**.) = POET *laureate*. E16. **b** *transf.* A person who is pre-eminent or worthy of special distinction in a certain sphere. E19. **c** A eulogist, a court panegyrist. M19. **d** A person awarded an honour for achieving distinction, a graduate. L19.

2b H. COLERIDGE Herrick was the laureate of flowers and perfumes. **d** *Nobel laureate*: see NOBEL 2.

laureateship *n.* the position or office of (poet) laureate L18.

laureate /ˈlɒrɪeɪt, ˈlɔː-/ *v.t.* LME. [In sense 1 f. med.L *laureare* (see prec.); in sense 2 f. the adj.: see -ATE[3].] **1** Crown with laurel as a mark of honour; crown as victor, poet, etc.; confer honourable distinction upon. LME. **2** *spec.* **a** Confer a university degree on; in *pass.*, graduate. M17. **b** Appoint to the office of poet laureate. E18.

laureation /lɒrɪˈeɪʃ(ə)n, lɔː-/ *n.* E17. [med.L *laureatio(n-)*, f. *laureat-* pa. ppl stem of *laureare*: see LAUREATE *a.* & *n.*, -ATION.] The action of crowning someone with laurel or making someone laureate; the creation of a poet laureate. In Scottish universities, graduation or admission to a degree, now *spec.* an honorary degree.

laurel /ˈlɒr(ə)l/ *n.* & *a.* Also (earlier) **†laurer.** ME. [OFr. *lorier* (mod. *laurier*) f. Prov. *laurier*, f. *laur* (= OFr. *lor*, Catal. *llor*, etc.) f. L *laurus*, prob. of Mediterranean origin. The later form is due to dissimilation of *r . . r* to *r . . l*: cf. Sp. *laurel*.] **A** *n.* **1** A tree or shrub of the genus *Laurus* (family Lauraceae); *spec.* (more fully *bay-laurel*) the bay tree, *L. nobilis*. ME. **2** *collect. sing.* & in *pl.* The foliage of this tree (real or imaginary) as an emblem of victory or of distinction in poetry etc. Esp. *reap* or *win one's laurels*. LME. **b** A branch or wreath of this tree (real or imaginary). LME. **†c** The dignity of poet laureate. E18–E19. **d** = *laurel-green* below. E20. **3 a** Any of various trees and shrubs having leaves resembling those of the bay tree; *esp.* (more fully *common laurel* or *cherry-laurel*) *Prunus laurocerasus*, an evergreen shrub of the rose family much grown in shrubberies. E17. **b** Any of various trees and shrubs of the family Lauraceae, related to the bay-tree. M17. **4** *Numism.* Any of various English gold pieces (esp. those of 20 shillings) on which the monarch's head was figured with a wreath of laurel. E17.

2 look to one's laurels beware of losing one's pre-eminence. **repose, rest,** or **retire on one's laurels** cease to strive for further glory. **3a** *Japanese laurel, mountain laurel, spurge laurel*, etc. **b** *camphor laurel*.

Comb.: **laurel-bottle** a bottle containing crushed laurel leaves, used by entomologists for killing insects; **laurel-cherry** = *cherry-laurel*, sense 3 above; **laurel-green** the medium green colour of bay tree leaves; **laurel magnolia** *US* either of two magnolias, the evergreen *Magnolia grandiflora* and the sweet bay, *M. virginiana*; **laurel oak** *US* either of two oaks, *Quercus laurifolia* and *Q. imbricaria*; **laurel-water** the water obtained by distillation from the leaves of the cherry-laurel and containing a small proportion of prussic acid.

†B *adj.* Crowned or wreathed with laurel; *fig.* renowned. L16–E17.

laurel /ˈlɒr(ə)l/ *v.t.* Infl. **-ll-**, ***-l-**. M17. [f. the n.] Wreathe with laurel, adorn with or as with laurel; *fig.* honour, acclaim.

laurelled /ˈlɒr(ə)ld/ *a.* Also ***-eled.** M17. [f. LAUREL *n.*, *v.*: see -ED[2], -ED[1].] Adorned, crowned, or wreathed with laurel; *fig.* honoured, illustrious. Also, covered with a growth of laurel, made of laurel.

Laurence /ˈlɒr(ə)ns/ *n.* Also **Lawrence.** L18. [Male forename.] **1** Laziness personified, a lazy person. Also *Lazy Laurence obs.* exc. *dial.* L18. **2** The shimmer reflected from the earth's surface on hot days; a mirage. *US colloq.* E20.

Laurentian /lɒˈrɛnʃ(ə)n/ *a.*[1] M19. [f. L *Laurentius* Laurence, Lawrence, f. the St Lawrence River + -AN.] *Geol.* Designating or pertaining to a geological region in eastern Canada of Precambrian age (the *Laurentian Shield*) or the period in which it was formed; *esp.* designating a group of granites found north-west of the St Lawrence River.

Laurentian /lɒˈrɛnʃ(ə)n/ *a.*[2] M19. [f. Lorenzo (*Laurentius*) de' Medici (1449–92), Florentine nobleman + -AN.] Designating or pertaining to the library in Florence founded by Lorenzo de' Medici, or manuscripts preserved there.

Laurentian *a.*[3] & *n.* var. of LAWRENTIAN.

†laurer *n.* & *a.* see LAUREL *n.* & *a.*

lauric /ˈlɔːrɪk/ *a.* L19. [f. mod.L genus name *Laurus* laurel + -IC.] Chem. *lauric acid*, a saturated fatty acid, $CH_3(CH_2)_{10}COOH$, which occurs as a glyceride in laurel oil, coconut oil, and other vegetable fats. Also called *dodecanoic acid*.

lauroyl /ˈlɔːrəʊʌɪl, -ɔɪl/ *n.* the radical $CH_3(CH_2)_{10}CO\cdot$ M20.

laurustine /ˈlɔːrəstʌɪn/ *n.* L17. [Anglicized f. next.] = next.

laurustinus /lɒrəˈstʌɪnəs, lɔː-/ *n.* E17. [mod.L *laurus tinus*, i.e. L *laurus* laurel + *tinus* laurustinus.] A Mediterranean evergreen winter-flowering shrub, *Viburnum tinus*, of the honeysuckle family.

lauryl /ˈlɒrɪl, -rʌɪl, ˈlɔː-/ *n.* E20. [f. LAURIC + -YL.] *Chem.* A radical $CH_3(CH_2)_{10}CH_2\cdot$, derived from lauric acid; dodecyl. Usu. in *comb.*

Comb.: **lauryl alcohol** a crystalline low-melting alcohol, $CH_3(CH_2)_{10}CH_2OH$, which is obtained by reduction of coconut oil and whose sulphate esters are used in detergents.

Lausitz /ˈlaʊsɪts/ *a.* E20. [Ger. name of Lusatia: see LUSATIAN *n.* & *a.*] *Archaeol.* Designating or pertaining to an urn-field culture which flourished in central Europe during the later Bronze Age.

lautenclavicymbel /ˈlaʊt(ə)nklavɪˌsɪmb(ə)l/ *n.* Also **-al.** L19. [G *Lautenklavizimbel*, f. *Laute* lute + *Klavizimbel* harpsichord, f. as CLAVICYMBAL.] *Hist.* A type of harpsichord with gut rather than metal strings. Also called *lute harpsichord*.

lauter /ˈlaʊtə/ *a.* & *v.* E20. [f. G *läutern* purify, refine, strain.] *Brewing.* **A** *adj.* Involved in, used in, or resulting from the refining process. E20.

Comb.: **lautermash** refined liquid, wort.

B *v.t.* Refine, filter. Chiefly as *lautering* vbl n. M20.

lauwine /laʊˈviːnə, ˈlɔːwɪn/ *n.* Now *rare.* Also ***lawine*** /ˈlɑːviːnə/. E19. [(Orig. Swiss) G *Lawine*, †*Lauwin*(*e*, etc., of unkn. origin.] An avalanche.

¶ Formerly more fully naturalized.

lav /lav/ *n. colloq.* E20. [Abbrev.] = LAVATORY *n.* 3. Cf. LAVVY.

lava /ˈlɑːvə/ *n.* M18. [It. (orig. Neapolitan dial.) = lava-stream from Vesuvius, (formerly) stream caused by sudden rain, f. L *lavare* to wash.] **1** The fluid or semifluid magma or molten rock which flows from a volcano or other fissure in the earth. M18. **2** A stream or flow of molten rock issuing from a volcanic crater or fissure. M18. **3 a** The hard igneous rock resulting from the cooling of volcanic lava. M18. **b** A kind of lava; a bed of solidified lava. L18.

1 *Scientific American* If the magma is erupted at the surface as lava, it forms extrusive igneous rocks such as basalt. **2** *Sunday Express* Composed of solidified lavas from ancient volcanoes, this . . mountain is the highest point in the land.

Comb.: *lava bomb*: see BOMB *n.* 4; **lava flow** a mass of flowing or solidified lava; **lava tube** (chiefly *US*) a tubular cave occurring naturally in some solidified lava flows; **lava ware** a type of stoneware with the semi-vitreous appearance of lava.

laval *a.* L19.

lavabo /ləˈveɪbəʊ, *in sense 2* ˈlavəbəʊ/ *n.* Pl. **-o(e)s.** M18. [L = I will wash.] **1** *Eccl.* **a** In the Eucharist: the ritual washing of a celebrant's hands at the offertory. M18. **b** The small towel used to wipe the celebrant's hands. M18. **c** The basin used for the washing. M18. **2 a** A washing-trough used in some medieval monasteries. L19. **b** A wash-hand basin. E20. **c** = LAVATORY *n.* 4. M20.

lavage /ˈlavɪdʒ, laˈvɑːʒ/ *n.* & *v.* L18. [Fr., f. *laver* to wash: see -AGE.] **A** *n.* **1** An act of washing, a wash. L18. **2** *Med.* The irrigation of an organ, either to cleanse it or to allow its contents to be examined. L19. **B** *v.t. Med.* Cleanse, irrigate, (an organ). M20.

lava-lava /ˈlɑːvəlɑːvə/ *n.* L19. [Samoan.] In Samoa and some other Pacific islands: a wrap-around skirtlike garment worn by either sex.

lavaliere /ləˈvaljɛː/ *n.* Also **-(l)lière, -lier** /-lɪə/, **L-.** L19. [Louise de *la Vallière* (1644–1710), French courtesan.] **1** Used *attrib.* to designate any of various items of women's clothing in styles associated with the reign of Louis XIV of France. L19. **2** A pendent necklace. E20. **3** A loosely tied cravat. M20. **4** A small microphone worn hanging around the neck. Also *lavaliere microphone*. M20.

†lavament *n.* LME–E19. [med.L *lavamentum*, f. L *lavare* to wash: see -MENT. Cf. LAVEMENT.] An act of washing; a wash, a lotion.

lavandera /lavanˈdera/ *n.* M19. [Sp.] In Spain and Spanish-speaking countries: a washer-woman.

lavaret /lavare (*pl. same*), ˈlav(ə)rət/ *n.* M19. [Fr.] A form of the freshwater houting, *Coregonus lavaretus*, occurring in central European lakes.

lavatera /lavəˈtɛːrə, ləˈvɑːt(ə)rə/ *n.* M18. [mod.L (see below), f. the brothers *Lavater*, 17th- and 18th-cent. Swiss physicians and naturalists.] Any of various herbs or shrubs constituting the genus *Lavatera*, of the mallow family, bearing pink, white, or purple flowers; *esp.* the tree mallow, *L. arborea*.

lavation /ləˈveɪʃ(ə)n/ *n.* LME. [L *lavatio(n-)* washing, f. *lavat-* pa. ppl stem of *lavare* wash: see -ATION.] The action of washing, an instance of this; water for washing.

lavatorial /lavəˈtɔːrɪəl/ *a.* M19. [f. next + -AL[1].] **1** Of or pertaining to washing. M19. **2** Of or pertaining to lavatories; *spec.* (*a*) designating or pertaining to a style of architecture or decoration alleged to resemble that used for public lavatories; (*b*) (of conversation, humour, etc.) making undue reference to lavatories and their use. M20.

2 A. ROSS Endless lavatorial town hall corridors. *Reader's Report* Many poets, when talking about their art, drop . . into . . obstetrical and even lavatorial imagery.

lavatory /ˈlavət(ə)ri/ *n.* LME. [Late L *lavatorium*, f. L *lavat-*: see LAVATION, -ORY[1].] 1 A vessel for washing; a laver, a bath. Also (*Eccl.*), a piscina. LME. †b *fig.* A means of spiritual cleansing or purification. LME–M17. †2 A lotion, a wash. LME–L17. 3 *Eccl.* The ritual washing of a celebrant's hands at the offertory (cf. LAVABO 1a) or (formerly) after the cleansing of the vessels following the Eucharist. E16. 4 Orig., a room with washing facilities. Now, a room, building, or compartment fitted for people to urinate and defecate in, usu. with facilities for washing the hands and face; also, any place or facility provided for urination and defecation. M17. b An appliance for urinating and defecating into, usu. flushed by water. M20. †5 A laundry. M17–L19.

4 J. P. DONLEAVY And a toilet bowl wedged between two walls, the lavatory. M. SPARK Freddy went to the lavatory, not from need, but in case there should be a long journey ahead. b *attrib.*: K. WILLIAMS You're sitting on this freshly painted lavatory seat and the cistern overflows.

Comb.: **lavatory humour** unsavoury or crude humour making undue reference to lavatories, lavatorial humour; **lavatory paper** = *toilet paper* s.v. TOILET *n.*; **lavatory style** a lavatorial style of architecture.

lavatory /ˈlavət(ə)ri, ləˈveɪt(ə)ri/ *a.* M19. [f. the n.] Of or pertaining to washing.

lave /leɪv/ *n. obs.* exc. *Sc.* [OE *lāf* = OFris. *lāva*, OLG *lēva*, OHG *leiba*, ON *leif*, Goth. *laiba* f. Gmc base also of LEAVE *v.*[1]] What is left; the remainder, the rest.

lave /leɪv/ *a. obs.* exc. in comb. below. LME. [Cf. ON *lafa* to droop.] Of ears: drooping, hanging.

Comb.: **lave-eared** *a.* having lave-ears; **lave-ears** drooping or hanging ears (esp. of a horse), lop-ears.

lave /leɪv/ *v.* Now chiefly *poet.* [OE *lafian* = (M)Du. *laven*, OHG *labōn*, G *laben* refresh, f. L *lavare* wash. Coalesced in ME w. forms f. (O)Fr. *laver* f. L *lavare*.] 1 *v.t.* Wash, orig. *spec.* by pouring water on; bathe. OE. b *v.i.* Bathe. E18. 2 *v.t.* Pour (out), sprinkle, ladle. Foll. by *into*, *on*, *upon*. OE. 3 *v.t.* Draw (water) out or up with a bucket, scoop, etc.; bale. (Foll. by *out*, *up*.) *obs.* exc. *dial.* ME. 4 *v.t.* Of a river or body of water: wash against, flow along or past. E17.

1 J. UPDIKE Several Tuareg women . . were laving Sheba's feet. 4 W. DE LA MARE When calm waters lave a rock-bound coast.

laveer /ləˈvɪə/ *v.i. obs.* exc. *literary.* L16. [Du. *laveeren*, earlier †*loveren* f. Fr. †*loveer* (now. *louvoyer*), f. *lof* windward, LUFF *n.*[1]: see -EER.] *Naut.* Beat to windward, tack.

lavement /ˈleɪvm(ə)nt/ *n.* M17. [(O)Fr., f. *laver* to wash: see LAVE *v.*, -MENT. Cf. LAVAMENT.] 1 The action of washing or cleansing. *rare.* M17. 2 *Med.* A cleansing solution, *esp.* an enema. Now *rare.* L18.

†**lavender** *n.*[1] ME–M16. [OFr. *lavandier* (masc.), *-iere* (fem.) f. Proto-Romance var. of L *lavanda* things to be washed, use as n. of neut. pl. of gerundive of *lavare* to wash: see -ER[2].] = LAUNDER *n.* 1.

¶Contr. to LAUNDER *n.*

lavender /ˈlav(ə)ndə/ *n.*[2] & *a.* ME. [AN *lavendre*, ult. dissimilated form of med.L *lavendula* etc., of unkn. origin.] A *n.* 1 Any of various small labiate shrubs constituting the genus *Lavandula*, with spikes of purple flowers and narrow oblong or lanceolate leaves, native to the Mediterranean region; *spec.* any of those grown in gardens or cultivated for perfume, esp. *Lavandula angustifolia*, *L. latifolia* and their hybrid. ME. 2 The flowers and stalks of cultivated lavender, dried and placed among linen, clothes, etc., to scent them and preserve them from moths. L16. 3 *ellipt.* Lavender-blue. M19. 4 *fig.* Effeminacy, homosexuality, homosexual tendencies. E20. 5 *Cinemat.* Positive stock, or a positive print, used for producing duplicate negatives; a print made from such a negative. M20.

Phrases: *French lavender*: see FRENCH *a.* **lay up in lavender** preserve carefully for future use. **oil of lavender** the oil obtained by distillation of the blossoms of cultivated lavender, used in medicine and perfumery. SEA *lavender*. *spike lavender*: see SPIKE *n.*[2]

Comb.: **lavender bag** a bag containing dried lavender; **lavender-blue** (of) the colour of lavender flowers, a pale blue with a trace of red; **lavender cotton** a greyish aromatic shrub of the composite family, *Santolina chamaecyparissus*, grown for ornament; **lavender oil** = *oil of lavender* above; †**lavender rays** ultraviolet radiation; **lavender soap** soap perfumed with lavender; **lavender water** perfume made from distilled lavender, alcohol, and ambergris.

B *adj.* 1 Of the colour or fragrance of lavender flowers. M19. 2 *fig.* Refined, genteel, sentimental. E20. b Of or pertaining to homosexuality; (of a man) homosexual, effeminate. *colloq.* M20.

lavendery *a.* perfumed with lavender, fragrant L19.

lavender /ˈlav(ə)ndə/ *v.t.* E19. [f. the n.] Perfume with lavender; put lavender among (linen etc.). Also, launder.

†**lavendry** *n.* ME–M16. [OFr. *lavanderie* (cf. L *lavandaria* things to be washed): see -RY.] = LAUNDRY *n.* 1, 2. Also, a washerwoman, a laundress.

¶Contr. to LAUNDRY *n.*

lave net /ˈleɪv nɛt/ *n. phr.* L19. [Origin of 1st elem. unkn.] A kind of fishing net used chiefly in shallow water.

laver /ˈleɪvə, ˈlɑːvə/ *n.*[1] LOE. [L.] †1 A water-plant mentioned by Pliny. Also called *sion*. LOE–E17. 2 Formerly, any of various marine algae. Now, one that is edible, *esp.* (more fully *purple laver*) *Porphyra umbilicaulis*. E17.

Comb.: **laver bread** a Welsh food made from the fronds of *Porphyra umbilicaulis*, which are boiled, dipped in oatmeal, and fried.

laver /ˈleɪvə/ *n.*[2] ME. [OFr. *laveor*, *laveoir* (mod. *lavoir*) f. as LAVATORY *n.*] 1 A basin or bowl for washing; (occas.) any vessel for water. Formerly also, a piscina or a washing-trough in a monastic cloister. Now only *poet.* & *rhet.* ME. b In biblical translations and allusions: a large bronze vessel used by Jewish priests for washing. M16. c The basin of a fountain. *arch.* E17. 2 The baptismal font. Also *fig.*, the spiritual purification of baptism; any spiritually cleansing agency. LME. †3 A process or instance of washing. Only in L17.

Comb.: **laver-pot** *Her.* a jug with a handle and a lid.

laver /ˈleɪvə/ *n.*[3] E19. [Perh. var. of LEVERS.] *Her.* A charge representing a ploughshare. Also *laver cutter*.

Laverack /ˈlav(ə)rak/ *n.* L19. [Edward *Laverack* (d. 1877), Eng. dog-breeder.] In full *Laverack setter*. (A dog of) a breed of English setter having long white fur flecked with other colours.

laverock *n.* see LARK *n.*[1]

Laves phase /ˈlɑːvəs feɪz/ *n. phr.* M20. [f. Fritz-Henning *Laves* (b. 1906), Ger. crystallographer + PHASE *n.*] *Metall.* Any of a group of intermetallic compounds of composition approximately AB_2 in which the relative sizes of the A and B atoms allow a stable packing arrangement with unusually high coordination numbers.

lavish /ˈlavɪʃ/ *a.* LME. [OFr. *lavasse* deluge of rain (cf. OFr. *lavis* torrent of words), f. *laver* wash, pour: see -ISH[1].] 1a Spending, producing, or giving without moderation; unstinting; extravagant, prodigal. (Foll. by *of*, *in*, *with*.) LME. b Spent, given, or produced in unstinted profusion; abundant. L16. c Sumptuous, rich, luxurious. L19. 2a Of speech etc.: unrestrained, effusive. L15. †b Of conduct or disposition: unrestrained, wild, licentious. L16–M17. c Of grass or wheat: rank, overgrown. *dial.* E18.

1a E. A. FREEMAN The people . . were . . most lavish in gifts to holy places. M. WEST Herman was lavish with compliments. b J. A. MICHENER The two Cobb boys . . passed among the guests, treating each with lavish deference. c *Which?* They've poured money into the pubs . . with large sums spent . . on lavish decor. S. NAIPAUL Their food was not only plentiful but lavish.

lavishly *adv.* LME. **lavishness** *n.* L15.

lavish /ˈlavɪʃ/ *v.* M16. [f. the n.] †1 *v.i.* Be extravagant, plunge *into* (excess); be excessive with words, exaggerate. M16–L17. b Of rain: pour *along* in torrents. Only in M19. 2 *v.t.* Give or spend profusely or excessively. (Foll. by *in*, *on*, *upon*.) M16.

2 W. S. CHURCHILL He was astonished at the vast sums which were being lavished upon the masonry. R. GRAVES If I lavished extravagant praise on her, she deserved it all.

lavishingly *adv.* (now *rare*) in a lavish manner L16. **lavishment** *n.* (now *rare*) the action of lavishing M17.

lavolta /ləˈvɒltə/ *n.* L16. [f. It. *la* the + *volta* turn.] *Hist.* A lively dance for couples in 3/4 time, in which each partner lifts the other clear of the ground in turn.

lavra *n.* var. of LAURA.

lavvy /ˈlavi/ *n.* M20. [Abbrev.] = LAVATORY *n.* 3. Cf. LAV.

law /lɔː/ *n.*[1] [OE *lagu* (pl. *laga*) f. ON pl. of *lag* something laid down or fixed, ult. f. Gmc base of LAY *v.*[1], LIE *v.*[1]] I A rule of conduct imposed by secular authority. 1 (Usu. w. *the.*) The body of rules, whether formally enacted or customary, which a particular State or community recognizes as governing the actions of its subjects or members and which it may enforce by imposing penalties. Orig. also, a code or system of rules of this kind. OE. †b What the law awards; what is due according to the law. LME–L16. c Personified as an agent uttering or enforcing the rules of which it consists. Also *colloq.* (orig. *US*), a police officer, the police; a sheriff. E16. 2 Any of the body of individual rules in force in a State or community. In early use only in *pl.*, w. a collect. sense approaching sense 1. OE. 3a Laws regarded as obeyed or enforced; controlling influence of laws; a state of respect for or observance of the laws. Freq. in *law and order*. ME. b Laws regarded collectively as a social system; rules or injunctions that must be obeyed; something which has the binding force or effect of laws. ME. c Laws regarded as a class of objects or as a subject of study; that department of knowledge of which laws are the subject-matter; (*sing.* & in *pl.*) jurisprudence. Also (w. specifying wd), any of the branches into which this collective body may be divided as it affects particular spheres of activity. LME. 4a (Usu. w. *the.*) The profession which is concerned with the exposition of the law, with pleading in the courts, and with the transaction of business requiring skilled knowledge of law; the profession of a lawyer. ME. b Legal knowledge; legal acquirements. M17. 5 The action of the courts, as a means of providing redress of grievances or enforcing claims; judicial remedy; recourse to the courts, litigation. ME. 6 The statute and common law. Opp. EQUITY 3. L16. 7 (Predicatively.) A correct decision or opinion on a legal matter; (with *good*, *bad*, etc.) a legal judgement considered from the point of view of correctness. M18.

1 SHAKES. *Merch. V.* The Venetian law Cannot impugn you as you do proceed. L. R. BANKS Even my dad, that's so strict, breaks the law sometimes. c DICKENS If the law supposes that, . . the law is a ass—a idiot. *Times* I enquired of the Law where I might cash a cheque. *Orlando (Florida) Sentinel* The students now know they could get . . in trouble with the law. 2 SHAKES. *Hen. VIII* His faults lie open to the laws; let them, Not you, correct him. R. CAMPBELL A stupid law prevents them entering town in their native garb. J. RATHBONE Laws are not for governments, they are for the governed. 3a V. SETH A nation . . In its own birth resisted law. *Proverb*: Necessity has (*or* knows) no law. b TENNYSON You knew my word was law, and yet you dared To slight it. G. ORWELL His actions are not regulated by law or by any clearly formulated code of behaviour. c J. H. NEWMAN Men learned in the law. W. CATHER He was going . . to read law in the office of a Swedish lawyer. 4a OED Three of his brothers are in the law. b R. CHURCH Coke thoroughly disliked Bacon. He thought lightly of his law. 7 W. BLACKSTONE If it be found that the former decision is manifestly absurd or unjust, it is declared, not that such a sentence was bad law, but that it was not law.

II Chiefly *Chr. Ch.* Divine commandments. 8 The body of commandments considered to express the will of God with regard to the conduct of intelligent creatures, whether revealed in Scripture, innate in the mind, or demonstrable by reason. Also, a particular commandment. Freq. in *God's law*, *law of nature* (cf. sense 15 below), *law of reason*, etc. OE. **9** The system of moral and ceremonial precepts contained in the Pentateuch; the ceremonial portion of the system considered separately. Also (in expressed or implied opposition to *the Gospel*), the Mosaic dispensation; the system of divine commands and penalties imposed for disobedience contained in the Scriptures. More explicitly *the law of Moses*, *the Mosaic law*, etc. OE. **b** (**L-**.) *The* five books of the Pentateuch taken together, in the Jewish religion constituting the first and most important of the three canonical divisions of the Hebrew Scriptures (the others being the Prophets and the Hagiographa or Writings). LME. †**10** A religious system; a faith or creed. ME–L17.

8 AV *Ps.* 1:2 His delight is in the Law of the Lord. 9 J. CUMMING By what he suffered, I escape the law's curse. C. RAPHAEL The sense of purpose which Moses unfolded found form in the 'Law', the Kings and the Prophets.

III A rule or procedure not derived from an external commanding authority. †**11** Custom, customary rule or usage; habit, practice. Also, a particular (esp. criminal) practice. ME–L16. †**12** What is or is considered right or proper; justice or correctness of conduct. Only in ME. **13** A rule of action or procedure; any of the rules defining correct procedure in an art or department of action, social context, or in a game etc. Also, the code or body of rules recognized in a specified department of action etc. ME. **14** An allowance in time or distance made to an animal that is to be hunted, or to one of the competitors in a race, in order to ensure equal conditions; a start; *gen.* indulgence, mercy. *arch.* E17.

13 T. JACKSON Unto Satan .. he did vouchsafe the benefit of the law of Armes or duel. L. ADDISON Contrary to all .. Laws of Hospitality. E. R. CONDER A moral law states what ought to be. 14 G. WHITE When the devoted deer was separated from his companions, they gave him .. law .. for twenty minutes. GEO. ELIOT I will never grant One inch of law to feeble blasphemies.

IV A regularity in the material world. **15** A principle deduced from observation, applicable to a defined group or class of phenomena, and generally expressible by the statement that a particular phenomenon always occurs if certain conditions are present; *esp.* (with specifying wd(s)) such a principle formulated in a particular case or associated with a particular discoverer. Also (w. ref. to the physical world) *law of nature* (cf. sense 8 above). M17. **b** A (freq. jocular) precept or rule of action, or statement of cause and effect in everyday life. M20. **16** *Math.* The rule or principle on which a series, or the construction of a curve, etc., depends. E19. **17** The state of being describable by natural laws; order and regularity in the natural world. M19.

15 J. TYNDALL As regards the motion of the surface of a glacier, two laws are to be borne in mind. B. STEWART A perfect gas obeys Gay Lussac's law. *Bode's law*, *Grassmann's law*, *Grimm's law*, *Kepler's laws*, *Ohm's law*, *Stefan-Boltzmann law*, *Trouton's law*, etc. b *New York Times* The first law for officeholders is .. 'Get re-elected.' H. MCCLOY I call this Julian's Law: a great man's intimates are never as great as he is. *Murphy's law*, *Parkinson's law*, *Sod's law*, etc. 17 J. B. MOZLEY In the argument against miracles the first objection is that they are against law.

Phrases etc.: **at law** according to the laws (*sue at law*: see SUE 12). *bad law*: see BAD *a.* **be a law unto oneself** be guided by one's own sense of what is right; habitually disregard custom or the usual norms. *blue laws*: see BLUE *a.* **both laws** *Hist.* the civil and the canon laws. *brother-in-law*: see BROTHER *n.* *canon law*: see CANON *n.*[1] *case-law*: see CASE *n.*[1] *civil law*: see CIVIL *a.* *court of law*: see COURT *n.*[1] 11. *criminal law*: see CRIMINAL *a.* 2. DAUGHTER-*in-law*. *father-in-law*: see FATHER *n.* *first law of* THERMODYNAMICS. **give law (to)** *arch.* exercise undisputed control (over); impose one's will (on). **go to law** take legal action, make use of the courts of law. **have the law on** or †**of** take legal action against. *international law*: see INTERNATIONAL *a.* *inverse square law*: see INVERSE *a.* *law of averages*: see AVERAGE *n.*[2] 5. *law of* GRAVITATION. *law of honour*: see HONOUR *n.* *law of nations*: see NATION *n.*[1] **law of nature** = *natural law* below. *law of parsimony*: see PARSIMONY 2b. *law of sewers*: see SEWER *n.*[1] **law of the jungle** the supposed code of survival in jungle life; a system in which brute force and self-interest are paramount. **law of the land** (*a*) *arch.* the custom of the country concerned; (*b*) the laws in force in the country concerned. **law of the Medes and Persians** [*Dan.* 6:12] a law, or system of laws, that cannot be altered. **lay down the law** be dogmatic or authoritarian. *limb of the law*: see LIMB *n.*[1] *lynch law*: see LYNCH *n.*[1] *man of law*: see MAN *n.* *martial law*: see MARTIAL *a.* *moral law*: see MORAL *a.* *mother-in-law*: see MOTHER *n.*[1] **natural law** (*a*) = sense 8 above; (*b*) an observable law relating to natural phenomena. †**new law** the Gospel. †**old law** the Mosaic dispensation; the Old Testament. *Oral Law*: see ORAL *a.* *periodic law*: see PERIODIC *a.*[1] 2. *personal law*: see PERSONAL *a.* *presumption of law*: see PRESUMPTION 2. *public law*: see PUBLIC *a.* & *n.* *Rejoicing of, over*, etc., *the Law*: see REJOICING 1b. *Roman law*: see ROMAN *a.* *rule of law*: see RULE *n.* *Salic law*: see SALIC *a.*[1] *second law of* THERMODYNAMICS. SERGEANT *of law*. *sister-in-law*: see SISTER *n.* *son-in-law*: see SON *n.*[1] *square law*: see SQUARE *a.* *strong arm of the law*: see STRONG *a.* **take the law into one's own hands** seek to redress a grievance by one's own methods, esp. by force. **take the law of** *arch.* = *have the law on* above. *third law of* THERMODYNAMICS. *wage one's* (or *the*) *law*: see WAGE *v.* 3a. *wager of law*: see WAGER *n.* 5a.

Comb.: **law-abiding** *a.* obedient to the law; **law-abidingness** obedience to the law; *law agent*: see AGENT *n.* 2; **law-book**: (*a*) containing a code of laws; (*b*) on the subject of law; **law-borrow**(s), **law-burrow**(s) *Sc. Law* (*a*) legal security required from a person that he or she will not injure the person, family, or property of another; (*b*) a person standing surety for another; **lawbreaker** a person who breaks the law; **lawbreaking** *n.* & *a.* (of, engaged in) breaking the law; *law-burrow(s)*: see *law-borrow(s)* above; **law centre** a publicly-funded centre providing legal advice; **law-church** *arch.* (*derog.*) the Established Church; **Law Commission** a body of legal advisers responsible for systematically reviewing the law of England and Wales or of Scotland and advising on reform; **Law Commissioner** a member of one of the Law Commissions; **lawcourt** a court of law; **law-day** (*a*) *Hist.* the day of the meeting of a sheriff's court, court leet, or other court; (the session of) such a court; (*b*) *Hist.* the day appointed for the discharge of a bond; (*c*) *US* a day on which educational publicity is given to legal matters in some States; **law French** the non-standard variety of Norman French used in English law-books from the medieval period to the 18th cent.; **lawgiver** a person who makes or codifies laws; **lawgiving** the making or codifying of laws, legislation; **law-hand** a style of handwriting formerly used for legal documents; **law-keeper** †(*a*) a guardian of the law; (*b*) a law-abiding person; **law Latin** the non-standard Latin of early English statutes; **Law Lord** (*a*) any of the members of the House of Lords qualified to take part in its judicial business; (*b*) *colloq.* (in Scotland) any of the judges of the Court of Session or High Court of Justiciary who have by courtesy the style of 'Lord'; **law-maker** = *law-giver* above; **law merchant** [med.L *lex mercatoria*] *Hist.* the body of rules regulating trade and commerce between different countries; **law office** *N. Amer.* a lawyer's office; **law-officer** a public functionary employed in the administration of the law, or to advise the Government in legal matters; *spec.* (more fully *law-officer of the Crown*), in England and Wales either the Attorney-General or the Solicitor-General, in Scotland either the Lord Advocate or the Solicitor-General for Scotland; **Law Society** a professional body representing solicitors (in the UK and some Commonwealth jurisdictions); **law station** *slang* a police station; **law stationer** a trader who stocks stationery etc. required by lawyers, formerly often also taking in documents for fair copying or engrossing; **lawsuit** an action in law; a prosecution of a claim by litigation; **law term** (*a*) a word or expression used in law; (*b*) each of the periods appointed for the sitting of the courts of law.

law-worthy *a.* (*Hist.*) having a standing in the courts of law; within the purview of the law: E19.

law /lɔː/ *n.*[2] *Sc.* & *north.* ME. [Var. of LOW *n.*[1]] A hill, *esp.* one more or less round or conical. Chiefly in names, as *North Berwick Law*, *Cushat Law*.

†**law** *n.*[3] *Sc.* LME–M16. [Prob. f. ON *lag* (see LAW *n.*[1]).] Share of expense; a charge, a bill.

¶ Survives in LAWING.

law /lɔː/ *v.* OE. [f. LAW *n.*[1]] **1** *v.t.* †**a** Ordain (laws); establish as a law; make lawful. OE–M17. **b** Command or impose as law; control (as) by law. *rare.* L18. **2a** *v.i.* & †*t.* (w. *it*). Go to law, litigate. L15. **b** *v.t.* Take legal action against. M17. **3** *v.t.* Expeditate (a dog) and so render incapable of doing mischief. *obs.* exc. *Hist.* M16.

2a J. FLETCHER Ye must law and claw before ye get it. GEO. ELIOT People who inherited estates that were lawed about.

law /lɔː/ *int.* Now *colloq.* Also **laws** /lɔːz/. L16. [Rel. to LO *int.*[1], LA *int.*, or alt. of LOR'. Cf. LAWK.] Expr. chiefly astonishment or admiration, or (often) surprise at being asked a question; orig. chiefly asseverative.

Also **lawsy** *int.* (chiefly *US*) L19.

lawdy *int.* var. of LORDY.

lawful /ˈlɔːfʊl, -f(ə)l/ *a.* ME. [f. LAW *n.*[1] + -FUL.] **1** Observant of law or duty; law-abiding, faithful, loyal. Now *rare.* ME. **2a** Appointed, sanctioned, or recognized by law; legally qualified or entitled. ME. **b** Of a marriage: legally valid. Of offspring: legitimate. LME. †**c** In exclamations as an intensive. *dial.* L18–M19. **3a** According or not contrary to law, permitted by law. Freq. *pred.* LME. †**b** Permissible; allowable, justifiable. L16–E18. †**4** Pertaining to or concerned with law. LME–M17. **5** Describable or governed by laws of nature. M20.

lawfully *adv.* ME. **lawfulness** *n.* ME.

lawine *n.* var. of LAUWINE.

lawing /ˈlɔːɪŋ/ *n.* *Sc. arch.* M16. [f. LAW *n.*[3] + -ING[1].] A reckoning or bill at a public house.

lawk /lɔːk/ *int. arch.* Also **lawks** /lɔːks/. M18. [Alt. of LORD *n.*, perh. also rel. to LACK *n.*[2] Cf. LAW *int.*] Expr. surprise, consternation, etc.

Comb.: **lawkadaisy** = LACKADAISY; **lawkamercy, -mussy** Lord have mercy!

lawless /ˈlɔːlɪs/ *a.* ME. [f. LAW *n.*[1] + -LESS.] **1a** Without law; having no laws, or enforcement of laws; ignorant of law. ME. **b** Exempt from law, not within the province of law. Formerly also, in the position of an outlaw. ME. **2** Regardless of or disobedient to law; uncontrolled by law, unbridled, licentious. ME.

1 W. IRVING Commercial feuds in the lawless depths of the wilderness. 2 LD MACAULAY He should be protected against lawless violence. R. K. NARAYAN Ramani was eccentric and lawless in his tastes. G. GORER One of the most lawless populations in the world has turned into one of the most law-abiding.

lawlessly *adv.* L16. **lawlessness** *n.* L16.

lawlike /ˈlɔːlʌɪk/ *a.* M16. [f. LAW *n.*[1] + -LIKE.] **1** Like law, having a resemblance to law, or to legal phraseology or proceedings. Now *rare.* M16. **2** Resembling a law of nature. Also, such as to be a law of nature if established as true. M20.

lawman /ˈlɔːmən/ *n.* Pl. **-men.** OE. [f. LAW *n.*[1] + MAN *n.*, partly after ON *lagamaðr*, *lǫgmaðr*.] **1** *Law* (now *Hist.*). An officer in Anglo-Saxon England, *spec.* (*a*) a person whose official duty it was to declare the law; (*b*) In the five Danish boroughs, any of a number of magistrates or aldermen. OE. **2** *Hist.* The president of the supreme court in Orkney or Shetland. M16. **3** A man of law, a lawyer. Now *rare.* M16. **4** A law-enforcement officer; a sheriff, a policeman. *colloq.* M20.

lawn /lɔːn/ *n.*[1] & *a.* LME. [Prob. f. *Laon*, a city in France, important for linen manufacture.] **A** *n.* **1** A kind of fine linen or cotton; in *pl.*, pieces or sorts of this. LME. **b** *spec.* This fabric used for the sleeves worn by a bishop. Hence, the dignity or office of a bishop. M17. †**2** A garment or other article made of lawn. L15–E19. **3** = *lawn sieve* below. M19.

B *attrib.* or as *adj.* Made of lawn. L15.

Special collocations & comb.: **lawn sieve** a fine sieve of silk or other fabric, used esp. for clay; **lawn-sleeved** *a.* wearing lawn sleeves; of or pertaining to a bishop or bishops; **lawn sleeves** sleeves of lawn as forming part of episcopal dress; the office or dignity of a bishop; a bishop or bishops.

lawned *a.* arrayed in lawn, wearing lawn sleeves L18.

lawn /lɔːn/ *n.*[2] & *v.* M16. [Alt. of LAUND *n.*] **A** *n.* **1** An open space between woods; a glade. = LAUND *n.* Now *arch.* & *dial.* exc. w. ref. to the New Forest. M16. **2** (A stretch of) untilled ground; (an extent of) grass-covered land. *obs.* exc. as passing into sense 3. E17. **3** An area of grass-covered ground which is kept mown and smooth, in a garden, park, etc.; such ground. Also, an area planted with low-lying herbs etc., esp. camomile. M18. 4 *Biol.* A layer of bacteria or other cells uniformly distributed over the surface of a culture medium. M20.

1 J. THOMSON The thistly lawn, the thick-entangled broom. 2 MILTON The Shepherds on the Lawn.. Sate simply chatting in a rustick row. 3 R. W. EMERSON The beautiful lawns and gardens of the colleges. B. RUBENS The neat square of lawn that fronted the house.

Comb.: **lawn chair** *N. Amer.* a folding chair for use out of doors; **lawn edger** a powered appliance for trimming the grass at the edge of a lawn; **lawn meet** the meeting of a hunt in the grounds of a private house; **lawnmower** a machine with a rotating blade or blades for cutting the grass on a lawn; **lawn party** a party held on a lawn, a garden-party; **lawn sand** a top-dressing of sand and other components, used as a fertilizer and weedkiller for lawns; *lawn tennis*: see TENNIS *n.* 2.

B *v.t.* Turn (ground) into lawn; lay with lawn. M18.

lawny /ˈlɔːni/ *a.*[1] L16. [f. LAWN *n.*[1] + -Y[1].] **1** Made of lawn. L16. **b** Dressed in lawn; of or pertaining to a bishop or bishops. M17. **2** Resembling lawn. E17.

lawny /ˈlɔːni/ *a.*[2] E17. [f. LAWN *n.*[2] + -Y[1].] Resembling a lawn; covered with smooth green turf. Formerly also, containing lawns or glades.

Lawrence *n.* var. of LAURENCE.

Lawrencian *a.* & *n.* var. of LAWRENTIAN.

lawrencium /lɒˈrɛnsɪəm/ *n.* M20. [f. Ernest O. *Lawrence* (1901–58), US physicist + -IUM.] A radioactive transuranic metallic element, atomic no. 103, produced artificially. (Symbol Lr, formerly Lw.)

Lawrentian /lɒˈrɛnʃɪən, -ʃ(ə)n/ *a.* & *n.* Also **Laurentian**, **Lawrencian**. E20. [f. *Lawrence* (see below), L *Laurentius* + -IAN.] **A** *adj.* **1** Of or pertaining to the British military leader and author Thomas Edward Lawrence ('Lawrence of Arabia') (1888–1935), his actions, or his works. E20. **2** Of or pertaining to the English author David Herbert Lawrence (1885–1930), or his work or style of writing. M20. **B** *n.* An admirer or student of T. E. or D. H. Lawrence or the work of either. M20.

Lawrentiˈana *n.pl.* [-ANA] publications or other items concerning or associated with D. H. Lawrence M20.

lawrightman /ˈlɔːrʌɪtmən/ *n. obs.* exc. *Hist.* Pl. **-men**. LME. [f. LAW *n.*[1] + RIGHT *n.*[1] + MAN *n.*, tr. ON *lǫgréttu-maðr*.] In Orkney and Shetland: a local official responsible mainly for the supervision of weights and measures (in Shetland) or for keeping the peace (in Orkney).

laws *int.* var. of LAW *int.*

Lawson cypress *n. phr.* var. of LAWSON'S CYPRESS.

lawsoniana /ˌlɔːsəʊnɪˈɑːnə/ *n.* M20. [mod.L specific epithet, f. as LAWSON'S CYPRESS.] = LAWSON'S CYPRESS.

Lawson's cypress /ˈlɔːs(ə)nz ˈsʌɪprəs/ *n. phr.* Also **Lawson cypress**. M19. [Peter (d. 1820) and his son Charles (1794–1873) *Lawson*, Sc. nurserymen, who first cultivated the plant.] A cypress, *Chamaecyparis lawsoniana*, native to the western US, that is widely planted as an ornamental shrub or tree.

lawting /ˈlɔːtɪŋ/ *n. obs.* exc. *Hist.* L15. [ON *lǫgþing*, f. *lǫg* LAW *n.*[1] + *þing* THING *n.*[2]] The former supreme court of judicature in Orkney and Shetland.

lawyer /ˈlɔːjə, ˈlɔɪə/ *n.* & *v.* LME. [f. LAW *n.*[1] + -YER.] **A** *n.* **1** A person with knowledge of the law; a member of the profession of the law; *esp.* a solicitor, a barrister. LME. **†2** A lawgiver. M16–M17. **3a** Either of two birds, the black-necked stilt, *Himantopus mexicanus*, and the avocet, *Recurvirostra americana*. *US.* E19. **b** Either of two fishes: the burbot, *Lota lota*, and the bowfin, *Amia calva*. *US.* M19. **4** A thorny creeping plant; a bramble, a briar. *dial.* & *NZ.* M19.

4 *bush lawyer*: see BUSH *n.*[1]

Phrases: COMMON LAWYER. *criminal lawyer*: see CRIMINAL *a.* 2. **lawyer's wig** = SHAGGY *ink-cap*. PENANG LAWYER. PHILADELPHIA *lawyer*. SEA-*lawyer*.

Comb.: **lawyer cane**, **-vine** *Austral.* a thorny climbing plant, esp. *Calamus australis*.

B *v.i.* Follow the profession of lawyer; act as a lawyer. Chiefly as *lawyering* vbl n. L17.

lawyer-like *a.* & *adv.* (*a*) *adj.* resembling a lawyer or the practice of a lawyer; (*b*) *adv.* in the manner of a lawyer: L16. **lawyerly** *a.* lawyer-like; of or pertaining to lawyers, suitable for lawyers: M17.

lax /laks/ *n.*[1] Now *rare.* [OE *læx*, (WS) *leax* = LG *las*, OHG *lahs* (G *Lachs*), ON (Sw., Da.) *lax*, f. Gmc. Cf. LOX *n.*[2]] A salmon; *esp.* a Swedish or Norwegian salmon.

lax /laks/ *n.*[2] *obs.* exc. *dial.* LME. [Perh. f. LAX *v.*] **†1** (Treatment of illness by) a laxative medicine, an aperient. LME–M16. **2** Looseness of the bowels, diarrhoea. LME. **†3** Relief, release. *rare.* Only in L18.

lax /laks/ *n.*[3] *colloq.* M20. [Contr.] = LACROSSE.

lax /laks/ *a.* & *adv.* LME. [L *laxus* loose, cogn. w. SLACK *a.*] **A** *adj.* **1** Of the bowels: loose. Formerly also, (of a person) having loose bowels. LME. **2a** Loose in texture; loosely cohering or compacted; porous. LME. **b** *Bot.* Esp. of an inflorescence: having the parts distant from each other or in an open or loose arrangement. L18. **3** Loose-fitting, worn loosely; careless of one's dress or appearance. *rare.* LME. **4** Not strict or severe; vague, not precise or exact. L15. **5** Slack; not tense or rigid; (of bodily constitution or mental powers) lacking in tone or tension. Now *rare.* M17. **b** Of the limbs etc.: relaxed, without muscular tension. M19. **c** *Phonet.* Of a speech sound: pronounced with the vocal muscles relaxed. Cf. TENSE *a.* 1b. E20.

2a T. H. GREEN Those organs which possess a lax structure.. as the lungs. 4 J. R. GREEN Richard [Cromwell] was known to be lax and godless in his conduct. M. EDWARDES Discipline was lax, and bad practices were widely in evidence. 5b R. WEST A two-day-old calf, lax on the ground, like a great skein of fawn-coloured silk.

†B *adv.* So as to have ample room. *rare* (Milton). Only in M17.

laxly *adv.* LME. **laxness** *n.* LME.

lax /laks/ *v.t.* LME. [L *laxare*, f. *laxus* LAX *a.*] **1** Make lax; loosen, relax. *obs.* exc. *Sc.* LME. **2** *Phonet.* Articulate (a speech sound) with the vocal muscles relaxed. M20.

laxation /lakˈseɪʃ(ə)n/ *n.* LME. [Late L *laxatio(n-)*, f. L *laxat-* pa. ppl stem of *laxare*: see prec., -ATION.] The action or an act of loosening or relaxing something; the state of being loosened or relaxed; *Med.* defecation. Also, administration of a laxative.

laxative /ˈlaksətɪv/ *a.* & *n.* LME. [(O)Fr. *laxatif*, *-ive* or late L *laxativus*, f. L *laxat-*: see prec., -ATIVE.] **A** *adj.* **1** Of medicine etc.: tending to cause evacuation of the bowels. LME. **2** Of the bowels etc.: loose. Of a disease: characterized by looseness of the bowels. Now *rare.* LME. **b** *transf.* Unable to contain one's speech or emotions. Now *rare* or *obs.* E17. **B** *n.* **1** A laxative medicine. LME. **†2** (A) looseness of the bowels. *rare.* LME–E16.

laxativeness *n.* E17.

laxist /ˈlaksɪst/ *n.* & *a.* M19. [f. LAX *a.* + -IST.] **A** *n.* A person who favours lax views or interpretation; a person who is not a rigorist. M19. **B** *attrib.* or as *adj.* Of or pertaining to laxists. L19.

laxity /ˈlaksɪti/ *n.* E16. [Fr. *laxité* or L *laxitas*, f. *laxus* LAX *a.*: see -ITY.] **1** Looseness, esp. of the bowels; slackness, absence of tension. E16. **2** Looseness of texture or cohesion. E17. **3** Lack of strictness or severity; vagueness; lack of precision. E17.

3 R. L. STEVENSON How are you, the apostle of laxity, to turn.. about into the Rabbi of precision. R. MACAULAY Laxity among the rich encourages immorality among the poor.

Laxton /ˈlakst(ə)n/ *n.* Also **Laxton's** /ˈlakst(ə)nz/. E20. [*Laxton* Brothers (see below).] Any of several varieties of fruit bred and introduced by Laxton Brothers, a firm of English nurserymen.

Laxton's Superb a popular, late-ripening variety of red-skinned eating apple.

laxy /ˈlaksi/ *a.* Long *rare.* E18. [f. LAX *a.* + -Y[1].] = LAX *a.* 2.

lay /leɪ/ *n.*[1] Long *obs.* exc. *dial.* [OE *lagu* f. Gmc, perh. also infl. by OFr. *lai* pool f. late L *lacus*.] A lake, a pool.

lay /leɪ/ *n.*[2] ME. [(O)Fr. *lai* corresp. to Prov. *lais*: ult. origin unkn.] **1** A short lyric or narrative poem intended to be sung; a narrative poem; a song. ME. **b** The song of birds. *poet.* LME. **†2** A tune. Only in 16.

1 E. HUXLEY: W. S. Gilbert's lay of the two Englishmen wrecked on a desert island. N. FRYE One can never spontaneously burst into song, however doleful a lay.

†lay *n.*[3] LME–L18. [Perh. aphet. f. ALLAY *n.*[1]] Alloy. Freq. in *lay metal*, a kind of pewter.

lay /leɪ/ *n.*[4] M16. [f. LAY *v.*[1]] **1** The action of imposing a tax; an assessment, a rate, a tax. Now *dial.* M16. **†2** A wager, a bet, a stake. L16–M18. **3** The resting-place of an animal. Also, an oyster- or mussel-bed. L16. **†4** A layer, a stratum; a course of masonry etc. L16–M18. **5** Rate or terms of purchase or remuneration. *local US.* E18. **6** A line or plan of business, occupation, etc.; a (particular) job. *slang.* E18. **7a** The position or direction in which something, esp. country, lies; lie of the land etc. E19. **b** The direction or amount of twist in the strands of a rope etc. E19. **c** *Printing.* The arrangement of type in a compositor's case. Also, the position of the print on a sheet of paper. L19. **8** A share in a venture; *esp.* an individual's proportion of the proceeds of a whaling voyage. M19. **9** The laying of eggs. Chiefly in *in lay*, (of a hen) in a condition to lay eggs; *point of lay* s.v. POINT *n.*[1] L19. **10** A woman (occas. a man) who is readily available for sexual intercourse; an act of sexual intercourse. Cf. LAY *v.*[1] 3b. *slang* (orig. *US*). M20.

2 DEFOE By venturing my life upon an even lay with him. 3 F. FRANCIS The boatman will probably know.. the lay of the trout. 6 G. B. SHAW So blackmail is the game... There's nothing to be got out of me on that lay. 7a N. MARSH Did she tell you anything that supports our theory or sets us off on another lay? 10 J. O'HARA Then you turn around and pay him back by giving his girl a lay. S. BELLOW She wanted to give her heart once and for all,.. and quit being an easy lay.

Comb.: **lay-edge** *Printing* the edge of a sheet of paper which is used to determine the correct position of the sheet in a press; **lay gauge** an attachment on a printing-press that keeps the paper in the correct position.

lay /leɪ/ *n.*[5] *dial.* L18. [Alt. of LATHE *n.*[4]] *Weaving.* The batten of a loom; = LATHE *n.*[4]

lay *n.*[6] var. of LEY *n.*[1]

lay /leɪ/ *a.* ME. [OFr. *lai* (now repl. by *laïque*) f. as LAIC.] **1** Of a person: non-clerical; not in ecclesiastical orders. ME. **2†a** Uninstructed, unlearned. *rare.* ME–M16. **b** Non-professional, not expert, not professionally trained or qualified, esp. in law or medicine. E19. **3** Pertaining to or characteristic of a lay person or the laity; done by a lay person or the laity. E17.

1 *New York Times* Particular attention must now be given to women, both lay and religious. 2b *Times* Any interest on the part of lay people in medical matters is regarded as.. interference. 3 W. COWPER With reverend tutor clad in habit lay.

Special collocations: **lay analysis** psychoanalysis undertaken by an analyst who has not been medically trained. **lay analyst** a person who practises psychoanalysis without medical training. **lay bishop** †(*a*) *derog.* a person who sets up as a teacher of morality; (*b*) a lay rector. **lay brother**, **sister** a man, woman, who has taken the habit and vows of a religious order, but is employed mostly in manual labour and is excused other duties. **lay clerk** (*a*) an adult singer in a cathedral or collegiate church; (*b*) a parish clerk. **lay communion** (*a*) membership of a Church as a lay person; (*b*) the communicating of the laity in the Eucharist. **lay deacon** a person in deacon's orders who also follows a secular employment. **lay elder** a non-clerical elder of a Church. **lay preacher** a preacher (esp. in the Methodist Church) who is not ordained. *lay reader*: see READER 1b. **lay rector** a layman receiving rectorial tithes. *lay sister*: see *lay brother* above. *lay* VICAR.

lay /leɪ/ *v.*[1] Pa. t. & pple **laid** /leɪd/. [OE *lećgan* = OFris. *ledza*, *leia*, OS *leggian* (Du. *leggen*), OHG *lecken*, *legen* (G *legen*), ON *legja*, Goth. *lagjan*, f. Gmc base also of LIE *v.*[1]] I Prostrate. **1** *v.t.* Bring or cast down from an erect position; strike down; make prostrate. Formerly also, abase, humble. Now only with compl. denoting prostration or extension on a surface. OE. **b** Of wind or rain: beat down (crops). L16. **2** *v.t.* Cause (the sea, a wind, a cloud of dust, etc.) to subside; allay (anxiety), appease (anger, appetite, etc.). Now chiefly *arch.* & *dial.* exc. in *lay the dust*. ME. **b** Cause (a ghost) to cease appearing. L16. **3** *v.t.* **a** Deliver (†oneself, a mother) of a child; bring to bed *of* a child. *obs.* exc. *dial.* LME. **b** Have sexual intercourse with (esp. a woman). Cf. LAY *n.*[4] 10. *slang* (orig. *US*). M20. **4** *v.t. Hort.* = LAYER *v.* 1a. Now *rare* or *obs.* M16. **b** Trim (a hedge) back, cutting the branches half through, bending them down, and interweaving them. Chiefly *dial.* M18. **5** *v.t.* Orig., bring down, reduce, (a swelling). Now, smooth down, cause to lie evenly. L16. **6** *v.t. Naut.* Sail out so far as to bring (land etc.) below the horizon. Opp. *raise*. L16.

1 BROWNING We check the fire by laying flat Each building in its path. TENNYSON Like flaws in summer laying lusty corn. 2 SHAKES. *Two Gent.* See how I lay the dust with my tears. A. F. DOUGLAS-HOME The mistrust of the Archbishop was never laid. b B. HARTE For now that the ghosts of my heart are laid. *transf.*: *Times* We must lay the myth that the RPO was .. more eligible for penalisation than .. other orchestras.

II Deposit. **7** *v.t.* Place in a position of rest *on* the ground or any other supporting surface; deposit in some specified place. OE. **b** In the British Parliament: place (documents) on the table in order to give information to the House of Commons. E20. **8** *v.t.* **a** Deposit *in* the grave; bury. Freq. in *lay one's bones* below. OE. **b** Place (a person etc.) in a recumbent posture in a specified place. ME. **9** *v.t.* & *i.* Of a hen bird etc.: eject (an egg) from its body. See also *lay an egg* below. OE. †**10** *v.t.* With advb. phr. as compl.: deposit as a pledge or in pawn; mortgage (lands). ME–L17. **b** Give up (a person) as a hostage; give up (a hostage). ME–M16. **11** *v.t.* Put down as a wager; stake (a sum, one's head, life, etc.). Also, stake something on (a wager, a bet). ME. **b** *v.i.* Wager, bet; announce one's readiness to bet. LME. **c** *v.t.* Bet on (a horse etc.). L19. †**12** *v.t.* Relinquish, sacrifice, (one's life). ME–M16. †**13** *v.t.* Lose the faculty of (speech). *north.* ME–M17.

7 G. GREENE I laid the newspaper flat on the table. DAY LEWIS At a level crossing I laid pins on the line. b *Hansard* His Majesty's Government have been willing to lay the complete records. 8a YEATS In Drumcliff churchyard Yeats is laid. TOLKIEN They had laid their fallen comrades in a mound. b M. ARNOLD The bent grass where I am laid. 9 ADDISON When she has laid her Eggs in such a manner that she can cover them. B. MACDONALD Black chickens which were supposed to lay as well as the White Leghorn. 11 ARNOLD BENNETT I lay anything he had opened the safe before and read the will before. J. COLVILLE The invasion may be pending (though I'll lay 10–1 against).

III Place, set, apply. **14** *v.t.* Place close *to*; put *to* for a purpose, apply. OE. †**b** Attach, add, annex *to*. OE–E19. †**c** Put *in* or commit *to* prison. ME–M16. **d** Put (hounds) *on* a scent. L18. **15** *v.t.* Place (one's hand or hands) on or apply (one's hand or hands) to a person or thing, esp. for purposes of appropriation or in violence. OE. **b** *gen.* Place (one's arms, legs, etc.) in a specified position. LME. **16** *v.t.* Place (affection, hope, confidence, value) *on* or *in* a person or thing. *arch.* ME. **17** *v.t.* Arrange (a snare, a trap, an ambush) ready for operation, set. ME. **b** *v.i.* Set an ambush or a trap *for*; lie in wait *for*. L15. †**c** *v.t.* Set watch or guard in (a place); search (a place) *for*. M16–M17. **18** *v.t.* Bring into a specified state, esp. of subjection, passivity, or exposure to view or danger. ME. **b** *Naut.* Foll. by *aboard*: run into or alongside (a ship), usu. for boarding. Also, bring (a ship) into a specified position, as *alongside* another vessel etc. L16. **19** *v.t.* †**a** Post or station (a body of soldiers etc.); station (post-horses) along a route. Also, beset (a place) with soldiers. LME–M19. **b** Locate (a scene) in a particular place. Formerly also, assign to a specified locality. L16. **20** *v.t. Mil.* Set (a gun, esp a large one) in the correct position to hit a mark, aim. L15. **21** *v.refl.* & *i.* Orig., set oneself *against*. Later, apply oneself *to*. M16.

14 SHAKES. *Macb.* By each at once her choppy finger laying Upon her skinny lips. E. M. FORSTER She laid her face against the tree. 15 *Book of Common Prayer* Or have laid violent hands upon themselves. DICKENS Laying hands on the article as if it were a Bottle. b D. H. LAWRENCE Louis .. laid his head a little on one side. 16 CONAN DOYLE Neither now or at any time have I laid great store upon my life. 17b M. KINGSLEY The men go and lay for a rubber-hunter. 18 J. COLLIER It lays him at the mercy of chance and humour. C. M. YONGE He was laid under orders to follow the commands of the Spanish king. 19b W. COWPER I never framed a wish or formed a plan .. But there I laid the scene. 20 K. DOUGLAS I crammed shells into the six-pounder as fast as Evan could lay and fire it. 21 CARLYLE When Friedrich laid himself to engineering, I observe, he did it well.

IV Impose as a burden. **22** *v.t.* Impose (a penalty, command, obligation, tax, etc.) as a burden. Also (*N. Amer. slang*), inflict (an experience, emotion, etc.). Freq. foll. by *on*. OE. †**b** Assess, rate, tax, (a person). ME–E18. **23** *v.t.* Cause (blame, †aspersions, †ridicule) to fall *on*. ME. **24** *v.t.* Bring (a stick etc.) down *on*; inflict (blows) *on*. ME. **25** *v.i.* Deal blows; make an attack. Chiefly foll. by preps.: see below. ME. †**26** *v.t.* Strike, beat (a person) *on* the face, *over* the head, etc. ME–E18.

22 H. L. MENCKEN Not many of them returned in taxes the extra expense they laid on the community. 23 W. IRVING The good wives .. never failed .. to lay the blame on Dame van Winkle. 24 J. A. FROUDE What if my son wishes to lay a stick on my back? 25 GOLDSMITH Rascal! replied the Tyrant, give me the Stick; and .. he laid on the unresisting Slave. 26 J. ARBUTHNOT The cook laid them over the pate with a ladle.

V Dispose or arrange in proper relative position over a surface. **27** *v.t.* Place (a foundation, a floor, bricks, a submarine cable, etc.) in the horizontal position; place (a carpet) in position on the floor. OE. **b** Set out (a table), spread (a tablecloth), place (plates, cutlery, etc.) in order in preparation for a meal; set out a table ready *for* (a meal) in this way. Also, place fuel ready for lighting (a fire). Formerly also, prepare (a bed) for sleeping in. ME. **c** *Printing.* Fill (a case) with new sorts. L17. **28** *v.t.* Orig., establish (a law), settle, lay down (a principle). Later, fix the outlines of, arrange, devise, (a plan, a plot, a scheme). OE. **b** *v.i.* Orig., make arrangements or plans *for*. Later (now *dial.* & *US*), plan or intend *to do*. LME. †**c** *v.t.* Contrive, arrange. E17–E18. **29** *v.t.* †**a** Direct (one's steps). Only in OE. †**b** Apply or devote (one's power, affection, possessions) *to*. Also foll. by *into*. ME–E17. **c** *Naut.* Set (a course *for*). M17. †**30** *v.t.* Set down *in* writing; put into or express *in* (a particular form of language). ME–L18. **31** *v.t.* Cover or coat (a material, an object, etc.), *with* something, esp. for ornamentation. LME. **32** *v.t.* Twist yarn to form (a strand), or strands to form (a rope). LME. **33** *v.t.* Sharpen (a cutting instrument) with a steel. *dial.* L15. **34** *v.t. Art.* Put (colour etc.) on a surface in layers; put or arrange (colours, †a picture) on canvas. L15.

27 W. BRONK Looking at stones the Incas laid. *fig.*: M. EDGEWORTH She laid the cornerstone of all her future misfortunes at that very instant. b G. GREENE No table was laid for dinner. P. H. JOHNSON You can come and lay the table. We'll eat in the kitchen. 28 C. THIRLWALL His schemes also were more artfully laid. 29c C. FRANCIS The wind freshened and shifted .., so that *Gulliver G* was able to lay her course. 31 J. A. FROUDE My bath-room is .. a part of the veranda laid with zinc.

VI Present, put forward. **35** *v.t.* Bring forward as a charge, accusation, or imputation; impute, attribute (a fault etc.) *to*. *arch.* ME. **36** *v.t.* Put forward, allege, (a claim, †reason, †example, etc.). LME. **b** Orig., assign (a date). Later (*Law*), state or describe *as*; fix (damages) *at* a certain amount. Now *rare*. LME. **c** Present (an information, indictment, etc.) in legal form. L18.

35 SOUTHEY That .. you should lay to me Unkind neglect. G. W. DASENT He had .. to lay his sleeplessness on something, .. so he laid it on the lobster salad. 36 W. S. MAUGHAM She was careful to make it plain .. that she laid no claims on him.

VII **37** *v.i.* = LIE *v.*[1] I, II. Now chiefly *dial.* & *non-standard*. ME. **b** *Naut.* Of a ship: lie in a specified position. M16.

37 *Word Study* I was just laying there minding my own business. R. ADAMS So even if you *was* to have to lay down for a bit. *Rescue News* The flints were .. just laying on the beach.

Phrases: *kill the goose that lays the golden eggs*: see GOOSE *n.* **lay about one** hit out on all sides (*lit.* & *fig.*). **lay a charge** make an accusation. *lay a finger* or *one's finger(s) on*: see FINGER *n.* **lay a ground** *Art* spread a coating over a surface, as a basis for colours. **lay an egg** *colloq.* (*a*) (of an aircraft) drop a bomb; (*b*) (orig. *US*) (of a performer or performance) fail badly. **lay an eye on** *US* = *lay eyes on* below. *lay by the heels*: see HEEL *n.*[1] *lay claim to*: see CLAIM *n.* 1. **lay dead** *colloq.* (chiefly *US*) remain inactive, lie low, do nothing in particular. **lay emphasis, stress, weight, on** emphasize, treat as being particularly important. **lay eyes on** set eyes on, look at; catch sight of. **lay hands on** (*a*) seize, appropriate; (*b*) do violence to (esp. oneself); (*c*) confirm or ordain by placing one's hands on the head of (a candidate). **lay hold of, on** seize, grasp, *fig.* benefit from (an opponent's weak point etc.). †**lay home to** assault, attack, (*lit.* & *fig.*). *lay in* (*to*) *pledge*: see PLEDGE *n.* **lay it on a person** *N. Amer. slang* give information to a person. *lay low*: see LOW *a.* & *n.*[4] *lay one's account with* (*on, for*): see ACCOUNT *n.* **lay one's bones** be buried *in* a specified place. *lay lay oneself wide open*: see WIDE *adv.* *lay one's finger(s)* on: see FINGER *n.* *lay one's hands on*: see HAND *n.* *lay on one's oars*: see OAR *n.* *lay on the line*: see LINE *n.*[2] *lay on the table*: see TABLE *n.* *lay open to*: see OPEN *a.* *lay pipe* or *pipes*: see PIPE *n.*[1] **lay siege to** besiege; attack (*lit.* & *fig.*). *lay something at a person's door*: see DOOR *n.* *lay stress on*: see *lay emphasis on* above. *lay the saddle upon the right horse*: see SADDLE *n.* *lay to heart*: see HEART *n.* **lay to rest** put to rest, bury, (*lit.* & *fig.*). *lay to sleep*: see SLEEP *n.* *lay to someone's charge*: see CHARGE *n.* *lay to wed*: see WED *n.* 2. *lay violent hands on* or *upon*: see VIOLENT *a.* *lay wait*: see WAIT *n.* 4. *lay waste*: see WASTE *a.* *lay weight on*: see *lay emphasis on* above.

With advs. in specialized senses: **lay abroad** *arch.* spread out; spread (a net). **lay aside** (*a*) put (a garment, weapon, etc.) away from one; put on one side; (*lay aside the tomahawk*: see TOMAHAWK *n.*); (*b*) cease to use or think of or practise; †(*c*) put out of the way, get rid of; (*d*) set (money etc.) apart *for* future use; (*e*) in *pass.*, be incapacitated for work by illness. **lay away** (*a*) = *lay aside* (a), (b) above; (*b*) *rare* bury; (*c*) place (hides) flat in a large vat or pit to steep in strong tan liquor, as the final stage in the tanning process. **lay back** (*a*) cause to slope back from the vertical; (*b*) *colloq.* (chiefly *US*) lie or lean back, recline, relax. **lay by** (*a*) = *lay aside* (a), (b) above; †(*b*) = *lay aside* (c) above; (*c*) put away in store; store up; save (money); (*d*) put away for future disposal or safety; (*e*) in *pass.* be incapacitated by illness; (*f*) *US* work (a crop or field) for the last time, before leaving it to grow without further husbandry. **lay down** (*a*) put down on the ground or other surface, after holding or carrying; put off, discard (a garment, armour); *lay down (one's) arms*: see ARM *n.*[2]; (*b*) resign, relinquish (office, power, dignity, hopes, etc.); cease to bear (a name); discontinue (a custom, a fashion); (*c*) place in a recumbent or prostrate position, cause to lie down; (*d*) put down (money) as a wager or a payment; †(*e*) cast down, overthrow; (*f*) *Naut.* (of the wind or sea) make (a ship etc.) lie on its side; (*g*) (begin to) construct (a road, a railway, etc.); *lay down a keel*, begin to construct a ship; (*h*) establish, formulate definitely (a principle, a rule); prescribe (a course of action, limits, etc.); *lay down the law*: see LAW *n.*[1]; (*i*) set down (a plan) on paper etc.; delineate; †(*j*) put down in writing; treat of; (*k*) *Needlework* (*arch.*) run and fell (a seam); trim, embroider; (*l*) convert (arable land) into pasture; put (land) *under* grass, clover, etc. (also foll. by *in*, *to*, *with*); (*m*) store (wine) in a cellar; (*n*) *US* give up; cease to act; fail; withdraw; (*o*) *Jazz slang* set up or establish (a certain beat); (*p*) make a recording of (esp. popular music). **lay fast** †(*a*) put in fetters, imprison (also *lay fast by the feet*); (*b*) make unable to proceed or escape. †**lay forth** (*a*) stretch out in a prostrate position; display openly; (*b*) put or bring forward in argument etc.; reveal, make clear. **lay in** (*a*) place in store; provide oneself with a stock of; †(*b*) put in (a claim); (*c*) enclose or reserve (a meadow) for hay; (*d*) *Hort.* place in position (the new wood of a trained tree); (*e*) paint (a picture etc.) in the first unfinished stage; (*f*) *Naut.* unship (oars); (*g*) *Basketball* bounce (the ball) off the backboard into the basket. **lay off** †(*a*) take off, take away; †(*b*) *Naut.* steer (a ship) away from the shore; (of a ship) remain stationary outside a harbour; (*c*) mark or separate off (land etc.), esp. for a specific purpose; (*d*) (orig. *dial.* & *US*) discontinue; discharge (an employee) permanently or temporarily, esp. owing to shortage of work; (*e*) in decorating, work over a painted etc. surface with brushstrokes going in the same direction; (*f*) desist from (doing something); abstain from or stop using (something); stop bothering (a person); freq. *absol.* in *imper.*: cut it out! stop it!; (*g*) *Naut.* & *Aeronaut.* indicate on a chart etc., work out (a course); (*h*) (of a bookmaker) insure against a substantial loss resulting from (a large bet) by placing a similar bet with another bookmaker; (*i*) (*Football, Hockey,* etc.) pass (the ball) to a team-mate who can make progress with it. **lay on** (*a*) impose (a command, a penalty, a tax); (*b*) deal blows with vigour; make a vigorous attack; (*c*) inflict (blows); ply (a lash etc.) vigorously; (*d*) *lay* (*it*) *on* increase the charge for goods etc.; formerly also, be lavish in expense; (*e*) apply a coat of (paint, varnish, etc.) to a surface; *lay* (*it*) *on thick, lay* (*it*) *on with a trowel*, do something to excess, flatter, eulogize, etc., lavishly; (*f*) *Printing* place (the sheets of paper) on the type to be printed; (*g*) put (hounds) on a scent; (*h*) *Needlework* place (thread) on a material before couching it down with a separate thread; (*i*) provide pipes, cables, etc., for the supply of (water, gas, electricity, telephonic communication, etc.); make available (refreshments, entertainment, a means of transport, etc.); (*j*) *N. Amer. slang* give (something) to a person; (*k*) (*Football, Hockey,* etc.) make (a pass) with accuracy so that a team-mate can readily make the next move; (*l*) *v.phr.t.* & *i.* (*Angling*) lower (a weight or shot) to rest with the hook and bait on the bed of the river, stream, etc. **lay out** (*a*) extend at length; take out and expose to view, the air, etc.; lay so as to project outwards; (*b*) stretch out and prepare (a body) for burial or cremation; *slang* kill (a person); *colloq.* put (a person) temporarily out of action; knock unconscious; *lay out cold*: see COLD *a.*; (*c*) spend (money); †(*d*) employ or exercise (powers, effort); (*e*) *lay oneself out*, take pains; (*f*) *lay out for* (now *rare* or *obs.*), look out for; take measures to win or get; (*g*) scheme, plan *to* effect some purpose; (*h*) (now *rare* exc. *US*) display, expose; set forth, expound, demonstrate; (*i*) apportion (land) for a purpose; dispose, arrange, (grounds, streets, a garden, etc.) according to a plan; (*j*) plan or map out; (*k*) *Naut.* occupy a position on a yard towards the yard-arms for the purpose of manipulating the sails. **lay over** (*a*) overlay; (*b*) *US colloq.* miss, allow to pass by; postpone; place a temporary embargo on; (*c*) *US colloq.* excel, outdo; (*d*) *N. Amer. colloq.* lie over; break one's journey and stop, esp. overnight. **lay to** (*a*) place in juxtaposition; †(*b*) put or bring into action; bring to bear; (*c*) *Naut.* come to a stationary position with the head towards the wind; = *lie to* s.v. LIE *v.*[1] **lay together** (*a*) place in juxtaposition; add together; *lay their heads together*: see HEAD *n.*; †(*b*) concoct, compose (a story). **lay up** †(*a*) vomit up; (*b*) *Agric.* throw up (land) in ridges as a preparation for sowing; reserve (land) for hay; (*c*) put away for safety; store up (goods, provisions); put by; save; *lay up in lavender*: see LAVENDER *n.*[2]; (*d*) confine to a house or bed through illness etc.; freq. in *pass.*, be (taken) ill; (*e*) take (a ship, vehicle, etc.) out of service; (*f*) = sense 32 above; (*g*) *Naut.* lay a course; (*h*) assemble or stack (plies or layers) in the arrangement required for the manufacture of plywood or other laminated material (usu. prior to bonding into a single structure).

With preps. in specialized senses: **lay at** (now chiefly *dial.*) aim blows or an attack at; attack, assail, (*lit.* & *fig.*). **lay before** place in front of (a person); bring to the notice of, submit to the consideration of. **†lay from** put away from (oneself); take *one's fingers* off (something). **lay into** *colloq.* belabour. **†lay off** = *lay from* above. **lay on** attack vigorously, beat soundly. **†lay to** assault, attack, press hard (*lit.* & *fig.*).

Comb.: **lay-back** (*a*) the receding position of the nose of certain breeds of dog, esp. the bulldog; (*b*) *Mountaineering* a method of climbing a crack in a rock etc. by leaning back with the feet against the (rock) face; (*c*) in various sports, the movement or position of leaning backwards or lying on one's back; **laybacking** *Mountaineering* the activity of climbing a crack by means of a lay-back; **laybarge** a barge designed for laying underwater pipelines; **lay-bed** (*a*) (now *dial.*) a grave; †(*b*) a layer, a stratum; **lay-down** *n.* (*a*) *slang* a certainty, a sure thing; (*b*) *slang* a remand in custody; (*c*) *dial.* & *non-standard* a lie-down, a rest; **lay-down** *a.* (*a*) designating a collar which is folded over and does not stand up; (*b*) designating a hand or contract at cards (esp. bridge) which is such that success is possible against any defence, so that no harm would be done by exposing the player's cards on the table; **layflat** *a.* & *n.* (designating) a tube, tubing, etc., that can lie or be laid flat; **lay-in** *Basketball* a shot made at the top of a jump, usu. by bouncing the ball off the backboard into the basket; **lay-off** (*a*) a rest, a respite; a period during which a worker is temporarily dismissed or given leave; (*b*) a part of the year during which activity in a particular business or game is partly or completely suspended; (*c*) the (esp. temporary) dismissal of a number of workers from a factory etc., usually for economic reasons; **lay-over** †(*a*) an additional cloth laid over a tablecloth; (*b*) *N. Amer.* a stop or stay in a place, esp. overnight; a halt, a rest, a delay; **lay-up** (*a*) a period during which a person or thing is (temporarily) out of employment or use; (*b*) the operation of laying up in the manufacture of laminated material; the assembly of layers ready for bonding so produced; (*c*) *Basketball* (also *lay-up shot*) an attempt to score from free play; a shot made directly into the basket without bouncing the ball off the backboard.

¶The use in branch VII, avoided in standard English, is probably encouraged by confusion with LAY *v.*[2], the pa. t. of LIE *v.*[1]

lay *v.*[2] pa. t. of LIE *v.*[1]

layabout /ˈleɪəbaʊt/ *n.* M20. [f. LAY *v.*[1] + ABOUT *adv.*] A habitual loafer or idler.

N. BAWDEN He wasn't lazy, not a layabout. *attrib.*: *Punch* Any old-fashioned plot about layabout art-lecturers getting mixed up with funny spies.

layaway /ˈleɪəweɪ/ *n.* L19. [f. *lay away* s.v. LAY *v.*[1]] **1** *Tanning.* = LAYER *n.* 5. Freq. *attrib.* L19. **2** = LAY-BY 2b. *N. Amer.* M20. **b** An article reserved for a customer who has paid a deposit. *N. Amer.* L20.

2b unclaimed layaway a reserved and partly paid-for article offered for sale at a reduced price on the customer's failing to complete the purchase.

lay-by /ˈleɪbʌɪ/ *n.* Pl. **lay-bys**. E19. [f. *lay by* s.v. LAY *v.*[1]] **1a** A part of a river, canal, etc., in which barges are put aside out of use. E19. **b** A railway siding. M19. **c** A length of roadway at the side of a carriageway on which vehicles can park without obstructing other traffic. M20. **2a** Something laid by or saved; savings. L19. **b** A system of paying a deposit to secure an article for later purchase. Chiefly *Austral.* & *NZ.* M20.

lay-day /ˈleɪdeɪ/ *n.* L18. [f. LAY *v.*[1] + DAY *n.*: cf. G *Liegetage* (pl.) lay-days, (days of) demurrage.] *Comm.* **1** Any of a certain number of days allowed for the loading and unloading of cargo. L18. **2** A day on which a boat is delayed in port, e.g. by bad weather. M20.

layer /ˈleɪə/ *n.* ME. [f. LAY *v.*[1] + -ER[1].] **1a** A person who lays stones; a mason. Long *obs.* exc. *Hist.* ME. **b** *gen.* A person who or thing which lays something or someone. M16. **c** A hen that lays eggs. Freq. w. specifying wd. E18. **d** = *gun-layer* s.v. GUN *n.* L19. **2** A region of matter that is thin in relation to its lateral extent, *esp.* one adjacent to or covering a surface; a thickness of clothing worn over or under another; a stratum, a course, a bed. E17. **b** A formation of aircraft, esp. bombers, flying at the same height. M20. **3** *Hort.* A shoot fastened down and partly covered with earth to take root while still attached to the parent plant. E17. **b** A crop of, or field containing, sown grass or clover; = LEY *n.*[1] Chiefly *dial.* L18. **c** *collect.* Plants of a specific kind forming part of a hedge. Chiefly *dial.* L18. **4** An oyster-bed. M17. **5** A large vat or pit in which hides are placed flat to steep in strong tan liquor as the final stage in the tanning process. L18. **6** *Cartography.* An area depicted in a particular tint chosen to represent all land between two specified heights. E20.

1b N. FAIRFAX Layers of plots and traps. R. LEIGHTON The Lord Himself is the layer of this corner stone. **c** *Poultry World* A..deep drinking trough essential for the adult layer. **2** P. DAVIES Old stars blast off an outer layer into space. MALPIGHIAN *layer.* NEPHELOID *layer.* PILIFEROUS *layer.* PLEXIFORM *layer.* PRISMATIC *layer.* REVERSING *layer. scattering layer*: see SCATTERING *ppl a.* 2. VISCERAL *layer. vitelline layer*: see VITELLINE 2.

Comb.: **layer-cake** a cake consisting of layers of sponge held together by a sweet filling, and usu. iced; **layer cloud** *Meteorol.* a sheetlike cloud having little vertical depth but considerable horizontal extent; **layer colour** *Cartography* a colour used in the layer system of showing relief; **layer-cut** *n.* & *v.* (*a*) *n.* a haircut with the hair in overlapping layers; (*b*) *v.t.* cut (hair) in overlapping layers; **layer dressing** the wearing of layers of clothes of varying lengths such that each layer shows beneath the one outside it; **layer-out** a person who prepares a body for burial or cremation; **layer pit** = sense 5 above; **layer-pudding** a steamed pudding consisting of layers of suet crust pastry with a sweet filling; **layer shading** *Cartography* the use of layer tints to show relief; **layer system** *Cartography* the representation of land between different heights or contours by different colours or tints that are graded so as to show relief at a glance; **layer tint** *Cartography* a layer colour, or a tint of such a colour; **layer vat** = sense 5 above.

layer /ˈleɪə/ *v.* E18. [f. the n.] **1** *Hort.* **a** *v.t.* Propagate (a plant) as a layer. E18. **b** *v.i.* Bend down a layer to the ground and cover it partly with earth to take root and propagate the plant. L18. **c** = LAY *v.*[1] 4b. L19. **2** *v.i.* Of crops: be laid flat as by wind or rain through weakness of growth. L19. **3** *v.t.* Place or insert as a layer; arrange in layers. E20. **b** Cut (hair) in overlapping layers. M20.

layered /ˈleɪəd/ *a.* M19. [f. LAYER *n.*, *v.*: see -ED[2], -ED[1].] Divided into layers; having layers (of a specified character or number); covered with layers; *Cartography* having relief shown by the layer system; (of dress) worn in layers; (of hair) cut in overlapping layers.

layering /ˈleɪərɪŋ/ *n.* E18. [f. LAYER *v.* + -ING[1].] The action of LAYER *v.*; *spec.* (*a*) *Hort.* the method or activity of propagating a plant as a layer; (*b*) *Cartography* = *layer shading* s.v. LAYER *n.*; the use on a distribution map of shading etc. to represent distribution in layers; (*c*) = *layer dressing* s.v. LAYER *n.*

layette /leɪˈjɛt/ *n.* M19. [Fr., dim. of OFr. *laie* drawer, box f. MDu. *laege*: see -ETTE.] A set of clothing, toilet articles, and bedclothing for a newborn child.

lay-fee /ˈleɪfiː/ *n. obs.* exc. *Hist.* ME. [AN *lai fe*: see LAY *a.*, FEE *n.*[2]] **1** A fee or estate in land held in consideration of secular services, as distinguished from an ecclesiastical fee. ME. **†2** The laity, lay people collectively. LME–M17.

lay figure /leɪ ˈfɪɡə/ *n. phr.* L18. [f. LAY(MAN *n.*[2] + FIGURE *n.*] **1** A jointed figure of a human body used by artists as a model for arranging drapery on etc. L18. **2** A person lacking in individuality, a nonentity; an unrealistic character in a novel etc. serving only to advance the plot. M19.

1 W. S. MAUGHAM The look of a lay figure in a studio. **2** G. GREENE She isn't a lay figure, the audience see enough of her..to feel the shock of her murder.

laygear /ˈleɪɡɪə/ *n.* M20. [f. LAY(SHAFT + GEAR *n.*] *Engin.* The set of gearwheels on a layshaft. Also *laygear cluster*.

laying /ˈleɪɪŋ/ *n.* ME. [f. LAY *v.*[1] + -ING[1].] **1** The action of LAY *v.*[1] ME. **2** A thing that is laid; a layer, a bed, a stratum. LME. **b** An oyster-bed. M19.

Comb.: **laying house** (*a*) a building in which rope is made; (*b*) a building in which laying hens are kept; **laying mash, meal** a special food for laying hens.

laying /ˈleɪɪŋ/ *a.* L16. [f. LAY *v.*[1] + -ING[2].] Esp. of a hen: that lays.

laylight /ˈleɪlʌɪt/ *n.* M20. [f. LAY *v.*[1] + LIGHT *n.*] A window or light made of glazed panels and set into a ceiling to provide natural or artificial light.

laylock *n.* & *a.* see LILAC.

layman /ˈleɪmən/ *n.*[1] Pl. **-men**. LME. [f. LAY *a.* + MAN *n.*] **1** A person who is not a cleric; a member of the laity. LME. **2** A person without professional or special knowledge in a particular subject, esp. law or medicine. L15.

1 T. S. ELIOT None of my people,..Whether layman or clerk, shall you touch. **2** G. STEINER There is no use trying to explain to the layman the reality-concepts of modern mathematics or physics. A. STORR Another feature of psychotherapy which the layman finds hard to understand.

†layman *n.*[2] Pl. **-men**. L17–L18. [Du. *leeman*, f. *led* (now *lid*) limb, joint (cf. LITH *n.*[1]) + *man* MAN *n.*] = LAY FIGURE.

laymen *n.*[1], *n.*[2] pls. of LAYMAN *n.*[1], *n.*[2]

layout /ˈleɪaʊt/ *n.* M19. [f. *lay out* s.v. LAY *v.*[1]] **1** The planning or disposition of land, streets, etc.; land laid out; the plan or disposition of a house, factory, garden, etc.; the way in which plans, printed matter, etc., are arranged or set out. M19. **b** A drawing showing the design of a proposed piece of printing, sometimes with specifications for production; the preparation of such drawings; the design details of a cartoon film. E20. **2** Something arranged or set out in a particular way; the tools or apparatus pertaining to some occupation etc.; *US slang* the equipment used for smoking opium. M19. **b** A scheme, a plan, an arrangement; a course of action. Orig. & chiefly *US*. M19. **c** A number of people associated in some way; a party or gang (of people); a family. Freq. *derog. US colloq.* & *dial.* M19. **3a** In faro, the representation in enamel etc. of a suit of cards on a green cloth, on which stakes are laid. M19. **b** The arrangement formed by the cards laid out on the table in any of various card-games, esp. patience; a tableau. M19.

Laysan /leɪˈzɑːn, -ˈzan/ *n.* L19. [An island in the Hawaiian archipelago.] Used *attrib.* to designate birds native to Laysan.

Laysan albatross an albatross, *Diomedea immutabilis*, of the N. Pacific. **Laysan duck** = *Laysan teal* below. **Laysan finch** a Hawaiian honeycreeper, *Telespyza cantans*, a large finchlike bird noted for its song. **Laysan rail** an extinct rail, *Porzanula palmeri*. **Laysan teal** a mallard of the subspecies *Anas platyrhynchos laysanensis*.

layshaft /ˈleɪʃɑːft/ *n.* L19. [Prob. f. LAY *v.*[1] + SHAFT *n.*] A short secondary or intermediate shaft driven by gearing from the main shaft of an engine; *spec.* one inside a gearbox that transmits the drive from the input shaft to the output shaft.

laystall /ˈleɪstɔːl/ *n. arch.* E16. [f. LAY *v.*[1] + STALL *n.*[1]] †**1** A burial place. E–M16. **2** A (public) refuse-heap. M16.

laywoman /ˈleɪwʊmən/ *n.* Pl. **-women** /-wɪmɪn/. E16. [f. LAY *a.* + WOMAN *n.*] A female member of the laity; a woman without professional or special knowledge in a particular subject, esp. law or medicine.

Laz /lɑːz/ *n.* & *a.* Also **Laze** /ˈlɑːzə/. M19. [Laz.] **A** *n.* Pl. **Laz, Lazes** /ˈlɑːzɪz, -zəz/. **1** A member of a group of Caucasian peoples of Lazistan in NE Turkey. M19. **2** The S. Caucasian language of this people. M20. **B** *attrib.* or as *adj.* Of or pertaining to the Laz or their language. M20.

Lazic *a.* M20.

lazar /ˈleɪzə/ *n.* & *a. arch.* ME. [med.L *lazarus*, an application of the name *Lazarus* (*Luke* 16:20), partly through OFr. *lasdre* (mod. *ladre*).] **A** *n.* **1** A poor and diseased person, *esp.* a leper. ME. †**2** Discoloured and decaying matter in cheese. L16–E18.

Comb.: **lazar-house** = LAZARETTO I.

B *adj.* Of a person: poor and diseased; leprous. LME.

lazarlike *a.* resembling a poor and diseased person, leprous E17.

lazaret /lazəˈrɛt/ *n.* Also **-ette**. E17. [Fr. f. as next.] **1** = LAZARETTO I. E17. **2** = LAZARETTO 2. E18. **3** = LAZARETTO 3. L19.

lazaretto /lazəˈrɛtəʊ/ *n.* Pl. **-os**. M16. [It., dim. of LAZZARO.] **1** A hospital for diseased people, esp. those with leprosy. M16. **2** A building or ship for quarantine. E17. **3** *Naut.* The after part of a ship's hold, used for stores. E18.

Lazarist /ˈlazərɪst/ *n.* M18. [Fr. *Lazariste*, f. *Lazare* Lazarus: see LAZAR, -IST.] *Chr. Ch.* A member of the Congregation of the Priests of the Mission founded by St Vincent of Paul in 1624, and established a few years later in the College of St Lazare at Paris.

Lazarite /ˈlazərʌɪt/ *n.* Now *rare* or *obs.* M16. [f. *Lazarus* (see LAZAR) + -ITE[1].] *Chr. Ch.* †**1** A member of a religious order taking its name from Lazarus. Only in M16. **2** = LAZARIST. E18.

Lazarus /ˈlaz(ə)rəs/ *n. rare.* L15. [Pers. name used allusively: see LAZAR.] A person with leprosy; a beggar.

laze /leɪz/ *n.*[1] *colloq.* M19. [f. LAZE *v.*] The action of lazing; an instance of this; a spell of lazing.

Laze *n.*[2] & *a.* var. of LAZ.

laze /leɪz/ *v.* L16. [Back-form. f. LAZY *a.*] **1** *v.i.* Lie, move, or act in a sleepy listless fashion; enjoy oneself lazily. L16. **2** *v.t.* Orig., indulge (oneself) in indolence. Later, pass (time) *away* lazily. E17.

1 D. WIGODER He . . shouted that I had lazed around for long enough. *Holiday Which?* You . . may spot a turtle or a manta ray, lazing on the sea bed.

†**lazo** *n.* & *v.* var. of LASSO.

lazule /ˈlazjuːl/ *n.* Now *rare* or *obs.* L16. [med.L *lazulum*: see LAPIS LAZULI.] More fully *lazule-stone*. = LAPIS LAZULI.

lazuli /ˈlazjʊlʌɪ, -li/ *n.* M17. [f. LAPIS) LAZULI.] = LAPIS LAZULI.

Comb.: **lazuli bunting, finch** a small cardinal grosbeak of western N. America, *Passerina amoena*, the male of which has a brilliant blue head and back.

lazulite /ˈlazjʊlʌɪt/ *n.* E19. [f. as prec. + -ITE[1].] *Min.* A hydrous phosphate of aluminium and magnesium, occurring as blue monoclinic crystals. Also (*poet.*), lapis lazuli.

lazuˈlitic *a.* M19.

lazurite /ˈlazjʊrʌɪt/ *n.* L19. [f. med.L *lazur* f. Arab. *lāzaward* (see AZURE *n.* & *a.*): see -ITE[1].] *Min.* A rare silicate of sodium and aluminium occurring as blue crystals of the cubic system and as the chief constituent of lapis lazuli.

lazy /ˈleɪzi/ *a.* M16. [Perh. of LDu. origin: cf. LG *lasich* languid, idle.] **1 a** Of a person etc.: disinclined to work, not disposed to action or effort; idle; inactive, slothful. M16. **b** *transf.* Of a thing, place, or condition: characterized by or inducing laziness. E17. **2** Orig. (of a literary style etc.), languid, having little energy. Later (now esp. of a river), sluggish, slow-moving. M16. †**3** Bad, worthless. *dial.* L17–L18.

1 R. LAWLER And you, yer lazy sod, lollin' there. Git on out into me kitchen. M. ROBERTS Bring the wine over, Helen. I'm too lazy to move. b LONGFELLOW The great dog . . Hangs his head in the lazy heat. 2 H. BELLOC In the courtyard . . a lazy fountain leaped and babbled. B. PEARSON Two lagoons fed by a creek that was lazy when it wasn't in flood.

Special collocations & comb.: **lazy arm** a type of boom from which a microphone may be slung. **lazy-back** †(*a*) a sluggard; (*b*) the place at the surface of a mine where coals are loaded and stacked for sale; (*c*) (chiefly *Hist.*) a high back-bar to a carriage-seat; a movable backrest on a gig etc.; (*d*) *lazy-back chair*, a chair with a reclining back. **lazy-bed** a bed about two metres or six feet wide, on which potatoes etc. for cultivation are laid, and covered with earth taken from a trench up to a metre or three feet wide on each side. **lazy-board** *US* a short board on the left side of a wagon, used by teamsters to ride on. **lazy daisy (stitch)** a petal-shaped embroidery stitch. **lazy dog** *US Mil. slang* a type of fragmentation bomb designed to explode in mid-air and scatter steel pellets at high speed over the target area. **lazy eight** an aerobatic manoeuvre in which an aircraft executes an S-shaped path which, when viewed laterally, resembles a figure 8 lying on its side. **lazy eye** an amblyopic eye in which underuse has contributed to its poor vision, *esp.* the unused eye in squint. **lazy-jack** (*a*) a device resembling a lazy-tongs; (*b*) *Naut.* any of various small ropes extending vertically from the topping-lifts to the boom for holding a fore-and-aft sail when taking it in. *Lazy* LAURENCE. **Lazy Susan** (orig. *US*) a revolving stand on a table to hold condiments etc.; a muffin-stand. **lazy-tongs** a device for grasping objects at a distance, comprising a system of several pairs of levers crossing and pivoted at their centres like scissors, so connected that the movement of the first pair is communicated to the last, which is fitted with ends like those of a pair of tongs.

lazyhood *n.* laziness M19. **lazily** *adv.* L16. **laziness** *n.* L16. **lazyish** *a.* somewhat lazy L19.

lazy /ˈleɪzi/ *v.* E17. [f. LAZY *a.*] **1** *v.i.* = LAZE *v.* I. E17. **2** *v.t.* = LAZE *v.* 2. L19.

lazybones /ˈleɪzɪbəʊnz/ *n. colloq.* Pl. same. L16. [f. LAZY *a.* + BONE *n.* + -S[1].] A lazy person.

lazzaro /ˈlazərəʊ/ *n.* Pl. **-ri** /-ri/. M17. [It., f. as LAZAR.] = LAZZARONE.

lazzarone /lazəˈrəʊni/ *n.* Pl. **-ni** /-ni/. L18. [It., augm. of LAZZARO.] In Naples and other Italian cities: a person who subsists on the proceeds of odd jobs, an idler, a beggar.

-le /(ə)l/ *suff.*[1] (not productive). [Repr. OE *-el*, *-ela*, *-(e)le* in ns. and *-ol*, *-ul*, *-el* in adjs., f. Gmc, w. many IE cognates. See also -EL[1].] Forming ns. from ns. w. (orig.) dim. sense, as *bramble*, or denoting an appliance, as *thimble*, *handle*; forming ns. f. vbs, denoting an agent, as *beadle*, or an instrument, as *bridle*, *girdle*, and adjs. f. vbs w. the sense 'apt or liable (to do)', as *brittle*, *fickle*, *nimble*. In some ns., as *riddle*, repr. a back-form. f. *-els*, taken as pl.

-le /(ə)l/ *suff.*[2] (not productive). Forming ns. w. (orig.) dim. sense, and repr. OFr. *-el* f. L *-ellum* dim. suff., as *castle*, *mantle*, OFr. *-el* f. L *-ale* neut. sing. of *-alis* adj. suff., as *cattle*, OFr. *-aille* f. L *-alia* neut. pl. of *-alis* adj. suff., as *battle*, and OFr. *-eille* f. L *-icula* dim. suff., as *bottle*. Cf. -EL[2].

-le /(ə)l/ *suff.*[3] (not productive). [Repr. OE *-lian* f. Gmc.] Forming vbs w. frequent. or dim. sense, as *babble*, *crumple*, *dazzle*, *giggle*, *nestle*, *twinkle*, *wrestle*.

lea /liː/ *n.*[1] Now chiefly *poet.* exc. in place-names. Also †**ley**. See also LEY *n.*[2] [OE *lēah*, *lēa* corresp. to OHG *lōh* grove (MHG = low brushwood, scrubland), f. Gmc f. IE base repr. also by L *lucus* grove, Lith. *laũkas* field, Skt *lokás* open space.] A tract of open ground, *esp.* grassland.

lea /liː/ *n.*[2] LME. [Perh. deriv. of Fr. *lier* bind, tie, f. L *ligare*, but cf. LEASE *n.*[2]] A measure of yarn of varying quantity.

lea *n.*[3] see LEY *n.*[1]

lea /liː, leɪ/ *a.* Now *dial.* Also **ley, lay** /leɪ/. OE. [Perh. f. base of LAY *v.*[1], LIE *v.*[1]] Of land: fallow, unploughed.

leach /liːtʃ/ *n.*[1] *arch.* LME. [OFr. *lesche* (mod. *lèche*).] †**1** A slice (of meat etc.); a strip. LME–E16. **2** A dish consisting of sliced meat, eggs, fruits, and spices in jelly etc. LME.

leach /liːtʃ/ *n.*[2] M17. [App. f. LEACH *v.*[1]] **1** The saturated brine which drains from the salt in salt extraction, or is left behind when salt is extracted. Earliest in †*leach-brine*. M17. **2** A perforated vessel or trough used for making lye from wood ashes by pouring water over them. *obs.* exc. *dial.* L17. **3** *Tanning.* A pit in which a tanning liquid is mixed. L18.

Leach /liːtʃ/ *n.*[3] M19. [William *Leach* (1790–1836), Eng. naturalist.] *Leach's (storm) petrel*, a storm petrel of the N. Atlantic and N. Pacific, *Oceanodroma leucorhoa*, which flies in a distinctive darting manner close to the sea.

leach /liːtʃ/ *v.*[1] [OE *leċċan* f. WGmc, f. base also of LAKE *n.*[1]] †**1** *v.t.* Water, wet. *rare.* OE–L16. †**2** *v.i.* Soften, melt. *rare.* Only in E17. **3a** *v.t.* Cause (a liquid) to percolate through some material. *rare.* L18. **b** *v.t.* Subject (soil, ores, etc.) to the action of percolating water etc. which removes soluble constituents; *fig.* slowly deprive *of.* M19. **4** *v.t.* Take (a substance) *away*, *out*, by percolation. M19. **5** *v.i.* Be subject to the action of percolating water; (of a liquid or solute) pass through or *out* by percolation. L19.

leachaˈbility *n.* ability to be leached out M20. **leachable** *a.* able to be leached out M20. **leachate** *n.* (a quantity of) liquid that has percolated through a solid and leached out some of the constituents M20. **leacher** *n.* (*a*) = LEACH *n.*[2] 3; (*b*) a person who leaches something: L19. **leachy** *a.* (of a soil) unable to hold water; very porous: L19.

leach /liːtʃ/ *v.*[2]*t. arch.* LME. [f. LEACH *n.*[1]] Cut (meat etc.) in slices; slice.

lead /lɛd/ *n.*[1] & *a.* [OE *lēad* = OFris. *lād*, MLG *lōd* (Du. *lood*) lead, MHG *lōt* (G *Lot*) plummet, solder, f. WGmc.] **A** *n.* **1** A soft, heavy, malleable, bluish-grey metal that is a chemical element, atomic no. 82, occurring in galena and other minerals. (Symbol Pb.) OE. **2a** A large pot, cauldron, or kettle, a large open vessel used in brewing and various other operations, (orig., one made of lead). Now *dial.* OE. **b** A lead milk-pan. *dial.* M18. **3** The metal made into an object, e.g. a seal, the plummet of a plumb-line, a pipe, a lead coffin. Now *esp.* (more fully *cold lead*) bullets. ME. **4** *Naut.* A lump of lead suspended on a line to discover the depth of water; a sounding-lead. ME. **5a** In *pl.* The sheets or strips of lead used to cover a roof; a lead roof. ME. **b** A strip of lead between panes in lattice or stained-glass windows, a came. Usu. in *pl.* E18. **6** Graphite, used as a material for pencils; a thin stick of graphite within a pencil, or for filling a propelling pencil. Cf. *blacklead* s.v. BLACK *a.* E19. **7** *Typogr.* A thin strip, usu. of type-metal, less than type-high, of varying thickness and length, used to separate lines of type. E19.

1 SHAKES. *Macb.* A heavy summons lies like lead upon me. COLERIDGE The ship went down like lead. *milled lead, pig-lead, pot-lead, sheet lead,* etc.

Phrases etc.: *arm the lead*: see ARM *v.*[1] **as heavy as lead** very heavy. *blacklead*: see BLACK *a.* **cast the lead** lower a sounding-lead from a ship. *cold lead*: see sense 3 above. **lead in one's pencil** *slang* (esp. male sexual) vigour. *mock lead*: see MOCK *a. potter's lead*: see POTTER *n.*[1] *red lead*: see RED *a. sugar of lead*: see SUGAR *n.* & *a.* **swing the lead** *slang* idle, shirk; malinger. **take the lead out of one's pants** *slang* hurry up, act promptly. TETRAETHYL *lead. white lead*: see WHITE *a.*

B *attrib.* or as *adj.* Made (wholly or partly) of lead, consisting of lead. LME.

Special collocations & comb.: **lead-acid** *a.* designating a secondary cell or battery in which the anode and cathode are plates or grids of lead (or lead alloy) coated with lead dioxide and spongy lead respectively, both immersed in dilute sulphuric acid. **lead-ash, -ashes** litharge. **lead-back** *US* the dunlin. **lead balloon** a failure, an unsuccessful venture. **lead bronze**: containing lead, used in bearings. **lead bullion** a mixture of lead and other heavy metals formed during the extraction of lead. **lead-burn** *v.t.* weld (pieces of lead). **lead-burning** the welding of lead. **lead cell** a lead-acid cell. **lead chamber** a large vessel made of welded sheet lead, used in the manufacture of sulphuric acid from sulphur dioxide, air, and steam using oxides of nitrogen as catalysts. **lead comb**: made of lead, used to darken the hair. **lead crystal** = *lead glass* below. **lead flat** a flat roof made of sheet lead laid across joists and boarding. **lead glance** galena. **lead glass** glass containing a substantial proportion of lead oxide, making it more refractive. **lead glaze** *Pottery*: containing lead oxide. **lead light** a window in which small panes are fixed in lead calms, a leaded light. **lead-line** (*a*) a sounding-lead, a plumb-line; (*b*) a line loaded with lead weights, running along the bottom of a net; (*c*) *Med.* a bluish-grey line along the gums at their junction with the teeth, indicating lead-poisoning; (*d*) a narrow strip of lead between two pieces of stained glass; a calm. **lead-line** *v.t.* put lead-lines in (stained-glass work). **leadman** (*a*) a dealer in lead; (*b*) a lead-miner. **lead-mill** (*a*) a factory for producing milled or sheet lead; (*b*) a lead plate used for grinding gemstones. **lead-nail**: used to fasten a sheet of lead on a roof (usu. in *pl.*). **lead ochre** = MASSICOT. **lead-paper** a test-paper treated with a preparation of lead. **lead-papered** *a.* covered with or containing lead-paper. **lead pencil**: of graphite, often enclosed in cedar or other wood. **lead-pipe cinch** *US colloq.* a complete certainty. **lead-plant** *US* a leguminous shrub, *Amorpha canescens*, formerly believed to indicate the presence of lead ore. **lead-plaster** = DIACHYLON. **lead-poisoning** acute or chronic poisoning by the absorption of lead into the body. **lead ratio** the ratio of the quantity of lead in a rock sample to that of its radioactive parents uranium and thorium, from which the age of the sample may be determined. *lead shot*: see SHOT *n.*[1] **lead-spar** = CERUSSITE. **lead-swing** *v.i.* (*slang*) = *swing the lead* above. **lead-swinger** *slang* a shirker, a malingerer. *lead* TETRAETHYL. **lead-tin** *n.* & *a.* (an alloy) containing lead and tin. **lead-tree** (*a*) a tropical leguminous tree, *Leucaena latisiliqua*; (*b*) a dendritic crystalline deposit of metallic lead or zinc in lead acetate solution. **lead-vitriol** = ANGLESITE. **lead-wash, -water** *Med.* a dilute solution of lead acetate. **lead wool** lead in a fibrous state, used for caulking pipe joints. **leadwort** (*a*) any of various mainly tropical perennial herbs and shrubs of the genus *Plumbago*, with tubular calyx and five-lobed corolla, esp. *P. europaea* of southern Europe; (*b*) any member of the family Plumbaginaceae, which includes this genus and also the thrifts and sea-lavenders.

lead /liːd/ *n.*[2] ME. [f. LEAD *v.*[1]] **1 a** The action of LEAD *v.*[1]; leading, direction, guidance. *obs.* exc. *dial.* ME. **b** Direction given by going in front; example, precedent. Esp. in *follow the lead of.* M19. **c** A guiding indication; a clue to the solution of something. M19. **d** *Journalism.* A summary or outline of a newspaper story; a guide to a story that needs further development or exploration; the first (often the most important) item in a newspaper etc. Cf. *lead story* below. E20. **2 a** A man-made watercourse, *esp.* one leading to a mill (also called *mill-leat*). M16. **b** A (garden) path; an alley. L16. **c** A channel in an ice-field. E19. **d** A thong, strap, or cord for leading or controlling a dog etc. L19. **3 a** The front or leading place; the place in front *of* (something); freq. in *take the* (or *a*) *lead*. Also, the position or function of leading, leadership. L16. **b** The front section of a flock of sheep. *Austral.* & *NZ.* M20. **4 a** *Curling.* The first player; the stone first played. Also, the course along which the stones are propelled. L17. **b** *Bowls.* The advantage of throwing the jack and bowling first. M18. **c** *Boxing.* The first punch delivered (of two or more). E20. **5 a** *Campanol.* The position of the first of a set of changing bells. L17. **b** *Mus.* The giving out of a phrase or passage by one of the voices or instruments in a piece, to be followed in harmony by the others. L19. **c** *Mus.* The most prominent part in a piece played by an orchestra, esp. a jazz band; the player or instrument that plays this; the leader of a section of an orchestra. Also, the start of a passage played by a particular instrument. Freq. *attrib.* M20. **6** *Cards.* The action, privilege, or obligation of playing the first card in a round or trick. Also, the card (to be) played first in a round or trick; the suit to which the first card belongs. M18. **7** *Mining.* **a** = LODE 5. E19. **b** An alluvial deposit of gold along the bed of an ancient river. M19. **8** *Theatr.* (A person who plays) the leading or principal part in a play. E19. **9** The distance which ballast, coal, soil, etc. has to be conveyed to its destination. M19. **10** *Naut.* The direction in which a rope runs fair to the deck. Cf. *fairlead* s.v. FAIR *a.* & *adv.* M19. **11** *Electr.* A conductor (usu. a wire) conveying electric current from a source to an appliance. L19. **12** *Electr.* The angle through which the brushes are shifted around a commutator from the neutral point. L19. **13** *Horology.* The action of a tooth of a toothed wheel in impelling another tooth or a pallet. L19. **14** A piece of railway track connecting a switch to a frog. E20. **15** *Mech.* The axial distance travelled by a screw in one turn. E20.

Phrases: **give a lead (to)** (*Hunting* etc.) go first in jumping a fence etc. to give encouragement (to the rest); *fig.* provide (with) a clue. **have, gain, a lead on** have, acquire, a position in front of or an advantage over. *juvenile lead*: see JUVENILE *a.* **leads and lags** the hastening or delaying of payment to take advantage of expected changes in the exchange rate. **return the lead** *Cards* lead the suit already led by one's partner.

Attrib. & comb.: In the sense 'leading,' as *lead guitarist, singer*, etc. Special combs., as **lead-bars** the bars to which the traces of front coach-horses are attached; **lead counsel** *US* the senior of two or more lawyers acting for the same party; **lead-horse, lead-mule** a horse or mule that is guided or controlled by a lead; **lead-reins** the reins of the front coach-horses; **lead-rope** a rope used as a lead for a horse etc.; **lead-screw**: that moves the carriage of a lathe; **lead sheet** *US slang* a sheet of music with the melodic line and lyric only; *transf.* an overcoat; **lead story**: given greatest prominence in a newspaper etc.; **lead time**: between the initiation and completion of a process of production or development.

lead /liːd/ *v.*[1] Pa. t. & pple **led** /lɛd/. [OE *lǣdan* = OFris. *lēda*, OS *lēdjan* (Du. *leiden*), OHG, G *leiten*, ON *leiða*, f. Gmc, f. base also of LOAD *n.*] **I** Conduct. **1** *v.t.* Cause to go along with oneself; *spec.* †(*a*) bring or take (a person or animal) to a place (also foll. by *away, down,* etc.); (*b*) convey, usu. in a cart or other vehicle; now only *north.*, cart (coal, corn, stones, turf, etc.). †(*c*) (of a natural agent, e.g. the wind) carry. OE. **b** Bring forward, adduce (testimony). Formerly also, initiate (an action) at law. Now only *Sc. Law.* ME. **2** *v.t.* Of a person or (*transf.*) a circumstance, motive, etc.: accompany and show the way to (a person); *esp.* direct or guide by going on in advance. Freq. with *away, in, out,* etc. OE. **3** *v.t.* Of a commander: march at the head of and direct the movement of (troops). Also foll. by *on.* OE. **4** *v.t.* Direct the course of (a person) by holding the hand or some part of the body or clothing; conduct (an animal) by means of a cord, halter, bridle, etc. Also foll. by *away, in, off,* etc. OE. **b** *v.t. fig.* Guide by persuasion as contrasted with commands or threats. L16. **c** *v.i.* Submit to being led. E17. **5** With inanimate thing as obj.: **a** *v.t.* Guide the course or direction of (something flexible); draw or pass (a rope etc.) *over* a pulley, *through* a hole, etc. Formerly also, trace (a line, a boundary). OE. **b** *v.t.* Conduct (water etc.) through a channel or pipe. Also foll. by *away, forth, off, out.* ME. †**c** *v.t.* Steer (a boat); drive (a carriage). LME–M16. **d** *v.i. Naut.* Of a rope: admit of being led. M19. **6** *v.t.* Guide with reference to action or opinion; bring by persuasion or counsel *to* or *into* a condition, bring by argument etc. *to* a conclusion; induce *to do.* ME. **b** *Law.* Put a question to (a witness) in such a way as to suggest the answer required. Cf. *leading question* s.v. LEADING *a.* Chiefly *US.* M19. **7 a** *v.t.* & *i.* Of a thoroughfare etc.: serve as a passage or approach for (a person) *to* or *into* a place. ME. **b** *v.i.* Foll. by *to*: tend towards as a consequence; end in. LME. **c** *v.i.* Form a channel *into*; form a connecting link *to* (something). M19. †**8** *v.t.* Conduct (affairs); manage, govern. ME–L16. †**9** *v.t.* Deal with, treat. As pa. pple: circumstanced, situated, in a specified condition. ME–L15.

1 JOSEPH HALL Causing the Clouds to lead in store of rain. W. B. STONEHOUSE One shilling a load is the price . . for leading a cart-load of warp. **b** *Times* It would be strange if evidence competent to prove the offender's guilt . . could not be led in a hearing. 2 C. RAYNER Mrs Miller led Freddy . . up the first flight of stairs. K. LAING Sackey's long strides led him far ahead. 3 H. BAILEY Victor . . had been blinded at Arras, leading his platoon into battle. 4 J. HERRIOT Five dogs were being led round the perimeter. B. BREYTENBACH The workers who can still see lead their blind comrades by the hand. **b** G. PUTTENHAM Princes may be lead but not driuen. **c** *Time* These people lead real easy. 6 *Law Reports* There was nothing in the prospectus to lead him to such a conclusion. M. BARING It was Master C. who had led him into mischief. W. ABISH Her appearance, her surname . . led him to assume that she was of German extraction. 7a J. STEINBECK The rutted sandy road that led through the brushy country. *fig.*: R. K. NARAYAN Staying in Malgudi would not lead him anywhere. **b** ANTHONY SMITH Damage to a part of the cortex invariably led to speech disorder. *Christian Aid News* These policies have led to increased bank lending.

II Carry on. †**10** *v.t.* Engage in, perform (a dance, a song); utter sounds of (joy or mournfulness). OE–L15. **11** *v.t.* Go through and experience, pass, (a period of time, now usu. a life or a particular kind of life). OE. †**b** Pass through (pain, suffering); bear, endure. ME–L15.

11 T. FULLER He led his old age in London. L. HELLMAN Julia was leading a strange life.

III Precede, be foremost. (Cf. sense 2.) **12** *v.t.* Have the first place in. LME. **b** *v.i.* & *t.* Have the lead (over) in a race, match, game, etc.; be ahead (of). L18. **c** *v.t.* Outnumber. L20. **13** *v.t.* Take the principal part in (proceedings of any kind); be at the head of (a party, a movement); have the official initiative in the proceedings of (a deliberative body). Also, set (a fashion). M17. **b** Perform one's part in (singing, a musical performance) so as to give the cue to others; give the cue to (other singers or performers) by performing one's part. M19. **14** *v.i.* **a** *Campanol.* Be the first of the changing bells. L17. **b** *Mus.* In a fugue etc.: introduce a subject which is taken up by the other parts successively. L19. **15** *Cards.* **a** *v.i.* Play the first card in a round or trick. Also foll. by *off.* L17. **b** *v.t.* Play (a specified card) as first player; play a card of (a specified suit). Also foll. by *out.* M18. **16 a** *v.t.* Of a barrister: act as leading counsel in (a case); act as leader to (another barrister). E19. **b** *v.i.* Appear as leading counsel (*for* the prosecution, defence, the plaintiff, the defendant). M19. **17** *v.i. Boxing.* Direct a punch at one's opponent, esp. as the first of a series of punches. Freq. with *with.* L19. **18** *v.t. Shooting.* Aim ahead of (a moving target) so that the target and the missile reach the same point simultaneously. L19. **19** *v.i.* Give prominence to an event, story, etc. Foll. by *on, with.* E20.

12 P. BAILEY May our country ever lead The world, for she is worthiest. *Harper's Magazine* Of the causes . . pneumonia led the list. **b** *Oxford Mail* An Abingdon side who led 6–3 at half-time. *Daily Telegraph* Northants, with seven wickets standing, lead Kent by 90 runs. **c** *Times* Advancing issues led declines by a ratio of only three to two. 13 T. FULLER They should

rather lead a fashion of thrift, than follow one of riot. D. DELILLO She led a more or less daily protest against . . her mother's habits. M. FOOT He lacked the . . sympathy to understand the Labour movement which he aspired to lead. **b** G. MANVILLE FENN He . . led the chorus. **15b** *Bridge Magazine* Now he leads a low spade which South wins. **16b** A. TROLLOPE Of course I must lead in defending her. **19** *Times* For Princess Margaret's wedding *The Times* . . did not even lead with the story.

Phrases: **lead a person a chase** give a pursuer trouble by one's speed or circuitous course. *lead a person a dance*: see DANCE *n.* **lead a person a (difficult, uncomfortable,** etc.) **life** subject a person to a life of constant difficulty, discomfort, etc. *lead apes (in hell)*: see APE *n.* **lead by the nose** cause to obey submissively. **lead captive** take away or escort as a prisoner. **lead in prayer** guide (a congregation) in public prayers. *lead large*: see LARGE *adv. lead the dance*: see DANCE *n.* **lead the prayers (of a congregation** etc.) = *lead in prayer* above. *lead the ring*: see RING *n.*[1] **lead the van** be in the forefront. **lead the way** go in advance of others, take the lead in an expedition or course of action. **lead up the garden (path)** lead on, entice; mislead, deceive. **lead with one's chin** (of a boxer) leave one's chin unprotected; *fig.* behave or speak incautiously.

With advs. & preps. in specialized senses: **lead away** induce to follow unthinkingly (usu. in *pass.*). **lead off** *v.phr.t.* & *i.* (*a*) take the first steps in (a dance, a ball); (*b*) begin (a performance), open (a conversation, a discussion) (freq. foll. by *with*). **lead on** (*a*) *v.phr.t.* induce gradually to advance; entice or beguile into going to greater lengths; (*b*) *v.phr.i.* direct conversation *to* a subject. **lead out** take the first steps in (a dance); conduct (a partner) into the dance. **lead through** (*a*) *v.phr.t.* (*Cards*) force to be played before an opponent; (*b*) *v.phr.i.* (of two climbers) act alternately as leader over successive stretches of rock. **lead up** (*a*) *v.phr.t.* (now *rare* or *obs.*) = *lead out* above; (*b*) *v.phr.i.* form a gradual introduction *to*; direct one's talk gradually *to* a topic or point; (*c*) *v.phr.i.* (foll. by *to*) lead a card and so allow the safe play of (a card held by another player).

lead /lɛd/ *v.*[2] LME. [f. LEAD *n.*[1]] **1** *v.t.* Cover with lead. Also foll. by *over.* LME. **2** *v.t.* Arm, load, or weight with lead. L15. **3** *v.t.* **a** Fix (glass in a window) with lead cames. Also foll. by *in, up.* M16. **b** Set or fasten *in* firmly with molten lead. L18. †**4** *v.t.* Line (pottery) with lead or lead glaze; glaze. Also foll. by *over.* M16–L17. **5** *v.t. Printing.* Separate (lines of type) by inserting leads; *loosely* in photocomposition or computer-assisted setting, space out (lines). M19. **6** *v.i. Naut.* Use a sounding-lead; take soundings. M19. **7** *v.t.* In *pass.* Of a gun barrel: become foul with a coating of lead. L19. **8** *v.t.* Smooth the inside of (a gun barrel) with a lap of lead. L19.

leadable /ˈliːdəb(ə)l/ *a. rare.* M19. [f. LEAD *v.*[1] + -ABLE.] Able to be led, amenable to being led.

leadableness *n.* L19.

leadbeater /ˈlɛdbiːtə, -bɛtə/ *n. Austral.* L19. [f. next.] = next.

Leadbeater's cockatoo /ˈlɛdbɛtəz kɒkəˈtuː, -biːt-/ *n. phr.* M19. [Benjamin *Leadbeater*, 19th-cent. Eng. naturalist.] The pink cockatoo, *Cacatua leadbeateri.*

Leadbeater's possum /ˈlɛdbɛtəz ˈpɒsəm, -biːt-/ *n. phr.* M20. [f. John *Leadbeater* (*c* 1832–88), Austral. taxidermist.] A small Australian possum, *Gymnobelideus leadbeateri*, which has grey and white fur with dark markings and is only found in eastern Victoria.

leaded /ˈlɛdɪd/ *a.* ME. [f. LEAD *n.*[1], *v.*[2]: see -ED[2], -ED[1].] **1** Covered, lined, loaded, or weighted with lead. ME. **2** Of a pane of glass: fitted into lead cames. M19. **3** *Typogr.* Having the lines of type separated by leads; *loosely* having extra space between lines. M19. **4** Affected by lead-poisoning. L19. **5** Containing added lead; *spec.* (of petrol) containing tetraethyl lead. M20.

leaden /ˈlɛd(ə)n/ *a.* OE. [f. LEAD *n.*[1] + -EN[4].] **1** Consisting or made of lead. OE. **2** Of a cold dull grey colour. LME. **3** *transf.* & *fig.* **a** Of base quality or composition; of little value. L16. **b** Weighing like lead; oppressively burdensome or numbing. Of the limbs: hard to drag along, moving slowly and heavily. L16. **c** Lacking animation; inert, spiritless, depressing. L16.

1 E. YOUNG Night . . stretches forth Her leaden sceptre o'er a slumb'ring world. **2** S. J. PERELMAN It was the season of the southwest monsoon, marked by leaden, overcast skies. **leaden fly-catcher** a small grey-green Australasian fly-catcher, *Myiagra rubecula.* **3a** C. MARLOWE Base leaden Earles, that glory in your birth. **b** POPE Leaden slumbers press his drooping eyes. O. MANNING The heat now had a leaden weight so even the flies were stilled. **c** *Opera Now* Some of the chorus singing . . is ill-defined and leaden.

leadenly *adv.* L19. **leadenness** /-n-n-/ *n.* E17.

leaden /ˈlɛd(ə)n/ *v. rare.* M16. [f. LEAD *n.*[1] + -EN[5] or f. LEADEN *a.*] †**1** *v.t.* Fasten with molten lead. Only in M16. **2** *v.i.* Press down like lead. Only as *leadening* ppl a. M19. **3** *v.t.* Make leaden or dull. L19.

Leadenhall Street /ˈlɛd(ə)nhɔːl striːt/ *n. phr.* E19. [A street in the City of London, which from 1648 to 1861 contained the headquarters of the East India Company.] *Hist.* The East India Company.

leader /ˈliːdə/ *n.* ME. [f. LEAD *v.*[1] + -ER[1].] **I** A person or an animal. **1** A person who conducts others, precedes others as a guide, leads a person by the hand or an animal by a cord, etc. ME. †**b** The driver of a vehicle. Latterly *dial.*, a carter. ME–L19. **2** A person who leads an armed body. ME. **3** A person who guides others in action or opinion; a person who takes the lead in a business, enterprise, or movement. Freq. *spec.*, the official head or chief spokesman of a nation, a political party, a deliberative body, etc. Formerly also, a chieftain, a ruler. LME. **b** A barrister whose status (in England, that of a King's or Queen's Counsel) entitles him to lead a case. Also, the senior counsel of a circuit. M19. **c** The foremost member of a profession; more widely, a person of eminent position and influence. M19. **d** *spec.* (Usu. **L-**.) [tr. G *Führer*, It. *Duce*, Sp. *Caudillo.*] The head of an authoritarian State. E20. **4** *Mus.* A person who leads a choir or band of dancers, musicians, or singers; *spec.* the first violin in an orchestra. Also (*US*), a conductor. M16. **5a** The first person in a file; any of the front people in a moving body. In *Surveying*, the person at the forward end of the chain. E17. **b** Any of the front horses, cattle, or dogs in a team; the front horse in a tandem. L17. **c** The player, team, etc., that has the lead in a race, match, etc. L20. **6a** *Cards.* The first player in a round. Also, a person who leads from a particular suit. L17. **b** *Curling.* The first player. L18. **7** *Methodism.* In full *class-leader.* The presiding member of a class. M18.

1 DRYDEN Ample Plains, Where oft the Flocks without a Leader stray. *follow-my-leader*: see FOLLOW *v.* **3** *Daily Telegraph* Mr. Brezhnev, the Soviet Communist party leader. M. ANGELOU Martin King had been a hero and a leader to me. **Leader of the House** (*a*) (in the House of Commons) an MP chosen from the party in office to plan the Government's legislative programme and arrange the business of the House; (*b*) (in the House of Lords) the peer who acts as spokesman for the Government. **Leader of the Opposition** the MP chosen to lead the main opposition party in the House of Commons.

II A thing. **8** A thing which leads; *colloq.* a remark or question intended to lead conversation, a feeler. ME. **b** *Comm.* An article that attracts buyers; *esp.* = *loss-leader* s.v. LOSS *n.* M19. **c** A share that is leading the movement of prices on a stock exchange. M20. **9** *Bot.* The growing tip of the main stem or of a principal branch of a tree or shrub. Also, a bine. L16. **10** *Mining.* A small and insignificant vein, which leads to or indicates the proximity of a larger and better one. M17. **11** A tendon. E18. **12a** *Engin.* The one of a set of wheels connected directly to the source of power. E19. **b** In *pl.* = *leading wheels* s.v. LEADING *a.* L19. **c** *Naut.* = *leading-block* s.v. LEADING *n.*[1] L19. **13** *Typogr.* Each of a series of dots or dashes to guide the eye in lists etc. Usu. in *pl.* E19. **14a** A main agricultural drain. M19. **b** A tributary. M19. **15** *Journalism.* = *leading article* (a) s.v. LEADING *a.* M19. **16** A quick-match enclosed in a paper tube for the purpose of conveying fire rapidly to an explosive. M19. **17** *Fishing.* A length of material connecting the end of a fishing-line to a hook or fly. M19. **b** A net so placed as to intercept fish and lead them into a pound, weir, trap-net, etc. L19. **18** A pipe to conduct water. *Sc.* & *US.* M19. **19** A short length of blank or uncoated film or recording tape attached at the beginning or end of a reel for purposes of threading or identification. E20. **20** *Meteorol.* In full *leader stroke.* A preliminary stroke of lightning that ionizes the path taken by the much brighter return stroke that follows. M20.

15 *Wales* The Welsh weeklies have often masterly leaders on politics and literature.

Comb.: **leader board** a scoreboard, esp. at a golf course, on which the names etc. of the leading competitors are displayed; *leader stroke*: see sense 20 above; **leader tape** (a length of) uncoated tape intended for use as a leader on a reel of magnetic tape.

leadered *ppl a.* made the subject of a leading article L19. **leaderene** *n.* (*joc.*) [with female ending after forenames like *Marlene*] a female leader, esp. of an autocratic character (orig. as a nickname given to Margaret Thatcher (b. 1925) when leader of the Conservative Opposition in Britain, 1975–9) L20. **leaderess** *n.* (now *rare*) a female leader L16. **leadeˈrette** *n.* a short editorial paragraph printed after the principal leader(s) in a newspaper L19. **leaderless** *a.* L19. **leaderly** *a.* (*rare*) having the qualities of a leader E20. **leadership** *n.* (*a*) the office or position of leader, esp. of a political party; (*b*) the action of leading or influencing; ability to lead or influence; (*c*) the leaders of a group collectively: E19.

leadhillite /ˈlɛdhɪlʌɪt, lɛdˈhɪlʌɪt/ *n.* M19. [f. *Leadhills*, Scotland + -ITE[1].] *Min.* A monoclinic basic sulphate and carbonate of lead occurring as whitish pearly crystals.

lead-in /ˈliːdɪn/ *n.* E20. [f. LEAD *v.*[1] + IN *adv.*] **1** In full *lead-in wire*: **a** A wire that leads in from outside, *esp.* one connecting an outdoor aerial with an indoor receiver or transmitter. E20. **b** A wire in an electric lamp that carries the current between the cap and the filament or electrode. E20. **2** An introduction, an opening. E20.

leading /ˈliːdɪŋ/ *n.*[1] ME. [f. LEAD *v.*[1] + -ING[1].] **1** The action of LEAD *v.*[1] ME. **2** A small or lateral vein in a lead-mine. Cf. LEADER 10. M17. **3** A directing influence or guidance; *spec.* (esp. in the Society of Friends) a spiritual indication of the proper course of action in any case. E19.

Comb.: **leading-block** *Naut.* a single block used to bring the hauling part of a rope or the fall of a tackle into a more convenient direction; **leading-rein**: to lead a horse or other animal; **leading-staff**: to lead a bull by means of a ring through its nose; **leading-string** (*a*) in *pl.*, strings for guiding and supporting children when learning to walk (*be in leading-strings* (fig.), be in a state of helpless dependence); (*b*) a cord for leading an animal.

leading /ˈlɛdɪŋ/ *n.*[2] LME. [f. LEAD *v.*[2] + -ING[1].] **1** The action of covering, framing, or mending something with lead. LME. **2** Leadwork; *spec.* the calms of a window collectively. E19. **3** *Typogr.* The placing of leads between lines of type; the result of such separation of lines; *loosely* the spacing of lines. M19. **4** Lead deposit on a surface; *esp.* fouling in a gun from lead bullets. L19.

leading /ˈliːdɪŋ/ *a.* L16. [f. LEAD *v.*[1] + -ING[2].] **1** That goes first or is in front. L16. **2** That guides, directs, or leads (*to* something). E17. **3** That takes the lead; chief, principal, prominent. E17.

3 E. KUZWAYO He . . was honoured . . to speak to a leading member of the Soweto community. *Financial Times* Barclays Bank, Britain's leading issuer of Visa credit cards.

Special collocations & *comb.*: **leading aircraftman**: holding the rank next above aircraftman. **leading article** (*a*) an article in a newspaper appearing as the expression of editorial opinion; (*b*) a principal article of trade. *leading case*: see CASE *n.*[1] **leading counsel** a King's or Queen's Counsel; the senior of two or more barristers appearing for the same party. **leading dog** *Austral.* & *NZ*: trained to run ahead of a flock of sheep to control its speed. **leading edge** (*a*) the forward edge of a moving body, esp. an aircraft wing or propeller blade; (*b*) *Electronics* the part of a pulse in which the amplitude increases; (*c*) *fig.* the forefront or vanguard, esp. of technological development (freq. *attrib.*). **leading-in wire** = LEAD-IN 1. **leading lady** the actress or film star who plays the principal female part in a play or film. **leading light** (*a*) *Naut.* a leading mark illuminated at night; (*b*) *fig.* a person of importance and influence in a specified sphere. **leading man** the actor or film star who plays the principal male part in a play or film. **leading mark**

Naut. any of a set of conspicuous objects on land which a pilot has to keep visually in line in order to bring a vessel safely in and out of harbour. **leading note** *Mus.* the seventh note of the diatonic scale (leading upwards to the tonic). **leading question** (*a*) (esp. *Law*) a question put in such a way as to suggest the answer required; (*b*) (in weakened use) an awkward or pointed question; an important point. **leading rating**, (*Hist.*) **seaman** a seaman in the Royal Navy holding the rank next below petty officer. **leading shoot** *Bot.* = LEADER 9. **leading tone** *Mus.* (*US*) = *leading note* above. **leading wheels** the front pair of wheels in a locomotive, placed before the driving-wheels. **leading wind** *Naut.* a fair wind, *esp.* one blowing abaft the beam.

leadingly *adv.* (*rare*) M19.

†leadish *a.* LME–L18. [f. LEAD *n.*[1] + -ISH[1].] Somewhat like lead.

leadless /ˈlɛdlɪs/ *a.* E19. [f. LEAD *n.*[1] + -LESS.] Containing or using no lead, devoid of lead.

lead-off /ˈliːdɒf/ *n.* L19. [f. *lead off* s.v. LEAD *v.*[1]] A commencement; a thing which leads off, the first of a series.

lead-out /ˈliːdaʊt/ *n.* & *a.* E20. [f. LEAD *v.*[1] + OUT *adv.*] A *n.* An act of leading something or someone out. E20. B *attrib.* or as *adj. Electronics.* Designating or pertaining to a conductor by which current may enter or leave an electronic device. M20.

leadsman /ˈlɛdzmən/ *n.* Pl. **-men**. L18. [f. LEAD *n.*[1] + -'S[1] + MAN *n.*] The sailor who casts the lead in taking soundings.

lead-up /ˈliːdʌp/ *n.* M20. [f. *lead up* s.v. LEAD *v.*[1]] A thing which leads up to something else.

leadwork /ˈlɛdwəːk/ *n.*[1] M17. [f. LEAD *n.*[1] + WORK *n.*] 1 Plumber's or glazier's work. M17. 2 In *pl.* (freq. treated as *sing.*). An establishment for smelting lead-ore. E18.

leadwork /ˈliːdwəːk/ *n.*[2] E20. [f. unkn. 1st elem. + WORK *n.*] *sing.* & in *pl.* Fancy stitches used as an ornamental filling in lace-making.

leady /ˈlɛdi/ *a.* LME. [f. LEAD *n.*[1] + -Y[1].] Resembling lead, esp. in colour.

leaf /liːf/ *n.*[1] Pl. **leaves** /liːvz/. [OE *lēaf*, corresp. to OFris. *lāf*, OS *lōf* (Du. *loof*), OHG *loup* (G *Laub*), ON *lauf*, Goth. *laufs*, f. Gmc.] I The organ of a plant etc. 1 Any of the relatively broad flat usu. green outgrowths of a vascular plant, produced laterally from a stem or branch or springing from the base of the stem, which function as the principal organ in photosynthesis (in their fullest form consisting of an expanded part, attached to the stem by a stalk); *pop.* the expanded part only. OE. 2 The leaves of a tree or plant collectively; foliage. OE. †b [Cf. Fr. *vin de deux feuilles*.] In the description of wine: a season, a year. L16–E18. 3 *pop.* A petal, esp. of a rose. LME. 4 A representation of a leaf; (esp. *Archit.*) an ornament in the form of a leaf. LME. 5 *spec.* a The dried leaves of the tobacco plant, or of other plants used for smoking. E17. b The green leaves of the tea plant. L19.

1 A. A. MILNE I was shaking like an aspen leaf. V. S. NAIPAUL The stacked-up, wet beech leaves slowly turning to compost. *five-leaf*: see FIVE *a.* FOLIAGE *leaf*. *juvenile leaf*: see JUVENILE *a.* *rough leaf*: see ROUGH *a.* *seed-leaf*: see SEED *n.* *true leaf*: see TRUE *a.* etc. *walking leaf*: see WALKING *ppl a.* 2 F. BROOKE The year began in March with the coming of the leaf. *fig.*: SHAKES. *Macb.* I have lived long enough. My way of life Is fall'n into the sear, the yellow leaf. *fall of the leaf*: see FALL *n.*[2] **in (full) leaf** having (all) its leaves expanded. *yellow leaf*: see YELLOW *a.* 5a **in the leaf** (of tobacco) unstemmed and uncut. *wrapper leaf*: see WRAPPER *n.* 1b.

II An object resembling a leaf. 6 Each of the subdivisions of a folded sheet of paper, parchment, etc., after trimming; *esp.* any of a number of such subdivisions (each containing one page on each side of the fold) which compose a book or manuscript, a folio; a single sheet of paper, esp. stationery. Also, the matter printed or written on a leaf. OE. 7 A layer of fat inside an animal; *esp.* that surrounding the kidneys of a pig. LME. 8 A very thin sheet of metal (esp. gold or silver) or other material produced by beating out or splitting; a lamina of horn, marble, wood, etc. Also, a thin piece of soap or other detergent (larger than a flake). LME. b Each of the metal strips of a leaf spring. E20. c Each of the solid layers of a cavity wall. M20. 9 A hinged part or any of a series of parts connected at one side or end by a hinge. Now usu. *spec.*, (*a*) each of two or more parts of a door, gate, or shutter turning on hinges; (*b*) a hinged flap at the side of a table, able to be raised when required for use; any movable addition to the top of a table; (*c*) the part of a drawbridge or bascule bridge which is raised on a hinge; (*d*) a hinged sight on the barrel of a rifle. LME. 10 Each of the teeth of a pinion. E18. 11 The brim of a hat. Chiefly *Anglo-Ir.* M18. 12 *Weaving.* A set of heddles stretched between the same two shafts. M19. 13 *Zool.* An organ or part resembling a leaf, as the external ear of a mammal or the nasal appendage of a leaf-nosed bat. M19. 14 *Math.* & *Computing.* = *leaf node* below. M20.

6 M. LEITCH He put the folded slip between the leaves of the book. *loose-leaf*: see LOOSE *a.* **take a leaf out of a person's book** base one's conduct on what a person does. **turn over a new leaf** adopt a different (now always a better) line of conduct. 8 *gold leaf*: see GOLD *n.*[1] & *a.* *silver leaf*: see SILVER *n.* & *a.* 9 V. SACKVILLE-WEST The table had been extended by the addition of several leaves. *Daily Telegraph* It takes two footmen to open a front door, one for each leaf. 12 **eight-** etc. **leaf twill**: woven on eight etc. leaves of heddles.

Comb.: **leaf-arrowhead** *Archaeol.* an arrowhead shaped like a leaf, usu. of the neolithic period and made of flint; **leaf-bed** a layer of leaves sometimes found in subsoil; **leaf beet** any of several varieties of beet (chard, seakale beet, spinach beet) of which the midribs or leaves are cooked as a vegetable; **leaf-beetle** any beetle of the very varied family Chrysomelidae, comprising usu. robust compact beetles with smooth elytra in bright or metallic colours; **leafbird** any bird of the southern Asian family Irenidae; *esp.* a bright green bird of the genus *Chloropsis*; **leaf blight** any of several plant diseases causing the death of foliage; **leaf blister** (*a*) a disease of certain fruit trees caused by a parasitic mite; (*b*) a disease of pear trees caused by the fungus *Taphrina bullata*, in which the leaves develop brown blisters; **leaf blotch** any of several plant diseases indicated by discoloured patches on foliage; *esp.* (*US*) = *black spot* (a) s.v. BLACK *a.*; **leaf-brown** *a.* & *n.* (having) the colour of dead leaves; **leaf-bud** a bud from which leaves are produced; **leaf-butterfly** a butterfly which resembles a leaf, e.g. one of the genus *Kallima*; **leaf cast** any of several fungal diseases causing conifers to shed their needles, e.g. *larch leaf cast*, due to *Meria laricis*, and *pine leaf cast*, due to *Lophodermium pinastri*; **leaf curl** any of several plant diseases characterized by curling leaves, *esp.* (more fully *peach leaf curl*) a disease of peach, almond, and nectarine trees caused by the fungus *Taphrina deformans*; **leaf-cutter** (*a*) (in full *leaf-cutter bee*) any of various solitary bees of the family Megachilidae which cut fragments from leaves to line their nests; (*b*) (in full *leaf-cutter ant*) any of various chiefly tropical American ants of the genus *Atta* which use pieces cut from leaves to cultivate fungus for food; **leaf-cutting** a leaf used as a cutting in the propagation of certain plants, e.g. begonias; **leaf-cutting ant, bee** = *leaf-cutter* (b), (a) above; **leaf-fall** the shedding of leaves by a plant; **leaf-fat** the fat occurring in layers round a pig's kidneys; **leaf-flea** a plant-louse; **leaf-folder** = *leaf-roller* below; **leaf-frog** any American tree frog of the genus *Phyllomedusa* or related genera; **leaf-gap** *Bot.* an area of parenchyma in the stem immediately above the point at which a leaf-trace diverges from it; **leaf gelatin**: manufactured in sheet form for cooking purposes; **leaf-gold** = *gold leaf* s.v. GOLD *n.*[1] & *a.* **leaf-green** *a.* & *n.* (having) the colour of green leaves; **leafhopper** any leaping homopteran insect of the superfamily Cicadelloidea, whose members suck the sap of plants and often spread disease; **leaf insect** any of various insects of the family Phyllidae (order Phasmida) which closely resemble leaves in shape and colour; **leaf-lard**: made from the leaf-fat of a pig; **leaf-louse** a plant-louse, an aphid; **leaf-miner** any insect (esp. a fly of the family Agromyzidae) whose larvae eat their way between the cuticles of leaves; **leaf-monkey** any of various monkeys of S. or SE Asia of the subfamily Colobinae (family Cercopithecidae); a colobine; **leaf-mould** (*a*) topsoil or compost consisting largely of decayed leaves; (*b*) a disease of tomatoes caused by the fungus *Cladosporium fulvum*; **leaf node** *Math.* & *Computing* a node or vertex in a tree connected to only one other node or vertex; **leaf-nosed** *a.* (esp. of a bat) having a leaflike appendage on the snout; *spec.* designating a bat of the Old World family Hipposideridae, or the New World family Phyllostomatidae; **leaf-opposed** *a.* (of a flower etc.) arising opposite a leaf; **leaf-point** *Archaeol.* a projectile point shaped like a leaf, made of flint or some similar rock, found in various palaeolithic and later cultures; **leaf protein** protein present in leaves, esp. when extracted for use as a possible dietary supplement; **leaf-roll** a virus disease of potatoes marked by upward curling of the leaves; **leaf-roller** any insect (esp. a tortricid moth) whose larvae roll up the leaves of plants which they infest; **leaf scald** (*a*) = *leaf scorch* below; (*b*) a disease of sugar cane caused by the bacterial pathogen *Xanthomonas albilineans*; **leaf-scale** a scale on a plant-stem which develops into a leaf; **leaf-scar** a cicatrix left on the bark by the separation of the leaf-stalk of a fallen leaf; **leaf scorch** (*a*) a plant disease caused by a deficiency of potassium, which makes leaves shrivel and turn brown at the edges; (*b*) any of several fungal diseases producing similar effects; **leaf-shaped** *a.* having the shape of a leaf; *leaf-shaped arrowhead* = *leaf-arrowhead* above; **leaf-sheath** a flattened expansion of the petiole in some plants, which embraces the stem; **leaf shutter** *Photogr.*: composed of a ring of thin plates which swivel to admit light through a central aperture (cf. *iris diaphragm* s.v. IRIS *n.* 4b); **leaf-soil** = *leaf-mould* (a) above; **leaf-spine**: formed from a modified leaf; **leaf-spot** any of numerous fungal and bacterial plant diseases which cause leaves to develop discoloured spots; **leaf spring**: consisting of a number of strips of metal curved slightly upwards and clamped together one above the other; **leaf-stalk** a petiole; **leaf-tendril**: formed from a modified leaf or part of a leaf; **leaf-tobacco** raw tobacco with the stalks still on it; **leaf-trace** *Bot.* a vascular bundle extending from the stele to the base of a leaf; **leaf warbler** any small green or yellow Old World woodland warbler of the genus *Phylloscopus*.

leaflike *a.* resembling (that of) a leaf E19.

leaf /liːf/ *n.*[2] *Mil. slang.* M19. [Var. of LEAVE *n.*[1]] Leave of absence; furlough.

leaf /liːf/ *v.* E17. [f. LEAF *n.*[1]] 1 *v.i.* Bear leaves or foliage, come into leaf. Also (*N. Amer.*) foll. by *out.* E17. 2 a *v.t.* Turn the leaves of (a book or papers), esp. in a casual manner. Also foll. by *over.* Now *US.* M17. b *v.i.* Turn the leaves of a book or papers, esp. in a casual manner. Usu. foll. by *through.* E20. 3 *v.t.* Cover or shade with foliage. *rare.* M19. 4 *v.t.* Give a number in sequence to (a leaf of a book). L19.

2b D. LESSING One tattered old magazine, the sort of thing you leaf through at the dentist.

leafage /ˈliːfɪdʒ/ *n.* L16. [f. LEAF *n.*[1] + -AGE.] 1 Leaves collectively; foliage. L16. 2 The representation of leaves or foliage, esp. as ornamentation. E18.

leafed /liːft/ *a.* M16. [f. LEAF *n.*[1] + -ED[2]: cf. LEAVED *a.*] 1 Having leaves or foliage; bearing (a specified kind of) foliage. Chiefly after a descriptive or numeral adj. M16. †2 Of a door, book, etc.: having (a specified number of) leaves. L16–E17. 3 Of a hat: (broad-)brimmed. M19.

leafery /ˈliːf(ə)ri/ *n.* M19. [f. LEAF *n.*[1] + -ERY.] Leafage, foliage.

leafit /ˈliːfɪt/ *n.* Now *rare.* L18. [f. LEAF *n.*[1] + *-it*, perh. = -ET[1].] = LEAFLET *n.* 1.

leafless /ˈliːflɪs/ *a.* Also (earlier) **†leaveless**. L15. [f. LEAF *n.*[1] + -LESS.] Without a leaf; destitute of leaves or foliage.

leafless tree *slang* the gallows.

leaflessness *n.* E19.

leaflet /ˈliːflɪt/ *n.* & *v.* L18. [f. LEAF *n.*[1] + -LET.] A *n.* 1 †a *Bot.* A sepal. L18–M19. b *Bot.* Each of the divisions of a compound leaf. E19. c *pop.* A young leaf. Also (*rare*), a petal. M19. 2 *Anat.* & *Zool.* An organ or part resembling a thin leaf or sheet; *spec.* the thin flap of a valve in the heart or a blood-vessel. E19. 3 A small sheet of paper or a sheet folded into two or more leaves but not stitched, containing printed matter (often advertisements), usu. distributed free of charge. M19.

1b A. T. THOMSON The leaves are . . pinnate, with a terminal leaflet a little larger than the rest. 3 *Which?* BAR publish a leaflet on their arbitration scheme.

Comb.: **leaflet raid** a raid in which leaflets are dropped from an aircraft.

B *v.i.* & *t.* Distribute printed leaflets to (a community, neighbourhood, etc.). M20.

leafle'teer *n.* (freq. *derog.*) a writer or distributor of leaflets L19.

leafy /ˈliːfi/ *a.* In sense 1 also (earlier, now *poet.*) **leavy** /ˈliːvi/. LME. [f. LEAF *n.*[1] + -Y[1]: cf. LEAVY.] 1 Covered with leaves, having many leaves; (of a place) rich in foliage from the abundance of trees or bushes. Also, made or consisting of leaves. LME. b Of a part of a plant: leaflike, foliaceous. L17. c Producing broad-bladed leaves, as distinct from other kinds of foliage. L19. 2 Of a substance: consisting of thin sheets; laminate. M18.

1 COLERIDGE In the leafy month of June. A. MILLER Brooklyn Heights was like a quiet, leafy village. *Power Farming* The leafy top growth of the plant.

leafiness *n.* E17.

league /liːɡ/ *n.*[1] *arch.* LME. [Either f. late L *leuca, leuga*, late Gk *leugē* (of Gaulish origin), or f. Prov. *lega* = (O)Fr. *lieue.*] A variable measure of distance, usu. estimated at about five kilometres or three miles.

league /liːɡ/ *n.*[2] LME. [Partly f. Fr. *ligue* f. It. *liga*, Latinized form of *lega*, f. *legare* bind f. L *ligare*; partly immed. f. It. *lega.*] 1 A military, political, or commercial compact made between parties for their mutual protection and assistance in matters of common interest; a body of States or people associated in such a compact. LME. b An association of individuals, clubs, or societies for some common political, sporting, or other purpose; *spec.* a group of sports clubs or a class of contestants who compete with one another for a championship. M19. c *transf.* & *fig.* A group showing a certain level of competence or ability. M20. 2 *gen.* A covenant, a compact, an alliance. Now *rare.* E16. 3 *Basket-making.* A single continuous cane used as a combined bottom stick and upright. E20.

1 R. WATSON Exciting the princes of the league of Munster to take the field against the Spaniards. b *Delian League, Gaelic League, Hanseatic League, Ivy League*, etc. *baseball league, cricket league, football league, rugby league*, etc. c M. AMIS She was fairly formidable, a bit out of my league really. J. HENNESSY They were .. moving into a new league, where they could command .. what music they wanted. *Bulletin (Sydney)* If East-West wants to play in the big league it must shape up to heavy competition.

Phrases: *big league*: see BIG *a.* **Holy League** any of several leagues in European history, as that formed by Pope Julius II against the French in 1511. **in league with** having a compact with, allied or conspiring with. *Land League*: see LAND *n.*[1] **League of Nations** an association of States, dominions, and colonies established by the treaty of peace of 1919 to promote international cooperation, peace, and security, now replaced by the United Nations. *Little League*: see LITTLE *a. major league*: see MAJOR *a. minor league*: see MINOR *a.* & *n. Muslim League*: see MUSLIM *a. Primrose League*: see PRIMROSE *n. Solemn League and Covenant*: see COVENANT *n.* 6. **the League** *Hist.* (*a*) a league formed in 1576 under the direction of the Guises, to prevent the accession of Henry IV to the French throne; (*b*) the League of Nations.

Comb.: **league football** football played in leagues, *spec.* (*Austral.*) rugby league or Australian Rules football; **league table** a list of the members of a competitive league in ranking order; any list of ranking order; *transf.* a systematic comparison of performance in any field of competitive activity.

leaguite *n.* = LEAGUER *n.*[2] M19.

league /liːɡ/ *v.t.* & *i.* L16. [f. LEAGUE *n.*[2] Cf. Fr. *liguer.*] Form (into) or join a league (*with*); confederate.

W. DRUMMOND To league a people is to make them know their strength of power. SHELLEY Where kings first leagued against the rights of men. H. ADAMS Count 'Loweis' .. leagued with the Counts of Flanders, .. and Toulouse, against Philip Augustus.

leaguer /ˈliːɡə/ *n.*[1] L16. [Du. *leger* camp, corresp. to OE *leger* LAIR *n.*[1] Cf. LAAGER *n.*] 1 A military camp, *esp.* one engaged in a siege; a besieging force. L16. 2 A military siege. L16.

1 R. CAPELL Here was the German leaguer, whither .. the Germans withdrew behind wire. 2 J. L. MOTLEY The Harlem siege, and .. the more prosperous leaguer of Alkmaar.

Phrases: **in leaguer** in camp, engaged in a siege. **lie leaguer** (now *rare*) be resident as an ambassador, agent, etc.

Comb.: **leaguer-lady, leaguer-lass** *euphem.* a woman attached to a military camp, providing various (esp. sexual) services.

leaguer /ˈliːɡə/ *n.*[2] L16. [f. LEAGUE *n.*[2] + -ER[1].] A member of a league.

M. L. DARLING In this year's election he stood as a Unionist, and .. was defeated by a Leaguer. *Cape Times* There are few American major leaguers earning less than $30 000 a year.

¶ See also TEXAS *leaguer.*

leaguer /ˈliːɡə/ *n.*[3] *obs.* exc. *S. Afr.* L17. [Perh. f. Du. *ligger* tun, f. *liggen* LIE *v.*[1] Cf. G *Leger* freshwater cask(s) on board ship.] A measure of liquid, as water, wine, oil, etc.; a cask of corresponding size.

Naval Chronicle The largest casks are called leaguers. *Cape Times* Two lorries .. carrying a 5-leaguer tank of wine (some 800 gallons).

leaguer /ˈliːɡə/ *v.* L16. [f. LEAGUER *n.*[1]] 1 *v.i.* & *refl.* Lodge, lie; *spec.* encamp, set one's leaguer. Now *rare.* L16. 2 *v.t.* Besiege, beleaguer. Chiefly as *leaguered, leaguering* ppl adjs. E18.

1 B. MONTGOMERY We were leaguering as an Army beyond that once-dreaded position. 2 COLERIDGE That the voice of truth .. though leagured round By envy .. Be heard. W. SARGENT His .. defence of Detroit against Pontiac and his leaguering hordes.

leak /liːk/ *n.* L15. [Prob. of LG or Du. origin, w. LEAK *v., a.*, ult. f. Gmc var. of base of LACK *n.*[1]: the n. is repr. by MDu. *lek*, G dial. *Lech* a crack, ON *leki.*] 1 a A hole, crack, etc. (orig. in a ship) through which a liquid, gas, powder, etc., enters or escapes. L15. b *transf.* & *fig.* A breach or defect which allows the gradual loss of valuable materials or qualities. L16. c *Physics.* A path or component of relatively high resistance through which a small (freq. controlled) flow of current, gas, etc., may occur. L19. d An improper or deliberate disclosure of (secret or confidential) information. E20. 2 a The action or an act of leaking; an escape of fluid, gas, radiation, flux, etc., through a hole or crack, or by permeation of an intended barrier; leakage of electric charge or current. E19. b An act of urinating. Cf. LEAK *v.* 2b. *slang.* M20.

1a SIR W. SCOTT Rent was the sail, and strain'd the mast, And many a leak was gaping fast. J. WILCOX The workmen will be here to fix a leak in the roof. *Chemical Engineering* The instrument is to test for leaks in sealed gas-filled objects. b P. G. HAMERTON An able finance minister .. has found means of closing a great leak in the treasury. d D. O. SELZNICK There have been leaks about previous discussions. *Encounter* What we have .. is security punctuated by leaks. 2a *Academy* In hydrogen the leak was slowest ... The rate of leak in the halogens is .. very rapid. *Times* Burst pipes .. caused a minor radiation leak at one of the country's .. nuclear power stations. **b take a leak** urinate.

†**leak** *a.* OE–L18. [OE (*h*)*lec*, later f. as LEAK *n.*: the adj. is repr. by MDu. *lek*, G dial. *lech*, ON *lekr.*] = LEAKY.

leak /liːk/ *v.* LME. [f. as LEAK *n.*; the vb is repr. by MDu. *lēken*, OHG *lēchen*, MHG, G dial. *lechen* crack, become leaky, ON *leka.*] 1 *v.i.* Pass (*out, away, forth*) by a leak or leakage. LME. 2 *v.i.* & *t.* Allow (fluid etc.) to pass in or out through a leak. E16. b *v.i.* Urinate. *slang.* L16. †3 *v.t.* In *pass.* Have sprung a leak; be emptied (*out*) by leakage. E17–M18. 4 *v.t. Brewing.* Cause (liquor) to run *over, on, off*, gradually. *obs.* exc. *dial.* L17. 5 a *v.i.* Of a secret etc.: transpire, become known. Also foll. by *out.* L18. b *v.i.* & *t.* Disclose or allow the disclosure of (secret or confidential information). M19.

1 J. WOODWARD A Crack, through which a small quantity of the Liquor leak'd forth. E. POLLARD A particle can 'leak' through any but an infinitely thick wall. 2 JOHN ROSS The starboard boiler began to leak. M. PIERCY The attic roof leaks .. into a pail. 5a *Time* They claimed the Campbell allegation had somehow leaked to the Atlanta newspaper. W. TREVOR We could get into terrible trouble .. if any of this leaked out. b J. COLVILLE An alarming communiqué to the effect that the French had leaked about the project. *Herald (Melbourne)* Daniel Ellsberg .. was charged with leaking the secret Pentagon papers.

leaker *n.* M20.

leakage /ˈliːkɪdʒ/ *n.* L15. [f. LEAK *v.* + -AGE.] 1 The action of leaking; admission or escape of fluid etc. through a leak; loss of fluid etc. by leaking. L15. 2 Allowance made for waste of fluid etc. by leakage. L16. 3 a *transf.* & *fig.* Diminution resulting from gradual waste or escape; unexplained continuous disappearance of something. M17. b *Physics.* The passage of radiation, magnetic flux, etc., across a boundary, or through an intended barrier; a gradual escape of electric charge or current. M19. c The improper or deliberate disclosure of (secret or confidential) information. L19. 4 Fluid etc. which leaks. M17.

1 G. ANSON Jars .. are liable to no leekage, unless they are broken. *Science* The leakage of helium through Pyrex glass at elevated temperatures has been noted. 2 S. SMILES The lightermen claimed as their right the perquisites of 'wastage' and 'leakage'. 3a C. WILSON The problem with neurotics .. is a kind of *leakage* of energy. b *Consumers Digest* One of the best companies hasn't yet built Appliance Leakage Current Interrupters. *Which?* We test for microwave leakage. 4 W. IRVING The drippings of the kitchen and the leakage of the tap-room.

leakance /ˈliːk(ə)ns/ *n.* L19. [f. LEAK *v.* + -ANCE, as contr. of *leakage conductance.*] *Electr.* Conductance attributable to leakage or imperfect insulation.

leaky /ˈliːki/ *a.* E17. [f. LEAK *n.* + -Y[1].] 1 a Having a leak or leaks; allowing fluid etc. to pass through a hole or fissure. E17. b *fig.* (Of a person) unable to keep a secret; (of memory) not retentive. L17. c Passing urine frequently or in large quantities; incontinent. E18. d Of a person: inclined to weep, lachrymose. E20. 2 *Electr.* Retaining electric charge only with gradual loss; connected to or having a high resistance that acts as a leak. E20. 3 *Genetics.* Designating a mutant gene that has some residual activity of the wild type; designating a protein with reduced activity compared with that produced by the wild type. Cf. HYPOMORPHIC. M20.

1a *US News & World Report* Hoang Nhu Tran and his Family fled Vietnam on a leaky boat. b W. SOMERVILLE But be thou, my Muse! No leaky Blab. M. WARNOCK Other people have memories 'like a sieve', .. notoriously leaky.

Comb.: **leaky-grid detection** *Electr.*: in which the signal is applied to the grid of a valve through a series capacitor and a resistor connected as a grid leak or in parallel with the capacitor.

leakiness *n.* E17.

leal /liːl/ *a.* & *adv.* Now *Sc.* & *north.* or *literary.* ME. [AN *leal*, OFr. *leel*: see LOYAL.] A *adj.* 1 Loyal, faithful, honest. ME. 2 True, genuine; real, actual; exact, accurate. ME. 3 Lawful; just, fair. LME.

1 R. GRAVES Now you vow to be leal and true. 2 J. LOUTHIAN The said Witnesses to bear leal and soothfast Witnessing.

Comb.: **leal-hearted** *a.* loyal, faithful, honest.

B *adv.* 1 Loyally, faithfully. ME. 2 Truly, exactly, accurately; perfectly, thoroughly. LME.

leally *adv.* loyally, faithfully, truly ME. **lealty** *n.* (*arch.*) faithfulness, loyalty M19.

lea-land /ˈliːland/ *n.* Now *dial.* Also **lay-** /ˈleɪ-/. ME. [f. LEA *a.* + LAND *n.*[1]] Fallow land; land laid down to grass.

leam /liːm/ *n.* & *v.* Now *Sc.* & *north.* [OE *lēoma* = OS *liom*, ON *ljómi*, f. Gmc n. whence also Goth. *lauhmuni* lighting, f. Gmc f. IE base also of L *lux, lumen* light.] A *n.* Light, flame; a flash, ray, or gleam of light; brightness, gleam. OE. B *v.i.* Shine, gleam; light *up.* ME.

†**leamer** *n.* var. of LIMER *n.*[1]

lean /liːn/ *n.*[1] LME. [f. the vb.] 1 A thing to lean or rest on; a support. Long *obs.* exc. *Sc.* LME. 2 The action or condition of leaning; inclination. L18.

lean /liːn/ *n.*[2] LME. [f. the adj.] The lean part of meat; lean meat.

Nursery rhyme: Jack Sprat could eat no fat, his wife could eat no lean.

lean /liːn/ *a.* [OE *hlǣne* f. Gmc, perh. rel. to Lith. *klýnas* scrap, fragment, Latvian *kleins* feeble.] 1 Thin, not plump or fat; not fleshed out. OE. b Of a ship: built on clean tapering lines. M18. 2 *fig.* Meagre, poor in quality; (of diet) not nourishing; (of employment) unremunerative. ME. 3 *techn.* Of various materials, as soil, mortar, fuel, etc.: low in essential or valuable elements or qualities. ME. 4 Scantily provided. Formerly also, short *of.*

ME. 5 Of meat: containing little or no fat. LME. 6 *Typogr.* Of (a stroke in) a letter: thin, slender. Now *rare.* L17. 7 Of industry, a company, etc.: economical, efficient. L20.

1 R. GRAVES The lean captain of a trading-vessel envies the big-paunched wine-shop proprietor. 2 E. BLUNDEN The day's meals . . were still substantial despite the lean supplies. *Times* He went through a lean patch . . but has since come back strongly. 5 M. PYKE Meat is made of . . the fat, and the lean or protein part. 7 *Observer* Industry was now leaner and fitter and in a much better position to compete.

Special collocations & comb.: **lean-burn** *a.* designating (the technology associated with) an internal-combustion engine designed to run on a lean mixture and so reduce pollution. **lean mixture** vaporized fuel containing a high proportion of air. **lean times, years**, etc., times, years, etc., of scarcity.

leanish *a.* M17. **leanly** *adv.* L16. **leanness** /-n-n-/ *n.* OE.

lean /liːn/ *v.* Pa. t. & pple **leaned** /liːnd/, **leant** /lɛnt/. [OE *hleonian, hlinian*, corresp. to OFris. *lena*, OS *hlinon* (Du. *leunen*), OHG *(h)linēn* (G *lehnen*), f. Gmc base rel. to that of Gk *klimax* ladder, CLIMAX, L *clivus* declivity, Skt *çri* lean, with *-n-* formative as in Gk *klinein* to lean, slope, L *inclinare* INCLINE *v.*] 1 *v.*†*i.* & *refl.* Recline, lie (*down*), rest. *obs.* exc. *Sc.* OE. 2 *v.i.* a Bend or incline in a particular direction. (Foll. by *back, over, towards*, etc.) OE. b Move or be situated obliquely; swerve (*aside*). LME. 3a *v.i.* Incline against an object for support; support oneself or be supported *on*, (*up*) *against* something. ME. b Press *upon*; lay emphasis *upon*. M18. 4 *v.i. fig.* Rely or depend *on*. ME. 5 *v.t.* a Cause to lean or rest, prop (*against, on*, etc.). ME. b Cause to bend or incline. LME. 6 *v.i.* Incline or tend *towards* or *to* some quality or condition. Also, have a tendency favourable *to*. LME. 7 *v.i.* a Incline or tend in thought, affection, or conduct; be disposed *to, towards*. M16. †b Defer *to* an opinion. M16–E17.

2a H. JACOBSON I leaned towards them so as not to miss a single word. b R. L. STEVENSON The gigs had leaned to their right. 3a G. GREENE She leant against the door and tried to steady herself. 4 P. CASEMENT Trainees . . often lean too heavily upon the advice or comments of a supervisor. 5a P. THEROUX Haddy rolled the barrel . . into the junkpile and leaned a log against it. b E. B. BROWNING I would lean my spirit o'er you. 6 POPE There's not a blessing Individuals find, But some way leans and hearkens to the Kind. 7a G. KEILLOR I lean toward this theory. b SHAKES. *Cymb.* You lean'd unto his sentence with what patience Your wisdom may inform you.

Phrases & comb.: **lean against** (chiefly *Law*) be unfavourable to, not countenance. **lean on** *colloq.* put pressure on (a person) in order to force him or her to do something. **lean-over** an inclination down or forward; something over which one can lean. *lean over backward(s)*: see BACKWARD *adv.* I. **lean to one side** *fig.* (*Polit.*) (of a political party, diplomatic policy, etc.) be biased towards a particular, esp. socialist, country, party, etc. **lean upon** *Mil.* be close up to something serving as a protection.

leaner *n.* M16.

leangle /ˈliːaŋg(ə)l/ *n. Austral.* Also **leeangle, liangle**, & other vars. M19. [Aborig.] A wooden club bent at the striking end.

leaning /ˈliːnɪŋ/ *n.* OE. [f. LEAN *v.* + -ING[1].] 1 The action of LEAN *v.* OE. 2 *fig.* An inclination, a bias; a tendency. L16.

2 W. TREVOR He had no political leanings himself, neither Republican nor imperialist.

Comb.: **leaning-note** *Mus.* = APPOGGIATURA; **leaning-stock** a support (*lit.* & *fig.*); *spec.* the ledge on which an organ-pipe rests.

leant *v.* pa. t. & pple: see LEAN *v.*

lean-to /ˈliːntuː/ *n.* & *a.* LME. [f. LEAN *v.* + TO *adv.*] A *n.* Pl. **-tos**. 1 A building whose roof leans against another building or against a wall; a penthouse. LME. 2 *transf.* A temporary shelter, supported or free-standing, of brushwood, canvas, etc.; a rudimentary tent or hut. Chiefly *Canad.* L19.

1 R. MACAULAY A small . . man crept out of a lean-to which was propped against a ruined wall.

B *attrib.* or as *adj.* Pertaining to or of the nature of a lean-to. Also, placed so as to lean against something. M17.

lean-to building, lean-to porch, lean-to room, lean-to shed, etc.

leap /liːp/ *n.*[1] Also (*Sc.* & *Ir.*) **lep** /lɛp/. [OE *hlȳp* f. Gmc base of LEAP *v.* Cf. OFris. *hlēp*, Du. *loop*, OHG *hlouf* (G *Lauf*), ON *hlaup*. Partly directly f. the vb.] 1 a An act or the action of leaping; a bound, a jump, a spring. OE. b *transf.* & *fig.* An abrupt change or movement (*from, to, up* etc.); a sudden transition. Later *spec.*, a sudden increase or advance (*to, up*, etc.). OE. 2 A thing to be leaped over or from. Also, a place or distance leaped. Freq. in place-names, as *Smuggler's Leap, Lover's Leap*. ME. 3 An act or the action of springing on a female in copulation; an act of copulation. Now *rare.* E17. 4 *Mus.* A passing from one note to another by an interval greater than one degree of the scale; an interval greater than one degree of the scale. Cf. STEP *n.*[1] 4b. L17. 5 *Mining.* A fault or dislocation of strata. M18. 6 The sudden fall of a river to a lower level. M18.

1a P. G. WODEHOUSE She sprang onto the pavement with a gay leap. b N. ARMSTRONG That's one small step for man, one giant leap for mankind. D. PRATER He began to prepare for his leap into the unknown. *Financial Times* The crucial factor was . . the leap in the oil price . . with rises in other . . prices. 6 H. I. JENKINSON The water makes five or six leaps in its descent.

Phrases: **by leaps (and bounds)** by sudden transitions; with startlingly rapid progress or increase. **leap forward** a marked or notable advance (*Great Leap Forward*: see GREAT *a.*). *leap in the dark*: see DARK *n.*[1]

Comb.: **leap day** an intercalary day in the calendar, *esp.* that of a leap year (29 February); **leap second** a second which on particular occasions is inserted into (or omitted from) the atomic scale of reckoning time in order to bring it into correspondence with solar time; **leap year** a year having one intercalary day (now 29 February) more than the common year of 365 days (perh. so called because fixed festivals after February in a leap year fall two days of the week, instead of the usual one day, later than in the preceding year).

leap /liːp/ *n.*[2] *obs.* exc. *dial.* [OE *lēap* = ON *lauper.*] A basket; *spec.* a basket in which to catch or keep fish.

leap /liːp/ *v.* Pa. t. & pple **leaped** /liːpt/, **leapt** /lɛpt/. Also (*Sc.* & *Ir.*) **lep** /lɛp/, pa. t. & pple **lept**. [OE *hlēapan* = OFris. *(h)lāpa*, OS *-hlōpan* (Du. *loopen*), OHG *loufan* (G *laufen* run), ON *hlaupa* (whence LOUP *v.*), Goth. *-hlaupan*, f. Gmc. Cf. WALLOP *v.*] 1 *v.i.* a Rise with both (or all) feet suddenly from a standing-place, alighting in some other position; jump, spring. Freq. foll. by *aside, down, in*, etc. OE. b Spring to one's seat *upon* a horse, *into* the saddle. (Foll. by *up.*) OE. c Of a fish: spring from the water. LME. 2 *v.i.* Spring sportively up and down; jump, esp. with joy, mirth, etc.; dance, skip. OE. 3 *v.i.* Run; rush, throw oneself. Also foll. by *forth, out*, etc. Long *rare.* LOE. 4 *v.i.* Spring suddenly *to* or *upon* one's feet; rise with a bound *from* a sitting or recumbent position. Freq. foll. by *up*. ME. 5 *v.i.* a *transf.* & *fig.* Of a thing: spring, move with a leap or bound; *esp.* fly, by explosive or other force. ME. b Of the heart, (*rare*) the pulse: beat vigorously, bound, throb. E16. c *Mining.* Of a vein of ore: be dislocated. M18. d Of frost: melt or thaw suddenly. *colloq.* M19. 6 *fig.* a *v.i.* Pass abruptly from one condition or position to another. Also foll. by *back, down, up*. ME. b *v.i.* Pass *over* without pausing. L16. c *v.i.* & *t. Mus.* Pass from one note to another (by an interval greater than one degree of the scale). L19. 7 *v.t.* Spring over; pass from one side to the other by leaping (*lit.* & *fig.*); *spec.* (of a bridge) span, extend across. LME. 8 *v.t.* & *i.* Spring on (a female) in copulation; copulate with (a female). Now *rare.* LME. 9 *v.t.* Cause (an animal) to take a leap. L17.

1a M. SCAMMELL They would leap naked into the Volga to swim. *Proverb*: Look before you leap. c J. MCPHEE A salmon . . leaps into the air . . ten pounds of fish jumping . . high into the air. 2 M. PIERCY I leap and twirl and prance. 4 G. VIDAL Burden leapt to his feet. 5a P. ABRAHAMS The high ceiling collapsed . . sending massive tongues of fire leaping at the sky. b H. ROTH David's heart leaped in secret joy. 6a H. KELLER The fire leaped into life. *Private Eye* Sir Michael . . leapt into the Press denouncing the sentences. b A. HAMILTON I can perceive several Things worth noticing, they have neglected or leapt over. 7 *New Yorker* A railroad bridge and two highway bridges leap the Atchafalaya. 8 J. BARTH Confronted with that battery of eager bosoms and delicious behinds, . . the urge to . . leap those fine girls was terrific. 9 W. H. RUSSELL [He] had leaped his horse across a deep nullah.

Phrases: **(be ready to) leap out of one's skin** be delighted, eager, or surprised. **leap at** make a spring at in order to seize; *fig.* exhibit eagerness for. **leap to the eye** be immediately apparent.

leapable *a.* E20.

leaper /ˈliːpə/ *n.* OE. [f. LEAP *v.* + -ER[1].] †1 A runner; a dancer. OE–L16. 2 A person who or animal which leaps or jumps; an animal which uses leaping as a mode of progression. ME.

leap-frog /ˈliːpfrɒg/ *n.* & *a.* L16. [f. LEAP *v.* + FROG *n.*[1]] A *n.* 1 A game in which one player places his or her hands on the bent back or shoulders of another and vaults over him or her with legs apart, typically then becoming the one, or the last of a line, to be leaped over while the (first) bent-over player becomes the leaper. Also, a vault of this kind. L16. 2 *fig.* The taking of turns in moving to the front, the action or process of leap-frogging; *spec.* (*a*) *Mil.* a method of maintaining constant communication with a moving command by keeping one instrument in operation while another moves past it to a position in front; (*b*) competition for higher wages by leap-frogging. E20.

B *attrib.* or as *adj.* Of the nature or style of leap-frog, a leap-frog, or leap-frogging. E17.

Time Sequential or 'leap-frog' bypasses around two blocked sections of the arteries.

leap-frog /ˈliːpfrɒg/ *v.* Infl. **-gg-**. L19. [f. the n.] 1 *v.i.* a Leap or vault as at leap-frog. L19. b *Mil.* Of detachments or units, esp. in an attack: go in advance of each other by turns. E20. c Demand higher wages every time a group of comparable wage-earners has succeeded in pulling level or getting ahead. Chiefly as *leap-frogging* vbl n. & ppl a. M20. 2 *v.t.* Leap or vault over as at leap-frog; move in front of by leap-frogging. L19.

1 R. KIPLING He . . tried to leapfrog into the saddle. *fig.* A. POWELL Through column-writing and minor editorships, he had . . leapfrogged into a . . promising position in Fleet Street. c *New York Times* Direct controls may check 'leapfrogging' by unions . . to . . maintain . . wages relative to those of other workers. 2 A. J. BARKER The two rear companies were picked up . . and leap-frogged to the head of the main column.

leaping /ˈliːpɪŋ/ *vbl n.* OE. [f. LEAP *v.* + -ING[1].] The action of LEAP *v.*

Comb.: **leaping-head, -horn** the lower pommel on a side-saddle, against which the left knee presses in leaping; †**leaping house** a brothel; **leaping time** *rare* the time of activity, youth.

leaping /ˈliːpɪŋ/ *ppl a.* OE. [f. LEAP *v.* + -ING[2].] That leaps. Formerly also, that runs or dances.

(Cape) leaping hare = SPRINGHAAS. **leaping ague** chorea.

leapt *v.* pa. t. & pple: see LEAP *v.*

lear /lɪə/ *n.*[1] Now *Sc.* & *north.* LME. [f. *lear* var. of LERE *v.* Cf. LORE *n.*[1]] Instruction, learning. Formerly also, a piece of instruction, a lesson; a doctrine, a religion.

Comb.: **lear-father** a master in learning; a person who has influenced others.

†**lear** *n.*[2] LME. [OFr. *loiure, lieure*, (also mod.) *liure* f. L *ligatura* LIGATURE *n.*] 1 Tape; binding for the edges of fabric. LME–M18. 2 A thickening for sauces, soups, etc.; a thickened sauce. LME–M19.

lear /lɪə/ *n.*[3] L15. [Perh. extended use of LAIR *n.*[1] 6.] Colour (of sheep or cattle) due to the nature of the soil.

lear *n.*[4] var. of LEER *n.*[4]

lear *v.* var. of LERE.

learn /ləːn/ *v.* Pa. t. & pple **learned** /ləːnd/, **learnt** /ləːnt/. Also (now *dial.* & *joc.*) **larn** /lɑːn/. [OE *leornian* = OFris. *lernia, lirnia*, OS *līnon*, OHG *lernēn, lirnēn* (G *lernen*) f. WGmc, f. base also of LORE *n.*[1]] I Acquire knowledge. 1 *v.t.* & *i.* Acquire knowledge of (a subject) or skill in (an art etc.) as a result of study, experience, or instruction; acquire or develop an ability *to do*. OE. 2 *v.t.* & *i.* Become acquainted with or informed of (a fact); hear (*of*), ascertain. ME.

1 G. STEIN Lena could first . . learn how to do things. B. MONTGOMERY We learnt by bitter experience. S. DELANEY Oh Jo, you're only a kid. Why don't you learn from my mistakes? R. P. JHABVALA She had learned a lot and was very wise and provident now. D. WIGODER From my clumsy fall I learned to be more cautious. 2 T. HARDY He . . held up his watch to learn the time. *Times* One learnt by chance that they were in lowly jobs. G. GREENE When Rembrandt wants to marry . . we learn for the first time of an impediment.

II Impart knowledge. Now *non-standard.* 3 *v.t.* Give instruction to, teach. ME. b Give instruction in, teach (a thing) *to* a person. *rare.* LME. †4 *v.t.* Inform (a person) of something. Foll. by obj. cl. or double obj. LME–L17.

3 H. MAYHEW My mother learned me to needlework and knit. 4 SHAKES. *Tr. & Cr.* Learn me the proclamation.

Phrases etc.: **I am** or **have yet to learn** I am unaware (usu. with implication of disbelief). **I'll learn you** *non-standard*: a warning of impending punishment. **learn by heart, learn by rote** commit to memory (a formulaic information, a passage of prose or verse). **learning machine** a computer etc. designed to improve its ability to solve problems or perform tasks by making use of information from previous attempts. *learn one's lesson*: see LESSON *n.* 6. **learn the hard way** learn by painful experience. *learn the ropes*: see ROPE *n.*[1] **learn-to-(read, ski, swim,** etc.) *attrib. a.* designating a course of lessons or step-by-step instructions in a subject or skill. *live and learn*: see LIVE *v.*

With advs. in specialized senses: **learn off** commit to memory, learn by heart. **learn out** (now *dial.*) find out, discover. **learn up** make oneself familiar with by study etc.

learna'bility *n.* the quality or fact of being learnable M20. **learnable** *a.* able to be learned, easily learned E17.

learned /'lɜːnɪd, *in branch II* lɜːnd/ *a.* Compar. (*arch.*) **learneder**; superl. (*arch.*) **learnedest**. ME. [f. LEARN + -ED[1].] I f. LEARN II. 1 Of a person: that has been taught; educated; now *spec.* having profound knowledge gained by study, deeply read, erudite. Foll. by *in*. ME. b *spec.* Knowledgeable in law. Now a courtesy title for lawyers in courts of law, the House of Commons, etc., esp. in *my* etc. *learned friend.* L15. 2 Pursued or studied chiefly by people of learning; (of a word) introduced into the language by people of learning; showing or characterized by learning; scholarly. L16.

1 R. DAHL Dr. Hugh Alderson Fawcett was a keen and learned archaeologist. 2 G. W. KITCHIN Words of very different origin . . the one popular, the other learned. E. WILSON Those . . learned families . . managed not merely to set up the classics but to edit and elucidate them too. *learned journal, learned paper, learned society*, etc.

II f. LEARN I. 3 That has been learned. (*rare* bef. M20). LME.

3 *Physiology & Behaviour* Replication was made of a study suggesting transfer of a learned response from 1 rat to another.

learnedly *adv.* M16. **learnedness** *n.* (earlier in UNLEARNEDNESS) M17.

learner /'lɜːnə/ *n.* OE. [f. LEARN + -ER[1].] 1 A person who is learning a subject or skill, a person under instruction; a disciple. In early use also, a scholar, a learned person. OE. 2 *spec.* A person who is learning a foreign language. L19. 3 A person who is learning to drive a motor vehicle and has not yet passed a driving test. M20.

Comb.: **learner-driver** = sense 3 above; **learner plate** a sign showing a red L, attached to a motor vehicle in order to designate the driver a learner (freq. in *pl.*); **learner's dictionary** a simple dictionary designed for the use of foreign students.

learning /'lɜːnɪŋ/ *n.* OE. [f. LEARN + -ING[1].] 1 The action of LEARN *v.* OE. b Education; schooling. *obs.* exc. *dial.* LME. 2 Knowledge acquired by systematic study; the possession of such knowledge. ME. †3 A thing learned or taught; a lesson, an instruction; information; a doctrine; a maxim; a branch of learning; an acquired skill. LME–E17.

2 *Proverb*: A little learning is a dangerous thing.

Phrases: *latent learning*: see LATENT *a.* *new learning*: see NEW *a.* *open learning*: see OPEN *a.* *revival of learning*: see REVIVAL 1a.

Comb.: **learning curve** a graph showing progress in learning; the rate at which something is learned or experience is acquired; **learning disability** a difficulty in learning caused by a physical or psychological dysfunction; **learning resource** a material for (esp. self-)education, e.g. a microfilm or audiovisual aid, made accessible in a library, school, etc. (freq. in *pl.*); **learning set** *Psychol.* an ability to solve problems of a particular type which is acquired through experience in solving such problems.

learnt *v.* pa. t. & pple: see LEARN.

leary *a.* var. of LEERY *a.*[2]

lease /liːz/ *n.*[1] *obs.* exc. *dial.* Also **leaze**. [OE *lǣs* f. Gmc, perh. f. base of LET *v.*[1] Occas. conf. w. pl. of LEA *n.*[1]] Pasture; meadowland; common.

lease /liːs/ *n.*[2] LME. [App. var. of LEASH *n.*, perh. partly f. Fr. *lisse, lice* (in sense 2a).] *Weaving.* 1 A certain quantity of thread. Long *obs.* exc. *Sc.* LME. 2 a = LEASH *n.* 7a. E19. b The crossing of the warp-threads in a loom; the place at which the warp-threads cross. Freq. in *keep the lease*, separate the threads alternately. M19.

lease /liːs/ *n.*[3] LME. [AN *les* = OFr. *lais, leis*, f. spec. use of *lesser, laissier* (mod. *laisser*) let, leave f. L *laxare*, f. *laxus* loose, LAX *a.*] 1 A contract between parties by which one conveys property, esp. lands (later also rights, services, etc.) to the other for a prescribed term, or at will, usu. in consideration of a periodic payment; the instrument by which such a conveyance is made. LME. 2 A piece of land held on lease. *Austral.* & *N. Amer.* L19.

1 *Law Times* The lease . . had been lent . . to the plaintiff . . for perusal. E. KUZWAYO The 99-year leases . . are now seen as an insecure piece of legislation. F. WYNDHAM My mother . . was . . trying to secure the lease of a small house in Knightsbridge. *fig.*: SHAKES. *Macb.* Our high-plac'd Macbeth Shall live the lease of nature. 2 M. MACHLIN There had also been several good shows of natural gas on neighbouring leases.

Phrases: *missive of lease*: see MISSIVE *n.* 2. **new lease of** or (*N. Amer.*) **on life** a substantially improved prospect of living, or of use after repair. *wet lease*: see WET *a.*

Comb.: **leaseman** an agent in the oil industry who negotiates leases of land for drilling and related matters.

†lease *a.* & *n.*[4] [OE *lēas*, f. Gmc base also of -LESS, LOOSE *a.*] A *adj.* Untrue, false; lying. OE–LME. B *n.* An untruth, a falsehood. OE–L16.

lease /liːz/ *v.*[1]*t.* & *i.* *obs.* exc. *dial.* [OE *lesan* = OFris. *lesa* read, OS, OHG *lesan* (Du. *lezen*, G *lesen* gather, read), ON *lesa*, Goth. *galisan* gather, f. Gmc.] 1 Glean. OE. 2 Pick, esp. in separating good seeds etc. from bad. LME.

leaser *n.*[1] ME.

lease /liːz/ *v.*[2]*i.* *obs.* exc. *Sc.* & *north.* OE. [f. LEASE *a.*] Tell lies.

leaser *n.*[2] OE. **leasing** *n.* lying, falsehood; a lie: OE.

lease /liːs/ *v.*[3] L15. [AN *lesser*: see LEASE *n.*[3]] 1 *v.t.* & (*rare*) *i.* Take a lease of (a property etc.); hold (a property etc.) by a lease. L15. 2 *v.t.* Grant the possession or use of by a lease; let *out* on a lease. L16.

1 J. P. HENNESSY The land . . did not belong to Mr. Trollope but was only leased from Lord Northwick. 2 A. MILLER Our landlord was . . planning to lease out our . . apartment to two families. *New York Times* T. Talbot Bond Co. . . sells and leases office equipment.

leasee *n.* (*rare*) = LESSEE L16. **leaser** *n.* (*rare*) = LESSOR L19. **leasor** *n.* (*rare*) = LESSOR L15.

lease /liːz/ *v.*[4]*t.* L19. [f. *leas* pl. of LEA *n.*[2]] Divide (yarn or thread) into leas.

leaseback /'liːsbak/ *n.* & *a.* M20. [f. LEASE *v.*[3] + BACK *adv.*] A seller's action in taking out a lease on a property from the buyer, as part of the terms of the sale. Freq. in *sale and leaseback*.

leasehold /'liːshəʊld/ *n.* & *a.* E18. [f. LEASE *n.*[3] after *freehold*.] A *n.* A tenure by lease; real estate so held. E18.

B *attrib.* or as *adj.* Held by lease. E18.

What Mortgage If you are buying a leasehold property—a flat, for instance.

leaseholder *n.* a person who possesses leasehold property M19.

lease-lend /liːs'lɛnd/ *a.*, *n.*, & *v.* M20. [f. LEASE *v.*[3] + LEND *v.*] A *adj.* & *n.* (Designating or pertaining to) an arrangement between parties for exchanging reciprocal aid, orig. *spec.* one of 1941 whereby armaments, supplies, and services were exchanged among the Allies during the war of 1939–45. M20. B *v.t.* Pa. t. & pple **-lent** /-lɛnt/. Supply by means of a lease-lend arrangement. M20.

leash /liːʃ/ *n.* & *v.* ME. [OFr. *lesse*, (also mod.) *laisse*, f. spec. (let (a dog) run on a slack lead) use of *lesser, laissier*: see LEASE *n.*[3]] A *n.* 1 A thong or lead by which a dog, orig. *spec.* a hound or hunting dog, is held. ME. b A harness for restraining a young child while walking etc. Chiefly *N. Amer.* M20. 2 A set of three hounds, hawks, hares, etc. ME. 3 *fig.* A restraint; control. Esp. in *in* or *out of leash*. ME. †4 A snare, a noose. *rare.* LME–E19. 5 *Falconry.* A thong or string passed through the varvels of the jesses to secure a hawk. LME. 6 A lash with a thong, whip, etc. *Sc.* Long *rare.* E16. 7 *Weaving.* a Any of the cords with an eye in the middle to receive the warp-thread, which run between the parallel laths of the heddle of a loom. M18. b = LEASE *n.*[2] 2b. L19.

1 SIR W. SCOTT She led three greyhounds in a leash. D. CARNEGIE What do you mean by letting that dog run loose . . without a . . leash? **strain at the leash** pull hard at a restraining leash; *fig.* be eager or impatient to begin (chiefly as *straining at the leash*). 2 *Hounds* Although the tally was a leash the last brave hare beat us. *transf.*: TENNYSON Then were I wealthier than a leash of Kings.

Comb.: **leash law** †(*a*) a regulation in hunting or coursing; (*b*) (chiefly *N. Amer.*) a regulation by which a dog etc. must be kept on a leash in public.

B *v.t.* 1 Orig., beat with a leash. Now (*dial.*), whip. E16. 2 Attach or tie by a leash. L16. 3 Link (*together*), esp in threes. M19.

leasow /'liːsəʊ, 'lɛzə/ *n.* & *v.* Now *dial.* [OE *lǣswe* obl. form of *lǣs* LEASE *n.*[1]] A *n.* = LEASE *n.*[1] OE. B *v.t.* & *i.* Pasture, graze. Long *rare.* OE.

least /liːst/ *a.*, *n.*, & *adv.* [OE *lǣst* contr. of *lǣsest* f. Gmc, f. bases of LESS *a.*, -EST[1].] A *adj.* 1 Smallest; less than any other in size or degree; *colloq.* fewest. OE. 2 Lowest in position or importance; meanest. *arch.* OE. 3 *the least*, any, however slight: usu. in neg. and hypothetical contexts. LME. 4 In the names of animals and plants: smallest among several bearing the same name. Cf. LESSER *a.* 2a. M17.

1 L. STERNE A fix'd star of the least magnitude. J. M. MURRY A part, and not the least part, of Keats' share of that burden. 2 P. SIDNEY I am poore and least of all. 3 T. MEDWIN The least noise often scares away . . game of the forest. *Times* Impolite men are not the least bit fanciable.

B *absol.* as *n.* 1 That which is least; the least quantity or amount. ME. b *the least* (advb.), = sense C.1 below. M17. †2 A most minute quantity or part. M17–E19.

1 SHAKES. *Mids. N. D.* Love, therefore, and tongue-tied simplicity In least speak most to my capacity. OED The very least I can do is to apologize for the mistake. 2 T. STANLEY There being in Nature no least which cannot be divided.

C *adv.* 1 In the lowest degree; less than any other, or than at any other time. ME. 2 = *at least* below. *colloq.* L19.

1 SHAKES. *Lear* Thy youngest daughter does not love thee least. MILTON Mammon, the least erected Spirit that fell From Heav'n. G. BERKELEY Alciphron has made discoveries where I least expected it. 2 M. TWAIN Yes, least I reckon so.

Phrases & special collocations: **at (the) least** (*a*) not less than, at the minimum; (*b*) at any rate, at all events; if nothing else. *circle of least confusion*: see CIRCLE *n.* 1. **in the least** at all; in the slightest degree. *last but not least*: see LAST *a.* **law of least action** *Physics* = *principle of least action* below. **least chipmunk** a small brown striped chipmunk, *Tamias minimus*, widespread in N. America. *least common denominator*: see DENOMINATOR 1. *least common multiple*: see MULTIPLE *n.* 1. **least flycatcher** a small migratory American flycatcher, *Empidonax minimus*, with grey and yellow plumage. **least of all** especially not. **least said, soonest mended** talking will not improve matters. *method of least squares*: see SQUARE *n.* *not least*: see NOT *adv.* **principle of least action** *Physics* the principle that an actual trajectory of a physical system is always such that, in comparison with any slightly different motion between the same end-points, the integral over the trajectory of the momentum with respect to distance has a minimum (or a maximum) value. **principle of least constraint** *Engin.* the principle that the motions of a set of interconnected masses vary as little as possible from those they would exhibit if separate. *principle of least squares*: see SQUARE *n.* **to say the least (of it)** to put it mildly.

leastways /ˈliːstweɪz/ *n.* & *adv.* Also (earlier) **-way**. LME. [f. LEAST *a.* + WAY *n.* + -S[1]: see -WAYS. Cf. next.] †**A** *n. at, in (the) least way(s)*, at least. LME–E17. **B** *adv.* Or rather, at least. *dial.* & *colloq.* E19.

leastwise /ˈliːstwʌɪz/ *n.* & *adv.* LME. [f. LEAST *a.* + -WISE. Cf. prec.] †**A** *n. at leastwise*, at least. LME–L17. **B** *adv.* = LEASTWAYS *adv.*. Now *rare.* E19.

leat /liːt/ *n.* Chiefly *dial.* & *techn.* L16. [Repr. in OE *wæter*) *gelǣt* water channel, f. base of *lǣtan* LET *v.*[1]] A channel made to carry water for a mill etc.

leath /liːθ/ *n.* & *v.* Long *obs.* exc. *dial.* ME. [Origin unkn.] **A** *n.* **1** Cessation, rest. ME. **2** *Mining.* A soft part in a vein. M18. **B** *v.* **1** *v.t.* Soften, relax. ME. †**2** *v.i.* Cease, abate. Only in ME.

leather /ˈlɛðə/ *n.* & *a.* [OE *leþer* (in compounds) = OFris. *lether*, OS *leþar* (Du. *leer*), OHG *ledar* (G *Leder*), ON *leðr*, f. Gmc f. IE base also of OIr. *lethar* (mod. *leathar*), Welsh *lledr*, Breton *ler*.] **A** *n.* **1** Animal skin treated by tanning or a similar process. OE. **b** A kind of leather. Usu. in *pl.* M19. **2** Skin (now *slang*); *spec.* the skin on the ear-flap of a dog. Formerly also, a bag or pouch of skin. ME. **3** A thing made wholly or largely of leather; a piece of leather, as one for polishing. LME. **b** *spec.* = *stirrup-leather* s.v. STIRRUP *n.* M16. **c** The ball in cricket or football. *slang.* M19. **d** A wallet, a purse. *slang.* L19. **4a** In *pl.* Articles of clothing made of leather, as shoes, leggings, breeches, etc.; *spec.* leather clothes for wearing on a motor cycle. M19. **b** Leather clothing, esp. as intended to express extreme masculinity, aggression, or sado-masochistic tendencies, or to arouse sexual (esp. homosexual) desire. M20. **5** A brown colour like that of leather. L19.

1 *buff leather, japanned leather, morocco leather, patent leather, Russia leather, Spanish leather, Turkey leather, upper leather* etc. **3** *chamois leather, wash-leather*, etc. *tough as leather*: see TOUGH *a.* **4a** R. RENDELL The boy .., dressed in leathers now and carrying a crash helmet. **b** J. EPSTEIN A homosexual man who takes part in sado-masochistic activity .. is 'into leather'.

Phrases: *hell for leather*: see HELL *n. leather and prunella*: see PRUNELLA *n.*[2] **lose leather** *slang* suffer abrasion of the skin. *pull leather*: see PULL *v.*

B *attrib.* or as *adj.* **1** Made of leather; resembling leather. OE. **2** Of, pertaining to, or wearing leather clothing. M20.

2 P. THEROUX She saw .. another gang of leather boys howling at a cornered Asian. W. BAYER You go to bars. Ever go to a leather bar?

Special collocations & *comb.*: **leatherback (turtle)** a large marine turtle, *Dermochelys coriacea*, with a thick leathery carapace; also called *trunk-turtle*. **leather beetle** a dermestid beetle, *Dermestes maculatus*; also called *hide beetle*. **leather breeches (beans)** *US dial.* dried beans or bean-pods; dried beans cooked in their shells. **leather-carp** an abnormal scaleless variety of the carp. **leathercloth** cloth coated on one side with a waterproof varnish; a synthetic product simulating leather. **leather-coat** a russet apple. **leather-flower** a N. American climbing plant, *Clematis viorna*, with thick leathery purplish sepals. **leather-head** (*a*) *slang* a stupid person; (*b*) *Austral.* any of various friar-birds. **leather-headed** *a.* (*slang*) stupid, slow-witted. **leather-headedness** *slang* stupidity. **leather-hunting** *Cricket slang* fielding, esp. when the batsman is hitting out freely. **leatherleaf** a N. American low evergreen shrub, *Chamaedaphne calyculata*, of the heath family, with leathery leaves. **leather medal** (orig. *US*) a derisory award. **leatherneck** *slang* (*a*) *Naut.* a soldier; (*b*) *US* a marine; (*c*) *Austral.* = ROUSEABOUT *n.* 2. **Leather-Stocking** a N. American frontiersman. **leather-turtle** = *leatherback* above. **leatherwood** a N. American shrub, *Dirca palustris* (family Thymelaeaceae), with a very tough bark; also called *moosewood*.

leathe'rette *n.* imitation leather made from cloth, paper, etc. L19. **leather-like** *adv.* & *a.* (*a*) *adv.* (*rare*) in the manner of leather; (*b*) *adj.* resembling leather, esp. in appearance: L16. **leatheroid** *n.* a fabric, resembling leather, made from chemically treated cotton paper L19.

leather /ˈlɛðə/ *v.* ME. [f. prec.] **1** *v.t.* Cover or fit with leather. ME. **2** *v.t.* Beat, flog, *spec.* with a leather belt. E17. **b** *v.i.* Foll. by *away, on*: work unremittingly (*at*). M19.

2 TENNYSON I'd like to leather 'im black and blue.

leathered *a.* (*a*) covered or fitted with leather(s); (*b*) made into, or like, leather: ME. **leathering** *n.* (*a*) the action of the vb; (*b*) *colloq.* a beating, a flogging; (*c*) a covering or strip of leather: E16.

leather-jacket /ˈlɛðədʒakɪt/ *n.* L18. [f. LEATHER *n.* & *a.* + JACKET *n.*] **1** Any of various thick-skinned marine fishes, as the carangid *Oligoplites saurus*, and various file-fishes and trigger fishes (family Balistidae). L18. **2** *Austral.* A kind of pancake. M19. **3** Any of various Australian trees with a tough bark, esp. *Ceratopetalum apetalum* (family Cunoniaceae). L19. **4** A burrowing crane-fly larva, *esp.* one of the genus *Tipula*. L19. **5** A person, esp. a member of a gang or a delinquent, wearing a leather jacket. M20.

leathern /ˈlɛð(ə)n/ *a. arch.* OE. [f. LEATHER *n.* + -EN[4].] Made of leather; leathery.

leathern convenience (latterly *joc.*) a large horse-drawn carriage.

leathery /ˈlɛð(ə)ri/ *a.* M16. [f. LEATHER *n.* + -Y[1].] Resembling leather in appearance or texture.

leathery-turtle = *leatherback (turtle)* s.v. LEATHER *n.* & *a.*

leatheriness *n.* E20.

leathwake /ˈliːθweɪk/ *a.* Long *obs.* exc. *north.* [OE *liþewāc, leoþuwāc*, f. as LITH *n.*[1] + *wāc* soft, pliant (see WEAK *a.*).] Having supple joints; *gen.* pliant, soft.

leave /liːv/ *n.*[1] [OE *lēaf* f. WGmc base also of MHG *loube*, G †*Laube*, f. Gmc base also of LIEF.] **1** Permission (*to do*). OE. **b** More fully *leave of absence*. Permission to be absent from one's normal duties, employment, etc.; (authorized) absence from work etc.; a period of such absence. L18. **2** Farewell, departure. Formerly also, permission to depart. Chiefly in *take (one's) leave (of)* below. ME.

1 W. H. IRELAND Upon which subject I shall beg leave to dwell a little. H. JAMES The young girl gave him gracious leave to accompany her. W. S. CHURCHILL Free to say what they like in print without prior leave of the Government. **b** R. K. NARAYAN I'll have to apply to my office for leave. A. WEST The .. platform was crowded with soldiers and airmen going home on leave from the camps. J. BERMAN Dick announces his plan to take a leave from the clinic. *compassionate leave, maternity leave, paternity leave, sabbatical leave, shore leave, sick leave*, etc. **2** MILTON And Satan bowing low .. Took leave. *fig.*: B. FRANKLIN I now took leave of printing, as I thought, for ever.

Phrases: **by your leave** (freq. *iron.*) with your permission. *French leave*: see FRENCH *a.* **get one's leave** (*obs.* exc. *Sc.*) be discharged or dismissed from one's job etc. **give a person his** or **her leave** (*obs.* exc. *Sc.*) discharge or dismiss a person from a job. *leave of absence*: see sense 1b above. **take leave of one's senses** have a mental aberration, go mad. **take leave to** venture to, presume to. **take (one's) leave (of)** †(*a*) obtain permission to depart (from a person); (*b*) say goodbye (to). TICKET OF LEAVE. **without so much as a by your leave** without even apologizing; brusquely. **with your leave** = *by your leave* above.

Comb.: **leave-breaker** a sailor who exceeds his leave of absence; **leave-taker** a person saying goodbye; **leave-taking** the action or an act of saying goodbye.

leave /liːv/ *n.*[2] L19. [f. the vb.] The position in which the balls are left for the next stroke in billiards, croquet, etc.

leave /liːv/ *v.*[1] Pa. t. & pple **left** /lɛft/. [OE *lǣfan* = OFris. *lēva*, OS *-lebian*, OHG *leiban* (cf. OHG *bilīban*, G *bleiban* remain), ON *leifa*, Goth. *-laibjan*, f. Gmc vb meaning 'remain', f. base also of LAVE *n.*] **1** *v.t.* **a** (Arrange to) transfer possession of at one's death *to* an heir or successor; bequeath (*to*). Also in *indirect pass.* OE. **b** Have remaining on one's death; be survived by. OE. †**2** *v.i.* Remain (*behind, over*); continue in one place. OE–M16. **3a** *v.t.* Allow to remain; let remain in the same place or in a specified condition by refraining from consuming or otherwise acting on. In *pass.*, remain. OE. **b** *v.t.* Of a mathematical operation: yield as a remainder. LME. †**c** *v.i.* Not to consume the whole of one's portion of food etc. Also foll. by *over*. Only in E17. **4** *v.t.* **a** Put down, deposit; place and keep; hand in and have kept; deposit and (deliberately or inadvertently) omit to remove; deposit or entrust (a thing or matter) to be attended to, delivered, collected, etc., in one's absence. ME. **b** Cause to be in a specified condition. LME. **c** Deposit or cause to remain as a trace or record. M18. **5** *v.t.* **a** Omit to do, abstain from dealing with, esp. so that another agent may be able to; commit, refer (something) *to* a person. ME. **b** Allow (a person or thing) *to do* something or something *to be done* or dealt with without interference or assistance or in one's absence; *colloq.* (chiefly *US*) let (a person or thing) do something. E16. **c** Postpone (a decision, action, etc.). M16. **6** *v.t.* Go away, depart, move away, from (a place, person, or thing); deviate from (a line of road, etc.); pass (an object) so that it is in a specified relative position or direction. ME. **7** *v.t.* Stop doing or resign from (a job etc.); terminate one's relation to or connection with (a place, person, institution, etc.); abandon. ME. †**b** Part with, lose (one's breath, life). ME–M17. **8** *v.t.* Cease, desist from (a habit, activity, etc.); drop (a subject). ME. †**b** *v.i.* Stop; cease (*to*); break off a narrative. ME–E17. **9** *v.i.* Depart, set off, go away; abandon one's place of residence etc.; stop doing or resign from one's job etc. M16.

1 ADDISON I was left a thousand pounds by an uncle. J. BUCHAN My father died a year ago and left me the business. L. WHISTLER He made a new will, leaving everything to me. **b** R. BROOKE Then they died. They left three children. E. BROCK When he died he left two meerschaum pipes / and a golden sovereign on a chain. **3** E. LINKLATER She pours her brother's whisky into what's left of her lager. H. MOORE The parts he disliked he would alter and the parts he didn't dislike he'd leave. **b** O. HENRY One from four leaves three. **4a** J. G. COZZENS He realized that he must have left his hat somewhere—in the taxi? L. HELLMAN Willy had phoned and left the name of a man who made fine riding boots. M. ANGELOU Some of the workers would leave their sacks at the store. **b** E. WAUGH I know I look awful ... The adjutant left me in no doubt on that subject. R. DAHL Two hours of writing fiction leaves this particular writer absolutely drained. E. FEINSTEIN His death left her an orphan. **c** I. MURDOCH My steps as I crossed the pavement left moist sticky traces. **5a** J. C. POWYS We'd better leave theology to people who're too old for anything else. *Observer* It is left to the New Parliament to make a European electoral law. **b** A. CHRISTIE I left her to have a wash and brush up. J. O'FAOLAIN Ah, leave her go. **6** J. GALSWORTHY It was enough to make a man get up and leave the table. G. GREENE Men who leave a bar unobtrusively when other people enter. **7** C. SIMMONS After nine years of marriage, Winifred left Buckram. *Sunday Express* Around this time South Africa was leaving the Commonwealth. **8** G. GREENE She said she had read my books and left the subject there. **9** J. LE CARRÉ She watched him leave, perhaps to make sure he really went. I. MURDOCH Adelaide was clever at school, but left at fifteen and became a clerk.

Phrases & *comb.*: **be well left** be well provided for by inheritance. **get left** *colloq.* be deserted or worsted. **leave a card on** make a formal call on (a person). *leave alone*: see ALONE 1. *leave a person cold, cool*: see COLD *a.*, COOL *a.* **leave a person to his or her own devices** let a person tackle a problem etc. without help or interference. **leave a person to it** *colloq.* let a person get on with a job etc. without help or interference. **leave away from** not bequeath to. **leave be** *colloq.* refrain from disturbing; not interfere with. *leave flat*: see FLAT *a.* 6. **leave for dead** (*a*) abandon as being beyond rescue; (*b*) *Austral. slang* outdistance, excel by far. **leave go** or **hold (of)** *colloq.* let go (of), cease holding. *leave in the lurch*: see LURCH *n.*[1] 2. **leave it at that** abstain from further comment or action. **leave it out** *slang* stop it. **leave it to** (or **with**) **a person** let a person deal with a matter etc.; put a person in charge of a matter etc. *leave much to be desired*: see *leave something to be desired* below. *leave no stone unturned*: see STONE *n.* **leave nothing to chance** arrange every detail carefully. *leave oneself wide open*: see WIDE *adv. leave one's visiting card*: see VISITING *vbl* *n. leave out of account*: see ACCOUNT *n.* **leave something, much,** etc., **to be desired** fail to meet a standard; be (very etc.) unsatisfactory. *leave standing*: see STANDING *a.* **leave the room** *euphem.* go to the lavatory. *leave to stew in one's own juice*: see STEW *v.* *leave to the* MERCY *of.* **leave up to** let (a choice, action. etc.) be the prerogative or responsibility of. *leave well alone*: see WELL *a.* **leave word (with)** entrust with a message. *left holding the baby*: see HOLD *v.* **left-luggage (office)** a place at a railway station etc. where luggage may be deposited for later retrieval.

With advs. & preps. in specialized senses: **leave aside** omit, ignore, not consider. **leave behind** (*a*) not take with one at one's departure, go away without; (*b*) cause to remain as a trace or record; (*c*) outstrip. **leave for** (*a*) set off to travel to (a place etc.); (*b*) abandon, depart from, in favour of a new (person or pursuit). **leave from** = *leave away from* above. **leave off** (*a*) cease from *doing*; not wear; discontinue (an action, habit, etc.); make an end, stop; (of a narrative) come to an end; (*b*) set (a person) down (from a vehicle), drop (a person) off. **leave out** (*a*) leave in a visible or accessible place; leave outdoors; (*b*) omit; ignore. **leave out of** exclude from. **leave over** (*a*) allow to remain; (*b*) postpone for subsequent consideration or action.

leavable *a.* L19. **leaver** *n.* a person who has just left or is about to leave a position etc., *spec.* a boy or girl who has just left or is about to leave school: M16.

leave /liːv/ *v.*[2]*i.* ME. [f. LEAF *n.*[1] w. voicing bef. the vbl inflection.] = LEAF *v.* I.

†leave *v.*[3]*t. rare* (Spenser). Only in L16. [(O)Fr. *lever*: see LEVY *n.*[1]] Raise (an army).

leaved /liːvd/ *a.* ME. [f. LEAF *n.*[1], LEAVE *v.*[2]: see -ED[2], -ED[1].] 1 Bearing leaves, in leaf; having leaves (of a specified number or kind). ME. †2 Reduced to a leaf or thin plate; laminated. M16–M17. 3 Resembling a leaf of a plant. M19.

1 C. BRONTË The great dining-room, whose two-leaved door stood open. E. DIEHL After the flat book form had become .. usual, papyrus .. was made up into leaved books.

†leaveless *a.* see LEAFLESS.

leaven /ˈlɛv(ə)n/ *n.* Also **levain**. ME. [OFr. *levain* f. Proto-Gallo-Romance use of L *levamen* lit. 'means of raising', only in sense 'alleviation, relief', f. *levare* lighten, relieve, raise, f. *levis* light.] 1 A substance or agent which produces fermentation; *spec.* (*a*) yeast added to dough to make it rise; (*b*) dough reserved from an earlier batch to start a later one fermenting. ME. 2 *fig.* a An agency which exercises a transforming influence from within (chiefly w. allusion to the Gospels, e.g. *Matt.* 13:33, 16:6). LME. b A tempering or modifying element; an admixture (of some quality etc.). L16.

2a M. L. KING You are to be that vitally active leaven in the lump of the nation. b A. C. SWINBURNE Pleasure with pain for leaven. *Manchester Examiner* We should remember their temptations and mix a large leaven of charity with our judgements.

Phrases: **of the same leaven** of the same sort or character. *the old leaven*: see OLD *a.*

leavenless *a.* L19.

leaven /ˈlɛv(ə)n/ *v.t.* LME. [f. the n.] 1 Ferment (dough etc.) with leaven. LME. 2 *fig.* Permeate with a transforming influence; imbue or mingle *with* some tempering or modifying element. Formerly also (*rare*), debase or corrupt by admixture. M16.

1 AV *1 Cor.* 5:6 Know ye not that a little leauen leaueneth the whole lumpe? 2 J. GROSS Those useful wealthy eccentrics who did so much to leaven the conformism of Victorian culture.

Leavers *n.* var. of LEVERS.

leaves *n.* pl. of LEAF *n.*[1]

leaving /ˈliːvɪŋ/ *n.* ME. [f. LEAVE *v.*[1] + -ING[1].] 1 In *pl.* & †*sing.* What is left or remains; things left over, esp. as worthless. ME. 2 The action of LEAVE *v.*[1] LME.

1 *Graphic* Their leavings—what they did not touch—made a luxurious supper for all my waiters. 2 *leaving certificate, examination, party*, etc.

Comb.: **leaving-shop** *slang* an unlicensed pawnshop.

Leavisian /liːˈvɪsɪən/ *n.* & *a.* M20. [f. *Leavis* (see below) + -IAN.] A *n.* An admirer, supporter, or student of the English literary critic Frank Raymond Leavis (1895–1978). M20. B *adj.* (Characteristic) of F. R. Leavis or his writings. M20.

Leavisite /ˈliːvɪsʌɪt/ *a.* & *n.* Freq. *depreciative.* M20. [f. as prec. + -ITE[1].] A *n.* = LEAVISIAN *n.* M20. B *adj.* (Characteristic of the work) of F. R. Leavis (see prec.) or his disciples. M20.

leavy *a.* see LEAFY.

leban *n.* var. of LABAN.

Lebanese /lɛbəˈniːz/ *n.* & *a.* E20. [f. *Lebanon* (see below) + -ESE.] A *n.* Pl. same. A native or inhabitant of Lebanon, a coastal country in the eastern Mediterranean. E20. B *adj.* Of or pertaining to Lebanon or its inhabitants. E20.

lebbek /ˈlɛbɛk/ *n.* Also **labakh** /ˈlabak/ & other vars. M18. [Arab. *labak̲*.] = KOKKO I.

leben *n.* var. of LABAN.

Lebensform /ˈleːbənsfɔrm; ˈleɪb(ə)nsfɔːm, -z-/ *n.* Pl. ***-en*** /-ən/. M20. [G, lit. 'form of life'.] A sphere of human social activity involving values; a style or aspect of life.

Lebenslust /ˈleːbənslʊst; ˈleɪb(ə)nslʊst, -nz-, -lʌst/. *n.* L19. [G.] Zest for life, *joie de vivre.*

lebensraum /ˈleːbənsraʊm; ˈleɪ-, -z-/ *n.* Also ***L-***. E20. [G.] Space for living, room to exist and function freely; *spec.* (*Hist.*) territory which many German nationalists in the mid 20th cent. claimed was needed for the survival and healthy development of the nation.

lebensspur /ˈleːbənsʃpuːr; ˈleɪb(ə)nspʊə, -z-/. *n.* Pl. ***-ren*** /-rən/. Also ***L-***. M20. [G, f. *Leben* life + *Spur* trace, track.] *Geol.* A small track, burrow, cast, etc., left in sediment by a living organism; *esp.* one preserved in fossil form in sedimentary rock, a trace fossil. Usu. in *pl.*

Lebenswelt /ˈleːbənsvɛlt, ˈleɪ-/ *n.* Pl. ***-en*** /-ən/. M20. [G.] = *life-world* s.v. LIFE *n.*

Leber /ˈleɪbə/ *n.* L19. [Theodor *Leber* (1840–1917), Ger. ophthalmologist.] Med. *Leber's atrophy, disease*, hereditary optic atrophy, a rare condition, in which partial blindness in both eyes sets in rapidly, typically affecting young men.

leberwurst /ˈleɪbəwəːst/ *n.* M19. [G.] (A) liver sausage.

lebes /ˈlɛbiːz/ *n.* M19. [Gk *lebēs.*] *Gk Antiq.* A deep round-bottomed bowl for holding wine.

Leboyer /ləˈbwajeɪ, *foreign* ləbwaje/ *n.* L20. [Frédérick *Leboyer* (b. 1918), Fr. obstetrician.] Used *attrib.* with ref. to a manner of childbirth involving gentle delivery and handling with minimum intervention and minimum stimulation of the baby.

lecanomancy /ˈlɛk(ə)nə(ʊ),mansi/ *n.* L16. [f. Gk *lekanomanteia*, f. *lekanē* dish, pan, pot: see -MANCY.] Divination by inspecting water in a basin.

leccer /ˈlɛkə/ *n. slang* (now *joc.*). Also **lecker**. L19. [Alt.: see -ER[6].] A lecture. Freq. in *pl.*

lech /lɛk/ *n.*[1] Now *rare.* M18. [Welsh *llech* (flat) stone. Cf. CROMLECH.] A Celtic monumental stone.

lech /lɛtʃ/ *n.*[2] Now *colloq.* Also **letch**. L18. [Origin uncertain: now interpreted as back-form. f. LECHER *n.* Cf. LECH *v.*] 1 A strong desire or longing, *esp.* a sexual one; a lustful look. L18. 2 A lecherous person. M20.

Lech /lɛk/ *n.*[3] & *a.* Also **Lekh**. M19. [G f. OPol.] A *n.* Pl. same, -s. A member of an early Slavonic people once inhabiting the region around the upper Oder and Vistula, whose descendants are the Poles. M19. B *attrib.* or as *adj.* Of or pertaining to the Lechs. L19.

Lechish *n.* & *a.* [G *lechisch*] = LECHITIC L19. **Le'chitic** *n.* & *a.* [G *lechitisch*] (*a*) *n.* a group of West Slavonic languages held by some to have once formed a single sub-dialect within the Slavonic group; (*b*) *adj.* = LECH *a.*: M20.

lech /lɛtʃ/ *v.i. colloq.* Also **letch**. E20. [Back-form. f. LECHER *n.*] Behave lecherously; feel (esp. sexual) desire (foll. by *after*); look lustfully (*at*).

lechaim *int.* var. of LECHAYIM.

Le Chatelier /lə ʃaˈteljeɪ/ *n.* E20. [Henry *Le Chatelier* (1850–1936), Fr. chemist.] 1 Chem. *Le Chatelier('s) principle*: if a constraint (such as a change in pressure, temperature, or concentration of a reactant) be applied to a system in equilibrium, the equilibrium will shift so as to tend to counteract the effect of the constraint. E20. 2 Used *attrib.* with ref. to a test for the soundness (freedom from expansion) of cement. E20.

lechatelierite /ləʃaˈtɛlɪərʌɪt, ləʃateˈlɪərʌɪt/ *n.* E20. [f. prec. + -ITE[1].] Naturally occurring vitreous silica, formed when siliceous material is intensely heated (as by lightning).

lechayim /ləˈxajim/ *int.* Also ***lechaim*** /ləˈxʌɪm/ & other vars. M20. [Heb. *lĕ-ḥayyīm.*] A drinking toast: to life!

leche *n.* var. of LECHWE.

lecheguilla *n.* var. of LECHUGUILLA.

lechenaultia *n.* var. of LESCHENAULTIA.

lecher /ˈlɛtʃə/ *n.*[1] & *v.* Also **†letcher**. ME. [OFr. *lichiere* (nom.), *lecheor, -ur* (accus.), f. *lechier* live in debauchery or gluttony (mod. *lécher* lick), f. Frank. f. WGmc base of LICK *v.*] A *n.* A man of lewd and promiscuous sexual desires or behaviour. ME. B *v.i.* Behave like a lecher; copulate. LME–M18.

Lecher /ˈlɛtʃə, *foreign* ˈlɛçər/ *n.*[2] L19. [Ernst *Lecher* (1856–1926), Austrian physicist.] *Physics.* Used *attrib.* and (formerly) in *possess.* to designate a device for measuring a high-frequency electric oscillation, consisting of two parallel wires joined by a sliding contact, positions of maximum response or absorption being separated by a distance equal to half the wavelength of the oscillation.

lecherous /ˈlɛtʃ(ə)rəs/ *a.* Also **†letcherous**. ME. [OFr. *lecheros*, f. *lecheor*: see LECHER *n.*[1], -OUS.] 1 Given to lechery, lewd and promiscuous; (of behaviour, thought, etc.) characteristic of a lecher. ME. †2 Of a person: fond of luxurious living, gluttonous. Of food: rich, mouth-watering. L15–M16.

lecherously *adv.* ME. **lecherousness** *n.* M16.

lechery /ˈlɛtʃ(ə)ri/ *n.* Also **†leachery, letcherie, -ery**. ME. [OFr. *lecherie*, f. *lecheor*: see LECHER *n.*[1], -Y[3].] Lewd and promiscuous sexual indulgence. Formerly also, an instance of this.

lechuguilla /lɛtʃəˈgɪl(j)ə/ *n.* Also **lecheg-**. M19. [Mex. Sp. f. Sp. = wild lettuce, dim. of *lechuga* LETTUCE.] Any of several fibrous agaves of Mexico and the southern US, esp. *Agave lecheguilla*, used as a source of istle.

lechwe /ˈlɛːtʃwi/ *n.* Also **leche** /ˈlɛtʃi/ & other vars. M19. [Prob. f. Bantu.] A grazing antelope, *Kobus leche*, of flood plains in central southern Africa.

NILE *lechwe.*

-lecithal /ˈlɛsɪθ(ə)l/ *suff.* [f. Gk *lekithos* yolk of an egg: see -AL[1].] *Embryol.* Forming adjs. with the sense 'having a yolk (of a specified type)', as *alecithal, homolecithal, telolecithal*, etc.

lecithin /ˈlɛsɪθɪn/ *n.* M19. [f. Gk *lekithos* yolk + -IN[1].] *Biochem.* Any of a group of natural phospholipids which are esters of a phosphatidic acid with choline; such phospholipids collectively; a mixture containing these, used commercially as a food emulsifier etc.

lecithinase /-z/ *n.* = PHOSPHOLIPASE E20.

lecithotrophic /ˌlɛsɪθəˈtrəʊfɪk, ˌlɛkɪ-, -ˈtrɒfɪk-/ *a.* M20. [f. as prec. + -O- + -TROPHIC.] *Zool.* Of the larvae of certain marine invertebrates: feeding on the yolk of the egg from which they have emerged.

lecker *n.* var. of LECCER.

Leclanché /ləˈklɑ̃ːʃeɪ/ *n.* L19. [Georges *Leclanché* (1839–82), Fr. chemist.] Physics. *Leclanché battery, cell*, a primary electrochemical cell with a zinc cathode in contact with zinc chloride, ammonium chloride as the electrolyte, and a carbon anode in contact with a mixture of manganese dioxide and carbon powder.

lect /lɛkt/ *n.* L20. [f. next.] *Ling.* A variety within a language; a form of speech defined by a homogeneous set of rules.

-lect /lɛkt/ *suff.* M20. [f. DIA)LECT.] Forming ns. denoting a variety within a language, a form of speech defined by a homogeneous set of rules, as *acrolect, basilect, idiolect, sociolect*, etc.

lectern /ˈlɛkt(ə)n, -əːn/ *n.* ME. [OFr. *letrun* f. med.L *lectrum*, f. L *legere* read.] A stand or desk, usu. with a sloping top or front that can hold an open book, notes, etc., from which a person can read: *esp.* (*a*) one in a church for use by a lector, cantor, or preacher; (*b*) one for a lecturer's notes.

lectin /ˈlɛktɪn/ *n.* M20. [f. L *lect-* pa. ppl stem of *legere* choose, select + -IN¹.] *Biochem.* Any of various proteins, usu. of plant origin, which bind specifically to certain sugars or saccharide residues and so cause agglutination of particular cell types.

lectio difficilior /ˌlɛktɪəʊ dɪfɪˈkɪlɪɔː/ *n. phr.* Pl. **lectiones difficiliores** /lɛktɪˌəʊneɪz dɪfɪkɪlɪˈɔːreɪz/. M20. [Word-order var.] = DIFFICILIOR LECTIO.

lection /ˈlɛkʃ(ə)n/ *n.* ME. [L *lectio(n-)*, f. *lect-* pa. ppl stem of *legere* read: see -ION. Cf. OFr. *lection*.] †1 = ELECTION. ME–M16. 2†a A particular way of reading or interpreting a passage. M16–E18. b *Textual Criticism.* A reading found in a particular copy or edition of a text. M17. 3 An extract from a sacred book, appointed to be read at religious services; a lesson. E17.

lectionary /ˈlɛkʃ(ə)n(ə)ri/ *n.* L18. [med.L *lectionarius*, *-arium*, f. L *lect-*: see prec., -ARY¹.] A book of extracts from sacred books appointed to be read at religious services. Also, a list of extracts to be so read.

lectiones difficiliores *n. phr.* pl. of LECTIO DIFFICILIOR.

lectisternium /lɛktɪˈstəːnɪəm/ *n.* Also (earlier) Anglicized as †**lectistern**. L16. [L, f. *lectus* couch, bed + -I- + *sternere* spread.] *Rom. Hist.* A sacrificial banquet at which food was set before images of gods, placed on couches.

lector /ˈlɛktɔː/ *n.* LME. [L, f. *lect-*: see LECTION, -OR.] 1 *Eccl.* A person commissioned as, or ordained to the office of, a liturgical reader. LME. 2 A person who reads; *spec.* a reader or lecturer in a college or university, now esp. one in a Continental country, as Germany or France, or in a foreign country teaching his or her native language. LME.

lectorate *n.* (*Eccl.*) the position or office of lector L19. **lectorship** *n.* the office of lector, a post as a lector E17.

lectotype /ˈlɛktətʌɪp/ *n.* E20. [f. Gk *lektos* chosen + TYPE *n.*] *Taxon.* A specimen from the material originally used to describe a species and later selected as the type in the absence of a holotype.

lectric /ˈlɛktrɪk/ *n.* & *a. colloq.* Also **'lectric**. M20. [Aphet.] = ELECTRIC.

lectrice /lɛkˈtriːs, ˈlɛktriːs/ *n.* L19. [Fr. f. L *lectrix* fem. of L LECTOR.] 1 A woman engaged as an attendant or companion to read aloud. L19. 2 A female lecturer. M20.

lecture /ˈlɛktʃə/ *n.* LME. [OFr., or med.L *lectura*, f. *lect-*: see LECTION, -URE.] 1 The action or an act of reading. Also, a text to be read. *arch.* LME. †2 = LECTION 2. LME–L17. 3a An address or discourse on a particular subject; *esp.* (*a*) a formal discourse delivered to students etc. by a teacher at a college or university; (*b*) an expository or catechetical sermon delivered outside the regular order of liturgical services. Also, the delivering of formal discourses as a method of instruction. M16. b (An endowment for) a regular series of lectures; a lectureship. Now *rare*. E17. 4 A lengthy reprimand, a reproving speech. Formerly also, a (moral) lesson or example. M16.

1 J. CONRAD He had evolved from the lecture of the letters a definite conviction. 3a R. ELLMANN Attending Ruskin's lectures on Florentine art. b J. BANDINEL The Lecture founded by the late rev. and pious John Bampton M.A. 4 E. YOUNG Heaven means to make one half of the species a moral lecture to the other. J. RULE His mother's . . little lectures about trying to be kinder to his sister. *wormwood lecture*: see WORMWOOD *a.*

Comb.: **lecture circuit** a regular itinerary for lecturers on tour; **lecture-recital** a lecture illustrated by music; *lecture theatre*: see THEATRE *n.* 5a.

lectu'rette *n.* a short lecture M19.

lecture /ˈlɛktʃə/ *v.* L16. [f. the n.] 1 *v.i.* & †*t.* w. *it.* Give a lecture or lectures; hold a post as a lecturer. L16. 2 *v.t.* Give a lecture or lectures to (an audience); instruct or entertain by lecture. Formerly also, stir *up* by lectures or sermons. L17. 3 *v.t.* Rebuke or reprimand at length. E18.

lectu'ree *n.* (*rare*) a person who attends or receives a lecture or lectures E20.

lecturer /ˈlɛktʃ(ə)rə/ *n.* L16. [f. LECTURE *v.* + -ER¹.] 1 *Anglican Ch.* An ordained stipendiary minister, usu. appointed locally to preach regular lectures (chiefly *Hist.*). Formerly also = LECTOR *n.* 1. L16. 2 A person who lectures, esp. in a college or university. Now also, (the grade of) a person with an academic teaching post below the rank of professor. E17.

2 *visiting lecturer*: see VISITING *ppl a.*

lecturership *n.* (*rare*) a lectureship L19.

lectureship /ˈlɛktʃəʃɪp/ *n.* M17. [f. LECTURE *n.* + -SHIP.] The position or office of lecturer; a post as a lecturer.

lecturess /ˈlɛktʃ(ə)rɛs/ *n.* Now *rare*. E19. [f. LECTURER: see -ESS¹.] A female lecturer, a lectrice.

lecythus /ˈlɛsɪθəs/ *n.* Pl. ***-thi*** /-θʌɪ/. M19. [Late L f. as LEKYTHOS.] *Gk Antiq.* = LEKYTHOS.

LED /ɛliːˈdiː/ *n.* Also **led**. M20. [Acronym, f. *l*ight-*e*mitting *d*iode.] A light-emitting diode, a semiconductor diode that emits light when a voltage is suitably applied.

led /lɛd/ *a.* L16. [pa. pple of LEAD *v.*¹] 1 That has been or is led. L16. 2 That follows slavishly or sycophantically. *arch.* L17.

led *v.* pa. t. & pple of LEAD *v.*¹

†**ledden** *n.* var. of LIDDEN.

ledeburite /ˈleɪdəbjʊrʌɪt/ *n.* E20. [f. Adolf *Ledebur* (1837–1906), Ger. metallurgist + -ITE¹.] *Metall.* The eutectic of the iron/iron carbide system, composed of austenite and cementite and occurring in cast iron.

†**leden** *n.* var. of LIDDEN.

lederhosen /ˈleɪdəhəʊz(ə)n/ *n.pl.* M20. [G, f. *Leder* leather + *Hosen* pl. of *Hose* trouser.] Leather shorts, esp. as traditionally worn in Alpine regions of Bavaria etc.

ledge /lɛdʒ/ *n.* & *v.*¹ ME. [Origin uncertain: perh. f. an early form of LAY *v.*¹] A *n.* 1 A bar or strip of wood or other material fixed across a door, gate, chair, etc. Now *dial.* ME. b *Naut.* Any of several pieces of timber fixed transversely across a wooden ship between beams supporting the deck. L17. 2 A raised edge around a board, tray, etc. Now *rare* or *obs.* M16. 3 A narrow horizontal surface projecting from a wall etc. or formed by the top of a vertical structure. M16. b A shelflike projection from the side of a rock, a mountain, etc. M18. c *Meteorol.* A layer in the ionosphere in which the ionization increases less rapidly with height than in the regions immediately above and below it. M20. 4 *Geol.* A ridge esp. of rocks, beneath the sea near the shore. Formerly also, a range of mountains or hills. M16. 5a *Archit.* A string-course; a moulding. E17. b *Mining.* A stratum of metal-bearing rock. Also, a vein of quartz etc. M19.

3 J. T. MICKLETHWAITE The ledge of the pulpit. I. MCEWAN Geraniums on window ledges.

Comb.: **ledge-door** = LEDGED *door*; **ledge-handle** *Archaeol.* a handle resembling a ledge, found on pottery.

B *v.i.* Form a ledge. *rare*. L16.

ledgeless *a.* E19. **ledging** *n.* a ledge; *collect.* ledges: E19. **ledgy** *a.* having many ledges, consisting of ledges (of rock) L18.

ledge /lɛdʒ/ *v.*²*t.* Long *obs.* exc. *dial.* Also †**lege**. ME. [Aphet.] Allege.

ledged /lɛdʒd/ *a.* M16. [f. LEDGE *n.* + -ED².] Having or provided with a ledge or ledges.

ledged door an unframed door consisting of vertical boards fixed to horizontal ledges.

ledgement /ˈlɛdʒm(ə)nt/ *n.* Also **-dgm-**. LME. [App. f. LEDGE *n.* + -MENT.] *Archit.* 1 A string-course. LME. 2 The representation of a structure in two dimensions as though the surfaces of the structure were laid flat in a manner revealing their relative dimensions and positions. M19.

ledger /ˈlɛdʒə/ *n.*, *a.*, & *v.* Also (now the usual form in *Angling* & *Mus.*) **leger**, (now only in sense A.3) **lieger** /ˈliːgə/. LME. [Some early forms corresp. in sense to Du. *legger*, *ligger* (f. *leggen* LAY *v.*¹, *liggen* LIE *v.*¹), on which the Eng. forms were prob. modelled w. phonet. accommodation to early forms of LAY *v.*¹, LIE *v.*¹ w. /dʒ/: see -ER¹.] A *n.* 1†a A large bible or breviary. LME–L17. b A record-book, a register. M16. c The principal book of a set of account-books used for recording financial transactions etc., containing debtor-and-creditor accounts. L16. 2a A flat stone slab covering a grave. E16. b A lower millstone. Now *dial.* E16. 3a A resident ambassador; a (permanent) representative. *obs.* exc. *Hist.* M16. †b A person permanently in a place; a resident. L16–M17. 4a A horizontal timber in a scaffolding, lying parallel to the face of the building. L16. b A wooden rod laid across a thatch to hold it in place. E20. 5 *Angling.* A bait fished on the bottom without a float. M17.

1c *nominal ledger*: see NOMINAL *a.*

B *attrib.* or as *adj.* Remaining or resting in a place; resident, esp. as an ambassador etc.; permanent; standing, stationary. *obs.* exc. as below. M16.

Special collocations & *comb.*: **ledger-bait** = sense A.5 above. **ledger book** a record-book, a register, an account-book. **ledger line** *Mus.* a line added above or below the staff for a note or group of notes higher or lower than the staff can accommodate. **ledger-millstone** (now *dial.*) = sense A.2b above. **ledger-pole** = sense A.4a above. **ledger space** *Mus.*: between the stave and a ledger line or between ledger lines. **ledger-stone** = sense A.2a above. **ledger-tackle** *Angling*: using a (lead) weight to keep the bait on the bottom.

C *v. Angling.* 1 *v.i.* Use a ledger-bait. L17. 2 *v.t.* Fix (tackle or bait) for fishing on the bottom without a float. L20.

ledgment *n.* var. of LEDGEMENT.

ledum /ˈliːdəm/ *n.* M19. [mod.L (see below) f. Gk *lēdon* mastic.] Any of several dwarf shrubs of the genus *Ledum*, of the heath family, native to cold north temperate regions; *esp.* Labrador tea.

lee /liː/ *n.*¹ & *a.* [OE *hlēo*, *hlēow-* = OFris. *hlī*, OS *hleo*, *hlea*, ON *hlé*, f. Gmc (whence also ON *hlý*).] Naut. use mainly f. ON. See also LEW, LUKE *a.*] A *n.* 1 *sing.* or (*rare*) in *pl.* Protection, shelter. OE. †2 A sheltered position or condition. Also, calmness, peace, tranquillity. LME–M17. 3 Chiefly *Naut.* The sheltered side of an object. Also, the side of a ship, the land, an eminence, etc., that is turned or faces away from the wind. LME. †4 A river. *rare* (Spenser). Only in L16.

1 J. WAIN In the lee of this behemoth, David was . . well hidden. 3 R. HUGHES Manoeuvring . . to the schooner's lee and clambering on board.

Phrases: **lee ho!**, **lee o!**: a helmsman's warning that the vessel is coming about. **on**, **under** (**the**) **lee** *Naut.* to leeward. **under the lee** (**of**) under the protection (of), under the shelter (of).

B *attrib.* or as *adj.* 1 Sheltered, esp. from the wind. *obs.* exc. *dial.* LME. 2 Situated or occurring on the sheltered side of a vessel or other object. E16. 3 Moving in the direction of the prevailing wind. Freq. in *lee tide*. E18.

Comb. & *special collocations*: **leeboard** a vertical wooden board, fixed to the side of a flat-bottomed sailing vessel and lowered into the water to diminish the drift to leeward; *lee gauge* (in *have the lee gauge of*): see GAUGE *n.* 2; *lee helm*: see HELM *n.*²; **lee-room** room for a ship to deviate from or manoeuvre within its course; a safety margin; **lee shore** a shore that the wind blows on, that is to the lee of a passing vessel; **lee side** (*a*) = sense A.3 above; (*b*) *Geol.* the downstream side of a mound of rock which has undergone erosion by a glacier; **lee wave** *Meteorol.* a standing wave generated on the sheltered side of an obstacle by an air current passing over or around it.

leemost *a.* furthest to leeward E17.

†**lee** *n.*² Pl. LEES. LME–E19. [OFr. *lie* = Prov., Port. *lia*, Sp. *lía*, med.L pl. *liae* f. Gaulish (cf. OIr. *lige*).] = LEES.

leeangle *n.* var. of LEANGLE.

leech /liːtʃ/ *n.*¹ *arch.* [OE *lǣće* = OFris. *letza*, *leischa*, OS *lāki*, OHG *lāhhi*, OSw. *läkir*, Goth. *lēkeis*, f. Gmc f. IE (cf. Ir. *liaigh*).] A physician, a healer.

Comb.: **leechcraft** the art of healing; medical science.

leechdom *n.* a medicine, a remedy OE.

leech /liːtʃ/ *n.*[2] [OE *lǣce*, (Kentish) *lȳce* = MDu. *lake, lieke, leke*, assim. to prec.] 1 Any annelid worm of the class Hirudinea, comprising forms with a sucker at each end; *esp.* one that sucks blood, as *Hirudo medicinalis*, formerly used for drawing blood. OE. 2 *fig.* A rapacious exploitative person. (See note below.) L18.

1 *horseleech, land leech, medicinal leech, sea leech, water leech*, etc.

Phrases: **like a leech** persistently.

Comb.: **leech-extract** an anticoagulant extract prepared from leeches, containing hirudin; †**leech-glass** *Med.* a glass tube to hold a leech when applying it to a particular spot.

¶ The parallel fig. use of *horseleech* is recorded M16.

leechlike *a.* resembling (that of) a leech L17.

leech /liːtʃ/ *n.*[3] L15. [Perh. rel. to ON *lik* a naut. term of uncertain meaning (cf. Sw. *lik*, Da. *lig* bolt-rope).] *Naut.* Either vertical edge of a square sail; the aft edge of a fore-and-aft sail.

after leech, mast leech, weather leech, etc.

Comb.: **leech-line** a rope attached to the leech, used to truss a sail up to a yard; **leech-rope** that part of a bolt-rope which borders the leech.

leech /liːtʃ/ *v.*[1]*t.* Now *arch. rare.* ME. [f. LEECH *n.*[1]] Cure, heal.

leecher *n.* a physician LME. **leechery** *n.* the art or practice of healing E17.

leech /liːtʃ/ *v.*[2] E19. [f. LEECH *n.*[2]] 1 *v.t.* Apply leeches to medicinally. E19. 2 *v.t. fig.* Drain of energy, money, etc. E20. 3 *v.i.* Attach oneself like a leech, be parasitic. Foll. by *on* (*to*). M20.

3 R. K. NARAYAN He left college, and . . was still leeching on his father.

Leech lattice /liːtʃ ˈlatɪs/ *n. phr.* L20. [J. *Leech* (1925–92), Brit. mathematician.] *Math.* A set of points in 24-dimensional Euclidean space regularly arranged such that each point has exactly 196,560 nearest neighbours.

Leeds /liːdz/ *n.* & *a.* M19. [A city in W. Yorkshire, England.] (Designating) creamware of a type originally made at Leeds.

Lee-Enfield /liːˈɛnfiːld/ *n.* & *a.* E20. [f. J. P. *Lee* (1831–1904), US designer of the bolt action + *Enfield* (see ENFIELD).] (Designating) a type of bolt-action rifle formerly used by the British army.

†**leeful** *a.* ME–E19. [f. LEAVE *n.*[1] + -FUL.] Permissible, right, lawful; just.

leegte *n.* var. of LAAGTE.

leek /liːk/ *n.* [OE *lēac*, corresp. to MDu. *looc* (Du. *look*), OHG *louh* (G *Lauch*), ON *laukr* f. Gmc base also of Finn. *laukka*, Old Ch. Slav. *lukŭ*.] 1 A culinary herb, *Allium porrum*, of the lily family, allied to the onion but with flat overlapping leaves forming an elongated cylindrical bulb. Also, this herb as the Welsh national emblem. OE. †**b** Used as a type of something of little value. ME–L18. 2 With specifying wds: any of various other plants of the genus *Allium* or (formerly) other genera. LME. 3 *green leek*, any of various green parrots, *esp.* the superb parrot, *Polytelis swainsoni*. M19.

1 **eat the** or **one's leek** submit to humiliation under compulsion. *houseleek*: see HOUSE *n.*[1] & *a.* 2 *sand leek*: see SAND *n. sectile leek*: see SECTILE 1. *wild leek*: see WILD *a., n.,* & *adv.*

Comb.: **leek-green** *n.* & *a.* (of) a very pale green.

leeky *a.* (*a*) leek-green; (*b*) full of leeks: M16.

lee-lone /ˈliːləʊn/ *n.* Chiefly *dial.* Also **-lane** /-leɪn/. L19. [Emphasized form of LONE *n.*[2]] *One's* individual self; *one's* own. Chiefly in *by one's lee-lone.*

Lee-Metford /liːˈmɛtfəd/ *n.* & *a.* L19. [f. J. P. *Lee* (see LEE-ENFIELD) + W. E. *Metford.*] (Designating) a type of rifle in use before the Lee-Enfield rifle.

leep /liːp/ *v.t.* L19. [Hind. *līp, līpna*, f. Skt *lip-* smear.] In the Indian subcontinent: wash with cow-dung and water.

†**leer** *n.*[1] [OE *hlēor* = OS *hleor* etc., ON *hlýr* pl.] 1 The face, the countenance. Also, the look or appearance of the face and skin, the complexion. OE–E19. 2 The cheek. OE–L16.

1 SHAKES. *Tit. A.* Fie, treacherous hue . . Here's a young lad framed of another leer.

leer /lɪə/ *n.*[2] Long *rare* exc. *dial.* LME. [Origin unkn. Cf. LIRE *n.*[1]] The flank, the loin; the hollow under the ribs.

leer /lɪə/ *n.*[3] L16. [f. the vb.] A sideways glance; a sly, malign, or lascivious smile or look.

P. TOYNBEE The old man looks . . appreciatively at the nurses; even manages a . . leer.

leer /lɪə, lɛː/ *n.*[4] Also **lear, lehr.** M17. [Origin unkn.] A slow-cooling heated tunnel for annealing glass.

Comb.: **leer man** a person who works at a leer.

leer /lɪə/ *a.*[1] [OE (earlier in *lǣrnes* LEERNESS) = OS, OHG *lāri* (Du. *laar*, G *leer*), f. WGmc.] 1 Empty. Formerly also, clear *of.* Long *arch. rare.* OE. 2 Having no burden or load; (of a horse) without a rider. *obs.* exc. *dial.* LME. 3 Having an empty stomach; hungry, faint through lack of food. *dial.* M19.

leerness *n.* (long *arch. rare*) emptiness OE.

†**leer** *a.*[2] E17–E19. [App. f. the vb.] Looking sideways or askance; indirect; sly.

leer /lɪə/ *v.i.* M16. [Perh. f. LEER *n.*[1], with the idea of glancing over one's cheek.] 1 Look sideways or askance. Now only, look or gaze with a sly, malign, or lascivious expression. M16. 2 Walk stealthily or with averted looks; slink *away, off.* Now *rare.* M16.

1 C. LAMB Slily leering down the table. S. KITZINGER A woman . . is leered at by men who look her body up and down. 2 *Landfall* The youth leering off to his first booze-up.

leeringly *adv.* in a leering manner E18.

leervis /ˈlɪəfəs/ *n. S. Afr.* Also **-fish** /-fɪʃ/. M19. [Afk., f. *leer* leather + *vis* fish.] A large carangid game-fish, *Hypacanthus amia*, found off the Atlantic coast of southern Africa.

leery /ˈlɪəri/ *a.*[1] *obs.* exc. *dial.* L17. [f. LEER *a.*[1] + -Y[1].] = LEER *a.*[1]

leery /ˈlɪəri/ *a.*[2] *slang.* Also **l(e)ary, lairy** /ˈlɛːri/. E18. [Perh. f. LEER *a.*[2] + -Y[1].] 1 Wide awake, knowing, sharp, street-wise. Also, shy, doubtful, suspicious, wary, (*of, about*). E18. 2 Flashily dressed; showy, trashy. *Austral.* & *NZ.* E20.

1 *New Yorker* If a hawk . . plows into a snowbank, he will be leery of snow.

leerily *adv.* M19. **leeriness** *n.* doubt, suspicion, mistrust L19.

lees /liːz/ *n.pl.* LME. [Pl. of LEE *n.*[2]] 1 The sediment of wine or some other liquids. LME. 2 *fig.* The basest part, dregs, refuse. L16.

1 H. MAYHEW The scum and lees of all broths and soups. 2 H. MELVILLE My body is but the lees of my better being.

Phrases: **drain** or **drink (to) the lees** drain or drink to the last drop, drain or drink to the very end. **(settle) on** or **upon the lees** *fig.* (become) sedentary.

leesome /ˈliːs(ə)m/ *a.*[1] *obs.* exc. *Sc.* ME. [f. LIEF *a.* + -SOME[1].] Lovable; pleasing; pleasant.

†**leesome** *a.*[2] Chiefly *Sc.* LME–M18. [f. LEAVE *n.*[1] + -SOME[1].] Lawful, permissible, right.

leet /liːt/ *n.*[1] *obs.* exc. *Hist.* ME. [AN *lete*, AL *leta*, of unkn. origin.] 1 A court of record which the lords of certain manors were empowered by charter or prescription to hold once or twice a year. Also *court leet.* ME. 2 The jurisdiction of a leet; the district over which this jurisdiction extended. LME.

leet /liːt/ *n.*[2] Now chiefly *Sc.* LME. [Prob. f. AN, OFr. *lit(t)e* var. of *liste* LIST *n.*[3]] A list of people designated as eligible for some office. Freq. in *short leet* s.v. SHORT *a.*

leet /liːt/ *n.*[3] Long *dial. rare.* E17. [Repr. OE *gelǣte* junction, f. Gmc base of LET *v.*[1]] A meeting of ways, a crossroads. Only in *two-, three-, four-way leet.*

leetle /ˈliːt(ə)l/ *a. joc.* L17. [Alt.] Little.

leeward /ˈliːwəd, ˈljuːəd/ *n., a.,* & *adv.* M16. [f. LEE *n.*[1] + -WARD.] A *n.* = LEE *n.*[1] 3. Chiefly in *to leeward.* M16. **B** *adj.* †1 Of a ship: that makes much leeway. E17–M18. 2 Situated on the side turned away from the wind; having a direction away from the wind. (Foll. by *of.*) Opp. *windward.* M17. **C** *adv.* Towards the lee or sheltered side. L18.

leewardly *a.* (of a ship) liable to drift to leeward when sailing close to the wind E17. **leewardmost** *a.* furthest to leeward L17.

leeway /ˈliːweɪ/ *n.* M17. [f. LEE *n.*[1] + WAY *n.*] 1 Lateral drift of a ship to leeward of the desired course; the amount of deviation produced by such drift. M17. 2 *fig.* Freedom of action within set limits; room allowed for this; a safety margin. L19.

1 F. CHICHESTER Because of the . . leeway caused by the gale, I had been driven back . . towards Europe. **make leeway** drift to leeward. **make up leeway** correct or compensate for leeway; *fig.* struggle out of a bad position, recover lost time. 2 J. HENNESSY For all the rigidity of the . . rules there was some leeway for personal expression. A. WEST She's . . late now and half an hour is her usual amount of leeway.

left /lɛft/ *a., adv.,* & *n.* [OE *lyft-* in *lyftādl* (disease) paralysis, Kentish *left*, corresp. to EFris. *luf*, Du. dial. *loof* weak, worthless, MDu., LG *luchter, lucht, luft*, NFris. *leeft, leefter* left: ult. origin unkn.] A *adj.* †1 Weak. Only in OE. 2 Designating that side of the body which is usually the weaker of the two and which is in the position of west if one is facing north, its individual parts, and (occas.) their clothing; designating the corresponding side of any other body or object. ME. 3 That has the relative position of the left side with respect to the right. (Sometimes w. ref. to the direction in which an object is considered to face, sometimes w. ref. to an object's appearance to a spectator.) In pred. use usu. foll. by *of*; in attrib. use now chiefly replaced by *left-hand*, exc. in certain special collocations (see below). ME. **b** *Math.* Designating an entity whose definition involves two elements in a conventionally defined order, opposite to that designated as right. M20. 4 (Also **L-**.) Of or pertaining to the left in politics, philosophy, etc. See sense C.2 below. M19.

2 MILTON Who stooping op'nd my left side, and took From thence a Rib. E. WAUGH Pins and needles in my left leg. G. GREENE Kay . . winked her left eye. **have two left feet** be awkward or clumsy. 3 I. MURDOCH Is he on the left side of the road or the right side? 4 T. E. LAWRENCE We are the more liberal ('left' in the Parliamentary sense).

Special collocations: **left arm** *Cricket* a player who bowls with the left arm. **left back** *Football, Hockey*, etc., (the position of) a back who plays primarily on the left of the pitch. *left bank*: see BANK *n.*[1] 1. *left bower*: see BOWER *n.*[5] **left centre** *Football, Hockey*, etc., (the position of) a player who plays primarily to the left of the centre of the pitch. **left defender** *Football, Hockey*, etc., a left half who plays deep. **left flank** = LEFT WING *n. phr.* 2. **left half(-back)** *Football, Hockey*, etc., (the position of) a half-back who plays primarily on the left of the pitch. **left midfield** *Football, Hockey*, etc., the midfield players who play primarily on the left of the pitch. **left turn** a turn that brings a person's front to face as his or her left side did before; a turn or turning to the left.

Comb.: **left-brained, -eyed, -footed** *adjs.* having the left as the dominant or more efficient part of the brain, eye, foot; **left-footer** *slang* (*derog.*) a Roman Catholic.

B *adv.* On or towards the left side; in the direction of the left; (of rotary motion) anticlockwise. ME.

Birmingham Post It is just a case of looking left and right. *eyes left*: see EYE *n.* **left, right, and centre,** (also) **right and left, right, left, and centre** in all directions; on all sides; indiscriminately. *stage left*: see STAGE *n.* 4.

Comb.: **left-leaning** *a.* sympathetic towards the left in politics.

C *n.* 1 The left-hand part, side, region, or direction. ME. 2 *Mil.* The left wing of an army. Also (in *pl.*), the soldiers whose place is on the left. E18. 3 Orig., those members of comparatively radical opinions in a Continental legislature, by custom seated on the left of the president. Now, (the views and aims of) any party or group favouring radical, reforming, or socialist views. Also, the more advanced or innovating section of a philosophical, religious, etc., group. M19. 4 A shoe etc. for the left foot; a glove etc. for the left hand. M19. 5 A shot fired at game with the left barrel of a double-barrelled shotgun; a creature hit by such a shot. Earliest in *right-and-left* s.v. RIGHT *n.*[1] M19. 6 Chiefly

Boxing. (A blow dealt with) the left hand. M19. **7** *Football, Hockey*, etc. (The position of) a player who plays primarily on the left side of the pitch. Chiefly in *inside left*, *outside left*. L19. **8** A left turn. L20.

1 G. GREENE Rimmer moved a hand to the left, a hand to the right. F. SWINNERTON Peters . . who sat on her left, was as tongue-tied as Turnbull on her right. *true left*: see TRUE *a.*, *n.*, & *adv.* 3 T. BENN He moved . . to the Left . . arguing for world peace, human rights and civil liberties. *New Left*: see NEW *a. Old Left*: see OLD *a.* 6 G. F. FIENNES Out shot a telescopic left, and I had the shiner of all time for weeks. 8 G. SIMS Straight on is Fort Mason. . . We make a left on to Lombard. *hang a left*: see HANG *v.*

¶ In most senses opp. *right*; in some also opp. *centre*.

leftish *a.* inclined to the political, philosophical, etc., views of the left M20. **leftishness** *n.* M20. **leftism** *n.* the political, philosophical, etc., views or principles of the left; profession of left-wing views: E20. **leftist** *n.* & *a.* (*a*) *n.* an adherent of the left; a person who professes to be left-wing; (*b*) *adj.* of or pertaining to leftism or the left: E20. **leftmost** *a.* situated furthest to the left M19. **leftness** *n.* the condition of being on the left M16.

left *v.* pa. t. & pple of LEAVE *v.*[1]

left field /lɛft 'fiːld/ *n.* & *a. phr.* As adj. also **left-field**. M19. [f. LEFT *a.* + FIELD *n.*] **A** *n. phr.* **1** *Baseball*. (A fielder in) the part of the outfield to the left of the batter when facing the pitcher. M19. **2** *fig.* A position away from the centre of activity or interest, or (*US*) from the left in politics; a state of ignorance, confusion, or unreality. *colloq.* M20.

2 *Time* An increasing number of candidates are emerging from left field to give voters surprising options.

B *adj.* That is outside the mainstream of fashion, unconventional. *colloq.* L20.

Christian Science Monitor Occasional left-field productions like . . 'Dr. Strangelove'.

left-fielder *n.* (*Baseball*) a fielder in the left field M19.

left hand /lɛft 'hand/ *n.* & *a. phr.* As adj. also **left-hand**. ME. [f. LEFT *a.* + HAND *n.*] **A** *n. phr.* **1** The hand of the left side. ME. **2** (The region or direction on) the left side of a person or thing. ME.

1 J. STEINBECK Kino carried a bundle in his left hand. **marry with the left hand** marry morganatically. 2 C. JONES Place of every Suit in your Hand the worst of it to the Left-hand.

B *adj.* **1** On or to the left side; done with the left hand. ME. **2** Ambiguous, questionable; sinister. Now *rare*. L16.

1 M. ATWOOD He drove with . . the left-hand window open. *Fleming's left-hand rule*: see FLEMING *n.*[2] **left-hand drive** a motor-vehicle steering-system with the steering-wheel and other controls fitted on the left side; a vehicle with such steering. **left-hand marriage** a morganatic marriage. **left-hand rope**: laid up and twisted anticlockwise. **left-hand rule** *Physics* = *Fleming's left-hand rule* s.v. FLEMING *n.*[2] **left-hand screw** a screw which rotates anticlockwise when inserted; any equivalent spiral.

left-handed /lɛft'handɪd, *esp. attrib.* 'lɛfthandɪd/ *a.* & *adv.* LME. [f. prec. + -ED[2].] **A** *adj.* **1** Having the left hand more serviceable than the right; using the left hand by preference. LME. **2** *fig.* †**a** Crippled, defective. LME–M17. **b** Clumsy, inept. LME. **3** Ambiguous, doubtful; questionable. E17. **4** Inauspicious, sinister, malign. Long *rare*. E17. **5** Of or pertaining to the left hand; *spec.* (*a*) designating or pertaining to a marriage in which the bridegroom gives the bride his left hand instead of his right (as was the custom at morganatic weddings in Germany), morganatic; (*b*) (of an implement) adapted or designed for use by a left-handed person; (*c*) (of an action) performed with the left hand. M17. **6** Characterized by a leftward direction or rotation; (of a screw) that is turned anticlockwise to drive it in; laevorotatory; (of a shell) sinistral. Cf. LAEVO-. E19.

1 *Pall Mall Gazette* A left-handed bowler is nearly always a right-handed bat. 2b A. BLOMFIELD Spiritual men are generally left-handed in secular affairs. 3 J. STEVENS 'Tis not safe trusting a Left Handed Man with Money. A. DOUGLAS 'I'm not trying to date you.' 'Well, that's a left-handed compliment,' she complained.

B *adv.* Towards the left; with the left hand. M19.

Horse & Hound The fox ran . . left-handed over the Waltham Lane.

left-handedly *adv.* L19. **left-handedness** *n.* M17.

left-hander /lɛft'handə/ *n.* M19. [f. as prec. + -ER[1].] **1** A blow delivered with the left hand. M19. **2** A left-handed person. L19. **3** A left-handed compliment. M20. **4** A left-hand turn or bend. L20.

3 *Times* 'Not bad' might appear a good enough specimen of the simplest type of left-hander.

leftie *n.* & *a.* var. of LEFTY *n.* & *a.*

leftover /'lɛftəʊvə/ *a.* & *n.* L19. [f. *left* pa. pple of LEAVE *v.*[1] + OVER *adv.*] **A** *adj.* Remaining over; not used up or disposed of. L19. **B** *n.* **1** A thing remaining over; *esp.* a portion of some article of food left over from a meal. Usu. in *pl.* L19. **2** A survivor. E20.

leftward /'lɛftwəd/ *adv.* & *a.* L15. [f. LEFT *a.* + -WARD.] **A** *adv.* On or in the direction of the left side; towards the left. L15.

Listener I was rather Conservative as a young man. I've moved gently leftward.

B *adj.* Situated on the left; directed or tending towards the left; executed from right to left. E19.

Times In the borough elections the leftward movement . . has been repeated.

leftwardness *n.* (*rare*) M20. **leftwards** *adv.* = LEFTWARD *adv.* L19.

left wing /lɛft 'wɪŋ/ *n.* & *a. phr.* As adj. also **left-wing**. M16. [f. LEFT *a.* + WING *n.*] **A** *n. phr.* **1** The division on the left side of an army or fleet in battle array. M16. **2** *Football, Hockey*, etc. (The position of) a player on the left side of the centre(s); the part of the field in which a left wing normally plays. L19. **3** The radical or socialist section of a group or political party; the more liberal or progressive section of a right-wing or conservative group or political party. L19.

3 J. WHITE A massive purge of the left wing of the fascist party.

B *adj.* Of or pertaining to the left wing, esp. in politics. L19.

P. ARROWSMITH She was too young, modern and Left Wing to hold conventional views about sex.

left-'winger *n.* (*a*) a player on the left wing; (*b*) *Polit.* an adherent of the left wing: L19. **left-'wingery** *n.* adherence to the left wing, the beliefs or practices of the left wing M20. **left-'wingism** *n.* = LEFT-WINGERY E20.

lefty /'lɛfti/ *a.* & *n. colloq.* Also **leftie**. L19. [f. LEFT *n.* + -Y[6].] **A** *adj.* **1** Left-handed. L19. **2** Of or pertaining to the left in politics etc. M20. **B** *n.* **1** A left-handed person, esp. a sportsperson. E20. **2** *Polit.* An adherent of the left. M20.

leg /lɛg/ *n.* ME. [ON *leggr* (cf. Lombardic *lagi* thigh, Sw. *lägg*, Da. *læg* calf of the leg, L *lacertus* muscles) f. Gmc. Superseded *shank*.] **I 1** Each of the limbs of support and locomotion in an animal body; *esp.* either of the two lower limbs of the human body. Also, the part of this from the hip to the ankle, or (*spec.* in *Anat.*) from the knee to the ankle. ME. **b** (A part of) a leg of an animal or bird used as food. LME. **c** *leg up*, *leg-up*, a lift by the leg to help a person climb up or get over an obstacle; a help in a difficulty, an aid to progress. Orig. & esp. in *give a person a leg up*. *colloq.* M19. **2** An obeisance made by drawing back one leg and bending the other; a bow, a scrape. Freq. in *make a leg*. Now *arch.* or *joc.* L16. **3** = BLACKLEG *n.* 2. *arch. slang.* E19. **4** *Cricket*. The side of the pitch on which the batsman stands, esp. the part which lies behind or roughly in line with him or her (also *leg side*). Also, (the area occupied by) a fielder who plays on this side of the pitch. E19. **5** A woman. *derog. slang* (chiefly *US*). M20.

1 C. STEAD His legs were shaking, and he stumbled at every step. A. HARDY A terrestrial animal . . larger than an elephant would have . . legs so thick . . it could not walk. I. MCEWAN Mary was . . scratching the calf and ankle of one leg. b D. LEAVITT I bought a leg of lamb to freeze. 4 *Times* His attempt to sweep to leg at a straight enough ball.

II A thing resembling a leg or acting as a support. **6** An artificial leg. Also *peg leg*, *wooden leg*, etc. LME. **7** Chiefly *Her.* A representation or figure of a leg, esp. bent at the knee. LME. **8** A part of a garment which covers a leg. LME. **9** †**a** The stem of an earthenware or glass vessel. Only in L15. **b** Each of the comparatively long and slender supports of a piece of furniture etc. E17. **c** Each of the columns extending below the main deck of an oil rig, used to float and stabilize the vessel or to rest it on the seabed. M20. **10** Esp. *Shipbuilding* & *Mining*. A bar, pole, etc., used as a support or prop. L15. **11** *Naut.* Any of various short ropes which branch out into two or more parts. E17. **12 a** Either of the sides of a triangle, viewed as standing on a base; either of the two parts on each side of the vertex of a curve. M17. **b** Each of the branches of a forked, jointed, or curved object. L17. **c** A strand of the network connecting the patterns in lace. Usu. in *pl.* M19. **d** *Gold-mining*. Either of the two nearly vertical lateral prolongations of the saddle of a quartz-reef. L19. **e** *Broadcasting*. A supplementary network attached to a main network and providing coverage for a particular region; a group of stations in a network. *US.* M20. **13 a** *Naut.* A run made on a single tack. M19. **b** *gen.* A part of, or stage in, a journey, race, competition, etc. E20. **c** *Stock Exch.* A stage or period of an account or market. L20.

8 DICKENS Put my hunk of bread-and-butter down the leg of my trousers. 9b M. BRADBURY A number of tables with gunmetal legs and bright yellow tops. 12b *Croquet* It cannot effect the stroke . . on account of the leg of a hoop intervening. 13a H. ALLEN Captain Bittern . . fetched a tremendous leg away across the Atlantic. b *Sunday Graphic* Mrs. Morrow-Tait . . arrives at Malta from Marseilles . . on the second leg of her round-the-world tour. c *Times* Equities ended the first leg of the two week account on a . . firm note.

Phrases: **abdominal leg** *Entomol.* = PROLEG. *a bone in one's leg*: see BONE *n. an arm and a leg*: see ARM *n.*[1] *cost an arm and a leg*: see COST *v.* I. **change leg** (of a horse) change step. **dance, run, walk**, etc. **a person off his** or **her legs** cause a person to dance, run, walk, etc., to exhaustion. **false leg** *Entomol.* = PROLEG. *feel one's legs*: see FEEL *v.* **get one's leg over** *slang* engage in sexual intercourse. *hang a leg*: see HANG *v. Harry long legs*: see HARRY *n.*[2] **have legs** *US colloq.* (of a book, film, play, etc.) have lasting popularity. **have no legs** *colloq.* have insufficient momentum to reach a desired point. **have the legs of** travel faster than. †**heave up the leg** = *lift* (*up*) *the leg* below. *keep one's legs*: see KEEP *v.* **lay one's leg over** *slang* = *get one's leg over* above. **leg before wicket** *Cricket* illegal obstruction of the ball by the batsman with a part of the body other than the hand, for which he or she can be given out. **legs eleven** *joc.* eleven orig. & esp. in the game of bingo. *leg up*: see sense 1c above. **lift (up) the leg** *slang* (esp. of a dog) urinate. **long leg** *Cricket* (the position of) a fielder on the leg side at a long distance from the wicket. *middle leg*: see MIDDLE *a.* **no** or **not a leg to stand on** no support whatever. *on one's hind legs*: see HIND *a.* **on one's last legs** at the end of one's life or resources. **on one's legs** (*a*) standing; (of a public speaker etc.) standing up and orating; (*b*) well enough to stand or walk; (*c*) *fig.* prosperous, established. **pull a person's leg** *colloq.* tease a person, deceive a person playfully or humorously. *red leg*: see RED *a. run a person off his* or *her legs*: see *dance a person off his* or *her legs* above. SEA *legs*. **shake a leg** (*a*) make a start; hurry up; (*b*) begin dancing. **shake a loose leg** lead an irregular life. **short leg** *Cricket* (the position of) a fielder on the leg side at a short distance from the wicket. **show a leg** get out of bed; make one's appearance. **square leg** *Cricket* (the position of) a fielder on the leg side about square with the wicket (*short square leg*: see SHORT *a.*). *straight leg*: see STRAIGHT *a.*[1] & *adv.*[1] **stretch one's legs** †(*a*) increase one's stride, walk fast; (*b*) exercise the legs by walking. **take to one's legs** run (away). *talk the hind legs off a* DONKEY. *walk a person off his* or *her legs*: see *dance a person off his* or *her legs* above. *walking leg*: see WALKING *vbl n. walking on* or *with two legs*: see WALKING *n. white leg*: see WHITE *a. with one's tail between one's legs*: see TAIL *n.*[1]

Comb.: **leg bail** (*a*) [BAIL *n.*[1]] *give leg bail* (joc.), run away; (*b*) [BAIL *n.*[2]] *Cricket* the bail nearest the batsman; **leg-bone** the shin-bone, the tibia; **leg break** *Cricket* a ball which deviates from the leg side after bouncing; such a deviation; *leg-bye*: see BYE *n.* 3; **leg-cutter** *Cricket* a fast leg break; **leg drive** (*a*) *Rowing* drive imparted by movement of the rower's legs; (*b*) *Cricket* a drive to the leg side; *leg glance*: see GLANCE *n.*[1] 2b; **leg-guard** a protection for the leg; *Cricket* a covering for the knee, shin, and ankle, worn as a protection against injury from the ball; †**leg-harness** armour for the leg; **leg-iron** a shackle or fetter for the leg; **leg man, woman** an assistant who does leg work; **leg-of-mutton** *a.* resembling a leg of mutton, esp. in shape; *leg-of-mutton sail,* a triangular mainsail; *leg-of-mutton sleeve,* a sleeve very full on the arm but close-fitting at the wrist; **leg-over** *slang* sexual intercourse; **leg-pad** *Cricket* a leg-guard; **leg-pull** a playful or humorous deception; **leg-puller** a person given to leg-pulling; **leg-pulling** the action or an act of deceiving a person playfully or humorously; **leg-rest** a support for the leg of a seated invalid; **leg-ring** an aluminium strip secured round a bird's leg to identify it; **leg-room** space for the legs, *spec.* in a car; **leg-rope** *v.* & *n.* (*Austral.* & *NZ*) (*a*) *v.i.* & *t.* catch (an animal) by the leg with a noosed rope; (*b*) *n.* a noosed rope used for catching animals; **leg-show** *colloq.* a theatrical production in which dancing girls display their legs; *leg side*: see sense A.4 above; **leg slip** *Cricket* (a fielder in) a position to stop a ball glancing off the bat to the leg side behind the wicket; **leg spin** *Cricket* a type of spin which causes the ball to turn from the leg side after bouncing; **leg-spinner** *Cricket* a ball bowled with a leg spin; a leg spin bowler; **leg stump** *Cricket* = *leg bail* (b) above; **leg theory** *Cricket* a theory that favours bowling to leg with a concentration of fielders on the leg side; **leg trap** *Cricket* a group of fielders stationed for catches near the wicket on the leg side; *leg-up*: see sense 1c above; **leg warmer** either of a pair of tubular (usu. knitted) garments, orig. worn by dancers at rehearsal, covering the leg from ankle to thigh, but often worn gathered from the ankle to below the knee (usu. in *pl.*); *leg woman*: see *leg man* above; **leg work** work which involves running errands, going from place to place gathering information, etc.; **leg-worm** = *Guinea worm* s.v. GUINEA I.

leglet *n.* (*a*) a little leg; (*b*) an ornament or band worn round the leg: E19.

leg /lɛg/ *v.t.* Infl. **-gg-**. E17. [f. the n.] **I 1** Foll. by *it*: use the legs; walk fast, run. E17. **2** Chiefly *Hist.* Propel (a boat) through a canal-tunnel by thrusting the legs against the walls; navigate (a tunnel) in this way. Also foll. by *through.* M19.

1 *Golf Illustrated* The.. coach broke down and.. David legged it up to the clubhouse to find.. alternative transport.

II 3a Hit with gunshot or otherwise injure on the leg. E19. **b** Seize or hold by the leg. L19.

3a *Shooting Times* I legged a hare and it went into that hedge.

legacy /ˈlɛgəsi/ *n.* LME. [OFr. *legacie* f. med.L *legatia* legateship, f. *legatus* LEGATE *n.*: see -CY. In Branch II repr. also med.L *legantia*, f. *legare* bequeath: cf. LEGANTINE *a.*] **I** Legateship, legation. †**1** The function or office of a delegate or deputy, esp. a papal legate. LME–E18. †**2** A body of people sent as a deputation to a monarch etc.; the act of sending such a body. LME–L16. †**3** The message or business committed to a delegate or deputy. LME–M17.

II 4 A sum of money, or a specified article, given to another by will; a bequest. LME. **b** *transf.* & *fig.* A tangible or intangible thing handed down by a predecessor; a long-lasting effect of an event or process. L16. †**5** The action or an act of bequeathing; bequest. L15–E17.

4 C. HOPE Perhaps a rich relative would die and leave him a legacy. b J. WAIN The legacy of Victorian industrialism—slums, ignorance, densely crowded streets. S. BRETT The scar on her thumb, legacy of an accident with a kitchen knife.

Comb.: **legacy-hunter, -monger** a person who is attentive to old and rich people in the hope of obtaining a legacy.

†**legacy** *v.t.* M16. [f. the n.] **1** Give or leave as a legacy. M16–M17. **2** Bequeath a legacy to. L18–L19.

legal /ˈliːg(ə)l/ *a.* & *n.* LME. [(O)Fr. *légal* or L *legalis*, f. *leg-, lex* law: see -AL^1. Cf. LEAL *a.*, LOYAL.] **A** *adj.* **1** *Chr. Ch.* **a** Of or pertaining to the Mosaic law. LME. **b** Of or pertaining to the law of works, i.e. salvation by works, as opp. to salvation by faith. Formerly also (of a person), upholding the law of works. M17. **2a** Of or pertaining to law; falling within the province of law. E16. **b** Belonging to or characteristic of the profession of the law. E19. **3a** Required or appointed by law; founded on or deriving authority from law. E17. **b** Recognized by law as distinguished from equity. E19. **4** Permitted, or not forbidden, by law; lawful. M17. **b** Allowed by or in accordance with a particular set of rules; permissible. M20.

2a C. ACHEBE The paper I signed has no legal force. b OED Whether he is a lawyer or not, he seems to have a legal mind. 3a K. WATERHOUSE He has not.. explicitly acknowledged her legal right to do it. *legal separation* etc. 4 F. ASTAIRE Betting on the animals away from the race course is legal in England. b *Pool Magazine* If you get a red and three yellows on the first legal shot.

Special collocations: **legal aid** official assistance allowed under certain conditions towards the expense of litigation. **legal beagle** *colloq.* a lawyer, *spec.* one who is keen and astute. **legal cap** *US* ruled writing paper used chiefly for drafting legal documents. **legal capacity** a person's authority under law to engage in a particular undertaking or maintain a particular status. **legal charity** *Hist.* relief dispensed under the Poor Laws. **legal eagle** *colloq.* = *legal beagle* above. **legal fiction** an assumption that something is true even though it may be untrue, made esp. in judicial reasoning to develop the law. **legal holiday** *US* a public holiday established by law. **legal man** [law L *legalis homo*] a man who has full legal rights. **legal memory** the period of legal prescription, in England reckoned from the commencement of the reign of Richard I (1189). **legal person** a person who has full legal rights. **legal proceedings** (steps taken in) a legal action or lawsuit. *legal separation*: see SEPARATION 5. **legal tender** coin or other money which a creditor is bound by law to accept when tendered in payment of a debt.

B *n.* **1** A thing connected with law; a legal formality; a legal notice. E16. **2** The exact taxi fare without any tip. *slang.* E20.

1 *Sunday Sun* (*Brisbane*) Do your own legals. Arrange your own divorce,.. will,.. estates & probate.

lega'lese *n.* (*colloq.*) the abstruse and complicated language of legal documents E20. **legally** *adv.* in a legal manner; lawfully; from the point of view of law: M16. **legalness** *n.* (*rare*) legality M17.

legalise *v.* var. of LEGALIZE.

legalism /ˈliːg(ə)lɪz(ə)m/ *n.* M19. [f. LEGAL *a.* + -ISM.] **1** *Chr. Ch.* Adherence to the Mosaic law as opp. to the gospel; the doctrine of justification by works; teaching influenced by that doctrine. M19. **2** Attribution of great importance to law or formulated rule; strict adherence to the letter rather than the spirit of law. L19.

legalist /ˈliːg(ə)lɪst/ *n.* M17. [f. LEGAL *a.* + -IST.] **1** *Chr. Ch.* An adherent of legalism. M17. **2** A person versed in the law; a person who views things from a legal standpoint. E19.

lega'listic *a.* of or pertaining to legalists or legalism; characterized by legalism: L19. **lega'listically** *adv.* M20.

legality /liːˈgalɪti, lɪ-/ *n.* LME. [Fr. *légalité* or med.L *legalitas*, f. L *legalis*: see LEGAL, -ITY.] **1** The quality or state of being legal or in conformity with the law. Also, observance of the law; strict adherence to law or rule, legalism. LME. **2** An obligation imposed by law; a legal procedure. Usu. in *pl.* M19.

1 A. BRIEN She had never doubted the legality of the union between the lady and the gentleman. 2 *Redbook* Buying a home.. is a transaction fraught with legalities.

legali'tarian *a.* advocating or insisting on conformity with the law M20. **legali'tarianism** *n.* (*a*) advocacy of or insistence on conformity with the law; (*b*) legal egalitarianism: M20.

legalize /ˈliːg(ə)lʌɪz/ *v. t.* Also **-ise**. E18. [f. LEGAL *a.* + -IZE.] Make legal or conformable to law; make authoritative under law; sanction.

legali'zation *n.* E19.

legantine /ˈlɛgəntɪn/ *a.* Now *rare.* M16. [Alt. of med.L *legatinus* (f. as LEGATE *v.*) after L *legant-* pres. ppl stem of *legare* bequeath: see -INE^1. Cf. med.L *legantia* for *legatio* LEGACY *n.*] = LEGATINE.

legatary /ˈlɛgət(ə)ri/ *n.* & *a.* Now *rare.* M16. [L *legatarius*, f. *legatum* bequest, f. as LEGATE *v.*: see -ARY^1.] **A** *n.* A person to whom a bequest is left; a legatee. M16. **B** *adj.* Of or pertaining to a bequest; of the nature of a bequest. L17.

legate /ˈlɛgət/ *n.* LOE. [(O)Fr. *légat* f. L *legatus* use as n. of pa. pple of *legare*: see next, -ATE^1.] **1** Orig., an ecclesiastic deputed to represent the Pope and vested with his authority. Now *spec.* a cardinal sent as papal ambassador extraordinary on special missions to States acknowledging the supreme spiritual authority of the Pope. LOE. **b** *Hist.* A governor of a province of the Papal States. M17. **2** *gen.* An ambassador, a delegate, a messenger. LME. **3** *Rom. Hist.* (The deputy of) a general or governor of a province. L15.

1 **legate a latere** /ɑː ˈlatəri/ [L = by a third party] a papal legate of the highest class and fullest powers.

legateship *n.* the office of legate, the dignity of a legate, a post as a legate M16.

legate /lɪˈgeɪt/ *v.t.* L15. [L *legat-* pa. ppl stem of *legare* bequeath, (also) send as an envoy: see -ATE^3.] Give by will, bequeath. Freq. in *give and legate.*

lega'tee *n.* a person to whom a legacy has been bequeathed (*residuary legatee*: see RESIDUARY I) L17.

legatine /ˈlɛgətɪn/ *a.* E17. [f. LEGATE *n.* + -INE^1. Cf. LEGANTINE.] Of or pertaining to a legate; having the authority of a legate.

legation /lɪˈgeɪʃ(ə)n/ *n.* LME. [(O)Fr. *légation* or L *legatio(n-)*, f. as LEGATE *v.*: see -ATION.] **1** The object for which a legate is sent, a legate's mission or commission. LME. **2** The action of sending a (papal) legate; the fact of being sent as a legate. LME. **3** A body of deputies sent on a mission; a diplomatic minister (now esp. one ranking below ambassador) and his or her entourage. E17. **b** The official residence or office of a diplomatic minister. M19. **4** The position or office of legate, a legateship. E17. **5** *Hist.* A province of the Papal States, governed by a legate. M19.

3 LD MACAULAY The report which the English legations made of what they had seen.. in Russia. 4 W. FORSYTH He wrote.. to request that he might have a legation given him.

legationary *a.* of or pertaining to a legation, qualified or ready to go on a legation M19.

legative /ˈlɛgətɪv/ *a.* M16. [Late L *legativus*, f. as LEGATE *v.*: see -IVE.] Of or pertaining to a legate; empowering a person as a representative conferring the authority of a legate.

legato /lɪˈgɑːtəʊ/ *a.*, *adv.*, & *n.* M18. [It., pa. pple of *legare* bind f. L *ligare.*] *Mus.* **A** *adj.* & *adv.* Smooth(ly) and connected(ly), with no breaks between successive notes. Freq. as a direction. M18. **B** *n.* A legato style of performance; a piece or passage (to be) played legato. L19.

legator /lɪˈgeɪtə/ *n.* M17. [L, f. as LEGATE *v.*: see -OR.] A person who gives something by will, a testator.

lega'torial *a.* of or pertaining to a legator or testator L19.

†**lege** *v.* var. of LEDGE *v.*^{2}

legend /ˈlɛdʒ(ə)nd/ *n.* & *a.* ME. [(O)Fr. *légende* f. med.L *legenda* lit. 'things to be read', neut. pl. of gerundive of *legere* read, taken as fem. sing.: see -END.] **A** *n.* **1** The story of the life of a saint. Long *rare.* ME. **2** A collection of saints' lives or similar stories. Now chiefly in *the* (*Golden*) *Legend*, a 13th-cent. collection of saints' lives written by Jacobus de Voragine, Archbishop of Genoa. ME. †**3** A story, a history, an account. LME–L17. †**4** A list, a record. LME–E17. **5** *Eccl.* A lectionary. *obs.* exc. *Hist.* LME. **6a** A writing, an inscription, a motto, *esp.* one on a coin or medal. L15. **b** A written explanation accompanying an illustration, map, etc. E20. **7a** A traditional tale popularly regarded as historical; an inauthentic story popularly regarded as true. E17. **b** Such stories collectively. M19. **c** A person about whom such stories are told; a subject of legend; a very famous or notorious person. Freq. in *be* or *become a legend in one's* (*own*) (*life*)*time.* M20. **8** An estimate or statement of legend displacement, speed, etc. See sense B.2 below. M20.

5 E. C. THOMAS The Legend containing Scriptures, Homilies, and Lives of the Saints. 6a B. MALAMUD Fidelman went among the graves, reading legends on tombstones. b P. KAVANAGH The principal legend on the note stated that all stuff delivered must be 'according to sample'. 7b JAN MORRIS Bishop Moberly.. whose wife only once, so legend says, called him by his Christian name. c W. RAEPER Hawker was.. a legend by this time in his work of seeking to rescue.. sailors. 8 W. S. CHURCHILL Ask your people to give you a legend for a 16-inch-gun ship.

B *attrib.* or as *adj.* **1** Of the nature of a legend. *rare* E17. **2** Designating the estimated or planned displacement, speed, etc., of a ship before construction or testing. E20.

¶ Misused in Shakes. and later writers for LEGION *n.*

legended *a.* (*rare*) (*a*) bearing a legend or inscription; (*b*) celebrated in legends: M19. **legendist** *n.* a writer of legends M17. **legendry** *n.* legends collectively M19.

legendary /ˈlɛdʒ(ə)nd(ə)ri/ *n.* & *a.* E16. [med.L *legendarius* adj., *-ium* n., f. *legenda*: see prec., -ARY[1].] **A** *n.* †**1** A collection of legends, esp. of lives of saints. Only in 16. **2** A writer of legends. E17.

B *adj.* **1** Pertaining to or of the nature of a legend; based on a legend; celebrated or related in legend, very famous or notorious. L16. **2** Of a writer: relating legends. M17.

1 D. ADAMS College porters are legendary for .. such feats of memory. **legendary age, period**: of which the accounts are mostly of the nature of legends.

legen'darily *adv.* according to legend, notably, notoriously M20.

Legendre /ləˈʒɑ̃drə/ *n.* L19. [A. M. *Legendre* (1752–1833), Fr. mathematician.] *Math.* Used *attrib.* and in *possess.* to designate various expressions investigated by Legendre, esp. the differential equation

$$(1-x^2)\,d^2y/dx^2 - 2x\,dy/dx + n(n+1)y = 0,$$

its solutions, and associated functions.

Legendre('s) coefficient, Legendre('s) function, Legendre('s) polynomial, etc.

Legendrian *a.* L19.

Leger /ˈlɛdʒə/ *n.*[1] L19. [Abbrev.] **1** = *St Leger* s.v. SAINT *n.* & *a.* L19. **2** A stand or section of a racecourse, *esp.* one some distance from the winning-post. *Austral.* L20.

leger *a.*, *n.*[2], & *v.* see LEDGER.

legerdemain /lɛdʒədɪˈmeɪn/ *n.* LME. [Fr. *léger de main*, f. *léger* light + *de* of + *main* hand.] **1** Sleight of hand; juggling; conjuring. LME. **2** *transf.* & *fig.* Trickery, deception. M16. †**3** An instance of legerdemain. M16–M17.

1 COLERIDGE The professors of legerdemain .. pull out ribbon after ribbon from their mouth. 2 M. ANDERSON The trial itself was shot full of legerdemain, prearranged to lead the jury astray.

legerdemainist *n.* a juggler, a conjuror, a trickster M19.

legerity /lɪˈdʒɛrɪti/*n.* Now *rare.* M16. [Fr. *légèreté*, f. *léger* f. Proto-Gallo-Romance f. L *levis* light: see -ITY.] Lightness (*lit.* & *fig.*); nimbleness.

M. BEERBOHM Alighting with the legerity of a cat, he .. was off, like a streak of .. lightning.

†**lege talionis** *adv. phr.* L16–M18. [L (*lege* abl. of *lex*): see LEX TALIONIS.] According to the *lex talionis*.

leggat *n.* var. of LEGGET.

legged /lɛgd, ˈlɛgɪd/ *a.* LME. [f. LEG *n.* + -ED[2].] Having legs, esp. of a specified kind, number, or (*Her.*) tincture. Freq. as 2nd elem. of comb., as *bow-legged*, *long-legged*, *two-legged*, etc.

legger /ˈlɛgə/ *n.*[1] M19. [f. LEG *v.* + -ER[1].] Chiefly *Hist.* A person who propels a barge through a canal-tunnel by thrusting his or her legs against the walls.

legger /ˈlɛgə/ *n.*[2] E20. [f. LEG *n.* + -ER[1].] In a slaughterhouse, a butcher who works on the legs of the carcasses.

legger /ˈlɛgə/ *n.*[3] *US colloq.* E20. [Abbrev.] = BOOTLEGGER. Also as 2nd elem. of comb., an illegal seller (of the thing specified).

leggero *a.* & *adv.* var. of LEGGIERO.

legget /ˈlɛgət/ *n.* Also **-at**. M16. [Origin unkn.] In thatching, a tool made from a flat board attached to a handle and studded with nails, used for dressing and driving reeds into place.

leggiero /lɛˈdʒɛːrəʊ, *foreign* lɛdˈdʒɛːro/ *a.* & *adv.* Also **leggero**. L19. [It.] *Mus.* Light(ly) and graceful(ly). Freq. as a direction.

legging /ˈlɛgɪŋ/ *n.* Also **-in** /-ɪn/. M18. [f. LEG *n.* + -ING[3].] **1** In *pl.* (an overgarment consisting of) protective coverings for the legs, usu. from ankle to knee; also, tight-fitting stretch trousers for women and girls; *sing.* (*rare*) either leg of a pair of leggings. M18. **2** *Cricket.* A leg-guard. Usu. in *pl.* Now *rare* or *obs.* M19.

legginged *a.* having leggings M19.

leggo /lɛˈgəʊ/ *v.i.* (*imper.*). *non-standard.* L19. [Contr.] Let go.

leggy /ˈlɛgi/ *a.* L18. [f. LEG *n.* + -Y[1].] **1** Having (particularly) long legs; *slang* (of a woman) attractive, sexy. L18. **2** Characterized by a display of legs. *slang.* M19. **3** Of a plant: long-stemmed. M19.

1 Z. TOMIN He squeezes his leggy body into what little space is left under the table. *Listener* A couple of leggy dollybirds. 2 *Daily Telegraph* Christmas .. concerts, leggy burlesques.

legh *n.* var. of LEIGH.

leghaemoglobin /ˌlɛghiːməˈgləʊbɪn/ *n.* Also ***-hemo-**. M20. [f. LEG(UME + HAEMOGLOBIN.] *Biochem.* A red pigment in the root nodules of legumes which facilitates nitrogen fixation and has a structure similar to haemoglobin.

Leghorn /lɛˈgɔːn, ˈlɛghɔːn/ *a.* & *n.* Esp. in sense 1 also **l-**. M18. [Anglicized f. It. *Legorno*, now *Livorno* (repr. L *Liburnus*), a port in Tuscany, western Italy.] **1** (Designating) a fine straw plaiting of a kind originally imported from Livorno; (designating) a hat made from such plaiting. M18. **2** (A bird of) a breed of small hardy domestic fowl. M19.

legible /ˈlɛdʒɪb(ə)l/ *a.* LME. [Late L *legibilis*, f. *legere* read: see -IBLE.] **1** Of writing: clear enough to be read; easily deciphered. LME. **2** Of a literary composition: accessible to readers; easy to read, readable. *rare.* LME. **3** *transf.* & *fig.* Clear, discernible. E17.

legi'bility *n.* the quality or condition of being legible L17. **legibleness** *n.* legibility E18. **legibly** *adv.* L16.

legion /ˈliːdʒ(ə)n/ *n.* & *a.* ME. [OFr. *legiun*, *-ion* (mod. *légion*) f. L *legio(n-)*, f. *legere* choose, levy: see -ION.] **A** *n.* **1 a** *Hist.* A body of infantry in the Roman army, ranging in number from 3,000 to 6,000 (at the time of Marius), and usu. combined with many cavalry. ME. **b** Any of various (esp. Continental) military bodies of modern times. L16. **2** *gen.* An armed host, (a part of) an army. *literary.* ME. **3** A vast host or multitude, esp. of angels or spirits. ME. **4** Any of various national associations of ex-servicemen and (now) ex-servicewomen instituted after the war of 1914–18. E20.

3 AV *Matt.* 26:53 He shall presently giue me more then twelue legions of Angels. M. L. KING We are marching no longer by ones and twos but in legions of thousands. 4 *American Legion*, (*Royal*) *British Legion*, *Canadian Legion*, etc.

Phrases: **foreign legion** a body of foreign volunteers in the French army, in the 19th and early 20th cents., employed in the colonies or on distant expeditions and famed for their audacity and endurance. **Legion of Honour** a French order of distinction, founded by Napoleon in 1802, conferred as a reward for civil or military services. **legion of the lost** (**ones**) people who are destitute or abandoned; *spec.* the elderly or mentally infirm.

Comb.: **Legion disease, fever**, etc. (*slang*, esp. *Journalists'*) = *legionnaires' disease* s.v. LEGIONNAIRE.

B *adj.* **1** Innumerable, widespread. Esp. (w. allus. to *Mark* 5:9) in *my*, *their*, etc. *name is legion*. L17. **2** *attrib.* Of or pertaining to a national legion of ex-servicemen and ex-servicewomen. M20.

1 *Times* The inaccuracies were so legion.

legioned *a.* (*poet.*) arrayed in legions E19.

legionaire *n.* var. of LEGIONNAIRE.

legionary /ˈliːdʒ(ə)n(ə)ri/ *a.* & *n.* LME. [L *legionarius*, f. *legio(n-)*: see LEGION, -ARY[1].] **A** *adj.* **1** Of or pertaining to a legion. LME. **2** Constituting or consisting of a legion or legions. M17. **B** *n.* **1** A soldier of a legion; a member of a legion. L16 **2** A member of the Legion of Honour. E19.

legionella /liːdʒəˈnɛlə/ *n.* Pl. **-llae** /-liː/. L20. [mod.L, f. LEGION + -ELLA.] A bacterium of the genus *Legionella*, comprising rod-shaped aerobic Gram-negative forms; *esp.* one that causes legionnaires' disease.

legionnaire /liːdʒəˈnɛː/ *n.* Also **legionaire**. E19. [Fr. *légionnaire*, f. *légion* LEGION *n.*] A member of a legion; *esp.* (usu. **L-**) a member of a named legion, as the American Legion, the Royal British Legion, or the French Foreign Legion.

legionnaires' disease [f. an outbreak at a convention of the American Legion in Philadelphia in 1976] a severe form of bacterial pneumonia (often accompanied by mental confusion) caused by *Legionella pneumophila* and associated esp. with infected water systems in buildings.

legislate /ˈlɛdʒɪsleɪt/ *v.* E18. [Back-form. f. LEGISLATOR, LEGISLATION.] †**1** *v.t.* Make laws for. *rare.* Only in E18. **2** *v.i.* Make or enact laws; make provision by laws *for.* E19. **3** *v.t.* Create or destroy by legislation; drive or change by legislation *into*, *out of.* M19.

2 *Which?* The Government should legislate for standard quantities of wine. 3 *Lancashire Life* It could be legislated out of existence.

legislation /lɛdʒɪsˈleɪʃ(ə)n/ *n.* M17. [f. late L *legis latio(n-)*, i.e. *legis* genit. of *lex* law + *latio(n-)* proposing (a law), f. *latus*: see LEGISLATOR, -ATION.] **1** The action of making or giving laws; the enactment of laws; an instance of this. M17. **2** The enactments of a legislator or legislature collectively; the whole body of enacted laws. M19.

1 *Guardian* The best legislation is not legislation which results in a lot of cases going to the High Courts. 2 M. BRETT The framework for the system .. is enshrined in legislation.

Phrases: *subordinate legislation*: see SUBORDINATE *a.* 2.

legislational *a.* E19.

legislative /ˈlɛdʒɪslətɪv/ *a.* & *n.* M17. [f. LEGISLATION, LEGISLATOR: see -ATIVE. Cf. Fr. *législatif.*] **A** *adj.* **1** That legislates, that has the function of legislating, that has the power to legislate. M17. **2** Of or pertaining to legislation. M17. **3** Enacted or appointed by legislation. L18.

1 A. TOFFLER Congresses, .. parliaments, city councils—legislative bodies in general. 2 H. D. THOREAU Those who go to soirees and legislative halls must have new coats. 3 J. MCPHEE The Homestead Act and other legislative provisions.

B *n.* The power of legislating; the body in which this power is vested, the legislature. Now *rare.* M17.

legislatively *adv.* in a legislative manner; by legislation: M17.

legislator /ˈlɛdʒɪsleɪtə/ *n.* L15. [f. L *legis lator*, i.e. *legis* genit. of *lex* law + *lator* proposer, mover, agent-n. f. *latus* pa. pple of *tollere* raise.] A person who makes laws (for a people or nation); a member of a legislative body.

legislatorial /ˌlɛdʒɪsləˈtɔːrɪəl/ *a.* (*a*) of or pertaining to a legislator or legislation; (*b*) having the power to legislate, acting as a legislator or legislature: L18. **legisla'torially** *adv.* E19. **legislatorship** *n.* the position of legislator M17. **legislatress** *n.* (now *rare*) a female legislator E18. **legis'latrix** *n.* (now *rare*) = LEGISLATRESS L17.

legislature /ˈlɛdʒɪslətʃə/ *n.* L17. [f. LEGISLATOR + -URE, after JUDICATURE.] **1** The power that makes or enacts laws; a body of people empowered to make or enact the laws of a country or State. L17. †**2** The exercise of the power of legislation. E–M18.

1 W. LIPPMANN The existing laws of property and contracts had not been formally enacted by a legislature.

legist /ˈliːdʒɪst/ *n.* LME. [(O)Fr. *légiste* or med.L *legista*, f. L *leg-*, *lex* law: see -IST.] **1** A person knowledgeable in the law. LME. **2** *spec.* A member of a group of legal philosophers in the early Han dynasty in China. M20.

†**legister** *n.* [OFr. *legistre* var. (infl. by *ministre* etc.) of *legiste* LEGIST] = LEGIST 1 ME–M16.

legit /lɪˈdʒɪt/ *n.* & *a.* *colloq.* L19. [Abbrev. of LEGITIMATE *a.* & *n.*] **A** *n.* **1** A legitimate actor. L19. **2** The legitimate theatre, legitimate drama. L19. **3** A legitimate child. M20. **4** *on the legit*, within the law. M20. **B** *adj.* **1** Of or pertaining to the legitimate theatre or legitimate drama. E20. **2** Lawful, legal. M20.

legitim *a.* & *n.* var. of LEGITIME.

legitimacy /lɪˈdʒɪtɪməsi/ *n.* L17. [f. LEGITIMATE *a.*: see -ACY.] **1** The fact of being a legitimate child. L17. †**b** Genuineness. Only in L17. **2** Legal right to govern or to sovereignty; *spec.* the fact or principle of strict hereditary succession to a throne. E19. **3** Conformity to law, rule, or principle; lawfulness; conformity to sound reasoning, logicality. M19.

legitimate /lɪˈdʒɪtɪmət/ *a.* & *n.* LME. [med.L *legitimatus* pa. pple of *legitimare* legitimize, f. L *leg-*, *lex* law: see -ATE².] **A** *adj.* **1** (Of a child) having the status of one born to parents lawfully married to each other, entitled in law to full filial rights; (of a parent) lawfully married to the other parent of a child; (of status, descent, etc.) of or through such parents or children. LME. †**b** Genuine, not spurious. M16–E19. **2a** Conformable to, sanctioned or authorized by, law or principle; lawful; justifiable; proper. M17. **b** Normal, regular; conformable to a recognized standard type; *Horse-racing* designating flat-racing as opp. to hurdle-racing or steeplechasing. M17. **c** Designating or pertaining to art considered to have aesthetic merit or serious intent, esp. (*a*) conventional theatre or drama as opp. to musical comedy, farce, etc.; (*b*) classical music as opp. to jazz or popular music. L18. **d** Sanctioned by the laws of reasoning; logically admissible or inferable. L18. **e** Of a monarch, sovereignty, etc.: justified or validated by the strict principle of hereditary right. E19.

1 R. ELLMANN Lady Wilde presented her husband with three legitimate offspring to match his three illegitimate ones. A. N. WILSON Sergey did the decent thing . . and married her, giving her children legitimate status. 2a H. KISSINGER The only legitimate war aim left for the United States was to get its prisoners back. W. VAN T. CLARK We must act in a reasoned and legitimate manner, not as a lawless mob. b *New Yorker* I grew up exposed to the wealthy . . and . . wealthy people became legitimate to me. c S. BRETT I am an act*or* in the legitimate theatre; these are mere variety artistes.

B *n.* **1** A legitimate child. L16. **2** A supporter or advocate of strict hereditary succession to a throne, a legitimist. Also, a legitimate monarch. E19. **3a** The legitimate theatre. L19. **b** An actor in the legitimate theatre. Cf. earlier LEGIT *n.* 1. M20.

legitimately *adv.* L16. **legitimateness** *n.* legitimacy E17.

legitimate /lɪˈdʒɪtɪmeɪt/ *v.t.* L15. [med.L *legitimat-* pa. ppl stem of *legitimare*: see prec., -ATE³.] **1** Make lawful, legalize; authorize by legal enactment. L15. **2** Give the status of a legitimate child to, as by subsequent marriage; establish the legitimacy of (a person) by an authoritative declaration or decree. L16. **3** Affirm or show to be legitimate; authorize or justify by word or example; serve as justification for. E17.

1 *Daily Colonist* No nation in world history has ever legitimated the use of marijuana. 2 *Daily Telegraph* The child of an adulterous union could be legitimated by the subsequent marriage of its parents. 3 J. N. ISBISTER He constantly makes appeal to . . science to justify and legitimate his theoretical conclusions.

legitimation /lɪˌdʒɪtɪˈmeɪʃ(ə)n/ *n.* LME. [med.L *legitimatio(n-)*, f. as prec.: see -ATION. Cf. (O)Fr. *légitimation.*] **1** An authoritative declaration or decree of legitimacy; a document of authorization. *rare.* LME. †**2** Legitimacy, authenticity. M16–L17. **3** The action or process of legitimating someone. M16. **4** The action or process of legitimating something. M16. **5** A legitimating authority; a justification. M20.

3 BOSWELL Legitimation by subsequent marriage.

legitimatize /lɪˈdʒɪtɪmətʌɪz/ *v.t.* Also **-ise.** L18. [f. LEGITIMATE *a.* + -IZE.] = LEGITIMIZE.

DICKENS He married her in good earnest, and legitimatized . . all the other children.

legitimatiˈzation *n.* L20.

legitime /ˈlɛdʒɪtɪm/ *a.* & *n.* Also **-im.** LME. [(O)Fr. *légitime* adj. & n. f. L *legitimus*, f. *leg-*, *lex* LAW *n.*¹] †**A** *adj.* **1** = LEGITIMATE *a.* 1. LME–E17. **2** = LEGITIMATE *a.* 1. LME–L18. **B** *n.* †**1** *pl.* Those of legitimate birth. Only in LME. **2** *Civil* & *Sc. Law.* The portion of a deceased person's estate to which a child of his or hers is legally entitled, regardless of the terms of the will. L17.

legitimise *v.* var. of LEGITIMIZE.

legitimism /lɪˈdʒɪtɪmɪz(ə)m/ *n.* L19. [Fr. *légitimisme*, f. as LEGITIME: see -ISM.] Support of legitimate authority, esp. of a claim to a throne on the grounds of strict hereditary succession; adherence to legitimist claims or views.

legitimist /lɪˈdʒɪtɪmɪst/ *n.* & *a.* M19. [Fr. *légitimiste*, f. as LEGITIME: see -IST.] **A** *n.* A supporter of legitimate authority, esp. of a claim to a throne on the grounds of strict hereditary succession; *spec.* in France, a supporter of the elder Bourbon line, driven from the throne in 1830. M19.

B *attrib.* or as *adj.* Of or pertaining to legitimists or legitimism. M19.

L. ADAMIC Washington . . was legitimist It wanted no revolution in Yugoslavia.

legitimity /lɛdʒɪˈtɪmɪti/ *n.* *rare.* E19. [Fr. *légitimité*, f. as LEGITIME: see -ITY.] Legitimacy.

legitimize /lɪˈdʒɪtɪmʌɪz/ *v.t.* Also **-ise.** M19. [f. L *legitimus* (see LEGITIME) + -IZE.] Make (esp. a child) legitimate; serve as a justification for.

legitimiˈzation *n.* M19.

leglen /ˈlɛglən/ *n.* *Sc.* E18. [Perh. alt. of LAGGIN.] A milk pail.

legless /ˈlɛglɪs/ *a.* LME. [f. LEG *n.* + -LESS.] **1** Having no legs. In early use also, lacking a leg. LME. **2** Drunk, *esp.* too drunk to stand. *slang.* L20.

leglessness *n.* M19.

Lego /ˈlɛgəʊ/ *n.* M20. [f. Da. *leg godt* play well, f. *lege* play.] (Proprietary name for) a constructional toy consisting of interlocking plastic building blocks.

legong /lɛˈgɒŋ/ *n.* E20. [Indonesian.] (A participant in) a stylized Balinese dance performed esp. by young girls.

legrandite /ləˈgrɑːndʌɪt/ *n.* M20. [f. *Legrand*, a 20th-cent. Belgian mine manager + -ITE¹.] *Min.* A hydrated arsenate of zinc occurring as yellow transparent monoclinic crystals.

leguan /ˈlɛgjʊən/ *n.* Also **leguaan.** L18. [Prob. f. Fr. *l'iguane* the iguana. Cf. LIKKEWAAN.] = IGUANA 2.

leguleian /lɛgjʊˈliːən/ *n.* & *a.* M17. [f. L *leguleius* pettifogger (f. *leg-*, *lex* law) + -AN.] **A** *n.* A lawyer. *derog.* M17. **B** *adj.* Of or pertaining to petty questions of law or law language. *rare.* L17.

leguleious *a.* (*rare*) = LEGULEIAN *a.* M17.

legume /ˈlɛgjuːm/ *n.* M17. [Fr. *légume* f. L *legumen*, f. *legere* gather: so called because the fruit may be gathered by hand.] **1** The fruit or edible portion of any leguminous plant (bean, pea, etc.) grown for food; any vegetable used as food. Usu. in *pl.* M17. **2** A leguminous plant. L17. **3** The pod or seed-vessel of a leguminous plant. L18.

legumen /lɪˈgjuːmən/ *n.* Pl. **-mens, -mina** /-mɪnə/. LME. [L: see prec.] **1** = LEGUME 1. LME. **2** = LEGUME 2. L17. **3** = LEGUME 3. M18.

legumin /lɪˈgjuːmɪn/ *n.* M19. [f. LEGUME + -IN¹.] *Biochem.* A protein resembling casein, found in leguminous and other seeds.

legumina *n.pl.* see LEGUMEN.

leguminose /lɪˈgjuːmɪnəʊs/ *a.* L17. [f. as next: see -OSE¹.] = next.

leguminous /lɪˈgjuːmɪnəs/ *a.* LME. [f. L *leguminosus*, f. *legumin-*, *legumen* LEGUME: see -OUS.] **1** Of or pertaining to pulse; (of a vegetable or crop) of the nature of pulse. LME. **2** *Bot.* Of or pertaining to the Leguminosae, a large family which includes peas, beans, mimosas, and other plants bearing legumes or pods, freq. with nitrogen-fixing nodules on the roots and pinnate or trifoliate leaves. L17. **b** Like that of a leguminous plant. L17.

¶In isolated use bef. M17.

lehr *n.* var. of LEER *n.*⁴

Lehrjahr /ˈleːrjaːr/ *n.* Pl. **-e** /-ə/. M19. [G, f. *lehr(en* teach + *Jahr* years.] A year of apprenticeship or learning. Usu. in *pl.*, one's apprenticeship.

lehua /leɪˈhuːə/ *n.* L19. [Haw.] An evergreen tree, *Metrosideros collina*, of the myrtle family, native to the Polynesian and Melanesian islands of the Pacific Ocean and bearing panicles of scarlet flowers. Cf. OHIA.

lei /leɪ/ *n.*¹ M19. [Haw.] A Polynesian garland made of flowers, feathers, shells, etc., often given as a symbol of affection.

lei /leɪ/ *n.*² E20. [Chin. *léi.*] *Archaeol.* An urn-shaped Chinese bronze wine-vessel of the Shang period to *c* 250 BC.

lei *n.*³ pl. of LEU.

Leibnitz *n.*, **Leibnitzian** *a.* & *n.* vars. of LEIBNIZ, -IAN.

Leibniz /ˈlʌɪbnɪts/ *n.* Also **-tz.** M19. [G. W. *Leibniz* (1646–1716), Ger. philosopher and mathematician.] **1** Math. *Leibniz('s) theorem*, the theorem that the *n*th derivative of a product of two functions may be expressed as a sum of products of the derivatives of the individual functions, the coefficients being the same as those occurring in the binomial theorem. M19. **2** Philos. *Leibniz's law*, the principle of the identity of indiscernibles. M20.

Leibnizian /lʌɪbˈnɪtsɪən/ *a.* & *n.* Also **-tz-.** M18. [f. as prec. + -IAN.] **A** *adj.* Pertaining to or characteristic of Leibniz or his philosophy; regarding matter as a multitude of monads and assuming pre-established harmony between everything. M18. **B** *n.* A follower or adherent of Leibniz. M18.

Leicester /ˈlɛstə/ *n.* L18. [A city in Leicestershire, central England.] **1** In full *Leicester sheep.* (An animal of) a valuable long-woolled variety of sheep orig. bred in Leicestershire, England. In *Austral.* & *NZ* freq. more fully *English Leicester.* See also *Border Leicester* s.v. BORDER *n.* L18. **2** (An animal of) a long-horned variety of cattle, orig. bred in Leicestershire. M19. **3** In full *Leicester cheese.* A firm-textured usu. orange-coloured full milk cheese of a type orig. made in Leicestershire. L19.

Leichhardt /ˈlʌɪkɑːt/ *n.* M19. [F. W. L. *Leichhardt* (1813–48), Ger. explorer of Australia.] In full *Leichhardt pine, Leichhardt tree.* A tree of the madder family, *Nauclea orientalis*, which is native to Australia and India and bears heads of yellow flowers.

Leidenfrost /ˈlʌɪd(ə)nfrɒst/ *n.* M19. [J. G. *Leidenfrost* (1715–94), Ger. physicist.] *Physics.* Used *attrib.* and in *possess.* with ref. to a phenomenon in which liquid, in contact with a surface whose temperature exceeds some critical value (the *Leidenfrost point*), forms a vapour layer which insulates it from the surface.

leigh /liː/ *n.* Also **legh.** L18. [Origin unkn.] = *Irish deer, elk* s.v. IRISH *a.*

†**leighton** *n.* OE–L18. [f. as LEEK + TOWN *n.*] A garden.

leio- /ˈlʌɪəʊ/ *comb. form* of Gk *leios* smooth, forming chiefly ns. and adjs. in *Biol.* & *Med.*: see -O-.

leiomyˈoma *n.*, pl. **-mas, -mata** /-mətə/, *Med.* a myoma arising from smooth muscle L19. **leiomyosarˈcoma** *n.*, pl. **-mas, -mata** /-mətə/, *Med.* a malignant sarcoma arising from smooth muscle, *esp.* a uterine fibroid E20. **leioˈphyllous** *a.* (*Bot.*) having smooth leaves L19. **leiotrichous** /lʌɪˈɒtrɪkəs/ *a.* smooth-haired; having straight lank hair: M19. **leiotrichy** /lʌɪˈɒtrɪki/ *n.* the fact or condition of being leiotrichous E20.

leir *v.* see LERE *v.*

Leishman /ˈliːʃmən/ *n.* E20. [W. B. *Leishman* (1865–1926), Brit. pathologist.] *Med.* **1** *Leishman('s) body*, an ovoid structure consisting of a single non-flagellated leishmania found in the macrophages of people with leishmaniasis. Also *Leishman–Donovan body.* E20. **2** *Leishman('s) stain*, a mixture of eosin and methylene blue used to stain blood smears. E20.

leishmania /liːʃˈmeɪnɪə/ *n.* Pl. **-ia, -iae** /-ɪiː/, **-ias.** E20. [mod.L (see below), f. prec. + -IA¹.] *Zool.* & *Med.* **1** Any protozoon of the genus *Leishmania* (family Trypanosomidae), comprising pathogenic species occurring as non-flagellated Leishman bodies in human macrophages, and as flagellated individuals in the alimentary canal of sandflies, which act as vectors. E20. **2** Any flagellate of the family Trypanosomidae when existing in a leishmanial form. E20.

leishmanial, **leishmanian** *adjs.* caused by leishmaniae; typical of a leishmania as it occurs in man and other mammals (i.e. as a Leishman body): E20.

leishmaniasis /-məˈnʌɪəsɪs/, *n.*, pl. **-ases** /-əsiːz/, infection with or a disease caused by species of *Leishmania*, principally kala-azar and oriental sore E20. **leishmaniˈosis** *n.*, pl. **-oses** /-ˈəʊsiːz/, = LEISHMANIASIS E20. **ˈleishmanoid** *n.* (in full *dermal leishmanoid*) a condition occurring as a sequel to kala-azar and characterized by an eruption of whitish patches on the skin E20.

Leisler's bat /ˌlʌɪzləz ˈbat/ *n. phr.* E20. [T. P. *Leisler*, 19th-cent. Ger. zoologist.] A small black vespertilionid bat, *Nyctalus leisleri*, of N. Africa and Eurasia. Also called *lesser noctule*.

leister /ˈliːstə/ *n.* & *v.* M16. [ON *ljóstr* (Norw. dial. *lioster*, Sw. *ljuster*, Da. *lyster*), f. *ljósta* to strike.] A *n.* A pronged spear for striking and catching fish, chiefly salmon. M16. B *v.t.* Spear with a leister. M19.

leisurable /ˈlɛʒ(ə)rəb(ə)l/ *a.* Now *rare.* L16. [f. next + -ABLE, after *comfortable*: cf. PLEASURABLE.] 1 Carried out without haste, deliberate; having leisure, leisurely. L16. 2 Of the nature of leisure, not requiring haste. E17.

leisurably *adv.* M16.

leisure /ˈlɛʒə/ *n.* & *a.* ME. [AN *leisour*, OFr. *leisir* (mod. *loisir*) f. Proto-Romance use as n. of L *licere* be allowed.] A *n.* 1a (The state of having) time at one's own disposal; free or unoccupied time. ME. b A period or spell of unoccupied time. Now *rare* or *obs.* LME. †2 Freedom or opportunity (*to do*). ME–M17. †3 Leisureliness, deliberation. ME–L17. 4 Opportunity afforded by freedom from occupations (*to do, for*). LME. 5 Time remaining, sufficient time. Now *rare* or *obs.* M16.

1a J. RUSKIN The first volume . . took the best of the winter's leisure. 4a P. G. WODEHOUSE The wolf at the door left little leisure for careful thought. W. STYRON He would also have the leisure to start a project which he had always cherished. 5 SIR W. SCOTT He found himself unexpectedly in Eachin's close neighbourhood, with scarce leisure to avoid him.

Phrases: **at leisure** (*a*) with free or unoccupied time at one's disposal; (*b*) without haste, with deliberation. **at one's leisure** when one has unoccupied time at one's disposal; at one's ease or convenience. **attend** or **stay (upon) a person's leisure** *arch.* wait until a person is unoccupied. †**by leisure** in a leisurely manner; at one's leisure; by degrees. **gentleman of leisure** = *man of leisure* below. **lady of leisure** a woman of independent means or whose time is free from obligations to others. **man of leisure** a man of independent means or whose time is free from obligations to others. *stay (upon) a person's leisure*: see *attend (upon) a person's leisure* above.

B *attrib.* or as *adj.* Of or pertaining to leisure, having leisure; free, unoccupied. LME.

W. T. MILLS The ancient priesthood gathered to itself all the functions of the leisure and professional classes. F. RAPHAEL A vermilion track-suit . . and Puma leisure shoes.

Special collocations & comb.: **leisure centre**, **complex** a building having sporting facilities, bars, etc. **leisurewear** informal clothes, *esp.* tracksuits, sportswear, etc.

leisureful *a.* having much leisure, leisurely LME. **leisureless** *a.* M16.

leisure /ˈlɛʒə/ *v. rare.* E20. [f. the n.] 1 *v.i.* Have or enjoy leisure. E20. 2 *v.t.* Make leisurely. E20.

leisured /ˈlɛʒəd/ *a.* E16. [f. LEISURE *n.* + -ED².] 1 Characterized by or having leisure; leisurely. E16. 2 Having ample leisure. Esp. in *the leisured class(es)*. L18.

1 Y. MENUHIN Tours were comparatively leisured; a few days were spent at each stopping place.

leisurely /ˈlɛʒəli/ *a.* E17. [f. LEISURE *n.* + -LY¹.] 1 Having leisure; able to proceed without haste. E17. 2 Of an action or agent: performed or operating at leisure or without haste; deliberate. E17.

1 F. DONALDSON One of those leisurely souls who believe in taking time over one's packing. 2 P. G. WODEHOUSE Her gaze was moving easily about the room, taking in each picture . . in a leisurely inspection.

leisureliness *n.* E19.

leisurely /ˈlɛʒəli/ *adv.* L15. [f. LEISURE *n.* + -LY².] At leisure, without haste; with deliberate motion or action.

J. K. TOOLE The slowly rocking streetcars . . seemed to be leisurely moving toward no special destination.

leitmotiv /ˈlʌɪtməʊtiːf/ *n.* Also **-if**. L19. [G, f. *leit-* leading + *Motiv* MOTIVE *n.*] 1 *Mus.* A theme associated throughout a work with a particular person, situation, or sentiment. L19. 2 *gen.* A recurrent idea or image in a literary work etc. L19.

2 H. ACTON She longed for a place of her own: this was the leitmotiv of her letters. J. BERMAN Staircase imagery functions as a leitmotif in Eliot's writings.

lek /lɛk/ *n.*¹ & *v.* L19. [Perh. f. Sw. *leka* to play: cf. LAIK.] *Zool.* A *n.* A patch of ground which the males of certain species of bird use solely for communal breeding displays and to which the females come to mate; such a gathering or display. L19. B *v.i.* Infl. **-kk-**. Take part in a lek. L19.

lek /lɛk/ *n.*² Pl. **lekë** /ˈlɛkə/, **-s**, same. E20. [Albanian.] The basic monetary unit of Albania, equal to 100 qintars.

lekach /ˈlɛkax/ *n.* M20. [Yiddish.] A Jewish cake traditionally made with honey.

lekane /lɛˈkɑːni/ *n.* E20. [Gk *lekanē* a bowl, a dish.] *Gk Antiq.* A shallow bowl, usu. with handles and a cover.

lekanis /lɛˈkɑːnɪs/ *n.* Pl. ***-ides*** /-ɪdiːz/. E20. [Dim. of prec.] = prec.

lekë *n.pl.* see LEK *n.*²

Lekh *n.* & *a.* var. of LECH *n.*³ & *a.*

lekker /ˈlɛkə/ *a. S. Afr. colloq.* E20. [Afk. f. Du. (cf. G *lecker*) rel. to Du. *likken* LICK *v.*] Pleasant, sweet, nice; good, excellent.

lekythos /ˈliːkɪθɒs, ˈlɛ-/ *n.* Pl. ***-thoi*** /-θɔɪ/. M19. [Gk *lēkuthos*. See also LECYTHUS.] *Gk Antiq.* A vase or flask with a narrow neck.

leman /ˈlɛmən, ˈliː-/ *n. arch.* Pl. **-s**. ME. [f. LIEF *a.* + MAN *n.*] 1 A lover, a sweetheart. Formerly (occas.), a husband or wife. ME. 2 An illicit lover, now *esp.* a mistress. ME.

lemanless *a.* (*rare*) M18. **lemanry** *n.* (now *rare*) illicit love L15.

lemel *n.* var. of LIMAIL.

lemma /ˈlɛmə/ *n.*¹ Pl. **lemmas**, **lemmata** /ˈlɛmətə/. L16. [L f. Gk *lēmma*, pl. *lēmmata*, something taken for granted or assumed, theme, argument, title, f. base also of *lambanein* take.] 1 An axiom or demonstrated proposition used in an argument or proof. L16. 2 The argument or subject of a literary work, prefixed as a heading; the heading or theme of a scholium or annotation. Also, a motto attached to a picture etc. E17. 3 A word or phrase defined in a dictionary, glossed in a glossary, entered in a word-list, etc.; the form of a word or phrase chosen to represent all inflectional and spelling variants in a dictionary entry etc. M20.

lemma /ˈlɛmə/ *n.*² Pl. **lemmas**, **lemmata** /ˈlɛmətə/. M18. [Gk, f. *lepein* to peel.] †1 The husk or shell of a fruit. Only in M18. 2 *Bot.* The lower bract of the floret of a grass. Cf. PALEA 2. E20.

lemmata *ns.pl.* see LEMMA *n.*¹, *n.*²

lemmatical /ləˈmatɪk(ə)l/ *a. rare.* M17. [f. L *lemmat-*, LEMMA *n.*¹ + -IC + -AL¹.] Of or pertaining to a lemma; of the nature of a lemma.

Also **lemmatic** *a.* (*rare*) M20.

lemmatize /ˈlɛmətʌɪz/ *v.t.* Also **-ise**. M20. [f. as prec. + -IZE.] Sort into lemmas, sort so as to group together inflected or variant forms of the same word.

lemmatiˈzation *n.* M20.

lemme /ˈlɛmi/ *v.i.* (*imper.*). *colloq.* L19. [Contr.: cf. GIMME.] Let me.

C. E. MONTAGUE Lemme alone. I'm an old man. C. WESTON Okay, man, lemme think.

lemming /ˈlɛmɪŋ/ *n.* E18. [Norw., Da. *lemming*, rel. to Sw. *lämmel*, Norw. *lemen(de)*, ON *lómundr*.] 1 Any of several small short-tailed Arctic rodents of the genus *Lemmus* and related genera of the family Muridae, noted for their fluctuating populations and, esp. in the Norway lemming (see below), periodic mass migrations. Also *lemming mouse, lemming rat.* E18. 2 *fig.* A person bent on a headlong rush, esp. towards disaster; a person unthinkingly joining a mass migration; an unthinking person. M20.

1 **bog lemming**: of the American genus *Synaptomys*. **collared lemming**: of the genus *Dicrostonyx*. **Norway lemming** a Scandinavian lemming, *Lemmus lemmus*. **steppe lemming** any central Asian vole of the genus *Lagurus*. 2 *Listener* Some lemmings . . learn sooner than others. The exodus to . . Yorkshire began several years ago. *attrib.*: D. F. HORROBIN This lemming unconcern may have dangerous consequences.

lemming-like *a.* resembling (that of) a lemming; headlong, suicidal, unthinking: M20.

lemna /ˈlɛmnə/ *n.* L18. [mod.L *Lemna* (see below) f. Gk *lemna*.] Any of various aquatic plants of the genus *Lemna* (family Lemnaceae); = *duckweed* s.v. DUCK *n.*¹

Lemnian /ˈlɛmnɪən/ *a.* L16. [f. L *Lemnius*, Gk *Lēmnios*, f. *Lēmnos* (see below) + -AN.] Of or pertaining to the Aegean island of Lemnos.

Lemnian earth a grey or yellowish-red clay formerly used in medicine.

†**lemnisc** *n. rare.* Only in E18. [f. as LEMNISCUS.] 1 A ribbon. E18. 2 = LEMNISCUS 1. E18.

lemniscate /lɛmˈnɪskət/ *n.* & *a.* L18. [f. mod.L *lemniscata* fem. of L *lemniscatus* adj., adorned with ribbons, f. as next: see -ATE².] *Math.* A *n.* A type of Cassinian oval with two symmetrical loops across a central node (as the figure 8), defined by the equation $r^2 = 2a^2 \cos 2\theta$. L18. B *adj.* Of or pertaining to lemniscates; of the nature of a lemniscate. L19.

lemniscus /lɛmˈnɪskəs/ *n.* Pl. **-sci** /-skʌɪ/, *in sense 1 also* -sʌɪ/. M19. [L f. Gk *lēmniskos* ribbon. Cf. earlier LEMNISC.] 1 The character ÷ used by ancient textual critics in their annotations. M19. 2 *Zool.* Either of the two ribbon-like internal appendages associated with the proboscis of acanthocephalans. M19. 3 *Anat.* A band or bundle of fibres in the central nervous system, *esp.* any of those connecting sensory nuclei to the thalamus. M19.

lemon /ˈlɛmən/ *n.*¹, *a.*, & *v.* LME. [(O)Fr. *limon* (now restricted to the lime), corresp. to Sp. *limón*, Port. *limão*, It. *limone*, med.L *limo*, *limon-*, f. Arab. *līmūn*, *laymūn* collect. (sing. *-ūna*) fruits of the citron kind. Cf. LIME *n.*³] A *n.* 1 The ovate pale yellow acid fruit of the tree *Citrus limon*, much used for making drinks and as a flavouring. LME. 2 The tree which bears this fruit, a widely cultivated member of the rue family. Also *lemon tree*. E17. 3 Preceded by specifying wd: any of several other plants bearing yellow fruit like lemons. M18. 4 The colour of a lemon; pale yellow. L18. 5a Formerly, a person with a tart or snappy disposition. Now usu., a simpleton, a loser; a person easily deluded or taken advantage of. *slang.* M19. b A thing which is bad, unsatisfactory, or disappointing; *esp.* a substandard or defective car. *slang* (orig. *US*). E20. c The head. *slang.* E20. d An informer, a person who turns State's evidence. *US slang.* M20. 6 A lemon-flavoured soft drink; lemonade, lemon juice. L19.

Phrases etc.: **hand a person a lemon** pass off a substandard article as good; swindle a person, do a person down. *oranges and lemons*: see ORANGE *n. salt of lemon*: see SALT *n.*¹ 2c. *sweet lemon*: see SWEET *a.* & *adv.* **the answer is a lemon** a reply is unsatisfactory or non-existent. *water lemon*: see WATER *n.*

B *adj.* Of or resembling the colour, flavour, or fragrance of a lemon; pale yellow. M17.

Comb. & special collocations: *lemon balm*: see BALM *n.*¹ 6; **lemon cheese** a conserve made from lemons, butter, eggs, and sugar; **lemon-colour** (of) a pale yellow; **lemon-coloured** *a.* pale yellow; **lemon curd** = *lemon cheese* above; **lemon drop** a boiled sweet flavoured with lemon; **lemon-game** *US slang* a type of confidence trick in which the victim is led to believe that he or she can win at pool against a player who is in fact expert; **lemon geranium** a pelargonium, *Pelargonium crispum*, grown for its lemon-scented leaves; **lemon grass** a lemon-scented grass, *Cymbopogon citratus*, native to southern India and Sri Lanka (Ceylon), which yields an oil used in perfumery and cookery; **lemon law** *N. Amer. colloq.* a law requiring the manufacturer or seller to repair or replace a defective car; **lemon meringue (pie)** an open pie consisting of a pastry case with a lemon filling and a topping of meringue; **lemon oil** an essential oil obtained from the rind of lemons, used in cooking and perfumery; **lemon plant** = *lemon verbena* below; **lemon-scented** *a.* having a smell suggestive of lemons; *lemon-scented verbena* = *lemon verbena* below; **lemon squash** a drink made from lemons and other ingredients, often sold in concentrated form; **lemon-squeezer** (*a*) an instrument for extracting the juice from a lemon; (*b*) *Austral.* & *NZ colloq.* a hat with a peaked crown and broad flat brim, worn by New Zealand troops; **lemon thyme** a lemon-scented cultivated variety of thyme, *Thymus × citriodorus*, grown as a herb; **lemon verbena** a S. American shrub of the verbena family, *Aloysia triphylla*, grown for its lemon-scented leaves; **lemonwood** (*a*) *NZ* a small New Zealand evergreen tree, *Pittosporum eugenioides* (family Pittosporaceae), with leaves that are fragrant when crushed; (*b*) (the light-coloured wood of) any of several tropical American trees, esp. the Cuban *Calycophyllum candidissimum*, of the madder family; **lemon yellow** (of) a pale yellow.

C *v.t.* Flavour with lemon. M18.

lemonish *a.* somewhat resembling the colour, flavour, or fragrance of a lemon E18.

lemon /ˈlɛmən/ *n.*[2] M19. [Fr. *limande*, beside *lime* (cf. It *lima*, *limanda*), of unkn. origin.] In full *lemon dab*, *lemon sole*. A common flatfish of the eastern N. Atlantic, *Microstomus kitt*, of the flounder family, an important food fish. Also (by assoc. w. LEMON *n.*[1]), any of various mostly yellowish flatfishes.

lemonade /lɛməˈneɪd/ *n.* M17. [Fr. *limonade*, f. *limon* lemon: see -ADE.] A drink made of lemon juice and water, sweetened with sugar; a synthetic carbonated drink flavoured with lemon.

lemony /ˈlɛməni/ *a.* M19. [f. LEMON *n.*[1] + -Y[1].] 1 Of or resembling the flavour or fragrance of a lemon. M19. 2 Irritated, angry. *Austral.* & *NZ slang.* M20.

2 **go lemony at** become angry with (someone).

lempira /lɛmˈpɪərə/ *n.* M20. [*Lempira*, 16th-cent. chieftain who opposed the Spanish conquest of Honduras.] The basic monetary unit of Honduras, equal to 100 centavos.

lemur /ˈliːmə/ *n.* Pl. (in sense 1) **lemures** /ˈlɛmjʊriːz/, (in sense 2) **lemurs.** M16. [(mod.L f.) L *lemures* (pl.) shades of the dead.] 1 Chiefly *Rom. Mythol.* In *pl.*, the spirits of the dead, ghosts. Now occas. *sing.*, a ghost. M16. 2 *Zool.* Any mammal of the prosimian family Lemuridae, comprising long-tailed, sharp-muzzled, arboreal animals found chiefly in Madagascar. Also, any related primate, as the indri and the loris. L18.

2 *flying lemur, mongoose lemur, ring-tailed lemur, woolly lemur*, etc.

lemurid /ˈliːmjʊrɪd, ˈlɛm-/ *n.* a member of the family Lemuridae L19. **lemuriform** /lɪˈmjʊərɪfɔːm/ *a.* & *n.* (an animal) resembling a lemur L19. **lemurine** /ˈliːm-, ˈlɛm-/ *a.* & *n.* = LEMUROID M19.

lemurian /lɪˈmjʊərɪən/ *a.* L19. [f. (as) prec. + -IAN.] 1 (**L-**.) Of or pertaining to Lemuria, a hypothetical continent formerly supposed to have existed in the Jurassic period, stretching from Africa to SE Asia. Now *rare* or *obs.* L19. 2 Of or pertaining to lemurs; characteristic of lemurs. L19.

lemuroid /ˈliːmjʊrɔɪd, ˈlɛm-/ *a.* & *n.* L19. [f. LEMUR + -OID.] A *adj.* Designating or pertaining to the prosimian suborder Lemuroidea, of which the genus *Lemur* is the type. Also, resembling the lemurs. L19. B *n.* A lemuroid animal. L19.

Lenape /ˈlɛnəpi/ *n.* & *a.* E18. [Lenape = people.] A *n.* Pl. same, **-s.** 1 A member of the Delaware or any of various subgroups of the Delaware. E18. 2 The Algonquian language of any of these peoples. L19. B *attrib.* or as *adj.* Of or pertaining to the Lenape or their language(s). M19.

lenate /ˈliːneɪt, lɪˈneɪt/ *v.t.* & *i.* E20. [f. L *lenis* soft + -ATE[3].] = LENITE.

leˈnation *n.* E20.

lend /lɛnd/ *n. Sc., dial.*, & *colloq.* L16. [f. the vb.] A loan.

lend /lɛnd/ *v.* Pa. t. & pple **lent** /lɛnt/. [OE *lǣnan* = OFris. *lēna*, *lēnia*, Du. *leenen*, OHG *lēhanōn* (G *lehnen* enfeoff), f. Gmc base also of LOAN *n.*[1]: inf. w. *-d* f. LME after vbs, as *bend*, *send*, having an analogous pa. t. & pple.] 1 *v.t.* Grant the temporary use of (a thing) on the understanding that it or its equivalent shall be returned. Now also foll. by *out.* OE. b *spec.* Grant the use of (money) at interest. OE. c *v.i.* Make a loan or loans. OE. 2 *v.t.* a Give, grant, or impart (something abstract or temporary). OE. †b Hold out (a hand) to be taken. LME–E17. c Give or deal (a blow). Now *dial.* LME. d Grant the use or support of (a part of the body). L16. 3 *v.refl.* Accommodate or adapt oneself *to*. Of a thing: admit of being applied *to* a purpose or subjected *to* a certain treatment. M19.

1 *Spectator* 20,000 books of reference (which are not, of course, to be lent out). A. MILLER Manny . . had a policy of never lending tools. R. ELLMANN Pater would get into trouble later for lending Flaubert's books to undergraduates. b C. HOPE The banks are falling over each other to lend him money. 2a R. CROMPTON He certainly lends an interest to life. M. FLANAGAN They found new ways of lending support to each other. 3 E. BOWEN Lewis did not lend himself to the subterfuge. M. WARNOCK Brain activity . . lends itself to being described as a series of happenings or events.

Phrases: *lend a hand*: see HAND *n.* **lend an ear** listen, pay attention. *lend colour to*: see COLOUR *n.* **lending library** (a part of) a library from which books may be borrowed (with or without direct payment). **lend one's ears** = *lend an ear* above. *lend wings to*: see WING *n. minimum lending rate*: see MINIMUM *a. Public Lending Right*: see PUBLIC *a.* & *n.*

lendable *a.* E17.

lender /ˈlɛndə/ *n.* LOE. [f. prec. + -ER[1].] A person who lends; *esp.* a person who or institution which makes a business of lending money at interest.

lender of last resort an institution that will lend money, usu. at a high rate of interest, to a borrower unable to obtain a loan elsewhere.

lending /ˈlɛndɪŋ/ *n.* ME. [f. LEND *v.* + -ING[1].] 1 The action of LEND *v.*; *esp.* the lending of money at interest. ME. 2†a In *pl.* Money advanced to soldiers when regular pay cannot be given. L16–M17. b *gen.* A thing lent. E17.

lend-lease /lɛndˈliːs/ *a.*, *n.*, & *v.* M20. [f. LEND *v.* + LEASE *v.*[3]] = LEASE-LEND.

lene /ˈliːn/ *a.* & *n.* Now *rare* or *obs.* E18. [f. as LENIS.] A *adj.* †1 *Heb. Gram.* Of a point within a Hebrew letter: denoting absence of aspiration. Only in E18. 2 *Phonet.* Of a consonant: voiceless and plosive; (occas. simply) plosive. M18. B *n. Phonet.* A (voiceless) plosive consonant. M18.

lenes *n.* pl. of LENIS *n.*

†**leng** *n.* see LING *n.*[1]

†**leng** *v.* var. of LING *v.*

†**lenger** *a.* & *adv.* [OE *lengra* f. Gmc compar. of base of LONG *a.*[1]: see -ER[3].] A *adj.* Longer. OE–M16. B *adv.* Longer. ME–L16.

length /lɛŋθ, lɛŋkθ/ *n.* [OE *lengþu* = Du. *lengte*, ON *lengd*, f. Gmc, f. base also of LONG *a.*[1]: see -TH[1].] 1 Extent from beginning to end, esp. of a period of time, a speech, etc. OE. b An instance of this; a period or duration of time, *esp.* a long period. LME. 2 The linear extent of any thing as measured from end to end; the greater of two or greatest of three dimensions of a body or figure. Also, the extent of a garment in a vertical direction when worn. LOE. b An instance of this. E18. 3 The distance or extent between the extremities of something specified. ME. b The full extent of one's body. L16. c *Sport.* The distance between the nose and tail of a horse etc., or between the bow and stern of a boat, used in expressing the winning-margin or lead in a race. M17. d *Swimming.* The distance from end to end of a swimming pool; this distance as an amount swum. Cf. WIDTH 1b. E20. 4a The quality or fact of being long; substantial duration or extent. Opp. *shortness.* LME. b Verbosity, lengthiness. Now *rare.* L16. 5a Distance to a location or destination; distance travelled. Now *Sc.* LME. b *fig.* A degree or extreme to which a course of action or an opinion can be taken. L17. †6 Reach, range. LME–E17. 7a A (long) stretch or extent of land, hair, etc. L16. b A piece of material etc. of a certain or distinct extent. M17. c The penis. Also, an act of sexual intercourse. *slang.* M20. 8 *Theatr.* A portion of an actor's part, consisting of forty-two lines. M18. 9 *Brewing.* The quantity of liquid drawn off from a certain amount of malt. M18. 10 *Pros.* Quantity, esp. long quantity, of a sound or syllable. Opp. *shortness.* M18. 11a *Cricket.* The distance from the batsman at which a (well-bowled) ball pitches; the consistent reaching of a (good) distance by the bowler. M18. b *Tennis*, *Badminton*, etc. The quality of making shots to the back of the court; the consistent achievement of such play. E20. 12 *Bridge.* Four or more cards of the same suit held in one hand. E20. 13 *Math.* The number of components in any connected sequence. M20.

1 I. WATT Sentences . . of fairly usual length. C. HOPE The length of military service was indefinite. b R. K. NARAYAN She was welcome to stay any length of time. 2 R. P. JHABVALA He looked down the length of the table. b J. AGEE The inward wall . . was hung solid with cassocks of all lengths. A. KOESTLER Relationship between the lengths of the sides of a right-angled triangle. 3b TENNYSON All her fair length upon the ground she lay. c *Horse & Hound* Holborn Head passed the post three lengths clear. 4a J. BAYLEY 'The Turn of the Screw' . . in spite of its length has . . the characteristics . . of a short story. 5b M. ANGELOU Disappointment drives our young men to some desperate lengths. 7b A. T. ELLIS She had posted off a length of pale blue silk. 11a P. WARNER Rhodes . . was accurate in his length.

Phrases: *at arm's length*: see ARM *n.*[1] *at full length*: see FULL *a.* **at length** (*a*) after a long time, at or in the end; (*b*) at (*great, some*, etc.) *length*, for a long time, in detail, fully. †**at the length** = *at length* above. †**draw out in length** prolong, protract. **draw out to a great** etc. **length** prolong, protract. *full length*: see FULL *a. measure (out) one's length*: see MEASURE *v. not the length of a street*: see STREET *n.* †**of length** long. **slip someone a length** (of a man) have sexual intercourse with someone. **the length and breadth** (throughout) the whole area, (in) all parts or directions. **the length of** *Sc.* as far as.

Comb.: **lengthman** a person appointed to maintain a certain stretch of road, railway, or canal; **length-mark** (*a*) a phonetic symbol used to indicate the length of a sound, esp. to indicate that a vowel sound is long; (*b*) a macron indicating length; **lengthsman** = *lengthman* above.

lengthful *a.* (*poet.*, now *rare*) long E17.

lengthen /ˈlɛŋθ(ə)n, -ŋkθ-/ *v.* LME. [f. LENGTH + -EN[5].] 1 *v.t.* Make longer, extend; prolong. Also foll. by *out.* LME. b Make phonetically or prosodically long. M17. 2 *v.i.* Become longer. LME.

1 J. WAIN A garrulous chairman lengthened out a . . meeting into nearly three hours. *lengthen one's grip*: see GRIP *n.*[1] *lengthen one's stride*: see STRIDE *n.* 1a. 2 C. MORGAN The young shoots were lengthening. DENNIS POTTER The awkward pause lengthened between them.

lengthened *a.* made longer; long: L16. **lengthener** *n.* M16.

lengthways /ˈlɛŋθweɪz, -ŋkθ-/ *adv.* L16. [f. LENGTH + -WAYS.] In the direction of or parallel to the length of something; along the length.

lengthwise /ˈlɛŋθwʌɪz, -ŋkθ-/ *adv.* & *a.* L16. [f. LENGTH + -WISE.] A *adv.* = LENGTHWAYS. L16. B *adj.* Following the direction of the length. L19.

lengthy /ˈlɛŋθi, ˈlɛŋkθi/ *a.* L17. [f. LENGTH + -Y[1].] 1 (Of a composition, speech, etc.) of unusual length, excessively detailed, prolix; (of a period of time) long, extended, tedious. L17. 2 Physically long. Now *rare.* M18.

¶ Orig. an Americanism.

lengthily *adv.* L18. **lengthiness** *n.* E19.

Lengua /ˈlɛŋgwə/ *n.* & *a.* E19. [Sp., lit. 'tongue'.] A *n.* Pl. same, **-s.** 1 A member of a S. American Indian people inhabiting the Paraguayan Gran Chaco area. E19. 2 The language of this people. E20. B *adj.* Of or pertaining to the Lengua. E20.

lenient /ˈliːnɪənt/ *a.* M17. [L *lenient-* pres. ppl stem of *lenire* soothe, f. *lenis* soft, mild, smooth: see -ENT. Cf. Fr. †*lénient.*] 1 Emollient, soothing, relaxing. *arch.* M17. 2 Merciful, mild, tolerant; not disposed to or characterized by severity. Also, (of punishment) mild. (Foll. by *to*, *towards*, *with.*) L18.

2 K. GRAHAME Supposing you were to say . . three years for the furious driving, which is lenient. *Daily Express* William's much-loved nanny . . was sacked for being too lenient with him.

lenience *n.* lenient action or behaviour, indulgence

L18. **leniency** *n.* the quality of being lenient L18. **leniently** *adv.* M19.

lenify /ˈliːnɪfʌɪ/ *v.t.* Now *rare.* M16. [Late L *lenificare*, f. L *lenis*: see prec., -FY.] 1 Alleviate, mitigate, soothe (suffering, emotion, etc.). M16. †2 Soothe, soften (a part of the body); relieve (an ailment). L16–E18.

Leninism /ˈlɛnɪnɪz(ə)m/ *n.* E20. [f. *Lenin*, the assumed name of Vladimir Il'ich Ulyanov (1870–1924), leader of the Bolsheviks and founder of the Soviet State, + -ISM.] The political and economic doctrines of Marx as interpreted and applied by Lenin to the governing of the Soviet Union, to international proletarian revolution, and to the dictatorship of the working class. See also *Marxism–Leninism* s.v. MARXISM *n.*[1] (also called *Marxist-Leninism*).

Comb.: **Leninism-Stalinism** Lenin's doctrines as interpreted and applied by Stalin.

Leninist /ˈlɛnɪnɪst/ *a.* & *n.* E20. [f. as prec. + -IST.] A *adj.* Of, pertaining to, or characteristic of Lenin, his followers, or his doctrines. E20. B *n.* A follower or adherent of Lenin or his doctrines. E20.

Comb.: **Leninist-Marxist** *a.* = *Marxist-Leninist* s.v. MARXIST *n.*[1] & *a.*[1]; **Leninist-Stalinist** *a.* of, pertaining to, or characteristic of Leninism-Stalinism.

Also **Leninite** *a.* & *n.* E20.

lenis /ˈliːnɪs, ˈleɪnɪs, ˈlɛnɪs/ *a.* & *n.* E20. [L: see LENIENT. Cf. LENE.] *Phonet.* A *adj.* Of a consonant: weakly articulated; *spec.* designating the less or least strongly articulated of two or more homorganic consonants. see also *spiritus lenis* s.v. SPIRITUS 1a. E20. B *n.* Pl. **lenes** /-iːz/. A lenis consonant. M20.

¶ Opp. *fortis.*

lenite /ˈliːnʌɪt, lɪˈnʌɪt/ *v.t.* & *i.* E20. [Back-form. f. LENITION.] Esp. in Celtic languages: make or become lenis in articulation.

leˈnitable *a.* M20.

lenitic /lɪˈnɪtɪk/ *a.* E20. [f. L *lenitas* mildness, f. *lenis* (see LENIENT): see -IC.] *Ecol.* Of freshwater organisms or habitats: inhabiting or situated in still water. Cf. LOTIC.

lenition /lɪˈnɪʃ(ə)n/ *n.* LME. [f. as LENIS + -ITION, in sense 2 after G *Lenierung*.] †1 A relief, a mitigation. *rare.* LME–M16. 2 In Celtic languages: the process or result of a consonant's becoming lenis or lost; weakening of articulation. E20.

lenitive /ˈlɛnɪtɪv/ *n.* & *a.* LME. [med.L *lenitivus*, f. L *lenit-* pa. ppl stem of *lenire* soften, f. as LENIS: see -IVE. Cf. (O)Fr. *lénitif, -ive*.] A *n.* 1 A soothing medicine or medical appliance. LME. 2 Anything that mitigates or soothes; a palliative. E17. B *adj.* 1 Of a medicine or medical appliance: soothing, gently laxative. Now *rare.* LME. 2 Of a person, a person's disposition, etc.: lenient, mild, gentle. Now *obs.* exc. *Sc.* E17.

lenitively *adv.* E17.

lenity /ˈlɛnɪti/ *n.* LME. [OFr. *lénité* or L *lenitas*, f. as LENIS: see -ITY.] Lenience, gentleness, mercifulness; an instance of this.

leno /ˈliːnəʊ/ *n.* & *a.* Also †**lino**. Pl. of n. **-os**. L18. [Fr. *linon*, f. *lin* flax: cf. LINE *n.*[1], LINEN.] (Of) a kind of cotton gauze, used for veils, curtains, etc.; (designating) the type of weave used for this fabric.

Comb.: **leno loom** a loom which produces leno weave.

lens /lɛnz/ *n.* L17. [L = lentil: so called on account of its shape.] 1 A piece of glass or other transparent substance with one or two surfaces curved or otherwise shaped to cause regular convergence or divergence of light passing through it; such a piece, or combination of pieces, as forming part of a camera etc. L17. b *spec.* A piece of glass or plastic enclosed in a frame for wearing in front of the eyes. Also, a contact lens. L19. 2a *Anat.* The transparent elastic biconvex structure behind the iris of the eye by which light is focused on to the retina. Also *crystalline lens.* E18. b *Zool.* Any of the facets of a compound eye. M19. 3 A biconvex body of any material, as rock, ice, water, etc. L19. 4 A structure or device analogous to a glass lens for focusing or otherwise modifying the direction of sound, electrons, radiation, etc. E20.

1 *contact lens*: see CONTACT *n.* 4. *simple lens*: see SIMPLE *a.* 9. *supplementary lens*: see SUPPLEMENTARY *a.* *zoom lens*: see ZOOM *n.* 4 *acoustic lens, gravitational lens,* etc.

Comb.: **lens cap** a protective cap that fits over the end of a lens tube; **lens coating** a thin transparent coating applied to a lens to reduce reflection of light at its surface; **lens hood** a tube with outwardly sloping sides fitted to a camera lens to shield it from unwanted light; **lensman** = *cameraman* s.v. CAMERA; **lens paper, lens tissue** a kind of soft thin absorbent paper suitable for wiping lenses; **lens turret** a rotatable mounting fitted to the front of a camera and carrying several lenses; **lens-work** = *camera-work* s.v. CAMERA.

lensless *a.* L19. **lenslet** *n.* a small lens, *esp.* one of many in a compound eye or lenticular film M20.

lens /lɛnz/ *v.* E20. [f. the n.] 1 *v.i. Geol.* Of a body of rock: become gradually thinner along a particular direction to the point of extinction. Usu. foll. by *out.* E20. 2 *v.t.* = FILM *v.* 2. *US slang.* M20.

lensing *n.* (*a*) the action of the vb; (*b*) *Astron.* & *Physics* an effect resembling that of a lens, *esp.* the bending of radiation by a strong gravitational field: E20.

lensed /ˈlɛnzd/ *a.* M19. [f. LENS *n.*, *v.*: see -ED[2], -ED[1].] 1 Provided with a lens or lenses. M19. 2 *Astron.* Of (an image of) a celestial object: having an appearance affected by a gravitational lens situated between the object and the observer. L20.

lensoid /ˈlɛnzɔɪd/ *a.* M20. [f. LENS *n.* + -OID.] = LENTOID *a.*

Lent /lɛnt/ *n.*[1] ME. [Abbrev. of LENTEN.] 1 The season of spring. *obs.* exc. in *comb.* below. ME. 2 *Eccl.* The period of 40 weekdays from Ash Wednesday to Easter Eve, devoted to fasting and penitence in commemoration of Jesus' fasting in the wilderness. ME. †3a A period of fasting prescribed by any religious system. LME–L18. b A period or indulgence of 40 days. L15–M16. 4 In *pl.* The boat races held in the spring term at Cambridge University. L19.

Comb.: **lent-lily** the wild daffodil, *Narcissus pseudonarcissus*; **Lent term** the term in some universities etc. in which Lent falls, the spring term.

lent /lɛnt/ *n.*[2] *obs.* exc. *dial.* LME. [pa. pple of LEND *v.*] The action of lending; a loan.

lent /lɛnt/ *a.* LME. [(OFr. f.) L *lentus* slow, calm.] †1 Chiefly of a fever or a fire: slow. LME–L18. 2 *Mus.* In slow time. Now *rare.* E18.

lent *v.* pa. t. & pple of LEND *v.*

-lent /lənt/ *suff.* (not productive). [L *-lentus* -ful.] In and forming adjs. w. the sense 'full of, characterized by', as *pestilent, violent.* Cf. -ULENT.

lentamente /lɛntəˈmɛnti/ *adv.* M18. [It., f. *lento* f. L *lentus* slow.] *Mus.* Slowly, in slow time.

lente /ˈlɛnti/ *a.* M20. [L = slowly.] *Med.* Of a substance, esp. insulin: that is metabolized or absorbed gradually when introduced into the body.

Lenten /ˈlɛnt(ə)n/ *n.* & *a.* Also **l-**. [OE *lencten* prob. f. base also of MLG, MDu., Du. *lente*, G *Lenz*, etc., spring, f. Gmc base of LONG *a.*[1] (w. ref. to the lengthening of the days in spring). As adj. now interpreted as f. LENT *n.*[1] + -EN[4].] †A *n.* 1 Spring; = LENT *n.*[1] 1. OE–ME. 2 = LENT *n.*[1] 2. OE–M17.

B *attrib.* or as *adj.* 1 Of or pertaining to Lent, observed or taking place in Lent. OE. 2 Appropriate to Lent; (of food etc.) meagre, plain; (of appearance or facial expression) mournful, dismal. L16.

1 H. R. LANDON The annual Lenten concerto, which took place on 16 and 17 April. 2 G. BRENAN Our cities are sad and sordid places, our food lenten.

Special collocations: **Lenten corn** corn sown about Lent. **Lenten face** a dismal look or countenance. **Lenten fare** food without meat. **Lenten-kail** *Sc.* broth made without meat. **Lenten pie** a pie containing no meat. **Lenten rose** a variety of *Helleborus orientalis*, blooming in late winter and early spring.

lentic /ˈlɛntɪk/ *a.* M20. [f. L *lentus* (see LENT *a.*) + -IC.] *Ecol.* = LENITIC.

lenticel /ˈlɛntɪsɛl/ *n.* M19. [mod.L *lenticella* (Fr. *lenticelle*) dim. of L *lent-*, *lens* lentil.] *Bot.* A pore in the bark of woody stems and in some roots which allows the passage of gases.

lentiˈcellate *a.* producing or bearing lenticels M19.

lenticle /ˈlɛntɪk(ə)l/ *n.* L19. [f. as LENTICULE.] *Geol.* A lenticular piece or mass of rock, a small lentil.

lenticular /lɛnˈtɪkjʊlə/ *a.* & *n.* LME. [L *lenticularis*, f. as LENTICULE: see -AR[1].] A *adj.* 1 Shaped like a lentil or a (usu. biconvex) lens. LME. 2 Of or pertaining to a lens; using a lens or lenses. L19. 3 *Photogr.* (Of a film, screen, etc.) embossed with minute, usu. cylindrical, lenses so that two or more images can be interspersed; designating a method of colour photography using such a film together with filters. M20.

Special collocations: **lenticular cloud** *Meteorol.* a lens-shaped cloud with sharp, occas. iridescent, outlines usu. associated with lee waves. **lenticular galaxy** *Astron.*: having a flattened shape and dense centre like a spiral galaxy, but without spiral arms. **lenticular gland** *Bot.* = LENTICEL. **lenticular nucleus** *Anat.* = LENTIFORM *nucleus.*

†B *n.* A surgical knife with a lenticular shape. LME–E19.

lenticuˈlarity *n.* lenticular form or quality E20.

lenticulated /lɛnˈtɪkjʊleɪtɪd/ *a.* E20. [f. LENTICULE + -ATE[3] + -ED[1].] Embossed with minute lenses; = LENTICULAR *a.* 3.

lenticulation /lɛn,tɪkjʊˈleɪʃ(ə)n/ *n.* E20. [f. LENTICULE + -ATION.] *Photogr.* 1 The condition of being lenticulated. E20. 2 Each of the minute lenses of a lenticular film. M20.

lenticule /ˈlɛntɪkjuːl/ *n.* L19. [L *lenticula*: see LENTIL, -CULE.] 1 A lentil-shaped object. L19. 2 *Photogr.* = LENTICULATION 2. M20.

lentiform /ˈlɛntɪfɔːm/ *a.* E18. [f. L *lent-*, *lens* lentil + -I- + -FORM.] Shaped like a lentil or a (usu. biconvex) lens; lenticular.

lentiform nucleus *Anat.* the lower of the two grey nuclei of the corpus striatum.

lentigo /lɛnˈtʌɪɡəʊ/ *n.* Pl. **lentigines** /lɛnˈtɪdʒɪniːz/. LME. [L, f. as prec.] A freckle, a pimple; *spec.* a small brown hyperpigmented patch of skin usu. occurring on the face or hands, esp. of elderly people. Also, the condition of having such patches.

lentiginous /lɛnˈtɪdʒɪnəs/ *a.* covered with freckles, affected with lentigo L16.

lentil /ˈlɛnt(ə)l/ *n.* ME. [(O)Fr. *lentille* f. Proto-Romance f. L *lenticula* dim. of *lent-*, *lens* lentil.] 1 Any of the small rounded seeds of a leguminous plant, *Lens culinaris*, used in soups, stews, etc. (usu. in *pl.*); the plant itself, cultivated for food in Mediterranean countries. ME. †b In *pl.* In full *water lentils, lentils of the water.* Duckweed (genus *Lemna*). E16–E17. †2 In *pl.* Freckles or spots on the skin. M16–L17. 3 *Geol.* A mass of rock shaped like a biconvex or planoconvex lens; *spec.* one regarded as a subdivision of a formation. L19.

lentiscus /lɛnˈtɪskəs/ *n.* Pl. **-sci** /-skiː/, **-scuses**. LME. [L: see next.] = next.

lentisk /lɛnˈtɪsk/ *n.* LME. [L *lentiscus*, prob. of alien origin.] The mastic tree, *Pistacia lentiscus*.

lentitude /ˈlɛntɪtjuːd/ *n.* E17. [L *lentitudo*, f. *lentus* slow: see -TUDE.] Slowness, lethargy.

lentivirus /ˈlɛntɪvʌɪrəs/ *n.* L20. [f. L *lentus* slow + -I- + VIRUS.] *Biol.* & *Med.* Any of a group of retroviruses producing illnesses characterized by a delay in the onset of symptoms after infection.

lento /ˈlɛntəʊ/ *adv.* & *a.* E18. [It.] 1 *adv.* & *adj.* *Mus.* (A direction:) in slow time, slower than adagio. E18. 2 *adj.* Pronounced more slowly than in normal speech. M20.

lentoid /ˈlɛntɔɪd/ *a.* & *n.* L19. [f. L *lent-*, *lens* lentil + -OID.] A *adj.* Shaped like a lens or lentil, biconvex. L19. B *n.* *Biol.* A lens-shaped or spherical structure composed of retinal cells adhering together. M20.

lentor /ˈlɛntə, -ɔː/ *n.* E17. [L = viscosity, f. *lentus*: see LENT *a.*, -OR. Sense 2 cf. (O)Fr. *lenteur.*] †1 Clamminess, tenacity, or viscidity of the blood etc. E17–M19. b A viscid component of the blood. Only in E18. 2 Slowness, lack of vitality. M18.

Lenz's law /ˈlɛntsɪz lɔː, ˈlɛnz-/ *n. phr.* M19. [f. H. F. E. *Lenz* (1804–65), Ger. physicist.] *Electr.*

The law that the direction of an induced current is always such as to oppose the change in the circuit or the magnetic field that produces it.

Leo /ˈliːəʊ/ *n.* In sense 1 **l-**. OE. [L: see LION.] †1 A lion. OE–ME. 2 (The name of) a conspicuous constellation on the ecliptic just north of the celestial equator, between Cancer and Virgo; *Astrol.* (the name of) the fifth zodiacal sign, usu. associated with the period 23 July to 22 August (see note s.v. ZODIAC); the Lion. OE. b *Leo Minor*, (the name of) an inconspicuous constellation immediately north of Leo; the Little Lion. E18. 3 *Astrol.* A person born under the sign Leo. L19.

2 *attrib.*: E. KIRK Leo people are fine conversationalists. 3 S. PLATH The astrologer at her elbow (a Leo).

Leonardesque /liːənɑːˈdɛsk/ *a.* M19. [f. *Leonardo* da Vinci (see below) + -ESQUE.] Characteristic of or resembling the works of the Tuscan artist Leonardo da Vinci (1452–1519).

Leonberg /ˈliːənbəːg/ *a.* & *n.* E20. [A town in SW Germany.] (Designating) a breed of large dog, a cross between a St Bernard and a Newfoundland, often golden in colour; (designating) a dog of this breed.

Leonberger *n.* a Leonberg dog M20.

leone /liːˈəʊn/ *n.* M20. [f. Sierra *Leone*, a country on the coast of W. Africa.] The basic monetary unit of Sierra Leone, equal to 100 cents.

Leonese /liːəˈniːz/ *a.* & *n.* M19. [f. *León* (see below) + -ESE.] A *adj.* Of or pertaining to the Spanish province and former kingdom of León or the town of León in this area. M19. B *n.* Pl. same. 1 A native or inhabitant of León. M19. 2 The Spanish dialect of León, having affinities with Portuguese. M19.

Leonid /ˈliːənɪd/ *n.* & *a.* L19. [f. L *leo(n-)*, lion + -ID².] *Astron.* (Designating) any of a shower of meteors seeming to radiate from the constellation Leo in November.

leonine /ˈliːənʌɪn/ *a.*¹ LME. [(O)Fr. *léonin*, *-ine* or L *leoninus*, *-ina*, f. *leo(n-)* LION: see -INE¹.] 1 Resembling a lion, like that of a lion, lion-like. LME. b *Med.* Designating the lion-like facial appearance characteristic of leontiasis. E19. 2 Of or pertaining to a lion. E16.

1 J. HELLER A splendid . . old man with a massive leonine head and an angry shock of wild white hair.

Leonine /ˈliːənʌɪn/ *a.*² & *n.* In senses A.2, B. also **l-**. LME. [f. male forename *Leo*, f. as prec.] A *adj.* 1 Of or pertaining to any of the popes named Leo. LME. 2 Designating or pertaining to a kind of medieval Latin verse in hexameter or elegiac metre with internal rhyme. Now also, designating English verse with internal rhyme. M17.

1 **Leonine City** the part of Rome in which the Vatican stands, walled and fortified by Pope Leo IV.

B *n.* In *pl.* Leonine verse. M19.

leontiasis /liːɒnˈtʌɪəsɪs/ *n. rare.* Pl. **-ases** /-əsiːz/. M18. [mod.L f. Gk, f. *leont-*, *leōn* LION: see -IASIS.] *Med.* Orig., a supposedly lion-like appearance of the face due to lepromatous leprosy. Now, a similar condition (more fully *leontiasis ossea* /ˈɒsɪə/ [L *osseus* bony]) arising from Paget's disease (of the facial bones).

leopard /ˈlɛpəd/ *n.* & *a.* Also (*arch.*) **libbard** /ˈlɪbəd/. ME. [OFr. (mod. *léopard*) f. late L *leopardus* f. late Gk *leopardos*, also *leontopardos*, f. *leōn*, *leont-* LION + *pardos* PARD *n.*¹] A *n.* 1 A large carnivorous mammal of the cat family, *Panthera pardus*, of Africa and southern Asia, having a yellowish-fawn coat with dark brown or black spots grouped in rosettes. Cf. PANTHER. ME. b Any of various other related animals. Usu. w. specifying wd. L18. 2a *Her.* In medieval blazon: lion passant guardant, as in the arms of England. ME. b A figure of a leopard in painting, heraldry (in post-medieval blazon), etc. ME. 3 The fur of the leopard. Also, the skin of the leopard; a coat made from this. L15.

1 AV *Jer.* 13:23 Can the Ethiopian change his skinne? or the leopard his spots? b **black leopard** a leopard of a black-coated variety found in SE Asia. *clouded leopard*: see CLOUD *v.* 3. *snow leopard*: see SNOW *n.*¹ 3 *Vogue* A suède coat lined and trimmed with leopard. E. MCBAIN Two furs. A leopard and an otter.

Comb.: **leopard cat** any of several small spotted cats, *esp.* the wild cat of SE Asia, Japan, and Taiwan, *Felis bengalensis*; **leopard frog** *US* a N. American frog, *Rana pipiens*, that is green with black pale-ringed blotches; also called *meadow frog*; **leopard lily** (orig. *US*) any of several spotted lilies, esp. *Lilium pardalinum* (cf. PANTHER-*lily*); **leopard-man** a member of a leopard society (see below); **leopard moth** a large European goat moth, *Zeuzera pyrina*, that is white with black spots; **leopard's bane** any of various yellow-rayed plants of the genus *Doronicum*, of the composite family, much grown in gardens for their early flowers, esp. *D. pardalianches*; **leopard seal** an Antarctic seal, *Hydrurga leptonyx*, with a partly spotted coat; **leopard-skin** *a.* (*a*) made of leopard skin or of material resembling leopard skin; (*b*) *leopard-skin chief*, *priest*, among the Nuer people of E. Africa, a mediator or arbitrator who settles disputes; **leopard snake** a colubrid snake of central Europe and western Asia, *Elaphe situla*, with blotched brown markings; **leopard society** in W. Africa, a secret society whose members dress as leopards and attack people in the manner of leopards; **leopard-tortoise** a large spotted African land tortoise, *Testudo pardalis*; **leopard-tree** (*a*) = *letter-wood* s.v. LETTER *n.*¹; (*b*) = *leopard-wood* (b) below; **leopard-wood** (*a*) (the wood of) a S. American tree of the fig family, *Brosimum guianense*; (*b*) *Austral.* (the wood of) either of two trees with spotted bark, *Flindersia maculosa* and *F. collina*, of the rue family.

B *adj.* Made of leopard skin or of material resembling leopard skin. L18.

leopardess *n.* a female leopard M16.

Leopardian /liːəˈpɑːdɪən/ *a.* L19. [f. *Leopardi* (see below) + -IAN.] Of, pertaining to, or characteristic of the Italian poet and scholar Count Giacomo Leopardi (1798–1837) or his work.

leopon /ˈlɛp(ə)n/ *n.* M20. [Blend of LEOPARD and LION.] *Zool.* An animal born of a mating between a leopard and a lion.

leotard /ˈliːətɑːd/ *n.* L19. [Jules *Léotard* (1830–70), French trapeze artist.] A close-fitting one-piece garment, usu. covering the torso and arms, worn by gymnasts, dancers, etc.; a similar fashion garment.

leotarded *a.* L20.

lep *n.*, *v.* see LEAP *n.*¹, *v.*

Lepcha /ˈlɛptʃə/ *n.* & *a.* E19. [Nepali *lāpche*.] A *n.* Pl. **-s**, same. 1 A member of a people of Sikkim in India. E19. 2 The Tibeto-Burman language of this people. M19. B *attrib.* or as *adj.* Of or pertaining to the Lepchas or their language. E19.

¶Also called *Rong*.

leper /ˈlɛpə/ *n.*¹ Now *rare* or *obs.* ME. [(O)Fr. *lèpre* f. late L LEPRA.] Leprosy.

leper /ˈlɛpə/ *a.* & *n.*² LME. [Prob. f. attrib. use of prec.] †A *adj.* Affected with leprosy, leprous. LME–L16.

B *n.* 1 A person with leprosy. Now usu. avoided in med. use. LME. 2 A person who is shunned, esp. on moral grounds; an outcast. E19.

2 E. WAUGH No one knows papa. He's a social leper. *Sunday Express* They are the lepers in every prison—child molesters, rapists.

Comb.: **leper-house** a refuge or hospital for people with leprosy.

lepid /ˈlɛpɪd/ *a.* Now *rare* or *obs.* E17. [L *lepidus*.] Witty, amusing; charming, elegant.

lepido- /ˈlɛpɪdəʊ/ *comb. form* of Gk *lepid-*, *lepis* scale: see -O-.

lepidocrocite /-ˈkrəʊsʌɪt/ *n.* [Gk *krokis* fibre] *Min.* a red to reddish-brown orthorhombic hydroxide of ferric iron, usu. occurring as scaly or fibrous dipyramidal crystals E19. **lepidoˈdendron** *n.* [Gk *dendron* tree] a fossil plant of the genus *Lepidodendron*, common in coal measures, and characterized by the presence on the trunk of leaf-scars M19. **lepidomelane** /-ˈmɛleɪn/ *n.* [Gk *melanos* black] *Min.* a ferroan variety of biotite, usu. occurring in aggregations of small black scales M19. **lepidoˈsaurian** *a.* & *n.* (*a*) *adj.* designating or pertaining to the large group of reptiles which have a scaly skin, including all living lizards and snakes; (*b*) *n.* a reptile of this group: L19. **lepidoˈsiren** *n.* the S. American lungfish, *Lepidosiren paradoxa* M19. **lepidotrichium** /-ˈtrɪk-/ *n.*, pl. **-trichia**, [Gk *trikh-*, *thrix* hair] *Ichthyol.* any of the bony rays supporting the outer part of the fins in most teleost fishes E20.

lepidolite /ˈlɛpɪdəlʌɪt, lɪˈpɪdəlʌɪt/ *n.* L18. [f. prec. + -LITE.] *Min.* A kind of mica containing lithium.

Lepidoptera /lɛpɪˈdɒpt(ə)rə/ *n.pl.* L18. [mod.L, f. LEPIDO- + Gk *pteron* wing: see -A³.] (Members of) a large order of insects having four scale-covered wings, comprising butterflies and moths.

lepidopter *n.* an insect of this order E19. **lepidopteral** *a.* lepidopteran E19. **lepidopteran** *a.* & *n.* (*a*) *adj.* of or pertaining to the order Lepidoptera; (*b*) *n.* a lepidopteran insect: M19. **lepidopterist** *n.* a person who studies Lepidoptera E19. **lepidopterous** *a.* lepidopteran L18. **lepidoptery** *n.* = next M20.

lepidopterology /ˌlɛpɪdɒptəˈrɒlədʒi/ *n.* L19. [f. prec. + -OLOGY.] The branch of entomology that deals with Lepidoptera.

lepidopteroˈlogical *a.* L19. **lepidopterologist** *n.* L19.

lepidote /ˈlɛpɪdəʊt/ *a.* Now *rare.* M19. [mod.L *lepidotus* f. Gk *lepidōtos*, f. *lepid-*, *lepis* scale.] Chiefly *Bot.* Covered with scurfy scales.

leporine /ˈlɛpərʌɪn/ *a.* M17. [L *leporinus*, f. *lepor-*, *lepus* hare: see -INE¹.] Of, pertaining to, or resembling a hare, harelike.

lepospondyl /lɛpəˈspɒndɪl/ *n.* M20. [f. mod.L *Lepospondyli* (see below), f. Gk *lepos* husk + *spondulos* vertebra.] Any amphibian of the fossil suborder Lepospondyli, distinguished by vertebrae shaped like hourglasses.

lepospondylous *a.* E20.

lepper /ˈlɛpə/ *n. dial.* & *slang.* E20. [Var. of LEAPER.] A horse or dog that jumps, *esp.* one used for hunting or racing.

lepra /ˈlɛprə/ *n.* LME. [Late L, cl.L *leprae* pl., f. Gk *lepra* use as n. of fem. of *lepros* scaly, f. *lepos*, *lepis* scale.] *Med.* Orig., any disease characterized by scaling of the skin, *esp.* psoriasis. Now, leprosy.

leprechaun /ˈlɛprəkɔːn/ *n.* E17. [Ir. *leipreachán* alt. of MIr. *luchrupán* alt. of OIr. *luchorpán*, f. *lu* small + *corp* body.] In Irish folklore, a small, usu. mischievous being of human form, often associated with shoemaking or buried treasure.

leprolin /ˈlɛprəlɪn/ *n.* E20. [f. LEPROSY + *-lin*, after TUBERCULIN.] *Med.* = LEPROMIN.

leprologist /lɪˈprɒlədʒɪst/ *n.* E20. [f. LEPRA + -OLOGIST.] A medical expert in leprous diseases.

leproma /lɛˈprəʊmə/ *n.* Pl. **-mas**, **-mata** /-mətə/. L19. [f. LEPRA + -OMA.] *Med.* Any of the swellings of the skin, nerves, or mucous membranes characteristic of one of the principal forms of leprosy.

lepromatous *a.* of the nature of a leproma; characterized by or exhibiting lepromas: L19.

lepromin /ˈlɛprəmɪn/ *n.* M20. [f. prec. + -IN¹.] *Med.* A boiled saline extract of lepromatous tissue, used in testing resistance to leprosy.

leprophil /ˈlɛprəfɪl/ *n.* M20. [f. LEPROSY + -PHIL.] A person who is attracted to people with leprosy.

leproˈphilia *n.* attraction to people with leprosy M20.

leprophobia /lɛprəˈfəʊbɪə/ *n.* L19. [f. LEPROSY + -PHOBIA.] Irrational fear of leprosy; *spec.* an irrational belief that one has leprosy.

leprosarium /lɛprəˈsɛːrɪəm/ *n.* Pl. **-ia** /-ɪə/. M19. [f. late L *leprosus* LEPROUS + -ARIUM.] A hospital for people with leprosy.

leprose /ˈlɛprəʊs/ *a.* M19. [f. as prec. or f. LEPRA: see -OSE¹.] *Bot.* Having a scaly or scurfy appearance; *esp.* (of lichen) in which the thallus adheres like a scurf.

leprosery /lɛˈprɒsəri/ *n.* Also **-rie**. L19. [Fr. *léproserie*, f. *lépreux* or late L *leprosus*: see LEPROUS, -ERY.] A leper-house; a leper-colony.

leprosy /ˈlɛprəsi/ *n.* M16. [f. next + -Y³, repl. LEPRY.] 1 = *Hansen's disease* s.v. HANSEN 2. In biblical translations and allusions, any disfiguring skin disease. M16. 2 *fig.* Moral corruption or contagion. L16.

leprous /ˈlɛprəs/ *a.* ME. [OFr. *lepro(u)s* (mod. *lépreux*) f. late L *leprosus*, f. as LEPRA: see -OUS.] 1 Affected with leprosy. Also (*fig.*), foul, obscene; morally corrupt or corrupting. ME. †b Causing or inducing leprosy. *rare.* M16–E17. c Pertaining to, resembling, or accompanying leprosy. M17. 2 Covered with whitish scales; *Bot.* = LEPROSE; pale, unhealthy-looking. E17.

1 F. W. FARRAR Her literature . . a leprous fiction which poisoned every virtue. 2 YEATS You that have no living light, but dropped from a last leprous crescent of the moon.

leprously *adv.* E17. **leprousness** *n.* L15.

†**lepry** *n.* ME–M17. [f. LEPER *n.*[2] + -Y[3].] = LEPROSY.

¶The earlier term.

lepta *n.pl.* see LEPTON *n.*[1]

lepto- /ˈlɛptəʊ/ *comb. form* of Gk *leptos* fine, small, thin, delicate: see -O-. Opp. PACHY-.

leptomenin'gitis *n.* inflammation of the leptomeninges M19. **leptomeninx** /-ˈmiːnɪŋks/ *n.*, pl. **-meninges** /-mɪˈnɪndʒiːz/, (*Anat.*) *sing.* & (usu.) in *pl.*, the arachnoid and pia mater considered together L19. **lepto'nema** *n.* [Gk *nēma* thread] *Cytol.* = LEPTOTENE E20. **leptopro'sopic** *a.* [Gk *prosōpon* face] having a long narrow face L19. **leptorrhine** /ˈlɛptərʌɪn/ *a.* [Gk *rhin-*, *rhis* nose] *Anthropol.* (of the nose) long and narrow; having such a nose: L19. **leptotene** *n.* [-TENE] *Cytol.* the first stage of the prophase of the first meiotic division, in which the chromosomes are visible as fine slender threads E20.

leptocaul /ˈlɛptəkɔːl/ *n.* & *a.* M20. [f. LEPTO- + Gk *kaulos* stem, stalk.] *Bot.* (A tree) having or characterized by a relatively thin primary stem and branches. Cf. PACHYCAUL.

lepto'caulous *a.* = LEPTOCAUL *a.* M20. **leptocauly** *n.* development of this type M20.

leptocephalus /lɛptə(ʊ)ˈsɛf(ə)ləs, -ˈkɛf-/ *n.* Pl. **-li** /-lʌɪ, -liː/. M18. [mod.L, f. LEPTO- + Gk *kephalē* head.] The transparent leaf-shaped larva of an eel or of certain other fishes.

¶Orig. erron. regarded as a fish of a distinct genus, *Leptocephalus*.

leptokurtic /lɛptə(ʊ)ˈkɔːtɪk/ *a.* E20. [f. LEPTO- + Gk *kurtos* bulging + -IC.] *Statistics.* Of a frequency distribution or its graphical representation: having greater kurtosis than the normal distribution.

leptokur'tosis *n.* the property of being leptokurtic E20.

leptome /ˈlɛptəʊm/ *n.* Now *rare.* L19. [G *Leptom*, f. Gk *leptos* thin: see -OME.] *Bot.* The conducting tissue of the phloem. Cf. HADROME.

leptomonad /lɛpˈtɒmənad/ *n.* & *a.* E20. [f. next + -AD[1].] *Zool.* (Designating) any trypanosome when existing in an elongated form (assumed only in the invertebrate host and in culture) with a flagellum emerging from the anterior end. Also = next.

leptomonas /lɛpˈtɒmənas/ *n.* & *a.* Pl. same. E20. [mod.L (see below), f. LEPTO- + Gk *monas* MONAD.] *Zool.* (Designating) any trypanosome of the genus *Leptomonas*, which includes species parasitic in insects etc. and existing in both leptomonad and leishmanial forms. Also = prec.

lepton /ˈlɛptɒn/ *n.*[1] Pl. **-ta** /-tə/, **-tons.** E18. [Gk (sc. *nomisma* coin), neut. of *leptos* small.] An ancient Greek coin of small value, a mite; in modern Greece, a monetary unit equal to one-hundredth of a drachma.

lepton /ˈlɛptɒn/ *n.*[2] M20. [f. Gk *leptos* small + -ON.] *Particle Physics.* Any of a class of subatomic particles (including electrons, muons, and neutrinos) which do not take part in the strong interaction. Cf. HADRON.

Comb.: **lepton number** a quantum number assigned to subatomic particles that is ±1 for leptons and 0 for other particles and is conserved in all known interactions.

lep'tonic *a.* of, pertaining to, or involving leptons M20.

leptoquark /ˈlɛptəʊkwɑːk/ *n.* L20. [f. LEPTON *n.*[2] + QUARK *n.*[2]] *Particle Physics.* Any of several hypothetical subatomic particles with some properties of a lepton and some of a quark.

leptosomic /lɛptə(ʊ)ˈsəʊmɪk/ *a.* M20. [f. LEPTO- + Gk *sōma* body + -IC.] Designating or possessing a type of physique characterized by leanness and tallness.

'leptosome *n.* (a person with) a leptosomic physique M20.

leptospira /lɛptə(ʊ)ˈspʌɪrə/ *n.* Pl. **-rae** /-riː/. E20. [mod.L (see below), f. LEPTO- + Gk *speira* coil.] *Bacteriol.* Any spirochaete bacterium of the genus *Leptospira*, which includes *L. icterohaemorrhagiae*, a parasite of rats and the cause of Weil's disease in humans.

leptospiral *a.* pertaining to, characteristic of, or caused by leptospirae; *leptospiral jaundice*, infectious or spirochaetal jaundice, Weil's disease: E20. **'leptospire** *n.* = LEPTOSPIRA M20. **leptospi'rosis** *n.*, pl. **-roses** /-ˈrəʊsiːz/, infection with, or a disease caused by, leptospirae E20.

Lepus /ˈlɛpəs/ *n.* L17. [L *lepus* hare, Lepus.] (The name of) a constellation of the southern hemisphere immediately south of Orion; the Hare.

lere /lɪə/ *v. obs.* exc. *Sc.* Also **lear,** (*Sc.*) **leir.** [OE *lǣran* = OFris. *lēra*, OS *lērian* (Du. *leeren*), OHG *lēren* (G *lehren*), ON *læra*, Goth. *laisjan*, f. Gmc base also of LORE *n.*[1], LEARN.] †1 *v.t.* Teach; = LEARN *v.* 3. OE–M19. †2 *v.t.* Inform, tell; = LEARN *v.* 4. ME–M17. †3 *v.t.* & *i.* Acquire knowledge of (something); = LEARN *v.* 1. ME–E19. 4 *v.i.* Acquire knowledge, become informed. ME.

lered *ppl a.* (*obs.* exc. *dial.*) = LEARNED ME.

lerky /ˈləːki/ *n. local.* E20. [Origin unkn.] A children's noisy outdoor game in which players hide and then come out to try and kick a tin can etc.

lerp /ləːp/ *n.* M19. [Aborig.] A sweet secretion produced by insect larvae on the leaves of eucalypts and other plants; the scales produced by its solidification, eaten by Australian Aborigines.

lerret /ˈlɛrɪt/ *n. dial.* E19. [Origin unkn.] A boat suitable for heavy seas, used around the Isle of Portland in Dorset, SW England.

T. HARDY The trip in the stern of the lerret had quite refreshed her.

les /lɛz/ *n.* & *a. slang.* Also **lez, L-.** E20. [Abbrev.: cf. LESBO, LEZZY.] = LESBIAN *a.* 2, *n.* 2.

Lesbian /ˈlɛzbɪən/ *a.* & *n.* In senses A.2, B.2 now usu. **l-.** M16. [f. L *Lesbius*, Gk *Lesbios*, f. *Lesbos* (see below) + -AN (senses A.2 & B.2 f. the alleged homosexuality of Sappho, poetess of Lesbos (*c* 600 BC): cf. SAPPHIC).] A *adj.* 1 Of or pertaining to the island of Lesbos in the northern Aegean. M16. 2 Of a woman: homosexual. Also, of, pertaining to, or characterized by female homosexuality. L19.

1 **Lesbian rule** *Hist.* a mason's rule made of lead, which could be bent to fit curved surfaces; *fig.* a principle allowing flexibility. 2 D. LESSING Thinking that two women, friends on a basis of criticism of men are Lesbian. *Atlantic Monthly* Two girls who discover in themselves the first stirrings of lesbian attraction.

B *n.* 1 A native or inhabitant of Lesbos. L16. 2 A female homosexual. L19.

lesbianism *n.* female homosexuality L19. **lesbic** *a.* = LESBIAN *a.* 2 L19.

lesbo /ˈlɛzbəʊ/ *n. slang.* Also **L-.** Pl. **-os.** M20. [Abbrev.: see -O. Cf. LES, LEZZY.] = LESBIAN *n.* 2.

leschenaultia /lɛʃəˈnəʊtɪə/ *n.* Also **lech-.** E19. [mod.L (see below), f. L. T. *Leschenault* de la Tour (1773–1826), Fr. botanist and traveller: see -IA[1].] Any of various herbaceous plants and evergreen shrubs of the Australian genus *Leschenaultia* (family Goodeniaceae), bearing red, blue, white, or yellow flowers.

Lesch–Nyhan syndrome /lɛʃˈnʌɪhən ˌsɪndrəʊm/ *n. phr.* M20. [f. Michael *Lesch* (b. 1939) and William L. *Nyhan* (b. 1926), US physicians.] *Med.* A rare hereditary syndrome which affects young boys (usu. causing early death) and is marked by compulsive self-mutilation of the head and hands, together with mental handicap and involuntary muscular movements.

lese /liːz/ *v. obs.* exc. *dial.* Pa. t. **lore** /lɔː/; pa. pple **lorn** /lɔːn/. ME. [Repr. OE *-lēosan* as in *forlēosan* FORLESE.] 1 *v.t.* Lose. ME. †2 *v.i.* Lose, be a loser. ME–E17. 3 *v.t.* Destroy; bring to ruin or perdition; spoil. ME. †4 *v.i.* Come to ruin; be ruined or lost. *rare.* ME–L15. †5 *v.t.* Forsake, desert, abandon. Cf. earlier LORN *a.* 2. *rare* (Spenser). Only in L16.

1 BACON Flowers Pressed or Beaten, do lese the Freshness and Sweetness of their Odour. 5 SPENSER Neither of them she found where she them lore.

lesed /liːzd/ *a. obs.* exc. (*rare*) *Sc. Law.* LME. [f. L *laesus* pa. pple of *laedere* injure, hurt + -ED[1].] Damaged, injured.

lese-majesty /liːzˈmadʒɪsti/ *n.* Also ***lèse-majesté*** /lɛzmaʒɛste/. LME. [Fr. *lèse-majesté* f. L *laesa majestas* hurt or violated majesty (i.e. of the sovereign people), f. *laesa* fem. pa. pple of *laedere* injure, hurt, *majestas* MAJESTY.] 1 The insulting of a monarch or other ruler. Also, treason. LME. 2 *transf.* Presumptuous behaviour, disrespect. M17.

Lesghian /ˈlɛzgɪən/ *n.* & *a.* Also **Lezgian.** M19. [f. Russ. *Lezgin*: see -IAN.] A *n.* 1 A member of a people of the NE Caucasus. Formerly also, a member of a mountain people of Dagestan. M19. 2 The Ibero-Caucasian language of these people. L19. B *adj.* Of or pertaining to the Lesghians or their language. L19.

lesion /ˈliːʒ(ə)n/ *n.* & *v.* LME. [(O)Fr. *lésion* f. L *laesio(n-)*, f. *laes-* pa. ppl stem of *laedere* injure, hurt: see -ION.] A *n.* 1 Injury, harm; a wound, a blemish. LME. 2 Orig., damage to property or rights. Now (chiefly *Sc. Law*), injury or loss used as grounds for annulling a contract. M16. 3 *Med.* & *Biol.* A pathological change in the functioning or structure of an organ, body, organism, etc. M18. B *v.t. Med.* & *Biol.* Cause a lesion or lesions in (an animal, organ, etc.). M20.

†**leskar** *n.* see LASHKAR.

lespedeza /lɛspɛˈdiːzə/ *n.* L19. [mod.L (see below), f. (by a misreading) V. M. de *Céspedes* (fl. 1785), Sp. governor of eastern Florida.] Any of various leguminous herbs and shrubs of the genus *Lespedeza*, native to N. America and eastern Asia; *esp.* a plant of this kind used in the southern US as a fodder crop and to control soil erosion. Also called *bush clover*, *Japan clover*.

less /lɛs/ *a.* (in mod. usage also classed as a *determiner*), *adv.*, *prep.*, *n.*, & *conj.* As conj. also **'less.** [OE *lǣssa* = OFris. *lēssa* f. Gmc (whence also OE *lǣs* = OFris. *lēs* adv.), f. IE base also of Gk *loisthos* last. As conj. partly abbrev. of UNLESS. Cf. LEAST.] A *adj.* A compar. of *little.* 1 a A smaller number of; fewer. Now *non-standard.* OE. b Of number, amount, degree, etc.: not so great (as something mentioned or implied). Formerly also of physical size and material objects: smaller. (In attrib. use *lesser* is more usual.) Opp. (in mod. Eng.) *greater.* LOE. c Of smaller quantity or amount; not so much. ME. 2 Of lower status or rank; inferior. *obs.* exc. in phrs. like *no less a person than.* OE. 3 Designating the smaller, inferior, or (after L use) younger of two persons or things of the same name. *obs.* exc. in *James the Less* and imitations of this. OE. †4 With wds expressing or implying a neg.: more. *rare* (Shakes.). Only in E17.

1b JOSEPH HARRIS 19 is less than 20. BYRON And then the sighs he would suppress . . grew less and less. A. N. WILSON Their number was less than ten. c G. GREENE Things would have been different . . if Margaret had been less artist, more woman. E. BOWEN Mrs. Kearney could do with a little less weight and Miss Kevin . . with a little more. P. THEROUX Going without food he needed less sleep. W. BOYD With less reluctance than usual . . Temple allowed his father-in-law to grasp his hand.

B *adv.* To a smaller extent; in a lower degree; to an inferior extent, amount, etc. OE.

M. ARNOLD The less practised eye of sanguine youth. H. JAMES It didn't matter if one was a little more or a little less understood. G. VIDAL It looked smaller and less tidy than he had expected. J. MITCHELL It . . applied less in Shrieve's colony than in others.

C *prep.* With the subtraction of; minus. Orig. following the quantity to be subtracted. OE.

Times Cost of paint . . Less VAT input tax . . £500.

D *n.* A smaller amount, quantity, or number (*than* one that is mentioned or implied, *of* something). OE.

C. H. SPURGEON The less said about her the better. J. CONRAD In less than two minutes he was back in the brig. W. FAULKNER The face . . showed less of the ravages of passions . . than his own.

E *conj.* Unless. Now *US dial.* & *colloq.* ME.

Phrases (of adj., adv., & n.): **do less than** do anything other than (freq. in neg. contexts). **do no**

less do nothing else or other (*than*). **in less than no time** *colloq.* very soon, very quickly. *know little* (or *nothing*) *and care less*: see KNOW *v.* †**less in** inferior in point of. **less of** †(*a*) = *less in* above; (*b*) *less of a* —, a — to a smaller extent; (*c*) *colloq.* (as imper.) let us have less of, desist from (an action). **less than** (*a*) not at all, by no means; †(*b*) unless. *more haste, less speed*: see HASTE *n. more or less*: see MORE *a.* etc. **much less**: introducing a statement or suggestion regarded as still more unacceptable than one that has just been denied. NE'ER *the less. no less*: see NO *adv.*[2] †**nothing less** least of all things, anything rather (than the thing in question). **nothing less than** †(*a*) far from being, anything rather than; (*b*) the very same thing as; quite equal to. *not the less*: see NOT *adv.* **still less** = *much less* above. **the less** a thing which or person who is smaller or less (of two things compared).

less /lɛs/ *v.* Long *rare.* ME. [f. LESS *a.*] †**1** *v.i.* = LESSEN *v.* 1. ME–E17. **2** *v.t.* = LESSEN *v.* 2. ME.

-less /lɪs/ *suff.* [OE *-lēas* devoid (of), free (from), f. Gmc base also of LOOSE *a.*] **1** Forming adjs. & advs. f. ns. w. the sense 'free from, lacking (a), without (a)', as *doubtless, fearless, hatless, powerless.* **2** Forming adjs. f. vbs w. the senses 'unable to be —ed', as *countless, tireless*; 'that does not —', as *fadeless.*

-lessly *suff.*: forming corresp. advs. **-lessness** *suff.*: forming corresp. ns.

lessee /lɛ'siː/ *n.* L15. [AN *lessee*, OFr. *lessé*, pa. pples of *lesser* (mod. *laisser*): see LEASE *n.*[3], -EE[1].] A person to whom a lease is granted; a person holding property under a lease, a tenant.

lesseeship *n.* the condition or position of a lessee E19.

lessen /'lɛs(ə)n/ *v.* LME. [f. LESS *a.* + -EN[5]; superseded LESS *v.*] **1** *v.i.* Become less in size, quantity, amount, scope, etc.; decrease. LME. **b** Decrease in apparent size as a result of increasing distance. E17. **2** *v.t.* Make less in size, quantity, amount, scope, etc.; diminish. LME. **3** *v.t.* Represent as less; extenuate, palliate (a fault); disparage, belittle. *arch.* LME. †**4** *v.t.* Lower the dignity, position, or character of; humble; degrade, demean. LME–L18. †**5** In *pass.* Suffer loss or curtailment *of*; be reduced *in* (some quality). LME–L18.

1 P. WHITE Amongst the lessening throng of dancers. D. JOHNSON Soon the rain lessened. **2** J. C. POWYS The car.. lessened its pace the moment he stood still. A. HARDING Only time would lessen my feeling for my cousin.

lessen /'lɛs(ə)n/ *conj. US dial.* L19. [Repr. a pronunc. of *less than.*] Unless.

lesser /'lɛsə/ *a.*, *n.*, & *adv.* ME. [f. LESS *a.* + -ER[3]: a double compar.] **A** *adj.* **1** Not so great or much (as something mentioned or implied); inferior, of lower status or worth; smaller. Chiefly, & now only, *attrib.* ME. **2** *spec.* **a** Designating the smaller of two similar or related plants, animals, anatomical parts, or places. Opp. *greater* (see GREAT *a.* 7e). Cf. LEAST *a.* 4. E17. **b** *Mus.* Designating a minor interval. Now *rare.* L17.

1 A. DESAI The lesser functionaries of the camp to whom the commandant left the daily routine. F. WELDON Lesser men do that, who don't have the same sensitivities. DENNIS POTTER He did not call out, nor make any lesser sign of distress. **2a** *Lesser Antilles, lesser celandine, lesser noctule, lesser omentum, lesser spotted woodpecker*, etc.

Special collocations: **Lesser Asia** *arch.* Asia Minor. *Lesser Bear*: see BEAR *n.*[1] 2. **lesser breed** people of inferior status. *lesser diesis*: see DIESIS 1. *Lesser Dog*: see DOG *n.* 5. *lesser doxology*: see DOXOLOGY 2. *Lesser Entrance*: see ENTRANCE *n. lesser evil*: see EVIL *n.*[1] *lesser fry*: see FRY *n.*[1] **lesser light** [*Gen.* 1:16] a person of less eminence or importance. *Lesser Wain*: see WAIN *n.*[1] 2.

B *absol.* or as *n.* The lesser person or thing. L15.

B. MONTGOMERY It was considered that this alternative would be the lesser of two evils. *lesser of two evils*: see EVIL *n.*[1]

C *adv.* = LESS *adv.* Long *obs.* exc. in *lesser-known* adj. L16.

lesserness *n.* (*rare*) M16.

lesses /'lɛsɪz/ *n.pl. arch.* LME. [(O)Fr. *laisses* (mod. also *laissées*), f. *laisser* to leave.] *Hunting.* The droppings of a beast of prey.

lessest /'lɛsɪst/ *a.* & *n. obs.* exc. *dial.* M16. [f. LESS *a.* + -EST[1].] (The) least.

lessive /'lɛsɪv/ *n. rare.* L18. [(O)Fr. f. late L *lixiva* use as n. of pl. of *lixivus* var. of *lixivius*: see LIXIVIUM.] A lye of wood ashes, soap suds, etc., used in washing.

lessness /'lɛsnɪs/ *n. rare.* LME. [f. LESS *a.* + -NESS.] The quality or condition of being less; inferiority.

lesson /'lɛs(ə)n/ *n.* ME. [(O)Fr. *leçon* f. as LECTION.] †**1** Matter intended to be read or listened to; a public reading, a lecture; a course of lectures. ME–E18. **2** *Chr. Ch.* A passage of Scripture or other religious writing (appointed to be) read during a liturgical service (usually, a passage other than the Gospel at the Eucharist); *esp.* either of two such passages (see *first lesson, second lesson* below) in Anglican matins and evensong. ME. †**3** The action of reading to oneself; study (*of*). ME–L15. **4** A portion of a book or dictated matter to be studied by a pupil for repetition to the teacher; something that is learned or intended to be learned. ME. **5** A continuous portion of teaching given to a pupil or class at one time; any of the portions into which a course of instruction is divided. ME. **6** An occurrence from which instruction may be gained; an instructive example; a rebuke or punishment calculated to prevent a repetition of an offence. LME. †**7** A musical exercise or composition. L16–E19.

2 first lesson: from the Old Testament and forming the first of two in matins and evensong. *proper lesson*: see PROPER *a.* 2. **second lesson**: from the New Testament and forming the second of two in matins and evensong. **4** R. K. NARAYAN I could hear my classmates shouting their lessons in unison. S. COOPER Knots had been another of her father's favourite lessons. **5** E. BLISHEN Every lesson was an hour long. N. HINTON The bell rang for the first lesson. **give lessons** give systematic instruction (*in* a subject) over a period. *take lessons*: see TAKE *v.* **6** G. STEIN It was a lesson to poor Mrs. Haydon not to do things any more for anybody. **learn one's lesson** *fig.* be wiser as a result of an unpleasant, painful, etc., experience. **read a person a lesson** *fig.* reprimand or punish a person. **teach a person a lesson** *fig.* punish a person.

Comb.: **lesson-piece** a piece of material on which to practise needlework.

lesson /'lɛs(ə)n/ *v.t. arch.* M16. [f. the n.] Give a lesson or lessons to, instruct, teach; admonish, rebuke. Also, bring *into* or *to* (a certain state) by giving a lesson or lessons.

lessor /lɛ'sɔː, 'lɛsɔː/ *n.* LME. [AN *lesso(u)r*, f. *lesser*: see LEASE *n.*[3], -OR.] A person who grants a lease.

lessy *n.* & *a.* var. of LEZZY.

lest /lɛst/ *conj.* [OE *þȳ lǣs þe* whereby less that (*þȳ* THE *adv.*, *lǣs* less, *þe* rel. particle), late OE *þe læste*, f. which the first wd was lost by aphesis in ME.] **1** A neg. particle of intention or purpose, introducing a subjunct. cl. expr. something to be prevented or guarded against: in order that.. not. Also †*lest that.* OE. **2** After vbs of fearing or phrs. indicating apprehension or danger, introducing a subjunct. cl. expr. the event that is feared: that. OE.

1 R. KIPLING Lord God of Hosts, be with us yet, Lest we forget, lest we forget. M. SINCLAIR She drew in her breath lest he should hear it now. **2** F. CLISSOLD I felt a strong inclination to sleep, and feared lest I should drop down.

leste /'lɛstə/ *n.* M19. [Port. = east wind.] A hot dry east wind in Madeira and the Canary Islands.

lestobiosis /ˌlɛstəʊbʌɪ'əʊsɪs/ *n.* E20. [f. Gk *lestēs* robber + -O- + Gk *biōsis* way of life, after *symbiosis* etc.] *Zool.* A form of symbiosis found among certain social insects in which a small species inhabits the nest of a larger one and feeds on the food stored there, or on the brood of the larger species.

lestobiotic /-'ɒtɪk/ *a.* exhibiting lestobiosis E20.

Lestrigon /'lɛstrɪg(ə)n/ *n.* Also **Lae-** /'liː-, 'lʌɪ-/. Pl. **Lestrigones** /lɛ'strɪgəniːz/, **Lestrigons.** L16. [(L *Laestrygones* pl. f.) Gk *Lestrugones.*] = LESTRIGONIAN *n.* Formerly also *transf.*, a cannibal, a monster.

Lestrigonian /lɛstrɪ'gəʊnɪən/ *n.* & *a.* Also **Lae-** /liː-, lʌɪ-/. M16. [f. as prec. + -IAN.] **A** *n.* A member of a cannibal people of southern Italy in Homer's *Odyssey.* M16. **B** *adj.* Of or pertaining to the Lestrigonians. E17.

let /lɛt/ *n.*[1] ME. [f. LET *v.*[2]] **1** Hindrance, obstruction; a thing that hinders, an impediment. *arch.* exc. in (*without*) *let or hindrance, without let.* ME. **2** *Tennis, Fives*, etc. Obstruction of the ball in a way specified in the rules, on account of which it must be served again; an instance of this. In *Tennis* also, (a ruling requiring) an additional serve when a line judge and umpire disagree on the outcome of the previous play. E19.

let /lɛt/ *n.*[2] L17. [f. LET *v.*[1]] The action or an act of letting accommodation or a property for hire or rent.

¶Rare bef. 19.

let /lɛt/ *v.*[1] Infl. **-tt-**. Pa. t. & pple **let.** [OE *lǣtan* = OFris. *lēta*, OS *lātan* (Du. *laten*), OHG *lāzan* (G *lassen*), ON *láta*, Goth. *lētan*, f. Gmc (orig. redupl.) vb f. base rel. to that of LATE *a.*] **I** Leave; allow to pass. †**1** *v.t.* Allow to remain, leave behind; refrain from taking away, using, consuming, occupying, etc. OE–M17. †**2a** *v.t.* Leave undone; leave out, omit; omit or forbear *to do.* Cf. LET *v.*[2] 2. OE–M17. **b** *v.i.* Desist, forbear. (Foll. by *of, from.*) Cf. LET *v.*[2] 2. ME–M16. †**3** *v.t.* Leave (a task, responsibility, bequest) *to* someone else. OE–E17. **4** *v.t.* Allow the escape of (confined fluid); shed (tears, blood); emit (breath, a sound, etc.). Now *rare* exc. in *let blood* s.v. BLOOD *n.* OE. **5a** *v.t.* Grant the possession and use of (land, a building, a room, movable property) to or *to* another in consideration of rent or hire; award (a contract). Formerly also, lend (money) at interest. OE. **b** *v.i.* Of property etc.: be let. L18. **6** *v.t.* Set free, liberate. Also w. adj. compl. Long *obs.* exc. in *let loose* below. OE. †**7** *v.t.* & *i.* (w. *of*). Omit or cease to speak of. Only in ME. †**8** *v.t.* Leave, abandon, forsake; abandon *to* the flames. ME–L16. †**9** *v.t.* Lose (one's life, virtue, honour, etc.). ME–L16. **10** *v.t.* Allow to pass or go. Foll. by *to, into*, etc. LME.

5a S. SPENDER The West End is full of shops to let. P. NORMAN So she gravitated upwards, letting the ground floor to tenants. *Daily Telegraph* The contract has been let for the M40.. road. **b** O. ONIONS That the old place should suddenly let over his head seemed .. the slightest of risks. **10** A. T. ELLIS She felt that she had let into her mind something evil.

II Uses w. a following inf. (usu. without *to*). **11a** Not prevent or forbid; permit, allow. Also *ellipt.* w. inf. understood. OE. †**b** *v.i.* Give permission. M16–E18. **12** *v.t.* Cause. Now only foll. by *know* exc. as passing into sense 11a above. OE. **13** *v.t.* In *imper.* (with n. or pron. as obj.) as aux. vb, w. inf. serving as 1st or 3rd person imper. of the following vb, in exhortations, commands, and assumptions to be made. Also *ellipt.* w. inf. understood. ME. **b** *ellipt.* Let *us* etc. go. *arch.* L16.

11a J. KEBLE If they be indulged and let to run wild. M. MORRIS They might march directly down upon Montrose's left flank—if Montrose would let them. J. STEINBECK He stood aside and let the doctor and his man enter. I. MURDOCH He never let himself doze in the mornings. *Daily Mirror* You're letting her spoil your sex life. **12** *Financial Times* He has let it be known that he might be available to help. **13** E. NESBIT 'There are steps down,' said Jimmy... 'Don't let's,' said Kathleen. R. P. JHABVALA Let us be thankful for small mercies. **b** SIR W. SCOTT Let us home ere the storm begins to rage.

III Behave, appear, think. †**14a** *v.t.* With compl.: regard as. With obj. and inf., or cl.: consider *to be, that* (a person or thing) *is.* OE–LME. **b** *v.i.* Think. ME–L15. †**15** *v.i.* Behave, conduct oneself; have (a particular) behaviour or appearance; make *as though*, pretend. LOE–L18. †**16** *v.i.* Think (highly, lightly, much, etc.) *of.* Also foll. by *by, to.* LOE–E17.

Phrases: (A selection of cross-refs. only is included: see esp. other vbs.) *let alone*: see ALONE 1. *let* (*a person*) *blood*: see BLOOD *n.* **let a person have it** *slang* direct a blow or shot at a person; assail with blows or words. **let at** (now *Sc.*) discharge missiles at, assail. **let be** (*a*) *v.phr.t.* = *let alone* (a) s.v. ALONE 1 above; (*b*) *v.phr.i.* desist; (*c*) *v.phr.t.* (chiefly *Sc.*) = *let alone* (b) s.v.

ALONE I above. *let drive*: see DRIVE *v.* II. **let drop** (*a*) = *let fall* (b) below; (*b*) *let it drop*, let the matter end there, not continue with the matter (freq. in *imper.*). **let 'em all come** *colloq.*: expr. cheerful defiance. **let fall** (*a*) lower, cause to fall; (*b*) = DROP *v.* II; †(*c*) allow to lapse; proceed no further with; (*d*) *Geom.* draw (a perpendicular) to a line from a point not on it (foll. by *on*); (*e*) shed (tears). *let fly*: see FLY *v.* **let go** (*a*) allow to escape or go free, set at liberty; release; (*b*) relax or relinquish (one's hold); (*c*) relax or relinquish one's hold (*of*); (*d*) dismiss from one's thoughts; cease to attend to or control; *let it go at that*: see GO *v.*; (*e*) cease to restrain; chiefly *refl.*, give way to enthusiasm, an impulse, etc.; also, cease to take trouble about one's appearance, habits, etc.; (*f*) drop (an anchor); (*g*) dismiss (an employee). **let know** inform (a person). **let loose** set free, set at large, (esp. something fierce or uncontrollable); *all hell let loose*: see HELL *n. let me see*: see SEE *v. let pass*: see PASS *v. let rip*: see RIP *v.*[1] **let's** *colloq.* let us; *let's pretend*, a game of pretence or make-believe; *let's you and me* (or *you and I*, or *us*) (US colloq.), let us *do*. **let slip** (*a*) *v.phr.t.* & *i.* loose (a hound) from the lease in order to begin the chase; (*b*) *v.phr.t.* allow to escape through carelessness; fail to take (an opportunity); *let slip through one's fingers*: see FINGER *n. let the world wag* (*as it will*): see WAG *v. let walk*: see WALK *v.*[1] *let well alone*: see WELL *a. let wit*: see WIT *v. not let the grass grow under one's feet*: see GRASS *n.*

With advs. in specialized senses: **let down** (*a*) *v.phr.t.* lower; cause or allow to descend by gradual motion or short stages; lower in status, intensity, or strength; *let a person down gently, easily* (colloq.), treat considerately so as to spare a person's self-respect; avoid humiliating a person abruptly; *let one's hair down*: see HAIR *n.*; (*b*) *v.phr.t.* disappoint; fail in supporting, aiding, or justifying (a person, team, etc.); freq. in *let the side down* s.v. SIDE *n.*; (*c*) *v.phr.i.* (*US*) diminish, deteriorate; relax; (*d*) *v.phr.t.* (of a cow) produce (milk); (*e*) *v.phr.i.* (of an aircraft or a pilot) descend prior to making a landing. (*f*) *v.phr.t.* lengthen (a garment); lower (a hem) in order to lengthen a garment; (*g*) *v.phr.t.* deflate (a tyre). **let in** (*a*) allow to enter; give admittance to (a person), esp. into a dwelling; open the door of a dwelling to; *refl.* enter the dwelling where one lives, usually by means of a key; (*b*) *let in on*, allow to share (confidential information, privileges, etc.); (*c*) insert into the surface or substance of a thing; (*d*) *arch.* give rise to; (*e*) *colloq.* involve in loss or difficulty by fraud, financial failure, etc.; *let in for*, involve in, commit to, (something unpleasant or unexpected); (*f*) *Motoring* engage (the clutch) by releasing one's pressure on the clutch pedal. **let off** (*a*) discharge (a gun, a firework) with an explosion; *fig.* crack (a joke); *let off steam*: see STEAM *n.*; (*b*) allow to go or escape; excuse from punishment, a duty, etc.; punish lightly *with* a specified punishment; (*c*) let or lease (property) in portions; (*d*) allow to alight from a bus etc. **let on** *colloq.* (*a*) reveal, divulge, disclose, or betray a fact by word or look (foll. by *to* a person, *that* or *why* something is the case); (*b*) pretend (*that, to do*). **let out** (*a*) *v.phr.t.* give egress to; cause, allow, or enable to go out or escape by an opening, esp. through a doorway; set free, liberate; release from prison or confinement; *fig.* excuse or release from an obligation; *let the cat out of the bag* : see CAT *n.*[1]; (*b*) *let out of*, permit to be absent from (esp. one's sight); (*c*) *v.phr.t.* give vent to (anger etc.); give expression to (a thought); (*d*) *v.phr.t.* release (a reef) so as to increase the size of a sail; make (a garment) fuller or looser by allowing extra material at the seams; alter (the seams) in order to increase the fullness or size of a garment; (*e*) *v.phr.t.* put out to hire or contract; distribute among several tenants or hirers; *arch.* lend (money) at interest; (*f*) *v.phr.t.* divulge, disclose; freq. with cl. as obj.; (*g*) *v.phr.i.* & *t.* strike out with (the fist, the heels, etc.); give way to invective, use strong language; (*h*) *v.phr.t.* & *i.* (*colloq.*) give (a horse) its head; drive (a motor vehicle) very fast; (*i*) *v.phr.t.* (*Motoring*) release (the clutch), (*j*) *v.phr.i.* (*N. Amer.*) (of a class, meeting, entertainment, etc.) finish, come to an end. **let through** allow to pass. **let up** *colloq.* (*a*) become less intense or severe; cease; *let up on* (US), cease to have to do with; (*b*) relax one's efforts.

With preps. in specialized senses: **let into** (*a*) allow to enter; (*b*) insert into the surface or substance of; (*c*) introduce to the knowledge of, make acquainted with. **let off** excuse from (a punishment, duty, etc.).

Comb.: **let's-pretend** *a.* pretended, counterfeit; imaginary.

letting *n.* (*a*) the action of the vb; an instance of this; freq. w. adv. or vb; (*b*) a property that is let or available for letting: LME.

let /lɛt/ *v.*[2] *arch.* Infl. **-tt-**. Pa. t. & pple **let, letted**. [OE *lettan* = OFris. *letta*, OS *lettian* (Du. *letten*), OHG *lezzen*, ON *letja*, Goth. *latjan*, f. Gmc base of LATE *a.*] **1** *v.t.* Hinder, prevent, obstruct. Now chiefly in *let and hinder*. (Foll. by *from*, †*of*, †*to do*, †*that*.) OE. †**2** *v.i.* & *t.* Check or withhold oneself, desist, forbear; omit *to do*. (Not always distinguishable from LET *v.*[1] 2.) Only in ME. †**3** *v.i.* Be a hindrance. LME–M17.

1 *Daily Telegraph* A Church let and hindered from striking out boldly on new paths.

-let /lɪt, lət/ *suff.* [Orig. f. OFr. *-elette*, f. *-et*(*e*) -ET[1] added to wds in *-el* -EL[2] I (also = L *-ale* -AL[1]).] Forming ns. f. ns. **1** Denoting a smaller or lesser kind, as *booklet, flatlet, starlet*. **2** Denoting an article worn on the part of the body signified by the base, as *anklet, necklet*.

¶Wds f. OFr. include *bracelet, chaplet, crosslet, frontlet, gauntlet, hamlet, mantelet*. Early Eng. formations are *armlet, ringlet, townlet* (all M16). The suff. became common only in 18 (*cloudlet, leaflet, streamlet*), and prolific in 19.

letch /lɛtʃ/ *n.*[1] Now *rare*. L18. [Perh. f. LATCH *v.*[1], infl. by LECH *n.*[2]] A craving, a longing.

letch *n.*[2], *v.*, †**letcher** *n.* & *v.*, etc., vars. of LECH *n.*[2] etc.

let-down /ˈlɛtdaʊn/ *n.* & *a.* M18. [f. *let down* s.v. LET *v.*[1]] **A** *n.* **1** A disappointment; a drawback, a disadvantage. M18. **2** The descent of an aircraft or spacecraft prior to landing. M20. **3** The action of a cow producing milk. M20.

1 A. LURIE They sent me to Fresh Air Camp. What a let-down. J. HELLER He felt a melancholy let-down at the thought she might not care.

B *attrib. adj.* Able to be let down or lowered. M20.

let-go /ˈlɛtgəʊ/ *n.* M17. [f. *let go* s.v. LET *v.*[1]] An act of letting go.

lethal /ˈliːθ(ə)l/ *a.* & *n.* L16. [L *lethalis*, f. *lethum* var. of *letum* death, by assoc. w. Gk *lēthē*: see LETHE, -AL[1].] **A** *adj.* **1** *Theol.* Causing or resulting in spiritual death; entailing damnation. Formerly esp. of sin: mortal. L16. **2** Causing or capable of causing death, deadly; resulting in death. E17. **b** *Genetics.* Of an allele or chromosomal abnormality (such as a deletion): resulting in the death of an individual possessing it before the normal span or before sexual maturity; capable of causing such premature death when homozygous. E20. **3** Of or pertaining to death. E17. **4** *fig.* Harmful, injurious; destructive. M19.

2 A. G. GARDINER I struck a swift, lethal blow with my right hand. 4 V. BROME An aching head—the result of one particularly lethal champagne party.

Special collocations: **lethal chamber**: in which to kill people or animals by means of a toxic gas. **lethal dose** the amount of a toxic substance that causes death in people or animals.

B *n. Genetics.* A lethal allele or chromosomal abnormality. E20.

lethally *adv.* M17.

lethality /lɪˈθalɪti/ *n.* M17. [f. prec. + -ITY.] The condition or quality of being lethal; ability to cause death.

¶Rare bef. 20.

lethargic /lɪˈθɑːdʒɪk/ *a.* & *n.* LME. [L *lethargicus* f. Gk *lēthargikos*, f. *lēthargos*: see LETHARGY, -IC.] **A** *adj.* **1** Affected with lethargy; of or pertaining to lethargy. LME. **2** Causing lethargy. E18.

1 O. MANNING The city was lethargic, the palace dormant. G. GORDON Edward, not an especially lethargic man, was worn out by the time he reached the office.

†**B** *n.* A lethargic person. LME–M18.

lethargical *a.* = LETHARGIC *a.* I E17. **lethargically** *adv.* M17. **lethargicalness** *n.* M17.

lethargize /ˈlɛθədʒʌɪz/ *v.t.* Also **-ise**. E17. [f. next + -IZE.] Affect with lethargy.

lethargy /ˈlɛθədʒi/ *n.* & *v.* LME. [OFr. *litargie* (mod. *léthargie*) f. late L *lethargia* (med.L *litargia*, after med.Gk pronunc.) f. Gk *lēthargia*, f. *lēthargos* forgetful, f. *lēth-* base of *lanthanesthai* forget.] **A** *n.* **1** A condition of torpor, inertness, or apathy; lack of vitality. LME. **2** *Med.* A pathological state of sleepiness or deep unresponsiveness and inactivity. Now *rare*. LME. **B** *v.t.* = LETHARGIZE. *rare*. E17.

Lethe /ˈliːθi, -iː/ *n.* M16. [L f. Gk *lēthē* forgetfulness, oblivion, f. *lēth-*: see prec.] **1** In Greek mythology, a river in Hades whose water produced, in those who drank it, forgetfulness of the past (freq. in allusive phrs.); oblivion, forgetfulness of the past. M16. †**2** Death. *rare* (Shakes.). Only in L16.

Lethean /liːˈθiːən/ *a.* E17. [f. L *Lethaeus* f. Gk *lēthaios*, f. *lēthē*: see prec., -AN.] Of or pertaining to the mythological River Lethe; pertaining to or causing oblivion.

lethed /liːθt/ *a. rare*. E17. [Perh. f. L *lethum* death + -ED[2].] Dead (*lit.* & *fig.*).

†**Lethe'd** *a. rare* (Shakes.). Only in E17. [f. LETHE + -ED[2].] Lethean.

lether *n.* see LADDER *n.*

lethiferous /lɪˈθɪf(ə)rəs/ *a.* M17. [f. L *let(h)ifer*, f. *let(h)um* death: see -FEROUS.] = LETHAL *a.* 2.

let-in /ˈlɛtɪn/ *a.* L19. [f. *let in* s.v. LET *v.*[1]] *Typogr.* Designating a note at the side of a text and protruding into it, next to a row of indented lines.

let-off /ˈlɛtɒf/ *n.* E19. [f. *let off* (a), (b) s.v. LET *v.*[1]] **1** A display of festivity, a festive occasion. *arch.* E19. **2** A release or exemption from punishment or duty. M19. **b** *Cricket.* A batsman's escape from dismissal when a fielder misses an opportunity to get him or her out. M19. **3** The action of pulling the trigger of a rifle. E20.

let-out /ˈlɛtaʊt/ *n.* & *a.* M19. [f. *let out* s.v. LET *v.*[1]] **A** *n.* **1** An entertainment on a large or lavish scale. *Anglo-Ir.* M19. **2** An opportunity of avoiding a difficulty, an embarrassing situation, etc.; an excuse. E20.

Comb.: **let-out clause**: specifying a circumstance in which the terms of an agreement, contract, etc., shall not apply.

B *adj.* Of a fur garment: made by cutting a fur and reassembling the pieces to make a longer narrower whole. M20.

le tout /lə tu/ *a. phr.* E20. [Fr.] The whole of, everyone in, all, (a place).

Times The talk of le tout Paris in the French business world.

let-pass /lɛtˈpɑːs/ *n.* M17. [f. *let pass* s.v. PASS *v.*] A permit allowing passage.

Lett /lɛt/ *n.* L16. [G *Lette* f. Latvian *Latvi.*] **1** A member of a people living near the Baltic, chiefly in Latvia; a Latvian. L16. **2** Latvian, Lettish. M19.

lettable /ˈlɛtəb(ə)l/ *a.* E17. [f. LET *v.*[1] + -ABLE.] Able to be let; suitable for letting.

letter /ˈlɛtə/ *n.*[1] ME. [(O)Fr. *lettre* f. L *littera* letter of the alphabet, (in pl.) epistle, document, literature, culture.] **I** An alphabetic character. **1** A character representing one or more of the elementary sounds of the speech of a language; any of the symbols that compose an alphabet. ME. **b** Such characters collectively. Long *obs.* exc. in *before the letter* below. LME. **c** In *pl.* (*colloq.*), a degree, qualification, or honour denoted by its initial letters following the name of the holder; such letters. In *sing.* (*US*), a school or college honour for achievement in sport, denoted similarly by an abbreviation or monogram representing the name of the school etc. L19. **2** *Printing.* In *pl.* & *sing.*, types. Also, a font of type; a particular style of printed characters. Now *rare*. M16.

1 R. HOGGART SILENCE, in letters nine inches high and four inches across. *block letters, capital letters*, etc.

II Something written. †**3** An inscription, a document, a text; a written warrant or authority; in *pl.*, writings, written records. ME–L18. **4** *sing.* & (*arch.*) in *pl.* A written, typed, or printed communication addressed to a person, organization, etc., and usually sent by post or messenger. ME. **b** *sing.* & (usu.) in *pl.* A formal or legal document of this kind. ME. **c** An article, report, etc., describing the social, political, or cultural situation of the correspondent, esp. for a newspaper. L18. **5** The precise terms or strict verbal interpretation of a statement or document; the signification that lies on the surface. Cf. SPIRIT *n.* 7c. ME. **6** In *pl.* Literature in general; acquaintance with literature;

learning, erudition. Also, authorship. ME. 7 In full *French letter*. A condom. M19.

4 *air letter, chain-letter, day letter, form-letter, love-letter,* etc. c K. MARTIN Dore was an excellent correspondent, who for many years had written paragraphs about Parliament, mainly for the London Letter. 5 *New Yorker* Even according to the strictest letter of the law, kissing and embracing are permitted. H. CARPENTER Ritual laws governed daily conduct, and religion was of the letter rather than the spirit. *Shetland Times* The council . . obliged BP to stick by the letter of its lease. 6 W. S. CHURCHILL It was . . the Augustan Age of English letters.

Phrases: ascending letter: see ASCENDING I. BEAUTIFUL *letters*. **before the letter** a proof before letters, = PROOF *n*. 13. *begging letter*: see BEG *v*. *black letter*: see BLACK *a*. **commonwealth** or **republic of letters** authors collectively; literature. *dead letter*: see DEAD *a*. etc. *Dear John letter*: see DEAR *a*.[1] *descending letter*: see DESCENDING *a*. I. *dominical letter*: see DOMINICAL *a*. 2. *French letter*: see sense 7 above. *initial letter*: see INITIAL *a*. **in letter and in spirit** in form and substance. *Latin letter*: see LATIN *a*. **letter by letter** taking each letter in its turn. *letter* CERTIFICATORY. *letter missive*: see MISSIVE *a*. I. **letter of advice** *Comm*. a letter notifying the drawing of a bill on or the consignment of goods to the recipient. *letter of attorney*: see ATTORNEY *n*. **letter of comfort** an assurance about a debt, short of a legal guarantee, given to a bank by a third party. *letter of credence*: see CREDENCE 2. *letter of credit*: see CREDIT *n*. **letter of intent** a document containing a declaration of the intentions of the writer. **letter of introduction**: written by one person and given to another to introduce him or her to the addressee. *letter of marque (and reprisal)* : see MARQUE *n*.[1] *letter of protection*: see PROTECTION 3. *letter of recommendation*: see RECOMMENDATION I. *letter of slains*: see SLAIN *n*. *letters* AVOCATORY. *letter of* TRANSMITTAL. *letters dimissory*: see DIMISSORY 2. *letters missive*: see MISSIVE *a*. I. *letters of administration*: see ADMINISTRATION 4. *Letters of Orders*: see ORDER *n*. *letters patent*: see PATENT *a*. I. *letter(s) testimonial*: see TESTIMONIAL *a*. I. **man of letters** a scholar, a writer. *missive letter*: see MISSIVE *a*. I. *nundinal letter*: see NUNDINAL. *open letter*: see OPEN *a*. *pastoral letter*: see PASTORAL *a*. **profession of letters** authorship. *proof before letters*: see PROOF *n*. 13. *red letter day*: see RED *a*. *republic of letters*: see *commonwealth of letters* above. *revival of letters*: see REVIVAL 1a. *Samian letter*: see SAMIAN *a*. *scarlet letter*: see SCARLET *a*. SUNDAY *letter*. *the will of the summons letters*: see WILL *n*.[1] **to the letter** with adherence to every detail; in accordance with a strict literal interpretation (*of*). *white letter*: see WHITE *a*. *woman of letters*: see WOMAN *n*.

Comb.: **letter-balance** a balance for weighing a letter; **letter-bomb** an explosive device sent through the post as a terrorist's weapon; **letter-box** (*a*) a box in which letters are kept; (*b*) a public receptacle into which letters are dropped for collection and subsequent delivery by post; a receptacle into which letters are dropped when delivered; a slit in a door through which letters may be put; (*c*) a person or place through which spies pass information; **letter-card** a card with a gummed edge which can be folded and sealed to serve in place of a letter and its envelope; **letter-carrier** a person who carries letters; *spec*. (*N. Amer*.) a postman, a postwoman; **letterform** the graphic form of a letter of an alphabet; **letter-founder** (now *rare*) a typefounder; **letterhead** a printed heading on a sheet of letter-paper containing the address etc. of an organization or individual; a sheet of paper with such a heading; **letter-heading** a printed heading on a letterhead; **letter-man** †(*a*) a Chelsea pensioner who was entitled to extra pay on the ground of a letter from the monarch; (*b*) *US* a person who has received a letter for sport; **letter-office** a post-office; **letter-paper** paper for writing letters, esp. business ones; **letter-perfect** *a*. (*a*) *Theatr*. knowing one's part to the letter; (*b*) literally correct, verbally exact; *fig*. flawless, unexceptionable; **letter-plate** a plate for fixing to the outside of a door or wall and having a rectangular aperture through which letters may be put; **letterpress** (*a*) printed text as opp. to or accompanying illustrations; (*b*) matter printed from a raised surface, as opp. to lithography etc.; **letter-quality** *a*. (esp. of a printer attached to a computer) producing print of a quality suitable for business letters; (of a letter etc.) printed to this standard; **letter-scale** a scale for weighing letters; **letter-space** *n*. & *v*. (*Typogr*.) (*a*) *n*. a space inserted between the letters of a word; (*b*) *v.i*. insert extra space between the letters of a word; **letter-spaced** *a*. (*Typogr*.) having extra space between the letters of a word; **letter-weight** a paperweight; **letter-wood** the wood of the S. American tree *Brosimum aubletii*, of the mulberry family, which is red-brown, marked with irregular black spots; the tree itself; also called *leopard-wood*; **letter-word** a runic symbol or ideogram signifying both the name for something and a specific single letter; a word wholly or partly consisting of a letter or letters which are abbreviations in themselves; **letter-writer** a person who writes letters.

letter /ˈlɛtə/ *n*.[2] LME. [f. LET *v*.[1] + -ER[1].] A person who lets something; (with suffixed adj., vb, etc.) a person who lets loose, lets go, etc.

JONSON A careless letter-go Of money. H. MAYHEW The letters of rooms are the most exacting in places crowded with the poor. *blood-letter* etc.

letter /ˈlɛtə/ *v*. LME. [f. LETTER *n*.[1]] †1 *v.t*. Instruct in letters or learning. Only in LME. 2 *v.t*. Exhibit, classify, or distinguish by means of letters. M17. 3 *v.i*. Write letters. Chiefly as LETTERING. M17. 4 *v.t*. Write, paint, etc., letters on; write, paint, etc., (a word or words) on; inscribe. E18.

4 J. GARDNER He drove an old blue Chevy truck with his name and phone number lettered on the door.

letterer *n*. a person who practises or is skilled in lettering; a calligrapher: E20.

lettered /ˈlɛtəd/ *a*. ME. [f. LETTER *n*.[1], *v*.: see -ED[2], -ED[1].] 1 Acquainted with or instructed in letters; learned, literate, educated. ME. b Of or pertaining to learning or learned people; characterized by learning or literary culture. E18. 2 Inscribed with letters; *spec*. (of a book) having the title etc. on the back or spine in gilt or coloured letters. M17.

1b DISRAELI A man of lettered tastes.

Letterer-Siwe /lɛt(ə)rəˈsiːvə/ *n*. M20. [f. Erich *Letterer* (b. 1895) & Sture *Siwe* (b. 1897), Ger. physicians.] *Med*. Used *attrib*. and in *possess*. to designate a usu. fatal histiocytosis of the reticulo-endothelial system, occurring in early childhood.

letteret /ˈlɛt(ə)rɪt/ *n*. E19. [f. LETTER *n*.[1] + -ET[1].] A little or short letter.

lettergram /ˈlɛtəgram/ *n*. E20. [f. LETTER *n*.[1] + TELE)GRAM.] Chiefly *Hist*. A telegram meant to be delivered with the ordinary mail.

lettering /ˈlɛt(ə)rɪŋ/ *n*. M17. [f. LETTER *v*., *n*.[1] + -ING[1].] 1 The action of writing letters; letter-writing. Now *rare*. M17. 2 Letters written, painted, etc., on something. Also, the action or art of forming letters; calligraphy. E19.

2 F. RAPHAEL Tasteful lettering pointed out the multi-storey car park.

Comb.: **lettering piece** a piece of leather on the spine of a book bearing the title.

letterless /ˈlɛtəlɪs/ *a*. L16. [f. LETTER *n*.[1] + -LESS.] †1 Not written down. Only in L16. 2 Unacquainted with letters or literature; illiterate. E17. 3 Having no letters or correspondence. M18. 4 Having no letters inscribed or appended. M19.

letterset /ˈlɛtəsɛt/ *n*. M20. [f. *letter(press* s.v. LETTER *n*.[1] + OFF)SET *n*.] A method of printing in which ink is transferred from a raised surface to a blanket wrapped round a cylinder and from it to the paper etc.

Lettic /ˈlɛtɪk/ *a*. & *n*. *arch*. M19. [f. LETT + -IC.] A *adj*. Of or pertaining to the Letts or Latvians; *spec*. = BALTIC *a*. 2. M19. B *n*. The Latvian language. M19.

lettiga /lɛˈtiːgə/ *n*. E19. [It. f. L *lectica* litter, f. *lectus* bed.] A kind of sedan-chair in which two people are carried facing one another.

Lettish /ˈlɛtɪʃ/ *a*. & *n*. *arch*. M18. [f. LETT + -ISH[1].] A *adj*. Of or pertaining to the Letts or Latvians or their language; Latvian. M18. B *n*. Latvian. M19.

Letto- /ˈlɛtəʊ/ *comb. form*. *arch*. M19. [mod.L *Letto*, f. LETT: see -O-.] Used with adjs. & ns. referring to other languages or peoples, w. the sense 'Lettish or Latvian and', as *Letto-Lithuanian*, *-Slavonic*, etc.

lettre /lɛtr/ *n*. Pl. pronounced same. E18. [Fr.: see LETTER *n*.[1]] The Fr. for 'letter', occurring in various phrases used in Eng.

lettre bâtarde /batard/ [Fr. = bastard] bastarda L19. **lettre de cachet** /də kaʃe/, pl. **lettres de cachet**, [lit. 'of seal'] (*a*) *Hist*. a warrant issued in the France of the *ancien régime* for the imprisonment of a person without trial at the pleasure of the monarch; (*b*) an official order for imprisonment, exile, etc.: E18. **lettre de forme** /də fɔrm/ [lit. 'of shape or form'] textura L19. **lettre de somme** /də sɔm/ [lit. 'of sum or total'] rotunda L19.

lettrine /lɛˈtriːn/ *n*. M20. [Fr., f. as LETTER *n*.[1]: see -INE[1].] An initial letter, *esp*. a decorated one; an initial letter standing out from a painted background.

lettrism /ˈlɛtrɪz(ə)m/ *n*. Also in Fr. form ***lettrisme*** /lɛtrism/. M20. [Fr., f. as LETTER *n*.[1]: see -ISM.] A movement in French art and literature characterized by a repudiation of meaning and the use of letters (sometimes invented) as isolated units.

lettrist, ***lettriste*** /lɛtrist (*pl. same*)/ *n*. & *a*. (*a*) *n*. an exponent or advocate of lettrism; (*b*) *adj*. pertaining to or characteristic of lettrism or lettrists: M20.

lettuce /ˈlɛtɪs/ *n*. ME. [OFr. *letuës*, *laituës* pl. of *laituë* (mod. *laitue*) f. L *lactuca*, f. *lac(t-)* milk, w. ref. to the milky juice of the plant.] 1 Any plant of the genus *Lactuca* of the composite family; *esp*. (also *garden lettuce*) the cultivated species *L. sativa*, whose leaves are much used as a salad; such plants or their leaves collectively. Also, any of various plants resembling true lettuces. ME. 2 Money. *slang* (orig. *US*). E20.

1 H. SPURLING Bowls of the lettuce and radishes . . began to appear on Ivy's table. *cabbage lettuce, cos lettuce, iceberg lettuce, sea lettuce*, etc.

Comb.: **lettuce green** a medium shade of green.

lettuce-like *a*. resembling (that of) a lettuce L19.

letty /ˈlɛti/ *n*. *slang*. M19. [It. *letto* f. L *lectus*.] A bed; a lodging.

scarper the letty: see SCARPER 2.

let-up /ˈlɛtʌp/ *n*. M19. [f. *let up* s.v. LET *v*.[1]] A diminution in intensity or severity; a cessation, a break. (Foll. by *in*.)

Nature There is little prospect of a letup in fuel shortages for the next few years.

Letzeburgesch /ˈlɛtsəˈbʊrgɛʃ/ *n*. & *a*. Also **-isch** /-ɪʃ/. E20. [f. local name for Luxembourg + *-esch* -ISH[1].] = LUXEMBURGISH.

leu /ˈleɪuː/ *n*. Pl. **lei** /leɪ/. L19. [Romanian = lion.] The basic monetary unit of Romania, equal to 100 bani.

Leucadian /l(j)uːˈkeɪdɪən/ *n*. & *a*. E17. [f. *Leucadia* (see below) + -IAN.] Chiefly *Hist*. A *n*. A native or inhabitant of Leucadia (mod. Leukas or Levkas), an island in the Ionian Sea. E17. B *adj*. Of or pertaining to Leucadia. M20.

leucine /ˈluːsiːn/ *n*. Also (now *rare*) **-in** /-ɪn/. E19. [f. Gk *leukos* white + -INE[5], -IN[1].] *Biochem*. A hydrophobic amino acid, $(CH_3)_2CHCH_2CH(NH_2)COOH$, which occurs in proteins and is essential in the human diet; 2-amino-4-methylpentanoic acid.

leucite /ˈluːsʌɪt/ *n*. L18. [f. as prec. + -ITE[1].] *Min*. A potassium aluminosilicate, crystallizing in the tetrahedral system and usu. found as grey or white glassy trapezohedrons in volcanic rocks.

leucitic /-ˈsɪtɪk/ *a*. containing or of the nature of leucite M19.

leuco- /ˈluːkəʊ/ *comb. form*. Bef. a vowel also **leuc-**. Also (esp. *Med*. & *US*) **leuk(o)-**. In sense 2 also as attrib. adj. **leuco**. [f. Gk *leukos* white: see -O-.] 1 Forming ns. and adjs. w. the sense 'white, pale'; *esp*. in *Med*., repr. LEUCOCYTE; in *Chem*., forming names of colourless compounds chemically transformable to coloured ones. 2 Chiefly *Dyeing*. Designating the reduced, water-soluble colourless form of a dye which is fixed on the fibre and subsequently oxidized to the dye proper by the air.

leucoblast *n*. (*Biol*.) a spheroidal cell from which a leucocyte develops L19. **leucoˈblastic** *a*. (*Biol*.) containing or involving leucoblasts E20. **leucoˈcidin** *n*. a bacterial leucotoxin L19. **leucoˈcratic** *a*. (*Petrogr*.) (of a rock) light-coloured; rich in felsic minerals: E20. **leucoderm** *n*. & *a*. (a person who is) white-skinned, Caucasian E20. **leucoˈderma**, **-ˈdermia** *ns*. (*Med*.) an acquired local depigmentation of the skin of unknown cause; cf. VITILIGO: L19. **leucoˈdermic** *a*. (*a*) pertaining to or exhibiting leucoderma; (*b*) (naturally) white-skinned, Caucasian: L19. †**leucopathy** *n*. = ALBINISM M-L19. **leucoˈpenia** *n*. (*Med*.) a reduction in the number of white cells in the blood L19. **leucophore** *n*. (*Zool*.) a type of guanophore, an iridocyte E20. **leucoˈplakia** *n*. [Gk *plak-*, *plax* flat surface] *Med*. white patches appearing on the tongue or on other mucous membranes L19. **leucoplast**,

leuco'plastid *ns.* (*Biol.*) a colourless starch-accumulating organelle found in plant cells L19. **leucopoiesis** /-pɔɪ'iːsɪs/ *n.* (*Physiol.*) the production of leucocytes in the bone marrow E20. **leucopoietic** /-'ɛtɪk/ *a.* (*Physiol.*) of or pertaining to leucopoiesis E20. **leucopterin** /luː'kɒptərɪn/ *n.* (*Chem.*) a white pterin pigment found esp. in certain butterflies E20. **leuco'tactic** *a.* (*Physiol.*) pertaining to or promoting leucotaxis M20. **leuco'taxin, -ine** *n.* (*Physiol.*) a substance found in injured tissue and inflammatory exudates which causes an increase in the permeability of capillaries, and attracts leucocytes M20. **leuco'taxis** *n.* (*Physiol.*) movement of leucocytes in a particular direction M20. **leuco'toxin** *n.* (*Med.*) a substance which destroys leucocytes E20.

leucocyte /'luːkə(ʊ)sʌɪt/ *n.* Also **leuko-**. L19. [f. LEUCO- + -CYTE.] *Physiol.* Any of various colourless nucleated amoeboid cells of the blood, lymph, connective tissue, etc; also called *white* (*blood*) *cell, corpuscle*.

leucocytic /-'sɪtɪk/ *a.* of or pertaining to leucocytes; characterized by the presence of leucocytes: L19. **leucocy'tosis** *n.*, pl. **-toses** /-'təʊsiːz/, an increase in the number of leucocytes in the blood M19.

leucoma /luː'kəʊmə/ *n.* Also **leuk-**. E18. [mod.L f. Gk *leukōma*, f. as LEUCO- + -OMA.] *Med.* (The condition of having) a white opacity in the cornea of the eye, usu. as a result of inflammation. Also called *albugo*.

leucomatous *a.* affected with leucoma L19.

leucon /'luːkɒn/ *n.* E20. [mod.L genus name, f. as LEUCO-.] *Zool.* A grade of sponge structure of the leuconoid type; a leuconoid sponge. Cf. ASCON, SYCON.

leuconoid *a.* & *n.* (*a*) *adj.* designating, of, or pertaining to a sponge of the most complex type, composed of a mass of flagellated chambers and water canals; (*b*) *n.* a sponge of this type: E20.

†leucophlegmacy *n.* Also in L form **-matia**. M16–M18. [med.L *leucophlegmasia*, f. as LEUCO- + late L *phlegma*: see PHLEGM, -ACY.] Dropsy.

†leucophlegmatic *a.* dropsical M17–M19.

leucorrhoea /luːkə'riːə/ *n.* Also ***-rrhea**. L18. [f. LEUCO- + -RRHOEA.] *Med.* A mucous or mucopurulent discharge from the vagina. Also called *the whites, white flux*.

leucorrhoeal, leucorrhoeic *adjs.* of, pertaining to, or affected with leucorrhoea E19.

leucoses *n.* pl. of LEUCOSIS.

leucosin /'luːkə(ʊ)sɪn/ *n.* Also **leuk-**. L19. [f. Gk *leukos* white + -IN[1].] *Biochem.* **1** An albumin found in some cereal grains. L19. **2** A polysaccharide found in storage vesicles in cells of some golden algae. E20.

leucosis /luː'kəʊsɪs/ *n.* In sense 2 **leuk-**. Pl. **-oses** /-əʊsiːz/. E18. [Gk *leukōsis*, f. *leukoun* make white, f. *leukos* white: see -OSIS.] *Med.* **1** Whiteness; the process of becoming white. *rare*. E18. **2** Chiefly *Vet. Med.* Leukaemia; a leukaemic disease of animals, *esp.* any of a group of malignant viral diseases of poultry (*avian* or *fowl leucosis*) or of cattle (*bovine leucosis*). E20.

leucotic /-'kɒtɪk/ *a.* of, pertaining to, or affected with leucosis L19.

leucotomy /luː'kɒtəmi/ *n.* E18. [f. LEUCO- + -TOMY.] **†1** Surgical cutting of the sclera of the eye. Only in E18. **2** Surgical cutting of tracts of white nerve fibres in the brain; orig. *spec.*, prefrontal lobotomy; an instance of this. E18.

'leucotome *n.* an instrument used to perform leucotomy M20. **leucotomize** *v.t.* perform leucotomy on M20.

leucotriene *n.* var. of LEUKOTRIENE.

leucous /'luːkəs/ *a.* Now *rare* or *obs.* M19. [f. Gk *leukos* white + -OUS.] Having a white skin; albino.

leud /l(j)uːd/ *n.* Pl. **leudes** /'l(j)uːdiːz/, **leuds**. M18. [Repr. med.L *leudes* f. OS *liudi* people, nation.] *Hist.* In the Frankish kingdoms: a person holding land by feudal tenure; a vassal.

leuk- *comb. form* see LEUCO-.

leukaemia /luː'kiːmɪə/ *n.* Also ***-kemia**. M19. [f. LEUK- + -AEMIA.] *Med.* Any of a group of malignant progressive diseases characterized by the gross overproduction of (freq. immature or abnormal) leucocytes, which accumulate and suppress other haemopoietic activity.

leukaemic /luː'kiːmɪk/ *a.* & *n.* Also ***-kemic**. L19. [f. prec. + -IC.] **A** *adj.* Affected with leukaemia; characteristic of or resembling leukaemia; *spec.* marked by an excess of leucocytes in the blood. L19. **B** *n.* An individual with leukaemia. M20.

leukaemogenic /luːˌkiːmə'dʒɛnɪk/ *a.* Also ***-kemo-**. M20. [f. LEUKAEMIA + -O- + -GENIC.] *Med.* Capable of producing leukaemia; pertaining to the production of leukaemia.

leu'kaemogen *n.* a leukaemogenic substance or agent M20. **leukaemogenesis** *n.* the production or development of leukaemia M20.

leukaemoid /luː'kiːmɔɪd/ *a.* Also ***-kemoid**. E20. [f. LEUKAEMIA + -OID.] *Med.* Of a symptom or condition: resembling (that found in) leukaemia but due to some other cause.

leukemia *n.*, **-mic** *a.* & *n.*, etc., see LEUKAEMIA etc.

leuko- *comb. form* see LEUCO-.

leukocyte *n.* var. of LEUCOCYTE.

leukosin *n.* var. of LEUCOSIN.

leukosis *n.* see LEUCOSIS.

leukotriene /luːkə'trʌɪiːn/ *n.* Also **leuco-**. L20. [f. LEUCO- + TRIENE.] *Biochem.* Any of a group of biologically active metabolites of arachidonic acid, orig. isolated from leucocytes, which contain three conjugated double bonds.

leukovirus /'luːkəʊvʌɪrəs/ *n.* M20. [f. LEUKO- + VIRUS.] Any of a group of pleomorphic retroviruses which cause leucosis or tumours in mammals and birds.

lev /lɛv/ *n.* Also **leva** /'lɛvə/. Pl. **leva, levas, levs**. L19. [Bulgarian, var. of *lăv* lion.] The basic monetary unit of Bulgaria, equal to 100 stotinki.

levada /lɛ'vɑːdə/ *n.* L19. [Port. = mill-stream, sluice.] In Madeira: a canal for irrigation.

levade /lə'vɑːd/ *n.* M20. [Fr., f. *lever* raise: see -ADE.] A dressage movement (superseding the *pesade*) in which the horse raises its forequarters with the forelegs drawn up, and balances on its hind legs which are placed well forward under the body and deeply bent.

levain *n.* var. of LEAVEN *n.*

Levallois /lə'valwɑː/ *n.* & *a.* E20. [A suburb of northern Paris.] *Archaeol.* (Designating or characterized by) a technique of working flint or other rocks, developed in the lower and middle palaeolithic periods, in which a block is trimmed so that a flake of predetermined size and shape can be struck from it.

Levall'oisian *adj.* designating, pertaining to, or characterized by this technique; pertaining to or characteristic of such a culture: M20.

levallorphan /liːvə'lɔːfan/ *n.* M20. [f. *levo-* var. of LAEVO- + ALL(YL + M)ORPHINE + -AN.] *Pharm.* A morphine analogue and opioid antagonist which is used to counteract the effects of some narcotics.

levan /'liːvan/ *n.* E20. [f. LEVO- + -AN, after *dextran*.] *Biochem.* A fructan, *esp.* any of a class of fructans produced by bacteria and grasses.

levancy /'lɛv(ə)nsi/ *n.* L17. [f. LEVANT *a.*[1]: see -ANCY.] *Law* (now *Hist.*). The fact of being levant. Only in *levancy and couchancy*.

Levant /lɪ'vant/ *n.*[1] In sense 3 also **l-**. L15. [Fr., pres. pple of *lever* raise, used as n. for the point where the sun rises: see -ANT[1].] **1** The countries of the East; *spec.* the eastern part of the Mediterranean, with its islands and neighbouring countries. Now *arch.* or *Hist.* L15. **2** = LEVANTER *n.*[1] 2. Now *rare* or *obs.* E17. **3** = *Levant morocco* s.v. LEVANT *a.*[2] L19.

†levant *n.*[2] *slang*. E18–E19. [Transf. use of prec. sense 1. Cf. Fr. *faire voile en Levant* be stolen or spirited away. Cf. LEVANT *v.*] An act of absconding after losing a bet, a bet made with the intention of absconding if it is lost. Only in *come the levant, run* or *throw a levant*.

levant /'lɛv(ə)nt/ *a.*[1] LME. [Fr., pres. pple of *lever* raise, *se lever* rise: see -ANT[1].] *Law* (now *Hist.*). Of an animal: rising. Only in *levant and couchant*, (*a*) (of cattle) turned out day and night on common land; (*b*) (of straying animals) having stayed for a day and a night (the necessary period before the landowner might distrain them).

Levant /lɪ'vant/ *a.*[2] Also **l-**. E16. [Attrib. use of LEVANT *n.*[1]] **1** Pertaining to or obtained from the Levant. Now chiefly *arch.* or *Hist.* E16. **2** East, eastern, easterly. Opp. PONENT *a.* 1. *arch.* L16.

1 Levant morocco a high-grade large-grained morocco leather. **Levant wormseed** = SANTONICA.

levant /lɪ'vant/ *v.i. slang*. E17. [f. as LEVANT *n.*[2]] Abscond, run away, esp. with (gambling) debts unpaid.

Levanter /lɪ'vantə/ *n.*[1] In sense 2 also **l-**. M17. [f. LEVANT *n.*[1] + -ER[1].] **1** = LEVANTINE *n. rare*. M17. **2** A strong easterly wind in the Mediterranean. L18.

levanter /lɪ'vantə/ *n.*[2] *slang*. L18. [f. LEVANT *v.* + -ER[1].] A person who absconds, esp. after losing a bet.

Levantine /lɪ'vantʌɪn, 'lɛv(ə)n-, -tɪn/ *n.* & *a.* Now chiefly *arch.* or *Hist.* E17. [f. LEVANT *n.*[1] + -INE[1].] **A** *n.* A native or inhabitant of the Levant. E17. **B** *adj.* Of or pertaining to the Levant or its inhabitants; (of a ship) trading to the Levant. In early use, pertaining to the east, eastern. E17.

Levantinism /lɪ'vantɪnɪz(ə)m/ *n.* the spirit or culture of the Levant M20. **levantinize** /lɪ'vantɪnʌɪz/ *v.t.* make Levantine in form or character E20.

levari facias /lɪˌvɑːrʌɪ 'feɪʃɪas/ *n. phr.* E17. [L = cause to be levied, f. *levari* be levied (f. *levare* raise) + *facias* cause, 2nd person sing. pres. subjunct. of *facere* do, make.] *Law* (now *Hist.*). A writ ordering a sheriff to distrain the defendant's goods and income from lands against payment of the sum for which judgement has been given.

levas *n.pl.* see LEV.

levator /lɪ'veɪtə/ *n.* E17. [L = a person who lifts, f. *levat-* pa. ppl stem of *levare* lift: see -OR.] **1** *Anat.* A muscle which raises a limb or organ. Also *levator-muscle*. E17. **†2** *Surg.* An elevator for lifting depressed broken bone. L17–L18.

leveche /lɛ'vɛtʃi/ *n.* L19. [Sp.] A hot, dry, more or less southerly wind of SE Spain, the local counterpart of the sirocco.

levee /'lɛvi, 'lɛveɪ/ *n.*[1] & *v.*[1] L17. [Fr. *levé* var. of *lever* rising, use as n. of *lever* (inf.) rise. Cf. COUCHEE.] **A** *n.* **1 a** *Hist.* A reception of visitors on rising from bed; a morning assembly held by a person of distinction. L17. **b** *Hist.* An afternoon assembly for men only held by (a representative of) the British monarch. M18. **c** A reception or assembly at any time of day. Now *arch.* exc. *N. Amer.* M18. **†2** The company assembled at a levee. Only in 18. **†3** The action of rising, *spec.* from one's bed. E18–E19. **†B** *v.t.* Attend the levees of; pursue at levees. Only in 18.

levee /'lɛvi, lɪ'viː/ *n.*[2] & *v.*[2] *US*. E18. [Fr. *levée* fem. of *levé* pa. pple of *lever* raise: see LEVY *n.*[1]] **A** *n.* **1** An embankment to prevent the overflow of a river. E18. **b** *Physical Geogr.* A low broad ridge of sediment running alongside a river channel. Also, any similar natural embankment, as one formed by a mud flow, lava flow, or submarine current. L19. **2** A landing-place, a pier, a quay. M19.

B *v.t.* Raise a levee or embankment along (a river) or in (a district). Also, shut or keep *off* by means of a levee. M19.

J. PALMER Islands in the river might be *leveed* and successfully cultivated.

leveed *a.* (of a district) surrounded by or provided with levees; (of a river) having a (natural) levee or levees: M20.

levée en masse /ləve ɑ̃ mas/ *n. phr.* Pl. ***levées en masse*** (pronounced same). E19. [Fr.] A mass mobilization (orig. in Revolutionary France) in response to the threat of invasion. Cf. *levy in mass* s.v. LEVY *n.*[1] 2.

Economist An immediate *levée en masse*, . . the calling up now of every able-bodied man.

level /'lɛv(ə)l/ *n.* ME. [OFr. *livel* (later *nivel*, mod. *niveau*) f. Proto-Romance var. of L *libella* dim. of *libra* balance, scales.] **I 1** An instrument which indicates a line parallel to the plane of the horizon, used to determine whether a surface is horizontal; *spec.* a surveying instrument for giving a horizontal line of sight. ME. **b** (Usu. **L-**.) *The* constellation Norma. L19. **2** A horizontal position; the condition of being horizontal. LME. **3a** A (nearly) horizontal passage or gallery in a mine, *esp.* one used for drainage. M16. **b** A level tract of land, a stretch of country without hills; *spec.* (in proper names) any of various large expanses of level country. E17. **c** A (more or less) level or flat surface. M17. **d** A floor or storey in a building; a stratum in the earth. M20. **4** Position as marked by a horizontal line; a (real or imaginary) horizontal line or plane in relation to which elevation is measured. M16. **b** A position (on a real or imaginary scale) in respect of amount, intensity, extent, etc.; a relative height, amount, or value. L19. **c** *Physics.* More fully *energy level* (The energy value associated with) each of a set of discrete states of a quantized system; *spec.* a state or group of states of an atom characterized by the quantum numbers *n, L, S,* and *J* (cf. STATE *n.* 3b, TERM *n.* 13c). E20. **d** *Statistics.* In full *level of confidence* or *significance.* A number chosen as the maximum (or minimum) value of the probability with which any statistical result must be false (or true) for that result to be accepted as having been demonstrated. E20. **e** *Broadcasting & Recording.* The volume of a sound or the strength of a signal as it shows up in different pieces of equipment. M20. **5** A plane or standard in social, moral, or intellectual matters. E17. **b** A layer or position in a hierarchy. M20. **c** A facet or layer of significance, esp. in a literary or artistic work; any of various shades of meaning which may be perceived. M20. **d** The aspect or aspects of a subject, situation, etc., being considered at any particular time. M20.

1 *spirit-level, stride-level,* etc. 2 DEFOE The rising of the water brought me a little more upon a level. 3c TENNYSON By zig-zag paths.. Came on the shining levels of the lake. d N. MOSLEY Our house is on four levels. *London Archaeologist* Post-medieval levels deserve greater attention. 4 M. BRADBURY It rains.. and the level of the lake rises. *sea level* etc. b *Nature* That could result in dangerous levels.. of sulphates in city air. *Daily Telegraph* New.. starts are down to 40 per cent. of their level.. last year. 5 C. STEAD This stupid conversation, which she thought beneath Miss Aiden's level. P. BROOK He is there, on our level, attainable. b *Guardian* On instructions from director-level, the estimates.. had been prepared. B. EMECHETA Professorial class,.. those on salary level sixteen. c *Books* On the surface, it is.. pacy... On another level, it explores.. agonizing moral decisions. d C. F. HOCKETT Selection and preliminary ordering of data determine the *range* of analysis; the choice of criteria fixes the *level* of analysis. K. WATERHOUSE Conversation,.. seemingly on a personal level, flows easily.

†II 6 That which a weapon is aimed at; a mark. Also (*fig.*), an aim, a purpose. E16–E17. **b** The action of aiming; aim. Also, the line of fire, the range of the missile. M16–E18.

Phrases: advanced level: see ADVANCED 2. *black level*: see BLACK *a. dumpy level*: see DUMPY *a.*² *energy level*: see sense 4c above. **find one's level** reach one's right (social, intellectual, etc.) place in relation to one's associates. *level of confidence* or *significance*: see sense 4d above. **on a level** on a horizontal line or plane. **on a level with** on the same plane as; *fig.* the equal of. **on the level** (*a*) on the flat, horizontal; (*b*) (*colloq.*, orig. *US*) honest(ly), truthful(ly), straightforward(ly). *ordinary level*: see ORDINARY *a.* **take a level** *Surveying* ascertain the elevation of a piece of land. *trophic level*: see TROPHIC *a.* 2. *white level*: see WHITE *a.*

Comb.: **level-free** *a.* (of a mine) able to be worked or drained by means of levels; **level test**: of a recording or broadcast signal level to determine whether the settings or positions of equipment should be changed; **level tube** the glass tube of a spirit-level.

level /ˈlɛv(ə)l/ *a.* & *adv.* LME. [f. the n.] **A** *adj.* **1** Horizontal; perpendicular to the plumb-line. LME. **b** Lying, moving, or directed in an (approximately) horizontal plane. M17. **2** Having an even surface; flat; not bumpy. M16. **b** Of a quantity of a dry substance or ingredient: even with the brim of the measure; not rounded or heaped. M20. **3a** Lying in the same horizontal plane as something else; on a level *with.* Also *fig.*, consistent *with*, equal *to.* M16. **b** Of two or more things: situated in the same level or plane. E17. **4†a** In equipoise, balanced, steady. L16–E17. **b** Of the head (as the seat of the mind): well balanced, not agitated or confused, sensible. Orig. *US.* M19. **5** Of even, equable, or uniform quality, tone, or style; of even tenor. M17. **6** Of a contest: even, with no competitor having the advantage. E19.

2 J. CONRAD A great plain as level as the sea. C. MACKENZIE Turf recently disturbed was trodden level again. b E. CRAIG A heaped spoonful equals 2 level or liquid spoonfuls. 3a R. DAHL The flame is absolutely level with my eyes. b B. BYARS She sat down.. so that their heads were level. 4b *Woman & Home* It's vital to keep a level head if you're to be of help. 5 J. RULE I've actually tried to meet your level gaze. *Running* Run at a level pace.

Comb., special collocations, & phrases: **level crossing** a place at which a road and a railway, or two railways, cross each other at the same level; **level-dyeing** a process designed to prevent uneven absorption of the colouring matter in dyeing; **level-headed** *a.* having a level head, mentally well balanced, cool, sensible; **level-headedness** the quality or state of being level-headed; **level pegging** equality in a contest, equality of scores or achievements, the fact of being neck and neck; *level* PLAYING *field*; **one's level best**, (*US colloq.*) **one's levelest** one's very best, the most one can possibly do.

B *adv.* With direct aim; on a level *with*; horizontally. E17.

levelly *adv.* E17. **levelness** *n.* M17.

level /ˈlɛv(ə)l/ *v.*¹ Infl. **-ll-**, ***-l-**. LME. [f. the n.] **I 1** *v.t.* Make (a surface) level or even; remove or reduce irregularities in the surface of. LME. **b** Foll. by *out*: extend on a level. M17. **c** *Ling.* Reduce or obliterate a phonetic or morphological difference between (related forms), esp. by analogy. L19. **2** *v.t.* Place (two or more things) on the same level or (horizontal) plane. M16. **3a** *v.t.* Bring or reduce to the level or standard of something else (foll. by *to*); put on a level *with.* E17. **b** *v.i.* Be on a level or par *with. rare.* E17. **c** *v.t.* & *i.* Bring or move *up* or *down* to the level of something (expressed or implied); standardize. M18. **4** *v.t.* Beat or knock down; lay low, raze to the ground. E17. **b** *transf.* & *fig.* Reduce or remove (inequalities) to produce evenness or equality; smooth *away, out.* M17. **5** *v.t.* & *i.* Foll. by *off, out*: bring (an aircraft) into horizontal flight; (of an aircraft) assume horizontal flight; *transf.* & *fig.* (cause to) cease ascending or descending, increasing or decreasing. M20.

1 W. GASS The land is flat because the winds have leveled it. 2 WENDELL PHILLIPS Gunpowder leveled peasant and prince. 3a W. H. PRESCOTT Aristocracy was levelled.. to the condition of the peasant. c F. R. LEAVIS The modern world of mass-production and levelling-down,.. hostile.. to all distinction of spirit. *Independent* Conservatives.. in favour of 'levelling up', not down. 4 P. EGAN Davis caught his adversary, and.. levelled him. *Independent* The earthquake levelled 90 per cent of the houses. b B. C. BRODIE Circumstances of trial, which.. level all artificial distinctions. *Times* The question of their co-operating.. to level out the production of cars. 5 *Literary Digest* A 'pancake landing' occurs when the ship is leveled off several feet above the ground. *Times* Yields have been tending to level off, or even fall.

II 6 *v.t.* Aim (a missile weapon); bring (a weapon) to the proper level for firing or striking. L15. **†b** Shoot (a missile) *out* (*of* a weapon). L16–M17. **c** *transf.* & *fig.* Direct (one's gaze) *at*, (satire, criticism, an accusation, etc.) *at* or *against.* L16. **†d** Aim or intend (a thing) *to do.* Usu. in *pass.* E18–E19. **7** *v.i.* Aim, take aim, (*lit.* & *fig.*). *arch.* L15. **†b** Guess *at.* Only in L16. **8** *v.i.* Be honest or truthful; tell the truth, speak frankly, behave honestly or deal straightforwardly (*with*). *slang* (orig. *US*). E20.

6 E. L. RICE He comes quickly down the steps.. levelling his revolver at the crowd. **level one's aim** take aim. c M. SINCLAIR A look through his glasses, leveled at each member of his household. M. FOOT The charge could never be.. levelled against Nye. 7 W. DAMPIER When they shoot.., they level, and fire. T. SHERIDAN The Author in this Satyr levels at Nero. 8 R. CRAWFORD I'll level with you, I've been paid to find your brother. S. BELLOW He wouldn't answer. Lawyers level only among themselves.

III 9 *v.t.* & *i.* *Surveying.* Ascertain the differences of level in (a piece of land); determine the height of a point or points relative to a given horizontal plane. L16.

level /ˈlɛv(ə)l/ *v.*² *obs.* exc. *dial.* E16. [Perh. alt. of LEVY *v.* by assoc. with prec.] = LEVY *v.*

leveler *n.*, **leveling** *n.*, *a.* see LEVELLER etc.

leveller /ˈlɛv(ə)lə/ *n.* Also ***leveler.** L16. [f. LEVEL *v.*¹ + -ER¹.] **1a** A person who takes soundings or levels. Also, an instrument for taking levels. L16. **b** A person who or thing which levels ground. E18. **c** *Boxing.* A knock-down blow. E19. **2** An advocate of the abolition of social distinctions. Orig. & *spec.* (**L-**) a radical dissenter in 17th-cent. England, professing egalitarian principles. M17. **3** A thing which brings all people to a common level. M17.

levelism *n.* the principle of abolishing distinctions in society; in early use *spec.* the principles advocated by the Levellers: M17.

levelling /ˈlɛv(ə)lɪŋ/ *vbl n.* Also ***leveling.** L16. [f. LEVEL *v.*¹ + -ING¹.] The action of LEVEL *v.*¹; an instance of this.

Comb.: **levelling instrument** an instrument used in surveying and consisting essentially of a telescope fitted with a spirit-level; **levelling pole, rod** an instrument consisting essentially of a graduated pole with a vane sliding upon it, used in levelling; **levelling-screw** a screw used to adjust parts of a contrivance to an exact level; **levelling staff** = *levelling pole* above.

levelling /ˈlɛv(ə)lɪŋ/ *ppl a.* Also ***leveling.** M17. [f. LEVEL *v.*¹ + -ING².] That levels something; *esp.* bringing all to the same social, moral, or intellectual level. Also, of or pertaining to levellers and their principles.

lever /ˈliːvə/ *n.* ME. [AN *lever*, (O)Fr. *levier* alt. of OFr. *leveor*, f. *lever* raise.] **1** A bar resting on a pivot, used to raise or dislodge some heavy or firmly fixed object; a crowbar; *Mech.* a simple machine consisting of a rigid bar which pivots about a fulcrum and may be used to transmit force applied at a second point to move a resistant load at a third, esp. with mechanical advantage. ME. **†b** *gen.* A bar, a pole, a rod. ME–E17. **2** A projecting arm or handle by which a mechanism is operated or adjusted. M19. **3** In full *lever watch.* A watch with a lever escapement. M19. **4** *fig.* A means of exerting moral force; a means of effecting something. M19.

2 *Toronto Sun* A simple flip of a lever will enable the bike to be folded. 4 *Christian Aid News* The Government has sometimes used our aid as a lever to coax countries.

Comb.: **lever escapement** *Watchmaking* an escapement in which the connection between the escape wheel and the balance is made by means of a separate lever; **lever frame** the frame in a railway signal-box in which the operating levers are mounted and interlocked; *lever watch*: see sense 4 above; **leverwood** the American hop hornbeam, *Ostrya virginica.*

lever /ˈliːvə/ *v.* M19. [f. the n.] **1** *v.i.* Apply a lever; work with a lever. M19. **2** *v.t.* Lift, push, or otherwise move with or as with a lever; move or raise (oneself, another) awkwardly or with difficulty. Also, bring into a specified condition by or as by applying a lever. L19.

2 C. MACKENZIE Joseph.. levered up the lid.. with a chisel. A. MACLEAN I levered Smithy into a sitting position.

leverage /ˈliːv(ə)rɪdʒ/ *n.* & *v.* E18. [f. LEVER *n.* + -AGE.] **A** *n.* **1** The action of levering; the way of applying a lever. Also, a system of levers. E18. **2** The power of a lever; the mechanical advantage gained by the use of a lever. M19. **b** *fig.* Advantage for accomplishing a purpose; increased power of action. M19. **3** *Comm.* **a** The proportion of a company's total capital to ordinary shares; the effect of this on share prices. M20. **b** The earning potential created by the ratio of capital to shares; the use of borrowed capital to enhance this. M20.

B *v.* **1** *v.t.* = LEVER *v.* 2. M20. **2** *v.t.* Use borrowed capital for. Chiefly as *leveraged* ppl a. M20. **3** *v.i.* Use borrowed capital for investment, expecting profits made to be greater than the interest payable. M20.

2 **leveraged buyout** the buyout of a company (by its management) using borrowed capital.

lever de rideau /ləve də rido/ *n. phr.* Pl. ***levers de rideau*** (pronounced same). M19. [Fr.] = *curtain-raiser* s.v. CURTAIN *n.*

leveret /ˈlɛv(ə)rɪt/ *n.* LME. [AN, dim. of *levre*, (O)Fr. *lièvre* f. L *lepus, lepor-* hare: see -ET[1].] 1 A young hare; *spec.* one in its first year. LME. †2 *transf.* & *fig.* A pet, a mistress. E-M17.

levers /ˈliːvəz/ *n.*[1] Long *obs.* exc. *dial.* [OE *læfer*. Cf. LAVER *n.*[3]] Any of various plants with long flat leaves; *esp.* the yellow flag, *Iris pseudacorus*.

Levers /ˈliːvəz/ *n.*[2] Also **Leavers**. E19. [John *Levers* (1786–1848).] Used *attrib.*, *absol.*, and in *possess.* in names of lace-making machinery developed by Levers, and of lace thus produced.

levers de rideau *n. phr.* pl. of LEVER DE RIDEAU.

†**levet** *n.* E17–E18. [Perh. f. It. *levata*, f. *levare* raise.] A trumpet call etc. to rouse soldiers and others in the morning; a reveille.

levi *n.* see LEVI'S.

leviable /ˈlɛvɪəb(ə)l/ *a.* Also **levy-**. L15. [f. LEVY *v.* + -ABLE.] 1 Of a duty, tax, etc.: able to be levied. L15. 2 Of a person: able to be called on for payment of a contribution. Of a thing: able to be seized in execution. L19.

leviathan /lɪˈvʌɪəθ(ə)n/ *n.* & *a.* As n. freq. also **L-**. LME. [late L (Vulgate) f. Heb. *liwyāṯān*.] A *n.* 1 An (imaginary or real) aquatic animal of enormous size; a sea-monster. LME. b *fig.* A man of vast and formidable power or enormous wealth. E17. c Anything very large of its kind; *esp.* a huge ship. E19. 2 [After *Isa.* 27:1.] Satan. LME. 3 [After a book by Hobbes, 1651.] The commonwealth, the State. In later use, a totalitarian or bureaucratic regime. M17.

1 MILTON Leviathan, Hugest of living Creatures. b DE QUINCEY So potent a defendant as this leviathan of two counties. 2 R. WEST As the Almighty pointed out to Job, nothing can be done about . . leviathan.

B *adj.* Huge, monstrous. E17.

leviaˈthanic *a.* (*rare*) huge as a leviathan M19.

Levied /ˈliːvʌɪd/ *a.* Also **Levi'd**. M20. [f. LEVI'S + -ED[2].] Clad in Levi's; wearing Levi's.

levier /ˈlɛvɪə/ *n.* Also **levy-**. L15. [f. LEVY *v.* + -ER[1].] A person who levies something.

levigate /ˈlɛvɪgeɪt/ *v.t.* Pa. pple †**-ate** (earlier), **-ated**. M16. [L *levigat-* pa. ppl stem of *levigare* make smooth, polish: see -ATE[3].] †1 Lighten, alleviate. Only in M16. †2 Make smooth; polish. M16–M19. 3 Reduce to a fine smooth powder; make a smooth paste of (*with* some liquid). M16.

levigator *n.* a thick metal polishing disc, used to smooth a lithographic stone E20.

levigation /lɛvɪˈgeɪʃ(ə)n/ *n.* L15. [f. L *levigatio(n-)*, f. as prec.: see -ATION.] The grinding of a substance in a mortar or on a slab, esp. with a liquid; the action of levigating something.

levin /ˈlɛvɪn/ *n. arch.* ME. [Prob. ON, perh. f. 1st elem. of OSw. *liughnelder* (Sw. *ljungeld*, Da. *lygnild*) lightning flash, f. Gmc base of LIGHT *n.*] Lightning; a flash of lightning. Also, any bright light or flame.

levir /ˈliːvə/ *n.* M19. [L, = OE *tācor*, Homeric Gk *daēr*, Skt *devr* husband's brother, brother-in-law.] *Anthropol.* A brother-in-law; a person acting as such under the custom of the levirate.

levirate /ˈliːvɪrət/ *n.* E18. [f. as prec. + -ATE[1].] The custom among ancient Hebrews and some other peoples, which obliged a dead man's brother or next of kin under certain circumstances to marry his widow.

leviˈratic *a.* pertaining to or in accordance with the levirate E20.

Levi's /ˈliːvʌɪz/ *n.pl.* Also **Levis, l-**, in attrib. use **levi**. E20. [*Levi* Strauss: see below.] (Proprietary name for) a type of blue denim jeans or overalls, with rivets to reinforce stress-points, patented and produced by Levi Strauss as working clothes in the 1860s and adopted as a fashion garment in the 20th cent. Now also, any garment made by Levi Strauss & Co.

levitate /ˈlɛvɪteɪt/ *v.* L17. [f. L *levis* light, after GRAVITATE: see -ATE[3].] 1 *v.i.* Rise by virtue of lightness. *rare* in *gen.* sense. L17. b Chiefly *Spiritualism.* Rise and float in the air through supernatural agency. L19. 2 *v.t.* Make lighter or of less weight. *rare.* L17. 3 *v.t.* a Chiefly *Spiritualism.* Cause to levitate. L19. b Cause (something heavier than the surrounding fluid) to rise or remain suspended without visible means (e.g. using magnetic forces). M20.

1b CARYL CHURCHILL Joy will cause the . . population to levitate two feet off the ground. 3a A. LANG The levitated boy . . flew over a garden. b *Observer* Levitated trains would hover five inches above a metal track, held aloft by advanced repelling magnets.

levitant *n.* = LEVITATOR L19. **levitative** *a.* adapted for or capable of levitation L19. **levitator** *n.* a person who believes in levitation or professes ability to practise it L19.

levitation /lɛvɪˈteɪʃ(ə)n/ *n.* M17. [f. prec. + -ATION.] 1 The action or process of levitating or being levitated; an instance of this. M17. †2 The action or process of becoming lighter. Also, the quality of being comparatively light; buoyancy. L17–M18.

1 H. G. WELLS The invisibility of all the machinery gave an extraordinary effect of independent levitation. *Listener* A standing offer of £1,000 to any medium who can produce physical phenomena such as . . levitation . . under test conditions. *Observer* 'Magnetic levitation' . . could turn out to be the most important advance in transport technology.

levitational *a.* E20.

Levite /ˈliːvʌɪt/ *n.* ME. [Chr.L *levita, levites*, f. Gk *levitēs*, f. *Levi*, f. Heb. *lēwī* Levi: see -ITE[1].] 1 A member of the ancient Hebrew tribe of Levi, esp. of that part of it which provided assistants to the priests in worship in the temple. ME. †2 A deacon. LME–E17. †3 A member of the clergy; a domestic chaplain. Usu. *derog.* M17–M19.

Levitic /lɪˈvɪtɪk/ *a.* M17. [f. as next: see -IC.] = next.

Levitical /lɪˈvɪtɪk(ə)l/ *a.* M16. [f. late L (Vulgate) *leviticus* f. Gk *levitikos* f. *levitēs*: see LEVITE, -ICAL.] 1 Of or pertaining to the Levites. M16. 2 Of or pertaining to the ancient Jewish system of ritual administered by the Levites. Also, of or pertaining to the biblical Book of Leviticus. M16.

2 **levitical degrees** the degrees of consanguinity within which marriage is forbidden (*Lev.* 18:6–18).

Leviticalism *n.* Levitical tenets and practice L19. **Levitically** *adv.* in a Levitical manner, according to Levitical law M17.

levity /ˈlɛvɪti/ *n.* M16. [L *levitas*, f. *levis* light: see -ITY.] 1 A tendency to make light of serious matters; frivolity; inappropriate jocularity. Now also, an instance of this. M16. b Lack of constancy or resolution; instability, fickleness. E17. c Undignified behaviour, impropriety; an instance of this. E17. 2 The quality or fact of having comparatively little weight; lightness. *arch.* L16. b A property formerly believed to exist in varying degrees in all substances and which made them tend to rise, as substances possessing gravity tend to sink. Cf. GRAVITY 4a. *obs.* exc. *Hist.* E17.

1 R. W. EMERSON But politics . . cannot be treated with levity. J. K. JEROME He had not meant to be funny, . . levity was not his failing. b GIBBON Forgot, with the levity of Barbarians, the services which they had . . received. c SWIFT Those . . little levities so commonly incident to young ladies. 2 M. SOMERVILLE Hydrogen . . rises in the air on account of its levity.

levo- *comb. form* see LAEVO-.

levodopa /liːvə(ʊ)ˈdəʊpə/ *n.* L20. [f. *levo-* var. of LAEVO- + DOPA.] *Biochem.* & *Pharm.* = L-*dopa* s.v. DOPA.

levorotatory *a.* see LAEVOROTATORY.

levulinic *a.* see LAEVULINIC.

levulosan, -lose *ns.* see LAEVULOSAN, LAEVULOSE.

levy /ˈlɛvi/ *n.*[1] ME. [(O)Fr. *levée* use as n. of fem. pa. pple of *lever*, f. L *levare* raise, f. *levis* light.] 1 a The collection of an assessment, duty, or tax (formerly also, of a debt or fine). ME. b A tax, *esp.* one raised for a particular purpose; a call for or contribution of so much per member of a society. M17. 2 The enrolling or conscription of men for war. E17. b A body of men enrolled; in *pl.*, the men enrolled. E17.

1 DISRAELI The sole object of the Government was to settle the legal levy of the duties. b W. E. COLLINSON The compulsory levy made by the Trade Unions. *capital levy*: see CAPITAL *a.* & *n.*[2] 2 **levy in mass** conscription of all able-bodied men (cf. LEVÉE EN MASSE). b E. A. FREEMAN The Danes put the irregular . . levies to flight.

Comb.: **levy-money** †(*a*) a gratuity paid to recruits on enlistment; (*b*) contributions called for from the members of a society.

levy /ˈlɛvi/ *n.*[2] *local US* (*arch.*). E19. [Contr. of *eleven* (*pence* or *-penny bit*).] = BIT *n.*[2] 4b.

levy /ˈlɛvi/ *v.t.* LME. [f. LEVY *n.*[1], or directly f. (O)Fr. *lever*.] 1 Raise (contributions, taxes) or impose (a rate, toll, fee, etc.) as a levy. Foll. by †*of, on, upon.* LME. b Impose (service) *upon*; demand (a person's attendance). M19. c Impose a levy on (a person). E20. 2†a Raise (a sum of money) as a profit or rent; collect (a debt). Also, take the revenues of (land). LME–M18. b Raise (a sum of money) by legal execution or process. Foll. by *on* (*the goods of*). E16. c Extort (esp. blackmail). M19. †3 Set up (a fence, weir, etc.); erect (a house). LME–M18. 4 Begin to wage (war), commence (hostilities). Foll. by *against, on, upon.* LME. 5 *Law.* a *levy a fine*, enter into a collusive suit for the transfer of land. *obs.* exc. *Hist.* L15. b Draw up (an objection, protest) in due form. M17. 6 Enlist (armed men), raise (an army). L15. †7 Raise (a siege); break up (a camp). M16–E17.

levyable *a.*, **levyer** *n.* vars. of LEVIABLE, LEVIER.

lew /ljuː, luː/ *n.*, *a.*, & *v.* Now *dial.* Also **loo** /luː/. [OE *hlēow-* stem of *hlēo*: see LEE *n.*[1] See also LEW-WARM.] A *n.* 1 Lee, shelter; something giving shelter. OE. 2 Warmth, heat. *obs.* exc. *Sc.* L16. B *adj.* †1 Warm; sunny. Only in OE. 2 Lukewarm, tepid. ME. 3 Sheltered from the wind. L17. C *v.* 1 *v.t.* & *i.* Make or become warm or tepid. OE. 2 *v.t.* Shelter. M17.

lewd /luːd, ljuːd/ *a.* OE. [Origin unkn.] †1 Lay, not in holy orders, not clerical. OE–E19. †2 Unlearned, unlettered, untaught. Of speech or art: crude, artless. ME–E17. 3 Belonging to or characteristic of the common people; common, low, vulgar. Long *rare.* LME. †4 Foolish, unskilful, bungling; ill-bred, ill-mannered. LME–E18. †5 Bad, worthless, poor, sorry. LME–L17. 6 Vile, evil, wicked, good-for-nothing, worthless. *obs.* exc. as passing into sense 7. LME. 7 Lascivious, unchaste; indecent, obscene. LME.

lewdly *adv.* LME. **lewdness** *n.* LME. **lewdster** *n.* (*rare*) a lascivious person L16.

lewis /ˈluːɪs/ *n.*[1] LME. [Prob. f. OFr. *lous*, pl. of *lou(p)* 'wolf', a kind of siege engine.] An iron contrivance for gripping heavy blocks of stone for lifting, consisting of three pieces arranged to form a dovetail, the outside pieces being fixed in a dovetail mortise by the insertion of the middle piece.

Lewis /ˈluːɪs/ *n.*[2] E20. [Col. Isaac Newton *Lewis* (1858–1931), US soldier.] In full *Lewis* (*machine-*)*gun*. A light magazine-fed, gas-operated, air-cooled machine-gun.

Lewis /ˈluːɪs/ *n.*[3] M20. [Gilbert Newton *Lewis* (1875–1946), US chemist.] *Chem.* Used *attrib.* and in *possess.* to designate the theory proposed by Lewis that atoms can combine to form molecules by sharing electrons.

Lewis acid a compound or ionic species which can accept an electron pair from a donor compound. **Lewis base** a compound or ionic species which can donate an electron pair to an acceptor compound.

lewis *n.*[4] see LOUIS *n.*[1]

lewis /ˈluːɪs/ *v.t.* M19. [f. LEWIS *n.*[1]] Fasten by means of, or after the manner of, a lewis.

lewisia /luːˈɪzɪə, -ˈɪsɪə/ *n.* M19. [mod.L (see below), f. Capt. Meriwether *Lewis* (1774–1809), US explorer + -IA[1].] Any plant of the genus *Lewisia*, of the purslane family, comprising small flowering perennials native to western N. America, with fleshy leaves in a basal rosette and thick starchy roots.

Lewisian /luːˈɪsɪən/ *a.* M19. [f. *Lewis* (see LEWISMAN) + -IAN.] *Geol.* Of, pertaining to, or characteristic of Lewis in the Outer Hebrides; *spec.* designating the oldest rocks in Britain, a group of Precambrian gneisses in NW Scotland.

lewisite /ˈluːɪsʌɪt/ *n.* E20. [f. Winford Lee *Lewis* (1878–1943), US chemist + -ITE[1].] A powerful vesicant and respiratory irritant developed for use in chemical warfare; 2-chlorovinyldichloroarsine, $ClCH{:}CHAsCl_2$, a dark oily liquid or vapour.

Lewisman /ˈluːɪsmən/ *n.* Pl. **-men**. E20. [f. *Lewis* (see below) + MAN *n.*] A native or inhabitant of Lewis, the northern section of the island of Lewis with Harris in the Outer Hebrides off the NW coast of Scotland.

lewth /luːθ/ *n. obs.* exc. *dial.* OE. [f. LEW *a.* + -TH[1].] Warmth; shelter.

lew-warm /ˈljuːwɔːm, ˈluː-/ *a.* Now *dial.* LME. [f. LEW *a.* + WARM *a.*] Lukewarm.

lex domicilii /ˌlɛks dɒmɪˈsɪlɪʌɪ/ *n. phr.* E19. [L = law of the domicile.] *Law.* The law of the country in which a person is domiciled, as determining the right to make a will, succeed to property, etc.

lexeme /ˈlɛksiːm/ *n.* M20. [f. LEX(ICON + -EME.] *Ling.* A lexical unit in the vocabulary of a language; a morpheme representing such a unit.

leˈxemic *a.* & *n.* (*a*) *adj.* of or pertaining to lexemes; (*b*) *n.* in *pl.*, the branch of linguistics that deals with lexemes: M20.

lex fori /lɛks ˈfɔːrʌɪ/ *n. phr.* E19. [L = law of the court.] *Law.* The law of the country in which an action is brought, as regulating procedure, evidence, execution of judgements, etc.

lexical /ˈlɛksɪk(ə)l/ *a.* M19. [f. Gk *lexikos* (see LEXICON) + -AL[1].] **1** Of or pertaining to the words or vocabulary of a language. Freq. opp. *grammatical.* M19. **2** Pertaining to or of the nature of a lexicon or dictionary. L19.

1 G. A. MILLER In the Oxford English Dictionary there are nearly half a million lexical units. **lexical meaning** the meaning of a base in a paradigm or abstracted from particular grammatical contexts, e.g. of *love* in or as represented by *loves, loved, loving*, etc.

lexically *adv.* (*a*) in respect of vocabulary; (*b*) according to lexicons of a language; in the manner of a lexicon: M19.

lexicalize /ˈlɛksɪk(ə)lʌɪz/ *v.t.* Also **-ise**. M20. [f. prec. + -IZE.] *Ling.* Represent by a unit or distinction in the lexicon or vocabulary of a language. Usu. in *pass.*

lexicaliˈzation *n.* M20.

lexico- /ˈlɛksɪkəʊ/ *comb. form.* M20. [Gk *lexiko-*, f. *lexikos*: see LEXICON, -O-.] *Ling.* Forming compounds w. the sense 'partly lexical and partly —', as in *lexico-grammatical, statistic* adjs.

lexicographer /lɛksɪˈkɒgrəfə/ *n.* M17. [f. late Gk *lexikographos*, f. as LEXICO-: see -GRAPHER.] A writer or compiler of a dictionary or dictionaries.

lexicography /lɛksɪˈkɒgrəfi/ *n.* L17. [f. as LEXICO- + -GRAPHY.] The art or practice of writing dictionaries.

lexicoˈgraphic *a.* = LEXICOGRAPHICAL E19. **lexicoˈgraphical** *a.* of or pertaining to lexicography L18. **lexicoˈgraphically** *adv.* L19. **†lexicographics** *n.pl.* lexicographical writings: only in E18.

lexicology /lɛksɪˈkɒlədʒi/ *n.* E19. [f. as LEXICO- + -LOGY.] The branch of knowledge that deals with words, their form, meaning, and (sometimes) history; the branch of linguistics that deals with the structure and content of the lexicon.

lexicoˈlogical *a.* of or pertaining to lexicology M19. **lexicoˈlogically** *adv.* M20. **lexicologist** *n.* L19.

lexicon /ˈlɛksɪk(ə)n/ *n.* E17. [mod.L f. Gk *lexikon* (sc. *biblion* book) neut. sing. of *lexikos* pertaining to words, f. *lexis* phrase, word, diction f. *legein* speak.] **1** A dictionary, *esp.* one of Greek, Hebrew, Syriac, or Arabic. E17. **b** The vocabulary of some department of knowledge or sphere of activity; the vocabulary or word-stock of a region, a particular speaker, etc. Also, a list of words or names. M17. **2** *Ling.* The complete set of elementary meaningful units in a language; the words etc. which would be in a complete dictionary (but without definitions). M20. **3** (**L-**.) (Proprietary name for) a game played with cards marked with the letters of the alphabet, the object being to form as long a word as possible. M20.

1b M. SCAMMELL That uniquely broad . . earthy lexicon that instantly identifies . . Solzhenitzyn's mature literary style. *New York Times* The President . . has decided to begin testing—'routine' testing—of immigrants. . . In Mr. Reagan's lexicon 'routine' means 'mandatory, compulsory'.

lexiconize *v.* (*a*) *v.i.* compile a lexicon; (*b*) *v.t.* reduce to the form of a lexicon: L19.

lexicostatistic /ˌlɛksɪkəʊstəˈtɪstɪk/ *a.* M20. [f. LEXICO- + STATISTIC *a.*] *Ling.* Of or pertaining to the statistics of vocabulary.

lexicostatistical *a.* M20. **lexicostatistically** *adv.* M20.

lexicostatistics /ˌlɛksɪkəʊstəˈtɪstɪks/ *n.* M20. [f. LEXICO- + STATISTICS.] The branch of linguistics that deals with the statistics of vocabulary; *spec.* = GLOTTOCHRONOLOGY.

lexigram /ˈlɛksɪgram/ *n.* L20. [f. Gk LEXIS + -GRAM.] A symbol representing a word; *esp.* one used in learning a language.

lexigraphy /lɛkˈsɪgrəfi/ *n.* E19. [f. Gk LEXIS + -GRAPHY.] A system of writing in which each character represents a word, as in Chinese. Also (*rare*), the art of defining words.

lexiˈgraphic *a.* pertaining to or characterized by lexigraphy M19. **lexiˈgraphical** *a.* (*a*) = LEXIGRAPHIC; †(*b*) giving a diagrammatic representation of items in a list: E19. **lexigraphically** *adv.* M19.

Lexiphanes /lɛkˈsɪf(ə)niːz/ *n. literary.* M18. [Gk *Lexiphanēs* phrase-monger (title of one of Lucian's dialogues), f. LEXIS + *phan-*, *phainein* to display.] A person who uses bombastic phraseology.

Lexiˈphanic *a.* indulging in or marked by bombastic phraseology M18. **Lexiˈphanicism** *n.* (an instance of) bombastic phraseology M18.

lexis /ˈlɛksɪs/ *n.* M20. [Gk: see LEXICON.] **1** The diction or wording, in contrast to other elements, of a piece of writing. M20. **2** *Ling.* Items of lexical, as opp. esp. to grammatical, meaning; the total word-stock of a language. Also, the branch of knowledge that deals with words as lexical items. M20.

lex loci /lɛks ˈləʊsʌɪ/ *n. phr.* L18. [L = law of the place.] *Law.* The law of the country in which some event material to a case took place. Freq. foll. by a defining wd or phr.

lex loci contractus /kɒnˈtraktjuːs/ [= of a contract] the law of the country in which a contract was made. ***lex loci delicti*** /dəˈlɪktʌɪ/ [= of an offense] the law of the country in which a tort was committed.

lexotactics /lɛksəʊˈtaktɪks/ *n.* M20. [Irreg. f. LEX(EME + -O- + TACTICS.] The branch of linguistics that deals with the ordering of lexemes in a language. Cf. MORPHOTACTICS, PHONOTACTICS.

lex talionis /ˌlɛks talɪˈəʊnɪs/ *n. phr.* M17. [L, f. *lex* law + *talionis* genit. of *talio(n-)* (see TALION). Cf. earlier LEGE TALIONIS.] The (supposed) law of retaliation; the retributive theory of punishment, based on the Mosaic principle 'an eye for an eye, a tooth for a tooth'.

ley /leɪ/ *n.*[1] Also **lay**, (now *rare*) **lea** /liː/. LME. [Absol. use of LEA *a.*] Land that has remained untilled for some years; *spec.* (*Agric.*) land put down to grass or clover for a limited period of years.

Comb.: **ley farming** the alternate growing of crops and grass.

ley /liː, leɪ/ *n.*[2] E20. [Specialized use of var. of LEA *n.*[1]] A hypothetical straight line connecting prehistoric sites etc., freq. regarded as the line of an ancient track and credited by some with paranormal properties. Now usu. more fully *ley-line*.

leycesteria /lɛˈstɪərɪə/ *n.* M19. [mod.L (see below), f. William *Leyster* (fl. 1820), Chief Justice of Bengal + -IA[1].] Any of several Himalayan shrubs of the genus *Leycesteria*, of the honeysuckle family, with flowers in the axils of conspicuous purple bracts; esp. *L. formosa*, sometimes planted as cover for game.

Leyden /ˈlʌɪd(ə)n, ˈleɪd(ə)n/ *n.* M18. [A city in the Netherlands (now *Leiden*).] Chiefly *Hist.* *Leyden jar* (†*bottle*, †*phial*), an early electrical capacitor consisting of a glass bottle partly coated inside and outside with tinfoil.

Leydig /ˈlʌɪdɪg/ *n.* E20. [Franz von *Leydig* (1821–1908), Ger. anatomist.] Anat. *Leydig('s) cell*, *cell of Leydig*, an interstitial cell of the testis, believed to be the site of androgen production. Usu. in *pl.*

Leyland cypress /ˈleɪlənd ˈsʌɪprəs/ *n. phr.* Also **Leyland's cypress** /-ləndz/. M20. [Christopher John *Leyland* (1849–1926), Brit. horticulturist.] A vigorous ornamental hybrid cypress, × *Cupressocyparis leylandii*, much grown as a screening plant.

lez *n.* & *a.* var. of LES.

Lezgian *n.* & *a.* var. of LESGHIAN.

lezzy /ˈlɛzi/ *n.* & *a. slang.* Also **lessy**. M20. [Abbrev.: see -Y[6]. Cf. LES, LESBO, LIZZIE 1b.] = LESBIAN *a.* & *n.*

Lhasa /ˈlɑːsə/ *n.* E20. [The capital of Tibet.] In full *Lhasa apso* /ˈapsəʊ/, pl. *-os*. (An animal of) a breed of small long-coated dog, often gold or grey and white, originating at Lhasa. Formerly also *lhasa terrier*.

lhiamba /lɪˈambə/ *n.* Also **li-**. M19. [Bantu (cf. Kikongo *diamba*).] In southern central Africa: marijuana, cannabis.

li /liː/ *n.*[1] Pl. same. L16. [Chin. *lǐ*.] A Chinese unit of distance, equal to about 0.6 km (0.4 mile).

li /liː/ *n.*[2] L17. [Chin. *lǐ*.] In Neo-Confucianism: correct observance of the rules governing behaviour to others, regarded as needed to maintain a person's harmony with the moral principles of nature.

li /liː/ *n.*[3] Pl. same. M20. [Chin. *lì*.] An ancient Chinese bronze or pottery cooking vessel, with (usu. three) hollow legs.

liability /lʌɪəˈbɪlɪti/ *n.* L18. [f. LIABLE *a.* + -ITY.] **1** *Law.* The condition of being liable or answerable by law or equity. L18. **2** The condition of being liable or subject *to* something, apt or likely *to do* or *to suffer*, something undesirable. E19. **3** A thing for which a person is liable; *esp.* in *pl.*, the debts or pecuniary obligations of a person or company. M19. **4** *transf.* & *fig.* A person who or thing which puts one at a disadvantage, a hindering responsibility, a handicap. Freq. opp. *asset.* M20.

1 *limited liability*: see LIMITED *a.* STRICT *liability*. 4 M. ATWOOD I had been twelve, which was a liability when other people were fifteen. *Lancaster Guardian* British Rail want to close it because it is a maintenance liability.

liable /ˈlʌɪəb(ə)l/ *a.* (*pred.*) LME. [Perh. f. AN, f. (O)Fr. *lier* bind (see LIAISON), but late and not in AN or AL records.] **1** *Law.* Bound or obliged by law or equity; answerable at law (*for*, †*to*); subject *to* a tax, penalty, etc.; bound in law *to do*. LME. **b** Of land: subject to taxation. Now *rare* or *obs.* E17. **2 a** Susceptible, exposed, or open *to* (something undesirable). Formerly also *gen.*, subject *to* (any influence or change). L16. **b** Apt or likely *to do* (exc. *dial.* & *N. Amer.* chiefly something undesirable), *to be* —*ed*. L17. **†3** Subject or subservient *to*; attached or belonging *to*. L16–E17. **†4** Suitable, apt, (*to do*). Only in L16. **†5** Incident *to*. M17–M18.

1 F. DONALDSON If I spend more than six months in this country I'm liable to pay income tax. *Woman & Home* All drug companies will become strictly liable for injuries caused by their products. *Which?* Goods brought in from a non-EC country are liable to import duty. 2a ADDISON He . . found that though they were Objects of his Sight, they were not liable to his Touch. A. STORR Although everyone, in varying degree, is liable to depression . . some persons are peculiarly susceptible. b *Farmer & Stockbreeder* Salesmanship . . is liable to be overrated. W. WHARTON Without his glasses, he's liable to smash into a tree. 4 SHAKES. *John* Finding thee . . Apt, liable to be employ'd in danger. 5 E. HAYWOOD The faults of inadvertency are liable to us all.

liableness *n.* (now *rare*) M17.

liaise /lɪˈeɪz/ *v.i. colloq.* E20. [Back-form. f. LIAISON.] Establish communication or cooperation, act as a link, (*with*, *between*).

¶ Orig. *Mil. slang.*

liaison /lɪˈeɪz(ə)n, -zɒn, -zɔ̃/ *n.* M17. [Fr., f. *lier* bind f. L *ligare* -ISON.] 1 *Cookery.* A binding or thickening agent for sauces, consisting chiefly of the yolks of eggs. Formerly, the process of binding or thickening. M17. 2 An intimate relation or connection; *spec.* an illicit sexual relationship, esp. between a man and a married woman. E19. 3 Communication and cooperation, orig. *spec.* between military forces or units, esp. during a battle or campaign. E19. 4 *Phonet.* The pronunciation of a normally silent final consonant before a vowel (or mute *h*) beginning the following word, esp. in French. L19.

2 R. THOMAS Her antidote .. had been party after party .. and dangerous, discreet liaisons. 3 B. B. SCHOFIELD The liaison between the two services was as good as it could be. A. W. MYERS Mind and body must be working in liaison. 4 *Daily Chronicle* The nightly false 'liaison' made by a clever actress... 'Take Lady Agatha-r-out,' she says.

Comb.: **liaison officer** an officer in the armed services concerned with the liaison of units etc.

liamba *n.* var. of LHIAMBA.

liana /lɪˈɑːnə/ *n.* Also **liane** /lɪˈɑːn/. L18. [Fr. *liane*, †*liène*, orig. = clematis, perh. f. dial. Fr. *liener* bind sheaves, f. Fr. *lien* bond, tie; alt. after L or Sp. models.] Any long woody climbing plant that twines round trees, esp. in a tropical rainforest; the stem of such a plant.

liang /ljaŋ/ *n.* Pl. same. E19. [Chin. *liǎng*.] A Chinese weight equal to about 38 gm (1⅓ oz.); this weight in silver as a monetary unit. Also called *tael*.

liangle *n.* var. of LEANGLE.

liar /ˈlʌɪə/ *n.* [OE *lēogere* (= OHG *liugari*, ON *ljúgari*), f. *lēogan* LIE *v.*[2] + -ER[1]: see -AR[3].] 1 A person who lies or tells a falsehood; an untruthful person. OE. 2 In *pl.*, or in full *liar dice*. A gambling game resembling poker-dice, in which the thrower conceals the dice thrown and sometimes declares a false score. M20.

1 **paradox of the liar, the liar (paradox)** *Logic* the paradox involved in a speaker's statement that he or she is lying or is a (habitual) liar.

liard /ljɑː, ljɑːd/ *n.* M16. [Fr., of unkn. origin.] *Hist.* A small coin formerly current in France, worth a quarter of a sou. Also, (the type of) a coin of small value.

lias /ˈlʌɪəs/ *n.* In sense 1 orig. **lyas**; in sense 2 usu. **L-**. LME. [OFr. *liais* hard limestone, prob. f. *lie* LEE *n.*[2]] 1 A kind of blue argillaceous limestone rock, esp. as it occurs in SW England. LME. 2 Geol. *the Lias*, a series of fossiliferous strata forming the lowest division of the Jurassic system, and including blue argillaceous limestones. E19.

liassic /lʌɪˈasɪk/ *a.* (*Geol.*) of or pertaining to the Lias M19.

liatris /lʌɪˈatrɪs, ˈlʌɪətrɪs/ *n.* E19. [mod.L (see below), of unkn. origin.] Any of various N. American plants of the genus *Liatris*, of the composite family, cultivated for their long spikes of purple or white flower-heads. Also called *blazing star*.

Lib /lɪb/ *n.*[1] & *a. colloq.* Also **l-**. L19. [Abbrev.] = LIBERAL *a.* 5, *n.* 2. See also LIB-LAB.

Lib Dem *colloq.* a Liberal Democrat, Liberal Democratic.

lib /lɪb/ *n.*[2] *colloq.* M20. [Abbrev.] Liberation, esp. from social discrimination.

Gay Lib: see GAY *a. Men's Lib*: see MAN *n. women's lib*: see WOMAN *n.*

lib /lɪb/ *v.*[1]*t. obs.* exc. *dial.* LME. [Perh. f. Gmc base repr. also by MDu. *lubben* maim, geld, and already in OE. See also GLIB *v.*[2]] Castrate, geld.

†lib *v.*[2]*i. Criminals' slang.* M16–M19. [Origin unkn.] Sleep.

libament /ˈlɪbəm(ə)nt/ *n. arch.* L16. [L *libamentum*, f. *libare*: see next, -MENT.] A drink-offering, a libation.

libate /lʌɪˈbeɪt/ *v.t.* & *i. literary.* M19. [L *libat-* pa. ppl stem of *libare* pour out, rel. to Gk *leibein* pour drop by drop: see -ATE[3].] Pour out (wine etc.) in honour of a god. Also, make a libation to (a god).

libation /lʌɪˈbeɪʃ(ə)n/ *n.* LME. [L *libatio(n-)*, f. as prec.: see -ATION.] 1 The action or an act of pouring out of wine or other liquid in honour of a god; liquid so poured out; a drink-offering. LME. 2 *transf.* Liquid poured out to be drunk; a potation. *joc.* M18.

1 T. O. ECHEWA Everyone pours libations .. to the spirits of the ancestors. 2 J. AGATE Further libations being indicated, my .. bottle of whiskey .. was now requisitioned.

libationary *a.* = LIBATORY *a.* L19. **libationer** *n.* a person who pours out libations to a god etc. E20.

libatory /ˈlʌɪbət(ə)ri/ *n.* & *a.* E17. [As n. f. eccl.L *libatorium*, f. as LIBATE; as adj. f. LIBATION after *vibratory*, *vibration*: see -ORY[1], -ORY[2].] †A *n.* A vessel used in libation. Only in E17. B *adj.* Pertaining to or consisting of libations. M19.

libbard *n.* & *a.* see LEOPARD.

†libbege *n. Criminals' slang.* M16–M19. [Origin uncertain: cf. LIB *v.*[2]] A bed.

libber /ˈlɪbə/ *n. colloq.* L20. [f. LIB *n.*[2] + -ER[1].] An advocate of liberation, a liberationist; *esp.* = *women's liberationist* s.v. WOMAN *n.*

libbet /ˈlɪbɪt/ *n.*[1] *obs.* exc. *dial.* M16. [Perh. rel. to OFr. *libe*, *libbe* block of stone: see -ET[1].] A thick length of wood; a stick used to beat or throw at something.

libbet /ˈlɪbɪt/ *n.*[2] *obs.* exc. *dial.* Also **lippet** /ˈlɪpɪt/. L16. [Origin uncertain: perh. var. of LAPPET.] A torn piece, a shred, a fragment. Formerly, the lobe of the ear.

libeccio /lɪˈbɛtʃəʊ/ *n.* M17. [It., f. L *Lib-*, *Libs* (also *Lips*) f. Gk *Lib-*, *Lips*.] (The Italian name for) the south-west wind.

libel /ˈlʌɪb(ə)l/ *n.* ME. [OFr. (mod. *libelle*) f. L *libellus* dim. of *liber* book: see -EL[2].] 1 A formal document, a written declaration or statement. *obs.* exc. *Hist.* (as occasional rendering of L *libellus*). ME. 2a *Civil & Admiralty Law.* A writing or document containing a plaintiff's allegations and instituting a suit. ME. b *Sc. Law.* A formal statement setting out the grounds on which either a civil or criminal prosecution is made; an indictment. LME. c *Eccl. Law.* The initial pleading, or the plaintiff's written declaration or charges, in a plenary case. M16. 3 A little book; a (short) treatise or piece of writing. Also (by confusion), = LABEL *n.* 8. Now only *Sc.* LME. †4 A leaflet, bill, or pamphlet posted up or publicly circulated; *spec.* one assailing or defaming the character of some person. E16–L18. 5a A false and defamatory statement; *transf.* a thing or circumstance that tends to bring undeserved discredit *on* a person, a country, etc. by misrepresentation etc. E17. b *Law.* A false and defamatory statement in writing, film, or other permanent form; the act or offence of publishing such a statement. Cf. SLANDER *n.* 1. M17.

2b *subsumption of the libel*: see SUBSUMPTION 1b. 5a R. RENDELL She bore not the least resemblance to the Marquise of Tai and it would have been a cruel libel to suggest it. b *criminal libel*: see CRIMINAL *a. public libel*: see PUBLIC *a.* & *n. seditious libel*: see SEDITIOUS 2.

libel /ˈlʌɪb(ə)l/ *v.* Infl. **-ll-**, ***-l-**. LME. [f. the n.: cf. med.L *libellare* in sense 2.] †1 *v.i.* Institute a suit against or *against* a person. LME–L16. 2 *v.t.* a *Eccl.* & *Sc. Law.* Specify in a libel; institute a suit against (a person) by means of a libel. L15. b *Admiralty Law.* Bring suit against (a vessel or cargo or its owner). E19. 3 *v.i.* Make libellous accusations or statements; spread defamation. Foll. by *against*, *on*. L16–M17. 4 *v.t.* Defame by the circulation of libellous statements; accuse falsely and maliciously; *spec.* (*Law*), publish a libel against. E17.

4 POPE But what so pure, which envious tongues will spare? Some wicked wits have libell'd all the fair.

libelee, -er *ns.*, etc., see LIBELLEE etc.

libellant /ˈlʌɪb(ə)l(ə)nt/ *n.* Also ***libelant**. E18. [f. LIBEL *v.* + -ANT[1], after *appellant* etc.] *Law.* A person who institutes a suit in an ecclesiastical or admiralty court.

libellee /lʌɪbəˈliː/ *n.* Also ***libelee**. M19. [f. LIBEL *v.* + -EE[1].] *Law.* A person against whom a libel has been filed. Also, a person who is the object of a libel.

libeller /ˈlʌɪb(ə)lə/ *n.* Also ***libeler**. L16. [f. LIBEL *v.* + -ER[1].] A person who publishes a libel or libels.

libellist /ˈlʌɪb(ə)lɪst/ *n.* Also ***libelist**. L18. [f. LIBEL *n.* + -IST.] = LIBELLER.

libellous /ˈlʌɪb(ə)ləs/ *a.* Also ***libelous**. E17. [f. LIBEL *n.* + -OUS.] Containing or constituting a libel, of the nature of a libel. Also, engaged in libels.

libellously *adv.* M19.

libellula /lɪˈbɛljʊlə/ *n.* M18. [mod.L (see below), dim. of *libella* dragonfly, perh. f. L *libella* scales (see LEVEL *n.*).] *Entomol.* Any of several dragonflies of the genus *Libellula* or the family Libellulidae.

libellulid *n.* a dragonfly of the family Libellulidae M19.

libelous *a.* see LIBELLOUS.

liber /ˈlʌɪbə/ *n.* Now *rare.* M18. [L = inner bark, parchment, book.] *Bot.* = PHLOEM.

liberal /ˈlɪb(ə)r(ə)l/ *a.* & *n.* ME. [(O)Fr. *libéral* f. L *liberalis*, f. *liber* free: see -AL[1].] A *adj.* 1 Orig., suitable for a free man or (in later use) a gentleman or person of social standing. Now only of education, culture, etc., usu. with an admixture of sense 4: directed to a general broadening of the mind, not restricted to the requirements of technical or professional training. ME. 2 Free in giving; generous, open-handed. (Foll. by *of*.) ME. b Given or offered unstintingly; (of a meal, a helping, etc.) ample, lavish. LME. c Of a part of the body, outline, etc.: full, large. E17. 3†a Free from restraint in speech or action; unrestrained by prudence or decorum. LME–E18. b Of passage etc.: freely permitted, not interfered with. Long *arch.* M16. c Of interpretation: inclining to laxity or indulgence; not rigorous. Of a translation: free, not literal. L18. 4 Unprejudiced, open-minded; *esp.* free from bigotry or unreasonable prejudice in favour of traditional opinions or established institutions, open to the reception of new ideas. Of a member or branch of a Church or religion: holding opinions less traditional than those accepted as orthodox. L18. 5 Favourable to or respectful of individual rights and freedoms; *spec.* (in politics) favouring free trade and gradual political and social reform that tends towards individual freedom or democracy. Also (usu. **L-**), belonging to the Liberal Party of Great Britain or any analogous party so named in another country. E19.

1 C. MIDDLETON Agriculture was held the most liberal employment in old Rome. BURKE They are permitted .. to emerge out of that low rank into a more liberal condition. LD MACAULAY Countries which neither mercantile avidity nor liberal curiosity had ever impelled any stranger to explore. 2 M. C. CLARKE With Cassio he is patronising, and liberal of his advice. R. K. NARAYAN He was very liberal in entertaining me. b J. WAIN It seemed big to us, with its liberal allowance of bedrooms. 3a SHAKES. *Haml.* Daisies, and long purples That liberal shepherds give a grosser name. 4 JAS. MILL Liberal enquiries into the literature .. of the Hindus. W. P. ROBERTS I maintain that Liberal Protestantism .. is not anti-dogmatic. 5 J. BARZUN The liberal doctrine that school children have rights to freedom and individuality. C. SAGAN Holland was the most liberal and least authoritarian nation in Europe during this time. A. STORR The conditions of his imprisonment were sufficiently liberal to allow him visits to his .. family.

Special collocations & comb.: *liberal arts*: see ART *n.*[1] **Liberal Christian** (*a*) *US* a Unitarian; also, a Universalist; (*b*) a Christian who rejects or considers unimportant many traditional beliefs. **Liberal Democrat** a member of a British political party (formerly the *Social and Liberal Democrats*) formed from the Liberal Party and members of the Social Democratic Party. **Liberal Democratic** *a.* of or pertaining to the Liberal Democrats. **Liberal Judaism** a progressive movement in Judaism that abandons many of the traditional observances of Judaic law. **Liberal-Labour** *a.* of or pertaining to (people associated with or sympathetic to) both Liberal and Labour parties. **Liberal Party** any of various political parties professing to favour progressive legislation; *esp.* (*Hist.*) a British political party which replaced the old Whig Party *c*1860 and was one of the two dominant parties in Britain until *c*1920 (in 1988 merged with the Social Democratic

Party under the title the *Social and Liberal Democrats*, now *Liberal Democrats*). **Liberal Unionist** a member of the party formed by those Liberals who would not support W. E. Gladstone's measure for Irish Home Rule in 1886.

B *n.* †**1** The principal in a hierarchy of rogues. *Criminals' slang.* Only in M17. **2** Orig. (*derog.*), an extreme Whig. Later, a person of liberal principles or ideas; *esp.* (usu. **L-**) a member of the Liberal Party of Great Britain or of an analogous party of another country. E19. **b** A person who holds liberal views in theology. E19.

2 ARNOLD BENNETT Every Briton is at heart a Tory—especially every British Liberal. *New Yorker* I don't think he's a liberal . . he wants to see the poor work for their money.

liberally *adv.* in a liberal manner; *esp.* lavishly, profusely: LME. **liberalness** *n.* LME.

liberalise *v.* var. of LIBERALIZE.

liberalism /ˈlɪb(ə)r(ə)lɪz(ə)m/ *n.* E19. [f. LIBERAL + -ISM.] (The holding of) liberal opinions in politics or theology; (**L-**) the political tenets characteristic of a Liberal.

liberalist *n.* & *a.* (*a*) *n.* an advocate of liberalism; (*b*) *adj.* of or pertaining to liberalists or liberalism: E19. **libera'listic** *a.* of or pertaining to liberalism, of the nature of or inclining towards liberalism M19.

liberality /lɪbəˈralɪti/ *n.* ME. [(O)Fr. *liberalité* or L *liberalitas*, f. *liberalis*: see LIBERAL, -ITY.] **1** The quality of being liberal or free in giving; generosity, munificence. ME. **b** An instance of this; a liberal gift or bounty. Now *rare*. E16. **2** Breadth of mind; freedom from prejudice; liberal-mindedness. E19.

1 R. ELLMANN He dispensed money with liberality. 2 F. RAPHAEL The rampant liberality of Sixties London.

liberalize /ˈlɪb(ə)r(ə)lʌɪz/ *v.* Also **-ise**. L18. [f. LIBERAL *a.* + -IZE.] **1** *v.t.* **a** Make liberal; imbue with liberal ideas or principles; make liberal-minded; free from narrowness; enlarge the intellectual range of. L18. **b** (Freq. **L-**.) Make Liberal in politics. M19. **c** Remove restrictions on (the import of goods, outflow of capital, etc.). M20. **2** *v.i.* Favour liberal opinions; be or become liberal in one's ideas or principles. E19.

liberali'zation *n.* M19. **liberalizer** *n.* M19.

liberate /lɪbəˈreɪti/ *n. obs.* exc. *Hist.* LME. [Use as n. of med.L imper. pl. of *liberare* to free, liberate (see next), the wd with which the writs began.] *Law.* Any of various writs requiring something to be paid or someone or something to be delivered up or handed over.

liberate /ˈlɪbəreɪt/ *v.t.* Pa. pple & ppl a. **-ated**, (earlier) †**-ate**. L16. [L *liberat-* pa. ppl stem of *liberare*, f. *liber* free: see -ATE[3].] **1** Set free, set at liberty; free, release *from* (something); *Chem.* set free from combination. L16. **2** Free (a country etc.) from enemy occupation. Also *iron.*, subject to a new tyranny. M20. **3** Loot (property); misappropriate. *slang.* M20. **4** Free from social conventions, esp. ones based on sex. Freq. as *liberated* ppl a. Cf. EMANCIPATE *v.* 2. M20.

1 G. F. KENNAN To liberate from every kind of slavery . . the toiling masses of the world. 2 R. WHELAN They found the town liberated and German prisoners rounded up. 3 J. DIDION She knows where they could liberate a Signal Corps generator. 4 U. BENTLEY You're all supposed to be liberated women, why leave it up to the man?

liberation /lɪbəˈreɪʃ(ə)n/ *n.* LME. [(O)Fr. *libération* or L *liberatio(n-)*, f. as prec.: see -ATION.] The action or an act of liberating someone or something or of setting someone free from bondage or oppression; the condition of being liberated.

Gay Liberation: see GAY *a. Men's Liberation*: see MAN *n. women's liberation*: see WOMAN *n.*

Comb.: **Liberation Society** a 19th-cent. society which campaigned for the disestablishment of the Church of England and the repeal of discriminatory legislation against Nonconformists; **liberation theologian** a person who teaches liberation theology; **liberation theology** a theory, originating among Latin American theologians, which interprets liberation from social, political, and economic oppression as an anticipation of eschatological salvation.

liberationism *n.* the principles or practice of liberationists L19. **liberationist** *n.* (*a*) a sympathizer with the aims of the Liberation Society; (*b*) an advocate of women's liberation: M19.

liberative /ˈlɪb(ə)rətɪv/ *a.* M19. [f. as LIBERATE *v.* + -IVE.] Liberating; favouring liberation.

liberator /ˈlɪbəreɪtə/ *n.* M17. [L, f. as LIBERATE *v.*: see -OR.] A person who liberates a people or country; a deliverer.

liberatory /ˈlɪb(ə)rət(ə)ri/ *a. rare.* L16. [f. as prec. + -ORY[2].] = LIBERATIVE.

liberatress /ˈlɪbəreɪtrɪs/ *n.* L18. [f. LIBERATOR + -ESS[1].] A female liberator.

liberi *n.* pl. of LIBERO.

Liberian /lʌɪˈbɪərɪən/ *a.*[1] L18. [f. *Liberius* (see below) + -AN.] Of or pertaining to Liberius (Pope, 352–66) or the period of his pontificate.

Liberian calendar a calendar attributed to the pontificate of Liberius. **Liberian catalogue** a list of the Popes up to and including Liberius.

Liberian /lʌɪˈbɪərɪən/ *a.*[2] & *n.* M19. [f. *Liberia* (see below), f. L *liber* free (as founded as a settlement for freed Black slaves from the US) + -AN.] **A** *adj.* Of or pertaining to the W. African State of Liberia or its people. M19. **B** *n.* A native or inhabitant of Liberia. Also, a Liberian ship. M19.

libero /ˈliːbero/ *n.* Pl. ***-ri*** /-ri/. M20. [It., lit. 'free'.] *Soccer.* = SWEEPER 7.

libertarian /lɪbəˈtɛːrɪən/ *n.* & *a.* L18. [f. LIBERTY *n.* + -ARIAN, after *unitarian* etc.] **A** *n.* **1** A person who holds the doctrine of the freedom of the will, as opp. to that of necessity. L18. **2** A person who approves of or advocates liberty. L19. **B** *adj.* **1** Believing in free will. L19. **2** Advocating liberty. E20.

libertarianism *n.* the principles or doctrines of libertarians M19.

liberticide /lɪˈbəːtɪsʌɪd/ *n.* & *a.* L18. [Fr., f. *liberté*: see LIBERTY *n.*, -CIDE.] **A** *n.* **1** A destroyer of liberty. L18. **2** The destruction of liberty. *rare.* E19. **B** *adj.* Destructive of liberty. L18.

liberti'cidal *a.* = LIBERTICIDE *a.* L18.

libertinage /ˈlɪbətɪnɪdʒ/ *n.* E17. [f. next + -AGE.] **1** = LIBERTINISM 1. E17. **2** = LIBERTINISM 2. M17.

libertine /ˈlɪbətiːn, -tɪn, -tʌɪn/ *n.* & *a.* LME. [L *libertinus*, f. *libertus* freedman, f. *liber* free; in sense 2 after Fr. *libertin*: see -INE[1].] **A** *n.* **1** *Rom. Hist.* A freedman; a person manumitted from slavery. Also, the son of a freedman. LME. **2** A member of any of various antinomian sects of the early 16th cent., which arose in France and elsewhere in Continental Europe (usu. in *pl.*); *gen.* a freethinker. M16. **3** *transf.* A person who follows his or her own inclinations; a person who is not restricted or confined by convention etc. L16. **4** A man (occas., a woman) who is not restrained by morality, esp. in sexual relations; a person who leads a dissolute life, a licentious person. L16.

2 J. PARKER The intellectual libertine who denies everything that cannot be certified by the senses. 3 CHARTERED *libertine*. 4 R. CHRISTIANSEN Don Giovanni is no mere libertine, but a man . . driven to excess by his contempt for the . . mediocrity around him.

B *adj.* **1** Acknowledging no law in religion or morals; freethinking. L16. **2** Free or unrestrained in disposition, habit, conduct or language. Now *rare* or *obs.* L16. †**b** Of literary composition, translation: extremely free. M17–M18. **3** Manumitted from slavery. *rare.* E17. **4** Characterized by habitual disregard of morality, esp. with regard to sexual relations; licentious, dissolute; characteristic of or resembling a libertine. E17.

4 A. S. BYATT One tends to think that those who are brought up libertine will compensate by growing strict.

libertinism /ˈlɪbətɪnɪz(ə)m/ *n.* E17. [f. prec. + -ISM.] **1** Disregard of moral restraint, esp. in sexual relations; licentious or dissolute practices or habits of life. E17. **2** Freethinking. M17. **3** Freedom of life or conduct; unrestrained liberty. *rare.* M17.

libertinous /lɪˈbəːtɪnəs/ *a. rare.* M17. [f. as LIBERTINE + -OUS.] = LIBERTINE *a.*

liberty /ˈlɪbəti/ *n.* LME. [(O)Fr. *liberté* f. L *libertat-*, *-tas*, f. *liber* free: see -TY[1].] **1** Exemption or release from captivity, bondage, or slavery. LME. **b** *Theol.* Freedom from the bondage of sin, or of the law. LME. **2** Exemption or freedom from arbitrary, despotic, or autocratic rule or control. LME. **3** The condition of being able to act in any desired way without restraint; power to do as one likes. LME. **b** *Philos.* The condition of being free from the control of fate or necessity. Now chiefly opp. *necessity*. M16. **4** Free opportunity, range, or scope *to do* (or †*of doing*) something; *gen.* leave, permission. LME. **b** Unrestricted use of a thing; access to or permission to go anywhere within the limits of a place. Chiefly in *have the liberty of*. (Cf. FREEDOM 8b.) Now *rare* or *obs.* E17. **c** *Naut.* Leave of absence. Cf. *liberty man* below. M18. **5** *Law.* **a** A privilege or exceptional right granted to a subject by the sovereign power. Cf. FRANCHISE *n.* 4b. LME. **b** In *pl.* Privileges, immunities, or rights enjoyed by prescription or by grant. LME. **c** *Hist.* A district having such privileges etc.; *spec.* (*a*) the district over which a corporation's privilege extended; (*b*) a district within the limits of a county, but exempt from the jurisdiction of the sheriff, and having a separate commission of the peace; (*c*) a district containing several manors held by a single lord; (*d*) *sing.* & in *pl.*, a district controlled by a city though outside its boundary; (*e*) an area outside a prison where some prisoners were sometimes allowed to reside. LME. **6** Formerly, unrestrained action, conduct, or expression; freedom of behaviour or speech, beyond what is granted or recognized as proper; licence. Now only, an instance of this, an overstepping or setting aside of rules or conventions. M16.

1 AV *Isa.* 61:1 To proclaime libertie to the captiues. 2 R. H. TAWNEY The theocracy of Massachusetts, merciless alike to religious liberty and to economic licence. ISAIAH BERLIN The liberty of some must depend on the restraint of others. *personified*: H. HALLAM Liberty never wore a more unamiable countenance than among these burghers, who abused the strength she gave them. 3 A. DE MORGAN We have a glorious liberty in England of owning neither dictionary, grammar nor spelling-book. 4 H. MARTINEAU Bid him come in and wait for liberty to talk. b DEFOE They allowed him the liberty of the town. 5b W. H. PRESCOTT The liberties of the commons were crushed at the fatal battle of Villalar. 6 J. KNOX John the Baptist, whom Herode . . had beheaded for the libertie of his tonge. B. JOWETT Thucydides has rarely . . allowed himself liberties not to be found somewhere in other writers.

Phrases: **at liberty** (*a*) not in captivity or confinement; esp. in *set at liberty*, liberate, set free; (*b*) free *to do, move, think*, etc.; (*c*) (of a person or thing) unoccupied, disengaged. †**at one's liberty** (*a*) at one's own choice, as one pleases; (*b*) in one's power, at one's disposal. *cap of liberty*: see CAP *n.*[1] *civil liberty*: see CIVIL *a. liberty of* CONSCIENCE. *liberty of the press*: see PRESS *n.*[1] **natural liberty** the state in which everyone is free to act as he or she thinks fit, subject only to the laws of nature. **take a liberty, take liberties** be unduly or improperly familiar *with* a person (sometimes *euphem.*); use freedom in dealing *with* rules, facts, etc. **take the liberty** presume or venture *to do*, take the presumptuous step *of doing*. *tree of liberty*: see TREE *n.*

Comb.: **liberty act** a circus act performed by liberty horses; **liberty boat** *Naut.* a boat carrying liberty men; **Liberty bodice** (proprietary name for) a girl's or woman's underbodice designed with reinforcing strips; **liberty bond** any of a series of interest-bearing war bonds issued by the US government in 1917–18; **liberty boy** a noisy zealot for liberty; *US* a supporter of a freedom movement; **liberty cabbage** *US* sauerkraut; **liberty cap** (*a*) = *cap of liberty* s.v. CAP *n.*[1]; (*b*) a common small European toadstool, *Psilocybe semilanceata*, which contains psilocybin; **liberty day** *Naut.*: on which part of a ship's crew are allowed to go ashore; **liberty hall** a place where one may do as one likes; **liberty horse** a horse that performs in a circus without a rider; **Liberty loan** any of the four issues of liberty bonds; **liberty man** *Naut.* a sailor having leave to go ashore; **liberty-pole** a tall mast or staff with a Phrygian cap or other symbol of liberty on the top; **Liberty ship** a type of merchant vessel built in the US by rapid mass-production methods during the war of 1939–45; **liberty tree** = *tree of liberty* s.v. TREE *n.*

Liberty /ˈlɪbəti/ *a.* L19. [Messrs *Liberty* & Co., a London drapery firm.] Designating materials,

styles, colours, etc., characteristic of textile fabrics or articles sold by Messrs Liberty.
¶A proprietary name.

liberty /ˈlɪbəti/ *v.t.* Long *obs.* exc. *dial.* LME. [f. the n.] †**1** Endow with liberties or privileges. Only in LME. **2** Give liberty to; allow to run loose. L15.

liberum arbitrium /ˌliːbərʊm ɑːˈbɪtrɪəm, ˌlʌɪbərəm/ *n. phr.* M17. [L (Livy) = free judgement, free will.] Full power to decide; freedom of action.

liberum veto /ˌliːbərʊm ˈviːtəʊ, ˌlʌɪbərəm/ *n. phr.* L18. [f. L *liberum* neut. of *liber* free + VETO *n.*] A veto possessed by each member of a legislative etc. body requiring unanimity.

libidinal /lɪˈbɪdɪn(ə)l/ *a.* E20. [f. L *libidin-*, LIBIDO lust + -AL[1].] *Psychoanalysis.* Of or pertaining to libido.
libidinally *adv.* M20.

libidinous /lɪˈbɪdɪnəs/ *a.* LME. [f. L *libidinosus*, f. as prec.: see -OUS.] Given to, full of, or characterized by lust or lewdness; lustful, lecherous, lewd.
libidinously *adv.* E17. **libidinousness** *n.* E17.

libido /lɪˈbiːdəʊ, lɪˈbʌɪdəʊ/ *n.* E20. [L = desire, lust.] *Psychoanalysis.* Psychic drive or energy, *esp.* that associated with the sexual instinct.

†**libken** *n. Criminals' slang.* M16–E19. [f. LIB *v.*[2] + KEN *n.*[2]] A place to sleep in.

Lib-Lab /lɪbˈlab/ *a.* & *n.* E20. [f. LIB *n.*[1] & *a.* + LAB *n.*[3] & *a.*] A *adj.* = *Liberal-Labour* s.v. LIBERAL *a.* E20. B *n.* A Liberal-Labour politician. E20.
Lib-Labbery *n.* Liberal-Labour politics M20.

Libra /ˈliːbrə, ˈlɪb-, ˈlʌɪb/ *n.* In sense 2 **l-**. OE. [L *libra* pound, balance, Libra.] **1** (The name of) a constellation of the southern hemisphere, on the ecliptic between Scorpio and Virgo; *Astrol.* (the name of) the seventh zodiacal sign, usu. associated with the period 23 September to 22 October (see note s.v. ZODIAC); the Scales, the Balance. OE. **b** *Astrol.* A person born under the sign Libra. M20. **2** *Rom. Hist.* A unit of weight, equivalent to a pound of 12 ounces (0.34 kg). LME.
1 *attrib.*: A. LEO This causes Libra persons to love harmony.

libral /ˈlʌɪbr(ə)l/ *a. rare.* M17. [L *libralis*, f. as prec.: see -AL[1].] Weighing a (Roman) pound.

Libran /ˈliːbrən, ˈlɪb-, ˈlʌɪb-/ *n.* E20. [f. LIBRA + -AN.] *Astrol.* = LIBRA *n.* 1b.

librarian /lʌɪˈbrɛːrɪən/ *n.* L17. [f. L *librarius* concerned with books, (as n.) bookseller, scribe, f. *libr-*, *liber* book, + -AN.] †**1** A scribe, a copyist. L17–E18. **2** A person in charge of a library; an assistant in a library; a person trained or qualified to work in a library. E18.
librarianess *n.* (*rare*) a female librarian M19. **librarianship** *n.* the profession or work of a librarian E19.

librarious /lʌɪˈbrɛːrɪəs/ *a. rare.* M17. [f. as prec. + -OUS.] Of or pertaining to books.

library /ˈlʌɪbrəri, -bri/ *n.* LME. [(O)Fr. *librairie* (mod. = bookshop, book trade) f. Proto-Romance alt. of L *libraria* bookshop, use as n. of *librarius*: see LIBRARIAN, -ARY[1], -Y[3].] **1** A large organized collection of books for reading or reference, for use by the public or by a specific group; an individual's collection of books. LME. **b** A mass of learning or knowledge; a source or the sources providing knowledge or learning. LME. **c** A collection of films, gramophone records, computer routines etc., esp. when organized or sorted for some specific purpose. E20. **d** *Genetics.* A collection of bacterial cultures each transfected with a piece of genetic material, esp. forming a complete set representing a chromosome or genome; a collection of genes so transfected. Also, the set of genes common to a group of organisms. L20. **2** A building or room containing such a collection of books, films, records, music, etc.; an institution or organization holding such a collection. LME. **b** A theatre-ticket agency. *slang.* E19. **3** A series of books, gramophone records, etc., issued by a publisher in similar bindings etc. as a set. L17.
1 R. GRAVES Collecting a library of the pagan Classics. K. CLARK His brother . . had a large library, but his books were chosen for their instructive texts. **b** J. HAWTHORNE Cards and men formed the library of the Duchess of Marlborough. **2** A. RADCLIFFE The library occupied the west side of the chateau. R. QUIRK Our bookshelves and libraries are full of books on the use of words.
Phrases: **circulating library** a small library with books lent to a group of subscribers in turn. *free library*: see FREE *a. lending library*: see LEND *v. public library*: see PUBLIC *a. reference library*: see REFERENCE *n. travelling library*: see TRAVELLING *ppl a. twopenny library*: see TWOPENNY *a.* 2.
Comb.: **library binding** a special strong binding of books for lending libraries; **library edition** an edition of good size and print and strongly bound; *spec.* a uniform edition of a writer's works; **library(-frame) glasses** spectacles with heavy frames suitable for use when reading; **library school** a college teaching librarianship; **library science** librarianship as a subject of study; **library spectacles** = *library(-frame) glasses* above; **library steps** a stepladder for use in a library.

librate /ˈlʌɪbreɪt/ *n.* E17. [med.L *librata* (*terrae*) a pound's worth (of land), f. *libra* pound: see -ATE[1].] *Hist.* A piece of land worth a pound a year.

librate /ˈlʌɪbreɪt/ *v.* E17. [L *librat-* pa. ppl stem of *librare*, f. *libra* balance: see -ATE[3].] †**1** *v.t.* Weigh. E–M17. **2** *v.i.* Oscillate like the beam of a balance; move from side to side or up and down. L17. **b** Oscillate or waver *between* one thing and another. E19. **3** *v.i.* Of a bird etc.: be poised, balance itself. L18.
libratory *a.* oscillatory M17.

libration /lʌɪˈbreɪʃ(ə)n/ *n.* E17. [L *libratio(n-)*, f. as prec.: see -ATION.] **1** The action of librating; (*a*) motion like that of the beam of a balance oscillating upon its pivot; the state of being balanced or in equilibrium. E17. **2** *Astron.* A real or apparent oscillating motion; *spec.* an irregularity of the moon's motion which makes it possible to see more than about 59 per cent of its surface from the earth. M17. †**3** The action of weighing. M17–L18.
librational *a.* of or pertaining to (the moon's) libration L19.

libretto /lɪˈbrɛtəʊ/ *n.* Pl. **-ttos**, **-tti** /-ti/. M18. [It., dim. of *libro* book.] The text of an opera or other long vocal composition.
librettist *n.* a writer of a libretto or librettos M19.

libriform /ˈlʌɪbrɪfɔːm/ *a.* L19. [f. L *libr-*, LIBER + -FORM.] *Bot.* Of certain xylem fibres: resembling the phloem or inner bark.

Librium /ˈlɪbrɪəm/ *n.* Also **l-**. M20. [Origin unkn.] *Pharm.* (Proprietary name for) the tranquillizer chlordiazepoxide.

Libyan /ˈlɪbɪən/ *n.* & *a.* L15. [f. L *Libya* + -AN.] A *n.* A native or inhabitant of Libya, a country in N. Africa. L15. B *adj.* Of or pertaining to Libya; *poet.* N. African. E16.
†**Libyc** *a.* [Gk *Libukos*] = LIBYAN *a.* M16–M17.

Libyo- /ˈlɪbɪəʊ/ *comb. form.* L19. [f. LIBY(AN + -O-.] Libyan and —, as *Libyo-Phoenician*.

licca /ˈlɪkə/ *n.* M18. [Origin unkn.] In full *licca tree.* A West Indian tree, *Zanthoxylum spinosum*, of the rue family.

lice *n.pl.* see LOUSE *n.*

licence /ˈlʌɪs(ə)ns/ *n.* Also ***license**. LME. [(O)Fr. f. L *licentia* liberty, freedom, licentiousness, (in med.L) authority, permission, f. *licent-* pres. ppl stem of *licere* be allowed: see -ENCE.] **1** Liberty, esp. *to do* something; leave, permission. Formerly also, exemption *from* something. LME. †**b** *spec.* Leave or permission to depart. Chiefly in *take one's licence.* L15–M16. **2** Formal, usu. printed or written, permission from an authority to do something (esp. marry, print or publish a book, preach, drive on a public road, or carry on some trade (esp. in alcoholic liquor)), or to own something (esp. a dog, gun, or television set); a document giving such permission; a permit. LME. **b** In some universities and colleges, a certificate of competence in a faculty. M16. **3** Liberty of action conceded or acknowledged; freedom; an instance of this. LME. **b** Excessive liberty or disregard for law or propriety; an instance of this. LME. **c** Licentiousness. E18. **4** A writer's or artist's irregularity in grammar, metre, perspective, etc., or deviation from fact, esp. for effect; an example of this. Freq. in *poetic licence.* M16.
1 W. BLACKSTONE The king . . may . . prohibit any of his subjects from going into foreign parts without licence. K. WATERHOUSE He seized on it as licence to raise . . the point of information. **2** G. ORWELL They had had a pub, but they had lost their licence for allowing gambling. *Shetland Times* They are also looking for people using black and white licences for colour television. *driving licence, marriage licence, road fund licence, television licence*, etc. *late licence*: see LATE *a.* **3** D. STOREY You . . put down your thoughts . . and allow your imagination a little licence. B. T. BRADFORD Old people believe . . age gives them the licence to say exactly what they think. **b** S. SASSOON The thriftless licence of war-time behaviour. A. BEVAN They . . warn us that 'we must distinguish between freedom and licence'. **c** G. M. TREVELYAN Churchmen and Dissenters co-operated against the licence of the age.
Comb.: **licence plate** (chiefly *N. Amer.*) a number plate of a licensed motor vehicle.
licenceless *a.* not possessing a licence E20.

licence *v.*, **licenced** *a.* vars. of LICENSE *v.*, LICENSED.

license *n.* see LICENCE *n.*

license /ˈlʌɪs(ə)ns/ *v.t.* Also **licence**. LME. [f. the n.: sp. w. *-s-* after *practice*/*practise* etc.] **1** Allow, give permission to, (a person) *to do*, †*that*; permit or allow (a thing) to be done. Now *rare.* LME. **2** Grant (a person) a licence or formal permission *for*, *to do*; grant formal permission for, authorize, (an action or practice). LME. **b** Authorize the publication of (a book) or the performance of (a play). E17. **c** Authorize the use of (a thing, esp. premises) for a specific purpose. L18. †**3** Give leave of departure to; dismiss *from*; send away *to*. LME–E19. **4** Allow complete freedom or liberty to. *obs.* exc. as LICENSED *a.* 1. E17.
1 A. W. KINGLAKE Lord Stratford was licensed to do no more than send a message to an Admiral. **2** M. PATTISON A patent of Henry II . . licenses the sale of Rhenish wine. V. S. NAIPAUL A little notice said that Beharry was licensed to sell spirituous liquors. *Which?* The Council ensures that all conveyances it licenses, have met its professional requirements. **c** M. E. BRADDON In which there is . . not even a cottage licensed for the sale of ale. J. LE CARRÉ An old . . hotel with a lift licensed for three persons at a time.
licensable *a.* E17. **licen'see** *n.* a person to whom a licence is granted, esp. to sell alcoholic liquor M19. **licenser** *n.* a person who licenses something; *esp.* an official who licenses the publication of books or the performance of plays according to censorship rules: M17. **licensor** *n.* (*Law*) = LICENSER M19.

licensed /ˈlʌɪs(ə)nst/ *a.* Also **licenced**. L16. [f. LICENSE *v.* + -ED[1] or LICENCE *n.* + -ED[2].] **1** Allowed complete freedom or liberty; privileged. L16. **2** To whom or for which a licence has been granted; having a licence; *esp.* (of premises) licensed for the sale of alcoholic liquor. M17.
2 licensed victualler an innkeeper licensed to sell alcoholic liquor etc.

licensure /ˈlʌɪs(ə)nsjʊə/ *n.* Chiefly *N. Amer.* M19. [f. LICENSE *v.* + -URE.] The granting of a licence esp. to carry on a trade or profession.

licentiate /lʌɪˈsɛnʃɪət/ *n.* L15. [med.L *licentiatus* use as n. of pa. pple of *licentiare*: see next, -ATE[1].] **1** The holder of a university or college licence; *spec.* & now only in some foreign universities, the holder of a particular degree between bachelor and master or doctor. Now usu., the holder of a certificate of competence from a particular body or college to practise a particular profession. L15. **2** Esp. in Presbyterian Churches, a person with a licence to preach but as yet no appointment. M19.
1 B. BAINBRIDGE A Fellow of the Royal College of Surgeons and a Licentiate of the Apothecaries' Company.
licentiateship *n.* the status or qualification of a licentiate L19.

licentiate /lʌɪˈsɛnʃɪeɪt/ *v.t.* Pa. pple & ppl a. **-ated**, (earlier) †**-ate**. LME. [Orig. pa. pple, f. med.L *licentiatus* pa. pple of *licentiare*, f. *licentia*: see LICENCE *n.*, -ATE[2], -ATE[3].] **1** Allow, permit, (something); allow (a person) *to do*, †*that*. Now *rare* or *obs.* LME. †2 Grant a licence to (a person), esp. to preach. Cf. LICENTIATION. Chiefly *Sc.* M17–M18.

ˌ**licenti'ation** *n.* (now *rare*) †(*a*) the action of allowing something; (*b*) the action of granting a licence to practise medicine: M17.

licentious /lʌɪ'sɛnʃəs/ *adv.* & *a.* LME. [f. L *licentiosus*, f. *licentia*: see LICENCE *n.*, -OUS.] †A *adv.* With licence or liberty; freely. Only in LME. B *adj.* 1 Lawless, lax, immoral. Now usu. *spec.*, immoral or promiscuous in sexual relations. M16. 2 Disregarding commonly accepted rules or conventions; deviating freely from grammatical or literary correctness. *arch.* M16.

licentiously *adv.* M16. **licentiousness** *n.* M16.

lich /lɪtʃ/ *n. arch.* exc. in LICH-GATE, (in var. form) LYKE-WAKE. Also **lych, lyke** /lʌɪk/. [OE *līc* = OFris. *līk*, OS *līc* (Du. *lijk*), OHG *lih* (G *Leiche*), ON *lík*, Goth. *leik*, f. Gmc.] †1 A living body. Also, the trunk, the torso. OE–LME. 2 A dead body, a corpse. Formerly also, a wake. OE.

Comb.: **lich-house** a mortuary; **lich-owl** a screech-owl (its cry supposedly portending a death); **lich-path** a path along which a corpse has been carried to burial, in some districts supposedly establishing a right of way; †**lich-rest** a burial place, a tomb; **lich-stone** a stone to place the coffin on at the lich-gate; †**lich-way** = *lich-path* above.

lichanos /'lɪkənɒs/ *n.* L17. [Gk *likhanos* lit. 'forefinger'.] In ancient Greek music, the third note up in a lower tetrachord, immediately above the parhypate.

lichee *n.* var. of LYCHEE.

lichen /'lʌɪk(ə)n/ *n.* Pl. **-s**, same. E17. [L f. Gk *leikhēn*.] 1 Any of a large group of composite organisms formed by association of algal cells with a fungus, and occurring as encrusting or branching friable growths on surfaces, to which they give a green, grey, or yellow colour; orig. also, a liverwort. Also *collect.*, such organisms growing as a crust or clump. E17. 2 *Med.* & *Vet.* Any of various unrelated skin conditions usu. characterized by (small) tough excrescences over a more or less limited area. E17.

2 **lichen planus** /'pluːnəs/ [L = flat] a skin disorder characterized by an eruption of wide, flat, shiny, purple pimples.

Comb.: **lichen-starch** lichenin; **lichen substance** any of about 65 compounds, mostly acids, which occur uniquely in lichens.

liche'nicolous *a.* inhabiting lichens M19. **lichenification** /lʌɪˌkɛnɪfɪ'keɪʃ(ə)n, ˌlʌɪk(ə)nɪfɪ-/ *n.* (*Med.* & *Vet.*) hardening and thickening of the skin caused by scratching or other continued irritation; an area of skin so affected: L19. **lichenin** *n.* a glucan resembling cellulose and occurring esp. in lichens M19. **lichenism** *n.* the symbiosis between alga and fungus which occurs in lichens L19. **lichenist** *n.* = LICHENOLOGIST M19. **liche'nivorous** *a.* lichen-eating M19. **lichenless** *a.* M19. **lichenoid** *a.* resembling (a) lichen M19. **lichenose** *a.* of the nature of a lichen M19. **licheny** *a.* overgrown with lichens; lichened: E19.

lichen /'lʌɪk(ə)n/ *v.t.* M19. [f. the n.] Cover with lichen. Chiefly as *lichened* ppl a.

lichenized /'lʌɪk(ə)nʌɪzd/ *a.* Also **-ised**. M19. [f. LICHEN *n.* + -IZE + -ED[1].] 1 Covered with lichens. *rare.* M19. 2 Of a fungus or alga: living or adapted to live as a component of a lichen. M20.

lichenology /lʌɪkə'nɒlədʒi/ *n.* M19. [f. LICHEN *n.* + -OLOGY.] The branch of botany that deals with lichens.

licheno'logical *a.* M19. **lichenologist** *n.* M19.

lichenometry /lʌɪkə'nɒmɪtri/ *n.* M20. [f. LICHEN *n.* + -O- + -METRY.] *Geol.* The dating of moraines or other recently exposed surfaces by measurement of the area of lichen growing on them.

licheno'metric, -ical *adjs.* M20.

lichenous /'lʌɪk(ə)nəs/ *a.* E19. [f. LICHEN *n.* + -OUS.] 1 *Med.* Pertaining to or of the nature of the skin condition lichen. E19. 2 Of, pertaining to, consisting of, or resembling lichen; covered with lichen. M19.

lich-gate /'lɪtʃgeɪt/ *n.* Also **lych-gate**. L15. [f. LICH + GATE *n.*[1]] A roofed gateway to a churchyard, formerly used for sheltering a coffin until the clergyman's arrival for a burial.

licit /'lɪsɪt/ *a.* L15. [L *licitus* pa. pple of *licere* be allowed.] Allowable, permitted; lawful.

licitly *adv.* L15. **licitness** *n.* L18.

licitation /lɪsɪ'teɪʃ(ə)n/ *n.* E17. [L *licitatio(n-)*, f. *licitat-* pa. ppl stem of *licitari* bid at an auction: see -ATION.] Now *US Law.* The action of putting something up for sale to the highest bidder.

¶ Only in Dicts. bef. 20.

lick /lɪk/ *n.* L16. [f. the vb.] 1 An act of licking; as much as may be taken by licking; *transf.* a small quantity or amount (*of* something). L16. b A place to which animals go to lick earth impregnated with salt; a block of salt for animals to lick, a lick-log. Also *salt-lick*. Chiefly *N. Amer.* M18. 2 A smart blow; *transf.* an attack, an attempt. L16. b In *pl.* A beating (*Sc.* & *north.*); *colloq.* critical or censorious remarks, criticism. L18. 3 (A) speed, (a) pace; a burst of speed, a spurt. *colloq.* E19. 4 In jazz, rock music, etc.: a short solo or phrase. Freq. in *hot licks*. M20.

1 **a lick** *N. Amer. colloq.* a bit (usu. in neg. contexts). **a lick and a promise** *colloq.* a hasty performance of a task, esp. of washing oneself. b D. TUKE Licks . . can be placed in a manger for greedy feeders. 2 R. L. STEVENSON I wish I had had a lick at them with the gun first. O. MANNING The man . . gave his horse a lick and the creature trotted for nearly a hundred yards. b P. ABRAHAMS I saw one take licks like that in slavery time; he died. *Time* A Star is Born does not deserve the licks it has got. 3 D. ADAMS Smoke billowed down out of it at an incredible lick. *Aviation News* The pilot . . took off down the aerodrome at a fair lick.

lick /lɪk/ *v.* [OE *liccian* = OS *liccon, leccon* (Du. *likken*), OHG *leckōn* (G *lecken*), f. WGmc, f. IE base repr. also by Gk *leikhein*, L *lingere*.] 1 *v.t.* Pass the tongue over (something), with the object of tasting, moistening, removing something, etc.; take *in, up, off*, etc., by licking; make *clean* etc. by licking. OE. †b *v.t.* & *i.* (w. *of, on*). Lap with the tongue, drink, sip, (a liquid). ME–L18. 2 *v.i.* & *t. transf.* & *fig.* Of an inanimate object (esp. a wave, flame, etc.): lap (*at*) like a tongue, play lightly over or *over*, etc. OE. 3 *v.t.* a Beat, thrash; drive (something) *out of* (a person) by beating. *slang.* M16. b Defeat, get the better of, surpass, (a person); solve (a problem), overcome (a difficulty). *slang* (chiefly *N. Amer.*). L18. 4 *v.t.* Paint with cosmetics; give a smooth or smart finish to (a picture). Now *rare* or *obs.* L16. 5 *v.i.* & *t.* (w. *it*). Run, ride, or move at full speed. *slang* (chiefly *N. Amer.*) & *dial.* M19.

1 A. CHAMBERS Morgan licked dribbling coffee from the side of his plastic mug. B. BYARS Simon had licked the icing off one of the Christmas cupcakes. L. CODY She watched one of the men licking cigarette papers and sticking them together. R. K. NARAYAN The goat . . licked the plate dry. C. HOPE Her face was chalky white, the lips dry and she licked them in her sleep. *Living* Two bad habits . . are cleaning lenses in tap water and licking them clean. b W. COWPER Lie there, and feed the fishes, which shall lick Thy blood. 2 J. H. NEWMAN The tide of human beings . . licking the base of the hill. V. CRONIN Flames from the fire . . were already licking at the staircase. G. M. FRASER The flames were licking towards the catwalk leading to the north-west tower. 3a C. DARWIN How these poor dogs must have been licked. b E. O'NEILL You've finally got the game of life licked. H. ROBBINS The guy had guts. 'Try not to worry,' he said. 'We'll find a way to lick the bastards yet.' 5 A. P. GASKELL He sped her along. Boy, she can lick.

Phrases: **lick a person's arse** (*coarse slang*) or **boots** or **shoes** behave sycophantically towards a person, be servile. *lick creation*: see CREATION 4. **lick into fits** defeat thoroughly. **lick into shape** make presentable or efficient. **lick one's chops** *fig.* (*a*) = *lick one's lips* below; (*b*) *Jazz slang* warm up before a session. **lick one's lips** *fig.* (*a*) look forward to something with relish; (*b*) show one's satisfaction. **lick one's wounds** *fig.* be in retirement after defeat. *lick the trencher*: see TRENCHER *n.*[1] †**lick whole** heal by licking.

Comb.: †**lick-dish** = *lickspittle* n. below; **lick-hole** *Austral.* a place where lick-logs are placed for stock to lick; **lick-log** a block of salt for stock, esp. cattle, to lick; *stand up to one's lick-logs*, make a firm stand; **lick-penny** a thing that uses up money; **lickpot** (long *obs.* exc. *W. Indies*) the first finger; **lickspittle** *n.* & *v.* (*a*) *n.* a sycophant, a parasite; (*b*) *v.t.* behave sycophantically towards; †**lick-trencher** = *lickspittle* n. above.

licking *n.* (*a*) the action of the vb; (*b*) *colloq.* a beating: LME. **licking** *a.* (*a*) that licks; (*b*) *slang* splendid: M17.

licken /'lɪk(ə)n/ *v.i.* Long *obs.* exc. *dial.* M16. [Alt. of LIPPEN *v.*] Foll. by *to*: trust to, depend on.

licker /'lɪkə/ *n.* LME. [f. LICK *v.* + -ER[1].] 1 A person who or thing which licks or (*spec.*) beats or defeats another. LME. 2 *licker-in*, the cylinder in a carding-machine which receives the cotton, wool, etc., from the feed-rollers and passes it on to the main cylinder. M19.

lickerish /'lɪkərɪʃ/ *a.* Also **liquorish**. L15. [Alt. of LICKEROUS, with -ISH[1] for -OUS.] 1 Fond of delicious food; greedy; *fig.* eagerly desirous, longing. (Foll. by †*after, for, to do.*) L15. b Lecherous, lustful. E17. 2 Pleasant to the palate; sweet; tempting. Formerly also, (of a cook) skilful. L16.

lickerishly *adv.* M17. **lickerishness** *n.* L16.

†**lickerous** *a.* ME. [AN var. of OFr. *lecheros* LECHEROUS: see -OUS.] 1 = LICKERISH 2. ME–L17. 2 = LICKERISH 1. LME–M17. b = LICKERISH 1b. LME–E17.

†**lickerously** *adv.* ME–L16. †**lickerousness** *n.* LME–M17.

lickety /'lɪkəti/ *n.* & *pref. colloq.* (chiefly *N. Amer.*). E19. [Fanciful extension of LICK *n.*, *v.*] †A *n. as fast as lickety*, at full speed, headlong. Only in E19. B *pref.* Forming advs., chiefly w. vb stems, w. the sense 'at full speed, headlong', as *lickety-cut*, (esp.) *lickety-split*, etc. M19.

licorice *n.* var. of LIQUORICE.

lictor /'lɪktə/ *n.* LME. [L, perh. rel. to *ligare* bind.] *Rom. Hist.* An officer attending a consul or other magistrate, bearing the fasces, and executing sentence on offenders.

licuala /lɪkjʊ'ɑːlə/ *n.* L19. [mod.L (see below), f. Makasarese *lekowala*.] Any of various small palm trees of the genus *Licuala* with fan-shaped leaves and prickly stalks, native to Malaysia, New Guinea, and northern Australia.

lid /lɪd/ *n.* [OE *hlid* = OFris. *hlid*, MLG *lit* (*lid-*) (Du. *lid*), OHG (*h*)*lit* (now in G (*Augen*)-*lid* eyelid), ON *hlið* gate, gateway, gap, f. Gmc, f. base meaning 'cover'.] 1 A hinged or detachable cover for an upward-facing opening or esp. the top of a container; *dial.* the top crust of a pie. OE. b A door, shutter, or similar means for closing an aperture. Now *dial.* exc. in *port-lid* s.v. PORT *n.*[3] 2b. ME. 2 Either of the upper and lower folds of skin that meet when the eye is closed; an eyelid. ME. 3 *transf.* a Either of the two sides or covers of a book. Chiefly *dial.* & *US.* L16. b *Bot.* & *Zool.* An operculum. L17. c *Mining.* A roof-stone covering a pipe or cylindrical vein of ore (also *lid-stone*). Also, a flat piece of wood reinforcing the roof of a shaft. Chiefly *dial.* M18. d A hat, a cap; *spec.* a motor cyclist's crash-helmet. *slang.* L19. e An ounce of marijuana. *slang.* M20.

1 E. WELTY A candy box with the picture of a pretty girl on the dusty lid. V. S. NAIPAUL Below the sloping lid of the desk . . were my father's records. *New Yorker* A greedy man in a good kitchen before dinner, lifting all the lids. 2 D. JACOBSON She will be wearing green eye-shadow . . on her lids. B. T. BRADFORD Her alert green eyes, wise and shrewd under the wrinkled lids, missed nothing.

Phrases: **put the (tin) lid on** *colloq.* (*a*) be the culmination of; (*b*) put a stop to. **take the lid off** *colloq.* expose (a scandal etc.).

lidless *a.* without a lid; *poet.* vigilant: LME.

lid /lɪd/ *v.t.* Infl. **-dd-**. ME. [f. the n.] Cover with a lid.

lidar /'lʌɪdɑː/ *n.* M20. [f. LIGHT *n.* + RADAR.] A detection system which works on the principle of radar, but uses light from a laser.

lidded /'lɪdɪd/ *a.* OE. [f. LID *n.*, *v.*: see -ED[2], -ED[1].] 1 Having a lid; covered (as) with a lid. OE. 2 *spec.* Of the eyes: having lids, covered with lids. Chiefly as 2nd elem. of comb., as *half-lidded, heavy-lidded, high-lidded*. E19.

lidden /'lɪd(ə)n/ *n.* Long *obs.* exc. *dial.* Also †**led(d)en**. [OE *lǣden* repr. a Celt. or early Proto-Romance pronunc. of L *Latinum* Latin, conf. w. OE *leden* (sense 2), f. *leode* people.] †**1** Latin. Only in OE. **2**†**a** The language of a people etc.; a tongue. OE–ME. †**b** (A form of) speech or utterance; a way of speaking, a language; *poet.* birdsong. ME–E17. **c** Noise, chatter. L17.

liddle /ˈlɪd(ə)l/ *a. dial., nursery, & non-standard.* L19. [Repr. a pronunc.] = LITTLE *a.*

Lide /lʌɪd/ *n. obs.* exc. *dial.* [OE *hlȳda*, cogn. w. *hlūd* LOUD *a.*] The month of March.

lidgate /ˈlɪdgeɪt, ˈlɪdʒɪt/ *n. obs.* exc. *dial.* OE. [f. LID *n.* + GATE *n.*[1]] A gate, *esp.* one set up between pasture and ploughed land or across a road to prevent cattle from straying.

lidia /ˈliðja/ *n.* L19. [Sp., lit. 'fight'.] A bullfight, esp. the earlier stages in which the *cuadrilla* prepares the bull for the *faena*.

lidiador /liðjaˈðɔr/ *n.*, pl. **-dores** /-ˈðɔːres/, a bullfighter L19.

lido /ˈliːdəʊ, ˈlʌɪ-/ *n.* Pl. **-os.** L17. [It. *Lido*, a bathing beach near Venice, f. *lido* shore, beach f. L *litus*.] A bathing beach, orig. *spec.* that near Venice; a resort; a public open-air swimming pool.

lidocaine /ˈlɪdəkeɪn/ *n.* M20. [f. ACETANI)LID(E + -O- + -CAINE.] *Pharm.* = LIGNOCAINE.

lie /lʌɪ/ *n.*[1] [OE *lyġe* f. Gmc, assim. to LIE *v.*[2]] **1** An act or instance of lying; an intentional false statement; an untruth. OE. **b** Something that deceives; an imposture. M16. **2** A charge of falsehood. *obs.* exc. in *give the lie to* below. L16. **3** An anecdote, a tale, a tall story. Orig. & chiefly *Black English*. M20.

1 J. CARY I had committed some fault and told a lie about it. b N. O. BROWN Sublimation . . is a lie and cannot survive confrontation with the truth. 2 SHAKES. *Rich. II* That lie shall lie so heavy on my sword.

Phrases: **act a lie** deceive without verbal lying. **give the lie to** accuse (a person) directly of lying; serve to show the falsity of (a supposition etc.). *nail a lie*: see NAIL *v.* OFFICIOUS *lie.* **tell a lie** utter a lie. *white lie*: see WHITE *a.*

Comb.: **lie-detector** an instrument intended to indicate when a person is lying by detecting changes in his or her physiological characteristics.

lie /lʌɪ/ *n.*[2] In sense 4 also **lye.** L17. [f. LIE *v.*[1]] **1** Manner of lying; direction or position in which something lies; direction and amount of slope or inclination; *fig.* the position or aspect (of affairs etc.). L17. **b** The position of a golf ball to be struck (freq. w. specifying wd). Also, the angle of the head of a golf club when the ball is to be struck. L18. **2** A mass that lies; a stratum, a layer. E18. **3a** Room to lie or take cover. *rare.* M19. **b** The place of cover of an animal or bird. L19. **4** A railway siding. Chiefly *Sc.* M19. **5** An act or period of lying. Chiefly w. advs. (see below). M19. **b** A *long* etc. period of resting or lying, esp. in bed. Cf. *lie-in* below. Chiefly *Sc.* E20.

1 S. BARING-GOULD The horizontal lie of the chalk beds. **lie of the land** *fig.* state of affairs, how matters are tending. b *Times* Pitching cleverly short of the green from an awkward lie. *hanging lie*: see HANGING *a.*

Comb.: **lie-down** *colloq.* a rest (on a bed etc.); **lie-in** *colloq.* (*a*) = a period or act of lying in bed in the morning after one's usual time for getting up (cf. sense 5 above); (*b*) a form of protest in which the participants lie down on the ground and refuse to move; **lie-up** the fact of lying inactive in a place. See also combs. s.v. LIE *v.*[1]

Lie /liː/ *n.*[3] M20. [Sophus *Lie* (1842–99), Norw. mathematician.] *Math.* **1** *Lie algebra*, a vector space over a field in which a product operation is defined such that, for all x, y, z in the space, $x \times y$ is bilinear, $x \times x = 0$, and $(x \times y) \times z + (y \times z) \times x + (z \times x) \times y = 0$. M20. **2** *Lie group*, a topological group in which it is possible to label the group elements by a finite number of coordinates in such a way that the coordinates of the product of two elements are analytic functions of the coordinates of those elements, and the coordinates of the inverse of an element are analytic functions of the coordinates of that element. M20.

lie /lʌɪ/ *v.*[1] Pa. t. **lay** /leɪ/, pres. pple **lying** /ˈlʌɪɪŋ/, pa. pple **lain** /leɪn/. Also (now *dial.*) **lig** /lɪg/. See also LIG. [OE *liċġan* = OFris. *lidz(i)a*, OS *liggian* (Du. *liggen*), OHG *liggen*, ON *liggja*, f. Gmc, f. IE base repr. also by Gk *lektron*, *lekhos*, L *lectus* bed.] **I** *v.i.* **1** Of a person or animal: have the body in a more or less horizontal position along the ground, a surface, etc. Freq. w. compl. expr. condition. OE. **b** Orig., be dead. Later, (of a dead body) be extended on a bier etc.; be buried (in a specified place). OE. †**c** Lie sick, stay in bed through illness etc. ME–L16. **d** Be in bed for the purpose of sleeping or resting. ME. **e** Have sexual intercourse *with*. *arch.* ME. **2** Be or remain in a specified state of subjection, misery, captivity, etc.; be kept *in* prison. OE. **3** Take a recumbent or prostrate position (chiefly w. advs.: see below). Formerly also, lean or hang *over* (a wall). ME. **4a** Reside, stay; *esp.* sleep or pass the night (in a place), lodge temporarily. *arch.* ME. **b** *spec.* Of troops etc.: be encamped *at*, *in*, *near*, a place; have or take up a position. ME. †**c** Live under specified circumstances or engaged in some specified occupation. (Foll. by *at*, *about*.) M16–E18. **5** Be or remain in a state of inactivity or concealment. Freq. w. compl. (adj. or pa. pple). ME. **b** Of a game-bird: not rise. L18. **6**†**a** Foll. by *at*, *on*: importune, urge. M16–M18. †**b** Foll. by *on*: oppress, harass. L16–L17. **c** Apply oneself vigorously and steadily *to* (also foll. by †*at*). L16.

1 SCOTT FITZGERALD A stretcher on which lies a drunken woman. DAY LEWIS The long white forenoons of childhood, as I lay ill or convalescent. G. GREENE The boy lay asleep . . in his teak bunk. b J. BETJEMAN Beneath the Abbey bells. . . Here, where England's statesmen lie. e P. O'BRIAN Woman, wilt thou lie with me? 2 LD MACAULAY The defendant . . was lying in prison as a debtor. 3 B. BAINBRIDGE He . . went upstairs to lie on the couch. 4 GOLDSMITH He was to lie that night at a neighbour's. b T. FAIRFAX At Wakefield . . lay three thousand of the enemy. 5 DICKENS Do you mean to . . let me lie here till this hunt is over? *Proverb*: Let sleeping dogs lie. *lie close*, *lie doggo*, *lie low*, *lie perdu*, etc.

II *v.i.* †**7** Of land, landed possessions: appertain *to*. OE–E17. **8** Be situated (in space), have a (specified) position, (of an event, experience, etc.) be disposed in time. Freq. with adj. or advb. compl. LOE. **b** Of a road, a course of travel, etc.: extend, have a (specified) direction; lead *through*, *by*, *along*, *among*, etc. LOE. **c** Of the wind: remain in a specified quarter. E17. **d** Be spread out or extended to the view; (of a period of time, a sequence of events, etc.) extend back into the past or forward into the future. M18. **e** Of a competitor in a race: occupy a specified ordinal position. M20. **9** *Naut.* **a** Of a ship: float in a berth or at anchor. LOE. **b** Steer in a (specified) direction. L16. **10** Of a material thing: be placed usu. more or less horizontally on the ground or other surface; (of a building etc.) be overthrown or fallen. ME. **b** Be deposited, remain permanently in a specified place. LME. **c** Of snow: settle and remain unmelted on the ground etc. L17. **11** Remain unworked, unused, untouched, or undiscovered. Freq. foll. by compl. ME. **12** Of an abstract thing: exist, be found, reside, be arranged or related, in some specified position or order. ME. †**b** Belong or pertain *to* a person (to do); pertain *to* a thing. ME–M17. **c** Rest or be imposed as a charge, obligation, etc., *on* a person; be incumbent *on*; weigh *on* (one's mind etc.). ME. **d** Be set *at stake*; hang or depend *on* a doubtful issue etc. Long *rare.* L16. †**e** Of thoughts, inclinations, activities, etc.: have a specified direction. M17–E19. **13** Chiefly *Law.* Of an action, charge, claim, etc.: be admissible or sustainable. ME. **14** Of the wind etc.: be or become still, subside. Long *obs.* exc. *dial.* L17.

8 G. GREENE I am not to this day absolutely sure of where . . Jones's home lay. A. MACLEAN A small village lay at the head of the lake. b CARLYLE Our course lay along the Valley of the Rhone. d J. PAYN What a future seemed to lie before him! e D. FRANCIS He took the first half mile without apparent effort, lying about sixth. 9a J. CONRAD The English ship . . was lying in Hyères Roads. 10 J. STEINBECK Boxes of lettuce lay on her porch. I. MURDOCH We tilted the cage until it lay entirely upon its side. c *Times* North London had its heaviest snowfall of the winter . . but the snow did not lie. 11 GLADSTONE Rarely within the living memory has so much skill lain barren. *lie fallow*, *lie idle*, *lie waste*, etc. 12 G. M. TREVELYAN His strongest appeal lay in the strength, beauty and accuracy of his pictures of nature. C. HILL There could no longer be any doubt where real power lay. c DEFOE These Things . . lay upon my Mind. CASTLEREAGH It lay upon them to offer terms to us. d SHAKES. *All's Well* He persists As if his life lay on't. 13 A. CRUMP In which case no action for damages would lie.

III *v.t.* **15** Cause to lie, lay. Now *rare.* OE. **b** *Naut.* Lay (a course). L16.

Phrases: *here lies our*, *your way*: see WAY *n.* *how the wind lies*: see WIND *n.*[1] **lie heavy on** be a weight on (one's stomach or conscience). *lie in one's way*: see WAY *n.* **lie in ruins** or **in the dust** be overthrown or fallen (*lit.* & *fig.*). *lie in state*: see STATE *n.* *lie in the bed one has made*: see BED *n.* *lie in the dust*: see *lie in ruins* above. *lie in wed*: see WED *n.* 2. *lie like a log*: see LOG *n.*[1] *lie on the stomach*: see STOMACH *n.* *lie on the table*: see TABLE *n.* *lie to wed*: see WED *n.* 2. *lie upon the wager*: see WAGER *n.* 3. *there lies your way*: see WAY *n.*

With advs. in specialized senses: **lie about** lie here and there; be left carelessly out of place or in disorder. **lie ahead** be going to happen, be in store. **lie along** (*a*) be prostrate at full length, lie outstretched on the ground (*arch.*); extend along a surface; (*b*) *Naut.* (of a ship) lean to one side under the pressure of a wind abeam. **lie around** = *lie about* above. **lie back** lean backwards against some support; recline so as to rest; *lie back and enjoy it* (iron.), relax and accept the inevitable. **lie by** †(*a*) have a concubine; (*b*) *Naut.* = *lie to* below; also, arrange the sails of a ship during a gale so that heavy seas do not break aboard; (*c*) remain unused, be laid up in store; (*d*) keep quiet or retired; remain inactive, rest. **lie down** (*a*) assume a lying position; have a brief rest in or on a bed etc.; *fig.* give up, be remiss or lazy; *take lying down*, receive (a beating, defeat, etc.) in an abject manner, without resistance or protest (chiefly in neg. contexts); *lie down and die*, give up completely; *lie down under*, accept without protest; †(*b*) be brought to bed *of* a child. **lie in** (*a*) be brought to bed in childbirth (*of* a child); †(*b*) amount to, cost, (a certain sum); (*c*) *colloq.* lie in bed in the morning after one's usual time for getting up. **lie off** *Naut.* (of a ship) stand some distance away from the shore or another ship. **lie over** (*a*) be held over or deferred to a future occasion; (*b*) *US* break one's journey; stop. **lie to** *Naut.* (of a ship) come almost to a stop with its head near the wind by backing or shortening sail. **lie up** (*a*) go into or be in hiding; take to one's bed or remain in one's room through illness; (of a ship) go into dock or be out of commission; (*b*) *Naut.* lay or shape one's course.

With preps. in specialized senses: **lie in** (*a*) rest or centre in; depend on; be in the power of (*to do*); *as far as in me* etc. *lies*, to the best of my etc. power; (*b*) consist in, have its ground or basis in; (*c*) be contained or comprised in (a specified room or compass). **lie under** be subject to (some disadvantage or obligation); *lie under sentence of death*, be condemned to death. **lie with** be the office or province of a person *to do* something; (see also sense 1e above).

Comb.: **lie-abed** *arch.* a person who lies in bed; a late riser; a sluggard; **lie-about** an idle person, a layabout; **lie-by** (*a*) a neutral; (*b*) (now *dial.*) a concubine, a mistress. (See also combs. of LIE *n.*[2])

lier *n.* M16.

lie /lʌɪ/ *v.*[2] Pa. t. & pple **lied** /lʌɪd/, pres. pple **lying** /ˈlʌɪɪŋ/. [OE *lēogan* = OFris. *liāga*, OS *liogan* (Du. *liegen*), OHG *liogan* (G *lügen*), ON *ljúga*, Goth. *liugan*, f. Gmc base also of LIE *n.*[1]] **1** *v.i.* Make an intentionally false statement, tell a lie or lies (*to* a person). OE. **2** *v.i.* Of a thing: present a false statement; convey a false impression; be deceptive. ME. **3** *v.t.* †**a** Utter (a falsehood); say or allege (something) falsely. ME–E16. **b** Get (oneself, a person, etc.) *into* or *out of* by lying. E18. †**4** *v.t.* Accuse of lying. Only in LME. **5** *v.i.* Talk, gossip; tell tall stories, exchange anecdotes. Orig. & chiefly *Black English*. M20.

1 G. GREENE The train was very full, he said, though Myatt knew he lied. I. MURDOCH It seems so terrible to lie to him . . about things which just aren't true. *lie in one's teeth*: see TOOTH *n.* *lie in one's throat*: see THROAT *n.* *lie like a trooper*: see TROOPER 1. 2 A. PRICE The ground never lies, you can't put a spade in it without leaving a mark. 3b *Punch* Go on tamely to allow yourself to be lied into Party blindness.

lié /lje, ˈliːeɪ/ *pred. a.* M19. [Fr., pa. pple of *lier* to bind.] Connected (*with*), intimately acquainted (*with*).

liebchen /ˈliːpçən, ˈliːbtʃ(ə)n/ *n.* Also ***L-***. L19. [G.] A person who is very dear to another; a sweetheart, a pet, a darling. Freq. used as a term of endearment.

lieber Gott /ˈliːbər gɒt/ *n. phr.* L19. [G.] Dear God. Chiefly as *int.*

Lieberkühn /ˈliːbəkyːn/ *n.* M19. [J. N. *Lieberkühn* (1711–56), Ger. anatomist.] Anat. *crypt* or *gland of Lieberkühn*, *Lieberkühn's gland* etc., any of the minute tubular glands found at the base of the villi in the small intestine. Usu. in *pl.*

Lieber'kühnian *a.* M19.

Liebestod /ˈliːbəstoːt/ *n.* Also ***l-***. L19. [G, lit. 'love's death'.] An aria or a duet in an opera etc. proclaiming the suicide of lovers; such a suicide.

Liebfraumilch /ˈliːbfraʊmɪlk, *foreign* ˈliːp fraʊmɪlç/ *n.* M19. [G, f. *lieb* dear + *Frau* lady, (i.e. the Virgin Mary, patroness of the convent where it was first made) + *Milch* MILK *n.*] A mild white Rhine wine.

Liebig /ˈliːbɪg/ *n.* M19. [Baron Justus von *Liebig* (1803–73), Ger. chemist.] 1 More fully *Liebig's extract* (*of beef*). A highly concentrated extract containing the soluble constituents of beef. Now *rare*. M19. 2 *Liebig*(*'s*) *condenser*, a common distillation device consisting of two concentric tubes, a coolant (usu. water) being passed through the outer tube to condense vapour in the inner one. M19.

liebling /ˈliːplɪŋ, ˈliːb-/ *n.* Also ***L-***. M19. [G.] = LIEBCHEN.

lied /liːd, -t/ *n.* Pl. **lieder** /ˈliːdə/. Also **L-**. M19. [G.] A song; *esp.* a song characteristic of the German Romantic period, usu. for solo voice with piano accompaniment.

Comb.: **liederabend** /-ɑːbənt/ [G *Abend* evening] an evening recital of such songs.

Liederkranz /ˈliːdəkrants/ *n. US.* E20. [G, lit. 'choral society'.] (Proprietary name for) a strong-flavoured soft cheese.

lief /liːf/ *a.*, *n.*, & *adv.* Now *arch.* & *dial.* [OE *lēof* = OFris. *liāf*, OS *liob*, *liof* (Du. *lief*), OHG *liub*, *liup* (G *lieb*), ON *ljúfr.*, Goth. *liufs*, f. Gmc, rel. to LEAVE *n.*[1], LOVE *n.*] **A** *adj.* 1 Beloved, dear, agreeable, acceptable, precious. OE. 2 Not disagreeable; not unwilling. Freq. in *lief or loath*. OE. †3 Desirous, willing, glad. (Foll. by *of*, *to do*.) ME–E16.

1 F. SHERIDAN I had as lief have let it alone. TENNYSON I charge thee, quickly go again As thou art lief and dear. E. POUND This most lief lady. 2 R. W. DIXON Now hence must I . . be I loth or lief.

†**B** *n.* A beloved, a dear person; a friend, a sweetheart; a wife. Also (as a form of respectful address), sir, lord. OE–M17.

C *adv.* Gladly, willingly. ME.

A. E. HOUSMAN Where shall one halt to deliver This luggage I'd lief set down? C. DAY He said . . he would as lief go around in a wheelbarrow.

liefly *adv.* †(*a*) beautifully; dearly, kindly; (*b*) *rare* willingly, gladly: OE.

liege /liːdʒ/ *a.*, *n.*, & *v.* ME. [(O)Fr. *lige* (OFr. also *liege*) f. med.L *leticus*, *laeticus* f. *letus*, *litus*, prob. f. Gmc.] **A** *adj.* 1a *Hist.* Of a superior: entitled to feudal allegiance and service (now *rare* exc. in *liege lord* below). Of a vassal: bound to give feudal service and allegiance (cf. LIEGEMAN). ME. b Loyal, faithful. *rare*. L15. 2 *Hist.* Of or pertaining to the bond between feudal superior and vassal. LME.

1 **liege lord** a feudal superior, a sovereign.

B *n.* 1 *Hist.* The superior to whom a vassal owes feudal allegiance and service; a liege lord. LME. 2 A vassal who owes feudal allegiance and service to a superior, a liegeman (*Hist.*); *transf.* a loyal subject of a sovereign. Usu. in *pl.* LME.

1 BROWNING My liege, do not believe it! I am yours. 2 SIR W. SCOTT Her Majesty, being detained by her gracious desire to receive the homage of her lieges. J. TEY The Chief Constable . . sent a request to the Home Office for troops to protect the lieges.

C *v.t.* †1 Give (homage etc.) as a liegeman. Only in L17. 2 Foll. by *it*: rule over like a liege lord. *rare*. M19.

liegedom *n.* the condition of being a liege E19. **liegeless** *a.* (*rare*) (*a*) not subject to a superior; free; (*b*) disregardful of obligations to a superior: E19.

liegeman /ˈliːdʒmən/ *n.* Pl. **-men**. LME. [f. LIEGE *a.* + MAN *n.*: cf. med.L *homo ligeus*, OFr. *home* (mod. *homme*) *lige*.] 1 *Hist.* A vassal owing feudal allegiance and service to a liege lord. LME. 2 A person who serves another as though sworn to do so, a faithful follower or subject. E19.

Liégeois /lɪˈeɪʒwɑː/ *n.* & *a.* Pl. of n. same. L16. [Fr., f. *Liège* (see below).] (A native or inhabitant) of Liège, a city and province in Belgium.

lieger *n.* & *a.* see LEDGER *n.* & *a.*

lien /liːn, ˈliːən, ˈlʌɪən/ *n.* M16. [Fr. f. OFr. *loien* f. L *ligamen* bond, f. *ligare* to tie.] *Law.* A right to keep possession of property belonging to another person until a debt due by that person is discharged.

fig.: T. LUNDBERG The assets are free of any lien or encumbrances. *Rolling Stone* A sport on which television already had a lien.

lieno- /lʌɪˈiːnəʊ/ *comb. form.* [f. L *lien* spleen: see -O-.] = SPLENO-, as *lieno-renal*.

lientery /ˈlʌɪənt(ə)ri/ *n.* Now *rare* or *obs.* Also (earlier) in mod.L form **lienteria** /lʌɪənˈtɪərɪə/. LME. [(O)Fr. *lientérie* or med.L *lienteria* f. Gk *leienteria*, f. *leios* smooth + *entera* bowels: see -Y[3].] *Med.* A form of diarrhoea in which the food passes through the bowels partially or wholly undigested; an instance or kind of this.

lien'teric *a.* L17.

lierne /lɪˈəːn/ *n.* LME. [Fr., perh. transf. use of *lierne* clematis, dial. var. of *liane*: see LIANA.] *Archit.* A short rib connecting the bosses and intersections of vaulting-ribs.

Liesegang /ˈliːzəgaŋ/ *n.* E20. [R. E. *Liesegang* (1869–1947), Ger. chemist.] Physical Chem. *Liesegang ring* (or *figure* etc.), each of a set of concentric rings of precipitate produced by the diffusion together of two solutions that react to form a slightly soluble precipitate. Usu. in *pl.*

lieu /ljuː, luː/ *n.* ME. [(O)Fr. f. L LOCUS *n.*[1] place.] *in lieu*, in the place, instead, (*of*).

lieutenancy /lɛfˈtɛnənsi, *l(j)uːˈtɛnənsi/ *n.* LME. [f. LIEUTENANT: see -ANCY.] 1 The position, rank, office, or authority of a lieutenant. LME. †2 The district or province governed by a lieutenant. L16–E18. 3 The term of a lieutenant's office. M17. †4 Delegated authority or command. Only in M17. 5 The body of deputy lieutenants in a county. Also, in the City of London, the body of commissioners (now usu. appointed annually) performing some of the duties of a Lord Lieutenant. L17.

lieutenant /lɛfˈtɛnənt, *l(j)uːˈtɛnənt/ *n.* LME. [(O)Fr., f. as LIEU + TENANT *n.* Cf. LOCUM TENENS.] 1 A person who takes the place of another; *esp.* an officer (civil or military) acting for a superior; a representative, a substitute; a trusty assistant, a henchman. LME. †b [tr. L *legatus*, *proconsul*, *suffectus*, etc.] A consul suffect, a legate, a proconsul. LME–M18. 2a An officer in the army or (US etc.) air force, ranking next below a captain. M16. b A naval officer ranking next below a lieutenant commander. L16. c An officer in the Salvation Army ranking next below a captain. L19. 3 In the US etc., a police or prison officer ranking next below a captain. E20.

1 E. LINKLATER With Rod were his two most trusted lieutenants. 2a R. KIPLING Lieutenant Corkram . . rode by. b F. MARRYAT The Admiralty . . had . . promoted him to the rank of lieutenant.

Phrases: DEPUTY *lieutenant*. **first lieutenant** (*a*) a naval officer with executive responsibility for a ship etc.; (*b*) in the US etc. army or air force, an officer ranking next below a captain. *flight lieutenant*: see FLIGHT *n.*[1] **Lieutenant of the Tower** the acting commandant of the Tower of London. *Lord Lieutenant*: see LORD *n.* **second lieutenant** a naval officer ranking next below a (first) lieutenant.

Comb.: **lieutenant colonel** an army officer ranking next below a colonel, having the actual command of a regiment; **lieutenant colonelcy** the office or rank of lieutenant colonel; **lieutenant commander** a naval officer ranking below a commander and above a lieutenant; **lieutenant-governor** the acting or deputy governor of a State, province, etc., under a governor or governor-general.

†**lieutenantry** *n.* lieutenancy M16–L18. **lieutenantship** *n.* (now *rare*) the rank or position of a lieutenant LME.

lieutenant general /lɛfˌtɛnənt ˈdʒɛn(ə)r(ə)l/ *n. phr.* L15. [f. LIEUTENANT + GENERAL *a.* (later taken as n.), after Fr. *lieutenant général*.] †1 *gen.* A person exercising a delegated rule or command over some extensive region or department; the vicegerent of a kingdom etc. L15–E18. 2 A person acting as deputy to a general; an army officer ranking below a general and above a major-general. L16.

life /lʌɪf/ *n.* Pl. **lives** /lʌɪvz/. [OE *līf* corresp. to OFris., OS *līf* life, person (Du. *lijf* body), OHG *līb* life (G *Leib* body), ON *líf* life, body, f. Gmc, f. base the weak grade of which appears in LIVE *v.*] **I** 1 The condition, quality, or fact of being a living organism; the condition that characterizes animals and plants (when alive) and distinguishes them from inanimate matter, being marked by a capacity for growth and development and by continued functional activity; the activities and phenomena by which this is manifested. OE. b Continuance or prolongation of animate existence (as opp. to death). OE. c Animate existence as dependent on sustenance or favourable physical conditions. Formerly also, a livelihood, a person's living. Long *rare* or *obs.* ME. 2 *fig.* A condition of power, activity, or happiness; *esp.* (chiefly in biblical and religious use) the condition of a person freed from the state of sin equated with spiritual death; salvation; regenerate condition. OE. 3 A being's, esp. a person's, animate existence viewed as a possession of which one is deprived by death. OE. 4 The cause or source of living; the animating principle; a person who or thing which makes or keeps a thing alive. ME. 5a A living being, a person. Long *rare* exc. as passing into sense 3. ME. b Vitality as embodied in an individual person or thing. *arch.* L16. c Living things and their activity; *spec.* human presence or activity. E18. 6 Energy; liveliness; animation, vivacity, spirit; *Cricket* that quality in the pitch which causes the ball to rise abruptly or unevenly after pitching. L16. 7 The or *the* living form or (esp. nude) model; living semblance; life-size. L16.

1 J. MILLER The start of life is traditionally identified with the first breath. P. DAVIES Today we understand how man, and even . . how life has arisen on Earth. *bird-life*, *pond-life*, etc. b BYRON No bugle awakes him with life-and-death call. c AV *Deut.* 20:19 The tree of the field is mans *life*. 2 CARLYLE If our Bodily Life is a burning, our Spiritual Life is a being-burnt, a Combustion. 3 P. S. BUCK Her Life would not easily pass from her body. *Financial Times* Political violence claims an average of almost nine lives a day. 4 T. TRYON Water and Air are the true life and Power of every Being. *Melody Maker* Offstage . . Dudley doesn't strike you as being the life and soul of the party. 5c DICKENS Very little life was to be seen on either bank. K. WATERHOUSE The office area, though brightly lit, is empty of life. D. ATTENBOROUGH It was only the dinosaurs that disappeared, not the whole of animal life. 6 LYTTON There was no lustre in her eye, no life in her step. M. CONEY She was full of life, full of vitality and youth. 7 W. HOLLAR He was drawing a figure after the life. *New Yorker* Unlike Acord, . . she preferred to draw from life.

II 8 The animate existence of an individual in respect of its duration; the period from birth to death, from birth to a particular time, or from a particular time to death. OE. b The time for which an inanimate thing exists or continues to function or be saleable or valid; *spec.* in *Physics* (more fully *mean life*), the average duration of existence of a type of particle or state (equal to the period in which the population decreases by a factor *e*, approx. 2.718). Cf. *half-life* s.v. HALF-. E18. c Imprisonment for life; a life sentence. *slang.* E20. 9 A chance to live after a narrowly escaped death. Chiefly w. ref. to the nine lives traditionally attributed to the cat. Usu. in *pl.* Cf. sense 11 below. M16. 10 A person considered with regard to the probable future duration of his or her life, esp. for insurance purposes; any particular amount of expectation of life. L17. 11 In various games, esp. card-games, any of a specified number of successive chances each player has before being put out. Also (*Cricket*, *Baseball*, etc.), the continuation of a batsman's innings or a batter's turn at bat after a chance has been missed of getting him or her out. E19.

8 E. BAKER Man's life can be separated into . . four stages of childhood, youth, middle years . . old age. b E. RUTHERFORD A radioactive life of less than a minute. c *Times* Its . . turbo-jet engines will be permitted an initial 'life' . . of 1,000 hours.J. C. OATES A backwoods woman come to visit her husband, sentenced to Powhatassie for life. **11** J. SNOW Walters . . was given a life by another blunder by Rowan.

III 12 The series of actions and occurrences constituting the history of an individual from birth to death; the course of (human) existence from birth to death. Also (*Theol.*), either of the two states of human existence separated by death. OE. **b** A particular manner or course of living. Freq. w. specifying wd. OE. **c** The active part of human existence; the business and active pleasures of the world. Also, the position of participating in the affairs of the world, of being a recognized member of society. L18. **13** A written account of a person's history; a biography. ME.

12 MILTON To know That which before us lies in daily life. b R. CAMPBELL Few people enjoyed *living* so much as Aunt Jessie . . though her life was . . truly tough. DAY LEWIS Living . . the same enclosed, garrison life . . as the Anglo-Indians in India. c C. MACKENZIE I've got a fancy . . to show you a bit of life. **13** S. SASSOON He had written the lives of several Generals. B. BAINBRIDGE The book was a life of Mozart.

Phrases: **a bad life** a person assessed for life-insurance purposes as not likely to exceed his or her expectation of life. **a good life** a person assessed for life-insurance purposes likely to exceed his or her expectation of life. **a matter of life and death** something on which it depends whether one shall live or die; *fig.* something of vital importance (cf. *life-and-death* adj. below). **anything for a quiet life** any concession to ensure that one is not disturbed. **(as) large as life** (*a*) life-size; (*b*) in person, esp. prominently. *book of life*: see BOOK *n. the* BREATH *of life.* **bring to life** recover from unconsciousness or inactivity, impart animation to. **come to life** emerge from unconsciousness or inactivity; become animated. *decrement of life*: see DECREMENT 2b. *depart from life*: see DEPART *v. dog's life*: see DOG *n. double life*: see DOUBLE *a.* & *adv. downhill of life*: see DOWNHILL *n.* I. ELIXIR *of life.* **eternal, everlasting, life**: in heaven. **expectation of life** the average period that a person at a specified age, in a known state of health, etc., may be expected to live, esp. as derived from statistics of the population at large. *fact of life*: see FACT *n. for dear life*: see DEAR *a.*[1] **for life** for the remaining period of the person's life. *for* ONCE *in one's life.* **for one's life** for dear life, (as if) to escape death. **for the life of me** even if my life depended on it (I could not etc.). **frighten the life out of** terrify. *future life*: see FUTURE *a.* & *n.* **get, have, the fright of one's life** be frightened as never before. **have the time of one's life** enjoy oneself as never before. *high life*: see HIGH *a.* **how's life?** *colloq.* how are things going? **in life** to be experienced anywhere. *large as life*: see *as large as life* above. **larger than life** more than life-size; exaggerated. *lead a person a* (*difficult, uncomfortable,* etc.) *life*: see LEAD *v.*[1] *life and limb*: see LIMB *n.*[1] *light of one's life*: see LIGHT *n. line of life*: see LINE *n.*[2] *live one's own life*: see LIVE *v. long of life*: see LONG *a.*[1] *lose one's life*: see LOSE *v. loss of life*: see LOSS *n.* **make life easy (for)** not create problems (for). *middle life*: see MIDDLE *a.* **my life** *arch.* my beloved, my dearest. *natural life*: see NATURAL *a. new lease of* or *on life*: see LEASE *n.*[3] **not on your life** *colloq.* most certainly not. **on life** *arch.* alive. *other life*: see OTHER *a. plague the life out of*: see PLAGUE *v. pride of life*: see PRIDE *n.*[1] *private life*: see PRIVATE *a.* **put some life into it** act, perform, more energetically. **save a person's life** prevent a person's dying or being killed; *hyperbol.* provide much-needed relief for a person, esp. oneself, from exhaustion, boredom, etc. *secret life*: see SECRET *a.* & *n. see life*: see SEE *v. sell one's life dear* or *dearly*: see SELL *v. slice of life*: see SLICE *n.*[1] 3. *staff of life*: see STAFF *n.*[1] *state of life*: see STATE *n. still life*: see STILL *a.* **take life** kill a person or an animal. **take one's life in one's hands** *colloq.* risk one's life. **take one's own life** kill oneself, commit suicide. *the change of life*: see CHANGE *n.* I. *the facts of life*: see FACT *n. the kiss of life*: see KISS *n.* **the life** *US slang* prostitution (freq. in *in the life*). *the life of* RILEY. **the life of the mind** intellectual or aesthetic pursuits, the realm of the imagination. *the story of my, his,* etc., *life*: see STORY *n.*[1] *the struggle for life*: see STRUGGLE *n.* **this life** [tr. Vulgate *haec vita*, in *1 Cor.* 15:19] life on earth; *depart from this life*: see DEPART *v.* **this is the life** *colloq.*: expr. contentment. *time of life, time of one's life*: see TIME *n.* **to the life** with lifelike representation; with fidelity to the original. *tree of life*: see TREE *n.* **true to life** providing an accurate representation of behaviour etc. *unitive life*: see UNITIVE *a.* I. *university of life*: see UNIVERSITY I. **upon my life!** *arch.*: expr. of asseveration. *walk in life, walk of life*: see WALK *n.*[1] *water of life*: see WATER *n. way of life*: see WAY *n.* **what a life!** *colloq.*: expr. discontent. *within an inch of one's life*: see INCH *n.*[1] *you bet your life*: see BET *v.* 2. *your money or your life*: see MONEY *n.*

Comb.: **life-and-death** *a.* involving life and death; vitally important (cf. *a matter of life and death* above); **life assurance** = *life insurance* below; **lifebelt** a belt of buoyant or inflatable material for supporting the body in water; **lifeblood** (*a*) the blood necessary to life; *fig.* the vitalizing influence, the vital factor; (*b*) *colloq.* an involuntary twitching of the lip or eyelid; **lifeboat** (*a*) a boat of special construction launched from land for rescuing those in distress at sea; a ship's small boat for abandoning ship in an emergency; (*b*) *US slang* a pardon, a commutation of sentence; (*c*) a system of support organization arranged by the Bank of England for secondary banks in danger of collapse; **life-breath** the breath which supports life; *fig.* an inspiring influence, a sustaining principle; *lifebuoy*: see BUOY *n.* 1b; **life cord** (*arch. rare*) = *life-string* below; **life cycle** (*a*) *Biol.* (an account of) the series of developmental stages through which an organism passes from its initial state (egg) to the same state in the next generation; (*b*) the course of human, cultural, etc., existence from beginning through development and productivity to decay and ending; **life-day** *arch.* a day etc. of a person's life; freq. in *pl.* (occas. *sing.*), a person's life or lifetime, (all) the days of (one's) life; **life-estate** property that a person holds for life but cannot dispose of further; **life-everlasting** an American everlasting, *Anaphalis margaritacea*, grown for ornament; **life expectancy, life expectation** = *expectation of life* above; **life-force** vital energy, a driving force or influence; **life-giver** a person who or thing which gives life; **life-giving** *n.* & *a.* (*a*) *n.* the giving of life; (*b*) *adj.* that gives life; **life-gun** a gun used for sending life-saving apparatus to ships; **life history** *Biol.* = *life cycle* above; *transf.* (an account of) the series of stages in the existence of an inanimate thing; the story of a person's life, esp. when told at tedious length; **life-hold** *a.* designating property which is held for life; **life imprisonment** imprisonment for life; **life-in-death** (*a*) a phantom state, a condition of being or seeming to be neither alive nor dead; something having the form or appearance of the supernatural, an apparition, a spectre; (*b*) = *death-in-life* s.v. DEATH *n.*; **life insurance** insurance for payment on the death of the insured person; **life interest** a right to a life estate; **life-jacket** a jacket of buoyant or inflatable material for supporting the body in water; **life list** *Ornith.* a list of the kinds of bird recorded by a person during his or her life; **life member** a person who has acquired lifelong membership of a society etc; **life membership** the status or position of a life member; **life net** *US* a safety net held to catch people forced by fire etc. to escape from buildings by jumping; **life-office** an office or company dealing in life insurance; **life-or-death** *a.* = *life-and-death* adj. above; **life peer** a peer whose title cannot be inherited; **life peerage**: held by a life peer; **life-plant** a plant of the stonecrop family, *Kalanchoe pinnata*, which will produce young plants from the leaves even after the leaves are removed from the plant; **life-policy** a life-insurance policy; **life-preserver** (*a*) (long *rare* or *obs.*) a person who preserves life; (*b*) a lifebuoy, lifebelt, or other contrivance used in saving life at sea; (*c*) a short stick with a heavily loaded end; **life-raft** a raft, usu. an inflatable one, for conveying people, esp. as a substitute for a boat in an emergency; **liferent** *n.* & *v.* (*Sc. Law*) (*a*) *n.* a rent or income which a person is entitled to receive for life, usually for support; a right to use and enjoy (property) during one's life; (*b*) *v.t.* assign in liferent; use and enjoy property during one's life; **liferenter** *Sc. Law* a person who is entitled to or enjoys a liferent; **liferentrix** a female liferenter; **life-ring** *N. Amer.* a lifebuoy; **life-save** *v.t.* save from death or serious difficulty, esp. drowning; act towards as a life-saver; **life-saver** (*a*) a person who or thing which may save a person etc. from death or serious difficulty; *esp.* (*Austral.* & *NZ*) = LIFEGUARD 4; (*b*) *fig.* a quality, characteristic, or circumstance that helps a person to endure adversity; **life-saving** *a.* & *n.* of or pertaining to, the action of, saving a person etc. from death or serious difficulty, esp. from drowning; **life science** any of the sciences (such as zoology, bacteriology, or physiology) which deal with living organisms; such sciences collectively; **life scientist** an expert in or student of a life science; **life sentence** a sentence of imprisonment for life; *transf.* an illness, obligation, etc.; **life-size** *a.* & *n.* (*a*) *adj.* of the size of life; (of a picture or statue) equal in size to the original; (*b*) *n.* the size of someone or something; a life-size portrait or statue; **life-sized** *a.* = *life-size* adj. above; **life span** a lifetime; the period of duration or existence (of an animate or inanimate thing); **life-spring** *arch.* the spring or source of life; **life-string** *arch.* a nerve etc. supposed to be essential to life; in *pl.*, things essential to the support of life; **lifestyle** (*a*) a person's basic character as established early in childhood which governs his or her reactions and behaviour; (*b*) an individual's or group's way of life; a way or style of living; **life-support** *a.* (of equipment) allowing vital functions to continue in an adverse environment or during severe disablement, as in giving assisted ventilation to a paralysed patient; **life's-work** the work of a lifetime; a task pursued throughout a person's whole life; **life-table** a table of statistics relating to expectation of life; **life tenancy**: terminating with the holder's death; **life tenant** the holder of a life tenancy; **life test**: made on a sample of components under specified conditions, over a set period or until failure occurs, to determine their reliability; **life-test** *v.t.* perform a life test on; **life-tide** *arch. rare* (*a*) a lifetime; (*b*) the tide or stream of life; **life-tree** = *tree of life* s.v. TREE *n.*; **life-vest** *US* = *life-jacket* above; **lifeway** (orig. *N. Amer.*) a way or manner of life; **life-while** *arch.* a lifetime; **life-work** = *life's-work* above; **life-world** *Philos.* [tr. G LEBENSWELT] all the immediate experiences, activities, and contacts that make up the world of an individual, or of a corporate, life; **life-writer** *rare* a biographer; **life-writing** (the writing of) biography.

lifeward *adv.* in the direction of life, towards life M19. **lifey** *a.* (*a*) characteristic of or belonging to life; (*b*) lively, spirited: LME.

life /lʌɪf/ *v.t. rare.* L19. [f. the n.] Give life to.

life-form /ˈlʌɪffɔːm/ *n.* L19. [f. LIFE *n.* + FORM *n.*] **1** *Biol.* A habit or vegetative form exhibited by any particular plant or which characterizes a group of plants. L19. **2** A living organism; any kind of living thing. E20.

lifeful /ˈlʌɪffʊl, -f(ə)l/ *a.* & *n.* Now *rare.* ME. [f. LIFE *n.* + -FUL.] **A** *adj.* Full of life; having much vitality or animation; giving or bestowing life or vitality. ME. **B** *n.* An amount sufficient to fill a lifetime. M19.

lifefully *adv.* LME. **lifefulness** *n.* M19.

lifeguard /ˈlʌɪfgɑːd/ *n.* M17. [f. LIFE *n.* + GUARD *n.*, prob. after Du. †*lijfgarde*, G *Leibgarde*, (1st elem. meaning body).] **1** A bodyguard of soldiers. M17. **2** The guard or protection of a person's life; a protecting agent or influence. Now *rare* or *obs.* M17. **3** A device attached to the front of a railway engine for sweeping small obstructions from the track. M19. **4** An expert swimmer employed to rescue bathers from drowning. Orig. *US.* L19.

1 The Life Guards in the British army, a regiment of the Household cavalry, now merged with the Horse Guards and the Dragoon Guards in the Household Cavalry.

Comb.: **lifeguardman** a member of a lifeguard; **Life Guardsman** a soldier belonging to the Life Guards.

lifeless /ˈlʌɪflɪs/ *a.* [OE, f. as LIFE *n.* + -LESS.] **1** That has ceased to live; no longer living; dead. OE. **b** Unconscious. Chiefly *hyperbol.* M17. **2** Not endowed with or possessing life; inanimate. OE. **3** Lacking animation, vigour, or activity. ME. **4** Devoid of life or living beings. M18.

1 M. SHADBOLT The bird lay limp. . . It was already quite lifeless. b DISRAELI Mrs. Felix Lorraine sank lifeless into his arms. **2** SHAKES. *A.Y.L.* That which here stands up Is but a quintain, a mere lifeless block. **3** E. BOWEN The flags had dropped and hung lifeless down their poles. B. PYM Marcia's short, stiff, lifeless hair. **4** BROWNING Treeless, herbless, lifeless mountain.

lifelessly *adv.* M19. **lifelessness** *n.* E18.

lifelike /ˈlʌɪflʌɪk/ *a.* & *adv.* E17. [f. LIFE *n.* + -LIKE.] **A** *adj.* **1** Likely to live. *rare.* E17. **2** Like or resembling life; exactly like a living or real original, closely resembling the person or thing represented. E18. **B** *adv.* With animation or liveliness. *rare.* M19.

lifelikeness *n.* M19.

lifeline /ˈlʌɪflʌɪn/ *n.* E18. [f. LIFE *n.* + LINE *n.*[2]] **1** A line or rope for use in life-saving, e.g. attached to a lifebuoy or used by fire-fighters. E18. **b** A diver's signalling line. L19. **2** *fig.* In *Class. Mythol.*, the thread supposedly spun by the

Fates, determining the length of a person's life (formerly also called *line of life*). Also, an essential supply route, a line of communication, etc. M19. 3 *Palmistry.* A line on the palm of the hand supposed to indicate one's length of life. L19.

1 *Ilkeston Advertiser* The lifelines—easier to use and more accurate than lifebelts—were provided. *fig.*: G. ORWELL The public schoolman . . clings to the Old School Tie as to a lifeline. 2 *Sun (Baltimore)* As they [the Japanese] went along, they . . got themselves into a position where they could threaten the American life line to Australia. B. UNSWORTH Battistella, his lifeline in this too, brought him the gossip of the coffee house. 3 M. MCCARTHY He felt a sharp pain in . . his palm, the part bounded by his lifeline.

lifelong /ˈlʌɪflɒŋ/ *a.* & *adv.* M18. [f. LIFE *n.* + LONG *a.*[1]] **A** *adj.* **1** = LIVELONG *a. rare.* M18. **2** Lasting a lifetime. E19. **B** *adv.* For a lifetime. *rare.* M19.

lifemanship /ˈlʌɪfmənʃɪp/ *n.* M20. [f. LIFE *n.* + -MANSHIP.] Skill in getting the edge over, or acquiring an advantage over, another person or persons.

lifer /ˈlʌɪfə/ *n. slang.* M19. [f. LIFE *n.* + -ER[1].] **1** A person serving a sentence of imprisonment for life. M19. **2** A sentence of imprisonment for life. M19. **3** A person who leads a life of a specified character. Freq. as 2nd elem. of comb. E20. **4** A life peer. M20.

1 J. C. HOLMES A letter from a lifer describing sex practices in the penitentiary. 2 E. WALLACE My husband got a lifer two years ago. 3 *Listener* Members may be 'arty-crafty' and 'simple-lifers'.

lifesome /ˈlʌɪfs(ə)m/ *a.* Now *rare.* L16. [f. LIFE *n.* + -SOME[1].] †**1** Fraught with life. Only in L16. **2** Full of life or animation, lively. L17.

lifesomely *adv.* L17. **lifesomeness** *n.* M19.

lifetime /ˈlʌɪftʌɪm/ *n.* ME. [f. LIFE *n.* + TIME *n.*] **1** The duration of a person's life, the (remaining) time during which a person is alive; *colloq.* an exceedingly long time. ME. **2** The duration of a thing or a thing's usefulness etc.; = LIFE *n.* 8b. M19.

1 C. ODETS My father never said one word to my mother in her whole lifetime. *attrib.*: *Country Life* The gifts tax . . would be a tax on lifetime gifts. **the chance** or **opportunity of a lifetime**: such as occurs only once in a person's life. 2 P. DAVIES Such clusters only have a finite lifetime, at the end of which they collapse.

lift /lɪft/ *n.*[1] *obs.* exc. *Sc.* & *poet.* [OE *lyft*, corresp. to OS, OHG *luft* (Du. *lucht*, G *Luft*), ON *lopt* (see LOFT *n.*), Goth. *luftus*, f. Gmc.] Orig., the air, the atmosphere. Later, the sky, the upper regions. Also in *pl.*, the (seven) heavens.

lift /lɪft/ *n.*[2] ME. [f. LIFT *v.*] **I 1** The quantity or weight, esp. of paper, that can be lifted at one time. Also (*Sc.*), a large quantity. ME. **2** A particular joint or cut of meat, esp. of beef. *dial.* E16. **3** A hingeless gate that is removed or opened by lifting. *dial.* L17. **4** An area of rising ground. E19. **5** A fingerprint that has been lifted. *US.* M20.

1 A. TROLLOPE I have used up three lifts of notepaper already. 4 J. R. GREEN A mere lift of higher ground with a few grey cottages dotted over it.

II 6 *Naut.* In *pl.* Ropes reaching from each masthead to their respective yard-arms to steady and suspend the ends. ME. **7** Any of the layers of leather etc. in the heel of a boot or shoe. Also, a built-up heel or device worn in a boot or shoe to make the wearer appear taller. L17. **8** An apparatus for raising or lowering people or things from one floor or level to another; an ascending chamber or compartment; a hoist. Also, the well or vertical opening in which such an apparatus works. M19. **b** An apparatus for carrying people up and down a mountain etc. M20. **9** A set of pumps in a mine; the section of a shaft occupied by one such set. M19.

8 ALDOUS HUXLEY Lenina Crowne shot up seventeen stories, turned to the right as she stepped out of the lift. *express lift*: see EXPRESS *a. paternoster lift*: see PATERNOSTER *n.* 4. **b** *chair-lift, ski-lift*, etc.

III 10 The action or an act of lifting; a raising, a rising; the distance through which a thing is lifted and moved; the distance or extent to which something rises. LME. **b** A free ride as a passenger in another person's vehicle. E18. **c** The removal of a corpse from a house for burial or cremation; the starting of a funeral procession. *Sc.* & *north.* L19. **11** An act of lifting or stealing. Formerly also, a shift, a trick. *obs.* exc. *dial.* & *slang.* L16. **12** *fig.* A rise in social status, prosperity, etc.; promotion; a rise in price; an act of helping, or a circumstance that helps, someone or something to a higher or more advanced position. E17. **b** An elevating influence or effect; a cheering or encouraging influence or effect, a sense of elation. L18. †**13** The action of cutting a pack of cards; each of the portions into which a pack is divided by cutting. L17–E18. **14** *Engin.* The action of lifting a load through a vertical distance, or one of several successive distances. Also (*Mining*), a set of inclined workings following the slope of the beds. E18. **15** The act or habit of carrying the head, neck, eyes, etc., aloft; elevated carriage. M19. **16** *Pros.* A stressed element in a line of alliterative verse. L19. **17a** The upward pressure which the air exerts on an aircraft etc. counteracting the force of gravity; the force on an aerofoil at right angles to its direction of motion through a fluid; upwardly-moving air which provides sufficient upward force to support a glider or carry it higher (freq. in *in lift*). E20. **b** The (maximum) weight that an aircraft can raise. E20. **18** *Dance.* A movement in which a dancer lifts another in the air. E20. **19** Transport by air; a number of people or an amount of supplies so transported. M20. **20** The establishment by a sheepdog of control over a flock of sheep. M20. **21** *Audio.* A relative amplification of signals within a particular part of the audible range, esp. the bass. M20. **22** *Sport.* A movement by which a weightlifter lifts a weight or a wrestler lifts an opponent. M20.

10 E. K. KANE We continue perched up, just as we were after our great lift of last December. J. R. LOWELL An almost imperceptible lift of the eyebrow. *dead lift*: see DEAD *a.* etc. **b** E. WAUGH A man in a newspaper van offered me a lift as far as Elstree. 12 LEIGH HUNT I shall set myself more on a level with these gentry . . by a lift in my fortunes. *Manchester Examiner* The extension of the franchise . . has given an incalculable forward lift to the principles of the Alliance. *Times* A lift in the dividend at Wilson (Connelly) earned its shares a rise. **b** *Practical Gardening* Fresh flowers are wonderful for . . giving us a lift when we feel a bit low. P. THEROUX The sugary breakfast . . gave him a lift. 15 R. D. BLACKMORE The proud lift of her neck was gone. 17a *Nature* Most flying insects depend, for their lift and thrust, on conventional aerofoil action. **b** *Daily Telegraph* The Puma . . helicopter, which has a total lift of up to 5,500 lb. 18 K. AMBROSE With the invention of each new ballet, new lifts are devised. 19 *air-lift.*

†**IV 23** A person who lifts or takes away and appropriates something; a thief. *slang.* L16–M17.

Comb.: **lift-bridge** a bridge on a canal etc. that may be raised to allow the passage of a boat; **lift coefficient** *Aerodynamics* a ratio representing the lift developed by unit area of an aerofoil in relation to the air speed; **lift-fan** a fan in a hovercraft which provides the air-cushion; **lift-gate** (*a*) = sense 2 above; (*b*) a gate opening on to a lift in a building etc.; (*c*) *US* in a motor vehicle, a hinged back panel that opens upwards, a hatchback; **lift-slab** *attrib. a.* designating a labour-saving system of building whereby precast components are raised by jacks to the position desired; **lift truck** = *fork-lift* (*truck* etc.) s.v. FORK *n.*; **lift valve** a valve which opens by the valve head moving (vertically) out of its (horizontal) seat; **lift-web** a strip of webbing joining the harness and the rigging lines of a parachute; **lift wire** *Aeronaut.* a wire on a biplane or light monoplane that extends from the wing to the fuselage and is designed to transmit part of the lift to the latter during flight.

liftless *a.* not provided with a lift E20.

lift /lɪft/ *v.* ME. [ON *lypta* = MHG, G *lüften*, f. Gmc base of LIFT *n.*[1]] **1** *v.t.* Raise into the air from the ground, or to a higher position, hoist (also foll. by *up*, *aloft*, etc.); pick up and bring to a lower position (usu. foll. by *down*); pick up and bring *out* etc. ME. †**b** Bear, support. *rare.* Only in L16. **c** Take up and hold or carry, pick up; *Golf* pick up (a ball) during play. See also sense 6 below. L16. **d** Help (sick or weak cattle) to stand up. Earlier as LIFTING *n.* 2. L19. **e** Perform cosmetic surgery on (esp. the face or breasts) to reduce sagging; perform a face-lift on. E20. **f** *Sport.* Win, carry off, (a prize, trophy, etc.). E20. **g** *Printing.* Raise (lines of type), esp. in moving types from a composing-stick to a galley, or in preparation for the distribution of used type. M20. **2** *v.t. fig.* Elevate to a higher plane of thought or feeling; stimulate morally or spiritually, uplift. Freq. foll. by *up*. ME. **b** Raise in dignity, rank, or estimation; exalt. Also foll. by *up*. Now *rare.* ME. **c** Cheer (*up*), encourage. Also (*arch.*), make arrogant, puff *up* (with pride). LME. **d** Raise in price, value, or amount. E20. **3** *v.i.* Rise; *esp.* (of a ship etc.) rise when riding on the waves. Also, admit of being raised (*up*). LME. **b** Be or become visible above or against a surrounding landscape. L16. **c** Of a floor etc.: swell or warp upwards; bulge. L18. **d** *Naut.* Of a sail: ruffle slightly when caught by the wind on the leech. E19. **e** Of clouds, fog, etc.: disperse, rise. Also (*N. Amer.*), of rain etc.: cease temporarily. M19. **f** *Printing.* Of a forme of type: stay in one piece when raised from the surface on which it has been assembled. M19. **g** Of an aircraft etc.: rise off or *off* the ground. L19. **h** Rise in tone or volume of sound. E20. **4** *v.t.* Take up or collect (rents or moneys) as due; levy (contributions, fines, etc.); draw (wages, profits, etc.). Now *dial.* LME. †**5** *v.t.* Carve (a swan). LME–E19. **6** *v.t.* Pick up (a portable object) with dishonest intentions; steal (esp. cattle); steal (something) from a shop etc. *slang.* E16. **b** Plagiarize (a passage, title, etc.). *colloq.* E20. †**7** *v.i.* Foll. by *at*: pull at (something) in an attempt at raising (*lit.* & *fig.*); rise in opposition to. M16–E18. **8** *v.t.* Take up and remove, take away; drive (cattle) away or to market; strike (a tent etc.); *Sc.* remove (a corpse) for burial or cremation; *fig.* discontinue, remove, (restrictions, an embargo, etc.). M16. **b** *v.t.* *Hunting.* Move (hounds) from a lost scent in order to find the scent again elsewhere. Also, disperse (scent). L18. **c** *v.t.* Get rid of, pay off (a mortgage). *US.* M19. **d** *v.t.* Give a lift to in a carriage, motor vehicle, etc. L19. **e** *v.t.* & *i.* *Artillery.* Increase (the range of fire) from that being used at a given point in an attack. E20. **f** *v.t.* Of a sheepdog: establish control over a flock of sheep. E20. **g** *v.t.* Arrest, take into custody. E20. **h** *v.t.* Evacuate (soldiers) from a beach etc.; air-lift. M20. **i** *v.t.* Take an impression of (fingerprints) for identification purposes. *US.* M20. **9** *v.i.* Cut a pack of cards to determine the dealer. Now *rare* or *obs.* L16. **10** *v.t.* Bear or carry in an elevated position; hold high. L17. **11** *v.t.* Take up out of the ground (*Sc.* in *gen.* sense); *Hort.* dig up (potatoes, bulbs, etc.). M19. **12** *v.t.* Hit (a ball) into the air; (of a batsman) hit a ball bowled by (a bowler) into the air. L19.

1 E. O'NEILL Lifting Mary to the floor. R. G. COLLINGWOOD I felt as if a veil had been lifted and my destiny revealed. A. PATON He . . lifts her from the floor to the chair. G. ORWELL He lay flat on his belly and tried to lift his weight by his hands. *Observer* This has to be lifted up and down when inserting paper. N. LUARD The Belgian unlocked the trunk, stood by the porter while he lifted out two suitcases. **c** D. STOREY Pulling at his mother's skirt and asking to be lifted. **f** *Belfast Telegraph* The third Second Division side in five years to lift the FA cup. 2 STEELE It lifts an heavy empty Sentence, when there is added to it a lascivious Gesture of Body. J. CARLYLE With so rich a husband she would be able to lift them out of all their difficulties. P. H. KOCHER He . . is lifted up to live above himself. **b** H. L. MENCKEN Those of the academic moiety seldom lift themselves above the level of mere pedagogues. **c** AV *2 Chron.* 26:16 But when he was strong, his heart was lifted vp to his destruction. G. BOYCOTT You take brilliant catches standing back, you lift and inspire the team. **d** *Times* Better than expected trading news from Reed International lifted the price 16p to 254p. 3 R. KIPLING The big liner rolled and lifted. *Daily Express* The window-seat top lifts up. *Times* Hopes of future Government contracts caused the shares to lift 3p to 63p. **b** H. BELLOC The chestnuts made a dark belt from which the tall graces of the birches lifted. **d** E. PEACOCK The thick fog had lifted. J. C. OATES One of those . . storms that can last for a week without lifting. **g** H. G. WELLS The aëropile . . lifted clean and rose. *Scientific American* On July 21, 1969, *Eagle* lifted off from the moon. **h** J. GALSWORTHY The sounds of conversation lifting round

him. 6 R. KIPLING He has lifted the Colonel's mare that is the Colonel's pride. T. KENEALLY She got six months for lifting a . . figurine from a store. E. REVELEY He had had to resort to . . lifting a wallet like a common pick-pocket. b CLIVE JAMES The lines about Leonidas are lifted straight from the *Imitations* version of Rauben's 'Die Tauben'. 7 J. LOCKE Like the Body strain'd by lifting at a Weight too heavy. 8 I. L. IDRIESS His gang lifted their cattle. . . and got safely across to the Paroo. *Nature* If the embargo is . . lifted, it will take . . weeks for the oil to reach United States ports. b J. MASEFIELD The hounds were lifted and on his line. d M. SHARP Up she drove, lifted by Mr. Simnel the chemist, Taunton-bound. e A. FARRAR-HOCKLEY Some aghast to see the supporting artillery fire already lifting ahead of them. g *Times* If you have a father who is lifted, he has sons . . who will take his place. h J. MASEFIELD The first men lifted were not always soldiers. *Daily Telegraph* Medical supplies . . were being lifted in by helicopter. 10 MILTON There the Capitol thou seest Above the rest lifting his stately head. 11 *Times* Nurseries . . cannot lift and pack all their orders in a month. 12 *Daily Telegraph* W. G. lifted Spofforth round to the leg boundary.

Phrases: *lift a finger*: see FINGER *n.* **lift one's elbow** = *crook one's elbow* s.v. CROOK *v.* 1. *lift one's eyes*: see *lift up one's eyes* below. **lift one's game** improve one's game, begin to play better. **lift one's hand** *spec.* raise one's hand in taking an oath, or in hostility *against* (a person); *slang* to do a stroke of work (usu. in neg. contexts). *lift one's hands*: see *lift up one's hands* below. *lift the leg*: see LEG *n. lift the roof*: see ROOF *n.* **lift (up) one's eyes** give an upward direction to the eyes, look up (*lit.* & *fig.*). **lift (up) one's hands**: esp. in prayer, thanksgiving, etc. **lift up one's head** (*a*) raise one's head; (*b*) *fig.* recover vigour after prostration. **lift up one's voice** (*a*) sing, speak; (*b*) cry out. †**lift up the head of** bring out from prison; restore to liberty, dignity, etc. **lift up the heart of** raise the thoughts or desires of; encourage. *lift up the horn*: see HORN *n. lift up the leg*: see LEG *n.*

Comb.: **liftback** a type of hatchback car; **lift-on** *a.* made to lift on; *lift-on, lift-off*, (designating) a method of hoisting containers from one vessel or vehicle to another; **lift-out** *a.* made to lift out; **lift-up** *a.* made to lift up.

liftable *a.* (earlier in UNLIFTABLE) M19.

lifter /ˈlɪftə/ *n.* M16. [f. LIFT *v.* + -ER[1].] 1 A person who lifts something (*lit.* & *fig.*). M16. b A person who takes something up dishonestly; a thief. L16. 2 A thing, esp. part of a contrivance or appliance, which lifts or is used for lifting. L16. b *Mining.* A beam to which the head of a stamp is fastened in a stamp-mill. L17. c *Cricket.* A ball, usu. one from a fast bowler, that rises sharply after striking the pitch. M20.

1b *cattle-lifter, shoplifter*, etc.

lifting /ˈlɪftɪŋ/ *n.* ME. [f. LIFT *v.* + -ING[1].] 1 The action of LIFT *v.*; an instance of this (*lit.* & *fig.*). ME. 2 The raising of sick or weak cattle to enable them to stand. E19. 3 In competitive walking, the raising of the rear heel before the front foot touches the ground. M19. 4 *Comm.* In *pl.* The amount of a product, esp. mineral oil, transported through or out of a particular place, or by a particular means. L20.

1 *shoplifting*.

Comb.: **lifting beam** a beam, fitted to a crane hook, to which a load may be attached in two or more places; **lifting plate** an iron plate fastened on to the face of a pattern and provided with a hole into which a lifting screw can be inserted; **lifting screw** *n.*[1] a hook with a threaded shank which can be screwed into an object to facilitate its lifting; (see also *lifting screw* s.v. LIFTING *ppl a.*); **lifting tape** *US* a kind of tape used for taking fingerprints.

lifting /ˈlɪftɪŋ/ *ppl a.* ME. [f. LIFT *v.* + -ING[2].] That lifts; *Aeronaut.* providing lift.

lifting body a (wingless) spacecraft with a shape designed to produce lift, so that aerodynamic control of its flight is possible within the atmosphere. **lifting-bridge** a bridge of which either a part or the whole may be raised at one end to allow boats to pass. **lifting screw** *n.*[2] a rotor operating in a horizontal plane so as to provide lift for an aircraft; (see also *lifting screw* s.v. LIFTING *n.*).

lift-off /ˈlɪftɒf/ *a.* & *n.* E20. [f. LIFT *v.* + OFF *adv.*] A *adj.* Removable by lifting. E20.

Country Life The lift off tray is divided into nine crenellated compartments. *lift-on, lift-off*: see *lift-on* s.v. LIFT *v.*

B *n.* 1 A parachutist's method of leaving an aircraft by opening the parachute while standing on a wing, so as to be carried away by the air current. M20. 2 The vertical take-off of a rocket, helicopter, etc.; the moment at which an aircraft begins to leave the ground; *fig.* initiation or commencement of activity; getting off the ground (of a project or scheme). M20.

2 J. A. MORRIS The launch vehicle exploded soon after lift-off. *Daily Telegraph* Shell has lift-off with its space promotion.

Lifu /ˈliːfuː/ *n.* & *a.* M19. [*Lifu* Island (see below).] (Of) a Melanesian language spoken on Lifu Island, the largest of the Loyalty Islands in the SW Pacific.

Lifuan *n.* & *a.* (a native or inhabitant) of Lifu Island L19.

lig /lɪg/ *v.i.* Infl. **-gg-**. OE. [Var. of LIE *v.*[1]] 1 See LIE *v.*[1] OE. 2 Idle or lie about; sponge; gatecrash or attend parties. *slang.* M20.

ligament /ˈlɪgəm(ə)nt/ *n.* LME. [L *ligamentum*, f. *ligare* bind, tie: see -MENT.] 1 A binding, a band, a tie; *Surg.* a bandage, a ligature. Long only *fig.* (*arch.*), a bond of union. LME. 2 *Anat.* A short band of tough flexible fibrous tissue which binds together bones or cartilages; any membranous fold which supports an organ and keeps it in position. LME. b *Zool.* Any similar part in lower organisms; *spec.* the elastic substance which holds together the valves of a bivalve shell. L18.

2 *cruciate ligament*: see CRUCIATE *a. nuchal ligament*: see NUCHAL *a.* THYRO-ARYTENOID *ligaments*.

ligaˈmental *a.* = LIGAMENTOUS L16. **ligaˈmentary** *a.* = LIGAMENTOUS M18. **ligaˈmentous** *a.* of, pertaining to, of the nature of, or characteristic of a ligament or ligaments; composed of fibrous connective tissue: L17.

ligan *n.* var. of LAGAN.

ligand /ˈlɪg(ə)nd/ *n.* M20. [f. L *ligandus* gerundive of *ligare* bind: see -AND.] *Chem.* A molecule, ion, atom, etc., (capable of) forming a coordination complex with a central (usu. a metal) atom.

Comb.: **ligand field** the electrostatic field produced by the ligands in the vicinity of the central atom.

ligancy *n.* = COORDINATION *number* (a) M20. **liganded** *a.* bound to a ligand or ligands M20.

ligase /ˈlɪgeɪz/ *n.* M20. [f. L *ligare* bind + -ASE.] *Biochem.* An enzyme which catalyses the linking together of two molecules, esp. with a simultaneous conversion of ATP to ADP. Cf. SYNTHASE.

ligate /lɪˈgeɪt/ *v.t.* L16. [L *ligat-* pa. ppl stem of *ligare* tie, bind: see -ATE[3].] Bind with a ligature or bandage; *esp.* in *Surg.*, tie up (an artery etc.) to stop bleeding.

ligation /lɪˈgeɪʃ(ə)n/ *n.* LME. [Late L *ligatio(n-)*, f. as prec.: see -ATION.] 1 The action or process of binding; the condition of being bound. Long *obs.* exc. as in *gen.* sense. LME. 2 The action or an act of binding with a ligature; *esp.* in *Surg.*, the operation of ligating a bleeding artery etc. LME. 3 A thing used in binding; a bandage, a tie. *arch.* L16.

2 *tubal ligation*: see TUBAL 2.

ligature /ˈlɪgətʃə/ *n.* & *v.* LME. [Late L *ligatura*, f. as LIGATE: see -URE.] A *n.* 1 A thing used in binding or tying; a band, a tie; *esp.* (*a*) *Surg.* a thread or cord used to tie up a bleeding artery etc.; (*b*) an adjustable band securing the reed to the mouthpiece in instruments of the clarinet family. LME. b *fig.* A bond of union. E17. †c Binding quality; something having this quality. L17–E18. 2 = LIGAMENT 2. Now *rare.* LME. 3 The action or an act of binding or tying; the result or place of such an action. M16. 4 *Mus.* A note-form representing two or more notes to be sung to one syllable; a tie, a slur. L16. 5 A character or type formed by two or more letters joined together; a monogram. Also, a stroke connecting two letters. L17. B *v.t.* = LIGATE. E18.

ligeance /ˈliːdʒ(ə)ns/ *n.* LME. [OFr. (also *legiance*) (in med.L *ligantia, -entia, leg-*), f. *lige* LIEGE: see -ANCE.] 1 The allegiance of a liegeman or subject. *arch.* LME. 2 The jurisdiction of a monarch over his or her subjects or lieges; the territories subject to a monarch. Now *rare* or *obs.* LME.

liger /ˈlʌɪgə/ *n.* M20. [Blend of LION and TIGER *n.*] An animal born of a mating between a lion and a tigress. Cf. TIGON.

ligger /ˈlɪgə/ *n. dial.* LME. [f. LIG + -ER[1].] 1 A coverlet; a mattress. LME. 2a A plank; a beam; *spec.* = LEDGER *n.* 4a. LME. b A branch laid on the top of a plashed hedge. E19. c = LEDGER *n.* 4b. M20. 3 *Angling.* A line with a float and bait which is left in the water, as used in pike-fishing. E19. 4 A person who gatecrashes parties; a sponger. *slang.* L20.

light /lʌɪt/ *n.* [OE *lēoht*, (Anglian) *līht* = OFris. *liacht*, OS, OHG *lioht* (Du., G *Licht*), f. WGmc, ult. f. IE base repr. also by Gk *leukos* white, L *lux* light. See also LITE *n.*[2]] 1 The natural agent which emanates from the sun, an intensely heated object, etc., and stimulates sight (now recognized as electromagnetic radiation: see sense e below); the medium or condition of space in which this is present and in which vision is possible (opp. *darkness*); *spec.* the illumination proceeding from the sun in daytime; daylight, daytime. OE. b An individual appearance of brightness as an object of perception. OE. c The quantity or quality of illumination in a place; a person's fair or usual share of this. M16. d Vivacity, enthusiasm, or inspiration in a person's face, esp. in the eyes. L16. e *Physics* etc. Electromagnetic radiation having a wavelength between about 400 and 750 nm, which is visible to the human eye; invisible electromagnetic radiation outside this range, *esp.* ultraviolet radiation. E18. f The sensation produced (as) by the impinging of visible radiation on the retina. E19. 2 The state of being visible or exposed. OE. 3 Power of vision, eyesight (now *poet.*); in *pl.* (now *slang*), the eyes. OE. 4 A source of illumination, as the sun or esp. a lighted candle, a (now usu. electric) lamp, a beacon, etc.; a lighthouse; in *pl.*, illuminations. Formerly also *collect.*, the candles etc. used to light a place. OE. b *spec.* A traffic light. Usu. in *pl.* E20. 5a Spiritual or religious illumination; in the Christian Church, God as the source of this; *spec.* in the Society of Friends, the inward revelation of Christ in the soul. OE. b Mental illumination; elucidation, enlightenment, knowledge. Freq. in *cast, shed*, or *throw light on*, help explain. OE. c In *pl.* Pieces of information, facts which explain a subject; the opinions, information, and capacities forming a person's intellect or mental ability. Freq. in *according to one's lights*. E16. d In a puzzle, the answer to a clue; *spec.* (*a*) a line in an acrostic puzzle; (*b*) the item filling the spaces in a crossword puzzle as the answer to a clue. M19. 6 A window or opening in a wall for the admission of light; *spec.* (*a*) any of the perpendicular divisions of a mullioned window; (*b*) a subdivision of a window with tracery. LME. b Any of the (usu. openable) panes of glass forming the roof or side of a greenhouse or the top of a frame. M18. 7 An eminent person; a person notable for virtue, intellect, etc. LME. 8 (Any of) the bright parts of a picture etc. suggesting illumination; comparative lightness as represented pictorially; *transf.* & *fig.* quieter or less dramatic passages in music or literature, providing artistic contrast (freq. in *light and shade*: cf SHADE *n.* 4). E17. b A lighter glint in the hair, a highlight. M20. 9 The aspect in which a thing is regarded or judged. L17. 10 A flame or spark serving to ignite a combustible substance; a device producing this, as a taper, match, etc. L17. 11 *Law.* The light falling on the windows of a house, the obstruction of which by a neighbour is illegal. M18. 12 *Mech.* An aperture, a clear space. L18.

1 A. RANSOME Coming out . . into the light after being . . in the darkness inside the hill. J. HERSEY After dark, they worked by the light of the city's fires. J. STEINBECK A match flared, and in its momentary light Kino saw . . the men were sleeping. FRANK THOMPSON Starting at early light from the old fort. H. E. BATES We skated . . on into the evening by the light of fires. J. FOWLES She had only a candle's light to see by. b DAY LEWIS The whole picture . . is bathed in a brooding, sub-aqueous light. J. BERGER The lamps cast bright distinct circles of light. c E. WAUGH In that kindly

light the stained . . paint of the bungalow and the plot of weeds . . lost their extreme shabbiness. F. WYNDHAM In some lights his markings appeared to be charcoal on cream. **d** J. B. PRIESTLEY Then the light died out of her face. S. BRETT The old light of paranoia gleamed in Alex's eye. **e** P. DAVIES Light takes an enormous length of time to travel between galaxies. **2** E. A. FREEMAN He breaks forth into full light in the course of the next year. **3** R. GRAVES The light of both his eyes was quenched . . with red-hot needles. R. B. PARKER How come somebody punched your lights out over her? **4** C. ISHERWOOD One by one, the lights go out and there is total blackness. M. SPARK He saw below . . the lights of a car. E. ARDIZZONE The light of the lighthouse was out. D. FRANCIS The lights shone bright in the early winter evening. *courtesy light, klieg light, obstruction light, reversing light, traffic-light,* etc. *attrib.* L. DUNCAN It lit up her face as though she had pressed a light switch. **b** R. MACAULAY As the lights changed I saw a bus dashing up. S. BRILL They crashed into a car that was stopped at a light. **5a** J. WESLEY I found such a light . . as I never remember to have had before. **b** A. BRINK The . . search for new light on the deaths of Gordon and Jonathan. *Music* The . . book . . throwing light on many areas of the profession hitherto surrounded in mystery. **6** M. GIROUARD Its row of first-floor oriel windows with arched central lights. *Do-It-Yourself* Fit locks on all ground floor lights. **b** *Gardener* Once the seedlings have germinated, remove the frame lights. **7** J. O'HARA In the 'prelims' one sees the lesser known lights of the boxing fraternity. **8** W. M. CRAIG A light is made brighter by being opposed to a dark. TENNYSON The lights and shadows fly! **9** T. S. ELIOT I am glad that you have come to see it in that light. J. HELLER We can't afford a situation that might put us in a bad light. H. MACMILLAN He tried to see matters in an objective light. **10** W. BESANT A jar of tobacco, and a box of lights. S. THEMERSON I struck a match and gave him a light for his cigarette.

Phrases: *ancient lights*: see ANCIENT *a.* 4. **appear in the light of** seem to be. *black light*: see BLACK *a.* **bring to light** reveal. *cast light on*: see sense 5b above. *cold light*: see COLD *a.* **come to light** (*a*) be revealed; (*b*) *NZ & Austral. colloq.* produce, come up, *with*. *Dutch light*: see DUTCH *a.* **festival of lights** (*a*) = HANUKKAH; (*b*) = DIWALI. FIRST *light*. *green light*: see GREEN *a.* *have one's name in lights*: see NAME *n.* *hide one's light under a bushel*: see BUSHEL *n.* *inner light*: see INNER *a.* **in the light of** having regard to; drawing information from. *leading light*: see LEADING *a.* *lesser light*: see LESSER *a.* *light at the end of the tunnel*: see TUNNEL *n.* **light of day** (*a*) daylight, sunlight; (*b*) general notice; public attention. **light of one's life** (chiefly *joc.*) a much-loved person. **lights out** (*a*) bedtime in a school etc.; (*b*) *Mil.* the last bugle-call of the day. NEON *light*. *New Light*: see NEW *a.* NORTH *light*. *northern lights*: see NORTHERN *a.* *Old Light*: see OLD *a.* **out like a light** deeply asleep or unconscious. *polar light*: see POLAR *a.* **put out** or **quench a person's light** kill a person. *raking light*: see RAKE *v.*[2] *red light*: see RED *a.* *rising of the lights*: see RISING *n.* **see the light** (*a*) come into the world, be brought out or published; (*b*) reach a full understanding or realization, esp. of Christianity. *shed light on*: see sense 5b above. SHINING *light*. *sound and light*: see SOUND *n.*[2] *southern lights*: see SOUTHERN *a.* **stand in a person's light** stand so as to cut out (some of) the light a person is seeing by; *fig.* prejudice a person's interests or chances. *strike a light!*: see STRIKE *v.* *strobe light*: see STROBE *a.* *sweetness and light*: see SWEETNESS 1. *throw light on*: see sense 5b above. *top light*: see TOP *a.* *Vauxhall light*: see VAUXHALL *a.* 1. *visible light*: see VISIBLE *a.* *Wood's light*: see WOOD *n.*[3] 2. *yellow light*: see YELLOW *a.*

Comb.: **light barrier** [after *sound barrier*] the speed of light as the limiting speed attainable by any object; **lightboat** = *lightship* below; **light-box** a box with a side of translucent glass and containing an electric light, so as to provide an evenly lighted flat surface; **light-bulb** a glass bulb containing gas and a metal filament, giving light when an electric current is passed through; **light-buoy**: equipped with a warning light which flashes intermittently; **light cone** *Physics* a surface in space-time, represented as a cone in three dimensions, comprising all the points from which a light signal would reach a given point (at the apex) simultaneously, and which therefore appear simultaneous to an observer at the apex; **light cord** a cord which operates an electric light when pulled; **light curve** *Astron.* a graph showing the variation in the light received over a period of time from a variable star or other celestial object; **light-day** *Astron.* the distance travelled by light in a day; **light-demander** a tree needing full light; **light-demanding** *a.* (of a tree) needing full light; **light due** a toll on ships for the maintenance of lighthouses and lightships; **light-fast** *a.* resistant to discoloration by light; **light-fastness** the quality of being light-fast; **light-fixture** a flex, socket, etc., for use with a light-bulb; **light-grasp** *Astron.* light-gathering power (of a telescope); **light guide** a transparent cylinder or strip along which light can travel with little loss by means of total internal reflection; an optical fibre; **light-gun** = *light-pen* below; **light-man** (*a*) a person in charge of the light in a lighthouse or lightship; (*b*) a linkman; **light meter** an instrument for measuring the intensity of light, esp. to show the correct photographic exposure; *light microscope*: see MICROSCOPE *n.* 1; **light-minute** *Astron.* the distance travelled by light in one minute; **light-money** money paid in light dues; **Lightmonger** a member of a City of London Livery Company representing the lighting industry (usu. in *pl.*); **light organ** the structure in a luminescent animal that emits light; **light-pen** a hand-held penlike photosensitive device that may be used to transmit information to a data-processing system by placing or moving the tip on a surface, esp. the screen of a terminal etc.; **lightproof** *a.* capable of resisting the harmful effects of (esp. intense) light; **light quantum** *Physics* = PHOTON 2; **light-scattering** scattering of light, *spec.* of monochromatic light by a solution as a method of investigating the molecular weight and conformation of dissolved polymers; **light-second** *Astron.* the distance travelled by light in one second; **lightship** a moored or anchored ship with a warning beacon light; **light show** a display of changing coloured lights for entertainment; **light station** a group of buildings comprising a lighthouse and associated housing for personnel, supplies, and equipment; **light-tight** *a.* impervious to light; **light-time** *Astron.* the time taken by light to travel from a distant source to the observer; **light trap** (*a*) *Photogr.* a device for excluding light from a room without preventing access into it; (*b*) a trap for night-flying insects; **light-trapped** *a.* provided with a light trap; **light value** *Photogr.* a number representing on an arbitrary scale the intensity of light from a particular direction; **light valve** an electrical device which regulates the amount of light passing through it, used esp. in cinematography; **light-well** a shaft designed to admit light from above into inner rooms or a staircase of a building; **light-year** (*a*) *Astron.* the distance light travels in a year, approximately 9.46×10^{12} km (5.88×10^{12} miles); (*b*) *sing.* & (usu.) in *pl.*, a long distance, a great amount.

light /lʌɪt/ *a.*[1] [OE *lēocht*, *līht* = OFris. *li(u)cht*, OS *-līht* (Du. *licht*), OHG *līht(i)* (G *leicht*), ON *léttr*, Goth. *leihts*, f. Gmc, f. IE base repr. also by LUNG. See also LITE *a.*[2]] **I** Not physically weighty. **1** Of little weight; relatively low in weight; of little weight due to lack of quality; (esp. of traffic) not abundant, sparse. OE. **b** Of low relative density; *spec.* (of bread, pastry, etc.) properly risen, not dense. ME. **c** Deficient in weight; below the standard or legal weight. L15. **2** (Of a vehicle, vessel, or aeroplane) lightly built; adapted for light loads and fast movement; bearing a small or comparatively small load; unladen, without cargo; (of a locomotive) with no train attached. ME. †**b** Delivered (*of* a child). *rare* exc. in compar. Chiefly *Sc.* ME–E20. **3** Chiefly *Mil.* Lightly armed or equipped. LME.

1 R. BRADBURY Their luggage . . was light enough to be entirely empty. R. BRAUTIGAN A girl in a light summer dress. B. GILROY She was so light, he could pick her up . . like a baby. *Los Angeles Times* Light traffic . . at the time of the accident was . . the reason more vehicles were not involved. **2** THACKERAY My Lord Mohun sent to London for a light chaise he had. *Aviation News* Among the cluster of American light types appeared a couple of sailplanes.

II Expressing the action or appearance of something physically light. **4** Having little momentum or force; acting or moving gently or without heavy pressure or violence. OE. **5** (Of food or drink) small in amount, easy to digest, not rich; (of wine, beer, etc.) containing little alcohol. Also, containing relatively few calories (cf. LITE *a.*[2]). OE. **6** (Of soil) friable, porous, workable; (of a cloud) fleecy, vaporous. ME. **7a** Of a building: having the appearance of lightness; graceful, delicate, elegant. M18. **b** *Printing*. Of type: having letters made up of thin strokes, not bold. L19. **8** (Of a syllable) unstressed, of little sonorousness; (of rhythm) consisting largely of unstressed syllables. L19.

4 J. RUSKIN A painter's light execution of a background. H. E. BATES Her feet were light, no one heard. I. MURDOCH The garden was being caressed . . by the light rain. B. PYM She's got a light hand with pastry. **5** LYTTON The . . family were assembled at the last and lightest meal of the day. P. V. PRICE These wines are light in terms of body character. *Super Marketing* The new Goodalls Dressings are . . 'lighter', containing only 190 calories.

III Of little importance; not serious. **9** Of little importance; slight, trivial. *spec.* (of a sin) venial. OE. **b** Of small value; cheap; (of a price) low. Now only *spec.* (*a*) *Comm.* (of a currency, investment, profit, etc.) low in value or price; (*b*) *Bridge* low, short of points for a traditional bid. ME. **10** Characterized by levity, frivolous, unthinking. Foll. by †*of*. ME. **b** Of a woman or a woman's behaviour: unchaste, wanton. LME.

9 LD MACAULAY Against the lighter vices the ruling faction waged war. I. MURDOCH To provide staff of any description in response to a department's lightest wish. *Financial Times* There are still a few operators whose lightest word can move individual stocks. **10** R. L. STEVENSON I made some light rejoinder. D. STOREY She was like a girl, or a woman just grown, light, uncaring. L. BLUE We touched many deep things in a light way.

IV Having the quick action resulting from lightness. **11** Moving readily; agile, nimble, quick. *arch.* OE. **12** *fig.* That moves or is moved easily; fickle, shifty; facile, ready (esp. of belief). Foll. by *of*, *to do*. Now *rare*. ME.

V That does not weigh heavily on or oppress the senses or feelings. **13** Easy to bear or endure. OE. **14** Of work, a task, etc.: easy to perform or accomplish; requiring little exertion. Also, slight in amount and so undemanding. OE. **15** Of sleep, a trance, or a person asleep: easily disturbed. OE. **16** Of literature, an artistic production, etc.: requiring little mental effort, not profound or serious; amusing, entertaining. ME.

14 *Chicago Tribune* This position is based in . . Chicago and requires light travel. V. BRITTAIN The nursing was now very light; most of our patients were convalescent. **15** DICKENS I am a light sleeper; and it's better to be up than lying awake. E. WAUGH I had roused Julia from the light trance in which she sat. **16** L. URIS A small orchestra played some light dinner music. A. BROOKNER I am not going to confide . . . Light conversation is all that is called for.

VI 17 Free from the weight of care or sorrow; cheerful, merry. ME. **18** Dizzy, giddy, delirious; = LIGHT-HEADED 1. Now chiefly *dial.* LME.

17 C. POTOK I felt light and happy and completely at ease. **18** C. ACHEBE He felt somewhat light in the head.

Phrases: **light o' love** a fickle woman; a prostitute. **light on** *colloq.* deficient in, short of. **make light of** treat as unimportant. **make light work of** do quickly and easily. *the light* FANTASTIC *toe*. *trip the light* FANTASTIC.

Special collocations & comb.: **light-armed** *a.* with light weapons or armour. *light-bob*: see BOB *n.*[5] **light bread** *US* (*a*) white bread; (*b*) any yeast-raised bread. **lighter-than-air** *a.* (of an aircraft) weighing less than the air it displaces. **light-fingered** *a.* given to stealing. *light flyweight*: see FLY *n.*[1] **lightfoot** *a.* & *n.* (*a*) *adj.* (*poet.*) light-footed; (*b*) *n.* (a name for) a hare or a deer. **light-footed** *a.* nimble. **light-footedly** *adv.* nimbly. **light hand** *fig.* a capacity for or instance of tactful management. **light-handed** *a.* having a light, delicate, or deft touch. **light-handedness** the quality of being light-handed. *light heavyweight*: see HEAVYWEIGHT. **light-heeled** *a.* nimble. **light horse** (a soldier of) the light-armed cavalry. **light horseman** a soldier of the light horse. **light infantry**: with light weapons. **light industry** the manufacture of small or light articles. **light-limbed** *a.* nimble. *light* MIDDLEWEIGHT. **light-minded** *a.* frivolous. **light-mindedness** the quality of being light-minded. **light oil** any of various fractions of relatively low relative density obtained by the distillation of coal tar, wood-tar, petroleum, etc. **light-skirts** *arch.* a promiscuous woman; a prostitute. **light touch** *fig.* a capacity for or instance of delicate or tactful treatment. **light water** (*a*) water containing the normal proportion (or less) of deuterium oxide (about 0.02 per cent); *light water reactor*, a nuclear reactor in which the moderator is light water; (*b*) a foam formed by water and a fluorocarbon surfactant which floats on flammable liquids lighter than water and is used in fire-fighting. *light* WELTERWEIGHT.

light /lʌɪt/ *a.*[2] [OE *lēoht*, *līht* = OFris. *liācht*, OS, OHG *lieht* (Du., G *licht*), ult. f. as LIGHT *n.*] **1** †**a** Bright, shining, luminous; *esp.* (of a fire) burning brightly, blazing. OE–M18. **b** Of a place, the time of day, etc.: having a considerable or sufficient amount of light, not dark. Formerly also, brightly illuminated. OE. 2 Pale, approaching white in colour. LME.

1a J. JORTIN He piled these ancient books together and set them all on a light fire. b R. HUGHES If only it had been light they could have been happy enough exploring. 2 G. VIDAL Not a dark sullen blue but a light and casual blue. J. BARNES The dining hall . . where the light pine of my youth had been darkened by time. *light knotgrass*: see KNOTGRASS 3. **light red** *spec.* (of) a pale red or reddish-orange pigment produced from iron oxide; *light red silver ore*: see SILVER *n.* & *a.* **Light Sussex** (a bird of) a white variety of domestic fowl.

light /lʌɪt/ *v.*[1] Pa. t. & pple **lighted, lit** /lɪt/. [OE *līhtan* = OFris. *lichta*, MDu. *lichten*, OHG *līhten*, ON *létta*, f. Gmc base also of LIGHT *a.*[1]] I Lighten. 1 *v.t.* Make light or lighter, lessen the weight of. Formerly also *fig.*, mitigate, assuage. Long *obs.* exc. *Sc.* OE. 2 *v.t.* Relieve *of* a material load or burden; unload (a ship); (latterly *dial.*) deliver *of* a child. Formerly also *fig.*, relieve *of* pain, sorrow, etc.; comfort, cheer. Now *rare* or *obs.* OE. †b *v.i.* Become (more) cheerful. Only in ME. †3 *v.t.* Lessen the effect or influence of; *Sc.*, slight, undervalue. E17–E19. 4 *v.t.* & *i.* *Naut.* Move or lift (a sail etc.) *along* or *over*. M19.

II Descend. Cf. ALIGHT *v.* 5 *v.i.* Descend *from* a horse or vehicle; dismount. Also foll. by *off*, *down*. *arch.* OE. †6 *v.i.* & *refl.* Of a person: descend, esp. from heaven or to hell. ME–M16. 7 *v.i.* Fall and settle or land on a surface. ME. 8 *v.i.* Of a blow, bullet, etc.: land, strike, (foll. by *on*, *upon*). Formerly also *gen.*, come *to* a person; arrive *at* a place; lodge or be situated *in* some position. Now *rare*. ME. b Come or fall *into* a person's possession or company. Now *rare* or *obs.* M16. c Turn out (*well*, *happily*, etc.); happen, occur. Now *dial.* E17. 9 Foll. by *on*, *upon*: (*a*) (of a thing) fall or descend upon as a piece of good or bad luck; (*b*) (of a person) happen to come across, chance upon. ME. †10 *v.i.* [Perh. in antithesis to sense 5, or merely transf. from sense 8.] Mount *on* horseback; climb *into* the saddle. LME–L16.

5 BYRON Stern Hassan . . from his horse Disdains to light. 7 SIR W. SCOTT A feather just lighted on the ground can scarce be less concerned. W. VAN T. CLARK One of the coins lit on its edge and started rolling. 9 E. A. FREEMAN I have . . only once lighted on the use of the word in the singular. P. SCOTT Luck had lighted on our shoulders.

III 11 *v.i.* Foll. by *out*: depart, get out. *colloq.* M19. 12 *v.i.* Foll. by *in*, *into*: attack. *colloq.* L19.

light /lʌɪt/ *v.*[2] Pa. t. & pple **lighted, lit** /lɪt/. [OE *līhtan* = OS *liuhtian*, Goth. *liuhtjan*, f. Gmc base also of LIGHT *n.*] 1 *v.i.* †a Be luminous; shine; be alight or burning. OE–L18. b Of day: grow light, break. Long *obs.* exc. *W. Indies*. OE. 2 *v.t.* Set burning (a candle, lamp, etc.); kindle (a fire); ignite. Also foll. by *up*, (rare) *off*. ME. b *v.i.* Begin to burn, be lighted. LME. c *v.i.* Foll. by *up*: set burning or begin to smoke a cigarette, pipe, etc. *colloq.* M19. 3 *v.t.* Provide with light or lighting; illuminate, esp. brightly or suddenly (freq. foll. by *up*). ME. b *v.t.* & *i.* *transf.* (Cause to) gleam or brighten with animation. Usu. foll. by *up*. M18. 4 *v.t.* Provide (a person) with light to see the way etc. ME. 5 *v.t.* Enlighten spiritually or intellectually. *arch.* ME.

1a GOLDSMITH The taper which was lighting in the room was burnt out. 2 D. H. LAWRENCE When dark fell, the vendors lighted their torch-lamps. J. STEINBECK George walked to the fire pile and lighted the dry leaves. R. GRAVES Four tallow candles had just been lighted. P. MORTIMER I lit the cigarette. J. BERGER Every winter afternoon a fire is still lit. *light a shuck*: see SHUCK *n.*[2] 1. b G. GREENE The gas-main . . had been hit, and the gas wouldn't light properly. *transf.*: A. CARY The eve had just begun to light. 3 J. STEINBECK One of them carried a lantern which lighted the ground. M. GIROUARD A Gothic-arched window was naturally adapted to light a vaulted building. J. BARNES The sun lit up that corner of the room. I. MURDOCH The scene was lit by oil lamps. F. SPALDING He . . saw life . . as if lit up on a stage. b DISRAELI A smile . . lighted up her face. W. BESANT I see the faces of all light up with satisfaction. 4 S. O'FAOLÁIN She took a candle and lit me upstairs to bed. B. CHUTE It's turned dark. I'll light you home.

lightable *a.* able to be lighted L19.

light /lʌɪt/ *adv.*[1] [OE *lēohte* = OS, OHG *līhto*, corresp. to the adjectival forms of LIGHT *a.*[1]] In a light manner; lightly as opp. to heavily; *esp.* with a light or the minimum load; *spec.* (of a locomotive running) with no rolling-stock attached.

C. ROBERTS To travel in America one must travel light. *Railway Magazine* His engine ran light from Orpington to Kent House.

†**light** *adv.*[2] OE–E18. [OE *lēohte* (= OHG *liohto*), f. as LIGHT *a.*[2]] Brightly, clearly.

lightage /ˈlʌɪtɪdʒ/ *n.* E17. [f. LIGHT *n.* + -AGE.] †1 A toll paid by a ship coming to a port where there is a lighthouse. E17–L18. 2 Provision of (artificial) light. M19.

lighted *v.*[1], *v.*[2] see LIGHT *v.*[1], *v.*[2]

lighten /ˈlʌɪt(ə)n/ *v.*[1] LME. [f. LIGHT *a.*[1] + -EN[5]; in sense 5 an extension of LIGHT *v.*[1]] I 1 *v.t.* Relieve of or *of* a load or burden; unload (a ship). *arch.* LME. 2 *v.t.* *fig.* Remove a burden from, relieve (the heart or mind). Formerly also, cheer, comfort. Now *rare*. LME. 3 *v.t.* Make lighter or less heavy; lessen the pressure of; alleviate, mitigate. Also foll. by *up*. L15. b *Equestrianism*. Make lighter or more free in movement. E18. 4 *v.i.* Become lighter or less heavy; ease up or *up*; (foll. by *up*) (of a person) become more cheerful (freq. in *imper.*). E18.

1 R. G. COLLINGWOOD This . . leaves the audience's mind . . not loaded with pity and fear but lightened of them. 2 *Christian Aid News* One day our hearts will be lightened. 3 A. MILLER Start off with a couple of your good stories to lighten things up. M. L. KING His ready good humor lightened many tense moments. L. DEIGHTON Lightened by the loss of the great twelve cylinder Merlin the port wing tilted upwards. Q. CRISP Something—anything—that will . . lighten the terrible financial burden. J. DIDION You might try lightening up the foot on the gas pedal. 4 O. E. RÖLVAAG His mood lightened and brightened as he figured things out. J. C. OATES The rain lightened; and then suddenly increased. *Irish Press* He does lighten up occasionally in the company of his . . underling. D. LEAVITT Just lighten up. . . Don't be so worried all the time.

II †5 Descend, light *upon*. LME–E18.

lightener *n.*[1] †(*a*) *north.* = LIGHTER *n.*[1]; (*b*) a person who or thing which lightens or alleviates something: M16.

lighten /ˈlʌɪt(ə)n/ *v.*[2] ME. [f. LIGHT *a.*[2] + -EN[5].] 1 *v.t.* Give light to; make bright or luminous; light up. ME. †b In biblical translations and allusions: remove blindness or dimness from (the eyes). ME–M16. 2 *v.t.* Shed spiritual light on; enlighten spiritually. *arch.* ME. †3 *v.t.* Kindle, ignite. ME–M17. 4 *v.i.* Shine, burn brightly; be or grow luminous or light; become paler. LME. 5 *v.i.* Flash lightning, emit flashes of lightning. Usu. *impers.* in *it lightens*, *it is lightening*, etc. LME. b *v.t.* Cause to flash *out* or *forth*. Now *rare*. L16. 6 *v.t.* & *i.* Light up with animation etc.; brighten. L18.

1 F. O'BRIEN No beam of sun lightened the dull blackness of the clouds. 4 HUGH MILLER The low-browed clouds that lightened and darkened . . as the flames rose and fell. A. WILSON A great rocky plateau . . lightening to a lemon yellow. E. LINKLATER Presently the sky began to lighten. 5 M. SINCLAIR It thundered and lightened. 6 E. K. KANE The gloom of several countenances was perceptibly lightened.

lightener *n.*[2] LME.

lightening /ˈlʌɪt(ə)nɪŋ/ *n.*[1] See also LIGHTNING *n.* ME. [f. LIGHTEN *v.*[2] + -ING[2].] 1 See LIGHTNING *n.* ME. 2 The action of LIGHTEN *v.*[2]; an instance of this. ME.

2 **lightening before death** a revival of the spirits supposedly occurring just before death.

lightening /ˈlʌɪt(ə)nɪŋ/ *n.*[2] LME. [f. LIGHTEN *v.*[1] + -ING[1].] The action of LIGHTEN *v.*[1]; an instance of this; *Med.* a drop in the level of the womb during the last weeks of pregnancy as the head of the foetus engages in the pelvis.

lighter /ˈlʌɪtə/ *n.*[1] & *v.* LME. [f. LIGHT *v.*[1] + -ER[1], or f. Du. *lichter*.] A *n.* A boat, usu. a flat-bottomed barge, used for transferring or transporting goods from a ship to a wharf or another ship. LME.

Comb.: **lighterman** a worker on a lighter.

B *v.t.* Transfer or transport (goods) in a lighter. E19.

lighterage *n.* (the charge made for) the transferral or transport of goods by a lighter L15.

lighter /ˈlʌɪtə/ *n.*[2] M16. [f. LIGHT *v.*[2] + -ER[1].] 1 A person who lights candles etc. Also *lighter-up*. M16. 2 A thing for lighting a candle, fire, etc.; a device for lighting a cigarette etc., a cigarette-lighter. E19.

lightful /ˈlʌɪtfʊl, -f(ə)l/ *a.* LME. [f. LIGHT *n.* + -FUL.] Full of light; bright.

lightfulness *n.* L16.

light-headed /lʌɪtˈhɛdɪd/ *a.* LME. [f. LIGHT *a.*[1] + HEADED *a.*] 1 Frivolous; thoughtless; fickle. LME. 2 Dizzy, giddy; delirious. M16.

light-headedly *adv.* L19. **light-headedness** *n.* E18.

light-hearted /lʌɪtˈhɑːtɪd/ *a.* LME. [f. LIGHT *a.*[1] + HEARTED.] 1 Having a light heart; cheerful. LME. 2 Not serious; (unduly) casual; thoughtless. M19.

light-heartedly *adv.* M19. **light-heartedness** *n.* E19.

lighthouse /ˈlʌɪthaʊs/ *n.* E17. [f. LIGHT *n.* + HOUSE *n.*[1]] A tower or other structure with a powerful light (orig. a beacon) at the top, situated on the coast or offshore to warn or guide ships.

lighting /ˈlʌɪtɪŋ/ *n.* OE. [f. LIGHT *v.*[2] + -ING[1].] 1 Illumination, the provision of light; *spec.* equipment in a room, street, etc. for producing light, lights collectively. OE. 2 Lightning. Long *dial.* ME. 3 Kindling, ignition. LME. 4 The arrangement or effect of light. M19.

Comb.: **lighting bridge** *Theatr.* a narrow platform over a stage, on which lights are operated; **lighting plot** *Theatr.* a diagrammatic list showing the lighting to be used in each scene; **lighting tower** *Theatr.* a tall structure on which lights are fixed; **lighting-up time** the time when lights are switched on; *esp.* the time when lights on vehicles are required by law to be switched on.

lightish /ˈlʌɪtɪʃ/ *a.* M17. [f. LIGHT *a.*[2] + -ISH[1].] Somewhat light.

lightless /ˈlʌɪtlɪs/ *a.* OE. [f. LIGHT *n.* + -LESS.] 1 Receiving no light; dark. OE. 2 Giving or producing no light. ME.

lightlessness *n.* M19.

lightly /ˈlʌɪtli/ *a.* Chiefly *Sc.* Long *rare* or *obs.* OE. [f. LIGHT *a.*[1] + -LY[1].] Frivolous, contemptible; contemptuous, disparaging.

lightly /ˈlʌɪtli/ *v.t.* Chiefly *Sc.* LME. [f. LIGHTLY *a.*] Make light of, despise, disparage.

lightly /ˈlʌɪtli/ *adv.* OE. [f. LIGHT *a.*[1] + -LY[2].] 1 With little weight; with little pressure, force, or violence; gently; in no great quantity or thickness; sparsely; in no great degree. OE. b Of sleeping: not deeply. OE. 2 Without careful consideration; without strong reason. OE. 3 With a lack of concern; carelessly, indifferently; slightingly. ME. 4 With agility, nimbly. Formerly also, quickly; promptly; immediately. ME. 5 Easily, readily. *arch.* ME. 6 Without depression; cheerfully, merrily, light-heartedly. LME. †7 As may easily or is apt to happen; probably; commonly. LME–L17.

1 SHAKES. *Rich. III* They love his Grace but lightly. M. SINCLAIR Leaning back in his armchair . . his hands joined lightly at the finger-tips. J. P. DONLEAVY I'll knock lightly so's not to be rude. DAY LEWIS The adult world pressed only lightly upon me. E. BOWEN Samples—only lightly wrapped . . in thin paper. J. LEASOR I then ordered black coffee . . and two lightly boiled eggs. J. M. COETZEE 'Cheer up!' said the man, . . punching him lightly on the shoulder. b J. CARLYLE I sleep lightly enough for such emergency. 2 J. BUCHAN Something in the . . voice . . forbade Vernon to dismiss lightly this extraordinary tale. T. CAPOTE I will request the judge to set the death penalty. This . . decision has not been arrived at lightly. 3 D. H. LAWRENCE She took her responsibilities lightly. B. PYM 'Oh, I don't suppose I shall see anything of her . .' I said lightly. 4 J. HAYWARD He lightly vaulting off his saddle, drew out his sword. O. MANNING Simon moved lightly among the stalls. 5 SIR W. SCOTT That's lightly said, but no sae lightly credited. 6 E. PEACOCK The old man . . chatted lightly with Basil.

Phrases: **get off lightly** be acquitted or escape with little or no punishment. **take lightly** not be serious about.

lightmans /ˈlʌɪtm(ə)ns/ *n. slang.* Now *rare* or *obs.* M16. [f. LIGHT *a.*[2]: for 2nd elem. cf. DARKMANS, TOGEMANS.] The day.

lightness /ˈlʌɪtnɪs/ *n.*[1] LOE. [f. LIGHT *a.*[2] + -NESS.] †**1** Brightness, light. LOE–E19. **2** The condition or state of being light or illuminated; the quality of being light or pale (in colour). ME.

1 H. LATIMER They were vnapte to receyue the bryghte lyghtnes of the truthe. **2** LYTTON The first thing that struck Walter in this apartment was its remarkable lightness. A. BROOKNER There was lightness in the sky that promised a change of season.

lightness /ˈlʌɪtnɪs/ *n.*[2] ME. [f. LIGHT *a.*[1] + -NESS.] **1** The quality or fact of having little weight; the fact of having a light load; smallness in quantity or amount. ME. **b** Of bread, pastry, etc.: the quality or fact of being properly risen. M19. **2** Levity, fickleness, frivolity, thoughtlessness. ME. †**b** Wantonness. E16–M17. **3** Agility, nimbleness, quickness. ME. †**4** Ease, facility, readiness, esp. of belief. ME–M18. **5** Freedom from depression or sorrow, cheerfulness, mirth, light-heartedness. ME. **6** Absence of force or pressure in action or movement. LME. **7** Grace, elegance, delicacy. E19.

lightning /ˈlʌɪtnɪŋ/ *n.* & *a.* ME. [Specialized use of LIGHTENING *n.*[1], now differentiated in spelling.] **A** *n.* **1** The sudden bright light produced by electric discharge between clouds or between a cloud and the ground; (now *rare*) a flash of lightning, a thunderbolt. ME. **2** Gin. Also, any strong, esp. low-quality, alcoholic spirit. Chiefly *US slang.* L18. **3** In *pl.* A top grade of white jute. E20.

1 Y. MENUHIN When we were safely in the studio . . lightning split the sky . . illuminating woods and mountains. MERLE COLLINS Two more quick stabs of lightning Thunder crashed again, insistently. *ball lightning, forked lightning, sheet lightning, summer lightning* etc. **like (greased) lightning** with the greatest conceivable speed. *ride the lightning*: see RIDE *v.* **2** *Jersey lightning*: see JERSEY *n.*[1] *white lightning*: see WHITE *a.*

B *attrib.* or as *adj.* Very quick. M17.

E. WELTY The trick was not to miss the lightning visits of Dr. Courtland. V. BROME They were given a lightning tour of New York.

Comb. & *special collocations*: **lightning-arrester** a device to protect telegraphic apparatus etc. from lightning or other voltage surges; **lightning beetle** *US* = *lightning-bug* below; **lightning box**: used to produce stage lightning; **lightning bug** *N. Amer.* a firefly; **lightning chess**: in which moves must be made at very short intervals; **lightning-conductor** a metallic rod or wire fixed to the top or other exposed point of a building, or the mast of a ship, to divert lightning into the earth or sea; **lightning-proof** *a.* protected from lightning; **lightning-rod** = *lightning conductor* above; **lightning-stone** = FULGURITE; **lightning strike** a strike by workers at short notice, esp. without official union backing.

lightning /ˈlʌɪtnɪŋ/ *v.i.* E20. [f. the n.] = LIGHTEN *v.*[2] 5.

lights /lʌɪts/ *n.pl.* ME. [Use as n. of LIGHT *a.*[1]: see -S[1]. See also LITE *n.*[2] Cf. LUNG.] The lungs. Now only, the lungs of sheep, pigs, bullocks, etc., used as food esp. for pets.

scare the (liver and) lights out of scare greatly.

lightsome /ˈlʌɪts(ə)m/ *a.*[1] ME. [f. LIGHT *a.*[1] + -SOME[1].] **1** Having the effect or appearance of lightness; *esp.* light, graceful, elegant. ME. **2** Light-hearted, cheerful, merry. ME. **b** Flighty, frivolous. M16. **3** Lively, nimble, quick. E17.

lightsomely *adv.* M16. **lightsomeness** *n.*[1] ME.

lightsome /ˈlʌɪts(ə)m/ *a.*[2] LME. [f. LIGHT *n.* + -SOME[1].] **1** Radiant with light; luminous. LME. **2** Esp. of a room, building, etc.: permeated with light; well lit, bright. LME. **3** Clear, manifest. Now *rare.* M16. †**4** Light-coloured. L16–L17.

lightsomeness *n.*[2] LME.

lightweight /ˈlʌɪtweɪt/ *n.* & *a.* L18. [f. LIGHT *a.*[1] + WEIGHT *n.*] **A** *n.* **1** A weight at which boxing etc. matches are made, intermediate between featherweight and welterweight, in the amateur boxing scale now being between 57 and 60 kg, though differing for professionals, wrestlers, and weightlifters, and according to time and place; a boxer etc. of this weight; *gen.* a person or thing of below average weight. Formerly also, a horse carrying a light weight in a handicap race. L18. **2** *fig.* An unimportant or superficial person or thing. L19. **3** A garment, usu. a suit, made from lightweight material. L20.

B *adj.* Light in weight; (of a coin) deficient in weight; (of a boxer etc.) that is a lightweight, of or pertaining to lightweights; *fig.* unimportant, superficial, trivial. E19.

Melody Maker Tastier than the lightweight singles of their past. *New Yorker* In the warmest weather our lightweight poplin suit maintains its . . crisp appearance.

Phrases: **junior lightweight** (of) a weight in professional boxing of between 57.1 and 59 kg; (designating) a boxer of this weight.

lightwood /ˈlʌɪtwʊd/ *n.*[1] M19. [f. LIGHT *a.*[1] + WOOD *n.*[1]] Any of various trees so called from the lightness of their wood; *esp.* (in Australia) *Acacia implexa* and *A. melanoxylon.*

lightwood /ˈlʌɪtwʊd/ *n.*[2] *N. Amer.* & *W. Indies.* L17. [f. LIGHT *n.* (or LIGHT *v.*[2]) + WOOD *n.*[1]] **1** Any wood used in lighting a fire; *esp.* (in the southern US) resinous pinewood. L17. **2** Any of various trees which burn with a brilliant flame; *esp.* candlewood, *Amyris balsamifera.* L19.

lign-aloes /lʌɪnˈaləʊz/ *n.* Also **lign-aloe**. LME. [Late L *lignum aloes* wood of the aloe (*aloes* genit. of *aloe*). Cf. LINALOE.] **1** The bitter drug aloes; = ALOE 3. LME. **2** Aloes wood; = ALOE 1. E17. **3** = LINALOE. M19.

ligneous /ˈlɪgnɪəs/ *a.* E17. [f. L *ligneus*, f. *lignum* wood: see -OUS, -EOUS.] **1** Of the nature of wood; woody. Chiefly of plants and their texture (opp. *herbaceous*). E17. **2** Made or consisting of wood, wooden. Chiefly *joc.* E19.

ligni- /ˈlɪgni/ *comb. form* of L *lignum* wood: see -I-. Cf. LIGNO-.

lig'nicolous *a.* (*Bot.* & *Zool.*) (*a*) living or growing on wood (as some mosses, fungi, etc.); (*b*) living in wood (as certain bivalves, termites, etc.): M19. **ligniform** *a.* of the form or appearance of wood L18. **lig'nivorous** *a.* wood-eating E19.

lignify /ˈlɪgnɪfʌɪ/ *v.t.* & *i.* E19. [f. L *lignum* wood + -I- + -FY.] *Bot.* Make or become woody. Chiefly as *lignified* ppl a.

lignifi'cation *n.* the process of becoming woody E19.

lignin /ˈlɪgnɪn/ *n.* E19. [f. as prec. + -IN[1].] *Bot.* & *Chem.* A cross-linked phenolic polymer which combines with cellulose to give woody plant tissue its rigidity.

Comb.: **lignin sulphonate** a salt of a lignosulphonic acid, used industrially as a dispersant, binder, etc.

lignite /ˈlɪgnʌɪt/ *n.* E19. [f. as prec. + -ITE[1].] *Geol.* A brown, fossil deposit of late Cretaceous or Tertiary age, having a visibly ligneous structure; brown coal.

lig'nitic *a.* pertaining to or of the nature of lignite M19. **ligni'tiferous** *a.* (of a bed or stratum) producing lignite M19.

ligno- /ˈlɪgnəʊ/ *comb. form* of L *lignum* wood, or of LIGNIN: see -O-. Cf. LIGNI-.

ligno'cellulose *n.* the complex of lignin and cellulose formed in woody plant cell walls E20. **lignocellu'losic** *a.* pertaining to or containing lignocellulose M20. **ligno'ceric** *a.* (*Chem.*): *lignoceric acid*, a long-chain fatty acid, $CH_3(CH_2)_{22}COOH$, which is a minor component of natural fats; *n*-tetracosanoic acid: L19. **ligno'sulphonate** *n.* = LIGNIN *sulphonate* E20. **lignosul'phonic** *a.*: *lignosulphonic acid*, any of various compounds in which sulphonic acid groups are attached to lignin molecules, formed in the sulphite process for producing wood pulp E20.

lignocaine /ˈlɪgnəkeɪn/ *n.* M20. [f. LIGNO- (w. ref. to earlier name XYLOCAINE) + -CAINE.] *Pharm.* An aromatic amide used as a local anaesthetic for the gums and mucous membranes.

lignose /ˈlɪgnəʊs/ *a.* & *n.* Now *rare* or *obs.* L17. [L *lignosus*, f. *lignum* wood: see -OSE[1].] **A** *adj.* = LIGNEOUS. L17. **B** *n.* = LIGNOCELLULOSE. L19.

lignous /ˈlɪgnəs/ *a.* Now *rare* or *obs.* M17. [f. as prec. + -OUS.] = LIGNEOUS.

lignum /ˈlɪgnəm/ *n.*[1] LME. [L = wood.] With specifying wd: a tree; wood.

Comb.: **lignum aloes** = LIGN-ALOES 2.

lignum /ˈlɪgnəm/ *n.*[2] *Austral. colloq.* L19. [Alt. of mod.L POLYGONUM *n.*[1]] Any of various tough wiry plants of the genus *Muehlenbeckia*, allied to the genus *Polygonum* (the knotweeds) and formerly included in it.

lignum vitae /lɪgnəm ˈvʌɪtiː, ˈviːtʌɪ/ *n.* L16. [L = wood of life.] **1** = GUAIACUM 1. Also, any of several other trees with hard heavy wood. L16. **2** = GUAIACUM 2. L16. **3** = GUAIACUM 3. Long *rare* or *obs.* E17.

ligroin /ˈlɪgrəʊɪn/ *n.* L19. [Origin unkn.] *Chem.* A volatile petroleum fraction with a boiling point between about 60 and 150°C, used as a solvent.

ligula /ˈlɪgjʊlə/ *n.* Pl. **-lae** /-lʌɪ, -liː/. M18. [L = strap, spoon, var. of LINGULA: see -ULE.] **1** A narrow strap-shaped part in a plant; *esp.* = LIGULE 2(a). Now *rare* or *obs.* M18. **2** A strap-shaped part in an insect; *spec.* the distal part of the labium, usu. lobed. M18.

ligular *a.* pertaining to or resembling a ligula L19.

ligularia /lɪgjʊˈlɛːrɪə/ *n.* M19. [mod.L (see below), f. L LIGULA (w. ref. to the shape of the ray-florets) + *-aria* -ARY[1].] Any of various ornamental herbaceous plants of the Eurasian genus *Ligularia*, of the composite family, grown for their showy yellow-rayed flowers.

ligulate /ˈlɪgjʊlət/ *a.* M18. [f. LIGULA + -ATE[2].] Having the form of a ligule, strap-shaped; *Bot.* (of a floret of a plant of the composite family) extended on one side to form a flat strap-shaped limb (opp. *tubular*).

Also **ligulated** *a.* M18.

ligule /ˈlɪgjuːl/ *n.* E17. [L LIGULA.] †**1** A Roman measure approximately equivalent to a small spoonful. Only in E17. **2** A narrow strap-shaped part of a plant; *spec.* (*a*) a membranous scale occurring on the inner side of the leaf-sheath at its junction with the blade in most grasses and sedges; also, a scale on the upper surface of a leaf in the selaginellas; (*b*) the blade formed by a ligulate floret. E19.

ligure /ˈlɪgjʊə/ *n. obs.* exc. *Hist.* Also †**ligury** & other vars. ME. [Late L (Vulgate) *ligurius*, f. Septuagint Gk *ligurion* one of the stones in the high priest's breastplate.] A kind of precious stone.

AV *Exod.* 28:19 And the third row a Lygure, an Agate, and an Amethist.

Ligurian /lɪˈgjʊərɪən/ *a.* & *n.* E17. [f. L *Liguria* (see below) + -AN.] **A** *n.* A native or inhabitant of Liguria, now a region in NW Italy, formerly an ancient country extending from NE Spain to NW Italy and including Switzerland and SE Gaul. Also, the pre-Italic Indo-European language of the ancient Ligurians; the Gallo-Italian dialect of modern Liguria. E17. **B** *adj.* Of or pertaining to Liguria, the Ligurians, or their language. M17.

†**ligury** *n.* var. of LIGURE.

ligustrum /lɪˈgʌstrəm/ *n.* M17. [L.] = PRIVET 1.

Lihyanite /liːˈjɑːnʌɪt/ *n.* & *a.* M20. [f. Arab. *lihyān* the name of an ancient tribe + -ITE[1].] (Of) an early form of Arabic known only from north Arabian inscriptions of the 2nd and 1st cents. BC, written in a southern Semitic alphabet.

Also **Lihyani** /liːˈjɑːniː/ *n.* & *a.* E20.

likable *a.* var. of LIKEABLE.

like /lʌɪk/ *n.*[1] ME. [f. LIKE *v.*[1]] †**1** *sing.* & in *pl.* (One's) good pleasure. ME–E17. **2** In *pl.* Feelings of affection or preference for particular things; things liked or preferred; predilections. Chiefly coupled w. *dislikes.* L18.

like /lʌɪk/ *n.*[2] ME. [f. LIKE *a.* etc.] **1** With qualifying possess.: a person or thing of the same kind, one's counterpart, one's equal, one's match. ME. **2** A thing considered in respect of its likeness to something else; an instance of similarity. Chiefly in proverbial expressions, as *like breeds like, like will to like.* LME. **3** *the like*, a similar thing or things. LME. **4** *sing.* & (usu.) in *pl.* Likelihood, probability. *rare* exc. *dial.* E17. **5** *Golf.* The same number of strokes as one's opponent; a stroke that makes one's score for a hole equal to that of one's opponent. Chiefly in *the like.* Cf. ODD *n.* 3. L18.

1 E. W. MACBRIDE 'Sports' . . which breed true when crossed with their like. *Guardian* The recent murder . . was the work of Mr Mohtashemi or his like. **3 and the like** and similar things, et cetera. **or the like** or another thing or other things of the same kind. **the likes of** *colloq.* such a person or such people as (*the likes of me*, persons as humble as I; *the likes of you*, persons as distinguished as you).

like /lʌɪk/ *a., prep., adv.,* & *conj.* ME. [ON *líkr* aphet. f. *glíkr*: see ALIKE *a.* Cf. earlier LIKENESS.] **A** *adj.* **1** Having the same characteristics or qualities as some other person or thing; of approximately identical shape, size, etc., with something else; similar. Now usu. *attrib.*; also (*arch.*) foll. by *to, with,* †*as*. ME. **b** Like each other, mutually similar. LME. **2** *pred.* **a** That may reasonably be expected *to do*, likely *to do*. Now chiefly *colloq.* ME. **b** Apparently about *to do*. Now *colloq.* M16. **3** Apt, suitable. Chiefly *pred.* Long *obs.* exc. *Sc.* LME. **4** In accordance with appearances, probable, likely. Now *dial.* LME. **5** Of a portrait etc.: bearing a faithful resemblance to the original. Now only *pred.* M16.

1 M. TWAIN Claws like to a bat's but broader. *Lancet* Farmer's lung and like conditions. **b** TENNYSON No two dreams are like. H. M. ROSENBERG There is a mutual repulsion between like charges. **2a** A. E. HOUSMAN We're like to meet no more. **b** SIR W. SCOTT The eldest man seemed like to choke with laughter. **4** SHAKES. *Rom. & Jul.* Is it not like that I, So early waking . . shall I not be distraught?

Comb.: **like-minded** *a.* having similar tastes, opinions, etc. **like-mindedness** the state of being like-minded.

B *prep.* (Retaining an adjectival character and able to be qualified by advs. of degree and compared.) **1** Having the same characteristics or qualities as; of approximately identical shape, size, etc., as; similar to. Orig. w. dat. obj. ME. **b** Similar to that or those of. *non-standard.* LME. **2** In the manner of, in the same way as; to the same degree as. (With obj. of prep. the subj. of the vbl action understood.) ME. **b** In the manner or to the extent that one would or could. (With obj. of prep. the obj. of the vbl action understood: cf. sense D. below.) *colloq.* L17. †**3** In accordance with. LME–L16. **4** With certain vbs of perception: having the perceived quality of (something) so as to suggest its presence or occurrence. L16. †**5** As well as, as also. *rare.* L16–M17. **6** Characteristic of; such as one might expect from. M17. **7** Of the kind represented by; such as. L19.

1 J. PRIESTLEY There was nothing like it in the philosophy of Plato. G. GREENE I think . . I am very like Napoleon IV. I. MURDOCH It was rather like the inside of a wardrobe. **b** J. BUCHAN The bent and heather of the Cheviots were like my domestic hills. **2** F. BURNEY She sings like her, laughs like her. *Punch* What was the use of his talking like that? D. HAMMETT 'You can't say that.' 'Like hell I can't.' DAY LEWIS Like flaming swords they barred my way. *like a lamb, like a red rag to a bull, like a shag on a rock, like a shot, like nothing on earth, like smoke, like stink, like steam,* etc. **b** R. KIPLING At least she did not treat me like a child. A. MAUPIN Why was this . . dowager talking to her like an equal. **4** SIR W. SCOTT That sounds like nonsense, my dear. **6** DICKENS It would be like his impudence . . to dare to think of such a thing. **7** J. B. PRIESTLEY It . . offers you fantastic little old streets like Mary-Le-Port Street and Narrow Wine Street.

C *adv.* **1** Foll. by *to*: in the manner of, in the same way as; to the same degree as. *arch.* LME. **2** Equally, alike. Now *poet.* & only qualifying adjs. & advs. LME. **3** Qualifying an adj.: in the manner of a person who or thing which is. Now only *colloq.* in certain phrs. E16. **4** Likely, probably. *rare* exc. in *like enough, very like,* (*as*) *like as not.* L16. **5** So to speak; as it were. Also used as a filler of little or no meaning. *colloq.* L18.

1 SHAKES. *Sonn.* Then my state, Like to the lark . . arising . . , sings hymns at heaven's gate. **3** *like crazy, like mad,* etc. **5** LYTTON If your honour were more amongst us, there might be more discipline like. ALAN BENNETT He hasn't passed his examinations like. *New Society* I'm just dreading the first day, like. *New Yorker* Some guy dumped a bucket of Gatorade on us, and then, like, everyone was screaming.

D *conj.* **1** As if, as though. Now *non-standard.* E16. **2** In the same way that; as. *colloq.* E16.

1 W. FAULKNER It looked like I was going to get shut of it. M. MACHLIN They all treat me like I was some weirdo. **2** D. L. SAYERS Like I was saying to your lady. G. GREENE He had to humiliate him like he humiliated my mother. M. MCCARTHY In the library there was . . a white piano, like in a night club.

Phrases (of all parts of speech): (A selection of cross-refs. only is included: see esp. other ns.) **anything like** in any way resembling (chiefly in neg. contexts). (**as**) **like as not** *colloq.* very likely. *as like as two peas*: see PEA *n.*[1] 1. **be like that** (*a*) be of the nature, character, or habit indicated; (*b*) (with stress on *that*, accompanied by or implying the crossing of fingers) be on very friendly or intimate terms. *feel like*: see FEEL *v.* *in like manner*: see MANNER *n.*[1] †**in like wise** in the same manner, similarly, likewise. *like a bird*: see BIRD *n. like a book*: see BOOK *n. like a house on fire*: see HOUSE *n.*[1] **like another** (of a thing) that is ordinary; that is only one of a number of similar things, possibilities, etc. *like anything*: see ANYTHING *pron.* **like as** *arch.* in the same way as (now only w. following cl.); just as if. *like as not*: see *as like as not* above. *like* BILLY-O. *like crazy*: see CRAZY *a.* **like enough** quite likely, very likely. *like hang*: see HANG *n.* **like — like — as — is,** so is —. *like mad*: see MAD *a.* **like so** *colloq.* in this way. *like the wind*: see WIND *n.*[1] *like the wrath of God*: see WRATH *n. like water*: see WATER *n. like wild*: see WILD *a., n.,* & *adv. like* WINKING. *like* WINKY. *look like*: see LOOK *v.* **more like** *colloq.* nearer (a specified number or quantity); (also *more like it*) nearer what is required or expected. **nothing like** in no way resembling, *esp.* in no way as good or effective as. *same like*: see SAME *adv.* *sleep like a log* or *top*: see SLEEP *v.* **something like** (*a*) in some way resembling, approximately; (*b*) *ellipt.* (*colloq.*) (with stress on *like*) what such a thing should be, a fine example; (*c*) *ellipt.* (*colloq.*) in a tolerably adequate manner. *tell it like it is*: see TELL *v.* **what is — like?** what is the nature or character of —?

like /lʌɪk/ *v.*[1] [OE *līcian* = OFris. *līkia*, OS *līkon* (Du. *lijken*), OHG *līhhēn*, ON *líka*, Goth. *leikan*, f. Gmc, f. base also of LICH *n.*] **1 a** *v.t.* (orig. w. dat. obj.). Be pleasing to, suit, (a person). Now *arch.* & *dial.* OE. †**b** *v.i.* Be pleasing, be liked or approved. OE–E17. †**2** *v.refl.* & *i.* Take pleasure; delight *in* something. ME–M16. **3** *v.i.* Be pleased, be glad. *obs.* exc. *Sc.* ME. †**4** *v.i.* Be in good condition; get on, thrive, (*well, better,* etc.). Latterly chiefly as *liking* ppl a. ME–L19. **5** *v.t.* **a** Find agreeable, congenial, or satisfactory; feel attracted to or favourably impressed by (a person); have a taste for, take pleasure in, (a thing, *doing, to be, to do,* etc.). Also *like well* (now *arch.* exc. w. qualification, e.g. *very*, or as compar. *better* or superl. *best*). ME. **b** Find it agreeable, feel inclined, (*to do, to be*). In conditional use (*should like* etc.) expr. desire, derision, or scepticism. ME. **c** Prefer, choose to have, (a thing, *to do,* †*that*; a person or thing *to do, to be,* adj. compl. (w. *to be* understood), (*to be*) *done*). M16. **d** In interrog. w. *how*: feel about, regard, (a person or thing, *doing*, (in conditional use) *to do*). L16. **e** With conditional aux.: wish to have. E19. **6** *v.i.* Derive pleasure *of*, a person or thing; approve *of*, become fond *of*. *obs.* exc. *dial.* LME. **7** *v.i.* Entertain feelings of affection. *arch.* L16.

1 SIR W. SCOTT At first . . it liked me ill. D. G. ROSSETTI I rode sullenly Upon a certain path that liked me not. **5a** H. B. STOWE I may *like* him well enough; but you don't *love* your servants. D. H. LAWRENCE He sang in the choir because he liked singing. T. F. POWYS An English gentleman never likes to be beaten. A. RANSOME Nobody much likes steak-and-kidney pudding . . eaten all cold and greasy at six. J. STEINBECK When there is a parade he likes to carry the flag. E. BOWEN They had from the first liked Rodney better than Edward. **b** J. LOCKE He may either go or stay, as he best likes. SHELLEY If you would like to go, We'll visit him. DICKENS I should like to see you do it, sir. E. WAUGH I should like to go with them and drink beer. **c** S. COLVIN The sonatas of Haydn were the music he liked Severn best to play to him. A. CARNEGIE He would like me to explain how I had been able to steer clear of these . . troubles. **d** C. LAMB The Chorics (how do you like the word?) of Samson Agonistes. LYTTON How do you like sharing the mirth of the groundlings? J. TICKELL How would you like to be half-starved for a bit? **e** S. T. WARNER Wouldn't Mr. Fortune like a girl too?

Phrases: **and like it** (after an imper.) and any complaint will be unheeded. **if you like** *colloq.* if you wish to express it or consider it in that way; indeed, perhaps. **I like that!** *iron.*: expr. surprise or disgust at another's impudence, conceit, etc. *know what one likes*: see KNOW *v.* **like it or not** *colloq.* whether it is acceptable or not. *like to hear oneself speak* or *talk*: see HEAR *v. not like the look of*: see LOOK *n. wouldn't you, he,* etc., *like to know*: see KNOW *v.*

like /lʌɪk/ *v.*[2] LME. [f. LIKE *a.* etc.] †**1** *v.t.* Make in a certain likeness; represent as like to; compare to; make a likeness of. LME–E17. **2** *v.i.* Orig., seem, pretend. Later, look like or be near to doing something or to being treated in a specified manner. Foll. by *to do*. Now *non-standard*, chiefly in *had liked to do*. LME.

2 SHAKES. *Much Ado* We had lik'd to have had our two noses snapp'd off.

-like /lʌɪk/ *suff.* [f. LIKE *a.* etc.] Forming (*a*) adjs. f. ns. & (chiefly *Sc.*) adjs., w. the sense 'similar to, characteristic of, befitting, (one who is)', as *doglike, ladylike, shell-like; gluey-like*; (*b*) (now *colloq.*) advs. f. ns. & adjs., w. the senses 'in the manner of', 'like one who is', as *coward-like; strange-like*.

¶A hyphen is usual in less common words of more than one syllable and in all words ending in *-l*.

likeable /ˈlʌɪkəb(ə)l/ *a.* Also **likable**. M18. [f. LIKE *v.*[1] + -ABLE.] Esp. of a person: easy to like; pleasant, agreeable.

likea'bility *n.* E19. **likeableness** *n.* M19.

likelihead /ˈlʌɪklɪhɛd/ *n.* Long *arch.* LME. [f. LIKELY + -HEAD.] **1** = LIKELIHOOD 2. Chiefly in *by likelihead*, in all likelihood. LME. †**2** = LIKELIHOOD 1. Only in LME.

likelihood /ˈlʌɪklɪhʊd/ *n.* LME. [f. LIKELY + -HOOD.] †**1** Likeness, similarity; an instance of this, a resemblance. LME–L17. **2** The quality or fact of being likely; an instance of this, a (good) chance. (Foll. by *of,* †*to do*.) LME. †**3** A thing that is likely, a probability; a ground of probable inference, an indication. Freq. in *pl.* M16–M17. **4** The quality of offering a prospect of success; promise. Now only as an echo of Shakes. M16. **5** *Statistics.* A function of the variable parameters of a family of probability distributions that depends on a fixed set of data and equals the probability of the data, if these are assumed to relate to a population whose distribution has the given parameters. E20.

2 H. CARPENTER There is every likelihood that she knew his books. A. STORR Association with other criminals carried the likelihood of reinforcing . . crime as a way of life. **in all likelihood,** †**in likelihood** in all probability, very probably. **the likelihood** the probable fact. **4** SHAKES. *1 Hen. IV* A fellow of no mark nor likelihood.

Comb.: **likelihood ratio** *Statistics* the ratio of two likelihoods based on alternative hypotheses about the parameters of a distribution, used in testing these hypotheses.

likeliness /ˈlʌɪklɪnɪs/ *n.* Now *rare.* LME. [f. LIKELY + -NESS.] †**1** = LIKELIHOOD 1. LME–E18. **2** = LIKELIHOOD 2. LME. †**3** = LIKELIHOOD 4. LME–M18.

likely /ˈlʌɪkli/ *a.* & *adv.* ME. [ON (*g*)*líkligr*, f. *líkr* LIKE *a.* etc. + *-ligr* -LY[1].] **A** *adj.* **1** Having an appearance of truth or fact; that looks as if it would happen, be realized, or prove to be what is alleged or suggested; probable; to be reasonably expected *to do, to be,* (w. impers. *it*) *that*. ME. †**2** Having a resemblance, similar; resembling an original. LME–M17. **3** Apparently suitable or qualified (*for* a thing); apparently able or fitted (*to do, to be*). LME. **4** Having the appearance or giving evidence of vigour or ability; giving promise of success or excellence. LME. †**5** Seemly, becoming, appropriate. LME–M18. **6** Good-looking. Chiefly *US* & *dial.* LME.

1 E. M. FORSTER I hope that none of your friends are likely to come in. *Listener* In a television studio, where the acoustic is liklier to be drier. A. THWAITE It seems likely that St Paul's was the church Edmund was going to. H. BAILEY Officers . . were six times as likely to be killed as their men. G. GREENE His life provided models for behaviour in any likely circumstance. *Lancaster Guardian* Surveys carried out last winter have helped to predict likely road conditions. **a likely story**: expr. disbelief of another's statement. **as likely as not** quite probably. **not likely** *colloq.* certainly not (more strongly *not bloody likely*; see also *not* PYGMALION *likely*). **3** C. BURNEY Lely gave me these papers as the likelyest man to get them perfected. G. LORD He made a wide arc . . until he came to a likely

camp site. 4 *Birmingham Post* The department has ten jobs on offer to likely boys and girls.

B *adv.* †**1** In a like or similar manner, similarly; (with ref. to portraiture) with close resemblance. LME–L16. **2** Probably, in all probability. Now chiefly *N. Amer., Sc., & dial.*, & in *most likely, very likely.* LME. †**3** In a fit manner, suitably, reasonably. LME–L17.

2 B. JOWETT You may be very likely right in that. D. MARQUIS A middle-aged person has likely learned how to have a little fun.

liken /ˈlʌɪk(ə)n/ *v.* ME. [f. LIKE *a.* etc. + -EN[5].] **1** *v.t.* Represent as similar, point out the similarity of. Foll. by *to.* ME. **b** In *pass.* Be associated by repute with another, esp. as a lover or future spouse. Foll. by *with, to.* Long *obs.* exc. *Sc.* M16. †**2** *v.i.* & *t.* Be or become similar *to*, be or become like. ME–M19. **3** *v.t.* Make like. *rare.* LME.

1 ANTHONY SMITH Plato likened memory to a wax tablet.

likening *n.* (*a*) the action of the vb; †(*b*) a comparison, a simile: ME.

likeness /ˈlʌɪknɪs/ *n.* [OE (*ge*)*līknes*, f. as ALIKE *a.* + -NESS.] †**1** A person's stature. Only in OE. **2** A visual representation of a person or thing; a copy, an image, a portrait. Also, a person who closely resembles another. OE. **3** A shape or form like or identified as something, a semblance or guise *of.* ME. **4** The quality or fact of being like; (a) resemblance, (a) similarity. (Foll. by *between, to,* †*with.*) ME. †**5** A comparison; a parable. Only in ME.

2 DYLAN THOMAS On receiving your photograph I went immediately to have my own likeness taken. 3 SHELLEY The likeness of a throned king came by. E. A. FREEMAN Spalato is putting on the likeness of a busy modern town. 4 H. JAMES She seemed to see a far-away likeness to the vaguely-remembered image of her mother. *catch a likeness*: see CATCH *v.*

liker /ˈlʌɪkə/ *n.* Now *rare.* M16. [f. LIKE *v.*[1] + -ER[1].] A person who likes something or someone.

Likert scale /ˈlʌɪkət skeɪl/ *n. phr.* M20. [Rensis *Likert* (1903–81), US psychologist.] *Psychol.* A scale used to represent people's attitudes to a topic.

likesome /ˈlʌɪks(ə)m/ *a. obs.* exc. *dial.* M16. [f. LIKE *v.*[1] + -SOME[1].] Agreeable, pleasant.

†**likeways** *adv.* M16–E18. [f. LIKE *a.* + -WAYS.] = LIKEWISE.

likewise /ˈlʌɪkwʌɪz/ *adv.* LME. [Abbrev. of *in like wise* s.v. LIKE *a.* etc.] **1** In the like manner, similarly. Now only in *do likewise.* LME. **2** Also, as well, moreover, too; in return, conversely. E16.

2 F. SWINNERTON On the floor above, young Bertram Thornycroft was likewise in high glee. *Sunday Express* That is what Denis gives .. me and, likewise, what I try to give to him.

liking /ˈlʌɪkɪŋ/ *n.* OE. [f. LIKE *v.*[1] + -ING[1].] †**1** The fact of being to one's taste or of being liked. OE–L16. †**2** Pleasure, enjoyment; an instance of this; *spec.* sensuality, sexual desire. ME–E18. **3** The bent of the will; what one wishes or prefers, (a person's) pleasure. Now *rare* exc. in *to one's liking* below. ME. **4** The condition of being fond of or not averse to a person or thing; favourable regard, a fondness, a taste, a fancy. (Foll. by *for, to* a person.) ME. †**5** Bodily condition, esp. good or healthy condition. ME–M18. †**6** An object liked, (one's) beloved. LME–M17.

3 **on** or **upon liking** (now *rare*) on approval or trial. **to one's liking** according to one's wish, to one's taste. 4 A. KOESTLER Sympathy for his own body, for which usually he had no liking, played over him. E. FERRARS He's too stiff and prickly for my liking. R. WHELAN Capa and Dinah took an immediate liking to him.

likkewaan /ˈlɪkəvɑːn/ *n.* E20. [Afk. f. as LEGUAN.] = IGUANA 2.

Likud /lɪˈkuːd, -ˈkʊd/ *n.* L20. [Heb. *likkūḏ* union, (mod.) coalition.] A nationalist coalition party in the State of Israel, formed to oppose Labour monopoly government.

likuta /lɪˈkuːtə/ *n.* Pl. **makuta** /məˈkuːtə/. M20. [Kikongo.] A monetary unit of Zaire (formerly of the Congo) equal to one-hundredth of a zaire.

lil /lɪl/ *n. slang & dial.* Also **lill.** E19. [Romany.] **1** A book. E19. **2** A currency note. M19.

lil /lɪl/ *a. colloq.* L19. [Repr. an informal pronunc.] Little.

lila /ˈliːlɑː/ *n.* E19. [Skt *līlā* play, amusement.] In Hindu mythology and theology, the spontaneous playful activity exercised by God in all his actions, esp. in the creation of the universe; a sacred dance-drama reenacting this.

lilac /ˈlʌɪlək/ *n.* & *a.* Also (now *dial.*) **laylock** /ˈleɪlɒk/. E17. [Obs. Fr. (now *lilas*) ult. f. Pers. *līlak* (whence also Turk. *leylâk*) var. of *nīlak* bluish, f. *nīl* blue + dim. suff. *-ak.*] **A** *n.* **1** A shrub or small tree, *Syringa vulgaris*, of the olive family, cultivated for its fragrant blossoms, which are typically of a pale pinkish-violet colour; *collect.* flowering sprays of this plant. Also (usu. w. specifying wd), (flowering sprays of) any of various other shrubs or trees belonging to this genus or thought to resemble the lilac. E17. **2** A pale pinkish-violet colour. L18. **3** The scent of lilac, esp. as used in cosmetics. L19.

1 **Persian lilac** the azedarac, *Melia azedarach.*

B *adj.* Of the colour lilac. E19.

Country Life Full-skirted lilac dress. **lilac-breasted roller** a roller, *Coracias caudata*, of eastern and southern Africa.

lilacky *a.* resembling or suggestive of lilac, of a colour resembling lilac M19.

lilangeni /liːlaŋˈgeɪni/ *n.* Pl. **emalangeni** /ˌɪmalaŋˈgeɪni/. L20. [Bantu, f. *li-* sing. pref. (*ema-* pl. pref.) + *-langeni* member of royal family.] The basic monetary unit of Swaziland, equal to 100 cents.

liliaceous /lɪlɪˈeɪʃəs/ *a.* M18. [f. late L *liliaceus*, f. *lilium* LILY: see -ACEOUS.] Pertaining to or characteristic of lilies, lily-like; *spec.* (*Bot.*) of or pertaining to the family Liliaceae, which includes the genus *Lilium*, the lilies.

lilied /ˈlɪlɪd/ *a.* E17. [f. LILY + -ED[2].] **1** Resembling a lily in fairness of complexion. E17. **2** Covered with lilies, having many lilies. M17. **b** Embellished with fleurs-de-lis. L18.

1 BROWNING Of just-tinged marble, like Eve's lilied flesh. 2 GEO. ELIOT Its lilied pool and grassy acres specked with deer.

lilipi /ˈlɪlɪpi/ *n.* L18. [Origin unkn.] Chiefly *NZ Hist.* Boiled flour as an article of food.

lilium /ˈlɪlɪəm/ *n.* E20. [L: see LILY.] = LILY *n.* 1.

lill /lɪl/ *n.*[1] *Sc.* E18. [Origin uncertain: cf. Du. *lul.*] Any of the holes of a woodwind instrument.

lill *n.*[2] var. of LIL *n.*

lill /lɪl/ *v.t.* & *i.* Long *obs.* exc. *dial.* M16. [Symbolic: cf. LOLL *v.*] Esp. of an animal: hang (the tongue) *out* or out.

Lille lace /liːl ˈleɪs/ *n. phr.* M19. [f. *Lille*, a city in northern France.] A kind of pillow or bobbin lace.

Lillet /ˈliːleɪ/ *n.* M20. [Fr. surname.] A French white wine aperitif resembling vermouth; a glass of this.

¶Proprietary name in the US.

lilli-pilli *n.* var. of LILLY-PILLY.

lilliput /ˈlɪlɪpʌt/ *attrib. a.* Also **L-.** M18. [*Lilliput*, an imaginary country in Swift's *Gulliver's Travels* (1726), peopled by pygmies six inches high.] Diminutive, lilliputian.

lilliputian /lɪlɪˈpjuːʃ(ə)n/ *n.* & *a.* Also **L-.** E18. [f. prec. + -IAN.] **A** *n.* (In Swift's *Gulliver's Travels*) an inhabitant of Lilliput; a person of diminutive size, character, or mind. E18. **B** *adj.* Of or pertaining to Lilliput or its inhabitants; of diminutive size; petty. E18.

lilliputianize *v.t.* dwarf L19.

lilly-pilly /ˈlɪlɪˌpɪli/ *n.* Also **lilli-pilli.** M19. [Origin unkn.] An Australian evergreen tree, *Acmena smithii*, of the myrtle family, with edible purplish to white berries; the timber or the fruit of this tree.

Li-Lo /ˈlʌɪləʊ/ *n.* Also **Lilo.** Pl. **-os.** M20. [Alt. of *lie low.*] (Proprietary name for) an inflatable plastic or rubber mattress.

lilt /lɪlt/ *n.* L17. [f. the vb.] **1** A song, a tune, *esp.* one of a cheerful or merry character. Chiefly *Sc.* L17. **2** The rhythmical cadence or swing of a tune or of verse; a characteristic inflection or rhythm in the voice. M19. **3** A springing action; a light springing step. M19.

lilt /lɪlt/ *v.* Orig. *Sc.* & *north.* LME. [Rel. to LG, Du. *lul* pipe (Du. *lullepijp* bagpipe).] †**1** *v.t.* Sound (an alarm); lift up (the voice). LME–E16. **2** *v.t.* Sing cheerfully or merrily; strike *up* (a song); tune *up* (pipes). E18. **3** *v.i.* Sing or sound cheerfully or merrily; sing or speak with a lilt. Freq. as *lilting* ppl a. E18. **4** *v.i.* Move with a lilt. Chiefly as *lilting* ppl a. L18. **5** *v.i.* Of music or speech: have a lilt. Chiefly as *lilting* ppl a. E19.

3 SIR W. SCOTT Jenny, whose shrill voice I have heard .. lilting in the Tartarean regions of the kitchen. 4 *Longman's Magazine* Swinging down the street with an easy lilting stride. 5 W. H. AUDEN Or west to the Welsh Marches; to the lilting speech and the magicians' faces.

lily /ˈlɪli/ *n.* & *a.* OE. [L *lilium* f. (as) Gk *leirion*, perh. of non-IE origin.] **A** *n.* **1** Any plant of the genus *Lilium* (family Liliaceae), comprising tall bulbous plants bearing large showy trumpet-shaped flowers on a tall slender stem, and often grown for ornament; *esp.* (without qualification) = MADONNA *lily.* Also, a flower or flowering stem of such a plant. OE. **b** In biblical translations: any of one or more conspicuous Palestinian flowers, variously identified as a lily, tulip, anemone, gladiolus, etc. LME. **c** With specifying wd: any of various plants of other genera of the family Liliaceae or of related families, esp. the Amaryllidaceae. Also, any of certain unrelated plants with similarly conspicuous flowers. M16. **2** *fig.* **a** A person or thing of exceptional whiteness, fairness, or purity; *sing.* & in *pl.*, the white of a beautiful complexion. LME. **b** A person one despises; *esp.* a man regarded as lacking masculinity. E20. **3** A representation of the flower; *spec.* the heraldic fleur-de-lis, esp. with ref. to the arms of the old French monarchy (also *golden lilies*); *the* royal arms of France, *the* French (Bourbon) dynasty. LME. †**b** The fleur-de-lis which was used to mark north on a compass. E–M17. **c** In *pl.* = *lily-feet* below. Also *golden lilies.* M19.

1 *martagon lily, tiger lily, Turk's-cap lily*, etc. **b** AV *Matt.* 6:28 Consider the lilies of the field... Euen Solomon in all his glory was not arayed like one of these. **c** *arum lily, belladonna lily, day lily, Guernsey lily, Kaffir lily, Lent lily, May lily, Peruvian lily, St Bruno's lily, water lily*, etc.

Phrases: **gild the lily** embellish excessively, add ornament where none is needed. **lily of the valley** or (*arch.*) **vale** [tr. Vulgate *lilium convallium* (*S. of S.* 2:1) tr. Heb., an unidentified plant] a May-flowering woodland plant, *Convallaria majalis*, of the lily family, with two large leaves and racemes of white bell-shaped fragrant flowers; the scent of this plant, esp. as used in cosmetics. **paint the lily** [Shakes. *John*] = *gild the lily* above.

B *adj.* **1** White or fair as a lily; lily-white. L15. **2** Pale, pallid, colourless, bloodless. L16.

Comb. (of n. & adj.): **lily bell, lily cup** the flower of the lily of the valley; **lily feet** the bound feet of a Chinese woman; **lily flower** the flower of the white lily; **lily-footed** *a.* having lily feet; **lily-iron** a harpoon with a detachable head used in killing sword-fish; **lily liver** the supposedly white liver of cowards; **lily-livered** *a.* cowardly; **lily-pad** the broad flat leaf of a water lily as it lies on the water; **lily-pond**: in which water lilies grow; **lily-pot** a flowerpot with a lily in it; a representation of this, esp. as a religious emblem of purity and innocence; an ornamental vase resembling the lily-pot of religious art, *esp.* a tobacco jar; **lily-trotter** a jacana, *esp.* an African one; **lily-turf** = MONDO *n.*[1]

lily-like *a.* resembling (that of) a lily M17.

lily-white /ˈlɪlɪwʌɪt/ *a.* & *n.* ME. [f. LILY + WHITE *a.*] **A** *adj.* **1** As white as a lily. ME. **2** In favour of, committed to, or pertaining to a policy of racial segregation. E20. **3** Irreproachable, lacking faults or imperfections. M20. **B** *n.* A chimney sweep. *slang.* Now *rare* or *obs.* L17.

Lima /ˈliːmə/ *n.* M18. [The capital of Peru.] In full *Lima bean.* A bean plant, *Phaseolus limensis* (or *P. lunatus*) native to tropical S. America; the large flat white edible seed of this plant; a butter-bean.

limaceous /lʌɪˈmeɪʃəs/ *a.* M17. [f. as LIMAX + -ACEOUS.] Of or pertaining to the genus *Limax* of slugs. Formerly, resembling a snail.

limaces *n.* pl. of LIMAX.

limaciform /lʌɪˈmeɪsɪfɔːm/ *a.* E19. [f. as LIMAX + -I- + -FORM.] Having the form of a slug.

limacine /ˈlʌɪməsʌɪn, -sɪn/ *a.* L19. [f. as LIMAX + -INE[1].] Resembling a slug or a snail.

limaçon /ˈlɪməsɒn/ *n.* Also **-con.** L16. [Fr. = snail shell, spiral staircase, etc., f. (O)Fr. *limace* f. as LIMAX: see -OON.] †**1** A kind of spiral military manoeuvre. Only in L16. **2** *Math.* Any of a series of closed curves represented by the formula $r = a\cos\theta + b$, which when $a = b$ gives a cardioid; the locus of a point on a line a fixed distance from the intersection of the line with a circle, as the line rotates about a fixed point on the circle. L19.

limail /ˈliːm(ə)l/ *n.* Now only *techn.* Also **lemel.** LME. [(O)Fr. *limaille*, f. *limer* to file f. L *limare*.] Metal filings.

liman /liːˈmɑːn/ *n.* M19. [Russ. = estuary, f. Turk. f. mod.Gk *limeni* f. Gk *limēn*.] A shallow lagoon at the mouth of a river behind a bar or spit, characteristic of the Black Sea.

limation /lʌɪˈmeɪʃ(ə)n/ *n.* Now *rare.* E17. [Late L *limatio(n-)*, f. L *limat-* pa. ppl stem of *limare* to file: see -ATION.] Filing; *fig.* the process of refining or improving the appearance of something.

limax /ˈlʌɪmaks/ *n.* Pl. **limaces** /lʌɪˈmeɪsiːz/. LME. [L *limax*, *limac-* slug, snail.] Orig., a slug. Now, a slug of the genus *Limax* or the family Limacidae containing it.

limb /lɪm/ *n.*[1] [OE *lim* corresp. to ON *limr*, prob. rel. to LITH *n.*[1]] **1** An organ or part of the body. Long *obs.* exc. *dial.* OE. **2** A projecting part of a human or animal body such as a leg, arm, or wing. OE. **b** *spec.* A leg of an animal or person; (now *joc.*) a leg of an object. LME. **3** Orig., a member; a section, a branch; an element, a component part. Now only, a member of something regarded metaphorically as a body. OE. **4** A large branch of a tree. OE. **5** *spec.* A projecting section of a building; each of the branches of a cross; a member or clause of a sentence; a spur of a mountain range; the part of a compound core of a transformer, electromagnet, etc., on which a coil is wound. L16. **6** [f. *devil's limb* etc. below] A mischievous person, esp. a child; a young imp or rascal. *colloq.* E17. **7** Either half of an archery bow. E19.

2 C. BLACKWOOD He had an artificial limb, for he had lost a leg in the war. M. SCAMMELL They climbed down from . . the lorries and stretched their stiff limbs. b J. F. COOPER His limbs were guarded with long leggings. 3 A. W. KINGLAKE An army is but the limb of a nation. 6 A. WEST Off it, you young limb, and out of there.

Phrases: **devil's** or **fiend's limb** †(*a*) an agent or scion of the Devil; (*b*) (now *dial.*) a mischievous wicked person. **life and limb** all the bodily faculties (*with life and limb*, without grave injury). **limb of the devil, Satan, hell** = *devil's limb* above. **limb of the law** *derog.* a legal functionary; a lawyer, a police officer. **out on a limb** in an isolated or stranded position; at a disadvantage. PHANTOM *limb.* **tear limb from limb** dismember violently.

Comb.: **limb-bud** a small protuberance in an embryo from which a limb develops.

limblike *a.* resembling (that of) a limb L19.

limb /lɪm/ *n.*[2] LME. [(O)Fr. *limbe* or L LIMBUS.] †**1** = LIMBO *n.*[1] I. *Sc.* LME–L18. **2** *Sci.* An edge; *spec.* (*a*) the graduated edge of a scientific instrument, esp. a quadrant; (*b*) the edge of the disc of a celestial object, esp. of the sun and moon. LME. **b** *Bot.* The lamina or expanded portion of a monopetalous corolla or of a petal or sepal. Also, the lamina or blade of a leaf. M18. †**3** A border. *rare.* LME.

Comb.: **limb-darkening** *Astron.* the apparent darkening of the face of the sun towards its edge.

limb /lɪm/ *v.t.* M17. [f. LIMB *n.*[1]] †**1** *refl.* Provide oneself with limbs. *rare* (Milton). Only in M17. **2** Dismember. L17. **3** Remove branches from (a tree). M19.

Limba /ˈlɪmbə/ *n.*[1] & *a.* E20. [Limba.] **A** *n.* Pl. **-s**, same. **1** A member of a W. African people inhabiting Sierra Leone and Guinea. E20. **2** The Niger-Congo language of the Limbas. E20. **B** *attrib.* or as *adj.* Of or pertaining to the Limbas or their language. E20.

limba /ˈlɪmbə/ *n.*[2] M20. [Gabon name *limbo*.] (The timber of) a tall W. African hardwood tree, *Terminalia superba*. Also called *afara*.

limbal /ˈlɪmb(ə)l/ *a.* M20. [f. LIMBUS + -AL[1].] Of or pertaining to the limbus of the cornea.

limbate /ˈlɪmbeɪt/ *a.* E19. [Late L *limbatus*, f. L LIMBUS: see -ATE[2].] *Biol.* Having an edge of a different colour from the rest.

limbeck /ˈlɪmbɛk/ *n.* & *v. arch.* LME. [Aphet. f. ALEMBIC.] **A** *n.* = ALEMBIC *n.* LME. †**B** *v.t.* = ALEMBIC *v.*; *fig.* rack (the brain). L16–M17.

limbed /lɪmd/ *a.* ME. [f. LIMB *n.*[1] + -ED[2].] Having limbs. Chiefly as 2nd elem. of comb., as *straight-limbed*, *well-limbed*, etc.

limber /ˈlɪmbə/ *n.*[1] Orig. †**lymo(u)r**; also †**limmer.** LME. [Perh. f. (O)Fr. *limon*, med.L *limo(n-)* shaft.] **1** The shaft of a cart or carriage. *obs.* exc. *dial.* LME. **2** *Mil.*, *sing.* & (orig.) †in *pl.* The detachable forepart of a gun-carriage, consisting of two wheels and an axle, a pole for the horses, and a frame which holds one or two ammunition boxes. L15.

Comb.: **limber-box, limber-chest** *Mil.* the ammunition box carried by a limber.

limber /ˈlɪmbə/ *n.*[2] E17. [(O)Fr. *lumière* light, limber, f. Proto-Romance, f. pl. of L *luminare* light, lamp, f. *lumin-*, *lumen* light.] *Naut.* Each of the holes made in the floor-timbers of a ship to allow bilge-water to run through to the lowest point for pumping (also more fully *limber hole*); in *pl.*, any passage serving the same purpose.

Comb.: **limber-chain**: used like a limber-rope; *limber hole*: see above; **limber-rope**: passing through the limber holes, and moved to and fro to clear them.

limber /ˈlɪmbə/ *a.* M16. [Perh. f. LIMBER *n.*[1] w. allus. to the to-and-fro motion of shafts and limbers.] **1** Easily bent; flexible, pliant, supple. M16. **2** Of a person, movement, etc.: bending or moving easily; lithe and nimble. L16. **3** Limp, flaccid; flabby. Now chiefly *dial.* L16.

1 *fig.*: SHAKES. *Wint. T.* You put me off with limber vows. 2 DISRAELI A limber and graceful figure. G. SANTAYANA Selling his polo-ponies, some of which . . were no longer quite keen and limber enough. 3 R. PRICE A sheriff that can't even serve his wife, limber as beeswax soon's he hits the bed.

Comb. & *special collocations*: †**limberham** (*a*) a supple-jointed person; *fig.* an obsequious person; (*b*) a foolish man who keeps a mistress, like the hero of Dryden's play *Mr Limberham*; **limber-neck** a kind of botulism affecting poultry; **limber pine** a small pine of the Rocky Mountains, *Pinus flexilis*, with flexible branches.

limberly *adv.* L19. **limberness** *n.* M16.

limber /ˈlɪmbə/ *v.*[1] M18. [f. prec.] **1** *v.t.* Make limber. Also foll. by *up.* M18. **2** *v.i.* Exercise to make oneself limber, esp. in preparation for athletic activity etc. Usu. foll. by *up.* E20.

2 *Successful Slimming* A gentle jog or on-the-spot limbering-up.

limber /ˈlɪmbə/ *v.*[2] M19. [f. LIMBER *n.*[1]] *Mil.* **1** *v.i.* Fasten together the two parts of a gun-carriage, as a preparation for moving away. Usu. foll. by *up.* M19. **2** *v.t.* Attach the limber to (a gun). Usu. foll. by *up.* M19.

limbi *n.* pl. of LIMBUS.

limbic /ˈlɪmbɪk/ *a.* L19. [Fr. *limbique*, f. as LIMB *n.*[2]: see -IC.] *Anat.* Designating or pertaining to a lobe of the cerebrum forming the edge of the medial part of the cortex; of or pertaining to the limbic system.

limbic system a part of the brain that includes the limbic lobe and is concerned with basic emotions and with autonomic and olfactory functions.

limbless /ˈlɪmlɪs/ *a.* L16. [f. LIMB *n.*[1] + -LESS.] Having no limbs, or fewer than the normal number of limbs.

limb-meal /ˈlɪmmiːl/ *adv. arch.* & *dial.* OE. [f. LIMB *n.*[1] + -MEAL.] Limb from limb, limb by limb; piecemeal.

limbo /ˈlɪmbəʊ/ *n.*[1] Pl. **-os.** LME. [L, abl. sing. of LIMBUS, in phrs. like *in limbo*, *e* (= out of) *limbo*.] **1** *Chr. Ch.* A region supposed in some beliefs to exist on the border of Hell as the abode of the just who died before Christ's coming and of unbaptized infants. LME. †**b** Hell, Hades. L16–M17. **2** Prison, confinement. Formerly also, pawn. *slang.* L16. **3** An unfavourable place or condition, likened to limbo; *esp.* a condition of neglect or oblivion to which people or things are consigned when regarded as superseded, useless, or absurd; an intermediate or indeterminate condition; a state of inaction or inattention pending some future event. M17.

3 E. HUXLEY Legally, the Irish occupy a curious limbo. U. LE GUIN A fever that . . left him in a limbo between reason and unreason. JAN MORRIS Hav remained in a kind of limbo until . . the League of Nations declared its mandate. *Independent* These prisoners are totally in limbo . . No one is responsible for their welfare.

Comb.: †**limbo-lake** the abode of spirits or tormented souls.

limbo /ˈlɪmbəʊ/ *n.*[2] Pl. **-os.** L19. [Zulu *ulembu* web, limbo.] *S. Afr. Hist.* A kind of coarse calico.

limbo /ˈlɪmbəʊ/ *n.*[3] Pl. **-os.** M20. [f. LIMBER *a.*, *v.*[1]] A W. Indian dance in which the dancer bends backwards and passes under a horizontal bar progressively lowered to just above the ground.

limbric /ˈlɪmbrɪk/ *n.* M20. [Origin unkn.: *-bric* perh. f. CAMBRIC.] A closely-woven cotton cloth of light to medium weight.

Limbu /ˈlɪmbuː/ *n.* & *a.* E19. [Limbu.] **A** *n.* Pl. **-s**, same. **1** A member of a people of eastern Nepal. E19. **2** The Tibeto-Burman language of this people. E20. **B** *attrib.* or as *adj.* Of or pertaining to the Limbus or their language. M19.

Limburger /ˈlɪmbəːɡə/ *n.* M19. [Du. & G, f. *Limburg*, a province of NE Belgium: see -ER[1].] A soft white cheese with a characteristic strong smell, orig. made in Limburg. Also *Limburger cheese.*

limburgite /ˈlɪmbəːɡʌɪt/ *n.* L19. [f. *Limburg*, a hamlet in Baden-Württemberg, Germany + -ITE[1].] *Geol.* A dark, very basic extrusive igneous rock consisting of phenocrysts of pyroxene and olivine in an alkali-rich glassy groundmass.

limbus /ˈlɪmbəs/ *n.* Pl. **-bi** /-bʌɪ/. LME. [L = edge, border, (in med.L) region on the border of hell.] **1** = LIMBO *n.*[1] I. Now *rare.* LME. **2** *techn.* A border, a margin; *spec.* (*Anat.*) the margin of the cornea; *Bot.* = LIMB *n.*[2] 2b. L17.

lime /lʌɪm/ *n.*[1] [OE *līm* corresp. to MDu. *līm* (Du. *lijm*), OHG *līm* (G *Leim*), ON *lím*, f. Gmc var. of base of LOAM *n.*, ult. rel. to L *limus* mud.] **1** Orig., any adhesive substance, e.g. glue, paste. Later *spec.* = BIRDLIME *n.* I; *fig.* a thing that entraps or holds a person. Now *poet.* OE. **2** Mortar or cement used in building. Freq. coupled w. *stone. obs.* exc. *Sc.* OE. **3** The alkaline earth, calcium oxide, a brittle white caustic solid which is obtained by heating limestone, combines with water with the evolution of much heat, and is used as a refractory and a constituent of mortar, a source of slaked lime, and in many industrial processes; also called *quicklime.* Also, slaked lime; (in phrs.) calcium; *Agric.* any calcium-containing fertilizer. OE. **4** A vat containing a solution of lime for removing the hair from skins; such a solution. L19.

2 SHAKES. *Rich. II* King Richard lies Within the limits of yon lime and stone. 3 L. MACNEICE No lime has been laid on the land for forty years.

Phrases: **carbonate of lime** *arch.* calcium carbonate (cf. LIMESTONE). **lime and hair** a kind of plasterer's cement to which hair is added to bind the mixture closely together. *white lime*: see WHITE *a.*

Comb.: **lime-ash** *dial.* a composition of ashes and lime used as a rough kind of flooring for kitchens etc.; **lime-burner** a person whose occupation is calcining limestone to obtain lime; **lime-cast** a covering or layer of lime mortar; **limekiln** a kiln in which limestone is calcined to obtain lime; **limepit** (*a*) a pit where limestone is quarried or calcined; (*b*) a pit containing lime for steeping hides to remove hair or fur; **lime-pot** (*a*) a pot for holding lime, birdlime, or limewash; †(*b*) a pot in which limestone was calcined; **lime-rock** limestone; **lime-rubbish** broken mortar from old walls etc. used as a dressing for land; **lime-**

sink a rounded depression in the earth found in limestone districts; **lime soap** a mixture of insoluble calcium salts of fatty acids formed as a precipitate when soap is used in hard water, manufactured for various industrial purposes; **lime-soda** *a.* designating a process for softening water by treatment with lime and sodium carbonate; **lime-sulphur** an insecticide and fungicide containing calcium polysulphides which is made by boiling lime and sulphur in water; **lime-twig** *n.* & *v.* (*a*) *n.* a twig smeared with birdlime for catching birds; †(*b*) *v.t.* entangle, ensnare; **limewash** *n.* & *v.* (*a*) *n.* a mixture of lime and water used for coating walls etc.; (*b*) *v.t.* whitewash with such a mixture; **lime water** a solution of calcium hydroxide, formerly used medicinally; **lime-work** †(*a*) stucco; (*b*) = *lime-works* below; **lime-works** a place where lime is made.

lime /lʌɪm/ *n.*[2] E17. [Alt. of *line* var. of LIND.] (More fully *lime tree*) any of various deciduous trees of the genus *Tilia* (family Tiliaceae), esp. *T.* × *vulgaris*, a common ornamental tree with heart-shaped leaves and many small fragrant yellowish flowers; also called *linden*. Also, the wood of these trees.

lime /lʌɪm/ *n.*[3] M17. [Fr. f. Sp. *lima* f. Arab. *līma*: cf. LEMON *n.*[1]] **1** A globular citrus fruit that is smaller and greener than the lemon and has a more acid taste; the small spiny tree, *Citrus aurantiifolia* (family Rutaceae), of tropical regions which bears this fruit. M17. **b** Any of various other trees, esp. of the family Rutaceae. M18. **2** *ellipt.* Lime-green. E20. **3** *ellipt.* Lime-juice. Earlier in LIMEY. M20.

1b sweet lime a tree, *Citrus limetta*, resembling the lemon but with an insipidly sweet fruit. **3** *gin and lime* etc.

Comb.: **lime-green** a pale green colour like that of a lime; **lime-juice** (a preparation of) the juice of the lime as a drink, formerly given to prevent scurvy on long sea voyages; **lime-juicer** (cf. LIMEY) †(*a*) *Austral. slang* a person who has recently emigrated to Australia from Britain; (*b*) *US* a British ship or sailor; **lime-marmalade**: made from limes; **lime-punch**: made with lime-juice instead of more usual lemon-juice; **lime-squash**: made with lime-juice.

lime /lʌɪm/ *n.*[4] *colloq.* L19. [Abbrev.] = LIMELIGHT. Freq. in *pl.*

lime /lʌɪm/ *v.*[1] LOE. [f. LIME *n.*[1]] **I 1** *v.t.* Join together, unite. LOE. **2** *v.t.* Smear with a sticky substance, *spec.* with birdlime to catch birds. ME. **3** *v.t.* Catch with birdlime. Freq. *fig.*, entrap, ensnare. *arch.* ME. †**4** *v.t.* Foul, defile. LME–L16. **II** †**5** *v.t.* Coat with limewash. LME–E17. †**6** *v.i.* Put lime into wine. *rare* (Shakes.). Only in L16 **7** *v.t.* & *i.* Dress (land, crops, etc.) with lime to improve growth. E17. **8** *v.t.* Steep (skins) in lime and water. L17. **9** *v.t.* Give (wood) a bleached effect by treating it with lime. Chiefly as *limed* ppl a. M20.

lime /lʌɪm/ *v.*[2]*i.* *W. Indies.* L20. [Origin unkn.: rel. to LIMER *n.*[3]] Spend one's time idly in the street.

limeade /lʌɪmˈeɪd/ *n.* L19. [f. LIME *n.*[3] + -ADE.] A drink made from lime-juice sweetened with sugar.

Limehouse /ˈlʌɪmhaʊs/ *v.i.* *slang.* E20. [A district of E. London, England, where Lloyd George made such speeches.] Make fiery speeches, esp. political ones.

limeless /ˈlʌɪmlɪs/ *a.* E18. [f. LIME *n.*[1] + -LESS.] Having or containing no lime (calcium oxide).

limelight /ˈlʌɪmlʌɪt/ *n.* & *v.* E19. [f. LIME *n.*[1] + LIGHT *n.*] **A** *n.* **1** The intense white light produced by heating lime in an oxyhydrogen flame, formerly used in theatres to light up important players and scenes and so direct attention to them; a lamp producing such light (cf. DRUMMOND LIGHT). E19. **2** *the limelight*, the full glare of publicity; people's full attention. L19.

2 E. LEWIS We earned . . a nice little sum out of Tutankhamen when he was in the limelight. P. USTINOV A puppy will steal the limelight from even a well-loved dog.

B *v.t.* Pa. t. & pple **-lighted**, **-lit**. Illuminate with limelight or other strong light; make a focus of publicity or attention. E20.

limen /ˈlʌɪmɛn, ˈliː-/ *n.* M17. [L = threshold; in sense 2 tr. G *Schwelle*.] †**1** A threshold. Only in M17. **2** *Psychol.* The minimum strength of a stimulus required to produce a sensation; the minimum amount by which one stimulus has to differ from another for the difference to be perceptible. L19.

Limenian /lɪˈmiːnɪən/ *n.* E19. [f. Amer.-Sp. *limeño*, *-ña*, f. *Lima*: see below, -IAN.] A native or inhabitant of Lima, the capital of Peru.

limeño /liˈmeɲo/ *n.*, pl. **-os** /-ɔs/, a male Limenian M20. *limeña* /liˈmeɲa/ *n.* a female Limenian L19.

limer /ˈliːmə/ *n.*[1] *obs.* exc. *Hist.* Also †**leam-**. ME. [AN = OFr. *liemier* (mod. *limier*), f. as LYAM.] A hound; a bloodhound; a mongrel.

limer /ˈlʌɪmə/ *n.*[2] E17. [f. LIME *v.*[1] + -ER[1].] A person who limes something; a person who sets snares with birdlime; a person who limewashes walls etc. Also, a brush used for limewashing.

limer /ˈlʌɪmə/ *n.*[3] *W. Indies.* L20. [Origin unkn.: rel. to LIME *v.*[2]] A person who spends time idly in the streets.

Limerick /ˈlɪm(ə)rɪk/ *a.* & *n.* E19. [The chief town of County Limerick, Ireland.] **A** *adj.* **1** Designating gloves of fine leather formerly made at Limerick. E19. **2** Designating (the pattern of) a fish-hook in which the wire is bent abruptly through a large angle behind the barb but thereafter is bent more shallowly to the point at which it continues as the straight shank. E19. **3** Designating a type of embroidered lace originally made at Limerick. M19. **B** *n.* **1** A Limerick fish-hook. M19. **2** Limerick lace. L19. **3** (Usu. **l-**.) A humorous or comic five-line stanza with the rhyme scheme *aabba*, there being three feet in the *a* lines and two in the *b* lines. L19.

limes /ˈlʌɪmiːz/ *n.* Pl. **limites** /ˈlʌɪmɪtiːz/ M16. [L = LIMIT *n.*] Now *Archaeol.* A boundary; *spec.* the boundary of the Roman Empire, esp. in the north of Europe.

limestone /ˈlʌɪmstəʊn/ *n.* & *a.* LME. [f. LIME *n.*[1] + STONE *n.*] **A** *n.* A sedimentary rock composed chiefly of calcium carbonate, which yields lime when calcined and is used as a building material and in the making of cement; a species or (formerly) a piece of this rock. LME.

B *attrib.* or as *adj.* Made or consisting of limestone. L17.

LITHOGRAPHIC *limestone*. MILIOLITE *limestone*.

Comb.: **limestone fern**, **limestone polypody** a fern of limestone rocks and screes, *Gymnocarpium robertianum*, with greyish glandular fronds.

Limey /ˈlʌɪmi/ *a.* & *n.* *colloq. derog.* Also **l-**. L19. [f. LIME *n.*[3] (w. ref. to *lime-juice*) + -Y[6].] **A** *adj.* In former British colonies and the US: English, British. L19.

D. LODGE Can't understand a word because of the guy's limey accent.

B *n.* **1** An English or British ship or sailor; an Englishman, a Briton. *N. Amer.* E20. **2** In some former British colonies: an English immigrant. M20.

limicole /ˈlʌɪmɪkəʊl/ *n.* M20. [f. L *limus* mud + -I- + -COLE.] An oligochaete worm living in mud or water.

limicoline /lʌɪˈmɪkəlʌɪn, -lɪn/ *a.* L19. [f. mod.L *Limicolae* (see below), f. as prec.: see -INE[1].] Of or pertaining to the suborder Charadrii of waders or shore-birds (formerly the order Limicolae).

liminal /ˈlɪmɪn(ə)l/ *a.* L19. [f. L *limin-* LIMEN + -AL[1].] **1** Of, pertaining to, or constituting a transitional or initial stage of a process. Also, marginal, incidental, insignificant. L19. **2** Of, pertaining to, or situated at a limen; occupying a position on, or on both sides of, a boundary or threshold. L19.

limiˈnality *n.* M20.

liminary /ˈlɪmɪn(ə)ri/ *a.* Now *rare.* E17. [Fr. *liminaire* f. L *liminaris*, f. as prec.: see -ARY[2].] Preliminary, preparatory.

liminess /ˈlʌɪmɪnɪs/ *n.* E20. [f. LIMY + -NESS.] The quality or state of being limy.

limit /ˈlɪmɪt/ *n.* LME. [L *limit-*, *limes*.] **1** Orig., a boundary, a frontier; an object serving to define a boundary, a landmark. Now *spec.* a boundary or terminal point considered as confining or restricting. Usu. in *pl.* LME. **2** Any of the fixed points between which the possible or permitted extent, amount, duration, etc., of something is confined; a bound which may not be passed or beyond which something ceases to be possible or allowable. LME. †**3** A tract, a region; in *pl.*, the bounds, territories. L15–L18. **4** Limitation, restriction within limits. Chiefly in *without limit.* L16. **5** Prescribed time; the prescribed period of repose after child-bearing. *rare* (Shakes.). E17. **6** *Astron.* The greatest heliocentric latitude of a planet. E18. **7** *Math.* A finite quantity to which the sum of a converging series progressively approximates; a fixed value to which a function can be made to approach continually, so as to differ from it by less than any assignable quantity; either of the two values of a variable between which a definite integral is taken. M18. **8** A greatest or smallest permitted or allowed amount; *spec.* (*a*) *Cards* an agreed maximum stake or bet; (*b*) the maximum concentration of alcohol in the blood that the law allows in the driver of a motor vehicle. M19. **9** The worst imaginable or tolerable. *colloq.* E20.

1 L. CODY They reached the lower limits of Hampstead Heath. JAYNE PHILLIPS After dusk you could get outside the city limits. **2** H. JAMES He had perhaps reached the limits of legitimate experimentation. R. MACAULAY There *is* a limit to the patience of bishops. H. MOORE There was no barrier, no limit to what a young provincial student could . . do. **8** L. DUNCAN Punished to the full limit of the law. R. LARDNER Two is my limit and I've already exceeded it. *Daily Express* Divorcee Lorna was double the legal limit. *age limit*, *speed limit*, *weight limit*, etc. **9** G. B. SHAW Really! your father does seem to be about the limit.

Phrases: *frozen limit*: see FROZEN *ppl a.* 2. **go the limit** behave in an extreme way; last the stated number of rounds or the full time, as in a boxing-match; allow sexual intercourse. *limit of* PROPORTIONALITY. **off limits** out of bounds; forbidden. **over the limit** having exceeded a prescribed limit. *proportional limit*: see PROPORTIONAL *a.* 1. *Rayleigh limit*: see RAYLEIGH 1. *Roche('s) limit*: see ROCHE *n.*[2] *territorial limit*: see TERRITORIAL *a. the sky is the limit*: see SKY *n.* **within limits** to a moderate extent; with some degree of freedom. **without limit** unrestrictedly.

Comb.: **limit bid** *Bridge* a call which shows that the strength of the caller's hand does not exceed a certain value; **limit dog**: shown in a class limited to dogs having certain required qualifications; **limit gauge** *Engin.*: used for determining whether a dimension of a manufactured item falls within the specified tolerance; **limit man**: who receives the longest start allowed in a handicap; **limit point** *Math.* a point every neighbourhood of which contains a point belonging to a given set; **limit switch** *Engin.* a switch preventing the travel of an object past some predetermined point and mechanically operated by the motion of the object itself.

limit /ˈlɪmɪt/ *v.* LME. [(O)Fr. *limiter* or L *limitare*, f. as prec.] **1** *v.t.* Assign, make *over*, within limits (also foll. by *away*); appoint, fix definitely; specify. (Foll. by *to*, *upon*, *to do*.) Now *rare* or *obs.* LME. †**b** Appoint (a person) *to* an office; assign (a duty) *to* a person. LME–M17. †**c** Allot, apportion. Usu. foll. by *out*. M16–M17. **2** *v.t.* Confine within limits, set bounds to; restrict. (Foll. by *to*.) LME. **3** *v.t.* Serve as a limit or boundary to; mark off *from*. Now *rare* exc. as *limiting* ppl a. L16.

1 MARVELL Neither do I believe we can finish it . . within the time limited us. **2** G. M. TREVELYAN The Ten Hours Bill limited the daily work of women and youths in textile factories. L. CODY Such space as there was further limited by green filing-cabinets. J. MCDOUGALL I shall limit mystery here to giving a glimpse into a psychic scene. **3** A. HOLMES Domes and basins represent the limiting cases in which the beds dip in all directions . . from, or . . towards, the centre. *Science News* This chamber is the limiting factor in rocket design.

limitable *a.* L16.

limitary /ˈlɪmɪt(ə)ri/ *a.* E17. [Senses 1, 3 f. LIMIT *n.* + -ARY[2]; sense 2 f. L *limitaris*, f. as LIMIT *n.*] **1** Subject to limits; limited, restricted. E17. **2** Of or pertaining to a limit or boundary; situated on a boundary. M17. **3** Serving as a limit or boundary; limiting, confining, containing. (Foll. by *of*.) E19.

limitate /ˈlɪmɪteɪt/ *pa. pple* & *ppl a.* L16. [L *limitatus* pa. pple of *limitare* LIMIT *v.*: see -ATE[2].] †**I** *pa. pple.* **1** Limited. Only in L16. **II** *ppl a.* **2**

Of land: divided up by boundaries. *rare*. M19. 3 *Bot.* Bounded by a distinct line. L19.

limitation /lɪmɪˈteɪʃ(ə)n/ *n.* LME. [L *limitatio(n-)*, f. *limitat-* pa. ppl stem of *limitare* LIMIT *v.*: see -ATION.] 1 The action or an act of limiting. LME. †**b** *spec.* The action of determining the boundaries of a country or the contour of a figure. L16–E18. †**2a** An allotted space; the district or circuit of an itinerant officer or preaching friar; the region belonging to a particular nation; *fig.* one's allotted sphere. LME–M16. **b** An allotted time. *rare* (Shakes.). Only in E17. 3 A point or respect in which a thing, esp. a person's ability, is limited; a limiting provision or circumstance. E16. 4 = LIMIT *n.* 1, 2. Freq. in *pl.* E16. 5 The condition of being limited. L16. 6 *Law.* The legal specification of a period within which an action must be brought or a period for which an estate shall continue or a law operate; a period so specified. L16.

3 H. J. S. MAINE He was heir to the earldom of Tyrone according to the limitations of the patent. E. F. BENSON 'He does love discussion,' said Lucia. 'I know... Don't you?'.. 'I like it, with limitations.' P. ROSE Mr Taylor.. considering his limitations, was behaving remarkably well. **have one's** or **its limitations** lack talent or ability in some respects. 5 C. LYELL The limitation of groups of distinct species to regions separated.. by certain natural barriers. 6 **statute of limitations**: prescribing a period of limitation for the bringing of actions of certain kinds.

limitative /ˈlɪmɪtətɪv/ *a.* M16. [med.L *limitativus*, f. *limitat-*: see prec., -IVE.] Tending to limit; limiting, restrictive.

limited /ˈlɪmɪtɪd/ *a.* & *n.* M16. [f. LIMIT *v.* + -ED[1].] **A** *adj.* †**1** Appointed, fixed. M16–M17. 2 Confined within definite limits; restricted in scope, extent, amount, etc.; (of an amount or number) small; (of an income) low; (of monarchy, government, etc.) exercised under limitations of power prescribed by a constitution. E17.

2 E. BOWEN Her time in London was limited. *New Yorker* The Bicentennial carpet is now being shown at a limited number of fine stores. M. HUNTER Because of the narrator's limited vocabulary, there is no scope for.. adventure in language. E. PIZZEY Like many young working-class girls.. the choices open to her were very limited. *Which?* A very limited amount of wine—say one white and one red.

Special collocations: **limited company**: whose members' liability for its debts are legally limited to the extent of their investment. **limited edition** an edition of a book, or reproduction of an object, limited to some specific number of copies. **limited liability** *Law* liability that is limited by law (*limited-liability company* = *limited company* above). **limited partner** a partner in a company etc. whose liability towards its debts is legally limited and who does not take an active part in its running. **limited partnership** a partnership in which the liability of some partners is legally limited to the extent of their investment. **limited train** *US* a train consisting of a small number of cars and making few stops; an express train. **limited war**: in which the weapons used, the nations or territory involved, or the objectives pursued, are restricted.

B *n.* 1 A limited train. *US colloq.* L19. 2 A limited company. E20.

¶Earlier in UNLIMITED.

limitedly *adv.* E17. **limitedness** *n.* M17.

limiter /ˈlɪmɪtə/ *n.* LME. [f. LIMIT *v.* + -ER[1].] 1 A friar licensed to beg within certain limits. Also *friar limiter. obs.* exc. *Hist.* LME. 2 A person who or thing which limits something or someone. L15. **b** *Electronics.* A device whose output is restricted to a certain range of values irrespective of the size of the input. E20.

limites *n.* pl. of LIMES.

limitless /ˈlɪmɪtlɪs/ *a.* L16. [f. LIMIT *n.* + -LESS.] Having or admitting of no limits; unlimited; unbounded, unrestricted.

JANET MORGAN The garden seemed limitless to Agatha, most of whose childhood world it composed. J. M. COETZEE There are times when I feel my strength to be limitless.

limitlessly *adv.* M19. **limitlessness** *n.* M19.

limitrophe /ˈlɪmɪtrəʊf/ *n.* & *a.* L16. [Fr. f. late L *limitrophus*, f. as LIMIT *n.* + Gk *-trophos* supporting, f. *trephein* support, nourish.] **A** *n.* A borderland. Long *rare.* L16. **B** *adj.* Situated on a frontier; adjacent *to* another country. M18.

limma /ˈlɪmə/ *n.* L17. [Late L f. Gk *leimma* remnant, lemma, f. *leipein* leave.] *Mus.* The semitone of the Pythagorean scale.

limmer /ˈlɪmə/ *n.*[1] & *a. Sc.* & *north.* LME. [Perh. rel. to LIMB *n.*[1]] **A** *n.* 1 A rogue, a scoundrel. LME. 2 A promiscuous woman; a jade, a hussy. M16. **B** *adj.* Knavish, scoundrelly. E16.

†**limmer** *n.*[2] var. of LIMBER *n.*[1]

limmu /ˈlɪmuː/ *n.* M19. [Assyr.] The year of office to which an Assyrian eponym gave his name; the office of an Assyrian eponym.

limn /lɪm/ *v.* Now *literary.* LME. [Alt. of LUMINE.] 1 *v.t.* & †*i.* Illuminate (a manuscript etc.). Now *rare.* LME. †**2** *v.t.* Adorn or embellish with gold or bright colour; depict *in* gold etc. M16–M17. 3 *v.t.* & †*i.* Paint (a picture or portrait); portray (a subject); *fig.* depict, make visible. Formerly *spec.*, paint in watercolour or distemper. L16. 4 *v.t.* Portray or represent (esp. a person) in words. L16.

3 H. ROBBINS Rocco's face was limned in the dim glow from the match. J. STRACHEY The image of the loosened rose-spray clearly limned in the rain pool. 4 *Publishers Weekly* Virginia Woolf's sharp wit, which could limn Ottoline Morell perfectly.

limner /ˈlɪmnə/ *n.* ME. [Alt. of †*luminer*, f. LUMINE + -ER[2].] 1 *Hist.* An illuminator of manuscripts. ME. 2 A painter, *esp.* a portrait painter. Now *literary.* L16.

limnetic /lɪmˈnɛtɪk/ *a.* L19. [f. Gk *limnētēs* living in marshes, f. *limnē*: see LIMNO-, -IC.] Of, pertaining to, or living in the open part of a freshwater lake or pond, away from the margin or bottom; = PELAGIC 4.

limnic /ˈlɪmnɪk/ *a.* M20. [G *limnisch*, f. Gk *limnē*: see LIMNO-, -IC.] *Geol.* Formed or laid down in an inland body of standing fresh water such as a lake or a swamp.

limning /ˈlɪmɪŋ, ˈlɪmnɪŋ/ *n.* LME. [f. LIMN + -ING[1].] **1a** Painting. LME. **b** A painting, a portrait. L17. 2 The action or art of illuminating manuscripts etc. L15.

limno- /ˈlɪmnəʊ/ *comb. form.* L19. [f. Gk *limnē* pool, marshy lake + -O-.] Of, pertaining to, or occurring in fresh water, esp. fresh standing water.

limnograph *n.* an apparatus for automatically recording the variations of level in a lake L19. **limˈnometer** *n.* an apparatus for measuring the variations of level in a lake M19. **limnoplankton** *n.* plankton found in fresh water L19.

limnology /lɪmˈnɒlədʒi/ *n.* L19. [f. LIMNO- + -LOGY.] The physical, chemical, geological, and biological aspects of lakes and other bodies of fresh standing water or (more widely) all inland water; the branch of science that deals with these.

limnoˈlogical *a.* L19. **limnoˈlogically** *adv.* from the point of view of limnology E20. **limnologist** *n.* E20.

limnoria /lɪmˈnɔːrɪə/ *n.* M19. [mod.L f. Gk *Limnoreia* water-nymph.] A marine isopod crustacean of the genus *Limnoria*, which includes *L. lignorum*, the gribble.

limo /ˈlɪməʊ/ *n. colloq.* Pl. **-os.** M20. [Abbrev.] = LIMOUSINE.

Limoges /lɪˈməʊʒ/ *a.* M19. [See below.] Designating painted enamels, porcelain, etc., made in Limoges, a city in central France.

limon /limɔ̃/ *n.* L19. [Fr. f. L *limus* mud.] *Geol.* A fine sandy soil, probably of similar origin to loess, which is widespread in northern France and Belgium.

limonene /ˈlɪməniːn/ *n.* E20. [G *Limonen*, f. *Limone* lemon: see -ENE.] A colourless liquid terpene, $C_{10}H_{16}$, occurring in lemon, orange, and other essential oils and used in flavouring, as a solvent and wetting agent, etc.

limonite /ˈlʌɪmənʌɪt/ *n.* E19. [G *Limonit*, prob. f. Gk *leimōn* meadow, after the earlier G name *Wiesenerz* lit. 'meadow-ore': see -ITE[1].] *Min.* An amorphous secondary material now recognized as a mixture of hydrous ferric oxides and important as an iron ore.

limoˈnitic *a.* containing or resembling limonite L19.

limonium /lɪˈməʊnɪəm/ *n.* M16. [mod.L = L *limonion* f. Gk *leimōnion* neut. of *leimōnios*, f. *leimōn* meadow: see -IUM.] Orig., any wintergreen of the genus *Pyrola*, esp. *P. rotundifolia*. Now, any plant of the genus *Limonium* (family Plumbaginaceae); sea lavender.

limous /ˈlʌɪməs/ *a.* Now *rare.* LME. [f. L *limosus*, f. *limus* mud: see -OUS.] Muddy; slimy.

Limousin /ˈlɪmʊzã/ *n.* & *a.* M17. [See below.] **A** *n.* 1 A native or inhabitant of the former province of Limousin in central France or of the region round Limoges; the dialect of this region. M17. 2 (An animal of) a French breed of beef cattle. L20. **B** *adj.* Of or pertaining to Limousin. E18.

limousine /ˈlɪməziːn, lɪməˈziːn/ *n.* E20. [Fr., f. fem. of prec.; orig. a caped cloak worn in Limousin.] 1 A large luxurious motor car, often with a separate compartment for the driver. Orig., a car with a roof that projected over an outside driving seat. E20. 2 A passenger vehicle for carrying people over a fixed route to and from an airport. *N. Amer.* M20.

Comb.: **limousine liberal** *US* a wealthy liberal.

limp /lɪmp/ *n.*[1] M18. [Origin unkn.] *Mining.* An instrument for separating refuse from ore in the operation of jigging.

limp /lɪmp/ *n.*[2] E19. [f. LIMP *v.*] The action of limping; a limping gait; a propensity to limp.

Daily Telegraph The little girl has a limp in one leg and will undergo physiotherapy.

limp /lɪmp/ *a.* E18. [Prob. of dial. origin; perh. ult. rel. to LIMP *v.*, the basic sense being 'hanging loose'.] 1 Lacking firmness or stiffness, flaccid; flexible, pliant; (of a fabric) unstiffened. E18. 2 Designating or having a book cover that is not stiffened with board. M19. 3 Lacking will, firmness, strictness, nervous energy, etc. M19.

1 E. WAUGH The Emperor's colours hung limp in the sultry air. K. KESEY His breath explodes out of him, and he falls back limp against the wall. 3 E. WAUGH He talked five hours and left me limp. P. KURTH The failure of the tribunal.. to confront its experts with these limp, layman's objections.

Special collocations & comb.: **limp wrist** *US slang* a homosexual or effeminate man; **limp-wrist, limp-wristed** *adjs.* (*slang*) homosexual, effeminate; weak, feeble.

limply *adv.* M19. **limpness** *n.* M18.

limp /lɪmp/ *v.i.* LME. [Prob. back-form. f. LIMPHALT: cf. MHG *limpfen.*] †**1** Fall short *of.* Only in LME. 2 Walk lamely. L16. 3 Of verse: be metrically defective. M17. 4 Of a damaged ship, aircraft, etc.: proceed slowly or with difficulty. E20.

2 J. CONRAD The man limped down the ladder. J. FRAME Tom eased himself from his bed and limped from the room. *fig.*: G. GREENE How slowly time limps by in childhood. 4 J. BARTH A divided rig.. would leave.. hope of limping bravely to port.

limper *n.* M17. **limping** *a.* that limps; *Law* (of a relationship or status) legal or recognized in one country but not in another: L16. **limpingly** *adv.* L16. **limpingness** *n.* M18.

limpet /ˈlɪmpɪt/ *n.* [OE *lempedu* (cf. OHG *lampfrida*) f. med.L *lampreda*, *-rida* limpet: see LAMPREY.] 1 Any of various marine gastropod molluscs with a shallow conical shell and a broad muscular foot that sticks tightly to rocks; *esp.* (more fully *common limpet*) *Patella vulgata*. OE. **b** *fig.* A clinging person. E20. 2 In full *limpet bomb, mine*, etc. A type of explosive device attached magnetically to a ship's hull. M20.

†**limphalt** *a.* OE–M16. [f. Gmc base f. IE base also of Skt *lámbate* hangs down or loose, sinks + HALT *a.*] Lame, limping.

¶Prob. the source of LIMP *v.*

limpid /ˈlɪmpɪd/ *a.* LME. [L *limpidus*, prob. rel. to *lympha* LYMPH.] 1 (Esp. of liquids) free from turbidity or suspended matter; clear, transparent. LME. 2 *transf.* & *fig.* Free from obscurity, complication, or guile; pure. M17.

1 WILKIE COLLINS The eyes are of that soft, limpid, turquoise blue. D. H. LAWRENCE The morning was of a lovely limpid gold colour. E. WAUGH Two corpses.. rotated slowly.. in the limpid morning sunlight. 2 B. PYM The limpid notes of a recorder playing 'Brother James's Air'.

lim'pidity *n.* M17. **limpidly** *adv.* L19. **limpidness** *n.* M17.

limpish /'lɪmpɪʃ/ *a.* L19. [f. LIMP *a.* + -ISH[1].] Somewhat limp.

limpkin /'lɪm(p)kɪn/ *n.* L19. [f. LIMP *v.* + -KIN, w. ref. to the bird's limping gait.] A wading bird, *Aramus guarauna*, of S. America and south-eastern N. America, similar to but larger than a rail and living chiefly in marshes.

limpsy /'lɪm(p)si/ *a. dial.* & *US.* E19. [f. LIMP *a.* + -SY.] Limp.

limulus /'lɪmjʊləs/ *n.* Pl. **-li** /-lʌɪ, -liː/. M19. [mod.L f. L *limulus* somewhat oblique, f. *limus* oblique.] A horseshoe crab of the genus *Limulus*.

limuloid *a.* & *n.* (a crustacean) resembling a horseshoe crab M19.

limy /'lʌɪmi/ *a.* M16. [f. LIME *n.*[1] + -Y[1].] **1** Besmeared with birdlime. M16. **2** Of the nature of lime (calcium oxide), resembling lime. M17. **3** Consisting of or containing lime. L17.

lin /lɪn/ *v.* Long *obs.* exc. *Sc.* & *north.* Infl. **-nn-**. [OE *linnan* = OHG *bilinnan*, ON *linna*, Goth. *aflinnan*, f. Gmc, f. base also of LITHE *a.*] **†1** *v.i.* Cease (*to do*), leave off; desist (*from*); (of the wind) drop. OE–E18. **b** Fail, omit, *to do*. Only in E18. **2** *v.t.* Cease from, leave off, discontinue. ME.

linable /'lʌɪnəb(ə)l/ *a.* Also **lineable**. L17. [f. LINE *n.*[2] or *v.*[2] + -ABLE.] (Able to be) ranged in a straight line.

linac /'lɪnak/ *n.* M20. [f. *lin*ear *ac*celerator.] *Physics.* A linear (i.e. straight) particle accelerator.

linage /'lʌɪnɪdʒ/ *n.* Also **lineage**. L19. [f. LINE *n.*[2] + -AGE.] **1** Position (of figures) in line. L19. **2** The number of lines in printed or written matter. L19. **3** Payment according to the number of lines in printed or written matter. Also, the charge made (by a newspaper etc.) according to the number of lines occupied by an advertisement etc. L19.

linaloe /lɪ'naləʊ/ *n.* Also **linaloa** /lɪnə'ləʊə/. L19. [Mex. Sp. *lináloe* f. Sp. = LIGN-ALOES.] The aromatic wood of several Mexican trees of the genus *Bursera* (family Burseraceae), esp. *B. aleoxylon*.

linalool /lɪ'naləʊɒl/ *n.* L19. [f. prec. + -OL.] *Chem.* A fragrant liquid alcohol, $C_{10}H_{18}O$, found in various natural oils (including those of linaloe, rose, and orange) and used in perfumery.

'linalyl *n.* the radical $C_{10}H_{17}$· present in ethers and esters of linalool E20.

linamarin /lɪnə'marɪn/ *n.* L19. [f. L *linum* flax + *amarus* bitter + -IN[1].] *Chem.* A bitter, toxic, cyanogenic glucoside which occurs in flax, cassava, and other plants.

linaria /lʌɪ'nɛːrɪə/ *n.* L16. [mod.L (see below), f. L *linum* flax (w. ref. to the leaf-shape) + *-aria* -ARY[1].] Any of several plants of the genus *Linaria*, of the figwort family, with spurred flowers and linear leaves; *esp.* yellow toad-flax, *L. vulgaris*.

linarite /lɪ'nɑːrʌɪt, 'lɪnərʌɪt/ *n.* M19. [f. *Linares*, a town in southern Spain + -ITE[1].] *Min.* A monoclinic sulphate of lead and copper, $PbCu(SO_4)(OH)_2$, occurring as brilliant blue prisms.

linch /lɪn(t)ʃ/ *n.*[1] Long *obs.* exc. in comb. [OE *lynis* = WFris. *lins*, OS *lunisa* (Du. *luns*, *lens*), MHG *luns(e)*, G *Lünse* rel. to OHG *lun(a)* (G dial. *lunn*, *lon*): cf. OHG *luning* linchpin.] A linchpin.

Comb.: **linch-drawer** *dial.* a tool for drawing out linchpins; **linch-hoop** a ring on the spindle of a carriage-axle, held in place by the linchpin; LINCHPIN.

linch /lɪn(t)ʃ/ *n.*[2] *dial.* Also **lynch**. L16. [Repr. OE *hlinc*: see LINK *n.*[1]] A rising ground; a ridge; a ledge, esp. on the side of a chalk down; an unploughed strip serving as a boundary between fields.

linch /lɪn(t)ʃ/ *v.t.* L19. [f. LINCH *n.*[1]] Fasten (as) with a linchpin.

linchpin /'lɪn(t)ʃpɪn/ *n.* LME. [f. LINCH *n.*[1] + PIN *n.*] **1** A pin passed through an axle-end to keep a wheel in position. LME. **2** A person or thing vital to an enterprise, organization, etc. L20.

Lincoln /'lɪŋk(ə)n/ *n.* ME. [The county town of Lincolnshire, a county in eastern England.] **I** *attrib.* **1** Designating things originating in or associated with Lincoln. ME.

1 **†Lincoln farthing** a hearth-tax payable at Lincoln. **Lincoln green** a bright green cloth of a kind originally made at Lincoln. **Lincoln imp** a grotesque carving in Lincoln cathedral; an ornament etc. representing this. **Lincoln Longwool** (an animal of) a breed of sheep characterized by its large size and long fleece. **Lincoln Red** (an animal of) a breed of red shorthorn cattle producing both milk and beef. **Lincoln wool** wool from a Lincoln Longwool.

II *ellipt.* **2** (An animal of) a variety of sheep originally bred in Lincolnshire. Also, a Lincoln Longwool, a Lincoln Red. M19.

Lincolnesque /lɪŋk(ə)n'ɛsk/ *a.* E20. [f. *Lincoln* (see below) + -ESQUE.] Resembling or having the qualities of Abraham Lincoln (1809–65), sixteenth president of the US.

Lincolnian /lɪŋ'kəʊnɪən/ *a.* M19. [f. as prec. + -IAN.] = LINCOLNESQUE.

Lincolniana /lɪŋkənɪ'ɑːnə, lɪŋˌkəʊnɪ-/ *n.pl.* [-ANA] publications or other items concerning or associated with Abraham Lincoln E20.

Lincoln rocker /'lɪŋk(ə)n ˌrɒkə/ *n. phr. US.* M20. [f. Abraham *Lincoln* (see LINCOLNESQUE) + ROCKER.] A type of rocking-chair with a straight upholstered back and seat and open arms, popular in the mid 19th cent.

Lincolnshire /'lɪŋk(ə)nʃə/ *n.* E20. [A county in eastern England.] Used *attrib.* to designate things originating in or associated with Lincolnshire.

Lincolnshire Curly-Coat(ed) (an animal of) an extinct breed of pig having a light-coloured curly or woolly coat. **Lincolnshire Longwool** = LINCOLN *Longwool*. **Lincolnshire Red** = LINCOLN *Red*.

lincomycin /lɪŋkə(ʊ)'mʌɪsɪn/ *n.* M20. [f. mod.L *lincolnensis* (see below) + -MYCIN.] *Pharm.* An antibiotic produced by the bacterium *Streptomyces lincolnensis* and effective against Gram-positive bacteria, esp. staphylococci and streptococci.

Lincrusta /lɪŋ'krʌstə/ *n.* Also **l-**. L19. [f. L *linum* flax + *crusta* rind, bark, after *linoleum*.] (Proprietary name for) a wallpaper covered with embossed linoleum.

linclure /'lɪŋktʃə/ *n.* Long *rare.* E17. [f. as next + -URE, or f. a med.L formation in *-ura*.] = next.

linctus /'lɪŋktəs/ *n.* L17. [med.L (cl.L = licking, f. *lingere* to lick), after late L *electuarium* ELECTUARY.] A syrupy liquid medicine, now *esp.* a soothing cough mixture.

†lind *n.* Also **line**. OE–L18. [OE *lind(e)* corresp. to OS *lind(i)a* (Du. *linde*), OHG *linta* (G *Linde*), ON *lind*, prob. rel. to Gk *elatē* silver fir. See also LINN *n.*[2]] A lime tree; *gen.* a tree of any kind.

Lindabrides /lɪn'dabrɪdiːz/ *n. arch.* M17. [A lady in the 16th-cent. romance 'Mirror of Knighthood'.] A lady-love, a sweetheart, a mistress.

lindane /'lɪndeɪn/ *n.* M20. [f. Teunis van der *Linden* (b. 1884) Du. chemist + -ANE.] A toxic colourless crystalline compound, the gamma isomer of benzene hexachloride, $C_6H_6Cl_6$, used chiefly as an insecticide powder or spray.

¶A proprietary name for this substance is GAMMEXANE.

Linde /'lɪndə/ *n.* E20. [Carl P. G. R. von *Linde* (1842–1934), Ger. physicist.] Used *attrib.* to designate a process for liquefying gases (esp. atmospheric oxygen and nitrogen) by means of repeated cycles of compression, cooling, and expansion.

linden /'lɪndən/ *n.* L16. [Partly f. LINDEN *a.*, partly (in comb. *linden tree*) f. Du. *lindeboom*, †*lindenboom*, G *Lindenbaum*, f. *linde* (see LIND) + *boom*, *Baum* tree.] A lime tree. Also *linden tree*.

†linden *a.* OE–ME. [f. LIND + -EN[4].] Made of the wood of the lime tree.

lindorm *n.* var. of LINDWORM.

lindworm /'lɪndwəːm/ *n.* Also **lindorm** /'lɪndɔːm/. E19. [Da. & Sw. *lindorm* a kind of mythical serpent, f. Sw. *lind* flexible + *orm* snake, serpent (cf. WORM *n.*). Cf. LINGWORM.] A monstrous and evil serpent or dragon of Scandinavian mythology.

lindy /'lɪndi/ *n.* Also **L-**. M20. [Nickname of C. A. *Lindbergh* (1902–74), the American pilot who in 1927 was the first to make a solo non-stop transatlantic flight: see -Y[6].] In full *Lindy Hop*. A dance originating as a form of the jitterbug among Blacks in Harlem, New York.

line /lʌɪn/ *n.*[1] Now chiefly *dial.* [OE *līn* = OS, OHG *līn* (Du. *lijn-*, G *Lein*), ON *lín*, Goth. *lein*, f. Gmc f. or corresp. to L *linum* rel. to Gk *linon*.] **1** The fibre of the flax-plant. Now only, flax fibre of a fine and long staple, which has been separated by the hackle from the tow; occas., a similar fibre of other plants. OE. **2** Flax spun or woven; linen thread or cloth. OE. **3** The flax-plant. LME. **†4** The seed of flax; linseed. M–L16.

line /lʌɪn/ *n.*[2] [OE *līne* = MDu. *līne* (Du. *lijn*), OHG *līna* (G *Leine* cord), ON *lína*, prob. f. Gmc f. L *linea*; partly f. (O)Fr. *ligne* f. Proto-Romance var. of L *linea*, *linia* orig. use as n. (sc. *fibra* FIBRE) of fem. of *lineus* pertaining to flax, f. *linum* flax: see prec.] **I 1** A (piece of) rope, cord, or wire, esp. as serving a specified purpose. OE. **b** A fishing-line. ME. **†c** In *pl.* Strings or cords for snaring birds. ME–M18. **d** A cord used for measuring, or for levelling or straightening. ME. **e** A clothes-line. M18. **f** In *pl.* Reins. *dial.* & *US.* E19. **g** A telegraph or telephone wire or cable; a connection by means of this; an individual telephone number or extension. Also, any wire or cable serving as a conductor of electric current. M19. **†2** Rule, canon, precept; standard of life or practice. *rare.* ME–E17. **3** In *pl.* One's appointed lot in life (orig. w. ref. to *Ps.* 16:6). E17. **†4** A cord in the body. *rare.* E17–L18. **5** A spider's thread. *poet.* M18.

1 I. SHAW In the bow, with the neat coiled spirals of lines. *clew-line*, *clothes-line*, *drag-line*, *fishing-line*, *jerk-line*, *plumb-line*, *shroud line*, *spurling line*, etc. **b** L. HELLMAN A line on a fishing reel that tangled and couldn't be untangled. *cod-line*, *dandy-line*, *fly-line*, *paternoster line*, etc. **d** W. C. BRYANT Trees then he felled . . and carefully He smoothed their sides, and wrought them by a line. **e** R. ADAMS Letting her drop, limp as an old garment fallen from a line. **f** *Budget* (*Ohio*) When the horses took off. . . He jumped on the wagon and grabbed the lines. **g** J. MASTERS Macaulay was on the line. A. BRINK The call came through. A very bad line, her voice . . almost unrecognisable. *chatline*, *helpline*, etc. **2** AV *Ps.* 19:4 Their line is gone out through all the earth, and their words to the end of the world. **3** J. G. WHITTIER My brother's lines have indeed fallen unto him in a pleasant place. **5** W. COWPER Spun as fine As bloated spiders draw the flimsy line.

II 6 A row of characters either written, printed, or displayed on a VDU; any of the rows of characters in a piece of text; in *pl.*, the contents or sense of what is written, printed, or displayed. OE. **b** A unit of poetry written etc. as continuous text, usu. on one line; a verse; in *pl.*, verses, poetry. Also (in *pl.*), a specified amount of text to be written out as a school punishment. M16. **c** *Printing.* A row of letterforms and spacing material produced by a composition system. M17. **d** A few words in writing; *esp.* a short letter. M17. **e** In *pl.* = MARRIAGE *lines*. Also (*dial.*), a certificate of church membership etc. E19. **f** In *pl.* The words of an actor's part. L19. **7** A row of people or things; *N. Amer.* a queue. M16. **b** In certain team games as American football, ice hockey, etc.: a row of players. L19. **c** A row of machines or workstations progressively assembling or performing a succession of operations on a product during manufacture or processing. E20. **d** In a business etc. organization, the chain of command or responsibility; the employees concerned directly with production as opp. to the provision of advisory and ancillary services. E20. **8** *Mil.* A trench, a rampart; in *pl.* (also *collect. sing.*), a connected series of fieldworks, defences, etc. Also, a row of huts or tents in a camp. M17. **b** *Hist.* In the war of 1914–18, the trenches collectively; the front line. Freq. in *up the line* below. E20. **9a** *Naut.* A body of ships in formation one after the other. E18. **b** *Mil.* A wide-fronted shallow formation of troops or armoured vehicles etc. in adjacent columns. E19. **10** A regular succession of buses, ships, aircraft, etc., plying between certain places; a company conducting a business providing this. Orig. *US.* L18.

6 C. WOLFE We carved not a line, and we raised not a stone. T. HARDY Not a line of her writing have I, Not a thread of her hair. S. PLATH My hand made big, jerky letters . . and the lines sloped down the page. b C. S. LEWIS If my lines rhymed and scanned and got on with the story I asked no more. E. BLISHEN One could cane them; give them lines. d D. L. SAYERS To write a few lines to the Dowager Duchess. e R. KIPLING I want . . The name, an' lines to show, An' not to be an 'ore. f M. AMIS I felt the uneasiness of a good actor with bad lines. 7 W. IRVING A line of trading posts from the Mississippi and the Missouri across the Rocky mountains. J. REED There was a long line of people waiting to be let in. *breadline* etc. c *assembly line, production line.* 8 SLOAN WILSON A hundred men dropped behind the German lines to destroy a bridge. b S. SASSOON Up in the line one somehow lost touch with such humanities. 9a T. CAMPBELL While the sign of battle flew On the lofty British line. b LYTTON Suddenly the lines of the Moors gave way. 10 *Scotsman* The first vessel of the new direct line to Jamaica from England. A. GRAHAM-YOOLL The Houlder Brothers Shipping line . . had been prominent in the meat trade for almost one century.

III 11 A long narrow stroke or mark drawn or engraved on a surface or shown on a visual display unit. ME. **b** A mark limiting an area of play on a court or pitch for a game; *spec.* a mark that must be crossed in order to score; in racing, a mark on the track (actual or imaginary) at the winning-post. M16. **c** *Mus.* Each of (usu. five) horizontal parallel equidistant strokes forming a stave in notation. E17. **d** *Fine Art.* Any of the lines employed in a picture; chiefly *collect.* or in *gen.* sense, character of draughtsmanship, method of rendering form. E17. **e** *Dance & Sport.* The total effect of the disposition of the limbs, body, and head of a dancer, gymnast, skater, fencer, etc., in movement or repose. E20. **f** *Mus.* Instrumental or vocal melody; a structured sequence of notes or tones. E20. **g** Each of the narrow horizontal strips forming a television picture. E20. **12a** A thing resembling a drawn stroke or mark, esp. in a natural object, as a thin band of colour; a suture, a ridge. ME. **b** A furrow or seam in the face or hands; *Palmistry* a mark on the palm of the hand supposed to indicate one's fate, temperament, or abilities. M16. **c** A narrow peak or trough of intensity in a spectrum, appearing as a fine straight black or bright band transverse to the length of the spectrum (cf. FRAUNHOFER(*'s*) *lines*). Also, a component of emitted radiation at a discrete wavelength or narrow range of wavelengths, represented by such a band. M19. **13** A circle of the terrestrial or celestial sphere. Now *rare.* LME. **14a** *Math.* A continuous extent of length without thickness, freq. repr. by a drawn line (sense 11); the track of a moving point. LME. **b** *Physics, Geogr.*, etc. A curve connecting all points having a common property. Usu. w. specifying wd. E19. **15** A straight line (sense 14) imagined as drawn between two points, or between some point and the observer; *spec.* the (usu. imaginary) continuous horizontal mark through the feet of most letters. LME. **16** A contour, an outline; lineament. LME. **b** *Fashion.* The outline or dominant features of composition of a dress or suit. E20. **17** A direction as indicated by marks on a surface, a row of people or things, etc. Freq. in *come, bring into line* below. L15. **b** *Mil.* An arrangement of companies side by side. L18. **c** A particular policy or set of policies which a politician may maintain or expect others to follow; = *party line* s.v. PARTY *n.* Orig. *US.* L19. **d** A marked tendency, a policy or trend; *colloq.* a glib or superficially attractive mode of address or behaviour, plausible talk. E20. **e** The point spread for a number of football games on which bets may be laid. *US colloq.* M20. **†18** Degree, rank, station. E16–L18. **19** A limit, a boundary. L16. **b** *Bridge.* A line across a score-card. Chiefly in *above, below, the line* below. E20. **c** The boundary between a credit and a debit in an account. M20. **20** One twelfth of an inch. M17. **21** In *pl.* **a** The outlines, plan, or draft of a building etc.; *spec.* in *Shipbuilding*, the outlines of a vessel as shown in its horizontal, vertical, and oblique sections. L17. **b** *fig.* Plan of action, procedure, etc. M18.

11 W. M. CRAIG An expression of forms only by simple lines. B. MALAMUD A heavy line was drawn on which to sign his name. b *goal-line, halfway line, penalty line, service line, 22 metre line*, etc. f R. H. MYERS His music has line . . and the enormous merit of condensation. *Melody Maker* I consider jazz to be a lot of horns and one of those top speed bass lines. 12a J. TYNDALL Along the faces of the sections the lines of stratification were clearly shown. b I. ZANGWILL There were lines of premature age on the handsome face. A. FRASER Already the characteristic deep lines . . had formed from nostril to chin. 13 MILTON Under the Ethiop Line By Nilus head. POPE Where spices smoke beneath the burning Line. 16 SHELLEY The dim long line before Of a grey and distant shore. b *Times* The curved line was seen in all the long coats. *Vogue* Overall, a clear narrowing of the silhouette, . . presaging an even sparer line for autumn. *A-line, empire-line*, etc. 17 E. HOYLE When your Adversary has a Bishop and one Pawn on the Rook's Line. G. A. LAWRENCE Get the horses in line, to start them for the farmer's Cup. b TENNYSON And he call'd 'Left wheel into line!' c G. F. KENNAN He had to follow . . the line his government had laid down for him. H. MACMILLAN His intervention followed the line of an article which had already appeared in the Daily Express. d A. L. ROWSE He has a fine line in Churchillian invective. *Globe & Mail* (*Toronto*) Try that line on your spouse. 'Dear, we're not going to save money.' 18 G. A. BELLAMY She had received a more liberal education than is usually bestowed upon English women in the middle line of life. 19 C. ISHERWOOD For her, the line between reality and hallucination is getting very thin. *Maginot Line, Mason-Dixon line, Plimsoll line, Wallace's line*, etc. 21 G. SEMPLE The principal Lines of my Design of a Bridge suitable to that Place. C. READE Her extravagant poop that caught the wind, and her lines like a cocked hat reversed. b L. STRACHEY He laid down the lines for a radical reform in the . . administration of the army.

IV 22 A lineage, a stock, a race. ME. **b** A breed or variety of animal or plant universally characterized by some feature whose strength is the criterion for continued selection by breeders. Cf. *line-bred, line-breeding* below. E19. **23** A continuous series of people in chronological succession, *esp.* several generations of a family. Freq. w. specifying wd. ME.

22 H. BELLOC His line survives to-day. J. CLAVELL Our Queen's the third of the Tudor line. 23 W. COWPER In the line Of his descending progeny. J. T. STORY The Gladstones originally came from a long line of East Anglian politicians. *direct line, female line, male line.*

V 24 A course of action, procedure, life, thought, or conduct. ME. **25** A track, a course, a direction; a route. LME. **b** A single track of a railway (freq. in *the up line, the down line*). Also, a branch or route of a railway or the whole system of railways under one management. E19. **c** A settlement road, a bush road. Chiefly *Canad.* & *NZ.* E19. **d** The straight or direct course in the hunting field or round a racetrack (also *racing-line*). M19. **e** A row of traps or of poison bait. M19. **f** A pipe or tube (of great or indefinite length in relation to its thickness). M19. **g** In *Golf*, the direction of the hole from the position of a player's ball. In *Cricket*, the direction of flight of the ball from the bowler's hand. L19. **†26** In *pl.* Goings on, caprices or fits of temper. *rare* (Shakes.). L16–E17. **27** A department of activity; a kind or branch of business or occupation. M17. **28** *Comm.* (An order for, the stock in hand of) a particular design or class of goods. M19. **b** The amount which one underwriter (or one company) accepts as his or her share of the total value of the subject matter covered by insurance. L19. **c** A dose of a powdered narcotic or hallucinatory drug, as cocaine, heroin, etc., laid out in a line for use. *slang.* L20.

24 DISRAELI I should then have inherited some family line of conduct, both moral, and political. G. C. LEWIS The Protectionists . . have taken no line in the matter. 25 W. COWPER Though . . the shaft . . err but little from the intended line. I. ZANGWILL They ran on parallel lines that never met. b J. MASTERS An engine whistling . . a mile up the line. *belt line, branch line, main line, shunt line*, etc. 27 DICKENS Mr Augustus Cooper was in the oil and colour line. B. PYM Memorial services were not much in Edwin's line. 28 S. UNWIN They are mostly content with quick-selling lines such as Annuals. H. FAST Fritz Alcheck . . carried a line of men's haberdashery. c *Observer* Everybody I know takes heroin. . . Every party . . has smack available, lines and lines of it.

Phrases: (A selection of cross-refs. only is included.) **above the line** (*a*) *Bridge* (of points) scored for game, honours, overtricks, rubber, or for the failure of opponents to fulfil their contract; (*b*) *Econ.* (spent etc.) on items of current expenditure; *Advertising* in the mass media; *Cinemat.* (incurred etc.) before filming begins. **all along the line, all (the way) down the line** at every point. **below the line** (*a*) *Bridge* (of points) scored for tricks bid and won, and counting towards the game; (*b*) *Econ.* (spent etc.) on items of capital expenditure; *Advertising* on means of promotion other than the mass media; *Cinemat.* (incurred etc.) during and after filming. *bottom line*: see BOTTOM *a.* **bring into line** cause to agree, conform, or cooperate. **by rule and line** with precision. **come into line** agree, conform, cooperate. *contour line*: see CONTOUR *n.* 2. **do a line with** *Austral.* & *NZ colloq.* (try to) enter into an amorous relationship with. DOTTED *line.* **draw the line at** refuse to go as far as or beyond. *equinoctial line*: see EQUINOCTIAL *a.* 1. FIRST *line. front line*: see FRONT *n.* & *a.* **get a line on** acquire information about (a thing), come to know. **get one's** or **the lines crossed** have a misunderstanding, become confused. **give a person line enough** let a person continue unhindered for a time in order to secure or detect him or her later. **hard lines** (usu. *colloq.*) bad luck, hardship. *heaving line*: see HEAVE *v. hold the line*: see HOLD *v. hook, line, and sinker*: see HOOK *n. hot line*: see HOT *a.* **in line** so as to form a straight line (*with*); *in line with*, in accordance with. **in one's line** suited to one's capacity, taste, etc. *lateral line*: see LATERAL *a.* etc. **lay** (or **put**) **it on the line** (*a*) hand over money; (*b*) state (something) clearly, plainly, or categorically. **lay,** (or **put**) **on the line** place (one's career etc.) at risk. **line abreast** *Naut.* a number of parallel ships ranged on a line crossing the keels at right angles. **line ahead** *Naut.* a number of ships following one another in a line. **line astern** (in) an aircraft formation in which a number of planes follow one another in a line. **line by line, line for line** from beginning to end, seriatim. *line of battle*: see BATTLE *n.* **line of beauty** the curve (resembling a slender elongated S) held by Hogarth to be a necessary element in all beauty of form. **line of business** *spec.* in the 18th- and 19th-cent. theatre, the kind of part for which an actor or actress was specifically engaged. *line of country* : see COUNTRY *n.* **line of credit** a loan by one country to another, to be utilized by the second for buying goods from the first; credit extended by a bank to a commercial concern to a certain amount; the amount so extended. *line of defence*: see DEFENCE *n.* 3. **line of fire** the expected path of gunfire, a missile, etc. *line of flotation*: see FLOTATION 1. **line of force** *Physics* a curve whose direction at each point is that of the electric etc. force there. **line of fortune** = *line of life* (b) below. *line of least* RESISTANCE. **line of life** (*a*) *Class. Mythol.* the thread spun and cut by the Fates, determining the length of a person's life (cf. LIFELINE 2); (*b*) = LIFELINE 3. *line of march*: see MARCH *n.*[3] *line of metal*: see METAL *n.* 7. *line of sight*: see SIGHT *n. line of vision*: see VISION *n. long line*: see LONG *a.*[1] *loxodromic line*: see LOXODROMIC *a. meridian line*: see MERIDIAN *a.* 3. **not one's line** not one's vocation or calling, not among one's pursuits or interests. **on the line** (*a*) at risk; (*b*) (of a picture) exhibited with its centre about level with the spectator's eye. *open line*: see OPEN *a.* **out of line** not in alignment with, discordant; *step, get*, etc., *out of line*, behave in an unconventional, discordant, or inappropriate manner. **out of one's line** unsuited to one's capacity, taste, etc. *outside line*: see OUTSIDE *a.* **pay on the line** pay promptly. *pure line*: see PURE *a. put (it) on the line*: see *lay it on the line* above. **read between the lines** discover a meaning or purpose in a piece of writing etc. not obvious or explicitly expressed. *red line*: see RED *a.* **ride the line** *US* make the circuit of the boundary of a cattle-drift in order to drive in stray cattle. *right line*: see RIGHT *a. second line*: see SECOND *a.* **ship of the line** a line-of-battle ship.

shoot a line *colloq.* put on an act, talk pretentiously, boast. *soft line*: see SOFT *a.* **somewhere along the line** at some point (in time). **stand in line** *N. Amer.* form a queue. **the end of the line** (*a*) = *the end of the road* s.v. END *n.*; (*b*) the last goods in stock of a particular design or class. **the line** (*a*) the equinoctial line; *spec.* (**L-**) *the* Equator; (*b*) *US* the Mason–Dixon line; (*c*) in the British army, the regular and numbered regiments as distinguished from the Guards and the auxiliary forces; in the US army, the regular fighting force of all arms; (*d*) *Canad.* the US-Canadian border. *thin blue line*: see THIN *a.* *toe the line*: see TOE *v.* 2. **up the line** *Mil.* to the battle-front. *visual line*: see VISUAL *a.* *wet one's line*: see WET *v.* *white line*: see WHITE *a.* *yellow line*: see YELLOW *a.* YRAST *line*. *Z line*: see Z, Z 6.

Comb.: **line angle** *Dentistry* the angle at the junction of two surfaces of a tooth or cavity; **line-at-a-time printer** = *line printer* below; **linebacker** *Amer. Football* a player just behind the defensive line (*middle linebacker*: see MIDDLE *a.*); **linebacking** *Amer. Football* playing as a linebacker; **line blanking** *Television* the suppression of signals that would contribute to the picture during fly-back of the scanning spot between the transmission of successive lines; **line block** a block bearing a design in relief from which an illustration made up of lines without variations in tone may be printed; an illustration printed in this way; **line-boat** a boat used for line-fishing; **line-book** (*a*) *Printing* (*obs.* exc. *Hist.*) a book in which compositors kept account of the lines of set type credited and debited to them; (*b*) *RAF slang* a record of boasts; **line-bred** *a.* produced by line-breeding; **line-breeding** selective breeding of animals for some desired feature by mating within a related line; **line-camp** *N. Amer.* a camp, esp. a cabin, for ranch hands in an outlying part of a large ranch; **line-casting** *a.* (of a composing-machine) that casts type a line at a time; **line-drawing** a drawing done with a pen or pencil, a drawing in which images are produced from variations of lines; **line-drawn** *a.* made by line-drawing; **line-drive** *Baseball* a ball driven straight and low above the ground; **line drop** *Electr. Engin.* the voltage drop between two points on a transmission line; **line editor** *Computing* a program that enables the editing of one line at a time on a VDU display; **line-ending** (*a*) = *line-filling* below; (*b*) the end of a line of poetry; **line-engraved** *a.* made by line engraving; **line-engraver** a practitioner of line engraving; **line engraving** the art of engraving, by lines incised on the plate, as distinguished from etching and mezzotint; an engraving executed in this manner; **linefeed** the action of advancing of paper in a printing machine by the space of one line; (a character or code causing) an analogous movement of text on a VDU screen; **line-fence** *N. Amer.* a boundary fence between two farms or ranches; **line-filling** a flourish or ornament in the blank space at the end of a line of manuscript; **line finder** *Teleph.* a selector which searches for the calling subscriber's line when he or she lifts the receiver so that the line can be connected to a group of selectors available to any caller; **line-finishing** = *line-filling* above; **line-firing** *Mil.* firing by a body of men in line; **line-fisherman** a person who practises line-fishing; **line-fishing** fishing with a line as opp. to a net; fishing with a long line with many baited hooks attached at intervals; **line frequency** *Television* the number of scanning lines produced per second; **line gale** *US* = *line-storm* below; **line gauge** *Printing* a ruler showing the size of a type or types; **line graph**: in which the values of the variables are represented by a (continuous) line (cf. *bar chart* s.v. BAR *n.*[1]); **line haul** *US slang* a scheduled truck route or movement of freight; **line-integral** *Math.* the integral, taken along a line, of any differential that has a continuously varying value along that line; **line-integration** the operation of finding a line-integral; **line judge** a linesman in a tennis match; **line loss** *Electr. Engin.* loss of electrical energy along a transmission line; **line manager** a manager to whom an employee is directly responsible; **line officer** an officer holding command in a line regiment; **line pin** any of the pins used to fasten a bricklayer's line; **line pipe** pipe specially manufactured for use in pipelines; **line printer** a machine that prints output from a computer a line at a time; **line regiment** a regular and numbered regiment in the British army, a regiment of the line; **line-ride** *v.i.* (*US*) perform the action of line-riding; **line-rider** *US* a person engaged in line-riding; **line-riding** *US* the action of riding the line (see *ride the line* above); **line scan** (a device or technique using or involving) the motion of a scanning beam or spot along a line, or over an object or scene line by line; **line-sequential** *a.* designating a system of colour television in which each line of the picture is in one of the three primary colours, the colour changing for each successive line; **line shaft, line shafting** a shaft, shafting, of relatively great length from which a number of separate machines are driven by countershafts or endless belts; **line-side** *a.* adjacent to a railway line; **line-soldier** a soldier of a line regiment, a linesman; **line space** the space between the rows of characters in text; a space equivalent to a line of text; *line-space lever, mechanism*, etc., a device that turns the platen of a typewriter to a new line of writing; **line-spacing** *n.* & *a.* (*a*) *n.* the space between successive lines of text; (*b*) *adj.* designating or pertaining to the device that moves the platen to a new line; **line spectrum** a spectrum consisting of separate isolated lines; an emission (of light, sound, or other radiation) composed of a number of discrete frequencies or energies; **line-squall** a squall, consisting of a violent straight blast of cold air with snow or rain, occurring along a cold front; **line standard** (*a*) a standard of length in the form of a bar marked with two lines, the distance between which (under specified conditions) is the standard length; (*b*) the number of lines constituting a complete television picture; **line-storm** *US* an equinoctial storm; **line-synchronizing** *a.* designating a pulse transmitted in a television signal which causes the scanning process in the receiver to remain in synchrony with that at the transmitter; **line-width** *Physics* the width of a spectral line as measured by the difference in wavelength, wave number, or frequency between its two limits; **line-wire** *Telegr.* the wire which connects the stations of a telegraph-line; **line-work** (*a*) drawing or designing executed with the pen or pencil (as opp. to wash etc.); (*b*) copy or reproduction consisting of solid elements as distinct from halftone; (*c*) work as a lineman.

†line *n.*[3] var. of LIND.

line /lʌɪn/ *v.*[1]*t.* LME. [f. LINE *n.*[1], w. ref. to the use of linen as a lining material. Cf. med.L *lineare, liniare.*] **1** Cover the inside surface of (a garment, box, etc.) with a layer of usu. different material; cover (a garment, box, etc.) on the inside; cover with an (adhesive) inside layer. LME. **b** *Cookery.* Cover the inside of (a dish, tin, etc.) *with* pastry etc. prior to baking. E19. **2** Fill the cavity of (one's purse, stomach, etc.), esp. plentifully; cram, stuff. E16. **†3** Strengthen by placing something alongside; reinforce, fortify. L16–M18. **4** Cover the outside of; overlay, drape, pad; *Naut.* add a layer of wood to. Now *rare* or *obs.* L16. **5** Serve or be used as a lining for. E18. **6a** *Bookbinding.* Glue on the back of (a book) a paper covering continuous with the lining of the back of the cover. L19. **b** *Cabinet-making.* Foll. by *up*: put a moulding round (the top of a piece of furniture). L19.

1 S. BELLOW His coat, once lined with fox, turned dry and bald. *fig.*: W. COWPER And poplar that with silver lines his leaf. **b** *Evening Post (Nottingham)* Line a flan dish with short crust pastry and bake blind. **2** J. G. WHITTIER No bridegroom's hand be mine to hold That is not lined with yellow gold. **line one's pocket** or **purse** make money esp. by corrupt means. **3** SHAKES. *Hen. V* To line and new repair our towns of war. **4** C. MARSHALL If the bed gets over cool, line it, or cover round with straw. **5** M. BRADBURY Howard's study is lined with bookshelves.

line /lʌɪn/ *v.*[2] LME. [f. LINE *n.*[2]] **1** *v.t.* Tie with a line, string, or cord. *rare.* LME. **2** *v.t.* Measure or test with a line, cut to a line. LME. **3** *v.t.* Trace *out* the outlines of (something to be constructed) (*lit.* & *fig.*); trace (as) with a line or lines; delineate, sketch; put *in* with a hard pencil the permanent lines of (a freehand drawing). LME. **4** *v.t.* Mark in, off, out, with a line or lines; impress lines on; cover with lines. M16. **5** *v.t.* **a** Post troops etc. along (a hedge, road, etc.); (of troops) form an open or close line along (a pass etc.); (of persons or things) stand at fairly short intervals along (a street, wall, etc.). L16. **b** Foll. by *out*: transplant (seedling trees) from beds into lines in a nursery for further growth. M20. **6a** *v.t.* Draw (persons or things) *up* or up in line (*with*); *US* assign (a person) *to* certain work; aim (a weapon) in a direct line *on* an object. Foll. by *up*: arrange, produce, or make ready, esp. *for* a particular person or purpose. L18. **b** *v.i.* Form a line with others; fall into line; spread *out* in line. Foll. by *up*: be arranged in a line or lines; measure up (*to*). L18. **c** *v.t.* & *i. Baseball.* Hit (a ball) straight and low above the ground; play (a shot) as a line-drive. Freq. foll. by *out.* L19. **7** *v.t.* Follow the line of flight of (bees). *US.* E19. **8** *v.t.* & *i.* **a** Catch (fish) with a hook and line. *US. rare.* M19. **b** Guide or control (a boat or canoe) from the bank or shore of a stretch of inland water by means of a rope or ropes. *N. Amer.* E20. **9** *v.t.* Read out (a metrical psalm, a hymn) line by line for a congregation to sing. Also foll. by *out.* M19.

3 SHAKES. *A.Y.L.* All the pictures fairest lin'd Are but black to Rosalinde. A. YARRANTON Here is a way plainly lined out to cheat the Rats and Mice. **4** DICKENS This entry was afterwards lined through. *Expositor* The pale wronged face, lined with melancholy resignation. **5a** GIBBON The ramparts were lined with trembling spectators. G. ORWELL The trees lined the road in close, dusty ranks. **6a** A. ALVAREZ The same bottles of hair lotion . . were lined above the basin in his father's dressing-room. K. AMIS You've got some scheme lined up for visiting places of . . historical interest. P. BARKER The women were lined up facing each other. **b** A. TROLLOPE She struggled to line up to the spirit of her promises and she succeeded. R. C. HUTCHINSON We all lined up outside the office to get our pay. **c** *Globe & Mail (Toronto)* Frank White lined a drive to centre field.

Comb.: **line-up** a line of people for inspection; an arrangement of people in a team, nations in an alliance, etc.; the personnel or configuration of a band etc.

line /lʌɪn/ *v.*[3]*t.* LME. [(O)Fr. *ligner, aligner* LINE *v.*[2], but sense-development obscure.] Of a dog, wolf, etc.: copulate with, cover, (a bitch).

linea /ˈlɪnɪə/ *n.* Pl. ***-eae*** /-ɪiː/. E17. [L = LINE *n.*[2]] *Anat.* With mod.L specifying wd: any of various (apparent) lines or linear structures in or on the body.

linea alba /ˈalbə/ [white] a tendinous line running from the breastbone to the pubis, where the flat abdominal muscles are attached.

lineable *a.* var. of LINABLE.

lineae *n.* pl. of LINEA.

lineage /ˈlɪnɪɪdʒ/ *n.*[1] ME. [(O)Fr. *lignage*, †*linage*, f. Proto-Romance, f. L LINEA: see -AGE.] **1** Lineal descent from an ancestor; ancestry, pedigree. ME. **2†a** The people through whom one's lineal descent is traced; one's ancestors collectively. ME–M16. **b** The descendants of a specified ancestor collectively. ME. **c** A family or people viewed with reference to its descent; a tribe, a clan; *spec.* in *Anthropol.*, a line of descent from a single ancestor, a social group tracing its descent from a single ancestor. LME. **3** *Biol.* A sequence of species each of which is considered to have evolved from its predecessor. M20.

1 TOLKIEN Aragorn is descended in direct lineage . . from Isildur Elendil's son himself. *transf.*: R. P. GRAVES His high lineage was that of the great classical scholars who had preceded him. **2b** H. COX The dignity of the peerage . . was confined to the lineage of the person ennobled. **c** R. FIRTH The Tikopia lineages are patrilineal.

lineage *n.*[2] var. of LINAGE.

lineal /ˈlɪnɪəl/ *a.* & *n.* LME. [(O)Fr. *linéal* f. late L *linealis*, f. L LINEA: see -AL[1].] **A** *adj.* **1** Of or pertaining to a line or lines; consisting of lines; (of writing) arranged in regular lines. LME. **b** Of a measure: relating to a single dimension of space; linear. L17. **2a** Of descent, ancestry, etc.: that is in the direct line (opp. *collateral*). LME. **b** Pertaining to or transmitted by the direct line of descent. L15. **c** Of a person: lineally descended (*from, to*, †*of*). *rare.* L16.

1 W. ROBERTS This way of writing may be as swift, lineal, and legible, as the operations of daylight. T. HOLCROFT They were not . . ignorant of lineal perspective. **b** R. RAYMOND The claim is 1,000 feet lineal measurement in length. **2a** J. LOCKE The Prime and Ancient Right of Lineal Succession to any thing. T. HARDY You are the lineal representative of the ancient and knightly family of the d'Urbervilles. S. BECKETT Seven male relations, lineal and collateral.

B *n.* **†1** Genealogy, pedigree. Only in LME. **2** A person who is related in the direct line. Usu. in *pl. rare.* M18.

line'ality *n.* the quality of being lineal; *esp.* uniformity of direction of a way of writing: E19.

lineally /ˈlɪnɪəli/ *adv.* LME. [f. prec. + -LY[2].] **1** In the direct line of descent; by lineal descent. LME. **2** In a (direct) line. Now *rare.* LME. **3** Orig., by means of lines; graphically. Later, with regard to the lines or outline of a thing; line for line. E17.

lineament /ˈlɪnɪəm(ə)nt/ *n.* LME. [L *lineamentum*, f. *lineare* make straight, (in med.L) delineate, f. LINEA: see -MENT.] **1** †**a** A part of the body, considered with respect to its contour or outline, a distinctive physical feature. LME–M18. **b** *fig.* In *pl.* Distinctive features or characteristics. Now chiefly as passing into sense 2. M17. **2** A part of the face viewed with respect to its outline; a facial feature. Usu. in *pl.* E16. †**3** A line; a delineation, a diagram, an outline, a sketch. L16–E19. **b** A minute portion, a trace; in *pl.*, elements, rudiments. L17–E19.

1a SWIFT What lineaments divine we trace Through all his figure, mien, and face! b LD MACAULAY Some lineaments of the character of the man were early discerned in the child. 2 F. O'CONNOR He made out the lineaments of the face—a mouth, . . a straight nose. 3 D. HUME The broken lineaments of the piece . . are carefully studied. b J. PINKERTON The paste . . encloses some lineaments of black mica.

†**lineamental** *a.* of the nature of a sketch or imperfect outline; pertaining to lineaments: E17–L18.

linear /ˈlɪnɪə/ *a.* M17. [L *linearis*, f. as LINEA + -AR[1].] **1** Of or pertaining to a line or lines. M17. **2** Resembling a line; very narrow in proportion to its length, and of uniform breadth; *Bot.* (of a leaf) long and narrow. M17. **3** Arranged or measured along a (straight) line; extended in a line or in length; *spec.* in *Math.* & *Physics*, involving measurement in one dimension only; able to be represented by a straight line on a graph (in Cartesian coordinates); involving or exhibiting directly proportional change in two related quantities. E18. **b** Progressing in a single direction by regular steps or stages, sequential. M20. **4** Consisting of lines; involving the use of lines; in lines; (of depiction) using clear outlines, expressed in lines rather than masses. M19. **b** *Mus.* = HORIZONTAL *a.* 4. M20.

1 *Pall Mall Gazette* That linear hardness which never appears in nature. 3 J. MCPHEE It is a linear community: cabins spaced along the river. b P. MATTHIESSEN The Australian aborigines distinguish between linear time and a 'Great Time' of dreams . . in which all is present in this moment. 4 *Crafts* Certain linear kinds of image . . are . . not suitable for tapestry.

Special collocations: **Linear A** the earlier and undeciphered form of two forms of Bronze Age writing found in Crete and parts of Greece and recording a form of Mycenean Greek (opp. *Linear B* below). **linear accelerator** a particle accelerator in which the particles travel in straight lines rather than in closed loops. **linear algebra** *Math.* a finite-dimensional vector space, with multiplication defined and distributive over addition, in which $(\lambda \mathbf{a})\mathbf{b} = \lambda(\mathbf{ab}) = \mathbf{a}(\lambda \mathbf{b})$ for any scalar λ of the associated field and any vectors **a** and **b**; the branch of algebra that deals with the properties of these entities. **Linear B** the later of two forms of Bronze Age writing found in Crete and parts of Greece and recording a form of Mycenean Greek (opp. *Linear A* above). **linear equation** an equation of the first degree (i.e. not having terms raised to higher than the first power). **linear motor**: producing linear rather than rotary motion by means of a magnetic field. **linear search** *Computing* a search carried out in the order in which items are stored in a file.

linearise *v.* var. of LINEARIZE.

linearity /lɪnɪˈarɪti/ *n.* M18. [f. LINEAR + -ITY.] **1** The quality or condition of being linear; a linear arrangement or formation. M18. **2** *Math.* & *Physics.* The property of being representable by a line; proportionality of two related quantities (such as input and output). E20.

linearize /ˈlɪnɪərʌɪz/ *v.t.* Also **-ise**. L19. [f. LINEAR + -IZE.] Represent in a linear form; transform *into* a linear figure; make linear.

lineariˈzation *n.* L19. **linearizer** *n.* a person who or thing which linearizes something; *esp.* a device which linearizes the response of a measuring instrument or other mechanism L20.

linearly /ˈlɪnɪəli/ *adv.* M19. [f. LINEAR + -LY[2].] **1** In a way that involves only terms of one dimension; in a linear or proportional manner. M19. **2** In a linear direction; by linear measurement; by means of lines. L19.

lineate /ˈlɪnɪət/ *ppl a.* M17. [L *lineatus* pa. pple, f. as next: see -ATE[2].] Marked with lines.

lineate /ˈlɪnɪeɪt/ *v.t.* Long *rare.* M16. [L *lineat-* pa. ppl stem of *lineare* reduce to a line, (in med.L) delineate, f. LINEA: see -ATE[3].] **1** Mark with lines. M16. †**2** Delineate; represent by drawing or by description. E–M17.

lineation /lɪnɪˈeɪʃ(ə)n/ *n.* LME. [L *lineatio(n-)*, f. as prec.: see -ATION.] **1** The action or process of drawing lines or marking something with lines; an instance of this; a contour, an outline. Also, a marking or line on a surface, esp. of the skin. LME. **b** Linear markings; an arrangement or group of lines. M16. **2** A division into lines. M19. **3** *Geol.* A linear feature observed in rock etc. M20.

lined /lʌɪnd/ *a.*[1] LME. [f. LINE *v.*[1] + -ED[1].] **1** That has been lined or given a lining. LME. **2** *Her.* Of the lining of a mantle etc.: of a different tincture from the garment itself. L17.

1 *fur-lined*, *silk-lined*, etc.

lined /lʌɪnd/ *a.*[2] E17. [f. LINE *n.*[2], *v.*[2]: see -ED[2], -ED[1].] **1** Marked with lines, having lines traced or impressed on the surface. Also (as 2nd elem. of comb.), composed of a certain kind or number of lines. E17. **2** *Her.* Of an animal: having a line or leash attached to its collar. E18.

1 J. STEINBECK Her face was hard and lined and leathery with fatigue. M. ATWOOD The pad of lined paper I was writing on. *five-lined*, *right-lined*, *straight-lined*, etc.

lineless /ˈlʌɪnlɪs/ *a.* L16. [f. LINE *n.*[2] + -LESS.] †**1** On whom no bounds can be set. *rare.* Only in L16. **2** Having no lines. L18.

lineman /ˈlʌɪnmən/ *n.* Pl. **-men**. M19. [f. LINE *n.*[2] + MAN *n.*] **1** A person employed for the maintenance of a railway, telegraph, or telephone line. M19. **2** A person who carries the line in surveying. *rare.* M19. **3** A line-fisherman. L19. **4** *Amer.* & *Canad. Football.* A forward. L19.

linen /ˈlɪnɪn/ *a.* & *n.* [OE *līnen*, *lĭnnen* = OFris. (Du.) *linnen*, OS, OHG *līnīn* (G *leinen*), f. WGmc, f. as LINE *n.*[1]: see -EN[4].] **A** *adj.* Made of flax or cloth woven from flax. OE.

W. WOOD Our Returns are chiefly in Linnen and Linnen Yarn. J. STEINBECK Alice patted the cuts with a linen handkerchief dipped in warm water.

B *n.* **1** *collect.* Garments or other articles made or originally usually made of linen, as sheets, cloths, shirts, undergarments, etc. ME. **2** Cloth woven from flax. LME. **b** A particular kind of such cloth. Usu. in *pl.* M18. **3** Something made of linen; a linen garment. Now usu. in *pl.* M16. **b** Orig., a piece or pieces of linen, *esp.* strips of linen for use as bandages. Later (in *pl.*), graveclothes. *obs.* exc. *Sc.* L16. **4** *ellipt.* = *linen-draper* (b) below. *slang.* M20.

1 KEATS And still she slept an azure-lidded sleep, In blanched linen, smooth, and lavender'd. *Birmingham Post* His linen is as carefully selected as his wine list. **wash one's dirty linen in public** be indiscreet about one's domestic quarrels, private disagreements, etc. 2 E. SAINTSBURY Chemical properties necessary for the bleaching of linen and other materials made from flax. 3 L. HELLMAN Dresses . . a tan linen, and . . a white net for Babbie. *Woman's Own* She personally saw to her husband and son's linens.

Comb. & *special collocations*: **linen-armourer** (*a*) (*obs.* exc. *Hist.*) a maker of gambesons and similar adjuncts to armour; † (*b*) *joc.* a tailor; **linen basket**: for soiled clothes; **linen-cupboard** a cupboard for bedlinen and table linen; the contents of such a cupboard; **linen-draper** (*a*) a trader who deals in linens, calicos, etc.; (*b*) *rhyming slang* a newspaper; **linen duster** a duster (see DUSTER 3) made of linen; **linenfold** carved or moulded ornament representing a fold or scroll of linen; **linen-hall** a market-hall for the sale of linens; **linen-panel**: one decorated with linenfold; **linen-press** a frame or receptacle for pressing or holding linen; **linen shower** *N. Amer.* a party at which a bride-to-be is given presents of household linen etc.; **linen tea** a tea arranged in order to provide house-linen for a crèche, day nursery, etc.

linenless *a.* M19.

lineolate /ˈlɪnɪəleɪt/ *a.* M19. [f. L *lineola* dim. of *linea* LINE *n.*[2] + -ATE[2].] *Bot.* & *Zool.* Marked with minute lines.

Also **lineolated** *a.* E19.

line-out /ˈlʌɪnaʊt/ *n.* L19. [f. LINE *v.*[2] + OUT *adv.*] *Rugby Union.* A formation of parallel lines of opposing forwards at right angles to the touch-line for the throwing in of the ball; a play in which the ball is thrown in to such a formation.

liner /ˈlʌɪnə/ *n.*[1] E17. [f. LINE *v.*[1] + -ER[1].] **1** A person who lines or fits a lining to something. E17. **2** A lining in an appliance, device, or container, *esp.* a removable one. M19. **b** A paper or board for covering another similar material by adhesion etc. as part of the finished product. E20. **3** A lining of a garment, *esp.* one made of a man-made fibre. M20. **b** A disposable lining for a baby's nappy. Also *nappy-liner*. M20. **4** In full *liner note*. The text printed on the sleeve of a gramophone record, a sleeve-note. Chiefly *N. Amer.* M20.

Comb.: **linerboard** a paperboard used as a facing on fibreboard; *liner note*: see sense 4 above.

liner /ˈlʌɪnə/ *n.*[2] LME. [f. LINE *n.*[2], *v.*[2] + -ER[1].] **I 1** An official appointed to mark out boundaries of properties in a burgh. *Sc.* LME. **2** A person employed to paint lines on the wheels etc. of a vehicle, esp. a carriage. E19. **3** A writer of miscellaneous news items paid for at so much per line. Now chiefly in PENNY-A-LINER. M19. **4** = LINESMAN 1. L19.

II 5 A threshed sheaf of corn. Long *obs.* exc. *dial.* E17. **6 a** A line-of-battle ship. E19. **b** A ship belonging to a line of passenger ships. M19. **c** An aircraft belonging to a regular line, used esp. for passenger transport. Also, a spaceship. E20. **d** Any of a fleet of lorries; a container-lorry. Also, a container-train (chiefly in *freightliner* s.v. FREIGHT *n.*, *liner train* below). M20. **7** *Baseball.* A ball which, when struck, flies through the air in a nearly straight line not far from the ground. M19. **8 a** A fine paintbrush used for outlining etc. L19. **b** A cosmetic used for tinting a part of the face; a brush or pencil for applying this; *spec.* = *eye-liner* s.v. EYE *n.* E20. **9** A picture exhibited on the line, with its centre about level with the spectator's eye. *colloq.* L19. **10** A boat engaged in sea-fishing with lines as opp. to nets. E20. **11** An advertisement occupying a specified number of lines of print; *colloq.* a spoken passage of a specified number of lines in a play etc. Usu. as 2nd elem. of comb., preceded by a numeral (cf. *one-liner* s.v. ONE *a.*). E20. **12** A ferret held on a leash or line while rabbiting. E20.

6b R. P. JHABVALA Both loved the fun to be had on an ocean liner. *Sunday Express* The supposedly unsinkable liner rammed an iceberg on . . her maiden voyage. c *New Scientist* The Boeing liner will have rather more than twice the capacity of the Concorde. 8b *Slimming* Her eyes aren't circled any more by hard black liner. 11 *one-liner*, *two-liner*, etc.

Comb.: **liner train** a fast through-running freight train made up of detachable containers on permanently coupled wagons.

linesman /ˈlʌɪnzmən/ *n.* Pl. **-men**. M19. [f. LINE *n.*[2] + -'S[1] + MAN *n.*] **1** A soldier belonging to a regiment of the line. M19. **2** = LINEMAN 1. L19. **3 a** An umpire's or referee's assistant who decides whether or not a ball falls within the area of play on a court or pitch. L19. **b** = LINEMAN 4. M20. **4** A person who attends to the upkeep of roadside verges. L19.

liney *a.* var. of LINY.

ling /lɪŋ/ *n.*[1] Also (earlier) †**leng**. ME. [Prob. of Du. or LG origin; cf. Du. *leng*, earlier *lenghe*, *linghe* rel. to LONG *a.*[1] (cf. ON *langa*, Sw. *långa*, Da. *lange*).] **1** Any of several long slender predacious gadoid fishes of the genus *Molva*, esp. *M. molva*, an important food fish found chiefly in the E. Atlantic. ME. **2** Any of various other usu. slender fishes; *spec.* (*a*) *US* the burbot; (*b*) *Austral.* the beardie; (*c*) *Austral.* & *NZ* the pinkish-white cusk-eel *Genypterus blacodes*. M19.

1 *blue ling*: see BLUE *a.*

Comb.: **lingcod** *N. Amer.* a large food and sporting fish, *Ophiodon elongatus*, of the greenling family, found in the N. Pacific; also called *cultus-cod*.

ling /lɪŋ/ *n.*[2] ME. [ON *lyng*, of unkn. origin.] Any of various plants of the heath family, esp. *Calluna vulgaris*, heather. Formerly also, ground having much heather, heathland.

Comb.: **ling-bird** the meadow-pipit, *Anthus pratensis*.

ling /lɪŋ/ *n.*[3] M19. [Chin. *ling*.] A water chestnut, *Trapa bicornis*, native to China, the seeds of which are much eaten as food.

†**ling** *v.* Also (earlier) **leng**. [OE *lengan* = MLG *lengen*, OHG *lengen* (G *längen*), ON *lengja*, f. Gmc, f. base also of LONG *a.*[1]] 1 *v.t.* Lengthen, prolong; delay. OE–ME. 2 *v.i.* Linger, remain; continue in some condition. ME–L16.

¶The base of LINGER.

-ling /lɪŋ/ *suff.*[1] [OE f. Gmc, f. as -LE[1] + -ING[3]. In sense 2 f. ON.] 1 (Not productive.) Forming ns. f. ns. w. the sense 'a person or thing belonging to or concerned with', as *hireling*, *sapling*, etc.; ns. f. adjs. w. the sense 'a person or thing having the quality of being', as *darling*, *youngling*, *sibling*, etc., (and similarly f. an adv., *underling*); and ns. f. vbs w. the sense 'a person or thing undergoing', as *shaveling*, *starveling*. 2 Forming ns. f. ns. w. the sense 'a diminutive person or thing', as *gosling*, *duckling*; now freq. *derog.*, as *godling*, *lordling*, *princeling*.

-ling /lɪŋ/ *suff.*[2] (not productive). Also **-lings** /-lɪŋz/. [OE *-ling* f. Gmc base = extend.] Forming advs. of direction or extent f. ns., as *grovelling*, and adjs. of condition or position f. advs., as *darkling*.

linga /ˈlɪŋgə/ *n.* Also **lingam** /ˈlɪŋgam/. E18. [Skt *liṅga* sign, (sexual) characteristic. Var. infl. by Tamil *iliṅkam*.] A Hindu sacred object constituting a symbol of the god Siva, *spec.* (the representation of) a phallus.

Lingala /lɪŋˈgɑːlə/ *n.* & *a.* Also **Ngala** /(ə)ŋˈgɑːlə/. E20. [Bantu.] (Of or pertaining to) a Bantu language of Zaire, widely used as a lingua franca in the north and east of that country.

lingam *n.* var. of LINGA.

lingberry *n.* var. of LINGONBERRY.

ling chih /ˈlɪŋ dʒə/ *n. phr.* E20. [Chin. *língzhī* (Wade-Giles *ling chih*), f. *ling* divine + *zhī* fungus.] A motif on Chinese ceramic ware, esp. a representation of the fungus *Polyporus lucidus*, symbolizing longevity or immortality.

linge /lɪndʒ/ *v.t. obs.* exc. *dial.* E17. [Origin unkn.] Beat, thrash.

lingel /ˈlɪŋg(ə)l/ *n.*[1] Now *dial.* Also **lingle**. LME. [OFr. *lignoel*, *ligneul* f. pop.L f. L *linea* LINE *n.*[2]] A shoemaker's waxed thread.

lingel /ˈlɪŋg(ə)l/ *n.*[2] Now *dial.* Also **lingle**. LME. [App. repr. AN f. L *lingula* strap etc. dim. of *lingua* tongue: see -EL[2].] †1 *collect. sing.* The leather straps etc. of a horse's harness. Only in LME. 2 A thong, a latchet. M16. †3 A flat blade or spoon, a spatula. L16–E17.

lingenberry *n.* var. of LINGONBERRY.

linger /ˈlɪŋgə/ *v.* ME. [Frequent. of LING *v.*: see -ER[5].] †1 *v.i.* Dwell, abide, stay (in a place). Only in ME. 2 *v.t.* a Foll. by *forth, on, out*: draw out, prolong, protract by loitering or dallying. Also, idle or fritter *away* (time etc.). L15. b Pass (life) sadly or wearily. *arch. rare.* E18. 3 *v.i.* Stay behind, postpone one's departure; stay on in or not leave a place at the expected or right time, esp. because of reluctance to go. M16. b Proceed at a slow pace; loiter, dawdle. E19. c *fig.* Spend a long time *over* or *on* a subject or *round* a place. M19. 4 *v.i.* Of a person: drag *on* one's existence in a state of illness, wretchedness, etc.; languish. M16. 5 *v.i.* Be slow to do or begin something; hesitate, delay. M16. 6 *v.t.* †a Cause to linger; prolong, draw out (the time etc.); delay, defer. M16–M17. †b Keep waiting, put (a person) *off*. M16–E17. 7 *v.i.* Have a longing or craving, hanker (*after*). M17. 8 *v.i.* Esp. of illness: be slow to pass away, be protracted; hang *on*. M18. b Be slow in coming or accruing. M19. c Of an action or condition: be protracted (tiresomely or painfully), drag on. M19.

2a T. BROWN The first linger away their lives in perpetual drudgery. SIR W. SCOTT Half measures do but linger out the feud. b POPE Far from gay cities, and the ways of men, I linger life. 3 D. H. LAWRENCE Kate lingered to hear the end of this hymn. W. S. CHURCHILL Leslie . . lingered in the city with the Scottish cavalry till the day was lost. E. J. HOWARD Emma stayed to clear the table, and Dan lingered with her. b DICKENS He was never lingering or loitering, but always walking swiftly. c A. P. STANLEY I linger round a subject. D. H. LAWRENCE They measured the rooms, and lingered over every consideration. 4 RIDER HAGGARD He lingered for nearly two years. 5 E. A. FREEMAN Malcolm lingered in his preparations. 6a SHAKES. *Oth.* He goes into Mauritania . . unless his abode be linger'd here by some accident. R. SANDERSON Secure ones may linger their repentance till it be too late. 7 N. BACON The Cardinal finding the King's mind to linger after another Bedfellow. 8 E. EDWARDS When the Plague had departed from most parts of London, it often lingered in the Tower. B. JOWETT But he has still a doubt lingering in his mind. M. L. KING The bitterly cold winter of 1962 lingered throughout the opening months of 1963. A. C. CLARKE These beliefs still survived, and would linger on for generations. b TENNYSON Knowledge comes, but wisdom lingers. c C. THIRLWALL As the siege of Ithome lingered, the Spartans called on their allies for aid.

lingerer *n.* M16.

lingerie /ˈlãʒ(ə)ri, *foreign* lɛ̃ʒri/ *n.* M19. [Fr., f. *linge* linen: see -ERY.] Orig., linen articles collectively; all the articles of linen, lace, etc., in a woman's wardrobe or trousseau. Now, women's underwear and nightclothes.

lingering /ˈlɪŋg(ə)rɪŋ/ *a.* M16. [f. LINGER *v.* + -ING[2].] 1 *gen.* That lingers. M16. 2 Esp. of illness: slow, painfully protracted. Formerly also, of a poison: characterized by slow action. L16.

lingeringly *adv.* L16.

lingle *n.*[1], *n.*[2] vars. of LINGEL *n.*[1], *n.*[2]

lingo /ˈlɪŋgəʊ/ *n.*[1] *colloq.* (orig. *joc.* & *derog.*). Pl. **-o(e)s**. M17. [Prob. f. Port. *lingoa* var. of *lingua* f. L LINGUA.] A foreign speech or language; the vocabulary of a special subject or class of people.

W. SAFIRE It was not until the 1960's that 'freak out' blossomed into drug lingo. E. FIGES 'German is a hideous lingo,' muttered Claude.

lingo /ˈlɪŋgəʊ/ *n.*[2] Pl. **-os**. M18. [Perh. var. of LINGOT.] *Weaving.* A weight in a Jacquard loom.

lingo *n.*[3] var. of LINGOA.

lingoa /lɪŋˈgəʊə/ *n.* Also ***lingo*** /ˈlɪŋgəʊ/. E19. [Moluccan Malay *linggua*.] A large SE Asian leguminous tree, *Pterocarpus indicus*; the wood of this tree (also called *Burmese rosewood*, *amboyna wood*).

lingoa geral *n. phr.* var. of LINGUA GERAL.

lingonberry /ˈlɪŋg(ə)nbɛri/ *n.* Also **lingberry** /ˈlɪŋbɛri/, **lingenberry**. M20. [f. Sw. *lingon* cowberry + BERRY *n.*[1]] The cowberry, *Vaccinium vitis-idaea*, esp. in Scandinavia, where the berries are much used in cookery. Also, an Arctic variety of this occurring in the USSR and N. America.

lingot /ˈlɪŋgət/ *n. arch.* L15. [Fr., f. *l'* the + INGOT.] 1 = INGOT 2. L15. †2 = INGOT 1. M16–L17.

-lings *suff.* var. of -LING [2].

lingua /ˈlɪŋgwə/ *n.* L17. [L = tongue, language.] 1 A language. L17. 2 = LINGO *n.*[2] *rare.* L18. 3 *Anat.* & *Zool.* The tongue; an organ resembling the tongue in form or function; *spec.* in *Entomol.*, the central portion of the hypopharynx. E19.

†**lingua-** *comb. form* see LINGUO-.

linguacious /lɪŋˈgweɪʃəs/ *a. rare.* M17. [L *linguaci-*, *linguax* loquacious, f. as LINGUA + -ACIOUS.] 1 Talkative, loquacious. M17. †2 Linguistic. Only in E19.

lingua franca /lɪŋgwə ˈfraŋkə/ *n. phr.* Pl. **lingua francas**, **lingue franche** /lɪŋgwɪ ˈfraŋki/. L17. [It. = Frankish tongue.] A mixture of Italian with French, Greek, Arabic, Turkish, and Spanish, used in the Levant (now *Hist.*). Also, any language serving as a medium between different nations etc. whose own languages are not the same; a system of communication providing mutual understanding.

K. A. PORTER Ric and Rac could not understand the words, but they knew . . the lingua franca of gallantry.

lingua geral /lɪŋgwə dʒəˈrɑːl/ *n. phr.* Also **lingoa geral**. M19. [Port. *lingua geral* general language.] A trade language based on Tupi and used as a lingua franca in Brazil.

lingual /ˈlɪŋgw(ə)l/ *a.* & *n.* LME. [med.L *lingualis*, f. as LINGUA + -AL[1].] A *adj.* †1 Tongue-shaped. Only in LME. 2 Chiefly *Anat.* & *Zool.* Of, pertaining to, or involving the tongue or a tongue-like part; situated on or towards the tongue. M17. 3 *Phonet.* Of a sound: formed by the tongue. M17. 4 Pertaining to the tongue as the organ of speech; pertaining to language or languages. L18.

2 **lingual nerve** a sensory nerve (a branch of the fifth cranial nerve) supplying the tongue. **lingual ribbon** the odontophore of a mollusc.

B *n.* 1 *Phonet.* A lingual sound. M17. 2 *Anat.* The lingual nerve. L19.

lingualize *v.t.* make lingual L19. **lingually** *adv.* (*Anat.*) towards the tongue L19.

Linguaphone /ˈlɪŋgwəfəʊn/ *n.* Also **l-**. E20. [f. LINGUA + *-phone*, after GRAMOPHONE.] (Proprietary name for) a language-teaching system based on the use of sound recordings in conjunction with textbooks.

linguatulid /lɪŋˈgwatjʊlɪd/ *n.* & *a.* E20. [mod.L *Linguatulida* former name of the group, f. *Linguatula* (see below), f. L *linguatus* lit. 'having a tongue', f. as LINGUA: see -ATE[2], -ID[3].] A *n.* = PENTASTOMID *n.*; *spec.* one of the genus *Linguatula*, which parasitizes carnivorous mammals, esp. canids. E20. B *adj.* = PENTASTOMID *a.* E20.

lingue franche *n. phr. pl.* see LINGUA FRANCA.

Linguet /ˈlɪŋgwət/ *n.* Also **l-**. M20. [f. L *lingua* tongue + -ET[1].] *Pharm.* A tablet that is retained in the mouth, usu. under the tongue, while its ingredients are absorbed through the oral tissues.

¶Proprietary name in the US.

linguiform /ˈlɪŋgwɪfɔːm/ *a.* M18. [f. LINGUA + -I- + -FORM.] *Bot.*, *Anat.*, & *Zool.* Shaped like a tongue.

linguine /lɪŋˈgwiːni/ *n.pl.* M20. [It., pl. of *linguina* dim. of *lingua* tongue f. L.] Pasta in the form of tongue-shaped ribbons; an Italian dish consisting largely of this and usu. a sauce.

linguist /ˈlɪŋgwɪst/ *n.* L16. [f. L LINGUA + -IST.] 1 A person skilled in foreign languages. Freq. w. specifying wd. L16. †2 A person who speaks freely and eloquently; a skilful speaker. L16–L17. 3 An expert in or student of language or linguistics. E17. 4 = INTERPRETER 2. Now *rare* or *obs.* E17.

1 P. GROSSKURTH Abraham, . . well known as a gifted linguist. R. DEACON Blackwell was . . a linguist with a command of twenty languages. 2 A. WOOD Richard Martin . . was a plausible Linguist, and eminent for Speeches spoken in Parliaments. 3 D. HARTLEY A Light in which Grammarians and Linguists alone consider Words. N. CHOMSKY A linguist studying English might propose several possible rules of question-formation. *mathematical linguist*: see MATHEMATICAL *a.* STRUCTURAL *linguist*. 4 P. THOMAS This Evening came . . a Chinese Interpreter or Linguist.

linguister /ˈlɪŋgwɪstə/ *n.* Now *US.* M17. [f. prec. + -ER[1].] 1 = LINGUIST 4. M17. 2 = LINGUIST 3. *rare.* L19.

linguistic /lɪŋˈgwɪstɪk/ *a.* & *n.* M19. [f. as LINGUIST + -IC. Cf. Fr. *linguistique*, G *Linguistik*.] A *adj.* Of or pertaining to the knowledge or study of languages; of or pertaining to language or languages. M19.

J. B. CARROLL The study of verbal behavior . . has . . been called . . *linguistic psychology*. V. S. NAIPAUL The knowledge I brought . . was linguistic I knew that 'avon' originally meant only 'river'. **linguistic analysis** (*a*) the analysis of language structures in terms of a particular theory of language; (*b*) *Philos.* analysis of language as the medium of thought. **linguistic analyst** a person who practises linguistic analysis. **linguistic anthropology** anthropological research based on the study of the language of a selected group. **linguistic atlas** a set of tables or maps recording regional or dialectal variations of pronunciation, vocabulary, or inflectional forms. **linguistic geography** the branch of knowledge that deals with the geographical distribution of languages, dialects, etc.

B *n.* = LINGUISTICS. *rare.* M19.

linguistical *a.* linguistic E19. **linguistically** *adv.* M19. **linguistician** /-ˈtɪʃ(ə)n/ *n.* an expert in or student of linguistics L19.

linguistics /lɪŋˈgwɪstɪks/ *n.* M19. [f. prec.: see -ICS.] The branch of knowledge that deals with language.

applied linguistics, *area(l) linguistics*, *historical linguistics*, *mathematical linguistics*, *structural linguistics*, *systemic linguistics, text linguistics, theoretical linguistics,* etc. *ethnolinguistics, psycholinguistics, sociolinguistics,* etc.

linguistry /ˈlɪŋgwɪstri/ *n. rare.* L18. [f. as LINGUIST + -RY.] Linguistics.

lingula /ˈlɪŋgjʊlə/ *n.* Pl. **-lae** /-liː/. M17. [L, partly f. *lingere* lick, partly dim. of LINGUA: see -ULE. Cf. LIGULA.] 1 A device or (now usu.) anatomical structure resembling a small tongue; *spec.* in *Anat.*, a projection from the anterior cerebellum. M17. 2 Any (extant or fossil) inarticulate brachiopod of the genus *Lingula*. Now chiefly as mod.L genus name. M19.

lingular *a.* (*Anat.*) of or pertaining to a lingula M19.

lingulate /ˈlɪŋgjʊleɪt/ *a.* M19. [L *lingulatus*, f. as prec. + -ATE[2].] Tongue-shaped.

linguo- /ˈlɪŋgwəʊ/ *comb. form* of L LINGUA tongue: see -O-. Also †**lingua-**.

¶The etymologically correct comb. form would be *lingui-*.

linguo'dental *a.* & *n.* = INTERDENTAL *a.* 2, *n.* M17.

lingworm /ˈlɪŋwəːm/ *n.* Also **lyngorm** /ˈlɪŋɔːm/. L19. [ON *lyngormr*, f. *lyng* heather + *ormr* serpent, snake (cf. WORM *n.*). Cf. LINDWORM.] A fabulous serpent of Scandinavian mythology.

lingy /ˈlɪŋi/ *a.* M17. [f. LING *n.*[2] + -Y[1].] Having much ling or heather; covered with ling.

linhay /ˈlɪni/ *n. dial.* L17. [Origin unkn.] A shed or other farm building open in front, usually with a lean-to roof.

liniment /ˈlɪnɪm(ə)nt/ *n.* LME. [Late L *linimentum*, f. L *linire* smear, anoint: see -MENT.] †1 Something used for smearing or anointing. LME–L17. 2 *spec.* An embrocation, usu. made with oil. LME.

linin /ˈlʌɪnɪn/ *n.* M19. [Gk *linon* thread + -IN[1].] *Cytol.* (now chiefly *Hist.*). A lightly staining substance which forms a network of fine threads around the chromatin in an interphase nucleus.

lining /ˈlʌɪnɪŋ/ *n.*[1] LME. [f. LINE *v.*[1] + -ING[1].] 1 The material with which a garment is lined; the inner or undersurface of material used to line a garment, esp. for protection or warmth. LME. b In *pl.* Knickers, underpants; underclothes. Chiefly *dial.* E17. 2 *fig.* Contents; what is inside. LME. 3 Any material occurring or placed next beneath an outer one; an inside layer or surface. E18. 4 The action of providing something with a lining. Also foll. by *up*. M19.

1 J. RATHBONE A black velvet coat with . . scarlet silk lining. 2 SHAKES. *Rich. II* The lining of his coffers shall make coats To deck our soldiers for these Irish wars. J. BURROUGHS I was sure to return at meal-time with a lining of berries in the top of my straw hat. 3 P. PARISH The stomach can get 'upset' if its lining is irritated (e.g. by aspirin or alcohol). *silver lining*: see SILVER *n.* & *a.*

lining /ˈlʌɪnɪŋ/ *n.*[2] L16. [f. LINE *v.*[2] + -ING[1].] 1 Chiefly *Mil.* Arranging in line, alignment. L16. 2 The official marking of the boundaries of burghal properties in a Scottish royal burgh. Also (more fully *decree of lining*), permission to erect or alter a building according to specified conditions. L16. 3 The use of a measuring line or of a stretched cord for alignment. E19. 4 The action of tracing (*out*) lines. E19. 5 The giving out of a hymn (by the precentor) line by line. Also foll. by *out*. M19. 6 Fishing with a line as opp. to a net. M19.

linish /ˈlɪnɪʃ/ *v.t.* L20. [f. LIN(EN *n.* + FIN)ISH *v.*] Polish or remove excess material from (an object) by contact with a moving continuous belt coated with abrasive material. Chiefly as *linishing* vbl n.

linisher *n.* a machine for linishing things M20.

link /lɪŋk/ *n.*[1] [OE *hlinc* (whence also LINCH *n.*[2]), perh. deriv. of base of LEAN *v.*] 1 Rising ground; a ridge, a bank. *obs.* exc. *dial.* OE. 2 In *pl.* Level or gently undulating sandy ground near a seashore, with turf, coarse grass, etc. (*Sc.*); (treated as *sing.* or *pl.*, more fully *golf-links*) a golf course, *esp.* one on such ground. LME.

Comb.: **linksland** ground suitable or used for a golf-links.

linky *a.* (*rare*) resembling a link or links M19.

link /lɪŋk/ *n.*[2] LME. [ON *hlekkr* (Icel. *hlekkur*, OSw. *lænker*), f. Gmc, rel. to MLG *lenkhake* pot-hook, MHG *gelenke* (collect.) flexible parts of the body, (also mod.) *gelenk* joint, link.] 1 Any of a series of rings or loops forming a chain. Formerly also (in *pl.*), chains, fetters. LME. b A chain. Long *obs.* exc. *dial.* L16. c Any of the hundred divisions of a surveyor's chain; a length equal to this (7.92 inches, approx. 20.1 cm.). M17. d = *cuff-link* s.v. CUFF *n.*[1] E19. 2 Something looped, or forming part of a chainlike arrangement; a loop. LME. b Any of the divisions of a chain of sausages or black puddings. Usu. in *pl.* Now chiefly *dial.* LME. c A joint of the body. Long *obs.* exc. *Sc.* E16. d In *pl.* The windings of a stream; the land along such windings. *Sc.* L18. 3 A connecting part; *esp.* a thing or a person serving to establish or maintain a connection; a member of a series; a means of connection or communication. LME. b A means of travel or transport between two places. M19. c A system or unit of contact by radio or telephone between two points. E20. d [tr. Russ. *zveno*.] A small labour unit on a collective farm in the countries of the former USSR. M20. e *Hockey* & *Football*. A linkman. M20. f *Computing*. = POINTER 3d. M20.

1 L. T. C. ROLT Short links between each of the main links of the suspension chains. *fig.*: R. V. JONES I had . . forged out every link in the chain of evidence. d S. BELLOW His shirt cuffs were soiled; he turned them underside up and transferred the links. 2 SHAKES. *2 Hen. IV* Now, Sir, a new link to the bucket must needs be had. b B. BAINBRIDGE Links of sausages coiled on a newspaper. 3 N. FRYE The connecting link between . . the poem . . and what unites it to other forms of poetic experience. A. BEVAN The last link with medieval society was broken. b P. THEROUX There is no road or rail link through the Darien Gap between Panama and Columbia.

Phrases: **let out the links** act with more power, put more into something. MISSING *link*. *weak* or *weakest link*: see WEAK *a.*

Comb.: **link buttons** a pair of buttons linked by a thread etc.; **link road** a road serving to link two or more major roads or centres; **link rod** (*a*) a rod which joins the levers on the steered stub axles of a motor vehicle; (*b*) each of the rods which connect pistons to wrist pins on the master rod in a radial internal-combustion engine; **linkspan** a bridge hinged at one end and used in loading and unloading a ship etc.; **link-verb** *Gram.* a copular verb; **link-word** *Gram.* any part of speech performing a linking function; **link-work** (*a*) work composed of or arranged in links; (*b*) a kind of gearing whereby motion is transmitted by links as opp. to wheels or bands.

link /lɪŋk/ *n.*[3] E16. [Perh. f. med.L *linchinus* alt. of *lichinus* wick, match f. Gk *lukhnos* light.] 1 *Hist.* A torch made esp. of tow and pitch for lighting the way along dark streets. E16. b A link-boy. M19. †2 The material of such a torch used as blacking. L16–E18.

Comb.: **link-boy**: employed to carry a link; LINKMAN *n.*[1]

Link /lɪŋk/ *n.*[4] M20. [Edward *Link*, its Amer. inventor.] In full *Link trainer*. A flight simulator on which pilots are trained.

link /lɪŋk/ *a.* L19. [Yiddish f. G = left.] Among Jews: not pious, not orthodox (in religion).

link /lɪŋk/ *v.*[1] LME. [f. LINK *n.*[2]] 1 *v.t.* Connect or join (two things or one thing to another) with or as with a link. (Foll. by *together, to, with.*) LME. b Clasp, intertwine, (hands or arms). M19. c Connect causally, associate in speech, thought, etc., *with* or *to*. M20. 2 *v.i.* Be joined or connected (as) with a link, esp. in friendship, marriage, etc. Also foll. by *together*. M16. b Go arm in arm, or hand in hand. E19.

1 D. ATTENBOROUGH A . . blood-vessel and a nerve cord run . . through all the segments, linking and coordinating them. R. DAVIES The automobile was linking the villages with towns, and the towns with cities. b P. H. JOHNSON His hands linked like an old man's behind his back. S. MIDDLETON They linked arms, filling the pavement. c E. L. DOCTOROW Her name was linked with dozens of men around town. 2 SHAKES. *3 Hen. VI* For I were loath To link with him that were not lawful chosen. BURKE No one generation could link with the other.

With advs. in specialized senses: **link up** connect, combine, (*with*).

Comb.: **link-up** an act or result of linking up.

linker *n.* M19.

link /lɪŋk/ *v.*[2]*i. Sc.* & *north.* E18. [Origin uncertain: perh. rel. to LINK *v.*[1] Cf. Norw. *linka* toss or bend the body.] Move nimbly, pass quickly along.

link off pass away, disappear quickly.

linkage /ˈlɪŋkɪdʒ/ *n.* L19. [f. LINK *n.*[2], *v.*[1] + -AGE.] 1 The state of being linked; a system of links. Also, a link; a connection; the process of linking or connecting. L19. b The linking together of different political issues as a negotiating tactic. M20. 2 *Genetics*. (An) association between characters in inheritance such that they tend to be inherited together, owing to the location of their respective alleles on the same chromosome; formerly called (*gametic*) *coupling*. Also, the amount or degree of this association (between 50 per cent and 100 per cent). Cf. REPULSION 3c. E20.

1 *Time* She had made the proper linkages to British Victorianism and German romantic philosophy. b *Time* The real stumbling block is 'linkage'—the relationship between an Egyptian-Israeli treaty and a wider Middle East settlement.

Comb.: *linkage map*: see MAP *n.*[1] 1b.

linked /lɪŋkt/ *a.* LME. [f. LINK *n.*[2], *v.*[1]: see -ED[2], -ED[1].] 1 Connected (as) by links; joined, associated. Formerly also, made or fashioned with links. LME. 2 *Mil.* Of two infantry battalions or regiments: joined together to form a regimental district. L19. 3 Of industries: allied to and dependent on one another. M20.

1 **linked list** *Computing* an ordered set of data elements, each of which contains a pointer to its successor.

linkedness *n.* (*rare*) interconnection E20.

linking /ˈlɪŋkɪŋ/ *a.* L19. [f. LINK *v.*[1] + -ING[2].] 1 That links or joins together; *Gram.* copulative. L19. 2 *Broadcasting* & *Cinemat.* Of music, camera shots, commentary, etc.: providing continuity between programmes, scenes, etc. M20.

1 **linking r** a word-final *r* sound, represented in spelling, that is pronounced before a vowel but in standard British English no longer before a consonant or pause, as in *bar opens* /bɑːr ˈəʊpənz/ as opp. to *bar closes* /bɑː ˈkləʊzɪz/ (cf. *intrusive r* s.v. INTRUSIVE *a.* 2).

linkman /ˈlɪŋkmən/ *n.*[1] Pl. **-men**. E18. [f. LINK *n.*[3] + MAN *n.*] *Hist.* A man employed to carry a link to light the way.

linkman /ˈlɪŋkmən/ *n.*[2] Pl. **-men**. E20. [f. LINK *n.*[2] + MAN *n.*] 1 A person serving as a link between groups of people etc. E20. 2 *Broadcasting*. A person providing continuity in a radio or television programme consisting of several items. M20. 3 *Hockey* & *Football*. A player between the forwards and half-backs or strikers and backs. M20.

lin-lan-lone /ˈlɪnlanləʊn, lɪnlanˈləʊn/ *n.* L19. [Imit.] Repr. the sound of a chime of three bells.

linn /lɪn/ *n.*[1] Chiefly *Sc.* [OE *hlynn*, but largely f. Gael. *linne*, Ir. *linn* (earlier *lind*) = Welsh *llyn* lake, pool, OCorn. *-lin*, Breton *lin*.] 1 A torrent running over rocks; a cascade, a waterfall. OE. 2 A pool, *esp.* one into which a cataract falls. M16. 3 A precipice, a ravine with precipitous sides. L18.

linn /lɪn/ *n.*[2] Now *dial.* & *US*. L15. [Alt. of LIND.] The linden or lime; the wood of this tree.

linnaea /lɪˈniːə/ *n.* M19. [mod.L (see below), f. *Linnaeus*: see next.] A slender trailing plant, *Linnaea borealis*, of the honeysuckle family, which bears two pink pendulous flowers and is found in coniferous woods in northern latitudes. Also called *twinflower*.

Linnaean /lɪˈniːən/ *a.* & *n.* Also **Linnean**. M18. [f. *Linnaeus*, Latinized form of *Linné* (see below) + -AN.] A *adj.* Of or pertaining to the Swedish naturalist Linnaeus (Carl von Linné, 1707–78), the founder of modern systematic botany and zoology, or his binomial system of nomenclature for the classification of plants and animals; instituted by Linnaeus; adhering to the system of Linnaeus. M18. B *n.* A follower of Linnaeus; a person who adopts the Linnaean system. L18.

¶Spelt *Linnean* in *Linnean Society*.

Linnean *a.* & *n.* var. of LINNAEAN.

linnet /ˈlɪnɪt/ *n.* E16. [OFr. (Walloon, Picard) *linette*, earlier *linot* (mod. *linot*, *linotte*), f. *lin* flax f. L *linum*. Cf. LINTWHITE.] A small common migratory Eurasian songbird, *Acanthis cannabina*, of the passerine family Fringillidae, with brown or grey plumage, formerly kept as a pet. Also (usu. w. specifying wd), any of several similar songbirds.

green linnet: see GREEN *a.* **mountain linnet** = TWITE. *pine linnet*: see PINE *n.*[2] *rose linnet*: see ROSE *a.*

linnet-hole /ˈlɪnɪthəʊl/ *n.* M17. [f. alt. of Fr. LUNETTE + HOLE *n.*[1]] *Glass-making.* = LUNETTE 9.

lino /ˈlʌɪnəʊ/ *n.*[1] Pl. **-os.** E20. [Abbrev.] = LINOLEUM.

lino /ˈlʌɪnəʊ/ *n.*[2] E20. [Abbrev.] = LINOTYPE.

†**lino** *n.*[3] var. of LENO.

linocut /ˈlʌɪnəʊkʌt/ *n.* E20. [f. LINO(LEUM + CUT *n.*[2]] (A print made from) a design cut in relief on a piece of linoleum.

linocutter *n.* a person who makes a linocut; a tool for making linocuts: E20. **linocutting** *n.* the making of linocuts E20.

linography /lʌɪˈnɒgrəfi/ *n.* L19. [f. L *linum* flax + -OGRAPHY.] A process of photographing on linen or calico to produce a representation to be coloured.

linograph *n.* a picture produced by linography L20.

linoleic /lɪnə(ʊ)ˈliːɪk, -ˈleɪɪk/ *a.* M19. [f. L *linum* flax + OLEIC.] Chem. *linoleic acid*, a polyunsaturated fatty acid, $C_{17}H_{31}COOH$, which occurs as a glyceride in linseed oil and other drying oils, and is essential in the human diet. Cf. next.

li'noleate *n.* a salt or ester of linoleic acid M19. **li'nolein** *n.* a glyceride of linoleic acid occurring in linseed oil E20.

linolenic /lɪnə(ʊ)ˈlɛnɪk, -ˈliːnɪk/ *n.* L19. [f. G *Linolen(saüre)*, f. *Linolsaüre* LINOLEIC *acid* w. inserted *-en* -ENE: see -IC.] Chem. *linolenic acid*, a polyunsaturated fatty acid, $C_{17}H_{29}COOH$ (with one more double bond than the related linoleic acid), which occurs as a glyceride in linseed oil and other drying oils, and is essential in the human diet.

li'nolenate *n.* a salt or ester of linolenic acid E20.

linoleum /lɪˈnəʊlɪəm/ *n.* L19. [f. L *linum* flax + *oleum* oil.] Canvas backing thickly coated with a preparation of linseed oil and powdered cork etc., used esp. as a floor-covering; a piece or example of this.

linoleumed *a.* L19.

Linotype /ˈlʌɪnə(ʊ)tʌɪp/ *n.* Also **l-**. L19. [Alt. of *line o' type.*] *Printing.* (Proprietary name for) a composing-machine producing lines of words as single strips of metal, used esp. for newspapers.

linotypist *n.* a person who uses a Linotype machine L20.

linoxyn /lɪˈnɒksɪn/ *n.* L19. [f. L *linum* flax + OXY- + -IN[1].] *Chem.* Any of various gelatinous or resinous substances obtained by oxidation of linseed oil by air.

linsang /ˈlɪnsaŋ/ *n.* E19. [Jav. *lingsang*, *wlingsang*, Malay *linsang*.] Either of two SE Asian forest animals related to civets, *Prionodon pardicolor* (more fully *spotted linsang*) and *P. linsang* (more fully *banded linsang*). Also (more fully *African* or *Guinea linsang*), the related W. African mammal *Poiana richardsonii*.

linseed /ˈlɪnsiːd/ *n.* OE. [f. LINE *n.*[1] + SEED *n.*] The seed of flax. Formerly also (*rare*), the flax-plant.

Comb.: **linseed cake** linseed pressed into cakes and used as cattle-food; **linseed meal** ground linseed; **linseed oil** a desiccant oil extracted from linseed and used in paint and varnish; **linseed poultice** a poultice made of linseed or linseed-meal.

linsey /ˈlɪnzi/ *n.* & *a.* LME. [Prob. f. *Lindsey* in Suffolk, southern England, said to be the original place of manufacture.] Orig., (made of) a coarse linen fabric. Later, (made of) linsey-woolsey.

linsey-woolsey /lɪnzɪˈwʊlzi/ *n.* & *a.* L15. [f. prec. + WOOL *n.* + *-sey* jingling termination. Cf. WINCEY.] A *n.* 1 Orig., a textile material of wool and linen. Now, a dress material of coarse inferior wool woven on a cotton warp. L15. b A garment of this material. L19. 2 *fig.* A strange medley in talk or action; confusion, nonsense. L16. B *attrib.* or as *adj.* Made of linsey-woolsey; *fig.* appearing to constitute a strange medley, confused, nonsensical. M16.

Linson /ˈlɪns(ə)n/ *n.* M20. [f. *Lin*wood, Scotland, where first made + R. & W. Wat*son*, the first manufacturers.] (Proprietary name for) a tough fibrous paper fabric used esp. in bookbinding as a cheaper substitute for cloth.

linstock /ˈlɪnstɒk/ *n. obs.* exc. *Hist.* L16. [Du. *lontstok*, f. *lont* match + *stok* stick, assim. to LINT.] A staff with a head to hold a lighted match, and used to fire a cannon.

lint /lɪnt/ *n.* LME. [Perh. f. OFr. *linette* linseed, f. *lin* flax: see -ETTE, -ET[1].] 1 The flax-plant. Now only *Sc.* LME. 2 Flax prepared for spinning. Also, the refuse of this, used as a combustible. Chiefly *Sc.* LME. 3 A soft material used esp. for dressing wounds, orig. made by ravelling or scraping linen cloth. Formerly also in *pl.*, pieces of this material. LME. b Orig., a particle of fluff. Later, fluff. E17. 4 Netting for fishing nets. Now *dial.* & *US.* E17. 5 The material which forms the bulk of the fibres in the cotton boll (cf. LINTER), which is separated from the cotton seeds by ginning and which after processing is the ordinary cotton of commerce. L19.

Comb.: **lint-head** *US dial.* a worker in a cotton-mill; *contempt.* a person of whom one disapproves; **lint-scraper** *Hist.* a person employed to scrape lint (for hospital use); *derog. slang* a young surgeon.

linty *a.* †(*a*) resembling lint (*lit.* & *fig.*); (*b*) full of lint or fluff: E17.

lintel /ˈlɪnt(ə)l/ *n.* ME. [OFr. (mod. *linteau*) f. Proto-Romance, infl. by late L *liminare*, f. L *limin-*, *limen* threshold.] *Archit.* A horizontal supporting timber, stone, etc., across the top of a door or window.

lintelled *a.* provided with a lintel E19.

linter /ˈlɪntə/ *n. US.* E20. [f. LINT + -ER[1].] 1 A machine for removing the short fibres from cotton seeds after ginning. E20. 2 In *pl.* The short fibres removed from the cotton seeds after ginning. E20.

lintern /ˈlɪntən/ *n.* Long *obs.* exc. *dial.* Also (earlier) **linton**. M16. [Alt.] = LINTEL.

lintie /ˈlɪnti/ *n. Sc.* L18. [f. LINT(WHITE + -IE, -Y[6].] = LINNET.

rose lintie: see ROSE *a.*

linton *n.* see LINTERN.

lintwhite /ˈlɪntwʌɪt/ *n.* Chiefly *Sc.* [OE f. LINE *n.*[1] + *-twige* as in OHG *zwigōn* pluck.] = LINNET.

linum /ˈlʌɪnəm/ *n.* M19. [mod.L (see below), use as genus name of L *linum* flax.] Any of various plants constituting the genus *Linum* (family Linaceae), which includes the cultivated flax, *L. usitatissimum*; *esp.* one grown for ornament.

linuron /ˈlɪnjʊrɒn/ *n.* M20. [f. *lin-* of unkn. origin + UR(EA + *-on* (arbitrary ending).] An agricultural herbicide consisting of a cyclic derivative of urea.

liny /ˈlʌɪni/ *a.* Also **liney**. E19. [f. LINE *n.*[2] + -Y[1].] 1 Of the nature of or resembling a line or streak, thin, meagre. E19. 2 Full of lines, marked with lines. E19.

Linzertorte /ˈlɪntsərtɔrtə, ˈlɪntsətɔːtə/ *n.* Pl. ***-ten*** /-t(ə)n/. E20. [G, f. *Linzer* adj. of the Austrian city *Linz* + *Torte* tart, pastry, cake (cf. TORTE).] A kind of pastry with a jam filling, decorated on top with strips of pastry in a lattice pattern.

lion /ˈlʌɪən/ *n.* & *a.* ME. [AN *liun* (Fr. *lion*) f. L *leo*, *leon* f. Gk *leōn*, replacing earlier LEO.] A *n.* 1 A large powerful carnivorous feline, *Panthera leo*, found in sub-Saharan Africa and parts of India (formerly more widely) and having a tawny or yellowish brown coat, a tufted tail, and (in the male) a shaggy mane; the male of this (cf. LIONESS); this animal as the type of strength, majesty, and courage, the 'king of beasts'. See also *ant-lion* s.v. ANT *n.*, SEA LION. ME. 2 *fig.* a A person who is strong, courageous, or fiercely brave. ME. b A fiercely cruel, tyrannical, or rapacious creature or person. ME. c (**L-**.) A member of a Lions Club (see below). E20. 3 An image or picture of a lion, esp. as a heraldic emblem, or as a sign for inns etc. ME. b (**L-**.) The lion as the national emblem of Great Britain; *fig.* the British nation. Also *British Lion.* L17. c (**L-**.) A member of a British Isles rugby union team touring abroad. Also *British Lion.* M20. 4 A gold coin current in Scotland down to the reign of James VI. Also = HARD-HEAD 5. *obs.* exc. *Hist.* LME. 5 (Usu. **L-**.) (The name of) *the* constellation and zodiacal sign Leo; *Little Lion*, (the name of) *the* constellation Leo Minor. LME. 6a In *pl.* Things of note, celebrity, or curiosity (in a town etc.); sights worth seeing. Esp. in *see* (or *show*) *the lions.* L16. b A person of note or celebrity who is much sought after. E17. †c A visitor to Oxford University. *slang.* L18–E19.

1 E. HALL We must . . fight together like lions. J. HOWELL Like the month of March, which entreth like a Lion. 3 R. WEST Let's stop off at the Red Lion . . they do a posh tea. 6a B. H. MALKIN The churches were the best lions we met with. b A. S. DALE At fifty Shaw was a literary lion with a colourful public image. B. MASON Whenever Glad could bag a visiting lion . . , she would command The Friends to entertain.

Phrases: **a lion in the way** (or **path**) [*Prov.* 26:13] a danger or obstacle, esp. an imaginary one. *beard the lion in his den* (or *lair*): see BEARD *v.* 1. *British Lion*: see senses 3b, c above. *Little Lion*: see sense 5 above. **mountain lion** = PUMA. NEMEAN *lion.* **the lion's mouth** (a type of) a place of great peril. **the lion's provider** the jackal. **the lion's share** the largest or principal portion. *twist the lion's tail*: see TWIST *v.*

Comb.: **lion-ant** = *ant-lion* s.v. ANT *n.*; **lion dance** a traditional Chinese dance in which the dancers are masked and costumed to resemble lions; **lion dog** (*a*) (a dog belonging to) any of several breeds resembling miniature lions in colour or type of fur; (*b*) = *ridgeback* s.v. RIDGE *n.*[1]; **lion-head** a variety of goldfish having an enlarged head; **lion-heart** a courageous person, freq. [tr. Fr. *Cœur de Lion*] as a sobriquet of Richard I, King of England 1189–99; **lion-hearted** *a.* having the heart or courage of a lion; courageous; magnanimously brave; **lion-hunter** a person who hunts lions; a person who is given to lionizing celebrities; **lion-huntress** a female lion-hunter; **Lions Club** any of numerous associated clubs devoted to social and international service, the first of which was founded in Chicago in 1917; **lion's ear** any of various plants of the African genus *Leonotis*, of the mint family, esp. *L. leonurus*, cultivated for its showy orange flowers borne in axillary clusters; **lion's foot** a plant of the Eurasian genus *Leontopodium*, of the composite family, *esp.* edelweiss, *L. alpinum*; **lion's heart** = *obedient plant* s.v. OBEDIENT 1; **lion's leaf** any plant of the Eurasian genus *Leontice*, of the berberis family, esp. *L. leontopetalum*; **lion's tail** the plant *Leonotis leonurus* (see *lion's ear* above); **lion's turnip** = *lion's leaf* above; **lion-tailed macaque** a SW Indian macaque, *Macaca silenus*; **lion tamarin** a golden tamarin, *Leontopithecus rosalia*, of SE Brazil, with long silky golden fur (more fully *golden lion tamarin*); **lion-tawny** *n.* & *a.* (of) the tawny colour characteristic of lions.

B *attrib.* or as *adj.* Like a lion, characteristic of a lion; strong, brave, or fierce as a lion. M16.

MILTON The bold Ascalonite Fled from his Lion ramp. TENNYSON Strong mother of a Lion-line.

lionhood *n.* the state or condition of being a lion M19. **lionish** *a.* resembling, characteristic of, or of the nature of a lion; brave or fierce as a lion: M16. **lionism** *n.* the practice of lionizing; the condition of being treated as a celebrity: M19. **lion-like** *a.* & *adv.* (*a*) *adj.* resembling a lion; characteristic or suggestive of a lion; (*b*) *adv.* in the manner of a lion: M16. **lionship** *n.* M18.

lioncel /ˈlʌɪənsɛl/ *n.* Now *rare.* E17. [OFr. (mod. *lionceau*), dim. of *lion* LION: see -EL[2].] Chiefly *Her.* A young or small lion; *spec.* each of two or more lions appearing together in arms.

lionel /ˈlʌɪən(ə)l/ *n.* Now *rare* or *obs.* M17. [OFr., dim. of *lion* LION: see -EL[2].] *Her.* = prec.

lioness /ˈlʌɪənɪs/ *n.* ME. [OFr. *lion(n)esse*, *leonesse* (mod. *lionne*), f. *lion* LION: see -ESS[1].] 1 A female lion. ME. 2†a A lady visitor to Oxford University. Cf. LION *n.* 6c. *slang.* E–M19. b A female celebrity; a woman who is lionized. Cf. LION *n.* 6b. L19.

lionet /ˈlʌɪənɪt/ *n.* Now *rare.* L16. [OFr., dim. of *lion* LION: see -ET[1].] A young lion.

lionize /ˈlʌɪənʌɪz/ *v.* Also **-ise.** E19. [f. LION + -IZE.] **1** *v.t.* Treat (a person) as a celebrity; make a lion of. E19. **2** *v.t.* & *i.* See the chief sights of (a place); visit or go over (a place of interest). Now *rare.* E19. **b** *v.t.* Show the chief sights of a place to (a person); show the chief sights of (a place). Now *rare.* E19.

lioniˈzation *n.* M19. **lionizer** *n.* E19.

lionly /ˈlʌɪənli/ *a. rare.* M17. [f. LION + -LY[1].] Lion-like.

lip /lɪp/ *n.* [OE *lippa* = OFris. *lippa*, MLG, MDu. *lippe* (whence G *Lippe*), f. Gmc, f. base also of synon. OS *lepor*, OHG *leffur*, *lefs* (G dial. *Lefze*), f. IE base also of L *labia*, *labra* lips.] **I 1** Either of the two fleshy parts which in humans and animals form the upper and lower edges of the mouth-opening. OE. **b** The condition or strength of a wind instrumentalist's lips; embouchure. L19. **†2** Language. Chiefly in *of one lip* (a Hebraism). LME–L17. **3a** Impertinent talk; impudence, cheek. *colloq.* E19. **b** A lawyer, *esp.* a criminal lawyer. *US slang.* E20.

1 SHAKES. *Mids. N. D.* When she drinks, against her lips I bob. MILTON From his Lip Not Words alone pleas'd her. R. L. STEVENSON A cry rose to his lips. DAY LEWIS The set of the lips suggests a certain inward firmness. A. GERAS She . . remembered his lips on the back of her neck. R. B. PARKER I . . licked a little salt off my upper lip. **b** E. LEONARD He could have this job if he promised not to play his horn anymore. Well, he had lost his lip anyway. **3a** B. ASHLEY You wanna watch your lip, son. G. NAYLOR You were standing there, handing him all that lip.

II A thing resembling the lips of the mouth. **4** The margin of a cup or other vessel, or of a bell; the edge of an opening or cavity, e.g. of the crater of a volcano; a (projecting) edge or rim. LME. **5** Each of the edges of a wound. LME. **6** = LABIUM 1, 2, LABRUM. LME. **7** Each of the edges of the aperture of a spiral shell. L17. **8** Either of the upper and lower edges of the aperture of an organ-pipe. E18. **9** *Bot.* Either of the two divisions of a two-lipped corolla or calyx (see *two-lipped* s.v. TWO *a.*). Also = LABELLUM 2. L18.

4 M. R. MITFORD A small brown pitcher with the lip broken. J. HILTON The moon . . swung over the lip of some shadowy eminence. J. S. HUXLEY A splendid waterfall with . . primroses growing near its lip. T. MORRISON The women . . shrieked at the lip of the open grave.

Phrases: **bite one's lip** †(*a*) show vexation, (*b*) repress an emotion, stifle laughter etc. *curl the* or *one's lip*: see CURL *v. hang on a person's lips*: see HANG *v. lick one's lips*: see LICK *v.* **†make (up) a lip** make a face *at*; pout or poke fun *at*. *pass a person's lips*: see PASS *v. seal a person's lips*: see SEAL *v.*[1] *stiff upper lip*: see STIFF *a.* **to the lips** (immersed etc.) very deeply.

Comb.: **lip-brush** a small brush used to apply lipstick; **lip-deep** *a.* (*a*) deeply immersed (chiefly *fig.*); (*b*) of the nature of lip-service; insincere, superficial; **lip gloss** a glossy cosmetic applied to the lips; **lip-labour** (*a*) empty or futile talk; †(*b*) kissing; **lip-line** the outline of a person's lips; **lip microphone**: for use close to a speaker's lips; **lip-read** *v.t.* & *i.* understand (a speaker, speech) solely by observing the movement of the lips; **lip-reader** a person who lip-reads; **lipsalve** (*a*) a preparation (now usu. in stick form) to prevent or relieve sore lips; (*b*) *fig.* flattering speech; **lip-service** service that is proffered but not performed; insincere expressions of support, respect, etc. (chiefly in *pay lip-service to*); **lip-strap**: passing from one cheek of a horse's bit through a ring in the curb chain to the other cheek; **lip-sync(h)** *n.* & *v.* (*a*) *n.* (in film etc. acting) movement of a performer's lips in synchronization with a pre-recorded soundtrack; (*b*) *v.t.* & *i.* perform (esp. a song) on film using this technique; **lip-work** = *lip-labour* above; **lip-worship** worship that consists only in words.

lipless *a.* LME. **liplike** *a.* resembling (that of) a lip M19.

lip /lɪp/ *v.* Infl. **-pp-**. E17. [f. the n.] **I 1** *v.t.* Touch with the lips, apply the lips to; *poet.* kiss; touch lightly, (of water) lap. E17. **2** *v.t.* Say, utter; *esp.* pronounce with the lips only, murmur softly. Also, (*colloq.*) sing. L18. **3** *v.t.* Insult, abuse, be impudent to (someone). *dial.* & *colloq.* L19. **4** *v.t.* Take to the lips; taste, sip, nibble. M20.

1 SHAKES. *Ant. & Cl.* A hand that kings Have lipp'd, and trembled kissing. *Chambers's Journal* Some little bay lipped by the Arctic current. 2 KEATS Salt tears were coming when I heard my name Most fondly lipp'd. B. HINES Billy opened his book, . . and began to lip the words. 4 B. BREYTENBACH Slowly we lipped and sipped our kümmel.

II †5 *v.t.* Edge or overlay the lip of (a vessel). Only in E17. **6** *v.i.* Rise to, cover, or flow over the lip or brim of a vessel; (of a vessel) have liquid flowing over its brim or edge. Chiefly *Sc.* E18. **7** *v.t.* Notch on the lip or edge. E19. **8** *v.t.* Fill in the interstices of (a wall). *Sc.* E19. **9** *v.t.* Serve as a lip or margin to. Cf. LIPPED *a.* M19. **10** *v.i.* Chiefly *Med.* Of bone: grow out (abnormally) or project at an extremity or edge. L19. **11** *v.t. Golf.* Drive the ball just to the lip or edge of (a hole); (of a ball) reach the edge of (a hole) but fail to drop in. L19.

6 R. L. STEVENSON The gunwale was lipping astern. J. MASEFIELD The water . . left a trail, Lipped over on the yard's bricked paving.

lip- *comb. form* see LIPO-.

lipaemia /lɪˈpiːmɪə/ *n.* Also ***-pem-**. L19. [f. LIPO- + -AEMIA.] *Med.* The presence in the blood of an abnormally high concentration of emulsified fat.

lipaemic *a.* characterized by lipaemia L19.

lipase /ˈlɪpeɪz, ˈlʌɪp-/ *n.* L19. [f. LIPO- + -ASE.] *Biochem.* An enzyme which catalyses the hydrolysis of fats and oils to fatty acids and alcohols.

lipemia *n.* see LIPAEMIA.

lipid /ˈlɪpɪd/ *n.* Also (earlier, now *rare*) **-ide** /-ʌɪd/. E20. [Fr. *lipide*, f. as LIPO- + -IDE.] *Biochem.* Any of the large group of fats and fatlike compounds (including oils, waxes, steroids, etc.) which occur in living organisms and are soluble in certain organic solvents but only sparingly soluble in water; (an ester or other derivative of) a fatty acid.

lipiˈdosis *n.*, pl. **-doses** /-ˈdəʊsiːz/, *Med.* a disorder characterized by an excessive accumulation of lipids in tissue M20.

Lipizzaner *n.* var. of LIPPIZANER.

lipo- /ˈlɪpəʊ, ˈlʌɪpəʊ/ *comb. form.* Bef. a vowel **lip-**. [f. Gk *lipos* fat: see -O-.] Chiefly *Biochem.* & *Med.* Forming ns. and adjs. w. the sense 'fat, lipid'.

lipochrome *n.* any naturally occurring pigment which is soluble in fats or fat solvents L19. **lipoˈdystrophy** *n.* any of various disorders of fat metabolism or of the distribution of fat in the body E20. **lipoˈfuscin** *n.* any of various brownish pigments, esp. those deposited in certain body tissues during old age E20. **lipoˈgenesis** *n.* the metabolic formation of fat L19. **liˈpolysis** *n.* the hydrolytic breakdown of fat E20. **lipoˈlytic** *a.* having the property of decomposing or hydrolysing fats L19. **lipoˈlytically** *adv.* as regards lipolysis E20. **lipophile, -ˈphilic** *adjs.* having an affinity for lipids; readily dissolving, or soluble in, lipids: M20. **lipoˈphobic** *a.* tending to repel lipids; not readily soluble in lipids: M20. **lipopolyˈsaccharide** *n.* a complex molecule containing both lipid and polysaccharide parts M20. **lipoprotein** *n.* any of a group of proteins, present esp. in blood plasma and lymph, that have a molecule including a lipid component E20. **liposarˈcoma** *n.*, pl. **-mas, -mata** /-mətə/, a sarcoma of fatty tissue L19. **lipoˈsuction** *n.* a technique of cosmetic surgery in which particles of excess fat are removed through incisions by a vacuum pump L20.

lipogram /ˈlɪpəgram/ *n.* E18. [Back-form. f. Gk *lipogrammatos*: see next, -GRAM.] A composition from which the writer systematically omits a certain letter or certain letters.

lipogrammatic /ˌlɪpə(ʊ)grəˈmatɪk/ *a.* M18. [f. Gk *lipogrammatos* lacking a letter, f. *lip-* wk stem of *leipein* leave, be lacking + *grammat-*, *gramma* letter: see -IC.] Of or pertaining to a lipogram; of the nature of a lipogram.

lipoˈgrammatist *n.* a writer of lipograms E18.

lipography /lɪˈpɒgrəfi/ *n.* L19. [f. Gk *lip-* (see prec.) + -OGRAPHY.] The omission of a letter or syllable in writing, *esp.* the scribal error of writing once what should be written twice.

lipoic /lɪˈpəʊɪk/ *a.* M20. [f. LIPO- + -IC.] Biochem. *lipoic acid*, a sulphur-containing cyclic carboxylic acid, $C_8H_{14}O_2S_2$, which is a cofactor in the metabolic decarboxylation of pyruvate.

lipoate /ˈlɪpəʊeɪt/ *n.* a salt or ester of lipoic acid M20.

lipoid /ˈlɪpɔɪd/ *a.* & *n.* L19. [f. LIPO- + -OID.] *Biochem.* & *Med.* **A** *adj.* Resembling or of the nature of fat. L19. **B** *n.* A fatlike substance; a lipid. E20.

liˈpoidal *a.* resembling or containing fat E20. **lipoiˈdosis** *n.*, pl. **-doses** /-ˈdəʊsiːz/, = LIPIDOSIS M20.

lipoma /lɪˈpəʊmə/ *n.* Pl. **-mas, -mata** /-mətə/. M19. [f. LIPO- + -OMA.] *Med.* A benign tumour of fatty tissue.

lipomaˈtosis *n.* abnormal deposition of fat in other tissue; growth of lipomas: L19.

liposome /ˈlɪpəsəʊm/ *n.* E20. [f. LIPO- + -SOME[3].] *Biol.* **1** A fatty globule suspended in the cytoplasm of a cell. Now *rare.* E20. **2** A minute artificial spherical sac consisting of one or more layers of phospholipid enclosing an aqueous core, used experimentally to represent biological membranes. M20.

lipothymy /lɪˈpɒθɪmi/ *n.* Now *rare* or *obs.* Also in L form **lipothymia** /lɪpəˈθʌɪmɪə/. E17. [f. mod.L *lipothymia* f. Gk *lipothumia*, f. *lip-* (see LIPOGRAMMATIC) + *-o-* + *thumos* animation, spirit: see -Y[3].] Fainting, swooning; an instance of this.

lipoˈthymic *a.* L17.

lipotropic /lɪpə(ʊ)ˈtrəʊpɪk, -ˈtrɒpɪk/ *a.* M20. [f. LIPO- + -TROPIC.] *Physiol.* Tending to prevent or remove an accumulation of excess fat in the liver.

lipotropism *n.* lipotropic property or phenomena M20.

lipped /lɪpt/ *a.* LME. [f. LIP *n.* + -ED[2].] Having or provided with a lip or lips; having lips of a specified kind; *Bot.* labiate.

lippen /ˈlɪpən/ *v.* Chiefly *Sc.* ME. [Origin unkn. See also LICKEN.] **1** *v.i.* Confide, rely, trust. Foll. by *to*, *till*, (occas.) *in*, *into*, *of*, *on*. ME. **2** *v.t.* Entrust. Foll. by *to*, *till*. LME. **3** *v.t.* Expect with confidence. LME.

lipper /ˈlɪpə/ *v.* & *n. dial.* & *Naut.* E16. [Perh. frequent. LAP *v.*[1]: see -ER[5].] **A** *v.i.* Of water: ripple. E16. **B** *n.* A rippling or slight ruffling of the surface of the sea. E16.

Lippes loop /ˈlɪpɪz luːp/ *n. phr.* M20. [Jack *Lippes* (1924–), US obstetrician.] An intrauterine contraceptive device in the shape of a double S.

lippet *n.* var. of LIBBET *n.*[2]

lipping /ˈlɪpɪŋ/ *n.* M19. [f. LIP *v.* + -ING[1].] **1** The action of LIP *v.* M19. **b** *Med.* Abnormal outgrowth of bone at a joint. L19. **2** An edging strip fixed to a board, door, etc.; the action of fixing such a strip. M20.

lippitude /ˈlɪpɪtjuːd/ *n.* Now *rare.* LME. [L *lippitudo*, f. *lippus* bleary-eyed: see -TUDE.] Soreness or bleariness of the eyes; an instance of this.

Lippizaner /lɪpɪtˈsɑːnə, lɪpɪˈzeɪnə/ *n.* Also **Lipizzaner**. E20. [G, f. *Lippiza* (see below).] (An animal of) a fine white breed of horse developed at the former Austrian Imperial stud at Lippiza near Trieste, and used esp. in dressage at the Spanish Riding School, Vienna.

lippy /ˈlɪpi/ *a.* L19. [f. LIP *n.* + -Y[1].] **1** Impertinent, insolent; talkative, verbose. *colloq.* & *dial.* L19. **2** Of a dog: having (unusually) hanging lips. L19.

lipstick /ˈlɪpstɪk/ *n.* & *v.* L19. [f. LIP *n.* + STICK *n.*[1]] **A** *n.* A stick of cosmetic for colouring the lips, usu. a shade of pink or red. L19. **B** *v.t.* & *i.* Apply lipstick to (the lips). E20.

lipsticky *a.* covered or sticky with lipstick M20.

Liptauer /ˈlɪptaʊə/ *n.* E20. [G, f. *Liptó* a place in Slovakia.] A soft cheese originally made in Hungary, usu. coloured and flavoured with paprika and other seasonings. Also *Liptauer cheese*.

†liquable *a.* L15–M18. [L *liquabilis*, f. *liquare*: see LIQUATE, -ABLE.] Able to be liquefied or melted.

†liquamen *n.* LME. [L, f. *liquare*: see next.] **1** A substance reduced to a liquid state. LME–E19. **2** A fluid for administering medicine. *rare.* Only in L19.

liquate /lɪˈkweɪt/ *v.* M17. [L *liquat-* pa. ppl stem of *liquare* make liquid, rel. to L LIQUOR *n.*: see

-ATE³.] †1 *v.t.* & *i.* Make or become liquid, melt. M17–E18. 2 *v.t.* *Metall.* Separate or purify (metals) by melting. M19.

liquation /lɪˈkweɪʃ(ə)n/ *n.* L15. [Late L *liquatio(n-)*, f. as prec.: see -ATION.] 1 *Metall.* The action or process of separating or purifying metals by melting. L15. 2 The process of making or becoming liquid; the condition of being melted; the capacity to be melted. E17–E18.

liquefaction /lɪkwɪˈfakʃ(ə)n/ *n.* LME. [Late L *liquefactio(n-)*, f. L *liquefact-* pa. ppl stem of *liquefacere* LIQUEFY: see -FACTION.] 1 The action or process of liquefying; the state of being liquefied; reduction to a liquid state. LME. †2 *fig.* A 'melting' of the soul by religious ardour. E16–E18.

liquefactive /lɪkwɪˈfaktɪv/ *a.* LME. [med.L *liquefactivus*, f. *liquefact-*: see prec., -IVE.] Having the effect of liquefying.

liquefy /ˈlɪkwɪfʌɪ/ *v.* Also **liquify**. LME. [(O)Fr. *liquéfier* f. L *liquefacere* make liquid, melt (pass. *liquefieri*), f. *liquere* rel. to L LIQUOR *n.*: see -FY.] 1 *v.t.* Make liquid; melt; convert (a gas) to a liquid state. Formerly also, dissolve. LME. 2 *v.i.* Become liquid. Formerly also, become dissolved. L16. b Become intoxicated. *joc.* E19. 3 *v.t.* Pronounce (a consonant) as a liquid. Now *rare* or *obs.* E18.

liquefiable *a.* M16. **liquefied** *a.* (*a*) that has (been) liquefied; (*b*) *joc.* drunk, intoxicated: L16. **liquefier** *n.* E19.

liquesce /lɪˈkwɛs/ *v.i.* *rare.* M19. [L *liquescere*: see next.] Become liquid; *fig.* merge *into.*

liquescent /lɪˈkwɛs(ə)nt/ *a.* E18. [L *liquescent-* pres. ppl stem of *liquescere* become liquid, f. *liquere* rel. to L LIQUOR *n.*: see -ESCENT.] That is in the process of becoming liquid (*lit.* & *fig.*); liable to become liquid.

B. MALAMUD A thin-faced boy with brown liquescent eyes out of Murillo.

liquescence *n.* L19. **liquescency** *n.* (*rare*) M17.

liqueur /lɪˈkjʊə/ *n.* M18. [Fr. = LIQUOR *n.*] 1 Any of various strong sweet alcoholic spirits flavoured with aromatic substances, usu. drunk after a meal. Also, a glass of such a drink. M18. 2 *ellipt.* A liqueur-glass; a liqueur chocolate. E20.

Comb.: **liqueur brandy, whisky**: of supposed special quality, intended to be drunk straight in small quantities like a liqueur; **liqueur chocolate** a chocolate with a liqueur filling; **liqueur-glass** a very small drinking-glass used for liqueurs; *liqueur whisky*: see *liqueur brandy* above.

liquid /ˈlɪkwɪd/ *a.* & *n.* LME. [L *liquidus*, f. *liquere*, rel. to LIQUOR *n.*: see -ID¹.] A *adj.* 1 Of a material substance: in that state (familiar as the normal condition of water, milk, etc.) in which it flows and takes a shape determined by its container while occupying the same volume (rather than dispersing like a gaseous substance); (of a gas) in such a state by reason of low temperature or high pressure. Also, composed of a substance in this condition. LME. b Watery; (occas.) filled with tears. *poet.* L16. 2 Not fixed or stable, fluid. Of movement: facile, unconstrained. LME. 3a Of an account or debt: undisputed. Now only *Sc. Law*, = LIQUIDATE *a.* E16. †b Of a proof, exposition, etc.: clear, evident, manifest. E17–E18. 4 Of light, fire, air, the eyes, etc.: clear, transparent, bright (like pure water). L16. 5 Of sound: flowing, pure and clear in tone; free from harshness or discord; *Phonet.* of the nature of a liquid (see sense B.1 below). E17. 6 (Of assets etc.) able to be easily converted into cash; (already) in the form of cash. Also, having ready cash or liquid assets. Cf. FROZEN *a.* 2c. L19.

1 SPENSER Which feedes each living plant with liquid sap. SHAKES. *Mids. N. D.* Decking with liquid pearl the bladed grass. G. GORDON He .. squirted liquid soap into the sink. b POPE Meanwhile our vessels plough the liquid plain. 2 E. O. M. DEUTSCH The liquid nature, so to speak, of its technical terms. *New Yorker* A tall Bedouin .. walking with long, liquid strides. 4 DRYDEN They That wing the liquid Air, or swim the Sea. T. GRAY The insect youth .., Eager to .. float amid the liquid noon. R. P. JHABVALA The Rawul's eyes were not the usual kind of liquid brown. 5 J. BURROUGHS The liquid and gurgling tones of the bobolink. H. SWEET 'Liquid' voiced consonants .. unaccompanied by buzz. R. THOMAS Laura tried to get her stiff tongue around the soft, liquid sounds. 6 N. FREELING Were they realizing assets, gathering up all the liquid money they could find?

B *n.* 1 *Phonet.* A voiced frictionless continuant consonant, *spec.* an oral rather than a nasal one (denoted by the letters *l*, *m*, *n*, and *r*, *spec.* the letters *l* and *r*). M16. 2 A liquid substance; liquid matter. In *pl.* freq., liquid food. E18.

2 *noble liquid*: see NOBLE *a.*

Special collocations & *comb.*: **liquid compass** a form of magnetic compass in which the card and needle are mainly supported by floating in a liquid. **liquid crystal** *Physical Chem.* a turbid liquid that exhibits double refraction (indicative of some degree of ordering in its internal structure) and exists as a distinct state of certain pure substances between the melting point and some higher temperature, at which it becomes an ordinary liquid; *liquid crystal display*, a visual display, esp. of segmented numbers or letters, in which liquid crystals are made visible by temporarily modifying their capacity to reflect light. **liquid drop** a small drop of liquid, *spec.* (*Physics*) as a model for the theoretical description of an atomic nucleus. **liquid fire** a very fiery (in taste) or highly combustible liquid; *esp.* one that can be sent as a burning jet in warfare. **liquid lunch** *colloq.* a midday meal at which alcoholic drink rather than food is consumed. **liquid manure** a water extract of manure used as a fertilizer. **liquid measure** a unit for expressing the volume of liquids. **liquid paper** (also **Liquid Paper**, US proprietary name) correction fluid. **liquid paraffin** *Pharm.* an almost tasteless and odourless oily liquid that consists of hydrocarbons obtained from petroleum and is used as a laxative and in dressings. **liquid petroleum** *US* = *liquid paraffin* above. **liquid rheostat**: that uses an electrolyte solution as the resistive element. **liquid starter** a liquid rheostat used as a starter of an electric motor. *liquid storax*: see STORAX 1.

liquidly *adv.* †(*a*) clearly, plainly; (*b*) in a liquid manner; after the manner of a liquid: E17. **liquidness** *n.* M16. **liquidy** *a.* (*rare*) of a liquid nature; somewhat liquid: LME.

liquidambar /lɪkwɪdˈambə/ *n.* L16. [mod.L, app. irreg. f. L *liquidus* LIQUID *a.* + med.L *ambar* AMBER.] 1 A resinous gum which exudes from the bark of trees of the genus *Liquidambar* (see below); liquid storax. Cf. AMBER *n.* 4. L16. 2 Any of various trees of the genus *Liquidambar* of the witch-hazel family, esp. *L. orientalis* of Asia Minor, and *L. styraciflua*, the sweet gum of N. America. M18.

liquidate /ˈlɪkwɪdeɪt/ *a.* Now only *Sc.* M16. [med.L *liquidatus* pa. pple, f. as next: see -ATE².] *Law.* Of a debt or other sum: ascertained and fixed in amount by written agreement or the decree of a court. Cf. LIQUID *a.* 3a.

liquidate /ˈlɪkwɪdeɪt/ *v.* Pa. pple **-ated**, (earlier) †**-ate**. M16. [med.L *liquidat-* pa. ppl stem of *liquidare*, f. L *liquidus*: see LIQUID, -ATE³. The financial senses are due to It. *liquidare*, Fr. *liquider*, sense 6 after Russ. *likvidirovat'*.] †1 *v.t.* Determine and apportion by agreement or by litigation; reduce to order, set out clearly (accounts). Cf. prec. M16–L18. †2 *v.t.* a Clear away, resolve (objections). *rare.* E17–M19. b Make clear or plain; render unambiguous; settle. M17–L18. 3 *v.t.* Liquefy, melt; *fig.* dissipate, waste. *rare.* M17. 4 *v.t.* Clear off, pay (a debt). E18. 5a *v.t.* Ascertain and set out clearly the liabilities of (a company or firm) and arrange the apportioning of the assets; wind up. Also, convert to liquid assets. L19. b *v.i.* Go into liquidation. L19. 6 *v.t.* Put an end to or get rid of, esp. by violent means; wipe out; kill. E20.

6 B. BETTELHEIM Even before an extermination policy went into effect, the Gestapo had been liquidating unfit persons. L. DEIGHTON Do German communities still exist in Russia? I thought Stalin liquidated them .. in the forties.

liquidator *n.* (*a*) a person appointed to conduct the winding up of a company; (*b*) a person who implements a policy of liquidation: M19.

liquidation /lɪkwɪˈdeɪʃ(ə)n/ *n.* M16. [Fr., f. *liquider* liquidate, or directly f. prec.: see -ATION. Cf. med.L *liquidatio(n-)* making clear, explaining.] †1 *Law.* The action or process of ascertaining and apportioning the amounts of a debt etc. M16–M18. 2 The clearing off or settling of a debt. L18. 3 The action or process of winding up the affairs of a company etc.; the state or condition of being wound up; esp. in *go into liquidation.* Also, the selling of certain assets in order to achieve greater liquidity. M19. 4 The action or fact of partaking of an alcoholic drink. *rare.* L19. 5 The action or process of abolishing or eliminating something or someone; the doing away with or killing of unwanted people. E20. 6 *Chess.* A rapid exchange of pieces leading to simplification of the position. M20.

liquidise *v.* var. of LIQUIDIZE.

liquidity /lɪˈkwɪdɪti/ *n.* E17. [Fr. *liquidité* or med.L *liquiditas*, or directly f. LIQUID *a.*: see -ITY.] 1 The quality or condition of being liquid. E17. 2 Clearness or purity of tone. E19. 3 The interchangeability of assets and money; availability of liquid assets. E20.

Comb.: **liquidity preference** the holding of assets in money or near money in preference to securities or interest-bearing investments; **liquidity ratio** the proportion of total assets which is held in liquid or cash form.

liquidize /ˈlɪkwɪdʌɪz/ *v.* Also **-ise**. M19. [f. LIQUID *a.* + -IZE.] 1 *v.t.* & *i.* Make or become liquid. M19. 2 *v.t.* Purée, emulsify, or blend (food), *esp.* in a liquidizer. M20.

liquidizer *n.* a machine used in the preparation of food, to make purées, emulsify, etc. M20.

liquidus /ˈlɪkwɪdəs/ *n.* E20. [L = LIQUID *a.*] A line or surface in a phase diagram, or a temperature (corresponding to a point on the line or surface), above which a mixture is entirely liquid and below which it consists of liquid and solid in equilibrium. Also *liquidus curve, surface, temperature.*

liquify *v.* var. of LIQUEFY.

liquor /ˈlɪkə/ *n.* ME. [OFr. *licur, licour* (mod. LIQUEUR) f. L *liquor* rel. to *liquare* liquefy, filter, *liqui* flow, *liquere* be fluid.] 1 A liquid; matter in a liquid state; a fluid. *obs.* exc. as below. ME. 2 Liquid for drinking; beverage, drink. Now usu. (a kind of) alcoholic drink, esp. produced by distillation. ME. b A drink of an intoxicating beverage. *slang* (chiefly *US*). M19. 3 The water in which meat has been boiled; broth, sauce; the fat in which bacon, fish, etc., has been fried; the liquid contained in oysters. LME. †4 Grease or oil for lubricating purposes. Cf. LIQUOR *v.* 1. *dial.* M–L16. 5 A liquid of a particular kind used or produced in a chemical or industrial process etc. Also, the liquid part of a secretion; *Med.* = *liquor amnii* below. M16. b *Brewing.* Water. M18. c *Pharm.* An aqueous solution of a particular substance. L18. d The liquid produced by infusion of a tea. L19.

1 SHAKES. *Temp.* Yond .. black cloud, .. looks like a foul bombard that would shed his liquor. 2 M. PUZO There was also plenty of liquor; champagne .., scotch, rye, brandy. 3 J. GRIGSON Simmer 4 oysters .. in their own liquor. 5 *Nature* Lignins are produced .. in waste liquors from pulping processes.

Phrases: **in liquor** intoxicated. ***liquor amnii*** /lɪkwɔːr ˈamnɪʌɪ, lʌɪkwɔːr, lʌɪkər/ [L] *Med.* amniotic fluid. *malt liquor*: see MALT *n.*¹ & *a.* *mother liquor*: see MOTHER *n.*¹ *spirituous liquor*: see SPIRITUOUS 3. VINOUS *liquor*.

liquorless *a.* M19. **liquorous** *a.* †(*a*) liquid; (*b*) full of (alcoholic) liquor; redolent of liquor: L17.

liquor /ˈlɪkə/ *v.* E16. [f. the n.] 1 *v.t.* Cover or smear with a liquor; *esp.* lubricate or dress with grease or oil. Now *rare.* E16. 2 *v.t.* Supply with liquor to drink; ply with liquor. Also *liquor up.* Now *slang.* M16. 3 *v.t.* Steep in, soak, or treat with a liquor; steep (malt) in water. M18. 4 *v.i.* Drink alcoholic liquor. Also *liquor up. slang.* M19. 5 *v.i.* Of tea: produce an infusion (of a specified quality). Chiefly as *liquoring* ppl a. L19.

1 †**liquor a person's hide** thrash or beat a person.

liquorice /ˈlɪk(ə)rɪs, -rɪʃ/ *n.* Also **licorice**. ME. [AN *lycorys*, OFr. *licoresse, -ece*, f. (w. assim. to *licor* LIQUOR *n.*) late L *liquiritia* f. Gk *glukurrhiza*, f. *glukus* sweet + *rhiza* root.] 1 The rhizome (also *liquorice-root*) of the plant *Glycyrrhiza glabra* (see below); a preparation made from the evaporated juice of this, used medicinally and as a sweet, usu. in the form of a black chewy substance. ME. 2 The leguminous plant *Glycyrrhiza glabra*, native to the Mediterranean region and central and SW Asia. ME. 3 With specifying wd: a preparation which resembles or is used as a substitute for the true liquorice; (the root of) a plant providing this. LME.

3 *Indian liquorice*: see INDIAN *a.* **wild liquorice** a Eurasian milk-vetch of calcareous hedge banks and scrub, *Astragalus glycyphyllus*, with axillary racemes of cream-coloured flowers.

Comb.: *liquorice-root*: see sense 1 above; **liquorice-stick** a stick of liquorice, as a sweet; **liquorice vetch** = *wild liquorice* above.

liquorish /ˈlɪkərɪʃ/ *a.*[1] L19. [f. LIQUOR *n.* + -ISH[1].] Fond of or indicating fondness for liquor.

liquorishly *adv.* M19. **liquorishness** *n.* L18.

liquorish *a.*[2] var. of LICKERISH.

liquorist /ˈlɪkərɪst/ *n.* M19. [Fr. *liquoriste*, f. as LIQUEUR: see -IST.] A person who makes liqueurs.

lira /ˈlɪərə, *foreign* ˈliːra/ *n.* Pl. **lire** /ˈlɪəri, ˈlɪəreɪ, *foreign* liːre/, (occas.) **liras**. E17. [It. f. Prov. *liura* = Fr. LIVRE, It. *libbra*, f. L *libra* pound.] 1 The basic monetary unit of Italy, used also in San Marino and the Vatican City State, equal to 100 centesimi; a coin or note of this value. Also, the basic monetary unit of Malta, equal to 100 cents. E17. 2 The basic monetary unit of Turkey, equal to 100 kurus. L19.

lirate /ˈlʌɪərət/ *a.* L19. [f. L *lira* ridge + -ATE[2].] *Zool.* Of a shell: having ridges.

li'ration *n.* lirate marking E20.

lire /lʌɪə/ *n.*[1] Long *obs.* exc. *Sc.* & *north.* [OE *līra* rel. to ON *lær*, Sw. *lår* thigh, ON *leggr* leg. Cf. LEER *n.*[2]] Flesh, muscle, brawn.

liry *a.* L15.

lire *n.*[2]*pl.* see LIRA.

lirella /lɪˈrɛlə/ *n.* M19. [mod.L (= Fr. *lirelle*), dim. of L *lira* furrow: see -ELLA.] *Bot.* The narrow apothecium, with a furrow along the middle, found in some lichens.

lirelliform *a.* shaped like a lirella M19.

†**liriconfancy** *n.* M16–M18. [Alt. of L *lilium convallium*, infl. by FANCY *n.* & *a.*] The lily of the valley, *Convallaria majalis*.

liriodendron /lʌɪrɪəˈdɛndrɒn/ *n.* E19. [mod.L (see below), f. Gk *leirion* lily + *dendron* tree.] Either of two trees of the genus *Liriodendron*, of the magnolia family; *esp.* the tulip tree, *L. tulipifera*, of the eastern US.

liripipe /ˈlɪrɪpʌɪp/ *n.* Also (the usual form in sense 1) **-poop** /-puːp/. M16. [med.L *liripipium*, *lero-* variously explained as 'tippet of a hood', 'cord', 'shoelace', of unkn. origin. Forms in *-poop* unexpl. See also LURRY *n.*] 1 A thing to be learned and acted or spoken; one's lesson, one's rôle. Chiefly in *know* or *have one's liripoop*, *teach a person his* or *her liripoop*. Long *arch. rare.* M16. 2 A silly person. Long *arch. rare.* E17. 3 A long tail of a hood, esp. in old academic or clerical dress or attached to a medieval chaperon; a very long tippet. E17.

lirk /ləːk/ *n.* & *v. Sc.* & *north.* LME. [Origin unkn.] A *n.* A fold in the skin; a wrinkle. LME. B *v.i.* & *t.* Wrinkle. L17.

lis /liːs/ *n.*[1] Pl. same, (*rare*) **lisses**. E17. [Fr. = lily.] *Her.* = FLEUR-DE-LIS 2.

lis /lɪs/ *n.*[2] M18. [L = quarrel, dispute.] *Law.* A lawsuit; a process or action at law.

lis pendens /ˈpɛndɛnz/ a suit (elsewhere) pending; a formal notice that legal action is pending.

lis /lɪs/ *n.*[3] Also **liss**. M19. [Ir. *lios*, OIr. *lis*, *less* = Welsh *llys*.] *Ir. Antiq.* A circular enclosure having an earthen wall, often used as a fort.

Lisbon /ˈlɪzb(ə)n/ *n.* M17. [The capital of Portugal, Port. *Lisboa*.] 1 *gen. attrib.* Designating things found or made in, associated with, or obtained from Lisbon, Portugal. M17. 2 *Hist.* More fully *Lisbon wine*. A Portuguese white wine imported from Lisbon. E18. †3 More fully *Lisbon sugar*. A kind of soft sugar. M18–E19. 4 A kind of lemon with a relatively sour taste. L19.

lisente *n.* pl. of SENTE.

li shu /ˈliː ʃu/ *n. phr.* L19. [Chin. *lì shū* clerical writing.] In Chinese calligraphy, a form of script developed during the Han dynasty and widely adopted for official and educational purposes.

lisk /lɪsk/ *n.* Long *obs.* exc. *dial.* ME. [Prob. of Scand. origin: cf. MSw. *liuske*, Da. *lyske*.] The loin or flank. Also, the groin.

lisle /lʌɪl, liːl/ *n.* Also (formerly usu.) **L-**. M16. [*Lisle*, former name of a town in NE France (now *Lille*).] 1 *attrib.* Made in, associated with, or obtained from Lille, France. Chiefly & now only *spec.* designating or made of a fine smooth cotton thread, used for stockings etc. M16. 2 (Cloth made from) lisle thread. M16.

lisp /lɪsp/ *n.*[1] E17. [f. the vb.] 1 The action or an act of lisping; a lisping pronunciation. E17. 2 *transf.* A sound resembling a lisp, as the rippling of water, the rustle of leaves. M19.

lispy *a.* characterized by a lisp, inclined to lisp M19.

Lisp /lɪsp/ *n.*[2] Also **LISP**. M20. [f. *list processor*: see s.v. LIST *n.*[3]] *Computing.* A high-level programming language devised for list processing.

lisp /lɪsp/ *v.* [OE *ā*)*wlyspian*, f. *wlisp*, *wlips* (adj.) lisping: cf. MLG *wilspen*, *wlispen* (Du. *lispen*), OHG *lisp* stammering, *lispen* lisp (G *lispeln*). Of imit. origin.] 1 *v.i.* Substitute sounds approaching /θ/ and /ð/ for the sibilants /s/ and /z/ in speaking; (esp. of a child) speak with imperfect pronunciation. OE. 2 *v.t.* Utter with a lisp or lispingly. Also foll. by *out*. E17.

1 *fig.*: W. DE LA MARE Each leaf to its sisters lisps softly.

lisper *n.* LME.

lisping /ˈlɪspɪŋ/ *ppl a.* M16. [f. LISP *v.* + -ING[2].] That lisps; (of a sound or utterance) characterized by a lisp or lisping.

lispingly *adv.* M17.

lispound /ˈlɪspaʊnd/ *n.* E16. [LG, Du. *lispund*, for *livsch pund* lit. 'Livonian pound'.] *Hist.* A unit of weight used in the Baltic trade, and in Orkney and Shetland, varying at different periods and in different localities from 12 to 30 pounds (approx. 5½ to 13½ kg).

†**liss** *n.*[1] [OE *līþs*, *liss*, f. *līþe* LITHE *a.*] 1 Remission, release; mitigation, abatement; cessation, end. OE–L19. 2 Tranquillity, peace, rest; joy, delight. OE–LME.

liss *n.*[2] var. of LIS *n.*[3]

liss /lɪs/ *v. obs.* exc. *Sc.* & *N. Ir.* [OE *lissian*, f. as LISS *n.*[1]] †1 *v.t.* Subdue; mitigate, relieve (pain etc.). OE–M16. †2 *v.t.* Relieve (*of* pain etc.); comfort. LME–L15. 3 *v.i.* Abate, cease; be relieved *of*. LME.

Lissajous /ˈlɪsaʒuː/ *n.* L19. [Jules Antoine *Lissajous* (1822–80), Fr. physicist.] Used *attrib.* and in *possess.* to designate the plane figures (mostly crossed loops and simple curves) traced by a point executing two independent simple harmonic motions at right angles to one another and with frequencies in a simple numerical ratio.

lisse /liːs (*pl. same*)/ *n.* & *a.* M19. [Fr. = smooth (in *crêpe lisse*).] (Of) a kind of silk or cotton gauze.

lissoir /ˈliːswɑː; *foreign* liswaːr (*pl. same*)/ *n.* E20. [Fr., f. *lisser* to smooth + *-oir*, -ORY[1].] *Archaeol.* A smoothing, polishing tool.

lissom /ˈlɪs(ə)m/ *a.* Also **lissome**. L18. [Contr. f. as LITHESOME.] Supple, limber; lithe and agile.

lissomly *adv.* E20. **lissomness** *n.* M19.

list /lɪst/ *n.*[1] & *a.* [OE *līste* = MDu. *lijste* (Du. *lijst*), OHG *līsta* (G *Leiste*), f. Gmc. In tilting repr. OFr. *lisse* (mod. *lice*).] A *n.* I Border, edging, strip. 1a *gen.* A border, a hem, a bordering strip. Long *rare*. OE. †b A lobe of an ear. M16–M17. 2 A strip of cloth or other fabric; *spec.* the selvage or edge of a cloth, usually of different material from the body of the cloth. ME. b Such selvages collectively; material used for the selvage of cloth. M16. 3†a A band or strip of any material; a line or band conspicuously marked on a surface. LME–L18. b A section of hair of a head or on a beard. M19. 4 A stripe of colour. L15. 5 *Archit.* A small square moulding or ring encircling the foot of a column, between the torus below and the shaft above (cf. LISTEL). Formerly also, a spiral line of a volute. M17.

II Boundary. †6 A limit, a boundary. Freq. in *pl.* LME–M17. 7a In *pl.* (†sometimes treated as *sing.*). The palisades or other barriers enclosing a space set apart for tilting; a space so enclosed for tilting-matches or tournaments. LME. b *transf.* & *fig.* A place or scene of combat or contest. L16. †8a *sing.* & in *pl.* An encircling palisade; a railed or staked enclosure. L16–M18. b In *pl.*, the starting-place of a race (= L *carceres*). Also *sing.*, a racecourse or exercising-ground for horses. L16–M18.

7b **enter the lists** make or accept a challenge, esp. to controversy (foll. by *against*).

B *attrib.* or as *adj.* Made of list or material used for selvages. M17.

list /lɪst/ *n.*[2] ME. [f. LIST *v.*[1]] †1 Pleasure, joy, delight. ME–L16. 2 Appetite, craving; desire, longing; inclination. Foll. by *to* a thing, *to do*. *arch.* ME. 3 (One's) desire or wish; (one's) good pleasure. *arch.* ME.

list /lɪst/ *n.*[3] L16. [Fr. *liste* = Sp., It. *lista*, presumably f. as LIST *n.*[1] (from a strip of paper).] A catalogue or roll consisting of a row or series of names, figures, words, etc.; *spec.* (*a*) in early use, a catalogue of the names of people engaged in the same duties or connected with the same object; (*b*) a catalogue of the soldiers of an army or of a particular arm; (*c*) a catalogue of the titles of the books (to be) published by a particular publisher; (*d*) an official register of buildings of architectural or historical importance that are statutorily protected from demolition or major alteration; (*e*) in the National Health Service, a general practitioner's register of patients; (*f*) *Computing* a formalized representation of the concept of a list, used for the storage of data or in list processing.

housing list, *reading list*, *transfer list*, *waiting-list*, *wine list*, etc. *active list*: see ACTIVE *a.* 5. *backlist*: see BACK-. *blacklist*: see BLACK *a.* *civil list*: see CIVIL *a.* *free list*: see FREE *a.* *linked list*: see LINKED *a.* 1. LLOYD'S *List*. *Reserved List*: see RESERVED 3. RETIRED *list*. *secret list*: see SECRET *a.* & *n.* *short list*: see SHORT *a.* *sick list*: see SICK *a.* *white list*: see WHITE *a.*

Comb.: **list broker** a trader in mailing lists; **list-broking** trading in mailing lists; **list price** the price shown for an article in a printed list issued by the maker, or by the general body of makers of the particular class of goods; **list processing** *Computing* the manipulation and use of chained lists and of data in them; **list processor** *Computing* a processing system, language, etc., for use in list processing; **list system** a system of voting, common in Continental western Europe, in which voters cast their vote for a list of candidates rather than for an individual candidate; **list vote, voting** a vote cast, voting, under a list system.

list /lɪst/ *n.*[4] M17. [Origin unkn.] 1 *Naut.* A careening or inclination of a ship to one side (owing to a leak, shifting cargo, etc.). M17. 2 *transf.* A leaning over (of a building etc.). L18.

1 S. J. PERELMAN The ship had developed a dangerous list to port. 2 E. HEMINGWAY The lovely *campanile* . . that has damn near as much list on it as the leaning tower of Pisa.

list /lɪst/ *v.*[1]*t.* *arch.* 3 sing pres. **list, listeth,** (*pers.*) **lists**; pa. **list, listed**. [OE *lystan* = OS *lustian* (Du. *lusten*), OHG *lusten* (G *lüsten*), ON *lysta*, f. Gmc, f. base of LUST *n.*] 1 *impers.* (In OE with *accus.* or *dat.*) Be pleasing to. OE. 2 *pers.* Desire, like, wish, (*to do*). ME.

1 W. RALEIGH When it listeth him to call them to an account. P. FLETCHER When me list to sadder tunes apply me. 2 S. RICHARDSON Let them think what they list. SIR W. SCOTT We will, if your ladyship lists, leave him. H. ALLEN We shall make as many detours as we list.

list /lɪst/ *v.*[2] *arch.* [OE *hlystan*, ult. f. Gmc base repr. also by LISTEN *v.*] 1 *v.i.* Listen (*to*, *unto*). OE. 2 *v.t.* Listen to, hear. ME.

list /lɪst/ *v.*[3]*t.* ME. [f. LIST *n.*[1] Cf. OFr. *lister* put a list on (cloth), Du. *lijsten*.] †1 Put a list or edge round (an object); put as a list *upon*; fix list on the edge of (a door). ME–L19. †2 Enclose; shut *in* with rails etc. L15–M16. 3 *Carpentry.* Cut away the sappy edge of (a board); shape (a block or stave) by chopping. M17. 4 *Agric.* Prepare (land) for a crop by making ridges and furrows with a lister or beds and alleys with a hoe. *US.* L18.

list /lɪst/ *v.*[4] In senses 3, 4 now also **'list**. E17. [f. LIST *n.*[3] In senses 3, 4 now aphet. f. ENLIST.] 1 *v.t.* Set down together or enter in a list; make a list of; catalogue, register; *spec.* (*a*) approve (a stock or other security) for dealing on a stock exchange (usu. in *pass.*); (*b*) *N. Amer.* place (a property) in the hands of a real-estate agent for sale or rent; add to the list of properties advertised by a real-estate agent; (*c*) enter (a name and address) in a telephone directory; (*d*) protect (a building etc.) by inclusion in a statutory preservation register; (*e*) *Computing* display or print out (a program, the contents of a file, etc.). E17. **b** *v.i.* Be specified in a list (*at*, *for* a price). M20. **2** *v.t.* Include as if in a list or catalogue; categorize *among, in, under, with*, etc.; report, mention. E17. **3** *v.t.* Enter on the list of a military body; appoint formally to a post in a military body. In later use *spec.* enlist (oneself, another) for military service. *arch.* M17. **4** *v.i.* Have one's name entered on the list of a military body; enlist for military service. *arch.* M17.

1 SCOTT FITZGERALD I tried . . to list the quotations on an interminable amount of stock. *Listener* The Stock Exchange now lists the Shares of the Houston Natural Gas Corporation. F. SPALDING Kenneth Clark, writing on the 'New Romanticism in British Painting' . . listed Sutherland, Piper and Moore as the leading figures. **2** SWIFT It is under this class I have presumed to list my present treatise. *Anderson (S. Carolina) Independent* McGee listed the time of death as approximately 10 a.m. Tuesday. *blacklist*: see BLACK *a.* **3** STEELE A Drum passing by, . . I listed myself for a Soldier. R. KIPLING There's a Legion that never was 'listed. *transf.*: J. BENTHAM Men whose affections are already listed against the law in question. **4** W. BLACKSTONE If any officer and soldier . . shall desert, or list in any other regiment. *transf.*: T. HOOD When first the scholar lists in learning's train.

list /lɪst/ *v.*[5]*i.* E17. [f. LIST *n.*[4]] (Of a ship) careen, heel, or incline to one side; *transf.* (of a building etc.) lean over.

A. SCHLEE The deck listed with the weight of passengers. J. C. OATES Sauntering about with the baby on her hip, listing to one side.

listable /ˈlɪstəb(ə)l/ *a.* Orig. *US.* M17. [f. LIST *v.*[4] + -ABLE.] Able to be listed or put on a list.

listed /ˈlɪstɪd/ *a.*[1] ME. [f. LIST *v.*[3], *n.*[1]: see -ED[1], -ED[2].] **I 1** Bordered, edged; striped; (of colours) arranged in bands or stripes. ME. **2** Provided with a list or selvage. M16. **3** Covered or edged with list. E19. **4** *Basket-making.* Having an extra (decorative) skein on a handle. E20. **II 5** Enclosed, fenced in; *spec.* (of ground) enclosed in or converted into lists for tilting; (of a combat) fought in the lists. LME **6** Engaged in the lists. *poet.* M18.

listed /ˈlɪstɪd/ *a.*[2] M17. [f. LIST *v.*[4] + -ED[1].] **1** Enlisted for military service. *arch.* M17. **2** Included in a list, directory, or catalogue; *spec.* (of a building) protected from demolition or major alteration by being included in an official list of buildings of architectural or historical importance. E20.

2 *Western Mail (Cardiff)* The thatched cottage . . is 18th century in part and it is a grade two listed building. M. BRETT The Stock Exchange . . requires that listed companies produce figures showing profits.

listel /ˈlɪst(ə)l/ *n.* L16. [It. *listello* (whence also Fr. *listel*) dim. of *lista* LIST *n.*[1]] *Archit.* A small list or fillet.

listen /ˈlɪs(ə)n/ *n.* LME. [f. the vb.] †**1** Hearing, sense of hearing. Only in LME. **2** The action or an act of listening; a spell of listening or attentive hearing. Also *listen-in*. L18.

2 G. MANVILLE FENN She was often on the watch, and always on the listen. P. BAIR 'Did you have a nice listen?' 'I had a long listen'.

listen /ˈlɪs(ə)n/ *v.* [OE *hlysnan* corresp. to MHG *lüsenen*, f. WGmc, f. Gmc base repr. also by LIST *v.*[2]] **1** *v.t.* Hear attentively; pay attention to (a person speaking or some utterance). Now *arch.* & *poet.* OE. **2** *v.i.* **a** Give attention with the ear to some sound or utterance or person speaking; make an effort to hear something. ME. **b** Give attention with the ear *to, unto*; (in extended use) pay heed *to*, yield *to* (a person furnishing) a temptation or request. ME. **3** *v.i.* Sound (in a certain way), convey a certain impression *to* a listener. *US.* E20.

1 TENNYSON Listening the lordly music. **2a** D. H. LAWRENCE She stood and listened, and it seemed to her she heard sounds from the back of the cottage. *Radio Times* We sat listening . . with a portable set. H. ROTH Listen, I have an idea. *listen good*: see GOOD *a.* **b** R. GRAVES Listen to those doors banging. D. LESSING I've listened to you two talk all my life. J. SIMMS My teacher is a fine critic and I listen carefully to him. *listen to reason*: see REASON *n.*[1]

With advs. & preps. in specialized senses: **listen for** be eager or make an effort to catch the sound of; endeavour to hear or to hear of. **listen in** use a radio receiving set to listen to a broadcast programme etc., listen secretly to or tap a telephonic communication, listen to the conversation etc. of others, (foll. by *to*, *on*). **listen out** listen eagerly or carefully, listen for a sound on a radio receiver etc.; *listen out for* = *listen for* above.

listenable /ˈlɪs(ə)nəb(ə)l/ *a.* E19. [f. LISTEN *v.* + -ABLE.] **1** Willing to listen. Now *rare.* E19. **2** Easy or pleasant to listen to. E20.

listenaˈbility *n.* M20.

listener /ˈlɪs(ə)nə/ *n.* E17. [f. LISTEN *v.* + -ER[1].] **1** A person who listens; an attentive hearer. Also *listener-in*. E17. **2** The ear. *arch. slang.* E19. **3** *Fortif.* = LISTENING *gallery*. E19.

1 LD MACAULAY The streets were stopped up . . by groups of talkers and listeners. *Daily Chronicle* By the magic of wireless it was, perhaps, the listeners-in who heard it first. R. JARRELL He was a remarkably polite listener, and nodded all the time you spoke. R. THOMAS You just sit there and listen. You're a pretty good listener, aren't you?

listenership *n.* the estimated number of listeners to a broadcast programme or to radio (*spec.* as opp. to television) M20.

listening /ˈlɪs(ə)nɪŋ/ *n.* ME. [f. LISTEN *v.* + -ING[1].] **1** The action of LISTEN *v.*; an instance of this. Also *listening-in*. ME. **2** With qualifying adj.: broadcast, recorded, or other matter for listening to, esp. with reference to its quality or kind. M20.

1 TENNYSON Lonely listenings to my mutter'd dream. *Saturday Evening Post* These telephones were connected with a listening-in device concealed behind a picture on the wall. **2** *Church Times* Other incidents in his life also made interesting listening.

Comb.: **listening gallery** *Fortif.* an advanced trench or gallery used to listen to the movements of an enemy; **listening post** *Mil.* an advanced position used to discover movements or the disposition of an enemy; *transf.* a station for intercepting electronic communications, a position from which to listen.

lister /ˈlɪstə/ *n.*[1] L17. [f. LIST *v.*[4] + -ER[1].] **1** A person who enlists others for military service. *arch.* L17. **2** A person who makes out a list. L17.

lister /ˈlɪstə/ *n.*[2] *US.* L19. [f. LIST *v.*[3] + -ER[1].] A double-mould-board plough which throws up ridges and at the same time plants and covers seed in the furrows.

listeria /lɪˈstɪərɪə/ *n.* Pl. **-s**, same. M20. [mod.L (see below), f. Joseph *Lister*, 1827–1912, Eng. surgeon: see -IA[1].] *Bacteriol.* A bacterium of the genus *Listeria*, esp. *L. monocytogenes*, a widespread pathogen of people and animals.

listerial, **listeric** /lɪˈstɛrɪk/ *adjs.* caused by or derived from listerias M20. **listeriˈosis** *n.* infection with, or a disease caused by, listerias (contracted esp. by the ingestion of contaminated food or silage) M20.

listful /ˈlɪstfʊl, -f(ə)l/ *a. arch.* L16. [f. LIST *v.*[2] + -FUL.] Inclined to listen, attentive.

listing /ˈlɪstɪŋ/ *n.*[1] LME. [f. LIST *n.*[1] + -ING[1].] **1** A selvage, a border; material used for the selvage of cloth. LME. **2** *Basket-making.* Extra (decorative) skeining on a handle. E20.

listing /ˈlɪstɪŋ/ *n.*[2] M17. [f. LIST *v.*[4] + -ING[1].] **1** The action of enlisting someone; enrolment. *arch.* M17. **2** The action of listing someone or something; the drawing up of a list. M17. **3** An entry in a catalogue, telephone directory, timetable, or other list or register (freq. in *pl.*); a list; *Computing* a printed or displayed copy of a program or of the contents of a file. E20.

3 *Times* The consortium says that it intends to retain a Stock Exchange listing. E. LEONARD He remembered from the TV listings that both movies first came out in 1957. *New Yorker* A real-estate agent . . who . . had a listing just a couple of houses down from Jennifer's.

listless /ˈlɪs(t)lɪs/ *a.* LME. [f. LIST *n.*[2] + -LESS.] Characterized by unwillingness to move, act, or make any exertion; marked by languid indifference. Formerly also, without relish or inclination for some specified object or pursuit (foll. by *of*).

S. RAVEN James' growing indifference was reflected in the boys' bored and listless play. N. BAWDEN She was so listless, all her old sparkle gone. A. HUTSCHNECKER Humiliation and a sense of futility caused apathetic, listless, states of mind.

listlessly *adv.* L17. **listlessness** *n.* M17.

Lisu /ˈliːsuː/ *n.* & *a.* L19. [Yi (Lisu).] **A** *n.* Pl. **-s**, same. A member of a Tibeto-Burman people of the mountainous south-west region of China; the Yi dialect of this people. L19. **B** *adj.* Designating or pertaining to the Lisu or their dialect. E20.

Lisztian /ˈlɪstɪən/ *a.* & *n.* L19. [f. *Liszt* (see below) + -IAN.] **A** *adj.* Of, pertaining to, or characteristic of the Hungarian pianist and composer Ferenc (Franz) Liszt (1811–86) or his music. L19. **B** *n.* An interpreter, student, or admirer of Liszt or his music. M20.

lit /lɪt/ *n. obs.* exc. *dial.* ME. [ON *litr*: cf. LITMUS.] **1** A colour, a dye; a stain. ME. **2** Dye stuff; a batch of dyeing. ME.

lit /lɪt/ *a.* E19. [pa. pple of LIGHT *v.*[2]] **1** That has been lit; lighted, illumined. Also foll. by *up*. E19. **2** Drunk, intoxicated. Freq. foll. by *up*. *slang.* E20.

lit /lɪt/ *v.*[1] *obs.* exc. *dial.* Infl. **-tt-**. Pa. pple & ppl a. **lit, litted**. ME. [ON *lita*, f. as LIT *n.*] **1** *v.t.* Colour, dye; stain. ME. **2** *v.i.* Blush deeply. E19.

lit *v.*[2], *v.*[3] pa. t. & pple: see LIGHT *v.*[1], *v.*[2]

lit. /lɪt/ *n.* & *a. colloq.* Also **Lit.**, & without point. M19. [Abbrev.] **A** *n.* Literature (earliest in ENG. LIT.). Also, a student or devotee of literature; a literary magazine. M19.

B *adj.* Literary. L19.

lit. crit. literary criticism. **lit. sup.** a literary supplement.

litaneutical /lɪtəˈnjuːtɪk(ə)l/ *a.* M19. [f. Gk *litaneutikos*, f. *litaneuein* pray: see next, -AL[1].] Of the nature of a litany.

litany /ˈlɪt(ə)ni/ *n.* ME. [OFr. *letanie* (mod. *litanie*) f. eccl.L *litania* f. Gk *litaneia* prayer, entreaty, f. *litaneuein* pray, f. *litanos* suppliant, f. *litē* supplication: see -Y[3].] **1** *Chr. Ch.* A series of supplications, deprecations, or intercessions in which the clergy lead and other people respond, the same formula of response usu. being repeated for several successive clauses (used either as part of a service or by itself, in the latter case often in procession). ME. **2** *transf.* A form of supplication (e.g. in non-Christian worship) resembling a litany; a continuous repetition or long enumeration, a repeated formula, a long series. LME.

1 the Litany that form of 'general supplication' appointed for use in the *Book of Common Prayer.* **2** W. GOLDING Our crew . . invoked Allah and a whole litany of what I supposed were saints. H. BAILEY 'A generation gone,' went the litany of the time. *Sunday Times* The reform of any socialist system is likely to involve a litany of words and phrases such as skills, market economy, mobility of labour.

Comb.: **litany-desk**, **-stool** a low movable prayer-desk at which a minister kneels while reciting the litany.

litchi *n.* var. of LYCHEE.

lite /liːt, lɪt/ *n.*[1], *a.*[1], & *adv.* Long *arch.* & *dial.* [OE *lȳt* (n., adj., & adv.) = OS *lūt* (n.). Partly f. ON *lítt* (adv.) contr. of *lítil* neut. of *lítill* LITTLE *a.*] **A** *n.* **1** Little, not much; *a* little. OE. **2** Few. OE. **B** *adj.* **1** Few; *a* few. OE. **2** Little in amount; not much of. ME. **3** Little in magnitude; small. ME. **C** *adv.* Little; in a small degree, to a small extent. OE.

lite /lʌɪt/ *n.*[2] & *a.*[2] Now *informal* (chiefly *commercial*). L16. [Var. of *light*. Now usu. a deliberate respelling.] **A** *n.* **1** In *pl.* = LIGHTS. Chiefly *dial.* L16. **2** A light; *esp.* a courtesy light in a motor vehicle. L20. **3** (Also **L-**.) (Proprietary name for) a light beer with relatively few calories. L20. **B** *adj.* Light; *spec.* (also **L-**, proprietary) designating a light beer with relatively few calories. L16.

-lite /lʌɪt/ *suff.* [= Fr. *-lite*, G *-lit(h)*, repr. Gk *lithos* stone. Cf. -LITH.] Forming names of minerals, rocks, mineral structures, etc., esp. as an alternative to -ITE[1] for stems ending in a vowel (*geikielite*, *phonolite*).

liter *n.* see LITRE.

literacy /ˈlɪt(ə)rəsi/ *n.* L19. [f. LITERATE: see -ACY. After earlier ILLITERACY.] The quality or state of being literate; knowledge of letters; condition in respect to education, *esp.* ability to read and write.
COMPUTER *literacy.*

literae humaniores /ˌlɪtərʌɪ hjuːˌmanɪˈɔːriːz/ *n. phr.* Also ***litterae humaniores***. M18. [L = more humane letters.] The humanities, secular learning as opp. to divinity; *esp.* at Oxford University, the school or subject of Greek and Roman classical literature, philosophy, and ancient history.

literal /ˈlɪt(ə)r(ə)l/ *a.* & *n.* LME. [(O)Fr. *littéral* or late L *lit(t)eralis*, f. *lit(t)era* LETTER *n.*[1]: see -AL[1].] A *adj.* **I 1** Designating or pertaining to a sense or interpretation of a text, orig. esp. the Bible, obtained by taking words in their primary or customary meaning, and applying the ordinary rules of grammar, without mysticism, allegory, or metaphor; designating or pertaining to the etymological or a primary sense of a word. LME. **2** (Of a translation, version, transcript, etc.) representing the very words of the original, verbally exact; (of a representation in art or literature) exactly copied, true to life, realistic. L16. **3** That is so in its literal sense, without metaphor, exaggeration, or inaccuracy; literally so called; *colloq.* so called with some exaggeration etc. M17. **4** Free from figures of speech, exaggeration, inaccuracy, distortion, or allusion. M18. **5** Of a person, a person's mind: apt to take literally what is spoken or written figuratively or with humorous exaggeration or irony; unimaginative, matter-of-fact. L18.
1 S. BECKETT True there was never much talk of the heart, literal or figurative. N. PODHORETZ The literal meaning of *Torah lishma* may be 'learning for its own sake', but the true, the theological meaning of the idea is 'studying the revealed word of God for the sake of heaven.' F. SPALDING His literal illustration of *The Song of Songs* aroused a Catholic controversy. 2 DRYDEN The common way . . is not a literal Translation, but a kind of Paraphrase. F. HOYLE These extremely literal animal forms are accompanied by symbolic human figures. 3 E. A. FREEMAN The literal extirpation of a nation is an impossibility. G. A. BIRMINGHAM Do you suppose that the Prime Minister, when he thinks he'll have to go to war with Germany, tells the literal truth? 4 A. N. WILSON It is not safe to take Tolstoy's diaries as a literal record of events. 5 H. ALLEN You assured ships with honest, literal, and unimaginative persons.
II 6 Of or pertaining to letters of the alphabet; of the nature of a letter or letters, alphabetical. LME. **b** Of a misprint or (occas.) scribal error: involving a letter or letters. E17. **c** *Math.* Performed by means of letters; denoted or expressed by a letter or letters; algebraic but not numerical. Now *rare.* L17. †**7** Of or pertaining to literature or letters; literary. LME–E17.
Comb.: **literal-minded** *a.* having a literal mind, characteristic of a person with a literal mind, unimaginative; **literal-mindedness** the quality or state of being literal-minded.
B *n.* **1** *Printing.* A misprint, a typographical error. E17. †**2** A literal interpretation or meaning. Only in M17. **3** *Computing.* An operand which directly specifies a value, or defines itself rather than serving as an address or label; a character that is treated as data rather than as a symbolic name. M20.

literalise *v.* var. of LITERALIZE.

literalism /ˈlɪt(ə)r(ə)lɪz(ə)m/ *n.* M17. [f. LITERAL *a.* + -ISM.] **1** The disposition to literal interpretation. M17. **2** The disposition to literal representation in art or literature. M19. **3** Literal translation as a principle; a peculiarity of expression due to this. L19.

literalist /ˈlɪt(ə)r(ə)lɪst/ *n.* M17. [f. as prec. + -IST.] A person who insists on or is given to literal interpretation. Also, in art or literature, a person who depicts or describes things realistically, an exact copyist.
litera'listic *a.* pertaining to or characteristic of a literalist or literalism L19.

literality /lɪtəˈralɪti/ *n.* M17. [f. as prec. + -ITY.] The quality or fact of being literal; literalness; an instance of this.

literalize /ˈlɪt(ə)r(ə)lʌɪz/ *v.t.* Also **-ise**. E19. [f. as prec. + -IZE.] Make literal; represent or accept as literal.
literali'zation *n.* M19. **literalizer** *n.* L19.

literally /ˈlɪt(ə)rəli/ *adv.* L15. [f. as prec. + -LY[2].] In a literal manner, in the literal sense; so as to represent the very words of the original; so as to depict or describe the thing realistically; (emphasizing the use of a word or phrase) without metaphor, exaggeration, distortion, or allusion, *colloq.* with some exaggeration etc., emphatically.
STEELE Others repeat only what they hear from others as literally as their parts or zeal will permit. T. HARDY A tone expressing that these words signified . . about one hundred times the amount of meaning they conveyed literally. G. GREENE He had only two pounds in his pocket—not literally in his pocket because . . they had been taken away from him. J. B. MORTON Though Tennyson's *Enoch Arden* was not literally inspired by her, yet he was staying with some friends of her great uncle's when it was published. K. AMIS Literally hundreds of men were always pestering her to marry them. R. M. PIRSIG He literally had to move heaven and earth to arrive at this systematic understanding.

literalness /ˈlɪt(ə)r(ə)lnɪs/ *n.* M17. [f. as prec. + -NESS.] The quality or fact of being literal.

literarily /ˈlɪt(ə)rərɪli/ *adv.* E19. [f. LITERARY + -LY[2].] In a literary manner or respect.

literariness /ˈlɪt(ə)rərɪnɪs/ *n.* L19. [f. as prec. + -NESS.] The quality or fact of being literary.

literarism /ˈlɪt(ə)rərɪz(ə)m/ *n.* M20. [f. next + -ISM.] = LITERARYISM.

literary /ˈlɪt(ə)r(ə)ri/ *a.* & *n.* M17. [L *lit(t)erarius*, f. *lit(t)era* LETTER *n.*[1]: see -ARY[1].] A *adj.* †**1** Pertaining to the letters of the alphabet. M17–L18. **2** Of, pertaining to, or of the nature of literature; of or pertaining to books and written compositions; (of a word or idiom) used chiefly in books or by writers, not colloquial; *esp.* pertaining to or having the characteristics of that kind of written composition valued on account of its qualities of form or emotional effect. Formerly also, of or pertaining to the humanities or polite learning. M18. **3** Acquainted with or versed in literature; *spec.* engaged in literature as a profession, occupied in writing books. Of a society etc.: consisting of people engaged or interested in literature. L18. **4** Of painting, sculpture, etc.: that depicts or represents a story. E20.
2 LD MACAULAY The parliamentary conflict on the great question of a standing army was preceded by a literary conflict. G. GREENE The long pompous literary oath full of words too difficult for Taylor to pronounce. B. EMECHETA She had already cultivated the taste for wide reading and . . was always in the mood for literary talk. D. HALBERSTAM He was not much interested in literary style and he did not care about good writing.
Special collocations & comb.: **literary adviser** a person who gives advice or information on literary matters. **literary agency**: that acts for authors in dealing with publishers etc. **literary agent**: who acts for an author in dealing with publishers etc. **literary critic** a person who engages in literary criticism. **literary-critical** *a.* pertaining to or of the nature of literary criticism. **literary criticism** the art or practice of estimating the qualities and character of literary works. **literary editor** (*a*) the editor of the literary section of a newspaper; (*b*) the editor of a book of collected writings. **literary-editorship** the post or function of a literary editor. *literary* EXECUTOR. **literary history** the history of the treatment of, and references to, a specified subject in literature. **literary property** (*a*) property which consists in written or printed compositions; (*b*) the exclusive right of publication as recognized and limited by law.
B *n.* A literary club or society; a literary person. *US.* E20.
literaryism *n.* addiction to literary forms; an instance of this, a form of expression belonging to literary language: L19.

litera scripta /lɪtərə ˈskrɪptə/ *n. phr.* M19. [L.] The written word.

literate /ˈlɪt(ə)rət/ *a.* & *n.* LME. [L *lit(t)eratus*, f. *lit(t)era* LETTER *n.*[1]: see -ATE[2].] A *adj.* **1** Acquainted with letters or literature; able to read and write; educated; (usu. as 2nd elem. of comb.) competent or knowledgeable in a specified area. LME. **2** Of or pertaining to literature or letters, literary. *arch.* M17.
1 COMPUTER-*literate.*
B *n.* **1** A liberally educated or learned person. M16. **2** *spec.* In the Anglican Church, a person admitted to holy orders without having obtained a university degree. E19. **3** A person who can read and write (opp. an *illiterate*); (usu. as 2nd elem. of comb.) a person who is competent or knowledgeable in a specified area. L19.
literately *adv.* M20.

literati /lɪtəˈrɑːtiː/ *n.pl.* E17. [L *lit(t)erati* pl. of *lit(t)eratus* LITERATE *a.* Cf. LITERATO, LITERATUS.] Men of letters; the learned class as a whole.

literatim /lɪtəˈreɪtɪm, -ˈrɑːtɪm/ *adv.* M17. [med.L *lit(t)eratim*, f. *lit(t)era* LETTER *n.*[1], after GRADATIM. Cf. VERBATIM.] Letter for letter; literally.

literation /lɪtəˈreɪʃ(ə)n/ *n.* E20. [f. L *lit(t)era* LETTER *n.*[1] + -ATION.] The representation of sounds or words by a letter or letters, spelling.

literatist /ˈlɪt(ə)rətɪst/ *n.* Now *rare.* M17. [f. LITERATE *a.* + -IST.] A person engaged in literary pursuits; a writer, an author.

literato /lɪtəˈrɑːtəʊ/ *n.sing.* Corresp. pl. LITERATI. E18. [It. *litterato* (now usu. *letterati*) f. as LITERATE.] A member of the literati; a man of letters, a learned man. Cf. LITERATUS.

literator /ˈlɪt(ə)reɪtə/ *n.* M17. [L *lit(t)erator* teacher of letters, grammarian, sciolist, f. *lit(t)era* LETTER *n.*[1]: see -ATOR.] †**1** A pretender to learning, a sciolist. Only in M17. †**2** A bibliographer. Also, a literary or textual critic. M18–M19. **3** = LITTÉRATEUR. L18.

literature /ˈlɪt(ə)rətʃə/ *n.* LME. [(Fr. *littérature* f.) L *lit(t)eratura*, f. *lit(t)era* LETTER *n.*[1]: see -URE.] **1** Acquaintance with books; polite or humane learning; literary culture. Now *arch. rare.* LME. **2** Literary work or production; the realm of letters. L18. **3a** Literary productions as a whole; the body of writings produced in a particular country or period. Now also *spec.*, that kind of written composition valued on account of its qualities of form or emotional effect. E19. **b** The body of books and writings that treat of a particular subject. M19. **c** Printed matter of any kind. *colloq.* L19.
1 S. JOHNSON His literature was unquestionably great. He read all the languages which are considered either as learned or polite. 2 LYTTON Ah, you make literature your calling, sir? 3a S. SPENDER Trying to distinguish the kind of writing which is literature from that which is worthless. J. PLAMENATZ The quality of a literature does not always improve . . as population increases and literacy spreads. *American literature, English literature, Russian literature*, etc. *Wisdom literature*: see WISDOM. b J. BARZUN It is possible to master the literature of a subject. *Holiday Which?* It's . . not as spectacular as the tourist literature suggests. c V. BRITTAIN A suitcase full of informative literature.

literatus /lɪtəˈrɑːtəs/ *n.sing. rare.* Corresp. pl. LITERATI. E18. [f. as LITERATE.] A member of the literati; a man of letters, a learned man. Cf. LITERATO.

literose /ˈlɪtərəʊs/ *a. rare.* L19. [Late L *lit(t)erosus*, f. *lit(t)era* LETTER *n.*[1]: see -OSE[1].] Studiedly or affectedly literary.
lite'rosity *n.* L19.

lith /lɪθ/ *n.*[1] Now *arch.* & *dial.* [OE *liþ* = OS *lið*, OFris. *lith* (Du. *lid*), OHG *lid* (G *Glied*), ON *liðr*, Goth. *liþus*, f. Gmc; prob. rel. to LIMB *n.*[1]] **1** A limb. OE. **2** A joint; *spec.* the last joint or the tip of a finger. OE. **3** A segment of an orange etc. Also, each of the rings at the base of a cow's horn. Chiefly *Sc.* L18.

lith /lɪθ/ *n.*[2] & *a.* M20. [Abbrev. of LITHOGRAPHY, LITHOGRAPHIC.] (Designating or pertaining to) a photographic film thinly coated with emulsion, for producing images of extremely high contrast and density and used extensively in lithographic printing.

-lith /lɪθ/ *suff.* [f. Gk *lithos* stone. Cf. -LITE.] *Palaeont., Archaeol.,* & *Med.* Forming ns. w. the sense 'stone, stony structure', as *batholith, coccolith, gastrolith, monolith, otolith.* Cf. -LITHIC.

lithaemia /lɪˈθiːmɪə/ *n.* Now *rare.* Also *‑**themia**. L19. [f. LITHIC *a.*[1] + -AEMIA.] = HYPERURICAEMIA.
lithaemic *a.* of, pertaining to, or affected with lithaemia L19.

litham /liːˈθɑːm/ *n.* M19. [Arab. *liṯām* veil for the mouth.] A cloth wound round the lower part of the face covering the mouth and sometimes part of the nose, worn by Bedouins.

litharge /ˈlɪθɑːdʒ/ *n.* ME. [OFr. *litarge* (mod. *lith‑*) f. L *lithargyrus* f. Gk *litharguros*, f. *lithos* stone + *arguros* silver.] *Chem.* **1** Lead monoxide, PbO, a toxic red or yellow solid prepared by oxidation of lead in air and used as a pigment and in making glass and ceramics. Also †*litharge of lead.* Cf. MASSICOT. ME. †**b** Any of various impure ores or mixtures containing lead monoxide. LME–L18. †**2** White lead; red lead. M16–E19.

lithe /lʌɪð/ *n.*[1] Long *obs.* exc. *Sc.* ME. [f. LITHE *a.*] **1** A calm, a lull. ME. **2** Shelter. M18.

lithe /lʌɪð/ *n.*[2] *obs.* exc. *dial.* L17. [f. LITHE *v.*[1]] Oatmeal and water used to thicken broth.

lithe /lʌɪð/ *a.* & *v.*[1] [OE *līþe* = OS *līþi*, OHG *lindi* (G *lind*) soft, gentle, f. WGmc, f. Gmc f. IE base also of ON *linr* soft, yielding, OE *linnan* LIN *v.*] **A** *adj.* **1** Of a person, action, etc.: gentle, meek, mild. Long *Sc. rare.* OE. **2** Of a thing: mild, soft; agreeable, mellow. *obs.* exc. *dial.* OE. †**b** Of weather: calm, serene. Of water: smooth, still. ME–L16. **c** Comfortable, sheltered. *Sc.* LME. **3** Easily bent, flexible; (of a person) supple, agile, (gracefully) slim and muscled. ME. **4** Of broth etc.: smooth, thick. Chiefly *dial.* M17.
3 D. H. LAWRENCE He had that fine, lithe physique, suggestive of much animal vigour. V. SETH John.. talking to a lithe nymphet.
B *v.t.* †**1** Make gentle or mild; assuage, relieve, soothe; make supple; subdue. OE–M17. **2** Make thick; thicken (broth etc.). Long *Sc. rare.* L17.
lithely *adv.* OE. **litheness** *n.* ME.

lithe /lʌɪð/ *v.*[2] Now *arch.* & *dial.* ME. [ON *hlýða*, f. *hljóð* listening, sound, rel. to Goth. *hliuma* sense of hearing, OE *hlēoþor* sense of hearing, music, OHG *hliudar*, f. Gmc var. of base of LIST *v.*[2], LISTEN *v.*] **1** *v.i.* Hearken, listen. ME. **2** *v.t.* Hear (something). LME.

lithemia *n.* see LITHAEMIA.

lither /ˈlɪðə/ *a.* & *adv.* Now *arch.* & *dial.* [OE *lȳþre* f. Gmc base also of 1st elem. of MHG, G *liederlich*: cf. MLG *lüder* lewd man.] **A** *adj.* †**1** Wicked, bad. OE–M16. †**2** Ill-looking, worthless, poor, sorry. Of a part of the body: withered, paralysed. OE–E17. **3** Lazy, sluggish, spiritless. LME. **4** Pliant, supple; (of the air) yielding, allowing (swift) movement. Also, agile, nimble. M16. †**B** *adv.* Badly, wickedly; ill, poorly. OE–ME.
†**litherly** *a.* (*a*) idle, lazy; (*b*) spiteful, mischievous: L16–E19. †**litherly** *adv.* OE–E17. †**litherness** *n.* ME–E18.

lithesome /ˈlʌɪðs(ə)m/ *a.* M18. [f. LITHE *a.* + -SOME[1]. See also LISSOM.] Supple, agile, lissom.

lithia /ˈlɪθɪə/ *n.*[1] E19. [Alt. of LITHION after *soda*, *potassa*, etc.] *Chem.* Lithium oxide, Li_2O, a white hygroscopic alkaline solid.
Comb.: **lithia-emerald** = HIDDENITE; **lithia-mica** = LEPIDOLITE; **lithia-tourmaline** any variety of tourmaline which contains lithium; **lithia water** mineral water containing dissolved salts of lithium.

lithia /ˈlɪθɪə/ *n.*[2] *rare.* E19. [mod.L, f. Gk *lithos* stone: see -IA[1].] *Med.* Lithiasis; *esp.* the formation of concretions in the sebaceous glands of the eyelid.

lithian /ˈlɪθɪən/ *a.* M20. [f. LITHIUM + -IAN.] *Min.* Having a constituent element partly replaced by lithium.

lithiasis /lɪˈθʌɪəsɪs/ *n.* Pl. **-ases** /-əsiːz/. M17. [med.L f. Gk, f. *lithos* stone: see -IASIS.] *Med.* The formation of stony concretions or calculi in the body, esp. in the gall bladder or the urinary system.

lithiated /ˈlɪθɪeɪtɪd/ *a.* L18. [In sense 1 f. LITHIC *a.*[1], in sense 2 f. LITHIA *n.*[1]: see -ATE[3], -ED[1].] †**1** *Chem.* Combined with uric acid. L18–L19. **2** Chiefly of mineral water: impregnated with lithium salts. E20.

lithic /ˈlɪθɪk/ *a.*[1] L18. [Gk *lithikos*, f. *lithos* stone: see -IC.] **1** *Chem.* & *Med.* Orig., = URIC. Now (*arch.*), of or pertaining to stones in the bladder. L18. **2** *gen.* Of, pertaining to, or resembling stone; consisting of stone; *Archaeol.* of or pertaining to stone artefacts. M19.
lithate *n.* = URATE *n.* E19.

lithic /ˈlɪθɪk/ *a.*[2] L19. [f. LITHIUM + -IC.] Chiefly *Chem.* Of, pertaining to, or containing lithium.

-lithic /ˈlɪθɪk/ *suff.* [f. as -LITH + -IC: cf. Gk *lithikos* of stone.] Forming adjs. w. the sense 'of or pertaining to stone', as *granolithic*, *megalithic*; *spec.* in *Archaeol.* designating or pertaining to a particular cultural period that is a division of the Stone Age, as *mesolithic*, *neolithic*, *palaeolithic*.

lithification /ˌlɪθɪfɪˈkeɪʃ(ə)n/ *n.* L19. [f. next + -FICATION.] *Geol.* The process of compaction of a sediment into stone.
Also **lithiˈfaction** *n.* L19.

lithify /ˈlɪθɪfʌɪ/ *v.t.* L19. [f. Gk *lithos* stone + -I- + -FY.] Form into stone. Chiefly as *lithified* ppl a.

†**lithion** *n.* E–M19. [Use as n. of neut. of Gk *lithios* stony, f. *lithos* stone.] *Chem.* = LITHIA *n.*[1]

lithiophilite /lɪθɪˈɒfɪlʌɪt/ *n.* L19. [f. LITHIUM + -O- + Gk *philos* friend + -ITE[1].] *Min.* A pink or brown orthorhombic phosphate of lithium and magnesium, often containing iron and forming a series with triphylite.

lithium /ˈlɪθɪəm/ *n.* E19. [f. LITHIA *n.*[1]: see -IUM.] A soft light highly reactive chemical element, atomic no. 3, which is a member of the alkali metal group and is found esp. in the minerals spodumene and lepidolite. (Symbol Li.)

litho /ˈlʌɪθəʊ, ˈlɪθ-/ *n.*, *a.*, & *v.* *colloq.* L19. [Abbrev.] **A** *n.* Pl. **-os**. = LITHOGRAPH *n.*, LITHOGRAPHY. L19. **B** *adj.* = LITHOGRAPHIC. E20. **C** *v.t.* = LITHOGRAPH *v.* M20.

litho- /ˈlɪθəʊ/ *comb. form.* Bef. a vowel **lith-**. [Gk *lithos* stone: see -O-.] Of or pertaining to stone or rock, or a calculus.
lithochroˈmatic *a.* of, pertaining to, or produced by lithochromatics L19. **lithochroˈmatics** *n.* the art of taking impressions from stone painted with oil colours M19. **lithochrome** *a.* lithochromatic M19. **lithochromy** *n.* painting on stone M19. **lithoclast** *n.* †(*a*) a stone-breaker; (*b*) *Surg.* (now *rare*) an instrument for breaking up stone in the bladder: E19. **lithofacies** *n.* (*Geol.*) a facies distinguished by its lithology M20. **lithoˈgenesis** *n.* (*Geol.*) the formation of (esp. sedimentary) rock E20. **liˈthogenous** *a.* (*a*) *Zool.* (of an animal) that secretes coral; (*b*) *Geol.* (of a sediment) resulting from the breakdown of rock: M19. **lithoglyph** *n.* an engraving on stone; the art of engraving on stone: M19. **liˈtholatrous** *a.* stone-worshipping L19. **liˈtholatry** *n.* stone-worship L19. **lithoneˈphrotomy** *n.* (*Med.*) = NEPHROLITHOTOMY L19. **lithoˈphagic** *a.* = LITHOPHAGOUS M20. **liˈthophagous** *a.* (*Zool.*) stone-eating; *esp.* (of a mollusc) that bores through stone; (of a bird etc.) that swallows stones to aid digestion: E19. **lithophane** *n.* [Gk *-phanēs* appearing] a kind of ornamentation of porcelain visible when held to the light, produced by pressing designs into it when soft; an object so decorated: E20. **lithophanic** /-ˈfanɪk/ *a.* pertaining to lithophanes or lithophany E19. ***lithophanie*** /lɪtɔfani (*pl. same*)/ *n.* [Fr.] (*a*) = LITHOPHANE; (*b*) = LITHOPHANY: M19. **liˈthophany** *n.* the art or process of making lithophanes M19. **lithophile** *a.* (*Geol.* & *Chem.*) designating an element which commonly occurs combined as a silicate, and is supposed to have become concentrated in the earth's outer layers E20. **liˈthophilous** *a.* (*Bot.* & *Zool.*) that thrives in stony places or on rocks M19. **lithopone** *n.* [Gk *ponos* (a thing produced by) work] a mixture of zinc sulphide and barium sulphate used as a white pigment in paints, leathers, etc. (now largely superseded by titanium dioxide) L19. **lithosere** *n.* (*Ecol.*) a plant succession originating on bare rock E20. **lithosol** *n.* (*Soil Sci.*) an azonal soil consisting largely of imperfectly weathered rock fragments M20. **lithoˈstatic** *a.* (*Geol.*) designating pressure exerted by overlying rock M20. **lithotint** *n.* (chiefly *Hist.*) the art or process of printing tinted pictures by lithography; a picture so printed: M19.

lithocyst /ˈlɪθəsɪst/ *n.* M19. [f. LITHO- + CYST.] **1** *Zool.* = STATOCYST. Now *rare* or *obs.* M19. **2** *Bot.* A cell containing a cystolith. L19.

lithodipyra /ˌlɪθə(ʊ)dɪˈpʌɪ(ə)rə/ *n.* L18. [f. LITHO- + DI-[2] + Gk *pur* fire, w. the sense 'stone twice fired'.] An artificial stone claimed to have greater frost and heat resistance than natural stone and formerly much used for statues, decorative work, etc.

lithodomous /lɪˈθɒdəməs/ *a.* M19. [f. mod.L *Lithodomus* (see below), f. Gk *lithodomos* mason, f. as LITHO- + *domos* building: see -OUS.] *Zool.* Living in rock; *spec.* designating or pertaining to stone-boring mussels of the genus *Lithodomus*.

lithograph /ˈlɪθə(ʊ)grɑːf, ˈlʌɪ-/ *n.* E19. [Back-form. f. LITHOGRAPHY.] **1** A lithographic print. E19. **2** An inscription on stone. *rare.* M19.

lithograph /ˈlɪθə(ʊ)grɑːf, ˈlʌɪ-/ *v.t.* E19. [f. as prec.] **1** Print, produce, or portray by lithography. E19. **2** Write or engrave on stone. *rare.* L19.

lithographer /lɪˈθɒgrəfə/ *n.* L17. [f. LITHO- + -GRAPHER.] †**1** A person who writes about stones. Only in L17. **2** A person who practises lithography. E19.

lithographic /lɪθə(ʊ)ˈgrafɪk/ *a.* E19. [f. LITHOGRAPHY + -IC.] Of, pertaining to, or produced by lithography; engraved on stone.
lithographic limestone a compact fine-grained yellowish limestone used in lithography. **lithographic offset** = OFFSET *n.* 7. **lithographic paper**: suitable for lithographic printing. **lithographic stone** = *lithographic limestone* above. **lithographic varnish** a preparation of linseed oil used in inks for lithographic printing.
lithographical *a.* (*rare*) = LITHOGRAPHIC E19. **lithographically** *adv.* by means of lithography E19.

lithography /lɪˈθɒgrəfi/ *n.* E18. [In sense 1 f. mod.L *lithographia*; in sense 2 f. G *Lithographie*, f. as LITHO- + -GRAPHY.] †**1** A description of stones or rocks. Only in E18. **2** The art or process of making a print using greasy ink on porous stone or (now usu.) a metal or plastic plate or roller which has been treated to accept the ink only where it is required for printing; an analogous process used in the manufacture of computer chips. E19.

lithoid /ˈlɪθɔɪd/ *a.* M19. [Gk *lithoeidēs*, f. as LITHO- see -OID.] Of the nature or structure of stone.
Also **liˈthoidal** *a.* M19.

Lithol /ˈlɪθɒl/ *n.* E20. [Origin unkn.] *Chem.* (Proprietary name for) any of various azo dyes. *Lithol red*, *yellow*, etc.

lithology /lɪˈθɒlədʒi/ *n.* E18. [f. LITHO- + -LOGY.] **1** *Geol.* The general physical characteristics of a rock, esp. as discernible without a microscope; the branch of geology that deals with these characteristics. Cf. PETROLOGY. E18. **2** The branch of medicine that deals with calculi. *rare.* E19.
lithoˈlogic *a.* E19. **lithoˈlogical** *a.* L18. **lithoˈlogically** *adv.* with regard to lithology M19. **lithologist** *n.* M18.

lithomancy /ˈlɪθə(ʊ)mansi/ *n.* M17. [f. LITHO- + -MANCY.] Divination by signs derived from a stone or stones, esp. a lodestone.

lithomarge /ˈlɪθə(ʊ)mɑːdʒ/ *n.* M18. [mod.L *lithomarga*, f. as LITHO- + L *marga* marl.] *Geol.* Orig., any of various soft claylike minerals, including kaolin. Now usu., a smooth hardened reddish deposit containing kaolinite and formed by the degradation of basalts.

lithontriptic /lɪθɒnˈtrɪptɪk/ *a.* & *n.* Now *rare* or *obs.* Also †**-thriptic**. M17. [Fr. *lithontriptique* or mod.L *lithontripticus* (later *-thrypticus*), f. Gk LITHO- + *thruptein* break up, infl. by Gk *tripsis* rubbing, grinding: cf. LITHOTRIPSY.] *Med.* (A medicine) having the property of breaking down calculi; lithotritic.

lithophone /ˈlɪθəfəʊn/ *n.* L19. [f. LITHO- + -PHONE.] †**1** *Med.* An instrument for rendering audible the contact of a sound or probe with a vesical calculus. *rare.* Only in L19. **2** *Mus.* Any of various percussion instruments made of marble or other stone. M20.

†**lithophyta** *n.* pl. of LITHOPHYTON.

lithophyte /ˈlɪθə(ʊ)fʌɪt/ *n.* L18. [f. LITHO- + -PHYTE.] **1** *Zool.* A polyp with a calcareous skeleton; a stony coral. L18. **2** *Bot.* A plant which grows on bare stone or rock. L19.
lithophytic /-ˈfɪtɪk/, **-phytous** /-ˈfʌɪtəs/ *adjs.* E19.

†lithophyton *n.* Pl. **-ta.** M17–M18. [mod.L, f. as LITHO- + Gk *phuton* plant.] A coral.

lithoprint /ˈlɪθə(ʊ)prɪnt, ˈlʌɪ-/ *v.t.* M20. [f. LITHO(GRAPHY + PRINT *v.*] Chiefly *Hist.* Print (esp. a typescript copy) by photolithography.

lithops /ˈlɪθɒps/ *n.* M20. [mod.L (see below), f. LITHO- + Gk *ops* face.] Any of various small succulent plants of the genus *Lithops* (family Aizoaceae), native to deserts in southern Africa and resembling small pairs of stones.

lithospermum /lɪθə(ʊ)ˈspəːməm/ *n.* Also (earlier) **†-mon.** M16. [(mod.L f.) Gk *lithospermon*, f. as LITHO- + *sperma* seed.] Any of various plants of the borage family included or formerly included in the genus *Lithospermum*, bearing white, yellow, or blue flowers and polished stony nutlets; *esp.* one grown for ornament.

lithosphere /ˈlɪθə(ʊ)sfɪə/ *n.* M19. [f. LITHO- + -SPHERE.] Formerly, the rocky part of the earth; the earth's crust. Now *spec.* the rigid outer portion of the earth including the crust and the outermost mantle, above the asthenosphere.
litho'spheric *a.* L20.

lithostratigraphy /ˌlɪθə(ʊ)strəˈtɪɡrəfi/ *n.* M20. [f. LITHO- + STRATIGRAPHY.] *Geol.* The branch of stratigraphy that deals with the relationship between lithology and stratigraphic position of strata.
lithostrati'graphic, -ical *adjs.* M20.

lithotomy /lɪˈθɒtəmi/ *n.* M17. [Late L *lithotomia* f. Gk *lithotomia*, f. as LITHO- + -TOMY.] **†1** A quarry. Only in M17. **2** Surgical incision into the bladder, kidney, etc., for the purpose of removing a stone; an instance of this. E18.
2 lithotomy position a supine position of the body, with the legs raised in stirrups, flexed and apart, used orig. for lithotomy and subsequently also in childbirth.
litho'tomic *a.* E19. **litho'tomical** *a.* L19. **lithotomist** *n.* M17.

lithotripsy /ˈlɪθə(ʊ)trɪpsi/ *n.* M19. [f. LITHO- + Gk *tripsis* rubbing, grinding + -Y[3]: cf. LITHONTRIPTIC.] *Med.* The operation of breaking or wearing down stones in the bladder, kidney, etc., by mechanical or ultrasonic means.
lithotripter *n.* a machine which generates and focuses ultrasonic waves to shatter stones in the bladder or kidney L20. **litho'triptic** *a.* M19. **lithotriptor** *n.* (*rare*) = LITHOTRITE E19.

lithotrity /lɪˈθɒtrɪti/ *n.* E19. [f. LITHO- + L *tritor* rubber (f. *terere* rub) + -Y[3]: cf. prec.] *Med.* The operation of crushing a stone in the bladder into minute particles which can be expelled through the urethra; mechanical lithotripsy.
'lithotrite *n.* an instrument for lithotrity M19. **litho'tritic** *a.* M19. **lithotritor** *n.* (now *rare* or *obs.*) = LITHOTRITE E19.

lithotype /ˈlɪθə(ʊ)tʌɪp, *in senses 1, 2 also* ˈlʌɪ-/ *n.* L19. [f. LITHO- + -TYPE.] **1** *Printing.* A stereotype made with shellac, sand, tar, and linseed oil, and pressed while hot on a plaster mould taken from type. L19. **2** A lithographed fingerprint. L19. **3** *Geol.* An individual lithological character or category; *esp.* any of several lithologically distinct types of coal. M20.

lithsman /ˈlɪθsmən/ *n.* Pl. **-men.** LOE. [ON *liðsmaðr* (accus. *-mann*), f. *liðs* genit. of *lið* host + *maðr* MAN *n.*] *Hist.* A sailor in the navy under the Danish kings of England.

Lithuanian /lɪθjʊˈeɪnɪən, lɪθʊ-/ *n.* & *a.* L16. [f. *Lithuania* (see below) + -AN.] **A** *n.* A native or inhabitant of Lithuania, the most southern of the three Baltic States; the language of Lithuania, belonging to the Baltic language group. L16. **B** *adj.* Of or pertaining to Lithuania, its people, or its language. L18.
Lithuanic *a.* & *n.* Lithuanian M19.

lithy /ˈlɪði/ *a.* Long *obs.* exc. *dial.* [OE *liþig* = ON *liðugr* yielding, nimble, MDu. *ledech*, G *ledig* unoccupied, vacant: ult. origin unkn.] **1** Flexible; supple; lithe; soft. OE. **†2** Weak, feeble. LME–M16.

litigable /ˈlɪtɪɡəb(ə)l/ *a.* M18. [f. LITIGATE + -ABLE.] That may become the subject of litigation.

litigant /ˈlɪtɪɡ(ə)nt/ *a.* & *n.* M17. [Fr., f. L *litigant-* pres. ppl stem of *litigare*: see next, -ANT[1].] **A** *adj.* Engaged in a lawsuit or dispute. Chiefly qualifying *party*. Freq. *postpositive.* M17. **B** *n.* A person engaged in a lawsuit or dispute. M17.

litigate /ˈlɪtɪɡeɪt/ *v.* E17. [L *litigat-* pa. ppl stem of *litigare*, f. *lit-*, *lis* strife, lawsuit: see -ATE[3].] **1** *v.i.* Be a party to or counsel in a lawsuit; carry on a lawsuit; go to law. Formerly also *gen.*, dispute. E17. **2** *v.t.* Make the subject of a lawsuit, contest at law; *gen.* contest (a point etc.). M18.

litigation /lɪtɪˈɡeɪʃ(ə)n/ *n.* M16. [Late L *litigatio(n-)*, f. as prec.: see -ATION.] **1** *gen.* Disputation. Now *rare.* M16. **2** The action or process of carrying on a lawsuit; legal proceedings. Also, an instance or (formerly) type of legal proceedings. M17. **b** The practice of going to law. L18.

litigator /ˈlɪtɪɡeɪtə/ *n.* L19. [f. LITIGATE + -OR.] A person who litigates; *spec.* (*US*) a trial lawyer.
S. BRILL The Solicitor General (the federal government's top litigator). *Guardian* A series of steps which allow solicitors to qualify as advocates and non-solicitors to become litigators.

litigiosity /lɪˌtɪdʒɪˈɒsɪti/ *n.* M19. [f. L *litigiosus* (see LITIGIOUS) + -ITY.] *Civil & Sc. Law.* The quality or fact of being litigious.

litigious /lɪˈtɪdʒəs/ *a.* LME. [(O)Fr. *litigieux* or L *litigiosus*, f. *litigium* litigation, rel. to *litigare*: see LITIGATE, -OUS.] **1** Fond of or given to litigation or carrying on lawsuits; *gen.* (now *rare*) fond of disputes, argumentative. LME. **2** Disputable, questionable, contentious. Long only *spec.* disputable at law; that is or is liable to become the subject of a lawsuit; (*Civil & Sc. Law*) (of property) respecting which an action or diligence is pending, and which therefore may not be alienated. LME. **3** Of or pertaining to lawsuits or litigation. L16.
litigiously *adv.* L16. **litigiousness** *n.* M17.

litiscontestation /ˌlʌɪtɪskɒntɛˈsteɪʃ(ə)n/ *n.* LME. [f. L *litis* (genit. of *lis* lawsuit) + *contestatio(n-)* (see CONTESTATION).] *Civil & Sc. Law.* The formal entry of a suit in a court of law. Also, the establishment and joinder of contentious issues.

litmus /ˈlɪtməs/ *n.* ME. [ON *lit-mosi* (f. as LIT *n.* + *mosi* moss), MDu. *lijkmoes*.] A soluble blue powder obtained from various lichens which turns red in acidic conditions and blue in alkaline over a range of pH 4.5–8.3.
Comb.: **litmus blue** a blue pigment prepared from litmus; **litmus paper** unsized paper stained blue with litmus, to serve as a test for acids, reddened by an acid, to serve as a test for alkalis; **litmus test** a test for acids or alkalis using litmus paper; *fig.* a simple test to establish true character.

litoptern /lɪˈtɒptəːn/ *n.* E20. [f. mod.L *Litopterna* (see below), f. Gk *litos* smooth + *pternē* heel-bone.] *Palaeont.* Any extinct S. American ungulate mammal of the order Litopterna.

litotes /lʌɪˈtəʊtiːz/ *n.* L16. [Late L f. Gk *litotēs*, f. *litos* single, simple, meagre.] *Rhet.* Ironical understatement, *spec.* in which an affirmative is expressed by the negative of the contrary, as *no small amount*, *no mean feat*, etc. Also called *meiosis*.

lit-par-lit /liparli, liːpɑːˈliː/ *a.* & *adv.* L19. [Fr., lit. 'bed by bed'.] *Geol.* **A** *adj.* Designating or resulting from the intrusion of innumerable narrow, more or less parallel, sheets or tongues of magma into the bedding of rocks. L19. **B** *adv.* In the manner of *lit-par-lit* intrusion. E20.

litre /ˈliːtə/ *n.* Also ***liter.** L18. [Fr., alt. of next.] A unit of capacity and volume in the metric system, now defined as one cubic decimetre (formerly as the volume of one kilogram of water under standard conditions) and equivalent to approx 1.75 pints.
Times Bruigi, driving a three-litre Ferrari.

¶The various definitions of the litre are very nearly but not quite equivalent to one another.

†litron *n.* E18–E19. [Fr. f. med.L *litra* f. Gk *litra* a Silician monetary unit.] A unit of volume equal to a sixteenth of an old French bushel.

litster /ˈlɪtstə/ *n.* Now *rare* or *obs.* LME. [f. LIT *v.*[1] + -STER.] A dyer.

litten /ˈlɪt(ə)n/ *n. obs.* exc. *dial.* OE. [f. LICH + TOWN *n.*, contr. in LME.] A graveyard, a churchyard. Also *church-litten*.

litten /ˈlɪt(ə)n/ *ppl a. pseudo-arch.* E19. [f. LIGHT *v.*[2] + -EN[6].] Lighted, lit. Usu. as 2nd elem. of comb., as *red-litten*, *star-litten*, etc.

litter /ˈlɪtə/ *n.* ME. [AN *litere*, (O)Fr. *litière* f. med.L *lectaria*, f. L *lectus* (whence Fr. *lit*) bed.] **†1** A bed. ME–L15. **2** A form of conveyance containing a couch shut in by curtains and carried on two or more persons' shoulders or by beasts of burden (now chiefly *Hist.*); *spec.* a stretcher or portable bed for transporting the sick or wounded. ME. **3** Straw, rushes, etc., used as bedding (now only for animals). Also, straw and dung together; *spec.* (in full *cat litter*) grains of an absorbent material for lining a box for a cat to urinate and defecate in. LME. **b** Straw etc. used for the protection of plants or (formerly) for thatch or as a component of plaster. LME. **c** Decomposing but still recognizable vegetable debris from plants etc. forming a distinct layer above the soil, esp. in a forest. E20. **4** A group of young (mammalian) animals comprising all those born at one birth. Formerly also, an act of giving birth to young. LME. **5** Odds and ends or discarded material lying about; a state of untidiness; an accumulation *of* (disordered things). Now *esp.* refuse or rubbish discarded in an open or public place. M18.
2 R. MACAULAY He was carried out on a golden litter. A. MASON A covered litter, borne by four slaves, its occupant quite invisible. F. NORRIS A litter was improvised, and throwing their coats over the body, the party carried it back. *attrib.*: *Sun* (*Baltimore*) First to be unloaded . . were the litter cases—seriously wounded and dying. **3** *deep litter*: see DEEP *a.* **4** P. NORMAN Then Melody had her second litter of puppies. **5** CONAN DOYLE The rack . . was covered with a formidable litter of rods, reels and baskets. V. WOOLF Cigarette ends, little bits of paper, orange peel, all the litter of the day.
Comb.: **litter-basket, -bin**: for the disposal of waste-paper and other litter; **litterbug** a person who carelessly leaves litter in a public place; **litterfall** *Ecol.* the fall of leaves and other vegetable matter from plants to form litter; **litter-lout** = *litterbug* above.
littery *a.* of or pertaining to litter; marked by the presence of litter; untidy: E19.

litter /ˈlɪtə/ *v.* LME. [f. the n.] **1** *v.t.* Provide (a horse etc.) with litter or straw as bedding. Also foll. by *down*. LME. **b** *v.i.* Lie down on litter as bedding. *rare.* M17. **2** *v.t.* & *i.* Of an animal or (occas., *derog.*) a person: give birth to (young). L15. **†3** *v.t.* Mix (plaster) (as) with litter; plaster. *rare.* M16–M19. **4** *v.t.* Carry in a litter. *rare.* E18. **5** *v.t.* Spread litter or straw on (the floor) or in (a stable). Also foll. by *down*. E18. **6** *v.t.* **a** Strew *with* objects scattered untidily; leave as litter, scatter untidily *about* or *on*. Usu. in *pass.* E18. **b** Of things: lie about untidily on. M19.
6a F. A. KEMBLE Firewood and shavings lay littered about the floors. W. GERHARDIE The table was littered with bottles of the very best wine. V. S. PRITCHETT A piece of waste ground littered with tins and rubbish. C. FRANCIS The entire south Cornish coast is littered with wrecks. *fig.*: J. P. HOWES I would not like anyone to imagine we litter the texts of our dictionaries with typesetting codes. **b** E. TAYLOR The room looked extremely neat, except for all the papers littering the table. I. BANKS Ruined arches, fallen lintels, collapsed walls littered the slopes of sand.
litterer *n.* a person who throws or drops litter E20.

litterae humaniores *n. phr.* var. of LITERAE HUMANIORES.

littérateur /lɪtərɑːˈtəː, *foreign* literatœːr (*pl. same*)/ *n.* E19. [Fr. f. L *litterator*: see LITERATOR.] A writer of literary or critical works, a literary person.

littering /ˈlɪt(ə)rɪŋ/ *n.* LME. [f. LITTER *n.* or *v.* + -ING[1].] **1** The straw of an animal's bed; a layer of this. LME. 2 The action of LITTER *v.* M16. **b** The action of throwing or dropping litter. M20. 3 *collect.* Odds and ends scattered about. L19.

little /ˈlɪt(ə)l/ *a.*, *n.*, & *adv.* [OE *lȳtel*, *lytel* = OS *luttil* (Du. *luttel*), OHG *luzzil* (MHG, G dial. *lützel*), f. WGmc adj., f. base repr. also by OE *lyt* adv. 'little'.] A *adj.* Compar. LESS *a.*, LESSER, **littler**; superl. LEAST, **littlest**. I Small; not great. 1 Of a material object, area of space, etc.: small in size, not large or big. Of a person: short in stature. OE. **b** *attrib.* Designating the smaller or smallest of things of the class specified; forming names of animals (esp. birds), towns, rivers, streets, districts, etc., that are less large or important, later established, or suggestive of another or others of that name. Opp. GREAT *a.* 7b. OE. **c** *iron.* Big, considerable. Usu. preceded by *some.* L16. 2 *spec.* Young; (esp. of a sibling) younger. OE. 3 Of a collective unity: having few members, inhabitants, etc.; small in number. OE. 4 Of distance or (a period of) time: short. Also qualifying a specific length of duration or distance w. emphatic force. *arch.* exc. in *a little while.* OE. 5 Of a thing: not of great importance or interest; trifling, trivial. Of a person: inferior in rank or condition (now *rare*). ME. **b** Paltry, mean, contemptible. L15. 6 Of an immaterial thing: small in quantity, duration, degree, intensity, etc. ME. †**b** Having the quality or performing the action indicated to a slight extent only. Foll. by *of.* LME–E16. **c** Of an agent or n. indicating occupation: that is such on a small scale. LME. 7 Used as an extension of various of the above senses to convey emotional overtones, as affection, amusement, condescension, disparagement, etc., not implied by *small.* ME.

1 L. STERNE Green taffeta, lined with a little bit of white quilted satin. J. CONRAD Depend on me to pick up the least little bit of a hint. HARPER LEE A big cake and two little ones on Miss Maudie's kitchen table. A. N. WILSON They had been talking . . of getting a little cottage. W. TREVOR I think we might have a little drink. D. DELILLO It's a little bitty thing but it shoots real bullets. **b** *little auk, little gull, little owl,* etc. *Little Clarendon Street, Little Malvern, Little Ouse,* etc. *Little Africa, Little England, Little Italy, Little Switzerland, Little Venice,* etc. **c** SHAKES. *Rich. III* Since I am crept in favour with myself, I will maintain it with some little cost. *Times* Movement out from . . London . . by teachers who have been there for some little time. 2 I. MURDOCH She recalled a little girl, but . . the years seemed to have brought about a young woman. *Rolling Stone* Her sister . . remembers her once beating up a bully to protect their little brother. K. GIBBONS When I was little I would think of ways of killing my daddy. 3 KEATS What little town by river or sea shore . . Is emptied of this folk, this pious morn? J. MORLEY In the realm of . . letters, Voltaire is one of the little band of great monarchs. 5 LD MACAULAY Every little discontent appears to him to portend a revolution. D. ROWE When you're depressed. . . Even the littlest thing hurts. **b** C. CLARKE They do this with the little cunning of little minds. 6 GOLDSMITH Upon that I proceed, . . though with very little hopes to reclaim him. DICKENS Tiny Tim . . had a plaintive little voice. E. C. STEDMAN A little poem, 'The Flower'. J. CONRAD Seating himself with a little spring on the . . parapet. SCOTT FITZGERALD She gave a little sigh . . so small that he did not notice it. M. MCCARTHY She did not seem to realize the little social nuances. **c** A. YOUNG A much larger capital than any little farmer can possess. 7 G. B. SHAW It was that awful little curate. G. B. SHAW Oh dear! My poor little brain is giving way. J. PORTER To sink or swim all on my little own! D. FRANCIS I have destroyed better things than your father's little racing stables. R. RENDELL They can't wait to get their hot little hands on rich capitalists' property. *New Yorker* Come and meet Mr. Haelkamp. He's the little painter we're beginning to collect.

II Opp. *much.* (In mod. usage also classed as a *determiner.*) 8 Not much; only a slight amount or degree of; scarcely any. OE. **b** That is scarce or absent. Now *rare.* OE. 9 Preceded by *a*: a small quantity of; some though not much. Also (*rare*, Shakes.) without *a.* ME. †10 Few, not many. ME–M17.

8 J. M. MURRY His poetic gift has little or no admixture of non-poetic elements. G. GREENE His own books took up so little room. W. GOLDING There had seemed little light all day. A. MCCOWEN My father . . was a man of . . very little education. Q. CRISP He seemed to have little difficulty in finding engagements for me. A. SCHLEE I . . had little idea how to conduct myself. **b** WORDSWORTH God help me for my little wit! 9 POPE A little learning is a dang'rous thing. LD MACAULAY By a little patience . . such a toleration might have been obtained. D. H. LAWRENCE Not even a little wind flickered the willows of the islets. R. K. NARAYAN Won't you come and have a little coffee with us? I. MURDOCH Mitzi had saved a little money. G. GORDON I was glad to have a little time . . to collect myself.

Special collocations, phrases, & comb.: *a little bird*: see BIRD *n.* *a little wee*: see WEE *a.* *great cry and little wool*: see CRY *n.* *have little scruple*: see SCRUPLE *n.* *hold little store by, on*: see STORE *n.* *Land of (the) Little Sticks*: see LAND *n.*[1] **laugh like little Audrey** laugh heartily (esp. at a serious situation). *Little Bear*: see BEAR *n.*[1] 2. **little black dress** a simple black dress suitable for most relatively formal social engagements. **little-boy, -boyish** *adjs.* pertaining to, suited to, or resembling (that of) a small boy. **little-boy-lost** *a.* resembling (that of) a small boy who has lost his way. **little boys' room** *euphem.* a men's lavatory. *little* CASSINO. **little chief hare** *N. Amer.* [tr. Chipewyan *bucka-thrae-ggayaze*] a N. American pika, *Ochotona princeps.* **little death** a weakening or loss of consciousness, *spec.* in sleep or during an orgasm. *Little Dipper*: see DIPPER 5a. *Little Dog*: see DOG *n.* 5. **little-ease** *Hist.* a prison-cell too small to stand or lie full-length in. **little end** *Mech.* the smaller end of a connecting-rod, attached to the piston. **Little Englander** (chiefly *Hist.*) a person opposed to an imperial role or policy for Britain. **Little Englandism** (chiefly *Hist.*) opposition to an imperial role or policy for Britain. *Little Entrance*: see ENTRANCE *n.* **little finger** either of the outermost and smallest fingers. **little-girl, -girlish** *adjs.* pertaining to, suited to, or resembling (that of) a little girl. **little-girl-lost** *a.* resembling (that of) a small girl who has lost her way. **little girls' room** *euphem.* a women's lavatory. **little go** (*a*) *Hist.* a private and illegal lottery; (*b*) *arch. slang* the first examination for the degree of BA at the Universities of Oxford and Cambridge. **little grebe** a small dumpy grebe, *Tachybaptus ruficollis*, with a trilling call, occurring widely in the Old World; also called *dabchick.* **little green man** an imaginary person of peculiar appearance, esp. from outer space. *little Hitler*: see HITLER *n.* 2. **Little Horse** *the* constellation Equuleus. **little house** (now *Austral.*, *NZ*, & *dial.*) a privy, a lavatory. **little ice age** *Meteorol.* any period of comparatively cold climate occurring outside the major glacial periods; *spec.* (freq. w. cap. initials) such a period which occurred in the 17th cent. **little Joe** in the game of craps, a throw of four. **Little League** *N. Amer.* a baseball league for children between the ages of 8 and 12. *Little Lion*: see LION *n.* 5. **little magazine** a literary magazine, usu. with experimental writing and in small format. **little man** (*a*) (esp. *joc.*) (as a form of address) a boy; (*b*) a person working or producing on a small scale; (*c*) the ordinary 'man in the street'; (*d*) (now *dial.*) the little finger. **Little Mary** *colloq.* the stomach. *little master*: see MASTER *n.*[1] 19. **Little Masters** a group of 16th-cent. German engravers, followers of Dürer, named from the size of their prints. *little mastery*: see MASTERY 5. **little neck (clam)** *US* [f. *Little Neck*, Long Island, NY State] a small variety of quahog. *little old*: see OLD *a.* **little ones** young children or animals. *little Parliament*: see PARLIAMENT *n.* **little people** (*a*) fairies; (*b*) children; (*c*) the poor; ordinary people. *little ray of sunshine*: see RAY *n.*[1] *Little Red Book*: see RED *a.* **Little Russian** *n.* & *a.* (*Hist.*) (*a*) *n.* a Ukrainian; the Ukrainian language; (*b*) *adj.* Ukrainian. *little scarlet*: see SCARLET *n.* 5. **little science** scientific or technological investigation not requiring large resources. **little season** the fashionable season in London in the winter. **little skate** a small rounded skate, *Raja erinacea*, which has a densely thorny black back and is common in the NW Atlantic. *little slam*: see SLAM *n.*[2] *little stranger*: see STRANGER *n.* 5c. **little theatre**: esp. for experimental productions. *little tin god*: see TIN *n.* & *a.* **little toe** either of the outermost and smallest toes. *little Turk*: see TURK *n.*[1] **little-worth** *a.* (now *arch.* & *Sc.*) of little worth. *much cry and little wool*: see CRY *n.* *no little*: see NO *a.* *one's little all*: see ALL *n.* 8. *poor little rich boy* or *girl*: see POOR *a.* *put, set, little store by, on*: see STORE *n.* *the little corporal*: see CORPORAL *n.*[2] 1. **the little woman** (*colloq.*, freq. *derog.*) one's wife. *the patter of little feet*: see PATTER *n.*[2] *this, that, little lot*: see LOT *n.* *turn, twist, wind,* or *wrap round one's little finger*: see FINGER *n.* *ye gods and little fishes*: see GOD *n.* *your little game*: see GAME *n.*

B *absol.* as *n.* I *absol.* 1 **a** Those that are little. Chiefly w. *the.* OE. **b** That which is little; the little qualities, aspects, etc. Chiefly w. *the.* L18. 2 Not much, only a small amount (*of the, my, this,* etc.). Qualified by a demonstr. or possess.: (the) small amount, (so) small a quantity. OE.

2 OED He showed little of the amiability which was ascribed to him. I. MURDOCH She knew little about jewels. B. MALAMUD A shrug that may mean much or little. C. RAYNER We ate so little. A. THWAITE She knew the value of education though she had little herself. K. WATERHOUSE There seems little else to be said.

II 3 *A* small quantity, piece, or portion (*of the, my, this,* etc.); *arch.* a small thing; a trifle (usu. in *pl.*). OE. 4 *A* short time or distance. Chiefly in *after a little, for a little, in a little.* OE.

3 T. GODWIN He drank a little of the wine. DISRAELI Let me recommend you a little of this pike! A. TATE Not a little of it comes from the comfortable habit of citing a passage in the Preface to *Lyrical Ballads.* N. COWARD Would you like some brandy? . . Just a little. I. MURDOCH Out of so much, can we not salvage a little.

Phrases: **a little** (*a*) to a little or slight extent; in a small degree; (*b*) for or at a short time or distance. **a little —** somewhat, rather. **by little and little** *arch.* = *little by little* below. **in little** (*a*) on a small scale; †(*b*) *spec.* (*Painting*) in miniature. *know little and care less*: see KNOW *v.* **little by little** by degrees, gradually. **little or nothing** hardly anything. *make little of*: see MAKE *v.* **not a little** a great deal. *say little for*: see SAY *v.*[1] *see little of*: see SEE *v.*

C *adv.* 1 To only a small extent or degree; not much. Also, infrequently, rarely. OE. 2 Not at all; hardly. Only w. vbs of knowing, thinking, or caring, etc. Freq. preceding the vb modified, w. periphrastic *do.* ME. †3 A little time (before); for only a little time. ME–E17.

1 W. S. MAUGHAM She cared little what he spoke of. J. BUCHAN He is old and can go about very little. S. BEDFORD They entertained their neighbours as little as possible. G. GREENE It is awful how little we change. E. BLISHEN We thought little of the concert hall, a university lecture room. *Cornwall Review* St. Just-in-Penwith . . seems to have been little influenced by the outside world. V. S. NAIPAUL I walked . . down little-used lateral lanes on the hillsides. 2 M. EDGEWORTH He little imagined of how much consequence it might be. T. HARDY You only knew me as a governess; you little think what my beginnings were. G. GREENE Little did they know that the story . . had already reached the ears of the drinkers. *New Yorker* 'Little did they imagine,' she said.

little /ˈlɪt(ə)l/ *v.t.* & *i.* *obs.* exc. *poet.* OE. [f. LITTLE *a.*] Make or become little; diminish.

littleness /ˈlɪt(ə)lnɪs/ *n.* OE. [f. LITTLE *a.* + -NESS.] 1 Smallness of quantity, stature, degree, extent, etc. OE. 2 Absence of greatness or importance; triviality; meanness, pettiness; an instance of this. LME.

littler *a.* see LITTLE *a.*

Littler's blue /lɪtləz ˈbluː/ *n. phr.* M20. [William *Littler* (1724–84), Eng. potter.] A rich blue colour applied to porcelain or stoneware.

Little's disease /ˈlɪt(ə)lz dɪˌziːz/ *n. phr.* L19. [William John *Little* (1810–94), Eng. physician.] *Med.* A form of congenital cerebral palsy causing bilateral spastic weakness of the limbs.

littlest *a.* see LITTLE *a.*

littlie *n.* var. of LITTLY.

littling /ˈlɪtlɪŋ/ *n.* *dial.* OE. [f. LITTLE *a.* + -LING[1].] A young child or animal.

littlish /ˈlɪtlɪʃ/ *a.* Chiefly *dial.* M19. [f. LITTLE *a.* + -ISH[1].] Rather little.

littly /ˈlɪtli/ *n.* Also **littlie.** L19. [f. LITTLE *a.* + -Y[6], -IE.] A small child or person; *esp.* (in *pl.*), small children, the young children of a family etc.

littoral /ˈlɪt(ə)r(ə)l/ *a.* & *n.* M17. [L *littoralis* var. of *litoralis*, f. *litor-*, *litus* shore: see -AL[1].] A *adj.* 1 Of or pertaining to the shore of the sea, a lake, etc.; existing or occurring on or adjacent to the shore. M17. 2 *Ecol.* & *Geol.* Designating, of, or pertaining to the zone of the shore extending from the high-water mark to the low-water mark (= INTERTIDAL), or (occas.) to the edge of the continental shelf; (of an organism) living in this zone; (of a sediment) deposited in this zone. Also, designating or pertaining to the region of a lake near the shore in which rooted vegetation occurs; = INFRALITTORAL (b). M17. **B** *n.* A littoral area; the coast. E19.

littorinid /lɪˈtɒrɪnɪd/ *n.* & *a.* M20. [mod.L *Littorinidae* (see below), f. *Littorina* genus name: see -ID[3].] **A** *n.* A marine snail of the family Littorinidae, which includes the periwinkles. M20. **B** *adj.* Of, pertaining to, or designating this family. M20.

litui *n.* pl. of LITUUS.

liturgic /lɪˈtəːdʒɪk/ *a.* & *n.* M17. [med.L *liturgicus* f. Gk *leitourgikos*, f. *leitourgia*: see LITURGY, -IC.] **A** *adj.* = LITURGICAL. M17. **B** *n.* †**1** A liturgical book. Only in L17. **2** In *pl.* (treated as *sing.*). The branch of knowledge that deals with liturgies, their form, origin, etc. Also called *liturgiology*. M19.

liturgical /lɪˈtəːdʒɪk(ə)l/ *a.* M17. [f. as prec.: see -ICAL.] Of or pertaining to (forms of) public worship or *spec.* the Liturgy or Eucharist. Also, of or pertaining to liturgics.

liturgical colours: used in ecclesiastical vestments, hangings for an altar, etc., varying according to the season, festival, or kind of service. **Liturgical Movement** a movement advocating the restoration of the active participation by the people in the official worship of the Church.

liturgically *adv.* from a liturgical point of view; in a liturgy, in liturgical worship: M19.

liturgiology /lɪˌtəːdʒɪˈɒlədʒi/ *n.* M19. [f. LITURGY + -OLOGY.] Liturgics.

liturgioˈlogical *a.* L19. **liturgiologist** *n.* M19.

liturgise *v.* var. of LITURGIZE.

liturgism /ˈlɪtədʒɪz(ə)m/ *n.* E20. [f. LITURGY + -ISM.] Excessive concern with liturgy or liturgical detail.

liturgist /ˈlɪtədʒɪst/ *n.* M17. [f. LITURGY + -IST.] **1** A person who uses or advocates the use of a liturgy. M17. **2** An authority on liturgies; a compiler of liturgies. M17. **3** A person who celebrates divine worship. M19.

liturˈgistical *a.* L19.

liturgize /ˈlɪtədʒʌɪz/ *v.i. rare.* Also **-ise**. E19. [f. LITURGY + -IZE.] Perform a liturgical act.

liturgy /ˈlɪtədʒi/ *n.* M16. [Fr. *liturgie* or late L *liturgia* f. Gk *leitourgia* public service, worship of the gods, f. *leitourgos* public servant, minister, f. var. of *lēitos* public, f. *lēos* Ionic form of *lāos* people + *-ergos* performing.] **1** (**L-**.) The service of the Eucharist of the Orthodox Church; a specified type or form of Eucharistic service. M16. **2** A form of public worship, esp. in the Christian Church; a set of formularies for the conduct of this. L16. **b** *the Liturgy*, the *Book of Common Prayer*. E17. **3** *Gk Hist.* A public office or duty performed gratuitously by a rich Athenian. M19.

1 *Liturgy of the Presanctified*: see PRESANCTIFY. **2** *transf.*: D. ACHESON The Council of Foreign Ministers . . had developed a liturgy and tradition of its own.

lituus /ˈlɪtjʊəs/ *n.* Pl. **litui** /ˈlɪtjʊʌɪ/. E17. [L.] **1** *Rom. Antiq.* The crooked staff or wand carried by an augur. Also, a curved trumpet, a clarion. E17. **2** *Math.* A plane spiral having (in polar coordinates) the formula $r^2\theta = a$, with a tail that approaches the polar axis asymptotically. M18.

Litvak /ˈlɪtvɒk/ *n.* L19. [Yiddish f. Pol. *Litwak* Lithuanian.] A Jew from Lithuania or its neighbouring regions.

litzendraht /ˈlɪtsəndraːt/ *n.* E20. [G, f. *Litze* braid, cord, lace, strand + *Draht* wire.] = next.

Litz wire /lɪts ˈwʌɪə/ *n. phr.* E20. [Partial tr. of prec.] *Electr.* Wire composed of many fine strands twisted together and individually insulated, so as to reduce the increase in resistance at high frequencies.

livable *a.* var. of LIVEABLE.

live /lʌɪv/ *a.* M16. [Aphet. f. ALIVE, repl. earlier LIVES *a.*] **1** **a** That is alive; living, as opp. to dead. Chiefly *attrib.* M16. **b** Actual, genuine; not pretended or pictured or toy. Chiefly in *a real live*. Usu. *joc.* L19. **c** Corresponding to actual facts. E20. **d** Of a performance etc.: heard or watched at the time of its occurrence, as opp. to recorded on film, tape, etc. Also, (of a recording, a film, etc.) made of a live performance. M20. **2** Of a coal, embers, etc.: flaming, glowing. E17. **3** *transf.* & *fig.* Full of life or active power; busy, lively; alert, energetic. Also, (of a question, an issue, etc.) of current interest, not obsolete or exhausted. M17. **4** (Of a mineral or rock) still forming part of the earth's mass, unwrought; (of air) in its native state, pure. M17. **5** Containing unexpended energy; (of a shell) unexploded; (of a match) unkindled. L18. **b** *Electr.* (Of a rail, wire, etc.) connected to a source of electrical power, carrying a voltage; (of a microphone etc.) switched on, receptive to sound. L19. **6** Of a machine part or piece of apparatus, esp. an axle: that moves or imparts movement. E19. **7** *Acoustics.* Of a room or enclosure: having a relatively long reverberation time. Cf. DEAD *a.* 15. M20.

1a P. THEROUX We had got used to Father looking like a live scarecrow. **d** A. ROAD Recording . . can never be quite as nail-biting as live transmission. *Guardian* No doubt the video is not quite the same as watching the race live. **2** Z. TOMIN There must be a live lump of coal somewhere, burning itself out. **3** M. ARNOLD All the live murmur of a Summer's day. *Sun (Baltimore)* Another live issue—the question of setting up a . . buffer zone in Korea.

Special collocations & comb.: **live action** *Cinemat.* action involving real people or animals, as opp. to animation, titles, etc. **live bait** *Angling* a living worm, small fish, etc., used as bait. **live-bearing** *a.* bearing live young, not laying eggs; viviparous. **live-birth**: in which the child is born alive. **live-born** *a.* born alive. **live fence** (orig. *US*) a hedge. **live load** a temporary or varying load on a structure, *esp.* the weight of people or goods in a building or vehicle (cf. *dead load* s.v. DEAD *a.*). **live oak**: of the evergreen species *Quercus virginiana*, of the southern US. **live steam**: from a boiler at full pressure. **livestock** animals kept or dealt in for use or profit. **live weight** the weight of an animal before it has been slaughtered and prepared as a carcass. **live wire** *fig.* an energetic or forceful person.

liveness *n.* L19.

live /lɪv/ *v.* [OE *libban* & *lifian*, corresp. to OFris. *libba*, *lifa*, OS *libian*, *lebon*, OHG *lebēn* (G *leben*), ON *lifa* live, remain, Goth. *liban*, f. Gmc base rel. to that of LIFE *n.*, LEAVE *v.*[1]] **1** *v.i.* **a** Be alive; have animal or vegetable life. OE. **b** *fig.* Of a thing: exist, be found. *poet.* L16. **2** *v.i.* Supply oneself with food; feed, subsist. Foll. by *by*, *on*, *upon*. OE. **3** *v.i.* Procure oneself the means of subsistence; depend on for a livelihood. Foll. by *by*, *off*, *on*, *upon*. OE. **4** *v.i.* Spend or lead one's life; conduct oneself in a specified way, esp. w. ref. to moral behaviour, personal aims or principles, or personal conditions. OE. **b** *v.t.* w. cognate obj. Lead (one's life) in a specified way. OE. **5** *v.i.* Continue in life; be alive for a longer or shorter period; have one's life prolonged. Also foll. by *on*. OE. **b** Escape spiritual death. Now *rare*. LME. **c** *fig.* Of a thing: survive, continue. *poet.* & *rhet.* M18. **6** *v.i.* Endure, last through; *spec.* (of a vessel) escape destruction, remain afloat. ME. **7** *v.i.* Make one's home; dwell, reside; *transf.* (of an object) have its place. Also, spend much non-working time *in* a room etc. ME. **8** *v.t.* Express in one's life; carry out in one's life the principles etc. of. M16. **9** *v.i.* Continue in the memory; escape obliteration or oblivion. L16. **10** *v.i.* Enjoy life intensely or abundantly. E17.

1 H. BAILEY She had only two more years to live. **2** AV *Matt.* 4:4 Man shall not live by bread alone. I. MURDOCH Carel was a vegetarian and lived on grated carrot and eggs and cheese. **3** A. JESSOPP Those luxuries which the big man consumes . . the small man lives by. C. ISHERWOOD He left him all his money, not very much, but enough to live on, comfortably. ANTHONY SMITH Primitive *Homo*, living off the countryside. **4** O. BLACKALL Rules . . to observe and live by. P. CAMPBELL The family lived in considerable comfort. I. MURDOCH Adelaide lived in a perpetual state of anxiety. J. C. OATES No intention whatsoever of living as their families had lived. **b** J. MORLEY Montaigne—content to live his life, leaving many questions open. **5** *Academy* Lord Carnarvon did not live to put the final touches to his translation. **c** P. KAVANAGH His pleasure did not live long. **7** D. H. LAWRENCE They'd lived next door to us when I was a little lad. J. CANNAN I couldn't find any brandy. Do you know where it lives? H. BAILEY The poor live in caravans, the bourgeoise in solid brick houses. **8** J. JORTIN To say who is the Lord . . is to deny God . . and live a lie. *Grimsby Evening Telegraph* How can a man like this hope to negotiate with Iceland . . whose people virtually live fish? **9** R. W. DIXON So would he . . give me those kind looks which live in me. C. H. SISSON To live in the memory of men is one of the most persistent . . wishes of mankind. **10** N. HINTON He couldn't wait to get out of school and really start living.

Phrases: **he'll**, **I'll**, etc., **live** (freq. *joc.*) no need for worry or concern. *how the other half lives*: see HALF *n.* *I'll live*: see *he'll live* above. **live and learn** continually discover new facts as life goes on. **live and let live** be tolerant of others and be so tolerated. *live by one's wits*: see WIT *n.* **live dangerously** take risks habitually. *live extempore*: see EXTEMPORE *adv.* *live for the* MOMENT. *live high off* or *on the hog*: see HOG *n.* *live in each other's pockets*: see POCKET *n.* **live in oneself** rely on oneself for company etc., live in isolation. *live in sin*: see SIN *n.*[1] *live in the* MOMENT. **live it up** live gaily and extravagantly. *live like a lord*: see LORD *n.* **live off the country** or **land** subsist on the produce of the land. **live on air** (appear to) eat nothing. **live one's own life** follow one's own plans or principles; live independently. *live on one's hump*: see HUMP *n.* *live on one's nerves*: see NERVE *n.* **live out of a suitcase** live temporarily with one's belongings still packed. *live over the brush*: see BRUSH *n.*[2] 3. *live over the shop*: see SHOP *n.* *live rough*: see ROUGH *adv.* *live tally*: see TALLY *n.* **live to oneself** = *live in oneself* above. *live to tell the tale*: see TALE *n.* **live within oneself** = *live in oneself* above. **live with oneself** retain one's self-respect. **long live** — *int.* expr. loyalty. **where one lives** *US slang* at or to the right or vital point. *well to live*: see WELL *a.* *will to live*: see WILL *n.*[1]

With preps. & advs. in specialized senses: **live down** overcome (a prejudice, scandal, etc.) by a blameless course of life. **live in**, **live out** reside in, away from, one's place of employment. **live through** survive, remain alive at the end of. **live to** survive and reach (a certain age etc.). **live together** cohabit, esp. as man and wife. **live up to** (*a*) act in full accordance with (principles, rules, etc.); (*b*) push expenditure to the full limits of (one's fortune). **live well** (*a*) have plenty; be in comfortable circumstances; (*b*) live a virtuous life. **live with** (*a*) reside with, *esp.* cohabit with as man and wife; (*b*) tolerate, accept.

Comb.: **lived-in** *a.* occupied, inhabited; comfortable, homely; **live-for-ever** = LIVELONG *n.*; **live-in** *a.* & *n.* (*a*) *adj.* resident, esp. in one's place of employment or as a person's lover, common-law spouse, etc.; (of an item of clothing) able to be worn continually; very comfortable or practical.; (*b*) *n.* a live-in employee, lover, etc. **live-out** *a.* residing away from one's place of employment.

liveable /ˈlɪvəb(ə)l/ *a.* Also **livable**. E17. [f. LIVE *v.* + -ABLE.] †**1** Likely to live. *rare.* Only in E17. †**2** Conducive to comfortable living. Only in M17. **3** Of a house, a room, a locality, etc.: that may be lived in; suitable for living in. E19. **4** Of life: that can be lived; bearable, supportable. M19. **5** Of a person: easy to live with or *with*; companionable, sociable. M19.

liveaˈbility *n.* (*a*) suitability for habitation; (*b*) survival expectancy, esp. of poultry: E20. **liveableness** *n.* M19.

lived /lʌɪvd/ *a.* LME. [f. *live* infl. form of LIFE *n.* + -ED[2].] Having a certain kind or length of life, as *low-lived*, etc.

¶ Earliest in LONG-LIVED; see also SHORT-LIVED.

†**livelihead** *n.* LME. [f. LIVELY *a.* + -HEAD.] **1** Liveliness; vivacity. LME–E18. **b** Living form. Also, condition of being alive. M–L16. **2** Means of living; inheritance; livelihood. L15–L16.

livelihood /ˈlʌɪvlɪhʊd/ *n.*[1] [OE *līflād*, f. *līf* LIFE *n.* + *lād* course, way (see LOAD *n.*, LODE), assim. in 16 to LIVELY *a.* and -HOOD.] †**1** Lifetime; kind or manner of life; conduct. OE–L16. **2** A means of living, a source of maintenance. Freq. in *earn*, *get*, *make*, etc., *a livelihood*. ME. †**b** Sustenance, food, nourishment. ME–L17. †**3** Income, revenue, a stipend; in *pl.*, emoluments. LME–E17. †**4** Property yielding an income, landed or inherited property; an estate, an inheritance. LME–E17.

†**livelihood** *n.*[2] M16–M17. [f. LIVELY *a.* + -HOOD.] Liveliness.

livelong /ˈlɪvlɒŋ/ *n.* L16. [f. LIVE *v.* + LONG *adv.*: cf. *live-for-ever* s.v. LIVE *v.*] Any of several plants which retain their form or greenness for a long time; *esp.* (*a*) orpine, *Sedum telephium*; †(*b*) pearly everlasting, *Anaphalis margaritacea*.

livelong /ˈlɪvlɒŋ/ *a. poet.* & *rhet.* LME. [Orig. f. LIEF *a.* + LONG *a.*[1] (cf. G *die liebe lange Nacht*). In 16 interpreted as f. LIVE *a.* or *v.* + LONG *a.*[1], and alt. in form.] Of a period of time: very long or apparently very long; whole, entire.

STEELE Here I sit moping all the live-long Night.

lively /ˈlʌɪvli/ *a.* OE. [f. LIFE *n.* + -LY[1].] **I** †**1** Having life; living, live, animate. OE–M17. **b** Of or pertaining to a living person; (of instruction etc.) delivered orally. M16–E18. †**2** Of or pertaining to life; necessary to life, vital. OE–M17. **3** Full of action or interest; lifelike, animated; vivid, stimulating. ME. **4** Full of life; vigorous, energetic, active, brisk. ME. **5** Of colour, light, etc.: vivid, bright, fresh. LME. **6** Vivacious, jolly, sociable. L16. **7** Exciting, dangerous, difficult. *joc.* L18.

3 J. GILMOUR A valley lively with flocks, herds, tents. M. WEST The discussion was so lively that it was a quarter to one before Mendelius was able to escape. *Holiday Which?* They are .. aimed at young people looking for a lively holiday in the sun. 4 B. TARKINGTON His mother took a lively interest in everything. **look lively** move (more) quickly or energetically (freq. in *imper.*). 6 D. WIGODER She was lively, laughed gaily, talked easily. 7 *Law Times* The Press is making things lively for Her Majesty's judges.

II 8 *Naut.* Of a boat etc.: rising lightly to the waves. L17.

livelily *adv.* M16. **liveliness** *n.* LME.

lively /ˈlʌɪvli/ *adv.* OE. [f. as LIFE *n.* + -LY[2].] †**1** So as to impart life. Only in OE. †**2** As a living person or thing. LME–L16. **3** With animation, actively, briskly, nimbly, vigorously. Now chiefly in *step lively*, = *look lively* s.v. LIVELY *a.* 4. LME. †**b** With feeling. L16–M18. **4** In a lifelike manner; vividly. Now *rare.* LME. †**b** Clearly, plainly. M16–L17.

liven /ˈlʌɪv(ə)n/ *v.t.* & *i.* *colloq.* E18. [f. LIFE *n.* + -EN[5]. Cf. ENLIVEN.] Make or become (more) lively; brighten, cheer. Also foll. by *up*.

A. BROOKNER Things livened up a little when the cousins .. arrived.

livener *n.* a thing that enlivens; *spec.* an alcoholic drink: L19.

liver /ˈlɪvə/ *n.*[1] & *a.* [OE *lifer* = OFris. *livere*, MDu. *lever* (Du. *lever*), OHG *libara* (G *Leber*), ON *lifr*, f. Gmc.] **A** *n.* **1** A large lobed glandular organ in the abdomen of vertebrate animals which secretes bile, detoxifies the blood, and is important in the metabolism and storage of major nutrients. Also, the flesh of the liver of some animals, used as food. OE. **b** Any of various analogous glandular organs or tissues in invertebrates. M19. **2** *fig.* & *allus.* **a** The seat of love or other passionate emotion, as anger, bitterness, etc. *arch.* LME. **b** The seat of cowardice. L16. **3** *Chem.* = HEPAR. *arch.* L17. **4** A diseased or disordered condition of the liver. Freq. w. specifying wd, e.g. *hobnail liver.* E19. **5** *ellipt.* = *liver colour* below. M19.

1 J. RULE Silver set down a plate of eggs, chicken livers, and toast. 2a DRYDEN When Love's unerring Dart Transfixt his Liver, and inflam'd his Heart.

Phrases: LILY *liver.* **liver of sulphur** a liver-coloured mixture containing potassium sulphide and used as a lotion to treat skin diseases. *scare the liver and* LIGHTS *out of*. *white liver*: see WHITE *a.*

B *adj.* Liver-coloured. M19.

Comb. & *special collocations*: **liver chestnut** a dark kind of chestnut horse; **liver colour** the colour of liver, dark reddish-brown; **liver-coloured** *a.* of liver colour; *liver fluke*: see FLUKE *n.*[1] 2; **liver-hearted** *a.* cowardly; **liverleaf** *N. Amer.* = HEPATICA 2; **liver pad** a pad or plaster for the area of the liver; **liver rot** disease of the liver; (*esp.* in *Vet. Med.*) a type of anaemia caused by the liver fluke; distomiasis; fascioliasis; **liver salts**: intended to be taken in water etc. to relieve dyspepsia or biliousness; **liver sausage** (a) soft sausage filled with cooked liver etc.; **liver-spot** any of several skin conditions causing brown spots or patches of melanin, *esp.* chloasma or (now usu.) lentigo; any of the brown spots on the skin characteristic of these conditions; **liver-spotted** *a.* having liver-coloured spots or liver-spots; †**liver-vein** (*a*) the basilic vein; (*b*) *allus.* the conduct of someone in love; **liver-wing** the right wing of a fowl etc. which, when dressed for cooking, has the liver tucked under it; *joc.* the right arm; **liverwurst** /-wəːst/ [G *Wurst* sausage: cf. LEBERWURST] = *liver sausage* above.

livered *a.* †(*a*) coagulated, clotted; (*b*) (as 2nd elem. of comb.) having a liver of a specified kind, as *lily-livered, white-livered*, etc.: ME. **liverless** *a.* L16.

liver /ˈlɪvə/ *n.*[2] LME. [f. LIVE *v.* + -ER[1].] **1** A person who lives or is alive (now *rare*). Also (chiefly *US*), a resident, a dweller. LME. **b** = LIVIER 1a. *Canad.* M18. **2** With qualifying adj.: a person who lives in a specified way, for a long time, etc. LME.

2 HUGH WALPOLE To be an artist was .. synonymous with being a loose liver and an atheist. D. HEWETT The Brewsters were long livers. The old man looked good for another thirty years.

Phrases: *free liver*: see FREE *a.* **good liver** (*a*) a virtuous person; (*b*) a person given to good living.

liver /ˈlɪvə/ *v.t.* & *i.* *obs.* exc. *dial.* ME. [Partly f. OFr. *livrer* (see LIVERY *n.*), partly aphet. f. DELIVER *v.*] = DELIVER *v.*

liverance /ˈlɪv(ə)r(ə)ns/ *n.* *obs.* exc. *dial.* ME. [Partly f. OFr. *livrance* delivery, sort of homage, f. *livrer* (see LIVERY *n.*). Partly aphet. f. DELIVERANCE.] Delivery, distribution; deliverance, release.

liverish /ˈlɪv(ə)rɪʃ/ *a.* M18. [f. LIVER *n.*[1] + -ISH[1].] **1** Resembling liver. M18. **2** Suffering from a disorder of the liver. Also, peevish, bad-tempered. L19.

liverishness *n.* E20.

Liverpool /ˈlɪvəpuːl/ *n.* & *a.* M19. [A city in NW England, on the River Mersey.] (Designating) delftware and porcelain manufactured in Liverpool in the 18th cent.

Liverpudlian /lɪvəˈpʌdlɪən/ *n.* & *a.* M19. [f. as prec. (w. joc. substitution of *puddle* for *pool*) + -IAN.] (A native or inhabitant) of the city of Liverpool in NW England.

liverwort /ˈlɪvəwəːt/ *n.* LOE. [f. LIVER *n.*[1] + WORT *n.*[1], tr. med.L *hepatica.*] **1** Orig., the thalloid bryophyte *Marchantia polymorpha*, lobed like the liver. Now, any bryophyte of the class Hepaticae, with a capsule splitting open into four valves and either thalloid or mosslike (foliose) in form. LOE. **2** = HEPATICA 2. Now *US.* L16.

livery /ˈlɪv(ə)ri/ *n.* & *v.* ME. [AN *liveré*, (O)Fr. *livrée*, use as n. of fem. pa. pple of *livrer* dispense, deliver, f. L *liberare* LIBERATE *v.*, (in med.L) deliver up, hand over: see -Y[5].] **A** *n.* **1 a** *Hist.* The dispensing of food, provisions, or clothing to retainers or servants; *gen.* provision, allowance. ME. **b** *Hist.* The food or provisions so dispensed; an allowance or ration of food served out. ME. **c** Allowance of provender for horses. Now *rare* exc. in *at livery, livery stable*, below. LME. **2** Orig., clothing, *esp.* distinctive clothing or a distinctive item of clothing worn by the retainers or servants of a particular employer, for recognition. More widely, a distinctive badge or outfit worn by a member of a City Company, a servant, an official, etc. ME. **b** *transf.* & *fig.* A distinctive guise, marking, or outward appearance. ME. **c** An emblem, device, or distinctive colour scheme on a vehicle, product, etc., indicating its owner or manufacturer. M20. **3** *collect.* **a** Retainers or servants in livery. Now *rare* or *obs.* LME. **b** A livery company; the members of a livery company. E16. **4** *Law* (now *Hist.*). The legal delivery of property into a person's possession; a writ allowing this. LME. †**5 a** *gen.* The action of handing over or conveying something into a person's hands; delivery of goods, money, a writ, etc. LME–M18. **b** Delivery or dealing of blows. Only in LME. **6 a** = *livery stable* below. *US.* M19. **b** A horse kept at livery; a horse (and carriage) hired from a livery stable. Also, stabling at a livery stable. L19.

2 A. SETON Two boys in white livery marched through the gate. A. CARTER The valet sat up on the box in a natty black and gold livery. b G. BERKELEY Clothing themselves in the livery of other men's opinions. c K. WARREN The 14 vehicles were in a new livery, basically light grey and green. 3b *Times* A dinner given by the Distillers' Company for the ladies and livery yesterday.

Phrases: **at livery** (of a horse) stabled, fed, and groomed for the owner at a fixed charge. **in livery** wearing a particular livery. **livery of seisin** *Law* (now *Hist.*) an early means of granting freehold land or property by any of a number of symbolic gestures, as giving the grantee a piece of turf from the land, standing on the land and inviting the grantee to enter, etc. **out of livery** not dressed in livery; wearing plain clothes. **take up one's livery** become a liveryman.

Comb.: **livery company** any of the London City companies which formerly had a distinctive costume; **livery cupboard** *Hist.* (*a*) a cupboard in which allowances of food were served out; (*b*) an ornamental buffet or sideboard; **livery servant** a servant who wears livery; **livery stable** a stable where horses are kept at livery or let out for hire.

B *v.t.* Array in a livery. *rare.* L16.

liveried *a.* dressed in or provided with a livery M17.

livery /ˈlɪvəri/ *a.* M18. [f. LIVER *n.*[1] + -Y[1].] **1** Of the consistency or colour of liver; (of soil) heavy, tenacious. M18. **2** = LIVERISH 2. *colloq.* M20.

liveryman /ˈlɪv(ə)rɪmən/ *n.* Pl. **-men.** L17. [f. LIVERY *n.* + MAN *n.*] **1** A liveried retainer or servant. Now *rare* or *obs.* L17. **2** A member of a livery company. L17. **3** A keeper of or attendant in a livery stable. M19.

lives *n.* pl. of LIFE *n.*

†**lives** *a.* OE–E17. [OE *līfes* genit. sing. of *līf* LIFE *n.*: see -'S[1]. Cf. LIVE *a.*] Alive; live, living.

liveware /ˈlʌɪvwɛː/ *n.* M20. [f. LIVE *a.* + WARE *n.*[2]] Working personnel, as distinct from the inanimate or abstract things they work with; *spec.* computer personnel or users.

liveyer(e) *ns.* see LIVIER.

livid /ˈlɪvɪd/ *a.* LME. [Fr. *livide* or L *lividus*, f. *livere* be bluish: see -ID[1].] **1** Of a bluish-leaden colour; discoloured as by a bruise; black and blue. LME. **2** Of a colour: having a bluish or greyish tinge. E19. **3** Furiously angry, as if pale with rage. *colloq.* E20.

1 J. UPDIKE Her left leg showed a livid ripple of varicose vein. 3 R. CHANDLER Orrin would be absolutely livid Mother would be furious too.

li'vidity *n.* LME. **lividness** *n.* M17.

livier /ˈlɪvjə, *in sense 3 also* ˈlʌɪ-/ *n.* *dial.* In sense 1a also (now usu.) **livyer, liveyer(e).** M19. [Prob. alt. of LIVER *n.*[2]: see -IER.] **1 a** A resident or a permanent settler in Newfoundland or Labrador. Cf. earlier LIVER *n.*[2] 1b. *Canad.* M19. **b** *gen.* An inhabitant, a dweller. L19. **2** A living person. L19. **3** A person who holds a tenement on a lease for a life or lives. L19.

living /ˈlɪvɪŋ/ *n.*[1] ME. [f. LIVE *v.* + -ING[1].] **1 a** The action of LIVE *v.*; the fact of being alive or of dwelling in a specified place. ME. **b** The action of leading one's life in a particular (moral, physical, etc.) manner. ME. †**c** One's lifetime. LME–L16. **2 a** A livelihood; a means of maintenance or support. Formerly also, an income, an endowment. ME. †**b** Food; in *pl.*, victuals. LME–M19. **c** The action, process, or method of gaining one's livelihood. M16. **3** †**a** Property, *esp.* landed estate. Also (in *pl.*), estates, possessions. LME–E19. **b** A holding of land, a tenement. *obs.* exc. *dial.* L16. **4** *Eccl.* A position as a vicar or rector with income or property or both. LME.

1a G. JOSIPOVICI The ordinary complements to daily living, the plates, the cups, the bowls. 2a N. GORDIMER This cocky miss who played the guitar .. as if the world owed her a living. E. LEONARD Maureen wouldn't've cared what you did for a living. *earn, get, make*, etc., *a living*. 4 R. MACAULAY On his last return to Anglicanism, he had accepted a country living.

Phrases: *cost of living*: see COST *n.*[2] **good living** a high standard of life, esp. with regard to food and drink. *gracious living*: see GRACIOUS *a.* **plain living and high thinking** frugal and philosophic life. *standard of living*: see STANDARD *n.*

Comb.: **living area** = *living space* (c) below; **living floor** *Archaeol.* a well-defined single horizon containing contemporary (esp. prehistoric) material suggesting domestic occupation; **living-in, living-out** residing in, out of, an employer's premises; **living-room** (*a*) a room for general day use; (*b*) = LEBENSRAUM; **living space** (*a*) = LEBENSRAUM; (*b*) space for accommodation; (*c*) an area in a room or house for general day use; **living standard** the level of consumption in terms of food, clothing, services, etc., estimated for a person, group, or nation; **living wage** a wage on which it is possible to live without undue hardship.

livingless *a.* (*rare*) without a living L19.

living /ˈlɪvɪŋ/ *a.* & *n.*[2] OE. [f. LIVE *v.* + -ING[2].] **A** *adj.* **1** *pred.* & *postpositive.* Not dead; alive, when alive. OE. **2** That lives or has life; that is real. Also, contemporary, now existent. OE. **b** *transf.*

(Of water) flowing, running; (of a coal, embers, etc.) live; (of a rock or stone) = LIVE *a.* 4. LME. c Of a language: still in vernacular use. L17. 3 With specifying wd.: that passes life in a specified manner. LME. 4 Of or pertaining to a living person or what is living. L17. 5 = LIVELY *a.* 4-7. E18.

1 R. B. PEAKE You are the only man living that can serve my brother. 2 DICKENS By the living Lord it flashed upon me . . that she had done it. T. K. WOLFE There was no way to explain this to a living soul. *Independent* He is living proof that the party can change its way. 4 J. CRACE She is . . interested in living folklore.

Special collocations: **living chess**: in which living people act as the chess-pieces. **living dead** (*fig.*) *the* class of people leading an empty or miserable existence. **living-dead** *a.* experiencing living death. **living death** an empty or miserable existence. **living fossil** a plant or animal that has survived relatively unchanged since the extinction of the others of its group, known only as fossils. *living image*: see IMAGE *n.* **living memory** the memories of some people still living. **living newspaper** a theatrical documentary consisting of a series of short social or political scenes. **living picture** (*a*) = TABLEAU *vivant*; (*b*) a motion picture. **living skeleton** a very emaciated person. **living theatre** theatre consisting of live stage performances, as opp. to cinema. **living will** a written declaration by a person setting out the circumstances in which artificial means of maintaining his or her life should be withdrawn.

B *n. collect. pl. The* class of living people. OE.

D. A. DYE Hey, Taylor. You back among the living? *in the land of the living*: see LAND *n.*[1]

livingly *adv.* LME. **livingness** *n.* L17.

Livingstone daisy /ˌlɪvɪŋstən ˈdeɪzi/ *n. phr.* M20. [f. unidentified proper name + DAISY.] A dwarf mesembryanthemum, *Dorotheanthus bellidiformis*, native to the Cape Province of South Africa, bearing daisy-like flowers in many colours.

Livonian /lɪˈvəʊnɪən/ *n.* & *a.* L16. [f. med.L *Livonia* (see below) + -IAN.] **A** *n.* 1 A native or inhabitant of Livonia, a former Baltic province of Russia, now divided between Estonia and Latvia. L16. 2 The Baltic language of the Livonians. E19. **B** *adj.* Of or pertaining to Livonia, the Livonians, or their language. M18.

livor /ˈlʌɪvɔː/ *n. arch.* LME. [L.] 1 Discoloration of the skin, as from bruising or in a corpse. LME. †2 Ill will, malignity, spite. Only in 17.

Livornese /lɪvɔːˈniːz/ *n.* & *a.* E19. [f. *Livorno* (see LEGHORN) + -ESE.] **A** *n.* Pl. same. A native or inhabitant of the city of Livorno (Leghorn) in W. central Italy. E19. **B** *adj.* Of or pertaining to Livorno. E19.

livraison /livrɛzɔ̃/ *n.* Pl. pronounced same. E19. [Fr. f. L *liberatio(n-)* LIBERATION.] A part, number, or fascicle of a work published by instalments.

livre /ˈliːvrə/ *n.* M16. [Fr. f. L *libra* pound: cf. LIRA.] An old French monetary unit, worth one pound of silver.

livre de chevet /liːvrə də ʃəvɛ/ *n. phr.* Pl. ***livres de chevet*** (pronounced same). E20. [Fr. lit. 'book of the bed-head'.] A bedside book; a favourite book.

livre de circonstance /liːvrə də sirkɔ̃stɑ̃ːs/ *n. phr.* Pl. ***livres de circonstance*** (pronounced same). M20. [Fr.] A book composed or adapted for the occasion.

livres de chevet, de circonstance *n. phrs.* pls. of LIVRE DE CHEVET, DE CIRCONSTANCE.

livret /ˈliːvrɪt/ *n. rare.* LME. [Fr. f. *livre* book: see -ET[1].] A small book.

livyer *n.* see LIVIER.

liwa /ˈliːwɑː/ *n.* E20. [Arab. *liwā'* banner, flag, province.] *Hist.* A province or large administrative district in any of several Arabic-speaking countries, esp. Iraq.

lixivia *n.* pl. of LIXIVIUM.

lixivial /lɪkˈsɪvɪəl/ *a.* & *n.* M17. [f. LIXIVI(UM + -AL[1].] **A** *adj.* Of, pertaining to, or of the nature of (a) lye. Also, alkaline. Now *rare.* M17. †**B** *n.* A lye; an alkali. Only in L17.

Also †**lixiviate** *a.* & *n.* M17-E19.

lixiviate /lɪkˈsɪvɪeɪt/ *v.t.* M17. [mod.L *lixiviat-* pa. ppl stem of *lixiviare*, f. as next: see -ATE[3].] 1 Impregnate with lye. Now *rare* or *obs.* M17. 2 Separate (a substance) into soluble and insoluble constituents by percolation of liquid, usu. water; leach. M18.

lixiviˈation *n.* M18.

lixivium /lɪkˈsɪvɪəm/ *n. arch.* Pl. **-ia** /-ɪə/. M17. [Late L, use as n. of L *lixivius* made into lye, f. *lix* ashes, lye.] A solution obtained by leaching; lye; *spec.* water containing alkaline salts leached from wood ashes.

lixivious *a.* (now *rare* or *obs.*) of, pertaining to, or of the nature of (a) lye M17.

lizard /ˈlɪzəd/ *n.* LME. [OFr. *lesard, -arde* (mod. *lézard, -arde*) repr. L *lacertus, lacerta*, app. identical w. *lacertus* muscle: see -ARD.] 1 Any of numerous mostly small reptiles which have an elongated body, a long tail, four legs, and a scaly or granulated skin, and belong to the order Lacertilia; *Zool.* any reptile of the order Lacertilia, which also includes limbless forms (e.g. slow worms). Also (now *loosely*), any related or similar animal, as a crocodilian or dinosaur; *arch.* a newt. LME. **b** With specifying wd: any of various species of the genus *Lacerta* or other lacertilian genera. L17. **c** Lizard skin. L19. 2 Chiefly *Her.* A figure or charge representing a lizard. LME. 3 (Usu. **L-**.) (The name of) *the* constellation Lacerta. L18. 4 *Naut.* A piece of rope having a thimble or block spliced into one or both ends. L18. 5 A fancy variety of canary. Also *lizard canary.* M19. 6 A musterer of sheep; a person who maintains boundary fences. *Austral.* & *NZ slang.* M20.

1 *flying lizard, monitor lizard, sleeping lizard, viviparous lizard*, etc.

Phrases: *lounge lizard*: see LOUNGE *n.*[1]

Comb.: *lizard canary*: see sense 5 above; **lizard cuckoo** any of several W. Indian lizard-eating cuckoos of the genus *Saurothera*; **lizardfish** any of various fishes of the family Synodontidae, found in warm seas and having large pelvic fins on which they rest; **lizard-green** *n.* & *a.* (of) a colour resembling that of the green lizard; **lizard orchid** a rare British orchid, *Himantoglossum hircinum*, having greenish flowers with a very long narrow central lobe to the labellum; **lizard-skin** *a.* made of the skin of a lizard; **lizard's tail** a US swamp plant, *Saururus cernuus* (family Saururaceae), with long tapering spikes of apetalous flowers.

lizard-like *adv.* & *a.* (*a*) *adv.* (*rare*) in the manner of a lizard; (*b*) *adj.* resembling (that of) a lizard: L16. **lizardly** *a.* (*rare*) resembling a lizard L19.

Lizzie /ˈlɪzi/ *n.* Also **l-**. E20. [Pet-form of the female forename *Elizabeth*. In sense 1b infl. by LEZZY; in sense 3 alt. of *Lisbon*.] **1a** An effeminate young man. Also *lizzie boy. slang.* E20. **b** A lesbian. *slang.* M20. **2** More fully *tin Lizzie*. A motor car, *esp.* an early model of a Ford. *slang.* E20. **3** Lisbon wine. *arch. slang.* M20. **4** *busy Lizzie*, any of several balsams with usu. red, pink, or white flowers much grown as house-plants, esp. *Impatiens walleriana* and *I. sultanii*, natives of East Africa, and their hybrids. M20.

'll *v.* see SHALL *v.*, WILL *v.*[1]

llama /ˈlɑːmə/ *n.* E17. [Sp. f. Quechua.] 1 A S. American cud-chewing mammal, *Llama glama*, which belongs to the same family as camels but is smaller and humpless, and is found only domesticated as a beast of burden and a source of soft woolly fur and meat. E17. 2 The wool of the llama; a material made from this. M19.

llanero /lɑːˈnɛːrəʊ, lj-/ *n.* Pl. **-os**. E19. [S. Amer. Sp., f. next.] An inhabitant of a llano.

llano /ˈlɑːnəʊ, ˈljɑː-/ *n.* Pl. **-os**. E17. [Sp. f. L *planum* PLANE *n.*[3]] A level treeless plain in the south-western US and the northern parts of S. America.

Lloyd-Georgian /lɔɪdˈdʒɔːdʒɪən/ *a.* & *n.* E20. [f. *Lloyd George* (see below) + -IAN.] *Hist.* **A** *adj.* Of, pertaining to, or associated with the British Liberal statesman and Prime Minister Lloyd George (1863-1945). E20. **B** *n.* A follower or adherent of Lloyd George or his policies. E20.

lloydia /ˈlɔɪdɪə/ *n.* M19. [mod.L (see below), f. Edward Lhwyd or *Lloyd* (1660-1709), Welsh antiquary + -IA[1].] Any of various small bulbous alpine plants constituting the genus *Lloydia* of the lily family, and bearing white or yellow flowers; *esp.* the Snowdon lily, *L. serotina*.

Lloyd Morgan /lɔɪd ˈmɔːg(ə)n/ *n.* M20. [C. *Lloyd Morgan* (1852-1936), Brit. psychologist.] *Lloyd Morgan('s) canon*, the principle that the behaviour of an animal should not be interpreted in terms of a higher psychological process if it can be explained in terms of a lower one.

Lloyd's /lɔɪdz/ *n.* E19. [f. Edward *Lloyd*, who supplied shipping information to clients meeting in his coffee-house in London from 1688.] An incorporated association of underwriters in London who undertake insurance (orig. marine insurance only) with individual liability.

Lloyd's List a daily publication devoted to shipping news. **Lloyd's Register** (**of Shipping**) an annual classified list of ships over a certain tonnage; the independent society which publishes this.

Lo /ləʊ/ *n. US.* Pl. **Los**. L19. [f. the line '*Lo*, the poor Indian' in Pope's *Essay on Man*, a use of LO *int.*[1]] An American Indian. Also *Mr* (or *Mrs*) *Lo.*

lo /ləʊ/ *int.*[1] [OE *lā* natural exclam. (cf. LA *int.*); from ME partly f. imper. of LOOK *v.*] Orig., oh! Later, used to direct attention to a surprising fact or sight; see! look! Now *arch.* exc. in *lo and behold* (chiefly *joc.*).

lo /ləʊ/ *int.*[2] *colloq.* Also **'lo**. E20. [Abbrev.] Hello.

loa /ˈləʊə/ *n.*[1] M19. [mod.L (see below), app. f. a Bantu lang. of Angola.] A filarial worm of the genus *Loa*, found in tropical Africa and infecting the eyes and subcutaneous tissues in humans; an eye-worm.

loa /ˈləʊə/ *n.*[2] Pl. same, **-s**. M20. [Haitian creole *lwa*, f. Yoruba *oluwa* lord, owner.] A god in the voodoo cult of Haiti.

loach /ləʊtʃ/ *n.* LME. [(O)Fr. *loche*, of unkn. origin.] Any of numerous small slender freshwater cyprinoid fishes of the family Cobitidae, found in Europe and Asia.

SPINED *loach. stone loach*: see STONE *n., a.,* & *adv.*

load /ləʊd/ *n.* Also †**lode**. See also LODE. [OE *lād* = OHG *leita* course, leading, procession (G *Leite*), ON *leið* way, course, f. Gmc, f. base also of LEAD *v.*[1]] **I 1** See LODE. OE.

II †**2** Carriage, carrying. Also, an act of placing a burden for carrying on or in something. OE-E16. **b** [f. the vb.] *Computing.* The action or an act of loading a program. Usu. *attrib.* M20. **3a** A thing laid on or taken up by a person or animal, or put in a vehicle or vessel, to be carried; a burden; (usu. with preceding n.) an amount which is usually or actually carried, or which can be carried, by a specified vehicle etc. ME. **b** The quantity of a particular substance which it is customary to load at one time; a unit of measure or weight based on this. LME. **c** The (amount of) material carried along by a stream; the material carried by various other natural agents of transportation, as glaciers, winds, and ocean currents. L19. **d** A quantity of items washed or to be washed in a washing machine or dishwasher at one time. M20. **4** *fig.* A burden of affliction, sin, responsibility, etc.; a thing which weighs down, oppresses, or impedes a person. LME. **5a** A material object or a force which acts or is conceived as a weight, clog, etc. L16. **b** The charge of a firearm. L17. **c** The resistance which machinery offers when driven by a dynamo or motor. L19. **d** *Building* & *Engin.* The force exerted on a structure or part of one. L19. **e** The electric power that a generating system is delivering or required to deliver at any moment. L19. **f** *Electronics.* An impedance or circuit that receives the output of a transistor or other device, or in which the output is developed. E20. **6** One's fill of alcoholic drink. Freq. in *get a load on* below. *colloq.* L16. **7** A great quantity or number (*of*); plenty, a lot. Freq. in *pl. colloq.* E17. **8** = DOSE *n.* 4. *slang.* M20. **9** An amount of work, teaching, etc., to be done by a person. Freq. w. preceding n. M20. **10** The quantity of semen ejaculated at orgasm. *slang.* L20.

3a R. K. NARAYAN She wasn't asking him to carry the load on his head. K. GIBBONS He . . picks up the next load of strangers. ALAN BENNETT I've got to pick up a load of . . windcheaters. *cart-load, horse-load, lorry-load*, etc. 4 D. W. JERROLD With this thought, a load was lifted from the old man's heart. 5b Z. GREY He had used up all the loads in Wright's gun. 7 K. ISHIGURO There's always loads on in London. *Independent* What a load of old cobblers. *New York Times* A rambling summer camp where you had loads of fun. 9 J. C. HEROLD His teaching load amounted to three and a half hours daily. *case-load* etc.

Phrases: **a load off a person's mind** a source of anxiety removed; *take a load off a person's mind*, bring a person relief from anxiety. *dead load*: see DEAD *a*. etc. **get a load of** *slang* look at, perceive, make oneself aware of, scrutinize; listen carefully to; freq. in *imper*. **get** or **have a load on** *slang* become or be drunk. †**lay on load** deal heavy blows; *fig*. speak with emphasis or exaggeration; emphasize (the fact) *that*; exaggerate; be extravagant. *like a load of bricks*: see BRICK *n*. *live load*: see LIVE *a*. **take a load off (one's feet)** sit or lie down. **under load** *Mech*. & *Electr*. subjected to a load. *useful load*: see USEFUL *a*. I.

Comb.: **load displacement, load draught** the displacement or draught of a vessel when laden; **load factor** (*a*) the ratio of the average or actual amount of work, power, etc., to the maximum possible; (*b*) the ratio of the weight of an aircraft to the maximum weight the wings can support; also, the reciprocal of this; (*c*) the ratio of the number of seats occupied in an aircraft to the number available; the weight of freight carried as a proportion of the maximum that can be carried; **load line** (*a*) a Plimsoll line; (*b*) *Electronics* a straight line that crosses the characteristic curves of a transistor or valve and has a gradient and position determined by the load, so that it represents the possible operating conditions of the device; **loadmaster** the member of an aircraft's crew who is responsible for the cargo; **load-shedding** a temporary curtailment of the supply of electricity to an area to avoid excessive load on the generating plant; **loadspace** space in a motor vehicle for carrying a load; **load-water-line** the line of flotation of a ship when fully laden; the Plimsoll line.

load /ləʊd/ *v*. Pa. pple **-ed**, (*arch*. & *dial*.) **-en**. L15. [f. the n.] **1a** *v.t*. Place on a person or animal, or on or in a vehicle, as a load for transport; put on board as cargo. Formerly, carry (hay etc.). L15. **b** *v.i*. Take on a load or cargo; (of a vehicle) fill with passengers. Also foll. by *up*. E18. **2** *v.t*. Put a load on or in; provide with a burden or cargo; charge *with* a load. Also foll. by *up*. E16. **3** *v.t. fig*. **a** Weigh down, burden, oppress *with* affliction, sin, responsibility, etc.; impede, encumber. E16. **b** Overwhelm *with* abuse, reproaches, etc. Formerly also, throw blame upon; charge *with* something opprobrious. M17. **4** *v.t*. **a** Add weight to; be a weight or burden on; bear down or oppress *with* a material weight; weight with lead; increase the resistance to the working of (a machine). L16. **b** Adulterate by adding something to increase weight or density; make (light or thin wine) appear full-bodied by adulteration. M19. **c** Give a bias to (dice, a roulette wheel). (Earlier as LOADED 1b.) E20. **d** *Electr*. Provide with additional inductance in order either to reduce the distortion and attenuation of signals (in the case of a telephone line etc.), or to reduce the resonant frequency (in the case of an aerial); provide with a load consisting of any kind of impedance. E20. **5** *v.t*. Supply in excess or overwhelming abundance *with*. Also foll. by *up with*. Usu. in *pass*. L16. **6** *v.t*. **a** Heap or pile *on*. *rare*. L16. **b** *Painting*. Lay (colour) on thickly in opaque masses. M19. **7a** *v.t*. & *i*. Put a charge of ammunition into (a firearm); in *pass*., have one's firearm loaded. E17. **b** *v.t*. Insert a photographic film or plate in (a camera); insert (a film etc.) *into* a camera. L19. **c** *v.t*. Fill (a pipe) with tobacco; place items for washing in (a washing machine or dishwasher). E20. **d** *v.t*. *Computing*. Transfer (a program or data) into memory, or into the central processor from a more remote part of memory. M20. **e** *v.t*. Take up a quantity of paint on (a paintbrush). L20. **8** *v.refl*. & *i*. Increase (an insurance premium) by adding a charge to provide for expenses, an increased risk, etc.; charge (a particular life) with a loaded premium. Chiefly as LOADING 3. M19. **9** *v.refl*. & *i*. *Stock Exch*. Buy in large quantities. L19. **10** *Psychol*. **a** *v.t*. Weight the relative contribution of (a factor). M20. **b** *v.i*. Be correlated. (Foll. by *on*.) L20.

1a *Beano* Load your goodies on my cart, Mr. Baker. A. BROOKNER The chauffeur loads the suitcases into the car. **b** *Australian Financial Review* More than 10 huge bulk carriers have waited . . to load at Port Hedland. **2** JAYNE PHILLIPS We are kept busy loading and unloading the supply ships. *Sunday Express* After loading up the Land Rover . . , Titus, our driver/guide, sped south. **3a** J. GALSWORTHY We load our houses with decoration. G. GREENE Every day . . had loaded her with something to decide. **4a** J. WAIN Two middle-aged women . . began to load the rack with parcels. **5** SIR W. SCOTT Old Torquil . . loaded him with praises. **7a** R. NICHOLS Soon we shall load and fire and load. **b** *SLR Camera* Take a roll of film . . and load it into your camera.

Phrases: **load the bases** *Baseball* place base-runners on all three bases. **loading dose** *Med*. a dose sufficiently large that increasing it produces no increase in its effects.

Comb.: **load-and-go** *Computing* an operating technique in which the loading and execution of a program, and any intervening processes, form one continuous operation.

loadability /ləʊdəˈbɪlɪti/ *n*. M20. [f. LOAD *v*. + -ABILITY.] The degree of ease with which goods may be loaded or transported.

loadberry /ˈləʊdb(ə)ri/ *n*. *dial*. M18. [Rel. to Norw. dial. *ladberg*, ON *hlaðberg*.] In Shetland: a flat rock forming a natural landing-place; *spec*. a small enclosed landing-place for the unloading of boats.

loaded /ˈləʊdɪd/ *a*. M17. [f. LOAD *v*. + -ED[1].] **1** That has been loaded; bearing or carrying a load; laden; charged. M17. **b** Weighted, esp. with lead; (of dice) weighted or biased so that some faces come uppermost more often than others. L18. **c** *fig*. Charged with some hidden implication or underlying suggestion; biased, prejudiced. M20. **2a** Drunk. Chiefly *pred*. *slang*. M19. **b** Drugged; under the influence of drugs. Chiefly *pred*. *US slang*. E20. **3** Well prepared (*for* a thing). Chiefly in *loaded for bear* s.v. BEAR *n*.[1] I. *US*. L19. **4** Wealthy. *slang*. M20. **5** Esp. of a car: well fitted out; having optional extras. *N. Amer*. *colloq*. M20.

1 loaded down weighed down with a load. **loaded with** having a load of, *colloq*., having much or many. **b** J. M. ROBERTSON One is flogged to death with loaded whips. **c** *Listener* An ill-prepared or a loaded question.

loaden /ˈləʊd(ə)n/ *v*.[1]*t*. *obs*. exc. *dial*. M16. [f. LOAD *n*. + -EN[5]. Cf. LADEN *v*.] Load.

loaden *v*.[2] pa. pple: see LOAD *v*.

loader /ˈləʊdə/ *n*.[1] ME. [f. LOAD *v*. + -ER[1].] **1a** A person who loads something; a person whose task it is to load guns; (*obs*. exc. *dial*.) a carrier. ME. **b** A machine or device for loading things; *Computing* a program which controls the loading of other programs. L19. **2** With preceding n. or adj.: a gun, machine, vessel, etc., that is loaded in the specified way. M19.

1a *Scottish Sunday Express* Passengers were delayed yesterday when loaders walked out at . . Heathrow Airport. **2** *Independent* The vessel . . is a stern loader. *front-loader* etc.

loading /ˈləʊdɪŋ/ *n*. LME. [f. LOAD *v*. + -ING[1].] **1** The action of LOAD *v*. LME. **b** *Med*. The administration of a large amount, esp. a loading dose, of a substance. M20. **2** The load or cargo of a vehicle, vessel, etc. Now *rare*. L15. **3a** An amount added to an insurance premium to load it. M19. **b** *Austral*. An amount added to a basic wage or salary in recognition of some special factor. M20. **4** A substance used to load another; *spec*. one added in the course of paper-making to modify the quality of the paper. L19. **5** *Building* & *Engin*. The loads collectively that act on a structure or part of one. E20. **6** The weight of an aircraft divided by its wing area (in full *wing loading*) or by the power of its engines (in full *power loading*). E20. **7** The maximum current or power that an electrical appliance is meant to take. M20. **8** *Psychol*. The extent to which a factor or variable contributes to or is correlated with some resultant quality or overall situation, usu. represented by a number arrived at by statistical analysis of test results. M20. **9** The concentration or amount of one substance in another. M20. **10** The number of passengers carried by a vehicle or vessel. M20.

1b *Journal of Neurochemistry* No 5-hydroxytryptophan was detected in the brain after tryptophan loading. **5** J. S. FOSTER Types of floor structure which impose an even distribution of loading on the wall. **9** *Nature* An increase in the stratospheric dust loading. **10** *Railway World* Apart from poor loadings on 6 September, patronage has been good.

Comb.: **loading bay** a bay or recess in a building where vehicles are loaded and unloaded; **loading coil** an inductance coil used in the loading of telephone lines or aerials; **loading gauge** (*a*) the maximum height and width allowed for railway vehicles to ensure adequate clearance through bridges and tunnels; (*b*) a device suspended over railway lines for checking the dimensions of rolling-stock; **loading rod** a ramrod; **loading shovel** a vehicle with a power-operated shovel for digging out material and carrying it short distances.

†**loadsome** *a*. *rare*. L16–M19. [f. LOAD *n*. + -SOME[1].] Burdensome.

loadstar *n*. var. of LODESTAR.

loadstone *n*. var. of LODESTONE.

loadum /ˈləʊdəm/ *n*. *obs*. exc. *Hist*. L16. [Perh. contr. of *load him*.] A card-game, an ancestor of hearts, the aim of which was to avoid taking tricks or penalty cards in tricks.

loaf /ləʊf/ *n*.[1] Pl. **loaves** /ləʊvz/. [OE *hlāf* = OHG *leip* (G *Laib*, †*Leib*), ON *hleifr* loaf, Goth. *hlaifs* bread, f. Gmc.] **1** Bread. *obs*. exc. *dial*. OE. **2** A portion of bread baked in one mass; any of the portions, of uniform size and shape, into which a batch of bread is divided. OE. **3** A moulded conical mass of sugar; a sugar loaf. LME. †**4** *gen*. A mass or lump of anything. LME–L17. **5** A head on a cabbage. E19. **6** (A mass of) minced or chopped meat moulded into the shape of a loaf and cooked, usu. to be eaten cold in slices. Usu. w. preceding n. L19. **7** A person's head; the mind, common sense. Esp. in *use one's loaf*. *slang*. E20.

2 *cottage loaf, fruit loaf, granary loaf, wholemeal loaf*, etc. **6** *beef loaf, ham loaf, meat loaf*, etc.

Phrases: **brown loaf**: of brown bread. *French loaf*: see FRENCH *a*. *holy loaf*: see HOLY *a*. **loaf of** or **o' bread** *rhyming slang* dead. **loaves and fishes** [after *John* 6:26] personal profit as a motive for religious profession or public service. **mushroom loaf, oyster loaf** the crust of a loaf or roll of bread filled with a stuffing of mushrooms or oysters. **white loaf**: of white bread.

Comb.: **loaf-bread** (now *dial*.) bread made in the form of loaves; ordinary bread as opp. to cake or wafers; **loaf-cake** a plain cake made in the form of a loaf; **loaf-eater** *Hist*. a household servant in pre-Conquest England; **loaf sugar** refined sugar made into a loaf-shaped mass.

loaf /ləʊf/ *n*.[2] M19. [f. LOAF *v*.[2]] An act or spell of loafing.

loaf /ləʊf/ *v*.[1]*i*. L16. [f. LOAF *n*.[1]] Of a cabbage: form a head.

loaf /ləʊf/ *v*.[2] M19. [Prob. back-form. f. LOAFER.] **1** *v.i*. Spend time idly, loiter; saunter. Freq. foll. by *about, around*. M19. **2** *v.t*. Fritter (time) *away*. M19.

1 G. B. SHAW He shuts the door; yawns; and loafs across to the sofa. M. J. BRUCCOLI He dressed in his slacks and a sweater and loafed while waiting. D. ADAMS He was a poet and preferred loafing about under trees with a bottle of laudanum.

loafer /ˈləʊfə/ *n*. M19. [Perh. f. G *Landläufer* tramp, f. *Land* LAND *n*.[1] + *laufen* (dial. *lofen*) to run. Cf. LAND-LOPER.] **1** A person who loafs. M19. **2** = LOBO. Also *loafer wolf*. *N. Amer*. L19. **3** (L-.) **a** (Proprietary name for) a shoe like a moccasin for casual wear. Usu. in *pl*. M20. **b** (Proprietary name for) a type of jacket for informal wear. M20.

loaferdom *n*. the state of being a loafer L19. **loaferism** *n*. (now *rare*) the practice of loafing M19.

loaiasis /ləʊəˈʌɪəsɪs/ *n*. Also **loasis** /ləʊˈeɪsɪs/, **loiasis** /ləʊˈʌɪəsɪs/. E20. [f. LOA *n*.[1] + -IASIS.] Infection with, or a disease caused by, loas.

loam /ləʊm/ *n*. & *a*. [OE *lām* = (M)Du. *leem*, MLG *lēm* (whence G *Lehm*) rel. to OHG *leimo* (G dial. *leimen*), f. WGmc, f. var. of base of LIME *n*.[1], rel. to L *limus* mud.] **A** *n*. †**1** Clay, clayey earth, mud. OE–M17. **2** Clay moistened with water so as to form a paste that can be moulded into shape; *spec.* a mixture of moistened clay, sand, chopped straw, etc., used in making bricks, plastering walls, grafting, etc. ME. 3 Earth, soil. *arch.* ME. 4 (A) very fertile soil composed chiefly of clay, sand, and humus; *Geol.* (a) friable mixture of sand, silt, clay, and usually humus. M17.

4 C. LYELL Cliffs, composed . . of alternating strata of blue clay, gravel, loam, and fine sand. F. NORRIS The Quien Sabe ranch—some four thousand acres of rich clay and heavy loams. *red loam*: see RED *a.*

B *attrib.* or as *adj.* Made or consisting of loam. E16.

loamless *a.* (esp. of potting compost) containing no loam L19.

loam /ləʊm/ *v.* E17. [f. the n.] †**1** *v.t.* Cover or plaster with loam. E17–E18. **2** *v.i.* & *t.* Search (a region) for gold by washing the loam from the foot of a hill until the increasing number of gold grains leads to the lode. *Austral.* E20.

Loamshire /ˈləʊmʃə/ *n.* M19. [f. LOAM *n.* + SHIRE *n.*] (The name of) an imaginary rural English county in some fiction; in *pl.*, a regiment from this county.

loamy /ˈləʊmi/ *a.* ME. [f. LOAM *n.* + -Y[1].] †**1** Formed of earth. *rare.* Only in ME. **2** Of or pertaining to loam; consisting of or resembling loam. L16.

loaminess *n.* E18.

loan /ləʊn/ *n.*[1] ME. [ON *lán* corresp. to OE *lǣn* LAEN, MDu. *lēne* (Du. *leen*), OHG *lēhan* (G *Lehn, Lehen*), f. Gmc base also of LEND *v.*] †**1** A gift or grant from a superior. ME–L15. **2** A thing that is lent; *esp.* a sum of money lent to an individual, organization, etc., often at interest. ME. **b** A word, custom, etc., adopted by one people from another. M18. **3a** The action or an act of lending; the state of being lent. Freq. in *on loan*, acquired or given as a loan. ME. †**b** The action of hiring or letting. E17–L18. **4a** A contribution of money, formerly often a forced one, from a private individual or public body towards the expenses of the State, the amount of which is acknowledged by the Government as a debt; a sum of money so contributed. LME. **b** An arrangement by which a Government receives advances of money on specified conditions, esp. the payment of stipulated interest. M18.

2 J. WILCOX She was in the middle of discussing a loan with a client at the bank. J. N. ISBISTER He remained very poor, dependent . . upon loans made to him by his wealthier friends. 3a J. ADAMS I am much obliged to you . . for the loan of this precious collection of memorials.

Phrases: *savings and loan*: see SAVING *n.* 3. *soft loan*: see SOFT *a.* *subordinated loan*: see SUBORDINATE *v.* 2.

Comb.: †**loan-bank** an establishment from which poor people could borrow money at low interest; **loan-blend** a compound word consisting of both native and foreign elements; **loan capital** the part of the capital of a company etc. that has to be repaid, usu. at a stipulated rate of interest, irrespective of profits; **loan-collection** a collection of works of art, curiosities, etc., lent by their owners for exhibition; **loan-farm** *S. Afr.* a piece of land loaned to a farmer by the Government; **loanholder** a person who holds debentures or other acknowledgements of a loan; a mortgagee; **loan-money** †(*a*) money payable as a contribution to a government loan; (*b*) money advanced as a loan; **loan-monger** *derog.* a person who negotiates loans; **loan-office** (chiefly *US*) (*a*) an office for lending money to private borrowers; (*b*) an office for receiving subscriptions to a government loan; **loan-place** *S. Afr.* = *loan-farm* above; **loan shark** *colloq.* a person who lends money at exorbitant rates of interest; **loan-sharking** *colloq.* the lending of money at exorbitant rates of interest; **loan-shift** a change in the meaning of a word resulting from the influence of a foreign language; a word so affected; **loan-translation** an expression adopted by one language from another in more or less literally translated form, a calque; **loanword** a word adopted or borrowed, usu. with little modification, from another language.

loan /ləʊn/ *n.*[2] *Sc.* & *north.* Also †**lone**. LME. [Var. of LANE *n.*[1] Earlier in LOANING.] **1** A lane, a narrow path; *spec.* (*a*) a green lane through unenclosed fields, esp. one leading to common open ground (now chiefly in surviving names); (*b*) a street, a roadway. LME. **2** An open uncultivated piece of ground near a farmhouse or village on which cows are milked etc. E18.

loan /ləʊn/ *v.t.* ME. [f. LOAN *n.*[1]] Grant the loan of; lend (esp. money).

J. RULE She liked loaning her car to Walt. J. WILCOX You said you'd loan me a few bucks.

loanable *a.* able to be loaned; available for loans: M19. **loanee** *n.* a person to whom a loan has been granted, a borrower M19. **loaner** *n.* (*a*) a lender; (*b*) (in full *loaner car*) a car lent by a garage to a customer whose own car is kept for repair or service: L19.

loaning /ˈləʊnɪŋ/ *n.* *Sc.* & *north.* Also **lonnin(g)** /ˈlɒn-/. ME. [f. LOAN *n.*[2] + -ING[1].] = LOAN *n.*[2] 1.

loasis *n.* var. of LOAIASIS.

†**loath** *n.* OE. [f. LOATH *a.* (orig. f. the neut.). In sense 2 f. LOATHE *v.*] **1** A hateful or harmful thing; evil, harm; an annoyance, a trouble. OE–LME. **2** Dislike, hatred, ill will; disgust, loathing. ME–E18.

loath /ləʊθ/ *a.* Also **loth**. [OE *lāþ* = OFris. *leed*, OS *lēþ* (Du. *leed*), OHG *leid* (cf. G *Leid* sorrow, pain, *leider* (compar. of adj.) unfortunately), ON *leiðr*, f. Gmc.] †**1** Hostile, angry, spiteful. OE–LME. †**2** Repulsive, loathsome, unpleasant. (Foll. by dat., *to* a person.) OE–L16. **3** Disinclined, reluctant, unwilling. Chiefly *pred.* (Foll. by *to do, that.*) ME. †**b** Displeased. *rare.* ME–L17. †**4** Ugly. ME–M16.

3 GEO. ELIOT Lammeter isn't likely to be loth for his daughter to marry into my family. A. JOHN I was loath to leave this delightful inn. E. BOWEN Antonia, loth to have them out of her sight, . . came down to follow the two. **nothing loath** not at all unwilling.

Comb.: **loath-to-depart** *arch.* a song expressing regret for departure; any tune played as a farewell.

loathe /ləʊð/ *v.* [OE *lāþian* = OS *lēþon*, ON *leiða*, f. Gmc, f. base of LOATH *a.*] †**1a** *v.i.* Be hateful, displeasing, or offensive. (Foll. by indirect obj., *to* a person). OE–L16. **b** *v.t.* Excite loathing or disgust in (a person); make (a person) loath *to do* or averse *from*. M16–M17. **2** *v.t.* Formerly, grow weary of; feel aversion or dislike for. Now, have an intense aversion for; regard with utter abhorrence and disgust; detest. ME. †**3** *v.i.* Be or become disgusted, feel disgust. ME–E17.

2 DAY LEWIS I still loathe artichokes. B. MASON From being generally disliked, Ginger Finucane was now loathed. JULIAN GLOAG If I didn't loathe taking pills . . I'd cheerfully swallow a few too many.

loather *n.* E17. **loathing** *n.* the action of the vb; (an) intense dislike, disgust: ME. **loathingly** *adv.* in the manner of a person who feels a loathing E17.

loathful /ˈləʊðfʊl, -f(ə)l/ *a.* LME. [f. LOATH *n.* + -FUL.] **1** Loathsome. Now *rare.* LME. **2** Retiring, bashful. Long *obs.* exc. *Sc.* M16.

loathly /ˈləʊðli/ *a.* OE. [f. LOATH *a.* + -LY[1]. See also LAIDLY.] Loathsome, repulsive, hideous, horrible.

¶Rare after 16 until revived as a literary wd in 19.

loathliness *n.* (now *rare*) LME.

loathly /ˈləʊðli/ *adv.* Now *rare.* OE. [f. LOATH *a.* + -LY[2].] †**1** In a manner to cause loathing; foully, hideously. OE–E17. **b** With abhorrence or detestation. ME–E17. **2** Reluctantly, unwillingly. LME.

loathness /ˈləʊθnɪs/ *a.* Long *rare.* ME. [f. LOATH *a.* + -NESS.] The quality or condition of being loath; reluctance, disinclination.

loathsome /ˈləʊðs(ə)m/ *a.* ME. [f. LOATH *n.* + -SOME[1].] Arousing disgust or loathing; offensive to the senses; hateful, distasteful, repulsive.

loathsomely *adv.* LME. **loathsomeness** *n.* (*a*) the quality of being loathsome; (*b*) a loathsome thing; †(*c*) a feeling of loathing, disgust: ME.

loathy /ˈləʊði/ *a.* *arch.* LME. [f. LOATH *n.* + -Y[1].] †**1** = LOATH *a.* 3. Only in LME. **2** = LOATHSOME. L15.

loaves *n.* pl. of LOAF *n.*[1]

lob /lɒb/ *n.*[1] & *a.* ME. [Prob. f. various LDu. wds: cf. EFris. *lob(be* hanging lump of flesh, Du. †*lobbe, lubbe* hanging lip, *lobbes* bumpkin.] **A** *n.* **1** A pollack; a saithe. Long *obs.* exc. *Sc.* ME. **2** A country bumpkin; a clown, a lout. Now *dial.* LME. **3** A pendulous object. *rare.* L17. **4** A lump, a large piece; a nugget of gold. Chiefly *dial.* E19.

Comb.: **lob-tail** *v.i.* (of a whale) raise its tail in the air and beat the water with it (chiefly as *lob-tailing* vbl n.).

B *attrib.* or as *adj.* Rustic; loutish; clumsy. Now *dial.* E16.

lob /lɒb/ *n.*[2] Also **lobb**. L17. [Origin unkn.] A step in a mine; any of a series of veins of ore descending stepwise. Usu. in *pl.*

lob /lɒb/ *n.*[3] *Criminals' slang.* Also **lobb**. E18. [Origin unkn.] A box; a till.

lob /lɒb/ *n.*[4] M19. [f. LOB *v.*] **1** *Cricket.* A slow underhand ball. M19. **2** In many ball games: a ball struck in a high arc, a stroke sending the ball in a high arc. L19.

lob /lɒb/ *v.* Infl. **-bb-**. L16. [f. LOB *n.*[1] Cf. LOP *v.*[2]] †**1** *v.i.* Behave like a lout. Only in L16. **2** *v.t.* Cause or allow to hang heavily. Now *rare.* L16. **3** *v.i.* Move heavily or clumsily; (of a cab-driver) travel slowly in search of a fare. E19. **4a** *v.t.* & *i.* Throw, esp. heavily or clumsily; toss or bowl with a slow movement; *spec.* in many ball games, strike (the ball) in a high arc. M19. **b** *v.t.* Deceive or defeat (an opponent) with a lobbed ball. E20. **5** *v.i.* Arrive; drop *in*. *Austral. slang.* E20.

3 B. HINES The hawk lobbed off her perch, and . . reached the shelf behind the door. 4a *Football News* Worrall quickly lobbed the ball in front of the empty goal. S. MIDDLETON He moodily lobbed three stones at the rock tower.

Lobachevskian /lɒbəˈtʃɛvskɪən, -ˈtʃɛf-/ *a.* L19. [f. Nikolai *Lobachevsky* (1793–1856), Russ. mathematician: see -IAN.] *Math.* Designating, of, or pertaining to a non-Euclidean hyperbolic geometry in which space is everywhere negatively curved. Cf. RIEMANNIAN.

lobar /ˈləʊbə/ *a.* M19. [f. LOBE + -AR[1].] Of or pertaining to a lobe; designating an acute form of pneumonia most commonly caused by pneumococcal infection and affecting one lobe of a lung.

lobate /ˈləʊbeɪt/ *a.* M18. [f. LOBE + -ATE[2].] Chiefly *Bot.*, *Zool.*, & *Geol.* Having or characterized by lobes, lobed.

Also **lobated** *a.* E18.

lobation /lə(ʊ)ˈbeɪʃ(ə)n/ *n.* M19. [f. LOBATE + -ATION.] The formation of lobes; the condition of being lobate.

lobato- /lə(ʊ)ˈbeɪtəʊ/ *comb. form.* M19. [f. LOBATE + -O-.] Lobate and —, as *lobato-digitate*, *lobato-foliaceous* adjs., etc.

lobb *n.* var. of LOB *n.*[2], *n.*[3]

lobbier *n.* var. of LOBBYER.

lobby /ˈlɒbi/ *n.* M16. [med.L *lobia*: see LODGE *n.*] †**1** A monastic cloister. Only in M16. **2** A passage or corridor connected with one or more apartments in a building; an anteroom, an entrance-hall; the foyer of a hotel. L16. **3a** In the Houses of Parliament, a hall adjacent to one or other debating chamber where members of the House concerned can meet non-members; (more fully *central lobby*) a hall between these two lobbies to which the public has access; in the Houses of Parliament and some other legislatures, either of two corridors either side of a debating chamber into which members go, and thereby vote, during a division (more fully *division lobby*). Also, the body of lobby correspondents. M17. **b** A body of people seeking to influence legislators or public opinion on behalf of a particular interest or cause; influence of this kind; an event at which people go to a house of legislature to lobby its members. E19. **4** *Agric.* A small enclosure for cattle adjoining a farmyard. L18.

2 J. THURBER I chanced to be in the lobby of the theatre between acts. G. MARKSTEIN In the lobby of the officers' club the wives were having a whist drive. 3b *Economist* American . . interests have maintained their effective lobby against the project. *Listener* The vested privileges and subsidies of the powerful alcohol lobby.

Comb.: **lobby chest** *Hist.* a low chest of drawers; **lobby correspondent** a political journalist who has access to MPs in the lobby of the House of Commons; any of a group of journalists who receive unattributable briefings from the Government.

lobby /ˈlɒbi/ *v.* Orig. *US.* M19. [f. the n.] **1** *v.t.* Seek to influence (members of a house of legislature) in the exercise of legislative functions, orig. by frequenting the lobby; seek to win over to a cause. Also, procure the passing of (a bill etc.) *through* a legislature by such means. M19. **2** *v.i.* Frequent the lobby of a house of legislature for the purpose of influencing members' votes; seek to gain support (*for* a cause). M19.

1 *Which?* Abroad, all Access/Visa can do is lobby their international organisations . . for a ban. A. BRIEN Write to the papers, organize petitions, lobby relatives, complain to the Governor. 2 S. BRILL From the day . . Hoffa went off to jail, Fitzsimmons had lobbied for his release. V. BROME Between meetings, considerable lobbying went on behind the scenes.

lobbyer /ˈlɒbɪə/ *n. US.* Also **lobbier**. M19. [f. prec. + -ER[1].] = LOBBYIST.

lobby-gow /lɒbɪˈgaʊ/ *n. US slang.* E20. [Origin unkn.] An errand-boy, a messenger; a hanger-on, an underling, esp. in an opium den or in the Chinese quarter of a town.

lobbyist /ˈlɒbɪɪst/ *n.* Orig. *US.* M19. [f. LOBBY *n.* + -IST.] A person who lobbies, a supporter of a lobby.

lobbyism *n.* the system of lobbying L19.

lobcock /ˈlɒbkɒk/ *n.* Now *dial.* M16. [f. LOB *n.*[1] + COCK *n.*[1]] A country bumpkin; a lout, a boor; a heavy dull creature; a blundering fool.

lobe /ləʊb/ *n.* LME. [Late L *lobus* f. Gk *lobos* lobe of the ear or liver, capsule, pod.] **1** A roundish projecting part, usually one of two or more similar portions into which an object is divided by a fissure; *esp.* one of the divisions of the liver, lungs, brain, or other organ. LME. **2** *Bot.* A (chiefly rounded) projection or division of a leaf, petal, or other organ of a plant; *esp.* one extending less than halfway to the centre. Formerly also, a pod, a capsule. L17. **3** = *ear lobe* s.v. EAR *n.*[1] E18. **4** The larger or most important and projecting part of a cam-wheel. M19. **5** *Geol.* A great marginal projection from the body of a continental ice sheet. L19. **6** A portion of the radiation pattern of an aerial which represents a group of directions of stronger radiation and is bounded on each side by directions in which there is minimum radiation. E20. **7** *Calligraphy.* A curved projecting part of a letter. M20.

1 J. BRONOWSKI The main organisation of the brain is in the frontal lobes and the prefrontal lobes. *Roche lobe*: see ROCHE *n.*[2]

Comb.: **lobe-fin** a crossopterygian fish; **lobe-finned** *a.* designating a crossopterygian fish.

lobed *a.* having a lobe or lobes L18. **lobeless** *a.* (*rare*) M19. **lobelike** *a.* resembling (that of) a lobe M19.

lobectomy /ləʊˈbɛktəmi/ *n.* E20. [f. LOBE + -ECTOMY.] Surgical removal of a lobe, esp. of a lung or the brain; an instance of this.

lobelia /ləˈbiːlɪə/ *n.* M18. [f. Matthias de *Lobel* (1538–1616), botanist to James I + -IA[1].] **1** Any of various chiefly tropical and subtropical herbaceous (rarely shrubby) plants of the genus *Lobelia* (family Lobeliaceae), of which many species are cultivated in gardens; *esp.* the common blue-flowered bedding plant *L. erinus* and the red-flowered *L. fulgens*. M18. **2** (The dried stem and leaves of) Indian tobacco, *Lobelia inflata*, used medicinally. M19.

lobeliˈaceous *a.* of or pertaining to the family Lobeliaceae M19. **ˈlobeline** *n.* (*Chem.*) an alkaloid, $C_{22}H_{27}NO_2$, obtained from Indian tobacco which has physiological effects similar to those of nicotine M19.

Lobel's catchfly /ləʊˈbɛlz ˈkatʃflʌɪ/ *n. phr.* M17. [f. M. de *Lobel*: see LOBELIA.] = *sweet-william catchfly* s.v. SWEET *a.*

†lobfish *n.* Pl. **-es** (usu.) same. M16–E19. [f. LOB *n.*[1] + FISH *n.*[1]] A kind of stockfish.

lobing /ˈləʊbɪŋ/ *n.* L19. [f. LOBE + -ING [1].] The formation or occurrence of lobes.

loblolly /ˈlɒblɒli/ *n.* L16. [Origin unkn.] **1** Thick gruel, esp. as a rustic or nautical dish or a simple medicinal remedy. Formerly also, the medicines of a ship's doctor. Now *dial.* L16. **b** A mudhole. *US colloq.* M19. **2** A country bumpkin, a boor. Now *dial.* E17. **3** In full *loblolly pine*. A long-leaved pine, *Pinus taeda*, of the southern US. M18.

Comb.: **loblolly bay** a small ornamental evergreen tree, *Gordonia lasianthus*, of the tea family, native to the southern US; **loblolly boy** an attendant who assists a ship's surgeon and his mates in their duties; *dial.* an errand-boy, a man of all work; *loblolly pine*: see sense 3 above; **loblolly tree** *W. Indies* any of several tropical American trees of the genus *Cupania* (family Sapindaceae), so called from the softness of their wood.

lobo /ˈləʊbəʊ/ *n. N. Amer.* Pl. **-os**. M19. [Sp. f. L *lupus* wolf.] A large grey wolf of the south-western US. Also called *loafer* (*wolf*).

lobola /ləˈbəʊlə/ *n.* Also **-lo** /-ləʊ/. M19. [Bantu: cf. Xhosa *lobola* give a bride-price.] The bride-price, usu. in cattle, given by many Black grooms in southern Africa to the parent or guardian of the bride; the custom of paying such a bride-price.

lobopod /ˈləʊbəpɒd/ *a.* & *n.* M20. [f. next.] *Zool.* **A** *adj.* Of a worm etc.: possessing a lobopodium. M20. **B** *n.* = LOBOPODIUM 2. M20.

lobopodium /ləʊbəˈpəʊdɪəm/ *n.* Pl. **-ia** /-ɪə/. E20. [f. mod.L *lobosus* having many or large lobes + PODIUM.] *Zool.* **1** A blunt or lobelike pseudopodium. E20. **2** A primitive blunt limb or limblike organ on some worms or wormlike animals. M20.

lobopodial *a.* of the nature of or possessing a lobopodium M20.

lobotomy /ləˈbɒtəmi/ *n.* M20. [f. LOBE + -O- + -TOMY.] Surgical incision into a lobe, esp. the frontal lobe of the brain, in the treatment of mental illness; an instance of this.

lobotomiˈzation *n.* the action of lobotomizing someone; the state of being lobotomized: L20. **lobotomize** *v.t.* perform a lobotomy on M20. **lobotomized** *a.* (*a*) that has been lobotomized; (*b*) *slang* sluggish, stupefied: M20.

lobscouse /ˈlɒbskaʊs/ *n. dial.* & *Naut.* E18. [Corresp. to Du. *lapskous*, Da., Norw., G *lapskaus*: ult. origin unkn. Cf. LOBLOLLY. See also SCOUSE.] A sailor's dish consisting of meat stewed with vegetables and ship's biscuit etc.

lobscouser *n.* a sailor L19.

Lob's pound /lɒbz ˈpaʊnd/ *n. phr. obs.* exc. *dial.* L16. [f. LOB *n.*[1] + -'S[1] + POUND *n.*[2]] Prison, the lock-up; *fig.* an entanglement, a difficulty.

lobster /ˈlɒbstə/ *n.*[1] & *v.* [OE *loppestre*, *lopystre*, *lopustre* f. L *locusta* crustacean, LOCUST, with *-stre* after agent-ns. in -STER.] **A** *n.* **1** Any of several large marine decapod crustaceans of the genus *Homarus*, with stalked eyes, a long tail, and large pincers as the first pair of limbs; (usu. w. specifying wd) any similar crustacean of the same family, Nephropidae. OE. **b** The flesh of a lobster as food. L18. **c** A freshwater crayfish, *esp.* one with claws eaten as food. *Austral.* & *NZ.* E19. **2** A British soldier or marine; orig. *spec.* a member of a regiment of Roundhead cuirassiers (from their wearing jointed plate armour suggestive of a lobster's tail, later use after the red coat of a soldier's uniform). Also *boiled lobster*. *derog.* M17. **3** (In full *lobster moth*) a brown moth, *Stauropus fagi*, of the prominent family (Notodontidae); (in full *lobster caterpillar*) the caterpillar of this, distinguished by some unusually long legs and a posterior end reflexed over the back. E19. **4** A slow-witted, awkward, or gullible person; a fool. a dupe; a bore. *US slang.* L19.

Phrases: *boiled lobster*: see sense 2 above. NORWAY *lobster*. **raw lobster** *slang* [w. allus. to the blue uniform, as opp. to the former red coats of 'boiled lobsters'] a police officer. SPINY *lobster*. **unboiled lobster** *slang* = *raw lobster* above.

Comb.: **lobster bisque** (the colour of) a thick cream soup made of lobster; **lobster-boat** a boat used in lobster-fishing, with a well in which to keep the lobsters alive; *lobster caterpillar*: see sense 3 above; *lobster moth*: see sense 3 above; **lobster Newburg** lobster cooked in a thick cream sauce containing sherry or brandy; **lobster-pot** a basket or similar structure serving as a trap to catch lobsters; **lobster shift** *US slang* = *lobster trick* below; **lobster-tail** a piece of armour jointed in the manner of a lobster's tail; **lobster thermidor** cooked lobster mixed with a cream sauce, returned to its shell, sprinkled with cheese, and browned; **lobster trick** *US slang* an overnight shift, esp. on a newspaper.

B *v.i.* Fish for lobsters. Chiefly as *lobstering* vbl n. L19.

lobsterish *a.* resembling a lobster; red-faced: E20. **lobsterling** *n.* a young lobster E20.

lobster /ˈlɒbstə/ *n.*[2] L19. [f. LOB *v.* + -STER.] A person who (habitually) lobs a ball.

lobstick *n.* var. of LOPSTICK.

lobular /ˈlɒbjʊlə/ *a.* E19. [f. LOBULE + -AR[1].] Pertaining to, having the form of, or affecting a lobule or lobules.

lobulated /ˈlɒbjʊleɪtɪd/ *a.* L18. [f. LOBULE + -ATE[2] + -ED[1].] Having lobules, consisting of lobules.

lobulate /-lət/ *a.* = LOBULATED M19. **lobuˈlation** *n.* the formation of lobules; a lobulated condition: L19.

lobulato- /lɒbjʊˈleɪtəʊ/ *comb. form.* M19. [f. LOBULATE + -O-.] Lobulated and —, as *lobulato-crenate*.

lobule /ˈlɒbjuːl/ *n.* L17. [f. LOBE + -ULE, after *globule* etc.] Chiefly *Anat.* A small lobe; a lobular subdivision of a lobe.

lobulus /ˈlɒbjʊləs/ *n.* Pl. **-li** /-lʌɪ, -liː/. M18. [mod.L dim. of L *lobus* LOBE, or Latinization of LOBULE.] = LOBULE.

lobworm /ˈlɒbwəːm/ *n.* M17. [f. LOB *n.*[1] + WORM *n.*] **1** A large earthworm used for bait by anglers. M17. **2** A lugworm. M19.

locable /ˈləʊkəb(ə)l/ *a. rare.* M16. [med.L *locabilis*, f. L *locare* to place, f. *locus* place: see -ABLE.] Able to be localized or placed.

†local *n.*[1] var. of LOCALE.

local /ˈləʊk(ə)l/ *a.* & *n.*[2] LME. [(O)Fr. f. late L *localis*, f. L LOCUS *n.*[1]: see -AL[1].] **A** *adj.* **1** Of or affecting a particular part of the body; of or pertaining to a particular place in a system, series, etc., or a particular part of an object. LME. **2** Belonging to or existing in a particular locality or neighbourhood, esp. a town, county, etc., as opp. to the country as a whole. L15. **b** Limited or peculiar to a particular place or places. E17. **3 a** Pertaining to or concerned with spatial position or extension. Now chiefly in *local situation*. L15. **†b** Having the attribute of spatial position. M16–E18. **c** *Gram.* Esp. of a case: relating to place or situation. M19. **4** Of or pertaining to places (in the geographical sense) or an individual place as such. E17. **5** *Math.* Of or pertaining to a locus. Now *rare*. E18.

2 D. WIGODER My local G.P. . . was waiting at the door of my house. L. CODY Anna dutifully followed her round the local shops. *USA Today* The history of the Cold War and local crises around the world. M. MILNER We took the plane to Athens, then the local bus to Delphi. 3 J. PRIESTLEY The Cartesians . . maintain . . that spirits have no extension, nor local presence. 4 RICHARD MORRIS The etymology of local names.

Special collocations: *local* ANAESTHESIA. *local anaesthetic*: see ANAESTHETIC *n.* **local area network** a network joining computers in the same building or nearby buildings, by which they can communicate with each other with enhanced quality and speed owing to their proximity. **local authority** an administrative body in British local government. **local call** a telephone call within a prescribed area around a caller's local exchange. **local cluster** *Astron.* a cluster of stars, within the Galaxy, to which the sun belongs. **local colour** (*a*) *Art* the actual colour of a thing in ordinary daylight and uninfluenced by the proximity of other colours; (*b*) the detailed representation of the characteristic features of a place or period in order to convey a sense of actuality; such features themselves in real life, picturesque qualities. **local content** the part of a manufactured product that is made, supplied, or assembled locally. *local derby*: see DERBY 2b. **local exchange** the telephone exchange to which a subscriber has a direct line. **local government** the administration of the affairs of a town, county, etc., by the elected representatives of those who live in it, as opp. to administration by the Government. **local group** *Astron.* the cluster of about twenty galaxies to which our own galaxy belongs. **†local motion** movement from place to place, motion of translation. **local option** (a) choice at local or district level whether to accept or reject State or national legislation, *spec.* any allowing or prohibiting the sale of alcoholic liquor. **local oscillator** an oscillator in a radio receiver etc. that generates oscillations for heterodyning with an incoming signal. **local paper** a newspaper distributed only in a certain area and usu. featuring local, as distinct from national, news. **local preacher** a lay member of the Methodist Church who is authorized to lead worship in the district in which he or she resides. **local pub** *colloq.* a public house convenient to a person's home, a public house serving a locality or community. **local radio** radio broadcasting that serves a local area only. **local talent** the talented people or (*colloq.*) the attractive women or men of a particular locality. **local time** (*a*) *Astron.* time as reckoned from the transit of the mean sun over the meridian of the place concerned; (*b*) time as reckoned throughout a particular country time zone, esp. w. ref. to an event reported from it. **local veto**: on the sale of alcoholic liquor in a district under the exercise of a local option.

B *absol.* as *n.* **1** A locally applied medicament. Only in LME. **2a** A person who is attached by occupation, function, etc., to some particular place or district; *esp.* = *local preacher* above. E19. **b** An inhabitant of a particular locality regarded w. ref. to that locality. M19. **3** An item of local interest in a newspaper; *collect.* matter of local interest. M19. **4** A postage stamp current only in a certain district. L19. **5** A train which serves the stations of a particular district or which stops at all or most of the stations on a line. L19. **6** A local branch of a trade union. *N. Amer.* L19. **7** = *local pub* above. *colloq.* M20. **8** = *local anaesthetic* s.v. ANAESTHETIC *n.* M20. **9** A person who trades in a financial market on his or her own account. M20.

2b H. JACOBSON She . . left him to bore the locals with his explanations of what everything in their village really meant. 6 S. BRILL He did legal work for the Teamsters, serving the Detroit local. 7 L. P. HARTLEY The first thing he usually does . . is to pay a visit to the local.

local /ˈləʊk(ə)l/ *v.t.* Infl. **-ll-**, **-l-**. L16. [f. LOCAL *a.*] *Sc. Law.* Apportion an increase in (a minister's salary) among different landholders; lay the charge of (such a salary) *on* a landholder or land.

lo-cal /ləʊˈkal/ *a. informal* (chiefly *commercial*). M20. [f. alt. of LOW *a.* + abbrev. of CALORIE.] = *low-calorie* s.v. LOW *a.*

locale /ləʊˈkɑːl/ *n.* Also †**local**. L18. [Fr. *local* n. (see LOCAL *a.* & *n.*[2]) respelt to indicate stress. Cf. MORALE.] A place, a locality, esp. w. ref. to some event or circumstances connected with it; a venue.

localisable *a.*, **-ise** *v.*, **-ised** *a.* vars. of LOCALIZABLE etc.

localism /ˈləʊk(ə)lɪz(ə)m/ *n.* E19. [f. LOCAL *a.* + -ISM.] **1** Something characteristic of a particular locality; a local idiom, custom, etc. E19. **2** Attachment to a locality, esp. to the place in which one lives; limitation of ideas, sympathies, and interests arising out of such attachment; preference for what is local; an instance of this state of mind. M19.

1 *Scientific American* Some of the varieties of speech are mere localisms. 2 C. LASCH The will to build a better society . ., along with traditions of localism, self-help, and community action.

localist /ˈləʊk(ə)lɪst/ *n.* & *a.* L17. [f. LOCAL *a.* + -IST.] **A** *n.* A person who tends to treat or regard things as local, to subject them to local conditions, etc.; a student of what is local. L17. **B** *adj.* Of or pertaining to localism or localists; parochial, provincial. M20.

loca'listic *a.* L19.

localitis /ləʊkəˈlʌɪtɪs/ *n. colloq.* M20. [f. LOCAL *a.* + -ITIS.] Undue concern for or attention to a particular place or region to the detriment of others.

locality /ləʊˈkalɪti/ *n.* E17. [Fr. *localité* or late L *localitas*, f. *localis* LOCAL *a.*: see -ITY.] **1** The fact or quality of having a position in space. E17. **2**†**a** An assessment, tax, or levy, *esp.* one for the expenses of war. *Sc.* M–L17. **b** The localling of a minister's stipend; a decree enacting this; a stipend that is localled. *Sc.* M17. †**3** The fact of belonging to a particular spot; in *pl.*, local characteristics, feelings, or prejudices. L18–E19. **4** In *pl.* The features or surroundings of a particular place. E19. **5** *Phrenol.* The faculty of recognizing and remembering places. E19. **6** The situation or position of an object; *esp.* the geographical place or situation of a plant, mineral, etc. E19. **7** An area or district considered as the site occupied by certain people or things or as the scene of certain activities; a neighbourhood. M19. **8** *Psychol.* The action of mentally locating a tactile stimulus. L19.

5 *bump of locality*: see BUMP *n.*[1] 7 W. TREVOR The girl's father . . was a man of some note in the locality. *Which?* Planning permission is intended to make sure a . . development fits in with the locality.

localizable /ˈləʊk(ə)lʌɪzəb(ə)l/ *a.* Also **-isable**. M19. [f. next + -ABLE.] Able to be localized.

localiza'bility *n.* M20.

localize /ˈləʊk(ə)lʌɪz/ *v.* Also **-ise**. L16. [f. LOCAL *a.* + -IZE.] **1** *v.i.* **a** Adapt oneself to a place, comply temporarily with the requirements of a particular place. *rare.* L16. **b** Be confined to or concentrated in one place, *spec.* (foll. by *in*, of a disease or a causative agent of disease) be confined to (a specified area of the body); *Austral.* settle down to live in one place. M20. **2** *v.t.* Make local in character; imbue with the characteristics of a particular place. Now *rare.* L18. **3** *v.t.* Fix in a particular place or district or in a particular part of a whole; *esp.* restrict or confine *to* a particular place, make local in range or currency. L18. **b** Concentrate (attention) *on* a particular spot. E19. **c** Identify with a particular locality. L19. **4** *v.t.* Attribute (in thought or statement) to a particular place; find or invent a locality for, ascertain the locality of. Also foll. by *to.* E19.

1b R. W. RAVEN The viruses of West Nile . . localized preferentially in the tumours of some patients. 3 *Annual Register* The policy of non-intervention . . had succeeded in its main object of localising the conflict. 4 *Brain* A patient . . was unable to localize an object seen.

¶In isolated use bef. L18.

locali'zation *n.* the action or an act of localizing; the state of being localized: E19. **localizer** *n.* a person who or thing which localizes something; *spec.* in *Aeronaut.*, a device for transmitting a narrow vertical radio beam along a runway by means of which an incoming aircraft can be brought into line with it and any lateral deviation automatically corrected: L19.

localized /ˈləʊk(ə)lʌɪzd/ *a.* Also **-ised**. E19. [f. prec. + -ED[1].] Confined to or concentrated in a particular place or part; that has been localized.

B. SPOCK A haematoma, a localized haemorrhage under the scalp that sticks out as a distinct bump. *Financial Times* Midland Bank is carrying out a localized experiment with these 'smart' cards at Loughborough.

locally /ˈləʊk(ə)li/ *adv.* LME. [f. LOCAL *a.* + -LY[2].] **1** In respect to place or to position in space. LME. **2** With regard to a particular place or part; in certain districts; *esp.* in the locality specified or alluded to. M19.

1 *Scientific American* The extraneous points that minimize the length of the network locally are . . called Steiner points. 2 *New York Times* Craftsmen were hired locally or flown in from Colorado.

localness /ˈləʊk(ə)lnɪs/ *n.* M18. [f. LOCAL *a.* + -NESS.] The quality of being local.

locanda /loˈkanda/ *n.* M18. [It. f. med.L (*camera, domus*) *locanda* (room, house) to be let.] In Italy: a lodging-house, an inn.

locant /ˈlɒk(ə)nt/ *n.* M20. [L *locant-* pres. ppl stem of *locare* LOCATE: see -ANT[1].] *Chem.* A number or letter in the name or cipher of a compound that indicates the position in its molecular structure of a constituent atom or group.

locate /lə(ʊ)ˈkeɪt/ *v.* E16. [L *locat-* pa. ppl stem of *locare* to place, let for hire, f. LOCUS *n.*[1] place: see -ATE[3].] †**1** *v.t. Law.* Let out on hire. *rare.* E16–L19. **2** *v.t.* Appoint the site of; assign (in thought or statement) to a particular place or position; station, position; *US Hist.* survey and demarcate (a tract of land etc.), take possession of (a land-claim, mine, etc.). L16. **3** *v.i.* Establish oneself or itself in a place; take up residence or business in a place; settle. Chiefly *N. Amer.* M17. **4** *v.t.* Fix or establish in a place (chiefly *N. Amer.*); in *pass.*, be situated, (of a quality etc.) be present *in.* E19. **b** *v.t.* Appoint (a minister) to a permanent pastoral charge of the Methodist Church. *US.* E19. **c** *v.i.* Of a Methodist minister: take up a permanent pastoral charge; retire. *US.* M19. **5** *v.t.* Allocate, apportion. E19. **6** *v.t.* Discover the exact place or locality of. L19.

3 *Fortune* Many of America's biggest blue-chip corporations have located here. 4 F. MARRYAT We packed up and located ourselves about two miles from the common. E. CALDWELL A large . . duck pond located on the north side of the park. *Oban Times* Their plans to locate the system at Invergarry. 6 J. BERMAN More than 3000 letters have been located, perhaps half the number he actually wrote.

locatable *a.* M20.

location /lə(ʊ)ˈkeɪʃ(ə)n/ *n.* L16. [L *locatio(n-)*, f. as prec.: see -ATION.] **1** The action or process of locating something. L16. **2** The fact or condition of occupying a particular place; local position, situation; position in a series. L16. **3** A site, a place; *US* a tract of land surveyed and demarcated, *esp.* a mining claim; *S. Afr.* an area set apart for Blacks, usu. on the outskirts of a town or city. L18. **b** A place of settlement or residence. Chiefly *US.* L18. **c** A farm, a sheep station. *Austral.* E19. **d** *Cinemat.* An actual place or natural setting where filming takes place, as opp. to one simulated in a studio. Freq. in *on location.* E20. **e** *Computing.* (A unit of memory occupying) a position in memory. M20.

1 W. H. PRESCOTT The Castilian officers, to whom the location of the camp had been intrusted. 2 M. SCAMMELL It was strictly forbidden to reveal the location of the camp. 3 S. BELLOW Alone on the Rue Bonaparte, such an enviable location.

locational *a.* E20.

locative /ˈlɒkətɪv/ *a.* & *n.* E19. [f. as LOCATE + -IVE, after *nominative*, *accusative*, etc.] **A** *adj.* **1** *Gram.* Designating, being in, or pertaining to a case in inflected languages expressing place or location. E19. **2** Of or pertaining to location; serving to locate something. *rare.* E19. **B** *n. Gram. The* locative case; a word, form, etc., in the locative case. E19.

locator /lə(ʊ)ˈkeɪtə/ *n.* Now *rare* or *obs.* E17. [f. LOCATE + -OR.] **1** *Law.* A person who lets something for hire. E17. **2** *US* & *Austral. Hist.* A person who takes up a grant of land, opens a mine, etc. L18. **3** A thing which locates or is used for locating something. E20.

loc. cit. /lɒk ˈsɪt/ *adv. phr.* M19. [Abbrev. of L *loco citato* or *locus citatus* (in) the place cited.] In the book etc. that has previously been quoted, in the passage already cited.

locellus /lə(ʊ)ˈsɛləs/ *n.* Pl. **-li** /-lʌɪ, -liː/. M19. [L, dim. of LOCULUS compartment.] *Bot.* A secondary cell; *esp.* a secondary compartment in the loculus of an anther or ovary.

locellate *a.* divided into locelli L19.

loch /lɒk, lɒx/ *n.*[1] LME. [Gael. Cf. LOUGH.] In Scotland: a lake; (more fully *sea loch*) an arm of the sea, esp. when narrow or partially land-locked.

Comb.: **lochside** *n.* & *a.* (situated or occurring at) the edge of a loch.

loch *n.*[2] var. of LOCHE.

Lochaber-axe /lɒˈkɑːbəraks, -ˈka-, -x-/ *n.* E17. [A district of the Highland region, NW Scotland.] *Hist.* A large halberd with a hook at the end.

lochage /ˈlɒkeɪdʒ/ *n.* E19. [Gk *lokhagos*, f. *lokhos* lochus + *agein* to lead.] *Gk Hist.* The commander of a lochus.

lochan /ˈlɒk(ə)n, -x-/ *n.* L17. [Gael., dim. of LOCH *n.*[1]] In Scotland: a small loch or lake.

loche /lɒʃ/ *n.* Chiefly *Canad.* Also **loch**, **losh**. E19. [Fr. = LOACH.] = BURBOT.

Loch Fyne /lɒk ˈfʌɪn, lɒx/ *a. phr.* E20. [A sea loch in W. Scotland.] Designating a type of fishing boat with a standing lug mainsail.

lochi *n.* pl. of LOCHUS.

lochia /ˈlɒkɪə, ˈləʊ-/ *n.pl.* (treated as *sing.* or †*pl.*). Orig. in Fr. form †**lochies**. L17. [mod.L f. Gk *lokhia* use as n. of neut. pl. of *lokhios* pertaining to childbirth, f. *lokhos* childbirth.] Matter discharged from the uterus and vagina following childbirth.

lochial *a.* M18.

Lochinvar /lɒkɪnˈvɑː, -x-/ *n.* L19. [The hero of a ballad in Sir Walter Scott's *Marmion*.] A young male eloper.

Lochlann /ˈlɒklan, -x-/ *n.* M19. [Ir. = Scandinavia, *Lochlannach* Scandinavian.] *Hist.* A Viking, a Norseman.

Loch Ness monster /lɒk nɛs ˈmɒnstə, lɒx/ *n. phr.* M20. [See below.] A monster alleged to exist in the waters of Loch Ness, in the Highland region of northern Scotland.

lochus /ˈlɒkəs/ *n.* Pl. **-chi** /-kʌɪ/. M19. [mod.L f. Gk *lokhos*.] *Gk Hist.* A division of the army in Sparta and some other States.

lochy /ˈlɒki, -x-/ *a. rare.* E19. [f. LOCH *n.*^{1} + -Y^1.] Full of lochs.

loci *n.*^{1} var. of LOCIE.

loci *n.*^{2} pl. of LOCUS *n.*^{1}

loci classici, desperati *n. phrs.* pls. of LOCUS CLASSICUS, DESPERATUS.

locie /ˈləʊki/ *n. N. Amer.* & *NZ colloq.* Also **loci, lokey.** M20. [Abbrev. of LOCOMOTIVE *n.*: see -IE. Cf. LOCO *n.*^{2}] A railway engine, a locomotive.

loci poenitentiae, standi *n. phrs.* pls. of LOCUS POENITENTIAE, STANDI.

lock /lɒk/ *n.*^{1} [OE *locc* = OFris., OS *lok*, MDu. *locke* (Du. *lok*), OHG *loc* (G *Locke*), ON *lokkr*, f. Gmc. Perh. identical w. next.] **1** Any of the portions into which a head of hair, a beard, etc., naturally divides itself; a curl, a tress; in *pl.* (*literary*), the hair of the head. OE. †**b** A lovelock; a tress of artificial hair. Only in 17. **2** A tuft or flock of wool, cotton, etc. ME. **3** A quantity, usually a small one, of any material, esp. hay or straw; a handful, an armful, a bundle. Now *dial.* LME.

1 D. CARNEGIE He wore his hair so long that his auburn locks almost touched his shoulders. J. CARY Long black locks streamed down her forehead. E. LONGFORD Though this . . hair was turning from grey to white, Mrs. Arbuthnot snipped off two locks. 3 T. HARDY I'll curl up to sleep in a lock of straw.

lock /lɒk/ *n.*^{2} [OE *loc* = OFris. *lok* lock, OS *lok* hole, OHG *loh* (G *Loch*) hole, ON *lok* lid, end, conclusion (Goth. has *usluk* opening), f. Gmc. Partly f. LOCK *v.*^{1}] **I** A fastener. **1** Orig., any fastener such as a bar, bolt, or latch. Later, a device for fastening a door, lid, etc., consisting of a bolt or system of bolts in a mechanism which can be operated only by means of a key of a particular shape; any fastener designed to be secure against people without the particular means or knowledge required to operate it. OE. †**2** A hobble or shackle on the foot of a horse or other animal to prevent it from straying. E16–L17. **3** The mechanism in a firearm by means of which the charge is detonated. Also *gunlock*. Earliest as 2nd elem. of comb. M16. **4** = ROWLOCK. M19. **5** A device to keep a wheel from revolving, or from turning to right or left. L19.

1 D. L. SAYERS He had new locks put on the doors. S. QUINN Her second diary . . had . . a lock, making it safer for private thoughts. *oarlock, rowlock,* etc. *combination lock, mortise lock, padlock, Yale lock,* etc. 3 *firelock, flintlock, matchlock, Miquelet lock,* etc.

II A barrier, an enclosure. †**6** A barrier on a river that can be opened or closed as required. ME–M18. †**7** The passage or waterway between the piers of a bridge. M16–E19. **8** On a canal or river: a portion of the channel shut off at each end by folding gates provided with sluices to let the water in or out, and so raise or lower boats from one water level to another. L16. **9** = *airlock* (a) s.v. AIR *n.*^{1} L19.

9 *vapour lock*: see VAPOUR *n.*

III Senses derived from LOCK *v.*^{1} **10** An interlocked or jammed state, esp. of traffic. Formerly, an unintelligible or ambiguous discourse. M16. **11a** A wrestling hold that prevents an opponent from moving the part held; *fig.* a stratagem, a dodge, *esp.* a means of ensuring a person's compliance or cooperation; a difficulty, a dilemma. E17. **b** *Rugby Football.* (The position of) either of two players in the second row of a scrum, behind the hooker. Also *lock forward*, LOCKMAN 3. E20. **12** A receiver of stolen goods; a house where stolen goods are received. *Criminals' slang.* L17. **13** The turning of the front wheels of a vehicle from the line of direction of the rear wheels, as when changing direction (also *steering lock*); the limit of such turning in each direction (more fully *full lock*). M19.

11a M. PUZO Gilly here has a lock on the federal judge who will try the case. b *Glasgow Herald* Catswell, six times at lock for Glasgow, will be making his first appearance as a district flanker. 13 L. MACNEICE The quick lock of a taxi. *Autocar* The 35ft. 3in. mean turning circle with 4.25 turns lock-to-lock is not excessive.

IV 14 (Also **L-**.) A hospital for the treatment of venereal disease. Also *Lock-hospital*. Now *arch.* or *Hist.* L16.

Comb. & phrases: **lock and block (system)** a system of railway signalling by which a train does not enter a section of line until the preceding train has left it, the signal being locked at 'danger' and only released when the preceding train leaves the section; **lock-and-key** *a.* involving structural complementarity or mutual specificity like that of a lock and its key; **lock-box** *N. Amer.* a delivery letter-box provided with a lock; *lock forward*: see sense 11b above; †**lock-hole** a keyhole; **lock-keeper** a person who looks after a lock on a canal or river; **lock-knit** *n.* & *a.* (fabric) knitted with an interlocking stitch; **lock-nut** (*a*) a nut screwed down on another to prevent its breaking loose; (*b*) a nut designed to prevent accidental loosening once it has been tightened; **lock-saw** a long tapering saw for cutting the seat for a lock in a door; **lock step** *n.* & *a.* (*a*) *n.* marching with each person as close as possible to the person in front; *fig.* rigidity of procedure or operation (*in lock step*, in exact synchronism, exactly parallel); (*b*) *adj.* not amenable to alteration; **lock stitch** a sewing-machine stitch in which two threads are locked firmly together; **lock, stock, and barrel, stock, lock, and barrel** (*a*) absolutely everything; (*b*) *advb.* in its entirety; **lock-washer** a washer which when compressed by the tightening of a nut exerts an outward force on the nut to prevent its becoming loose; **under lock and key** securely locked up.

lockful *n.* as much or as many as will fill a lock (on a canal etc.) E19. **lockless** *a.* L16.

lock /lɒk/ *v.*^{1} ME. [f. LOCK *n.*^{2}] **I 1a** *v.t.* Fasten (a door, drawer, etc.) with a lock and key; secure (a room, building, etc.) by locking the doors (usu. foll. by *up*). ME. **b** *v.i.* Of a door etc.: have the means of being locked. L16. **2** *v.t.* Confine in a room, building, etc., with a lock; (foll. by *up, away* (US) *down*) put under lock and key, make secure or inaccessible (as) in a locked receptacle. ME. **3** *v.t.* **a** Esp. of hills, ice, etc.: enclose, surround. Usu. in *pass.* LME. **b** Of sleep, enchantment, etc.: overpower completely. Usu. foll. by *up*. E18. **4a** *v.t.* Fix or join firmly by fitting of parts into each other. Also foll. by *together*. LME. **b** *v.t.* Engage in a close embrace or close combat. Now only in *pass.* E17. **c** *v.i.* Interlock, intertwine. L17. **5** *v.t.* Shut off (as) with a lock *from* a person; preclude or prevent *from* something (as) by locking. Also foll. by *up*. Now *rare.* E17. **6** *v.i.* Of a vehicle: allow the front wheels to turn to right or left. Of wheels: be capable of turning to right or left. M17. **7a** *v.t.* Fasten, make fast, fix; *techn.* fasten or engage (one part of a machine) *to* another. L17. **b** *v.t.* Immobilize (esp. a wheel). L17. **c** *v.i.* Of a mechanism or joint: become locked, jam. M19. **8** *v.t.* & *i. Electronics.* (Cause to) keep *to* a particular frequency of operation. M20.

1a LD MACAULAY The reformers locked up the church and departed with the keys. G. GREENE Then he closed, locked, bolted and chained the door. 2 T. WILLIAMS I have all these treasures locked in my heart. *Peace News* Prison officers . . refused to lock up a frail 75 year old man. G. NAYLOR He locked the circulars up in his desk. *Time* He was locked in the same Montluc prison. J. UGLOW Mrs. Pullet's medicines all have to be priced, valued and above all locked away. 3a W. H. DIXON The vessel was locked in ice. 4a T. HEGGEN He sat down in the chair . . locked his hands behind his head. **lock horns** (of cattle) entangle the horns mutually in fighting; *fig.* (*N. Amer.*) engage in combat (*with*). b R. GRAVES They stood there, . . locked in each other's arms. *fig.*: *Times* Mrs. Thatcher is locked in disagreement with other member states over future EEC spending. 6b *Daily Telegraph* Letting in the clutch gently so as not to lock the driving wheels. c *Which?* Brakes satisfactory but front wheels lock early. 7 R. BROUGHTON The road is narrow and the coach will not lock.

II 9 *v.i.* Provide locks for the passage of vessels. M18. **10** *v.i.* (Of a canal) pass by a lock *into*; (of a vessel) pass *down, in*, etc., through a lock; take a boat into a lock; (of a person) go *out* through an airlock. M18. **11** *v.t.* **a** Pass (a vessel) *down, in*, etc., by means of a lock. M18. **b** Provide (a canal etc.) with locks; shut *off* (part of a river) by means of a lock. M18.

With advs. in specialized senses: **lock in** trap or fix firmly or irrevocably. **lock on** (cause to) locate and then track automatically as a target or reference object (foll. by *to*). **lock out** (*a*) prevent the entry of (a person) by locking a door; (*b*) (of an employer) submit (employees) to a lockout; (*c*) *Electronics* temporarily prevent the operation or use of. **lock up** (*a*) *Mil.* take a position in line or in file as close as possible to the next person; (*b*) invest (capital) in something that is not easily convertible into money; (*c*) *Printing* fix the type or pages in (a forme) ready for press; (*d*) make certain of (an outcome, prize, etc.); (see also senses 1a, 2, etc., above).

lockable *a.* L19.

†**lock** *v.*^{2}*t.* L15–M19. [Du. *lokken* = G *locken*.] Allure, entice.

-lock /lɒk/ *suff.* (not productive). [OE *-lac*.] Forming ns., mostly long obs., now only in *wedlock*, w. the sense 'actions or proceedings, practice'.

lockage /ˈlɒkɪdʒ/ *n.* L17. [f. LOCK *n.*^{2}, *v.*^{1} + -AGE.] **I** †**1** The means of locking or fitting pieces of timber together. Only in L17. **II 2** The amount of rise or fall effected by a (canal etc.) lock or series of locks. L18. **3** Payment levied for going through a lock. L18. **4** The construction and working of locks; locks collectively. E19. **5** The passage of a vessel through a lock. E20.

Lockean /ˈlɒkɪən/ *a.* & *n.* Also **Lockian.** E19. [f. *Locke* (see below) + -AN, -IAN.] **A** *adj.* Of, pertaining to, or characteristic of the English empiricist philosopher and political theorist John Locke (1632–1704) or his ideas. E19. **B** *n.* A follower or adherent of Locke. L19.

Lockeanism *n.* the philosophical doctrines of Locke or his followers M19.

locked /lɒkt/ *a.*^{1} LME. [f. LOCK *n.*^{1} + -ED^2.] Having locks of hair.

locked /lɒkt/ *a.*^{2} LME. [f. LOCK *v.*^{1}, *n.*^{2}: see -ED^1, -ED^2.] **1** That has been locked; that has locked; *esp.* (also foll. by *up*) closed with a lock and key. LME. **2** Provide with a (pad)lock. L15. **3** Of a canal: provided with locks. E19.

1 *British Medical Journal* Limited movement in knee which becomes locked if moved much. A. JUDD The people . . had retreated behind locked doors and put out their lights.

Special collocations & *comb.*: **locked-coil** *a.* designating a rope or cable which has the outer strands of such a shape as to lock together and form a smooth cylindrical surface. **locked groove** on a gramophone record, a circular groove into which the normal spiral groove runs. **locked jaw** (*a*) a jaw shut fast by spasmodic contraction of the muscles; (*b*) = LOCKJAW.

locker /ˈlɒkə/ *n.* ME. [f. LOCK *n.*^{2}, *v.*^{1} + -ER^1; sense 2 prob. of LDu. origin (cf. Flem. *loker*).] **I 1** A thing that locks, closes, or fastens something. Now *rare* or *obs.* exc. *techn.* ME.

II 2 A box, chest, or compartment with a lock, *esp.* any of a number for public use in a pavilion, gymnasium, sports centre, etc.; *Naut.* a chest or compartment for clothes, stores, ammunition, etc. Also, a small cupboard attached to a bench, under a window-seat, etc. LME. †**3** *Eccl.* An aumbry in a church. Only in 16. **4** A compartment in a dovecot. E17.

2 E. PIZZEY They made their beds and tidied their lockers.

III 5 A person who locks something; *spec.* an official in charge of a bonded warehouse, under the warehouse-keeper. Also w. advs. E18.

Phrases: **a shot in the** or **one's locker** money in one's possession; a chance left; a thing in reserve but ready for use. DAVY JONES's *locker*.

Comb.: **locker room** a room containing a number of lockers in a pavilion, gymnasium, sports centre, etc.

locker /ˈlɒkə/ *v.i.* Chiefly *Sc.* & *north.* Now *rare* or *obs.* LME. [Perh. f. LOCK *n.*^{1} + -ER^5.] Curl. Chiefly as *lockered, lockering* ppl adjs.

locket /ˈlɒkɪt/ *n.* LME. [OFr. *locquet* (mod. *loquet* latch) dim. of (chiefly AN) *loc* latch, lock, f. Gmc base also of LOCK *n.*^{2}: see -ET^1.] †**1** An iron crossbar in a window. LME–L16. 2 A metal plate or band, esp. on a scabbard. LME. †3 A group of small jewels set in a pattern. M17–E18. 4 A small ornamental case containing a miniature portrait, a lock of hair, etc., and usually hung round the neck. Formerly also, a small lock on a necklace etc. L17.

locketed *a.* ornamented with a locket; set in a locket: L19.

lockfast /ˈlɒkfɑːst/ *a.* LME. [Sense 1 f. LOCK *n.*[2] + FAST *a.*; sense 2 f. LOCK *v.*[1] + FAST *adv.*] 1 Fastened or secured by a lock. Chiefly *Sc.* LME. 2 Adapted for locking something securely. L19.

Lockian *a.* & *n.* var. of LOCKEAN.

lock-in /ˈlɒkɪn/ *n.* E20. [f. *lock in* s.v. LOCK *v.*[1]] The act or fact of locking in a person or thing; the state of being locked in.

locking /ˈlɒkɪŋ/ *n.* E17. [f. LOCK *v.*[1] + -ING[1].] 1 The action of LOCK *v.*[1]; an instance of this. Also w. advs. E17. 2 A mechanism for locking something. M17.

1 P. O'DONNELL I'll see to the locking-up. *Motor Boat & Yachting* The steel hull will take all the knocks and bumps of continual locking. B. MOORE Heavy doors clanged shut and he heard a locking sound. attrib.: *locking plate, ring*, etc.

Lockist /ˈlɒkɪst/ *n.* Now *rare.* E18. [f. *Locke* (see LOCKEAN) + -IST.] = LOCKEAN *n.*

lockjaw /ˈlɒkdʒɔː/ *n.* E19. [Alt. of *locked jaw* s.v. LOCKED *a.*[2]] Trismus tetanus.

lockjawed *a.* unable to speak, speechless E19.

lockman /ˈlɒkmən/ *n.* Pl. **-men.** LME. [f. LOCK *n.*[2] + MAN *n.*] 1 *Sc. Hist.* A public executioner. LME. 2 In the Isle of Man, a coroner's summoner. M17. 3 *Rugby Football.* = LOCK *n.*[2] 11b. E20.

lock-on /ˈlɒkɒn/ *n.* M20. [f. *lock on* s.v. LOCK *v.*[1]] 1 (The commencement of) automatic tracking. M20. 2 The establishment of a rigid physical connection. M20.

lockout /ˈlɒkaʊt/ *n.* M19. [f. *lock out* s.v. LOCK *v.*[1]] 1 The exclusion of employees by their employer from their place of work until certain terms are agreed to. M19. 2 *Electronics.* The automatic temporary prevention of the operation or use of a relay or other device. Usu. *attrib.* E20.

lockram /ˈlɒkrəm/ *n.*[1] & *a.*[1] *obs.* exc. *Hist.* L15. [Fr. *locrenan* f. *Locronan* (lit. 'cell of St Ronan'), a village in Brittany where the fabric was formerly made. For the change of final *n* to *m* cf. *buckram.*] A *n.* (An article made of) linen fabric for clothing and household use. L15. B *attrib.* or as *adj.* Made of lockram. M16.

lockram /ˈlɒkrəm/ *a.*[2] & *n.*[2] *dial.* E19. [Perh. fig. use of prec.] A *adj.* Nonsensical. E19. B *n.* Nonsense. M19.

locksman /ˈlɒksmən/ *n.*[1] Pl. **-men.** E18. [f. LOCK *n.*[2] + -'S[1] + MAN *n.*] †1 A turnkey, a jailor; a public executioner. *Sc.* E18–E19. 2 A lock-keeper. M19.

locksman /ˈlɒksmən/ *n.*[2] Pl. **-men.** M20. [f. LOCK *n.*[1] + -S[1] + MAN *n.*] In Jamaica, a Rastafarian who wears his hair long and plaited.

locksmith /ˈlɒksmɪθ/ *n.* ME. [f. LOCK *n.*[2] + SMITH *n.*] A person who makes or mends locks.

locksmithery *n.* the locksmith's art E19.

lockspit /ˈlɒkspɪt/ *v.* & *n.* M17. [f. LOCK *n.*[2], *v.*[1] + SPIT *n.*[3]] A *v.t.* & *i.* Mark out (ground) by a lockspit. M17. B *n.* A cut or trench in the ground indicating the line further work should follow (in mining, fortifications, etc.). E18.

lock-up /ˈlɒkʌp/ *a.* & *n.* M18. [f. *lock up* s.v. LOCK *v.*[1]] A *adj.* Esp. of a building or room: able to be locked up. M18.

Morecambe Guardian The accommodation provides lock-up shop plus freezer room.

B *n.* 1 The action or an act of locking something up, esp. a building for the night; the time at which a building is locked up. M19. b The action of locking up capital; the unrealizable state of capital that is locked up; an amount of capital locked up. M19. 2 A place that can be locked up; *spec.* a building or room for the detention (usually temporary) of offenders. M19. b A lock-up garage. E20.

locky /ˈlɒki/ *a.* E17. [f. LOCK *n.*[1] + -Y[1].] Of or pertaining to locks of hair; having many locks of hair.

loco /ˈləʊkəʊ/ *n.*[1] Pl. **-os.** M19. [Abbrev. of LOCOFOCO.] *US Hist.* A Locofoco Democrat.

loco /ˈləʊkəʊ/ *n.*[2] *colloq.* Pl. **-os.** M19. [Abbrev. of LOCOMOTIVE *n.* Cf. LOCIE.] A railway engine, a locomotive.

Comb.: **locoman** an engine-driver; a man who works on the railways.

loco /ˈləʊkəʊ/ *n.*[3] & *a.* L19. [Sp. = insane.] A *n.* Pl. **-o(e)s.** 1 Any of several leguminous plants (chiefly species of *Astragalus*) found in the western and south-western US which cause loco disease (see below). L19. 2 = *loco disease* (a) below. L19.

Comb.: **loco disease** (*a*) a disease in cattle, horses, etc., affecting the brain, caused by eating loco-weed; (*b*) *Austral.* a similar disease affecting stock eating Darling pea, *Swainsona galegifolia*; **loco-weed** (*a*) = sense 1 above; (*b*) *US slang* marijuana.

B *adj.* Crazy, insane, off one's head. *slang* (orig. *US*). L19.

loco-descriptive /ˌləʊkəʊdɪˈskrɪptɪv/ *a.* E19. [f. L LOCUS *n.*[1] place + -O- + DESCRIPTIVE.] Descriptive of local scenery.

locoed /ˈləʊkəʊd/ *a.* *US.* L19. [f. LOCO *n.*[3] & *a.* + -ED[2].] Affected with or poisoned by loco; (of a person) = LOCO *a.*

locofoco /ˌləʊkəʊˈfəʊkəʊ/ *n.* & *a.* *US.* Pl. of n. **-os.** M19. [Invented wd, perh. f. LOCO *n.*[2] + alt. of It. *fuoco*, Sp. *fuego* fire.] †1 (Designating) a self-igniting cigar or match. M–L19. 2 (Usu. **L-.**) (Designating, pertaining to, or characteristic of) a member of the Democratic Party, esp. (*Hist.*) the radical wing of it in and after 1835. M19.

locofocoism *n.* (*Hist.*) the principles of the Locofoco party M19.

locomobile /ləʊkəˈməʊbɪl/ *n.* Now *rare.* L19. [f. L *loco* (see LOCOMOTIVE) + *mobilis* MOBILE *a.*] A steam-powered road vehicle.

locomote /ˈləʊkəməʊt/ *v.i.* *slang* exc. *Sci.* M19. [Back-form. f. next.] Move about from place to place.

locomotion /ləʊkəˈməʊʃ(ə)n/ *n.* M17. [f. L *loco* (see next) + *motio(n-)* MOTION *n.*] 1 The action or power, on the part of an organism or vehicle, of moving from place to place. M17. 2 Movement from place to place, esp. by artificial means; travel. L18.

1 V. GORNICK Her legs were attached to her torso for the strict purpose of useful locomotion. 2 D. JACOBSON For you riding is a sport, . . not a serious means of locomotion.

locomotive /ləʊkəˈməʊtɪv/ *a.* & *n.* E17. [mod.L *locomotivus*, f. L *loco* abl. of LOCUS *n.*[1] place + late L *motivus* MOTIVE *a.*, after med.L *in loco moveri* move by change of position in space.] A *adj.* 1 Of, pertaining to, or effecting progressive motion by an organism or vehicle. E17. b Of or pertaining to travel. *joc.* L18. 2 Having the power of progressive motion. M17. b Of a person: constantly travelling from place to place. *joc.* M18.

2 **locomotive engine** an engine designed to travel under its own power, *esp.* one for drawing railway vehicles; a railway engine.

B *n.* 1 A locomotive engine, a railway engine; a mechanically propelled vehicle not designed to carry a load (other than its own fuel etc.) and with a weight greater than a legally specified minimum. E19. 2 In *pl.* The legs. *slang.* M19. 3 A cheer. *US slang.* E20.

locomotively *adv.* with regard to locomotion M19. **locomotiveness** *n.* the quality or fact of being locomotive; power of or fondness for locomotion: E19.

locomotor /ˈləʊkəməʊtə/ *n.* & *a.* E19. [f. L *loco* (see prec.) + MOTOR *n.*. As adj. f. Fr. *locomoteur.*] A *n.* A person or thing which can move from place to place. E19.

B *adj.* Chiefly *Biol.* Of or pertaining to locomotion. L19.

locomotor ATAXIA.

locomotory /ləʊkəˈməʊt(ə)ri/ *a.* M19. [f. as prec. + MOTORY.] Pertaining to or having the power of locomotion.

locoum *n.* var. of LOKUM.

Locrian /ˈləʊkrɪən/ *a.* & *n.* M16. [f. L *Locris* (see below) + -AN.] A *n.* A native or inhabitant of Locris, a division of ancient Greece. M16.

B *adj.* Of or pertaining to Locris or the Locrians. M17.

Locrian mode *Mus.* an (unidentified) ancient Greek mode; (occas.) one of the church modes.

loculament /ˈlɒkjʊləm(ə)nt/ *n.* Now *rare.* M17. [L *loculamentum*, f. as LOCULUS.] A little cell; *spec.* (*Bot.*) any of the cells or compartments of a capsule or pericarp.

locular /ˈlɒkjʊlə/ *a.* M19. [f. LOCUL(US + -AR[1].] = LOCULATED. Cf. earlier BILOCULAR.

loculated /ˈlɒkjʊleɪtɪd/ *a.* E19. [f. LOCUL(US + -ATE[2] + -ED[1].] Having or divided into loculi.

locule /ˈlɒkjuːl/ *n.* L19. [Fr. f. as LOCULUS.] Chiefly *Biol.* = LOCULUS.

loculicidal /ˌlɒkjʊlɪˈsʌɪd(ə)l/ *a.* E19. [f. L LOCULUS + -I- + *caedere*, *-cid-* to cut (cf. -CIDE) + -AL[1].] *Bot.* (Of the dehiscence of a fruit) occurring through the back or dorsal suture of the loculus; (of a carpel of fruit) that undergoes such dehiscence. Cf. SEPTICIDAL.

loculicidally *adv.* M19.

loculus /ˈlɒkjʊləs/ *n.* Pl. **-li** /-lʌɪ, -liː/. LME. [L, dim. of LOCUS *n.*[1] place: see -CULE.] †1 A purse. Only in LME. 2 A small chamber or cell in an ancient tomb. L17. 3 *Biol.* Any of a number of small cavities or cells separated from one another by septa; *esp.* (*Bot.*) a cavity of an ovary or anther. M19.

locum /ˈləʊkəm/ *n.*[1] E20. [Abbrev. of LOCUM TENENS, LOCUM-TENENCY.] 1 A person who undertakes the professional duties of someone else in his or her absence, *esp.* a physician or member of the clergy who stands in for another; a person who holds office temporarily. E20. 2 The situation of a locum; a post as a locum. E20.

locum *n.*[2] var. of LOKUM.

locum-tenency /ləʊkəmˈtɛnənsi/ *n.* M19. [f. next: see -CY.] = LOCUM *n.*[1] 2.

locum tenens /ləʊkəm ˈtiːnɛnz, ˈtɛn-/ *n. phr.* Pl. **locum tenentes** /tɪˈnɛntiːz/. M17. [med.L, f. L *locum* accus. of LOCUS *n.*[1] place + *tenens* pres. pple of *tenere* hold.] 1 = LOCUM *n.*[1] 1. M17. 2 = LOCUM *n.*[1] 2. L19.

locuplete /ˈlɒkjʊpliːt/ *a.* *rare.* L16. [L *locuplet-*, *locuples*, f. LOCUS *n.*[1] place + *plere* fill.] Well-stored, rich.

locus /ˈləʊkəs, ˈlɒkəs/ *n.*[1] Pl. **loci** /ˈləʊsʌɪ, ˈlɒkiː/. E18. [L = place.] 1 A place, a site; a position, a point, esp. in a text. E18. b *Genetics.* A position on a chromosome at which a particular gene is located; a gene. E20. 2 *Math.* The curve or other figure composed of all the points which satisfy a particular equation or are generated by a point, line, or surface moving in accordance with defined conditions. E18. 3 A subject, a topic. M18. 4 = LOCUS STANDI. E20.

1 M. H. ABRAMS The realm of Ideas is the ultimate locus not only of reality but of value. *Times Lit. Suppl.* Sind had been the locus of one of man's earliest urban societies. 4 *Daily Telegraph* He had 'no locus' . . and . . action against the council would now have to come . . from a ratepayer.

Phrases: *genius loci*: see GENIUS 5. ***locus in quo*** /ɪn ˈkwəʊ/ [L = in which] the locality of an event; *Law* the land on which a trespass has been committed. **locus of control** *Psychol.* the perceived site of the controlling influence in a person's life and environment.

locus /ˈləʊkəs/ *n.*[2] & *v.* *slang.* L17. [Perh. f. Sp. *loco*: see LOCO *n.*[3] & *a.*] A *n.* A stupefying drink or ingredient. L17. B *v.t.* Stupefy with drink; get *away* under the influence of drink. Cf. HOCUS *v.* 2. M19.

locus ceruleus /ləʊkəs sɪˈruːlɪəs, ˌlɒkəs/ *n. phr.* Also **caer-, coer-.** L19. [L *locus caeruleus* blue place.] *Anat.* An area on the floor of the fourth ventricle of the brain.

locus classicus /ˌləʊkəs ˈklasɪkəs, ˌlɒkəs/ *n. phr.* Pl. ***loci classici*** /ˌləʊsʌɪ ˈklasɪsʌɪ, ˌlɒkiː ˈklasɪkiː/. M19. [L = classical place.] A passage regarded as the principal authority on a subject or the origin of a quotation or saying; the best known occurrence of an idea or theme.

locus desperatus /ˌləʊkəs dɛspəˈreɪtəs, ˌlɒkəs dɛspəˈrɑːtəs/ *n. phr.* Pl. ***loci desperati*** /ˌləʊsʌɪ dɛspəˈreɪtʌɪ, ˌlɒkiː dɛspəˈrɑːtiː/. E20. [L = hopeless place.] A corrupt manuscript reading that defies interpretation.

locus poenitentiae /ˌləʊkəs piːnɪˈtɛnʃiː, ˌlɒkəs piːnɪˈtɛnʃɪʌɪ/ *n. phr.* Pl. ***loci poenitentiae*** /ˌləʊsʌɪ piːnɪˈtɛnʃiː, ˌlɒkiː piːnɪˈtɛnʃɪʌɪ/. M18. [L = place of penitence.] A place of repentance; *Law* an opportunity for a person to withdraw from a commitment or contract, esp. an illegal one, so long as some particular step has not been taken.

locus standi /ləʊkəs ˈstandʌɪ, lɒkəs ˈstandiː/ *n. phr.* Pl. ***loci standi*** /ləʊsʌɪ ˈstandʌɪ, lɒkiː ˈstandiː/. E19. [L = place of standing.] A recognized or identifiable status, esp. in law; the right to be heard in a court of law.

locust /ˈləʊkəst/ *n.* & *v.* ME. [(O)Fr. *locuste* f. L *locusta* locust, crustacean (cf. LOBSTER *n.*[1] & *v.*).] **A** *n.* **1** Any grasshopper of the family Acrididae (the short-horned grasshoppers); *esp.* any of several species of Africa and the warm parts of Asia and the Americas that form large migratory swarms highly destructive to vegetation. ME. **b** *fig.* A person of devouring or destructive propensities. M16. **c** A grasshopper of the family Tettigoniidae (long-horned grasshoppers). Chiefly *Austral.* M19. **d** A cicada, esp. *Cicada septendecim*, the seventeen-year locust. *US* & *Austral.* M19. **2** The pod of the cassia, *Cassia fistula*; the pod of the carob tree, thought to resemble a locust. E17. **3** In full *locust tree*. Any of various leguminous trees; *esp.* (*a*) = CAROB 2; (*b*) a tree of the W. Indies and Guyana, *Hymenaea courbaril*; (*c*) *N. Amer.* = ACACIA 2 (also *black locust*); (*d*) *NZ* a kowhai, *Sophora tetraptera*. E17. **b** A club of the wood of the N. American locust tree, formerly carried by US police. *US.* M19.

3 *honey locust tree*: see HONEY *n.*

Comb.: **locust bean** the fruit of the carob tree; **locust-berry** the fruit of a W. Indian tree, *Byrsonima coriacea* (family Malpighiaceae); the tree itself; **locust-bird** *S. Afr.* any of various birds (esp. certain pratincoles) that eat locusts, *spec.* (more fully *great locust-bird*) the European white stork, *Ciconia ciconia*; **locust-eater** *S. Afr.* = *locust-bird* above; *locust tree*: see sense 3 above; **locust years** years of poverty and hardship.

B *v.i.* Swarm (and devour) as locusts do. *rare.* L19.

locusta /ləˈkʌstə/ *n.* Now *rare* or *obs.* Pl. **-stae** /-stiː/. LME. [L: see prec.] †**1** A locust. Only in LME. **2** *Bot.* The spikelet of a grass. E18.

locution /ləˈkjuːʃ(ə)n/ *n.* LME. [(O)Fr., or L *locutio(n-)*, f. *locut-* pa. ppl stem of *loqui* talk, speak: see -ION.] **1** A form of expression; a phrase, an expression. LME. †**2** The action of speaking, utterance. L15–M18. **3** Speech as the expression of thought; style of discourse, expression. Now *rare.* E16.

1 J. UPDIKE Critical prose, like the prose of business letters, has its set locutions and inevitable rhythms.

locutionary *a.* (*Philos.* & *Ling.*) designating, pertaining to, or of the nature of an act of speaking or writing considered with reference only to its sense and reference (cf. ILLOCUTIONARY, PERLOCUTIONARY) M20.

locutor /ləˈkjuːtə/ *n. rare.* M19. [L, f. *loqui*: see prec., -OR.] A speaker.

locutory /ˈlɒkjʊt(ə)ri/ *n.* L15. [med. L *locutorium*, f. L *locut-*: see LOCUTION, -ORY[1].] An apartment in a monastery set apart for conversation.

Also **locutorium** /lɒkjʊˈtɔːrɪəm/ *n.* L18.

lod /lɒd/ *n.* M20. [f. *l*ogarithmic *od*ds.] *Statistics.* The logarithm of the odds in favour of or against an event; the logarithm of the ratio of two odds. Usu. in *pl.* or more fully *lod score*.

Loddon lily /ˈlɒd(ə)n ˈlɪli/ *n. phr.* L19. [The *Loddon*, a tributary of the River Thames near Reading in southern England, on the banks of which the plant was once common.] The summer snowflake, *Leucojum aestivum*.

lode /ləʊd/ *n.* Also (now *rare*) **load**. [OE *lād*: see LOAD *n.*] **I 1** Orig., a course, a way, a journey. Later (*dial.*), a road, a lane. OE. †**2** Guidance. Only in ME. **3** A watercourse, a (natural or man-made) channel; an open drain in fenny districts. Now *local.* LME. **4** A lodestone; *fig.* an object of attraction. E16. **5** *Mining.* A vein of metal ore. E17.

5 *masterly lode*, *scovan lode*, etc.

II See LOAD *n.*

†**lodeman** *n.* Pl. **-men**. OE–M16. [f. prec. + MAN *n.*] = LODESMAN.

lodemanage /ˈləʊdmanɪdʒ/ *n.* ME. [AN *lodmanage*, f. prec.: see -AGE.] Pilotage; skill in navigation. Also, the cost of pilotage.

†**lodemen** *n.* pl. of LODEMAN.

loden /ˈləʊd(ə)n/ *n.* & *a.* Also **L-**. E20. [G.] **A** *n.* **1** A heavy waterproof woollen cloth. E20. **2** A coat or cloak made of this. M20. **3** A dark green colour in which the cloth is often made. M20. **B** *adj.* Made of this cloth. E20.

lodesman /ləʊdzmən/ *n.* Pl. **-men**. ME. [Alt. of LODEMAN after *doomsman* etc.] †**1** A leader, a guide. ME–L16. **2** *Hist.* A pilot; a steersman. ME.

lodestar /ˈləʊdstɑː/ *n.* Also **load-**. ME. [f. LODE + STAR *n.*[1]: cf. ON *leiðastjarna*, MHG *leit(e)sterne*.] **1** A star that serves as a guide for navigation etc.; *esp.* the polestar. ME. **2** *fig.* A person or thing on which one's attention or hopes are fixed; a guiding principle. Also, an object of pursuit. LME.

2 D. PARKER One who murmurs that his wife Is the lodestar of his life.

lodestone /ˈləʊdstəʊn/ *n.* Also **load-**. E16. [f. LODE + STONE *n.*] **1** Magnetite that is naturally magnetized; a piece of this used as a magnet. E16. **2** *fig.* A thing that is a focus of attention or attraction. L16.

1 *variation of the lodestone*: see VARIATION 8.

lodge /lɒdʒ/ *n.* ME. [OFr. *loge* arbour, summer-house, hut (in mod.Fr. hut, cottage, theatre box, etc.) f. med.L *laubia*, *lobia* f. Gmc (whence G *Laube* arbour), perh. f. base of LEAF *n.*[1] Cf. LOBBY *n.*] **I 1** A small house or dwelling, *esp.* a temporary one; a hut; a tent; an arbour. Now *dial.* ME. †**b** A prison, a cell. ME–E18. **c** A shed, an outhouse. *dial.* E18. **2** A workshop, *esp.* a mason's workshop. Long *obs.* exc. *Hist.* ME. **3** A house in a forest, on a moor, etc., used for temporary accommodation by people hunting or shooting game. LME. **4** A small house, at the entrance of a park or in the grounds of a mansion, occupied by a gate-keeper, gardener, etc.; a room or kiosk occupied by a porter at the entrance of a college, factory, etc. LME. **5** The den or lair of an animal, now *esp.* that of a beaver or otter. M16. **6** *gen.* A lodging, an abode; *esp.* a temporary one. Formerly also, a place where something can lodge. L16. **7** A meeting-place for members of a branch of the Freemasons or some other societies; (the members of) a branch of Freemasons etc., a local branch of a trade union. Also, a meeting of a lodge of Freemasons etc. L17. **8** The residence of the head of a college, esp. at Cambridge University. M18. **9 a** A sump or pump room in a mine shaft. M18. **b** A mill dam. *dial.* M19. **10** A large house; a hotel. Chiefly as 2nd elem. of proper names. E19. **11** The tent of a N. American Indian; a wigwam, a tepee. Also, the number of Indians accommodated in one tent as a unit of enumeration, reckoned from four to six. E19.

2 H. BRAUN Quarries having their own lodges capable of supplying ready-made such simple features as doorways. 3 R. MACAULAY The Maxwells' shooting lodge stood in a fold of the moors. 7 *Daily Mail* Men at 25 miners' union lodges . . have already defied a recommendation from their area delegates. **Grand Lodge** the governing body of the Freemasons (and of some other societies), presided over by the grand-master. *Orange Lodge*: see ORANGE *a.*[2] **10** *motor lodge*: see MOTOR *n.* & *a.*

II Rendering related mod. Romance wds. †**12** = LOGGIA. M17–E19. **13** = LOGE *n.* 2. *rare.* M18. **14** [Cf. Port. *loja*.] A storage room for wine. L19.

lodge /lɒdʒ/ *v.* ME. [OFr. *logier* (mod. *loger*), f. as prec.] **I** *v.t.* †**1** Place in tents or other temporary shelter; station (an army); *refl.* pitch one's tent, take up a military position. ME–L16. **2** Provide with sleeping-quarters; receive into one's house for the night; provide with accommodation, establish as a resident (*in*). Formerly also, entertain (a guest). LME. **b** *refl.* Establish oneself, take up one's quarters. Formerly also, pass the night. LME. **c** Of a room, house, etc.: serve as a lodging or habitation for. Of a thing: contain; in *pass.*, be contained *in*. LME. †**d** *fig.* Harbour or entertain (a feeling or thought) in one's mind or heart. L16–E18. **e** Have as a lodger. M18. **3** Discover the lair of (a buck or stag). L16. **4** Of rain or wind: flatten or bend (a standing crop). L16. **5 a** Get (a thing) into an intended place; *esp.* succeed in causing (a weapon or blow) to reach a target. E17. **b** Throw (a thing) so as to be caught in flight; cause to become embedded, caught, or fixed in something; (of a current etc.) deposit in passing. E17. **c** Deposit in a specified place of custody or security. M17. **d** Vest or represent as residing *in* a specified person or thing; place (power etc.) *with* or *in the hands of* a person or body. L17. **e** Deposit in court or with an official a formal statement of (a complaint, objection, etc.); bring forward, allege, (an objection etc.). E18. †**f** Set or fasten in a socket etc. E18–E19.

2 LYTTON You lodge your horses more magnificently than yourself. M. COX The old Christopher Inn, where the . . boys were lodged. c T. CLARK The backwindow / lodges six housesparrows in the bricks Under the sill. 4 *Scientific American* Lodged plants often end up lying in the mud. 5b W. ABISH They inspected . . the bullets still lodged in the ceiling. E. RHODE This incident . . lodged itself in my mind. c B. STEWART Four authorized copies were made and lodged at the office of the Exchequer. d E. ARBER Selden lodges the Civil Power of England in the King and the Parliament. e W. GERHARDIE He would lodge a vigorous protest through the usual channels.

II *v.i.* †**6** Encamp. LME–E17. **7** Remain or live in a place, esp. temporarily; *spec.* pass the night; (of a thing) have its seat, reside. Now *rare.* LME. **b** *spec.* Reside or live in another person's house, paying a sum of money periodically in return; be a lodger, live in lodgings. M18. **8** Of a buck or stag: go to its lair. L15. **9** Become embedded, caught, or fixed in something. E17. **10** Of a standing crop: be bent or flattened by wind or rain. M17.

7b R. MACAULAY Any cheap room where I could lodge for a few days. 9 L. DURRELL The machine flew into the apricot-tree where it lodged precariously. **10** *New Yorker* The wheats . . tended to lodge.

lodgeable *a.* able to be lodged in, suitable for lodging in L16. **lodged** *a.* that has lodged; *Her.* (of a beast of the chase, as a buck, hart, etc.) represented as lying on the ground with the head up: ME.

lodgement /ˈlɒdʒm(ə)nt/ *n.* Also **-dgm-**. L16. [(O)Fr. *logement*, f. *log(i)er*: see prec., -MENT.] **1** A place in which persons or things are lodged, located, or deposited, *esp.* a lodging-house, lodgings; a place of shelter or protection; *Mil.* quarters for soldiers. Now *rare.* L16. **2** *Mil.* A temporary defensive work made on a captured part of an enemy's fortifications to make good a position and provide protection. L17. **3 a** *Mil.* The action of establishing oneself or making good a position in enemy territory; an area of enemy territory that is captured and held. E18. **b** A stable position gained, a foothold; the state or fact of being lodged. E18. **4** The action of lodging something, esp. a sum of money, securities, etc.; a deposit of money. E18. **5** The fact or process of becoming lodged; a place where something becomes lodged; a mass of matter that has become lodged. M18. **6** Accommodation in or provision of lodgings; lodging. *rare.* E19.

3a C. RYAN Throughout the 82nd's vast lodgment . . a series of wild . . enemy attacks threatened disaster. b L. J. JENNINGS An intention which seems . . never to have held more than a temporary lodgment in his mind. W. DE LA MARE The claw of the tender bird Finds lodgement here. 4 T. WOGAN Some unfortunate customer entering the bank with a large lodgment would . . find the place deserted. 5 J. S. FOSTER They do not protrude into the cavity and provide lodgement for mortar droppings.

lodge-pole /ˈlɒdʒpəʊl/ *n.* & *v.* E19. [f. LODGE *n.* + POLE *n.*[1]] **A** *n.* A pole used to support a wigwam or tepee. *N. Amer.* E19.

Comb.: **lodge-pole pine** a pine native to mountainous regions of north-west N. America, *Pinus contorta* var. *latifolia*.

B *v.t.* Beat with a lodge-pole. M19.

lodger /ˈlɒdʒə/ *n.* ME. [f. LODGE *v.* + -ER[1].] †**1** A person who lives in a tent. Only in ME. **2** A person who remains or lives in a place, esp. temporarily; a person who passes the night in a place. *arch.* E16. †**3** A person who lodges another, a host. M16–M17. **4** A person who lodges in another person's house, now esp. in part of a house that remains under the general control of the landlord. L16. **5** A thing that lodges or becomes lodged. M19.

4 P. H. JOHNSON The top two floors of the house were kept furnished for lodgers.

Comb.: **lodger-franchise** *Hist.* a right to vote conferred in 1867 on people in boroughs (and later in counties) occupying lodgings of an annual rental value of at least £10.

lodgerdom *n.* lodgers collectively; a district where many people live as lodgers: E20.

lodging /ˈlɒdʒɪŋ/ *n.* ME. [f. LODGE *v.* + -ING[1].] **I1a** A place or building in which a person lodges or resides; a dwelling; *Sc.* a self-contained house. Formerly also, a bedroom; a (military) encampment. ME. †**b** A prison, a hospital; a prison cell. LME–L17. †**c** The lair of a buck or stag. L16–E17. †**2** Dwelling, abode, esp. of a temporary nature. Chiefly in *make, take (up), (one's) lodging*. LME–E17. **3** Accommodation in hired rooms or a lodging-house (freq. in *board and lodging*); temporary or overnight accommodation. Formerly, permanent residential accommodation. LME. †**b** Material to lie or sleep on. L17–E18. **4** In *pl.* †**a** Military quarters; a defensive position. LME–L17. **b** A room or set of rooms in another person's house or (formerly) an inn or hotel where a person lodges. M17. **c** An official residence; *esp.* that of the head of certain Oxford colleges. M17.

3 *board and lodging*: see BOARD *n.* 4c **Judges' lodgings** a house which was the residence of the assize judge when he came for the assizes.

II5 The action of LODGE *v.* E16.

Comb.: **lodging-house** a house in which lodgings are let (*model lodging-house*: see MODEL *a.* 1). **lodging-room** (now *local*) a bedroom. **lodging turn** an occasion or period for which a railway employee has to lodge at the destination before returning to the place of departure.

lodgment *n.* var. of LODGEMENT.

lodh /ləʊd/ *n.* L18. [Hind. f. Skt *lodhra*.] The bark of a shrub, *Symplocos racemosa* (family Symplocaceae), of Southern and SE Asia used in dyeing (also *lodh-bark*); the shrub itself.

lodicule /ˈlɒdɪkjuːl/ *n.* M19. [L *lodicula* dim. of *lodic-*, *lodix* coverlet: see -CULE.] *Bot.* A green or white scale forming the lowest part of a grass flower.

loellingite *n.* var. of LÖLLINGITE.

loerie /ˈlʊəri/ *n. S. Afr.* Also **lourie**. L18. [Afk. f. Du. *lori* f. as LORY.] Any of several South African turacos.

loess /ˈləʊɪs, ləːs/ *n.* M19. [G *Löss* f. Swiss G *lösch* loose, f. *lösen* loosen.] *Geol.* A fine yellowish-grey loam composed of material transported by the wind during and after the glacial period which forms extensive deposits from north central Europe to eastern China, in the American Midwest, and elsewhere.

loessial, loessic *adjs.* composed of loess E20.

lo-fi /ˈləʊfʌɪ/ *n.* & *a. colloq.* M20. [f. alt. of LOW *a.* + *-fi*, after HI-FI: cf. *low fidelity* s.v. LOW *a.*] *Audio.* (Designating, pertaining to, or characterized by) sound reproduction inferior to that produced by hi-fi.

loft /lɒft/ *n.* LOE. [ON *lopt* air, sky, upper room, f. Gmc. Cf. ALOFT, LIFT *n.*[1]] **I**†**1** The air, the sky, the upper region. LOE–L16. **2** An upper room, an attic, esp. for storage etc. rather than living accommodation; *US* any upstairs room. Formerly also, an apartment or room. ME. **b** A room over a stable esp. for the storage of hay and straw; a hayloft. M16. †**3a** A floor or storey in a house. LME–M17. **b** A layer, a stratum. M16–L17. **4** Orig., a room or gallery at the top of a rood-screen, a rood-loft. Later (now chiefly *Sc.* in *gen.* sense) a gallery in a church or public room; *spec.* an organ-loft. LME. **5** A ceiling. Formerly also, a floor of a room. *obs.* exc. *Canad. dial.* L16. **6** An upper storey; an upper level in a house. *N. Amer.* E18. **7** Chiefly *Shipbuilding* & *Naut.* A large room or gallery where something can be spread out for working on. Chiefly w. specifying wd. E18. **b** A place where sails are made; a sail-loft. M20. **8** A pigeon-house, a dovecot, (also *pigeon-loft*). Also *collect.*, the pigeons kept in a loft. M18.

1 SPENSER And ever-drizling raine upon the loft. 2 *Which?* The Mansfield's house has .. 25mm of insulation in the loft. *hayloft*, *rood-loft*, etc. 4 THACKERAY The two schools had their pews in the loft on each side of the organ. 7 *mould-loft*, *rigging-loft*, *sail-loft*, etc.

II9 Backward slope in the head of a golf club. L19. **10** The action of lofting a ball in golf etc.; a lofting hit or stroke. L19.

Comb.: **loft conversion** the alteration of a loft, attic, etc., from storage space into a room suitable for living accommodation.

loft /lɒft/ *v.t.* LME. [f. the n.] †**1** Insert a layer of planks etc. in (a building) so as to separate the storeys; fit with a ceiling or floor. Also, furnish with a loft or upper storey. LME–M17. **2** Store (goods or produce) in a loft. *rare.* E16. **3** Gently hit, throw, kick, or otherwise send (a ball etc.) high up; hit high up so as to clear (an obstacle); hit a delivery of a ball from (a bowler, pitcher, etc.) high up. Also, raise (something) to a higher position. M19. **4** Keep (pigeons) in a loft or flock. L19.

3 *Scientific American* The denser crystals sink and the pumice dust is lofted. *Times* He was seen suddenly to loft both fists skywards.

lofted /ˈlɒftɪd/ *a.* M16. [f. LOFT *n.*, *v.*: see -ED[2], -ED[1].] **1** Orig., fitted with an inner ceiling, floored. Later (*Sc.* & *north.*), having one or more storeys above the ground floor. M16. **2a** Of a golf club: made with a backward slope in the head. L19. **b** Of a stroke etc.: that lofts a ball. Also (of a ball), that has been lofted. L19.

lofter /ˈlɒftə/ *n.*[1] Now *rare.* L19. [f. LOFT *v.* + -ER[1].] A golf club, *spec.* a number 8 iron, for lofting the ball.

lofter /ˈlɒftə/ *n.*[2] L20. [f. LOFT *n.* + -ER[1].] A decoy placed in a tree etc. to attract pigeons.

lofting /ˈlɒftɪŋ/ *n.* E16. [f. LOFT *n.*, *v.* + -ING[1].] **1** A roofing, ceiling, or flooring, esp. in a mine. Now chiefly *dial.* E16. **2** The action of LOFT *v.* M19. **3** *Shipbuilding* & *Aeronaut.* The activity of a loftsman, a loftsman's work. M20.

Comb.: **lofting-iron** (now *rare*) = LOFTER *n.*[1]; **lofting pole** a pole used to position a decoy for pigeons in a tree etc. (cf. LOFTER *n.*[2]).

loftsman /ˈlɒf(t)smən/ *n.* Pl. **-men**. E20. [f. LOFT *n.* + -'S[1] + MAN *n.*] *Shipbuilding* & *Aeronaut.* A person who reproduces a draughtsman's specifications for a ship or aircraft in full size on the floor of a mould-loft.

lofty /ˈlɒfti/ *a.* & *n.* ME. [f. LOFT *n.* + -Y[1], infl. by ALOFT.] **A** *adj.* **1a** Exalted in dignity, character, or quality; of high rank; (of an expectation, aim, or wish) directed to a high object. ME. **b** Consciously haughty, proud, aloof, dignified. L15. **c** Of written or spoken language (and occas. of a writer or speaker): elevated in style or sentiment; sublime. M16. **d** Majestic in sound, producing a majestic sound. L16. **2** Of a mountain, tree, building, etc.: extending to a great height in the air; of imposing altitude, towering. L16. **b** Of flight: soaring to a great height. Of the brow: imposingly high. M18. †**3** Of the wind, the sea: violent, high. E17–M18. **4** Massive, superior. Formerly also (of sheep), in good condition. *dial.* M17. **b** Of wool and woollen fabrics: bulky and springy, resilient. L19.

1a E. JENKINS Heir to one of the loftiest of the English peerages. E. JONES Those who have set themselves lofty goals and had great expectations. b F. BURNEY He appeared very lofty, and highly affronted. W. W. JACOBS Mr. John Blows stood listening to the foreman with an air of lofty disdain. c POPE The shades where .. lofty Denham sung. B. JOWETT I am willing to speak in your lofty strain. 2 K. AMIS It was a lofty room with an immense window. M. L. KING The South's beautiful churches with their lofty spires pointing heavenward. b J. WESLEY Ye birds of lofty Wing, On high his Praises bear. W. S. LANDOR The kingly brow, arched lofty for command.

B *absol.* as *n.* **1** *collect. pl.* *The* class of lofty people. *rare.* L16. **2** (**L-**.) (A nickname for) a very tall or (*iron.*) short person. M20.

1 AV *Isa.* 5:15 The eyes of the loftie shall be humbled. *Sunday Telegraph* Scottie, Windmill and Lofty had all got themselves nicked.

loftily *adv.* M16. **loftiness** *n.* (*a*) the state of being lofty; (*b*) *rare* (with possess. adj., as *your* etc. *loftiness*) a mock title of respect given to a tall person: M16.

log /lɒg/ *n.*[1] ME. [Origin unkn.] **I1** A bulky mass of wood; *esp.* an unhewn portion of a felled tree, or a length cut off for use as firewood. ME. **b** *Surfing.* A large or heavy surfboard. M20. **2a** A heavy piece of wood, fastened to the leg of a person or an animal to impede movement. L16. **b** *Mil. Hist.* A form of punishment whereby a heavy weight was chained to an offender's leg to be dragged or carried around as the person moved. M19. **3** A piece of quarried slate before it is split into layers. E18. **4** In *pl.* A jail, a lock-up. *Austral. slang.* L19.

1 D. L. SAYERS He walked up to the fire and kicked the logs moodily. P. GALLICO He .. pulled her down between two logs of fallen trees. 2a DICKENS Here I am tied like a log to you. 3 *Times* Collyweston slate is .. produced by the action of frost on the stone logs. 4 R. BOLDREWOOD Ten minutes in the logs.

II5 An apparatus for ascertaining the speed of a ship, consisting of a float attached to a line wound on a reel. Also, any other apparatus for the same purpose. L16. **6a** A book containing a detailed daily record of a ship's voyage; a logbook. E19. **b** A systematic record of things done, found, experienced, etc., as (*a*) a record of discoveries or variations at successive depths in drilling a well; a graph or chart displaying this information; (*b*) a record with details of journeys kept by a lorry driver; (*c*) a record of what is broadcast by a radio or television station; (*d*) *Computing* a sequential file of the transactions on a database. E20. **c** A list or summary of claims for a wage increase etc. Freq. more fully *log of claims*. *Austral.* E20.

5 F. CHICHESTER An old-fashioned log, which worked by timing the run-out of a given length of line. 6a *Yachting World* In theory, a navigator keeps everything in his log. b K. G. FENELON A daily log .. showing the nature of the work performed. *National Observer* (*US*) Newspapers run their own TV logs.

Phrases: (*as*) *easy as falling off a log*: see FALLING *vbl n.* **fall like a log** fall in a helpless or stunned state. **heave, stream, throw, the log** use a log to ascertain a ship's speed. **in the log** (of wood) unhewn. *King Log*: see KING *n.* **lie like a log** lie motionless, lie in a helpless or stunned state. *log of claims*: see sense 6c above. *patent log*: see PATENT *a.* *rough log*: see ROUGH *a.* *round log*: see ROUND *a.* **sail by the log** calculate a ship's position by the log. *sleep like a log*: see SLEEP *v.* *stream, throw the log*: see *heave the log* above.

Comb.: **log-basket** a basket for holding logs by a fire; **log-board** a hinged pair of boards on which the particulars of a ship's log are noted for transcription into the logbook; **log cabin** (orig. *US*) (*a*) a cabin or small house built of logs; (*b*) a pattern in patchwork, quilting, etc., in which pieces of material are arranged to give the effect of pieces of wood formed into adjoining squares; **log canoe**: hollowed out of a single tree; **log-cock** *N. Amer.* = PILEATED *woodpecker*; **log flume** (*a*) a channel built to convey water for transporting logs or timber; (*b*) = FLUME *n.* 2b; **loghead** a stupid person; **logheaded** *a.* stupid, dull, obtuse; **log-house** (*a*) a house etc. built of logs; *US Hist.* a prison; (*b*) = *log-cabin* (b) above; **log-line** a line of 100 fathoms or more forming part of a log for ascertaining the speed of a ship; the kind of line used for this purpose; **log-man** †(*a*) *gen.* a person who carries logs; (*b*) *US local* a person employed to cut and carry logs to a mill; **logrunner** any of various mainly Australasian ground-dwelling songbirds of the family Orthonychidae; *spec.* (also called *chowchilla*) either of two birds of the genus *Orthonyx*, which have stiffened tail feathers; **log sheet** a logbook in which the driver of a commercial motor vehicle enters particulars of working and rest hours; **log-work** (*a*) the arrangement of logs in the walls of a house or other building; (*b*) the keeping of a log or logbook.

log /lɒg/ *n.*[2] & *a.* M17. [Abbrev.] A *n.* = LOGARITHM (freq. used preceding a number or algebraic quantity the logarithm of which is to be indicated). M17.

log$_e$ natural logarithm (of).

B *adj.* = LOGARITHMIC. L18.

Comb. & *special collocations*: **log-log** *a.* (of a graph or graph paper) having or using a logarithmic scale along both axes; **log-normal** *a.* (*Statistics*) such that the logarithm of the variate is distributed according to a normal distribution; **log-normally** *adv.* according to a log-normal distribution; **log table** a table of logarithms (usu. in *pl.*).

log /lɒg/ *v.*[1] Infl. **-gg-**. E17. [f. LOG *n.*[1]] †1 *v.i.* Be like a log, be sluggish. Only in E17. 2 *v.t.* Orig., bring (a tree) to the state of a log; deprive of branches. Later, cut (timber) into logs; (chiefly *N. Amer.*) clear (a region) of logs or trees (also foll. by *off, over, up*). L17. b *v.i.* Fell timber and cut the wood into logs. Cf. earlier LOGGING *n.* 1. Orig. *US.* M19. c *v.t.* Foll. by *up*: pile (logs, debris, etc.) together for final clearance by burning after an initial bush burn has taken place. *NZ colloq.* L19. 3 *v.i.* Orig. (of water), lie heavily in a ship. Later, lie motionless like a log. M18. 4 *v.t. Mil. Hist.* Inflict on (an offender) the punishment of the log (LOG *n.*[1] 2b). E19. 5 *v.t.* a Orig. *Naut.* Enter (esp. the distance made by a ship) as information in a log or logbook; *gen.* enter (information) in a regular record. Also foll. by *down, up.* E19. b Esp. of a ship: achieve or cover (a certain distance); travel at (a certain speed). Also, attain as a cumulative total of time, distance, etc., which is entered in a regular record. L19. c *Naut.* Fine. (From the entering of details of offenders and offences committed in a logbook.) L19. 6 *v.t.* Lay *out* (a road) with a layer of logs. L19. 7 *v.i. Mining.* Make a log support for a windlass. Foll. by *up.* *Austral.* L19. 8 *v.i.* & *t.* a Foll. by *in, on*: go through the procedure, as entering a password or identification number at a terminal, which gives access to a computer system; gain access for (a person) by logging in. (Foll. by *to.*) M20. b Foll. by *off, out*: go through the procedure, as entering a command at a terminal, which ends access to a computer system; end access for (a person) by logging off. M20.

2 H. D. THOREAU Only a little spruce and hemlock beside had been logged here. b C. L. SKINNER They always went upstream to log, and let the current bring down the timber. 3 T. WOOLNER The logging crocodiles' Outrageous bulk. 5a N. H. BISHOP Logging with pleasure my day's run at sixty-seven miles. D. CAUTE Female cousins . . neatly logged in Elizabeth's address book as Aunt This and Aunt That. b *Listener* The *Graf Zeppelin* was the first aircraft to log over a million miles. H. ALLEN She logs about ten knots in this breeze.

Comb.: LOG-IN; **log-off** the action or an act of logging off; LOG-ON; **log-out** = *log-off* above.

log /lɒg/ *v.*[2]*t.* & *i.* Chiefly *dial.* Infl. **-gg-**. E19. [Origin unkn. Earlier as LOGAN.] Rock, move to and fro; oscillate. Chiefly as *logging* ppl a.

logging-rock, -stone = LOGAN.

-log *suff.* see -LOGUE.

logan /ˈlɒg(ə)n/ *a.* & *n.* M18. [Var. of *logging* ppl a. of LOG *v.*[2]] (Designating, in *logan-stone*) a poised heavy stone which rocks at a touch.

loganberry /ˈləʊg(ə)nb(ə)ri/ *n.* L19. [f. J. H. *Logan* (1841–1928), US horticulturist + BERRY *n.*[1]] A soft fruit resembling a blackberry but longer and reddish; the plant bearing this fruit, *Rubus loganobaccus*, apparently resulting from a cross between the Pacific dewberry, *Rubus ursinus*, and an American variety of raspberry. Cf. TAYBERRY, TUMMELBERRY, VEITCHBERRY.

logaoedic /lɒgəˈiːdɪk/ *a.* & *n.* M19. [Late L *logaoedicus* f. Gk *logaoidikos*, f. *logos* saying, speech (see LOGOS) + *aoidē* song: see -IC.] *Pros.* A *adj.* Designating any of various metres in which dactyls are combined with trochees. M19. B *n.* A logaoedic verse. Usu. in *pl.* M19.

logarithm /ˈlɒgərɪð(ə)m, -rɪθ-/ *n.* E17. [mod.L *logarithmus*, f. Gk *logos* relation, ratio (see LOGOS) + *arithmos* number.] *Math.* The power to which a fixed number or base must be raised in order to produce any given number; any of a series of such exponents tabulated as a means of simplifying computation by making it possible to replace multiplication and division of numbers by addition and subtraction of their corresponding exponents; *spec.* (more fully = *common logarithm*) a logarithm to the base 10.

common logarithm: see above. **Napierian** or **natural logarithm** a logarithm to the base *e* (2.71828...).

loga'rithmal *a.* (*rare*) = LOGARITHMIC M17. †**logarithmetical** *a.* = LOGARITHMIC E17–M19.

logarithmic /lɒgəˈrɪðmɪk/ *a.* L17. [f. prec. + -IC.] *Math.* Of or pertaining to logarithms; involving or employing logarithms; expressed by or as a logarithm; exponential.

logarithmic amplifier: that produces an output in logarithmic proportion to the input. **logarithmic cosine, sine, tangent**, etc. the logarithm of a cosine etc. **logarithmic curve**: which forms a straight line when plotted against a logarithmic scale; an exponential curve. *logarithmic decrement*: see DECREMENT 3c. **logarithmic scale**: along which distances are proportional to the logarithms of the marked indices. *logarithmic sine*: see *logarithmic cosine* above. **logarithmic spiral** = EQUIANGULAR *spiral*. *logarithmic tangent*: see *logarithmic cosine* above.

logarithmical *a.* M17. **logarithmically** *adv.* by the use of logarithms; in logarithmic proportions: M18.

logatom /ˈlɒgatəm/ *n.* M20. [Arbitrary.] *Teleph.* A meaningless syllable formed usu. from initial and final consonants and a vowel, for use in testing telephone systems.

logbook /ˈlɒgbʊk/ *n.* L17. [f. LOG *n.*[1] + BOOK *n.*] 1 *Naut.* A book containing a detailed daily record of a ship's voyage (including the rate of progress as indicated by the log); *Aeronaut.* a book in which particulars of aircraft flights, flying hours, etc., are recorded; *gen.* any book containing a detailed record. L17. 2 In the UK, a document (now officially called the *vehicle registration document*) recording the registration details of a motor vehicle. M20.

loge /lɔːʒ (*pl. same*), ləʊʒ/ *n.* M18. [Fr.: see LODGE *n.*] 1a A booth, a stall. M18. b A concierge's lodge. M20. 2 A box in a theatre, opera-house, etc. M18.

-loger /lədʒə/ *suff.* [f. (as) -LOGY: see -ER[1].] Forming ns. w. the sense 'a person skilled in a specified branch of knowledge', as *astrologer, campanologer*, etc.; = -LOGIST.

loggat /ˈlɒgət/ *n. obs.* exc. *Hist.* Also **logget**. M16. [App. f. LOG *n.*[1]] 1 A game in which thick sticks were thrown as close as possible to a mark (usu. in *pl.*); a missile used in this game. M16. †2 A pole, a heavy stake. E–M17.

logger /ˈlɒgə/ *n.*[1] M18. [f. LOG *v.*[1] + -ER[1].] 1 A person who fells timber or cuts timber into logs; a lumberjack. *N. Amer.* M18. 2 More fully *data-logger*. An instrument for making a (continuous or intermittent) recording of the successive values of a number of different physical quantities. M20.

logger /ˈlɒgə/ *n.*[2] *dial.* L18. [Symbolic, f. LOG *n.*[1] Prob. earlier as 1st elem. of LOGGERHEAD.] 1 A block of wood for hobbling a horse. L18. 2 Lumpy matter. L19.

logger /ˈlɒgə/ *a. obs.* exc. *dial.* L17. [App. back-form. f. LOGGERHEAD.] Thick, heavy, stupid.

loggerhead /ˈlɒgəhɛd/ *n.* L16. [Prob. f. LOGGER *n.*[2] + HEAD *n.*] 1 A stupid person. *arch.* L16. 2 A head out of proportion to the body; a large or thick head. *colloq.* L16. 3a In full *loggerhead turtle*. A large-headed sea turtle, *Caretta caretta*, of warm seas worldwide. M17. b In full *loggerhead kingbird*. A W. Indian kingbird, *Tyrannus caudifasciatus*. M17. c Any of various large-headed fishes, such as the bullhead. *dial.* L17. d In full *loggerhead shrike*. A shrike, *Lanius ludovicianus*, of the southern US and Mexico. E19. e Any of various large moths. *dial.* M19. 4 An iron instrument with a long handle and a ball at the end heated for melting pitch etc. L17. 5 In *pl.* (treated as *sing.*). Knapweed. *dial.* E19. 6 A rounded wooden upright near the stern of a whaling boat to which a turn of the line may be caught. M19.

Phrases: **at loggerheads** disagreeing or disputing (*with*).

loggerheaded *a.* (*a*) stupid; (*b*) (esp. of an animal) having a large head: L16.

logget *n.* var. of LOGGAT.

loggia /ˈləʊdʒə, ˈlɒ-, -dʒɪə/ *n.* M18. [It. = LODGE *n.*] 1 A gallery or arcade having one or both of its sides open to the air. M18. 2 An open-sided extension to a house, a veranda. E20.

logging /ˈlɒgɪŋ/ *n.* E18. [f. LOG *v.*[1] + -ING[1].] 1 The action of felling timber or hewing timber into logs. Also, a quantity of timber felled. E18. 2 = LOGROLLING 1. E19. 3 The process of taking and recording information about something. M20.

loggy /ˈlɒgi/ *a.* E17. [f. LOG *n.*[1] + -Y[1].] †1 Of a crop: of strong growth, rank. E–M17. 2 Heavy; sluggish in movement. M19. 3 Having many logs. M19.

logginess *n.* a state of heaviness or sluggishness E20.

logia *n.* pl. of LOGION.

logic /ˈlɒdʒɪk/ *n.* LME. [(O)Fr. *logique* f. late L *logica* f. Gk *logikē* (*tekhnē* art) of reason, f. *logos* reasoning, discourse: see LOGOS, -IC.] 1 *sing.* & (now *arch. rare*) in *pl.* (treated as *sing.* or *pl.*). The branch of philosophy that deals with forms of reasoning and thinking, esp. inference and scientific method. Also, the systematic use of symbolic techniques and mathematical methods to determine the forms of valid deductive argument. LME. b In Hegelian philosophy, the fundamental science of thought and its categories (including metaphysics or ontology). M19. 2a A system or scheme of logic. Also, an instance of the application of science or the art of reasoning to some particular branch of knowledge or investigation. LME. b The inferential procedures or structure *of* some field of inquiry. M19. 3a Logical argumentation; a chain of reasoning; the correct or incorrect use of reasoning. Also, ability in reasoning. LME. b A means of convincing someone or proving something; the inexorable force or compulsion *of* a thing. Also, the necessary consequence *of* an argument, a decision, etc. L17. 4 *Computing* & *Electronics*. The system or principles underlying the representation of logical operations and two-valued variables by physical signals, esp. as in a computer; the (esp. conceptual) forms and interconnections of logic elements in a computer etc.; logical operations collectively, as performed by computers etc. M20.

1 J. S. MILL Logic is not the science of Belief, but . . of Proof, or Evidence. 2a R. ADAMSON The metaphysical logic of Hegel, the empirical logic of Mill, the formal logic of Kant. *mathematical logic*: see MATHEMATICAL *a.* *modal logic*: see MODAL *a.* 1. *symbolic logic*: see SYMBOLIC *a.* b R. G. COLLINGWOOD As mathematics is the logic of physics, so law is the logic of politics. 3a LD MACAULAY We should be sorry to stake our faith in a higher Power on Mr. Robert Montgomery's logic. E. V. NEALE Sir William Hamilton argues with overpowering learning and logic. *chop logic*: see CHOP *v.*[2] b J. EADIE The logic of their facts was irresistible.

Comb.: **logic circuit** a circuit for performing logical operations, consisting of one or more logic elements; **logic element** a device (usu. electronic) for performing a logical operation, in which the past or present values of one or more inputs determine the values of one or more outputs according to a simple scheme usu. involving only two possible values for the signals; *logic gate*: see GATE *n.*[1] 11b; **logic-tight** *a.* impervious to logic or reason.

-logic /ˈlɒdʒɪk/ *suff.* [f. or after Gk *-logikos*, f. adjs. & ns. in *-logos, -logia* -LOGY: see -IC.] Forming adjs. corresp. esp. to ns. in *-logy*, w. the sense 'pertaining to or derived from a particular branch of knowledge or experience'; = -LOGICAL.

logical /ˈlɒdʒɪk(ə)l/ *a.* & *n.* LME. [med.L *logicalis*, f. late L *logica* LOGIC: see -ICAL.] A *adj.* 1 Of or pertaining to logic or formal argument. LME. b *Computing* & *Electronics*. Of or pertaining to the logic of computers and similar equipment or the conceptual arrangement of software or data; designed to carry out processes which can be expressed in terms of symbolic logic. M20. 2 Not contravening the principles of logic; correctly reasoned. L16. 3 Of a person:

capable of reasoning correctly. M17. 4 Characterized by reason; rational, reasonable. *rare.* M17. 5 That follows as a reasonable inference or natural consequence; deducible or defensible on the ground of consistency; reasonably believed or done. M19.

3 *Edinburgh Review* The strong and logical-minded Manning. 5 M. M. ATWATER Harold was the logical suspect—plenty of motive, the opportunity, it all checked. G. BROWN It would scarcely seem logical to have a Deputy Leader not in the Government.

Special collocations: **logical addition** the formation of a logical sum. *logical atom*: see ATOM *n.* 7. *logical atomism*: see ATOMISM 2. **logical empiricism** = *logical positivism* below. **logical empiricist** = *logical positivist* below. **logical form** the form, as distinct from the content, of a proposition, argument, etc., which can be expressed in logical terms. **logical grammar** the rules of word-use in a proposition on which its logical, as distinct from its purely grammatical, sense or meaning is held to depend. **logical implication** implication which is based on the formal and not the material relationship between propositions. **logical multiplication** the formation of a logical product. **logical necessity** the compulsion to believe that of which the opposite is inconceivable. **logical operation** an operation of the kind used in logic (such as conjunction or negation); any analogous (non-arithmetical) operation on numbers, esp. binary numbers, in which each digit of the result depends on only one digit in each operand. *logical paradox*: see PARADOX *n.* 2c. **logical positivism** a form of positivism regarding all valid philosophical problems as solvable by logical analysis. **logical positivist** an adherent or student of logical positivism. **logical product** the conjunction of two or more propositions; the intersection of two or more sets; (written $p \vee q$, $p \cap q$, $p.q$, pq, p and q). **logical structure** the formal framework of logical rules to which a theory, language, proposition, etc., must conform in order to have truth-value. **logical subject** the subject which is implied in a sentence or proposition, or which exists in the deep structure of a sentence. **logical sum** the disjunction of two or more propositions; the union of two or more sets; (written $p \wedge q$, $p \cup q$, p or q, $p + q$). **logical syntax** the system of sentence-construction in a proposition on which its logical, as distinct from its purely grammatical sense or meaning, is held to depend. **logical truth** that which is true in logical or formal terms regardless of material meaning. **logical word** a word of the type which gives logical context or form to a proposition but which, by itself, is non-representational and without meaning.

B *n.* In *pl.* The subjects studied in a course of instruction in logic. *obs.* exc. *Hist.* M16.

logi'cality *n.* the quality of being logical M19. **logicalize** *v.t.* make logical M19. **logically** *adv.* in a logical manner, according to the principles of logic or the laws of sound reasoning; *logically perfect language*, a language in which the grammatical structure of sentences would be identical with their logical structure: L16. **logicalness** *n.* (*rare*) logicality E18.

-logical /ˈlɒdʒɪk(ə)l/ *suff.* [f. as -LOGIC: see -ICAL.] Forming adjs. corresp. esp. to ns. in *-logy*, w. the sense 'pertaining to or derived from a particular branch of knowledge or experience', as *pathological*, *theological*, etc.

¶An adj. in *-logical* may exist alongside an adj. in *-logic* formed from the same base, but in such a case the adj. in *-logical* is likely to be more commonly used and to have a wider application (cf. -IC, -ICAL).

logician /ləˈdʒɪʃ(ə)n/ *n.* LME. [(O)Fr. *logicien*, f. as LOGIC + -ICIAN.] **1** A writer on logic; a student of logic. LME. **2** A person skilled in reasoning. L16.

1 *mathematical logician* etc.

logicise *v.* var. of LOGICIZE.

logicism /ˈlɒdʒɪsɪz(ə)m/ *n.* M20. [f. LOGIC + -ISM.] The theory that a set of axioms for mathematics can be deduced from a primitive set of purely logical axioms.

logicist /ˈlɒdʒɪsɪst/ *n.* & *a.* E20. [f. LOGIC + -IST.] **A** *n.* A (mathematical) logician; an adherent or student of logicism. E20. **B** *attrib.* or as *adj.* Of or pertaining to logicists or logicism. M20.

logicize /ˈlɒdʒɪsʌɪz/ *v.* Also **-ise**. M19. [f. LOGIC + -IZE, after *criticize*.] **1** *v.i.* Use logical argument, employ logic. M19. **2** *v.t.* Turn into logic. M19.

logico- /ˈlɒdʒɪkəʊ/ *comb. form.* [f. LOGIC, LOGIC(AL *a.*: see -O-.] Forming adjs. w. the sense 'logical and —', as *logico-mathematical*, *logico-philosophical*, etc., and occas. ns. w. the sense 'of logic, employing logic', as *logico-analyst*.

logie /ˈləʊgi/ *n.* M19. [App. f. David *Logie*, the inventor.] *Theatr.* An ornament made of zinc, intended to give the effect of jewellery.

log-in /ˈlɒgɪn, lɒgˈɪn/ *n.* & *a.* Also **login**. M20. [f. LOG *v.*[1] + IN *adv.*: see LOG *v.*[1] 8a.] *Computing.* **A** *n.* The action or an act of logging in. M20. **B** *attrib.* or as *adj.* Designating a procedure which is carried out every time a user logs in. L20.

logion /ˈlɒgɪɒn/ *n.* Pl. **logia** /ˈlɒgɪə/. L19. [Gk = oracle, f. *logos* word (see LOGOS).] A traditional maxim of a religious teacher or sage; *esp.* in *pl.* (also **L-**), a supposed collection of the sayings of Jesus circulating in the early Church.

Logian *a.* (of a document etc.) containing the Logia of Jesus E20.

†**logist** *n.* L16–M18. [L *logista* or Gk *logistēs*, f. *logizesthai*: see LOGISTIC *a.*[1] & *n.*, -IST.] An expert reckoner or accountant; *spec.* a member of a board of Athenian officials whose function was to examine the accounts of those who had completed a term of office in the magistracy.

-logist /lədʒɪst/ *suff.* [f. (as) -LOGY: see -IST.] Forming ns. w. the sense 'an expert in or student of the specified branch of knowledge, a person skilled in *—logy*', as *etymologist*, *geologist*, *heresiologist*, *ideologist*, *zoologist*, etc.

logistic /ləˈdʒɪstɪk/ *a.*[1] & *n.* E17. [Late L *logisticus* f. Gk *logistikos*, f. *logizesthai* reckon, f. as LOGOS: see -ISTIC. Cf. earlier LOGISTICAL *a.*[1]] **A** *adj.* †**1** Of or pertaining to reasoning; logical. E–M17. **2** Of or pertaining to reckoning or calculation. *rare.* E18. **3a** *Math.* Logarithmic, exponential. Now *rare* or *obs.* exc. in *logistic curve* below. E18. **b** Of or pertaining to mathematical or symbolic logic. E20.

3a **logistic curve** a sigmoidal curve used in population studies, which increases approximately exponentially for small values of the variable and approaches a constant value asymptotically for large values.

B *n.* †**1** = CALCULATOR 1. Only in M17. **2** = LOGISTICS *n.*[1] Now *rare* or *obs.* M17. **b** Mathematical or symbolic logic. E20. **3** *Math.* A logistic curve. E18.

logistician /-ˈstɪʃ(ə)n/ *n.* an expert in or student of mathematical or symbolic logic M20.

logistic /ləˈdʒɪstɪk/ *a.*[2] M20. [f. (as) LOGISTICS *n.*[2]] Of or pertaining to logistics; = LOGISTICAL *a.*[2]

logistical /ləˈdʒɪstɪk(ə)l/ *a.*[1] L16. [f. as LOGISTIC *a.*[1]: see -ICAL.] **1** Of or pertaining to calculation. Long *rare.* L16. **2** Pertaining to or based on reasoning or disputation. Now *rare.* M17. **3** *Math.* = LOGISTIC *a.*[1] 3a. Long *rare* or *obs.* M17. **4** Of or pertaining to logicism. M20.

logistical /ləˈdʒɪstɪk(ə)l/ *a.*[2] M20. [f. (as) LOGISTIC *a.*[2]: see -ICAL.] Of or pertaining to logistics; = LOGISTIC *a.*[2]

logistically /ləˈdʒɪstɪk(ə)li/ *adv.*[1] E20. [f. LOGISTIC *a.*[2] or LOGISTICAL *a.*[2]: see -ICALLY.] From the point of view of logistics, with regard to logistics.

logistically /ləˈdʒɪstɪk(ə)li/ *adv.*[2] *rare.* M20. [f. LOGISTIC *a.*[1] or LOGISTICAL *a.*[1]: see -ICALLY.] With regard to mathematical or symbolic logic; in the manner of mathematical or symbolic logic.

logistics /ləˈdʒɪstɪks/ *n.*[1] Now *rare* or *obs.* E18. [f. LOGISTIC *n.*: see -ICS.] The art of arithmetical calculation; the elementary processes of calculation.

logistics /ləˈdʒɪstɪks/ *n.*[2]*pl.* L19. [f. Fr. *logistique*, f. *loger* quarter, LODGE *v.*: see -ICS.] The organization of moving, lodging, and supplying troops and equipment; *transf.* the detailed organization and implementation of a plan or operation.

LADY BIRD JOHNSON The vast logistics of deciding who was going to stay where. *Guardian* The logistics of interviewing the six women were tough.

logit /ˈlɒgɪt/ *n.* M20. [Contr. of *logarithmic unit*.] *Statistics.* The natural logarithm of the quotient of a probability and its complement.

Comb.: **logit analysis** a form of regression analysis which makes use of logits.

log-jam /ˈlɒgdʒam/ *n.* L19. [f. LOG *n.*[1] + JAM *n.*[4]] **1** A crowded mass of logs in a river; a place where logs become jammed. L19. **2** *fig.* An obstruction, a blockage; a delay; a deadlock. L19.

2 *Listener* Nothing is likely to break the Arab-Israeli log-jam until the Arabs achieve . . unity.

logo /ˈlɒgəʊ, ˈləʊgəʊ/ *n.* Pl. **-os**. M20. [Abbrev.] = LOGOGRAM 3, LOGOTYPE 2.

S. KNIGHT In Italy the logo of the Brotherhood is the figure of a Black Friar. *Marketing Week* LWT's logo, previously orange, turquoise and white, now a crisp red, white and blue.

logocentric /lɒgə(ʊ)ˈsɛntrɪk/ *a.* M20. [f. Gk *logos* word, reason (see LOGOS) + -CENTRIC.] **1** Centred on reason. M20. **2** Centred on language; regarding the word as a fundamental expression of reality. L20.

logocentrism *n.* concentration on language; the belief that the word is a fundamental expression of reality: L20.

logodaedalist /lɒgəˈdiːd(ə)lɪst/ *n.* *rare.* E18. [f. mod.L *logodaedalus* f. Gk *logodaidalos*, f. *logos* word (see LOGOS) + *daidalos* skilful: see -IST.] A person skilled in the use of words.

logodaedaly *n.* skill in using words E18.

logodiarrhoea /ˌlɒgədʌɪəˈrɪə/ *n.* *rare.* E18. [f. Gk *logos* word (see LOGOS) + DIARRHOEA. Cf. LOGORRHOEA.] = *verbal diarrhoea* s.v. VERBAL *a.*

Earlier †**logodiarrhe** *n.* [cf. Fr. *logodiarrhée*]: only in E17.

logogram /ˈlɒgəgram/ *n.* E19. [f. Gk *logos* word (see LOGOS) + -GRAM.] **I 1** = LOGOGRIPH. *rare.* E19. **II 2** A sign, symbol, or character representing a word, as in shorthand or some ancient writing systems. Also, such a sign etc. used to represent part of a word. M19. **3** *gen.* A symbol or device designed to represent in simple graphic form an object, concept, or attitude; an organization's emblem or badge, a logotype. M20.

logograph /ˈlɒgəgrɑːf/ *n.* L18. [f. Gk *logos* word (see LOGOS) + -GRAPH.] †**1** = LOGOGRIPH. Only in L18. **2** = LOGOGRAPHER 2. *rare.* M19. **3** = LOGOGRAM 2. L19. **4** = LOGOTYPE 1. L19. **5** An instrument for giving a graphic representation of speech sounds. L19.

logographer /ləˈgɒgrəfə/ *n.* M17. [f. late L *logographus* accountant f. Gk *logographos* prose-writer, f. *logos* word: see LOGOS, -GRAPHER.] †**1** A lawyer's clerk; an accountant. M17–M18. **2** An early writer of (esp. Greek) traditional history in prose. M19. **3** A professional speech-writer in ancient Greece. M19.

logography /ləˈgɒgrəfi/ *n.* L18. [f. Gk *logos* word (see LOGOS) + -GRAPHY.] **1** *Printing.* A method of composition involving the arrangement and composition of groups of letters or complete words as opp. to single letters. L18. **2** A method of long-hand reporting employing several reporters each taking down a few words in succession. M19.

logo'graphic *a.* (*a*) of or pertaining to logography; (*b*) consisting of characters or signs, each of which singly represents a group of characters, which may constitute a complete word: L18. **logo'graphical** *a.* (*rare*) logographic E19. **logo'graphically** *adv.* L18.

logogriph /ˈlɒgəgrɪf/ *n.* L16. [Fr. *logogriphe*, f. Gk *logos* word (see LOGOS) + *griphos* fishing-basket, riddle.] A kind of enigma in which a certain word and other words that can be formed out of all or any of its letters are to be guessed from synonyms of them introduced into a set of verses. Also, an anagram, a puzzle involving anagrams.

logo'griphic *a.* (*rare*) of or pertaining to logogriphs, of the nature of a logogriph E19.

logolatry /ləˈgɒlətri/ *n.* E19. [f. Gk *logos* word (see LOGOS) + -LATRY.] Excessive admiration for words; unreasonable regard for words or for verbal truth.

logology /ləˈgɒlədʒi/ *n.* E18. [f. Gk *logos* word (see LOGOS) + -LOGY.] †**1** The doctrine of the Logos. *rare.* E–M18. **2** The branch of knowledge that deals with words. E19.

logomachy /lə'gɒməki/ *n.* M16. [Gk *logomakhia*, f. *logos* word (see LOGOS) + -MACHY.] Contention about words; controversy turning on merely verbal points; an instance of this.

logomachist *n.* a person given to logomachy, a person who disputes about verbal subtleties E19.

logomaniac /lɒgə(ʊ)'meɪnɪak/ *n.* L19. [f. Gk *logos* (see LOGOS) word + -MANIAC.] A person who is obsessively interested in words.

log-on /'lɒgɒn, lɒg'ɒn/ *n.* & *a.* Also **logon**. L20. [f. LOG *v.*[1] + ON *adv.*: see LOG *v.*[1] 8a.] *Computing.* A *n.* The action or an act of logging on. L20. B *attrib.* or as *adj.* Designating a procedure which is carried out every time a user logs on. L20.

logopaedics /lɒgə'piːdɪks/ *n.* Also *__-ped-__. E20. [f. Gk *logos* word (see LOGOS), after ORTHOPAEDICS.] The branch of medicine that deals with speech disabilities and their treatment; speech therapy.

logophile /'lɒgəfɪl, -fʌɪl/ *n.* M20. [f. Gk *logos* word (see LOGOS) + -PHILE.] A lover of words.

logophobia /lɒgə'fəʊbɪə/ *n.* E20. [f. Gk *logos* word (see LOGOS) + -PHOBIA.] Irrational fear or distrust of words.

logorrhoea /lɒgə'rɪə/ *n.* Also *__-rrhea__. E20. [f. Gk *logos* word (see LOGOS) + -RRHOEA, prob. after DIARRHOEA.] Abnormally rapid and voluble speech, as a symptom of mental illness; *gen.* an excessive flow of words, prolixity; = *verbal diarrhoea* s.v. VERBAL *a.*

logorrhoeic *a.* of, pertaining to or affected with logorrhoea M20.

Logos /'lɒgɒs/ *n.* L16. [Gk = account, relation, ratio, reason(ing), argument, discourse, saying, speech, word, rel. to *legein* choose, collect, gather, say, used in a mystic sense by Hellenistic and Neoplatonist philosophers and by St John.] 1 *Philos.* & *Chr. Theol.* The Word of God, the second person of the Trinity. L16. 2 A pervading cosmic idea or spirit of creativity or rationality. M17.

logothete /'lɒgəθiːt/ *n.* L18. [med.L *logotheta* or its source Gk *logothetēs* auditor, f. *logos* account (see LOGOS).] *Hist.* Any of various functionaries under the Byzantine emperors; *esp.* (also in the Norman kingdom of Sicily) a high official with the function of a chancellor.

logotype /'lɒgə(ʊ)tʌɪp/ *n.* E19. [f. Gk *logos* word (see LOGOS) + TYPE *n.*] 1 *Printing.* A type containing a word, or two or more letters, cast in one piece. E19. 2 An emblem or device used as the badge of an organization in display material. M20. 3 *Printing.* A single piece of type that prints such an emblem. M20.

logroll /'lɒgrəʊl/ *v.* Chiefly *US.* M19. [Back-form. f. LOGROLLING.] 1 *v.t.* Procure the passing of (a bill) by logrolling. M19. 2 *v.i.* Practise logrolling. M19.

logroller /'lɒgrəʊlə/ *n.* Chiefly *N. Amer.* M19. [f. LOG *n.*[1] + ROLLER *n.*[1]] 1 A person who practises logrolling. M19. 2 A device for transporting logs in a sawmill. L19.

logrolling /'lɒgrəʊlɪŋ/ *n.* Chiefly *US.* E19. [f. LOG *n.*[1] + ROLLING *n.*] 1 The practice of exchanging favours, esp. (*a*) in politics, of exchanging votes to mutual benefit, (*b*) of providing reciprocally favourable reviews, notices, etc., in literary publications. *colloq.* E19. 2a The action of rolling logs to a required spot; the action of causing a floating log to rotate by treading, esp. as a competitive sport. M19. b A meeting for cooperation in rolling logs for transportation etc. M19.

¶From the expression *You roll my log and I'll roll yours.*

-logue /lɒg/ *suff.* Also *__-log__. [f. or after Fr. f. Gk *-logos*, *-logon* speaking or treating of, f. *logos*: see LOGOS.] 1 Forming ns. w. the senses 'talk, kind of discourse', as *dialogue*, *monologue*, etc., and (occas.) 'compilation', as *catalogue* etc. 2 = -LOGIST, as *ideologue*, *Sinologue*, etc.

logwood /'lɒgwʊd/ *n.* L16. [f. LOG *n.*[1] + WOOD *n.*[1]] 1 (The heartwood of) a Central American and W. Indian leguminous tree, *Haematoxylum campechianum*. L16. 2 An extract of this wood, used for colouring and dyeing. L19.

logy /'ləʊgi/ *a.* *N. Amer.* M19. [Origin uncertain: cf. Du. *log* heavy, dull.] Dull and heavy in motion or thought.

-logy /lədʒi/ *suff.* E19. [Fr. *-logie* or med. L *-logia* f. Gk, f. *logos*: see LOGOS, -Y[3].] Forming ns. w. the senses 'discourse' as *tetralogy*, *trilogy*, etc.; 'a characteristic of speech or language', as *battology*, *cacology*, *dittology*, *eulogy*, *tautology*, etc.; 'a subject of study or interest, a branch of knowledge' (usu. with -o-: see -OLOGY), as *archaeology*, *geology*, *sociology*, *theology*, *zoology*, etc.

Lohan /'ləʊhaːn/ *n.* M19. [Chin. *luóhàn* (Wade-Giles *Lo-han*).] = ARHAT.

†**lohoch** *n.* Also **looch**. M16–M19. [med.L *lohoc* f. Arab. *la'ūk* electuary, f. *la'ika* lick.] *Med.* A linctus.

loiasis *n.* var. of LOAIASIS.

loi-cadre /lwakadr/ *n.* Pl. ***lois-cadres*** (pronounced same). M20. [Fr.] *Fr. Pol.* A general outline law, the principles of which can be applied by the government in succeeding parallel situations.

loid /lɔɪd/ *n.* & *v.* *Criminals' slang.* Also **'loid**. M20. [Abbrev. of CELLULOID *n.*] A *n.* A celluloid strip used by thieves to force open a spring lock. M20. B *v.t.* Break open (a lock) by this method. M20.

loin /lɔɪn/ *n.* ME. [OFr. *loigne* eastern var. of *longe* (mod. = loin of veal) f. Proto-Romance, f. L *lumbus* loin.] *sing.* & (usu.) in *pl.* The part or parts of a human being or quadruped situated on both sides of the vertebral column, between the ribs and the pelvis (*biblical*, *arch.*, & *literary* as the part of the body that should be covered by clothing or as the seat of physical strength and of reproductive power). Also, a joint of meat which includes the vertebrae of the loins.

DAY LEWIS His satisfaction at inheriting blood which had not passed through any huckster's loin. M. AMIS His loins were rich in sons. *gird* (*up*) *one's loins*: see GIRD *v.*[1]

Comb.: **loincloth** a cloth worn round the loins, esp. as the sole garment.

loined *a.* having loins (of a specified kind) M19.

loir /lɔɪə, *foreign* lwaːr (*pl. same*)/ *n.* Now *rare* or *obs.* L18. [(O)Fr. f. pop.L var. of L *glir-*, *glis* dormouse.] The fat or edible dormouse, *Glis glis*.

Loire /lwaː/ *n.* M20. [The longest river in France.] In full *Loire wine*. (A) wine from grapes grown in the Loire valley, France.

lois-cadres *n.* pl. of LOI-CADRE.

loiter /'lɔɪtə/ *v.* LME. [Perh. f. MDu. *loteren* wag about, Du. *leuteren* shake, totter, dawdle, f. base repr. also by MDu. *lutsen* wag about. Cf. G *lottern*.] 1 *v.i.* Waste time in idleness. Now *spec.* linger indolently on the way when on an errand, journey, etc.; linger idly about a place; dawdle. LME. b Travel or proceed indolently and with frequent pauses. Foll. by adv. or advb. phr. E18. 2 *v.t.* Allow (time etc.) to pass idly; waste carelessly or on trifles. Now only foll. by *away*, (occas.) *out*. M16.

1 J. LE CARRÉ People . . loiter outside the house with nothing to do. b O. WISTER I loitered here and there, . . watching the cowboys. 2 OED We loitered away the rest of the day. *loiter with intent* (to commit a felony).

loiterer *n.* M16. **loiteringly** *adv.* in a loitering manner M16.

lokal /lo'kal/ *n.* E20. [G.] In Germany or Austria: a local bar, a nightclub.

lokanta /lo'kanta, lə(ʊ)'kantə/ *n.* M20. [Turk. f. It. *locanda*.] In Turkey: a restaurant.

lokey *n.* var. of LOCIE.

lokoum *n.* var. of LOKUM.

Lok Sabha /ləʊk sə'baː/ *n.* M20. [f. Skt *lok* people + *sabhā* SABHA.] The lower house of the Indian parliament. Cf. RAJYA SABHA.

lokshen /'lɒkʃ(ə)n/ *n.pl.* L19. [Yiddish, pl. of *loksh* noodle.] Noodles (in Jewish cookery).

lokum /lɒ'kuːm/ *n.* Also ***-koum***, ***-c-***, ***la-*** /lə-/. E20. [Abbrev. of Turk. RAHAT *lokum*.] Turkish delight.

loligo /lə'lʌɪgəʊ/ *n.* Pl. **-os**. E17. [mod.L f. L *lolligo*.] A squid, *esp.* one of the genus *Loligo*. Now chiefly as mod.L genus name.

Lolita /lə'liːtə/ *n.* M20. [The main character in a novel (1958) of the same name by Vladimir Nabokov (1899–1977).] A sexually precocious schoolgirl.

loll /lɒl/ *n.* L16. [f. the vb.] 1 A person who lolls. Formerly also, a thing that lolls, e.g. a tongue. L16. 2 The action or posture of lolling. E18. 3 A pet, a spoilt child. *dial.* E18.

loll /lɒl/ *v.* LME. [Symbolic: cf. LILL *v.*] 1 *v.i.* Hang down loosely, droop, dangle, (also foll. by *down*). Now usu. lean idly, recline or rest in a relaxed attitude against something. LME. 2 *v.t.* Let droop or dangle. Later *spec.* allow to rest idly or in a relaxed attitude. Formerly also foll. by *up*: hang. Now *rare*. LME. 3a *v.t.* Stick out (the tongue) in a pendulous manner. Also foll. by *out*. E17. b *v.i.* Of the tongue: stick out pendulously, hang out. Usu. foll. by *out*. L17.

1 V. SACKVILLE-WEST The housekeeper never lolled. She sat . . upright. P. H. JOHNSON The tired waiters lolled against the wall. G. SWIFT The boys are lolling about, reading comics. D. M. THOMAS Kolya . . was asleep, his head lolling on her shoulder. 3a D. WELCH The boy . . lolled out his tongue. b DENNIS POTTER Her tongue lolling out between her teeth.

loller *n.* LME. **lolling** *a.* (*a*) that lolls; (*b*) *Her.* (of a falcon or hawk) with wings raised and hanging down: M16. **lollingly** *adv.* M19.

lollapaloosa, -za, -zer *ns.* vars. of LALLAPALOOSA.

Lollard /'lɒləd/ *n.* LME. [MDu. *lollaerd* lit. 'mumbler, mutterer,' f. *lollen* mumble: see -ARD.] 1 *Hist.* Any of the heretics, from the 14th-cent. to the Reformation, who were either followers of John Wyclif or held opinions similar to his, esp. on the necessity for the Church to aid people to live a life of evangelical poverty and imitate Jesus. LME. 2 [Assoc. w. prec.] A person who lolls; an idler. *rare*. M17.

2 E. B. BROWNING Learn to be a *Loll*ard like me, and establish yourself on a sofa.

Lollardism *n.* the tenets and practice of the Lollards E19. **Lollardry** *n.* = LOLLARDISM LME. **Lollardy** *n.* = LOLLARDISM LME. **Lollardy** *a.* (*rare*) characteristic of the Lollards E16.

löllingite /'ləːlɪŋgʌɪt/ *n.* Also **loe-**. M19. [f. *Lölling*, Austria + -ITE[1].] *Min.* An arsenide of iron occurring as brilliant white bipyramidal crystals of the orthorhombic system.

lollipop /'lɒlɪpɒp/ *n.* L18. [Perh. f. LOLLY *n.*[3] (though recorded earlier) + POP *n.*[1]] 1 Orig. (*dial.*), a sweet confection of a particular kind; in *pl.*, sweets in general. Now *spec.* a large sweet (esp. a boiled sweet), water-ice, or similar confection, on a stick. L18. 2 *fig.* A showy or non-serious composition or performance. M19. 3 A circular sign used by a lollipop man etc. (see below). *colloq.* M20.

2 *Gramophone* The choice of music is admirable (no lush lollipops).

Comb.: **lollipop lady, man, woman** *colloq.* an official using a circular sign on a stick to stop traffic so that children may cross a road, esp. near a school.

lollop /'lɒləp/ *v.* & *n.* *colloq.* M18. [Prob. f. LOLL *v.*, by assoc. w. TROLLOP.] A *v.i.* Lounge, sprawl; move or proceed in a lounging or ungainly way; bob or heave up and down; bound clumsily. M18.

B. PYM His old sealyham, who lolloped along like a little rocking-horse. M. BRADBURY The sea lolloped against the side of the ship. B. BAINBRIDGE I'm supposed to be her companion. Why else should I be lolloping about the Soviet Union?

B *n.* 1 The action or an act of lolloping. M19. 2 A trifling lazy person. L19.

lollopy *a.* disposed to lollop, characterized by lolloping M19.

lolly /'lɒli/ *n.*[1] *Canad.* *rare*. L18. [Abbrev. of LOBLOLLY.] Soft ice formed in turbulent water along a shore etc.; = FRAZIL. Also *lolly ice*.

lolly /'lɒli/ *n.*[2] M19. [Abbrev. of LOLLIPOP.] 1 A sweet. Exc. *Austral.* & *NZ* now *spec.* a lollipop. *colloq.* M19. 2 An easy catch in cricket. E20. 3 Money. *slang.* M20.

1 **ice(d) lolly** a water-ice or ice-cream on a small stick.

lolly /ˈlɒli/ *n.*[3] *dial.* L19. [Origin uncertain: perh. f. use in pronunc. of *l* or f. LOLL *v.*] The tongue.

¶Prob. much earlier and perh. the 1st elem. of LOLLIPOP.

lollygag *n.* & *v.* var. of LALLYGAG.

Lolo /ˈləʊləʊ/ *n.* & *a.* M18. [Lolo.] A *n.* Pl. **-os**, same. A member of an aboriginal people of SW China; the Tibeto-Burman language of these people. M18. B *attrib.* or as *adj.* Of or pertaining to the Lolos or their language. E20.

¶Also called *Yi*.

loma /ˈləʊmə/ *n.*[1] *US.* M19. [Sp. f. *lomo* back, loin, ridge.] In the south-western US, a broad-topped hill or ridge.

Loma /ˈləʊmə/ *n.*[2] & *a.* M20. [Loma.] A *n.* Pl. **-s**, same. A member of a people inhabiting the border regions of Liberia, Sierra Leone, and Guinea; the Mande language of this people. M20. B *attrib.* or as *adj.* Of or pertaining to the Loma or their language. M20.

Lombard /ˈlɒmbəd, -bɑːd/ *n.*[1] & *a.* ME. [MDu., MLG *lombaerd* or Fr. *lombard* f. It. *lombardo* (med.L *lombardus*) repr. late L *Langobardus*, *Longo-*, L *langobardi* (Tacitus) f. Gmc, f. base of LONG *a.*[1] + ethnic name *Bardi*. Cf. LANGOBARD, LONGOBARD. See also LUMBER *n.*[2]] A *n.* 1 *Hist.* A member of a Germanic people from the lower Elbe who invaded Italy in the 6th cent. and founded a kingdom named Lombardy after them. ME. 2 A native or inhabitant of the region of Lombardy in north central Italy. Formerly *spec.*, one engaged in banking, money-changing, or pawnbroking; hence any banker, money-changer, or pawnbroker. LME. 3 The Italian dialect of modern Lombardy. L16. †4 A bank, a money-changer's or moneylender's office; a pawnshop. Cf. LUMBER *n.*[2] E17–L18.

B *adj.* Of or pertaining to the Lombards or Lombardy; Lombardic. ME.

Special collocations & comb.: **Lombard band** *Archit.* a shallow pilaster dividing a wall into bays. **Lombard Street** [a street in London, orig. occupied by Lombard bankers and still containing many of the principal London banks] the money market, financiers as a body; *Lombard Street to a China orange*, great wealth against one ordinary object, virtual certainty.

Lomˈbardian *a.* = LOMBARDIC *a.* M19. **Lombardism** *n.* a Lombardic idiom E19. **Lomˈbardo-** *comb. form.* [after It. *Lombardo-Veneto*] Lombardic and —: L19.

lombard /ˈlɒmbəd/ *n.*[2] M19. [Sp. †*lombarda*.] *Hist.* A light cannon used in Spain in the 16th cent.

Lombardic /lɒmˈbɑːdɪk/ *a.* L17. [f. LOMBARD *n.*[1] + -IC.] Of or pertaining to Lombardy or the Lombards; *spec.* designating or pertaining to the style of architecture which prevailed in northern Italy from the 7th to the 13th cent., a style of handwriting common in Italian manuscripts during the same period, and the school of painters, represented esp. by Leonardo da Vinci, Mantegna, and Luini, which flourished at Milan and other Lombard cities during the 15th and 16th cents.

Lombardy poplar /ˈlɒmbədi ˈpɒplə/ *n. phr.* M18. [A region of north central Italy: see LOMBARD *n.*[1]] A fastigiate variety of the black poplar, *Populus nigra* var. *italica*, widely planted in Europe and N. America, and orig. introduced to lowland Britain from Italy.

Lombrosian /lɒmˈbrəʊzɪən/ *n.* & *a.* E20. [f. *Lombroso* (see below) + -IAN.] A *n.* An adherent or student of the Italian physician and criminologist Cesare Lombroso (1836–1909) and his theories of the physiology, psychology, and treatment of criminals. E20. B *adj.* Of or pertaining to Lombroso or his theories. M20.

loment /ˈləʊmɛnt/ *n.* LME. [L *lomentum* bean-meal (orig. a cosmetic made of bean-meal), f. *lavare* to wash.] †1 Bean-meal. Only in LME. 2 *Bot.* = LOMENTUM. E19.

lomentum /lə(ʊ)ˈmɛntəm/ *n.* Pl. ***-ta*** /-tə/. M19. [L: see LOMENT.] *Bot.* A legume which is narrower in the spaces between the seeds, breaking up when mature into sections each containing one seed.

lomi-lomi /ləʊmɪˈləʊmi/ *n.* M19. [Haw., lit. 'masseur, masseuse', redupl. of *lomi* massage, f. *lomi* rub with the hand.] A type of massage practised among the Hawaiians.

London /ˈlʌndən/ *n.* ME. [The capital of England, and now of the UK.] Used *attrib.* to designate things from or associated with London.

London bridge: a children's singing game (more fully *London bridge is falling down*). **London broil** *N. Amer.* a grilled steak served cut diagonally in thin slices. **London clay** *Geol.* a clay formation of the lower Eocene in SE England, esp. around London. **London fog** a dense fog once peculiar to London and large industrial towns. **London gin** a dry gin. **London ivy** *arch.* (*a*) the smoke of London, as clinging to and blackening buildings; (*b*) a thick London fog. *London particular*: see PARTICULAR *n.* *London plane*: see PLANE *n.*[2] 1. **London pride** (*a*) (now *dial.*) sweet william, *Dianthus barbatus*; (*b*) a commonly cultivated saxifrage, *Saxifraga × urbium*, with panicles of white red-spotted flowers and rosettes of leathery leaves. **London purple** an insecticide containing arsenic trioxide and aniline. **London rocket** [so named f. its springing up on the ruins after the Great Fire of London (1666)] a cruciferous plant, *Sisymbrium irio*, with yellow flowers. **London shrinking** a finishing process applied to fabric to prevent shrinkage. **London-shrunk** *a.* finished by London shrinking.

Londoner *n.* a native (or inhabitant) of London LME. **Londonian** /lʌnˈdəʊnɪən/ *n.* & *a.* (*a*) *n.* (*rare*) a Londoner; (*b*) *adj.* pertaining to or characteristic of London: E19. **Londonish** *a.* pertaining to or characteristic of London, exhibiting features or aspects of London M19. **Londonism** *n.* a word, idiom, or pronunciation peculiar to London speech E19. **Londoniˈzation** *n.* the action or process of Londonizing something or someone L19. **Londonize** *v.t.* make like London or its inhabitants, give a Londonish character to L18. **Londony** *a.* suggestive of London or its characteristics L19.

†lone *n.*[1] var. of LOAN *n.*[2]

lone /ləʊn/ *a.*, *adv.*, & *n.*[2] Also (*Sc.*) **lane** /leɪn/. LME. [Aphet. f. ALONE.] A *adj.* & *adv.* I *attrib.* 1 (Of a person, personal situation, etc.) companionless, solitary (chiefly *literary*). Also, standing apart from others, isolated. LME. b Having a feeling of loneliness; lonesome. M19. 2 Now esp. of a woman: unmarried, single or widowed. M16. 3 Only, sole. *rare.* E17. 4 Of a place: lonely; unfrequented, uninhabited. *poet.* E17.

1 E. M. FORSTER Two lone females in an unknown town. M. ESSLIN A lone outsider, cut off and isolated. P. FERGUSON A lone sock curled amidst the dust. *Daily Express* Charles spent a lone holiday. 2 *Which?* Lone parents . . are likely to lose out. 4 POPE In some lone isle, or distant Northern land.

II *pred. a.* & *adv.* 5 Alone, by oneself or itself. Now *dial.* E17.

Special collocations & comb.: **lone hand** in card-games, esp. euchre, a hand played, or a player playing, against all the other players, or against the opposite side without help; *play a lone hand* (fig.), act on one's own without help. **lone pair** *Physical Chem.* a pair of electrons in the outer shell of an atom which are not involved in bonding. **lone ranger** [f. the hero of a western] a person acting alone, esp. to uphold the right. **Lone Scout** a Scout who does not have a regular access to a Scout troop. **lone star** the single star on the State flag of Texas; *the Lone Star State*, Texas. **lone wolf** a person who mixes little with others, a person who prefers to act alone. **lone-wolf** *v.i.* live, work, or act alone.

B *n.* (Also **lones**.) *One's* self, *one's* own. Chiefly in *by* or *on one's lone*. Chiefly *Sc.* & *north.* LME.

W. M. RAINE Why for do they let a sick man . . travel all by his lone.

loneful *a.* (long *obs.* exc. *dial.*) lonely, forlorn M16. **loneness** *n.* (now *rare*) solitariness; loneliness; lonesomeness: L16.

lonelihood /ˈləʊnlɪhʊd/ *n. poet.* M19. [f. LONELY + -HOOD.] Loneliness.

lonelily /ˈləʊnlɪli/ *adv.* M19. [f. LONELY + -LY[2].] In a lonely fashion.

loneliness /ˈləʊnlɪnɪs/ *n.* L16. [f. next + -NESS.] 1 The condition of being alone or solitary; isolation. L16. 2 The condition of being unfrequented; desolateness. M18. 3 Sadness at being alone; the sense of solitude; dejection arising from lack of friends or company. E19.

lonely /ˈləʊnli/ *a.* L16. [f. LONE *a.* + -LY[1].] 1 Of a person, personal situation, etc.: companionless, unaccompanied, solitary. L16. 2 Of a place: unfrequented; desolate. L16. 3 Of a thing: isolated, standing apart. Chiefly *poet.* M17. 4a Imparting a feeling of loneliness; dreary. M17. b Dejected because of lack of friends or company; sad at the thought that one is alone; having a feeling of solitariness. E19.

1 R. K. NARAYAN The Temptress Devil, who waylaid lonely wayfarers. C. C. TRENCH Frederick had spent a lonely childhood, with no relatives . ., no friends. 2 J. A. MICHENER One of the loneliest and gloomiest sections of Texas. 3 M. ARNOLD That lonely tree against the western sky. *plough a lonely furrow*: see PLOUGH *v.* 4a CONAN DOYLE My house is lonely I . . and my bees have the estate all to ourselves. b A. MCCOWEN My Grandma Walkden died . ., and my grandfather was very lonely.

Comb.: **lonely-heart** a person suffering from loneliness; *Miss Lonelyhearts*, (a pseudonym used by) a journalist giving advice in a newspaper or magazine to people who are lonely or in difficulties.

loner /ˈləʊnə/ *n.* M20. [f. LONE *a.* + -ER[1].] A person who avoids company and prefers to be alone; an animal of solitary habits.

lones *n.* var. of LONE *n.*[2]

lonesome /ˈləʊns(ə)m/ *a.* & *n.* M17. [f. LONE *a.* + -SOME[1].] A *adj.* 1 Of a person etc.: solitary, lonely; now *esp.* having a feeling of solitude or loneliness, feeling lonely or forlorn. Also foll. by *for*. M17. 2 Of a place etc.: unfrequented, desolate; now *esp.* causing feelings of loneliness, making one feel forlorn. M17.

1 M. WEBB It seemed lonesome that night without Gideon. A. BEATTIE I got lonesome for you tonight.

B *n. One's* self, *one's* own. Chiefly in *by* or *on one's lonesome*. *colloq.* L19.

lonesomely *adv.* L18. **lonesomeness** *n.* E18.

long /lɒŋ/ *a.*[1] & *n.* [OE *lang*, *long* = OFris., OS *lang*, *long*, OHG *lang* (Du., G *lang*), ON *langr*, Goth. *laggs*, f. Gmc.] A *adj.* I With ref. to spatial measurement. 1 Great in measurement from end to end; not soon traversed. OE. b Tall. Now *colloq.*, esp. *Sc.* OE. c Designating a measure of length greater than the standard measure of that name. E17. d Of action, vision, etc.: acting at or extending to a great distance. E17. 2 Having (a relative or specified) extension from end to end. Freq. w. adv. or adv. phr. expressing the amount of length. OE. 3 Having the length much greater than the breadth; elongated. OE.

1 T. HARDY She could not have come a very long distance. I. MURDOCH Annette walked quickly, taking long strides. E. CALDWELL She has long brown hair hanging down her back. W. BOYD The long stretch of Government Road. 2 THOMAS HUGHES Pike, three inches long.

II With ref. to serial extent or duration. 4 Of a series, enumeration or succession, a speech, a sentence, a word, a literary work, etc.: having a great extent from beginning to end; not soon finished. OE. b Of a number or thing numerically estimated: large; expressed by many digits; consisting of many individuals; *Cards* (of a suit) of which a large number of cards (4 or more) are held or have been played, (of a card) of such a suit. M18. 5 (Of a period of time, or a process, state, or action) having a great extent in duration; that has continued or will continue in action, operation, or obligation for a long period, lasting. OE. 6 *Phonet.* & *Pros.* (Of a vowel (in mod. use also of a consonant or syllable)) having the greater of two recognized contrastive durations; (of a vowel or syllable) stressed; (of a vowel letter) representing in context a vowel with such duration (in English the sound of its alphabetical name, as *i* in *pile*, *u* in *cute*). OE. 7 Having (a relative or specified) extension serially or temporally. ME. 8 Continuing too long; lengthy, prolix, tedious. ME. 9 Of a point in time: distant, remote. Now only in *long date* below, and in legal phr. *a long day*. LME. b Of a bill of exchange, promissory note, etc.: maturing at a distant date, having a long time to run. M19. 10 Designating a period of time, a number, a weight, or a quantity greater than the usual period etc. of that name. Also, felt as excessive or unusual in duration.

L16. **11** *Comm.* Designating or pertaining to the buying of stocks, commodities, etc., in large quantities in expectation of a coming scarcity and rise in price. M19.

4 G. VIDAL The treaty was very long. **b** *Black World* I'd quit pushing tomorrow, baby, but the money is so long. **5** SCOTT FITZGERALD There was such a long pause. D. DUNN In the afternoon twilight of a long lunch in London. I. MURDOCH From long experience Barney could tell the . . boats apart. A. THWAITE I am not doomed to a long exile here. **7** J. WILCOX I'm not going to do any paper longer than five pages. **8** POPE He is apt to be too long in his descriptions. **10** G. GREENE The law has . . , impressed it on me through three long days. A. ALVAREZ A long fortnight, sixteen days.

Phrases: *a long row to hoe*: see ROW *n.*[1] *as broad as it is long*: see BROAD *a.* 1. *at a long stay*: see STAY *n.*[1] 1. *at long last*: see LAST *adv., a.,* & *n.*[5] *at long range*: see RANGE *n.*[1] *by a long way*: see WAY *n. come a long way*: see WAY *n. cut a long story short*: see SHORT *a. for a long season*: see SEASON *n. go a long way*: see WAY *n.* **go long (on)** *Comm.* buy in large quantities in expectation of a coming scarcity and rise in price. *have a face as long as a fiddle*: see FIDDLE *n. Land of the Long White Cloud*: see LAND *n.*[1] **long in the tooth** (orig. of a horse) displaying the roots of the teeth owing to the recession of the gums with increasing age; *gen.* old. **long of life** (now *rare*) of long life. **long on** *colloq.* well supplied with, having plenty of. **the long robe** *fig.* (*arch.*) the legal profession (chiefly in *of the long robe*); cf. *the short robe* s.v. SHORT *a., n.,* & *adv. think (it) long*: see THINK *v.*[2]

Special collocations & *comb.*: **long acre** †(*a*) a long narrow field of an acre; (*b*) *NZ* a grass verge between a roadway and a fence. **long-acuminate** *a.* (*Bot.*) having a long tapering point. **long-and-short** *a.* (*a*) *long-and-short stitch*, in embroidery, a flat stitch used for shading; (*b*) *long-and-short work* (Archit.), alternation of tall quoins horizontal with slabs. **long arm** (*a*) an arm fully extended to reach something; *make a long arm* (colloq.), reach out the arm a long way; (*b*) a far-reaching power (freq. in *the long arm of coincidence, of the law*); (*c*) (w. hyphen or as one wd) a long-barrelled gun, as a musket, rifle, etc.; (*d*) (w. hyphen or as one wd) a pole fitted with a hook, shears, etc., for use at a height beyond the ordinary reach of the arm. **long barrow** *Archaeol.* an elongated neolithic grave-mound. **long-beard** (*a*) *rare* [pseudo-etymol. rendering] a Lombard; (*b*) Spanish moss, *Tillandsia usneoides*. **longbill** a bird with a long bill, *esp.* a woodcock. **long bill** a bill containing a great number of items; a bill in which the charges are excessive. **long blow** *Austral.* & *NZ* a stroke of the shears in sheep-shearing which cuts away the fleece from rump to neck. **longboard** a type of long surfboard. **longboat** the largest boat belonging to a sailing vessel. **long bone** any of the main limb bones, *esp.* (in *pl.*) the femur, tibia, humerus, and radius. **longbow** a large bow drawn by hand and discharging a long feathered arrow, the chief weapon of English armies from the 14th cent. until the introduction of firearms (*draw* or *pull the longbow*, make exaggerated statements, tell invented stories). *long*-BREATHED. **long card** in whist or bridge, a card of a suit held only by one player (usu. in *pl.*); (see also sense 4b above). **long-case (clock)** a weight-and-pendulum clock in a tall wooden case; also called *grandfather clock*. **long chain** *Chem.* a relatively large number of atoms (usu. of carbon) linked together in a line (freq. *attrib.* w. hyphen). **long chair** = CHAISE LONGUE. *long chalk(s)*: see CHALK *n.* **long chance**: involving considerable uncertainty or risk. **long cist** *Archaeol.* a type of megalithic tomb having a long and narrow chamber to which there is direct entry. *long clam*: see CLAM *n.*[2] 1(c). **long clay** *colloq.* a churchwarden pipe. **long cloth** cloth woven in unusually long pieces, *esp.* cotton or calico cloth of this kind made in the Indian subcontinent. **long clothes** the garments of a baby in arms. **long-coat** a coat reaching to the ankles; in *pl.* also (*arch.*) = *long clothes* above. **long corner** *Hockey* a penalty hit taken from a spot on the back line within 5 yards of the corner flag (opp. *short corner*). **long cross** (*a*) *Printing* in a hand-press, a bar dividing a chase the longest way; (*b*) *Numism.* a cross of which the limbs extend to the outer circle on a coin. **long date** a distant date for the maturing of a bill etc. **long-dated** *a.* †(*a*) that has existed from a distant date; (*b*) extending to a distant date in the future; *esp.* not due for early payment or redemption, designating fixed-interest securities having redemption dates more than 15 years away. **long-day** *a.* (*a*) having a long working day; (*b*) (of a plant) needing a long daily period of light to induce flowering. **long dog** *dial.* a greyhound. *long dozen*: see DOZEN *n.* 1. *long division*: see DIVISION 5. **long drawer** a drawer extending the full width of a chest, wardrobe, etc. **long dress** a floor- or ankle-length dress, usu. worn as evening dress. **long drink** a drink served in a tall glass; a large measure of liquid to drink. **long dung** = *long manure* below. **long ear** (*a*) *arch.* an ass (*lit.* & *fig.*); (*b*) [tr. of local name] a member of the people who once inhabited Easter Island and were distinguished by artificially lengthened ears. **long-eared** (*a*) having long ears; *long-eared owl*, an owl, *Asio otus*, widespread in the northern hemisphere, having two earlike tufts on top of the head; (*b*) asinine, stupid. **long-ells** *Hist.* a kind of coarse woollen cloth. *Longer Catechism*: see CATECHISM 2. **long face** *colloq.* a dismal or exaggeratedly solemn facial expression. **long-faced** *a.* (*colloq.*) having a dismal or exaggeratedly solemn facial expression. **long family**: having many children. **long field** *Cricket* (*a*) long off or long on; (*b*) part of the field behind the bowler. **long figure** a heavy cost. **long finger** the middle finger; in *pl.* also the three middle fingers. *long firm*: see FIRM *n.* 3. **long-footed** *a.* having long feet; *long-footed* POTOROO. *long Forties*: see FORTY *n.* 1. **long-fours** long candles, four of which weighed a pound. **long game** *Golf* driving and other play to reach the green. **long glass** a full-length looking-glass. **long grass** *spec.* grass or grasslike growth, typical of certain areas in Africa, tall enough to conceal large animals. *long green*: see GREEN *n.* **longhair** a person or animal (esp. a cat) with longer hair than usual (RUSSIAN *longhair*); a person of a type regarded as characteristically having long hair; *spec.* (*a*) (freq. *derog.*) a clever person, an aesthete, an intellectual; a devotee of classical (as opp. to popular) music; (*b*) a hippy, a beatnik. **longhaired** *a.* (*a*) having longer hair than usual; of a kind or breed characterized by relatively long hair; (*b*) (freq. *derog.*) that is a 'longhair', with aesthetic or intellectual pretensions. **longhand** ordinary handwriting, as distinguished from shorthand or typing or printing. **long handle** (*Cricket*) *the* action or practice of hitting freely. **long-haul** *a.* designating or pertaining to travel, transport of goods, or any effort made, over a long distance. **longhead** (*a*) a person who has a skull of more than average length; *spec.* in *Anthropol.* a dolichocephalic person; (*b*) *colloq.* a shrewd person. **long-headed** *a.* (*a*) of great discernment or foresight; shrewd; (*b*) having a long head; dolichocephalic. **long-headedness** the quality or state of being long-headed. **long hop** a ball bowled or thrown so that it makes a long flight after pitching or bouncing. **long-horned** *a.* having long horns; *long-horned beetle*, = LONGHORN 2; *long-horned grasshopper*, = *bush-cricket* s.v. CRICKET *n.*[1] **long hour**: indicated by any of the higher number of strokes on a clock etc. **longhouse** †(*a*) a privy, a lavatory; (*b*) a house of unusual length, *spec.* a long communal dwelling among certain peoples, as some N. American Indians and Indonesians. *long* HUNDREDWEIGHT. **long ink** *Printing*: of a consistency such that it can be drawn out. **long john** (*a*) *sing.* & (usu.) in *pl.* (*colloq.*) underpants with full-length legs; (*b*) (also w. caps.) a long coffee table (also *long john table*); (*c*) (*longjohn*) a tropical S. American tree of the knotgrass family, *Triplaris surinamensis*, so called from its long inflorescence. **long jump** an activity or athletic contest of jumping as far as possible along the ground in one leap from a running start. **long-jump** *v.i.* make or take part in a long jump. **long-jumper** a person who long-jumps. **Long Knife** (*a*) a knife with a long blade, esp. used as a weapon; *night of the long knives*: see NIGHT *n.*; (*b*) *N. Amer. Hist.* (a name given by N. American Indians to) White settlers, esp. of Virginia, or White soldiers, in Canada, *spec.* a citizen of the US, (freq. in *pl.*). **long-leaf pine** a pine of the southern US, *Pinus palustris*, with long leaves and cones. *long leg*: see LEG *n.* **long-legged** *a.* (*a*) having long legs; *fig.* speedy; (*b*) *Naut.* (of a ship) drawing a great deal of water. **long-legs** (*a*) *longshanks* (b) below; (*b*) = DADDY-*long-legs*. **long lens**: with a great focal length. **long-life** *a.* remaining usable or serviceable for an unusually long time. **long line** (*a*) a line of manuscript or type that runs across the page without columnar division; (*b*) in Old English verse, two half-lines considered as a unit; (*c*) (usu. *long-line*) a deep-sea fishing-line. **long-liner** (chiefly *N. Amer.*) a person who fishes with a long-line; a fishing vessel which uses long-lines. **long-lining** fishing with long-lines. **long-lugged** *a.* (*Sc.*) having long ears; *fig.* eager to listen to secrets or scandal. **long-lunged** *a.* = LONG-WINDED 2. **long manure** manure containing unclipped straw undecayed. **Long March** (*Hist.*) *the* year-long retreat of the Chinese Communists across SW China during the period of Nationalist government. **long mark** a macron (placed over a vowel letter to indicate long quantity). **long measure** linear measure, the measure of length (metres, miles, etc.). **long memory**: that retains the recollection of events for a long period. **long metre** (*a*) a hymn stanza of four lines each containing eight syllables; (*b*) a quatrain of iambic tetrameters with alternate lines rhyming. **long mirror** = *long glass* above. **long-moss** = *long-beard* (b) above. **long-nebbed** *a.* (*Sc.*) having a long nose; *fig.* curious, prying. **longneck** (*a*) an earthenware retort or still with a long neck; (*b*) a bird with a long neck, *esp.* a heron or a pintail duck; (*c*) *longneck clam*: see CLAM *n.*[2] 1(c). **long-necked** *a.* having a long neck; *long-necked clam* = *longneck* (c) above. **long nine** *Hist.* a kind of long cheap cigar. **long nose** (*a*) *slang* the thumb to the nose, as a gesture of mockery (chiefly in *make a long nose*); (*b*) (*long-nose*) any of various fishes having an elongated snout. **long-nosed** *a.* having a long nose; *long-nosed* POTOROO. **long odds** very unequal stakes or chances in betting. *long off*: see OFF *n. long on*: see ON *n. Long Parliament*: see PARLIAMENT *n. long pepper*: see PEPPER *n.* **long-persistence** *a.* designating a screen of a cathode-ray tube on which a spot remains luminous for some time after the beam has moved away. **long pig** [f. Polynesian name] human flesh as food. **long-pod** a variety of broad bean which produces a very long pod. **long price** a heavy cost; high odds in betting. *long primer*: see PRIMER *n.*[1] 3. **long pull** (*a*) *Printing* a pull on the bar of a wooden hand-press almost to its fullest extent; (*b*) a practice in public houses of giving overmeasure to attract custom. **long purples** *dial.* any of several plants with long spikes or racemes of purple flowers; *esp.* (*a*) early purple orchid, *Orchis mascula*; (*b*) purple loosestrife, *Lythrum salicaria*. **long purse** *colloq.* (a purse containing) plenty of money. **long rains** in tropical countries, the rainy season. **long-range** *a.* having a long range, of or pertaining to a long period of future time. *long rape*: see RAPE *n.*[3] 2. **long room** an assembly room in a private house or public building. **long rope** a skipping game using a rope of considerable length. *long rough dab*: see ROUGH *a.* **long run** (*a*) a long period of continuous presentation (of a play, a broadcast programme, etc.); (*b*) *in the long run*, in the end, over a long period of time, as the ultimate outcome (after all vicissitudes). **long-run** *a.* taken or considered in the long run. **long s** a lower-case form of the letter s, written or printed ſ, not in general use after the early 19th cent. *long sea*: see SEA *n.* **long service** prolonged service in one post, *esp.* (*Mil.*) enlistment for a long or the maximum period. **longshanks** (*a*) a tall or long-legged person, orig. *spec.* (**L-**) Edward I of England (1239–1307); (*b*) the black-winged stilt, *Himantopus himantopus*. **long ship** *Hist.* a ship accommodating a large number of rowers; a ship of war, a galley. **long-short** a long short story. **long short story** a short story of more than average length, a novella. **long shot** (*a*) a shot fired at a distance; a distant range; (*b*) something incredible or very unlikely; a far-fetched explanation; a wild guess; a bet laid against considerable odds; (*c*) a cinema or television shot which includes figures or scenery at a distance. **long sight** (*a*) capacity for seeing distant objects; (*b*) the defect of sight by which only comparatively distant objects are seen distinctly; hypermetropia. **long-sighted** *a.* (*a*) having long sight; unable to distinguish nearby objects clearly; hypermetropic; (*b*) *fig.* having great foresight; far-seeing. **long-sightedly** *adv.* in a long-sighted manner. **long-sightedness** the condition of being long-sighted. **long sixes** long candles, six of which weighed a pound. **long sleeve** a sleeve extending below the elbow, esp. fully to the wrist. **long-sleeved** *a.* having long sleeves. **long-sleever** *Austral. slang* a tall glass, a long drink. **long-spined** *a.* having long spines; *long-spined sea scorpion*: see SEA *n.* **long-splice** a splice without significant thickening of the rope at the join. **longspur** any of several N. American buntings of the genus *Calcarius*; LAPLAND *longspur*. **long-staple** *a.* & *n.* (designating) cotton having a long fibre. **longstop** *Cricket* (the position of) a fielder who stands behind the wicket-keeper to stop the balls that pass him or her; *fig.* a last resort in an emergency etc. **long straw** *Thatching* unclipped straw (esp. as opp. to reed). **long stroke** a piston or pump-rod stroke which is longer than the average. **long sufferance** *arch.* patient endurance of a provocation or trial. **long suit** *fig.* [f. sense 4b above] one's strong point. **long sweetening** *US* molasses or other liquid sweetening. **long-tackle** *Naut.* a light two-block tackle for hoisting sails etc. **long-term** *a.* & *adv.* (*a*) *adj.* lasting for or pertaining to a relatively long period of time; maturing or becoming effective only after a long period; (*b*) *adv.* over or at the end of a long period of time. **long-termer** a prisoner serving a long sentence. **long time** (advb.) (*a*) *a long time*, for a long time; also without *a* (*arch.* exc. *Jamaican* & in *long time no see* (colloq.) [joc. imitation of broken English], used as a greeting after prolonged separation); (*b*) *this long time*, for a long time down to the present. **long-time** *a.* that has been such for a long time; extending for a long time into the future, requiring a long time. **long-timer** = *long-termer* above. **long togs** *Naut.* clothes worn on shore. **Long Tom** (*a*) *Hist.* a gun of large size and long range; (*b*) a trough for washing gold-bearing deposits; (*c*) *Austral.* any marine fish of the family Belonidae, with elongated jaws; (*d*) *slang* a particularly high-powered telephoto camera lens. *long ton*: see TON *n.*[1] 4. **long tongue** *fig.* a capacity to talk a lot. **long-tongued** *a.* having much to say, loquacious, chattering, babbling. **long trousers**: reaching to the ankle. **long twelves** *Printing* (chiefly *Hist.*) a duodecimo imposition scheme with the forme arranged in two rows of six long narrow type pages (as opp. to the standard three rows of four shorter and broader pages). **long vacation**, (*colloq.*) **vac** the summer vacation of courts of law and universities, and similar institutions; a regular long holiday. **long verse** (*a*) = *long-line* (b) above; (*b*) hexametric verse. **long view(s)** consideration of remote effects; *take the long view*, have regard for more than current needs or concerns; plan for the future. **long waist** a low or deep waist of a dress or body. **long-waisted** *a.* having a long waist. **longwall** *n.*, *a.*, & *adv.* (*Mining*) (*a*) *n.* & *a.* (pertaining to or involving) a single long face worked (usu. mechanically) along its whole length; (*b*) *adv.* by the longwall method. **long wave** a wave of relatively long wavelength; *spec.* in *Broadcasting*, a radio wave with a wavelength between about one and ten kilometres. **long weekend** a weekend holiday of more than the usual length; *fig.* the period between the wars of 1914–18 and 1939–45. *long whist*: see WHIST *n.*[2] **long-wings** the swift. **long-wool** (*a*) long-stapled wool, suitable for combing or carding; (*b*) (usu. *longwool*) a sheep of a breed with long wool (LINCOLN *Longwool*). **long-woolled** *a.* (of a sheep) having long wool. **long word** (*colloq.* or *proverbial*) a word that indicates a long time. **long years** *rhet.* many years. (See also combs. of LONG *adv.*)

B *n.* **I** *absol.* **1** Much time; a long interval or period. (Passing into adv., having a comparative & superlative, & modifiable by advs. of degree). OE. **2** *The* long explanation or recital. Chiefly in *the long and the short of it*, the sum total or substance, the upshot. E16.

1 *Engineering* It will take . . ten times that long to get a train ready. E. O'NEILL Life at its longest is brief enough. B. PYM It seems to take so long to get everything.

II As count n. **3** A long note in music; a long flash or dash in Morse code etc.; a long syllable or vowel; a mark indicating that a vowel or (formerly) a note is long. LME. **4** *Archit.* Each of a series of long blocks placed alternately with short ones in a vertical line. M19. **5** A long vacation. M19. **6** In *pl.* a Long clothes. M19. **b** Long trousers. *colloq.* E20. **7** In *pl.* Long whist. *obs.* exc. *Hist.* M19. **8** *Comm.* **a** A person who has bought stocks, commodities, etc., in expectation of a coming scarcity and rise in price. L19. **b** In *pl.* Long-dated stocks. M20.

Phrases: **at (the) longest** on the longest estimate. **before long** before a long time has elapsed, soon, (also *before much longer* etc.). ERELONG. **for long** for a long time, esp. projecting into the future (also *for a little longer* etc.). **longs and shorts** (*a*) quantitative (esp. Latin or Greek) verses or versification; (*b*) *Archit.* (the style of masonry with) alternate short and long blocks in a vertical line. **that long** *colloq.* that length of time, (in neg. contexts) much time. *the long and the short of it*: see sense B.2 above.

longish *a.* somewhat long E17.

long /lɒŋ/ *a.*[2] Now *arch.* & *dial.* ME. [Aphet. f. ALONG *a.*[1] Cf. LONG *v.*[2]] *long of* (†*long on*), attributable to, owing to, on account of, because of.

long /lɒŋ/ *v.*[1] [OE *langian* = OS *langon*, MDu. *langen* seem long, desire, extend, offer (Du. *langen* offer, present), OHG *langēn* (impers.) (G *langen* reach, extend, suffice), ON *langa* (impers. & pers.) desire, long, f. Gmc, f. base of LONG *a.*[1]] †**I 1** *v.i.* & *t.* Lengthen. OE–L15.

II †**2** *v.i. impers. me longs* (*longeth*), etc., I have etc. a yearning desire. Foll. by *after, to, to do.* OE–LME. **3** *v.i.* Have a yearning desire; wish earnestly. Foll. by *for* (*after*), *to do.* ME. †**b** Foll. by adv. or advb. phr. w. a vb of motion implied: long to go. ME–M16.

3 E. L. DOCTOROW She longed to have her ambitions aroused. M. AMIS He longed for him to be taken into care.

long /lɒŋ/ *v.*[2]*i.* Now *arch. rare.* Also **'long**. ME. [f. as LONG *a.*[2]; later taken as abbrev. of BELONG *v.*] **1** Be appropriate; pertain, refer or relate, *to, unto*; belong *to, unto* as a member, part, inhabitant, dependent, etc. ME. †**b** Be of concern *to* (a person); be fitting *to.* LME–M16. †**2** Foll. by *to, unto*: be the property or rightful possession of; = BELONG *v.* 3. ME–L19.

long /lɒŋ/ *adv.* [OE *lange, longe* = OFris. *lang(e, long(e*, OS, OHG *lango* (Du. *lang*, G *lange*), f. Gmc base of LONG *a.*[1]] **1** For or during a long time; in *compar.* and *superl.* or preceded by advs. of comparison (*as, how, so, thus, too*, etc.), for or during the specified or implied length of time. OE. **2** *pred.* after *be* (passing into adj. & n.). (Occupied or delayed for) a long time. Foll. by *doing, in* (†*of*, †*a*) *doing*, (colloq.) *absol.* ME. **3** At, from, or to a distant point of time (usu. followed by *after, before*, (arch.) *ere, since* (advs., conjs., or preps.)); in *compar.* (chiefly preceded by advs. of degree, as *any, no, much, a little*, etc.), after the specified or implied point of time. ME. **4** Subjoined to n. phrs expressing duration: throughout the length of (the period specified or implied). ME. **5** At or to a great or a specified distance in space; far. Now chiefly *Sport*, of a ball etc. ME.

1 J. BUCHAN 'Have you known her long?' I asked. . . 'Since she was a child.' J. MITCHELL A series of . . kindly housekeepers (none of whom stayed very long). D. PRATER He . . would long remember their talk. N. GORDIMER I don't know how much longer I'll . . keep on that job. 2 SIR W. SCOTT They were not long of discovering the *tête-du-pont*. G. B. SHAW I shan't be long (He goes out). 3 SCOTT FITZGERALD I'll have a new score on Broadway long before you've finished. G. ORWELL He had long grown used to sleeping . . on his face. G. VIDAL The roof of the temple had long since fallen in. S. COOPER By the time he . . found what he was looking for, his shirt was long dry. 4 B. JOWETT He was . . working all his life long. E. O'NEILL Unable to bear the thick silence a minute longer. 5 W. MORRIS The fisher sits . . with a rod that reaches long.

Phrases: *all (the) day* or *night long*: see DAY *n.*, NIGHT *n.* **as** or **so long as**, (*colloq.*) **long as** during the whole time that; provided that, if only. *long live*: see LIVE *v.* **no longer** not now as formerly. **not be long for this world** have only a short time to live. **so long** *colloq.* goodbye, *au revoir. so long as*: see *as long as* above.

Comb. (not always clearly distinguishable f. combs. of LONG *a.*[1]): **long-acting** *a.* (*Pharm.*) having effects that last a long time; **long-ago** *a.* & *n.* (belonging to) the distant past; **long-continued** *a.* continued or that has continued for a long period or space; **long-drawn** *a.* (*a*) prolonged to a great or inordinate length (also *long-drawn-out*); (*b*) (chiefly *poet.*) having great longitudinal extension; **long-fed** *a.* (of cattle) fed a special diet to complete fattening for a long period before slaughter; **long-keeping** *a.* able to be kept for a long time; **long-lasting** *a.* that lasts for a long time; **long-living** *a.* that lives for a long time; **long-play** *a.* = *long-playing* below; **long-player** a long-playing record; **long-playing** *a.* that plays for a long time; *spec.* designating or pertaining to a microgroove gramophone record designed to be played at 33⅓ revolutions per minute and lasting for about 10 to 30 minutes on each side; abbrev. *LP*; **long-running** *a.* continuing for a relatively long period of time; *spec.* (of a play) having a large number of consecutive performances.

-long /lɒŋ/ *suff.* Also †**-longs**. [f. LONG *a.*[1]] Forming advs. and adjs. w. the senses '-wise', 'foremost', (= -LING[2]), as *headlong, sidelong*, and 'lasting or throughout the specified time', as *daylong, life-long*. (Earliest in ENDLONG.)

longaeval, **-aevous** *adjs.* vars. of LONGEVAL, -EVOUS.

longan /ˈlɒŋg(ə)n/ *n.* M18. [Chin. *lóngyǎn* lit. 'dragon's eye', f. *lóng* dragon + *yǎn* eye.] The edible fruit of an evergreen tree, *Dimocarpus longan* (family Sapindaceae), cultivated in China and SE Asia; the tree itself.

longanimity /lɒŋgəˈnɪmɪti/ *n.* Now *rare.* LME. [Late L *longanimitas, -tat-*, f. *longanimus*, f. *longus* LONG *a.*[1] + *animus* mind, after Gk *makrothumia*: see -ITY.] Long-suffering; forbearance or patience under provocation etc.

longanimous /lɒŋˈganɪməs/ *a.* (*rare*) long-suffering; enduring, patient: E17.

long-distance /lɒŋˈdɪst(ə)ns/ *a.*, *n.*, *adv.*, & *v.* L19. [f. LONG *a.*[1] + DISTANCE *n.*] **A** *adj.* To or from a long distance; (of a weather forecast) long-range; (of a telephone call, public transport, etc.) between distant places. L19. **B** *n.* A long-distance telephone (call); a race distance of the longest category, now usu. 10,000 metres or 6 miles and longer. E20. **C** *adv.* By long-distance telephone. M20. **D** *v.t.* Make a long-distance telephone call to (a person); report long-distance. M20.

longe *n.*, *v.* vars. of LUNGE *n.*[1], *v.*[2]

longer /ˈlɒŋə/ *n.*[1] *rare.* LME. [f. LONG *v.*[1] + -ER[1].] A person who longs for someone or something.

longer /ˈlɒŋə/ *n.*[2] *Canad.* L18. [f. LONG *a.*[1] + -ER[1].] A long pole or piece of timber used for fencing, a fishing stage, etc.

longeron /ˈlɒndʒərɒn/ *n.* E20. [Fr.] *Aeronaut.* A frame member running lengthways along a fuselage.

longeval /lɒnˈdʒiːv(ə)l/ *a.* Also **-aeval**. L16. [f. L *longaevus* (see next) + -AL[1].] Long-lived, long-lasting.

longevity /lɒnˈdʒɛvɪti/ *n.* E17. [Late L *longaevitas, -tat-*, f. L *longaevus*, f. *longus* LONG *a.*[1] + *aevum* age: see -ITY.] Long life; long duration of existence.

longevous /lɒnˈdʒiːvəs/ *a.* Now *rare.* Also **-aevous**. L17. [f. L *longaevus* (see prec.) + -OUS.] Long-lived; living or having lived to a great age.

longhorn /ˈlɒŋhɔːn/ *n.* M19. [f. LONG *a.*[1] + HORN *n.*] **1** (An animal of) a breed of beef cattle, often reddish, with long curved horns. M19. **2** In full *longhorn beetle*. Any of numerous usu. elongate beetles of the family Cerambycidae, having very long, slender, backwardly flexed antennae, and found worldwide esp. in woodland. M19. **3** = *long-eared owl* s.v. LONG *a.*[1] M19. **4** In full *longhorn grasshopper*. = *bush-cricket* s.v. CRICKET *n.*[1] L19.

1 TEXAS *longhorn*.

longi- /ˈlɒndʒi/ *comb. form* of L *longus* LONG *a.*[1]: see -I-.

longi'pennate *a.* long-winged M19.

longicorn /ˈlɒndʒɪkɔːn/ *a.* & *n.* M19. [f. mod.L *Longicornia* former taxonomic name, f. L *longus* LONG *a.*[1] + -I- + L *cornu* horn.] (Designating or pertaining to) a longhorn beetle; = CERAMBYCID.

longie /ˈlʌŋi/ *n. Sc.* E19. [Norn *longvi* f. ON *langvi* rel. to LOOM *n.*[3] (cf. Norw. *lomvi*).] The common guillemot, *Uria aalge*.

longiloquence /lɒnˈdʒɪləkw(ə)ns/ *n. rare.* M19. [f. LONGI-, after BREVILOQUENCE.] Speaking at great length.

longimanous /lɒnˈdʒɪmənəs/ *a. rare.* M17. [f. late L *longimanus*, f. *longus* LONG *a.*[1] + *manus* hand: see -OUS.] Long-handed. Formerly also *fig.*, far-reaching.

†**longimetry** *n.* L17–L18. [f. LONGI- after ALTIMETRY.] The art or process of measuring distances.

longing /ˈlɒŋɪŋ/ *n.* OE. [f. LONG *v.*[1] + -ING[1].] The action of LONG *v.*[1]; (a) yearning desire. (Foll. by *for, after, to do.*)

OCEANIC *longing. save one's longing*: see SAVE *v.*

longing /ˈlɒŋɪŋ/ *a.* E16. [f. LONG *v.*[1] + -ING[2].] That longs for someone or something; characterized by yearning desire.

longingly *adv.* in a longing manner, with yearning desire LME. **longingness** *n.* (*rare*) M16.

longinquity /lɒnˈdʒɪŋkwɪti/ *n.* Now *rare.* M16. [L *longinquitas, -tat-*, f. *longinquus* distant, f. *longus* LONG *a.*[1]: see -ITY.] **1** Long distance; remoteness. M16. **2** Remoteness of time, long continuance. E17.

longitude /ˈlɒndʒɪtjuːd, ˈlɒŋgɪ-/ *n.* LME. [L *longitudo, -din-*, f. *longus* LONG *a.*[1]: see -TUDE. Cf. (O)Fr. *longitude*.] **I 1 a** Length, longitudinal extent. Formerly also, tallness, height. Now chiefly *joc.* LME. **b** Length of time; long continuance. Now *rare.* E17.

II *techn.* (opp. LATITUDE). **2** *Geogr.* The angular distance of any place on the earth's surface, east or west of a standard meridian (e.g. that of Greenwich), measured in degrees up to 180° east or west, or in units of time (1 hour = 15°); distance east or west measured as the angle between two meridians. Also (*esp.* in *Astron.*), angular distance measured from a similar line of reference, e.g. on the surface of a celestial object. LME. **3** *Astron.* Angular distance measured eastward on the ecliptic from the vernal equinoctial point to a circle at right angles to the ecliptic through a given point. LME.

2 *galactic longitude, heliographic longitude*, etc. 3 *geocentric longitude, heliocentric longitude*, etc.

longitudinal /lɒndʒɪ'tjuːdɪn(ə)l, lɒŋɡɪ-/ *a.* & *n.* LME. [f. prec. + -AL[1].] A *adj.* 1 Extending or proceeding in the direction of the length of a body; running lengthwise. LME. b *Physics*. Of a vibration, wave, etc.: involving displacement parallel to the direction of propagation. M19. 2 Of or pertaining to length as a dimension; (of extent) in length. M18. 3 Of or pertaining to longitude; measured from east to west. L19. 4 Involving information about an individual or group at different times throughout a long period. M20.

1 C. DARWIN Several of the species are beautifully coloured with longitudinal stripes. R. F. CHAPMAN Running through the neck are longitudinal muscles. 2 W. COBBETT The number of longitudinal inches of the foot measure. 3 *Scholarly Publishing* The accurate relocation of the longitudinal position of France. 4 B. J. UNDERWOOD We are interested in the longitudinal aspects, i.e., how they developed.

B *n.* †1 *Anat.* Either of two muscles of the epigastrium. Only in M16. 2 A longitudinal member; *spec.* (*a*) in iron and steel ships, a plate parallel or nearly so to the vertical keel; (*b*) a longeron, *esp.* one in an airship. M19.

¶As adj. opp. *transverse*.

longitudinally *adv.* in a longitudinal direction; in the direction of the length of an object; lengthways: E18.

long-lived /lɒŋ'lɪvd/ *a.* LME. [Orig. f. LONG *a.*[1] + *live* infl. form of LIFE *n.* + -ED[1], later also taken as f. LONG *adv.* + *lived* pa. pple of LIVE *v.*] Having a long life or existence; living or lasting a long time, durable.

longlivedness *n.* longevity L19.

longly /'lɒŋli/ *adv.* Now *rare*. ME. [f. LONG *a.*[1] + -LY[2].] †1 For a long while. ME–E17. 2 At considerable length, using many words. ME. 3 To a considerable length (in space). M17.

longness /'lɒŋnɪs/ *n.* Now *rare*. OE. [f. LONG *a.*[1] + -NESS.] Length; long continuance.

Longobard /'lɒŋɡəbɑːd/ *n.* & *a.* LME. [Late L *Longobardus*: see LOMBARD *n.*[1] & *a.* Cf. LANGOBARD.] *Hist.* A *n.* Pl. **-bards, -bardi** /-bɑːdiː/. = LOMBARD *n.*[1] I. LME. B *adj.* Of or pertaining to the (Germanic) Lombards. M19.

Longo'bardian *a.* & *n.* M19. **Longo'bardic** *a.* M19.

longo intervallo /ˌlɒŋɡəʊ ɪntə'valəʊ/ *adv. phr.* L17. [L = at a distance.] At some remove; in spite of the gulf between.

†-longs *suff.* var. of -LONG.

longshore /'lɒŋʃɔː/ *a.* E19. [Aphet. f. *alongshore*: see ALONG *a.*[2], *prep.*, & *adv.*] 1 Existing on, frequenting, or directed along a shore; found or employed along a shore. E19. 2 *Physical Geogr.* Moving, taking place, or laid down more or less parallel to a shore. M19.

Comb.: **longshoreman** a person who frequents or is employed along a shore; a landsman engaged in loading and unloading cargoes, or in fishing for oysters etc., along a shore.

longshoring *n.* the type of work done at a port; the occupation of a longshoreman: E20.

longsome /'lɒŋs(ə)m/ *a.* Now *dial.* & *arch.* OE. [f. LONG *a.*[1] + -SOME[1]. Cf. OS, OHG *langsam* (Du. *langzaam*, G *langsam*).] Long, lengthy; long-lasting; *esp.* tediously long.

longsomely *adv.* LME. **longsomeness** *n.* OE.

long standing /lɒŋ 'standɪŋ, *as attrib. adj.* 'lɒŋstandɪŋ/ *n. phr.* & *a.* As adj. usu. **long-standing**. M16. [f. LONG *a.*[1] + STANDING *n.* As adj. partly attrib. use of n., partly f. LONG *adv.* + STANDING *a.*] A *n. phr.* Continuance for a long time in a settled and recognized position, rank, etc.; (now *rare*) an instance of this. Chiefly in *of long standing*. M16. B *adj.* Of long standing; that has existed for a long time, not recent. E19.

long-suffering /lɒŋ'sʌf(ə)rɪŋ, *as attrib. adj.* 'lɒŋsʌf(ə)rɪŋ/ *n.* & *a.* E16. [f. LONG *a.*[1] + SUFFERING *n.* As adj. largely f. LONG *adv.* + SUFFERING *a.*] A *n.* Patient endurance of provocation or trial. E16. B *adj.* Enduring provocation or trial with patience. M16.

longsufferingly *adv.* L19.

long-tail /'lɒŋteɪl/ *n.* L16. [f. LONG *a.*[1] + TAIL *n.*[1]] 1 A long-tailed animal; formerly, a dog or horse with the tail uncut; a long-tailed bird, *spec.* (*a*) the long-tailed duck, *Clangula hyemalis*; (*b*) the white-tailed tropic bird, *Phaethon lepturus*; (*c*) *dial.* a pheasant. L16. 2 A native of the county of Kent in SE England (in allusion to the jocular imputation that the people of Kent had tails). Long *obs.* exc. *dial.* E17.

Comb.: **long-tail pair** *Electronics* orig., a pair of matched valves connected to a common large resistor; now usu., a pair of matched bipolar transistors with their emitters so connected.

long-tailed /'lɒŋteɪld/ *a.* L15. [f. as prec. + -ED[2].] 1 Having a long tail. L15. 2 Of a word: having a long termination. Formerly also (of a speech etc.), long-winded. *joc.* M16.

Special collocations: **long-tailed duck** a marine duck, *Clangula hyemalis*, of Arctic regions, the male of which has elongated tail feathers. *long-tailed jaeger*: see JAEGER *n.*[2] *long-tailed mag*: see MAG *n.*[1] 2. **long-tailed pair** *Electronics* = LONG-TAIL *pair*. *long-tailed* SKUA. *long-tailed tailor-bird*: see TAILOR *n.* **long-tailed tit** any of several small tits of the family Aegithalidae, esp. *Aegithalos caudatus*.

longueur /lɔ̃gœːr (*pl. same*), lɔ̃(ŋ)'gɜː/ *n.* L18. [Fr. = length.] A lengthy or tedious passage of writing, music, etc.; a tedious stretch of time.

longwards /'lɒŋwədz/ *adv.* L20. [f. LONG *a.*[1] + -WARDS.] *Physics*. Towards longer wavelengths; on the long-wavelength side *of*.

Also **longward** *adv.* L20.

longways /'lɒŋweɪz/ *prep.* & *adv.* M16. [f. LONG *a.*[1] + -WAYS.] †A *prep.* In the direction of the length of, along. M16–M17. B *adv.* In the direction of the length of a thing; longwise, lengthways; longitudinally. L16.

long-winded /lɒŋ'wɪndɪd/ *a.* L16. [f. LONG *a.*[1] + WIND *n.*[1] + -ED[2].] 1 Capable of continuing in action for a long time without being out of breath; long-breathed. L16. 2 (Of a person) given to tedious lengthiness in speech or writing, or to dilatoriness in action; (of speech etc.) tediously long. L16.

long-windedly *adv.* M19. **long-windedness** *n.* M19.

longwise /'lɒŋwʌɪz/ *adv.* M16. [f. LONG *a.*[1] + -WISE.] Lengthwise, longitudinally, longways.

†longwort *n.* var. of LUNGWORT.

lonicera /lɒ'nɪs(ə)rə/ *n.* L18. [mod.L (see below), f. Adam *Lonicer* (1528–86), Ger. botanist.] Any of various climbing shrubs of the genus *Lonicera* (family Caprifoliaceae), which includes the common honeysuckle, *L. periclymenum*; *esp.* a dense evergreen shrub, *L. nitidum*, much used as hedging.

Lonk /lɒŋk/ *n.* M19. [Dial. var. of 1st syll. of *Lancashire*.] (An animal of) a variety of large mountain sheep which originated in Lancashire or Yorkshire in northern England; the wool of such sheep.

lonnin(g) *n.* var. of LOANING.

Lonsdale belt /lɒnzdeɪl 'belt/ *n. phr.* E20. [The title of Hugh Cecil Lowther (1857–1944), fifth earl of *Lonsdale*, who presented the first one.] Any of various belts conferred on professional boxing champions of the UK.

lontar /'lɒntɑː/ *n.* E19. [Malay.] = PALMYRA. Also, a manuscript written on leaves of this palm.

loo /luː/ *n.*[1] L17. [Abbrev. of LANTERLOO.] 1 A round card-game in which a player who fails to take a trick or breaks any of the laws of the game is required to pay a certain sum to a pool; the fact of having to pay a sum to the pool at loo; the sum deposited in the pool. L17. 2 A party playing at loo; a social gathering for playing loo. Now *rare*. M18.

Comb.: **loo-table** a round table for playing loo on or resembling one for this purpose.

loo /luː/ *n.*[2] *obs.* exc. *Hist.* L17. [f. as LOUP *n.*[2]] More fully *loo mask*. A half-mask covering the upper part of the face, worn by women in the 17th cent.

loo /luː/ *n.*[3] L19. [Hind. *lūh*, *lū*, also *lūk(h)*, f. Skt *lūkṣa*, Prakrit *lūha*, *lukkha* dry.] In Bihar and the Punjab: a hot dust-laden wind.

loo /luː/ *n.*[4] *colloq.* M20. [Origin unkn.] A water-closet, a lavatory.

loo *n.*[5], *a.* var. of LEW *n.*, *a.*

loo /luː/ *v.*[1]*t.* Long *obs.* exc. *dial.* Pa. t. & pple **looed, loo'd.** M17. [Aphet. f. HALLOO *v.*] Incite by shouting 'halloo!'; urge *on* by shouts.

loo /luː/ *v.*[2]*t.* Pa. t. & pple **looed,** (usu.) **loo'd.** L17. [f. LOO *n.*[1]] 1 Subject to a forfeit at the game of loo. L17. 2 *fig.* Defeat, thwart. Now *dial.* E18.

loo *v.*[3] var. of LEW *v.*

loo /luː/ *int.* E17. [Aphet. f. HALLOO *int.*] Inciting a dog to the chase; = HALLOO *int.*

looby /'luːbi/ *n.* Now chiefly *dial.* LME. [Origin uncertain: perh. rel. to LOB *n.*[1]] A lazy hulking fellow; a lout; an awkward, stupid, clownish person.

†loobily *a.* loutish, awkward, clumsy: M17–L18.

looch *n.* var. of LOHOCH.

looey /'luːi/ *n. N. Amer. slang.* Also **looie.** E20. [Abbrev. of LIEUTENANT (in N. Amer. pronunc.): see -Y[6], -IE.] A lieutenant.

loof /luːf/ *n.*[1] *Sc.* & *north.* LME. [ON *lófi* = Goth. *lofa*.] The palm of the hand.

loof /luːf/ *n.*[2] Now *rare*. M19. [Arab. *lūf*: see LOOFAH.] = LOOFAH.

loofah /'luːfə/ *n.* Also **luffa** /'lʌfə/. L19. [Arab. *lūfa* the plant, *lūf* the species.] A coarse sponge made from the bleached vascular system of the fruit of a tropical gourd, *Luffa aegyptiaca*, used to cleanse and scrub the skin. Also, the gourd itself.

loogan /'luːɡ(ə)n/ *n. arch. US slang.* E20. [Origin unkn.] A stupid or despicable person.

looie *n.* var. of LOOEY.

look /lʊk/ *n.* ME. [f. the vb.] 1 The action or an act of looking; a glance of the eyes; a particular direction of the eyes in order to look at someone or something (foll. by *at*, for the purpose of examining or considering); *transf.* an examination, a consideration, (foll. by *at*). ME. 2 *sing.* & in *pl.* Personal appearance or aspect; an expression in the eyes or on the face; (now usu. in *pl.*) an impression given by a person's general appearance; in *pl.* sometimes *spec.* good looks. LME. 3 The appearance of an inanimate or immaterial thing, esp. as expressive of its quality or nature; a way in which a thing appears. M16. b An appearance, style, or effect (usu. of a specified kind) of dress, toilette, or decoration. M20.

1 A. LOOS Mons. Broussard . . took a good look at us. V. WOOLF The hat she stuck on without giving a look in the glass. K. TENNANT Then she saw me . . and if looks could have killed! D. EDEN 'What are you doing with that torch?' 'Just having a look round.' B. MONTGOMERY The whole question of mobilisation requires a new look. W. WHARTON She gives me a couple of long looks. 2 J. GALSWORTHY The moustache, which imparted a somewhat military look to his face. RADCLYFFE HALL She had looks, too; he thought her a lovely creature. C. POTOK The look of surprise was gone from his face. R. L. FOX A venerable old man with a look of Homer. W. MAXWELL I studied the look in his hazel eyes. 3 E. WAUGH By the look of them, they were . . cheap cigars. K. AMIS The table had . . a cheap, hasty look. b C. ACHEBE The crew . . aspire to the military look. *Hairdo Ideas* If you are considering a longer look, here's how to grow your hair.

Phrases: *dirty look*: see DIRTY *a.* **for the look of the thing** *colloq.* for the sake of appearances. *good looks*: see GOOD *a.* **have a look of** resemble vaguely, remind the spectator of the appearance of (a person or thing). *new look*: see NEW *a.* **not like the look of** find (a situation etc.) disconcerting or alarming. *throw a look*: see THROW *v.* *wet look*: see WET *a.*

look /lʊk/ *v.* [OE *lōcian* = OS *lōkon*, MDu. *loeken*, f. WGmc, rel. to OHG *luogēn* (G dial. *lugen*) see, look, spy.] I Direct one's sight. 1 a *v.i.* Give a certain direction to one's sight; use one's ability to see; direct one's eyes to some person or object (foll. by *at*, (arch.) *on*, *upon*); occas. (now *colloq.*), give a look of surprise, stare; make a visual search or examination. Also of the eye: be directed to some person or object. OE. b *v.i.* Direct or apply one's mind; turn or fix one's attention or regard. (Foll. by *at*, (arch.)

on, upon.) OE. **c** *v.i.* In *imper.* Demanding attention or expostulating. Also *look you*, (arch.) *look ye* (repr. pop. speech *look'ee*), (more brusque) *look here*. See also LOOKIT, LOOKY. OE. **d** *v.t.* Direct (a look etc.) with the eyes; express by a look or glance, or by one's countenance; show or threaten by one's looks. L16. **2** *v.t.* Take care, make sure, see, *that* or *how* something is done (*arch.*); use one's sight to ascertain or observe (now *spec.* at a glance) *who, what, how, whether*, etc. Formerly also, consider, ascertain, *who, when, whether*, etc.; try *if* something can be done etc. OE. †**3** *v.t.* Take care of, keep, guard, watch over, preserve in safety; observe (a day). OE–LME. **4** *v.t.* (Chiefly synonymous w. *v.i.* w. prep.) Look at or towards; view, inspect, examine visually or (formerly) mentally; (now *rare*) bring by one's looks into a certain place or condition; search for, seek out. Now *dial.* exc. in *look a person in the eye* or *face* & in certain phrs. (see below). ME. †**b** Consult or refer to (an author, a book, or a place in a text); search for (a word etc.) in a book of reference. ME–E19. **5** *v.t.* Expect *to do*, †*that*, †*a thing*; intend, seek, try, *to do*. Formerly also, wait for the time *when*, be curious to see *how, whether*, etc. E16.

1a G. BERKELEY When we look only with one eye. OED Yes, you may look! W. S. MAUGHAM Though the police looked with care, they had discovered no fingerprints. E. O'NEILL They'd run over you as soon as look at you. J. C. POWYS Resplendently dressed ladies looked significantly at each other. C. ISHERWOOD Looking grimly into the mirror. B. RUBENS He looked straight ahead of him. M. SARTON Go into the study and look at TV. E. WELTY Roy looked from one man to the other. V. S. NAIPAUL I liked to look; I noticed everything. **b** SHAKES. *Haml.* He that made us with such large discourse, Looking before and after. M. PATTISON The . . manner of looking at things varies. **c** R. CROMPTON 'Look here!' began one outlaw in righteous indignation. I. MURDOCH Look, there isn't anything to say, is there? **d** J. THOMSON They . . sigh'd, and look'd unutterable Things. A. E. HOUSMAN Look your last at me, For I come home no more. A. CHRISTIE Poirot looked a question. The lady explained. **2** SHELLEY When I call, Look ye obey the masters. J. H. NEWMAN He glanced from one article to another, looking who were the University-preachers. **4** SHAKS. *Cymb.* Thou hast look'd thyself into my grace. A. RAMSAY He frown'd and look'd his watch. G. NORTH I was looking the sheep when the station rang. **5** S. DANIEL His fortune gives him more than he could looke. A. E. HOUSMAN Two lovers looking to be wed.

II Have a certain appearance. **6** *v.i.* (In some uses as copular vb.) Have the appearance of being; seem to the sight or the mind. Foll. by n. or adj. compl., inf., adv. (now chiefly *well, ill*, or indefinite in *how*). ME.

6 *Manchester Examiner* Miss Anderson looked the part to perfection. J. CONRAD She doesn't look just a girl. I. MURDOCH He remained . . , looking the picture of health. J. BETJEMAN A gun-emplacement . . Looks older than the hill fort. P. CAMPBELL Calais to Troyes looked about 250 miles. E. REVELEY They even looked alike, both tall willowy . . types. P. FERGUSON It wasn't often that Lily looked beaten. A. BROOKNER How do you think she's looking? *good-looking, ill-looking*, etc.

III Have an outlook, face a particular way. **7** *v.i.* Have or afford a particular outlook; face or turn (in a particular direction); face, front, or be turned *towards, into, on to*, etc. Cf. *look out* (c) below. M16. **8** *v.i.* Show a tendency; tend, point, (in a particular direction). Formerly also (*rare*), tend or promise *to do*. E17.

7 P. V. PRICE A vineyard that looks south . . will give wines that smile. **8** P. GREG All the facts look the other way.

Phrases etc.: **here's looking at you**, (*arch.*) **towards you** *colloq.*: used as a toast. *look a gift-horse in the mouth*: see GIFT *n.* *look alive*: see ALIVE 4. *look a person in the eye, the face*: see EYE *n.*, FACE *n.* **look as if** or (*colloq.*) **though** have an appearance suggesting the belief that; freq. *impers.* in *it looks as if, it looked as if*, etc. *look babies*: see BABY *n.* 3. *look big*: see BIG *adv.* *look daggers*: see DAGGER *n.*[1] **look down one's nose at** be scornful or dismissive of, feel oneself to be superior to. *look for trouble*: see TROUBLE *n.* *look good*: see GOOD *a.* **look like** (*a*) have the appearance of being; seem to be; (*b*) give promise of (esp. *doing*), threaten, show a likelihood of; usu. *impers.* in *it looks like, it looked like*, etc. *look lively*: see LIVELY *a.* 4. *look one's age*: see AGE *n.* 1. **look oneself** appear to be in one's usual health. *look on the bright side*: see BRIGHT *a.* 1b. **look sharp** †(*a*) keep strict watch; (*b*) bestir oneself briskly, lose no time. *look sick*: see SICK *a.* *look small*: see SMALL *a.* **look the other way** ignore what one should notice. *look the part*: see PART *n.* †**look what** whatever. **look what you've done!** *colloq.*: rebuking a person immediately after an action. **look who's here!** *colloq.*: expr. surprise or pleasure at an arrival. *look who's talking*: see TALK *v.* **not know which way to look** be embarrassed. *way of looking at it* (or *things*): see WAY *n.*

With advs. in specialized senses: **look about** be on the watch, be on the lookout; make a search *for*; let one's eyes rove. **look around** look about, look round (*for*). **look back** (*a*) turn and look at something in the direction from which one is going or from which one's face is turned; (*b*) direct the mind to something that is past, think on the past, (foll. by *into, on, upon, to*); (*c*) *colloq.* show signs of reversal, decline, or interrupted progress, be regretful or half-hearted about an enterprise one has begun, (usu. in neg. contexts). **look down** (*a*) foll. by *on, upon*: hold in contempt, scorn, consider oneself superior to; (*b*) *Comm.* tend downwards in price; (*c*) *arch.* quell or overcome by one's looks. **look forward to** await (an expected event), esp. with pleasure. **look in** (*a*) enter a room etc. for the purpose of seeing something; make a short call or visit (foll. by *on, upon* a person); (*b*) *colloq.* watch a television programme. **look on** direct one's looks towards an object in contemplation or observation; *esp.* be a mere spectator (and not a participator in the action). **look out** (*a*) look from within a building etc. to the outside; put one's head out of an aperture, e.g. a window, to look; (*b*) be on the watch, keep one's eyes open, (*for*); exercise vigilance, be prepared *for*, have care *for*; (*c*) have or afford an outlook (*on, over*, etc.); †(*d*) make a brief excursion; (*e*) find by looking, select by inspection. **look over** *v.phr.t.* cast one's eyes over (a person or thing); scrutinize; inspect one by one or part by part. **look round** look about in every direction; look in another direction; go round looking at the features of a place; examine the possibilities etc. with a view to deciding on a course of action; search about *for*. **look sideways** look (*at*) or regard furtively or improperly; *spec.* glance amorously or suspiciously. **look through** (*a*) *v.phr.t.* give (a person) a searching look or glance; examine or survey exhaustively or successively; †(*b*) become visible or obvious. **look up** (*a*) raise the eyes, turn the face upward; *look up to* (fig.), have a feeling of respect or veneration for; †(*b*) cheer up, take courage, be cheerful; (*c*) improve, esp. in price or prosperity; (*d*) search for; now *esp.* search for (something) in a dictionary or work of reference, among papers, etc., consult (a book etc.) in order to gain information; (*e*) *colloq.* call on, go to visit (a person), esp. for the first time or after loss of contact; (*f*) *arch.* direct vigilance to; (*g*) *look up and down*, scrutinize the appearance of (a person) from head to foot. †**look upon** = *look on* above.

With preps. in specialized senses: **look about —** turn one's eyes to or make searches in various parts of (a room etc.); go about observing in (a country, town, etc.); *look about one*, turn one's eyes or attention to surrounding objects, consider or take account of one's position and circumstances. **look after —** (*a*) follow with the eye; look in the direction of (a person or thing departing); *fig.* think regretfully of (something past); †(*b*) anticipate with desire or fear; look forward to; (*c*) seek for, demand (qualities); (*d*) concern oneself with; attend to, take care of; (*e*) *rare* keep watch over. **look against —** look and be dazzled by. **look around —** = *look round* below. **look at —** (*a*) take or accept (a thing), become involved in, find (a person) attractive, show sexual interest in, (usu. in neg. contexts); (*b*) *to look at*, in respect of appearance; *not* MUCH *to look at*; (*c*) *to look at —* (colloq.), judging from the appearance of —; (see also senses 1a, b above). **look for —** (*a*) expect, hope for, anticipate, be on the watch for; (*b*) seek, search for; *look for a needle in a haystack, a bottle of hay*: see NEEDLE *n.*; (*c*) *Sc.* look at, observe. **look into —** (*a*) direct one's sight to the interior of, examine the inside of, consult (a book etc.) in a cursory manner; (*b*) examine (a matter) minutely; investigate (a question); (*c*) enter (a house etc.) for a few moments in passing. **look on —** †(*a*) pay regard to; hold in esteem, respect; (*b*) regard or consider *as*; (*c*) regard with a specified expression or feeling; (see also senses 1a, b above). **look over —** (*a*) peruse or inspect cursorily; †(*b*) ignore, leave out of consideration; (*c*) *arch.* overlook, pardon, (a fault); (*d*) *Sc.* look after, take care of. **look round —** (*a*) inspect, scrutinize, search; go round looking at the features of (a place); (*b*) put one's head round (a door etc.) to look. **look through —** (*a*) direct one's sight through (an aperture, a transparent body, or something having interstices); pretend not to see (freq. *look right* or *straight through*); penetrate the dishonesty or pretence of; †(*b*) be visible through; (*c*) direct one's view over the whole of or to every one of; peruse cursorily from end to end; glance through (a book etc.). **look to —** (*a*) direct one's attention to; select for consideration; (in biblical translations) regard with favour; (*b*) attend to, take care of; concern oneself with guarding, preserving, or improving; *look to it*, be careful, beware, take care or see *that*; *look to one's hits*: see HIT *n.*; *look to one's laurels*: see LAUREL *n.* 2; (*c*) keep watch over; (*d*) direct one's expectations to; rely on (a person etc.) *for* something; look forward to, expect, count on, aim at. **look unto —** *arch.* = *look to* above. **look upon —** = *look on* above; (see also senses 1a, b above).

Comb. (partly f. the n.): **look-ahead** *n.* & *a.* (designating) an action of judging what can happen or is likely to happen in the (immediate) future; **look-and-say** *n.* & *a.* (designating) a method of teaching reading by identifying each word as a whole (as opp. to treating a word as a series of separate letters); **look-around, -round** an inspection, a scrutiny, a search; **look-on** *a.* designating a fishing net pulled up as a test of the condition of others. **look-through** *Paper-making* the appearance of paper when held up to light.

look-alike /ˈlʊkəlʌɪk/ *n.* & *a.* M20. [f. LOOK *v.* + ALIKE *a.*] **A** *n.* A person or thing closely resembling another in appearance, a double; a product closely similar to or meant to be identified with another. (Freq. following the name of the person or thing resembled.) M20.

L. GREENBAUM Except for the wife's stomach, the two women were look-alikes. M. PIERCY Burt Reynolds look-alikes in pick-up trucks. *Practical Computing* This Japanese PC look-alike has nothing new to offer.

B *adj.* Closely similar, esp. in appearance; identical. L20.

look-down /ˈlʊkdaʊn/ *n.* M19. [f. LOOK *v.* or *n.* + DOWN *adv.*] **1** A view or prospect downwards. *rare.* M19. **2** A silvery carangid fish, *Selene vomer*, of the tropical Atlantic, which has a distinctive high blunt forehead. Also called *horse-head*. *US.* L19.

looked /lʊkt/ *a. obs.* exc. *Sc.* L16. [f. LOOK *n.* + -ED[2].] Having a look or appearance of a specified kind (usu. preceded by defining adj. or adv.). Now only in *well-looked*.

looker /ˈlʊkə/ *n.* & *v.* ME. [f. LOOK *v.* + -ER[1].] **A** *n.* **1** A person who looks after or has charge of something; a shepherd, a farm-bailiff, a steward; (as 2nd elem. of comb.) an official inspector of the specified thing. Now *dial.* ME. **2** A person who looks or directs the eyes. Also foll. by adv. or prep. LME. **3** A person (occas. a thing) having an appearance or looks of a specified kind. L15. **b** A good-looking person, esp. a woman; a strikingly attractive thing. *colloq.* L19.

2 looker-in (*a*) a person who looks in on another, a casual visitor; (*b*) a viewer of television. **looker-on** a person who looks on, a mere spectator, (cf. *onlooker*). **looker-out** in the book-trade, a person who looks out wanted volumes from stock. **looker-upper** *colloq.* a person who looks something up. **3** *good-looker*: see GOOD *a.*

B *v.t.* & *i.* Tend and guard (farm animals). *dial.* L19.

look-in /ˈlʊkɪn/ *n.* M19. [f. LOOK *v.* or *n.* + IN *adv.*] **1** A hasty glance; a peep. *rare.* M19. **2** An informal call, a short visit. M19. **3** An opportunity to take part in something, esp. with a chance of success; a share of attention. *colloq.* L19.

looking /ˈlʊkɪŋ/ *n.* ME. [f. LOOK *v.* + -ING[1].] **1** The action of LOOK *v.*; an instance of this. Also foll. by adv. or prep. ME. †**2** A person's look, expression, or appearance. ME–E17.

1 looking-forward an act of looking forward, an anticipation of future events. **looking-over** an inspection.

looking-glass /ˈlʊkɪŋɡlɑːs/ *n.* E16. [f. prec. + GLASS *n.*] **I 1** A glass to look in, in order to see one's own face or figure; a mirror made of silvered glass. E16. **2** Plate glass; glass silvered for use as a mirror. Now *rare*. L17. **II 3** A chamber-pot. *arch. slang*. E17.

Comb. & *phrases*: **looking-glass carp** = *mirror carp* s.v. MIRROR *n.*; **looking-glass world** (or **land**) an imaginary world or land in which everything is as it would be if seen reversed, through a looking-glass; *Venus's looking-glass*: see VENUS.

lookit /ˈlʊkɪt/ *v.* (*imper.*). *N. Amer. colloq.* E20. [Extension of LOOK *v.* Cf. LOOKY.] **1** *v.i.*

Demanding attention or expostulating. Cf. LOOK *v.* IC. E20. 2 *v.t.* Look at (something or someone). E20.

lookout /ˈlʊkaʊt/ *n.* L17. [f. LOOK *v.* or *n.* + OUT *adv.*] **1a** A person or party employed or stationed to look out; a reconnoitring boat or vessel. L17. **b** A station or building from which a person or party can look out. Orig. *Naut.* E18. **2** The action or an act of looking out. Chiefly in *keep a* (*good* etc.) *lookout* (*for*), *on* or *upon the lookout* (*for*). Orig. *Naut.* M18. **3** A more or less distant view; a prospect; a prospective condition, an outlook. L18. **4** With possess.: a person's own concern, which others are not bound to consider. Chiefly after *be.* L18.

1a A. NICOL 'Someone!' the look-out called. 2 S. BECKETT Parts would . . get lost if he did not keep a sharp look-out. R. INGALLS Advise residents . . to be on the look-out for this highly dangerous animal. 3 DICKENS 'He's going at the knees.' 'That's a bad look-out.' C. MACKENZIE I remember the look-out . . to an ocean of blue sky. 4 T. S. ELIOT If they haven't any contingency fund . . , that's their look-out.

look-over /ˈlʊkəʊvə/ *n.* E20. [f. LOOK *v.* or *n.* + OVER *adv.*] An examination, a survey.

look-see /ˈlʊksiː/ *n. slang.* L19. [f. LOOK *v.* or *n.* + SEE *v.*, f. or imit. of pidgin Eng.] A survey; a tour of inspection, a reconnaissance; an investigation.

look-up /ˈlʊkʌp/ *n.* M19. [f. LOOK *v.* + UP *advs.*] **1** A call, a visit. *rare.* M19. **2** The action of looking something up in a dictionary, file, etc.; a facility for this; retrieval of information about items in an ordered collection. Freq. *attrib.* M20.

looky /ˈlʊki/ *v.i.* (*imper.*). *N. Amer. colloq.* L19. [Extension of LOOK *v.*, perh. repr. *look ye* (see LOOK *v.* IC). Cf. LOOKIT.] Demanding attention or expostulating. Chiefly in *looky here.*

loom /luːm/ *n.*[1] [OE *ġelōma*, f. as Y- + base also in *andlōman* (pl.) apparatus, furniture. Aphet. in ME.] **1** *gen.* An implement, a tool. *obs.* exc. *Sc.* & *north.* OE. †**b** The penis. LME–M16. †**c** = HEIRLOOM. LME–E19. **2** An open vessel, as a bucket, tub, vat, etc. *obs.* exc. *Sc.* ME. **3** A machine in which yarn or thread is woven into fabric by the crossing of vertical and horizontal threads (called respectively the warp and weft). LME. **4** The art, business, or process of weaving. Chiefly *literary.* L17. **5** *Electr.* **a** Flexible tubing fitted over an ordinary insulated wire to provide additional protection. E20. **b** A group of parallel insulated wires bound together into a bundle. M20.

3 *fig.*: T. NASHE Spiders . . wont to set vp their loomes in euery windowe. *circular loom, hand loom, Jacquard loom, power loom*, etc. 4 TENNYSON Display'd a splendid silk of foreign loom.

loom /luːm/ *n.*[2] L17. [Scand.: cf. Norw. *lom*, *lumm*, Icel. *hlummur* (ON *hlumr*).] The part of an oar between the rowlock and the grip for hands; *loosely* the handle of an oar.

loom /luːm/ *n.*[3] Orig. *Shetland.* L17. [ON *lómr.*] Any of several diving birds of northern seas, *esp.* a guillemot or a diver (cf. LOON *n.*[2]). Also, the flesh of these birds used as food.

loom /luːm/ *n.*[4] M19. [f. LOOM *v.*[2]] Chiefly *Naut.* An indistinct and exaggerated appearance or outline of an object or of land on the horizon, caused by refraction of light through mist etc. Also, a glow in the sky caused by reflection of light from a lighthouse etc.; a mirage over water or ice.

loom /luːm/ *v.*[1]*t. rare.* M16. [f. LOOM *n.*[1]] **1** Weave (a fabric). M16. **2** *loom the web*, mount the warp on a loom. E19.

loom /luːm/ *v.*[2]*i.* M16. [Prob. of LDu. origin: cf. EFris. *lōmen* (whence Sw. dial. *loma*) move slowly, rel. to MHG *lüemen* be weary, f. *lüeme* slack, soft.] **1** Appear indistinctly, come into view in an enlarged and indefinite form, freq. threateningly, (*lit.* & *fig.*). Also foll. by *up.* Freq. w. adj. compl., as *loom large.* M16. †**2** Of a ship, the sea: move slowly up and down. *rare.* Only in 17.

1 S. BARSTOW The bandstand . . looms up out of the dark. CLIVE JAMES Big ships loom at the ends of city streets. D. MURPHY The grey school buildings loomed out of the rain. R. SCRUTON Taxation has always loomed large among political issues.

loomer /ˈluːmə/ *n.* L19. [f. LOOM *v.*[1] + -ER[1].] In weaving, an operative who mounts the warp on a loom.

loomery /ˈluːməri/ *n.* M19. [f. LOOM *n.*[3] + -ERY.] A place where looms or guillemots breed; a colony of looms.

looming /ˈluːmɪŋ/ *n.* E17. [f. LOOM *v.*[2] + -ING[1].] The action or an act of looming or coming indistinctly into view; a mirage over water or ice (cf. LOOM *n.*[4]).

loon /luːn/ *n.*[1] Chiefly *Sc.* & *north.* LME. [Origin unkn.] **1** A worthless person; a rogue, a scamp; a sluggard, an idler. LME. **b** A prostitute, a concubine. M16. **2** A man of low birth or condition: contrastive with *lord. arch.* M16. **3** *gen.* A fellow, a man; a boy, a youth. M16. **4** A boor, a lout. E17.

loon /luːn/ *n.*[2] M17. [Prob. f. (as) LOOM *n.*[3], alt. perh. by assim. to prec. In sense 2 perh. infl. by LOONY *n.*[2]] **1** Any bird of the diver family, *esp.* (more fully *common loon*) the great northern diver, *Gavia immer.* Cf. LOOM *n.*[3] Chiefly *N. Amer.* M17. **b** The great crested grebe; the little grebe. L17. **2** A crazy person; a simpleton. L19.

1 (*as*) *crazy as a loon* (w. allus. to the bird's actions in escaping from danger and its wild cry).

loon /luːn/ *n.*[3] *colloq.* L20. [f. the vb.] In *pl.* & more fully *loon pants, trousers.* Close-fitting casual trousers widely flared from the knees to the ankles.

loon /luːn/ *v.i. slang.* M20. [Origin unkn.] Esp. of a young person: spend one's leisure time in a pleasurable way, e.g. by dancing to popular music; lie or wander *about.*

looney *a.* & *n.* var. of LOONY *a.* & *n.*[2]

loonie /ˈluːni/ *n.*[1] *Canad. colloq.* Also **-ny.** L20. [f. LOON *n.*[2] + -IE, -Y[6].] The Canadian one-dollar coin introduced in 1987; the Canadian dollar.

loonie *a.* & *n.*[2] var. of LOONY *a.* & *n.*[2]

loony *n.*[1] var. of LOONIE *n.*[1]

loony /ˈluːni/ *a.* & *n.*[2] *colloq.* Also **looney, loonie,** (now *rare*) **luny.** M19. [Abbrev. of LUNATIC: see -Y[6].] **A** *adj.* Lunatic, crazed, daft, dazed, demented, foolish, silly; holding unacceptably radical political views. M19.

Truck & Driver A fractured leg didn't stop the madman . . pulling his loony stunts. L. MCMURTRY Nobody would be loony enough to hire you to cook. *Times* The loony left has been disastrous for the Labour Party.

B *n.* A person who is mentally ill; an eccentric or foolish person. L19.

Comb.: *loony bin*: see BIN *n.* 7. **loony-doctor** *slang* a doctor who treats mental illnesses, a psychiatrist.

loop /luːp/ *n.*[1] ME. [Origin unkn.] **1** = LOOPHOLE. ME. †**2** An opening in the parapet of a fortification; an embrasure. L15–L17.

loop /luːp/ *n.*[2] LME. [Origin uncertain: cf. Ir. *lúb*, Gael. *lūb* a loop, a bend, etc.] **I** **1** A portion of a string, rope, thread, etc., doubled or crossing itself so as to form an aperture, commonly fastened at the point of crossing or juncture (used e.g. as an ornament for dress or as part of a fastener taking a hook or button). LME. **2** A thing, course, or figure having more or less the shape of a loop, as a curved line that crosses itself traced or written on paper, a part of the apparent path of a planet, a deep bend of a river; a ring or curved piece of metal etc., as one employed for the insertion of a bolt, ramrod, or rope, as a handle for lifting. LME.

1 E. LINKLATER Round his neck was the running loop of a rope. P. BOWLES He swung the box on one finger by the little loop . . in the string. R. INGALLS The dragon had his tail curled into loops. *Vogue* Shirt . . with loop for buttoning collar up. 2 M. HUGHES The river meandered in a wide lazy loop. *Tennis* His fear of losing made him hit the ball in higher and higher loops. *New Yorker* Her handwriting was neat and sloping, loops on the letters that demanded them.

II *spec.* **3** (A looped part of) a stitch in knitting, crochet, etc. L18. **4** *Anat.* & *Zool.* A looped vessel, fibre, or other structure. M19. **5** *Math.* A closed curve (on a graph etc.). M19. **6a** A complete circuit or path for an electrical signal or current. M19. **b** A railway or telegraph line diverging from, and afterwards returning to, the main line or circuit. L19. **7** *Skating.* A curve crossing itself, or any of several elaborations upon this, made on a single edge. Also (in full *loop jump*), a jump in which the skater makes a full turn in the air, taking off from and landing on the same edge. M19. **8** *Physics.* The portion of a standing wave between two nodes. L19. **9** A configuration in fingerprints with lines shaped like simple loops. L19. **10** A vertically curved path described by an aeroplane, (orig.) a fairground machine, etc., with a climb and a dive between which the body of the plane etc. is upside down; a manoeuvre in which such a path is taken. E20. **11** A slack length of film etc. left between two mechanisms to allow for a difference between the supply and take-up motions; an endless strip of film or magnetic tape allowing continuous repetition. E20. **12** = *loop aerial* below. E20. **13** A sequence of control operations or activities in which each depends on the result of the previous one; *esp.* (more fully *closed loop*) one in which there is feedback. M20. **14** *Computing.* A sequence of instructions which is executed repeatedly (usu. with an operand that changes in each cycle) until some previously specified criterion is satisfied. M20. **15** A type of intrauterine contraceptive coil. M20.

4 *Henle's loop, loop of Henle*: see HENLE. **10** *loop the loop*: see LOOP *v.*[1] 6. *outside loop*: see OUTSIDE *a.* **13** *open loop*: see OPEN *a.* **15** LIPPES LOOP.

Comb.: **loop aerial, loop antenna** an aerial consisting of one or more loops of wire; **loop film** an endless loop of cinematographic film; *loop jump*: see sense 7 above; **loop-knit** *a.* knitted with loop yarn; **loop-knot** †(*a*) a reef-knot; (*b*) a single knot tied in a doubled cord etc., so as to leave a loop beyond the knot; **loop-lace** (*a*) a kind of ornament consisting of a series of loops; (*b*) a kind of lace consisting of patterns worked on a ground of fine net; **loop-line** = sense 6b above; **loop pile** carpet pile with uncut loops; **loop-stitch** *n.* & *v.* (*a*) *n.* a kind of fancy stitch consisting of loops; (*b*) *v.t.* connect or attach by means of loop-stitches; **loop system** a method of connecting electrical supply points (as lamp roses) by taking the wires to each point from terminals at its switch and at the previous supply point, instead of making a separate joint elsewhere in the circuit; **loop-work** work consisting of loops or looped stitches; **loop-worm** = LOOPER *n.*[1] 1; **loop yarn** yarn with one thread fastened in loops around another (usu. finer) thread.

loop /luːp/ *n.*[3] Now *rare* or *obs.* Also **loup.** L17. [f. as LOUPE.] *Founding.* A soft mass of wrought iron taken from the finery for hammering into a bloom.

loop /luːp/ *v.*[1] LME. [f. LOOP *n.*[2]] **1** *v.t.* Draw through a loop; encircle or enclose *in* or *with* a loop. LME. **2** *v.i.* Form a loop; *spec.* (of a caterpillar etc.) move by successive curving and straightening actions. Cf. earlier LOOPER *n.*[1] 1. E19. **3** *v.t.* Put or form loops on; provide (a garment etc.) with loops. M19. **4** *v.t.* Form into a loop or loops. M19. **5** *v.t.* Fasten (*back, up*) by forming into a loop, or by means of an attached loop; join (*together*) or connect by means of a loop or loops; (foll. by *in*) connect (a wire, appliance, etc.) into an electric circuit by the loop system. L19. **6** *v.t. loop the loop*, (of an aeroplane or (orig.) a fairground machine) perform the feat of circling in a vertical loop (see LOOP *n.*[2] 10). E20. **7** *v.i. Computing.* Execute a loop. M20.

Comb.: **loop-in** a connection between two lengths of wire made at a terminal in the loop system; *loop-in system* = *loop system* s.v. LOOP *n.*[2] **loop-the-loop** an act of looping the loop.

¶Rare bef. M19.

loop /lʊəp/ *v.*[2]*i. S. Afr.* E19. [Afk. f. Du. *lopen* to walk.] Walk. Freq. in *imper.*, commanding an animal to start moving or (now usu.) a person or animal to leave.

looped /luːpt/ *a.*[1] E16. [f. LOOP *n.*[2], *v.*[2]: see -ED[2], -ED[1].] **1** Coiled or wreathed in loops. Formerly also, intertwined. E16. †**2** Having or fastened with a loop. L16–E17. **3** Of lace: worked on a ground of fine net. L17. **4** Held in a loop, held *up* by a loop. M19. **5** Intoxicated, drunk. *slang* (chiefly *N. Amer.*). M20.

looped /luːpt/ *a.*[2] *rare.* E17. [f. LOOP *n.*[1] + -ED[2].] Having loopholes.

looper /ˈluːpə/ *n.*[1] M18. [f. (as) LOOP *v.*[1] + -ER[1].] 1 The caterpillar of a geometrid moth, which moves by successive curving and straightening actions. M18. 2 A contrivance for making loops in a sewing-machine etc.; an implement for looping strips together in making rag-carpets. M19. 3 A person who loops the loop, or who has done so. E20.

looper /ˈlʊəpə/ *n.*[2] *S. Afr.* (now *Hist.*). E19. [Afk. f. Du., lit. 'runner'.] Any of the lugs or pellets of buck shot, usu. made by cutting a ball in four. Usu. in *pl.*

loopful /ˈluːpfʊl, -f(ə)l/ *n.* L19. [f. LOOP *n.*[2] + -FUL.] Chiefly *Microbiol.* The quantity of fluid, esp. of a bacterial suspension, which is contained in a loop of (platinum) wire.

loophole /ˈluːphəʊl/ *n.* & *v.* L16. [f. LOOP *n.*[1] + HOLE *n.*[1]] A *n.* 1 A narrow vertical slit in a wall etc. for shooting or looking through or for the admission of light and air. Formerly also, a porthole. L16. 2 *fig.* An outlet, a means of escape; *esp.* an ambiguity or omission in a statute, contract, etc. which affords opportunity for evading its intention. M17.

2 B. GELDOF We would have to find some legal loophole .. to get supplies .. here quickly.

B *v.t.* Cut loopholes in the walls of; provide with loopholes. M17.

loopy /ˈluːpi/ *a.* L18. [f. LOOP *n.*[2] + -Y[1].] 1 Crafty, deceitful. *Sc.* L18. 2 Full of loops; characterized by loops. M19. 3 Crazy. *slang.* E20.

loose /luːs/ *n.* E16. [f. LOOSE *v.*, *a.*] I 1 *Archery.* The action or an act of discharging an arrow. E16. †2 The conclusion or close of a matter. L16–M17. 3 A state or condition of looseness, laxity, or unrestraint; free indulgence; unrestrained action or feeling; abandonment. Now only in *give a loose* (occas. *give loose*) *to*, allow (a person) unrestrained freedom; give full vent or expression to (feelings etc.) L16. †4 An act of letting go or parting with something. E–M17. †5 The action or an act of getting free, liberation, release. M17–M18. †6 An impetuous course or rush. E–M19. II 7 *The* state of being loose. Chiefly in *on the loose*, (*a*) *arch.* living by prostitution; (*b*) having a spree, free from ties or commitments; (*c*) escaped from confinement or imprisonment. L18. 8 *Rugby Football. The* part of the play in which the ball travels freely from player to player. Chiefly in *in the loose.* L19.

loose /luːs/ *a.* & *adv.* ME. [ON *lauss* = OFris. *lās*, OS, OHG *lōs* (Du., G *los*), Goth. *laus*, f. Gmc, f. base also of LEASE *a.*, -LESS.] A *adj.* 1 a Free or released from bonds, fetters, or physical restraint; not confined or tethered; (of a horse etc.) running free. ME. †b Loosely clothed; naked. LME–E18. c Not bound together; not forming a bundle or package; not tied up or secured; having an end or ends hanging free; (of money, cash, etc.) in coins as opp. to notes, in relatively small denominations. L15. d Free for disposal or acquisition; unattached, unappropriated, unoccupied. Now *esp.* (of a football or hockey ball) not in any player's possession. L15. e Freed from an engagement, obligation, etc. Long *obs.* exc. *dial.* M16. f Of ideas, speech, etc.: unconnected, rambling, stray, random. Now *rare.* L17. g Of an inanimate thing: not fastened or attached to that to which it belongs as a part or appendage, or with which it has previously been connected; detached. E18. h Not joined to anything else. E19. i *Gram.* Of a modifying clause or phrase: dispensable without loss of semantic or grammatical completeness. M20. 2a Not rigidly or securely attached or fixed in place; ready to move in or come apart from the body to which it is joined or on which it rests. ME. †b Of the eyes: not fixed, roving. E17–M19. c Of a cough: producing phlegm or sputum with little difficulty. M19. 3 Not tightly drawn or stretched; slack, relaxed, not tense; limber; *slang* uninhibited. ME. b Of clothes: not clinging close to the figure or body; loosely fitting. LME. c Of a person's build: ungainly, looking unsuited for brisk movement. M19. 4a Lacking in retentiveness or power of restraint; (of the tongue) likely to speak indiscreetly; lax in principle, conduct, or speech, *esp.* promiscuous, dissolute, immoral. ME. b Of the bowels, a person: tending to diarrhoea. E16. 5 Not close or compact in arrangement or structure; not dense or serried; straggling. LME. b *Bot.* = LAX *a.* 2b. L18. c Designating or pertaining to exercise or play (esp. in football or hockey) in which those engaged are not close together or in which there is free movement. E19. 6 Not rigid, strict, correct, or careful; marked by inaccuracy or carelessness; inexact, indeterminate, vague; (of a translation) not close; (qualifying an agent-n.) doing the specified act loosely. M16. †b Not providing security, unsettled. Only in 17. 7 Designating a stable etc. in which animals are kept untethered or in which they can move about freely. E19.

1a A. PRICE There was a mass murderer loose. J. MCPHEE Cook's loose ones [dogs], running amok, could be counted on to .. drive the tied ones berserk. c G. GREENE He drew a loose match from his pocket. I. MCEWAN She tucked some loose strands of hair behind her ear. g *come loose, get loose*, etc. 2a R. DAHL He was up on the roof .. replacing some loose tiles. B. MOORE Loose chippings of stone rattled against the .. undercarriage. 3 MILTON What time the labour'd Oxe In his loose traces from the furrow came. P. ROTH Standing there as loose and as easy, as happy as I will ever be. *Running* The runners .. will need to keep loose and warm. J. WILCOX The loose flesh on the old woman's throat quivered. b R. CHANDLER The violet scarf was loose enough to show that he wore no tie. A. BROOKNER A loose sweater and a long jersey skirt. c DICKENS He was a strong, loose, round-shouldered, shuffling shaggy fellow. 4a DRYDEN The scandal I have given by my loose writings. CARLYLE A rash young fool; carries a loose tongue. *International Herald Tribune* Senators, so loose when it comes to their own behavior, suddenly become twitching watchdogs for virtue. 5 SHELLEY The loose array Of horsemen o'er the wide fields. J. A. MICHENER Instead of the compact bales .., large, loose stacks .. now went to St. Louis. G. LORD The last census, .. had contained fifteen households scattered in a wide, loose circle. Z. TOMIN A cohesive body, not just a loose collection of signatories. 6 W. D. WHITNEY We are loose thinkers and loose talkers. R. G. COLLINGWOOD The problems of philosophy were, even in the loosest sense of that word, eternal. *Times* McGlew was getting methodically behind .. every ball and hitting anything loose. A. BURGESS Staid conservatism is as much an enemy of the language as loose slanginess.

Phrases: (A small selection of cross-refs. only is included: see esp. other vbs.) *all hell let loose*: see HELL *n. a screw loose*: see SCREW *n.*[1] *cast loose*: see CAST *v.* **cut loose** (*a*) free oneself, escape, (*from*); (*b*) begin to act freely. *fast and loose*: see FAST *a. have a tile loose*: see TILE *n. let loose*: see LET *v.*[1]

Special collocations & comb.: **loose back** a method of binding the spine of a book to make it open more easily. **loose-bodied** *a.* (of a dress) loose-fitting. **loose box** a stall for a horse in which the animal can move about. **loose cannon** *fig.* a person or thing causing unintentional or misdirected damage. **loose change** a quantity of coins for casual use, kept or left in one's pocket etc. **loose coupling** *Electr.*: in which the interdependence between circuits is weak. **loose cover** a detachable cover for a chair, couch, or car seat. **loose end** *fig.* (*a*) a disconnected or uncompleted part, a final outstanding matter, (usu. in *pl.*); (*b*) *at a loose end*, (N. Amer.) *at loose ends*, without a definite occupation, with nothing to do. **loose-ended** *a.* ended or finished off in a slack, untidy, or inconclusive way. **loose-endedness** the quality or state of being loose-ended. **loose-fill** loose insulating material, as vermiculite, for filling spaces between rafters etc. **loose fish** (*a*) *Whaling* a whale not attached to a harpoon and line and free for any person to take; (*b*) *slang* a person of irregular habits, a dissipated person. **loose-footed** *a.* (*Naut.*) (of a sail) not tightly held in at the foot, (of a boat) having such a sail. **loose head** *Rugby Football* the forward in the front row of a scrummage closest to the scrum half as he (or she) puts the ball into the scrummage. **loose-housed** *a.* kept in loose-housing. **loose-housing** (a method of housing cattle unconfined in) partly covered barns with access to a feeding area. **loose ice** ice through which a ship etc. can pass. **loose-knit** *a.* connected in a tenuous or ill-defined way; not closely linked. **loose-leaf** *a.* (of a notebook, ledger, etc.) made with each leaf separate for ready insertion or removal. **loose-limbed** *a.* having supple limbs. **loose-lipped** *a.* (*a*) = *loose-mouthed* below; (*b*) having full lips. **loose-mouthed** *a.* loose-tongued; uninhibited in speech. **loose order** an arrangement of soldiers etc. with wide intervals between them. **loose rein** a rider's relaxed control of a horse, a control that is not rigorous, (chiefly in *on a loose rein*). **loose scrum(mage)** *Rugby Football* a scrum formed by the players round the ball during play, and not ordered by the referee. †**loose shot** marksmen not attached to a company. **loose-skinned** *a.* having skin wrinkled or hanging in folds. **loose smut** any of several diseases of cereals, esp. barley and wheat, caused by smut fungi of the genus *Ustilago*. **loose-tongued** *a.* likely to speak indiscreetly, blabbing.

B *adv.* Loosely; with a loose hold. L15.

sit loose (**to**) be independent (of), be indifferent (to).

loosely *adv.* LME. **looseness** *n.* LME.

loose /luːs/ *v.* ME. [f. the adj.] 1 *v.t.* Let loose or set free (*from*); release (*lit.* & *fig.*) from bonds, fetters, or physical restraint; free (the lips, tongue, etc.) from constraint. ME. b *v.i.* In biblical allusions: set people free, release people. Chiefly in *to bind and to loose.* LME. 2a *v.t.* Undo, untie, unfasten (fetters, a knot); break (a seal). ME. b *v.t.* Unlock or unpack (a chest etc.); unpack (goods) from a container. Chiefly *Sc.* LME. c *v.t.* Detach, cast loose, let go, (chiefly *Naut.*, from moorings etc.). Formerly also, remove (an article of clothing) from the body. LME. d *v.t.* & *i.* Detach the team from (a plough etc.). *Sc.* L15. †e *v.t.* Unjoin or unclasp (hands). M–L16. 3 *v.t.* Weaken the adhesion or attachment of; make unstable or insecure in position. Now *arch.* & *Sc.* ME. †4 *v.t.* Break up, dissolve, do away with. Chiefly *fig.* ME–E19. †5 *v.t.* Break (faith); violate (a peace). LME–M16. 6 *Naut.* †a *v.t.* Weigh (an anchor). LME–M16. b *v.i.* Weigh anchor. E16. 7a *v.t.* Shoot or let fly (an arrow); let off (a gun); *transf.* & *fig.* give vent to, emit, cause or allow to proceed from one. LME. b *v.i.* Shoot, let fly. Now usu. foll. by *off.* LME. 8 *v.t.* Make loose or slack; relax. *arch.* exc. in *loose hold* (colloq.), let go. LME. †b Relax or loosen (the bowels). LME–M17. 9 *v.t.* Redeem, release or obtain by payment; pay for. *Sc.* LME. 10 *v.t. Sc. Law.* Withdraw (an arrestment). E16. †11 *v.t.* Solve, explain. L16–M17. 12 *v.i.* Finish working; (of a school, factory, etc.) close, disperse, break up. *dial.* L17.

1 AV *Isa.* 51:14 The captiue exile hasteneth that he may be loosed. W. DE LA MARE Loosed from remorse and hope and love's distress. *New Yorker* The industry's reluctance to loose information on the non-expert world. 2a SHELLEY Throw back their heads and loose their streaming hair. J. BUCHAN I broke one of the bootlaces .. and loosed the other. 3 AV *Ecclus* 22:16 As timber girt and bound together in a building, cannot be loosed with shaking. 7a C. CAUSLEY Occasionally he looses a scared glance. K. CROSSLEY-HOLLAND He .. loosed an arrow at a luckless bird. b *Daily News* Artillerymen dashed forward .. and loosed on the foe.

looser *n.* E16.

loosen /ˈluːs(ə)n/ *v.* ME. [f. LOOSE *a.* + -EN[5].] I *v.t.* 1 Set free (*lit.* & *fig.*), release from bonds or physical restraint. Now chiefly (*fig.*) make (a person's tongue) talk more freely. ME. 2 Undo, untie, unfasten (bonds, a knot, etc.). Now *esp.* make looser or less tight, relax, slacken, *fig.* relax in point of severity or strictness. LME. 3 Weaken the adhesion or attachment of; unfix, detach. LME. †b *fig.* Detach in affection, make a breach between. Only in E17. 4a Relieve the costiveness of, cause a free evacuation of (the bowels). L16. b Make (a cough) produce phlegm or sputum with less difficulty. M19. 5 Make less coherent; separate the particles of. L17.

1 F. TUOHY Tongues loosened .. by .. the urgency of getting their say. 2 J. G. COZZENS Ernest relaxed more .., consciously loosening each muscle. H. WILLIAMSON He dismounted to loosen the curb-chain, which had been hooked too tight under the animal's jaw. D. ATHILL Pain and exhaustion had loosened her grip on life. *loosen the purse-strings*: see PURSE-STRING. 3 LD MACAULAY A wall which time .. had so loosened that it shook in every storm. M. M. KAYE A breeze blowing through the branches loosened the petals and sent them floating down. 5 DRYDEN Iron Teeth of Rakes .. to move The crusted Earth and loosen it.

II *v.i.* 6 Become loose or looser; relax. L17. 7 Foll. by *up*: a Give money willingly, talk freely.

N. Amer. colloq. E20. **b** Exercise the muscles before concentrated physical effort, limber up. M20.

6 A. P. HERBERT The taut rope, loosening, scattered a shower of brilliant rain. M. PIERCY He had begun to warm towards me, to loosen. A. LURIE Garrett's tongue seemed to be loosening. 7a R. D. PAINE Someone will have to loosen up to pay for the damage. b M. RUSSELL I'll be twenty minutes loosening up... I'm after the exercise.

loosener *n.* (*a*) a thing which or person who loosens something; (*b*) *Cricket* a (not very good) ball delivered before the bowler is fully loosened or warmed up: M17.

loosestrife /ˈluːsstrʌɪf/ *n.* M16. [f. LOOSE *v.* + STRIFE *n.*, mistr. L *lysimachia*, *-ion*, as if f. Gk *lusimakhos* 'loosing (i.e. ending) strife', instead of f. *Lusimakhos* Lysimachus, its discoverer.] Either of two tall upright summer-flowering plants growing by ponds and rivers, (*a*) (in full *yellow loosestrife*) *Lysimachia vulgaris*, of the primrose family, bearing racemes of golden-yellow flowers; (*b*) (in full *purple loosestrife*) *Lythrum salicaria* (family Lythraceae), with a long showy spike of purplish-red flowers. Also (usu. w. specifying wd), any of various other plants of the genus *Lysimachia* or the family Lythraceae.

loosish /ˈluːsɪʃ/ *a.* E19. [f. LOOSE *a.* + -ISH[1].] Somewhat loose.

loot /luːt/ *n.*[1] M19. [Hind. *lūṭ*, *lūṭnā*, f. Skt *luṇṭ(h)-* rob.] **1** Goods (esp. articles of considerable value) taken from an enemy, a captured city, etc.; booty, plunder, spoil; illicit gains made by a public servant. Also, the action or process of looting. M19. **2** Money. *slang.* M20.

loot /luːt/ *n.*[2] *US Mil. slang.* L19. [Abbrev. of LIEUTENANT (in N. Amer. pronunc.).] A lieutenant.

loot *n.*[3] see LUTE *n.*[3]

loot /luːt/ *v.* E19. [f. LOOT *n.*[1]] **1** *v.t.* & *i.* Plunder, sack (a city, a building, etc.); rob (a house, shop, etc.) left unprotected after violent events. E19. **2** *v.t.* Carry off as loot or booty; steal (goods). E19.

lootable *a.* (*rare*) that may be looted or taken as loot, desirable as loot L19. **looter** *n.* M19.

lootie /ˈluːti/ *n.* M18. [Hind. *lūṭī*, f. as LOOT *n.*[1]] *Hist.* In the Indian subcontinent: a member of a body of native irregulars whose chief object in warfare was plunder; a member of a band of marauders or robbers. Usu. in *pl.*

lop /lɒp/ *n.*[1] Now *dial.* LME. [Prob. f. ON f. base also of *hlaupa* LEAP *v.*] A flea.

lop /lɒp/ *n.*[2] LME. [Origin uncertain: perh. ult. rel. to Lith. *lùpti* to strip, to peel; later partly f. LOP *v.*[1] Cf. earlier LOPPED *a.*, AL *loppa* (pl.).] **1** *collect.* The smaller branches and twigs of a tree; faggot-wood. Also, a branch that has been lopped off. LME. †**2** The action or process of lopping a tree or boughs. Only in L16.

1 **lop and top, lop and crop** the trimmings of a tree.

Comb.: **lop-wood** branches and twigs lopped from a tree.

lop /lɒp/ *n.*[3] E19. [Imit.: cf. LOP *v.*[3]] *Naut.* A state of the sea in which the waves are short and lumpy.

lop /lɒp/ *n.*[4] M19. [Abbrev. of *lop-eared* s.v. LOP *v.*[2]] A variety of rabbit with long drooping ears.

lop /lɒp/ *v.*[1] Infl. **-pp-**. E16. [f. or rel. to LOP *n.*[2] Cf. earlier LOPPED *a.*, AL *loppare*.] **1** *v.t.* Cut off the branches, twigs, etc., from (a tree); cut away the superfluous growth of, trim; occas., cut the top off (a tree). E16. **b** *transf.* & *fig.* Cut off the head or a limb of (a person). (Foll. by †*away*, †*off*.) *arch.* E17. **2** *v.t.* Cut off (the branches, twigs, etc.) from a tree. Freq. foll. by *away*, *off*. L16. **b** *transf.* & *fig.* Cut off (a limb, the head) from the body; cut off from a whole, remove (items) as superfluous. (Foll. by *away*, *off*.) L16. **3** *v.i.* Lop branches and twigs from a tree; cut off a limb, the head or a part of any whole; make strokes *at* with the purpose of cutting something off. L16.

1 S. JOHNSON A few strokes of an axe will lop a cedar. 2 G. GREENE Somebody had lopped the branches for firewood. D. WIGODER To.. lop branches from overgrown trees. b *Times* Brownhills, which has been lopped off Miss Jennie Lee's constituency. A. HALEY The flash of a long knife lopped off his head cleanly at the shoulders. 3 R. HAWKINS One plowing,.. another sowing, and lopping.

lop /lɒp/ *v.*[2] Infl. **-pp-**. L16. [Prob. symbolic: cf. LOB *v.*] **1** *v.i.* Hang loosely or limply; droop; flop *about*; stick *out* ungracefully or in a lopsided way. L16. **b** *v.t.* Of an animal: let (the ears) hang or droop. E19. **2** *v.i.* Slouch, dawdle, hang *about*. L16. **3** *v.i.* Move with short bounds. L19.

Phrases: **lop down** *US colloq.* sit down, lie down.

Comb.: **lop-ear** (*a*) a drooping ear; (*b*) = LOP *n.*[4]; **lop-eared** *a.* (esp. of an animal) having drooping ears; **lop-ears** drooping ears; **lop-grass** *dial.* = *soft brome* s.v. SOFT *a.*; **lop-rabbit** = LOP *n.*[4]

lop /lɒp/ *v.*[3]*i.* Infl. **-pp-**. L19. [Imit.: cf. LOP *n.*[3]] Of water: break in short lumpy waves.

lope /ləʊp/ *n.* LME. [Var. of LOUP *n.*[1]] **1** A leap. *obs.* exc. *Sc.* LME. **2** A long bounding stride, a loping gait. E19.

1 R. NORTH I cannot do the Author Justice.. without taking a large Lope, over the next Reign. 2 E. L. DOCTOROW He.. ran along the top of the train in a kind of simian lope.

lope /ləʊp/ *v.i.* ME. [Var. of LOUP *v.*] **1** Leap, jump, spring, (*about*). *obs.* exc. *dial.* ME. **2** Run (away). Now only *slang* & *dial.* LME. **3** Run with a long bounding stride. (Foll. by *along*, *away*.) E19.

3 V. WOOLF As I lay in the grass a hare loped past me. H. WILLIAMSON He went for long runs, loping along.

loper /ˈləʊpə/ *n.* L15. [f. LOPE *v.* + -ER[1].] †**1** A leaper, a dancer. Only in L15. **2** *Ropemaking.* A swivel on which yarns are hooked at one end while being twisted into cordage. L18. **3** *Cabinet-making.* A sliding rail to be pulled out to support the leaf of a bureau etc. M19.

loperamide /ləʊˈpɛrəmʌɪd/ *n.* L20. [Prob. f. CH)LO(RO-[2] + PI)PER(IDINE + AMIDE.] *Pharm.* An opiate drug which inhibits peristalsis and is used to treat diarrhoea.

lopez-root /ˈləʊpɛz,ruːt/ *n.* L18. [= mod.L *radix lopeziana*, orig. applied to the root of a related E. African plant discovered by Juan Lopez Pinheiro.] The root of a SE Asian plant, *Toddalia asiatica*, of the rue family, used as a remedy for diarrhoea.

lophiodon /ləˈfʌɪədɒn/ *n.* M19. [mod.L (see below), f. Gk *lophion* dim. of *lophos* crest + -ODON.] *Palaeont.* A fossil ungulate mammal of the Eocene genus *Lophiodon* (cf. next).

lophiodont /ˈləʊfɪədɒnt, ˈlɒf-/ *a.* & *n.* M19. [f. as prec.] *Palaeont.* **A** *adj.* Pertaining to or resembling a lophiodon; of or characteristic of the family Lophiodontidae of Eocene ungulates, probably related to tapirs. M19. **B** *n.* An animal of the family Lophiodontidae. L19.

lophioid /ˈləʊfɪɔɪd, ˈlɒf-/ *a.* & *n.* M19. [f. mod.L *Lophius* genus name, app. f. Gk *lophia* or *lophos* mane, dorsal fin: see -OID.] *Zool.* **A** *adj.* Of or pertaining to the family Lophiidae, which includes certain angler-fishes. M19. **B** *n.* A lophioid fish. M19.

lopho- /ˈləʊfəʊ, ˈlɒfəʊ/ *comb. form* of Gk *lophos* crest, as *lophobranchiate*, *lophophore*, etc.: see -O-.

lophobranch /ˈləʊfə(ʊ)braŋk, ˈlɒf-/ *a.* & *n.* M19. [f. as next.] *Zool.* = next.

lophobranchiate /ləʊfə(ʊ)ˈbraŋkɪət, lɒf-/ *a.* & *n.* M19. [f. LOPHO- + Gk *bragkhia* gills: see -ATE[2].] *Zool.* **A** *adj.* Belonging to or having the characteristics of the order Lophobranchii of bony fishes (e.g. sea horses and pipefishes) in which the gills are arranged in small lobes or tufts. M19. **B** *n.* A lophobranchiate fish. M19.

lophodont /ˈləʊfə(ʊ)dɒnt, ˈlɒf-/ *a.* & *n.* L19. [f. LOPHO- + -ODONT.] *Zool.* **A** *adj.* (Of a molar tooth) having (esp. transverse) ridges between the cusps; (of a dentition) characterized by such molar teeth. L19. **B** *n.* A herbivore with a lophodont dentition. L19.

lophophorate /ləˈfɒfəreɪt, ləʊfə(ʊ)ˈfɔːreɪt/ *n.* & *a.* M20. [f. next: see -ATE[2].] *Zool.* **A** *n.* Any of a group of sessile or sedentary coelomate invertebrates possessing a lophophore, including brachiopods, bryozoans, and phoronids. M20. **B** *adj.* Designating, pertaining to, or characteristic of a lophophorate. M20.

lophophore /ˈləʊfə(ʊ)fɔː, ˈlɒf-/ *n.* M19. [f. LOPHO- + -PHORE.] **1** *Zool.* A feeding organ in lophophorates, pterobranchs, etc., consisting of a circular, crescentic, or spiral ridge surrounding the mouth and bearing ciliated tentacles, usu. hydraulically linked to the coelom. M19. **2** A bird of the genus *Lophophorus*; = MONAL. *rare.* L19.

lophoˈphoral *a.* of or pertaining to a lophophore L19.

lophotrichous /ləˈfɒtrɪkəs/ *a.* E20. [f. LOPHO- + -TRICH + -OUS.] *Microbiol.* Designating or characteristic of a bacterium in which several flagella occur as a crest or bundle at one end of the cell.

lopolith /ˈlɒpəlɪθ/ *n.* E20. [f. Gk *lopas* basin + -O- + -LITH.] *Geol.* A large intrusive mass similar to a laccolith but having the base centrally sunken.

lopoˈlithic *a.* M20.

loppage /ˈlɒpɪdʒ/ *n. rare.* L17. [f. LOP *v.*[1] + -AGE.] The loppings from trees collectively; lop.

lopped /lɒpt/ *a.* ME. [f. LOP *n.*[2] or *v.*[1]: see -ED[2], -ED[1].] **1** That has been lopped; *Bot.* & *Zool.* (now *rare* or *obs.*) truncate. ME. **2** *Her.* Of a branch etc.: couped to show the cross-section. *rare.* E19.

1 G. GREENE The lopped arm came into view.. the stump like a bludgeon of wood. I. MURDOCH A lopped tree trunk.. served as a seat.

lopper /ˈlɒpə/ *n.* M16. [f. LOP *v.*[1] + -ER[1].] A person who lops the branches, twigs, etc., off trees; a person who lops something off.

lopper /ˈlɒpə/ *a. obs.* exc. *Sc.* ME. [Prob. f. LOPPER *v.*] = LOPPERED.

lopper /ˈlɒpə/ *v.* Now only *Sc.* & *north.* ME. [Perh. f. ON *hlaup* coagulation (of milk or blood): see -ER[5].] **1** *v.i.* Esp. of milk: curdle, clot. ME. **b** *v.t.* Turn to curds; curdle; cause to clot. L19. **2** *v.i.* Dabble, besmear, cover with clotted matter. E19.

loppered *a.* (esp. of milk or blood) clotted, coagulated, curdled ME.

lopping /ˈlɒpɪŋ/ *n.* E16. [f. LOP *v.*[1] + -ING[1].] **1** The action of LOP *v.*[1] E16. **2** In *pl.* Branches and shoots lopped from a tree; material for lopping. L16.

loppy /ˈlɒpi/ *n. Austral. slang.* L19. [Perh. f. LOP *v.*[2] (see -Y[1]) or LOPPY *a.*[1]] A handyman on a rural station, a roustabout.

loppy /ˈlɒpi/ *a.*[1] *obs.* exc. *dial.* L15. [f. LOP *n.*[1] + -Y[1].] Full of or infested with fleas.

loppy /ˈlɒpi/ *a.*[2] M19. [f. LOP *v.*[2] + -Y[1].] That hangs loosely; limp.

loppy /ˈlɒpi/ *a.*[3] L19. [f. LOP *v.*[3] + -Y[1].] Of the sea: lumpy, choppy.

lopseed /ˈlɒpsiːd/ *n. N. Amer.* E19. [f. LOP *v.*[2] + SEED *n.*] A plant of NE Asia and eastern N. America, *Phryma leptostachya*, of the verbena family, with spikes of small white or purplish flowers which droop against the stem when in seed.

lopsided /lɒpˈsʌɪdɪd/ *a.* E18. [f. LOP *v.*[2] + SIDE *n.* + -ED[2].] That (appears to) lean on or towards one side; having one side lower or smaller than the other; (of a ship) disproportionately heavy on one side; unevenly balanced.

G. W. TARGET The boy trailed in, lopsided with the weight of the bag. E. BLISHEN This charming church, of which I'd made lopsided drawings in childhood. *fig.*: G. GREENE The novelist's philosophy will always be a little lopsided.

lopsidedly *adv.* L19. **lopsidedness** *n.* M19.

lopstick /ˈlɒpstɪk/ *n. Canad.* Also **lob-** /ˈlob-/. E19. [f. LOP *n.*[2] or *v.*[1] + STICK *n.*[1]] A tree which has had its branches lopped, usu. with the name of the lopper cut in its trunk.

loq. /lɒk/ *v.i.* (*3 sing. pres.*). M19. [Abbrev.] = LOQUITUR.

loquacious /lɒˈkweɪʃəs/ *a.* M17. [f. L *loquaci-*, *loquax*, f. *loqui* speak: see -ACIOUS.] **1** Given to much talking; talkative. M17. **2** Of birds, water, etc.: chattering, babbling. Chiefly *poet.* L17.

1 R. K. NARAYAN Twenty words where one would do... He was becoming loquacious. B. GILROY His

grief made him loquacious He talked on about everything. 2 POPE The chough, the sea-mew, the loquacious crow.

loquaciously *adv.* M19. **loquaciousness** *n.* E18.

loquacity /lɒˈkwasɪti/ *n.* ME. [Fr. *loquacité* or L *loquacitas*, f. as prec.: see -ACITY.] The condition or quality of being loquacious; talkativeness; an instance of this.

loquat /ˈləʊkwɒt/ *n.* E19. [Chin. (Cantonese) *luh kwat* lit. 'rush orange'.] The fruit of a tree of the rose family, *Eriobotrya japonica*, native to China and Japan and cultivated in many warm countries; (in full *loquat tree*) the tree itself. Also called *Japanese medlar*.

loquency /ˈləʊkw(ə)nsi/ *n. rare.* E17. [Late L *loquentia*, f. as next: see -ENCY.] Talking, speech. Also **loquence** *n.* L17.

loquent /ˈləʊkwənt/ *a. rare.* L16. [L *loquent-* pres. ppl stem of *loqui* speak: see -ENT.] That speaks.

loquently *adv.* L19.

loquitur /ˈlɒkwɪtə/ *v.i.* (*3 sing. pres.*). M19. [L.] Speaks (with the speaker's name added, as a stage-direction or to inform a reader). Abbrev. LOQ.

lor' /lɔː/ *int. colloq.* Also **lor.** M19. [Alt. of LORD *n.* Cf. LORS.] Expr. surprise, dismay, etc. Cf. LORD *n.* 5, LORDY.

TAFFRAIL Lor'! . . I do look a sight, and no mistake!

lora *n.* pl. of LORUM.

loral /ˈlɔːr(ə)l/ *a.* & *n.* L19. [f. LORE *n.*^{2} + -AL^1.] *Zool.* = LOREAL.

loran /ˈlɔːran, ˈlɒ-/ *n.* M20. [f. *lo*ng-*ra*nge *n*avigation.] A radar navigation system by which a position is calculated from the time delay between signals from two pairs of synchronized radio transmitters. Cf. SHORAN.

lorate /ˈlɔːreɪt/ *a.* M19. [f. L LORUM + -ATE^2.] *Bot.* Strap-shaped.

lorazepam /lɔːˈreɪzɪpam, -ˈrazə-/ *n.* M20. [f. CH)LOR(O-^{2} + *azepam*, after *diazepam* etc.] *Pharm.* A drug of the benzodiazepine group, given as a tranquillizer and hypnotic.

lorcha /ˈlɔːtʃə/ *n.* Also **lorch** /lɔːtʃ/. M17. [Port., of unkn. origin.] A fast sailing vessel with a hull of European shape but a Chinese rig.

lord /lɔːd/ *n.* [OE *hlāford* f. contr. of *hlāfweard* f. Gmc, f. base of LOAF *n.*^{1} + WARD *n.* See also LUD.] **I** A master, a ruler. †**1** A master in relation to servants; the male head of a household. OE–E17. **2** A man (or boy) who has dominion over others as his subjects, or to whom service and obedience are due; a master, a ruler, a chief, a prince, a monarch. Now chiefly *rhet.* OE. **b** *fig.* A pre-eminent person or thing. ME. **c** An owner, a possessor, a proprietor (of land, houses, etc.). Cf. LANDLORD. Now only *poet.* & *rhet.* ME. **d** A magnate in some particular trade. E19. **3** *spec.* A feudal superior; the proprietor of a fee, manor, etc. OE. **4** A husband. Now only *poet.* & *joc.* OE. **5** *Lord* (*God*) (usu. w. *the*, exc. as *voc.*), God. Freq. as int. and in exclamatory phrs. expr. surprise (originating from the use in invocations), dismay, etc. Cf. LAND *n.*^{1} 9, LOR', LORDY, LORS, LUD. OE. **6** Jesus Christ. Freq. in *Our Lord*, *the Lord*. ME. **7** *Astrol.* The planet that has a dominant influence over an event, period, region, etc. LME.

1 AV *Matt.* 24:46 Blessed is that seruant, whome his Lord when he cometh, shall finde so doing. 2 MILTON Man over men He made not Lord. LD MACAULAY A race which reverenced no lord, no king but himself. b J. G. STRUTT The attribute of strength by which the lord of the woods is more peculiarly distinguished. c R. KIPLING He was . . lord of a crazy fishing-boat. d *tobacco lord* etc. 3 T. KEIGHTLEY The rights of the Lord of a town extended to the levying of tolls. 4 C. PATMORE Love-mild Honoria . . With added loves of lord and child. 5 SHAKES. *Rich. II* The breath of worldly men cannot depose The deputy elected by the Lord. C. SIMEON This is the Lord's work and fit for a Sabbath-day. E. LEONARD They said, 'Oh, my Lord,' if he happened to mention he'd served time. 6 TENNYSON How loyal in the following of thy Lord!

II As a designation of rank or official dignity. **8** Orig., any man (or boy) of exalted position in a kingdom or commonwealth, *spec.* (*Hist.*) a feudal tenant who derived a title, by military or other honourable service, directly from the king (cf. BARON 1). Now, a nobleman, a peer of the realm, or a person (as an archbishop or bishop) entitled by courtesy, office, etc., to the title *Lord*, or some higher title. ME. **9** Used preceding a name to form part of the designation of a man (or boy) of rank, (*a*) as a less formal substitute for Marquess (of), Earl (of), Viscount, Baron, (never followed by *of*, e.g. *the Earl of Derby* but *Lord Derby*); (*b*) preceding the forename, with or without the surname, of the younger son of a duke or marquess. LME. **10** Forming part of the title of office of any of various high officials in the law, government, armed services, etc., holding authority deputed from the monarch. Also, given as part of a title to individual members of a board appointed to perform the duties of some high office of State that has been put in commission. LME. **11** A mock title of dignity given to the person appointed to preside on certain festive occasions. Chiefly in *Lord of Misrule* s.v. MISRULE *n.* M16. **12** A hunchback. *arch. slang.* L17.

9 C. C. F. GREVILLE I dined with Lord and Lady Frederick Fitz Clarence and Lord Westmoreland. H. WILSON Commoners, including Lord North, whose barony was a courtesy title.

Phrases & comb.: *by the Lord Harry* see HARRY *n.*^{2} *drunk as a lord*: see DRUNK *a.* *First Lord of the Treasury*: see TREASURY 4. *First Sea Lord*: see SEA. **House of Lords** (*a*) the upper legislative chamber of the UK, composed of peers and bishops; (*b*) a committee of specially qualified members of this assembly appointed as the ultimate appeal court; (*c*) the building where these bodies meet; (*d*) *slang* a lavatory. *(in the) year of Our Lord*: see YEAR *n.*^{1} *liege lord*: see LIEGE *a.* 1. **live like a lord** live sumptuously, have a high standard of living. *Lord Advocate*: see ADVOCATE *n.* 1. **lord and lady**, pl. **lords and ladies**, (orig. & chiefly *Canad.*) a harlequin duck (usu. in *pl.*). **lord and master** (*a*) (now chiefly *rhet.*) = sense 2 above; (*b*) *poet.* & *joc.* = sense 4 above. **Lord Bishop**: the formal title of a bishop, esp. a diocesan bishop of the Church of England. **Lord bless me, my soul, you**, etc. *int.*: expr. surprise. *Lord Chamberlain* (*of the Household*): see CHAMBERLAIN 1. *Lord Chancellor*: see CHANCELLOR. *Lord Chief Justice*: see JUSTICE *n.* *Lord Clerk Register*: see REGISTER *n.*^{1} *Lord Commissioner*: see COMMISSIONER 1. **Lord Derby** a large green- and yellow-skinned variety of cooking apple; the tree that produces it. *Lord God*: see sense 5 above. *Lord God of hosts*: see HOST *n.*^{1} *Lord Great Chamberlain* (*of England*): see CHAMBERLAIN 1. **Lord have mercy (on us)** *int.* expr. astonishment. *Lord High Admiral*: see ADMIRAL 2. *Lord High Chancellor*: see CHANCELLOR. *Lord High Commissioner*: see COMMISSIONER 1. *Lord High Steward of England, Scotland*: see STEWARD *n.* 8. *Lord High Treasurer*: see TREASURER 1. **lord-in-waiting** a nobleman holding a certain office in attendance on the monarch. *Lord Justice* (*Clerk, General, of Appeal*): see JUSTICE *n.* *Lord Keeper* (*of the Great Seal*): see KEEPER *n.* **lord-lieutenancy** the position or office of a Lord Lieutenant. **Lord Lieutenant** (*a*) an official holding deputed authority from the monarch; *spec.* the chief executive authority and head of the magistracy in each county (formerly also having extensive powers with regard to the militia etc.); (*b*) *Hist.* the viceroy of Ireland. *Lord love you, me, a duck*: see LOVE *v.* 1. *Lord Lyon*. *Lord Marcher*: see MARCHER *n.*^{1} **Lord Mayor** (the title of) the head of the municipal corporation of London, Dublin, or York, later also of any of several other large cities; *Lord Mayor's Day*, the day on which a Lord Mayor of London comes into office; *Lord Mayor's Show*, a procession of decorated vehicles etc. in London on Lord Mayor's Day. **Lord Muck** *slang* a pompous self-opinionated man, a socially pretentious man. **Lord of Appeal (in Ordinary)** a member of the House of Lords committee appointed as the ultimate judicial appeal court. *Lord of hosts*: see HOST *n.*^{1} *Lord of Misrule*: see MISRULE *n.* *lord of regality*: see REGALITY 2a. *Lord of Sabaoth*: see SABAOTH 1. *Lord of the ascendant*: see ASCENDANT *n.* 1. **lord of the bedchamber** a nobleman holding a certain office in personal attendance on the monarch. **Lord of the Flies** (*a*) Beelzebub; (*b*) with allusive ref. to the title of the book (1954) by William Golding (1911–), in which a group of schoolboys marooned on an uninhabited tropical island revert to savagery and primitive ritual. **lord of the manor** the lord or master of a manor house. *lord of the soil*: see SOIL *n.*^{1} *Lord Ordinary*: see ORDINARY *n.* *lord paramount*: see PARAMOUNT *a.* 1. *Lord President of the Council*: see PRESIDENT *n.* *Lord Privy Seal*: see PRIVY *a.* *lord proprietary*: see PROPRIETARY *n.* 3. *lord proprietor*: see PROPRIETOR 2. *Lord Protector* (*of the Commonwealth*): see PROTECTOR 2b. *Lord Provost*: see PROVOST *n.* *Lord Rector*: see RECTOR 3b. **lords and ladies** (*a*) the cuckoo-pint or wild arum, *Arum maculatum*; (*b*) see *lord and lady* above. **Lords Appellant**(**s**) *Hist.* a group of nobles who brought charges of treason against certain supporters of Richard II. *Lord's day*: see *the Lord's day* below. *lords of creation*: see *lords of the creation* below. *Lords of the Articles*: see ARTICLE *n.* 2. **lords of (the) creation** (*a*) humankind; (*b*) *joc.* men as opp. to women. *Lords triers*: see TRIER 5. *Lord Treasurer*: see TREASURER 1. *Lord Warden*: see WARDEN *n.*^{1} 11. *mesne lord*: see MESNE *a.* **my lord** (*a*) *arch.* the ordinary title used in speaking to or of a nobleman; (*b*) *voc.* preceding a title or rank or office; (*c*) in *pl.* (not preceding a title), the form of address to a number of noblemen or bishops or to two or more judges of the Supreme Court sitting together in a court of law; (*d*) in *pl.* (not preceding a title), in official correspondence, the ministers composing a department of State collectively; (*e*) (not preceding a title) the polite or respectful form of address to a nobleman under the rank of duke, a bishop, or a judge of the Supreme Court. *Our Lord*: see OUR *a.* 1b. *swear like a lord*: see SWEAR *v.* **the Lords** the temporal and spiritual peers of Parliament, constituting the upper legislative body of the UK; the House of Lords. **(the) Lord's day** Sunday. *the Lord's house*: see HOUSE *n.*^{1} **the Lord's Prayer** the prayer taught by Jesus to his disciples (*Matt.* 6:9–13, *Luke* 11:2–4). **the Lords spiritual**, the bishops and archbishops sitting in the House of Lords. **the Lord's Supper** the Eucharist. *the Lord's table*: see TABLE *n.* 13. **the Lords temporal**, the peers of the realm sitting in the House of Lords. **treat like a lord** entertain sumptuously, treat with profound deference.

lord-dom *n.* †(*a*) the position of being a lord, lordship; (*b*) *rare* the state of things characterized by the existence of lords: OE. **lordful** *a.* (*rare*) having the bearing of a lord, lordly LME. **lordless** *a.* OE. **lordlet** *n.* (*joc.*) a young, small, or minor lord L19. **lordlike** *a.* & *adv.* (*a*) *adj.* resembling, befitting, or characteristic of a lord; lordly; †(*b*) *adv.* in the manner of a lord; domineeringly; sumptuously: LME. **lorˈdolatry** *n.* (*joc.*) excessive admiration for a lord or lords M19.

lord /lɔːd/ *v.* ME. [f. the n.] †**1** *v.i.* Exercise lordship, have dominion. ME–L15. **2** *v.t.* Be or act as lord of; control, manage, rule. Now *rare.* LME. **3** *v.i.* & (chiefly) *t.* w. *it.* Behave in a lordly manner, assume airs of grandeur; domineer. Freq. foll. by *over.* M16. **4** *v.t.* Confer the title of *Lord* on; ennoble; address or speak of as 'lord'. E17.

3 P. USTINOV A mad monk lording it over an alleged parliament. A. BURGESS Laurence . . from the second class . . was able to observe Magnus lording it in first.

lording /ˈlɔːdɪŋ/ *n.* OE. [f. LORD *n.* + -ING^3.] **1** = LORD *n.* 2. Usu. in *pl.*, esp. as a form of address. *arch.* OE. **2** A little lord, a petty or minor lord. Chiefly *derog.* L16.

lordling /ˈlɔːdlɪŋ/ *n.* ME. [f. LORD *n.* + -LING^1.] = LORDING 2 (freq. *derog.*). Also occas. (*arch.*) = LORDING 1.

lordly /ˈlɔːdli/ *a.* & *n.* OE. [f. LORD *n.* + -LY^1.] **A** *adj.* **1** Of or pertaining to a lord or lords; consisting of lords; administered by lords. Now *rare.* OE. **2** Of a person: having the character, attributes, appearance, or demeanour of a lord. Of an action: befitting a lord; honourable, noble. LME. **b** Haughty, imperious, lofty, disdainful. LME. **3** Of a thing: fit for a lord; grand, magnificent, noble. L15.

1 JOHN HALL Lordly or absolute Monarchy is the best and most natural Government. E. MIALL Pensioning off supernumerary members of lordly houses. 2 C. H. SPURGEON He is more lordly than all emperors and kings. F. RAPHAEL Byron's name is associated with lordly excess and romantic adventure. b L. STEPHEN A lordly indifference to making money by his writings. 3 H. G. DAKYNS Cyrus was flying at lordlier game than certain irrepressible hill tribes. C. MACKENZIE The lordly spread, of which a magnificent lobster was the *pièce de résistance*.

B *absol.* as *n.* A lordly person or thing. Now usu., *the* lordly people as a class. L15.

lordlily *adv.* E17. **lordliness** *n.* †(*a*) lordly state or condition; (*b*) lordly disposition; grandeur; arrogance: LME.

lordly /ˈlɔːdli/ *adv. arch.* LME. [f. LORD *n.* + -LY^2.] After the manner of a lord; in a lordly manner.

R. SAVAGE Lordly neglectful of a worth unknown. W. MORRIS In a land where few were poor, if none Were lordly rich.

lordosis /lɔːˈdəʊsɪs/ *n.* Pl. **-doses** /-ˈdəʊsiːz/. E18. [mod.L f. Gk *lordōsis*, f. *lordos* bent backwards: see -OSIS.] **1** *Med.* (Abnormal) inward curvature of the spine causing increased concavity of the back. Cf. KYPHOSIS, SCOLIOSIS. E18. **2** *Zool.* A posture assumed by some female mammals during mating, in which the back is arched downwards; the assumption of such a posture. M20.

lordotic /-ˈdɒtɪk/ *a.* M19.

lordship /ˈlɔːdʃɪp/ *n.* & *v.* OE. [f. LORD *n.* + -SHIP.] **A** *n.* **1** The dignity and functions of a lord; dominion, rule, ownership *of*, *over*. OE. **2** The land or territory belonging to or under the jurisdiction of a lord; a domain, an estate, a manor. LME. †**b** A government, a province, a district. LME–L16. **3** With possess. adj. (as *your* etc. *lordship*): a title of respect given to a nobleman below the rank of a duke, to a judge, and to a bishop; *joc.* a mock complimentary or respectful designation for an ordinary person. LME. **4** A percentage on the sale of a book; a royalty (on a mine or a book). *Sc.* M18.

1 G. BANCROFT Parliament had asserted an absolute lordship over the colonies. H. WILSON The first lordship of the Treasury. **2** LD MACAULAY The new envoy . . bore a title taken from the lordship of Zulestein. **3** W. CRUISE We must call that case to the consideration of your Lordships. RACHEL ANDERSON The stone dogs on his Lordship's terrace.

B *v.* Infl. **-pp-**. †**1** *v.i.* & *t.* Exercise lordship (over); be a lord or ruler (of). ME–L15. **2** *v.t.* Address as 'your lordship'. M18.

lordy /ˈlɔːdi/ *int.* Orig. *US.* Also **lawdy**. M19. [f. LORD *n.* + -Y[6].] Expr. surprise, dismay, etc. Cf. LORD *n.* 5, LOR'.

N. MAILER Well, Lordy-me. N. FREELING A kidnapping. . . And lordy, it's the child of a magistrate.

lore /lɔː/ *n.*[1] [OE *lār* = OFris. *lāre*, OS, OHG *lēra* (Du. *leer*, G *Lehre*), f. WGmc base also of LEARN.] **1** The act of teaching; the condition of being taught; instruction, education; a piece of instruction; a lesson. Now *arch.* & *dial.* OE. **2** That which is taught; doctrine, teaching, *esp.* religious doctrine. Now *poet.* & *arch.* OE. †**b** A doctrine, a precept; a creed, a religion. OE–L16. **3** Advice, counsel; an instruction, a command. Now *rare* or *obs.* ME. **4** Orig., that which is learned; learning, scholarship, erudition; (now only *arch.* & *Sc.*: cf. LEAR *n.*[1]). Later, the body of traditional facts, anecdotes, or beliefs relating to some particular subject or held by a specific group. ME. †**b** A branch of knowledge, a science. ME–M16.

1 COLERIDGE We have learnt A different lore. J. M. NEALE In the Cross we found our pulpit, In the Seven great Words, our lore. **2** SIR W. SCOTT Can piety the discord heal . . Can Christian lore, can patriot zeal? **3** MILTON Understanding rul'd not, and the Will Heard not her lore. **4** R. C. A. WHITE Typical jury lore suggests that women are less likely to convict than men. R. MANNING Edith was very knowledgeable in country lore.

lored *a.* (*rare*) learned; stored with knowledge: M19. **loreless** *a.* (*rare*) without learning or knowledge ME.

lore /lɔː/ *n.*[2] E17. [L LORUM.] †**1** A strap, a thong, a rein. *rare.* E–M17. **2** *Zool.* A long flat appendage or surface; *spec.* (*a*) a mouthpart in certain insects, as homopterans and hymenopterans; (*b*) the region between the eye and the side of the beak in a bird, or between the eye and the nostril in a snake; = LORUM. E19.

lore *v.* pa. pple of LESE.

loreal /ˈlɔːrɪəl/ *a.* & *n.* M19. [f. prec. + -AL[1].] *Zool.* **A** *adj.* Of, pertaining to, or in the region of the lore; loral. M19. **B** *n.* A loreal plate, shield, etc. M19.

Lorelei /ˈlɔːrəlʌɪ, ˈlɒ-/ *n.* E20. [In German legend, a siren with long blonde hair who sat on the *Lorelei* rock on the Rhine, and whose song lured boatmen to destruction.] A dangerously fascinating woman, a temptress, a siren.

Lorentz /ləˈrɛnts/ *n.* E20. [H. A. *Lorentz* (1853–1928), Du. physicist.] *Physics.* Used *attrib.* to designate various concepts and phenomena described by Lorentz or arising from his work.

Lorentz-covariant *a.* covariant under a Lorentz transformation. **Lorentz (-FitzGerald) contraction** = FITZGERALD *contraction.* **Lorentz force**: exerted on a charged particle by a magnetic field through which it is moving. **Lorentz-invariant** *a.* invariant under a Lorentz transformation. **Lorentz transformation** the set of equations which in the special theory of relativity relate the space and time coordinates of one frame of reference to those of another moving rectilinearly with respect to it. **Lorentz triplet** a group of three spectral lines produced by the Zeeman effect.

Lorentzian *a.* & *n.* (*a*) *adj.* of or pertaining to Lorentz or his theories, or the concepts arising out of his work; *spec.* designating (the graph of) a function having the same form as the expression, in classical radiation theory, for the intensity of a spectral emission line in terms of frequency; (*b*) *n.* a Lorentzian curve or function: M20.

Lorenz /ləˈrɛnts/ *n.*[1] E20. [L. V. *Lorenz* (1829–91), Da. physicist.] Physics. *Lorenz('s) constant, Lorenz number*, the ratio $k/\sigma T$ (where k = thermal conductivity, σ = electrical conductivity, T = temperature), which has approximately the same value for many metallic elements over a wide range of temperatures.

Lorenz /ləˈrɛnts/ *n.*[2] M20. [M. O. *Lorenz* (1876–*c* 1970), US statistician.] *Lorenz curve*, a curve in which cumulative percentage of the total of some variable (esp. national income) is plotted against cumulative percentage of a corresponding population ranked in increasing order of the size of share, so illustrating any inequality of distribution.

lorgnette /lɔːnˈjɛt, *foreign* lɔrɲɛt (*pl. same*)/ *n.* E19. [Fr., f. *lorgner* to squint, ogle: see -ETTE.] *sing.* & in *pl.* A pair of eyeglasses to be held in the hand, usu. by a long handle. Also, a pair of opera-glasses.

lorgnon /ˈlɔːnjən, lɔrɲɔ̃ (*pl. same*)/ *n.* M19. [Fr., f. *lorgner*: see prec., -OON.] *sing.* & in *pl.* A single or double eyeglass; a lorgnette. Also, a pair of opera-glasses.

lorica /ləˈrʌɪkə/ *n.* Pl. **-cae** /-siː, -kiː/, **-cas**. E18. [L = breastplate f. as LORUM.] **1** *Rom. Antiq.* A cuirass or corslet of leather. E18. †**2** The coping or protecting head of a wall. Only in E18. **3** A kind of cement or paste for coating a vessel before subjecting it to heat. Now *rare* or *obs.* M18. **4** *Zool.* The stiff protective case or shell of some protozoans and rotifers. M19.

loricate /ˈlɒrɪkeɪt/ *a.* & *n.* E19. [L *loricatus* pa. pple, f. as next: see -ATE[2].] *Zool.* **A** *adj.* Covered with protective plates or scales; having a lorica. E19. **B** *n.* A loricate animal. Formerly *spec.* (*a*) a crocodilian; (*b*) an armadillo, a pangolin. *rare.* M19.

loricate /ˈlɒrɪkeɪt/ *v.t.* E17. [L *loricat-* pa. ppl stem of *loricare*, f. as LORICA: see -ATE[3].] Enclose in or cover with a protective coating.

loriˈcation *n.* (*a*) the action or an act of loricating something; (*b*) a defensive covering or casing: E18.

loricated /ˈlɒrɪkeɪtɪd/ *a.* E17. [f. as prec. + -ED[1].] Enclosed in or covered with a protective coating; *Zool.* = LORICATE *a.*

lorikeet /ˈlɒrɪkiːt/ *n.* L18. [f. LORY + *-keet*, after *parakeet*.] Any of various small brightly coloured lories of Australia and the Indo-Pacific islands, chiefly of the genera *Charmosyna, Glossopsitta*, and *Trichoglossus*.

lorilet /ˈlɒrɪlət, lɒrɪˈlɛt/ *n. Austral.* M20. [f. LORY + -LET.] Any of several very small, mainly green, short-tailed parrots of the genera *Opopsitta* and *Psittaculirostris*, native to rainforests in NE Australia and New Guinea. Also called *fig-parrot*.

lorimer *n.* var. of LORINER.

loriner /ˈlɒrɪnə/ *n.* Also **-mer** /-mə/. ME. [OFr. *lorenier, -mier*, f. *lorain* strap of a harness, f. Proto-Romance, f. L *lorum* strap, thong: see -ER[2].] A maker of bits and metal mountings for horses' bridles and of stirrup-irons; a spurrier; *gen.* a maker of small ironware, a worker in wrought iron. Now only in the title of one of the London livery companies.

†**loring** *n. rare* (Spenser). Only in L16. [f. LORE *n.*[1] + -ING[1].] Teaching, instruction.

loriot /ˈlɒrɪət/ *n.* Long *rare.* L16. [Fr., f. *l'* the + *oriot* var. of *oriol* ORIOLE.] The golden oriole, *Oriolus oriolus.*

loris /ˈlɔːrɪs/ *n.* L18. [Fr., perh. f. Du. †*loeris* clown, booby.] Any of several small slow-moving nocturnal primates of the subfamily Lorisinae, with small ears, very short tails, and opposable thumbs, *esp.* (more fully *slender loris*) *Loris tardigradus* of Sri Lanka (Ceylon) and southern India, and (more fully *slow loris*) *Nycticebus coucang* of SE Asia.

lorisid *n.* & *a.* (*a*) *n.* a member of the family Lorisidae, which includes lorises, pottos, and bushbabies; (*b*) *adj.* of or pertaining to the family Lorisidae: M20. **lorisoid** *n.* & *a.* (an animal) resembling a loris or related to the lorises M20.

lormery /ˈlɔːməri/ *n. obs.* exc. *Hist.* LME. [OFr. *lormerie*, f. *loremier*: see LORINER, -ERY.] The small ironware produced by lorimers; a place for the making or selling of such ware.

lorn /lɔːn/ *a.* Now *arch.* & *joc.* ME. [pa. pple of LESE.] **1** Lost, perished, ruined; doomed to destruction. *obs.* exc. *dial.* ME. **2** Abandoned, left alone; bereft *of*; lonely, desolate; forlorn. L15.

1 SIR W. SCOTT If thou readest, thou art lorn! Better hadst thou ne'er been born! **2** W. OWEN Uncle . . has made overtures to me to add my lorn voice to the choir. D. PARKER Mrs. Ewing never vaunted her lorn condition, never shut herself within the shaded chambers of bereavement.

lornness /-n-n-/ *n.* forlornness M19.

lorn *v.* pa. pple of LESE.

Lorraine /lɒˈreɪn/ *n.* M19. [A region and former province in NE France.] Chiefly Her. *Lorraine cross, cross (of) Lorraine*, a cross with two horizontal limbs.

¶Cf. QUICHE *Lorraine.*

Lorrainer /lɒˈreɪnə/ *n.* M18. [f. as prec. + -ER[2].] A native or inhabitant of Lorraine in NE France.

lorry /ˈlɒri, ˈlʌri/ *n.* M19. [Perh. f. the pers. name *Laurie.*] **1 a** A long flat low wagon without sides. Also, a truck or wagon used on a railway or tramway. M19. **b** A large strong motor vehicle for transporting goods, troops, etc., *esp.* an open one with a flat platform. E20. **2** *Mining.* A running bridge over a pit. L19.

1b *army lorry, articulated lorry, goods lorry*, etc. **fall off (the back of) a lorry** (of goods etc.) be acquired in dubious circumstances from an unspecified source.

Comb.: **lorry-bus** a lorry used as a vehicle for public transport; **lorry-hop** *v.* hitchhike by lorry; **lorry park** an open space or lot reserved for the parking of lorries.

lorry /ˈlɒri/ *v.t.* E20. [f. prec.] Transport or convey by means of a lorry or lorries.

lors /lɔːz/ *int. colloq.* M19. [Alt. of LORD *n.* Cf. LOR'.] Expr. surprise, dismay, etc.

lorum /ˈlɔːrəm/ *n.* Pl. **lora** /ˈlɔːrə/. L19. [L = strap, thong.] *Zool.* = LORE *n.*[2] 2.

lory /ˈlɔːri/ *n.* L17. [Malay *lori, luri*, dial. var. of *nuri*: cf. Du. *lori*, Fr. *lori.*] Any of various parrot-like birds with brilliant plumage of the family Loriidae, found in SE Asia and Australasia and feeding mainly on nectar with brush-tipped tongues. Cf. LOERIE.

losable /ˈluːzəb(ə)l/ *a.* Also **loseable**. LME. [f. LOSE *v.* + -ABLE.] Able to be lost.

Los Angelino /lɒs andʒəˈliːnəʊ/ *n.* Pl. **-os**. M20. [f. *Los Angeles* after ANGELENO.] = ANGELENO.

†**lose** *n.*[1] ME–E19. [OFr. *los, loz, loos* f. L *laudes* pl. of *laus* praise.] Praise; renown, fame; reputation.

lose /luːz/ *n.*[2] *slang.* L19. [f. LOSE *v.*] An instance of losing a race.

Comb.: **lose bet, game**: in which the loser of the game wins the stakes.

lose /luːz/ *v.* Pa. t. & pple **lost** /lɒst/. [OE *losian*, f. *los* LOSS, later sense-development infl. by cognate LESE, pronunc. prob. infl. by LOOSE *a.* etc.] †**1** *v.i.* Perish; be lost or missing. OE–LME. **2** *v.t.* †**a** Destroy, bring to perdition; be the ruin of. OE–E17. **b** In *pass.* Be brought to destruction or ruin; perish, die or be dead; (of the soul) be damned; (of a ship etc.) disappear, perish at sea. ME. **c** Ruin (a person) in another's estimation. Now *rare* or *obs.* E17. **3** *v.t.* Become unable to find; cease to know the whereabouts of. OE. †**b** Fail to retain in the mind or memory; forget. M16–E18. **c** Cease to follow (the right track). Freq. in *lose one's way* below. M16. **d** Fail to keep in sight; *poet.* cease to hear (a song etc.). L16. **e** Draw away from, be no longer near or among; leave (another competitor) hopelessly behind in a race. L17. **4** *v.t.* Suffer the privation of (a possession, an attribute, a faculty, etc.); cease to possess or have through negligence or misadventure; be or become separated from by death or estrangement; be deprived of; *spec.* (*a*) suffer the loss of (blood) from one's blood-vessels; (*b*) (of an army commander etc.) suffer the loss of (troops) by death, capture, etc.; (*c*) (of a doctor) fail to preserve the life of (a patient); (*d*) (of a woman) suffer the loss of (a child) in childbirth, miscarry (a child). ME. **b** Of a thing: be deprived of or part with (a portion of itself, a quality, an appendage). Also foll. by *off.* ME. **c** Fail to maintain (a position, a state of mind or body, etc.). L15. †**d** Be deprived of the power or opportunity *to do*. Only in 17. **e** Cease to suffer from, get rid of (a cold etc.); undergo a reduction of, shed (weight). Also, vomit up (a recently eaten meal). M17. **f** In *pass.* Of an art: cease to be known or practised. Of a quality etc.: cease to be present. M17. **5** *v.i.* Suffer loss or detriment; cease to possess something wholly or partly; incur disadvantage (foll. by *in*, †*of*); be worse off, esp. financially, as the result of a transaction (foll. by *by*, *on*). ME. **6** *v.t.* Spend (time, opportunities, etc.) to no purpose; waste. ME. **7** *v.t.* Fail to obtain (something one might have had); miss (a train etc.); fail to catch (a quarry). ME. **b** Fail to apprehend by sight or hearing; not catch (words etc.). L16. †**c** Fail to attend. E18–M19. **8** *v.t.* **a** Cause the loss of. ME. **b** Cause (a person) to miss the course of an argument etc.; bewilder. Chiefly *colloq.* M17. **c** Dispose of or discard as unnecessary or superfluous; kill. *colloq.* M20. **9** *v.t.* **a** Be deprived of (something) in a contest or game; forfeit (a stake); be defeated in (a game, a battle, a lawsuit); fail to carry (a motion). Also in *Cricket*, have (a wicket) taken by an opponent. (Foll. by *to*.) ME. **b** *v.i.* Be defeated; forfeit money, a stake, etc., by defeat in a game. M16. **10** *v.refl.* (& in *pass.*). **a** Lose one's way, go astray, (*lit.* & *fig.*). M16. **b** Lose identity, become merged (*in* something else), (*lit.* & *fig.*). E17. **c** Become deeply absorbed or engrossed (*in* thought etc.); be bewildered, be overwhelmed (*in*). Formerly also, be or become distracted (from emotion or excitement). E17. **d** Become hidden from view, become obscured, (*in* clouds etc.). L17. **11** Of a clock etc: **a** *v.i.* Run (increasingly) slow; indicate a time earlier than the correct time. M19. **b** *v.t.* Run slow by (a specified amount of time). M19.

2a SHAKES. *Haml.* What to ourselves in passion we propose, The passion ending, doth the purpose lose. **b** *Law Times* The vessel . . sank in a short time, all hands being lost. **c** C. SEDLEY 'Twas I that lost you in each Roman mind. **3** TENNYSON Since her horse was lost I left her mine. J. MORLEY Humanity had lost its title-deeds and he had recovered them. **c** D. H. LAWRENCE He . . stumbled blindly . . , having lost the path in the complete darkness. **d** T. HERBERT Wee . . got sight of the Carracke, and lost her for euer, in two houres after. TENNYSON Losing her carol I stood pensively. **e** POPE Here where the mountains less'ning as they rise Lose the low vales. **4** E. WAUGH My papa has just put all his money into a cinema film and lost it all. E. BOWEN They lost their colours and had five or six hundred slain. L. URIS For five consecutive years she lost children through early miscarriages. L. HELLMAN They had lost a brother in a yellow fever epidemic. **b** H. CAINE Her household duties had lost their interest. **c** MILTON They astonisht all resistance lost, All courage. **e** WILKIE COLLINS O! let me teach my heart to lose its fears. OED I have not yet lost my rheumatism. **5** TENNYSON 'Tis better to have loved and lost Than never to have loved at all. OED Both armies lost heavily. J. CLEARY I've lost on every race so far. **6** F. MARRYAT There is no time to be lost. G. BOOTHBY A . . fellow who never lost a chance of making himself objectionable. A. AYCKBOURN Of all the working days lost . . half are due to strikes and illness. **7** JAS. HARRIS The swift-footed Salius lost the prize to young Euryalus. OED I did not lose a word of his speech. S. LEACOCK No, not the fish they caught; this was the big one that they lost. **b** SWIFT I lost church today. **8a** E. A. FREEMAN The crimes of John lost him all the northern part of his French possessions. **b** P. CAREY I'm sorry . . but you've lost me. What was what deal? **9a** DICKENS The motion was lost by a majority of two. R. CAMPBELL I lost only one fight out of eight. G. BOYCOTT Bob Willis had lost his battle against a knee injury. **b** SHAKES. *Lear* Who loses and who wins; who's in, who's out. SWIFT She lost at one Sitting to the Tune of a hundred Guineas. **10a** MILTON In wandring mazes lost. J. C. POWYS His mind went faster still . . losing itself in infinite perspectives. **b** J. AUSTEN All surprise was shortly lost in other feelings. C. LAMB I love to lose myself in other men's minds. **c** W. IRVING As I . . lose myself in melancholy musings. B. JOWETT He seemed to be lost in the contemplation of something great. **d** DRYDEN When the setting Stars are lost in Day. W. COWPER Rills that . . lose themselves at length In matted grass.

Phrases: *heads I win, tails you lose*: see HEAD *n.* *lose an eye*: see EYE *n.* *lose caste*: see CASTE 3. *lose count*: see COUNT *n.*[1] I. *lose countenance*: see COUNTENANCE *n.* *lose face*: see FACE *n.* *lose flesh*: see FLESH *n.* *lose ground*: see GROUND *n.* *lose heart*: see HEART *n.* **lose height** (of an aeroplane etc.) descend to a lower level in flight. *lose interest*: see INTEREST *n.* *lose leather*: see LEATHER *n.* **lose nothing in the telling** = *not lose in the telling* below. *lose no time*: see TIME *n.* *lose one's balance*: see BALANCE *n.* *lose one's block*: see BLOCK *n.* 6b. *lose one's grip*: see GRIP *n.*[1] *lose one's hair*: see HAIR *n.* *lose one's head*: see HEAD *n.* *lose one's heart*: see HEART *n.* **lose one's life** be killed. *lose one's market*: see MARKET *n.* *lose one's mind*: see MIND *n.*[1] *lose one's nerve*: see NERVE *n.* *lose one's rag*: see RAG *n.*[1] *lose one's seat*: see SEAT *n.* *lose one's shirt*: see SHIRT *n.* *lose one's stirrups*: see STIRRUP *n.* *lose one's temper*: see TEMPER *n.* *lose one's touch*: see TOUCH *n.* *lose one's voice*: see VOICE *n.* **lose one's way** go astray (*lit.* & *fig.*). *lose one's wool*: see WOOL *n.* *lose patience*: see PATIENCE *n.* *lose sight of*: see SIGHT *n.* *lose sleep over*: see SLEEP *n.* *lose the number of one's mess*: see MESS *n.* *lose the scent*: see SCENT *n.* **lose the way** = *lose one's way* above. *lose touch* (*with*): see TOUCH *n.* *lose track of*: see TRACK *n.* **lose way** (of a ship or boat) begin to move less quickly. *lose weight*: see WEIGHT *n.* **nothing to lose** *colloq.* no possibility of further loss. **not lose in the telling** (of a story) be, if anything, exaggerated. *win the saddle or lose the horse*: see SADDLE *n.* **you** etc. **can't lose** you etc. must inevitably profit.

With advs. in specialized senses: **lose out** *colloq.* be unsuccessful, suffer a loss, not get a fair chance or advantage, (foll. by *on*).

loseable *a.* var. of LOSABLE.

losel /ˈləʊz(ə)l/ *n.* & *a.* Now *arch.* & *dial.* LME. [App. f. *los-* stem of LESE + -EL[1].] **A** *n.* A worthless person; a profligate, a rake; a ne'er-do-well. LME. **B** *adj.* Good-for-nothing, worthless. E17.

loselry *n.* worthless or profligate behaviour LME.

loser /ˈluːzə/ *n.* ME. [f. LOSE *v.* + -ER[1].] †**1** A destroyer. ME–E17. **2** A person who loses or suffers loss; *esp.* a person, horse, etc., that loses a race etc., an unsuccessful competitor. M16. **b** A consistently unsuccessful person, a failure. M20. **3** *Billiards.* A losing hazard. L19. **4** A convicted criminal, a person who has served a sentence in prison, esp. for a specified number of times. *US slang.* E20. **5** *Bridge.* A card that will not take a trick. E20.

2 SHAKES. *Haml.* You will draw both friend and foe, Winner and loser? LD MACAULAY He . . declared that he had been a loser by his mission. **a bad, poor,** (or **good**) **loser** a person who is (not) dejected or angered by losing a game etc. **b** E. FEINSTEIN Seryosha was a sick man, as well as a hopelessly weak one, a born loser. **4** E. S. GARDNER He's a two-time loser.

losh /lɒʃ/ *n.*[1] Now *rare.* L16. [Russ. *los'*.] An elk. Long *obs.* exc. in *losh hide, leather*, the untanned hide of the elk, and later of the buffalo and ox, prepared with oil; a soft buff-coloured leather.

losh *n.*[2] var. of LOCHE.

†**losh** *v.i.* E17–M19. [Perh. imit.] Fall with a splash; go stumbling.

losh /lɒʃ/ *int. Sc.* L18. [Alt. of LORD *n.* Cf. LOR', LORS.] Expr. surprise, dismay, etc.

losing /ˈluːzɪŋ/ *n.* OE. [f. LOSE *v.* + -ING[1].] The action of LOSE *v.*; an instance of this. In early use *spec.* perdition, destruction; the action of being lost or destroyed.

(*on*) *a losing streak*: see STREAK *n.*

losing /ˈluːzɪŋ/ *ppl a.* E16. [f. LOSE *v.* + -ING[2].] That loses, that results in loss.

losing battle a battle in which defeat seems inevitable (*lit.* & *fig.*). **losing game** (*a*) a game in which defeat seems inevitable; (*b*) a game in which the loser of the game wins the stakes, a test of skill in forcing one's opponent to win. *losing hazard*: see HAZARD *n.*

loss /lɒs/ *n.* [OE *los* corresp. to ON *los* breaking up of the ranks of an army, f. Gmc f. base also of LESE, LEASE *a.*, LOOSE *a.*; later back-form. f. *lost* pa. pple of LOSE *v.*] **1** Perdition, ruin, destruction; the state or fact of being destroyed or ruined. *obs.* exc. as passing into later senses. OE. **2a** Orig., the state of being a loser, defeat. Later, the losing of, or defeat in, a battle, game, or contest. ME. **b** The fact of losing someone or something, deprivation of or failure to keep a possession, attribute, faculty, etc. Also, the fact of being deprived of a person by death, estrangement, etc.; the death of a person regretted; *spec.* miscarriage of a child. LME. **c** Failure to take advantage or make good use of time, opportunities, etc. LME. **d** Failure to gain or obtain something sought. E17. **3** *Mil.* The losing (by an army commander etc.) of troops by death, capture, etc.; *sing.* & in *pl.*, the number of troops so lost. ME. †**4** A cause or occasion of ruin or deprivation. *rare.* LME–M16. **5** A particular instance of losing; a person, thing, or amount lost; *spec.* an instance of losing blood. LME. **6** Diminution of one's possessions or advantages; detriment or disadvantage involved in being deprived of something, or resulting from a change of conditions; an instance of this. (Opp. *gain*.) LME. †**7** *Real Tennis.* A lost chase. L16–E17. †**8** Lack, default, want. E–M17.

1 MILTON Thou hast . . quitted all to save A world from utter loss. **2a** C. HOPE The Brahm family regarded the loss of the Great War as a tragedy. **b** LD MACAULAY The Papists of Ireland attributed to him the loss of their lands. M. N. COX King Lear's is the archetypal cry of devastating loss 'Thou'lt come no more.' J. MCDOUGALL The loss of control that is entailed in letting their thoughts wander freely. *Which?* Insurance which covers loss of luggage. **c** SIR W. SCOTT Instant reimbursement for loss of time. J. TYNDALL This error caused us the loss of an hour. **d** D. DYKE A word that signifieth . . losse of victory. OED I do not wish to risk the loss of my train. **3** D. A. THOMAS The losses were horrific . . about 8,000 men. **5** EVELYN Thus ended this incomparable Lady: our never to be sufficiently lamented losse. *Holiday Which?* Nowadays people who try to sell their timeshare commonly make a sizeable loss. **6** AV *Phil.* 3:7 What things were gaine to me, those I counted losse for Christ. *Bella* A terrible sense of loss and grief filled Hilary.

Phrases: **a great loss** a person or thing whose loss is a severe blow (freq. in neg. contexts). **at a loss** (*a*) (of a hound) having lost the track or scent of a quarry, at fault; (*b*) (of a person) puzzled, not knowing what to do, (freq. foll. by *for, to do*); *be at a loss for words*, not know what to say; (*c*) (of something sold) for less than the purchase price. *consequential losses*: see CONSEQUENTIAL *a.* I. *cut one's losses*: see CUT *v.* *dead loss*: see DEAD *a.* etc. *loss of face*: see FACE *n.* **loss of life** (*a*) the fact of being put to death, esp. as a punishment; (*b*) *gen.* the destruction of human lives. *profit and loss*: see PROFIT *n.*

Comb.: **loss adjuster** an insurance agent who assesses the amount of compensation arising from a loss; **loss-leader** an article put on sale at a non-profit-making price in order to attract potential buyers of other articles; **loss-maker** a business etc. consistently working at a loss; **loss-making** *vbl n.* the making of a loss (in business, etc.); **loss-making** *ppl a.* that makes a loss; **loss-proof** *a.* guaranteed against loss, inflation, fluctuation in market value, etc.

losset /ˈlɒsɪt/ *n.* Chiefly *dial.* M17. [Ir. *losaid* (OIr. *losat*) kneading-trough.] A wooden tray.

lossless /ˈlɒslɪs/ *a.* L16. [f. LOSS *n.* + -LESS.] †**1** Without loss. L16–M17. **2** *Electr.* Characterized by or causing no dissipation of electrical or electromagnetic energy. M20.

lossy /ˈlɒsi/ *a.* M20. [f. LOSS *n.* + -Y[1].] *Electr.* Characterized by or causing dissipation of electrical or electromagnetic energy.

lost /lɒst/ *a.* & *n.* LME. [pa. pple of LOSE *v.*] **A** *adj.* **1** Of time, effort, opportunities, etc.: not used advantageously; spent in vain; wasted. LME. 2 Having gone astray, having lost the way; *fig.* bewildered, puzzled. Also, of which a person has been deprived; not retained in possession; no longer to be found. LME. 3 That has perished or been destroyed; ruined, esp. morally or spiritually; (of a soul) damned. M16. 4 Of a battle, game, etc.: in which a defeat has been sustained. E18.

Phrases: **be lost on** fail to influence or draw the attention of, not be noticed or appreciated by. **be lost without** be unable to cope without, have great difficulty if deprived of. **get lost** *slang* cease to be annoying, go away (usu. in *imper.*). *legion of the lost (ones)*: see LEGION *n.* *lost in the shuffle*: see SHUFFLE *n.* 3b. *lost in thought*: see THOUGHT *n.*[1] **lost to** (*a*) that has passed from the possession of, that has been taken from; (*b*) no longer affected by a sense of duty, shame, etc., with regard to.

Special collocations: *lost cause*: see CAUSE *n.* **lost generation** the generation reaching maturity *c*1915–25, a high proportion of whose men were killed in the war of 1914–18; any culturally or emotionally unstable generation. *lost labour*: see LABOUR *n.* **lost motion** imperfect transmission of motion between two parts of a machine which communicate one with the other, owing to faulty construction or looseness of the parts. **lost property** lost articles found but not claimed; *lost property department, office*, an office, department, dealing with (the disposal of) lost property. **lost river** *US* a river which disappears into the ground and re-emerges elsewhere. **lost rock, stone** *US* an erratic boulder. *Lost Tribes*: see TRIBE *n.* **lost wax** = CIRE PERDUE. **lost weekend** a weekend spent in dissolute living.

B *absol.* as *n.* 1 An advertisement of a lost article. *rare.* M18. 2 *The* lost persons or things as a class. M19.

2 LEGION *of the lost.*

lostly *adv.* (*rare*) M17. **lostness** *n.* E18.

lost *v.* pa. t. & pple of LOSE *v.*

los von Rom /loːs fɔn 'roːm/ *n. phr.* L19. [G = free from Rome.] *Hist.* A policy seeking to reduce the political influence of the Roman Catholic Church in Austria and Germany at the end of the 19th cent.; the movement concerned with this.

lot /lɒt/ *n.* [OE *hlot* corresp. to OFris. *hlot*, MLG, (M)Du. *lot*, ON *hlutr*, *hluti*, also OE *hlȳt*, f. Gmc. Rel. to G *Loos*, *Los*.] 1 Any of a set of objects used in a method of random selection to secure a decision in deciding disputes, dividing goods, choosing people for an office or duty, etc., by an appeal to chance or the divine agency supposed to be concerned in the results of chance. Now chiefly in *cast, draw*, etc., *lots* (usu. *between, for, who*, etc.). OE. 2 The action or an act of casting, drawing, etc. lots, to obtain a decision. Chiefly in *by lot*. OE. b The choice resulting from a casting, throwing, etc., of lots. ME. †c *sing.* & in *pl.* A game of chance. Also, a divinatory appeal to chance. L16–L18. 3 A portion, a share; *spec.* what is assigned by lot as a person's share or portion in an inheritance or a distribution of property; a division or share of property made by lot. OE. †b A person's turn *to do* something (orig., as determined by lot). ME–M17. 4 What is given to a person by fate or divine providence; *esp.* a person's destiny, fortune, or condition in life. OE. 5 *Hist.* a An amount to be paid, a tax, a due. Chiefly in *scot and lot, lot and scot* s.v. SCOT *n.*[2] OE. b A payment of lead ore as a royalty to the owner of a mine. L15. †6 A part, portion, or division of something; a number of things or persons forming part of a larger whole. (Cf. sense 10 below.) Only in ME. 7 Orig., a prize in a lottery. Later in the card-game lottery, a card obtaining a prize for the holder. M16. 8 A number of persons or things of the same kind, or associated in some way; a quantity, a collection, a set. Now chiefly *colloq.* L16. 9 A plot or portion of land assigned to a particular owner; a piece of land divided off or set apart for a particular purpose (freq. w. specifying wd). Also, each of the plots or portions into which a tract of land is divided when offered for sale. Chiefly *N. Amer.* M17. b Land round a film studio where outside filming may be done. Chiefly *N. Amer.* E20. c A car park; a plot of land used for parking vehicles for sale or hire. Chiefly *N. Amer.* M20. 10 An article, or set of articles, offered separately at a sale; *esp.* each of the items at a sale by auction. E18. b A person of a specified (usu. bad) kind. M19. 11 A considerable number, quantity, or amount; *a* good or great deal; *sing.* & in *pl.*, a great quantity. (Foll. by *of*.) *colloq.* E19.

1 G. CHAPMAN Each markt his lot, and cast it in, to Agamemnons caske. TOLKIEN They now drew lots for the watches. *Virgilian lots*: see VIRGILIAN *a.* 1. 2 R. HARRIS Let's put it to the Lot. b W. H. PRESCOTT The lot fell on Egmont to devise some suitable livery. 3 F. W. ROBERTSON When the revenues of a cathedral.. fell to the lot of a monastery. 4 L. STRACHEY A child of the eighteenth century whose lot was cast in a new,.. unsympathetic age. S. BRETT It is the actor's lot to have his performances dissected by ill-informed critics. 8 W. BENHAM Their crew seem to have been a lazy lot. E. WAUGH They are a very decent generous lot of people. 9 H. GEORGE A house and the lot on which it stands are alike property. SLOAN WILSON The possibility of subdividing her land into one-acre lots. *building lot, parking lot*, etc. b *Tucson Magazine* She is under contract with Universal and cannot do a series off the lot. 10 J. B. MORTON An auction of a job lot of vegetables. B. BAINBRIDGE The catalogue comprised 228 lots. 11 A. H. CLOUGH You see lots of villas, six or seven at least, in ruins. *Listener* Mr Donoghue.. doesn't mean us, he means you lot. *Economist* Luddites who would halt technology and therefore a lot of economic growth.

Phrases: *a lot on one's plate*: see PLATE *n.* 25. **across lots** *N. Amer. dial.* & *colloq.* over fields etc. as a short cut. **bad lot** a disreputable or vicious person. **cast** (or **throw**) **in one's lot with** associate oneself with, decide to share the fortunes of. **call to the lot of** become the duty, business, obligation, etc., of. **fall to the lot of** become the responsibility of (a person) *to do*. *have a lot of time for*: see TIME *n.* **have no** (or **neither**) **part nor lot in** (w. ref. to *Acts* 8:21) have no share in. *lot and scot*: see SCOT *n.*[2] *odd lot*: see ODD *a.* *round lot*: see ROUND *a.* *say a lot for*: see SAY *v.*[1] *scot and lot*: see SCOT *n.*[2] *set a lot by*: see SET *v.*[1] **that's the lot** *colloq.* there is no more to come, that is all there is. **that's your lot** *colloq.* there is no more to come to you, that is all you are going to get. **the (whole) lot** *colloq.* the whole of a certain number or quantity. **that, this, lot**, (chiefly *derog.* & *joc.*) **little lot** *colloq.* that, this, particular group or set. *this (little) lot*: see *that lot* above. *throw in one's lot with*: see *cast in one's lot with* above. **us lot, you lot**, etc. *colloq.* we, you, etc., as a group.

Comb.: **lot attendant** (chiefly *N. Amer.*) a car park attendant; **lot-jumper** *US* a person who appropriates another's plot or allotment of land; †*lot-lead*: see sense 3b above; **lot-man** †(*a*) a pressed seaman; †(*b*) *rare* a pirate; (*c*) *Sc.* a person who threshes grain etc.; **lot-mead, -meadow** a common meadow, the shares in which are apportioned by lot.

lot /lɒt/ *v.* Infl. **-tt-**. [OE *hlēotan* = OS *hliotan*, OHG *liozan*, ON *hlýta* cast lots, obtain by lot, f. Gmc base also of LOT *n.* Latterly directly f. LOT *n.* (cf. Fr. *lotir* cast lots etc.).] I *v.i.* 1 Cast lots *who, whether, for. rare.* OE. †2 Pay a lot or assessment. Only in *scot and lot, lot and scot* s.v. SCOT *v. Sc.* LME–E18. 3 Foll. by *on*: count on; rely on; look for, expect. Now *US.* M17. II *v.t.* †4 Obtain by lot, acquire a share in. Only in OE. 5 Divide (land) into lots, esp. for assignment to a private owner; portion *out* and allot (land *to* a person etc.). LME. 6 Assign *to* as a share or portion; assign as a person's lot or destiny. Also foll. by *out*. LME. †b Appoint or allot to *do* or *be*. L16–M17. †7 Impose a tax or due on. Only in M16. 8 Divide or group into lots for sale. Also foll. by *out*. E18. 9 Cast lots for; divide, apportion, or distribute by lot. Now *rare.* E18. 10 Choose (pressed men) by lot for service. *obs.* exc. *Hist.* M18. 11 Portion *off* by lot. M19.

¶Not recorded between OE and LME.

lota /'ləʊtə, -tɑː/ *n.* Also **lotah**. E19. [Hind. *loṭā*.] In the Indian subcontinent: a spheroidal water-pot, usually made of polished brass.

lotaustralin /ləʊ'tɑʊstrəlɪn/ *n.* M20. [f. mod.L *Lot(us) austral(is* (see below) + -IN[1].] *Chem.* A toxic cyanogenic glucoside which occurs in various plants, esp. *Lotus australis* and *Trifolium repens* (white clover).

lote /ləʊt/ *n. arch.* E16. [Anglicization.] = LOTUS (esp. sense 2).

Comb.: **lote-tree** (*a*) the nettle-tree, *Celtis australis*; (*b*) the jujube tree, *Ziziphus lotus*.

loth /ləʊt/ *n.* L17. [G = lead.] *Hist.* A unit of weight in the Netherlands, Germany, Austria, and Switzerland, equal to half the local ounce.

loth *a.* var. of LOATH *a.*

Lotharingian /ləʊθə'rɪndʒɪən/ *n.* & *a.* E17. [f. *Lotharingia* (see below) + -AN.] A *n.* A native or inhabitant of the ancient duchy of Lotharingia in northern Europe, situated between the Rhine and the Scheldt from Frisia to the Alps. E17. B *adj.* Of or pertaining to Lotharingia or its inhabitants, or modern Lorraine, a region in NE France. L19.

Lothario /lə'θɛːrɪəʊ, -'θɑː-/ *n.* Pl. **-os**. M18. [A character in Rowe's *Fair Penitent* (1703).] A libertine, a rake.

D. L. SAYERS Men like Crutchley, with quantities of large white teeth, are practically always gay Lotharios.

loti /'ləʊti, 'luːti/ *n.* Pl. **maloti** /mə'ləʊti, -'luːti/. L20. [Sesotho.] The basic monetary unit of Lesotho, equal to 100 lisente.

lotic /'ləʊtɪk/ *a.* E20. [f. L *lotus* washing, f. *lot-* (see LOTION) + -IC.] *Ecol.* Of freshwater organisms or habitats: inhabiting or situated in rapidly moving water. Cf. LENITIC *a.*

lotiform /'ləʊtɪfɔːm/ *a.* L19. [f. LOT(US + -I- + -FORM.] *Archit.* Of a pillar, column, etc.: shaped like a lotus.

lotion /'ləʊʃ(ə)n/ *n.* LME. [(O)Fr., or L *lotio(n-)* washing, f. *lot-*, *laut-* pa. ppl stem of *lavare* wash: see -ION.] 1 A liquid medicinal or cosmetic preparation applied externally. LME. †2a = LAVATORY *n.* 3. Only in 16. b *gen.* The action of washing the body, ablution, esp. a medicinal or cosmetic preparation. M16–L18. †3 The passing of metals, medicines, etc., through water for cleansing or purification. E17–L18. 4 Alcoholic drink. *arch. slang.* L19.

Lotka-Volterra /ˌlɒtkəvɒl'tɛrə/ *n.* M20. [A. J. *Lotka* (1880–1949), US statistician, and V. *Volterra* (1860–1940), It. mathematician.] *Math.* & *Biol.* Used *attrib.* with ref. to a mathematical model which uses coupled differential equations to predict the variation in time of two populations, *spec.* of a predator species and a prey species.

lotment /'lɒtm(ə)nt/ *n. obs.* exc. *dial.* M17. [f. LOT *v.* + -MENT.] An allotment of land.

loto *n.* see LOTTO *n.*[1]

lotong /ləʊ'tɒŋ/ *n.* E19. [Malay.] A leaf-monkey of the genus *Presbytis*, esp. *P. obscura*.

Lotophagi /ləʊ'tɒfədʒʌɪ/ *n.pl.* E17. [L f. Gk *Lōtophagoi*, f. *lōtos* LOTUS + *phagein* eat.] The lotus-eaters of Greek legend.

lotophagous *a.* (*rare*) lotus-eating, resembling the lotus-eaters M19.

lotos *n.* see LOTUS.

lotos-eater *n.* var. of LOTUS-EATER.

lottery /'lɒt(ə)ri/ *n.* M16. [Prob. f. Du. *loterij*, f. *lot* LOT *n.* + *-erij* -ERY. Cf. Fr. *loterie*, It. *lotteria*.] 1 A means of raising money by selling numbered tickets and giving prizes to the holders of numbers drawn at random. M16. 2 *transf.* & *fig.* An enterprise or process whose success is governed by chance. L16. †3 Decision by casting or drawing of lots. Also, chance, issue of events as determined by chance. L16–L17. †4 A thing which comes to a person by lot or fortune. Only in E17. 5 A card-game in which prizes are obtained by the holders of certain cards. M19.

Comb.: **lottery-wheel** a revolving mechanism used to shuffle the tickets in a lottery before the winning tickets are drawn.

lotto /'lɒtəʊ/ *n.*[1] Also (earlier, now *rare*) **loto** /'ləʊtəʊ/. L18. [(Fr. *loto* f.) It. *lotto*.] 1 A game of chance resembling bingo, in which numbers drawn as in a lottery are to be matched with numbers on a card, the winner being the first to have a card with a row of numbers all of which have been drawn. L18. 2 A lottery (in Italy). E19.

Lotto /'lɒtəʊ/ *n.*[2] M20. [Lorenzo *Lotto* (*c*1480–1556), It. painter.] In full *Lotto rug*. A kind of oriental rug characterized by a pattern based on a design of octagons, as depicted in paintings by Lorenzo Lotto.

lotus /'ləʊtəs/ *n.* Also (esp. in sense 2) **lotos**. L15. [L f. Gk *lōtos*.] 1 Some kind of clover or trefoil (referred to by Homer as food for horses). *obs.* exc. *Hist.* & *poet.* L15. 2 A plant yielding a fruit represented by Homer as producing in those who ate it a state of dreamy forgetfulness and loss of all desire to return home, identified by later Greek writers with a N. African shrub (probably the jujube tree, *Ziziphus lotus*). M16. 3 A tree mentioned by classical writers, having a hard black wood (probably the nettle-tree, *Celtis australis*). M16. 4 Any of several exotic water-lilies; *esp.* (*a*) *Nymphaea lotus*, sacred in ancient Egypt, which has white flowers and pink outer petals; (*b*) *Nelumbo nucifera*, sacred in parts of southern Asia (and treated symbolically in Hindu and Buddhist thought), which has white or pink flowers; (*c*) (more fully *American lotus*) the N. American water-lily *Nelumbo lutea*, which has fragrant yellow flowers. L16. **b** In full *lotus position*. In Yoga, a cross-legged bodily position with the feet resting on the thighs, said to resemble the lotus blossom. Also called *padmasana*. M20. 5 Any of various leguminous plants of the genus *Lotus*; *spec.* bird's-foot trefoil, *L. corniculatus*. M18.

Comb.: **lotus-bird** *Austral.* the jacana; **lotus capital**, **lotus-column** *Egyptian Archit.*: shaped like a lotus, ornamented with lotuses; **lotus-land** the fabled land of the lotus-eaters; a land of ease and delight; *lotus position*: see sense 4b above.

lotus-eater /ˈləʊtəsˌiːtə/ *n.* Also **lotos-**. M19. [f. prec. + EATER.] 1 A member of a people represented by Homer as living on the fruit of the lotus and living in a state of dreamy forgetfulness and idleness. M19. 2 A person given up to indolent enjoyment. M19.

lotus-eat *v.i.* give oneself up to indolent enjoyment (chiefly as *lotus-eating* vbl n. & ppl a.) M19.

louche /luʃ, luːʃ/ *a.* E19. [Fr. = cross-eyed, squinting.] Not straightforward. Now usu., dubious, shifty, disreputable.

E. WAUGH I knew of a louche little bar quite near here. *Time* She plays loose—and even louche—types.

Loucheux /luːˈʃəː, -ˈʃuː/ *n.* & *a.* E19. [Canad. Fr., f. as prec.] A *n.* Pl. same. An Athapaskan Indian people inhabiting the Yukon and Mackenzie River areas in Alaska and NW Canada; the language of this people. E19. **B** *attrib.* or as *adj.* Of or pertaining to the Loucheux or their language. E19.

loud /laʊd/ *a.* [OE *hlūd* = OFris. (*h*)*lūd*, OS *hlūd* (Du. *luid*), OHG *hlūt* (G *laut*), f. WGmc f. IE, f. base meaning 'hear', whence also Gk *kluein* hear, *klutos* famous, L *cluere* be famed.] 1 (Of a sound or voice) strongly audible, noisily or oppressively audible, making a powerful impression on the sense of hearing; that makes, or is able or liable to make, strongly audible sounds. OE. **b** Of a place etc.: full of noise, re-echoing. L16. 2**a** Clamorous, noisy; noisily aggressive; emphatic or vehement in expression. M16. †**b** Chiefly of a lie: manifest, palpable, flagrant. M16–L17. †**c** Of motives: pressing, urgent. Only in E17. 3 Of smell or flavour: powerful, offensive. Now chiefly *US*. M17. 4 Esp. of colour, pattern, dress, etc.: vulgarly obtrusive, flashy. L18.

1 G. LYTTELTON Down the Steep it falls, In loud Cascades. A. RADCLIFFE The storm was now loud. T. CAMPBELL The loud waves lash'd the shore. C. POTOK A straight, loud voice that rang through the terrible silence. A. DAVIS An explosion a hundred times louder than the loudest .. thunderclap. B. ASHLEY Vibrations from a loud electric bell. **b** *Guardian* In a wood which had previously been loud with bird-song, an eerie silence prevailed. 2**a** TENNYSON Men loud against all forms of power. S. BRILL Hoffa became louder and more bad-tempered. 3 MILTON The strong breath and loud stench of avarice. 4 D. LODGE He is wearing his loudest check sports jacket.

Special collocations & comb.: **loud-hail** *v.t.* & *i.* speak, call, or address through a loud-hailer. **loud-hailer** a megaphone or other electronic device for amplifying the voice, so that it can be heard at a distance. **loud-mouth** *a.*, *n.*, & *v.* (*a*) *adj.* loud-mouthed, noisy; (*b*) *n.* a person given to loud and self-assertive talk; (*c*) *v.i.* talk loudly and self-assertively, bluster. **loud-mouthed** *a.* noisily self-assertive, vociferous. **loud pedal** = *sustaining pedal* (a) s.v. SUSTAINING. **loudspeaker** an instrument for converting variations in applied electrical impulses into corresponding sound waves (usu. music or voice) that are able to be heard at a distance from the instrument.

loudish *a.* somewhat loud E19. **loudly** *adv.* L15.

loud /laʊd/ *adv.* [OE *hlude*, f. the adj.] 1 Loudly, with a loud noise or voice; aloud. OE. †2 With *lie*: openly, blatantly. LME–E17. 3 Of smell: strongly, offensively. Chiefly *US*. L19.

1 G. GREENE Better not talk so loud He may be listening. P. BOWLES They could hear the storm blowing louder than before. **loud and clear** (esp. in radio or telecommunication) (heard or received) loudly and clearly; *gen.* without misunderstanding or uncertainty. †**loud and still** under all circumstances. **out loud** aloud, so as to be widely heard.

Comb.: **loud-spoken** *a.* given to loud speaking.

louden /ˈlaʊd(ə)n/ *v.* M18. [f. LOUD *a.* + -EN^{5}.] 1 *v.t.* Make loud or louder. M18. 2 *v.i.* Become loud, grow louder. E19.

2 M. PEAKE Steerpike .. could hear the loudening of the rain.

loudness /ˈlaʊdnɪs/ *n.* LOE. [f. LOUD *a.* + -NESS.] The quality or condition of being loud; an instance of this. Also, the (great or small) extent to which a sound is heard as loud.

Comb.: **loudness control** a device on an audio amplifier which corrects for the change in quality of reproduced sound at low volumes by boosting the bass (and often also the treble) relative to the middle frequencies.

Lou Gehrig's disease /luː ˈgɛːrɪgz dɪˌziːz/ *n. phr.* M20. [Henry Louis *Gehrig* (1903–41), US baseball player, who died from the disease.] *Med.* A progressive degeneration of the motor neurones of the central nervous system, leading to muscle wasting and paralysis; amyotrophic lateral sclerosis.

lough /lɒk, lɒx/ *n.* OE. [Ir. *loch* = Gael. LOCH *n.*^{1}] 1 A lake, a pool. In early use also, a strait, a gulf. Now *rare* or *obs.* OE. 2 In Ireland: a lake, an arm of the sea. LME.

louis /ˈluːi/ *n.*^{1} Pl. same /-z/. Also (*arch.*) Anglicized as **lewis** /ˈluːɪs/, pl. same, **lewises**. M17. [Fr. f. next.] *Hist.* In full *louis d'or* /dɔː/ [= gold]. A French gold coin issued in the reign of Louis XIII (1640) and subsequently until the time of Louis XVI (1793). Later also, a 20-franc piece or Napoleon.

Louis /ˈluːi/ *n.*^{2} & *a.* Usu. in fuller phrs. as below. M19. [Fr. (see below).] (Designating or pertaining to) any of the styles in architecture, furniture, decorative art, etc., characteristic of the reigns of several kings of France named Louis; *spec.* and in full: *Louis Treize* /treɪz/, Louis XIII, 1610–43; *Louis Quatorze* /kaˈtɔːz/, Louis XIV, 1643–1715; *Louis Quinze* /kãz/, Louis XV, 1715–74; *Louis Seize* /seɪz/, Louis XVI, 1774–93.

Louisianian /lʊˌiːzɪˈanɪən, -ˈɑː-/ *a.* & *n.* L18. [f. *Louisiana* (see below), f. *Louis* XIV (see prec.) + -IAN.] A *n.* A native or inhabitant of Louisiana, a State of the south-western US at the mouth of the Mississippi. L18. **B** *adj.* Of or pertaining to the State of Louisiana. M19.

Louis-Philippe /ˌluːɪfiˈliːp/ *n.* & *a.* E20. [See below.] (Designating or pertaining to) the style of architecture, furniture, and interior decoration characteristic of the reign of Louis-Philippe, King of France 1830–48.

lounder /ˈlʌndə/ *n.* & *v.* *Sc.* E18. [Perh. symbolic.] A *n.* A heavy swingeing blow. E18. **B** *v.t.* Beat, cudgel, thrash. Also, hurl with violence *on*. L18.

loundering *a.* (of a blow etc.) swingeing, severe E18.

lounge /laʊn(d)ʒ/ *n.*^{1} L18. [f. LOUNGE *v.*^{1}] 1 An act or spell of lounging; a leisurely walk, a saunter, stroll. Also, a lounging gait or manner of reclining. L18. 2**a** A place for lounging; a gathering of loungers. Now *rare*. L18. **b** A sitting-room of a house; a public sitting-room in a hotel etc.; a waiting-room with seats at an airport etc. L19. 3 A kind of sofa or easy chair on which a person can lie at full length. M19.

1 LYTTON Our life is a lounge from the cradle to the grave. W. BLACK When we went out for a lounge after luncheon. 2**b** J. BETJEMAN It's ever so close in the lounge dear. J. MUNRO They were in the departure lounge, waiting for their flight call. M. BRADBURY The English department faculty lounge, wherein the faculty were .. assembled. J. RULE There was no one she knew in the employees' lounge.

Comb.: **lounge bar** a separate bar in a public house which is more comfortably furnished than the public bar; **lounge lizard** (*slang*, orig. *US*), a man who spends his time idling in fashionable society, esp. in search of a wealthy patroness; **lounge suit** a man's formal suit for ordinary day wear.

lounge *n.*^{2} see LUNGE *n.*^{2}

lounge /laʊn(d)ʒ/ *v.*^{1} Orig. *Sc.* E16. [Perh. symbolic.] 1 *v.i.* Move indolently; slouch. Freq. w. adv. E16. 2 *v.i.* Pass time indolently or without definite occupation; idle. L17. 3 *v.i.* Recline casually or comfortably, loll. M18. 4 *v.t.* Pass (time etc.) *away* (rarely *out*) in idleness. L18.

1 LYTTON Vargrave lounged into the billiard-room. 2 G. K. CHESTERTON Like all ingrainedly idle men, he was very fond of lounging. 3 J. CARY He lounged across the bed, propped on one elbow. H. G. WELLS The vicar ceased to lounge and sat up.

lounger *n.* (*a*) a person who lounges, an idler; (*b*) an article of furniture or dress designed for use in relaxation: E16.

lounge *v.*^{2} see LUNGE *v.*^{1}

loup /laʊp/ *n.*^{1} *Sc.* See also LOPE *n.* LME. [ON *hlaup*: see LEAP *n.*^{1}] = LEAP *n.*^{1}

loup /lu/ *n.*^{2} Pl. pronounced same. M18. [Fr., lit. 'wolf', f. L *lupus*.] 1 In full *loup de mer* /də mɛːr/ [= sea wolf]. The sea-bass, *Dicentrarchus labrax*, found off the coasts of western Europe and in the Mediterranean. M18. 2 A woman's light mask or half-mask for the face. Cf. earlier LOO *n.*^{2} M19.

loup *n.*^{3} var. of LOOP *n.*^{3}

loup /laʊp/ *v.i.* & *t.* *Sc.* & *north.* See also LOPE *v.* ME. [ON *hlaupa*: see LEAP *v.*] = LEAP *v.*

loupe /luːp/ *n.* LME. [(O)Fr. See also LOOP *n.*^{3}] †1 A precious stone of imperfect brilliancy; *esp.* a sapphire. LME–M16. 2 A kind of small magnifier used by watchmakers or jewellers. L19.

loup-garou /ˈluːgəruː/ *n.* L16. [Fr., f. *loup* wolf (see LOUP *n.*^{2}) + *garou* (f. OHG antecedent of MHG *werwolf* WEREWOLF).] = WEREWOLF.

louping-ill /ˈlaʊpɪŋˌɪl/ *n.* LME. [f. LOUP *v.* + -ING^{1} + ILL *n.*] *Vet. Med.* A viral disease of animals, esp. sheep, which causes a staggering gait often with spasmodic jumps.

lour /ˈlaʊə/ *n.*^{1} Also **lower**. ME. [f. the vb.] 1 A gloomy or sullen look; a frown, scowl. ME. 2 Gloominess of the sky, weather, etc.; threatening appearance; an instance of this. L16.

lour /ˈlaʊə/ *n.*^{2} *slang*. Now *rare* or *obs.* Also **lower**. M16. [Origin unkn.] Money.

lour /ˈlaʊə/ *v.i.* Also **lower**. ME. [Origin unkn.] 1 Frown, scowl; look angry or sullen. Formerly, also, be depressed or mournful. ME. **b** Of the clouds, sky, a tempest, etc.: look dark and threatening. L16. 2 Crouch, lurk, skulk. Chiefly *Sc.* Now *rare*. LME.

1 JAS. GRANT His brows knit and his eyes loured. S. NAIPAUL Carmen lowered at the mob. **b** SHAKES. *Rich. III* The clouds that lour'd upon our house.

lourd /lʊəd/ *a.* & *n.* Now *rare*. LME. [(O)Fr. = heavy, (formerly) foolish.] A *adj.* Orig., sluggish, dull, coarse, stupid. Later, heavy; gloomy. LME. †**B** *n.* A coarse fellow, a lout. Only in L16.

loure /lʊə/ *n.* E18. [Fr., also = kind of bagpipe.] *Hist.* A kind of rustic dance thought to have had a bagpipe accompaniment. Also, a slow baroque dance in 3/4 or 6/4 time.

lourie *n.* var. of LOERIE.

louring /ˈlaʊərɪŋ/ *a.* Also **lowering**. LME. [f. LOUR *v.* + -ING^{2}.] 1 Frowning, scowling; angry-looking, gloomy, sullen. LME. 2 Of the clouds, sky, weather, circumstances, etc.: gloomy, dark, threatening. LME. †3 Lurking, skulking. LME–L16.

1 D. H. LAWRENCE His boisterous humour gave way to lowering silences. 2 G. SANTAYANA Rather autumnal with lowering clouds and rain. *Daily Telegraph* The louring threat of nuclear warfare.

louringly *adv.* L16.

louro /ˈlʊərəʊ/ *n.* Pl. **-os**. E19. [Port., lit. 'laurel', f. L *laurus* LAUREL *n.*] Any of several tropical S. American hardwood timber trees belonging to the genera *Ocotea*, *Nectandra*, and related genera of the laurel family, *esp.* (in full *red louro*) *Ocotea rubra*; the dense wood of these trees. Also (the wood of) any of several similar Brazilian trees of the genus *Cordia*, of the borage family.

loury /ˈlaʊəri/ *a.* Also **lowery**. M17. [f. LOUR *n.*[1] + -Y[1].] Of the sky etc.: dull, gloomy, threatening.

louse /laʊs/ *n.* Pl. **lice** /lʌɪs/; in sense 2 usu. **louses**. [OE *lūs*, pl. *lȳs* = MLG, MDu., OHG *lūs*, (Du. *luis*, G *Laus*), ON *lús*.] **1** Any small wingless insect of the order Siphunculata (or Anoplura) (more fully *sucking louse*), parasitic on mammals, or the order Mallophaga (more fully *biting louse*), parasitic mainly on birds; spec. *Pediculus humanus*, which infests the hair and skin of humans and has two forms living respectively on the head (more fully *head louse*) and body (more fully *body louse*). Also, any of various other small creatures held to resemble these. OE. **b** As the type of something worthless or contemptible. L16. **2** A contemptible or unpleasant person. M17.

1 M. KINGSLEY Sleep impossible—mosquitoes! lice!! *book-louse, crab-louse, water-louse, woodlouse*, etc. **b** SWIFT 'Tis not that I value the money three skips of a louse. CHESTERFIELD I.. don't care a louse if I never see it again. **2** R. KIPLING Why hast thou allowed this louse Lutuf to live so long? R. SILVERBERG Is he worth risking your life for? I thought you said he was a louse.

Comb.: **louse-borne** *a.* (of a disease) transmitted by lice; **louse-trap** *dial.* & *slang* a comb; **lousewort** any plant of the genus *Pedicularis*, of the figwort family; esp. *P. sylvatica* and (N. Amer.) *P. canadensis*, which bear pink or red flowers.

louse /laʊz, -s/ *v.* LME. [f. the n.] **1** *v.t.* & *i.* Clear (a person, oneself, a garment) of lice, remove lice (from). LME. †**2** *v.i.* Be infested with lice. *rare* (Shakes.). Only in E17. **3** *v.t.* Foll. by *up*: infest with lice; spoil, mess up. *slang.* M20.

louser *n.* (*a*) a person who louses; (*b*) *slang* (also *louser-up*) a person who spoils things; a contemptible person: L16.

louses *n.pl.* see LOUSE *n.*

lousy /ˈlaʊzi/ *a.* ME. [f. LOUSE *n.* + -Y[1].] **1** Full of lice, infested with lice. ME. †**b** Characterized by the presence of lice. E16–M19. **2** Vile, contemptible; disgusting; inferior, very bad; ill; in low health or spirits. LME. **3** Teeming *with*; abundantly supplied *with*. *slang.* M19.

2 THACKERAY I've been trying to write today & only squeezed out one lousy page. S. BECKETT The patients did sometimes feel as lousy as they sometimes looked. M. GEE I'm a lousy pianist. A. LURIE Polly would be able to take taxis when the weather was lousy. **3** V. M. YEATES Were not shipping magnates lousy with shekels? *Field & Stream* The lilies were lousy with pickerel.

lousily *adv.* E17. **lousiness** *n.* M16.

lout /laʊt/ *n.* M16. [Perh. f. LOUT *v.*[1]] A rough, crude, or ill-mannered person (esp. a man).

A. F. DOUGLAS-HOME The lout who tries to throw his weight about at the expense of weaker brethren. J. IRVING The sort of louts who hung around the station all day. *lager lout, litter-lout*, etc.

lout /laʊt/ *v.*[1]*i.* Now *arch.* & *dial.* [OE *lūtan* = ON *lúta* (Sw. *luta*, Da. *lude*), f. Gmc.] Bend, bow, make an obeisance (*to*); stoop; *fig.* submit (*to*).

lout /laʊt/ *v.*[2] M16. [f. LOUT *n.* (but sense 2 may be a separate wd).] †**1** *v.t.* Treat with contempt, mock. M16–M17. **2** *v.i.* Act loutishly; lounge (*about, off*, etc.). E19.

loutish /ˈlaʊtɪʃ/ *a.* M16. [f. LOUT *n.* + -ISH[1].] Characteristic of a lout; ill-mannered, crude or rough in behaviour.

loutishly *adv.* L16. **loutishness** *n.* M16.

loutrophoros /luːtrəˈfɔːrɒs/ *n.* L19. [Gk, f. *loutron* water for a bath + *-phoros* -bearing.] *Class. Antiq.* A tall two-handled vessel used for carrying water to the nuptial bath.

louvre /ˈluːvə/ *n.* Also **-ver**. ME. [OFr. *lover*, *lovier* skylight, prob. f. Gmc form rel. to base of LODGE *n.*] **1** A structure like a turret on the roof of a medieval building, with side openings for ventilation etc. ME. **2** A hole in a roof for the passage of smoke; a chimney. *obs.* exc. *dial.* LME. **3** *sing.* & (earlier) in *pl.* An arrangement of overlapping slats placed across an opening and usu. designed to admit air and some light but exclude rain. Also (*sing.*), an individual slat of such an arrangement. M16.

Comb.: **louvre-board** each of the slats making up a louvre (usu. in *pl.*).

louvred *a.* (*a*) arranged like louvres; (*b*) provided with a louvre or louvres: M19.

lovable /ˈlʌvəb(ə)l/ *a.* Also **loveable**. LME. [f. LOVE *v.* + -ABLE.] Inspiring or deserving love or affection; amiable; attractive, pleasing.

lovaˈbility *n.* M19. **lovableness** *n.* E19. **lovably** *adv.* E19.

lovage /ˈlʌvɪdʒ/ *n.* LME. [Alt., by assoc. w. LOVE *n.* and ACHE *n.*[2] (=parsley), of OFr. *levesche*, *luvesche* (mod. *livèche*) f. late L *levisticum* (sc. *apium* parsley), for earlier *ligusticum* neut. of *ligusticus* Ligurian.] An umbelliferous plant, *Levisticum officinale*, native to southern Europe, used as a culinary and medicinal herb. Also (more fully *Scots* or *Scotch lovage*), a white-flowered umbellifer, *Ligusticum scoticum*, which grows on European rocky coasts.

lovat /ˈlʌvət/ *n.* & *a.* E20. [*Lovat*, a place in Highland, Scotland.] (Designating or made of) tweed of a muted green colour; (of) a muted green colour (also *lovat-green*).

love /lʌv/ *n.* [OE *lufu* = OFris. *luve*, OHG *luba*, Goth. (*brōþru*) *lubō* (brotherly) love, f. Gmc, f. wk grade of base repr. also by OS *lubig* loving, OHG *gilob* precious, OE, OS, ON *lof*, OHG *lob* praise, f. IE base also of L *lubet* it is pleasing, *lubido* desire, Old Ch. Slav. *ljubŭ* dear, *ljubiti* love, Skt *lubhyati* desires. Rel. also to LIEF, LEAVE *n.*[1]] **1** That state of feeling with regard to a person which manifests itself in concern for the person's welfare, pleasure in his or her presence, and often also desire for his or her approval; deep affection, strong emotional attachment. (Foll. by *of, for, to, towards*.) OE. **b** An instance of affection (now *rare*). Formerly also, an act of kindness. OE. **c** Affectionate greetings (freq. as a closing formula in letters). M17. **2** In Christian use: the benevolence and affection of God; the affectionate devotion due to God; regard and consideration prompted by a sense of a common relationship to God. OE. **3** Strong predilection, liking, or fondness for, or devotion to something. Foll. by *of, for*, (arch.) *to*. OE. **4** That feeling of attachment which is based on sexual qualities; sexual passion combined with liking and concern for the other. OE. **b** An instance of being in love; in *pl.*, amatory relations, love affairs. L16. **5a** (**L-**.) The personification of sexual affection, usu. masculine and more or less identified with Eros, Amor, or Cupid of classic mythology. ME. **b** A cupid; a god of love; a figure or representation of a god of love. L16. **6** A beloved person; *esp.* one's sweetheart. Freq. (with or without *possess.*) as a form of intimate or (*colloq.*) friendly address. ME. †**b** An illicit or clandestine lover. LME–E17. **c** *gen.* An object of love; a person who or thing which is loved. M18. **d** A charming or delightful person or thing. *colloq.* E19. **7** Amorous sexual activity, sexual intercourse. Now chiefly in *make love, lovemaking* below. LME. †**8** A game of chance: = MORA *n.*[2] L16–E18. †**9** A material worn in mourning; mourning-crape; a border of this. E17–E19. **10** In various games, esp. tennis, squash, etc.: no score, nil, nothing. M18.

1 SHAKES. *L.L.L.* My love to thee is sound, sans crack or flaw. J. HUXLEY I secretly adored my father and longed to be able to show him my love. B. GILROY The grandchildren's clothes washed and ironed with love. *brotherly love, mother love, platonic love, romantic love*, etc. **c** SCOTT FITZGERALD I'd been writing letters .. and signing them: 'Love, Nick.' **2** AV *1 John* 4:16 God is loue, and hee that dwelleth in loue, dwelleth in God. **3** C. A. LINDBERGH The army Air Corps is built up of men who fly for the love of flying. E. FEINSTEIN Marina's interest in gypsies was part of her love of everything exotic. **4** MILTON Haile wedded Love, mysterious Law, true sourse Of human ofspring. S. JOHNSON It is commonly a weak man who marries for love. K. WATERHOUSE Love was a taboo subject in our country. **b** SWIFT The Colonel was cross'd in his first Love. **5b** W. M. PRAED Wher'er her step in beauty moves, Around her fly a thousand loves. **6** C. MARLOWE Liue with me and be my Loue. SHAKES. *Merch. V.* Whether Bassanio had not once a love. ALAN BENNETT Wash your hands, love, we're all ready. **c** D. WIGODER He introduced me to one of my greatest loves—classical music. J. RULE You were the great love of her life. **d** J. AUSTEN The garden is quite a love. P. CAREY Be a love and get back into your own bed.

Phrases etc.: **apple of love** *arch.* = *love-apple* below. *boy's-love*: see BOY *n.* **fall in love** develop a great (esp. sexual) love (mutually or *with* another). FIRST *love*. **for love** without stakes, for nothing; for pleasure rather than profit. †**for** (or **of**) **all love(s)**: expr. strong adjuration or entreaty. **for the love of** for the sake of; on account of; *for the love of Mike*: see MIKE *n.*[2] 3. *free love*: see FREE *a.* **give one's love to** (*a*) send one's affectionate greeting to; (*b*) fall or be in love with. **in love (with)** enamoured (of), imbued with love (for); *transf.* very fond (of), much addicted (to). *labour of love*: see LABOUR *n.* *light o' love*: see LIGHT *a.*[1] **love at first sight** the action or state of falling in love with a person who or *transf.* a thing which one has not previously seen. **love in a cottage** *arch.* marriage with insufficient means. **love's young dream** the relationship of young lovers; the object of someone's love; a man regarded as a perfect lover. **make love** (*a*) *arch.* pay amorous attention (*to*); (*b*) have sexual intercourse (foll. by *to, with*). **no love lost between** (two people etc.) †(*a*) mutual affection; (*b*) mutual dislike. **not for love or money** not at any price, by no means. *of all love(s)*: see *for all love(s)* above. **out of love (with)** by no means or no longer in love (with); disgusted (with). *tug of love*: see TUG *n.*[1] 3. *tunnel of love*: see TUNNEL *n.* 4.

Comb.: **love affair** †(*a*) in *pl.*, the experiences connected with being in love; (*b*) a romantic or sexual relationship between two people in love; *fig.* an intense enthusiasm or liking for something; **love-apple** *arch.* a tomato; **love beads** (a necklace of) coloured beads worn as a symbol of universal love; **love-begotten** *a.* (*arch.*) (of a child) illegitimate; **love-bird** (*a*) any of various small parrots said to display remarkable affection for their mates; *esp.* any member of the chiefly African genus *Agapornis*; *Austral.* a budgerigar; (*b*) *joc.* & *colloq.* in *pl.*, an affectionate couple, lovers; **lovebite** (a bruise on the skin due to) a sucking kiss; **love bush** *W. Indies* dodder; **love-child** an illegitimate child; **love-curl** a lovelock, esp. on the forehead; **love-dart** *Zool.* a calcareous dart secreted by a snail's reproductive organs which is projected into the body of the snail's partner prior to copulation; †**loveday** a day appointed for a meeting to settle a dispute amicably; an agreement made on such a day; †**love-draught** a philtre; **love-feast** among early Christians, a meal affirming brotherly love (cf. AGAPE *n.*); a religious service (esp. of Methodists) imitating this; **love game** a game in tennis etc. in which the loser fails to score a point; **love-hate** *attrib. a.* designating a relationship etc. marked by ambivalent feelings of love and hate existing towards the same object; **love-in-a-mist** (*a*) a blue-flowered garden plant, *Nigella damascena*, with many delicate green bracts; (*b*) a W. Indian passion-flower, *Passiflora foetida*; **love-in-idleness** heartsease, *Viola tricolor*; **love-interest** a theme or episode in a story, film, etc., of which the main element is the affection of lovers; **love-juice** (*a*) a love-potion, an aphrodisiac; (*b*) a sexual secretion; **love-knot** a knot or bow tied as a token of love; **love-lay** *poet.* a love-song; **love-letter** a letter written to express love; **love-lies-bleeding** an amaranth, *Amaranthus caudatus*, with drooping purple-red flowering spikes, cultivated as a garden plant; **love-life** the aspect of a person's life involving relationships with lovers; **love-light** radiance (of the eyes) expressing love; **lovelock** a curl or lock of hair worn on the temple or forehead, or (formerly) in some other special way; **lovemaking** (*a*) *arch.* courtship; (*b*) amorous sexual activity, *esp.* sexual intercourse; **love-match** a marriage or engagement of which the motive is love, not worldly advantage or convenience; **love-mate** a sweetheart, a lover; **love-nest** a secluded retreat for (esp. illicit or clandestine) lovers; **love-object** the object on which love is centred; **love-pass(age)** *arch.* an incident involving love; **love-pat** a pat expressing or motivated by love; **love-play** wooing, caressing; *spec.* foreplay; **love-potion** a philtre supposed to excite love; **love-scene** an intimate scene between lovers, esp. in a story or play; **love-seat** an armchair or small sofa designed for two occupants; **love-song** a song of (romantic) love; **love-spoon** a wooden spoon, sometimes with a double bowl, carved for presentation to an intended wife; **love-story** a story in which the main theme is the affection of lovers; **love-tap** a tap or gentle blow expressing or motivated by love; **love-token** a thing given as a sign or token of love; **love-tree** the Judas tree, *Cercis* *siliquastrum*; **love-vine** *US* (*a*) dodder; (*b*) = CORALLITA.

lovelike *a.* (*rare*) (*a*) of a nature appropriate to love; †(*b*) lovely: E17.

love /lʌv/ *v.* OE. [f. the n.] **1** *v.t.* Feel love for (a person, a thing personified); be very fond of, hold dear. OE. **b** *spec.* Feel sexual love for; be in love with. OE. **c** *v.i.* Feel love; *esp.* be in love. ME. **2** *v.t.* **a** Be strongly attached to (a thing), be unwilling to part with or allow to perish (life, honour, etc.). OE. **b** Take great pleasure in, be devoted or addicted to; *colloq.* like very much. Foll. by simple obj. *to do, doing* a person or thing *to do*. ME. **c** Take pleasure in the existence of; admire greatly. ME. **3** *v.t.* Of a plant or (less usually) an animal: have a tendency to thrive in (a certain kind of situation). LME. **4** *v.t.* Embrace or caress affectionately. Freq. foll. by *up*. *colloq.* L19.

1 J. A. FROUDE A man who loved England well, but who loved Rome better. J. GARDAM He had loved the king and had ridden . . from the fells to Westminster for a coronation. J. NAGENDA Your old mother who loves you with all her heart. **I must** etc. **love you and leave you** *colloq.*: a formula of departure. **Lord love you, me, a duck**, etc. *int.* expr. surprise, emphasis, etc. **loved one** a person beloved; *esp.* in *pl.*, one's family or relations. *love paramour*: see PARAMOUR *adv.* 2. **b** SHAKES. *Oth.* I never knew woman love man so. *love to pieces*: see PIECE *n.* **c** SHAKES. *Jul. Caes.* Love, and be friends. TENNYSON 'Tis better to have loved and lost, Than never to have loved at all. **2a** MARVELL As you loue your own affairs . . be pleased . . to let me know your minds. **b** H. GLASSE Some love a pig brought whole to table. P. V. WHITE He loved her to need him. MERLE COLLINS The Christmas plays she also loved. M. MILNER I have always loved drawing goats. *San Francisco Chronicle* He loves to bat, especially if he can put the ball out of the park. **c** BURKE I love firm government. **3** B. TAYLOR The violet loves a sunny bank. **4** K. S. PRICHARD Why don't you give her a hug . . love her up a bit? B. HOLIDAY That dog . . began lapping me and loving me like crazy.

Comb.: **love-in** a gathering for the purpose of establishing and enjoying love relationships; **love-up** *slang* an act of caressing, hugging, or kissing.

loveable *a.* var. of LOVABLE.

loveful /ˈlʌvfʊl, -f(ə)l/ *a.* Now *rare*. ME. [f. LOVE *n.* + -FUL.] **1** Full of love. ME. †**2** Lovable. LME–L16.

Lovelace /ˈlʌvleɪs/ *n.* M19. [Robert *Lovelace*, a character in S. Richardson's novel *Clarissa Harlowe* (1747–8).] A seducer.

loveless /ˈlʌvlɪs/ *a.* ME. [f. LOVE *n.* + -LESS.] **1** Without love; unloving; unloved. ME. **2** Unlovely. *rare*. E17.

lovelessly *adv.* E17. **lovelessness** *n.* M19.

loveling /ˈlʌvlɪŋ/ *n. rare*. E17. [f. LOVE *n.* or *v.* + -LING^1.] A lovely creature; an object of love; a darling.

lovelorn /ˈlʌvlɔːn/ *a.* M17. [f. LOVE *n.* + LORN *a.*] Forsaken by one's love; pining from unrequited love.

lovely /ˈlʌvli/ *a.* & *n.* OE. [f. LOVE *n.* + -LY^1.] **A** *adj.* †**1a** Loving, kind, affectionate. Also, amicable. OE–M17. **b** Amorous. LME–L16. **2** Worthy of love; suited to attract love; spiritually or morally beautiful. OE. **3** Lovable or attractive on account of beauty; beautiful; *colloq.* delightful, pleasing, excellent, exquisitely beautiful. Also as *int.*, expr. pleasure, commendation, etc. ME.

2 SOUTHEY The life and death of that man were equally lovely. J. RUSKIN If his mind be . . sweetly toned, what he loves will be lovely. **3** SHAKES. *Tam. Shr.* Till the tears that she hath shed . . Like envious floods o'er-run her lovely face. E. WAUGH You do know a lovely lot of stories. DYLAN THOMAS Thank you so much . . ; it was lovely of you. J. F. LEHMANN It was a hauntingly lovely September morning. A. CROSS 'I'll bring some wine . . . ' 'Lovely' J. SIMMS There was a lovely smell of rock cakes. E. PIZZEY It's lovely to see you looking so well. **lovely and —** *colloq.* delightfully —, very —.

B *n.* A lovely person or thing. Now usu., a glamorously beautiful woman or girl. LME.

T. PYNCHON One of the girls, . . brown-haired lovely in a black knit leotard.

lovelify *v.t.* (*rare*) make lovely L19. **lovelihead** *n.* (*arch. rare*) loveliness M17. **lovelily** *adv.* ME. **loveliness** *n.* the quality of being lovely, exquisite beauty: ME.

lovely /ˈlʌvli/ *adv.* Now only *poet.* & *non-standard*. OE. [f. LOVE *n.* + -LY^2.] †**1** Lovingly, affectionately. OE–L16. **2** Lovably, beautifully; in a lovely manner, delightfully, excellently, commendably. LME.

2 A. E. HOUSMAN How clear, how lovely bright. C. FREMLIN *Your* mummy has taught you to eat up lovely.

lover /ˈlʌvə/ *n.* ME. [f. LOVE *v.* + -ER^1.] **1** A person who feels fondness or kindly regard towards another. Now *rare* exc. in Christian use (cf. LOVE *n.* 2). ME. **2** A person (esp. a man) who is in love with someone; either of two people involved in a sexual relationship (outside of or without marriage), *spec.* an illicit or clandestine one. Freq. in *pl.*, a couple in love, sexual partners. Also (*colloq.*) as a form of intimate or friendly address. ME. **b** A pimp. *US slang*. E20. **3** A person who has an affection, predilection, fancy, or liking for a specified thing, activity, idea, etc. ME.

1 C. WESLEY Jesu, Lover of my Soul. H. BROOKE A stranger, but a very warm lover of yours. **2** AV *Jer.* 3:1 Thou hast played the harlot with many louers. R. F. BURTON I am a lover separated from her beloved. D. HEYES 'You got it, lover,' the waitress said. P. THEROUX There were lovers on this heath, plainly copulating. R. INGALLS She never has had lovers? She's always been alone? **3** D. HUME Lovers of Liberty, but greater Lovers of Monarchy. L. GRIFFITHS We're all horse lovers but we're not daft as well. E. SAINTSBURY Lewis Carroll . . a great lover of children.

Comb.: **lover boy** *slang* a (male) lover, an attractive man, a woman-chaser; freq. as a form of address; **lover's knot** = *love-knot* s.v. LOVE *n.*; **lovers' lane** a road or other secluded place to which lovers resort; **lover's** or **lovers' quarrel**, **tiff**, etc., a dispute between lovers (which therefore will not last long).

lovered *a.* (*rare*) provided with or having a lover (of a specified kind) L16. **lovering** *n.* (*colloq.*) amorous activity, fondling; courting: L19. **loverless** *a.* E19. **loverlike** *a.* & *adv.* like or as befits a lover M16.

loverly /ˈlʌvəli/ *a.*^{1} E16. [f. LOVER + -LY^1.] Like or befitting a lover.

¶Only in isolated Sc. use bef. L19.

loverly /ˈlʌvəli/ *a.*^{2} *joc.* & *colloq.* E20. [Repr. a Cockney pronunc.] Lovely.

loverly /ˈlʌvəli/ *adv. rare*. L15. [f. LOVER + -LY^2.] In the manner of a lover.

lovesick /ˈlʌvsɪk/ *a.* LME. [f. LOVE *n.* + SICK *a.*] Languishing with romantic love.

J. M. MURRY Endymion's lovesick wanderings in search of the moon-goddess. L. GILLEN Idiotic of her to behave like a lovesick schoolgirl.

lovesickness *n.* E18.

lovesome /ˈlʌvs(ə)m/ *a.* Now *literary*. OE. [f. LOVE *n.* + -SOME^1.] **1** Worthy of or inspiring love; lovable. OE. **2** Lovable on account of beauty; lovely, beautiful. ME. **3** Loving, friendly. ME. **4** Amorous. M16.

lovesomeness *n.* OE.

loveworthy /ˈlʌvwəːði/ *a.* ME. [f. LOVE *n.* + -WORTHY.] Worthy to be loved, deserving love.

loveworthiness *n.* M19.

lovey /ˈlʌvi/ *n. colloq.* M18. [f. LOVE *n.* + -Y^6.] Used as a term of endearment: love, sweetheart. Cf. DOVEY.

lovey-dovey /ˈlʌvɪˌdʌvi, ˌlʌvɪˈdʌvi/ *n.* & *a. colloq.* E19. [f. LOVEY + DOVEY.] **A** *n.* Used as a term of endearment: love, sweetheart. E19.

B *adj.* Fondly affectionate, *esp.* unduly so; sentimental. L19.

T. CALLENDER Everything went back lovey-dovey again between the two of them. D. FRANCIS She was never a lovey-dovey sort of mother.

lovey-doveyness *n.* E20.

loving /ˈlʌvɪŋ/ *n.* LME. [f. LOVE *v.* + -ING^1.] The action of LOVE *v.*; active love, affection.

loving /ˈlʌvɪŋ/ *a.* OE. [f. LOVE *v.* + -ING^2.] That loves; feeling or showing love; affectionate. Freq. as 2nd elem. of comb.

ALDOUS HUXLEY Every loving word was treasured as a word . . from the depths of the heart. G. JEKYLL The rock-loving Campanulas. *Times* 20 fun-loving people to share Christmas. **loving-cup** a large, often silver, two-handled drinking-cup passed round at banquets, the guests successively drinking from it. **loving-kindness** kindness arising from a deep personal love, as (in Christian use) the active love of God for his creatures; affectionate tenderness and consideration. *tender loving care*: see TENDER *a.*

lovingly *adv.* LME. **lovingness** *n.* L16.

low /ləʊ/ *n.*^{1} Now chiefly *dial.* See also LAW *n.*^{2} [OE *hlāw*, *hlǣw*, corresp. to OS *hlēo*, *hlēw-*, OHG *hleo*, Goth. *hlaiw*, f. Gmc, ult. f. IE base meaning 'slope' (whence also LEAN *v.*).] **1** = LAW *n.*^{2} OE. **2** A grave-mound; a tumulus. OE.

low /ləʊ/ *n.*^{2} Chiefly *Sc.* & *north.* Also **lowe**. ME. [ON *logi* = OFris. *loga*, f. Gmc (rel. to G *Lohe* (also in *lichterloh* in a blaze)) f. IE base also of LIGHT *n.*] **1** (A) flame. ME. **2** A light. E19.

1 in, on a low on fire. **put the low to** set fire to. **take a low** catch fire.

low /ləʊ/ *n.*^{3} M16. [f. LOW *v.*^{1}] The action or an act of lowing; a bovine animal's deep subdued resonant sound.

low /ləʊ/ *a.* & *n.*^{4} ME. [ON *lágr* = OFris. *lēge*, *lēch*, MDu. *lage*, *laech*, *lege*, *leech* (Du. *laag*), MHG *læge* (G dial. *läg*) flat, f. Gmc base rel. to base of LIE *v.*^{1}] **A** *adj.* **I 1** Of small or less than average upward extent; little; short. Now *rare* of a person exc. *Sc.* ME. **b** Chiefly of clothing: cut so as to extend below the normal level; *esp.* = *low-cut* below. M19. **2** Situated not far above the ground or a specified level or (formerly) under the earth's surface; not elevated in position. Also, designating a country or a district near the sea or not far above sea level (now only in fixed collocations, as *the Low Countries*, *Low German*, etc.: cf. LOWER *a.* 2). ME. **b** Dead (and buried). *arch.* ME. **c** Of a curtsy, bow, etc.: in which the body is brought (relatively) close to the ground. M16. **d** Of the sun, moon, a star, etc.: near the horizon. L17. **3** Esp. of a river, a lake, etc.: below the usual vertical measurement; shallow. LME. **4** *Phonet.* Of a sound: produced with (part of) the tongue in a lowered position. M19.

1 D. H. LAWRENCE The kitchen, a long, low room. DAY LEWIS Five steps, flanked by low stone balustrades. **b** SCOTT FITZGERALD She wore a low gown which displayed the bright eczema of her chest and back. **2** G. BERKELEY Trẹes . . in low and shady places do not yield so good tar.

II *transf.* & *fig.* **5** Of or in a humble rank or position (now *derog.* of a person, passing into sense 5c); humble in disposition, meek (now *rare*). ME. **b** Base, mean. ME. **c** Coarse, vulgar; disreputable. L16. **6** Of inferior quality, character, or style; unrefined, commonplace. ME. **b** Chiefly *Biol.* Advanced to a lesser degree; having a simple or primitive organization. Usu. in compar.: see LOWER *a.* 2c. M19. **7a** (Of a quality, condition, etc.) small or reduced in quantity, degree, or intensity; *spec.* (*a*) (of sound) not loud (see also sense 9 below); (*b*) (of heat) not of a high temperature; (of temperature) less likely to promote melting and the emission of radiation. LME. **b** Of price, rate, quantity, value, etc.: not high, below what is regarded as normal or average; numerically small. E17. **c** Of latitude: at a short distance from the equator. M18. **8** Lacking physical strength or vigour; weak (through illness or poor nourishment). Now *esp.* dejected, dispirited, depressed. LME. **b** Of diet etc.: providing little nourishment, poor. E18. **9** Of a voice, musical sound, etc.: not high or acute in pitch, not shrill; producing or produced by relatively slow vibrations. LME. **10** Of a stock of a commodity etc.: small or reduced in quantity; nearly exhausted. E18. **11** = LOW CHURCH *a. phr. colloq.* M19. **12** Of a date: relatively recent. Usu. in *compar.* & *superl.* E20.

5 C. THIRLWALL A young man of low birth . . had been . . acknowledged as king. E. WAUGH You are a distinguished man, . . not like these low soldiers. **b** J. ROBERTSON Flattery or fawning or other low arts. **c** B. WEBB There is nothing that is low or bad broadcasted. L. BLUE I also like low things such as liver and lights. **6** C. KINGSLEY To discriminate between high art and low art they must have seen both. **7a** W. FAULKNER White faces . . sharp in the low light. M. FRAYN The air temperature was low, but the woods . . were filled with . . sunlight. G. VIDAL Her voice became so low that he could barely hear her. M. GORDON I have a rather low tolerance for horrors. **b** *Manchester*

Examiner Chinese workmen . . work for low wages. D. MURPHY The rent was so low . . because of the previous tenant's suicide. 8 T. DREISER He was exceedingly low and not expected to live. P. BARKER She came out of hospital so low that for the first time . . she thought about suicide. b L. STRACHEY The low diet and constant bleedings . . were an error. 10 TOLKIEN The food would not last for ever: it was . . beginning to get low.

III After a vb, as the result of an action or process. 13 So as to be in a low position or on or to a low level. Chiefly in *lay low, lie low* below. Passing into *adv.* ME.

Phrases: *burn low*: see BURN *v. high and low*: see HIGH *a, adv.*, & *n.* **lay low** (*a*) lay flat; bring to the ground; *fig.* humble; (*b*) bury. **lie low** (*a*) crouch; be prostrate, be dead; *fig.* be humbled; (*b*) *colloq.* keep quiet or out of the way; make no intervention; bide one's time. **low on** *colloq.* short of. **low to paper** *Printing* (of type) of less than normal height. *run low*: see RUN *v. the low toby*: see TOBY *n.*[2]

Special collocations & *comb.*: **low-alloy** *a.* (*Metall.*) containing a small proportion of alloying elements. **low-born** *a.* of humble birth. **lowboy** *N. Amer.* (*a*) a table with drawers and fairly short legs; (*b*) a low-slung trailer for transporting very tall or heavy loads. **low-bred** *a.* having or characterized by vulgar manners. **low-browed** *a.* (*a*) (of a person) having a low forehead; (*b*) (of rocks) overhanging; (of a doorway etc.) low, dark. **low-bush** *a.* (*N. Amer.*) designating or pertaining to a plant that grows low to the ground; *low-bush blackberry*, the N. American dewberry, *Rubus flagellaris*. **low-calorie** *a.* designating food or drink that is low in calories. **low-class** *a.* (*a*) of low quality; (*b*) of low social class. **low comedian** an actor of low comedy. **low comedy**: in which the subject and treatment border on farce. **low-cut** *a.* cut with a neckline that exposes the neck and upper part of the breast. **low-definition** *a.* designating or providing a relatively unclear or indistinct image. **low-down** *n.* & *a.* (*a*) *n.* (*colloq.*) the relevant information or fundamental facts *on*; (*b*) *adj.* abject, mean, despicable. *Low Dutch*: see DUTCH *a.*, *n.*[1] **low-end** *a.* (*Comm.*) of, pertaining to, or associated with the cheaper end of the market for a particular product. **low enema**: delivered into the rectum. *lowest common* DENOMINATOR. *lowest common multiple*: see MULTIPLE *n.* I. *lowest terms*: see TERM *n.* **low fidelity** *Audio* (the reproduction of) low-fidelity sound. **low-fidelity** *a.* (*Audio*) designating, pertaining to, or characterized by sound reproduction inferior to high fidelity (cf. LO-FI). **low frequency** *spec.* a frequency of vibration or oscillations having a relatively small number of cycles per second; in *Telecommunications* etc., a radio frequency in the range 30-300 kilohertz, *loosely* an audio (as opp. to a radio) frequency. **low gear** a gear of a motor vehicle providing a low ratio between the speed of the driven wheels and that of the driving mechanism and so a low speed of the vehicle itself. *Low German*: see GERMAN *n.*[1] & *a.*[1] **low grade** *Philol.* a reduced form in an ablaut series, usu. pronounced /ə/. **low-grade** *a.* of low quality. **low-headed** *a.* (of a tree) having a low crown of foliage. **low heels** low-heeled shoes. *low keep*: see KEEP *n.* **low-key** *a.* (*a*) *Photogr.* consisting of dark tones; (*b*) *fig.* muted, restrained, not intense or prominent. **low-keyed** *a.* = *low-key* (b) above. **Low Latin** [tr. Fr. *bas-latin*] late and medieval Latin. **low-level** *a.* (*a*) situated near or below ground level; *fig.* low-ranking, unobtrusive; (*b*) designating mild radioactivity or mildly radioactive waste; (*c*) *Computing* (of a programming language) containing only relatively simple instructions, close to machine language in form. **low-lived** *a.* of, pertaining to, or living a low or disreputable life. **low-loader** a lorry with a low floor and (usu.) no sides for heavy loads. **low-loss** *a.* (*Electr.*) characterized by or causing little dissipation of electric or electromagnetic energy. **low-lying** *a.* at low altitude (above sea level etc.). *low mass*: see MASS *n.*[1] **low-melting** *a.* melting at a relatively low temperature, esp. at little more than room temperature. **low men** dice loaded to turn up low numbers. **low-minded** *a.* vulgar or ignoble in mind or character. **low-mindedness** the quality or state of being low-minded. **low-molecular** *a.* (*Chem.*) having a low molecular weight. **low-necked** *a.* (of a garment) having a low-cut neck. **low opinion** a very unfavourable opinion. **low-pass** *a.* (*Electr.*, *Acoustics*, etc.) designating a filter that attenuates only those components with a frequency greater than some cut-off frequency. **low-pitched** *a.* (*a*) (of a sound) low in pitch; (*b*) (of a roof) not very steep. **low point** the minimum or worst state reached. **low-powered** *a.* having little power or energy. **low pressure** (*a*) a low degree of activity or exertion; (*b*) an atmospheric condition with pressure below average. **low profile** a low-keyed and unobtrusive policy or attitude, a condition of behaving in a restrained or inconspicuous way. **low-profile** *a.* (*a*) designating a motor-vehicle tyre which is wide in proportion to its height; (*b*) designating, having or maintaining a low profile. *low relief*: see RELIEF *n.*[2] I. **low-residue** *a.* (of a meal or diet) designed to produce relatively little faeces and urine. **low-rise** *a.* & *n.* (a building) of one storey or few storeys. **low season** the period of fewest visitors at a resort etc. **low side window** *Archit.* a small window lower than the other windows, found in some medieval churches. **low-spirited** *a.* dejected, depressed. **low-spiritedness** the quality or condition of being low-spirited. **low spirits** dejection, depression. **Low Sunday** the Sunday after Easter. **low tech** *n.* & *a.* (*a*) *n.* = *low technology* below; (*b*) *adj.* involved in, employing, or requiring only low technology. **low technology** less advanced or relatively unsophisticated technological development or equipment. **low tension** low voltage. **low tide** the time or level of the tide at its ebb. **low water** the tide at its lowest. **low-water mark** (*a*) the level reached at low water or on a drought or dry season; (*b*) a minimum recorded level or value. **Low Week** the week beginning with Low Sunday. **low-wines** the first spirit that comes off in the distillation process. **low-yield** *a.* producing little, giving a low return; *spec.* (of a nuclear weapon) having a relatively low explosive force.

B *n.* I *absol.* 1 That which is low; those who are low or of humble birth. ME. †2 After *at, in, on* preps. The ground, the earth. Only in ME.

II 3 A piece of low-lying land; *spec.* in East Anglia, a hollow or valley between dunes; a pool left by the tide in such a hollow. ME. 4 The lowest trump card dealt or drawn. Chiefly in *high-low-jack* (*and the game*), = ALL FOURS 2. E19. 5 An area of low barometric pressure. Also, an area of low gravitational field strength. L19. 6 A low point or minimum in price, temperature, etc.; *spec.* a depression, a state of dejection. E20. 7 = *low gear* above. M20.

3 *Rolling Stone* The peaks, lows and riffs of these . . Nevada California border ranges. 6 F. L. ALLEN The Boston *literati* . . sank . . to new lows for all time. *New York Times* The United States dollar plunged yesterday to another post-war low. C. THUBRON Easy does it, Daniel, you're having one of your lows. 7 A. HALL I dragged the manual into low to kill the rest of the speed.

low /ləʊ/ *v.*[1] [OE *hlōwan* = OS *hlōian* (Du. *loeien*) (whence *hlōwinga* roaring), OHG *hluoen*, f. Gmc redupl. str. vb, f. IE repr. base also of L *clamare* shout.] 1 *v.i.* Of a bovine animal: (orig.) bellow; (now) utter a deep subdued resonant sound, moo. OE. 2 *v.i. transf.* Make a loud noise, bellow. Now *rare.* OE. 3 *v.t.* Orig., utter with a bellow. Now, utter with a deep murmur. M16.

1 W. VAN T. CLARK We could hear the cows lowing . . , a mellow sound at that distance. A. BRINK A single calf in a pen, lowing wretchedly at regular intervals.

low /ləʊ/ *v.*[2]*t. obs.* exc. *dial.* ME. [f. LOW *a.*] 1 Make or bring low. Chiefly *fig.*, abase, humble. ME. 2 Diminish, lessen, esp. in value. ME. 3 Hold or put in a lower position. LME.

low /ləʊ/ *v.*[3]*i.* Chiefly *Sc.* & *north.* ME. [ON *loga*, f. *logi* LOW *n.*[2]] Flame, blaze, (*up*); glow; *fig.* burn with passion.

low /laʊ/ *v.*[4]*t. colloq.* Also (now usu.) **'low**. LME. [Partly f. (O)Fr. *louer* f. L *laudare* praise, approve; partly aphet. f. ALLOW.] = ALLOW I.

G. V. GALWEY Wind's backed four points. . . We've got to 'low for it.

low /ləʊ/ *adv.* ME. [f. LOW *a.*] 1 In a low position; on or not much above the ground or some other level. ME. b *fig.* Humbly; in a low condition or rank; at a low rate. LME. 2 To a low point or position. Also, in a low direction. ME. 3 In a low tone; not loudly, softly; with not much intensity. Also of singing etc.: at a low pitch, on low notes. ME. 4 (To a point) far down in time; late. M17.

1 J. MITCHELL They flew quite low over the bush. J. M. COETZEE He . . gathered the next tuft of lucerne, and cut it clean and low. *high and low*: see HIGH *a., adv.*, & *n.* 2 J. STEINBECK The sun dropped low toward the horizon. G. GREENE They stoop low slipping between the tables. 3 OED I can't sing so low as that. *blow high, blow low*: see BLOW *v.*[1]

Comb.: **low-flung** *a.* (*arch. US colloq.*) of low character or standing.

¶ In some uses indistinguishable from LOW *a.* 13.

lowan /ˈləʊən/ *n. Austral.* M19. [Aborig. *lauan.*] The mallee fowl.

lowance /ˈlaʊəns/ *n.* Now *dial.* M16. [Aphet. f. ALLOWANCE.] A limited portion of food or drink or its equivalent in money given in addition to wages.

lowball /ˈləʊbɔːl/ *n.* & *v.* Chiefly *US.* M19. [f. LOW *a.* + BALL *n.*[1]] A *n.* 1 *Baseball.* A ball pitched so as to pass over the plate below the level of the batter. M19. 2 *Comm.* (The action of offering) a deceptively or unrealistically low price or estimate. M20. B *v.t. Comm.* Reduce to a deceptive or unrealistically low price or level. M20.

lowballer *n.* L20.

lowbell /ˈləʊbɛl/ *n.* & *v.* L16. [Perh. f. LOW *a.* + BELL *n.*[1]] †A *n.* 1 A small bell; *esp.* a cow-bell, a sheep-bell. L16–M17. 2 A bell used at night in fowling, to stupefy the birds with terror. L16–E19. B *v.t.* †1 Capture (birds) by the use of a lowbell; scare or bewilder as with a lowbell. L16–M17. 2 Deride by the jangling of tins, kettles, etc. *dial.* M19.

lowbeller *n.* L16.

lowbrow /ˈləʊbraʊ/ *n.* & *a. colloq.* (orig. *US*). E20. [f. LOW *a.* + BROW *n.*[1], after HIGHBROW.] A *n.* A person who is not, or does not claim or aim to be, highly intellectual or cultured. E20.

B *adj.* Not highly, or not pretentiously, intellectual or cultured. E20.

H. CARPENTER Chapbooks, which played much the same part in society as lowbrow television drama does now.

lowbrowism *n.* lack of interest in intellectual or cultural matters M20.

Low Church /ləʊ ˈtʃəːtʃ/ *n.* & *a. phr.* E18. [f. LOW *a.* + CHURCH *n.*, after next.] A *n. phr.* (The principles of) a section of the Church of England or (now also) any of various Nonconformist Churches laying little emphasis on ritual, priestly authority, and sacraments. E18. B *adj. phr.* Of, pertaining to, or characteristic of (the principles of) this section or such a Church. E18.

Low-'Churchism *n.* Low-Church principles, doctrine, or practice M19.

Low Churchman /ləʊ ˈtʃəːtʃmən/ *n. phr.* Pl. **Low Churchmen**. E18. [f. LOW *a.* + CHURCHMAN.] An advocate of Low Church principles.

low-country /ˈləʊkʌntri/ *n.* & *a.* Also (in sense A.2 only) without hyphen. L15. [f. LOW *a.* + COUNTRY.] A *n.* 1 A region or district whose level is lower than that of the surrounding country. L15. 2 *the Low Countries*, the Netherlands, Belgium, and Luxembourg. M16. 3 = LOWVELD. *S. Afr.* L19. B *attrib.* or as *adj.* 1 (With cap. initials.) Of, pertaining to, or from the Low Countries. E17. 2 Of or pertaining to the low-country or (*S. Afr.*) the lowveld. M19.

lowe *n.* var. of LOW *n.*[2]

lower *n.*[1], *n.*[2] vars. of LOUR *n.*[1], *n.*[2]

lower /ˈləʊə/ *a.*, *n.*[3], & *adv.* ME. [f. LOW *a.* + -ER[3].] A *adj.* 1 Compar. of LOW *a.* ME. 2 *spec.* Designating a thing or person less high in position, degree, or status than, or situated below, another of the same. L16. b Designating (part of) a region, river, etc., situated on less high land, or to the south, or towards the sea. Usu. opp. *upper.* E17. c *Biol.* Of an organism or group: less advanced, primitive in organization. Opp. *higher.* L18. d *Geol.* & *Archaeol.* (Freq. L-.) Designating an older, and hence usu. deeper, part of a stratigraphic division, archaeological deposit, etc., or the period in which it was formed or deposited. Opp. *upper.* M19.

2 *lower intestine, lower lip*, etc. b *Lower California, Lower Egypt, the lower Danube*, etc. d *Lower Carboniferous, Lower Triassic*, etc.

Special collocations, comb., & *phrases*: *lower case*: see CASE *n.*[2] **Lower Chamber** = *Lower House* below. **lower-class** *a.* of or pertaining to the lower or working class; *derog.* common, vulgar. **lower class(es)** (the members of) the working class. **lower court** a court subject to overruling by another on appeal etc. **lower deck** (*a*) the deck of a ship situated immediately above the orlop deck; (*b*) the petty officers and men of a ship collectively. **lower fourth,**

lower fifth a lower division of a fourth, fifth, form in a secondary school. **Lower House** one of the houses of a legislature consisting of two houses, usu. the larger and more representative one, often dealing with legislation before the Upper House; *esp.* the House of Commons. *lower jaw*: see JAW *n.*[1] 1. **lower orders** = *lower classes* above. *lower pastern*: see PASTERN 2c. **lower regions** = *lower world* below. **lower school** in a secondary school, (the pupils in) the forms below the fifth. **lower second** the lower division of a second-class honours degree. **lower sixth** a lower division of a sixth form in a secondary school. **lower world** (*a*) earth as opp. to heaven; (*b*) hell; the realm of the dead. *lower yield point*: see YIELD *v. the lower criticism*: see CRITICISM 2.

B *n.* **1** An inferior person or thing. ME. **2** A lower plate of artificial teeth. L19.

C *adv.* Compar. of LOW *adv.* M16.

lowermost *a.* & *adv.* lowest M16.

lower /ˈləʊə/ *v.*[1] E16. [f. LOWER *a.*] **1** a *v.t.* Make lower, reduce the level of. E16. **b** *v.t.* Cause or allow to descend, let down gradually (a drawbridge, a person or thing suspended from above, etc.); haul down (a sail, a flag) (also (*Naut.*) foll. by *away*). M17. **c** *v.i. Naut.* Haul down a sail. Also foll. by *away*. M18. **d** *v.t.* Cause (one's eyes) to look downwards, cause (one's head, eyelids, etc.) to droop, esp. as an expression of humility, modesty, evasion, etc. M19. **e** *v.t.* Drink (beer etc.); empty (a bottle or glass of beer etc.) by drinking. *colloq.* L19. **2** *v.i.* Descend, sink. Formerly also, cower, crouch. Freq. foll. by *down*. M16. **b** Slope downwards. E19. **3** *v.t.* & *i.* Diminish, reduce, esp. in price. L17. **4** *v.t.* Make lower in quality or degree; lessen the intensity of. Formerly also, reduce the strength of, dilute (a liquid, the air, etc.). M18. **b** *Mus.* Depress in pitch, flatten. L19. **c** *Phonet.* Modify (a sound) by articulation with a lower tongue position. L19. **5** *v.t.* Bring down in rank or estimation, degrade, dishonour, (esp. oneself). L18. **6** *v.t.* Bring down to a lower position on a graduated scale. M19.

1a D. LARDNER The water escapes .. until the level of C has been lowered to that of B. **b** B. PYM Adam Prince lowered himself carefully on to the ground. K. WILLIAMS He lowered the blinds in his car. M. ATWOOD He .. lowered the outboard motor into the water. **d** R. P. JHABVALA He had lowered his eyes as if afraid of embarrassing me. **e** L. GREX He could lower a whole bottle of three-star brandy. **3** B. SPOCK It looks as though teething lowers resistance. *Lancaster Guardian* The committee decided to lower the entrance fee. **4** I. MURDOCH Bruno had lowered his voice to a confidential whisper. *Which?* The 'flash-freeze' button .. lowers the temperatures in the freezer. **5** LYTTON In marriage a man lowers a woman to his own rank. R. K. NARAYAN We have a status .. to keep. We can't lower ourselves unduly. **6** B. STEWART It is possible to lower the freezing-point by various means.

Phrases: *lower one's sights*: see SIGHT *n.* **lower the boom** *N. Amer. slang* inflict a physical defeat *on* (a person), treat severely.

lowerable *a.* L19. **lowerer** *n.* L19.

lower *v.*[2], **lowering** *a.*, **lowery** *a.* vars. of LOUR *v.*, LOURING, LOURY.

Lowestoft /ˈləʊstɒft/ *n.* & *a.* L18. [A town in Suffolk, England.] (Made from) a soft-paste porcelain made orig. in Lowestoft from 1757. Also *Lowestoft porcelain*.

Oriental Lowestoft: see ORIENTAL *a.*

lowish /ˈləʊɪʃ/ *a.* L17. [f. LOW *a.* + -ISH[1].] Somewhat low.

lowland /ˈləʊlənd/ *n.* & *a.* L15. [f. LOW *a.* + LAND *n.*[1] See also LALLAN.] **A** *n.* In sense 2 **L-**. **1** Low-lying or level land; the low-lying part of a country or district. Usu. in *pl.* L15. **2** *spec.* a In *pl.* & †*sing. The* less mountainous southern and eastern region of Scotland. L15. **b** In *pl. The* Low Countries. L17. **3** In *pl.* (treated as *sing.*). The dialect of the Scottish Lowlands, Lallans. *Sc.* M19. **B** *adj.* Of, pertaining to, or inhabiting lowland; *spec.* (**L-**) of, pertaining to, or characteristic of (the people of) the Scottish Lowlands. E16.

lowlander *n.* a native or inhabitant of the low-lying part of a country or district; *spec.* (**L-**) a native or inhabitant of the Scottish Lowlands: L17.

low-life /ˈləʊlʌɪf/ *a.* & *n.* L18. [f. LOW *a.* + LIFE *n.*] **A** *adj.* Disreputable, vulgar. Now also, of or pertaining to the (criminal) underworld or an underclass. L18. **B** *n.* Pl. **-lifes**, (occas.) **-lives** /-lʌɪvz/. A coarse vulgar person; a member of the (criminal) underworld or an underclass; such people collectively. E20.

lowlight /ˈləʊlʌɪt/ *n.* & *a.* E20. [f. LOW *a.* + LIGHT *n.*, after *highlight*.] **A** *n.* **1** A dark (esp. artificial) streak in lighter hair. E20. **2** A moment or feature of low interest or activity; a low point; a poor performance etc. L20. **B** *attrib.* or as *adj. Photogr.* Designating devices for use in conditions of little light, and operations performed in such conditions. L20.

low-lives *n.pl.* see LOW-LIFE.

lowly /ˈləʊli/ *a.* Now chiefly *arch.* or *rhet.* LME. [f. LOW *a.* + -LY[1].] **1** Humble in feeling or behaviour; humble in condition or quality; modest. LME. **b** Low, mean, base. *rare.* M18. **2** Low in position (usu. w. allus. to sense 1). L16. **3** Of a plant or animal: primitive, simple. L19.

1 R. OWEN Her parents would not .. consider allowing their daughter to marry a man .. of lowly origin. D. ROWE The lowly status of children .. in poverty. **2** E. K. KANE The sun, albeit from a lowly altitude, shone out.

lowlihead *n.* (*arch.*) humility, lowliness LME. **lowlily** *adv.* ME. **lowliness** *n.* LME.

lowly /ˈləʊli/ *adv.* Now chiefly *arch.* or *rhet.* ME. [f. LOW *a.* + -LY[2].] **1** In a lowly manner; humbly, modestly, meekly. ME. **2** In a low position or posture (in later use w. allus. to sense 1). ME. **b** In a low voice. Now *poet.* LME. †**c** In an inferior manner, meanly. *rare* (Shakes.). Only in E17. **d** With a low opinion. *rare.* M18.

lowmost /ˈləʊməʊst/ *a.* & *adv.* Now *dial.* M16. [f. LOW *a.*, *adv.* + -MOST.] Lowest.

lown /laʊn/ *a.*, *adv.*, & *n. Sc.* & *north.* LME. [ON (dial.) *logn*, earlier *lygn*.] **A** *adj.* **1** Of the weather, water, a place: calm, quiet, still. Of a person, action, etc.: calm, gentle, silent, still. LME. **2** Sheltered; cosy, snug. E18. **B** *adv.* Quietly, softly. M16. **C** *n.* Quiet, calm, stillness. Also, shelter. L18.

lownly *adv.* calmly, quietly; in shelter: L18.

lown /laʊn/ *v.i. Sc.* & *north.* LME. [f. LOWN *a.*] **1** Become calm, calm. LME. **2** Shelter. LME.

lowness /ˈləʊnɪs/ *n.* ME. [f. LOW *a.* + -NESS.] **1** The quality or condition of being low. ME. **2** (**L-**.) With possess. adj. (as *his* etc. *Lowness*): a mock title of rank. L18.

Lowry /ˈlaʊri/ *a.* M20. [See below.] Reminiscent or characteristic of the work of the British painter Lawrence Stephen Lowry (1887–1976); *esp.* matchstick, involving matchstick figures.

Lowry'esque *a.* M20.

lowveld /ˈləʊvɛlt, -f-/ *n.* L19. [Partial tr. Afk. *Laeveld* low country.] (A region of) veld situated at a low altitude; *spec.* the low-lying region of the eastern Transvaal and Swaziland.

lowy /ˈləʊɪ/ *n. obs.* exc. *Hist.* L16. [OFr. *louée*, *lieuée* f. med.L *leucata*, *leugata*, f. late L *leuca*, *leuga*: see LEAGUE *n.*[1], -Y[5].] A district or area extending for about a league outside a town but still under its control.

¶Probably dating back to ME.

lox /lɒks; ɛləʊˈɛks/ *n.*[1] Also **LOX**. E20. [Orig. f. *l*iquid *o*xygen e*x*plosive; later interpreted as repr. *l*iquid *ox*ygen.] **1** An explosive device which uses liquid oxygen as an oxidant. E20. **2** Liquid oxygen, esp. when used as a rocket propellant. M20.

lox /lɒks/ *n.*[2] Chiefly *N. Amer.* M20. [Yiddish *laks* f. G *Lachs* salmon.] Smoked salmon.

Loxa /ˈlɒksə/ *n.* L18. [A province (now Loja) of Ecuador.] More fully *Loxa bark*. Cinchona bark.

loxia /ˈlɒksɪə/ *n.* E18. [mod.L, f. Gk *loxos* oblique: see -IA[1].] A crossbill. Now chiefly as mod.L genus name.

loxodon /ˈlɒksədɒn/ *n.* Now *rare.* M19. [mod.L *Loxodonta* genus name, f. Gk *loxos* oblique + -ODON (w. ref. to the oblique ridges on the worn molars).] *Zool.* An African elephant.

Also **loxodont** *n.* L19.

loxodromic /lɒksəˈdrɒmɪk/ *n.* & *a.* L17. [Fr. *loxodromique*, f. Gk *loxos* oblique + *dromos* course: see -IC.] *Naut.* & *Math.* **A** *n.* **1** A loxodromic line or table. L17. **2** In *pl.* The art or practice of sailing to a constant compass bearing. E18.

B *adj.* Of or pertaining to motion or alignment at a constant angle to the meridians, esp. sailing by the rhumb (on a constant compass bearing). E18.

loxodromic curve, **line**, **spiral** a rhumb-line, a path which cuts the meridians at a constant angle (not a right angle).

loxodrome /ˈlɒksədrəʊm/ *n.* a loxodromic line, a rhumb-line L19. **loxodromism** *n.* the tracing of or movement in a loxodromic line or curve M19. **loxodromy** /lɒkˈsɒdrəmi/ *n.* loxodromism; loxodromics; a loxodrome: M17.

loy /lɔɪ/ *n.* M18. [Ir. *lái*.] A long narrow asymmetric spade used in Ireland. Also, a similar tool for digging with a broad chisel point.

loyal /ˈlɔɪəl/ *a.* & *n.* M16. [Fr. f. OFr. *loial* later var. of *leial*, *leel* f. L *legalis* LEGAL. Cf. LEAL.] **A** *adj.* **1** Faithful or steadfast in allegiance, *spec.* to the legitimate monarch or government of one's country. Also, enthusiastically reverential to (the family of) the monarch. M16. **b** *gen.* True or faithful to the obligations of duty, love, friendship, etc. L16. **2** Of a thing, action, etc.: characterized by or exhibiting loyalty. L16. †**3** Legal; *spec.* (of a child) legitimate. Only in 17.

1 W. S. CHURCHILL Charles set up his standard .. and called his loyal subjects to his aid. N. CHOMSKY A peasant-based guerilla force loyal to Sihanouk that will restore him to power. **b** M. ANGELOU One white New York club owner who had been a loyal friend to me. P. GROSSKURTH However loyal .. to Freud, he had a strong mind of his own. **2 loyal toast** a toast proposed and drunk to the monarch of one's country.

B *n.* Orig., a person bound by allegiance, a liege subject. Now *gen.*, a loyal subject. M16.

loyalize *v.t.* make or keep loyal E17. **loyally** *adv.* E16. **loyalness** *n.* L16.

loyalist /ˈlɔɪəlɪst/ *n.* & *a.* L17. [f. LOYAL *a.* + -IST.] **A** *n.* A loyal person; a person who actively maintains allegiance to a monarch, government, cause, etc. Now chiefly (usu. **L-**), a supporter of political union with, or an opponent of political separation from, a particular State; *spec.* (*a*) *Hist.* any of the colonists of the American revolutionary period who supported the British cause, many of whom afterwards migrated to Canada; (chiefly *Canad.*) a descendant of such a person; (*b*) an Irish or Northern Irish advocate or supporter of union between Great Britain and Northern Ireland or (before partition) the whole of Ireland. L17.

THACKERAY This resolute old loyalist .. was with the King whilst his house was .. being battered down. *Tribune* If re-elected she would .. be a strong Kinnock loyalist.

B *attrib.* or as *adj.* (Freq. **L-**.) Of or pertaining to a loyalist or Loyalists, characterized by loyalism. L19.

News on Sunday The bonfire was the first of dozens .. lit in Loyalist areas as part of the pre-July 12 celebrations.

loyalism /ˈlɔɪəlɪz(ə)m/ *n.* the principles, practices, or actions of a loyalist or (usu. **L-**) Loyalists M19.

loyalty /ˈlɔɪəlti/ *n.* LME. [OFr. *loialté* (mod. *loyauté*), f. *loial* LOYAL: see -TY[1].] **1** The fact or condition of being loyal; faithfulness to duty or in love, friendship, etc; faithful allegiance to the legitimate monarch or government of one's country. LME. **2** A feeling or example of this. Freq. in *pl.* E17.

1 J. W. KRUTCH Brand loyalty, or the refusal to be seduced from your devotion to a particular mark of goods. S. HASTINGS His love of France was fierce, his loyalty to the General absolute. P. LOMAS In times of crisis .. group loyalty is vital. **2** M. ARNOLD Home of lost causes .. and impossible loyalties. J. HUXLEY For me it was a battle of loyalties between my family and Julian's exacting demands.

†**loyn(e)** *n.* var. of LUNE *n.*[1]

Loyolite /ˈlɔɪəlʌɪt/ *n.* M17. [mod.L *Loyolita*, f. St Ignatius *Loyola* (1491–1556), one of the founders of the Society of Jesus: see -ITE[1].] A Jesuit.

lozen /ˈlɒz(ə)n/ *n.* & *a.* Chiefly *Sc.* LME. [Prob. f. OFr. *loseingne* var. of *losenge* LOZENGE.] **A** *n.* †**1** A thin cake made from pastry. Only in LME. †**2** A lozenge-shaped figure. L15–L18. **3** A pane of glass, orig. a lozenge-shaped one. L16. B *attrib.* or as *adj.* = LOZENGE *a.* E16.

lozened *a.* = LOZENGED M16.

lozenge /ˈlɒzɪndʒ/ *n.* & *a.* ME. [OFr. *losenge* (mod. *losange*), prob. deriv. of wd repr. by Prov. *lausa*, Sp. *losa*, Port. *lousa* slab, tombstone, and late L *lausiae (lapides)* stone slabs, slates, ult. of Gaulish or Iberian origin.] A *n.* 1 A rhombus or diamond-shaped figure. In *Her.*, a charge consisting of such a figure, less elongated than a fusil, and placed with its longer axis vertical; also, a lozenge-shaped shield upon which the arms of a spinster or widow are emblazoned. ME. b Any of the lozenge-shaped facets of a cut precious stone. M18. †2 *Cookery.* A lozenge-shaped cake; a lozenge-shaped ornament as a garnish. ME–L15. 3 A small (orig. lozenge-shaped) sweet or medicinal tablet made of flavoured sugar, for dissolving in the mouth. M16. 4 Any of the lozenge-shaped panes of glass in a casement. Cf. LOZEN 3. M17. B *attrib.* or as *adj.* Lozenge-shaped; of, composed of, or ornamented with lozenges. Cf. LOZEN *a.* M17.

lozenged *a.* ornamented with lozenge-shaped figures of alternate colours; divided into lozenge-shaped spaces: LME. **lozenger** *n.* †(*a*) = LOZENGE 1; (*b*) *US* & *north.* = LOZENGE 3: E16. **lozengewise** *adv.* (esp. *Her.*) so as to form a lozenge or in a lozenge pattern LME.

lozengy /ˈlɒzɪndʒi/ *a.* M16. [OFr. *losengié*, f. as prec.: see -Y⁵.] 1 *Her.* Of a field: covered with lozenges of alternate tinctures; divided into lozenges. Formerly also, (of a bearing) shaped like a lozenge. M16. 2 Resembling or shaped like a lozenge; composed of or divided into lozenges. E17.

Lozi /ˈləʊzi/ *n.* & *a.* In sense A.1 also (sing.) **Mulozi** /mʊ-/, (pl.) **Malozi** /mə-/. M20. [Bantu.] A *n.* Pl. **-zi**, **Lozis**. 1 A member of a Bantu-speaking people inhabiting Zambia. M20. 2 The language of this people, Silozi. M20. B *attrib.* or as *adj.* Of or pertaining to the Malozi or their language. M20.

¶Earlier called *Barotse*.

LSD /ɛlɛsˈdiː/ *n.* M20. [Abbrev.] Lysergic acid diethylamide (see LYSERGIC *a.*), a synthetic derivative of lysergic acid which is a powerful hallucinogenic drug able to produce profound changes in perception and mood.

lü /ljuː/ *n.* Pl. same. M17. [Chin. *lǜ*.] In Chinese music: each of a series of standard bamboo pitch-pipes used in ancient music; a fundamental pitch, each of the twelve semitone pitch notes within the octave (represented by these pitch-pipes).

luau /ˈluːaʊ/ *n.* M19. [Haw. *lū'au*.] A Hawaiian party or feast usu. accompanied by some form of entertainment.

Luba /ˈluːbə/ *n.* & *a.* L19. [Bantu.] A *n.* Pl. same, **-s**. A member of a Bantu-speaking people of Zaire; the language of this people. L19. B *attrib.* or as *adj.* Of or pertaining to the Luba or their language. E20.

lubbard /ˈlʌbəd/ *n. obs.* exc. *Sc.* & *north.* M16. [Alt. of next: see -ARD.] = next.

lubber /ˈlʌbə/ *n.*, *a.*, & *v.* LME. [Perh. f. OFr. *lobeor* swindler, parasite, f. *lober* deceive, sponge on, mock (perh. f. Frank. *lobon* praise) w. assim. in sense to LOB *n.*¹] A *n.* 1 A big, clumsy, esp. idle person; a lout. Formerly also, a drudge. *arch.* & *dial.* LME. 2 *Naut.* A clumsy sailor; a person not used or suited to sea life. Cf. LANDLUBBER. L16.

Comb.: **lubber fiend** a beneficent goblin supposed to perform chores etc. round the house or farm at night; **lubber-grasshopper** either of two large clumsy grasshoppers of the southern US, *Brachystola magna* and *Romalea microptera*; **Lubberland** an imaginary land of idleness and plenty; **lubber line, mark, point** *Naut.* a vertical line marked on a compass, indicating a ship's forward direction; **lubber's hole** *Naut.* a hole in the platform of a ship's top, used to avoid climbing the futtock shrouds.

B *attrib.* or as *adj.* Clumsy, stupid; loutish. M16.

C *v.i.* Behave as a lubber; loaf about; *Naut.* navigate a boat like a lubber. M16.

lubberlike *a.* of, pertaining to, or characteristic of a lubber L16.

lubberly /ˈlʌbəli/ *a.* & *adv.* L16. [f. LUBBER *n.* + -LY¹.] A *adj.* 1 Of the nature or characteristic of a lubber; loutish, clumsy, lazy, stupid. L16. 2 *Naut.* Resembling, pertaining to, or characteristic of a lubber; unseamanlike. L18. B *adv.* In a lubberly manner; unskilfully, clumsily. L16.

lubberliness *n.* L16.

lube /luːb, ljuːb/ *n.* & *v.* Chiefly *N. Amer.* & *Austral. colloq.* M20. [Abbrev.] A *n.* 1 = LUBRICANT *n.* M20. 2 = LUBRICATION. M20. B *v.t.* = LUBRICATE. M20.

Lubecker /ˈluːbɛkə, ˈljuː-/ *n.* E17. [f. *Lübeck* (see next) + -ER¹.] *Hist.* A merchant vessel from Lübeck in northern Germany.

Lubish /ˈluːbɪʃ, ˈljuː-/ *a. obs.* exc. *Hist.* M16. [G *lübisch*, f. *Lübeck* (see below) + *-isch* -ISH¹.] Of or pertaining to Lübeck, a town in northern Germany; *spec.* designating a money of account formerly in extensive mercantile use in northern Germany.

lubra /ˈluːbrə, ˈljuː-/ *n.* Chiefly *Austral.* Occas. *derog.* M19. [Aborig.] An Aboriginal woman of Australia; *gen.* (*slang*) a woman.

lubric /ˈluːbrɪk, ˈljuː-/ *a.* Now *rare.* L15. [(O)Fr. *lubrique* or L *lubricus* slippery: see -IC.] 1 Smooth and slippery. Formerly also *fig.*, unsteady, unsettled. L15. 2 Lascivious; wanton. L15.

Also **lubrical** *a.* E17.

lubricant /ˈluːbrɪk(ə)nt, ˈljuː-/ *n.* & *a.* E19. [L *lubricant* pres. ppl stem of *lubricare*: see next, -ANT¹.] A *n.* A substance, usu. an oil, used to lubricate machinery etc.; a substance used to make motion or action smooth or to remove friction. E19. B *adj.* Lubricating. E19.

lubricate /ˈluːbrɪkeɪt, ˈljuː-/ *v.* E17. [L *lubricat-* pa. ppl stem of *lubricare*, f. *lubricus* slippery: see -ATE³.] 1 *v.t.* Make slippery or smooth; make smooth the motion or action of (something) by applying a fluid or unguent; *spec.* apply oil etc. to (a machine part etc.) so as to minimize friction and allow smooth running. E17. b *gen.* Oil, grease. L18. 2 *v.i.* Act as a lubricant. E18. 3 *v.t.* Affect, esp. make convivial or tipsy, with liquor; accompany (a meal etc.) with drink. Usu. in *pass.* Cf. OILED 3. E20.

1 R. TATE All molluscous animals secrete a mucous fluid to lubricate the skin. *Practical Woodworking* Wax is used to lubricate the moving parts. 2 *Practical Hairstyling & Beauty* Conditioner.. coats each hair with a small amount of oil which protects and lubricates. 3 *Independent* Dinners prepared by juvenile amateur cooks and lubricated by cheap supermarket plonk.

lubriˈcation *n.* the action of lubricating; the condition of being lubricated: E19. **lubriˈcational** *a.* of, pertaining to, or for lubrication E20. **lubricative** *a.* having the property of lubricating L19.

lubricator /ˈluːbrɪkeɪtə, ˈljuː-/ *n.* M18. [f. prec. + -OR.] 1 A lubricating substance; a lubricant; *spec.* (*Photogr.*, now *rare*) an agent for glazing prints before burnishing. M18. 2 A device for lubricating a machine or instrument. M19. 3 A person who lubricates. L19.

lubricious /luːˈbrɪʃəs, ljuː-/ *a.* L16. [f. L *lubricus* slippery + -IOUS. Cf. (earlier) LUBRICOUS.] 1 Lewd; wanton; licentious. L16. 2 Slippery, smooth; slimy, oily. M17. b *fig.* Shifty; unstable, fickle, elusive. Formerly also, (*rare*), voluble, glib. M17.

1 *Observer* Displaying.. well-turned ankles to the lubricious gaze of the multitude. J. HELLER They fell immediately into an orgy of lubricious kissing. 2 R. FERGUSON How Lubricious a Friend and Changeable a Partizan he will be.

lubricity /luːˈbrɪsɪti, ljuː-/ *n.* L15. [(O)Fr. *lubricité* or late L *lubricitas*, f. as prec.: see -ITY.] 1 Lewdness, wantonness, licentiousness. Also, an instance of this. L15. †2 Looseness of the bowels. M16–M18. 3 Slipperiness, smoothness; oiliness. E17. 4 *fig.* Shiftiness; unsteadiness, instability; elusiveness. E17. †b Volubility, glibness. E–M17.

lubricous /ˈluːbrɪkəs, ˈljuː-/ *a.* M16. [f. as LUBRICIOUS + -OUS.] = LUBRICIOUS.

lubrify /ˈluːbrɪfʌɪ, ˈljuː-/ *v.t.* Now *rare.* LME. [med.L *lubrificare*, f. L *lubricus* slippery: see -FY.] Make slippery or smooth; lubricate.

lubritorium /luːbrɪˈtɔːrɪəm, ljuː-/ *n.* Chiefly *US.* M20. [f. LUBRICATE etc. after *auditorium*, *sanatorium*, etc.: see -ORIUM.] A greasing bay in a service station; a service station.

Lucan /ˈluːk(ə)n, ˈljuː-/ *a.* L19. [f. eccl.L *Lucas*, Gk *Loukas* Luke + -AN.] *Chr. Ch.* Of, pertaining to, or characteristic of the evangelist St Luke or the Gospel attributed to him.

Lucanian /luːˈkeɪnɪən, ljuː-/ *a.* & *n.* E17. [f. *Lucania* (see below) + -AN.] Chiefly *Rom. Hist.* A *adj.* Of, pertaining to, or belonging to Lucania, a region in southern Italy (now also called Basilicata). E17.

Lucanian cow, ox *Hist.* an elephant.

B *n.* A member of a Samnite tribe formerly inhabiting Lucania. E18.

lucanid /luːˈkeɪnɪd, ljuː-/ *a.* & *n.* E20. [mod.L *Lucanidae* (see below), f. *Lucanus* genus name, f. L *Lucania*: see prec., -ID³.] (Of, pertaining to, or designating) a stag beetle of the family Lucanidae.

lucarne /ˈluːkɑːn, ˈljuː-, *foreign* lykarn (*pl. same*)/ *n.* M16. [(O)Fr. (also †*lucane*) f. Prov. *lucana*, of unkn. origin. See also LUTHERN.] A skylight; a dormer window.

Lucas /ˈluːkəs, ˈluːkɑː, *foreign* lyka/ *n.* M20. [F. Édouard A. *Lucas* (1842–91), Fr. mathematician.] Math. *Lucas sequence, series*, the sequence of integers 1, 3, 4, 7, . . . , formed in the same way as the Fibonacci numbers; a generalization of this series and the Fibonacci series, in which the *n*th term $u_n = pu_{n-1} - qu_{n-2}$ (where *p* and *q* are constants); *Lucas number*, a number of the Lucas series.

Lucca /ˈluːkə, ˈlʌ-/ *a.* E18. [A city in Tuscany, western Italy (formerly also a province).] 1 Designating a variety of olive oil of a superior quality. E18. 2 Designating a type of processed lambskin used chiefly to make headwear. M20.

Luccan /ˈluːk(ə)n, ˈlʌ-/ *a.* & *n.* E20. [f. prec. + -AN. Cf. earlier LUCCHESE.] A *adj.* Of or pertaining to the city or former province of Lucca, in northern Italy. E20. B *n.* A native or inhabitant of Lucca. E20.

Lucchese /luːˈkiːz, -ˈkeɪsi, lʌ-/ *n.* & *a.* M17. [It., f. LUCCA + *-ese* -ESE.] A *n.* Pl. same, **Lucchesi** /luːˈkeɪsi, lʌ-/. A native or inhabitant of the city or (formerly) province of Lucca in northern Italy. M17. B *adj.* Of or pertaining to Lucca or the Lucchese. L19.

luce /luːs, ljuːs/ *n.* Pl. same. LME. [OFr. *lus*, *luis* f. as LUCY.] 1 A pike, *esp.* a full-grown one; (occas.) this as a heraldic charge; = LUCY. LME. 2 *luce of the sea*, *sea-luce*, the European hake. L16.

lucence /ˈluːs(ə)ns, ˈljuː-/ *n.* L15. [f. LUCENT: see -ENCE.] = next.

J. STEINBECK The pearly lucence of platinum or old pewter.

lucency /ˈluːs(ə)nsi, ˈljuː-/ *n.* M17. [f. next: see -ENCY.] Luminosity, brilliance.

W. BOYD The skyscrapers.. were hazy and indistinct against the soft lucency of the mid-afternoon sky.

lucent /ˈluːs(ə)nt, ˈljuː-/ *a.* LME. [L *lucent-* pres. ppl stem of *lucere* shine: see -ENT.] 1 Shining, bright, luminous. LME. 2 Translucent, clear. E19.

1 L. ADAMIC The alpine sun had burnished their faces and naked forearms to a deep, lucent brown. *Holiday Which?* It's on a beautiful site and built from lucent pink stone.

lucently *adv.* E19.

lucern /luːˈsəːn, ljuː-/ *n.*¹ Long *rare* or *obs.* M16. [Prob. f. early mod.G *lüchsern* adj., f. *Luchs* lynx.] The lynx; the fur of this (formerly freq. in *pl.*), formerly held in high esteem.

lucern *n.*² var. of LUCERNE *n.*²

lucernal /luːˈsəːn(ə)l, ljuː-/ *a.* Now *rare* or *obs.* L18. [f. as next + -AL¹.] Designating a microscope in which the object is illuminated by a lamp or other artificial light.

lucerne /luːˈsəːn, ljuː-/ *n.*¹ Long *obs.* exc. *Hist.* LME. [L *lucerna*, f. *luc-* *lux* light.] A lamp, a lantern.

lucerne /luːsəːn, ljuː-/ *n.*² Also **-ern**. M17. [Fr. *luzerne* f. mod.Prov. *luzerno* transf. use of *luzerno* glow-worm, w. ref. to the shiny seeds.] A leguminous plant, *Medicago sativa*, cultivated for fodder, which bears blue to violet flowers and trifoliate leaves. Also called *alfalfa*.

TOWNSVILLE *lucerne*.

lucet /ˈluːsɪt, ˈljuː-/ *n.* M17. [Origin unkn.] A lyre-shaped tool formerly used in making cords and laces.

Lucianic /luːʃɪˈanɪk/ *a.*¹ E19. [f. L *Lucianus* f. Gk *Loukianos* Lucian (see below) + -IC.] Of, pertaining to, or characteristic of Lucian (fl. AD 160), a Greek writer of satyrical dialogues, or his witty scoffing style.

†**Lucianical** *a.* = LUCIANIC *a.*¹ M16–M17. **Lucianically** *adv.* L16.

Lucianic /luːʃɪˈanɪk/ *a.*² L19. [f. as LUCIANIST *n.*² + -IC] *Eccl. Hist.* Of or pertaining to St Lucian of Antioch; *spec.* designating or pertaining to the text of the Greek Bible revised by him.

Lucianist /ˈluːʃ(ə)nɪst/ *n.*¹ L16. [f. as LUCIANIC *a.*¹ + -IST.] A student, follower, or imitator of the Greek satirist Lucian.

Lucianist /ˈluːʃ(ə)nɪst/ *n.*² E18. [f. L *Lucianus* (see below) + -IST.] *Eccl. Hist.* **1** A follower or adherent of Lucianus, a Marcionite of the 2nd cent. AD. Now *rare*. E18. **2** A follower or adherent of St Lucian of Antioch, a subordinationist theologian and teacher martyred in 312. E18.

lucible /ˈluːsɪb(ə)l, ˈljuː-/ *a. rare*. E17. [L *lucibilis*, f. *lucere* shine: see next, -IBLE.] Bright, lucent.

lucid /ˈluːsɪd, ˈljuː-/ *a.* L16. [Fr. *lucide* or It. *lucido* f. L *lucidus*, f. *lucere* shine, be evident, f. *luc-*, *lux* light: see -ID¹.] **1** Bright, luminous, resplendent (now *poet.*); *Entomol.* & *Bot.* smooth and shining; *Astron.* (of a star) visible to the naked eye. L16. **2** Translucent, clear. E17. **3** [tr. med.L (pl.) *lucida intervalla*.] Designating or pertaining to an interval of sanity between periods of insanity or dementia, or (formerly) a temporary remission in a disease. Also *transf.*, designating an interval of calm or normality. E17. **4** Marked by clearness of reasoning or expression; easily understood. L18. **5** Of a person: rational; sane. M19.

2 C. AIKEN In the cold blue lucid dusk before the sunrise, One yellow star sings. 4 L. MACNEICE Housman . . is usually a lucid poet but the poem below is one of his few obscure ones. N. FREELING The notebooks are tangled but . . perfectly lucid. 5 J. HIGGINS 'How's Malone?' . . 'Is he lucid?' 'Some of the time.'

lucidly *adv.* E18. **lucidness** *n.* M17.

lucida /ˈluːsɪdə, ˈljuː-/ *n.* E18. [L *lucida* (sc. *stella* star) fem. of *lucidus*: see LUCID.] *Astron.* The brightest star of a constellation.

lucidity /luːˈsɪdɪti, ljuː-/ *n.* M17. [L *luciditas*, f. *lucidus*: see LUCID, -ITY.] The quality or condition of being lucid; brightness, luminosity (now *poet.*); rationality; clarity of thought or expression.

lucifee /ˈluːsɪfiː/ *n. Canad.* & *local US*. Also **-vee** /-viː/. L18. [Alt. of Fr. *loup cervier* f. L *lupus cervarius*, f. *lupus* wolf + *cervarius* that hunts stags (f. *cervus* stag).] The Canadian lynx, *Lynx canadensis*.

Lucifer /ˈluːsɪfə, ˈljuː-/ *n.* In sense 3 **l-**. OE. [L *lucifer* adj. light-bringing, f. *luc-*, *lux* light, after Gk *phōsphoros* (see PHOSPHORUS): see -FER.] **1** The morning star; the planet Venus when in the sky before sunrise. Now *poet.* OE. **2** The rebel angel whose fall from heaven Jerome and other early Christian writers considered was alluded to in *Isa.* 14:12 (where the wd is an epithet of the king of Babylon); Satan, the Devil. Formerly also *allus.*, a person seeking to dethrone God. Now chiefly in *as proud as Lucifer*. OE. **3** A friction match. Also more fully *lucifer match*. *arch.* M19.

luciferase /luːˈsɪfəreɪz, ljuː-/ *n.* L19. [f. as prec. + -ASE.] *Biol.* An enzyme which catalyses a reaction by which a luciferin produces light.

Luciferian /luːsɪˈfɪərɪən, ljuː-/ *n.* & *a.*¹ M16. [f. L *Lucifer* (see below) + -IAN.] *Eccl. Hist.* **A** *n.* An adherent of the sect founded by Lucifer, bishop of Cagliari in the 4th cent. AD, who opposed the supposed leniency of the Church towards repentant Arians. M16. **B** *adj.* Of or pertaining to this sect. E17.

Luciferian /luːsɪˈfɪərɪən, ljuː-/ *a.*² Now *rare* or *obs.* L16. [f. LUCIFER + -IAN.] Of or pertaining to Lucifer; Satanic, devilish; *esp.* excessively proud.

luciferin /luːˈsɪf(ə)rɪn, ljuː-/ *n.* L19. [f. as LUCIFER + -IN¹.] *Biol.* A substance in an organism such as the glow-worm which can produce light when oxidized in the presence of a specific enzyme.

luciferous /luːˈsɪf(ə)rəs, ljuː-/ *a.* M17. [f. as LUCIFER + -OUS.] Bringing, conveying, or emitting light. Now chiefly *fig.*, affording illumination or insight; illuminating.

lucific /luːˈsɪfɪk, ljuː-/ *a.* E18. [Late L *lucificus*, f. L *luc-*, *lux* light: see -FIC.] Light-producing.

luciform /ˈluːsɪfɔːm, ˈljuː-/ *a.* Now *rare*. L17. [med.L *luciformis* (repr. Gk *augoeidēs*), f. L *luc-*, *lux* light: see -FORM.] Having the quality of light, luminous, (*spec.* as a quality of the body which is the vehicle of the soul in Neoplatonic philosophy).

lucifugous /luːˈsɪfjʊgəs, ljuː-/ *a.* M17. [f. L *lucifugus*, f. *luc-*, *lux* light + *fugere* to fly: see -OUS.] *Zool.* & *Bot.* Shunning the light.

Lucina /luːˈsʌɪnə, -ˈsiːnə, ljuː-/ *n.* LME. [L, use as n. of fem. of *lucinus* adj. f. *luc-*, *lux* light: see -INE¹.] The Roman goddess who presided over childbirth; *transf.* (*literary*, now *rare*) a midwife.

Lucite /ˈluːsʌɪt, ˈljuː-/ *n.* M20. [f. L *luc-*, *lux* light + -ITE¹.] (Proprietary name for) a solid transparent plastic that is a methyl methacrylate resin (see PERSPEX).

¶Another proprietary name for this substance is PLEXIGLAS.

lucivee *n.* var. of LUCIFEE.

luck /lʌk/ *n.* L15. [LG *luk* aphet. f. *geluk*, in MDu. *ghelucke* (Du. *geluk*) = MHG *gelücke* (G *Glück* good fortune, happiness), f. *ge-* Y- + base of unkn. origin. Prob. orig. a gambling term.] **1** The action or effect of casual or uncontrollable events; the sum of fortuitous events affecting (favourably or unfavourably) a person's interests or circumstances; a person's apparent tendency to have good or ill fortune; the imagined tendency of chance to bring a succession of (favourable or unfavourable) events. L15. †**b** A piece of *good*, *bad*, etc., fortune. M16–E17. **c** Chance regarded as a cause or bestower of good or ill fortune. (Sometimes personified: cf. *Lady Luck* s.v. LADY *n.* 5a.) M16. **d** An action or event regarded as bringing or presaging *good* or *bad* fortune. E20. **2** Good fortune; success, prosperity, or advantage coming by chance rather than as the consequence of merit or effort. L15. **b** An object, esp. an heirloom, on which the prosperity of a family etc. supposedly depends. L18. **c** A piece of good fortune. Also, a lucky find. *Sc.* M19.

1 SHAKES. *Com. Err.* I have but lean luck in the match. J. DAVIDSON I don't allow it's luck and all a toss. E. O'NEILL I've tried to keep things going in spite of bad luck. c I. FLEMING As luck would have it, there were no vacancies and I had to turn him down. *Evening Telegraph* (*Grimsby*) Valentinos Joy . . had luck on his side. d OED You should never put boots on the table: it's bad luck. 2 V. WOOLF What luck to find you alone. M. FITZHERBERT For an amateur journalist it was a great piece of luck. Z. TOMIN She had had all the luck She had never had to get her hands dirty.

Phrases: **bad luck to you!, it!**, etc. *colloq.*: expr. ill will, disappointment, etc. *beginner's luck*: see BEGINNER 2. **devil's own luck** uncannily good luck. **down on one's luck** in a period of ill fortune. **for luck** to bring good luck. **good luck to you!, it!**, etc. *colloq.*: expr. good-will, encouragement, etc. **hard luck** worse fortune than one deserves. *ill luck*: see ILL *a.* & *adv.* **in luck** fortunate, enjoying good luck. **just my, his, our**, etc., **luck** typical of my, his, our, etc., bad luck. **luck of the draw**: expr. resignation at the chance outcome of events etc. *nigger luck*: see NIGGER *a.* & *n.* **no such luck** *colloq.* unfortunately not. **(one's) luck is in** luck is on one's side. **out of luck** having bad luck, in misfortune. **press** or **push one's luck** *colloq.* take undue risks. **ride one's luck** *colloq.* let favourable events take their course, not take undue risks. SALTASH LUCK. *the best of British luck*: see BRITISH *a.* 2. **the luck of the Irish** very good luck. *tough luck*: see TOUGH *a.* **try one's luck** make a venture or attempt. **worse luck** *colloq.* unfortunately.

Comb.: **luck-money**, **luck-penny** (*a*) a piece of money given or kept for luck; (*b*) *Hist.* a certain sum required by local custom to be returned by the seller to the buyer, esp. in the sale of live-stock.

luck /lʌk/ *v.i.* LME. [Perh. f. Du. *lukken*, f. as prec.] **1** Chance, happen; turn out *well*, *ill*, etc. Also *impers.* in (*it*) *lucks* etc. *obs.* exc. *dial.* LME. **b** Be lucky; prosper, succeed. *obs.* exc. *dial.* L16. **2a** Foll. by *upon*, *up on*: chance to find or meet with. *colloq.* L17. **b** Foll. by *into*, *on to*: acquire by good fortune. *colloq.* M20. **3** Foll. by *out*: achieve success or advantage by good luck, esp. in a difficult or adverse situation. *N. Amer. colloq.* M20.

luckie *n.* var. of LUCKY *n.*¹

luckily /ˈlʌkɪli/ *adv.* L15. [f. LUCKY *a.* + -LY².] In a lucky manner; with good luck, fortunately. Formerly also, successfully, prosperously. Now chiefly modifying a sentence or clause.

E. BOWEN Luckily for Francis, he had been left on shore. A. S. BYATT Luckily you never realise what you've let yourself in for until afterwards.

luckiness /ˈlʌkɪnɪs/ *n.* M16. [f. LUCKY *a.* + -NESS.] The quality or condition of being lucky.

luckless /ˈlʌklɪs/ *a.* M16. [f. LUCK *n.* + -LESS.] **1** Having no luck or good fortune; unlucky, ill-starred, unfortunate. M16. †**2** Presaging evil, ominous. L16–M17.

lucklessly *adv.* M19. **lucklessness** *n.* M19.

lucky /ˈlʌki/ *n.*¹ *Sc.* (now *dial.*). Also **-ie**. E18. [f. the adj.] (A name for) an elderly woman, *spec.* a grandmother; *joc.* a woman of any age; *spec.* the landlady of an ale-house. Used as a form of address and as a title preceding the proper name.

lucky /ˈlʌki/ *n.*² *slang*. E19. [Origin unkn.] An act of escaping. Only in *cut* or *make one's lucky*, get away, escape.

lucky /ˈlʌki/ *a.* LME. [f. LUCK *n.* + -Y¹.] **1** Having good luck, attended by good luck; *spec.* successful through luck as distinct from skill, design, or merit. Formerly also *gen.*, successful, prosperous. LME. **b** Of a literary composition: unstudied in expression. E18. **2** Of an event, circumstance, etc.: of the nature of good luck; occurring by chance and producing a happy or good result. Also (*rare*), occurring by chance, fortuitous. M16. **3** Of an object: supposedly presaging or bringing good luck. M16. **4** Of an amount: full, good. *dial.* M17.

1 G. B. SHAW He will be lucky to have any pay at all. L. DUNCAN You're a lucky boy to have the opportunity of growing up in her home. W. ABISH Lovely children, lovely husband, lovely house. . . You're a lucky woman. A. N. WILSON She was lucky . . if she saw anyone, apart from the congregation at church. J. NAGENDA She was like a gambler, . . and her lucky streak held throughout. H. JACOBSON A German pilot had been lucky with his aim. P. CUTTING We regarded ourselves as among the lucky few who had escaped a kidnap attempt. 2 P. THEROUX It had been a lucky find at the Northampton dump. M. MOORCOCK A lucky V2 rocket destroyed the school. 3 QUEEN VICTORIA The new house seems to be lucky indeed. A. L. ROWSE He was born under a lucky star. W. BOYD 'I wasn't expecting you for two months.' 'Well, it's your lucky day, then.'

Phrases: **Lucky Country** Australia. **lucky him, you**, etc.: expr. envy at another's good fortune. *strike lucky*: see STRIKE *v. thank one's lucky stars*: see STAR *n.*¹ & *a.*

Comb.: **lucky-bag** (*a*) a bag of sweets etc. with (wholly or partly) unspecified contents; (*b*) a bag containing different articles to be chosen as from a lucky dip; **lucky dip** a tub containing different articles concealed in wrapping or bran etc., and chosen at random by participants; *fig.* a miscellany or medley from which one obtains something by chance.

†**lucration** *n.* M17–E19. [Late L *lucratio(n-)*, f. L *lucrat-*: see next, -ATION.] The action or an act of gaining.

lucrative /ˈluːkrətɪv, ˈljuː-/ *a.* LME. [L *lucrativus*, f. *lucrat-* pa. ppl stem of *lucrari* to gain, f. *lucrum* gain: see -ATIVE.] **1** Yielding financial gain or profit; profitable. LME. †**2** Of a person, action, etc.: intent on or directed towards profit; avaricious, covetous. M16–L18.

1 J. S. HUXLEY Aldous .. was busy writing film scripts, which he found more lucrative than essays and novels.

lucratively *adv.* M19. **lucrativeness** *n.* E18.

lucre /ˈluːkə, ˈljuː-/ *n.* Now *derog.* LME. [Fr., or L *lucrum* gain.] Financial gain or profit. Also, money. Formerly also, acquisition *of* or greed for profit or gain.

A. BLOND The only incentive to perform is the lure of lucre. *filthy lucre*: see FILTHY *a.*

Lucretian /luːˈkriːʃ(ə)n, ˈljuː-/ *a.* E18. [f. *Lucretius* (see below) + -AN.] Of, pertaining to, or characteristic of the Roman didactic poet Lucretius (Titus Lucretius Carus, *c* 94–*c* 55 BC) or his Epicurean philosophy.

†**lucriferous** *a.* M17–E18. [f. L *lucrum* LUCRE + -I- + -FEROUS.] Lucrative.

†**lucrous** *a.* E16–L18. [f. L *lucrosus*, f. *lucrum* LUCRE: see -OUS.] Of or pertaining to lucre. Also, avaricious.

†**luctiferous** *a. rare.* M17–E19. [f. L *luctifer*, f. *luctus* sorrow + *-ifer* bearing: see -FEROUS.] Bringing sorrow; mournful.

lucubrate /ˈluːkjʊbreɪt, ˈljuː-/ *v.i. literary.* E17. [L *lucubrat-* pa. ppl stem of *lucubrare*, f. *luc-*, *lux* light: see -ATE[3].] Work or study, esp. by artificial light at night. Also, express one's thoughts in writing, esp. laboriously and elaborately.

lucubrator *n.* L18. **lucubratory** *a.* of or pertaining to lucubration; elaborately meditative: M17.

lucubration /luːkjʊˈbreɪʃ(ə)n, ljuː-/ *n. literary.* L16. [L *lucubratio(n-)*, f. as prec.: see -ATION.] 1 The action or an act of lucubrating. L16. 2 The product of (esp. nocturnal) study or work; *spec.* a literary work, esp. of a pedantic or overelaborate nature. Usu. in *pl.* E17.

luculent /ˈluːkjʊl(ə)nt, ˈljuː-/ *a.* LME. [L *luculentus*, f. *luc-*, *lux* light: see -ENT.] 1 Full of light; bright, clear, shining. Now *rare.* LME. 2 Of evidence, an argument: clear, convincing. Of an explanation: lucid. Formerly also, (of oratory, an orator, etc.) brilliant, admirable. M16.

luculently *adv.* E17.

luculia /lʊˈkuːlɪə/ *n.* E19. [mod.L (see below), f. local name of *Luculia gratissima*.] Any of several evergreen shrubs of the genus *Luculia*, of the madder family, native to the Himalayas and Yunnan (SW China), with leathery leaves and corymbs of fragrant pink or white flowers.

Lucullan /luːˈkʌlən, lʊ-/ *a.* M19. [L *Lucullanus*, f. *Lucullus* (see below): see -AN.] Of, pertaining to, or characteristic of Licinius Lucullus, a wealthy Roman general of the 1st cent. BC famous for his lavish banquets; profusely luxurious.

Also **Lucullean** *a.* [f. L *Lucullеus*: see -EAN] E17. **Lucullian** *a.* [f. L *Lucullianus*: see -IAN] L19.

lucuma /ˈluːkjʊmə, ˈljuː-/ *n.* L16. [Sp. *lúcuma* f. Quechua *loqma*.] Any of various tropical American trees of the former genus *Lucuma*, now *Pouteria* (family Sapotaceae), which bear sweet fruit.

lucumo /ˈluːkjʊməʊ, ˈljuː-/ *n.* Pl. **-os.** M19. [L f. an Etruscan title.] *Rom. Hist.* Any of a group of Etruscan nobles, combining the character, status, and duties of priest and prince.

lucumony /ˈluːkjʊmənɪ, ˈljuː-/ *n.* M18. [Fr. *lucumonie*, f. as prec: see -Y[3].] *Rom. Hist.* Each of the twelve States of the Etruscan federation.

lucus a non lucendo /ˌluːkʌs ɑː nɒn luːˈkɛndəʊ, ˌl(j)uːkʌs eɪ nɒn l(j)uːˈsɛndəʊ/ *n. phr.* E18. [L, lit. 'a grove from its not shining', i.e. *lucus* (a grove) is derived from *lucere* (shine) because there is no light there.] A paradoxical or otherwise absurd derivation; something of which the qualities are the opposite of what its name suggests. Also abbrev. *lucus a non.*

lucy /ˈluːsi/ *n.* E17. [Late L *lucius*.] *Her.* A pike (fish).

lud /lʌd/ *n.* E18. [Repr. a pronunc.] 1 = LORD *n.* 5. Chiefly as *int. arch.* E18. 2 *m'lud*, *my lud* = *my lord* (e) s.v. LORD *n.*, used as a form of address to a judge in a court of law. M19.

Luddism /ˈlʌdɪz(ə)m/ *n.* E19. [f. as next + -ISM.] 1 *Hist.* The practices of the Luddites. E19. 2 *transf.* (Also **l-**.) Intense dislike of or opposition to increased industrialization or the introduction of new technology, esp. in a place of work. M20.

Luddite /ˈlʌdʌɪt/ *n.* & *a.* E19. [Perh. f. Ned *Lud* an insane person who destroyed two stocking-frames *c* 1779: see -ITE[1].] A *n.* 1 *Hist.* A member of the bands of English artisans who (1811–16) rioted against mechanization and destroyed machinery. E19. 2 *transf.* (Also **l-**.) A person opposed to increased industrialization or the introduction of new technology, esp. into a place of work. L20. B *adj.* 1 *Hist.* Of or pertaining to the Luddites or their beliefs. E19. 2 *transf.* (Also **l-**.) Characterized by opposition to increased industrialization or the introduction of new technology. M20.

Ludditism *n.* = LUDDISM M19.

luderick /ˈluːd(ə)rɪk, ˈlʌdrɪk/ *n.* L19. [Aborig.] An edible herbivorous percoid fish, *Girella tricuspidata* (family Kyphosidae), of Australasian coastal waters and estuaries. Cf. PARORE.

Ludian /ˈluːdɪən, ˈljuː-/ *n.* & *a.* M20. [f. as LUDIC *n.* & *a.*[1] + -IAN.] = LUDIC *n.* & *a.*[1]

ludibrious /luːˈdɪbrɪəs, ljuː-/ *a.* Now *rare.* L16. [f. L *ludibriosus*, f. *ludibrium* sport, jest, f. *ludere* play: see -OUS.] †1 Apt to be a subject of jest or mockery. L16–L17. 2 Scornful, mocking. M17.

†**ludibry** *n.* E17–E18. [L *ludibrium*: see prec., -Y[4].] Derision, contempt; an object of derision.

Ludic /ˈluːdɪk, ˈljuː-/ *n.* & *a.*[1] E20. [f. Olonetsian *lüüdi* (perh. f. Russ. *lyudi* people) + -IC.] (Of) a language of the Finnish group of the Finno-Ugrian language family, used by a small number of speakers in the Olonets region of NW Russia.

ludic /ˈluːdɪk, ˈljuː-/ *a.*[2] M20. [Fr. *ludique*, f. L *ludere* to play, f. *ludus* sport: see -IC.] (Of play) spontaneous and without purpose; (of behaviour) undirected and spontaneously playful.

ludicro- /ˈluːdɪkrəʊ, ˈljuː-/ *comb. form.* M18. [f. as next: see -O-.] Ludicrous and —.

ludicrous /ˈluːdɪkrəs, ˈljuː-/ *a.* E17. [f. L *ludicr-*, *ludi(cer)*, perh. f. *ludicrum* source of fun, witticism, sporting or theatrical show, f. *ludere*: see LUDIC *a.*[2], -OUS.] †1 Sportive; intended in jest, jocular; derisive. E17–L18. †2 Given to jesting; frivolous. Also, witty, humorous. L17–E19. 3 Ridiculous, laughably absurd. L18.

3 S. J. PERELMAN The effect of the trousers, at least three sizes too large for him, was .. ludicrous. B. PYM One of those ludicrous things that happen sometimes, reducing everything to the level of farce.

ludiˈcrosity *n.* ludicrousness M19. **ludicrously** *adv.* L17. **ludicrousness** *n.* the state or quality of being ludicrous M17.

ludification /ˌluːdɪfɪˈkeɪʃ(ə)n/ *n.* Now *rare.* LME. [L *ludificatio(n-)*, f. *ludificat-* pa. ppl stem of *ludificare* delude, f. *ludus* sport: see -FICATION.] A deception; a mocking jest.

ludo /ˈluːdəʊ, ˈljuː-/ *n.* L19. [L = I play.] A simple board game played with dice and counters in which the aim is to be the first to reach a destination.

Ludolph's number /ˈluːdɒlfs ˌnʌmbə/ *n. phr.* L19. [*Ludolph* van Ceulen (1540–1610), German-born teacher.] The number π, which Ludolph evaluated to 35 decimal places.

Luˈdolphian *a.* of or pertaining to Ludolph; chiefly in *Ludolphian number*, = LUDOLPH'S NUMBER L19.

Ludwig's angina /ˌlʊdvɪgz anˈdʒʌɪnə/ *n. phr.* M20. [W. F. von *Ludwig* (1790–1865), Ger. surgeon.] Severe inflammation of the tissues of the floor of the mouth (usu. caused by streptococci).

lues /ˈluːiːz, ˈljuː-/ *n.* M17. [L = plague.] Syphilis (also more fully *lues venerea* /vəˈnɪərɪə/). Formerly also, a plague, a pestilence.

lues Boswelliana /-ˌbɒzwɛlɪˈeɪnə, -ˈɑːnə/ *joc.* [mod.L, f. as BOSWELL + *-iana* (fem.) -IAN] a biographer's tendency to magnify his or her subject, regarded as a disease.

luetic /-ˈɛtɪk/ *a.* L19.

luff /lʌf/ *n.*[1] ME. [OFr. *lof*, prob. f. LG or Du.] *Naut.* †1 A device for altering the course of a ship, as a spar operating on a sail etc. ME–L15. †2 The part or side of a ship facing the wind. LME–E17. 3 The edge of a fore-and-aft sail next to the mast or stay. E16. 4 The broadest part of a ship's bow, where the sides begin to curve in towards the stem. E17. 5 In full *luff-tackle*. A purchase composed of a double and a single block. M17.

Phrases: **spring a, one's, luff** bring the ship's head closer to the wind.

luff /lʌf/ *n.*[2] *colloq.* E19. [Repr. a pronunc. of the 1st syll.] = LIEUTENANT.

luff /lʌf/ *v.* LME. [f. LUFF *n.*[1], perh. through Du. *loeven*.] 1 *v.i.* Bring the head of a ship nearer to the wind; steer or sail nearer the wind. Also foll. by *in*, *off*, *up*, etc. LME. 2 *v.t.* Bring the head of (a ship) nearer to the wind; turn (the helm) to achieve this. E17. 3 *v.t. Yacht-racing.* Obstruct (an opponent passing windward) by sailing closer to the wind. L19. 4 *v.t.* Alter the inclination of (the jib of a crane or derrick); raise by moving (the jib) *in*; lower by moving (the jib) *out.* E20.

4 **luffing crane** a crane whose jib can be luffed in operation.

luffa *n.* var. of LOOFAH.

luftmensch /ˈlʊftmɛnʃ/ *n.* Also **-mensh.** Pl. **-mens(c)hen** /-mɛnʃ(ə)n/. E20. [Yiddish *luftmensh*, f. *luft* (G *Luft*) air + *mensh* (G *Mensch*) person.] An impractical visionary.

Luftwaffe /ˈlʊftvafə/ *n.* M20. [G, f. *Luft* air + *Waffe* weapon.] *Hist.* The German air force up to the end of the war of 1939–45.

lug /lʌg/ *n.*[1] Now *dial.* ME. [Origin unkn.] 1 A long stick or pole; a branch of a tree. ME. 2 A unit of length, more or less equal to a pole or perch, varying between 15 and 21 feet, but usu. 16½ feet (approx. 5.03 m). Also, a unit of area more or less equal to a square pole or perch. M16.

lug /lʌg/ *n.*[2] L15. [Prob. of Scand. origin: cf. Sw. *lugg* forelock, nap of cloth.] 1 Either of two flaps of a hat, for covering the ears. *Sc.* & *north.* L15. 2 An ear. Formerly also, the lobe of an ear. *Sc.*, *north.*, & *colloq.* E16. 3 A projection resembling an ear on an object by which it may be carried, fixed in place, etc. E17. b Pressure used to extort money. Esp. in *put the lug on. US slang.* E20. 4 The side-wall of a recessed fireplace; a (chimney) corner. *Sc.* & *north.* L18. 5 A tobacco leaf of low quality. M19. 6 In *pl.* Airs, affected manners. Chiefly in *put on lugs. US slang.* L19 7 A lout; a sponger. Chiefly *N. Amer. slang.* M20.

3 E. LINKLATER The stack was stitched up so as to leave two lugs to carry it by. K. CLARK With pots .., such as casseroles, lugs .. facilitate easy gripping and lifting. 7 R. CHANDLER The girl snapped at me: 'Is this lug your partner?'

Comb.: **lug-chair** an easy-chair with side-pieces for the head; **lughole** *dial.* & *colloq.* the orifice of the ear (cf. *earhole* s.v. EAR *n.*[1]); **lug-mark** *n.* & *v.t.* = EARMARK; **lug sole** *N. Amer.* a shoe sole with deep indentations designed for a good grip.

†**lug** *n.*[3] Only in M16. [Cf. LUG *v.*, LG *lug*, Du. *log* slow, heavy, LOG *n.*[1]] A heavy clumsy thing.

¶Perh. surviving in FUSTILUGS.

lug /lʌg/ *n.*[4] E17. [Origin unkn.] = LUGWORM.

lug /lʌg/ *n.*[5] E17. [f. the vb.] 1 The action or an act of lugging; a rough or hard pull. E17. 2 A thing which is or needs to be lugged; *spec.* a box or crate used for shipping fruit. *US.* E19.

1 J. K. JEROME You give your ropes a lug that pulls all his pegs out.

lug /lʌg/ *n.*[6] M19. [Abbrev.] = LUGSAIL.

lug /lʌg/ *v.* Infl. **-gg-.** LME. [Prob. of Scand. origin: cf. Sw. *lugga* pull a person's hair & LUG *n.*[2]] 1 *v.t. gen.* Pull, give a pull to; pull *by* the ear, hair, etc.; *fig.* tease, worry, bait. *obs.* exc. *dial.* LME. 2 *v.t.* Pull along with violent effort; drag, tug (something heavy). Also, carry with difficulty (something heavy) *around* or *about* with one. LME. b *fig.* Introduce (a subject etc.) in a forced manner or irrelevantly. Usu. foll. by *in.* E18. 3 *v.i.* Pull (hard), tug, (*at*, *on*). LME. b Move heavily and slowly; drag. Now *rare.* LME. 4 *v.i.* Foll. by *out*: draw one's sword; pull out money or a purse. *arch.* L17.

1 POPE Mr. Lintott lugg'd the reins, Stopt Short, [etc.]. 2 ALDOUS HUXLEY Spandrell had to .. push and lug the heavy body on to its side. G. GREENE He bent and heaved and .. lugged it ashore. A. MCCOWEN He

lugged furniture about in a shop in Tonbridge. G. SWIFT I used to trail behind Dad, lugging his bag of clubs. b *Scotsman* Counsel for the other side had lugged in everything he could to prejudice the case. 3 BROWNING A whip awaits shirkers.. Who slacken their pace, sick of lugging At what don't advance for their tugging.

luggable *a.* able to be lugged; *spec.* (of a computer) barely portable: L20.

Luganda /luːˈgandə, ljuː-/ *n.* & *a.* L19. [Bantu, f. *lu-* pref. + *ganda*. Cf. MUGANDA, BAGANDA.] (Of) the Bantu language of the Baganda people, widely used in Uganda.

Lugbara /lʊgˈbɑːrə/ *n.* & *a.* Also **Lugwari** /lʌgˈwɑːri/. E20. [Lugbara.] A *n.* Pl. same, **-s.** 1 A member of a people inhabiting the border area of Uganda and Zaire. E20. 2 The Sudanic language of this people. M20. B *attrib.* or as *adj.* Of or pertaining to the Lugbara or their language. E20.

luge /luːʒ/ *v.* & *n.* L19. [Swiss Fr.] A *v.i.* Toboggan; ride or race on a luge. L19. B *n.* A light toboggan for one or two people usu. ridden in a supine position; the sport in which these are raced. E20.

Luger /ˈluːgə/ *n.* & *a.* E20. [George *Luger* (1849–1923), Ger. engineer and firearms expert.] (Proprietary name designating) a German type of automatic pistol.

luggage /ˈlʌgɪdʒ/ *n.* L16. [f. LUG *v.* + -AGE, after *baggage*.] 1 Orig., what has to be lugged about; inconveniently heavy baggage. Now (*sing.* & (*rare*) in *pl.*), the baggage of a traveller or passenger; also, the baggage of an army. L16. 2 Bags, suitcases, etc., designed to hold the belongings of a traveller or passenger. E20.

1 E. M. FORSTER Frieda and Helen and all their luggages had gone. JO GRIMOND The bus had to.. take the luggage—usually including a large trunk—to the station.

Comb.: **luggage locker** a locker at a railway station, air terminal, etc., for use by passengers. **luggage-van** a railway carriage for travellers' belongings.

luggaged *a.* loaded with luggage M19. **luggageless** *a.* M19.

†**luggard** *n. rare.* E16–M19. [f. LUG *v.* + -ARD.] A sluggard.

lugged /lʌgd/ *a. obs.* exc. *dial.* L15. [f. LUG *n.*[2] + -ED[2].] Having lugs or ears.

luggee /lʌˈgiː/ *n. rare.* M19. [f. LUG *v.* + -EE[1].] A person who is lugged or pulled.

lugger /ˈlʌgə/ *n.*[1] E17. [f. LUG *v.* + -ER[1].] A person who lugs something.

lugger /ˈlʌgə/ *n.*[2] M18. [f. (as) LUG *n.*[6] + -ER[1].] A small ship carrying two or three masts with a lugsail on each.

lugger /ˈlʌgə/ *v.t. obs.* exc. *dial.* M17. [f. LUG *v.* + -ER[5].] Drag or carry about; *fig.* burden, tease.

luggie /ˈlʌgi/ *n. Sc.* E18. [f. LUG *n.*[2] + -IE.] A small wooden vessel with a lug or handle.

Lugol /ˈluːgɒl/ *n.* L19. [Jean *Lugol* (1786–1851), Fr. physician.] *Lugol's iodine, solution*, a solution of iodine and potassium iodide in water, used to administer iodine internally and as a biological stain.

lugsail /ˈlʌgseɪl/ *n.* L17. [Prob. f. LUG *n.*[2] + SAIL *n.*[1]] *Naut.* A four-cornered sail bent on a yard slung at a third or quarter of its length from one end.

lugubrious /lʊˈguːbrɪəs/ *a.* E17. [f. L *lugubris*, f. *lugere* mourn: see -IOUS.] Characterized by, expressing, or causing mourning; mournful; doleful, dismal.

T. HEGGEN Pulver was.. depressed by the news, and he lay in Robert's bunk.. and made lugubrious conversation. C. BLACKWOOD The usual pained expression on her long lugubrious face. S. CHITTY Aunt Leah was the cheerful one while Aunt Rosina.. was lugubrious and suffered from indigestion.

†**lugubre** *a.* [Fr.] = LUGUBRIOUS E18–M19. **lugubri'osity** *n.* (*rare*) M19. **lugubriously** *adv.* M19. **lugubriousness** *n.* L19. †**lugubrous** *a.* = LUGUBRIOUS M17–E18.

Lugwari *n.* & *a.* var. of LUGBARA.

lugworm /ˈlʌgwəːm/ *n.* E19. [f. LUG *n.*[4] + WORM *n.*] A polychaete worm of the genus *Arenicola*, which burrows in sandy beaches and is much used as fishing-bait.

Luing /lɪŋ/ *n.* & *a.* L20. [An island in the Hebrides, Scotland.] A *n.* Pl. same. (An animal of) a breed of cattle derived from a crossing of the beef shorthorn and the Highland. L20. B *adj.* Designating this breed of cattle. L20.

Luiseño /luːɪˈseɪnjəʊ/ *n.* & *a.* Also (earlier) **San Luiseño** /sɑːn/. M19. [Sp., f. *San Luis Rey*, a mission in southern California.] A *n.* Pl. same, **-os.** A member of a Shoshone Indian people of SW California; the language of this people. M19. B *attrib.* or as *adj.* Of or pertaining to the Luiseño or their language. L19.

luke /luːk, ljuːk/ *a.* Now *dial.* ME. [Perh. f. as LEE *n.*[1] & *a.*, LEW. Cf. ON *hlyr* warm, mild, rel. to OHG *lāo* (G *lau*).] = LUKEWARM *a.*

lukewarm /ˈluːkwɔːm, luːkˈwɔːm, lj-/ *a.* & *n.* LME. [f. prec. + WARM *a.*] A *adj.* 1 Moderately warm, tepid. LME. 2 Of a person, action, attribute, etc.: having little warmth or depth of feeling; lacking enthusiasm; indifferent. LME.

1 J. STEINBECK He scooped lukewarm mush into two bowls. D. LEAVITT Celia is treading the lukewarm blue water of Nathan's parents' swimming pool. 2 M. MEYER The play.. attracted little notice, and such reviews as did appear were lukewarm.

B *n.* A lukewarm or unenthusiastic person. L17.

lukewarmly *adv.* E17. **lukewarmness** *n.* M16. **lukewarmth** *n.* the quality or state of being lukewarm L16.

lukiko /luːˈkiːkəʊ/ *n.* L19. [Luganda = audience-hall, council.] The council or parliament of the Baganda people of Uganda.

lulav /ˈluːlɑːv, ˈlʊləv/ *n.* Also **-b.** Pl. **-s, -im** /-ɪm/. L19. [Heb. *lūlāḇ* branch.] A palm branch traditionally carried at the Jewish festival of Succoth.

lull /lʌl/ *n.*[1] M17. [f. LULL *v.*] 1 †a Soothing drink. Only in M17. b A thing which lulls; *spec.* a lulling sound. E18. 2 A brief period of intermission or quiescence in a storm (*lit.* & *fig.*) or in any activity. E19. 3 A lulled or stupefied condition. M19.

2 P. L. FERMOR Even in a momentary lull, the rain was fierce. A. BROOKNER We were not busy in the shop: it was the lull before.. Christmas. J. NAGENDA All this was very much the lull before the storm.

lull /lʌl/ *n.*[2] M19. [Du. *lul* tube.] *Whaling.* A tube to convey blubber into the hold of a whaling-ship.

lull /lʌl/ *v.* ME. [Imit. of sounds used to sing a child to sleep: cf. LULLABY etc. & Sw. *lulla*, Da. *lulle* hum a lullaby, Du. *lullen*, also MDu. *lollen* mutter, L *lallare* sing to sleep.] 1 *v.t.* Soothe with sounds or caresses; induce to sleep or to pleasing quiescence. ME. b Quiet (suspicion) by deception; delude into a sense of security (usu. in *pass.*). E17. †2 *v.i.* Be lapped in soothing slumbers. LME–L16. 3 *v.t.* Bring to a state of comparative quiescence (winds, sea, etc.). L17. 4 *v.i.* (Of the sea or wind) become lulled, or gradually diminished in force or power; become quiescent or inactive. E19.

1 V. NABOKOV I would lull and rock.. Lolita in my marble arms. T. ROETHKE I'm lulled into half-sleep By the lapping of water. b *Truck & Driver* Mantova.. had been lulled into a false sense of security.

lullingly *adv.* in a lulling manner, with lulling effect M19.

lulla /ˈlʌlə/ *int. arch.* Also **lullay** /ˈlʌleɪ/. ME. [Imit.: see prec.] = LULLABY *int.* Now only in traditional songs.

lullaby /ˈlʌləbʌɪ/ *int.*, *n.*, & *v.* M16. [f. as prec. + *-by* as in BYE-BYE *n.*, *int.*. Cf. *hushaby*, *rock-a-bye*.] A *int.* Used to please or pacify a child or to send a child to sleep. (Sometimes preceded by *lulla*.) M16. †b Goodbye, goodnight. L16–E17. B *n.* A song or soothing refrain to pacify or put a child to sleep. L16. C *v.t.* & *i.* Soothe (a child) with a lullaby; sing (a child) to sleep. L16.

lullay *int.* var. of LULLA.

Lullian /ˈlʌlɪən/ *a.* M17. [f. *Lullius* (see below) + -AN.] Of or pertaining to the Christian mystic Lullius (Ramón or Raymond Lull, 1234–1315) his writings, or his beliefs.

†**Lullianist** *n.* = LULLIST: only in E17.

Lullist /ˈlʌlɪst/ *n.* M16. [f. *Lull* (see prec.) + -IST.] A follower of the Christian mystic Lullius (see prec.).

Lullism *n.* the beliefs of Lull or his followers E20.

lulu /ˈluːluː/ *n. slang.* Freq. *iron.* L19. [Origin uncertain: perh. f. *Lulu* pet-form of female forename *Louise*.] A remarkable or wonderful person or thing.

luluai /ˈluːluːʌɪ/ *n.* E20. [Tolai.] *Hist.* In New Guinea: a man appointed by the (colonial) government to be responsible for the maintenance of order in a village; a village headman.

Lulworth skipper /ˈlʌlwəθ ˈskɪpə/ *n. phr.* M19. [f. *Lulworth* Cove, Dorset + SKIPPER *n.*[1]] A hesperiid butterfly, *Thymelicus acteon*, found along the Dorset and Devon coast of SW England and in central and southern Europe and NW Africa.

lum /lʌm/ *n. Sc.* & *north.* E16. [Perh. f. OFr. *lum* light (f. L *lumen*): cf. Fr. *lumière* in sense 'aperture, passage'.] †1 An opening in a roof; a skylight. Only in E16. 2 A chimney; a chimney-top. E17.

lumachelle /luːməˈkɛl, ljuː-/ *n.* Also †**-lla**, †**-lli.** L18. [(Fr. f.) It. *lumachella* little snail, f. *lumaca* snail: see -EL[2].] A dark-coloured compact limestone containing fossil shells which make it iridescent.

lumbago /lʌmˈbeɪgəʊ/ *n.* & *v.* L17. [L *lumbago*, *lumbagin-*, f. *lumbus* loin.] A *n.* Rheumatic pain in the lower muscles of the back. L17. B *v.t.* Affect with lumbago. L18.

lumbaginous /-dʒɪnəs/ *a.* of, pertaining to, or affected with lumbago M17.

†**lumbal** *a.* & *n.* L17–E19. [mod.L *lumbalis*, f. L *lumbus* loin: see -AL[1].] = LUMBAR.

lumbar /ˈlʌmbə/ *n.* & *a.* LME. [med.L *lumbaris*, f. L *lumbus* loin: see -AR[1].] A *n.* †1 A bandage used for a rupture. Only in LME. 2 An artery, vein, nerve, or vertebra situated in the lumbar region. M19.

B *adj.* Situated in or designating the region of the loins, esp. the small of the back; of, pertaining to, or performed on or within the spinal cord in this region. M17.

lumbar puncture the insertion of a cannula into the lumbar part of the spinal cord to withdraw cerebrospinal fluid or introduce a drug.

lumbardar *n.* var. of LAMBARDAR.

lumber /ˈlʌmbə/ *n.*[1] M16. [Perh. f. LUMBER *v.*[1], but at one time assoc. w. LUMBER *n.*[2]] 1 Disused articles of furniture etc. taking up room inconveniently, or removed to be out of the way; useless odds and ends; useless or cumbrous material. M16. 2 Timber sawn into rough planks or otherwise partly prepared. Chiefly *N. Amer.* M17. 3 Superfluous fat, esp. in horses. E19.

1 POPE Loads of learned lumber in his head. R. GITTINGS An immense amount of accumulated lumber to pack and dispose.

Comb.: **lumber baron** *N. Amer.* a leading or wealthy timber merchant; **lumber-camp** (chiefly *N. Amer.*) a camp in which lumberjacks live; **lumberjack** (chiefly *N. Amer.*) a person who works with rough timber or lumber, *esp.* a feller and dresser of forest timber; **lumber-jacket** a warm hip-length jacket fastening up to the neck, of a type worn by lumberjacks; **lumberman** (chiefly *N. Amer.*) a lumberjack; **lumber-port** (*a*) a porthole in the bow or stern of a ship for loading or unloading timber; (*b*) a seaport from which timber is shipped; **lumber-raft** a raft made of logs, boards, etc.; **lumber-room** a room in which disused articles of furniture etc. are kept, a room for useless odds and ends; **lumber town** *N. Amer.* a town chiefly engaged in the timber trade; **lumber trade** (chiefly *N. Amer.*) the trade in rough timber; **lumber-wagon** *N. Amer.* a springless wagon of a type used for hauling timber; **lumber-yard** *N. Amer.* a timber-yard.

lumber /ˈlʌmbə/ *n.*[2] *slang.* E17. [Alt. of LOMBARD *n.*[1]] †1 A pawnbroking establishment. E17–M18. 2 *in lumber*, in pawn, in pledge; *transf.* in prison, in trouble, in difficulties. L17. 3 A house or room, *spec.* where stolen property is hidden; a house used by criminals. M18.

lumber /ˈlʌmbə/ *v.*[1]*i.* LME. [Perh. symbolic. Isolated ME use may be rel. to LAME *a.* Cf. LUMPER *v.*] 1 Move in a clumsy or blundering manner; now *esp.* move heavily on account of unwieldiness of bulk and mass. Now chiefly with adv. or advb. phr. LME. 2 Rumble, make a rumbling noise. *obs.* exc. *US.* L15.

1 R. K. NARAYAN I . . paused to observe . . a country cart lumbering along. G. VIDAL When he walks he sort of lumbers. C. THUBRON Water buffalo lumbered down sodden tracks.

lumber /ˈlʌmbə/ *v.*[2] M17. [f. LUMBER *n.*[1]] 1 *v.t.* Orig., cover, fill *up*, or obstruct with lumber; burden uselessly, encumber. Now usu., leave (someone) *with* something unwanted or unpleasant; get (someone) into trouble or difficulties; freq. in *pass.* M17. 2 *v.t.* Heap or place together as lumber, without order or method; deposit as lumber. L17. 3 a *v.i.* Perform the labour or carry on the business of cutting and preparing forest timber. (Earlier as LUMBERING *n.*) Chiefly *N. Amer.* E19. b *v.t.* Go over (ground) cutting down timber. M19.

1 E. WALLACE If they lumbered you with the crime, it was because you was a mug. *Daily Mail* If you're lured into parting with your lolly, you could be lumbered.

lumber /ˈlʌmbə/ *v.*[3]*t. slang.* E19. [f. LUMBER *n.*[2]] Deposit (property) in pawn; imprison, arrest.

lumberer /ˈlʌmb(ə)rə/ *n.*[1] L16. [f. LUMBER *v.*[1] + -ER[1].] A person who moves clumsily or blunderingly; a person who moves heavily on account of unwieldiness of bulk and mass.

lumberer /ˈlʌmb(ə)rə/ *n.*[2] Chiefly *N. Amer.* E19. [f. LUMBER *v.*[2] + -ER[1].] A person engaged in the lumber or timber trade.

lumberer /ˈlʌmb(ə)rə/ *n.*[3] *slang.* E19. [f. LUMBER *v.*[3] + -ER[1].] A pawnbroker.

lumbering /ˈlʌmb(ə)rɪŋ/ *n.* Chiefly *N. Amer.* M18. [f. LUMBER *v.*[2] + -ING[1].] The lumber or timber trade; dealing or working in timber.

lumbering /ˈlʌmb(ə)rɪŋ/ *a.* L16. [f. LUMBER *v.*[1] + -ING[2].] Ponderous in movement, inconveniently bulky.

lumberingly *adv.* M19.

lumberly /ˈlʌmbəli/ *a.* E19. [f. LUMBER *v.*[2] + -LY[1].] Clumsy, cumbrous.

†lumber-pie *n.* M17–M19. [f. var. of LOMBARD *a.* (cf. LUMBER *n.*[2]) + PIE *n.*[2]] A savoury pie made of meat or fish and eggs.

lumbersome /ˈlʌmbəs(ə)m/ *a.* E19. [f. LUMBER *v.*[1] + -SOME[1].] Cumbrous, unwieldy.

lumbo- /ˈlʌmbəʊ/ *comb. form.* L19. [f. L *lumbus* loin + -O-.] Pertaining to or situated in the lumbar and — regions, or the lumbar region and —, as *lumbo-aortic*, *lumbosacral* adjs.

lumbrical /lʌmˈbrʌɪk(ə)l/ *a.* & *n.* L17. [mod.L *lumbricalis*, f. L LUMBRICUS: see -AL[1].] A *adj.* 1 *Anat.* Designating certain fusiform muscles in the hand and the foot which assist in flexing and extending the digits. L17. 2 Pertaining to or resembling a worm. L17. B *n.* = LUMBRICALIS. L19.

lumbricalis /lʌmbrɪˈkeɪlɪs/ *n.* Pl. **-les** /-liːz/. E18. [mod.L: see prec.] *Anat.* A lumbrical muscle.

lumbriciform /lʌmˈbrʌɪsɪfɔːm, -ˈbrɪs-/ *a.* E19. [f. L LUMBRICUS + -I- + -FORM.] Vermiform.

lumbricine /ˈlʌmbrɪsʌɪn/ *a.* L19. [mod.L *lumbricina*, f. L LUMBRICUS: see -INE[1].] *Zool.* Of, pertaining to, or characteristic of the family Lumbricidae or the suborder Lumbricina of earthworms.

lumbricoid /ˈlʌmbrɪkɔɪd/ *a.* & *n.* M19. [f. LUMBRICUS + -OID.] *Zool.* (An organism) resembling a lumbricus.

lumbriculus /lʌmˈbrɪkjʊləs/ *n.* Pl. **-li** /-lʌɪ, -liː/. E20. [mod.L, dim. of L LUMBRICUS: see -CULE.] *Zool.* An aquatic oligochaete worm of the genus *Lumbriculus*, resembling an earthworm.

lumbricus /lʌmˈbrʌɪkəs, ˈlʌmbrɪkəs/ *n.* Pl. **-ci** /-sʌɪ, -siː/. LME. [L = worm.] *Zool.* An earthworm, *esp.* one of the genus *Lumbricus*. Also (now *rare*), an intestinal roundworm.

lumen /ˈluːmɛn, ˈljuː-/ *n.* Pl. (in sense 1) **-mina** /-mɪnə/, (in sense 2) **-mens.** L19. [L *lumen*, *lumin-* (a) light, an opening.] 1 a *Anat.* & *Biol.* A tubular passage or cavity in an organism or cell; the central space in an intestine, blood-vessel, etc. L19. b A tubular passage in a catheter or other surgical instrument. L19. 2 *Physics.* The SI unit of luminous flux, equal to the flux emitted by a uniform point source of intensity one candela (formerly, one candle) into a solid angle of one steradian. (Symbol lm.) L19.

lumen siccum /luːmɛn ˈsɪkəm, ˈljuː-/ *n. phr.* E17. [L, lit. 'dry light'.] The objective light of rational knowledge or thought.

lumeter /ˈluːmiːtə, ˈljuː-/ *n.* E20. [f. L LUMEN + -METER.] = LUXMETER.

lumi- /ˈluːmi, ˈljuː-/ *comb. form* of L *lumin-*, LUMEN light: see -I-.

lumichrome *n.* (*Chem.*) a compound, $C_{12}H_{10}N_4O_2$, formed by ultraviolet irradiation of riboflavin in acidic solution and showing a blue fluorescence M20. **lumiˈflavin** *n.* (*Chem.*) a compound, $C_{13}H_{12}N_4O_2$, formed by ultraviolet irradiation of riboflavin in alkaline solution and showing a yellow-green fluorescence M20. **lumirhoˈdopsin** *n.* (*Biochem.*) an orange intermediate that is formed when rhodopsin is bleached by light and changes spontaneously to metarhodopsin M20. **luˈmisterol** *n.* (*Biochem.*) a steroid alcohol, $C_{28}H_{44}O$, which is a stereoisomer of ergosterol and occurs as an intermediate when this is converted to vitamin D_2 by ultraviolet irradiation and warming M20.

lumina *n.pl.* see LUMEN.

luminaire /ˈluːmɪnɛː, ˈljuː-/ *n.* E20. [Fr.: see LUMINARY *n.*] (A lighting unit consisting of) an electric light and its fittings.

Luminal /ˈluːmɪn(ə)l, ˈljuː-/ *n.* E20. [Prob. f. L LUMEN (as a rendering of PHEN-) + -AL[2].] *Pharm.* (Proprietary name for) the drug phenobarbitone.

luminal /ˈluːmɪn(ə)l, ˈljuː-/ *a.* L19. [f. as LUMEN + -AL[1].] Of or pertaining to a lumen.

luminance /ˈluːmɪn(ə)ns, ˈljuː-/ *n.* L19. [f. (as) next: see -ANCE.] 1 Luminousness. L19. 2 *Physics.* The amount of luminous flux emitted by unit area of a source into unit solid angle (the objective analogue of subjective brightness). M20. 3 The component of a television signal which carries information on the brightness of the image. M20.

luminant /ˈluːmɪn(ə)nt, ˈljuː-/ *n.* & *a.* Now *rare.* L19. [L *luminant-* pres. ppl stem of *luminare*, f. *lumin-*, LUMEN: see -ANT[1].] A *n.* An illuminant. L19. B *adj.* Illuminating, luminous. L19.

luminarist /ˈluːmɪn(ə)rɪst, ˈljuː-/ *n.* Now *rare.* L19. [Fr. *luminariste*, f. L *lumin-*, LUMEN: see -IST.] *Art.* An adherent or practitioner of luminism.

luminarism *n.* the art or practice of luminarists, = LUMINISM 1 E20.

luminary /ˈluːmɪn(ə)ri, ˈljuː-/ *n.* LME. [OFr. *luminarie* (mod. *-aire*) or late L *luminarium*, f. L *lumin-*, LUMEN: see -ARY[1].] 1 a A lamp, an artificial light. LME. b A natural light-giving body; *esp.* a celestial object, the sun or the moon. L15. 2 A source of intellectual, moral, or spiritual light; a prominent or influential person. LME.

2 P. GROSSKURTH The leading luminaries sat around the . . table, the lesser figures . . behind them. *News on Sunday* A leading criminal lawyer said to be a luminary in the libel field.

luminate /ˈluːmɪneɪt, ˈljuː-/ *v.t. arch.* Pa. pple & ppl a. **-ated**, (earlier) **†-ate.** M16. [L *luminat-* pa. ppl stem of *luminare*: see LUMINANT, -ATE[3].] Light up, illuminate.

lumiˈnation *n.* (*rare*) a shedding or emission of light M17.

lumine /ˈluːmɪn, ˈljuː-/ *v.t.* Now *rare.* LME. [OFr. *luminer* f. L *luminare*: see LUMINANT. See also LIMN *v.*] Light up, illumine. In early use, illuminate (a manuscript etc.).

†luminer *n.* (see also LIMNER) ME–L15.

luminesce /luːmɪˈnɛs, ljuː-/ *v.i.* L19. [Back-form. f. LUMINESCENT.] Be or become luminescent.

luminescence /luːmɪˈnɛs(ə)ns, ljuː-/ *n.* L19. [f. (as) next: see -ENCE.] 1 The property of some substances of emitting light without being heated, as in fluorescence and phosphorescence. L19. 2 Light emitted by a luminescent object or surface. E20.

luminescent /luːmɪˈnɛs(ə)nt, ljuː-/ *a.* L19. [f. L *lumin-*, LUMEN + -ESCENT.] Exhibiting or pertaining to luminescence.

luminiferous /luːmɪˈnɪf(ə)rəs, ljuː-/ *a.* E19. [f. as prec.: see -FEROUS.] Producing or transmitting light. Chiefly *Hist.* in *luminiferous ether.*

luminise *v.* var. of LUMINIZE.

luminism /ˈluːmɪnɪz(ə)m, ˈljuː-/ *n.* E20. [f. L *lumin-*, LUMEN + -ISM.] *Art.* 1 A movement in painting concentrating on representing the effects of light. E20. 2 Use of light to produce an object of art. M20.

luminist *n.* & *a.* (*a*) *n.* an adherent or practitioner of luminism; (*b*) *adj.* of or pertaining to luminists or luminism: E20.

luminize /ˈluːmɪnʌɪz, ˈljuː-/ *v.t.* Also **-ise.** M20. [f. as prec. + -IZE.] Make luminous; apply a luminous substance to.

luminizer *n.* M20.

luminol /ˈluːmɪnɒl, ˈljuː-/ *n.* M20. [f. L *lumin-*, LUMEN + -OL.] *Chem.* A bicyclic hydrazide, $C_8H_7N_3O_2$, which gives a blue luminescence when oxidized in alkaline solution and is used in the determination of oxidizing agents and metal ions.

luminophore /ˈluːmɪnəfɔː, ˈljuː-/ *n.* Also **-phor.** E20. [f. as prec. + -O- + -PHORE.] 1 A luminescent substance. E20. 2 A group of atoms in a molecule which is responsible for its luminescence. E20.

luminosity /luːmɪˈnɒsɪti, ljuː-/ *n.* M17. [f. next: see -OSITY.] 1 The quality or condition of being luminous. M17. b The effectiveness of light of any particular wavelength in producing the sensation of brightness. L19. c *Astron.* The intrinsic brightness of a celestial object (as distinct from its apparent brightness, diminished by distance); the rate of emission of electromagnetic radiation within any part of the spectrum. E20. d *Physics.* A parameter of a colliding-beam accelerator equal to the ratio of the rate of interactions to the cross-section for the interaction. M20. 2 A luminous thing; a luminous point or area. M19.

Comb.: **luminosity curve**: showing how emitted energy or perceived brightness varies with wavelength; **luminosity function** *Astron.*: giving the number or proportion of celestial objects with an absolute magnitude equal to or greater than any value.

luminous /ˈluːmɪnəs, ˈljuː-/ *a.* LME. [(O)Fr. *lumineux* or L *luminosus*, f. *lumin-*, LUMEN: see -OUS.] 1 Full of light; emitting or casting light; shining, bright; luminescent. LME. b Of a room etc.: well lit. Now *rare.* E17. 2 Shedding intellectual, moral, or spiritual light; (of a writer, literary style, etc.) clear and illuminating. LME.

1 A. C. CLARKE In the lightless abyss, many creatures carry constellations of luminous organs. M. SHADBOLT Tim's pale shirt, vaguely luminous in the gloom. J. CHEEVER Her skin had a luminous and pearly whiteness. 2 *Women's Review* Luminous prose, acute intellect and the insight of a spiritual healer.

luminously *adv.* E19. **luminousness** *n.* M17.

lumme /ˈlʌmi/ *int. colloq.* L19. [Alt. of (*Lord*) *love me.*] Expr. surprise or emphasis.

lummox /ˈlʌməks/ *n. dial.* & *N. Amer. colloq.* E19. [Origin unkn.] A large, heavy, or clumsy person; an ungainly or stupid lout.

lummy /ˈlʌmi/ *a. arch. slang.* M19. [Origin unkn.] First-rate.

lump /lʌmp/ *n.*[1] ME. [Origin unkn. Cf. Da. *lump(e* lump, Norw., Sw. dial. *lump* block, stump, log; but what may be the original sense, 'shapeless piece', is seen also in Du. *lomp*, †*lompe* rag, Du. *lomp*, LG *lump* coarse, rude (whence G *Lumpen* rag).] 1 A compact, shapeless, or unshapely piece or mass. ME. b *ellipt.* A lump of sugar. L19. 2 a A mass of clay taken up by a potter or sculptor for one operation, a mass of dough intended for one baking. ME. b A mass of malleable iron. E16. 3 A heavy dull person, a lazy person; an ungainly person; a big sturdy person. ME. †4 An aggregate of units; a heap, a clump, a cluster. LME–L18. 5 A protuberance, a swelling, an excrescence, *esp.* one caused by disease or injury in an animal body. LME. **b** A feeling of tightness or pressure in the throat due to emotion. Chiefly in *a lump in one's throat, bring a lump to a person's throat. colloq.* M19. **6** A great quantity, a lot. *slang & dial.* E16. †**7** The whole mass or quantity of something; the great majority. L16–E18. **8** A nipple on the barrel of a musket; an iron block under the barrel of certain types of breech-loading gun descending into a recess in the action. M19. **9** *Naut.* A wave of a choppy sea. M19. **10** *The* workhouse. *arch. slang.* L19. **11** A parcel of food given to a tramp or vagrant. *US slang.* E20. **12** In *pl.* Hard knocks, attacks. *slang.* M20. **13** *The* class of people in building or other trades who contract to do work for a lump sum, or who work as self-employed individuals for payment without deduction of tax. M20.

1 J. T. STORY The police . . had seen Maria feeding lumps of sugar to the racehorse. P. ABRAHAMS A woman gave each person a lump of thick porridge. 3 L. CODY She makes me feel like a big lump. 5 E. NESBIT There was a lump on his young brow as big as a turkey's egg. D. DELILLO Steffie was routinely examining her chest for lumps. 6 R. D. BLACKMORE Colonel Harding owed him a lump of money. 12 J. H. GRAY My father would . . take his verbal lumps, saying nothing.

Phrases: **by** or **in the lump** as a whole, in a general manner; without breaking down into units, in the mass; wholesale; for a lump sum. **lump of clay** the human body regarded as purely material, without a soul. *lumps of delight*: see DELIGHT *n.* 4.

Comb.: **lump-account** an account in which items are treated together without particulars or details; **lump coal** coal in lumps as mined; **lump sugar** loaf sugar broken into lumps or cut into cubes; **lump sum** (*a*) a sum covering or including a number of items; (*b*) a sum of money paid to cover the complete cost of something; **lump work** work contracted for as a single job for a lump sum.

lump /lʌmp/ *n.*[2] M16. [MLG *lumpen*, MDu. *lumpe*, perh. identical w. LUMP *n.*[1]] = LUMPFISH.

lump /lʌmp/ *v.*[1]*t. obs.* exc. *dial.* M16. [Perh. rel. to Du. *lompen.*] Beat, thresh.

lump /lʌmp/ *v.*[2] L16. [Symbolic: cf. *dump, grump, mump,* etc.] **1** *v.i.* Look sulky or disagreeable. (In early use esp. in collocation w. *lour.*) Long *obs.* exc. *dial.* L16. **2** *v.t.* Be displeased at (something that must be endured), put up with ungraciously, tolerate reluctantly. (Freq. in antithesis with *like.*) *colloq.* E19.

2 W. S. MAUGHAM If they don't like it they can lump it. J. S. HUXLEY There was no alternative accommodation . . ; we just had to lump it.

lump /lʌmp/ *v.*[3] E17. [f. LUMP *n.*[1]] **1** *v.t.* Put together in one mass, sum, or group, without discrimination or regard for particulars or details; treat as alike or like. Foll. by *together, with, in with, under,* etc. E17. **b** *v.t.* & *i. Taxon.* Classify (plants or animals) disregarding minor variations as a basis for more taxa; conflate (taxa) in this way. L19. **2** *v.i.* Collect *together* into a lump; be formed or raised into lumps; coagulate. E17. **3** *v.t.* †**a** Pay in a lump sum. *rare.* Only in M18. **b** Lay the whole of (a particular sum of money) *on* a single object. M19. **4** *v.t.* Melt down into a lump; form or raise into lumps; cover with lumps. L18. **5** *v.i.* Move heavily *along*; drop or sit heavily *down.* M19. **6a** *v.i.* Act as a lumper, load or unload cargoes. Chiefly as *lumping* vbl n. (Cf. earlier LUMPER *n.* 1.) M19. **b** *v.t.* Load or unload (a ship, a cargo); *colloq.* carry or shift (something heavy) *about* etc. with effort or difficulty or roughly. L19.

1 J. W. KRUTCH Under this designation is lumped without discrimination any aspiration toward distinction. G. PRIESTLAND Pop (in which I lump, indiscriminately, . . all kinds of electronic bumping and grinding). J. BARZUN Jung's lumping of dreams, legends and hearsay with recorded fact. J. UPDIKE In the present volume, the footnotes are cumbersomely lumped at the back. J. WAIN In that district all of us who were not Welsh were inevitably lumped together as foreigners. 6 A. BRIEN Can't keep lumping your favourite books backwards and forwards.

lumpectomy /lʌm'pɛktəmi/ *n.* L20. [f. LUMP *n.*[1] + -ECTOMY.] Surgical removal of a lump from a woman's breast in a case of suspected or diagnosed cancer, the remainder of the breast being left intact; an instance of this.

lumped /lʌmpt/ *a.* LME. [f. LUMP *n.*[1], *v.*[3]: see -ED[2], -ED[1].] **1** Made, shaped, or raised into a lump. LME. **2** *Electr.* (Containing impedances or circuit elements) localized at a particular point or points, rather than distributed uniformly throughout part of a circuit. E20.

lumpen /'lʌmpən/ *a.* & *n. derog.* M20. [Back-form. f. next.] **A** *adj.* Ignorantly contented, boorish, stupid; uninterested in revolutionary advancement. Also joined to the n. qualified. M20.

A. BROOKNER Her lumpen immobility, her absorption in the cat. *Spectator* A lumpen-intelligentsia of déclassé students.

B *n. collect. pl. The* class of those who are lumpen. L20.

lumpenproletariat /ˌlʌmpənprəʊlɪ'tɛːrɪət/ *n. derog.* E20. [G, f. *Lumpen* rag (cf. LUMP *n.*[1]) + PROLETARIAT. Orig. used by Karl Marx.] The poorest and least cohesive section of the proletariat, making no contribution to the workers' cause; the ignorantly contented lower orders of society uninterested in revolutionary advancement.

lumpenproletarian *a.* & *n.* of or pertaining to, a member of, the lumpenproletariat M20.

lumper /'lʌmpə/ *n.* L18. [f. LUMP *v.*[3] or *n.*[1] + -ER[1].] **1** A labourer employed in loading and unloading cargoes, a docker; a person employed in unloading fish. L18. **2** A small contractor, a person who contracts for lump work. *slang.* M19. **3** A person (esp. a taxonomist) who attaches importance to similarities rather than differences in classification or analysis and so favours inclusive categories. Cf. SPLITTER *n.* 1b. M19.

lumper /'lʌmpə/ *v.i. obs.* exc. *dial.* E16. [Perh. symbolic. Cf. LUMBER *v.*[1]] Move clumsily; stumble or blunder along.

lumpers /'lʌmpəz/ *n.pl. slang.* M20. [f. *lump sum* s.v. LUMP *n.*[1]: see -ER[6].] A lump sum paid as compensation for loss of employment.

lumpfish /'lʌmpfɪʃ/ *n.* Pl. **-es** /-ɪz/, (usu.) same. E17. [f. LUMP *n.*[2] + FISH *n.*[1]] A spiny-finned heavy-bodied fish, *Cyclopterus lumpus*, of the N. Atlantic, with modified pelvic fins forming a disc-shaped sucker with which it clings to objects with great force.

lumping /'lʌmpɪŋ/ *a.* LME. [f. LUMP *v.*[3] + -ING[2].] **1** †**a** Weighing heavy. Only in LME. **b** Great, big. *colloq.* E18 **2** *gen.* That lumps (something). M18.

1b R. CAMPBELL A most melancholy fellow with a great lumping text-book in his fist. **a lumping pennyworth** (now *dial.*) plenty for one's money.

lumpish /'lʌmpɪʃ/ *a.* LME. [f. LUMP *n.*[1] (& partly LUMP *v.*[3]) + -ISH[1].] **1** Stupidly dull or lethargic in action, thought, or feeling. Formerly also, low-spirited, dejected, melancholy. LME. **2** Of cumbersome weight or bulk; not easily moved; *esp.* heavy and clumsy in appearance, shape, or movement. M16. **3** Full of lumps, in lumps, lumpy. E18. **4** Of sound: dull and heavy. M18.

1 POPE The lumpish husband snoar'd away the night. F. DONALDSON The earlier letters . . were . . of that lumpish kind everyone writes to school-children. 2 SIR W. SCOTT Swelling lumpish hills. 3 A. N. WILSON Tugging away the soft bread . . in lumpish handfuls. 4 H. FIELDING He fell prostrated on the floor with a lumpish noise.

lumpishly *adv.* LME. **lumpishness** *n.* L16.

lumpless /'lʌmplɪs/ *a.* E20. [f. LUMP *n.*[1] + -LESS.] Having no lumps.

lumpsucker /'lʌmpsʌkə/ *n.* M18. [f. LUMP *n.*[2] + SUCKER *n.*] = LUMPFISH.

lumpy /'lʌmpi/ *a.* E18. [f. LUMP *n.*[1] + -Y[1].] **1** Full of lumps; (of water) cut up by the wind into small waves. E18. **2** Having an outline or shape characterized by lumps or roundish protuberances; having a heavy and clumsy appearance. E18. **3** Intoxicated, drunk. *arch. slang.* E19.

1 *Listener* A lumpy swell and a Force Eight wind. P. BAILEY If there's one thing I can't abide, it's lumpy porridge. 2 N. GORDIMER The legs had the ex-dancer's hard lumpy calves.

Special collocations: **lumpy jaw** actinomycosis affecting the jaw, common in cattle.

lumpily *adv.* L19. **lumpiness** *n.* E19.

luna /'luːnə/ *n.* LME. [L = moon.] **1** (**L-**.) The moon (personified). LME. **2** †**a** *Alch.* The metal silver. LME–M17. **b** *Her.* The tincture argent in the fanciful blazon of the arms of sovereign princes. E18. **c** *luna cornea* /'kɔːnɪə/ [= horn], fused silver chloride. E18. **3** In full *luna-moth*. A large grey-green N. American saturniid moth, *Actias luna*, with crescent-shaped spots and long curved tails on the wings. L19.

lunabase /'luːnəbeɪs/ *n.* M20. [f. L LUNA moon + BASE *n.*[1] (with ref. to BASIC *a.* 2b).] *Astron.* The maria or lowlands of the moon (the dark-coloured regions as seen from the earth); the basaltic rock of which these are composed. Cf. LUNARITE.

lunacy /'luːnəsi/ *n.* M16. [f. LUNATIC: see -ACY.] **1** Insanity, orig. of an intermittent kind supposed to be brought about by the changes of the moon. Formerly in *Law*, such mental unsoundness as interferes with civil rights or transactions. M16. **2** Mad folly, great foolishness. L16.

1 commission of lunacy *Hist.* a commission, issuing from a court, authorizing an inquiry as to the soundness of a person's mind. **Master in Lunacy** *Hist.* a legal officer with the duty of investigating the mental condition of people alleged to be insane.

Luna Park /luːnə 'pɑːk/ *n. phr.* E20. [An amusement centre on Coney Island, Brooklyn, New York.] An amusement centre, an entertainment park.

lunar /'luːnə/ *a.* & *n.* LME. [L *lunaris*, f. as LUNA: see -AR[1].] **A** *adj.* **1** Crescent-shaped; marked with crescent-shaped spots. LME. **2** Of or pertaining to the moon; situated in or on the moon; of or pertaining to travel to the moon. Formerly also, (supposedly) influenced by or dependent on the moon. E17. **b** Monthly, menstrual. *rare.* L17. **c** Having the character of the moon as opp. to that of the sun; not warmly bright; pale, pallid. M18. **3** [So called because the class includes *ḳ*, the initial letter of Arab. *ḳamar* moon.] Of an Arabic consonant: before which the *l* of the article is not assimilated. Opp. SOLAR *a.*[1] 4. L18. **4** Of or containing silver. E19.

Special collocations & comb.: **lunar caustic** fused silver nitrate. **lunar cycle** the Metonic cycle. **lunar day** the interval of time between two successive crossings of the meridian by the moon. **lunar distance** the angular distance of the moon from the sun, a planet, or a fixed star, used in calculating longitude at sea. **lunar-diurnal** *a.* pertaining to the lunar day. *lunar eclipse* see ECLIPSE *n.* 1. **lunar (excursion) module** a module designed to take an astronaut from an orbiting spacecraft to the moon's surface and back. **lunar month** (*a*) = SYNODIC *month*; (*b*) a period of 28 days (four weeks). **lunar node** either of the two points at which the orbit of the moon cuts the ecliptic. **lunar observation** an observation of lunar distances in finding longitude at sea. **lunar orbit** (*a*) the orbit of the moon around the earth; (*b*) an orbit around the moon. *lunar regular*: see REGULAR *n.* 4. **lunarscape** a picture or view of the moon's surface; the lunar landscape. **lunar year** a period of twelve lunar months (about 354⅓ days).

B *n.* †**1** A moonlike body, a satellite. Only in M17. **2a** A lunar distance; a lunar observation. M19. **b** A look. *colloq.* E20. **3** The lunate bone. M19.

lunarnaut *n.* [after ASTRONAUT etc.] a person who travels or has travelled to the moon M20.

lunaria /luː'nɛːrɪə/ *n.* Also (earlier, now *rare* or *obs.*) **lunary** /'luːnəri/. LME. [med.L *lunaria*, f. L LUNA moon + *-aria* -ARY[1].] Any of several plants having a feature associated with the moon; *esp.* (*a*) the garden plant honesty, *Lunaria annua* (with ref. to the round shiny seed-vessels); (*b*) *arch.* the fern moonwort, *Botrychium lunaria* (with ref. to the crescent-shaped segments of the barren fronds).

lunarian /luː'nɛːrɪən/ *n.* Now *rare.* E18. [f. as LUNAR + -IAN.] **1** A (supposed) dweller in or on the moon. E18. **2** An observer or describer of the moon; a user of lunar observations in finding longitude. E19.

lunarite /'luːnəraɪt/ *n.* M20. [f. as LUNAR + -ITE[1].] *Astron.* The uplands of the moon (the light-coloured regions as seen from the earth);

the siliceous rock of which these are composed. Cf. LUNABASE.

lunarium /luːˈnɛːrɪəm/ *n.* L18. [mod.L, f. as LUNAR + -IUM.] An instrument representing the phases and motions of the moon.

lunary *n.* see LUNARIA.

lunary /ˈluːnəri/ *a.* Now *rare.* M16. [f. as LUNAR: see -ARY[2].] 1 = LUNAR *a.* 2. M16. 2 = LUNAR *a.* 1. E17.

lunate /ˈluːneɪt/ *a.* & *n.* L18. [L *lunatus*, f. LUNA moon: see -ATE[2].] A *adj.* Chiefly *Zool.* & *Bot.* Crescent-shaped; *spec.* (*Anat.*) designating one of the bones of the wrist. L18. B *n.* A small prehistoric crescent-shaped stone (usu. flint) artefact or implement. M20.

lunated *a.* (now *rare*) = LUNATE *a.* L17.

lunatic /ˈluːnətɪk/ *a.* & *n.* ME. [(O)Fr. *lunatique* f. late L *lunaticus*, f. L LUNA moon: see -ATIC.] A *adj.* 1 Insane; orig., affected by an intermittent kind of insanity supposed to be brought about by the changes of the moon. Formerly in *Law*, affected by such mental unsoundness as interferes with civil rights or transactions. ME. b Madly foolish, wildly eccentric, frantic, idiotic; (of an action, appearance, etc.) indicating lunacy or mad folly. E16. †2 a Influenced by the moon. LME–L16. b Of a horse: affected with moon-blindness; moon-blind. L16–M18.

B *n.* 1 An insane person; a person of unsound mind; a madman. LME. 2 A madly foolish or idiotic person. E17.

Comb. & *special collocations*: **lunatic asylum** (chiefly *Hist.*) a mental home or hospital; *lunatic fringe*: see FRINGE *n.*

lunatical /luːˈnatɪk(ə)l/ *a. rare.* L16. [f. prec. + -AL[1].] = LUNATIC *a.*

lunatically *adv.* L19.

lunation /luːˈneɪʃ(ə)n/ *n.* LME. [med.L *lunatio(n-)*, f. LUNA moon: see -ATION.] 1 The time from one new moon to the next, constituting a lunar or synodic month. LME. 2 The time of full moon. M16.

lunch /lʌn(t)ʃ/ *n.* & *v.* L16. [In sense 1 perh. f. Sp. *lonja* slice. In sense 2 abbrev. of next.] A *n.* †1 A (thick) piece; a hunk. L16–L19. 2 A meal taken around midday or early in the afternoon, *spec.* one lighter or less formal than the evening meal; a light refreshment taken between breakfast and a midday dinner or main meal; in some places, a light meal at any time of the day. E19.

2 *Dutch lunch*: see DUTCH *a.* LIQUID *lunch.* **out to lunch** *N. Amer. slang* insane; stupid, unaware; disorganized, incompetent; socially unacceptable. *ploughman's lunch*: see PLOUGHMAN 2. SUNDAY *lunch. working lunch*: see WORKING.

Comb.: **lunch-box** a container for a packed meal; **lunch-dinner** a meal that might be called either lunch or dinner, a midday dinner; **lunch-hour** a break of an hour or so for lunch, the hour at which lunch is (usually) taken; **lunch-room** a restaurant with quick service of lunches; **lunch-time** the time at which lunch is (usually) taken.

B *v.* 1 *v.i.* Take lunch. E19. 2 *v.t.* Provide lunch for. L19.

¶As a synonym of LUNCHEON *n.* 2, *v.*, now the usual word exc. in specially formal use & in certain combs., though formerly objected to as vulgar.

luncher *n.* M19. **lunchless** *a.* E20.

luncheon /ˈlʌn(t)ʃ(ə)n/ *n.* & *v.* L16. [In sense A.1 prob. an extension of LUNCH *n.* 1 after *punch, puncheon, brunch, bruncheon.* Other uses of unkn. origin.] A *n.* †1 = LUNCH *n.* 1. L16–L19. 2 Orig., a light refreshment or lunch taken between two of the ordinary mealtimes, esp. between breakfast and a midday dinner or main meal. Now usu., a lunch taken around midday or early in the afternoon (now *formal*). Also (*US*), a late supper or other light meal. M17.

Comb.: **luncheon-car** on a railway train, a restaurant-car where lunches are provided; **luncheon meat** a type of precooked meat containing preservatives, in loaf form for slicing etc.; **luncheon voucher** a money voucher given to an employee which is exchangeable for meals at certain restaurants or food from certain shops.

B *v.i.* Take luncheon, lunch. M19.

luncheo'nette *n.* a small restaurant or snack bar serving light lunches E20. **luncheonless** *a.* L19.

Lunda /ˈlʌndə/ *n.* & *a.* Pl. of n. same, **-s**. L19. [Bantu.] Of or pertaining to, a member of, a Bantu-speaking people of Angola and Zambia; (of) the language of this people.

lundum /ˈlʊndəm/ *n.* M20. [Port.] A simple Portuguese song and dance originating from Africa, probably one of the sources from which the *fado* developed.

Lundyfoot /ˈlʌndɪfʊt/ *n.* E19. [f. *Lundy Foot*, a tobacconist in Dublin, Ireland, *c* 1776.] A kind of snuff.

lune /luːn/ *n.*[1] Also †**loyn(e)**. LME. [OFr. *loigne* var. of *longe* shortening of *allonge* lengthening, drawing out, f. *allonger*, f. *long* LONG *a.*[1]] A length of cord etc.; *spec.* a leash for a hawk.

lune /luːn/ *n.*[2] *arch.* E17. [L LUNA moon, in med.L sense, whence also Fr. *lune*, MHG *lûne* (G *Laune* whim, caprice).] A fit of frenzy or lunacy; a mad freak or tantrum. Usu. in *pl.*

lune /luːn/ *n.*[3] E18. [Fr. f. L LUNA moon.] 1 *Geom.* A figure formed on a plane by arcs of two circles intersecting at two points; a figure formed on a sphere by two semicircles intersecting at diametrically opposite points. Also called *lunule, lunula.* E18. 2 Anything in the shape of a crescent or half moon. Now *rare.* E18.

lunel /luːˈnɛl/ *n.* L18. [f. *Lunel* (see below).] A sweet muscat wine produced around Lunel in the department of Hérault, southern France. Also *lunel-wine.*

lunette /luːˈnɛt, ljuː-/ *n.* L16. [Fr., dim. of *lune* moon f. L LUNA: see -ETTE.] 1 *Farriery.* A semicircular horseshoe for the front of the hoof only. Also *lunette-shoe.* L16. 2 *Archit.* a An arched aperture in a concave ceiling for the admission of light. E17. b A crescent-shaped or semicircular space in a ceiling, dome, etc., decorated with paintings or sculptures; a piece of decoration filling such a space. E18. 3 A blinker for a horse. M17. 4 In *pl.* Spectacles. Now *rare.* L17. 5 *Fortif.* A work larger than a redan, consisting of two faces forming a salient angle and two flanks. E18. 6 The figure or shape of a crescent moon. L18. 7 A watch-glass of flattened shape. Also *lunette (watch-)glass.* M19. 8 In the guillotine, the circular hole which receives the neck of the victim. M19. 9 Any of the flues connecting a glass furnace and its arch. (Earlier in LINNET-HOLE.) M19. 10 A crescent-shaped ornament. M19. 11 A ring or forked plate to or by which a field-gun carriage or other vehicle for towing is attached. L19. 12 *RC Ch.* A circular case, fitting into an aperture in a monstrance, for holding the consecrated host. L19. 13 *Physical Geogr.* A broad shallow mound of wind-blown material along the leeward side of a lake or dry lake basin, esp. in arid parts of Australia, and typically crescent-shaped with the concave edge along the lake shore. M20.

lung /lʌŋ/ *n.* [OE *lungen* = OFris. *lungen*, MLG *lunge*, MDu. *longe* (Du. *long*), OHG *lungun* (G *Lunge*), corresp. to ON *lunga*, f. Gmc f. IE base repr. also by LIGHT *a.*[1] Named for their lightness: cf. LIGHTS.] 1 The respiratory organ which brings air into contact with the blood in many vertebrates, occurring usually in pairs in the thorax and communicating through bronchi with the windpipe; a respiratory organ in some invertebrates. See also *iron lung* s.v. IRON *n.* & *a.* OE. b *fig.* A place where fresh air can be breathed; in *pl.*, the parks and open spaces in or close to a city. Foll. by *for, of.* E19. †2 *sing.* & in *pl.* A person who blows a fire; a chemist's assistant. E–M17.

1 P. BARKER She was aware of the movement of her lungs, sucking in and expelling air. b L. MUMFORD The urban park . . the 'lungs' of the city. *South Wales Echo* The planners . . want the land to the west of Caerphilly to remain as a lung for the town.

Phrases: *black lung*: see BLACK *a.* **lungs of (the) oak** a tree lichen, *Lobaria pulmonaria*, formerly reputed to be of value in treating disorders of the lung. *miner's lung*: see MINER.

Comb.: **lung book** = *book-lung* s.v. BOOK *n.*; **lung-fever** pneumonia; **lung fluke** a parasitic trematode flatworm of the genus *Paragonimus*; **lung-power** strength of voice; **lungworm** any of various nematode worms parasitic in the lungs of mammals, esp. of some farm and domestic animals. See also LUNGFISH.

lungful *n.* as much as will fill the lungs; *spec.* a quantity of inhaled cigarette-smoke: M19. **lungless** *a.* E17.

lunge /lʌn(d)ʒ/ *n.*[1] Also **longe** /lʌn(d)ʒ, lɒn(d)ʒ/. E17. [(O)Fr. *longe* var. of OFr. *loigne*: see LUNE *n.*[1]] †1 *gen.* A thong, a cord. Only in E17. 2 A long rope or rein used in training or exercising horses, by which a horse is held while being made to circle the trainer at a walk, trot, or canter. E18. 3 = *lungeing-ring* s.v. LUNGE *v.*[2] M19.

lunge /lʌn(d)ʒ/ *n.*[2] Also (now *rare* or *obs.*) **lounge** /laʊn(d)ʒ/. M18. [Aphet. f. (as) ALLONGE.] 1 A thrust with a sword (*spec.* in *Fencing*) or other weapon. M18. 2 A sudden forward movement; a plunge, a rush. M19. 3 An act of thrusting one foot forward with the knee bent while keeping the other foot fixed, as an exercise or gymnastic movement. L19.

lunge /lʌn(d)ʒ/ *n.*[3] *N. Amer.* M19. [Abbrev. of *muskellunge* var. of MASKINONGE.] Either of two large N. American freshwater fishes, *Esox masquinongy*, a pike found in the Great Lakes, and (now *rare*) the N. American lake trout, *Salvelinus namaycush.*

lunge /lʌn(d)ʒ/ *v.*[1] Also (now *rare* or *obs.*) **lounge** /laʊn(d)ʒ/. M18. [f. LUNGE *n.*[2]] 1 *v.t.* Deliver (a kick, a thrust) with a lunge. M18. 2 *v.i.* Make a lunge; *Fencing* make a thrust with a foil or rapier; *Boxing* deliver a blow from the shoulder. (Foll. by *at.*) E19. 3 *v.t.* Drive or thrust (as) with a lunge. M19.

2 M. S. POWER Poppy Burn lunged to her feet and fled. J. FULLER A stallion tethered by each foot strained and lunged. *New York Times* He lunged at me, and I stabbed him. 3 F. T. BUCKLAND The scorpion instantly lunged his sting into him. R. B. PARKER I . . lunged the door inward.

lunge /lʌn(d)ʒ/ *v.*[2]*t.* Also **longe** /lʌn(d)ʒ, lɒn(d)ʒ/. E19. [f. LUNGE *n.*[1]] Train or exercise (a horse, occas. a rider) with a lunge or in a lungeing-ring.

lungeing-ring *a.* a circular exercising-ground in which a lunge is used.

lunged /lʌŋd/ *a.* L17. [f. LUNG + -ED[2].] Having lungs, or something resembling lungs. Of a person usu. with prefixed adj., as *small-lunged, weak-lunged.*

lungeous /ˈlʌn(d)ʒəs/ *a. dial.* L17. [f. LUNGE *n.*[2] or *v.*[1] + -OUS.] †1 Of a fall: heavy. Only in L17. 2 Of a person: rough-mannered, violent (in play). L18.

lunger /ˈlʌn(d)ʒə/ *n.*[1] M19. [f. LUNGE *v.*[1] + -ER[1].] A person who lunges.

lunger /ˈlʌŋə/ *n.*[2] *arch. colloq.* L19. [f. LUNG + -ER[1].] A person diseased or wounded in the lungs.

lungfish /ˈlʌŋfɪʃ/ *n.* Pl. **-es** /-ɪz/, (usu.) same. L19. [f. LUNG *n.* + FISH *n.*[1]] A fish able to breathe air using primitive lungs, a dipnoan; *esp.* any of the extant genera *Lepidosiren* of S. America, *Protopterus* of Africa, and *Neoceratodus* of Australia, having long thick bodies and filamentous fins, and living in shallow fresh water or swamps.

QUEENSLAND *lungfish.*

lung-gom-pa /ˈlʊŋgompa/ *n.* M20. [Tib.] A Tibetan monk able to walk many miles at great speed without stopping.

lungi /ˈlʊŋgiː/ *n.* E17. [Hind. *lungī*: cf. LANGOTI.] In the Indian subcontinent: a cloth worn wound round the lower body with the end passed between the legs and tucked into the waist; cotton material of which such cloths are made. Also, a length of cotton cloth worn as a skirt in Myanmar (Burma), where it is part of the national dress of both sexes.

lungwort /ˈlʌŋwəːt/ *n.* Also †**long-**. OE. [f. LUNG + WORT *n.*[1], f. the reputed power of such plants to cure lung disorders.] †1 Any of a group of hawkweeds (*Hieracium murorum* and related forms) with leaves mostly in a basal rosette. In later use more fully *French lungwort, golden lungwort.* OE–L18. †2 White hellebore,

Veratrum album; black hellebore, *Helleborus niger*. ME–E17. 3 Any of several spring-flowering plants of the genus *Pulmonaria*, of the borage family, with flowers of pink, blue, or white (often changing with age); *esp.* the common garden flower *P. officinalis*, with white spots on the leaves supposed to resemble the spots in a diseased lung. M16. b With specifying wd: any of various chiefly N. American plants of the allied genus *Mertensia*. L18. †4 Great mullein, *Verbascum thapsus*. M16–E18. †5 = ANGELICA *n.*[1] 1. M16–M18. 6 A lichen, *Lobaria pulmonaria*, which grows on trees; = *lungs of (the) oak* s.v. LUNG. L16.

3b **sea lungwort** = *oyster-plant* (a) s.v. OYSTER *n.*

lungy /ˈlʌŋi/ *a. colloq.* L19. [f. LUNG + -Y[1].] 1 Affected with a disease of the lungs. L19. 2 Coming from the lungs. E20.

lunisolar /luːnɪˈsəʊlə/ *a.* L17. [f. L LUNA moon + -I- + SOLAR *a.*[1]] *Astron.* Of or pertaining to the mutual relations of the sun and moon; resulting from the combined action of the sun and moon.

lunisolar period a cycle of 532 years, containing a whole number of both lunar cycles and solar cycles. *lunisolar precession*: see PRECESSION 2a. **lunisolar year**: with divisions regulated by phases of the moon and an average length made to agree with the solar year.

lunitidal /luːnɪˈtʌɪd(ə)l/ *a.* M19. [f. L LUNA moon + -I- + TIDAL.] Designating the interval between the time when the moon crosses a given meridian and the time of the following high tide at that meridian.

lunk /lʌŋk/ *n. colloq.* (orig. *US*). M19. [Abbrev.] = LUNKHEAD.

lunker /ˈlʌŋkə/ *n. N. Amer. colloq.* E20. [Origin unkn.] An animal, esp. a fish, which is an exceptionally large example of its species.

lunkhead /ˈlʌŋkhɛd/ *n. colloq.* (orig. *US*). M19. [Prob. f. alt. of LUMP *n.*[1] + HEAD *n.*] A slow-witted unintelligent person, a blockhead.

lunkheaded *a.* L19

lunt /lʌnt/ *n.* & *v. Sc.* E16. [Du. *lont* match.] A *n.* 1 A slow-burning match; a torch. E16. 2 Smoke (with flame), *esp.* the smoke from a pipe. Also, hot vapour. L18. B *v.* 1 *v.i.* Smoke, emit smoke; blaze, glow; (of smoke) rise in wreaths, curl. L18. 2 *v.t.* Kindle, light *up*; smoke (a pipe). E19.

lunula /ˈluːnjʊlə/ *n.* Pl. **-lae** /-liː/. L16. [L, dim. of LUNA moon: see -ULE.] 1 *Geom.* = LUNE *n.*[3] 1. L16. 2 *Archaeol.* A gold crescent-shaped neck ornament of the early Bronze Age. E18. 3 *Anat., Zool., & Bot.* = LUNULE 3. E19. b *Anat.* A crescent-shaped region of thin tissue on each side of the nodule on each cusp of a valve in the heart or aorta. M19. 4 *Conchol.* = LUNULE 4. M19.

lunular /ˈluːnjʊlə/ *n.* & *a.* L16. [f. prec. + -AR[1].] *Geom.* †A *n.* A crescent-shaped figure. L16–L18. B *adj.* Of or pertaining to a lunule; of the form of a lunule, crescent-shaped. E18.

lunulate /ˈluːnjʊleɪt/ *a.* M18. [mod.L *lunulatus*, f. as LUNULA: see -ATE[2].] *Zool.* & *Bot.* 1 Crescent-shaped. M18. 2 Having crescent-shaped markings. M19.

lunulated /ˈluːnjʊleɪtɪd/ *a.* E18. [f. as prec. + -ED[1].] †1 = LUNULATE 1. Only in 18. 2 = LUNULATE 2. L18.

lunule /ˈluːnjuːl/ *n.* L16. [f. as LUNULA: see -ULE.] †1 A mark shaped like a half moon. Only in L16. 2 *Geom.* = LUNE *n.*[3] 1. M18. 3 *Anat., Zool., & Bot.* A crescent-shaped mark, spot, etc.; *spec.* the pale area at the base of a fingernail. Cf. LUNULA 3. E19. 4 *Conchol.* The crescent-shaped depression in front of the umbo of a shell; = LUNULA 4. E19.

lunulet /ˈluːnjʊlɪt/ *n.* E19. [f. (as) prec. + -ET[1].] *Zool.* & *Bot.* A small crescent-shaped mark.

luny *a.* & *n.* see LOONY *a.* & *n.*[2]

Luo /ˈluːəʊ/ *n.* & *a.* E20. [Luo.] A *n.* Pl. same, -s. 1 A member of an E. African people of Kenya and the upper Nile valley. E20. 2 The Nilotic language of this people. M20. B *attrib.* or as *adj.* Of or pertaining to the Luo or their language. M20.

lupanar /luːˈpeɪnɑː/ *n. literary.* M19. [L, f. *lupa* prostitute, she-wolf, fem. of *lupus* wolf.] A brothel.

lupara /luˈpaːra, luːˈpɑːrə/ *n.* M20. [It. (slang), f. *lupa* she-wolf.] A sawn-off shotgun as used by the Mafia.

Lupercal /ˈluːpəkal/ *n.* Pl. **Lupercalia** /luːpəˈkeɪlɪə/, **Lupercals**. L16. [L, n. form of *lupercale* neut. of *lupercalis* pertaining to Lupercus (see below).] †1 An orgy. Only in L16. 2 *Rom. Hist. sing.* & in *pl.* A festival held annually in February in honour of Lupercus, the Roman equivalent of the Greek god Pan. E17.

Lupercalian /luːpəˈkeɪlɪən/ *a.* of or pertaining to the Lupercalia L19.

lupin /ˈluːpɪn/ *n.* Also **lupine**. LME. [L *lupinus*, *lupinum*.] 1 Any of various leguminous plants of the genus *Lupinus*, with palmate leaves and showy flowers in long terminal racemes; a flowering stem of such a plant. In early use, *esp.* the Mediterranean *Lupinus albus*, cultivated for its seed and for fodder; now usu., any of the ornamental kinds, with flowers in many colours, mainly derivatives and hybrids of the N. American *L. polyphyllus* and *L. arboreus*. LME. 2 In *pl.* The seeds of this plant. LME.

1 *Nootka lupin*: see NOOTKA *a.* 1. RUSSELL LUPIN. *tree lupin*: see TREE *n.*

lupine *n.* var. of LUPIN.

lupine /ˈluːpʌɪn/ *a.* M17. [L *lupinus*, f. *lupus* wolf: see -INE[1].] Having the nature or qualities of a wolf.

lupinosis /luːpɪˈnəʊsɪs/ *n.* Pl. **-oses** /-əʊsiːz/. L19. [f. LUPIN + -OSIS.] Poisoning of animals, esp. sheep, after ingestion of lupins, usu. caused by toxins produced by a fungus of the genus *Phomopsis* growing on the plants.

lupoid /ˈluːpɔɪd/ *a.* M19. [f. LUPUS + -OID.] *Med.* = LUPOUS 2.

lupous /ˈluːpəs/ *a.*[1] M19. [f. (as) LUPUS + -OUS.] 1 = LUPINE *a. rare.* M19. 2 *Med.* Pertaining to or resembling lupus. L19.

lupulin /ˈluːpjʊlɪn/ *n.* E19. [f. mod.L use as specific epithet (see below) of L *lupulus* a plant mentioned by Pliny (perh. wild hops): see -IN[1].] A fine yellowish powder found under the scales of the calyx of the hop, *Humulus lupulus*; the bitter principle contained in this.

lupuˈlinic *a.* M19.

lupulone /ˈluːpjʊləʊn/ *n.* Also **-on** /-ɒn/. E20. [f. as prec. + -ONE.] *Chem.* A crystalline cyclic ketone, $C_{26}H_{38}O_4$, that is one of the bitter-tasting constituents of hops and has strong antibiotic activity. Cf. HUMULONE.

lupus /ˈluːpəs/ *n.* In sense 3 **L-**. L16. [L = wolf.] †1 A wolf. Only in L16. 2 Any of various ulcerous or erosive diseases of the skin; now *esp.* lupus vulgaris and lupus erythematosus (see below). Also called *noli me tangere*. L16. 3 (The name of) a constellation of the southern hemisphere, lying partly in the Milky Way between Scorpius and Centaurus; the Wolf. L17. 4 The pike (fish). E18.

2 **lupus erythematosus** /ˌɛrɪθiːməˈtəʊsəs/ [mod.L, f. Gk *eruthēma*: see ERYTHEMA] an inflammatory disease of the skin giving rise to scaly red patches, esp. on the face, and sometimes also involving internal organs. **lupus vulgaris** /vʌlˈɡɑːrɪs/ [L = common] a chronic tuberculous disease of the skin giving rise to brownish nodules.

lur /lʊə/ *n.*[1] Pl. **lurer** /ˈlʊərə/, **lurs**. L19. [Da., Norw., & Sw. Cf. LURE *n.*[2]] A Bronze Age musical instrument of the horn family found in Scandinavia.

Lur /lʊə/ *n.*[2] M19. [Prob. f. Iranian.] A member of an aboriginal people inhabiting Luristan in western Iran.

lurch /ləːtʃ/ *n.*[1] M16. [App. f. Fr. †*lourche* (also *l'ourche*) a game resembling backgammon, also in *demeurer lourche* be discomfited (originally in the game), prob. f. MHG *lurz* (mod. dial. *lurtsch*) left (hand), wrong. Cf. earlier LURCH *v.*[1]] †1 A cheat, a swindle. M16–E17. 2 A state of discomfiture. Long *obs.* exc. in *leave in the lurch*, leave (a friend, an ally) in adverse circumstances without assistance or in a position of unexpected difficulty. M16. 3 In various games, a concluding state of the score in which one player is greatly ahead of the other; a game or set of games in which the loser scores nothing; at cribbage, a game in which the winner scores 61 before the loser has scored 31 or 121 before the loser has scored 91; in whist, a treble. Now *rare* or *obs.* L16. †4 A game resembling backgammon. Only in 17.

lurch /ləːtʃ/ *n.*[2] Now *rare* or *obs.* M16. [f. LURCH *v.*[2]] †1 An opportunity for eating more than others. Only in M16. 2 A state of concealment. Only in *lie at lurch*, *lie on the lurch*, lie concealed, lie in wait (*lit.* & *fig.*). L16.

lurch /ləːtʃ/ *n.*[3] Orig. *Naut.* Also (earlier) †**larch**, †**latch**. L17. [Origin unkn.] 1 A ship's sudden leaning over to one side; *gen.* a sudden unsteady movement or lean to one side, a stagger; a staggering gait. L17. 2 A propensity, a penchant, a leaning. *US.* L18.

1 M. SCAMMELL Every lurch . . sent a spasm of agonizing pain coursing through his body. K. WATERHOUSE A lurch of panic as he realises he may be about to hear her voice.

¶Rare, and only in *la-* forms, bef. 19.

lurch /ləːtʃ/ *v.*[1]*t.* ME. [Rel. to LURCH *n.*[1]] 1 Beat in a game of skill, sometimes by a specified number or proportion of points. (Cf. LURCH *n.*[1] 3.) ME. b *fig.* Defeat. Now *rare* or *obs.* E18. 2 Leave in the lurch, disappoint, deceive. Now *rare* or *obs.* M17.

¶In isolated use bef. 17.

lurch /ləːtʃ/ *v.*[2] LME. [Perh. var. of LURK *v.*, infl. in meaning by LURCH *n.*[1]] †1 *v.i.* Remain in or about a place furtively or secretly, esp. with evil intent. Also, avoid company, sulk. LME–L18. b Of a dog, esp. a greyhound: run from the line, not pursue a quarry energetically. Chiefly as *lurching* vbl n. Only in 19. 2 *v.t.* Orig., start before and prevent (a person) from obtaining a fair share of food, profit, etc. Later, defraud, cheat, rob. *arch.* M16. †3 *v.t.* Secure (something) beforehand; engross, monopolize (a commodity). Also, get hold of by stealth, pilfer, steal. M16–M17. †b *v.i.* Get hold of something by stealth; pilfer, steal. L16–M17. 4 *v.t.* Pursue (rabbits etc.) with a lurcher. E18.

lurch /ləːtʃ/ *v.*[3]*i.* Orig. *Naut.* M19. [f. LURCH *n.*[3]] Make a lurch; lean suddenly over to one side; progress lurchingly; move suddenly, unsteadily, and without purpose; stagger.

D. H. LAWRENCE The car lurched and bumped in the great gaps. A. MACLEAN Halliday was . . lurching unsteadily in my direction, bottle in one hand and glass in the other. P. L. FERMOR In the fickle fashion of the very drunk, they lurched away into the night. J. FULLER The boat lurched dangerously in the rocky inlet.

lurchingly *adv.* in a lurching manner M19.

lurcher /ˈləːtʃə/ *n.* E16. [f. LURCH *v.*[2] + -ER[1].] 1 A petty thief, a swindler. *arch.* E16. †2 A person who starts before and prevents another from obtaining a fair share, esp. of food; a glutton. M16–E17. 3 A crossbred dog, esp. the offspring of a greyhound and a collie or retriever, used esp. by poachers for pursuing hares and rabbits. M17. 4 A person who loiters or lies hidden in a suspicious manner; a spy. E18. 5 = BUM *n.*[1] 3. *slang. obs.* exc. *Hist.* L18.

lurdan /ˈləːd(ə)n/ *n.* & *a. arch.* ME. [OFr. *lourdin*, f. *lourd* heavy, *lort* foolish f. L *luridus* LURID.] A *n.* A dull, incapable, idle, or rascally person; a sluggard, a vagabond, a loafer. ME. B *adj.* Worthless, ill-bred, lazy. LME.

lure /lʊə, ljʊə/ *n.*[1] ME. [OFr. *luere* (mod. *leurre*), f. Gmc, prob. rel. to MHG *luoder*, G *Luder* bait.] 1 A falconer's apparatus for recalling a hawk, consisting of a bunch of feathers attached to a long cord or thong, within which the hawk finds its food while being trained. ME. 2 A thing which allures, entices, or tempts; the enticing quality *of* a pursuit etc. LME. 3a A trap, a snare. Chiefly *fig.* LME. b A means of enticing fish or animals to be caught; a decoy. L17. 4 *Her.* a A charge representing a hawk's lure, consisting of two birds' wings with the points directed downwards, and joined above by a ring attached to a cord. L16. b *in lure*, (of wings) with the points downwards and joined at the top. E17. 5

The cry of a falconer recalling a hawk; *fig.* an alluring cry. M17.

1 B. HINES Billy . . began to swing the lure The hawk turned and stooped at it. 2 C. MCCULLOUGH The sound of his piper drawing him into battle was the sweetest lure in the world. D. LEAVITT There was the lure of the unknown, the unknowable. 3a DISRAELI The colonel fell into the lure only through his carelessness. b *National Observer* (*US*) I have fished with a good many lures.

lure /lʊə/ *n.*[2] M19. [Da. & Norw. *lur*, ON *lur*. Cf. LUR *n.*[1]] A long curved trumpet, used for calling cattle. Also called *velour*.

lure /lʊə, ljʊə/ *v.* LME. [f. LURE *n.*[1]] 1 *v.t.* Recall (a hawk) by casting the lure; call (a hawk) to the lure. LME. 2 *v.t.* Allure, entice, tempt. Also foll. by *out of*, *away from*, etc. LME. †3 *v.t.* Train (a hawk) to come to the lure. Now *rare*. L15–L16. 4 *v.i.* Call to a hawk while casting the lure. Now *rare*. M16. †b Call loudly (*at*). Only in 17. †5 *v.i.* Set a trap (*for*); entrap. L16–E18.

2 S. BELLOW It was a mistake to be drawn or lured out of his taciturnity. C. SANDBURG Painted women under the gas lamp luring the farm boys.

luringly *adv.* in a luring or enticing manner L19.

lurement /ˈlʊəm(ə)nt, ˈljʊə-/ *n. rare.* L16. [f. LURE *v.* + -MENT.] Allurement.

lurer *n.pl.* see LUR *n.*[1]

Lurex /ˈljʊərɛks/ *n.* Also **l-**. M20. [Origin unkn.] (Proprietary name for) a type of yarn which incorporates a metallic thread; fabric made from this yarn.

Lurgi /ˈlʊəgi, ˈləːgi/ *n.* M20. [f. the *Lurgi* Gesellschaft für Wärmetechnik m.b.H., of Frankfurt, Germany.] Used *attrib.* to designate a method of gasification suitable for low-grade coal such as lignite by reaction with steam and oxygen at high pressure.

Lurgi gas, plant, process.

lurgy /ˈləːgi/ *n. joc.* M20. [Origin unkn.] A (non-existent) highly infectious disease frequently referred to in the radio comedy series the Goon Show (see GOON *n.* 5); an unspecified minor illness. Chiefly in *the dreaded lurgy*

H. MACINNES I had caught the dreaded swamp lurgy.

lurid /ˈlʊərɪd, ˈljʊə-/ *a.* M17. [L *luridus*, f. base also of *luror* wan or yellow colour: see -ID[1].] 1 Pale and dismal in colour; wan and sallow; of a ghastly hue. M17. 2 Shining with a red glow or glare amid darkness. Also, vivid or glowing in colour. E18. b *hyperbol.* Having an unnatural glare. M18. 3 *Bot.* & *Zool.* Yellowish- or dingy brown. Now *rare*. M18. 4 *fig.* Ominous; sensational, horrifying; showy, gaudy. M19.

1 J. A. SYMONDS A leaden glare . . makes the snow and ice more lurid. 2 T. WILLIAMS The kitchen now suggests that sort of lurid nocturnal brilliance. I. MCEWAN The first course was in place, each melon slice with its lurid cherry. b DISRAELI The lurid glare of the anaconda's eye. 4 M. ANGELOU The lurid tales we read. E. SAINTSBURY Macdonald paints a picture of poverty . . equalled only by Dickens in its lurid detail.

luridly *adv.* L18. **luridness** *n.* M18.

lurk /ləːk/ *n.* Now chiefly *slang.* E19. [f. LURK *v.*] 1 The action of prowling about. Chiefly in *on the lurk. rare.* E19. 2a A method of fraud. M19. b A scheme, a dodge; a plan of action, a racket; a method of profitable business. Chiefly *Austral.* & *NZ.* E20. c A job. *Austral.* & *NZ.* E20. 3 An idle person, a loafer. *dial.* M19. 4 A hiding place; a place frequented by a particular person or class of people. E20.

lurk /ləːk/ *v.i.* ME. [Perh. f. LOUR *v.* + frequent. suff. *-k* as in *talk*. Cf. LG *lurken* shuffle along, Norw. *lurka* sneak away.] 1 Be hidden; lie in ambush; conceal oneself, esp. furtively, *in*, *under*, *about*, etc. Formerly also, live in concealment or retirement. ME. †b Shirk work; idle. M16–L18. 2 Move about secretively and furtively; steal *along*, *away*, *out*. Now *rare*. ME. 3 Escape notice, exist unobserved, be latent. LME. †4 Peer furtively or slyly. LME–E16. 5 Defeat in a game of chance. Chiefly as *lurked* ppl a. *slang.* E20.

1 A. UTTLEY Something was behind the oak tree, hidden, lurking. A. SILLITOE Scorpions lurk under loose stones. **lurking-place** a hiding place. 2 THACKERAY The main thoroughfare . . up which John lurks to bed. 3 R. BURNS Where the bluebell and gowan lurk lowly unseen. G. CLARE Behind the imposing façade of imperial splendour lurked defeat, poverty and fear. 5 C. MORGAN Four straight aces. Good enough? You're lurked, Sandford.

lurking *a.* that lurks; concealed, latent, semi-conscious: LME. **lurkingly** *adv.* M16. **lurky** *a.* (*rare*) tending to lurk L19.

lurker /ˈləːkə/ *n.*[1] ME. [f. LURK *v.* + -ER[1].] 1 A person who lurks. ME. 2 A begging impostor; a petty thief. *slang.* M19.

lurker /ˈləːkə/ *n.*[2] E19. [Origin unkn.] One of a group of three boats used in pilchard fishing, from which the fishing operation is directed.

lurry /ˈlʌri/ *n. obs.* exc. *dial.* L16. [Alt. of LIRIPIPE.] 1 Something said by rote; a lesson, a set speech, patter. L16. 2 A confused assemblage or mass. E17. 3 A confusion of voices; a babel, a hubbub, an outcry. M17.

Lusatian /luːˈseɪʃ(ə)n/ *n.* & *a.* M16. [f. med.L *Lusatia* (see below) + -AN.] A *n.* 1 A native or inhabitant of Lusatia, an area of eastern Germany between the Elbe and the Oder; *esp.* a Sorb. M16. 2 The West Slavonic language of Lusatia, Sorbian. L19. B *adj.* Of or pertaining to Lusatia or its inhabitants or language, Sorbian. M19.

luscious /ˈlʌʃəs/ *a.* & *n.* LME. [Perh. alt. of shortened form of DELICIOUS. Cf. also LUSH *a.*] 1 Richly sweet in taste or smell; *colloq.* delicious. LME. 2 Excessively sweet, cloying, sickly; (esp. of language or literary style) overrich in sound, imagery, or voluptuous suggestion. M16. 3 Orig., appealing to a lascivious taste, salacious, voluptuous. Later, voluptuously attractive, sexually desirable. E17.

1 A. G. GARDINER Pears that . . melted rich and luscious in the mouth. J. HUXLEY Fellows comfortably digested their luscious meal. 2 T. BIRCH A luscious Style stuffed with gawdy Metaphors and Fancy. HAZLITT A stream of luscious panegyrics. M. DONOVAN Without the addition of water . . the resulting wine would be luscious and heavy. 3 POPE Cantharides . . Whose use old Bards describe in luscious rhymes. E. PIZZEY A mole . . highlighted her luscious mouth.

lusciously *adv.* M16. **lusciousness** *n.* L16.

†**lush** *n.*[1] *rare.* LME–L19. [f. LUSH *v.*[1]] A stroke, a blow.

lush /lʌʃ/ *n.*[2] *slang.* L18. [Origin uncertain: perh. joc. f. LUSH *a.*] 1 Liquor, alcoholic drink. L18. 2 A drinking-bout. M19. 3 A drunkard, *N. Amer.* an alcoholic. L19.

1 N. MAILER Stoned with lush, with pot. 3 A. LURIE His wife's a lush and she screws around. R. JAFFE For him to make her mother stay dry he first had to admit she was a lush.

Comb.: **lushbum** a drunkard; **lush drum** a disreputable drinking-resort; **lush-head** a drunkard, an alcoholic.

lush /lʌʃ/ *a.* LME. [Perh. alt. of LASH *a.* by assoc. w. LUSCIOUS.] 1 Lax, flaccid; soft, tender. *obs.* exc. *dial.* LME. 2a Of vegetation, esp. grass: succulent and luxuriant. E17. b Characterized by luxuriance of vegetation. Also foll. by *with*. E19. c Luxurious; (of a woman) voluptuously attractive. M19. 3 Of a colour: deep and rich. M18.

1 T. BLUNDEVILLE The flesh of . . all his bodie is lush and feeble. 2a SHELLEY In the warm hedge grew lush eglantine. E. HEMINGWAY The grass was lush underfoot. b KEATS The year Grows lush in juicy stalks. LYTTON Hedges . . all lush with convolvulus and honeysuckle. c T. HARDY The aesthetic, sensuous, pagan pleasure in natural life and lush womanhood. D. LESSING The former hotel dining room, lush to the point of lubricity.

lushly *adv.* LME. **lushness** *n.* E20.

lush /lʌʃ/ *v.*[1] *obs.* exc. *dial.* ME. [Perh. var. of LASH *v.*[1]] 1 *v.i.* Rush, dash; come *down* with a rush. ME. 2 Strike. ME.

lush /lʌʃ/ *v.*[2] *slang.* E19. [f. LUSH *n.*[2]] 1 *v.t.* Ply with alcoholic liquor. E19. 2a *v.i.* & *t.* (w. *it*). Drink alcoholic liquor. E19. b *v.t.* Drink (alcoholic liquor). M19. 3 Foll. by *up*: a *v.i.* Get drunk. E20. b *v.t.* Ply with drink, make (a person) drunk. E20. c *v.t.* Provide with a luxurious standard of living. E20.

lusher *n.* an excessively self-indulgent person, *esp.* one who drinks to excess L19.

Lushai /ˈluːʃʌɪ/ *n.* & *a.* M19. [Lushai.] A *n.* Pl. same, **-s**. 1 A member of a people inhabiting a mountainous region in the Indian subcontinent between Myanmar (Burma) and Bangladesh. M19. 2 The Tibeto-Burman language of this people. L19. B *adj.* Of or pertaining to the Lushai or their language. M19.

lushburg /ˈlʌʃbəːg/ *n.* Long *obs.* exc. *Hist.* ME. [Alt. of *Luxembourg*: see LUXEMBOURGER.] A base coin made in imitation of the sterling or silver penny and imported from Luxembourg in the reign of Edward III.

Lushington /ˈlʌʃɪŋtən/ *n. arch. slang.* E19. [The 'City of *Lushington*', a convivial society which met at the Harp Tavern, Russell Street, London, prob. w. punning allus. to LUSH *n.*[2]] Drunkenness. Also, a drunkard.

lushy /ˈlʌʃi/ *a.*[1] & *n. slang.* E19. [f. LUSH *n.*[2] + -Y[1], -Y[6].] A *adj.* Intoxicated, drunk. E19. B *n.* A drunkard, an alcoholic. M20.

lushy /ˈlʌʃi/ *a.*[2] *rare.* E19. [f. LUSH *a.* + -Y[1].] 1 = LUSH *a.* 3. E19. 2 = LUSCIOUS *a.* L19.

Lusian /ˈluːsɪən/ *a.* & *n. poet.* L18. [L *Lusi-* in *Lusitania* (see next) etc. + -AN.] = LUSITANIAN.

Lusitanian /luːsɪˈteɪnɪən/ *a.* & *n.* L16. [f. L *Lusitania* (see below) + -AN.] A *adj.* 1 Of or pertaining to Lusitania, an ancient province of Hispania, mainly corresponding to modern Portugal; (chiefly *poet.*) of or pertaining to Portugal. L16. 2 *Bot.* & *Zool.* Of, pertaining to, or designating a part of the flora and fauna of the British Isles found particularly also in SW Europe, esp. Portugal. E20. B *n.* A native or inhabitant of Lusitania or (chiefly *poet.*) Portugal. E17.

lusk /lʌsk/ *a. obs.* exc. *dial.* L18. [f. next.] Lazy, sluggish.

†**lusk** *v.* & *n.* ME. [Origin unkn.] A *v.i.* Lie hidden; lie idly or at ease; skulk. ME–M17. B *n.* An idle or lazy person, a sluggard. LME–L17.

†**luskish** *a.* E16–E19. [f. LUSK *n.* + -ISH[1].] Slothful, lazy, sluggish.

†**luskishly** *adv.* M16–M17. †**luskishness** *n.* M16–M17.

lusky /ˈlʌski/ *a.* Long *obs.* exc. *dial.* E17. [f. LUSK *n.* + -Y[1].] Lazy, sluggish.

Luso- /ˈluːsəʊ/ *comb. form.* [f. *Lusitania*: see LUSITANIAN, -O-.] Forming adjs. and ns. w. the senses 'of Lusitania or Portugal', 'Lusitanian or Portuguese and —', as *Luso-Brazilian*, *Luso-Hispanic*, etc.

lusophone /ˈluːsəfəʊn/ *a.* L20. [f. LUSO- + -PHONE.] Portuguese-speaking.

lusory /ˈluːs(ə)ri/ *a.* Now *rare.* M17. [L *lusorius* belonging to a player, f. *lusor* player, f. *lus-* pa. ppl stem of *ludere* play: see -ORY[2].] Used as a pastime; playful, sportive; (of a composition) written in a playful style.

lust /lʌst/ *n.* [OE *lust* corresp. to OFris., OHG, G *lust*, ON *losti*, Goth. *lustus*, f. Gmc base repr. also by LIST *v.*[1]] †1 Pleasure, delight (also foll. by *in*, *to*, *unto*). Also (*poet.*), a source of pleasure or delight. OE–E17. b In *pl.* Pleasures. OE–LME. c Liking towards a person. Foll. by *to*. LME–M16. †2 Desire, appetite, inclination; an instance of this. Foll. by *of*, *to*, *to do*. *obs.* exc. as passing into sense 6. OE. 3 A sensuous appetite or desire considered as sinful or leading to sin. Usu. in *pl.* OE. 4 Strong (esp. uncontrollable) sexual appetite or desire. OE. †5 Vigour, life. ME–L17. 6 A passionate desire *for*, *to do*; a passionate enjoyment *of*. L17.

2 W. SCLATER I have neither lust nor leasure to enter the question. 3 R. NIEBUHR Man's lusts are fed by his imagination. 4 C. S. FORESTER He was hot with desire, dizzy with lust. S. KITZINGER So intensely sexual, that, driven by lust, they ravaged men's bodies and souls. R. CHRISTIANSEN Hogg had taken the noble principle of free love as an excuse to indulge mere lust. 6 H. J. LASKI The lust of power sets man against his neighbour to the profit of the rich. A. J. TOYNBEE The lust for taking human life had become obsessive—indeed, maniacal. J. WAIN They punched, elbowed, kicked and tore each other with a real lust to hurt.

lust /lʌst/ *v.* ME. [f. the n.] †1 *v.t.* Please, delight. ME–M16. †2 *v.i.* Desire, choose, wish, (*to do*). LME–E17. **3** *v.i.* Have a strong or excessive (*spec.* sexual) desire, feel lust. Foll. by *after, for*. E16.

3 M. S. POWER I've seen them lusting for blood once they start hunting. P. D. JAMES He had a wife he lusted after but didn't love.

luster /ˈlʌstə/ *n.*[1] Now *rare*. L16. [f. LUST *v.* + -ER[1].] A person who lusts.

luster *n.*[2], *n.*[3], *v.* see LUSTRE *n.*[1], *n.*[2], *v.*

lustered *a.* see LUSTRED.

lustering *n.* see LUSTRING *n.*[2]

lustful /ˈlʌstfʊl, -f(ə)l/ *a.* OE. [f. LUST *n.* + -FUL.] **1** Having a strong or excessive desire; eagerly or inordinately desirous *of, to do*. *arch.* OE. †**2** Delightful, pleasurable. Only in ME. **3** Vigorous, lively. *arch.* M16. **4** Full of or characterized by lust; pertaining to or manifesting lust. L16.

4 DENNIS POTTER Arthur was indeed a lustful psychotic, . . perpetually hard in the loins.

lustfully *adv.* OE. **lustfulness** *n.* OE.

lust-house /ˈlʌsthaʊs/ *n.* Now *rare*. L16. [Du. *lusthuis*, G *Lusthaus*, f. *Lust* pleasure + *Haus* HOUSE *n.*[1]] A German or Dutch country house.

†**lustick** *a.* & *adv.* Also **-ig**. E17. [Du. *lustig*.] A *adj.* Merry. E–M17. **B** *adv.* Merrily. Only in 17.

lustihead /ˈlʌstɪhɛd/ *n. arch.* LME. [f. LUSTY + -HEAD.] = LUSTINESS.

lustihood /ˈlʌstɪhʊd/ *n. arch.* L16. [f. LUSTY + -HOOD.] Lustiness, vigour.

lustily /ˈlʌstɪli/ *adv.* ME. [f. LUSTY + -LY[2].] †**1** With pleasure or delight. ME–M16. **2** With vigour or energy; heartily. ME. †**3** With lust or sexual desire; carnally. LME–L16.

2 J. B. MORTON The twelve dwarfs cheered lustily, waving their nondescript hats in the air. B. REID I learned to sing . . lustily enough for both of us, because he was too shy.

lustiness /ˈlʌstɪnɪs/ *n.* ME. [f. LUSTY + -NESS.] **1** Vigour; liveliness. ME. †**2** Pleasure, delight. LME–M16. †**3** Sexual desire, lustfulness. LME–E17.

lustless /ˈlʌs(t)lɪs/ *a.* ME. [f. LUST *n.* + -LESS.] †**1** Without vigour or energy. ME–E17. †**2** Without pleasure or delight. Only in 16. **3** Without lust or sexual desire. Now chiefly *joc.* L16.

lustly /ˈlʌstli/ *a.* Now *rare* or *obs.* ME. [f. LUST *n.* + -LY[1].] **1** Pleasant, delightful. ME. †**2** Lustful; carnal. ME–E17.

lustra *n.pl.* see LUSTRUM.

lustral /ˈlʌstr(ə)l/ *a.* M16. [L *lustralis*, f. as LUSTRUM + -AL[1].] **1** Pertaining to, of the nature of, or used in purification rites; purificatory. M16. **2** Occurring every five years; quinquennial. L18.

lustrate /ˈlʌstreɪt/ *v.* E17. [L *lustrat-* pa. ppl stem of *lustrare* purify by lustral rites, go round, etc., f. as LUSTRUM: see -ATE[3].] †**1** *v.t.* View, survey. E–M17. †**2** *v.i.* & *t.* Pass or go *through* or through (a place). M17–E18. **3** *v.t.* Purify by expiatory sacrifice, ceremonial washing, or other religious rite. M17.

lustrative *a.* of or pertaining to ritual purification L19. **lustratory** /ˈlʌstrət(ə)ri/ *a.* (*rare*) lustral, expiatory M18.

lustration /lʌˈstreɪʃ(ə)n/ *n.* E17. [L *lustratio(n-)*, f. as prec.: see -ATION.] **1** The action or an act of lustrating something or someone. E17. **b** *fig.* Spiritual or moral purification. M17. **c** *gen.* Washing. Chiefly *joc.* E19. **2** The action or an act of viewing or surveying a place, an army, etc. E17.

lustre /ˈlʌstə/ *n.*[1] Also ***luster**. E16. [Fr. f. It. *lustro*, f. *lustrare* f. L = illuminate, f. LUSTRUM.] **1** The quality or condition of shining by reflected light; a sheen, a gloss. Also occas., a glint. Freq. w. qualifying adj. E16. **b** A substance used to impart a sheen or gloss to an object. E18. **c** An iridescent metallic decorative surface on ceramics; the glaze used to produce this; *gen.* any shining or reflective finish (as on a photograph etc.). E19. **d** In full *lustreware*. Pottery or porcelain with an iridescent metallic glaze. E19. **2** Luminosity, brilliance, bright light. M16. **b** A shining object. M18. **3** *fig.* Brilliance, splendour, glory, distinction, (of character, achievement, etc.); radiance, splendid appearance. M16. †**b** Something giving glory or splendour. E–M17. **4** Any of a decorative group of prismatic glass pendants attached to a chandelier or other ornament; a cut-glass chandelier or candelabrum. L17. **5** A thin dress-fabric with a fine cotton (formerly also silk or mohair) warp and worsted weft, and a glossy surface; any fabric with a sheen or gloss. M19.

1 C. DARWIN A coating of a hard glossy substance with a pearly lustre. W. H. G. KINGSTON The wool appeared very long, soft, fine, and of a silky lustre. N. FREELING Even the gilt picture frames had lost all their lustre. c *moonlight lustre*: see MOONLIGHT *n.* & *a.* VITREOUS *lustre*. 2 DICKENS The sun was shining with uncommon lustre. 3 H. JAMES He had never been dazzled by his sister's intellectual lustre. R. GRAVES Restore the old lustre to the Roman military name. K. CLARK The men through whose greatness . . our own lives have received some occasional lustre. 4 B. MASON The roar was . . deafening, and all the lustres in the big chandelier were tinkling.

lustreful *a.* lustrous M19. **lustreless** *a.* E19.

lustre /ˈlʌstə/ *n.*[2] Also ***luster**. LME. [Anglicized f. LUSTRUM.] A period of five years.

lustre /ˈlʌstə/ *v.* Also ***luster**. L16. [f. LUSTRE *n.*[1]] †**1** *v.t.* Make illustrious; make attractive. L16–M17. **2** *v.i.* Be or become lustrous. Now *rare*. L16. **3** *v.t.* Give a lustre to (cloth, pottery, etc.). L19.

lustred /ˈlʌstəd/ *a.* Also ***lustered**. L16. [f. LUSTRE *n.*[1], *v.*: see -ED[2], -ED[1].] Esp. of cloth or pottery: having a lustre.

†**lustrifical** *a.* M17–M18. [f. L *lustrificus* (f. as LUSTRUM + -FIC) + -AL[1].] Purificatory.

lustring /ˈlʌstrɪŋ/ *n.*[1] & *a. arch.* Also **-trine** /-triːn/. L17. [f. Fr. *lustrine* or its source It. *lustrino*, f. *lustro* lustre, w. assim. to -ING[3]. Cf. earlier LUTESTRING *n.*[1] & *a.*] **A** *n.* A glossy silk dress-fabric. Also, a similar satin-weave fabric made of silk, wool, or rayon, or a combination of these. L17. **B** *adj.* Made of lustring. E20.

lustring /ˈlʌstrɪŋ/ *n.*[2] Also ***luster-**. L19. [f. LUSTRE *v.* + -ING[1].] The action of LUSTRE *v.*; the manner in which something is lustred.

†**lustrious** *a. rare*. M17–M18. [f. LUSTRE *n.*[1] after *illustrious*.] Splendid, lustrous.

lustrous /ˈlʌstrəs/ *a.* E17. [f. LUSTRE *n.*[1] + -OUS.] Having a lustre or a sheen; shining; *fig.* splendid.

lustrously *adv.* M19. **lustrousness** *n.* M19.

lustrum /ˈlʌstrəm/ *n.* Pl. **-tra** /-trə/, **-trums**. L16. [L, orig., a purificatory sacrifice after a quinquennial census, later also, a period of five years: ult. origin unkn.] A period of five years.

lusty /ˈlʌsti/ *a.* ME. [f. LUST *n.* + -Y[1].] **1** Of singing, a festivity, etc., (formerly also of a person): merry, cheerful, lively. Now *arch.* & *dial.* ME. †**2** Pleasing, pleasant, agreeable; attractive. ME–E17. †**3** Full of desire, desirous, (*to, to do, for*); *spec.* full of lust or sexual desire, lustful. ME–L17. **4** Healthy, strong, physically vigorous. LME. †**b** Of an inanimate agency: very effective, strong, powerful. L16–L17. †**5** Insolent, arrogant. E16–L17. **6** Of a physical action, esp. one involving effort: energetic, vigorous. Of a meal etc.: hearty, abundant. M17. †**7** Of a thing: massive, large. M17–M19. **8** Of a person: massively built; stout, fat. *arch.* L18.

1 SIR W. SCOTT The lusty banqueting with sweetmeats and comfits. 4 R. CROMPTON Singing 'Christians Awake!' at the top of his lusty young voice. *News on Sunday* She was delivered of a lusty black-haired boy. 6 S. W. BAKER She gave her a maternal welcome . . bestowing lusty blows on her back.

lusus /ˈluːsəs, ˈljuː-/ *n.* Pl. same /-suːs/, **-suses**. E17. [L *lusus naturae* a sport of nature.] In full *lusus naturae* /nəˈtjʊəriː, -rʌɪ/. A freak of nature, an abnormal formation, a natural curiosity.

lutaceous /luːˈteɪʃəs, ljuː-/ *a.* E20. [f. L *lutum* mud + -ACEOUS.] *Geol.* Of sedimentary rock: of the nature of a lutite, of argillaceous composition.

lutanist *n.* var. of LUTENIST.

lute /luːt, ljuːt/ *n.*[1] ME. [OFr. *leüt*, *lut* (mod. *luth*), prob. f. Prov. *laüt*, f. Arab. *al-ʿūd* wood (prob. repr. a Hispano-Arab. or N. Afr. pronunc.): see AL-[2]. Cf. LAUD *n.*[2], OUD.] **1** A musical instrument having a body with rounded pear-shaped back and a neck, and having six to thirteen pairs of strings which are plucked (much used from the 14th to the 17th cents.). Also, any of a large class of stringed musical instruments having a body with a neck, including the classic lute and also bowed and flat-backed instruments. ME. **2** A stop in some types of harpsichord. ME.

Comb.: **lute harpsichord** *Hist.* = LAUTENCLAVICYMBEL; **lute-pin** each of the pegs or screws for tuning the strings of a lute.

lute /luːt, ˈljuːt/ *n.*[2] LME. [(O)Fr. *lut* or med.L *lutum*, spec. use of L *lutum* mud, potter's clay.] **1** Clay or cement used to stop a hole, make a joint airtight, coat a crucible, protect a graft, etc.; a particular kind of this substance. LME. †**2** Mud. L17–M18. **3** An airtight rubber seal or washer for a jar etc. L19.

lute /luːt, ljuːt/ *n.*[3] In sense 1 also **loot**. L19. [Du. *loet*.] **1** A ladle or skimmer used in the production of salt to remove scum from a brine-pan. *dial.* L19. **2** A straight-edged piece of wood for removing excess clay from a brick-mould. *US*. L19.

lute /luːt, ljuːt/ *v.*[1] Now *rare*. LME. [f. LUTE *n.*[1]] **1** *v.i.* Play the lute. LME. **2** *v.t.* Play (a tune) on the lute. LME.

lute /luːt, ljuːt/ *v.*[2]*t.* LME. [L *lutare* daub with mud, f. *lutum* LUTE *n.*[2]] **1** Coat or cover with lute; seal or stop (as) with lute. LME. **2** Fasten, fix, cement (as) with lute. Freq. w. advs., as *down, on, together*, etc. LME.

luteal /ˈluːtɪəl, ˈljuː-/ *a.* E20. [f. L *luteus* yellow + -AL[1].] *Physiol.* Of or pertaining to the corpus luteum.

lutecium *n.* see LUTETIUM.

lutein /ˈluːtɪɪn, ˈljuː-/ *n.* M19. [f. L *luteum* egg-yolk (use as n. of neut. of *luteus* yellow) + -IN[1].] *Biochem.* A yellow xanthophyll pigment present in the leaves of plants, in egg-yolk, and in the corpus luteum.

luteinize /ˈluːtɪnʌɪz/ *v.t.* Also **-ise**. E20. [f. prec. + -IZE.] *Physiol.* Cause to produce lutein; cause to form a corpus luteum. Chiefly as *luteinized*, *luteinizing* ppl adjs.

luteinizing hormone: secreted by the adenohypophysis and (in females) promoting ovulation and the formation of the corpus luteum, (in males) promoting secretion of androgens.

luteiniˈzation *n.* the formation of the corpus luteum from the cells that remain of the Graafian follicle after expulsion of the ovum, with accompanying production of lutein E20.

lutenist /ˈluːt(ə)nɪst, ˈljuː-/ *n.* Also **lutanist**. E17. [med.L *lutanista*, f. *lutana* lute: see -IST.] A person who plays the lute.

luteo- /ˈluːtɪəʊ, ˈljuː-/ *comb. form* of L *luteus* (neut. *luteum*) yellow, esp. w. the sense 'of the corpus luteum': see -O-.

luteolysis /-ˈɒlɪsɪs/ *n.* degeneration of the corpus luteum, as when a discharged ovum is not fertilized M20. **luteoˈlytic** *a.* relating to or effecting luteolysis M20.

luteotrophic /ˌluːtɪə(ʊ)ˈtrəʊfɪk, -ˈtrɒfɪk; ˌljuː-/ *a.* Also **-tropic** /-ˈtrəʊpɪk, -ˈtrɒpɪk/. M20. [f. LUTEO- + -TROPHIC.] *Physiol.* Acting to maintain the corpus luteum during pregnancy.

luteotrophin /-ˈtrəʊfɪn/ *n.* a luteotrophic hormone M20.

luteous /ˈluːtɪəs, ˈljuː-/ *a.*[1] M17. [f. L *luteus* yellow + -OUS.] Chiefly *Bot.* & *Zool.* Of a deep orange-yellow colour.

†**luteous** *a.*[2] M17–M18. [f. L *luteus*, f. *lutum* mud: see -OUS.] Of or pertaining to mud.

luter /ˈluːtə, ˈljuː-/ *n.* Now *rare*. ME. [f. LUTE *v.*[1] + -ER[1].] A lutenist.

lutescent /luːˈtɛs(ə)nt, ljuː-/ *a.* E19. [f. L *luteus* yellow + -ESCENT.] Chiefly *Bot.* & *Zool.* Inclining to yellow; yellowish.

lutestring /ˈluːtstrɪŋ, ˈljuː-/ *n.*[1] & *a.* M17. [Alt. f. as LUSTRING *n.*[1] after next.] **A** *n.* A glossy silk fabric; a ribbon made of this fabric. M17. **B** *adj.* Made of lutestring. E18.

lutestring *n.*[2] see next.

lute-string /ˈluːtstrɪŋ, ljuː-/ *n.* Also (esp. in sense 2) **lutestring**. L15. [f. LUTE *n.*[1] + STRING *n.*] 1 A string of or for a lute. L15. 2 Any of several noctuid moths, esp. of the genus *Tethea*, having lines resembling the strings of a lute on their wings. E19.

2 POPLAR *lutestring*.

Lutetian /luːˈtiːʃ(ə)n, ljuː-/ *a.* & *n.* M18. [f. L *Lutetia* (see below) + -AN.] A *adj.* 1 Of or pertaining to Lutetia, an ancient city on the site of modern Paris, France; of or pertaining to Paris. M18. 2 *Geol.* Designating or pertaining to a stage of the middle Eocene typified by formations in the Paris basin. L19. B *n. Geol.* The Lutetian stage of the Eocene. E20.

lutetium /luːˈtiːʃɪəm, -sɪəm, ljuː-/ *n.* Also (earlier, now *rare*) **-cium**. E20. [Fr. *lutécium*, f. *Lutèce* L *Lutetia*: see prec., -IUM.] A metallic chemical element, atomic no. 71, that is the heaviest member of the lanthanide series. (Symbol Lu.)

luth /luːθ/ *n.* L19. [Fr., perh. = *luth* LUTE *n.*[1]] The leatherback turtle, *Dermochelys coriacea*.

Lutheran /ˈluːθ(ə)r(ə)n, ˈljuː-/ *n.* & *a.* E16. [f. *Luther* (see below) Ger. religious leader + -AN.] A *n.* A follower of the German Protestant theologian Martin Luther (1483–1546) or his doctrines; *spec.* a member of any of the (chiefly German and Scandinavian) Churches founded on the doctrines of Luther, which accept the Augsburg Confession of 1530, with justification by faith alone as a cardinal doctrine. E16. B *adj.* Of or pertaining to Luther or his theology; adhering to the doctrines of Luther. M16.

Lutheranize *v.t.* & *i.* make or become Lutheran M19.

Lutheranism /ˈluːθ(ə)r(ə)nɪz(ə)m, ˈljuː-/ *n.* M16. [f. prec. + -ISM.] The body of doctrine taught by Luther and his followers; adherence to Lutheran doctrines.

Lutherism /ˈluːθərɪz(ə)m, ˈljuː-/ *n.* L17. [f. as prec. + -ISM.] = LUTHERANISM.

Lutherist *n.* L19.

luthern /ˈluːθ(ə)n, ˈljuː-/ *n.* M17. [Perh. alt. of LUCARNE.] More fully *luthern-window*. A dormer window.

luthier /ˈluːtɪə, ˈljuː-/ *n.* L19. [Fr., f. *luth* LUTE *n.*[1]: see -IER.] A maker of stringed instruments, *spec.* of the violin family.

lutidine /ˈluːtɪdiːn, ˈljuː-/ *n.* M19. [Partial anagram of TOLUIDINE, a similar substance.] *Chem.* Any of a number of isomeric bases having the formula $C_6H_3(CH_3)_2NH_2$, which are dimethyl derivatives of aniline, and some of which occur in coal tar.

luting /ˈluːtɪŋ, ˈljuː-/ *n.* E16. [f. LUTE *v.*[2] + -ING[1].] 1 = LUTE *n.*[2] 1. E16. 2 The action of LUTE *v.*[2] E17. 3 A seal for closing an aperture, keeping out air or water, etc. E19.

lutino /luːˈtiːnəʊ/ *n.* & *a.* Pl. of n. **-os**. E20. [f. L *luteus* yellow, after ALBINO.] (A bird, usu. a cage-bird) having more yellow in its plumage than is usual for the species.

lutist /ˈluːtɪst, ljuː-/ *n.* E17. [f. LUTE *n.*[1] + -IST.] A lutenist. Also, a luthier.

lutite /ˈluːtʌɪt, ˈljuː-/ *n.* E20. [f. L *lutum* mud + -ITE[1].] *Geol.* A shale, mudstone, or other sedimentary rock made up very largely of argillaceous sediment.

Lutomer /ˈluːtəmə, ˈljuː-/ *n.* & *a.* M20. [*Ljutomer* (see below).] (Designating) any of various white wines, esp. riesling, produced in Ljutomer, a region in Slovenia, SE Europe.

luton /ˈluːtən/ *n.* Also **L-**. L20. [A town in Bedfordshire, England, where such vehicles are made.] 1 A part of the container of a lorry, van, horsebox, etc., which projects forwards over the cab. Also more fully *luton roof*. L20. 2 A vehicle with this type of container. Also more fully *luton van*. L20.

lutrine /ˈluːtrʌɪn, ˈljuː-/ *a.* L19. [f. L *lutra* otter: see -INE[1].] *Zool.* Of, pertaining to, or designating the mustelid subfamily Lutrinae, which comprises the otters.

lutulent /ˈluːtjʊl(ə)nt, ˈljuː-/ *a. literary.* Now *rare*. L16. [L *lutulentus*, f. *lutum* mud: see -ULENT.] Muddy, turbid.

lutulence *n.* (*rare*) E18.

Lutyenesque /lʌtjənˈɛsk/ *a.* M20. [f. *Lutyens* (see below) + -ESQUE.] Resembling or characteristic of the style of the English architect Sir Edwin Lutyens (1869–1944).

lutz /lʊts/ *n.* M20. [Prob. f. Gustave *Lussi* (b. 1898), Swiss figure-skater who introduced it.] A jump in ice-skating in which the skater takes off from the outside back edge of one skate and lands, after a complete rotation in the air, on the outside back edge of the opposite skate.

luv /lʌv, lʊv/ *n.* & *v. non-standard.* M19. [Respelling to suggest a dial. or colloq. pronunc.] A *n.* = LOVE *n.*; *esp.* = LOVE *n.* 6 (freq. as a form of address). M19. B *v.t.* & *i.* = LOVE *v.* M19.

Luvian /ˈluːvɪən/ *n.* & *a.* Also **Luwian** /*also* ˈluːɪən/. E20. [f. *Luvia* a part of Asia Minor: see -IAN.] A *n.* A member of an ancient Anatolian people contemporary with the Hittites, known from cuneiform inscriptions; the language of this people. E20. B *adj.* Of or pertaining to the Luvians or their language. M20.

lux /lʌks/ *n.* Pl. **lux**. L19. [L = light.] *Physics.* The SI unit of illumination, equal to the illumination of a surface all of which is one metre from a uniform point source of light of unit intensity (now one candela), i.e. (as now defined) one lumen per square metre. (Symbol lx.)

luxmeter *n.* an instrument for measuring the brightness or illumination of a surface E20.

†**lux** *v.t.* Only in 18. [Fr. *luxer* or L *luxare*: see next.] = next.

luxate /ˈlʌkseɪt/ *v.t.* Now *rare*. E17. [L *luxat-* pa. ppl stem of *luxare*, f. *luxus* dislocated: see -ATE[3].] *Med.* Dislocate, put out of joint.

luxation /lʌkˈseɪʃ(ə)n/ *n.* M16. [L *luxatio(n-)*, f. as prec.: see -ATION.] *Med.* (A) dislocation.

luxe /lʌks, lʊks/ *n.* M16. [Fr. f. L *luxus*: see LUXURY.] (A) luxury. Cf. DE LUXE.

Luxembourgeois /ˈlʌks(ə)mbʊəʒwɑː/ *a.* & *n.* E20. [Fr., f. *Luxembourg* (see next) + *-ois* -ESE.] A *adj.* Of or pertaining to Luxembourg or its inhabitants. E20. B *n.* Pl. same. A native or inhabitant of Luxembourg, = next. M20.

Luxembourger /ˈlʌks(ə)mbəːgə/ *n.* Also **-burger**. E20. [f. *Luxembourg* (see below) + -ER[1]. Cf. G *Luxemburger*.] A native or inhabitant of the State of Luxembourg, which lies between Belgium, Germany, and France.

Luxemburgish /lʌks(ə)mˈbəːgɪʃ/ *n.* & *a.* Also **-isch**. M20. [G *Luxemburgisch*, f. *Luxemburg* Luxembourg + *-isch* -ISH[1].] (Of) the German dialect spoken by natives of Luxembourg. Also called *Letzeburgesch*.

luxullyanite /lʌkˈsʌlɪənʌɪt/ *n.* L19. [f. *Luxullian* (*Luxulyan*), a village in Cornwall + -ITE[1].] *Petrogr.* A porphyritic granite containing tourmaline in radiating clusters of needle-shaped crystals.

luxuriant /lʌgˈʒʊərɪənt, lʌgˈzjʊə-, lʌkˈsjʊə-/ *a.* M16. [L *luxuriant-* pres. ppl stem of *luxuriare* grow rank, f. *luxuria*: see LUXURY, -ANT[1].] 1 Producing abundantly, prolific. Now *rare*. M16. 2 Of invention, genius, etc.: exuberantly productive. Of speech, style, etc.: florid, richly ornate. E17. †b Excessively prosperous. M17–M18. 3 Of a plant, hair, etc.: growing profusely; lush. M17. 4 Luxurious. L17.

2 A. BAIN A luxuriant imagination implies the facility of retaining scenes of every description. 3 F. KING Her once luxuriant black hair had gone thin and grey. *Holiday Which?* The steep slopes are covered with luxuriant vegetation, . . a profusion of vines, . . and brilliantly coloured flowers. 4 C. GIBBON It was a splendid apartment, . . luxuriant to a degree.

luxuriance *n.* E18. **luxuriancy** *n.* (now *rare*) M17. **luxuriantly** *adv.* E18.

luxuriate /lʌgˈʒʊərɪeɪt, lʌgˈzjʊə-, lʌkˈsjʊə-/ *v.i.* E17. [L *luxuriat-* pa. ppl stem of *luxuriare*: see prec., -ATE[3].] 1 Of a plant, hair, etc.: grow profusely. Formerly also, (of a writer) be exuberantly productive. E17. †b *fig.* Grow or develop exuberantly *into*. M17–E19. 2 Revel *in*, take self-indulgent delight *in*; take one's ease, relax in comfort. E17.

1 SCOTT FITZGERALD Two fine growths of hair which luxuriated in either nostril. 2 E. FITZGERALD I had a long letter from Morton . . —he is still luxuriating at Venice. R. MACAULAY Mrs Cox told her the story . . , luxuriating in the tragic tale. C. MILNE I lay there luxuriating in the comfort.

luxuriˈation *n.* M19.

luxurious /lʌgˈʒʊərɪəs, lʌgˈzjʊə-, lʌkˈsjʊə-/ *a.* ME. [OFr. *luxurios* (mod. *-rieux*) f. L *luxuriosus*, f. *luxuria*: see LUXURY, -OUS.] †1 Lascivious, lecherous. ME–L17. †2 Outrageous, excessive. LME–M17. 3 Fond of luxury, self-indulgent, voluptuous. E17. 4 Characterized by luxury; of the nature of a luxury; sumptuously comfortable; supplied with luxuries. M17. 5 = LUXURIANT 3. Now *rare*. M17.

3 GLADSTONE A wealthy country, with a large leisured class, in a luxurious age. V. S. NAIPAUL Someone who felt her beauty entitled her to luxurious sensations. 4 A. WEST The polished mahogany . . seemed wonderfully luxurious to me. P. FITZGERALD A luxurious home was maintained in Hendon. J. HUXLEY Shops flaunted luxurious temptations after the austere essentials of wartime. 5 G. GISSING March rains had brought the vegetation into luxurious life.

luxuriously *adv.* M16. **luxuriousness** *n.* M16.

luxurist /ˈlʌkʃərɪst/ *n. rare.* L17. [f. next + -IST.] A person addicted to luxury.

luxury /ˈlʌkʃəri/ *n.* & *a.* ME. [OFr. *luxurie* var. of (also mod.) *luxure* f. L *luxuria*, f. *luxus* abundance, sumptuous enjoyment: see -Y[3].] A *n.* †1 Lechery, lust. ME–E19. †2 Luxuriance. Only in 17. 3 (Habitual indulgence in) choice or costly surroundings, possessions, food, etc.; luxuriousness. M17. 4 A means or source of luxurious enjoyment; *spec.* something desirable for comfort or enjoyment, but not indispensable. E18.

3 A. S. DALE He had grown up in upper-class luxury—taught by governesses. *Kuwait Times* People today want . . luxury and they want comfort. *in the lap of luxury*: see LAP *n.*[1] 4 C. S. LEWIS Luxuries . . such as first-class railway carriages and sleeping-cars. J. KRANTZ Valentine lay . . revelling in the luxury of putting her feet up. J. RULE Her expensive sports car, her one luxury always. P. TOYNBEE The guilty luxury of a day in bed.

B *adj.* Providing great comfort; expensive. E20.

R. P. JHABVALA We took suites of rooms on one floor of a high, huge luxury hotel. *Holiday Which?* It's not worth paying luxury prices to stay here.

lwei /ləˈweɪ/ *n.* L20. [Angolan name.] A monetary unit of Angola equal to one-hundredth of a kwanza.

-ly /lɪ/ *suff.*[1] [OE *-lić* = OFris., OS *-līk*, OHG *-līh* (Du. *-lijk*, G *-lich*), ON *-ligr*, *-legr*, Goth. *-leiks*, f. Gmc, f. base also of LICH.] Forming adjs. usu. f. ns. w. the senses (*a*) having the qualities of, characteristic of, befitting, as *beastly*, *cowardly*, *knightly*, *queenly*, *rascally*, *scholarly*, *womanly*; †(*b*) of or pertaining to, as (in early sense) *manly*; (*c*) recurring at intervals of, as *daily*, *hourly*, *weekly*, *yearly*.

-ly /lɪ/ *suff.*[2] [OE *līće* = OFris. *-like*, OS *-līko*, OHG *-līhho* (Du. *-lijk*, G *-lich*), ON *-liga*, Goth. *-leikō*, f. Gmc base of -LY[1] + adv.-forming suff.] Forming advs. (*a*) f. adjs. w. the senses 'in a — manner' or 'to a — degree', as *amusingly*, *deservedly*, *firstly*, *fully*, *greatly*, *happily*, *hourly*, *truly*; (*b*) f. ordinal numerals, denoting serial order, as *firstly*, *secondly*; (*c*) (now *rare*) f. adjs. ending in *-ly*, as *godlily*, *livelily*.

Lyaeus /lʌɪˈiːəs/ *n. literary. rare.* E17. [L f. Gk *Luaios* a surname of the god Bacchus.] Wine.

lyam /ˈlʌɪəm/ *n. obs.* exc. *Hist.* & *dial.* Also **lyme** /lʌɪm/. LME. [OFr. *liem* (mod. LIEN), f. L *ligamen* bond, f. *ligare* to tie. Cf. LIMER *n.*[1]] 1 A leash for a dog; *Her.* a charge representing this. LME. 2 More fully *lyam-hound*. A bloodhound. L15.

lyart /ˈlʌɪət/ *n.* & *a. obs.* exc. *dial.* Also **-ard** /-əd/. ME. [OFr. *liart* or med.L *liardus*.] A *n.* (A name for) a horse spotted with white or grey, a dapple grey. Long *rare*. ME. B *adj.* Of a horse: spotted with white or grey; dapple grey. Of hair: grey. LME.

lycaenid /lʌɪˈsiːnɪd/ *n.* & *a.* L19. [mod.L *Lycaenidae* (see below), f. *Lycaena* genus name, app. f. Gk *lukaina* she-wolf: see -ID[3].] A *n.* A butterfly of the family Lycaenidae, which includes the blues and the hairstreaks. L19. **B** *adj.* Of, pertaining to, or designating this family. E20.

lycanthrope /ˈlʌɪk(ə)nθrəʊp/ *n.* E17. [mod.L *lycanthropus* f. Gk *lukanthrōpos*: see next.] **1** A person with lycanthropy. E17. **2** A werewolf. M19.

lycanthropy /lʌɪˈkanθrəpi/ *n.* L16. [mod.L *lycanthropia* f. Gk *lukanthrōpia*, f. *lukanthrōpos*, f. *lukos* wolf + *anthrōpos* man: see -Y³.] **1** A form of madness in which a person believes himself or herself to be an animal (esp. a wolf) and behaves accordingly. L16. **2** The mythical transformation of a person into a wolf. Also called *werewolfery*, *werewolfism*. M19.

lycanˈthropic *a.* of or pertaining to lycanthropy; affected with lycanthropy: E19. **lycanthropist** *n.* = LYCANTHROPE E18.

lycaon /lɪˈkeɪɒn/ *n.* E19. [mod.L genus name f. Gk *lukaōn*, L *lycaon* wolflike animal.] = *hunting dog* (b) s.v. HUNTING *n.*

Lycaonian /lɪkeɪˈəʊnɪən/ *a.* & *n.* L16. [f. L *Lycaonia*, Gk *Lukaonia* (see below) + -AN.] **A** *adj.* Of or pertaining to Lycaonia, an ancient region in southern Asia Minor, its inhabitants, or the language used there. L16. **B** *n.* **1** The language of Lycaonia. L19. **2** A native or inhabitant of Lycaonia. E20.

lycée /lise (*pl. same*), ˈliːseɪ/ *n.* M19. [Fr. f. L LYCEUM.] A State secondary school in France.

lycéen /liseɛ̃ (*pl. same*)/ *n.* a pupil at a *lycée* L19.

Lyceum /lʌɪˈsiːəm/ *n.* L16. [L f. Gk *Lukeion* (sc. *gumnasion* GYMNASIUM) neut. of *Lukeios* epithet of Apollo (from whose neighbouring temple the Lyceum was named).] **1** The garden at Athens in which Aristotle taught his philosophy; Aristotelian philosophy and its adherents. L16. **2** = LYCÉE. E19. **3** *US Hist.* (**l-**.) An institution in which popular lectures were delivered on literary and scientific subjects. E19. **4** *Theatr.* [A theatre near the Strand in London, England.] Used *attrib.* to denote a melodramatic performance or style, formerly characteristic of this theatre. L19.

lych *n.* var. of LICH.

lychee /ˈlʌɪtʃiː, ˈlɪ-/ *n.* Also **lichee**, **litchi** /ˈlɪ-/. L16. [Chin. *lìzhī*.] The fruit of the Chinese tree *Litchi chinensis* (family Sapindaceae), a large berry with a rough brown skin, sweet white pulp, and a single smooth stone, eaten fresh or preserved; the tree itself, widely cultivated in tropical countries.

lych-gate *n.* var. of LICH-GATE.

lychnis /ˈlɪknɪs/ *n.* E17. [L f. Gk *lukhnis* a red flower, f. *lukhnos* lamp.] Any of various plants of the genus *Lychnis*, of the pink family, including ragged robin (*L. flos-cuculi*) and some campions. Also (w. specifying wd), any of certain similar plants.

evening lychnis *N. Amer.* the Old World white campion, *Silene alba*, introduced in N. America. **scarlet lychnis** *N. Amer.* a red-flowered Russian lychnis, *L. chalcedonica*, introduced in N. America.

lychnoscope /ˈlɪknəskəʊp/ *n.* M19. [f. Gk *lukhnos* lamp + -SCOPE (so called from its supposed purpose to allow lepers to see the altar lights).] *Archit.* A low side window.

lychnoscopic *a.* M19.

Lycian /ˈlɪsɪən/ *n.* & *a.* L16. [f. L *Lycia*, Gk *Lukia* Lycia (see below) + -AN.] **A** *n.* **1** A native or inhabitant of Lycia, an ancient region in SW Asia Minor. L16. **2** The language of Lycia. M19. **B** *adj.* Of or pertaining to Lycia, its inhabitants, or language. E17.

lycid /ˈlɪsɪd/ *n.* & *a.* M20. [mod.L *Lycidae* (see below), f. *Lycus* genus name, f. Gk pers. name *Lukos*, L *Lycus*: see -ID³.] **A** *n.* Any of various beetles, often conspicuously coloured, of the family Lycidae. M20. **B** *adj.* Of, pertaining to, or designating this family. M20.

lycium /ˈlɪsɪəm/ *n.* M16. [Late L f. Gk *lukion*, orig. neut. sing. of *Lukios* Lycian.] A box-thorn (genus *Lycium*). Formerly also, a juice extracted from a box-thorn.

lycopene /ˈlʌɪkəpiːn/ *n.* M20. [f. LYCOPIN + -ENE.] *Chem.* A polyunsaturated hydrocarbon, $C_{40}H_{56}$, which is a red carotenoid pigment present in tomatoes and many berries and fruits.

lycoperdon /lʌɪkəˈpəːdən/ *n.* M18. [mod.L (see sense 1 below), irreg. f. Gk *lukos* wolf + *perdesthai* break wind.] **1** A puffball fungus of the genus *Lycoperdon*. Now chiefly as mod.L genus name. M18. **2** *lycoperdon nut*, = DEER-*ball*. M19.

lycopin /ˈlʌɪkəpɪn/ *n.* E20. [f. mod.L *Lycop(ersicon*, a genus including the tomato, f. Gk *lukos* wolf + *persikos* peach: see -IN¹.] *Chem.* = LYCOPENE.

lycopod /ˈlʌɪkəpɒd/ *n.* M19. [f. next.] *Bot.* A pteridophyte of the family Lycopodiaceae; a clubmoss.

lycopodiˈaceous *a.* of or pertaining to the family Lycopodiaceae M19.

lycopodium /lʌɪkəˈpəʊdɪəm/ *n.* E18. [mod.L (see below), f. Gk *lukos* wolf + *pod-*, *pous* foot, -POD (from the clawlike root of *L. clavatum*).] **1** A clubmoss of the genus *Lycopodium*, orig. spec. *L. clavatum*. E18. **2** In full *lycopodium powder*, *lycopodium dust*. A fine flammable powder consisting of ripe spores of *Lycopodium clavatum* or other species, formerly used as a surgical absorbent and in fireworks etc. M19.

Lycra /ˈlʌɪkrə/ *n.* Also **l-**. M20. [Origin unkn.] (Proprietary name for) an elastic polyurethane fibre and fabric used esp. for hosiery, underwear, and close-fitting sports clothing.

lyctus /ˈlɪktəs/ *n.* E20. [mod.L (see below) f. Gk *Luktos*, L *Lyctus* a city in Crete.] In full *lyctus beetle*. A wood-boring beetle of the genus *Lyctus*; a powder-post beetle.

lyctid *n.* & *a.* (*a*) *n.* a beetle of the family Lyctidae, which includes powder-post beetles; (*b*) *adj.* of, pertaining to, or designating this family: M20.

Lycurgan /lʌɪˈkəːg(ə)n/ *a.* M20. [f. L *Lycurgus* (see below), Gk *Lukourgos* + -AN.] Of, pertaining to, or characteristic of Lycurgus, the reputed founder of the ancient Spartan constitution (prob. about the end of the 9th cent. BC) or the constitutional innovations attributed to him; harsh, severe.

Lycurgean *a.* = LYCURGAN M19. **Lycurgian** *n.* (*rare*) an adherent of Lycurgus or his methods L16.

lyddite /ˈlɪdʌɪt/ *n.* L19. [f. *Lydd* a town in Kent, SE England, where the explosive was tested + -ITE¹.] Chiefly *Hist.* A high explosive consisting chiefly of picric acid, much used by the British in the war of 1914–18.

Lydian /ˈlɪdɪən/ *a.* & *n.* L15. [f. L *Lydius*, Gk *Ludios* Lydia (see below) + -AN.] **A** *n.* A native or inhabitant of Lydia, an ancient country in Asia Minor. Also, the language used there. L15.

B *adj.* **1** Of or pertaining to Lydia, its inhabitants, or language. L16. **2** *Mus.* Designating or pertaining to an ancient Greek mode, characterized as soft and effeminate. Also (since the Middle Ages), designating or pertaining to the scale whose notes are at intervals as represented by F–F on the white notes of a piano. L16.

1 Lydian stone a black variety of jasper (basanite), formerly used as a touchstone for gold.

lydite /ˈlɪdʌɪt/ *n.* E19. [f. prec. + -ITE¹.] = *Lydian stone* s.v. LYDIAN *a.* 1.

lye /lʌɪ/ *n.*¹ & *v.* [OE *lēaġ* = MDu. *lōghe* (Du. *loog*), OHG *louga* (G *Lauge*) lye, ON *laug* hot bath, f. Gmc base repr. also by LATHER *n.*¹, f. IE.] **A** *n.* **1** Water made alkaline, esp. by the lixiviation of vegetable ashes; any strong alkaline solution for washing etc. OE. **b** Any detergent material. Long *rare*. ME. **2** The fluid which forms in a blister etc. or collects in the body in dropsy. Long *dial.* E17. **3** Water impregnated with salts by decoction or lixiviation. Now *rare*. M17.

Comb.: **lye corn**: steeped in weak lye to remove the husk.

B *v.t.* Treat with lye. L18.

lye *n.*² see LIE *n.*²

lygaeid /lʌɪˈdʒiːɪd, -ˈgʌɪɪd/ *n.* & *a.* L19. [mod.L *Lygaeidae* (see below), f. *Lygaeus* genus name, f. Gk *lugaios* shadowy, gloomy: see -ID³.] *Entomol.* **A** *n.* Any of various dark or brightly coloured heteropteran bugs of the family Lygaeidae, some of which are agricultural pests. L19. **B** *adj.* Of, pertaining to, or designating this family. E20.

lygus /ˈlʌɪgəs/ *n.* Pl. same. E20. [mod.L (see below) f. Gk *lugos* chaste-tree, withy.] *Entomol.* Any of various plant-sucking mirid bugs of the genus *Lygus*, some of which transmit plant diseases. Also *lygus bug*.

lying /ˈlʌɪɪŋ/ *n.* ME. [f. LIE *v.*¹ + -ING¹.] **1** The action of LIE *v.*¹ ME. **b** *lying-in*, confinement in childbirth. LME. **2** A place to lie. Usu. w. qualifying adj. M19.

1 K. AMIS Just lying in the sun and no more, strikes me as a terrible thing to do. 2 J. T. NETTLESHIP A poet from his birth, nursed in Nature's softest lying.

Comb.: **lying-in-state** the display of the corpse of a public figure for public tribute before burial or cremation.

lying /ˈlʌɪɪŋ/ *a.*¹ OE. [f. LIE *v.*¹ + -ING².] **1** That lies (in a more or less horizontal position, etc.); that remains or rests. OE. **2** *spec.* Of money, goods, etc.: put by. *Sc.* E18.

1 J. BUCHAN The frost had gone, and the lying snow was as soft as butter.

lying /ˈlʌɪɪŋ/ *a.*² ME. [f. LIE *v.*² + -ING².] That tells lies; untruthful, deceitful.

E. PIZZEY She'd go .. potty waiting for your next lying 'phone call.

lyingly *adv.* LME.

lying *v.*¹, *v.*² pres. pple of LIE *v.*¹, *v.*²

lyke *n.* var. of LICH.

lyke-wake /ˈlʌɪkweɪk/ *n.* Also **lykewake**. LME. [f. *lyke* var. of LICH + WAKE *n.*¹ See also LATE-WAKE.] A watch kept at night over a dead body.

Lyle gun /ˈlʌɪl gʌn/ *n. phr.* L19. [D. A. *Lyle* (d. 1937), US army officer and engineer.] A cannon designed to project a rope to a stranded ship to facilitate salvaging and rescue operations.

Lylian /ˈlɪlɪən/ *a.* E20. [f. John *Lyly* (*c*1554–1606), Eng. dramatist and novelist + -AN.] Of, pertaining to, or characteristic of John Lyly or his works; euphuistic.

Lyman series /ˈlʌɪmən sɪəriːz/ *n. phr.* E20. [Theodore *Lyman* (1874–1954), US physicist.] *Physics.* A series of lines in the ultraviolet spectrum of atomic hydrogen, between 122 and 91 nanometres.

Lyme /lʌɪm/ *n.*¹ L20. [A town in Connecticut, USA, where an outbreak occurred.] Med. *Lyme disease* (or *arthritis*), a form of arthritis which mainly affects the large joints and is preceded by an erythematous rash, caused by a spirochaete bacterium transmitted by ticks.

lyme *n.*² var. of LYAM.

lyme-grass /ˈlʌɪmgrɑːs/ *n.* L18. [Perh. f. LIME *n.*¹: see GRASS *n.*] **1** A blue-green grass of sandy coasts, *Leymus* (formerly *Elymus*) *arenarius*, often planted to stabilize dunes. L18. **2** A noctuid moth, *Photedes elymi*, the caterpillars of which feed on lyme-grass. M19.

†lymo(u)r *n.* see LIMBER *n.*¹

lymph /lɪmf/ *n.* Also in L form **†lympha**. L16. [Fr. *lymphe* or L *lympha* water-nymph, water, prob. dissimilated form of *nympha*, Gk *numphē* nymph.] **1** (Pure) water. Also, a stream. *poet.* L16. **†2** *Bot.* A colourless fluid in plants; sap. L17–M19. **3** A colourless alkaline fluid, resembling blood but lacking red cells, which bathes various tissues and organs of the body and drains into the bloodstream through a network of vessels (the lymphatic system). L17. **4** The exudation from an inflamed tissue, a sore, etc; *spec.* a vaccine obtained from diseased tissue. E19.

Phrases & comb.: **lymph gland**, **lymph node** any of several small masses of tissue situated on the lymphatic vessels, responsible for removing foreign bodies from the lymph and for producing lymphocytes and antibodies. *plastic lymph*: see PLASTIC *a.* 5.

lymph- *comb. form* see LYMPHO-.

†lympha *n.* see LYMPH.

lymphad /ˈlɪmfad/ *n. obs.* exc. *Hist.* & *Her.* Also (earlier) **†langfad**. M16. [Gael. *longfhada*, f. *long* ship + *fhada* long.] A one-masted galley propelled by oars.

†lymphaeduct *n.* M17–M18. [mod.L

lymphaeductus, f. L *lymphae* genit. of *lympha* LYMPH + *ductus* DUCT *n*.] A lymphatic vessel.

lymphangiectasis /ˌlɪmfandʒɪˈɛktəsɪs/ *n*. Pl. **-ases** /-əsiːz/. M19. [f. LYMPHO- + ANGIO- + mod.L ECTASIS.] *Med.* Dilatation of the lymphatic vessels.

lymphangiography /ˌlɪmfandʒɪˈɒɡrəfi/ *n*. M19. [f. LYMPHO- + ANGIOGRAPHY.] *Med.* †1 A description of the lymphatic vessels. *rare* (Dicts.). Only in M19. 2 Radiography of the lymphatic vessels, carried out after introduction of a radio-opaque substance. M20.

lymˈphangiogram *n*. a radiograph made by lymphangiography M20. **lymphangioˈgraphic** *a*. M20. **lymphangioˈgraphically** *adv*. M20.

lymphangioma /ˌlɪmfandʒɪˈəʊmə/ *n*. Pl. **-mas**, **-mata** /-mətə/. L19. [f. LYMPHO- + ANGIOMA.] *Med.* A tumour-like mass resulting from a proliferation of lymphatic vessels.

lymphangiomatous *a*. of the nature of or characterized by a lymphangioma L19.

lymphangiosarcoma /lɪmˌfandʒɪəʊsɑːˈkəʊmə/ *n*. Pl. **-mas**, **-mata** /-mətə/. E20. [f. as next + SARCOMA.] *Med.* A sarcoma of the lymphatic vessels.

lymphangitis /lɪmfanˈdʒʌɪtɪs/ *n*. M19. [f. LYMPHO- + ANGIO- + -ITIS.] *Med.* Inflammation of the walls of lymphatic vessels.

†**lymphate** *v.t. rare*. Pa. pple & ppl a. **-ated**, (earlier) **-ate**. LME. [Orig. pa. pple, f. L *lymphatus* pa. pple of *lymphare*, f. *lympha*: see LYMPH, -ATE², -ATE³.] 1 Dilute with water. LME–L16. 2 Drive mad. Chiefly as *lymphated* ppl a. E17–E18.

†**lymphation** *n*. E17–E18.

lymphatic /lɪmˈfatɪk/ *a*. & *n*. M17. [L *lymphaticus* mad (f. as LYMPH: see -ATIC), after Gk *numpholēptos* seized by nymphs.] A *adj*. †1 Frenzied, mad. M17–E19. 2 Of or pertaining to lymph; involved in the secretion or conveyance of lymph. M17. †b *Bot.* Containing or conveying sap. L17–M19. 3 Sluggish, flabby, (formerly supposed to be as a result of an excess of lymph in the system). L18.

2 **lymphatic system** the network of vessels conveying lymph.

B *n*. 1 Any of the network of vessels which convey lymph. Formerly also (*Bot.*), a sap-vessel in a plant. Usu. in *pl*. M17. †2 An insane person. E–M18.

†**lymphatical** *a*. frenzied E17–E18.

lymphedema *n*. see LYMPHOEDEMA.

lympho- /ˈlɪmfəʊ/ *comb. form* of LYMPH: see -O-. Bef. a vowel **lymph-**. Chiefly *Med.*

lymphadeˈnectomy *n*. (an instance of) surgical removal of lymph nodes M20. **lymphadeˈnitis** *n*. inflammation of one or more lymph nodes L19. **lymphadenopathy** /ˌlɪmfadɪˈnɒpəθi/ *n*. diseased condition of lymph nodes E20. **lymphoblast** *n*. an abnormal cell, resembling a large lymphocyte, produced in large numbers in a form of leukaemia E20. **lymphoˈblastic** *a*. of the nature of or pertaining to lymphoblasts; (of leukaemia) in which lymphoblasts are produced: E20. **lymphoˈgenic** *a*. = LYMPHOGENOUS E20. **lymphogenous** /lɪmˈfɒdʒɪnəs/ *a*. (*a*) producing lymph or lymphocytes; (*b*) arising in, produced by, or disseminated via the lymphatic system: L19. **lymphokine** *n*. [Gk *kinein* move] any of various soluble substances released by lymphocytes which are thought to be involved in cell-mediated immunity but to lack the antigen-specificity of antibodies M20. **lymphoˈpenia** *n*. a decrease in the number of lymphocytes in the blood E20. **lymphopoiesis** /ˌlɪmfəʊpɔɪˈiːsɪs/ *n*. the formation of lymphocytes E20. **lymphopoietic** /ˌlɪmfəʊpɔɪˈɛtɪk/ *a*. of or pertaining to lymphopoiesis E20. **lymphoreˈticular** *a*. = RETICULOENDOTHELIAL M20. **lymphoˈrrhagia** *n*. the discharge of lymph from a damaged lymphatic vessel L19. **lymphosarˈcoma** *n*., pl. **-mas**, **-mata** /-mətə/, a sarcoma of lymphoid tissue L19. **lymphotropic** /-ˈtrəʊpɪk, -ˈtrɒpɪk/ *a*. affecting the lymphatic system L20.

lymphocyte /ˈlɪmfə(ʊ)sʌɪt/ *n*. L19. [f. prec. + -CYTE.] *Physiol.* A kind of small leucocyte which has a single round nucleus and little or no granulation in the cytoplasm, constitutes about a quarter of the total leucocytes, and is found in large numbers in the lymph nodes etc.

lymphocytic /-ˈsɪtɪk/ *a*. of or pertaining to, or characterized by the presence of lymphocytes L19. **lymphocyˈtosis** *n*., pl. **-toses** /-ˈtəʊsiːz/, an abnormal increase in the number of lymphocytes L19. **lymphocytoˈtoxic** *a*. (*a*) toxic towards lymphocytes; (*b*) pertaining to or involving lymphocytotoxins: M20. **lymphocytotoˈxicity** *n*. M20. **lymphocytoˈtoxin** *n*. a substance toxic towards lymphocytes E20.

lymphoedema /lɪmfɪˈdiːmə/ *n*. Also ***lymphedema**. L19. [f. LYMPHO- + OEDEMA.] *Med.* Oedema resulting from obstruction of lymph vessels or lymph nodes.

lymphoeˈdematous *a*. M20.

lymphogranuloma /ˌlɪmfəʊɡranjʊˈləʊmə/ *n*. Pl. **-mas**, **-mata** /-mətə/. E20. [f. LYMPHO- + GRANULOMA.] *Med.* Any of several diseases involving swelling or inflammation of lymph nodes, *spec*. (*a*) (in full *lymphogranuloma inguinale* /ɪŋɡwɪˈnɑːli/, also *lymphogranuloma venereum* /vɪˈnɪərɪəm/) a venereal disease, esp. of the tropics, caused by chlamydial infection and resulting in destructive inflammation of lymph nodes and lymph vessels, particularly in the inguinal region; (*b*) Hodgkin's disease; (*c*) sarcoidosis.

Also **lymphogranulomaˈtosis** *n*., pl. **-toses** /-ˈtəʊsiːz/, E20.

lymphography /lɪmˈfɒɡrəfi/ *n*. E19. [f. LYMPHO- + -GRAPHY.] †1 A description of the lymphatic system. *rare* (Dicts.). Only in E19. 2 = LYMPHANGIOGRAPHY. M20.

lymphoid /ˈlɪmfɔɪd/ *a*. M19. [f. LYMPH + -OID.] *Physiol.* & *Med.* Of or pertaining to lymph or the lymphatic system; *esp.* (of tissue) that produces lymphocytes.

lymphoma /lɪmˈfəʊmə/ *n*. Pl. **-mas**, **-mata** /-mətə/. L19. [f. LYMPH + -OMA.] *Med.* Any of several malignant disorders involving lymphoid tissue.

lymphomaˈtosis *n*., pl. **-toses** /-ˈtəʊsiːz/, any of various diffuse neoplastic or hyperplastic disorders originating in lymphoid tissue E20. **lymphomatous** *a*. of the nature of or characterized by a lymphoma L19.

lymphous /ˈlɪmfəs/ *a*. *rare*. L17. [f. LYMPH + -OUS.] †1 Of sap: watery. Only in L17. 2 *Physiol.* & *Med.* Of the nature of or resembling lymph. L19.

lymphy /ˈlɪmfi/ *a*. Now *rare*. M19. [f. LYMPH + -Y¹.] *Physiol.* & *Med.* = LYMPHOUS 2.

lyncean /lɪnˈsiːən/ *a*. E17. [f. L *lynceus* (f. Gk *lugkeios*, f. *lugx* LYNX) + -AN.] Lynx-eyed, keen-sighted.

D. DELILLO Precision was one of the raptures he allowed himself, the lyncean skill for selection and detail.

lynch /lɪn(t)ʃ/ *n*.¹ & *v*. Orig. *US*. E19. [f. Capt. William *Lynch* (1742–1820), head of a self-constituted judicial tribunal first organized in 1780 in Virginia, US.] A *n*. *lynch law*, (in early use also) *Lynch's law*, the practice of summary punishment and esp. execution of an alleged offender carried out by a self-constituted illegal court. E19.

B *v.t.* Of a mob or group of people: condemn and put (a person) to death (esp. by hanging) for an alleged offence without a legal trial. M19.

D. FRANCIS If you don't win they will likely lynch you. J. WAIN The white American was ready first to enslave and later to lynch.

Comb.: **lynch mob**: intent on lynching someone.

lyncher *n*. M19. **lynching** *n*. the action of the vb; an execution, esp. a hanging, without a legal trial: M19.

lynch *n*.² var. of LINCH *n*.²

lynchet /ˈlɪn(t)ʃɪt/ *n*. L17. [Prob. f. LINCH *n*.²] 1 An unploughed strip as a boundary between two fields. L17. 2 A slope or terrace along the face of a chalk down; *spec*. (*Archaeol.*) a cultivation terrace. L18.

lynchetted, **-eted** *a*. (of land) cultivated by using terraces E20.

Lyngby /ˈlɪŋbi/ *n*. & *a*. E20. [*Norre-Lyngby* in Denmark, where first discovered.] (Designating or pertaining to) a mesolithic culture of the Baltic area.

lyngorm *n*. var. of LINGWORM.

lynx /lɪŋks/ *n*. ME. [L f. Gk *lugx* rel. to OE *lox*, OHG *luhs* (G *Luchs*), OSw. *lō*.] 1 Any of various small to medium-sized members of the cat family typically having a short tail, tufted ears, and mottled or spotted fur; spec. *Lynx lynx*, which inhabits forest in NW Europe and northern Asia, and (more fully *Canadian lynx*) the larger *L. canadensis* of northern N. America. Formerly esp. = CARACAL. ME. b The fur of such an animal. M19. 2 (Usu. **L-**.) (The name of) a constellation of the northern hemisphere between Ursa Major and Gemini. Also *the Lynx*. E18.

Comb.: **lynx-eye** a keen eye; **lynx-eyed** *a*. keen-sighted.

lynxlike *a*. resembling (that of) a lynx L16.

Lyon /ˈlʌɪən/ *n*. LME. [Archaic var. of LION: named f. the lion on the royal shield.] In full *Lord Lyon* or *Lyon King of Arms*. (The title of) the chief herald in Scotland.

Comb.: **Lyon Court** the court over which the Lyon King of Arms presides.

Lyonese *a*. & *n*. var. of LYONNESE.

lyonization /lʌɪənʌɪˈzeɪʃ(ə)n/ *n*. Also **-isation**. M20. [f. Mary F. *Lyon* (b. 1925), Eng. biologist + -IZATION.] *Genetics*. The inactivation of one of the two X chromosomes in each cell of a developing female mammalian embryo.

Lyonnais /liːəˈneɪ, *foreign* ljɔnɛ/ *a*. & *n*. Fem. **-aise** /-eɪz, *foreign* -ɛːz/. E19. [Fr., f. as LYONS. Cf. next.] A *adj*. Of, pertaining to, or characteristic of the city of Lyons (Lyon) or the former province of Lyonnais, in SE France; *spec*. (*-aise*) in *Cookery*, designating food, esp. sliced potatoes, cooked with onions or with white wine and onion sauce. E19. B *n*. Pl. **-ais**, fem. **-aises**, (pronounced as sing.). 1 A native or inhabitant of Lyons. M20. 2 The French dialect of the area of Lyons. M20.

Lyonnois /liːəˈnwɑː/, fem. **-oise** /-wɑːz/ *n*. (now *rare* or *obs.*), pl. **-ois**, **-oises**, (pronounced same), = LYONNAIS *n*. 1 M17.

Lyonnese /liːəˈniːz/ *a*. & *n*. Also **Lyonese**. E19. [f. as next + -ESE.] A *adj*. Of or pertaining to Lyons, Lyonnais. E19. B *n*. Pl. same. = LYONNAIS *n*. 1. M19.

Lyons /ˈliːɔ̃ː, ˈlʌɪənz/ *a*. M18. [Fr. *Lyon* a city in SE France.] Designating various products, esp. fabrics, made in or associated with Lyons.

ARNOLD BENNETT She bought . . coffee, Lyons sausage, dried prunes. P. WENTWORTH Great ladies . . had bought changeable silks there, and fine Lyons velvet.

lyophile /ˈlʌɪəfʌɪl/ *a*. In sense 2 also **-phil** /-fɪl/. E20. [f. Gk *luein* loosen + -PHIL, -PHILE.] 1 *Physical Chem.* = LYOPHILIC *a*. E20. 2 *Biol.* & *Med.* Of, pertaining to, or employing freeze-drying; freeze-dried. M20.

lyophiliˈzation *n*. freeze-drying M20. **lyophilize** *v.t.* freeze-dry M20.

lyophilic /lʌɪə(ʊ)ˈfɪlɪk/ *a*. E20. [f. as prec. + -IC.] *Physical Chem.* Of a colloid: having an affinity for the dispersion medium, and not readily precipitated out by small quantities of electrolyte. Of a sol: containing such a phase, and generally having lower surface tension and a higher viscosity than the dispersion medium, and giving a gel on evaporation or cooling. Cf. next.

lyophobic /lʌɪə(ʊ)ˈfəʊbɪk/ *a*. E20. [f. Gk *luein* loosen + -O- + -PHOBIA + -IC.] *Physical Chem.* Of a colloid: not having an affinity for the dispersion medium, and readily precipitated out by small quantities of electrolyte. Of a sol: containing such a phase, and generally having a similar surface tension and viscosity to the dispersion medium, and on evaporation or cooling giving a solid which cannot readily be reconverted into a sol. Cf. prec.

Also **lyophobe** *a*. E20.

lyotropic /lʌɪə(ʊ)ˈtrəʊpɪk, -ˈtrɒpɪk/ *a*. E20. [f. Gk *luein* loosen + -O- + -TROPIC.] *Physical Chem.* 1 Associated with the change of internal pressure in a solvent caused by addition of a solute. E20. 2 Designating or pertaining to a mesophase which has its phase transitions readily effected by a change of concentration. M20.

1 **lyotropic series**: in which ions are arranged in order of their lyotropic effects, esp. their ability to cause precipitation of a lyophilic sol.

lyra /ˈlʌɪrə/ *n*. LME. [L f. Gk *lura*.] 1 A lyre. Also, any of various other musical instruments descended from or resembling the lyre. LME. 2 (**L-**.) (The name of) a small constellation of the northern hemisphere, lying on the edge of the Milky Way between Hercules and Cygnus; the Lyre. M16. †3 A gurnard, the piper *Trigla lyra*. E18–M19. 4 *Anat.* The triangular portion of the undersurface of the corpus callosum lying between the crura of the fornix. M18.

1 *bell lyra*: see BELL *n.*[1]

Comb.: *lyra glockenspiel*: see GLOCKENSPIEL 2; **lyra viol** a bass viol tuned and played according to a system of tablature; also called *viola bastarda*.

lyrate /ˈlʌɪreɪt/ *a.* M18. [f. L LYRA + -ATE[2].] Chiefly *Bot.* & *Zool.* Shaped like a lyre.

lyrated *a.* = LYRATE M18. **lyrately** *adv.* in a lyrate form L18.

lyre /lʌɪə/ *n.* ME. [OFr. *lire* (mod. *lyre*) f. L LYRA.] 1 A plucked stringed musical instrument having strings fixed between a crossbar supported by two arms; *spec.* such an ancient Greek instrument with outwardly curved arms, usu. played with a plectrum and used to accompany song and recitation. ME. 2 (Usu. **L-**.) (The name of) *the* constellation Lyra. M19.

Comb.: **lyre-bird** either of two mainly ground-dwelling Australian birds forming the family Menuridae, *Menura novaehollandiae* and *M. alberti*, which have a lyre-shaped tail; **lyre-flower** the plant bleeding heart, *Dicentra spectabilis*; **lyre-shaped** *a.* shaped like a lyre with outwardly curved arms; **lyre-tail** any of a number of cyprinodont fishes with coloured tails suggesting lyres.

lyric /ˈlɪrɪk/ *a.* & *n.* L16. [(O)Fr. *lyrique* or L *lyricus* f. Gk *lurikos*, f. *lura* lyre: see -IC.] A *adj.* 1 Of or pertaining to the lyre; pertaining to or characteristic of song, meant to be sung; *spec.* (*a*) (of poetry, whether or not intended to be sung) expressing the writer's emotions, usu. briefly and in stanzas or strophes, (of a poet) writing such poems; (*b*) (of a singing voice) using a light register. L16. 2 Given to song; singing. Chiefly *poet.* M17.

1 V. LEE Poetry which is lyric in spirit as well as in metre. F. FERGUSSON His great speech, 'O wealth and power', is a far more lyric utterance than the ordered exposition. *Opera Now* The American tenor . . is not quite the lyric tenor for the role. **lyric drama** opera. **lyric stage** the production or performance of opera.

B *n.* 1 *the lyric*, lyric poetry. L16. †2 A lyric poet. L16–M19. 3 A lyric poem; a song; in *pl.*, lyric verses. L16. 4 *sing.* & (usu.) in *pl.* The words of a song (or songs). L19.

3 N. FRYE The poet can express himself in a lyric only by dramatizing the mental state or mood. 4 M. ANGELOU A joy about the tune that changed the meaning of its sad lyrics. P. B. CLARKE Not all the lyrics and melodies used by Rastas are their own.

†**lyric** *v.t. rare.* L17–E18. [f. the adj.] Sing (*over*) in a lyrical manner.

lyrical /ˈlɪrɪk(ə)l/ *a.* E16. [f. as LYRIC *a.* & *n.* + -AL[1].] 1 = LYRIC *a.* 1. E16. 2 Characteristic of, expressed in, or using language appropriate to lyric poetry. E19. 3 Excitedly effusive; highly enthusiastic. Freq. in *wax lyrical*. *colloq.* M20.

2 M. TIPPETT The search for lyrical simplicity was . . the hardest thing of all. D. MURPHY A thousand-word lyrical description of the landscape, the birds and the ever-changing . . sky. 3 *Washington Post* Exley . . will wax lyrical on the subject, sharing . . remembrances which only great literature imparts.

lyrically *adv.* E19. **lyricalness** *n.* L19.

†**lyrichord** *n.* M18–L19. [f. LYRE after *harpsichord*.] A kind of harpsichord with wire and catgut strings sounded by rotating wheels.

lyricise *v.* var. of LYRICIZE.

lyricism /ˈlɪrɪsɪz(ə)m/ *n.* M18. [f. LYRIC *n.* & *a.* + -ISM.] Lyric character or style; a lyrical expression; high-flown sentiments or enthusiasm.

lyricist /ˈlɪrɪsɪst/ *n.* L19. [f. LYRIC *a.* & *n.* + -IST.] 1 A person skilled in lyric composition. L19. 2 A person who writes the words of songs. E20.

lyricize /ˈlɪrɪsʌɪz/ *v. rare.* Also **-ise**. M19. [f. LYRIC *a.* & *n.* + -IZE.] 1 *v.i.* Sing lyrics. M19. 2 *v.t.* Express or depict lyrically. M19.

Lyrid /ˈlʌɪrɪd/ *a.* & *n.* L19. [f. LYRA 2 + -ID[3].] *Astron.* (Designating) any of a shower of meteors seeming to radiate from the constellation Lyra in April.

lyriform /ˈlʌɪrɪfɔːm/ *a.* M19. [f. LYRE + -I- + -FORM.] Lyre-shaped.

lyrism /ˈlʌɪərɪz(ə)m, ˈlɪrɪz(ə)m/ *n.* M19. [Fr. *lyrisme* or Gk *lurismos* playing on the lyre, f. *lura* lyre: see -ISM.] = LYRICISM. Also (*rare*), a lyrical performance.

lyrist /ˈlɪrɪst/ *n.* M17. [L *lyrista* f. Gk *luristēs*, f. *lura* lyre: see -IST.] 1 A person who plays on the lyre. M17. 2 A lyric poet. E19.

lysarden /ˈlɪzəd(ə)n/ *n.* Also **lyz-**. E17. [f. LIZARD, from its shape.] *Early Mus.* A wind instrument of the cornett family, predating the serpent.

lysate /ˈlʌɪzeɪt/ *n.* E20. [f. LYSIS + -ATE[2].] *Biol.* A solution or preparation containing the products of lysis of cells.

lyse /lʌɪz/ *v.* E20. [Back-form. f. LYSIS after *analysis*, *analyse*, etc.] *Biol.* 1 *v.t.* Bring about lysis of (a cell etc.). E20. 2 *v.i.* Undergo lysis. M20.

Lysenkoism /lʌɪˈsɛŋkəʊɪz(ə)m/ *n.* M20. [f. *Lysenko* (see below) + -ISM.] Belief in or advocacy of the views of the Russian agronomist T. D. Lysenko (1898–1976), who opposed modern genetics and advocated neo-Lamarckian views and for a time exerted great influence in Soviet Russia.

Lysenkoist *n.* & *a.* (*a*) *n.* an adherent of Lysenkoism; (*b*) *adj.* of or pertaining to Lysenkoists or Lysenkoism: M20.

lysergic /lʌɪˈsəːdʒɪk/ *a.* M20. [f. *lys* (in HYDROLYSIS) + ERG(OT + -IC.] 1 Chem. *lysergic acid*, a crystalline tetracyclic compound, $C_{16}H_{16}N_2O_2$, orig. produced by the hydrolysis of ergot alkaloids, which contains the indole nucleus, and of which the hallucinogenic drug LSD is a derivative. M20. 2 *ellipt.* LSD. M20.

2 lysergic acid diethylamide = LSD.

lysigenous /lʌɪˈsɪdʒɪnəs/ *a.* L19. [f. Gk *lusis* loosening + -GENOUS.] *Bot.* Esp. of intercellular spaces: produced by the breaking down of adjoining cells. Cf. SCHIZOGENOUS.

lysimachia /lʌɪsɪˈmeɪkɪə/ *n.* L16. [L f. Gk *lusimakhion*, f. *Lusimakhos* Lysimachus: see LOOSESTRIFE, -IA[1].] A plant of the genus *Lysimachia* (family Primulaceae); loosestrife.

lysimeter /lʌɪˈsɪmɪtə/ *n.* L19. [f. Gk *lusis* loosening + -METER.] An apparatus for measuring mass changes due to leaching, evaporation, etc., undergone by a body of soil.

lysin /ˈlʌɪsɪn/ *n.* E20. [f. LYSIS + -IN[1].] *Biol.* A substance capable of lysing cells; *spec.* an antibody with this ability.

lysine /ˈlʌɪsiːn/ *n.* L19. [G *Lysin*, ult. f. Gk *lusis* loosening: see -INE[5].] *Biochem.* A basic amino acid which occurs in proteins and is essential in the human diet; 2,6-diaminohexanoic acid, $COOH{\cdot}CH(NH_2)(CH_2)_3CH_2NH_2$.

lysis /ˈlʌɪsɪs/ *n.* Pl. **lyses** /ˈlʌɪsiːz/. M16. [L f. Gk *lusis* loosening. In sense 2 prob. f. ending of HAEMOLYSIS etc.: cf. -LYSIS.] 1 *Med.* A gradual resolution of a disease without apparent phenomena (opp. *crisis*). Now *rare* or *obs.* M16. 2 *Biol.* The disintegration or dissolution of cells or cell organelles; *esp.* the dissolution of bacterial cells brought about by bacteriophages. E20.

-lysis /lɪsɪs/ *suff.* Pl. **-lyses** /lɪsiːz/. [f. as prec.] Forming ns. (esp. in *Biol*, *Med.*, & *Chem.*) w. the sense 'decomposition, disintegration, dissolution', the first elem. indicating the agent (*electrolysis*, *hydrolysis*), the substance or object affected (*glycolysis*, *haemolysis*, *frontolysis*), or some other characteristic of the process (*autolysis*, *heterolysis*).

lyso- /ˈlʌɪsəʊ/ *comb. form* of LYSIS: see -O-.

lyso'somal *a.* (*Biol.*) of or pertaining to a lysosome or lysosomes M20. **lysosome** *n.* (*Biol.*) a cytoplasmic cell organelle containing hydrolytic enzymes enclosed in a membrane M20. **lysozyme** *n.* (*Biochem.*) a low-molecular-weight enzyme capable of hydrolysing a particular mucopolysaccharide found in the cell walls of certain Gram-positive bacteria and hence of lysing such bacteria E20.

lysogenic /lʌɪsəˈdʒɛnɪk/ *a.* L19. [f. prec. + -GENIC.] *Biol.* Of or pertaining to lysis; capable of producing or undergoing lysis; *spec.* (of a bacterium) capable, without being attacked by a phage, of lysing and liberating a phage normally integrated with the bacterial genome.

lysogenicity /-ˈnɪsɪti/ *n.* = LYSOGENY M20. **lysogeni'zation** *n.* the process of lysogenizing a bacterium M20. **ly'sogenize** *v.t.* (of a phage) become stably integrated into the genome of (a bacterium) M20. **ly'sogeny** *n.* the property of being lysogenic; the lysis of a lysogenic bacterium with the subsequent release of phage: M20.

Lysol /ˈlʌɪsɒl/ *n.* Also **l-**. L19. [f. Gk *lusis* loosening + -OL.] (Proprietary name for) a solution of coal tar oil in soap.

lysopine /ˈlʌɪsəpiːn/ *n.* M20. [f. LYS(INE + OCT)OPINE *n.*] *Biochem.* An opine, $C_9H_{18}N_2O_4$, related to octopine and of similar origin. Cf. NOPALINE.

lyssa /ˈlɪsə/ *n. rare.* E18. [mod.L f. Gk *lussa*: cf. LYTTA.] *Med.* Rabies, hydrophobia.

lythe /lʌɪð/ *n. Sc.* & *Ir.* E16. [Perh. f. ON *lýr* pike.] The pollack.

lytic /ˈlɪtɪk/ *a.* L19. [Gk *lutikos* able to loose: see -IC.] 1 *Med.* Of, pertaining to, or causing gradual resolution of a disease (cf. LYSIS 1). Now *rare* or *obs.* L19. 2 *Biol.* Of, pertaining to, or causing lysis of a bacterium etc. E20.

lytically *adv.* M20.

-lytic /ˈlɪtɪk/ *suff.* [f. or after Gk *-lutikos*: cf. -IC.] Forming adjs. corresp. to ns. in *-lysis*, as *analytic*, *catalytic*, *haemolytic*.

lytta /ˈlɪtə/ *n.* E17. [mod.L f. Gk *lutta* Attic form of *lussa* LYSSA (w. allus. to its formerly supposed connection with liability to rabies).] A small ligament in a dog's tongue. Cf. WORM *n.* 11.

lyxose /ˈlɪksəʊz, -s/ *n.* L19. [f. XYLOSE by reversal of 2nd syll.] *Chem.* A crystalline pentose sugar isomeric with xylose and rare in nature.

lyzarden *n.* var. of LYSARDEN.

M

M, m /ɛm/, the thirteenth letter of the modern Eng. alphabet and the twelfth of the ancient Roman one, corresp. to Gk *mū*, Semitic *mēm*. The sound normally represented by the letter is a bilabial nasal consonant, usu. voiced, though with an unvoiced ending when followed by an unvoiced consonant, and able to be used syllabically (/-(ə)m/), particularly after /ð/ and /z/ at the end of words (of Gk etymology), as *rhythm*, *spasm*, *schism*, and the suffix *-ism*. The letter can be silent initially before *n* in Gk derivatives, as *mnemonic*. Pl. **M's**, **Ms**. See also EM.

I 1 The letter and its sound. 2 The shape of the letter. 3 *Typogr.* = EM 2.

2 **M-roof**: formed from two ordinary gable roofs with a valley between them, the section resembling the letter M.

II Symbolical uses. 4 Used to denote serial order; applied e.g. to the thirteenth (or often the twelfth, either I or J being omitted) group or section, sheet of a book, etc. 5 The roman numeral for a thousand. 6 *Physics*. a (Cap. M.) Designating the series of X-ray emission lines of an excited atom of longer wavelength than the L-series (cf. L, L 5b), arising from electron transitions to the atomic orbit of third lowest energy, with principal quantum number 3; hence *M-shell*, this orbit; *M-electrons*, electrons in this shell; *M-capture*, the capture by an atomic nucleus of one of the M-electrons. b Denoting magnetic quantum numbers (*m* for a single particle, *M* for an assemblage of particles), corresponding to the component of an angular momentum (often indicated by a subscript) in some physically distinguished direction.

III 7 Abbrevs.: (A small selection only is given here. Those all in caps. or small caps. also occur with a full stop after each letter; some of those all in caps. also occur (i) with initial cap. only, (ii) in small caps.) **M.** = Master (now only in academic degrees, = L *magister*); †*carry an M under one's girdle*, use a respectful prefix (Mr, Mrs) when addressing someone; Member (of); [Fr.] *Monsieur*. **M** = medium; (as *pref.*) mega-; (*Astron.*) Messier (number); (of paper quality) middling; million(s); (*Chem.*) molar; (*Econ.*) money (w. following numeral, in measures of money supply); morphine; (in road numbers) motorway. **m.** = (*Cricket*) maiden (over); male; mare; married; masculine; mile(s); minute(s). **m** = mark(s) (as monetary unit); mass; metre(s); (*Mus.*) (as *pref.*) mezzo; (as *pref.*) milli-; million(s). **m-** (*Chem.*) = meta-. **MA** = Massachusetts; Master of Arts. **ma.** /meɪ/ *colloq.* (in some schools) = major (elder of two namesakes). **Macc.** = Maccabees (Apocrypha). **MAD** = magnetic anomaly detection or detector; mutual assured destruction. **MAFF** /maf/ = Ministry of Agriculture, Fisheries, and Food. **Maj.** = Major. **Mal.** = Malachi (in the Bible). **Man.** = Manitoba. **M. and V.** = meat and vegetable(s). **Manit.** = Manitoba. **MAO** = monoamine oxidase. **Mar.** = March. **Mass.** = Massachusetts. **Matt.** = Matthew (esp. New Testament). **max.** = maximum. **MB** = [L] *Medicinae Baccalaureus* Bachelor of Medicine; (*Computing*) megabyte. **MBA** = Master of Business Administration. **MBE** = Member of (the Order of) the British Empire. **MC** = Master of Ceremonies (see also EMCEE); Member of Congress; Military Cross; music cassette. **Mc** = megacycle(s); megacycles per second; **MCC** = Marylebone Cricket Club (formerly, the governing body of English cricket and the official title of touring teams representing England). **M.Ch(ir).** = [L] *Magister Chirurgiae* Master of Surgery. **mCi** = millicurie(s). **M.Com.** = Master of Commerce. **MCP** = male chauvinist pig. **MCR** = middle common-room. **Mc/s** = megacycles per second. **MD** = [L] *Medicinae Doctor* Doctor of Medicine; Managing Director; Maryland; mentally deficient; Mini Disc; Musical Director. **Md.** = Maryland. **Md** (*Chem.*) = mendelevium. **MDA** (*Pharm.*) = 3,4-methylenedioxyamphetamine, a synthetic hallucinogenic drug. **MDMA** (*Pharm.*) = 3,4-methylenedioxymethamphetamine, a derivative of amphetamine that causes euphoria and hallucinations, orig. produced as an appetite suppressant; also called *ecstasy*. **MDT** (*N. Amer.*) = Mountain Daylight Time. **ME** = Maine; Middle English; myalgic encephalomyelitis. **Me.** = Maine; [Fr.] *maître* (French advocate). **M.Econ.** = Master of Economics. **M.Ed.** = Master of Education. **med.** = medium. **M.Eng.** = Master of Engineering. **MEP** = Member of the European Parliament. **MeV** = mega-electronvolt(s). **MF** = medium frequency. **mf** (*Mus.*) = mezzo forte. **MFH** = Master of Foxhounds. **MG** = machine-gun. **Mg** (*Chem.*) = magnesium. **mg** = milligram(s). **MGB** = [Russ.] *Ministérstvo Gosudárstvennoĭ Bezopásnosti* Ministry of State Security. **MGM** = Metro-Goldwyn-Mayer (film company). **Mgr.** = manager; [Fr.] *Monseigneur*, Monsignor. **MH** = Medal of Honor. **MHC** (*Biochem.*) = major histocompatibility complex (of proteins involved in immunity). **MHD** = magnetohydrodynamic(s). **MHR** = Member of the House of Representatives (in the US and Australia). **MHz** = megahertz. **MI** = Michigan; Military Intelligence (*M.I.5.*, *M.I.6.*, respectively British security service and espionage departments, until 1964); Mounted Infantry. **mi.** = mile(s). **MIA** = missing in action. **Mic.** = Micah (in the Bible). **MICE** = Member of the Institution of Civil Engineers. **Mich.** = Michaelmas; Michigan. **Middx.** = Middlesex. **MIEE** = Member of the Institution of Electrical Engineers. **Min.** = Minister; Ministry. **min.** = minim; minimum; minute(s). **Minn.** = Minnesota. **MIRAS** /ˈmʌɪrəs/ = mortgage interest relief at source. **misc.** = miscellaneous. **Miss.** = Mississippi. **MIT** = Massachusetts Institute of Technology. **MJI** = Member of the Institute of Journalists. **M.Juris** /ˈdʒʊərɪs/ = [L] *Magister Juris* Master of Law. **Mk.** = mark (German currency); Mark (esp. New Testament). **Mk** = mark (I, II, III, etc.). **mks** = metre-kilogram-second (system). **Mkt.** = Market. **ml** = mile(s); millilitre(s). **MLA** = Member of the Legislative Assembly; Modern Language Association (of America). **MLC** = Member of the Legislative Council. **MLD** = minimum lethal dose. **M.Litt.** = [L] *Magister Litterarum* Master of Letters. **Mlle** = [Fr.] *Mademoiselle*. **Mlles** = [Fr.] *Mesdemoiselles*. **MLR** = minimum lending rate. **MLRS** = multiple launch rocket system. **MM** = Maelzel's metronome; [Fr.] *Messieurs*; Military Medal. **mm** = millimetre(s). **Mme** = [Fr.] *Madame*. **Mmes** = [Fr.] *Mesdames*. **m.m.f.** = magnetomotive force. **M.Mus.** = Master of Music. **MN** = Merchant Navy; Minnesota. **Mn** (*Chem.*) = manganese. **MO** = medical officer; Missouri; (*Chem.*) molecular orbital; money order. **Mo.** = Missouri. **Mo** (*Chem.*) = molybdenum. **mo.** = month. **m.o.** = [L] *modus operandi*. **MOD** = Ministry of Defence. **MOH** = Medical Officer of Health. **Mon.** = Monday; Monmouthshire (a former county in Wales). **Mont.** = Montana. **MOR** = middle-of-the-road. **MORI** /ˈmɒri/ = Market & Opinion Research International. **MOS** = metal-oxide semiconductor. **MOT** = Ministry of Transport; [ellipt. for *MOT test*] a compulsory annual test of the roadworthiness of a motor vehicle of above a specified age, or a certificate of passing such a test. **MP** = Member of Parliament; military police(man). **mp** (*Mus.*) = mezzo piano. **m.p.** = melting point. **m.p.g.** = miles per gallon. **m.p.h.** = miles per hour. **M.Phil.** = Master of Philosophy. **MPS** = Member of the Pharmaceutical Society. **MR** = Master of the Rolls. **MRA** = Moral Re-Armament. **MRBM** = medium-range ballistic missile. **MRC** = Medical Research Council. **MRCA** = multi-role combat aircraft. **MRI** = magnetic resonance imaging. **mRNA** (*Biochem.*) = messenger RNA. **MS** = manuscript; Master of Science; Master of Surgery; Mississippi; motor ship; multiple sclerosis. **MSC** = Manpower Services Commission. **M.Sc.** = Master of Science. **MS-DOS** /ɛmɛsˈdɒs/ (*Computing*) = Microsoft disc operating system (a proprietary name). **MSF** = Manufacturing, Science, and Finance (Union). **MSG** = monosodium glutamate. **Msgr.** = [Fr.] *Monseigneur*, Monsignor. **MSH** = melanocyte-stimulating hormone. **MSS** /ɛmˈɛsɪz/ = manuscripts. **MST** (*N. Amer.*) = Mountain Standard Time. **M.St.** = Master of Studies. **MT** = machine translation; mechanical transport; Montana; motor transport. **Mt.** = Mount. **MTB** = motor torpedo-boat. **M.Tech.** = Master of Technology. **Mus.B.**, **Mus. Bac.** = [L] *Musicae Baccalaureus* Bachelor of Music. **Mus.D.**, **Mus. Doc.** = [L] *Musicae Doctor* Doctor of Music. **MV** = megavolt(s); motor vessel; muzzle velocity. **MVO** = Member of the Royal Victorian Order. **MVP** = most valuable player. **MW** = medium wave; megawatt(s). **mW** = milliwatt(s). **M-way** = motorway. **Mx.** = maxwell(s); Middlesex. **MY** = motor yacht. **MYOB** = mind your own business.

'm *n.* see MA'AM *n.*

m' *possess. a.* see MY *possess. a.*

ma /mɑː/ *n. colloq.* E19. [Abbrev. of MAMMA *n.*[2]] Mother. Also, Mrs; used as a form of address to a middle-aged or elderly woman other than one's mother.

P. G. WODEHOUSE Did Ma Purkiss make a speech? A. CARTER They all scattered in fright, bawling for their mas. R. BARNARD Cheery cries of 'Come on, Ma' to elderly ladies.

Comb.: **ma-in-law**, pl. **mas-in-law**, = *mother-in-law* s.v. MOTHER *n.*[1]

maa /mɑː/ *v.i.* E19. [Imit. Cf. BAA.] Esp. of a sheep: bleat.

ma'am /mɑːm, mam, *unstressed* məm/ *n.* & *v.* M17. [Contr. See also MARM, MAUM, MEM *n.*[1], MUM *n.*[4]] A *n.* Also (*colloq.*) **'m** /(ə)m/. 1 Madam. Chiefly as a respectful form of address: now usu. to a member of royalty or to a superior officer in the women's armed forces, but formerly used more generally to any (esp. married) equal or superior. M17. †2 A person addressed as 'ma'am'. M–L18.

1 DICKENS 'Mrs Sparsit ma'am', said Mr. Bounderby. 'I am going to astonish you.' *Guardian* Do you call the Queen . . 'Ma'am' or 'Marm' . . ? (Correct answer: Ma'am to rhyme with Pam). THANK-YOU-*ma'am*.

B *v.t.* Address as 'ma'am'. E19.

G. R. SIMS Don't ma'am me—I'm a miss.

maar /mɑː/ *n.* Pl. **maars**, *maare* /ˈmɑːrə/. E19. [G dial.] 1 (Usu. **M-**.) A crater-lake in the Eifel district of Germany. E19. 2 *Geol.* A broad low-rimmed usu. lake-filled volcanic crater of a kind exemplified by the Eifel Maars, formed by an explosive event with little lava. L19.

maas /mɑːs/ *n. S. Afr.* Also in Zulu form **amasi** /əˈmɑːsi/. E19. [Afk. f. Zulu (pl.) *amasi* curdled milk.] Thick sour milk.

Maasai *n.* var. of MASAI.

maasbanker /masˈbaŋkə, mɒsˈbɒŋkə/ *n. S. Afr.* M19. [Afk. f. Du. *marsbanker*. Cf. MOSSBUNKER.] The scad, *Trachurus trachurus*.

mab /mab/ *n.* Long *obs.* exc. *dial.* See also MOB *n.*[2] M16. [Origin unkn.] A slattern; a promiscuous woman.

mabele /məˈbiːli/ *n. S. Afr.* E19. [Bantu: cf. Zulu, Xhosa *ibele*, pl. *amabele*.] Kaffir corn, *Sorghum bicolor* var. *caffrorum*; meal or porridge made from this.

mac /mak/ *n.*[1] Also (earlier) †**mack**. E17. [*Mac-* (also written *Mc-*) patronymic pref. in many Sc. & Ir. names = Ir., Gael. *mac* son.] **1** A person whose name contains the prefix *Mac-*; *gen.* a Scotsman, (formerly also) an Irishman of Celtic origin. E17. **2** Used as a familiar form of address to a (male) stranger. *colloq.* (chiefly *N. Amer.*). M20.

2 J. WAINWRIGHT The bouncer . . tapped him on the shoulder and said: 'Hey, mac'.

mac /mak/ *n.*[2] *colloq.* Also **mack**. E20. [Abbrev.] = MACKINTOSH 1.

macabre /məˈkɑːbr(ə)/, *foreign* makɑːbr/ *n.* & *a.* LME. [f. OFr. *macabré* adj. (mod. *macabre*), perh. alt. of *Macabé* Maccabaeus, Maccabee, w. ref. to a miracle play containing the slaughter of the Maccabees. In early use perh. regarded as a proper name.] **A** *n.* **1** *dance of macabre*, = DANSE MACABRE. Long *obs.* exc. *Hist.* LME. **2** A macabre happening. *rare.* E20.

B *adj.* Grim, gruesome. Orig. in *dance macabre*. Cf. DANSE MACABRE. M19.

H. ACTON With macabre humour—somewhat sinister in retrospect—Nancy wrote . . about her tomb and burial. GODFREY SMITH The macabre pull of the Chamber of Horrors still exercises its malevolent thrall.

macabrely *adv.* M20.

macaco /məˈkeɪkəʊ/ *n.*[1] Now *rare* or *obs.* Pl. **-os**. L18. [Port.: see MACAQUE. Cf. MACAUCO.] A macaque; a monkey resembling a macaque.

macaco *n.*[2] var. of MACAUCO.

macadam /məˈkadəm/ *a.* & *n.* E19. [John Loudon *McAdam* (1756–1836), Brit. surveyor.] **A** *adj.* Of a roadway: of the kind laid down by McAdam; macadamized. See also TARMACADAM. E19. **B** *n.* The material of which a macadamized road is made. E19.

macadamia /makəˈdeɪmɪə/ *n.* E20. [mod.L (see below), f. John *Macadam* (1827–65), Scottish-born chemist.] Any of various Australian evergreen trees of the genus *Macadamia* (family Proteaceae), esp. *M. integrifolia* and *M. tetraphylla* (both also called *Queensland nut*) which yield edible nuts (also *macadamia nut*, *macadamia tree*); the nut of any of these trees.

macadamize /məˈkadəmʌɪz/ *v.t.* Also **-ise**. E19. [f. MACADAM + -IZE.] **1** Make or repair (a road) according to McAdam's system, by laying down successive layers of broken stone of nearly uniform size, each layer being consolidated by pressure before the next is laid. Freq. as *macadamized* ppl a. E19. **b** *fig.* Make level or even; raze. Now *rare*. E19. **2** Convert into road-metal; break up into pieces. Now *rare* or *obs.* E19.

macadamiˈzation *n.* the action of macadamizing a road; the process, practice, or system of making macadamized roads: E19. **macadamizer** *n.* (*a*) a person who makes macadamized roads; †(*b*) a person who rides on roads when hunting: E19.

macana /məˈkɑːnə/ *n.* M16. [Sp., Port. *macaná* f. Taino.] An ironwood club used by some indigenous S. American peoples.

Macanese /makəˈniːz/ *n.* & *a.* Also (earlier) **Macaoese** /makaʊˈiːz/, **Macaonese** /makaʊˈniːz/. E20. [f. *Macao* (see below), Port. *Macau*, after *Japanese* etc.: see -ESE.] **A** *n.* Pl. same. **1** A native or inhabitant of Macao, a Portuguese city and territory on the south coast of China, *esp.* one of mixed Chinese and Portuguese descent. E20. **2** The Portuguese creole language used in Macao. M20. **B** *adj.* Of or pertaining to Macao or the Macanese. E20.

†**macao** *n.*[1] Also **macco**. L18–L19. [f. as prec.] A game related to baccarat, in which each player receives only one card.

†**macao** *n.*[2] see MACAW *n.*[1]

Macaoese, **Macaonese** *ns.* & *adjs.* see MACANESE.

macaque /məˈkɑːk, -ˈkak/ *n.* L17. [Fr. f. Port. *macaco* f. Bantu *makaku* some monkeys, f. *ma* numerical sign + *kaku* monkey. Cf. MACACO *n.*[1], MACAUCO.] †**1** A kind of monkey native to Brazil. Only in L17. **2** Any of numerous monkeys of the Old World genus *Macaca*, including the rhesus monkey, *M. mulatta*, and the Barbary ape, *M. sylvanus*. M18.

2 JAPANESE *macaque*. *pigtailed macaque*: see PIGTAILED (a). *rhesus macaque*: see RHESUS 1.

Macaronesian /ˌmakərə(ʊ)ˈniːzjən, -ʒ(ə)n/ *a.* E20. [f. *Macaronesia* (see below), f. Gk *makarōn nēsoi* Islands of the Blessed (mythical islands later identified with the Canaries etc.), f. *makar* blessed or happy man + *nēsos* island, after *Polynesia* etc.: see -IAN.] Chiefly *Bot.* Of or pertaining to Macaronesia, a biogeographical region which embraces islands in the eastern N. Atlantic (principally the Azores, Madeira, Canary Islands, and Cape Verde Islands).

macaroni /makəˈrəʊni/ *n.* Pl. **-ies**. L16. [It. †*mac(c)aroni*, later *maccheroni*, pl. of †*mac(c)a-*, *maccherone* f. late Gk *makaria* barley food.] **1** Pasta in the form of tubes; an Italian dish consisting largely of this and usu. a sauce. L16. **2** A fop, a dandy; *spec.* one belonging to an 18th-cent. group who imitated extravagant Continental fashions. *obs.* exc. *Hist.* M18. **3** *Hist.* A West Indian coin worth a quarter of a dollar or (later) one shilling. E19. **4** In full *macaroni penguin*. A penguin, *Eudyptes chrysolophus*, apparently so called from its orange crest. M19. **5** An Italian. *slang. derog.* M19. **6** Nonsense, meaningless talk. *slang* (chiefly *Austral.*). E20.

Comb.: **macaroni cheese** a savoury dish consisting of macaroni baked or served with a cheese sauce; **macaroni tool** a square-cutting wood-carving chisel used for finishing recesses.

†**macaronian** *a.* = MACARONIC *a.*: only in 18. **macaronism** *n.* (now *rare* or *obs.*) behaviour characteristic of a macaroni; dandyism: L18.

macaronic /makəˈrɒnɪk/ *a.* & *n.* E17. [mod.L *macaronicus* f. It. †*macaronico*, later *maccheronico*, joc. f. *macaroni*: see prec., -IC.] **A** *adj.* †**1** Of the nature of a jumble or medley. E17–E19. **2** (Of verse) of a burlesque form in which vernacular words are introduced into the context of another language, esp. Latin, with appropriate inflections etc.; resembling the mixed jargon of such poetry. M17. †**3** Pertaining to a macaroni; foppish, conceited. *rare.* Only in E19. **B** *n.* †**1** A jumble, a medley. Only in E17. **2** Macaronic language or composition; in *pl.*, macaronic verses. M17.

macaronically *adv.* E19.

macaroon /makəˈruːn/ *n.* L16. [Fr. *macaron* f. It. *maccarone*: see MACARONI, -OON.] †**1** A buffoon, a dolt. Also (*dial.*), a fop. L16–E19. **2** A small cake or biscuit consisting chiefly of ground almonds, white of egg, and sugar; the mixture used to bake this. E17. †**3** = MACARONI 1. E–M18.

Macartney /məˈkɑːtni/ *n.* E19. [George, Earl *Macartney* (1737–1806), Brit. ambassador to China.] **1** *Macartney rose*, an evergreen white-flowered climbing rose, *Rosa bracteata*, native to China. E19. **2** In full *Macartney pheasant*. A fireback pheasant, esp. *Lophura ignita*. Now *rare* or *obs.* M19.

Macassar /məˈkasə/ *a.* & *n.* W. ref. to people or language now usu. **Makasar**. M17. [Earlier form of *Makasar*: see below.] **A** *adj.* Obtained from or associated with Makasar, a district of the island of Sulawesi (Celebes), Indonesia. Also = MAKASARESE *a.* M17.

Macassar ebony a form of ebony from Sulawesi and neighbouring islands. **Macassar oil** = sense B.1 below.

B *n.* **1** A kind of oil for the hair, orig. represented as consisting of ingredients obtained from Makasar. Cf. ANTIMACASSAR *n.* E19. **2** = MAKASARESE *n.* E19.

Macassarese *n.* & *a.* see MAKASARESE.

macauco /məˈkɔːkəʊ/ *n.* Now *rare* or *obs.* Also **macaco** /məˈkeɪkəʊ/. Pl. **-os**. M18. [Fr. *mococo*, perh. ult. f. Malagasy *maka*, *maki* lemur. Cf. MACACO *n.*[1], MACAQUE.] A lemur.

Macaulayesque /məkɔːlɪˈɛsk/ *a.* M19. [f. *Macaulay* (see below) + -ESQUE.] Characteristic of or resembling the historical method or (esp.) literary style of Thomas Babington, Lord Macaulay (1800–59), English historian.

macaw /məˈkɔː/ *n.*[1] Also (earlier) †**macao**. E17. [Port. *macao*, of unkn. origin.] Any of various large long-tailed parrots belonging to the genus *Ara* and other genera, native to tropical and subtropical America.

scarlet macaw: see SCARLET *a.*

macaw *n.*[2] see MACCA.

macca /ˈmakə/ *n.* Also (earlier) **macaw** /məˈkɔː/. M17. [Carib: cf. Arawak *mocoya*, *macoya*.] A spiny West Indian palm tree, *Acrocomia aculeata*, the nuts of which yield a fragrant oil; *gen.* any prickly shrub; prickles.

Comb.: **macca-fat (tree)** an oil-bearing palm, esp. *Acrocomia aculeata* or the oil palm, *Elaeis guineensis*.

Maccabee /ˈmakəbiː/ *n.* LME. [L *Maccabaeus*, Gk *Makkabaios*, epithet of Judas (see below), perh. f. Heb. *maqqeḇeṯ* hammer.] *Jewish Hist.* Any of a Jewish family (or their supporters), members of which (esp. Judas Maccabaeus) led a religious revolt in Judaea against the Syrian Seleucid king Antiochus IV, in 165 BC. Usu. in *pl.*

(**Books of**) **the Maccabees** four books of Jewish history and theology, of which the first two are included in the Apocrypha.

Maccaˈbean *a.* & *n.* (*a*) *adj.* of or pertaining to Judas Maccabaeus or the Maccabees; (*b*) *n.* = MACCABEE: M17.

macchia /ˈmɑːkɪə/ *n.* E20. [Corsican It. f. L *macula* spot.] = MAQUIS 1.

†**macco** *n.* var. of MACAO *n.*[1]

maccoboy /ˈmakəbɔɪ/ *n.* Also †**-baw**, **macouba** /məˈkuːbə/, & other vars. M18. [*Macouba*, a district in Martinique.] A kind of snuff, usu. scented with attar of roses.

mace /meɪs/ *n.*[1] ME. [OFr. *masse*, *mace* (mod. *masse* large hammer etc.) f. Proto-Romance.] **1** *Hist.* A weapon consisting of a heavy staff or club, either entirely of metal or having a metal head, often spiked. Formerly also *gen.*, a club. ME. †**b** The trident of Neptune. L16–L18. **2** A sceptre or staff of office, resembling the weapon of war, which is carried before (or was formerly carried by) certain officials; *spec.* that which lies on the table in the House of Commons when the Speaker is in the chair, viewed as a symbol of the authority of the House. LME. **b** A mace-bearer. M17. **3** A stick with a flat square head, used for propelling the ball in bagatelle or (formerly) billiards. E18.

1 *fig.*: LONGFELLOW The loud and ponderous mace of Time knocks at the golden portals of the day. 2 *Sergeant-at-mace*: see SERGEANT.

Comb.: **mace-bearer** a person who carries a mace, esp. as a symbol of authority ceremonially preceding a high dignitary.

mace /meɪs/ *n.*[2] ME. [AN *macis* or (O)Fr. *macis*, f. L *macir* red spicy bark from India: *mace* formed as sing. of *macis*, erron. taken as pl.] A spice consisting of the dried fleshy aril surrounding the seed (nutmeg) of the fruit of the nutmeg tree.

mace /meɪs/ *n.*[3] L16. [Malay *mās* prob. f. Skt *māṣa* weight of about 17 grains or 1.1 grams.] *Hist.* **1** In Malay countries: a small gold coin weighing 9 grains or .6 gram. L16. **2** *Hist.* A monetary unit of China equal to one-tenth of a silver liang or tael. E17.

mace /meɪs/ *n.*[4] *slang.* M18. [Origin unkn.] Swindling, robbery by fraud.

on mace on credit.

Mace /meɪs/ *n.*[5] Also **m-**. M20. [Prob. a use of MACE *n.*[1]] (Proprietary name for) an irritant chemical preparation used in aerosol form as a disabling weapon.

mace /meɪs/ *v.*[1]*t.* & *i. slang.* L18. [f. MACE *n.*[4]] Swindle, cheat.

mace /meɪs/ *v.*[2]*t. rare.* M19. [f. MACE *n.*[1]] Strike (as) with a mace.

Macedo- /ˈmasɪdəʊ/ *comb. form.* M19. [f. MACEDONIAN *a.*[1]] Forming names of dialects spoken in Macedonia, as *Macedo-Bulgarian, -Romanian*, etc.

macédoine /ˈmasɪdwɑːn/ *n.* E19. [Fr. f. *Macédoine* Macedonia, w. ref. to the diversity of peoples in the Macedonian empire of Alexander the Great.] Mixed fruit or vegetables cut up into small pieces; *fig.* a medley, a mixture.

†**Macedon** *n.* & *a.* LME–E18. [L *Macedon-, Macedo*, Gk *Makedōn, -don-* Macedonia.] A *n.* A Macedonian. LME–E18.
the Macedon: Alexander the Great.
B *adj.* Macedonian. LME–E18.

Macedonian /masɪˈdəʊnɪən/ *n.*[1] & *a.*[1] ME. [f. L *Macedonius*, Gk *Makedonios*, f. as prec.: see -AN.] A *n.* 1 A native of Macedonia, in ancient times a country corresponding to parts of northern Greece, Bulgaria, and present-day Macedonia; a native of present-day Macedonia, north of Greece. ME. 2a The language of ancient Macedonia, usu. regarded as a variety of Greek. M16. b The Slavonic language of present-day Macedonia and adjacent areas of Bulgaria and Greece. M20. B *adj.* Of or pertaining to (ancient or present-day) Macedonia or Macedonian. M16.

Macedonian /masɪˈdəʊnɪən/ *n.*[2] & *a.*[2] L15. [eccl.L *Macedonianus* adj., f. *Macedonius* (see below): see -AN.] *Eccl. Hist.* A *n.* A follower of the Pneumatomachian doctrine attributed to Macedonius, a bishop of Constantinople in the 4th cent. AD L15. B *adj.* Of or pertaining to Macedonians or their beliefs. L16.

macer /ˈmeɪsə/ *n.*[1] ME. [OFr. *maissier, massier*, f. *masse* MACE *n.*[1]: see -ER[2].] A mace-bearer; *spec.* in Scotland, an official who keeps order in courts of law.

macer /ˈmeɪsə/ *n.*[2] *slang.* E19. [f. MACE *v.*[1] + -ER[1].] A swindler, a cheat.

†**macerable** *a. rare.* M17–M18. [f. as next + -ABLE.] Able to be macerated.

maceral /ˈmas(ə)r(ə)l/ *n.* M20. [f. L *macerare* MACERATE *v.* + -AL[1], after *mineral.*] *Geol.* Any of the microscopic structural constituents of coal.

macerate /ˈmasərеɪt/ *n.* M20. [f. the vb, after *filtrate* etc.] A product obtained by maceration.

macerate /ˈmasəreɪt/ *v.* M16. [L *macerat-* pa. ppl stem of *macerare*, prob. cogn. w. Gk *massein* knead: see -ATE[3].] 1 *v.t.* Soften by steeping in a liquid, with or without heat; wear *away* or separate the soft parts of, by steeping. M16. b *v.i.* Undergo maceration in a liquid. E17. 2 *v.t.* Cause to grow thinner or to waste away, esp. by fasting. M16. †3 *v.t.* Fret, vex, worry. L16–M18.
1 R. B. TODD More complete mastication is performed after the food has been long macerated in the paunch. 2 I. D'ISRAELI Her frame was macerated by her secret sorrows. 3 L. STERNE A city so macerated with expectation.
macerator *n.* a person who or thing which macerates something; *esp.* a vessel or machine used for macerating a substance: L19.

maceration /masəˈreɪʃ(ə)n/ *n.* L15. [L *maceratio(n-)*, f. as prec.: see -ATION.] 1 The process of wasting away through fasting etc.; mortification of the flesh; an instance of this; the condition so produced. L15. 2 The action or process of softening by steeping in a liquid; the state of being subjected to this process; an instance of this. M16. †3 Fretting, vexation, worry; an instance of this. E–M17.

macfarlane /məkˈfɑːlən/ *n.* E20. [Prob. f. the surname *Macfarlane.*] A kind of caped overcoat with slits in the sides to allow access to pockets in the clothing underneath.

Mach /mɑːk, mak, *foreign* maːx/ *n.* E20. [Ernst *Mach* (1838–1916), Austrian physicist and philosopher.] 1 *Mach's principle*, the hypothesis that a body's inertial mass results from its interaction with the rest of the matter in the universe. E20. 2 *Mach number*, the ratio of the speed of a body to the speed of sound in the surrounding medium; *Mach ˈone, two* (or *1, 2*), etc., a speed corresponding to a Mach number of one, two, etc. M20. 3 *Mach('s) bands*, illusory bright or dark bands perceived where the spatial rate of variation of surface brightness abruptly increases or decreases (as at the edge of an indistinct shadow). M20.
Comb.: **Machmeter** an air-speed indicator that reads directly in Mach numbers.
Machian *a.* & *n.* (*a*) *adj.* of, pertaining to, or characteristic of Ernst Mach or his philosophical ideas, in which the principles of mechanics were based on an extreme sensationalist empiricism; (*b*) *n.* a follower or adherent of Mach: E20. **Machism** *n.* the theories of Ernst Mach, *esp.* his concept of empiro-criticism E20.

machaerdont *n.* & *a.* var. of MACHAIRODONT.

machair /ˈmakə, -x-/ *n. Sc.* L17. [Gael.] In Scotland: a flat or low-lying coastal strip of arable or grassland; land of this nature.

machairodont /məˈkʌɪrədɒnt/ *n.* & *a.* Also **-chaer-**. L19. [f. Gk *makhaira* sword, sabre + -ODONT. Cf. next.] *Palaeont.* A *n.* An extinct sabre-toothed felid of the subfamily Machairodontinae. L19. B *adj.* Of or pertaining to this subfamily; sabre-toothed. L19.
machairodus *n.* a machairodont of the genus *Machairodus* M19.

machan /mʌˈtʃɑːn/ *n.* L19. [Hind. *macān* f. Skt *mañcaka.*] In the Indian subcontinent: an elevated platform, esp. for use in hunting.

Machangana *n.pl.* see SHANGAAN *n.*

mâche /mɑːʃ/ *n.* Orig. Anglicized (only in *pl.*) as †**maches**. L17. [Fr.] Lamb's lettuce, cornsalad.

†**machecole** *v.t.* LME–M16. [OFr. *machecoller, machicoler*: see MACHICOLATE.] = MACHICOLATE.

macher /ˈmaxə/ *n. US* (freq. *derog.*). M20. [Yiddish f. G = maker, doer.] A man of importance, a bigwig; a braggart.

†**maches** *n.* see MÂCHE.

machete /məˈtʃɛti, -ˈʃɛti/ *n.* Also Anglicized as **matchet** /ˈmatʃɪt/. L16. [Sp., f. *macho* hammer f. L *marcus.*] A broad and heavy knife or cutlass, used, esp. in Central America and the W. Indies, as a tool or a weapon.

Machiavel /ˈmakɪəvɛl/ *n.* L16. [Anglicized f. *Machiavelli*: see next.] A person who acts on the principles of Machiavelli; an unscrupulous schemer.
machiaˈvellic *a.* = MACHIAVELLIAN *a.* M19. **machiaˈvellism** *n.* = MACHIAVELLIANISM L16. **machiaˈvellist** *n.* = MACHIAVELLIAN *n.* L16.

machiavellian /ˌmakɪəˈvɛlɪən/ *n.* & *a.* Also (esp. as n.) **M-**. M16. [f. Niccolò dei *Machiavelli* (1469–1527), Florentine statesman (see below) + -IAN.] A *n.* A person who adopts the principles recommended by Machiavelli in his treatise on statecraft; a person preferring expediency to morality. M16. B *adj.* Of, pertaining to, or characteristic of Machiavelli or his principles; adopting unscrupulous methods; duplicitous, deceitful; cunning, scheming. L16.
machiavellianism *n.* the principles and practice of Machiavelli; (an instance of) cunning or duplicity in behaviour: E17. **machiavellianly** *adv.* (*rare*) in a machiavellian manner M17.

machicolate /məˈtʃɪkəleɪt/ *v.t.* L18. [AL *machicollare*, f. OFr. *machicoler*, ult. f. Prov. *machacol*, f. *macar* beat, crush + *col* neck: see -ATE[3]. Cf. earlier MACHECOLE.] *Archit.* Provide with machicolations. Chiefly as *machicolated* ppl a.

machicolation /mətʃɪkəˈleɪʃ(ə)n/ *n.* L18. [f. prec. + -ATION.] *Archit.* An opening between the corbels which support a projecting parapet, or in the vault of a portal, through which combustibles, molten lead, stones, etc., could be dropped on assailants below. Also, a projecting structure containing a range of such openings.

machicoulis /mɑːtʃɪˈkuːli/ *n.* Now *rare* or *obs.* L18. [Fr. *mâchecoulis, mâchi-* f. OFr. *maschecoulis* rel. to Prov. *machacol*: see MACHICOLATE.] = prec.

machila /məˈʃiːlə/ *n.* Also **-ll-**. L19. [Port. f. as MUNCHEEL.] A conveyance, usu. for one person, used in Africa and consisting of a hammock slung between two poles, carried by bearers.

machinable /məˈʃiːnəb(ə)l/ *a.* E20. [f. MACHINE *v.* + -ABLE.] 1 Able to be cut by machine tools. E20. 2 Able to be processed by a computer or other machine. M20.
machinaˈbility *n.* E20.

machinal /ˈmakɪn(ə)l/ *a.* Now *arch. rare.* L17. [L *machinalis*, f. *machina* MACHINE *n.*: see -AL[1].] Of or pertaining to a machine or machines; mechanical.

machinate /ˈmakɪneɪt, ˈmaʃ-/ *v.* Pa. pple **-ated**, (earlier) †**-ate**. L16. [L *machinat-* pa. ppl stem of *machinari*, f. *machina* MACHINE *n.*: see -ATE[3].] 1 *v.t.* Contrive, plan, plot, (usu. in a bad sense). Now *rare.* L16. 2 *v.i.* Lay plots; intrigue, scheme. E17.
machinating *ppl a.* that machinates; given to scheming: M18. **machinator** *n.* a person who machinates; an intriguer, a plotter, a schemer: E17.

machination /makɪˈneɪʃ(ə)n, maʃ-/ *n.* LME. [(O)Fr., or L *machinatio(n-)*, f. as prec.: see -ATION.] 1 An instance of plotting or contrivance; an intrigue, a plot, a scheme. LME. 2 The action or process of contriving or planning; intrigue, plotting. Now *rare.* M16. †3 Something contrived or constructed; a machine (esp. of war), a framework, an apparatus. Only in 17. †4 The use or construction of machinery. M17–E18.
1 W. RAEPER Through the machinations of the evil Fairy . . the level of the lake begins to subside. M. FORSTER All the machinations of the complicated plot. 2 G. GISSING A schemer endeavouring to encompass vulgar ends by machination.

machine /məˈʃiːn/ *n.* M16. [(O)Fr. f. L *machina* device, contrivance, engine f. Gk *makhana* (Doric), *mēkhanē*, f. *mēkhos* contrivance, ult. f. Gmc base of MAY *v.*[1]] 1 A structure of any kind, material or immaterial; something constructed. Now *rare.* M16. †b A scheme, a plot. L16–E18. †c A ship, a boat. M17–E19. d A vehicle, a (wheeled) conveyance; formerly *esp.* a stagecoach, a mailcoach; *ellipt.* = BATHING-*machine. obs.* exc. *Hist.* L17. 2 The human and animal frame. Chiefly *fig.*: cf. sense 5 below. E17. 3 [L *machina*] a A military engine or siege-tower. *obs.* exc. *Hist.* M17. b *Theatr.* A contrivance for the production of stage effects; in *pl.*, stage machinery. *obs.* exc. *Hist.* M17. c In literature etc.: a contrivance for the sake of effect; a supernatural agency, personage, or incident introduced into a narrative; the interposition of one of these. L17. 4 An apparatus, an appliance; a device for applying mechanical power and having a number of interconnected parts, each with a definite function, *esp.* one that does not utilize human strength; an apparatus of a particular (specified or understood) kind; a bicycle, a motor vehicle; an aircraft; a computer; a typewriter. M17. b *Mech.* Any instrument that transmits force or directs its application. E18. c The penis. Also, a condom. *slang.* M18. 5 *fig.* A thing regarded as a combination of parts moving mechanically, often as contrasted with a being exercising free will; a person who acts mechanically or without thought, or with unfailing regularity. L17. b The controlling organization of a political party or similar body; a well-organized group acting with (ruthless) efficiency. M19.
1 BROWNING To each mortal peradventure earth becomes a new machine. d BURKE Your very kind letter . . I received by the machine. 2 ADDISON Cheerfulness is . . the best Promoter of Health. Repinings . . wear out the machine insensibly. 3b *god from the machine*: see GOD *n.* c ADDISON The changing of the Trojan fleet into Water-Nymphs . . is the most violent Machine of the whole Aeneid. 4 W. THOMSON Windmills as hitherto made are very costly machines. J. K. JEROME We were riding our machines . . in the company of many other cyclists. O. DOPPING A company which changes computers normally changes to a machine which is considerably faster. D. ROWE We no longer send five-year-olds into the factory to tend the machines. *Bella* Machines can measure the amount of stress you are under. *answering machine, flying-machine, gaming-machine, sewing-machine, vending machine, washing machine*, etc. *rotary machine, spindle machine*, etc. *Turing machine* etc. *infernal machine*: see INFERNAL *a.* b G. D. CAMPBELL A man's arm is a machine. **compound machine**: the efficiency

of which depends on the combined action of two or more parts. **simple machine**: in which there is no combination of parts, e.g. a lever. c J. CLELAND With that formidable machine of his, he lets the fury loose. 5 A. HAMILTON The nearer the soldiers approach to machines, perhaps the better. COLERIDGE To what purpose was he made a spirit of reason..not a machine of instinct? *fig.*: P. BOWLES The vast beautiful machine of which the air and the mountainside were parts. b I. MCEWAN People with connections in the Party machine.

Comb.: **machine age** an era notable for its extensive use of mechanical devices; esp. *the* present era so considered; **machine code** *Computing* = *machine language* below; **machine finish** a moderately smooth finish given to paper by the machine on which it is made; **machine-head** a head for a guitar etc. having worms and pinions, instead of pegs, for tightening the strings; **machine instruction** *Computing* an instruction in a machine language; **machine language** *Computing* a language that a particular computer can handle or act on directly, without further translation; **machine-pistol** a sub-machine-gun; **machine-readable** *a.* in a form that a computer can process; **machine room** a room in which machines, *spec.* printing-presses, are operated; **machine shop** a workshop for making or repairing machines or parts of machines; **machine tool** a mechanically-operated tool for cutting or shaping wood, metals, etc.; **machine translation**: by a computer; **machine-wash** *v.t.* wash in a washing machine; *machine word*: see WORD *n.* 12c.

machineless *a.* that does not use or require a machine or machines E20. **machine-like** *a.* & *adv.* (*a*) *adj.* resembling (that of) a machine, esp. in smoothness or independence of operation; (*b*) *adv.* in the manner of a machine: E18. **machiner** *n.* (*a*) a person who operates a machine; †(*b*) a horse employed to draw a stagecoach or other 'machine' (see MACHINE *n.* 1d): E19.

machine /məˈʃiːn/ *v.* LME. [In branch I f. (O)Fr. *machiner* f. L *machinari* MACHINATE; in branch II f. the n.] †I **1** *v.t.* & *i.* Contrive, plot. LME–L17.

II **2** *v.t.* Form, make, or operate on by means of a machine; cut, engrave, shape, print, or sew (something) by means of a machine. M19. **3** *v.i.* Operate a machine. *rare.* L19. **4** *v.i.* Undergo shaping etc. by machine (in a specified way). M20.

2 *Arena* Rather than mould the cap and barrel..we machine them..from a solid block. 4 *Practical Woodworking* Some woods do machine better than others.

machine-gun /məˈʃiːngʌn/ *n.*, *v.*, & *a.* L19. [f. MACHINE *n.* + GUN *n.*] **A** *n.* A (mounted or portable) gun which is mechanically loaded and fired, and is capable of continuous fire. L19.

Lewis machine-gun, *Maxim machine-gun*, *sub-machine-gun*, etc.

B *attrib.* or as *adj.* Like (that of) a machine-gun, esp. in rapidly (and noisily) repeated action. E20.

H. J. LASKI They cross-examined me with machine-gun rapidity. M. PUZO That machine-gun typing.

C *v.t.* Fire at with a machine-gun; hit with machine-gun fire. E20.

machine-gunner *n.* E20.

machinery /məˈʃiːn(ə)ri/ *n.* L17. [f. MACHINE *n.* + -ERY.] **1** The assemblage of contrivances employed for effect in literary work; supernatural personages and incidents, or other contrivances for effect, introduced in a narrative. L17. **2** Machines, or the constituent parts of a machine, taken collectively; the mechanism of a machine or machines. Freq. *transf.* & *fig.*, functional equipment; means or procedures available for action (foll. by *for*, *of*). M18. **3** A system or kind of machinery. M19.

1 HANNAH MORE Those who..deny the immortality of the soul..introduce the machinery of ghosts. ALDOUS HUXLEY Entangled in a novel I can't quite find a satisfactory machinery for. 2 LD MACAULAY The whole machinery of government was out of joint. J. W. KRUTCH Nuclear weapons and all the machinery of war. *Guardian* The machinery for salary-fixing in the universities is complicated. H. WILSON The industries producing plant and machinery cannot meet the orders. J. GARDAM Then away went the horses and in came the machinery. *Scientific American* The most central molecular machinery of modern organisms. 3 E. M. FORSTER All these tubes and buttons and machineries.

machinist /məˈʃiːnɪst/ *n.* E18. [Fr. *machiniste*, f. *machine*; later directly f. MACHINE *n.* + -IST.] **1** A person who invents, makes, or controls machines or machinery; an engineer. E18. **2** *spec.* A person who constructs or manages the stage machinery in a theatre. Now *rare.* M18. **3** A person who operates a machine, esp. a sewing-machine or machine tool. L19.

machinofacture /məˌʃiːnə(ʊ)ˈfaktʃə/ *n.* E20. [f. MACHINE *n.* + -O- + FACTURE, after *manufacture*.] The making of articles by machine; mechanization.

machismo /məˈtʃɪzməʊ, -ˈkɪz-/ *n.* M20. [Mex. Sp., f. as MACHO + *-ismo* -ISM.] The quality of being macho; male virility, masculine pride; a show of this.

attrib.: *Listener* Tough machismo exteriors,.. hovering towards hostility, yet not hostile.

macho /ˈmatʃəʊ/ *n.* & *a.* Orig. *US.* E20. [Mex. Sp. = male animal or plant, (as adj.) masculine, vigorous.] **A** *n.* Pl. **-os**. **1** A man; *spec.* an assertively vigorous man, a 'tough guy'. E20. **2** = MACHISMO. M20.

1 *Sunday Express* The machos and poseurs drink their lager straight out of the can now. 2 E. JONG She does love him... His blue-collar macho.

B *adj.* Ostentatiously or notably manly and virile. E20.

B. T. BRADFORD The glamorous macho Hollywood movie star. P. D. JAMES A macho enthusiasm for selective violence.

machree /məˈkriː/ *n.* *Anglo-Ir.* E19. [Ir. *mo chroidhe* (of) my heart.] As a form of address: my dear, darling.

Macht-politik /ˈmaxtpolitiːk/ *n.* E20. [G, f. *Macht* power, strength + *Politik* policy, politics.] Power politics; strength as a potential factor to use in gaining a desired result.

-machy /məki/ *suff.* [Gk *-makhia*, f. *-makhos* that fights, f. base of *makhē* battle: see -Y[3].] Used, w. medial -o-, in adoptions of Gk words and analogous Eng. formations w. the sense 'fighting, warfare', as *iconomachy*, *logomachy*.

Machzor /ˈmɑːkzɔː, -x-/ *n.* M19. [Heb. *maḥzōr* cycle.] A Jewish prayer book for use at festivals. Cf. SIDDUR.

macilent /ˈmasɪl(ə)nt/ *a.* Now *rare.* LME. [L *macilentus*, f. *macer* thin, MEAGRE *a.*: see -LENT.] Lean, shrivelled, thin; *fig.* jejune.

macilence *n.* LME. **macilency** *n.* M17.

MacIntosh *n.* var. of MCINTOSH.

mack /mak/ *n.*[1] *slang.* L19. [Abbrev. of MACKEREL *n.*[2]] A pander.

†**mack** *n.*[2] see MAC *n.*[1]

mack *n.*[3] var. of MAC *n.*[2]

Mackay *n.* var. of MCCOY.

mackerel /ˈmak(ə)r(ə)l/ *n.*[1] Pl. **-s**, same. ME. [AN *makerel*, OFr. *maquerel* (mod. *maquereau*), of unkn. origin (cf. -EL[2]). Cf. med.L (Flanders) *macarellus* (12).] **1** Any of various swift-swimming pelagic fishes of the family Scombridae, of which several are commercially important as food fishes; esp. *Scomber scombrus*, of the N. Atlantic and Mediterranean, which approaches the shore in shoals in summer for spawning; (w. specifying wd) any of certain other fishes resembling these. Also, the flesh of any of these fishes as food. ME. **2** *Angling.* (An artificial fly imitating) a kind of mayfly. Also *mackerel-fly*. Now *rare* or *obs.* L18.

1 *a sprat to catch a mackerel*: see SPRAT *n.*[1] FRIGATE *mackerel*. *holy mackerel*: see HOLY *a.* 5. *horse-mackerel*: see HORSE *n.* *Monterey (Spanish) mackerel*: see MONTEREY 3. *Spanish mackerel*: see SPANISH *a.*

Comb.: **mackerel-back(ed)** *a.* †(*a*) *slang* long-backed; (*b*) *mackerel-back(ed) sky*, = *mackerel sky* below; **mackerel-boat**: for mackerel-fishing; **mackerel breeze, gale** a breeze that ruffles the water, said to favour the catching of mackerel; **mackerel clouds**: in a mackerel sky; *mackerel-fly*: see sense 2 above; *mackerel gale*: see *mackerel breeze* above; **mackerel gull** *N. Amer.* a tern; **mackerel shark** a shark of the family Lamnidae, esp. the porbeagle, *Lamna nasus*, or the mako, *Isurus oxyrinchus*; **mackerel sky** a sky dappled with rows of small white fleecy clouds, resembling the pattern on a mackerel's back.

mackereling *n.* (*a*) fishing for mackerel; (*b*) a patterned effect like that of a mackerel sky or mackerel's back: M19.

mackerel /ˈmak(ə)r(ə)l/ *n.*[2] *slang.* LME. [OFr. *maquerel* (mod. MAQUEREAU, *-elle*), f. MDu. *makelaer* (Du. *-aar*) broker, whence also OFr. *makelare*.] A procurer or procuress; a pimp.

Mackinaw /ˈmakɪnɔː/ *n.* E19. [*Mackinaw* City, Michigan, USA, formerly an important trading post.] **1** In full *Mackinaw boat* (or *skiff*). A large flat-bottomed sharp-ended boat, used on the Great Lakes of N. America. E19. **2** In full *Mackinaw blanket*. A thick blanket, such as used to be distributed to Indians of the North-West by the US government. E19. **3** A heavy woollen cloth, now usu. with a plaid design; a garment made of this; *esp.* (also *Mackinaw coat, jacket*) a thick double-breasted jacket. M19. **4** *Mackinaw trout*, the N. American lake trout, *Salvelinus namaycush*. M19.

mackintosh /ˈmakɪntɒʃ/ *n.* In sense 1 also †**M-**. M19. [Charles *Macintosh* (1766–1843), Sc. inventor.] **1** Orig. (also *Mackintosh coat* etc.), a coat, cloak, etc., made of waterproof material consisting of two or more layers of cloth stuck together with rubber. Now, a rainproof coat made of this or any other material. Cf. MACK *n.*[2] M19. **2** Cloth made waterproof by a layer of rubber. L19.

mackintoshed *a.* wearing or protected by a mackintosh M19.

mackle /ˈmak(ə)l/ *n.* Also **macle**. E18. [Fr. *macule* f. L *macula* spot. Cf. next, MACULE *n.*] A blurred impression in printing. Also, a blurred sheet.

mackle /ˈmak(ə)l/ *v.* Also **macle**. L16. [Prob. f. the n. (although recorded earlier). Cf. MACULE *v.*] †**1** *v.i.* Of a page: become blurred. Only in L16. **2** *v.t.* Orig., blur or spot (a sheet of paper). Now only *spec.*, print (a page) blurred or double. E18.

Maclaurin /məˈklɒrɪn/ *n.* E19. [C. *Maclaurin* (1698–1746), Sc. mathematician.] *Math.* **1** *Maclaurin('s) theorem*, Taylor's theorem in the special case of a function whose argument is zero. E19. **2** *Maclaurin('s) series*, a representation of a function *f*(*x*) as a Taylor series about the origin. E20.

macle /ˈmak(ə)l/ *n.*[1] M18. [Fr. f. L *macula* spot, mesh.] **1** *Her.* = MASCLE. *rare.* M18. **2** *Cryst.* A twinned crystal. E19. **3** *Min.* **a** = CHIASTOLITE. E19. **b** *Min.* A darker inclusion in a mineral. M19.

macled *a.* (of a crystal) twinned E19.

macle *n.*[2], *v.* vars. of MACKLE *n.*, *v.*

maclura /məˈkl(j)ʊərə/ *n.* E19. [mod.L (see below), f. William *Maclure* (1763–1840), US geologist.] A N. American deciduous tree, *Maclura pomifera* (family Moraceae), bearing an inedible fruit resembling an orange. Also called *Osage orange*.

macock /ˈmeɪkɒk/ *n.* *US* (now *Hist.*). Also **maycock**. L16. [Algonquian *mahcawq*.] An inferior kind of melon, formerly cultivated by some N. American Indians.

Mâcon /ˈmakɔ̃ː/ *n.* M19. [See below.] A red or white burgundy, produced in the district around Mâcon, a city in eastern France.

Maconochie /məˈkɒnəki/ *n.* *Mil. slang.* E20. [*Maconochie* Brothers of London, makers of such food.] Meat stewed with vegetables and tinned, esp. as supplied to soldiers on active service. Also, the stomach.

macouba *n.* var. of MACCOBOY.

macr- *comb. form* see MACRO-.

macramé /məˈkrɑːmi/ *n.* & *a.* M19. [Turk. *makrama* handkerchief, tablecloth, towel f. Arab. *mikrama* bed-cover, bedspread.] **A** *n.* A fringe, trimming, or lace of knotted thread or cord; knotted-work; the art of making this. M19.

B *attrib.* or as *adj.* Made of or by macramé. L19.

D. LEAVITT The canvas bases her mother uses for her macramé wall-hangings.

macrauchenia /makrɔːˈkiːnɪə/ *n.* M19. [mod.L (see below), f. Gk *makraukhēn* long-necked, f.

makros long + *aukhēn* neck: see -IA[1].] *Palaeont.* A long-necked perissodactyl of the genus *Macrauchenia*, known from fossil remains. Now only as mod.L genus name.

macro /ˈmakrəʊ/ *n.* & *a.* M20. [Independent use of next.] A *n.* Pl. **-os.** 1 *Computing.* A macro-instruction. M20. 2 *Photogr.* Macrophotography; a macro lens. M20.

B *adj.* Macroscopic, large-scale; overall, comprehensive; *Chem.* of macroanalysis; *Photogr.* pertaining to or used in macrophotography. Freq. contrasted w. *micro.* M20.

D. WILSON The logic for the individual programs is expressed in terms of macro and micro block-diagrams. *Language* His attention is primarily focused on sociolinguistic research on a fairly macro level.
macro lens: suitable for taking photographs unusually close to the subject.

macro- /ˈmakrəʊ/ *comb. form.* Bef. a vowel also **macr-**. [Gk *makro-*, f. *makros* long, large: see -O-.] Used in wds adopted f. Gk and in Eng. wds modelled on these, and as a freely productive pref., w. the senses 'long, large, large-scale, comprehensive', *Med.* 'abnormally enlarged or elongated'. Freq. contrasted w. *micro-*.

macroˈbenthic *a.* of or pertaining to the macrobenthos M20. **macroˈbenthos** *n.* the macrofauna of the benthos M20. **macroclimate** *n.* the general climate of a relatively large area M20. **macrocliˈmatic** *a.* of or pertaining to a macroclimate or macroclimates M20. **macrocyst** *n.* an unusually large cyst L19. **macrodiˈagonal** *n.* & *a.* (pertaining to or designating) the longer of the diagonals of a rhombic prism M19. **macro-engiˈneering** *n.* the design and construction of very large-scale engineering projects M20. **macro-evoˈlution** *n.* major evolutionary change, usu. over a long period; the evolution of genera or higher taxa: M20. **macro-evoˈlutionary** *a.* of or pertaining to macro-evolution M20. **macrofauna** *n.* (*Biol.*) (a) fauna made up of animals visible to the naked eye; (a) fauna not confined to a microhabitat: E20. **macrofossil** *n.* a fossil large enough to be discerned by the naked eye M20. **macrogamete** *n.* the larger (female) sex cell of a protozoan L19. **macroˈglobulin** *n.* (*Biochem.*) any immunoglobulin of very high molecular weight (about 1,000,000 or more) M20. **macroglobuliˈnaemia** *n.* an excess of macroglobulins in the blood M20. **macroˈglossia** *n.* abnormal enlargement of the tongue M19. **macroˈgnathic, -ˈgnathous** *adjs.* having one or both jaws long or protruding M19. **macro-instruction** *n.* (*Computing*) an instruction in a programming or source language which is equivalent to a specified set of ordinary instructions in an object language (which may be the source language or machine language) M20. **macrolinˈguistic** *a.* of or pertaining to macrolinguistics M20. **macrolinˈguistics** *n.* the branch of linguistics that deals with language and all its related aspects as a whole M20. **macromere** *n.* [Gk *meros* part] *Biol.* a large cell formed by unequal division of an ovum or embryo, e.g. in sea urchins, and appearing at the vegetative pole L19. **macroˈmeric** *a.* (*Biol.*) of or pertaining to a macromere or macromeres L19. **macroˈnodular** *a.* (*Med.*) (of cirrhosis) characterized by the presence of large nodules M20. **macroˈnucleus** *n.*, pl **-nuclei**, *Zool.* the larger of two nuclei in ciliated protozoans, concerned esp. with feeding L19. **macroˈnutrient** *n.* any of the chemical elements (as potassium, nitrogen, calcium, sulphur, phosphorus, or magnesium) which are normally taken up by plants as inorganic salts and are required for growth and development in relatively large amounts (rather than trace amounts) M20. **macrophagous** /məˈkrɒfəgəs/ *a.* (*Zool.*) feeding on relatively large pieces of food M20. **macroˈphallic** *a.* having a large phallus L20. **macroˈphysical** *a.* of or pertaining to macrophysics E20. **macrophysics** *n.* the part of physics that deals with bodies and phenomena on a macroscopic scale E20. **macrophyte** *n.* any plant, esp. any aquatic plant, large enough to be discerned by the naked eye E20. **macrophytic** /-ˈfɪtɪk/ *a.* of the nature of a macrophyte; of or pertaining to macrophytes: E20. **maˈcropterous** *a.* long-winged M19. **macro-scale** *n.* a large or macroscopic scale; *Chem.* the scale of macroanalysis: M20. **macrosegment** *n.* (*Ling.*) a continuous unit of speech between two pauses, with a single intonation M20. **macroseism** /-sʌɪz(ə)m/ *n.* orig., a major earthquake; now, any earthquake, as opp. to a microseism: E20. **macroˈseismic** *a.* of, pertaining to, or of the nature of a macroseism; (of data) obtained other than with a seismometer: E20. **macrosocioˈlogical** *a.* of or pertaining to macrosociology M20. **macrosociˈology** *n.* the part of sociology that deals with large social groups and large-scale features of human society M20. **macrospore** *n.* (*Bot.*) = MEGASPORE M19. **macroˈtrichium** *n.*, pl. **-trichia**, in certain insects, any of the larger hairs on the body M20.

macroanalysis /ˌmakrəʊəˈnalɪsɪs/ *n.* M20. [f. prec. + ANALYSIS.] *Chem.* Quantitative analysis of samples of the size for which the older chemical techniques were usually developed, commonly 0.1–1 gram.

macrobian /məˈkrəʊbɪən/ *a. rare.* E18. [f. Gk *makrobios*, f. as MACRO- + *bios* life: see -AN.] Long-lived.

macrobiotic /ˌmakrə(ʊ)bʌɪˈɒtɪk/ *a.* L18. [f. Gk *makrobiotos*, f. as MACRO- + *biotos* life: see -IC.] 1 Inclined or tending to prolong life; relating to the prolongation of life. L18. 2 Of or pertaining to a Zen Buddhist dietary system intended to prolong life, comprising pure vegetable foods, brown rice, etc. M20.

macrobiotics *n.* (*a*) *rare* the science of prolonging life; (*b*) the use or theory of a macrobiotic diet: M19.

macrocarpa /makrə(ʊ)ˈkɑːpə/ *n.* E20. [mod.L (see below), f. as MACRO- + *karpos* fruit.] A cypress, *Cupressus macrocarpa*, native to the Monterey peninsula of California and widely cultivated elsewhere, esp. as a fast-growing hedge or wind-break. Also called *Monterey cypress*.

macrocephalic /ˌmakrə(ʊ)sɪˈfalɪk, -kɛˈfalɪk/ *a.* M19. [f. MACRO- + CEPHALIC.] (Of a person) having a long or large head; (of a head or skull) relatively long or large.

macroceˈphalia *n.* = MACROCEPHALY L19. **macroˈcephalous** *a.* = MACROCEPHALIC M19. **macroˈcephaly** *n.* macrocephalic condition; abnormal length or size of the head: L19.

macrocosm /ˈmakrə(ʊ)kɒz(ə)m/ *n.* E17. [med.L *macrocosmus*, f. as MACRO- + Gk *kosmos* world.] 1 The universe; the world of all nature. E17. 2 A complex structure or whole, *esp.* one considered to be epitomized by some constituent portion or microcosm. M19.

macroˈcosmic *a.* of or pertaining to the macrocosm; of the nature of a macrocosm: M19. **†macrocosmical** *a.* = MACROCOSMIC E17–M19. **macroˈcosmically** *adv.* in relation to the macrocosm L19.

macrocyclic /makrə(ʊ)ˈsʌɪklɪk, ˈ-sɪk-/ *a.* E20. [f. MACRO- + CYCLIC.] 1 *Bot.* Of a rust fungus: having a long life cycle. E20. 2 *Chem.* Containing or being a ring composed of a relatively large number of atoms. M20.

ˈmacrocycle *n.* (*Chem.*) a macrocyclic compound or molecule M20.

macrocyte /ˈmakrə(ʊ)sʌɪt/ *n.* L19. [f. MACRO- + -CYTE.] *Med.* An abnormally large red blood cell found in some forms of anaemia.

macrocytic /-ˈsɪtɪk/ *a.* of the nature of, pertaining to, or characteristic of a macrocyte; characterized by the presence of macrocytes: M20. **macrocytosis** /-sʌɪˈtəʊsɪs/ *n.* the presence of macrocytes in the blood L19.

macro-economics /ˌmakrəʊiːkəˈnɒmɪks, -ɛk-/ *n.* M20. [f. MACRO- + ECONOMICS.] The branch of economics that deals with large-scale economic factors; the economics of a national economy as a whole. Cf. MICRO-ECONOMICS.

macro-economic *a.* M20. **macro-eˈconomist** *n.* M20.

Macrolepidoptera /ˌmakrəʊlɛpɪˈdɒpt(ə)rə/ *n.pl.* L19. [f. MACRO- + LEPIDOPTERA.] The families of butterflies and moths whose members are large enough to be of interest to collectors. Cf. MICROLEPIDOPTERA.

macrolide /ˈmakrə(ʊ)lʌɪd/ *n.* M20. [f. MACRO- + L(ACTONE + -IDE.] *Pharm.* Any of a class of antibiotics containing macrocyclic lactone rings. Also *macrolide antibiotic*.

macrology /maˈkrɒlədʒi/ *n.* Now *rare* or *obs.* Also (earlier) in L form **†-logia**. M16. [Late L *macrologia* f. Gk *makrologia*, f. as MACRO- + -LOGY.] In *Rhet.*, the use of redundant words or phrases; *gen.* prolixity of speech.

macromolecule /makrə(ʊ)ˈmɒlɪkjuːl/ *n.* L19. [f. MACRO- + MOLECULE.] *Chem.* †1 A group of molecules in a crystal bound together in a characteristic shape, supposed to account for the symmetry of the crystal. Only in L19. 2 A molecule composed of a very large number of atoms and having a high molecular weight (e.g. a molecule of a polymer, protein, or nucleic acid). E20.

macromoˈlecular *a.* of, pertaining to, or consisting of a macromolecule or macromolecules M20.

macron /ˈmakrɒn/ *n.* M19. [Gk *makron* neut. of *makros* long.] A straight horizontal line ¯ written or printed over a vowel to indicate length or stress.

macrophage /ˈmakrə(ʊ)feɪdʒ/ *n.* L19. [f. MACRO- + Gk *phagein* eat.] *Physiol.* A large phagocytic cell, present in many organs and tissues in both stationary and mobile forms.

macroˈphagic *a.* E20.

macrophotography /ˌmakrə(ʊ)fəˈtɒgrəfi/ *n.* L19. [f. MACRO- + PHOTOGRAPHY.] Photography in which objects are reproduced larger than or at their actual size but without the degree of magnification that use of a microscope would give. Also called *photomacrography*.

macroˈphotograph *n.* a photograph produced by macrophotography E20.

macropodid /məˈkrɒpədɪd/ *n.* & *a.* L19. [mod.L *Macropodidae* (see below), f. *Macropus* genus name f. Gk *makropous* large foot, f. as MACRO- + *pous* foot: see -POD, -ID[3].] *Zool.* A *n.* A marsupial of the family Macropodidae, which includes the kangaroos and wallabies. L19. B *adj.* Of, pertaining to, or designating this family. M20.

ˈmacropod *n.* & *a.* = MACROPODID L19.

macropsia /maˈkrɒpsɪə/ *n.* L19. [f. MACRO- + Gk *-opsia* seeing.] *Ophthalm.* A condition of the eyes in which objects appear enlarged.

macroscopic /makrə(ʊ)ˈskɒpɪk/ *a.* L19. [f. MACRO- after *microscopic.*] Visible to the naked eye, as opp. *microscopic*; using the naked eye; *fig.* general, comprehensive, concerned with large units.

G. DANIEL A straight old-fashioned archaeologist . . trained in the macroscopic examination of artifacts.

macroscopical *a.* = MACROSCOPIC L19. **macroscopically** *adv.* L19.

macrosmatic /makrɒzˈmatɪk/ *a.* L19. [f. MACRO- + Gk *osmē* smell + -ATIC.] *Zool.* Having well-developed olfactory organs.

macrostructure /ˈmakrə(ʊ)strʌktʃə/ *n.* E20. [f. MACRO- + STRUCTURE *n.*] 1 Large-scale or overall structure; structure visible to the naked eye or under low magnification. E20. 2 A thing having such structure. M20.

macroˈstructural *a.* L19.

macrurous /məˈkrʊərəs/ *a.* E19. [f. mod.L *Macrura* former suborder name, f. Gk *makros* long + *oura* tail: see -OUS.] *Zool.* Of, pertaining to, or designating a group of decapod crustaceans having a relatively long abdomen, including the lobsters and crayfish.

macruran *n.* & *a.* (*a*) *n.* a macrurous crustacean; (*b*) *adj.* = MACRUROUS: M19.

mactation /makˈteɪʃ(ə)n/ *n.* M16. [Late L *mactatio(n-)*, f. L *mactat-* pa. ppl stem of *mactare* slay: see -ATION.] (A) sacrificial killing.

macula /ˈmakjʊlə/ *n.* Pl. **-lae** /-liː/, **-las.** LME. [L.] 1 Chiefly *Sci.* A spot, a stain; *Med.* a permanent spot or stain in the skin. LME. 2 *Anat.* Any of various structures which have the appearance of a spot. M19.

2 **macula lutea** /ˈluːtɪə/, pl. **maculae luteae** /ˈluːtiiː/, [L *luteus* yellow] an oval yellowish area surrounding the fovea near the centre of the retina, where visual acuity is most pronounced; also called *yellow spot*.

macular *a.* of or pertaining to maculae; characterized by the presence of maculae; *spec.* of or pertaining to the macula lutea: E19.

maculate /ˈmakjʊlət/ *a.* L15. [L *maculatus* pa. pple, f. as next: see -ATE[2].] Spotted, stained; *fig.* defiled, polluted. Now chiefly *literary*, in expressed or implied antithesis to *immaculate*.

H. FERGUSSON Her long black hair . . now hung wet and maculate with clay and sand.

maculate /ˈmakjʊleɪt/ *v.t.* Now *rare*. Pa. pple **-ated, †-ate.** LME. [L *maculat-* pa. ppl stem of *maculare*, f. *macula* spot: see -ATE[3].] Spot, stain, soil; *fig.* defile, pollute.

maculated *a.* (*a*) = MACULATE *a.*; (*b*) marked with maculae: M17.

maculation /makjʊ'leɪʃ(ə)n/ *n.* L15. [L *maculatio(n-)*, f. as prec.: see -ATION.] **1** The action of spotting or defiling; the condition of being spotted or defiled. L15. **2** The state of being marked with maculae; a particular arrangement or pattern of maculae. E19.

maculature /'makjʊlətʃə/ *n.* M17. [f. as MACULATE *v.* + -URE.] †**1** A sheet of waste or blotting-paper. *rare* (only in Dicts.). M17–E18. **2** A print taken from a block or print without re-inking, to remove traces of ink from it. E20.

macule /'makjuːl/ *n.* L15. [Fr., or its source L *macula* spot.] **1** A blemish, a spot; *esp.* (*Med.*) a macula on the skin. L15. **2** *Printing.* = MACKLE *n.* M19.

macule /'makjuːl/ *v.t. rare.* L15. [Fr. *maculer*, f. as prec.] Spot, stain; *Printing* = MACKLE *v.* 2.

maculopapule /,makjʊləʊ'papjuːl/ *n.* E20. [f. MACULA + -O- + PAPULE.] *Med.* A lesion having characteristics of both a macule and a papule.

maculopapular *a.* E20.

maculose /'makjʊləʊs/ *a.* LME. [L *maculosus*, f. *macula* spot: see -OSE[1].] Full of spots; spotted.
Also **maculous** *a.* (*rare*) LME.

macumba /mə'kʊmbə/ *n.* M20. [Port.] A Black religious cult practised in Brazil, characterized by sorcery, ritual dancing, and the use of fetishes.

macushla /mə'kʊʃlə/ *n. Anglo-Ir.* L19. [f. Ir. *mo* my + *cuisle* pulse: see ACUSHLA. Cf. CUSHLA-MACHREE.] As a form of address: my dear, darling.

mad /mad/ *n.* E18. [Absol. use of next.] **1** *pl. The* people who are mad. E18. **2** Madness, fury, anger; a fit of anger. *dial.* & *US slang.* M19.

mad /mad/ *a.* Compar. & superl. **-dd-**. [OE *ġemǣd(d*, *ġemǣded*, pa. pple of vb meaning 'make insane', f. *ġemād* insane = OS *gimēd* foolish, OHG *gameit* foolish, vain, boastful, Goth. *gamaiþs* crippled, f. Gmc.] **1** Insane; suffering from a psychotic illness. Now also, maniacal, frenzied. OE. †**b** Causing madness. *rare.* M16–L17. **2** Foolish, unwise. Now *spec.* extravagantly or wildly foolish; ruinously imprudent. OE. **3** Carried away by enthusiasm or desire; wildly excited; infatuated. Foll. by *about, for, on*, etc. ME. **b** Wildly desirous *to do* something. Now *rare.* E17. **4** Beside oneself with anger; moved to uncontrollable rage; furious. Now also, annoyed, exasperated. (Foll. by *at, with*, etc.) Chiefly *colloq.* ME. **5** Of an animal: abnormally furious, rabid; *spec.* suffering from rabies. ME. **6** Uncontrolled by reason; (wildly) irrational in demeanour or conduct. LME. **b** Of a storm, a wind: wild, violent. L16.

1 TENNYSON And then to hear a dead man chatter Is enough to drive one mad. *mad as a hatter, a March hare*, etc. 2 LD MACAULAY The chief justice . . was not mad enough to risk a quarrel on such a subject. 3 H. JACOBSON Despite myself I was mad about her. She was so good at what she did. *music-mad, poetry-mad, sex-mad*, etc. 4 C. BROWN I was mad . . I was going to beat both of their asses. J. J. HENNESSY I was so mad with her . . that I walked out of the room. 6 D. DELILLO Has my life been a mad dash for pleasure?

Phrases: **go mad** become insane; become wildly or frenziedly abnormal. **like mad** furiously, with excessive violence or enthusiasm. **run mad** = *go mad* above. *staring mad*: see STARING *a.* I.

Special collocations & comb.: **mad-apple** *arch.* [tr. L *malum insanum*, alt. of an oriental wd] an aubergine. **mad-brain** *n.* & *a.* (*a*) *n.* a mad-brained person, a scatterbrain; (*b*) *adj.* mad-brained. **mad-brained** *a.* hotheaded, uncontrolled; scatterbrained. **mad cow disease** *colloq.* = *bovine spongiform encephalopathy* s.v. BOVINE *a.* I. **mad-doctor** *arch.*: who treats the insane. *mad Greek*: see GREEK *n.* 5. **madhead** (*obs.* exc. *dial.*) an insane or wildly foolish person. **mad-headed** *a.* = *mad-brained* above. **madhouse** (*a*) (*arch.* or *colloq.*) a mental home or hospital; (*b*) *fig.* a scene of extreme confusion or uproar. **mad keen** *a.* (*slang*) extremely eager. **madman** an insane or wildly foolish man. *mad mick*: see MICK *n.*[1] **mad minute** *Mil. slang* a short period of rapid rifle-fire or frenzied bayonet-practice. **mad money** *colloq.* money for use in an emergency. **mad scientist** an eccentric or dangerously insane scientist (a stock figure of melodramatic horror-stories). **madstone** *US* a stone supposedly having the power to counteract the effect of the bite of a rabid animal. **madtom** any catfish of the N. American freshwater genus *Noturus*, comprising small forms resembling tadpoles and with poisonous pectoral fins. **madwoman** an insane or wildly foolish woman.

maddish *a.* †(*a*) of or pertaining to a mad person; resembling a mad person in behaviour; (*b*) somewhat mad: L16. **madling** *n.* (now *rare*) a mad person; a person who acts insanely or foolishly: M17.

mad /mad/ *v.* Infl. **-dd-**. ME. [f. the adj.] **1** *v.i.* Be or become mad; act like a mad person, rage, behave furiously. *arch.* ME. **2** *v.t.* Make mad; madden, make insane; infuriate, enrage. Now chiefly *US colloq.*, exasperate. LME.

Madagascan /madə'gask(ə)n/ *a.* & *n.* L19. [Irreg. f. next + -AN. Cf. MALAGASH, MALAGASY.] **A** *adj.* Of or pertaining to Madagascar. L19. **B** *n.* A native or inhabitant of Madagascar. L19.

Madagascar /madə'gaskə/ *n.* E19. [A large island off the east coast of Africa.] Used *attrib.* to designate things found in or associated with Madagascar.

Madagascar jasmine = STEPHANOTIS I. *Madagascar periwinkle*: see PERIWINKLE *n.*[1] I.

Madagascarian /madəga'skɛːrɪən/ *n.* & *a.* As n. also **-gascrian** /-'gaskrɪən/. E19. [f. prec. + -IAN.] = MADAGASCAN *a.* & *n.*

Madagass /'madəgas/ *n. arch.* L18. [Var. of MALAGASH.] A Madagascan.

madal /mə'dɑːl/ *n.* E20. [Origin unkn.] A double-headed drum used in Nepal and the eastern Indian subcontinent. Cf. MRIDANGAM.

madam /'madəm/ *n.* Also **M-**, **madame**. See also MADAME. ME. [OFr. *ma dame* (mod. *madame*) lit. 'my lady'.] **I 1** Used as a form of respectful or polite address or mode of reference, orig. by a servant to or of his or her mistress, or by any person addressing a lady of rank; later used more widely to address or refer to a woman of any rank or position, *spec.* by a sales assistant to or of a female customer or (more fully *dear madam*) at the beginning of a letter to a woman. Corresp. to *sir.* ME. **2** As a title: **a** Used preceding a woman's forename. *arch.* LME. **b** Used preceding a woman's surname, a woman's designation of rank or (occas.) office, or (formerly) playfully or derisively preceding any noun personified as a woman. E17. **3** A woman usually addressed or referred to as 'madam', e.g. a lady of rank, the mistress of a house, etc. M16. **b** An affected fine lady. *derog.* L16. **c** A conceited or precocious girl or young woman. *colloq.* E19. **d** A female brothel-keeper. L19. **4** Nonsense, humbug. *slang.* M20.

1 H. FIELDING 'If you will have patience, madam', answered Mrs. Miller, 'I will acquaint you who I am'. *Vogue* Madam comes to look. . . She is so astonished at the absurdly low prices. *Woman's Journal* Shall I have Madame's tray? 2b SHAKES. *Meas. for M.* Behold, behold, where Madam Mitigation comes! GOLDSMITH Good people all, with one accord Lament for Madam Blaize. 3b M. CHARLTON What should I care what those fine Madams says of me! c M. BINCHY She was a proper little madam that one.

II See MADAME.

Comb.: **madam-shop** a small shop selling up-market ready-to-wear ladies' clothes.

madam /'madəm/ *v.t.* E17. [f. the n.] Address as 'madam'.

Madame /madam; mə'dɑːm, 'madəm/ *n.* Also ***m-***, ***madam.*** See also MADAM *n.* Pl. ***Mesdames*** /medam, mɛ-, meɪ'dam/ (see also MESDAMES). ME. [OFr.: see MADAM *n.* Partly var. of MADAM *n.*] **I 1** See MADAM *n.* ME.

II 2 a Used as a title (preceding the surname) of or as a respectful form of address to a French married woman or (more widely) a married woman of any non-British nationality (corresp. to English *Mrs*, *Lady*, etc.), or in literal renderings of French speech. M16. **b** *Fr. Hist.* (A title of) a female member of the French royal family, *spec.* the eldest daughter of the French king or the dauphin (cf. MADEMOISELLE 3). L16. **c** Used as a title (preceding a name) by a businesswoman, fortune-teller, etc., esp. to imply skill and sophistication, or foreign origin. M19. †**3** A woman usually addressed or referred to as '*Madame*'; a French married woman; a Frenchman's wife. L16–M18.

2c JOYCE The window of Madame Doyle, court dress milliner, stopped him. N. COWARD Don't you think, Madame Arcati, that perhaps we've had enough seances?

¶As a title freq. abbrev. *Mme.*

madapollam /madə'pɒləm/ *n.* E19. [*Madapollam*, a suburb of Narsapur in Andhra Pradesh, India.] A kind of cotton cloth, orig. manufactured at Madapollam.

madar *n.* var. of MUDAR.

madarosis /madə'rəʊsɪs/ *n.* Pl. **-oses** /-'rəʊsiːz/. L17. [mod.L, f. Gk *madarōsis*, f. *madaros* bald: see -OSIS.] *Med.* Congenital deficiency or loss of the eyelashes (and eyebrows).

¶Only in Dicts. bef. 20.

madcap /'madkap/ *n.* & *a.* L16. [f. MAD *a.* + CAP *n.*[1]] **A** *n.* †**1** A madman; a maniac. *rare.* L16–E17. **2** A person who acts like a maniac; a reckless, wildly impulsive person. Now also, a lively and impulsive young woman. L16.

2 MABEL COLLINS On the boards she was the merriest, gayest, madcap in the world.

B *attrib.* or as *adj.* Mad, crazy; reckless, wildly impulsive. L16.

R. DEACON A madcap project in Kenya for creating a disease in the sacred baobab trees.

madcapery *n.* the behaviour of a madcap; lively or reckless conduct: E20.

madden /'mad(ə)n/ *v.* E18. [f. MAD *a.* + -EN[5].] **1** *v.t.* Make mad; infuriate, excite to frenzy. Also, irritate, annoy, vex. E18. **2** *v.i.* Become mad. M18.

maddening *a.* that makes a person mad; irritating, vexing: E19. **maddeningly** *adv.* M19.

madder /'madə/ *n.*, *v.*, & *a.* [OE *mædere*, corresp. to OHG *matara*, ON *maðra* in place-names (Sw. *madra*, Norw. *modra*, *maure*), obscurely rel. to synon. WFris. *miede*, MLG, MDu. *mēde* (Du. *mede*, *mee*).] **A** *n.* **1** A climbing plant, *Rubia tinctorum* (family Rubiaceae), with rough stems, rough whorled leaves, and panicles of small yellowish flowers, formerly cultivated for the reddish-purple dye obtained from the root. Also (w. specifying wd), any of several related plants. OE. **2** The root of *Rubia tinctorum*, employed medicinally or as a source of colouring matter; the dyestuff or pigment prepared from this. ME. **3** A reddish-purple colour, *esp.* one produced by madder dyes or pigments. L19.

1 *field madder*: see FIELD *n.* **Indian madder** a dye-plant of the Indian subcontinent, *Rubia cordifolia.* 3 *rose madder*: see ROSE *n.* *Rubens madder*: see RUBENS 2b.

B *v.t.* Treat or dye with madder. LME.

C *adj.* Of the colour produced by madder dyes; reddish-purple. M19.

madder brown, madder red, etc.

madding /'madɪŋ/ *ppl a.* Now *poet.* & *rhet.* L16. [f. MAD *v.* + -ING[2].] **1** Becoming mad; acting madly; frenzied. Now chiefly in *far from the madding crowd*, (of a place) secluded, removed from public notice. L16. **2** That makes a person mad; maddening. L16.

maddle /'mad(ə)l/ *v. obs.* exc. *dial.* M16. [f. MAD *a.* + -LE[3].] **1** *v.i.* Be or become mad; be confused in mind; be dotingly fond *of.* M16. **2** *v.t.* Make mad; confuse in mind, bewilder. E19.

†**maddock** *n.* ME. [Corresp. to ON *maðkr* (Da. *madike*, Sw. *mask*), MLG *medeke*, dim. of base of MATHE: see -OCK. Cf. MAGGOT, MAWK.] **1** An earthworm; a maggot. ME–L17. **2** A whim. *north.* Only in L18.

made /meɪd/ *ppl a.* LME. [pa. pple of MAKE *v.*] **I** *gen.* **1** That has been made. Also *made-out*, *-over*, etc. LME.

1 *home-made, man-made, self-made*, etc. *made to measure*: see MEASURE *n.*

II *spec.* †**2** (Of a story) invented, fictitious; (of a word) coined; (of an errand) invented for a pretext; made-up. LME–M19. **3** Artificially constructed or produced; contrived, arranged.

LME. 4 That has undergone a process of manufacture; (of a person) having success in life assured. LME. 5 Of a horse, hound, etc.: fully trained. L15. 6 Foll. by *-up*: that has been made up; *spec.* †(*a*) consummate, accomplished; (*b*) put together; composed of parts from various sources; (*c*) artificially contrived or prepared, invented, fabricated; (of a book) made good by the insertion of a leaf etc. from another copy; (*d*) ready-made, not made to measure; (*e*) wearing cosmetics or make-up. E17.

Special collocations: **made dish** a dish of food composed of several separate foods. **made man** a man whose success in life is assured; *slang* a member of the Mafia. **made mast** a ship's mast composed of several pieces of timber. **made-up tie** a tie, esp. a bow-tie, with a fixed bow or knot. **made wine** *arch.* a home-made esp. fruit wine.

¶For *pred.* uses see MAKE *v.* Earlier (ME) in UNMADE *a.*

made *v.* pa. t. & pple of MAKE *v.*

madefaction /madɪˈfakʃ(ə)n/ *n.* Long *rare* or *obs.* L16. [Fr. *madéfaction* f. L *madefactio(n-)*, f. *madefact-* pa. ppl stem of *madefacere*, f. *madere* be wet: see -FACTION.] The action or process of making wet or moist; a wetting.

Madeira /məˈdɪərə/ *n.*[1] L16. [An island in the Atlantic Ocean (f. Port. *madeira* timber f. Sp. *madera* f. L *materia* MATTER *n.*, so called because formerly thickly wooded).] 1 A fortified wine made in Madeira; a drink of this. L16. 2 Used *attrib.* to designate things found in, made in, or associated with Madeira. M17.

2 **Madeira cake** a kind of plain sponge cake. **Madeira embroidery** broderie anglaise. **Madeira nut** *US* the walnut, *Juglans regia.* **Madeira sauce** a rich brown sauce made with madeira and served with braised or roast meats. **Madeira wine** = sense 1 above.

madeira /məˈdɪərə/ *n.*[2] Also (earlier) †**madera**. M17. [Sp. *madera* timber: see prec. Sp. assim. to MADEIRA *n.*[1]] The Cuban mahogany, *Swietenia mahagoni.* Also *madeira wood.*

madeleine /ˈmadleɪn/ *n.* M19. [Fr., prob. f. *Madeleine* Paulmier, 19th-cent. Fr. pastry-cook.] A (kind of) small rich cake, in French cookery baked in a fluted tin, and in English cookery usu. baked in a dariole mould and decorated with coconut and jam.

Madelung /ˈmad(ə)lʊŋ/ *n.* M20. [Erwin *Madelung* (1881–1972), Ger. physicist.] *Physical Chem.* 1 *Madelung constant*, a value associated with an ionic crystalline solid and representing the sum of the potential energy of electrostatic attraction between all the ions of the lattice. M20. 2 *Madelung potential*, the potential at any point in an ionic lattice due to the combined electric field of all the ions in the lattice. M20.

Mademoiselle /madmwazɛl, madəmwəˈzɛl/ *n.* Also ***m-***. Pl. ***Mesdemoiselles*** /medmwazɛl, mɛdmwazɛl, meɪdəmwəˈzɛl/, ***Mademoiselles*** /madmwazɛl, madəmwəˈzɛlz/. LME. [OFr.: see MADAM *n.*, DEMOISELLE.] 1 Used as a title (preceding a name) of or as a respectful form of address to an unmarried Frenchwoman or (more widely) an unmarried woman of any non-British nationality (corresp. to English *Miss*), or in literal renderings of French speech. Also used as a respectful form of address to a French governess or a female French teacher in an English-speaking school. LME. 2 A woman usu. addressed or referred to as '*Mademoiselle*'; an unmarried Frenchwoman; a French governess. M17. 3 *Fr. Hist.* (A title of) the eldest daughter of the eldest brother (known as '*Monsieur*') of the French king. Later, (a title of) the French king's eldest daughter or (if he had no daughter) the unmarried princess most closely related to him (cf. MADAME 2b). L17. 4 A croaker (fish), *Bairdiella chrysoura*, of the southern US. Also called *silver perch*, *yellowtail. US.* L19.

¶As a title freq. abbrev. *Mlle.*

†**madera** *n.* see MADEIRA *n.*[2]

maderisation *n.* var. of MADERIZATION.

madérisé /maderize/ *a.* M20. [Fr., pa. pple of *madériser*: see next.] Of wine: affected with maderization.

maderization /madərʌɪˈzeɪʃ(ə)n/ *n.* Also **-isation**. M20. [Fr. *madérisation*, f. *madériser*, f. *Madère* MADEIRA *n.*[1]: see -IZATION.] A brown discoloration in white wines, often appearing after overlong or unsuitable storage.

ˈ**maderize** *v.i.* [Fr. *madériser*: see -IZE] (of wine) be or become *madérisé* M20.

madge /madʒ/ *n.* L16. [Prob. f. *Madge*, pet-form of female forename *Margaret*.] 1 The barn-owl. Also *madge-owl.* Now *rare.* L16. 2 The magpie. Cf. MARGARET 3. E19.

madia /ˈmeɪdɪə/ *n.* M19. [mod.L (see below), f. Chilean Sp. *madi* f. Araucanian.] A coarse hairy Chilean plant, *Madia sativa*, allied to the sunflower, which is cultivated for its oil-rich seeds.

madid /ˈmadɪd/ *a.* Now *rare.* E17. [L *madidus*, f. *madere* be wet: see -ID[1].] Wet, moist.

Madison /ˈmadɪs(ə)n/ *n.* M20. [Origin unkn.] (The name of) a dance popular in the early 1960s.

Madison Avenue /ˌmadɪs(ə)n ˈavənjuː/ *n. phr.* M20. [A street in New York City, centre of the American advertising business.] (American) advertising, the (American) advertising business; American advertising agents collectively.

madly /ˈmadli/ *adv.* ME. [f. MAD *a.* + -LY[2].] 1 In a mad, insane, or foolish manner. ME. 2 Passionately, fervently; extremely, very. *colloq.* M18.

2 B. REID I fell madly in love with him. N. MARSH She's madly keen on criminology.

madness /ˈmadnɪs/ *n.* LME. [f. MAD *a.* + -NESS.] 1 Mental illness, insanity; *esp.* insanity characterized by wild frenzy, mania. Also, (in an animal) rabies. LME. 2 Imprudence or (wild) foolishness resembling insanity. LME. 3 Wild excitement or enthusiasm; ecstasy. L16. 4 Uncontrollable anger, rage, or fury. M17.

1 *canine madness*: see CANINE *a.* 1. 2 RACHEL ANDERSON It seemed madness to spend . . money paying . . to go where I didn't want to be. METHOD *in one's madness.* 4 *transf.*: W. C. SMITH Then I see . . the waves lashed into madness.

mado /ˈmɑːdəʊ/ *n. Austral.* Pl. **-os**. L19. [Aborig.] A small marine percoid fish, *Atypichthys mado* (family Kyphosidae), found off eastern Australia and New Zealand.

Madonna /məˈdɒnə/ *n.* Also **m-**. L16. [It., f. *ma* old unstressed form of *mia* my (f. L *mea*) + *donna* lady (f. L *domina*): cf. MADAM *n.*] 1 a Used as a respectful form of address to an Italian woman, or in literal renderings of Italian speech. L16. b An Italian woman. *rare.* E17. 2 The or *the* Virgin Mary; a picture or statue of the Virgin Mary. M17. 3 More fully *Madonna braid.* A hairstyle in which the hair is parted in the centre and arranged smoothly on either side of the face, as in Italian representations of the Madonna. M19.

1a Y. CARTER 'Take my advice and do it now'. He . . shook his head. 'In a minute, madonna'. 2 R. WEST A single picture hung between two doors . . a Madonna and child painted in flat bright colours.

Comb.: **Madonna blue** *n.* & *a.* (of) a shade of deep blue; *Madonna braid*: see sense 3 above; **Madonna lily** a white-flowered lily, *Lilium candidum*, traditionally regarded as a symbol of purity and often shown with the Madonna in pictures.

Madonnaish *a.* resembling a Madonna E19.

madoqua /ˈmadəʊkwə/ *n. rare.* L18. [Amharic.] A dik-dik, esp. *Madoqua satiana* of Ethiopia.

Madras /məˈdrɑːs, -ˈdras/ *n.* & *a.* E19. [A seaport on the east coast of India, now capital of Tamil Nadu (formerly also the name of a province).] A *n.* 1 Used *attrib.* to designate things made in or associated with Madras. E19. b *ellipt.* A Madras handkerchief; a Madras curry. M19. 2 A cotton fabric with brightly coloured or white stripes, checks, etc., orig. produced in Madras. L19.

1 **Madras handkerchief** a brightly coloured handkerchief of silk and cotton, formerly often worn as a turban in the W. Indies. **Madras curry** a hot curry usu. containing chicken or beef.

B *adj.* Made of the fabric Madras. M20.

madrasah /məˈdrasə/ *n.* Also ***medresseh*** /mɛˈdrɛseɪ/ & other vars. E17. [Arab. *madrasa*, n. of place f. *darasa* to study.] A Muslim college.

Madrasi /məˈdrasi/ *a.* & *n.* Also **-ss-**. M19. [Urdu, f. MADRAS: see -I[2].] A *adj.* Of or pertaining to Madras, in India. M19. B *n.* A native or inhabitant of Madras. M19.

madre /ˈmadre/ *n.* E19. [Sp.] Mother. Chiefly in exclamatory phrs., as *madre de dios* /de ˈdios/ [lit. 'mother of God'], *madre mia* /ˈmia/ [lit. 'mother mine'], etc.

madreporarian /ˌmadrɪpɔːˈrɛːrɪən/ *a.* & *n.* L19. [f. mod.L *Madreporaria* former taxonomic name, f. as next: see -IAN.] *Zool.* A *adj.* Of, pertaining to, designating, or characteristic of a stony or true coral (order Scleractinia). L19. B *n.* A stony coral. L19.

madrepore /ˈmadrɪpɔː/ *n.* M18. [Fr. *madrépore* or mod.L *Madrepora* (see below) f. It. *madrepora*, presumably f. *madre* mother (perh. w. allus. to the prolific growth of the coral) + *poro* f. L *porus* PORE *n.* or L *porus* f. Gk *pōros* calcareous stone, stalactite.] 1 A stony coral, *esp.* one of the genus *Madrepora* or a related genus. M18. b The polyp of a madreporarian coral. M19. 2 = MADREPORITE 1. E19.

madreporic /madrɪˈpɒrɪk/ *a.* E19. [f. prec. + -IC.] 1 *Geol.* Produced by madrepores; consisting of madreporarian coral. Now *rare.* E19. 2 *Zool.* Pertaining to or designating the madreporite of echinoderms, or structures associated with it or resembling it. M19.

madreporite /madrɪˈpɔːrʌɪt/ *n.* E19. [f. MADREPORE + -ITE[1] (in sense 2 with ref. to the resemblance to madreporarian coral).] 1 *Geol.* A columnar calcareous rock with a radiating prismatic structure, resembling coralline limestone. E19. b *Palaeont.* Fossil madreporarian coral. *rare.* E19. 2 *Zool.* In echinoderms, the pore or perforated plate by which seawater enters the stone canal of the water vascular system. L19.

madrich /ˈmadrɪx, maˈdrix/ *n.* Pl. ***-im*** /-ɪm/. M20. [Heb. *madrīḵ*.] A group leader, a supervisor, esp. on a kibbutz.

madrier /madrije/ *n.* Pl. pronounced same. E18. [Fr.] A thick wooden plank used as a support in fortification work, or along with a petard to breach a gate etc.

madrigal /ˈmadrɪg(ə)l/ *n.* L16. [It. f. med.L *matricalis* mother: cf. med.L *ecclesia matrix* mother church, MATRIX *n.*] 1 A short lyrical love poem. L16. 2 *Mus.* A part-song for several voices, *spec.* one of a 16th- or 17th-cent. Italian style, arranged in elaborate counterpoint, and sung without instrumental accompaniment. Also, a 14th-cent. Italian pastoral song of several stanzas. L16. 3 *gen.* A song, a ditty. L16.

2 C. BURNEY The most chearful species of secular Music . . was that of madrigals. 3 J. CLARE Thrushes chant their madrigals.

madrigaˈlesque *a.* having the features or characteristics of a madrigal E20. **madrigalian** /-ˈgeɪlɪən/ *a.* pertaining to, consisting or characteristic of, or dealing with madrigals M19. **madriˈgalianism** *n.* = MADRIGALISM L20. **madrigalism** *n.* a musical feature characteristic of a madrigal, *esp.* the illustration of lyrics through vocal composition M20. **madrigalist** *n.* a writer or composer of madrigals L18.

madrilene /madrɪˈliːn, -ˈlɛn/ *n.* E20. [Fr. (*consommé à la*) *madrilène*, f. as next.] A clear soup usually served cold.

Madrilenian /madrɪˈleɪnɪən/ *a.* & *n.* M19. [f. Sp. *madrileño*, (fem.) *-leña* of Madrid (see below) + -IAN.] A *adj.* Of or pertaining to Madrid, the capital of Spain. M19. B *n.* A native or inhabitant of Madrid. M19.

Madrileño /madrɪˈlɛnjəʊ, *foreign* madriˈleɲo/ *n.* Pl. **-os** /-əʊz, *foreign* -os/. Fem. **-ña** /-njə, *foreign* -ɲa/. M19. [Sp.: see MADRILENIAN.] = MADRILENIAN *n.*

madroño /məˈdrəʊnjəʊ/ *n.* Pl. **-os**. Also **-na** /-nə/. M19. [Sp.] An evergreen tree of the heath family, *Arbutus menziesii*, of western N. America, with glossy leaves, white flowers, and orange or red berries.

Madura foot /'madʊrə fʊt/ *n. phr.* M19. [f. *Madura*, a city in southern India, now called Madurai.] *Med.* Maduromycosis of the foot.

Madurese /madjʊ'riːz/ *n.* & *a.* E19. [f. *Madura* (see below) + -ESE.] A *n.* Pl. same. 1 A native or inhabitant of Madura, an island off the north-east coast of Java. E19. 2 The Austronesian language of Madura. E19. B *adj.* Of or pertaining to Madura or its language. L19.

Maduran *n.* = MADURESE *n.* M19.

maduro /mə'duːrəʊ/ *n.* Pl. **-os**. L19. [Sp. = ripe, mature.] A dark-coloured cigar.

maduromycosis /,madʊrəʊmʌɪ'kəʊsɪs/ *n.* Pl. **-coses** /-'kəʊsiːz/. E20. [f. *Madura(i)* (see MADURA FOOT) + -O- + MYCOSIS.] *Med.* A chronic destructive fungal infection of the foot (rarely of other parts). Cf. MADURA FOOT.

madwort /'madwəːt/ *n.* L16. [App. f. MAD *a.* + WORT *n.*[1], tr. mod.L ALYSSUM.] Orig., any of several plants said to cure the bites of mad dogs, esp. the crucifer *Alyssum alyssoides*. Now (more fully *German madwort*), a hispid procumbent blue-flowered plant of the borage family, *Asperugo procumbens*, found as an alien in Britain.

maeander *n.* & *v.* see MEANDER.

maeandrine *a.* see MEANDRINE.

maeandrous *a.* see MEANDROUS.

Maecenas /mʌɪ'siːnəs/ *n.* M16. [Gaius *Maecenas* (d. 8 BC), Roman friend of Augustus, statesman, and patron of Horace and Virgil.] A generous patron of literature or art. Formerly also, any patron.

Maecenatism *n.* (long *rare*) patronage E17.

maedi /'meɪdi/ *n.* M20. [Icel. *mæði* lit. 'shortness of breath'.] *Vet. Med.* A slowly progressive form of interstitial pneumonia in sheep and goats, caused by the maedi-visna virus. Cf. VISNA.

Comb.: **maedi-visna** *n.* & *a.* (*a*) *n.* maedi; visna; (*b*) *adj.* designating the lentivirus that causes both these diseases.

maelstrom /'meɪlstrəm/ *n.* L17. [Early mod.Du (now *maalstroom*), f. *maalen* grind, whirl round + *stroom* STREAM *n.*, whence the Scand. forms (eg. Sw. *malström*, Da. *malstrøm*).] 1 A great whirlpool, orig. one in the Arctic Ocean off the west coast of Norway, formerly supposed to suck in and destroy all vessels within a long radius. L17. 2 *fig.* A state of turbulence or confusion. M19.

1 *American Poetry Review* They have pulled oars while caught in maelstroms. 2 L. CODY Simon . . succeeded in penetrating the maelstrom round the bar. *Times* The meeting . . is taking place amid a maelstrom of rumours about imminent changes.

Maelzel's metronome /'mɛlts(ə)lz 'mɛtrənəʊm/ *n. phr.* L19. [Johann N. *Maelzel* (Mälzel) (d. 1838), the inventor.] A metronome (as invented and designed by Maelzel).

maenad /'miːnad/ *n.* Also **menad, M-**. L16. [L *Maenad-*, *Maenas* f. Gk *Mainad-*, *Mainas*, f. *mainesthai* rave.] A Bacchante; *gen.* a frenzied woman.

mae'nadic *a.* characteristic of or resembling a maenad; frenzied: M19. **maenadism** *n.* wild or frenzied behaviour E20.

maestoso /mʌɪ'stəʊzəʊ/ *adv.*, *a.*, & *n.* E18. [It. = majestic, f. *maestà* f. L *majestas*, *-tat-* MAJESTY + *-oso* -OUS.] *Mus.* A *adv.* & *adj.* (A direction:) majestic(ally). E18. B *n.* Pl. **-os**. A majestic piece or movement. L19.

maestrale /mʌɪ'strɑːleɪ/ *n.* M18. [It. f. L *magistralis* (sc. *ventus* wind): see MAGISTRAL. Cf. MISTRAL.] Any of several mainly north-westerly winds which blow in the Mediterranean, esp. a summer wind in the Adriatic, and a winter wind, milder than a mistral, in the west.

maestri *n.pl.* see MAESTRO.

maestria /mʌɪ'striːə/ *n.* L19. [It. f. L *magisterium*, f. *magister* MASTER *n.*[1]] Skill, mastery.

maestro /'mʌɪstrəʊ, *foreign* ma'ɛstro/ *n.* Pl. **maestri** /'mʌɪstriː, *foreign* ma'ɛstri/, **maestros** E18. [It. f. L *magister* MASTER *n.*[1]] 1 a An expert in music; a great musical composer, teacher, or conductor. E18. b *transf.* A great performer or leader in any art, profession, etc. M20. 2 = MAESTRALE. E20.

1a E. HEATH Toscanini was conducting, but I could not afford the cost of a seat to hear the maestro. **maestro di capella** /diː kə'pɛla, *foreign* di kap'pɛlla/ [lit. 'of the chapel'] a choirmaster; a musical director, a conductor. b T. H. WHITE He was a better fencer than his maestro.

Maeterlinckian /meɪtə'lɪŋkɪən, 'mɑːtə-/ *a.* L19. [f. *Maeterlinck* (see below) + -IAN.] Of, pertaining to, or characteristic of the Belgian author Maurice Maeterlinck (1862–1949), or his writings.

Mae West /meɪ 'wɛst/ *n. slang.* M20. [The professional name of an American film actress and entertainer (1892–1980), noted for her large breasts.] An inflatable life-jacket, orig. one issued to Royal Air Force men in the war of 1939–45.

mafeesh /mə'fiːʃ/ *int.* & *a. colloq.* M19. [Colloq. Arab. *ma fī-š* there are none.] A *int.* Nothing doing! M19. B *adj.* Finished, done. E20.

Maffia *n.* var. of MAFIA.

maffick /'mafɪk/ *v.i. arch.* E20. [f. *Mafeking* (see below), treated joc. as a pres. pple, whence other parts of the vb.] Celebrate uproariously, rejoice extravagantly, esp. on an occasion of national celebration (orig. the relief of the British garrison besieged in Mafeking, South Africa, in May 1900).

Maffiosa, -so *ns.* see MAFIOSO.

maffle /'maf(ə)l/ *v. obs.* exc. *dial.* LME. [Cf. early mod.Du. *maffelen* move the jaws.] 1 *v.i.* Stammer; speak indistinctly, mumble. LME. 2 *v.i.* Blunder, bungle; delay, waste time. L18. 3 *v.t.* Confuse, bewilder, muddle. E19.

Mafia /'mafɪə/ *n.* Also **m-, -ff-**. M19. [It. (Sicilian) = bragging, spec. hostility towards the law and its upholders, freq. as manifested in vindictive crimes.] 1 *the Mafia*, an organized secret society of criminals, originating in Sicily but now operating internationally, esp in the US. Cf. UNIONE SICILIANA. M19. 2 *gen.* Any group regarded as exerting a secret and often sinister influence. M20.

1 A. CHRISTIE One of these secret societies, the Mafia, or the Camorra . . is on their track. A. HAILEY The game is Mafia-controlled, demonstrably crooked. 2 *New Society* The scientific mafia got to work as soon as Immanuel Velikovsky's book . . was announced.

mafic /'mafɪk/ *a.* E20. [Contr. of MAGNESIUM and FERRIC.] *Petrogr.* Of, pertaining to, or designating a group of dark-coloured, mainly ferromagnesian minerals; (of a rock) containing a high proportion of such minerals. Cf. FELSIC.

Mafioso /mafɪ'əʊsəʊ/ *n.* Pl. **-si** /-si/, **-sos**. Fem. **-sa** /-sə/. Also **m-, -ff-**. L19. [It., f. as MAFIA.] A member or supporter of the Mafia.

ma foi /ma fwa/ *int.* LME. [Fr., lit. 'my faith'.] Heavens! Goodness!

mafoo /'mɑːfuː/ *n.* M19. [Chin. *mǎ-fū*, f. *mǎ* horse + *fū* servant, labourer.] A Chinese groom, stable-boy, or coachman.

Mag /mag/ *n.*[1] LME. [Pet-form of female forename *Margaret*.] 1 †a *Mag('s) tales*, nonsense, trifling. Only in LME. b *Mag's diversion*, a foolish action, foolish behaviour. *arch.* M19. 2 A magpie. Also *long-tailed mag* (rare), the long-tailed tit. *colloq.* & *dial.* E19.

mag /mag/ *n.*[2] & *v. colloq.* (now chiefly *Austral.*). L18. [f. MAGPIE.] A *n.* 1 Chatter, talk; (a) chat. L18. 2 A chatterbox. L19. B *v.i.* Infl. **-gg-**. Chatter (*away*). E19.

E. LANGLEY Hurry up! Don't be magging there all day!

mag /mag/ *n.*[3] *arch. slang.* L18. [Origin unkn. Cf. MAKE *n.*[3]] A halfpenny.

mag /mag/ *n.*[4] *colloq.* E19. [Abbrev.] = MAGAZINE *n.* 5.

A. BROOKNER Pink harem pants . . as they say in the fashion mags.

mag /mag/ *n.*[5] Pl. same, **-s**. M19. [Abbrev.] *Astron.* = MAGNITUDE 4. Usu. w. preceding numeral.

mag /mag/ *n.*[6] *colloq.* E20. [Abbrev.] = MAGNETO.

mag /mag/ *n.*[7] *colloq.* M20. [Abbrev.] Magnesium; magnesium alloy.

Maga /'magə/ *n. colloq.* Now *rare* or *obs.*. Also **m-**. E19. [Abbrev.] A magazine, a periodical; *spec.* Blackwood's Magazine.

magadis /'magədɪs/ *n.* E18. [Gk.] An ancient Greek stringed musical instrument.

magadize /'magədʌɪz/ *v.i.* Also **-ise**. L18. [Gk *magadizein*, f. as prec. + -IZE.] *Hist.* 1 Play or sing in octaves. L18. 2 Play on the magadis. L19.

magalogue /'magəlɒg/ *n.* L20. [f. MAG(AZINE *n.* + CAT)ALOGUE.] A (free) promotional catalogue or sales-brochure designed to resemble a high-quality magazine.

Magar /'mɑːgɑː/ *n.* & *a.* E19. [Magar.] A *n.* A member of a people of central Nepal; the Tibeto-Burman language of this people. E19. B *attrib.* or as *adj.* Of or pertaining to the Magars or their language. M19.

magatama /'mɑːgətɑːmə/ *n.* L19. [Jap.] A curved ornament or jewel forming part of the Japanese imperial regalia.

magazine /magə'ziːn/ *n.* L16. [Fr. *magasin* f. It. *magazzino* f. Arab. *makzan*, *-in* storehouse, f. *kazana* store up.] 1 A place where goods are kept in store; a storehouse for merchandise; a warehouse, a depot; *transf.* a country or district rich in natural products, a centre of commerce. Now *rare*. L16. b A portable receptacle for articles of value. Now *rare*. M18. 2 *Mil.* A building for the storage of arms, ammunition, and provisions for use in war; *spec.* a store for large quantities of explosives. L16. 3a *Mil.* The contents of a magazine; a store (*of*). Formerly also *sing.* & in *pl.*, stores, provisions, equipment. L16. b *gen.* A store of provisions, materials, etc. E17. †4 A book providing information on a specified subject or for a specified group of people. (Freq. as part of the title.) M17–E19. 5 A periodical publication with articles by various writers; *esp.* one with stories, articles on general subjects, etc., and usu. illustrated with pictures or photographs. M18. b More fully *magazine programme*. A regular television or radio broadcast comprising a variety of entertainment or news items. M20. 6 A compartment for holding essential supplies in an apparatus; *spec.* a chamber in a repeating rifle, machine-gun, etc., containing a supply of cartridges which are fed automatically to the breech; a similar device in a camera, slide projector, etc. M18.

1 BURKE No magazine, from the warehouses of the East India Company to the . . baker's shop, possesses the smallest degree of safety. b L. RITCHIE The . . bourg of Chouzé, set down in a perfect magazine of fruit and vegetables. 2 N. NYE A barrell of the best powder in the Magazine. 3a GIBBON He used . . a large magazine of darts and arrows. b T. BEWICK Each Beaver forms its bed of moss, and each family lays in its magazine of winter provisions. 5 DAY LEWIS Short stories . . she had written for parish magazines. A. JUDD They emerged with a bundle of old pornographic magazines. *little magazine*: see LITTLE *a.* b *Listener* The extended Saturday magazine called Sport on 2.

Comb.: **magazine cover** the (usu. pictorial) cover of a magazine; *magazine programme*: see sense 4b above; **magazine rights**: of publishing matter in a magazine; **magazine section** a section in a newspaper the contents of which resemble a magazine; **magazine story**: written for publication in a magazine.

magazinedom *n.* the world or sphere of magazines L19. **magaziner** *n.* (*rare*) a person who writes articles for magazines M18. **magazinery** *n.* (*rare*) the profession of a writer for magazines; material of the nature of or suitable for a magazine: M19. **magazinish** *a.* = MAGAZINY L18. **magazinist** *n.* = MAGAZINER E19. **magaziny** *a.* of the nature of or suitable for a magazine L19.

magazine /'magəziːn/ *v.t.* Now *rare*. M17. [f. the n.] Store up (goods etc.) as in a magazine or storehouse. Also foll. by *up*.

magcon /'magkɒn/ *n.* L20. [f. *mag*netic *con*centration.] *Astron.* Any of several regions of the moon's surface having an anomalously high magnetic field strength.

magdalen /'magdəlɪn/ *n.* Also (esp. in sense 1) **M-, -lene** /-liːn/. LME. [eccl.L (*Maria*) *Magdalena*, *-lene* f. Gk (*Mariaē*) *Magdalēnē* (Mary) of *Magdala*, a town in ancient Palestine.

Cf. MAUDLIN *n.*] 1 Chr. Ch. *the Magdalen, Mary Magdalen*, a follower of Jesus to whom he appeared after his resurrection (*John* 20:1–18), in the West commonly identified with the sinner of *Luke* 8:37 and represented in hagiology as a reformed prostitute elevated to sanctity by repentance and faith. Cf. MAUDLIN *n.* 1. LME. **b** A representation of Mary Magdalen in art. M17. **2** *transf.* A repentant female sinner; *esp.* a reformed prostitute. M16. **b** *Hist.* A home for the refuge and reformation of prostitutes. Also *magdalen home, hospital*, etc. Cf. MAUDLIN *n.* 3. M18. **3** An old variety of peach. Cf. MAUDLIN *n.* 4. Long *rare.* E18.

magdalenism *n.* prostitution M19.

Magdalenian /magdə'liːnɪən/ *a.* & *n.* L19. [Fr. *Magdalénien*, f. La *Madeleine* (see below) + -IAN.] *Archaeol.* **A** *adj.* Designating or pertaining to a culture of the late upper palaeolithic period in Europe characterized by fine bone and antler artefacts and a strong artistic tradition, named after a site at La Madeleine in the Dordogne, France. L19. **B** *n.* (A person of) this culture. E20.

†magdaleon *n.* LME–M18. [med.L *magdaleo(n-)* f. Gk *magdalia* dough, breadcrumb.] A cylindrical roll of plaster, salve, or other medicinal substance.

Magdeburg hemisphere /'magdəbəːg 'hɛmɪsfɪə/ *n. phr.* E19. [f. *Magdeburg*, a city in Germany, home of the inventor, Otto von Guericke (1602–86).] Either of a pair of brass hemispheres exhausted of air to show atmospheric pressure by their cohesion.

mage /meɪdʒ/ *n.* Now *arch.* & *literary.* LME. [Anglicized f. MAGUS. Cf. (O)Fr. *mage.*] **1** A magician; a person of exceptional wisdom and learning. LME. **2** *spec.* = MAGUS 1. LME.

1 J. I. M. STEWART I might be in the presence of a mage or wizard in disguise.

Magellan /mə'gɛlən/ *n.* E17. [Anglicized f. Fernão de *Magalhães* (Sp. *Magallanes*), Port. explorer (d. 1521).] Used *attrib.* and in *possess.* = next.

Magellanic /madʒɪ'lanɪk, magɪ-/ *a.* E17. [f. prec. + -IC.] Pertaining to or named after Magellan (see prec.).

Magellanic Cloud *Astron.* either of two small galaxies (*large, small, Magellanic Cloud*) associated with the Milky Way and visible at night in the southern hemisphere as cloudy spots.

Magen David /mɑː'gɛn dɑː'viːd/ *n. phr.* E20. [Heb., lit. 'shield of David' (king of Israel from *c* 1000 BC).] = *Star of David* s.v. STAR *n.*[1] & *a.*

magenta /mə'dʒɛntə/ *n.* & *a.* M19. [*Magenta* in N. Italy, site of a battle (1859) shortly before the dye was discovered.] **A** *n.* A brilliant purple-pink aniline dye, fuchsine; the colour of this dye. M19. **B** *adj.* Of the colour of magenta. L19.

magg /mag/ *v.t.* *Sc.* M18. [Perh. f. MAG *n.*[1], MAGPIE.] Pilfer, steal.

magged /magd/ *a.* M19. [Origin unkn.] **1** *Naut.* Of rope etc.: worn, frayed. M19. **2** Irritated; exhausted, jaded. *colloq.* & *dial.* M19.

Maggid /'mɑːgɪd/ *n.* Pl. **-im** /-ɪm/. L19. [Heb. *maggīd* narrator.] An itinerant Jewish preacher.

maggie /'magi/ *n.* Also **M-**. See also MOGGY. E17. [*Maggie*, f. as MAG *n.*[1]: see -IE.] **1** A girl. *Sc.* E17. **2a** A magpie. *dial.* & *Austral.* E19. **b** A common guillemot. *Sc.* L19. **3** In full *Maggie Ann.* Margarine. *slang.* M20. **4** [*Margaret* Thatcher, Brit. Prime Minister 1979–1990.] A pound coin. *slang.* L20.

maggot /'magət/ *n.* LME. [Perh. f. AN alt. of MADDOCK.] **1** Any soft-bodied limbless larva, esp. of a housefly, blowfly, or other dipteran fly, typically found in decaying organic matter. LME. **2** A whimsical or perverse fancy. E17. **3** A whimsical or capricious person. L17.

maggotry *n.* (*rare*) †(*a*) folly, absurdity; (*b*) a place where maggots live and are reared: E18.

maggot-pie /'magətpʌɪ/ *n. obs.* exc. *dial.* L16. [f. Fr. *Margot*, pet-form of female forename *Marguerite* Margaret + PIE *n.*[1]] A magpie.

maggoty /'magəti/ *a.* M17. [f. MAGGOT + -Y[1].] **1** Full of whims and foolish fancies; capricious. M17. **2** Full of maggots. E18. **3** Angry, bad-tempered. Freq. in *go maggoty*, lose one's temper. *slang* (chiefly *Austral.* & *NZ*). E20.

maggotiness *n.* E18.

maghemite /mag'hiːmʌɪt/ *n.* E20. [f. MAG(NETITE + H(A)EM(ATITE + -ITE[1].] *Min.* A highly ferromagnetic mineral of the spinel group which is a form of ferric oxide, Fe_2O_3, formed principally by alteration of magnetite and crystallizing in the cubic system.

Maghreb *a.*, **Maghrebi** *n.* & *a.* vars. of MAGHRIB, MAGHRIBI.

Maghrebine /magrə'biːn/ *a.* E20. [Fr. *Maghrébine*, f. Arab. *Maġribīn* pl. of *Maġribī*: see MAGHRIBI. Cf. MAUGRABIN.] = MAGHRIBI *a.*

Maghrib /ma'griːb/ *n.* Also **Maghreb.** M20. [f. Arab. *Maġribī*: see next.] Of or pertaining to the Maghrib or the Maghribi.

Maghribi /ma'grɪbiː/ *n.* & *a.* Also **Maghrebi.** M19. [Arab. *Maġribī* lit. 'place of setting (of the sun)': see -I[2].] **A** *n.* Pl. same. A native or inhabitant of the Maghrib, a region of NW Africa including Morocco, Algeria, and Tunisia; the variety of Arabic spoken in this region. M19. **B** *attrib.* or as *adj.* Of or pertaining to the Maghribi or their language. M19.

Maghzen /'mɑːgz(ə)n, *foreign* 'mɑːx-/ *n.* M19. [Arab. *makzan*, *-in* treasury (see MAGAZINE *n.*), perh. repr. a Judaeo-Arab. pronunc.] **1** *Hist.* A body of Algerian horsemen in the service of France. M19. **2** (The seat of) the Moroccan government; the dominant official class in Morocco. L19.

magi *n.pl.* see MAGUS.

magian /'meɪdʒɪən/ *n.* & *a.* Also **M-.** M16. [f. L MAGUS + -IAN.] **A** *n.* A magus; *spec.* each of the three Magi. M16. **B** *adj.* Of or pertaining to the Magi or magi. E18.

magianism *n.* the doctrine of the magi E18.

magic /'madʒɪk/ *n.* Also (*arch.*) **-ck.** LME. [OFr. *magique* (mod. *magie*) f. late L *magica* f. Gk *magikē* use as n. (sc. *tekhnē* art) of *magikos*, f. *magos* MAGUS: see -IC.] **1** The supposed art of influencing the course of events and of producing extraordinary physical phenomena by the occult control of nature or of spirits; sorcery, witchcraft. Also, the practice of this art. LME. **†b** A magical procedure or rite; a magical object, a charm. LME–E19. **2** *fig.* An inexplicable and remarkable influence producing surprising results. Also, an enchanting quality; *colloq.* exceptional skill or talent. E17. **3** The art of producing (by sleight of hand, optical illusion, etc.) apparently inexplicable phenomena; conjuring. M19.

1 GIBBON The arts of magic and divination were strictly prohibited. P. LOMAS The Greek army.. would never defeat the Trojans without the help of.. magic. 2 DISRAELI What mourner has not felt the magic of time? E. A. FREEMAN Won over by the magic of his personal presence. P. NICHOLS I want to bring back the magic to our marriage. *Soccer* The Italians.. could not.. live with that special brand of Brazilian magic. 3 R. DAVIES To teach me magic,.. a few things with cards and coins.

Phrases: **black magic** [Fr. *magie noire*] magic involving the supposed invocation of evil spirits, harmful or malevolent magic. **like magic** without any apparent explanation; with incredible rapidity. **natural magic** magic involving no invocation of spirits. *sympathetic magic*: see SYMPATHETIC *a.* **white magic** [Fr. *magie blanche*] magic involving the supposed invocation of good spirits, beneficent or harmless magic.

magic /'madʒɪk/ *a.* Also (*arch.*) **-ck.** LME. [(O)Fr. *magique* f. L *magicus* f. Gk *magikos*: see prec.] **1** *attrib.* **a** Of or pertaining to magic; working or produced by magic. LME. **b** Of a material object: used or usable in magic rites, endued with supernatural powers. L17. **2** Producing surprising results, like those attributed to magic. Also, having a quality of enchantment. L17. **3** *Nuclear Physics.* (Of each of a set of numbers) corresponding to the number of protons or neutrons in nuclei of exceptional stability (the set now taken to be 2, 8, 20, 28, 50, 82, 126, and perhaps 184); (of a nucleus) containing such a number of protons or neutrons, or (*doubly magic*) such a number of each. M20. **4** Superlatively good, excellent, fantastic. *colloq.* M20.

1 SHAKES. *1 Hen. VI* Sorcerers.. By magic verses have contriv'd his end. I. MURDOCH He murmured her name like a magic charm to protect.. himself. **b** R. BURNS Where Pleasure is the Magic-wand That, wielded right, Maks Hours like Minutes. 2 JOYCE Timidity and inexperience would fall from him in that magic moment. R. DAHL The summer holidays! Those magic words! C. ACHEBE He never failed once in anything. Had the magic touch. 4 *Weekend Television* I found myself agreeing with our producer's favourite comment: magic.

Special collocations: **magic bullet** *colloq.* any (usu. undiscovered) highly specific therapeutic agent. **magic carpet** a mythical carpet able to transport a person on it to any desired place. **magic (chain-) stitch**: worked with two colours in one needle. **magic circle** (*a*) an arrangement of numbers in concentric circles, with properties similar to the magic square; (*b*) a circle used in magic as a protection against evil; (*c*) (with cap. initials) a society of conjurors; (*d*) a small group of people privileged to receive confidential information, make important decisions, etc. **magic eye** (*a*) (also w. cap. initials) (*US* proprietary name for) a miniature cathode-ray tube used esp. to indicate the strength of an electrical signal; (*b*) a photo-electric cell or similar electrical device used for identification, detection, or measurement. **magic glass, mirror**: in which future events or distant scenes are supposedly displayed. **magic lantern** a simple optical device using slides to display a magnified image on a white screen, wall, etc., in a darkened room. **magic-lanterned** *a.* (of an image etc.) displayed using a magic lantern. **Magic Marker** (proprietary name for) an indelible marker pen. *magic mirror*: see *magic glass* above. **magic mushroom** a mushroom with hallucinogenic properties, *esp.* one (e.g. the liberty cap) containing psilocybin. **magic realism** a literary or artistic genre in which realism and narrative are combined with surreal, fantastic, dreamlike, or mythological elements. **magic realist** *n.* & *a.* (*a*) *n.* an exponent of magic realism; (*b*) *adj.* of or pertaining to magic realists or magic realism. **magic square** a diagram consisting of a square divided into smaller squares, each containing a number, so arranged that the sum of the figures in each vertical, horizontal, or diagonal row is the same. *magic stitch*: see *magic chain-stitch* above. *magic wand*: see WAND *n.* 7.

magic /'madʒɪk/ *v.t.* Also (*arch.*) **-ck.** Infl. **-ck-.** E20. [f. the n.] Change, make, or produce (as if) by magic.

D. FRANCIS He magicked some huge open sandwiches. *Photography* Your.. brief allows you to magic vices into virtues. **magic away** cause to disappear (as if) by magic.

magical /'madʒɪk(ə)l/ *a.* M16. [f. MAGIC *n.* + -AL[1].] **1** Of or pertaining to magic; = MAGIC *a.* 1a. M16. **†b** = MAGIC *a.* 1b. E17–M18. **2** Resembling magic in action or effect; produced as if by magic. Also, having an enchanting quality. E17.

1 J. A. FROUDE The service of God was.. of the mind and heart, and not a magical superstition. E. GELLNER Nothing magical is being offered—no mysterious transformation of reality. 2 W. BLACK The magical disappearance of about fifty or sixty rabbits. A. CARTER 'Enter these enchanted woods..' Who could resist such a magical invitation?

Special collocations: **magical realism** = *magic realism* s.v. MAGIC *a.* **magical realist** *n.* & *a.* = *magic realist* s.v. MAGIC *a.*

magi'cality *n.* magical power or quality E20. **magically** *adv.* in a magical manner; (as if) by magic: E17.

magician /mə'dʒɪʃ(ə)n/ *n.* LME. [(O)Fr. *magicien*, f. late L *magica* MAGIC *n.*: see -ICIAN.] **1** A person skilled in or practising magic or sorcery. Also, a conjuror. LME. **2** *fig.* A person who exercises an influence like that of magic; a person of exceptional skill. E19.

1 BYRON A wise magician who has bound the devil. A. MASON Her magician had astonished the townspeople by floating.. from the roof of a high building. 2 J. BERMAN The myth of the psychiatrist as a modern magician.. in the psychic landscape of life.

magico- /'madʒɪkəʊ/ *comb. form.* E20. [f. MAGICAL *a.*: see -O-.] Forming adjs. w. the sense 'magical and —', as *magico-erotic, magico-religious*, etc.

magilp *n.* var. of MEGILP.

Maginot Line /ˈmadʒɪnəʊ lʌɪn/ *n. phr.* M20. [f. André *Maginot* (1877–1932), Fr. minister of war + LINE *n.*[2]] A line of fortifications along the north-eastern border of France, begun in 1920 as a defence against German invasion but overrun in 1940; *fig.* a line of defence on which one relies excessively or blindly.

magister /məˈdʒɪstə/ *n.* Also **M-**. LME. [L: see MASTER *n.*[1]] Chiefly *Hist.* Used as a title of respect preceding the name of a man of academic rank; master.

magisterial /madʒɪˈstɪərɪəl/ *a.* E17. [med.L *magisterialis*, f. late L *magisterius*, f. L *magister* MASTER *n.*[1]: see -IAL.] 1 Of, pertaining to, or befitting a master, teacher, or someone qualified to speak with authority; authoritative; dictatorial; (of a person) invested with authority. E17. †2 Of, pertaining to, or displaying the skill of a master artist. M–L17. 3 Of, pertaining to, or befitting a magistrate or magistrates; (of a person) holding the office of a magistrate; (of an inquiry) conducted by a magistrate or magistrates. M17. †4 Pertaining to a magistery (*Alch.*). Also (*Pharm.*) = MAGISTRAL *a.* 2a. M17–E18.

1 GODFREY SMITH Jeeves is.. naturally magisterial (he takes the chair at.. the.. club for gentlemen's gentlemen). B. CHATWIN These researches.. had culminated in his magisterial paper 'The Mammoth and His Parasites'. 3 *Times* He announced the setting up of a magisterial inquiry.

magisterially *adv.* M17. †**magisterialness** *n.* M17–E18.

magisterium /madʒɪˈstɪərɪəm/ *n.* L16. [f. as next.] †1 *Alch.* = MAGISTERY 3a. L16–L17. 2 *RC Ch.* The teaching function of the Church. M19.

magistery /ˈmadʒɪst(ə)ri/ *n. obs.* exc. *Hist.* L15. [L *magisterium* office of master, (in med.L) philosopher's stone, f. as MAGISTER: see -ERY.] †1 The quality, position, or function of a master; authority. L15–E18. †2 The office or position of a magistrate; magistrates collectively. M–L16. 3 *Alch.* & *Med.* a A master principle of nature; a potent transmuting or curative quality or agency; a substance, such as the philosopher's stone, capable of changing the nature of other substances. Also, a product of such transmutation. L16. b A precipitate, esp. from an acid solution. E17. c The concentrated essence of a substance. M17. d A specially prepared medicine. M17. 4 = MAGISTERIUM 2. L19.

magistracy /ˈmadʒɪstrəsi/ *n.* L16. [f. MAGISTRATE: see -ACY.] †1 The existence of magisterial power; the state of being a magistrate. L16–L17. 2 The position or office of magistrate; magisterial power or dignity. Now *rare.* L16. 3 *spec.* The office, dignity, and function of a particular type of magistrate identified contextually. E17. 4 Magistrates collectively; a body of magistrates. E17. 5 A district under the government of a magistrate; a magistrate's residence. L19.

2 LD MACAULAY Literature and science were, in the academical system of England.. armed with magistracy. 4 P. COLQUHOUN Checks established under the control of a vigilant magistracy.

magistral /ˈmadʒɪstr(ə)l, məˈdʒɪstr(ə)l/ *a.* & *n.* L16. [Fr. *magistral* or L *magistralis*, f. *magister* MASTER *n.*[1] + -AL[1].] A *adj.* 1†a Of a problem or a point of instruction: handed down from the masters of a branch of knowledge; forming part of the accepted course of teaching. L16–M17. b Of, pertaining to, or befitting a master; authoritative, dogmatic. Now *rare.* E17. 2 *Med.* a Of a remedy etc.: devised by a physician for a particular case; not included in the pharmacopoeia. Cf. OFFICINAL *a.* L16. †b Sovereign, supremely effective. L16–L17. 3 *Fortif.* Leading, principal; *spec.* designating a principal line in fieldworks which determines the direction and position of other lines. E19. 4 Having the title of 'Master'; of or pertaining to a particular master or masters contextually identified. M19. B *n.* †1 *Pharm.* A magistral preparation. Only in 17. 2 *Fortif.* A magistral line. M19.

magistrand /ˈmadʒɪstrand/ *n. Sc.* E17. [med.L *magistrandus* gerundive of *magistrari* become a Master (of Arts): see -AND.] An undergraduate, orig. *spec.* in an Arts faculty, in the fourth or final year at a Scottish University (now only St Andrews).

magistrate /ˈmadʒɪstrət, -streɪt/ *n.* LME. [L *magistratus*, f. as *magister* MASTER *n.*[1] + -ATE[1].] †1 The office or dignity of a magistrate. LME–L16. 2 *gen.* A civil officer administering the law, a member of the executive government. LME. 3 *spec.* A person conducting a court of summary jurisdiction (see *magistrates' court* below); a justice of the peace; (freq. w. specifying wd) a salaried official carrying out such duties. In *pl.* also, the provost and councillors of a Scottish burgh, as forming a court for police jurisdiction and the granting of licences. L17. 4 In full *Glasgow magistrate.* A herring. *Sc. slang.* M19.

2 D. HUME The king was too eminent a magistrate to be trusted with discretionary powers. 3 B. EMECHETA She imagined herself at a court and the magistrate sending her to jail. *Daily Telegraph* He had the whip confiscated by magistrates at Tottenham. **magistrates' court**: conducted by a magistrate and dealing with minor cases and preliminary hearings. *metropolitan magistrate*: see METROPOLITAN *a. resident magistrate*: see RESIDENT *a. stipendiary magistrate*: see STIPENDIARY *a.*

magistrateship *n.* the dignity, function, or (term of) office of a magistrate L16. **magisˈtratical** *a.* of, pertaining to, or befitting a magistrate or magistrates M17. **magisˈtratically** *adv.* M17.

magistrature /ˈmadʒɪstrətʃə/ *n.* L17. [Fr., f. *magistrat*, f. as prec. + -URE.] 1 The dignity or office of a magistrate; *sing.* & in *pl.*, the office of a particular magistrate identified contextually. L17. b A magistrate's term of office. E18. 2 Magistrates collectively; a body of magistrates. L17.

Maglemose /magləˈməʊsə/ *a.* E20. [f. as next.] = MAGLEMOSIAN *a.*

Maglemosian /magləˈməʊsɪən/ *a.* & *n.* E20. [f. *Maglemose* near Mullerup on the west coast of Denmark: see -IAN.] A *adj.* Designating or pertaining to a mesolithic culture of Europe represented by bone and stone implements found at Maglemose. E20. B *n.* (A person of) the Maglemosian culture. E20.

maglev /ˈmaglɛv/ *n.* L20. [f. *magnetic levitation.*] The use of magnetic repulsion to support a train above the rail(s) on which it runs. Usu. *attrib.*

magma /ˈmagmə/ *n.* LME. [L f. Gk, f. base of *massein* knead.] †1 The dregs remaining after a semi-liquid substance has been pressed or evaporated. LME–M19. 2 A mixture of mineral or organic substances having the consistency of paste; a viscous suspension. Now *rare.* L17. 3 *Geol.* A hot fluid or semifluid material beneath the crust of the earth or other planet, from which igneous rocks are formed by cooling and which erupts as lava. M19.

3 *fig.*: H. G. WELLS The social magma that arose out of this dissolution.

Comb.: **magma-chamber** a reservoir of magma within the planetary crust, esp. below a volcano.

magˈmatic *a.* (*Geol.*) of or pertaining to magma L19. **magˈmatically** *adv.* (*Geol.*) as regards magma; from or by means of magma: M20. **magmatism** *n.* (*Geol.*) (*a*) the theory advocated by magmatists; (*b*) motion or solidification of magma; magmatic activity: M20. **magmatist** *n.* (*Geol.*) a person who holds that most plutonic rocks, esp. granites, were formed from magma rather than by metamorphic granitization M20.

Magna Carta /magnə ˈkɑːtə/ *n. phr.* Also **Magna Charta**. L15. [med.L, lit. 'great charter'.] The charter of English personal and political liberty obtained from King John in 1215; *transf.* any similar document establishing rights.

H. G. WELLS Nationalisation will be the Magna Carta of the twentieth century. LD DENNING The delay of justice is a denial of justice. Magna Carta will have none of it.

magna cum laude /magnə kʌm ˈlɔːdiː, ˌmagnɑː kʊm ˈlaʊdeɪ/ *adv.* & *a. phr.* Chiefly *N. Amer.* L19. [L, lit. 'with great praise'.] With or of great distinction; *spec.* (of a degree, diploma, etc.) of a higher standard than the average (though not the highest). Cf. CUM *laude*, SUMMA CUM LAUDE.

magnae matres *n. phr.* pl. of MAGNA MATER.

Magnaflux /ˈmagnəflʌks/ *n.* & *v.* Also **m-**. M20. [f. MAGN(ETIC *a.* + *-a-* + FLUX *n.*] A *n.* (Proprietary name for) a method of testing metal parts for defects by magnetizing them and applying a magnetic powder which adheres to regions of flux leakage; the magnetic powder so used. M20. B *v.t.* Test (a part) by the Magnaflux method. M20.

magna mater /magnə ˈmeɪtə, ˈmɑːtə/ *n. phr.* Pl. ***magnae matres*** /magniː ˈmeɪtriːz, magnʌɪ ˈmɑːtreɪz/. E18. [L, lit. 'great mother'.] A mother-goddess; a fertility goddess.

magnanerie /maɲanri/ *n.* Pl. pronounced same. L19. [Fr., f. *magnan* silkworm + *-erie* -ERY.] A place for keeping or breeding silkworms.

magnanimity /magnəˈnɪmɪti/ *n.* ME. [(O)Fr. *magnanimité* f. L *magnanimitas*, f. *magnanimus*: see next, -ITY.] 1 Well-founded high regard for oneself manifesting as generosity of spirit and equanimity in the face of trouble etc.; loftiness of thought or purpose; grandeur or nobility of designs or ambition. Now *rare.* ME. †2 Great courage; fortitude. LME–E19. 3 Superiority to petty resentment or jealousy, generous disregard of slights; an instance of this. M17.

1 D. HUME The queen's magnanimity in forming such extensive projects was the more remarkable. 2 A. WILLET In courage and magnanimitie superior to Hercules. 3 V. SACKVILLE-WEST 'You have no notion of my generosity.'.. He began to see himself.. full of magnanimity. D. LESSING A largeness in them, a magnanimity, a.. sweep of understanding.

magnanimous /magˈnanɪməs/ *a.* L16. [f. L *magnanimus*, f. *magnus* great + *animus* mind: see -OUS.] 1 Of great courage; nobly valiant; (of a quality, action, etc.) proceeding from or manifesting high courage. Now *rare* or *obs.* L16. 2 Showing magnanimity; generous in feeling or conduct; not petty; *arch.* nobly ambitious. L16.

1 D. HUME When she saw an evident necessity she braved danger with magnanimous courage. 2 LD MACAULAY The magnanimous frankness of a man.. who could well afford to acknowledge some deficiencies. M. WEST His holiness was relieved enough to be magnanimous.

magnanimously *adv.* E17. **magnanimousness** *n.* (*rare*) E17.

magna opera *n. phr. pl.* see MAGNUM OPUS.

magnate /ˈmagneɪt/ *n.* LME. [Late L *magnat-*, *magnas*, f. L *magnus* great, perh. infl. in 18 by Fr. *magnat*: see -ATE[1].] 1 A great or noble person. Now *esp.* a wealthy and influential person, esp. in business (freq. w. specifying wd). LME. 2 *Hist.* In Hungary and Poland, a member of the Upper House in the Diet. L18.

1 BYRON Born of high lineage.. He mingled with the Magnates of his land. *Sunday Times* The Italian television magnate who has three channels in Italy.

¶Rare bef. L18.

magnateship *n.* the dignity or position of a magnate E20.

†**magnes** *n.* LME–M18. [L f. Gk *Magnēs*, *-ētos* (*lithos*) (stone) of Magnesia: see MAGNESIA.] In full *magnes stone.* A magnet, a lodestone.

magnesia /magˈniːʒə, -zjə, -ʃə/ *n.* LME. [med.L f. Gk *magnēsia* mineral from Magnesia in Asia Minor.] †1 *Alch.* A mineral supposed to be one of the ingredients of the philosopher's stone. LME–M17. †2 = MANGANESE 1. Also *black magnesia.* L17–L18. 3 Orig., & still in non-*techn.* use, hydrated magnesium carbonate, a white earthy powder (†*white magnesia*) used as an antacid and laxative. Now also (chiefly *Chem.*), magnesium oxide, MgO, a white refractory solid used in ceramics etc. M18.

3 *Milk of Magnesia*: see MILK *n.*

magnesian /magˈniːʒ(ə)n, -zjən/ *a.* L18. [f. prec. + -AN.] 1 Chiefly *Geol.* Of, pertaining to, or containing magnesium salts. L18. 2 *Min.* Having a constituent element partly replaced by magnesium. M20.

magnesic /mag'ni:zɪk/ *a. rare.* L19. [f. MAGNESIA + -IC.] Containing magnesium salts; (of a salt) containing magnesium.

magnesiochromite /mag,ni:zɪəʊ'krəʊmʌɪt/ *n.* L19. [f. MAGNESIUM + -O- + CHROMITE.] *Min.* Orig., a mineral analogous to chromite with magnesium replacing much of the iron. Now usu., any spinel of the general formula $(Mg,Fe)(Cr,Al)_2O_4$, *spec.* the end-member picro-chromite.

magnesite /'magnɪsʌɪt/ *n.* E19. [f. MAGNESIA + -ITE[1].] *Min.* Magnesium carbonate, crystallizing in the trigonal system and usu. occurring as compact white microcrystalline masses.

magnesium /mag'ni:zɪəm/ *n.* E19. [f. MAGNESIA + -IUM.] *Chem.* †1 The element manganese. Only in E19. 2 A light silvery metallic chemical element of the alkaline earth group, atomic no. 12, which burns with an intense white light and is a major constituent of rock-forming minerals. (Symbol Mg.) E19.

magnet /'magnɪt/ *n.* LME. [OFr. *magnete* or its source L *magneta* accus. of MAGNES.] 1 *Min.* A rock that is naturally magnetic; magnetite; = LODESTONE I. *arch.* LME. 2 Orig., a piece of iron, steel, alloy, ore, etc., which has the properties of attracting iron and of aligning roughly north–south when freely suspended. Now also, any object which has been given these properties; an object that produces a magnetic field. E17. 3 *fig.* A thing which attracts. M17.

1 MILTON In midst of this white City stands a Castle built of Magnet. 2 D. FRANCIS Three powerful . . magnets distorting the programs on the tapes. **bar magnet**: in the form of a straight bar. **horseshoe magnet**: in the shape of a bar bent until the ends nearly meet. *permanent magnet*: see PERMANENT *a.* 3 *Resurgence* Any new institution . . critical of the existing order . . became a magnet for the disaffected. S. QUINN The Berlin Institute acted as a magnet for a great array of people.

magnetician /-'tɪʃ(ə)n/ *n.* an expert in magnetism M19. †**magnetify** *v.t.* magnetize M17–L18.

magnetic /mag'nɛtɪk/ *a.* & *n.* E17. [Late L *magneticus*, f. L *magneta* MAGNET: see -IC.] A *adj.* 1 Having powers of attraction; very attractive or alluring. E17. 2a Having the properties of a magnet; pertaining to a magnet or to magnetism; producing, caused by, or operating by means of magnetism. M17. b *Naut.* & *Aeronaut.* Of a bearing: measured relative to magnetic north. Freq. *postpositive.* L18. c Capable of acquiring the properties of or of being attracted by a magnet; capable of undergoing an alignment of electron spins. M19. †3 = MAGNETICAL 2. M–L17. 4 Pertaining to animal magnetism; mesmeric. *arch.* E19.

1 L. DUNCAN There was something almost magnetic about those eyes. A. LURIE As if drawn by a magnetic force, Polly crossed the floor. 2c H. E. ROSCOE The ferrous salts are magnetic. 4 DICKENS As if he had been in a magnetic slumber.

Special collocations: **magnetic anomaly** a local deviation from the general pattern of a magnetic field, esp. that of the earth. **magnetic bottle** a magnetic field that confines a plasma to a restricted region within it. *magnetic bubble*: see BUBBLE *n.* 7. **magnetic compass** a ship's compass card with magnets attached for reading bearings and courses relative to magnetic north. *magnetic drum*: see DRUM *n.*[1] 7c. *magnetic equator*: see EQUATOR 3b. **magnetic field** a field of force produced by a magnetic object or particle or by a changing electric field. *magnetic flux*: see FLUX *n.* 7b. **magnetic lens** (a device producing) a magnetic field capable of focusing a beam of charged particles. **magnetic memory** (*a*) a dependence of the magnetic state of a body on its previous magnetic history; (*b*) *Computing* a memory that employs the magnetic properties of its components. *magnetic meridian*: see MERIDIAN *n.* **magnetic mine** a submarine mine detonated by the magnetic field of an approaching ship. **magnetic mirror** a magnetic field that causes approaching charged particles to be reflected. **magnetic moment** the property of an object or particle by virtue of which it experiences a torque in an applied magnetic field. *magnetic needle*: see NEEDLE *n.* 2. *magnetic* NORTH. *magnetic permeability*: see PERMEABILITY 2. *magnetic pole*: see POLE *n.*[2] **magnetic resonance** = RESONANCE 1i (*magnetic resonance imaging*, an imaging technique used in medicine that employs nuclear magnetic resonance of protons in the body; abbrev. *MRI*). *magnetic Reynolds(')* *number*: see REYNOLDS I. **magnetic storm** a large-scale disturbance of the magnetic field of the earth (or of a star or planet). *magnetic stripe*: see STRIPE *n.*[2] 1c. *magnetic* SUSCEPTIBILITY. *magnetic tape*: see TAPE *n.* 4. **magnetic termite** an Australian termite, *Amitermes meridionalis*, which builds mounds aligned north–south.

B *n.* †1 A magnet (*lit.* & *fig.*). M–L17. 2 In *pl.* The branch of knowledge that deals with magnetism. L18. 3 In *pl.* Magnetic devices or materials. M20. 4 In *pl.* Magnetic properties or phenomena collectively. L20.

magnetical /mag'nɛtɪk(ə)l/ *a.* Now *rare.* L16. [f. as prec.: see -ICAL.] 1 = MAGNETIC *a.* 2a. L16. †2 Designating a remedy for which a magical or occult virtue was claimed. E17–E18. 3 = MAGNETIC *a.* 1. M17. 4 = MAGNETIC *a.* 4. *arch.* L18.

magnetically /mag'nɛtɪk(ə)li/ *adv.* E17. [f. MAGNETIC *a.* or prec.: see -ICALLY.] In a magnetic manner; by means or in respect of magnetism.

magnetics *n.pl.* see MAGNETIC *n.*

magnetisable *a.*, **magnetisation** *n.*, **magnetise** *v.* vars. of MAGNETIZABLE, MAGNETIZATION, MAGNETIZE.

magnetism /'magnɪtɪz(ə)m/ *n.* E17. [mod.L *magnetismus*, f. L *magneta*: see MAGNET, -ISM.] 1 The characteristic properties of a magnet; magnetic phenomena, esp. attraction; the property of matter producing these. Cf. FERROMAGNETISM. E17. 2 *fig.* (An) attractive power or influence, *esp.* personal charm. M17. 3 The branch of knowledge that deals with magnetic phenomena. M18. 4 = ANIMAL *magnetism*, MESMERISM. *arch.* L18.

1 J. TYNDALL A blue flame . . being usually bent by the earth's magnetism. *permanent magnetism*: see PERMANENT *a.* **terrestrial magnetism** the magnetic properties of the earth as a whole. 2 R. P. JHABVALA She felt drawn to him by a strength, a magnetism. M. SEYMOUR Fullerton . . whose magnetism was at odds with his modest appearance.

magnetist *n.* an expert in magnetism M18.

magnetite /'magnɪtʌɪt/ *n.* M19. [f. MAGNET + -ITE[1].] *Min.* An oxide of ferrous and ferric iron, Fe_3O_4, which occurs as grey-black crystals of the cubic system, is strongly magnetic, and is an important ore of iron. Cf. LODESTONE.

magnetization /,magnɪtʌɪ'zeɪʃ(ə)n/ *n.* Also **-isation.** E19. [f. next + -ATION.] The action of magnetizing; the condition of being magnetized.

Comb.: **magnetization curve** a graph of magnetic induction against magnetic field strength in the same region.

magnetize /'magnɪtʌɪz/ *v.* Also **-ise.** L18. [f. MAGNET + -IZE.] 1 *v.t.* Influence by animal magnetism; mesmerize. *arch.* L18. 2 *v.t.* Make magnetic; induce magnetism in. E19. 3 *v.t.* Attract as a magnet does (*lit.* & *fig.*). M19.

1 E. B. BROWNING Her own maid magnetizes her twice a day— . . the learned say . . she will recover. 2 *Discovery* A natural ore which exists in a magnetized state. 3 E. BOWEN Bligh, as though magnetized, could not help glancing back . . again at the cottage.

magnetizable *a.* able to be magnetized L18. **magnetiza'bility** *n.* ability to be magnetized L19. **magnetizer** *n.* E19.

magneto /mag'ni:təʊ/ *n.* Pl. **-os.** L19. [Abbrev. of *magneto-electric machine.*] A small electric generator which uses permanent magnets; *spec.* one used for ignition in an internal-combustion engine.

magneto- /mag'ni:təʊ/ *comb. form.* [f. MAGNET, MAGNETIC, MAGNETISM: see -O-.] Forming wds designating processes, devices, phenomena, etc., involving (the use of) magnetism.

magneto'caloric *a.* designating or pertaining to the reversible change of temperature that accompanies a change in the magnetization of a paramagnetic or ferromagnetic material E20. **magneto'cardiogram** *n.* (*Med.*) a chart or record produced by a magnetocardiograph M20. **magneto'cardiograph** *n.* (*Med.*) an instrument that records or displays the variations in the body's magnetic field resulting from the activity of the heart M20. **magnetocardio'graphic** *a.* (*Med.*) involving or pertaining to magnetocardiography L20. **magnetocardi'ography** *n.* (*Med.*) the practice or technique of using a magnetocardiograph or magnetocardiograms M20. **magneto'chemical** *a.* of or pertaining to magnetochemistry E20. **magneto'chemistry** *n.* the branch of science that deals with the interrelation of magnetism and chemical phenomena, structure, etc. E20. **magnetograph** *n.* a recording magnetometer M19. **magneto'graphic** *a.* of or pertaining to a magnetograph L19. **magneto-i'onic** *a.* of or pertaining to the joint effect of a magnetic field and ionized gas (e.g. in the ionosphere) on the propagation of radio waves E20. **magneto-me'chanical** *a.* pertaining to the interrelation of magnetic and mechanical properties; *spec.* = MAGNETOGYRIC 2: E20. **magneto-'optical** *a.* of or pertaining to magneto-optics M19. **magneto-'optics** *n.* the branch of physics that deals with the optical effects of magnetic fields E20. **magnetopause** *n.* the outer limit of a magnetosphere M20. **magnetore'sistance** *n.* dependence of the electrical resistance of a body on an external magnetic field M20. **magnetosphere** *n.* the region (not nesessarily spherical) surrounding the earth or another astronomical body in which its magnetic field is effective and prevails over other magnetic fields M20. **magneto'spheric** *a.* of or pertaining to a magnetosphere M20. **magneto'static** *a.* of or pertaining to an unchanging magnetic field L19. **magneto'statics** *n.* the branch of physics that deals with unchanging magnetic fields L19. **magneto'striction** *n.* a dependence of the state of strain of a body (and hence its dimensions) on its state of magnetization L19. **magneto'strictive** *a.* of, exhibiting, or using magnetostriction E20. **magnetotail** *n.* the broad elongated extension of the earth's magnetosphere on the side away from the sun L20. **magnetote'lluric** *a.* pertaining to or designating a technique for investigating the electrical conductivity of the earth by measuring simultaneously fluctuations in its magnetic and electric fields at the surface M20. **magnetote'llurics** *n.* the branch of geophysics that deals with magnetotelluric investigation M20.

magneto-electric /mag,ni:təʊɪ'lɛktrɪk/ *a.* M19. [f. MAGNETO- + ELECTRIC.] Of, pertaining to, or involving electric currents induced in a conducting material by its motion in a magnetic field.

magneto-electric machine *Hist.* = MAGNETO.

magneto-electrical *a.* magneto-electric M19. **magneto-elec'tricity** *n.* electricity generated by the movement of electrical conductors in a magnetic field M19.

magnetogyric /mag,ni:tə(ʊ)'dʒʌɪrɪk/ *a.* E20. [f. MAGNETO- + Gk *guros* ring, circle + -IC.] *Physics.* 1 Pertaining to or exhibiting the Faraday effect. E20. 2 Designating the ratio of the magnetic moment of an atom or particle to its angular momentum. M20.

magnetohydrodynamic /mag,ni:təʊ hʌɪdrə(ʊ)dʌɪ'namɪk/ *a.* M20. [f. MAGNETO- + HYDRO- + DYNAMIC.] Of, pertaining to, or involving an electrically conducting fluid (as a plasma or molten metal) acted on by a magnetic field; hydromagnetic.

magnetohydrodynamical *a.* M20. **magneto-hydrodynamics** *n.* the branch of physics that deals with magnetohydrodynamic phenomena (also called *hydromagnetics*) M20.

magnetoid /mag'ni:tɔɪd/ *a.* & *n.* M19. [f. MAGNET + -OID.] A *adj.* Having properties like those of a magnet. M19. B *n.* A magnetoid body; *spec.* (*Astron.*) a massive rotating body of magnetized plasma, postulated to account for the energy emission of quasars. M20.

magnetometer /magnɪ'tɒmɪtə/ *n.* E19. [f. MAGNETO- + -METER.] An instrument for measuring magnetic forces, esp. the strength of terrestrial magnetism.

magnetometric /mag,ni:tə(ʊ)'mɛtrɪk/ *a.* of, pertaining to, or measured by a magnetometer M19. **magnetometry** *n.* L19.

magnetomotive /mag,ni:tə(ʊ)'məʊtɪv/ *a.* L19. [f. MAGNETO- after *electromotive.*] Pertaining to or producing magnetic flux.

magnetomotive force a scalar quantity representing the line integral of the magnetic field intensity around a closed line.

magneton /'magnɪtɒn/ *n.* E20. [f. MAGNETIC *a.* + -ON.] *Physics.* Any of several units of magnetic moment (see below).

Bohr magneton a unit equal to $eh/4\pi m$ (where e and m are the charge and mass of the electron, and h is Planck's constant, in SI units), i.e. about

9.27 × 10⁻²⁴ joule per tesla. **nuclear magneton** a unit of nuclear magnetic moment, analogous to the Bohr magneton with the mass of the proton replacing that of the electron, equal to about 5.05 × 10⁻²⁷ joule per tesla.

magnetophone /magˈniːtə(ʊ)fəʊn/ *n.* In sense 3 also in G form **-phon** /-fɒn/. L19. [f. MAGNETO- + -PHONE.] †1 An instrument for producing musical tones by means of a perforated disc that is rotated between a magnet and a induction coil connected to a telephone receiver. Only in L19. 2 An early form of moving-coil microphone. E20. 3 A tape recorder (chiefly w. ref. to early German machines). M20.

magnetron /ˈmagnɪtrɒn/ *n.* E20. [f. MAGNETIC *a.* + -TRON.] *Electronics.* A diode with a cylindrical anode surrounding a coaxial cathode in which the current is controlled by a magnetic field applied parallel to the axis, now usu. designed to produce microwave pulses of high power.

magnific /magˈnɪfɪk/ *a. arch.* L15. [(O)Fr. *magnifique* or L *magnificus*, f. *magnus* great: see -FIC.] †1 Renowned, glorious. L15–M17. 2 Sumptuous, splendid. L15. 3 Imposing by vastness or dignity; (of language etc.) exalted, sublime; *derog.* pompous, grandiloquent. M16. †4 Of a title, expression, etc.: serving to magnify or extol; highly honorific or eulogistic. M16–E18. †5 Nobly lavish or munificent. L16–M17.

magnifical /magˈnɪfɪk(ə)l/ *a. arch.* M16. [f. as prec. + -AL¹.] †1 = MAGNIFIC 1. M–L16. 2 = MAGNIFIC 2. M16. 3 Exalted, sublime; honorific, eulogistic. M16. †4 = MAGNIFIC 5. L16–E17.

magnifically /magˈnɪfɪk(ə)li/ *adv. arch.* M16. [f. MAGNIFIC or prec.: see -ICALLY.] Magnificently, splendidly; in eulogistic terms.

magnificat /magˈnɪfɪkat/ *n.* ME. [L, 2nd person sing. pres. indic. of *magnificare* MAGNIFY: see below.] 1 (**M-**.) A canticle forming part of the Christian liturgy at evensong and vespers, and comprising the hymn of the Virgin Mary in *Luke* 1:46–55 (in the Vulgate beginning *Magnificat anima mea Dominum*). Also, the music to which this is set. ME. 2 *transf.* A song of praise; a paean. E17.

magnification /ˌmagnɪfɪˈkeɪʃ(ə)n/ *n.* LME. [Partly f. eccl.L *magnificatio(n-)*, f. L *magnificat-* pa. ppl stem of *magnificare* MAGNIFY (see -ATION); partly directly f. MAGNIFY (see -FICATION).] 1 *gen.* The action or an act of magnifying; the condition of being magnified; the result of magnifying. LME. 2 A magnified reproduction. M19.

1 A. C. CLARKE He .. expanded the image as far as the screen magnification would allow. *Which Micro?* 32 sprites in two sizes and two magnifications allowing .. '3D' graphics.

magnificence /magˈnɪfɪs(ə)ns/ *n.* ME. [(O)Fr., or L *magnificentia*, f. *magnificent-*: see MAGNIFICENT, -ENCE.] 1 In Aristotelian and scholastic ethics, liberality of expenditure combined with good taste. ME. †2 Supreme bounty or munificence. LME–M17. †3 Glory; greatness of nature or reputation. LME–M17. 4 Sumptuousness or splendour of surroundings or adornments. Formerly also, an instance or particular display of this. LME. 5 Grandeur or imposing beauty of appearance. Formerly also (in *pl.*), features constituting this. LME. 6 With possess. adj. (as *your* etc. *magnificence*): a title of respect given to a monarch or other distinguished person. *obs.* exc. *Hist.* and as repr. a foreign title. LME.

4 G. HARRIS O-grak swirled round to display the full magnificence of his cloak. 5 *Sunday Express* The .. scene is dominated by the .. magnificence of Kilimanjaro.

magnificency /magˈnɪfɪs(ə)nsi/ *n.* Long *arch.* M16. [L *magnificentia*: see prec., -ENCY.] 1 Magnificence. M16. 2 A magnificent object, ceremony, etc. L16.

magnificent /magˈnɪfɪs(ə)nt/ *a.* LME. [(O)Fr., or L *magnificent-* stem (in compar. and superl.) of *magnificus* MAGNIFIC: see -ENT.] 1 Of an immaterial thing: exalted, sublime. LME. 2 Characterized by greatness of achievement or by conduct befitting high position. *obs.* exc. (*Hist.*) in *the Magnificent*, used postpositively to designate a particular distinguished ruler etc. E16. 3 Of a state of existence: characterized by grandeur or stateliness. Of a person: characterized by display of wealth and ceremonial pomp. M16. 4 Sumptuously constructed or decorated; imposingly beautiful, splendid. M16. 5 Characterized by expenditure or munificence on a grand scale. Now *rare.* L16. 6 Excellent, splendid, fine. Now chiefly *colloq.* E18. 7 In names of animals, esp. birds: having an imposing or splendid appearance. L18.

1 W. COWPER The song magnificent—the theme a worm! 2 *Lorenzo the Magnificent, Suleiman the Magnificent*, etc. 3 LD MACAULAY The magnificent king who .. represented France. 4 S. LEWIS Our magnificent new hotels .. and the paintings .. in their lobbies. 5 T. FULLER Hampton Court was built by .. Cardinal Wolsey; once so magnificent in his expenses. 6 R. LYND A magnificent attack was beaten by a still more magnificent defence. 7 **magnificent frigate-bird** a very large frigate-bird, *Fregata magnificens*, found in the tropical Atlantic and eastern Pacific. **magnificent fruit-dove** = WOMPOO. *magnificent* RIFLE BIRD.

magnificently *adv.* LME.

magnifico /magˈnɪfɪkəʊ/ *n.* Pl. **-o(e)s.** L16. [It. (adj.) = magnificent.] A magnate (orig. a Venetian one); a grandee.

P. ZIEGLER Three rear-admirals made a respectable tally of naval magnificos.

magnify /ˈmagnɪfʌɪ/ *v.* LME. [(O)Fr. *magnifier* or L *magnificare*, f. *magnificus*: see MAGNIFIC, -FY.] 1 *v.t.* Praise highly; glorify, extol; *esp.* render honour to (God). *arch.* LME. 2 *v.t.* Make greater in size, status, importance, etc.; enlarge, augment. Now *rare.* LME. 3 *v.t.* Increase the apparent size of (a thing) as with a lens or microscope. M17. 4 *v.i.* Have effect; signify. Now *dial.* E18. 5 *v.t.* Represent (a thing) as greater than in reality; exaggerate, intensify. (Now freq. assoc. w. sense 3 above.) M18.

1 AV *Luke* 1:46 And Marie said, My soule doth magnifie the Lord. 2 W. COWPER Her head, adorned with lappets .. And magnified beyond all human size. 3 W. WITHERING When magnified they appear like ill-formed warts. JAYNE PHILLIPS Her glasses magnified her eyes. **magnifying glass** (a device with) a convex lens used to increase the apparent size of an object viewed through it. 5 G. GREENE Every lie I would magnify into a betrayal. R. THOMAS Isolation magnified feelings that she would have dismissed outside.

magnifier *n.* M16.

magniloquent /magˈnɪləkwənt/ *a.* M17. [f. L *magniloquus* (f. *magnus* great + *-loquus* speaking) + -ENT.] Lofty or ambitious in expression, grandiloquent. Also, boastful.

T. R. LOUNSBURY To describe so slight a performance in so magniloquent a manner. F. DONALDSON Psmith .. is elegant in appearance, imperturbable by nature, a magniloquent tease.

magniloquence *n.* the quality of being magniloquent E17. **magniloquently** *adv.* M19. **magniloquy** *n.* (*rare*) [L *magniloquium*] magniloquence M17.

magnipotent /magˈnɪpət(ə)nt/ *a.* Long *rare* or *obs.* L17. [f. L *magnus* great + POTENT *a.*², after *omnipotent.*] Possessing great power.

magnipotence *n.* M19.

magnitude /ˈmagnɪtjuːd/ *n.* LME. [L *magnitudo*, f. *magnus* great, large, rel. to Gk *megas* and Gmc base also of MUCH: see -TUDE.] †1 Greatness of character, rank, or position. LME–M17. 2 Great size or extent; great degree or importance. LME. 3 Size; geometrical measure or extent. LME. b A quantity, an amount. L16. c The intrinsic size of an earthquake or underground explosion (as distinct from its local intensity), usu. expressed by a logarithmic function of the peak seismometric deflection, adjusted for distance. M20. 4 *Astron.* Each of a set of classes into which stars are arranged according to their brilliance, stars of the first magnitude being the most brilliant, those of the sixth barely visible to the naked eye. Now regarded as a value on a continuous scale representing the negative logarithm of the brightness, such that a decrease of one magnitude represents an increase in brightness of 2.512 times. M17.

2 J. TYNDALL As our eye ranged over .. the mountain .. the conception of its magnitude grew. C. HAYFORD I cannot see the magnitude of the offence. J. BARZUN We can never forget the magnitude of the difficulties. 3 D. BREWSTER The creations of the material world, whether they be of colossal or atomic magnitude.

Phrases: **absolute magnitude**: of a star as from a standard distance of 10 parsecs. **apparent magnitude**: of a star as seen from the earth. BOLOMETRIC *magnitude.* **of the first magnitude**: of the utmost importance. *order of magnitude*: see ORDER *n.*

magnitudinous /magnɪˈtjuːdɪnəs/ *a.* E19. [f. prec. after *platitudinous* etc.] Characterized by magnitude.

magnolia /magˈnəʊlɪə/ *n.* & *a.* M18. [mod.L (see below), f. Pierre *Magnol* (1638–1715), Fr. botanist: see -IA¹.] A *n.* 1 Any of various usu. large Asian and N. American trees of the genus *Magnolia* (family Magnoliaceae), much cultivated for their showy cup-shaped flowers produced in spring before the leaves. M18. 2 The colour of some magnolia blossom, a pale pinkish white. M20.

1 **Magnolia State** *US* the State of Mississippi.

B *adj.* Of the colour of some magnolia blossom; pale pinkish-white. M20.

magnolious /magˈnəʊlɪəs/ *a. slang.* M19. [f. MAGNOLIA + -OUS.] Magnificent, splendid, large.

magnon /ˈmagnɒn/ *n.* M20. [f. MAGN(ETIC + -ON.] *Physics.* A quantum or quasiparticle associated with a spin wave in a magnetic material.

magnoperate /magˈnɒpəreɪt/ *v. rare.* E17. [Partly f. L *magnopere* greatly (contr. of *magno opere*), partly f. L *magnus* great + *oper-*, *opus* work, after *operate*: see -ATE³.] †1 *v.t.* Make greater. Only in E17. †2 *v.i.* Work at a magnum opus. Only in E19. 3 *v.i.* Act in a grand manner. E20.

Magnox /ˈmagnɒks/ *n.* M20. [f. *mag*nesium *no* *ox*idation.] Any of various magnesium-based alloys containing a small proportion of aluminium, developed for the fuel containers of nuclear reactors. Freq. *attrib.*

magnum /ˈmagnəm/ *n.* & *a.* L18. [L, use as n. of neut. sing. of *magnus* large.] A *n.* 1 A bottle for wine, spirits, etc., twice the standard size, now usu. containing 1½ litres; the quantity of liquor held by such a bottle. L18. 2 (Also **M-**.) A Magnum revolver or cartridge (see sense B. below). M20. 3 *Zool.* The section of a bird's oviduct which secretes albumen. M20.

1 J. GLASSCO There was a magnum of bad champagne waiting in an ice bucket.

B *attrib.* or as *adj.* (Also **M-**.) Of a cartridge: adapted so as to be more powerful than its calibre suggests. Of a gun: designed to fire such cartridges. M20.

¶Proprietary name in the US in senses A.2, B.

magnum bonum /magnəm ˈbəʊnəm, ˈbɒnəm/ *n. phr.* E18. [f. as prec. + use as n. of neut. sing. of L *bonus* good.] 1 A variety of large yellow cooking plum. Also *magnum bonum plum.* E18. †2 = MAGNUM *n.* 1. *Sc.* M–L18. 3 A large-barrelled steel pen. M19.

magnum opus /magnəm ˈəʊpəs, ˈɒpəs/ *n. phr.* Pl. ***magnum opuses, magna opera*** /magnə ˈəʊpərə, ˈɒpərə/. L18. [L = great work.] A great and usu. large work of art, literature, etc.; *spec.* the most important work of an artist, writer, etc. Cf. *opus magnum* s.v. OPUS *n.*

Magnus effect /ˈmagnəs ɪˌfɛkt/ *n. phr.* E20. [Heinrich G. *Magnus* (1802–70), Ger. scientist.] The effect of rapid spinning on a cylinder or sphere moving through a fluid in a direction at an angle to the axis of spin, which results in a sideways force at right angles to both the direction of motion and the axis of spin.

Magosian /maˈgəʊsɪən/ *a.* & *n.* M20. [f. *Magosi* in Uganda + -AN.] *Archaeol.* A *adj.* Designating or pertaining to a Stone Age culture in sub-Saharan Africa, thought to be represented by certain finds made in Uganda. M20. B *n.* The Magosian culture. M20.

magot /ˈmagət, *foreign* mago (*pl. same*)/ *n.* E17. [Fr.] **1** The Barbary ape. E17. **2** A small grotesque Chinese or Japanese figurine of porcelain, ivory, wood, etc. M19.

magpie /ˈmagpʌɪ/ *n.* & *a.* L16. [f. MAG *n.*[1] + PIE *n.*[1]] **A** *n.* **1a** A common bird of the northern hemisphere, *Pica pica* of the crow family, with a long pointed tail, black and white plumage, and a noisy chattering call, proverbial for its habit of taking and hoarding bright objects. Also (w. specifying wd), any of several other long-tailed birds of the crow family. L16. **b** More fully *Australian magpie*. Any of several black and white Australian birds of the butcher-bird family Cracticidae, esp. *Gymnorrhina tibicen*. L18. **2** *transf.* An idle or impertinent chatterer; a petty pilferer; a person who collects and hoards objects, information, etc. M17. **3** Orig., an Anglican bishop (from the ceremonial episcopal costume of black chimere and white rochet). Now only, the episcopal costume consisting of these vestments. Chiefly *joc.* or *derog.* E18. **4** A fancy coloured breed of pigeon. M19. **5** A halfpenny. *arch. slang.* M19. **6** A shot from a rifle which strikes the outermost division but one of a target, and is signalled by a black and white flag. *Mil. slang.* L19.

1a **green magpie**: of the SE Asian genus *Cissa*.

B *attrib.* or as *adj.* Of black and white colouring. L19.

Daily Telegraph Ermine that imparts the fashionable magpie effect.

Comb.: **magpie diver, duck** (*a*) the goldeneye, *Bucephala clangula*; (*b*) the smew, *Mergus albellus*; (*c*) the tufted duck, *Aythya fuligula*; **magpie goose** a long-legged, black and white gooselike bird, *Anseranas semipalmata*, of New Guinea and N. Australia; also called *pied goose*; **magpie-lark** any of several Australian birds of the family Grallinidae, *esp.* the common, black and white, stilt-legged *Grallina cyanoleuca*; **magpie moth** a white geometrid moth with black and some yellow spots, *Abraxas grossulariata*, whose caterpillars attack fruit bushes; **magpie-robin** (*a*) a long-tailed black and white bird of the thrush family, *Copsychus saularis*, of the Indian subcontinent and SE Asia; also called *dial-bird*; (*b*) either of two similar birds, *Copsychus sechellarum* of the Seychelles, and *C. albospecularis* of Madagascar.

magslip /ˈmagslɪp/ *n.* M20. [App. f. *magnetic slip*-ring.] Chiefly *Naut.* An electric motor designed to receive and transmit data concerning the angular position of mechanical equipment by means of the position of its rotor. Cf. SELSYN, SYNCHRO.

magsman /ˈmagzmən/ *n. slang.* Pl. **-men**. E19. [f. MAG *n.*[2] + -'S[1] + MAN *n.*] **1** A street swindler, a confidence man. E19. **2** A storyteller, a raconteur. *Austral.* M20.

magtig /ˈmaxtɪx/ *int. S. Afr.* L19. [Afk. abbrev. of *allemagtig* almighty.] Expr. astonishment, awe, etc.

maguari /məˈgwɑːri/ *n.* L17. [Port. f. Tupi *mauári*.] More fully *maguari stork*. A S. American stork, *Ciconia maguari*, with a forked tail.

maguey /ˈmagweɪ, *foreign* maˈgej/ *n.* M16. [Sp. f. Taino.] Any of various fleshy-leaved agaves; *esp.* the American aloe, *Agave americana*.

magus /ˈmeɪgəs/ *n.* Also **M-**. Pl. **magi** /ˈmeɪdʒʌɪ/. ME. [L f. Gk *magos* f. OPers. *maguš*. Cf. MAGE.] **1** A member of an ancient Persian priestly caste (*Hist.*); *transf.* a magician, a sorcerer. ME. **2** *the* (*three*) *Magi*, the three 'wise men' from the East who brought gifts to the infant Jesus (*Matt.* 2:1), a representation of these. LME.

Magyar /ˈmagjɑː/ *n.* & *a.* L18. [Hungarian.] **A** *n.* **1** A member of a people now forming the predominant section of the inhabitants of Hungary. L18. **2** The language of this people; Hungarian. E19. **3** A garment in the Magyar style (see sense B.2 below). E20. **B** *attrib.* or as *adj.* **1** Of or pertaining to the Magyars or their language. E19. **2** Designating a style of blouse, bodice, etc., in which the sleeves are cut in one piece with the main part of the garment. E20.

Magyarization *n.* the action of Magyarizing; the state of being Magyarized: L19. **Magyarize** *v.t.* make Magyar in form or character L19.

mah /mɑː, *unstressed* mə/ *possess. a. Black English.* M20. [Repr. a pronunc.] = MY *possess. a.*

†Maha *n.* & *a.* see OMAHA.

mahaila /məˈhʌɪlə/ *n.* E20. [Iraqi Arab. *muhayla*.] A kind of large river sailing boat used in Iraq.

mahal /ˈmah(ə)l/ *n.* E17. [In sense 1 f. Urdu & Pers. *mahal(l)* f. Arab. *mahall*, f. *hall* stopping-place, abode, alight; in sense 2 f. Urdu & Pers. *mahāl(l)* f. Arab. *mahāll* pl. of *mahall*; in sense 3 transf. use of Pers. *mahal(l)*.] **1** In the Indian subcontinent: a house or palace for use in summer; also private apartments. E17. **2** In the Indian subcontinent: a territorial division; a ward of a town; also, a division of an estate or tract of land forming a unit let out for farming, hunting, etc. L18. **3** (**M-**.) A type of coarse-woven carpet made near Arak in Iran. E20.

mahaleb /ˈmɑːhəlɛb/ *n.* M16. [Fr. *macaleb* (now *mahaleb*) f. Arab. *mahlab*: later assim. to Arab.] A Eurasian cherry, *Prunus mahaleb*, with a hard scented wood (also called *St Lucie cherry*). Also, the fragrant kernels of its fruits, used in perfumery.

Mahamad /ˈmahəmad/ *n.* Also **m-**. M19. [Heb. *ma'ămad*, f. *a'āmad* to stand.] The body of trustees ruling a Sephardic synagogue. Freq. in *gentlemen of the Mahamad*.

mahant /məˈhʌnt/ *n.* E19. [Hind.] In the Indian subcontinent, a religious superior.

maharaja /mɑː(h)əˈrɑːdʒə, məhɑː-/ *n.* Also **-ah, maharaj** /-ˈrɑːdʒ/, **M-**. L17. [Skt *mahārāja*, f. *mahā* great + *rājan* RAJA *n.*[1]] (The title of) an Indian prince of high rank.

transf.: *Beano* I, Ali Tiger, am the new maharaja of this safari park.

maharana /mɑː(h)əˈrɑːnə, məhɑː-/ *n.* Also **M-**. E19. [Hind. *mahārānā*, f. Skt *mahā* great + *rājan* RAJA *n.*[1]] *Hist.* (The title of) the ruler of Udaipur, a State in India until 1947, when it became part of Rajasthan.

maharani /mɑː(h)əˈrɑːni, məhɑːˈrɑːniː/ *n.* Also **-nee, M-**. M19. [Hind. *mahārānī*, f. Skt *mahā* great + *rājñī* RANEE.] (The title of) the wife or widow of a maharaja.

Maharashtri /mɑː(h)əˈrɑːʃtri/ *n.* & *a.* L19. [Skt *Māhārāṣṭrī*, f. *Mahārāṣṭra* Maharashtra (see next), lit. 'great kingdom'. Cf. MARATHA.] (Of) the Prakrit language of Maharashtra (see next), the ancestor of Marathi.

Maharashtrian /mɑː(h)əˈrɑːʃtriən/ *a.* & *n.* M20. [f. *Maharashtra* (see below) + -IAN. Cf. prec.] **A** *adj.* Of, pertaining to, or characteristic of Maharashtra, a region of central and south-western India, since 1960 a State of India. M20. **B** *n.* A native or inhabitant of Maharashtra. M20.

maharishi /mɑː(h)əˈrɪʃi/ *n.* Also **M-**. L18. [Alt. of Skt *maharṣi*, f. *mahā* great + *ṛṣi* RISHI.] (The title of) a Hindu sage or holy man; *gen.* (the title of) a popular leader of spiritual thought. Cf. GURU.

K. PLATT Testimonials of faith and gratitude to Guru Maharishi Viparina.

mahatma /məˈhatmə, məˈhɑː-/ *n.* L19. [Skt *mahātman*, f. *mahā* great + *ātman* soul.] **1** In the Esoteric Buddhism of members of the Theosophical Society: any of a class of people with preternatural powers, supposed to exist in the Indian subcontinent and Tibet; *transf.* a sage, an adept. L19. **2** (**M-**.) In the Indian subcontinent, (the title of) a revered person regarded with love and respect. M20.

2 the Mahatma, Mahatma Gandhi: Mohandas Karamchand Gandhi (1869–1948).

Mahayana /mɑː(h)əˈjɑːnə, məhɑː-/ *n.* M19. [Skt *mahāyāna*, f. *mahā* great + *yāna* vehicle.] A form of Buddhism with syncretistic features, practised in China, Japan, and Tibet. Also *Mahayana Buddhism*. Cf. THERAVADA.

Mahdi /ˈmɑːdi/ *n.* E19. [Arab. (*al-*)*mahdī* lit. 'he who is rightly guided', f. pass. pple of *hadā* lead on the right way, guide aright.] In Muslim belief: the restorer of religion and justice who will rule before the end of the world; a claimant of this title, *esp.* (*Hist.*) Muhammad Ahmad of Dongola in Sudan who proclaimed himself such in 1881 and launched a political and revolutionary movement which overthrew the Turco-Egyptian regime.

Mahdism *n.* belief in or adherence to the Mahdi or a Mahdi L19. **Mahdist** *n.* a believer in or adherent of the Mahdi or a Mahdi L19.

Mahican /ˈmahɪk(ə)n/ *n.* & *a.* E17. [Mahican *muhheakunneuw* lit. 'people of the tidal waters'.] **A** *n.* A member of an Algonquian Indian people formerly inhabiting parts of Connecticut, Massachusetts, and New York State; the language of this people. E17. **B** *attrib.* or as *adj.* Of or pertaining to the Mahicans or their language. L18.

¶ Freq. confused with the Mohicans (Mohegans).

mah-jong /mɑːˈdʒɒŋ/ *n.* & *v.* Also **-ngg**. E20. [Chin. dial. *ma jiang* sparrows.] **A** *n.* A game (orig. Chinese) for four, played with 136 or 144 pieces called tiles, divided into five or six suits. E20. **B** *v.i.* Complete one's hand at mah-jong; win a game of mah-jong. E20.

Mahlerian /mɑːˈlɪərɪən/ *a.* & *n.* M20. [f. *Mahler* (see below) + -IAN.] **A** *adj.* Of, pertaining to, or characteristic of the Austrian composer Gustav Mahler (1860–1911) or his music. M20. **B** *n.* An interpreter, student, or admirer of Mahler or his music. M20.

mahmudi /mɑːˈmuːdiː/ *n.* Pl. same. E17. [Pers. *mahmūdī*, f. the name of Shah *Mahmūd*.] *Hist.* A Persian silver coin. Also, an Indian gold coin.

mahoe /məˈhəʊ/ *n.*[1] M17. [Fr. *mahot* f. Carib *mahou*.] Any of various tropical trees and shrubs, chiefly of the mallow family, with a fibrous bast; esp. *Hibiscus tiliaceus*, widespread in the tropics, and (more fully *blue mahoe*) the W. Indian *H. elatus*, whose wood is shot with blue. Also, the wood or fibre of such a tree. Cf. PURAU.

mahoe /məˈhəʊi/ *n.*[2] M19. [Maori.] A small bushy New Zealand tree, *Melicytus ramiflorus*, of the violet family, with whitish bark and clusters of small greenish flowers.

mahogany /məˈhɒgəni/ *n.* & *a.* M17. [Origin unkn.] **A** *n.* **1a** The hard, fine-grained, chiefly reddish-brown wood of a W. Indian and Central American tree, *Swietenia mahagoni* (family Meliaceae), often used for furniture. Also, the colour of this wood when polished; a rich reddish brown. M17. **b** The tree itself. M18. **2** A Cornish drink made of gin and treacle; *slang* a strong mixture of brandy and water. L18. **3** *transf.* Any of various trees, esp. (*Austral.*) eucalypts, with hard reddish-brown timber like mahogany; *spec.* (*Austral.*) the jarrah, *Eucalyptus marginata*. Also, the wood of these trees. Usu. w. specifying wd. L18. **4a** A table, *esp.* a dining-table. *arch. colloq.* M19. **b** = BAR *n.*[1] 19. *colloq.* M20.

3 *African mahogany, forest mahogany, Natal mahogany, swamp mahogany*, etc.

Comb.: **mahogany birch** *US* = *mountain mahogany* (a) s.v. MOUNTAIN *n.*

B *adj.* **1** Made of mahogany. M18. **2** Of the colour of polished mahogany; rich reddish-brown. M18.

mahoitre /məˈhɔɪtə/ *n.* Long *obs.* exc. *Hist.* M19. [OFr.] A pad placed in the upper part of a sleeve to give added breadth to the shoulders.

Mahomet /məˈhɒmɪt/ *n.* Now *arch. rare.* ME. [(O)Fr. *Mahomet*, †*Mach-* f. med.L *Ma(c)hometus* MUHAMMAD. Cf. MAUMET.] **1** = MUHAMMAD. Formerly also, an idol. ME. **†2** A Muslim. E16–M18. **3** A breed of pigeon. Now *rare* or *obs.* M18.

†Mahometical *a.* Muslim M16–E18. **†Mahometism** *n.* the Muslim religion, Islam L16–L18.

Mahometan /məˈhɒmɪt(ə)n/ *n.* & *a.* Now *arch. rare.* E16. [med.L *Ma(c)hometanus*, f. *Ma(c)hometus*: see prec., -AN.] **A** *n.* = MUSLIM *n.* E16. **B** *adj.* = MUSLIM *a.* E17.

Mahometanism *n.* the Muslim religion, Islam E17.

Mahometry /məˈhɒmɪtri/ *n.* Now *arch. rare.* L15. [f. MAHOMET + -RY. Cf. MAUMETRY.] The Muslim religion, Islam. Formerly also, idolatry.

†mahone *n.* L16–M19. [Fr. *mahonne*, Sp. *mahona*, It. *maona*, Turk. *mavuna*, *mavna*, f. Arab. *ma'ūna* provisions.] A flat-bottomed Turkish sailing vessel.

mahonia /mə'həʊnɪə/ *n.* E19. [mod.L (see below), f. Bernard McMahon (d. 1816), US botanist + -IA[1].] Any of various freq. cultivated Asian and N. American shrubs of the genus *Mahonia*, of the barberry family, with yellow flowers and prickly pinnate leaves; *esp.* Oregon grape, *M. aquifolium*.

mahorka /mə'hɔːkə/ *n.* E20. [Russ. *makhórka*.] A kind of coarse Russian tobacco.

Mahound /mə'huːnd, mə'haʊnd/ *n.* ME. [OFr. *Mahun*, *-um* contr. of MAHOMET. Cf. MAUMET.] 1 = MAHOMET 1. Now *arch.* & *poet.* ME. †2 A monster; a hideous creature. LME–L16. 3 The Devil. Chiefly *Sc.* Now *rare* or *obs.* LME.

mahout /mə'haʊt/ *n.* M17. [Hind. *mahāut*, *mahāvat* f. Skt *mahāmātra* high official, elephant-keeper, f. *mahā* great + *mātra* measure.] In the Indian subcontinent: an elephant-driver.

Mahratta *n.* & *a.* var. of MARATHA.

Mahratti *n.* var. of MARATHI.

mahseer /'mɑːsɪə/ *n.* M19. [Hind. *mahāser*, f. Skt *mahā* great + *śaphara* carp.] Any of various large Indian freshwater cyprinoid fishes, esp. *Barbus tor*, which resembles the barbel.

Mahsud /'mɑːsuːd/ *n.* & *a.* L19. [Pers. & Arab. *Mahsūd* envied.] A *n.* A member of a Pathan people of Waziristan in NW Pakistan. L19. B *adj.* Of or pertaining to this people. L19.

†Mahu *n.* Only in E17. [Perh. rel. to MAHOUND.] A devil.

mahua /'mɑhʊə/ *n.* Also **mahwa(h)**, **mohwa** /'məʊwə/, **mowra** /'məʊrə/ & other vars. L17. [Hind. *mahūā*, *mo(h)ā*, Bihari *mahuar*, Gujarati *mahuṛo*, *mauṛo* f. Skt *madhūka*, f. *madhu* sweet. Cf. MOHUR *n.*[2]] Any of several Indo-Malayan trees of the genus *Madhuca* (family Sapotaceae), esp. *M. latifolia*, with sweet fleshy edible flowers and oily seeds. Also *mahua-tree*.

mahwa(h) *n.* var. of MAHUA.

mai /mʌɪ/ *n. NZ.* M19. [Contr.] = MATAI *n.*[1]

maid /meɪd/ *n.* ME. [Abbrev. of MAIDEN *n.* For similar loss of *n* cf. *clew*, *game*, *eve*.] 1 A girl; a young (unmarried) woman. Now *arch.*, *poet.*, & *dial.* ME. 2a A virgin; *spec.* the Virgin Mary. *arch.* ME. †b A man who has not had sexual intercourse. ME–E18. 3 A female servant (esp. for indoor work) or attendant. Freq. w. specifying wd. ME. 4 A young skate or thornback. Also, a twait shad. L16. 5 An unmarried woman, a spinster. Now chiefly in OLD MAID. E17. 6 Any of various objects or contrivances; *spec.* (*a*) = MAIDEN *n.* 5; (*b*) = MAIDEN *n.* 7; (*c*) = MAIDEN *n.* 6. L17.

1 COLERIDGE Sweet maid . . Thy sire and I will crush the snake! P. S. BUCK The seeking of a maid who might be his son's wife. 2b JONSON Two noble Maids Of either sexe, to Union sacrificed. 3 C. ISHERWOOD She . . kept a maid to do the housework. J. BARTH Jane reappeared . . and behind her came the maid with our cocktails. *barmaid*, *chambermaid*, *dairymaid*, *housemaid*, *nursemaid*, etc. *waiting-maid*: see WAITING *ppl a.* 1. 5 SIR W. SCOTT Miss Lucy St. Aubin lived and died a maid for his sake.

Phrases: *French maid*: see FRENCH *a.* **Maid Marian** a female character in the traditional morris dance, in later tradition the companion of Robin Hood. **maid of all work** a female servant doing general housework; *fig.* a person doing many jobs. **maid of honour** (*a*) an unmarried lady attending a queen or princess; (*b*) a kind of custard tartlet; (*c*) *N. Amer.* a principal bridesmaid. OLD MAID. **the Maid (of Orleans)** [tr. Fr. *la Pucelle*] Joan of Arc. *universal maid*: see UNIVERSAL *a.*

Comb.: **†maid-child** a female child; **maid-fish** = sense 7 above; **maidservant** = sense 3 above.

maidhood *n.* maidenhood OE. **maidish** *a.* maidenish L19. **maidkin** *n.* (long *rare* or *obs.*) a young or small maid LME. **maidless** *a.* not having, without, a maidservant L19. **maidling** *n.* (*rare*) a young or small maid M19. **maidy** *n.* (*dial.*) a young or small maid L19.

maid /meɪd/ *v.* L19. [f. the n.] 1 *v.t.* = MAIDEN *v.* 2. *dial.* L19. 2 *v.i.* Do maids' work; act as a maid. E20. 3 *v.t.* Wait on (a person) as a maid. E20.

2 M. MITCHELL My Prissy been maidin' fo' Miss India fo' a year now. 3 A. CHRISTIE Susanne . . used to look after my clothes and maid me.

maidan /mʌɪ'dɑːn/ *n.* E17. [Urdu & Pers. *maidān* f. Arab. *maydān*] An open space in or near a town; a parade-ground.

maiden /'meɪd(ə)n/ *n.* & *a.* [OE *mæġden* = OHG *magatīn* f. Gmc dim. = maid, virgin, repr. also by OE *mæġ(e)þ*, OS *magaþ*, OHG *magad* (G *Magd*, whence dim. *Magdchen*, now *Mädchen* girl), Goth. *magaþs*, and rel. to Gmc f. IE base also of OE, OS *magu*, ON *mǫgr*, Goth. *magus* son, young man, OIr. *mug* boy, servant: see -EN[1]. Cf. MAC *n.*[1], MAY *n.*[1]] A *n.* 1 = MAID *n.* 1. OE. 2a = MAID *n.* 2a. OE. b = MAID *n.* 2b. Now *dial.* ME. 3 A maidservant, a female attendant. (Cf. MAID *n.* 3.) Now *arch.* & *dial.* OE. 4 = MAID *n.* 5. Long *obs.* exc. *dial.* LME. 5 *Hist.* A kind of guillotine, *esp.* one used for executions in Edinburgh. M16. 6 An apparatus or instrument used in washing clothes, a dolly. Also, a clothes-horse. Chiefly *dial.* M18. 7a The last handful of corn cut in a harvest-field, often roughly shaped into the figure of a girl and decorated with ribbons. Also *harvest maiden*. L18. b The harvest home and the feast with which it was celebrated. *Sc.* E19. 8a *ellipt.* A maiden horse, a maiden race, a maiden over, a maiden tree. E19. b A strawberry plant bearing its first crop. E20.

2a A. DUGGAN I have never . . seduced a virtuous woman . . the wife I have married . . came to me a maiden. G. GREENE The definition of a maiden in common use . . is an unbroken hymen. 3 AV *Ps.* 123:2 As the eyes of a maiden [looke] vnto the hand of her mistresse.

Phrases: *iron maiden*: see IRON *n.* & *a.* *Rhine maiden*: see RHINE *a.* **the answer to a maiden's prayer** an eligible bachelor.

B *attrib.* or as *adj.* I 1 Unmarried; virgin. Formerly also, (of a child) female. ME. 2 Of or pertaining to a maiden or maidenhood; suitable for a maiden, having the qualities of a maiden. L16. 3 Of a female animal: unmated. M19.

1 D. ROCK The girl-like maiden-mother bowed down before the crib. V. S. PRITCHETT There are three maiden aunts—an extinct genus now. 2 SHAKES. *Mids. N. D.* And the imperial vot'ress passed on, In maiden meditation fancy-free. DISRAELI Not . . a word that could call forth a maiden blush.

II 4 That is the first of its kind; made, used, etc., for the first time. Freq. in *maiden speech* below. M16. 5 That has yielded no results. a (Of a game) in which no points are scored; *spec.* in *Cricket* (of an over) in which no runs are scored. L16. b Of an assize, circuit, or session: orig., at which no capital conviction occurred; now, at which there are no cases for trial. L17. c Of a horse etc.: that has never won a prize. Of a race: open to a horse etc. that has never won a prize. M18. d *Founding*. Of a bell: that needs little or no tuning after it has been cast. E20. 6a Of a town, fortress, etc.: that has never been captured. L16. b Of a soldier, sword, etc.: untried. L16. c Of soil, metal, etc.: that has never been disturbed; unworked. E17. d Of a plant or tree: grown from seed as opp. to a stock; not pruned or transplanted. M17.

4 J. HENNESSY Other westerners in the party were making their maiden voyages. 6a WORDSWORTH She was a maiden City, bright and free. b L. RITCHIE He had not as yet fleshed his maiden sword.

Special collocations & *comb.*: **maiden name** the surname of a girl or woman before marriage. **maiden pink** a wild pink, *Dianthus deltoides*, of gravelly pastures. **maiden plum (tree)** any of various W. Indian trees of the genus *Comocladia* (family Anacardiaceae). **maiden-servant** (long *rare* or *obs.*) = sense A.3 above. **maiden speech** the first speech delivered in the House of Commons by a Member of Parliament. **maiden's wreath** an ornamental pink- or white-flowered plant, *Francoa sonchifolia*, of the saxifrage family; = *bridal wreath* s.v. BRIDAL *a.* **maiden thought** *poet.* the stage of human development after infancy; a period of innocent untarnished hope. **maiden-widowed** *a.* (*rare*, Shakes.) widowed while still a maiden.

maidenhood *n.* (*a*) the condition or period of being a maiden; †(*b*) = MAIDENHEAD *n.*[1]: OE. **maidenish** *a.* (chiefly *derog.*) resembling a maiden, characteristic of a maiden M18. **maidenlike** *a.* & *adv.* (*a*) *adj.* resembling (that of) a maiden, suitable for a maiden; (*b*) *adv.* (*rare*) in the manner of a maiden: E16. **maidenship** *n.* (with possess. adj., as *your* etc. *maidenship*) a playful title of respect given to a maiden E17.

maiden /'meɪd(ə)n/ *v.t. obs.* exc. *dial.* L16. [f. the n.] †1 Foll. by *it*: act like a maiden; be coy. Only in L16. 2 Wash clothes with a maiden or dolly. M19.

2 **maidening pot, tub** a washtub.

maidenhair /'meɪd(ə)nhɛː/ *n.* LME. [f. MAIDEN *n.* + HAIR *n.*] 1 Any of various ferns of the genus *Adiantum*, of warmer regions of the world, with delicate pale green fan-shaped pinnules; *esp.* (orig. more fully *black* or *true maidenhair*) *A. capillus-veneris*, a rare British native of sheltered sea-cliffs, frequently cultivated. Also *maidenhair fern*. LME. 2 Either of two spleenworts, ferns of the genus *Asplenium*, (*a*) (more fully *English maidenhair*) *A. trichomanes*, with simply pinnate fronds, frequent on old walls and rocks; (*b*) *white maidenhair*, wall rue, *A. ruta-muraria*. Now *rare* or *obs.* LME. 3 *golden maidenhair*, a fine-leaved moss, *Polytrichum commune*. L16.

Comb.: **maidenhair-spleenwort** any of several ferns of the genus *Asplenium*; *spec.* = *English maidenhair* (see sense 2(a) above); **maidenhair tree** the ginkgo, the leaves of which resemble the segments of an *Adiantum*.

maidenhead /'meɪd(ə)nhɛd/ *n.*[1] *arch.* ME. [f. MAIDEN *n.* + -HEAD.] The state or condition of a maiden; virginity. Also, the hymen.

maidenhead /'meɪd(ə)nhɛd/ *n.*[2] L15. [f. MAIDEN *n.* + HEAD *n.*] A representation of the head or head and shoulders of the Virgin Mary, *spec.* (*a*) as an ornamental finish to the handle of a spoon (occas., a spoon with such a handle), (*b*) *Her.* as a charge on a shield etc.

maidenly /'meɪd(ə)nli/ *a.* LME. [f. MAIDEN *n.* + -LY[1].] 1 Of or pertaining to a maiden; virginal. LME. †2 Of a person: like a maiden in behaviour or appearance; gentle, modest, shy. E16–L17. 3 Of a quality, action, etc.: regarded as appropriate to or characteristic of a maiden. M16.

1 R. ELLIS Her maidenly bloom fresh-glowing. 2 MARVELL Our author is very maidenly, and condescends to his Bookseller not without some reluctance. 3 L. GORDON Maidenly innocence, sweetness, chastity . . might suffer if women were allowed to read Latin and Greek.

maidenliness *n.* M16.

maidenly /'meɪd(ə)nli/ *adv.* L16. [f. as prec. + -LY[2].] After the fashion of a maiden; in a maidenly manner.

HUGH WALPOLE He stopped by Jeremy, who was maidenly conscious of his nudity.

maiden's blush /meɪd(ə)nz 'blʌʃ/ *n. phr.* L16. [f. MAIDEN *n.* + -'S[1] + BLUSH *n.*] 1 A delicate pink colour. Also (in full *maiden's blush rose*), a rose of this colour, one of the *Rosa* × *alba* group. L16. 2 A small geometrid moth, *Cyclophora punctaria*. M19. 3 Either of two Australian trees with pinkish wood, *Sloanea australis* (family Elaeocarpaceae) and *Euroschinus falcatus* (family Anacardiaceae). L19.

maieutic /meɪ'juːtɪk/ *a.* M17. [Gk *maieutikos*, f. *maieuesthai* act as midwife, f. *maia* midwife: see -IC.] Of a mode of inquiry: Socratic, serving to bring out a person's latent ideas into clear consciousness.

maieutics /meɪ'juːtɪks/ *n.* L19. [f. as prec.: see -ICS.] The maieutic method.

maigre *n.* var. of MEAGRE *n.*[1]

maigre /'meɪgə, *foreign* mɛgr/ *a.* M16. [(O)Fr.: see MEAGRE *a.*] I †1 = MEAGRE *a.* I. M16–L17. II *RC Ch.* 2 Designating a day on which abstinence from meat is ordered. L17. †3 *eat, keep, live maigre*, live on a maigre diet. M–L18. 4 Of food, esp. soup: not containing meat; suitable for eating on maigre days. L18.

maihem *n.* & *v.* var. of MAYHEM.

maiko /'mʌɪkəʊ, *foreign* 'maiko/ *n.* Pl. same, **-os**. E20. [Jap.] A girl who is being trained to become a geisha.

mail /meɪl/ *n.*[1] Now only *Sc.* [OE *mæl*, prob. contr. of OE *mæþel* meeting, discussion, OS,

OHG *mahal* assembly, judgement, treaty, Goth. *maþl* meeting-place, repl. by forms f. ON *mál* speech, agreement. In sense corresp. to ON *máli* stipulation, stipulated pay. Cf. BLACKMAIL.] †**1** Speech. Only in OE. **2** Payment, tax, tribute, rent. OE.

2 mails and duties the rents of an estate. **silver mail** rent paid in money.

mailing *n.* (*a*) a rented farm; (*b*) the rent paid for a farm: LME.

mail /meɪl/ *n.*[2] ME. [(O)Fr. *maille* f. L *macula* spot, mesh.] †**1** Any of the metal rings or plates composing mail-armour. ME–E18. **2** Armour composed of interlaced rings or chains or of overlapping plates fastened on some material. ME. †**b** A piece of such armour. Only in E17. **c** The protective shell or scales of certain animals. E18. **3**†**a** A small hole for a lace, clasp, or other fastening of a garment to pass through; an eyelet-hole, an eye. LME–M17. **b** *Weaving.* A ring in a loom through which the warp thread passes. M18. **4** A film over the eye; a defect in vision. Long *obs.* exc. *dial.* LME. **5** *Falconry.* The breast-feathers of a hawk collectively, when the feathers are full-grown. Also, the plumage of certain other birds. L15. **6** A section of interlinked pieces of metal used in rope-making for rubbing loose hemp off cordage. M18.

2 MILTON Mangl'd with gastly wounds through Plate and Maile. W. MORRIS Through the glimmering thicket the linked mail rang out. *chain-mail. fig.*: G. MACDONALD She was clad in the mail of endurance. *coat of mail*: see COAT *n.* *frock of mail*: see FROCK *n.* *shirt of mail*: see SHIRT *n.* **b** SHAKES. *Tr. & Cr.* To hang Quite out of fashion, like a rusty mail. **c** M. ARNOLD The sea-snakes coil and twine, Dry their mail and bask in the brine.

Attrib. & comb.: In the senses 'made of mail', 'in mail', as *mail-armour, -shirt, -clad*, etc.

mailless /-l-l-/ *a.* E19.

mail /meɪl/ *n.*[3] ME. [OFr. *male* (mod. *malle* bag, trunk) f. Gmc (cf. OHG *mal(a)ha* wallet, bag, MDu. *male*, Du. *maal*).] **1** Orig., a bag, a pack, a wallet; a travelling bag. Now (*Sc.* & *US*) in *pl.*, baggage. ME. **2** A bag or packet of letters for conveyance by post; the postal matter so conveyed; all that is so conveyed on one occasion. Also, the letters etc. delivered at one place or to one person on one occasion. Freq. in titles of newspapers. M17. **3** A person or vehicle to carry postal matter; *ellipt.* a mail boat, a mail train, etc. Also, the system of conveyance of letters etc. by post; the official conveyance or dispatch of postal matter; the post. M17.

1 R. L. STEVENSON He . . emptied out his mails upon the floor that I might have a change of clothes. **2** D. HAMMETT When I got the mail this morning there was a letter for him. M. DE LA ROCHE They watched the mails and no letter came from her. Z. TOMIN I sent it out with the diplomatic mail. *Daily Mail, Oxford Mail*, etc. **3** L. T. C. ROLT The night mail from Paddington. P. GROSSKURTH The mail was good in those days. Alix Strachey received the letter on Jan. 1 1925. *airmail, sea-mail, surface mail*, etc.

Phrases: CERTIFIED *mail*. *direct mail*: see DIRECT *a.* *electronic mail*: see ELECTRONIC *a.*

Attrib. & comb.: Designating people and vehicles employed to carry mail, as *mail boat, -boy, ship, train*, etc. Special combs., as **mailbag** a large bag for mail; **mail-box** (*a*) *Hist.* a box in which the mailbags were placed on a mail-coach; (*b*) *N. Amer.* a box for delivery of mail; **mail-car** (*a*) a railway carriage in which mail is carried; (*b*) *Ir. Hist.* a jaunting car used for the conveyance of mail; (*c*) *Austral.* & *NZ* a motor vehicle used for the conveyance of mail (and also sometimes of passengers); **mail carrier** *US* a postman or postwoman; **mail cart** (*a*) a cart for carrying mail by road; (*b*) a light vehicle for carrying children, made with shafts so as to be drawn or pushed by hand; **mail-coach** (*a*) *Hist.* a stagecoach used primarily for the conveyance of mail; *spec.* a coach used by the Post Office for carrying parcels by road; (*b*) = *mail-car* (a) above; **mail cover** *US* the monitoring of all mail sent to a specified address; **mail-day** *US* the day on which mail is dispatched or received; **mail drop** *N. Amer.* a place where mail may be left to be collected by another person; **mailman** *N. Amer.* a postman; **mail order** (orig. *US*) an order for goods to be sent by post; *mail-order firm, business*, etc., a firm, business, etc., operating mainly by this system; **mail-rider** *US Hist.* a mail carrier; **mailroom** a room where mail is collected, sorted, or otherwise dealt with; **mailshot** material posted to potential customers as part of an advertising campaign; **mail-time** the time mail takes to pass from one place to another.

mail /meɪl/ *n.*[4] *obs.* exc. *Hist.* Also **maille**. L16. [AN *mayle*, OFr. *m(e)aille* (whence MDu. *mealge*), f. late L: see MEDAL *n.*] A coin; *spec.* a halfpenny.

maille noble a gold coin of the reign of Edward III; a half-noble.

mail /maːj/ *n.*[5] Now *rare* or *obs.* Pl. pronounced same. M17. [OFr. f. L *malleus* hammer. Cf. MAUL *n.*, MALL *n.*] Orig., the game of pall-mall; a place where the game was played. Later (from the *Mail* in Paris), a public promenade bordered by trees.

the Mail = *the Mall* s.v. MALL *n.*

¶Reintroduced f. Fr. in E20.

†**mail** *v.*[1]*t.* Also **meal**. OE–E19. [f. as MOLE *n.*[1]] Spot, stain.

mail /meɪl/ *v.*[2]*t.* ME. [Origin unkn.] †**1** Tie (*up*), wrap up (goods, a parcel, etc.); envelop. ME–M17. **2** *Falconry.* Cover (a hawk) with a cloth etc. to promote tameness or to ensure passivity during an operation. L16.

mail /meɪl/ *v.*[3]*t. arch.* LME. [Partly f. MAIL *n.*[2], partly back-form. f. MAILED *a.*] †**1** Make (a piece of armour) out of mail (*lit.* & *fig.*). Only in LME. **2** Clothe or arm (as) with mail. L18.

¶Rare bef. L18.

mail /meɪl/ *v.*[4]*t.* Orig. *US.* E19. [f. MAIL *n.*[3]] Send (letters etc.) by post, post.

L. HELLMAN I . . never had an answer to the letter I had mailed from New Orleans. J. WILCOX I want to mail out personalized appeals.

Comb.: **mail-in** *n.* & *a.* (*a*) *n.* an item, as a promotion brochure, postal vote, etc., sent out or returned by post; (*b*) *adj.* (of an item, as a promotion brochure, postal vote, etc.) that is or can be sent through the post; (of a ballot, survey, etc.) conducted by post; **mail-out** *a.* & *n.* (*a*) *adj.* = *mail-in* adj. above; (*b*) *n.* the action of sending out a number of items such as promotion brochures etc. at one time.

maila'bility *n.* the condition of being mailable L19. **mailable** *a.* acceptable for conveyance by post M19. **mailer** *n.* (*a*) *US* a person or thing which dispatches (letters etc.) by mail; (*b*) a mail-boat; (*c*) *S. Afr.* a middleman who buys liquor legitimately and resells it to an illicit liquor dealer or shebeen keeper; (*d*) a container for the conveyance of items by post; (*e*) an advertising pamphlet, brochure, etc., sent out by post; freq. in *self-mailer*: M19.

mailed /meɪld/ *a.* LME. [f. MAIL *n.*[2] + -ED[2].] **1** Covered with or composed of mail or plates of metal. LME. **2** Armed with mail, mail-clad; (of a ship) ironclad. LME. **3** Of a hawk: having mail or breast-feathers (of a specified colour). Formerly also, (of a bird's plumage etc.) speckled, spotted. LME. **4** Of an animal etc.: having a skin or protective covering resembling mail-armour. LME.

1 JOYCE With his mailed gauntlet he brushed away a furtive tear. **2** T. WOOLNER With charge of mailèd horse and showers Of steel. *fig.*: *Guardian* Accused . . of being the silk glove that masks the mailed fist. **3** J. JOSSELYN The Osprey, which in this Country is white mail'd. **4** R. OWEN The ball-proof character of the skin of the largest of these mailed examples.

mailgram /ˈmeɪlɡram/ *n.* *US.* Also **M-**. M20. [f. MAIL *n.*[3] or *v.*[4] + -GRAM.] A message transmitted electronically from one post office to another and then delivered by ordinary post; the service providing this form of transmission.

mailing /ˈmeɪlɪŋ/ *n.* Orig. *US.* L19. [f. MAIL *v.*[4] + -ING[1].] **1** The action of sending something by mail; posting. L19. **2** Something sent by mail; *spec.* a number of items posted at one time, esp. as part of a publicity campaign, a survey, etc. E20.

1 *direct mailing*: see DIRECT *a.*

Comb.: **mailing list**: of people to whom advertising matter etc. is to be posted; **mailing shot** = *mailshot* s.v. MAIL *n.*[3]

maille *n.* var. of MAIL *n.*[4]

maillot /majo/ *n.* Pl. pronounced same. L19. [Fr.] **1** Tights. L19. **2** A tight-fitting, usu. one-piece, swimsuit. E20. **3** A jersey, a top. M20.

Mailmerge /ˈmeɪlməːdʒ/ *n.* Also **m-**. L20. [f. MAIL *n.*[3] + MERGE *v.*] *Computing.* (Proprietary name for) a program that draws on a file of names and addresses and a text file to produce multiple copies of a letter each addressed to different recipients.

maim /meɪm/ *n.*[1] Long *arch.* ME. [OFr. *mayhem, mahaing, main(e*, f. *mahaignier, mayner*: see MAIM *v.* Cf. MAYHEM.] Orig., a serious loss or permanent bodily hurt or disfigurement. Later, loss or permanent disablement of a limb etc.; an injury to the body causing this; a mutilation. Also *fig.*, the loss of an essential part, a grave defect or blemish.

T. FULLER They are so eminent . . that their omission would make a maim in history. G. BANCROFT A crowd gathered round the scaffold when Prynne and Bastwick and Burton were to suffer maim. T. H. WHITE Oh, defend us from death and horrible maims.

maim /meɪm/ *a.* & *n.*[2] Long *rare.* L15. [Prob. rel. to prec. Cf. OFr. *mehaigne*, mod.Fr. dial. *mécaigne*.] **A** *adj.* Maimed. L15.

R. L. STEVENSON His own life being maim, some of them are not admitted in his theory.

B *n. collect. pl. The* class of maimed people. M19.

Granta We thrashed these representatives of the maim, the halt and the blind.

maim /meɪm/ *v.t.* ME. [OFr. *mahaignier, mayner* f. Proto-Romance: ult. origin unkn. Cf. MAIM *n.*[1]] Orig., disable, wound, cause bodily hurt or disfigurement to. Now, deprive of (the use of) a limb etc.; mutilate, cripple; *fig.* render powerless or essentially incomplete.

BURKE Pulling down hedges, . . firing barns, maiming cattle. P. WARNER Most were maimed for life by having a hand or foot cut off. J. WYNDHAM To deprive a gregarious creature of companionship is to maim it, to outrage its nature.

maimer *n.* M16.

maimai /ˈmʌɪmʌɪ/ *n.* *NZ.* M19. [Alt. of Australian Aborig. MIA-MIA.] A makeshift shelter of sticks, grass, etc. Also, a hide or stand for a person shooting ducks.

maimed /meɪmd/ *a.* & *n.* ME. [f. MAIM *v.* + -ED[1].] **A** *adj.* That has been maimed (*lit.* & *fig.*). ME.

J. GARDNER He'd end up maimed, a brace on one boot, no arm in one sleeve.

B *n. collect. pl. The* class of maimed people. ME.

A. B. JAMESON The sick and maimed who are healed by her intercession.

maimedly /ˈmeɪmɪdli/ *adv.* (long *rare* or *obs.*) L16. **maimedness** /ˈmeɪmɪdnɪs/ *n.* E17.

Maimonidean /mʌɪˌmɒnɪˈdiːən, mʌɪməʊˈnɪdɪən/ *a.* & *n.* Also **-ian**. E19. [f. L *Maimonides* (see below): see -AN, -EAN, -IAN.] **A** *adj.* Of or pertaining to the Jewish philosopher and theologian Maimonides (Moses ben Maimon, 1135–1204), or his teaching. E19. **B** *n.* An adherent or student of Maimonides or his teaching. M19.

main /meɪn/ *n.*[1] [OE *mægen* = OS *megin*, OHG *magan, megin*, ON *magn, meg(i)n*, f. Gmc base meaning 'have power': cf. MAY *v.*[1] In branch II f. MAIN *a.*] **I 1** Physical strength, force, or power. Now only in *with might and main* s.v. MIGHT *n.*[1] OE. †**2** A host of soldiers etc.; a (military) force. OE–ME.

II 3a The mainland. Now *arch.* & *poet.* M16. **b** *Hist.* = *Spanish Main* s.v. SPANISH *a.* L19. **4** A mainsail; a mainmast. M16. **5a** The high seas, the open ocean. Now *poet.* M16. †**b** A broad expanse. L16–M17. **6a** The chief or principal part *of* a whole; the important or essential point *of. arch.* exc. in *in the main* below. L16. **b** The most important part of some business, subject, argument, etc.; the chief matter or principal thing in hand. E17. †**7** The object aimed at; a particular end or purpose. E–M17. **8** A principal channel, duct, or conductor for conveying water, sewage, gas, or (usu. in *pl.*) for the supply of electricity. Also, in *pl.*, the public supply of water, electricity, etc., collectively. E17. **9** A principal seam of coal; a coalmine. Also, a main line of a railway. M19.

3a C. THIRLWALL The island . . was separated from the main by a channel. **b** J. CLAVELL He wanted to go . . south along the Main then back across the Atlantic. **4** *Practical Boat Owner* Her main and jib gave us 194 square feet of sail. **5a** GOLDSMITH To traverse climes beyond the western main. **b** SHAKES. *Sonn.* Nativity, once in the main of light, Crawls to maturity. 6a S. JOHNSON The main of life is composed of small incidents. b A. COWLEY Frugal, and grave, and careful of the main. 7 J. WEBSTER 'Tis the very main of my ambition. 8 G. ORWELL The lights would be switched off at the main. *Listener* There were lights—not from the mains, but from a generator. *attrib.*: *Soviet Weekly* You rent a cottage with mains water and a gas cooker.

Phrases: **in the main** for the most part; in all essential points; mainly. *rising main*: see RISING *a.* *Spanish Main*: see SPANISH *a.* *with might and main*: see MIGHT *n.*[1]

main /meɪn/ *n.*[2] *Sc.* & *north.* LME. [Aphet. f. DOMAIN.] *sing.* (*obs.*) & in *pl.* treated as *sing.* or (usu.) *pl.* The farm attached to a mansion-house; a home farm; a demesne. Freq. in *the Mains of —* as the name of a farm.

main /meɪn/ *n.*[3] M16. [Prob. f. *main chance* s.v. MAIN *a.*] **1** †**a** A principal object or undertaking. M16–L18. **b** In the game of hazard, a number (5, 6, 7, 8, or 9) called by a player before throwing the dice. L16. †**2** A match (at archery, boxing, bowls, etc.). L16–L19. **3** A match between fighting cocks; occas., a number of fighting cocks engaged in a match. M18.

1a SHAKES. *1 Hen. IV* To set so rich a main On the nice hazard of one doubtful hour. G. TOWERSON Recreations . . must consequently be . . used as things on the by and not as the main. 3 **Welsh main** a series of cock-fighting matches organized as a knockout competition.

main /meɪn/ *a.* OE. [Partly repr. MAIN *n.*[1] in comb., partly f. ON *megenn*, *megn* (in comb. *megin*) strong, powerful.] **1** †**a** Of an action etc.: manifesting or requiring great force or energy. OE–L17. **b** Of strength etc.: exerted to the full, sheer. Now chiefly in *by main force*. OE. **c** Strong, potent; *esp.* (of a sound) loud. Long *arch. rare.* LME. †**d** Of motion etc.: swift, speedy, rapid. L16–M17. †**2** (Of an army) large, powerful; *esp.* designating a complete and fully equipped force as opp. to a small or irregular one. Also, designating a pitched battle as opp. to a skirmish. OE–M17. **3a** Of a material object: of great size or bulk. *obs.* exc. *dial.* OE. **b** Of a quantity or amount: large. *obs.* exc. *dial.* E17. **4a** Esp. of an action, a quality, etc.: very great in degree, value, etc.; highly remarkable for a specified quality; very great or considerable of its kind. (Occas. with *compar.* & *superl.*) *obs.* exc. *dial.* OE. **b** Of a person, an agent: great, remarkable, or pre-eminent for the quality or characteristics indicated. *obs.* exc. *dial.* LME. †**5a** Of a person: powerful, high in rank or position. *rare.* OE–E17. **b** Of an affair, event, etc.: highly important; having great results or important consequences; momentous. L16–L17. †**6** Of a body of flowing water: in flood; large, full-flowing. Also, designating the ocean or the open sea. ME–E17. **7** *Naut.* Pertaining to, connected with, or near the mainmast or mainsail. LME. **8a** Chief or principal in permanent relation to others of the same kind. L15. **b** Greater or more important than others of the same kind; pre-eminent; leading. L16. **9a** Designating a considerable, uninterrupted stretch of land, water, space, etc. M16. †**b** Of earth, rock: forming the principal or entire mass; solid. M16–M17. **10a** Chief in size or extent; constituting the bulk or principal part; designating the chief part of the thing specified. L16. †**b** Referring or pertaining to all or the majority; general. L16–M17.

1a H. FOULIS She also gave a main stroke against Cecchino. b SIR W. SCOTT Yet with main strength his strokes he drew. c JOYCE And he answered with a main cry: *Abba! Adonai!* d J. FLETCHER Making with all maine speed to th' port. 2 R. CAREW To withstand any great Navie or maigne invasion. T. SHELTON This Giant . . would pass with a main power into my Land. 3a MILTON Themselves invaded next, and on their heads Main Promontories flung. 4a D. FEATLEY This is one of our mainest exceptions against the Roman Church. R. L. STEVENSON It [an island] were a main place for pirates once. b R. B. SHERIDAN I am a main bungler at a long story. 5a J. FLETCHER So main a person, A man of so much Noble note and honour. b MILTON All commit the care And management of this main enterprise To him their great Dictator. 6 SHAKES. *Merch. V.* And bid the main flood bate his usual height. 7 JOHN ROSS The main and fore hatchway. 8a W. IRVING After turning from the main road up a narrow lane. *Encycl. Brit.* A rate of fall of 1 in 120 . . is desirable . . for a main sewer. b H. ROGERS I went carefully over all the main points of the argument. E. A. FREEMAN The statements may be grouped under two main heads. 9a MILTON Over all the face of Earth Main Ocean flow'd. 10a WELLINGTON The main body of the allied army. LD MACAULAY The sturdy country gentlemen who formed the main strength of the Tory party. b SHAKES. *Hen. VIII* By the main assent Of all these learned men, she was divorced.

Phrases: **main and —** *dial.* = MAIN *adv.* **the Main Plot** *Hist.* the more important of two plots against the government of James I (opp. *the Bye Plot*).

Special collocations & comb.: **main beam** (*a*) a principal beam which transmits a load directly to a column; (*b*) the undipped beam of the headlights of a motor vehicle. **main body** the body of troops forming the chief part of an army or armed force, occupying the space between the vanguard and the rear. **main brace** *n.*[1] [BRACE *n.*[2]] *Naut.* the brace attached to the main yard; *splice the main brace* (Hist.), serve an extra rum ration. **main brace** *n.*[2] [BRACE *n.*[1]] a principal brace; *Mech.* in a system of braces, the one that takes the principal strain. **main breadth** *Naut.* the broadest part of a ship at a particular timber or frame. **main chance** †(*a*) = MAIN *n.*[3] 1b; chiefly *fig.*, the likely outcome, the most important point risked or at stake; (*b*) something which is of principal importance, *esp.* the opportunity of enriching or otherwise benefiting oneself; *an eye to the main chance*, consideration for one's own interests. **main chancer** an opportunist, a person who has an eye to the main chance. **main couple** the principal truss in a roof. **main course** (*a*) any of a number of substantial dishes in a large menu; the principal dish of a meal; (*b*) *Naut.* (now *rare* or *obs.*) a mainsail. **main crop** the chief crop, excluding the early and late varieties or sections. **maincrop** *a.* of or pertaining to the main crop. **main deck** *Naut.* (*a*) the deck next below the spar-deck in a man-of-war; (*b*) the upper deck between the poop and the forecastle in a merchantman. **main dish** = *main course* (a) above. *main drag*: see DRAG *n.* 11. **mainframe** *Computing* orig., the central processing unit of a computer; now usu., any large or general-purpose computer, *esp.* one supporting numerous peripherals etc. **main guard** *Hist.* (*a*) *Fortif.* the keep of a castle; the part of the building in which the main guard (sense (b) below) is lodged; (*b*) a body of troops constituting a guard, *esp.* a body of cavalry posted on the wings of a camp towards the enemy; a guard in a fortress taking custody of disturbers of the peace etc. **main half-breadth** *Naut.* a section of the broadest part of a ship. **main line** (*a*) a chief railway line; (*b*) a principal route, a connection, conduit, etc.; (*c*) *slang* a principal vein, esp. as a site for (illicit) drug injection; (the action or habit of making) such an injection (cf. MAINLINE); (*d*) *US* a chief road or street. **main-line** *a.* of or pertaining to a main line. **mainmast** the principal mast in a ship. **mainplane** *Aeronaut.* a principal supporting surface of an aircraft (as distinguished from a tailplane). **main range** *Austral.* & *NZ* the principal ridge of a chain of mountains. **mainsail** *Naut.* the principal sail of a ship; *esp.* the lowest sail on the mainmast in a square-rigged vessel; the sail set on the after part of the mainmast in a fore-and-aft rigged vessel. **main sea** *arch.* the high sea; = MAIN *n.*[1] 5a. **main sequence** *Astron.* a series of star types represented on a Hertzsprung–Russell diagram (of stellar magnitude against surface temperature) as a continuous band extending from the upper left (hot bright stars) to the lower right (cool dim stars), to which most stars belong (cf. DWARF *n.* 3). **mainsheet** (*a*) *Naut.* the rope which controls the boom of the mainsail when set; (*b*) *slang* in Jamaica, a drink of rum and water. **mainspring** (*a*) the principal spring in a piece of mechanism, esp. in a watch, clock, etc.; (*b*) *fig.* the chief motive power, the main incentive. **main squeeze** *N. Amer. slang* (*a*) an important person; (*b*) a person's principal friend of the opposite sex. **mainstay** (*a*) *Naut.* the stay which extends from the maintop to the foot of the foremast; *mainstay sail*, a storm-sail set on the mainstay; (*b*) *fig.* a chief support. **main stem** (*a*) the principal stem (*lit.* & *fig.*); (*b*) *US slang* the main street of a town etc. **mainstream** *n.*, *a.*, & *v.* (*a*) *n.* the principal stream or river etc.; the prevailing trend of opinion, fashion, etc.; *Education* the stream or class for those without special needs; (*b*) *adj.* of or pertaining to the mainstream; (of jazz) neither traditional nor modern; belonging to or characteristic of an established field of activity; (*c*) *v.t.* & *i.* incorporate *into* the mainstream; *spec.* in *Educ.*, place (a pupil) in a class for those without special needs. **main street** (as a name also w. cap. initials) the principal street of a town; *fig.* (after Sinclair Lewis's novel *Main Street*, 1920) the mediocrity, parochialism, or materialism regarded as typical of small-town life. **mainstreeting** *N. Amer.* political campaigning in main streets to win electoral support. **maintop** *Naut.* the top of a mainmast; the platform above the head of the lower mainmast. **main-topgallant** *a.* (*Naut.*) designating the mast, sail, yard, etc., above the maintopmast and maintopsail. **maintopmast** *Naut.* the mast above the lower mainmast. **maintopsail** *Naut.* the sail above the mainsail. **main-ward** (*a*) the main body of an army; (*b*) the principal ward of a lock. **mainway** the gangway or principal passage in a mine. **main-yard** *Naut.* the yard on which the mainsail is extended.

main /meɪn/ *v.t.* E20. [f. MAIN *a.*] **1** Convert (a road) into a main road. E20. **2** = MAINLINE. *slang.* L20.

main /meɪn/ *adv.* Long chiefly *dial.* M17. [f. MAIN *a.* Cf. MIGHTY *adv.*] Very, exceedingly.

W. GODWIN It is main foolish of me to talk to you thus.

Maine Law /'meɪn lɔː/ *n. phr.* M19. [f. as MAINER.] *US Hist.* A law forbidding the manufacture or sale of intoxicating liquors; *spec.* the prohibitory law passed in Maine in 1851.

Mainer /'meɪnə/ *n.* L19. [f. *Maine* (see below) + -ER[1].] A native or inhabitant of the State of Maine in the north-eastern US.

Also **Mainite** *n.* M19.

mainferre /'meɪnfɛː/ *n. obs.* exc. *Hist.* LME. [Perh. repr. Fr. *main ferrée* ironclad hand or *main-de-fer* hand of iron.] A piece of medieval armour; *esp.* a gauntlet for the left arm.

mainland /'meɪnlənd, -land/ *n.* LME. [f. MAIN *a.* + LAND *n.*[1]] **1** A large continuous extent of land, including the greater part of a country or territory and excluding outlying islands, peninsulas, etc. Formerly also, land as opp. to sea, *terra firma*; *poet.* great extent of country, wide territory. LME. **2a** (**M-**.) The largest island in Orkney and in Shetland. M16. **b** The South Island of New Zealand. *NZ colloq.* M20.

1 T. H. HUXLEY Pillars of chalk have . . been separated from the mainland. V. S. NAIPAUL Venezuelans flew over from the mainland to shop.

Comb.: **Mainland China** the People's Republic of China, as opp. to Taiwan.

mainlander *n.* a native or inhabitant of the mainland M19.

mainline /'meɪnlʌɪn/ *v.t.* & *i. slang* (orig. *US*). M20. [f. *main line* s.v. MAIN *a.*] Inject (heroin or another narcotic drug) intravenously, esp. illicitly.

mainliner *n.* M20.

mainly /'meɪnli/ *adv.* ME. [f. MAIN *a.* + -LY[2].] †**1** With force; vigorously, violently. ME–M17. **b** In a loud voice, loudly. ME–L19. †**c** Vehemently, strongly; earnestly, eagerly. LME–E17. **2**†**a** In a great degree; greatly, considerably, very much, a great deal. Also, entirely, perfectly. LME–E19. **b** Very, exceedingly. Cf. MAIN *adv. obs.* exc. *dial.* L17. **3** For the most part; in the main; as the chief thing, chiefly, principally. M17.

2a SHAKES. *Haml.* As by your safety, wisdom, all things else, You mainly were stirr'd up. C. LAMB I think we should suit one another mainly. b SMOLLETT The captain was mainly wroth, and would . . have done him a mischief. 3 E. SAINTSBURY Then, cottages were mainly of stone. S. PLATH Blackberries on either side, though on the right mainly.

mainmortable /meɪn'mɔːtəb(ə)l/ *a.* & *n.* E18. [Fr., f. *mainmorte* dead hand: see -ABLE. Cf. MORTMAIN.] *Hist.* **A** *adj.* Of, pertaining to, or designating (the possessions of) serfs childless at death, who under French feudal law were not at liberty to alienate their possessions. E18. **B** *n.* A mainmortable serf. E18.

mainour /'meɪnə/ *n.* Now *arch.* or *Hist.* Also **manner** /'manə/. L15. [AN *mainoure*, *meinoure*, *main oevere*, OFr. *manuevre*: see MANOEUVRE *n.*] *Law.* A stolen object found in the possession of a thief when arrested. Chiefly in *taken* or *found with the mainour*

in the mainour in the act of doing something unlawful, *in flagrante delicto*.

mainpast /'meɪmpɑːst, -past/ *n.* M19. [AN *meynpast* f. med.L *manupastus*, f. *manu* abl. of *manus* hand + *pastus* pa. pple of *pascere* feed (cf.

opinions held by Georg Major (1502–74), a German Protestant, who maintained that good works are necessary for salvation.

Majorist *n.* a follower of Georg Major L19. **Majo'ristic** *a.* pertaining to Majorism or to the Majorists M19.

Majorism /'meɪdʒərɪz(ə)m/ *n.*[2] L20. [f. John *Major* (see below) + -ISM.] The political and economic policies of the British Conservative politician John Major (b. 1943), who became Prime Minister in 1990.

majoritarian /mə,dʒɒrɪ'tɛːrɪən/ *a.* & *n.* E20. [f. next + -ARIAN.] (A person) governed by or believing in decision by a majority; (a person) supporting the majority party.

majoritarianism *n.* belief in, or the existence of, rule or decisions by a majority M20.

majority /mə'dʒɒrɪti/ *n.* M16. [Fr. *majorité*, in branch I f. med.L *majoritas*, f. as MAJOR *a.*, in branch II f. as MAJOR *n.*[1]: see -ITY.] **I** †**1** The state or fact of being greater; superiority; pre-eminence. M16–E18. **2** The state of being of full age. M16. **3** The greater number or part; a number which is more than half the whole number; *spec.* the larger party voting together in a deliberative assembly or electoral body. L17. **4** The number by which the votes cast for one party etc. exceed those for the next in rank. M18.

2 L. STRACHEY A few days before her eighteenth birthday—the date of her majority. *Listener* It is sad that, as it approaches its majority, this organisation should have run into deep waters. 3 BYRON The majority In council were against you. F. H. A. SCRIVENER Nor in the vast majority of instances does it exist. N. CHOMSKY The large majority of its population . . is Khmer . . but there are substantial Chinese and Vietnamese minorities. J. NAGENDA These friends, the majority of whom had been at school with him. 4 J. MCCARTHY A majority of forty-six was given for the resolution. V. BRITTAIN Mr. Harris won the election with a comfortable majority.

II 5 The rank or office of a major. L18.

5 R. CAPELL This redoubtable sapper, risen from the ranks to a majority, is a type such as makes empires.

Phrases: *absolute majority*: see ABSOLUTE *a.* 8. **in the majority** belonging to or constituting the majority. *silent majority*: see SILENT *a. the great majority*: see GREAT *a.* **the majority** *spec.* the dead; *join the majority*, die. *the vast majority*: see VAST *a.* 5.

Comb.: **majority carrier** *Electronics* in a semiconductor, a charge carrier (electron or hole) of the kind carrying the greater proportion of the current; **majority rule** the principle that the greater number should exercise greater power; **majority verdict** a verdict given by more than half of a jury, but not unanimous.

majuscule /'madʒəskjuːl/ *a.* & *n.* E18. [Fr., f. L *majuscula* (*littera*) dim. of *major*: see MAJOR *a.*, -CULE.] **A** *adj.* **1** *Typogr.* Of a letter: capital. *rare.* E18. **2** *Palaeogr.* Of a letter: large (whether capital or uncial); pertaining to, of, or written in large lettering; designating or pertaining to a script having every letter bounded by the same two (imaginary) lines. M19. **B** *n.* **1** *Typogr.* A capital letter. *rare.* E19. **2** *Palaeogr.* A large letter, whether capital or uncial; (a manuscript in) large lettering or majuscule script. M19.

majuscular /mə'dʒʌskjʊlə/ *a.* †(*a*) *gen.* large; (*b*) of the nature of a majuscule; written in majuscules: E19.

makable /'meɪkəb(ə)l/ *a.* LME. [f. MAKE *v.* + -ABLE.] That can be made.

makai /mə'kʌɪ/ *adv.* & *a.* M20. [Haw., f. *ma* toward + *kai* the sea.] In Hawaii: in the direction of the sea, seaward.

makan /'makan/ *n.* E20. [Cf. Malay *makan* to eat, *makanan* food.] In Malaysia, food.

makar /'makə/ *n. Sc.* LME. [Var. of MAKER.] = MAKER. Now only, a poet writing in Scots.

makara /'mʌkərə/ *n.* L19. [Skt: cf. MUGGER *n.*[2]] A crocodile, variously represented in Indian art; the equivalent of Capricorn in the signs of the zodiac.

Makasar *a.* & *n.* see MACASSAR.

Makasarese /məkasə'riːz/ *n.* & *a.* Also (*arch.*) **Macassar-**. L19. [f. *Makasar* (see MACASSAR) + -ESE.] **A** *n.* Pl. same. A member of a Malay people of Makasar in the island of Sulawesi (Celebes), Indonesia. Also, the language of this people. L19. **B** *adj.* Of or pertaining to the Makasarese or their language. M20.

make /meɪk/ *n.*[1] *obs.* exc. *dial.* [OE *gemaca* corresp. to OS *gimaco* fellow, equal, OHG *gimahho*, f. WGmc: rel. to MATCH *n.*[1]] **1** An (or one's) equal, a match; (one's) like. OE. **2** An animal's, esp. a bird's, breeding-partner, a mate; a person's husband or wife, a person's lover or mistress. OE. **3** A companion. ME.

make /meɪk/ *n.*[2] ME. [f. the vb.] **1** The manner in which a thing (natural or manufactured) is made; style of construction, kind of composition; build of body; (particular) origin or type of manufacture, a brand. ME. **b** Of an immaterial thing: form, fashion; sort, character, nature; *dial.* a kind, a sort, a species. M17. **c** Mental or moral constitution, disposition, or character. L17. †**2** Doing, action; *esp.* (*Sc.*) manner of action or behaviour. LME–M16. **3a** The action or process of making or manufacture. Now *rare.* M18. **b** An amount manufactured; the quantity produced. M19. **4** *The* action of making profit or of advancing oneself. Only in *on the make* below. *slang.* M19. **5** The act of making electrical contact; the position or condition in which contact is made. L19. **6** *Bridge.* A declaration. E20. **7** A (sexual) conquest. *slang.* M20. **8** An identification or profile of, or information about, a person or thing from police records, fingerprints, etc. *slang.* M20.

1 H. MARTINEAU Look at his delicate hands and slight make. J. CARY He was crowned by a helmet of French make. E. BRUTON A stone which is near the ideal is said to be of good make or fine make. *Motor Sport* They confine their purchases to one make of car or commercial vehicle. 8 N. THORNBURG Let me give you a short make on our witness here. N. MAILER 'What's your make on Pangborn?' 'Corporate lawyer. Sharp.'

Phrases: **make and mend** the action of making and repairing clothes; *Naut.* a period set apart for repairing clothes, a period of leisure, a half-holiday. **on the make** *slang* (*a*) intent on profit or advancement; (*b*) intent on winning someone's affections, seeking sexual pleasure; (*c*) improving, advancing, getting better. **put the make on** *N. Amer. slang* make sexual advances towards.

make /meɪk/ *n.*[3] *arch. slang* & *dial.* M16. [Origin unkn. Cf. MAG *n.*[3]] A halfpenny.

make /meɪk/ *v.* Pa. t. & pple **made** /meɪd/. [OE *macian* = OFris. *makia*, OS *makon* (Du. *maken*), OHG *mahhōn* (G *machen*), f. WGmc, f. Gmc base meaning 'fitting'. Rel. to MATCH *n.*[1]] **I 1** *v.t.* Produce by combination of parts or ingredients, by giving a certain form to matter, by extraction, or by modification of some other substance; construct, frame, fashion. (Foll. by *of, out of, with.*) OE. **b** *v.t. spec.* Produce (an article of food or drink) by culinary or other operations; put together and set alight materials for (a fire); set apart and prepare the site for (a garden, park, road, etc.). OE. **c** *v.t.* & †*i.* Compose, write as the author (a book, a poem, verses, etc., †a letter, †a work of a specified title); draw up (a legal document, esp. one's will). ME. **d** *v.i.* Produce an article (*for*). Freq. in *make or mend.* M19. **2** *v.t.* Cause the material or physical existence of; produce by action, bring about (a condition of things, a state of feeling); inflict (a wound); produce (a hole, a mark, a sound, etc.); create or take part in the creation of (a sound recording, film, etc.). OE. †**b** Foll. by double obj. (orig. dat. of the person) or *to, unto*: cause to happen to or fall to the lot of; cause to experience. OE–E18. **c** *Gram.* Of a word: form (a certain case, tense, etc.) in a specified manner; change into (a specified form) when inflected. OE. **d** Establish (a rule, an ordinance); enact (a law); impose (a rate). Formerly also, found, institute (a religious order etc.); arrange, fix the time and place for (a match), institute (games). OE. **e** Prepare or provide (a meal, a feast) for guests; give (a dinner etc.). *arch.* OE. **f** Give rise to; have as a result or consequence; be the cause of. ME. **g** Bring (a crop etc.) to maturity, grow. *US.* E18. **h** *Electr.* Complete, close, (a circuit). Opp. *break.* M19. **3** *v.t.* **a** Create by election, appointment, or ordination; appoint (an officer), ordain (a priest etc.). OE. **b** *gen.* Cause a person or persons to become (what is specified by the object). ME. **c** Fix (a price). Now only *Comm.* LME. †**d** Translate, render. E16–E17. **e** *Naut.* Promote in rank. L18. **4** *v.t.* Form by collection of individuals, get together (in early use *spec.* a party, a force, troops). ME. **5** *v.t.* Foll. by *of* or (esp. in physical sense) *out of*: cause what is denoted by the object of the prep. to become what is denoted by the object of the vb; create (one thing) *of* or *out of* another; regard what is denoted by the object of the prep. as being what is denoted by the object of the vb, arrive at (a particular amount or quantity) as the result of calculation or estimation, assign (a meaning) to a statement, expression, representation, etc., or (a cause, motive, or reason) for actions or phenomena, (freq. with interrog. or indef. pron. as object). ME. †**b** *v.i.* Foll. by *of*: (*a*) esteem (*well, ill*); (*b*) value highly, treat with great consideration. LME–E19. **6** *v.t.* Produce from one's body or organically (now *spec.* urine, water, formerly also fruit, blossom); (now *dial.*) give birth to, beget. ME. **7** *v.t.* Amount to; (of the latest item in an enumeration) bring up the sum to (a certain amount); be sufficient to constitute, be the essential criterion of, (in proverbial or quasi-proverbial uses, mainly in neg. contexts); avail (now *rare*) or signify (much, little, nothing, etc.). ME. †**b** *v.t.* & *i.* Of arguments or evidence: avail (much, little, etc.) *for, against* (an opinion or a disputant). L16–E18. **8** *v.t.* **a** Gain, acquire, or earn (money, reputation, etc.) by labour, business, etc. (foll. by *of, out of*); *slang* & *dial.* steal, acquire, manage to get; be sold for or fetch (a certain price). ME. **b** In *Cards*, win or take (a trick), play to advantage (a certain card), win the number of tricks that fulfils (a contract). M16. **c** In various games, secure a score of, score (a point, a run, etc.); (passing into sense 2f) play so as to enable another to score (a goal etc.). M16. **9** *v.t.* Form within the mind; give conceptual existence or recognition to; entertain (a doubt, scruple, question, etc.) in the mind; formulate mentally. LME. **b** Formulate and set out (a case, a legal title, etc.). M19. **10** *v.t.* Count as, have the position of, form, (a part or unit in an aggregate, a particular member in a series). LME. **11** *v.t.* Be the material or components of, constitute, be made or converted into, serve for; admit of being made into; (of a person) become by development or training, (with obj. a n. qualified by *good, bad,* etc.) perform (*well, ill,* etc.) the part or function of. LME. **12** *v.t. Naut.* Descry or discern (as) from the top of a mast or tower; come in sight of. M16.

1 R. PECOCK God that made the world and alle thingis that ben in it. GOLDSMITH As birds sometimes are seen to make their nests. A. URE The patent plan of Mr William Onions of making cast steel. P. MORTIMER The factory made many things beside rope mats. **b** L. HELLMAN That night I was making her saffron rice. S. HARVESTER Who can make tea with a bloody bag like a lavendar sachet? **c** C. C. F. GREVILLE In 1810 the king made another will. P. KAVANAGH I make a lot of ballads. *Punch* He has made only a couple of dozen short stories. **2a** R. H. MOTTRAM The shell had fallen . . and made a hole the size of the midden at home. J. RHYS They made a hell of a row for a week. G. PRIESTLAND The car was sold to make room in the garage for rabbits. R. ELLMANN Miles . . made a small sketch of Wilde. *make a commotion, a fuss, an impression, a noise, a sensation, a stir,* etc. **f** V. WOOLF One word of affection . . would have made all the difference. DAY LEWIS It made a stanza in my poem, 'The Innocent'. I. MURDOCH He would have liked a coal-fire now, only it made so much work. **3b** LD MACAULAY He . . tried . . to make as few enemies as possible. J. HUXLEY Oxford, where we had so naturally made many friends. **5** H. JAMES I didn't know at first quite what to make of it. D. H. LAWRENCE Of her own kerchief she made a pad for the wound. M. BRADBURY For the mass of men . . you can't make a silk purse out of a sow's ear. M. WARNOCK Jean Smith who made sense of my manuscript. T. TANNER Too much has perhaps been made of the notion that the English novel is obsessed with . . class. *make a habit of, a practice of,* etc. *make an example of, an exhibition of oneself, a fool of (oneself),* etc.

6 S. T. Warner Small proud boys making water against notices that say they're not to. L. Niven How many children do you expect to die before they grow to make children? 7 Shakes. *Ant. & Cl.* The policy of that purpose made more in the marriage than the love of the parties. R. Lovelace Stone walls doe not a prison make, Nor iron bars a cage. Defoe All which did not make thirty thousand men. L. Griffiths Because you are an instinctive entrepreneur you know that two plus two makes whatever you want. 8 H. Roth He has a very good job and he makes good money. G. Millar Potatoes and onions I had 'made' from the food-dumps round Alexandria. C. Chaplin With my bonus I was making two hundred dollars a week. J. Gardam I'd say the lad took off somewhere and made his fortune. F. Wyndham He made quite a name for himself as an amateur jockey. c *Rebound* He made 47 and 41 points in the semi-final and final. *Cricketer* In the first 15 minutes of his innings, they made only four. 10 Dickens To see that sort of people together, and to make one of 'em. 11 W. Beckford They [frogs] make a good soup, and not a bad fricassée. J. Conrad The ridge of his backbone made a chain of small hills. Anthony Smith The last two quotations make particularly pertinent reading. M. Amis I was nice, extremely friendly, and would make a fine husband.

II †**13** *v.t.* Handle, manage, deal with in a particular way; bring *to* a specified condition, reduce *to*. OE–L17. **14** *v.t.* Prepare (a bed) for sleeping in, arrange bedclothes on (a bed) for future use. Orig. branch I, as the n. meant not a permanent article of furniture, but a prepared place for rest, which does not exist until 'made'. ME. **15** *v.t.* Shut, close, bar (a door). Long *arch.* & *dial.* ME. †**16** *v.refl.* Get ready *to do*; prepare *for*. Chiefly *Sc.* LME–M17. **17** *v.t.* **a** Hew or shape (timber); cut up (wood) into faggots or for firewood. *dial.* LME. **b** Prepare (fish) by curing or packing. E16. **c** Shuffle (cards) for dealing. L19. **18** *v.t.* Effect or secure the success or advancement of; *esp.* endow (a person) with fortune or prosperity; render independent, set up (usu. in *pass.*). LME. **19** *v.*†*refl.* & *i.* Prepare to go or proceed in a specified direction. LME. **20** *v.t.* Turn over and expose (hay or another crop) to the sun. LME. **21** Train (a hawk, a dog, a horse, *for*). LME.

18 G. Berkeley What one man loses another gets.. as many are made as ruined. O. Manning His voice is the very voice of Pandarus. He could make my production. S. Bellow A piece of research that made his reputation decades ago. 19 *Shetland Times* We made towards her and when we got close we saw smoke and flames coming from the galley.

III **22** *v.t.* Cause (another person, oneself, a thing) to be or become. As compl. n., adj., pa. pple (now chiefly *known, acquainted, felt, heard, understood*), †pred. phr. OE. **b** *v.t. spec.* With n. as compl.: appoint to the office of, raise to the dignity of; *arch.* transform, transmute, or fashion into (usu. in *pass.*); determine (a thing, occas. a person) to be, establish or set down as (a law, penalty, etc.), take as (one's business, abode, object, etc.). ME. **c** *v.i.* With adj. as compl.: cause oneself or another or something to be. ME. **23** *v.t.* Regard (another person, †oneself, a thing) as, consider or compute to be; describe or represent as; cause to appear as. As compl. n., adj., †pa. pple, †prep. phr. ME. **24** *v.t.* Foll. by *into*: convert into something else; work on (materials) so as to produce something; arrange, divide, or combine so as to form. L16.

22 I. Murdoch Please don't mention this.. not till it's officially made public. A. S. Dale The fact that Scott is an uneven writer does not make him a bad one. J. Nagenda The grandmother started shrieking and it was impossible to make yourself heard. J. Berman She usually remains silent, making it difficult .. to determine the extent of her knowledge. b J. Wain If Ned had known.. he'd have made it his business to help you. J. Rathbone After the battle of Talavera, Wellesley was made Viscount Wellington. 23 Dickens What time may you make it, Mr Twemlow? M. J. Guest Macbeth is not half so bad as the play makes him. E. Blishen What do you make the answer to Number 10, Johnson? A. Haley He was only seventeen when he had won the bird. That would make him around fifty-six or fifty-seven now. Janet Morgan Agatha made Hercule Poirot a retired Belgian police officer. 24 G. Gissing The shopman put them aside, to be made into a parcel. E. Jenks The wife and daughters of the shepherd.. make the milk of the herds into butter and cheese. *Observer* Lambeth Palace is rather difficult to make into a home.

IV **25** *v.t.* Bring it about *that. arch.* OE. **26** *v.t.* Cause or compel (a person or thing) to do something (foll. by *do* (now usu. only when both *make* and the dependent vb are in the active voice), *to do* (now usu. only when *make* is in the passive voice)); cause (a thing) *to be done*. ME. **b** Compel, force, (a person or thing). *colloq.* M17. **27** *v.t.* †**a** Show or allege *that*. M–L16. **b** Consider, represent, or allege (a person or thing) *to be, (to) do*. L16. **28** *v.t.* Recognize, identify. *US Criminals' slang*. E20.

26 E. Pound The snow makyth me to remember her. Scott Fitzgerald Wind.. blew the wires and made the lights go off and on again. S. Chitty Gwen had.. often made her carry the heavy sack of equipment. C. Peters He wanted to be made to write. b *Times* The enemy will not play the game.. and there are none to make him. 27b E. A. Freeman Most of the Chronicles make Richard die in 1026.

V Do, perform, accomplish: chiefly idiomatically with ns. of action. **29** *v.t.* †**a** Work (a miracle); commit (a sin, a crime, a fault), tell (a lie); do (justice, mercy); give (alms). OE–E18. **b** Wage (war). Formerly also, do (battle), join (a fight), take part in (a campaign). ME. **c** Enter into, conclude, (a bargain, contract); (now *Law*) enter into a contract of (marriage). ME. **d** Go on (a journey etc.). ME. **e** Perform or execute (a bodily movement or gesture, e.g. one expressive of respect or of contempt); deliver orally (a speech). ME. **30** *v.t.* In questions introduced by an objective *what*: have as one's business or purpose, do (as *what make you here?*); (by inversion, as *what makes you here?*) cause to be or do. *arch.* ME. **31** *v.t.* With ns. expressing the action of vbs (whether etymologically cognate or not) forming innumerable phrases approximately equivalent in sense to those vbs: see examples below and the ns. ME. **32** *v.t.* Offer, present, render, (now esp. amends, *Law* (chiefly *US*) a decision or judgement). Formerly *spec.*, do (homage, fealty); pay (some mark of respect); render (support, aid); present (a person's compliments); propound (a question); give (an instance, notice, a reason, warning). Foll. by *to* or indirect obj. ME. †**33** *v.t.* Entertain or manifest (a specified emotion). ME–L16. **34** *v.t.* Exert (an effort). LME. **35** *v.t.* Incur, suffer, (something undesirable). Formerly also (chiefly *Sc.*) defray, provide for (expenses, costs). *arch.* LME. **36** *v.t.* Eat (a meal). M16. **37** *v.t.* Accomplish (a distance, a speed) by travelling etc.; reach (a place) in travelling, come to, arrive at; *colloq.* catch (a train etc.), manage (an appointment, date, etc.); achieve, accomplish, reach; (chiefly *N. Amer.*) attain the rank of. M16. **b** Be successful in sexual advances to; win the affection of; *spec.* persuade (a person) to consent to sexual intercourse, seduce. *slang* (orig. *US*). E20.

29d *make an excursion, a tour, a trip, a voyage*, etc. e *make a bow, a curtsy, a leg*, etc. 31 *make an acknowledgement, an acquisition, an advance, an allegation, (an) allowance, (an) answer, an appeal, an (also one's) appearance, (an) application, an ascent, an assault, an assertion, (an) assurance, atonement, an attack, an attempt, (an) avowal, an award, a beginning, a bid, a blunder, a calculation, a call, a change, (a) claim, a climb, a comment, a comparison, a complaint, conversation, a dash, a defence, delay, a discovery, a donation, an endeavour, an entrance, an error, (an) exception, (an) excuse, an experiment, a find, a gift, a grant, haste, an incision, (an) inquiry, intercession, a joke, mention, a mistake, a move, (an) objection, an observation, an offer, (a) pretence, (a) proclamation, (a) profession, progress, a promise, proof, a proposal, a protest, provision, a recovery, a remark, (a) reply, (a) request, resistance, restitution, (a) retreat, a sacrifice, a sale, (a) search, a shot, a stand, a start, a surrender, a transition, a translation, (a) trial, use, a venture, a vow*, etc. 37 A. Lovell When the Wind blew so hard, that we made nine or ten Miles an hour. W. Faulkner He graduated.. with the highest marks ever made at the Academy. J. Barth I made the bus with two minutes to spare, and was soon off to Baltimore. T. Roethke I could still make the deadline, if I get my manuscript off today. N. Monsarrat It took the ship another five hours to make the last forty miles. *Observer* Ferrari believes he has the talent ultimately to make the top. K. Amis They can't make Boxing Day. They'll be down with us. *Ships Monthly* I managed to make the upturned dinghy.. and.. clambered in. S. Rushdie The murders barely made the newspapers; they were not reported on the radio.

VI †**38** *v.t. make it* (with adv. or advb. phr. of manner or with adj.): act, behave. OE–E17. **39** *v.i.* In early use (with adv. or advb. phr. of manner), behave, act, (now only as in sense 40 below). Later (with adj.), be (now chiefly in *make bold, free*). OE. **40** *v.i.* Behave or act *as if, as though*, (colloq.) *like*. LME. **b** Act as if with the intention *to do*. L19. **41** *v.i.* Have to do *with*; interfere *in*. Chiefly in collocation w. *meddle*. *dial.* M16. **42** *v.i. Naut.* Of a tide: begin to flow or ebb, rise, flow in a specified direction. M17. **43** *v.i.* †**a** *Naut.* Have a certain form or appearance; look *like*. M–L18. **b** Of land, landscape, etc.: extend in a certain direction. *US* & *Austral.* L18. **44** *v.i.* Of ice: form. *N. Amer.* L18. **45** *v.i.* Of an argument, evidence, influence, etc.: be effective, tell (on one side or the other). L19.

40 AV *Josh.* 8:15 And Ioshua and all Israel made as if they were beaten before them, and fled. M. Woodhouse You aren't making much noise... For a guy who was making like an avalanche an hour back. b S. Phillips He makes to follow, then stops.

Phrases: (A selection of cross-refs. only is included: see esp. other ns.) **as — as they make them** *colloq.* as — as possible, thoroughly —. **be made** (*a*) be naturally fitted or destined (*for, to do*); *be made for each other* (or *one another*), form an ideal combination, be ideally suited; (*b*) have been fashioned out *of*, consist *of*, be composed *of*; *be made of money* (colloq.), be extremely rich; (*c*) (of a person) be built in a specified manner (*well* etc.), have a bodily build of a specified kind. **have (got) it made** *colloq.* be sure of success, have it easy, have no more obstacles to overcome. **make a bag** kill a number of game on a shooting expedition. **make a book** arrange a series of bets referring to one and the same race or event. **make a day, night**, etc., **of it** continue doing something, esp. enjoying oneself, throughout the day, night, etc. *make a habit of*: see HABIT *n. make a hash of*: see HASH *n.*[1] *make a head*: see HEAD *n. make a House*: see HOUSE *n.*[1] *make a meal of*: see MEAL *n.*[2] 2. *make (a) mock of*: see MOCK *n. make a monkey (out) of*: see MONKEY *n. make a mountain (out) of a* MOLEHILL. *make a night of it*: see *make a day of it* above. **make a person's day, evening**, etc. be the essential factor in the pleasure of a day etc., redeem a day etc. from routine, dullness, or banality. *make a work*: see WORK *n. make (beautiful) music (together)*: see MUSIC *n.* **make believe** pretend *that, to do*, esp. (of a child in play, etc.) for enjoyment. *make (both) ends meet*: see END *n. make certain*: see CERTAIN *a. make default*: see DEFAULT *n.* **make do** manage with or *with* what is available, esp. as an inferior or temporary substitute; *make do and mend*, repair for continued use, proceed by expedients. *make eyes at*: see EYE *n. make friends*: see FRIEND *n. make fun of*: see FUN *n. make game of*: see GAME *n. make good*: see GOOD *a.* **make good time** accomplish a distance in a short time, keep to or ahead of a schedule on a journey etc. *make hay*: see HAY *n.*[1] *make head or tail of*: see HEAD *n. make heavy weather of*: see WEATHER *n. make history*: see HISTORY *n.* **make in one's way** *arch.* direct one's journey so as to pass by or through (a place). **make it** †(*a*) see sense 38 above; (*b*) succeed in covering an intended distance or reaching an intended place; achieve a desired object; be successful (*make it big* (slang), be very successful, become very prominent); *slang* achieve sexual intercourse (*with*); (*c*) (with compl.) in *imper.*, select or provide (a particular drink, time, place, etc.) from the possibilities. *make its way*: see WAY *n. make light of*: see LIGHT *a.*[1] *make light work of*: see LIGHT *a.*[1] *make love*: see LOVE *n. make merry*: see MERRY *a. make mischief*: see MISCHIEF *n. make money*: see MONEY *n.* **make much, little**, etc., **of** (*a*) have a high, low, etc., opinion of; treat with much, no, etc., consideration or affection; (*b*) derive much, little, etc., advantage from; make much, little, etc., effort to mark (an occasion etc.). *make no bones about*: see BONE *n. make no mistake*: see MISTAKE *n.* **make nothing of** (*a*) have a very low opinion of, rate or treat as valueless; (*b*) derive no advantage from; make no effort to mark (an occasion etc.); (*c*) find no difficulty in *doing*, feel no scruples at *doing*. *make oneself scarce*: see SCARCE *a. make one's mark*: see MARK *n.*[1] **make one's soul** (orig. *Anglo-Ir.*) devote one's efforts to the saving of one's soul; repent and be converted. *make one's way*: see WAY *n.* **make or break, make or mar**, cause either the complete success or the ruin of (a person or thing). *make peace*: see PEACE *n. make room*: see ROOM *n.*[1] **make sail** (*a*) spread a sail or sails; start on a voyage, set sail; (*b*) spread additional sails in order to increase a ship's speed. **make something of** derive some advantage from; make an effort to mark (an occasion etc.). *make sure*: see SURE *a.* **make the bag** contribute most to the total of game killed on a shooting expedition. *make the worst of*: see WORST *a., adv.,* & *n.* **make time** (*a*) find an occasion when time is available (*for, to do*); (*b*) *N. Amer. slang* (foll. by *with*) make sexual advances to; be successful in sexual advances to; court or flirt with. *make to measure*: see MEASURE *n. make use of*: see USE *n. make war*: see WAR *n.*[1] *make water*: see WATER *n. make waves*: see WAVE *n. make way*: see WAY *n. make welcome*: see WELCOME *a.* I. *make wing*: see WING *n.*

With preps. in specialized senses: **make after** — *arch.* go in pursuit of, follow. **make against** — be unfavourable to; militate or tell against. **make at** — *arch.* approach (as if) to attack or seize. **make for** — (*a*) operate in favour of, conduce to; tend to the advancement or progress of; confirm (a view etc.); (*b*) proceed or direct one's course towards; go in the direction of; (*c*) assail, make to attack. †**make to, unto** — (*a*) = *make for* — above; (*b*) be pertinent or applicable to. **make upon** — *arch.* = *make at* — above. **make with** — †(*a*) side with, make common cause with; (of a thing) tell in favour of; (*b*) *slang* [partly tr. Yiddish *mach mit*] bring into operation; use, affect; concern oneself with.

With advs. in specialized senses: **make away** †(*a*) = *make away with* below; (*b*) *arch.* go away suddenly or hastily, make off. **make away with** (*a*) put out of the way; kill; (*b*) remove from its rightful place or ownership; get rid of; dissipate, squander; destroy fraudulently. **make down** (*a*) (chiefly *Sc.*) fold down the sheets etc. on (a bed) to make it ready for use; (*b*) *colloq.* refashion so as to fit a smaller wearer. **make in** go in towards a particular point; intervene in an action; join in a fray. **make off** (*a*) fatten (lambs etc.) for the market; (*b*) depart or leave a place suddenly or hastily, run away, decamp (*with* something in one's possession). **make on** (*a*) *dial.* put together and set alight materials for (a fire); (*b*) go or hasten forward, proceed. **make out** (*a*) draw up (a list, a document, etc.); make a draft of; write out (a bill, cheque, etc., *to* or *in favour of* a person); (*b*) succeed in accomplishing, effect, achieve, (now *Sc.*); *make it out* (slang), achieve sexual intercourse (*with*); (*c*) *colloq.* manage, make shift, (*to do*), get along, fare, succeed, thrive, get on (well, badly, etc.); *slang* achieve sexual intercourse (*with*); †(*d*) compensate for (a defect etc.); supply the lack or the deficiencies of; (*e*) make complete; get together with difficulty or by degrees; †(*f*) fill up or while away (the time) with some occupation; (*g*) (now only in *Art*) represent or delineate clearly or in detail; (*h*) establish by evidence, argument, or investigation; demonstrate, prove; claim to have proved, try to prove (a thing, a thing to be, *that*); represent *as*, pretend *to be*; (*i*) find out the meaning of; arrive at an understanding of; decipher; succeed in reading; understand the character or behaviour of (a person); (*j*) discern, discover, find out; distinguish by sight or hearing; (*k*) (now only *dial.*) start, set out, sally forth; get away, escape. **make over** (*a*) hand over (by a formal agreement); transfer the possession of (a thing) from oneself *to* another; (*b*) remake, refashion (a garment etc.); refurbish, reorganize. **make up** †(*a*) erect; build up (a bank etc.); (*b*) serve or act to overcome or supply (a deficiency); make complete; raise (a sum) *to* a larger sum; make good, compensate for; *make it up to*, compensate (a person *for*); also, compensate *for*, atone *for*; (*c*) (now chiefly *dial.*) fill up (an opening or gap); stop up (a hole or passage); shut or fasten up (a door, a house); (*d*) wrap up (an article); put together into a parcel or package; (*e*) put together, construct, compound, by combination of parts or ingredients; sew together the parts of (a garment etc.), fit together (pieces of material) to form a garment etc., make (cloth) into clothing; get together, collect (a company, a sum of money), furnish by contributions from different sources; *Typogr.* arrange into columns or pages; add fuel to (a fire) to keep it burning; also admit of being made up into a garment etc.; (*f*) compose, compile, draw up (a list, document, etc.); concoct, invent, fabricate (a story, a lie); compose (verses etc.) impromptu, improvise; (*g*) (of component parts) constitute, compose, (a whole, (now *rare*) a total), (freq. in *pass.*, foll. by *of* the parts); (*h*) prepare (a person, esp. oneself) for a theatrical performance or other public appearance by means of an appropriate costume, false hair, cosmetics, etc., apply cosmetics to (the face, a facial feature), (chiefly *refl.* or in *pass.*); (now *US*) get (a horse etc.) into good condition for selling; fatten; put in order (a bed, a room, etc.) for a particular occasion; (*i*) set out the items of (an account) in order; add up and balance (an account); (*j*) *make up one's mind*, come to a decision or conclusion, resolve, (*that, to do*); (*k*) arrange (a marriage etc.), conclude (a treaty); settle (a dispute etc.), end (a quarrel) by reconciliation (freq. *make it up*); also, be reconciled after a dispute or quarrel, become friends again (also in *kiss and make up*); (*l*) advance in a certain direction; now only foll. by *to*: draw near to, approach, make advances to (a person), court, curry favour with.

make-and-break /meɪk(ə)nd'breɪk/ *a.* & *n.* M19. [f. MAKE *v.* + AND *conj.*[1] + BREAK *v.* (sc. *contact*).] **A** *adj.* That alternately makes and breaks electrical contact. M19. **B** *n.* **1** The alternate making and breaking of electrical contact. E20. **2** An apparatus for automatically making and breaking electrical contact. E20.

makebate /'meɪkbeɪt/ *n. arch.* E16. [f. MAKE *v.* + BATE *n.*[1]] A person who or (occas.) thing which creates contention or discord; a fomenter of strife.

make-belief /'meɪkbɪliːf/ *n.* M19. [f. MAKE *v.* + BELIEF *n.*] Make-believe.

make-believe /'meɪkbɪliːv/ *n.* & *a.* E19. [f. *make believe* s.v. MAKE *v.*] **A** *n.* **1** The action of making believe; pretence. E19. **2** A person who makes believe or pretends. *rare.* M19. **B** *adj.* Of the nature of make-believe, pretended. E19.

make-do /meɪk'duː/ *n.* & *a.* L19. [f. *make do* s.v. MAKE *v.*] **A** *n.* Pl. **-dos, -do's**. A makeshift; a temporary expedient. Also *make-do-and-mend.* L19. **B** *adj.* Characterized by makeshift methods. E20.

make-game /'meɪkgeɪm/ *n.* Now *arch. rare.* M18. [f. *make game (of)* s.v. GAME *n.*] A source of amusement; a laughing-stock.

make-hawk /'meɪkhɔːk/ *n.* L16. [f. MAKE *v.* + HAWK *n.*[1]] *Falconry.* A hawk employed to teach young ones.

makeless /'meɪklɪs/ *a. obs.* exc. *dial.* ME. [f. MAKE *n.*[1] + -LESS.] **1** Without an equal; matchless, peerless. ME. **2** Without a mate; wifeless, husbandless, widowed. LME.

make-over /'meɪkəʊvə/ *n.* Chiefly *N. Amer.* M20. [f. *make over* s.v. MAKE *v.*] A reorganization, a reshaping; *esp.* (*a*) a thorough refashioning of a person's appearance by beauty treatment; (*b*) a deliberate alteration of the public image of an organization etc.

make-peace /'meɪkpiːs/ *n.* & *a. arch.* E16. [f. *make peace* s.v. PEACE *n.*] (That is) a peace-maker.

maker /'meɪkə/ *n.* See also MAKAR. ME. [f. MAKE *v.* + -ER[1].] **1** A person who makes something; a creator or producer (*of*). ME. **2** A poet. Cf. MAKAR. *arch.* LME. **3** Foll. by *-up*. A person who makes something or someone up; *esp.* a person who makes up garments. M16.

1 AV *Isa.* 45:16 They shall goe to confusion together that are makers of idoles. I. MURDOCH The maker and breaker of many a film career. A. BRIEN Recorders of trivia can become makers of history. *Which?* No guarantee that the name of a maker is a . . guide to the car's . . origin. *clockmaker, mapmaker, shoemaker*, etc. **one's** or **the Maker** God (*meet one's Maker*, die).

makeready /'meɪkrɛdi/ *n.* M19. [f. *make ready* s.v. READY *a.*] **1** A position of being ready to fire a gun etc. M19. **2** *Printing.* The final preparation and adjustment for printing; material used in making ready; a sheet on which overlays are pasted for printing a particular forme of type. L19.

makeshift /'meɪkʃɪft/ *n.* & *a.* M16. [f. *make shift* s.v. SHIFT *n.*] **A** *n.* †**1** A shifty person, a rogue. M16–M19. **2** A temporary substitute, esp. of an inferior kind, an expedient. E19. **3** The action of making shift; the state of being a temporary substitute, expediency. L19.

2 C. LAMB The cottage was a sorry antediluvian make-shift of a building. A. WEST Quinbury wouldn't do, even as a temporary makeshift. 3 J. GALSWORTHY His marriage with herself but domestic makeshift. D. WELCH The air of poverty and makeshift which hangs round expensive private schools in England.

B *adj.* †**1** Shifty, roguish. Only in L16. **2** Of the nature of a makeshift, serving as a temporary substitute, esp. of an inferior kind; formed haphazardly; characterized by makeshifts. L17.

2 W. S. CHURCHILL A makeshift administration . . struggled ineptly with the situation. F. ASTAIRE There were makeshift repairs with temporary fences and holes covered over with boards. H. CARPENTER Temporary offices . . had been found . . and things were very makeshift there. G. LORD She'd made a makeshift stretcher out of the blanket.

makeshifty *a.* of the nature of a makeshift, characterized by makeshift M19.

make-up /'meɪkʌp/ *n.* E19. [f. *make up* s.v. MAKE *v.*] **1** The manner in which something is made up, put together, or composed; composition, constitution; a person's character or temperament. E19. **2a** An appearance of face, dress, etc., adopted for a theatrical performance or other public appearance; the action or process of making up with cosmetics etc. M19. **b** Cosmetics (as lipstick, powder, etc.) used in making up the face etc. L19. **c** In a television studio, on a film-set, etc.: the place where performers etc. are made up; (the work of) the people who make up performers etc. *colloq.* M20. **3** *Printing.* The process of organizing text and other matter into pages; matter so made up; (preparation of) the layout of a page. Also, an editor's selection of articles to form a number of a periodical. M19. **4** A made-up story; an invention, a fiction. M19. **5** Something (esp. food) made up from odds and ends. *colloq.* & *dial.* M19. **6** Replacement of water lost from a boiler etc. by evaporation, leakage, etc.; water added for this purpose. M20. **7** The adding up and balancing of accounts at the end of a certain period. M20. **8** A resit. *US.* M20.

1 H. SPENCER Something in the pattern or make-up of their clothes. J. ARCHER Roy Jenkins had announced the make-up of his shadow team. 2a GEO. ELIOT The Zouaves, with their wondrous make-ups as women. b R. JARRELL Her lips were painted a purplish maroon; she had put on no other make-up. 4 N. MARSH I'm quite sure it's all a make-up They think it's true.

makeweight /'meɪkweɪt/ *n.* Also **make-weight**. L17. [f. MAKE *v.* + WEIGHT *n.*] **1** A comparatively small quantity added to make up a certain weight. Formerly *spec.*, a small candle. L17. **2** *fig.* A person or thing of insignificant value thrown in to make up a deficiency or fill a gap. L18. **3** A counterbalancing weight, a counterpoise. L18.

make-work /'meɪkwɔːk/ *n.* Orig. *US.* M20. [f. MAKE *v.* + WORK *n.*] Work or activity of little or no value devised mainly to keep someone busy.

makimono /maki'moːno, makɪ'məʊnəʊ/ *n.* Pl. same, **-os**. L19. [Jap. = something rolled up, a scroll.] A Japanese scroll containing a narrative, usu. in pictures with explanatory writing, designed to be examined progressively from right to left as it is unrolled. Cf. EMAKIMONO.

making /'meɪkɪŋ/ *n.* OE. [f. MAKE *v.* + -ING[1].] **1** The action of MAKE *v.*; production, preparation, appointment, doing, performance (of a specified action), conversion into something. Freq. w. possess., attributing responsibility to a specified agent. Also *making-up* etc. OE. †**2** Poetical composition; versifying. Also in *pl.*, poetical compositions, poems. ME–E17. **3** Something that has been made; a product of manufacture; (formerly) a creature. Also, the quantity made at one time. ME. **b** In *pl.* Earnings, profits. *colloq.* M19. **4** Advancement, success. Now only in *be the making of*, be what ensures the success or favourable development of. LME. †**5** The way in which a thing or person is made; conformation, form, shape, build. LME–M17. **6** The material out of which something may be made; the potentiality of becoming something. Chiefly in *have* or *be the makings* (*of*). E17. **b** In *pl.* The materials or ingredients for making something; *spec.* paper and tobacco for rolling a cigarette. *N. Amer., Austral.,* & *NZ colloq.* L19.

1 CARLYLE Any making-up of his mind. TENNYSON Since the making of the world. *Conservation News* Mutual sacrifice and making do . . outweigh the hardships and problems. V. S. NAIPAUL I was involved in the slow making of this story. A. N. WILSON A spiritual wilderness of his own making. *bookmaking, haymaking, merry-making*, etc. 6 D. FRANCIS He's too young really. But he's got the makings. A. WEST She obviously had the makings of a successful writer. A. PRICE He's a good copper. With the makings of a very good one.

Phrases: *be the making of*: see sense 4 above. **in the making** *postpositive a. phr.* in the course of being developed or formed.

making /'meɪkɪŋ/ *ppl a.* LME. [f. MAKE *v.* + -ING[2].] That makes something or someone. Now chiefly as 2nd elem. of comb., as *sick-making*.

mako /'mɑːkəʊ/ *n.*[1] Pl. **-os**, same. M19. [Maori.] In full *mako shark*. A large blue mackerel shark, *Isurus oxyrinchus*, of tropical and temperate oceans worldwide. Also called *blue pointer*.

mako /'mɑːkəʊ/ *n.*[2] *NZ.* Also **makomako** /ˌmɑːkəʊ'mɑːkəʊ/. Pl. **-os**. M19. [Maori.] A small New Zealand tree, *Aristotelia racemosa* (family Elaeocarpaceae), bearing clusters of small pink flowers and dark red berries.

Makololo /makə'ləʊləʊ/ *n.* & *a.* M19. [Bantu.] A *n.* Pl. same, **-os**. A member of an African people now living in Zambia near the junction of the Zambezi and Kafue rivers. M19. B *adj.* Of or pertaining to this people. M19.

makomako /mɑːkəʊ'mɑːkəʊ/ *n.*[1] *NZ.* Pl. **-os**. M19. [Maori.] = KORIMAKO.

makomako *n.*[2] var. of MAKO *n.*[2]

Makonde /mə'kəʊndi/ *n.* & *a.* E20. [Bantu.] A *n.* Pl. same, **-s**. A member of a people inhabiting the border area of Tanzania and Mozambique; the Bantu language of this people. E20. B *adj.* Of or pertaining to this people or their language. E20.

makoré /makə'reɪ/ *n.* E20. [App. W. Afr.] A large W. African tree, *Tieghemella heckelii* (family Sapotaceae); the dark red-brown wood of this tree.

makuta *n.* pl. of LIKUTA.

makutu /mə'kuːtuː/ *v.* & *n.* *NZ.* M19. [Maori.] A *v.t.* Put a spell on, bewitch. *rare.* M19. B *n.* Sorcery, witchcraft; a magic spell. E20.

mal- /mal/ *pref.* Also †**male-**. [Fr. *mal* adv. f. L *male* ill, badly, or (occas.) OFr. *mal* adj. f. L *malus* bad.] In senses 'bad(ly), wrong(ly), improper(ly)', as *malformation*, *malodorous*, *malpractice*, *maltreat*, and 'not', as *maladroit*, *malcontent*.

Malabar /'maləbɑː/ *n.* & *a.* L16. [A coastal district of SW India.] A *n.* Chiefly *Hist.* 1 A native or inhabitant of the Malabar coast, SW India. Also, a Tamil. L16. 2 The language of the Malabar coast, Malayalam. Also, Tamil. E19. 3 A brightly coloured cotton handkerchief. L19.

B *attrib.* or as *adj.* Of or pertaining to the Malabar coast; Tamil. L17.

Malabar nightshade: see NIGHTSHADE. **Malabar plum** (the fruit of) the rose apple, *Syzygium jambos*. **Malabar spinach** = *Malabar nightshade* s.v. NIGHTSHADE.

Malabaric /malə'bɑːrɪk/ *a.* & *n.* (now *rare*) (*a*) *adj.* = MALABAR *a.*; (*b*) *n.* = MALABAR *n.* 2: E18.

malabathrum /malə'baθrəm/ *n.* M16. [L *malabathrum*, *malo-*, *-on* f. Gk *malabathron*, *malo-* f. Skt *tamālapatra*, f. *tamāla* a kind of tree + *patra* leaf.] *Hist.* (A perfumed ointment prepared from) an aromatic leaf mentioned by ancient writers.

malabsorption /maləb'zɔːpʃ(ə)n/ *n.* M20. [f. MAL- + ABSORPTION.] *Med.* Imperfect absorption of nutrients from the intestines.

Malacca /mə'lakə/ *n.* M19. [A town and district on the Malay peninsula, SE Asia.] 1 Used *attrib.* to designate things, esp. plants and vegetable products, found in or obtained from Malacca. M19. 2 *ellipt.* A Malacca cane. M19.

1 **Malacca cane** a walking-cane of a rich brown colour, often clouded or mottled, usu. made from a stem of the palm *Calamus scipionum*.

malachite /'maləkʌɪt/ *n.* & *a.* LME. [OFr. *melochite* (mod. *malachite*) f. L *molochites* f. Gk *molokhitis*, f. *molokhē* var. of *malakhē* MALLOW.] A *n.* 1 A monoclinic basic copper carbonate, usu. occurring as bright-green masses or fibrous aggregates, which is used ornamentally and as an ore of copper. LME. 2 A bright green colour like that of malachite. E20. B *attrib.* or as *adj.* Made of or resembling malachite; of the colour of malachite, bright green. L19.

Special collocations & comb.: **malachite-green** (*a*) a dye of the colour of malachite; (*b*) = sense A.2 above. **malachite kingfisher** a small blue, green, and red kingfisher, *Alcedo cristata*, found in sub-Saharan Africa.

malacia /mə'leɪʃə/ *n.* *rare.* M17. [L = Gk *malakia* softness, f. *malakos* soft.] *Med.* 1 Abnormal craving for particular kinds of food. Now *rare* or *obs.* M17. 2 Abnormal softening of a tissue or part. E18.

malaco- /'maləkəʊ/ *comb. form* of Gk *malakos* soft: see -O-.

malacopterygian /ˌmaləkɒptə'rɪdʒɪən/ *a.* & *n.* [Gk *pterugion* fin, dim. of *pterux* wing] (*Ichthyol.*) (designating) a soft-finned fish, i.e. a bony fish that is not an acanthopterygian M19.

malacology /malə'kɒlədʒi/ *n.* M19. [f. prec. + -LOGY.] The branch of zoology that deals with molluscs.

malaco'logical *a.* L19. **malacologist** *n.* M19.

malacon /'malək(ə)n/ *n.* M19. [G *Malakon* f. Gk *malakon* neut. of *malakos* soft.] *Min.* A soft brown altered form of zircon.

malacostracan /malə'kɒstrək(ə)n/ *n.* & *a.* M19. [f. mod.L *Malacostraca* (see below), Gk *malakostraka*, f. *malakos* soft + *ostrakon* shell: see -AN.] A *n.* Any crustacean of the class Malacostraca, which includes shrimps, crabs, lobsters, isopods, and amphipods. M19. B *adj.* Of or pertaining to the class Malacostraca. M19.

malacostracous *a.* = MALACOSTRACAN *a.* M19.

†**malactic** *a.* & *n.* M16. [Gk *malaktikos*, f. *malak-* stem of *malassein* soften: see -IC.] A *adj.* Adapted to soften; emollient. M16–E18. B *n.* An emollient medicine. M–L17.

maladaptation /ˌmaladəp'teɪʃ(ə)n/ *n.* L19. [f. MAL- + ADAPTATION.] Faulty or imperfect adaptation.

maladaptive /malə'daptɪv/ *a.* M20. [f. MAL- + ADAPTIVE.] Faultily or imperfectly adaptive; not characterized by or given to adaption.

maladaptively *adv.* M20.

malade imaginaire /malad imaʒinɛːr/ *n. phr.* Pl. ***-s -s*** (pronounced same). E19. [Fr., after the title of a play by Molière (1673).] A person with an imaginary illness.

maladif /maladif/ *a.* M19. [Fr., f. *malade* (see MALADY) + *-if* -IVE.] = next.

maladive /'malədɪv/ *a.* L15. [f. as prec.] Of, pertaining to, or affected with sickness, sickly. Cf. prec.

maladjusted /malə'dʒʌstɪd/ *a.* L19. [f. MAL- + *adjusted* pa. pple of ADJUST.] Inadequately adjusted; exhibiting or characterized by psychological maladjustment.

maladjustment /malə'dʒʌs(t)m(ə)nt/ *n.* M19. [f. MAL- + ADJUSTMENT.] Faulty or imperfect adjustment; *spec.* unsuccessful or unsatisfactory adaptation to one's social environment.

maladminister /maləd'mɪnɪstə/ *v.t.* E18. [f. MAL- + ADMINISTER.] Administer, execute, or manage inefficiently or badly.

maladministration /ˌmalədmɪnɪ'streɪʃ(ə)n/ *n.* M17. [f. MAL- + ADMINISTRATION.] Faulty or imperfect administration; inefficient or improper management of (esp. public) affairs.

maladministrator *n.* a person who is guilty of maladministration M19.

maladresse /maladrɛs, malə'drɛs/ *n.* E19. [Fr., f. as next after *adroit*, *adresse*.] Lack of dexterity or tact; awkwardness.

maladroit /'malədrɔɪt/ *a.* L17. [Fr., f. as MAL- + ADROIT.] Lacking in adroitness or dexterity; awkward, bungling, clumsy.

F. WYNDHAM The self-consciousness which made her so socially maladroit. *Sunday Express* His maladroit fumbling had been honed to a streamlined accuracy.

maladroitly *adv.* L17. **maladroitness** *n.* L18.

†**maladventure** *n.* LME–E19. [f. MAL- + ADVENTURE *n.*] A lawless proceeding, an escapade; an unlucky undertaking, a misadventure, misfortune.

malady /'malədi/ *n.* ME. [(O)Fr. *maladie*, f. *malade* sick, ill, f. Proto-Romance, f. L *male* badly + *habitus* pa. pple of *habere* have, hold.] 1 An ailment, a disease. Formerly also, ill health, disease. ME. 2 *fig.* A bad quality, habit, or disposition; a condition that calls for a remedy. LME.

1 D. JACOBSON He was suffering from a malady neither he nor his doctors could explain. ANTHONY SMITH It is not known . . how the malady should be managed. 2 CARLYLE Our spiritual maladies are but of Opinion.

mala fide /meɪlə 'fʌɪdiː, malə 'fiːdeɪ/ *adv.* & *a. phr.* E17. [L = with bad faith (abl. of next).] (Acting or done) in bad faith; insincere(ly), not genuine(ly).

mala fides /meɪlə 'fʌɪdiːz, malə 'fiːdeɪz/ *n. phr.* L17. [L = bad faith.] Chiefly *Law*. Bad faith, intent to deceive.

Malaga /'maləgə/ *n.* E17. [*Málaga* (see below).] A white or (now usu.) red fortified wine from Málaga, a seaport in southern Spain. Also *Malaga wine*.

malagas /malə'gas/ *n.* *S. Afr.* Also **malgas** /mal'gas, *foreign* -x-/. M18. [Du. *mallegas* f. Port. *mangas(-de-velludo)* lit. 'velvet sleeves', the wandering albatross.] The Cape gannet, *Sula capensis*.

Malagash /'maləgaʃ/ *a.* & *n.* Now *rare* or *obs.* E18. [f. as next. Cf. MADAGASS.] A *n.* Pl. same, **-es**. A native or inhabitant of Madagascar. E18. B *adj.* Of or pertaining to Madagascar. L18.

Malagasy /malə'gasi/ *a.* & *n.* M19. [Var. of MADAGASCAR. Cf. MADAGASCAN.] A *adj.* Of or pertaining to Madagascar, its inhabitants, or its language. M19. B *n.* Pl. **-sies**, same. 1 A native or inhabitant of Madagascar. M19. 2 The Austronesian language of Madagascar. M19.

†**malagma** *n.* Pl. **-gmata**. M16–M18. [Late L f. Gk, f. *malassein* assuage.] *Med.* An emollient plaster.

Malagueña /malə'geɪnjə/ *n.* In sense 2 also **m-**. M19. [Sp., f. as MALAGA.] 1 A woman or girl of Málaga in S. Spain. M19. 2 A Spanish dance resembling the fandango. Also, an emotional Spanish gypsy song. L19.

malaguetta /malə'getə/ *n.* M16. [Fr. *maniguette*, †*-guete* alt. of *malaguette* f. Sp. *malagueta*: cf. med.L *melegeta*, perh. dim. of It. *melica* millet.] = *grains of Paradise* s.v. GRAIN *n.*[1] 3a.

mala in se *n. phr.* pl. of MALUM IN SE.

malaise /ma'leɪz/ *n.* M18. [Fr., f. OFr. *mal* bad, ill (f. L *malus*) + *aise* EASE *n.* Cf. earlier MALEASE.] A condition of bodily discomfort, *esp.* one without the development of specific disease; a feeling of uneasiness.

J. HERSEY Suddenly ill with a general malaise, weariness, and feverishness. R. ELLMANN His spiritual malaise which involved anxiety over his future.

malalignment /malə'lʌɪnm(ə)nt/ *n.* M20. [f. MAL- + ALIGNMENT.] Misalignment.

malambo /mə'lambəʊ/ *n.* E19. [Amer. Sp., perh. of Afr. origin.] The aromatic bark of *Croton malambo*, a shrub (family Euphorbiaceae) of northern S. America, used in medicine and perfumery. Also *malambo bark*.

malamute /'maləmjuːt/ *n.* Also **male-**. L19. [Eskimo (Inuit) *malimiut*, a people of the Kolzebue Sound, Alaska who developed the breed.] (A dog of) a spitz breed developed in Alaska, with a thick grey or black and white coat, pointed ears, and a plumed tail curling over the back.

malander, -ders *ns.* see MALLENDERS.

malanga /mə'laŋgə/ *n.* E20. [Amer. Sp., prob. f. Kikongo, pl. of *elanga* water lily.] Any of several plants grown in the Caribbean and in Central and S. America for their edible tubers.

malapert /'maləpəːt/ *a.* & *n.* *arch.* ME. [OFr., f. *mal-* (indicating the opposite) + *apert* var. of *espert* EXPERT *a.*, but taken as if f. MAL- improperly + *apert* bold, pert.] (A person who is) presumptuous, impudent, saucy.

malapertly *adv.* LME. **malapertness** *n.* LME.

malapportionment /malə'pɔːʃ(ə)nm(ə)nt/ *n.* Chiefly *US.* M20. [f. MAL- + APPORTIONMENT.] Bad or inequitable apportionment, *spec.* of representation in a political assembly.

malapportioned *a.* M20.

malappropriate /malə'prəʊprɪət/ *a.* M19. [f. MAL- + APPROPRIATE *a.*] Ill-suited, inappropriate.

malappropriate /malə'prəʊprɪeɪt/ *v.t.* M19. [f. MAL- + APPROPRIATE *v.*] Misapply.

malappropri'ation *n.* M19.

mala praxis /meɪlə 'praksɪs/ *n. phr.* M18. [mod.L, f. L *mala* fem. of *malus* bad + PRAXIS. Cf. MALPRAXIS.] *Law.* Medical malpractice.

malaprop /'maləprɒp/ *n.* & *a.* E19. [f. Mrs *Malaprop* (after MALAPROPOS) in Sheridan's play *The Rivals* (1775).] A *n.* = MALAPROPISM. E19. B *adj.* = MALAPROPIAN. E19.

malapropian /malə'prɒpɪən, -'prəʊpɪən/ *a.* M19. [f. (as) prec. + -IAN.] Of the nature of a malapropism; given to malapropisms.

malapropism /'maləprɒ,pɪz(ə)m/ *n.* M19. [f. as prec. + -ISM.] Ludicrous misuse of words, esp. in mistaking a word for another resembling it; an instance of this.

malapro'pistic *a.* of the nature of a malapropism L20.

malapropos /,malaprə'pəʊ/ *adv.*, *a.*, & *n.* Also **mal-à-propos** & other vars. M17. [Fr. *mal à propos*, f. *mal* ill + *à* to + *propos* purpose: see MAL-, APROPOS.] A *adv.* In an inopportune or awkward manner; at an inopportune or awkward time; inappropriately. M17. B *adj.* Inopportune, inappropriate. E18. C *n.* An inopportune or inappropriate thing. M19.

malar /'meɪlə/ *a.* & *n.* L18. [mod.L *malaris*, f. L *mala* jaw, cheek-bone: see -AR[1].] *Anat.* A *adj.* Of or pertaining to the cheek. L18. B *n.* = *cheekbone* (a) s.v. CHEEK *n.* M19.

malaria /mə'lɛːrɪə/ *n.* M18. [It. *mal' aria* = *mala aria* bad air.] Orig., an unwholesome condition of the atmosphere in hot countries due to the exhalations of marshes, to which fevers were ascribed. Now (also *malaria fever*), any of a class of intermittent and remittent febrile diseases formerly supposed to result from this cause, but now known to be due to infection with parasitic protozoans of the genus *Plasmodium*, transmitted by the bite of a mosquito of the genus *Anopheles*.

fig.: T. C. GRATTAN A sort of moral malaria pervading society and carrying off many victims. *quartan malaria*: see QUARTAN *a.* *tertian malaria*: see TERTIAN *a.* I.

Comb.: *malaria fever*: see above; **malaria parasite** a parasitic protozoan of the genus *Plasmodium*, causing malaria.

malarial /mə'lɛːrɪəl/ *a.* M19. [f. prec. + -AL[1].] 1 Infected with malaria; infested with malaria-bearing mosquitoes. M19. 2 Of, pertaining to, or of the nature of malaria. M19.

malarian *a.* pertaining to or causing malaria; malarial: M19.

malariology /məlɛːrɪ'ɒlədʒi/ *n.* E20. [f. MALARIA + -OLOGY.] The scientific study of malaria.

malariologist *n.* E20.

malarious /mə'lɛːrɪəs/ *a.* M19. [f. MALARIA + -OUS.] = MALARIAL.

malarkey /mə'lɑːki/ *n. slang.* E20. [Origin unkn.] Humbug, nonsense, foolishness.

malarrangement /malə'reɪndʒm(ə)nt/ *n.* M19. [f. MAL- + ARRANGEMENT.] Faulty or imperfect arrangement.

malassimilation /,maləsɪmɪ'leɪʃ(ə)n/ *n.* M19. [f. MAL- + ASSIMILATION.] Imperfect assimilation; *esp.* (*Med.*) = MALABSORPTION.

malate /'meɪleɪt/ *n.* L18. [f. MALIC + -ATE[1].] *Chem.* A salt or ester of malic acid.

malathion /malə'θʌɪən/ *n.* M20. [f. MAL(EATE + -*a*- + THIO- + -*on*.] An organophosphorus insecticide, with relatively low toxicity to plants and animals.

Malawi /mə'lɑːwi/ *a.* & *n.* M20. [See below.] (A native or inhabitant) of Malawi, a country in south central Africa (formerly Nyasaland).

Malawian *n.* & *a.* M20.

†malax *v.t.* LME. [L *malaxare*: see next.] 1 Rub or knead (a plaster etc.) to softness. LME–M18. 2 Of a material agent: soften. M17–M18.

malaxate /'maləkseɪt/ *v.t.* M17. [L *malaxat-* pa. ppl stem of *malaxare* f. Gk *malassein* make soft: see -ATE[3].] Knead to softness; make soft by mixing or rubbing.

mala'xation *n.* the action of reducing to a soft mass by kneading or rolling; a form of kneading in massage: M17.

Malay /mə'leɪ/ *n.* & *a.* L16. [Malay †*Malayu* (now *Me-*).] A *n.* 1a A member of a people inhabiting Malaysia, Brunei, parts of Indonesia, and other areas. L16. b In South Africa, a member of the Muslim community of Cape Town and adjoining districts (chiefly descendants of slaves and immigrants from Malaysia etc.). Also *Cape Malay*. L18. 2 The Austronesian language of the Malays of Malaysia etc., the official language of the Federation of Malaysia. L16. 3 *ellipt.* A Malay fowl. M19.

B *adj.* 1 Of, pertaining to, or characteristic of, the Malays or parts of Malaysia and Indonesia inhabited by them. L18. 2 Of, pertaining to, or characteristic of the Cape Malays. L19.

1 **Malay apple** (the edible fruit of) a tree of the myrtle family, *Syzygium malaccense*, native to the Malay peninsula. **Malay fowl** (a bird of) a large variety of domestic fowl introduced from the Malay peninsula. **Malay peninsula** a peninsula of SE Asia, forming (in the south) the continental part of Malaysia and (in the north) part of Thailand. **Malay tapir** = *Malayan tapir* s.v. MALAYAN *a.*

Malayic *a.* (*rare*) = MALAY *a.* I E18.

Malayalam /malə'jɑːləm/ *n.* & *a.* E19. [Malayalam *Malayālam*, f. *mala* (Tamil *malai*) mountain + *āḷ* man.] (Of) a Dravidian language, closely related to Tamil, spoken in the State of Kerala and adjacent parts of SW India.

Malayali /malə'jɑːli/ *n.* & *a.* Also **-lee**. M19. [Irreg., f. prec. + -I[2].] A member of, of or pertaining to, a Malayalam-speaking people chiefly inhabiting the State of Kerala in SW India.

Malayan /mə'leɪən/ *n.* & *a.* L16. [f. MALAY or (in sense 1b) *Malaya* + -AN.] A *n.* 1a = MALAY *n.* 1a. L16. b During the existence of the Federation of Malaya (from 1948 until 1963), a native or inhabitant of Malaya (regardless of race or creed). M20. 2 = MALAY *n.* 2. Now *rare*. E17.

B *adj.* = MALAY *a.* I. Also, of or pertaining to Malaya (see sense A.1b above). E17.

Malayan tapir a black and white tapir, *Tapirus indicus*, native to SE Asia and Sumatra.

Malayani'zation *n.* the action or process of Malayanizing something, as by introducing Malayan personnel M20. **Malayanize** *v.t.* make Malayan in character or composition, employ Malayans in M20.

Malayo- /mə'leɪəʊ/ *comb. form* of MALAY: see -O-.

Malayo-Polynesian *a.* & *n.* (*a*) *adj.* of or pertaining to the Malays and the Polynesians; *spec.* of or pertaining to the family of agglutinative languages including Malay and Polynesian languages, Austronesian; (*b*) *n.* the Malayo-Polynesian family of languages, Austronesian: M19.

Malaysian /mə'leɪzɪən, -ʒ(ə)n/ *n.* & *a.* E17. [f. *Malaysia* a name for the Malay archipelago, f. root of Malay *Melayu* after *Asia* etc.: see -AN.] A *n.* A native or inhabitant of the Malay archipelago in SE Asia or *spec.* (now) of the Federation of Malaysia (formed in 1963 from the States of Malaya, Sabah, Sarawak, and the now independent State of Singapore). E17. B *adj.* Of, pertaining to, or characteristic of the Malay archipelago or (now) Malaysia. L19.

Malaysiani'zation *n.* the action or process of Malaysianizing something, as by introducing Malaysian personnel L20. **Malaysianize** *v.t.* make Malaysian in character or composition, employ Malaysians in L20.

malaysianite /mə'leɪzɪənʌɪt, -ʒ(ə)nʌɪt/ *n.* M20. [f. prec. + -ITE[1].] *Geol.* A tektite from the strewn field of the Malay peninsula.

malbehaviour /malbɪ'heɪvjə/ *n. rare.* Also **†male-**, ***-or**. E18. [f. MAL- + BEHAVIOUR.] Bad or improper behaviour.

malcoha /'malkəʊə/ *n.* Also **-koha**. L20. [Origin unkn.] Any of several long-tailed cuckoos of the genus *Rhopodytes* and related genera, found in SE Asia and the Indian subcontinent.

malconduct /mal'kɒndʌkt/ *n.* Also **†male-**. L17. [f. MAL- + CONDUCT *n.*[1]] Improper conduct; *esp.* improper or dishonest administration of a public office, business, etc.

malconformation /,malkɒnfə'meɪʃ(ə)n/ *n.* L18. [f. MAL- + CONFORMATION.] Faulty or imperfect conformation.

malconstruction /malkən'strʌkʃ(ə)n/ *n.* E19. [f. MAL- + CONSTRUCTION.] Faulty or imperfect construction.

malcontent /'malkəntɛnt/ *a.* & *n.* Also **†male-**. L16. [(O)Fr., f. as MAL- + CONTENT *pred. a.* & *n.*[3] In sense B.2 f. MAL- + CONTENT *n.*[2]] A *adj.* Discontented, dissatisfied; inclined to rebellion or mutiny; restless and disaffected. L16.

B *n.* 1 A malcontent person. L16. †2 A state of discontentment. L16–L17.

1 A. N. WILSON There was every reason for Russian dissidents and malcontents to rejoice.

malcontented /malkən'tɛntɪd/ *a.* Now *rare*. Also **†male-**. L16. [f. MAL- + CONTENTED.] = MALCONTENT *a.*

J. UPDIKE A group of suspect liberals and malcontented expatriates.

malcontentedly *adv.* M17. **malcontentedness** *n.* L16.

mal de mer /mal də mɛːr/ *n. phr.* L18. [Fr.] Seasickness.

maldescended /maldɪ'sɛndɪd/ *a.* E20. [f. MAL- + *descended* pa. pple of DESCEND.] *Med.* Of a testis: not having descended all the way into the scrotum from the abdominal cavity during development of the foetus, or having descended ectopically.

maldescent *n.* the state of being maldescended; incomplete or ectopic descent of a testis: E20.

maldevelopment /maldɪ'vɛləpm(ə)nt/ *n.* L19. [f. MAL- + DEVELOPMENT.] Faulty or imperfect development.

maldistribution /,maldɪstrɪ'bjuːʃ(ə)n/ *n.* L19. [f. MAL- + DISTRIBUTION.] Faulty or imperfect distribution.

maldi'stributed *ppl a.* M20.

Maldivian /mɒl'dɪvɪən, mɔːl-/ *n.* & *a.* L18. [f. *Maldives* or *Maldive* islands (see below) + -IAN.] A *n.* A native or inhabitant of the Maldives, a country consisting of a chain of islands in the Indian Ocean; the form of the Sinhalese language used in the Maldives. L18. B *adj.* Of or pertaining to the Maldives or the Sinhalese language used there. M19.

maldonite /'mɔːld(ə)nʌɪt/ *n.* L19. [f. *Maldon*, a place in Victoria, Australia + -ITE[1].] *Min.* A native alloy of gold and bismuth, crystallizing in the cubic system.

mal du pays /mal dy pe(j)i/ *n. phr.* L18. [Fr.] †1 A country's or region's prevalent illness. *rare*. Only in L18. 2 Homesickness. E19.

mal du siècle /mal dy sjɛkl/ *n. phr.* E20. [Fr.] World-weariness, weariness of life, deep melancholy because of the condition of the world.

male /meɪl/ *a.* & *n.* LME. [OFr. *ma(s)le* (mod. *mâle*) f. L *masculus*, f. *mas* male (person). Cf. MASCULINE.] A *adj.* 1 Of, pertaining to, or designating the sex which can beget offspring; in organisms which undergo sexual reproduction, designating, pertaining to, or producing gametes (as spermatozoa) that can fertilize female gametes (ova). LME. b Of a plant, flower, etc.: bearing stamens but lacking functional pistils. LME. 2 Of a plant, mineral, or other object: having a colour or other property associated with maleness, esp. as being superior to a corresponding female property etc. Now *rare* exc. in certain collocations (see below). LME. 3 Of, pertaining to, or characteristic of men or boys or male animals or plants. E17. 4 Composed or consisting of men or boys or of male animals or plants. L17. 5 Of a mechanical instrument etc.: adapted to penetrate or fill a corresponding female part. L18.

1 W. CRUISE An estate in tail male was vested in Edmund Hicks, as heir male of . . Launcelot Hicks. F.

WELDON Men visitors were only allowed . . if they described themselves as close male relatives. R. K. NARAYAN A male tiger hardly ever lives with the family. C. SIMMONS The male nurse arrived with a wheelchair. 3 C. DARWIN The common drake . . after the breeding season is well known to lose his male plumage. R. WEST Through the thudding of the engines came the sound of Chris' great male voice. *Rage* Concerned with . . male bonding and buddy movies.

B *n.* 1 A male person, animal, or plant; (the member(s) of) the male sex; a man or boy as distinguished from a woman or girl. LME. †2 A male precious stone (cf. sense A.2 above). LME–M18.

1 N. TINBERGEN Such an aggressive bird is always a male. D. FRANCIS About two thirds of the best seats in the Members' stands were reserved for males. P. LOMAS The traditional role of the male has not . . included empathetic caring.

Special collocations & comb.: **male chauvinism** prejudice against women, inconsiderate treatment of women. **male chauvinist** a man who is prejudiced against or inconsiderate of women (freq. in *male chauvinist pig*). **male-chauvinistic** *a.* characteristic of a male chauvinist, of the nature of male chauvinism. **male fern** a common woodland fern, *Dryopteris filix-mas*. **male gauge** the outer gauge or screw of a printing-press. **male impersonator** a female performer dressed and acting as a man. †**male incense** a superior quality of incense, frankincense. *male* MENOPAUSE. *male organ*: see ORGAN *n.*[1] 4d. **male pill** a contraceptive pill for men. **male rhyme** = *masculine rhyme* s.v. MASCULINE *a. male screw*: see SCREW *n.*[1] I. *tail male*: see TAIL *n.*[2] 4.

maleness *n.* M17.

†**male-** *pref.* var. of MAL-.

malease /ma'liːz/ *n.* ME. [f. as MALAISE. In mod. use f. MAL- + EASE *n.*] 1 Absence of ease; uneasiness, discomfort; inconvenience, annoyance; distress, trouble. ME. †2 Disease, sickness. ME–E16.

¶Not recorded between E16 and E20.

maleate /mə'liːeɪt/ *n.* M19. [f. MALEIC + -ATE[1].] *Chem.* A salt or ester of maleic acid.

†**malebehaviour** *n.* var. of MALBEHAVIOUR.

malebolge /malɪ'bɒldʒeɪ, *foreign* male'bɔldʒe/ *n. literary.* M19. [It. *Malebolge*, f. *male* fem. pl. of *malo* evil + †*bolge* pl. of *bolgia* lit. 'sack, bag', the name given in Dante's *Inferno* to the eighth circle in hell, consisting of ten rock-bound concentric circular trenches, esp. w. allus. to Canto xviii.] A pool of filth; a hellish place or condition.

Malecite /'maləsiːt/ *n.* & *a.* Also **Maliseet**. M19. [Micmac *mali:sit* lit. 'a person who speaks poorly'.] **A** *n.* Pl. same, **-s**. 1 A member of a N. American Indian people of New Brunswick and Maine, nearly identical in language and culture to the Passamaquoddy. M19. 2 The eastern Algonquian language of this people. E20. **B** *adj.* Of or pertaining to the Malecite or their language. L19.

†**maleconduct** *n.*, **-content** *a.* & *n.*, etc., vars. of MALCONDUCT etc.

maledicent /malɪ'dʌɪs(ə)nt/ *a.* Now *rare.* L16. [L *maledicent-* pres. ppl stem of *maledicere*: see MALEDICTION, -ENT.] Given to speaking evil. Of an utterance: slanderous.

maledict /'malɪdɪkt/ *a.* & *n. arch.* M16. [L *maledictus* pa. pple, f. as next.] (A person who is) accursed.

maledict /'malɪdɪkt/ *v.t.* E17. [L *maledict-*: see next.] 1 = BACKBITE. *rare.* E17. 2 Address with maledictions, curse, execrate. E18.

malediction /malɪ'dɪkʃ(ə)n/ *n.* LME. [L *maledictio(n-)*, f. *maledict-* pa. ppl stem of *maledicere* speak evil of, f. *male* ill, badly + *dicere* say: see -ION. Cf. Fr. *malédiction.*] 1 (The utterance of) a curse; the condition of being under a ban or curse. LME. 2 Reviling, slander; the condition of being reviled or slandered. M16.

maledictive /malɪ'dɪktɪv/ *a.* M19. [f. L *maledict-* (see prec.) + -IVE.] Characterized by cursing or curses; uttering maledictions.

maledictory /malɪ'dɪkt(ə)ri/ *a.* E19. [f. as prec. + -ORY[2].] Of the nature of or resembling a malediction.

maleducation /ˌmalɛdjʊ'keɪʃ(ə)n/ *n.* M19. [f. MAL- + EDUCATION.] Imperfect or misdirected education.

maleesh /'mɑːliːʃ/ *int.* & *n.* E20. [Colloq. Arab. *mā 'alē-š* never mind.] **A** *int.* No matter! never mind! E20. **B** *n.* Indifference, slackness. M20.

malefaction /malɪ'fakʃ(ə)n/ *n.* E17. [med.L *malefactio(n-)*, f. *male facere* do evil (to), after *benefactio(n-)* BENEFACTION; partly f. MALEFACTOR: see -FACTION.] (An instance of) evildoing, a criminal act.

malefactor /'malɪfaktə/ *n.* LME. [L, f. *male facere*: see prec., -OR. Partly through OFr. *malfaiteur.*] 1 A person guilty of a heinous offence against the law; a felon, a criminal. LME. 2 An evildoer; a person who behaves badly or wickedly towards another. LME.

malefactress *n.* a female malefactor M17.

maleffect /malɪ'fɛkt/ *n. rare.* L17. [f. MAL- + EFFECT *n.*] A bad or injurious effect.

malefic /mə'lɛfɪk/ *a.* M17. [L *maleficus*, f. *male* ill, badly: see -FIC.] Esp. of a stellar influence or magical art or practice: productive of disaster or evil, harmful; baleful in effect or purpose.

†**malefical** *a.* (*rare*) E–M17. **malefically** *adv.* M17.

malefice /'malɪfɪs/ *n. arch.* LME. [L *maleficium* evil deed, sorcery, f. as prec.] 1 A wicked enchantment; sorcery. LME. 2 An evil deed; mischief. L16.

maleficence /mə'lɛfɪs(ə)ns/ *n.* M16. [L *maleficentia*, f. as MALEFIC: see -ENCE.] 1 Evildoing; *rare* an evil act. M16. 2 Malefic character; harmfulness. L18.

maleficent /mə'lɛfɪs(ə)nt/ *a.* L17. [f. prec.: see -ENT.] 1 Harmful, malefic (*to*). L17. 2 Criminal. M18.

maleficial /malɪ'fɪʃ(ə)l/ *a.* Now *rare.* E17. [f. (as) MALEFICE: see -IAL. In later use after BENEFICIAL.] Malefic, maleficent.

maleic /mə'liːɪk/ *a.* M19. [Fr. *maléique* alt. of *malique* MALIC.] *Chem.* 1 *maleic acid*, a crystalline unsaturated dibasic acid, *cis*-$HOOC{\cdot}CH{=}CH{\cdot}COOH$, which is isomeric with fumaric acid and is obtained in the dry distillation of malic acid; *cis*-butenedioic acid. M19. 2 *maleic anhydride*, the anhydride, $C_4H_2O_3$, of maleic acid, used in synthesis to form addition compounds with substances containing conjugated carbon–carbon double bonds. M20.

mal élevé /mal el(ə)ve/ *a. phr.* Fem. **-ée**. L19. [Fr. = badly brought up.] Bad-mannered, ill-bred.

malemute *n.* var. of MALAMUTE.

malengin /'malɛndʒɪn/ *n.* Long *arch.* Also **-engine**. LME. [(O)Fr. (obs.), f. *mal* evil + *engin* contrivance, ENGINE *n.*] Evil machination, ill intent; fraud, deceit, guile.

mal-entendu /malɑ̃tɑ̃dy/ *a.* & *n.* E17. [Fr., f. *mal* ill + *entendu* pa. pple of *entendre* hear, understand.] †**A** *adj.* Mistaken, misapprehended. Only in E17. **B** *n.* Pl. pronounced same. A misunderstanding. L18.

maleo /'malɪəʊ/ *n.* Pl. **-os**. M19. [Moluccan Malay.] More fully *maleo fowl*. A megapode bird, *Macrocephalon maleo*, inhabiting Sulawesi.

Maler /'mɑːlə/ *n.* & *a.* E19. [Maler = hillmen, ult. f. Dravidian *mala* mountain.] **A** *n.* Pl. **-s**, same. A member of a Dravidian people of the Rajmahal hills of northern India; the language of this people (also called *Malto, Rajmahali*). E19. **B** *attrib.* or as *adj.* Of or pertaining to the Maler or their language. E19.

malerisch /'maːlərɪʃ/ *a.* M20. [G = painterly, f. *Maler* painter + *-isch* -ISH[1].] (Of painting) characterized more by the merging of colours than by a formal linear style; painterly.

†**maletolt** *n.* ME–E20. [AN *maletoute*, OFr. *maletote, maltolte, maletoute* (mod. *maltôte*), repr. med.L *mala tolta* bad tax.] *Law.* An unjust or burdensome tax.

malevolence /mə'lɛv(ə)l(ə)ns/ *n.* LME. [OFr. *malivolence, male-* f. L *malevolentia*, f. *malevolent-*: see next, -ENCE.] The quality of being malevolent; the wishing or the disposition to wish evil to others; ill will.

Also **malevolency** *n.* M17.

malevolent /mə'lɛv(ə)l(ə)nt/ *a.* & *n.* E16. [OFr. *malivolent* or L *malevolent-*, f. *male* ill, badly + *volent-* pres. ppl stem of *velle* will, wish: see -ENT.] **A** *adj.* 1 Desirous of evil to others; feeling, arising from, or indicative of ill will; disposed or addicted to ill will. E16. 2 *Astrol.* Exercising an evil or baleful influence. L16.

1 I. MURDOCH That she's completely malevolent, that she enjoys destroying things? C. BLACKWOOD She was eerie; she was evil; her intentions were entirely malevolent.

†**B** *n.* A malevolent person. L16–L17.

malevolently *adv.* E17.

†**malevolous** *a.* E16–E18. [f. L *malevolus*, f. *male* ill, badly + *vol-*, *velle* wish, will + -OUS.] Malevolent.

malexecution /ˌmalɛksɪ'kjuːʃ(ə)n/ *n.* L17. [f. MAL- + EXECUTION.] Bad execution or administration.

malfeasance /mal'fiːz(ə)ns/ *n.* L17. [AN *malfaisance*, f. *mal-* MAL- + (O)Fr. *faisance*: see FEASANCE. Cf. MISFEASANCE.] *Law.* Evildoing, illegal action; an illegal act; *spec.* official misconduct by a public servant.

malfeasant /mal'fiːz(ə)nt/ *a.* & *n.* E19. [Fr. *malfaisant*, f. *mal-* MAL- + *faisant* pres. pple of *faire* do: see -ANT[1].] **A** *adj.* Evildoing. E19. **B** *n.* An evildoer, a criminal. L19.

malformation /malfɔː'meɪʃ(ə)n/ *n.* E19. [f. MAL- + FORMATION.] Faulty or anomalous formation or structure of parts; *esp.* congenital abnormality of a part of the body.

malformed /mal'fɔːmd/ *a.* E19. [f. MAL- + *formed* pa. pple of FORM *v.*[1]] Badly formed; marked or characterized by malformation.

malfunction /mal'fʌŋ(k)ʃ(ə)n/ *n.* M20. [f. MAL- + FUNCTION *n.*] Bad or faulty functioning; an instance of this.

malfunction /mal'fʌŋ(k)ʃ(ə)n/ *v.i.* E20. [f. MAL- + FUNCTION *v.*] Function badly or faultily.

malgas *n.* var. of MALAGAS.

malgovernment /mal'gʌv(ə)nm(ə)nt, -v(ə)m(ə)nt/ *n.* M17. [f. MAL- + GOVERNMENT.] Bad government.

malgrace /mal'greɪs/ *n.* ME. [Orig. two wds, f. OFr. *male grace* lit. 'evil grace'.] †1 Disfavour. ME–E18. 2 Something unbecoming. *pseudo-arch. rare.* L19.

malgré /malgre/ *prep.* E16. [Fr.: see MAUGRE.] In spite of, notwithstanding.

malgré lui /lɥi/ in spite of himself or herself. ***malgré tout*** /tu/ despite everything.

†**malheur** *n.* L15–L18. [Fr. (earlier *maleur*), f. *mal* evil + *eur* fortune.] Misfortune.

mali /'mɑːliː/ *n.*[1] M18. [Hind. *mālī* f. Skt *mālin*, f. *mālā* garland.] A member of a caste in the Indian subcontinent whose traditional occupation is gardening; any non-European gardener.

Mali /'mɑːli/ *a.* & *n.*[2] E20. [See below.] **A** *adj.* Of or pertaining to Mali, an ancient empire (of the 13th and 14th cents.) and a modern republic (founded in 1960) in W. Africa. E20. **B** *n.* A native or inhabitant of modern Mali. M20.

Also **Malian** *a.* & *n.* M20.

Malibu /'malɪbuː/ *n.* Chiefly *Austral.* & *NZ*. Also **m-**. M20. [*Malibu* beach, California, USA.] In full *Malibu* (*surf*)*board*. A short lightweight surfboard.

malic /'meɪlɪk/ *a.* L18. [f. L *malum* apple + -IC.] *Chem.* 1 *malic acid*, a colourless crystalline acid, $HOOC{\cdot}CH_2CH(OH){\cdot}COOH$, present in apples, rowan berries, and many other fruits. L18. 2 Of an enzyme: that acts on malic acid. M20.

malice /'malɪs/ *n.* & *v.* ME. [(O)Fr. f. L *malitia*, f. *malus* bad: see -ICE[1].] **A** *n.* †1 Badness; *esp.* wickedness. ME–M17. 2 The desire to injure another person; active ill will or hatred. In later use also, the desire to tease. ME. †3 Malicious conduct; a malicious act or device. ME–M17. †4 Power to harm, harmful action or effect, malignancy; *Astrol.* the baleful influence of certain stars. LME–L17. 5 *Law.* Wrongful intention, esp. as aggravating guilt in certain offences or depriving some act of a justification or excuse that might otherwise have been allowed. M16.

2 **bear malice** feel ill will, now usu. on account of some injury (foll. by *against, to, toward(s)*). 5 *malice* AFORETHOUGHT. *malice prepense*: see PREPENSE *a.* 1. *malice prepensed*: see PREPENSE *v. stand mute of malice*: see MUTE *a.* 2.

B *v.t.* Bear malice towards. Long *arch.* & *dial.* M16.

maliceful *a.* (chiefly *dial.*) malicious M17.

malicho *n.* var. of MALLECHO.

malicious /mə'lɪʃəs/ *a.* & *n.* ME. [OFr. *malicius* (mod. *malicieux*) f. L *malitiosus*, f. *malitia*: see prec., -OUS.] A *adj.* 1 Given to, arising from, or characterized by malice. ME. †b Wicked. ME–L15. c *Law.* Characterized by malice prepense. LME. †2 Harmful, malignant. LME–E18. †3 Clever, artful. LME–L16.

1 MILTON Thou knowst . . what malicious Foe . . seeks to work us woe and shame. E. M. FORSTER Mr Vyse . . took a malicious pleasure in thwarting people. V. BROME Clearly . . a great deal of gossip, backbiting and malicious talk went on. c L. SOUTHWORTH He did have a couple of arrests. One for malicious damage and the other for G.B.H. *Daily Telegraph* Guilty verdicts . . for causing an affray and malicious wounding were unsafe and unsatisfactory.

B *n.* A malicious person. *rare.* M16.

maliciously *adv.* LME. **maliciousness** *n.* LME.

maliferous /mə'lɪf(ə)rəs/ *a.* Now *rare.* E18. [f. L *malus* bad: see -FEROUS.] Bringing or producing evil; unwholesome, insalubrious.

malign /mə'lʌɪn/ *a.* ME. [(O)Fr. *maligne* fem. of (O)Fr. *malin* or its source L *malignus*, f. *malus* bad.] 1 Of a thing: evil in nature and effects; baleful, gravely injurious; (chiefly *Astrol.*) having an evil influence or effect. Formerly also, of sin: heinous. ME. 2 Characterized by ill will; desiring or rejoicing in the suffering of others; malevolent. LME. 3 Of a disease etc.: malignant. Now *rare.* LME.

1 LONGFELLOW A poison malign Is such Borgia wine. 2 A. STORR To discover that the person one believed was on one's side is actually malign.

malignly *adv.* M16.

malign /mə'lʌɪn/ *v.* LME. [OFr. *malignier* f. late L *malignare* contrive maliciously, f. *malignus*: see prec.] †1 *v.i.* Speak ill, inveigh; plot, contrive. (Foll. by *against.*) LME–E17. †2 *v.i.* Feel malice or ill will. Foll. by *against, at.* LME–M17. †3 *v.t.* Regard with hatred or envy. Also, resent, take amiss. L15–E18. 4 *v.t.* Speak ill or wrongly of, traduce, slander. M16.

4 G. GREENE He sounded professional, and I wondered whether perhaps I had maligned him. L. CODY You're maligning all my varied professions.

maligner *n.* LME.

malignance /mə'lɪgnəns/ *n.* M17. [f. as next: see -ANCE.] = next.

malignancy /mə'lɪgnənsi/ *n.* E17. [f. next: see -ANCY.] 1 Malign or baleful character; great injuriousness. E17. 2 Disaffection to constituted authority, *obs.* exc. *Hist.* (*derog.*) sympathy with the royalist cause during the English civil war. M17. 3 Malignant or intensely malevolent disposition; envenomed hostility; desire to inflict injury or suffering. M17. 4 An instance of malignancy; a malignant quality. M17. 5 *Med.* Malignant quality, now esp. of a cancer or tumour (cf. MALIGNANT *a.* 2). L17. b A malignant tumour. M20.

malignant /mə'lɪgnənt/ *a.* & *n.* M16. [Late L *malignant-* pres. ppl stem of *malignare*: see MALIGN *v.*, -ANT[1].] A *adj.* 1 Disposed to rebel against God or against constituted authority; disaffected. Now only *Hist.* (*derog.*), sympathetic to the royalist cause during the English civil war. M16. 2 Orig., (of a disease) liable to become progressively more severe; extremely virulent; very infectious. Now chiefly of a cancer or tumour: tending to spread to other parts of the body, or to recur after removal; cancerous. M16. 3 Chiefly *Astrol.* Having an evil influence or effect. L16. 4 Characterized by intense ill will; keenly desirous of the suffering or misfortune of others. L16.

2 *malignant pustule*: see PUSTULE 1.

B *n.* A person who is disaffected towards constituted authority or (in early use) an accepted true religion; a malcontent; *Hist.* (*derog.*) a supporter of the royalist cause during the English civil war. L16.

malignantly *adv.* M16.

malignation /malɪg'neɪʃ(ə)n/ *n.* LME. [f. late L *malignat-* pa. ppl stem of *malignare*: MALIGN *v.*, -ATION.] †1 Feeling of dislike or ill will. LME–L15. †2 A malefic incantation. Only in M17. 3 The action of maligning or slandering. *rare.* M19.

malignify /mə'lɪgnɪfʌɪ/ *v.t. rare.* E17. [f. L *malignus* MALIGN *a.*: see -I-, -FY.] Make malign.

malignity /mə'lɪgnɪti/ *n.* LME. [OFr. *malignité* or L *malignitas*, f. *malignus* MALIGN *a.*: see -ITY.] 1 Wicked and deep-rooted ill will or hatred; intense and persistent desire to cause suffering to another person; propensity to this feeling. LME. b In *pl.* Malignant feelings or actions. E16. 2 Wickedness, heinousness. *arch.* M16. 3 Noxiousness, deleteriousness. *arch.* E17. 4 *Med.* = MALIGNANCY 5. M17.

malihini /mɑːlɪ'hiːni/ *n.* E20. [Haw.] In Hawaii: a stranger, a newcomer; a beginner, a novice.

malik /'malɪk/ *n.* E19. [Arab. *mālik* use as n. of act. pple of *malaka* possess, rule.] The chief or headman of a village or other community in parts of the Indian subcontinent and the Middle East.

Maliki /'malɪki/ *n.* & *a.* E18. [Arab. *mālikī*, f. *Malik* (see below).] A *n.* A member of one of the four sects of Sunni Muslims, following the rite of the Muslim jurist Malik ibn Anas (713–795). E18. B *adj.* Of or pertaining to the Malikis. L19.

Also **Malikite** *n.* & *a.* M19.

malimbi /mə'lɪmbi/ *n.* L20. [Origin unkn.] Any of several weaver-birds of the genus *Malimbus*, found in west and central Africa.

Malines /ma'liːn/ *n.* & *a.* Also **m-**. M19. [Fr. name of *Mechelen* in Belgium: see MECHLIN.] 1 (Designating or made of) bobbin lace of a type or floral pattern produced at Mechelen. M19. 2 (Designating or made of) a net for millinery or veils. L19. 3 (Of or designating) a Belgian breed of the domestic fowl. E20.

malinfluence /mal'ɪnflʊəns/ *n.* L18. [f. MAL- + INFLUENCE *n.*] Evil influence.

malinger /mə'lɪŋgə/ *v.i.* E19. [Back-form. f. next.] Pretend or exaggerate illness in order to escape duty or work.

malingerer /mə'lɪŋg(ə)rə/ *n.* L18. [App. f. (O)Fr. *malingre*, perh. f. as MAL- + *haingre* weak, thin, prob. of Gmc origin.] A person who malingers.

Malinke /mə'lɪŋkeɪ/ *n.* & *a.* L19. [Malinke.] A *n.* Pl. same, **-s**. A member of a people of W. Africa; the Mande language of this people. L19. B *attrib.* or as *adj.* Of or pertaining to the Malinke or their language. L20.

¶Also called *Mandinka*. Cf. also MANDING.

Malinowskian /malɪ'nɒfskɪən/ *a.* M20. [f. *Malinowski* (see below) + -AN.] Of, pertaining to, or characteristic of the Polish-born anthropologist Bronislaw K. Malinowski (1884–1942) or his works.

malintegration /ˌmalɪntɪ'greɪʃ(ə)n/ *n.* M20. [f. MAL- + INTEGRATION.] Bad or faulty integration, esp. into society.

Maliseet *n.* & *a.* var. of MALECITE.

malism /'meɪlɪz(ə)m/ *n.* L19. [f. L *malus* bad + -ISM.] The doctrine that this world is an evil one.

malison /'malɪz(ə)n, -s-/ *n.* Now *arch.* & *dial.* ME. [OFr. f. as MALEDICTION.] A curse, a malediction.

malist /'meɪlɪst/ *n.* L19. [f. L *malus* bad + -IST.] A person who holds the doctrine of malism.

ma'listic /mə'lɪstɪk/ *a.* pertaining to or holding the doctrine of malism L19.

malkin /'mɔːkɪn/ *n. obs.* exc. *dial.* Also **mawkin**. ME. [Dim. of *Malde* early form of female forenames Maud or Matilda: see -KIN. Cf. MAUX, MERKIN.] 1 (Formerly used as a typical name of) a lower-class, untidy, or sluttish woman, esp. a servant, or country girl. ME. †2 (A name for) a female spectre or demon. (In later use app. associated w. sense 5a.) ME–E17. 3 A mop; a bundle of rags fastened to the end of a stick, esp. for cleaning out a baker's oven. LME. 4 A scarecrow; a ragged puppet, a grotesque effigy. M16. 5a (A name for) a cat. Cf. earlier GRIMALKIN. L17. b (A name for) a hare. *Sc.* & *north.* E18.

malkoha *n.* var. of MALCOHA.

mall /mal, mɔːl/ *n.* ME. [Earlier form of MAUL *n.* In branch II cf. PALL-MALL.] I 1 See MAUL *n.* ME. II *spec.* 2 *Hist.* a A mallet used in the game pall-mall. M17. b The game pall-mall. M17. c An alley for the game of pall-mall. M17. 3a A sheltered walk serving as a promenade. Orig. in *the Mall*, a walk bordered by trees in St James's Park, London, orig. a mall in sense 2c. L17. b A shopping-precinct closed to vehicles; a large shopping-centre. Also more fully *shopping mall.* Chiefly *N. Amer.*, *Austral.*, & *NZ.* M20.

†mall *v.* var. of MAUL *v.*

Mallaby-Deeley /maləbɪ'diːli/ *n. arch. slang.* E20. [Harry *Mallaby-Deeley* (1863–1937), Eng. clothing manufacturer.] A cheap suit of clothes.

mallam /'maləm/ *n.* M20. [Hausa *mālam(i)*.] In Nigeria and other parts of Africa, a learned man, a scribe, a teacher.

mallard /'malɑːd, -ləd/ *n.* Pl. **-s**, same. ME. [OFr. *mallard*, (also mod.) *malart* mallard drake, prob. f. as MALE *a.* & *n.* + -ARD.] 1 The male of the common holarctic wild duck *Anas platyrhynchos*. Now also, the male or female of this duck. ME. 2 The flesh of this duck as food. LME.

mallardite /'malədʌɪt/ *n.* L19. [f. Ernest *Mallard* (1833–94), Fr. crystallographer + -ITE[1].] *Min.* A monoclinic hydrated sulphate of manganese, usu. occurring as rose-coloured fibrous masses.

malleable /'malɪəb(ə)l/ *a.* LME. [OFr. f. med.L *malleabilis*, f. L *malleare* to hammer, f. as MALLEUS + -ABLE.] 1 Esp. of a metal: able to be hammered or pressed out of shape without a tendency to return to the original shape or to fracture. LME. 2 *transf.* & *fig.* Able to be fashioned or adapted; adaptable, pliable. E17.

1 **malleable (cast) iron** cast iron which has been decarburized by oxidation under prolonged heat and made somewhat malleable. 2 JOHN BROOKE He saw the Prince as undeveloped and malleable and he tried to shape his character. V. BROME Neither the media universe nor the events of everyday life were malleable to his will.

mallea'bility *n.* L17. **malleableize** *v.t.* make malleable L19. **malleableness** *n.* (now *rare*) M17.

malleate /'malɪət/ *a.* L19. [f. MALLEUS + -ATE[2].] *Zool.* Having a malleus or mallei.

malleate /'malɪeɪt/ *v.t.* Now *rare.* L16. [L *malleat-* pa. ppl stem of *malleare*: see MALLEABLE, -ATE[3].] Beat with a hammer; *spec.* beat (metal) thin or flat.

malleation /malɪ'eɪʃ(ə)n/ *n.* Now *rare.* L15. [med.L *malleatio(n-)*, f. as prec.: see -ATION.] 1 The action of beating something with a hammer; the condition of being beaten with a hammer. L15. 2 *Med.* A convulsive hammering of one part of the body against another, as a symptom of mental illness. E19.

mallecho /'malɪkəʊ/ *n. rare.* Also **malicho**. E17. [Origin uncertain: perh. f. Sp. *malhecho* misdeed.] Mischief. Only in *miching mallecho* (in and after Shakes.).

SHAKES. *Haml.* Marry, this is miching mallecho; it means mischief.

¶The meaning and origin of the phr. are uncertain: it is usu. taken to mean 'skulking (= MITCH *v.*) mischief'.

mallee /'maliː/ *n.* M19. [Aborig.] Any of various low-growing eucalypts which have many slender stems rising from a large underground stock; scrub or thicket formed by such trees, typical of some arid parts of Australia.

Comb.: **mallee fowl** (also **bird, hen**) an Australian megapode, *Leipoa ocellata*, inhabiting mallee scrub.

mallei *n.* pl. of MALLEUS.

malleiform /ˈmaliːɪfɔːm/ *a.* M19. [f. as MALLEUS + -I- + -FORM.] Having the form of a hammer.

mallemuck *n.* var. of MOLLYMAWK.

mallenders /ˈmal(ə)ndəz/ *n.* Also (earlier) †**-der, malan-**. LME. [(O)Fr. *malandre* f. L *malandria* pl., pustules on the neck.] *Vet. Med.* A dry scabby eruption behind the knee in horses. Cf. SALLENDERS.

malleo- /ˈmalɪəʊ/ *comb. form.* [f. MALLEUS: see -O-.] Forming ns. and adjs. w. the sense 'of the bone of the ear'.

malleo-inˈcudal *a.* (*Anat.*) pertaining jointly to the malleus and the incus of the ear L19.

malleolus /maˈliːələs/ *n.* Pl. **-li** /-lʌɪ, -liː/. E17. [L, dim. of MALLEUS.] †1 *Antiq.* A kind of burning dart. E17–L18. 2 *Anat.* A protuberance of the tibia (in full *internal* or *medial malleolus*) or of the fibula (in full *external* or *lateral malleolus*) at the side of the ankle. L17.

malleolar /maˈliːələ, ˈmalɪələ/ *a.* M19.

†**maller** *n.* var. of MAULER.

mallet /ˈmalɪt/ *n.*[1] LME. [(O)Fr. *maillet*, f. *mailler* to hammer, f. *mail* hammer, MAUL *n.*: see -ET[1].] 1 A kind of hammer, usu. with a relatively large head and of wood, used for various purposes, as driving a chisel etc. LME. †2 A heavy club, a mace. L15–E16. †3 *fig.* A person or agency that hits, beats down, or crushes. E16–E19. 4 *Anat.* The malleus of the ear. *rare.* L16. 5 A long-handled implement like a hammer used for striking the balls in croquet, (formerly) pall-mall, or polo. M19. 6 *Mus.* A light hammer used for playing the vibraphone, xylophone, etc. M20.

Comb.: **mallet finger** *Med.* (the condition of having) a finger permanently flexed at the distal joint; **mallet-shoot** a hammer-shaped slip of a tree or shrub for planting.

†**mallet** *n.*[2] *rare.* E17–M19. [Sp. *maleta* = Fr. *mallette* dim. of *maille* MAIL *n.*[3]: see -ET[1].] A little bag or portmanteau.

mallet /ˈmalɪt/ *n.*[3] M19. [Aborig.] (The timber of) any of various eucalypts with tannin-rich bark, *esp.* yate, *E. cornuta*.

mallet /ˈmalɪt/ *v.t.* L16. [f. MALLET *n.*[1]] Beat or hammer (as) with a mallet.

malleus /ˈmalɪəs/ *n.* Pl. **mallei** /ˈmalɪʌɪ/. M17. [L = hammer (from its shape).] 1 *Anat.* & *Zool.* The outermost of the three small bones which conduct sound through the mammalian ear, transmitting the vibrations of the tympanum to the incus. Cf. INCUS, STAPES. M17. 2 *Zool.* In rotifers, either of two parts of the chitinous mouth-apparatus, which masticate food by working on the incus. M19.

Malling /ˈmɔːlɪŋ/ *n.* E20. [Two villages, East and West *Malling*, in Kent, England.] 1 Used *attrib.* to designate a rootstock for fruit trees developed at the East Malling Research Station. E20. 2 Used *attrib.* to designate (articles, esp. tin-enamelled jugs, of) a type of English stoneware of the late 16th cent. M20.

Mallorcan /məˈlɔːk(ə)n, məˈljɔː-/ *n.* & *a.* M19. [f. *Mallorca* Majorca + -AN. Cf. next.] = next.

Mallorquin /məˈlɔːkɪn, məˈljɔː-/ *n.* & *a.* M19. [Sp. *Mallorquín*, f. *Mallorca* Majorca: see MAJORCAN. Cf. prec.] A *n.* 1 A Majorcan. M19. 2 The Catalan dialect of Majorca. M19. B *adj.* Majorcan. M19.

mallow /ˈmaləʊ/ *n.* Also †**mallows**. OE. [L *malva* rel. to Gk *malakhē*, *molokhē*. Cf. MAUVE.] Any of various plants of the family Malvaceae and esp. of the genus *Malva*, typically with hairy stems and leaves and deeply-cleft purple flowers; spec. *Malva sylvestris* (also *common*, *field*, or *wild mallow*).

curled(-leaved) mallow a variety of *Malva verticillata*, grown as a salad plant. **dwarf mallow** a low-growing Eurasian mallow, *Malva neglecta*, common in waste ground. *glade mallow*: see GLADE *n.*[2] *Indian mallow*: see INDIAN *a.* *Jew's mallow*: see JEW *n.* MARSHMALLOW. *musk mallow*: see MUSK *n.* **rose-mallow** = HIBISCUS. *tree mallow*: see TREE *n.*

†**mallowe** *n.* see MULLOWAY.

†**mallows** *n.* var. of MALLOW.

malm /mɑːm/ *n.* & *v.* [OE *mealm-* (in *mealmstān*) = ON *malr* ore, metal, Goth. *malma* sand, f. Gmc base also of MEAL *n.*[1]] A *n.* 1 (More fully *malm rock*, *malmstone*) a soft friable rock consisting largely of chalky material; light loamy soil formed by the disintegration of this rock. OE. 2 More fully *malm-brick*. A fine-quality brick made orig. from malm, marl, or similar chalky clay. E19. B *v.t.* †1 Treat (land) with malm. Only in E17. 2 Convert (clay) into artificial malm for brick-making; cover (brick earth) with artificial malm. M19.

malmy *a.* of a loamy character L17.

Malmaison /malˈmeɪzɒn/ *n.* L19. [Short for Fr. *Souvenirs de Malmaison* 'recollections of Malmaison' (château of the Fr. empress Josephine), name of a variety of rose which the carnation was held to resemble.] *Hort.* In full *Malmaison carnation*. A kind of carnation variety with a sturdy, large-flowered habit.

malmsey /ˈmɑːmzi/ *n.* Also **M-**. LME. [MDu., MLG *malmesie*, *-eye*, in med.L *malmasia* f. Gk place-name *Monemvasia* in the Peloponnese. Cf. MALVASIA, MALVOISIE.] 1 A strong (now fortified) sweet wine, orig. from around Monemvasia in the Peloponnese, Greece, now also from Spain, the Azores, the Canary Islands and (esp.) Madeira. Also *malmsey wine*. LME. 2 A kind of grape, orig. from the eastern Mediterranean, from which malmsey was originally made. E16.

Comb.: †**malmsey-face** a face inflamed by alcoholic drink; **malmsey madeira** malmsey from Madeira; †**malmsey-nose** a nose inflamed by alcoholic drink; *malmsey wine*: see sense 1 above.

malnourished /malˈnʌrɪʃt/ *a.* E20. [f. MAL- + *nourished* pa. pple of NOURISH *v.*] Suffering from malnutrition; not provided with adequate nourishment.

malnourishment /malˈnʌrɪʃm(ə)nt/ *n.* M20. [f. MAL- + NOURISHMENT.] = MALNUTRITION.

malnutrition /malnjʊˈtrɪʃ(ə)n/ *n.* M19. [f. MAL- + NUTRITION.] Nutrition which is not adequate to maintain good health, whether through insufficient quantity of food, lack of essential dietary components, unbalanced diet, or malabsorption; the condition of poor health resulting from this.

malobservance /maləbˈzəːv(ə)ns/ *n.* E19. [f. MAL- + OBSERVANCE.] Observance of a wrong kind.

malobservation /ˌmalɒbzəˈveɪʃ(ə)n/ *n.* M19. [f. MAL- + OBSERVATION.] Faulty or imperfect observation.

maloca /məˈləʊkə/ *n.* M19. [Port. = large hut f. Amer. Sp. (raid, attack), f. Araucanian *malocan* to fight.] A large hut in certain Indian settlements in S. America.

malocclusion /maləˈkluːʒ(ə)n/ *n.* L19. [f. MAL- + OCCLUSION.] *Dentistry.* Faulty or imperfect occlusion of the teeth.

malodorous /malˈəʊd(ə)rəs/ *a.* M19. [f. MAL- + ODOROUS.] Evil-smelling. (*lit.* & *fig.*).

R. MANNING A strong whiff of these malodorous views hung in the air.

malodorously *adv.* E20. **malodorousness** *n.* L19.

malodour /malˈəʊdə/ *n.* E19. [f. MAL- + ODOUR *n.*] An evil smell, a stench.

malolactic /maləˈlaktɪk/ *a.* E20. [f. MAL(IC + -O- + LACTIC.] Designating bacterial fermentation which converts malic acid (in wine) to lactic acid.

malonic /məˈlɒnɪk/ *a.* M19. [Fr. *malonique* alt. of *malique* MALIC.] *Chem.* 1 *malonic acid*, a crystalline acid, $CH_2(COOH)_2$, obtained by the oxidation of malic acid. M19. 2 *malonic ester*, the liquid diethyl ester, $CH_2(COOC_2H_5)_2$, of malonic acid, widely used in a method for synthesizing carboxylic acids. L19.

malonate /ˈmalәneɪt/ *n.* a salt or ester of malonic acid M19. ˈ**malonyl** *n.* the divalent radical $\cdot COCH_2CO\cdot$ derived from malonic acid L19.

maloperation /ˌmalɒpəˈreɪʃ(ə)n/ *n.* E19. [f. MAL- + OPERATION.] Faulty or imperfect operation.

malorganization /ˌmalɔːgənʌɪˈzeɪʃ(ə)n/ *n.* Also **-isation**. M19. [f. MAL- + ORGANIZATION.] Faulty or imperfect organization.

Malorian /maˈlɔːrɪən/ *a.* Also **Maloryan**. E20. [f. *Malory* (see below) + -AN.] Of, pertaining to, or in the manner of the English writer Sir Thomas Malory (d. 1471) or his translations of Arthurian legend.

Malo-Russian /mɑːləʊˈrʌʃ(ə)n/ *n.* & *a.* *arch.* M19. [f. Russ. *Malorossiya* lit. 'Little Russia', Ukraine or *Malorossiyánin* a 'Little Russian', a Ukrainian: see -AN.] = UKRAINIAN.

Maloryan *a.* var. of MALORIAN.

maloti *n.* pl. of LOTI.

Malozi *n.pl.* see LOZI.

malpais /malpɑːˈiːs/ *n.* *US.* M19. [Sp., f. *malo* bad + *país* country, region.] Rugged or difficult country of volcanic origin.

malperformance /malpəˈfɔːməns/ *n.* M20. [f. MAL- + PERFORMANCE.] Faulty or imperfect performance.

Malpighian /malˈpɪgɪən/ *a.* M19. [f. Marcello *Malpighi* (1628–94), It. physician + -AN.] Designating certain anatomical structures discovered by Malpighi or connected with structures discovered by him.

Malpighian body, corpuscle *Anat.* (*a*) a glomerulus of the kidney together with the Bowman's capsule surrounding it; (*b*) any of the lymphoid follicles of the spleen. **Malpighian layer** *Anat.* the innermost layer of the epidermis, in which cell division occurs. *Malpighian pyramid*: see PYRAMID *n.* 7. **Malpighian tubule** *Zool.* a tubular excretory organ, numbers of which open into the gut in certain insects and other arthropods.

malposition /malpəˈzɪʃ(ə)n/ *n.* M19. [f. MAL- + POSITION *n.*] Misplacement; the condition of being wrongly placed; *Med.* faulty position of a part or organ, esp. of a foetus in the uterus.

malpractice /malˈpraktɪs/ *n.* L17. [f. MAL- + PRACTICE *n.*] 1 *Law.* Improper treatment or culpable neglect of a patient by a physician or of a client by a lawyer. L17. 2 *gen.* A criminal or illegal action; wrongdoing, misconduct. M18.

malpraxis /malˈpraksɪs/ *n.* M19. [f. MAL- + L PRAXIS. Cf. MALA PRAXIS.] *Law.* = MALPRACTICE 1.

malpresentation /ˌmalprɛz(ə)nˈteɪʃ(ə)n/ *n.* M19. [f. MAL- + PRESENTATION.] *Med.* Abnormal presentation at parturition.

malt /mɒlt, mɔːlt/ *n.*[1] & *a.* [OE *malt* (*mealt*) = OS *malt* (Du. *mout*), (O)HG *malz*, ON *malt*, f. Gmc, rel. to base of MELT *v.*] A *n.* 1 Barley or other grain prepared for brewing or distilling or vinegar-making, esp. by steeping, germinating, and drying. OE. 2 Malt liquor; (now *esp.*) malt whisky; an example or drink of this. *colloq.* E18.

1 *brown malt*: see BROWN *a.* 2 *single malt*: see SINGLE *a.* & *adv.*

B *attrib.* or as *adj.* Prepared or distilled from malt. L17.

single malt whisky: see SINGLE *a.* & *adv.*

Comb. & *special collocations*: **malt-comb(s)** (now *dial.*) = COMB *n.*[2]; **malt-distiller** a distiller of malt spirits; **malt-distillery** †(*a*) the action or art of the malt-distiller; (*b*) a place where malt spirits are distilled; **maltdust** refuse falling from grain in the process of malting; **malt extract** a sweet sticky substance obtained from wort; **malt-floor** a floor upon which barley etc. is spread to germinate; †**malt-horse** *arch.* a heavy kind of horse used by maltsters (used occas. as a term of abuse); **malt-house** a building for preparing and storing malt, a malting; **malt-kiln** a kiln in which barley etc. is dried after steeping and germinating; **malt liquor** liquor made from malt by fermentation as opp. to distillation, as ale, beer, stout, etc.; **malt-maker** (now *rare*) a maltster; **maltman** a maltster; **malt shop** *N. Amer.* a shop where malted milk is sold; **malt spirits** spirits distilled from malt; **malt sugar** = MALTOSE; **malt-tax** *Hist.* a tax on malt, imposed by Parliament in 1697, repealed in 1880; **malt vinegar** vinegar made from the fermentation of malt; **malt whisky**: made only from malted barley; cf. *grain whisky* s.v. GRAIN *n.*[1]; **maltworm** †(*a*) a weevil infesting malt; (*b*) *arch.* a lover of malt liquor, a heavy drinker; **maltwort** (now *rare*) = WORT *n.*[2]

Malt /mɒlt, mɔːlt/ *n.*[2] *slang* (usu. *derog.*). M20. [Abbrev.] A Maltese.

malt /mɒlt, mɔːlt/ *v.* LME. [f. MALT *n.*[1]] 1 *v.t.* & *i.* Convert (barley or other grain) into malt. LME. 2 *v.t.* Make (liquor) with malt; combine with malt. Chiefly as MALTED *ppl a.* E17. 3 *v.i.* Admit of being malted. M18. 4 *v.t.* in *pass.* & *i.* Of seeds: become malt owing to germination being checked by drought. M18. 5 *v.i.* Drink malt liquor. *colloq.* Now *rare.* E19.

malter *n.* (*obs.* exc. *dial.*) a maltster ME.

Malta /ˈmɒltə, mɔːltə/ *n.* M17. [An island in the central Mediterranean, given to the Knights Hospitallers in the 16th cent., later a dependency of Great Britain, now an independent republic.] Used *attrib.* to designate things found in or associated with Malta.

†**Malta cross** a Maltese cross. **Malta fever** *Med.* undulant fever caused by *Brucella melitensis*, as formerly prevalent in Malta and other places in the Mediterranean.

maltalent /ˈmaltal(ə)nt/ *n.* & *a.* ME. [OFr., f. *mal* evil + *talent* disposition, temper (see TALENT *n.*[1]).] A *n.* †1 Ill will, malevolence. ME–E19. 2 An ill-tempered person. *rare.* M20. †B *adj.* Ill-tempered. Only in L16.

maltase /ˈmɒlteɪz, ˈmɔːlt-/ *n.* L19. [f. MALT *n.*[1] + -ASE.] *Biochem.* An enzyme which hydrolyses maltose and similar glycosides, forming glucose.

malted /ˈmɒltɪd, ˈmɔːlt-/ *ppl a.* & *n.* L17. [f. MALT *v.* + -ED[1].] A *ppl a.* 1 Converted into malt. L17. 2 Esp. of (powdered) milk: combined with malt. L19. B *n.* A drink of malted milk. M20.

¶Earlier in UNMALTED.

Maltese /mɒlˈtiːz, mɔːl-/ *n.* & *a.* E17. [f. MALTA + -ESE.] A *n.* Pl. same. 1 A native or inhabitant of Malta, an island in the central Mediterranean. Formerly also, a member of the Knights Hospitallers (with headquarters in Malta). E17. 2 The Semitic language of Malta, much influenced by Italian. E19. 3 A breed of white toy dog; a dog of this breed. M19. 4 *ellipt.* Maltese lace. M19.

B *adj.* Of or pertaining to Malta or its inhabitants. L18.

Maltese cat (an animal of) a bluish-grey short-haired breed of cat. **Maltese cross** (*a*) a cross with the limbs broadened outwards and often indented at the ends (formerly worn by Knights Hospitallers); (*b*) *Philately* a cross-shaped postmark used on British stamps from their introduction in 1840 until 1844; (*c*) a Geneva mechanism in a cinematographic projector. **Maltese dog** = sense A.3 above. **Maltese lace** a fine bobbin-lace associated with Malta. **Maltese terrier** = sense A.3 above.

maltha /ˈmalθə/ *n.* Now *rare.* LME. [L f. Gk.] 1 A kind of cement made by mixing pitch and wax, or lime and sand, with other ingredients. LME. 2 A viscid form of natural asphalt. Also called *mineral tar.* E17.

malthoid /ˈmalθɔɪd/ *n. Austral.* & *NZ.* Also **M-**. M20. [f. prec. + -OID.] (Proprietary name for) a bituminous material made from wood fibre and used esp. as a roof- or floor-covering.

Malthusian /malˈθjuːzɪən/ *a.* & *n.* E19. [f. *Malthus* (see below) + -IAN.] A *adj.* Of, pertaining to, or characteristic of the English clergyman and economist Thomas Robert Malthus (1766–1834), the population control advocated by him (see MALTHUSIANISM), or his followers. E19. B *n.* An adherent of Malthus in his views on population. E19.

Malthusianism /malˈθjuːzɪənɪz(ə)m/ *n.* M19. [f. prec. + -ISM.] The doctrine of T. R. Malthus and his followers that the rate of increase of the population tends to be out of proportion to the increase of its means of subsistence and therefore should be checked, mainly by sexual restraint.

malting /ˈmɒltɪŋ, ˈmɔːlt-/ *n.* ME. [f. MALT *v.* + -ING[1].] 1 The action of MALT *v.* ME. 2 A malt-house. E18.

Malto /ˈmaltəʊ/ *n.* & *a.* L19. [Maler (Malto) = language of the Maler.] (Of) the Dravidian language of the Maler, also called *Maler, Rajmahali.*

maltodextrin /mɒltəʊˈdɛkstrɪn, mɔːlt-/ *n.* E20. [f. MALTO(SE + DEXTRIN.] *Chem.* A dextrin containing maltose, used as a food additive.

maltol /ˈmɒltɒl, ˈmɔːlt-/ *n.* L19. [f. MALT *n.*[1] + -OL.] *Chem.* A crystalline pyranone derivative, $C_6H_6O_3$, present in larch bark and chicory and prepared by roasting malt.

maltose /ˈmɒltəʊz, -s, mɔːlt-/ *n.* M19. [f. MALT *n.*[1] + -OSE[2].] *Chem.* A disaccharide consisting of two glucose residues, produced by the hydrolysis of starch under the action of malt, saliva, etc.

maltreat /malˈtriːt/ *v.t.* E18. [Fr. *maltraiter*, f. as MAL- + TREAT *v.*] Abuse, ill use; handle roughly or rudely; ill-treat.

maltreater *n.* E20.

maltreatment /malˈtriːtm(ə)nt/ *n.* E18. [Fr. *maltraitement*, f. as prec.: see -MENT.] The action of maltreating someone or something; the state of being maltreated.

maltster /ˈmɒltstə, mɔːlt-/ *n.* ME. [f. MALT *n.*[1] + -STER.] A person whose occupation it is to make malt.

malty /ˈmɒlti, ˈmɔːlti/ *a.* E19. [f. MALT *n.*[1] + -Y[1].] 1 Addicted to, affected by, or pertaining to malt liquor. *joc. arch.* M19. 2 Of the nature of or resembling malt. M19.

maltiness *n.* M20.

malum in se /maləm ɪn ˈsiː, ˈseɪ/ *n.* & *a. phr.* Pl. of n. ***mala in se*** /ˈmalə/. E17. [med.L = bad in itself.] (A thing) intrinsically evil or wicked.

malvaceous /malˈveɪʃəs/ *a.* L17. [f. L *malvaceus*, f. *malva* MALLOW: see -ACEOUS.] *Bot.* Like mallow; of or pertaining to the family Malvaceae to which the mallows belong.

malvasia /malvəˈsiːə, -z-/ *n.* Also **M-**. M19. [It. form of *Monemvasia*: see MALMSEY. Cf. MALVOISIE.] = MALMSEY.

Malvern /ˈmɒlv(ə)n, ˈmɔːl-/ *n.* M18. [A town in Hereford and Worcester, England: cf. next.] In full *Malvern water.* A mineral water from springs near Malvern.

Malvernian /mɒlˈvəːnɪən, -ˈmɔːl-/ *a.* L19. [f. *Malvern* Hills, a range of hills in Hereford and Worcester, England: see -IAN. Cf. prec.] Chiefly *Geol.* Of, pertaining to, or characteristic of the Malvern Hills; *spec.* designating (*a*) a Precambrian series of plutonic rocks forming most of the hills; (*b*) a north-south orientation like that of the hills.

malversate /malˈvəːseɪt/ *v.t.* L19. [Back-form. f. next.] Use (funds) for an improper purpose, misappropriate.

malversation /malvəˈseɪʃ(ə)n/ *n.* M16. [Fr., f. *malverser* f. L *male versari* behave badly: see -ATION.] 1 Corrupt behaviour in a commission, office, employment, or position of trust; an instance of this. M16. 2 Corrupt administration *of* (public money etc.). E18.

†**malverse** *v.i.* Chiefly *Sc.* M17–M18. [Fr. *malverser*: see prec.] Act corruptly in a position of trust.

Malvi /ˈmɑːlvi/ *n.* & *a.* L19. [Rajasthani.] (Of) a Rajasthani dialect of NW Madhya Pradesh, India.

malvoisie /ˈmalvɔɪzi, malvɔɪˈziː/ *n. arch.* Also **M-**. LME. [Fr. form of *Monemvasia*: see MALMSEY. Cf. MALVASIA.] = MALMSEY.

mal vu /mal vy/ *a. phr.* E20. [Fr., lit. 'badly seen'.] Held in low esteem, looked down on.

mam /mam/ *n. colloq.* & *dial.* L16. [Perh. imit. of infants' first speech: see MAMMA *n.*[2] Cf. MUM *n.*[3]] Mother.

mama *n.* var. of MAMMA *n.*[2]

mamaliga /mæməˈliːgə/ *n.* L19. [Romanian *mămăligă*.] Polenta, maize porridge, as a staple food in Romania.

mamaloi /ˈmam(ə)lwɑː/ *n.* Pl. **-s**, same. L19. [Haitian creole *mamalwa*, f. *mama* mother + *lwa* LOA *n.*[2]] A voodoo priestess. Cf. PAPALOI.

†**Mamamouchi** *n.* L17–M18. [The mock-Turkish title pretended to have been conferred by the Sultan upon M. Jourdain, in Molière's play *Le Bourgeois Gentilhomme.*] A pompous-sounding title. Also, a person assuming such a title, a ridiculous pretender to elevated dignity.

mama-san /ˈmaməsan/ *n.* Pl. ***-s***, same. M20. [Jap., f. *mama* mother + SAN *n.*[3]] In Japan and the Far East: a woman in a position of authority, *spec.* one in charge of a geisha-house; the mistress of a bar.

mamba /ˈmambə/ *n.* M19. [Zulu *imamba.*] Any of several large venomous semi-arboreal elapid snakes of the tropical African genus *Dendroaspis*; esp. *D. angusticeps*, which occurs in green and black colour phases (*green, black, mamba*).

mambo /ˈmambəʊ/ *n.* & *v.* M20. [Amer. Sp., prob. f. Haitian creole, f. Yoruba, lit. 'to talk'.] A *n.* Pl. **-os**. 1 A kind of rumba, a ballroom dance of Latin American origin; a piece of music for this dance. M20. 2 A voodoo priestess. M20. B *v.i.* Dance the mambo. M20.

†**mambu** *n.* M17–L18. [Port.: see BAMBOO.] = BAMBOO I.

mamelière /mamɛljɛːr/ *n.* Pl. pronounced same. E19. [Fr., f. as next.] *Hist.* A piece of armour consisting of a circular plate of metal covering either breast.

mamelle /maˈmɛl/ *n.* LME. [(O)Fr. f. L MAMILLA: see -EL[1].] †1 A woman's breast. LME–L15. 2 A rounded hill, esp. as one of a pair. *N. Amer.* L18.

mamelon /ˈmamɪlən/ *n.* M19. [Fr. = nipple, f. as prec.] 1 A small rounded eminence or hillock. M19. 2 *Zool.* A small rounded structure, esp. the central knob of an echinoid tubercle. L19.

mamelonated *a.* covered with rounded protuberances M19.

Mameluco /maməˈluːkəʊ/ *n.* Pl. **-os**. M19. [Port., prob. f. Arab. *mamlūk*: see next.] A person with one White and one Brazilian Indian parent; a Brazilian mestizo.

Mameluke /ˈmaməluːk/ *n.* & *a. obs.* exc. *Hist.* Also **Mamluk** /ˈmaml(j)uːk/. E16. [Fr. *mameluk* f. Arab. *mamlūk* object of possession, slave, use as n. of pass. pple of *malaka* possess.] A *n.* 1 A member of a regime established and maintained by (emancipated) white military slaves (orig. Kipchaks, later Circassians) which ruled Egypt as a sultanate from 1250 until 1517, continuing as a ruling military caste under Ottoman sovereignty until 1812, and in Syria from 1260 to 1516. E16. 2 A slave in a Muslim country. E16. 3 A member of any military body of slaves; a slavish champion or supporter. M16. B *attrib.* or as *adj.* Of or pertaining to the Mamelukes. L18.

mamenchisaurus /məmɛntʃɪˈsɔːrəs/ *n.* Pl. **-ri** /-rʌɪ/, **-ruses**. L20. [mod.L (see below), f. *Mamenchi*, a place in Sichuan province, China, where fossil remains were found + Gk *sauros* lizard.] *Palaeont.* A large Jurassic dinosaur of the genus *Mamenchisaurus*, related to the diplodocus and having an extremely long neck.

Also **maˈmenchisaur** *n.* L20.

mamey *n.* var. of MAMMEE.

mamilla /maˈmɪlə/ *n.* Also ***-mm-**. Pl. **-llae** /-liː/, **-llas**. L17. [L, dim. of *mamma* breast, teat.] 1 *Anat.* & *Zool.* The nipple of the mamma or mammary gland. L17. 2 *transf.* (*Anat., Bot.,* etc.) Any nipple-shaped organ or protuberance; a papilla. E19.

mamillar, -ary *adjs.* see MAMMILLAR, -ARY.

mamillate *a.* var. of MAMMILLATE.

mamillated *a.* see MAMMILLATED.

mamillation *n.*, **mamilliferous, -iform** *adjs.* vars. of MAMMILLATION etc.

Mamluk *n.* & *a.* var. of MAMELUKE.

mamma /ˈmamə/ *n.*[1] Pl. **mammae** /ˈmamiː/. OE. [L.] *Anat.* & *Zool.* The milk-secreting organ of the female in humans and other mammals; the breast; the mammary gland. Also, the corresponding vestigial structure in males.

mamma /məˈmɑː, ˈmamə/ *n.*[2] Also **mama**. L16. [Redupl. of *ma* in infants' natural first speech. See also MAMMY *n.*[1], MOMMA, MUMMY *n.*[2] Cf. MA, MAUMA, MOMMA.] 1 Mother. Used also, chiefly among Blacks, as a form of address to a mature or older woman. L16. 2 A wife, a girlfriend; a sexually attractive (esp. mature) woman. *slang* (chiefly *US*). E20.

1 **Mamma mia!** /mamə ˈmiːə/ [It. = mother mine]: expr. surprise or astonishment. **mamma's boy** = *mother's boy* s.v. MOTHER *n.*[1] 2 *sweet mamma*: see SWEET *a.* & *adv.*

¶In Britain in the 18th cent., although probably commonly used by young children, app. confined to the higher classes; in the 19th cent. in much extended use, and among the lower middle class a mark of 'gentility'; in the 20th cent. unfashionable, even as used by children.

mammae *n.* pl. of MAMMA *n.*[1]

mammal /'mam(ə)l/ *n.* E19. [First used in pl. as an Anglicized form of MAMMALIA.] A furred, warm-blooded, amniote animal of the vertebrate class Mammalia, members of which are characterized by the possession of mammary glands in the female (from which the young are fed) and a four-chambered heart, are typically viviparous (but see MONOTREME; cf. also MARSUPIAL, PLACENTAL), and include humans, rodents, bats, whales, ungulates, carnivores, etc.

mamma'liferous *a.* (*Palaeont.*) containing mammalian remains M19. **mammal-like** *a.* resembling (that of) a mammal; *mammal-like reptile*, spec. = SYNAPSID *n.*: M20.

Mammalia /ma'meɪlɪə/ *n.pl.* Also **m-**. L18. [mod.L, use as n. of neut. pl. of late L *mammalis* adj., f. *mamma*: see MAMMA *n.*[1], -IA[2].] *Zool.* A class of vertebrate animals comprising the mammals; mammals collectively.

mammalian /ma'meɪlɪən/ *a.* & *n.* M19. [f. prec. + -AN.] A *adj.* Of, belonging to, or characteristic of the Mammalia; of, pertaining to, or of the nature of a mammal or mammals. M19. B *n.* A mammal. *rare.* M19.

mammalogy /ma'malədʒi/ *n.* M19. [Irreg. f. MAMMAL + -LOGY.] The scientific study of mammals.

mamma'logical *a.* of or pertaining to mammalogy M19. **mammalogist** *n.* M19.

mammaplasty /'mamәplasti/ *n.* Also **mammo-**. M20. [f. MAMMA *n.*[1] + -PLASTY.] Alteration of the shape or size of a breast by plastic surgery; an instance of this.

mammary /'mamәri/ *a.* & *n.* L17. [f. MAMMA *n.*[1] + -ARY[1].] A *n.* 1 A mammary artery, gland, etc. L17. 2 A breast. Usu. in *pl. slang.* L20.

B *adj.* 1 Of or pertaining to the mamma or breast. E18. †2 Of a tumour: resembling a mammary gland in structure. Only in 19.

1 **mammary gland** the milk-secreting gland in the mamma of a female mammal.

mammee /ma'miː/ *n.* Also **mamey**. L16. [Sp. *mamei* (whence Fr. *mamey*) f. Taino.] 1 More fully *mammee apple*. A large tropical American tree, *Mammea americana* (family Guttiferae); its edible fruit, which has a sweet yellow aromatic flesh. L16. 2 In full *mammee sapote, sapota*, or *zapote*. A Central American tree, *Pouteria sapota* (family Sapotaceae); the oval russet edible fruit of this tree, which has a spicy red flesh (also called *marmalade plum*). M17.

mammer /'mamә/ *v.i. obs.* exc. *dial.* LME. [Imit., w. frequent. suff. -ER[5].] Stammer, mutter. Also, vacillate, waver, be undecided.

mammering *n.* (*a*) the action of the vb; (*b*) a state of doubt, hesitation, or perplexity: M16.

mammet, mammetry *ns.* see MAUMET, MAUMETRY.

mammiferous /ma'mɪf(ә)rәs/ *a.* Now *rare.* E19. [f. MAMMA *n.*[1] + -I- + -FEROUS.] 1 = MAMMALIAN *a.* E19. 2 *Anat.* Of a part of the body: bearing the mammae. L19.

mammifer /'mamɪfә/ *n.* (now *rare*) = MAMMAL *n.* M19.

mammiform /'mamɪfɔːm/ *a.* E18. [f. as prec. + -I- + -FORM.] Breast-shaped; having the form of a dome or rounded cone.

mammilla *n.* see MAMILLA.

mammillar /'mamɪlә/ *a.* Also **mamill-**. L16. [f. as next: see -AR[1].] = MAMMILLARY 1.

mammillary /'mamɪlәri/ *a.* Also (earlier) **mamill-**. LME. [f. as MAMILLA + -ARY[2]: alt. to *-mm-* by assim. to MAMMARY.] 1 a Breast-shaped; of the form of a dome or rounded cone; mammiform. LME. b Chiefly *Min.* Having several smoothly rounded convex surfaces; botryoidal. E19. 2 Of or pertaining to the nipple or (formerly) the breast. M17.

1 **mammillary body** [L *corpus mamillare*] either of a pair of small rounded structures on the ventral surface of the hypothalamus in vertebrates.

¶Only in isolated use bef. E17, translating L *mamillare*.

mammillate /'mamɪleɪt/ *a.* Also **mamill-**. E19. [f. as prec. + -ATE[2].] Mammillated; mammiform.

mammillated /'mamɪleɪtɪd/ *a.* Also (earlier) **mamill-**. M18. [f. as prec. + -ED[2].] 1 Characterized by or covered with rounded mounds or lumps; now chiefly *Geol.*, (of a glaciated landform) worn into smooth convexities. Also (*Min.*), = MAMMILLARY 1b. M18. 2 *Bot.* & *Zool.* Having a nipple-shaped process or part. M19.

mammillation /mamɪ'leɪʃ(ә)n/ *n.* Also **mamill-**. M19. [f. as prec. + -ATION.] 1 The condition of being mammillated. M19. 2 A rounded protuberance. M19.

mammilliferous /mamɪ'lɪf(ә)rәs/ *a.* Also **mamill-**. M19. [f. as prec. + -I- + -FEROUS.] Chiefly *Zool.* Having or bearing mamillae.

mammilliform /ma'mɪlɪfɔːm/ *a.* Also **mamill-**. M19. [f. as prec. + -I- + -FORM.] *Anat.* & *Zool.* Shaped like or resembling a mamilla; nipple-shaped.

mammitis /ma'mʌɪtɪs/ *n.* L19. [f. MAMMA *n.*[1] + -ITIS.] *Med.* Inflammation of a mammary gland.

mammo- /'mamәʊ/ *comb. form* of MAMMA *n.*[1]: see -O-.

mammogen *n.* any substance having (supposed) mammogenic activity M20. **mammo'genesis** *n.* the stimulation of the growth of the breasts, esp. at puberty M20. **mammo'genic** *a.* of, pertaining to, or causing mammogenesis M20. **mammogram, mammograph** *ns.* (*Med.*) a radiograph taken by mammography M20. **mammo'graphic** *a.* of, pertaining to, or designating mammography L20. **ma'mmography** *n.* a technique or procedure for diagnosing and locating abnormalities of the breasts using X-rays; an examination by this technique: M20.

mammock /'mamәk/ *n.* & *v.* Now *arch.* & *dial.* E16. [f. unkn. 1st elem. + -OCK.] A *n.* A scrap, a shred, a broken or torn piece. E16. B *v.t.* Break, cut, or tear into fragments or shreds. E17.

Mammon /'mamәn/ *n.* Also **m-**. LME. [Late L *mam(m)ona, mam(m)on* f. New Testament Gk *mam(m)ōnas* (*Matt.* 6:24, *Luke* 16:9, 11, 13) f. Heb. *māmōn* money, wealth.] In early use, (the proper name of) the devil of covetousness. Later, (usu. with more or less personification) wealth regarded as an idol or as an evil influence.

A. N. WILSON The worship of Mammon blatantly overrode any questions of justice, fairness or human kindness. **the Mammon of unrighteousness** wealth ill-used or ill-gained.

Mammondom *n.* the realm or domain of Mammon E19. **Mammonish** *a.* influenced by or devoted to Mammon M17. **Mammonism** *n.* devotion to the pursuit of riches M19. **Mammonist** *n.* a worshipper of Mammon, a person devoted to the pursuit of riches M16. **Mammo'nistic** *a.* of or pertaining to Mammonists or Mammonism L19. **Mammonite** *n.* = MAMMONIST E18. **Mammonitish** *a.* resembling Mammon; characteristic of a Mammonist: E17.

mammoplasty *n.* var. of MAMMAPLASTY.

mammoth /'mamәθ/ *n.* & *a.* E18. [Russ. *mámo(n)t*, prob. of Siberian origin.] A *n.* 1 Pl. **-s**, same. Any of several very large extinct mammals of the Pleistocene genus *Mammuthus*, related to the elephants and known from fossil and mummified remains in northern Eurasia and N. America. E18. b A mastodon. *US.* E19. 2 A thing of huge size. L19.

1 *imperial mammoth, Siberian mammoth, woolly mammoth.*

B *adj.* Comparable to the mammoth in size; huge, gigantic. E19.

LYNDON B. JOHNSON The mammoth task of preparing a $100 billion budget. **mammoth tree** the Wellingtonia, *Sequoiadendron giganteum.*

mammotrophic /mamә(ʊ)'trәʊfɪk, -'trɒf-/ *a.* Also **-tropic** /-'trәʊpɪk, -'trɒp-/. M20. [f. MAMMO- + -TROPHIC, -TROPIC.] *Physiol.* Of a hormone or its activity: regulating the growth or milk secretion of the breasts.

'mammotroph /-trәʊf/ *n.* a cell of the mammalian adenohypophysis which secretes prolactin M20. **mammotrophin, -tropin** *ns.* = PROLACTIN M20.

mammy /'mami/ *n.*[1] E16. [f. (as) MAM + -Y[6]. Cf. MOMMY, MUMMY *n.*[2]] 1 Mother. *colloq.* & *dial.* E16. 2 In the southern US, esp. before the abolition of slavery, a Black woman having the care of White children (cf. earlier MOMMA 1); *gen.* (usu. considered *offensive*) a Black woman. Cf. MAUMA. M19.

Comb.: **mammy-sick** *a.* (*arch.*, *contempt.*) distressed at being separated from one's mother.

mammy /'mami/ *n.*[2] *W. Afr.* E20. [Origin unkn.] 1 *mammy boat, chair*, a (wicker) basket or chair used on ships for conveying people to and from surf-boats. E20. 2 *mammy-cloth*, a cotton cloth or robe wrapped around the body. M20. 3 *mammy lorry, wagon*, a small open-sided vehicle for transporting passengers or goods. M20. 4 *mammy trader*, a woman market-trader. M20.

mamo /'meɪmәʊ/ *n.* Pl. **-os**. L19. [Haw.] Either of two Hawaiian honey-creepers, the black and yellow *Drepanis pacifica* and (more fully *black mamo*) the black *D. funerea*, both extinct since the early 20th cent.

mamoty /'mamәti/ *n.* Also **mamootie**. L18. [Tamil *mammaṭṭi* alt. of *maṇveṭṭi*, f. *man* earth + *veṭṭi* spade.] A digging tool shaped like a hoe with the blade at an acute angle to the handle, used mainly in India.

mampus /'mampәs/ *n. dial.* E18. [Origin unkn.] A great number, a crowd.

Mam'selle /mam'zɛl; *foreign* mamzɛl/ *n. colloq.* Pl. same. E19. [Fr., contr.] = MADEMOISELLE.

mamur /ma'muːr/ *n.* M19. [Arab. *ma'mūr* use as n. of pass. pple of *'amara* to order.] An Egyptian official governing a district.

mamzer /'mʌmzә/ *n.* Also **momser, momzer**, /'mɒmzә/. Pl. **-rim** /-rɪm/, **-ers**. M16. [Late L f. Heb. *mamzēr*.] A person conceived in a forbidden sexual union, esp. as defined by rabbinical tradition. Also used as a term of abuse or familiarity.

man /man/ *n.* Pl. **men** /mɛn/. [OE *man(n)*, *mon(n)* corresp. to OFris. *man, mon*, OS *man*, OHG *man* (Du. *man*, G *Mann*), ON *maðr*, Goth. *manna*, f. Gmc bases rel. to Skt *manu* man, mankind.] I 1 A human being (formerly explicitly irrespective of sex or age), a person. Now chiefly in general or indefinite applications, as in *every man, any man, no man*, (in pl.) *all men, some men, many men*, etc. OE. 2 (Also **M-**.) (Without article.) The human race or species, humankind, mankind; *Zool.* the human race viewed as a genus (*Homo*) or species (*H. sapiens*) of animal. OE.

1 D. HUME There is in all men, both male and female, a desire and power of generation. TENNYSON For men may come and men may go, but I go on for ever. J. PLAMENATZ A man, in order to be a man, must know that he is one. *Proverb*: When the wind is in the east, 'tis neither good for man nor beast. 2 CARLYLE Man is not only a working but a talking animal. M. ESSLIN Winnie's cheerfulness in the face of death . . is an expression of man's courage. *Cornwall Review* Bodmin Moor bears traces of very early man.

II 3 An adult male person, as opp. to a woman or boy or both; (non-contrastively, passing into sense 1) an individual (male) person. OE. b An adult male eminently endowed with manly qualities. Also, a (male) person of importance. ME. c As *voc.* introducing a remark or parenthetically, now sometimes implying contempt or impatience, or as a form of address to both men and women (esp. among Blacks, among jazz musicians and enthusiasts, and *S. Afr. colloq.*), as a meaningless expletive, or as *int.* expr. surprise, delight, deep emotion, etc. LME. 4 A member of a fighting force; now *esp.* a rank-and-file soldier or sailor as distinguished from an officer. Usu. in *pl.* OE. 5 *Hist.* A vassal, a liegeman. OE. 6 a A manservant; a valet; a workman as distinguished from his employer (usu. in *pl.*). ME. b At a university or public school, an undergraduate or student, as distinguished from a graduate or don. *arch.* E19. 7 a A husband. Exc. in *man and wife*, now chiefly *Sc., dial., S. Afr.*, & *Blacks'*. ME. b A lover, a suitor. Long *dial.* ME. †8 A non-human being likened to or a thing personified as a male human, e.g. God, the Devil, death. E16–E18. 9 (Without article.) The male human being. L16.

3 SHAKES. *Temp.* Misery acquaints a man with strange bedfellows. WORDSWORTH The Child is father

to the Man. T. S. ELIOT Mr Simpkins is a man who knows his own mind. B. RUBENS He had seen old men cry, and little boys, but never a man. *man of feeling, honour, peace, property, sense, wisdom*, etc. c C. BROWN He said, 'Man, you Claude Brown?' 'Yeah, man, like, I'm the one.' J. NAGENDA He had to leave in a hurry. But . . man, what an achievement!

III *transf.* **10** Any of the pieces used in playing chess, draughts, backgammon, etc. LME. **11** (A cairn or pile of stones marking) a summit or prominent point of a mountain. *north.* LME. **12** The obverse of a coin used in tossing (as the side of a penny having the king's head as opp. to Britannia). Cf. WOMAN *n.* 6. *arch.* E19.

IV As 2nd elem. of comb. (in many w. pronunc. /mən/). **13** A person, esp. a male, having a specified nationality, place of origin, abode, or education, profession, occupation, or interest; a person, esp. a male, using or skilled in the use of a specified implement; a person, esp. a male, associated with something specified or described as something specified. OE. **b** (An individual of) a prehistoric type of man named from the specified place where remains were found. M19. **14** A piece used in playing a specified game. L15. **15** A ship of a specified type. Cf. MAN-OF-WAR. L15.

13 *axeman, badman, barman, bondsman, brakeman, chairman, churchman, clergyman, coalman, countryman, craftsman, Englishman, exciseman, freeman, Frenchman, gentleman, Harvard man, highwayman, journeyman, layman, liegeman, middleman, milkman, Oxford man, penman, postman, rag-and-bone man, Renaissance man, salesman, swordsman, trencherman, university man*, etc. **b** *Cro-Magnon man, Java man, Neanderthal man, Peking man, Piltdown man*, etc. **14** *chessman, draughtsman*, etc. **15** *Indiaman, merchantman*, etc.

Phrases & comb.: (A selection of cross-refs. only is included: see esp. other ns.) Appositional (pl. *men*) with the sense 'male', esp. in names of professions etc. more usually pursued by women, as *man cook, nurse*, etc. **a man and a brother** a fellow human being. **as a man** (considered) in respect of his personal character, as distinguished e.g. from his achievements, wealth, etc. **as one man** in unison, unanimously, with one accord. **be a man** be manly, not show fear. **become** or **be made man** assume human nature. **be man** have human nature. **be one's own man** (*a*) have command or control of oneself; be in full possession of one's senses, faculties, or powers; (*b*) be free to act, be independent. *best man*: see BEST *a.*, *n.*, & *adv.* *every man Jack*: see JACK *n.*[1] *good man!*: see GOOD *a.* *grand old man*: see GRAND *a.*[1] *high men*: see HIGH *a.* *in-and-out man*: see IN AND OUT. *inner man*: see INNER *a.* & *n.* *little green man*: see LITTLE *a.* *little man*: see LITTLE *a.* *low men*: see LOW *a.* & *n.*[4] *man about town*: see TOWN *n.* *man alive!*: see ALIVE. **man and boy** *adv. phr.* throughout life from boyhood. **man-ape** an extinct primate intermediate between ape and man; an australopithecine. *man-at-arms*: see ARM *n.*[2] **man-bites-dog** *a.* designating a situation in which the usual sufferer is the aggressor. **manbote** (*obs.* exc. *Hist.*) a fine paid to an overlord for the loss of a man. **man-boy** a youth, an immature man. **man-child**, pl. **men-children**, *arch.* a male child. **man-crazy** *a.* = *man-mad* below. **man-day** a day of work etc. by one person, as a unit of measure. **man-eater** (*a*) a person who eats human flesh, a cannibal; (*b*) an animal, esp. a shark or tiger, that eats or has a propensity for eating human flesh; (*c*) *colloq.* a woman who has many men as lovers. **man-eating** *a.* (*a*) that eats or has a propensity for eating human flesh; (*b*) (of a woman) having many men as lovers. **man-for-man** = *man-to-man* (b) below. *Man Friday*: see FRIDAY *n.* 1. **man-god** a being (*spec.* Jesus) who is both man and God; a being who is both a man and a god. **man-hater** a hater of humankind, a misanthrope; a hater of the male sex. **man-haul** *v.t.* haul or draw along (a sledge etc.) by human exertion rather than by dog etc. **manhole** a hole or opening in a floor, pavement, boiler, etc., through which a person may pass; a shaft, usu. with a cover, giving access to a sewer etc. for inspection or repair. **man-hour** an hour of work etc. by one person, as a unit of measure. **manhunt** an organized search for a person, esp. a criminal. **manhunter** a hunter of men; a cannibal, a slave-dealer, a brigand. **man in motion** *Amer. Football* an offensive back allowed to move during a scrimmage before the ball is put in play. **man-in-space** an astronaut. **man-keen** *a.* (now *dial.*) (*a*) (of an animal) inclined to attack people, fierce, savage; (*b*) (of a woman) very fond of men. **man-killer** a killer of humans; a homicide. **man-mad** *a.* madly desirous of a man or men. **man-made** *a.* & *n.* (*a*) *adj.* made or devised by human effort, not existing in nature; artificially made; (of a fibre) manufactured (from regenerated or synthetic polymer); (*b*) *n.* a man-made fibre or fabric. **man-midwife** (now *rare*) a male midwife, an obstetrician. **man-midwifery** (now *rare*) the practice or occupation of a male midwife, obstetrics. **man-milliner** (*a*) a male milliner; (*b*) *arch.* a man who busies himself with trifling occupations. **man-mountain** an enormously large person; now *esp.* a large wrestler. **man of action** a man whose life is characterized by physical activity or deeds rather than by thoughts and ideas. **man-of-all-work** a male servant who does all kinds of domestic work. **man of blood** *arch.* [a Hebraism] a man who has been responsible for murder or death. **man of destiny** a man looked upon as an instrument of destiny; *spec.* Napoleon I. **man of distinction** a man distinguished in looks, manners, and bearing. *man of fortune*: see FORTUNE *n.* *man of his hands*: see HAND *n.* **man of God** a man devoted to the service of God, a saint, an ecclesiastic. *man of ideas*: see IDEA *n* **man of law** *arch.* a lawyer. *man of leisure*: see LEISURE *n.* *man of letters*: see LETTER *n.*[1] **man of men** a man of supreme excellence. *man of* SCIENCE. **man of sense** a sagacious or sensible man. *man of straw*: see STRAW *n.* **man of the cloth** a clergyman, an ecclesiastic. **man of the house** the chief male of a household. **man of the match** the player adjudged to have played best in a particular game of football, cricket, etc. **man of the people** a man who comes from or identifies himself with ordinary people; a working-class man. **man of the world** (*a*) a secular person; a worldly or irreligious person; (*b*) a man experienced in the ways of the world and prepared to accept its conventions, a practical tolerant man with experience of life and society. **man-of-the-worldish, man-of-the-worldly** *adjs.* pertaining to or characteristic of a man of the world. *man of virtu*: see VIRTU *n.* 1. *man of wax*: see WAX *n.*[1] **man orchid** a rare British orchid of chalk grassland, *Aceras anthropophorum*, the labellum of which resembles a dangling greenish-yellow human figure. **manpack** a compact package containing equipment or supplies, designed to be carried easily by one man. **manqueller** (long *arch.*) a murderer. **man-rate** *v.t.* make (a rocket, spaceship, etc.) suitable for manned flight; certify as safe for manned flight. **man-rem** a unit of radiation exposure equal to one rem incident on one person. **man-riding** the vehicular transport of miners underground. **man-rope** *Naut.* a rope on the side of a gangway or ladder, held in ascending and descending a ship's side, etc. **man's best friend** *spec.* the dog. *man's estate*: see ESTATE *n.* 1b. **man-shift** (the amount of work done in) a single shift worked by one man. **man-size(d)** *adjs.* of the size of a man; large, full-size; large enough to occupy, suit, or satisfy a man. **manslayer** *arch.* a murderer; occas., a manslaughterer. **manslaying** *arch.* murder. **man's man** a man who is popular with or who prefers the company of other men. **man-sty** [after *pig-sty*] a dwelling-house or hut used for but unfit for human habitation. **man's woman** a woman who is popular with or who prefers the company of men. **man-tailored** *a.* (of a woman's garment) tailored after the fashion of a man's garment. **man-tiger** (*a*) a man resembling a tiger in ferocity; (*b*) a person believed to transform into a tiger. **man to man, man-to-man** *a.* & *adv.* (*a*) straight-forward(ly), frank(ly); (*b*) *attrib.* designating a type of defensive strategy in a team ball game in which each player is responsible for marking one member of the opposing team. **man-trade** the slave-trade. **mantrap** *n.* & *v.* (*a*) *n.* a trap for catching people, esp. trespassers; (*b*) *v.t.* beset with a mantrap or mantraps. **manway** a small passage used by miners etc. **man-week** a week of work etc. by one person, as a unit of measure. **man-woman** (*a*) a hermaphrodite; (*b*) a mannish woman. **man-year** a year of work etc. by one person, as a unit of measure. **menfolk(s)** men in general, the men of a family or in a company. **menkind** (now *rare*) men in general. **men-only** *a.* restricted for the use of men. **Men's Liberation, Men's Lib.** (a movement aimed at) the freeing of men from traditional views of their character and role in society. **men's room** a lavatory for males. **men's wear, menswear** clothes for men. **my (good) man**: used as a patronizing form of address. *new man*: see NEW *a.* OLD MAN. **one's man** the person who can fulfil one's requirements or with whom one can deal; *spec.* one's representative or envoy *in* a particular place. **play the man** act in a manly fashion, not show fear. **rights of man** human rights. **separate** or **sort out the men from the boys** *colloq.* distinguish which people in a group are truly mature, manly, or competent. *strong man*: see STRONG *a.* **the man** (*a*) the person in his human (as distinguished from his professional, etc.) capacity or character; (*b*) (also *the Man*) a person in authority; such persons collectively; a prison governor; a policeman, a detective; the police; one's employer or boss; *Black slang* a White man; White people collectively; *US slang* a drug-pusher; (*c*) (also *the very man*) the man most suitable *for* some office, work, or need; the kind of man qualified or likely *to do* something. **the man for me,** (*colloq.*) **for my money** the man whom I should choose to employ or support. **the man in the boat** *slang* the clitoris. **the man in the moon** the semblance of a human face seen in the full moon (also as the type of an imaginary person). **the man in** (or *US* **on**) **the street** the ordinary person, esp. as opp. to an expert. *the man on the* CLAPHAM *omnibus*. **the man who** he who, the person who. **the man X** the man previously known or mentioned as bearing the specified name. **the men's** the men's lavatory. **to a man** without exception. *utility man*: see UTILITY *a.* *waiting-man*: see WAITING *ppl a.* 1. *White man*: see WHITE *a.* *write oneself man*: see WRITE *v.* *yesterday's man*: see YESTERDAY *n.* *young man*: see YOUNG *a.*

manness /-n-n-/ *n.* (*rare*) †(*a*) human nature; (*b*) maleness: ME. **manward** *adv.* & *a.* (*a*) *adv.* [orig. †*to manward*] towards man, in the direction of man; in relation to man; (*b*) *adj.* tending or directed towards man: LME. **manwise** *adv.* & *pred. a.* in the fashion or way of men; in respect of a man; concerning individual men: E20.

man /man/ *v.t.* Infl. **-nn-**. [Late OE (*ġe*)*mannian*, w. corresp. forms in other Gmc langs., f. as the n.] **I 1** Act as or provide the person(s) required to serve or defend (a fort, ship, etc.), be ready for action at or in (a particular position or place), undertake (an industrial enterprise, etc.), fulfil the function or work of (a job etc.). LOE. †**b** Equip and send (a boat, occas. an army) *out*, *forth*, *after*, etc. L15–L18. †**2 a** Supply with inhabitants; people. LME–L16. †**b** Fill up with men. *rare* (Spenser). Only in L16. †**3 a** Provide with followers or attendants; escort (a person, esp. a woman). LME–M18. **b** Provide (a horse) with a rider. M16–M17.

1 J. CONRAD The ship of which I knew nothing, manned by men of whom I knew very little. J. K. GALBRAITH The greatest industrial enterprises . . were manned principally by men who could speak no English. D. M. FRAME Well fortified and manned, the town held out stoutly. *Country Quest* A cousin of mine volunteered to man a machine-gun post. **man up** provide with the full complement of people, esp. workers, required.

II 4 †**a** *refl.* Put on a show of manliness. Only in ME. **b** Make (esp. oneself) manly or courageous; brace (oneself or another) *up*; fortify the spirits or courage of (esp. oneself). E17. **5** Be the master of; manage, rule. *obs.* exc. *dial.* ME. **6** Invest with manly qualities or appearance; make manlike or (formerly, of God) into a man. Now *rare.* L16.

III 7 Accustom (a hawk or other bird) to human presence or handling; *gen.* make tame or tractable. L16.

¶ Orig. military & nautical.

manned *ppl a.* that has been manned; now *esp.* designating or pertaining to aviation or space travel with a human crew: E17.

mana /ˈmɑːnə/ *n.*[1] M19. [Maori.] Power, authority, prestige (chiefly *NZ*); *Anthropol.* an impersonal supernatural power which can be associated with people or with objects and which can be transmitted or inherited.

†**mana** *n.*[2] var. of MAUND *n.*[2]

manacle /ˈmanək(ə)l/ *n.* & *v.* ME. [(O)Fr. *manicle* handcuff, (as in mod.Fr.) gauntlet f. L *manicula* dim. of *manus* hand.] **A** *n.* **1** A fetter for the hand; a handcuff; *fig.* a bond, a restraint. Usu. in *pl.* ME. †**2** A tether or shackle for a horse. M16–E17. **B** *v.t.* Fetter or confine (the hands); fetter with handcuffs; *fig.* bind, restrain. ME.

manage /ˈmanɪdʒ/ *n. arch.* L16. [It. *maneggio* (whence Fr. MANÈGE), f. as next.] **1 a** = MANÈGE 2. L16. **b** = MANÈGE 1. M17. †**2** The action or manner of managing; management. L16–M18. **3** The skilful handling *of* (a weapon etc.). E17.

manage /ˈmanɪdʒ/ *v.* M16. [It. *maneggiare* f. Proto-Romance, f. L *manus* hand.] **I** *v.t.* **1** Handle, train, or direct (a horse) in its paces; put through the exercises of the manège. *obs.* exc. as passing into sense 4. M16. **2** Handle, wield, make use of (a weapon, tool, implement, etc.); control the sailing of (a ship or boat). L16. 3 Conduct or carry on (a war, a business, an undertaking, an operation); control the course of (affairs) by one's own action; control and direct the affairs of (a household, institution, State, etc.); be the manager of (a team etc.); take charge of, attend to (cattle, etc.). L16. b Work out in literary treatment. L17. 4 Cause to submit to one's rule or direction (a person, animal, etc.). L16. 5 Administer, regulate the use or expenditure of (finances, provisions, etc.); (now *rare*) deal with or treat carefully, use sparingly or with judgement, husband (one's health, life, money, etc.). L16. †b Treat with indulgence or consideration. Only in E18. 6 Control the use or exploitation of (land etc.); manipulate for a purpose. Formerly also, till. M17. 7 Bring (a person) to consent to one's wishes by artifice, flattery, or judicious suggestion of motives. L17. 8 Bring about by contrivance; succeed in accomplishing or acquiring; find a way *to do*; (freq. *iron.*) be so unskilful or unlucky as *to do*. E18. 9 With *can* or *be able*: cope with the difficulties of; succeed in using, dealing with, etc. E19.

2 R. L. STEVENSON He carried a crutch, which he managed with wonderful dexterity. G. A. BIRMINGHAM Like a man who might make a wreck of a boat through incapacity to manage her. 3 D. LESSING The liquor shop that Mr and Mrs Danderlea had been managing for . . twenty years. *Economist* Fulham are managed by an elderly asthmatic who foresaw football's slump. *Washington Post* The saxophonist's career has been managed by his wife. T. BENN If we are to have a managed economy . . 'In whose interests is it to be managed?'. H. R. LANDON As Grand Duke of Tuscany he had managed his Duchy wisely. b DRYDEN How a tragedy should be contrived and managed, in better verse . . than I could teach others. 4 G. STEIN This daughter who was always a hard child to manage. 6 *Bird Watching* Heather moorlands, still managed for grouse shooting. 7 GEO. ELIOT Managing one's husband is some pleasure. 8 G. VIDAL I was miserable, wondering in what I had managed to offend him. D. ATHILL I struggled to get the sails up, but I managed it. G. HARRIS Huddled in the narrow aisle, Gidjabolgo and Gwerath did manage a little sleep. 9 C. LAMB I had more time on my hands than I could ever manage.

II *v.i.* †10 Of a horse: perform the exercises of the manège. L16–E18. 11 Conduct affairs; act as a manager. Formerly also, plot, scheme, intrigue. E17. 12 Succeed (under disadvantages) in one's aim; cope with one's life or situation; contrive to get on *with* (esp. what is hardly adequate). *colloq.* M19.

11 F. NIGHTINGALE As impossible in a book to teach a person . . how to manage, as . . to teach her how to nurse. 12 A. CARNEGIE I have a good . . wife who manages well. We . . buy our supplies wholesale . . and save one third. G. CLARE She walked slowly and always used a stick, but she managed quite well. R. DAHL They simply amputated . . and . . my father had to manage with one arm.

mana'gee *n.* (*rare*) the person who is managed (correl. to *manager*) M19.

manageable /ˈmanɪdʒəb(ə)l/ *a.* L16. [f. prec. + -ABLE.] That can be managed; amenable to control or guidance, tractable; admitting of being wielded, manipulated, or administered, workable; able to be accomplished by contrivance.

managea'bility *n.* L18. **manageableness** *n.* M17. **manageably** *adv.* M19.

managed /ˈmanɪdʒd/ *ppl a.* L16. [f. as prec. + -ED[1].] 1 Trained to the manège. *arch.* L16. 2 Controlled, conducted, administered. E17. 3 Of demeanour, expressions, etc.: nicely restrained, measured. Now *rare*. L18.

2 *well-managed, ill-managed,* etc. **managed currency** a currency system which is not tied to the gold standard but is regulated by the government of the country concerned. **managed economy** an economy in which the framework and general policies are regulated or controlled by the government.

management /ˈmanɪdʒm(ə)nt/ *n.* L16. [f. as prec. + -MENT.] 1 The action of managing; the manner of managing; the application of skill or care in the manipulation, use, treatment, or control of things or persons, or in the conduct of an enterprise, operation, etc.; the administration of (a group within) an organization or commercial enterprise; *Med.* the technique of treating all the manifestations of a disease etc. L16. †b An instance of managing; an administrative act. Only in 17. 2 The use of contrivance, prudence, ingenuity, or (esp.) deceit or trickery for effecting some purpose. M17. †b A contrivance, a device; a piece of trickery. Only in M18. †3 A negotiation. Only in E18. †4 Indulgence or consideration shown towards a person; politic moderation in the conduct of a case; an instance of this. E18–E19. 5 *collect.* A governing body of an organization or business, as a board of directors; that group of employees administering and controlling an organization, business, etc., the group or class of managers. M18.

1 LD MACAULAY In the management of the heroic couplet Dryden has never been equalled. W. S. MAUGHAM She had never been used to the management of money. H. I. ANSOFF Management of a business firm is a very large complex of activities. J. ARGENTI Management by Exception . . , 'don't tell someone if everything is O.K.—only . . if something has gone wrong'. N. SEDAKA Leba began to help with the management of my career. 2 B. JOWETT We rely not upon management or trickery, but upon our own hearts and hands. 5 J. PLAMENATZ Powerful workers' organizations make demands that neither managements nor governments can ignore. *Broadcast* Management decided it could not afford to replace him. *middle management*: see MIDDLE *a.*

manage'mental *a.* L19.

manager /ˈmanɪdʒə/ *n.* L16. [f. as prec. + -ER[1].] 1 A person who manages something. Now *rare* in *gen.* sense. L16. 2 Any of several members of either House of Parliament appointed for the performance of some specified duty connected with the functions of the two Houses. M17. 3 A person skilled in managing household affairs, money, etc. Chiefly w. qualifying adj. as *good, poor,* etc. L17. 4 A person whose office it is to manage an organization, business establishment, or public institution, or part of one; a person with a primarily executive or supervisory function within an organization etc.; a person controlling the activities of a person or team in sports, entertainment, etc. E18. 5 *Law.* A person appointed, ordinarily by a Court of Chancery, to control and account for a business for the benefit of creditors etc. L18.

4 *bank manager, factory manager, floor manager, football manager, hotel manager, personnel manager, stage-manager, team manager, theatre manager,* etc. *middle manager*: see MIDDLE *a.*

managership *n.* the office or position of a manager; managerial control; (a) management: E19.

manageress /ˌmanɪdʒəˈrɛs, ˈmanɪdʒərɪs/ *n.* L18. [f. prec. + -ESS[1].] A woman manager; *esp.* a woman who has charge of a shop, hotel, canteen, etc.

managerial /manɪˈdʒɪərɪəl/ *a.* M18. [f. as prec. + -IAL.] Of, pertaining to, or characteristic of a manager, esp. a professional manager of or within an organization, business, establishment, etc.

managerialism *n.* (belief in) the use of professional managers in conducting or planning business or other enterprises M20. **managerialist** *n.* & *a.* (*a*) *n.* an adherent of managerialism; (*b*) *adj.* of or pertaining to managerialists or managerialism: M20. **managerially** *adv.* in the manner or capacity of a manager, in relation to a manager L19.

†**managery** *n.* L16. [f. MANAGE *n.*, *v.* + -ERY, infl. by Fr. *ménagerie.*] 1 Management; administration; economy. L16–M18. 2 = MANÈGE. L17–L18.

managing /ˈmanɪdʒɪŋ/ *ppl a.* E18. [f. MANAGE *v.* + -ING[2].] That manages; *spec.* (*a*) having executive control or authority; (*b*) fond of scheming or assuming the direction of affairs; (*c*) *arch.* skilful and diligent in management, economical.

managing director, managing editor, etc.

manaia /məˈnʌɪə/ *n.* L19. [Maori.] A motif in Maori carving with a birdlike head and a human body.

manakin /ˈmanəkɪn/ *n.* E17. [Var. of MANIKIN *n.*] 1 = MANIKIN *n.* 1, 2. *rare.* E17. 2 Any of various small fruit-eating passerine birds of the tropical American family Pipridae, the males of which are brightly coloured and have complex courtship displays. Cf. MANIKIN *n.* 3. M18.

mañana /maˈɲana, manˈjɑːnə/ *adv.* & *n.* M19. [Sp. = morning, tomorrow (in this sense f. OSp. *cras mañana* lit. 'tomorrow early') ult. f. L *mane* in the morning.] Tomorrow, (on) the day after today; (in) the indefinite future (from the supposed easy-going procrastination of Spain and Spanish-speaking countries).

mananosay /manəˈnəʊseɪ/ *n. US.* Also **mananose** /ˈmanənəʊz/ & other vars. E18. [Prob. f. an eastern Algonquian lang.] The soft-shelled clam, *Mya arenaria.*

manatee /ˈmanətiː/ *n.* Also **-ti.** M16. [Sp. *manatí* f. Carib *manáti.*] A sirenian mammal; *spec.* any of several tropical sirenians of the genus *Trichechus*, inhabiting Atlantic coasts and adjacent rivers.

Comb.: **manatee-grass** *W. Indies* a flowering plant, *Cymodocea manatorum* (family Cymodoceaceae), which grows submerged in the sea.

†**manation** *n. rare.* LME–E19. [L *manatio(n-),* f. *manat-* pa. ppl stem of *manare* flow: see -ATION.] A flowing out.

manavilins /məˈnavɪlɪnz/ *n.pl. slang.* Now *rare.* Also **manavlins** /məˈnavlɪnz/. M19. [Origin unkn.] Small matters, odds and ends; extra articles.

mancala /manˈkɑːlə/ *n.* M19. [Colloq. Arab. *mankala*, f. *nakala* remove, take away.] A board game for two players, originally Arabic but now common throughout Africa and Asia, played on a special board with rows of holes or hollows, and having as its object the capture of the opponent's pieces.

mancando /manˈkando, manˈkandəʊ/ *a.* & *adv.* E19. [It. = lacking, failing.] *Mus.* (A direction:) becoming even softer, dying away.

Manchegan /manˈtʃeɪg(ə)n/ *a.* & *n.* M19. [f. Sp. *manchego, -ga*, f. *La Mancha* (see below): see -AN.] (A native or inhabitant) of La Mancha, a region (formerly a province) of central Spain.

Manchester /ˈmantʃɪstə/ *n.* M16. [A large city in (Lancashire) NW England, historically the chief centre of cotton manufacture.] Used *attrib.* to designate things from or associated with Manchester, esp. cotton goods.

Manchester cotton: see COTTON *n.*[2] **Manchester goods** cotton textiles. **Manchester School** *Hist.* a body of politicians (meeting in Manchester) who advocated the principles of free trade and laissez-faire in the mid 19th cent. **Manchester terrier** (a dog of) a breed of small, short-coated, black and tan terrier. **Manchester warehouse** *arch.* a warehouse for cotton textiles. **Manchester warehouseman** *arch.* a storer of cotton textiles. **Manchester wares** = *Manchester goods* above.

Manchesterian /mantʃɪˈstɪərɪən/ *a.* & *n.* = MANCUNIAN L18. **Manchesterism** *n.* (*Hist.*) the principles advocated by or attributed to the Manchester School L19. **Manchesteri'zation** *n.* the action or process of Manchesterizing M20. **Manchesterize** *v.t.* make representative or typical of Manchester E20.

manchet /ˈmantʃɪt/ *n.* LME. [Perh. f. elem. of AN *pain demeine, demaine,* med.L *panus dominicus* lit. 'lord's bread' + CHEAT *n.*[2]] 1 (A small loaf or roll of) the finest kind of wheaten bread. *obs.* exc. *dial.* & *Hist.* LME. 2 *Her.* A small circular loaf or manchet used as a charge. M17.

manchette /mɑ̃ʃɛt/ *n.* Pl. pronounced same. M19. [Fr., dim. of *manche*: see MAUNCH, -ETTE.] *Hist.* A kind of trimming worn round the lower part of the sleeve of a woman's dress.

manchineel /man(t)ʃɪˈniːl/ *n.* M17. [Fr. *mancenille* f. Sp. *manzanilla* dim. of *manzana* apple, alt. form of OSp. *mazana* f. L *matiana* (neut. pl., sc. *poma, mala*) a kind of apple.] 1 A poisonous W. Indian tree, *Hippomane mancinella*, of the spurge family, with a highly caustic latex and an acrid fruit. Also *manchineel tree.* M17. 2a The wood of this tree. L17. b Poison from this tree. L19.

Manchu /man'tʃu:/ *n.* & *a.* L17. [Manchu = pure.] A *n.* 1 A member or descendant of a non-Chinese people of Manchuria, who conquered China and formed the last imperial dynasty (1644–1912). L17. 2 The language of the Manchus, a member of the Tungusic group in the Altaic language family. E19. B *attrib.* or as *adj.* Of or pertaining to the Manchus or their language. M18.

Comb.: **Manchu-Tungus** *n.* & *a.* (of) the language family comprising Manchu and Tungus.

Manchurian /man'tʃʊərɪən/ *a.* E18. [f. *Manchuria* (see below) + -AN.] Of or pertaining to Manchuria, a region forming the north-eastern portion of China (formerly a separate country).

Manchurian crane a crane of eastern Asia, *Grus japonensis*, black and white with a red crown. **Manchurian tiger** the Siberian tiger.

mancia /'mantʃə/ *n.* M20. [It.] A gratuity, a tip.

mancipable /'mansɪpəb(ə)l/ *a. rare.* L19. [f. MANCIPATE + -ABLE.] *Rom. Law.* That may be conveyed or transferred by mancipation.

mancipate /'mansɪpeɪt/ *v.t.* Pa. pple & ppl a. **-ated**, (earlier) †**-ate**. L15. [L *mancipat-* pa. ppl stem of *mancipare*, f. *manceps* purchaser, f. *manus* hand + base of *capere* take: see -ATE[3].] †1 Make subject, enslave (*lit.* & *fig.*). Chiefly foll. by *to*, *unto*. L15–E19. 2 *Rom. Law.* Convey or transfer by the formality of mancipation. M17. †3 Devote or consecrate *to*. E18–E19.

mancipation /mansɪ'peɪʃ(ə)n/ *n.* L16. [L *mancipatio(n-)*, f. as prec.: see -ATION.] 1 The action of enslaving; the state of being enslaved. L16. 2 *Rom. Law.* A ceremonial process by which certain kinds of property were transferred, children emancipated, etc. M17.

mancipatory /'mansɪpət(ə)ri/ *a. rare.* M19. [f. MANCIPATE + -ORY[2].] *Rom. Law.* Pertaining to or involving mancipation.

manciple /'mansɪp(ə)l/ *n.* ME. [AN & OFr. var. of *mancipe* f. L *mancipium* purchase, slave, f. *manceps*: see MANCIPATE.] 1 An officer or servant responsible for purchasing provisions for a college, an Inn of Court, a monastery, etc. ME. †2 A bondslave, a servant. LME–L16.

Mancunian /maŋ'kju:nɪən/ *n.* & *a.* E20. [f. L *Mancunium* Manchester + -AN.] (A native or inhabitant) of the city of Manchester in NW England.

mancus /'maŋkəs/ *n. obs.* exc. *Hist.* [OE *mancus* = OS *mancus*, OHG (accus. pl.) *manchussa* f. med.L *mancusus* f. Arab. *mankūš* use as n. (sc. *dīnār* DINAR) of pass. pple of *nakaša* engrave, inscribe.] An Anglo-Saxon monetary unit of the value of thirty pence.

-mancy /mansi/ *suff.* [Repr. OFr. *-mancie*, late L *-mantia*, Gk *manteia* divination, f. *manteuesthai* prophesy, f. *mantis* prophet, diviner: see -CY.] Forming ns. w. the sense 'divination by', as *chiromancy*, *geomancy*, *hydromancy*, *necromancy*, etc.

Mandaean /man'di:ən/ *a.* & *n.* Also **-dean**. L18. [f. Mandaean Aram. *mandaia*, f. *manda* knowledge, + -AN.] A *adj.* Designating or pertaining to a Mesopotamian Gnostic sect (now Iraqi) regarding St John the Baptist as the Messiah, or the Aramaic dialect in which the sect's sacred books are written. L18. B *n.* A member of the Mandaean sect; the Aramaic dialect of the Mandaean sect. L19.

Also **Mandaite** /'mandeɪʌɪt/ *a.* & *n.* L19.

mandala /'mandələ, 'mʌn-/ *n.* M19. [Skt *mándala* disc, circle.] A symbolic circular figure, usu. with symmetrical divisions and figures of deities, etc., in the centre, used in Buddhism and other religions as a representation of the universe; *Jungian Psychol.* an archetype of a similar circle, held to symbolize a striving for unity of self and completeness.

mandamus /man'deɪməs/ *n.* & *v.* M16. [L = we command.] *Law.* A *n.* Orig., any of a number of writs, mandates, etc., issued by the monarch, directing the performance of a certain act. Later, a judicial writ or order issued in the name of the Crown or the government directing an inferior court, a corporation, an officer, etc., to perform a public or statutory duty. M16. B *v.t.* Serve with a mandamus. E19.

Mandan /'mand(ə)n/ *a.* & *n.* L18. [N. Amer. Fr. *Mandane*, prob. f. Dakota Sioux *mawátāna*.] A *adj.* Designating or pertaining to a Sioux Indian people of North Dakota. L18. B *n.* Pl. **-s**, same. A member of this people; the Siouan language of this people. E19.

mandant /'mand(ə)nt/ *a.* & *n.* M16. [L *mandant-* pres. ppl stem of *mandare*: see MANDATE *n.*, -ANT[1].] †A *adj. Physiol.* Of an organ, esp. the brain: that is the source of impulse. M16–L17. B *n. Law.* = MANDATOR. L17.

mandarin /'mand(ə)rɪn/ *n.*[1] & *a.* Also †**-ine**; (esp. in sense A.2) **M-**. L16. [Port. *mandarim* alt. of Malay *menteri* f. Skt *mantrī*, *mantrin* counsellor, minister. Cf. MANTRI, MENTRI.] A *n.* 1 a *Hist.* A member of each of the nine grades of Chinese officials under the Empire, selected by examination. Formerly also, any of various other Asian officials. L16. b A toy figure in Chinese costume, so contrived as to continue nodding for a long time after being shaken. L18. c A person of much importance; *esp.* a leading government official or politician, a reactionary or secretive bureaucrat. E20. 2 (**M-**.) The form of the Chinese language formerly used by officials and educated people generally; any of the varieties of this used as a standard language in China, *spec.* the northern variety. E18. b Obscure or esoteric language. M20. 3 *ellipt.* = *mandarin duck* below. M19.

1c *Mail on Sunday* Civil servants dropping into private . . jobs with salaries . . three times what they earned as Whitehall mandarins.

B *attrib.* or as *adj.* 1 Of or pertaining to mandarins or a Mandarin. E17. 2 Esoteric, consciously superior, (of style) affectedly ornate or complex. E20.

1 P. GOODMAN A mandarin bureaucracy is valuable . . because of the vastness of the underlying population. 2 *Listener* The conventionally acceptable accents and Mandarin prose we learn at school.

Special collocations & comb.: **mandarin coat** a loose silk coat with a mandarin collar. **mandarin collar** a narrow collar standing up from a close-fitting neckline and not quite meeting in front. **mandarin duck** a duck with bright and variegated plumage, *Aix galericulata*, native to eastern Asia and naturalized in Britain. **mandarin jacket**: with a mandarin collar. **mandarin porcelain** oriental (esp. Japanese) porcelain decorated with figures of mandarins. **mandarin sleeve** a wide loose sleeve. **mandarin vase** a vase of mandarin porcelain.

mandarinism *n.* (*a*) the mandarin system, government by mandarins; (*b*) (an example of) pedantry, highbrow or esoteric study: M19. **mandarinship** *n.* the position, office, or rank of a mandarin L17.

mandarin /'mand(ə)rɪn/ *n.*[2] Also **-ine** /-i:n/. L18. [Fr. *mandarine* (sc. *orange*: cf. Sp. *naranja mandarina*) fem. of *mandarin*, prob. f. as prec. after the yellow of mandarins' costume.] 1 More fully *mandarin orange*. A citrus fruit resembling a small flattened orange, but with sweet pulp and easily detached peel; *esp.* one with yellow or pale orange peel. Also, the tree bearing this fruit, *Citrus reticulata*, widely grown in subtropical regions. Cf. SATSUMA, TANGERINE. L18. 2 An orange colour. Also *mandarin-orange*. L19. 3 A mandarin-flavoured liqueur. L19.

mandarinate /'mand(ə)rɪneɪt/ *n.* E18. [f. MANDARIN *n.*[1] + -ATE[1].] The position or office of a mandarin; the body of mandarins, mandarins collectively; government by mandarins.

F. FITZGERALD Their aristocracy sent its sons to compete for the mandarinate in the regional examinations. *Citizen* (*Ottawa*) The upper mandarinate where access to such information ahead of the rest of the world is a status symbol.

†**mandarine** *n.*[1] & *a.* var. of MANDARIN *n.*[1] & *a.*

mandarine *n.*[2] var. of MANDARIN *n.*[2]

mandat /mɑ̃da (*pl. same*), 'mandat/ *n.* M19. [Fr. f. as MANDATE *n.*] 1 *Hist.* A paper money issued by the revolutionary government of France from 1796 to 1797. Cf. ASSIGNAT. M19. 2 In France, a money order. L19.

mandatary /'mandət(ə)ri/ *n.* LME. [L *mandatarius*, f. as next: see -ARY[1].] 1 Chiefly *Law.* A person to whom a mandate is given; *Hist.* a State receiving a mandate from the League of Nations. LME. †2 A person appointed to a benefice by a papal mandate. E17–E18.

mandate /'mandeɪt/ *n.* E16. [L *mandatum* use as n. of neut. pa. pple of *mandare* command, send out, enjoin, commit, f. *manus* hand + base of *dare* give: see -ATE[1].] 1 *gen.* A command, an order, an injunction. Now *literary.* E16. 2 a A judicial or legal command from a superior to an inferior; in early English law, a command of the monarch to a court relating to a private suit; in US law, a document conveying a decision of a court of appeal to a court below for the enactment of judgement. E16. b A papal rescript, esp. with reference to preferment to a benefice. E17. c *Hist.* A command from the monarch to elect a fellow of a college or to confer a degree. E17. †d A pastoral letter. M18–E19. 3 a *Sc. Law.* A contract by which a person undertakes to act gratuitously for another. L17. b *Rom. Law.* A commission by which one person (the mandator) requests another (the mandatary) to perform gratuitously some service, undertaking to indemnify the mandatary for expenses. M18. c A contract of bailment by which a mandatary undertakes to perform gratuitously some service in respect of a thing committed to his or her keeping by the mandator. L18. 4 a The commission as to policy supposed to be given by the electors to their elected representatives; support for a policy or measure regarded by a victorious party, candidate, etc., as derived from the wishes of the people in an election; *gen.* a commission. L18. b *Hist.* A commission issued by the League of Nations (1919–1946) authorizing a selected power to administer, control, and develop a territory for a specified purpose; the territory so allocated. E20.

4a *Tucson Magazine* It's all right to screw the people as long as you were given a large mandate in the previous election. **doctor's mandate** a mandate from the people empowering the government to take extreme measures in the national interest.

mandate /man'deɪt/ *v.t.* E17. [L *mandat-* pa. ppl stem of *mandare*: see prec., -ATE[3].] 1 Command, require by mandate; necessitate. Now chiefly *US* (*rare* bef. L20). E17. 2 Commit (one's sermon) to memory. *Sc.* E18. 3 *Hist.* Assign (territory) under a mandate of the League of Nations. E20. 4 Give a mandate to, delegate authority to (a representative, group, organization, etc.). Freq. as *mandated* ppl a. M20.

mandative /'mandətɪv/ *a.* M17. [Late L *mandativus*, f. as prec.: see -IVE.] Of or pertaining to command; *Gram.* imperative.

mandator /man'deɪtə/ *n.* L17. [L, f. as MANDATE *v.*: see -OR.] Chiefly *Law.* A person who gives a mandate.

mandatory /'mandət(ə)ri/ *a.* & *n.* L15. [Late L *mandatorius* (adj.), f. as MANDATE *v.*: see -ORY[2]. As n. f. med.L: see -ORY[1].] A *adj.* 1 Of the nature of, pertaining to, or conveying a command or mandate. L15. 2 Of an action: obligatory in consequence of a command, compulsory. (Foll. by *upon*.) E19. 3 *Hist.* Designating a power or State in receipt of a mandate from the League of Nations, or the system of rule by mandate. E20. B *n.* 1 A person to whom a mandate is given; = MANDATARY. M17. 2 *Hist.* A power or State in receipt of a mandate from the League of Nations to administer and develop a territory. E20.

Mande /'mɑ:ndeɪ/ *n.* & *a.* L19. [Mande.] A *n.* Pl. **-s**, same. 1 A member of a large group of peoples of W. Africa. L19. 2 The group of Niger-Congo languages of these peoples. L19. B *attrib.* or as *adj.* Of or pertaining to these peoples or their group of languages. L19.

¶Also called *Mandingo*.

Mandean *a.* & *n.* var. of MANDAEAN.

Mandelbrot set /ˈmand(ə)lbrɒt sɛt/ *n. phr.* L20. [Benoit B. *Mandelbrot* (b. 1924), Polish-born US mathematician.] *Math.* The set of all complex numbers c such that under repeated application of the mapping $z \rightarrow z^2 + c$ any complex variable z converges to some finite value.

mandelic /manˈdɛlɪk/ *a.* M19. [f. G *Mandel* almond + -IC.] Chem. *mandelic acid*, a colourless crystalline acid, $C_6H_5CH(OH)COOH$, obtainable from amygdalin and used to treat bacterial infection; α-phenylhydroxyacetic acid.
mandeloˈnitrile *n.* a yellow oily liquid which is the nitrile of mandelic acid and of which amygdalin is a glycoside L19.

Mandevilla /mandəˈvɪlə/ *n.* M19. [mod.L (see below), f. John Henry *Mandeville* (1773–1861), Brit. minister in Buenos Aires.] Any of various woody climbing plants of the S. American genus *Mandevilla* (family Apocynaceae), with fragrant white, pink, or red flowers, grown for ornament esp. in tropical and subtropical regions; *esp.* Chilean jasmine, *M. laxa*.

mandible /ˈmandɪb(ə)l/ *n.* Also in L form **mandibula** /manˈdɪbjʊlə/, pl. **-lae** /-liː/. LME. [OFr., or directly f. late L *mandibula*, f. *mandere* chew.] Now only *Anat.* & *Zool.* 1 A jaw, a jawbone; *esp.* the lower jaw or jawbone in mammals and fishes. LME. 2 In birds, either of the two parts, upper and lower, of the beak. L17. 3 In insects and other arthropods, either of the appendages forming the main or anterior mouthparts. Also, in other invertebrates, any of various parts functioning as or resembling jaws. E19.
¶Cf. MAXILLA.

mandibular /manˈdɪbjʊlə/ *a.* M17. [f. L *mandibula*: see prec., -AR[1].] *Anat.* & *Zool.* Belonging to, connected with, or forming part of a mandible.
Also **mandibulary** *a.* (*rare*) M17.

mandibulate /manˈdɪbjʊleɪt/ *a.* E19. [f. as prec.: see -ATE[2].] *Zool.* 1 Esp. of an arthropod: having a mouth adapted for mastication (rather than for sucking), or provided with mandibles (rather than a haustillum or chelicerae). E19. 2 Of a mouth or mouthparts: adapted for mastication; formed as mandibles. M19.
mandibulated *a.* = MANDIBULATE *a.* I M19.

mandibulo- /manˈdɪbjʊləʊ/ *comb. form.* L19. [f. as prec.: see -O-.] Forming adjs. w. the sense 'pertaining to the mandible', as *mandibulo-hyoid*, *-maxillary*, etc.

mandil /ˈmandɪl/ *n.* Now *rare.* M17. [(Sp. f.) Arab. & Pers. *mandīl*, *mindīl* sash, turban, cloth, handkerchief, f. med.Gk *mantēlion* f. L *mantelium*, *mantelum*: see MANTLE *n.*] A turban.

mandilion /manˈdɪlɪən/ *n. obs.* exc. *Hist.* L16. [Fr. (obs.) dim. of *mandil* (now *mandille*), f. as prec.] A loose coat or cassock, in later times sleeveless, worn by soldiers and menservants as a kind of overcoat.

Manding /ˈmandɪŋ/ *n.* & *a.* M20. [Mande: cf. next.] A *n.* Pl. same. 1 The Mande language of the Malinke (also called *Malinke*, *Mandinka*). Also, a group of closely related and largely mutually intelligible Mande languages, including Malinke, widely spoken in W. Africa. M20. 2 *pl.* The speakers of any of these languages collectively. M20. B *attrib.* or as *adj.* Of or pertaining to Manding or its speakers. M20.

Mandingo /manˈdɪŋgəʊ/ *n.* & *a.* E17. [Mande: cf. prec.] A *n.* Pl. same, **-o(e)s**. 1 = MANDE *n.* I. E17. 2 = MANDE *n.* 2. M18. B *adj.* = MANDE *a.* L18.

Mandinka /mənˈdɪŋkə/ *n.* & *a.* Pl. of n. **-s**, same. M20. [Mande.] = MALINKE.

mandola /manˈdəʊlə/ *n.* Also **-dora** /-ˈdɔːrə/. E18. [It. Cf. MANDORE.] A large early form of mandolin.

mandolin /ˈmandəlɪn/ *n.* Also (the usual form in sense 2) **-ine**. E18. [Fr. *mandoline* f. It. *mandolino* dim. of MANDOLA: see -INE[1].] 1 A musical instrument of the lute kind having from four to six paired metal strings stretched on a deeply-rounded body, usu. played with a plectrum. E18. 2 A kitchen utensil fitted with cutting blades and used for slicing vegetables. M20.
mandolinist *n.* a performer on the mandolin L19.

mandor /ˈmandɔː/ *n.* L19. [Malay f. Port. *mandador* a person who gives orders.] A foreman or overseer in Malaysia or Indonesia.

mandora *n.* var. of MANDOLA.

mandore /manˈdɔː/ *n.* M17. [Fr. f. as MANDOLA.] = MANDOLA.

mandorla /manˈdɔːlə/ *n.* L19. [It. = almond.] An almond-shaped panel or decorative space in religious art.

mandragora /manˈdragərə/ *n.* Also Anglicized as **-dragore** /-drəˈgɔː/. OE. [((O)Fr. *mandragore* f.) med.L *mandragora*, cl.L *-as* f. Gk *mandragoras*, prob. of pre-Hellenic origin.] = MANDRAKE I (*arch.*). Now only (*Bot.*), any of the various plants of the genus *Mandragora*.
fig.: J. GALT Earnest employment is the best mandragora for an aching heart.

mandrake /ˈmandreɪk/ *n.* ME. [Prob. f. MDu. *mandrag(r)e* f. med.L MANDRAGORA, assoc. w. MAN *n.* (w. allus. to the shape of the root) and DRAKE *n.*[1]] 1 A poisonous and narcotic Mediterranean plant of the nightshade family, *Mandragora officinarum*, with a very short stem and solitary purple or whitish flowers, which was formerly credited with magical and medicinal properties because of the supposedly human shape of its forked fleshy root, and reputed to shriek when taken from the ground. ME. †b *fig.* Something or someone unpleasant or unwanted; something to be rooted up, a pestilential growth. E16–M17. 2 The may-apple, *Podophyllum peltatum*. *US.* E19.

Mandrax /ˈmandraks/ *n.* M20. [Origin unkn.] *Pharm.* (Proprietary name for) a sedative containing methaqualone and diphenhydramine hydrochloride; a tablet of this. Cf. MANDY.

mandrel /ˈmandr(ə)l/ *n.* Also **-dril** /-drɪl/. E16. [Origin unkn.] 1 A miner's pick. E16. 2 A shaft or spindle to which work is secured while being turned in a lathe; a cylindrical rod round which metal or other material is forged or shaped. M17.

mandrill /ˈmandrɪl/ *n.* M18. [App. f. MAN *n.* + DRILL *n.*[3]] †1 = CHIMPANZEE. Only in M18. 2 A large W. African forest baboon, *Mandrillus sphinx*, the adult of which has a bright red and blue face and blue buttocks. L18.

†mandritta *n.* L16–M19. [It. *mandritto* f. *mandritta* right hand.] *Fencing.* A cut from right to left.

manducable /ˈmandjʊkəb(ə)l/ *a. literary.* Now *rare.* E17. [Late L *manducabilis*, f. *manducare*: see next, -ABLE.] Edible; chewable.

manducate /ˈmandjʊkeɪt/ *v.t. literary.* E17. [L *manducat-* pa. ppl stem of *manducare* chew: see -ATE[3].] Chew, eat.

manducation /mandjʊˈkeɪʃ(ə)n/ *n. literary.* L15. [L *manducatio(n-)*, f. as prec.: see -ATION.] The action of eating or chewing; *spec.* participation in the Eucharist.

manducatory /ˈmandjʊkət(ə)ri/ *a.* E19. [f. as MANDUCATE: see -ORY[2].] Chiefly *Zool.* Pertaining to or concerned with eating or chewing.

mandy /ˈmandi/ *n. slang.* Also **M-**. L20. [Abbrev.] A tablet of the sedative Mandrax.

mane /meɪn/ *n.* [OE *manu* = OFris. *mana*, MDu. *mane* (Du. *manen* pl.), OHG *mana* (G *Mähne*), ON *mǫn*, f. Gmc.] 1 A growth of long hair on the back of the neck and the shoulders, characteristic of various animals, esp. the horse and lion. OE. 2 A person's long hair. LME. 3 A ridge or tuft of grass or stubble, left by mowers. Now *dial.* E16. †4 The hackles on the neck of a game cock. E17–E18.
maneless *a.* E19.

-mane /meɪn/ *suff.* [Fr. Cf. -MANIAC.] In or (occas.) after wds from Fr. in sense 'a person who has a mania for (something)', as *balletomane*, *bibliomane*, etc.

maneaba /maˈneɪəbə/ *n.* M20. [Micronesian.] In Kiribati and Tuvalu (formerly the Gilbert and Ellice Islands): a meeting-house.

maneb /ˈmanɛb/ *n.* M20. [f. MAN(GANESE + E(THYLENE + BIS-, elems. of systematic name (see below).] A cyclic organosulphur compound used as a fungicidal powder on vegetables and fruit; manganese ethylene bisdithiocarbamate, $C_4H_6MnN_2S_4$.

maned /meɪnd/ *a.* ME. [f. MANE + -ED[2].] Having a mane.
maned wolf a wild dog, *Chrysocyon brachyurus*, of S. American grasslands, resembling a shaggy long-legged fox.

manège /maˈneɪʒ/ *n.* Also **manege**. M17. [Fr. f. as MANAGE *n.*] 1 A riding-school. M17. 2 The movements in which a horse is trained in a riding-school; the art or practice of training and managing horses; horsemanship. L18.

maneh /ˈmɑːneɪ/ *n.* E17. [Heb. *māneh* prob. f. Babylonian or Akkadian (cf. MAUND *n.*[2]), whence also MINA *n.*[1]] *Antiq.* A Hebrew coin and weight of between 50 and 60 shekels.

manerial /məˈnɪərɪəl/ *a.* Now *rare.* M18. [med.L *manerialis*, f. *manerium* MANOR: see -AL[1].] = MANORIAL *a.*

manes /ˈmɑːneɪz, ˈmeɪniːz/ *n.* LME. [L.] 1 *pl.* The deified souls of dead ancestors (as beneficent spirits). LME. 2 *sing.* The spirit or shade of a dead person, considered as an object of reverence or as demanding to be propitiated. L17.

maness /ˈmanɛs/ *n. rare.* L16. [f. MAN *n.* + -ESS[1].] Woman as the feminine of man.

maneton /ˈmanɪt(ə)n/ *n.* E20. [Fr. = crankpin.] *Aeronaut.* In a rotary or radial engine, the detachable short end of the crankshaft.

Manetti /maˈnɛti/ *n.* M19. [Xavier *Manetti* (1723–84), It. botanist.] In full *Manetti rose*. A dwarf variety of rose much used as a stock.

maneuver *n.*, *v.* see MANOEUVRE *n.*, *v.*

maneuverable *a.* see MANOEUVRABLE.

manful /ˈmanfʊl, -f(ə)l/ *a.* LME. [f. MAN *n.* + -FUL.] Characterized by manly courage and resolution; brave, resolute.
manfully *adv.* LME. **manfulness** *n.* LME.

manga /ˈmaŋgə/ *n.*[1] E19. [Sp., lit. 'sleeve', f. L *manica*: see MAUNCH.] A Mexican and Spanish-American cloak or poncho.

†manga *n.*[2] var. of MANGO.

mangabey /ˈmaŋgəbeɪ/ *n.* L18. [A region in Madagascar (erroneously applied).] Any of several small long-tailed forest-dwelling monkeys of the genus *Cercocebus*, of central and west Africa.
sooty mangabey: see SOOTY *a.*

mangal /maŋˈgal/ *n.* E19. [Turk. f. Arab. *mankal*.] A kind of Turkish brazier.

mangan- /ˈmaŋg(ə)n/ *comb. form.* [G *Mangan* MANGANESE.] *Min.* Forming names of minerals or mineral varieties containing (a large amount of) manganese, as *manganbrucite*, *manganhedenbergite*, etc. Cf. MANGANO-.
manganˈapatite *n.* a fluorescent yellow variety of apatite containing up to 10.5 per cent manganese replacing calcium L19.

manganate /ˈmaŋgənət, -neɪt/ *n.* M19. [f. MANGANESE + -ATE[1].] *Chem.* A salt containing oxyanions of manganese; *spec.* a salt of the anion MnO_4^{2-}. Cf. PERMANGANATE.

†manganeous *a.* see MANGANOUS.

manganese /ˈmaŋgəniːz/ *n.* L17. [Fr. *manganèse* f. It. *manganese*, unexpl. alt. of med.L *magnesia*, *mangnesia* MAGNESIA.] 1 A black mineral substance consisting largely of the dioxide of manganese (sense 2), used from ancient times in glass-making, and now in many industrial processes. Also *black manganese*. L17. 2 A hard grey brittle chemical element, atomic no. 25, which is one of the transition metals and is used in steels and magnetic alloys. (Symbol Mn.) L18.
Comb. & phrases: *black manganese*: see sense I above; **grey manganese** = MANGANITE I; **manganese bronze** an alloy of copper and zinc with manganese; **manganese nodule** a small friable concretion of manganese and iron oxides, found on or in sediments on the ocean floor worldwide; **manganese-purple** = *manganese violet* below; **manganese spar** (*a*) = RHODONITE; (*b*) = RHODOCHROSITE; **manganese steel**

any of various hard steels containing manganese; **manganese violet** a purple manganese-containing phosphate pigment used in the decoration of ceramics.

manganesian /maŋgəˈniːzjən, -ʒ(ə)n/ *a.* (chiefly *Min.*) of or containing manganese L18.

†manganesium *n.* Also **-sum**. L18–L19. [f. MANGANESE + -IUM.] *Chem.* = MANGANESE 2.

mangani- /ˈmaŋgəni/ *comb. form.* [f. MANGANESE, MANGANIC: see -I-.] *Chem.* Forming names of compounds (chiefly cyanides) containing trivalent manganese. Cf. MANGANO- 2.

manganic /maŋˈganɪk/ *a.* M19. [f. MANGANESE + -IC.] *Chem.* Of or containing manganese in a higher valency. Cf. MANGANOUS.

manganic acid a (hypothetical) parent acid of manganates.

manganiferous /maŋgəˈnɪf(ə)rəs/ *a.* M19. [f. as prec. + -FEROUS.] *Geol.* & *Min.* Containing or yielding manganese.

manganin /ˈmaŋgənɪn/ *n.* E20. [f. as prec. + -IN¹.] *Metall.* (Proprietary name for) an alloy of copper, manganese, and nickel, used esp. in electrical apparatus.

manganite /ˈmaŋgənʌɪt/ *n.* E19. [f. as prec. + -ITE¹.] **1** *Min.* Basic manganese(II) oxide, MnO(OH), occurring massive or as grey or black striated prismatic crystals of the orthorhombic system. E19. **2** *Chem.* A salt of an oxyanion containing divalent manganese. Now *rare* or *obs.* M19.

mangaˈnitic *a.* containing manganite L19.

Manganja /mənˈgandʒə/ *n.* M19. [Bantu.] **A** *n.* Pl. same, **-s**. A member of a Bantu-speaking people inhabiting southern Malawi; the language of this people. M19. **B** *attrib.* or as *adj.* Of or pertaining to the Manganja or their language. M19.

mangano- /ˈmaŋgənəʊ/ *comb. form.* [f. MANGANESE, MANGANOUS: see -O-.] **1** *Min.* Forming names of minerals or mineral varieties containing (a large amount of) manganese, as *manganocolumbite*, *manganotantalite*, etc. Cf. MANGAN-. **2** *Chem.* Forming names of compounds (chiefly cyanides) containing divalent manganese. Cf. MANGANI-.

manganoan /maŋgəˈnəʊən/ *a.* M20. [f. prec. + -AN: cf. FERROAN.] *Min.* Having a constituent element partly replaced by divalent manganese.

manganolite /ˈmaŋgənəlʌɪt/ *n.* L19. [f. MANGANO- + -LITE.] **1** *Min.* = RHODONITE. Now *rare* or *obs.* L19. **2** *Geol.* Any rock composed predominantly of manganese minerals. L19.

manganous /ˈmaŋgənəs/ *a.* Also (earlier) **†-eous**. E19. [f. MANGANESE + -OUS.] Chiefly *Chem.* Of or containing manganese, *spec.* in the divalent state.

mange /meɪndʒ/ *n.* LME. [OFr. *manjue*, *mangeue* itch, f. *manju-* pres. indic. sing. stem of *mangier* (mod. *manger*) eat f. L *manducare*: see MANDUCATE.] **1** Any of various itching cutaneous diseases of hairy and woolly animals, and also poultry, caused by parasitic mites which burrow into the skin. Also (*loosely*), scabies in humans. LME. **†2** *fig.* A restless desire. M17–L18.

Comb.: **mange mite** any parasitic mite which causes mange.

mangeao /maŋˈgiːəʊ, *foreign* maŋiˈaʊ/ *n.* M19. [Maori.] A New Zealand tree, *Litsea calicaris*, of the laurel family, with tough, light brown wood.

mangel /ˈmaŋg(ə)l/ *n.* Also **-gold** /-g(ə)ld/. M19. [Abbrev.] = MANGEL-WURZEL.

Comb.: **mangel beetle** a small blue-black beetle, *Aclypea opaca*, whose larvae feed on the root of the beet; **mangel-fly** a small dipteran fly, *Pegomya hyoscyami*, whose larvae feed on beet leaves.

mangel-wurzel /ˈmaŋg(ə)lˌwəːz(ə)l/ *n.* Also **mangold-wurzel** /ˈmaŋg(ə)ld-/. L18. [G *Mangoldwurzel*, f. *Mangold* beet + *Wurzel* root.] A variety of beet with a root larger than that of the garden beet, cultivated as food for cattle.

Comb.: **mangel-wurzel fly** = MANGEL-*fly*.

manger /ˈmeɪndʒə/ *n.* ME. [(O)Fr. *mangeoire*, f. *mangeure* f. Proto-Romance, f. L *manducat-*: see MANDUCATE.] **1** A long open box or trough in a stable, barn, etc., for horses and cattle to eat out of. ME. **2** *Naut.* (chiefly *Hist.*). A small space in the bows of a ship enclosed by a low board or coaming, intended to keep the water entering the hawse-holes from flooding the deck. E17.

1 *at heck and manger*: see HECK *n.*¹ *at rack and manger*: see RACK *n.*² *dog in the manger*: see DOG *n.*

mangerful *n.* a quantity that fills a manger L16.

mange-tout /ˈmɑ̃ʒtuː, mɑ̃ʒˈtuː/ *n.* Pl. same, **-s** (pronounced same). E19. [Fr., lit. 'eat-all'.] A variety of pea of which the pods are eaten whole with the seeds they contain. Also *mange-tout pea*. Also called *sugar-pea*.

mangey *a.* var. of MANGY.

mangle /ˈmaŋg(ə)l/ *n.*¹ E17. [Sp.: see MANGROVE.] = MANGROVE.

mangle /ˈmaŋg(ə)l/ *n.*² L17. [Du. *mangel* abbrev. of synon. *mangelstok*, f. *mangelen* to mangle + *stok* staff, roller, STOCK *n.*¹, ult. f. Gk *magganon*: see MANGONEL.] **1** A machine for squeezing water from and pressing linen, clothing, etc., after washing, latterly consisting of two or more cylinders working on each other, formerly of a heavy chest on two cylinders, worked backwards and forwards over wet clothing etc. spread on a table; a wringer. L17. **2** A bicycle. *Austral. slang.* M20.

mangle /ˈmaŋg(ə)l/ *v.*¹*t.* LME. [AN *mangler* (cf. med.L *mangulare*) prob. frequent. of *mahaignier* MAIM *v.*: see -LE³.] Hack, cut, lacerate, or mutilate by repeated blows; cut or hack roughly so as to damage and disfigure; reduce to a more or less unrecognizable condition; spoil (esp. a text) by gross blundering or falsification; make (words) almost unrecognizable by mispronunciation.

T. CAPOTE On his left hand . . what remained of a finger once mangled by a piece of farm machinery. A. CARTER She fell beneath . . a brewer's dray and was mangled to pulp. G. NAYLOR She threw it on the floor and tried to mangle the pictures with her heels. JULIAN GLOAG It was torture to listen to her mangling the language.

mangler *n.*¹ M16.

mangle /ˈmaŋg(ə)l/ *v.*²*t.* L18. [f. MANGLE *n.*²] Press (linen, clothing, etc.) in a mangle.

mangler *n.*² M19.

mango /ˈmaŋgəʊ/ *n.* Pl. **mango(e)s**. Also (earlier) **†manga**. L16. [Port. *manga* f. Malay *mangga* f. Tamil *māṅkāy*, f. *mā* mango tree + *kāy* fruit.] **1** The sweet orange-fleshed fruit of an Indian and Myanmar (Burmese) tree, *Mangifera indica* (family Anacardiaceae), which is eaten as dessert or used in its unripe state to make chutney or jam. L16. **2** The tree producing this fruit, widely cultivated in tropical countries. L17. **3** A pickle, esp. of melons or cucumbers, resembling that made of green mangoes. Now *rare.* L17. **4** In full *mango-(humming)bird*. Any of several hummingbirds of the genus *Anthracothorax*, of tropical America and the Caribbean. M18.

Comb.: **mango-bird** (*a*) in the Indian subcontinent, a golden oriole; (*b*) see sense 4 above; **mango-fish** = TUPSEE; **mango-fly** (*a*) = TUMBU *fly*; (*b*) any of various African tabanid flies of the genus *Chrysops*, which are carriers of loaiasis; **mango-ginger** (the pungent root of) an Indian plant, *Curcuma amada*, closely related to turmeric; *mango-hummingbird*: see sense 4 above.

mangold(-wurzel) *ns.* vars. of MANGEL, MANGEL-WURZEL.

mangonel /ˈmaŋgən(ə)l/ *n. obs.* exc. *Hist.* ME. [OFr. *mangonel(le)* (mod. *mangonneau*) f. med.L *manganellus*, *-gon-* dim. of late L *manganum* f. Gk *magganon* engine of war, axis of a pulley.] A military engine for throwing stones and other missiles.

mangosteen /ˈmaŋgəstiːn/ *n.* L16. [Malay *manggustan* dial. var. of *manggis*.] **1** The fruit of a Malaysian tree, *Garcinia mangostana* (family Guttiferae), with a thick reddish-brown rind enclosing a sweet white juicy pulp; the tree producing this fruit. L16. **2** In the W. Indies, a kind of jujube tree, *Ziziphus mauritiana*. M18.

mangrove /ˈmaŋgrəʊv/ *n.* E17. [Prob. ult. f. Port. *mangue*, Sp. *mangle*, f. Taino, w. 2nd elem. assim. to GROVE.] **1** Any of various tropical trees or shrubs of the genera *Rhizophora* and *Bruguiera* (family Rhizophoraceae) with interlacing aerial roots, which form dense thickets in muddy swamps subject to tidal inundation; *esp.* (in full *common* or *red mangrove*) *Rhizophora mangle*. E17. **2** Any of various other tropical trees or shrubs of similar habit and appearance, esp. of the genus *Avicennia* (of the verbena family). L17.

2 **black mangrove** (*a*) *Avicennia marina*, of Florida and the W. Indies; (*b*) *Aegiceras majus*, a similar and related Australian mangrove. **white mangrove** (*a*) a W. African and tropical American mangrove, *Laguncularia racemosa* (family Combretaceae); (*b*) a mangrove of the Pacific region, *Avicennia officinalis*, with leaves white beneath.

Comb.: **mangrove crab** any of various small grapsoid crabs of tropical American mangrove swamps; **mangrove cuckoo** a cuckoo, *Coccyzus minor*, of Florida and the W. Indies; **mangrove fly** a W. African tabanid fly, esp. *Chrysops dimidiatus*; **mangrove-hen** (in Jamaica) the clapper rail, *Rallus longirostris*; **mangrove jack** an edible Indo-Pacific snapper fish, *Lutjanus argentimaculatus*, which frequents mangrove swamps; **mangrove oyster** a small edible Caribbean oyster, *Ostrea frons*, which grows on submerged mangrove roots; **mangrove snapper** an edible Atlantic snapper fish, *Lutjanus griseus*, which frequents mangrove swamps; also called *grey snapper*.

mangy /ˈmeɪndʒi/ *a.* Also **-ey**. E16. [f. MANGE + -Y¹.] **1** Having the mange; of the nature of or caused by the mange. Formerly also, scabby. E16. **2** Squalid, poverty-stricken, shabby; contemptible. E16.

1 E. BLYTON A dreadful animal . . all sort of mangy and moth-eaten. 2 R. CROMPTON A mangy fur rug was tied round his arms. J. RABAN That would be a mangy compromise unfair . . even to George.

mangily *adv.* E17. **manginess** *n.* LME.

manhandle /ˈmanhand(ə)l/ *v.t.* LME. [f. MAN *n.* + HANDLE *v.*¹] **†1** Handle or wield (a tool). Only in LME. **2†a** Attack (an enemy). Only in LME. **b** Handle (a person) roughly; pull or hustle about. *slang.* M19. **3** Move by human effort alone; move slowly or with difficulty. M19.

manhattan /manˈhat(ə)n/ *n.* Also **M-**. L19. [f. as next.] A cocktail made with vermouth and a spirit, as whisky or brandy, sometimes with a dash of bitters.

Manhattanese /manˌhatəˈniːz/ *n.* & *a.* E19. [f. *Manhattan* (see below) + -ESE.] **A** *n.* Pl. same. **1** A native or inhabitant of Manhattan, (the borough including) the island on which the older part of New York City is built, or (*loosely*) New York City. E19. **2** The English dialect of Manhattan or New York City. E20. **B** *adj.* Of or pertaining to Manhattan or New York City. M19.

Manhattanite /manˈhat(ə)nʌɪt/ *n.* M20. [f. as prec. + -ITE¹.] A native or inhabitant of Manhattan or (*loosely*) New York City.

manhood /ˈmanhʊd/ *n.* ME. [f. MAN *n.* + -HOOD.] **I1** The state or condition of being human; human nature. ME. **†2** Humaneness ME–L16. **II3** The state of being a man, as opposed to a boy or a woman, or both. LME. **4** Manliness, courage; (now *esp.*) virility, male sexual potency. LME. **b** The male external genitals; the penis. M20. **5** Men collectively; the adult male members of a population, country, etc. L16.

mani /ˈmɑːni/ *n.*¹ E17. [Sp. *maní* f. Taino.] In S. America: the groundnut, *Arachis hypogaea*.

mani /ˈmɑːni/ *n.*² M19. [Tib. *mani* f. Skt = precious stone.] A Tibetan wall of stones with religious inscriptions. Also *mani wall*. Cf. MENDANG.

mania /ˈmeɪnɪə/ *n.* LME. [Late L f. Gk, rel. to *mainesthai* be mad, ult. f. IE base of MIND *n.*¹: see -IA¹.] **1** *Psychiatry.* Mental disturbance characterized by great excitement or elation, extravagant delusions, and overactivity. LME. **2** Excessive excitement or enthusiasm; (usu.) an excessive enthusiasm or passion (*for*), a temporary enthusiasm or craze (*for*). L17.

2 M. BRADBURY Building mania or, as it was put, an Edifice Complex. JANET MORGAN It was as well that the house was spacious, since Frederick had a mania for collecting.

-mania /ˈmeɪnɪə/ *suff.* [f. as prec.] Forming ns. w. the sense 'a particular kind of mania', as *Anglomania*, *bibliomania*, *kleptomania*, *megalomania*, *nymphomania*, etc.

†**maniable** *a.* L15. [(O)Fr., f. *manier* to handle, ult. f. L *manus* hand: see -ABLE.] **1** Easy to handle or work; flexible, pliable; (of a person etc.) manageable, tractable. L15–E18. **2** That may be handled or felt, palpable. L15–L17.

maniac /ˈmeɪnɪak/ *a.* & *n.* L16. [Late L *maniacus* f. late Gk *maniakos*, f. Gk MANIA: see -AC.] **A** *adj.* **1** Affected with mania; raving mad. L16. **2** Of, pertaining to, or characterized by mania or excessive enthusiasm. E18. **B** *n.* A person affected with mania, a mad person; a person with a mania for something. M18.

-maniac /ˈmeɪnɪak/ *suff.* [f. as prec. Cf. -MANE.] Forming adjs. and ns. w. the sense '(a person) affected by a particular kind of mania', as *kleptomaniac*, *nymphomaniac*, etc.

maniacal /məˈnʌɪək(ə)l/ *a.* L17. [f. MANIAC + -AL[1].] **1** = MANIAC *a.* 1. L17. **2** = MANIAC *a.* 2. E18.

maniacally *adv.* M19.

manic /ˈmanɪk/ *a.* E20. [f. MANIA + -IC.] Of, pertaining to, or resembling mania; affected with or characteristic of mania.

Comb.: **manic depression** the condition of manic-depressive illness; **manic-depressive** *a.* & *n.* (*a*) *adj.* characterized by or affected with alternating periods of elation and mental depression; (*b*) *n.* a manic-depressive person.

manically *adv.* M20.

Manichaean /manɪˈkiːən/ *a.* & *n.* Also **-chean**. M16. [f. as next + -AN.] **A** *adj.* Of, pertaining to, or characteristic of Manichaeism or its adherents; *transf.* of or pertaining to dualism, dualistic. M16. **B** *n.* An adherent of Manichaeism; *transf.* a dualist. M16.

Manichaeism /manɪˈkiːɪz(ə)m/ *n.* Also **-cheism**. E17. [f. late L *Manichaeus* (late Gk *Manikhaios*), f. *Mani*, *Manes* (*c* 216–76), Persian founder of the system: see -ISM.] A religious system with Christian, Gnostic, and pagan elements, founded in the 3rd cent. AD and widespread in the Roman Empire and Asia until the 5th (surviving until the 13th), based on a supposed primeval conflict between light and darkness, and representing Satan as coeternal with God; *transf.* dualism.

Manichae'istic *a.* of, pertaining to, or of the nature of Manichaeism E20.

Manichean *a.* & *n.* var. of MANICHAEAN.

Manichee /ˈmanɪkiː/ *n.* LME. [f. as MANICHAEISM.] = MANICHAEAN *n.*

Manicheism *n.* var. of MANICHAEISM.

manichord /ˈmanɪkɔːd/ *n. obs.* exc. *Hist.* Also (earlier) †**-dion**. E17. [Fr. *manichordion*, †*manicorde* f. med.L *monochordium* f. late Gk *monokhordion*, cl.Gk *-khordon* MONOCHORD, assoc. w. L *manus* hand.] = CLAVICHORD.

manicotti /manɪˈkɒti/ *n.pl.* M20. [It., pl. of *manicotto* sleeve, muff.] Large tubular pasta shells; an Italian dish consisting largely of these and usu. a sauce.

manicou /ˈmanɪkuː/ *n.* M20. [Fr.] Any of various small opossums of the genus *Marmosa*, of Central and S. America. Also called *mouse opossum*.

manicure /ˈmanɪkjʊə/ *n.* & *v.* L19. [Fr., f. L *manus* hand + *cura* care.] **A** *n.* **1** = MANICURIST. Now *rare*. L19. **2** The cosmetic treatment and care of the hands and fingernails, by shaping the nails, removing cuticles, etc.; an instance of such treatment, esp. by a manicurist. L19.

2 R. DAHL His hairdresser trimmed his hair . . and he always took a manicure at the same time. *attrib.*: A. J. CRONIN She took her manicure set and began to do her nails.

B *v.t.* **1** Apply manicure treatment to (the nails, a person, etc.). L19. **2** *transf.* & *fig.* Trim or cut neatly. E20.

2 J. BRAINE Big houses with drives . . and manicured hedges.

manicurist /ˈmanɪkjʊərɪst/ *n.* L19. [f. prec. + -IST.] A person who gives manicure treatment, esp. professionally.

†**manier** *a.* see MANY.

maniéré /manjere/ *a.* M18. [Fr.] Affected or characterized by mannerism, mannered.

manière criblée /manjɛːr krible/ *n. phr.* E20. [Fr.: see MANNER *n.*[1], CRIBLÉ.] *Criblé* engraving.

†**maniest** *a.* see MANY.

manifest /ˈmanɪfɛst/ *n.* M16. [It. MANIFESTO.] **1** A manifestation, an indication. Now *rare*. M16. **2** A public proclamation or declaration; a manifesto. Now *rare*. E17. **3** A list of a ship's cargo for the information and use of Customs officers; a list of freight or passengers carried by a train or aeroplane; *gen.* an inventory. E18. **b** A fast freight train. Also *manifest train*. Chiefly *N. Amer.* E20.

1 A. MILLER She swears that she never saw . . apparitions, nor any manifest of the Devil.

manifest /ˈmanɪfɛst/ *a.* ME. [(O)Fr. *manifeste* or L *manifestus*, earlier *manufestus*, f. *manus* hand + *festus* struck (only in compounds, as *infestus* dangerous), f. base of *defendere* DEFEND, *offendere* OFFEND.] **1** Clearly revealed to the eye, mind, or judgement; open to view or comprehension; obvious. ME. †**2** Having evident signs *of*; evidently possessed *of* or guilty *of*. *literary*. L17–E18.

1 **manifest destiny** (the doctrine of) the (supposed) inevitability of the supremacy or expansion of power of a people or State, orig. esp. of the US or of those of European origin in or over the entire western hemisphere.

manifest /ˈmanɪfɛst/ *v.* LME. [(O)Fr. *manifester* or L *manifestare*, f. *manifestus*: see prec.] **1** *v.t.* Make evident to the eye or to the understanding; show plainly, reveal; display (a quality, condition, feeling, etc.) by action or behaviour; evince; be evidence of, prove, attest. LME. †**2** *v.t.* Expound, unfold, clear up (a matter). M16–M17. **3** *v.t.* Record or enumerate in a manifest. M16. **4** *v.i. Spiritualism.* Of a ghost or spirit: make an appearance. L19. **5** *v.i.* = DEMONSTRATE *v.* 6. Now *rare*. L19.

1 SHAKES. *2 Hen. IV* Thy life did manifest thou lov'dst me not. M. MEAD The Balinese manifest less fatigue than any people of whom we have a record. E. H. GOMBRICH Royal patronage, to manifest the interest which the King took in the arts. D. FRANCIS Guilt and remorse can manifest themselves in excess of mourning. A. SILLITOE If God manifested Himself . . He would be quickly disowned.

mani'festable *a.* (now *rare*) E16. **mani'festant** *n.* (now *rare*) = DEMONSTRATOR 3 L19. **manifester** *n.* L15. **manifestive** *a.* (*rare*) M19. **manifestly** *adv.* (*a*) (now *rare*) in a manifest manner; (*b*) (qualifying a statement) as is manifest, evidently, unmistakably: LME. **manifestness** *n.* L16.

manifestation /ˌmanɪfɛˈsteɪʃ(ə)n/ *n.* LME. [Late L *manifestatio(n-)*, f. *manifestat-* pa. ppl stem of *manifestare*: see prec., -ATION.] **1** The action of manifesting; the fact of being manifested; the demonstration, revelation, or display of the existence, presence, qualities, or nature of some person or thing. LME. **2** An instance of this; a means or thing by which something is manifested. L18. **b** *spec.* = DEMONSTRATION 6. Now *rare*. L19. **3** *Spiritualism.* A phenomenon or number of phenomena by which the presence of a spirit is supposed to be rendered perceptible. M19.

manifestational *a.* (*rare*) L19. **manifestationist** *n.* (*rare*) a believer in manifestation M19.

manifestative /manɪˈfɛstətɪv/ *a.* M17. [med.L *manifestativus*, f. *manifestat-*: see prec., -IVE.] Having the function or quality of manifesting something.

manifestatively *adv.* in a manifestative manner; in respect of manifestation: M17.

manifesto /manɪˈfɛstəʊ/ *n.* & *v.* M17. [It., f. *manifestare* f. L: see MANIFEST *v.*] **A** *n.* Pl. **-o(e)s**. **1** A public declaration or proclamation; *esp.* a printed declaration or explanation of policy (past, present, or future) issued by a monarch, State, political party or candidate, or any other individual or body of individuals of public relevance. M17. †**2** A proof, a piece of evidence. M–L17.

1 P. B. CLARKE The Association's main aims as expressed in the manifesto. M. FOOT She knew what . . the party manifesto committed her to achieve. J. UGLOW A manifesto for a literalism in art and a commitment to describing the mundanities of life.

B *v.i.* Issue a manifesto or manifestos. *rare*. M18.

manifold /ˈmanɪfəʊld/ *a.*, *adv.*, & *n.* [OE *manigfeald* = OFris. *manichfald*, OHG *managfalt* (G *mannigfalt*), Goth. *managfalþs*, f. Gmc, f. as MANY + -FOLD. Cf. MANYFOLD.] **A** *adj.* Now chiefly *literary*. **1** Varied or diverse in appearance, form, or character; having various forms, features, component parts, relations, applications, etc.; performing several functions at once. OE. **b** That is the specified thing in many ways or in many relations; entitled to the specified name on many grounds. Now *rare*. ME. **2** Numerous and varied; of many kinds or varieties. Formerly simply, numerous, many. OE. †**3** *Math.* = MULTIPLE *a.* 3. ME–M17.

1 LD MACAULAY A manifold hatred, theological and political, hereditary and personal. W. G. PALGRAVE Coffee though one in name is manifold in fact. b W. CONGREVE Secure that manifold villain. 2 H. READ This belief that behind manifold appearances there is one enduring reality. O. SITWELL The Bowes Museum is vast, its exhibits are manifold. 3 **manifold to** a multiple of.

†**B** *adv.* **1** In many ways or degrees. ME–L16. **2** In the proportion of many to one. Cf. MANYFOLD. Only in E17.

C *n.* †**1** *by* (occas. *on*) *manifold*, many times over, in the proportion of many to one. ME–L16. **2** That which is manifold; *spec.* in *Kantian Philos.*, the sum of the particulars furnished by sense before they have been unified by the synthesis of the understanding. M19. **3** *Math.* A topological space each point of which has a neighbourhood homoeomorphic to the interior of a sphere in a Euclidean space of given dimension. L19. **4** = *manifold paper* below. L19. **5** *Engin.* A pipe or chamber that has a number of branches, or inlets or outlets; *spec.* (in an internal-combustion engine) that which delivers air and fuel from the carburettor to the cylinders (in full *inlet*, *intake manifold*), and that leading from the cylinders to the exhaust pipe (in full *exhaust manifold*). L19.

Comb.: **manifold paper** lightweight paper for making carbon copies, copying paper; **manifold writer** (chiefly *Hist.*) a machine with carbon paper for multiplying copies of a document etc.

manifoldly *adv.* (now *literary*) (*a*) in manifold ways; †(*b*) in the proportion of many to one: OE. **manifoldness** *n.* OE.

manifold /ˈmanɪfəʊld/ *v.t.* OE. [f. the adj.] **1** Make manifold, multiply. *rare* in *gen.* sense. OE. **2** *spec.* Multiply impressions or copies of, esp. mechanically. *arch.* M19.

¶Became obs. in ME. Re-formed in 18.

manifolding *n.* (*a*) the action of the vb; (*b*) = MANIFOLD *n.* 5: M18. **manifolder** *n.* E20.

maniform /ˈmanɪfɔːm/ *a.*[1] *rare.* E19. [f. L *manus* hand + -I- + -FORM.] Having the form of a hand; *Entomol.* chelate.

maniform /ˈmanɪfɔːm/ *a.*[2] M19. [f. MANY + -FORM, after *manifold*.] Multiform.

maniformly *adv.* (*rare*) in many or various ways LME.

manify /ˈmanɪfʌɪ/ *v.t. rare.* L18. [f. MAN *n.* + -I- + -FY.] Make manlike.

manihot *n.* see MANIOC.

manikin /ˈmanɪkɪn/ *n.* & *a.* Also (the only form in sense A.3b) **-nn-**. See also MANAKIN. M16. [Du. *manneken* dim. of *man* MAN *n.*: see -KIN. Cf. MANNEQUIN.] **A** *n.* **1** A little man (freq. *contempt.*); a dwarf, a pygmy. M16. **2** A small figure or statue of a man; *spec.* (*a*) an artist's lay figure; (*b*) a model of the human body used for exhibiting the anatomical structure or for demonstrating surgical operations. M16. **3a** = MANAKIN 2. L18. **b** Any of various small finchlike birds of the genus *Lonchura* (family Estrildidae), which are found in Africa, Asia, and Australasia and are popular as cage-birds. M20. **B** *attrib.* or as *adj.* Diminutive, dwarf; puny. M19.

Manila /məˈnɪlə/ *a.* & *n.* Also **-ll-**, **m-**. L17. [The capital and chief port of the Philippines.] **A** *adj.* **1** *attrib.* Designating things produced in or associated with Manila or the Philippines. L17. 2 Made from Manila hemp or manila paper; of the light yellow-brown colour of manila paper. M19.

1 **Manila cheroot, cigar**: of a kind manufactured in Manila. *Manila* ELEMI. **Manila hemp** the fibres of the pseudostem of the plant *Musa textilis* (family Musaceae), used to make ropes, matting, paper, etc. **manila paper**: of a light yellow-brown colour made from Manila hemp or other material, used esp. as wrapping paper. *Manila tamarind*: see TAMARIND 3. 2 P. HIGHSMITH He put on old manila trousers. D. LODGE The brown manila envelope . . already . . used twice for the circulation of internal mail.

B *n.* 1 Manila hemp; Manila rope; manila paper. M19. 2 A Manila cheroot or cigar. M19.

manilla /mə'nɪlə/ *n.*[1] M16. [Sp., prob. dim. of *mano* hand f. L *manus*.] A ring of metal worn on the arm or wrist by some African peoples and used as a medium of exchange.

Manilla *a.* & *n.*[2] var. of MANILA.

manille /mə'nɪl/ *n.* L17. [Fr. f. Sp. *malilla* dim. of *mala* fem. (sc. *carta* card) of *malo* bad.] *Cards.* In quadrille and ombre, the second best trump or honour (being the two of a black suit or the seven of a red suit). Also, a French card-game in which the ten or manille is the highest card in each suit.

maninosay, maninose *ns.* vars. of MANANOSAY.

manioc /'manɪɒk/ *n.* Also (earlier) **manihot** /'manɪhɒt/. M16. [Fr. (also †*manihot*), repr. Tupi *manioca*.] The cassava plant, *Manihot esculenta*. Also, the meal made from its starchy root.

maniple /'manɪp(ə)l/ *n.* ME. [OFr. (mod. *manipule*) or L *manipulus* handful, troop of soldiers, f. *manus* hand + elem. of unkn. origin.] 1 *Eccl.* In the Western Church, one of the Eucharistic vestments, consisting now of a strip worn suspended from the left arm near the wrist. Also called *fanon*. ME. 2 *Rom. Hist.* A subdivision of the Roman legion, of which a cohort contained three, numbering 120 or 60 men. M16. †b *transf.* A small band of soldiers of more or less definite number. L16–M17. †3 A handful. L16–E19. 4 A hand. *joc.* E19.

manipulable /mə'nɪpjʊləb(ə)l/ *a.* L19. [f. MANIPUL(ATE + -ABLE. Cf. MANIPULATABLE.] Able to be manipulated.

manipula'bility *n.* M20.

manipulandum /mənɪpjʊ'landəm/ *n.* Pl. **-da** /-də/. M20. [f. MANIPUL(ATE + L *-andum*: see -AND.] A thing (to be) manipulated, esp. in a psychological test or experiment.

manipular /mə'nɪpjʊlə/ *a.* & *n.* E17. [L *manipularis*, f. *manipulus*: see MANIPLE, -AR[1]. In sense A.2 assoc. w. MANIPULATE.] A *adj.* 1 *Rom. Hist.* Of or pertaining to a maniple of a legion. E17. 2 Of or pertaining to manipulation or handling. E19. B *n. Rom. Hist.* A soldier of a maniple. M19.

manipulatable /mə'nɪpjʊleɪtəb(ə)l/ *a.* M20. [f. next + -ABLE.] = MANIPULABLE.

manipulate /mə'nɪpjʊleɪt/ *v.t.* E19. [Back-form. f. next, after Fr. *manipuler*: see -ATE[3].] Handle, esp. with (physical or mental) dexterity; manage, work, or treat by manual or mechanical means; manage by (esp. unfair) dexterous contrivance or influence; stimulate sexually with the hand(s); *Med.* treat (part of the body, a fracture, etc.) by manual action; *Computing* carry out operations on (numbers, text, etc.).

E. FERBER Old Eusebio . . was manipulating four cooking vessels at once. JOHN BROOKE A stupid man, manipulated by minds sharper and cleverer than his own. C. TOMALIN She manipulates her . . friends and admirers, using the devotion she inspires for her own ends. *Which?* The burglar usually forced or manipulated the window catch.

manipulation /mənɪpjʊ'leɪʃ(ə)n/ *n.* E18. [Fr., f. L *manipulus*: see MANIPLE, -ATION.] †1 The method of digging silver ore. Only in Dicts. E18–E19. 2 *Chem.* Experimental procedure or technique. *arch.* L18. 3 *gen.* The action or an act of manipulating something or somebody; manual management or action, *spec.* (*Med.*) the manual treatment of a part of the body; management by (esp. unfair) contrivance or influence. E19.

3 H. B. STOWE In . . her manipulations, the young disciple had contrived to snatch . . gloves and a ribbon. *Nation* Manipulation signifies a common . . design . . to raise or depress values in order to get other people's money. A. E. STEVENSON Evidence of the distortion and manipulation of the news. *Annabel* Expert advice on caring for your spine, exercise, physiotherapy, and manipulation . . are all available.

manipulative /mə'nɪpjʊlətɪv/ *a.* M19. [f. MANIPULATE: see -ATIVE.] Of, pertaining to, concerning, or involving manipulation; given to manipulation.

S. SMILES Workmen . . executing machinery requiring manipulative skill. R. KYLE Lillian had just completed a manipulative session and was wearing only a wrapper. *Glasgow Herald* Manipulative television has little to do with informing, educating or entertaining. M. M. R. KHAN Benjamin, even though manipulative, rarely lied.

manipulatively *adv.* M20. **manipulativeness** *n.* M20.

manipulator /mə'nɪpjʊleɪtə/ *n.* M19. [f. as prec.: see -ATOR.] 1 A person who manipulates something or someone. M19. 2 A device used for or in manipulation, as a remote-controlled device for handling radioactive material behind a protective shield. M19.

manipulatory /mə'nɪpjʊlət(ə)ri/ *a.* E19. [f. as prec. + -ORY[2].] Pertaining to or involving manipulation.

Manipuri /mʌnɪ'pʊəri/ *a.* & *n.* M19. [f. *Manipur* (see below) + -I[2].] A *adj.* Of or pertaining to Manipur, a State in the region of Assam in NE India. M19. B *n.* Pl. **-s**, same. 1 A member of the people of Manipur. M19. 2 The Tibeto-Burman language of the Manipuri. E20.

manis /'meɪnɪs/ *n.* L18. [mod.L, perh. a spurious sing. of MANES.] *Zool.* = PANGOLIN. Now only as mod.L genus name.

ma nishtana /ma niʃ'tana/ *n. phr.* E20. [Heb. = how different (*sc.* from all other nights!), the opening wds.] *Judaism.* The four questions in the Passover Haggadah, traditionally asked by the youngest member of a Jewish household on Seder Night; this part of the Passover celebrations.

manism /'mɑːnɪz(ə)m, 'meɪ-/ *n.* E20. [f. MANES + -ISM.] The worship of the manes or shades of the dead; ancestor-worship.

ma'nistic *a.* M20.

manito *n.* var. of MANITOU.

manitoka /manɪ'təʊkə/ *n. S. Afr.* E20. [Prob. invented.] A tall Australian evergreen white-flowered shrub, *Myoporum insulare* (family Myoporaceae), used in South Africa for hedges.

manitou /'manɪtuː/ *n.* Also **-tu**; **-to**, pl. **-tos**. L16. [Narragansett *manittówock* (pl.) or Delaware *manə̆tːu* supernatural being, reinforced by similar cognates in other Algonquian langs.] Among some N. American Indians, a spirit (of good or evil) which is an object of religious awe or reverence; anything regarded as having supernatural power, as a fetish.

manjak /'mandʒak/ *n.* Orig. *W. Indies*. Also (earlier) †**mountjack**. M17. [Origin unkn.] *Geol.* A form of asphalt which occurs in Barbados.

manjee /'mɑːndʒi/ *n.* L17. [Hind. *mā̃jhī*.] In the Indian subcontinent: the captain or steersman of a boat.

†**mank** *a.* Chiefly *Sc.* E16–E18. [OFr. *manc*, *manque* f. L *mancus* maimed.] Maimed, mutilated, defective.

¶ Prob. 1st elem. of MANKY.

mank /maŋk/ *v.t. obs.* exc. *Sc.* ME. [Late L (chiefly Frank.) *mancare*, f. *mancus*: see prec.] Maim, mangle, mutilate.

mankin /'mankɪn/ *n.* E19. [f. MAN *n.* + -KIN.] A diminutive or puny man; a manikin.

mankind /man'kʌɪnd, *in sense A.3* 'mankʌɪnd/ *n.* & *a.* ME. [f. MAN *n.* + KIND *n.*] A *n.* 1 The human species; human beings in general. ME. †2 Human nature; human feeling, humanity. ME–E17. 3 The male sex; men or male people in general. LME. †B *adj.* 1 Human. Only in L16. 2 Of a woman: masculine. L16–M17. 3 Male. Only in M17.

manky /'maŋki/ *a. dial.* & *colloq.* M20. [Prob. f. MANK *a.* + -Y[1], perh. infl. by Fr. *manqué*.] Bad, inferior, defective; dirty.

manless /'manlɪs/ *a.* OE. [f. MAN *n.* + -LESS.] 1a Having no men; having no human beings. OE. b Of a woman: lacking the company of men, *spec.* having no husband or lover. E20. †2 Unmanly, effeminate. E16–M17.

manlessness *n.* †(*a*) cowardice; (*b*) the state or condition of being manless: M17.

manlike /'manlʌɪk/ *a.* & *adv.* LME. [f. MAN *n.* + -LIKE.] A *adj.* 1 Having (good or bad) qualities or characteristics associated with men as distinguished from women or children; (of a woman) mannish. LME. 2 Of an animal: resembling a man or human being. L16. B *adv.* Manfully. L16.

manlikely *adv.* (*rare*) LME. **manlikeness** *n.* (*rare*) M18.

manling /'manlɪŋ/ *n. rare.* L16. [f. MAN *n.* + -LING[1].] A little man.

manly /'manli/ *a.* ME. [f. MAN *n.* + -LY[1].] †1 Belonging to human beings; human. ME–E17. 2 Having good qualities or characteristics associated with men as distinguished from women or children; *esp.* courageous, independent in spirit, frank, upright. ME. b Of a woman: mannish. E16. 3 Of a thing, quality, etc.: befitting or belonging to a man; masculine. LME. †4 Adult, mature. L16–L17.

2 T. O. ECHEWA He stored his grief and prided himself in his manly ability to store it. 3 L. F. BAUM His manly beauty was so great that Gayelette loved him dearly. A. N. WILSON His silk display handkerchiefs, his manly striped ties.

manlihood *n.* (*rare*) manliness M17. **manlily** *adv.* LME. **manliness** *n.* LME.

manly /'manli/ *adv. arch.* OE. [f. MAN *n.* + -LY[2].] 1 In a manly manner; like a man; manfully, courageously. OE. †2 Like a human being. OE–M16. †3 Excellently. Only in E17.

manna /'manə/ *n.* OE. [Late L f. Hellenistic Gk f. Aram. *mannā* f. Heb. *mān* corresp. to Arab. *mann* exudation of the tamarisk *Tamarix mannifera*.] I 1 The edible substance described as miraculously supplied to the Israelites in the wilderness (*Exod.* 16). OE. 2 Spiritual nourishment, *esp.* the Eucharist; something beneficial provided unexpectedly (freq. *manna from heaven*). ME. II 3 A sweet hardened flaky exudation obtained from the manna-ash (see below), rich in mannitol and used as a mild laxative. Also, a similar exudation from other plants (e.g. a Middle Eastern tamarisk, *Tamarix mannifera*, a Middle Eastern legume, *Alhagi maurorum*, and the larch) and certain insects. LME. †4 (A grain of) frankincense. LME–M18. †5 *Chem.* A fine white precipitate. L17–E18. 6 In full *Polish manna*. The seeds of the floating sweet-grass, *Glyceria fluitans*, used as food. L18.

3 TREHALA *manna*.

Comb.: **manna-ash** a white-flowered ash, *Fraxinus ornus*, of southern Europe; **manna-grass** floating sweet-grass, *Glyceria fluitans*; **manna-gum** *Austral.* a manna-yielding eucalyptus, *Eucalyptus viminalis*; **manna-lichen** any of several edible lichens of the genus *Sphaerothallia* (esp. *S. esculenta*) sometimes identified with the manna of the Bible; **manna sugar** = MANNITOL; **manna-tree** = *manna-ash* above.

mannan /'manan/ *n.* L19. [f. MANNOSE + -AN.] *Chem.* Any of a group of polysaccharides composed chiefly of mannose residues, occurring widely in plants esp. as reserve foods.

mannequin /'manɪkɪn, -kwɪn/ *n.* M18. [Fr. f. as MANIKIN.] 1 A model of a human figure; an artist's lay figure; a dummy for the display of clothes etc. M18. 2 A woman (or occas. a man) employed by a dressmaker, costumier, etc., to display clothes by wearing them; a model. E20.

manner /'manə/ *n.*[1] ME. [AN *manere*, (O)Fr. *manière*, f. Proto-Romance use as n. of fem. of L *manuarius* pertaining to the hand, f. *manus* hand: see -ER[2].] 1 The way in which something is done or happens; a method of action; a mode of procedure. ME. †2 The state, character, disposition, or nature *of*. ME–M17. 3 Customary mode of acting or behaviour; habitual practice; usage, custom, fashion. Now *literary*. ME. 4 In *pl.* †a A person's habitual behaviour or conduct; morals; conduct in its moral aspect; morality. ME–L18. b The prevailing modes of life, the customary rules of behaviour, the conditions of society. Sometimes *spec.* good customs or social conditions. ME. †c An animal's habits. LME–L18. †d The distinctive varieties of disposition and temperament portrayed in a work of literature. L17–L18. 5 Outward bearing, deportment; a person's characteristic style of attitude, gesture, or utterance. ME. b A distinguished or fashionable air. *arch.* L17. 6 In *pl.* & †*sing.* a External social behaviour, estimated according to its degree of politeness or of conformity to the accepted standards of behaviour or propriety; (of an animal) trained behaviour, action. ME. b Polite social behaviour or deportment; habits indicative of good breeding; (*obs.* exc. *dial.*) forms of politeness or respect (now only in *do* or *make one's manners*, curtsy, bow, etc.). LME. 7 A species, kind, or sort *of*; qualified by *all, many, these*, or a numeral as *pl.*, kinds or sorts *of*. (Formerly often with ellipsis of *of*.) Now only in *all manner of*, (arch.) *what manner of?* ME. 8 A method or style of execution in art, literature, etc.; style. LME. b Mannerism. E18. †9 Measure, moderation. LME–E16.

1 *New Yorker* Not to dispose of these documents or destroy them in any manner. A. BLEASDALE Driving in a manner likely to cause an accident. A. DESAI She leant against the door in the theatrical manner that came naturally to her. 3 B. JOWETT Here Ctesippus, as his manner was, burst into a roar of laughter. W. TREVOR Culture is the byword in our villa, but otherwise we live in the local manner. P. B. CLARKE West Indian Pentecostal congregations are distinguishable by their manner of worship. 4a S. JOHNSON A change of fortune causes a change of manners. GIBBON Divorces were prohibited by manners rather than by laws. b SHAKES. *1 Hen. IV* Defect of manners, want of government. J. E. T. ROGERS Contemporary novels are good evidence of manners. d ADDISON This is Aristotle's Method of considering, first the Fable, and secondly the Manners. 5 A. LURIE She had developed a special effusive manner. M. FITZHERBERT His sheltered life had led to a singularity of manner. C. SIMMONS What it was in my speech, actions, or manner that provoked these feelings. b GOLDSMITH Who can have a manner, who has never seen . . such places where the nobility chiefly resort? 6 D. EDEN Don't you know it's very bad manners to read other people's letters? M. SPARK Trevor threw half a crown backwards on to the counter. 'Manners,' the barmaid said. M. FOOT Sometimes Gaitskell refers self-mockingly to his immaculate Wykehamist manners. b Q. CRISP Manners . . are a means of getting what we want without appearing to be absolute swine. 7 SHAKES. *Wint. T.* What manner of fellow was he that robb'd you? L. APPIGNANESI All manner of food and basic commodities were in short supply. 8 N. MITFORD An oil painting . . by Boy or Lady Montdore. . . It was in their early manner. P. MEDAWAR People more affected by manner than by matter. M. GIROUARD Nesfield designed his first known building in a post-Gothic manner.

Phrases: **adverb of manner**: which answers or asks the question how? *by all (any, no) manner of means*: see MEAN *n.*[1] COMEDY *of manners. do one's manners*: see sense 6b above. **in a manner** (*a*) in some way, in some degree, so to speak, as it were; †(*b*) to a considerable degree, almost entirely, very nearly. **in a manner of speaking** in some sense, to some extent, so to speak. **in like manner** in a similar way, similarly. **in the manner of** after the style or fashion of, in the guise of, in the same way as. *make one's manners*: see sense 6b above. *manner of articulation*: see ARTICULATION *n.* 5. **no manner of — *arch.*** no — whatever. **to the manner born** [Shakes. *Haml.*] destined by birth to be subject to some custom; *colloq.* naturally fitted for some position or employment.

manner *n.*[2] var. of MAINOUR.

mannerable /ˈman(ə)rəb(ə)l/ *a. obs.* exc. *dial.* LME. [f. MANNER *n.*[1] + -ABLE.] Well-mannered, polite.

mannered /ˈmanəd/ *a.* LME. [f. MANNER *n.*[1] + -ED[2].] 1 Having manners of a specified kind (indicated by an advb. phr., or by a prefixed adj. or adv.). LME. b Well-behaved, well-mannered. Long *dial. rare.* LME. 2 Characterized by or given to mannerism. E19.

1 *ill-mannered, rough-mannered, well-mannered*, etc. 2 H. R. HAWEIS That Spohr was too doctrinaire and mannered, . . most musicians will allow. M. FORSTER She began . . to drop the rather mannered style of her first letters.

mannerise *v.* var. of MANNERIZE.

mannerism /ˈmanərɪz(ə)m/ *n.* E19. [f. MANNER *n.*[1] + -ISM.] 1 Excessive or affected adoption of a distinctive manner or method of treatment, esp. in art and literature; *spec.* (freq. **M-**) a style of art which originated in Italy and preceded the baroque, characterized by stylistic exaggeration and distortion of figures etc. E19. 2 A habitual peculiarity of style or manner; a trick or gesture of speech or action, esp. of an actor. E19.

2 *Times* He has abandoned his mannerisms and been content to make a beautiful picture. N. GORDIMER She fell again into the mannerism of holding her head to one side. P. ACKROYD I detest the critical mannerism that professes to find good in everything.

mannerist /ˈmanərɪst/ *n.* & *a.* L17. [f. MANNER *n.*[1] + -IST, orig. after Fr. *maniériste*.] A *n.* A person who adopts or adheres to mannerism; *spec.* an exponent or adherent of Mannerism in art. L17. B *adj.* Of or pertaining to mannerism or mannerists. M20.

manne'ristic *a.* characterized by mannerism M19. **manne'ristical** *a.* M19.

mannerize /ˈmanəraɪz/ *v.t. rare.* Also **-ise**. L19. [f. MANNER *n.*[1] + -IZE.] Make manneristic.

mannerless /ˈmanəlɪs/ *a.* L15. [f. MANNER *n.*[1] + -LESS.] Without manners; ill-mannered, unmannerly.

mannerlessness *n.* M20.

mannerly /ˈmanəli/ *a.* LME. [f. MANNER *n.*[1] + -LY[1].] 1 Characterized by good manners; well-mannered; polite. Formerly also, seemly, decent, respectable, modest. LME. †2 Moral, well-conducted. LME–M16.

mannerliness *n.* L15.

mannerly /ˈmanəli/ *adv.* LME. [f. MANNER *n.*[1] + -LY[2].] With good manners; politely, courteously. Formerly also, in a seemly manner, decently, becomingly.

¶Earlier in UNMANNERLY *adv.*

Mannesmann /ˈmanɪsmən/ *n.* E20. [Reinhard M. *Mannesmann* (1856–1922), Ger. industrialist and inventor.] Used *attrib.* to designate a method of making thick-walled seamless metal tubes by drawing a heated cylinder of metal lengthwise on to a pointed mandrel.

mannie /ˈmani/ *n.* Orig. & chiefly *Sc.* Also **manny**. L17. [f. MAN *n.* + -IE, -Y[6].] A little man. Freq. as a term of endearment to a little boy.

mannikin *n.* & *a.* see MANIKIN.

mannish /ˈmanɪʃ/ *a.* [OE *mennisċ*, f. as MAN *n.* + -ISH[1]. Later re-formed on or infl. by MAN *n.*] 1 Of, pertaining to, or characteristic of the human species. Long *rare.* OE. 2 Of a woman, a woman's attributes, etc.: resembling (those of) a man, masculine. Chiefly *derog.* LME. 3 Of, pertaining to, or characteristic of an adult male person, as opp. to a boy or woman or both. M16.

mannishly *adv.* M19. **mannishness** *n.* LME.

mannite /ˈmanaɪt/ *n.* M19. [f. MANNA + -ITE[1].] *Chem.* = MANNITOL.

mannitic /maˈnɪtɪk/ *a.* derived from mannite M19.

mannitol /ˈmanɪtɒl/ *n.* L19. [f. prec. + -OL.] *Chem.* A colourless sweet-tasting crystalline alcohol, $CH_2OH(CHOH)_4CH_2OH$, which is found in many plants and is used in various foods and medical products. Also called *manna sugar, mannite*.

Mannlicher /ˈmanlɪkə, *foreign* ˈmanlɪçər/ *n.* L19. [Ferdinand Ritter von *Mannlicher* (1848–1904), Austrian inventor.] A type of sporting rifle. Also more fully *Mannlicher rifle*.

mannose /ˈmanəʊz, -s/ *n.* L19. [f. MANNITE + -OSE[2].] *Chem.* A hexose sugar which occurs as a component of many natural polysaccharides, esp. mannans.

Mann-Whitney /manˈwɪtni/ *n.* M20. [f. Henry Berthold *Mann* (b. 1905), Austrian-born US mathematician + Donald Ransom *Whitney* (b. 1915), US statistician.] *Statistics.* Used *attrib.* with ref. to a method of comparing samples from two unmatched groups of subjects, based on the rank ordering. Chiefly in *Mann-Whitney (U) test*.

manny *n.* var. of MANNIE.

mano /ˈmano, ˈmɑːnəʊ/ *n.* Pl. **-os** /-ɒs, -əʊz/. E20. [Sp. = hand.] *Anthropol.* A primitive hand-held stone implement, used in the Americas for grinding cereals etc.

mano a mano /ˌmɑːnəʊ ə ˈmɑːnəʊ *foreign* ˌmano a ˈmano/ *a., adv.,* & *n. phr.* Also **mano-a-mano**. L20. [Sp. = hand to hand.] A *adj.* & *adv. phr.* Hand to hand; one to one; face to face. L20. B *n. phr.* A confrontation, a duel. L20.

manoao /ˈmanəʊˌəʊ/ *n.* Also **mon-** /ˈmɒn-/. M19. [Maori.] A New Zealand coniferous tree, *Halocarpus kirkii* (family Podocarpaceae).

Manoeline *a.* var. of MANUELINE.

manoeuvrable /məˈnuːvrəb(ə)l/ *a.* Also ***maneuver-**. E20. [f. MANOEUVRE *v.* + -ABLE.] Able to be manoeuvred, (esp. of an aircraft or motor vehicle) easily manoeuvred.

manoeuvra'bility *n.* E20.

manoeuvre /məˈnuːvə/ *n.* Also ***maneuver**. L15. [Fr. *manœuvre* (OFr. *manuevre*), f. as next.] †1 Work using the hands. *rare.* Only in L15. 2 (A) planned or regulated movement of one or more military, naval, etc., units; (a) tactical or strategic movement or change of position. Now often in *pl.*, large-scale tactical exercises involving various fighting units. M18. 3 *gen.* (A) deliberate movement, esp. to deceive or elude; a move or act of control requiring some skill; an ingenious expedient or artifice. L18.

2 B. JOWETT The manoeuvres suited to fast-sailing vessels . . cannot be practised in a narrow space. D. FRASER In any siege manoeuvre ceases. M. FITZHERBERT He left . . to go on manoeuvres with the Japanese Army. 3 H. MACMILLAN The Chancellor was at first inclined to regard my visit as . . an election manoeuvre. D. FRANCIS The furniture had been pushed back . . to give the fat man clear space for manoeuvre. K. M. E. MURRAY To dismount . . by falling sideways, a manoeuvre apt to take by surprise any unwary cyclist following. *Valsalva('s) manoeuvre*: see VALSALVA I.

manoeuvre /məˈnuːvə/ *v.t.* & *i.* Also ***maneuver**. L18. [Fr. *manœuvrer* f. med.L *man(u)operare* for L *manu operari* work with the hand, f. *manus* hand.] (Cause to) perform a manoeuvre or manoeuvres; move or steer by an act of control requiring some skill; employ or effect by stratagem or artifice; act or manipulate schemingly or adroitly. (Foll. by *into, out of*, etc.)

C. STEAD She manoeuvred the car round a tricky corner. J. C. OATES They maneuver him into the foyer and into the elevator. J. RABAN A scallop boat manoeuvered alongside. R. K. NARAYAN Rann was manoeuvring to elope with the girl. M. FLANAGAN You get what you want. You manoeuvre everyone. J. DISKI He had manoeuvered the conversation from the general to a personal confrontation.

manoeuvrer *n.* E19. **manoeuvring** *n.* the action of the vb; an instance of this, a manoeuvre: L18.

man-of-war /manəvˈwɔː/ *n.* Also **man o'war** /man əˈwɔː/. Pl. **men-** /mɛn-/. LME. [In sense 1 app. after Fr. *homme de guerre*; in sense 2 cf. MAN *n.* 15.] 1 A fighting man; a soldier, a warrior. Now *arch.* or *joc.* LME. 2 A vessel equipped for warfare; a warship belonging to the recognized navy of a country. Now chiefly *Hist.* L15. 3 A sailor serving on a man-of-war. More usu. *man-of-war's-man*. Now chiefly *Hist.* L16. 4 More fully *man-of-war bird*. A large sea bird; *spec.* a frigate-bird. M17. 5 In full *Portuguese man-of-war*. A large pelagic siphonophore of the genus *Physalia*, with a float like a sail and numerous stinging tentacles. E18. 6 *Hist.* Used *attrib.* to designate a boy's garment resembling that worn by a sailor. L19.

Comb.: **man-of-war fish** any of various tropical marine fishes of the family Nomeidae, esp. *Nomeus gronovii*, which is often found among the tentacles of Portuguese men-of-war.

manoir /manwaːr/ *n.* Pl. pronounced same. M19. [Fr.: see MANOR.] A French manor-house; a country house built in the style of a French manor-house.

manoletina /ˌmanoleˈtina, ˌmanə(ʊ)ləˈtiːnə/ *n.* Pl. **-as** /-as, -əz/. M20. [Sp., f. *Manolete* professional name of the Sp. bullfighter Manuel L. R. Sánchez (1917–47) + *-ina* -INE[4].] *Bullfighting.* A decorative pass in which the muleta is held behind the back in the left hand. Also called *orteguina*.

manometer /məˈnɒmɪtə/ *n.* M18. [Fr. *manomètre*, f. Gk *manos* thin, rare: see -METER.] An instrument for measuring the pressure in a fluid; *esp.* one consisting of a U-tube containing mercury or other liquid, a difference in the pressures acting on the two ends of the liquid column being indicated by a difference in the levels reached by the liquid in the two arms of the U-tube.

manoˈmetric *a.* of or pertaining to a manometer or manometers; made with a manometer: L19. **manoˈmetrical** *a.* = MANOMETRIC L18. **manoˈmetrically** *adv.* by means of a manometer L19. **manometry** *n.* the use of manometers E20.

manool /məˈnəʊɒl/ *n.* Also **manoöl**. M20. [f. MANOAO + -OL.] *Chem.* A bicyclic diterpenoid alcohol, which occurs in the oil of manoao wood and is used as a base for perfumes.

manor /ˈmanə/ *n.* ME. [AN *maner*, OFr. *maneir*, (also mod.) *manoir* dwelling, habitation, use as n. of inf. *maneir* dwell f. L *manere* remain.] 1 A mansion, a house; the principal house of an estate. Also, such a house with the land belonging to it; a landed possession. Now *Hist.* exc. in names of or with ref. to specific (ancient) manor-houses and in *lady* or *lord of the manor* s.v. LADY *n.* & *a.*, LORD *n.* ME. †b *fig.* An abode, a resting-place. LME–L16. 2 A unit of English territorial organization, orig. of the nature of a feudal lordship, now consisting of a lord's demesne and lands from whose holders the lord may extract certain fees etc. M16. 3 *N. Amer. Hist.* An estate held in fee-farm, *esp.* one granted by royal charter in a British colony or by the Dutch governors of what is now New York State. M17. 4 A police district; a local unit of police administration; *transf.* one's home ground, one's own particular territory. *slang.* E20.

1 *steward of the manor*: see STEWARD *n.* 4 B. FORBES His own Chief Constable.. deeply resented any intrusion into his manor.

Comb.: **manor-house**, (*arch.*) **manor-place** the mansion of the lord of a manor.

manorship *n.* = MANOR 2 L18.

manorial /məˈnɔːrɪəl/ *a.* L18. [f. prec. + -IAL. Cf. MANERIAL.] Of or pertaining to a manor or manors; incidental to a manor.

manorialiˈzation *n.* the process of making or becoming manorial E20. **manorialize** *v.t.* make manorial L19.

manoscope /ˈmanəskəʊp/ *n. rare.* M18. [f. *mano-* as in MANOMETER + -SCOPE.] = MANOMETER.

manostat /ˈmanəstat/ *n.* E20. [f. as prec. + -STAT.] A device for automatically maintaining a constant pressure in an enclosed space.

manoˈstatic *a.* M20.

man o'war *n. phr.* var. of MAN-OF-WAR.

manpower /ˈmanpaʊə/ *n.* & *v.* M19. [f. MAN *n.* + POWER *n.*] A *n.* 1 The power or agency of man in work; (power as measured in terms of) a unit of rate of performing work, approximately equal to one-tenth of a horsepower. M19. 2 The body of people available or needed for military service, work, or other purpose; workers viewed as a quantifiable resource, labour. E20.

1 G. CLARK The mere transport of these by manpower would have involved 100,000 levies. 2 A. J. TOYNBEE The invaders found the entire manpower of Macedon arrayed against them. *London Daily News* The company has reduced manpower in glass by 30%. *attrib.*: A. MILLER You would think.. that with the manpower shortage they'd economize on personnel.

B *v.t. Hist.* Conscript for non-military service as part of the war effort. *Austral.* & *NZ colloq.* M20.

manque /mɑ̃ːk/ *n.* M19. [Fr., f. *manquer* fall short (of), lack, fail (from the numbers' failing to be higher).] In roulette, that section of the cloth covering the numbers 1 to 18; a bet placed on this section.

manqué /mɑ̃ke, ˈmɒŋkeɪ/ *a.* Fem. also **-ée**. L18. [Fr., pa. ppl a. of *manquer*: see prec.] 1 *postpositive.* That might have been but is not, that has missed being. L18. 2 *pred.* Defective, spoilt, missing, lacking. L18.

1 *Saturday Review* 'The History of Anthony Waring' is a poem manqué. G. VIDAL He chose to be a dentist, that last resort of the rabbi manqué.

mansard /ˈmansɑːd, -səd/ *n.* Also (esp. in sense 2) **-de**. M18. [Fr. *mansarde* (*toit en mansarde*), f. François *Mansard* (1598–1666), Fr. architect.] 1 More fully *mansard roof*. A roof in which each face has two slopes, the lower one steeper than the upper, a curb roof. M18. 2 A storey or apartment under a mansard roof. L19.

mansarded *a.* E20.

manse /mans/ *n.* L15. [med.L *mansus*, *-sa*, *-sum*, f. *mans-*: see MANSION.] †1 The principal house of an estate. L15–L18. 2 An ecclesiastical residence; a house allocated to or occupied by a minister, esp. in the Church of Scotland. M16. 3 A measure of land regarded as sufficient for the support of a family, *spec.* as an ecclesiastical endowment. *obs.* exc. *Hist.* L16.

2 **child, daughter, son**, etc., **of the manse** the child etc. of a Protestant minister, esp. in the Church of Scotland.

manservant /ˈmansəːv(ə)nt/ *n.* Pl. **menservants** /ˈmɛnsəːv(ə)nts/. LME. [f. MAN *n.* + SERVANT *n.*] A male servant.

manship /ˈmanʃɪp/ *n.* Long *rare.* OE. [f. MAN *n.* + -SHIP.] †1 Humanity, kindness; courtesy. OE–LME. †2 Homage; honour. Only in ME. 3 Manly courage, manliness. Long *obs.* exc. *dial.* ME. 4 The condition of being a man. ME.

-manship /mənˈʃɪp/ *suff.* [f. MAN *n.* + -SHIP, after *churchmanship*, *craftsmanship*, etc. In mod. spec. sense orig. in GAMESMANSHIP.] Forming ns. denoting skill in a subject or activity; *spec.* skill so deployed as to disconcert a rival or opponent, as *brinkmanship*, *gamesmanship*, *oneupmanship*, etc.

mansion /ˈmanʃ(ə)n/ *n.* ME. [(O)Fr. f. L *mansio(n-)* stay, station, abiding-place, quarters (whence Fr. *maison* house), f. *mans-* pa. ppl stem of *manere* remain, stay. In sense 6 rendering med.L *mansus*, *-sa*: cf. MANSE.] †1 The action of remaining, living, or staying in a place. Also, continuance in a position or state. ME–E18. 2 A place in which to live or lodge, a place of abode; in *pl.* formerly *spec.*, in a larger house or delimited area. *arch.* ME. 3 A structure or building serving as a place in which to live or lodge. Now only *spec.* a manor-house, a large and stately residence. ME. b In *pl.* (treated as *sing.*). A large building divided into flats. Chiefly in proper names. L19. †4 A stopping-place in a journey; the distance between two stopping-places; a stage. LME–M18. 5 *Astrol.* = HOUSE *n.*[1] 9b. Also, each of the twenty-eight divisions of the ecliptic, occupied by the moon on successive days. LME. 6 *Hist.* A hide of land. LME.

1 H. SYDENHAM Sitting presupposes stabilitie and mansion. 2 TINDALE *John* 14:2 In my fathers housse are many mansions. S. JOHNSON Oxford, the mansion of the liberal arts. 3 W. VAN T. CLARK He'd built a white wooden mansion.. like a Southern plantation home. *Sunday Express* Plas Mawr.. is a fascinating Elizabethan mansion.

Phrases: **have, keep, make**, or **take one's mansion** dwell, abide.

Comb.: **mansion-house** (*a*) *gen.* a dwelling-house; (*b*) an official residence; formerly *esp.* that belonging to the benefice of an ecclesiastic; now *spec.* (*the Mansion House*) the official residence of the Lord Mayor of London; (*c*) the house of the lord of a manor, the chief residence of a landed proprietor; (now *US*) a large house of good appearance; †**mansion-seat** (*a*) a place of abode; (*b*) the chief residence of a landed proprietor.

mansionry *n.* (*rare*) mansions collectively E17.

mansionary /ˈmanʃ(ə)n(ə)ri/ *a.* & *n. rare.* LME. [med.L *mansionarius*, f. L *mansio(n-)*: see prec., -ARY[1].] †A *adj.* Living or lodging in a place, resident. LME–E18. B *n.* †1 A resident. Only in LME. †2 *Eccl.* An endowment for a chantry priest. Only in M17. 3 A custodian of a church. E18.

manslaughter /ˈmanslɔːtə/ *n.* & *v.* ME. [f. MAN *n.* + SLAUGHTER *n.*] A *n.* †1 The killing of a human being by a human being; (esp. criminal) homicide, murder. ME–E17. 2 The slaughtering of human beings; destruction of human life. ME. 3 *Law.* The unlawful killing of a human being in circumstances not amounting to murder; criminal homicide without malice aforethought. ME. B *v.* 1 *v.i.* Slaughter human beings. Chiefly as *manslaughtering* ppl a. & vbl n. E18. 2 *v.t.* Kill (a person) without malice aforethought. *colloq.* E20.

manslaughterer *n.* (*a*) a person who slaughters human beings; (*b*) a person who commits manslaughter: M19. **manslaughterous** *a.* L19.

manso /ˈmanso/ *n.* & *a.* Pl. **-os** /-ɔs/. M19. [Sp.] (A person who or animal which is) meek, tame, or cowardly.

mansonia /manˈsəʊnɪə/ *n.* M20. [mod.L (see below), f. F. B. *Manson* (fl. 1905), forester in Burma (Myanmar): see -IA[1].] Any of several large trees of the genus *Mansonia* (family Sterculiaceae), esp. the W. African *M. altissima*; the hardwood obtained from such a tree.

mansuete /manˈswiːt, ˈmanswiːt/ *a.* Now *arch. rare.* LME. [L *mansuetus*, f. *manus* hand + *suetus* accustomed.] Gentle, mild; tame, not wild or fierce.

mansuetude /ˈmanswɪtjuːd/ *n. arch.* LME. [(O)Fr. *mansuétude* or L *mansuetudo*, f. as prec.: see -TUDE.] Gentleness, meekness, docility.

manswear /ˈmanswɛː/ *v.* Long *obs.* exc. *Sc.* & *north.* Pa. t. **-swore** /-swɔː/; pa. pple **-sworn** /-swɔːn/. [OE *mānswerian*, f. *mān* wickedness (= OFris., OS *mēn*, OHG *mein* (surviving in G *Meineid* perjury), ON *mein*) + *swerian* SWEAR *v.*] 1 *v.i.* Swear falsely. OE. 2 *v.t.* a As *mansworn* ppl a. Perjured. ME. b *refl.* Perjure oneself. LME. †3 *v.t.* Swear falsely by (a god etc.); take (a god's name etc.) in vain. LME–M16. †4 *v.t.* Renounce on oath, forswear. LME–M17.

†**mant** *n.* M17. [Sense 1 f. Sp. MANTO; sense 2 f. Fr. *mante*, ult. f. late L *mantus*: see MANTLE *n.*] 1 A mantilla. Only in M17. 2 = MANTEAU. L17–M18.

manta /ˈmantə/ *n.* L17. [Sp. = blanket.] 1 In Spain and Spanish-speaking countries: a wrap, a cloak. L17. 2 More fully *manta ray*. A very large tropical ray of the genus *Manta* or the family Mobulidae. Also called *devilfish*. M18.

manteau /ˈmantəʊ/ *n.* L17. [Fr.: see MANTLE *n.* Cf. MANTUA.] *Hist.* A loose gown worn by women in the 17th and 18th cents.; a robe. Also, a cloak.

Comb.: **manteau-maker** a maker of women's robes; a dressmaker.

manteca /manˈtɛkə/ *n. obs.* exc. *US dial.* M17. [Sp., of unkn. origin.] Butter, lard, fat.

†**manteel** *n.* L15–M19. [App. f. Fr. *mantille* f. Sp. MANTILLA. Cf. MANTLE *n.*] A cloak or similar garment; a cape; a mantle.

mantel /ˈmant(ə)l/ *n.* Also **mantle**. L15. [Specialized use of MANTLE *n.*] †1 = MANTELET 2. L15–M16. 2 a = MANTELTREE 1 (earlier). E16. b = MANTELPIECE 1. M16. c = MANTELSHELF 1. M18.

Comb.: **mantel clock** a clock designed to sit on a mantelpiece; **mantelplace** *dial.* = MANTELPIECE 1.

¶ Earlier in MANTELTREE.

mantelet /ˈmantlɪt/ *n.* Also **mantlet**. LME. [OFr., dim. of *mantel* MANTLE *n.*: see -ET[1].] 1 A kind of short loose sleeveless cape, cloak, or mantle. LME. †b A woollen covering for a horse. LME–M16. †c = MANTELLETTA. E17–E18. 2 *Mil.* A movable shelter or protective screen, *esp.* (*Hist.*) one used to cover the approach of soldiers when besieging a fortified place. Cf. earlier MANTEL 1. E16.

mantelletta /mantɪˈlɛtə/ *n.* Pl. **-ttas, -tte** /-ti/. M19. [It., prob. f. med.L *mantelletum* f. L *mantellum* MANTLE *n.*] *RC Ch.* A sleeveless vestment reaching to the knees, worn by cardinals, bishops, and other high-ranking ecclesiastics.

mantelpiece /ˈmant(ə)lpiːs/ *n.* Also **mantle-**. L17. [f. MANTEL + PIECE *n.*] 1 The ornamental structure of wood, marble, etc., above and around a fireplace; the manteltree of a fireplace with its supports. L17. 2 = MANTELSHELF 1. E19.

mantelshelf /ˈmant(ə)lʃɛlf/ *n.* Also **mantle-**. Pl. **-shelves** /-ʃɛlvz/. E19. [f. MANTEL + SHELF *n.*[1]] 1 A projecting part of a mantelpiece serving as a shelf. E19. 2 *Mountaineering* & *Rock-climbing*. A projecting shelf of rock. L19.

Comb.: **mantelshelf technique** *Mountaineering* & *Rock-climbing* a technique for climbing on to a ledge using the heels of the hands.

manteltree /ˈmant(ə)ltriː/ *n.* Also **mantle-**. LME. [f. MANTEL + TREE *n.*] 1 A beam across the opening of a fireplace, supporting the masonry above. In later use, a stone or arch serving the same purpose. LME. 2 = MANTELPIECE. M17.

mantic /ˈmantɪk/ *a.* M19. [Gk *mantikos*, f. *mantis* prophet, f. *man-* as in MANIA: see -IC.] Of or pertaining to divination or prophecy.

mantical *a.* = MANTIC L16. **mantically** *adv.* E19. **manticism** /-sɪz(ə)m/ *n.* the practice of divination M19.

-mantic /ˈmantɪk/ *suff.* [f. as prec.] Forming adjs. corresponding to ns. in -MANCY, as *geomantic* etc.

manticore /ˈmantɪkɔː/ *n.* Also **-cora** /-kɔːrə/, **-ger** /-gə/. ME. [L *manticora* repr. Gk *mantikhōras*, corrupt reading in Aristotle for *martikhoras*, f. an OPers. wd for 'man-eater'.] 1 A fabulous monster having the body of a lion, the head of a man, porcupine's quills, and the tail or sting of a scorpion. ME. 2 *Her.* A monster represented with the body of a beast of prey, the head of a man, sometimes with spiral or curved horns, and sometimes the feet of a dragon. L15.

mantid /ˈmantɪd/ *n.* L19. [f. MANTIS + -ID[3].] A mantis; an insect of the family Mantidae.

mantiger *n.* var. of MANTICORE.

mantilla /manˈtɪlə/ *n.* E18. [Sp., dim. of *manta* MANTLE *n.*] 1 A light scarf, freq. of black lace, worn over the head and shoulders, esp. by Spanish women. E18. 2 A small cape or mantle. M19.

Mantinean /mantɪˈniːən/ *n.* & *a.* M16. [f. Gk *Mantineia*, L *Mantinea* (see below) + -AN.] (A native or inhabitant) of the ancient city of Mantinea in Arcadia, Greece.

mantis /ˈmantɪs/ *n.* Pl. **-ises**, same. M17. [mod.L f. Gk, lit. 'prophet': see MANTIC.] Any of various predatory insects of the family Mantidae, usu. slender and cryptically coloured, with a mobile triangular head and large raptorial forelimbs held raised and folded like hands in prayer. Also *praying mantis*.

Comb.: **mantis shrimp** any of various predatory marine crustaceans of the order Stomatopoda (Hoplocarida), having a pair of large spined raptorial front legs resembling those of a mantis.

mantissa /manˈtɪsə/ *n.* M17. [L *mantis(s)a* makeweight, perh. f. Etruscan.] †1 An addition of comparatively small importance, esp. to a text or discourse. M–L17. 2 *Math.* a The part of a logarithm after the decimal point. M19. b The number or quantity to which an exponent is appended; *spec.* in *Computing*, a number (usu. of a fixed number of digits) which is multiplied by a specified power of a base to represent any number by floating-point representation. M20.

mantle /ˈmant(ə)l/ *n.* See also MANTEL. OE. [L *mantellum* var. of *mantelum* rel. to *mantelium*, *-ele*, *-til-* towel, napkin, tablecloth, whence also late L *mantus*, med.L *mantum* short cloak. Replaced in ME by forms f. OFr. *mantel* (mod. *manteau*) f. L.] 1 A loose sleeveless cloak, now usu. one worn by a woman. Now freq. *fig.*, repr. responsibility, authority, etc., handed down (from the passing of Elijah's mantle to Elisha (*2 Kings* 2:13)). OE. b More fully *Irish mantle*. A kind of blanket or plaid worn until the 17th cent. by the rustic Irish. Now *rare* or *obs.* L15. c *Her.* = MANTLING *n.* 3. Also, an unslashed robe of estate borne behind an achievement. L16. d *transf.* With qualifying colour adj. A person, *spec.* a herald, wearing a mantle of the specified colour. E17. †2 a A blanket, a cover. ME–L18. b A measure of quantity of furs, containing from 30 to 100 skins. LME–M17. 3 *transf.* & *fig.* A thing that enfolds, enwraps, or encloses; a covering. ME. 4 *Zool.* In molluscs, cirripedes, and brachiopods, the layer of epidermal tissue which encloses the body and secretes the shell. Also, any of various similar enclosing structures, as the body-wall of an ascidian. LME. 5 The plumage of the back and folded wings of a bird, esp. if distinct in colour. M19. 6 A fragile lacelike covering fixed over a gas-jet to give an incandescent light when heated. Also *gas-mantle*. L19. 7 *Bot.* The outer layer of cells in an apical meristem. L19. 8 *Anat.* & *Zool.* = PALLIUM 3b. L19. 9 *Geol.* The layer in the interior of the earth which extends between the crust and the core, and is physically and chemically distinct from each. Formerly *gen.*, that part of the earth outside the core. M20.

1 R. DAHL He had taken upon himself the mantle of Health Officer. V. BROME Since Freud's death the mantle had mutually descended on Anna Freud and Ernest Jones. d *Bluemantle* etc. 3 SHAKES. *Lear* Poor Tom; that . . drinks the green mantle of the standing pool. MILTON The Moon . . unvaild her peerless light And o're the dark her Silver Mantle threw. J. CONRAD Ribs of grey rock under the dank mantle of matted leafage.

Phrases & comb.: *lady's mantle*: see LADY *n.* & *a.* **mantle-cavity** the space enclosed between the mantle and the body of a mollusc, brachiopod, etc., containing respiratory organs. **mantle fibre** *Cytol.* any spindle fibre which is attached to a chromosome. *mantlepiece*: see MANTELPIECE. *mantleshelf*: see MANTELSHELF. *mantletree*: see MANTELTREE. WATTEAU *mantle*.

mantlewise *adv.* in the manner of a cloak or mantle M16.

mantle /ˈmant(ə)l/ *v.* ME. [Partly f. the n., partly f. OFr. *manteler*.] 1 *v.t.* Clothe or wrap in or as in a mantle; cover, conceal; obscure; enfold, embrace; encircle, surround; envelop. ME. 2 *v.i.* & †*refl.* Of a perched bird of prey: spread the wings over the outstretched legs, spread the wings and tail so as to cover food. L15. 3 *v.i.* Of a liquid: be or become covered with a coating or scum; form a head. L16. 4 *v.i.* Form a mantle or covering; spread or be extended over a surface. M17. 5 *v.i.* & *t.* Suffuse (the cheeks, the face) with a blush; (of a blush etc.) suffuse the cheeks; flush. E18.

1 M. ARNOLD The mourning-stole no more Mantled her form. M. AMIS This frenzy of solitude which mantles me now. R. CARVER Clouds mantled the white hills. 4 SIR W. SCOTT Seldom o'er a breast so fair, Mantled a plaid with modest care. 5 DISRAELI Her rich face mantling with emotion. W. S. CHURCHILL The blood mantled his cheek.

mantled /ˈmant(ə)ld/ *a.* LME. [f. MANTLE *n.*, *v.*: see -ED[2], -ED[1].] 1 Wearing a mantle; covered (as) with a mantle. LME. 2 *Her.* Having the outside of mantling of a specified tincture. L16.

mantlepiece *n.* var. of MANTELPIECE.

mantleshelf *n.* var. of MANTELSHELF.

mantlet *n.* var. of MANTELET.

mantletree *n.* var. of MANTELTREE.

mantling /ˈmantlɪŋ/ *n.* E16. [f. MANTLE *n.*, *v.* + -ING[1].] 1 †a The action of making a mantle. Only in E16. b The action of MANTLE *v.* E17. 2 Orig., a kind of cloth. Later, material for making mantles. Now *rare*. M16. 3 *Her.* An ornamental accessory of slashed drapery issuing from a helmet and sometimes resembling acanthus leaves flowing from the helmet; a lambrequin. L16. 4 A mantle; a protective or ornamental covering. Now *rare*. M17. 5 A blush or suffusion of colour produced by emotion. M18.

manto /ˈmantəʊ/ *n.* Pl. **-os**. L17. [It. & Sp. f. late L *mantus*, med.L *mantum*: see MANTLE *n.*] A (Spanish etc.) cloak or mantle.

†**mantoa** *n.* var. of MANTUA.

†**Mantoan** *n.* & *a.* var. of MANTUAN.

mantology /manˈtɒlədʒi/ *n.* *rare*. L18. [Irreg. f. Gk *mantis* (see MANTIC) + -OLOGY.] The art or practice of divination.

Manton /ˈmant(ə)n/ *n.* E19. [See below.] *Hist.* More fully *Joe Manton*. A fowling-piece or other firearm made by the London gunsmith Joseph Manton.

man-t'ou /ˈmantəʊ/ *n.* Also ***mantou***. M20. [Chin. *mántou*.] Steamed bread, as eaten in N. China.

Mantoux /ˈmɑ̃tuː, ˈmantuː/ *n.* M20. [Charles *Mantoux* (1877–1947), Fr. physician.] *Med.* Used *attrib.* to designate a type of intradermal tuberculin test.

mantra /ˈmantrə/ *n.* Also (*rare*) **-tram** /-trəm/. L18. [Skt, lit. 'thought', f. *man* think.] A sacred Hindu text or passage, *esp.* one from the Vedas used as a prayer or incantation; in Hinduism and Buddhism, a holy name or word, for inward meditation; *transf.* & *fig.* a repeated phrase or sentence, a formula, a refrain.

mantri /ˈmantri/ *n.* L18. [Skt *mantrī*: see MANDARIN *n.*[1]] 1 In India etc.: a minister, a counsellor. L18. 2 In Indonesia (including the former Netherlands East Indies): a minor official or subordinate functionary vested with some authority. E19.

mantric /ˈmantrɪk/ *a.* L20. [f. MANTRA + -IC.] Of, pertaining to, or of the nature of a mantra.

mantua /ˈmantjʊə/ *n.* Also **M-**, †**-toa**. M16. [See sense 1. In sense 2 alt. of MANTEAU after this.] 1 (**M-**.) Used *attrib.* to designate things made in or associated with the city of Mantua in northern Italy. M16. 2 *Hist.* = MANTEAU. L17. †3 A material of a type made in Mantua. Only in 18.

Comb.: **mantua-maker** *Hist.* a person who makes mantuas, a dressmaker; **mantua-making** *Hist.* the making of mantuas, dressmaking.

Mantuan *n.* & *a.* (a native or inhabitant) of Mantua LME.

Manu /ˈmanuː/ *n.* L18. [Skt *manu*: see MAN *n.*] In Hindu cosmology: the first man; any of the series of cosmic deities and progenitors of humankind presiding over a distinct period of time or manvantara.

manual /ˈmanjʊ(ə)l/ *a.* & *n.* LME. [(O)Fr. *manuel* f. L *manualis*, f. *manus* hand: see -AL[1]. Later assim. to L.] A *adj.* 1 Of or pertaining to the hand or hands; done or performed with the hands, involving physical rather than mental effort; worked by hand, not by automatic equipment or with electronic etc. assistance. LME. b Of a signature etc.: autograph. Chiefly in SIGN-MANUAL. LME. 2 *Law.* Of occupation, possession: actual, in one's own hands, not merely prospective. M16. 3 That works with the hands; engaged in labour involving physical rather than mental effort. M17.

1 E. B. TYLOR I expressed my ideas by manual signs. M. MEYER Ibsen hated seeing his wife doing anything manual such as knitting. *Farm Machinery* A manual over-ride to allow the driver to guide the machine into the crop. **manual alphabet** the finger alphabet. **manual exercise** *Mil.* exercise or drill in handling a rifle or musket. 3 G. GREENE Do you believe . . that a manual labourer should be paid less than a man who works with his brains?

B *n.* 1 A small book for handy use; a concise treatise, an abridgement, a handbook, a textbook; a book of instructions for operating a machine, learning a subject, etc.; *Eccl. Hist.* a book containing the forms to be observed by priests in the administration of the sacraments etc. LME. 2 *ellipt.* Anything distinguished by manual operation, as (a vehicle with) a manual gearbox, a manual typewriter, etc. L17. 3 *Mil.* = *manual exercise* above. M18. 4 An organ keyboard played with the hands, as opp. to one operated by the feet. M19.

1 B. TRAPIDO Roger had duly acquired us an antiquated sex manual. P. ROSE A great number of domestic manuals about women's place appeared in the 1830s. *Practical Motorist* The manual is very comprehensive and is in three volumes.

manualism *n.* (*rare*) the action or process of teaching by means of the manual alphabet L19. **manualist** *n.* †(*a*) a person who works or labours with the hands; (*b*) a user or advocate of the manual alphabet: L16. **manually** *adv.* L15.

manuary /ˈmanjʊ(ə)ri/ *a.* & *n.* Long *rare*. M16. [L *manuarius*, f. *manus* hand: see -ARY[1].] A *adj.* 1 Of or pertaining to the hand; performed by or with the hands; manual. M16. †2 That works with the hands. M–L17. †B *n.* 1 A manual worker. L16–M17. 2 (People engaged in) manual work. L16–E17.

manubrium /mə'n(j)uːbrɪəm/ *n.* Pl. **-ia** /-ɪə/, **-iums**. M17. [L.] †1 A handle, a haft. *rare.* Only in M17. 2 *Anat.* & *Zool.* A projection like a handle, esp. (*a*) on the malleus of the mammalian ear; (*b*) in some birds, on the keel of the sternum; (*c*) in rotifers, forming the lower part of the malleus; (*d*) in coelenterates, forming the tube which bears the mouth. M19. b The broad upper part of the sternum of mammals, with which the clavicles and first ribs articulate. M19.

manubrial *a.* M19.

manucaption /manjʊ'kapʃ(ə)n/ *n. obs.* exc. *Hist.* L16. [med.L *manucaptio(n-)*, f. *manucapt-* pa. ppl stem of *manucapere* lit. 'take by the hand': see -ION.] *Law.* 1 = MAINPRIZE *n.* 1. L16. 2 A writ directing the bringing in of a person charged with a felony. L16.

manucaptor *n.* = MAINPERNOR L16.

manucode /'manjʊkəʊd/ *n.* M19. [Fr. f. mod.L *manucodiata* f. Malay *manuk dewata* bird of the gods. Cf. next.] A bird of paradise; *spec.* any of several blue-black birds of the genus *Manucodia*, of New Guinea, *esp.* the trumpet-bird (also found in Queensland, Australia).

†**manucodiata** *n.* M16–M18. [mod.L: see prec.] A bird of paradise.

manuduction /manjʊ'dʌkʃ(ə)n/ *n.* E16. [med.L *manuductio(n-)*, f. *manu ducere* lead by the hand, guide: see -ION.] 1 The action or an act of leading, guiding, or introducing. E16. 2 A means or instrument of guidance or introduction. Now *rare.* E17.

†**manuductor** *n.* M17–M19. [f. L *manu* by the hand + L DUCTOR leader.] A guide, a director; *spec.* the conductor of a band or choir.

manuductory /manjʊ'dʌkt(ə)ri/ *a. rare.* L17. [f. as prec.: see -ORY[2].] Leading (as) by the hand; that leads up to or towards something; introductory.

Manueline /'manjʊəlʌɪn/ *a.* Also **Manoel-** /'manəʊəl-/. E20. [f. *Manuel* I (b. 1469), king of Portugal + -INE[1].] Of, pertaining to, or designating a style of Portuguese architecture developed during the reign of Manuel I (1495–1521) and characterized by ornate elaborations of Gothic and Renaissance styles.

†**manufaction** *n.* E17–M18. [f. L *manu* by hand + *factio(n-)* making, FACTION *n.*[1]] Manufacture.

†**manufactor** *n.* M17–E19. [f. L *manu* by hand + *factor* maker, FACTOR *n.*] A manufacturer, an artificer.

manufactory /manjʊ'fakt(ə)ri/ *n.* E17. [Alt. of MANUFACTURE *n.*, *v.* after FACTORY: see -ORY[1].] †1 A product of labour, a manufactured article. E17–L18. †2 The production of manufactured goods. E17–M19. 3 A place where a product is manufactured, a factory, a workshop. M17.

†**manufactory** *a.* M17–M18. [f. as MANUFACTOR: see -ORY[2].] Pertaining to or of the nature of manufacture; engaged in manufacture.

manufacture /manjʊ'faktʃə/ *n.* M16. [Fr. f. It. *manifattura* w. refashioning after L *manu factum* made by hand: see FACT, -URE.] 1 †a An article made by hand; a person's handiwork. M16–E18. b An article or material produced by physical labour or machinery, now *spec.* one produced on a large scale. E17. c *depreciative.* A product of mere mechanical labour; an article produced merely to supply the demand of the market. L19. 2†a The action or process of making something by hand. Only in E17. b The action or process of making articles or material by physical labour or machinery, now *spec.* on a large scale. E17. c A particular branch or form of productive industry. L17. d *depreciative.* Production involving mere mechanical labour, as contrasted with that requiring intellect or imagination. Also, deliberate fabrication of false statements etc. on a large scale. E19. †3 Working with the hands; a manual occupation, handicraft. Only in 17. 4 A manufacturing establishment or business; a factory. Long *rare.* M17.

2b of home, foreign, English, etc. **manufacture** manufactured at home, abroad, etc. c *linen manufacture, woollen manufacture,* etc.

manufactural *a.* of or pertaining to manufacture L18.

manufacture /manjʊ'faktʃə/ *v.t.* L17. [f. the n.] 1 Bring (material) into a form suitable for use. L17. 2 Make or fabricate from material; produce by physical labour or machinery, now *spec.* on a large scale. M18. b Produce by natural agency. L19. 3 *depreciative.* Invent fictitiously, deliberately fabricate. Also, produce by mere mechanical labour rather than by intellect or imagination. M18.

2 R. CROMPTON Throwing paper pellets at her (manufactured previously for the purpose). E. LANGLEY Dried tea leaves from which he manufactured reconditioned tea. C. THUBRON China . . still manufactures steam engines. b ANTHONY HUXLEY Unique characteristic of plants is their capacity to manufacture energy from light. 3 D. MACDONALD His books seem to have been manufactured rather than composed. R. DEACON Attempts to manufacture evidence against . . Western politicians.

manufactura'bility *n.* ability to be manufactured L20. **manufacturable** *a.* able to be manufactured L18.

manufacturer /manjʊ'faktʃ(ə)rə/ *n.* E18. [f. prec. + -ER[1].] †1 A factory worker. E18–M19. 2 An employer of workers for manufacturing; a factory-owner; a manufacturing company or group. M18. 3 *depreciative.* A producer of something by mere mechanical labour; a deliberate fabricator of false statements etc. E19.

manuka /'mɑːnʊkə, mə'nuːkə/ *n.* M19. [Maori.] Any of several Australasian trees and shrubs of the genus *Leptospermum*, of the myrtle family, with a hard dark close-grained wood and an aromatic leaf used as a substitute for tea; esp. *L. scoparium*, of New Zealand and Tasmania.

manul /'mɑːnʊl/ *n.* L18. [App. f. Kirghiz.] A small wild cat, *Felis manul*, of the mountains and steppes of central Asia. Also called *Pallas's cat.*

manumise /'manjʊmʌɪz/ *v.t.* Now *rare.* Also **-miss** /-mɪs/, **-ize**. E16. [L *manumiss-*: see next. Form in *-ise* after *promise* etc., in *-ize* after *-ise*, *-ize* variation.] Chiefly *Hist.* = MANUMIT.

manumission /manjʊ'mɪʃ(ə)n/ *n.* LME. [(O)Fr., or L *manumissio(n-)*, f. *manumiss-* pa. ppl stem of *manumittere* MANUMIT.] Chiefly *Hist.* The action of manumitting, the fact of being manumitted; formal release from slavery or servitude; an act or instance of this.

manumit /manjʊ'mɪt/ *v.t.* Infl. **-tt-**. LME. [L *manumittere*, pre-cl.L *manu emittere* lit. 'send out from one's hand'.] Chiefly *Hist.* Release from slavery; release from bondage or servitude; set free.

M. MITCHELL Old Angus had never manumitted a single slave. S. HEANEY Subjugated yearly under arches, Manumitted by parchments and degrees.

manumitter *n.* M19.

manumize *v.* var. of MANUMISE.

manumotive /manjʊ'məʊtɪv/ *a.* E19. [f. L *manu* by hand + MOTIVE *a.*] Of a vehicle: propelled by a mechanism worked by hand.

manurable /mə'njʊərəb(ə)l/ *a.* E17. [f. MANURE *v.* + -ABLE.] †1 *Law.* Admitting of being held in corporeal possession. E17–M18. 2 Of land: that can be worked or cultivated. Long *rare.* M17. 3 Able to be manured or fertilized. E19.

†**manurage** *n. rare.* L16–L18. [f. MANURE *v.* + -AGE.] Occupation or cultivation of land.

manurance /mə'njʊər(ə)ns/ *n.* Now *rare.* LME. [f. MANURE *v.* + -ANCE.] †1 Tenure, occupation (of land or other property); control, management. LME–E18. 2 Formerly, cultivation (of land), tillage. Later, manuring. L16. †b *fig.* Cultivation or training of the character or faculties. L16–E17.

manure /mə'njʊə/ *n.* M16. [f. the vb.] 1 Dung or compost (to be) spread over or mixed with soil to fertilize it. Also, (an) artificial fertilizer. M16. †2 The action of MANURE *v.*; cultivation. M16–L17.

1 *green manure*: see GREEN *a. liquid manure*: see LIQUID *a.* & *n. long manure*: see LONG *a.*[1] *short manure*: see SHORT *a.*

Comb.: **manure-heap** a heap of manure and sometimes other organic refuse kept for fertilizer.

manur(e)y *a.* splashed or littered with manure L19.

manure /mə'njʊə/ *v.* LME. [AN *mainoverer*, OFr. *mano(u)vrer* (mod. *manœuvrer*): see MANOEUVRE *v.* Assim. to -URE.] †1 *v.t.* Hold or occupy (land, property); have the tenure of; administer, manage. LME–M17. †b *v.t.* & *i.* Live in or *in* (a place). L16–L17. 2 *v.t.* Orig., till, cultivate (land). Later *spec.*, enrich (land) with manure; apply manure to; supply with fertilizing material. LME. †b Improve or develop (the body, mind, etc.) by training. M16–L18. †c Promote the growth of, cultivate (a plant). L16–M18. d *v.i.* Apply manure. M19. †3 *v.t.* Work on with the hands; handle. LME–L16.

†**manurement** *n.* cultivation (*lit.* & *fig.*) M17–E18. **manurer** *n.* L15.

manurial /mə'njʊərɪəl/ *a.* M19. [Irreg. f. MANURE *n.* + -IAL.] Of, pertaining to, or of the nature of manure.

manus /'meɪnəs/ *n.* Pl. same /-'nuːs/. E16. [L = hand.] †1 *manus Christi* [lit. 'hand of Christ'], sugar boiled in rose-water etc., as a drink for invalids. E16–E18. 2 *Anat.* & *Zool.* The terminal or distal segment of the forelimb, esp. of a vertebrate; the hand. Cf. PES. E19. 3 *Rom. Law.* The power or authority which certain husbands had over their wives. M19.

†**manuscribe** *v.t. rare.* M17–E19. [f. L *manu* by hand + *scribere* write.] Write with one's (own) hand.

manuscript /'manjʊskrɪpt/ *a.* & *n.* L16. [med.L *manuscriptus*, f. L *manu* by hand + *scriptus* pa. pple of *scribere* write. Cf. med.L *manuscriptum* document in a person's own hand.] A *adj.* Written by hand, not printed; (of paper) printed with staves for writing music by hand. L16.

B *n.* 1 A book, document, etc., written by hand; a book, document, etc., written before the general adoption of printing in a country; a written composition which has not been printed, an author's written or (now) typed copy of a work for printing and publication. E17. 2 A person's (style of) handwriting. M19. 3 The state of being in written form; writing as opp. to print. L19.

1 M. COWLEY Sheets of typewritten manuscript, with words crossed out. K. CLARK Only three or four antique manuscripts of the Latin authors are still in existence. R. V. JONES Written in longhand, it was typed . . direct from my manuscript. J. BERMAN Freud usually destroyed all the . . original manuscripts after a work was published. 3 H. CARPENTER Strong did not recommend that *'Outlines'* . . be published, and the book remained in manuscript.

Comb.: **manuscript paper** paper ruled for writing music on.

¶ Abbrev. *MS*, pl. *MSS*.

manuscriptal *a.* (*rare*) L17. **manu'scriptural** *a.* (*rare*) [after SCRIPTURAL] E19.

manvantara /man'vantərə/ *n.* M19. [Skt, f. as MANU + *antara* period.] In Hindu cosmology: any of the fourteen periods, each presided over by a special Manu or cosmic god, which make up a *kalpa*.

Manx /maŋks/ *a.* & *n.* E16. [ON, assumed metath. alt. of *Man-* (nom. *Mǫn*) f. OIr. *Manu* Isle of Man + *-skr* -ISH[1].] A *adj.* Of or pertaining to (the inhabitants or language of) the Isle of Man in the Irish Sea. E16. B *n.* 1 The Celtic language of the Isle of Man, not now learned as a first language but still in use for ceremonial purposes. M17. 2 As *pl. The* people of the Isle of Man. L17. 3 A Manx cat. L19.

Special collocations & *comb.*: **Manx cat** a tailless variety of the domestic cat, originating in the Isle of Man. **Manxman** a (male) native of the Isle of Man. **Manx shearwater** a shearwater of Atlantic and Mediterranean waters, *Puffinus puffinus*, brownish black with white underparts. **Manxwoman** a female native of the Isle of Man.

many /'mɛni/ *a.* (in mod. usage also classed as a *determiner*), *pron.*, & *n.* Compar. †**manier** (now served by MORE *a.* etc.), †**maniest** (now served by MOST). [OE *manig*, *monig*, later *mænig*, corresp. to OFris. *man(i)ch*, *monich*, *menich*, OS *manag*, MDu. *menech* (Du. *menig*), OHG *manag*, *menig* (G *manch*), OSw. *mangher*, Goth. *manags*, f. Gmc.] A *adj.* 1 A great (indefinite) number of. Preceding *n.sing.* with the indef. article *a(n)* or *another* (now *literary* or *rhet.*), *n.sing.* without article (long *obs.* exc. *Sc.*), *n.pl.* (†and any determiners); following *n.pl.* (*poet.* & *arch.*). OE. 2 As subj. or compl. of *be*: (indefinitely) great in number. Treated as *sing.* (only in *many is*, *was*, *the* — (esp. *time*)) or *pl.* Now *literary* or *rhet.* ME. 3 *A* great number of; (now usu.) *a good*, *great*, etc., number of. L16.

1 SHAKES. *Ant. & Cl.* Letters . . of many our contriving friends. DICKENS We must drink many happy returns to her. R. ELLIS Many a wistful boy, and maidens . . desire it. BROWNING In its hope that for many and many a year we may have your very self among us. A. WILSON She dearly loved . . a gentleman at her feet, and many a one . . she'd had. R. GORDON It's going to be many a long day before I get involved. M. L. KING Errands to be run, phone calls to be made, typing, so many things. C. JACKSON There weren't many Cadillacs around in those days. *comb.*: SHELLEY Like a dome of many-coloured glass. A. N. WHITEHEAD And space is many-dimensional. 2 E. BOWEN Though they were still many, the lamps were fewer. *Encounter* Many were the times we went out to hunt. J. NAGENDA Many's the time I've asked myself, 'Why me?'

B *pron.* & *n.* 1 *absol.* Many people or things understood contextually; many people; a great number *of*, a lot *of*. OE. 2 *The* great body of persons or things (specified or understood); *the* majority. E16. 3 *A* great number (*of*); (now usu.) *a good*, *great*, etc., number (*of*). E16. †4 [App. by confusion with MEINIE.] A company, a host, a flock (*of*); one's retinue or following. L16–E18.

1 J. MORLEY Many of his ideas . . did not belong to him peculiarly. T. HARDY When . . the audience withdrew, many chose to find their way out. O. MANNING He was only one knave of many. G. GREENE Many served very gallantly in the Red Cross. 2 COLERIDGE The . . foolish self-opinion of the half-instructed many. 3 THACKERAY Catholic gentry, of whom there were a pretty many in the country. J. HUXLEY A good many were separated at birth from their mothers.

Phrases: **as many** the same number of, that number of. **as many again** the same number additionally. †**as many as** all who. *have many strings to one's bow*: see STRING *n.* *how many*: see HOW *adv.* *in so many words*: see WORD *n.* *many's the time*: see TIME *n.* *of many words*: see WORD *n.* **one too many** something not wanted, something repeated to excess. **the one and the many** *Philos.* unity and plurality. **too many for** more than a match for.

Comb.: **many-body** *a.* pertaining to or involving three or more bodies or particles, *spec.* w. ref. to the problem of predicting their future positions and motions given their present states and manner of interacting; **many-headed** *a.* having many heads; *the many-headed* (*beast*, *monster*), the people, the populace; **many-many** *a.* designating or pertaining to a correspondence or relation between two sets such that each member of either set is associated with or related to two or more members of the other; **many-one** *a.* designating or pertaining to a correspondence or relation such that two or more members of one set are associated with or related to each member of a second set; **many-sided** *a.* having many sides, aspects, bearings, capacities, or possibilities; **many-sidedness** the condition of being many-sided; **many-valued** *a.* (*Math.*) having more than one value for some or all of its argument(s); that maps to more than one point, number, etc.; **many-where** *adv.* (*rare*) in many places.

manyness *n.* (*rare*) †(*a*) a great number; (*b*) plurality, numerousness: LME.

manyatta /man'jatə/ *n.* E20. [Masai.] Among certain African peoples, esp. the Masai: a group of huts forming a unit within a common fence.

manyfold /'mɛnɪfəʊld/ *adv.* L19. [f. MANY + -FOLD. Cf. MANIFOLD *adv.*] In the proportion of many to one.

manyogana /manjə'gɑːnə/ *n.* Also **-kana** /-'kɑːnə/. M19. [Jap. *man'yōgana*, f. *Man'yōshū* lit. 'collection of a myriad leaves', an 8th-cent. poetry anthology in which the system is found + KANA.] A system of writing in use in Japan in the 8th cent. in which Chinese characters represented Japanese sounds.

manyplies /'mɛnɪplʌɪz/ *n.* Chiefly *dial.* L18. [f. MANY + *plies* pl. of PLY *n.* (from its many folds).] The omasum or third stomach of a ruminant. Also (*joc.*), a person's stomach.

manzanilla /manzə'nɪlə, -'niːljə; *foreign* manθa'niʎa/ *n.* M19. [Sp., lit. 'camomile'.] 1 A kind of pale very dry sherry; a drink or glass of this. M19. 2 A variety of olive, distinguished by small thin-skinned fruit. E20.

manzanita /manzə'niːtə, *foreign* manθa'nita/ *n.* M19. [Sp., dim. of *manzana* apple.] (The fruit of) any of various bearberries of the south-western US.

manzello /man'zɛləʊ/ *n.* Pl. **-os**. M20. [Origin unkn.] A musical instrument resembling a soprano saxophone.

manzil /'mʌnzɪl/ *n.* Also **men-** /'mɛn-/. M17. [Arab., f. *nazala* descend, alight.] In the Middle East: a stopping-place; the distance between two stopping-places, a stage.

Mao /maʊ/ *a.* M20. [f. *Mao* Zedong: see next.] Designating a garment or article of clothing characterized by a simplicity of style based on dress formerly worn in Communist China.

J. MITCHELL Mao boiler suit to show he was one of the righteous.

Maoism /'maʊɪz(ə)m/ *n.* M20. [f. *Mao* Zedong (Tse-Tung) (1893–1976), Chairman of the Central Committee of the Chinese Communist Party + -ISM.] The Marxist-Leninist theories of Mao Zedong developed and formerly practised in China.

Maoist *n.* & *a.* (*a*) *n.* a follower of Mao or his theories; (*b*) *adj.* of or pertaining to Maoism or Maoists: M20.

maomao /'maʊmaʊ/ *n.* *NZ.* L19. [Maori.] An edible blue marine fish, *Scorpis aequipinnis* (family Kyphosidae), of New Zealand and Australian waters. Also *blue maomao*.

Maori /'maʊri, 'mɑː(ə)ri/ *n.* & *a.* M19. [Maori.] A *n.* Pl. **-s**, same. 1 A member of the Polynesian aboriginal people of New Zealand. M19. 2 The language of this people. M19. 3 (Also **m-**.) Each of three brightly coloured wrasses, *Ophthalmolepsis lineolatus*, of the S. Australian coast, and *Cheilinus undulatus* and *C. fasciatus* of the tropical Indian and Pacific Oceans. Also *Maori wrasse*. L19.

B *attrib.* or as *adj.* Of or pertaining to the Maoris or their language. M19.

Special collocations, comb., & phrases: KOPA MAORI. **Maori bug** *NZ* a large cockroach, *Platyzosteria novaeseelandiae*, which emits an unpleasant smell when disturbed. **Maori dog** *NZ* a dog of Polynesian origin first introduced to New Zealand by the Maoris and now extinct. **Maori-hen** = WEKA. **Maoriland** (*colloq.*, chiefly *Austral.*) New Zealand; **Maorilander** (*colloq.*, chiefly *Austral.*) a White New Zealander; **Maori oven** = KOPA MAORI. **Maori PT** *NZ slang* taking it easy and doing nothing. *Maori wrasse*: see sense A.3 above.

Maoridom *n.* the Maori world; Maori culture: L19.

Maoritanga /maʊrɪ'taŋə/ *n.* M20. [Maori.] The culture, traditions, and heritage of the Maori people; the individuality of the Maoris; the fact of being a Maori.

maormor *n.* var. of MORMAOR.

Mao-tai /maʊ'tʌɪ/ *n.* M20. [A town in SW China.] A strong sorghum-based liquor distilled in SW China.

map /map/ *n.*[1] E16. [med.L *mappa* (*mundi*) lit. 'sheet (of the world)', f. L *mappa* tablecloth, napkin + *mundi* genit. of *mundus* world.] 1 A (flat) representation of the earth's surface or a part of it, showing physical, geographical, or political features, as mountains, roads, relative rainfall, territorial divisions, etc.; a similar representation of the sky showing the relative positions of stars etc., or of the surface of a planet etc. Also, a diagrammatic representation of a route etc. E16. b A diagram representing the spatial distribution of anything or the relative positions of its components; *spec.* (*Genetics*) a diagram which represents the linear order and relative distance apart of the known genes of (part of) a chromosome (also *linkage map*). M19. 2 A representation or account of a state of things (now *rare* or *obs.*); the embodiment *of* a quality etc.; the very picture or image *of*. Now *rare*. L16. 3 A person's face. *slang*. E20. 4 *Math.* = MAPPING 2. M20.

1 A. FRASER The King had to be shown where Tangier was on the map. J. RABAN Finding Qatar . . on a map of Arabia requires . . perseverance. R. B. PARKER The Holiday Inn . . had a map of downtown Portland in its lobby. *Sunday Times* A small, bearded Armenian whose face is a map of worry lines. b W. L. BRAGG Electron density map of the phthalocyanine molecule. 2 BURKE I don't know the map of their situation.

Phrases: CONTOUR *map*. KARNAUGH *map*. *linkage map*: see sense 1b above. *moving map*: see MOVING *a.* **off the map** into (or in) oblivion or an insignificant position; of no account. **on the map** in an important or prominent position; of some account or importance; freq. in *put on the map*. *video map*: see VIDEO *a.* & *n.*

Comb.: **map butterfly** a small nymphalid butterfly, *Araschnia levana*, with prominent white veins on the underside of the wings; **map-fire** artillery-fire in which maps are used for laying the guns; **map lichen** a lichen, *Lecidea geographica*, whose thallus has markings resembling a map; **map-maker** a person who makes maps, a cartographer; **map-making** the making of maps, cartography; **map-measurer**, **map-meter** an instrument for measuring distances on maps; **map-net** = GRATICULE 1; **map projection** a geometrical or cartographic method of representing on a flat surface (part of) the earth's surface; **map-read** *v.i.* consult and interpret a map (chiefly as *map-reading* vbl n.); **map reference** a set of numbers or letters specifying a location as represented on a map; **map turtle** any of several freshwater turtles of the genus *Graptemys* (family Emydidae), which have prominent markings on the head and shell; esp. *G. geographica*, of the central US and the Great Lakes.

mapless *a.* without a map or maps M17. **mappy** *a.* like a map M19.

†**map** *n.*[2] see MOP *n.*[2]

map /map/ *v.* Infl. **-pp-**. L16. [f. MAP *n.*[1]] 1 *v.t.* Make a map of; represent or delineate (as) on a map; establish the relative positions, or the spatial relations or distribution, of (an object or its components). L16. b Associate with each element of (a set) one or more elements of another set in accordance with a mapping; associate (an element) with one or more others in this way; *Computing* associate (an item of data) with a specified location in memory; associate (a memory location) with a data item; *Ling.* convert *into* by the application of a rule. Foll. by *to*, *into*, *onto*. M20. 2 *v.t.* Foll. by *out*: a Orig., record in detail. Later, plan; envisage; outline. E17. b Represent in detail on a map. M17. c Divide into districts, as by lines on a map. M19. 3 *v.i.* Fall into place on a map or plan; *spec.* have a specified position on a genetic map. L19.

1 P. CAREY Cartographers were still able to map the questionable parts of the nether regions. W. BRONK To explore / and map a surrounding country. b N. CHOMSKY The transformational rules map deep structures into surface structures. 2a H. CARPENTER He mapped out the imaginative territory . . he would explore in closer detail. *Daily Express* Robson maps out plan for 1990.

mappable *a.* that may be represented on or by a map E20. **mapper** *n.* a map-maker M17. **mappery** *n.* (*derog.*) map-making E17. **mappist** *n.* (*rare*) = MAPPER E17.

mapau /'mɑːpaʊ/ *n.* *NZ.* Also **mapou**. M19. [Maori.] Any of several New Zealand trees; esp. *Rapanea australis* (family Myrsinaceae), an evergreen tree with reddish twigs and clusters of small white flowers (also called *red matipo*).

mape /'mɑːpeɪ/ *n.* Also **mapé**. L19. [Polynesian.] = IVI.

Mapharsen /ma'fɑːs(ə)n/ *n.* M20. [f. *meta-amino para-hydroxyl* + ARSEN(IC *n.* & *a.*[1]] An organic arsenical drug formerly used to treat syphilis.

¶ Proprietary name in the US.

maple /'meɪp(ə)l/ *n.* & *a.* [OE *mapel-* (in *mapeltrēow*, *mapulder* corresp. to OS *mapulder*, MLG *mapeldorn*). Simple form recorded from LME.] A *n.* 1 A Eurasian tree, *Acer campestre* (family Aceraceae), with fruit in the form of two winged samaras joined together and palmately lobed leaves (more fully *common* or *hedge maple*). Also (w. specifying wd), any of numerous similar trees of this or other genera. Also *maple tree*. OE. 2 The wood of these trees. Also *maple-wood*. LME. b The colour of maple-wood, a light brown. M19. 3 In full *maple pea*. A variety of field pea with mottled seeds. E18.

1 *Japanese maple, mountain maple, Norway maple, soft maple*, etc.

B *attrib.* or as *adj.* Made of or resembling maple-wood; of the colour of maple-wood, light brown. M17.

Special collocations & comb.: **maple beer** an alcoholic drink made from maple sap. **maple bush** a shrubby maple, *Acer spicatum*, of mountains in N. America (also called *mountain maple*). **maple candy** a sweet made from maple sap. **maple-honey** *US* the uncrystallized part of the sap of the sugar maple. **maple key** the fruit of a maple. **maple-leaf** (*a*) the leaf of the maple, used as an emblem of Canada; (*b*) a Canadian gold coin traded as an item for collectors and investors. **maple molasses** *US* = *maple syrup* below. *maple pea*: see sense A.3 above. **maple sugar** *N. Amer.* sugar obtained by evaporation from the sap of certain maples, *esp.* the sugar maple. **maple syrup** a syrup obtained by evaporating maple sap or dissolving maple sugar; *maple syrup (urine) disease*, a rare metabolic disorder leading to diminished intelligence and usu. fatal at a very early age, in which the urine has a characteristic smell of maple syrup owing to the presence of certain amino acids. *maple tree*: see sense A.1 above. *maple-wood*: see sense A.2 above.

mapou *n.* var. of MAPAU.

†mapp *n.* see MOP *n.*[2]

mappemonde /map'mɔ̃d/ *n.* LME. [(O)Fr. f. med.L *mappa mundi*: see MAP *n.*[1]] *Hist.* A map of the world. Formerly also, the world itself.

mapping /'mapɪŋ/ *n.* L18. [f. MAP *v.* + -ING[1].] 1 The action of MAP *v.* L18. 2 *Math., Ling.*, etc. A correspondence by which each element of a given set has associated with it one or more elements of a second set; a transformation; *spec.* a continuous transformation. Cf. MAP *n.*[1] 4. M20.

1 *video mapping*: see VIDEO *a.* & *n.*

maprotiline /mə'prəʊtɪliːn/ *n.* L20. [f. unidentified 1st elem. + alt. of *-tyline* after AMITRIPTYLINE etc.] *Pharm.* A tetracyclic antidepressant.

Mapuche /ma'pʊtʃi/ *n.* & *a.* E20. [Mapuche, f. *mapu* country + *che* people.] A *n.* Pl. same, **-s**. 1 A member of any of the Araucanian Indian peoples of central Chile and Argentina. E20. 2 The language of these peoples. M20. B *attrib.* or as *adj.* Of or pertaining to the Mapuche or their language. M20.

maquereau /makro/ *n.* Pl. **-eaux** /-o/. L19. [Fr.] = MACKEREL *n.*[2]

maquette /ma'kɛt/ *n.* E20. [Fr. f. It. *macchietta* speck, little spot, dim. of *macchia* spot, f. *macchiare* to spot, stain, f. L *maculare* MACULATE *v.*] A small preliminary sketch or wax or clay model from which a sculpture is elaborated.

maqui /mɑː'kiː/ *n.* E18. [Sp. *maquí* f. Mapuche.] A Chilean evergreen shrub, *Aristotelia chilensis* (family Elaeocarpaceae), whose berries are sometimes used to adulterate wine.

maquiladora /makija'dora/ *n.* L20. [Mex. Sp., f. *maquilar* assemble.] A factory in Mexico run by a foreign company and exporting its products to the country of that company.

maquillage /makijaʒ/ *n.* L19. [Fr., f. *maquiller* make up one's face, f. OFr. *masquiller* to stain, alt. of *mascurer* darken: see -AGE.] Make-up, cosmetics; the application of this.

maquillé(e) /makije/ *a.* wearing cosmetics, made up E20.

maquis /'mɑːkiː/ *n.* Pl. same. M19. [Fr. f. as MACCHIA.] 1 The dense scrub characteristic of certain Mediterranean coastal regions, esp. in Corsica. M19. 2 *Hist.* (Usu. **M-**.) A member of the French resistance movement during the German occupation (1940–5). M20. b A member of any resistance group or army. M20.

maquisard /mɑːkiː'zɑː/ *n.* a member of the Maquis M20.

mar /mɑː/ *n.*[1] ME. [f. the vb.] 1 A hindrance, an obstruction; a speech impediment. *obs.* exc. *Sc.* ME. 2 A thing which mars or impairs something, a drawback *to*. Formerly also, a fault. M16.

2 P. S. BUCK Almost a mar to his beauty were his two black brows, too heavy . . for his young, pale face.

Mar /mɑː/ *n.*[2] L17. [Aram.] An honorific title for a saint or a member of the higher clergy, chiefly in the Nestorian and Jacobite Churches.

mar /mɑː/ *v.* Infl. **-rr-**. [OE *merran*, (WS) *mierran* = OFris. *meria*, OS *merrian* hinder (Du. *marren* fasten, tie up, loiter), OHG *marren*, *merren* hinder, ON *merja* bruise, crush, Goth. *marzjan* cause to stumble (tr. Gk *skandalizein*).] 1 *v.t.* Hinder, interrupt, or stop (a person, event, etc.). *obs.* exc. *Sc.* OE. 2 *v.t.* Damage so as to render useless, ruin, impair the quality. Now chiefly, detract from or impair the perfection of, disfigure. OE. †b *v.i.* Deteriorate, spoil. ME–E17. 3†a *v.i.* Be or become bewildered or confused. OE–E16. b *v.t.* Confuse, bewilder; trouble; annoy. Long *obs.* exc. *Sc.* ME. 4 *v.t.* a Do bodily harm to. *arch.* ME. b *fig.* Ruin (a person, a person's fortunes, etc.); ruin morally, corrupt. Now only (*dial.*), spoil (a child) by indulgence. ME.

2 R. W. HAMILTON The vessel is so marred that it cannot be repaired. W. S. MAUGHAM Not a wrinkle marred the smoothness of her skin. D. LODGE She led a busy, enjoyable life, only slightly marred by occasional twinges of anxiety. D. FRASER Brooke, complete with a streaming cold which had marred the weekend. P. LOMAS His interesting ideas are rather marred by a self-indulgent . . style. *make or mar*: see MAKE *v.*

Comb.: **mar resistance**, **mar-resistant** *a.* resistance, resistant, to loss of gloss by abrasion.

mara /'mɑːrə/ *n.* M19. [Amer. Sp. *mará*.] = *Patagonian cavy* s.v. PATAGONIAN *a.*

Mara /'mɑːrə/ *n.*[2] L19. [Skt *Māra* = death, f. *mṛ-* die.] *Buddhism.* The personification of evil.

marabou /'marəbuː/ *n.* & *a.* Also **mari-** /'marɪ-/, **-bout**. E19. [Fr. f. Arab. *murābiṭ* holy man (see next), the stork being regarded as holy.] A *n.* 1 A tropical African stork, *Leptoptilos crumeniferus*, which has an inflatable pendent pouch on the neck and feeds on carrion. Also *marabou stork*. E19. 2 A tuft of soft white down from the wings or tail of this stork, used for trimming hats etc.; *collect.* trimming made of this down. E19. 3 An exceptionally white kind of raw silk which can be dyed without first removing the natural gum and is used in crêpe weaving. M19. B *adj.* Made of marabou. E19.

marabout /'marəbuːt/ *n.*[1] E17. [Fr. f. Port. *marabuto* f. Arab. *murābiṭ*, f. *ribāṭ* frontier station, where merit could be acquired by combat against the infidel. Cf. MARAVEDI.] 1 A Muslim holy man or mystic, esp. in N. Africa. E17. 2 A shrine marking the burial place of a marabout. M19.

marabout *n.*[2] & *a.* var. of MARABOU.

marabunta /marə'bʌntə/ *n.* L19. [Guyanan name.] In Guyana and the Caribbean islands, a social wasp.

†marabuto *n.* E17–M19. [Sp.] *Naut.* A jib-sail.

maraca /mə'rakə/ *n.* Also **-cc-**. E17. [Port. *maracá* f. Tupi *maráka*.] A Latin American percussion instrument made from a hollow gourd or gourd-shaped container filled with beans etc., and usu. shaken in pairs. Usu. in *pl.*

maracock /'marəkɒk/ *n. obs.* exc. *Hist.* E17. [Algonquian.] (The fruit of) any of certain American passion-flowers, esp. the May-pop, *Passiflora incarnata*, of the southern US.

marae /mə'rʌɪ/ *n.* L18. [Polynesian.] Orig. (now *Hist.*), a Polynesian sacrificial altar or sacred enclosure. Now, the courtyard of a Maori meeting-house, esp. as a forum or centre for ceremonies and social functions.

marage /'mɑːreɪdʒ/ *v.t.* M20. [f. MAR(TENSITE + AGE *v.*] *Metall.* Strengthen (a steel alloy) by a process of slow cooling involving the transformation of austenite to martensite and subsequent age-hardening.

maraging steel: suitable for or hardened by maraging, usu. containing up to 25 per cent nickel and smaller amounts of other metals.

marah /'mɑːrə/ *n.* & *a.* LME. [Heb. *mārāh* (fem. of *mar* bitter) used as a proper name in *Exod.* 15:23 and *Ruth* 1:20.] In biblical allusions: bitter(ness).

maral /'mɑːr(ə)l/ *n.* M19. [Turkic.] A red deer, *Cervus elaphus*, of the Caspian subspecies.

Maranao /'marənaʊ/ *n.* & *a.* M20. [Maranao *Maranáw*, f. *ranaw* lake.] A *n.* Pl. same. 1 A member of a Moro people inhabiting the province of Lanao del Sur and parts of central Cotabato province on the island of Mindanao in the Philippines, and some areas of northern Borneo. M20. 2 The Austronesian language of this people. M20. B *attrib.* or as *adj.* Of or pertaining to the Maranao or their language. M20.

maranatha /marə'naθə/ *adv.*, *n.*, & *int.* Also **M-**. LME. [Gk, f. Aram. *māran ʾᵃṯā* our Lord has come, or *māranā ṯā* O Lord, come.] A *adv.* In translations of *1 Cor.* 16:22.: at the coming of the Lord. LME. B *n.* [By a misunderstanding of *1 Cor.* 16:22.] More fully *anathema maranatha*. A portentously intensified anathema; a terrible curse. M17. C *int.* In the early Church: expr. a deep longing for the coming of the Lord. L19.

Marangoni /maraŋ'gəʊni/ *n.* M20. [Carlo G. M. *Marangoni* (1840–1925), It. physicist.] *Physics.* 1 *Marangoni effect*, small-scale turbulence at a liquid interface owing to local variations in surface tension. Hence *Marangoni instability*, instability in a liquid interface associated with such variations. M20. 2 *Marangoni number*, a dimensionless number equal to the ratio of the surface tension gradient in a liquid to the product of viscous drag and the rate of heat diffusion. M20.

maranta /mə'rantə/ *n.* E19. [mod.L (see below) f. Bartollomeo *Maranta*, 16th-cent. It. herbalist.] Any of various tropical American monocotyledonous plants of the genus *Maranta* (family Marantaceae), which includes the arrowroot; *esp.* the prayer plant, *M. leuconeura*, of Brazil, which has variegated leaves, and is grown as a house-plant.

marantic /mə'rantɪk/ *a.* L19. [Gk *marantikos*, f. *marainein* waste away: see -IC.] *Med.* Pertaining to or of the nature of marasmus.

marasca /mə'raskə/ *n.* M19. [It., aphet. f. *amarasca*, f. *amaro* bitter.] A small black Dalmatian cherry, a variety of morello cherry grown for the distilling of maraschino. Also *marasca cherry*.

maraschino /marə'skiːnəʊ/ *n.* Pl. **-os**. L18. [It., f. as prec. + *-ino* -INE[1].] A strong sweet liqueur distilled from the marasca cherry.

Comb.: **maraschino cherry**: preserved in real or imitation maraschino and used esp. to decorate cocktails etc.

†marasme *n.* E17–E18. [Fr.] = MARASMUS.

marasmic /mə'razmɪk/ *a.* L19. [f. MARASMUS + -IC.] Pertaining to or arising from marasmus; affected with marasmus.

marasmus /mə'razməs/ *n.* M17. [mod.L f. Gk *marasmos*, f. *marainein* waste away.] Severe loss of weight in a person, esp. an undernourished child; *Med.* the condition in a child of having a weight less than 60 per cent of the normal for his or her age.

Maratha /mə'rɑːtə/ *n.* & *a.* Also **Mahratta**. M18. [Marathi *Marāṭhā*, Hind. *Marhaṭṭā* f. Skt *Mahārāṣṭra* great kingdom. Cf. MAHARASHTRI.] Chiefly *Hist.* A *n.* A member of the princely and military classes of the former Hindu kingdom of Maharashtra in central India (now the modern Indian State of Maharashtra). M18. B *attrib.* or as *adj.* Of or pertaining to the Marathas. M18.

Marathi /mə'rɑːti/ *n.* & *a.* Also **Mahratti**. L17. [f. as prec.: see -I[2].] (Of or pertaining to) the Indo-Aryan language of the Marathas, now the official language of the Indian State of Maharashtra.

marathon /'marəθ(ə)n/ *n.* & *a.* L19. [*Marathōn* in Greece, site of an Athenian victory over an invading Persian army in 490 BC, news of the victory traditionally being said to have been announced in Athens by a messenger who ran all the way from the battlefield and fell dead on arrival.] A *n.* 1 A long-distance running race, usu. of 26 miles 385 yards (42.195 km). L19. 2 Any race, competition, or activity of long distance or duration requiring endurance. E20.

1 J. HOPKINS British runners are to be found among the leaders in almost every international Marathon. 2 G. PRIESTLAND The gradual conversion of Christmas . . into a TV-watching marathon. *Packet* (*Camborne*) Leukaemia sufferer Louise . . will benefit from a 72 hour sponsored CB marathon.

B *attrib.* or as *adj.* Of, pertaining to, or designating a marathon or marathons; of long distance or duration. E20.

F. WILT Regarded as one of the world's premier marathon runners. *Christian Aid News* Agriculture Ministers . . emerged from 90-hour, marathon talks in Brussels.

marathoner *n.* a person who competes in a marathon E20.

Marathonian /marəˈθəʊnɪən/ *a.* M17. [f. L *Marathonius*, f. as prec. + -IAN.] Of or pertaining to Marathon or the battle of Marathon.

maraud /məˈrɔːd/ *n. rare.* M19. [Fr. *maraude*, f. as next.] The action of raiding or plundering.

maraud /məˈrɔːd/ *v.* L17. [Fr. *marauder*, f. *maraud* rogue, vagabond, scoundrel.] 1 *v.i.* Make a plundering raid (*on*); plunder; raid. Also, pilfer systematically. L17. 2 *v.t.* Plunder (a place). E19.

1 P. S. BUCK Robbers who . . marauded. . . Many houses they had burned and women . . carried away. E. FIGES Perched in the bottom branch of a tree to escape marauding tigers.

marauder *n.* L17.

maravedi /marəˈveɪdi/ *n.* LME. [Sp. *maravedí* f. Arab. *murābiṭīn* (obl. case pl. of *murābiṭ*: see MARABOUT *n.*[1]) name of the N. African Berber rulers of Muslim Spain from the late 11th cent. to 1145.] *Hist.* A former Spanish copper coin and monetary unit.

marble /ˈmɑːb(ə)l/ *n.* & *a.* Orig. also †**marbre**. ME. [OFr., dissimilated form of (O)Fr. *marbre* f. L *marmor* f. Gk *marmaros* shining stone, orig. (block of) stone, but later assoc. with *marmairein* shine.] A *n.* 1 Limestone that has been recrystallized by metamorphism and is capable of taking a polish; *esp.* one that is pure white or has a mottled surface. Also, a kind or variety of this. ME. b *fig.* As a type of something hard, inflexible, or durable. L16. 2 A piece, block, or slab of marble; a marble monument. ME. †b *spec.* A tomb or tombstone made of marble. ME–M18. c The stone as a material used for making tombs and tombstones. *poet.* E17. d *Antiq.* In *pl.* A collection of sculpture made of marble. Freq. w. specifying wd. M17. e A slab of marble on which to grind paints etc. L17. †3a A mottled or dappled colour resembling that of variegated marble; a cloth of such a colour. LME–E18. b The marbled pattern or paper used in ornamenting books. L17–E19. 4 A small ball orig. made of marble, now usu. of glass, clay, etc., used in a (children's) game; in *pl.*, the game itself. L17. b [tr. Fr. *meubles*.] In *pl.* Furniture, movables, personal effects. *slang.* M19. c In *pl.* Mental faculties; brains; common sense. *slang.* E20.

1 *Connemara marble*, *forest marble*, *landscape marble*, *statuary marble*, etc. b M. E. BRADDON Clarice had made up her mind . . , and she was marble. 2d *Oxford marbles*, *Elgin marbles*, etc. 4 HARPER LEE Children were playing marbles in Tom's front yard. DENNIS POTTER Its eyeballs changed colour and fell at my feet like squashy marbles. c *Daily Telegraph* At 91, Mr. Schotz not only has all his marbles, he is gifted with concentration.

Phrases: FOREST *marble*. ISTRIAN *marble*. KILKENNY *marble*. **make one's marble good** *NZ* & *Austral. slang* make a good impression on a person, ingratiate oneself. *pass in one's marble*: see PASS *v.*

B *adj.* 1 Made of or consisting of marble. LME. 2 Of a variegated or mottled colour; marbled. LME. 3 *fig.* Hard, cold, or rigid like marble; enduring as marble; smooth as marble. M16.

1 G. GREENE The beer slopped over on to the marble top of the table. 3 SHAKES. *3 Hen. VI* Her tears will pierce into a marble heart.

Special collocations & comb.: **marble bone** (*a*) *sing.* & in *pl.* = OSTEOPETROSIS; (*b*) a bone affected by osteopetrosis. **marble cake** (orig. *US*) a cake with a mottled appearance like that of marble. **marble gall** a hard, dark brown gall formed on the common oak by the gall wasp *Andricus kollari*. **marble orchard** *US slang* a cemetery. **marble-paper** paper coloured in imitation of marble. **marble-stone** (*obs.* exc. *dial.*) = senses A.1, 2 above. **marble-wood** any of various trees with mottled or banded wood, esp. *Diospyros marmorata* (family Ebenaceae) of the Andaman Islands, and the native olive *Olea paniculata*, of Australia; the timber of such a tree.

marble /ˈmɑːb(ə)l/ *v.t.* M17. [f. the n.] †1 Pickle (fish). Only in M17. 2 Cause to resemble marble; *spec.* (*a*) stain or colour (paper, the edge of a book, soap, etc.) to look like variegated marble; (*b*) *rare* make white like marble. Cf. earlier MARBLED 2. L17.

marbled /ˈmɑːb(ə)ld/ *a.* L16. [f. MARBLE *n.*, *v.*: see -ED[2], -ED[1]. Cf. MARL *n.*[3]] 1 Made of marble; portrayed in marble; decorated with marble. L16. 2 (Of paper, the edge of a book, soap, etc.) coloured or stained with a variegated pattern; mottled, dappled. E17. b *spec.* Of meat: having the lean streaked with thin layers of fat. L18.

1 M. CHABON The marbled steps of the library. 2 *Art & Craft* The children used . . marbled paper to represent the water. A. LURIE Wiping the worn marbled vinyl with a wet wadded paper towel.

marbled beauty a noctuid moth, *Cryphia domestica*, with white wings mottled with grey. **marbled green** a noctuid moth, *Cryphia muralis*, with wings of varying colours. **marbled newt** a large green newt, *Triturus marmoratus*, with blach blotches, found in SW Europe. **marbled white** (**butterfly**) a satyrid butterfly, *Melanargia galathea*, with creamy wings with black markings.

marbleize /ˈmɑːb(ə)lʌɪz/ *v.t.* Orig. *US.* Also **-ise**. M19. [f. MARBLE *n.* + -IZE.] Stain or colour to look like variegated marble; give a variegated appearance to, esp. by an artificial process. Chiefly as *marbleized* ppl a.

marbler /ˈmɑːblə/ *n.* ME. [f. MARBLE *n.*, *v.* + -ER[1].] 1 A person who quarries or carves marble. Now *rare* or *obs.* ME. 2 A person who marbles paper etc. Also, an instrument for marbling paper. M19.

marblet /ˈmɑːblɪt/ *n.* M19. [f. MARBLE *n.* + -ET[1], after Fr. *marbré* pa. pple of *marbrer* to marble.] A S. American iguanid lizard, *Polychrus marmoratus*.

marbling /ˈmɑːblɪŋ/ *n.* L17. [f. MARBLE *n.*, *v.* + -ING[1].] 1 The action of MARBLE *v.* L17. 2 Colouring or marking resembling that of marble. E18. b *spec.* In meat, the quality or state of being streaked with thin layers of fat. E20.

marbly /ˈmɑːbli/ *a.* LME. [f. MARBLE *n.* + -Y[1].] Resembling marble; rigid or cold like marble.

†**marbre** *n.* & *a.* see MARBLE *n.* & *a.*

Marburg /ˈmɑːbəːg/ *n.* M20. [A city in Germany.] Used *attrib.* to designate (the virus causing) an acute, often fatal, haemorrhagic febrile disease.

marc /mɑːk/ *n.* E17. [Fr., f. as MARCH *v.*[2] Cf. MURK *n.*[2]] 1 The refuse of processed grapes etc. E17. 2 A brandy made from this. Also *marc brandy*. M19.

Marcan /ˈmɑːk(ə)n/ *a.* E20. [f. L *Marcus* Mark + -AN.] *Chr. Ch.* Of, pertaining to, or characteristic of the evangelist St Mark or the Gospel attributed to him.

†**marcantant** *n. rare* (Shakes.). Only in L16. [Repr. It. *mercatante*.] A merchant.

marcasite /ˈmɑːkəsʌɪt, -ziːt/ *n.* & *a.* LME. [med.L *marcasita* f. Arab. *marḳašīta* f. Pers.: assoc. w. -ITE[1].] A *n.* 1 Orig., a metallic sulphide (as pyrites) or similar compound, *esp.* one which physically resembled the (specified) metal which it was (often erroneously) believed to contain. Now, iron pyrites, esp. as used in jewellery; *Min.* the orthorhombic form of iron pyrites, occurring as bronze-yellow crystals (white on freshly exposed faces) with a metallic lustre. LME. 2 A piece of marcasite, esp. as used in jewellery; an ornament made of marcasite. LME. B *attrib.* or as *adj.* Made or consisting of marcasite; set or ornamented with a marcasite or marcasites. L16.

marcaˈsitical *a.* pertaining to or containing marcasite L17.

marcassin /mɑːˈkasɪn/ *n.* Now *rare* or *obs.* E18. [Fr.] *Her.* A young wild boar with a limp tail, as a charge.

marcato /mɑːˈkɑːtəʊ/ *adv.* & *a.* M19. [It., pa. pple of *marcare* mark, accent, of Gmc origin.] *Mus.* (With each note) emphasized.

marcel /mɑːˈsɛl/ *n.* & *v.* L19. [François *Marcel* Grateau (1852–1936), Fr. hairdresser.] A *n.* Also **M-**. In full *marcel wave*. A deep artificial wave in the hair produced by heated curling-tongs. L19. B *v.t.* Infl. **-ll-**. Wave (hair) in this way. E20.

marcella /mɑːˈsɛlə/ *n.* & *a.* L18. [Repr. a pronunc. of MARSEILLES.] (Made of) an imitation of Marseilles quilting, used for coverlets, petticoats, etc.

marcescent /mɑːˈsɛs(ə)nt/ *a.* E18. [L *marcescent-* pres. ppl stem of *marcescere* inceptive of *marcere* wither, be faint: see -ESCENT.] *Bot.* Withering but not falling off.

marcescence *n.* marcescent condition M19.

March /mɑːtʃ/ *n.*[1] ME. [OFr. *march(e)* north-eastern var. of *marz*, (also mod.) *mars* f. L *Martius* (*mensis*) (month) of Mars.] The third month of the year in the Gregorian calendar.

Proverb: March comes in like a lion and goes out like a lamb.

Comb.: **March brown** *Angling* (an artificial fly) imitating a kind of large brown mayfly; **March court, meeting** *US* a court or town-meeting held in March, being the principal one of the year; **March fly** (*a*) any dark-coloured hairy fly of the family Bibionidae; (*b*) *Austral.* any bloodsucking tabanid horsefly; **March hare** a hare in the breeding season, characterized by much leaping, chasing, etc.; freq. in *mad as a March hare*; *March meeting*: see *March court* above; **March moth** a drab geometrid moth, *Alsophila aescularia*, whose larvae feed on plum and cherry trees.

march /mɑːtʃ/ *n.*[2] ME. [(O)Fr. *marche* f. Proto-Romance (cf. MARQUIS), med.L *marca* f. OFrank., f. Gmc base of MARK *n.*[1] Cf. MERCIAN.] 1 Chiefly *Hist.* The border or frontier of a country; *sing.* & (now usu.) in *pl.*, a tract of land on the border of a country, a disputed tract separating one country from another. ME. b The boundary of an estate. Chiefly *Sc.* LME. c A boundary mark, a landmark. Long *obs.* exc. *dial.* L15. †2 A country, a territory. ME–L15. 3 [G *Mark*, It. *marca*] Any of various (specified) German or Italian territories or principalities. Cf. MARK *n.*[1] 2. Now *Hist.* & *arch.* E18.

1 **the Marches** the parts of England along the border with Wales (and formerly Scotland).

Comb.: **march-land** (chiefly *Hist.*) land comprising the marches of a country; a border district; **march-man** *Hist.* an inhabitant of the marches or borders; **march stone** (chiefly *Sc.* & *north.*) a stone marking the boundary of an estate.

march /mɑːtʃ/ *n.*[3] LME. [In branch I f. (O)Fr. *marche*, f. *marcher* MARCH *v.*[2]; in branch II f. MARCH *v.*[2]] I †1 In *pl.* The footprints or tracks of an animal, esp. an otter. *rare.* Cf. MARK *n.*[1] 13b. LME–L16.

II 2 Advance, forward movement, progress. Also, the course or direction of advance. M16. b A move of a chess-piece etc. L16. 3 The action or an act of marching; the regular forward movement together and in time of a body of troops; the similar orderly forward movement of an exploring party, a procession, etc.; the distance covered by marching for a (specified) period. L16. b A long difficult walk. L17. c A procession organized as a protest or demonstration. Also *protest march*. E20. 4 *Mil.* A beating of a drum in a particular rhythm as an accompaniment to the marching of troops. L16. 5 *Mus.* A tune or composition of marked rhythm and esp. characterized by rhythmical drum beats, designed to accompany the marching of troops etc.; any composition of similar character and form. E17. 6 The regular and uniform step of a body of troops etc. Freq. w. specifying adj. M17. 7 *Euchre.* The winning of all five tricks by one side. M19.

2 A. WEST I was a problem for her . . in the course of her march towards some goal. J. K. GALBRAITH The enemy of the conventional is not ideas but the march

of events. H. JACOBSON Harry's quick sketch of the march of history. 3 SHAKES. *1 Hen. VI* Two mightier troops.. Which join'd with him and made their march for Bordeaux. W. IRVING A march of three or four days.. brought Captain Bonneville.. to Jackson's Hole. J. G. FARRELL Relief comes nearer.. as much as twenty miles nearer with every day's march. c J. MORTIMER Newspapers had ridiculed.. supporters of C.N.D. for not turning out on the march. *Lilith* Feminism.. isn't a part-time practice that happens only at meetings or marches. 6 *quick march, slow march*, etc.

Phrases & comb.: *dead march*: see DEAD *a.* etc. **gain, get a march on** get ahead of to the extent of a march. **line of march** the direction or route of marching. *Long March*: see LONG *a.*[1] **march fracture** *Med.* a stress fracture of the metatarsal. **march past** the marching of troops past a saluting point at a review. **steal a march on** get ahead of by stealth; gain an advantage on.

march /mɑːtʃ/ *v.*[1] ME. [OFr. *marchir*, f. as MARCH *n.*[2]] 1 *v.i.* & *t.* Border (*on*); have a common frontier or boundary with or *with*. ME. †2 *v.t.* Fix or mark the boundaries of with landmarks. *Sc.* LME–L17.

1 *Times* The frontiers of Dakota, Montana and Washington march with the Canadian dominion. M. BORWICK The Ainsty country proper which marches the Branham Moors on the western end.

march /mɑːtʃ/ *v.*[2] LME. [(O)Fr. *marcher* walk, (orig. tread, trample) f. Proto-Gallo-Romance, f. late L *marcus* hammer.] 1 *v.i.* Walk in a military manner with a regular and measured tread; (of a body of troops) walk in step and in time with a regular and uniform movement. Also, start on a march. Also w. advs. LME. b Take part in a protest march. M20. 2 *v.i.* Walk or proceed in a steady or deliberate manner. Also w. advs., as *off, on, out*, etc. M16. 3 *v.t.* Cause to march or walk in a military manner. Now also *gen.*, cause (a person) to walk or go; force to go, conduct. Freq. w. advs. L16. †4 *v.i.* Have a specific position in a series; rank *with, after*, etc. E–M17. 5 *v.i.* Advance, make progress; continue unrelentingly. M17. 6 *v.t.* Traverse (a distance or area) in marching. E19.

1 R. MACAULAY Near to where.. the Ten Thousand marched down from the mountains. P. F. BOLLER He had difficulty keeping step when his company.. marched to music. 2 C. RAYNER She.. marched away down the corridor.. with what shreds of dignity she could. *Stamps* March along to your local dealer for further details. 3 D. H. LAWRENCE The officer spoke two words, they saluted and marched off their prisoner. J. M. COETZEE They march me out of the yard. 6 *Freedomways* Civil rights workers.. face screaming mobs.. as they peacefully march to end housing discrimination. G. GREENE No one has protested, no one has marched.

Phrases: *march in a net*: see NET *n.*[1] **marching girl** *NZ & Austral.*: trained to march in formation.

marchantia /mɑːˈkantɪə/ *n.* M19. [mod.L (see below), f. N. *Marchant* (d. 1678), Fr. botanist: see -IA[1].] Any of various liverworts of the genus *Marchantia*; esp. *M. polymorpha*, one of the most representative liverworts and the one to which the name liverwort was first applied.

Märchen /ˈmɛːrçən/ *n.* Pl. same. Also **m-**. L19. [G = fairy tale f. MHG *merechyn* short verse narrative, f. MHG *mære* (OHG *māri*) news, famous, ult. f. Gmc, + *-chīn*, -KIN dim. suff.] A folk-tale, a fairy tale.

marcher /ˈmɑːtʃə/ *n.*[1] ME. [f. MARCH *n.*[2] + -ER[1].] *Hist.* †1 A person with territory adjoining that of another. Only in ME. 2 An inhabitant or a lord of a march or border district. LME. †3 A border territory or march. LME–L15

Phrases: **Lord Marcher**, pl. **-s -s**, a lord who enjoyed royal liberties and had exclusive jurisdiction over territory in the marches obtained by border warfare.

marchership *n.* the position or office of a Lord Marcher M19.

marcher /ˈmɑːtʃə/ *n.*[2] L16. [f. MARCH *v.*[2] + -ER[1].] 1 A person who marches or walks. L16. 2 *spec.* A person who takes part in a protest or demonstration march. E20.

marchesa /marˈkeːza/ *n.* Pl. ***-se*** /-ze/. L18. [It., fem. of MARCHESE *n.*[1]] In Italy, a marchioness.

marchese /marˈkeːze/ *n.*[1] Pl. ***-si*** /-zi/. E16. [It.] In Italy, a marquis.

marchese *n.*[2] pl. of MARCHESA.

marchesi *n.* pl. of MARCHESE *n.*[1]

marching /ˈmɑːtʃɪŋ/ *n.* M16. [f. MARCH *v.*[2] + -ING[1].] 1 The action of MARCH *v.*[2]; an instance of this. M16. †2 The move of a chess-piece. *rare.* Only in M16. 3 The action of performing a march past. M19.

Comb.: **marching order** (*a*) equipment or a formation for marching; (*b*) in *pl.*, the direction for troops to depart for war etc.; *fig.* a dismissal (freq. in *get one's marching orders*).

marchioness /ˈmɑːʃ(ə)nɪs/ *n.* L16. [med.L *marchionissa*, f. *marchio(n-)* captain of the marches, f. *marca* MARK *n.*[1], MARCH *n.*[2]: see -ESS[1].] 1 The wife or widow of a marquess; a woman holding the rank of marquess in her own right. L16. b A maid-of-all-work. *joc.* L19. 2 A variety of pear. E18.

marchpane *n.* & *a.* see MARZIPAN.

marcid /ˈmɑːsɪd/ *a.* Now *rare.* LME. [L *marcidus* withered, f. *marcere* wither: see -ID[1].] Withered, wasted; weak, feeble.

Marcionist /ˈmɑːʃ(ə)nɪst, -ʃɪən-/ *n.* LME. [Late L *Marcionista*, late Gk *Markiōnistēs*, f. *Marcion*: see next, -IST.] *Eccl. Hist.* = next.

Marcionite /ˈmɑːʃ(ə)nʌɪt, -ʃɪən-/ *n.* & *a.* M16. [eccl.L *Marcionita*, f. *Marcion*: see below, -ITE[1]. Cf. prec.] *Eccl. Hist.* **A** *n.* An adherent of the rigorously ascetic sect founded in Rome in the 2nd cent. AD by Marcion of Sinope, who rejected the authority of the Old Testament. M16. **B** *attrib.* or as *adj.* Of or pertaining to the Marcionites. M18.

Marcionitism *n.* the doctrines of the Marcionites L19.

Marcomanni /ˈmɑːkə(ʊ)maniː/ *n.pl.* E17. [L, of Gmc origin: cf. MARK *n.*[1], MARCH *n.*[2], MAN *n.*] *Hist.* An ancient Germanic people of the Suevian group who lived in central Europe north of the Danube until the 4th cent. AD.

Marconi /mɑːˈkəʊni/ *n.* L19. [Guglielmo, Marchese *Marconi* (1874–1937), It. physicist.] 1 *Hist.* Used *attrib.* to designate (things connected with) the system of radiotelegraphy invented by Marconi. L19. 2 *Naut.* Used *attrib.* to designate (a part of) a type of rig, so called after its resemblance to a radio mast. E20.

marconigram *n.* (*Hist.*) a radiotelegram E20. **marconigraph** *n.* & *v.* (*Hist.*) (*a*) *n.* an apparatus used for transmitting radiotelegrams; (*b*) *v.t.* & *i.* send (a message) by radiotelegraphy: E20. **marcoˈnigraphy** *n.* (*Hist.*) radiotelegraphy E20. **Marconist** *n.* (*Hist.*) an operator of a Marconi system E20.

marcor /ˈmɑːkɔː/ *n.* Long *rare* or *obs.* M17. [L, f. *marcere* waste away.] Orig., decay. Later *spec.*, emaciation.

marcot /ˈmɑːkɒt/ *n.* & *v.* E20. [Back-form. f. next.] *Hort.* **A** *n.* A plant propagated by marcottage. E20. **B** *v.i.* Infl. **-tt-**. Propagate by marcottage. E20.

marcottage /mɑːkɒˈtɑːʒ, mɑːˈkɒtɪdʒ/ *n.* E20. [Fr. = layering.] *Hort.* A method of propagating plants in which an incision is made below a joint or node and covered with a thick layer of moss etc., into which new roots grow.

Marcusian /mɑːˈk(j)uːzɪən/ *a.* & *n.* M20. [f. *Marcuse* (see below) + -IAN.] **A** *adj.* Of or pertaining to Herbert Marcuse (1898–1979), US philosopher and writer, or his political views. M20. **B** *n.* A supporter of the political views of Marcuse. M20.

mard /mɑːd/ *a. dial.* E20. [Repr. pronunc. of *marred* pa. pple of MAR *v.* Cf. next.] Of a child: spoilt; peevish.

mard /mɑːd/ *v.t. dial.* L19. [Cf. prec., MAR *v.*] Spoil (a child) by indulgence.

Mardi gras /mɑːdɪ ˈgrɑː/ *n. phr.* L17. [Fr., lit. 'fat Tuesday'.] Shrove Tuesday, celebrated in some Roman Catholic countries with a carnival; the last day of a carnival etc., esp. in France; *Austral.* a carnival or fair at any time.

mardy /ˈmɑːdi/ *a. dial.* E20. [f. MARD *a.* + -Y[1].] (Esp. of a child) spoilt, sulky, whining.

mare /mɛː/ *n.*[1] [OE *mearh* = OFris., MLG, MDu. *mer(r)ie*, OHG *mar(i)ha*, Du. *merrie*, G *Mähre*, ON *merr*, f. Gmc, f. base repr. also by Gael. *marc*, Welsh *march* stallion, Corn. *margh*.] 1 In early use, the horse. Later, the female of a horse, ass, zebra, or other equid; *esp.* the female of a horse. OE. 2 A woman. Usu. *derog.* ME. †3 A see-saw. Also = HORSE *n.* 5(a). Also *wild mare*. L16–E19. 4 A kind of trestle used by masons. M17.

Phrases: *flying mare*: see FLYING *ppl a.* *grey mare*: see GREY *a.* **mare's nest** a (wonderful) discovery which proves or will prove to be illusory. **mare's tail** (*a*) an aquatic plant, *Hippuris vulgaris* (family Hippuridaceae), having an erect stem with leaves in whorls and small greenish axillary flowers; (*b*) in *pl.*, long straight streaks of cirrus cloud, often believed to herald stormy weather. *Shanks'* (or *Shanks's*) *mare*: see SHANK *n.* †**two-** (or **three-**)**legged mare** the gallows. *wild mare*: see sense 3 above.

mare /mɛː/ *n.*[2] Long *obs.* exc. *dial.* & in NIGHTMARE *n.* & *a.*, *v.* [OE *mære*, corresp. to MLG *mar*, MDu. *mare*, *maer*, OHG *mara* (G *Mahr*), ON *mara*, f. Gmc.] 1 = NIGHTMARE *n.* 1, 2. OE. †b The blues, melancholy. E16–E17. †2 A spectre, a hag. LME–E16.

mare /ˈmɑːreɪ, -ri/ *n.*[3] Pl. **-ria** /-rɪə/, (occas.) **-res** /-reɪz, -riːz/. M19. [L = sea.] *Astron.* Any of the extensive areas of flat terrain ('seas') on the surface of the moon, which appear dark and were once thought to be seas; a similar area on Mars etc.

¶From 17 in mod.L proper names, as *M. Imbrium*, *M. Tranquillitatis*, etc.

†**marechal** *n.* Also **-ale**; (earlier) **marshal**. L17–E20. [App. f. as next.] A scent, a perfume; a hair powder scented with this.

maréchal /mareʃal/ *n.* Pl. ***-chaux*** /-ʃo/. L17. [Fr.: see MARSHAL *n.*[1]] A French marshal or field-marshal.

¶Formerly naturalized.

†**marechale** *n.* var. of MARECHAL.

Maréchal Niel /ˌmareɪʃ(ə)l ˈniːl/ *n. phr.* M19. [Fr., f. as prec. + Adolphe *Niel* (1802–69), Marshal of France.] A climbing noisette rose of a variety bearing large well-formed fragrant yellow flowers.

maréchaussée /mareʃose/ *n.* Also ***M-***. Pl. pronounced same. L18. [Fr. f. OFr. *mareschaucie*: see MARSHALCY.] A French military force under the command of a marshal (*Hist.*). Also (*joc.* & *colloq.*), the French police, the gendarmerie.

maréchaux *n.* pl. of MARÉCHAL.

mare clausum /mɑːreɪ ˈklaʊsʊm, mɛːrɪ ˈklɔːzəm/ *n. phr.* Pl. **maria clausa** /mɑːrɪə ˈklaʊsə, mɛːrɪə ˈklɔːzə/. M17. [L = closed sea, title of a work by John Selden (1584–1654), Eng. jurist, written in answer to Grotius (see MARE LIBERUM).] A sea under the jurisdiction of a particular country. Cf. MARE LIBERUM.

Maree *n.* & *a.* var. of MARIA.

Marek's disease /ˈmarɛks dɪˌziːz/ *n. phr.* M20. [Josef *Marek* (fl. 1907), Hungarian veterinary surgeon.] *Vet. Med.* An infectious disease of poultry caused by a herpesvirus, which attacks nerves, causing paralysis, or initiates widespread tumour formation.

mare liberum /mɑːreɪ ˈliːbərʊm, mɛːrɪ ˈlʌɪbərəm/ *n. phr.* Pl. **maria libera** /mɑːrɪə ˈliːbərə, mɛːrɪə ˈlʌɪbərə/. M17. [L = free sea, title of a treatise by Hugo Grotius (1583–1645), Du. jurist.] A sea open to all nations. Cf. MARE CLAUSUM.

maremma /məˈrɛmə/ *n.* Pl. **-me** /-mi/. M19. [It. f. L *maritima* fem. of *maritimus* MARITIME.] In Italy: low marshy unhealthy country by the seashore; an area of this.

Comb.: **maremma sheepdog** an Italian breed of sheepdog; a dog of this breed.

Marengo /məˈrɛŋgəʊ/ *n.* M19. [A village in N. Italy, scene of Napoleon's victory over the Austrians in 1800, after which the dish is said to have been served to him.] Cookery. *chicken* etc. (*à la*) *Marengo*, chicken sautéed in oil, served with a tomato sauce, and traditionally garnished with eggs and crayfish.

mareogram /ˈmarɪə(ʊ)gram/ *n.* E20. [f. L *mare* sea + -O- + -GRAM.] A graphical record of variations in sea level.

mareograph *n.* = MARIGRAPH L19. **mareoˈgraphic** *a.* pertaining to or concerned with the (automatic) recording of variations in sea level M20.

Marfan /ˈmɑːfã(ŋ)/ *n.* M20. [A. B. J. *Marfan* (1858–1942), Fr. paediatrician.] Med. *Marfan('s) syndrome*, a hereditary disorder of connective tissue resulting in abnormally long and thin digits and frequently in optical and cardiovascular defects.

marg *n.* var. of MARGE *n.*[2]

Margaret /ˈmɑːg(ə)rɪt/ *n.* LME. [Female forename.] 1 A daisy. Cf. MARGUERITE. *obs.* exc. *dial.* LME. †2 A variety of apple. L16–M19. 3 A magpie. Cf. MADGE 2, MAG *n.*[1] 2. *dial.* M19.

margaric /mɑːˈgarɪk/ *a.* E19. [Fr. *margarique*, f. Gk *margaron* pearl, in ref. to the pearly lustre of the crystals: see -IC.] Chem. *margaric acid*: orig., a fatty acid obtained from animal fat, now known to be a mixture of palmitic and stearic acids; now, a crystalline fatty acid, $C_{17}H_{35}COOH$; also called *heptadecanoic acid*.

ˈmargarate *n.* a salt or ester of margaric acid E19.

margarin /ˈmɑːgərɪn/ *n.* M19. [f. prec. + -IN[1].] *Chem.* A glyceryl ester of margaric acid.

margarine /mɑːdʒəˈriːn, ˈmɑːgəriːn/ *n.* & *v.* L19. [Fr., misapplication of *margarine* = prec.] A *n.* A substance made by emulsifying vegetable oils or animal fats with water, milk, etc., and used as a substitute for butter. L19. B *v.t.* Spread (esp. bread) with margarine. E20.

margarita /mɑːgəˈriːtə/ *n.* Also **M-**. E20. [Sp. equiv. of female forename Margaret.] 1 A kind of Spanish wine. Now *rare*. E20. 2 A cocktail made with tequila and citrus fruit juice. M20.

margaritaceous /mɑːg(ə)rɪˈteɪʃəs/ *a.* E19. [f. L *margarita* (see next) + -ACEOUS.] *Zool.* Pearly.

margarite /ˈmɑːgərʌɪt/ *n.* ME. [In branch I f. OFr. (mod. *marguerite*) f. L *margarita* f. Gk *margaritēs* f. *margaron* pearl, *margaros* pearl-oyster, in branch II f. Gk *margaron* pearl: see -ITE[1].] I 1 A pearl. Long *arch.* ME. II 2 *Min.* A calcium aluminosilicate of the mica group, usu. occurring as scales having a pearly lustre. E19. 3 *Petrogr.* A line of globulites resembling a string of pearls. L19.

margaritiferous /mɑːg(ə)rɪˈtɪf(ə)rəs/ *a.* M17. [f. L *margaritifer*, f. *margarita*: see prec., -I-, -FEROUS.] Producing pearls.

margate /ˈmɑːgɪt/ *n.* M18. [Origin unkn.] In full *margate-fish*. A grunt, *Haemulon album*, largely grey in colour, found in the western Atlantic, important as a food fish.

margay /ˈmɑːgeɪ/ *n.* L18. [Port. *maracaj'a* f. Tupi *marakaya*.] A Central and S. American felid, *Felis wiedii*.

marge /mɑːdʒ/ *n.*[1] Now *poet.* M16. [(O)Fr., f. as MARGIN *n.*] A margin; *esp.* the edge of a body of water.

marge /mɑːdʒ/ *n.*[2] *colloq.* Also **marg.** E20. [Abbrev.] = MARGARINE *n.*

†**margeline** *n.* L16–L18. [Fr. *morgeline*.] Scarlet pimpernel, *Anagallis arvensis*.

margent /ˈmɑːdʒ(ə)nt/ *n.* Now *arch.* & *poet.* LME. [Alt. of MARGIN *n.* as in *ancient*, *pageant*, etc.] = MARGIN *n.* 1, 2.

margin /ˈmɑːdʒɪn/ *n.* LME. [L *margin-*, *margo* rel. to MARK *n.*[1] Cf. prec.] 1 That part of a surface which lies immediately within its boundary, esp. when in some way distinguished from the rest of the surface; *esp.* the space immediately adjacent to a river or piece of water; an edge, a border, a brink. LME. b *Bot.* & *Zool.* A contour or boundary line of a body, or a distinct border differing in texture etc. from the main body. M18. 2 The space on a page between the extreme edge and the main body of written or printed matter, sometimes containing notes, references, illuminations, etc.; *esp.* the border at either side of the page as distinguished from the head and foot. Also, an annotation made in such a border; a ruled line marking off such a border. LME. 3 *Carpentry.* The flat part of the stiles and rails of framed work. E19. 4a A condition near the limit below or beyond which something ceases to be possible or desirable. M19. b An amount of space, time, money, material, etc., by which something exceeds or falls short of what is required; *spec.* = *profit margin* s.v. PROFIT *n.* M19. c *Stock Exch.* A sum deposited by a speculative seller or buyer with a broker to cover the risk of loss on a transaction on account. M19. d An addition to a person's wage or salary for extra skill or responsibility. *Austral.* M20.

1 SOUTHEY Between the mountain-base And the green margin of the waters. R. C. HUTCHINSON Here the road was rough, its margins indistinct. *fig.*: P. FITZGERALD The margin between alarm and fascination was soon crossed. b D. MORRIS A sharp margin between the lips and the surrounding face. 2 J. IRVING Both sides of the page . . were . . filled. Dr Larch was not a man for leaving margins. 4a J. BUCHAN The working classes . . being nearer the margin of subsistence . . are . . likely to be content with what meets their immediate needs. b A. LURIE He realizes by what a narrow margin he has been saved. P. AUSTER All investigations of this sort must make allowances for a certain margin of error.

Phrases: **margin of safety** an allowance made for safety; *spec.* a number equal to the factor of safety minus one.

Comb.: **margin call** a demand by a broker that an investor deposit further cash or securities to guarantee the margin on an investment; **margin release** a mechanism on a typewriter which allows typing in the margin previously set; the key operating this.

marginless *a.* M19.

margin /ˈmɑːdʒɪn/ *v.* M16. [f. the n.] 1 *v.t.* Provide with marginal notes; annotate in the margin. M16. 2 *v.t.* Specify in the margin of a page. M17. 3 *v.t.* Provide with a margin, edge, or border. Usu. in *pass.* E18. 4 *Stock Exch.* a *v.t.* Deposit a margin on (an account etc.). L19. b *v.i.* Foll. by *up*: provide additional margin when what has been paid is insufficient. *US.* L19.

marginal /ˈmɑːdʒɪn(ə)l/ *a.*, *n.*, & *v.* L16. [med.L *marginalis*, f. as MARGIN *n.*: see -AL[1].] A *adj.* 1 Written or printed in the margin of a page. L16. 2 Pertaining to an edge, border, or boundary; situated at or affecting the extreme edge of an area, body, etc.; not central. M17. 3a That is on or close to the margin below or beyond which something ceases to be possible or desirable; *esp.* of or pertaining to goods produced and marketed at a small margin of profit. L19. b Of land, ore, etc.: barely worth developing. Of a farmer etc.: working such land. E20. c *Sociol.* Of an individual or group: partly belonging to two differing societies or cultures but not fully integrated into either. E20. d Of minor importance, small, having little effect. (Foll. by *to*.) E20. e Of a constituency etc.: held by a very small majority, in which an election is likely to be very closely contested. M20. 4 *Stock Exch.* Of or pertaining to margins; of the nature of a margin. L19.

1 J. HUTCHINSON The earliest books left spaces for . . marginal decorations. 2 W. BLACK A marginal growth of willow and flag. C. LLOYD If its leaves start marginal browning . . I'm in trouble. 3a **marginal cost** the cost added by making one extra item of a product. b *Which?* Large areas of marginal land . . have been ploughed up. d P. ZWEIG His reputation was at best that of a marginal poet. K. ISHIGURO Our contribution was always marginal No-one cares . . what the likes of you and me once did. e *Times* Redistribution can make a safe seat marginal.

B *n.* 1 A marginal note, reference, or decoration. Now *rare.* E17. 2 *Ornith.* A feather on the edge of a bird's wing. L19. 3 A marginal constituency or seat. M20.

†C *v.t.* Enter in the margin of a book; add marginal notes to. E17–L18.

marginalism *n.* economic analysis which gives prominence to marginal factors in the economy E20. **marginalist** *n.* & *a.* (*a*) *n.* an adherent or practitioner of marginalism; (*b*) *adj.* of or pertaining to marginalists or marginalism: E20. **margiˈnality** *n.* E20. **marginally** *adv.* (*a*) in the margin of a page; as a marginal note; (*b*) at, in, or towards the margin or edge; (*c*) by a small margin, slightly: E17.

marginalia /mɑːdʒɪˈneɪlɪə/ *n.pl.* M19. [med.L, neut. pl. of *marginalis*: see prec., -IA[2].] Marginal or incidental notes.

marginalize /ˈmɑːdʒɪn(ə)lʌɪz/ *v.* Also **-ise**. M19. [f. MARGINAL + -IZE.] 1 *v.t.* & *i.* Make marginal notes (on). *rare.* M19. 2 *v.t.* Make marginal; remove from the centre; *esp.* move to the margin of a sphere of activity, make economically marginal, impoverish. L20. b Treat as marginal; depreciate, undervalue. L20.

marginaliˈzation *n.* L20.

marginate /ˈmɑːdʒɪnət/ *a.* L18. [L *marginatus*, f. *marginat-* (see next) + -ATE[2].] Chiefly *Bot.* & *Zool.* Having a distinct margin.

marginate /ˈmɑːdʒɪneɪt/ *v.t.* E17. [Sense 1 f. L *marginat-* pa. ppl stem of *marginare*, f. as MARGIN *n.* Senses 2, 3 directly f. MARGIN *n.*: see -ATE[3].] 1 Chiefly *Bot.* & *Zool.* Provide with a margin or border. Chiefly as *marginated* ppl a. E17. 2 Annotate with marginal notes. *rare.* E17. 3 = MARGINALIZE *v.* 2. M20.

margiˈnation *n.* (*a*) a marginated appearance or marking; (*b*) *rare* annotation with marginal notes: L19.

margined /ˈmɑːdʒɪnd/ *a.* E19. [f. MARGIN *n.*, *v.*: see -ED[2], -ED[1].] Chiefly *Bot.* & *Zool.* Having a margin, esp. of a specified kind; marginate.

margo /ˈmɑːgəʊ/ *n.* Pl. **-os**. M20. [L = MARGIN *n.*] *Bot.* The network of cellulose strands surrounding the torus of the pit membrane in a bordered pit of a gymnosperm.

margosa /mɑːˈgəʊsə/ *n.* E19. [Port. *amargosa* fem. of *amargoso* bitter.] = NEEM.

margrave /ˈmɑːgreɪv/ *n.* Also (esp. in titles) **M-**. LOE. [MDu. *markgrave* = OHG *marcgrāvo* (G *Markgraf*), f. *marca* MARK *n.*[1] + *grāve* GRAVE *n.*[2]] *Hist.* Orig., a military governor of a German border province. Later, a hereditary prince in any of certain states of the Holy Roman Empire.

margravate *n.* = MARGRAVIATE E19. **marˈgravial** *a.* of or pertaining to a margrave M18. **marˈgraviate** *n.* the territory ruled by a margrave E18.

margravine /ˈmɑːgrəviːn/ *n.* Also (esp. in titles) **M-**. L17. [Du. *markgravin* fem. of *markgraaf* MARGRAVE.] *Hist.* The wife of a margrave; the female ruler of a margraviate.

marguerite /mɑːgəˈriːt/ *n.* E17. [Fr. equiv. of female forename *Margaret*.] Orig. (*rare*), the common daisy. Now, (a flower or flowering stem of) any of various (cultivated) plants with flowers like those of the daisy; *esp.* (*a*) the ox-eye daisy, *Leucanthemum vulgare*; (*b*) the Paris daisy, *Chrysanthemum frutescens*.

blue marguerite a blue-flowered plant of the composite family, *Felicia amelloides*, native to southern Africa.

Marheshvan /mɑːˈhɛʃvən/ *n.* Also **-ches-** /-ˈxɛs-/, **-chesh-** /-ˈxɛʃ-/. M18. [Heb.: see HESVAN.] *Hist.* = HESVAN.

Mari /ˈmɑːri/ *n.* Pl. same, **-s**. E20. [Cheremiss (Russ. *mariets*, pl. *-ïtsy*).] = CHEREMISS.

Maria /ˈmarɪə/ *n.*[1] & *a.* Also **Maree** /ˈmari/. E19. [Gond *maria*.] A *n.* Pl. **-s**, same. A member of a jungle-dwelling Dravidian people of central India; the Dravidian language of this people. E19. B *attrib.* or as *adj.* Of or pertaining to the Marias or their language. L19.

maria *n.*[2]*pl.* see MARE *n.*[3]

mariachi /marɪˈɑːtʃi/ *n.* M20. [Mex. Sp. *mariache*, *-chi*.] An itinerant Mexican folk band (also *mariachi band*); a member of such a band.

maria clausa *n. phr.* pl. of MARE CLAUSUM.

mariage blanc /marjaʒ blɑ̃/ *n. phr.* Pl. ***-s -s*** (pronounced same). E20. [Fr., lit. 'white marriage'.] An unconsummated marriage.

mariage de convenance /marjaʒ də kɔ̃vnɑ̃s/ *n. phr.* Pl. ***mariages de convenance*** (pronounced same). M19. [Fr.] A marriage of convenience.

mariages blancs, de convenance *n. phrs.* pls. of MARIAGE BLANC, DE CONVENANCE.

Marial /ˈmɛːrɪəl/ *a.* E20. [Fr.] = MARIAN *a.*[2] 2.

maria libera *n. phr.* pl. of MARE LIBERUM.

marialite /ˈmarɪəlʌɪt, məˈriːəl-, məˈrʌɪəl-/ *n.* M19. [G *Marialit*, f. *Marie* wife of Gerhard vom Rath, 19th-cent. Ger. mineralogist + *-lit* -LITE.] *Min.* An aluminosilicate mineral, the sodium- and chloride-rich end-member of the scapolite series. Cf. MEIONITE.

Marian /ˈmɛːrɪən/ *n.*[1] & *a.*[1] L16. [L *Marianus*, f. *Marius*: see below, -AN.] A *n.* An adherent or supporter of the famous Roman general Gaius Marius (d. 86 BC). L16. B *adj.* Of or pertaining to Marius or his party. L17.

Marian /ˈmɛːrɪən/ *a.*[2] & *n.*[2] E17. [f. L *Maria* MARY + -AN.] A *adj.* 1 a Of or pertaining to Mary Queen of England (1516–58), or her reign (1553–8). E17. b Of or pertaining to Mary Queen of Scots (1542–87). E20. 2 *Chr. Ch.* Of or pertaining to the Virgin Mary; characterized by special veneration for her. E18. B *n.* 1 A person who has a special veneration for the Virgin Mary. M17. 2 *Hist.* A supporter of Mary Queen of England; an English Catholic during her reign. M19. 3 *Hist.* A supporter of Mary Queen of Scots. L19.

Marianism /ˈmɛːrɪənɪz(ə)m/ *n.* M19. [f. MARIAN *a.*[2] + -ISM.] Particular or excessive veneration of the Virgin Mary; *rare* (*derog.*) a religious system based on this.

Marianist /ˈmɛːrɪənɪst/ *n.* E20. [f. as prec. + -IST.] *RC Ch.* A member of the Society of Mary, founded in Bordeaux in 1817 by W. J. Chaminade and devoted to missionary work and the veneration of the Virgin Mary. Cf. MARIST.

Mariavite /ˈmɛːrɪəvʌɪt/ *n.* & *a.* E20. [Pol. *Mariawita*, f. L *qui Mariae vitam imitantur* who copy the life of Mary.] A *n.* A member of a Polish Christian sect founded in 1906. E20. B *adj.* Of or pertaining to this sect. E20.

maribou(t) *n.* & *a.* var. of MARABOU.

mari complaisant /mari kɔ̃plɛzɑ̃/ *n. phr.* Pl. **-s -s** (pronounced same). L19. [Fr.] A husband tolerant of his wife's adultery.

mariculture /ˈmarɪkʌltʃə/ *n.* E20. [f. L *mari-*, *mare* sea + CULTURE *n.*] The cultivation of the resources of the sea; *esp.* the cultivation of fish for food.

mariˈcultural *a.* E20. **mariˈculturist** *n.* a person engaged in or specializing in mariculture M20.

marid /ˈmarɪd/ *n.* M19. [Arab. *mārid* act. pple of *marada* to rebel.] A very powerful wicked jinnee in Arabian stories and Muslim mythology.

marie /ˈmɑːri/ *n.* L19. [Fr. equiv. of female forename *Mary*.] More fully *marie biscuit*. A type of plain sweet biscuit.

Marie Celeste /ˌmarɪ sɪˈlɛst/ *n.* M20. [Alt. of *Mary Celeste*, a ship found in the N. Atlantic in 1872, in perfect condition but abandoned.] A building, vessel, etc., suddenly and inexplicably deserted.

Marie Louise /ˌmarɪ luːˈiːz/ *n.* E19. [*Marie Louise* of Austria (1791–1847), second wife of Napoleon.] A variety of yellow-skinned pear.

marigenous /məˈrɪdʒɪnəs/ *a.* L16. [f. L *mari-*, *mare* sea + -GENOUS.] Produced in or by the sea.

marigold /ˈmarɪgəʊld/ *n.* & *a.* ME. [f. female forename *Mary* (prob. w. ref. to the Virgin Mary) + GOLD *n.*[2]] A *n.* 1 A common garden flower, *Calendula officinalis*, of the composite family, with large orange-yellow daisy-like flowers (also *pot marigold*); a flowering stem of this plant. Also, (a flowering stem of) either of two related garden plants, *Tagetes patula* (more fully *French marigold*) and *T. erecta* (more fully *African marigold*), with feathery leaves and flowers in various shades of yellow, maroon, etc. ME. b Any of various other related or similar plants. Freq. w. specifying wd. L16. 2 A variety of cider apple, with a striped skin. Also *marigold apple*. Long *rare* or *obs.* L16. 3 The colour of a marigold flower, bright orange-yellow. M19.

1b *Cape marigold, corn marigold, marsh marigold*, etc.

B *adj.* Of the colour of a marigold flower, bright orange-yellow. L18.

Special collocations & comb.: *marigold apple* see sense A.2 above. **marigold window** *Archit.* a rose-window.

marigot /ˈmarɪgɒt/ *n.* Pl. pronounced same. M18. [Fr.] In W. Africa, a side channel of a river.

marigraph /ˈmarɪgrɑːf/ *n.* M19. [f. L *mari-*, *mare* sea + -GRAPH.] A tide-gauge.

marijuana /marɪˈhwɑːnə, marjʊˈɑːnə/ *n.* Also **-huana**. L19. [Amer. Sp. Cf. JU-JU *n.*[1]] 1 = CANNABIS 2, *esp.* cannabis in a form for smoking. L19. 2 = CANNABIS 1. E20.

marikina /marɪˈkiːnə/ *n.* L18. [Fr. f. Tupi *murikina* (cf. Port. *mariquinâ*).] = LION *tamarin*.

marimba /məˈrɪmbə/ *n.* E18. [Congolese.] A kind of deep-toned xylophone, originating in Africa and consisting of wooden keys on a frame with a tuned resonator beneath each key.

marimbaphone /məˈrɪmbəfəʊn/ *n.* E20. [f. prec. + -PHONE.] = prec.

marimonda /marɪˈmɒndə/ *n. rare.* M18. [Amer. Sp., prob. f. a local name.] The long-haired spider monkey, *Ateles belzebuth*.

marina /məˈriːnə/ *n.* E19. [It. & Sp. fem. of *marino* f. L *marinus* MARINE *a.*] A harbour, usu. specially designed or located, with moorings for yachts and other small craft.

Holiday Which? A sandy beach with watersports, a marina full of smart yachts, and a lido.

marinade /marɪˈneɪd/ *n.* E18. [Fr. f. Sp. *marinada*, f. *marinar* to pickle in brine (= It. *marinare*, Fr. *mariner*), f. *marino* (see prec.). Cf. MARINATE *a.*, *v.*] A flavouring and tenderizing mixture of wine, vinegar or other acidic liquid, with oil, herbs, spices, etc., in which meat, fish, etc., may be soaked before cooking; the meat, fish, etc., thus soaked.

marinade /ˈmarɪneɪd/ *v.t.* & *i.* L17. [f. as prec.] Soak in a marinade.

marinara /mɑːrɪˈnɑːrə, ˈmar-/ *a.* M20. [It. *alla marinara* sailor-fashion, f. fem. of *marinero* seafaring.] Designating a sauce made from tomatoes, onions, herbs, etc., usu. served with pasta.

†marinate *a.* M17–L19. [It. *marinato* pa. pple of *marinare* = Sp. *marinar*: see MARINADE *n.*, -ATE[2].] Marinaded.

marinate /ˈmarɪneɪt/ *v.* M17. [It. *marinare* or Fr. *mariner* = Sp. *marinar*: see MARINADE *n.*, -ATE[3].] 1 *v.t.* & *i.* = MARINADE *v.* M17. †2 Prepare (poultry) by a certain method of stuffing. E18–E19.

marine /məˈriːn/ *n.* & *a.* ME. [(O)Fr. *marine* fem. of *marin* f. L *marinus*, f. *mari-*, *mare* sea: see -INE[1].] A *n.* †1 The coast or shore by the sea; a harbour. ME–E18. 2 A soldier trained to serve at sea, or on shore under specified circumstances; in *pl.*, a body of such soldiers. Formerly also *gen.*, a sailor. L16. b More fully *dead marine*. An empty bottle. *slang* (chiefly *Austral.*). M19. 3 The collective shipping, fleet, or navy of a country; seagoing vessels collectively, esp. with reference to nationality or class. M17. 4 The department concerned with the navy in the French and some other foreign governments. L18. 5 A seascape. M19.

2 W. CRUISE A commission in the marines. D. A. THOMAS The destroyer *Anthony* landed 50 marines. *Royal Marine*: see ROYAL *a.* **tell that to the marines** *colloq.*: indicating incredulity. 3 G. BORROW To this inconsiderable number of vessels is the present war marine of Spain reduced. *mercantile marine*: see MERCANTILE *a.* 1. *merchant marine*: see MERCHANT *n.* & *a.*

B *adj.* 1 Of, pertaining to, found in, or produced by the sea; inhabiting or originating in the sea. LME. †b *Chem.* Of a substance: obtainable from the sea. E17–E19. c Of an artist etc.: that depicts sea subjects. L19. 2 Of or pertaining to shipping, a navy, or naval matters. M16. 3 Of, pertaining to, or situated on the coast. M17. 4 Of or pertaining to the marines; trained to serve at sea. L17. 5 Esp. of an instrument: used or adapted for use at sea. E18.

1 F. HOYLE Marine waters are in general deeper than freshwater systems. A. LURIE Umbrellas bobbed and dodged like multicolored marine plants. b **†marine salt** common salt, sodium chloride, (later) any chloride. **†marine acid** hydrochloric acid. 2 J. MARRYAT The petitioners pray that they may have the privilege of.. effecting marine insurance as a company. *Sunday Express* According to marine records, 20,000 vessels foundered in this century alone. 3 I. MURDOCH I see you in a cosy marine bungalow on the sea front. 4 *marine barracks, marine captain, marine officer, marine regiment*, etc.

Special collocations & comb.: *marine architecture*: see ARCHITECTURE *n.* 1. **marine band** *Geol.* a thin bed containing marine fossils, situated between non-marine strata. **marine-biological** *a.* of or pertaining to marine biology. **marine biologist** a person engaged in or expert in marine biology. **marine biology** the biology of plants and animals living in the sea. **marine blue** *n.* & *a.* [from the colour of the Royal Marines' uniform] (of) a dark blue. **marine glue** an adhesive mixture of shellac and rubber used in ship carpentry. **marine iguana** a large marine lizard, *Amblyrhynchus cristatus*, of the Galapagos Islands. **marineland** a zoo designed to exhibit and preserve marine animals. **marine railway** a slipway to facilitate the handling of boats for repair etc. **marine science** the science of the sea and the life, minerals, etc., contained in it; any of the individual disciplines involved in this. **marine scientific** *a.* of or pertaining to marine science. **marine scientist** a person engaged or expert in marine science. **marine soap** a soap which lathers well with seawater. **marine store** (*a*) in *pl.*, new or old ships' materials etc. sold as merchandise; (*b*) a shop selling these. **marine toad** = *cane toad* s.v. CANE *n.*[1] *marine trumpet*: see TRUMPET *n.*

marined /məˈriːnd/ *a.* Now *rare* or *obs.* E19. [f. MARINE *a.* + -ED[1].] *Her.* Designating an animal whose lower body is represented as a fishtail.

mariner /ˈmarɪnə/ *n.* ME. [AN, or (O)Fr. *marinier* f. med.L *marinarius*, f. L *marinus*: see MARINE, -ER[2].] 1 A person who navigates or assists in navigating a ship; a sailor; *Law* any person employed on a ship. ME. †2 *spec.* A fighting man on board ship. M–L17.

1 **master mariner** (*a*) the commander of a ship; (*b*) *spec.* the captain of a merchant vessel.

Comb.: **mariner's compass** (*a*) a compass showing magnetic or true north and the bearings from it; (*b*) *the* southern constellation Pyxis Nautica. *mariner('s) portage*: see PORTAGE *n.*[1] 3.

†marinership *n.* the skill or art of a mariner M16–E17.

marinera /mariˈnera/ *n.* E20. [Sp., fem. of *marinero* marine, seafaring.] = CUECA.

marinescape /məˈriːnskeɪp/ *n.* E20. [f. MARINE *a.* + SCAPE *n.*[3], after *landscape*.] A picturesque view of the sea, a seascape.

marinise *v.* var. of MARINIZE.

Marinism /məˈriːnɪz(ə)m/ *n.* M19. [f. *Marini* (see below) + -ISM.] The affected style of writing characteristic of the Italian poet Giovanni Battista Marini (d. 1625).

Marinist *n.* an imitator of Marini M19.

marinize /məˈriːnʌɪz/ *v.t.* Also **-ise**. M20. [f. MARINE *a.* + -IZE.] Modify, convert, or adapt for marine use. Chiefly as *marinized* ppl a.

Mariolatry /mɛːrɪˈɒlətri/ *n. derog.* E17. [f. L *Maria* MARY + -OLATRY.] Excessive reverence for the Virgin Mary.

Mariolater *n.* a person who practises Mariolatry M19. **Mariolatrous** *a.* characterized by Mariolatry M19.

Mariology /mɛːrɪˈɒlədʒi/ *n.* M19. [f. as prec. + -OLOGY.] That part of Christian theology dealing with Mary as the virgin mother of Jesus.

Marioˈlogical *a.* M20.

marionette /ˌmarɪəˈnɛt/ *n.* E17. [Fr. *marionnette*, f. *Marion* dim. of *Marie* MARY: see -ETTE.] 1 A puppet with jointed limbs operated by strings. E17. 2 The bufflehead, *Bucephala albeola*. Now *rare* or *obs. US.* M19.

marionettish *a.* E20. **marionettist** *n.* a person who operates marionettes E20.

Mariotte /ˈmarɪət/ *n.* M19. [Edme *Mariotte* (*c*1620–84), Fr. physicist.] 1 *Mariotte('s) bottle, flask*, a bottle with an outlet near the bottom and an adjustable tube passing through a cork in the neck, which if filled above the bottom of the tube gives a flow of constant head equal to the height of the bottom of the tube above the outlet. M19. 2 *Mariotte's law*, = BOYLE'S LAW. M19. 3 *Mariotte's tube*, a U-tube with one arm short and sealed and the other long and open to the air. M19.

mariposa /marɪˈpəʊsə, *in sense 2 also foreign* mariˈposa/ *n.* M19. [Sp., lit. 'butterfly'.] 1 In full *mariposa lily* or *tulip*. Any plant of the genus *Calochortus*, of the lily family, the members of which have brightly coloured flowers and are native to western N. America; *spec.* any with large cup-shaped flowers. M19. 2 *Bullfighting*. A movement in which the bullfighter draws the bull by flapping the cape behind his or her back. M20.

mariposite /marɪˈpəʊzʌɪt, -sʌɪt/ *n.* M19. [f. *Mariposa* County, California + -ITE[1].] *Min.* A green or greenish-yellow variety of muscovite, containing a relatively high proportion of silica and up to 1 per cent chromic oxide.

mariscal /məˈrɪsk(ə)l/ *a.* Now *rare* or *obs.* E19. [f. mod.L *marisca* haemorrhoids (f. L, lit. 'coarse fig': cf. FIG *n.*[1] 2a) + -AL[1].] *Med.* Of the nature of haemorrhoids.

maris complaisants *n. phr.* pl. of MARI COMPLAISANT.

marish /ˈmarɪʃ/ *n.* & *a.*[1] Now *arch.* & *dial.* ME. [(O)Fr. *marais*, †*mareis* f. med.L *mariscus* MARSH *n.*[1]] A *n.* = MARSH *n.*[1] ME. B *adj.* Marshy; found or produced in a marsh. Now only *attrib.* LME.

†**marishy** *a.* = MARISH *a.*[1] E17–E18.

marish /ˈmɛːrɪʃ/ *a.*[2] *rare.* L17. [f. MARE *n.*[1] + -ISH[1].] Characteristic of a mare.

marisma /maˈrisma/ *n.* L19. [Sp. = marsh, mud flats.] The marshy waste lands near the Guadalquivir river in southern Spain.

Marist /ˈmɛːrɪst/ *n.* & *a.* L19. [Fr. *Mariste*, f. *Marie* MARY: see -IST.] (A member) of any of various Roman Catholic missionary and teaching orders, esp. the Society of Mary founded in Lyons in the early 19th cent. Cf. MARIANIST.

marital /ˈmarɪt(ə)l/ *a.* L15. [L *maritalis*, f. *maritus* husband: see -AL[1].] 1 Of or pertaining to marriage or the relations between (people living as) husband and wife. L15. 2 Of or characteristic of a husband. E17.

1 R. INGALLS Isabelle gave no hint as to the marital status of the next four people. R. P. JHABVALA Our parents were having marital squabbles. R. DINNAGE My husband was feeling very threatened .. so we went to marital therapy together.

Special collocations: **marital rape** sexual intercourse forced on a woman by her husband, knowingly against her will.

mariˈtality *n.* excessive affection of a wife for her husband M19. **maritally** *adv.* as if married, as a married person M19.

maritime /ˈmarɪtʌɪm/ *a.* & *n.* M16. [(Fr. f.) L *maritimus*, f. *mari-*, *mare* sea + *-timus*, as in *finitimus* neighbouring etc.] A *adj.* 1 Living or found near the sea; (of a country, district, etc.) bordering on the sea. M16. 2 Of a fighting force: intended for service at sea. M16. 3 Connected with the sea in relation to navigation, commerce, etc. L16. 4 Of, pertaining to, arising from, or existing in the sea. Now *rare* or *obs.* E17. 5 Characteristic of a sailor; nautical. M18.

1 *Bird Watching* More maritime than the common tern, it is less inclined to nest away from the coast. *Sunday Express* Rock gardens include many maritime plants like thrift. **maritime pine** a southern European pine, *Pinus pinaster*, distinguished by its clustered cones and often planted in coastal areas to bind the sand. **Maritime Provinces** = sense B.2 below. 3 GIBBON Britain .. already assumed its natural and respectable station of a maritime power. J. BRIGHT Maritime law .. consists of opinions and precedents for the most part. E. HEATH Hundreds of ships .. loading and unloading; where else .. can one see maritime trade on that scale? 4 JOHN ROSS An interesting maritime landscape.

B *n.* †1 The sea-coast; a region adjoining the sea. L16–M17. 2 (**M-**.) In *pl.* *The* eastern provinces of Canada adjoining the Atlantic Ocean (Nova Scotia, New Brunswick, and Prince Edward Island). E20.

Maritimer *n.* a native or inhabitant of the Maritimes M20.

Marivaudage /marivodaʒ/ *n.* M18. [Fr., f. P. C. de *Marivaux* (1688–1763), Fr. novelist and dramatist.] Exaggeratedly sentimental or affected style, language, etc., characteristic of Marivaux.

marjoram /ˈmɑːdʒ(ə)rəm/ *n.* LME. [OFr. *marjorane* (mod. *marjolaine*) = Prov., Sp., It. *majorana*, Romanian *măgheran* f. med.L *majorana*, of unkn. origin.] Any of various labiate plants of the genus *Origanum*, aromatic herbs much used in cooking; esp. *O. vulgare* (more fully *wild marjoram*), native on chalk and limestone and the source of oregano, and the less pungent *O. majorana* (more fully *sweet* or *knotted marjoram*), and *O. onites* (more fully *pot marjoram*). Also, the leaves of such a plant as used to flavour meat dishes etc.

mark /mɑːk/ *n.*[1] [OE (Anglian) *merc*, (WS) *mearc* = OFris. *merke*, OS *marka* (Du. *mark*), OHG *marc(h)a* (G *Mark*), ON *mǫrk*, Goth. *marka*, f. Gmc n. rel. to L *margo* MARGIN *n.* In branch IV f. MARK *v.* Cf. MARCH *n.*[2]] I A boundary. 1 A boundary, a frontier, a limit. Now only *arch.* & *poet.* OE. 2 [G *Mark*, It. *marca*.] Any of various (specified) German or Italian territories or principalities. Cf. MARCH *n.*[2] 3. Now *arch.* or *Hist.* E18. 3 *Hist.* A communal tract of land held by a Germanic or medieval German village community. M19.

II Something indicating a boundary, position, etc. †4 A standard, a banner. OE–ME. 5 A stone or other monument serving as a memorial or as a guide. Long *spec.*, an object on shore or at sea whose position serves to guide or warn a passing traveller. OE. b A fishing-ground. M20. †6 A post, stone, fence, etc., indicating a boundary; = LANDMARK *n.* 1. ME–M18. 7 A target, butt, or other object to be aimed at with a missile or projectile; *slang* an intended victim of a swindler etc. ME. †b The quarry of a hawk etc. L16–L17. c The jack in bowls. Also, a position allowed for this resulting from the initial delivery. M17. d *Boxing.* The pit of the stomach. M18. 8 An object indicating the terminal point of a race. Chiefly *fig.*, an object desired or striven for, a goal, a standard for attainment. ME. 9 A line, notch, post, attached object, etc., intended to record or indicate position, esp. for measurement. ME. b *fig.* A fixed or recognized standard; (preceded by a numeral) (an approximation of) a limit or total. M18. c The height or distance achieved by an athlete's throw, jump, etc.; the measurement representing this; *transf.* a best performance, a record. E20. 10 *spec.* a *Naut.* A piece of material or a knot used to indicate a position on a sounding-line. M18. b In rugby football, a heel-mark on the ground made by a player who has caught the ball direct from a kick or knock-on or throw-forward by an opponent. In Australian Rules football, the catching of a ball direct from a kick of at least ten metres; the spot from which the subsequent kick is taken. M19. c *Athletics.* A competitor's starting point in a race; a line drawn to indicate this. L19.

5 HOBBES Men that have past by a Rock at Sea, set up some mark, thereby to remember their former danger, and avoid it. 7 G. ORWELL Perched on the hill-tops .. we should have made lovely marks for artillery. T. H. WHITE Shooting one arrow each at any agreed mark. *fig.*: G. J. WHYTE-MELVILLE Gilbert's efforts to amuse her often fell short of the mark. 8 T. NORTON Let this be our perpetual marke, to aide all men faithfully. 9 M. BRIDGMAN She slips the letter in her novel for a mark. *Daily Chronicle* The floods .. call attention to the little interest .. taken by local authorities as regards erecting flood-marks. b F. W. ROBINSON He made the sum come pretty near the mark. J. I. M. STEWART Mr. Gender is asking whether we can borrow a sum somewhere near the million mark. S. KNIGHT Only by the criticism .. of an Opposition can a government be kept up to the mark. c *Sun* (*Baltimore*) The victor's time was one of the best marks of the meeting. 10c G. MITCHELL 'On your marks,' said the starter. The swimmers were poised and ready.

III A sign, a token, an indication. 11 An appearance, action, etc., indicating something; a sign, a token. OE. †b A vestige, a trace. ME–L16. c A characteristic property, a distinctive feature. ME. d *spec.* A depression in each of a horse's incisor teeth, which by its appearance and gradual disappearance gives some indication of the animal's age; the age when this is apparent. Freq. in *mark of mouth*. LME. 12a A written character, as an asterisk etc.; *spec.* such a character, usu. a cross, made in place of a signature by an illiterate person. OE. b A stamp, seal, label, inscription, etc., on an article, identifying it or indicating its ownership, origin, good quality, etc. ME. c A visible sign, as a badge, brand, etc., identifying a person's occupation, status, etc. ME. d *Her.* A small charge added to a coat of arms as a sign of distinction, esp. cadency. E17. e A point awarded for a pupil's correct answer etc.; *esp.* a written symbol or a numeral representing the number of such points gained, esp. out of a given possible total, awarded as an assessment of proficiency or conduct. E19. 13 A visible trace or impression on a surface, produced by nature, accident, or design, as a stain, blemish, scar, fleck, stroke, dot, etc. ME. b *spec.* In *pl.* The footprints or tracks of an otter. Cf. MARCH *n.*[3] 1. Long *dial.* ME. c *Telecommunications.* Each of a succession of strokes, dots, etc., on or holes in a paper strip whose relative duration and separation convey telegraphic information; any signal that conveys information by its intermittent presence rather than by its magnitude. Opp. *space.* M19. †14 A flock of swans marked with the same identifying brand. LME–M16. †15 A particular type or class of person. LME–M16. 16 A particular brand, make, or design of an article; *esp.* (freq. **M-** and followed by a numeral) a manufactured product (as a car, aeroplane, etc.) as represented at a particular stage in its design and development. M17. 17 That which suits or pleases one particularly. *colloq.* M18. 18 A die or stamp for impressing on goods a symbol identifying the manufacturer. L18.

11 R. GRAVES The broad-headed halberd and the long sword are marks of high rank. A. GRAY All .. bowed their heads as a mark of respect. R. K. NARAYAN I could invite him to have a group photo with me as a mark of friendship. c R. CROMPTON That disregard for consequences which is the mark of youth. 12a H. SWEET The stress-marks are put before the element on which the stress begins. JOYCE He visited the chief factory .. and signed his mark in the visitors' book. *exclamation mark*, *question mark*, etc. b J. FRYER The Company's Mark upon all their Goods. *earmark*, *hallmark*, *trade mark*, etc. e *Nature* No marks out of 10. J. HUXLEY My highest mark was for composition for which the Director commended me. *fig.*: H. JAMES Sculpture .. uninjured as if .. under glass. One good mark for the French Revolution! 13 R. K. NARAYAN She .. renewed the vermilion mark on her forehead. W. TREVOR There was a dark mark, a smudge or a bruise, on her left cheek. J. GARDAM You can probably pick out their spade marks. M. HUGHES She .. noticed an ink mark on her finger. 16 J. WAMBAUGH Philo was peeking up over the hood of a red Mark V when Tutu saw him. 17 T. PARKER This cottage was going, so I took it. .. It's just about my mark this is.

IV†19 Attention, notice, heed. ME–E19. 20 Importance, note. Chiefly in *of mark*. L16.

19 SIR W. SCOTT Little matter worthy of mark occurred. 20 R. WEST This French tutor was a man of mark .. who had .. held a lectureship in Paris.

Phrases: **be quick off the mark** lose no time in starting. **beside the mark** = *wide of the mark* below. **be slow off the mark** waste time in starting. *black mark*: see BLACK *a.* *bless the mark*: see (*God*) *save* or *bless the mark* below. *full marks*: see FULL *a.* **get off the mark** start. **(God) save** or **bless the mark** *int.* (freq. *iron.*) apologizing for or disagreeing with a preceding word or phrase. *high-water mark*: see HIGH *a.* etc. *late mark*: see LATE *a.* & *n.*[2] *leading mark*: see LEADING *a.* **leave** or **make a mark** leave or make a permanent, important, or obvious impression. *long mark*: see LONG *a.*[1] *low-water mark*: see LOW *a.* & *n.*[4] *make a mark*: see *leave* or *make a mark* above. **make one's mark** attain distinction. *mark twain*: see TWAIN *n.* 1b. *mason's mark*: see MASON *n.* 1. **overshoot** or **overstep the mark** *fig.* go beyond a fixed or accepted standard or limit; behave improperly. *save the mark*: see (*God*) *save* or *bless the mark* above. *short mark*: see SHORT *a.* *the mark of the Beast*: see BEAST *n.* *wide of the mark*: see WIDE *a.*

Comb.: **mark-boat** a boat moored at a particular spot and serving as a guide; **mark man**, **mark mason**, **mark master** a Freemason holding a certain rank; **mark-vessel** = *mark-boat* above.

mark /mɑːk/ *n.*[2] [OE *marc* corresp. to OFris. *merk*, MDu. *marc*, (Du. *mark*), MHG *marke* (G *Mark*), ON *mǫrk*, prob. all f. med.L *marcus*, *marca* (whence also Fr., Prov. *marc*, Sp. *marco*, It. *marco*, *-a*): perh. ult. identical with MARK *n.*[1]] 1 A measure of weight, chiefly for gold and silver, formerly used throughout western Europe and usu. equal to 8 ounces (226.8 grams). Now only, any of various similar foreign measures of weight. OE. **2** A monetary unit, orig. representing the value of a mark weight of pure silver, equal to thirteen shillings and fourpence in the (English and Scottish) currency of the day. *obs.* exc. *Hist.* OE. **b** A Scottish coin of this value. *obs.* exc. *Hist.* ME. **3** Any of various foreign coins and monetary units (*obs.* exc. *Hist.*). Now *spec.* the basic monetary unit of Germany, equal to 100 pfennigs; a coin of this value; (see also DEUTSCHMARK, OSTMARK). ME. **4** In Orkney and Shetland: a division of land originally representing the value of one Scottish mark. Also *markland*. *obs.* exc. *Hist.* L15.

2 *mark (of) sterling*: see STERLING *n.*[1] 1a.

mark /mɑːk/ *v.* [OE *mearcian* = OFris. *merkia*, OS (*gi*)*markon* appoint, observe (Du. *marken*), OHG *marchōn* plan, ON *marka* mark, observe, f. WGmc, f. Gmc base of MARK *n.*[1]] **I** Put a mark on. **1** *v.t.* Trace out boundaries for; plot or plan out. Now usu. foll. by *out.* OE. **†b** Fashion, frame. *poet.* Only in LME. **2** *v.t.* Make a mark or marks on (a thing or person) by drawing, stamping, cutting, hitting, etc.; form or represent by making marks. OE. **b** Orig., embroider. Now *spec.* put a person's initials or other identifying mark on (clothing, linen, etc.) by means of embroidery, ink, etc. ME. **c** In *pass.* Have or bear natural marks. LME. **d** Attach a price to (an article or goods). M19. **e** Draw or cut lines on (an object) to act as a guide during subsequent machining, cutting, aligning, etc. Foll. by *off.* L19. **f** Earmark (a lamb or calf); castrate (a lamb). *Austral.* & *NZ.* M20. **3** *v.t. fig.* **a** Designate as if by placing a mark on; characterize; destine. Foll. by *as, down, for, out,* (now *rare*) *to do.* OE. **†b** Mete out, allot. *poet.* ME–L15. **c** Separate *from* something else as by drawing a boundary line or imposing a distinctive mark. Usu. foll. by *off, out.* E18. **4a** *v.t.* Note down, indicate in writing (long *obs.* exc. *Sc.*); indicate or represent by a mark, symbol, or marker. OE. **b** *v.i.* Of a horse: indicate its age by its mark of mouth (MARK *n.*[1] 11d). M18. **c** *v.t.* & *i.* Record (points) in a game. E19. **d** *v.t.* & *i.* Award marks to or grade (an examination, pupil, etc.). L19. **e** *v.t. Stock Exch.* Record the price at the making of (a bargain or transaction). E20. **†5** *v.t.* Make (the sign of the cross) with the hand. ME–L16. **6** *v.t.* Be a distinguishing mark of, characterize; be a noteworthy feature or attendant circumstance of. Freq. in *pass.* M17. **b** Indicate the position or course of; be an indication of. L17. **c** In *pass.* Of a feature etc.: be (more or less) strikingly noticeable. E19. **7** *v.t.* Show or manifest (one's approval, displeasure, etc.) by some significant action. L18. **8** *v.t. Mil.* Indicate (the pivots, formations, etc.) in military evolutions. L18.

1 BROWNING All that time stood Rosamund Page.. on the turf marked out for the party's firing-place. A. CHRISTIE William is the gardener. He keeps the paths and marks the tennis courts. 2 W. TREVOR Throwing her fork down, marking the white tablecloth. Z. TOMIN She scratched me, the stupid cow has marked me for life. *fig.*: E. FEINSTEIN Those pains of childhood never leave us. We are marked by them for ever. b J. PAYN We are marking the house linen. c W. S. DALLAS The species of the genus *Argynnis*.. are elegantly marked with silvery spots. 3a R. H. MOTTRAM Only the boots and the hatless head marked her for a follower of the continental tradition. J. BETJEMAN Pedestrians and dogs and cats—we mark them down for slaughter. M. BRAGG His boots, his cap, his heavy flapping jacket all marked him out as a miner. c T. E. HARVEY Her son's serious ways, by which he was marked out from his.. brothers and sisters. A. BULLOCK This was an attitude.. which marked him off from Morrison. 4a R. MACAULAY Some of the rivers and small lakes that I saw marked on the map. A. MOOREHEAD Mark your routes as permanently as possible, by leaving records, sowing seeds, building cairns. R. K. NARAYAN They made Jaggu return to the starting point, marked it with white paint. d G. GREENE He marked him 100% for Classics. *Today* The anguished expression of a man who has marked too many misspelt exam papers. 6 W. S. MAUGHAM He came towards her with the springy gait which marked his eager vitality. S. UNWIN The official end of the Congress was marked by a Dinner. A. BRIEN Mother does nothing to mark the occasion. b J. C. POWYS They had been planted to mark the spot where the Vikings had landed. D. STOREY The grave was marked by a small round-headed stone. M. ESSLIN This homecoming marked the beginning of the most productive period in Beckett's life. 7 E. GASKELL Sitting down herself on a.. stool to mark her sense of the difference in their conditions.

II Direct one's course or aim. **†9** *v.t.* & *i.* Direct, continue on, (one's way). ME–L16. **10†a** *v.t.* Aim a blow or missile at; strike, hit. ME–E16. **b** *v.i.* Take aim, aim a blow. (Foll. by *to.*) Long *obs.* exc. *Sc.* ME.

III Notice, observe. **11** *v.t.* Notice; observe, watch. ME. **12** *v.t.* & *i.* Consider; give one's attention (to); take notice (of). LME. **13** *v.t.* Note the place of going to cover of (game) after it has been put up. Also foll. by *down.* LME. **14** *v.t.* & *i. Sport.* Keep close to and so hamper (a player in an opposing team). L19. **b** *Austral. Rules Football.* Catch (the ball). M20.

11 DISRAELI I looked up, I marked the tumultuous waving of many torches. F. HERBERT She marked how he fingered his beard. 12 K. WATERHOUSE There is, mark you, no guarantee. R. WEST Mark my words, he'll come back.

Phrases, & with advs. in specialized senses: *mark a person's card*: see CARD *n.*[2] 3b. **mark down** (*a*) reduce the price of; (*b*) make a written note of; (see also sense 3 above). **mark time** (*a*) *Mil.* march on the spot, without moving forward; (*b*) act routinely; go through the motions; (*c*) await an opportunity to advance. **mark up** (*a*) correct or annotate (copy or proofs) for typesetting, printing, etc.; (*b*) raise the price of. *mark with a white stone*: see WHITE *a.*

Comb.: **mark-down** a reduction in price; **mark-up** (*a*) the amount added to the cost price of goods to cover overheads and provide profit; (*b*) the process or result of marking up copy or proofs; (*c*) *Computing* the process of assigning tags to elements of a text to indicate their relation to the structure of the text; the tags so assigned.

markable *a.* (*rare*) †(*a*) remarkable; (*b*) able to receive a mark or imprint: LME.

marked /mɑːkt/ *a.* OE. [f. MARK *n.*[1], *v.*: see -ED[2], -ED[1].] **1** Having a visible mark; *spec.* (of a playing-card) having a distinctive mark on the back to enable or facilitate cheating or conjuring. OE. **2** Clearly defined, clearly noticeable; evident. L18. **3** *Ling.* Of a form, entity, etc., in a binary pair: carrying or distinguished by a (specified) distinctive feature; less frequent or usual of the two. M20.

2 D. BREWSTER We slightly resented a piece of marked incivility. M. DRABBLE The resemblance between mother and daughter was marked. S. KITZINGER Fear of miscarriage also has a marked effect on the physical expression of sexual feelings.

Special collocations: **marked cheque**: whose value is guaranteed by a bank. **marked man** (*a*) a person whose conduct is watched with suspicion or hostility; a person on whom vengeance will be taken; (*b*) a person destined to succeed. **marked price** the price of an article for sale indicated by an attached label etc.

markedly /ˈmɑːkɪdli/ *adv.* E19. **markedness** /ˈmɑːkɪdnɪs/ *n.* M19.

marker /ˈmɑːkə/ *n.* LME. [f. MARK *v.* + -ER[1].] **1a** A person who marks boundaries. *rare.* LME. **b** A person who marks game. *rare.* L15. **c** A person who records the score in a game (esp. billiards or squash), or at target practice; a scorer. Also, a scoreboard or card etc. to record a score. M16. **d** A person who puts a mark, stamp, etc., on something. M16. **e** *Mil.* A person placed as a formation mark in military evolutions. L18. **f** *Sport.* A player whose function is to mark or guard a player of the opposing team. L20. **2** An implement, tool, or device for making a mark or marks. E18. **b** *spec.* More fully *marker pen.* A broad-tipped felt pen used esp. for highlighting or for marking indelibly. M20. **3a** A bookmark. M19. **b** An object acting as a guide to direction or indicating a route, boundary, etc.; *spec.* a flare dropped from an aircraft to illuminate or mark a target. M19. **c** A distinctive feature, characteristic, etc., *esp.* one aiding recognition. E20. **d** A monument, memorial stone, etc., marking a place of special interest. E20. **4** Something worthy to be compared. Usu. in neg. contexts. *slang.* L19. **5** A promissory note; an IOU. *US slang.* L19. **6** *Genetics.* An allele used to identify a chromosome or to locate other genes on a genetic map. M20. **7** *Ling.* A word, affix, etc., which distinguishes or determines the class or function of the form, construction, etc., with which it is used. M20.

2b *Magic Marker*: see MAGIC *a.* 3a M. R. MITFORD I had no marker, and the richly bound volume closed. b C. BONINGTON Marker flags are essential.. to ensure that sherpas follow the selected route safely. J. ARCHER As they approach the six-furlong marker—Rosalie and Crown Princess come up on the stand side. c *Gainesville Daily Sun* We added a number of plants that were very good markers of wetlands. 4 W. HUNT The early days of Montana were not a marker to what I have gone through.

Comb.: **marker crude** a grade of (usu. light) crude oil whose price, fixed by agreement between oil producers, is used as a guideline for other oil prices; *marker pen*: see sense 2b above.

market /ˈmɑːkɪt/ *n.* [Late OE *-markett* in *gēarmarkett* year market (cf. OE *gēares ċīeping* year's market) f. OS *iārmarket* = OHG *iārmarchāt*, 2nd elem. of which is f. L *mercatus* (whence (through Proto-Romance) OFr. *marchiet* (mod. *marché*), OProv. *mercat* (mod. *marcatz*)), f. *mercārī* buy, f. *merc-*, *merx* merchandise. Cf. MART *n.*[1]] **1** A meeting or gathering together of people for the purchase and sale of provisions or livestock, publicly displayed, at a fixed time and place; the occasion or time of this. Also, a company of people so gathered. LOE. **b** *Law* (now *Hist.*). The right granted to the lord of a manor, a municipality, etc., to establish such a meeting. LOE. **c** *The* stock market. L19. **2** An open space or covered building in which provisions, livestock, etc., are displayed for sale. Now also, a supermarket. ME. **3** The action or business of buying and selling; an instance of this, a commercial transaction; a (*good* or *bad*) bargain. *obs.* exc. *dial.* & in phrs. ME. **†b** The marketing or selling *of* a commodity. Only in 17. **4** The rate of purchase and sale of a commodity, share, etc.; market value. Also, a share performing in a specified way in the stock market. M16. **5** An opportunity for buying or selling. Chiefly in phrs. below. Now *rare* or *obs.* L16. **6** A place or group with a demand for a commodity or service. E17. **7** Sale as controlled by supply and demand; *esp.* a demand *for* a commodity or service. L17. **8** *The* trade in a specified commodity. L17.

1 DAY LEWIS The rest of the flat cart was filled with hens for the market. C. THUBRON Markets spilling over the pavements with sacks of bananas, improvised stalls piled with cheap clothes. c *Sunday Times* The market's initial reaction to the Benlox bid was incredulous. 2 M. L. KING The largest cattle market east of Fort Worth,.. marketing approximately $30 million worth of cattle annually. 4 T. HARDY Just when I sold the markets went lower. P. KAVANAGH The market rose sixpence after I had sold first time. *Times* Bulmer shares have certainly been a strong market in recent weeks. 6 D. MACDONALD The important change was the replacement of the individual patron by the market. M. EDWARDES The United States of America—our major sports car market. 7 *Times Lit. Suppl.* A market surely exists for an esoteric study of Wittgenstein's notoriously recondite ideas.

Phrases: **be in the market for** wish to buy. *black market*: see BLACK *a.* **bring to market** offer for sale (*bring one's pigs to market*: see PIG *n.*[1]). *buyer's* or *buyers' market*: see BUYER 1. *Common Market*: see COMMON *a.* *drive one's pigs to market*: see PIG *n.*[1] *free market*: see FREE *a.* **go to market** *colloq.* (*a*) make an attempt; (*b*) *Austral.* & *NZ* behave in an angry manner, become angry. *grey market*: see GREY *a.* *idols of the market*: see IDOL *n.* **lose one's market** miss one's chance of doing business. **make a market** *Stock Exch.* induce active dealing in a stock or share by being both a buyer and a seller of it. **make a** or **one's market of** make a profit out of. **†make market** trade. *make one's market*: see *make a market* above. **market overt** *Law* (offering for sale goods in) an open and legally constituted market. *mass market*: see MASS *n.*[2] & *a.* *milk the market*: see MILK *v.* *open market*: see OPEN *a.* *parallel market*: see PARALLEL *a.* *play the market*: see PLAY *v.* *price out of the market*: see PRICE *v.* 1. *rig the market*: see RIG *v.*[4] *seller's* or *sellers' market*: see SELLER. *single market*: see SINGLE *a.* & *adv.* *stand the market*: see STAND *v.* *straddle the market*: see STRADDLE *v.* *vertical market*: see VERTICAL *a.*

Comb.: **market basket** a large basket usu. with a lid, used to carry provisions etc.; **market cross**: erected in a market-place; **market-day**: on which a market is regularly held, usu. weekly; **market economy** an economy subject to and determined by free competition; **market garden** a piece of land on which fruit and vegetables are grown to be sold at a market; **market gardener** a person who owns or is employed in a market garden; **market-house** a building in which a market is held; **market hunter** a person who hunts game to sell at a market; **market-maker** a member of a stock exchange who buys and sells continuously within prescribed regulations; **market mammy** *colloq.* an African woman stallholder; **market man** (*a*) a man who buys or sells in a market; (*b*) a man who works in a stock exchange; **market-peace** *Hist.* a peace or truce prevailing in a market on market-days; **market-place** (*a*) an open space in a town where a market is held; (*b*) the world of commerce or trade; *fig.* any place or environment where ideas etc. are exchanged; **market potential** the estimated potential demand for and sales of a commodity or service; **market-price** the current price which a commodity or service fetches in the market; **market-rate** the current value of a commodity or service; **market research** the study of consumers' needs and preferences, esp. for a particular commodity or service; **market researcher** a person engaged in market research; **market shooter** a person who shoots game to sell at a market; **market socialism** an economic system in which a country's resources are publicly owned but production is determined by the private customer; **market square** an open square in which a town market is held; **market stall** a trader's stand or booth in a market; **marketstead** *arch.* = *market-place* above; **market town**: where a market is held regularly; **market value** the current or saleable value of a commodity or service; **market woman**: who buys or sells in a market.

market /ˈmɑːkɪt/ *v.* LME. [f. the n.] **1** *v.t.* Sell in a market; bring or send to a market. LME. **2** *v.i.* Deal in a market, buy and sell; purchase provisions, shop. M17. **3** *v.t.* Promote and distribute (a product etc.) for sale. E20.

2 R. CHANDLER Then I have to go uptown and market. 3 *Lancaster Guardian* It is . . important that the resort continues to be marketed as a seaside holiday destination.

marketable /ˈmɑːkɪtəb(ə)l/ *a.* L16. [f. prec. + -ABLE.] **1** Able to be marketed; that finds a ready market; saleable. L16. **2** Of or pertaining to trade; *spec.* (of price, value) that may be obtained in buying or selling. E17.

marketa'bility *n.* L19. **marketableness** *n.* E19. **marketably** *adv.* M19.

marketeer /mɑːkɪˈtɪə/ *n.* M19. [f. MARKET *n.* + -EER.] **1** A person who sells in a market. M19. **2** A supporter of the Common Market and Britain's membership of it. M20. **3** A specialist in marketing. L20.

marketer /ˈmɑːkɪtə/ *n.* Chiefly *US.* L18. [f. MARKET *v.* + -ER[1].] **1** A person who buys or sells in a market. E16. **2** A person who promotes and distributes a product for sale. M20.

marketing /ˈmɑːkɪtɪŋ/ *n.* M16. [f. MARKET *v.* + -ING[1].] **1** The action of MARKET *v.*; an instance of this. M16. **b** *spec.* The action, business, or process of promoting and selling a product etc., including market research, choice of product, advertising, and distribution. L19. **2a** Something bought at a market; a purchase. *rare.* E18. **b** Produce to be sold at market. *rare.* L19.

1b P. PARISH Many over-the-counter preparations contain vitamins and these are the subject of intense marketing.

Comb.: **marketing research** the study of the factors involved in marketing a product.

markhor /ˈmɑːkɔː/ *n.* Also **-ore**. M19. [Pers. *mār-ḵwār* lit. 'serpent-eater'.] A large wild goat, *Capra falconeri*, with a slate-grey coat and long spiral horns, found in mountain woodlands in central Asia.

marking /ˈmɑːkɪŋ/ *n.* ME. [f. MARK *v.* + -ING[1].] **1** The action of MARK *v.*; an instance of this. ME. †**2** Notice, consideration. LME–E17. **3** A mark; a pattern of marks, esp. on an animal (freq. in *pl.*). LME.

3 R. DAHL The shape and colour and markings of perhaps several hundred different but very similar dogs. C. PHILLIPS Despite the markings on their tickets people just took whatever cabin they could find.

Comb.: **marking board** (*a*) a scoreboard; (*b*) a board in a stock exchange for registering transactions; **marking cotton** coloured cotton thread for marking linen etc.; **marking ink** indelible ink for marking linen etc.; †**marking iron** (*a*) a branding iron; (*b*) a device for making patterns on pastry; **marking-nut** the fruit of a tropical Asiatic tree, *Semecarpus anacardium* (family Anacardiaceae), the juice of which is used to mark linen; **marking stitch** a stitch used in marking linen etc.

markka /ˈmɑːkɑː/ *n.* E20. [Finn.] The basic monetary unit of Finland, equal to 100 penniä.

markless /ˈmɑːklɪs/ *a.* M19. [f. MARK *n.*[1] + -LESS.] Without a mark or marks.

markman /ˈmɑːkmən/ *n.* Pl. **-men**. L16. [f. MARK *n.*[1] + MAN *n.*] †**1** = MARKSMAN 1. L16–M17. **2** *Hist.* A person living in a mark (MARK *n.*[1] 3). L19.

Markov /ˈmɑːkɒf/ *n.* Also **Markoff**. M20. [A. A. *Markov* (1856–1922), Russ. mathematician.] *Math.* Used *attrib.* to designate (the characteristic property of) any stochastic process for which the probabilities of the different future states depend only on the existing state and not on how that state was arrived at.

Markov chain a Markov process in which there are a denumerable number of possible states or in which transitions between states occur at discrete time intervals (freq. with constant transition probabilities).

Markovian /mɑːˈkəʊvɪən/ *a.* pertaining to or of the nature of a Markov process M20.

marksman /ˈmɑːksmən/ *n.* Pl. **-men**. M17. [f. MARK *n.*[1] + -S[1] + MAN *n.*] **1** A person skilled or practised in shooting or aiming at a mark or target; *spec.* a person who attains a certain standard of proficiency in rifle practice. Cf. earlier MARKMAN 1. M17. **2** A person who makes a mark in place of a signature. L18. **3** A person who ranges competitors in a race. L19.

marksmanship *n.* the skill or art of a marksman M19.

markswoman /ˈmɑːkswʊm(ə)n/ *n.* Pl. **-women**. E19. [f. as prec. + WOMAN *n.*] A woman skilled or practised in shooting or aiming at a mark or target.

markworthy /ˈmɑːkwəːði/ *a.* E19. [f. MARK *n.*[1] + -WORTHY, after G *merkwürdig.*] Worthy of note, notable.

marl /mɑːl/ *n.*[1] ME. [OFr. *marle* (mod. *marne*, dial. *marle*) f. med.L *margila* f. L *marga* (after *argilla* white clay).] **1** Soil consisting principally of clay mixed with calcium carbonate and forming a loose unconsolidated mass, valuable as a fertilizer. ME. **2** Earth, soil. *poet.* L16. **3** A brick made from marl. E19.

1 **burning marl** [after Milton *Paradise Lost*] the torments of hell.

Comb.: **marl-pit**: from which marl is dug; **marl slate** *Geol.* fissile, usu. calcareous, shale. **marlstone** *Geol.* argillaceous and ferruginous limestone such as lies between the Upper and Lower Lias of England.

marl /mɑːl/ *n.*[2] *obs.* exc. *dial.* E17. [Contr.] = MARVEL *n.*[1]

marl /mɑːl/ *n.*[3] & *a.* L19. [Contr. of MARBLED.] **A** *n.* A mottled yarn made from two or more differently coloured threads twisted together; fabric produced from this yarn. L19. **B** *attrib.* or as *adj.* Made or consisting of marl. E20.

marl /mɑːl/ *v.*[1]*t.* ME. [f. MARL *n.*[1]] Apply marl to (land); fertilize (as) with marl; *fig.* (*arch.*) enrich.

marler *n.* now *dial.* a person who digs or spreads marl ME.

marl /mɑːl/ *v.*[2]*t.* LME. [Du. *marlen*: see MARLINE.] †**1** Tie, noose. Only in LME. **2** *Naut.* Fasten with marline or other light rope; secure *together* by a succession of half-hitches; wind serving round (a parcelled rope), securing it with a half hitch at each turn. E18.

marl /mɑːl/ *v.*[3] *obs.* exc. *dial.* L16. [Contr.] = MARVEL *v.*

marlberry /ˈmɑːlbəri/ *n.* *US.* L19. [Prob. f. dial. var. of MARBLE *n.* + BERRY *n.*[1]] An evergreen shrub or small tree, *Ardisia escallonoides* (family Myrsinaceae), with white flowers and black berries, found in the W. Indies and Central America.

marled /mɑːld/ *a.* Orig. *Sc.* Also **merled**, **mirled**, /məːld/. E16. [Perh. f. OFr. *merelé*, f. *merelle* counter, game played with counters (mod. *marelle* hopscotch): see -ED[2]. Cf. MARLY *a.*[2]] Mottled, variegated, streaked.

†**marlet** *n.* M16–M17. [(O)Fr. *merlette* martlet, app. dim. of *merle* blackbird: see MERLE *n.*[1], -ET[1].] A martin; *Her.* a martlet.

marlin /ˈmɑːlɪn/ *n.*[1] *US.* M19. [Origin unkn.] A godwit.

marlin /ˈmɑːlɪn/ *n.*[2] E20. [App. f. MARLIN(SPIKE.] Any of several large marine game-fishes and food fishes of the genera *Makaira* and *Tetrapterus* with the upper jaw elongated to form a pointed snout.

marline /ˈmɑːlɪn/ *n.* LME. [Du. *marlijn* (f. *marren* to bind + *lijn* LINE *n.*[1]) & *marling* (f. *marlen* frequent. of MDu. *marren* + *-ing* -ING[1]).] *Naut.* Light rope of two strands.

marlinspike /ˈmɑːlɪnspʌɪk/ *n.* Also **-line-**. Orig. (now *rare*) **marling-** /ˈmɑːlɪŋ-/. E17. [App. f. *marling* pres. pple of MARL *v.*[2] + SPIKE *n.*[2], the 1st elem. being later interpreted as prec. Cf. MARLIN *n.*[2]] *Naut.* A pointed iron tool used to lift the strands of rope in splicing, as a lever in marling, etc.

marlion *n.* var. of MERLION.

marlite /ˈmɑːlʌɪt/ *n.* L18. [f. MARL *n.*[1] + -ITE[1].] A variety of marl which resists the decomposing action of air.

marloes /ˈmɑːləʊz/ *n.* Chiefly *dial.* E19. [Perh. f. MAR(BLE *n.* + arbitrary *-loes*.] The game of marbles.

Marlovian /mɑːˈləʊvɪən/ *a.* & *n.* L19. [f. mod.L *Marlovia* Marlowe (see below) + -IAN.] **A** *adj.* Pertaining to or characteristic of the English dramatist Christopher Marlowe (1564–93). L19. **B** *n.* An admirer or student of Marlowe or his writing. L19.

marly /ˈmɑːli/ *a.*[1] ME. [f. MARL *n.*[1] + -Y[1].] Resembling marl; composed of marl; having much marl.

marly /ˈmɑːli/ *a.*[2] *Sc.* & *dial.* E18. [Rel. to MARLED: see -Y[1].] = MARLED.

marm /mɑːm, mam/ *n.* Chiefly *US.* M19. [Respelling of MA'AM. Cf. MAUM.] **1** = MA'AM. M19. **2** Mother (also as a form of address). M19.

marmalade /ˈmɑːməleɪd/ *n.* & *a.* L15. [Fr. *marmelade* f. Port. *marmelada*, f. *marmelo* quince, dissimilated form of L *melimelum* f. Gk *melimēlon* kind of apple grafted on a quince, f. *meli* honey + *mēlon* apple.] **A** *n.* **1** A preserve made by boiling fruits (orig. quinces, now citrus fruit, *spec.* oranges) with sugar to form a consistent mass. L15. **2** (The fruit of) the marmalade tree. Also *natural marmalade*. L18.

1 OXFORD *marmalade.*

Comb.: **marmalade box** (the fruit of) the genipap tree, *Genipa americana*; **marmalade plum** (the fruit of) the marmalade tree; **marmalade tree** the mammee sapota tree, *Pouteria sapota*.

B *adj.* †**1** Sweet. Only in E17. **2** Made with or consisting of marmalade. L19. **3** Of the colour of marmalade; orange, ginger. E20.

3 S. T. WARNER Jim was . . a mottled marmalade cat.

marmalady *a.* resembling marmalade esp. in sweetness, stickiness or colour E17.

marmalade /ˈmɑːməleɪd/ *v.t.* M20. [f. prec.] Spread with marmalade.

marmem /ˈmɑːmɛm/ *n.* L20. [f. MAR(TENSITE + MEM(ORY.] *Metall.* = *shape memory* s.v. SHAPE *n.*[1]

marmennill /mɑːˈmɛnɪl/ *n.* *rare.* E19. [Icel., dim. of *mar* sea + *mann-*, *maður* man.] A merman.

marmite /ˈmɑːmʌɪt; *in sense 1 also foreign* marmit (*pl. same*)/ *n.* E19. [Fr.] **1** An earthenware cooking-vessel. E19. **2** (Also **M-**.) (Proprietary name for) a savoury extract made from fresh brewer's yeast, used esp. in sandwiches and for flavouring. E20.

1 *petite marmite*: see PETITE *a.* 2.

marmiton /marmitɔ̃/ *n.* Pl. pronounced same. *rare.* M18. [Fr., f. as prec.] A servant in a kitchen doing menial work.

marmolite /ˈmɑːm(ə)lʌɪt/ *n.* E19. [f. Gk *marmairein* to shine + -O- + -LITE.] *Petrogr.* A pale green laminated serpentine with a pearly lustre.

marmoraceous /mɑːmə'reɪʃəs/ *a. rare.* L17. [f. L *marmor* MARBLE *n.* + -ACEOUS.] Pertaining to or resembling marble.

marmorate /'mɑːm(ə)reɪt/ *a.* M16. [L *marmoratus* pa. pple of *marmorare* overlay with marble, f. *marmor* MARBLE *n.*: see -ATE[2].] †**1** Overlaid with or enclosed in marble. Only in M16. **2** *Bot.* & *Zool.* Variegated or veined like marble. E19.

marmoreal /mɑː'mɔːrɪəl/ *a.* Chiefly *poet.* & *rhet.* L18. [f. L *marmoreus*, f. *marmor* MARBLE *n.*: see -AL[1].] **1** Resembling marble or a marble statue; cold, smooth, white, etc., like marble. L18. **2** Made or composed of marble. E19.

marmoreally *adv.* M19.

marmorean /mɑː'mɔːrɪən/ *a. poet.* & *rhet.* M17. [f. as prec. + -AN.] = prec.

marmoset /'mɑːməzɛt/ *n.* LME. [(O)Fr. *marmouset* grotesque image, young boy, (dial.) ape, of unkn. origin.] †**1** A grotesque figure; an idol; a gargoyle. LME–M18. **2** Orig., any small monkey. Now, any of several small neotropical monkeys with fine silky coats and long bushy tails which together with tamarins constitute the family Callitricidae; *spec.* any of the genus *Callithrix*. LME. †**3a** A man one despises. L15–E19. **b** A woman, a child, (used as a term of endearment or playful reproach). E16–M18.

2 SILVERY *marmoset*.

marmot /'mɑːmət/ *n.* E17. [Fr. *marmotte*, prob. alt. of Romansch *murmont* f. Proto-Romance wd meaning 'mountain mouse'.] Any of several burrowing colonial rodents of the genus *Marmota*, belonging to the same family (Sciuridae) as squirrels and found on high grassland in Europe, Asia, and N. America. Also (w. specifying wd), any of various similar mammals.

hoary marmot: see HOARY 4. **Polish marmot** = BOBAC. PRAIRIE *marmot*. *whistling marmot*: see WHISTLING *ppl a.*

maro /'marəʊ/ *n.* Pl. **-os**. L18. [Polynesian.] A loincloth worn by certain South Sea Islanders.

marocain /marə'keɪn/ *n.* & *a.* E20. [Fr., f. *Maroc* (see MOROCCO) + *-ain* -AN. Cf. MAROQUIN.] **A** *n.* (A garment made from) a crêpe fabric of silk or wool or both. E20. **B** *adj.* Made of marocain. L20.

maroela *n.* var. of MARULA.

Maronite /'marənʌɪt/ *n.* & *a.* E16. [med.L *Maronita*, f. *Maron* reputed 5th-cent. AD founder of the sect: see -ITE[1].] **A** *n.* A member of a sect of Syrian Christians living chiefly in Lebanon and now in communion with the Roman Catholic Church. E16. **B** *adj.* Of or pertaining to the Maronites. E17.

maroodi /mə'ruːdi/ *n.* E19. [Arawak *marodi*.] In Guyana, a guan.

maroon /mə'ruːn/ *n.*[1] M17. [Fr. *marron*, †*maron* f. Sp. *cimarrón*: see CIMARRON, -OON.] **1** (Also **M-**.) Any of the Blacks in the mountains and forests of Suriname and the W. Indies who are descended from runaway slaves. M17. **2** In full *maroon* †*frolic*, *party*. A pleasure party, *esp.* a hunting or fishing trip of the nature of a picnic but of longer duration. *Southern US.* L18. **3** A person who is marooned. L19.

maroon /mə'ruːn/ *n.*[2] & *a.* L17. [Fr. *marron* f. It. *marrone* f. med.Gk *maraon*. Cf. MARRON *n.*[1]] **A** *n.* †**1** = MARRON *n.*[1] I. Only in L17. **2** A brownish-crimson or claret colour. L18. **3** A firework intended to imitate the noise of a cannon, used esp. as a warning. E19. **B** *adj.* Of the colour maroon. E19.

maroon /mə'ruːn/ *v.* L17. [f. MAROON *n.*[1]] †**1** *v.t.* As *marooned* ppl a. Lost in the wilds. Only in L17. **2** *v.t.* Put (a person) ashore and leave on a desolate island or coast (as was done by buccaneers and pirates) by way of punishment. Freq. as *marooned* ppl a. E18. **b** Cause (a person) to be unable to leave a place. Freq. as *marooned* ppl a. E20. **3** *v.i.* Camp out for several days on a pleasure party. *Southern US.* L18. **4** *v.i.* Idle, loiter. E19.

2b F. ASTAIRE We ran into a snow bank and were marooned for twenty-four hours.

marooner *n.* (*a*) a buccaneer, a pirate; (*b*) a person who maroons someone: M17.

†**maroquin** *a.* & *n.* E16. [Fr., f. alt. (prob. after Sp. *marroquín*) of *Maroc* (see MOROCCO) + *-in* -INE[1]. Cf. MAROCAIN.] **A** *adj.* = MOROCCO *a.* I, 2. E16–E19. **B** *n.* = MOROCCO *n.* L16–E19.

maror /mɑː'rɔː/ *n.* L19. [Heb. *mārōr*.] Bitter herbs eaten at the Passover Seder service as a reminder of the bitterness of the Israelites' captivity in Egypt.

marotte /marɔt/ *n.* Pl. pronounced same. E17. [Fr.] A fool's bauble.

marouflage /maruflaʒ/ *n.* Pl. pronounced same. L19. [Fr., f. *maroufler* attach (canvas) to a wall, f. *maroufle* (layer of) adhesive used for the purpose.] *Art.* **1** The act or process of pasting a painted canvas to a wall, traditionally using an adhesive made of white lead ground in oil. L19. **2** A piece of leather or other material used as a backing to show off decorative ironwork. M20.

Marplan /'mɑːplan/ *n.* M20. [Origin uncertain: perh. rel. to MARSILID.] *Pharm.* (Proprietary name for) the drug isocarboxazid.

marplot /'mɑːplɒt/ *n.* E18. [f. MAR *v.* + PLOT *n.*] A person who spoils a plot or hinders the success of any undertaking.

marque /mɑːk/ *n.*[1] LME. [Fr. f. Prov. *marca*, f. *marcar* seize as a pledge, perh. ult. f. Gmc base of MARK *n.*[1] Cf. MART *n.*[3]] *Hist.* Reprisals. Long only as below.

letter of marque (*a*) (in full *letter of marque and reprisal*) orig., a licence granted by a monarch authorizing a subject to take reprisals on the subjects of a hostile State; later, legal authority to fit out an armed vessel and use it in the capture of enemy merchant shipping and to commit acts which would otherwise have constituted piracy; usu. in *pl.*; (*b*) a ship carrying letters of marque; a privateer.

marque /mɑːk/ *n.*[2] E20. [Fr., back-form. f. *marquer* to mark or brand, alt. of OFr. *merchier*, f. *merc* limit, of Scand. origin (cf. OHG *marc(h)a* MARK *n.*[1]).] A make or brand of something, esp. a motor vehicle.

Autosport Lancia won the day in Madeira, when examples of their marque filled the first six places.

marquee /mɑː'kiː/ *n.* L17. [f. MARQUISE, taken as a pl. & assim. to -EE[1].] **1** A tent large enough to hold many people, used esp. for social or commercial functions. L17. **2** = MARQUISE 3b. *N. Amer.* M20.

marquench /'mɑːkwɛn(t)ʃ/ *v.t.* M20. [f. MAR(TENSITE + QUENCH *v.*] *Metall.* Temper (steel) by martempering, esp. with the constant-temperature stage too short to allow the austenite/martensite transformation to be isothermal. Chiefly as *marquenching* vbl n.

marquesa /mar'kesa, mɑː'keɪzə/ *n.* M19. [Sp., fem. of *marqués* MARQUIS.] A Spanish marchioness.

Marquesan /mɑː'keɪs(ə)n, -z-/ *n.* & *a.* L18. [f. *Marquesas* (see below) + -AN.] **A** *n.* A native or inhabitant of the Marquesas Islands in the S. Pacific; *spec.* a member of the aboriginal Polynesian people of these islands. Also, the Polynesian language of this people. L18. **B** *adj.* Of or pertaining to the Marquens or their language. M19.

marquess, **marquessate** *ns.* see MARQUIS etc.

marquetry /'mɑːkɪtri/ *n.* M16. [Fr. *marqueterie*, f. *marqueter* variegate, f. as MARQUE *n.*[2]: see -ERY.] Inlaid work in wood, ivory, etc., esp. as used for the decoration of furniture.

marquis /'mɑːkwɪs/ *n.* Also **marquess**, (esp. in titles) **M-**. ME. [OFr. *marchis* (later altered to *marquis* after Prov. *marques*, Sp. *marqués*) f. Proto-Romance base of MARCH *n.*[2]] **1** In some Continental countries: orig. (now *Hist.*), a ruler of certain territories (originally marches or frontier districts); later, a nobleman (or, in the 16th and 17th cents., a noblewoman) ranking below a duke and above a count. ME. **2** (Now usu. **marquess**.) A British or Irish hereditary nobleman of the second rank of the peerage, below a duke and above an earl. LME.

marquisate /'mɑːkwɪsət/ *n.* Also (now usual in sense 1) **-quess-**. E16. [f. prec. + -ATE[1], after Fr. *marquisat*, It. *marchesato*, etc.] **1** The rank or dignity of a marquess. Formerly also, a place from which a marquess takes his title. E16. **2** In some Continental European countries: the territorial lordship or possessions of a marquis or margrave. L16.

marquise /mɑː'kiːz, *foreign* markiz (*pl. same*)/ *n.* E17. [Fr., fem. of *marquis*: see MARQUIS.] **1** (The title of) a marchioness in Continental Europe or (formerly) Britain. E17. **2** A variety of pear. E18. **3a** = MARQUEE I. Now *rare* or *obs.* L18. **b** A permanent canopy projecting over the entrance to a hotel, theatre, etc. Cf. MARQUEE 2. L19. **4** A finger-ring set with a pointed oval gem or cluster of gems. Also more fully *marquise ring*. L19.

marquisette /mɑːkɪ'zɛt/ *n.* & *a.* E20. [Fr., dim. of *marquise*: see prec., -ETTE.] (Of) a plain gauze dress fabric orig. made from silk, later from cotton.

marquois scale /'mɑːkwɔɪz skeɪl/ *n. phr.* M19. [f. alt. of Fr. *marquoir* ruler used by tailors, f. *marquer* (see MARQUE *n.*[2]) + *-oir* -ORY[1], + SCALE *n.*[4]] An apparatus for drawing equidistant parallel lines.

¶*Marquois* sometimes erron. written *Marquoi's*, *Marquois's*, as if the possess. of a personal name.

marra *n.* & *a.* var. of MARROW *n.*[2] & *a.*

marram /'marəm/ *n.* M17. [ON *marálmr*, f. *marr* sea + *hálmr* HAULM.] **1** A coastal grass, *Ammophila arenaria*, with long dense spikes and far-creeping roots, often planted in order to bind sand. Also *marram-grass*. M17. **2** A sand-hill grown over with this grass. *local.* M19.

Marrano /mə'rɑːnəʊ/ *n.* Pl. **-os**. L16. [Sp., of unkn. origin.] *Hist.* In medieval Spain: a christianized Jew or Moor, *esp.* one who merely professed conversion in order to avoid persecution.

Marranism *n.* the practice of Marranos of professing Christianity to avoid persecution M18.

marrer /'mɑːrə/ *n.* LME. [f. MAR *v.* + -ER[1].] A person who mars something.

marri /'mari/ *n.* M19. [Aborig.] (The timber of) a western Australian red gum tree, *Eucalyptus calophylla*.

marriable /'marɪəb(ə)l/ *a.* Now *rare.* LME. [(O)Fr. *mariable*, f. *marier* MARRY *v.*: see -ABLE.] Able to be married; marriageable.

marriage /'marɪdʒ/ *n.* ME. [(O)Fr. *mariage*, f. *marier* MARRY *v.*: see -AGE.] **1** Legally recognized personal union entered into by a man and a woman usu. with the intention of living together and having sexual relations, and entailing property and inheritance rights; the condition of being a husband or wife; the relation between persons married to each other. ME. **2** The action or an act of getting married; the ceremony or procedure by which two persons are made husband and wife. ME. **b** This ceremony together with the accompanying festivities; a wedding. *arch.* LME. †**3** A dowry. ME–L16. **4** An intimate union. LME. **5** *Hist.* The right of a feudal superior (in England *spec.* the monarch) to exact a fine for the marriage of a vassal; the sum of money so acquired. LME. **6** A particular union between a husband and wife. LME. †**7** A person viewed as a prospective husband or wife; a (good or bad) match. LME–E17. **8** In bezique, pinochle, and similar card-games, the declaration of a king and queen of the same suit. In patience, two consecutive cards of the same suit. M19. **9** A married antique. M20.

1 D. ROWE Most of us enter into marriage with romantic ideas. **4** *Dance Theatre Journal* The marriage of art and industry is back in fashion. **6** S. KITZINGER The marriage started to crack under the impact of . . 'appalling rows'. *Woman & Home* She had a son and a daughter by her first marriage.

Phrases: *arranged marriage*: see ARRANGE *v.* 3. *civil marriage*: see CIVIL *a.* *common-law marriage*: see COMMON LAW. **communal marriage** the system in some cultures by which, in a small community, all the men are regarded as married to all the women, and vice versa. *fleet marriage*: see FLEET *n.*[2] **group marriage** = *communal marriage* above. **in marriage** (*a*) in the matrimonial state, in wedlock; (*b*) as husband or wife (freq. in *give* or *take in marriage*). *in (the) way of marriage*: see WAY *n. jactitation of marriage*: see JACTITATION I. *left-hand marriage*: see LEFT HAND *a. phr. marriage of convenience*: see CONVENIENCE *n.* MIXED *marriage. open marriage*: see OPEN *a.* **plural marriage** polygamy. *propose marriage*: see PROPOSE *v.* 4a. PUTATIVE *marriage. secondary marriage*: see SECONDARY *a.* SHOTGUN *marriage. steal a marriage*: see STEAL *v.*

Comb.: **Marriage Act** any of the Acts of Parliament regulating marriages; **marriage articles** an antenuptial agreement about rights of property and succession; **marriage-bed** (the rights and duties of) the sexual relationship of a husband and wife; **marriage broker** (*a*) *derog.* a matchmaker; (*b*) in a culture in which arranged marriages are the norm, a person who arranges marriages for a fee; **marriage bureau** an agency which arranges introductions for people wishing to marry; **marriage certificate** a copy of the record of a legal marriage which is given to the persons concerned, with details of names, date, etc.; **marriage counselling, guidance** the counselling of married people who are having problems in their relationship; **marriage licence** (*a*) a document giving official permission to marry; (*b*) a marriage certificate; **marriage lines** *colloq.* one's marriage certificate; **marriage market** the supply of and demand for eligible partners for marriage; **marriage payment** *Anthropol.* = *bride-price* s.v. BRIDE *n.*[1]; **marriage portion** a portion or dowry given to a bride at her marriage; **marriage-ring** a wedding ring; **marriage settlement** a legal arrangement securing certain property for an intended wife and sometimes also for any children of the marriage; **marriage-song** = EPITHALAMIUM.

marriageable /ˈmarɪdʒəb(ə)l/ *a.* M16. [f. prec. + -ABLE.] 1 Able to be married, *esp.* old or rich enough for marriage, eligible. M16. 2 Of a person's age or (formerly) qualities: befitting marriage or the married state. L16.

marriageaˈbility *n.* L19.

married /ˈmarɪd/ *a.* & *n.* LME. [f. MARRY *v.* + -ED[1].] A *adj.* 1 United to another person in marriage. LME. 2 Pertaining to or characteristic of married people or marriage. L16. 3 Of an antique: put together from parts of two or more different articles, sometimes of different dates. M20.

2 *married bliss, married life, married quarters*, etc.

Special collocations: **married print** *Cinemat.* a positive film carrying both pictures and a soundtrack.

B *n.* A married person; *collect. pl.*, *the* class of married people collectively. Freq. in *young marrieds*. L19.

¶ Earlier in UNMARRIED.

marrier /ˈmarɪə/ *n.* L16. [f. MARRY *v.* + -ER[1].] A person who marries someone or something.

Marrism /ˈmɑːrɪz(ə)m/ *n.* M20. [f. *Marr* (see below) + -ISM.] (Advocacy of) the linguistic theories advocated by the Russian linguist and archaeologist N. Y. Marr (1865–1934), in which language is regarded as a phenomenon of social class rather than of nationality.

Marrist *a.* M20.

marron /ˈmarɒn; *foreign* marɔ̃, ma-/ *n.*[1] L16. [Fr.: see MAROON *n.*[2] & *a.*] 1 A large and particularly sweet kind of chestnut. Now chiefly in *marron glacé* below. L16. †2 = MAROON *n.*[2] 3. Only in M18.

1 **marron glacé** /ˈglaseɪ, *foreign* glase/, pl. **-s -s** (pronounced same), a chestnut preserved in and coated with sugar or syrup, as a sweet.

marron /ˈmar(ə)n/ *n.*[2] M20. [Aborig.] A large freshwater crayfish, *Cherax tencrimanus*, of western Australia.

marrot /ˈmarət/ *n.* Chiefly *Sc.* E18. [Origin unkn. Cf. MURRE.] An auk; *esp.* the guillemot.

marrow /ˈmarəʊ/ *n.*[1] [OE *mærh, mærg* (WS) *mearh, mearg*, corresp. to OFris. *merg, merch*, OS *marg* (Du. *merg*), OHG *mar(a)g* (G *Mark*), ON *mergr*, f. Gmc.] 1 The soft vascular fatty substance in the cavities of bones (also *bone marrow*); this as the type of vitality and strength or (freq. w. biblical allusion) of rich and nutritious food. OE. †2 The pith of a plant; the pulp of a fruit. OE–L18. 3 The substance of the spinal cord. Now always *spinal marrow*. LME. 4 The vital or essential part, = GOODNESS 4; the in most or central part. Freq. w. *the*. LME. 5 In full *vegetable marrow*. The long cylindrical green, white, or striped fruit of a kind of gourd, *Cucurbita pepo*, eaten as a vegetable; the plant producing this, a trailing annual with deep yellow flowers. E19.

Phrases: **to the marrow** right through, to the centre of one's being.

Comb.: **marrow pudding**: made with beef or vegetable marrow; **marrow squash** *N. Amer.* a vegetable marrow; **marrow-stem (kale)** a coarse kind of kale grown esp. in Australia and New Zealand as fodder.

marrowed *a.* full of marrow ME. **marrowy** *a.* full of marrow; of the nature of marrow: LME.

marrow /ˈmarəʊ/ *n.*[2] & *a.* Now *dial.* Also **marra** /ˈmarə/. LME. [Prob. f. ON *margr* many, (fig.) friendly, communicative.] A *n.* 1 A companion, a fellow-worker, a partner. LME. 2 A thing which makes a pair with another, a counterpart. E16. 3 One's equal or like; a match. Formerly also, an opponent. M16. 4 A husband, a wife. L16. B *adj.* Similar, corresponding. L16.

marrow /ˈmarəʊ/ *v. Sc.* & *north.* L15. [f. MARROW *n.*[2]] 1†a *v.t.* Join, associate; pair. L15–E19. b *v.i.* Be a partner or fellow-worker (*with*). M16. 2 *v.t.* Be a companion to; marry. E16. 3 *v.t.* Resemble, be equal to; produce something equal to, match. M16.

marrowbone /ˈmarə(ʊ)bəʊn/ *n.* ME. [f. MARROW *n.*[1] + BONE *n.*] 1 A bone containing edible marrow. ME. 2 *sing.* & (usu.) in *pl.* The knees. *joc.* M16. 3 In *pl.* Fists as weapons; pugilists. *slang.* E17. 4 In *pl.* Crossbones. M19.

marrowfat /ˈmarə(ʊ)fat/ *n.* E18. [f. MARROW *n.*[1] + FAT *n.*[2]] 1 A substance like tallow prepared by boiling down marrow. *N. Amer.* E18. 2 In full *marrowfat pea*. A kind of large rich pea. M18.

marrowless /ˈmarə(ʊ)lɪs/ *a.*[1] E17. [f. MARROW *n.*[1] + -LESS.] Having no marrow.

marrowless /ˈmarə(ʊ)lɪs/ *a.*[2] Now *dial.* M17. [f. MARROW *n.*[2] + -LESS.] Companionless; unmarried; unequalled; lacking the other member of the pair.

marrowsky /məˈraʊski/ *n.* M19. [Origin unkn.] A variety of slang, or a slip in speaking, characterized by transposition of initial letters, syllables, or parts of two words; an instance of this, a spoonerism.

marrowskying *n.* the transposition of initial letters etc. M19.

Marrucinian /maruːˈsɪnɪən/ *a.* & *n.* L16. [f. L *Marrucini* Marrucinians + -AN.] *Hist.* A *adj.* Designating, of, or pertaining to an Oscan-Umbrian people living near Teate in ancient E. Italy. L16. B *n.* 1 A member of this people. M19. 2 The language of this people. M20.

Maˈrrucian *n.* (long *rare* or *obs.*) = MARRUCINIAN *n.* I L16. **Maˈrrucine** *n.* (long *rare* or *obs.*) = MARRUCINIAN *n.* I E17.

marry /ˈmari/ *v.* ME. [(O)Fr. *marier* f. L *maritare*, f. *maritus* married, (as n.) husband, prob. f. IE.] I *v.t.* 1 Join (two persons, one person *to* another) in marriage; constitute as husband and wife according to law or custom. ME. 2 Of a parent or guardian: give in marriage, cause to be married. ME. †3 *v.refl.* = sense 6 below. ME–E19. 4 Take as one's husband or wife. LME. b Obtain (something) by getting married. Freq. in *marry money*. M19. 5 *transf.* & *fig.* a Unite intimately, join closely or permanently; correlate. LME. b *Naut.* Splice (two ropes) together without increasing girth. Also, bring together (two ropes) so as to haul them together equally. E19. c In *pass.* Of the king or queen in certain card-games: be declared as held in the same hand with the queen or king of the same suit. M19. d *Stock Exch.* Set (one transaction) against another transaction. M20.

1 SHAKES. *A.Y.L.* You shall be the priest, and marry us. A. LIVINGSTONE She became engaged to him and the following June they were married. 2 R. PLAYER Her parents married her to . . a wealthy landowner. H. R. LANDON Ferdinand IV and his consort . . had just been to Vienna to marry off two of their daughters. 4 F. HUME He had added to his crime by marrying a pretty girl. 5a G. SAINTSBURY This hybrid and bizarre vocabulary is . . admirably married to the substance of the writing. *Annabel* Some men found it difficult to marry their objective views with their own situations.

II *v.i.* 6 Enter into marriage, get married; take a husband or wife. Also foll. by *on* (Sc.), *with* (now *US*). ME. b *transf.* & *fig.* Enter into intimate union; join, so as to form one; (of wine etc.) mature. E16. 7 Of a minister etc.: conduct a marriage ceremony. M16.

Phrases, & with advs. & preps. in specialized senses: **marry above, below,** or **beneath oneself** marry a person of higher, or lower, social position. *marry a fortune*: see FORTUNE *n.* **marry into** become a member of (a family) as a result of marrying one of its members. *marry (into) money*: see MONEY *n.* **marry off** (of a parent or guardian) find a husband or wife for (a child or ward). **marry out** marry a person of a different clan, group, religion, etc. *marry over the broomstick*: see *broomstick* s.v. BROOM. **marry up** (*a*) *colloq.* tie up or preoccupy in marriage; (*b*) join or link up *with*. **marry well** have or make a successful marriage in terms of harmony, material gain, or social standing. *marry with the left hand*: see LEFT HAND *n. phr.* I.

marry /ˈmari/ *int.* Now *arch.* & *dial.* L16. [Alt. of (the Virgin) MARY.] Expr. asseveration, surprise, indignation, etc., esp in response to a question. Cf. MARY I.

marry come up: expr. indignant or amused surprise or contempt.

Mars /mɑːz/ *n.* ME. [L *Mars, Mart-* (reduced form of *Mavors, Mavort-*) the Roman god of war (see below). Cf. MAVORS.] 1 The fourth planet in order of distance from the sun, whose orbit lies between those of the earth and Jupiter. ME. 2 The god of war of the ancient Romans, ranking in importance next to Jupiter and identified from an early period with the Greek Ares. Also *fig.* (*arch.*), warfare, warlike prowess, fortune in war. LME. b A great warrior. *arch.* M16. †3 *Alch.* The metal iron. LME–M18. 4 *Her.* The tincture gules in the fanciful blazon of arms of sovereign princes. *obs.* exc. *Hist.* L16.

Comb.: **marsquake** [after *earthquake*] a tremor or violent shaking of part of the surface of the planet Mars.

Marsala /mɑːˈsɑːlə/ *n.* E19. [See below.] In full *Marsala wine*. A white wine resembling a light sherry that is exported from Marsala, a town on the west coast of Sicily.

Marse *n.* see MAS *n.*[1]

Marseillais /mɑːseɪˈjeɪ, *foreign* marsejɛ/ *a.* & *n.* L17. [Fr., f. *Marseille* (see MARSEILLES) + *-ais* -ESE.] A *adj.* Belonging or pertaining to Marseilles, a port in SE France. L17. B *n.* Pl. same. A native or inhabitant of Marseilles. M19.

Marseillaise /mɑːseɪˈjeɪz, -s(ə)ˈleɪz, *foreign* marsejɛːz/ *n.* L18. [Fr., f. fem. adj. of prec.] The national anthem of France, composed in 1792 on the declaration of war against Austria and first sung in Paris by Marseilles patriots. Also more fully *Marseillaise hymn*.

Marseilles /mɑːˈseɪlz/ *n.* M18. [Anglicized f. *Marseille*, a port in SE France.] 1 In full *Marseilles quilting*. A stiff cotton fabric, similar to piqué. M18. 2 In full *Marseilles ware*. A type of pottery produced in Marseilles during the 17th and 18th cents. L19.

marsh /mɑːʃ/ *n.*[1] [OE *mersć, merisć* = MLG *mersch, marsch*, MDu. *mersch(e*, f. WGmc base also of L *mariscus*. Cf. MARISH *n.* & *a.*[1]] 1 (A tract of) low-lying land that is flooded in wet weather and usually more or less watery at all times. OE. 2 A meadow; a stretch of grassland near a river or the sea. *local.* L18.

1 J. BUCHAN Out of the marshes a fog crept. P. DICKINSON The awkward sploshing of his paddle . . had been the loudest sounds in the marsh.

Comb.: **Marsh Arab**: from the marsh area of southern Iraq; *marsh arrow-grass*: see *arrow-grass* s.v. ARROW *n.*; **marshbird** (*a*) either of two streaked warblers of the genus *Megalurus* (family Sylviidae) found in Australia, New Guinea, and Indonesia, *M. timoriensis* and *M. gramineus*; (*b*) either of two small birds of the genus *Pseudoleistes* (family Icteridae), having yellow and brown plumage and found in S. American swamps and marshes; **marsh blackbird** the American red-winged blackbird, *Agelaius phoeniceus*; **marshbuck** = SITATUNGA; **marsh elder** (*a*) (now *dial.*) the guelder rose, *Viburnum opulus*; (*b*) any of various plants of the genus *Iva*, of the composite family, native to salt-marshes in N. America; **marsh fern** a delicate fern of fens, *Thelypteris palustris*; **marsh fever** malaria; **marsh fritillary** a tawny nymphalid butterfly, *Eurodryas aurinia*; **marsh frog** a large frog,

Rana ridibunda, with a loud chuckling call, native to SW and eastern Europe; **marsh gas** gas consisting chiefly of methane, emanating from stagnant water; methane; **marsh grass** any of various grasses growing in marshy ground or salt-marshes; *spec.* (*US*) a cord-grass, *Spartina patens*; **marsh harrier** a large harrier, *Circus aeruginosus*, of Old World wetlands; **marsh hawk** *US* = *hen-harrier* s.v. HEN *n.*; **marsh hay**: made from marsh grasses; **marshman** a person who lives in marshy country; **marsh marigold** a plant of wet places, *Caltha palustris*, of the buttercup family, bearing yellow flowers; **marsh orchid** any of a group of European orchids of the genus *Dactylorhiza* (esp. *D. praetermissa* and *D. incarnata*) which have unspotted leaves and purple or pink flowers and occur in damp and marshy ground; *marsh pennywort*: see *pennywort* (b) s.v. PENNY; **marsh pink** = SABBATIA; **marsh quail** *US* a meadow lark; **marsh samphire** = *glasswort* (a) s.v. GLASS *n.* & *a.*; **marsh spot** a deficiency disease of garden peas, caused by a lack of manganese; **marsh tacky** *US* a small pony bred in marshy districts; **marsh tern** the gull-billed tern, *Gelochelidon nilotica*, found near water in temperate and subtropical parts of the western Palaearctic; **marsh tit(mouse)** a tit, *Parus palustris*, of deciduous woods and hedges in Europe and the Far East; **marsh treader** *US* a water bug of the family Hydrometridae; **marsh trefoil** = BUCKBEAN; **marsh violet** = *bog violet* s.v. BOG *n.*[1]; **marsh warbler** a Eurasian warbler, *Acrocephalus palustris*, with plain brown plumage and a song involving much mimicry of other birds; **marsh worm** a kind of worm used as a bait in angling; **marshwort** any of several creeping aquatic umbelliferous plants of the genus *Apium*; *esp.* fool's watercress, *A. nodiflorum*; **marsh wren** a N. American wren, *Cistothorus palustris*, which frequents marshes and swamps.

Marsh /mɑːʃ/ *n.*[2] M19. [James *Marsh* (1794–1846), Brit. chemist.] Used in *possess.* and *attrib.* to designate a test for the presence of arsenic in which nascent hydrogen is used to reduce any arsenic present to the gas arsine, which is then converted into a dark stain of metallic arsenic by heat.

marshal /ˈmɑːʃ(ə)l/ *n.*[1] ME. [OFr. *mareschal* (mod. MARÉCHAL) f. Frank. L *mariscalcus* f. Gmc (whence also OHG *marahscalh*, G †*Marschalk*, *Marschall*), f. two wds meaning 'horse' (repr. by MARE *n.*[1]) and 'servant' (repr. by OE *sċealc*).] †**1** A person who tends horses; a smith; *esp.* a person who treats diseases of horses, a farrier. ME–E18. **2** One of the chief functionaries of a royal household or court (in the middle ages usually entrusted with the military affairs of the monarch); a high officer of State. Formerly *spec.* (now *Hist.*) = *Earl Marshal* s.v. EARL. ME. **3a** Orig., any senior army officer; a commander, a general. Later (esp. in *marshal of the field* or *camp*), a (senior) officer of a definite rank, which varied according to period and country. Now *obs.* exc. in *Field Marshal* s.v. FIELD *n.* & *a.* ME. **b** An officer of the highest rank in any of various armies. ME. **4** An officer of a court of law responsible for the custody of prisoners and for the keeping of order, and frequently entrusted with the keeping of a prison. Also *Marshal of the Exchequer, of the King's* or *Queen's Bench*. *obs.* exc. *Hist.* ME. **b** An official (now usually a barrister) who accompanies a judge on circuit to act as secretary and personal assistant. Also *judge's marshal*. M19. **5** A person responsible for arranging ceremonies or controlling people at a race, banquet, etc. ME. **b** In full *City marshal*. An officer of the corporation of the City of London. M17. **6a** Orig., an official with certain police duties, or in charge of the infliction of punishment. Now (*US*), a police officer or sheriff with responsibility for a designated area; the administrative head of a police or fire department. L16. **b** A legal officer in each judicial district responsible for executing court precepts. *US.* L18. **7** The chief of the proctors' attendants at Oxford University; either of two officials appointed by the Vice-Chancellor of Cambridge University to act as his messengers, to summon meetings, etc. E19.

5 *Bike Events* Marshals along the route . . to guide the way and help you to get there.

Phrases: *Air (Chief) Marshal*: see AIR *n.*[1] *City marshal*: see sense 5b above. *Earl Marshal*: see EARL *n. judge's marshal*: see sense 4b above. **knight marshal** †(*a*) a military officer acting as a quartermaster; (*b*) *Hist.* an officer in the royal household with judicial functions (see MARSHALSEA). **Marshal of the Admiralty (Court)** an officer of the Court of Admiralty concerned with executing warrants issued by the court etc. *Marshal of the Exchequer, the King's* or *Queen's Bench*: see sense 4 above. **Marshal of the Royal Air Force** the highest rank in the Royal Air Force, equivalent to Field Marshal and Admiral of the Fleet.

Comb.: **marshal-man** any of a number of men (formerly under the orders of the knight marshal) belonging to the royal household, and going before the British monarch in processions to clear the way; a similar officer under the orders of the marshal of the City of London.

marshaˈless *n.* the wife of a marshal L18. **marshalship** *n.* = MARSHALCY 1 M16.

†**marshal** *n.*[2] see MARECHAL.

marshal /ˈmɑːʃ(ə)l/ *v.* Infl. **-ll-**, ***-l-**. LME. [f. MARSHAL *n.*[1]] †**1** *v.t.* Tend (a horse) as a farrier. Also, fake up (a horse) for sale. LME–E16. **2** *v.t.* Arrange, place, or rank in order at a banquet, table, etc. LME. †**b** Arrange (a banquet). Also foll. by *up*. L16–E17. **3** *v.t.* Arrange or draw up (armed forces) in order for fighting, exercise, or review; arrange in a body or procession; arrange (competitors) for a race etc. LME. **b** *v.refl.* & *i.* Take up positions in a due arrangement. L17. **4** *v.t.* Dispose, arrange, or set (things, material or immaterial) in methodical order. LME. **b** *Finance.* Arrange (assets or securities) according to availability to meet various kinds of claims. L18. **5** *v.t.* Usher or guide (a person) on his or her way; conduct ceremoniously. L16. **6** *v.t. Her.* Combine (two or more coats of arms) in one escutcheon to form a single composition; associate (accessories) with a coat of arms to form a complete achievement. L16.

3 D. A. THOMAS Jan Evertsen and Cornelis Tromp marshalled the Dutch fleet into a controlled withdrawal. 4 *Law Times* Clients . . need to be represented by those who are adepts in marshalling facts and handling witnesses. **marshalling yard** an area of branching and interconnected railway lines where trains can be assembled from individual trucks etc. 5 R. CROMPTON Eglantine saw a hedge with a gate in it and marshalled her party through that.

marshaller *n.* E17.

Marshalate /ˈmɑːʃ(ə)leɪt/ *n.* L19. [f. MARSHAL *n.*[1] + -ATE[1].] **1** *Hist.* The period of the rule of Marshal MacMahon as President of the French Republic (1873–9). L19. **2** The position or rank of Marshal in the French army. M20. **3** (**m-**.) The position or rank of a marshal. *US.* M20.

marshalcy /ˈmɑːʃ(ə)lsi/ *n.* ME. [AN *mareschalcie*, OFr. *mareschaucie* f. Frank. L *mariscalcia* (AL *marescalcia*), f. *mariscalcus* MARSHAL *n.*[1] + *-ia* -Y[3]. Cf. MARSHALSEA, MARÉCHAUSSÉE.] **1** The position or rank of marshal. ME. †**2** A military force under the command of a marshal. Chiefly as tr. Fr. *maréchaussée*. LME–M18. †**3** Farriery. LME–E18.

Marshall /ˈmɑːʃ(ə)l/ *n.* M20. [See below.] Used *attrib.* to designate (aid provided under) a plan initiated in 1947 by George C. Marshall (1880–1959), US Secretary of State, to supply financial assistance to certain western European countries to further their recovery after the war of 1939–45.

Marshallese /mɑːʃəˈliːz/ *n.* & *a.* M20. [f. *Marshall* (see below) + -ESE.] **A** *n.* **1** The Micronesian language of the Marshall Islands, a group of islands in the NW Pacific administered by the US under trusteeship of the United Nations. M20. **2** (Pl. same.) A native or inhabitant of the Marshall Islands. L20. **B** *adj.* Of or pertaining to the Marshall Islands or Marshallese. M20.

Marshallian /mɑːˈʃalɪən/ *a.* M20. [f. *Marshall* (see below) + -IAN.] Of or pertaining to the English political economist Alfred Marshall (1842–1924) or his work, esp. his concepts of marginal utility and elasticity of demand.

marshalsea /ˈmɑːʃ(ə)lsiː/ *n.* LME. [f. as MARSHALCY, w. assim. to SEA *n.*] *Hist.* **1** A court formerly held before the steward and the knight marshal of the royal household of England (latterly before a barrister appointed by the knight marshal), orig. to hear cases between the monarch's servants, but afterwards with wider jurisdiction. LME. **2** (**M-**.) A former prison in Southwark, London, under the control of the knight marshal. LME.

marshland /ˈmɑːʃlənd/ *n.* OE. [f. MARSH *n.*[1] + LAND *n.*[1]] Land consisting of marshes; marshy country.

marshlander *n.* a person or animal that lives on marshland L18.

marshmallow /mɑːʃˈmaləʊ/ *n.* OE. [f. MARSH *n.*[1] + MALLOW.] **1** A shrubby herb, *Althaea officinalis*, of the mallow family, which grows in brackish ditches and has ovate leaves, pale pink flowers, and a mucilaginous root. OE. **2** A soft sweet confection made orig. from the root of this plant, but now from albumen, gelatin, sugar, etc.; a small cake of this. Also (*fig.*), something or someone that is soft at the centre; a sentimental person. L19.

Comb.: **marshmallow roast** a party at which marshmallows are roasted and served.

marshmallowy *a.* sentimental, cloying E20.

marshy /ˈmɑːʃi/ *a.* LME. [f. MARSH *n.*[1] + -Y[1].] **1** Pertaining to or of the nature of a marsh; consisting of or containing marshes. LME. **2** Produced in or characteristic of marshland. L17.

marshiness *n.* E18.

Marsi /ˈmɑːsiː/ *n.pl.* L16. [L.] *Hist.* A Sabine people who lived near the Fucine Lake in ancient central Italy.

Marsian /ˈmɑːsɪən/ *n.* & *a.* L16. [f. prec. + -IAN.] *Hist.* **A** *n.* **1** A member of the Marsi. L16. **2** The language of the Marsi. M19. **B** *adj.* Of or pertaining to the Marsi or their language. M17.

Also **Marsic** *a.* M18.

†**marsilian** *n.* L17–M19. [It. *marsigliana*, f. *Marsiglia* Marseilles.] A square-sterned Venetian ship.

Marsilid /ˈmɑːsɪlɪd/ *n.* M20. [Origin unkn.] (Proprietary name for) the drug iproniazid phosphate.

marsipobranch /ˈmɑːsɪpəbraŋk/ *n.* & *a.* L19. [mod.L *Marsipobranchii* (alternative name for the class Agnatha), f. Gk *marsipos* (see MARSUPIUM) + *bragkhia* gills.] *Zool.* = AGNATHAN.

Also **marsipoˈbranchiate** *n.* & *a.* L19.

marsouin /marswɛ̃/ *n.* Pl. pronounced same. M16. [Fr. f. OHG *meriswīn* cognate w. Eng. *mereswine* s.v. MERE *n.*[1]] Any of various cetaceans of the family Delphinidae, *esp.* a beluga or (formerly) a porpoise.

marsupial /mɑːˈsuːpɪəl/ *a.* & *n.* L17. [mod.L *marsupialis*, f. as MARSUPIUM: see -AL[1].] **A** *adj.* **1** Pertaining to or resembling a marsupium or pouch. L17. **2** Designating, of, or pertaining to a marsupial or the order Marsupialia. E19. **b** Of or pertaining to the pouch of a marsupial. E19.

2 *marsupial mole*: see MOLE *n.*[2] 1. **marsupial mouse** any of numerous mouselike carnivorous marsupials of Australia and New Guinea, members of the family Dasyuridae. **b marsupial bone** an epipubic bone.

B *n.* A mammal (e.g. a kangaroo or an opossum) of the order Marsupialia, characterized by young that are born imperfectly developed and are usu. carried after birth in a pouch on the mother's belly, over the mamillae. M19.

marsupialiˈzation *n.* (*Med.*) the action of marsupializing a cyst etc.; the surgical formation of a pouch: L19. **marsupialize** *v.t.* (*Med.*) surgically convert (a cyst etc.) into a pouch by making a permanent wide opening to the exterior L19. **marsupian, marsupiate** *adjs.* & *ns.* = MARSUPIAL M19.

marsupite /ˈmɑːsjʊpʌɪt/ *n.* E19. [mod.L *marsupites*, f. as next: see -ITE[1].] *Palaeont.* A fossil crinoid whose shell resembles a purse.

marsupium /mɑːˈsuːpɪəm/ *n.* Pl. **-ia** /-ɪə/. M17. [L (also *-pp-*) f. Gk *marsupion*, *-sipion* dim. of *marsipos* purse.] *Zool.* & *Med.* A structure resembling a bag or pouch; *spec.* (*a*) the pouch of a marsupial; (*b*) the pecten of a bird's eye.

mart /mɑːt/ *n.*[1] ME. [Du. †*mart* var. of *markt* MARKET *n.*] **1** A periodical gathering of people for the purpose of buying and selling, esp. (in early use) in the Low Countries; a market. ME. †**2** Buying and selling; trade. Also, a bargain. M16–M17. **3** An auction room; a tradesman's shop or stall; (now *poet.* & *rhet.*) any public place for buying and selling. L16. 4 A city, region, or locality where things are bought and sold; a centre of trade. E17.

1 M. BINCHY He went to Mass on a Sunday as regularly as . . to the marts to buy sheep. 3 D. H. LAWRENCE She puts me away like a saleswoman whose mart is Endangered by the pilferer.

mart /mɑːt/ *n.*[2] *Sc.* & *north.* ME. [Gael. & Ir.] **1** An ox or cow fattened for slaughter. ME. †**2** A carcass, a slaughtered animal. Only in LME.

†**mart** *n.*[3] L16–M18. [Alt., app. infl. by MART *n.*[1]] = MARQUE *n.*[1]

mart /mɑːt/ *n.*[4] Chiefly *dial.* E18. [Back-form. f. FOUMART.] A marten; *esp.* (also *sweet-mart*) the pine marten. Cf. FOUMART.

mart /mɑːt/ *v.* Long *rare.* M16. [f. MART *n.*[1]] †**1** *v.i.* Do business at a mart; bargain. M16–E17. **2** *v.t.* Make merchandise of, deal in. L16.

Martaban /ˈmɑːtəban/ *n.* Also **-bani** /-ˈbani/. L16. [See below.] (Designating) a kind of glazed pottery, used esp. for jars or pots, made at Martaban, a town in the district of Pegu in Myanmar (Burma)).

martagon /ˈmɑːtəg(ə)n/ *n.* L15. [Fr. f. Turk. *martağān* form of turban worn by Sultan Mehmed I.] More fully *martagon lily.* A Eurasian lily, *Lilium martagon*, bearing dull purplish-red nodding flowers with reflexed perianth segments (also called *Turk's-cap lily*). Also, any of several similar lilies.

martel /ˈmɑːt(ə)l/ *n.* & *v.* ME. [OFr. (mod. *marteau*) f. med.L *martellus* f. L *martulus* var. of *marculus* small hammer: see -EL[2].] **A** *n. Hist.* A hammer, *esp.* one used in war. ME. †**B** *v.i.* Rain blows *on. rare* (Spenser). Only in L16.

martelé /ˈmɑːt(ə)leɪ/ *a.*, *adv.*, & *n.* L19. [Fr., pa. pple of *marteler* to hammer.] *Mus.* = MARTELLATO.

¶Used only w. ref. to bowed stringed instruments (unlike *martellato*).

martellato /mɑːtɪˈlɑːtəʊ/ *a.*, *adv.*, & *n.* L19. [It., pa. pple of *martellare* to hammer.] *Mus.* **A** *adj.* & *adv.* (Played) with notes heavily accented and left before their full time has expired. L19. **B** *n.* Martellato playing. E20.

Martello /mɑːˈtɛləʊ/ *n.* Pl. **-os**. E19. [Alt. (by assoc. w. It. *martello* hammer) of Cape *Mortella* in Corsica, where such a tower proved difficult for the English to capture in 1794.] In full *Martello tower.* A small circular fort with very thick walls, *esp.* any of those erected in Britain as a coastal defence during the Napoleonic Wars.

martemper /ˈmɑːtɛmpə/ *v.t.* M20. [f. MAR(TENSITE + TEMPER *v.*[1]] *Metall.* Temper (steel) by quenching rapidly to a temperature just above that at which martensite begins to form, allowing the temperature to stabilize, and then cooling slowly, esp. so that the austenite/martensite transformation is isothermal. Chiefly as *martempering* vbl n.

marten /ˈmɑːtɪn/ *n.* ME. [MDu. *martren* f. OFr. *martrine* use as n. (sc. *peau* skin) of *martrin*, f. *martre* f. WGmc (whence also OHG *mardar*, G *Marder*), extended form of Gmc base of OE *mearþ*, ON *mǫrðr*. Cf. MARTER.] **1** The fur or dressed skin of a marten. Formerly freq. in *pl.* ME. **2** Any of several bushy-tailed arboreal mustelid mammals of the genus *Martes*, found in forests of Eurasia and N. America. Also †*marten cat.* LME.

2 *pine marten*: see PINE *n.*[2] *stone marten*: see STONE *n.*, *a.*, & *adv.*

Martenot /ˈmɑːt(ə)nəʊ/ *n.* Pl. same, **-s**. M20. [f. *Martinot*: see ONDES MARTENOT.] = ONDES MARTENOT.

martensite /ˈmɑːtɪnzʌɪt/ *n.* L19. [f. A. *Martens* (1850–1914), Ger. metallurgist + -ITE[1].] *Metall.* A hard, very brittle solid solution of carbon in iron, formed from austenite when steel is quenched very rapidly.

martensitic /mɑːtɪnˈzɪtɪk/ *a.* pertaining to or containing martensite; involving the formation of martensite (from austenite): E20. **marten'sitically** *adv.* L20.

†**marter** *n.* ME–L16. [Fr. *martre*: see MARTEN.] (The fur or dressed skin of) a marten.

Martha /ˈmɑːθə/ *n.* L19. [Female forename, w. allus. to *Luke* 10:38–42.] An active or busy woman, much concerned with domestic affairs; in Christian allegory, used as a symbol of the active life. Opp. MARY 4.

Martha Gunn /mɑːθə ˈgʌn/ *n.* E20. [*Martha Gunn* (1727–1815), a female bathing-attendant celebrated for having dipped the Prince of Wales in the sea at Brighton.] A jug in the form of a woman, analogous to a toby jug. Also *Martha Gunn jug.*

martial /ˈmɑːʃ(ə)l/ *a.* LME. [(O)Fr., or L *martialis*, f. *Mart-*, MARS: see -AL[1], -IAL.] **1** a Of or pertaining to war or battle; (of music) appropriate to warfare. LME. **b** Of sports, exercises, etc.: serving as training for warfare. LME. **2** Warlike; brave, valiant; fond of fighting. LME. **3** Of or pertaining to the army or the military profession; military rather than civil. *obs.* exc. in COURT MARTIAL. L15. **4** Characteristic of or suitable for a warrior. L16. †**5** Of, pertaining to, or characteristic of the Roman god Mars. *rare* (Shakes.). Only in E17. **6** (Usu. **M-**.) Of or pertaining to the planet Mars, Martian; *Astrol.* influenced by Mars; (of an animal or plant) poisonous, stinging. Now *rare* or *obs.* E17. †**7** *Chem.* Of or pertaining to iron; containing iron. L17–L19.

Special collocations: **martial art** any of various sports or skills, mainly of Japanese origin, which originated as forms of self-defence or attack, such as judo, karate, and kendo (usu. in *pl.*). **martial eagle** a large crested eagle, *Polemaetus bellicosus*, of central and southern Africa. **martial law** (*a*) government of a country or district by military authority, with ordinary civil laws suspended; †(*b*) military law.

martialism *n.* warlike quality E17. **martialist** *n.* (*a*) a person skilled in war; a military man; †(*b*) *Astrol.* a person born under the influence of Mars: M16. **marti'ality** *n.* martial quality or state M17. **martialize** *v.t.* (*rare*) make martial E17. **martially** *adv.* L16. **martialness** *n.* E18.

Martian /ˈmɑːʃ(ə)n/ *a.* & *n.* LME. [OFr. *martien* or L *Martianus*, f. *Marti-*, MARS: see -IAN.] **A** *adj.* †**1** Of or pertaining to war or battle. LME–L16. **2** Of or pertaining to the month of March. E17. **3** Of or pertaining to the planet Mars or its (imagined) inhabitants. L19. **B** *n.* An (imagined) inhabitant of Mars. L19.

martin /ˈmɑːtɪn/ *n.*[1] LME. [Male forename, prob. a use of the name of St *Martin* of Tours: see MARTINMAS. Cf. next.] **1** Any of various typically short-tailed birds belonging to the swallow family Hirundinidae or (*dial.*) otherwise resembling the swallow. LME. †**2** A dupe. L16–E17.

1 *bank martin*, *bee-martin*, *fairy martin*, *house martin*, *sand martin*, etc.

Comb.: **martin-box** *US* a box or coop for martins to build in; **martin bug** a bloodsucking bug, *Oeciacus hirundinis*, whose principal host is the house martin; **martin-house** *US* = *martin-box* above.

Martin /ˈmɑːtɪn/ *n.*[2] M17. [f. St *Martin*: see MARTINMAS. Cf. prec.] Orig. more fully †*dry Martin*, †*Martin dry*. A variety of pear, so called from being ripe at Martinmas.

†**martinet** *n.*[1] LME. [Fr., dim. of male forename *Martin*: see -ET[1]. Cf. MARTLET *n.*[1]] **1** A martin; a swift. LME–M19. **2** A student at the medieval University of Paris who did not belong to a college. M–L19.

martinet /ˈmɑːtɪnɪt/ *n.*[2] L15. [(O)Fr. in various unconnected senses, perh. belonging to etymologically distinct wds.] †**1** A water-mill for an iron forge. Only in L15. †**2** A small cart. Only in L15. **3** A military engine for throwing large stones. *obs.* exc. *Hist.* E16. **4** *Naut.* A leech-line of a square sail. L16.

martinet /mɑːtɪˈnɛt/ *n.*[3] L17. [*Martinet* (see below).] †**1** The system of drill invented by J. Martinet, 17th-cent. French drill-master. Only in L17. **2** A military or naval officer who is a stickler for strictness of discipline; a rigid disciplinarian. M18.

martinetism *n.* the spirit or action characteristic of a martinet E19.

martineta /mɑːtɪˈneɪtə/ *n.* L19. [Amer. Sp. prob. f. Sp. *martinete* night heron.] A tinamou, *Eudromia elegans*, of S. Argentina.

martinettish /mɑːtɪˈnɛtɪʃ/ *a.* Also **-etish**. M19. [f. MARTINET *n.*[3] + -ISH[1].] Having the characteristics of a martinet.

martingale /ˈmɑːtɪŋgeɪl/ *n.* & *v.* L16. [Fr., in *chausse à la martingale* kind of hose fastening at the back, perh. f. mod.Prov. *marte(n)galo* fem. of *marte(n)gal* inhabitant of Martigues in Provence.] **A** *n.* **1** A strap or arrangement of straps fastened at one end to the noseband, bit, or reins of a horse and at the other to its girth, to prevent it from rearing or throwing back its head and to strengthen the action of the bit. L16. **2** *Naut.* A stay which holds down the jib-boom of a square-rigged ship, running from the boom to the dolphin-striker (also *martingale-stay*); a dolphin-striker. Also, in a dinghy, a rope running from the boom to the foot of the mast, to prevent the boom from rising when it swings outwards. L18. **3** A gambling system in which a player who is losing repeatedly doubles the stake in the hope of eventual recoupment. E19.

1 *Irish martingale*, *running martingale*, *standing martingale*, etc.

B *v.* **1** *v.i.* Gamble according to a martingale. E19. **2** *v.t. Naut.* Secure with a martingale or guy. L19.

martingana /mɑːtɪŋˈgɑːnə/ *n.* E19. [Sicilian It.] A kind of boat used in Sicily.

Martini /mɑːˈtiːni/ *n.*[1] L19. [See below.] In full *Martini rifle* (also *Martini-Henry* (*rifle*) [see HENRY *n.*[1]]). A rifle used in the British army from 1871 to 1891, combining a breech-mechanism invented by Friedrich von Martini with a .45-calibre barrel devised by Benjamin Tyler Henry.

Martini /mɑːˈtiːni/ *n.*[2] Also **m-**. L19. [*Martini* & Rossi, It. firm selling vermouth; as cocktail perh. of different origin.] (Proprietary name for) a type of vermouth. Also, a cocktail consisting of gin and dry vermouth, sometimes with the addition of orange bitters.

dry martini *spec.* a martini containing more gin than vermouth.

Martiniquan /mɑːtɪˈniːk(ə)n/ *n.* & *a.* Also **-ican**. L19. [f. *Martinique* (see below) + -AN.] **A** *n.* A native or inhabitant of Martinique, an island in the W. Indies. L19. **B** *adj.* Of or pertaining to Martinique or the Martiniquans. L19.

Martiniquais /mɑːtɪˈniːkeɪ/ *n.* & *a.* (*a*) *n.* (pl. same) = MARTINIQUAN *n.*; (*b*) *adj.* = MARTINIQUAN *a.*: L19.

Martinist /ˈmɑːtɪnɪst/ *n.* L16. [f. *Martin* (see below) + -IST.] **1** *Hist.* A supporter of 'Martin Marprelate', the writer or writers of certain controversial tracts published in 1588–9. L16. **2** A member of a school of mystics founded by L. C. de Saint-Martin (1743–1803). L19.

Martinism *n.* (*a*) *Hist.* the tenets of 'Martin Marprelate'; (*b*) the system of L. C. de Saint-Martin: L16.

Martinmas /ˈmɑːtɪnməs/ *n.* ME. [f. St *Martin* (see sense 1) + MASS *n.*[1]] **1** (The date, 11 November, of) the feast of St Martin, 4th-cent. Bishop of Tours and patron saint of France, formerly the usual time in England for hiring servants and slaughtering cattle to be salted for the winter. ME. †**2** A person one despises. *rare* (Shakes.). Only in L16.

Comb.: †**Martinmas beef, flesh, meat** the meat of an ox salted at Martinmas.

Martinware /ˈmɑːtɪnwɛː/ *n.* L19. [f. *Martin* (see below) + WARE *n.*[2]] A type of brown, salt-glazed, freq. elaborately modelled pottery made by the Martin brothers in Southall, now part of London, in the late 19th and early 20th cents.

martlet /ˈmɑːtlɪt/ *n.*[1] LME. [Fr. *martelet* alt. of *martinet*: see MARTINET *n.*[1]] **1** A swift; a swallow, a house martin. *arch.* LME. **2** *Her.* A bird with tufts of feathers for legs and no feet, borne as a charge. LME.

†**martlet** *n.*[2] LME–E19. [Alt. of MARTRET.] (The fur or dressed skin of) a marten.

†**martly** *adv.* L16–E18. [f. MART *n.*[1] + -LY[2].] At the time of each mart or fair.

†martret *n.* Only in LME. [f. MARTER + -ET[1].] A polecat.

martynia /mɑːˈtɪnɪə/ *n.* M18. [mod.L (see below), f. John *Martyn* (1699–1768), Eng. botanist: see -IA[1].] A Mexican plant, *Martynia annua* (family Pedaliaceae), with viscid hairy stems, campanulate corollas, and long-beaked fruits which are sometimes pickled.

martyr /ˈmɑːtə/ *n.* & *v.* [OE *martir* = OFris., OS, OHG *martir*, f. eccl.L *martyr* f. Gk *martur*.] **A** *n.* **1** A person who voluntarily undergoes the death penalty for refusing to renounce the Christian faith or a Christian doctrine, for persevering in a Christian virtue, or for obeying a law of the Church. OE. **2** A person who undergoes death or great suffering on behalf of any religious or other cause, or as a consequence of devotion to some object. (Foll. by *to*.) OE. **3** A person who suffers tortures comparable to those described in the legends of martyrs; a constant sufferer. (Foll. by *to* an ailment, etc.) M16. **4** A person who dies a victim *to* something. L18.

Phrases: **make a martyr of** (now freq. *joc.*) subject to hardship or inconvenience. **make a martyr of oneself** make a real or pretended sacrifice of one's inclinations in order to be more highly thought of.

B *v.t.* **1** Put to death as a martyr; make a martyr of. OE. **†2** Kill, esp. by a cruel death. ME–L18. **3** Inflict severe suffering or pain on; torment. ME. **4a** Spoil; bespatter; bungle, mismanage. Long *obs.* exc. *Sc.* & *dial.* LME. **†b** Inflict wounds or disfiguring blows on; mutilate; disfigure. M16–M17.

martyred *a.* that has been martyred, made to suffer martyrdom; expressive of martyrdom: L16. **martyrial** /mɑːˈtɪrɪəl/ *a.* (*rare*) befitting a martyr L17. **martyrish** *a.* having the air of a martyr L19.

martyrdom /ˈmɑːtədəm/ *n.* OE. [f. MARTYR + -DOM.] **1** The sufferings and death of a martyr; the act of becoming or the condition of being a martyr. OE. **†2** Slaughter. Esp. in *make martyrdom*. ME–L15. **3** Severe pain or suffering; torment. ME.

1 J. A. FROUDE Encouraging catholics to persevere to martyrdom for their faith. B. GELDOF 'That's what I'm giving up,' I said with an expression of insufferable martyrdom.

martyrion /mɑːˈtɪrɪən/ *n.* Also in L form **-ium** /-ɪəm/. Pl. of both **-ia** /-ɪə/. E18. [Gk.] A shrine, oratory, or church built in memory of a martyr; a building marking the place of a martyrdom or the site of a martyr's relics.

martyrize /ˈmɑːtərʌɪz/ *v.* Also **-ise**. LME. [Late L *martyrizare*, f. eccl.L *martyr*: see MARTYR, -IZE.] **1** *v.t.* = MARTYR *v.* 1. Now *rare*. LME. **2** *v.i.* Be or become a martyr. *rare*. LME. **3** *v.t.* = MARTYR *v.* 3. M17. **†4** *v.t.* = MARTYR *v.* 4b. M17–E18. **5** *v.t.* Cause to suffer hardship on behalf of a cause. M19.

3 E. BOWEN He looked at me and said: 'Go!' . . I saw that my presence martyrised him. 5 A. MORRISON She proceeded to martyrize herself by a show of 'setting to rights' in the room.

martyriˈzation *n.* the action of making a martyr of someone LME.

martyrly /ˈmɑːtəli/ *a. rare*. M17. [f. MARTYR + -LY[1].] Resembling or characteristic of a martyr.

martyrly /ˈmɑːtəli/ *adv. rare*. E19. [f. MARTYR + -LY[2].] In a manner befitting a martyr.

martyrolatry /mɑːtəˈrɒlətri/ *n.* L19. [f. MARTYR + -O- + -LATRY.] Excessive reverence for martyrs.

martyrology /mɑːtəˈrɒlədʒi/ *n.* L16. [In sense 1 f. med.L *martyrologium* f. eccl.Gk *marturologion*, f. *martur* (see MARTYR) + *logos* discourse: see -LOGY. In sense 2 f. MARTYR + -OLOGY.] **1** A list or account of martyrs; *spec.* a book listing Christian martyrs and other saints in the order of their commemoration, with a description of their lives and sufferings. L16. **2** The branch of history or literature that deals with the lives of martyrs; histories of martyrs collectively. E19.

†martyrologe *n.* [Fr.] = MARTYROLOGY E16–E18. **martyroˈlogical** *a.* M17. **martyrologist** *n.* L17.

martyry /ˈmɑːtəri/ *n.* ME. [med.L *martyrium* f. Gk *marturion* witness, martyrdom, f. *martur*: see MARTYR, -Y[4].] **†1** Martyrdom; suffering, torment. ME–L17. **2** = MARTYRION. E18.

marula /məˈruːlə/ *n.* Also **maroela**, **merula**, & other vars. M19. [Afk. f. Setswana, North Sesotho *morula*.] A central and southern African tree, *Sclerocarya birrea* subsp. *caffra* (family Anacardiaceae), bearing an oval yellow fruit used locally to make beer; the fruit of this tree.

marum /ˈmɛːrəm/ *n. arch.* M17. [L f. Gk *maron*.] Either of two aromatic labiate plants of the Iberian peninsula, *Thymus mastichina* (see MASTIC *n.* 3) and *Teucrium marum*, formerly used in medicine to induce sneezing.

marv /mɑːv/ *a. slang.* M20. [Abbrev.] Marvellous.

marvel /ˈmɑːv(ə)l/ *n.*[1] ME. [(O)Fr. *merveille* f. Proto-Romance use as sing. n. of L *mirabilia* neut. pl. of *mirabilis* wonderful, f. *mirari* wonder at. Cf. MARL *n.*[2]] **1** A wonderful or astonishing thing; a cause of surprise, admiration, or wonder. ME. **†2** A wonderful story or legend. ME–L15. **3** Wonder, astonishment, surprise, admiration. *arch.* ME. **†4** A miracle. ME–L16.

1 G. HARRIS The blind singer who spoke so vividly of the marvels of the north. R. INGALLS She's a marvel at discipline.

Phrases: **marvel of Peru** a tropical American plant, *Mirabilis jalapa* (family Nyctaginaceae), with funnel-shaped flowers of various colours which open at dusk; also called *false jalap, four o'clock flower, pretty-by-night*.

marvel /ˈmɑːv(ə)l/ *n.*[2] Chiefly *dial.* M18. [Alt.] A marble.

marvel /ˈmɑːv(ə)l/ *v.* Now *literary*. Infl. **-ll-**, ***-l-**. ME. [(O)Fr. *merveiller*, f. as MARVEL *n.*[1] Cf. MARL *v.*[3]] **1** *v.i.* & **†***t.* (*refl.* & in *pass.*) Be filled with wonder or astonishment; be struck with surprise. (Foll. by *at, that, to do*.) ME. **2** *v.i.* & **†***t.* (*refl.* & in *pass.*) Feel astonished curiosity; ask oneself wonderingly. Foll. by interrog. cl. LME. **†3** *v.t.* Wonder or be astonished at. Freq. in *pass.* with cl. attached. LME–E19. **†4** *v.t.* Cause to wonder; astonish. LME–M19.

1 G. HARRIS Kerish marvelled to find this ancient custom . . still kept. M. FORSTER Elizabeth . . marvelled at his self-control.

marveller *n.* a person given to marvelling E17. **marvellingly** *adv.* in a marvelling manner, with wonder or astonishment L19.

marvellous /ˈmɑːv(ə)ləs/ *a.*, *n.*, & *adv.* Also ***marvelous**. ME. [OFr. *merveillos* (mod. *merveilleux*), f. *merveille*: see MARVEL *n.*[1], -OUS.] **A** *adj.* **1** Such as to excite wonder or astonishment; wonderful, astonishing; excellent. ME. **2** Of poetry etc.: concerned with the supernatural. E18.

1 A. GERAS Yasha looks like a child opening a marvellous gift. E. O'NEILL The play was such a marvelous success!

Special collocations: **marvellous apple** = *balsam apple* s.v. BALSAM *n.*

B *adv.* Marvellously; excellently. *arch.* ME.

C *n. the marvellous*, that which is marvellous; *esp.* the prodigious or extravagantly improbable. *arch.* M18.

marvellously *adv.* ME. **marvellousness** *n.* M16.

marver /ˈmɑːvə/ *n.* & *v.* M19. [Fr. *marbre* MARBLE *n.*] **A** *n.* A polished slab of marble or iron on which glass-blowers roll and shape hot glass under the blowpipe. M19. **B** *v.t.* Roll (glass) on a marver. M19.

Marwari /mɑːˈwɑːri/ *n.* & *a.* E19. [Hind. *Mārvār*, f. Skt *maru* desert, wilderness.] **A** *n.* Pl. **-s**, same. **1** A native or inhabitant of Marwar, a region now part of the state of Rajasthan in NW India. E19. **2** The dialect of Rajasthani used in Marwar. L19. **B** *adj.* Of or pertaining to Marwar. M19.

Marxian /ˈmɑːksɪən/ *a.*[1] & *n.*[1] L19. [f. *Marx* (see MARXISM *n.*[1]) + -IAN.] **A** *adj.* Of or pertaining to the political and economic theories of Karl Marx; = MARXIST *a.*[1] L19. **B** *n.* = MARXIST *n.*[1] L19.

Marxianism *n.* adherence to Marxian doctrines or theories, = MARXISM *n.*[1] L19.

Marxian /ˈmɑːksɪən/ *a.*[2] & *n.*[2] M20. [f. *Marx* (see below) + -IAN.] **A** *adj.* Of, pertaining to, or characteristic of the Marx Brothers (Chico, Harpo, Groucho, and Zeppo), 20th-cent. US comedians. M20. **B** *n.* An admirer or student of the Marx Brothers or their films. M20.

Marxisant /marksizɑ̃/ *a.* Also **m-**. M20. [Fr., f. *Marxiste* MARXIST *n.*[1] & *a.*[1] + *-ant* -ANT[1].] Having Marxist leanings.

Marxise *v.* var. of MARXIZE.

Marxism /ˈmɑːksɪz(ə)m/ *n.*[1] L19. [f. *Marx* (see below) + -ISM, perh. through Fr. *Marxisme*, G *Marxismus*.] The political and economic theories of the German-born writer Karl Marx (1818–83), esp. that, as labour is basic to wealth, historical development must lead to the violent overthrow of the capitalist class and the taking over of the means of production by the proletariat, in accordance with scientific laws determined by dialectical materialism.

Comb.: **Marxism-Leninism** the doctrines of Marx as interpreted and put into effect by Lenin; Leninism; official Communist interpretation of the doctrines of Marx as implemented by Lenin, developed as a set of principles to guide policy and behaviour.

Marxism /ˈmɑːksɪz(ə)m/ *n.*[2] M20. [f. as MARXIAN *a.*[2] & *n.*[2] + -ISM.] The type of comedy performed by the Marx Brothers; a witticism typical of the Marx Brothers.

Marxist /ˈmɑːksɪst/ *n.*[1] & *a.*[1] L19. [f. as MARXISM *n.*[1] + -IST.] **A** *n.* A follower of Karl Marx's political and economic theories; a member of a political organization, with international affiliations, based on Marxism. L19.

B *adj.* Of or pertaining to Marxism or Marxists. L19.

Comb.: **Marxist-Leninism** = *Marxism-Leninism* s.v. MARXISM *n.*[1]; **Marxist-Leninist** *a.* of, pertaining to, or characteristic of Marxism-Leninism.

Marˈxistically *adv.* M20.

Marxist /ˈmɑːksɪst/ *n.*[2] & *a.*[2] M20. [f. as MARXIAN *a.*[2] & *n.*[2] + -IST.] = MARXIAN *a.*[2] & *n.*[2]

Marxite /ˈmɑːksʌɪt/ *a.* & *n.* Now *rare*. L19. [f. as MARXISM *n.*[1] + -ITE[1].] = MARXIST *n.*[1] & *a.*[1]

Marxize /ˈmɑːksʌɪz/ *v.* Also **-ise**. M20. [f. as prec. + -IZE.] **1** *v.t.* Form or adapt in accordance with the doctrines of Karl Marx; give a Marxist character to. M20. **2** *v.i.* Follow or advocate Marxism. M20.

Mary /ˈmɛːri/ *n.* Pl. **Marys**. ME. [Female forename f. eccl.L *Maria* (partly through (O)Fr. *Marie*) f. Gk *Maria*, *Mariam* f. Heb. *miryām* Miriam.] **1** The name of the mother of Jesus, also called the (Blessed) Virgin Mary, or Saint Mary, used in asseverations. Cf. MARRY *int.* ME. **2** In full *Mary Ann*. An effeminate or homosexual man. Also, a domesticated man. *slang*. L19. **3** A woman, *esp.* an Aboriginal woman. *Austral. slang*. L19. **4** [W. allus. to *Luke* 10:38–42.] A contemplative or intellectual woman; in Christian allegory, used as a symbol of the contemplative life. Opp. MARTHA. E20.

1 *Holy Mary!*, *by Saint Mary!*, etc.

Comb. & phrases: *Joseph and Mary*: see JOSEPH *n.* 1(b); *Little Mary*: see LITTLE *a.*; **Mary Ann** (*a*) *Taxi-drivers' slang* a taximeter; (*b*) *slang* marijuana; (*c*) see sense 2 above; **†Mary-bud** the bud of a marigold; **Mary Jane** *slang* marijuana; **Mary lily** the Madonna lily, *Lilium candidum*; **Mary Queen of Scots cap** a Mary Stuart cap; **Mary Warner** *slang* marijuana; *Queen Mary*: see QUEEN *n.*; *Typhoid Mary*: see TYPHOID *a.*; *Virgin Mary*: see VIRGIN *n.*

Maryland /ˈmɛːrɪland/ *n.* M19. [f. prec. (after Henrietta *Maria* (1609–69) Queen Consort of King Charles I) + LAND *n.*[1]] **1** Tobacco from Maryland. M19. **2** Used *attrib.* to designate things found in or associated with Maryland, a State of the eastern US. E20.

2 **Maryland chicken** (also **chicken (à la) Maryland**) a piece of chicken covered in breadcrumbs and fried, and served with sweetcorn and bacon. *Maryland yellowthroat*: see *yellowthroat* s.v. YELLOW *a.*

Marylander *n.* a native or inhabitant of Maryland M17.

Marymass /ˈmarɪmas/ *n.* Now *Sc. dial.* OE. [f. MARY + MASS *n.*[1]] *Chr. Ch.* **1** A festival of the Virgin Mary, esp. the Assumption, 15 August, or (formerly) Candlemas, 2 February OE. **†2** A mass in honour of the Virgin Mary. Chiefly in the asseveration *by the Marymass*. M16–M19.

Marys *n.* pl. of MARY.

Mary Stuart /mɛːrɪ ˈstjuːət/ *n.* & *a.* M19. [See below.] (Designating) a style of clothes, hair, etc., similar to those worn by Mary Stuart, Queen of Scots (1542–87), *spec.* headwear with a central dip or peak over the forehead.

marzacotto /mɑːtsəˈkɒtəʊ, mɑːz-/ *n.* Pl. **-os.** L19. [It.] A transparent glaze used by Italian majolica workers.

marzipan /ˈmɑːzɪpan, mɑːzɪˈpan/ *n.* & *a.* Also (*arch.*) **marchpane** /ˈmɑːtʃpeɪn/. L15. [G, earlier *marcipan* alt. (as if f. L *Marci panis* Mark's bread) of *marczapan* f. It. *marzapane.*] **A** *n.* A paste of ground almonds, sugar, etc., made up into small cakes or used as a coating on large cakes; a cake or shaped piece of this. L15. †**B** *adj.* Dainty, superfine. L16–M17.

Mas /mas/ *n.*[1] Also **Mas'**, (esp. repr. *Black English*) **Marse** /mɑːs/. L16. [Abbrev. of MASTER *n.*[1]] Master; mister.

Comb.: **Mas John** *joc.* & *derog. arch.* a Scottish Presbyterian minister, in contrast to an Anglican or Roman Catholic one.

mas /mɑs/ *n.*[2] Pl. same. E20. [Prov.] A farm, house, or cottage in the south of France.

mas /mɑːs/ *n.*[3] *W. Indies.* M20. [Abbrev. of MASQUERADE.] (A) carnival, (a) festival; a procession, a parade.

Mas' *n.* see MAS *n.*[1]

masa /ˈmasa/ *n.* E20. [Sp.] In Central and S. American cuisine, a type of dough made from cornmeal and used to make tortillas etc.

Masai /ˈmɑːsʌɪ, məˈsʌɪ, mɑːˈsʌɪ/ *n.* & *a.* Also **Maas-**. M19. [Masai.] **A** *n.* Pl. same. **1** A member of a pastoral people inhabiting parts of Kenya and Tanzania. M19. **2** The Nilotic language of this people. M19. **B** *attrib.* or as *adj.* Of or pertaining to the Masai or their language. M19.

masala /məˈsɑːlə/ *n.* L18. [Urdu *maṣālaḥ* f. Pers. & Urdu *maṣāliḥ* f. Arab. *maṣāliḥ*.] Any of various spice mixtures ground into a paste or powder for use in Indian cookery; a dish flavoured with this. Cf. GARAM MASALA.

masalchi *n.* var. of MUSSALCHEE.

Masarwa /məˈsɑːwə/ *n.* & *a. S. Afr.* L19. [Afr. name.] **A** *n.* Pl. same. A member of a Bushman people inhabiting the N. Kalahari desert. L19. **B** *adj.* Of or pertaining to this people. L19.

mascara /maˈskɑːrə/ *n.* & *v.* L19. [It. *mascara, maschera* MASK *n.*[2]] **A** *n.* A cosmetic for darkening and colouring the eyelashes. L19. **B** *v.t.* Put mascara on. M20.

mascaret /maskare/ *n.* Pl. pronounced same. M19. [Fr. f. Gascon dial. = spotted cow, f. *mascara* (cf. Prov. *mascarar*, OFr. *mascurer*, Fr. *mâchurer* daub, black the face), app. w. allus. to the bore's resemblance to the movement of running cattle.] In France, a tidal bore.

mascaron /maskarɔ̃ (*pl. same*), ˈmaskər(ə)n/ *n.* M17. [Fr. f. It. *mascherone*, f. *maschera* MASK *n.*[2]] In decorative art, a grotesque face or mask.

mascarpone /maskarˈpoːne/ *n.* M20. [It.] A soft mild Italian cream cheese.

mascle /ˈmɑːsk(ə)l/ *n.* ME. [AN f. AL *ma(s)cula* alt. of L *macula* MAIL *n.*[2] by assoc. w. MASK *n.*[1]] †**1** A spot, a speck. Only in ME. †**2** The mesh of a net. ME–L17. **3** *Her.* A charge in the form of a lozenge with a lozenge-shaped opening through which the field appears. LME. **4** *Hist.* Any of the perforated lozenge-shaped plates of metal fastened to the outer surface of 13th-cent. military tunics. E19.

mascled *a.* covered with mascles LME.

mascon /ˈmaskɒn/ *n.* M20. [f. *mass concentration.*] *Astron.* Any of the concentrations of denser material thought to exist under some lunar maria; a similar thing on another planet.

mascot /ˈmaskɒt/ *n.* L19. [Fr. *mascotte* f. mod.Prov. *mascotto* fem. of *mascot* dim. of *masco* witch: see -OT[1].] A thing, animal, or person supposed to bring luck.

mascotry *n.* attachment to or belief in mascots; the use of mascots: E20.

masculate /ˈmaskjʊleɪt/ *v.t. rare.* E17. [f. L *masculus* MALE *a.* + -ATE[3].] Make masculine.

masculine /ˈmaskjʊlɪn/ *a.* & *n.* ME. [(O)Fr. *masculin*, fem. *-ine* f. L *masculinus, -ina*, f. *masculus* MALE *a.*: see -INE[1].] **A** *adj.* **1** *Gram.* Designating the gender to which belong words classified as male on the basis of sex or some arbitrary distinction, such as form; (of a word) belonging to this gender; (of a suffix, inflection, etc.) used with or to form words of this gender. ME. **2** Of a person or animal: male. Now *rare.* LME. **3**†**a** Of an object to which sex was attributed: male. LME–E19. **b** Designating a variety of apricot. E17. **4** Of or pertaining to men; peculiar to or assigned to men; characteristic or regarded as characteristic of men; manly, virile; vigorous, powerful. L16. †**b** Of a material thing or physical quality: powerful in action, strong. M17–E18. **5** Of a woman or a woman's qualities or attributes: having capacities, manners, appearance, or tastes regarded as characteristic of or appropriate to men. E17.

4 W. COWPER Or if in masculine debate he shared. L. DUNCAN 'Hello, Sue?' a masculine voice said. . . 'This is David Ruggles.' S. WEINTRAUB Her interest in masculine good looks remained undiminished.

Special collocations: **masculine protest** in Adlerian psychology, the adoption of overtly masculine behaviour by a person of either sex in (unconscious) reaction to the stereotypical association of femininity and submissiveness. **masculine rhyme**: between lines ending in stressed syllables.

B *n.* **1** A man. Formerly also, man, men. Now *rare.* LME. **2** *Gram.* A masculine word, form, etc.; the masculine gender. M16.

masculinely *adv.* E17. **masculineness** *n.* M17.

masculinise *v.* var. of MASCULINIZE.

masculinism /ˈmaskjʊlɪnɪz(ə)m/ *n.* L19. [f. MASCULINE + -ISM.] **1** The qualities of a male; *spec.* in *Med.*, the development of masculine sexual characteristics in a female, masculinization. L19. **2** Advocacy of the rights of men. *rare.* E20.

masculinist /ˈmaskjʊlɪnɪst/ *n.* & *a.* E20. [f. as prec. + -IST.] **A** *n.* An advocate of the rights of men. E20. **B** *adj.* Of or pertaining to the advocacy of the rights of men; characterized by or designating attitudes, values, etc., held to be typical of men. M20.

masculinity /maskjʊˈlɪnɪti/ *n.* M18. [Fr. *masculinité*, f. as MASCULINE: see -ITY.] The state or fact of being masculine; the characteristic quality or qualities of men; manliness.

M. MOORCOCK The occasional intrusion of his masculinity into a world predominantly filled by women and children. E. SHOWALTER The public image of the Great War was one of strong unreflective masculinity.

masculinize /ˈmaskjʊlɪnʌɪz/ *v.t.* Also **-ise**. E20. [f. MASCULINE + -IZE.] **1** Make masculine or more masculine. E20. **2** Induce male physiological characteristics in. E20.

masculiniˈzation *n.* the action of masculinizing a person or thing; the process of becoming masculinized; the state of being masculinized: L19.

masculinoid /ˈmaskjʊlɪnɔɪd/ *a.* E20. [f. as prec. + -OID.] Masculine (but not male); of male form or appearance.

masculist /ˈmaskjʊlɪst/ *n.* & *a.* L20. [f. as prec. + -IST, after FEMINIST.] = MASCULINIST.

masculy /ˈmaskjʊli/ *a.* M16. [f. MASCLE + -Y[5].] *Her.* Covered with mascles.

mase /meɪz/ *v.i.* M20. [Back-form. f. next, as though this were an agent-n. in -ER[1].] = LASE; *esp.* lase in the microwave part of the spectrum.

maser /ˈmeɪzə/ *n.* M20. [Acronym, f. *m*icrowave *a*mplification by *s*timulated *e*mission of *r*adiation. Cf. LASER *n.*[2]] A laser; *spec.* one that emits microwaves. Also (*Astron.*), an interstellar gas cloud which emits microwaves naturally by stimulated emission.

mash /maʃ/ *n.*[1] Also †**mask.** [OE *māsc* = MLG *mēsch, māsch*, MHG *meisch* crushed grapes (G *Maisch*), f. WGmc, perh. ult. rel. to OE *miscian* mix. Cf. MUSH *n.*[1]] **I 1** *Brewing.* Malt mixed with hot water to form wort. OE. **2** A mixture of boiled grain, bran, etc., given as a warm food to animals. E16. **3** Anything reduced to a soft pulpy consistency, by beating or crushing, by mixing with or steeping in water, etc. L16. **b** *fig.* A confused mixture; a muddle. Cf. MISHMASH. L16. **c** The state of being mashed or reduced to a soft mass. M17. **4** Mashed potatoes, esp. as served with sausages. *colloq.* E20.

2 G. LORD She went to mix up some mash for the chooks. D. TUKE A supply of bran . . as it is essential in the time of sickness, when a horse needs mashes. 3 SMOLLETT One of his great toes was crushed into a mash. W. SOYINKA A pawpaw turned to red mash. b G. W. THORNBURY His will is an extraordinary mash of grammar. c DRYDEN Buy me a sieve-full [of damsons] to preserve whole, and not in mash. 4 M. DICKENS The chap had bought him tea and bangers and mash.

II [f. MASH *v.*[2] II] **5 a** The action of MASH *v.*[2]; an infatuation, a crush. *arch. slang.* L19. **b** A person who is the object of infatuation. *arch. slang.* L19.

Comb.: **mash note** *arch. slang* a love letter; **mash-roll, -staff** an instrument used to stir the malt in a mash tub; **mash-tub, -vat**: in which malt is mashed;

¶Not recorded bef. E16 exc. in *comb.*

mash /maʃ/ *n.*[2] *Sc.* & *north.* L17. [f. MASH *v.*[2] or Fr. *masse* MACE *n.*[1]] A heavy hammer for breaking stone.

†**mash** *n.*[3] & *v.*[1] var. of MESH *n.* & *v.*

mash /maʃ/ *v.*[2]*t.* Also (*Sc.* & *north.*) **mask** /mask/. ME. [f. MASH *n.*[1] In branch II back-form. f. MASHER.] **I 1 a** *Brewing.* Mix (malt) with hot water to form wort. ME. **b** Brew (beer etc.). Now only *fig.* in *be masking*, (of a storm etc.) be brewing. *obs.* exc. *dial.* M16. **c** Infuse (tea). *dial.* L18. **2** Beat into a soft mass; crush, pound, or smash to a pulp. Also foll. by *up.* ME. **b** *spec.* Reduce (food) to a homogeneous mass by crushing, beating, or stirring. E17. †**c** Make a hash of. M17–M18. †**3** Mix, mingle. LME–E18. **4** Feed with a mash. *rare.* M19.

1c B. HINES There's some tea mashed if you want a cup. 2 S. O'FAOLÁIN The sound of feet mashing the gravel outside. S. BRILL He mashed his cigar out on the man's desk. G. KEILLOR The front of the car was mashed in back to the engine block. b A. TYLER I mashed my peas with my spoon. M. ANGELOU The Irish accent was as palpable as mashed potatoes. *fig.*: SIR W. SCOTT I can clear the ground better now by mashing up my old work . . with new matter.

II 5 Excite sentimental admiration in (a person of the opposite sex); *be mashed on*, be infatuated with, have a crush on. *arch. slang.* L19.

mashed *n.* (*colloq.*) mashed potatoes; = MASH *n.*[1] 4: E20.

masha /ˈmaʃə/ *n.* M19. [Hind. *māśā* f. Skt *māsa.*] In the Indian subcontinent: a unit of weight equal to about 0.97 gram.

mashallah /maˈʃalə, mɑːʃɑːˈlɑː/ *int.* E19. [Arab. *mā šā'llāh.*] (This is) what God wills (as an expression of praise or resignation).

masher /ˈmaʃə/ *n.* L15. [f. MASH *v.*[2] + -ER[1].] †**1** A person who mashes or mixes wine. L15–E17. **2** A machine, vessel, or utensil for mashing malt, fruit, vegetables, etc. M19. **3** A dandy frequenting music halls etc.; a beau, a lady-killer. *arch. slang.* L19.

2 R. CROMPTON One held aloft a rusty potato masher of ancient design. 3 *Sunday Australian* Brighton's West Pier, once the trysting place for Edwardian mashers and their ladyloves. *Daily Telegraph* Imagine the office masher . . sidling up to the sweet innocent . . in the typing pool.

mashie /ˈmaʃi/ *n.* L19. [Origin uncertain: perh. f. Fr. *massue* club.] *Golf* (now chiefly *Hist.*). An iron-headed club used for lofting or for medium distances.

attrib.: A. BLOND We work in rooms not a mashie shot from Gray's Inn.

Comb.: **mashie-niblick** a club combining the features of mashie and niblick, now called a number 7 iron.

mashlum *n.* see MASLIN *n.*[2]

Mashona /məˈʃɒnə, -ˈʃəʊ-/ *n.* & *a.* M19. [Bantu. Cf. SHONA.] **A** *n.* Pl. **-s**, same. A member of the Shona people. M19. **B** *attrib.* or as *adj.* Of or pertaining to this people. L19.

masjid /ˈmʌsdʒɪd, ˈmas-/ *n.* M19. [Arab.: see MOSQUE.] A mosque.

mask /mɑːsk/ *n.*[1] Long *obs.* exc. *dial.* [OE *max*, perh. metath. alt. of MESH *n.*, or f. cognate ON *mǫskve*.] In early use, a net. Later, a mesh.

mask /mɑːsk/ *n.*[2] Also †**masque**. See also MASQUE *n.* E16. [Fr. *masque* f. It. *maschera*, perh. f. Arab. *maskara* buffoon, f. *sakira* ridicule.] †**I 1** See MASQUE *n.* E16.

II 2a A covering, usu. of velvet or silk, with holes for seeing, concealing the face or the upper part of it, worn for disguise at balls etc. M16. **b** A covering worn on the face for protection; *esp.* a screen of wire, gauze, etc., to protect the face from injury, e.g. in fencing; a face-covering worn by a surgeon, dentist, etc., to prevent infection. L16. **c** *Class. Antiq.* A hollow figure of a human head worn by actors, to identify the character represented and to amplify the voice. E18. **d** A likeness of a person's face in clay, wax, etc.; *esp.* one made by taking a mould from the face itself. L18. **e** A grotesque or comical representation of a face worn at carnivals, parties, etc., to frighten or amuse. M19. **3** *fig.* **a** A disguise, a pretence; a pretended appearance or expression. L16. **b** A thing which covers something or hides something from view. M18. **4** A masked person; a person in masquerading dress. *arch.* L16. **5a** *Archit.* A representation in stone of a face, often grotesque in nature, used in panels, keystones, etc. M18. **b** *Entomol.* The enlarged labium of a dragonfly larva, which can be extended to seize prey. L18. **c** The face or head of an animal; *esp.* that of a fox (displayed as a hunting trophy). E19. **d** *Fortif.* A screen to protect men engaged in constructing a work, to conceal a battery, etc. E19. **e** *Photogr.* A screen used to cover any part of an image which it is desired to exclude. L19. **f** A cosmetic preparation spread on the face, a face-pack. M20. **g** *Electronics.* In the manufacture of microcircuits, a thin surface layer that is removed in parts allowing selective modification of the underlying material. M20.

2a DEFOE I had no Mask but I ruffled my Hoods . . about my face. **in mask** disguised behind a mask. *iron mask*: see IRON *n.* & *a.* *loo mask*: see LOO *n.*[2] *vizard-mask*: see VIZARD 1, 2. b P. PARISH Doctors . . nurses and anyone who handles the drug frequently should wear masks and rubber gloves. *gas mask*: see GAS *n.*[1] d DEATH-*mask*. 3a GOLDSMITH A base, ungenerous wretch who under the mask of friendship has undone me. J. BUCHAN He hadn't a face, only a hundred masks that he could assume when he pleased. b KEATS The new soft-fallen mask Of snow upon the mountains.

Comb.: **mask jug** a jug with a lip or front shaped like a face.

†**mask** *n.*[3] var. of MASH *n.*[1]

mask /mɑːsk/ *v.*[1]*t.* Long *obs.* exc. *dial.* LME. [f. MASK *n.*[1]] Mesh, enmesh (*lit.* & *fig.*).

mask /mɑːsk/ *v.*[2] Also †**masque**. M16. [f. MASK *n.*[2]] **I** *v.i.* †**1** Take part in a masque or masquerade. M16–M18. †**2** Be or go in disguise; hide one's real nature under an outward show. L16–M17.

II *v.t.* **3** Cover or provide with a facial mask. Freq. in *pass.*, wear or be disguised with a mask. L16. **b** *gen.* Disguise. *rare.* M19. **4** Conceal from view by interposing something, cover. L16. **b** *Mil.* Conceal (a battery etc.) from the view of the enemy; hinder (a force etc.) from action by watching with sufficient strength; hinder (a friendly force) by standing in its line of fire. E18. **c** *Photogr.* etc. Cover, shade, or mount with a mask. L19. **d** Of a sound or other object of perception: diminish or prevent the perception of (another stimulus). E20. **e** *Chem.* Prevent (a compound etc.) from taking part in a certain reaction by causing it to undergo another preliminary reaction. M20. **5** *fig.* Disguise (feelings etc.) under an assumed outward show; conceal (intentionally or otherwise) the real nature, intent, or meaning of. L16.

3 SHAKES. *Lucr.* I have no one to blush with me . . To mask their brows and hide their infamy. b TENNYSON A rout of saucy boys Brake on us . . Mask'd like our maids. 4 A. WEST His eyebrows almost masked his eyes. A. CARTER No paint nor powder . . can mask that red mark on my forehead. **masking tape** adhesive tape used in painting to cover areas on which paint is not wanted. c R. K. NARAYAN Don't worry that you may also be in the picture—I'll mask you. d *Encycl. Brit.* The substantially greater intensity of one odour may mask another. 5 R. B. SHERIDAN He has been obliged to mask his pretensions. R. BUSH A world-renowned writer whose celebrity masked a ruined marriage and a barren pen. *Independent* The figures mask an erratic progress. R. CHRISTIANSEN Her depression set in . . masked from friends and acquaintances, but painfully communicated to Shelley.

masked *a.* (*a*) having, wearing, or provided with a mask; (*b*) concealed or disguised with a mask or by a masking process; (*c*) *Zool.* having facial markings or features suggesting a mask (*masked owl*, any of several Australasian and Indonesian barn owls of the genus *Tyto*); (*d*) *masked ball*, a ball at which masks are worn: L16.

mask *v.*[3] see MASH *v.*[2]

maskelynite /ˈmask(ə)lɪnʌɪt/ *n.* L19. [f. Neville Story-*Maskelyne* (1823–1911), Eng. mineralogist + -ITE[1].] *Min.* A colourless aluminosilicate glass which occurs in some meteorites and in rocks subjected to intense shock.

masker *n.* var. of MASQUER.

masker /ˈmɑːskə/ *v.t.* Long *obs.* exc. *dial.* [OE (in *malscrung* vbl n.), app. w. isolated Gmc cognates.] Bewilder. Usu. in *pass.*

maskinonge /ˈmaskɪnɒn(d)ʒ/ *n. N. Amer.* Also **muskellunge** /ˈmʌsk(ə)lʌn(d)ʒ/ & other vars. Pl. **-s**, same. L18. [Ojibwa.] A large pike, *Esox masquinongy*, of the Great Lakes of N. America, valued as a game-fish. Also called *musky*.

maslin /ˈmazlɪn/ *n.*[1] *obs.* exc. *dial.* [OE *mæstling*, *mæslen*, prob. rel. to MHG *mess(e* brass (early mod. & dial. G *mess*, *mesch*, *möss*, *mösch*) and cognates with suffixes, MDu., MHG *messinc*, *missinc* (Du., G *Messing*).] **1** A kind of brass. Now only *attrib.* in *maslin kettle* a large pan for boiling fruit for preserve. OE. **2** A vessel made of this brass; *spec.* = *maslin kettle* above. OE.

maslin /ˈmazlɪn/ *n.*[2] Now *dial.* Also (*Sc.*) **mashlum** /ˈmaʃləm/, & other vars. ME. [OFr. *mesteillon* f. Proto-Romance f. L *mistus* pa. pple of *miscere* MIX *v.*: Cf. MDu. *mastelūn* (Du. *masteluin*).] **1** Mixed grain, *esp.* rye mixed with wheat. Also, bread made from this. ME. †**2** *fig.* A mixture, a medley. L16–M19.

masochism /ˈmasəkɪz(ə)m/ *n.* L19. [f. Leopold von Sacher- *Masoch* (1835–95), Austrian novelist, who described the practice + -ISM.] The condition or state of deriving (esp. sexual) gratification from one's own pain or humiliation; *colloq.* enthusiasm for doing what appears to be painful or tiresome. Cf. SADISM.

SADO-MASOCHISM.

masochist /ˈmasəkɪst/ *n.* L19. [f. as prec. + -IST.] A person who is given to masochism.

maso'chistic *a.* of, pertaining to, resembling, or characterized by masochism E20. **maso'chistically** *adv.* M20.

mason /ˈmeɪs(ə)n/ *n.* ME. [ONFr. *machun* or (later) OFr. *masson* (later *maçon*) f. Proto-Romance, prob. f. Gmc (whence also OHG (*stein*) *mezzo*, G *Steinmetz* stonemason), perh. rel. to MATTOCK.] **1** A builder and worker in stone; a worker who dresses and lays stone in building. ME. **2** (Usu. **M-**.) = FREEMASON. L15.

1 **mason's mark** a distinctive device carved on stone by the mason who dressed the stone. MONUMENTAL *mason*.

Comb.: **mason-bee, -wasp** any of numerous solitary bees and wasps belonging to the families Megachilidae and Eumenidae respectively, which lay eggs in hard cells made out of clay, earth, etc.; **mason-work** stonework, masonry.

mason /ˈmeɪs(ə)n/ *v.t.* LME. [OFr. *maçoner* (mod. *maçonner*), f. *maçon*: see prec.] **1** Build of masonry; strengthen with masonry. LME. †**2** Build *in(to)* a wall. Only in 16. **3** *Her.* As *masoned* pa. pple: marked with lines representing the joints in masonry. L17.

masoner *n.* (*obs.* exc. *dial.*) a mason, a bricklayer E17.

Mason-Dixon line /meɪs(ə)nˈdɪks(ə)n lʌɪn/ *n. phr.* Also (earlier) **Mason and Dixon('s) line**. L18. [Charles *Mason* & Jeremiah *Dixon*, Eng. astronomers, who surveyed the line in 1763–7.] The boundary between Maryland and Pennsylvania, taken as the northern limit of the slave-owning States before the abolition of slavery in the US.

masonic /məˈsɒnɪk/ *a.* L18. [f. MASON *n.* + -IC.] **1** (Usu. **M-**.) Of, pertaining to, or characteristic of Freemasons or Freemasonry. L18. **2** Of or pertaining to stonemasons or stonemasonry. *rare.* E19.

Masonite /ˈmeɪs(ə)nʌɪt/ *n.* Also **m-**. E20. [f. *Mason* Fibre Co., Laurel, Mississippi, US + -ITE[1].] (Proprietary name for) fibreboard made from wood-fibre pulped under steam at high pressure.

Mason jar /ˈmeɪs(ə)n dʒɑː/ *n. phr.* Orig. *US.* L19. [John *Mason* (fl. 1858), US inventor.] A wide-mouthed glass jar with an airtight screw top, used in home bottling.

masonry /ˈmeɪs(ə)nri/ *n.* LME. [OFr. *maçonerie* (mod. *-nn-*), f. *maçon*: see MASON *n.*, -ERY.] **1** The art, skill, or occupation of a mason; the art or work of building in stone. Now *rare.* LME. **2** Work executed by a mason; stonework. LME. **3** (Usu. **M-**.) = FREEMASONRY. L17.

2 J. BUCHAN By the use of out-jutting stones and gaps in the masonry . . I got to the top. *attrib.*: *New York Times* A 14-story masonry and glass building.

masonried *a.* built or strengthened with masonry M19.

Masorah /masəˈrɑː, məˈsɔːrə/ *n.* Also **-ss-**, **-ra**. E17. [Heb. var. of *māsōreṯ* bond (*Ezek.* 20:37), f. *ʾāsar* bind (later interpreted as 'tradition' as if f. *māsar* hand down).] The body of traditional information and comment relating to the text of the Hebrew Scriptures, compiled by Jewish scholars in the 10th cent. and earlier; the collection of critical notes in which this information is preserved.

Masorete /ˈmasəriːt/ *n.* Also **-ss-**. L16. [Fr. *Massoret* & mod.L *Massoreta*, orig. misuse of Heb. *māsōreṯ* (see prec.), with subsequent assim. of the ending to L *-eta*, Gk *-ētēs*.] Any of the Jewish scholars who contributed to the formation of the Masorah.

Masoretic /masəˈrɛtɪk/ *a.* of, pertaining to, or proceeding from the Masoretes L17. **Maso'retical** *a.* (now *rare*) = MASORETIC L17. **Masorite** *n.* (now *rare*) = MASORETE E17.

masque /mɑːsk/ *n.* Also †**mask**. See also MASK *n.*[2] E16. [f. as MASK *n.*[2]] **I 1** A masquerade, a masked ball. Now *rare.* E16. †**b** A set of masquers. L16–E17. **2** A form of amateur dramatic entertainment, popular at Court and amongst the nobility in 16th- and 17th-cent. England, consisting of dancing and acting performed by masked players, orig. in dumb show, later with metrical dialogue. E16. **b** A dramatic composition intended for this. E17. **II** See MASK *n.*[2]

†**masque** *v.* var. of MASK *v.*[2]

masquer /ˈmɑːskə/ *n.* Also **masker**. M16. [f. *masque* MASK *v.*[2] + -ER[1].] A person who takes part in a masquerade or a masque; a person in masquerade.

masquerade /mɑːskəˈreɪd, mas-/ *n.* & *v.* L16. [Fr. *mascarade* (whence Sp. *mascarada*) f. It. *mascherata*, f. *maschera* MASK *n.*[2]: see -ADE.] **A** *n.* **1** A ball at which the guests wear masks and other disguises (often of a rich or fantastic kind); a masked ball. L16. **b** *transf.* & *fig.* A gathering or procession of fantastic or ill-assorted characters. L16. **2a** Disguise worn at or suitable for a masquerade; *gen.* disguise; *fig.* pretended outward appearance. Chiefly in *in masquerade*. M17. **b** A false outward show, a pretence; the action of masquerading. M19. †**3** A masquer. M17–E18. †**4** A kind of textile fabric. L17–M19.

1b POPE Visits to ev'ry Church we daily paid, And march'd in ev'ry holy Masquerade. 2a BYRON And, after all, what is a lie? 'Tis but The truth in masquerade. b S. BRETT His masquerade of pretending that the phone was being answered . . by . . a horde of underlings.

B *v.* †**1** *v.t.* Disguise as at a masquerade. *rare.* M17–E18. **2** *v.i.* Appear or go about in disguise; have or assume a false appearance. Usu. foll. by *as*. L17.

2 C. JACKSON I feel fifty-five when I look at that sophomoric adolescent masquerading as a man. A.

BRIEN Paris is a huge fairground or amusement park masquerading as a capital city.

masquerader *n.* a person who takes part in a masquerade; a person who masquerades or assumes disguise: L17.

mass /mas, mɑːs/ *n.*[1] Also **M-**. [OE *mæsse*, *messe*, corresp. to OFris., OS *missa*, OHG *messa*, *missa* (G *Messe*), ON *messa*, f. eccl.L *missa* vbl n. (whence (O)Fr. *messe*, It. *messa*, Sp. *misa*), f. *miss-* pa. ppl stem of *mittere* send (away), perh. f. the formula of dismissal (*Ite, missa est*) at the end of the service.] **1** (Freq. **M-**.) The Eucharist, *esp.* (in post-Reformation use) that of the Roman Catholic Church, or as administered and doctrinally viewed by Roman Catholics; a particular celebration of this. OE. **2** A feast-day or festival of a specified saint etc. Long *obs.* exc. as 2nd elem. of comb. (*Candlemas*, *Christmas*, *Lammas*, etc.). OE. **3** A rite used in a celebration of the Eucharist, esp. in the Roman Catholic Church. LME. **4** A musical setting of those invariable parts of the Mass which are usually sung (the Kyrie, Gloria, Credo, Sanctus, Benedictus, and Agnus Dei). L16.

1 B. MOORE Where every Catholic went to Mass of a Sunday. P. TOYNBEE His priest at Cwmbran celebrated mass. D. CUPITT It was important to assist souls in purgatory with Masses, indulgences and prayers. M. SPARK Wanda had been to the one o'clock Polish mass at Brompton Oratory.

Phrases: *Black Mass*: see BLACK *a.* **by the mass**: expr. asseveration, imprecation, outrage, etc. **dry mass** *Hist.* an abbreviated form of mass without either consecration or communion. **high mass** (a) mass celebrated with the assistance of a deacon and subdeacon, with incense and music. **low mass** (a) mass said without music and with the minimum of ceremony. *mass of requiem*: see REQUIEM *n.*[1] 1. *Mass of the Presanctified*: see PRESANCTIFY. MIDNIGHT *mass*. *nuptial mass*: see NUPTIAL *a.* 1. *pontifical mass*: see PONTIFICAL *a.* 1. *red mass*: see RED *a.* *sacring of (the) mass*: see SACRING 1. **solemn mass** = *high mass* above. *votive mass*: see VOTIVE *a.* 1.

Comb.: **mass-book** a missal; **mass-day** *arch.* a saint's feast-day; **mass-house** *derog.* (*obs.* exc. *Hist.*) a Roman Catholic place of worship; **mass-monger** *derog.* (*arch.*) a Roman Catholic; **mass-penny** *arch.* an offering of money made at mass; **mass-priest** *arch.* a priest whose function is to celebrate mass, *esp.* (*derog.*) a Roman Catholic priest.

mass /mas/ *n.*[2] & *a.* LME. [(O)Fr. *masse* f. L *massa* f. Gk *maza* barley-cake, perh. rel. to *massein* knead.] **A** *n.* **1** A coherent body of fusible or plastic material (as dough or clay), not yet fashioned into objects of definite shape; a lump of raw material for moulding, casting, etc. *obs.* exc. as passing into sense 2. LME. †**b** A kind of matter able to be fashioned or moulded. L15–E18. **c** An amorphous quantity of material used in or remaining after a chemical or pharmaceutical operation. M16. **2** A coherent body of matter of unspecified shape, often one of relatively large bulk; a solid physical object; *Med.* a tumour or growth that is palpable or visible. LME. †**b** *Med.* The whole quantity *of* blood in an animal body. E17–M18. **3** A dense aggregation of objects apparently forming a continuous body; a large quantity, amount, or number (of material or immaterial things); an oppressively or bewilderingly large amount. Freq. in *pl.* L15. †**b** *spec.* A large sum *of* money, treasure, etc.; *ellipt.* a stock, a fund. M16–E18. **c** Foll. by *of*: a person or thing viewed (hyperbolically) as consisting of a large number of the things specified. E17. **d** An extensive unbroken expanse of colour, light, shadow, etc.; any of the several main portions each having some unity in colour, lighting etc., which the eye distinguishes in a painting etc. M17. **e** A volume or body of sound; *Mus.* the effect of a large number of instruments or voices of the same character. L19. **4a** Solid bulk, massiveness. E17. **b** *Physics.* The quantity of matter which a body contains, as measured by its acceleration under a given force or by the force exerted on it by a gravitational field. E18. **5** A large number of people collected closely together or viewed as forming an aggregate in which their individuality is lost; *the* generality of humankind, *the* main body of a nation, people, etc.; (usu. in *pl.*) *the* ordinary people. E18.

2 W. R. GROVE When the magnet as a mass is in motion. J. TYNDALL Adjacent to us rose the mighty mass of the Finsteraarhorn. 3 LD MACAULAY They removed a vast mass of evil. J. IRVING The mass of logs .. moved swiftly downstream. S. BELLOW Uncle knew masses of stuff about plants. b T. FULLER Keeping their money for them till it amounted to a mass. c S. SMILES The Church itself was seen to be a mass of abuses. L. CODY This shoulder's going to be .. a mass of bruises in the morning. d I. ZANGWILL The occasional fineness of line, the masterly distribution of masses. 4a SHAKES. *Haml.* This army of such mass and charge. b E. RUTHERFORD The helium nucleus has a mass nearly four times that of hydrogen. 5 C. CONNOLLY What illness performs for the individual, war accomplishes for the mass. J. HIGGINS Cussane liked seaside towns, especially the ones that catered for the masses. M. FOOT Some hours later he stood on tiptoe amid a heaving, breathless mass.

Phrases: ATOMIC *mass*. *centre of mass*: see CENTRE *n.* CRITICAL *mass*. GRAVITATIONAL *mass*. **in mass** *en masse*, bodily, all at once. **in the mass** without distinction of component parts or individuals. *levy in mass*: see LEVY *n.*[1] 2. MISSING *mass*. *relative atomic* or *molecular mass*: see RELATIVE *a.* *solar mass*: see SOLAR *a.*[1] **the (great) mass of** the greater part or majority of.

B *attrib.* or as *adj.* Relating to, done by, or affecting large numbers of people or things; large-scale. M18.

D. DELILLO A brief pause before the mass wailing recommenced. E. LONGFORD George V had had to support his Prime Minister .. with a mass creation of Liberal peers. *City Limits* You can't blame the communities for not coping with mass unemployment.

Comb. & special collocations: **mass action** (*a*) *law of mass action* (Chem.), the principle that the rate of a chemical reaction is proportional to the masses of the reacting substances; (*b*) the action of a mass of people; **mass defect** *Physics* the sum of the masses of the constituent particles of an atomic nucleus, as free individuals, minus the mass of the nucleus (a quantity which effectively represents the binding energy of the nucleus); **mass effect** (*a*) *Metall.* the effect of size and shape in causing different rates of cooling in different parts of an object following heat treatment; (*b*) *sing.* & (usu.) in *pl.*, a total or grand effect; (*c*) an effect due to or dependent on mass; **mass-energy** *Physics* mass and energy regarded as interconvertible manifestations of the same phenomenon, according to the laws of relativity; the mass of a body regarded relativistically as energy; **mass man** a hypothetical average man; *esp.* one regarded as lacking individuality and being dominated by the mass media; **mass market** the market for mass-produced goods; **mass-market** *v.t.* market (a product) on a large scale; **mass medium** a medium of communication (such as radio, television, newspapers) that reaches a large number of people; usu. in *pl.*, such media collectively; **mass meeting** a meeting of a large body of people; *esp.* a meeting of all or most of the members of a workforce etc.; **mass noun** *Gram.* a noun denoting something (as a substance or quality) which cannot be counted, in English usu. a noun which in common usage lacks a plural and is not used with an indefinite article, (opp. *count noun*); **mass number** *Nuclear Physics* the total number of protons and neutrons in an atomic nucleus; **mass observation** (chiefly *Hist.*) the study and recording of the social habits and opinions of ordinary people; **mass-point** *Physics* an entity conceived as having mass but (like a geometrical point) lacking spatial extension; **mass-produce** *v.t.* manufacture by mass production; **mass production** the production of manufactured articles in large quantities by a standardized process; **mass radiography** radiography of the chests of large numbers of people by a quick routine method; **mass-ratio** the ratio of the mass of a fully fuelled rocket to that of the same rocket without fuel; **mass society**: in which the population is largely homogeneous and is strongly influenced by the mass media; **mass spectrograph** a mass spectrometer which employs photographic detection of the deflected ions; **mass spectrometer**, **mass spectroscope** an apparatus which ionizes material, forms the ions into a beam, separates the ions according to the ratios of their mass to their net electric charge (e.g. by deflecting them in a magnetic field or accelerating them in an electric field), and detects them, usu. electrically, producing a mass spectrum; **mass spectrometry**, **mass spectroscopy** the use of the mass spectrometer to analyse substances; **mass spectrum** a record obtained with a mass spectrometer, in which ions from a sample are represented as dispersed according to their mass-to-charge ratio.

mass /mas/ *v.*[1]*i.* Now *rare* or *obs.* OE. [f. MASS *n.*[1]] Celebrate mass; say or sing mass.

mass /mas/ *v.*[2] M16. [(O)Fr. *masser*, f. *masse* MASS *n.*[2]] **1** *v.t.* Form or gather into a mass; bring together in masses; *esp.* concentrate (troops etc.) in a particular place. Also (now *rare*) foll. by *up*. M16. **2** *v.i.* Collect, assemble, or come together in masses. M19.

1 J. RUSKIN But all these virtues mass themselves in the Greek mind into the two main ones. *Boston Sunday Herald* A nationwide movement designed to mass anti-war support. 2 DAY LEWIS The compulsive force of waters that have stealthily massed behind a dam. A. BULLOCK The German forces were massing for the invasion of the United Kingdom.

mass /mas/ *v.*[3]*t. rare.* L18. [Fr. *masser*: see MASSAGE.] Massage.

masser *n.* a masseur, a masseuse L18.

Massa /ˈmasə/ *n.* L18. [Repr. a pronunc.] In representations of Black speech: master.

massacre /ˈmasəkə/ *n.* L16. [(O)Fr. (also †*maçacre* etc.) shambles, butchery, of unkn. origin.] **1** A general slaughter of people or (less usu.) animals; carnage. L16. **b** *fig.* A great destruction or downfall. Now *esp.* (*colloq.*), a crushing defeat in sport. L16. †**2** A cruel or atrocious murder. L16–E17.

1 SHAKES. *Tit. A.* For I must talk of murders, rapes, and massacres. G. BORROW Plunder and massacre had been expected.

massacre /ˈmasəkə/ *v.t.* L16. [(O)Fr. *massacrer*, f. as prec.] **1** Cruelly or violently kill (people, less usu. animals) in numbers; make a general slaughter of. L16. **2** Mutilate, mangle. Long *obs.* exc. *dial.* L16. **3** Murder (one person) cruelly or violently. E17. **4** *fig.* Defeat heavily, esp. in a sporting event; trounce. *colloq.* M20.

1 P. WARNER He marched them out bound .. and massacred them with sword and spear. 3 G. P. R. JAMES He would be massacred the moment he showed his face amongst the infuriated mob. 4 *Scotsman* Ipswich .. should massacre Norwich on Wednesday at home in the East Anglian derby.

massacrer *n.* L16.

massage /ˈmasɑːʒ, maˈsɑːʒ, -dʒ/ *n.* & *v.* L19. [Fr., f. *masser* apply massage to, perh. f. Port. *amassar* knead.] **A** *n.* **1** The application (usu. with the hands) of pressure and strain on the muscles and joints of the body by rubbing, kneading, etc., in order to stimulate their action and increase their suppleness; an instance or spell of such manipulation. L19. **2** *euphem.* The services of prostitutes. Chiefly in *massage parlour* below. E20.

1 *Swedish massage*: see SWEDISH *a.*

Comb.: **massage parlour** an establishment providing massage; *euphem.* a brothel operating under the guise of providing massage.

B *v.t.* **1** Apply massage to; treat by means of massage. L19. **b** Rub (lotion etc.) *into* by means of massage. L20. **2** Manipulate (data, figures, etc.), esp. in order to give a more acceptable result. M20.

1 I. MCEWAN Mary massaged his back .. with convergent movements of her thumbs. *fig.*: P. D. JAMES He wasn't looking for a female subordinate to massage his ego. b L. CODY She massaged some warmth into her cramped fingers.

massager *n.* (*a*) a masseur, a masseuse; (*b*) a machine used for massaging: L19. **massagist** *n.* a masseur, a masseuse L19.

Massagetae /masəˈgiːtʌɪ/ *n.pl.* E17. [L f. Gk *Massagetai*, perh. f. Scythian name *Masakata* Great Sakas.] *Hist.* An ancient Scythian people who lived to the east of the Caspian Sea.

Massalian *n.* & *a.* var. of MESSALIAN.

Massaliot /maˈsalɪət/ *n.* & *a.* Also **-ssil-** /-ˈsɪl-/. M19. [f. Gk *Massalia*, L *Massilia* (see below), after *Cypriot* etc. Cf. earlier MASSILIAN.] **A** *n.* A native or inhabitant of Massalia (or Massilia, mod. Marseilles), a Greek colony founded *c* 600 BC to the east of the mouth of the Rhône on the Mediterranean coast of southern France. M19. **B** *adj.* Of or pertaining to Massalia or its inhabitants. M19.

massasauga /masəˈsɔːgə/ *n.* M19. [Alt. of MISSISAUGA.] A small spotted venomous N. American rattlesnake, *Sistrurus catenatus*. Also *massasauga rattler*.

massé /ˈmaseɪ/ *a.* & *n.* L19. [Fr., pa. pple of *masser* play a massé stroke, f. *masse* MACE *n.*[1]] *Billiards* etc. (Designating) a stroke made with the cue more or less vertical, so as to impart extra swerve to the cue-ball.

massecuite /masˈkwiːt/ *n.* L19. [Fr., lit. 'cooked mass'.] The juice of sugar cane after concentration by boiling.

massed /mast/ *ppl a.* L19. [f. MASS *v.*[2] + -ED[1].] 1 Gathered into a mass; assembled in a mass. L19. 2 Of an inscription: having the words arranged to form a solid column of lettering. E20. 3 *Psychol.* Designating conditioning or training in which practice is concentrated with very short intervals between repetitions. M20.

1 O. MANNING There was shade from the massed foliage of palms, sycamores, banyans and mangoes. A. LIVELY The serried ranks of young girls, and the massed drums that drove them on.

masseter /maˈsiːtə/ *n.* L16. [Gk *masētēr*, f. *masasthai* chew.] *Anat.* More fully *masseter muscle*. Either of a pair of muscles passing from the maxilla and zygomatic arch on each side of the head to the ramus of the mandible, and used in mastication.

masseˈteric *a.* M19.

masseur /maˈsəː/ *n.* Fem. **masseuse** /maˈsəːz/. L19. [Fr., f. *masser* (see MASSAGE) + *-eur* -OR.] A person who provides massage (professionally).

Swedish masseur: see SWEDISH *a.*

Massic /ˈmasɪk/ *a.* & *n.* M17. [L *Massicus* a mountain in Campania.] (Designating) a wine produced in Campania, Italy, in classical times.

massicot /ˈmasɪkɒt/ *n.* L15. [Fr. (also †*masticot*), obscurely rel. to It. *marzacotto* unguent, Sp. *mazacote* kali, mortar, prob. through med.L f. Arab.] Yellow lead monoxide or litharge used as a pigment.

massif /ˈmasɪf, maˈsiːf, *foreign* masif (*pl. same*)/ *n.* E16. [Fr., use as n. of *massif* MASSIVE.] 1 A block of building. Passing into *fig.* use of sense 2. E16. 2 A large mountain-mass; a compact group of mountain heights. L19. 3 *Hort.* A mass or clump of plants. L19.

1 *Times* There must, dear God, be something between slums and concrete massifs. 2 A. N. WILSON The Russians made inroads into the main Caucasus massif. *transf.*: T. KENEALLY Her path took her over the sandstone under the cliffs . . massifs taller than she.

¶ Only in isolated use bef. L19.

massify /ˈmasɪfʌɪ/ *v.t.* M20. [f. MASS *n.*[2] + -I- + -FY.] Form into a mass society.

massifiˈcation *n.* M20.

Massilian /məˈsɪlɪən/ *n.* & *a.* E17. [f. L *Massilia* (see MASSALIOT) + -AN] = MASSALIOT.

Massiliot *n.* & *a.* var. of MASSALIOT.

Massim /ˈmasɪm/ *n.* & *a.* L19. [Alt. of *Misima*, offshore island of Papua New Guinea.] **A** *n.* Pl. same. A member of a people of SE Papua New Guinea. L19. **B** *adj.* Of or pertaining to this people. M20.

massive /ˈmasɪv/ *a.* LME. [Fr. *massif*, *-ive* alt. of OFr. *massiz* MASSY *a.*: see -IVE.] 1 Forming or consisting of a large mass; having great size and weight or solidity; large in scale physically. LME. b Of (an article of) gold or silver: solid, not hollow or plated. LME. c Of architectural or artistic style: presenting great masses, solid. M19. 2 Forming a solid or continuous mass; compact, dense, uniform; existing in compact continuous masses. Now *esp.* (*a*) (of a mineral) not definitely crystalline; (*b*) (of a rock formation) lacking structural divisions. M16. 3 (Of an immaterial thing) solid, substantial; impressive, great or imposing in scale. Now freq. in weakened sense: very large, great, far-reaching. L16. 4 Of or pertaining to masses (as distinct from molecules). *rare.* L19. 5 *Physics.* Of a particle: having non-zero mass, not massless. M20.

1 J. A. MICHENER They had built a massive wall nine feet high and four feet thick. W. S. BURROUGHS She is a massive woman with arms like a wrestler. O. MANNING The wall enclosed a row of palms from which hung massive bunches of red dates. 3 L. STEPHEN Scott was a man of more massive and less impulsive character. *Word* He died suddenly of a massive heart attack. B. GELDOF Slotted between the news and *Top of the Pops*—giving us a massive captive audience. M. BRETT America runs a massive trade deficit.

¶ Cf. MASSY *a.*

massively *adv.* M16. **massiveness** *n.* M16. **maˈssivity** *n.* E20.

massless /ˈmaslɪs/ *a.* L19. [f. MASS *n.*[2] + -LESS.] Having no mass.

masslessness *n.* M20.

massoola /məˈsuːlə/ *n. obs.* exc. *Hist.* Also **-ah**. L17. [Origin unkn.] A large surf-boat used on the Coromandel coast of India. Also *massoola-boat*.

Massorah *n.* see MASORAH.

Massorete *n.* var. of MASORETE.

massoy /ˈmasɔɪ/ *n.* E19. [Malay *mesui*.] The bark of a tree, *Cryptocarya aromatica* (family Lauraceae), native to New Guinea. Also *massoy-bark*.

massula /ˈmasjʊlə/ *n.* Pl. **-lae** /-liː/. M19. [mod.L, dim. of L *massa* MASS *n.*[2]] *Bot.* 1 In certain orchids, a cluster of pollen grains developed from a single cell. M19. 2 In certain heterosporous ferns, the tissue surrounding the maturing microspores. L19.

massy /ˈmasi/ *n. dial.* (chiefly *US*). E19. [Repr. a pronunc.] In interjections: mercy.

massy /ˈmasi/ *a.* Exc. in sense 5, now *literary* or *arch.* LME. [Perh. orig. f. OFr. *massiz* (whence *massif* MASSIVE) f. pop.L f. L *massa* MASS *n.*[2], or directly f. MASS *n.*[2]: see -Y[1].] 1 Solid and weighty; heavy as consisting of compact matter; (esp. of precious metals) occurring in mass, solid, not hollow or alloyed. LME. †b Compact, dense. E16–E19. †c Solid, having three dimensions. M16–M17. 2 Consisting of a large mass or masses of heavy material; of great size and weight; (of a building) consisting of great blocks of masonry. LME. b Of architectural or artistic style: presenting great masses. E19. 3 Of large size; voluminous, bulky; spreading in a mass or in masses. LME. 4 Of an immaterial thing: great, substantial, impressive. L16. 5 *Physics.* = MASSIVE 5. M20.

1 M. TWAIN Its furniture was all of massy gold. 2 LD MACAULAY The massy remains of the old Norman castle. b *Modern Painters* This predilection for massy stability of form is present in Moore's earliest life-drawings. 3 J. UPDIKE Brick pinnacles and massy trees.

¶ Superseded by MASSIVE in ordinary use.

massily *adv.* (long *rare*) massively LME. **massiness** *n.* massiveness L16.

mast /mɑːst/ *n.*[1] [OE *mæst* = (M)LG, (M)Du., (O)HG *mast*, f. WGmc (ON *mastr* etc. being f. MLG) f. IE, whence perh. L *malus* mast, OIr. *maite*, *matán* club.] 1 A long pole or spar, often one of a number, set up more or less vertically on the keel of a sailing vessel to support its sails. In other vessels, a similar structure (often taking the form of a slender lattice-work tower, a tripod, etc.) erected for any of various purposes. OE. b *Naut.* A piece of timber suitable for use as a mast. L15. 2 *gen.* A pole; a tall pole or other slender structure set upright for any purpose; *esp.* (*a*) a flag-pole; (*b*) a post or lattice-work upright supporting a radio or television aerial; (*c*) (in full *mooring-mast*) a strong steel tower to the top of which an airship can be moored. E16.

1 LYTTON Afar off you saw the tall masts of the fleet. G. BENNETT The funnels and masts of warships. *foremast*, *mainmast*, *mizen-mast*, *royal mast*, *topmast*, etc. **before** (or **afore**) **the mast** *Naut.* as an ordinary seaman (quartered in the forecastle). *dolphin of the mast*: see DOLPHIN 4b. *made mast*: see MADE *ppl a.* *nail one's colours to the mast*: see COLOUR *n.* 2 J. WYNDHAM The tower was flying two flags on one mast. S. HYLAND The enormous meccano structure of the television mast on top of Sydenham Hill.

Comb.: **mast coat** *Naut.* a covering of painted canvas round the foot of a mast and secured to the deck, to prevent ingress of water; **mastman** (chiefly *US*) a sailor whose duty is to oversee the working of halyards etc. in sailing; **mast-step** *Naut.* a block fixed to the keelson in which a mast is set.

mastless *a.* L16.

mast /mɑːst/ *n.*[2] [OE *mæst* = MLG, MDu., OHG *mast*, f. WGmc, prob. f. base of MEAT *n.*] *collect.* & (*rare*) in *pl.* The fruit of beech, oak, chestnut, and other forest trees, esp. when fallen, as food for pigs etc.

A. HIGGINS He could see the beech tree . . and the pheasants rooting in the beech mast.

Comb.: **mast cell** [G *Mast* = fattening, feeding] *Physiol.* a cell filled with basophil granules, found in numbers in the connective tissue and releasing histamine and other substances in inflammatory and allergic reactions; **mast year**: in which forest trees produce a good crop of mast.

†mast *n.*[3] M–L18. [Alt. of Fr. *masse* MACE *n.*[1] by confusion w. MAST *n.*[1]] A heavy billiard cue, of which the broad end was used for striking.

mast /mɑːst/ *v.t.* E16. [f. MAST *n.*[1]] Provide with masts.

mastaba /ˈmastəbə/ *n.* Also **-ah**. E17. [Arab. *mistaba*, *maṣ-*.] 1 In Islamic countries: a (stone) bench or seat attached to a house. E17. 2 *Archaeol.* An ancient Egyptian flat-topped tomb, rectangular or square in plan and with sides sloping outward to the base. Also *mastaba tomb*. L19.

mastage /ˈmɑːstɪdʒ/ *n. obs.* exc. *Hist.* E17. [f. MAST *n.*[2] + -AGE.] The mast of trees; the right of feeding animals on mast.

mastalgia /maˈstaldʒə/ *n.* M19. [f. Gk *mastos* breast + -ALGIA.] *Med.* Pain in the breast.

mastax /ˈmastaks/ *n.* M19. [Gk = mouth.] *Zool.* The muscular pharynx of a rotifer, containing the masticatory jaws.

mastectomy /maˈstɛktəmi/ *n.* E20. [f. Gk *mastos* breast + -ECTOMY.] Surgical removal of a breast; an instance of this.

masted /ˈmɑːstɪd/ *a.* E17. [f. MAST *n.*[1], *v.*: see -ED[2], -ED[1].] 1 Provided with a mast or masts. Freq. as 2nd elem. of comb., as *two-masted* etc. E17. 2 Of a harbour etc.: thronged with masts. *rare.* M18.

master /ˈmɑːstə/ *n.*[1] & *a.* Also (esp. in titles) **M-**. [OE *mægister*, *magister* (corresp. to OFris. *māster*, (also OS) *mēster*, (O)HG *meister*, ON *meistari*), a Gmc adoption from L; reinforced by OFr. *maistre* (mod. *maître*) f. L *magister*, *magistr-*, usu. referred to *magis* adv. = more.] **A** *n.* **I** A person (orig. & usu. a man) having control or authority. 1 *gen.* A man (occas. an animal or thing) having direction or control over the action of another or others; a director, a leader, a chief, a commander; a ruler, a governor. *obs.* exc. as below. OE. 2a The captain of a merchant vessel (also *master mariner*). Orig. also (in *pl.*), the officers, the crew. ME. b *Hist.* A naval officer (ranking next below a lieutenant) responsible for the navigation and sailing of a warship during warlike operations. See also *master and commander* below. L16. 3 A person who employs another; one's superior in a business, hierarchy, etc.; a monarch in relation to a minister etc.; the owner of a slave. ME. b The owner of an animal; the person whom an animal is accustomed to obey; (more fully *master of* (*fox*)*hounds*, *beagles*, etc.) the person who owns or controls a pack of foxhounds, beagles, etc.; a member of a hunt who supervises the kennels and hunting arrangements generally. LME. c A device or component which directly controls another. Opp. *slave*. Cf. sense B.2b below. M20. 4a The male head of a house or household; w. *possess.* (now *joc.* exc. *dial.*) a woman's husband. ME. b The head or presiding officer of a society, institution, etc., e.g. of certain colleges (in Oxford, Cambridge, and elsewhere), guilds, livery companies, masonic lodges, etc. LME. c In titles of various officials; *spec.* in *Law* (in full *Master in Chancery*) until 1852, each of twelve assistants to the Lord Chancellor, the chief of whom was Master of the Rolls; since 1897, each of four chief clerks of the Chancery Division of the Supreme Court. LME. 5 The possessor or owner of something (now usu. of a quality, skill, etc.); a person highly accomplished in a particular activity (foll. by *of*). ME. 6 A person (or thing personified) having the power to control, use, or dispose of something at will. Chiefly *pred.*, foll. by *of*. ME. 7 A person who overcomes another, a victor; a person who gets the upper hand. ME. **b** *Bridge*. = *master card* (a) below. M20. **8** The jack in bowls. Long *rare*. M16. **9** A thing from which a number of copies are made; the original copy of a sound recording, film, data file, etc.; *spec*. a disc with ridges in place of grooves, used to manufacture gramophone records. Cf. sense B.2c below. E20.

1 SHAKES. *Tit. A.* Like stinging bees . . Led by their master to the flow'red fields. 3 G. BORROW I have lived in many houses and served many masters. A. WILSON The manservant . . was as old as his master. b M. MAETERLINCK The dog who meets with a good master is the happier of the two. 4a DICKENS I'm a-watching for my master. R. K. NARAYAN The master of the house rose to his feet. b *Times* The first woman to hold office as Master of the United College. 5 J. TRUSLER I was master of more than twenty pounds. W. CRUISE Judgement and discretion, which an infant was not master of. J. AGATE Barrie was a master of plot and invention. 6 JOSEPH HALL An honest man's word must be his master. J. R. GREEN To secure a landing at all, the Spaniards had to be masters of the Channel. 7 TENNYSON If they quarrell'd, Enoch stronger-made Was master. 9 *Melody Maker* Band requires record company/label to release high quality master.

II A teacher; a person qualified to teach. **10** A male tutor or teacher; *esp*. one in a school, a schoolmaster. OE. **11** A man of whom one is a disciple; a revered male teacher in religion, philosophy, etc.; the (male) teacher from whom one has chiefly learned, or whose doctrines one accepts. ME. **12** A skilled workman, orig. one qualified by training and experience to teach apprentices; a workman who is in business on his own account. ME. **13** A holder of a specific degree of a university or other academic institution, orig. of a level which conveyed authority to teach in the university. LME. **b** In *possess*.: = *master's degree* below. *N. Amer. colloq*. M20. **14** An artist of great skill, one regarded as a model of excellence; a work of painting or sculpture by such an artist (chiefly in *old master* s.v. OLD *a*.). LME. **15a** *Chess*. A player of proved ability at international or national level. Cf. GRAND MASTER 3. M19. **b** In *pl*. In some sports, a class for competitors over the usual age for the highest level of competition. Usu. *attrib*. L20.

10 E. BLISHEN Mr. Oakes, the P. T. master, was our captain. D. STOREY A master came from the school to talk of Richard's university chances. 11 G. BORROW Why should I be ashamed of their company when my Master mingled with publicans and thieves? G. SAINTSBURY John Keats . . and his master Leigh Hunt. 12 R. H. TAWNEY Gilds . . appear to have included 5,000 masters, who employed not more than 6,000 to 7,000 journeymen. 14 T. GRAY With a Master's hand, and Prophet's fire. K. CLARK When one compares the figures by the master himself . . with those of his assistants.

III As a title of rank or compliment. **16** As *voc*. (*obs*. exc. *dial*.): sir. Also (now *arch*. & *rhet*.) in *pl*., often with *my*: sirs, gentlemen (freq. *iron*.). ME. **17** Used preceding the name or designation of a man of high social rank or of learning, accomplishment, etc.' *arch*. ME. **†b** Used preceding a title of office or profession, etc. ME–M17. **18** (*Master of* —.) As a courtesy title of the heir-apparent to a Scottish baron, viscount, or (formerly) earl. L15. **19** Used preceding the name of a boy not old enough to be called *Mr*. Hence (freq. as a form of address), a boy; also *young master, little master*. L16. **b** Used, with disparaging implication, preceding the name of an adult. L19.

16 SHAKES. *Haml.* You are welcome, masters; welcome, all. N. GORDIMER they had tried to train him to drop the 'master' for the ubiquitously respectful 'sir'. 17 M. PATTISON Two allegorical pieces by Master Hans Holbein. 18 D. DUNNETT When her husband died . . the elder boy . . became third Baron Culter, and . . his brother received the heir's title of Master of Culter. 19 SWIFT Maids, misses, and little master . . in a third [coach]. DICKENS Wait a bit Master Davy, and I'll—I'll tell you something.

Phrases: **be one's own master** be independent or free to do as one wishes. GRAND MASTER. **†great master** = GRAND MASTER 1, 2. *little master*: see sense 19 above. *little Masters*: see LITTLE *a*. *lord and master*: see LORD *n*. **make oneself master of** acquire a thorough knowledge of or facility of. **master and commander** *Hist*. (until 1814) the full title of the rank of Commander in the Royal Navy. *master-at-arms*: see ARM *n*.[2] *Master in Chancery*: see sense 4c above. *Master in Lunacy*: see LUNACY 1. *Master of Arts*: see ART *n*.[1] *master of beagles*: see sense 3c above. *Master of Ceremonies*: see CEREMONY *n*. *master of (fox)hounds*: see sense 3c above. *Master of Misrule*: see MISRULE *n*. *Master of Science*: see SCIENCE. **Master of the Horse** (the title of) the third official of the British royal household, attending the monarch on State occasions. *Master of the (King's* or *Queen's) Music*: see MUSIC *n*. 4. *Master of (the) Request(s)*: see REQUEST *n*. *master of the revels*: see REVEL *n*.[1] 2. *Master of the Rolls*: see ROLL *n*.[1] **master's degree** a degree of Master of Arts, Master of Science, etc. **master's mate** *Hist*. a petty officer rated as an assistant to the master of a warship. *old master*: see OLD *a*. *young master*: see sense 19 above.

B *attrib*. or as *adj*. **1** That is a master; chief, leading, commanding; great, powerful. ME. **b** Chiefly *Hist*. Designating an official with authority over others of the same kind. ME. **c** Designating a workman who is a master as distinguished from an apprentice or journeyman, or who employs others. ME. **d** Supremely or consummately skilled; accomplished, expert. ME. **e** *Chess*. Of the standard of master (cf. sense A.15 above). L19. **2** Of a (material or immaterial) thing: main, principal; controlling, supreme. ME. **b** *spec*. Designating a device or component which directly controls the action of others. Opp. *slave*. E20. **c** Designating the copy of a tape, disc, file, etc., which is the authoritative source for copies. E20. **3** Of, pertaining to, or characteristic of a master. E17.

1 SHAKES. *Jul. Caes.* The choice and master spirits of this age. POPE The master Ram at last approach'd the gate. c C. KINGSLEY He would be a man and a master-sweep. M. MOORCOCK A master baker, he had written for the trade journals. d TENNYSON And last the master-bowman, he, Would cleave the mark. T. S. ELIOT He's the master criminal who can defy the Law. L. DEIGHTON Champion was some kind of master spy. 2 POPE One master Passion in the breast, Like Aaron's serpent, swallows up the rest. c A. MILLER It all goes into the master file in the governor's office.

Comb. & *special collocations*: **Master Aircrew** an Royal Air Force rank equivalent to warrant-officer; **masterbatch** a concentrated mixture used in the production of synthetic rubbers and plastics; **master-builder** (*a*) a skilled builder or architect; (*b*) a builder who employs other workmen; **master card** (*a*) *Bridge* a card that cannot be beaten unless trumped; (*b*) a record card which summarizes the information recorded on a number of other cards; **master-class** (*a*) the most powerful or influential class in society; (*b*) a class receiving instruction from a distinguished musician etc.; an advanced class given by a distinguished musician etc.; **master clock** a clock which transmits regular pulses of electricity for controlling other devices; **master-craftsman** a craftsman who is a master; an expert worker; *Master Gunner*: see GUNNER 1; **master-hand** (*a*) the hand or agency of a master; (*b*) a highly skilled worker; **master-key** a key that will open a number of different locks, each of which has its own key that will not open any of the rest; **master-man** †(*a*) (chiefly *Sc*.) a chief, a leader; (*b*) a master with apprentices or employees; *master* MARINER; **master mason** (*a*) a skilled mason; a mason who employs other workers; (*b*) (*Master Mason*) a fully qualified Freemason, who has passed the third degree; **master oscillator** *Electronics*: used to produce a constant frequency, esp. the carrier frequency of a radio etc. transmitter; **master race** a race of people considered or claiming to be pre-eminent; *spec*. (in Nazi Germany) the 'Aryans' regarded as a superior people; **master-singer** = MEISTERSINGER; **master-spring** (now *rare* or *obs*.) a mainspring (chiefly *fig*.); **master-stroke** an act or touch worthy of a master; an outstandingly skilful act of policy etc.; one's cleverest move; **master-touch** a touch worthy of a master; a masterly manner of dealing with something; **master-work** (*a*) a masterpiece; (*b*) an action of chief importance; †(*c*) a main drainage or irrigation channel.

¶ Cf. MISTER *n*.[2]

masterhood *n*. LME.

master /ˈmɑːstə/ *n*.[2] E19. [f. MAST *n*.[1] + -ER[1].] With numeral prefixed: a vessel having the specified number of masts.

three-master, seven-master, etc.

master /ˈmɑːstə/ *v.t.* ME. [f. MASTER *n*.[1] & *a*. Cf. OFr. *maistrier*.] **1** Get the better of in a contest or struggle; overcome, defeat. ME. **2** Reduce to subjection, compel to obey; break, tame. ME. **3** Temper, season; modify. *obs*. exc. *Dyeing*, season or age (dyestuffs); in *Tanning*, subject (skins) to the action of an astringent lye. LME. **†4** Have at one's disposal; own, possess. L16–M17. **5 †a** Execute with skill. Only in E17. **b** Make oneself master of (an art, science, etc.); acquire complete knowledge or understanding of, acquire complete facility in using. L17. **6** Act the part of master towards; rule as a master; be the master of (a school etc.). E17. **7** Record the master disc or tape for (a sound recording); make a recording of (a performance) from which a master can be created. M20.

1 J. BERESFORD Lord Edward was mastered, brought to the Castle, and committed to Newgate. G. P. R. JAMES Deep grief masters me. 2 GOLDSMITH The Zebra . . could never be entirely mastered. GEO. ELIOT A woman who would have liked to master him. 4 SHAKES. *Merch. V.* The wealth That the world masters. 5b R. G. COLLINGWOOD I have never been able to master the piano. K. WATERHOUSE We had mastered the mysteries of foreplay, contraception, climax. A. MACLEAN Captain Imrie had long mastered the art of dining gracefully at sea.

masterer *n*. (*rare*) E17. **mastering** *n*. (*a*) the action of the vb; (*b*) *Tanning* a kind of lye made of lime etc. (cf. MASTER *v*. 3): L15.

masterate /ˈmɑːstərət/ *n*. E20. [f. MASTER *n*.[1] & *a*. + -ATE[1].] The status or dignity of a person holding a master's degree.

masterdom /ˈmɑːstədəm/ *n*. OE. [f. MASTER *n*.[1] & *a*. + -DOM.] **†1** The position or office of master or teacher; the degree of master. *rare*. OE–LME. **2** The position of being master; dominion, absolute control, supremacy. LME. **†b** Masterful behaviour. *rare* (Spenser). Only in L16. **†3** With *possess*.: = MASTERSHIP 3. L16–E17.

masterful /ˈmɑːstəfʊl, -f(ə)l/ *a*. LME. [f. MASTER *n*.[1] & *a*. + -FUL.] **1** Given to acting the part of master; accustomed to insist on having one's own way; imperious, overbearing; (of an action) high-handed, despotic, arbitrary. LME. **†b** *Law* (chiefly *Sc*.). Of (the action of) a robber etc.: using violence or threats. LME–E19. **†c** Of natural agency: violent, overwhelming. E16–M17. **2** Having the capacities of a master; commanding; powerful and vigorous in rule; (in weakened sense) self-confident, assured, assertive. Also, indicative of authority, command, or confidence. LME. **3** Characterized by the skill that constitutes a master; masterly. Freq. with some admixture of sense 2. E17.

1 HUGH WALPOLE Mrs. Moy-Thompson . . had long ago been crushed into a miserable negligibility by her masterful husband. P. GAY Freud knew what he wanted, and his masterful impetuosity carried her with him. 2 J. HUTCHINSON This masterful disregard of logical thought. V. SACKVILLE-WEST He was . . growing more . . masterful, and arranged his life as it pleased him. DENNIS POTTER Her change of tone allowed him to play the smoothly masterful role which pleased him most. 3 *Aviation Week* The Arabs did a masterful job of concealing their true intentions.

masterfully *adv*. LME. **masterfulness** *n*. L16.

masterless /ˈmɑːstəlɪs/ *a*. LME. [f. MASTER *n*.[1] & *a*. + -LESS.] **1** Having no master. Of an animal: deprived of a controlling hand. LME. **b** Having no reputable means of living; vagrant, vagabond. Long *obs*. exc. *Hist*. L15. **c** Of unknown authorship or provenance. L19. **†2** Unable to be mastered; ungovernable. E17–M18.

masterlessness *n*. E19.

masterly /ˈmɑːstəli/ *a*. M16. [f. MASTER *n*.[1] & *a*. + -LY[1].] **†1** Belonging to, characteristic of, or resembling a master or lord; arbitrary, despotic, imperious, domineering. M16–M18. **2** Resembling, characteristic of, or worthy of a master or skilled workman; skilfully exercised or performed. M16. **3** Mining. *masterly lode*, a main lode. L19.

1 DRYDEN You are a saucy, masterly companion; and so I leave you. 2 J. M. MURRY Time and again he marshals the evidence, in his masterly fashion, so that the conclusion . . appears inevitable. H. ACTON Wilson Steer painted a masterly portrait of her in her heyday.

masterliness *n*. E18.

masterly /ˈmɑːstəli/ *adv*. Now *rare*. LME. [f. MASTER *n*.[1] & *a*. + -LY[2].] In a masterly manner.

SHAKES. *Wint. T.* Masterly done! The very life seems warm upon her lip.

mastermind /ˈmɑːstəmʌɪnd/ *n.* & *v.* Also **master-mind**. E18. [f. MASTER *n.*[1] & *a.* + MIND *n.*[1]] **A** *n.* **1** (A person with) an outstanding or commanding intellect. E18. **2** The person (or other body) directing an intricate, esp. criminal, enterprise. L19.

1 P. G. WODEHOUSE You can't expect two masterminds like us to pig it in that room downstairs. E. JENKINS Hers was one of the earliest master-minds in advertising. **2** A. TROLLOPE The police thought that I had been the master-mind among the thieves.

B *v.t.* Be the mastermind behind (an enterprise, a crime, etc.); plan and direct. M20.

S. BRILL Sammy Pro was indicted for masterminding a counterfeiting operation. A. BRIGGS Sweeping changes in the power . . of the Church masterminded by Thomas Cromwell were effected.

masterpiece /ˈmɑːstəpiːs/ *n.* E17. [f. MASTER *n.*[1] & *a.* + PIECE *n.*, after Du. *meesterstuk*, G *Meisterstück*.] **1** A work of outstanding artistry or skill; a masterly production; a consummate example *of* some skill or other kind of excellence; (with *possess.*) a person's best piece of work. E17. **b** A remarkable or singular person or thing. *colloq.* E20. †**2** The most important feature, or the chief excellence, of a person or thing. Only in 17.

1 SHAKES. *Macb.* Confusion now hath made his masterpiece. F. QUARLES Man is heav'n's Masterpiece. K. CLARK It is . . a masterpiece of Gothic architecture. A. LURIE A dealer can't always fill his gallery with masterpieces. *fig.*: JONSON Here, we must rest; this is our maister-piece; We cannot thinke to goe beyond this.

mastership /ˈmɑːstəʃɪp/ *n.* LME. [f. MASTER *n.*[1] & *a.* + -SHIP.] **1** The condition of being a master or ruler; dominion, rule, ascendancy, control. LME. **b** Mastery, the upper hand. Now *rare* or *obs.* LME. **c** The authority of a master or teacher. L16. **2** The function, office, or dignity of a master, esp. a schoolmaster; the term of office of a master. LME. †**3** With possess. adj. (as *your* etc. *mastership*): a title of respect given to a master. LME–E17. **4** The skill or knowledge of a master; mastery, thorough knowledge *of* a subject. E17. **b** The status of a recognized master in a craft; the holding of a master's degree. L17. **5** The existence of masters or employers in industrial organization. M19.

masterwort /ˈmɑːstəwəːt/ *n.* M16. [f. MASTER *n.*[1] & *a.* + WORT *n.*[1]] Any of various umbellifers used as pot-herbs or medicinally; *spec.* (*a*) any of the genus *Astrantia*, comprising perennial plants of woods and damp meadows in Europe and western Asia; (*b*) *Peucedanum ostruthium*, a perennial native to southern Europe and naturalized in moist places elsewhere.

mastery /ˈmɑːst(ə)ri/ *n.* ME. [OFr. *maistrie*, f. *maistre* MASTER *n.*[1] & *a.*: see -Y[3].] **1** The state or condition of being master, controller, or ruler; authority, dominion; an instance of this. ME. †**b** Predominance; prevailing character. L15–M17. **2** Superiority or ascendancy in competition or strife; the upper-hand; victory (leading to domination). ME. †**3** Superior force or power. ME–E19. **4** Masterly skill or knowledge; supreme talent; skilful use or intellectual command *of* a technique, subject, instrument, etc. ME. **b** The action of mastering a subject etc. L18. †**5** An action demonstrating skill or power; a feat, a trick; a test of strength or skill. ME–L17.

1 J. R. GREEN Edward's aim . . was . . to save English commerce by securing the mastery of the Channel. A. TOFFLER Science first gave man a sense of mastery over his environment. **2** S. AUSTIN He . . always gained the mastery in the end. K. LINES There were many battles between the two armies . . yet neither side gained mastery. **4** H. KELLER I am surprised at the mastery of language which your letter shows. K. AMIS After half an hour of further attempts . . he considered he had a fair mastery of the weapon. M. FOOT Lloyd George returned to the platform with all his old mastery and relish. **b** SIR W. SCOTT It is matter beyond my mastery. **5** †**great** (or **little** etc.) **mastery** a great (or little etc.) achievement, a matter of great (or little etc.) difficulty. †**try masteries** engage in a trial of skill, strength, etc., (*with*).

masthead /ˈmɑːsthɛd/ *n.* & *v.* L15. [f. MAST *n.*[1] + HEAD *n.*] **A** *n.* **1** The head or highest part of a mast; *esp.* that of the lower mast as a place of observation or punishment, or of the whole mast as the place for flying flags etc. L15. **b** A person stationed at the masthead. M19. **2** The title, colophon, motto, etc., of a newspaper or journal, printed conspicuously esp. above the editorial or at the top of the first page. Orig. *US*. M19.

1 *fig.*: R. L. STEVENSON He was . . enjoying to the mast-head the modest pleasures of admiration. **2** *Oxford Art Journal* Another of his designs . . was the masthead of a . . theatrical column in a magazine.

B *v.t.* **1** Send (a sailor) to the masthead as a punishment. E19. **2** Raise (a yard, sail, etc.) to its position on the mast or at the masthead. M19.

†**mast-holm** *n.* L16–E18. [f. MAST *n.*[2] + HOLM *n.*[2]] The holm-oak.

mastic /ˈmastɪk/ *n.* & *a.* LME. [(O)Fr. f. late L *mastichum*, *masticha*, vars. of *mastiche* f. Gk *mastikhē*, presumed to be f. *mastikhan*: see MASTICATE.] **A** *n.* **1** A gum or resin which exudes from the bark of mastic trees (see sense 2), used in making varnish and (formerly) medicinally. Also *mastic gum*, *gum mastic*. LME. **2** In full *mastic tree*. An evergreen shrub, *Pistacia lentiscus* (family Anacardiaceae), yielding mastic gum, native to the eastern Mediterranean region. Also, any of certain related trees and shrubs yielding similar gums, *esp.* (more fully *American mastic*) *Schinus molle*, native to tropical America. LME. **b** A timber tree of the W. Indies and Florida, *Sideroxylon foetidissimum* (family Sapotaceae). M17. †**3** In full *herb mastic*. A labiate shrub, *Thymus mastichina*, native to Iberia and N. Africa. Cf. MARUM. L16–M19. **4** Orig., a kind of resinous or bituminous cement. Now, any waterproof, plastic, putty-like substance used as a filler, sealant, etc. E18. **5** A liquor flavoured with mastic gum; = MASTIKA. L19. **6** The colour of mastic; a shade of pale yellow. L19. **B** *attrib.* or as *adj.* **1** Of a cement, adhesive, etc.: of the nature or consisting of mastic (sense A.4 above). E19. **2** Of the colour of mastic; pale yellow. L19.

masticable /ˈmastɪkəb(ə)l/ *a. rare.* M19. [f. next + -ABLE.] Able to be masticated.

mastica'bility *n.* M19.

masticate /ˈmastɪkeɪt/ *v.t.* M17. [Late L *masticat-* pa. ppl stem of *masticare* f. Gk *mastikhan* grind the teeth, rel. to *masasthai* chew and perh. to synon. L *mandere*: see -ATE[3].] **1** Grind (food) to a pulp in the mouth; grind with the teeth, chew. M17. **2** Mechanically reduce (rubber etc.) to a pulp. M19.

mastication /mastɪˈkeɪʃ(ə)n/ *n.* LME. [Late L *masticatio(n-)*, f. as prec.: see -ATION.] The action or process of masticating something.

masticator /ˈmastɪkeɪtə/ *n.* L17. [f. prec. + -OR.] **1** In *pl.* The teeth, the jaws. *joc.* L17. **2** A person or animal that chews. E19. **3** A machine for grinding or pulping. M19.

masticatory /ˈmastɪkət(ə)ri/ *a.* & *n.* E17. [mod.L *masticatorius*, *-um*, f. *masticare*: see MASTICATE, -ORY[1], -ORY[2].] **A** *adj.* **1** Of, pertaining to, or concerned with mastication. E17. **2** *Med.* Affecting the organs of mastication. M19. **B** *n.* A medicinal substance to be chewed. E17.

mastiff /ˈmastɪf, ˈmɑː-/ *n.* ME. [Obscurely repr. OFr. *mastin* (mod. *mâtin*) f. Proto-Romance f. L *mansuetus* (earlier *mansues*) tamed, tame: see MANSUETE.] A breed of large strong dog with a large head, drooping ears, and pendulous lips, used as a watchdog; a dog of this breed. Also *mastiff dog*.

bull-mastiff: see BULL *n.*[1] & *a.* *Tibetan mastiff*: see TIBETAN *a.*

Comb.: **mastiff bat** any of numerous heavily built bats with a broad muzzle that belong to the family Molossidae and occur in warmer parts of the world; *esp.* an American bat of the genus *Molossus* or the genus *Eumops*.

†**mastiff** *a.* LME. [Alt. of MASTY by assoc. w. prec. and *massive*.] **1** Of a swine: fattened. Only in LME **2** Massive, solid, bulky; burly. L15–M18.

mastigoneme /ˈmastɪgəniːm/ *n.* M20. [f. Gk *mastigo-*, *mastix* whip + *nēma* thread.] *Biol.* Any of the hairlike structures situated, usu. in rows, on the flagellum of some unicellular eukaryotes.

mastigophore /ˈmastɪgəfɔː/ *n.* M17. [f. as next: see -PHORE.] †**1** *Gk Hist.* An usher carrying a whip for dispersing crowds. *rare* (Dicts.). Only in M17. **2** *Zool.* = FLAGELLATE *n.* L19.

mastigophorous /mastɪˈgɒf(ə)rəs/ *a.* E19. [f. Gk *mastigophoros*, f. *mastig-*, *mastix* whip: see -PHOROUS.] **1** That carries a scourge. *joc.* E19. **2** *Zool.* Having flagella; flagellate. L19.

Also **mastigo'phoric** *a.* E19.

mastigure /ˈmastɪgjʊə/ *n.* M19. [mod.L *mastigura*, *-urus*, f. Gk *mastig-*, *mastix* whip + *oura* tail.] A N. African agamid lizard of the genus *Uromastix*, with a spiny tail.

mastika /maˈstiːkə/ *n.* E20. [mod.Gk *mastikha*.] A liquor flavoured with mastic gum; = MASTIC *n.* 5.

masting /ˈmɑːstɪŋ/ *n.* E17. [f. MAST *n.*[1], *v.* + -ING[1].] **1** The action or process of fitting a ship etc. with masts. E17. **2** Masts collectively. E18. **3** The action of felling trees for masts. *N. Amer.* E18.

mastitis /maˈstʌɪtɪs/ *n.* M19. [f. Gk. *mastos* breast + -ITIS.] *Med.* Inflammation of the mammary gland in people or animals.

summer mastitis: see SUMMER *n.*[1]

-mastix /ˈmastɪks/ *suff.* [f. Gk *mastix* scourge, after *Homeromastix* scourge of Homer (the name given to the grammarian Zoïlus on account of the severity of his censure of the Homeric poems).] Forming quasi-Gk combs. designating persons or books etc. violently hostile to some person, class, institution, etc., as *Puritanomastix*, *Satiromastix*, etc.

¶Used esp. in 17.

masto- /ˈmastəʊ/ *comb. form*. [In sense 1 f. MASTOID; in sense 2 f. Gk *mastos* breast: see -O-.] **1** Pertaining jointly to the mastoid process or bone and some other part of the skull, as *mastoparietal* etc. **2** Affecting or involving the mammary gland.

masto'dynia *n.* (*Med.*) neuralgia of the female breast E19. **ma'stopathy** *n.* any disease or dysfunction of the female breast M19.

mastodon /ˈmastədɒn/ *n.* E19. [f. Gk *mastos* breast + -ODON.] *Palaeont.* A large extinct mammal of the genus *Mammut*, resembling the elephant but having nipple-shaped tubercles in pairs on the crowns of the molar teeth.

masto'donic *a.* (*rare*) = MASTODONTIC M19. **masto'dontic** *a.* of or pertaining to a mastodon; resembling the mastodon: M19.

mastoid /ˈmastɔɪd/ *a.* & *n.* M18. [Fr. *mastoïde* or mod.L *mastoides* f. Gk *mastoeidēs*, f. *mastos* breast: see -OID.] **A** *adj.* Chiefly *Anat.* & *Zool.* Shaped like a female breast. Also, of or pertaining to the mastoid process or bone. M18.

mastoid bone (*a*) the mastoid process; (*b*) in fishes and reptiles, a bone of the skull homologous with this. **mastoid process** a conical prominence of the temporal bone behind the ear.

B *n.* **1** *Anat.* = *mastoid process*, *mastoid bone* above. M19. **2** = MASTOIDITIS. *colloq.* M20.

ma'stoidal *a.* of or pertaining to the mastoid process M19. **mastoi'dectomy** *n.* (an instance of) surgical incision of the mastoid process, in order to relieve infection within its cavities L19. **mastoi'ditis** *n.* inflammation of (the cavities of) the mastoid process L19.

†**mastuprate** *v.i.* E–M17. [Alt. of L *masturbat-* (see next) as if f. L *manus* hand + *stuprare* defile: see -ATE[3].] = next.

†**mastupration** *n.*: only in E17. †**mastuprator** *n.*: only in M19.

masturbate /ˈmastəbeɪt/ *v.* M19. [L *masturbat-* pa. ppl stem of *masturbari*, of unkn. origin: see -ATE[3]. Cf. prec.] **1** *v.t.* Stimulate the genitals of (oneself, another person) manually for sexual pleasure. M19. **2** *v.i.* Stimulate one's own genitals for sexual pleasure. L19.

masturbator *n.* a person who masturbates M19. **masturbatory** *a.* of, pertaining to, or involving masturbation M19.

masturbation /mastəˈbeɪʃ(ə)n/ *n.* M18. [L *masturbatio(n-)*, f. as prec.: see -ATION. Cf. MASTUPRATION.] The action or practice of masturbating; manual stimulation of the genitals for sexual pleasure.

mutual masturbation manual stimulation of each other's genitals by two people for sexual pleasure.

masty /ˈmɑːsti/ *a.* Long *obs.* exc. *dial.* LME. [f. MAST *n.*[2] + -Y[1]. Cf. MASTIFF *a.*] **1** †**a** Of a pig: fattened. LME–M16. **b** Burly, big-bodied. M16. †**2** Producing mast. L16–M17.

†**masures** *n.pl. rare.* E17–L18. [Fr.] Ruins (of buildings); ramshackle habitations.

masurium /məˈz(j)ʊərɪəm/ *n.* E20. [f. G *Masuren*, a region of NE Poland + -IUM.] *Hist. Sci.* The element of atomic no. 43 (later named *technetium*), mistakenly claimed to have been discovered spectroscopically.

mat /mat/ *n.*[1] Also †**-tt.** [OE *matt*, *meatt(e)*, corresp. to MDu. *matte*, OHG *matta* (Du. *mat*, G *Matte*), f. WGmc f. late L *matta*.] **1** A piece of a coarse material, usu. woven or plaited, used for lying, sitting, or kneeling on, or as a protective covering for floors, walls, etc. Also, a small rug. OE. **b** *spec.* An article of this kind, or of material such as rubber or cork, placed on the floor near a door for people entering to wipe their shoes on. Cf. *doormat* s.v. DOOR. M17. **c** *Bowls.* = FOOTER *n.*[1] 2. L19. **d** A piece of padded material, canvas, etc., on which wrestling bouts, gymnastic displays, etc., take place. E20. **2** A coarse piece of sacking on which a feather bed is laid. Also, a bed-covering, a quilt. Now *dial.* ME. **3** *Naut.* A thick web of rope yarn used to protect standing rigging from the friction of other ropes. ME. **4 a** Material of which mats are made; plaited or woven rushes, straw, etc.; matting. *obs.* exc. *attrib.* E16. **b** A bag made of matting. L17. **5** A thin flat article (orig. of plaited straw, but now usu. of cork, plastic, etc., and often ornamental) to be placed under a dish, plate, etc., in order to protect the surface beneath from heat, moisture, etc. E19. **6** *transf.* A thick tangled mass of hair, vegetation, etc., esp. forming a layer. E19. **b** *Engin.* A flat interwoven or lattice structure used as a foundation or support. L19. **7** A type of cloak or cape worn by Maoris; hence, *the* Maori way of life. *NZ.* E19. **8** The closely-worked part of a lace design. M19.

1 S. PEPYS A very fine African mat, to lay upon the ground under a bed of state. C. ACHEBE Joy was now having her hair done, seated on a mat on the floor. *bath-mat*, *collision-mat*, *prayer-mat*, etc. **on the mat** *colloq.* in trouble with some authority; ≈ *on the carpet* (b) s.v. CARPET *n.* **b** *Independent* The excitement . . on seeing an envelope, the address handwritten, on the mat. **d go to the mat** contend in wrestling etc. (*with*); *fig.* argue, struggle, (*with*). **5** *beer-mat*, *drip-mat*, *place-mat*, *table-mat*, etc. **6** A. DESAI His chin sank down into the mat of black hair on his chest. **7** KOROWAI *mat*.

Comb.: **mat-grass** a wiry grass of moorland and mountainside, *Nardus stricta*; **mat-man** *slang* a wrestler; **matweed** any of various rushlike grasses, as marram; **mat-work** (*a*) matting; a structure like a mat; (*b*) physical exercises performed on a mat.

mat /mat/ *n.*[2] M18. [Abbrev.] *Cards.* = MATADOR 2.

mat /mat/ *n.*[3] *colloq.* E20. [Abbrev.] = MATINÉE 1.

mat /mat/ *n.*[4] E20. [Abbrev.] = MATRIX *n.* 3a.

mat *n.*[5] var. of MATT *n.*[1]

mat *a.* var. of MATT *a.*

mat /mat/ *v.*[1] Infl. **-tt-.** LME. [f. MAT *n.*[1]] †**1** *v.i.* Make mats. *rare.* Only in LME. **2** *v.t.* Cover or provide with mats or matting. M16. **3** *v.t.* Cover with something resembling a mat; cover with an entangled or hardened mass. L16. **4** *v.t.* Form into a mat; entangle or entwine (*together*) in a thick mass. L16. **b** Make by interlacing, form into a mat. E19. **5** *v.i.* Become entangled (*together*), form tangled masses. M18. **6** *v.t.* Put 'on the mat'; reprimand; = CARPET *v.* 2. *colloq.* M20.

3 F. W. ROBERTSON A temple . . matted with ivy. A. MASON Clods of earth still matted the hair. **4** A. TUCKER To . . disentangle the boughs where they had matted themselves together.

mat *v.*[2] var. of MATT *v.*

-mat /mat/ *suff.* [Abbrev. of -MATIC.] Forming names (freq. proprietary) of equipment that works automatically, or establishments operating such equipment, as *Laundromat*.

Matabele /matəˈbiːli, -ˈbeɪli/ *n.* & *a.* E19. [f. Bantu *ma-* tribal pref. + Sesotho *(le)tebele*: see NDEBELE.] **A** *n.* Pl. **-s**, same. A Ndebele, esp. in Zimbabwe. E19.

B *attrib.* or as *adj.* Of or pertaining to the Indebele, esp. in Zimbabwe. M19.

Matabele ant a large black stinging ant, *Megaponera foetens*, found in Zimbabwe.

matachin /matəˈʃiːn/ *n. obs.* exc. *Hist.* L16. [Fr. (now *matassin*) f. Sp. *matachin* or It. *mattaccino*, of unkn. origin.] **1** A kind of sword dancer in an extravagantly fanciful costume. L16. †**2** A masked dance performed by matachins (usu. three). L16–L17.

matador /ˈmatədɔː/ *n.* Also (esp. senses 2, 3) **-ore.** L17. [Sp., f. *matar* kill.] **1** A bullfighter whose task is to kill the bull. L17. **2** In some card-games (as quadrille, ombre, solo): any of the highest trumps so designated by the rules of the game. L17. **3** A domino game in which halves are matched so as to make a total of seven; any of the dominoes which have seven spots altogether, together with the double blank. M19.

Comb.: **matador pants** = TOREADOR *pants*.

mata'dora *n.* a female matador M20.

mataeology /matɪˈɒlədʒi/ *n. rare.* M17. [f. Gk *mataios* vain + -O- + -LOGY.] Vain or unprofitable discourse.

matagouri /matəˈgʊəri, -ˈgaʊri/ *n. NZ.* M19. [Alt. of Maori TUMATAKURU.] A thorny New Zealand shrub, *Discaria toumatou* (family Rhamnaceae). Also called (*wild*) *Irishman*, *tumatakuru*.

Mata Hari /mɑːtə ˈhɑːri/ *n.* M20. [The name taken by Margaretha Gertruida Zelle (1876–1917), Du. courtesan and spy, f. Malay *matahari* sun, f. *mata* eye + *hari* day.] A beautiful and seductive woman spy.

matai /ˈmatʌɪ/ *n.*[1] M19. [Maori.] A New Zealand coniferous tree, *Podocarpus spicata* (also called *black pine*); the light-coloured wood of this tree.

matai /məˈtʌɪ/ *n.*[2] E20. [Samoan.] In a Samoan extended family, the person who is chosen to succeed to a chief's or orator's title and honoured as the head of the family.

matamata /matəˈmatə/ *n.* M19. [Prob. of S. American origin.] A S. American turtle, *Chelus fimbriatus*, with a lumpy carapace, long neck, and broad flat head.

matapi /ˈmatəpiː/ *n.* L18. [Arawak.] A pliable basket used in Guyana for expressing the poisonous juice from the root of the cassava or manioc.

matata /ˈmatətə/ *n. NZ.* M19. [Maori.] = *fern-bird* s.v. FERN *n.*

match /matʃ/ *n.*[1] [OE *ġemæċċa* f. Gmc, rel. to base of *ġemaca* MAKE *n.*[1]] †**1** A husband, a wife, a partner, a lover. Also, an animal's mate. OE–M17. †**2** An equal in age, rank, position, etc.; a fellow, a companion. OE–L16. **3a** A person (occas. a number of persons or a thing) able to contend with another as an equal. ME. †**b** An opponent, a rival. LME–L16. **4a** A person, thing, action, etc., equal to another in some quality. LME. **b** A person or thing that exactly corresponds to or resembles another, or that forms a matching pair with another; *Computing* a record, string, etc., that matches the requirements of a search or is identical with a given record etc. E16. **c** A more or less matching pair; two persons, things, or sets each the counterpart of the other. M16. †**5** A matching of adversaries against each other; a contest viewed with regard to the equality or inequality of the parties. LME–E17. **6** A contest or competitive trial of skill in some sport, exercise, or operation, in which two or more people or teams compete against each other; an engagement or arrangement for such a contest. Also, a contest in which animals are made to compete. M16. †**7** An agreement, a bargain. M16–E18. **8a** A marriage, a marriage agreement, *esp.* one viewed as more or less advantageous with regard to wealth or status. L16. †**b** The action of marrying; relationship by marriage. L16–M17. **c** A person viewed with regard to his or her eligibility for marriage, esp. on the grounds of wealth or rank. L16. †**d** A heraldic representation of a marriage. Only in 17. **9** *Electr.* An equality of impedance between two coupled devices. M20.

3a K. ISHIGURO Sometimes, even Father's no match for Mother. **4a** E. GASKELL I don't believe there is his match anywhere for goodness. **b** J. PALMER You've got two nice creatures, they are right elegant matches. **6** *Economist* In the cricket match, the 'Windies' scraped home in a nail-biting finish. *ploughing-match*, *return match*, *slanging-match*, *test match*, etc. **8a** H. ALLEN Although Don Luis was . . older than his bride . . the match seemed a fortunate one. **c** G. MEREDITH He's the great match of the county.

Phrases: **be a match for** be equal to. **find** or **meet one's match** encounter or come up against one's equal, esp. in strength or ability. *game, set, and match*: see GAME *n. hatches, matches, and dispatches*: see HATCH *n.*[2] **make a match** bring about a marriage. *man of the match*: see MAN *n. meet one's match*: see *find one's match* above. **more than a match for** superior to in strength, ability, etc. *steal a match*: see STEAL *v. varsity match*: see VARSITY *a.*

Comb.: **match ball** (*a*) in cricket etc., a ball of the standard specified by the laws of the game; (*b*) in tennis, a ball that may decide a match; **match-book** (*a*) a book containing dates and details of horse-races; (*b*) *Cricket* a book containing the scores etc. of matches played by a club or an eleven; **match-card** *Cricket* a card summarizing the score and listing the players in batting order, a score-card; **match-fit** *a.* in good physical condition for a match, sufficiently fit to play in a match; **match-play** (*a*) the play in a match; (*b*) *Golf* play in which the score is reckoned by counting the holes gained on each side; **match-point** (*a*) the state of a game when one side or player needs only one point to win the match; this point; (*b*) *Bridge* a unit of scoring in tournament play; **match race** orig., a race run between two horses; more widely, a race run as a competition; **match-rifle** a rifle used in shooting competitions; **match-winner** a person whose skill etc. contributes to or brings about victory in a match; **match-winning** *a.* (of a player, style of play, etc.) contributing to or bringing about victory in a match.

match /matʃ/ *n.*[2] LME. [OFr. *meiche*, *mesche* (mod. *mèche*) corresp. to Sp., Port. *mecha*, It. *miccia*, which have been referred to L *myxa* (f. Gk *muxa*) nozzle of a lamp, (in med.L) lamp-wick.] †**1** The wick of a candle or lamp. LME–M17. **2** A piece of wick, cord, etc., designed to burn steadily when lit at the end, and used to fire a cannon, ignite a trail of gunpowder etc. M16. **b** The material of which this is made; cord etc. prepared for ignition. L16. **3** A piece of cord, cloth, paper, etc., dipped in melted sulphur so as to be readily ignited with a tinder-box, and used to light a candle or lamp, or to set fire to fuel. *obs.* exc. *Hist.* M16. **b** A similar object used for fumigation. E18. **4** A short slender piece of wood, wax, etc., tipped with a composition which bursts into flame when rubbed on a rough or specially prepared surface or, formerly, when brought into contact with a chemical reagent. M19.

4 M. LOWRY Three cigarettes were lit on one match. P. BOWLES Give me a match . . My candle's gone out. *Congreve match*, *lucifer match*, *safety match*, *slow match*, etc.

Phrases: **put a match to** set fire to.

Comb.: **matchbook** a book (BOOK *n.* 8) containing matches; **match-head** the mass of flammable composition forming the tip of a match; **match-safe** *US* a container for holding matches and keeping them dry or preventing accidental ignition.

match /matʃ/ *a. obs.* exc. *techn.* L15. [f. attrib. & appositive uses of MATCH *n.*[1]] That matches; corresponding.

Special collocations & comb.: **match dissolve** *Cinemat.* & *Television* a fade from one picture to another in which a similar or identical object appears in the same place in each picture. **match-plane** either of two planes used respectively to form the groove and tongue in grooving and tonguing boards.

match /matʃ/ *v.*[1] LME. [f. MATCH *n.*[1]] **1** **a** *v.t.* Encounter with equal power, be a match for; equal, rival. Formerly also, encounter as an adversary. LME. †**b** *v.i.* Meet in combat, fight (*with*). LME–L16. **2** *v.t.* Place in opposition or conflict *against* or *with*. Also, place in competition or comparison *with*. LME. **3** *v.t.* **a** Arrange (persons or things) according to fitness or equality; place in a suitable or equal pair or set; provide with an adversary or competitor of equal power. Also foll. by *up*. Usu. in *pass.*, esp. in *ill-*, *well-matched*. LME. **b** Proportion, make to correspond *to* or *with*. L17. **c** *Carpentry.* Provide (a board) with a tongue and a groove on opposite edges, to allow interlocking with other boards. M19. **d** *Electr.* Equalize (two coupled impedances) so as to bring about the maximum transfer of power from one to the other; make (a device) equal in effective impedance *to*. E20. **4** **a** *v.t.* Join in marriage (esp. w. ref. to the suitability or otherwise of the partnership); procure a match for; connect (a family) by marriage. Also foll. by *to*, *with*. *arch.* LME. **b** *v.i.* Join oneself in marriage, marry. Foll. by *into*, *with*. Now *rare* exc. *dial.* M16. †**5** *v.t.* Associate, join in companionship or cooperation; put together so as to form a pair or set *with* another person or thing. L15–M17. **6** **a** *v.i.* Be equal *with*; be suitably coupled (*with*); correspond, harmonize, go. M16. **b** *v.t.* Be equal to; correspond to, go with, be the match or counterpart of. L16. †**7** *v.t.* Regard, treat, or speak of as equal. L16–E17. **8** *v.t.* **a** Find or produce an equal to. Also, find (a person or thing) suitable for another. L16. **b** Provide with a suitable addition or counterpart; *spec.* (seek to) find material, a garment, etc., that complements or accords with (another). E17. †**9** *v.t.* Procure as a match. *rare* (Shakes.). Only in L16.

1a K. ISHIGURO We are now a mighty nation, capable of matching any of the Western nations. 2 SHAKES. *Rom. & Jul.* That fair.. With tender Juliet match'd, is now not fair. W. S. MAUGHAM The prospect of matching his wits with such an antagonist excited him. 3b M. ARNOLD God doth match His gifts to man's believing. 4a J. TIPPER I am heartily glad your dear Sister is so happily match'd to Mr. Stevens. 6a OED These patterns do not match. b A. C. BOULT His knowledge of Westminster Abbey was exceeded by none and matched by few. W. TREVOR She put on her red and black dress, with a hat that perfectly matched it. 8a J. PORY Excellent wines, and sugars which cannot be matched. b J. HAWTHORNE As if it were a question of matching knitting-yarns.

Phrases: ill-matched: see ILL *a.* & *adv.* **matched orders** *Comm.* systems of manipulation on a stock exchange involving artificial treatment of orders to buy and sell shares etc. **match up to** attain the standard of, equal. *mix and match*: see MIX *v.* **to match** corresponding in a particular respect with something already mentioned. *well-matched*: see WELL *adv.*

Comb.: **match-up** the action of pairing or setting in opposition, esp. in sport or politics, two suited or equal persons or things (cf. sense 3 above); a pair so matched; a contest between such a pair.

matcher *n.* E17.

match /matʃ/ *v.*[2]*t.* E18. [f. MATCH *n.*[2]] Fumigate (wine, liquor, or casks) by burning sulphur matches (MATCH *n.*[2] 3).

matchable /ˈmatʃəb(ə)l/ *a.* M16. [f. MATCH *v.*[1] + -ABLE.] **1** Able to be matched, equalled, or rivalled. M16. †**2** Comparable, equal, similar. Foll. by *to*, *with*. L16–L17. †**3** Suitable, accordant. E17–E19.

¶Earlier in UNMATCHABLE.

matchableness *n.* E17.

matchboard /ˈmatʃbɔːd/ *n.* & *v.* M19. [f. MATCH *a.* + BOARD *n.*] *Carpentry.* **A** *n.* A board which has a tongue along one edge and a groove in the opposite edge, so that it interlocks with other similar boards. M19. **B** *v.t.* Cover or provide with matchboards. L19.

matchboarding *n.* matchboards fitted together to form a building material M19.

matchbox /ˈmatʃbɒks/ *n.* L18. [f. MATCH *n.*[2] + BOX *n.*[2]] †**1** *Mil.* A metal tube full of small holes, in which a soldier carried a lighted match (MATCH *n.*[2] 2). Only in L18. **2** A box for holding matches M19. **3** Something very small, *esp.* a very small house or flat. E20.

3 JOYCE Got notice to quit this match-box and am.. looking for a flat.

Comb.: **matchbox bean** *Austral.* a leguminous climbing plant, *Entada phaseoloides*; the seed-pod of this, used to make matchboxes.

matchcoat /ˈmatʃkəʊt/ *n. obs.* exc. *Hist.* Orig. †**matchco** (pl. **-os**). M17. [Virginia Algonquian *matchkore*, alt. by pop. etym. as if f. MATCH *n.*[1], *v.*[1] + COAT *n.*] A kind of mantle formerly worn by American Indians, orig. made of fur skins and later of coarse woollen cloth; the cloth used for this.

matchet *n.* see MACHETE.

matchless /ˈmatʃlɪs/ *a.* M16. [f. MATCH *n.*[1] + -LESS.] **1** Having no match, without an equal, incomparable. M16. †**2** That are not a match or pair. *rare* (Spenser). Only in L16. †**3** Unmarried. E–M17.

1 H. AINSWORTH There she stood before him, in all her matchless beauty.

matchlock /ˈmatʃlɒk/ *n.* M17. [f. MATCH *n.*[2] + LOCK *n.*[2]] *Hist.* A gunlock in which a match (MATCH *n.*[2] 2) is placed to ignite the powder; a gun having such a lock.

matchmake /ˈmatʃmeɪk/ *v.i.* Infl. as MAKE *v.* E17. [Back-form. f. MATCHMAKER *n.*] Scheme or contrive to bring about a marriage. Chiefly as *matchmaking* vbl n. & ppl a.

matchmaker /ˈmatʃmeɪkə/ *n.* M17. [f. MATCH *n.*[1] + MAKER.] **1** A person who schemes or enjoys scheming to bring about a match or marriage. M17. **2** A person who arranges a boxing-match or other sporting contest. E18.

1 *Woman & Home* The Princess of Wales, reportedly an incorrigible matchmaker during Sarah's and Andrew's courtship.

match-maker /ˈmatʃmeɪkə/ *n.* M17. [f. MATCH *n.*[2] + MAKER.] A person who makes matches (MATCH *n.*[2]).

matchstick /ˈmatʃstɪk/ *n.* & *a.* L18. [f. MATCH *n.*[2] + STICK *n.*[1]] **A** *n.* **1** (The stick of) a wooden match. L18. **2** A thin person. *slang.* M20.

1 E. PIZZEY She.. looked down at her legs. 'They're not like matchsticks any more.'

B *attrib.* or as *adj.* Very thin, skeletal. Also, (of a drawing, a drawn figure, etc.) executed with short straight lines. M20.

Guardian Matchstick men—taught by adults, copied by infants—can be death to child art.

matchwood /ˈmatʃwʊd/ *n.* L16. [f. MATCH *n.*[2] + WOOD *n.*[1]] †**1** Touchwood. Only in L16. **2** Wood suitable for matchsticks. L16.

2 (**break** etc.) **into matchwood** (break) into minute pieces.

mate /meɪt/ *n.*[1] ME. [(O)Fr. *mat* in *eschec mat* CHECKMATE.] *Chess.* = CHECKMATE.

fool's mate: see FOOL *n.*[1] *scholar's mate*: see SCHOLAR *n.* See also SELFMATE, STALEMATE.

mate /meɪt/ *n.*[2] ME. [MLG *mate*, *gemate* (Flem. *gemaat*, Du. *maat*) = OHG *gimmazzo*, f. WGmc bases of Y- (denoting association), MEAT *n.*, the lit. sense being 'messmate'.] **1** †**a** A creature, a fellow, a chap. Freq. *contempt.* ME–E17. **b** A companion, a fellow, a comrade, a friend; a fellow worker. LME. **c** (With specifying wd.) A person with whom one shares accommodation. M17. **d** A helper or assistant to a more skilled worker. L19. **2** Used as a form of address to an equal. *colloq.* LME. **3** *Naut.* **a** The rank of officer on a merchant ship next below that of master, divided into *first*, *second*, *third*, etc., *mate*, according to seniority; an officer of this rank. L15. **b** An assistant to an officer on board ship. L15. **c** An assistant to a warrant officer in the US navy. L19. **4** A suitable associate or (formerly) adversary; an equal, a match. *arch.* M16. **5** **a** A partner in marriage. Formerly also (*rare*), a lover. M16. **b** Either of a pair of animals. L16. **6** Either of a pair of things; a counterpart, a parallel; *spec.* a solid or fixed point on a railway line which pairs or mates with the movable tongue or switch on the other rail. L16.

1b P. BARKER She expected to see two of his mates but no, the men were strangers. *New Society* I was with my mate, John's brother. *playmate*, *running mate*, *schoolmate*, etc. **be** or **go mates with** be an associate or partner of. c *cabin-mate*, *cell-mate*, *flat-mate*, *room-mate*, etc. 2 S. L. ELLIOTT Well, well—pleased to meet you mate. *Listener* Look, mate, we *live* here. 3a W. H. GRAY An old scholar, who was first mate on board a ship. b BOATSWAIN*'s mate. master's mate*: see MASTER *n.*[1] 5b B. GILROY Like a bird calling for its mate she called and called for Danny. 6 N. MARSH The glove is Mrs. Wilde's... She wore the mate yesterday.

matehood *n.* = MATESHIP I E20. **mateless** *a.* L16.

mate *n.*[3] var. of MATY *n.*

†**mate** *a.* ME. [(O)Fr. *mat* mated at chess f. Pers. *māt* in phr. (used in chess) *šāh māt*: see CHECKMATE, MATE *n.*[1]] **1** Overcome, vanquished; exhausted, worn out. ME–M16. **2** Dejected, downcast; alarmed, distraught. ME–M16. **3** Mated in chess. LME–L16.

mate /meɪt/ *v.*[1] ME. [Fr. *mater*, f. as prec.] **1** *Chess.* **a** *v.t.* Checkmate. ME. †**b** *v.i.* Be checkmated. LME–L16. †**2** *v.t.* Overcome, defeat, subdue. ME–E17. **3** *v.t.* Nonplus, confound; make powerless or worthless. *obs.* exc. *dial.* ME. †**4** *v.t.* Put out of countenance; make helpless; daunt, abash; stupefy. LME–E19. **5** *v.t.* Exhaust, weary; dull (passion). *obs.* exc. *Sc. dial.* LME.

1a G. ORWELL It was like trying to make a move at chess when you were already mated.

mate /meɪt/ *v.*[2] E16. [f. MATE *n.*[2]] **1** **a** *v.t.* Be a match for; equal, rival. Now *poet.* E16. **b** *v.i.* Claim equality *with*. *arch.* L17. **2** *v.i.* & *t.* = MATCH *v.*[1] 4. L16. **3** *v.t.* Join suitably *with*; associate, treat as comparable *with*. L16. **4** **a** *v.t.* Pair (animals) for breeding. Also foll. by *up*. E17. **b** *v.i.* Of animals: come together for breeding; copulate (*with*). M19. **5** **a** *v.i.* Associate or keep company *with*. M19. **b** *v.t.* Accompany suitably. *rare.* L19. **6** *Mech.* **a** *v.i.* Of a part: make a good or proper fit *with*. E20. **b** *v.t.* Fit or join (a part) *with* or *to*. M20.

1a SIR W. SCOTT In speed His galley mates the flying steed. 2b LYTTON I fear that the king will be teased into mating my sister with the Count of Charolois. 4a *Oban Times* The first common seal in Scotland to give birth in captivity.. was mated last April. b D. H. LAWRENCE Dark, like a lair where strong beasts had lurked and mated. 5a G. NAYLOR Contempt mates well with pity. 6b *Time* The orbiter will be 'mated' to a carrier plane.

Phrases: **mating call** a characteristic call used by an animal during the mating season, esp. by males to attract potential mates. **mating season** a period of the year during which members of an animal species mate, often adopting a special coloration and characteristic behaviour.

maté /ˈmateɪ/ *n.* E18. [Sp. *mate* f. Quechua *mati.*] **1** A gourd, calabash, etc., in which the leaves of the shrub maté are infused. Also *maté-cup*. E18. **2** (An infusion of) the leaves of a S. American shrub, *Ilex paraguariensis* (family Aquifoliaceae); the shrub itself. Also more fully *yerba maté*. M18.

matelassé /mat(ə)ˈlaseɪ, *foreign* matlase (*pl. same*)/ *n.* & *a.* Also **-lasse**. L19. [Fr., pa. pple of *matelasser* to quilt, f. *matelas* MATTRESS.] **A** *n.* A silk or wool fabric with a raised design. L19. **B** *adj.* Having a raised design like quilting. L19.

matelot /ˈmatləʊ/ *n.* E20. [Fr. = sailor. Cf. MATLOW.] **1** A sailor. *Naut. slang.* E20. **2** A shade of blue. E20.

matelote /ˈmat(ə)ləʊt, *foreign* matlɔt (*pl. same*)/ *n.* E18. [Fr., f. as prec.] A dish of fish etc. served in a sauce of wine, onions, etc.

mater /ˈmeɪtə/ *n.* L16. [L, lit. 'mother'.] **1** The thickest plate of an astrolabe. *obs.* exc. *Hist.* L16. **2** Mother. Cf. PATER. Chiefly *joc.* & *School slang* M19.

¶Earlier in DURA MATER, PIA MATER.

†**materas** *n.* var. of MATRASS *n.*[1]

Mater Dolorosa /ˌmeɪtə dɒləˈrəʊsə/ *n. phr.* Pl. **Matres Dolorosae** /ˌmeɪtriːz dɒləˈrəʊsiː/. E19. [med.L, lit. 'sorrowful mother'.] (A title of) the Virgin Mary, as having a role in the Passion of Christ; a representation, in painting or sculpture, of the Virgin Mary sorrowing; *transf.* a woman resembling the sorrowful Virgin in appearance, manner, etc.

materfamilias /meɪtəfəˈmɪlɪas/ *n.* M18. [L, f. MATER + *familias* old genit. of *familia* FAMILY.] The female head of a family or household.

material /məˈtɪərɪəl/ *a.* & *n.* ME. [(O)Fr. *matériel*, †*-ial* f. late L *materialis*, f. L *materia* matter: see -AL^1.] A *adj.* 1 Of or pertaining to matter or substance; formed or consisting of matter; corporeal. ME. †b Forming the material or substance of a thing. *rare* (Shakes.). Only in E17. 2a *Philos.* Of or pertaining to matter as opp. to form. LME. b *Logic.* Concerned with the matter, not the form, of reasoning. E17. c *Philos.* & *Theol.* That is so by conduct or matter, rather than by motive or form. M17. 3a Serious, important; of consequence. L15. b Pertinent, relevant; essential *to*; *US Law* having a logical connection with the facts at issue. L15. c Chiefly *Brit. Law.* Of evidence or a fact: significant, influential, esp. to the extent of determining a cause, affecting a judgement, etc. L16. †d Full of sense or sound information. Only in 17. 4 Of conduct, a point of view, etc.: not elevated or spiritual. L16. 5 Concerned with or involving matter or the use of matter; relating to the physical, as opp. to the intellectual or spiritual, aspect of things; concerned with physical progress, bodily comfort, etc. M17. †6 Physically bulky, massive, or solid. M17–M18.

1a J. BUTLER The material world appears to be .. boundless and immense. *Annabel* The accumulation of material things has never been of great significance to me. 3a G. GROTE The Athenians had a material interest in the quarrel. b SIR W. SCOTT Certain passages material to his understanding the rest of this important narrative. 4 C. BRONTË What I saw struck me .. as grossly material, not poetically spiritual. 5 M. MCCARTHY No nation with any sense of material well-being would endure the food we eat.

Special collocations & comb.: *material cause*: see CAUSE *n. material culture*: see CULTURE *n.* **material implication** *Logic* a relationship which always holds between two propositions except when the first is true and the second false. **material noun** *Gram.* = *mass noun* s.v. MASS *n.*^{2} & *a.* **material object** *Philos.* an object regarded as having a physical existence independent of consciousness. **material-objectness** *Philos.* the state of existing as a material object. **material thing** = *material object* above.

B *n.* 1 *sing.* & in *pl.* a The matter of which a thing is or may be made. LME. b The constituent parts of something. M17. 2 *sing.* & in *pl.* Information, evidence, ideas, etc., for use in writing a book or script, drawing a conclusion, etc. LME. 3 In *pl.* Items needed for an activity. L16. 4 Cloth, fabric. M19. 5 With specifying wd: a person or thing suitable for a specific role or purpose. L19.

1a SWIFT A palace may be built .. of materials so durable as to last for ever. K. CLARK The new material that was going to transform the art of building—iron. **raw material** unmanufactured material, material from which something is or may be made. 2 H. MOORE A painter .. must be continually gathering material from his experience of things seen. E. KUZWAYO I returned to Thabu' Nehu to seek out material for my book. 3 *building materials, cleaning materials, writing materials*, etc. 4 S. PLATH The girls had pocket-book covers made out of the same material as their dresses. 5 *academic material, officer material.*

Comb.: **material(s) clerk**: who controls the supply of materials in a business; **material(s) control**: of working materials in relation to production plans; **material(s) handling** the movement and storage of materials in a factory; **material(s) man** a man responsible for the materials required in building or manufacturing; **material(s) science** the branch of science that deals with the structure and properties of materials, esp. with relation to their (potential) usefulness.

materialise *v.* var. of MATERIALIZE.

materialism /məˈtɪərɪəlɪz(ə)m/ *n.* M18. [f. prec. + -ISM.] 1 *Philos.* The doctrine that nothing exists except matter and its movements and modifications. Also, the doctrine that consciousness and will are wholly due to the operation of material agencies. M18. 2 *Art.* A tendency to lay stress on the material aspect of the objects represented. M19. 3 A tendency to prefer material possessions and physical comfort to spiritual values; a way of life based on material interests. M19. 4 *Chr. Ch.* An excessive emphasis on the material aspects of the sacraments at the expense of the spiritual. *contempt.* M19.

3 A. N. WILSON The materialism of the modern world .. washing machines, glass and steel, and a Comprehensive School.

Phrases: *dialectical materialism*: see DIALECTICAL *a.* 2.

materialist /məˈtɪərɪəlɪst/ *n.* & *a.* M17. [f. as prec. + -IST.] A *n.* 1 *Philos.* An adherent of materialism. M17. 2 A person who takes a material view of things or who favours material possessions and physical comfort. M19.

1 D. HUME The materialists, who conjoin all thought with extension. 2 P. MORTIMER My mother's family, stern materialists who believed devoutly in success.

B *attrib.* or as *adj.* Materialistic. M19.

materialistic /məˌtɪərɪəˈlɪstɪk/ *a.* M19. [f. prec. + -IC.] Pertaining to, characterized by, or devoted to materialism.

P. B. CLARKE A highly industrialized, materialistic society like Britain.

materialistically *adv.* M19.

materiality /mətɪərɪˈalɪti/ *n.* E16. [Orig. f. med.L *materialitas* material quality or embodiment. Later f. MATERIAL + -ITY.] 1 That which constitutes the matter or material of something. Long *rare.* E16. 2a The quality of being composed of matter. L16. b That which is material; in *pl.*, material things. E19. 3 Material aspect or character. L16. 4 Now chiefly *Law.* The quality of being relevant or significant. M17.

2a G. ADAMS The decomposition of the rays of light proves their materiality. 3 DENNIS POTTER It .. cannot release the smallest breath of life out of the suffocatingly dead materiality of things.

materialize /məˈtɪərɪəlʌɪz/ *v.* Also **-ise**. E18. [f. MATERIAL *a.* + -IZE.] 1 *v.t.* Make material; represent in material form. Also, make materialistic. E18. 2 *Spiritualism.* a *v.t.* Cause (a spirit etc.) to appear in bodily form. M19. b *v.i.* Of a spirit etc.: appear in bodily form. L19. 3 *v.i.* Come into perceptible existence; become actual fact. Also (*colloq.*), arrive or be present when expected. L19.

1 N. HAWTHORNE I had the glimmering of an idea, and endeavoured to materialize it in words. 2a A. MASON He had astonished thousands by materializing objects out of nothing. 3 HENRY MILLER I was always being promised things which never materialized. W. TREVOR Words formed on her lips but did not materialize.

materiali'zation *n.* M19. **materializer** *n.* (*rare*) E19.

materially /məˈtɪərɪəli/ *adv.* LME. [f. MATERIAL *a.* + -LY^2.] 1 Chiefly *Philos.* & *Logic.* With regard to matter as opp. to form. LME. 2 In respect of matter or material substance. L16. †3 Of speaking or writing: with an appropriate use of matter; soundly; pertinently. E17–M18. 4 In a material degree; substantially, considerably. Also, in respect of material interests. M17.

2 L. HOWELL As he created all Men out of the same matter, they are materially equal. 4 G. GROTE Tribes differing materially in habits and civilization. H. JAMES She .. had even contributed materially to the funds required.

materialness /məˈtɪərɪəlnɪs/ *n.* L16. [f. MATERIAL *a.* + -NESS.] The quality of being material.

materia medica /məˈtɪərɪə ˈmɛdɪkə/ *n. phr. pl.* M17. [mod.L tr. Gk *hulē iatrikē* healing material.] The remedial substances used in the practice of medicine; (treated as *sing.*) the branch of medicine that deals with their origins and properties.

materia prima /məˈtɪərɪə ˈprʌɪmə/ *n. phr.* M16. [L.] = *first matter* s.v. MATTER *n.*

materiate /məˈtɪərɪeɪt/ *v.t.* Now *rare* or *obs.* M17. [L *materiat-* pa. ppl stem of *materiare* (in cl.L construct of wood, in scholastic use, as in sense 2 below), f. *materia* MATTER *n.*] *Scholastic Philos.* 1 Make (a form) inherent in a particular matter. M17. 2 Supply or be the matter or material part of. L17.

matériel /materjɛl, mətɪərɪˈɛl/ *n.* E19. [Fr., use as n. of adj.: see MATERIAL.] 1 Available means or resources. Also (*rare*), technique. E19. 2 The equipment, supplies, etc., used in an army, navy, or business. Opp. *personnel.* E19.

2 *Time* The U.S. tacitly backed the rebellion, encouraging the Shah to supply the Kurds with arms and matériel.

mater lectionis /ˌmeɪtə lɛktɪˈəʊnɪs/ *n. phr.* Pl. ***matres lectionis*** /ˌmeɪtriːz lɛktɪˈəʊniːz/. M17. [mod.L, lit. 'mother of reading'.] A letter which has the function of a diacritical mark; *spec.* in Hebrew writing, a sign indicating a vowel sound.

maternal /məˈtəːn(ə)l/ *a.* L15. [(O)Fr. *maternel* or f. L *maternus*, f. *mater* MOTHER *n.*^{1}: see -AL^1.] 1 Of or pertaining to a mother or mothers; motherly. L15. b Having the instincts of motherhood. L18. c *spec.* Of or pertaining to the mother in pregnancy and childbirth; uterine (as opp. *foetal*). E19. 2 That is a mother. Now *rare.* E16. 3 Belonging to a mother. E17. 4 Inherited from or related through a mother or the mother's side. M17.

1 J. ROSENBERG Mothers .. tired from their exhausting maternal duties. b G. F. ATHERTON She is not maternal .. I never saw a baby held so awkwardly. c A. S. NEILL Who can say what effect .. maternal rigidity has on the newborn baby? 3 DICKENS Interposed Lavvy, over the maternal shoulder. 4 H. BAILEY Vera's maternal grandfather .. was Welsh.

Special collocations: **maternal language, tongue** (now *rare*) a mother tongue, one's native language.

maternalism *n.* maternal instincts; the characteristics or state of motherhood: M20. **materna'listic** *a.* motherly, maternal M20. **maternally** *adv.* M17.

maternity /məˈtəːnɪti/ *n.* & *a.* E17. [Fr. *maternité* f. med.L *maternitas*, f. L *maternus*: see -ITY.] A *n.* 1 The quality or condition of being a mother; motherhood. E17. 2 The qualities or conduct characteristic of a mother; motherliness. E19. 3 A maternity ward or hospital. L19.

1 S. KITZINGER She feels tied down by maternity and domesticity. 2 H. DRUMMOND The tender maternity of the bird.

B *attrib. adj.* 1 For a woman during and just after childbirth. L19. 2 Of a garment etc.: suitable for a pregnant woman. L19.

1 *maternity benefit, maternity hospital, maternity leave*, etc. 2 *maternity dress, maternity wear*, etc.

mateship /ˈmeɪtʃɪp/ *n.* L16. [f. MATE *n.*^{2} + -SHIP.] 1 The condition of being a mate; companionship, fellowship. Formerly also, equality. Now chiefly *Austral.* L16. 2 *Zool.* Pairing of one animal with another. E20.

matey /ˈmeɪti/ *n. colloq.* M19. [Dim. of MATE *n.*^{2}: see -Y^6.] A companion, a mate.

DOCKYARD *matey.*

matey /ˈmeɪti/ *a.* Also **maty**. Compar. **matier**, superl. **matiest**. E20. [f. MATE *n.*^{2} + -Y^1.] Like a mate or mates; friendly, familiar, sociable.

mateyness /ˈmeɪtɪnɪs/ *n.* Also **matiness**. E20. [f. MATEY *a.* + -NESS.] Friendliness, sociableness.

matfellon /ˈmatfɛl(ə)n/ *n. obs.* exc. *dial.* LME. [OFr. *matefelon*, app. f. *mater* MATE *v.*^{1} + *felon* FELON *n.*^{2}] Knapweed.

math /mɑːθ, maθ/ *n.*^{1} *obs.* exc. *dial.* and in AFTERMATH, LATTERMATH. [OE *mǣþ* corresp. to MHG *māt, mād-* (G *Mahd*), f. Gmc base also of MOW *v.*^{1}: see -TH^1.] A mowing; the amount of a crop mowed.

math /mʌt/ *n.*^{2} E19. [Hind. *maṭh* f. Skt *maṭha* hut, cell.] In the Indian subcontinent, a Hindu convent of celibate mendicants.

math /maθ/ *n.*^{3} *N. Amer. colloq.* M19. [Abbrev.] = MATHEMATICS. Cf. MATHS.

new math: see NEW *a.*

¶In British English used in writing only, *maths* being used in speech.

mathe /meɪð/ *n.* Long *rare* or *obs.* exc. *Sc.* [OE *maþa, maþu*, cogn. w. OS *maþo*, OHG *mado* (Du., G *Made*), ON *maðkr* (see MADDOCK), Goth. *maþa*, f. Gmc: ult. origin unkn.] A maggot, a grub, a worm.

mathematic /maθ(ə)ˈmatɪk/ *n.* & *a.* LME. [(O)Fr. *mathématique* or L *mathematicus* f. Gk *mathēmatikos*, f. *mathēma(t-)* something learned, science, f. base of *manthanein* learn. As n. repr. ellipt. uses of the fem. adjs. (*sc.* L *ars, disciplina*, Gk *tekhnē, theōria*).] A *n.* See also MATHEMATICS. 1 Each of the sciences or disciplines of the quadrivium, i.e. geometry, arithmetic, astronomy, and music; these disciplines collectively. *obs.* exc. *Hist.* LME. †2 A mathematician; an astrologer. M16–L17. †3 In *pl.* Dice which roll true. L17–E18. 4 =

MATHEMATICS. *rare*. M19. **B** *adj*. = MATHEMATICAL *a*. Now *rare*. LME.

¶Gradually superseded as n. between 16 and 18 by MATHEMATICS in the modern sense (f. which sense 4 is a late back-form. emphasizing the unity of the subject, app. after G *Mathematik*).

mathematical /maθ(ə)ˈmatɪk(ə)l/ *a.* & *n.* LME. [f. as prec.: see -ICAL.] **A** *adj.* **1a** Of, pertaining to, or of the nature of mathematics. LME. **b** Of a person: expert in mathematics; studying or teaching mathematics. E16. **c** Of a concept, object, etc.: as understood or defined in mathematics. M16. †**2a** Astrological. M16–L17. **b** Mechanical. Only in M16. **3** *transf.* **a** Rigorously exact. M17. **b** Exactly regular. L18.

3a COLERIDGE A theory conducted throughout with mathematical precision. b J. HAWTHORNE Straight paths and mathematical grass-plots.

Special collocations: *mathematical* GEOGRAPHY. *mathematical induction*: see INDUCTION 1c. **mathematical instrument** an instrument used in drawing geometrical figures (usu. in *pl.*). **mathematical linguist** an expert in or student of mathematical linguistics. **mathematical linguistics** a branch of linguistics that deals with the application of mathematical models and procedures to the analysis of linguistic structure. **mathematical logic** logic that is mathematical in its method, manipulating symbols according to definite and explicit rules of derivation; symbolic logic. **mathematical logician** an expert in or student of mathematical logic. **mathematical philosophy** the branch of philosophy that deals with the nature of mathematics. **mathematical point**: having a position but no extension in any dimension. **mathematical table** a table of the values of a mathematical function (e.g. logarithms) for different values of the variable.

B *n.* In *pl.* Mathematical objects or entities. *obs.* exc. *Hist.* M16.

mathematically /maθ(ə)ˈmatɪk(ə)li/ *adv.* M16. [f. MATHEMATIC *a.* or prec.: see -ICALLY.] **1** With mathematical accuracy or exactness. M16. **2** By mathematical methods; according to mathematical principles; in terms of mathematics. L16.

mathematician /maθ(ə)məˈtɪʃ(ə)n/ *n.* LME. [(O)Fr. *mathématicien*, f. L *mathematicus* MATHEMATIC: see -IAN.] **1** An expert in or student of mathematics. LME. †**2** Chiefly *Hist.* An astrologer. L16–E18.

mathematicise *v.* var. of MATHEMATICIZE.

mathematicism /maθ(ə)ˈmatɪsɪz(ə)m/ *n.* M20. [f. MATHEMATIC *a.* + -ISM.] *Philos.* The opinion that everything can be described ultimately in mathematical terms, or that the universe is fundamentally mathematical.

mathematicize /maθ(ə)ˈmatɪsʌɪz/ *v.* Also **-ise**. M19. [f. MATHEMATIC *a.* + -IZE.] **1** *v.i.* = MATHEMATIZE 1. *rare*. M19. **2** *v.t.* Consider or treat (a subject) in mathematical terms; reduce to mathematics. Chiefly as *mathematicized*, *mathematicizing* ppl adjs. M19.

mathematiciˈzation *n.* the action of mathematicizing; the state of being mathematicized: M20.

mathematico- /maθ(ə)ˈmatɪkəʊ/ *comb. form.* [f. MATHEMATICAL, MATHEMATICS: see -O-.] Partly mathematical and partly —, as *mathematico-logical*.

mathematics /maθ(ə)ˈmatɪks/ *n.pl.* L16. [Pl. of MATHEMATIC *n.*, prob. after Fr. (*les*) *mathématiques*, repr. L *mathematica* neut. pl., Gk (*ta*) *mathēmatika*: see -ICS.] Orig. (treated as *pl.*, freq. with *the*), the sciences or disciplines of the quadrivium collectively; later, these and optics, architecture, navigation, etc. Now (treated as *sing.*), the abstract deductive science of space, number, quantity, and arrangement, including geometry, arithmetic, algebra, etc., studied in its own right (more fully *pure mathematics*), or as applied to various branches of physics and other sciences (more fully *applied mathematics*). Colloq. abbrev. *maths*, (N. Amer.) *math*.

higher mathematics: see HIGH *a.*, *adv.*, & *n.* *new mathematics*: see NEW *a.*

mathematize /ˈmaθ(ə)mətʌɪz/ *v.* Also **-ise**. E18. [f. MATHEMAT(IC + -IZE.] **1** *v.i.* Reason mathematically; perform mathematical calculations. E18. **2** *v.t.* Regard or treat (a problem, object, etc.) in mathematical terms; mathematicize. L19.

mathematiˈzation *n.* mathematical treatment; the state of being mathematized: M20.

mathemeg /ˈmaθəmɛg/ *n.* L18. [Cree dial. *ma:ðame:k*. Cf. TITTYMEG.] A catfish of the genus *Ictalurus*, of N. American lakes.

mathern *n.* var. of MAYTHEN.

mathesis /məˈθiːsɪs/ *n.* *arch.* LME. [Late L f. Gk *mathēsis*, f. base of *manthanein* learn.] Mental discipline; learning or science, *esp.* mathematical science. Also, the personification of this.

mathetic /məˈθɛtɪk/ *a.* E19.

maths /maθs/ *n.* *colloq.* E20. [Abbrev.] = MATHEMATICS. Cf. MATH *n.*[3]

new maths: see NEW *a.*

Mathurin /ˈmaθjʊrɪn/ *a.* & *n.* E17. [The chapel of St *Mathurin* in Paris.] *Eccl. Hist.* **A** *adj.* Of or pertaining to an order of regular canons (officially called Trinitarians) founded in 1198 by St John of Matha for the redemption of Christian captives. E17. **B** *n.* A Mathurin canon. L17.

-matic /ˈmatɪk/ *suff.* M20. [f. AUTO)MATIC *a.*] Forming ns. (usu. proprietary names) w. the sense 'a device which works automatically or mechanically,' as *Instamatic*.

matico /məˈtiːkəʊ/, *foreign* maˈtiko/ *n.* M19. [Sp. *yerba Matico*, f. *yerba* herb + *Matico* dim. of *Mateo* Matthew: reputedly named after a soldier who discovered its medicinal properties.] A Peruvian wild pepper, *Piper angustifolium*; the dried leaves of this plant, formerly used as a styptic.

matie /ˈmeɪti/ *n.* Chiefly *Sc.* Also **mattie** /ˈmati/ & other vars. E18. [Du. *maatjes* (*haring* herring), earlier *maetgens-*, *maeghdekins-*, f. *maagd* maid (cf. MAIDEN *n.*) + *-ken* -KIN. See also MATJE.] A herring in the condition considered best for food, when the roe or milt is not fully developed.

matier, matiest *adjs.* see MATEY *a.*

matière /matjɛːr/ *n.* E20. [Fr.] The quality an artist gives to the pigment used.

Matilda /məˈtɪldə/ *n.* L19. [Female forename.] **1** A bushman's bundle, a swag. *Austral. slang.* L19. **2** A British tank in use in the war of 1939–45. M20.

1 waltz Matilda, walk Matilda carry a swag.

matily /ˈmeɪtɪli/ *adv.* L20. [f. MATEY *a.* + -LY[2].] In a friendly, familiar, or sociable fashion.

matin /ˈmatɪn/ *n.* Pl. **matins, mattins** (treated as *sing.* or *pl.*). ME. [(O)Fr. *matines* pl. (sing. *matin*) f. eccl.L *matutinas* use as n. of fem. accus. pl. (prob. sc. *vigilias* watches) of *matutinus* MATUTINE.] **I** In *pl.* **1** *Eccl.* **a** (The canonical hour of) an office appointed in the breviary, properly a night office, but also said at daybreak (with the following office, lauds) or on the previous evening. ME. **b** The entire public service preceding the first mass on Sunday. Long *obs.* exc. *Hist.* ME. **c** An Anglican service held in the morning with a set form similar to that of evensong, based on the earlier matins with elements from lauds and prime. M16. **2** More fully *devil's matins*. A service of devil-worship attributed to witches; *transf.* an uproar. E17–E19. **3** A morning duty, occupation, or performance. *arch.* M17. **II** *sing.* †**4** A morning. *rare.* LME–M19. **III** In *pl.* & *sing.* **5** The morning song of birds. *poet.* E16.

Phrases: *Parisian matins*: see PARISIAN *a.*

matin /ˈmatɪn/ *a.* *literary.* M17. [f. prec.] Belonging to the early morning; = MATINAL *a.*

mâtin /mɑtɛ̃/ *n.* Pl. pronounced same. L16. [Fr.: see MASTIFF *n.*] A watchdog; a mastiff.

matinal /ˈmatɪn(ə)l/ *a.* Now *rare.* E19. [(O)Fr., f. *matin*: see MATIN *n.*, -AL[1].] Belonging to or taking place in the morning; early. Also, early-rising.

matinée /ˈmatɪneɪ, *foreign* matine (*pl. same*)/ *n.* Also **-nee**. M19. [Fr. = morning, what occupies a morning, f. *matin*: see MATIN *n.*, -EE[1].] **1** An afternoon performance at a theatre, cinema, or concert hall. Abbrev. MAT *n.*[3] M19. **2** A woman's lingerie jacket. L19.

Comb.: **matinée coat** a baby's short outer garment; **matinée idol** a handsome actor of a type supposed to be admired chiefly by women; **matinée jacket** = *matinée coat* above.

matiness *n.* var. of MATEYNESS.

matins *n.pl.* see MATIN *n.*

matipo /ˈmatɪpəʊ/ *n.* Pl. **-os**. M19. [Maori.] Either of two New Zealand evergreen trees, *Pittosporum tenuifolium* (family Pittosporaceae), which bears clusters of purple flowers (also *black matipo*), and *Rapanea australis*, the mapau (also *red matipo*).

matje /ˈmatjə/ *n.* Also **-jes** /-jəs/. L19. [f. as MATIE, reintroduced f. Du.] More fully *matje herring*. A young herring, esp. salted or pickled.

matless /ˈmatlɪs/ *a.* L19. [f. MAT *n.*[1] + -LESS.] Not provided with a mat or mats.

matlo *n.* var. of MATLOW.

matlow /ˈmatləʊ/ *n.* *slang.* Also **-lo**, pl. **-loes**. E20. [Repr. a pronunc. of MATELOT.] A sailor.

matoke /maˈtəʊkeɪ/ *n.* M20. [Bantu.] A preparation of the flesh of bananas, used as food in Uganda; bananas.

matra /ˈmɑːtrə/ *n.* L19. [Skt *mātrā*.] In Indian music, a beat or a subdivision of a beat within a rhythmic phrase.

matraca /məˈtrɑːka/ *n.* E20. [Sp.] In Spain, a mechanical wooden rattle used instead of church bells on Good Friday.

matrass /ˈmatrəs/ *n.*[1] Orig. **materas**. LME. [OFr. *materas*, *matelas* (later *matras*) f. late L *mattaris* f. cl.L *mataris*, of Gaulish origin.] A quarrel or bolt for a crossbow.

matrass /ˈmatras/ *n.*[2] E17. [Fr. *matras*, perh. f. prec. (w. allus. to the shape), infl. by Arab. *maṭra* leather bottle, or ult. f. Gk *metrētēs* a liquid measure.] *Chem.* A glass vessel with a round or oval body and a long neck, formerly used in distillation.

Matres Dolorosae *n. phr.* pl. of MATER DOLOROSA.

matres lectionis *n. phr.* pl. of MATER LECTIONIS.

matri- /ˈmatri, ˈmeɪtri/ *comb. form.* [f. L *matr-*, *mater* MOTHER *n.*[1] + -I-.] Forming ns. and adjs., esp. in *Anthropol.* & *Sociol.*, w. the sense '(of or pertaining to) relationship through a female line'.

matriˈcentred, matriˈcentric *adjs.* centred on the mother, having a mother as the head of the family or household M20. **matriclan** *n.* a matrilineal clan M20. **matriˈfocal** *a.* matricentric M20. **matriˈlateral** *a.* (esp. of marriage between cousins) pertaining to or designating a relationship in which a mother and one of her siblings or other relatives are both involved as parents M20.

matriarch /ˈmeɪtrɪɑːk/ *n.* E17. [f. as prec. on false anal. of *patriarch*: see -ARCH.] A woman who is the head of a family or tribe, or who dominates an organization; an elderly woman who is highly respected.

L. WOOLF Mrs. Eckhard was one of those immensely energetic, dominating Jewish matriarchs.

matriarchal /meɪtrɪˈɑːk(ə)l/ *a.* M19. [f. as prec. + -AL[1], after *patriarchal*.] Of or pertaining to a matriarch or maternal rule; pertaining to, of the nature of, or based on matriarchy; *Anthropol.* designating or exhibiting a form of social organization characterized by matriarchy.

B. JOWETT They .. are getting too old for the matriarchal form of government. E. B. TYLOR The Indian tribes further south are largely matriarchal.

matriarchalism *n.* the condition or state of having a matriarchal organization or rule L19.

matriarchate /meɪtrɪˈɑːkət/ *n.* & *a.* L19. [f. as prec. + -ATE[1], after *patriarchate*.] *Anthropol.* **A** *n.* A matriarchal community; a matriarchal form of social organization. L19. **B** *adj.* Matriarchal. L19.

matriarchy /ˈmeɪtrɪɑːki/ *n.* L19. [f. as prec. + -Y[3], after *patriarchy*.] A form of social organization in which the mother is the head of the family and descent and relationship are reckoned through the female line; a society, organization, etc., governed by a woman or women; government by a woman or women.

Matric /məˈtrɪk/ *n.* *colloq.* Also **m-**. L19. [Abbrev.] Matriculation.

matric /ˈmeɪtrɪk/ *a.* E20. [f. MATR(IX *n.* + -IC.] *Math.* Of or pertaining to a matrix or matrices.

matrical /ˈmatrɪk(ə)l, məˈtrʌɪk(ə)l/ *a. rare.* E17. [Late L *matricalis*, f. as MATRIX *n.*: see -AL¹.] Pertaining to a matrix or womb.

matricaria /matrɪˈkɛːrɪə/ *n.* L16. [med.L *matricaria*, f. L *matric-* MATRIX *n.* + *-aria* -ARY¹.] Orig., feverfew, *Tanacetum parthenium*. Later (*Bot.*), any of various plants of the composite family belonging or formerly belonging to the genus *Matricaria*, which originally included feverfew.

†matrice *n.* var. of MATRIX *n.*

matrices *n.pl.* see MATRIX *n.*

matricide /ˈmʌɪtrɪsʌɪd, ˈmeɪtrɪ-/ *n.* L16. [In sense 1 f. L *matricidium*, in sense 2 f. L *matricida*, both f. *matr-*, *mater* mother: see -CIDE.] **1** The action of killing one's mother. L16. **2** A person who kills his or her mother. M17.

matriˈcidal *a.* M19.

matricula /məˈtrɪkjʊlə/ *n. obs.* exc. *Hist.* Pl. **-lae** /-liː/. M16. [Late L *matricula* dim. of L MATRIX *n.*: see -CULE.] A list or register of people belonging to an order, society, etc.; a certificate of enrolment in such a register.

matriculability /məˌtrɪkjʊləˈbɪlɪti/ *n.* E20. [f. MATRICUL(ATE *v.* + -ABILITY.] Ability or fitness to matriculate.

matriculae *n.* pl. of MATRICULA.

matriculant /məˈtrɪkjʊl(ə)nt/ *n.* M19. [med.L *matriculant-* pres. ppl stem of *matriculare*: see MATRICULATE *v.*, -ANT¹.] A person who matriculates; a candidate for matriculation.

matricular /məˈtrɪkjʊlə/ *a.* & *n.* L16. [med.L *matricularius*, *-aris*, f. as MATRICULA: see -AR¹, -AR². In branch A.II also infl. by MATRIX *n.*] A *adj.* **I1** Pertaining to or of the nature of a matricula, esp. (*Hist.*) the one listing the contributions that member States were required to make to the Holy Roman (later the German) Empire. L16. **II†2** Of a language: original; from which others are derived. Only in L18. **3** Of or belonging to the womb. L19. **†B** *n.* = MATRICULA. Only in E17.

matriculate /məˈtrɪkjʊlət/ *a.* & *n.* L15. [med.L *matriculatus* pa. pple of *matriculare*: see next, -ATE².] A *adj.* **†1** Matriculated. L15–E18. **2** Of, pertaining to, or for a person who has been matriculated. L19. **B** *n.* A person who has been matriculated. E18.

matriculate /məˈtrɪkjʊleɪt/ *v.* L16. [med.L *matriculat-* pa. ppl stem of med.L *matriculare*, f. as MATRICULA: see -ATE³.] **1a** *v.t.* Enter (a name) in the register of a university, college, or polytechnic; admit as a member of a university, college, or polytechnic. L16. **b** *v.i.* Be admitted as a member of a university, college, or polytechnic. M19. **†2** *v.t. gen.* Insert (a name) in a register or official list; admit or incorporate into a society etc. by this means; enrol (a soldier). L16–E18. **b** Adopt (a child, a foreign custom); naturalize; consign *to* maternal care. L16–M18. **3** *v.t. Her.* (chiefly *Sc.*). Record (arms) in an official register. L16.

matriculation /mətrɪkjʊˈleɪʃ(ə)n/ *n.* L16. [med.L *matriculatio(n-)*, f. as prec.: see -ATION.] **1** The action or an act of matriculating; *esp.* formal admission into a university, college, or polytechnic. Also, an examination to qualify for this. L16. **†b** A certificate of matriculation. Only in M17. **2** *Her.* (chiefly *Sc.*). A registration of armorial bearings. E19.

matrilineal /matrɪˈlɪnɪəl/ *a.* E20. [f. MATRI- + LINEAL *a.*] Of, pertaining to, or based on (kinship with) the mother or the female line; recognizing kinship with and descent through females.

ˈmatriline /-lʌɪn/ *n.* a matrilineal line of descent M20. **matrilineage** *n.* matrilineal lineage M20. **matrilineˈality** *n.* M20. **matrilineally** *adv.* E20. **matrilinear** *a.* = MATRILINEAL E20. **ˈmatriliny** *n.* the observance of matrilineal descent and kinship E20.

matrilocal /matrɪˈləʊk(ə)l/ *a.* E20. [f. MATRI- + LOCAL *a.*] Designating or pertaining to a pattern of marriage in which a married couple settles in the wife's home or community.

matriloˈcality *n.* the custom of matrilocal residence M20. **matrilocally** *adv.* M20.

matrimonial /matrɪˈməʊnɪəl/ *a.* LME. [(O)Fr., or L *matrimonialis*, f. *matrimonium*: see next, -AL¹.] **1** Of or pertaining to marriage. LME. **2** Derived from marriage. M16. **3** Tending or calculated to promote marriage; inclining towards marriage. M18.

1 T. HARDY There were hardly two houses in Little Hintock unrelated by some matrimonial tie. A. KENNY My parents sold their matrimonial home and made a formal agreement of separation. 2 J. H. BURTON Conferring on the Dauphin the 'crown matrimonial'. 3 H. FIELDING She had matrimonial charms in great abundance.

Special collocations: **matrimonial agency** = MARRIAGE *bureau*. **matrimonial agent** a person who works in a matrimonial agency. **matrimonial bureau** = MARRIAGE *bureau*.

matrimonially *adv.* (*a*) according to the manner or laws of marriage; (*b*) by right of marriage; (*c*) as regards the married state: E17. **†matrimonious** *a.* = MATRIMONIAL *a.* M17–M19.

matrimony /ˈmatrɪməni/ *n.* ME. [AN *matrimonie* = OFr. *matremoi(g)ne* f. L *matrimonium*, f. *matr-*, *mater* MOTHER *n.*¹: see -MONY.] **1** The rite or institution of marriage; the action of marrying. ME. **†b** A marriage; an alliance by marriage. LME–M18. **†c** The marriage service. Only in E18. **2** The state of being married; the relation between married persons. ME. **†3** A husband, a wife. Only in 17. **4** *Cards.* An obsolete game played with a full pack of cards and resembling Newmarket. Also, the marriage of a king and queen. E19. **5** A mixture of two different items of food or drink. *slang* & *dial.* E19.

Comb.: **matrimony-vine** either of two kinds of boxthorn, *Lycium barbarum* and *L. chinense*, shrubs of the nightshade family sometimes grown in gardens.

matriotism /ˈmeɪtrɪətɪz(ə)m/ *n.* M19. [Alt. of PATRIOTISM after L *matr-*, *mater* MOTHER *n.*¹] Love of one's mother country, university, school, etc.

matrist /ˈmatrɪst/ *n.* & *a.* M20. [f. MATRI- + -IST, after *patrist*.] *Psychol.* A *n.* A person whose behaviour or attitude is influenced or dominated by the mother. M20. **B** *attrib.* or as *adj.* Of or pertaining to such influence or domination. M20.

matrix /ˈmeɪtrɪks/ *n.* Also **†matrice**. Pl. **-trixes**, **-trices** /-trɪsiːz/. LME. [L = breeding-female, register, (in late L) womb, f. *matr-*, *mater* MOTHER *n.*¹: see -TRIX.] **1** The uterus, the womb. *arch.* LME. **2** A place or medium in which something is bred, produced, or developed; a setting or environment in which a particular activity or process occurs or develops; a place or point of origin and growth. M16. **b** *Anat.* & *Zool.* The formative tissue from which a tooth, hair, feather, nail, etc., arises. M19. **c** *Bot.* The substrate on which a fungus or a lichen grows. M19. **3a** A mould in which something is cast or shaped; *Printing* a metal block in which a character is stamped or engraved so as to form a mould for casting a type; an engraved die used to strike a coin or medal. L16. **b** The bed or hollowed place in a slab in which a monumental brass is fixed. M19. **c** A (positive or negative) copy of an original disc recording that is used in the making of other copies. E20. **d** *Photogr.* A dyed print in relief used for transferring colour to a final colour print. M20. **4a** The rock material in which a fossil, gem, etc., is embedded. M17. **b** Any relatively fine or homogeneous substance in which coarser or larger particles are embedded; *spec.* in *Building*, lime, fine cement. M19. **5** *Math.* An array of symbols or mathematical expressions arranged in a rectangle of rows and columns, treated as a single entity and now usu. written within round brackets. M19. **b** *transf.* A rectangular arrangement or tabulation of words, data, etc.; *spec.* in *Logic*, (a part of) a truth-table, a set of basic truth-tables. E20. **c** *Logic.* An expression that would become a statement if its variables were replaced by constants (i.e. by names of individuals, classes, or statements, as appropriate). E20. **d** *Computing.* An interconnected array of elements that has a number of inputs and outputs and resembles a lattice in its design. M20. **e** *Television* & *Broadcasting.* A circuit designed to produce outputs that are linear combinations, in different proportions, of a number of inputs. Freq. *attrib.* M20. **f** An organizational structure in which two or more lines of command, responsibility, or communication may run through the same individual. M20. **g** *Computing.* A rectangular array of potential image points. Chiefly in *dot matrix* s.v. DOT *n.*¹, *matrix printer* below. M20. **6** *Dentistry.* A plate of metal or composition to serve as a temporary wall for a cavity of a tooth during filling. L19.

2 H. E. MANNING The root and matrix of the Catholic Church. H. GEORGE This is the matrix in which mind unfolds. A. W. READ The family is the matrix in which we see the bubbling up of linguistic experimentation. 3a *Archaeological Journal* Matrix of the seal of William Picard. 4b J. E. GORDON The function of the matrix is simply to glue together a number of strong fibres. 5 *diagonal matrix*, *row matrix*, *unitary matrix*, etc. b PAY-OFF *matrix*. *progressive matrices*: see PROGRESSIVE *a.*

Comb.: **matrix mechanics** *Physics* a form of quantum mechanics in which the operators corresponding to physical coordinates (position, momenta, etc.) are represented by matrices with time-dependent elements; **matrix number** a number assigned by a record company to a matrix in the manufacture of records; **matrix printer** a printer in which each printed character is made up of a pattern of tiny dots; **matrix sentence** *Ling.* in transformational grammar, a sentence into which subordinate sentences are introduced.

matrix /ˈmeɪtrɪks/ *v.t.* M20. [f. the n.] Combine (signals) in different proportions so as to obtain one or more linear combinations of them.

matroclinous /matrəˈklʌɪnəs/ *a.* E20. [f. L *matr-*, *mater* MOTHER *n.*¹ + -O- + Gk *klinein* to lean, slope + -OUS.] *Genetics.* Resembling the female more closely than the male parent; involving or possessing a tendency to inherit a character or characters from the female parent only.

ˈmatrocliny *n.* matroclinous inheritance E20.

matron /ˈmeɪtr(ə)n/ *n.* Also (esp. as a title) **M-**. LME. [(O)Fr. *matrone* f. L *matrona*, f. *matr-*, *mater* MOTHER *n.*¹] **1** A married woman, *esp.* one characterized by dignity, staid discreet behaviour, and plump motherly appearance. LME. **2** *spec.* A married woman considered as having expert knowledge in matters of childbirth, pregnancy, etc. Now only (*Hist.*) in *jury of matrons* s.v. JURY *n.* LME. **3a** Orig., a woman in charge of the domestic arrangements of a public institution. Later, a woman (occas. a man) in charge of the nurses in a hospital (now also called *senior nursing officer*); a woman managing the domestic arrangements of a school etc., esp. the care of the sick. M16. **b** A female prison warder. *US.* M20. **4** A female dog or horse used for breeding. M20.

1 R. K. NARAYAN She would grow into a bulky matron. R. CHRISTIANSEN A Roman matron, exerting influence from the family hearth by force of her incorruptible virtue. *transf.*: SHAKES. *Rom. & Jul.* Come, civil night, Thou sober-suited matron, all in black. **matron of honour** a married woman who attends the bride at a wedding. 3a *Beano* Now I shall visit matron and get my sore finger bandaged. R. MANNING She obtained a post at Great Ormond Street Hospital. . . She would have ended up as matron.

matronage *n.* (*a*) a body of matrons; matrons collectively; (*b*) guardianship by a matron; (*c*) matronhood: L18. **matronhood** *n.* the condition of being a matron M19. **matronism** *n.* (*rare*) (*a*) qualities regarded as befitting a matron; (*b*) guardianship by a matron: E17. **matronlike** *a.* resembling or regarded as befitting a matron; matronly: L16. **matronship** *n.* (*a*) (with possess. adj., as *your* etc. *matronship*) *joc.* a mock title of respect given to a matron; (*b*) matronhood; (*c*) the position or office of matron: L16.

matronal /ˈmeɪtr(ə)n(ə)l/ *a.* E17. [Fr. f. L *matronalis*, f. *matrona*: see prec., -AL¹.] **1** Of or pertaining to a matron; regarded as befitting a matron. E17. **2** Having the characteristics of a matron. M18.

Matronalia /matrəˈneɪlɪə/ *n.* E18. [L *Matronalia* use as n. of neut. pl. of *matronalis*: see prec.]

Rom. Hist. A festival in honour of the goddess Juno and her son Mars, celebrated by married women.

matronize /ˈmeɪtr(ə)nʌɪz/ *v.* Also **-ise**. M18. [f. MATRON + -IZE.] **1** *v.t.* Render matronly. M18. **2** *v.i.* Become or be made a matron. E19. **3** *v.t.* **a** Act as a female chaperon to. E19. **b** *US.* Preside as a matron over, act as hostess to, (a party etc.). L19. **4** *v.t.* Of a woman: patronize. *joc.* M19.

matronly /ˈmeɪtr(ə)nli/ *a.* M17. [f. as prec. + -LY[1].] Like a matron; characteristic of or regarded as befitting a matron.

M. R. MITFORD She was making a handsome matronly cap. W. WHARTON The nursing supervisor. . A big matronly type.

matronliness *n.* M19.

matronly /ˈmeɪtr(ə)nli/ *adv.* L16. [f. as prec. + -LY[2].] In the manner of a matron.

matronymic /matrəˈnɪmɪk/ *n.* & *a.* L18. [f. L *matr-*, *mater* MOTHER *n.*[1], after *patronymic.*] **A** *n.* A metronymic; a metronymic suffix. L18. **B** *adj.* = METRONYMIC *a.* L19.

matross /məˈtrɒs/ *n.* M17. [Du. *matroos* f. Fr. *matelots* pl. of *matelot* sailor.] *Mil. Hist.* An artillery soldier next in rank below a gunner.

matsu /ˈmatsuː/ *n.* E18. [Jap.] Any of several Japanese pine trees, *esp.* the Japanese red pine, *Pinus densiflora*, and the black pine, *P. thunbergii*.

matsuri /matˈsuːri/ *n.* E18. [Jap.] A solemn festival celebrated periodically at Shinto shrines in Japan.

matt /mat/ *n.*[1] Also **mat.** M19. [Fr. *mat* use as n. of *mat* MATT *a.*] **1** In gilding, (the appearance of) unburnished gold; a dull lustreless appearance. M19. **2** A border of dull gold round a picture. Also, a sheet of cardboard placed on the back of a print etc. and covered by a mount forming a margin round the print; the mount itself. M19. **3** In glass-painting, a layer of colour matted on the glass (see MATT *v.* 2). L19. **4** A punch for producing a matt finish on metal. L19.

†matt *n.*[2] var. of MAT *n.*[1]

matt /mat/ *a.* Also **mat, matte**. M17. [Fr. *mat*, sometimes identified with (O)Fr. *mat* MATE *a.*] Of a colour, surface, etc.: without lustre, dull.

matt /mat/ *v.t.* Also **mat** (infl. **-tt-**). E17. [In senses 1 and 2 f. Fr. *mater*, f. *mat* MATT *a.* In sense 3 f. MATT *n.*[1]] **1** Make (colours etc.) dull; give a matt appearance to; frost (glass). E17. **2** In glass-painting, cover (glass) with a layer of colour smoothed over with a soft brush. L19. **3** Mount (a print etc.) on a cardboard backing; provide (a print etc.) with a border. Chiefly as *matted* ppl a., *matting* vbl n. M20.

mattamore /ˈmatəmɔː/ *n.* L17. [Fr. *matamore* f. Arab. *maṭmūra*, f. *ṭamara* put underground, bury.] In N. Africa, an underground storehouse, granary, or habitation (esp. a prison).

matte /mat/ *n.* M19. [Fr., use as n. of fem. of *mat* MATT *a.*] **1** *Metall.* A molten mixture of impure metal sulphides produced during the smelting of sulphide ores of copper, nickel, etc. M19. **2** *Cinemat.* A mask used to obscure or shade an image or part of one. M19.

matte *a.* var. of MATT *a.*

matted /ˈmatɪd/ *a.* E17. [f. MAT *n.*[1], *v.*[1]: see -ED[2], -ED[1].] **1** Laid or spread with matting or mats. E17. **b** Made of plaited rushes; (of a chair etc.) rush-bottomed. L17. **c** Formed of mats as a covering. E18. **2** Esp. of plants, hair, etc.: tangled and interlaced; covered with a tangled layer; compressed into the semblance of a mat. E17. **b** Covered with a dense growth. L18. **3** Enclosed or wrapped in matting. M17.

1 *Daily Telegraph* The bedrooms have traditional matted floors. b J. A. MICHENER Rushes from the wadi . . to be woven into a tightly matted roof. c DEFOE We pitched our matted tents. 2 T. ROETHKE The briary hedge, the tangle of matted underbrush. R. P. JHABVALA He had long hair, all tangled and matted. *Florist's Journal* The roots are very apt to get matted in the pots. b E. DARWIN By thee the plowshare rends the matted plain.

mattedly *adv.* (*rare*) L19.

matter /ˈmatə/ *n.* ME. [AN *mater(i)e*, (O)Fr. *matière* f. L *materia* (also *materies*) timber, stuff of which a thing is made, subject of discourse.] **I 1** The substance or the substances collectively of which a physical object consists; constituent material, esp. of a particular kind. *obs.* exc. as passing into senses 3, 4. ME. **2** A substance used or acted on in a physical operation. *obs.* exc. as passing into sense 3. LME. **3** A physical substance. Freq. w. specifying adj. LME. **4** That which has mass and occupies space; physical substance as distinct from spirit, mind, qualities, etc. LME. **5** Pus. LME.

1 T. ELYOT He vsed no golde but pure beryll and christall, and other like mattier to drinke in. 2 J. PALSGRAVE I make the printe of a thyng in any mater or stuffe. 3 P. ABRAHAMS Jacob recognized the familiar farming community smells of animal dung, vegetable matter. *colouring matter, faecal matter*, etc. 4 *Scientific American* It explodes when it drags matter from a companion star. 5 HUGH MILLER My injured foot . . discharged great quantities of blood and matter.

II 6 †a In scholastic philosophy: the result of the first act of creation, substance without form. ME–E17. **b** In Aristotelian and scholastic philosophy, the component of a thing which has bare existence but requires an essential determinant (*form*) to make it a thing of a determinate kind. LME. **c** In Kantian philosophy: the element of knowledge supplied by feeling, as distinct from that (*form*) supplied by the mind. M19. **7** *Theol.* The essential substance employed in a sacrament, as water in baptism, the bread and wine in the Eucharist, as distinct from the required words of the rite. ME. **8** *Logic.* The particular content of a proposition or syllogism as distinct from its form. L17.

8 F. BOWEN In respect to their Matter, both the Premises and the Conclusion may be false.

III 9 Material for expression; fact or thought as material for a book, speech, etc. ME. **†10** The subject of a book, speech, etc.; a theme, a topic. ME–E18. **†11** That with which a branch of knowledge deals; what belongs to a subject of study. ME–L16. **12** Orig., ground, reason, or cause for doing or being something. Later, what is or may be the occasion *of* or *for* a specified feeling. ME. **13 a** The substance of a book, speech, etc.; the contents of a composition in respect of the facts or ideas expressed, as distinct from the form of words used to express them. ME. **†b** Sense, substance, as distinct from nonsense. *rare* (Shakes.). L16–E17. **14 a** An event, circumstance, question, etc., which is or may be an object of consideration or practical concern; in *pl.*, events, circumstances, etc., generally. Formerly w. *possess.*, an event etc. of concern to the person specified, (one's) affair. ME. **b** In *pl.* Physical objects. Now *rare* or *obs.* E18. **15** A thing or things collectively of a particular kind or related to a particular thing. Usu. foll. by *for* or *of*, or w. specifying wd. LME. **b** A subject of contention, dispute, etc.; *Law* a thing which is to be tried or proved; statements or allegations which come under the consideration of a court; *US Law* a case. LME. **†16** Material cause; elements of which something consists or out of which it arises. L16–E19. **17** A quantity or amount (*of*). Usu. w. specifying adj., esp. *small*. Now *rare* or *obs.* M17. **18** Things printed or written, or to be printed or written (freq. w. specifying wd); *Typogr.* the body of a printed work as distinct from the titles, headings, etc. L17.

9 STEELE Whether they have Matter to talk of or not. 10 SPENSER Thee, O Queene! the matter of my song. 12 MILTON This is the matter why Interpreters . . will not consent it to be a true story. A. E. HOUSMAN 'Tis sure small matter for wonder If sorrow is with one still. 13a DRYDEN Though I cannot much commend the style . . there is somewhat in the matter. b SHAKES. *Much Ado* I was born to speak all mirth and no matter. 14a J. BARTH There was one final matter to be settled before I could call myself really free. W. ABISH Lunch, a serious matter. W. TREVOR I have been thinking about many of the matters we discussed. 15 SHAKES. *Merry W.* I will make a Star Chamber matter of it. N. WANLEY Mens Consciences are not to be forced in matters of Religion. J. DORAN This new-fangled scholarism was a very sad matter indeed. *hanging matter, money matters*, etc. b E. L. LINTON They rarely met without crossing swords on one matter if not another. 16 BACON The matter of seditions is of two kindes, Much povertye and much discontent. 17 M. NEEDHAM At first an easie matter was demanded by the King of Denmark. H. FIELDING I . . sent a small matter to his wife. 18 J. CARLYLE We have printed half the matter. M. LEITCH Under the cushioned seat he knew there would be reading matter. *printed matter, written matter*, etc.

Phrases: *a matter*: see *a small matter* below. **a matter of** (*a*) approximately; (*b*) a circumstance that involves, a circumstance depending (*only*) etc. on. **a matter of fact** (*a*) what pertains to the realm of fact (as distinct from probability, opinions, etc.); *as a matter of fact*: see FACT *n.*; (*b*) *Law* the part of a judicial inquiry concerned with the truth of the alleged facts (as distinct from *a matter of law* below). *a matter of form*: see FORM *n.* **a matter of law** the part of a judicial inquiry concerned with the correctness of the legal procedure (as distinct from *a matter of fact* above). *a matter of life and death*: see LIFE *n. a matter of opinion*: see OPINION *n. a matter of record*: see RECORD *n.* **a (small) matter** *adv. phr.* (*arch.*) somewhat, slightly. *be of no matter*: see *no matter* below. *dark matter*: see DARK *a. dry matter*: see DRY *a.* **first matter** a formless primordial substance considered as the original material of the universe. **for that matter** (*a*) so far as that is concerned; (*b*) and indeed also (something further). **for the matter of that** *arch.* = *for that matter* above. *front matter*: see FRONT *n.* & *a. grey matter*: see GREY *a.* **in the matter of** [Law L *in re*] (chiefly *Law*) in relation to, with regard to. *make no matter*: see *no matter* below. **†matter in it** some importance attaching to it. *matter of breviary*: see BREVIARY 1. *matter of course*: see COURSE *n.*[1] *matter of record*: see RECORD *n. matter subject*: see SUBJECT *a. mend matters*: see MEND *v. mince matters, the matter*: see MINCE *v. mind over matter*: see MIND *n.*[1] *no laughing matter*: see LAUGHING *vbl n.* **no matter** (*a*) *make no matter, be of no matter*, be of no consequence or importance; (*b*) *colloq.* it is of no consequence or importance, never mind. **the matter** (*a*) the circumstance or state of things involving or concerning a person or thing, *esp.* one calling for remedy or explanation (freq. in *what is the matter?*); *what is the matter with?* (colloq.) what is troubling, what is wrong with?, *joc.* what is the objection to, what is there to complain of in?; †(*b*) something contemplated, intended, or desired; *to the matter*, to the point, relevant(ly); *from the matter*, irrelevant(ly); †(*c*) *on the* (*whole*) *matter*, taking the thing as a whole, speaking generally, for all practical purposes. **what matter?** that need not disquiet us. *white matter*: see WHITE *a.*

Comb.: **matter-of-fact** *a.* pertaining to, having regard to, or depending on actual fact as distinct from what is speculative or fanciful; unimaginative; prosaic; **matter-of-factly** *adv.* in a matter-of-fact manner; **matter-of-factness** matter-of-fact quality or character; **matter wave** *Physics* a particle considered in terms of its wavelike properties, a de Broglie wave.

matterful *a.* (esp. of a book etc.) full of matter or substance E19. **†matterish** *a.* of the nature of pus, mattery L16–E18. **mattery** *a.* (*a*) full of, forming, or discharging pus; purulent; †(*b*) full of sense or meaning: LME.

matter /ˈmatə/ *v.* E16. [f. the n.] **1** *v.i.* Secrete or discharge pus; suppurate. *obs.* exc. *dial.* E16. **2** *v.i.* & (*poet.*, *rare*) *t.* w dat. obj. Be of importance (*to*), signify. Usu. in neg. & interrog. contexts. L16. **3 a** *v.t.* Be concerned about, care for, regard, mind; approve of, like. *obs.* exc. *dial.* M17. **b** *v.i.* Care, mind. Now *rare* or *obs.* L17.

2 V. BROME He was still unpersuaded that his own fate mattered very much. R. INGALLS She hadn't brought her glasses with her; not that it really mattered.

†matterative *a.* M17–E18. [Irreg. f. MATTER *n.* or *v.* after *maturative*: see -ATIVE.] Of the nature of or containing pus.

matterless /ˈmatəlɪs/ *a.* LME. [f. MATTER *n.* + -LESS.] **†1** Without materials. *rare.* Only in LME. **2** Having no matter; not embodied in matter. Now *rare.* LME. **†3** Devoid of sense or meaning. E17–M18. **4** Of no concern or importance; immaterial. Now *arch.* & *dial.* M17. **b** Of a person: of no consequence; incompetent, shiftless, helpless. *dial.* L18.

Matthean /maˈθiːən/ *a.* Also **-aean**. L19. [f. L *Matthaeus* Matthew + -AN, -EAN.] *Chr. Ch.* Of, pertaining to, or characteristic of the evangelist St Matthew or the Gospel attributed to him.

Matthew principle /ˈmaθjuː ˌprɪnsɪp(ə)l/ *n. phr.* L20. [St *Matthew* (see prec.)] The principle that more will be given to those who already have (w. ref. to *Matt.* 25:29).

Matthew Walker /maθjuː ˈwɔːkə/ *n.* M19. [Pers. name.] *Naut.* More fully *Matthew Walker knot.* A knot tied in the separated strands of the end of a rope.

mattie *n.* var. of MATIE.

matting /ˈmatɪŋ/ *n.*[1] & *a.* E17. [f. MATT *v.*, *n.*[1] + -ING[1].] **A** *n.* **1** Material for mats, mats collectively. E17. **2** A thing that has become matted; the action of becoming matted; the state of being matted. E17. **3** The covering of a floor etc. with mats or matted fabric; the process of making mats or material for mats. E18.

1 JAN MORRIS The windows are covered with loose matting to keep the sun out. 2 P. H. GOSSE The matting of the vegetation, impeding the flow of the water.

B *attrib.* or as *adj.* Covered with or made of matting. M19.

matting /ˈmatɪŋ/ *n.*[2] L17. [f. MATT *v.* + -ING[1].] **1** (The production of) a matt surface. L17. **2** The action of providing a print etc. with a matt as a backing or border; such a matt. M19.

mattins *n.pl.* see MATIN *n.*

mattock /ˈmatək/ *n.* & *v.* OE. [f. unkn. 1st elem. + -OCK.] **A** *n.* A tool similar to a pick but with one arm of the head curved like an adze and the other ending in a chisel edge or a point, used for breaking up hard ground, grubbing up trees, etc. OE. **B** *v.t.* Dig *up* (as) with a mattock. M17.

mattoid /ˈmatɔɪd/ *a.* & *n.* *rare.* L19. [It. *mattoide*, f. *matto* insane: see -OID.] *Psychol.* (Designating) a person of erratic behaviour, approaching the psychotic.

mattress /ˈmatrɪs/ *n.* ME. [OFr. *materas* (mod. *matelas*) cogn. w. or f. It. *materasso*, parallel w. OCatal. *almatratzt*, OPort. *almatrá* (mod. *almadraque*), OSp. *almatraque* (mod. *almadraque*), f. Arab. *al-matrah* carpet, cushion, seat, bed, f. *taraḥa* throw.] **1** A large case of strong fabric for sleeping on, with a soft or firm filling, or filled with air or water; any of various devices used similarly and containing or consisting of springs. Freq. w. specifying wd. ME. **†2** A protective covering, *esp.* one for plants; a mat. M17–E18. **3** A place where sugar cane is grown or stored. *US.* E19. **4** *Engin.* A strong mat consisting of pieces of brushwood fastened together, used in the construction of dykes, piers, etc., and placed on river-banks to prevent scour. L19.

1 *air mattress, flock-mattress, hair mattress, spring mattress, wire mattress*, etc.

Matura /ˈmɑːtərə/ *n.* L19. [A town in Sri Lanka (Ceylon), now called Matara.] *Matura diamond*, a colourless or smoky variety of zircon used as a gem; = JARGON *n.*[2]

maturant /ˈmatjʊr(ə)nt/ *n.* & *a.* Now *rare* or *obs.* M17. [L *maturant-* pres. ppl stem of *maturare*: see MATURATE, -ANT[1].] **A** *n.* = MATURATIVE *n.* M17. **B** *adj.* = MATURATIVE *a.* M19.

maturase /ˈmatjʊreɪz/ *n.* L20. [f. MATURE *a.* or *v.* + -ASE.] *Biochem.* Any of a group of enzymes which catalyse the excision of introns from mitochondrial mRNA, and may themselves be coded for by intronic sequences.

maturate /ˈmatjʊreɪt/ *v.* M16. [L *maturat-* pa. ppl stem of *maturare*, f. as MATURE *a.*: see -ATE[3].] **1** *v.t.* Mature, ripen; *esp.* cause (a boil, abcess, etc.) to come to a head. Now *rare* or *obs.* M16. **†2** *v.t. Metall.* & *Alch.* Purify (esp. a metal); change by purification *into*; convert (an ore) *into* pure metal; *spec.* convert (base metal) into gold. M17–M18. **3** *v.i.* Esp. of a boil or abscess: undergo maturation; mature, ripen. M17.

maturation /matjʊˈreɪʃ(ə)n/ *n.* LME. [(O)Fr., or med.L *maturatio(n-)*, f. as prec.: see -ATION.] **1** *Med.* The formation or encapsulation of pus; suppuration; the process of causing this. LME. **†2** The forwarding of a business, enterprise, etc. L16–M17. **†3** *Alch.* Purification; *esp.* conversion of a base metal into gold. Only in 17. **4** The action of becoming or making ripe or matured; an instance of this. E17. **5** The process of coming to full growth or development; the completing or perfecting of a plan, work, etc. M17. **†6** *Physics.* The (supposed) natural ripening or development of material substances by the operation of heat and motion. M17–M18.

4 W. JAMES A flaw in white wines caused by their absorption of too much oxygen during . . maturation. 5 W. O. WEIGLE Acquired early in life before maturation of the immune mechanisms.

Comb.: **maturation division** *Biol.* either of the two divisions of meiosis.

maturational *a.* E20.

maturative /məˈtjʊərətɪv/ *a.* & *n.* Now *rare* or *obs.* LME. [(O)Fr. *maturatif, -ive* or med.L *maturativus*, f. as MATURATE *v.*: see -ATIVE.] **A** *adj.* **1** *Med.* Causing the formation of pus; suppurative. LME. **†2** Having the power or function of ripening fruit etc.; of or pertaining to maturation. M–L17. **B** *n. Med.* A maturative remedy. LME.

mature /məˈtjʊə/ *a.* LME. [L *maturus* ripe, timely, early, perh. rel. to *mane* early, in the morning. Cf. MATUTINE.] **1** Of thought or deliberation: suitably careful and adequate. Of a plan, conclusion, etc.: formed after adequate deliberation. LME. **2** Complete in natural development or growth; fully developed, fully grown; (of wine, cheese, etc.) ready for consumption; (of fruit) ripe (now *rare*). LME. **†b** *fig.* Ripe or ready *for.* E–M17. **3a** Having the powers of body and mind fully developed, adult; (of personal qualities etc.) fully developed. Also foll. by *in.* E16. **b** Of or pertaining to maturity or manhood. *rare* (Shakes.). E17. **†4** That takes place early; prompt. (Cf. earlier & later MATURELY *adv.*2) Only in 17. **†5** Of an event: occurring at the fitting time. Of time: due. E–M17. **6** *Med.* (Of a boil or abscess) that has come to a head; (of a progressive cataract) completely opaque. E19. **7** Of a bill etc.: due for payment. L19.

1 BURKE On a full and mature view and comparison of the historical matter. LYTTON The interval . . allowed no time for mature and careful reflection. 2 *Christian Science Monitor* Use a mature Cheddar with a lot of taste. *Natural World* The loss of mature oak and beech. 3a H. A. L. FISHER A society more . . mature than the western Europe of the early middle ages. H. GUNTRIP A relationship between two fully mature adult persons. L. CODY The hair was young, but the style was mature. 4 MARVELL Carrying things on with the maturest expedition.

Special collocations: **mature economy**: that is fully developed or established; that is at the highest point of expansion after which further development is unlikely or impossible. **mature student**: who undertakes a course of study at a later age than normal.

matureness *n.* the state of being mature, maturity E18.

mature /məˈtjʊə/ *v.* LME. [L *maturare*, f. as prec.] **1** *v.t.* & *i.* Bring to or reach a mature state; develop fully; ripen. LME. **2** *v.t. fig.* Make ready; perfect, bring to full development, (a plan, a course of action, etc.); develop *into.* M17. **3** *v.i. fig.* Ripen or develop *into* or *to.* E19. **4** *v.i.* Of a bill etc.: reach the time fixed for payment; become due. M19.

1 J. LUBBOCK In some cases the stigma has matured before the anthers are ripe. A. TOFFLER Our children mature physically more rapidly than we did. *Country Living* The ancient practice of maturing wines in oak casks. 4 *What Mortgage* When the policy matures, it will pay off your loan.

maturely /məˈtjʊəli/ *adv.* L15. [f. MATURE *a.* + -LY[2].] **1** With full deliberation, after mature consideration. L15. **†2** Promptly; in good time; not too late; early. M16–L18. **3** With complete natural development or growth; in a manner indicative of maturity. M19.

maturity /məˈtjʊərɪti/ *n.* LME. [L *maturitas*, f. as MATURE *a.*: see -ITY.] **†1** Deliberateness of action; mature consideration, due deliberation. LME–M18. **2** The state of being mature; fullness or perfection of natural development or growth; ripeness. LME. **†3** Due promptness. M16–L17. **4** The state of being complete, perfect, or ready. M16. **5** The state of being due for payment; the time at which a bill etc. becomes due. E19.

2 T. S. ELIOT I do not mean the impressionable period of adolescence, but the period of full maturity. 4 H. H. WILSON Measures which . . were nearly brought to maturity. 5 *Moneypaper* The stocks . . run the range of maturities from a few months time to well into the next century.

matutinal /matjʊˈtʌɪn(ə)l, məˈtjuːtɪn(ə)l/ *a.* M16. [Late L *matutinalis*, f. as next: see -AL[1].] Of or pertaining to the morning, occurring or performed in the morning, early.

matutine /ˈmatjʊtʌɪn, -tɪn/ *a.* LME. [L *matutinus*, f. *Matuta* goddess of the dawn, rel. to *maturus* MATURE *a.*: see -INE[1]. Cf. MATIN *a.*] **1** = prec. LME. **2** Of a celestial object: that rises above the horizon before sunrise. E16.

maty /ˈmeɪti/ *n.* Also **mate** /meɪt/. E19. [Origin unkn.] In the Indian subcontinent: a servant, *esp.* an assistant or subordinate one.

maty *a.* var. of MATEY *a.*

matzo /ˈmʌtsə, ˈmatsəʊ/ *n.* Pl. **-os, -oth** /-əʊt/. Also **matzah** /ˈmʌtsə, ˈma-/. M19. [Yiddish *matse* f. Heb. *maṣṣāh*.] (A wafer of) unleavened bread for Passover.

mauby /ˈməʊbi/ *n.* *W. Indies.* L18. [f. as MOBBIE.] A drink made from the bark of trees of the genus *Gouania* or related plants of the buckthorn family.

maud /mɔːd/ *n.* L18. [Origin unkn.] A grey striped plaid worn by shepherds in Scotland, esp. in the south. Also, a travelling-rug, a wrap.

maudit /modi/ *n.* & *a.* M20. [Fr., lit. 'cursed', f. *maudire* to curse. Cf. POÈTE MAUDIT.] **A** *n.* Pl. pronounced same. A person who is cursed; a despicable or deeply unpleasant person. M20.

B *adj.* Cursed; (of an artist etc.) insufficiently appreciated, forgotten. Usu. *postpositive.* L20.

Times Lit. Suppl. As fits an artist *maudit*, there is no exact record of his birth.

maudle /ˈmɔːd(ə)l/ *v.* *rare.* E18. [Back-form. f. MAUDLIN *a.*] **1** *v.t.* Make maudlin. E18. **2** *v.i.* Talk in a maudlin way. E19.

maudlin /ˈmɔːdlɪn/ *n.* In branch I also **M-**. ME. [(O)Fr. *Madeleine* f. eccl.L *Magdalena*: see MAGDALEN. In branch II f. the adj.] **I †1** = MAGDALEN 1. ME–L16. **b** A penitent resembling Mary Magdalen. Cf. MAGDALEN 2. E–M17. **2** (More fully *sweet maudlin*) the plant sweet yarrow, *Achillea ageratum.* Formerly also, costmary, *Tanacetum balsamita.* LME. **†3** = MAGDALEN 2b. Only in E17. **†4** An old variety of peach, = MAGDALEN 3. Also, an old variety of pear. M17–E18. **II 5** Weak or mawkish sentiment. M19.

Comb.: **maudlin tide** the period of some days around 22 July, the feast of St Mary Magdalen.

maudlin /ˈmɔːdlɪn/ *a.* E16. [f. the n., w. allus. to pictures of the Magdalen weeping.] **1** Tearful and emotional as a result of drink. (Earliest in *maudlin-drunk* below.) E16. **2** Weeping, tearful. *arch.* M17. **3** Characterized by tearful sentimentality; mawkishly emotional; weakly sentimental. M17.

1 G. VIDAL Wine made him maudlin, affectionate, confused. 3 J. A. MICHENER 'I have the best wife in the world,' he said with maudlin sentiment.

Comb.: **maudlin-drunk** in the maudlin stage of intoxication.

maudlinism *n.* the state of being maudlin-drunk M19. **maudlinly** *adv.* M19.

Maugrabee /ˈmɔːgrəbiː/ *n.* *literary.* E18. [f. as MAGHRIBI.] An African Moor.

Maugrabin /ˈmɔːgrəbɪn/ *n.* & *a.* E19. [Arab. *maġribīn* pl. of *maġribī*: see MAGHRIBI. Cf. MAGHREBINE.] **A** *n.* An African Moor. E19. **B** *attrib.* or as *adj.* Of or pertaining to Moors. L19.

maugre /ˈmɔːgə/ *n.*, *prep.*, & *adv.* ME. [(O)Fr. *maugré* (mod. *malgré* prep.), f. *mal* f. L *malum* bad, evil + *gré* pleasure f. L *gratum* use as n. of neut. of *gratus* pleasing.] **A** *n.* **†1** Ill will, displeasure, spite. ME–M16. **†2** The state of being regarded with ill will; an instance of this. ME–M16. **3** *in* (*the*) *maugre of*, in spite of, notwithstanding the power of. Long *rare* or *obs.* exc. *Sc.* LME.

B *prep.* In spite of, notwithstanding the power of. *arch.* ME.

HUGH MILLER I continued my rounds, maugre the suspicion.

†C *adv.* Notwithstanding. LME–E17.

maul /mɔːl/ *n.* Also (earlier) **†mall**. See also MALL *n.* ME. [(O)Fr. *mail* f. L MALLEUS. Cf.

MAIL *n.*[5], MALLET *n.*[1], MELL *n.*[1] In senses 3, 4 f. MAUL *v.*] I 1 *Hist.* = MACE *n.*[1] 1. Also, a wooden club. ME. 2 Orig. *gen.*, a massive hammer. Now, any of various special kinds of heavy hammer or beetle used in pile-driving, shipbuilding, mining, etc. LME. †b *fig.* A person regarded as the irresistible enemy or terrible oppressor of a particular class, institution, etc. LME–E18. †3 A heavy blow, as struck with a hammer. Only in M17. 4 In *Rugby League*, an act of mauling or tackling a player. In *Rugby Union*, a loose scrum in which the ball is off the ground (opp. *ruck*). M19. II See MALL *n.*

maul /mɔːl/ *v.* Also †**mall**. ME. [f. the n. In sense 7 perh. a different wd.] †1 *v.t.* Strike with a heavy weapon; knock *down*. ME–M17. b *v.i.* Hammer. LME–E17. c *v.t.* Split (rails) with a maul and wedge. *US.* L17–L19. 2 *v.t.* Subject to damaging criticism, injure by criticizing. L16. 3 *v.t.* Beat and bruise (a person); maltreat, knock about. E17. 4 *v.t.* Damage seriously, shatter, mangle; *esp.* (of an animal) tear and mutilate (a prey etc.). L17. 5 *v.t.* Handle roughly or carelessly (usu. foll. by *about*); damage by rough handling. Also *dial.*, lift *down*. M18. 6 *v.i.* Toil, work hard. *dial.* E19. 7 *v.t. Rugby Football.* Tackle. M19.

3 J. DORAN Thrashing the bishop and terribly mauling his body of followers. 4 V. WOOLF They worried him, they mauled him with their great yellow teeth.

Maulana /maʊˈlɑːnə/ *n.* M19. [Arab. *mawlānā* our master.] (A title given to) a Muslim man revered for his religious learning or piety.

mauler /ˈmɔːlə/ *n.* Also †**maller**. ME. [f. MAUL *v.* + -ER[1].] 1 Orig., a massive hammer. Later, a person who mauls something. Also = MAUL *n.* 2b. ME. 2 A hand, a fist. Cf. next. *slang.* E19.

mauley /ˈmɔːli/ *n. slang.* L18. [Origin uncertain, perh. f. prec., perh. f. Shelta *malya* (itself perh. f. transposition of Gael. *lámh* hand).] A hand, a fist.

maul oak /ˈmɔːl əʊk/ *n. phr.* L19. [Perh. f. Sp. *maula* sham + OAK.] An evergreen oak, *Quercus chrysolepis*, of the south-western US.

maulstick /ˈmɔːlstɪk/ *n.* M17. [Du. *maalstok*, f. *malen* to paint + *stok* stick.] A light stick with a padded leather ball at one end, held by a painter in one hand as a support for the hand used for painting.

maulvi *n.* var. of MOULVI.

maum /mɔːm/ *n. US colloq.* Also **mawm**. E19. [Var. of MA'AM or MAM. Cf. MARM.] Madam; mother.

mauma /ˈmɔːmə/ *n.* M19. [Var. of MAMMA *n.*[2] Cf. MAMMY *n.*[1]] = MAMMY *n.*[1] 2.

Mau Mau /ˈmaʊmaʊ/ *n.* & *a.* M20. [Kikuyu.] A *n.* Pl. **-s**, same. An African secret society originating among the Kikuyu and active in the 1950s, having as its aim the expulsion of European settlers and the ending of British rule in Kenya; (treated as *pl.*) members of this society. M20. B *attrib.* or as *adj.* Of or pertaining to (a member of) the Mau Mau. M20.

mau-mau /ˈmaʊmaʊ/ *v.t. US slang.* L20. [f. prec.] Terrorize, threaten.

maumet /ˈmɔːmɪt/ *n.* Now *arch.* & *dial.* Also **mamm-** /ˈmam-/, **momm-** /ˈmɒm-/, & other vars., and w. cap. initial. ME. [OFr. *mahomet* idol, MAHOMET.] †1 A false god, an idol. Cf. MAHOMET 1. ME–M17. 2a A dressed-up figure; a doll, a puppet. Also, a person of grotesque appearance, esp. in dress. LME. b *fig.* A person who is the tool of another. LME. c A baby, a child. M20. 3 A contemptible or hateful person. E16. †4 = MAHOMET 3. Now *rare* or *obs.* L17.

maumetry *n.* (*a*) idolatry; heathenism; †(*b*) in *pl.*, idolatrous beliefs or practices; †(*c*) idols collectively; (*d*) = MAHOMETRY: ME.

maun /mɒn, mɔːn/ *aux. v. Sc.* LME. [ON *man* pres. t. of *munu* MUN *v.*] = MUST *v.*[1] II, III, IV, MUN *v.*

maunch /mɑːn(t)ʃ, mɔːn(t)ʃ/ *n.* Also **manche** /mɑːn(t)ʃ/. LME. [(O)Fr. *manche* f. L *manica*, f. *manus* hand.] A sleeve. Now only *Hist.* & *Her.*, a loose straight hanging sleeve of a kind worn in the late Middle Ages.

maund /mɔːnd/ *n.*[1] *obs.* exc. *dial.* [OE *mand*, partly (O)Fr. *mande* f. MLG, MDu. (Du. *mand*): ult. origin unkn.] 1 A woven basket with a handle or handles. OE. 2 A measure of capacity. ME. 3 A utensil for moving grain or hops. M19.

maundful *n.* as much as a maund will hold, a basketful E19.

maund /mɔːnd/ *n.*[2] L16. [Arab. *mann* f. Akkadian *mana* (whence Gk *mna*, L *mina*): cf. Heb. *māneh* MANEH.] A unit of weight in the Indian subcontinent and western Asia, varying greatly in value according to locality.

†**maund** *n.*[3] *slang.* E17–L18. [f. MAUND *v.*] Begging.

†**maund** *v.t.* & *i. slang.* M16–M19. [Perh. f. (O)Fr. *mendier* beg, f. L *mendicare*: see MENDICANT.] Beg.

†**maunder** *n.*[1] *slang.* E17–M19. [f. MAUND *v.* + -ER[1].] A beggar.

maunder /ˈmɔːndə/ *n.*[2] M19. [f. MAUNDER *v.*] (A piece of) idle incoherent talk or writing.

maunder /ˈmɔːndə/ *v.* E17. [Perh. frequent. of MAUND *v.*: see -ER[5].] †1 *v.i.* Grumble, mutter, growl. E17–M19. 2 *v.i.* Move or act in a dreamy, idle, or inconsequent manner; dawdle. M18. b *v.t.* Fritter *away* (one's time, life, etc.). M19. 3 *v.i.* & *t.* Say (something) in a dreamy and rambling manner. M19.

3 A. TROLLOPE Men . . had heard the old Major maunder on for years past.

maunderer *n.* M18. **maundering** *n.* the action of the vb; an instance of this; rambling or drivelling talk; dotage: E17. **maunderingly** *adv.* in a maundering manner; inconsequently: E20.

Maunder minimum /ˈmɔːndə ˈmɪnɪmʌm/ *n. phr.* L20. [E. W. *Maunder* (1851–1928), Eng. astronomer.] A prolonged minimum in sunspot activity on the sun between about 1645 and 1715, which coincided with the Little Ice Age in the northern hemisphere.

†**maunding** *n. slang.* E17–E19. [f. MAUND *v.* + -ING[1].] The action or an act of begging; an abusive demand.

†**maunding** *a. slang.* M17–E18. [f. MAUND *v.* + -ING[2].] Mendicant.

Maundy /ˈmɔːndi/ *n.* Also **m-**. ME. [OFr. *mandé* f. L *mandatum* commandment, MANDATE *n.*, in *mandatum novum* a new commandment (with ref. to *John* 13:34), the opening of the first antiphon sung at the Maundy ceremony (see below).] 1 Orig., the ceremony of washing the feet of a number of poor people, performed by royal or other eminent people or by ecclesiastics, on the Thursday before Easter, and commonly followed by the distribution of clothing, food, or money. Now, the distribution by the British monarch of specially minted silver coins (*Maundy money* below) to a number of chosen recipients. ME. †b *fig.* Almsgiving, bounty, largesse. L16–M17. c The money distributed by the British monarch at the Maundy ceremony. Also *Royal Maundy*. M19. †2 The Last Supper. Also (*rare*), the Eucharist. LME–M17.

Comb.: **Maundy coin** a specially minted coin given as Maundy money; **maundy dish, purse**: used to hold the money to be distributed at a Maundy ceremony; **Maundy money** silver money distributed by the British monarch on Maundy Thursday; *maundy purse*: see *maundy dish* above; **Maundy Thursday** the Thursday before Good Friday.

Mauretanian *a.* & *n.* see MAURITANIAN.

Maurist /ˈmɔːrɪst/ *a.* & *n.* L18. [f. St *Maur* (see below) + -IST.] *Hist.* A *adj.* Of or pertaining to the French Benedictine congregation founded in 1621 by St Maur, a disciple of St Benedict, and famous for its scholarship. L18. B *n.* A member of this congregation. L19.

Mauritanian /mɒrɪˈteɪnɪən/ *a.* & *n.* Also (now usu. in senses A.1, B.1) **Mauretanian**. L16. [Partly f. *Mauretania*, f. L *Maurus* (see MOOR *n.*[2]), partly f. *Mauritania*: see below, -IAN.] A *adj.* 1 Of or pertaining to the ancient region of Mauretania in N. Africa, corresponding to parts of present-day Morocco and Algeria. L16. 2 Of or pertaining to the modern State of Mauritania on the west coast of Africa, between Morocco and Senegal. M20. B *n.* 1 A native or inhabitant of ancient Mauretania. *rare.* E17. 2 A native or inhabitant of the modern State of Mauritania. L20.

Mauritian /məˈrɪʃ(ə)n/ *a.* & *n.* M19. [f. *Mauritius* (see below) + -AN.] A *adj.* Of or pertaining to the island of Mauritius in the Indian Ocean. M19. B *n.* A native or inhabitant of Mauritius. M19.

mauryah *int.* var. of MOYA.

Mauryan /ˈmaʊrɪən/ *a.* L19. [f. *Maurya* (see below) + -AN.] *Hist.* Of or pertaining to the dynasty founded by Candragupta Maurya, which ruled northern India from 321 to *c*184 BC.

Mauser /ˈmaʊzə/ *n.* L19. [Paul von *Mauser* (1838–1914), Ger. inventor.] (Proprietary name for) a type of firearm, orig. a repeating rifle, now also a pistol.

mausoleum /mɔːsəˈlɪəm/ *n.* Pl. **-lea** /-ˈlɪə/, **-leums**. LME. [L f. Gk *Mausōleion*, f. *Mausōlos* Mausolos (see below).] 1 The magnificent tomb of Mausolus, King of Caria, erected in the 4th cent. BC at Halicarnassus by his queen Artemisia. LME. 2 *gen.* A large and stately place of burial. LME. †3 = CATAFALQUE 1. L17–E18.

2 *fig.*: H. BROOKE O! London, London! thou mausoleum of dead souls!

mausolean *a.* M16.

mauther /ˈmɔːðə/ *n.* Chiefly *dial.* Also **mawther**. LME. [Origin unkn.] A young girl.

mauvais /movɛ/ *a.* Fem. **-aise** /-ɛz/. E18. [Fr.] Bad. Only in Fr. phrs.

mauvais coucheur /kuʃœːr/, pl. ***mauvais coucheurs*** (pronounced same), [*coucheur* bedfellow] a difficult, uncooperative, or unsociable person. ***mauvaise honte*** /movɛz ɔ̃t/ [lit. 'ill shame'] false shame; painful diffidence. ***mauvaise langue*** /lɑ̃g/, pl. ***mauvaises langues*** (pronounced same), [*langue* tongue] an evil tongue; a vituperative gossip, a scandalmonger. ***mauvais pas*** /pɑ/, pl. same, [*pas* step] *Mountaineering* a place that is difficult or dangerous to negotiate. ***mauvais quart d'heure*** /kar dœːr/, pl. ***mauvais quarts d'heure*** (pronounced same), [lit. 'bad quarter of an hour'] a brief but unpleasant period of time. ***mauvais sujet*** /syʒɛ/, pl. ***mauvais sujets*** (pronounced same), [*sujet* subject] a worthless person, a bad lot. ***mauvais ton*** /tɔ̃/, pl. ***mauvais tons*** (pronounced same), [*ton* taste] (now *rare*) what is disapproved by good society; bad form.

mauve /məʊv/ *n.* & *a.* M19. [Fr. f. L *malva* MALLOW.] A *n.* 1 *Hist.* A bright but delicate purple aniline dye that was one of the earliest synthetic dyes. Also called *mauveine*, *Perkin's mauve* etc. (see PERKIN 1). M19. 2 The colour of this dye; any of a range of dull shades of purple between lilac and maroon. M19.

B *adj.* Of the colour mauve. M19.

mauvish *a.* somewhat mauve L19.

mauveine /ˈməʊviːn/ *n.* Also **-in** /-ɪn/. M19. [f. prec. + -INE[5], -IN[1].] *Chem.* = MAUVE *n.* 1.

maux /mɔːks/ *n. obs.* exc. *dial.* Pl. **-xes**, same. L16. [Perh. rel. to MALKIN *n.*] A low woman, a slattern. Formerly also, a prostitute.

maven /ˈmeɪv(ə)n/ *n. N. Amer.* M20. [Heb. *mēbīn* understanding.] An expert, a connoisseur.

maverick /ˈmav(ə)rɪk/ *n.*, *a.*, & *v.* M19. [Samuel A. *Maverick* (1803–70), Texas engineer who owned but did not brand cattle.] A *n.* 1 An unbranded calf or yearling. *N. Amer.* M19. 2 An unorthodox or independent-minded person; an individualist; *US* a politician who will not affiliate with a regular political party. L19.

2 A. HAILEY He was an original thinker, a maverick who would not be silenced. M. SARTON Minna . . had always been a maverick, the odd one out in a solid, conservative family.

B *attrib.* or as *adj.* That is a maverick; unorthodox, independent-minded. L19.

CLIVE JAMES A maverick scientist who treats science as an art. B. GELDOF It was the kind of maverick scheme which a single permanent charity could not have afforded.

C *v.* 1 *v.t.* Seize or brand (an animal) as a maverick. Also, take possession of without any legal claim; steal. L19. 2 *v.i.* Stray or wander like a maverick. E20.

mavis /ˈmeɪvɪs/ *n.* Now *poet.* & *dial.* LME. [(O)Fr. *mauvis*.] A song thrush.
red mavis: see RED *a.*

Mavors /ˈmeɪvɔːz/ *n. literary.* L16. [L: see MARS.] = MARS 2.

mavourneen /məˈvʊəniːn/ *n. Anglo-Ir.* E19. [Ir. *mo mhuirnín*, f. *mo* my + *muirnín* dim. of *muirn* affection: see -EEN[2].] My darling.

mavrodaphne /mavrəˈdafni/ *n.* E20. [mod.Gk f. late Gk *mauros* dark (Gk *amauros*) + *daphnē* laurel.] A dark-red sweet Greek wine; the grape from which this is made.

mavrone /məˈvrəʊn/ *int. Anglo-Ir.* L19. [Ir. *mo bhrón*, f. *mo* my + *brón* grief.] Expr. sorrow.

maw /mɔː/ *n.*[1] [OE *maga* corresp. to OFris. *maga*, MDu. *maghe* (Du. *maag*), OHG *mago* (G. *Magen*), ON *magi*, f. Gmc.] 1 The stomach of an animal or (now *joc.*) a person; the cavity of the stomach. Formerly *spec.*, the abomasum or fourth stomach of a ruminant. OE. 2†a Any of various internal organs, as (*a*) the abdominal cavity as a whole; the belly; (*b*) the womb; (*c*) the liver. ME–E16. b The swim-bladder of a fish. LME. 3 The throat, the gullet; *esp.* the jaws or mouth of a voracious mammal or fish. LME. †4 Appetite, inclination, liking. L16–E18.

1 N. HAWTHORNE Destined to glut the ravenous maw of that detestable man-brute. 3 *Trout & Salmon* It stuck its head up out of the river . . and it opened its great maw wide. *transf.*: K. KESEY We'll face the terrible maw of a muzzle-loading shotgun. 4 C. CIBBER I have no great Maw to that Business, methinks.

maw /mɔː/ *n.*[2] Long *obs.* exc. *Sc.* & *north.* LME. [Reduced form of MALLOW.] *sing.* & (usu.) in *pl.* (treated as *sing.*). A mallow.

maw /mɔː/ *n.*[3] *obs.* exc. *dial.* LME. [ON *már* = OE *mǣw*: see MEW *n.*[1]] A gull, *esp.* the common gull, *Larus canus*.

maw /mɔː/ *n.*[4] *obs.* exc. *Hist.* M16. [Origin unkn.] A Gaelic card-game from which twenty-five and spoil five developed.

maw /mɔː/ *n.*[5] *colloq.* & *dial.* (chiefly *US*). E20. [Repr. a pronunc. of MA *n.*: cf. PAW *n.*[2]] = MA *n.*

mawk /mɔːk/ *n. obs.* exc. *dial.* LME. [ON *maðkr*: see MADDOCK.] A maggot.

mawkin *n.* var. of MALKIN.

mawkish /ˈmɔːkɪʃ/ *a.* M17. [f. MAWK + -ISH[1].] 1 Inclined to sickness; without appetite. *obs.* exc. *dial.* M17. 2 Having a nauseating, sickly, or insipid taste. L17. 3 Feebly sentimental; imbued with sickly or false sentiment. E18.

2 P. V. WHITE She reached out for the . . barley water . . and tried to find comfort in . . that mawkish stuff. 3 C. P. SNOW Dickens made a mawkish cult of Mary Hogarth, and idolised her.

mawkishly *adv.* M18. **mawkishness** *n.* E18.

mawky /ˈmɔːki/ *a. obs.* exc. *dial.* L18. [f. MAWK + -Y[1].] 1 Maggoty (*lit.* & *fig.*). L18. 2 = MAWKISH 3. M19.

mawm *n.* see MAUM.

†**mawmish** *a.* M17–M19. [f. base of MALM *n.* + -ISH[1].] = MAWKISH 2, 3.

mawseed /ˈmɔːsiːd/ *n. arch.* M18. [Partial tr. G dial. *Mahsaat*, *Mohsamen*, f. *Mah*, *Moh* poppy (G *Mohn*) + *Saat*, *Samen* seed.] The seed of the opium poppy, *Papaver somniferum*.

mawther *n.* var. of MAUTHER.

mawworm /ˈmɔːwəːm/ *n.*[1] Now *rare* or *obs.* E17. [f. MAW *n.*[1] + WORM *n.*] A parasitic worm, esp. a nematode, infesting the gut of humans and other mammals.

mawworm /ˈmɔːwəːm/ *n.*[2] M19. [*Mawworm*, a character in Isaac Bickerstaffe's play *The Hypocrite*, 1769.] A hypocritical pretender to sanctity.

†**max** *n.*[1] E–M19. [Origin unkn.] Gin.

max /maks/ *n.*[2] & *a. N. Amer. colloq.* M19. [Abbrev. of MAXIMUM.] A *n.* 1 A maximum figure, achievement, etc. M19. 2 A maximum security prison. M20.

1 GRODY *to the max.*

B *attrib.* or as *adj.* Maximum. M20.

max q *Aeronaut.* the maximum dynamic pressure exerted on an aircraft or spacecraft in the course of its flight; the part of a flight during which the highest aerodynamic pressures are encountered.

max /maks/ *v. US colloq.* L19. [f. prec.] 1 *v.t.* & *i.* (usu. foll. by *out*). Do (a thing) well; perform to the limit of one's capacity, endurance, etc. L19. 2 *v.i.* Complete a maximum prison sentence. L20.

max /maks/ *adv. US colloq.* L20. [f. as prec.] At the maximum, at the most.

maxi /ˈmaksi/ *n. colloq.* M20. [f. next.] A thing that is large or long of its kind; *spec.* (*a*) a maxi-skirt; (*b*) *Austral.* & *NZ* a maxi-yacht.

maxi- /ˈmaksi/ *comb. form.* M20. [f. MAXI(MUM: cf. MINI-.] Forming chiefly ns. denoting a thing that is large or long of its kind, esp. a garment or (*Austral.* & *NZ*) a racing yacht, as *maxi-coat*, *maxi-skirt*, etc.

maxilla /makˈsɪlə/ *n.* Pl. **-llae** /-liː/. LME. [L = jaw.] 1 A jaw, a jawbone; *spec.* either of a pair of bones forming (part of) the upper jaw in vertebrates. LME. 2 In insects and other arthropods, either of a pair of mouthparts posterior to and accessory to the mandibles. L18.

¶Cf. MANDIBLE.

†**maxillar** *a.* & *n.* (a) maxillary L16–E18. **maxillary** *a.* & *n.* (*a*) *adj.* of, pertaining to, or designating a maxilla; forming part of a maxilla; (*b*) *n.* a maxillary bone; a maxilla: E17.

maxilliped /makˈsɪlɪpɛd/ *n.* Also **-pede** /-piːd/. M19. [f. MAXILLA + -I- + L *ped-*, *pes* foot.] *Zool.* In crustaceans, an appendage modified for feeding and occurring in pairs behind the maxillae.

maxillo- /makˈsɪləʊ, ˈmaksɪləʊ/ *comb. form.* [f. MAXILLA: see -O-.] Forming adjs. w. the sense 'pertaining to the maxilla and —', as *maxillo-facial*, *maxillo-mandibular*, etc., and ns. etc. derived from them.

maxim /ˈmaksɪm/ *n.*[1] LME. [Fr. *maxime* or its source med.L *maxima* use as n. (sc. *propositio* proposition) of fem. of *maximus*: see MAXIMUM. Cf. MAXIMA *n.*[1]] †1 A self-evident proposition assumed as a premiss in mathematical or dialectical reasoning. LME–L17. 2 A proposition, esp. a pithily-worded one, expressing a general truth drawn from science, law, or experience. Cf. earlier MAXIMUM I. L16. 3 A rule or principle of conduct; a pithily-expressed precept of morality or prudence. L16.

1 R. BENTLEY It is urged as an universal Maxim, That Nothing can procede from Nothing. 2 *Weekly Notes* He considered at length the meaning of the maxim, 'a man's house is his castle.' J. BERMAN She acts out the psychoanalytic maxim that wishes and fears are often inextricably related. 3 D. M. FRAME The maxim 'Know thyself' was on the temple of Apollo at Delphi.

maximist *n.* a person who makes or coins maxims M19.

Maxim /ˈmaksɪm/ *n.*[2] L19. [Sir Hiram S. *Maxim* (1840–1916), US-born Brit. inventor.] In full *Maxim* (*machine-*)*gun*. A single-barrelled quick-firing machine-gun with a barrel surrounded by an outer casing filled with water to keep the parts cool.

†**maxima** *n.*[1] M16. [med.L: see MAXIM *n.*[1]] 1 = MAXIM *n.*[1] M–L16. 2 *Mus.* = LARGE *n.* 4. M18–E19.

maxima *n.*[2] pl. of MAXIMUM *n.*

maximal /ˈmaksɪm(ə)l/ *a.* L19. [f. MAXIMUM + -AL[1].] Consisting of or relating to a maximum; of the greatest possible size, duration, or capacity.

maxiˈmality *n.* the property of being maximal M20. **maximally** *adv.* L19.

maximalist /ˈmaksɪm(ə)lɪst/ *n.* & *a.* Also **M-**. E20. [f. prec. + -IST, after Russ. *maksimalist*. Cf. BOLSHEVIK.] A *n.* A person who holds out for the maximum of his or her demands and rejects compromises; *spec.* (*Hist.*) a member of the part of the Russian Social-Democratic Party which favoured extreme methods; a member of any similar group outside the former USSR. E20. B *attrib.* or as *adj.* Of, pertaining to, or characteristic of maximalists or maximalism. M20.

maximalism *n.* the beliefs or practices of maximalists E20.

maximand /ˈmaksɪmand/ *n.* M20. [f. MAXIM(IZE *v.* + -AND.] A thing which is to be maximized.

maximin /ˈmaksɪmɪn/ *n.* & *a.* M20. [f. MAXI(MUM + MIN(IMUM, after *minimax*.] *Math.* A *n.* The largest of a set of minima. M20. B *attrib.* or as *adj.* Of, pertaining to, or of the nature of a maximin; *spec.* in *Game Theory*, designating a strategy that maximizes the smallest gain that can be relied on by a participant in a game or other situation of conflict. Cf. MINIMAX *n.* & *a.* M20.

maximize /ˈmaksɪmʌɪz/ *v.* Also **-ise**. E19. [f. L *maximus* (see MAXIMUM) + -IZE.] 1 *v.t.* Increase to the highest possible degree; enhance to the utmost. E19. 2 *v.i.* Chiefly *Theol.* Maintain the most rigorous or comprehensive interpretation possible of a doctrine or an obligation. L19. 3 *v.i.* Reach a maximum value. L20.

1 A. S. DALE He . . went to his father for advice on how to maximize his income. 2 W. S. LILLY I am far from wishing to maximize upon this matter. 3 *Globe & Mail* (*Toronto*) If emissions were curtailed now, the resultant ozone destruction would maximize around 1990.

maximiˈzation *n.* E19. **maximizer** *n.* M19.

maximum /ˈmaksɪməm/ *n.* & *a.* M16. [(Fr. f.) mod.L use as n. of neut. of L *maximus* superl. of *magnus* great.] A *n.* Pl. **maxima** /ˈmaksɪmə/, **maximums**. I †1 = MAXIM *n.*[1] 2. Only in M16.

II †2 The largest portion in which matter can exist. Only in M17. 3 *Math.* The greatest value which a variable may have; the largest element in a set; a point at which a continuously varying quantity ceases to increase and begins to decrease. M18. 4 *gen.* The highest possible magnitude or quantity of something attained, attainable, or customary; an upper limit of magnitude or quantity. M18. b The highest amount (esp. of temperature, barometric pressure, etc.) attained or recorded within a particular period. M19. 5 A superior limit imposed by authority; *esp.* in *Fr. Hist.*, a limit of price for corn. E19.

4 T. M. LINDSAY A strange compound of minimum of fact and maximum of theory. A. STORR Dependence is at its maximum at birth, when the human infant is most helpless.

Comb.: **maximum thermometer**: which records the highest temperature attained since it was last set.

B *attrib.* or as *adj.* Of or pertaining to a maximum, that is a maximum. M19.

Z. TOMIN It was a game requiring maximum concentration. **maximum price**: that may not by law etc. be exceeded.

maxina /ˈmaksɪnə/ *n.* E20. [Origin unkn.] A kind of ballroom dance in common time, first introduced in England in 1917.

maxixe /makˈsiːks, *foreign* məˈʃiʃə/ *n.* E20. [Port.] A dance for couples, of Brazilian origin, resembling the polka and the local tango.

Maxwell /ˈmakswɛl/ *n.* L19. [James Clerk *Maxwell* (1831–79), Sc. physicist.] *Physics.* 1 Used in *possess.* and *attrib.* to designate concepts originated by Maxwell. L19. 2 (**m-**.) A unit of magnetic flux in the cgs system, equal to the flux through an area of one square centimetre normal to a uniform induction of one gauss, and equivalent to 10^{-8} weber. E20.

1 **Maxwell('s) demon** a device (or imaginary being) conceived as allowing only fast-moving molecules to pass through a hole in one direction and only slow-moving ones in the other direction, so that if the hole is in a partition dividing a gas-filled vessel into two parts, one side becomes warmer and the other cooler, in violation of the second law of thermodynamics. **Maxwell('s) distribution** (a formula describing) the distribution of molecular velocities predicted by Maxwell's law, the number with a velocity between v and $v + dv$ being proportional to $\exp(-\frac{1}{2}mv^2/kT)v^2\,dv$ (where m is the mass of a molecule, k is Boltzmann's constant, and T is the absolute temperature). **Maxwell('s) equation** each of a set of four linear partial differential equations which summarize the classical properties of the electromagnetic field and relate space and time derivatives of the electric and

magnetic field vectors, the electric displacement vector, and the magnetic induction vector, and also involve the electric current and charge densities. **Maxwell('s) law** a law in classical physics giving the probabilities of different velocities for the molecules of a gas in equilibrium.

Maxwellian /maksˈwɛlɪən/ *a.* of, pertaining to, or originated by J. C. Maxwell; in accordance with Maxwell's law or equations: L19.

Maxwell-Boltzmann /makswɛlˈbəʊltsmən/ *n.* E20. [f. MAXWELL + BOLTZMANN.] *Physics.* Used *attrib.* to designate certain concepts in the kinetic theory of gases.

Maxwell-Boltzmann distribution = *Maxwell('s) distribution* s.v. MAXWELL 1, BOLTZMANN *distribution*.

Maxwell's duiker /ˈmakswɛlz ˈdʌɪkə/ *n. phr.* E20. [Charles *Maxwell*, 19th-cent. Eng. soldier and explorer.] A small grey or brown duiker, *Cephalophus maxwelli*, of W. African forests.

may /meɪ/ *n.*[1] *poet. arch.* [OE *mæġ* reinforced or replaced in ME by forms f. ON *mær* (genit. *meyjar*) maid = Goth. *mawi*, f. Gmc fem. of base of Goth. *magus* boy. Cf. MAIDEN *n.*] A maiden, a virgin.

May /meɪ/ *n.*[2] In sense 2 also **m-**. LOE. [(O)Fr. *mai* f. L *Maius* (sc. *mensis* month) pertaining to the Italic goddess *Maia*.] **1** The fifth month of the year in the Gregorian calendar. Also *fig.*, w. allus. to May's position at the beginning of summer in the northern hemisphere; *poet.* one's bloom, one's prime, the heyday. LOE. **b** The festivities of May Day. L15. **2** Hawthorn blossom; (occas.) the hawthorn tree. LME. **3** At Cambridge University: an examination or (in *pl.*) examinations held in May; in *pl.*, boat races held during May Week (see below). M19.

Phrases: **May and January** a young woman and an old man as husband and wife. *nuts in May*: see NUT *n.* **Queen of the May** (**†of May**) a girl chosen to be queen of games on May Day, usu. being gaily dressed and crowned with flowers.

Comb.: **May-apple** a N. American plant, *Podophyllum peltatum*, of the barberry family, with a solitary waxy flower; the yellowish egg-shaped fruit of this plant, produced in May; **May beetle** = *May-bug* below; **May-bird** a whimbrel; **May-blob** marsh marigold, *Caltha palustris*; **May-bug** any of various beetles of the scarab family which appear in late spring, *esp.* (in Europe) the cockchafer, (in N. America) the June bug, *Phyllophaga*; **May-bush** (a branch of) hawthorn; **†May butter** unsalted butter preserved in the month of May for medicinal use; **May-cherry** (*a*) a small early kind of cherry; (*b*) *US* (the fruit of) any of various shrubs of the genus *Amelanchier*, = *Juneberry* s.v. JUNE *n.*; **May Day** 1 May, esp. as marked by festivities or as an international holiday in honour of workers; **mayday** [repr. pronunc. of Fr. *m'aider* help me] an international radio distress signal; *transf.* a call for help; **May dew** dew gathered in the month of May, esp. on 1 May, popularly supposed to have medicinal and cosmetic properties; **mayduke** an early-ripening variety of duke cherry; **mayfish** (*a*) the twaite shad; (*b*) *US* the striped killifish, *Fundulus majalis*, of the Atlantic coast of N. America; **mayflower** (*a*) *dial.* any of various plants flowering in May, *esp.* the cowslip, *Primula veris*, and lady's smock, *Cardamine pratensis*; (*b*) *N. Amer.* the trailing arbutus, *Epigaea repens*; **May game** (*a*) in *pl.*, the merrymaking and sports associated with 1 May; (*b*) a performance or entertainment in May Day festivities; *gen.* a frolic, an entertainment; a foolish or extravagant action or performance; (*c*) *arch.* an object of sport, jest, or ridicule, a laughing-stock; **May lady** (*obs.* exc. *Hist.*) a Queen of the May; **May lily** orig., lily of the valley; now, a rare allied woodland plant, *Maianthemum bifolium*; **May morn** (*poet.*), **May morning** the morning of 1 May; **May-pop** *US* (the fruit of) the passion-flower, *Passiflora incarnata*; **May queen** the Queen of the May; **May-rose** any of various roses flowering in May; **May Week** at Cambridge University, a week in late May or early June when intercollegiate boat races are held. See also MAYFLY.

may /meɪ/ *n.*[3] M19. [f. MAY *v.*[1]] An instance of what is expressed by the auxiliary verb *may*; a possibility.

may /meɪ/ *v.*[1] Pres.: 1, 2, 3, sing. & pl. **may**; 2, sing. (*arch.*) **mayst** /meɪst/, **mayest** /ˈmeɪəst/. Pa.: 1, 2, 3, sing. & pl. **might** /mʌɪt/, (now *dial.*) **mought** /mɔːt/; 2, sing. (*arch.*) **mightest** /ˈmʌɪtɪst/. Neg. **may not**, (*informal*) **mayn't** /meɪnt/; **might not**, (*informal*) **mightn't** /ˈmʌɪt(ə)nt/. No other parts used. [OE *mæġ* (1st person sing.) = OFris. *mei*, OS, OHG *mag* (Du., G *mag*), ON *má*, Goth. *mag*: a Gmc preterite-present vb w. primary meaning 'have power'.] **I** As full vb. **†1** *v.i.* Be strong; have power or influence; prevail (*over*). OE–LME. **b** *v.t.* With cognate obj.: have (might, power). ME–L15.

II As auxiliary vb (often *ellipt.* with vb understood or supplied from the context). **2** Have ability or power to; = CAN *v.*[1] 4. *arch.* OE. **3** As *may* or (rejecting or qualifying a hypothesis etc. or implying improbability) in pa. form *might*: have the possibility, opportunity, or suitable conditions to; be likely to; (*may be* or *do*, perhaps is, will, or does; *may have been* or *done*, (now *rare*) *might be* or *do*, perhaps was or did, perhaps has been or done, perhaps can or could). (Pa. indic. now *rare* as tending to be interpreted as subjunct.) OE. **b** In pa. form *might*: used to. *poet.* E19. **c** In pa. form *might* (subjunct.) w. perf. inf.: would not have found it difficult to (perform an omitted act of duty or kindness). In pa. form *might* w. pres. inf.: ought not find it difficult to (perform a similar omitted act). *colloq.* M19. **4** As *may* or (rejecting or qualifying a hypothesis etc. or implying improbability) in pa. form *might*: be allowed by authority, law, rule, morality, reason, etc., to. OE. **b** *Law.* In the interpretation of some statutes: shall, must. E18. **5** In pa. form *might* as subjunct. in conditional sentences: were or would be or have been able to, were or would be or have been allowed to, were or would perhaps. OE. **6** In clauses of purpose or result: as part of a periphrastic subjunct. expressing virtually the same meaning as the subjunct. of the principal vb, which this combination has largely superseded. OE. **7** In exclamations: expr. a wish (usu. *may*; *might* also when its realization is thought hardly possible). LME. **8** In questions: *may* with inf. is sometimes substituted for the indic. of the principal vb to render the question less abrupt or pointed. E16.

2 M. DRAYTON Thy mighty strokes who may withstand. M. ARNOLD We . . have endured Sunshine and rain as we might. 3 STEELE The Improvement of our Understandings may, or may not, be of Service to us, according as it is managed. SIR W. SCOTT He joyed to see the cheerful light, And he said Ave Mary, as well he might. B. JOWETT I dare say . . that you may be right. SCOTT FITZGERALD I thought you might want to know. *Times Lit. Suppl.* Twenty years ago you might hear a sixpence described as a 'Lord'. S. SASSOON She had hoped and prayed that I might get a home-service job. *Atlantic Monthly* Any outside disturbance . . may well bring disaster to the whole region. *National Observer* (*US*) One theory . . was that frozen plumbing may have caused . . a contamination of the water system. P. THEROUX It might have been sisal, but more likely was the tequila plant. P. NIESEWAND A flypast might be nice. How about some sky-divers? c G. B. SHAW Really, . . you might at least join your flats. W. CATHER You might have told me there was a snake behind me! 4 THACKERAY May we take your coach to town? A. E. HOUSMAN 'Twill do no harm to take my arm. 'You may, young man, you may'. 5 BYRON Oh! might I kiss those eyes of fire, A million scarce would quench desire. E. RICKERT One might see in her withered . . face the wreckage of a great beauty. *Times* If a grave crisis were ever to arise on the western borders of Russia, the isolationists might be swept off their feet. E. A. CARLSON If Weldon had stopped here he might have won the battle. N. GORDIMER If we'd still been children, I might have been throwing stones at him in a tantrum. 6 S. JOHNSON Lest my appearance might draw too many compliments. LD MACAULAY It was not easy to devise any expedient which might avert the danger. 7 DICKENS May the present moment . . be the worst of our lives! 8 WORDSWORTH Sisters and brothers, little maid, How many may you be?

Phrases etc.: **be that as it may** irrespective of the situation regarding that, that may well be so (but there are other considerations). *may I have the pleasure?*: see PLEASURE *n.* *may it* PLEASE *you. may your shadow never grow less!*: see SHADOW *n.* **that is as may be** the truth of that is not yet determined, that may well be so (but it is not a significant consideration).

may /meɪ/ *v.*[2]*i. arch.* LME. [f. MAY *n.*[2]] Take part in the festivities of May Day or in the pleasures of the month of May; gather flowers in May. Chiefly as *maying* vbl n.

mayer *n.* M18.

maya /ˈmɑːjə/ *n.*[1] L18. [Skt *māyā*, f. *mā* create.] In *Hindu Philos.*, illusion, magic, the supernatural power wielded by gods and demons. In *Hindu* & *Buddhist Philos.*, the power by which the universe becomes manifest, the illusion or appearance of the phenomenal world.

Maya /ˈmʌɪ(j)ə, ˈmeɪ(j)ə/ *n.*[2] & *a.* Also (earlier) **†Maye**. Pl. of n. **-s**, same. E19. [Sp. f. Maya.] **A** *n.* **1** A member of an Indian people of Yucatan and Central America having an ancient civilization which reached its peak from the 4th to the 8th cents. E19. **2** The language of this people. M19. **B** *adj.* = MAYAN *a.* L19.

Mayan /ˈmʌɪ(j)ən, ˈmeɪ(j)ən/ *a.* & *n.* L19. [f. prec. + -AN.] **A** *adj.* Of or pertaining to the Mayas. L19. **B** *n.* **1** = MAYA *n.*[2] 1. E20. **2** = MAYA *n.*[2] 2. M20.

Mayanist *n.* an expert in or student of Mayan culture M20.

maybe /ˈmeɪbiː, -bi/ *adv.* & *n.* Also (*colloq.* & *dial.*) **mebbe** /ˈmɛbi/. LME. [f. *it may be*. Cf. MAYHAP.] **A** *adv.* Possibly, perhaps. LME.

JOYCE I'll make it worth while. And I don't mean may-be. *New Yorker* I wanted to think maybe she was different now.

B *n.* What may be; a possibility. Now *rare*. L16.

maycock *n.* var. of MACOCK.

†Maye *n.* & *a.* see MAYA *n.*[2] & *a.*

mayest *v.* see MAY *v.*[1]

Mayfair /ˈmeɪfɛː/ *n.* & *a.* E18. [f. MAY *n.*[2] + FAIR *n.*[1]] **A** *n.* A fair held in May, *esp.* (*Hist.*) that held annually from the 17th cent. until the end of the 18th cent. in Brook fields near Hyde Park Corner in London; the fashionable and opulent district in the West End of London occupying the site of the old fairground. E18. **B** *attrib.* or as *adj.* Of, pertaining to, or characteristic of Mayfair. M18.

Mayfairish *a.* of the nature or character of Mayfair M20.

mayfly /ˈmeɪflʌɪ/ *n.* Pl. **-flies**, same. M17. [f. MAY *n.*[2] + FLY *n.*[1]] **1** Any of various insects of the order Ephemeroptera, having aquatic larvae and short-lived adults with three long abdominal cerci and a characteristic bobbing mating flight; an ephemerid; *spec.* in *Angling*, (an artificial fly imitating) an adult of the genus *Ephemera*. M17. **2** Any of various other relatively large insects found near water, as a dragonfly, an alder-fly, a caddis-fly. Now *rare* or *obs.* M18.

mayhap /meɪˈhap, ˈmeɪhap/ *adv.* Now *arch.* & *dial.* M16. [f. *it may hap* (HAP *v.*[1]). Cf. MAYBE.] Perhaps, possibly.

Also **mayhappen** *adv.* E16.

mayhem /ˈmeɪhɛm/ *n.* & *v.* Also **†maihem**. L15. [AN *mahem*, OFr. *mahaing* MAIM *n.*[1]] **A** *n.* **1** Malicious injury to or maiming of a person, orig. (now *Hist.*) so as to impair or destroy the victim's capacity for self-defence. L15. **2** *transf.* & *fig.* Violent and damaging action; violent destruction; (in weakened sense) rowdy confusion, disruption, chaos. L19.

2 H. CARPENTER The ability to work at his desk in the middle of domestic mayhem. *Daily Express* It was mayhem on the motorway, which was blocked off to allow emergency services to reach the scene.

Phrases: **commit mayhem** maliciously injure or maim a person, be violently destructive, create chaos.

B *v.t.* Infl. **-m-**, ***-mm-**. Injure or maim maliciously. Now *rare*. M16.

mayn't *v.* see MAY *v.*[1]

mayo /ˈmeɪəʊ/ *n.* *colloq.* M20. [Abbrev.] Mayonnaise.

mayonnaise /meɪəˈneɪz/ *n.* E19. [Fr., also *magnonaise*, *mahonnaise*, perh. fem. of *mahonnais* adj., f. *Mahon* capital of Minorca.] A thick sauce consisting of yolk of egg beaten up with oil and vinegar and seasoned with salt etc., used as a dressing esp. for salad, eggs, cold meat, or fish; a dish (of meat etc.) having this sauce as a dressing.

mayonnaised *a.* dressed with mayonnaise M20.

mayor /mɛː/ *n.* In sense 2 usu. **mair**. ME. [(O)Fr. *maire* f. L MAJOR *a.*, used as n. in late

L.] 1 The head or chief officer of the municipal corporation of a city or borough in England, Wales, Ireland, parts of the British Commonwealth, the US, and formerly in Scotland (where now *provost*); in England and Wales now also, the head of a district council with the status of a borough. Occas., a French *maire* or (formerly) a similar municipal officer in other European towns; any of various administrative officers in other European countries, as the Netherlands and Switzerland. ME. 2 *Hist.* In Scotland, any of various officers with delegated jurisdiction or executive functions under the monarch or under some judicial authority. ME.

Phrases: *Lord Mayor*: see LORD *n.* **mayor of the palace** [Fr. *maire du palais* tr. med.L *major domus*] *Hist.* (orig. under the later Merovingian kings) a nominal subordinate wielding the power of his titular superior.

mayordom *n.* (*obs.* exc. *Hist.*) = MAYORALTY 1 M16. **mayorlet** *n.* (*rare*) a petty mayor M19.

mayoral /maːjəˈrɑːl, *foreign* majoˈral/ *n.* L16. [Sp., f. *mayor* greater f. L MAJOR *a.*] In Spain and Spanish-speaking countries, a conductor in charge of a train of animals or group of people.

mayoral /ˈmɛːr(ə)l/ *a.* L17. [f. MAYOR + -AL¹.] Of or pertaining to a mayor or mayoralty.

mayoralty /ˈmɛːr(ə)lti/ *n.* LME. [OFr. *mairalté*, f. *maire* MAYOR: see -TY¹.] 1 The status or office of a mayor. LME. 2 The period during which a mayor holds office. LME.

mayoress /ˈmɛːrɪs/ *n.* LME. [f. MAYOR + -ESS¹.] 1 The wife of a mayor; a woman fulfilling the ceremonial duties of a mayor's wife. LME. 2 A woman holding the office of mayor. L19.

1 *Lady Mayoress*: see LADY *n.* 5b.

mayorship /ˈmɛːʃɪp/ *n.* L15. [f. MAYOR + -SHIP.] = MAYORALTY 1.

mayory /ˈmɛːri/ *n.* Now *rare.* L17. [f. MAYOR + -Y⁵, after Fr. *mairie* etc.] The district over which a (Continental) mayor has jurisdiction; the place of business of a mayor.

maypole /ˈmeɪpəʊl/ *n.* M16. [f. MAY *n.*² + POLE *n.*¹] 1 A high pole, traditionally painted with spiral stripes and decorated with flowers, set up on a green or other open space, around which people dance on May Day holding long ribbons attached to the top. M16. 2 A tall object or (esp.) person. *joc.* L16.

mayst *v.* see MAY *v.*¹

maythe /meɪð/ *n. arch.* Also **maythes** /meɪðz/. [OE *magoþe* weak fem., *maegþa* weak masc., of unkn. origin.] 1 Any of various kinds of mayweed or camomile; *esp.* stinking camomile, *Anthemis cotula*. OE. †2 *red maythe*, pheasant's eye, *Adonis annua*. L16–E18.

maythen /ˈmeɪð(ə)n/ *n. obs.* exc. *dial.* Also **mathern**. ME. [Repr. OE *mæg(e)þan*, *magoþan*, obl. cases and pl. of *mægeþa*, *magoþa*: see prec.] = MAYTHE 1.

maythes *n.* var. of MAYTHE.

mayweed /ˈmeɪwiːd/ *n.* M16. [f. MAYTHE, MAYTHEN + WEED *n.*¹] Any of various kinds of wild camomile found as weeds of cultivated ground; *esp.* (more fully *scentless mayweed*) *Tripleurospermum inodorum* and (more fully *stinking mayweed*) *Anthemis cotula*.

mazagan /ˈmazəgan/ *n.* M18. [*Mazagan* in Morocco, where it grows wild.] In full *mazagan bean*. A small early variety of the broad bean, *Vicia faba*.

Mazahua /məˈzɑːwə/ *n.* & *a.* L18. [The Mazahua name for themselves.] A *n.* Pl. **-s**, same. 1 A member of an American Indian people of Mexico. L18. 2 The language of this people. M20. B *adj.* Of or pertaining to this people or their language. L20.

mazame /məˈzeɪm, məˈzɑːmeɪ/ *n.* L18. [Aztec *maçame* pl. of *maçatl* deer, mistaken for sing.] Any of various American deer; *spec.* = BROCKET 2. Also (occas.), a Rocky Mountain goat.

mazar /məˈzɑː/ *n.* E20. [Arab. *mazār* place visited, f. *zāra* to visit.] A Muslim tomb revered as a shrine.

mazard /ˈmazəd/ *n.*¹ *dial.* & *US*. Also **-zz-**. L16. [Perh. a use of next.] More fully *mazard cherry*. The wild form of the sweet cherry, *Prunus avium*, esp. when used as a stock for grafting; the small black or dark red fruit of this tree.

mazard /ˈmazəd/ *n.*² Also **-zz-**. E17. [Alt. of MAZER by assoc. of *-er* with -ARD. Perh. earlier in prec.] †1 A cup, a bowl, a drinking-vessel. Also *mazard bowl*. E17–L18. 2 The head; the face. *joc.* (*arch.*). E17.

mazarine /mazəˈriːn, ˈmazəriːn/ *n.* & *a.* Also **mazarin** /ˈmazərɪn/. L17. [Perh. f. Cardinal Jules *Mazarin* (1602–61) or the Duchesse de *Mazarin* (d. 1699). In sense A.1 perh. a different wd.] A *n.* 1 *Hist.* A deep plate, usually of metal, *esp.* one placed as a strainer inside a serving-dish. Formerly also *mazarine dish*, *plate*. L17. 2 In full *mazarine blue*. A deep rich blue. L17. b A fabric or garment of a mazarine blue colour. Now *rare*. L17. 3 In full *mazarine blue*. A Eurasian blue (lycaenid) butterfly, *Cyaniris semiargus*. E19. B *adj.* Of a mazarine blue colour. L17.

Mazatec /ˈmazətɛk/ *n.* & *a.* Also **Mazateco** /mazəˈtɛkəʊ/. E20. [Mazatec.] A *n.* Pl. **-s**, same. 1 A member of an Indian people of north Oaxaca in southern Mexico. E20. 2 The language of this people. M20. B *attrib.* or as *adj.* Of or pertaining to the Mazatecs or their language. M20.

Mazdaean /ˈmazdɪən/ *a.* & *n.* Also **-dean**. L19. [f. as next + -EAN.] A *adj.* Zoroastrian. L19. B *n.* A Zoroastrian. L19.

Mazdaism /ˈmazdəɪz(ə)m/ *n.* Also **Mazde-**. L19. [f. Avest. *mazdā*, the supreme god (Ahura Mazdā, Ormuzd) of ancient Persian religion + -ISM.] Zoroastrianism.

Mazdaist *n.* a Zoroastrian E20.

Mazdean *a.* & *n.* var. of MAZDAEAN.

Mazdeism *n.* var. of MAZDAISM.

maze /meɪz/ *n.*¹ ME. [f. MAZE *v.*] †1 *the maze*, delirium, delusion, disappointment. Only in ME. †2 A delusive fancy; a trick, a deception. Only in LME. 3 A state of bewilderment. *obs.* exc. *dial.* LME. 4 A structure consisting of a network of winding and intercommunicating paths and passages arranged in bewildering complexity (freq. with a correct path concealed by blind alleys), esp. formed by hedges in a garden or represented on paper by a pattern of lines, and designed as a puzzle or as a device to study intelligence and learning. Also, a structure with a single winding path much greater in distance from beginning to end than the direct line. LME. 5 *transf.* & *fig.* Any confusing or complex network, route, or mass. M16. b A winding movement, esp. in a dance. Now *dial.* E17.

5 E. MUIR And all the roads ran in a maze Hither and thither, like a web. A. BLOND In a maze of back alleys, we finally climbed a fire escape. *Guns & Weapons* The average bloke is put through a maze of paperwork.

mazeful *a.* (*arch.*) bewildering, confusing L16. **mazelike** *a.* resembling (that of) a maze L16.

maze *n.*² var. of MEASE.

maze /meɪz/ *v.* ME. [Aphet. f. AMAZE *v.*] 1 *v.t.* Stupefy, daze. Formerly also, craze, infatuate. Usu. in *pass.* Now *arch.* & *dial.* ME. †b *v.i.* Be stupefied or delirious. LME–M16. 2 *v.t.* Bewilder, perplex, confuse. ME. 3 *v.i.* Move in a mazelike course, wander (as) in a maze. L16.

mazedly *adv.* in a bewildered, confused, or stupefied manner ME. **mazedness** *n.* the state of being bewildered, confused, or stupefied LME.

mazel tov /ˈmaz(ə)l toːv, tɒf/ *int.* M19. [mod.Heb. *mazzāl ṭōḇ* lit. 'good star', f. Heb. *mazzāl* star, f. as MOZZLE.] Among Jews: good luck, congratulations.

mazement /ˈmeɪzm(ə)nt/ *n.* L16. [Partly f. MAZE *v.* + -MENT, partly aphet. f. AMAZEMENT.] A state of stupor or trance. Now usu., amazement.

mazer /ˈmeɪzə/ *n. obs.* exc. *Hist.* ME. [OFr. *masere* of Gmc origin, perh. reinforced f. MDu. *maeser* maple.] 1 A hardwood, esp. maple, used as a material for drinking-cups. Also *mazer wood*. ME. †b The tree yielding this wood; a maple. Also *mazer tree*. ME–M16. 2 A bowl, drinking-cup, or goblet without a foot, orig. one made of mazer wood. Also *mazer bowl*, *cup*. ME. †3 The head. L16–M17.

mazey *a.* var. of MAZY.

Mazhabi /ˈmʌzhəbiː/ *n.* M19. [Urdu & Pers. *mazhabī* religious, sectarian, f. Arab. *maḏhab* way, doctrine, creed, f. *ḏahaba* go.] In the Indian subcontinent, esp. the Punjab: a Sikh.

mazout *n.* var. of MAZUT.

mazuma /məˈzuːmə/ *n. US* & *Austral. slang.* E20. [Yiddish, f. Heb. *mĕzummān*, f. *zimmēn* prepare.] Money, cash; *esp.* betting money.

mazurka /məˈzəːkə, məˈzʊəkə/ *n.* E19. [Fr. or f. G *masurka* f. Pol. *mazurka* woman of the province Mazovia.] 1 A Polish dance in triple time, usu. with a slide and hop. E19. 2 A piece of music for this dance or composed in its rhythm, usu. with accentuation of the second or third beat. M19.

mazut /məˈzuːt/ *n.* Also **mazout**. L19. [Russ.] A viscous liquid left as residue after the distillation of petroleum, used in Russia as a fuel oil and coarse lubricant.

mazy /ˈmeɪzi/ *a.* Also **-ey**. E16. [f. MAZE *n.*¹ + -Y¹.] 1 Giddy, dizzy, confused in the head. *dial.* E16. 2 Resembling or of the nature of a maze; full of windings and turnings. L16. 3 Moving in a mazelike course, twisting and turning. E18.

mazily *adv.* ME. **maziness** *n.* E19.

mazzard *n.*¹, *n.*² vars. of MAZARD *n.*¹, *n.*²

Mazzinian /matˈsiːnɪən/ *a.* & *n.* M19. [f. *Mazzini* (see below) + -AN.] A *adj.* Of or pertaining to the Italian patriot and revolutionary Giuseppe Mazzini (1805–72) or his policies, esp. advocacy of a united republican Italy. M19. B *n.* An adherent of Mazzini. M19.

mbira /(ə)mˈbɪərə/ *n.* L19. [Bantu.] A musical instrument of southern Africa consisting of a set of keys or tongues attached to a resonator, which are plucked with the thumb and forefingers. Also called *sansa*.

mbongo /(ə)mˈbɒŋgəʊ/ *n. S. Afr. slang.* Pl. **-os**. E20. [Alt. of IMBONGI.] A political stooge or apologist, a 'yes-man'.

Mbuti /(ə)mˈbuːti/ *n.* & *a.* M20. [Mbuti.] A *n.* Pl. **-s**, same. A member of a pygmy people of western Uganda and adjacent areas of Zaïre; a language of this people. M20. B *attrib.* or as *adj.* Of or pertaining to the Mbutis or their languages. M20.

McBurney's point /məkbəːnɪz ˈpɔɪnt/ *n. phr.* L19. [Charles *McBurney* (1845–1913), US surgeon.] *Med.* The point on the surface of the abdomen which lies on a line from the tip of the hip-bone to the navel and one-third of the way along it, which is the point of maximum tenderness in appendicitis.

McCarthyism /məˈkɑːθɪɪz(ə)m/ *n.* M20. [f. *McCarthy* (see below) + -ISM.] The policy of hunting out (suspected) Communists and removing them from Government departments or other positions, *spec.* as pursued by Senator Joseph R. McCarthy (1908–57) in the US in the 1950s.

McCarthyite *n.* & *a.* (*a*) *n.* a supporter of this policy; (*b*) *adj.* of McCarthy or McCarthyism: M20.

McCoy /məˈkɔɪ/ *n. colloq.* Also **Mackay** /məˈkʌɪ/. L19. [Origin unkn.] *the real McCoy*, the genuine article, the real thing.

McGuffin /məˈgʌfɪn/ *n.* L20. [Origin unkn.] A thing in a film or story which appears to the characters and the audience to be of great significance but is actually only an excuse for the plot; a thing in a film etc. which misleads the characters and audience.

McIntosh /ˈmakɪntɒʃ/ *n.* Also **MacIntosh**. L19. [John *McIntosh* (b. 1777), Canad. farmer.] In full *McIntosh Red*. A red-skinned variety of eating apple.

McKenzie /məˈkɛnzi/ *n.* L20. [Name of the litigants in the case (*McKenzie* v. *McKenzie*) in which the English Court of Appeal ruled that any party in a trial is entitled to non-professional assistance in court.] *Law.* A non-professional person who attends a trial as a helper or adviser of one of the parties. Also *McKenzie man* etc.

McLuhanism /məˈkluːənɪz(ə)m/ *n.* M20. [f. *McLuhan* (see below) + -ISM.] The social ideas of the Canadian writer H. Marshall McLuhan (1911–80), such as that the effect of the introduction of the mass media is to deaden the critical faculties of individuals.

McLuhaˈnesque *a.* resembling or characteristic of McLuhan or his ideas M20.

McNaughten rules /məkˈnɔːt(ə)n ruːlz/ *n. phr. pl.* Also **McNaghten, M'-.** L19. [Daniel *M'Naghten*, acquitted of murder in 1843: the rules arose out of the consideration of his case by the House of Lords.] The British rules or criteria for judging criminal responsibility where there is a question of insanity.

me *n.*[1] var. of MI *n.*

me /miː, *unstressed* mɪ/ *pers. pron., 1 sing. objective (accus. & dat.), n.*[2], *& possess. a.* [OE *mē̆* (i) accus. corresp. to OFris. *mi*, OS *mī*, *mē* (Du. *mij*) & further to L *me*, Gk (*e*)*me*, OIr. *mé* (Ir. *mi*, *mi*), Welsh *mi*, Skt *mā*, (ii) dat. corresp. to OFris. *mi*(*r*), OS *mī* (Du. *mij*), (O)HG *mir*, ON *mér*, Goth. *mis*, f. IE base (in all IE langs.). As adj. prob. f. unstressed var. of MY *a.*] A *pron.* 1 Objective (direct & indirect) of I *pron.*: the speaker or writer himself or herself. OE. **b** Myself. Now *arch.* & *poet.* exc. *N. Amer. colloq.* OE. 2 Subjective: I. In standard use esp. pred. after *be* & after *as*, *than*. Now *colloq.* LME. 3 With less definite syntactical relation to the context. (Chiefly exclamatory.) L16.

1 SHAKES. *Per.* And make a conquest of unhappy me. C. LAMB He enters me his name in the book. T. HARDY Can I ask you to do me one kindness? SCOTT FITZGERALD There aren't any caddies here except me. I. MCEWAN Why did you take that picture of me? J. SIMMS So he reluctantly gave me absolution of my sins. M. AMIS My flat is small and also costs me a lot of money. See also MESEEMS, METHINKS. **b** I. MURDOCH I should steadfastly hold me in the Faith. P. GRACE I've got me a job down at the timber yard. 2 BYRON Lord Delawarr is considerably younger than me. E. WAUGH Edith and Olive and me have talked it over. 3 MILTON Me miserable! which way shall I flie Infinite wrauth. F. BURNEY 'Don't you dance?' he said. 'Me?' cried she, embarrassed. M. EDGEWORTH Which would be hard on us and me a widow. A. S. NEILL I'm going to start to-day to learn to read. 'Me too,' said Donald. D. BARNES Jed would say North, and Jod would say South, and me sitting between them going mad. *Listener* Me, I like fighting too.

Phrases: *ay me!*: see AY *int.*[2] **be me** be suited to me, represent my real self. *dear me!*: see DEAR *int. mighty me!*: see MIGHTY *a. riddle me a riddle*: see RIDDLE *v.*[1] 2. *search me*: see SEARCH *v.*[1] *stone me*: see STONE *v. the laugh is on me*: see LAUGH *n.*

Comb.: **me-and-you** *slang* a menu; **me-too** *a.* & *v.* (*a*) *adj.* designating or pertaining to views, policies, etc., adopted from, or products etc. copied from, an opponent or rival; (*b*) *v.t.* adopt or appropriate (a policy etc.) from an opponent or rival; **me-tooer** a person who adopts or appropriates a policy etc. from an opponent or rival; **me-tooism** the adoption or appropriation of a policy etc. from an opponent or rival.

B *n.* One's personality, the ego. E19.

C *adj.* My. *colloq.* & *dial.* M19.

me-ward(s) *adv.* towards me M19.

meacock /ˈmiːkɒk/ *n.* & *a.* Now *arch. rare.* E16. [Perh. orig. the name of some bird.] A *n.* An effeminate person; a coward, a weakling. E16. †B *adj.* Effeminate, cowardly, weak. L16–M17.

mea culpa /meɪə ˈkʊlpə, miːə ˈkʌlpə/ *int.* & *n. phr.* LME. [L, lit. '(through) my own fault': from the prayer of confession in the Latin liturgy of the Church.] A *int.* Acknowledging one's guilt or responsibility for an error. LME. B *n. phr.* An utterance of '*mea culpa*'; an acknowledgement of one's guilt or responsibility for an error. E19.

mead /miːd/ *n.*[1] [OE *medu*, *meodu* = OFris., MLG (Du.) *mede*, OHG *metu*, *mitu* (G *Met*), ON *mjǫðr*, f. Gmc f. IE base also of Gk *methu* wine, Skt *madhu* honey, sweet drink.] Alcoholic liquor produced by fermenting a mixture of honey and water; a type of this; a drink of this.

Comb.: **mead-bench** *Gmc Antiq.* a seat at a feast when mead was drunk; **mead-hall** *Gmc Antiq.* a banqueting-hall.

mead /miːd/ *n.*[2] Now *poet.* & *dial.* [OE *mǣd*: see next.] 1 = MEADOW 1. OE. †2 = MEADOW 2. ME–L17.

meadow /ˈmɛdəʊ/ *n.* & *v.* [OE *mǣdwe* etc., obl. cases of *mǣd*, f. Gmc, f. base also of MOW *v.*[1]] A *n.* 1 Orig., a piece of land permanently covered with grass to be mown for use as hay; later, any piece of cultivated grassland. Also, a tract of low well-watered ground, esp. near a river. OE. 2 Land used for the cultivation of grass, esp. for hay. OE. 3 *beaver meadow*, a fertile tract of land left dry above a demolished beaver dam. *N. Amer.* M17. 4 A low level tract of uncultivated grassland, esp. along a river or in a marshy region near the sea. *N. Amer.* L17. 5 A feeding-ground of fish. M19.

1 *water-meadow*: see WATER *n.*

Comb.: **meadow beauty** any of several N. American plants of the genus *Rhexia* (family Melastomataceae), with four-petalled pink flowers; **meadow bird** = BOBOLINK; **meadow brown** a common brown and orange satyrid butterfly, *Maniola jurtina*; **meadow buttercup** a Eurasian buttercup, *Ranunculus acris*, common in grassland; **meadow cat's-tail** = TIMOTHY; **meadow crake** = CORNCRAKE; **meadow fescue** a tall Eurasian fescue with flat leaves, *Festuca pratensis*, which is grown for pasture in Europe and N. America; **meadow foam** *US* the poached-egg flower, *Limnanthes douglasii*; **meadow frog** = *leopard frog* s.v. LEOPARD *n.* **meadow grass** a grass of the genus *Poa*; **meadow ground** a piece of ground used for the cultivation of grass, esp. for hay; **meadowland** (a stretch of) land used for the cultivation of grass, esp. for hay; **meadowlark** *N. Amer.* any of several American songbirds of the genus *Sturnella*, speckled brown with yellow underparts, *esp.* the eastern *S. magna* or the western *S. neglecta*; **meadow mouse** = *meadow vole* below; **meadow mushroom** an edible fungus, *Agaricus campestris*; **meadow parsnip** a yellow-flowered umbelliferous plant, *Thaspium trifoliatum*, of the US; **meadow pipit** a common European pipit, *Anthus pratensis*, inhabiting open country, heath, and moorland; also called *titlark*; **meadow rue** any of various plants constituting the genus *Thalictrum*, of the buttercup family, having leaves like those of rue and apetalous flowers; *spec.* (more fully *common meadow rue*) *Thalictrum flavum*, a plant of riversides; **meadow saffron** a plant of the lily family, *Colchicum autumnale*, producing pale purple flowers like crocuses in autumn and broad leaves the following spring; also called *naked ladies*; *meadow soft-grass*: see *soft-grass* s.v. SOFT *a.*; *meadow* VETCHLING; **meadow vole** a N. American vole, *Microtus pennsylvanicus*.

B *v.t.* Devote (land) to the production of grass, esp. for hay; use as meadow. M18.

meadowed *a.* (*a*) provided with meadows (chiefly as 2nd elem. of comb., as *well-meadowed*); (*b*) devoted to the production of grass, esp. for hay; used as meadow: M17. **meadowing** *n.* (*a*) land used or suitable for the cultivation of grass; (*b*) the action of the vb: L16. **meadowless** *a.* L19. **meadowy** *a.* resembling a meadow L16.

meadowsweet /ˈmɛdəʊswiːt/ *n.* M16. [f. prec. + SWEET *a.*] A plant of the rose family, *Filipendula ulmaria*, of wet meadows and stream banks, with panicles of creamy-white fragrant flowers; *US* any of several shrubs of the allied genus *Spiraea*.

meadstead *n.* var. of MIDSTEAD.

†**meadsweet** *n.* LME–M18. [f. MEAD *n.*[2], *n.*[1] (cf. next) + SWEET *a.*] Meadowsweet, *Filipendula ulmaria*.

†**meadwort** *n.* OE–L18. [f. MEAD *n.*[1] + WORT *n.*[1]: perh. the flowers were used for flavouring mead. Later assoc. with MEAD *n.*[2]] = prec.

meager *a.*, *n.*, & *v.* see MEAGRE *a.*, *n.*[2], & *v.*

meagre /ˈmiːgə/ *n.*[1] Also (earlier) **maigre** /ˈmeɪgə/. M19. [Fr. *maigre*: see next.] A large edible carnivorous sciaenid fish, *Argyrosomus regius*, of the Mediterranean, the E. Atlantic, and the SW Indian Ocean. Also called *kabeljou*, *kob*.

meagre /ˈmiːgə/ *a.*, *n.*[2], & *v.* Also ***meager**. ME. [AN *megre*, (O)Fr. *maigre*, f. L *macer*, *macr*- rel. to Gk *makros* long, *makethnos* tall, slender, *mēkos* length. See also MAIGRE *a.*] A *adj.* I 1 Of a person, animal, limb, etc.: having little flesh; lean, thin, emaciated. ME. 2 Deficient or inferior in quantity, size, or quality; lacking fullness, richness, or elaboration; poor, scanty; inadequate, unsatisfying. E16.

1 W. COWPER He calls for Famine, and the meagre fiend Blows mildew from between his shrivelled teeth. SIR W. SCOTT The meagre condition of his horse. W. IRVING A meagre wiry old fellow. 2 E. K. KANE The meagre allowance of two pounds of raw flesh every other day. K. AMIS The .. notes of a recorder playing a meagre air were distantly audible. D. HALBERSTAM Gas had ignited the building because Otis took such meager and inadequate safety precautions. L. AUCHINCLOSS A pompous beaux-arts facade much too grand for the meager, three-window frontage. E. KUZWAYO It augmented my meagre income.

II 3 = MAIGRE *a.* II. E18.

B *absol.* as *n.* †1 Leanness, emaciation. LME–M16. 2 Maigre diet. Now *rare.* M19.

†C *v.t.* Make meagre or lean. L16–E19.

meagrely *adv.* L16. **meagreness** *n.* LME.

meal /miːl/ *n.*[1] [OE *melu* = OFris. *mel*, OS *melo* (Du. *meel*), OHG *melo* (G *Mehl*), ON *mjǫl*, f. Gmc, f. IE base also of L *molere* grind.] 1 The edible part of any grain or pulse, now usu. other than wheat, ground to a powder. Also (*spec.*), in Scotland and Ireland oatmeal, in the US, maize flour. Cf. FLOUR *n.* OE. †**b** The finer part of ground grain, in contrast with *bran.* L16–E17. 2 *transf.* A powder produced by grinding; a powdery substance resembling flour; *Bot.* the powder covering the surface of the leaves etc. of certain plants. M16.

1 *Indian meal*: see INDIAN *a.* OATMEAL. *round meal*: see ROUND *a. whole meal*: see WHOLE *a.* 2 *bone-meal* etc.

Comb.: **meal-beetle** any beetle of the family Tenebrionidae whose larval or adult forms infest granaries etc.; **mealberry** the bearberry, *Arctostaphylos uva-ursi*; **mealman** a dealer in meal; **meal moth** any of several moths which infest mills, granaries, etc., esp. *Pyralis farinalis*; **meal-worm** the larva of a meal-beetle; *meal-worm beetle* = *meal-beetle* above.

meal /miːl/ *n.*[2] Also †**mele**. [OE *mǣl* corresp. to OFris. *mēl*, *māl*, OS *-māl* sign, measure (Du. *maal*), OHG *māl* time (G *Mal* time, *Mahl* meal), ON *mál* point or portion of time, mealtime, Goth. *mēl* time, f. Gmc, f. IE base meaning 'to measure'.] 1 A measure. Long *obs.* exc. as -MEAL. OE. 2 An occasion of taking food, *esp.* a customary one at a more or less fixed time of day; the food eaten at or provided for such an occasion. OE. 3 The quantity of milk given by a cow at one milking; the time of milking. Now *dial.* E17.

2 **make a meal of** (*a*) consume as a meal, devour; (*b*) treat in an overfussy manner, make (a task etc.) seem unduly laborious.

Comb.: **meal-pennant**: displayed during mealtimes in the US navy and on yachts; a red pennant; **meals-on-wheels** *n.* & *a.* (designating) a service, usually provided by a women's voluntary organization, whereby meals are delivered to old people, invalids, etc.; **meal-ticket** a ticket entitling a person to a meal, esp. at a specified place for a reduced cost; *fig.* a source of income or livelihood, *esp.* a husband or wife regarded merely as such; **mealtide** (*obs.* exc. *Sc.*) mealtime; one's food; **mealtime** the (usual) time for eating a meal.

mealless /-l-l-/ *a.* L19.

meal /miːl/ *v.*[1] Chiefly *Sc.* LME. [f. MEAL *n.*[1]] 1 *v.t.* & *i.* Grind or be ground into meal; reduce to meal or fine powder. LME. 2 *v.t.* Cover with meal; powder with meal; add meal to. E17. 3 *v.i.* Yield or be plentiful in meal. L18.

mealable *a.* E19.

meal /miːl/ *v.*[2]*i.* E17. [f. MEAL *n.*[2]] Make a meal; eat meals; feed.

†**meal** *v.*[3] var. of MAIL *v.*[1]

-meal /miːl/ *suff.* [OE *mǣlum* instr. pl. of *mǣl* MEAL *n.*[2]] Forming advs. f. ns. w. the sense 'measure, quantity taken at one time', as *flockmeal*, *inchmeal*, *piecemeal*.

mealer /ˈmiːlə/ *n.* M19. [f. MEAL *n.*[2], *v.*[2] + -ER[1].] 1 As 2nd elem. of comb.: a person who eats a specified number of meals a day. M19. 2 A person who takes meals at one place and lodges at another. *US colloq.* L19.

mealie /ˈmiːli/ *n. S. Afr.* Also **mielie**. E19. [Afk. *mielie* f. Port. *milho* maize, millet, f. L *milium*.] Maize; a corn-cob (usu. in *pl.*).

green mealie a corn-cob gathered and cooked while it is still green. *stamped mealies*: see STAMP *v.*

Comb.: **mealie-cob** a corn-cob; *mealie-cob worm*, the caterpillar of the corn ear worm, *Heliothis armigera*, a noctuid moth; **mealie meal** coarse meal of maize (a staple food); **mealiepap** [Afk. *pap* porridge] mealie meal porridge; **mealie rice** finely stamped grains of maize used instead of rice.

mealy /ˈmiːli/ *a.* M16. [f. MEAL *n.*[1] + -Y[1].] **1** Resembling meal, having the qualities of meal or flour, powdery; (of boiled potatoes) dry and powdery. M16. **2** Covered with or as with meal, flour, or any fine dust or powder. M16. **b** Of colour, a horse: spotty, interspersed with whitish specks. L17. **c** Of complexion: pale. M19. **3** Containing meal or flour; farinaceous. L16. **4** Not outspoken, afraid to speak plainly; mealy-mouthed. L16.

Special collocations & comb.: **mealy bug** any of various scale insects of the family Pseudococcidae, which are covered with a waxy powder. **mealy-mouth** *n.* & *v.* (*a*) *n.* a mouth which never speaks plainly; a soft, indirect, or reticent manner of speaking; a mealy-mouthed person; (*b*) *v.t.* & *i.* avoid speaking plainly (about), be mealy-mouthed (about). **mealy-mouthed** *a.* not outspoken, afraid to speak one's mind or to use plain terms; soft-spoken. **mealy-mouthedly** *adv.* in a mealy-mouthed manner. **mealy-mouthedness** the quality of being mealy-mouthed. **mealy pudding** = *white pudding* s.v. WHITE *a.*; *mealy redpoll*: see REDPOLL *n.*[1] **mealy tree** = *wayfaring-tree* s.v. WAYFARING *n.*

mealiness *n.* E17.

mean /miːn/ *n.*[1] ME. [Partly f. MEAN *a.*[2], partly f. OFr. *meien*, *moien* use as n. of adj.: see MEAN *a.*[2]] **I** That which is in the middle. **1** *Mus.* A middle or intermediate part in a harmonized composition or performance, *esp.* the tenor and alto. Also, a person performing such a part; an instrument on which such a part is played. *obs.* exc. *Hist.* ME. **2** That which is intermediate; a condition, quality, disposition, or course of action, that is equally removed from two opposite (esp. blameable) extremes; a medium. Freq. w. laudatory adj., as *golden mean*. LME. †**b** Absence of extremes; moderation. M16–E18. †**3** The middle (of something). LME–L17. †**4** Something interposed or intervening. LME–L16. **5a** *Math.* A term intermediate in position between the first and last terms of a progression; a term such that performing an operation on it *n* times is equivalent to operating similarly on of a set of *n* items; a mean value, an average; *spec.* = *arithmetic mean* s.v. ARITHMETIC *a.* L15. **b** An average amount or value; the mean pressure, temperature, etc. E19.

2 P. TILLICH Aristotle's doctrine of courage as the right mean between cowardice and temerity. N. GORDIMER The climate of each day the same cool mean, neither summer nor winter. 5 *Nature* Englishmen are normally distributed in height with a mean of 5 feet 8 inches.

II An intermediary agent or instrument. †**6** A mediator, an intermediary, a negotiator, an ambassador, an intercessor. LME–E17. **b** *sing.* & in *pl.* Mediation, intercession; instigation. LME–M17. **7** *sing.* (*arch.*) & in *pl.* (usu. treated as *sing.*). An instrument, agency, method, or course of action, by which some object is or may be attained, or some result is or may be brought about. Formerly also, a condition permitting or conducing to something, an opportunity. LME. †**b** In *pl.* Stratagem, trickery. LME–E17. **8** In *pl.* The resources available for effecting some object; *spec.* financial resources, esp. in relation to requirements or habits of expenditure. Also, money, wealth. M16.

7 W. SCLATER Vncharitable is that sentence . . that Baptisme is necessarie as a meane to saluation. T. OVERBURY In warre, there is no meane to erre twice. G. ORWELL Power is not a means, it is an end. DAY LEWIS How deeply the loss impoverished my growing years . . there is no means of telling. G. GREENE Try other means first. B. CHATWIN A solitary gas-ring was her only means of cooking. 8 C. P. SNOW There was plenty of money. . . Proust could draw on substantial private means. R. ELLMANN He declined . . to live within his means.

Phrases: *arithmetic mean*: see ARITHMETIC *a.* **by all (manner of) means** (*a*) in every possible way; (*b*) at any cost, without fail; (*c*) (emphasizing a permission, request, or injunction) certainly. **by any (manner of) means** in any way, at all. *by fair means or foul*: see FAIR *a.* **by means** (or †**mean**) **of** (*a*) by the agency or instrumentality of (a person or thing, *doing*); †(*b*) in consequence of, by reason of, owing to. **by no (manner of) means** (*a*) in no way, not at all; (*b*) on no account. **by this** or **that means** (or †**mean**) by means of this or that, in this or that way, thus. **find (the) means** (or †**mean**) find out a way (*to do*), contrive or manage (*to do*, †a thing). *geometric mean*: see GEOMETRIC 1. *golden mean*: see GOLDEN *a.* †**in the mean** in the meantime. **man, person, woman,** etc., **of means**: having a substantial income, being wealthy. *means and ways*: see WAY *n.* **means of grace** *Chr. Theol.* the sacraments and other religious agencies viewed as the means by which divine grace is imparted to the soul, or by which growth in grace is promoted. *private means*: see PRIVATE *a.* *regression to the mean*: see REGRESSION 4b. *ways and means*: see WAY *n.*

Comb.: **means-end(s)** *attrib. a.* of or pertaining to the ways of achieving a result considered together with the result; **means test** an official inquiry into an applicant's private resources, determining or limiting a grant or allowance of money from public funds; **means-test** *v.t.* subject (a person) to a means test, assess (a grant etc.) by a means test; **means-testable** *a.* subject to a means test.

†**mean** *n.*[2] ME–E19. [f. MEAN *v.*[2]] A lament, a complaint.

mean /miːn/ *a.*[1] & *adv.*[1] [OE *mǣne* (rare) for *ġemǣne* = OFris. *gemēne*, OS *gimēni* (Du. *gemeen*), OHG *gimeini* (G *gemein*), Goth. *gamains*, f. Gmc, f. as Y- + base repr. also by antecedent form of L *communis* COMMON *a.*] **A** *adj.* **I 1** Common to two or more persons or things; possessed jointly. Long *obs.* exc. *dial.* OE.

II Inferior. **2** Of a person, rank, etc.: low in the social hierarchy, not noble or gentle. Also, poor, badly off. *obs.* exc. as passing into sense 4. OE. **3** Inferior in ability, learning, or perception; having or exhibiting little mental power. Now chiefly in (*to*) *the meanest understanding, capacity*, etc. LME. **4** Poor in quality or condition; of little value, contemptible; comparatively worthless. Now chiefly *N. Amer. colloq.* LME. **b** In low spirits, in poor health, not quite well. *US colloq.* M19. **5** Undignified, low; not elevated or sublime. LME. **6** Not imposing in appearance, shabby; characterized by poverty. E17. **7** Lacking moral dignity, ignoble, small-minded; given to or exhibiting uncooperativeness, unkindness, or unfairness; *colloq.* (orig. *N. Amer.*) vicious, nasty, difficult to handle or deal with, unpleasant. Also (*colloq.*), ashamed of one's conduct. M17. **8** Niggardly, not generous or liberal, stingy. M18. **9** Remarkably clever or adroit; excellent; formidable. *slang* (orig. *US*). E20.

2 BUNYAN Thou shalt not steal, though thou be very mean. 4 C. M. KIRKLAND You've had a pretty mean time. 5 MARVELL He nothing common did or mean, Upon that memorable scene. 6 E. A. FREEMAN The robes . . made all that France . . had beheld of the same kind seem mean by comparison. E. JOLLEY Very different from the mean dirty streets they had come from. 7 I. D'ISRAELI Charles . . was mean enough to suspend her pension. R. T. COOKE It would be awful mean of me to leave you here alone. *Motocross Rider* Sittendorf . . is a mean, treacherous course mixing . . steep climbs, and menacing rocks. 8 A. MASSIE She was kept short of money, for Willy . . was mean. 9 *Golf* Many of the women . . play a mean game of golf.

Special collocations & phrases: **mean streets** (*a*) streets where the poor or socially deprived live or work; (*b*) streets where people exploit or show no consideration for others, streets noted for violence and crime. **mean White** (chiefly *US*, *derog.*) (of) a poor and landless Southern White, = *poor White* s.v. POOR *a.* **no mean —** a very good —, a not inconsiderable —.

B *adv.* Meanly. Now *non-standard.* E17.

mean /miːn/ *a.*[2] & *adv.*[2] ME. [AN *me(e)n*, OFr. *meien*, *moien* (mod. *moyen*) f. L *medianus* MEDIAN *a.*] **A** *adj.* †**1a** Occupying a middle or an intermediate place in sequential order or spatial position. ME–E19. **b** *Mus.* Designating the tenor and alto parts and the tenor clef, as intermediate between the bass and treble. L16–E18. **2** Intermediate in kind, quality, or degree. Now *rare.* ME. **3** Intermediate in time; coming between two points of time or two events; intervening. Now only in MEANTIME, MEANWHILE. LME. **4** *Law.* = MESNE *a.* LME. †**5** Used as an intermediary; serving as a means or instrument; intervening as part of a process. LME–E17. **6** Not far above or below the average; moderate, mediocre, middling. Later only disparagingly and so coincident w. MEAN *a.*[1] LME. **7** *Math.* Of a value: so related to a given set of values that the sum of their differences from it is zero; that is an arithmetic mean; average. LME.

Special collocations & phrases: *extreme and mean ratio*: see EXTREME *a.* 2. **mean free path** *Physics* the mean distance travelled by a particle between interactions (e.g. by a gas molecule between collisions). **mean moon** a hypothetical moon assumed to move uniformly in the ecliptic in the same time as the actual moon. **mean proportional** a quantity related to two given quantities in such a way that dividing it by the smaller gives the same result as dividing the larger by it; the geometric mean of the quantities. **mean solar day** *Astron.* the time between successive passages of the mean sun across the meridian. **mean solar time**: as calculated by the motion of the mean sun (i.e. as shown by an ordinary clock). **mean square** the (arithmetic) mean of the squares of a set of numbers; *mean-square deviation, error*, the mean of the squares of the differences between a set of values and some fixed value. **mean sun** a hypothetical sun conceived as moving uniformly through the sky throughout the year, used in calculating time. MEANTIME. **mean time** = *mean solar time* above (GREENWICH *Mean Time*); **mean tone** *Mus.* the averaged or standard interval (halfway between a greater and less major second) used as a basis for tuning keyboard instruments before the adoption of equal temperament.

B *adv.* †**1** Moderately; comparatively less. LME–E17. **2** Intermediately. Long *rare.* LME.

mean /miːn/ *v.*[1] Pa. t. & pple **meant** /mɛnt/, †**meaned**. [OE *mǣnan* = OFris. *mēna* signify, OS *mēnian* intend, make known (Du. *meenen*), (O)HG *meinen* (now usu. 'have an opinion'), f. WGmc, f. IE base of MIND *n.*[1]] **1a** *v.t.* Have as one's purpose or intention, have in mind, (esp. *to do*). OE. †**b** *v.t.* Aim at, direct one's way to. *rare.* LME–E18. **c** *v.t.* Design (a thing) for a definite purpose, intend (a person or thing) to have a particular future, nature, or use, destine to a fate, (foll. by *for, to be, to do,* †*to*); expect or require *to be, to do*. Freq. in *pass.* LME. **d** *v.i.* Be *well* (occas. *ill* etc.) intentioned or disposed. (Foll. by *to, towards, by*, or indirect obj.) LME. **e** *v.t.* Intend (a remark, allusion, etc.) to have a particular reference. Foll. by †*at*, †*by*, *for, of,* †*to*. Now *rare.* E16. **2** *v.t.* Intend to indicate (a certain object), convey (a certain sense) or refer to (a certain person or thing) when using some word, sentence, significant action, etc., (in interrog. contexts) have as a motive or justification, (now freq. foll. by *by* a thing, *doing*); (in emphatic contexts) be sincere or serious in saying. OE. **3** *v.t.* Have as signification; signify, import; have as an equivalent in another language; entail, necessitate, involve; portend. OE. **b** Be of a specified degree of account or importance *to* (a person), esp. as a source of benefit or as an object of regard or affection; matter (a lot, nothing, etc., *to*). L19. **4**†**a** *v.t.* & *i.* foll. by *of*. Say, tell, mention. OE–L18. †**b** *v.i.* & *t.* Think, imagine. ME–M17. **c** *v.t.* In *pass.* Be reputed or reported *to be, to do.* M20. †**5** *v.t.* & *i.* foll. by *of, on, upon.* Have in mind, remember. ME–E16.

1a M. TWAIN I didn't know I was doing any harm; I didn't *mean* to do any harm. S. T. WARNER I have been meaning . . to write and thank you. T. CONNOR For much he never got round to doing, but meant to, when the weather bucked up. G. VIDAL She had meant to speak . . humorously but somehow the words had come out all wrong. c R. KIPLING Roads were meant to be walked upon. G. B. SHAW All progress means war with Society. T. S. ELIOT I am not Prince Hamlet, nor was meant to be. M. BARING His plays are meant for drawing rooms. A. D. HOPE They begot me in their bed Meaning me to be a boy. *New Yorker* The worst . . is that I'm meant to give a speech. d RIDER HAGGARD I do not think that your cousin means kindly by you. S. B. JACKMAN He means well . . and you can't say worse than that about anyone. e H. STURGIS There is a young don in the story, and . . someone . . decided it was meant for me. 2 W. COBBETT And what is meaned by 'The fear of the Lord'? MRS H. WARD No top-coat in such weather!

What do you mean by that, sir? L. M. MONTGOMERY When I tell you to come in at a certain time I mean that time. E. WAUGH When Lady Metroland said half past one she meant ten minutes to two. I. MURDOCH By freedom we mean absence of external restraint. E. BOWEN 'You're not coming in?' asked Henry, meaning, into the vicarage. 3 J. BUCHAN Autumn meant the thick, close odour of rotting leaves. P. KAVANAGH The wind's over Brannagan's, now that means rain. V. SCANNELL You wouldn't know what the word beautiful means. G. GREENE A suicide always means an inquest. R. ELLMANN He was prizeman . . which meant he was excused from the annual examinations. b C. P. SNOW She meant much to me, much more than any other human being. J. RHYS It means a lot, a friendly word just now.

Phrases etc.: **do you mean to say, tell me**, etc., **that —?** *colloq.* are you sincere or serious in saying etc. that —, will you confirm that it is indeed true that —? **(if) you know, see, understand, what I mean** *colloq.*: expr. a hope that one has been understood in spite of not having expressed oneself clearly. **I mean** *colloq.*: used as a mere conversational filler. *mean* BUSINESS. **mean it** be sincere or serious, not be joking or exaggerating. *mean mischief*: see MISCHIEF *n.* **you don't mean to say, tell me**, etc., **that —?** *colloq* you are surely not sincere or serious in saying etc. that —, it is surely not true that —?

†**meanless** *a.* meaningless M18–M19.

mean /miːn/ *v.*[2] Long *obs.* exc. *Sc.* [OE *mǣnan* rel. to MOAN *n.*] **1** *v.t.* Complain of, lament for; pity. OE. **2** *v.i.* & †*refl.* Lament, mourn; complain. OE. †**3** *v.t.* State as a grievance; represent by way of formal complaint or petition. L15–M18.

mean /miːn/ *v.*[3]*t.* L19. [f. MEAN *n.*[1]] Calculate the arithmetic mean of; average. Also foll. by *up*.

meander /mɪˈandə, miː-/ *n.* & *v.* Also (now *rare*) **maeander**. L16. [(Fr. *méandre* f.) L *maeander* f. Gk *maiandros* transf. use of name of a winding river in Phrygia.] **A** *n.* **1** Any of the curves or bends in the course of a winding river etc.; any of the crooked or winding paths of a maze or passages of a labyrinth; a convolution. Usu. in *pl.* L16. †**2** A labyrinth, a maze. L16–L18. **3** A circuitous journey or movement; a deviation. Usu. in *pl.* M17. **4** An ornamental pattern of lines winding in and out with rectangular turnings, or crossing one another at right angles. E18.

1 W. BECKFORD Springs whose frequent meanders gave . . the appearance of a vast green carpet shot with silver. *Natural History* The *Jorge Carlos* rounds a meander of the Amazon River and the Peruvian city of Iquitos comes into view. *fig.*: J. ARBUTHNOT Ten long years did Hocus steer his Cause through all the meanders of the law.

B *v.* **1** *v.i.* (Of a river, stream, etc.) flow in meanders; take a winding course, wind about. L16. **2** *v.t.* Pass or travel deviously along or through (a river etc.). *US.* E19. **3** *v.i.* Of a person: wander deviously or aimlessly. M19.

1 G. E. HUTCHINSON Any river flowing in an easily eroded flood plain is . . apt to meander. *Sunday Express* The road . . meanders along the lush Conwy valley. **3** K. GRAHAME He thought his happiness was complete . . as he meandered aimlessly along. K. WATERHOUSE I meandered around the outside of the library building.

meandered *a.* (now *rare*) winding, labyrinthine E17. **meandering** *n.* (*a*) the action of the vb; (*b*) a meander (usu. in *pl.*): M17.

meandrine /mɪˈandrɪn, miː-/ *a.* Also (now *rare*) **maean-**. M19. [f. MEANDER *n.* + -INE[1].] Characterized by convolutions; *esp.* designating or describing brain-corals.

meandrous /mɪˈandrəs, miː-/ *a.* Also (now *rare*) **maean-**. M17. [f. as prec. + -OUS.] Full of or characterized by meanders; winding.

meaner /ˈmiːnə/ *n.* LME. [f. MEAN *v.*[1] + -ER[1].] A person who means, intends, or purposes. Chiefly w. qualifying adv. (as *well-meaner*) or (formerly) adj.

meanie /ˈmiːni/ *n. colloq.* Also **meany**. E20. [f. MEAN *a.*[1] + -IE, -Y[6].] A mean-minded or stingy person.

meaning /ˈmiːnɪŋ/ *n.* ME. [f. MEAN *v.*[1] + -ING[1].] **1** That which is or is intended to be expressed or indicated by a sentence, word, dream, symbol, action, etc.; a signification, a sense; an equivalent in another language; (in interrog. contexts) a motive, a justification. ME. **b** Significance, importance. L17. †**2** Remembrance; a commemoration, a memorial. ME–E16. **3** An intention, a purpose. *arch.* LME.

1 AV *Dan.* 8:15 When I . . had seene the vision, and sought for the meaning. T. HARDY What's the meaning of this disgraceful performance? R. K. NARAYAN Will you kindly make your meaning clearer? J. GARDNER Simon seemed unable to make sense of the words, but then their meaning came through. J. GARDAM First meaning of row with us seems to be quarrel. P. GROSSKURTH Whenever Melanie asked . . the meaning of a French . . expression, he never had to consult a dictionary. *double meaning*: see DOUBLE *a.* & *adv.* GRAMMATICAL *meaning*. *lexical meaning*: see LEXICAL I. **b** R. P. GRAVES There is no God, and therefore there is no meaning or purpose in life.

meaning /ˈmiːnɪŋ/ *a.* LME. [f. MEAN *v.*[1] + -ING[2].] **1** Having an intention or purpose. Chiefly w. qualifying adv. (as *well-meaning*). LME. **2** Conveying or expressing meaning or thought; expressive, meaningful, significant; suggestive. E18.

2 R. HOGGART She gave me a meaning look. R. DAVIES Willard . . gently stroked my left buttock. Gave it a meaning squeeze.

meaningly *adv.* LME. **meaningness** *n.* M18.

meaningful /ˈmiːnɪŋfʊl, -f(ə)l/ *a.* M19. [f. MEANING *n.* + -FUL.] Full of meaning or expression; significant; amenable to interpretation; having a recognizable function in a language or sign system; able to function as a term in such a system.

Physics Bulletin The phoneme is the smallest meaningful unit of sound a listener can perceive. J. HENNESSY Chris and Jayne turned to each other with raised eyebrows and meaningful looks. G. JOSIPOVICI There were no precious objects that had been particularly meaningful to him.

meaningfully *adv.* L19. **meaningfulness** *n.* E20.

meaningless /ˈmiːnɪŋlɪs/ *a.* L18. [f. as prec. + -LESS.] Without meaning or signification; devoid of expression; without purpose. Also, having no recognizable function in a language or sign system, unable to function as a term in such a system.

L. NKOSI The girl spoke a language that was meaningless to me. *Independent* The law is meaningless if it is not implemented.

meaninglessly *adv.* M19. **meaninglessness** *n.* M19.

meanly /ˈmiːnli/ *adv.*[1] LME. [f. MEAN *a.*[1] + -LY[2].] In an inferior manner; indifferently, poorly, badly; with mean attire or equipment; humbly, basely; shabbily; sordidly, niggardly, stingily.

†**meanly** *adv.*[2] LME–M18. [f. MEAN *a.*[2] + -LY[2].] In a middling degree or manner; intermediately; tolerably; fairly; (only) moderately.

meanness /ˈmiːnnɪs/ *n.* M16. [f. MEAN *a.*[1] + -NESS.] **1** The state or quality of being mean; inferiority; slightness, smallness; lowness or humbleness of rank, birth, etc.; insignificance; lack of dignity or grandeur; poorness of appearance or equipment, shabbiness; pettiness; niggardliness, stinginess. M16. **2** An instance of meanness; a deficiency; a mean act. Usu. in *pl.* E18.

meant *v.* pa. t. & pple of MEAN *v.*[1]

meantime /ˈmiːntʌɪm/ *n.* & *adv.* Also **mean time**. ME. [f. MEAN *a.*[2] 3 + TIME *n.* Cf. MEANWHILE.] **A** *n.* The time intervening between one particular period or event and another: in *for the meantime*, so long as the interval lasts, intended to serve for the interim; *in the meantime*, †*in meantime*, †*the meantime*, (*a*) = MEANWHILE *adv.* I, †(*b*) = MEANWHILE *adv.* 2. ME.

D. EDEN In the meantime that hundred pounds must be sent. H. ACTON Other books on the same subject are liable to be published in the meantime. *Which?* The telephone will . . redial the number, even if you've hung up in the meantime.

B *adv.* **1** = MEANWHILE *adv.* I. LME. †**2** = MEANWHILE *adv.* 2. L16–L17.

1 *Times Lit. Suppl.* Meantime . . the numbers of people . . increased immensely.

meanwhile /ˈmiːnwʌɪl/ *n.* & *adv.* Also **mean while**. LME. [f. MEAN *a.*[2] 3 + WHILE *n.* Cf. MEANTIME.] **A** *n.* The time intervening between one particular period or event and another: in *in the meanwhile*, †*in meanwhile*, (arch.) *the meanwhile*, (*a*) = sense B.1 below; (*b*) (now *rare* or *obs.*) = sense B.2 below. LME.

Daily Telegraph In the meanwhile, the Government is effectively admitting that state spending is out of control.

B *adv.* **1** During or within the time intervening between one particular period or event and another; while a particular thing is going on, at the same time; for the present. LME. **2** Nevertheless, still. L16.

1 S. BEDFORD Meanwhile, she had seen that they were given everything. E. WAUGH I shall be saying a few words after dinner. Meanwhile I expect you can all do with a drink. J. HUXLEY My mother meanwhile arrived from Neuchâtel. **2** L. STEPHEN Meanwhile, however, one characteristic . . must be noticed.

meany *n.* var. of MEANIE.

mear *n.* & *v.* var. of MERE *n.*[2] & *v.*

mearing *n.* var. of MERING.

mease /miːz/ *n. dial.* Also **maze** /meɪz/. ME. [OFr. *meise*, *maise* barrel for herrings, of Gmc origin: cf. MHG *meise*, MLG, MDu. *mēse*.] A measure for herrings, equal to five hundreds, esp. long hundreds.

measle *n.* see MEASLES.

†**measle** *a.* see MESEL *a.* & *n.*

measle /ˈmiːz(ə)l/ *v.t.* E17. [f. MEASLE(S).] **1** Infect with measles. E17. **2** Cover (a part of the body etc.) with blotches or spots. M17.

measled /ˈmiːz(ə)ld/ *a.* ME. [f. MEASLE(S, MEASLE *v.*: see -ED[2], -ED[1].] **1** Infected with measles. ME. **2** Blotchy, spotted. Now *rare*. M17.

measles /ˈmiːz(ə)lz/ *n.pl.*, also used as *sing.* Also (in some senses) in sing. form **measle**. ME. [Prob. f. MLG *masele*, MDu. *masel* pustule, spot on the skin (Du. *mazelen* measles) = OHG *masala* blood-blister, f. Gmc: see -S[1].] **1** *pl.* (now usu. treated as *sing.*) & (now *joc.*) as *sing.*, *measle*. An infectious viral disease characterized by a blotchy pink rash preceded and accompanied by catarrh and fever, freq. occurring in epidemics. ME. **b** *pl.* The inflamed spots characteristic of this disease. Formerly also, the pustules of any eruptive disease. LME. **2a** *pl.* (treated as *sing.*) & † as *sing.*, *measle*. A disease of pigs caused by invasion of muscle tissue by the scolex of the tapeworm; a similar disease of cattle etc. L16. **b** (*measle*.) The scolex or cysticercus which causes this disease. M19. **3** Orig. (as *sing.*, *measle*), a blister or excrescence on a tree. Later (*pl.*), a disease of certain trees which causes the bark to become rough and irregular. Now *rare* or *obs.* E17.

1 *German measles*: see GERMAN *a.*[1]

measly /ˈmiːzli/ *a.* L16. [f. prec. + -Y[1].] **1** Infected with measles, suffering from measles. L16. **2** Of or pertaining to measles; resembling measles. L18. **b** Blotchy, spotty. L19. **3** Inferior, contemptible, of little value. *slang.* M19.

1 *Woman's Realm* The measly child . . needs . . tender, loving care. **2b** F. RAPHAEL A mauve Mini, measly with rust, drew his attention. **3** *Sunday Telegraph* They have mastered only a measly five batting points all season.

measurable /ˈmɛʒ(ə)rəb(ə)l/ *a.* ME. [(O)Fr. *mesurable* f. late L *mensurabilis* MENSURABLE.] **1** Able to be measured or perceived; susceptible of measurement or computation; *Math.* (of a set) having a defined measure. Formerly also, of moderate size, dimensions, quantity, duration, or speed. ME. †**2** Of a person, action, etc.: characterized by moderation; moderate, temperate. ME–E18. †**3** Uniform in movement; metrical, rhythmical; *Mus.* in strict time. M16–L17.

1 within a measurable distance of near to (some undesirable condition or event).

measuraˈbility *n.* L17. **measurableness** *n.* LME.

measurably /ˈmɛʒ(ə)rəbli/ *adv.* LME. [f. prec. + -LY[2].] †**1** Moderately, in moderation. LME–L19. **2** In due measure or proportion; proportionably. Now *rare*. LME. **3** In some measure, to some extent. *US.* M18. **4** To a measurable extent. M19.

†**measurage** *n.* LME–M18. [(O)Fr. *mesurage*, f. as MEASURE *v.*: see -AGE.] A duty payable on the cargo of a ship.

measure /ˈmɛʒə/ *n.* ME. [(O)Fr. *mesure* f. L *mensura*, f. *mens-* pa. ppl stem of *metiri* to measure: see -URE.] **I 1** Size or quantity as ascertained or ascertainable by measuring (now chiefly in *made to measure* below); *spec.* (*a*) *Fencing* the distance of one fencer from another as determined by the length of his or her reach when lunging or thrusting; (*b*) the width of a full line of type or print, esp. as measured in picas; (*c*) the width of an organ-pipe. ME. **b** *fig.* State, character, or ability as assessed or assessable by judgement or observation, what is estimated to be expected (chiefly in *get, take*, etc., *the measure of* below). Formerly also, an estimate, an opinion, a notion. M17. †**c** Duration. M17–E18. **2** An instrument for measuring; *spec.* (*a*) a vessel of standard capacity used for separating and dealing out fixed quantities of various substances, as grain, liquids, coal, etc.; (*b*) a graduated rod, line, tape, etc., for taking measurements. ME. **3** A unit or denomination of measurement; the quantity indicated by any such unit. Also, (the quantity indicated by) any of various specific units of capacity (formerly also of length) understood from context or usage, as a bushel. ME. **4** A quantity, degree, or proportion (of something), esp. as granted to or bestowed on a person; an extent, an amount. LME. **5** A method of measuring; *esp.* a system of standard denominations or units of length, surface, or volume. Usu. w. specifying wd. LME. **6** The action or process of measuring, measurement. Now *rare*. LME. **7** That by which something is computed, estimated, judged, or regulated, or with which something is compared in respect of quantity or quality; a criterion, a test. Chiefly in *be the measure of*. L16. **8** *Math.* **a** = DIVISOR 2. L16. **b** A number assigned to a set under a specified rule such that the number assigned to the union of non-overlapping sets is equal to the sum of the numbers assigned to each of the sets; the rule itself. E20. **9** A stratum or bed of mineral. Now only in *pl.* M17.

1 *fig.*: SHAKES. *Two Gent.* Come not within the measure of my wrath. 2 *tape-measure, yard-measure*, etc. 3 W. C. BRYANT These Brought wine, a thousand measures. A. C. CLARKE A furlong is an obsolete measure of length. 4 P. GALLICO He was shocked by the measure of . . hatred of him he caught in her expression. A. BULLOCK Attlee found a surprising measure of agreement with Truman. 5 *linear measure, liquid measure*, etc. 7 BACON Time is the measure of businesse, as money is of wares. G. M. TREVELYAN The busy life of the rivers was a measure of the badness of the roads. C. MILNE Customers such as this . . whose measure of a book lay in how much they had paid for it. 9 *coal measures, Culm Measures*.

II †**10** That which is commensurate or adequate; satisfaction. ME–E17. **11** Moderation, temperance. Also, an extent not to be exceeded, a limit. Now only in certain phrs. (see below). ME. **12** †**a** Proportion; due proportion, symmetry. LME–M17. **b** *in measure as* [after Fr. *à mesure que*], in proportion as. L18. **13** Treatment handed out to a person, esp. by way of punishment or retribution. *arch.* L16.

13 W. COWPER Such hard and arbitrary measure here.

III 14 (A kind of) poetical rhythm, metre; a metrical group or unit, as of a dactyl or two iambuses, trochees, spondees, etc.; a metre. LME. **15** An air, a tune, a melody. Now *poet.* LME. **16** (A step of) a dance; *esp.* a grave or stately dance. *arch.* LME. **17** The quantitative relation between notes determining the kind of rhythm (duple, triple, etc.) of a piece of music; the time of a piece of music; a bar of music. L16. **18** Rhythmical motion, esp. as regulated by music; the rhythm of a movement. L16.

15 LYTTON Strange wild measures, on his violin. 16 SIR W. SCOTT Now tread we a measure!

IV 19 A plan or course of action intended to attain some object, a suitable action; *spec.* a legislative enactment proposed or adopted. L17.

19 W. S. CHURCHILL His second measure, a Land Act to prevent uncompensated eviction, had been passed in 1870. R. K. NARAYAN We are only trying some new measures to meet the competition. H. MACMILLAN The increase in the Bank Rate as a short-term measure.

Phrases: **above measure** = *beyond measure* below. **a measure of** some degree of. *apothecaries' measure*: see APOTHECARY I. **beyond measure** excessively, extremely. BINARY *measure*. **by measure** as determined by measuring (as opp. to weighing or counting). COAL *measures*. *Culm Measures*: see CULM *n.*[1] 4. **fill up the measure of** *arch.* complete the sum of, add what is lacking to the completeness of. **for good measure** as something beyond the minimum, as a finishing touch. *full measure*: see FULL *a.* **get the measure of** = *take the measure of* (b) below. **have the measure of** have an (accurate) opinion of the abilities or character of, have taken the measure of. **in a great** or **large measure** to a considerable extent or degree, largely. **in a measure** to a certain extent, to some degree, somewhat. **in measure** *arch.* to a limited extent, in part. *in measure as*: see sense 12b above. **in some measure** to a certain extent, in some degree, somewhat. **in the same measure** to the same extent. **keep measure** (*a*) observe strict time; (*b*) (also †*keep measures*) be moderate or restrained in action (usu. in neg. contexts). *long measure*: see LONG *a.*[1] **made to measure** (of a garment etc.) made in accordance with measurements taken, as opp. to ready-made; *transf.* & *fig.* fashioned to fulfil specified requirements, appropriate for a particular purpose. *optic measure*: see OPTIC *a.* **out of all measure** *arch.* excessively, extremely. POULTER'*s measure*. **set measures to** limit. *short measure*: see SHORT *a. square measure*: see SQUARE *a.* **take the measure of**, †**take measure of** (*a*) measure (a person) for clothes etc.; (*b*) form an estimate of; *esp.* weigh or gauge the abilities or character of, assess what to expect from (a person). *tread a measure*: see TREAD *v. Winchester measure*: see WINCHESTER I.

measure /ˈmɛʒə/ *v.* ME. [(O)Fr. *mesurer* f. L *mensurare*, f. *mensura*: see prec.] **I** *v.t.* †**1** Regulate, moderate, restrain. ME–L16. **2** Apportion by measure, deal *out*, now esp. to some known capacity or in some fixed unit. ME. **3** Ascertain or determine the spatial magnitude or quantity of (something), ascertain or determine (a spatial magnitude or quantity), by the application of some object of known size or capacity or by comparison with some fixed unit. ME. †**b** Form of, raise or reduce to, certain dimensions or proportions. ME–E16. **c** Mark off or *off* (a line of definite length) in a certain direction. M19. **4** Estimate the amount, duration, value, etc., of (an immaterial thing) by comparison with some standard; judge or estimate the greatness or value of (a person, a quality, etc.) by a certain standard or rule; appraise by comparison with something else. ME. **5** Travel over, traverse (a certain distance, a tract of country). Chiefly *poet.* LME. †**6** Encircle, encompass. LME–L17. **7** Mark the boundary or course of; delimit. Usu. foll. by *out. poet.* E16. **8a** Be the measure of, be a means of measuring. L16. **b** *Math.* Of a quantity: be a factor or divisor of (another quantity). Formerly also *refl.*, be exactly divisible *by*. Now *rare* or *obs.* L16. **9a** Adjust (something) *to* an object or *by* a standard. *arch.* L16. †**b** Be commensurate with. L16–M17. †**10** Turn into metre. L16–L18. **11** Have a measurement of (so much). L17. **12** Bring into competition, opposition, or comparison *with*; *refl.* try one's strength *against*. E18. **13** Take the measure of (a person, *for* clothes etc.); form an estimate of; look (a person) up and down. M18.

2 L. STEPHEN Sermons were measured out with no grudging hand. G. GREENE She had carefully measured out a quadruple whisky. 3 GOLDSMITH Instruments called anemometers . . made to measure the velocity of the wind. G. ORWELL He could walk three kilometres, measured by pacing the cell. A. GRAY The doctor measured this with a pocket ruler. 4 W. COWPER Measure life By its true worth, the comfort it affords. R. LYND It is, of course, extremely difficult to measure the happiness of any animal. 5 SHAKES. *Merch. V.* For we must measure twenty miles to-day. 8a J. N. LOCKYER For common purposes, time is measured by the Sun. 9a JER. TAYLOR You must measure your desires by your fortune . . not your fortunes by your desires. 11 J. C. LOUDON Each shutter measuring four feet six inches. 13 A. E. HOUSMAN In many an eye that measures me. R. P. JHABVALA The little tailor . . measured me right there . . in his open shop.

II *v.i.* **14** Take measurements; use a measuring instrument. E17. **15a** Vie in measurement *with*; be comparable *with*. E18. **b** Foll. by *up*: be equal in ability etc., have the necessary qualifications, meet the required standard, (foll. by *to*). E20. **16** Admit of measurement. M18.

14 B. JOWETT The young carpenter should be taught to measure and use the rule. 15b S. I. LANDAU A free-lancer who does not measure up is easily dismissed.

Phrases: †**measure back** retrace (one's steps, the road). **measure** (†**out**) **one's length** fall flat on the ground (accidentally). **measure swords** (of duellists) ascertain that the swords being used are of equal length (*Hist.*); meet in a contest or battle, try one's strength *with*.

measured /ˈmɛʒəd/ *a.* LME. [f. MEASURE *n.*, *v.*: see -ED[2], -ED[1].] †**1** Moderate, temperate. LME–L15. **2** That has been measured to determine spatial magnitude or quantity; apportioned or dealt out by measure; (of work) paid according to the amount done. LME. **b** Accurately regulated, correctly proportioned. E17. **3** Written in metre; metrical; having a marked or fixed rhythm; rhythmical; regular in movement. L16. **4** Esp. of language: carefully weighed or calculated; deliberate and restrained. E19.

2 **measured mile** a distance of one mile carefully measured, esp. for determining the speed of a ship.

measuredly *adv.* E19. **measuredness** *n.* M19.

measureless /ˈmɛʒəlɪs/ *a.* LME. [f. MEASURE *n.* + -LESS.] Having no bounds or limits; unlimited, immeasurable, infinite.

measurelessly *adv.* M19. **measurelessness** *n.* M19.

measurely /ˈmɛʒəli/ *adv.* Long *rare.* LME. [f. MEASURE *n.* + -LY[2].] Moderately.

measurement /ˈmɛʒəm(ə)nt/ *n.* E17. [f. MEASURE *v.* + -MENT.] †**1** = ADMEASUREMENT I. Only in E17. **2** The action or an act of measuring; mensuration. M18. **3** A dimension ascertained by measuring; a size, quantity, or extent measured by a standard. M18. **4** A system of measuring or of measures. M19.

3 J. GASKELL Her bust measurement must be all of 34 inches. *Which?* Our rating includes measurements for sharpness, . . sound frequency range.

Comb.: **measurement cargo, freight, goods**: on which freight is charged by measurement of bulk rather than by weight.

measurer /ˈmɛʒ(ə)rə/ *n.* LME. [f. MEASURE *v.* + -ER[1].] **1** A person who measures or takes measurements; *esp.* a person whose duty or office it is to see that goods or commodities are of the proper measure. LME. **2** An instrument used for measuring. M18.

measuring /ˈmɛʒ(ə)rɪŋ/ *n.* ME. [f. MEASURE *v.* + -ING[1].] **1** The action of MEASURE *v.*; the process of taking measurements; measurement, mensuration. ME. †**2** A dimension. Only in 16.

Attrib. & comb.: Designating vessels or instruments used for measuring, esp. with graduations, as *measuring-cup, -jug, -rod, -spoon, -tape, -yard*, etc. Special combs., as **measuring cast** (now *rare* or *obs.*) a competitive throw so nearly equal to another that measurement is required to decide the superiority; *fig.* a subtle question, a difficult point, a doubtful matter.

measuring /ˈmɛʒ(ə)rɪŋ/ *a.* L16. [f. MEASURE *v.* + -ING[2].] **1** That measures. L16. **2** *measuring worm*, the larva of a geometrid moth. M19.

meat /miːt/ *n.* [OE *mete* = OFris. *met(e*, OS *meti*, ON *matr*, Goth. *mats*, f. Gmc, f. base of METE *v.*] **I 1** Food; nourishment for people or animals; *esp.* solid food, as opp. to drink. Now *arch.* & *dial.* OE. **2** A kind of food, an article of food. *obs.* exc. in *sweetmeat*. OE. **3** A meal; (occas.) the principal meal of a day, dinner. *obs.* exc. in *after, at, before, meat* (arch.), after, at, before, a meal, after, in the process of, before, eating. ME. **4** The flesh of animals used as food, now esp. excluding fish and poultry; (usu. w. specifying wd) the edible soft part of a shellfish; *US dial.* bacon; animal flesh prepared for eating. ME. **b** *collect.* Living animals such as are killed for food; game, animals; *US* one's quarry or prey. E16. **5** The edible part of a fruit, nut, or egg; the pulp, kernel, yolk and white, etc., as opp. to the rind, peel, or shell. Now chiefly *US*. LME. 6 A kind of meat. Usu. in *pl.* L17.

1 S. JOHNSON The horses could not travel all day without rest or meat. SHELLEY He had . . meat and drink enough. *Proverb*: One man's meat is another man's poison. 2 *bake-meat*, *milkmeat*, etc. 4 *butcher-meat*, *carcass meat*, *crabmeat*, *horsemeat*, *mincemeat*, *pigmeat*, etc. *duck's meat*, *duckmeat*: see DUCK *n.*[1] b N. GORDIMER The third one had gone off, early, to shoot some meat—a family of wart-hogs. 5 SHAKES. *Rom. & Jul.* Thy head is as full of quarrels as an egg is full of meat. D. JOHNSON Belinda ate coconut meat off the shell. 6 W. TREVOR There was . . ham and pork and other meats.

II *transf.* & *fig.* 7 *sing.* & *collect. pl.* The penis; the female genitals; the human body regarded as an instrument of sexual pleasure. *coarse slang.* L16. 8 Human flesh; the human body regarded as large or powerful; muscle or fat on a person. *colloq.* M19. 9 Something enjoyable or advantageous; matter of importance or substance; the gist or main part (of a story, situation, etc.). L19. 10 The centre of a cricket bat, of the head of a golf club, etc. Esp. in *hit* (a ball) *on* or *with the meat. slang.* E20.

7 SHAKES. *2 Hen. IV* Away, you mouldy rogue, away! I am meat for your master. G. DAVIS I kept Maxine's . . younger brothers outside while Teddy slipped the meat to her in the bedroom. 8 F. O'CONNOR He liked women with meat on them, so you didn't feel . . their old bones. 9 M. MCLUHAN Send the enclosed article to Al. . . It is full of meat. *Rally Sport* The meat of the rally was in seven stages in Kielder Forest.

Phrases: *after meat*, *at meat*: see sense 3 above. **beat the meat** *coarse slang* (of a male) masturbate. *before meat*: see sense 3 above. **be meat and drink to** be a source of intense enjoyment to. *butcher's meat*: see BUTCHER *n.* *cold meat*: see COLD *a.* *cry roast meat*: see ROAST *a.* *cuckoo's meat*: see CUCKOO *n.* *duck's meat*: see DUCK *n.*[1] *easy meat*: see EASY *a.* **green meat** grass or green vegetables used as food or fodder. **make meat of** kill. **meat and potatoes** *fig.* basics, ordinary but fundamental things. **piece of meat** *slang* a person regarded as a purely physical specimen; a woman regarded as an instrument of sexual pleasure. *plates of meat*: see PLATE *n.* 25c. *pounded meat*: see POUND *v.*[1] *red meat*: see RED *a.* *strong meat*: see STRONG *a.* *white meat*: see WHITE *a.*

Comb.: **meat-and-potato(es)** *a.* basic, fundamental, down to earth; **meat-ant** *Austral.* any of several ants of the genus *Iridomyrmex*, *esp.* the large reddish-purple *I. purpureus*; **meat-axe** a butcher's cleaver; **meatball** (*a*) a ball of minced or chopped meat; (*b*) *slang* an unintelligent or boring person; **meat breakfast** a breakfast that includes a meat dish; **meat cube** a small cube of concentrated meat extract; **meat-fly** a fly that breeds in meat, a bluebottle; **meat-grinder** a mincing-machine; *fig.* a destructive action or process; **meathead** *slang* a stupid person; **meat-headed** *a.* (*slang*) stupid; **meat-hook** (*a*) a hook on which to hang meat carcasses etc.; (*b*) *slang* an arm, a hand; **meat-house** (*a*) a building in which to hang meat; (*b*) *slang* a brothel; **meat jelly** a jelly prepared from meat; **meat loaf** a loaf of minced or chopped meat; **meatman** †(*a*) a person who provides food, a caterer; †(*b*) a person who eats meat; (*c*) a person who sells or supplies meat; a butcher; **meat-market** †(*a*) a market where food of any kind is sold; (*b*) a market for butcher's meat; (*c*) *slang* a rendezvous for prostitutes, homosexuals, or others seeking sexual encounters; **meat-offering** in biblical translations, a sacrifice consisting of food; **meat-packer** a meat-packing business; **meat-packing** the business of processing and packing meat and distributing it to retailers; **meat poisoning** food poisoning caused by meat; **meat rack** *slang* = *meat-market* (c) above; **meat-rail** a rail for supporting meat in a larder, refrigerated container, etc.; **meat safe** a ventilated cupboard for storing meat, usu. made of wire gauze or perforated zinc; **meat tea** a tea at which meat is served, a high tea; **meat ticket** *Mil. slang* an identity disc; **meat-wagon** *slang* (chiefly *N. Amer.*) an ambulance; a police van; a hearse; **meat-works** (chiefly *Austral.* & *NZ*) (*a*) an establishment where meat is processed and packed; (*b*) a slaughterhouse.

meatless *a.* (*a*) *arch.* having no food; (*b*) without meat; (of prepared food) containing no meat: OE. **meatlessness** *n.* E20.

meat /miːt/ *v. obs.* exc. *dial.* LME. [f. the n.] 1 *v.i.* Feed, partake of food. LME. 2 *v.t.* Feed, supply with food or provender. M16.

2 **well-meated** *a.* (of an animal) well fed, having plenty of flesh.

meato- /mɪˈeɪtəʊ/ *comb. form* of MEATUS: see -O-.

meatotomy /miːəˈtɒtəmi/ *n.* (an instance of) surgical incision into the urethral meatus L19.

meatus /mɪˈeɪtəs/ *n.* Pl. **-es**, same /mɪˈeɪtjuːs/. LME. [L, lit. 'passage, course', f. *meare* go, pass.] †1 A channel, a passage. LME–L17. 2 *spec.* in *Anat.* A tubular passage in the body, *esp.* the external auditory meatus. Usu. w. specifying wd. LME.

2 (**external**) **auditory meatus** the channel leading into the ear. **nasal meatus**, **olfactory meatus** a deep groove in the nasal cavity. **urethral meatus**, **urinary meatus** the external orifice of the urethra.

meatal *a.* M19.

meaty /ˈmiːti/ *a.* L18. [f. MEAT *n.* + -Y[1].] 1a Full of meat; fleshy. L18. b *fig.* Full of substance. L19. 2 Of or pertaining to meat; like meat. M19.

1a J. T. FARRELL A girl whose slim, tall but meaty figure. b J. IRVING There were good heroes and their meaty adventures. *Times* The star of countless comic films plays a meatier role in . . *Long Day's Journey Into Night*.

meatiness *n.* L19.

mebbe *adv.* & *n.* see MAYBE.

mebos /ˈmiːbɒs, *foreign* ˈmeːbɔs/ *n. S. Afr.* L18. [Afk., prob. f. Jap. *umeboshi* dried and salted plums.] A confection made from dried flattened apricots, preserved in salt and sugar.

Mebyon Kernow /mɛbjɒn ˈkɔːnəʊ/ *n. phr.* (treated as *sing.* or *pl.*). M20. [Corn., lit. 'Sons of Cornwall'.] A Cornish nationalist party.

mecamylamine /mɛkəˈmʌɪləmiːn, -ˈmɪl-/ *n.* M20. [f. ME(THYL + CAM(PHOR *n.* + -YL + AMINE.] *Pharm.* A ganglionic blocking agent used to treat extreme hypertension.

mecate /meɪˈkɑːteɪ/ *n.* Chiefly *US*. M19. [Mex. Sp. f. Nahuatl *mecatl*.] A rope made of horsehair or of maguey fibre, used esp. to tether or lead a horse.

Mecca /ˈmɛkə/ *n.* Also **m-**. E19. [Arab. *Makka*, birthplace of Muhammad in Saudi Arabia, and place of pilgrimage for Muslims (cf. KAABA).] 1 *Mecca balm*, = *balm of Gilead* s.v. BALM *n.*[1] *rare.* E19. 2 A place regarded as supremely sacred or valuable; a place where a faith, policy, truth, etc., originated. Also, a place regarded as fashionable or desirable. M19.

2 W. GOLDING Once the airfield was a Mecca for children. C. CHAPLIN Hollywood was fast becoming the Mecca of writers, actors and intellectuals.

Meccan *a.* & *n.* (*a*) *adj.* of or pertaining to Mecca; (*b*) *n.* a native or inhabitant of Mecca: L17.

Meccano /mɪˈkɑːnəʊ/ *n.* Also **m-**. E20. [Invented wd, after *mechanic* etc.] (Proprietary name for) a system for constructing model machines, vehicles, etc., from reusable metal components, and for components of this.

mech /mɛk/ *n. slang.* M20. [Abbrev.] = MECHANIC *n.* 3.

mechanic /mɪˈkanɪk/ *a.* & *n.* LME. [((O)Fr. *mécanique* f.) L *mechanicus*, f. Gk *mēkhanikos* f. *mēkhanikē* MACHINE *n.*: see -IC.] A *adj.* 1 Pertaining to or involving manual labour or skill. Now *rare* or *obs.* LME. 2 Pertaining to or of the nature of a machine or machines; worked by machinery. Now *arch.* exc. *poet.* LME. 3 Of a person: having a manual occupation; working at a trade. Formerly also, low in the social scale; vulgar, coarse. Now *rare.* M16 4 = MECHANICAL *a.* 5a. Now *rare* or *obs.* M17. 5 Worked or working like a machine; automatic, unthinking. Cf. MECHANICAL *a.* 4. *arch.* M17.

B *n.* See also MECHANICS. 1 A manual worker; an artisan. *arch.* M16. b A person of low status, a vulgar person. *derog.* Now *rare.* E17. †2 A mechanical art. Also, manual labour, skill. Only in 17. 3 A skilled manual worker, *esp.* one who makes, uses, or repairs machinery. M17. 4 A person who cheats at gambling games, esp. cards; a card-sharp, *esp.* one who manipulates cards. *US* & *Austral. slang.* L19. 5 A hired assassin. *slang.* L20.

1 **mechanics' institute**, **institution** *Hist.* any of various societies providing education for working people. 3 A. MACLEAN The overalled mechanic was still at work on the helicopter's engine. DENTAL *mechanic.*

mechanical /mɪˈkanɪk(ə)l/ *a.* & *n.* LME. [f. as prec.: see -ICAL.] A *adj.* 1 Concerned with or involving machinery or tools; involving manual work; of the nature of handicraft. LME. 2 Of the nature of a machine or machines; acting, worked, or produced by a machine or mechanism. M16. 3 = MECHANIC *a.* 3. Now *rare.* L16. 4 Of a person or action: performing or performed without thought; lacking spontaneity or originality; machine-like; automatic, routine. E17. 5a Physical; of, pertaining to, or caused by physical properties, forces, agents, etc. Now freq. opp. *chemical.* E17. b Pertaining to mechanics as a science. Now *rare.* M17. 6 Concerned with or involving material objects or physical conditions, practical. M17. 7 Of a theory, an advocate of a theory: explaining phenomena in terms of physical properties only. M17. 8 *Math.* Of a curve: (drawable but) not expressible by an equation of finite and rational algebraical form. E18.

1 H. CARPENTER You must allow *some* good in mechanical science, such as the invention of printing. *Daily Telegraph* Three . . jets were grounded by mechanical faults and an accident. 2 R. INGALLS A story about a girl who danced with a mechanical robot. F. HOYLE James Croll calculated these results without the aid of any mechanical or electronic calculator. 4 A. S. NEILL When invention is left out, dancing becomes mechanical and dull. M. ESSLIN The mechanical exchange of platitudes that might as well be spoken into the wind. 5a J. E. GORDON Almost anything . . added to a metal will affect its mechanical properties. B. W. SPARKS It is convenient to differentiate between physical, or mechanical, weathering and chemical weathering.

Special collocations: **mechanical advantage** the ratio of the force produced by a machine to the force applied to it. **mechanical construction** *Geom.*: of a curve as a whole, without the calculation of individual points. **mechanical drawing**: performed with the help of instruments, as compasses, rulers, etc. **mechanical engineer** an expert in mechanical engineering. **mechanical engineering** the branch of engineering that deals with the design, construction, and maintenance of machines. *mechanical equivalent of heat*: see EQUIVALENT *n.* *mechanical mixture*: see MIXTURE 6. *mechanical power*: see POWER *n.* 13. **mechanical pulp**: prepared without chemical degradation. *mechanical stoker*: see STOKER 1. **mechanical twin** *Metall.* a twinned crystal produced by mechanical deformation. **mechanical zero** the state or position in which a measuring instrument remains when the quantity which it measures is absent.

B *n.* 1 = MECHANIC *n.* 1. *arch.* L16. 2 In *pl.* †a = MECHANICS 1. Only in E17. b = MECHANICS 2. E19. 3 *Printing.* A completed assembly of artwork and copy. M20.

mechaniˈcality *n.* the quality of being mechanical or like a machine L18. **mechanicaliˈzation** *n.* the action, process, or fact of making or becoming mechanical E20. **mechanicalize** *v.t.* make mechanical E17. **mechanically** *adv.* L16. **mechanicalness** *n.* E17.

mechanicalism /mɪˈkanɪk(ə)lɪz(ə)m/ *n.* L19. [f. prec. + -ISM.] 1 *Philos.* The doctrine that all natural phenomena are produced by mechanical forces; = MECHANISM 4. L19. 2 Machine-like procedure; routine. E20.

mechanicalist *n.* an adherent of the doctrine of mechanicalism L19.

mechanician /mɛkəˈnɪʃ(ə)n/ *n.* L16. [f. MECHANIC + -IAN.] A person skilled in a manual occupation, an artisan. Now also, a person skilled in the construction of machinery, a mechanic.

mechanicism /mɪˈkanɪsɪz(ə)m/ *n.* E18. [f. as prec. + -ISM.] = MECHANICALISM 2.

mechanicist /mɪˈkanɪsɪst/ *n.* M20. [f. as prec. + -IST.] *Philos.* An adherent of the doctrine of mechanicalism, a mechanicalist.

mechanico- /mɪˈkanɪkəʊ/ *comb. form.* [f. L *mechanicus* MECHANIC: see -O-.] Mechanical and —.

mechanico-ˈchemical *a.* pertaining partly to mechanics and partly to chemistry M19. **mechanico-corˈpuscular** *a.* designating a doctrine viewing all phenomena as explicable by the movement of atoms according to mechanical laws E19. **mechanico-ˈmorphic** *a.* = MECHANOMORPHIC M20. **mechanico-ˈmorphism** *n.* = MECHANOMORPHISM M20. **mechanico-ˈphysical** *a.* of or pertaining to the philosophy which explains all phenomena as the outcome of the motions and interactions of matter in accordance with physical laws L19.

mechanics /mɪˈkanɪks/ *n.* M17. [Pl. of MECHANIC: see -ICS.] **1** Treated as *sing.* or (occas.) *pl.* **a** The body of theoretical and practical knowledge concerned with the invention and construction of machines, the explanation of their operation, and the calculation of their efficiency; mechanical engineering. M17. **b** The branch of applied mathematics that deals with the motion and equilibrium of bodies and the action of forces, and includes statics, dynamics, and kinematics. Now distinguished as *classical mechanics* (as opp. to *quantum mechanics* s.v. QUANTUM *a.*). L17. **2** *pl.* The working parts of a machine; the technical or procedural details, the practicalities, (*of* something). E20.

1b *celestial mechanics, fluid mechanics, statistical mechanics, wave mechanics*, etc. **2** *Punch* It is a pity the mechanics of the story take up so much of the time. *Which?* We explain the mechanics of buying and selling.

mechanise *v.* var. of MECHANIZE.

mechanism /ˈmɛk(ə)nɪz(ə)m/ *n.* M17. [mod.L *mechanismus*, f. Gk *mēkhanē* MACHINE *n.*: see -ISM.] **1** The structure or way of working of the parts in a machine or natural system; the mode of operation of a process. M17. **2** A system of mutually adapted parts working together (as) in a machine; a piece of machinery; a means by which a particular effect is produced. Also (*collect.*), machinery, mechanical appliances. L17. **b** *Psychol.* An unconscious, structured set of mental processes underlying a person's behaviour or responses. L19. †**3** Mechanical action; action according to the laws of mechanics. L17–L18. **4** *Philos.* The doctrine that all natural (esp. biological or mental) phenomena are produced by mechanical forces. Cf. MECHANICALISM I. L17. **5** In painting, sculpture, music, etc.: the mechanical or physical execution of a work of art, technique. M19.

2 J. IMISON The part of the mechanism of a watch which shows the hour. P. BOWLES A part of the mechanism that held his being together. *Physics Bulletin* Some mechanism must be found for judging the quality of the work.

Phrases: *defence mechanism*: see DEFENCE *n.* ISOLATING *mechanism*. *tilt mechanism*: see TILT *n.*[2] 7.

mechanist /ˈmɛk(ə)nɪst/ *n.* E17. [f. MECHANIC + -IST.] **1** A person skilled in constructing machinery. Formerly also, an artisan. E17. **2** *Philos.* An adherent of the doctrine of mechanicalism. M17. **3** An expert in or student of mechanics. E18.

mechaˈnistic *a.* (*a*) of, pertaining to, or connected with mechanics or mechanism; (*b*) pertaining to or holding mechanical theories: L19. **mechaˈnistically** *adv.* in a mechanistic manner; on mechanistic principles: E20.

mechanize /ˈmɛk(ə)nʌɪz/ *v.* Also **-ise**. L17. [f. as prec. + -IZE.] **1** *v.t.* Make mechanical, give a mechanical character to. Also, introduce machinery in or into (a factory, process, industry, etc.); *spec.* in *Mil.*, equip (an army or force) with mechanical weapons and vehicles, orig. as substitutes for horse-drawn vehicles and cavalry. Freq. as *mechanized* ppl a. L17. **2** *v.i.* Work as a mechanic; move mechanically. *poet. rare.* L19. **3** *v.i.* Introduce machinery or mechanization into an industry etc. L20.

1 W. GOLDING A sweet factory . . small enough not to be mechanised. **3** *New Society* The labour intensive character of the Post Office could be reduced with a . . drive to mechanize.

mechaniˈzation *n.* M19. **mechanizer** *n.* (*a*) a person who mechanizes; (*b*) = MECHANICIST: M19.

mechano- /ˈmɛk(ə)nəʊ/ *comb. form.* [Gk *mēkhano-* comb. form of *mēkhanē* MACHINE *n.*: see -O-.] Of or pertaining to machines or mechanical phenomena, properties, etc.

mechanoˈcaloric *a.* (*Physics*) designating a phenomenon by which a linear flow of superfluid liquid helium (helium II) generates a temperature difference between its ends M20. **mechanoˈchemical** *a.* of or pertaining to mechanochemistry M20. **mechanoˈchemically** *adv.* in accordance with the laws of mechanochemistry L20. **mechanoˈchemistry** *n.* the branch of science that deals with the relation between mechanical and chemical phenomena and the interconversion of these forms of energy E20. **mechano-eˈlectric(al)** *adjs.* pertaining to or producing a conversion of mechanical movement into corresponding electrical effects M20. **mechaˈnology** *n.* (*rare*) the science or a treatise that deals with machines or mechanisms M19. **mechanoreception** *n.* (*Biol.*) (the mechanism of) the detection of a mechanical stimulus by means of mechanoreceptors; sensitivity to mechanical stimuli: M20. **mechanoreceptive** *a.* (*Biol.*) capable of performing mechanoreception; sensitive to mechanical stimuli: M20. **mechanoreceptor** *n.* (*Biol.*) a sensory receptor that responds to mechanical stimuli, such as pressure changes resulting from touch or sound E20. **mechanoˈsensitive** *a.* (*Biol.*) mechanoreceptive M20. **mechanoˈtherapy** *n.* (*Med.*) physiotherapy; *esp.* that involving the use of mechanical apparatus, e.g. to provide exercise: L19.

mechanomorphic /mɛk(ə)nə(ʊ)ˈmɔːfɪk/ *a.* L19. [f. as prec. + Gk *morphē* form + -IC.] Having the form or qualities of a machine or mechanism; of the nature of mechanomorphism.

mechanomorphism *n.* the concept or conceiving of something, esp. a god, as mechanomorphic E20.

méchant /meʃɑ̃/ *a.* Fem. **-ante** /-ɑ̃ːt/. E19. [Fr.] Malicious, spiteful.

mechatronics /mɛkəˈtrɒnɪks/ *n.* L20. [f. MECHA(NICS + ELEC)TRONICS.] The branch of technology which combines mechanical engineering with electronics.

¶Used chiefly w. ref. to Japanese industry.

Mechlin /ˈmɛklɪn/ *n.* & *a.* L15. [Former name of *Mechelen* (or Malines) in Belgium. Cf. MALINES.] (Designating or made of) a lace or other fine fabric orig. produced at Mechelen.

mechoacan /meˈtʃəʊək(ə)n/ *n.* Also **M-**. L16. [*Mechoacan*, a Mexican province.] **1** Any of several plants related to morning glory which have purgative roots, esp. *Ipomoea pandurata* of the southern US; the root of such a plant. L16. †**2** A purgative drug obtained from the roots of the mechoacan. E17–M18.

mecholyl /ˈmɛkəlʌɪl, -lɪl/ *n.* M20. [f. ME(THYL + CHOL(INE + -YL.] *Pharm.* = METHACHOLINE.

Meckel /ˈmɛk(ə)l/ *n.* M19. [J. F. *Meckel* (1714–74), or his grandson J. F. *Meckel* (1781–1833), Ger. anatomists.] *Anat.* & *Med.* **1** *Meckel's diverticulum*, a sacciform appendage of the ileum in some individuals; a pathological condition in which gastric acid is secreted by cells associated with this. M19. **2** *Meckel's cartilage*, a cartilaginous rod or bar in the mandibular region of a vertebrate embryo, around which the malleus and parts of the jaw arise. L19.

meclozine /ˈmɛkləzɪn, -iːn/ *n.* Also ***meclizine**. M20. [f. ME(THYL + C(H)LO(RINE *n.* + PIPERA)ZINE.] *Pharm.* An antihistamine drug derived from piperazine which is taken mainly as an anti-emetic, esp. to prevent motion-sickness.

meconin /ˈmiːkənɪn/ *n.* Also **-ine** /-iːn/. M19. [f. Gk *mēkōn* poppy + -IN[1], -INE[5].] *Chem.* A crystalline aromatic lactone which is one of the alkaloid components of opium.

meconium /mɪˈkəʊnɪəm/ *n.* E17. [L f. Gk *mēkōnion*, f. *mēkōn* poppy.] †**1** (Thickened) juice from the opium poppy; opium. E17–E19. **2** A dark, greenish, sticky substance found in the intestine of a foetus in the later part of gestation and forming the first faeces of a newborn infant. E18. **b** *Entomol.* The first faeces of an insect newly emerged from the pupa. L18.

meconopsis /miːkəˈnɒpsɪs/ *n.* M19. [mod.L *Meconopsis* (see below), f. Gk *mēkōn* poppy + *opsis* appearance.] Any of various ornamental plants of the genus *Meconopsis*, of the poppy family, which includes the Welsh poppy, *M. cambrica*, and the blue poppies, *M. betonicifolia* etc., of China and the Himalayas.

Mec Vannin /mɛk ˈvanɪn/ *n. phr.* (treated as *sing.* or *pl.*). M20. [Manx, lit. 'Sons of (the Isle of) Man'.] A Manx nationalist party.

med /mɛd/ *n.*[1] & *a. colloq.* Also **med.** (point). M19. [Abbrev.] **A** *n.* **1** = MEDIC *n.*[1], MEDICAL *n.* I. M19. **2** = MEDICINE *n.*[1] M20. **B** *adj.* = MEDICAL *a.* M20.

Med /mɛd/ *n.*[2] *colloq.* M20. [Abbrev.] The Mediterranean Sea.

médaillon /medajɔ̃/ *n.* Pl. pronounced same. E20. [Fr.: see MEDALLION.] A small, flat, round or oval cut of meat or fish.

medal /ˈmɛd(ə)l/ *n.* L16. [Fr. *médaille* f. It. *medaglia* = OFr. *m(e)aille*, Sp. *medalla*, ult. f. pop.L *medialia* small coin.] **1** A metal disc bearing a figure or an inscription, used as a charm or trinket or as a religious symbol. L16. **2** A piece of metal, usu. in the form of a coin, struck or cast with an inscription or image, *spec.* (*a*) to commemorate a person, action, or event, (*b*) to recognize the bravery or service of a soldier etc., (*c*) to reward merit, proficiency, or excellence in any art or subject. L16.

1 JOYCE A pious medal he had that saved him. **2** *Field* The Mayor . . presented the cup and medals to the winning team. *bronze medal, George Medal, gold medal, Military Medal*, etc.

Phrases: **the reverse of the medal** = *the other side of the coin* s.v. COIN *n.*

Comb.: **medal chief** *N. Amer. Hist.* an Indian chief who received a medal from the colonial or US authorities; **medal-play** *Golf* play in which the score is reckoned by counting the number of strokes taken to complete a round by each side (opp. *match-play* s.v. MATCH *n.*[1]); **medal ribbon** a ribbon of specific colours and design for attaching a particular medal or for wearing without a medal; **medal round** *Golf* a round of medal-play.

medalet *n.* a small medal L18. **meˈdallic** *a.* of, pertaining to, or resembling a medal; represented on a medal: E18.

medal /ˈmɛd(ə)l/ *v.t.* Infl. **-ll-**, ***-l-**. E19. [f. the n.] Decorate or honour with a medal. Usu. in *pass.*

New Yorker He was eulogized . . renowned and medalled for his war record.

medalled *a.* decorated with a medal; (of a picture etc.) for which a medal has been awarded: M19.

medalist *n.* see MEDALLIST.

medalize *v.* see MEDALLIZE.

medallion /mɪˈdaljən/ *n.* & *v.* M17. [Fr. *médaillon* f. It. *medaglione* augm. of *medaglia* MEDAL *n.*] **A** *n.* **1** A large medal. M17. **2** A thing resembling a medallion; *spec.* (*a*) a round or oval tablet or panel, usu. decorated in relief; (*b*) a round or oval portrait, design, etc. M18. **b** = MÉDAILLON. E20. **c** A permit licensing a taxi. *US colloq.* M20.

Comb.: **medallion man** *slang* a flashily dressed overconfident man, characterized as wearing a shirt open to reveal a medallion.

B *v.t.* Ornament with a medallion or medallions. E19.

medallionist *n.* (*rare*) a maker of medallions L19.

medallise *v.* var. of MEDALLIZE.

medallist /ˈmɛd(ə)lɪst/ *n.* Also ***medalist**. L17. [f. MEDAL *n.* + -IST.] **1** A person who is knowledgeable about or interested in medals. L17. **2** An engraver, designer, or maker of medals. M18. **3** A recipient of a (specified) medal awarded for merit. L18.

3 *bronze medallist, gold medallist*, etc.

medallize /ˈmɛd(ə)lʌɪz/ *v.t. rare.* Also **-ise**, ***medalize**. E18. [f. MEDAL *n.* + -IZE.] Represent or illustrate on a medal.

medano /ˈmɛdənəʊ/ *n. rare.* Pl. **-os**. M19. [Sp. *médano*.] A shifting crescent-shaped sand-dune, a barchan.

meddle /ˈmɛd(ə)l/ *v.* ME. [OFr. *medler*, *mesdler* vars. of *mesler* (mod. *mêler*) f. Proto-Romance f. L *miscere* mix. Cf. MELL *v.*] †**1** *v.t.* Mix, mingle, combine, (esp. *with*, *together*). ME–M17. **b** Mix (goods) fraudulently. LME–E17. †**2** *v.i.* Of things: mingle, combine. ME–E17. †**3** *v.i.* Have sexual intercourse (*with*). ME–M17. †**4** *v.i.* Engage in conflict, fight, (*with*). ME–E17. †**5** *v.refl.* Concern or busy oneself (*with*). ME–M16. †**6** *v.i.* Mingle or associate *with*. LME–L16. **7** *v.i.* Orig., concern oneself or deal *with*, take part *in*. Now, concern oneself unduly (*with*), interfere (*in*). LME.

7 A. CARY She had better attend her own affairs, and I will tell her so if she comes here meddling. J. P. DONLEAVY Who's been meddling with the dresser? J.

RULE I don't want you to think I'm meddling in your private affairs.

meddler *n.* LME. **meddlesome** *a.* given to meddling or interfering E17. **meddlesomely** *adv.* M19. **meddlesomeness** *n.* L17. **meddlingly** *adv.* in a meddling manner M18.

Mede /miːd/ *n.* LME. [L *Medi* pl. = Gk *Mēdoi*.] A member of an ancient Indo-European people who established an empire in Media, south-west of the Caspian Sea and including most of Persia (now Iran), in the 7th cent. BC. Cf. MEDIAN *n.*[1]

law of the Medes and Persians: see LAW *n.*[1]

medevac /ˈmɛdɪvak/ *n.* & *v.* *US.* Also **medi-**. M20. [f. MED(ICAL *a.* + EVAC(UATION.] **A** *n.* A military helicopter for transporting wounded soldiers etc. to hospital. M20. **B** *v.t.* Transport by medevac. M20.

medfly /ˈmɛdflʌɪ/ *n.* Chiefly *US.* Also **M-**. M20. [f. MED *n.*[2] + FLY *n.*[1]] *Agric.* & *Hort.* = *Mediterranean fruit fly* s.v. MEDITERRANEAN *a.* 1b.

media /ˈmiːdɪə/ *n.*[1] Pl. **-iae** /-iiː/, same. M18. [L, fem. of *medius* MID *a.*, used ellipt.] †**1** = MESE *n.*[2] Only in M18. **2** *Phonet.* A voiced stop in Greek; a (voiced) unaspirated stop. M19. **3** *Anat.* = TUNICA *media*. L19.

media /ˈmiːdɪə/ *n.*[2] E20. [Pl. of MEDIUM *n.*] **1** *pl.* & *collect. sing.* The main means of mass communication (also *mass media*), *esp.* newspapers, radio, and television; the reporters, journalists, etc., working for organizations engaged in such communication. E20. **2** *sing.* A means of mass communication, = MEDIUM *n.* 5. E20.

1 *Survey* The media of today . . are quite incapable of presenting sustained argument. *Packet (Camborne)* A special press seminar staged to help the media understand the issues involved. *attrib.*: *Times* He had his own television show . . and became a considerable media personality. *trial by the media*: see TRIAL *n.* 2 F. ZWEIG The calculating tactics of political parties and medias. *Guardian* A media capable of informing the public about issues which arise. MIXED *media*.

Comb.: **media event** an event intended to attract publicity.

¶The sing. uses are freq. regarded as erroneous.

mediagenic *a.* (*colloq.*, chiefly *US*) (of a thing, person, or action) apt to convey a favourable impression when reported by the media, esp. by television L20.

media *n.*[3]*pl.* see MEDIUM *n.*

mediacy /ˈmiːdɪəsi/ *n.* M19. [f. MEDIATE *a.*: see -ACY.] The quality of being mediate.

mediaeval *a.* & *n.* var. of MEDIEVAL.

medial /ˈmiːdɪəl/ *a.* & *n.* L16. [Late L *medialis*, f. *medius* MID *a.*: see -AL[1].] **A** *adj.* **1** *Math.* Pertaining to or designating a mathematical mean, or a line or area which is a mean proportional. L16. **2** Situated in the middle, intermediate, (foll. by *to*); (of a letter etc.) occurring in the middle of a word or between words. E18. **b** *Anat.* & *Zool.* Situated in or relating to the median plane of the body or the midline of an organ; towards the median plane. (Foll. by *to*.) Opp. *lateral*. E19. **3** Of average or ordinary dimensions, average. L18.

Special collocations: **medial cadence** *Mus.* a cadence in which the leading chord is inverted. *medial malleolus*: see MALLEOLUS 2.

B *n.* **1** A medial letter; a form of a letter used in the middle of a word. L18. **2** *Phonet.* = MEDIA *n.*[1] 2. M19.

medially *adv.* in or towards a medial or central position M19.

Median /ˈmiːdɪən/ *n.*[1] & *a.*[1] ME. [f. *Media* + -AN or MEDE + -IAN.] **A** *n.* = MEDE. Also, the language of the Medes, related to Old Persian (cf. MEDIC *n.*[2]). ME. **B** *adj.* Of or pertaining to the Medes or their language. Cf. MEDIC *a.*[2] E17.

median /ˈmiːdɪən/ *n.*[2] & *a.*[2] LME. [Fr. (*veine*) *médiane* or med.L *medianus* (in *mediana vena*) f. L, f. *medius* MID *a.*: see -AN.] **A** *n.* **1** *Anat.* A median vein or nerve. Formerly *spec.*, the antecubital vein. Now *rare* or *obs.* LME. **2** *Geom.* A line drawn from a vertex of a triangle to the midpoint of the opposite side. L19. **3** *Statistics.* A median quantity, term, or value. Cf. MEAN *n.*[1] 5a, MODE *n.* II. E20. **4** = *median strip* below. M20.

B *adj.* **1** *Anat.*, *Bot.*, & *Zool.* Of, pertaining to, or designating the plane which divides a body, organ, or limb into (roughly) symmetrical (e.g. right and left) halves; sagittal; situated in or directed towards this plane, medial. Formerly also, designating certain structures in the arm, as the antecubital vein. L16. **2** *gen.* (Situated in the) middle; intermediate, central. M17. **3** *Statistics.* Designating or pertaining to the midpoint of a frequency distribution, such that the variable has an equal probability of falling above or below it; designating the middle term of a discrete series arranged in order of magnitude, or if there is no middle term, the mean of the middle two terms. L19.

1 **median fin** *Zool.* in fishes, an unpaired fin on the median line (dorsal, caudal, or anal). 4 : **median strip** *N. Amer.* a strip of ground, paved or landscaped, dividing a street or highway.

medianly *adv.* in a median direction or position L19.

mediant /ˈmiːdɪənt/ *n.* M18. [Fr. *médiante* f. It. *mediante*, f. *mediare* come between f. late L *mediare* be in the middle, f. *medius* MID *a.*] *Mus.* The third note of a diatonic scale. Also, one of the regular modulations of a church mode.

mediant /ˈmiːdɪənt/ *a.* *rare.* M19. [Late L *mediant-* pres. ppl stem of *mediare*: see prec., -ANT[1].] Intervening.

mediastinum /ˌmiːdɪəˈstʌɪnəm/ *n.* Pl. **-na** /-nə/. Orig. also Anglicized as †**mediastine**. LME. [Neut. of med.L *mediastinus* medial, f. L = a low class of slave, f. *medius* MID *a.*] *Anat.* A partition between two body cavities or two parts of an organ; *esp.* that dividing the thorax, separating the right and left pleural cavities. Also, the space in the thorax between the pleural sacs, containing the heart, aorta, trachea, oesophagus, thymus, etc.

mediastinal *a.* E19. **mediastiˈnitis** *n.* inflammation of the mediastinum of the thorax M19.

mediate /ˈmiːdɪət/ *a.* LME. [L *mediatus* pa. pple of *mediare*: see next, -ATE[2].] **1** Intermediate or intervening *between* in state, position, time, etc. Now *rare*. LME. **2a** *spec.* (*Hist.*) (Of a feudal lord or tenant) related through an intermediary; (of a feudal relationship between lord and tenant) effected through an intermediary. LME. **b** *gen.* Dependent on or involving an intermediate person, thing, or action; (of a person or thing in relation to another) connected indirectly through another. L16. **3** *Med.* Of auscultation or percussion: performed with some object or instrument placed against the body. E19.

2b mediate inference: arrived at through a middle term. **mediate knowledge**: obtained by means of inference or testimony rather than by intuition or perception.

mediately *adv.* with an intermediary agency, with a person or thing intervening, indirectly LME. **mediateness** *n.* E18.

mediate /ˈmiːdɪeɪt/ *v.* M16. [L *mediat-* pa. ppl stem of *mediare*, f. *medius* MID *a.* Partly back-form. f. MEDIATION.] †**1** *v.t.* Divide (a thing) into two equal parts. M16–E17. **2** *v.t.* **a** Settle or soothe (a dispute etc.) by mediation. M16. **b** Bring about or obtain (an agreement etc.) by acting as mediator. L16. **3** *v.i.* †**a** Take a moderate position, avoid extremes. *rare*. Only in E17. **b** Occupy an intermediate position, be *between*; form a connecting link *between* one thing and another. M17. **4** *v.i.* Act as a mediator; intervene (*between* parties in dispute) to produce agreement or reconciliation. E17. **5** *v.t.* Act as an intermediary in facilitating (a result) or conveying (a gift etc.); in *pass.*, be imparted mediately; *Psychol.* bring about by acting as an intermediate stage between stimulus and response, or an intention and its realization; act as or make use of a mediator. M17.

4 L. NAMIER As for the King's advisers, he considered it their task to mediate between . . King and Parliament. 5 H. JOHNSON The United States pledged to mediate Guatemala's claim to British Honduras territory. R. D. LAING My experience of you is always mediated through your behaviour.

mediated *a.* interposed, intervening; *Psychol.* involving or arrived at by mediation: M19. **mediative** *a.* (*rare*) that mediates, pertaining to mediation or a mediator E19.

mediation /miːdɪˈeɪʃ(ə)n/ *n.* LME. [Late L *mediatio(n-)* (f. as prec.) or f. MEDIATOR: see -ATION.] **1** Mediative action; the process or action of mediating between parties in dispute to produce agreement or reconciliation; intercession on behalf of another. LME. **2a** The state or fact of serving as an intermediary; means, agency, medium. LME. **b** *Psychol.* The interposition of stages or processes between stimulus and result, or intention and realization. E20. †**3** Division by two, halving, bisection. LME–E18. **4** *Mus.* The part of a plainsong or Anglican chant which lies between the two reciting notes. M19.

1 H. KISSINGER They . . offered their mediation to break the . . deadlock. 2a A. BROOKNER A will to overcome . . translated, without the mediation of her mind, into excellent bodily health.

mediational *a.* M20.

mediatize /ˈmiːdɪətʌɪz/ *v.t.* Also **-ise**. E19. [Fr. *médiatiser*, f. *médiat* f. L *mediatus*: see MEDIATE *a.*, -IZE.] Annex (a State), leaving the former government or ruler a title and (usu.) some authority.

mediatiˈzation *n.* the action of mediatizing a State; the state of being mediatized: E19.

mediator /ˈmiːdɪeɪtə/ *n.* ME. [(O)Fr. *médiateur*, †*-our* f. Chr.L *mediator*, f. L *mediare* (see MEDIATE *v.*) or directly f. *medius* MID *a.* after Gk *mesitēs* as used in the New Testament: see -OR.] **1** *Chr. Theol.* A person, esp. Jesus, who mediates between God and humanity. ME. **2** A person who intervenes between two parties, esp. to effect reconciliation; an intercessor; a person who brings about (an agreement) or settles (a dispute) by mediation. LME. †**3** A go-between; a messenger, an agent. LME–L17. **4** A thing which effects a transition between one stage and another; *spec.* in *Psychol.*, an agent in mediation, an intermediate stage. M20.

2 D. ROWE She had to act as a mediator between her mother and father whenever they quarrelled.

mediaˈtorial *a.* of, pertaining to, or characteristic of a mediator or mediation M17. **mediatorship** *n.* the office or position of a mediator L16. **mediatory** /ˈmiːdɪət(ə)ri/ *a.* having the function of mediating; pertaining to or of the nature of mediation: E17.

mediatrix /miːdɪˈeɪtrɪks/ *n.* Pl. **-trices** /-trɪsiːz/, **-trixes**. LME. [Late L, fem. of *mediator*: see prec., -TRIX.] A female mediator.

Also **ˈmediatress** *n.* (now *rare*) E17. **ˈmediatrice** *n.* (now *rare*) LME.

media vuelta /ˈmedja ˈvwelta/ *n. phr.* M20. [Sp., lit. 'half-turn'.] *Bullfighting.* A method of killing a bull by approaching and stabbing it from behind.

medic /ˈmɛdɪk/ *n.*[1] & *a.*[1] M17. [L *medicus*, f. *mederi* heal (n. perh. infl. by OFr. *médique* physician): see -IC. Partly also abbrev. of MEDICAL.] **A** *n.* A physician, a medical practitioner; a medical student. *colloq.* M17.

K. BOYLE Our medics are up there shooting the people full of inoculations.

B *adj.* = MEDICAL *a. poet.* E18.

Medic /ˈmiːdɪk/ *n.*[2] & *a.*[2] L19. [L *Medicus* f. Gk *Mēdikos* Median: see -IC.] = MEDIAN *n.*[1] & *a.*[1]

†**medica** *n.* LME–M18. [L: see MEDICK.] = MEDICK.

medicable /ˈmɛdɪkəb(ə)l/ *a.* L16. [L *medicabilis*, f. *medicare*, *-ari*: see MEDICATE, -ABLE.] †**1** Possessing medicinal properties. L16–M17. **2** Able to be treated or cured medically. E17.

2 J. ARMSTRONG For want of timely care Millions have died of medicable wounds.

Medicaid /ˈmɛdɪkeɪd/ *n.* Also **m-**. M20. [f. MEDIC(AL *a.* + AID *n.*] In the US, a scheme providing State and Federal funds for people needing assistance with medical expenses. Cf. MEDICARE.

medical /ˈmɛdɪk(ə)l/ *a.* & *n.* M17. [Fr. *médical* or med.L *medicalis*, f. L *medicus* physician, f. *mederi* heal: see -AL[1]. Cf. MEDIC *n.*[1] & *a.*[1]] **A** *adj.* **1** Of or pertaining to the science or practice of medicine in general; of or pertaining to medicine as opp. to surgery. M17. **b** Of or pertaining to conditions requiring medical (esp. as opp. to surgical) treatment or diagnosis. L19. **2** Curative; medicinal. *rare*. M17.

1 R. INGALLS He isn't the kind to go flipping through medical dictionaries. *Daily Telegraph* The drug epidemiology unit of Boston University Medical Centre. b E. KUZWAYO And this sudden new medical condition—was it caused by prison conditions?

Special collocations: **medical board** a body of medical experts responsible for the medical examination of soldiers, the maintenance of public health, etc. **medical certificate** a certificate from a doctor giving the state of a person's health. **medical examination** = sense B.2 below. **medical examiner** (*a*) a doctor who carries out an examination for physical health or fitness; (*b*) *US* a medically qualified public officer who investigates unusual or suspicious deaths, performs post-mortems, and initiates inquests. **medical garden** (an area of) a garden devoted to the cultivation of medicinal plants. **medical hall** in Ireland, a pharmacy, a chemist's shop. **medical jurisprudence** the law as it relates to the practice of medicine. **medical officer** a doctor appointed by a company or public authority to attend to matters relating to health. **medical practitioner** a person who practises medicine; *esp.* (in Britain) one who has a registered qualification in medicine. **medical register** a register of all doctors legally in practice. **medical school** (a school or faculty of) a college or university in which medicine is studied.

B *n.* 1 A student or practitioner of medicine. *colloq.* E19. 2 An examination to determine the state of a person's physical health or fitness. E20.

2 A. MCCOWEN I didn't pass the Medical owing to my bad sight.

medically *adv.* in a medical manner; with respect to medical science or practice or the medical profession: M17.

medicalize /ˈmɛdɪk(ə)lʌɪz/ *v.t.* Also **-ise**. L20. [f. prec. + -IZE. Cf. Fr. *médicaliser*.] Give a medical character to; involve medicine in, view in medical terms, esp. unwarrantedly.

medicaliˈzation *n.* L20.

medicament /mɪˈdɪkəm(ə)nt, ˈmɛdɪk-/ *n.* & *v.* LME. [Fr. *médicament* or L *medicamentum*, f. *medicari*: see MEDICATE, -MENT.] A *n.* A substance used for medical treatment; a medicine, a remedy. LME.

MORTIMER COLLINS There are few medicaments equal to walking at your fastest pace.

B *v.t.* Administer medicaments to. *rare.* E19.

medicaˈmental *a.* (long *rare*) of the nature of a medicament, medicinal M17. **medicaˈmentally** *adv.* (now *rare*) M17. **medicaˈmentary** *a.* (long *rare*) of the nature of or pertaining to a medicament or medicaments L16.

Medicare /ˈmɛdɪkɛː/ *n.* Also **m-**. M20. [f. MEDI(CAL *a.* + CARE *n.*] In the US, a health insurance scheme for people over 65 years of age; in Canada and Australia, a national health care scheme financed by taxation. Cf. MEDICAID, DENTICARE.

medicaster /ˈmɛdɪkastə/ *n.* Now *rare.* E17. [Fr. *médicastre* or its source It. *medicastro*, ult. f. L *medicus*: see MEDIC *n.*[1] & *a.*[1], -ASTER.] A pretender to medical skill, a quack.

medicate /ˈmɛdɪkeɪt/ *v.t.* E17. [L *medicat-* pa. ppl stem of *medicari* administer remedies to, f. *medicus*: see MEDIC *n.*[1] & *a.*[1], -ATE[3].] 1 Treat medically; administer remedies to, heal, cure. E17. 2a Impregnate *with* a medicinal substance. Freq. as *medicated* ppl a. E17. †b Treat or mix (a thing) *with* drugs or other substances; adulterate (food etc.). M17–M19.

2a *Lancet* The soap is pleasantly medicated with . . eucalyptus. *Trade Marks Journal* A medicated preparation in tablet form for human use as a sedative and hypnotic.

medicative *a.* (now *rare*) curative, healing M17.

medication /mɛdɪˈkeɪʃ(ə)n/ *n.* LME. [L *medicatio(n-)*, f. as prec.: see -ATION. Cf. Fr. *médication*.] 1 The action of treating medically; treatment with a medicinal substance. LME. 2 The action of impregnating with a medicinal substance. M18. 3 A drug or drugs prescribed or given as medical treatment. M20.

3 D. W. GOODWIN Nor is there evidence that antidepressant medications are useful in the treatment of alcoholism. B. SPOCK The doctor can prescribe medication to relieve the symptoms.

Medicean /mɛdɪˈtʃiːən, -siːən, mɛˈdiːtʃɪən/ *a.* M17. [mod.L *Mediceus*, f. It. *Medici* (see below) + -AN.] Of or pertaining to the Medici family, rulers of Florence during the 15th cent.

Medici /ˈmɛdɪtʃi, mɛˈdiːtʃi/ *a.* L18. [See prec.] Of, pertaining to, or associated with the Medici family.

Medici collar a large pleated fan-shaped collar standing upright at the rear and sloping to meet a low neckline at the front. **Medici lace** a type of fine intricately worked lace, scalloped on one edge.

medicinable /ˈmɛdsɪnəb(ə)l, ˈmɛdɪsɪn-/ *a.* Now *arch.* or *poet.* LME. [OFr. *medecinable*, f. *medeciner*: see MEDICINE *v.*, -ABLE.] = MEDICINAL *a.* 1.

medicinal /məˈdɪsɪn(ə)l/ *a.* & *n.* ME. [(O)Fr. *médicinal* f. L *medicinalis*, f. *medecina*: see next, -AL[1].] A *adj.* 1 Having healing or curative properties or attributes; therapeutic. ME. 2 Of or pertaining to the science or the practice of medicine. LME. b Resembling (that of) medicine. *colloq.* E19.

1 J. BETJEMAN Your medicinal springs where their wives took the waters. JULIAN GLOAG A glass of Burgundy to go with it—purely for medicinal purposes, of course. **medicinal leech** a leech, *Hirudo medicinalis*, used (now infrequently) for blood-letting.

B *n.* A medicinal substance. LME.

medicinally *adv.* for a medicinal purpose, with a medicinal effect LME.

medicine /ˈmɛds(ə)n; ˈmɛdɪsɪn/ *n.*[1] ME. [OFr. *medecine*, *-icine* (mod. *médecine*) f. L *medicina*, f. *medicus*: see MEDIC *n.*[1] & *a.*[1], -INE[4].] 1 The science or practice of the diagnosis and treatment of illness and injury and the preservation of health; *spec.* the science or practice of restoring and preserving health by drugs and the regulation of diet, habits, etc., rather than by surgical methods. ME. 2 A substance or preparation used in the treatment of illness; a medicament, a drug; *esp.* one taken orally. Also, such substances generally. ME. b *fig.* A remedy, *esp.* one which is necessary but disagreeable or unwelcome. ME. †3 A drug used for other than remedial purposes, as a cosmetic, poison, potion, etc. LME–E17. 4 Among N. American Indians, (an object or practice thought to possess) magical, esp. healing or protective, power. E19. b = *medicine man* below. E19. 5 Alcoholic drink. Now also, narcotic, esp. addictive, drugs. *slang.* M19.

1 J. T. FLEXNER Morgan apprenticed himself to an experienced doctor; there was no other way of studying medicine. J. RABAN Traditional Arab medicine—the herbal remedies which were now banned in the new hospitals. 2 J. WESLEY One of the mistresses . . near death . . found no help from all the medicines she had taken. b M. R. MITFORD He finds in constant employment a medicine for great grief.

Phrases: **a dose, taste**, etc., **of one's own medicine** repayment or retaliation in kind, tit for tat. **bad medicine** (*a*) among N. American Indians, bad luck (regarded as able to be inherited or acquired); (*b*) *slang* a thing or person regarded as being sinister or ill-omened. *clinical medicine*: see CLINICAL I. *forensic medicine*: see FORENSIC *a.* *fringe medicine*: see FRINGE *a.* *nuclear medicine*: see NUCLEAR *a.* *patent medicine*: see PATENT *a.* *preventive medicine*: see PREVENTIVE *a.* *social medicine*: see SOCIAL *a.* *socialized medicine*: see SOCIALIZE *v.* 2. **take one's medicine** submit to or endure something necessary or deserved but disagreeable; learn a lesson.

Comb.: **medicine ball** a large heavy stuffed usu. leather ball thrown and caught for exercise; **medicine chest** a box containing medicines, items for first aid, etc.; **medicine glass** a small drinking-glass graduated for use in measuring medicines; **medicine line** (now *rare*) among N. American Indians, the border between Canada and the US; **medicine lodge** a structure used for religious ceremonies by certain N. American Indian peoples; a religious society among these peoples; **medicine man** (*a*) a healer or shaman among N. American Indians and other peoples; (*b*) *colloq.* a doctor; **medicine murder** murder committed to obtain parts of the body for medicine; ritual murder; **medicine seal** *Archaeol.* a small cubical or oblong stone with inscriptions in intaglio, apparently used by Roman physicians for marking their drugs; **medicine show** *N. Amer.* a travelling show in which entertainers attract customers to whom medicine can be sold; **medicine stamp** = *medicine seal* above; **medicine tree** the horseradish tree; **medicine wolf** *US* = COYOTE; **medicine woman** a N. American Indian female healer or shaman.

†**medicine** *n.*[2] LME–M17. [(O)Fr. *médecin* or its source med.L *medicinus* physician, use as n. of L *medicinus* adj., f. *medicus*: see prec.] A medical practitioner.

medicine /ˈmɛds(ə)n; ˈmɛdɪsɪn/ *v.t. arch.* LME. [(O)Fr. *médeciner*, f. as MEDICINE *n.*[1]] 1 Treat or cure by means of medicine; give medicine to. LME. †2 Bring *to* a certain state by medicinal means. *rare.* E17–E19.

2 SHAKES. *Oth.* Not poppy, nor mandragora . . Shall ever medicine thee to that sweet sleep.

mediciner /mɪˈdɪsɪnə, ˈmɛdsɪnə/ *n. arch.* (orig. *Sc.*). LME. [f. MEDICINE *n.*[1], *v.* + -ER [1]. Cf. OFr. *medecineur*.] A physician, a healer.

medick /ˈmiːdɪk/ *n.* LME. [L *medica* f. Gk *Mēdikē* (*poa*) lit. 'Median (grass)'.] Any of various leguminous plants of the genus *Medicago*, sometimes grown as fodder; *esp.* (*a*) (more fully *purple medick*) lucerne, *M. sativa*; (*b*) (more fully *black medick*) *M. lupulina*.

medico /ˈmɛdɪkəʊ/ *n.* Now *slang* or *joc.* Pl. **-o(e)s**. L17. [It. f. L *medicus* MEDIC *n.*[1]] A medical practitioner; a medical student.

medico- /ˈmɛdɪkəʊ/ *comb. form.* M17. [f. L *medicus* MEDIC *n.*[1] + -O-.] Forming chiefly adjs. w. the sense 'designating or pertaining to medicine and —', as *medico-botanical*, *medico-legal*, *medico-social*, etc.

mediety /mɪˈdʌɪɪti/ *n.* LME. [Late L *medietas* half (in cl.L middle), f. L *medius* MID *a.*: see -ITY. Cf. MOIETY.] 1†a A half. LME–L17. b *Law.* Either of two parts into which something (esp. an ecclesiastical benefice) is divided, a moiety. E17. †2 A middle or intermediate state, position, or quality. L16–M17. †3 *Math.* (The quality of being) a mean. L16–L17.

medieval /mɛdɪˈiːv(ə)l, miː-/ *a.* & *n.* Also **mediaeval**. E19. [f. mod.L *medium aevum* middle age + -AL[1]. Cf. earlier MIDDLE AGE *n.* 2, MIDDLE-AGED 2.] A *adj.* Of, pertaining to, or characteristic of the Middle Ages. Also (*colloq.*), old-fashioned, archaic, primitive; *spec.* barbarous, cruel. E19.

Edinburgh Review The economic difference between ancient, medieval and modern society. J. GATHORNE-HARDY It was a medieval farmhouse, and it hadn't been modernised. M. MCCARTHY It was medieval of Macy's to fire her because she'd had a breakdown. *Medieval Greek*, *Medieval history*, *Medieval Latin*, etc.

B *n.* A person who lived in the Middle Ages. M19.

medievalism *n.* (*a*) belief and practice characteristic of the Middle Ages; medieval thought, religion, art, etc.; (*b*) adherence to or interest in medieval ideals or styles; an instance of this: M19. **medievalist** *n.* (*a*) a person who lived in the Middle Ages; (*b*) an expert in or student of medieval history, culture, etc.; a person practising medievalism in art, religion, etc.: M19. **medievalize** *v.* (*a*) *v.t.* make medieval in character; (*b*) *v.i.* favour medieval ideas or styles: M19. **medievally** *adv.* in a medieval manner; in medieval times; in accordance with medievalism: L19.

medimnus /mɪˈdɪmnəs/ *n.* Pl. **-ni** /-nʌɪ/. Also Anglicized as **medimn(e)** /mɪˈdɪm/. L16. [L f. Gk *medimnos*. Cf. Fr. *médimne*.] An ancient Greek unit of capacity equivalent to approx. 55 litres, or 12 gallons.

medina /mɪˈdiːnə/ *n.* Also **M-**. E20. [Arab., lit. 'town'.] The old Arab or non-European quarter of a N. African town.

Medinal /ˈmɛdɪn(ə)l/ *n.* Also **m-**. E20. [Perh. f. MEDI(CAL + *Na* sodium + -AL[2].] *Pharm.* (Proprietary name for) the drug barbitone sodium.

medine /mɛˈdiːn/ *n.* L16. [Fr. *médin*, It. *medino* f. colloq. Arab. *maydī* f. the Sultan al-*Mu'ayyad Šayḵ* (see below): see -INE[1].] *Hist.* A coin of low denomination, orig. of silver (and issued by the 15th-cent. Sultan al-Mu'ayyad Šayḵ) and later of bronze, used in Egypt and corresponding to the Turkish para.

medio /ˈmɛdɪəʊ/ *n.* Pl. **-os**. E19. [Sp. = half.] *Hist.* A coin of low denomination used in Mexico and Cuba.

medio- /ˈmiːdɪəʊ/ *comb. form.* M19. [f. L *medius* MID *a.* + -O-.] Of or relating to the middle (of an organ or part), as *mediodorsal*, *medio-occipital*, *mediopassive*.

mediocre /miːdɪˈəʊkə/ *a.* Also †**médiocre.** L16. [(Fr. *médiocre* f.) L *mediocris* of middle height or degree, f. *medius* MID *a.* + *ocris* rugged mountain.] Of middling quality, neither bad nor good, average; indifferent, of poor quality, second-rate.

Observer Television—all it has ever done is to teach people how to tolerate mediocre entertainment. D. ROWE You cannot bear the thought of being mediocre and ordinary. *absol.*: *Law Times* The mediocre . . always form numerically the largest portion of every profession.

mediocracy *n.* (a group or State having) rule by mediocre people; a ruling body consisting of mediocre people: M20. ˈ**mediocrist** *n.* (now *rare*) a person of mediocre talents or ability L18.

mediocrity /miːdɪˈɒkrɪti/ *n.* LME. [(O)Fr. *médiocrité* f. L *mediocritas*, f. *mediocris*: see prec., -ITY.] †**1** Moderate fortune or condition in life. LME–E19. **2** The quality or condition of being intermediate between two extremes. Formerly also, a thing equally removed from two opposite extremes; a mean. M16. †**3** A middle course of action; moderation, temperance. M16–L18. †**4** The possession of attributes in a medium or moderate degree; moderate degree, quality, or amount. L16–E19. **5** The quality or condition of being mediocre. L16. **6** A person of mediocre talents or ability. L17.

5 D. PARKER There are certain things . . beside which even distinguished, searching, passionate novels pale to mediocrity. **6** C. C. TRENCH A worthy mediocrity of great application and dignity, but no talent save for time-serving.

medi͵ocritiˈzation *n.* (orig. *US*) the action or process of making mediocre; reduction to a common level of mediocrity: L20. **mediocritize** *v.t.* make mediocre, reduce (good and bad) to a common level L20.

mediopalatal /͵miːdɪəʊˈpalət(ə)l/ *a.* E20. [f. MEDIO- + PALATAL *a.*] *Phonet.* Articulated with the tongue against the middle part of the hard palate; designating this part of the palate.

mediopassive /͵miːdɪəʊˈpasɪv/ *a.* & *n.* E20. [f. MEDIO- + PASSIVE.] *Gram.* (Pertaining to or designating) the middle voice of a verb or a voice equivalent to the middle and passive voices.

Medise *v.* var. of MEDIZE.

Medism /ˈmiːdɪz(ə)m/ *n.* M19. [Gk *mēdismos*, f. *Mēdizein* MEDIZE.] **1** *Gk Hist.* Sympathy with or favouring of the Medes or Persians, enemies of Greece in the 6th and 5th cents. BC, on the part of a Greek. M19. **2** A word or idiom belonging to the language of the Medes. M19.

meditate /ˈmɛdɪteɪt/ *v.* M16. [L *meditat-* pa. ppl stem of *meditari* frequent. f. IE stem meaning 'measure': see -ATE[3]. Cf. METE *v.*, MODE.] **1** *v.i.* Exercise the mental faculties in (esp. religious or spiritual) thought or contemplation. (Foll. by *on*, *upon*, *over*.) M16. **2** *v.t.* Muse over, reflect on; consider, study, ponder. Also, plan by turning over in the mind, conceive mentally, (a thing, †*to do*). L16. **b** Fix one's attention on; observe intently or with interest. E18.

1 R. K. NARAYAN He has renounced the world; he does nothing but meditate. J. R. ACKERLEY My study was understood to be private ground where the Great Mind could meditate undisturbed. A. BELL He frequently meditated on the moral qualities of sound diet. **2** G. SARTON We ought to meditate the immortal words of Pericles. J. CONRAD The cat . . seemed to meditate a leap. W. S. CHURCHILL The British had remained at Halifax awaiting reinforcements . . and meditating their strategy.

meditant *a.* & *n.* (*rare*) (*a*) *adj.* meditating; (*b*) *n.* a person who meditates: E17. **meditater** *n.* = MEDITATOR E19. **meditatingly** *adv.* meditatively M18. **meditator** *n.* a person who meditates M17.

meditation /mɛdɪˈteɪʃ(ə)n/ *n.* ME. [(O)Fr. *méditation* f. L *meditatio(n-)*, f. as prec.: see -ATION.] **1 a** The action or practice of profound spiritual or religious reflection or mental contemplation. ME. **b** Continuous thought on one subject; (a period of) serious and sustained reflection or mental contemplation. LME. **2** A written or spoken discourse, freq. on a religious subject, arising from considered thought. ME.

1a J. HEWITT Buddhist meditation utilizes Yoga . . which lays emphasis on the trance. J. DISKI I imagine myself walking silent cloisters, my head bent in meditation. *Transcendental Meditation*: see TRANSCENDENTAL. **b** K. J. DOVER Philosophy . . was not the product of solitary meditation, to be communicated by a spell-binding orator. **2** *Sunday Express* These ideas are often meditations on a theme, rather than jokes or anecdotes.

meditative /ˈmɛdɪtətɪv, -teɪtɪv/ *n.* & *a.* E17. [f. MEDITATE + -IVE; partly f. (O)Fr. *méditatif*, *-ive* (n. f. late L *meditativus*).] †**A** *n.* *Gram.* = DESIDERATIVE *n.* E17–M19.

B *adj.* **1** Of a person, disposition, or state of mind: inclined or accustomed to meditation. Also, engaged in the meditation *of*. M17. **2** Of an action, appearance, etc.: accompanied by or indicative of meditation. M18. †**3** *Gram.* = DESIDERATIVE *a.* I. Only in M18.

1 J. R. GREEN The melancholy and meditative Jaques.

meditatively *adv.* E19. **meditativeness** *n.* M19.

Mediterranean /͵mɛdɪtəˈreɪnɪən/ *a.* & *n.* Also **m-.** M16. [L *mediterraneus* inland, f. *medius* MID *a.* + *terra* land, earth; in late L applied to the Mediterranean Sea, *Mare Mediterraneum*: see -AN, -EAN.] **A** *adj.* **1 a** *Mediterranean Sea*, the almost land-locked sea separating southern Europe from Africa, connected with the Atlantic Ocean by the Strait of Gibraltar, with the Black Sea by the Bosphorus, and (now) with the Red Sea by the Suez Canal. M16. **b** Of, pertaining to, or characteristic of the Mediterranean Sea; of, pertaining to, or characteristic of countries bordering the Mediterranean Sea or their inhabitants. M16. **2** (Of water) nearly or entirely surrounded by land, land-locked; (of land) inland, remote from the coast. E17.

1b Mediterranean climate the climate of countries around the Mediterranean Sea, characterized by hot dry summers and mild wet winters; any similar climate elsewhere. **Mediterranean fruit fly** a tephritid fruit fly, *Ceratitis capitata*, whose maggots burrow into citrus and other fruits; also called *medfly*.

B *n.* **1** *The* Mediterranean Sea. Also, an inland sea or lake, a body of water nearly or entirely surrounded by dry land. E17. **2** A human physical type found especially in countries bordering the Mediterranean Sea, characteristically dark-complexioned and not tall; a person of this physical type. L19.

Mediterraneanize *v.t.* make Mediterranean in character or attributes E20.

meditullium /mɛdɪˈtʌlɪəm/ *n.* Now *rare* or *obs.* E17. [L, f. *medius* MID *a.* + 2nd elem. perh. cogn. w. *tellus* earth.] A middle part or substance; *spec.* †(*a*) *Anat.* = DIPLOE; (*b*) *Bot.* an inner layer in a leaf, root, etc.

medium /ˈmiːdɪəm/ *n.* & *a.* Pl. of n. **-ia** /-ɪə/, **-iums.** See also MEDIA *n.*[2] L16. [L, lit. 'middle, midst', med.L 'means', use as n. of *medius* MID *a.* Cf. Fr. *médium*.] **A** *n.* **1** A middle quality, degree, or condition; something intermediate in nature or degree. L16. †**b** Moderation. L17–L18. †**2** *Logic.* The middle term of a syllogism; a ground of proof or inference. L16–E19. **3 a** An intervening substance through which a force acts on objects at a distance or through which impressions are conveyed to the senses, as air, water, etc. L16. **b** A pervading or enveloping substance; the substance in which an organism lives or is cultured; *fig.* one's environment, one's usual social setting. M17. †**4** A (geometric or arithmetic) mean; an average. E17–E19. **5** An intermediate agency, instrument, or channel; a means; *spec.* a channel of mass communication, as newspapers, radio, television, etc. See also MEDIA *n.*[2] E17. **6 a** A person acting as an intermediary, a mediator. *rare.* E19. **b** (Pl. **-iums.**) A person thought to be in contact with the spirits of the dead and to communicate between the living and the dead. M19. **7** A liquid substance with which a pigment is mixed for use in painting. Also, anything used as a raw material by an artist etc.; a style or variety of art, as determined by the materials or artistic form used. M19. **b** *Photogr.* A varnish used as a material in retouching. L19. **8** *Theatr.* A screen fixed in front of a light source in order to throw a coloured light on a stage. M19. **9** *Comm.* A medium-dated security. M20.

1 I. MILNER Is there no medium between going to Court, and going a hunting? **3a** *fig.*: H. JAMES The intensely habitual stillness offered a submissive medium to the sound of a distant church bell. D. JACOBSON What a strange medium time is: transparent when you look back . . opaque when you . . look forward. **b** G. GROTE You cannot thus abstract any man from the social medium by which he is surrounded. A. HARDY The shape of a fish is . . all-important in a fluid medium. **5** SLOAN WILSON Television is developing into the greatest medium for mass education and entertainment. H. READ If we have ideas to express, the proper medium is Language. **7** H. BELLOC Four pictures were set in the walls . . mosaics, they seemed—but he did not examine their medium closely. *Sunday Express* Water colour is his medium. R. MANNING Despite my occasional wish that I had been a painter . . words are my medium.

Phrases: *circulating medium*: see CIRCULATE. *contrast medium*: see CONTRAST *n.* *happy medium*: see HAPPY *a.* *mass medium*: see MASS *n.*[2] & *a.* **medium of circulation** or **exchange** a thing serving as the instrument of commercial transactions, as coin, notes, etc. *TYRODE's medium*.

B *adj.* †**1** Average, mean. L17–E19. **2** Intermediate between two or more degrees in size, character, amount, quality, etc.; *spec.* (*a*) (of paper) between royal and demy in size, usu. 600 × 470 mm; (*b*) (of wine etc.) having a flavour midway between dry and sweet; (*c*) (of meat) cooked between well done and rare. E18.

2 A. JUDD He was of medium height, slightly built. T. BERGER You don't want a violent boil; just . . firm and medium, a little higher than a simmer.

Special collocations & comb.: **medium bowler** *Cricket* a bowler who bowls at a medium pace. **medium bowling** *Cricket*: in which the ball travels at a medium speed. **medium close-up** a cinematic or television shot intermediate between a medium shot and a close-up. **medium-dated** *a.* (*Comm.*) (of a security) having between five and fifteen years until expiry. **medium frequency** an intermediate frequency (of oscillation); *spec.* a frequency of a medium wave, between 300 and 3000 kilohertz. **medium-pacer** *colloq.* (*Cricket*) = *medium bowler* above. **medium-range** *a.* (of an aircraft etc.) able to travel a medium distance. **medium rare** (of meat) cooked between medium and rare. **medium shot** a cinematic or television shot intermediate between a close-up and a long shot. **medium wave** *Telecommunications* a radio wave with wavelength between a hundred metres and a kilometre.

mediumism *n.* the practices or profession of a spiritualistic medium M19. **mediuˈmistic** *a.* of, pertaining to, or having the characteristics of a spiritualistic medium M19. **mediumly** *adv.* moderately, to a medium or average extent E20. **mediumship** *n.* (*a*) the state or condition of being or acting as a spiritualistic medium; (*b*) intervening agency, intermediation: M19.

medius /ˈmiːdɪəs/ *n.* Long *rare.* M16. [L, lit. 'middle'.] *Mus.* = MEAN *n.*[1] I.

¶See also GLUTEUS *medius*.

medivac *n.* var. of MEDEVAC.

Medize /ˈmiːdʌɪz/ *v.i.* Also **-ise, m-.** M19. [Gk *Mēdizein*, f. *Mēdoi* Medes: see MEDE, -IZE.] *Gk Hist.* Of a Greek: sympathize with or favour the interests of the Medes or Persians, enemies of Greece in the 6th and 5th cents. BC. Cf. MEDISM.

medjidie /mɛˈdʒiːdɪeɪ/ *n.* M19. [Turk. *mecidiye* silver coins, f. *Mejid* (see below).] **1** *the Medjidie*, a Turkish order or decoration instituted by the Sultan Abdul-Mejid (1823–61). M19. **2** A Turkish silver coin first minted by the Sultan Abdul-Mejid, equal to 20 piastres. L19.

medlar /ˈmɛdlə/ *n.* LME. [OFr. *medler* f. var. of *mesle* f. L *mespila*, *-us*, *-um* f. Gk *mespilē*, *mespilon*: for the ending cf. *cedar*, *poplar*.] **1** The tree *Mespilus germanica*, of the rose family, grown for its fruit (also *medlar tree*). Also (w. specifying wd), any of several related trees. LME. **2** The fruit of the medlar tree, like a small brown-skinned apple with a large cup-shaped 'eye' between the persistent calyx-lobes, which is eaten when half-rotten. LME.

1 *Japanese medlar*: see JAPANESE *a.* **Neapolitan medlar, oriental medlar** the azarole, *Crataegus azarolus*.

medley /ˈmɛdli/ *n.*, *a.*, & *v.* ME. [OFr. *medlee* var. of *meslee* MÊLÉE f. Proto-Romance use as n. of fem. pa. pple of med.L *misculare* mix. Cf.

MEDDLE.] A *n.* **1** Combat, conflict; fighting, esp. hand-to-hand. *arch.* ME. **2** A combination, a mixture, a collection, now *esp.* a heterogeneous one, a miscellany; *spec.* (*a*) a cloth woven with wools of different colours or shades; (*b*) a musical composition consisting of parts or subjects of a diverse or incongruous nature; a group of (parts of) songs or instrumental pieces performed together as a continuous whole; (*c*) a literary miscellany or collection; (*d*) a relay race in which team-members swim sections in different strokes, run distances of unequal length, etc. ME.

2 M. DE LA ROCHE A strange medley of bowls, vases, and boxes—Eastern and English, ancient and Victorian. R. MACAULAY A medley of harsh . . voices, raised in dispute. R. P. JHABVALA The string quartet had struck up a medley of old Broadway show tunes.

B *adj.* †**1** Of a mixed colour; variegated, motley. ME–L17. **2** Composed of diverse or incongruous parts or elements; mixed, motley. (Earlier in CHANCE-MEDLEY.) L16.

C *v.t.* Pa. t. & pple **medleyed, medlied**. Make a mixture of; intermix. Usu. in *pass.* L15.

Medo- /ˈmiːdəʊ/ *comb. form.* M18. [f. L *Medus* f. Gk *Mēdos*, f. *Medoi*: see MEDE, -O-.] Forming ns. and adjs. in the sense 'Median and —', as *Medo-Persian*.

Médoc /meɪˈdɒk, *foreign* medɔk (*pl. same*)/ *n.* Also **Medoc**. M19. [Fr.: see below.] (A) red wine produced in Médoc, the area along the left bank of the Gironde estuary in SW France.

medresseh *n.* var. of MADRASAH.

medrinaque /mɛdrɪˈnaki, *foreign* medriˈɲake/ *n.* Now *rare* or *obs.* E18. [Sp. *medriñaque*, of unkn. origin.] Fibre from the sago palm and other trees of the Philippines; cloth made from this fibre.

medulla /mɛˈdʌlə/ *n.* LME. [L = pith, marrow, perh. f. *medius* MID *a.*] *Biol.* **1** *Anat.* **a** The (inner) substance of the brain and spinal cord. Now *rare* or *obs.* M17. **b** *Anat.* & *Zool.* The central part or substance of various organs or structures where distinguishable from a cortex, e.g. of a kidney, adrenal gland, hair, or feather; pith. Also, the marrow of a bone. LME. **c** In full *medulla oblongata* /ɒblɒŋˈgɑːtə/ [L, lit. 'prolonged marrow']. The continuation of the spinal cord within the cranium, forming the hindmost part of the brain and containing regulatory centres for the heart, lungs, swallowing reflex, etc. L17. **d** The myelin sheath of a nerve. Now *rare.* M19. **2** *Bot.* The pith or soft internal tissue of a plant. M17. †**3** *fig.* The essential or central matter of a subject. Also, a compendium, a summary. M17–M18.

1b ADRENAL *medulla.*

medullar /mɪˈdʌlə/ *a.* Now *rare* or *obs.* M16. [Late L *medullaris*, f. as prec.: see -AR¹.] = next.

medullary /mɛˈdʌl(ə)ri, ˈmɛd(ə)l-/ *a.* E17. [f. as prec.: see -ARY².] **1** †**a** Of or pertaining to the soft pulp of a fruit. E17–E19. **b** *Bot.* Of, pertaining to, or designating the pith of a plant. M19. **2** *transf.* & *fig.* Pertaining to the inner part of anything. Long *rare.* M17. **3** *Anat.* & *Zool.* Pertaining to or designating the medulla of an organ or structure or the medulla oblongata. L17. **4** *Med.* = ENCEPHALOID. E19.

1b **medullary ray** each of the sheets of tissue in the stem of a dicotyledonous plant that extend radially from the pith to the cortex between the vascular bundles. **medullary sheath** in some higher plants, a layer of cells surrounding the pith of the stem. 3 **medullary plate** *Embryol.* = *neural plate* s.v. NEURAL *a.*

medullated /ˈmɛd(ə)leɪtɪd, mɛˈdʌl-/ *a.* (of a nerve or nerve fibre) myelinated M19.

medulloblastoma /mɛˌdʌləʊblaˈstəʊmə/ *n.* Pl. **-mas, -mata** /-mətə/. E20. [f. MEDULLA + -O- + BLASTO- + -OMA.] *Med.* A malignant brain tumour in children.

medusa /mɪˈdjuːzə, -sə/ *n.* In sense 1 usu. **M-**. Pl. **-sae** /-ziː, -siː/, **-sas**. LME. [L f. Gk *Medousa* the only mortal one of the three Gorgons in Gk mythol., with snakes for hair and a gaze which turned any beholder to stone: in sense 2 orig. as mod.L genus name.] **1** A terrifying or ugly woman, a gorgon. LME. **2** A jellyfish; *spec.* in *Zool.*, a coelenterate in the medusoid stage of its life cycle. M18.

Comb.: **medusa-fish** the stromateoid fish *Icichthys lockingtoni* (family Centrolophidae) of the N. Pacific, the young of which often swim close to jellyfishes.

medusal *a.* = MEDUSAN *a.* M19. **medusan** *a.* & *n.* (*a*) *adj.* of, pertaining to, or resembling a medusa, or (occas.) the Gorgon Medusa; (*b*) *n.* a medusoid coelenterate: M19.

Medusa's head /mɪˌdjuːzəz ˈhɛd, -səz/ *n. phr.* M16. [f. prec. + -'S¹ + HEAD *n.*] **1** *Astron.* A cluster of stars including the bright star Algol, in the constellation Perseus. M16. **2a** A succulent southern African spurge, *Euphorbia caput-Medusae*, with many long drooping branches. M18. **b** A Malayan orchid, *Bulbophyllum medusae*, with lateral sepals prolonged into threadlike processes. M19. **3** Any of various brittle-stars with long, flexible, freq. branched arms; a basket fish. L18.

medusiform /mɪˈdjuːsɪfɔːm/ *a.* M19. [f. prec. + -I- + -FORM.] *Zool.* = MEDUSOID *a.*

medusoid /mɪˈdjuːsɔɪd/ *a.* & *n.* M19. [f. MEDUSA + -OID.] *Zool.* A *adj.* Resembling a jellyfish or medusa; designating or pertaining to the reproductive, usu. free-swimming, stage of many coelenterates, in which the animal has a more or less domed shape with a central, downward-facing mouth and one or more rings of tentacles. M19. B *n.* A medusoid coelenterate; in some hydrozoans, a medusoid reproductive bud. Cf. HYDROID. M19.

mee /miː/ *n.* M20. [Chin. *miàn* (Wade–Giles *mien*) flour.] A Chinese dish made with noodles and other ingredients, popular in Malaysia.

meech /miːtʃ/ *v.i.* Now chiefly *US.* E17. [Dial. var. of MITCH *v.*] Retire from view; slink *off*; skulk *around*. Chiefly as *meeching* ppl a.

meed /miːd/ *n.* [OE *mēd* = OFris. *mēde*, OS *mēda*, *mieda*, OHG *mēta*, *mieta* (G *Miete*), f. WGmc, rel. to OE *meord*, Goth. *mizdō* (f. Gmc), Gk *misthos* reward.] **1** Orig., something given in return for labour or service, or for (good or ill) desert; recompense, reward. Later, a reward or prize given for excellence or achievement; one's merited portion *of* praise, honour, etc. Now *literary* & *arch.* OE. †**b** A gift. *rare.* Only in E17. †**2** Reward dishonestly offered or accepted; bribery. ME–E19. †**3** Merit, excellence, worth. LME–L18. **4** A fair share or proportion *of*. E20.

1 B. M. CROKER All the . . senior ladies, had received their due meed of attention. b SHAKES. *Timon* No meed but he repays Sevenfold above itself. 3 SHAKES. *3 Hen. VI* My meed hath got me fame. 4 *Daily Telegraph* The Golden Age had its meed of tin goods.

†**meedless** *a.* LME–L18.

meeja /ˈmiːdzə/ *n. slang.* Also **-jer**. L20. [Repr. a pronunc.] = MEDIA *n.*² 1.

meek /miːk/ *a.* & *adv.* ME. [ON *mjúkr* soft, pliant, gentle, rel. to Goth. form attested in *mūkamōdei* meekness.] A *adj.* **1** †**a** Courteous, kind; merciful, indulgent. ME–E17. **b** Not proud or self-willed; piously gentle in nature; humble, submissive. Also (now freq. *derog.*), inclined to submit tamely to oppression or injury, easily imposed on. ME. †**2** Of an animal: tame, gentle, not fierce. ME–M16. **3** Not violent or strong; mild. *arch.* ME.

1a SHAKES. *Jul. Caes.* I am meek and gentle with these butchers! b J. WAINWRIGHT He was no longer the meek, apologetic Barker of a few months ago. A. T. ELLIS 'He'll think you're dying.' I was too meek to tell her that I wished I was. *absol.*: AV *Matt.* 5:5 Blessed are the meeke: for they shall inherit the earth. **as meek as a lamb, as Moses**, etc., very meek. 3 S. E. FERRIER A meek, gray, autumnal day.

†**B** *adv.* Meekly. *rare.* ME–E17.

SHAKES. *Macb.* This Duncan Hath borne his faculties so meek.

meekly *adv.* ME. **meekness** *n.* ME.

meek /miːk/ *v.* Long *rare* or *obs.* ME. [f. prec.] **1** *v.t.* Make meek. ME. †**2** *v.i.* Be or become meek. Only in ME.

meeken /ˈmiːk(ə)n/ *v.* Now *rare.* ME. [f. MEEK *a.* + -EN⁵.] **1** *v.t.* Make meek; humble, tame; lessen the violence of; abase. ME. **2** *v.i.* Become meek or submissive; submit meekly (*to*). L15.

meemie /ˈmiːmi/ *n. slang* (orig. *US*). In sense 2 also **mimi**. E20. [Origin unkn.] **1** Orig., a state of drunkenness, delirium tremens. Later, hysterics; a hysterical person. Freq. in *the (screaming) meemies.* E20. **2** Hist. *screaming meemie*, a German rocket mortar in use in the war of 1939–45. M20.

meerkat /ˈmɪəkat/ *n.* L15. [Du. f. MLG *meerkatte* (OHG *merikazza*, G *Meerkatze*) lit. 'sea-cat', perh. orig. alt. of an oriental name: cf. Hindi *markaṭ*, Skt *markaṭa* ape.] †**1** A monkey. L15–M16. **2** Any of several mongooses of southern Africa, *esp.* the suricate or grey meerkat (see below). Orig. *S. Afr.* E19.

2 **grey meerkat** (*a*) a gregarious diurnal mongoose, *Suricata suricatta*, sometimes kept as a pet (also called *suricate*, *zenick*); (*b*) a solitary nocturnal mongoose, *Paracynictis selousi*. **red meerkat** a diurnal mongoose, *Cynictis penicillata*, with a tan coat. **slender-tailed meerkat** = *grey meerkat* (a) above.

meerschaum /ˈmɪəʃɔːm, -ʃəm/ *n.* L18. [G, f. *Meer* sea (see MERE *n.*¹) + *Schaum* foam (see SCUM), tr. Pers. *kef-i-daryā* foam of sea, w. ref to its frothiness.] **1** Hydrated magnesium silicate occurring as a soft white or yellowish claylike mineral; sepiolite. L18. **2** A tobacco-pipe with a bowl made from this. L18.

meese /miːz/ *n. obs.* exc. *dial.* Also **mese**. [OE *méos* = Flem. *mies*, OHG *mios*, ON *mýrr* (see MIRE *n.*¹), f. Gmc, whence also ON *mosi* MOSS *n.*] Moss.

meet /miːt/ *n.* M19. [f. MEET *v.*] **1** A meeting of hounds and people for a hunt. Also, a meeting of cyclists, athletes, etc., for a competition. M19. **b** A meeting; an assignation or appointment, esp. with an illicit supplier of narcotic etc. drugs. Also, a meeting-place, *esp.* one used by thieves. *slang.* M19. **2** *Math.* **a** A point, line, or surface of intersection. L19. **b** The intersection of two or more sets; the infimum of two or more elements of a lattice. M20.

1 *Tucson Magazine* The University of Arizona tracksters host two triangular meets. *Horse & Hound* The Clifton Foot arrived with . . their hounds to join . . the Ilminster pack at a joint meet.

meet /miːt/ *a.* & *adv. arch.* [OE (WS) *ġemǣte* = OHG *gamāzi* (G *gemäss*), f. as Y- + METE *v.*] A *adj.* †**1** Commensurate. Only in OE. **2** Having the proper dimensions; made to fit. Also, close-fitting, barely large enough. Long *rare* or *obs.* exc. *Sc.* ME. **3** Suitable, fit, proper (*for*, *to do*). Also, (usu. *pred.*, of an action) fitting, becoming, proper. ME. †**4** Equal (*to*), on the same level. Only in LME. **b** *be meet with*, be even with, be revenged on. L16–L17.

3 AV *Mark* 7:27 It is not meet to take the childrens bread, and to cast it vnto the dogges. V. SACKVILLE-WEST I should never suggest coming to tea. It would not be meet. S. DONALDSON They could not accept gifts without making meet return.

B *adv.* In a meet, fit, or proper manner; sufficiently. Also, exactly. Long *obs.* exc. *dial.* ME.

meetly *adv.* fittingly, suitably; moderately: ME. **meetness** *n.* fitness, suitability; moderation: ME.

meet /miːt/ *v.* Pa. t. & ppl **met** /mɛt/. [OE *mētan*, (Northumb.) *mœta*, *ġemētan* (see Y-) = OFris. *mēta*, OS *mōtian* (Du. *moeten*), ON *mœta*, Goth. *gamotjan*, f. Gmc base also of MOOT *n.*¹] I *v.t.* **1** Come on, come across, fall in with, find. Now *dial.* exc. as passing into sense 4 or as *meet with* (a) below. OE. **2a** Come face to face with (a person) from the opposite or a different direction. ME. **b** Arrive intentionally in the presence of (an approaching person etc.) from the opposite or a different direction (freq. in *go*, *run*, etc., *to meet*). Also, go somewhere to be present at the arrival of and welcome etc. (a person, a train, etc.). ME. **c** Of an object: come into contact or association with (a person or thing moving on a different course). Also, (of a line, road, etc.) reach a point of contact or intersection with (another line, road, etc.). ME. **d** Of an object of attention: present itself to, come to the notice of, (the hearing, sight, etc.). M17. **e** *Naut.* Control the sheer of (a ship) by putting the helm towards the opposite side. L18. **3a** Confront or oppose in battle, a contest, etc.;

fight a duel with. ME. **b** *fig.* Oppose or grapple with (an objection, difficulty, evil, etc.). M18. **4** Come accidentally or intentionally into the company of or into personal relations with (a person); come across (a person) in the course of social or business dealings. LME. **5** Experience, receive, suffer (one's death, a certain fate or treatment, etc.). Now *rare* or *poet.*, exc. as in *meet with* below. LME. **6** Come into conformity with (a person, a person's wishes or opinions). L17. **7** Satisfy (a demand or need); satisfy the requirements of (a particular case); be able or sufficient to discharge (a financial obligation). M19.

2a JAS. HOGG They perceived the two youths coming, as to meet them, on the same path. b OED An omnibus from the hotel meets all trains. G. GREENE I will arrange that he shall meet you here tomorrow. c LD MACAULAY The gibbet was set up where King Street meets Cheapside. H. ROTH The raw night air met him at the . . doorway. d G. M. TREVELYAN All that met his ear or eye. R. H. MOTTRAM The first object that met the gaze of the little party . . was Leon's garden ladder. 3a F. E. SMEDLEY I should be forced to meet him . . if he were to challenge me. b J. R. GREEN The threats of Charles were met by Offa with defiance. D. ROWE We struggle on, meeting . . an endless stream of difficulties. 4 LD MACAULAY The king did not then wish to meet them. S. HASTINGS She loved meeting new people. 5 M. PATTISON This generous appeal met no response. A. S. BYATT The awesome Flamborough Head, where so many have met terrible deaths. 6 LD MACAULAY The Estates . . would go as far as their consciences would allow to meet His Majesty's wishes. 7 H. MACMILLAN We received generous help to meet our urgent needs. K. M. E. MURRAY He had . . more demands on him than he could possibly meet. *Which?* All radial car tyres in this country must meet . . regulation standards.

II *v.i.* **8** Of two or more people: come from opposite or different directions to the same place or so as to be in each other's presence or company, either accidentally or intentionally; come face to face. Also foll. by *together*. ME. **†b** Come to or be present at a meeting; keep an appointment. LME–E18. **c** Of the members of a society, group, etc.: assemble for purposes of conference, business, etc. M16. **d** Arrive at mutual agreement. *rare.* M19. **9a** (Of things) come into contact, come together so as to occupy the same place; (of a line, road, etc.) reach a point of contact or intersection with another; (of a person's gaze, eyes, etc.) encounter the gaze, eyes, etc., of another. ME. **b** Of qualities etc.: unite in the same person etc. L16. **†c** Agree, tally. *rare.* L16–E19.

8 J. GAY We only part to meet again. E. PEACOCK They had not met for years. G. VIDAL She came towards him and they met beneath a portrait of her. b SHAKES. *Coriol.* The people . . are summon'd To meet anon, upon your approbation. c J. COLVILLE The House met, and . . Hore-Belisha rose to make his resignation speech. d *Methodist Recorder* Believers meet constantly for the apostles' teaching . . and the prayers. 9a R. KIPLING East is East, and West is West, and never the twain shall meet. V. WOOLF Their eyes met for a second. E. BOWEN Plaits were strained round her skull to meet at the top. P. LARKIN Where sky and Lincolnshire and water meet. b J. T. FOWLER The nobility of two races met in the child.

Phrases & comb.: *hail-fellow-well-met*: see HAIL *int.* *make (both) ends meet*: see END *n.* **meet a person's eye, gaze,** etc. (*a*) see that a person is looking at one; (*b*) reciprocate a person's look without turning away. **meet halfway** †(*a*) forestall, anticipate; (*b*) respond to the friendly advances of; (*c*) come to a compromise with. *meet one's maker*: see MAKER 1. *meet one's match*: see MATCH *n.*[1] *meet on one's own ground*: see GROUND *n.* **meet the case** be adequate. **meet the eye** (or **ear**) be visible (or audible). **meet-the-people** *a.* (orig. *US*) designating a tour etc. made by a public personage, esp. a politician, to meet members of the general public. **meet trouble halfway** distress oneself needlessly about what may happen. **more than meets the eye** hidden qualities or complications. *well met*: see WELL *adv.*

With advs. & preps. in specialized senses: **meet in with** *Sc.* meet, encounter. **meet up** (*a*) happen to meet; (*b*) *meet up with* (colloq.), overtake or fall in with; meet, encounter; become acquainted with. **meet with** (*a*) come on, come across, fall in with, find; †(*b*) = senses 2a, b above; †(*c*) = senses 3a, b above; †(*d*) come into or be in physical contact with; (of a garment) extend to (a certain point); (*e*) experience, receive, suffer (one's death, a certain fate, etc.); (*f*) have a business etc. meeting with. *pleased to meet you*: see PLEASE.

meeter *n.* (*a*) a person who attends or takes part in a meeting, *esp.* a participant in a meeting of the Society of Friends; (*b*) a person who meets someone: M17.

meeten /ˈmiːt(ə)n/ *v.t. arch. rare.* E19. [f. MEET *a.* + -EN[5].] Make meet or fit (*for*).

meeterly /ˈmiːtəli/ *adv.* Chiefly *north.* L16. [Perh. rel. to MEET *a.*: see -LY[2].] Tolerably, moderately; handsomely, agreeably.

meeting /ˈmiːtɪŋ/ *n.* [OE *gemēting*, re-formed in ME f. MEET *v.* + -ING[1].] **1** A private or (now often) public gathering or assembly of people for entertainment, discussion, legislation, etc.; an assembly of people, esp. the Society of Friends, for worship; a Nonconformist congregation, esp. of the Society of Friends. Also, the people attending a meeting, collectively. OE. **b** = *race meeting* s.v. RACE *n.*[1] L17. **2** The action of MEET *v.*; the action or an act of coming together, encountering, assembling, etc. ME. **3** A duel. Formerly also, a fight, a battle. ME. **4a** The junction, intersection, confluence, etc., of two or more things. LME. **b** A joint in carpentry or masonry. M17. **5** = *meeting-place* below. *poet.* L16.

1 L. R. BANKS We had a meeting . . to decide what to do. *Friends' Quarterly* We do require that the prospective member attend our Meetings. M. SPARK Turning up once a month for a directors' meeting. b R. DAHL Amber Flash nearly beat him on three legs last meeting. c *Shetland Times* The meeting heard a report . . on a year with some successes. 2 H. P. BROUGHAM The peoples' right of Meeting in large bodies. H. CARPENTER At a first meeting he would talk as if he had known you for years. 4a T. MOORE The Meeting of the Waters. 5 SHAKES. *1 Hen. IV* On Thursday we ourselves will march. Our meeting Is Bridgenorth.

Phrases: **go to meeting** attend a Nonconformist assembly for worship, esp. one of the Society of Friends. *mass meeting*: see MASS *n.*[2] & *a.* *mothers' meeting*: see MOTHER *n.*[1] & *a.* *parents' meeting*: see PARENT *n.* *preparative meeting*: see PREPARATIVE *a.* *protracted meeting*: see PROTRACT *v.* 2. STATUTORY *meeting*. *take the sense of the meeting*: see SENSE *n.* *Yearly Meeting*: see YEARLY *a.* 2.

Comb.: **meeting-house** †(*a*) a (private) house used for a meeting; (*b*) a place of worship (*US* or *derog.* exc. as used for meetings of the Society of Friends); (*c*) in Polynesia, a public hall; **meeting-place** (*a*) a place at which a meeting occurs; †(*b*) = *meeting-house* (b) above.

¶In sense 1 in OE glosses only bef. E16.

meetinger *n.* (*arch. derog.*) a member of a Nonconformist congregation E19.

mefenamic /mɛfəˈnamɪk/ *a.* M20. [f. ME(THYL + *-fen-* alt. of PHEN(YL + AM(INO- + BENZO)IC.] Pharm. *mefenamic acid*, a drug which inhibits prostaglandin synthesis and is used as an anti-inflammatory agent and analgesic, *N*-2,3-xylylanthranilic acid.

méfiance /mefjɑ̃s/ *n.* L19. [Fr.] Mistrust.

mefloquine /ˈmɛfləkwiːn/ *n.* L20. [f. ME(THYL + FL(UOR)O- + QUIN(OLIN)E.] *Pharm.* A fluorinated derivative of quinoline used as an antimalarial drug.

Meg /mɛg/ *n.*[1] Now *dial.* M16. [Pet-form of female forename *Margaret*.] (A name for) a hoyden, a coarse woman.

Meg Dorts: see DORT *n.*

meg /mɛg/ *n.*[2] *slang* & *dial.* L17. [Origin unkn.] †**1** A guinea. L17–M18. **2** Any of various coins of low value. L18.

meg /mɛg/ *n.*[3] L20. [Abbrev.] **1** *Electr.* Megohm(s). L20. **2** *Computing.* Megabyte(s). L20.

mega /ˈmɛgə/ *a. colloq.* (orig. *US*). L20. [Independent use of next.] Large, great. Also, brilliant, excellent.

New Yorker I was mega, but not mega enough for the job.

mega- /ˈmɛgə/ *comb. form.* Bef. a vowel also **meg-**. [Gk, comb. form of *megas* great. Cf. MEGALO-.] **1** Used in wds adopted f. Gk, in Eng. wds modelled on these, and as a freely productive pref., w. the sense 'very large'. **b** *Med.* Involving gross dilatation or hypertrophy of a part, as *megacolon*, *megaureter*. **2** Used in names of units of measurement etc. to denote a factor of one million (10^6), as *megahertz*, *megawatt*, also (in *Computing*) a factor of 2^{20} (1,048,576), as *megabyte*. Abbrev. *M*.

megabit *n.* (*Computing*) one million (or 1,048,576) bits, as a unit of data size or memory capacity M20. **megabuck** *n.* (*colloq.*) a million dollars, in *pl.*, very large sums of money M20. **megabyte** *n.* (*Computing*) one million (or 1,048,576) bytes, as a unit of data size or memory capacity L20. **megacycle** *n.* one million cycles (of an oscillatory or periodic phenomenon); *esp.* one million cycles per second, a megahertz: E20. **megadeath** *n.* the death of a million people, esp. as a unit in estimating the possible effects of nuclear war M20. **megadont** *a.* (*Anthropol.*) having or designating teeth of a large size, esp. as measured by a recognized dental index L19. **megafauna** *n.* (*Biol.*) the large or macroscopic animals or animal life, esp. the large vertebrates, of a given area, habitat, or epoch M20. **megaˈgamete** *n.* (*Biol.*) the larger (usu. female) gamete in an organism where the male and female gametes differ in size L19. **megagaˈmetophyte** *n.* (*Bot.*) a gametophyte that develops from a megaspore, a female gametophyte M20. **megamachine** *n.* a social system dominated by technology and functioning without regard for specifically human needs M20. **†megameter** *n.* an instrument for taking large measurements, esp. for calculating logitude from the position of the stars M18–L19. **megamillioˈnaire** *n.* a multimillionaire M20. **megaˈnucleus** *n.* (*Zool.*) the larger of two nuclei in ciliated protozoa, concerned with vegetative processes L19. **megaphyll** *n.* (*Bot.*) a usu. large type of leaf (esp. the frond of a fern) marked by branching veins and usu. associated with leaf gaps in the stele M20. **meˈgaphyllous** *a.* (*Bot.*) having megaphylls E20. **megaripple** *n.* (*Physical Geogr.*) an extensive undulation in a sandy beach or seabed, usu. of the order of tens of metres from crest to crest and tens of centimetres in height M20. **megashear** *n.* (*Geol.*) a transcurrent fault in which the displacement is greater than the thickness of the crust M20. **megastar** *n.* a very famous person, esp. in the world of entertainment L20. **megastardom** *n.* the condition of being a megastar; the world of megastars: L20. **megastore** *n.* a large store selling wares from its own factory to the customer L20. **megaˈstructural** *a.* of or pertaining to a megastructure M20. **megastructure** *n.* a massively large construction or complex, *esp.* one consisting of many buildings M20. **megaunit** *n.* (*Biol.* & *Med.*) a million international units M20. **megaˈvitamin** *a.* (*Med.*) designating or pertaining to therapy based on the taking of large doses of vitamins L20.

megacephalic /mɛgəsɪˈfalɪk, -kɛˈfalɪk/ *a.* L19. [f. MEGA- + -CEPHALIC.] = MACROCEPHALIC.

Also **megacephalous** *a.* M19.

megachiropteran /mɛgəkʌɪ(ə)rˈɒpt(ə)rən/ *a.* & *n.* L19. [f. mod.L *Megachiroptera* (see below), f. as MEGA- + *Chiroptera*: see CHIROPTERAN.] *Zool.* **A** *adj.* Of or pertaining to the chiropteran suborder Megachiroptera, which includes flying foxes and other fruit-bats. L19. **B** *n.* A megachiropteran bat. L19.

megacosm /ˈmɛgəkɒz(ə)m/ *n.* E17. [f. MEGA- after *microcosm*.] = MACROCOSM.

megaflop /ˈmɛgəflɒp/ *n.* L20. [f. MEGA- + acronym f. *f*loating-point *op*erations per *s*econd (w. *-s* taken as pl. suff. -S[1]).] *Computing.* A unit of computing speed equal to one million or 2^{20} floating-point operations per second.

megakaryocyte /mɛgəˈkarɪəsʌɪt/ *n.* L19. [f. MEGA- + KARYO- + -CYTE.] *Physiol.* A giant cell of the bone marrow, which has a large irregularly lobed nucleus and from which blood platelets are formed.

megakaryoblast *n.* a cell which develops into a megakaryocyte L20. **ˌmegakaryoˈcytic** *a.* M20. **ˌmegakaryocytopoiˈesis** *n.* production of megakaryocytes L20.

megalith /ˈmɛgəlɪθ/ *n.* M19. [Back-form. f. next: see -LITH.] *Archaeol.* A large stone, *esp.* one forming (part of) a prehistoric monument; a megalithic monument.

megalithic /mɛgəˈlɪθɪk/ *a.* M19. [f. MEGA- + -LITHIC.] *Archaeol.* Designating prehistoric monuments constructed of large stones; designating or pertaining to a culture, people, etc., characterized by the erection of such monuments.

C. DAWSON In Europe the Megalithic Culture as a whole belongs to the last phase of the neolithic period.

megalo- /ˈmɛɡələʊ/ *comb. form.* Bef. a vowel also **megal-**. [Gk, comb. form of *megas* great: see -O-. Cf. MEGA-.] = MEGA- 1.

megaloblast *n.* (*Med.*) a large abnormally developed erythroblast typical of certain forms of anaemia L19. **megaloˈblastic** *a.* (of anaemia) characterized by megaloblasts E20. **megaloˈcardia** *n.* (*Med.*) abnormal enlargement of the heart M19. **megalocyte** *n.* (*Med.*) a macrocyte L19. **megalopod** *a.* & *n.* (a person or creature) having large feet E20. **megalosphere** *n.* (*Zool.*) the initial chamber of a megalospheric foraminifer L19. **megaloˈspheric** *a.* (*Zool.*) designating certain foraminifera having a large initial chamber and a single large nucleus L19.

megalocephalic /ˌmɛɡ(ə)lə(ʊ)sɪˈfalɪk, -kɛˈfalɪk/ *a.* L19. [f. MEGALO- + -CEPHALIC.] = MACROCEPHALIC.

megaloˈcephalous *a.* = MEGALOCEPHALIC L19. **megaloˈcephaly** *n.* macrocephalic condition L19.

megalomania /mɛɡ(ə)lə(ʊ)ˈmeɪnɪə/ *n.* L19. [f. MEGALO- + -MANIA.] Delusions of grandeur or self-importance, esp. resulting from mental illness; a passion for grandiose schemes; lust for power.

megalomaniac *a.* & *n.* (*a*) *adj.* affected by or characteristic of megalomania; (*b*) *n.* a megalomaniac person: L19. **megalomaniacal** /-məˈnʌɪək(ə)l/ *a.* megalomaniac L19. **megalomanic** /-ˈmanɪk/ *a.* megalomaniac L20.

megalomartyr /mɛɡ(ə)lə(ʊ)ˈmɑːtə/ *n.* M18. [Late Gk *megalomartur*, f. as MEGALO- + Gk *martur* MARTYR *n.*] In the Orthodox Church, a martyr to whom particular veneration is given.

megalopa /mɛɡəˈləʊpə/ *n.* E19. [mod.L (orig. as genus name), f. Gk *megalōpos* large-eyed, or f. L MEGALO- + *ops* eye.] *Zool.* A larval stage in the development of crabs, following the nauplius stage and having the adult number of trunk segments and legs; a crab in this stage. Also called *megalops*. Freq. *attrib.*

megalopolis /mɛɡəˈlɒp(ə)lɪs/ *n.* Also **M-**. M19. [f. MEGALO- + -POLIS.] A very large city; the way of life of a very large city. Also, the practice of building very large cities.

megalopolitan /mɛɡ(ə)lə(ʊ)ˈpɒlɪt(ə)n/ *n.* & *a.* Also **M-**. M17. [f. as prec. + Gk *politēs* citizen: see -AN.] **A** *n.* A native or inhabitant of a megalopolis. M17. **B** *adj.* Of or pertaining to (the way of life characteristic of) a megalopolis. E20.

¶Rare bef. E20.

megalops /ˈmɛɡəlɒps/ *n.* M19. [mod.L (orig. as genus name), alt. of MEGALOPA.] *Zool.* = MEGALOPA. Freq. *attrib.*

megalosaurus /mɛɡ(ə)lə(ʊ)ˈsɔːrəs/ *n.* Pl. **-ri** /-rʌɪ/. Also Anglicized as **megalosaur** /ˈmɛɡ(ə)lə(ʊ)sɔː/. E19. [mod.L, f. MEGALO- + Gk *sauros* -SAUR.] A large bipedal carnivorous theropod dinosaur of the genus *Megalosaurus*, of the Eurasian Jurassic and Cretaceous.

megaloˈsaurian *a.* & *n.* (*a*) *adj.* of, pertaining to, or resembling (that of) a megalosaurus; (*b*) *n.* a megalosaurus; an animal resembling a megalosaurus: M19.

megamouth /ˈmɛɡəmaʊθ/ *n.* L20. [f. MEGA- + MOUTH *n.*] A shark, *Megachasma pelagios*, with a very large wide mouth, first captured in 1976 off the Hawaiian Islands. Also *megamouth shark*.

megaphone /ˈmɛɡəfəʊn/ *n.* & *v.* L19. [f. MEGA- + -PHONE.] **A** *n.* An instrument for carrying the sound of a voice over a distance; *spec.* a large speaking-trumpet. L19. **B** *v.i.* & *t.* Speak or utter (as) through a megaphone. E20.

megaphonic /-ˈfɒnɪk/ *a.* L19. **megaphonist** *n.* a person who speaks through a megaphone E20.

megapode /ˈmɛɡəpəʊd/ *n.* Also **-pod** /-pɒd/. M19. [mod.L *Megapodius* genus name, f. MEGA- + -POD.] Any of various brown or black gallinaceous birds of the Australasian family Megapodiidae, which have large strong feet and incubate their eggs in mounds of sand, leaves, etc., by solar or fermentative heat.

megapolis /məˈɡap(ə)lɪs/ *n.* M17. [f. MEGA- + -POLIS.] A major city.

Megarian /mɛˈɡɛːrɪən/ *a.* & *n.* Also **-ean**. E17. [Partly f. L, Gk *Megara* a city in Greece, partly f. L *Megareus* of Megara: see -IAN, -EAN.] **A** *adj.* **1** Of or pertaining to the school of philosophy founded *c*400 BC by Euclides of Megara. E17. **2** Designating a type of bowl of the Hellenistic period, usu. hemispherical with relief ornament. E20. **B** *n.* A member or adherent of the Megarian school of philosophy. M17.

Megaric /mɛˈɡarɪk/ *a.* & *n.* M17. [Gk *Megarikos* of or belonging to Megara: see prec., -IC.] **A** *adj.* =MEGARIAN *a.* 1. M17. **B** *n.* = MEGARIAN *n.* M19.

megaron /ˈmɛɡər(ə)n/ *n.* L19. [Gk.] In ancient Greece, the great central hall of a type of house characteristic esp. of the Mycenaean period.

megascope /ˈmɛɡəskəʊp/ *n.* M19. [f. MEGA- + -SCOPE.] A modification of the camera obscura or magic lantern which throws a reflected magnified image of an object upon a screen.

megascopic /-ˈskɒpɪk/ *a.* (*a*) visible to the naked eye, macroscopic; (*b*) of or pertaining to a megascope or its use; (*c*) *spec.* (of a photographic image etc.) enlarged, magnified: L19. **megascopically** /-ˈskɒp-/ *adv.* L19.

megasea /mɛˈɡasɪə/ *n.* L19. [mod.L *Megasea* (see below), f. Gk *megas* large, w. ref. to the size of the leaves.] Any of various ornamental plants of the former genus *Megasea*, now called *Bergenia*; a bergenia.

megaspore /ˈmɛɡəspɔː/ *n.* M19. [f. MEGA- + SPORE.] *Bot.* The larger of the two kinds of spores in heterosporous cryptogams, which develop into female gametophytes; the analogous structure (the immature embryo sac) in seed plants.

megaspoˈrangium *n.*, pl. **-gia**, a sporangium containing megaspores L19. **megaˈsporophyll** *n.* a leaf or modified leaf which bears megasporangia E20.

megass /mɛˈɡas/ *n.* M19. [Origin unkn. Cf. BAGASSE.] The fibrous residue left after the extraction of sugar from sugar cane.

megatherium /mɛɡəˈθɪərɪəm/ *n.* Pl. **-ia** /-ɪə/. Also Anglicized as **megathere** /ˈmɛɡəθɪə/. E19. [mod.L, as if Gk *mega thērion* great animal: see MEGA-.] *Palaeont.* **1** Any of several large extinct edentate mammals (ground sloths) of the genus *Megatherium* and related genera of the Upper Tertiary of S. America. E19. **2** *transf.* & *fig.* A thing of huge or ungainly proportions. M19.

megatherial *a.* resembling a megatherium, ponderous, unwieldy L19. **megatherian** *a.* & *n.* (of, pertaining to, resembling, or designating) a megatherium M19. **megatherioid** *a.* & *n.* (resembling or pertaining to) a megatherium or similar extinct edentate mammal M19.

megaton /ˈmɛɡətʌn/ *n.* & *a.* M20. [f. MEGA- + TON *n.*[1]] **A** *n.* A unit of explosive power, equal to that of one million tons of TNT. M20.

B *attrib.* or as *adj.* Of or pertaining to a megaton; of the size or power of a megaton. M20.

City Limits A single aircraft armed with binary warheads would kill as many civilians as a single megaton nuclear bomb. *fig.*: *Daily Telegraph* Another British spy scandal of 'megaton proportions' was forecast yesterday.

megatonnage *n.* explosive power of nuclear weapons, as expressed in megatons M20.

Megger /ˈmɛɡə/ *n.* Also **m-**. E20. [Origin uncertain: perh. f. MEGOHM.] (Proprietary name for) an instrument designed mainly for measuring electrical insulation resistance.

Megillah /məˈɡɪlə/ *n.* Also **m-**. M17. [Heb. *mĕgillāh*, lit. 'roll, scroll'.] **1** Each of five books of the Hebrew Scriptures (the Song of Solomon, Ruth, Lamentations, Ecclesiastes, and Esther) appointed to be read on certain Jewish notable days; *esp.* the Book of Esther, read at the festival of Purim. Also, a copy of all, or any, of these books. M17. **2** A long, tedious, or complicated story. Freq. in *a* or *the whole megillah*. *slang.* M20.

2 *High Times* Drooped leading edges, cupped wingtips, . . the whole megillah. S. BELLOW He tried to brief me. . . the main part of what he said was a regular megillah.

megilp /məˈɡɪlp/ *n.* Also **magilp** & other vars. M18. [Origin unkn.] A mixture, usu. of linseed oil with turpentine or mastic varnish, used as a vehicle for oil colours.

megimide /ˈmɛɡɪmʌɪd/ *n.* M20. [App. f. ME(THYL + G(LUTARIC + IMIDE.] *Pharm.* A cyclic organic compound which acts as a medullary respiratory stimulant and has been used to counteract the effects of barbiturates; 3-ethyl-3-methylglutarimide.

megohm /ˈmɛɡəʊm/ *n.* M19. [f. MEGA- + OHM.] *Electr.* A million ohms.

megrim /ˈmiːɡrɪm/ *n.*[1] *arch.* LME. [Var. of MIGRAINE.] **1** Migraine. LME. **2** Vertigo. L16. **3** A whim, a fancy, a fad. L16. **4** In *pl.* Low spirits; depression. M17. **5** In *pl.* The staggers in horses etc. M17.

4 G. R. SIMS Having as many dislikes as a fashionable lady with the megrims.

megrim /ˈmiːɡrɪm/ *n.*[2] M19. [Origin unkn.] Either of two flatfishes of European waters, the scald-fish, *Arnoglossus laterna*, and the sail-fluke, *Lepidorhombus whiffiagonis*.

mehari /məˈhɑːri/ *n.* M18. [Fr. *méhari*, pl. *méhara* f. Arab. *mahrī* (pl. *mahārī*, *mahārā*), use as n. of adj. = of Mahra (a region of southern Arabia).] In N. Africa and the Middle East: a dromedary, a riding camel.

mehmandar /ˈmeɪmændɑː/ *n.* E17. [Pers. *mihmāndār*, f. *mihmān* guest.] In Persian-speaking countries and the Indian subcontinent, an official appointed to act as courier to an important traveller.

mehtar /ˈmeɪtə/ *n.* M17. [Urdu, f. Pers. *mihtar* headman, prince, occurring esp. in titles, compar. of *mih* great.] **1** Orig., (the title of) any of several important officers of the Persian royal household. Later, a groom or a stable-boy in Persia (Iran). M17. **2** In the Indian subcontinent: a house-sweeper, a scavenger; the lowest-ranking house-servant. E19. **3** *Hist.* (The title of) the ruler of Chitral (in NW Pakistan). L19.

meibomian /mʌɪˈbəʊmɪən/ *a.* E19. [f. H. *Meibom* (1638–1700), Ger. anatomist: see -IAN.] *Anat.* Pertaining to or designating various large sebaceous glands of the human eyelid, whose infection results in chalazia.

meibomian cyst = CHALAZION.

Meiji /ˈmeɪdʒi/ *n.* & *a.* L19. [Jap., lit. 'enlightened government'.] **A** *n.* The period of the rule of the Japanese emperor Mutsuhito (1868–1912), marked by the modernization and westernization of Japan. L19. **B** *adj.* Of, pertaining to, or characteristic of this period. E20.

mein Gott /maɪn ˈɡɒt/ *int.* M19. [G.] = *my God* s.v. GOD *n.* 5(c).

mein Herr /maɪn ˈhɛr/ *n. phr.* E20. [G, f. *mein* my + HERR.] Used as a German form of address to a man; a German man.

meinie /ˈmeɪni/ *n.* Now chiefly *arch.* ME. [(O)Fr. *meinée*, *mesnée* = Prov. *mesnada* f. Proto-Romance, f. L *mansio(n-)* MANSION: see -Y[5]; later also infl. by MANY *n.*] **1** A family, a household. *obs.* exc. *Sc.* ME. **2** A body of retainers or followers; a retinue. ME. †**3** A body of people employed together or united by a common purpose; an army, a ship's crew, a congregation, etc. ME–L16. **4** A crowd of people; *derog.* a crew, a set. LME. **5** A number or collection of things. *obs.* exc. *Sc.* LME. †**6** A herd or flock of animals. L15–M16.

meio- /ˈmʌɪəʊ/ *comb. form* of Gk *meiōn* less, smaller: see -O-.

meioˈbenthic *a.* (*Biol.*) of or pertaining to the meiobenthos M20. **meioˈbenthos** *n.* (*Biol.*) the section of the benthos that includes animals of intermediate or meiofaunal size M20. **meiofauna** *n.*, pl. **-nae** /-niː/, **-nas**, (*Biol.*) the medium-sized (esp. the small but not microscopic) animals or animal life of a given area, habitat, or epoch M20. **meioˈfaunal** *a.* (*Biol.*) of or pertaining to meiofauna M20. **meionite** *n.* (*Min.*) an aluminosilicate mineral, the calcium- and carbonate-rich end-member of the scapolite series; cf. MARIALITE: E19. **meiophylly** *n.* [Gk *phullon* leaf] *Bot.* the suppression of one or more leaves in a whorl M19. **meiotaxy** *n.* (*Bot.*) the suppression of an entire whorl of floral organs M19.

meiosis /mʌɪˈəʊsɪs/ *n.* Pl. **-oses** /-ˈəʊsiːz/. M16. [mod.L f. Gk *meiōsis*, f. *meioun* lessen, f. *meiōn* less: see -OSIS.] **1** *Rhet.* **a** A figure of speech by which something is intentionally presented as smaller, less important, etc., than it really is. Now *rare*. M16. b = LITOTES. M17. 2 *Biol.* The division of a diploid cell nucleus into four haploid nuclei; this division together with the accompanying cell division giving rise to gametes (or in some organisms, a haploid generation), the diploid chromosome number being regained at a subsequent fertilization. Cf. MITOSIS. E20.

2 **meiosis I** the first of the two divisions of meiosis, in which homologous chromosomes pair, exchange material, and separate, one of each pair going to each daughter nucleus. **meiosis II** the second division of meiosis, in which each nucleus divides as in mitosis, without pairing of chromosomes.

meiotic /mʌɪˈɒtɪk/ *a.* E20. [Gk *meiōtikos* diminishing, f. *meioun* lessen.] 1 *Biol.* Of, pertaining to, or occurring during meiosis. E20. 2 *Rhet.* Characterized by meiosis. E20.

meiotically *adv.* L17.

mei ping /meɪ ˈpɪŋ/ *n. phr.* E20. [Chin. *méi píng* prunus vase.] A kind of Chinese porcelain vase with a narrow neck designed to hold a single spray of flowers.

meisie /ˈmeɪsi/ *n.* L19. [Afk., f. Du. *meisje*.] In South Africa, a girl, a young woman.

Meissen /ˈmʌɪs(ə)n/ *n.* M19. [A town in Germany near Dresden.] More fully *Meissen china*. Dresden china.

J. WADE Her face . . had the smooth, pleased prettiness of Meissen.

Meissner /ˈmʌɪsnə/ *n.* L19. [Georg *Meissner* (1829–1905), Ger. anatomist.] *Anat.* 1 *Meissner's corpuscle*, a mechanoreceptive sensory nerve ending found in the dermis in various parts of the body. L19. 2 *Meissner's plexus*, a network of parasympathetic nerve fibres serving the muscles and mucous membranes in the wall of the gut. L19.

Meissner effect /ˈmʌɪsnər ɪˌfɛkt/ *n. phr.* M20. [F. W. *Meissner* (1882–1974), Ger. physicist.] *Physics.* The existence of zero, or very low, magnetic induction in a superconducting material even in the presence of a magnetic field; *esp.* the expulsion of magnetic flux when a material becomes superconducting in a magnetic field.

Meistersinger /ˈmʌɪstəzɪŋə, -sɪŋ-/ *n.* Pl. same. M19. [G, f. *Meister* MASTER *n.*[1] + *Singer* SINGER *n.*[1]] A member of any of the German guilds for lyric poets and musicians in the 14th to 16th cents.

meith /miːθ/ *n. Sc.* L15. [App. f. ON *mið* mark, but assoc. w. L *meta* METE *n.*[1]] 1 A landmark, a sea-mark; a boundary, a goal. L15. 2 A measurement. E18.

Mekhitarist /ˈmɛkɪtɑːrɪst/ *n.* & *a.* M19. [f. *Mekhitar* (see below) + -IST.] A *n.* A member of a congregation of Roman Catholic Armenian monks originally founded at Constantinople in 1701 by Mekhitar, an Armenian, and finally established by him in 1717 in the island of San Lazzaro, south of Venice. M19. B *adj.* Of or pertaining to the Mekhitarists. L19.

mekometer /mɪˈkɒmɪtə/ *n.* L19. [f. Gk *mēkos* length + -OMETER.] 1 *Mil.* An instrument for finding the range for infantry fire. L19. 2 A device for the accurate measurement of distance in which light polarized at a microwave frequency is beamed at a reflector and the polarization of the reflected light analysed. M20.

mel /mɛl/ *n.* M20. [f. MEL(ODY.] *Acoustics.* A unit of subjective pitch, defined so that the number of mels is proportional to the pitch of a sound, and the pitch of a 1000-hertz note is 1000 mels.

mela /ˈmeɪlɑː, -lə/ *n.* E19. [Skt *melā* assembly, f. *mil-* to meet.] A Hindu festival and assembly.

melaena /mɪˈliːnə/ *n.* Also *-lena. E19. [mod.L f. Gk *melaina* fem. of *melas* black.] *Med.* Dark sticky faeces containing partly digested blood; (a condition characterized by) the production of such faeces, following internal bleeding or the swallowing of blood.

melaleuca /mɛləˈl(j)uːkə/ *n.* E19. [mod.L (see below), f. Gk *melas* black + *leukos* white.] Any of numerous mostly Australian shrubs and trees of the genus *Melaleuca*, of the myrtle family, with bundles of protruding brightly coloured stamens. Also called *honey-myrtle*.

melam /ˈmɛlam/ *n.* Now *rare*. M19. [G, of arbitrary formation.] *Chem.* A buff, insoluble amorphous organic substance obtained by distilling ammonium thiocyanate.

melamed /mɪˈlɑːməd/ *n.* L19. [Heb. *mělammēd*] A teacher of elementary Hebrew.

melamine /ˈmɛləmiːn/ *n.* In sense 2 also **M-**. M19. [f. MELAM + AMINE.] 1 *Chem.* A crystalline heterocyclic compound made esp. by heating cyanamide; 2,4,6-triamino-1,3,5-triazine, $(CNH_2)_3N_3$. M19. 2 A melamine resin, or a plastic derived from one. M20.

Comb.: **melamine resin** any of various thermosetting resins made by condensing melamine with aldehydes, used for moulded items, adhesives in laminates, and coatings for textiles and paper.

†**melampod** *n.* Also (later) in L form **melampodium**. L16–E19. [L *melampodium* f. Gk *melampodion*, f. *melan-*, *melas* black + *pod-*, *pous* foot.] Black hellebore, *Helleborus orientalis*.

melan- *comb. form* see MELANO-.

melanaemia /mɛləˈniːmɪə/ *n.* Also *-nemia. M19. [f. MELANO- + -AEMIA.] *Med.* A condition in which the blood contains melanin or other dark pigment, as in haemochromatosis.

melanaemic *a.* L19.

melancholia /mɛlənˈkəʊlɪə/ *n.* E17. [Late L: see MELANCHOLY *n.*] *Med.* = DEPRESSION 3b. Also (*gen.*), melancholy, depression.

Guardian A . . bitter-sweet operetta, which fuses Scandinavian melancholia and introversion with Manhattan stringency, and cynicism.

melancholiac *a.* & *n.* (a person) affected with melancholia M19.

melancholic /mɛlənˈkɒlɪk/ *a.* & *n.* LME. [(O)Fr. *mélancolique* f. L *melancholicus* f. Gk *melankholikhos*, f. *melankholia* MELANCHOLY *n.*: see -IC.] A *adj.* †1 Of or pertaining to choler adust, one of the cardinal humours; attributed to or believed to contain this humour. LME–M17. 2 Characterized by melancholy; constitutionally or habitually liable to melancholy. LME. 3 Causing or expressing sadness and depression; saddening, melancholy. Now *rare*. E17.

2 L. STRACHEY Melancholic by temperament, he could yet be lively on occasion. 3 E. GRIFFITH I wrote a long, and of course, a melancholic letter to you.

B *n.* A person affected with melancholy; a melancholiac. L16.

melancholically *adv.* L19.

melancholious /mɛlənˈkəʊlɪəs/ *a.* Now *rare*. LME. [OFr. *melancolieus*, f. *mélancolie* MELANCHOLY *n.*: see -IOUS.] 1 = MELANCHOLIC *a.* 2, 3. LME. †2 = MELANCHOLIC *a.* 1. LME–M16.

melancholiousness *n.* L16.

melancholise *v.* var. of MELANCHOLIZE.

melancholist /ˈmɛlənk(ə)lɪst/ *n.* Now *rare* or *obs.* L16. [f. MELANCHOLY *n.* + -IST.] A person liable to melancholy, a melancholiac.

melancholize /ˈmɛlənk(ə)lʌɪz/ *v.* Now *rare* or *obs.* Also **-ise**. L16. [f. as prec. + -IZE.] 1 *v.i.* & *refl.* Be or become melancholy. L16. 2 *v.t.* Make melancholy. M17.

melancholy /ˈmɛlənk(ə)li/ *n.* ME. [(O)Fr. *mélancolie* f. late L *melancholia* f. Gk *melankholia*, f. *melan-*, *melas* black + *kholē* bile: see -Y[3].] 1 *Med.* Orig. (*obs.* exc. *Hist.*), a pathological condition attributed to a supposed excess of choler adust, one of the cardinal humours, and distinguished esp. by sullenness, irascibility, and sadness. Later, (now *rare*) pathological depression, melancholia. ME. b *Hist.* = *choler adust* s.v. CHOLER 2. LME. †2 Irascibility, anger, sullenness. LME–L16. 3 Sadness, dejection, depression; *esp.* pensive or meditative sadness. Also, inclination or tendency to this. LME. b An annoyance, a vexation. Now chiefly *literary*. L15. c A state, episode, or mood of (pensive or meditative) sadness etc. L16.

1 H. LYTE The disease called choler or melancholy. W. H. O. SANKEY Cases of melancholy which are accompanied by great restlessness. 2 *personified*: SHAKES. *John* If that surly spirit, melancholy, Hath bak'd thy blood. 3 M. W. MONTAGU It gives me too much melancholy to see so agreeable a young creature buried alive. E. L. DOCTOROW Melancholy had taken the will out of her muscles. S. HASTINGS The autumnal countryside induced in her a pervasive feeling of melancholy. b H. JAMES These melancholies haven't prevented the London season from roaring and elbowing along. c BURKE In spite of all my efforts, I fall into a melancholy which is inexpressible.

melancholy /ˈmɛlənk(ə)li/ *a.* LME. [f. the n.] 1 Affected with or characterized by melancholy; liable to melancholy. Now *esp.* (inclined to be) sadly thoughtful or meditative. LME. †b = MELANCHOLIC *a.* 1. E–M17. †2 Irascible, angry; sullen. LME–E17. 3 Suggestive of or expressing sadness; depressing, dismal. L16. 4 Of a fact, event, etc.: lamentable, deplorable. E18.

1 J. THOMSON A certain music, never known before, Here soothed the pensive, melancholy mind. W. IRVING There is no more melancholy creature . . than a mountebank off duty. R. HUGHES He felt acutely melancholy, not very far from tears. 3 W. LITHGOW Padua is the most melancholy City of Europe. H. JACOBSON They cannot read a word of the melancholy poems. **melancholy thistle** a thistle of upland pastures, *Cirsium lenoides*, with a thornless stem and a single drooping head. 4 L. STERNE Melancholy! to see such sprightliness the prey of sorrow.

melancholily *adv.* M16. †**melancholiness** *n.* E16–E18. †**melancholish** *a.* (*a*) = MELANCHOLIC *a.* 1; (*b*) somewhat melancholy: M16–L18.

†**melancholy** *v.t.* LME–E19. [OFr. *melancolier*, f. as MELANCHOLY *n.*] Make melancholy.

Melanchthonian /mɛlaŋkˈθəʊnɪən/ *a.* & *n.* M18. [f. *Melanchthon* Graecized form of surname of Philipp Schwarzerd (lit. 'black earth') + -IAN.] A *adj.* Of or pertaining to (the beliefs of) the German Protestant reformer Philipp Melanchthon (1497–1560). M18. B *n.* An adherent or student of Melanchthon or his beliefs. M19.

melanemia *n.* see MELANAEMIA.

Melanesian /mɛləˈniːzjən, -ʒ(ə)n/ *a.* & *n.* M19. [f. *Melanesia* (see below), f. Gk *melas* black + *nēsos* island + -IA[1], after *Polynesia*: see -AN.] A *n.* A native or inhabitant of Melanesia, an island-group in the SW Pacific including the Solomon Islands, the Bismarck archipelago, Santa Cruz, Vanuatu, New Caledonia and Fiji; *spec.* a member of the dominant people of Melanesia, characteristically Negroid in appearance and of relatively small stature. Also, the group of Austronesian languages spoken in Melanesia. M19. B *adj.* Of or pertaining to Melanesia, the Melanesians, or their group of languages. M19.

Melanesoid /mɛləˈniːzɔɪd/ *a.* M20. [f. as prec.: see -OID.] Similar in physical type to the typical Melanesian; resembling a Melanesian.

mélange /meɪlɑ̃ːʒ (*pl. same*), meɪˈlɒ̃ʒ/ *n.* M17. [Fr., f. *mêler* mix: see MELL *v.*] 1 A mixture; a collection of heterogeneous items or elements, a medley. M17. 2 Yarn, esp. woollen yarn, to which dye has been applied unevenly so as to leave some areas undyed; a fabric of such a yarn. L19. 3 Coffee made with sugar and whipped cream; a drink of this. E20.

Melanian /mɪˈleɪnɪən/ *a.* M19. [Fr. *mélanien*, f. Gk *melan-*, *melas* black: see -IAN.] *Anthropol.* Orig., Negrito. Later, Negroid.

melanic /mɪˈlanɪk/ *a.* & *n.* E19. [f. Gk *melan-*, *melas* black + -IC.] A *adj.* 1 *Anthropol.* Having black hair and a black or dark complexion. E19. 2a Of or pertaining to melanin; containing melanin. M19. b Of a variety of animal: characterized by (esp. industrial) melanism. L19.

2b *Nature* The murk of nineteenth century Manchester fostered the melanic form . . of the peppered moth.

B *n.* A melanic variety of an animal. M20.

melanin /ˈmɛlənɪn/ *n.* M19. [f. as prec. + -IN[1].] *Biochem.* Any of various dark brown or black pigments present in the hair, skin, eyes, etc. of people and animals, derived from tyrosine by polymerization and produced in increased amounts during tanning and in certain diseases.

melanism /ˈmɛlənɪz(ə)m/ *n.* M19. [f. as prec. + -ISM.] 1 *Physiol.* & *Zool.* Darkness of colour, hereditary or (less commonly) pathological, resulting from an excess of melanin in the skin, fur, feathers, scales, etc. Cf. MELANOSIS. M19. 2 Chiefly *Ornith.* A melanic variety *of* a bird etc. M19.

1 **industrial melanism** the prevalence of dark-coloured varieties of animals (esp. moths) in industrial areas where they are better camouflaged against predators than paler forms.

mela'nistic *a.* characterized by melanism L19. **melani'zation** *n.* the process or result of developing melanism; the development of melanin: M20. **melanized** *a.* having undergone melanization L19.

melanite /'mɛlənʌɪt/ *n.* E19. [f. Gk *melan-*, *melas* black + -ITE[1].] *Min.* A velvet-black variety of andradite garnet.

melano /'mɛlənəʊ/ *n. rare.* Pl. **-os**. E20. [f. MELANISM after *albino*.] = MELANIC *n.*

melano- /'mɛlənəʊ/ *comb. form.* Bef. a vowel also **melan-**. [f. Gk *melan-*, *melas* black; in many scientific terms, f. MELANIN: see- O-.] Dark-coloured; *spec.* of or pertaining to melanin.

melanoblast *n.* (*Anat.* & *Zool.*) (a cell that develops into) a melanocyte E20. **melano'cratic** *a.* (*Petrogr.*) (of a rock) dark-coloured, rich in dark-coloured minerals E20. **melanoderm** *n.* & *a.* (a person who is) dark-skinned, Negroid E20. **melano'derma, -'dermia** *n.* (*Med.*) melanosis; chloasma: L19. **melano'dermic** *a.* (*a*) pertaining to or exhibiting melanodermia; (*b*) (naturally) dark-skinned, Negroid: L19. **melano'genesis** *n.* (*Physiol.*) the formation of melanin E20. **melanophore** *n.* (*Zool.*) a cell containing melanin, *esp.* such a cell in the lower vertebrates which is contractile and confers the ability to change the depth of colour E20. **melanosome** *n.* (*Physiol.*) a particle in the cytoplasm of melanocytes in which melanin is thought to be formed M20. **melano'vanadite** *n.* (*Min.*) a black opaque monoclinic oxide of calcium and vanadium occurring as bunches of needle-like crystals E20.

melanocomous /mɛlə'nɒkəməs/ *a.* M19. [f. Gk *melanokomēs*, f. as MELANO- + *komē* hair + -OUS.] Chiefly *Anthropol.* Black-haired.

melanocyte /'mɛlənə(ʊ)sʌɪt, mɪ'lanə(ʊ)-/ *n.* L19. [f. MELANO- + -CYTE.] *Anat.* & *Zool.* A mature melanin-forming cell, esp. in the skin. Also, a melanophore.

Comb.: **melanocyte-stimulating hormone** a hormone that stimulates melanocytes or melanophores and causes darkening of the skin; abbrev. *MSH.*

melanoid /'mɛlənɔɪd/ *a.* M19. [f. MELANO- + -OID.] *Med.* Resembling melanin; resembling or of the nature of melanosis.

melanoma /mɛlə'nəʊmə/ *n.* Pl. **-mas, -mata** /-mətə/. M19. [f. MELANO- + -OMA.] *Med.* A melanotic growth; *esp.* a tumour which contains or produces melanin, a tumour of melanocytes, (in its malignant form associated with skin cancer). Also the condition of having a melanoma or melanomas.

melanophlogite /mɛlə'nɒflədʒʌɪt/ *n.* L19. [f. MELANO- + Gk *phlog-*, *phlox* flame (w. ref. to the mineral's turning black when heated) + -ITE[1].] *Min.* A form of silica containing organic impurities, occurring in minute cubes on sulphur and formerly thought to be a polymorph of quartz.

melanose /'mɛlənəʊs/ *n.* L19. [Fr. *mélanose* MELANOSIS.] A disease of grapes, citrus fruit, etc., caused by the fungus *Septoria ampelina*.

melanose /'mɛlənəʊs/ *a.* Now *rare.* E19. [f. as MELANIC + -OSE[1].] *Med.* = MELANIC 2a.

melanosis /mɛlə'nəʊsɪs/ *n.* Pl. **-noses** /-'nəʊsiːz/. E19. [mod.L, f. Gk *melan-*, *melas* black + -OSIS.] *Med.* 1 Abnormal or excessive development of melanin in the skin or other tissue; a discoloration due to this. E19. 2 = MELANOMA. M19.

melanotic /mɛlə'nɒtɪk/ *a.* E19. [f. prec. + -OTIC.] 1 *Med.* Characterized by or of the nature of melanosis. E19. 2 *Zool.* = MELANISTIC. L19.

melanous /'mɛlənəs/ *a.* M19. [f. Gk *melan-*, *melas* black + -OUS.] *Anthropol.* Having or designating dark or blackish hair and complexion.

melanterite /mɪ'lantərʌɪt/ *n.* M19. [f. Gk *melantēria* black metallic dye or ink, f. *melan-*, *melas* black: see -ITE[1].] *Min.* Ferrous sulphate heptahydrate occurring as a colourless or blue-green monoclinic mineral, freq. with marcasite; native copperas.

melanuria /mɛlə'njʊərɪə/ *n.* L19. [f. MELANO- + -URIA.] *Med.* The production of urine which contains dark pigments such as melanin, or which darkens on standing.

melanuric *a.* of, pertaining to, or characterized by melanuria; *melanuric fever*, blackwater fever: L19.

melaphyre /'mɛləfʌɪə/ *n.* Now *rare* or *obs.* M19. [Fr. *mélaphyre*, f. Gk *melas* black + PORPHYRY.] *Geol.* Any of various dark-coloured porphyritic (esp. basaltic) rocks.

melasma /mɪ'lazmə/ *n.* Pl. **-mata** /-mətə/. E19. [mod.L f. Gk ult. f. *melas* black.] *Med.* = CHLOASMA.

†melasses *n.* see MOLASSES.

melastoma /mɪ'lastəmə/ *n.* Pl. **-mae** /-miː/, **-mas**. M18. [mod.L (see below), f. Gk *melas* black + *stoma* mouth, because the fruit of some species blackens the mouth.] Any of various shrubs of the genus *Melastoma* (family Melastomataceae) of SE Asia, with white or purple flowers and sweet edible berries.

melatonin /mɛlə'təʊnɪn/ *n.* M20. [f. MELA(NO- + SERO)TONIN.] *Biochem.* An indole derivative formed in the pineal gland of various mammals (principally from serotonin), which inhibits melanin formation and is thought to be concerned with regulating the reproductive cycle.

Melba /'mɛlbə/ *n.* Also **m-**. E20. [Nellie *Melba* (f. as next) stage name of the Austral. operatic soprano Helen Mitchell (1861–1931).] 1 *peach Melba*, *pêche(s) Melba* /pɛʃ/, a confection of ice-cream and peaches flavoured with raspberry sauce. E20. 2 *Melba sauce*, a raspberry sauce for desserts. E20. 3 *Melba toast*, *toast Melba*, thinly-sliced bread toasted or baked to crispness. E20.

Melburnian /mɛl'bəːnɪən/ *n.* Also **-bournian**. M19. [f. (Latinized alt. of) *Melbourne* (see below) + -IAN.] A native or inhabitant of Melbourne, the capital city of Victoria, Australia.

melch *a.* var. of MELSH.

Melchite /'mɛlkʌɪt/ *n.* Also **Melkite**. E17. [eccl.L *Melchitae* (pl.) f. Byzantine Gk *Melkhitai* repr. Syriac *malkāyā* royalist (in agreement with the Byzantine Emperor: see below), f. *malkā* king: see -ITE[1].] *Eccl.* Orig., an Eastern Christian adhering to the Orthodox faith as defined by the councils of Ephesus (AD 431) and Chalcedon (AD 451) and as accepted by the Byzantine Emperor. Now, an Orthodox or Uniate Christian belonging to the patriarchates of Antioch, Jerusalem, or Alexandria.

meld /mɛld/ *v.*[1] & *n.*[1] L19. [G *melden* announce, declare (at cards).] *Cards.* A *v.t.* & *i.* Declare (a combination of cards) in pinochle, canasta, rummy, and other card-games. L19. B *n.* A combination of cards to be declared in pinochle, canasta, rummy, and other card-games. L19.

meld /mɛld/ *v.*[2] & *n.*[2] Orig. *US.* M20. [Perh. f. MELT *v.* + WELD *v.*] A *v.t.* & *i.* Merge, blend together. M20.

Time He has plans to meld his eleven departments into five. *National Geographic* Then cloud and grey sea melded and a steady rain slanted across . . the island.

B *n.* A thing formed by merging or blending. L20.

Black World A spectacular meld of rock music, drama, film, poetry and song.

melded /'mɛldɪd/ *a.* M20. [Blend of MELT *v.* and WELDED *a.*: cf. prec.] Formed from or using man-made fibres that have an outer sheath which has been melted to bind the fibres together into a fabric.

melder /'mɛldə/ *n. Sc.* LME. [ON *meldr* f. base of *mala* to grind.] 1 A quantity of meal ground at one time. LME. 2 An occasion of taking corn to be ground. *rare.* L18.

†mele *n.* var. of MEAL *n.*[2]

mêlée /'mɛleɪ/ *n.* Also **melée, melee**. M17. [Fr. f. OFr. *mellée* pa. ppl a. of *meller* var. of *mesler* MEDDLE *v.* Sense 2 prob. a different wd. Cf. MEDLEY, MELLAY.] 1 A battle at close quarters, a hand-to-hand fight; a confused struggle or skirmish, esp. involving many people; a crush, turmoil; a muddle. M17. 2 *collect.* Small diamonds less than about a carat in weight. E20.

melena *n.* var. of MELAENA.

melezitose /mɪ'lɛzɪtəʊz, -s/ *n.* Also **-liz-** /-'lɪz-/. M19. [f. Fr. *mélèze* larch, after *melitose*.] *Biochem.* A trisaccharide sugar, containing one fructose and two glucose units, originally isolated from the sap of larches.

Melian /'miːlɪən/ *n.* & *a.* M16. [f. Gk *Mēlos* Melos (see below) + -IAN.] A *n.* A native or inhabitant of Melos, the most south-easterly of the Cycladic islands in the Aegean Sea. M16. B *adj.* Of or pertaining to the island of Melos. M19.

melianthus /mɛlɪ'anθəs/ *n.* M18. [mod.L (see below), f. Gk *meli* honey + *anthos* flower.] A plant of the genus *Melianthus* (family Melianthaceae); now *spec.* = *honey-flower* (a) s.v. HONEY *n.*

melibiose /mɛlɪ'bʌɪəʊz, -s/ *n.* L19. [f. Gk *meli* honey + BI- + -OSE[2].] *Chem.* A disaccharide sugar, $C_{12}H_{22}O_{11}$, composed of a glucose and a galactose unit, obtainable by partial hydrolysis of raffinose.

melibiase *n.* an enzyme which hydrolyses melibiose L19.

Meliboean /mɛlɪ'biːən/ *a. rare* (Milton). M17. [f. L *Meliboeus* (designating a purple dye) + -AN.] Of or pertaining to Meliboea, an island forming part of ancient Syria, colonized from Thessaly, and famous for its purple dye.

melic *n.*[1] var. of MELICK.

melic /'mɛlɪk/ *a.* & *n.*[2] L17. [L *melicus* f. Gk *melikos*, f. *melos* song: see -IC.] A *adj.* (Of poetry) intended to be sung; of or pertaining to strophic Greek lyric verse. L17. B *n.* Melic poetry. L19.

meliceris /mɛlɪ'sɪərɪs/ *n.* Pl. **-cerides** /-'sɛrɪdiːz/. Now *rare* or *obs.* M16. [mod.L f. Gk *melikēris* some eruptive disease, f. *meli* honey + *kēros* wax.] *Med.* A cyst containing matter which resembles honey; such matter.

melick /'mɛlɪk/ *n.* Also **melic**. L18. [mod.L *melica* (see below), perh. f. It. *melica*, *meliga* sorghum.] Any of several grasses of the genus *Melica*; *esp.* either of two woodland grasses, *M. uniflora* and *M. nutans*, with racemes or panicles of plump purplish spikelets. Also *melick-grass*.

†melicrate *n.* M16–L18. [Late L *melicratum* f. Gk *melikraton*, f. *meli* honey + *karannunai*, *ker-* mix.] A drink made with honey and water.

melilite /'mɛlɪlʌɪt/ *n.* Also **mell-**. L18. [f. Gk *meli* honey + -LITE.] *Min.* 1 = MELLITE. Now *rare* or *obs.* L18. 2 A tetragonal calcium aluminosilicate, also containing magnesium, found in igneous and metamorphic rocks and in slags. E19.

melilot /'mɛlɪlɒt/ *n.* LME. [(O)Fr. *mélilot* f. L *melilotos* f. Gk *melilōtos*, f. *meli* honey + *lōtos* LOTUS.] Any of various leguminous plants of the genus *Melilotus*, which smell of newly mown hay when dry, and have trifoliate leaves and long racemes of small yellow or white flowers.

meline /'miːlʌɪn/ *a.* L19. [mod.L *Melinae* (see below), f. L *meles* marten, badger (in mod.L genus name of the Eurasian badger): see -INE[1].] *Zool.* Of, pertaining to, or designating the mustelid subfamily Melinae, which includes the badgers; resembling or characteristic of a badger.

melinite /'mɛlɪnʌɪt/ *n.* M19. [f. Gk *mēlinos* (of the colour) of quince, f. *mēlon* quince, apple: see -ITE[1]. In sense 2 f. Fr. *mélinite*.] 1 *Min.* A clay resembling yellow ochre. M19. 2 A high explosive based on picric acid; lyddite. L19.

melioidosis /ˌmɛlɪɔɪ'dəʊsɪs/ *n.* Pl. **-doses** /-'dəʊsiːz/. E20. [f. Gk *mēlis* a disease of asses (prob. glanders) + -OID + -OSIS.] *Med.* An infectious disease of (chiefly tropical) rodents, similar to glanders, caused by the bacterium *Pseudomonas pseudomallei* and occasionally transmitted to people (in whom it is often fatal) and animals.

meliorate /'miːlɪəreɪt/ *v.* M16. [Late L *meliorat-* pa. ppl stem of *meliorare* improve, f. L *melior* better: see -ATE[3].] 1 *v.t.* = AMELIORATE *v.* 1. Also, mitigate (suffering etc.). M16. 2 *v.i.* = AMELIORATE *v.* 2. M17. 3 *v.i. Sc. Law.* Make meliorations. M19.

meliorater *n.* (now *rare* or *obs.*) M19. **meliorator** *n.* (*rare*) L19.

melioration /ˌmiːlɪəˈreɪʃ(ə)n/ *n.* LME. [f. as prec.: see -ATION.] 1 Amelioration, improvement; *Ling.* development of a more favourable meaning or connotation (opp. *pejoration*). LME. 2 A change for the better; a thing or an action by which something is made better; an improvement. M17. b *Sc. Law* In *pl.* Improvements made on rented property, esp. by the tenant. Now *rare.* M18.

meliorative /ˈmiːlɪərətɪv/ *a.* & *n.* E19. [f. as prec.: see -ATIVE.] A *adj.* Ameliorating, improving; *Ling.* giving or acquiring a more favourable meaning or connotation (opp. *pejorative*). E19. B *n. Ling.* A meliorative word, affix, etc. M20.

meliorism /ˈmiːlɪərɪz(ə)m/ *n.* L19. [f. L *melior* better + -ISM.] The doctrine that the world may be made significantly better by rightly-directed human effort.

meliorist *n.* & *a.* (*a*) *n.* an adherent of meliorism; (*b*) *adj.* of or pertaining to meliorists or meliorism: M19.

meliority /miːlɪˈɒrɪti/ *n.* Now *rare.* L16. [OFr. *meliorité* or med.L *melioritas*, f. as prec.: see -ITY.] The quality or condition of being better; superiority.

meliphagine /mɛˈlɪfədʒʌɪn/ *a.* L19. [f. mod.L *Meliphaga* genus name, f. as next: see -INE[1].] *Ornith.* Of, pertaining to, or designating the family Meliphagidae or the subfamily Meliphaginae of honeyeaters.

meliphagous /mɛˈlɪfəgəs/ *a.* E19. [f. Gk *meli* honey + *phagos* eater + -OUS.] Mellivorous; *Ornith.* meliphagine.

melisma /mɪˈlɪzmə/ *n.* Pl. **-mata** /-mətə/, **-mas.** L19. [Gk, lit. 'song'.] *Mus.* Orig., a melodic tune, melodic music. Now, in singing, the prolongation of one syllable over a number of notes.

melismatic /-ˈmatɪk/ *a.* of, pertaining to, or characteristic of melisma; florid: E20.

melissa /mɪˈlɪsə/ *n.* LME. [Gk = bee.] Lemon balm, *Melissa officinalis*, esp. as a source of a volatile oil.

melissic /mɪˈlɪsɪk/ *a.* M19. [f. next + -IC.] Chem. *melissic acid*, a straight-chain fatty acid, $CH_3(CH_2)_{28}COOH$, found in various plant and animal waxes.

melissin /mɪˈlɪsɪn/ *n.* M19. [f. as MELISSA + -IN[1].] *Chem.* Melissyl alcohol.

melissyl /mɪˈlɪsʌɪl, -sɪl/ *n.* M19. [f. as prec. + -YL.] *Chem.* The straight-chain hydrocarbon radical $C_{30}H_{60}$', found in various compounds derived from waxes. Usu. in *comb.*

Comb.: **melissyl alcohol** a straight-chain alcohol, $CH_3(CH_2)_{28}CH_2OH$, obtained from beeswax and other waxes; also called *melissin.*

melitose /ˈmɛlɪtəʊz, -s/ *n.* Now *rare* or *obs.* M19. [f. Gk *melit-*, *meli* honey + -OSE[2].] *Chem.* = RAFFINOSE.

melittin /mɪˈlɪtɪn/ *n.* M20. [f. Gk *melitta* bee + -IN[1].] *Biochem.* & *Pharm.* A polypeptide present in bee venom and used against penicillin-resistant bacteria and in the treatment of rheumatism.

meliturla /mɛlɪˈtjʊərɪə/ *n.* Now *rare* or *obs.* M19. [f. Gk *melit-*, *meli* honey + -URIA.] *Med.* Glycosuria.

melizitose *n.* var. of MELEZITOSE.

melkbos /ˈmɛlkbɒs/ *n. S. Afr.* Also **-bosch** /-bɒʃ/. M19. [Afk. *melkbosch*, f. *melk* milk + *bosch* bush.] Any of several shrubs or small trees with milky latex; *esp.* (*a*) the Transvaal rubber tree, *Diplorhynchus condylocarpon* (family Apocynaceae); (*b*) any of various shrubby or tree-sized spurges, esp. *Euphorbia mauritanica.*

Melkite *n.* var. of MELCHITE.

melktert /ˈmɛlktɛːt/ *n. S. Afr.* M20. [Afk., f. *melk* milk + *tert* tart, pie.] A kind of open tart with a custard filling sprinkled with cinnamon.

mell /mɛl/ *n.*[1] Now only *Sc.* & *north.* ME. [Var. of MAUL *n.*] Orig., a mace, a club. Later, a heavy hammer or beetle (= MAUL *n.* 2), esp. as a token given to the loser of a competition; a gavel.

†**mell** *n.*[2] L16–M19. [L *mel*, *mell-* = Gk *meli*, *melit-*.] Honey.

mell /mɛl/ *v.* Now chiefly *arch.* & *dial.* ME. [OFr. *meller*: see MÊLÉE. Cf. MEDDLE.] 1 *v.t.* & †*i.* Mix, mingle, combine. Also foll. by *together*, *with.* ME. 2 *v.i.* Associate, have dealings *with.* ME. 3 *v.i.* Come together, mingle, in combat. ME. 4 *v.refl.* Concern or busy oneself. *arch.* ME. †5 *v.i.* Copulate. LME–M17. 6 *v.i.* Concern, busy, oneself; deal *with*, treat; interfere, meddle. LME.

mellaginous /mɛˈladʒɪnəs/ *a.* L17. [f. mod.L *mellagin-*, *mellago* a preparation resembling honey, f. *mell-*, *mel* honey: see -OUS.] Pertaining to or of the nature of honey.

mellah /ˈmɛlə/ *n.* L19. [Origin unkn.] A Jewish quarter in a Moroccan or Turkish city.

mellay /ˈmɛleɪ/ *n.* Now *rare.* LME. [OFr. *mellée*: see MÊLÉE, -Y[5]. Cf. MEDLEY.] 1 Orig., a battle, a quarrel. Later = MÊLÉE 1. LME. †2 A cloth of a mixture of colours or shades of colour; a mixed colour. LME–L16.

melleous /ˈmɛlɪəs/ *a.* M17. [f. L *melleus*, f. *mell-*, *mel* honey: see -EOUS.] Of the nature of or resembling honey; containing honey.

melliferous /mɛˈlɪf(ə)rəs/ *a.* M17. [f. L *mellifer*, f. *mell(i)-*, *mel* honey: see -FEROUS.] Yielding or producing honey.

†**mellification** *n.* M17–M18. [L *mellificatio(n-)*, f. *mellificat-* pa. ppl stem of *mellificare*, f. *mellificus*, f. *mell(i)-*, *mel* honey: see -FICATION.] The action or process of making honey.

mellifluence /mɛˈlɪflʊəns/ *n.* M17. [f. as next + -ENCE.] The state or quality of being mellifluent.

mellifluent /mɛˈlɪflʊənt/ *a.* E17. [Late L *mellifluent-*, f. L *mell(i)-*, *mel* honey + *fluent-*: see FLUENT.] = MELLIFLUOUS.

mellifluous /mɛˈlɪflʊəs/ *a.* LME. [f. OFr. *melliflue* or its source late L *mellifluus*, f. L *mell(i)-*, *mel* honey + *-fluus* flowing, f. *fluere* flow: see -OUS.] 1 Esp. of the voice, words, etc.: sweetly flowing, pleasing, musical. LME. 2 Flowing with honey, honey-dropping; sweetened (as) with honey. Now *rare.* L15.

1 C. P. SNOW He was, underneath his mellifluous and sensitive apologies, remarkably selfish. G. S. FRASER Sidney's lines move with a mellifluous sweetness. 2 THACKERAY No one lacked . . of raspberry open-tarts, nor of mellifluous bull's-eyes.

mellifluously *adv.* E19. **mellifluousness** *n.* E19.

mellilite *n.* var. of MELILITE.

mellisonant /mɛˈlɪsənənt/ *a. arch.* M17. [f. L *mell(i)-*, *mel* honey + *sonant-*, pres. ppl stem of *sonare* to sound: see -ANT[1].] Sweet-sounding.

mellite /ˈmɛlʌɪt/ *n.* E19. [mod.L *mellites*, f. L *mell-*, *mel* honey: see -ITE[1].] *Min.* Aluminium mellitate, a tetragonal mineral occurring naturally as honey-yellow crystals, esp. in lignite; honeystone.

mellitic /mɛˈlɪtɪk/ *a.* L18. [f. MELLITE + -IC.] Chem. *mellitic acid*, a soluble crystalline acid, $C_6(COOH)_6$, obtainable from mellite or by oxidizing carbon with nitric acid; benzenehexacarboxylic acid.

'**mellitate** *n.* a salt or ester of mellitic acid E19.

mellivorous /mɛˈlɪv(ə)rəs/ *a.* E19. [f. mod.L *mellivorus*, f. L *mell(i)-*, *mel* honey: see -VOROUS.] Of an animal: feeding naturally on honey.

mellophone /ˈmɛləfəʊn/ *n.* Chiefly *US.* E20. [f. MELLO(W *a.* + -PHONE.] A type of brass instrument similar to the orchestral horn; an alto or tenor horn.

¶Distinguished f. MÉLOPHONE.

mellotron /ˈmɛlətrɒn/ *n.* M20. [f. MELLO(W *a.* + ELEC)TRON(IC.] *Mus.* An electronic device simulating the sounds of orchestral instruments.

mellow /ˈmɛləʊ/ *a.* LME. [Perh. f. attrib. use of OE *melu* (*melw-*) MEAL *n.*[1]] 1 Of fruit: soft, sweet, and juicy with ripeness. Now chiefly *literary.* LME. b Rich, soft, and suggestive of ripeness; (of wine) well-matured, smooth; (of sound, colour, light, etc.) full and pure without harshness. M16. c Of soil: soft, rich, and loamy. M16. d Soft and smooth to the touch. L18. 2 *fig.* Mature, ripe in age; (esp. of a person's character) softened by age, experience, etc.; having the gentleness or dignity of maturity. L16. 3 Affected by liquor, esp. pleasantly; slightly drunk. E17. 4a Good-humoured, genial, jovial; relaxed, easy. E18. b Satisfying; attractive; skilful; pleasant. *US slang.* M20.

1 SHAKES. *Coriol.* As Hercules Did shake down mellow fruit. SIR W. SCOTT Mellow nuts have hardest rind. b KEATS Season of mists and mellow fruitfulness. T. JONES A mellow voice said 'Rhonda, this is Joel speaking'. *Annabel* A beautifully-polished, mellow wooden floor. R. P. JHABVALA In a mellow evening light, the scene was dignified. c DRYDEN Hoary Frosts . . will rot the Mellow Soil. 2 SMOLLETT In florid youth or mellow age. M. ARNOLD The mellow glory of the Attic stage. C. CONNOLLY A raw and intolerant nation eager to destroy the tolerant and mellow. 3 W. S. MAUGHAM Bartolomeo . . was, if not drunk, at least mellow. 4a ADDISON In all thy Humours, whether grave or mellow. R. SILVERBERG He was . . always wondrously relaxed: truly the mellow man.

mellowly *adv.* E19. **mellowness** *n.* M16. **mellowspeak** *n.* (*US slang*) [-SPEAK] bland or euphemistic language L20. **mellowy** *a.* (*arch. rare*) mellow LME.

mellow /ˈmɛləʊ/ *v.* L16. [f. the adj.] 1 *v.t.* Make mellow. L16. 2 *v.i.* Become mellow. L16. b Foll. by *out*: relax, become less intense. *N. Amer. colloq.* L20.

1 S. ROGERS Its colours mellow'd, not impair'd, by time. LYTTON The year . . had mellowed the fruits of the earth. TENNYSON There he mellow'd all his heart with ale. E. BOWEN Age may have mellowed him, for he . . made a benevolent grandfather. F. FORSYTH The sun was blistering, but mellowed by a light wind. C. THUBRON It was a brutal city, and its past did nothing to mellow it. 2 SHAKES. *Rich. III* So now prosperity begins to mellow And drop into the rotten mouth of death. EVELYN Those which attain not their full ripeness . . but must be laid up to mellow in the House. A. E. W. MASON The sunlight mellowed and reddened. *My Weekly* She has mellowed and finds being a good wife and mother . . important. P. D. JAMES High summer was browning and mellowing into autumn.

melo /ˈmɛləʊ/ *n. colloq.* Pl. **-os.** L19. [Abbrev.] = MELODRAMA.

melocactus /mɛlə(ʊ)ˈkaktəs/ *n.* Pl. **-ti** /-tʌɪ/, **-tuses.** M18. [mod.L (see below), f. late L *melo* MELON *n.*[1] + CACTUS.] *Bot.* Any of various cacti of the genus *Melocactus*, native to Central and S. America. Also called *melon-thistle.*

melocoton /ˈmɛlə(ʊ)kɒt(ə)n/ *n. obs.* exc. *Hist.* E17. [Sp. *melocotón* f. It. *melocotogno* quince f. med.L *melum cotoneum* (= late L *malum cotoneum*) f. Gk *mēlon kudōnion* lit. 'apple of Cydonia' (in ancient Crete).] A late-ripening, thickly downy variety of peach. Also *melocoton peach.*

melodeon /mɪˈləʊdɪən/ *n.* Also **-ion.** M19. [Alt. of MELODIUM; in sense 3 perh. f. MELODY after *accordion.*] 1 A wind instrument with a keyboard, the bellows being moved by means of pedals worked by the performer's feet (an earlier form of the American organ). M19. 2 (Also **M-.**) A music hall. *arch. US.* M19. 3 A kind of accordion. L19.

melodia /mɪˈləʊdɪə/ *n.* L19. [Late L: see MELODY.] A kind of organ-stop with a flutelike tone.

melodial /mɪˈləʊdɪəl/ *a.* E19. [f. MELODY + -AL[1].] Of or pertaining to melody.

melodially *adv.* E19.

melodic /mɪˈlɒdɪk/ *a.* E19. [Fr. *mélodique* f. late L *melodicus* f. Gk *melōidikos*, f. *melōidia* MELODY: see -IC.] Of or pertaining to melody; having or producing melody.

melodic minor *Mus.* a scale with a major sixth and seventh ascending and a minor sixth and seventh descending.

melodically *adv.* in a melodic manner, with regard to melody L19.

melodion *n.* var. of MELODEON.

melodious /mɪˈləʊdɪəs/ *a.* LME. [OFr. *melodieus* (mod. *mélodieux*) = med.L *melodiosus*, f. L *melodia* MELODY: see -IOUS.] 1 Characterized by melody; sweet-sounding, tuneful. LME. 2

Producing melody; singing sweetly. L16. †3 Susceptible to melody. L16–E17. 4 Having a melody; pertaining to or of the nature of melody. E18.

1 DRYDEN A music more melodious than the spheres. I. MCEWAN Her voice was melodious. 2 SHAKES. *Tit. A.* Where like a sweet melodious bird it sang.

melodiously *adv.* LME. **melodiousness** *n.* M16.

melodise *v.* var. of MELODIZE.

melodist /ˈmɛlədɪst/ *n.* L18. [f. MELODY + -IST.] 1 A singer. L18. 2 A composer of melodies; a person skilled in melody. E19.

melodium /mɪˈləʊdɪəm/ *n.* M19. [f. MELODY after *harmonium*.] = MELODEON 1.

melodize /ˈmɛlədʌɪz/ *v.* Also **-ise**. M17. [f. MELODY + -IZE.] 1 *v.i.* Make melody, produce sweet music; *poet.* blend melodiously *with*. M17. 2 *v.t.* Make melodious. M18. 3 *v.t.* Compose a melody for (a song). L19.

melodrama /ˈmɛlə(ʊ)drɑːmə/ *n.* E19. [Alt. of MELODRAME after *drama*.] 1 Orig. (now *Hist.*), a (usu. romantic and sensational) play with songs interspersed and orchestral music accompanying the action. Now, a sensational dramatic piece with crude appeals to the emotions and usu. a happy ending. E19. 2 The genre of drama of this type; the mode of dramatic treatment characteristic of a melodrama. E19. 3 A series of incidents, a story, etc., resembling the plot of a melodrama; an occurrence suggestive of a melodrama; melodramatic language or behaviour. E19.

melodramatic /mɛlə(ʊ)drəˈmatɪk/ *a.* E19. [f. MELODRAMA after *dramatic*.] Of or pertaining to melodrama; having the characteristics of melodrama; characterized by sensationalism and spurious pathos.

B. GELDOF A big campaign to raise money for rather melodramatic 'mercy flights' to Ethiopia.

melodramatically *adv.* M19.

melodramatics /mɛlə(ʊ)drəˈmatɪks/ *n.pl.* E20. [f. prec.: see -ICS.] Melodramatic behaviour, action, or writing.

melodramatise *v.* var. of MELODRAMATIZE.

melodramatist /mɛlə(ʊ)ˈdramətɪst/ *n.* E19. [f. MELODRAMA after *dramatist*.] A writer of melodramas.

melodramatize /mɛlə(ʊ)ˈdramətʌɪz/ *v.t.* Also **-ise**. E19. [f. as prec., after *dramatize*.] Make melodramatic; adapt (a novel etc.) into a melodrama.

melodrame /ˈmɛlə(ʊ)dram/ *n.* Now *rare* or *obs.* E19. [Fr. *mélodrame*, f. Gk *melos* song, music + Fr. *drame* DRAMA.] A melodrama.

melody /ˈmɛlədi/ *n.* & *v.* ME. [(O)Fr. *mélodie* f. late L *melodia* f. Gk *melōidia* singing, choral song, f. *melōidos* musical, f. *melos* song, music + *ōidē* ODE: see -Y[3].] A *n.* 1 Sweet music, either vocal or instrumental; beautiful arrangement of musical sounds; tunefulness. ME. †2 A song or other musical performance. ME–M16. 3a A series of single notes arranged in musically expressive succession; an air. E17. b A poem, song, etc., written to be sung to a particular arrangement of single notes in expressive succession. E19. c The principal part in a harmonized piece of music. L19. 4 *Mus.* (The branch of music that deals with) the arrangement of single notes in expressive succession. Cf. HARMONY 3. E18.

1 SHAKES. *Mids. N. D.* Philomel with melody, Sing in our sweet lullaby. SHELLEY Whilst all the winds with melody are ringing. 3a DAY LEWIS From childhood I could pick up a melody by ear. S. RUSHDIE A glade filled with the gentle melodies of song-birds. b W. CARLETON The touching and inimitable Melodies of my countryman Thomas Moore. c W. S. ROCKSTRO Arrangements with the melody, as usual, in the Tenor. 4 F. BURNEY Melody and Harmony . . had been cultivated for the use of the church.

B *v.i.* Make melody; sing. *rare*. L16.

meloe /ˈmɛləʊiː/ *n.* M17. [mod.L *Meloe*, *Meloë*, perh. conn. w. L *mel* honey.] *Entomol.* Any of various oil-beetles mainly of the genus *Meloe*, several of which spend the larval stage within the brood cells of wild bees. Now chiefly as mod.L genus name.

meloid /ˈmɛlɔɪd, -əʊɪd/ *n.* & *a.* L19. [mod.L *Meloidae* (see below), f. as prec.: see -ID[3].] *Entomol.* A *n.* A beetle of the family Meloidae, which includes oil-beetles and blister-beetles. L19. B *adj.* Of, pertaining to, or designating this family. L19.

melologue /ˈmɛlə(ʊ)lɒg/ *n.* E19. [f. Gk *melos* song, music + -LOGUE.] A musical composition of verses in which some are sung and others recited.

melomane /ˈmɛlə(ʊ)meɪn/ *n.* L19. [Fr. *mélomane*, f. Gk *melos* song, music: see -MANE.] An enthusiast for music, a melomaniac.

melomania /mɛlə(ʊ)ˈmeɪnɪə/ *n.* L19. [Fr. *mélomanie*, f. Gk *melos* song, music: see -MANIA.] An enthusiasm, passion, or craze for music.

melomaniac *n.* a passionate or obsessive enthusiast for music L19. **melomanic** /-ˈmanɪk/ *a.* (now *rare* or *obs.*) characterized by melomania E19.

melon /ˈmɛlən/ *n.*[1] & *a.* LME. [(O)Fr. f. late L *melon-*, *melo* contr. of L *melopepo* MELOPEPON.] A *n.* 1 The fruit of a gourd, *Cucumis melo*, with sweet green, yellowish-pink, etc., flesh; the plant bearing this. Also, a watermelon. LME. b *fig.* A large profit to be divided among a number of people. *slang*. E20. c = *melon pink* below. M20. 2 *Zool.* In many toothed whales, a mass of waxy material in the head, thought to focus acoustic signals; the dome this forms on the forehead. L19.

1 *cantaloup melon*, *honeydew melon*, *musk melon*, etc. **cut the melon** *slang* (*a*) decide a question; (*b*) divide a large profit among a number of people.

B *adj.* Of a melon pink colour. L20.

Comb.: **melon-caterpillar** = *melonworm* below; **melon-oil** oil from the melon of a cetacean; **melon pink** (of) a yellowish-pink colour; **melon-seed** a seed from a melon; *melon-seed body* (Med.), a small loose rounded mass found in the cavities of inflamed joints and in certain types of cyst (usu. in *pl.*); **melon-shell** (the shell of) any of various very large smooth-shelled volutes of the tropical Indo-Pacific, *esp.* one of the genus *Melo*; **melon-thistle** = MELOCACTUS; **melon-wood** a yellow Mexican wood resembling sandalwood, used for furniture; **melonworm** the greenish caterpillar of an American pyralid moth, *Diaphania hyalinata*, which is a pest of pumpkins, melons, and other cucurbits.

†**meloniere** *n.* [Fr. *melonnière*] a melonry M17–E18. **melonist** *n.* (long *rare*) a person who cultivates melons M17. **melonry** *n.* a place for the cultivation of melons E18.

melon /ˈmɛlən/ *n.*[2] *Austral.* M19. [Abbrev.] = PADDYMELON.

Comb.: **melon-hole** = GILGAI.

melongena /mɛlənˈdʒiːnə/ *n.* L18. [mod.L f. as next.] (The fruit of) the aubergine, *Solanum melongena*.

melongene /ˈmɛləndʒiːn/ *n.* *W. Indies.* M20. [Fr. *mélongène*, ult. f. as AUBERGINE.] = prec.

†**melopepon** *n.* M16–E18. [L *melopepon-*, *melopepo* f. Gk *mēlopepōn*, f. *mēlon* apple + *pepōn* a kind of gourd.] A kind of pumpkin.

mélophone /ˈmɛlə(ʊ)fəʊn; *foreign* melɔfɔn (*pl. same*)/ *n.* Also **mel-** /ˈmɛl-/. M19. [Fr. f. Gk *melos* song, music: see -PHONE.] A kind of portable reed-organ with a hand bellows and keys, shaped like a guitar or a hurdy-gurdy.

¶Distinguished f. MELLOPHONE.

meloplasty /ˈmɛlə(ʊ)plasti/ *n.* *rare*. L19. [f. Gk *mēlon* apple, (poet.) cheek + -PLASTY.] Surgical repair of a cheek by grafting and plastic surgery; an instance of this.

melo'plastic *a.* M19.

melopoeia /mɛlə(ʊ)ˈpiːə/ *n.* M18. [Gk *melopoiia*, f. *melopoios* maker of songs, f. *melos* song, music + *poiein* make.] Chiefly *Class. Hist.* The art of composing melodies; the branch of dramatic art that deals with music.

melopoeic *a.* of, pertaining to, or characterized by melopoeia E20.

melos /ˈmɛlɒs, ˈmiːlɒs/ *n.* M18. [Gk = song, music.] *Mus.* Song, melody; *spec.* the succession of tones considered apart from rhythm; an uninterrupted flow of melody.

melo-tragedy /mɛlə(ʊ)ˈtradʒədi/ *n.* *rare*. E19. [f. Gk *melos* song, music + -O- + TRAGEDY.] A tragic play in which songs occur; an operatic tragedy.

melphalan /ˈmɛlfəlan/ *n.* M20. [Arbitrary formation, partly f. L-*ph*enyl*alan*ine.] *Pharm.* A nitrogen mustard used intravenously to treat cancers, esp. myelomatosis; 4-bis(2-chloroethyl)-amino-L-phenylalanine, $C_{13}H_{18}N_2O_2Cl_2$.

melpomenish /mɛlˈpɒmɪnɪʃ/ *a.* *literary. rare.* E19. [f. Gk *Melpomenē* (lit. 'singer') the Muse of tragedy + -ISH[1].] Tragic.

melsh /mɛlʃ/ *a.* Long *dial.* Also **melch** /mɛltʃ/. [OE *mel(i)sć*, *mylsć*, f. base also of MHG *molwic*, G *mollig*, *mollecht*, *molsch*, *mulsch* soft, OHG *molawēn* be soft, cogn. w. L *mollis* tender: see -ISH[1]. Cf. MULSH.] Mellow, soft, tender; (of weather) mild.

melt /mɛlt/ *n.*[1] M19. [f. MELT *v.*] 1 Metal etc. in a melted condition. M19. 2 A quantity of metal etc. melted at one operation. L19. 3 The process of melting. Freq. in *on the melt*. L19.

Comb.: **melt-spin** *v.t.* prepare by melt-spinning (freq. as *melt-spun* ppl a.); **melt spinning** the extrusion of a heat-softened substance (esp. a polymer) through a spinneret to form a fibre; **melt water** water resulting from the melting of ice or snow, esp. that of a glacier.

melt *n.*[2] var. of MILT *n.*

melt /mɛlt/ *v.* Pa. t. **melted**; pa. pple **melted**, **molten** /ˈməʊlt(ə)n/. [OE (i) str. vb *meltan*, (ii) (Anglian) wk vb *meltan*, (WS) *mieltan* = ON *melta*, f. base also of MALT *n.*, repr. IE base also of Gk *meldein* melt, L *mollis*, Skt *mṛdu* soft. Cf. MILD, SMELT *v.*[1]] I *v.i.* 1 Become liquefied by heat; (foll. by *away*) be destroyed by liquefaction; (foll. by *down*) become liquid and lose structure. OE. b Of a person: perspire excessively, suffer extreme heat. *colloq.* L18. 2a Orig., (of food) be digested. Later, become disintegrated, liquefied, or softened, esp. by the agency of moisture; dissolve. OE. b Of clouds etc.: be dispersed; break *into* rain. LME. c Vanish, disappear; (foll. by *away*) depart unobtrusively. E17. 3†a Be overwhelmed with dismay or grief. OE–E17. b Become softened by pity, love, etc.; yield to entreaty; dissolve *into* tears or laughter. ME. c Foll. by *away*: become ecstatic. *rare*. E18. 4 Waste *away*, become gradually smaller; dwindle *down to* a particular point or condition. ME. 5 Filter in, become absorbed *into*. LME. 6 Of sound: be soft and liquid. E17. 7 Pass by imperceptible degrees *into* another form. L18.

1 E. WAUGH The frost broke; the snow melted away. I. MCEWAN He stared ahead at the large flakes melting on contact with the windscreen. *Scientific American* There would be no possibility that the fuel core would melt down. 2b W. BLACK The clouds had melted into a small and chilling rain. c A. THIRKELL David . . melted from the room. E. WAUGH Popotakis's old clients melted away to other . . resorts. M. UNDERWOOD He didn't hang around afterwards . . he melted away. 3a AV *Josh.* 2:11 Our hearts did melt, neither did there remaine any more courage in any man. b STEELE She melted into a Flood of Tears. J. W. BURGON At sight of the dusty . . urchins, his heart evidently melted. c WILLIAM COLLINS There let me oft, retir'd by day In dreams of passion melt away. 4 SHAKES. *Ant. & Cl.* Authority melts from me. LD MACAULAY The host which had been the terror of Scotland melted away. M. TWAIN When one . . sees his resources melt down to a two-months' supply. 5 SHELLEY Like fiery dews that melt Into the bosom of a frozen bud. 6 S. ROGERS The enchanting serenade . . melts along the moonlight-glade. 7 W. COWPER Downs . . That melt and fade into the distant sky. HUGH WALPOLE Cool brown colours melting into the blue or grey of the sky.

II *v.t.* 8a Liquefy by heat; (foll. by *away*) cause to disappear by liquefaction; (foll. by *down*) change (coin, plate, etc.) by heat into liquid metal for use as raw material; (foll. by *up*) fashion (an object) from molten metal. OE. †b Liquefy by heat and refashion (an object) *into* another shape; form (an image etc.) out of molten material. LME–E17. c Cause (a person) to perspire excessively, subject to extreme heat. *colloq.* L17. 9a Orig., digest. Later, dissolve, make a solution of. OE. †b Disintegrate, loosen (soil). E17–E18. 10 Disperse, cause to disappear. Also foll. by *away*. ME. 11a Foll. by *away*: cause to become ecstatic. *rare*. ME. b Soften (a person, the feelings, etc.) by appealing to pity, love, etc.; touch. Freq. as *melted* ppl a. LME. †12 Weaken, enervate. Also, foll. by *down*. L16–E18. 13 Spend, squander (money). Also, cash (a cheque etc.). Chiefly *arch. slang*. E17. 14 Blend (individual components) *into* one mass of colour, sound, etc. L18.

8a J. TYNDALL A sun or planet once molten, would continue for ever molten. G. GREENE I am melting down some old family silver. F. HOYLE If all that ice were melted, the resulting water would raise sea level by perhaps 80 metres. *Holiday Which?* Workshops contain furnaces for melting the blister steel. *melted butter*: see BUTTER *n.*[1] 1. b AV *Isa.* 40:19 The workeman melteth a grauen image, and the goldsmith spreadeth it ouer with golde. 9a P. BARROUGH A Syrupe is of medicines a juyce with Sugar or Hony molten therin. 10 F. PARKMAN Cold, disease, famine, thirst, and the fury of the waves melted them away. 11a ADDISON Alas, thy Story melts away my Soul. b R. K. NARAYAN The thought of her melted him. M. FITZHERBERT His heart was melted. 12 SHAKES. *Much Ado* Manhood is melted into curtsies, valour into compliment. 14 W. BLACK Mist . . melted whole mountains into a soft dull grey.

melta'bility *n.* (*rare*) ability to be melted M19. **meltable** *a.* able to be melted E17. **melty** *a.* melting E20.

meltdown /ˈmɛltdaʊn/ *n.* M20. [f. MELT *v.* + DOWN *adv.*] 1 The action or process of melting; *spec.* the melting of part of a nuclear reactor, esp. the core or its metal shielding. M20. b An uncontrolled and usu. disastrous incident with far-reaching repercussions; *Comm.* a sudden rapid drop in the value of a currency, shares, etc., a crash. L20. 2 A mass of melted-down material. L20.

meltemi /mɛlˈtɛmi/ *n.* E20. [mod.Gk *meltémi*, Turk. *meltem*.] = ETESIAN *n.*

melter /ˈmɛltə/ *n.* E16. [f. MELT *v.* + -ER[1].] 1 A person or thing which melts something; *spec.* a person whose employment involves the melting of metals, esp. in a factory, a mint, etc. E16. 2 = FREESTONE 2. M18.

melting /ˈmɛltɪŋ/ *n.* ME. [f. MELT *v.* + -ING[1].] 1 The action of MELT *v.*; an instance of this. ME. 2 In *pl.* Melted material; a substance produced by melting. Now *rare* or *obs.* M16.

Comb.: **melting-house** a building for the process of melting, esp. at a mint; **melting point** the temperature at which a solid melts; **melting-pot** a vessel for melting metals etc.; *fig.* a place of reconstruction or vigorous mixing (freq. in *in the melting-pot*).

melting /ˈmɛltɪŋ/ *a.* LME. [f. MELT *v.* + -ING[2].] That melts or is in the process of melting (*lit.* & *fig.*); *esp.* (of a person, a mood, etc.) feeling or showing pity, love, etc., yielding to emotion; (of food) that dissolves easily in the mouth; (of fruit) sweet and tender.

SHAKES. *Oth.* Albeit unused to the melting mood. MILTON The melting voice through mazes running. R. DAHL The heavy rich smell of melting chocolate!

meltingly *adv.* L16. **meltingness** *n.* E17.

melton /ˈmɛlt(ə)n/ *n.* Also **M-**. E19. [*Melton* Mowbray, a town in central England.] 1 In full *Melton jacket, coat*, etc. A jacket, coat, etc., made of Melton cloth. E19. 2 More fully *Melton cloth*. A kind of cloth with a close-cut nap used esp. for jackets, coats, etc. M19. 3 *Melton* (*Mowbray*) *pie*, a kind of raised meat pie. L19.

melty /ˈmɛlti/ *a.* E20. [f. MELT *v.* + -Y[1].] Apt to melt.

Melungeon /mɪˈlʌndʒ(ə)n/ *n. US.* L20. [Perh. f. alt. of MÉLANGE.] A member of a people of mixed Black, White, and Amerindian descent inhabiting the southern Appalachian mountains in the eastern US.

melusine /mɛl(j)ʊˈsiːn/ *n.* & *a.* Also **M-**. E20. [Fr. *mélusine*, perh. conn. w. *Mélusine*, a fairy in Fr. folklore.] A *n.* A silky long-haired felt, used for making hats. E20. B *attrib.* or as *adj.* Made of this material. M20.

melvie /ˈmɛlvi/ *v.t. Sc.* Long *rare* or *obs.* L18. [Prob. ult. f. MEAL *n.*[1]] Cover with meal.

Melvillian /mɛlˈvɪlj(ə)n/ *a.* M20. [f. *Melville* (see below) + -IAN.] Of, pertaining to, or characteristic of the US novelist and poet Herman Melville (1819–91), or his work.

Also **Melvillean** *a.* M20.

mem /mɛm/ *n.*[1] E18. [Repr. a pronunc. of MA'AM *n.* In sense 2 abbrev.] 1 = MA'AM *n.* 1. E18. 2 = MEMSAHIB. E20.

mem /mɛm/ *a.* & *n.*[2] Also **mem.** (point). M18. [Abbrev.: cf. MEMO.] A *adj.* = MEMORANDUM *a.* M18. B *n.* = MEMORANDUM *n.* 1. E19.

¶Now less usual than MEMO.

member /ˈmɛmbə/ *n.* ME. [(O)Fr. *membre* f. L *membrum* limb.] 1 A part or organ of the body; *esp.* a limb or other separable portion. ME. b *spec.* In *pl.*, the genitals; *sing.* the penis. ME. c *Biol.* Any part of a plant or animal viewed with regard to its form and position. L19. 2 Each of the individuals, countries, etc., belonging to or forming a society or assembly; *spec.* (*a*) (usu. **M-**, more fully *Member of Parliament*, *Member of Congress*, etc.) a person who has been formally elected to take part in the proceedings of a parliament; (*b*) a person admitted to the lowest grade of an order, as the 5th class of the Order of the British Empire. Formerly also, a native or inhabitant (of a country or city). ME. b *ellipt.* A member of the community, a person. Now *slang* & *dial.* E16. †c A participant. M16–E17. d A Black. *US slang.* M20. 3 Each of the constituent portions of a complex structure. LME. b *Archit.* Each of the parts of a building, each of the mouldings in a collection of mouldings, as in a cornice, capital, base, etc. L17. 4 A component part or branch of a political body or, formerly, of a trade, art, profession, etc. LME. 5 A section or district, esp. an outlying part, of an estate, manor, parish, port, etc. LME. 6 A division or clause of a sentence; a branch of a disjunctive proposition. M16. 7 *Math.* A group of figures or symbols forming part of a numerical expression or formula; either of the sides of an equation. E17. 8 Each of the items forming a series. E18.

1 D. MORRIS Vultures, who plunge their heads and necks into gory carcasses, have lost their feathers from these members. S. BELLOW Leprosy—you lose a toe now and then; none of the main members have to be affected. *fig.*: ADDISON The Body of the Law is no less encumbered with superfluous Members. b J. HELLER The first time I laid eyes on Abigail . . my member grew hard as hickory. 2 THACKERAY Captain Raff, the honourable member for Epsom. W. S. CHURCHILL Austria was still a member of the German Confederation. C. IVES The action of a mob does not necessarily mean that a majority of its members are stupid. *Daily Mirror* Members of our swimming club were involved in rescuing three people. R. GUY All the members of the Maldoon family were assembled.

Phrases: **carnal member** *arch.* = sense 1b above. *private member*: see PRIVATE *a.* **privy member**(**s**) *arch.* = sense 1b above. *secret members*: see SECRET *a.* & *n.* *sitting member*: see SITTING *ppl a.* 4. *unofficial member*: see UNOFFICIAL *a.* 2. **unruly member** [after *James* 3:5–8] the tongue. **virile member** *arch.* the penis.

Comb.: Esp. in the sense 'that is a member of a society, assembly, (esp.) international organization, etc.', as *member country, society, State*, etc. **member bank** *US* a bank which holds shares in, and has representation on the board of directors of, a Federal Reserve Bank.

memberess *n.* (*rare*) a female member, *spec.* a female Member of Parliament M19. **memberless** *a.* having no member or members E17.

member /ˈmɛmbə/ *v.t. colloq.* Also **'member**. L19. [Aphet.] Remember.

membered /ˈmɛmbəd/ *a.* ME. [f. MEMBER *n.* + -ED[2].] 1 Having members, esp. a specified kind or number; divided into members. ME. 2 *Her.* Of a bird: having legs of a different tincture from the body. L16.

membership /ˈmɛmbəʃɪp/ *n.* M17. [f. MEMBER *n.* + -SHIP.] 1 The condition or status of a member of a society, assembly, or other (organized) body. (Foll. by *of*, (now esp. US) *in*.) M17. 2 The number of members in a particular body; the body of members. M19.

1 P. GROSSKURTH Klein was elected to full membership in the Berlin Society. *church-membership* etc. 2 *Brownie* Our Pack has a membership of 20 keen Brownies. *Times Educ. Suppl.* Teachers' leaders, who . . were out of touch with their membership.

membra disjecta /mɛmbrə dɪsˈjɛktə/ *n. phr. pl.* M20. [Alternative wd order.] = DISJECTA MEMBRA.

membral /ˈmɛmbr(ə)l/ *a.* E17. [f. MEMBER *n.* + -AL[1].] Pertaining to or characteristic of a member or members. Now chiefly *Anat.* & *Zool.*, appendicular.

membranaceous /mɛmbrəˈneɪʃəs/ *a.* L17. [f. late L *membranaceus*, f. *membrana* MEMBRANE: see -ACEOUS.] *Biol.* Resembling or of the nature of a membrane; membranous.

membranate /ˈmɛmbrənət/ *a. rare.* L18. [f. next + -ATE[2].] Having a membrane or membranes; of the nature of a membrane.

membrane /ˈmɛmbreɪn/ *n.* LME. [(Fr. *membrane* f.) L *membrana* skin covering part of the body, use as n. of fem. adj. (sc. *cutis* skin) f. *membrum* limb, MEMBER *n.*] 1a *Anat.* & *Biol.* Any thin, pliable, usu. fibrous sheet or layer of tissue, freq. serving to separate other structures or to line a part or organ; the tissue of which this is formed. LME. b *Med.* A thin sheetlike structure formed as a result of disease. M18. c *Cytol.* Any of various thin, fluid, semipermeable lipid bilayers with included proteins which form structures within living cells, *esp.* more fully (*cell membrane*) that which bounds the cell. L19. 2 Orig., parchment. Now, each of the parts of a parchment roll. LME. 3 Any thin extended sheetlike barrier of material. L19.

1a *basement membrane, mucous membrane, pit membrane*, etc. c PLASMA *membrane*. 3 P. DAVIES The surface of a balloon . . is a membrane of rubber.

Comb.: **membrane-bone** a bone which develops from membranous connective tissue, not cartilage; **membrane filter**: made of cellulosic material and capable of retaining objects as small as bacteria, used in microbiology and water purification; **membrane filtration**: by means of a membrane filter.

membraneless *a.* L19. **membranoid** *a.* resembling or consisting of membrane M19.

membranella /mɛmbrəˈnɛlə/ *n.* Pl. **-llae** /-liː/. Also Anglicized as **-nelle** /-ˈnɛl/. L19. [mod.L, dim. of L *membrana* MEMBRANE.] *Zool.* In some ciliates, a long flattened locomotory organ formed from fused cilia.

membraneous /mɛmˈbreɪnɪəs/ *a.* M17. [f. late L *membraneus*, f. L *membrana* MEMBRANE: see -OUS.] = MEMBRANOUS.

membraniform /mɛmˈbreɪnɪfɔːm/ *a.* E19. [f. MEMBRANE + -I- + -FORM.] Having the character or structure of a membrane.

membrano- /ˈmɛmbrənəʊ/ *comb. form* of MEMBRANE: see -O-.

membrano'genic *a.* producing (a) membrane L19. **membra'nology** *n.* the branch of science that deals with membranes (now esp. cell membranes) L18. **membranophone** *n.* a musical instrument which employs a stretched membrane to produce the sound M20.

membranous /ˈmɛmbrənəs/ *a.* L16. [Fr. *membraneux*, f. as MEMBRANE: see -OUS.] 1 Consisting of, resembling, or of the nature of (a) membrane; membranaceous; *esp.* in *Bot.*, thin and more or less translucent. L16. 2 *Med.* Of a disease: involving the formation or expulsion of (a) membrane. L19.

1 **membranous labyrinth** the soft structures of the inner ear, including the cochlea, utricle, saccule, and semicircular canals.

membranula /mɛmˈbreɪnjʊlə/ *n.* Pl. **-lae** /-liː/, **-las**. Also Anglicized as **-ule** /-juːl/. E19. [L, dim. of *membrana* MEMBRANE: see -ULE.] *Biol.* Any of various small membranes or membranous structures; *spec.* in *Entomol.*, a small opaque region at the base of the forewing in some dragonflies.

membrification /ˌmɛmbrɪfɪˈkeɪʃ(ə)n/ *n. rare.* L17. [f. L *membrum* MEMBER *n.*: see -FICATION.] Formation of members or limbs.

membrillo /mɛmˈbriʎo, mɛmˈbriːljəʊ/ *n.* E20. [Sp. = quince.] A Spanish preserve of quinces.

membrum virile /mɛmbrəm vɪˈrʌɪli, vɪˈriːli/ *n. phr. arch.* or *euphem.* M19. [L = male member.] The penis.

meme /miːm/ *n.* L20. [f. Gk *mimēma* that which is imitated, after GENE.] *Biol.* An element of a culture or system of behaviour that may be considered to be passed from one individual to another by non-genetic means, esp. imitation.

memento /mɪˈmɛntəʊ/ *n.* Pl. **-o(e)s.** LME. [f. L, imper. of *meminisse* remember, ult. redupl. of base of MIND *n.*[1]] 1 *Chr. Ch.* Either of the two prayers (beginning with *Memento*) in the canon of the Mass, in which the living and the dead are respectively commemorated; the commemoration of the living or the dead in these prayers. LME. 2 A reminder, warning, or hint as to future conduct or events. Now *esp.* an object serving as such a reminder or warning. L16. 3 A reminder of a past event or condition, of an absent person, or something that once existed. Now *esp.* an object kept as a memorial of some person or event, a souvenir. M18.

Phrases: ***memento mori*** /ˈmɔːrʌɪ, ˈmɔːri/ [L = remember that you have to die] a warning or reminder of death, *esp.* a skull or other symbolical object. ***memento vivere*** /ˈviːvəri/ [L = remember that you have to live, after *memento mori*] a reminder of life; a reminder of the pleasure of living.

Memnonian /mɛmˈnəʊnɪən/ *a. literary.* E17. [f. L *Memnonius* (f. Gk *Memnoneios*, f. *Memnōn* Memnon) + -AN.] Of or pertaining to Memnon, a mythical demigod said to have erected the citadel or palace at the ancient city of Susa in SW Iran (also thought to be represented by a statue at Thebes in Egypt believed to give out a musical sound when touched by the dawn); Persian, Iranian.

memo /ˈmɛməʊ/ *a., n.,* & *v.* E18. [Abbrev. Cf. MEM *a.* & *n.*[2]] A *adj.* = MEMORANDUM *a.* E18.

B *n.* Pl. **-os.** = MEMORANDUM *n.* 1, esp. 1e. E18.

M. BRADBURY Can I draw the chair's attention to the departmental memo, circulated this very morning. S. QUINN The Department of State issued a memo in response to Horney's renewed application for a passport.

C *v.t.* Send a memo to. M20.

memoir /ˈmɛmwɑː, -wɔː/ *n.* M16. [Fr. *mémoire* (masc.) specific use of fem. n. = MEMORY.] 1 A note, a memorandum, a record, now *spec.* an official one. M16. 2 *sing.* & in *pl.* A record of events or history from personal knowledge or from special sources of information; an autobiographical or (occas.) biographical record. M17. 3 An essay or dissertation on a learned subject specially studied by the writer. In *pl.* also, (the record of) the proceedings or transactions of a learned society. L17.

2 J. FOWLES Gosse was.. immortalized half a century later in his son Edmund's famous and exquisite memoir. E. PAWEL His memoirs, though.. based on notes made at the time, were never submitted for publication.

memoirist *n.* a writer of memoirs or of a memoir M18.

memomotion /ˈmɛməʊməʊʃ(ə)n/ *n.* M20. [Alt. of MICROMOTION, perh. after L *memor* mindful & related wds.] Movement of the body recorded by time-lapse photography for purposes of work study. Usu. *attrib.*

memorabilia /mɛm(ə)rəˈbɪlɪə/ *n.pl.* L18. [L, neut. pl. of *memorabilis*: see next, -IA[2].] 1 Memorable or noteworthy things. L18. 2 Souvenirs. L19.

memorable /ˈmɛm(ə)rəb(ə)l/ *a.* & *n.* LME. [Fr. *mémorable* or L *memorabilis*, f. *memorare*: see MEMORANDUM, -ABLE.] A *adj.* Worthy of remembrance or note, worth remembering, not to be forgotten; able to be remembered, easy to remember. LME.

J. RUSKIN The easily memorable root 'dab', short for dabble. R. SCRUTON Our century is memorable for nothing so much as its violence. E. FEINSTEIN Was there anything special about you? I don't remember a single memorable thing.

B *n.* In *pl.* = MEMORABILIA 1. Now *rare.* E17.

memoraˈbility *n.* M17. **memorableness** *n.* E18. **memorably** *adv.* in a memorable manner; so as to be remembered: M18.

†memorand *a.* & *n.* ME. [L *memorandus*: see MEMORANDUM.] A *adj.* Serving as a memorial. Only in ME. B *n.* 1 A memorial. Only in ME. 2 = MEMORANDUM *n.* L17–E18.

memorandum /mɛməˈrandəm/ *a., n.,* & *v.* LME. [L, neut. sing. of *memorandus* gerundive of *memorare* bring to mind, f. *memor* mindful. Cf. MEM *a.* & *n.*[2], MEMO.] A *adj.* To be remembered: placed at the beginning of a note of something to be remembered or a record (for future reference) of something done. Now only *Law.* LME.

B *n.* Pl. **-da** /-də/, **-dums.** 1 a A note to help the memory, a record of events or of observations on a particular subject, esp. for future consideration or use. L15. b *Law.* A writing or document summarizing or embodying the terms of a transaction, contract, agreement, establishment of a company etc. In *Marine Insurance*, a clause in a policy enumerating the articles in respect of which underwriters have no liability. L16. c A record of a money transaction. E17. d An informal diplomatic message, esp. summarizing the state of a question or justifying a decision. M17. e An informal written communication of a kind conventionally not requiring a signature, as within a business or organization, usu. written on paper headed 'Memorandum'. L19. †2 An injunction to remember something. L16–M17. 3 A reminder; a memento, a souvenir. *obs.* exc. *Sc. dial.* L16.

1b *memorandum of* ASSOCIATION.

C *v.t.* Make a memorandum of. L18.

memorate /ˈmɛməreɪt/ *v.t.* Long *rare.* E17. [L *memorat-* pa. ppl stem of *memorare*: see MEMORANDUM, -ATE[3].] Bring to mind; mention; remember.

memorative /ˈmɛm(ə)rətɪv/ *a.* & *n.* Now *rare.* LME. [(O)Fr. *mémoratif*, *-ive* or late L *memorativus*, f. as prec.: see -IVE.] A *adj.* 1 Preserving or reviving the memory of some person or thing; commemorative. LME. 2 Of or pertaining to memory. LME. †3 Having a good memory; retentive. L15–L17. †B *n.* A memorial. L16–L17.

memorial /mɪˈmɔːrɪəl/ *a.* & *n.* LME. [(O)Fr. *mémorial* or L *memorialis* adj. (late L *memoriale* n., sign of remembrance, memorial, monument), f. *memoria* MEMORY: see -AL[1].] A *adj.* 1 Preserving or intended to preserve the memory of a person or thing; commemorative. LME. †2 Remembered; worthy to be remembered, memorable. LME–M17. 3 Of or pertaining to memory. Formerly also, intended to assist the memory, mnemonic. LME.

1 *Times* A memorial service for General Grant will be held in Westminster Abbey. *Morning Star* The memorial reunion of resistance fighters. 3 F. BOWERS A memorial lapse, but not a misreading, must be posited.

B *n.* †1 Remembrance, recollection; (a person's) memory or power of recollection. LME–L18. 2 A memorial act; an act of commemoration; *spec.* = COMMEMORATION 1b. LME. 3 A thing, as a monument, a custom, etc., by which the memory of a person, thing, or event is preserved. LME. 4 A record, a chronicle; esp. in *pl.*, memoirs. LME. †5 A note, a memorandum. E16–E19. 6 Any of various informal diplomatic papers. M16. 7 A statement of facts forming the basis of or expressed in the form of a petition or remonstrance to a person in authority, a government, etc. L17. 8 *Law.* a *Sc. Law.* A statement of facts drawn up to be submitted for counsel's opinion. Also, an advocate's brief. E18. b An abstract of the particulars of a deed etc. serving for registration. E19.

Comb.: **Memorial Day** any of various days set aside for the commemoration of those who died in war; *spec.* in the US, 30 May, or the last Monday in May, set aside for the commemoration of those who died on active service and observed as a public holiday in many States.

memorial /mɪˈmɔːrɪəl/ *v.* M18. [f. the n.] 1 *v.t.* Address a memorial to (a person); memorialize. M18. 2 *v.i.* Draw up a memorial; petition *for.* M18.

memorialise *v.* var. of MEMORIALIZE.

memorialist /mɪˈmɔːrɪəlɪst/ *n.* E18. [f. MEMORIAL *n.* + -IST.] 1 A person who gives a memorial address or presents a memorial. E18. 2 A writer of biographical or historical memorials, a memoirist. M18.

memorialize /mɪˈmɔːrɪəlʌɪz/ *v.t.* Also **-ise.** L18. [f. as prec. + -IZE.] 1 Preserve the memory of; be or supply a memorial of; commemorate. L18. 2 Address or present a memorial to. L18.

memorialiˈzation *n.* L19. **memorializer** *n.* M19.

memorially /mɪˈmɔːrɪəli/ *adv.* M17. [f. MEMORIAL *a.* + -LY[2].] 1 By heart, from memory. M17. 2 As a memorial; so as to preserve a memory. *rare.* L19.

memoria technica /mɪˌmɔːrɪə ˈtɛknɪkə/ *n. phr.* M18. [mod.L (= technical memory) repr. Gk *to mnēmonikon tekhnēma.*] A method of assisting the memory by artificial contrivances; a system of mnemonics, a mnemonic aid.

memoried /ˈmɛmərɪd/ *a.* LME. [f. MEMORY + -ED[2], -ED[1].] 1 Remembered. *rare.* LME. 2 Having a memory, esp. of a specified kind, as *long-memoried, short-memoried.* LME. 3 Full of or fraught with memories. M19.

memorious /mɪˈmɔːrɪəs/ *a.* L16. [f. OFr. *memorieux* f. med.L *memoriosus*, f. *memoria*: see MEMORY, -OUS.] Having or showing a good memory.

memorise *v.* var. of MEMORIZE.

memorist /ˈmɛm(ə)rɪst/ *n. rare.* L17. [f. MEMORY or MEMORIZE: see -IST.] †1 A person who prompts the memory. Only in L17. 2 A person who memorizes things; a person with a retentive memory. L19.

memoriter /mɪˈmɒrɪtə/ *adv.* & *a.* E17. [L, f. *memor* mindful.] A *adv.* From memory, by heart. E17. B *adj.* Spoken or speaking from memory. E19.

memorize /ˈmɛmərʌɪz/ *v.* Also **-ise.** L16. [f. next + -IZE.] 1 *v.t.* Keep alive the memory or recollection of; cause to be remembered, make memorable. Now *rare.* L16. 2 *v.t.* Perpetuate the memory of in writing; relate, record, mention. Now *rare.* L16. 3 *v.t.* Commit to memory, learn by heart. M19. 4 *v.i.* Learn things by heart. L19.

3 B. PYM Groping for the light switch, whose position he had not yet memorized perfectly. G. NAYLOR The great slave poet, Jupiter Hammon, who memorized thousands of verses.

memorizable *a.* L19. **memoriˈzation** *n.* L19. **memorizer** *n.* M19.

memory /ˈmɛm(ə)ri/ *n.* ME. [OFr. *memorie*, (also mod.) *mémoire* f. L *memoria*, f. *memor* mindful: see -Y[3].] 1 The faculty by which things are remembered; the capacity for retaining, perpetuating, or reviving the thought of things past; an individual's faculty to remember things. ME. b The capacity of a body or substance for manifesting effects of its previous state, behaviour, or treatment, or for returning to a previous state when the cause of the transition from that state is removed; such effects, such a state. L19. c A device (usu. part of a computer) in which data or program instructions may be stored and from which they may be retrieved when required; capacity for storing data etc. in this way. M20. 2 The fact or condition of being remembered; remembrance, commemoration. Now only in *in memory of* below. ME. b *Chr. Ch.* A commemoration, esp. of the dead. *obs.* exc. *Hist.* LME. 3 The perpetuated knowledge or recollection (*of* something); what is remembered *of* a person, object, or event; (good or bad) posthumous reputation. ME. 4 The knowledge which a person can recover or has recovered by mental effort; the function of the mind regarded as a store for this. LME. b An act or instance of remembering; a representation in the memory; a person or thing as remembered; a recollection. E19. †5 A memorial account or record; a history. LME–M18. 6 A memorial object or act; a memento; a monument. Long *obs.* exc. *Canad. dial.*, an embroidered memorial wall-hanging. LME. 7 The length of time over which the recollection of a person or a number of persons extends. M16.

1 H. B. STOWE Topsy had an uncommon verbal memory. F. GALTON One favourite expedient was to associate the sight memory with the muscular memory. O. HENRY 'I've seen that fellow somewhere,' said Littlefield, who had a memory for faces. T. CAPOTE The prisoner.. proud of.. a brilliant memory, recited the names and addresses. W. TREVOR Memory fails me when I think about the men of the mill. c C. STOLL Other computer folks measure size in megabytes of memory. 3 SWIFT His late Majesty King William the Third, of ever glorious and immortal Memory. E. M. FORSTER I have my children and the memory of my dear wife to consider. J. MILLER Acute head injuries.. can rob the patient of any memory of the events.. leading up to the accident. 4 G. GROTE A considerable portion of the Greeks of Olbia could repeat the Iliad from memory. R. HARLING Perhaps.. it has slipped your memory. F. WYNDHAM A grim experience, which I later managed to blot out almost completely from my memory. C. SIMMONS I searched my memory for an instance of parental betrayal. b G. ORWELL His mother's memory tore at his heart because she had died loving him. E. FEINSTEIN My earliest memories turn around a room with a huge wooden table.

Phrases: *commit to memory*: see COMMIT *v.* I. **in memory of** so as to keep alive the remembrance of; as a record of. *legal memory*: see LEGAL *a.* *living memory*: see LIVING *a.* *long memory*: see LONG *a.*[1] *magnetic memory*: see MAGNETIC *a.* PHOTOGRAPHIC *memory*. **the Immortal Memory**: a toast to the Scottish poet Robert Burns (1759–96). †**to the memory of** = *in memory of* above.

Comb.: **memory bank** the memory device of a computer; *fig.* the human memory; **memory-belief** a memory implicitly believed in though probably unverifiable; **memory board** (*a*) a board on which is fixed or written something which is to be remembered; (*b*) *Theatr.* a programmable console for the semi-automatic control of stage lighting; (*c*) *Computing* a flat, freq. detachable, array of memory devices in a computer; **memory book** *US* a blank book in which cuttings from newspapers etc. are pasted for preservation; a scrapbook; an autograph album; **memory cycle** *Computing* (the time taken by) the process of replacing one unit of data in a memory by another; **memory drug** a drug supposed to improve the memory; **memory drum** (*a*) *Psychol.* a revolving device on which items to be learned are successively presented; (*b*) a drum-shaped memory device in a computer; **memory effect** an effect in a body or substance arising from memory; **memory lane** *fig.* a succession of sentimental memories deliberately pursued (chiefly in *down memory lane*); **memory span** *Psychol.* the maximum number of items that can be recalled in the correct order immediately after a single presentation of them; **memory trace** *Psychol.* a hypothetical trace left in the nervous system by the act of memorizing.

memoryless *a.* M19.

Memphian /ˈmɛmfɪən/ *n.* & *a.* Chiefly *literary.* L16. [f. *Memphis* (see below) + -AN.] A *n.* A native or inhabitant of the ancient Egyptian city of Memphis; an Egyptian. L16. B *adj.* Of or pertaining to Memphis; Egyptian. E17.

Memphitic /mɛmˈfɪtɪk/ *a.* LME. [L *Memphiticus* f. Gk *Memphitikos*, f. *Memphitēs* inhabitant of Memphis: see -ITE[1], -IC.] Of or pertaining to the ancient Egyptian city of Memphis or the dialect of Coptic spoken there.

memsahib /ˈmɛmsɑːɪb/ *n.* *Anglo-Ind.* M19. [f. MEM *n.*[1] (= MA'AM) + SAHIB.] A European married woman as spoken of or to by Indians.

men *n.* pl. of MAN *n.*

menaccanite /məˈnakənʌɪt/ *n.* L18. [Irreg. f. *Manaccan*, a village in Cornwall + -ITE[1].] *Min.* A ferrian variety of ilmenite.

menace /ˈmɛnəs/ *n.* ME. [L *minacia* (pl. in cl.L), f. *minac-*, *minax* threatening, f. base of *minari* threaten.] 1 A declaration or indication of hostile intention, or of a probable evil or catastrophe; a threat; the action of threatening. Now *literary.* ME. 2 A thing threatening danger or catastrophe; a dangerous or obnoxious thing or person; a great inconvenience. M19.

1 J. A. FROUDE The fierce menace was delivered amidst frowning groups of.. nobles. J. NAGENDA The voice.. had menace and the contempt which the power of the gun gave its owner. 2 J. R. GREEN The old social discontent.. remained a perpetual menace to public order. A. SILLITOE They said I was a menace to honest lads like Mike. *public menace*: see PUBLIC *a.* & *n.* *red menace*: see RED *a.*

menaceful *a.* threatening M19.

menace /ˈmɛnəs/ *v.* ME. [AN *manasser*, OFr. *menacier* (mod. *menacer*) f. Proto-Romance, f. as prec.] 1 *v.t.* Utter menaces against; threaten. ME. 2 *v.i.* Utter menaces; be threatening. ME. 3 *v.t.* Hold out as a punishment, penalty, or danger; threaten to inflict. ME.

1 E. L. RICE Maurrant.. menaces the man with his revolver. R. K. NARAYAN I was.. knocked down and hurt by bigger animals and menaced by lesser ones. A. STORR We are menaced by the possibility of a nuclear holocaust. 2 BURKE Earth below shook; heaven above menaced. 3 H. H. MILMAN No threatened excommunication is now menaced. J. MARTINE The solitary dissentient was menacing to leave the meeting-house.

menacement *n.* (now *rare*) menacing, threatening E17. **menacer** *n.* M17. **menacing** *n.* (now *rare*) (*a*) the action of the vb; (*b*) a threat, a menace: ME. **menacing** *ppl a.* that menaces or threatens, threatening LME. **menacingly** *adv.* L16.

menad *n.* var. of MAENAD.

menadione /mɛnəˈdʌɪəʊn/ *n.* Orig. *US.* M20. [f. ME(THYL + NA(PHTHALENE + -DIONE.] *Pharm.* A synthetic yellow derivative of naphthoquinone used to treat haemorrhage by stimulating prothrombin production; 2-methyl-1,4-naphthoquinone, $C_{11}H_8O_2$. Also called *menaphthone*, *vitamin* K_3. Cf. MENAQUINONE.

ménage /meɪˈnɑːʒ; *foreign* menaːʒ (*pl. same*)/ *n.* Also **menage**. ME. [OFr. *menaige*, *man-* (mod. *ménage*) f. Proto-Romance, f. L *mansio(n-)*: see MANSION, -AGE.] 1 A domestic establishment, a household. Formerly also, the members of a household. ME. b A sexual relationship; an affair. M20. 2 The management of a household, housekeeping. E19. 3 A benefit society or savings club of which every member pays in a fixed sum weekly; an arrangement for paying for goods by instalments. *Sc.* & *north.* E19.

1 ***ménage à deux*** /a dø, ɑː ˈdəː/ [= of two] an arrangement or relationship of two people living together. ***ménage à quatre*** /a katr, ɑː ˈkɑːtrə/ [= of four] an arrangement or relationship of four people living together. ***ménage à trois*** /a trwa, ɑː ˈtrwɑː/ [= of three] an arrangement or relationship in which three people live together, usually consisting of a husband, and wife, and the lover of one of these.

menagerie /məˈnadʒ(ə)ri/ *n.* L17. [Fr. *ménagerie*, f. *ménage*: see prec., -ERY.] 1 A collection of wild animals in cages or enclosures, *esp.* one kept for exhibition; a place or building in which such a collection is kept. L17. b A collection of strange or outlandish people. M19. †2 An aviary. M18–M19.

menagerist *n.* a keeper of a menagerie M19.

menald /ˈmɛn(ə)ld/ *a.* Also **mennal** /ˈmɛn(ə)l/. E17. [Origin unkn.] Of an animal: spotted, speckled. Of a deer: of a dappled chestnut colour.

menalty /ˈmɛn(ə)lti/ *n.* *rare.* M16. [f. MEAN *a.*[2] + -AL[1] + -TY[1].] The middle class.

W. H. AUDEN Sons of the menalty Divining their future from plum stones.

menaphthone /məˈnafθəʊn/ *n.* M20. [f. ME(THYL + NAPHTH(ALENE + -ONE.] *Pharm.* = MENADIONE.

Menapian /mɪˈnapɪən/ *a.* & *n.* M20. [f. L *Menapii* a people of northern Gaul in Roman times + -IAN.] *Geol.* (Designating or pertaining to) a middle Pleistocene glaciation in northern Europe preceding the Elster and Saale glaciations, and possibly corresponding to the Günz of the Alps.

menaquinone /mɛnəˈkwɪnəʊn/ *n.* M20. [f. ME(THYL + NA(PHTHALENE + QUINONE.] *Biochem.* An isoprenoid derivative of menadione synthesized in the body by (esp. intestinal) bacteria and essential for blood-clotting. Also called *vitamin* K_2.

menarche /məˈnɑːki/ *n.* E20. [f. Gk *mēn* month + *arkhē* beginning.] The first appearance of menstruation; the age at which this occurs.

menarcheal *a.* M20.

menazon /ˈmɛnəz(ə)n/ *n.* M20. [f. ME(THYL + AMI)N(O- + AZ(O- + THI)ON(ATE.] An organic compound containing sulphur, phosphorus, and a triazine ring, used as an insecticide and acaricide.

mench *v.* var. of MENSH.

mend /mɛnd/ *n.* ME. [Partly aphet. f. AMEND *n.*, partly f. the vb. Cf. MENDS.] †1 Reparation, restoration, recompense. ME–M17. 2 *on the mend*, recovering from sickness, improving in health or condition. E19. 3 An act of mending, a repair; a repaired hole etc. in a fabric. L19.

3 *make and mend*: see MAKE *n.*[2]

mend /mɛnd/ *v.* ME. [AN *mender* aphet. f. *amender* AMEND *v.* Partly directly aphet. f. AMEND *v.*] I With reference to defects. 1a *v.t.* Free (a person, character, habits) from sin or fault; improve morally; reform. Now *arch.* & *dial.* exc. in *mend one's manners, one's ways.* ME. b *v.i.* Reform. Now *rare* exc. in proverb *it is never too late to mend.* ME. 2a *v.t.* Remove the defects of (a thing); improve by correction or alteration. *obs.* exc. as passing into sense 5. ME. b *v.i.* Become less faulty. Of conditions: become less unfavourable, improve. LME. 3a *v.t.* Rectify, remedy, remove (an evil); correct, put right (a fault, something wrong). ME. b *v.i.* Of a fault: undergo rectification. E18. 4 *v.t.* Make amends or reparation for, atone for (a misdeed, an injury). *obs.* exc. in proverb *least said, soonest mended.* ME. 5 *v.t.* a Restore to a complete or sound condition (something broken, decayed, worn, torn, etc.); repair or make good (a defective part); add fuel to (a fire). ME. b Adjust, set right. *obs.* exc. *Naut.* E16. c Repair the garments of (a person). *arch. colloq.* L19. 6a *v.t.* Restore to health, cure, heal. *arch.* ME. b *v.i.* Regain health, recover from sickness, heal. E16.

3a SHELLEY Poverty, the which I sought to mend By holding a poor office in the state. R. K. NARAYAN He tried to mend his previous statement. 5a STEELE A blind Beggar.. with a Needle and thread thriftily mending his Stockings. KEATS A vile old pen... The fault is in the Quill: I have mended it. DAY LEWIS He mended his nets. S. CHITTY The stove would not work and she was too miserable to get it mended. c W. S. GILBERT She will tend him, nurse him, mend him. 6b H. WILLIAMSON No bones broken.. but he has some way to go to mend. R. D. LAING Even broken hearts have been known to mend.

II Without distinct reference to defects. 7 *v.t.* Improve the condition or fortune of. Now *rare* or *obs.* ME. 8 *v.t.* Improve on, surpass, better. Now *rare.* ME. 9 *v.t.* & *i.* Improve physically, fatten. *obs.* exc. *Sc.* & *N. Ir.* LME. †10a *v.t.* Improve by additions; supplement. LME–E18. b *v.i.* Improve in amount or price. E17–E19. 11 *v.*†*i* & *t.* Improve in quality. Now *rare.* M16.

Phrases: *end or mend*: see *mend or end* below. LEAST *said, soonest mended. make or mend*: see MAKE *v.* **mend matters** rectify or improve the state of affairs. **mend one's pace** walk more quickly, travel faster. **mend or end, end or mend** either improve or (if that is impossible) put an end to.

mendable *a.* M16. **mender** *n.* LME.

mendacious /mɛnˈdeɪʃəs/ *a.* E17. [f. L *mendac-*, *mendax* prob. orig. speaking incorrectly or falsely, f. *mendum* defect, fault + -OUS.] Lying; untruthful; false.

mendaciously *adv.* E19. **mendaciousness** *n.* mendacity L19.

mendacity /mɛnˈdasɪti/ *n.* M17. [eccl.L *mendacitas*, *-tat-*, f. as prec.: see -ACITY.] 1 The quality of being mendacious; habitual lying or deceiving. M17. 2 An instance of this; a lie, a falsehood. M17.

mendang /mɛnˈdaŋ/ *n.* Also **-dong** /-ˈdɒŋ/, **-dung** /-ˈdʌŋ/. E20. [Tib.] A Tibetan sacred wall composed of flat stones with religious inscriptions. Also *mendang wall.* Cf. MANI *n.*[2]

Mende /ˈmɛndi/ *n.* & *a.* Also **-di.** M18. [Mende.] A *n.* 1 The Mande language of the Mende. M18. 2 Pl. **-s**, same. A member of a people inhabiting Sierra Leone and Liberia in W. Africa. L19. B *attrib.* or as *adj.* Of or pertaining to the Mende or their language. E20.

mendee *n.* var. of MENDHI.

mendelevium /mɛndəˈliːvɪəm, -ˈleɪvɪəm/ *n.* M20. [f. Dmitri Ivanovich *Mendeleev* (1834–1907), Russ. chemist + -IUM.] A radioactive metallic chemical element of the actinide series, atomic no. 101, which is produced artificially. (Symbol Md.)

Mendelian /mɛn'diːlɪən/ *a.* & *n.* Also **m-**. E20. [f. Gregor Johann *Mendel* (1822–84), Moravian monk & botanist + -IAN.] *Biol.* A *adj.* Pertaining to or designating the theory of heredity first propounded by Mendel; following the laws or principles of Mendelism. E20. B *n.* A person who accepts or advocates Mendel's principles of heredity. E20.

Mendelianism *n.* = MENDELISM E20.

Mendelism /'mɛnd(ə)lɪz(ə)m/ *n.* E20. [f. *Mendel* (see prec.) + -ISM.] *Biol.* The theory that the inheritance of any particular character is controlled by the inheritance of discrete units (now called genes) which occur in pairs in somatic cells and separate (largely) independently of each other at meiosis; (Mendelian) genetics.

Mendelist *n.* (*rare*) = MENDELIAN *n.* E20. **Mendelize** *v.i.* behave or be inherited in accordance with Mendelian principles E20.

Mendelssohnian /mɛnd(ə)l'səʊnɪən/ *a.* L19. [f. *Mendelssohn* (see below) + -IAN.] Of, pertaining to, or characteristic of the German composer Felix Mendelssohn-Bartholdy (1809–47) or his music, esp. its quality of being expressive and picturesque without passion.

Also **Mendelssohnic** *a.* L19.

mendhi /'mɛndiː/ *n.* Also **-dee**. E19. [Hindi *mendhī*.] In the Indian subcontinent: the henna plant, *Lawsonia inermis*.

Mendi *n.* & *a.* var. of MENDE.

mendicancy /'mɛndɪk(ə)nsi/ *n.* L18. [f. next: see -ANCY.] The state or condition of being a mendicant or beggar; the habit or practice of begging.

mendicant /'mɛndɪk(ə)nt/ *n.* & *a.* LME. [L *mendicant-* pres. ppl stem of *mendicare* beg, f. *mendicus* beggar, f. *mendum* defect, fault: see -ANT[1].] A *n.* 1 A mendicant friar (see sense B.1 below). LME. 2 A beggar; a person who lives by begging. L15. B *adj.* 1 Designating or belonging to any of the religious orders whose members (known as friars) lived solely on alms. L15. 2 Begging; given to or characterized by begging. Also, characteristic of a beggar. E17.

mendicate /'mɛndɪkeɪt/ *v.t.* & *i.* *rare.* E17. [L *mendicat-* pa. ppl stem of *mendicare*: see prec., -ATE[3].] Beg (for), ask (for) like a beggar.

mendi'cation *n.* begging M17.

mendicity /mɛn'dɪsɪti/ *n.* LME. [(O)Fr. *mendicité* f. L *mendicitas*, *-tat-*, f. *mendicus*: see MENDICANT, -ITY.] 1 The state or condition of a mendicant or beggar, beggary. Also, the existence or numbers of mendicants. LME. 2 The practice or habit of begging. E19.

mending /'mɛndɪŋ/ *n.* ME. [f. MEND *v.* + -ING[1].] 1 The action of MEND *v.* ME. 2 a In *pl.* Articles to be repaired. *rare.* M19. b Clothing requiring or in the process of repair. L19.

1 *invisible mending*: see INVISIBLE *a.*

mendipite /'mɛndɪpʌɪt/ *n.* M19. [f. the *Mendip* Hills, Somerset + -ITE[1].] *Min.* Native lead oxychloride, an orthorhombic mineral usu. occurring as massed white crystals.

mendment /'mɛndm(ə)nt/ *n.* ME. [Aphet. f. AMENDMENT.] 1 Amendment, improvement, reparation, correction, reformation. Now *rare.* ME. 2 *spec.* Improvement of the soil; fertilizer, manure; = AMENDMENT 3b. *obs.* exc. *dial.* M17.

mendong *n.* var. of MENDANG.

mends /mɛndz/ *n.* *obs.* exc. *Sc.* ME. [Aphet. f. AMENDS. Cf. MEND *n.*] 1 Amends; recompense, reparation. ME. †2 Means of obtaining restoration or reparation; a remedy; a cure. LME–M17.

mendung *n.* var. of MENDANG.

meneer *n.* see MYNHEER.

meneghinite /mɛnɪ'giːnʌɪt, mɛ'nɛgɪn-/ *n.* M19. [f. G. G. A. *Meneghini* (1811–89), It. mineralogist + -ITE[1].] *Min.* A monoclinic sulphide and antimonide of lead and copper, usu. occurring as greyish-black prisms and in fibrous masses.

Menevian /mə'niːvɪən/ *a.* & *n.* M19. [f. *Menevia*, med.L name of St David's, S. Wales + -AN.] *Geol.* A *adj.* Of, pertaining to, or designating a group of fossiliferous rocks of Cambrian age found in Wales. M19. B *n.* The Menevian formation. L19.

meng /mɛŋ, mɛn(d)ʒ/ *v.t.* & *i.* Long *obs.* exc. *dial.* [OE *meng̣an* = OFris. *menza*, OS *mengian*, OHG *mengen* (Du., G *mengen*), ON *menga*, f. Gmc, f. base repr. also in AMONG.] Mix, mingle, blend.

mengkuang /mɛŋ'kwaŋ/ *n.* E20. [Malay.] Any of various large SE Asian trees of the genus *Pandanus* (family Pandanaceae), providing leaves that can be woven into matting, etc.; (matting made from) such leaves.

mengkulang /'mɛŋkuːlaŋ/ *n.* M20. [Malay.] Any of various Malayan timber trees of the genus *Heritiera* (family Sterculiaceae), esp. *H. simplicifolia*; the wood of these trees.

mengovirus /'mɛŋgəvʌɪrəs/ *n.* Also **Mengo virus**. M20. [f. *Mengo* district, Uganda + VIRUS.] *Biol.* A picornavirus originally found in monkeys but capable of infecting other species and causing encephalomyelitis in humans.

menhaden /mɛn'heɪd(ə)n/ *n.* L18. [Algonquian, perh. f. a base meaning 'fertilize'.] A fish of the herring family, *Brevoortia tyrannus*, of the Atlantic coast of N. America, an important source of fish guano and oil.

menhir /'mɛnhɪə/ *n.* M19. [Breton *maen-hir* (*maen* stone, *hir* long) = Welsh *maen hir*, Corn. *mênhere*.] *Archaeol.* A single tall upright monumental stone, esp. of prehistoric times.

menial /'miːnɪəl/ *a.* & *n.* LME. [AN *menial*, *meignial*, f. *meinie* MEINIE: see -AL[1].] A *adj.* 1 Pertaining to the household, domestic. *obs.* in *gen.* sense. LME. 2 Of a servant: forming one of the household, domestic, latterly *spec.* w. implication of employment for show rather than use. LME. 3 Proper to or performed by a menial or domestic servant; now *spec.* of the nature of drudgery, servile, degrading. L17.

3 S. SPENDER His nature was so menial that he was unhappy without dust-pan and brush. B. PYM He could hardly ask her to do such menial work.

B *n.* A domestic servant; latterly *esp.* a liveried manservant employed for show rather than use, a pompous or arrogant servant. LME.

menially *adv.* like a menial L19.

Ménière /mɛn'jɛː/ *n.* Also **Menière, -iere**. L19. [Prosper *Ménière* (1799–1862), Fr. physician.] *Med. Ménière's disease, syndrome*, a disease of the membranous labyrinth of the ear associated with tinnitus, progressive deafness, and intermittent vertigo.

meninges /mɪ'nɪndʒiːz/ *n.pl.* Also (*rare*) in sing. **meninx** /'miːnɪŋks/. E17. [mod.L f. Gk *mēnigx*, *mēnigg-* membrane.] The three membranes enveloping the brain and spinal cord: the dura mater, arachnoid, and pia mater.

meningeal *a.* of or pertaining to the meninges E19. **meningic** *a.* (*rare*) = MENINGEAL *a.* E19.

meningioma /mɪˌnɪndʒɪ'əʊmə/ *n.* Pl. **-mas**, **-mata** /-mətə/. E20. [f. MENING(O- + ENDOTHEL)IOMA.] *Med.* A tumour, usu. benign, arising from meningeal tissue (usu. that of the brain).

meningism /mɪ'nɪndʒɪz(ə)m, 'mɛnɪn-/ *n.* E20. [f. next + -ISM.] *Med.* Stiffness of the neck, esp. in fevers of children, resembling that caused by meningitis.

meningitis /mɛnɪn'dʒʌɪtɪs/ *n.* Pl. **-tides** /-tɪdiːz/. E19. [f. as MENINGES + -ITIS.] *Med.* (An) inflammation of the meninges of the brain or spinal cord.

meningitic /-'dʒɪtɪk/ *a.* L19.

meningo- /mɪ'nɪŋgəʊ, mɪ'nɪndʒəʊ/ *comb. form.* [f. MENINGES + -O-.] *Med.* Of or involving the meninges.

meningocele *n.* a protrusion of the meninges through a gap in the spine due to a congenital defect M19. **meningo'coccal** *a.* of, pertaining to, involving, or caused by a meningococcus E20. **meningo'coccus** *n.*, pl. **-cocci** /-'kɒk(s)ʌɪ, -iː/, a bacterium, *Neisseria meningitidis*, involved in cerebrospinal fever and meningitis L19. **meningoencepha'litis** *n.* inflammation of the membranes of the brain and the adjoining cerebral tissue L19. **meningoen'cephalocele** *n.* = CEPHALOCELE L19. **meningomye'litis** *n.* inflammation of the spinal cord and its membranes L19. **meningo'myelocele** *n.* = MYELOMENINGOCELE L19.

meninx *n.* sing. of MENINGES.

Menippean /mɪ'nɪpɪən/ *a.* E18. [f. *Menippus* (see below) + -EAN.] Characteristic of or resembling the satirical style of the Greek philosopher Menippus (fl. 3rd cent. BC).

meniscal /mɪ'nɪsk(ə)l/ *a.* *rare.* M19. [f. MENISCUS + -AL[1].] Of the nature of or resembling a meniscus.

Also **meniscate** *a.* M19.

menisci *n.* pl. of MENISCUS.

meniscoid /mɪ'nɪskɔɪd/ *a.* E19. [f. next + -OID.] *Bot.* Resembling a meniscus in form; thin, domed, and thickest in the middle.

Also **meni'scoidal** *a.* L19.

meniscus /mɪ'nɪskəs/ *n.* Pl. **-sci** /-sʌɪ/. L17. [mod.L f. Gk *mēniskos* crescent, dim. of *mēnē* moon.] 1 A lens convex on one side and concave on the other; *esp.* a convexo-concave lens (i.e. one thickest in the middle, with a crescent-shaped section). L17. 2 A crescent moon. *rare.* E18. 3 The convex or concave upper surface of a column of liquid in a tube, caused by surface tension or capillarity. E19. 4 *Anat.* A disclike interarticular fibrocartilage situated between the articular surfaces of certain joints, as those of the wrist and knee. M19. 5 A figure in the form of a crescent. L19.

meniscectomy /mɛnɪ'sɛktəmi/ *n.* (an instance of) surgical removal of a meniscus, esp. that of the knee M20.

mennal *a.* var. of MENALD.

Mennecy /'mɛnəsi/ *a.* & *n.* M19. [A town near Paris, France.] (Designating) a soft-paste porcelain made at Mennecy.

Mennist /'mɛnɪst/ *n.* & *a.* *US.* L18. [f. as next.] = MENNONITE.

Mennonist /'mɛnənɪst/ *n.* M17. [f. as next + -IST.] = MENNONITE *n.*

Mennonite /'mɛnənʌɪt/ *n.* & *a.* M16. [f. *Menno* Simons (1496–1561), their early leader + -ITE[1].] A *n.* A member of a Christian sect which arose in Friesland in the 16th cent. maintaining such principles as opposition to infant baptism, the taking of oaths, military service, and the holding of civic offices. M16. B *attrib.* or as *adj.* Of or pertaining to the Mennonites. M18.

meno /'mɛnəʊ, 'meɪnəʊ/ *adv.* L19. [It.] *Mus.* Less: used in directions, as *meno mosso*.

meno- /'mɛnəʊ/ *comb. form.* Bef. a vowel **men-**. [f. Gk *mēn*, *mēnos* month: see -O-.] Forming ns. w. the sense 'menstruation, menses', as *menorrhoea*.

men-of-war *n.* pl. of MAN-OF-WAR.

menologia *n.pl.* see MENOLOGY.

menologist /mɪ'nɒlədʒɪst/ *n.* L19. [f. as next.] A compiler of a menologium.

menology /mɪ'nɒlədʒi/ *n.* Also in L form **menologium** /mɛnə(ʊ)'ləʊdʒɪəm/, pl. **-ia** /-ɪə/, **-iums**. E17. [mod.L *menologium* f. eccl.Gk *mēnologion*, f. *mēn* month + LOGOS account.] An ecclesiastical calendar of the months; *spec.* a calendar of the Greek Orthodox Church containing biographies of the saints in the order of the dates on which they are commemorated.

Menominee /mɪ'nɒmɪniː/ *n.* & *a.* Also **-ni**. M18. [Ojibwa *manōminī* lit. 'wild-rice person'.] A *n.* Pl. same, -s. 1 A member of an Algonquian Indian people of Michigan and Wisconsin. M18. 2 The language of this people. E20. 3 = *Menominee whitefish* below. E20.

B *attrib.* or as *adj.* Of or pertaining to the Menominee or their language. M19.

Menominee whitefish a whitefish, *Prosopium cylindraceum*, of lakes in northern N. America.

menopausal /mɛnə(ʊ)'pɔːz(ə)l/ *a.* E20. [f. next + -AL[1].] Of, pertaining to, or characteristic of the menopause; undergoing the menopause.

M. WEST Lotte was at the low point of one of her menopausal depressions. *Which?* The typical shoplifter is not the muddled, middle-aged, menopausal woman many would have us believe. W. TREVOR Roy, have your menopausal fling with the girl.

menopause /ˈmɛnə(ʊ)pɔːz/ *n.* L19. [f. MENO- + *pausis* cessation, PAUSE *n.*] The final cessation of the menstrual cycle; the period of a woman's life when this occurs, usu. between the ages of 40 and 50. Also (in full *male menopause*), a supposedly corresponding stage in a man's life; a crisis of identity, confidence, etc., experienced by a middle-aged man.

menopausic *a.* (*rare*) = MENOPAUSAL L19.

menorah /mɪˈnɔːrə/ *n.* L19. [Heb. *mĕnōrāh* candlestick.] A holy candelabrum with seven branches that was used in the temple in Jerusalem; a candelabrum having any number of branches, but usually eight, used in Jewish worship, esp. during Hanukkah; a representation of either as a symbol of Judaism.

menorrhagia /mɛnəˈreɪdʒɪə/ *n.* L18. [mod.L, f. MENO- + -RRHAGIA.] *Med.* Excessively heavy bleeding at menstruation.

menorrhagic /-ˈradʒɪk/ *a.* pertaining to or suffering from menorrhagia M19.

menorrhoea /mɛnəˈriːə/ *n.* Also ***-rrhea**. M19. [Back-form. f. AMENORRHOEA.] *Med.* Normal bleeding at menstruation. Also, menorrhagia.

mensa /ˈmɛnsə/ *n.* L17. [L = table.] **1** The grinding surface of a molar tooth. *rare.* L17. **2** *Eccl.* The upper surface, esp. the top slab, of an altar: an altar-table. M19. **3** (**M-**.) (The name of) an inconspicuous constellation of the southern hemisphere, lying between Dorado and the South Pole; the Table. M20. **4** (**M-**.) (The name of) an organization of people with high intelligence quotients. M20.

mensal /ˈmɛns(ə)l/ *n.*[1] & *a.*[1] L15. [f. L *mensis* month + -AL[1].] †**A** *n.* A monthly account. L15–E16. **B** *adj.* Monthly. M19.

mensal /ˈmɛns(ə)l/ *a.*[2] & *n.*[2] LME. [Late L *mensalis*, f. *mensa* table: see -AL[1].] **A** *adj.* **1** Of, pertaining to, or used at the table. LME. **2a** *Ir.* & *Sc. Hist.* Designating land set aside to provide food for the royal table. E17. **b** Designating a church, benefice, etc., appropriated to defray some of the expenses of a (Roman Catholic) bishop or other cleric, *spec.* in Ireland and in Scotland before the Reformation. E17. **B** *n. Sc.* & *Ir. Hist.* A mensal church or benefice. L17.

mensch /mɛnʃ/ *n.* M20. [Yiddish f. G = person.] A person of integrity or rectitude; a just, honest, or honourable person.

mense /mɛns/ *n.* & *v. obs.* exc. *Sc.* & *north.* Orig. †**mensk**. ME. [ON *mennska* humanity, corresp. to OS, OHG *menniskī*, f. Gmc base of MANNISH. Later form repr. Sc. pronunc.] **A** *n.* **1** Humanity, kindness; courtesy, hospitality; propriety, decorum. ME. †**2** Honour, credit. ME–L17. **3** An honour, a credit. ME. **B** *v.t.* Grace; adorn, decorate; be a credit to, do honour to. ME.

menseful *a.* proper, decorous, discreet L17. **menseless** *a.* without propriety, decorum, or seemliness E16.

menservants *n.* pl. of MANSERVANT.

menses /ˈmɛnsiːz/ *n.pl.* L16. [L, pl. of *mensis* month.] The menstrual discharge. Also, the time of menstruation.

mensh /mɛnʃ/ *v.i. colloq.* Also **-ch**. M20. [Abbrev. of MENTION *v.*] Mention something. Chiefly in *don't mensh*, = *don't mention it* s.v. MENTION *v.* 1.

Menshevik /ˈmɛnʃɪvɪk/ *n.* & *a.* E20. [Russ. *men'shevik* = member of the minority, f. *men'shiĭ* less, compar. of *malyĭ* little.] *Hist.* **A** *n.* A member of a minority faction of the Russian Social-Democratic Party who opposed the Bolshevik policy of non-cooperation with other opponents of the tsarist regime and violent revolutionary action by a small political élite. Cf. BOLSHEVIK *n.* 1. E20. **B** *attrib.* or as *adj.* Of or pertaining to Mensheviks or Menshevism. E20.

Menshevism *n.* the doctrine and practices of the Mensheviks E20. **Menshevist** *n.* & *a.* = MENSHEVIK E20.

†**mensk** *n.* & *v.* see MENSE.

mens rea /mɛnz ˈriːə/ *n. phr.* M19. [L = guilty mind.] *Law.* The state of mind accompanying an illegal act which makes the act a crime; criminal state of mind.

mens sana in corpore sano /mɛns ˈsɑːnə ɪn ˌkɔːpərə ˈsɑːnəʊ/ *n. phr.* E17. [L (Juvenal).] A sound mind in a sound body, esp. regarded as the ideal of education. Also *ellipt.* as *mens sana.*

menstrua *n.pl.* see MENSTRUUM.

menstrual /ˈmɛnstrʊəl/ *a.* LME. [L *menstrualis*, f. *menstruus* monthly, f. *mensis* month: see -AL[1].] **1** Of or pertaining to menstruation. LME. **2** Monthly; happening once a month, varying in monthly periods. Now *rare* or *obs.* L16.

1 menstrual cycle the process of ovulation and menstruation in sexually mature women and female primates.

menstruant /ˈmɛnstrʊənt/ *a.* & *n. rare.* M17. [Late L *menstruant-* pres. ppl stem of *menstruare*: see next, -ANT [1].] (A woman who is) menstruating.

menstruate /ˈmɛnstrʊeɪt/ *v.* M17. [Late L *menstruat-* pa. ppl stem. of *menstruare*, f. L *menstrua*: see MENSTRUUM, -ATE[3].] †**1** *v.t.* Soil as with menstrual blood. Only in M17. **2** *v.i.* Undergo menstruation; undergo the menstrual cycle. E19.

menstruation /mɛnstrʊˈeɪʃ(ə)n/ *n.* L18. [f. prec. + -ATION.] The process of discharging blood and other material from the lining of the uterus through the vagina, which occurs in sexually mature women (except during and for a time after pregnancy) normally at intervals of about one lunar month, until the menopause.

menstruous /ˈmɛnstrʊəs/ *a.* LME. [OFr. *menstrueus* or late L *menstruosus*, f. L *menstrua*: see next, -OUS.] **1** Undergoing menstruation. LME. **2** Of or pertaining to menstruation; = MENSTRUAL 1. LME. †**3** Soiled (as) with menstrual blood; horribly filthy or polluted. LME–L17. †**4** = MENSTRUAL 2. *rare.* M17–M19.

menstruum /ˈmɛnstrʊəm/ *n.* Pl. **-strua** /-strʊə/, **-struums**. LME. [L, use as n. of *menstruus* monthly, f. *mensis* month. In cl.L (in sense 1) only as pl. *menstrua*.] **1** *sing.* & in *pl.* Menses. Now *rare.* LME. **2** *Chem.* & *Pharm.* A solvent; a liquid medium. *arch.* E17.

¶ Sense 2 arose from alchemical analogy between the supposed agency of a solvent in the transmutation of metals and the supposed function of the menses in nurturing a developing foetus.

mensual /ˈmɛnsjʊəl, -ʃʊəl/ *a.* L18. [Late L *mensualis*, irreg. f. L *mensis* month after *annualis* annual: see -AL[1].] Of or relating to a month; monthly.

mensur /mɛnˈzuːr, mɛnˈsʊə/ *n.* Pl. **-ren** /-rən/, **-rs**. E20. [G, lit. 'measure'.] Chiefly *Hist.* In Germany, a fencing duel between students fought with partially blunted weapons.

mensurable /ˈmɛnʃ(ə)rəb(ə)l, -sjə-/ *a.* LME. [Fr., or late L *mensurabilis*, f. *mensurare*: see MENSURATE, -ABLE.] †**1a** Moderate. Only in LME. **b** Just, fair. Only in M17. **2** Able to be measured; having assigned limits. L16. **3** *Mus.* Having fixed rhythm with notes and rests indicating a definite duration, *spec.* as characterizing the style succeeding simple plainsong. L18.

mensuraˈbility *n.* (*rare*) L17. **mensurableness** *n.* (*rare*) E18.

mensural /ˈmɛnʃ(ə)r(ə)l, -sjə-/ *a.* L16. [L *mensuralis*, f. *mensura* MEASURE *n.*: see -AL[1].] **1** *Mus.* = MENSURABLE 3. L16. **2** Of or pertaining to measuring. M17.

mensuralist *n.* & *a.* (*a*) *n.* a composer or advocate of mensurable music, *spec.* plainsong; (*b*) *adj.* of or pertaining to mensurable music or mensuralists: E20.

mensurate /ˈmɛnʃəreɪt, -sjə-/ *v.t.* M17. [Late L *mensurat-* pa. ppl stem of *mensurare*, f. L *mensura* MEASURE *n.*: see -ATE [3].] Measure; ascertain the size, extent, or quantity of.

mensurative *a.* capable of measuring; adapted for taking measurements: M19. **mensurator** *n.* a means of or apparatus for measuring E18.

mensuration /mɛnʃəˈreɪʃ(ə)n, -sjə-/ *n.* L16. [Late L *mensuratio(n-)*, f. as prec.: see -ATION.] **1** The action or an act of measuring. L16. **2** *Math.* The part of geometry that deals with the measurement of lengths, areas, and volumes. E18.

mensurational *a.* L19.

mensuren *n.pl.* see MENSUR.

-ment /m(ə)nt/ *suff.* [Repr. Fr. *-ment* or (its source) L *-mentum*.] Used in ns. adopted f. Fr. or L and in Eng. formations modelled on these and as a productive suff., expr. the result, product, or means of an action, usu. f. vbs and vb stems, as *abridgement*, *accomplishment*, *banishment*, *bereavement*, *commencement*, *embodiment*, *enhancement*, *excitement*, *fragment*, *garment*, *implement*, *ligament*, *ornament*, *treatment*, *wonderment*, etc., but also f. adjs., as *betterment*, *merriment*, *oddment*.

mental /ˈmɛnt(ə)l/ *a.*[1] & *n.* LME. [(O)Fr., or late L *mentalis*, f. *ment-*, *mens* mind: see -AL[1].] **A** *adj.* **1** *gen.* Of or pertaining to the mind. LME. **2** Carried on or performed by the mind; taking place in the mind. E16. **3** Of or pertaining to the mind as an object of study; concerned with the phenomena of mind. E19. **4** Characterized by the possession of mind, intellectual. *rare.* M19. **5** Of or pertaining to disorders or illnesses of the mind. L19. **b** Mentally ill; mentally handicapped. *colloq.* E20.

1 R. C. HUTCHINSON One whose mental growth had stunted the physical. M. WARNOCK Memory is a mental phenomenon. *mental breakdown*, *mental disorder*, *mental handicap*, *mental retardation*, etc. **2** *Listener* Hearing it I could not help directing a mental kick at all those other . . plays. K. WATERHOUSE His mental calculations . . seemed to be giving him trouble. *mental restriction*: see RESTRICTION 5. **4** J. JONES This young man is also very mental His being is riddled with theory and hypothesis. **5** *mental asylum*, *mental hospital*, *mental nurse*, *mental patient*, etc.

Special collocations: **mental age** the degree of mental development of a person, expressed as the age at which a similar level is attained by an average person. **mental arithmetic**: performed without the use of written figures or other visible symbols. *mental block*: see BLOCK *n.* 10c. **mental cruelty** conduct which inflicts suffering on the mind of another person, esp. (*US*) as constituting grounds for legal separation or divorce. *mental defective*: see DEFECTIVE *n.* 2. *mental deficiency*: see DEFICIENCY 1. **mental handicap** the condition of being of such low intelligence, or having the intellectual capacities so underdeveloped, esp through illness or injury, as to inhibit normal social functioning; an instance of this. **mental healer** a practitioner of mental healing. **mental healing** healing effected by mental effort. *mental health*: see HEALTH 5. **mental hygiene** (measures directed towards the preservation or improvement of) mental health. *mental note*: see NOTE *n.*[2] 14. **mental ratio** = INTELLIGENCE *quotient.* **mental set** the set or predisposition of the mind which governs reactions to stimuli. **mental test** = INTELLIGENCE *test.* **mental year** the average mental attainment of each year of growth, used as a unit of measurement of mental development.

B *n.* †**1** An intellectual faculty. *rare.* Only in L17. †**2** A mental reservation. *rare.* Only in E18. **3** A mentally ill person; a mental patient. *colloq.* E20.

mentalize *v.t.* develop or cultivate mentally; give a mental quality to: E19.

mental /ˈmɛnt(ə)l/ *a.*[2] E18. [Fr., f. L *mentum* chin: see -AL[1].] **1** Of or pertaining to the chin. E18. **2** *Biol.* Of, pertaining to, or situated on the mentum. M19.

mentalism /ˈmɛnt(ə)lɪz(ə)m/ *n.* L19. [f. MENTAL *a.*[1] + -ISM.] **1** A mental process. *rare.* L19. **2** The theory that physical events are ultimately explicable only as aspects or functions of the mind; belief in the primacy of mind. L19.

mentalist /ˈmɛnt(ə)lɪst/ *n.* & *a.* M17. [f. as prec. + -IST.] **A** *n.* **1** *rare* **a** A person who conceals his or her real thoughts. M17. **b** A person whose tastes are for mental rather than for material pleasures. L18. **c** A person whose artistic aim is the expression of thought. M19. **2** An adherent of mentalism. L19. **B** *attrib.* or as *adj.* Of or pertaining to mentalists or mentalism. M20.

mentaˈlistic *a.* of, pertaining to, or of the nature of mentalism L19. **mentaˈlistically** *adv.* M20.

mentality /mɛnˈtalɪti/ *n.* L17. [f. as prec. + -ITY.] **1** A mental action. *rare.* L17. **2** Mental ability; intellectual quality, intellectuality. M19. **3**

Mental character or disposition; (an) outlook; a kind or degree of intelligence. L19.

3 R. MACAULAY We should not be at all friendly with a government so little liberal in mentality. U. LE GUIN These Port managers . . tended to acquire the bureaucratic mentality: they said No automatically. J. BAYLEY Hardy and D. H. Lawrence . . use the story . . as a kind of safety-valve, for things in their mentalities which demanded direct . . expression.

mentally /ˈmɛnt(ə)li/ *adv.* LME. [f. as prec. + -LY[2].] In the mind, by a mental operation; as regards the mind.

M. KLINE Leonardo da Vinci. . . Incredibly endowed both physically and mentally. A. HUTSCHNECKER People who commit suicide are mentally sick people. D. MADDEN Mentally, she recited a fragment of poetry. *mentally defective*: see DEFECTIVE *a.* 1c. *mentally deficient*: see DEFICIENT *a.* 3. **mentally handicapped** having a mental handicap.

mentation /mɛnˈteɪʃ(ə)n/ *n.* M19. [f. L *ment-*, *mens* mind + -ATION.] Mental activity.

menthol /ˈmɛnθɒl, -θ(ə)l/ *n.* L19. [f. L *mentha* mint + -OL.] *Chem.* An optically active crystalline terpenoid alcohol with a characteristic cooling odour and taste, obtainable from peppermint and other oils, or by hydrogenation of thymol, and used in medicines (esp. decongestants), perfumes, cigarettes, etc.; 2-isopropyl-5-methylcyclohexanol, $C_{10}H_{19}OH$.

mentholated *a.* treated or impregnated with menthol; containing menthol: M20.

menthone /ˈmɛnθəʊn/ *n.* L19. [f. prec. + -ONE.] *Chem.* An optically active cyclic ketone which is a colourless oily liquid occurring in peppermint and other oils; 2-isopropyl-5-methylcyclohexanone, $C_{10}H_{18}O$.

menticide /ˈmɛntɪsʌɪd/ *n.* M20. [f. L *menti-*, *mens* mind + -CIDE.] The (esp. institutionalized) undermining or destruction of the mind or will.

menticulture /ˈmɛntɪkʌltʃə/ *n. rare.* M19. [f. L *menti-*, *mens* mind + -CULTURE.] The cultivation of the mind.

mentiˈcultural *a.* M19.

mention /ˈmɛnʃ(ə)n/ *n.* ME. [(O)Fr. f. L *mentio(n-)*, f. base of *meminisse* remember, ult. redupl. of base of MIND *n.*[1]: see -ION.] **1** The action or an act of referring to, remarking on, or introducing the name of a person or thing, now *spec.* incidentally, as not obviously essential to the context (foll. by *of*). Orig. in *make mention of* below. ME. **b** [abbrev. of *honourable mention*, *mention in dispatches*, etc.] A formal or official commendatory reference, as in a military dispatch. L19. **2** An indication, a vestige, a trace, a remnant. *obs.* exc. *Sc.* M16.

1 R. L. STEVENSON The mention of his name leads me on to speak of our ship's cook. D. J. ENRIGHT: Q. D. Leavis comes in for favourable mention, too, as an 'astringent and serious reviewer'. E. KUZWAYO There is no mention of the circumstances which preceded my ill-health. S. HASTINGS He distinguished himself by winning a mention in despatches for valour at Sedan. *Marketing Week* There will be no straight advertising . . although any of the shows or places featured will pay a set fee for a mention. HONOURABLE *mention*. **make mention of** refer to, introduce the name of, (in general use now usu. in neg. contexts, as *make no mention of*).

mention /ˈmɛnʃ(ə)n/ *v.* M16. [Fr. *mentionnier*, f. as prec.] **1** *v.t.* Refer to or remark on incidentally; specify by name or otherwise; state incidentally *that*. M16. †**2** *v.i.* Foll. by *of*: refer to, speak of. M16–L18.

1 J. OSBORNE Letters in which I'm not mentioned at all because my name is a dirty word. P. O'DONNELL I wouldn't mind a drink, though, now you mention it. J. BERMAN When Freud's name was mentioned for the Nobel Prize, it was more often for literature. R. ELLMANN He forebore to mention that he planned to stop in Rome. **don't mention it** *colloq.*: indicating that one considers offered thanks or apology to be inappropriate or excessive. *mentioned in dispatches*: see DISPATCH *n.* **not to mention** *rhet.*: introducing a fact or making a reference of primary importance.

mentionable *a.* that can or may be mentioned, worthy of mention, (earlier & more usual in *unmentionable*) M19. **mentioned** *ppl a.* of which mention has been made (now chiefly as 2nd elem. of comb., as *before-mentioned*, *undermentioned*, etc.) L16. **mentioner** *n.* (now *rare*) E17.

mento /ˈmɛntəʊ/ *n.* Pl. **-os**. E20. [Origin unkn.] A Jamaican style of popular music and dance; a song or dance in this style.

mento- /ˈmɛntəʊ/ *comb. form* of L *mentum* chin: see -O-.

mento-Meckelian /-mɛˈkiːlɪən/ *a.* & *n.* (*Anat.*) (designating) a bone in the jaw formed in part by the ossification of Meckel's cartilage L19. **mento-ˈvertical** *a.* & *n.* (designating or pertaining to) the diameter of the head from the menton to the highest point of the vertex L20.

menton /ˈmɛnt(ə)n/ *n.* M20. [Fr., f. as MENTUM.] *Anat.* = GNATHION.

mentor /ˈmɛntɔː/ *n.* M18. [Fr. f. L *Mentor* f. Gk *Mentōr* the guide and adviser of Odysseus' son Telemachus (prob. chosen as a name as f. base meaning 'remember, think, counsel').] An experienced and trusted adviser or guide; a teacher, a tutor.

W. S. CHURCHILL One who possesses unique claims to be our guide and mentor. M. N. COX The trainee will always modify what he learns from his mentors.

mentorial /mɛnˈtɔːrɪəl/ *a.* of or pertaining to a mentor, containing advice M19.

mentri /ˈmɛntri/ *n.* Also (as a title) ***M-***. M19. [Malay f. Skt *mantrī* nom. sing. of *mantrin*: see MANTRI.] In parts of Malaysia and Indonesia: a government minister.

mentri besar /bɪˈsɑː/ a chief minister.

mentum /ˈmɛntəm/ *n.* E19. [L = chin.] **1** *Entomol.* A part of the base of the labium in some insects. E19. **2** *Anat.* The chin. M19. **3** *Bot.* A projection formed by the sepals and the base of the column in some orchids. M19.

menu /ˈmɛnjuː/ *n.* M17. [Fr. = detailed list, use as n. of adj. = small f. L *minutus* MINUTE *a.* In branch I short for *menu peuple*.] **I** †**1** The common people. *rare.* Only in M17.

II 2 A list of the dishes to be served at a banquet or meal or available at a restaurant etc.; a card etc. on which a menu is written or printed. Also, the food served or available. M19. **3** *transf.* A list of things available or for completion. L19. **b** *Computing.* A computer-generated list of available commands, facilities, or other options, usu. displayed onscreen, for selection by the operator. M20.

2 *Journal of Home Economics* Exactly the same menu was served in a large college dining room and at the cafeteria. D. JOHNSON The waiter brought me a menu. 3 H. G. WELLS All the intelligent ones feel baffled at the menu of these degree courses.

Comb.: **menu card** a card on which a menu is written or printed; **menu-driven** *a.* (of a program or computer) operated by making selections from menus.

menudo /mɪˈnuːdəʊ/ *n.* M20. [Mex. Sp., use as n. of adj. = small f. L *minutus* MINUTE *a.*] A spicy Mexican soup made from tripe.

menuet *n.* & *v.* var. of MINUET.

menura /mɪˈn(j)ʊərə/ *n.* Chiefly *Austral.* M19. [mod.L (see below), f. Gk *mēnē* crescent moon + *oura* tail (from the crescent-shaped spots on the tail).] A bird of the genus *Menura*; a lyre-bird.

menus plaisirs /məny plezɪːr/ *n. phr. pl.* L17. [Fr. = small pleasures.] Simple pleasures; small personal expenses or gratifications; fanciful or trifling objects bought with pocket money.

menzil *n.* var. of MANZIL.

Meo /ˈmeɪəʊ/ *n.*[1] & *a.*[1] M19. [Rajasthani.] **A** *n.* Pl. **-os**, same. A member of a people of the Mewat region in NW India (now called Alwar and part of Rajasthan) and neighbouring areas; a Mewati; *spec.* one professing Hinduism. M19. **B** *attrib.* or as *adj.* Of or pertaining to this people. L19.

Meo *n.*[2] & *a.*[2] var. of MIAO.

meow *n.*, *v.*, & *int.* var. of MIAOW.

mepacrine /ˈmɛpəkrɪn, -iːn/ *n.* M20. [f. ME(THOXY- + *-p-* (perh. f. PENTANE) + ACR(ID)INE.] *Pharm.* A tricyclic base derived from acridine, used as an anthelmintic and antimalarial drug. Also called *quinacrine*.

¶A proprietary name for this drug is ATEBRIN.

meperidine /məˈpɛrɪdiːn, -iːn/ *n.* Chiefly *US.* M20. [f. ME(THYL + PI)PERIDINE.] *Pharm.* = PETHIDINE.

mephenesin /məˈfɛnəsɪn/ *n.* M20. [f. ME(THYL + PHEN(YL + CR)ES(OL + -IN[1].] *Pharm.* A phenoxy compound, $CH_3{\cdot}C_6H_4O{\cdot}CH_2CH(OH){\cdot}CH_2OH$, used as a muscle relaxant and tranquillizer.

Mephistophelean /ˌmɛfɪstəˈfiːlɪən/ *a.* Also **-ian**. M20. [f. as next + -AN, -IAN.] Of, pertaining to, or resembling Mephistopheles; fiendish; fatally tempting.

Mephistopheles /mɛfɪˈstɒfɪliːz/ *n.* Also (earlier) †**Mephostophilis, -us**. L16. [The evil spirit to whom Faust in German legend sold his soul, esp. as represented in Marlowe's *Doctor Faustus* (*c* 1590) and Goethe's *Faust* (1808–32).] A fiendish person, a person who entraps another to destruction, a fatal tempter.

Mephistophelian *a.* var. of MEPHISTOPHELEAN.

mephitic /mɪˈfɪtɪk/ *a.* E17. [Late L *mephiticus*, f. as next: see -IC.] Offensive to the smell; (of a vapour or exhalation) pestilential, noxious, poisonous.

Also **mephitical** *a.* E18.

mephitis /mɪˈfʌɪtɪs/ *n.* E18. [L.] A noxious or pestilential emanation, esp. from the earth; an obnoxious or poisonous stench.

mephitism *n.* (now *rare*) evil-smelling poisoning of the air E19.

†**Mephostophilis, -us** *n.* see MEPHISTOPHELES.

meprobamate /mɪˈprəʊbəmeɪt/ *n.* M20. [f. ME(THYL + PRO(PYL + CAR)BAMATE.] *Pharm.* A bitter-tasting carbamate, $CH_3CH_2CH_2C(CH_2{\cdot}O{\cdot}CO{\cdot}NH_2)_2CH_3$, used as a mild tranquillizer.

¶A proprietary name for this drug is MILTOWN.

mepyramine /mɪˈpɪrəmiːn/ *n.* M20. [f. ME(THYL + PYR(IDINE + AMINE.] *Pharm.* A polycyclic substituted amine with antihistamine properties, used to treat allergic conditions.

mer /məː/ *n.* M20. [Back-form. f. POLYMER. Cf. -MER.] *Chem.* The repeating unit in a polymeric molecule.

mer- /məː/ *pref.* [After MERMAID.] Of the mermaid kind, as *merbaby*, *merchild*, *merman*, *merwoman*, etc.

-mer /mə/ *suff.* [Repr. Gk *meros* part, after *isomer*, *polymer*.] Forming ns. chiefly denoting particular kinds of polymer, as *dimer*, *elastomer*, or isomer, as *epimer*, *tautomer*. Also used with prefixed numeral to denote polymers of a given number of units, as *9-mer*, *16-mer*.

meranti /məˈranti/ *n.* L18. [Malay.] (The hardwood timber of) any of various trees of the genus *Shorea* (family Dipterocarpaceae), native to Indonesia and parts of Malaysia.

merbau /ˈməːbaʊ/ *n.* L18. [Malay.] (The hardwood timber of) either of two leguminous trees, *Intsia bijuga* and *I. palembanica*, native to Malaysia and Indonesia.

merbromin /məˈbrəʊmɪn/ *n.* M20. [f. MER(CURIC + BROM(O- + -IN[1].] *Pharm.* A fluorescein derivative containing bromine and mercury, obtained as greenish iridescent scales which dissolve in water to give a red solution used as an antiseptic.

¶A proprietary name for this drug is MERCUROCHROME.

merc /məːk/ *n. colloq.* M20. [Abbrev. of MERCENARY.] A mercenary soldier.

mercado /məːˈkɑːdəʊ, *foreign* merˈkaðo/ *n.* Pl. **-os** /-əʊz, *foreign* -os/. M19. [Sp. f. L *mercatus* MARKET *n.*] A market in Spain and Spanish-speaking countries.

Mercalli scale /məːˈkalɪ skeɪl/ *n. phr.* E20. [Giuseppe *Mercalli* (1850–1914), It. geologist.] *Geol.* An arbitrary 12-point scale for expressing the intensity of an earthquake at any place.

mercantile /ˈməːk(ə)ntʌɪl/ *a.* M17. [Fr. f. It., f. *mercante* MERCHANT *n.*: see -ILE.] **1** Of or pertaining to merchants or their trade; concerned with the exchange of merchandise; of or pertaining to trade or commerce; commercial. M17. **2** Having payment or gain as the motive; mercenary; fond of bargaining. M18.

1 J. ARBUTHNOT The Expedition of the Argonauts.. was partly mercantile, partly military. G. CRABBE A bill That was not drawn with true mercantile skill. G. J. GOSCHEN Putting aside.. the.. currency altogether, and confining ourselves to the more mercantile part of the question. G. STEINER The new mercantile society.. followed hard on the decay of feudalism. **mercantile marine** the shipping employed in commerce as opp. to war, the merchant navy. 2 **mercantile system** *Hist.*: based on the principles of mercantilism.

mercantilely *adv.* from a mercantile point of view; with regard to business transactions: E19.

mercantilism /ˈməːk(ə)ntʌɪlɪz(ə)m/ *n.* L19. [f. prec. + -ISM.] 1 The mercantile spirit; the principles or practice characteristic of merchants; commercialism. L19. 2 *Hist.* The economic theory that trade generates wealth and is stimulated by the accumulation of bullion, which a government should encourage by promoting exports and restricting imports. L19.

mercantilist *n.* & *a.* (*Hist.*) (*a*) *n.* an advocate of mercantilism; (*b*) *adj.* of or pertaining to mercantilism or mercantilists: M19. **mercantiˈlistic** *a.* of the nature of mercantilism L19.

mercaptan /məˈkapt(ə)n/ *n.* M19. [f. mod.L (*corpus*) *mercurium captans* lit. 'seizing mercury'.] *Chem.* Any of a series of organic compounds containing a sulphydryl group, ·SH, many of which have a strong, unpleasant odour; a thioalcohol, a thiol.

mercaptide *n.* a salt of a mercaptan, containing the anion RS^- where R is an alkyl or aryl group M19.

mercapto- /məˈkaptəʊ/ *comb. form.* Bef. a vowel also **mercapt-**. Also as attrib. adj. **mercapto**. [f. MERCAPTAN + -O-.] *Chem.* Designating or containing the radical ·SH (or a substituted form of this).

mercaptoˈpurine *n.* (*Pharm.*) any of various mercapto derivatives of purine; *spec.* 6-mercaptopurine, $C_5H_4N_4S$, a yellow cytotoxic agent used esp. to treat leukaemia in children: M20. **mercapturic** /məːkapˈtjʊərɪk/ *a.*: *mercapturic acid*, any of various acids of formula $RSCH_2CH(NH{\cdot}CO{\cdot}CH_3)COOH$ (where R is an aryl group), some of which are excreted in the urine as detoxication products of aromatic compounds L19.

Mercator /məːˈkeɪtə/ *n.* M17. [Gerhardus *Mercator*, Latinized name of Gerhard Kremer (1512–94), Flemish cartographer.] 1 Used *attrib.* and in *possess.* with ref. to an orthomorphic cylindrical map projection in which meridians are represented by equidistant straight lines at right angles to the equator and any course that follows a constant compass bearing is represented by a straight line. M17. 2 (A map drawn on) Mercator's projection. L19.

1 R. HINKS The great distortion in the north and south makes Mercator's projection.. unsuitable for a land map. *transverse Mercator*: see TRANSVERSE *a.* 2 A. H. ROBINSON The poles.. are 'at' infinity on the conventional Mercator.

mercatorial /məːkəˈtɔːrɪəl/ *a.*[1] Now *rare.* L17. [f. L *mercatorius*, f. *mercator*, f. *mercari* to trade + -AL[1].] Of or pertaining to merchants or merchandise; mercantile.

Mercatorial /məːkəˈtɔːrɪəl/ *a.*[2] L19. [f. MERCATOR + -IAL.] Of, pertaining to, or derived from Mercator or Mercator's projection.

mercatory /ˈməːkət(ə)ri/ *a. rare.* M17. [f. as MERCATORIAL *a.*[1]: see -ORY[2].] = MERCATORIAL *a.*[1]

mercement /ˈməːsm(ə)nt/ *n.* Long *obs.* exc. *Sc.* Also **merci-** /ˈməːsɪ-/, **†mercia-**. ME. [Aphet. f. AMERCEMENT, AMERCIAMENT.] = AMERCEMENT. Also, judgement, mercy.

mercenary /ˈməːsɪn(ə)ri/ *n.* & *a.* LME. [L *mercenarius*, earlier *-nn-*, f. *merces, merced-* reward, wages: see MERCY, -ARY[1].] A *n.* 1 A person who works merely for money or other material reward; a hireling, a mercenary person. Now *rare* or *obs.* LME. 2 A person who receives payment for his or her services; *spec.* a professional soldier serving a foreign power. E16.

B *adj.* 1 Working or done merely for money or other material reward; actuated or characterized by self-interest; motivated by desire for money or other material reward. M16. 2 Hired, serving for wages or hire, now *spec.* as a soldier for a foreign power. L16. †3 Salaried, stipendiary. M17–L18.

1 H. JAMES I might improve my fortune by some other means than by making a mercenary marriage. A. E. HOUSMAN These.. Followed their mercenary calling, And took their wages and are dead. A. WEST The activities of mercenary and unscrupulous journalists. 2 JOHN BROOKE As the British could not raise their own army they had to use mercenary troops.

mercenarian /məːsɪˈnɛːrɪən/ *a.* & *n.* (*rare*) †(*a*) *n.* a mercenary, a hired soldier; (*b*) *adj.* of or pertaining to mercenaries: L16. **mercenarily** *adv.* E17. **mercenariness** *n.* E17. **mercenarism** *n.* service as a mercenary L20.

mercer /ˈməːsə/ *n.* ME. [AN *mercer*, (O)Fr. *mercier* f. Proto-Romance, f. L *merc-*, *merx* merchandise: see -ER[2].] A dealer in textile fabrics, esp. silks, velvets, and other costly materials.

mercerize /ˈməːsərʌɪz/ *v.t.* Also **-ise**. M19. [f. John *Mercer* (d. 1866) of Accrington, NW England, said to have discovered the process in 1844 + -IZE.] Treat (cotton fabric or thread) under tension with a solution usu. of sodium or potassium hydroxide to give greater strength and impart lustre.

merceriˈzation *n.* E20.

mercery /ˈməːs(ə)ri/ *n.* ME. [(O)Fr. *mercerie*, f. *mercier*: see MERCER, -Y[3].] 1 *collect.* The wares sold by a mercer. ME. †2 *the Mercery*, the Mercers' Company; the trade in mercery; the part of a city where this is carried on. LME–M17. 3 A mercer's shop. L19.

merchandise /ˈməːtʃ(ə)ndʌɪz/ *n.* ME. [(O)Fr. *marchandise*, f. *marchand* MERCHANT *n.*: see -ISE[2].] 1 The action of buying and selling goods or commodities for profit; the business of a merchant; commerce, trading. *arch.* ME. 2 *sing.* & †*pl.* The commodities of commerce; goods to be bought and sold. ME. †b A kind of merchandise; a saleable commodity. LME–M19.

Phrases: **make (a) merchandise of** *arch.* deal or traffic in, esp. inappropriately in something which should not be the subject of trade.

merchandise /ˈməːtʃ(ə)ndʌɪz/ *v.* LME. [f. the n.] 1 *v.i.* Trade, traffic; engage in the business of a merchant. *arch.* LME. 2 *v.t.* Buy and sell; barter; traffic in. *arch.* M16. 3 *v.t.* Put on the market, promote the sale of (goods etc.); *transf.* advertise (an idea or person), publicize. E20.

3 A. E. STEVENSON That you can merchandise candidates.. like breakfast cereal.. is.. the ultimate indignity to the democratic process.

merchandisable *a.* = MERCHANTABLE (*rare* bef. 20) L15. **merchandiser** *n.* (*a*) a person who merchandises something or someone; (*b*) a display stand for merchandise: L16.

merchandry /ˈməːtʃ(ə)ndri/ *n.* Long *arch.* LME. [(O)Fr. *march(ë)anderie*, f. *marchand* MERCHANT *n.*: see -RY.] Trade, commerce; the business of a merchant.

merchant /ˈməːtʃ(ə)nt/ *n.* & *a.* ME. [OFr. *march(ë)ant*, later (& mod.) *marchand*, f. Proto-Romance pres. ppl stem of vb f. L *mercari* to trade, f. *merc-*, *merx* merchandise: see -ANT[1].] A *n.* 1 A person whose occupation is the purchase and sale of goods or commodities for profit; (without specifying wd usu.) a wholesale trader, esp. dealing with foreign countries; (esp. *Sc.*, *north.*, *US*, & as 2nd elem. of comb.) a retail trader, a shopkeeper. ME. b A buyer, a customer. *Sc.* L17. 2 A fellow, a person. Now usu. w. specifying wd, a person with an interest in or partiality for the thing specified. *slang.* M16. 3 A trading vessel, a merchantman. L16. †4 A supercargo. Only in 17.

1 *coal-merchant, corn-merchant, wine-merchant*, etc. 2 G. SIMS Sorry to be such a gloom merchant. *speed merchant* etc.

Phrases: **merchant of death** a person who makes a profession of war; *spec.* (*a*) a dealer in armaments; (*b*) a mercenary soldier.

B *adj.* (*attrib.* & *postpositive*). 1 Connected with merchandise; relating to trade or commerce. Chiefly in *law-merchant, statute-merchant*. LME. 2 (Of a ship) serving for the transport of merchandise; of or pertaining to the mercantile marine. LME. 3 (Of a town) occupied in commerce, commercial; consisting of merchants. LME.

Special collocations & comb.: **merchant-adventurer** *Hist.* a merchant engaged in the organization and dispatch of trading expeditions overseas and the establishment of factories and trading stations in foreign countries; a member of an association of such merchants incorporated by royal charter or other lawful authority. **merchant bank** a bank whose main business is the providing of long-term credit and the support and financing of commercial enterprises. **merchant banker** a person engaged in merchant banking; in *pl.* also, a merchant bank as a firm. **merchant banking** the activity of a merchant bank; the provision of commercial loans and financing. **merchant-bar** a bar of merchant iron. **merchant fleet** a fleet of merchant ships, a merchant navy. **merchant guild** a (medieval) guild of merchants. **merchant iron** iron in finished bars, ready for sale. **merchantman** (*a*) *arch.* a merchant, a trader; (*b*) a ship conveying merchandise, a vessel of the mercantile marine. **merchant marine** (chiefly *US*) the merchant navy, the mercantile marine. **†merchant mill** *US* a mill engaged in the grinding of grain for wholesale selling. **merchant navy** a fleet or number of ships used in trade and not for purposes of war, a country's mercantile marine. **merchant prince** a merchant of princely wealth and munificence. **merchant-princely** *a.* characteristic of a merchant prince. **merchant seaman**: serving in a merchant ship or merchant navy. **merchant service** the merchant navy, the mercantile marine. *merchant stapler*: see STAPLER *n.*[1] 1. **†merchant-stranger** a merchant from another country; a foreign trader. **merchant-tailor** *Hist.* a tailor who supplies the materials of which his goods are made; a member of the company of such tailors. **merchant-venturer** *Hist.* = *merchant-adventurer* above.

merchanthood *n.* (*rare*) the quality or condition of being a merchant M19. **merchantlike** *a.* & *adv.* (*a*) *adj.* resembling or befitting a merchant; formerly also, of or pertaining to merchants or commerce, mercantile; (*b*) *adv.* after the manner of a merchant: LME. **†merchantly** *a.* of, pertaining to, or characteristic of a merchant L16–M18. **merchantry** *n.* (*a*) the business of a merchant; trade, commercial dealings; (*b*) merchants collectively: L18.

merchant /ˈməːtʃ(ə)nt/ *v.* LME. [(O)Fr. *march(ë)ander* (mod. *marchander*), f. as prec.] 1 *v.i.* Trade as a merchant. Formerly also, bargain, haggle. Now chiefly as *merchanting* vbl n. & ppl a. LME. 2 *v.t.* Trade or deal in; buy and sell. Now *rare.* E16.

merchantable /ˈməːtʃ(ə)ntəb(ə)l/ *a.* L15. [f. prec. + -ABLE.] 1 Suitable or prepared for purchase or sale; that may or can be bought or sold; saleable; marketable. L15. †2 Of or pertaining to trade; commercial. E–M17.

merchantaˈbility *n.* L19. **merchantableness** *n.* M18.

merchet /ˈməːtʃɪt/ *n. obs.* exc. *Hist.* ME. [AN = ONFr. MARKET *n.*] A fine paid by a tenant or bondsman to his overlord for liberty to give his daughter in marriage.

merciable /ˈməːsɪəb(ə)l/ *a.* Long *arch. rare.* ME. [OFr., f. as MERCY: see -ABLE.] Merciful, compassionate.

†merciament *n.* see MERCEMENT.

Mercian /ˈməːsɪən, ˈməːʃ(ə)n/ *n.* & *a.* E16. [f. med.L *Mercia* f. OE *Merċe, Mierċe* (pl.) lit. 'borderers', f. Gmc base of MARCH *n.*[2], MARK *n.*[1]: see -AN.] A *n.* 1 A native or inhabitant of the Anglo-Saxon kingdom of Mercia in central England. E16. 2 The (Anglian) dialect of Old English spoken in Mercia. L19. B *adj.* Of or pertaining to Mercia or its dialect. E17.

merciful /ˈməːsɪfʊl, -f(ə)l/ *a.* ME. [f. MERCY + -FUL.] Having, feeling, or exercising mercy; characterized by mercy; compassionate; affording relief from misery etc.

DRYDEN God is infinitely merciful. G. K. CHESTERTON The world was growing more merciful and therefore no one would ever desire to kill. E. PIZZEY When you get to my age, death really is a merciful release. J. MORTIMER There was a merciful gap in Leslie's speech, into which the Chairman hurried to pour oil.

mercifully *adv.* (*a*) in a merciful manner; as a mercy, through (God's) mercy; (*b*) *colloq.* (modifying a sentence) it is a mercy (that), fortunately: ME. **mercifulness** *n.* LME.

†mercify *v.t. rare.* L16–M18. [f. MERCY + -FY.] Pity, extend mercy to.

merciless /ˈməːsɪlɪs/ *a.* & *adv.* LME. [f. MERCY + -LESS.] **A** *adj.* **1** Without mercy; showing no mercy; pitiless, unrelenting. LME. **†2** Obtaining no mercy. LME–M16.

1 L. STEPHEN A doggrel epitaph . . turned his fine phrases into merciless ridicule. A. HUTSCHNECKER The merciless demands of reality. U. BENTLEY A merciless creature, glorying in the heartache of her rivals.

†B *adv.* Mercilessly. LME–M16.

mercilessly *adv.* E17. **mercilessness** *n.* L16.

merciment *n.* see MERCEMENT.

Merckani *n.* var. of AMERICANI.

mercurate /ˈməːkjʊreɪt/ *v.t.* E20. [f. MERCURY + -ATE[3].] *Chem.* Convert into a mercury derivative; introduce mercury into as a substituent, esp. in an aromatic ring.

mercuˈration *n.* the process of mercurating or of becoming mercurated E20.

mercurial /məːˈkjʊərɪəl/ *a.* & *n.* Also (now chiefly in senses A.1, 2) **M-**. LME. [(O)Fr. *mercuriel* or (in sense B.1) *mercurial* or L *mercurialis*, f. *Mercurius*: see MERCURY, -AL[1].] **A** *adj.* **1** Of or pertaining to the planet Mercury; *Astrol.* influenced by Mercury, proceeding from the influence of Mercury. Cf. MERCURIAN *a.* 3. LME. **2** Of or pertaining to the god Mercury. Now *rare.* L15. **3** Born under the planet Mercury; having the qualities (identical with those assigned to or supposed to be inspired by the god Mercury) supposed to result from such a nativity, as eloquence, ingenuity, aptitude for commerce. Now *esp.* lively, sprightly, ready-witted, volatile, changeable, (commonly understood as alluding to the properties of the metal mercury). L16. **†4** *Alch.* Pertaining to or consisting of mercury, the elementary principle. E–M17. **5** Of or pertaining to the metal mercury or quicksilver; consisting of or containing mercury; *Med.* (now *rare*, of a disease, a symptom) produced by the presence of mercury. M17.

3 J. K. GALBRAITH The most mercurial source of spending . . has . . been recognised to be that for business investment. C. PRIEST She was mercurial, able to change her mind or her mood.

B *n.* **†1** Any of the plants called mercury (see MERCURY 6). LME–M17. **†2** A person born under the planet Mercury or having the qualities supposed to result from such a nativity; a lively, sprightly, ready-witted, or volatile person. L16–L17. **3** Any compound, esp. a drug or medicine, that contains mercury. L17.

mercurialism *n.* (*Med.*) (chronic) mercury poisoning E19. **mercurialist** *n.* †(*a*) = MERCURIAL *n.* 2; (*b*) (*obs.* exc. *Hist.*) a medical practitioner who advocated the use of drugs containing mercury, esp. in the treatment of syphilis: M16. **mercuriˈality** *n.* †(*a*) that part of something consisting of or containing mercury; (*b*) the condition of being mercurial; liveliness, volatility: L15. **mercurialiˈzation** *n.* (now *rare*) the action of treating something with mercury; the condition of being mercurialized: M19. **mercurialize** *v.* (now *rare*) †(*a*) *v.i.* & *t.* (w. *it*) behave in a mercurial manner; (*b*) *v.t.* subject to the action of mercury; treat with mercury: E17. **mercurially** *adv.* (*a*) in a mercurial manner, volatilely; (*b*) by a mercurial process: M17. **mercurialness** *n.* (*rare*) E19.

Mercurian /məːˈkjʊərɪən/ *a.* & *n.* Also **m-**. L16. [f. MERCURY + -AN.] **A** *adj.* **†1** = MERCURIAL *a.* 3. L16–L17. **2** Of or pertaining to the god Mercury; = MERCURIAL *a.* 2. E18. **3** *Astron.* Of or pertaining to the planet Mercury. Cf. MERCURIAL *a.* 1. L19. **B** *n.* **1** A person born under the planet Mercury. L16. **2** An (imagined) inhabitant of the planet Mercury. M19.

mercuric /məːˈkjʊərɪk/ *a.* E19. [f. MERCURY + -IC.] *Chem.* Of or containing mercury in the divalent state.

mercurification /məːˌkjʊrɪfɪˈkeɪʃ(ə)n, məːˌkjʊə-/ *n.* Now *rare* or *obs.* L17. [f. MERCURY + -FICATION.] **1** Orig. (*Alch.*), the action or process of obtaining the mercurial principle of a metal. Later, the extraction of metallic mercury from its ore. L17. **2** Treatment with mercury. M19.

†mercurified *a.* that has undergone mercurification L17–L18.

Mercurochrome /məːˈkjʊərəkrəʊm/ *n.* Chiefly *N. Amer.* Also **m-**. E20. [f. MERCURY + -O- + Gk *khrōma* colour.] *Pharm.* (Proprietary name for) the drug merbromin.

mercurous /ˈməːkjʊrəs/ *a.* M19. [f. MERCURY + -OUS.] *Chem.* Of or containing mercury in the monovalent state.

mercury /ˈməːkjʊri/ *n.* In branches I, IV usu. **M-**. ME. [L *Mercurius* (f. *merc-*, *merx* merchandise), a Roman god, identified from an early period with the Greek Hermes, the god of eloquence and dexterity, protector of traders and thieves, presider over roads, messenger of the gods, etc.] **I 1** The planet which is the nearest of the major planets to the sun. ME. **2** *Her.* The tincture purpure in the fanciful blazon of arms of sovereign houses. *obs.* exc. *Hist.* M16. **II 3** A heavy silvery-white metallic chemical element, atomic no. 80, which is liquid at room temperature, dissolves other metals to form amalgams, and is used in thermometers and barometers (symbol Hg). Also called *quicksilver*. LME. **b** The column of mercury in a barometer or thermometer; atmospheric pressure or temperature indicated by this, esp. as rising or falling. E18. **c** The metal or one of its compounds prepared for medicinal use. L18. **4** *Alch.* One of the elementary principles of which all substances were supposed to be compounded. L15. **†5** *fig.* Spirit, liveliness; volatility of temperament, inconstancy; wittiness. M17–L18. **III 6a** The pot-herb Good King Henry. LME. **b** Either of two plants of the spurge family, with inconspicuous greenish flowers and opposite toothed leaves, *Mercurialis perennis* (in full *dog's mercury*), a perennial woodland plant, and *Mercurialis annua* (in full *annual mercury*), a garden weed. M16. **IV 7** A statue or image of the god Mercury, usu. represented as a young man with winged sandals and hat, bearing a caduceus. Formerly *spec.*, = HERM. L16. **8a** A messenger, a bringer of news. Also, a go-between. L16. **b** A guide or conductor on the road. Now *rare* or *obs.* L16. **†c** A nimble person; a dexterous thief. L16–E17. **†d** A hawker of pamphlets etc. M17–E18. **9** A newspaper. Freq. (now only) in titles. M17.

3b MILLIMETRE *of mercury*.

Comb.: **mercury arc** (*a*) an electric discharge through mercury vapour; (*b*) = *mercury vapour lamp* below; **mercury gilding**: using an amalgam of gold and mercury from which the mercury is driven off by heat; **mercury lamp** = *mercury vapour lamp* below; **mercury pool** a mass of liquid mercury, esp. used as an electrode; *mercury sublimate*: see SUBLIMATE *n.* 1. **mercury vapour** a vapour of mercury atoms or ions above liquid mercury or at low pressure; *mercury vapour lamp*, a lamp in which bluish light (rich in ultraviolet) is produced by a mercury arc, the envelope often being coated with a phosphor to produce more visible light (cf. FLUORESCENT *lamp*); *mercury vapour pump*, a pump for producing high vacuums by entraining molecules of the gas to be evacuated in a jet of mercury vapour.

mercy /ˈməːsi/ *n.* & *a.* ME. [(O)Fr. *merci* f. L *merces*, *merced-* reward, wages, revenue, in Chr.L used for *misericordia* pity.] **A** *n.* **1** Forbearance and compassion shown to a powerless person, esp. an offender, or to one with no claim to receive kindness; kind and compassionate treatment in a case where severity is merited or expected. ME. **b** *spec.* God's pitiful forbearance and forgiveness of sins. ME. **c** *spec.* Clemency or forbearance shown by a conqueror or absolute ruler. ME. **2** Disposition to forgive or show compassion; compassionateness, mercifulness. ME. **3** In *ellipt.* & as *int.* Asking for mercy or (also *mercy me!*, *mercy on us!*, *for mercy's sake!*, *God-a-mercy!*, *lord-a-mercy!*) expr. surprise, fear, etc. ME. **4** An act of mercy; an event or circumstance calling for special thankfulness; a blessing, a relief. ME. **5** = AMERCEMENT. *obs.* exc. *Hist.* ME.

1 BURKE Their enemies will fall upon them . . and show them no mercy. 2 D. HAMMETT I've thrown myself on your mercy, told you that without your help I'm utterly lost. *Times* The process of sovietization has been applied to the Baltic States without mercy. 4 C. BRONTË What a mercy you are shod with velvet, Jane! JOYCE Its a mercy we werent all drowned.

Phrases: **†at mercy** absolutely in the power of a victor or superior; liable to punishment or hurt at the hands of another; on sufferance. **at the mercy of** wholly in the power of, at the discretion or disposal of; liable to danger or harm from. **†cry (a person) mercy** beg the pardon or forgiveness of. **†deed of mercy** = *work of mercy* below. ERRAND *of mercy*. **have mercy on** or **upon** show mercy to. **†in mercy** absolutely in one's power as the victor or superior. **leave to the mercy of** leave at the mercy of, expose to probable danger or harm from. *Lord have mercy (on us)*: see LORD *n.* **mercy sakes!** *US* (expr. surprise, fear, etc.) for mercy's sake! *prerogative of mercy*: see PREROGATIVE *n.* 1. *sin one's mercies*: see SIN *v.* 2. **Sister of Mercy** a member of a Roman Catholic sisterhood dedicated to works of mercy; *pop.* a member of any nursing sisterhood. **small mercy** a minor piece of good fortune (usu. in *pl.*). *tender mercies*: see TENDER *a.* & *n.*[3] *thankful for small mercies*: see THANKFUL 1. **work of mercy** an act of compassion towards a suffering fellow-creature, *spec.* each of seven spiritual and seven corporal works enumerated in medieval theology.

Comb.: **mercy-seat** the golden covering placed upon the Ark of the Covenant, regarded as the resting-place of God; the throne of God in Heaven.

B *attrib.* or as *adj.* Administered or performed out of mercy or desire to relieve suffering; motivated by compassion. M20.

Guardian Prisoners of war freed by the Communists were making mercy flights home . . to be with their families. P. DEVLIN A murderer . . can be one of many types ranging from the sadist to the mercy-killer.

merd /məːd/ *n.* L15. [f. as next.] A piece or ball of excrement.

merde /mɛrd/ *n.* M20. [Fr. f. L *merda*.] Excrement, dung. Also (*slang*) as *int.*, expr. annoyance, exasperation, surprise, etc.

merdeka /məːˈdeɪkə/ *n.* M20. [Malay.] In Malaysia and Indonesia: freedom, independence.

merdivorous /məːˈdɪv(ə)rəs/ *a. rare.* M19. [f. L *merda* excrement + -VOROUS.] Chiefly *Entomol.* Coprophagous.

mere /mɪə/ *n.*[1] [OE *mere* corresp. to OS *meri* sea (Du. *meer* sea, pool), OHG *mari*, *meri* (G *Meer*), ON *marr* sea, Goth. *mari-*, f. Gmc f. IE base also of Old Ch. Slav. *morje* (Russ. *more*), L *mare*.] **1** The sea. Long *obs.* exc. in *comb.* (cf. MER-). OE. **†b** An arm of the sea. L16–L17. **2** A sheet of standing water; a lake, a pond. Now chiefly *literary* & *dial.* OE. **3** A marsh, a fen. *obs.* exc. *dial.* E17.

Comb. (cf. MER-): **†mereswine** a dolphin, a porpoise.

mere /mɪə/ *n.*[2] & *v.* Now chiefly *dial.* Also **mear**. [OE (*ġe*)*mǣre* = MDu. *mēre*, ON (*landa*)*mæri* landmark, f. Gmc, perh. rel. to L *murus* wall.] **A** *n.* A boundary; an object indicating a boundary, a landmark; *spec.* a ridge of uncultivated land or a road serving as a boundary. OE.

Comb.: **meresman** a person appointed to find out the exact boundaries of a parish etc.; **merestone** a stone set up as a landmark.

B *v.* **1** *v.t.* Mark *out* boundaries on (land). Now usu., record the position of (a boundary) by specifying its relation to or *to* a visible feature on the ground. OE. **†2** *v.i.* Abut *upon*; be bounded *by*. L16–E18.

mere /ˈmɛri/ *n.*[3] E19. [Maori.] A Maori war-club, *esp.* one made of greenstone.

mere /mɪə/ *a.* & *adv.* LME. [AN *meer* (in legal uses), OFr. *mier* or its source L *merus*.] **A** *adj.* **†1** Pure, unmixed; undiluted. LME–M19. **2** Done, performed, or exercised without help; sole. LME. **3** That is what it is in the full sense of the term; absolute, entire, sheer, perfect, downright. Now *rare*. LME. **4** Having no greater extent, range, value, power, or importance than the designation implies; that is barely or only what it is said to be; (chiefly *pred.*) insignificant, ordinary, foolish, inept. L16.

3 C. ISHERWOOD It is a mere waste of time even pretending to teach Frl. Hippi anything. 4 J. M. MURRY The mere remembering of great works is not knowledge of them. M. DICKENS Sissons, who didn't count, because she was the Junior and mere. C.

MILNE A tiny push, the merest fraction of my full weight. J. BARNES The great Gothic cathedrals .. had the power to convert by their mere presence. T. PARKS A mere piece of foil paper.

Special collocations: **mere right** *Law* (a) right as distinguished from possession.

†**B** *adv.* Merely. LME–M17.

mereness *n.* (*rare*) †(*a*) purity; (*b*) the state or quality of being merely something or of being small or insignificant: M17.

-mere /mɪə/ *suff.* [Repr. Gk *meros* part.] Chiefly *Biol.* Forming ns. w. the sense 'part, segment', as *blastomere, centromere, metamere.*

mère /mɛːr, mɛː/ *n.* M19. [Fr. = mother.] The mother, elder: appended to a name to distinguish between a mother and daughter of the same name.

M. LOWRY Taskerson mère had taken a fancy to the French boy.

Meredithian /mɛrɪˈdɪθɪən/ *a.* & *n.* Also **-ean**. L19. [f. *Meredith* (see below) + -IAN, -EAN.] **A** *adj.* Of, pertaining to, or characteristic of the English novelist and poet George Meredith (1828–1909) or his work. L19. **B** *n.* An admirer or student of Meredith or his work. L19.

mereing *n.* var. of MERING.

merel *n.* var. of MERRILL.

merely /ˈmɪəli/ *adv.* LME. [f. MERE *a.* + -LY².] †**1** Without admixture or qualification; purely; without the help of others. LME–M17. †**2** Absolutely, entirely; quite, altogether. E16–L18. **b** As a matter of fact, actually. L16–E17. **3** Without any other quality, reason, purpose, view, etc.; only (what is referred to) and nothing more. Often preceded by *not.* L16.

2 SHAKES. *Haml.* Things rank and gross in nature Possess it merely. 3 C. P. SNOW The interests I have been describing merely add glow and savour to .. a pleasant time. D. FRANCIS The contents looked merely like ordinary files. Z. TOMIN I am .. shivering and .. not merely because the weather has changed. D. ATHILL Some of his activities had a purpose beyond that of merely passing the time. M. BRETT This process constituted .. theft rather than merely .. market custom.

merengue /məˈrɛŋgeɪ/ *n.* Also **meringue** /məˈraŋ/. M20. [Amer. Sp. f. Haitian creole *méringue* lit. 'meringue' f. Fr.] A dance of Dominican and Haitian origin, with alternating long and short stiff-legged steps; a piece of music for this dance, usu. in duple and triple time.

mereology /mɛrɪˈɒlədʒi/ *n.* M20. [Fr., irreg. f. Gk *meros* part + -OLOGY.] *Philos.* The abstract study of the relations between parts and wholes.

merese /məˈriːz/ *n.* E20. [Origin unkn.] A rib, flange, or collar on the stem of a glass vessel.

merestead *n.* see MIDSTEAD.

meretrices *n.pl.* see MERETRIX.

meretrician /mɛrɪˈtrɪʃ(ə)n/ *n.* & *a. rare.* M17. [f. as next + -AN.] **A** *n.* A prostitute. M17. †**B** *adj.* = MERETRICIOUS 1. Only in E18.

meretricious /mɛrɪˈtrɪʃəs/ *a.* E17. [f. L *meretricius* (f. *meretric-*, MERETRIX) + -OUS.] **1** Of, pertaining to, characteristic of, or befitting a prostitute; having the character of a prostitute. E17. **2** Showily but falsely attractive. M17.

2 R. MANNING It is possible to be sentimental, meretricious and even downright dishonest in painting or in music. A. LURIE Like a stage set after the lights have been turned off, Key West had lost its meretricious charm.

meretriciously *adv.* M18. **meretriciousness** *n.* E18.

meretrix /ˈmɛrɪtrɪks/ *n. literary.* Pl. **-trices** /-trɪsiːz/, **-trixes**. ME. [L, f. *mereri* serve for hire: see MERIT *n.*, -TRIX.] A prostitute.

merganser /məːˈganzə, -s-/ *n.* M17. [mod.L, f. *mergus* diver + *anser* goose.] Any of a group of large holarctic diving ducks of the genus *Mergus*, with long narrow serrated bills hooked at the tip. Cf. *sawbill* s.v. SAW *n.*¹

common merganser = GOOSANDER. **hooded merganser** a crested N. American merganser, *Mergus cucullatus*. **red-breasted merganser** a crested merganser, *Mergus serrator*, of N. America and northern Eurasia. **white merganser** = SMEW.

merge /məːdʒ/ *v.* & *n.* M17. [L *mergere* dip, plunge; in legal senses through AN *merger.*] **A** *v.* †**1** *v.t.* Immerse (esp. oneself). Foll. by *in.* M17–M19. **2** *v.t.* In *Law*, incorporate or embody (an estate, title, etc.) in a greater or superior one; *gen.* cause (something) to be absorbed into something else, so as to lose its own character or identity; join or blend, esp. gradually; combine, amalgamate. Foll. by *in*, (occas.) *into, with.* E18. **3** *v.i.* In *Law*, be incorporated or embodied in a greater title, estate, etc.; *gen.* be absorbed and disappear, lose character or identity by absorption into something else; join or blend, esp. gradually; combine, amalgamate. Foll. by *in, into, with.* E18.

2 COLERIDGE The patriotism of the citizen ennobles, but does not merge, the individual energy of the man. W. S. CHURCHILL The war between Britain and Spain .. was soon merged in a general European struggle. B. BAINBRIDGE His face was a mess. The stings and constellations of pimples were merged. B. PYM As if trying to merge herself with the rows of books behind her. *Independent* Bromley Council wants to merge the school with nearby Ramsden Boys'. 3 M. RENAULT The next few evenings all merged for him later into a common memory. M. BRADBURY The groups that began as separate and compartmentalized begin to merge and mix. H. WILSON The two departments merged in November .. and, inevitably, it became a virtual takeover. T. K. WOLFE So he took that street, but it quickly merged with a narrow side street.

B *n.* An act or instance or merging, a merger. E19.

merˈgee *n.* a participant in a merger M20. **mergence** *n.* the action of merging, the condition of being merged M19.

merger /ˈməːdʒə/ *n.* E18. [AN use as n. of inf.: see prec., -ER⁴.] **1** *Law.* Incorporation or embodiment of a right, estate, contract, action, etc., in another. E18. **2** The combination or consolidation of two commercial companies, organizations, institutions, etc., into one. M19. **3** *gen.* An act of merging; the fact of being merged. L19.

mericarp /ˈmɛrɪkɑːp/ *n.* M19. [Fr. *méricarpe*, irreg. f. Gk *meros* part + *karpos* fruit.] *Bot.* A portion of a fruit which divides to form a perfect fruit; *esp.* either of the two one-seeded carpels which together constitute the cremocarp or fruit in umbelliferous plants.

meridian /məˈrɪdɪən/ *n.* LME. [(O)Fr. *méridien* or L *meridianum* noon, the south, med.L *meridiana* noon, siesta, uses as n. of L *meridianus*: see next. In sense 5 ult. for L *circulus meridianus* meridian circle, tr. Gk *kuklos merēmbrinos.*] **1** Midday, noon. Long *rare.* LME. **2a** A midday rest, a siesta. *obs.* exc. *Hist.* LME. **b** A midday drink. *Sc. obs.* exc. *Hist.* L18. **3** The point at which the sun or a star attains its highest altitude; the zenith. *arch.* LME. **b** *fig.* The point or period of highest development or perfection; full splendour; one's prime of life. L16. †**4** The south. LME–E17. **5** *Astron.* & *Geogr.* A great circle of the celestial sphere which passes through the celestial poles and the zenith of a given place on the earth's surface, or the great circle of the earth which lies in the same plane; that half of the latter circle which extends from pole to pole through a place, corresponding to a line of longitude. Also, a line (on a map, globe, etc.) representing one of these. LME. **b** A graduated ring or half-ring within which an artificial globe is suspended. M17. **c** *Geom.* Any great circle of a sphere that passes through the poles; any line on a surface of revolution that is in a plane with its axis. E18. **6** *transf.* & *fig.* A distinctive locality, situation, or character; *the* tastes, habits, capacities, etc., *of* a particular set of people etc. L16. **7** *Acupuncture.* Any of the pathways in the body along which energy is said to flow, *esp.* each of a set of twelve associated with specific organs. M20.

Phrases: GREENWICH *meridian. inferior meridian*: see INFERIOR *a.* **magnetic meridian** the great circle of the earth that passes through a given point on its surface and the magnetic poles. *prime meridian*: see PRIME *a.*

Comb.: **meridian circle** *n.*¹ a telescope fitted with a graduated circle, by which the right ascension and declination of a star may be determined; **meridian-mark** a mark fixed due north or south of an astronomical instrument, by which it is aligned in the meridian.

meridian /məˈrɪdɪən/ *a.* LME. [(O)Fr. *méridien* or L *meridianus*, f. *meridies* midday, south, f. (by dissimilation) *medius* middle + *dies* day: see -AN.] **1** Of or pertaining to midday or noon. Now *literary.* LME. **2** Of or pertaining to the position, strength, etc., of the sun at midday. LME. †**b** Of supreme excellence; consummate. M17–M18. **c** *fig.* Pertaining to or characteristic of the point or period of highest development or splendour (of a person, institution, etc.). L17. **3** Of, pertaining to, or of the nature of a meridian. LME. **4** Southern, meridional. *rare.* LME.

3 **meridian altitude** the angle between the horizon and a celestial object as it crosses the meridian. **meridian circle** *n.*², **meridian line** = MERIDIAN *n.* 5.

meridional /məˈrɪdɪən(ə)l/ *a.* & *n.* Also **-dia-**. LME. [(O)Fr. *méridional* f. late L *meridionalis*, irreg. f. *meridies* (see prec.) after *septentrionalis* SEPTENTRIONAL.] **A** *adj.* **1** Of or pertaining to the south; situated in the south; southern, southerly. LME. **b** *spec.* Pertaining to or characteristic of the inhabitants of southern Europe. M19. †**2** Of or pertaining to the position of the sun at midday; pertaining to or characteristic of midday. LME–M19. **3** Of, pertaining to, or aligned with a meridian. M16. **4** Of a marking or structure on a roundish body: lying in a plane with the axis of the body. Cf. MERIDIAN *n.* 5c. M17. **B** *n.* A native or inhabitant of the south. Now *spec.* a native or inhabitant of the south of France. L16.

meridioˈnality *n.* the state of being on the meridian, or aligned along a meridian M17. **meridionally** *adv.* in or along a meridian or meridians; north and south; in the direction of the poles (of a magnet): E17.

mering /ˈmɪərɪŋ/ *n.* Now chiefly *dial.* Also **mear-, mere-**. M16. [f. MERE *v.* + -ING¹.] = MERE *n.*²

meringue /məˈraŋ; *foreign* mərɛ̃g (*pl. same*)/ *n.*¹ E18. [Fr., of unkn. origin.] A confection made chiefly of sugar and whites of eggs whipped together and baked crisp; a small cake or shell of this, usu. decorated or filled with cream.

meringue (à la) Chantilly a meringue filled with sweetened whipped cream.

meringue *n.*² var. of MERENGUE.

merino /məˈriːnəʊ/ *n.* & *a.* Pl. of n. **-os**. L18. [Sp., of unkn. origin.] **1** (Designating or pertaining to) a breed of sheep prized for the fineness of its wool, originating in Spain; (designating) a sheep of this breed. L18. **b** *pure merino*, (*a*) an early immigrant to Australia with no convict origins, a member of a leading family in Australian society, a person of fine breeding or good character; (*b*) *attrib.* first-class, well-bred, excellent. *Austral. slang.* E19. **2** (Of) a soft fine material resembling cashmere, made of wool (orig. merino wool) or wool and cotton. E19. **b** A garment, esp. a dress or shawl, made of this; *W. Indies* a vest. M19. **3** (Of) a fine woollen yarn used in the manufacture of hosiery and knitwear. L19.

merise /məˈriːz/ *n.* E18. [Fr., perh. blend of *amer* bitter, *cerise* cherry. Cf. earlier MERRY *n.*] A kind of small black cherry; the tree that bears this.

merisis /ˈmɛrɪsɪs/ *n.* M20. [f. Gk *meris* (also *meros*) part, after *auxesis.*] *Biol.* Growth by cellular multiplication.

merismatic /mɛrɪzˈmatɪk/ *a.* M19. [f. Gk *merismat-*, *merisma* separated part, f. *merizein* divide into parts, f. *meros* part: see -ATIC.] *Biol.* Of, pertaining to, exhibiting, or designating division into portions by the formation of internal partitions.

merismoid /məˈrɪzmɔɪd/ *a.* M19. [f. Gk *merisma* (see prec.) + -OID.] *Bot.* Of a sporophore, esp. an agaric: having a branched or laciniate pileus.

merispore /ˈmɛrɪspɔː/ *n.* L19. [Irreg. f. Gk *meros* part + SPORE.] *Mycol.* A spore cell in a compound spore.

merissa /məˈrɪsə/ *n.* L19. [Afr. name.] A Sudanese drink made from fermented maize.

meristele /mɛrɪˈstiːl, -ˈstiːli/ *n.* L19. [f. Gk *meris* (also *meros*) part + STELE.] *Bot.* A strand of vascular tissue made up of xylem surrounded by phloem.

meristelic *a.* E20.

meristem /ˈmɛrɪstɛm/ *n.* L19. [Irreg. f. Gk *meristos* divided, divisible, f. *merizein* divide into parts, f. *meros* part, with ending after *phloem*, *xylem*.] *Bot.* A tissue which continues to undergo cell division and differentiation throughout the life of a plant, found esp. in root and shoot apices and in the cambium; merismatic tissue.

meriste'matic *a.* of, pertaining to, or of the nature of meristem L19. **meriste'matically** *adv.* after the manner of meristem L19.

meristic /məˈrɪstɪk/ *a.* L19. [f. Gk *meris* (also *meros*) part + -ISTIC.] *Biol.* Of or relating to the presence or number of similar units, parts, or segments making up a structure.

meristically *adv.* L19.

merit /ˈmɛrɪt/ *n.* ME. [(O)Fr. *mérite* f. L *meritum* price, value, service rendered, use as n. of neut. pa. pple of *merere*, *-ri* earn, deserve, rel. to Gk *meiresthai* obtain as a share, *moira* share, fate, *meros* part.] †1 Deserved reward or punishment. ME–E18. 2 The quality of deserving well or of being entitled to reward or gratitude; claim or title to commendation or esteem; excellence, worth; *spec.* (*a*) *Chr. Theol.* the quality, in actions or persons, of being entitled to future reward from God; (*b*) *Buddhism* & *Jainism* the quality of actions in one of a person's states of existence which helps determine a better succeeding state. ME. b Claim to gratitude, the honour or credit of bringing about (something). Foll. by *of*. Now *rare*. E18. 3 *sing.* & in *pl.* The condition or fact of deserving, deserts. Now *rare*. LME. 4 A thing entitling a person to reward or gratitude. Usu. in *pl.*, *spec.* in *Chr. Theol.*, good works viewed as entitling a person to future reward from God. LME. 5 A point of intrinsic quality; a commendable quality, an excellence, a good point. Earliest in *pl.*, the intrinsic rights and wrongs *of* a matter, esp. a legal case, the intrinsic excellences or defects of something. M16.

2 C. ACHEBE I had had scholarships . . without any godfather's help but purely on my own merit. C. MILNE A single book, one that we feel to have some special merit, not an obvious bestseller but one . . deserving our support. **Order of Merit** an order whose members are admitted for distinguished achievement. 3 A. G. MORTIMER His superabundant merits, which are laid up as a rich treasure for His Church. 5 R. K. NARAYAN Talking about the picture, its merits and demerits. M. N. COX Each case must be judged on its merits. *Observer* It at least has the merit of a certain rough honesty. **make a merit of** account or represent (some action of one's own) as meritorious.

Comb.: **merit increase** an increase in pay for personal ability or achievement; **merit money** money awarded as a merit increase; **merit monger** *arch.* (*contempt.*) a person who seeks to merit salvation or eternal reward by good works; **merit pay** pay awarded as a merit increase; **merit rating** the assessment of an employee's ability to do his or her job; a measurement of this ability; **merit system** the system of giving (promotion in) public office according to the competence of the candidates rather than because of their political affiliations etc.

meritless *a.* L16.

merit /ˈmɛrɪt/ *v.* L15. [(O)Fr. *mériter*, f. as prec.] †1 *v.t.* Reward, recompense. *rare*. L15–E17. 2 *v.t.* Be or become entitled to or worthy of, deserve, (a thing, *to do*); earn by merit. E16. 3 *v.i.* Acquire merit; become entitled to reward, gratitude, or commendation. Now *rare*. E16. 4 *v.i.* Deserve, esp. *well* (*of* a person). L16.

2 R. HOOKER Did they think that men doe merit rewards in heaven by the workes they performe on earth? R. DAHL I asked whether the story was really interesting enough to merit being put on paper. A. HARDING He had been harsh . . to Peter, who had surely done nothing to merit such treatment. *Which?* This iron doesn't merit a recommendation.

meritable *a.* meritorious LME. **meritedly** *adv.* deservedly M17. **meriting** *ppl a.* (now *rare*) that merits (something indicated in the context); deserving, meritorious: E17.

meritocracy /mɛrɪˈtɒkrəsi/ *n.* M20. [f. MERIT *n.* + -O- + -CRACY.] Government or the holding of power by people selected on the basis of merit, *spec.* in a competitive educational system; a society governed by such people or in which such people hold power; a ruling or influential class of educated people.

'meritocrat *n.* & *a.* (*a*) *n.* an adherent of meritocracy, a member of a meritocracy; (*b*) *adj.* belonging to a meritocracy: M20. **merito'cratic** *a.* characterized by meritocracy; of or pertaining to meritocrats or meritocracy: M20.

meritorious /mɛrɪˈtɔːrɪəs/ *a.* LME. [f. L *meritorius*, f. *merere*, *-ri* (see MERIT *n.*) + *-orius* -ORY[2]: see -OUS.] 1 Entitling a person to reward, *spec.* in *Chr. Theol.* future reward from God; deserving reward or gratitude; well-deserving, meriting commendation, having merit (freq. w. implication, though of a limited kind). LME. †2 Earning or deserving some specified good or evil. Foll. by *of*. M16–M18. †3 Given in accordance with merit; merited. L16–M17.

1 B. JOWETT Well-conducted and meritorious citizens. E. F. BENSON This performance, very meritorious in itself, for he played well, had been quite sufficient for him. R. A. KNOX The good works done by the heathen were good works done without the grace of Christ; they could not, therefore, be meritorious.

Special collocations: **meritorious cause** *Chr. Theol.* an action or agent that causes some good or evil result by meriting it.

meritoriously *adv.* (*a*) in a meritorious manner; so as to deserve commendation; †(*b*) so as to acquire merit; †(*c*) deservedly: L15. **meritoriousness** *n.* M17.

Merkani *n.* var. of AMERICANI.

merkin /ˈməːkɪn/ *n.* E17. [App. var. of MALKIN.] 1 An artificial covering of hair for the pubes. Also, an artificial vagina. E17. 2 The female external genitals. M17.

merle /məːl/ *n.*[1] *poet.* Orig. *Sc.* LME. [(O)Fr. f. L *merula*, (post-classical) *-ulus*.] The blackbird, *Turdus merula*.

merle /məːl/ *a.* & *n.*[2] E20. [f. *merled*, *mirled* vars. of MARLED *a.*] (A dog, esp. a collie) having blue-grey fur speckled or streaked with black.

merled *a.* var. of MARLED.

merlin /ˈməːlɪn/ *n.* ME. [AN *merilun* aphet. f. OFr. *esmirillon* (mod. *émirillon*) augm. of *esmiril* f. Frank. wd corresp. to OHG *smerlo*, *smiril* (G *Schmerl*).] A small falcon, *Falco columbarius*, of N. America and northern Eurasia, with pale brown streaked underparts, a barred tail, and (in the male) a slate-blue and (in the female) a deep brown back.

Merlin chair /ˈməːlɪn tʃɛː/ *n. phr.* L18. [f. J. J. *Merlin* (1735–1803), its inventor.] *Hist.* A type of wheelchair.

†**merling** *n.* ME–M18. [OFr. *merlenc* (mod. *merlan*) f. L *merula* a kind of fish: see -ING[3].] A (European) whiting.

merlion /ˈməːlɪən/ *n.* Also **mar-** /ˈmɑː-/. L15. [Prob. var. of MERLIN.] *Her.* A bird with either no feet (identical with the heraldic martlet) or neither feet nor beak.

merlon /ˈməːlən/ *n.* E18. [Fr. f. It. *merlone* augm. of *merlo* battlement.] A part of an embattled parapet between two embrasures; a similar structure on a battleship.

Merlot /ˈməːləʊ, -lɒt, *foreign* mɛrlo/ *n.* E19. [Fr.] (The vine bearing) a black grape used in wine-making; red wine made from these grapes.

mermaid /ˈməːmeɪd/ *n.* ME. [f. MERE *n.*[1] + MAID *n.*] 1 An imaginary partly human sea creature with the head and trunk of a woman and the tail of a fish or cetacean (in early use often identified with the siren of classical mythology); a representation of such a creature, esp. (*Her.*) depicted with long flowing golden hair and a comb in the left hand and a mirror in the right. ME. 2†a A sweet singer, a siren. Also, a prostitute. L16–E17. b A woman who is at home in water. *joc.* L19.

Comb.: **mermaid's glove**(s) a marine organism somewhat resembling a glove; *esp.* a sponge, *Halichondria palmata*; **mermaid's hair** a dark green filamentous seaweed, *Lyngbya majuscula*; **mermaid's purse** the horny egg-case of a skate, ray, or shark; a sea purse; **mermaid-weed** any of various N. American aquatic plants of the genus *Proserpinaca* (family Haloragaceae), having leaves toothed like a comb.

Also **mermaiden** *n.* (now *rare*) LME.

merman /ˈməːman/ *n.* Pl. **-men** /-mɛn/. E17. [f. MER- + MAN *n.*, after prec.] A male of the mermaid kind, an imaginary partly human sea creature with the head and trunk of a man and the tail of a fish or cetacean; a representation of such a creature, esp. (*Her.*) depicted with a trident in the right hand and a conch-shell trumpet in the left.

mermithid /məːˈmɪθɪd/ *n.* & *a.* L20. [f. mod.L *Mermithoidea*, f. *Mermis* (see below): see -ID[3].] *Zool.* A *n.* Any of various nematode worms of the genus *Mermis* or the order Mermithoidea, whose larvae are parasites of insects. L20. B *adj.* Of, pertaining to, or designating such worms. L20.

mero /ˈmɛːrəʊ/ *n.* Pl. **-os**. Also **merou** /ˈmɛruː/. M18. [Sp. *mero*, Fr. *mérou*.] Any of various groupers; *esp.* the dark brown *Epinephelus guaza*, of the Mediterranean and E. Atlantic (also called *dusky perch*).

mero- /ˈmɛrəʊ/ *comb. form*[1]. Bef. a vowel also **mer-**. [f. Gk *meros* part, fraction: see -O-.] Part, partly. Freq. opp. HOLO-.

mero'blastic *a.* (*Biol.*) (of an ovum) undergoing partial cleavage, usu. on the surface of a large yolk L19. **merocrine** *a.* (*Physiol.*) of, pertaining to, or designating a gland in which cytoplasm is not lost during secretion E20. **mero'cyanine** *a.* & *n.* (*Chem.*) (designating) any of a class of neutral dyes (many used as photographic sensitizers) in which a nitrogen atom and a carbonyl group (both usu. parts of heterocycles) are linked by a conjugated chain of carbon atoms M20. **mero'diploid** *a.* & *n.* (*Bacteriol.*) (*a*) *adj.* (made up of cells) having second copies of part of the normal chromosome complement; (*b*) *n.* a merodiploid organism: M20. **merogamete** *n.* (*Biol.*) a gamete formed by fission of a vegetative cell in some protists and usu. smaller than an ordinary individual M20. **me'rogamy** *n.* (*Biol.*) a mode of reproduction in some protists involving the fusion of merogametes E20. **mero'gonic** *a.* (*Biol.*) of, pertaining to, or of the nature of merogony L19. **me'rogony** *n.* (*Biol.*) (*a*) the production of an embryo from a portion of an ovum; (*b*) = SCHIZOGONY: L19. **mero'hedral** *a.* (of a crystal or crystal form) less symmetrical than is possible for its crystal class L19. **mero'istic** *a.* [Gk *ōion* egg] *Biol.* (of an ovariole) having nurse-cells L19. **mero'mictic** *a.* (of a lake) in which water below a certain depth does not circulate with the upper layers, usu. as a result of high salt concentration M20. **mero'morphic** *a.* (*Math.*) (of a complex function) analytic in a given domain except for a finite number of poles L19. **mero'myosin** *n.* (*Biochem.*) either of the two components of myosin which correspond roughly to the rod-shaped and globular parts of the molecule M20. **mero'plankton** *n.* (*Biol.*) meroplanktonic organisms E20. **meroplank'tonic** *a.* (*Biol.*) (of an aquatic organism) passing only part of its life cycle as plankton L19. **merosy'mmetrical** *a.* = MEROHEDRAL L19. **mero'symmetry** *n.* the condition or quality of being merohedral L19. **merosyste'matic** *a.* = MEROHEDRAL L19. **mero'zoite** *n.* (*Zool.*) any of the cells produced by multiple fission (schizogony) of a schizont E20. **mero'zygote** *n.* = MERODIPLOID *n.* M20.

mero- /ˈmɪərəʊ/ *comb. form*[2]. [f. Gk *mēros* thigh: see -O-.] *Anat.* & *Zool.* Forming ns. and adjs. w. the sense 'of the thigh or an analogous structure'.

merocele *n.* (now *rare* or *obs.*) a femoral hernia E19.

Meroitic /mɛrəʊˈɪtɪk/ *a.* & *n.* M19. [f. *Meroë* (see below) + -ITIC.] A *adj.* Of or pertaining to the ancient Nubian kingdom of Meroë in NE Africa or its language. M19. B *n.* The language of this kingdom, of uncertain affiliation. E20.

Meroite /ˈmɛrəʊʌɪt/ *n.* & *a.* (*a*) *n.* a native or inhabitant of Meroë; (*b*) *adj.* = MEROITIC *a.*: M19.

merops /ˈmɛrɒps/ *n.* L17. [L f. Gk.] The bee-eater, *Merops apiaster*. Now only as mod.L genus name.

meros /ˈmɪərɒs/ *n.* E19. [Gk *mēros* thigh.] 1 *Archit.* The plane surface between the grooves of a triglyph. E19. 2 *Anat.* The thigh. E19. 3 *Zool.* One of the joints of a maxilliped. M19.

merostome /ˈmɛrəstəʊm/ *n.* L19. [f. mod.L *Merostomata* (see below), f. as MERO-[1] + Gk *stomat-*, *stoma* mouth.] *Zool.* Any arthropod of the class Merostomata; a horseshoe crab.

merou *n.* var. of MERO.

-merous /mərəs/ *suff.* L19. [Extracted f. DIMEROUS etc.] Chiefly *Bot.* Forming adjs. in sense 'having (a specified number of) parts', as *pentamerous, tetramerous.* Also used with prefixed numeral, as *2-merous, five-merous.*

Merovingian /mɛrəˈvɪndʒɪən/ *n.* & *a.* L17. [Fr. *mérovingien*, f. med.L *Merovingi* (pl.), f. L *Meroveus* their reputed founder: see -ING[3], -IAN.] **A** *n.* A member of the first dynasty of Frankish kings founded by Clovis and reigning in Gaul and Germany from about 500 to 751–2. Also, the style of handwriting developed from Roman cursive during this period and characteristic of it. L17. **B** *adj.* Designating or pertaining to this dynasty or the style of handwriting characteristic of the period of its rule. L18.

merrie *a.* & *adv.* see MERRY *a.* & *adv.*

merrill /ˈmɛr(ə)l/ *n.* Also **merel, merril.** LME. [OFr. (mod. *méreau*) token, coin, counter, f. Proto-Romance.] **1** In *pl.* A game played on a board between two players, each with an equal number of pebbles, discs of wood or metal, pegs, or pins. Also called *(nine men's) morris.* LME. **2** Each of the counters or pieces used in this game. LME.

merrily /ˈmɛrɪli/ *adv.* ME. [f. MERRY *a.* + -LY[2].] **1** In early use, pleasantly, agreeably, cheerfully, happily. In later use, with exuberant gaiety, joyously, mirthfully. ME. †**2** Jocularly, facetiously, wittily, in jest. LME–M18. **3** With alacrity; briskly. LME.

merriment /ˈmɛrɪm(ə)nt/ *n.* L16. [f. MERRY *a.* + -MENT.] †**1** A thing that contributes to mirth; a jest; a brief comic dramatic entertainment; a humorous or scurrilous publication. L16–E19. **2** The action of making merry; animated enjoyment or jocularity; mirth, fun. L16. †**3** Entertainment, amusement. Only in L16.

merriness /ˈmɛrɪnɪs/ *n.* Now *rare.* ME. [f. MERRY *a.* + -NESS.] The quality or condition of being merry.

merry /ˈmɛri/ *n.* Now chiefly *dial.* L16. [f. as MERISE.] The wild cherry tree, *Prunus avium* (also *merry-tree*); the small black fruit of this tree.

merry /ˈmɛri/ *a.* & *adv.* Also (now *pseudo-arch.*) **merrie.** [OE *myr(i)ġe* f. Gmc base also of MIRTH.] **A** *adj.* **1** Of a thing: pleasing, agreeable, delightful. *obs.* exc. as passing into senses 3, 5. OE. **2** Of looks, appearance: (orig.) pleasant, agreeable, bright; (later) expressive of cheerfulness, mirthful. *obs.* exc. as passing into sense 3. OE. **3** Of a person, action, attribute, etc.: full of animated enjoyment (in early use chiefly with reference to feasting or sport); full of laughter or gaiety; joyous, mirthful; (of general disposition) given to joyousness or mirth. OE. †**b** Happy. LME–M17. **c** Slightly tipsy. *colloq.* L16. **d** Pleasantly amused; being facetious. Foll. by *with, on, upon* (a person). *arch.* E17. **4** Of a saying, jest, etc.: amusing, diverting, funny. Passing into sense 5. *arch.* LME. **5** Designating or pertaining to a time, season, etc., characterized by festivity or rejoicing. M16.

3 W. IRVING His memory was always cherished as that of a merry companion. J. L. WATEN From within came the sound of merry voices. *Proverb:* The more the merrier. c N. HINTON They'd finished the champagne and started on the wine so they were all a bit merry. 4 R. K. NARAYAN The men . . made a few merry jokes. 5 M. WEBB It was a merry scene, with the bright holly and mistletoe.

Phrases, special collocations, & comb.: *lead a person a merry dance* : see DANCE *n.* **make merry** be festive or jovial; indulge in feasting and jollity. **make merry over,** (†**with**) make fun of, ridicule. **merry Andrew** a comic entertainer; a buffoon, a clown, a mountebank's assistant. **merry Christmas!**: a conventional salutation just before or at Christmas. *merry dancers*: see DANCER 3. **merry England,** (esp. *iron.*) **merrie England** England characterized by (orig.) pleasant landscape etc. or (later, freq. *iron.*) the cheerfulness or animation of its people. †**merry-go-down** *slang* strong ale. **merry-go-round** *n.* & *a.* (*a*) *n.* a revolving machine on which people ride round and round for amusement, as one with horses, cars, etc., at a fair or one in a playground; a roundabout; *fig.* a cycle of bustling activity, a pointless circular course; (*b*) *adj.* designating or pertaining to a railway system whereby a train of coal hoppers runs perpetually on a circular route between consignor and consignee. *merry Greek*: see GREEK *n. merry hell*: see HELL *n.* **merrymake** *n.* & *v.* (*a*) *n.* (*arch.*) (*a*) merrymaking; (*b*) *v.i.* make merry, be festive, revel. **merrymaker** a person who makes merry, a participant in festivities, a reveller. **merrymaking** (*a*) the action of making merry, revelling; conviviality; (*b*) an occasion of festivity, a convivial entertainment. **merryman** a jester, a buffoon. **merry-meeting** (now *arch.* & *dial.*) a festive or convivial gathering. **merry men** the companions in arms or followers of a knight, an outlaw chief, etc.; *joc.* a person's followers or assistants. **merry thought** the forked bone between the neck and breast of a bird, the wishbone; the portion of a bird when carved that includes this. **Merry Widow** [the English name of Franz Lehár's operetta *Die Lustige Witwe*] an amorous or designing widow; *Merry Widow hat,* a type of ornate wide-brimmed hat. **the Merry Monarch**: Charles II.

B *adv.* Merrily. Now *rare.* OE.

merry /ˈmɛri/ *v.* Long *rare.* [OE *myrġan*, f. Gmc base of MERRY *a.*; later directly f. MERRY *a.*] **1** *v.i.* Be merry; act or play merrily. OE. †**2** *v.t.* Make (a person etc.) merry. ME–E17.

mersalyl /ˈməːsəlɪl/ *n.* M20. [f. MER(CURY + SAL(IC)YL.] *Pharm.* An organomercury compound, $C_{13}H_{16}NO_6HgNa$, which is a powerful diuretic formerly used to treat oedema.

Mersenne /məːˈsɛn, *foreign* mɛrsɛn/ *n.* L19. [Marin *Mersenne* (1588–1648), Fr. mathematician and musician.] *Math.* Used *attrib.* and in *possess.* to designate numbers of the form $2^p - 1$ (where *p* is a prime number).

mersion /ˈməːʃ(ə)n/ *n.* Long *rare.* M17. [Late L *mersio(n-)*, f. L *mers-* pa. ppl stem of *mergere* dip, MERGE *v.*: see -ION.] Immersion, in early use *spec.* in baptism.

Mertensian /məːˈtɛnzɪən/ *a.* Also **m-.** M20. [f. R. *Mertens* (1894–1975), Ger. zoologist + -IAN.] Zool. *Mertensian mimicry*, a form of mimicry in which a mildly noxious animal is imitated by both harmless Batesian and poisonous Müllerian mimics.

Merthiolate /məːˈθʌɪəleɪt/ *n.* Also **m-.** E20. [f. MER(CURY + THIO- + SALICY)LATE.] *Pharm.* (US proprietary name for) thiomersal.

Mertonian /məːˈtəʊnɪən/ *n.* & *a.* L19. [f. *Merton* College (named from its founder Walter de Merton) + -IAN.] **A** *n.* A member of Merton College, Oxford. L19. **B** *adj.* Of or pertaining to Merton College or its members; *spec.* designating or pertaining to a school of mathematics and astronomy that existed there in the 14th cent. L19.

Meru /ˈmɛruː/ *n.* & *a.* E20. [A town and district in central Kenya.] **A** *n.* Pl. same, **-s. 1** A member of a people inhabiting the Meru region of Kenya. E20. **2** The Bantu language of this people. E20. **B** *attrib.* or as *adj.* Of or pertaining to the Meru or their language. E20.

merula *n.* var. of MARULA.

merveille du jour /mɛːˌveɪ dʊ ˈʒʊə/ *n. phr.* E20. [Fr. = wonder of the day.] A noctuid moth, *Dichonia aprilina,* with pale green and black wings.

merwoman /ˈməːwʊmən/ *n.* Pl. **-women** /-wɪmɪn/. E19. [f. MER- + WOMAN *n.*, after MERMAID.] A mermaid when older or married.

merycism /ˈmɛrɪsɪz(ə)m/ *n.* M19. [mod.L *merycismus* f. Gk *mērukismos* rumination, f. *mērukizein* ruminate: see -ISM.] *Med.* A rare condition in which food is returned to the mouth after a short period in the stomach. Cf. RUMINATION 2.

mesa /ˈmeɪsə/ *n.* M18. [Sp. = table f. L *mensa.*] **1** A high rocky tableland or plateau; a flat-topped hill with precipitous sides. Earliest in names of particular plateaux or hills. Orig. *US.* M18. **2** *Electronics.* A raised flat-topped portion of *n-* or *p*-type semiconductor in a transistor or diode surrounded by an area in which the underlying *p-* or *n*-type material (respectively) has been exposed by etching. Usu. *attrib.*, as *mesa diode, transistor.* M20.

mesad /ˈmɛsad/ *adv.* L19. [f. Gk *mesos* middle + -AD[3].] *Anat.* = MESIAD.

mésalliance /mezaljɑ̃s (*pl. same*), mɛˈzalɪəns/ *n.* L18. [Fr., f. *més-* MIS-[1] 2 + *alliance* ALLIANCE. Cf. MISALLIANCE.] A marriage with a person thought to be of inferior social position; an unsuitable union.

Q. BELL When . . Julia's relations did make a really disastrous *mésalliance* the young couple were firmly . . removed to the colonies.

mes ami(e)s *n. phr. pl.* see MON AMI.

mesangium /mɪˈsandʒɪəm/ *n.* M20. [f. as MESO- + Gk *aggeion* vessel + -IUM.] *Anat.* The part of a renal glomerulus where the afferent and efferent arterioles are closest together.

mesangial *a.* of or pertaining to the mesangium; *spec.* pertaining to or designating cells of the glomerulus between the capillary endothelium and the basement membrane: M20.

mesaortitis /ˌmɛseɪɔːˈtʌɪtɪs, ˌmiːz-/ *n.* E20. [f. MESO- + AORTA + -ITIS.] *Med.* Mesarteritis of the aorta.

†**mesaraic** *a.* & *n.* Also **-ser-.** LME–M19. [med.L *mesaraïcus* f. Gk *mesaraïkos*, f. *mesaraïon*, f. *meson* middle + *araia* flank, belly: see -IC.] *Anat.* **A** *adj.* = MESENTERIC. LME–M19. **B** *n.* A mesenteric vein. Usu. in *pl.* LME–M19.

mesarch /ˈmɛzɑːk, ˈmiːz-, -s-/ *a.* L19. [f. MESO- + Gk *arkhē* beginning, origin.] **1** *Bot.* Of primary xylem: developing both from the centre of the stem and the periphery. L19. **2** *Ecol.* Of a succession of plant communities: originating in a mesic or moderately moist habitat. E20.

mesarteritis /ˌmɛsɑːtəˈrʌɪtɪs, ˌmiːz-/ *n.* L19. [f. MESO- + ARTERITIS.] *Med.* Inflammation of the middle layer (tunica media) of the wall of an artery.

mesarteritic /-ˈrɪtɪk/ *a.* L19.

mesati- /ˈmɛsəti, ˈmiːz-/ *comb. form.* [f. Gk *mesatos* midmost (superl. of *mesos* middle): see -I-.] Chiefly *Anat.* Intermediate. Cf. MESO-.

mesatice'phalic *a.* = MESOCEPHALIC L19. **mesati'pellic** *a.* [Gk *pella* bowl] having or designating a pelvis of a proportion intermediate between dolichopellic and platypellic L19.

mesaxon /mɛˈsaks(ə)n/ *n.* M20. [f. MES(ENTERY + AXON.] *Anat.* A membranous structure linking the outside of a Schwann cell to the central axon, in myelinated nerve fibres having a spiral cross-section and forming the myelin sheath.

mesaxonic /miːzakˈsɒnɪk, mɛz-/ *a.* L19. [f. MESO- + Gk *axōn* axis + -IC.] *Zool.* Of a foot (of an ungulate): having the axis running through the central toe.

mescal /ˈmɛskal, mɛˈskal/ *n.* E18. [Sp. *mezcal* f. Nahuatl *mexcalli.*] **1** Any of several plants of the genus *Agave* found in Mexico and the south-western US, used as sources of fermented liquor, food, or fibre; *esp.* the American aloe, *Agave americana.* E18. **b** The cooked root, head, or other parts of such a plant eaten as food. M18. **2** A strong intoxicating spirit distilled from the fermented sap of the American aloe or allied species. Cf TEQUILA. E19. **3** A small desert cactus, *Lophophora williamsii*, of Mexico and Texas, having a soft segmented body a few inches high in the form of a flattened globe; a preparation of this used as a hallucinogenic drug. Cf. MESCALINE, PEYOTE. L19.

Comb.: **mescal button** the dried disc-shaped crown of the cactus *Lophophora williamsii*, consumed for its hallucinogenic effects; this plant.

'mescalism *n.* the practice of consuming mescal buttons or mescaline; intoxication resulting from this: E20.

mescaline /ˈmɛskəlɪn, -iːn/ *n.* Also **-in** /-ɪn/. L19. [G *Mezcalin, Mesc-*, f. as prec.: see -IN[1], -INE[5].] An alkaloid derived from mescal buttons, having intoxicating and hallucinogenic properties similar to but milder than those of LSD; 3,4,5-trimethoxyphenethylamine, $(CH_3O)_3{\cdot}C_6H_2{\cdot}CH_2CH_2NH_2$.

Mesdames /meɪˈdam, *foreign* medam/ *n.pl.* L16. [Fr., pl. of MADAME.] **1** Pl. of MADAME. L16. **2** Used as pl. of MRS. L18.

Mesdemoiselles *n.* pl. of MADEMOISELLE.

†mese *n.*[1] LME–E18. [OFr., fem. of *mes* f. late L *mansum*, *-us*: see MANSE. Cf. MIDSTEAD.] = MESSUAGE.

mese /ˈmɛsiː/ *n.*[2] E17. [Gk *mesē* (sc. *khordē* string) fem. of *mesos* middle.] In ancient Greek music, the fixed note which is the highest note of a lower tetrachord or lower pair of tetrachords, and in some scales is identical with the lowest note of a higher tetrachord (cf. PARAMESE), sometimes regarded as the keynote of a scale or system.

mese *n.*[3] var. of MEESE.

meseems /mɪˈsiːmz/ *v.i. impers. arch.* Also **meseemeth** /mɪˈsiːmɪθ/. Pa. t. **meseemed**. LME. [Orig. two wds, ME *pron.* (*dat.*) & 3rd person sing. of SEEM *v.* Cf. METHINKS.] It seems to me. (With noun cl., with or without *that*.)

CARLYLE Meseems I could discover fitter objects of piety!

†mesel *a.* & *n.* In sense A.2b also **measle**. ME. [OFr. f. med.L *mesellus*, *mis-* f. L *misellus* wretched, wretch, dim. of *miser* wretched: see -EL[2]. Assoc. w. MEASLES.] A *adj.* 1 Leprous. ME–E17. 2a Of a fish: diseased. LME–M16. b Of a pig: afflicted with measles. LME–M17. B *n.* 1 A leper. ME–M16. b *fig.* A foul person. LME–M18. 2 Leprosy; *transf.* any affliction. LME–M16.

meself /mɪˈsɛlf/ *pron. non-standard.* M19. [Repr. a pronunc.] = MYSELF.

mesembryanthemum /mɪˌzɛmbrɪˈanθɪməm/ *n.* L18. [mod.L (see below), f. (ult.) Gk *mesēmbria* noon + *anthemon* flower, with subsequent misspelling.] Any of numerous chiefly southern African succulent plants of or formerly included in the genus *Mesembryanthemum* (family Aizoaceae), freq. cultivated for their colourful daisy-like flowers which open only in bright sunshine.

mesencephalon /mɛsɛnˈsɛf(ə)lɒn, miːz-, -ˈkɛf-/ *n.* M19. [f. MESO- + ENCEPHALON.] *Anat.* & *Zool.* The midbrain.

mesencephal *n.* = MESENCEPHALON M19. **mesencephalic** /-sɪˈfalɪk/ *a.* M19.

mesenchyme /ˈmɛsəŋkʌɪm, ˈmiːz-/ *n.* Also **mesenchyma** /mɪˈsɛŋkɪmə/. L19. [f. Gk *mesos* middle + *egkhuma* infusion.] *Anat.* & *Zool.* A loosely organized, mainly mesodermal embryonic tissue which develops into connective and skeletal tissues, blood, etc.

mesenchymal /mɪˈsɛŋkɪm(ə)l/, **mesenchymatous** /mɪsɛnˈkɪmətəs, -ˈkʌɪm-, miːz-/ *adjs.* L19.

mesenteron /mɪˈsɛntərɒn/ *n.* L19. [f. Gk *mesos* middle + *enteron* intestine.] *Anat.* & *Zool.* The midgut.

mesentery /ˈmɛs(ə)nt(ə)ri/ *n.* LME. [mod.L *mesenterium* f. Gk *mesenterion*, f. *mesos* middle + *enteron* intestine: see -Y[3].] 1 *Anat.* A fold of peritoneal tissue which attaches an organ, esp. the small intestine, to the posterior wall of the abdomen. LME. 2 *Zool.* Any of various animal structures which serve to attach organs, esp. the gut, to the body wall; *esp.* each of the longitudinal sheets of tissue which divide the body cavity of many coelenterates. M19.

mesenterial /mɛs(ə)nˈtɪərɪəl/ *a.* E17. **mesenteric** /mɛs(ə)nˈtɛrɪk/ *a.* M17. **mesenteritis** /mɪˌsɛntəˈrʌɪtɪs/ *n.* (*Med.*) inflammation of the mesentery E19.

†meseraic *a.* & *n.* var. of MESARAIC.

†mesestead *n.* see MIDSTEAD.

meseta /meˈseta/ *n.* E20. [Sp., dim. of MESA.] In Spain and Spanish-speaking countries: a plateau; spec. *the* high plateau of central Spain.

mesethmoid /mɛˈsɛθmɔɪd/ *a.* & *n.* L19. [f. MESO- + ETHMOID.] *Anat.* (Of, pertaining to, or designating) the ethmoid bone or the cartilage from which this develops.

mesh /mɛʃ/ *n.* & *v.* Also **†mash**. LME. [Prob. f. MDu. *maesche*, *masche* (Du. *maas*) f. Gmc.] A *n.* 1 Any of the open spaces or interstices between the strands of a net, sieve, etc. LME. b In *pl.*, the strands between the interstices of a net etc.; *collect.* netting. E17. c *Electr.* A closed loop in a network. L19. d The coarseness or spacing of the strands of a grid, net, or screen; (with preceding numeral) a measure of this (representing the number of openings per unit length) or of the size of particles which will (just) pass through such a grid etc. M20. 2 An interlaced fabric or structure, a network, netting; a grid, a framework; *fig.* a thing or situation which holds or constrains; an entanglement, a snare. M16 b *Building.* A steel network used as reinforcement in concrete. E20. 3 *Engin.* A state of engagement between (the teeth of) gearwheels, toothed racks, etc. Chiefly in *in, out of, into mesh.* L19.

1 A. HARDY Birds . . swoop down to peck at the fish through the meshes of the net. b *fig.*: J. HUXLEY Ottoline and Bertie remained, bound still in the meshes of their great love affair. 2 F. NORRIS He was entangled; already his foot was caught in the mesh that was being spun. T. CAPOTE The cell windows are . . not only barred but covered with a wire mesh. M. BRADBURY Fitting her toes into the light, stretchable mesh of the tights. C. THUBRON Roads sliced through the mesh of alleys and courtyards.

Comb.: **meshwork** meshes collectively; structure consisting of meshes; a network.

B *v.* I 1 *v.t.* Catch (a thing or person) in the meshes of a net; *fig.* entangle, involve inextricably. M16. 2 *v.refl.* & *i.* Become enmeshed or entangled. L16. 3 *v.i.* Of the teeth of a wheel etc.: be engaged *with* another piece of machinery. M19. 4 *v.t.* Cause (gears, esp. those of a motor vehicle) to become engaged; put into mesh. L19. 5 *v.i.* Fit in, be harmonious; combine. (Foll. by *together, with.*) M20. 6 *v.t.* Bring *together*, harmonize, reconcile. M20.

5 E. BLISHEN Our strange young lives so uneasily failing to mesh with the lives of our teachers. *Women's Review* Historical meanings in practice often mesh together in a way which may confuse modern viewers.

II 7 *v.t.* Construct the meshes of (a net, snare, etc.). Chiefly *Canad. dial.*. E17.

meshed *a.* having the form or appearance of mesh; tangled, intricate: M17. **meshing** *n.* (*a*) the action of the vb, *spec.* the making of meshes in a net; (*b*) a meshed structure, meshwork: E17. **meshy** *a.* consisting of meshes, resembling mesh E17.

meshuga /mɪˈʃʊɡə/ *a. slang.* Also **-gga(h)** & other vars. L19. [Yiddish *meshuge* f. Heb. *mĕshuggā'*. Cf. G *meschugge* crazy.] Mad, crazy; stupid. Chiefly *pred.* (cf. MESHUGENER).

meshugaas /mɪˈʃʊɡɑːs/ *n. slang.* Also **mishugas** & other vars. E20. [Yiddish f. Heb. *mĕshuggā'*: see prec.] Madness, craziness; nonsense, foolishness.

meshugener /mɪˈʃʊɡənə/ *attrib. a.* & *n. slang.* Also **-gg-**, **-nah**, & other vars. E20. [Positional var. of MESHUGA.] (A person who is) mad, crazy, or stupid.

meshugga(h) *a.* var. of MESHUGA.

meshuggenah, -ner *ns.* vars. of MESHUGENER.

meshumad /mɪˈʃʊmad/ *n.* Also **-mm-**. Pl. **-im** /-ɪm/. L19. [Yiddish f. Heb. *mĕshummāḏ* lit. 'a person who is destroyed', or *mĕšu'māḏ* baptized, f. Aramaic *'maḏ* be baptized.] An apostate from Judaism.

mesiad /ˈmiːzɪad, ˈmɛsɪad/ *adv.* E19. [f. next + -AD[3].] *Anat.* Towards the median line of a body.

mesial /ˈmiːzɪəl, ˈmɛsɪəl/ *a.* E19. [Irreg. f. Gk *mesos* middle + -IAL.] Chiefly *Anat.* Pertaining to, situated in, or directed towards the middle line of a body; median. Also, situated mesially with respect *to*.

mesially *adv.* in a mesial position or direction M19.

mesic /ˈmiːzɪk, ˈmɛzɪk/ *a.*[1] E20. [f. Gk *mesos* middle + -IC.] *Ecol.* Of a habitat: containing a moderate amount of moisture.

mesic /ˈmiːzɪk, ˈmɛzɪk/ *a.*[2] M20. [f. MESON *n.*[3] + -IC.] *Particle Physics.* Of, pertaining to, or of the nature of a meson; *spec.* designating a system analogous to an atom in which a meson takes the place of either an orbital electron or the nucleus.

†mesite *n.* Only in M19. [Fr. *mésite* f. Gk *mesitēs* go-between (as being intermediate between alcohol and ether): see -ITE[1].] *Chem.* Acetone.

mesityl /ˈmɛsɪtʌɪl, -tɪl/ *n.* M19. [f. prec. + -YL.] *Chem.* A hypothetical radical derived from acetone.

Comb.: **mesityl oxide** a colourless oily flammable ketone, $CH_3CO{\cdot}CH{:}C(CH_3)_2$, used as a solvent; 4-methyl-3-penten-2-one.

mesitylene /mɪˈsɪtɪliːn/ *n.* a colourless liquid hydrocarbon, 1,3,5-trimethylbenzene, obtainable from petroleum M19.

meslé /ˈmɛzleɪ/ *a.* Long *rare* or *obs.* Fem. **-ée**. M17. [OFr., pa. ppl a. of *mesler* (mod. *mêler*) mix.] *Her.* Of a field: composed equally of a metal and a colour.

mesmerian /mɛzˈmɪərɪən/ *n.* & *a. rare.* E19. [f. as MESMERISM + -IAN. Cf. Fr. *mesmérien.*] A *n.* A follower of the Austrian physician Mesmer; a mesmerist. E19. B *adj.* Mesmeric. M19.

mesmeric /mɛzˈmɛrɪk/ *a.* E19. [f. as next + -IC.] Pertaining to, characteristic of, producing, or produced by mesmerism; hypnotic, fascinating.

O. MANNING Odd experiences, induced perhaps by the mesmeric dazzle of the light.

mesmerical *a.* (*rare*) M19. **mesmerically** *adv.* M19.

mesmerise *v.* var. of MESMERIZE.

mesmerism /ˈmɛzmərɪz(ə)m/ *n.* L18. [f. F. A. *Mesmer*, Austrian physician (1734–1815) who popularized the practice + -ISM.] The process or practice of inducing a hypnotic state, usu. accompanied by insensibility to pain and muscular rigidity, by the influence of an operator over the will of a patient; the state so induced; *fig.* fascination. Also, belief in this process; an influence producing such a state. Formerly also called (*animal*) *magnetism*.

mesmerist *n.* a person who practises mesmerism; (occas.) a believer in mesmerism: M19.

mesmerize /ˈmɛzmərʌɪz/ *v.t.* Also **-ise**. E19. [f. as prec. + -IZE.] Subject to the influence of mesmerism, hypnotize; lead *into* something as if by mesmerism; *fig.* fascinate, hold spellbound. Freq. as *mesmerized* ppl a.

I. COMPTON-BURNETT I am mesmerized into silence; Dulcia fascinates me like a snake. P. PEARCE They stood at the window . . watching the snow . . mesmerized by it.

mesmeriza'bility *n.* the extent to which a person may be mesmerized M19. **mesmerizable** *a.* able to be mesmerized M19. **mesmeri'zation** *n.* E19. **mesmerizer** *n.* E19.

mesnalty /ˈmiːn(ə)lti/ *n.* M16. [Law Fr. *mesnalte*, f. *mesne* (see next) after *comunalte* COMMONALTY.] *Law* (now *Hist.*). The estate of a mesne lord; the condition of being a mesne lord.

mesne /miːn/ *n.* & *a.* LME. [Law Fr., var. of AN *meen* MEAN *a.*[2]: for the unetymological *s* cf. DEMESNE.] †A *n.* 1 = MEAN *n.*[1] 2, 7. LME–E19. 2 = *mesne lord* below. M16–E18.

B *adj.* 1 Occurring or performed at a time intermediate between two dates. *obs.* exc. *Law.* M16. 2 *Law* (now *Hist.*). Of a person: intermediate, intervening. E19.

1 **mesne process** *Hist.* any writ or process issued between the primary and the final process. **mesne profits** the profits of an estate received by a tenant in wrongful possession and recoverable by the landlord. 2 **mesne lord** a lord holding an estate from a superior feudal lord.

meso- /ˈmɛsəʊ, ˈmɛzəʊ, ˈmiːsəʊ, ˈmiːzəʊ/ *comb. form.* In sense 1, bef. a vowel also **mes-**. In sense 2 also as attrib. adj. **meso**. [f. Gk *mesos* middle (in some anat. terms extracted f. MESENTERY): see -O-.] 1 Forming chiefly scientific terms, w. the sense 'middle, intermediate'. 2 *Chem.* (As pref. usu. italicized.) Designating an isomer which has one or more pairs of enantiomorphic structural units so arranged that the molecule as a whole is optically inactive.

meso-a'ppendix *n.* (*Anat.*) the mesentery of the appendix L19. **mesoblast** *n.* (*Embryol.*) the mesoderm, esp. in the earliest stages M19. **meso'blastic** *a.* (*Embryol.*) of or pertaining to the mesoblast L19. **mesocarp** *n.* (*Bot.*) the middle layer of the pericarp of a fruit, between the endocarp and the exocarp M19. **mesocolic** /-ˈkɒlɪk/ *a.* (*Anat.*) of or relating to the mesocolon M19. **mesocolon** *n.* (*Anat.*) a fold of peritoneum which supports the colon L17. **mesoconch** /-kɒŋk/, **meso'conchic** *adjs.* (*Anthropol.*) in which the orbit of the eye is of moderate height in relation to its width E20. **meso'conchous** *a.* (*Anthropol.*) = MESOCONCHIC L19. **mesoconchy** *n.* the condition of being mesoconchic E20. **mesocyclone** *n.* (*Meteorol.*) a rotating column of rising air, associated with a small area of low pressure, which may develop into a tornado M20. **meso'dorsal** *a.* (*Zool.*) situated on the middle of the back L19. **mesoform** *n.* (*Physical Chem.*) = MESOPHASE M20. **mesogaster** *n.* (*Anat.*) the mesentery which supports the stomach E19. **mesogloea, *-glea** /-'gliːə/ *n.* [Gk *gloia* glue] *Zool.* a gelatinous layer between the endoderm and ectoderm of a coelenterate L19. **meso'gloeal, *-gleal** *a.* (*Zool.*) of, pertaining to, or of the nature of (a) mesogloea L19. **meso'gnathic** *a.* (*Anthropol.*) = MESOGNATHOUS L19. **mesognathism** /mɪ'sɒgnəθɪz(ə)m/ *n.* (*Anthropol.*) = MESOGNATHY L19. **meso'gnathous** *a.* (*Anthropol.*) having or designating an intermediate facial profile, neither prognathous nor orthognathous L19. **mesognathy** /mɪ'sɒgnəθi/ *n.* (*Anthropol.*) mesognathous condition L19. **meso-i'nositol** *n.* (*Biochem.*) = MYO-INOSITOL M20. **meso'kurtic** *a.* [Gk *kurtos* bulging] *Statistics* of, pertaining to, or designating a frequency distribution having the same kurtosis as the normal distribution E20. **mesokur'tosis** *n.* (*Statistics*) the property of being mesokurtic E20. **mesolect** *n.* [-LECT] *Ling.* the dialect or variety of any language with an intermediate level of prestige; an intermediate form between the acrolect and the basilect: L20. **meso'lectal** *a.* (*Ling.*) of, pertaining to, or of the nature of a mesolect L20. **meso'limbic** *a.* (*Anat.*) situated in or pertaining to the middle of the limbic system of the brain L20. **mesomere** *n.* (*Embryol.*) a medium-sized cell produced by some forms of embryonic cleavage E20. **mesome'tritis** *n.* (*Med.*) inflammation of the mesometrium L19. **mesometrium** /-'mɛt-/ *n.* [Gk *mētra* womb] *Anat.* & *Zool.* the fold of peritoneum which supports the uterus or (in birds) the oviduct M19. **meso'notum** *n.* (*Entomol.*) the dorsal portion of the mesothorax of an insect M19. **mesopause** *n.* (*Meteorol.*) the upper boundary of the mesosphere, at an altitude of about 80 km (50 miles), where the temperature begins to increase with height M20. **mesope'lagic** *a.* pertaining to or inhabiting the intermediate depths of the sea, *spec.* those between 200 and 1000 metres (approx. 660 and 3280 ft) down M20. **mesophase** *n.* (*Physical Chem.*) a mesomorphic phase, a liquid crystal E20. **mesophile** *n.* (*Biol.*) a mesophilic organism E20. **meso'philic** *a.* (*Biol.*) (of an organism, esp. a bacterium) flourishing at moderate temperatures L19. **meso'plankton** *n.* (*a*) plankton in the region between about 200 metres (approx. 660 ft) from the sea floor and 200 metres from the surface; (*b*) relatively large microplankton: L19. **mesoplank'tonic** *a.* of, pertaining to, or of the nature of mesoplankton L19. **mesopodium** /-'pəʊdɪəm/ *n.* (*Zool.*) the middle lobe of the foot of a mollusc M19. **mesorrhine** /-'rʌɪn/ *a.* [Gk *rhin-*, *rhis* nose] *Anthropol.* (of the nose) moderately long and wide; having such a nose: L19. **meso'salpinx** *n.*, pl. **-salpinges** /-sal'pɪndʒiːz/, [Gk *salpinx*: cf. SALPINGO-] *Anat.* a peritoneal fold above the mesovarium which encloses the Fallopian tubes L19. **meso'saprobe, mesosa'probic** *adjs.* (of running water) partially polluted E20. **mesoscale** *n.* (*Meteorol.*) an intermediate scale, between that of weather systems and that of microclimates, on which such phenomena as storms occur M20. **mesoscaph(e** *n.* a bathyscaphe designed for use at moderate depths M20. **meso'scopic** *a.* on a medium scale; *spec.* in *Geol.*, large enough for examination with the naked eye but not too large to allow inspection of the whole: M20. **meso'seismal** *a.* pertaining to or designating the region near the epicentre of an earthquake L19. **mesospore** *n.* (*Bot.*) the middle layer of a spore L19. **mesostasis** /mɪ'sɒstəsɪs/ *n.* (*Petrogr.*) the most recently formed interstitial substance in an igneous rock L19. **meso'sternal** *a.* (*Entomol.* & *Anat.*) of, pertaining to, or of the nature of a mesosternum E19. **meso'sternum** *n.* (*a*) *Entomol.* the sternum of the mesothorax of an insect; (*b*) *Anat.* the part of the breast-bone between the manubrium and the xiphisternum: E19. **mesosuchian** /-'sjuːkɪən/ *a.* & *n.* [Gk *soukhos* crocodile] *Palaeont.* (*a*) *adj.* of, pertaining to, or designating the extinct suborder Mesosuchia of Jurassic and Cretaceous crocodiles; (*b*) *n.* a crocodile of this suborder: L19. **mesotherm** *n.* (*Bot.*) a plant requiring a moderate temperature L19. **meso'thermal** *a.* (*Petrogr.*) of, pertaining to, or designating mineral and ore deposits formed by hydrothermal action at intermediate temperature and pressure E20. **meso'thermic** *a.* (*Bot.*) of, pertaining to, or of the nature of a mesotherm E20. **mesotho'racic** *a.* (*Entomol.*) of, pertaining to, or of the nature of a mesothorax M19. **meso'thorax** *n.*(*Entomol.*) the middle segment of the thorax of an insect E19. **meso'tonic** *a.* (*Mus.*) designating or pertaining to the mean tone M19. **meso'varium** *n.* (*Anat.*) a peritoneal fold above the mesometrium which supports the ovaries L19.

Meso-American /ˌmɛsəʊə'mɛrɪk(ə)n, ˌmɛz-, ˌmiːs-, ˌmiːz-/ *a.* & *n.* Also **Mesoamerican**. M20. [f. *Meso-America* (see below, MESO-, AMERICAN) + -AN.] **A** *adj.* Of or pertaining to Meso-America, the region of America from central Mexico to Nicaragua, or any of several advanced pre-Columbian cultures which flourished there; *loosely* Central American. M20. **B** *n.* A member of a Meso-American people. L20.

mesocephalic /ˌmɛsə(ʊ)sɪ'falɪk, ˌmɛz-, ˌmiːs-, ˌmiːz-, -kɛ'falɪk/ *a.* M19. [f. MESO- + -CEPHALIC.] Having a medium-sized head; *spec.* having a cranial index between 75 and 80.

'mesocephal *n.*, pl. **-s**, [back-form. f. mod.L pl.] a mesocephalic person E20. **meso'cephali** *n.pl.* (now *rare* or *obs.*) [mod.L] mesocephals M19. **meso'cephalism, meso'cephaly** *ns.* mesocephalic condition L19.

mesocracy /mɛ'sɒkrəsi/ *n. rare.* L19. [f. MESO- + -CRACY.] Government or the holding of power by the middle classes; a society governed by the middle classes, or in which the middle classes hold power.

mesocratic /mɛsə(ʊ)'kratɪk, mɛz-, miːs-, miːz-/ *a.* M19. [f. MESO- + *-cratic* as in *democratic* etc.] **1** Of or pertaining to the middle classes. *rare.* M19. **2** *Petrogr.* Of a rock: intermediate in composition between leucocratic and melanocratic rock. E20.

mesode /'mɛsəʊd/ *n.* M19. [Gk *mesōdos*, f. as MESO- + *ōdē* ODE.] A part of a Greek choral ode coming between the strophe and antistrophe.

me'sodic *a.* pertaining to or of the nature of a mesode L19.

mesoderm /'mɛsə(ʊ)dəːm, 'mɛz-, 'miːs-, 'miːz-/ *n.* L19. [f. MESO- + Gk *derma* skin.] *Biol.* The middle germ layer of the embryo in early development, between endoderm and ectoderm; cells or tissues derived from this.

meso'dermal, meso'dermic *adjs.* of, pertaining to, or derived from the mesoderm L19.

mesogastrium /mɛsə(ʊ)'gastrɪəm, mɛz-, miːs-, miːz-/ *n.* M19. [mod.L, f. as MESO- + Gk *gastr-*, *gastēr* stomach: see -IUM.] *Anat.* **1** The middle region of the abdomen between the epigastrium and the hypogastrium. M19. **2** = MESOGASTER. M19.

mesogastric *a.* M19.

mesolabe /'mɛsə(ʊ)leɪb, 'mɛz-, 'miːs-, 'miːz-/ *n.* *obs.* exc. *Hist.* L16. [L *mesolabium*, f. Gk *mesolabos*, *-on*, f. *mesos* middle + *lab-* base of *lambanein* take: cf. ASTROLABE.] An instrument used to find mean proportional lines.

mesolithic /mɛsə(ʊ)'lɪθɪk, mɛz-, miːs-, miːz-/ *a.* & *n.* M19. [f. MESO- + -LITHIC.] *Archaeol.* **A** *adj.* Designating or pertaining to part of the Stone Age intermediate between the palaeolithic and the neolithic periods. M19.

B *n.* *The* mesolithic period. M20.

R. BRADLEY In Ireland . . microliths do not occur in the late Mesolithic.

mesomerism /mɪ'sɒmərɪz(ə)m, mɪ'zɒm-/ *n.* E20. [f. MESO- after *tautomerism*.] *Chem.* The property exhibited by certain molecules of having a structure which cannot adequately be represented by a single structural formula but is intermediate between two or more graphical structures which differ in the distribution of electrons. Also called *resonance*.

meso'meric *a.* of, pertaining to, exhibiting, or arising from mesomerism M20.

mesomorph /'mɛsə(ʊ)mɔːf, 'mɛz-, miːs-, 'miːz-/ *n.* M20. [f. MESO- + -MORPH.] **1** A person whose build is powerful, compact, and muscular (with noticeable development of tissue derived from embryonic mesoderm, as bones, muscles, and connective tissue). M20. **2** *Physical Chem.* A mesophase or liquid crystal. *rare.* M20.

mesomorphy *n.* the state or property of being a mesomorph M20.

mesomorphic /mɛsə(ʊ)'mɔːfɪk, mɛz-, miːs-, miːz-/ *a.* E20. [f. as prec. + -IC.] **1** *Physical Chem.* Of, pertaining to, or of the nature of a liquid crystal, intermediate between the ordered state of matter in crystals and the disordered state in ordinary liquids. E20. **2** Having the bodily build of a mesomorph; of, pertaining to, or characteristic of a mesomorph. M20.

mesomorphism *n.* (*Physical Chem.*) the state or property of being mesomorphic M20. **mesomorphous** *a.* (*Physical Chem.*) = MESOMORPHIC 1 M20.

meson /me'sɒn/ *n.*[1] E19. [Sp. *mesón*.] An inn or lodging-house in Mexico or the south-western US.

meson /'mɛsɒn/ *n.*[2] L19. [Use as n. of neut. of Gk *mesos* middle.] *Anat.* The median plane, which divides a body into two roughly symmetrical halves.

meson /'miːzɒn, 'mɛzɒn/ *n.*[3] M20. [f. MESO- + -ON.] *Particle Physics.* Orig., any of a group of subatomic particles intermediate in mass between an electron and a proton. Now *spec.* any such particle that has zero or integral spin and can take part in the strong interaction.

mu-meson, omega meson, phi meson, etc.

Comb.: **meson factory** *colloq.* an establishment with a high-energy accelerator etc. for producing and experimenting with an intense beam of mesons.

mesonephros /mɛsə(ʊ)'nɛfrɒs, mɛz-, miːs-, miːz-/ *n.* Pl. **-nephroi** /-'nɛfrɔɪ/. Also (now *rare*) **-nephron** /-'nɛfrɒn/, pl. **-nephra** /-'nɛfrə/. L19. [f. MESO- + Gk *nephros* kidney.] *Anat.* & *Zool.* The second of the three segments of the embryonic kidney in vertebrates, which becomes the adult kidney of fishes and amphibians and survives in humans and other amniotes as the epididymis (in males) and the epoophoron (in females). Also called *Wolffian body*. Cf. METANEPHROS, PRONEPHROS.

mesonephric *a.* L19.

mesonic /miː'zɒnɪk, mɛ-/ *a.* M20. [f. MESON *n.*[3] + -IC.] *Particle Physics.* = MESIC *a.*[2]

mesophyll /'mɛsə(ʊ)fɪl, 'mɛz-, 'miːs-, 'miːz-/ *n.* M19. [f. Gk *mesos* middle + *phullon* leaf.] *Bot.* The parenchyma of a leaf, between the upper and lower layers of epidermis.

meso'phyllic *a.* L19.

mesophyte /'mɛsə(ʊ)fʌɪt, 'mɛz-, 'miːs-, 'miːz-/ *n.* L19. [f. MESO- + -PHYTE.] *Bot.* A plant of a group intermediate between hydrophytes and xerophytes, i.e. one avoiding extremes of moisture and dryness.

mesophytic /-'fɪtɪk, mɛz-, miːs-, miːz-/ *a.* L19.

Mesopotamia /mɛsəpə'teɪmɪə/ *n.* M19. [Gk (sc. *khōra* country), f. *mesos* middle + *potamos* river: see next.] (A name for) an area between two rivers.

Mesopotamian /mɛsəpə'teɪmɪən/ *n.* & *a.* L16. [f. *Mesopotamia* (see below) + -AN.] **A** *n.* A native or inhabitant of Mesopotamia, a region in SW Asia between the Tigris and the Euphrates rivers, site of the ancient civilizations of Sumer, Babylon, and Assyria, and now in Iraq. L16. **B** *adj.* Of or pertaining to Mesopotamia. L18.

mesosiderite /mɛsə(ʊ)'sɪdərʌɪt, mɛz-, miːs-, miːz-, -sʌɪ'dɪərʌɪt/ *n.* M19. [f. MESO- + SIDERITE.] *Geol.* A stony-iron meteorite in which the principal silicates are pyroxene and plagioclase.

mesosome /'mɛsəsəʊm, 'mɛz-, 'miːs-, 'miːz-/ *n.* In sense 1 also **-soma** /mɛsə'səʊmə/. L19. [f. MESO- + Gk *sōma* body.] **1** *Zool.* The middle region or segment of the body of various invertebrates (as scorpions, lophophorates). L19. **2** *Bacteriol.* A membranous structure in many bacteria that is associated with respiratory and photosynthetic activity. M20.

mesosphere /'mɛsə(ʊ)sfɪə, 'mɛz-, 'miːs-, 'miːz-/ *n.* M20. [f. MESO- + -SPHERE.] **1** *Meteorol.* The layer of the earth's atmosphere above the stratopause and below the mesopause, in which temperature decreases with height. M20. **2** *Geol.* The lower layer of the earth's mantle, which is resistant to plastic flow and not involved in tectonic processes. M20.

mesospheric /mɛsə(ʊ)'sfɛrɪk, mɛz-, miːs-, miːz-/ *a.* of, pertaining to, or occurring in the mesosphere M20.

mesothelia *n.* pl. of MESOTHELIUM.

mesothelioma /ˌmɛsə(ʊ)θiːlɪ'əʊmə, ˌmɛz-, ˌmiːs-, ˌmiːz-/ *n.* Pl. **-mas, -mata** /-mətə/. E20. [f. next + -OMA.] *Med.* A tumour of mesothelial tissue, associated esp. with exposure to asbestos.

mesothelium /mɛsə(ʊ)'θiːlɪəm, mɛz-, miːs-, miːz-/ *n.* Pl. **-lia** /-lɪə/. L19. [f. MESO- + EPI)THELIUM.] *Anat.* Epithelium that forms the surface layer of the mesoderm and lines the embryonic body cavity; (a body of) tissue derived from this, which lines the pleurae, peritoneum, and pericardium.

mesothelial *a.* L19.

mesothorium /mɛsə(ʊ)'θɔːrɪəm, mɛz-, miːs-, miːz-/ *n.* E20. [f. MESO- + THORIUM.] *Nuclear Physics.* Either of two radioactive nuclides produced during the decay of thorium, radium 228 (*mesothorium I*), produced by α-decay of thorium 232, and actinium 228 (*mesothorium II*), produced by β-decay of mesothorium I.

mesotron /'miːzətrɒn, 'mɛz-, 'miːs-, 'mɛs-/ *n.* *obs.* exc. *Hist.* M20. [f. MESO- + *-tron*, after *electron, neutron*.] *Particle Physics.* = MESON *n.*[3]

mesozoan /mɛsə'zəʊən, miːz-/ *n.* & *a.* E20. [f. MESOZOON + -AN.] *Zool.* **A** *adj.* Of or pertaining to mesozoa or the phylum Mesozoa. E20. **B** *n.* A member of the phylum Mesozoa, comprising minute animals with no organs or body cavity which are parasitic on marine invertebrates. M20.

Mesozoic /mɛsə(ʊ)'zəʊɪk, mɛz-, miːs-, miːz-/ *a.* & *n.* M19. [f. MESO- + -ZOIC.] *Geol.* **A** *adj.* Designating or pertaining to the second era of the Phanerozoic eon, following the Palaeozoic and preceding the Cenozoic, and comprising the Triassic, Jurassic, and Cretaceous periods. M19. **B** *n.* The Mesozoic era; the rocks collectively dating from this time. L19.

mesozoon /mɛsə(ʊ)'zəʊən, mɛz-, miːs-, miːz-/ *n.* Pl. **-zoa** /-'zəʊə/. L19. [mod.L *Mesozoa* pl., f. Gk MESO- + *zōia* pl. of *zōion* animal.] *Zool.* Orig., an animal intermediate in structure between protozoans and metazoans. Now *spec.* = MESOZOAN *n.* Usu. in *pl.*

mespilus /'mɛspɪləs/ *n.* M18. [mod.L (see below) f. L: see MEDLAR.] Any of various trees and shrubs now or formerly belonging to the genus *Mespilus*, of the rose family, e.g. the medlar, *M. germanica*.

snowy mespilus a kind of Juneberry, *Amelanchier lamarckii*.

mesquin /mɛskɛ̃/ *a.* Now *rare.* E18. [Fr.] Mean, sordid, shabby.

mesquite /'mɛskiːt, mɛ'skiːt/ *n.* Also **-it**. M18. [Mex. Sp. *mezquite* f. Nahuatl *mizquitl*.] **1** Any of various thorny pinnate-leaved leguminous shrubs and small trees of the genus *Prosopis*, of arid regions of Mexico, the south-western US, etc., esp. *P. glandulosa*; vegetation or terrain in which these plants predominate. M18. **2** = *mesquite-grass* below. M19.

Comb.: **mesquite bean** the pod of the mesquite, used as fodder; **mesquite-grass** any of various grasses, esp. of the genus *Bouteloua*, that grow in association with the mesquite.

mess /mɛs/ *n.* ME. [OFr. *mes* portion of food, mod. *mets* (infl. by *mettre* place) f. late L *missus* course of a meal, f. L *miss-* pa. ppl stem of *mittere* send (out). See also MUSS *n.*[2]] **I1a** A serving of food; a course of a meal; a prepared dish (of a specified kind of food). *arch.* ME. **b** A quantity (of food) sufficient to make a dish; the quantity of milk given by a cow at one milking. Now *dial.* & *US.* E16. **c** A (large) quantity or number *of* something. *N. Amer. colloq.* M19. **2** A portion or kind of liquid, partly liquid, or pulpy food; a quantity of this for an animal, esp. a hound. LME. **b** An unappealing concoction or pulp, esp. of foodstuffs. E19. **3a** A state or situation of confusion or muddle; a condition of embarrassment or trouble. E19. **b** A dirty or untidy state of things or of a place; a thing or collection of things causing such a state; dirty or misplaced things collectively. M19. **c** Excrement, esp. of a domestic animal or a child. *colloq.* E20. **d** A person whose life or affairs are confused; a dirty or untidy person. Also, an objectionable, ineffectual, or stupid person. *colloq.* M20.

1 A. UTTLEY Beautiful copper saucepans filled with savoury messes which they put on the stove. 3a M. WEST With the world in such a mess . . you were wise to retire from it. W. GOLDING Anyone . . after a month . . in a boat will know what a mess we were in. b D. FRANCIS The overturned mess of paints and easel which the young man had left. J. CANNAN Oh, the mess they leave on our little common . . in spite of the litter baskets. d T. K. WOLFE His hair felt like a bird's nest. He was a mess.

II4a Orig., each of the groups, usu. of four people, into which the guests at a banquet were commonly divided. Now, a company of esp. legal professional people who regularly take meals together. LME. **b** In the armed forces, each of the groups into which a regiment etc. is divided and whose members take meals together. Also, the place where meals are taken in such groups, a place for communal recreation for the members of a mess. M16. **c** (Without article.) The taking of a meal in such a group. L18. **†5** *gen.* A company or group of four persons or things. E16–L19.

4b B. REID Lance bombardiers couldn't drink in the officers' mess.

Phrases: **lose the number of one's mess** *Mil. slang* die, be killed. **make a mess** (*a*) put things into a disorderly, untidy, or dirty state; (*b*) (esp. of a domestic animal or a child) defecate. **make a mess of** (*a*) mishandle (an undertaking), spoil or botch (a job of work); (*b*) make disorderly, untidy, or dirty. **mess of pottage** [*Gen.* 25:29–34] a material or trivial comfort gained at the expense of something more important.

Comb.: **mess-boy** *Naut.* a man or boy who waits at table in a mess; **mess-jacket** a short tailless jacket reaching just below the waistline, worn esp. at a mess; **mess kit** (*a*) a soldier's cooking and eating utensils; (*b*) (military) uniform designed to be worn at meals; **mess-room** a dining- or recreation room for the members of a mess; **mess tin** a small oval bucket, part of a mess kit. See also MESSMATE.

mess /mɛs/ *v.* LME. [f. the n.] **1** *v.t.* Serve up (food); divide (food) into portions. *obs.* exc. *dial.* LME. **†2** *v.t.* Divide (a ship's company) into messes. Only in 17. **3** *v.i.* Take one's meals, esp. as a member of a mess; share accommodation or facilities. E18. **4** *v.t.* Provide with food in a mess, supply with food. E19. **5** *v.i.* Mix or associate *with*. Only in *mess or* (or *and*) *mell*. *Sc.* E19. **6** *v.i.* **a** Busy oneself in an untidy or desultory way, act with no definite purpose or result, dabble, (usu. foll. by *about, around*). Also, make a mess, put things into a disorderly or untidy state; (esp. of a domestic animal or a child) defecate. *colloq.* M19. **b** Foll. by *with*: interfere or get involved with; make a mess of; trouble, annoy. *N. Amer. colloq.* E20. **c** Foll. by *up*: make a mess of a situation; get into trouble. *N. Amer. colloq.* M20. **7** *v.t.* **a** Make a mess of; disorder, make dirty or untidy; mishandle (an undertaking); spoil, ruin. (Foll. by *up*.) M19. **b** Handle roughly or interferingly; treat unfairly or inconsistently; inconvenience, annoy. Usu. foll. by *about, around*. *colloq.* L19.

6a K. GRAHAME What boy has ever passed a bit of water without messing in it? R. K. NARAYAN A guest would mean a great deal of messing about with oil and frying-pan. E. BLYTON The children messed about that day, doing nothing at all. N. HINTON And don't go messing round with drugs. b J. MALCOLM He was playing with fire when he messed with you. 7a T. HILLERMAN Tell me more about how these sand paintings got messed up. P. LOMAS I would have had to behave in a very silly way to have messed up the interview. A. GERAS The wind tears at your hair and messes your clothes. b *Essex Weekly News* Defendant . . had never been messed about by policemen before. *Jackie* He's been messing her about for ages.

Comb.: **mess-up** a mess, a muddle; a confused situation.

messing *n.* (*a*) the action of the vb; (*b*) participation in a mess or common meal; (*c*) the food served to an individual in a mess: ME.

messa di voce /'messa di 'votʃe, 'mɛsə dɪ 'vəʊtʃi/ *n. phr.* Pl. ***messe di voce*** /'messe, 'mɛseɪ/. L18. [It., lit. 'placing of the voice'.] In singing, a gradual crescendo and diminuendo on a long-held note.

message /'mɛsɪdʒ/ *n.* & *v.* ME. [(O)Fr. f. Proto-Romance f. L *missus* pa. pple of *mittere* send: see -AGE.] **A** *n.* **1** A usu. brief communication transmitted through a messenger or other agency; an oral, written, or recorded communication sent from one person or group to another. ME. **b** A communication by a prophet or preacher or from God. Also, the central import of something; an implicit esp. polemical meaning in an artistic work etc. M16. **c** An official or formal communication, as between a ruler or parliament and a lower authority or the public. M16. **2** The carrying of a communication; a mission, an errand. ME. **b** In *pl.* Articles bought on an errand, shopping. Chiefly *Sc.* E20.

1 J. VAN DRUTEN I left a message at my hotel telling him to come . . and pick me up. R. K. NARAYAN He remembered the message he had been entrusted with. S. BELLOW I . . left a haughty message on the answering machine. b J. LOGAN His oracles of truth proclaim the message brought to man. *Times* His real gifts for story-telling and satirical observation are . . obscured by too heavy an insistence on the 'message' implicit in the plot. c LD MACAULAY A royal message authorizing the Commons to elect another Speaker.

Phrases: **get the message** *colloq.* understand a position stated or implied. **†on** or **of message** carrying a communication, doing an errand.

Comb.: **message-boy** *Sc.* an errand-boy; **message card** a card on which a message may be written; *Hist.* a card of invitation to a reception or entertainment; **message-stick** a wooden stick carved with significant marks and used as a means of communication or identification among Australian Aborigines.

B *v.t.* Send or communicate as a message; transmit (a plan etc.) by signalling etc. Also, send a message to. L16.

Sun (*Baltimore*) General MacArthur messaged them by radio: 'Thanks for a grand ride.' J. H. VANCE Lindbergh . . messaged that he would visit.

messageless *a.* E20.

messagerie /mesaʒri/ *n.* Pl. pronounced same. L18. [Fr.: see next.] The transportation or delivery of goods, messages, or people; a conveyance for these. In *pl.* also, goods, messages, or people for transportation or delivery.

messagery /'mɛsɪdʒ(ə)ri/ *n.* Long *arch. rare.* LME. [Fr. *messagerie*, f. *messager* MESSENGER + *-erie* -ERY.] The occupation or function of a messenger; the carrying of a message or errand.

Messalian /mɛ'seɪlɪən/ *n.* & *a.* Also **Ma-** /ma-/. L16. [Late Gk *Messalianos*, *Mass-* f. Syriac *mṣalyānā* person who prays, f. *ṣallī* pray.] *Eccl. Hist.* **A** *n.* = EUCHITE. Formerly also = HESYCHAST. L16. **B** *adj.* Of or pertaining to the Messalians. L16.

Messalina /mɛsə'liːnə/ *n.* L19. [Valeria *Messalina*, third wife of the Roman Emperor Claudius.] A licentious and scheming woman.

messaline /'mɛsəliːn/ *n.* & *a.* E20. [Fr., f. as prec.] (Made of) a soft lightweight and lustrous silk or rayon fabric.

messan /'mɛs(ə)n/ *n.* *Sc.* Also **-in**. L15. [Gael. *measan* = Ir. *measán*, MIr. *mesán*.] A small pet dog, a lap-dog. Also *messan-dog*.

Messapian /mə'seɪpɪən/ *n.* & *a.* E17. [f. L *Messapius*, f. *Messapia* (see below) + -AN.] *Hist.* **A** *adj.* Of or pertaining to the ancient district of Messapia, in southern Italy (now Apulia and Calabria), its inhabitants, or their language. E17. **B** *n.* **1** A native or inhabitant of Messapia. L18. **2** The language of the Messapians. L19.

Messapic *n.* & *a.* (of) the language of the Messapians M20.

messe di voce *n. phr.* pl. of MESSA DI VOCE.

Messeigneurs *n.* pl. of MONSEIGNEUR.

messenger /'mɛsɪndʒə/ *n.* & *v.* ME. [(O)Fr. *messager*, f. as MESSAGE: see -ER[2]. For the intrusive *n* cf. *passenger, scavenger*, etc.] **A** *n.* **1** A person who carries a message or goes on an errand for another; a person employed to carry messages. ME. **b** A bearer *of* (a specified message). ME. **c** *Biol.* A molecule or substance that carries (esp. genetic) information. Freq. *attrib.* M20. **2** A person sent forward to prepare the way; a herald, a precursor, a harbinger. *arch.* ME. **3** A government official employed to carry dispatches and formerly to apprehend State prisoners; a courier. LME. **4a** Esp. *Naut.* An endless rope, cable, or chain used with a capstan to haul a cable or to drive a powered winch etc. Also, a light line used to haul or support a larger cable. M17. **b** A device able to be sent down a line, esp. in order to trip a mechanism. M18.

1 D. CARKEET You can't shoot the messenger for bringing bad news. M. FLANAGAN Jason asked for a cheque to be sent round by messenger. 2 *fig.*: SHAKES. *Jul. Caes.* Yon grey lines That fret the clouds are messengers of day.

Phrases: *express messenger*: see EXPRESS *a.* **King's** or **Queen's messenger** a courier employed by the British Government to carry important official papers within Britain and abroad. *second messenger*: see SECOND *a.*

Comb.: **messenger-at-arms** *Sc.* an official employed to execute writs from the Court of Session and the High Court of Justiciary; **messenger cable** a cable used to support a power cable or other conductor of electricity; a suspension cable or wire; **messenger RNA** *Biol.* RNA which is synthesized in a cell nucleus with a nucleotide sequence complementary to the coding sequence of a gene (transcription), and passes from the nucleus to a ribosome, where its nucleotide sequence determines the amino-acid sequence of a protein synthesized there (translation); abbrev. *mRNA*; **messenger wire** = *messenger cable* above.

B *v.t.* Send by messenger. (*rare* before. L20.) E19.

messengership *n.* the position or function of a messenger E17.

Messenian /mɛˈsiːnɪən/ *n.* & *a.* M16. [f. L *Messenius* f. Gk *Messēnios* of Messenia (see below) + -AN.] A *n.* 1 A native or inhabitant of (esp. ancient) Messenia, a region in the SW Peloponnese in Greece. M16. 2 The dialect of ancient Greek spoken in Messenia. E20. B *adj.* Of or pertaining to Messenia, the (ancient) Messenians, or their dialect. M19.

messer /ˈmɛsə/ *n.*[1] M17. [f. MESS *v.* + -ER[1].] †1 A supplier of meat to ships. M17–M18. 2 A person who makes a mess; a muddler, a bungler. *colloq.* E20.

Messer /ˈmɛsə/ *n.*[2] L17. [It. *messere.*] Used as a title preceding the name of an Italian man: = MR.

Messiah /mɪˈsʌɪə/ *n.* Also (earlier) †**-ias.** ME. [(O)Fr. *Messie* f. pop.L *Messias* f. Gk *Messias* f. Aram. *mĕšīḥā*, Heb. *māšīăḥ* anointed, f. *māšhaḥ* anoint. Mod. form *Messiah* created by the Geneva translators of 1560 as looking more Hebraic than *Messias.*] The promised deliverer of the Jewish nation prophesied in the Hebrew Scriptures; Jesus regarded as the saviour of humankind. Also (*transf.*), an actual or expected liberator of an oppressed people or country etc.; a leader or saviour of a specified group, cause, etc.

Guardian Howard Jarvis . . the Messiah of taxpayers. P. B. CLARKE Haile Selassie, former emperor of Ethiopia and the Rastafarian messiah.

Messiahship *n.* the character or position of the Messiah or of a Messiah; the fact of being the Messiah: E17.

Messianic /mɛsɪˈanɪk/ *a.* Also **m-.** M19. [Fr. *messianique*, f. *Messie* MESSIAH after *rabbinique* RABBINIC: see -IC.] Of, pertaining to, or characteristic of the Messiah or a Messiah; inspired by hope of or belief in the Messiah or a Messiah.

A. S. DALE Fanatics who wanted to lead messianic cults to replace Christianity. *Daily Telegraph* An almost messianic approach to making herbs better known and better grown.

Messianically *adv.* with reference to the Messiah or a Messiah, as referring to the Messiah or a Messiah M19. **Meˈssianism** *n.* belief in a coming Messiah L19.

Messidor /ˈmɛsɪdɔː, *foreign* mesidɔːr/ *n.* M19. [Fr., f. L *messis* harvest + Gk *dōron* gift: see -OR.] *Hist.* The tenth month of the French Republican calendar (introduced 1793), extending from 19 June to 18 July.

Messier /ˈmɛsɪə/ *n.* M19. [Charles *Messier* (1730–1817), Fr. astronomer.] *Astron.* Used *attrib.* to designate a catalogue of 109 non-stellar objects visible in the northern sky, first published in 1774, and (usu. w. an identifying numeral) objects listed in the catalogue.

Listener The Great Nebula (Messier 31).

Messieurs *n.* pl. of MONSIEUR.

messin *n.* var. of MESSAN.

messire /mesiːr/ *n.* Now *arch.* or *Hist.* L15. [OFr., f. *mes* my (f. L *meus*) + SIRE *n.* Cf. MONSIEUR.] Used *voc.* or preceding the name of a high-ranking French noble or any important man: my lord, sir.

messmate /ˈmɛsmeɪt/ *n.* M18. [f. MESS *n.* + MATE *n.*[2]] 1 A regular companion at meals; a member of a mess, esp. in the armed forces. M18. 2 (The wood of) any of several rough-barked eucalypts, esp. *Eucalyptus cloeziana* and *E. obliqua*. *Austral.* M19.

Messrs /ˈmɛsəz/ *n.pl.* Also **Messrs.** (point). L18. [Abbrev.] Messieurs. Now usu. as pl. of MR and in addressing a private firm or company by name.

J. SMEATON I returned with Messrs. Jessop and Richardson to Plymouth. J. H. MAPLESON Messrs. Steinway now . . undertook to supply each leading member of the Company with pianos.

messuage /ˈmɛswɪdʒ/ *n.* LME. [AN *mes(s)uage*, prob. orig. misreading of *mesnage* MÉNAGE: see -AGE.] Orig., the portion of land intended to be or actually occupied as a site for a dwelling-house and its appurtenances. Now (*Law*), a dwelling-house with its outbuildings and the adjacent land assigned to its use.

messy /ˈmɛsi/ *a.* M19. [f. MESS *n.* + -Y[1].] 1 Of the nature of a mess; involving, accompanied by, or causing mess or disorder; untidy, dirty. Also, difficult to deal with, full of awkward complications. M19. 2 Immoral, unethical. *colloq.* E20.

1 J. B. PRIESTLEY A messy, dribbling, pie-faced urchin. A. LURIE I should warn you . . they're kind of messy to eat. J. DISKI How do they fit in? Messy old emotions.

messily *adv.* in a messy manner, so as to make a mess E20. **messiness** *n.* L19.

mestee *n.* var. of MUSTEE.

mesteque /ˈmɛstɛk/ *n.* Now *rare* or *obs.* M17. [Origin unkn.] A kind of fine cochineal.

mesterolone /mɛˈstɛrələʊn/ *n.* M20. [f. ME(THYL + STEROL + -ONE.] *Pharm.* A synthetic androgen used to treat male hypogonadism.

mestizo /mɛˈstiːzəʊ/ *n.* & *a.* Pl. of. n. **-os.** Fem. **-za** /-zə/. L16. [Sp. f. Proto-Romance f. L *mixtus* pa. pple of *miscere* mix.] A *n.* A Spanish or Portuguese person with parents of different races, *spec.* one with a Spaniard as one parent and an American Indian as the other; *gen.* any person of mixed blood. Also, a Central or S. American Indian who has adopted European culture. L16.

B *attrib.* or as *adj.* That is a mestizo or mestiza. E17.

J. A. MICHENER He was one of the first of Mexico's mestizo children, half Spanish, half Indian.

mesto /ˈmɛsto/ *adv.* & *a.* E19. [It. f. L *maestus* sad.] *Mus.* A direction: sad(ly), mournful(ly).

mestome /ˈmɛstəʊm/ *n.* Also **mestom** /ˈmɛstəm/. L19. [f. Gk *mestōma* filling up, f. *mestoun* fill up, f. *mestos* full.] *Bot.* The conducting part of a fibrovascular bundle. Now only in *mestome sheath*, the inner thick-walled sheath which surrounds the vascular tissue in some grasses. Cf. STEREOME I.

mestranol /ˈmɛstrənɒl/ *n.* M20. [f. ME(THYL + O)ESTRA(DIOL + -*n*- + -OL.] *Pharm.* A synthetic oestrogen, the 3-methyl ether of ethynyloestradiol, which is more potent than oestradiol and is commonly used in oral contraceptives.

met /mɛt/ *n.*[1] *obs.* exc. *dial.* [OE *ġemet* = OS *gimet*, OHG *gamez*, ON *mét* (neut. pl.) weight of a balance, f. Gmc base also of MEET *a.*, METE *v.*] †1 Size, dimension, or quantity as determinable by measurement. OE–E16. 2 = MEASURE *n.* 3. OE. 3 = MEASURE *n.* 2. OE. †4 = MEASURE *n.* II. OE–LME. †5 The action of measuring. Only in ME. †6 = MEASURE *n.* 5. ME–E17.

met /mɛt/ *n.*[2] *colloq.* Also **met.**, **M-.** L19. [Abbrev.] 1 *The* Metropolitan Line or (*Hist.*) Railway in London, *the* Metropolitan Opera House in New York, *the* Metropolitan Police in London. L19. 2 *The* Meteorological Office. M20.

met /mɛt/ *a. colloq.* Also **met.**, **M-.** M20. [Abbrev.] 1 Meteorological. Esp. in *the Met. Office.* M20. 2 Metropolitan. M20.

met *v.* pa. t. & pple of MEET *v.*

met- *pref.* var. of META-.

meta /ˈmiːtə/ *n.*[1] Pl. **-tae** /-tiː/. L16. [L.] *Rom. Antiq.* A conical column placed at each end of a racetrack to mark the turning-place; a boundary, a boundary-marker.

Meta /ˈmɛtə/ *n.*[2] Also **m-.** E20. [Abbrev.] (Proprietary name for) metaldehyde, esp. as used in block form.

meta /ˈmɛtə/ *a.* & *adv.* Freq. italicized. L19. [f. META-.] *Chem.* A *adj.* Characterized by or relating to (substitution at) two carbon atoms separated by one other in a benzene ring; at a position next but one *to* some (specified) substituent in a benzene ring. L19. B *adv.* So as to form meta-substituted compounds. M20.

meta- /ˈmɛtə/ *pref.* Bef. a vowel or *h* also **met-.** [Gk *met(a)-* (*meth-*), occurring separately as the prep. *meta* with, after. In sense I after METAPHYSICS.] 1 Denoting a nature of a higher order or more fundamental kind, as *metalanguage*, *metatheory*. 2 Chiefly *Anat.* & *Zool.* Denoting position behind, at the back, or after. 3 *Biol.* Denoting occurrence or development at a later stage or time. 4 *Chem.* a Denoting derivation from, metamerism with, or resemblance to a given compound; *spec.* in names of salts and acids containing fewer molecules of water. b (Freq. italicized.) Denoting substitution in a benzene ring at carbon atoms separated by one carbon atom. Cf. ORTHO- 2b, PARA-[1] 3. 5 *Geol.* Denoting metamorphism. 6 Denoting change, alteration, or effect generally.

meˈtabasis *n.*, pl. **-ases** /-əsiːz/, a transition, *spec.* (*a*) *Rhet.* from one subject or point to another; (*b*) *Med.* from one remedy etc. to another: M16. **metabioˈlogical** *a.* of or pertaining to metabiology E20. **metabiˈology** *n.* a hypothetical science supposed to deal with phenomena of living organisms in a manner beyond the scope of conventional biology E20. **metaˈchrosis** *n.* [Gk *khrōsis* colouring] *Zool.* ability to change colour L19. **metaˈcinnabar(ite)** *ns.* (*Min.*) mercuric sulphide, occurring as a black mineral crystallizing in the cubic system, dimorphous with cinnabar L19. **metacommuniˈcation** *n.* communication taking place with or underlying a more obvious form of communication; principles or theories about communication derived from the study of communication: M20. **metacommuniˈcational**, **metacoˈmmunicative** *adjs.* concerned with or pertaining to metacommunication M20. **metaˈconal** *a.* (*Zool.*) of, pertaining to, or of the nature of a metacone L19. **metacone** *n.* (*Zool.*) a cusp on the posterior buccal corner of a tribosphenic upper molar tooth L19. **metaˈconid** *n.* (*Zool.*) a cusp on the posterior lingual corner of the trigonid of the tribosphenic lower molar tooth L19. **metaˈcontrast** *n.* (*Psychol.*) a change, esp. a diminution, in the after-effect of a visual stimulus as a result of a rapidly succeeding second stimulus M20. **metaconule** /-ˈkɒnjuːl/ *n.* (*Zool.*) an intermediate cusp between the hypocone and the metacone of a mammalian upper molar tooth L19. **metacryst** *n.* (*Petrogr.*) a large crystal formed in a metamorphic rock by recrystallization E20. **meta-ˈethical** *a.* of or pertaining to meta-ethics M20. **meta-ˈethics** *n.* the branch of knowledge that deals with the foundations of ethics, esp. of ethical statements M20. **metafiction** *n.* (a work of) fiction which does not rely on traditional ideas of realism or does not conform to experience of the world M20. **metaˈfictional** *a.* pertaining to or of the nature of metafiction L20. **metagaˈlactic** *a.* (*Astron.*) of, pertaining to, or designating the (or a) metagalaxy M20. **metaˈgalaxy** *n.* (*Astron.*) the entire system of galaxies and other bodies which makes up the universe; a cluster or group of galaxies: M20. **metageoˈmetrical** *a.* of or pertaining to metageometry L19. **metageˈometry** *n.* non-Euclidean geometry L19. **metagnathism** /mɛˈtagnəθɪz(ə)m/ *n.* (*Ornith.*) metagnathous condition L19. **metagnathous** /mɛˈtagnəθəs/ *a.* (*Ornith.*) having or designating a beak with crossed tips L19. **metalaw** *n.* a hypothetical legal code based on the principles underlying existing legal codes and designed to provide a framework of agreement between diverse legal systems M20. **metaˈlegal** *a.* of or pertaining to (the principles of) metalaw M20. **metamessage** *n.* an ulterior or underlying massage, an innuendo; *Advertising* a statement that relies on implication rather than exhortation, a message conveyed in this way: L20. **metamict** *a.* [Gk *miktos* mixed] (of a mineral) made amorphous through the radioactive decay of atoms contained in it E20. **metamictiˈzation** *n.* the process of becoming or state of being metamict M20.

metamictness *n.* metamict character M20. **metane'phridial** *a.* (*Zool.*) of or pertaining to a metanephridium M20. **metane'phridium** *n.* (*Zool.*) a nephridium whose inner end opens into a coelom, as in many worms M20. **meta'notum** *n.* (*Entomol.*) the dorsal part of the metathorax of an insect M19. **metaphone** *n.* (*Ling.*) each of two or more equally acceptable variants of a phoneme (e.g. the first vowel /ʌɪ/ or /iː/ of *either*) M20. **meta'phonic** *a.* (*Philol.*) affected by or involving metaphony M20. **me'taphonized** *a.* (*Philol.*) affected by metaphony L20. **me'taphony** *n.* (*Philol.*) umlaut (the vowel change) L19. **meta'podial** *n.* (*Anat.* & *Zool.*) a metacarpal or metatarsal bone L19. **meta'podium** *n.* (*Zool.*) the posterior lobe of the foot of a mollusc M19. **metarho'dopsin** *n.* (*Biochem.*) either of two interconvertible intermediates (the orange *metarhodopsin I* and the yellow *metarhodopsin II*) that are formed from lumirhodopsin when rhodopsin is bleached by light and undergo spontaneous hydrolysis to retinal and opsin M20. **metarule** *n.* a convention or universal rule in a symbolic system, esp. a linguistic system M20. **metascience** *n.* the branch of philosophy that has science as its subject M20. **metascien'tific** *a.* of or pertaining to metascience M20. **metascien'tifically** *adv.* in a metascientific manner M20. **meta'sternal** *a.* (*Entomol.* & *Anat.*) of, pertaining to, or of the nature of a metasternum E19. **meta'sternum** *n.* (*a*) *Entomol.* the ventral piece of the metathorax of an insect; (*b*) *Anat.* = XIPHISTERNUM: E19. **meta-talk** *n.* talk in which there are hidden meanings M20. **metatho'racic** *a.*(*Entomol.*) of, pertaining to, or of the nature of a metathorax M19. **meta'thorax** *n.*(*Entomol.*) the third, posterior segment of the thorax of an insect E19. **metavol'canic** *n.* & *a.* (*Geol.*) (designating) a volcanic rock that has been subjected to metamorphosis M20. **metaxylem** /mɛtə'zʌɪləm/ *n.* (*Bot.*) the later-formed part of the primary xylem, maturing after elongation of the plant tissue is complete E20.

metabiosis /mɛtəbʌɪ'əʊsɪs/ *n.* L19. [f. next after *symbiosis*, *symbiotic*.] *Biol.* A form of ecological dependence in which one organism must modify the environment before the second is able to live in it.

metabiotic /-'ɒtɪk/ *a.* of, pertaining to, or of the nature of metabiosis L19.

metabolic /mɛtə'bɒlɪk/ *a.* M18. [Gk *metabolikos* changeable, f. as METABOLISM: see -IC.] **1** Pertaining to or involving transition. *rare.* M18. **2** *Biol.* & *Biochem.* Pertaining to, involving, characterized or produced by, metabolism. M19. **3** *Biol.* Pertaining to, of the nature of, or exhibiting metaboly. E20.

2 metabolic pathway any sequence of chemical, usu. enzyme-catalysed reactions undergone by a compound within a living cell or organism.

metabolically *adv.* as regards or by means of metabolism E20.

metabolise *v.* var. of METABOLIZE.

metabolism /mɛ'tabəlɪz(ə)m/ *n.* L19. [f. Gk *metabolē* change, f. *metaballein* to change, f. as META- + *ballein* throw + -ISM.] *Biol.* & *Biochem.* The sum of the chemical processes, in a cell or organism, by which complex substances are synthesized and broken down, and growth and energy production sustained; anabolism and catabolism considered together; the overall rate at which these processes occur; the sum of the chemical changes undergone in the body by any particular substance.

basal metabolism: see BASAL *a.* 1.

metabolite *n.* any substance produced during or necessary to metabolism L19.

metabolize /mɛ'tabəlʌɪz/ *v.* Also **-ise**. L19. [f. Gk *metabolē* change (see prec.) + -IZE.] *Biol.* & *Biochem.* **1** *v.t.* Cause (a substance) to undergo metabolism; process by metabolism. L19. **2** *v.i.* Perform or undergo metabolism. M20.

metaboliza'bility *n.* ability to be metabolized E20. **metabolizable** *a.* (*a*) (of a substance) able to be processed in metabolism; (*b*) (of energy) that can be made available or produced by metabolic processes: E20. **metabolizer** *n.* an individual or organism that metabolizes a particular substance L20.

metaboly /mɛ'tabəli/ *n.* L19. [f. Gk *metabolē* change (see METABOLISM) + -Y[3].] *Biol.* The changes of shape characteristic of protists with a firm but flexible pellicle; euglenoid movement.

†metacarp *n.* see METACARPUS.

metacarpal /mɛtə'kɑːp(ə)l/ *a.* & *n.* M18. [f. METACARPUS + -AL[1].] *Anat.* A *adj.* Of or pertaining to the metacarpus. M18. **B** *n.* A metacarpal bone. M19.

metacarpi *n.* pl. of METACARPUS.

metacarpo- /mɛtə'kɑːpəʊ/ *comb. form* of next: see -O-.

metacarpophalan'geal *a.* (*Anat.*) of, pertaining to, or (esp.) connecting the metacarpus and the phalanges M19.

metacarpus /mɛtə'kɑːpəs/ *n.* Pl. **-pi** /-pʌɪ, -piː/. Formerly also Anglicized as **†metacarp**. LME. [mod.L, alt. of Gk *metakarpion* after CARPUS: see META-.] *Anat.* & *Zool.* The part of the skeleton between the carpus or wrist and the phalanges, consisting of e.g. the five long bones of the hand in humans, and the cannon bone of the foreleg in horses and other quadrupeds.

metacentre /'mɛtəsɛntə/ *n.* Also ***-center**. L18. [Fr. *métacentre*, f. as META- + CENTRE *n.*] *Physics* & *Shipbuilding.* The point of intersection between a line (vertical at equilibrium) through the centre of buoyancy of a floating body, esp. a ship, and the vertical line through the centre of buoyancy of the body when slightly tilted away from equilibrium, which point must be above the centre of gravity if the body is to return to equilibrium. Also called *shifting centre*.

metacentric /mɛtə'sɛntrɪk/ *a.* & *n.* L18. [f. as prec. + -IC.] **A** *adj.* **1** *Physics* & *Shipbuilding.* Of or pertaining to the metacentre of a ship etc. L18. **2** *Cytol.* Of a chromosome: having the centromere at or near the centre. M20.

1 metacentric height the height of the metacentre of a floating body above the centre of gravity.

B *n.* A metacentric chromosome. M20.

metacercaria /mɛtəsəː'kɛːrɪə/ *n.* Pl. **-iae** /-iiː/. E20. [f. META- + CERCARIA.] *Zool.* A parasitic trematode in encysted form.

metacetone /mɛ'tasɪtəʊn/ *n.* M19. [f. MET(A- + ACETONE.] *Chem.* A colourless flammable liquid ketone, $(C_2H_5)_2C{:}O$, obtained by distillation of sugar in excess lime; pentan-3-one.

metachromasia /mɛtəkrə'meɪzɪə/ *n.* M20. [f. as next: see -CHROMASIA.] *Biol.* The property of certain biological materials of staining a different colour from that of the stain solution used; the property of certain stains of changing colour in the presence of certain biological materials.

Also **metachromasy** /-'krəʊməsi/ *n.* E20.

metachromatic /mɛtəkrə'matɪk/ *a.* L19. [f. META- + Gk *khrōmat-*, *khrōma* colour + -IC.] **1** Of or pertaining to metachromatism. L19. **2** *Biol.* Of, pertaining to, exhibiting, or involving metachromasia. Cf. ORTHOCHROMATIC 2. L19.

metachromatically *adv.* E20.

metachromatism /mɛtə'krəʊmətɪz(ə)m/ *n.* L19. [f. as prec. + -ISM.] **1** Change or variation of colour. L19. **2** *Biol.* = METACHROMASIA. L19.

metachrome /'mɛtəkrəʊm/ *n.* & *a.* L19. [f. META- + Gk *khrōma* colour.] *Chem.* **A** *n.* A body or substance that changes colour. *rare.* L19. **B** *adj.* (Of a mordant dye) able to be applied simultaneously with the mordant in the same bath; pertaining to or involving dyes of this kind. E20.

metachromism /mɛtə'krəʊmɪz(ə)m/ *n.* *rare.* L19. [f. as prec. + -ISM.] *Chem.* Change of colour.

metachronism /mɛ'takrənɪz(ə)m/ *n.* E17. [med.L *metachronismus*, f. Gk *metakhron(i)os* happening later, f. as META- + *khronos* time: see -ISM.] **1** An error in chronology consisting in placing an event later than its real date (opp. PROCHRONISM). Cf. PARACHRONISM. E17. **2** *Biol.* The coordination of the movement of cilia or similar parts into a progressive wave. E20.

metachronal /mɛtə'krəʊn(ə)l/ *a.* (*Biol.*) exhibiting or characteristic of metachronism E20. **meta'chronally** *adv.* E20.

metacism /'mɛtəsɪz(ə)m/ *n.* *rare.* M17. [Late L *metacismus* f. late Gk *mutakismos* fondness for the letter m, f. *mu*, name of the letter: see -ISM.] The placing of a word with final *m* before a word beginning with a vowel, regarded as a fault in Latin prose composition. Also, the pronouncing of a final *m* which ought to be elided before a following vowel.

metacyclic /mɛtə'sʌɪklɪk, -'sɪk-/ *a.* & *n.* L19. [f. META- + CYCLIC.] **A** *adj.* **1** *Math.* Of or pertaining to the permutation of a set of elements in a cycle. L19. **2** *Biol.* & *Med.* Designating the form that some trypanosomes assume in the intermediate (invertebrate) host, in which they are infective for the vertebrate host. E20. **B** *n.* *Biol.* & *Med.* A metacyclic trypanosome. M20.

metadyne /'mɛtədʌɪn/ *n.* M20. [f. META- + Gk *dunamis* force, power.] *Electr.* A rotary direct-current generator in which the output voltage can be varied by a control field perpendicular to the main field, used in position or speed control systems.

metae *n.* pl. of META *n.*[1]

metage /'miːtɪdʒ/ *n.* E16. [f. METE *v.* + -AGE.] The action of measuring officially the content or weight of a load of grain, coal, etc.; the duty paid for such measuring (cf. MEASURAGE).

metagenesis /mɛtə'dʒɛnɪsɪs/ *n.* L19. [f. META- + -GENESIS.] *Biol.* Alternation between sexual and asexual reproduction; alternation of generations.

metage'netic *a.* of, pertaining to, characterized by, or involving metagenesis M19. **metage'netically** *adv.* by metagenesis M19.

metagnomy /mɛ'tagnəmi/ *n.* E20. [Fr. *métagnomie*, f. as META- + Gk *gnōmē* thought.] The supposed acquisition of information by supernormal means; divination, clairvoyance. Also, the power of acquiring information in this way.

'metagnome *n.* a person having the power of metagnomy, a medium M20. **metag'nomic** *a.* of or pertaining to metagnomy E20.

metagram /'mɛtəgram/ *n.* M19. [f. Gk META- + -GRAM, after *anagram*.] A kind of puzzle in which a word is changed by replacing some of its letters.

metagrobolize /mɛtə'grɒbəlʌɪz/ *v.t.* *joc.* Now *rare.* Also **-ise**. M17. [Fr. †*metagraboulizer*.] Puzzle, mystify; puzzle out.

métairie /meteri/ *n.* Pl. pronounced same. E19. [Fr., f. as MÉTAYER.] A farm held on the *métayage* system.

metake /'mɛtəkeɪ/ *n.* L19. [Jap.] A tall slender Japanese bamboo, *Pseudosasa japonica*. Also called *arrow bamboo*.

metakinesis /mɛtəkʌɪ'niːsɪs, -kɪ-/ *n.* Pl. **-neses** /-'niːsiːz/. L19. [f. META- + KINESIS.] **1** *Cytol.* **a** The separation of chromatids during anaphase. L19. **b** The process of alignment of chromosomes on the equator of the spindle. M20. **2** A manifestation of consciousness or mental phenomena. *rare.* L19.

metakinetic /-kɪ'nɛtɪk/ *a.* L19.

metal /'mɛt(ə)l/ *n.* & *a.* Also **†mettle**. See also METTLE. ME. [(O)Fr. *métal*, †*metail* or its source L *metallum* mine, quarry, metal f. synon. Gk *metallon*.] **A** *n.* **I 1 a** Any of the class of substances including the elements gold, silver, copper, iron, lead, and tin, and certain alloys (as brass and bronze), characteristically lustrous, ductile, fusible, malleable solids that are good conductors of heat and electricity; *Chem.* an element that readily forms positive ions. ME. **b** Material of this nature; *spec.* (*a*) as that of arms and armour; (*b*) cast iron. ME. **†c** Precious metal, gold. *rare* (Shakes.). L16–E17. **2** Ore. ME. **3 †a** An object made of metal; *spec.* (*a*) a medal, a coin; (*b*) a metal reflector of a telescope. LME–L18. **b** In *pl.* The rails of a railway or tramway. M19. **4** *Her.* Either of the tinctures or and argent. LME. **5** Material, matter, substance; *esp.* earthy matter. M16. **6** Molten glass before it is blown or cast. L16. **7** The metal composing the barrel of a gun; (also *line of metal*) a gunner's line of sight (chiefly in *under*, *over metal*); the guns or fire-power of a warship etc. (chiefly in *weight of metal*). L16. **8** A specific alloy used in any particular craft or trade. Freq. w. preceding adj. or n. E18. **9** Hardened clay, shale; rock met with in the course of mining; in *pl.*, strata containing minerals. Chiefly *Sc.* E18. **10** Broken stone for use in making roads (also *road-metal*) or as ballast for railway lines. L18. **11** *ellipt.* = *heavy metal* s.v. HEAVY *a.* & *n.* L20.

1 ADAM SMITH The durableness of metals is the foundation of this steadiness of price. *base metal*: see BASE *a. precious metal*: see PRECIOUS *a.* **b** SHAKES. *John* That I must draw this metal from my side To be a widow-maker! RACHEL ANDERSON We heard the metal click as the latch on the big gate was lifted. M. BRETT A contract for delivery of a ton of metal. *Britannia metal, gun-metal, Wood's metal*, etc. **3b** N. WOOLER Oil gas.. remained in use right up until the 1960s, particularly on London Midland metals.

†**II** See METTLE *n.*

B *attrib.* or as *adj.* †**1** Var. of METTLE *a.* Only in L16. **2** Made or consisting of metal; metallic. E17.

2 M. S. POWER She washed him in the big metal tub in front of the fire.

Comb. & *special collocations*: **metal age** a period when weapons and tools were commonly made of copper, bronze, or iron; **metal arc welding** arc welding in which the melting of a metal electrode provides the joining material; **metal-detector** an instrument for detecting metallic objects under the ground from their magnetic effects above ground; *metal fatigue*: see FATIGUE *n.* 2b; *metal* GUITAR; **metalmark** any butterfly of the predominantly S. American family Riodinidae, many members of which have brilliant metallic markings on the wings; **metal thread** = METALLIC *thread*; **metalwork** (*a*) work, esp. artistic work, in metal; the art of working in metal; (*b*) in *pl.*, a factory where metal is produced; **metalworker** a worker in metal, a craftsman or -woman who works in metal.

metal /ˈmɛt(ə)l/ *v.t.* Infl. **-ll-**, ***-l-**. E17. [f. the n.] **1** Provide or fit with metal. E17. **2** Make or mend (a road) with road-metal. E19.

metalanguage /ˈmɛtəlaŋgwɪdʒ/ *n.* M20. [f. META- + LANGUAGE *n.*[1]] A language used for the description or analysis of another language; a system of propositions about other propositions.

metalation /mɛtəˈleɪʃ(ə)n/ *n.* M20. [f. METAL *n.* + -ATION.] *Chem.* The introduction into an organic compound of a metal atom in place of a hydrogen atom.

ˈ**metalate** *v.t.* bring about metalation in M20.

metalaxyl /mɛtəˈlaksɪl/ *n.* L20. [f. META- + A)LA(NINE + XYL(ENE.] A fungicide that is effective against mildew on some crops.

metaldehyde /mɪˈtaldɪhʌɪd/ *n.* M19. [f. META- + ALDEHYDE.] *Chem.* A solid that is a low polymer of acetaldehyde and is used to kill slugs and snails and as a fuel for cooking and heating. Cf. META *n.*[2]

metaled *a.* see METALLED.

metalepsis /mɛtəˈlɛpsɪs/ *n.* M16. [L, f. Gk *metalēpsis*, f. *metalambanein* to substitute, f. as META- + *lambanein* take.] A rhetorical figure consisting in the metonymical substitution of one word for another which is itself figurative.

metaleptic *a.* M17.

metalik /mɛˈtalɪk/ *n.* L19. [Turk., prob. f. mod.Gk *metallikos* METALLIC.] *Hist.* A former Turkish coin worth 10 paras.

metalimnion /mɛtəˈlɪmnɪən/ *n.* Pl. **-nia** /-nɪə/. M20. [f. META- + Gk *limnion* dim. of *limnē* lake.] The layer of water in a stratified lake beneath the epilimnion and above the hypolimnion, in which the temperature decreases rapidly with depth.

metalimnetic /-lɪmˈnɛtɪk/ *a.* of or within a metalimnion M20.

metaling *n.* see METALLING.

metalingual /mɛtəˈlɪŋgw(ə)l/ *a.* M20. [f. META- + LINGUAL.] = next.

metalinguistic /mɛtəlɪŋˈgwɪstɪk/ *a.* M20. [f. META- + LINGUISTIC.] Of or pertaining to a metalanguage or metalinguistics.

metaˈlinguist *n.* M20. **metalinguistically** *adv.* from the point of view of metalinguistics M20. **metalinguistics** *n.* (*a*) the branch of linguistics that deals with metalanguages: (*b*) *rare* the branch of linguistics that deals with the relation of language to the other elements of a culture; M20.

metalist *n.* see METALLIST.

metalize *v.* see METALLIZE.

metalled /ˈmɛt(ə)ld/ *a.* Also ***metaled**. L16. [f. METAL *n.*, *v.* + -ED[2], -ED[1].] **1**†**a** Made or consisting of metal; containing metal. L16–M17. **b** Having a covering or fittings of metal. E19. **2** Of a road: made with road-metal; having a specially made hard surface. E19.

metalleity /mɛtəˈliːɪti, -ˈleɪɪti/ *n.* M18. [Fr. *métalléité*, f. L *metalleus* of the nature of metal, f. *metallum* METAL *n.*: see -ITY.] The quality of being metallic; metallic qualities collectively.

metallic /mɪˈtalɪk/ *a.* & *n.* LME. [L *metallicus* f. Gk *metallikos*, f. *metallon* METAL *n.*: see -IC.] **A** *adj.* **1** Of, pertaining to, consisting of, or containing a metal or metals; of the nature of or resembling a metal. LME. **b** Involving or consisting of coin as distinguished from paper money. L18. **2** Yielding metal, metalliferous. L17. †**3** Connected with mining or metallurgy. L17–M19. **4** Having the form or outward characters of a metal; (of a metal) uncombined with other substances. M18. **5** Resembling a metal in appearance; *esp.* having or designating the peculiar sheen characteristic of metals; iridescent, glossy. L18. **6** Of taste: suggestive of metal. E19. **7** Of sound: resembling that produced by metal when struck; sounding sharp and ringing; (esp. of the voice or a cry) harsh and unmusical. M19.

1 *Scientific American* Metallurgists were able to make a number of accurate predictions about metallic behaviour. Z. TOMIN A large metallic sign rattled incessantly on a swaying post. **2** R. KIRWAN Metallic veins are never found in beds of lava. **4** R. RAYMOND The ore is.. free from base metals, and carries metallic silver. F. HOYLE At high temperatures, iron condenses in its metallic form. **5** I. MURDOCH Her reddish brown hair, to which a.. scattering of grey gave a metallic patina. *Practical Motorist* The En Vogue has metallic blue paintwork. **7** E. LUCIE-SMITH And fifty miles away the Channel gale Beats in the bays; / with loud metallic cries.

Special collocations: **metallic arc welding** = *metal arc welding* s.v. METAL *n.* **metallic bond** *Chem.* the kind of bond that exists between the atoms in a metal, with electrons delocalized throughout the crystal lattice rather than shared. **metallic circuit** a telegraphic circuit in which the return is through a wire rather than the earth. **metallic soap** any of a class of soaps (containing an alkaline-earth or heavy metal instead of an alkali metal) which are soluble in organic solvents but not in water and are used in waterproofing and in making antioxidants, lubricants, and fungicides. **metallic thread**: made from metal or a synthetic material resembling metal. *metallic tractors*: see TRACTOR 1. **metallic yarn** = *metallic thread* above.

B *n.* **1** An article or substance made of or containing metal. Usu. in *pl.* E17. **2** A metallic paint or colour. L20.

metallically *adv.* by means of a metal or metals; in the manner of a metal or metals: M19. **metallicity** /mɛtəˈlɪsɪti/ *n.* (*a*) the quality of being metallic; (*b*) *Astron.* the proportion of the material of a star that is an element other than hydrogen or helium: M19.

metallide /ˈmɛt(ə)lʌɪd/ *v.t.* M20. [f. METAL *n.* & *a.* + -IDE.] Deposit as an electroplated metal coating by a method involving immersion in a bath of molten fluoride salts, so that the metal forms a surface layer whose composition varies from the surface inwards. Chiefly as *metalliding* vbl n.

metalliferous /mɛtəˈlɪf(ə)rəs/ *a.* M17. [f. L *metallifer*, f. *metallum* METAL *n.*: see -FEROUS.] Containing or yielding metal.

metalline /ˈmɛtəlʌɪn/ *a.* LME. [OFr. *metalin* (mod. *métallin*), f. *métal*: see METAL *n.*, -INE[1].] **1** = METALLIC *a.* 1. LME. **2** Made of metal. L16. **3** Resembling metal in appearance, lustre, etc. L16. **4** Impregnated with metallic substances; (of vapour) arising from or produced by metal. E17. **5** Metalliferous. E17.

metalling /ˈmɛt(ə)lɪŋ/ *n.* Also ***metaling**. E19. [f. METAL *v.* + -ING[1].] **1** Road-metal. E19. **2** The action of METAL *v.* L19.

metallise *v.* var. of METALLIZE.

metallist /ˈmɛt(ə)lɪst/ *n.* Also ***metalist**. M17. [f. METAL *n.* + -IST.] **1** A person who is skilled in or works in metals. Now *rare.* M17. **2** An advocate of the use of a particular metal as currency or of metal as the principal or sole currency. L19.

metallize /ˈmɛt(ə)lʌɪz/ *v.t.* Also **-ise**, ***metalize**. L16. [f. METAL *n.* + -IZE.] **1** Make metallic; give a metallic form or appearance to. L16. **2** Coat or cover with metal. E20.

metalliˈzation *n.* M17. **metallizer** *n.* a machine or plant for metallizing something; a person or organization involved in metallizing something: M20.

metallo- /mɪˈtaləʊ, ˈmɛt(ə)ləʊ/ *comb. form* of Gk *metallon* METAL *n.*: see -O-.

metalloˈcarborane *n.* (*Chem.*) a compound consisting of metal ions complexed with ligands containing carbon, boron, and hydrogen M20. **meˈtallocene** *n.* (*Chem.*) any of a group of organometallic compounds with a sandwich structure, typified by ferrocene M20. ˈ**metallochrome** *n.* a prismatic tinting imparted to polished steel plates by depositing a film of lead oxide on them M19. **meˈtallochromy** *n.* the application of metallochromes for decorative purposes M19. **meˈtalloenzyme** *n.* (*Biochem.*) an enzyme which is a metalloprotein M20. **metalloˈgenesis** *n.* = METALLOGENY E20. **metallogeˈnetic** *a.* of or pertaining to metallogeny E20. **metallogeˈnetically** *adv.* as regards metallogeny E20. ˌ**metalloˈgenic** *a.* (*a*) (of an element) occurring in ores or as the native metal, rather than in rocks; (*b*) = METALLOGENETIC: E20. **metaˈllogeny** *n.* the origin of mineral deposits, esp. as related to petrographic and tectonic features; the branch of geology that deals with this: E20. ˌ**metallo-orˈganic** *a.* (*Chem.*) = ORGANOMETALLIC *a.* L19. **meˈtallophone** *n.* a musical instrument in which the sound is produced by striking metal bars of varying pitches L19. **metalloprotein** *n.* (*Biochem.*) a protein whose molecule contains a metal atom M20. **metallothionein** /mɪˌtaləʊˈθʌɪəniːn/ *n.* (*Biochem.*) any of a group of proteins in some organisms which bind toxic heavy metals such as cadmium and mercury and so provide protection against these metals M20.

metallography /mɛtəˈlɒgrəfi/ *n.* E18. [f. METALLO- + -GRAPHY. Cf. Fr. *métallographie*.] †**1** A treatise or description of metals. *rare.* Only in E18. **2** The branch of science that deals with the structure of metals, esp. on a microscopic scale; the metallographic features of something. L19.

metallographer *n.* E20. **metalloˈgraphic** *a.* (*a*) of or pertaining to metallography; (*b*) of or pertaining to the description of coins: M19. **metalloˈgraphical** *a.* = METALLOGRAPHIC (a) E20. **metalloˈgraphically** *adv.* by metallographic methods M20.

metalloid /ˈmɛt(ə)lɔɪd/ *n.* & *a.* E19. [f. METAL *n.* + -OID.] *Chem.* **A** *n.* Orig., (*a*) a solid non-metallic element; (*b*) an alkali metal or an alkaline-earth metal. Now, an element intermediate in its properties between a typical metal and a typical non-metal (e.g. boron, silicon, germanium). E19. **B** *attrib.* or as *adj.* Of, pertaining to, or of the nature of a metalloid. M19.

metaˈlloidal *a.* M19.

metallurgical /mɛtəˈlɜːdʒɪk(ə)l/ *a.* E19. [f. next + -ICAL.] Of or pertaining to metallurgy; concerned with metallurgy.

metallurgic *a.* = METALLURGICAL L18. **metallurgically** *adv.* L19.

metallurgy /mɪˈtalədʒi, ˈmɛt(ə)lɜːdʒi/ *n.* E18. [f. Gk *metallon* METAL *n.* + *-ourgia* work, working (as in *kheirourgia* SURGERY).] The art of working metals, comprising the separation of them from other substances in the ore, smelting, and refining; *spec.* the process of extracting metals from their ores. Also, the branch of science that deals with the structure, properties, and behaviour of metals.

metallurgist *n.* an expert in or student of metallurgy; a worker in metal: L17.

metally /ˈmɛt(ə)li/ *a.* LME. [f. METAL *n.* & *a.* + -Y[1].] **1** Metallic, metalline. *obs.* exc. *poet.* LME. **2** Mixed with shale. *dial.* L19.

metalogic /mɛtəˈlɒdʒɪk/ *n.* M19. [f. META- + LOGIC.] **1** The part of metaphysics which relates to the foundations of logic. Now *rare.* M19. **2** The field of study that deals with the processes and structures of logic. M20.

metalogical *a.* (*a*) of or pertaining to metalogic; (*b*) that is outside the province of logic: M19. **metalogically** *adv.* in terms of or by means of metalogic M20. **metalogician** /-ˈdʒɪʃ(ə)n/ *n.* an expert in or student of metalogic E20.

metamathematics /ˌmɛtəmaθ(ə)ˈmatɪks/ *n.* L19. [f. META- + MATHEMATICS.] The field of study that deals with the structure and formal properties of mathematics and similar formal systems.

metamathematical *a.* (*a*) of or pertaining to metamathematics; (*b*) *rare* that is outside the province of mathematics: M19. **metamathematically** *adv.* by means of metamathematics; from the point of view of metamathematics: M20. **metamathematician** /-'tɪʃ(ə)n/ *n.* an expert in or student of metamathematics M20.

metamer /'mɛtəmə/ *n.* L19. [Back-form. f. METAMERIC.] *Chem.* A compound which exhibits metamerism; a compound metameric with another.

Also **me'tameride** *n.* (now *rare* or *obs.*) M19.

metamere /'mɛtəmɪə/ *n.* L19. [f. META- + Gk *meros* part.] *Zool.* A body segment of a metameric organism; = SOMITE.

metameric /mɛtə'mɛrɪk/ *a.* M19. [f. as prec. + -IC.] **1** *Chem.* Characterized by metamerism. M19. **2** *Zool.* (Of an organism) having a body consisting of several similar segments or metameres; of, pertaining to, or characterized by metamerism. L19.

metamerically *adv.* with metameric segmentation L19.

metamerism /mɪ'tamərɪz(ə)m/ *n.* M19. [f. as prec. + -ISM.] **1** *Chem.* Orig., the relationship of two or more compounds that have the same molecular formula but different properties (i.e. isomerism). Later, the relationship between organic compounds that have similar molecular structures and differ only in the alkyl groups or other substituents they contain. M19. **2** *Zool.* The condition of consisting of several similar segments or metameres; metameric segmentation; an instance of this. L19.

metamerous /mɪ'tam(ə)rəs/ *a.* L19. [f. METAMERE + -OUS.] *Zool.* = METAMERIC 2.

meta-metalanguage /mɛtə'mɛtəlaŋgwɪdʒ/ *n.* M20. [f. META- + METALANGUAGE.] A language used in the description of another language which is itself a metalanguage; the universal linguistic or symbolic system from which a particular metalanguage derives.

metamorphic /mɛtə'mɔːfɪk/ *a.* & *n.* E19. [f. META- + Gk *morphē* a form + -IC, after METAMORPHOSIS.] **A** *adj.* **1** Characterized by or exhibiting metamorphosis. E19. **2** *Geol.* Pertaining to, characterized by, or formed by metamorphism; (of rock) that has undergone transformation by means of heat, pressure, or other natural agencies. M19. **3** That causes metamorphism or metamorphosis. M19.

3 *Scientific American* Metamorphic water plays a major role in the genesis of ores.

B *n.* A metamorphic rock. Usu. in *pl.* L19.

metamorphise *v.* var. of METAMORPHIZE.

metamorphism /mɛtə'mɔːfɪz(ə)m/ *n.* M19. [f. as prec. + -ISM.] *Geol.* Alteration of the composition or structure of a rock by heat, pressure, or other natural agencies.

dynamic metamorphism: see DYNAMIC *a.* *progressive metamorphism*: see PROGRESSIVE *a.* *regional metamorphism*: see REGIONAL *a.*

metamorphize /mɛtə'mɔːfʌɪz/ *v.t.* Also **-ise**. L16. [f. as prec. + -IZE.] = METAMORPHOSE *v.* 1, 2, 3.

metamorphopsia /mɛtəmɔː'fɒpsɪə/ *n.* E19. [f. METAMORPH(OSIS + Gk *-opsia* seeing, f. *opsis* sight: see -IA[1].] *Ophthalm.* A defect of vision characterized by distortion of things seen.

metamorphose /mɛtə'mɔːfəʊs, -z/ *n.* Now *rare.* E17. [Anglicization.] = METAMORPHOSIS.

metamorphose /mɛtə'mɔːfəʊz/ *v.* L16. [Fr. *métamorphoser*, f. *métamorphose* (n.) f. as next.] **1** *v.t.* Change *into* or to something else by supernatural means. L16. **2** *v.t.* Change the form or character of; alter the nature or disposition of; transform. Foll. by *into*, *to*. L16. **3** *v.t.* Subject to metamorphosis or metamorphism. M17. **4** *v.i.* Undergo metamorphosis or metamorphism; change. (Foll. by *into*.) E19.

1 GEO. ELIOT Perhaps they metamorphose themselves into a tawny squirrel. 2 T. HARDY The waves rolled in furiously.. and were metamorphosed into foam. 3 A. H. GREEN The rocks.. are highly metamorphosed Lower Silurian beds. 4 P. NORMAN Photographs of the grown up men into whom these two.. little boys have metamorphosed. J. MAY The monster scorpion metamorphosed into a handsome young ogre. S. RUSHDIE She sees the Parsee ayah metamorphosing, becoming liquid, flowing outwards until she fills the room.

metamorphoser *n.* L16.

metamorphosis /mɛtə'mɔːfəsɪs, mɛtəmɔː'fəʊsɪs/ *n.* Pl. **-phoses** /-fəsiːz, -'fəʊsiːz/. M16. [L f. Gk *metamorphōsis*, f. *metamorphoun* transform, f. as META- + *morphē* a form: see -OSIS.] **1** The action or process of changing in form, shape, or substance; *esp.* transformation by supernatural means. M16. **b** A metamorphosed form. L16. **2** A complete change in appearance, circumstances, condition, or character. M16. **3a** *Biol.* Normal change of form of a living organism, part, or tissue; *spec.* the transformation that some animals undergo in the course of becoming adult (e.g. from tadpole to frog, or pupa to adult insect), in which there is a complete alteration of form and habit. M17. **b** *Chem.* The change of a compound to a new form, esp. by catalytic action. Now *rare.* M19.

2 H. T. BUCKLE By a singular metamorphosis, the secular principle was now represented by the Catholics, and the theological.. by the Protestants. M. BEERBOHM Do not fear that I.. should demand a metamorphosis of your present self.

metamorphosic *a.* L18.

metamorphosize /mɛtə'mɔːfəsʌɪz/ *v.t.* & *i.* Also **-ise**. E20. [f. prec. + -IZE.] = METAMORPHOSE *v.*

†**metamorphostical** *a.* *rare.* E18–L19. [f. as prec. after Gk wds in *-ostikos*: see -ICAL.] Of or pertaining to metamorphosis.

metamorphotic /mɛtəmɔː'fɒtɪk/ *a.* E19. [f. as prec. + -OTIC.] Pertaining to or based on metamorphosis; causing metamorphosis.

metanalysis /mɛtə'nalɪsɪs/ *n.* E20. [f. META- + ANALYSIS.] *Philol.* Reinterpretation of the division between words or syntactic units (e.g. of *a naddre* as *an addre* in ME to give mod. *adder*).

me'tanalyse *v.t.* subject to or alter by metanalysis M20.

metanephros /mɛtə'nɛfrɒs/ *n.* Pl. **-nephroi** /-'nɛfrɔɪ/. Also (now *rare*) **-nephron** /-'nɛfrɒn/, pl. **-nephra** /-'nɛfrə/. L19. [f. META- + Gk *nephros* kidney.] *Zool.* & *Anat.* The third of the three segments of the embryonic kidney in vertebrates, which develops into the kidney and ureter in adult reptiles, birds, and mammals but disappears in lower animals. Cf. MESONEPHROS, PRONEPHROS.

metanephric *a.* L19.

metanoia /mɛtə'nɔɪə/ *n.* L19. [Gk, f. *metanoein* change one's mind, repent.] Penitence; reorientation of one's way of life, spiritual conversion.

metaphase /'mɛtəfeɪz/ *n.* L19. [G, f. as META- + Gk PHASIS.] *Biol.* The stage of mitotic or meiotic nuclear division when the chromosomes become attached to the spindle fibres; a dividing nucleus at this stage.

Comb.: **metaphase plate** the equatorial plane of a spindle during metaphase, with the centromeres of the chromosomes on or near the plane.

metaphor /'mɛtəfə, -fɔː/ *n.* L15. [(O)Fr. *métaphore* or L *metaphora* f. Gk, f. *metapherein* transfer, f. as META- + *pherein* to bear.] **1** A figure of speech in which a name or descriptive word or phrase is transferred to an object or action different from, but analogous to, that to which it is literally applicable; an instance of this, a metaphorical expression. L15. **2** A thing considered as representative of some other (usu. abstract) thing; a symbol. M19.

1 R. A. KNOX It is a metaphor if you describe Oxford as a hive of industry. MIXED *metaphor*.

metaphoric /mɛtə'fɒrɪk/ *a.* = METAPHORICAL L16. **metaphorical** /mɛtə'fɒrɪk(ə)l/ *a.* characterized by the use of metaphor; of the nature of metaphor; used metaphorically; not literal, figurative: M16. **metaphorically** /mɛtə'fɒrɪk(ə)li/ *adv.* in a metaphorical sense; by the use of metaphor: L16. **metaphorist** *n.* (*rare*) a person who uses metaphors E18. **metaphorize** *v.t.* (*a*) change metaphorically *into*; (*b*) ply with metaphor: M18.

metaphosphoric /mɛtəfɒs'fɒrɪk/ *a.* M19. [f. META- + PHOSPHORIC.] Chem. *metaphosphoric acid*, a glassy deliquescent solid, $(HPO_3)_n$, obtained by heating orthophosphoric acid.

meta'phosphate *n.* a salt of metaphosphoric acid M19.

metaphrase /'mɛtəfreɪz/ *n.* & *v.* As n. also (earlier) in L form †**-phrasis**. M16. [mod.L *metaphrasis* f. Gk, f. *metaphrazein* translate, f. as META- + *phrazein* tell.] **A** *n.* †**1** A metrical translation. M16–M18. **2** (A) translation. Now *spec.* (a) word-for-word translation as opp. to (a) paraphrase. M17. **B** *v.t.* †**1** Translate, esp. in verse. E–M17. **2** Alter the phrasing or language of; reword. M19.

metaphrast /'mɛtəfrast/ *n.* E17. [Gk *metaphrastēs*, *metaphrazein*, f. as prec.] A person who puts a composition into a different literary form, e.g. by turning prose into verse or one metre into another. Formerly also, a translator.

meta'phrastic *a.* [Gk *metaphrastikos*] of the nature of (a) metaphrase L18. **meta'phrastically** *adv.* by way of a metaphrase L16.

metaphysic /mɛtə'fɪzɪk/ *n.*[1] LME. [(O)Fr. *métaphysique* f. med.L *metaphysica* fem. sing., for earlier neut. pl. repr. by METAPHYSICS.] **1** = METAPHYSICS 1. LME. **2** = METAPHYSICS 2. M19.

metaphysic /mɛtə'fɪzɪk/ *a.* & *n.*[2] Now *rare.* E16. [med.L *metaphysicus* adj., f. *metaphysica* n.pl.: see METAPHYSICS.] **A** *adj.* Metaphysical. E16. †**B** *n.* A metaphysician. L16–E17.

metaphysical /mɛtə'fɪzɪk(ə)l/ *a.* & *n.* LME. [f. METAPHYSIC *n.*[1] + -AL[1].] **A** *adj.* **1a** Of, belonging to, or of the nature of metaphysics; such as is recognized by metaphysics. LME. **b** Excessively subtle or abstract. Long *rare.* M17. **c** Not empirically verifiable. M19. **2a** Immaterial, incorporeal, supersensible; supernatural. L16. **b** *Christian Science.* That transcends matter or the physical. Esp. in *metaphysical healing.* L19. **3** Fond of or suited to the study of metaphysics. E17. **4** Based on abstract general reasoning or a priori principles. M17. **5** Fanciful, imaginary. E18. **6** Of certain 17th-cent. poets: exhibiting subtlety of thought and complex imagery. Of poetry: typical of the metaphysical poets; expressing emotion within an intellectual context. M18.

1a A. KOESTLER Traversed the frontier between metaphysical speculation and empirical science. D. ROWE As metaphysical.. as believing that death is a doorway to another life. *metaphysical philosophy*: see PHILOSOPHY *n.* 2c. c A. J. AYER The metaphysical thesis that philosophy affords us knowledge of a reality transcending the world of science. 4 SIR W. SCOTT Wars have been waged for points of metaphysical right.

B *n.* A metaphysical poet. Freq. in *pl.* L19.

metaphysi'cality *n.* the quality of being metaphysical M18. **metaphysically** *adv.* (*a*) in a metaphysical manner or sense; according to the principles of metaphysics; from a metaphysical point of view; †(*b*) supernaturally; preternaturally: L16.

metaphysician /mɛtəfɪ'zɪʃ(ə)n/ *n.* LME. [Prob. f. METAPHYSIC *n.*[1] after *physic*, *physician.* Cf. OFr. *methafisicien.*] An expert in or student of metaphysics.

metaphysicize /mɛtə'fɪzɪsʌɪz/ *v.i.* Also **-ise**. L18. [f. METAPHYSICS + -IZE.] Indulge in metaphysical speculation; think, talk, or write metaphysically.

metaphysico- /mɛtə'fɪzɪkəʊ/ *comb. form.* M18. [f. METAPHYSIC *a.* & *n.*[2], METAPHYSIC(AL *adj.* + -O-.] Metaphysical and —, as *metaphysico-ethical*, *metaphysico-theological*, etc.

metaphysics /mɛtə'fɪzɪks/ *n.pl.* (treated as *sing.* or *pl.*). M16. [Pl. of METAPHYSIC *n.*[1], repr. med.L *metaphysica* neut. pl., med.Gk (*ta*) *metaphusika* for earlier *ta meta ta phusika* 'the (works of Aristotle) after the Physics'.] **1** The branch of philosophy that deals with the first principles of things, including such concepts as being, substance, essence, time, space, cause, and identity; theoretical philosophy as the ultimate science of being and knowing. M16. **2** The theoretical principles or higher philosophical rationale of a particular branch of knowledge. M19. **3** The philosophy of mind. M19. **4** Abstract or subtle talk; mere theory. L20.

metaphysis /mɪ'tafɪsɪs/ *n.* Pl. **-physes** /-fɪsiːz/. M18. [mod.L, f. Gk *metaphuesthai* become by change, f. as META- + *phu-* grow; in sense 2 after

DIAPHYSIS, EPIPHYSIS.] †1 Transformation; metamorphosis. *rare*. Only in M18. 2 *Anat.* The site of advancing ossification at one or both ends of a growing long bone, between the diaphysis and the epiphysial cartilage. E20.

metaphyseal /mɛtəˈfɪzɪəl, mɛtəfɪˈziːəl/ *a.* E20. **metaphysial** /mɛtəˈfɪzɪəl, mɛtəfɪˈziːəl/ *a.* M20.

metaplasia /mɛtəˈpleɪzɪə/ *n.* L19. [f. Gk *metaplassein* mould into a new form, f. as META- + *plassein* to mould: see -PLASIA.] *Biol.* & *Med.* Transformation of one kind of differentiated adult tissue into another.

metaplastic /-ˈplastɪk/ *a.* pertaining to or characterized by metaplasia L19.

metaplasm /ˈmɛtəplaz(ə)m/ *n.* L16. [In sense 1 f. L *metaplasmus*, Gk *metaplasmos*, f. *metaplassein*: see prec. In sense 2 f. META- + PROTO)PLASM.] 1 In *Rhet.*, the transposition of words from their usual or natural order; in *Gram.*, the alteration of a word by addition, removal, or transposition of letters or syllables. L16. 2 *Biol.* The non-living constituents of cytoplasm, such as pigment granules. L19.

metapolitical /mɛtəpəˈlɪtɪk(ə)l/ *a.* M17. [f. META- + POLITICAL.] 1 Lying outside the sphere of politics. M17. 2 Relating to metapolitics; given to the study of metapolitics. E19.

metapolitics /mɛtəˈpɒlɪtɪks/ *n.* Also (*rare*) **-ic**. L18. [f. META- + POLITIC *n.*] Abstract political science; *derog.* unpractical political theorizing.

metapolitician /ˌmɛtəpɒlɪˈtɪʃ(ə)n/ *n.* a person who holds or advocates theories of metapolitics E19.

metapsychics /mɛtəˈsʌɪkɪks/ *n.* E20. [f. META- + PSYCHIC *n.* + -S[1], after METAPHYSICS.] The field of study that deals with phenomena beyond the scope of orthodox psychology.

metapsychic(al) *adjs.* E20. **metapsychist** *n.* an expert in or student of metapsychics E20.

metapsychology /mɛtəsʌɪˈkɒlədʒi/ *n.* E20. [f. META- + PSYCHOLOGY.] Speculative inquiry regarding the ultimate nature of the mind and its functions which cannot be studied experimentally. Also, the field of study that deals with the theories and practice of psychology.

ˌmetapsychoˈlogical *a.* E20.

metapsychosis /mɛtəsʌɪˈkəʊsɪs/ *n. rare.* Pl. **-choses** /-ˈkəʊsiːz/. L19. [f. META- + PSYCHOSIS.] The supposed psychic action of one mind on another.

metasequoia /mɛtəsɪˈkwɔɪə, -ˈkɔɪə/ *n.* M20. [mod.L, f. META- + SEQUOIA.] A Chinese deciduous coniferous tree, *Metasequoia glyptostroboides*, belonging to a genus known at first only from fossil remains. Also called *dawn redwood*.

metasoma /mɛtəˈsəʊmə/ *n.* L19. [f. META- + Gk *sōma* body.] *Zool.* 1 The hinder portion of the abdomen of an arachnid or other arthropod. L19. 2 The posterior portion of the body of a cephalopod, enveloped in the mantle. L19.

metasomatic /mɛtəsəˈmatɪk/ *a.* L19. [f. prec. & next + -IC.] 1 *Zool.* Pertaining to the metasoma. L19. 2 *Geol.* Pertaining to or of the nature of metasomatism. L19.

metasomatically *adv.* E20.

metasomatism /mɛtəˈsəʊmətɪz(ə)m/ *n.* L19. [f. META- + Gk *sōma(t-)* body + -ISM.] *Geol.* Change in the composition of a rock as a result of the introduction or removal of chemical constituents.

metasomatize *v.t.* change as a result of metasomatism M20.

metastable /mɛtəˈsteɪb(ə)l/ *a.* L19. [f. META- + STABLE *a.*] *Physics* etc. 1 (Of equilibrium) stable only under small disturbances and capable of changing to a more stable state; of, pertaining to, or existing in such equilibrium. L19. 2 Of an excited state of an atom, nucleus, etc.: having an exceptionally long lifetime; passing to another state so slowly as to appear stable. E20.

metastaˈbility *n.* E20. **metastably** *adv.* M20.

metastases *n.* pl. of METASTASIS.

Metastasian /mɛtəˈsteɪsɪən, -zɪən/ *a.* M20. [f. *Metastasio* (see below) + -AN.] Of, pertaining to, or characteristic of the Italian poet and librettist, Pietro Metastasio (1698–1782).

metastasis /mɪˈtastəsɪs/ *n.* Pl. **-ases** /-əsiːz/. L16. [Late L f. Gk = removal, change, f. *methistanai* remove, change.] 1 *Rhet.* A rapid transition from one point to another. Long *rare*. L16. 2a *Med.* The transference of a bodily function, pain, or disease, or of diseased matter, from one site to another; *spec.* the occurrence or development of secondary foci of disease at a distance from the primary site, as in many cancers. M17. b *Biol.* Metabolism. *rare*. L19. 3 *gen.* Transformation; change from one condition to another. *rare*. M19.

metastasize *v.i.* (of a disease, esp. a tumour) undergo metastasis, spread to other sites in the body E20. **metaˈstatic** *a.* (*Med.*) pertaining to, characterized by, or produced by metastasis E19.

metasyncrisis /mɛtəˈsɪŋkrɪsɪs/ *n.* Now *rare*. M16. [mod.L f. Gk *metasugkrisis*, f. *metasugkrinein* use diaphoretics, f. as META- + *sugkrinein* compare.] *Med.* The evacuation of diseased matter, esp. through the pores of the skin.

metasynˈcritic *a.* of the nature of, pertaining to, or producing metasyncrisis M19. **metasynˈcritical** *a.* (long *rare* or *obs.*) = METASYNCRITIC M17.

metatarsal /mɛtəˈtɑːs(ə)l/ *a.* & *n.* M18. [f. METATARSUS + -AL[1].] *Anat.* A *adj.* Of or pertaining to the metatarsus. M18. B *n.* A metatarsal bone. M19.

metatarsi *n.* pl. of METATARSUS.

metatarso- /mɛtəˈtɑːsəʊ/ *comb. form* of next: see -O-.

metatarsophalanˈgeal *a.* (*Anat.*) of, pertaining to, or (esp.) connecting the metatarsus and the phalanges M19.

metatarsus /mɛtəˈtɑːsəs/ *n.* Pl. **-tarsi** /-ˈtɑːsʌɪ, -siː/. LME. [mod.L, f. as META- + TARSUS.] 1 *Anat.* & *Zool.* The group of five long bones of the human foot (and of the hind foot of quadrupeds) between the tarsus and the phalanges or toes; the tarsometatarsus of a bird. LME. 2 *Entomol.* The basal joint of the tarsus, esp. when much developed. E19.

ˌmetatarˈsalgia *n.* (*Med.*) pain in the metatarsus L19.

metate /məˈtɑːteɪ/ *n.* E17. [Amer. Sp. f. Nahuatl *métatl*.] In Central America, a flat or somewhat hollowed oblong stone on which grain, cocoa, etc., are ground by means of a smaller stone. Also *metate-stone*.

metatherian /mɛtəˈθɪərɪən/ *a.* & *n.* L19. [f. mod.L *Metatheria* (see below), f. as META- + Gk *thēria* pl. of *thērion* wild animal: see -AN.] A *adj.* Of, pertaining to, or designating the mammalian infraclass Metatheria, comprising the single order Marsupialia (the marsupials). L19. B *n.* A metatherian mammal, a marsupial. L19.

metathesis /mɛˈtaθɪsɪs, mɪ-/ *n.* Pl. **-theses** /-θɪsiːz/. L16. [Late L f. Gk, f. *metatithenai* transpose, change, f. as META- + *tithenai* put, place.] 1 *Ling.* The transposition of sounds or letters in a word; the result of such a transposition. Formerly also, the transposition of words. L16. †2 *Med.* Spread of a disease within the body, metastasis; movement of diseased matter to another part of the body. L17–M19. 3 *gen.* Change or reversal of condition. E18. 4 *Chem.* (An) interchange of an atom or atoms between two different molecules; *esp.* double decomposition. L19.

metathesize *v.i.* & *t.* (*Ling.*) undergo or subject to metathesis E20. **metathetic** /mɛtəˈθɛtɪk/, **-thetical** /-ˈθɛtɪk(ə)l/ *adjs.* characterized by or involving metathesis M19.

metatony /mɪˈtatəni/ *n.* M20. [Fr. *métatonie*, f. as META- + Gk *tonos* sound, TONE *n.*: see -Y[3].] *Philol.* In Baltic and Slavonic languages, any of certain kinds of substitution of one distinctive intonation for another in a given syllable; these substitutions collectively.

metaˈtonic *a.* M20.

Metatron /mɪˈtatrɒn/ *n.* M19. [Origin unkn.] In Jewish mystical theology, a supreme angelic being, usually identified with either Michael or Enoch.

metatrophic /mɛtəˈtrəʊfɪk, -ˈtrɒf-/ *a.* E20. [f. META- + -TROPHIC.] *Biol.* Of an organism: dependent on the presence of organic substances for nutrition.

Metawileh /mɛˈtɑːwɪleɪ/ *n.* L18. [Arab. *matāwila* pl. of *mutawālī*.] A sect of Shiite Muslims in Lebanon and Syria.

Metaxa /mɪˈtaksə/ *n.* M20. [Gk surname and company name.] (Proprietary name for) a dark Greek brandy; a drink or glass of this brandy.

métayer /meteje/ *n.* Pl. pronounced same. L18. [Fr. f. med.L *medietarius*, f. *medietas* half: see MOIETY.] A farmer who holds land on the *métayage* system.

métayage /metejaːʒ (*pl. same*)/ *n.* a system of land tenure in western Europe and the US, in which the farmer pays a certain proportion (generally half) of the produce to the owner as rent, and the owner generally provides stock and seed L19.

metazoan /mɛtəˈzəʊən/ *n.* & *a.* L19. [mod.L *Metazoa* (see below), f. META- + Gk *zōia* pl. of *zōion* animal: see -AN.] *Zool.* A *n.* An animal of the group Metazoa (comprising all animals except protozoa and sponges), members of which have bodies composed of more than one cell and display differentiation of tissue. L19. B *adj.* Of, pertaining to, or designating this group of animals. L19.

metazoic *a.* = METAZOAN *a.* L19. **metazoon** *n.*, pl. **-zoa**, = METAZOAN *n.* (usu. in *pl.*) L19.

mete /miːt/ *n.*[1] LME. [OFr. f. L *meta*: see META *n.*[1]] †1 A goal, a destination. LME–L15. 2 A boundary, a limit, (material or immaterial); a boundary stone or mark. Freq. (esp. *Law*) in *metes and bounds*. L15.

mete /miːt/ *n.*[2] M18. [f. METE *v.*] Size, quality, character, etc., as ascertainable by measuring; measure.

mete /miːt/ *v.* [OE *metan* = OFris. *meta*, OS *metan*, OHG *mezzan* (Du. *meten*, G *messen*), ON *meta*, Goth. *mitan*, f. Gmc, f. IE base repr. also by L *meditari* MEDITATE, Gk *medesthai* care for.] 1 *v.t.* Ascertain or determine the dimensions or quantity of, measure. Now *poet.* & *dial.* exc. in allus. to *Matt.* 7:2. Cf. MEASURE *v.* 3. OE. †b Complete the full measure or amount of. Also foll. by *forth*, *out*. E17–L18. †2 *v.t.* Mark (*out*) the boundary or course of; = MEASURE *v.* 7. OE–E19. 3 *v.t.* Estimate the greatness or value of. Cf. MEASURE *v.* 4. *arch.* OE. †4 *v.t.* & *i.* Travel or go (a distance). Cf. MEASURE *v.* 5. OE–L17. 5 *v.t.* Apportion by measure, allot; *esp.* allot (punishment, praise, reward, etc.). Usu. foll. by *out*. Now *literary*. OE. †6 *v.i.* Take measurements; measure distances *for* shooting at a mark; aim *at*. LME–M17.

1 AV *Matt.* 7:2 With what measure ye mete, it shall be measured to you againe. 5 T. COLLINS I meted out half a pint of water to him. S. NAIPAUL Blakey described the punishments meted out to refractory children.

metecious *a.* see METOECIOUS.

metel /ˈmiːt(ə)l/ *n.* Also †**methel**. E16. [mod.L *methel*, f. Arab. *jawz* (= nut) *māṯil*.] †1 *metel nut*, *nut metel*, a narcotic fruit covered with small spines, prob. that of the thorn-apple, *Datura stramonium*. Only in 16. 2 (The fruit of) the hairy thorn-apple, *Datura metel*. M18.

metempiric /mɛtɛmˈpɪrɪk/ *n.* In sense 1 also **-ics**. L19. [f. META- 1 + EMPIRIC.] 1 The branch of philosophy that deals with things outside the sphere of knowledge derived from experience. L19. 2 A metempiricist. L19.

metempirical *a.* pertaining to matters outside the sphere of knowledge derived from experience; (of opinions and their advocates) maintaining the validity of concepts and beliefs based other than on experience: L19. **metempirically** *adv.* L19. **metempiricism** /-sɪz(ə)m/ *n.* = METEMPIRIC 1 L19. **metempiricist** /-sɪst/ *n.* a person who believes in or advocates metempiricism L19.

metempsychosis /ˌmɛtɛmpsʌɪˈkəʊsɪs/ *n.* Pl. **-choses** /-ˈkəʊsiːz/. L16. [Late L, f. Gk *metempsukhōsis*, f. as META- + *en* in + *psukhē* soul: see -OSIS.] Transmigration of the soul; *esp.* the passage of the soul of a person or animal at or after death into a new body of the same or a different species (a tenet of the Pythagoreans and certain Eastern religions).

metempsychose *n.* & *v.* †(*a*) *n.* [Fr. *métempsycose*] = METEMPSYCHOSIS; (*b*) *v.t.* transfer (a soul) from one body to another: L16. **metempsychosic** *a.* E20. †**metempsychosical** *a.*: only in E17. **metempsychosist** *n.* a person who believes in metempsychosis M19.

metencephalon /mɛtɛn'sɛfəlɒn, -'kɛf-/ *n.* L19. [f. META- + ENCEPHALON.] *Anat.* The part of the hindbrain comprising the cerebellum and the pons, between the myelencephalon and the mesencephalon; the part of the embryonic brain that develops into this.

ˌ**metence'phalic** *a.* L19.

met-enkephalin /mɛtɛn'kɛfəlɪn/ *n.* L20. [f. MET(HIONINE + ENKEPHALIN.] *Biochem.* The enkephalin whose peptide chain ends with a methionine unit.

metensomatosis /ˌmɛtɛnsəʊmə'təʊsɪs/ *n.* M17. [Late L f. Gk *metensōmatōsis*, f. as META- + *en* in + *sōma(t-)* body: see -OSIS.] Re-embodiment of the soul.

meteor /'miːtɪə, -tɪɔː/ *n.* & *a.* L15. [mod.L *meteorum* f. Gk *meteōron* use as n. of neut. of *meteōros* raised up, lofty, f. as META- + alt. of base of *aeirein* raise.] **A** *n.* **1** Any atmospheric phenomenon. Now *techn.* L15. **2 a** A small mass of rock or metal that enters the earth's atmosphere and as a result of friction with it becomes sufficiently incandescent to be visible; a shooting star. Formerly also, a comet. L16. **b** Any of various other luminous atmospheric appearances, as the aurora borealis, the ignis fatuus, etc. Now *poet.* L16. **c** A meteoroid. L18. †**3** In *pl.* A treatise on atmospheric phenomena. L16–M17.

Comb.: **meteor shower** a group of meteors that seem to come from the same point in the sky, appearing when the earth passes through a meteor swarm; **meteor swarm** a group of meteoroids moving together in the same orbit; **meteor trail** a bright streak of ionized gas formed by a meteor passing through the upper atmosphere, which can provide a reflector for radio communication.

B *attrib.* or as *adj.* Blazing or flashing like a meteor; of short duration, transient. Chiefly *poet.* E18.

meteoric /miːtɪ'ɒrɪk/ *a.* M17. [Partly f. med.L *meteoricus* f. Gk *meteōros* (see prec.), partly f. prec.: see -IC.] †**1** Pertaining to the region midway between earth and heaven; elevated, lofty. M17–M19. **2** (Of a plant) dependent on atmospheric conditions; (esp. of water) produced by or derived from the atmosphere. L18. **3** Of, pertaining to, or derived from meteors; consisting of meteors. Also, meteoritic. E19. **4** *fig.* Transiently or irregularly brilliant, flashing or dazzling like a meteor; sudden and rapid. M19.

2 C. OLLIER The water emitted by hot springs is usually of meteoric origin. 4 C. CHAPLIN Maurice had a meteoric rise as a theatrical entrepreneur. A. C. BOULT The years 1931 to 1939 saw a meteoric development in broadcasting.

meteorically *adv.* (*a*) in accordance with atmospheric conditions; (*b*) with the suddenness and speed of a meteor: L19.

meteorise *v.* var. of METEORIZE.

meteorism /'miːtɪərɪz(ə)m/ *n.* Now *rare.* Also in mod.L form **meteorismus** /miːtɪə'rɪzməs/. M19. [Gk *meteōrismos* elevation, f. *meteōrizein*: see METEORIZE, -ISM.] *Med.* Flatulent distention of the abdomen with gas in the alimentary canal.

meteo'ristic *a.* pertaining to or affected by meteorism L19.

meteorite /'miːtɪərʌɪt/ *n.* E19. [f. METEOR + -ITE[1].] A fallen meteor; a mass of rock or metal that has fallen to the earth from beyond the atmosphere. Cf. AEROLITE, SIDERITE.

meteoritic /miːtɪə'rɪtɪk/ *a.* of or pertaining to meteorites; of the nature of a meteorite: M19. **meteo'ritical** *a.* M20. **meteo'ritically** *adv.* E20. **meteo'riticist** /-sɪst/ *n.* an expert in or student of meteoritics M20. **meteo'ritics** *n.* the branch of science that deals with meteors and meteorites M20.

meteorize /'miːtɪərʌɪz/ *v.* Now *rare.* Also **-ise**. M17. [Gk *meteōrizein* elevate, f. *meteōros*: see METEOR, -IZE.] †**1** *v.t.* & *i.* Vaporize. M–L17. **2** *v.i.* Resemble a meteor; flash, sparkle. E19. **3** *v.t.* *Med.* Affect with meteorism. E19.

meteorograph /'miːtɪərəgrɑːf/ *n.* L18. [Fr. *météorographe*, f. Gk *meteōron*: see METEOR, -O-, -GRAPH.] An apparatus for automatically recording several different kinds of meteorological phenomena at the same time.

meteorogram *n.* a chart or record produced by a meteorograph E20.

meteoroid /'miːtɪərɔɪd/ *a.* M19. [f. METEOR + -OID.] A small body of rock or metal moving through space, of the same nature as those which become visible as meteors when they pass through the atmosphere.

meteo'roidal *a.* L19.

meteorolite /'miːtɪərəlʌɪt/ *n.* E19. [Fr. *météorolithe*, f. Gk *meteōron*: see METEOR, -O-, -LITE.] A meteorite.

meteorolitic /ˌmiːtɪərə'lɪtɪk/ *a.* E19.

meteorology /miːtɪə'rɒlədʒi/ *n.* M16. [Gk *meteōrologia*, f. *meteōron*: see METEOR, -OLOGY.] **1** The branch of science that deals with phenomena and processes of the atmosphere, esp. with a view to forecasting the weather. M16. **2** The character *of* a particular region as regards weather, atmospheric changes, etc. L17.

meteoro'logic *a.* meteorological M18. **meteoro'logical** *a.* [Gk *meteōrologikos*] of or pertaining to meteorology or atmospheric phenomena L16. **meteoro'logically** *adv.* according to or by means of the science of meteorology; with regard to meteorological facts: L17. **meteorologist** *n.* M17.

meteoroscopy /ˌmiːtɪə'rɒskəpi/ *n. rare.* M17. [f. METEOR + -O- + -SCOPY, or f. METEOROSCOPE + -Y[3].] Observation of the celestial objects.

†**meteoroscope** *n.* [Gk *meteōroskopion*] an instrument for taking observations of celestial objects: only in E17. **meteoroscopist** *n.* an observer of celestial objects E18.

meteorous /'miːtɪərəs/, *poet.* miː'tiːərəs/ *a.* M17. [f. Gk *meteōros*: see METEOR, -OUS.] = METEORIC.

meter /'miːtə/ *n.*[1] ME. [f. METE *v.* + -ER[1].] A person who measures; a measurer; *esp.* a person responsible for seeing that commodities are of the proper measure.

meter /'miːtə/ *n.*[2] E19. [First in *gas meter*: perh. a use of prec. suggested by GASOMETER (L18).] **1** An instrument for automatically measuring or indicating the quantity, degree, or rate of something (e.g. electricity consumed or flowing, speed of travel, fuel remaining); *spec.* (identified contextually) a taximeter. E19. **b** A parking meter. M20. **2** A 25-cent coin. *US slang.* M20.

1 J. H. GOODIER The gloss meter works on the principle of directing a beam of light on to a painted panel. *Sunday Express* The taxi's meter ticked away expensively. *exposure meter, frequency meter, gas meter, moisture meter, tuning meter, water meter, wet meter*, etc.

Comb.: **meter-feeder** a motorist who usu. or habitually illicitly extends his or her parking time by putting more money in the meter instead of moving away; **meter maid** (orig. *US*) a female traffic warden; **meter-reader** a person responsible for reading gas or electricity meters.

meterless *a.* having no meter; done without the use of a meter: L20.

meter *n.*[3], *n.*[4] see METRE *n.*[1], *n.*[2]

meter /'miːtə/ *v.*[1] L19. [f. METER *n.*[2]] **1 a** *v.t.* & *i.* Measure by means of a meter; supply through a meter. L19. **b** *v.t.* Regulate the flow of; deliver (fluid) in regulated amounts *to*. M20. **2** *v.t.* Provide with a meter or meters. M20.

1a *Practical Photography* Meter from the highlights so that the shadow detail is underexposed. b *Scientific American* The water is metered to each plant through the drip-irrigation installation. 2 M. BRADBURY The terrace has been metered for parking. *Liverpool Echo* TV lounge, colour TV, metered fires in bedrooms.

meter *v.*[2] see METRE *v.*

-meter /'mɪtə/ *suff.* [Gk *metron* measure.] **1** *Pros.* Forming ns. denoting a line of poetry with a specified number of measures, as *hexameter*, *pentameter*. **2** Forming ns. denoting measuring instruments: orig. (as in *barometer*, *hydrometer*, *hygrometer*, *thermometer*) repr. mod.L forms in *-metrum*, with the ending intended to represent the Gk *metron* measure (see METRE *n.*[1]); later in wds with the same ending *-ometer* formed on Gk bases, as *anemometer*, *chronometer*, and in hybrid formations, some imitating the form of Gk compounds, as *gasometer*, *galvanometer*, *pedometer*, others with the combining vowel *i* of the L first elem., as *calorimeter*, *gravimeter*. In some late formations *-meter* is appended to mod. wds without any attempt to assimilate the form of the first elem. to that of a Gk or L comb. form, as in *voltameter*, *ammeter*.

metestrus *n.* see METOESTRUS.

metethereal /mɛtɪ'θɪərɪəl/ *a.* E20. [f. META- + ETHEREAL.] Spiritual, transcendental.

metewand /'miːtwɒnd/ *n.* LME. [f. METE *v.* or MET *n.*[1] + WAND *n.*] **1** A measuring rod. Now *dial.* LME. **2** A standard of measurement or estimation. *literary.* M16.

Also **meteyard** *n.* (*a*) (now *dial.*) = METEWAND 1; (*b*) *literary* = METEWAND 2: LME.

metformin /mɛt'fɔːmɪn/ *n.* M20. [f. METH(YL + FORM(ALDEHYDE + IM)IN(O-.] *Pharm.* A biguanide derivative, $C_4H_{11}N_5$, used in the oral treatment of diabetes.

meth /mɛθ/ *n.*[1] *colloq.* M20. [Abbrev.] (A tablet of) the drug Methedrine or methamphetamine.

meth *n.*[2] var. of METHS.

meth- /mɛθ, miːθ/ *comb. form.* [f. METHYL.] Used in forming names of substances, esp. drugs, containing methyl groups.

methacholine /mɛθə'kəʊliːn/ *n.* M20. [f. METH- + -*a*- + CHOLINE.] *Pharm.* A parasympathomimetic agent with effects similar to those of histamine, used to treat some heart arrhythmias.

methacrylic /mɛθə'krɪlɪk/ *a.* M19. [f. METH- + ACRYLIC.] Chem. *methacrylic acid*, 1-methylacrylic acid, $CH_2{:}C(CH_3)COOH$, a colourless compound melting at 15°C, which polymerizes when distilled and is used in the manufacture of methacrylate resins.

methacrylate /mɪ'θakrɪlət/ *n.* a salt or ester of methacrylic acid, *esp.* any of the esters of methacrylic acid used in making resins by polymerization; POLYMETHYL *methacrylate*: M19.

methadone /'mɛθədəʊn/ *n.* M20. [f. METH- + A(MINO- + DI-[2] + -ONE, elems. of the systematic name.] *Pharm.* A powerful synthetic analgesic which is similar to morphine in its effects but less sedative and is used as a substitute drug in the treatment of morphine and heroin addiction.

¶A proprietary name for this drug is PHYSEPTONE.

methaemoglobin /ˌmɛθiːmə'gləʊbɪn, -θiː-/ *n.* Also *-**hem-**. L19. [f. META- + HAEMOGLOBIN.] *Biochem.* A stable oxide of haemoglobin in which the iron of the haem group is in a ferric rather than a ferrous state, and so unable to combine with oxygen.

methaemoglobi'naemia *n.* (*Med.*) presence of methaemoglobin in the blood L19. **methaemoglobi'nuria** *n.* (*Med.*) presence of methaemoglobin in the urine L19.

methamphetamine /mɛθam'fɛtəmiːn, -ɪn/ *n.* M20. [f. METH- + AMPHETAMINE.] *Pharm.* A methyl derivative of amphetamine with effects that are more rapid in onset and longer lasting, used as a stimulant of the central nervous system. Cf. METHEDRINE.

methanal /'mɛθənal/ *n.* L19. [f. METHANE + -AL[2].] *Chem.* = FORMALDEHYDE.

methanation /mɛθə'neɪʃ(ə)n/ *n.* M20. [f. METHAN(E + -ATION.] Conversion (esp. of carbon monoxide and hydrogen) into methane.

'methanate *v.t.* [back-form.] convert into methane, subject to methanation M20.

methane /'miːθeɪn, 'mɛθeɪn/ *n.* M19. [f. METH- + -ANE.] *Chem.* A colourless odourless flammable gas, CH_4, the simplest of the alkanes, which occurs in natural gas, coal gas, and decaying organic matter, forms an explosive mixture with air, and is used as a fuel. Cf. *firedamp* s.v. FIRE *n.*

methano- /'mɛθənəʊ, mɛ'θanəʊ/ *comb. form* of prec.: see -O-.

me'thanogen *n.* a methanogenic bacterium L20. **methano'genesis** *n.* the production of methane by living organisms, esp. bacteria M20. **methano'genic** *a.* producing methane; pertaining to or involving methanogenesis; *spec.* designating archaebacteria etc. which reduce carbon dioxide to methane: M20. **methanometer** /mɛθə'nɒmɪtə/ *n.* an instrument for measuring the concentration of methane, esp. in mines

L19. **methanotroph** /-trəʊf/ *n.* a micro-organism that derives its carbon and energy from methane L20.

methanoic /mɛθəˈnəʊɪk/ *a.* L19. [f. METHANE + -OIC.] *Chem.* = FORMIC I.

methanol /ˈmɛθənɒl/ *n.* L19. [f. as prec. + -OL.] *Chem.* A colourless volatile flammable liquid alcohol, CH_3OH, used as an intermediate in the synthesis of formaldehyde, as a solvent, and as a denaturant for ethyl alcohol; methyl alcohol.

methaˈnolic *a.* in or of methanol M20.

methapyrilene /mɛθəˈpɪrɪliːn/ *n.* M20. [f. METH- + *-a-* + alt. of PYR(ID)YL + -ENE.] *Pharm.* An antihistamine agent also used to induce sleep.

methaqualone /mɛˈθakwələʊn/ *n.* M20. [f. METH- + *-a-* + QU(ININE + A(ZO- + -O)L + -ONE, elems. of the systematic name.] *Pharm.* A hypnotic and sedative drug derived from quinazoline.

¶A proprietary name for this drug is QUAALUDE; cf. also MANDRAX.

Methedrine /ˈmɛθədrɪn, -iːn/ *n.* M20. [f. METH- + BENZ)EDRINE.] *Pharm.* (Proprietary name for) the drug methamphetamine.

metheglin /mɪˈθɛɡlɪn, ˈmɛθəɡlɪn/ *n. obs.* exc. *Hist.* & *dial.* M16. [Welsh *meddyglyn*, f. *meddyg* medicinal (f. L *medicus*: see MEDIC *n.*[1] & *a.*[1]) + *llyn* liquor (= Ir. *lionn*, Gael. *leann*).] A spiced or medicated variety of mead, originally peculiar to Wales.

methel *n.* var. of METEL.

methemoglobin *n.* see METHAEMOGLOBIN.

methenamine /mɛˈθiːnəmiːn, -ˈθɛn-/ *n.* Chiefly *US.* E20. [f. next + AMINE.] *Chem.* = HEXAMETHYLENETETRAMINE.

methene /ˈmɛθiːn/ *n.* L19. [f. METH- + -ENE.] *Chem.* = METHYLENE.

methicillin /mɛθɪˈsɪlɪn/ *n.* M20. [f. METH- + PEN)ICILLIN.] *Pharm.* A semisynthetic penicillin used against staphylococci which produce penicillinase.

methide /ˈmɛθʌɪd, ˈmiːθ-/ *n.* M19. [f. METH- + -IDE.] *Chem.* A binary compound of methyl, esp. with a metal.

methimazole /mɛˈθɪməzəʊl/ *n.* M20. [f. METH- + IM(ID)AZOLE.] *Pharm.* An imidazole derivative with antithyroid properties, used to treat hyperthyroidism.

methinks /mɪˈθɪŋks/ *v.i. impers.* Now *arch.*, *poet.*, & *joc.* Also **methinketh** /mɪˈθɪŋkəθ/. Pa. t. **methought** /mɪˈθɔːt/. OE. [Orig. two wds, ME *pron.* (*dat.*) + 3rd person sing. of THINK *v.*[1] Cf. MESEEMS.] It seems to me. (W. noun cl., with or without *that*.)

TENNYSON At last methought that I had wander'd far In an old wood. *Times* Someone will, methinks, have to invent low-alcohol champagne.

methiocarb /mɪˈθʌɪəkɑːb/ *n.* M20. [f. METH- + THIO- + CARB(AMATE.] *Chem.* A carbamate used as an insecticide, molluscicide, and acaricide, common in garden preparations.

methionine /mɪˈθʌɪəniːn/ *n.* E20. [f. METH- + THION- + -INE[5].] *Biochem.* A hydrophobic sulphur-containing amino acid, $CH_3S(CH_2)_2$-$CH(NH_2)COOH$, which occurs in proteins and is essential in the human diet; 2-amino-4-(methylthio)butyric acid.

methisazone /mɪˈθɪsəzəʊn/ *n.* M20. [f. METH- + IS(ATIN + SEMICARB)AZONE.] *Pharm.* A thiosemicarbazone, $C_{10}H_{10}N_4OS$, with prophylactic activity against smallpox.

metho /ˈmɛθəʊ/ *n.*[1] *Austral.* & *NZ colloq.* Pl. **-os.** M20. [f. *methylated spirits* s.v. METHYLATE *v.* + -O.] **1** Methylated spirits. M20. **2** A person addicted to drinking methylated spirits. M20.

Metho /ˈmɛθəʊ/ *n.*[2] & *a. Austral. colloq.* M20. [Abbrev.] **A** *n.* Pl. **-os.** = METHODIST *n.* 4. M20. **B** *adj.* = METHODIST *a.* M20.

method /ˈmɛθəd/ *n.* LME. [L *methodus* f. Gk *methodos* pursuit of knowledge, mode of investigation, f. *meta* (see META-) + *hodos* way.] **I** Procedure for attaining an object. **1** The recommended or prescribed medical treatment for a specific disease. *obs.* exc. as in sense 2 below. LME. **b** *Hist.* (**M-.**) The system of medicine practised by the ancient school of Methodists. LME. **2** A mode of procedure; a (defined or systematic) way of doing a thing, *esp.* (w. specifying wd or wds) in accordance with a particular theory or as associated with a particular person. L16. **b** Any of various ordered sets of changes in bell-ringing. M17. **c** *Theatr.* An acting theory and technique in which an actor aspires to complete emotional identification with a part. Freq. *attrib.* E20.

2 B. JOWETT The theses of Parmenides are expressly said to follow the method of Zeno. ISAIAH BERLIN Some believe in coercion, others in gentler methods. W. S. CHURCHILL New methods of smelting brought a tenfold increase in the output of iron. W. RAEPER MacDonald followed the usual Congregational method of delivering his sermons extempore. c *attrib.*: F. HOWERD Although George may only have been playing a eunuch, I nearly turned him into a method actor. K. WILLIAMS 'I suppose it's all instinct with me.' 'That is better than method acting,' said Alfred.

II Systematic arrangement, order. **3** The branch of logic that deals with the description and arrangement of arguments or propositions for the investigation or exposition of a truth. M16. **4** Order in thinking or expressing thoughts; the orderly arrangement of ideas; *gen.* orderliness, regularity, or planning in doing anything. M16. **5** The order and arrangement of a literary work, speech, etc.; an author's design or plan. Long *rare* or *obs.* L16. †**b** A written systematically-ordered collection of rules, observations, etc., on a particular subject. L16–E19. †**c** The summary of the contents of a book, esp. as a list. E–M17. †**d** *Bot.* & *Zool.* A scheme of classification. E–M19. †**6** A particular orderly arrangement according to a regular plan or design. M17–M18.

4 V. S. NAIPAUL That briefcase suggested method, steadiness, many commissions. 6 ADDISON I would have all the knives and forks . . laid in a method.

Phrases: *direct method*: see DIRECT *a.* **method in one's madness** sense or reason in what appears to be foolish or abnormal behaviour. *method of* EXCLUSION. *method of least squares*: see SQUARE *n.* ORGANIZATION *and methods*. *scientific method*: see SCIENTIFIC *a.*

Comb.: **methods engineer** a person whose occupation is methods engineering; **methods engineering** the organization or improvement of business and management methods by method study; **method(s) study** the systematic study of business and management methods with a view to increasing efficiency.

methodless *a.* E17.

méthode champenoise /metɔd ʃɑ̃pənwɑːz/ *n. phr.* E20. [Fr., lit. 'champagne method'.] The method of introducing a sparkle into wine by allowing the last stage of fermentation to take place in the bottle; a sparkling wine made in this way.

Methodenstreit /meˈtoːdənʃtraɪt/ *n.* Pl. **-e** /-ə/. M20. [G, lit. 'methods struggle'.] (A) discussion or dispute concerning the methodology of a field of study.

methodic /mɪˈθɒdɪk/ *a.* & *n.* M16. [Late L *methodicus* f. Gk *methodikos*, f. *methodos* METHOD: see -IC.] **A** *adj.* †**1** (**M-.**) = METHODICAL 1. M16–M18. **2** = METHODICAL 2. E17. **B** *n.* **1** *Hist.* (**M-.**) = METHODIST *n.* 1. M16. **2** In *pl.* (treated as *sing.*) or †*sing.* Methodology, esp. of language teaching. M19.

methodical /mɪˈθɒdɪk(ə)l/ *a.* L16. [f. as prec. + -ICAL.] **1** *Hist.* (**M-.**) Of, pertaining to, or designating the ancient school of Methodists. L16. **2** Characterized by method or order; (of a person) acting with or observant of method or order. L16. **b** Of a material thing: arranged in a neat or orderly manner. *rare.* M17.

2 V. WOOLF Painters live lives of methodical absorption, adding stroke to stroke. SLOAN WILSON They had been methodical, they had done things According to Plan.

methodicalness *n.* L17.

methodically /mɪˈθɒdɪk(ə)li/ *adv.* L16. [f. METHODIC *a.* or prec.: see -ICALLY.] In a methodical manner.

R. K. NARAYAN She was steadily, definitely, methodically working herself up into a breakdown. D. FRANCIS I went methodically round the house . . locking and bolting all the outside doors.

methodise *v.* var. of METHODIZE.

Methodism /ˈmɛθədɪz(ə)m/ *n.* In sense 2 **m-.** M18. [f. METHOD + -ISM.] **1** The system, faith, and practice of the Methodist Churches. M18. **2** Adherence to or excessive regard for fixed methods. M19. **3** *Hist.* The doctrine and practice of the ancient school of Methodists. L19.

Methodist /ˈmɛθədɪst/ *n.* & *a.* In sense 2 **m-.** L16. [mod.L *methodista*, f. L *methodus* METHOD: see -IST.] **A** *n.* **1** *Hist.* A physician of an ancient school of medical thought that attributed disease either to narrowing or relaxation of the body's internal 'pores'. L16. **2** An advocate or follower of the use of a (particular or specified) method. L16. **b** *Bot.* & *Zool.* A person who classifies or arranges according to a particular (esp. artificial) method or scheme. *obs.* exc. *Hist.* M18. **3** *Hist.* A member of a 17th-cent. group of Roman Catholic apologists. L17. **4** A member of any of several Protestant denominations (now chiefly united) originating in the 18th-cent. evangelistic movement founded by John and Charles Wesley and George Whitefield. M18. **b** A person of strict religious views. *derog.* Now *rare* or *obs.* M18.

4 G. GORER The most sizable Protestant group after the Church of England are the Methodists. S. PLATH My mother had been a Catholic before she was a Methodist. *Primitive Methodist*: see PRIMITIVE *a.* *Wesleyan Methodist*: see WESLEYAN *a.*

B *adj.* Of or pertaining to (the denomination of) the Methodists. M18.

Harper's Magazine Judson Noth, a local Methodist preacher. E. P. THOMPSON The evangelical revival resulted in the distinct Methodist Church.

Methoˈdistic *a.* of, pertaining to, or characteristic of the Methodists or their doctrines, methods, or appearance L18. **Methoˈdistical** *a.* = METHODISTIC M18. **Methodistically** *adv.* in accordance with the principles or practice of Methodists L18.

methodize /ˈmɛθədʌɪz/ *v.t.* Also **-ise.** L16. [f. METHOD + -IZE.] **1** Reduce to method or order; arrange (ideas etc.) in an orderly manner. L16. **b** Make (a person) orderly or methodical. L18. **2** Convert to Methodism. *rare.* M19.

methodiˈzation *n.* the action or process of reducing to method or order; the state of being methodized or ordered: E19. **methodizer** *n.* L17.

methodology /mɛθəˈdɒlədʒi/ *n.* E19. [mod.L *methodologia* or Fr. *méthodologie*, f. as METHOD + -OLOGY.] **1** The branch of knowledge that deals with method and its application in a particular field. Also, the study of empirical research or the techniques employed in it. E19. **2** A body of methods used in a particular branch of study or activity. M19.

methodoˈlogical *a.* M19. **methodoˈlogically** *adv.* in a methodological manner or respect L19. **methodologist** *n.* M19.

Methody /ˈmɛθədi/ *n.* & *a. colloq.* & *dial.* M18. [f. METHOD(IST + -Y[6].] **A** *n.* = METHODIST *n.* 4. M18. **B** *adj.* = METHODIST *a.* L18.

methohexitone /mɛθəˈhɛksɪtəʊn/ *n.* M20. [f. METH- + -O- + HEX(A- + BARB)IT(URIC + -ONE.] *Pharm.* A derivative of barbituric acid, given intravenously as an anaesthetic.

Also **methohexital** *n.* (chiefly *US*) M20.

methomania /mɛθəˈmeɪnɪə/ *n. rare.* M19. [f. Gk *methē* strong drink + -O- + -MANIA.] *Med.* Dipsomania.

methonium /mɪˈθəʊnɪəm/ *n.* M20. [f. METH- + -ONIUM.] *Pharm.* Any of various (salts of) polymethylene bistrimethylammonium cations, $[(CH_3)_3N(CH_2)_xN(CH_3)_3]^{2+}$, some of which are ganglionic blocking agents used to treat hypertension. Chiefly in *methonium compound.*

methoprene /ˈmɛθəpriːn/ *n.* L20. [f. METH- + IS)OPRENE.] A derivative of an isoprene polymer, $C_{19}H_{34}O_3$, which causes arrest of development in various insects and is used as an insecticide.

methotrexate /mɛθəˈtrɛkseɪt, miːθə-/ *n.* M20. [f. METH- + elems. of unkn. origin.] *Pharm.* A cytotoxic orange-brown powder which is a folic acid antagonist used to treat certain cancers; 4-amino-10-methylfolic acid.

methought *v.* pa. t. of METHINKS.

methoxide /mɪˈθɒksʌɪd/ *n.* L19. [f. METHOXY- + -IDE.] *Chem.* A salt or simple compound containing the methoxyl radical, as *sodium methoxide*, $NaOCH_3$.

methoxy- /mɪˈθɒksi/ *comb. form*. Also as attrib. adj. **methoxy**. [f. METH- + OXY-.] *Chem.* Designating or containing a methoxyl group.

methoxychlor *n.* a crystalline compound, $(C_6H_4OCH_3)_2CHCCl_3$, related to DDT and used as an insecticide, esp. for veterinary hygiene M20.

methoxyl /mɪˈθɒksʌɪl, -sɪl/ *n.* M19. [f. as prec. + -YL.] *Chem.* The radical $CH_3O\cdot$, derived from methanol. Usu. in *comb.*

meths /mɛθs/ *n. colloq.* Also **meth** /mɛθ/. M20. [Abbrev.] = *methylated spirits* s.v. METHYLATE *v.*

attrib.: M. TRIPP I'd seen a meths drinker spewing blood the night before.

Methuen /ˈmɛθjuɪn/ *n. arch. rare.* M18. [Paul *Methuen* (1672–1757), Eng. diplomat who negotiated a commercial treaty between England and Portugal in 1703.] Portuguese wine.

Methuselah /mɪˈθ(j)uːz(ə)lə/ *n.* Also **-lem** /-ləm/. LME. [Heb. *mĕtūšelaḥ*, a pre-Noachian patriarch, stated to have lived 969 years (*Gen.* 5:27).] **1** A very old person or thing, esp. as a type or representation of extreme longevity. LME. **2** (Usu. **m-**.) A very large wine bottle, equivalent to eight ordinary bottles. M20.

methyl /ˈmiːθʌɪl, ˈmɛθ-, -θɪl/ *n.* M19. [Fr. *méthyle*, G *Methyl*, back-form. f. Fr. *méthylène*, G *Methylen* METHYLENE.] *Chem.* The radical $CH_3\cdot$ derived from methane, present in methanol, methanoic (formic) acid, etc. Usu. in *comb.*

Comb.: **methyl alcohol** = METHANOL; **methylbenzene** = TOLUENE; **methylcellulose** any of a range of white, tasteless compounds produced by etherifying cellulose and used as thickening, emulsifying, and stabilizing agents, esp. in foods, laxatives, and adhesives; **methyldopa** *Pharm.* a whitish powder, $C_{10}H_{13}NO_4$, used as a hypotensive agent; **methyl ethyl ketone** a colourless volatile liquid, $CH_3COCH_2CH_3$, used as a solvent for organic materials; butanone; **methyl green** a green dye used in microscopy to stain chromatin; **methyl isobutyl ketone** a liquid ketone, $(CH_3)_2CHCH_2COCH_3$, used as a solvent; hexone, 4-methylpentan-2-one; **methyl isocyanate** a toxic gas, CH_3NCO, used in making certain pesticides; **methyl methacrylate** a volatile colourless liquid, $CH_2{:}C(CH_3)COOCH_3$, that readily polymerizes to form resinous glassy materials such as Perspex and Plexiglas; such a polymeric material; **methyl orange** an orange crystalline compound which is the sodium salt of a sulphur-containing azo dye, chiefly used in solution as an acid-base indicator, giving a pink colour at pH 3 and yellow at pH 4.4; **methylphenidate** a sympathomimetic drug used as a CNS stimulant to treat various depressive and lethargic conditions; **methyl red** a red crystalline acidic azo dye, $(CH_3)_2N{\cdot}C_6H_4{\cdot}N{:}N{\cdot}C_6H_4{\cdot}COOH$, used in solution as an acid-base indicator, giving a red colour at pH 4.4 and yellow at pH 6; **methyl rubber** an early synthetic rubber made by polymerizing dimethylbutadiene; **methyl salicylate** a colourless or pale yellow liquid, $C_6H_4(OH)CO{\cdot}OCH_3$, the chief constituent of oil of wintergreen and sweet birch oil, which is used as a flavouring, in perfumery, and in analgesic liniments and ointments; **methyltestosterone** *Pharm.* any of the methyl derivatives of testosterone; *esp.* (more fully *17-methyltestosterone*) a synthetic androgen used to treat hormonal imbalances and certain cancers; **methylthiouracil** a drug which inhibits thyroid activity and is used to control thyrotoxicosis; 6-methyl-2-thiouracil; **methyl violet** gentian violet.

methylal /ˈmɛθɪlal/ *n.* M19. [f. prec. + -AL².] *Chem.* A colourless volatile fragrant liquid, $(CH_3O)_2CH_2$, used as a solvent and formerly as an anaesthetic.

methylate /ˈmɛθɪleɪt/ *n.* M19. [f. as next + -ATE¹.] *Chem.* = METHOXIDE.

methylate /ˈmɛθɪleɪt/ *v.t.* M19. [f. METHYL + -ATE³.] *Chem.* Introduce one or more methyl groups into (a compound or group). Also, adulterate with methanol. Chiefly as *methylated* ppl a.

methylated spirit(s) ethyl alcohol containing methanol; *esp.* that sold for general use, being made unfit for drinking by addition of about ten per cent methanol, and usu. also some pyridine and a violet dye. **methyˈlation** *n.* the process of methylating (esp. alcohol) L19. **methylator** *n.* a person who methylates alcohol L19.

methylene /ˈmɛθɪliːn/ *n.* M19. [Fr. *méthylène*, irreg. f. Gk *methu* wine + *hulē* wood (see -YL, -ENE).] *Chem.* The radical $\cdot CH_2\cdot$, which is the basic unit of hydrocarbon chains. Also *methylene group*.

Comb.: **methylene blue** a green crystalline compound, blue in aqueous solution, used in dyeing, as an antiseptic, and as a microscopic stain for bacteria.

methylic /mɛˈθɪlɪk/ *a.* Now *rare* or *obs.* M19. [f. METHYL + -IC.] *Chem.* Of, pertaining to, or including methyl.

¶Replaced by attrib. use of *methyl*.

methysergide /mɛθɪˈsəːdʒʌɪd/ *n.* M20. [f. METH- + L)YSERG(IC + AM)IDE.] *Pharm.* A lysergic acid derivative with serotonin-blocking properties, used as a preventive drug for recurrent migraine.

metic /ˈmɛtɪk/ *n.* E19. [Irreg. f. Gk *metoikos*, f. as META- + *-oikos* dwelling, f. *oikein* dwell: see -IC.] *Hist.* A resident alien in a Greek city with some of the privileges of citizenship.

metical /mɛtɪˈkal/ *n.* L20. [Port., f. as MISKAL.] The basic monetary unit of Mozambique, equal to 100 centavos.

meticulous /mɪˈtɪkjʊləs/ *a.* M16. [f. L *meticulosus*, f. *metus* fear: see -ULOUS.] †**1** Fearful, timid. M16–L17. **2** Overcareful about minute details. Now also simply, careful, precise. E19.

2 R. LEHMANN A letter written in a minute and meticulous hand.

meticuˈlosity *n.* M17. **meticulously** *adv.* L17. **meticulousness** *n.* E20.

métier /metje, ˈmeɪtɪeɪ/ *n.* L18. [Fr., f. Proto-Romance alt. of L *ministerium* service, MINISTRY, prob. infl. by *mysterium* MYSTERY *n.*¹] One's occupation or department of activity. Now usu., a field in which one has special skill or ability; one's forte.

W. A. PERCY Power? I knew nothing about it and it certainly wasn't my métier.

metif /meɪˈtiːf/ *n.* E19. [Fr. *métif* alt. of *métis*: see METIS.] A person with one White and one quarter Black parent.

metis /meɪˈtiːs; *Canad.* meɪˈtiː, ˈmeɪti/ *n.* Pl. same /meɪˈtiː(s), ˈmeɪti, ˈmeɪtɪz/). Also (fem.) **métisse** /meɪˈtiːs, *Canad. also* ˈmeɪtiːs/, pl. **-s**. E19. [Fr. *métis* f. OFr. *mestis* f. Proto-Romance, f. L *mixtus*: see MESTIZO.] A person of mixed descent; *esp.* (in Canada) a person with one White and one American Indian parent.

metoclopramide /mɛtəˈkləʊprəmʌɪd/ *n.* M20. [f. MET(H)O(XY)- + C(H)L(OR)O-² + PR(OCAIN)AMIDE.] *Pharm.* An amide with dopamine-receptor blocking properties, used to treat hypothyroidism and as an anti-emetic.

metoecious /mɪˈtiːʃəs/ *a.* Also ***metec-**. L19. [f. META- + Gk *oikia* house: see -IOUS.] *Bot.* = HETEROECIOUS.

metoecism /-sɪz(ə)m/ *n.* = HETEROECISM L19.

metoestrus /mɛˈtiːstrəs/ *n.* Also ***metest-**. E20. [f. META- + OESTRUS.] *Biol.* The short period following oestrus in many mammals during which sexual activity subsides.

metoestrous *a.* E20.

metol /ˈmɛtɒl/ *n.* L19. [Arbitrary.] *Photogr.* A soluble white crystalline compound, the sulphate of *p*-methylaminophenol, used as a photographic developer. Also, the free base, *p*-methylaminophenol.

Metonic /mɪˈtɒnɪk/ *a.* L17. [f. Gk *Metōn* Athenian astronomer + -IC.] *Metonic cycle, period, †year*, the cycle of 19 Julian years in which the moon returns (nearly) to the same apparent position with regard to the sun, so that the new and full moons occur at the same dates in the corresponding year of each cycle.

metonym /ˈmɛtənɪm/ *n.* M19. [Back-form. f. next: see -NYM.] A word used metonymically.

metonymy /mɪˈtɒnɪmi/ *n.* M16. [Late L *metonymia* f. Gk *metōnumia* lit. 'change of name', f. as META- + *onuma* name: see -NYM, -Y³.] **1** The substitution of a word denoting an attribute or adjunct of a thing for the word denoting the thing itself; an instance of this. M16. **2** A thing used or regarded as a substitute for or symbol of something else. M20.

1 *Athenaeum* 'Stokes', the name of the inventor.. has, by metonymy, come to mean the trench mortar gun itself.

metoˈnymic *a.* of, involving, or used in metonymy L18. **metoˈnymical** *a.* = METONYMIC M16. **metoˈnymically** *adv.* L16.

metope /ˈmɛtəʊp, ˈmɛtəpi/ *n.* M16. [L *metopa* f. Gk *metopē*, f. *meta* between + *opē* hole in a frieze for a beam-end.] *Archit.* A square space between triglyphs in a Doric frieze.

metopic /mɪˈtɒpɪk/ *a.* L19. [f. Gk *metōpon* forehead + -IC.] Of or pertaining to the forehead; frontal; (of a skull) exhibiting metopism.

ˈmetopism *n.* continued presence in the skull of an open frontal suture beyond infancy L19.

metoposcopy /mɛtəˈpɒskəpi/ *n.* M16. [Fr. *métoposcopie* f. L *metoposcopus* f. Gk *metōposkopos*, f. *metōpon* forehead: see -SCOPY.] **1** The art of judging character or telling a person's fortune from the forehead or face. M16. **2** The appearance or physical features of a person's forehead. M17.

metopoˈscopic *a.* (*rare*) M19. **metopoˈscopical** *a.* (*rare*) E19. **metoposcopist** *n.* a person skilled in metoposcopy L16.

metoprolol /mɪˈtɒprəlɒl/ *n.* L20. [f. MET(H- + -O- + PRO(PRANO)LOL.] *Pharm.* A beta blocker used to treat hypertension and angina.

Metran /ˈmɛtran/ *n.* M19. [Ethiopic.] = ABUNA.

metre /ˈmiːtə/ *n.*¹ Also ***meter**. OE. [((O)Fr. *mètre* f.) L *metrum* f. Gk *metron* measure, f. IE base + instr. suff.] **1** *Pros.* Poetic rhythm or scheme as determined by the number and length of the feet in a line; a (specified) form of this. OE. **2** Poetic composition, verse. Formerly also, a verse, a poem. ME. **3** *Pros.* A metrical group or measure. L19. **4** The basic pattern of beats in a piece of music. L19.

1 W. EMPSON The demands of metre allow the poet to say something which is not normal colloquial English. G. S. FRASER The metre of Michael Alexander's rendering is.. easy and pleasant to read.

Phrases: *common metre*: see COMMON *a.* *long metre*: see LONG *a.*¹ *short metre*: see SHORT *a.*

Comb.: **metre psalm** = *metric psalm* s.v. METRIC *a.*¹

metreless *a.* L19.

metre /ˈmiːtə/ *n.*² Also ***meter**. L18. [Fr. *mètre* f. as prec.] The fundamental unit of length in the metric system, approximately equal to 39.37 inches, and now, as an SI unit, defined as equal to the distance travelled by light in free space in 1/299,792,458 second. (Symbol m.)

superficial metre: see SUPERFICIAL *a.* 1.

Comb.: **metre-angle** *Ophthalm.* a unit of convergence equal to the angle between the line of sight of either eye and the median line passing between the eyes when fixating a point on the median line one metre away; **metre-candle** = LUX *n.*; **metre-kilogram-second** *a.* designating or pertaining to a system of measurement in which these three elements form the basic units of length, mass, and time respectively.

¶Orig. intended to represent one ten-millionth of the length of a quadrant of the meridian, and defined by reference to a platinum-iridium standard kept in Paris; later defined in terms of the wavelength (605.8 nanometres) of a particular orange line in the spectrum of krypton 86.

metre /ˈmiːtə/ *v.* Also ***meter**. LME. [f. METRE *n.*¹] **1** *v.t.* Compose in or put into metre. LME. **2** *v.i.* Versify. Now *rare* or *obs.* LME.

metrete /mɪˈtriːt/ *n.* ME. [L *metreta* f. Gk *metrētēs*, f. *metrein* to measure, f. *metron* METRE *n.*¹] An ancient Greek liquid measure equivalent to approx. 41 litres, or 9 gallons.

metric /ˈmɛtrɪk/ *n.*¹ & *a.*¹ L15. [L *metricus* f. Gk *metrikos*, f. *metron* METRE *n.*¹: see -IC, -ICS.] **A** *n.* **1** In *pl.* (treated as *sing.*) or (now *rare*) *sing.* The branch of study that deals with metre. L15. **2** *Math. & Physics.* A metric function. E20. **3** *Pros.* = METRE *n.*¹ 1. M20. **4** Esp. *Psychol. & Ling.* A system or standard of measurement. M20. **B** *adj.* = METRICAL *a.*¹ 2; *esp.* in *Math. & Physics*, pertaining to, involving, or defining distance (or an abstract quantity analogous to distance). M19.

Special collocations: **metric psalm** a biblical psalm translated into verse. **metric space** *Math.* a set together with a metric defined for all pairs of elements of the set.

metric /ˈmɛtrɪk/ *a.*[2] & *n.*[2] M19. [Fr. *métrique*, f. *mètre* METRE *n.*[2]: see -IC.] **A** *adj.* **1** Of, pertaining to, or based on the metre; *spec.* designating the decimal measuring system having the metre, litre, and gram (or kilogram) as its respective units of length, volume, and mass. M19. **2** Having the metric system as the principal system of weights and measures. E20.

1 *metric* HUNDREDWEIGHT. *metric ton*: see TON *n.*[1] 4. 2 D. FRANCIS The Australians had already gone metric, to the confusion of my mental arithmetic.

B *n.* The metric system of measurement. M20.

-metric /ˈmɛtrɪk/ *suff.* [f. or after Fr. *-métrique* f. (as) L *metricus* METRIC *n.*[1] & *a.*[1]] Forming adjs. corresp. to ns. in *-meter* or *-metry*, as *barometric*, *gravimetric*.

metrical /ˈmɛtrɪk(ə)l/ *a.*[1] LME. [f. as METRIC *n.*[1] & *a.*[1]: see -ICAL.] **1** *Pros.* Of, pertaining to, or composed in metre. LME. **2** Of, involving, or determined by measurement. M17.

metrical /ˈmɛtrɪk(ə)l/ *a.*[2] Now *rare*. L18. [Fr. *métrique* METRIC *a.*[2] & *n.*[2] + -AL[1].] = METRIC *a.*[2] 1.

metrically /ˈmɛtrɪk(ə)li/ *adv.*[1] L18. [f. METRIC *a.*[1] or METRICAL *a.*[1] + -ICALLY.] *Pros.* With regard to metre; (translated) into metre.

metrically /ˈmɛtrɪk(ə)li/ *adv.*[2] M20. [f. METRIC *a.*[2] or METRICAL *a.*[2] + -ICALLY.] In or with the metric system of weights and measures.

metricate /ˈmɛtrɪkeɪt/ *v.* M20. [Back-form. f. next.] **1** *v.i.* Change to or adopt the metric system of weights and measures. M20. **2** *v.t.* Convert or adapt to the metric system. L20.

metrication /mɛtrɪˈkeɪʃ(ə)n/ *n.* M20. [f. METRIC *a.*[2] + -ATION.] Conversion to the metric system of weights and measures; the adoption of the metric system.

metrician /mɪˈtrɪʃ(ə)n/ *n.* LME. [f. as METRIC *n.*[1] & *a.*[1] + -ICIAN.] *Pros.* †**1** A person writing in metre. LME–M16. **2** An expert in or student of metre. M19.

metrification /ˌmɛtrɪfɪˈkeɪʃ(ə)n/ *n.* LME. [In sense 1 f. med.L *metrificatio(n-)*, f. L *metrificat-* pa. ppl stem of *metrificare*: see next, -ATION. In sense 2 f. METRI(C *a.*[2] + -FICATION.] **1** *Pros.* Metrical composition or structure. LME. **2** = METRICATION. M20.

metrify /ˈmɛtrɪfʌɪ/ *v.t.* L15. [OFr. *metrifier* or med.L *metrificare*, f. L *metrum* METRE *n.*[1]: see -FY.] *Pros.* Put into metre, make a metrical version of.

metrisable *a.* var. of METRIZABLE.

metrisation *n.* var. of METRIZATION.

metrist /ˈmɛtrɪst/ *n.* M16. [med.L *metrista*, f. L *metrum* METRE *n.*[1]: see -IST.] A person who writes or composes (esp. skilfully) in metre.

metritis /mɪˈtrʌɪtɪs/ *n.* M19. [f. Gk *mētra* womb + -ITIS.] *Med.* Inflammation of the uterus.

metritic /mɪˈtrɪtɪk/ *a.* M19.

metrizable /mɪˈtrʌɪzəb(ə)l/ *a.* Also **-isable**. F20. [f. as next + -ABLE.] *Math.* Of a topological space: able to be assigned a metric which makes it a metric space whose topology is identical to that of the original space.

metriza'bility *n.* E20.

metrization /mɛtrʌɪˈzeɪʃ(ə)n/ *n.* Also **-isation**. E20. [f. METRIC *n.*[1] + -IZATION.] *Math.* The process of assigning a metric to a metrizable topological space.

metro /ˈmɛtrəʊ, ˈmeɪ-/ *n.*[1] *colloq.* Also **M-**. Pl. **-os**. E20. [Fr. *métro* abbrev. of (*Chemin de Fer*) *Métropolitain* Metropolitan (Railway).] An underground railway system in a city, *esp.* that in Paris.

metro /ˈmɛtrəʊ/ *a.* & *n.*[2] Also **M-**. M20. [Abbrev. of METROPOLITAN *a.*] **A** *adj.* = METROPOLITAN *a.* 2a, b. M20.

Economist The metro counties are Labour's territory.

B *n.* Pl. **-os**. The metropolitan area of a city. *Canad.* L20.

metrocracy /mɪˈtrɒkrəsi/ *n.* L19. [f. Gk *mētr-*, *mētēr* mother: see -CRACY.] = MATRIARCHY.

metroland /ˈmɛtrə(ʊ)land/ *n.* Also **M-**. E20. [f. METRO(POLITAN *a.* + LAND *n.*[1]] The area surrounding a metropolis, *spec.* that around London, esp. to the north-west, served by the underground railway.

metrolander *n.* E20.

Metroliner /ˈmɛtrəʊlʌɪnə/ *n.* Also **metro-liner**. M20. [f. METRO(POLITAN *a.* + LINER *n.*[2]] A high-speed intercity train in the US.

metrology /mɛˈtrɒlədʒi/ *n.* E19. [f. Gk *metron* METRE *n.*[1] + -OLOGY.] The branch of science that deals with measurement.

metro'logical *a.* M19. **metrologist** *n.* M19.

metromania /mɛtrəˈmeɪnɪə/ *n.* L18. [f. Gk *metron* METRE *n.*[1] + -MANIA.] A mania for writing poetry.

metromaniac *n.* & *a.* M19.

metronidazole /mɛtrəˈnʌɪdəzəʊl/ *n.* M20. [f. ME(THYL + NITRO- + IM)IDAZOLE, elems. of the systematic name (see below).] *Pharm.* An imidazole derivative used to treat infection by some anaerobic organisms, esp. trichomoniasis; 2-(2-methyl-5-nitroimidazol-1-yl)ethanol, $C_6H_9N_3O_3$.

metronome /ˈmɛtrənəʊm/ *n.* E19. [f. Gk *metron* METRE *n.*[1] + *nomos* law, rule.] *Mus.* A device for marking time which emits a regular tick at a selected rate, esp. by means of an oscillating rod or pendulum.

metro'nomic *a.* of or pertaining to a metronome; *fig.* resembling the action of a metronome: L19. **metro'nomically** *adv.* in a metronomic way; according to a metronome: E19.

metronymic /mɛtrəˈnɪmɪk/ *n.* & *a.* M19. [f. Gk *mētr-*, *mētēr* mother, after PATRONYMIC.] **A** *n.* A name derived from that of a mother or maternal ancestor, esp. by addition of an affix indicating such descent. M19. **B** *adj.* Designating such a name or such an affix; (of a group or culture) using such names. L19.

me'tronymy *n.* the practice of using metronymics L19.

metrop /mɪˈtrɒp/ *n. colloq.* Also **M-**. L19. [Abbrev.] = METROPOLIS 3a.

metroplex /ˈmɛtrəʊplɛks/ *n.* Chiefly *N. Amer.* M20. [f. METRO(POLITAN *a.* + COM)PLEX *n.*] A very large metropolitan area, *spec.* one which is an aggregation of two or more cities.

Times The whole metroplex of Houston ranks as an enterprise zone.

metropole /ˈmɛtrəpəʊl/ *n.* Also **M-**. LME. [(O)Fr. *métropol* f. as next.] **1a** A chief town or city. Now *rare*. LME. **b** The parent State of a colony. Cf. METROPOLIS 2. M20. **2** = METROPOLIS 1. M19. **3** A luxury hotel. L19.

1b *Survey* No longer were all the colonies economically indebted to the metropoles.

metropolis /mɪˈtrɒp(ə)lɪs/ *n.* Also **M-**. Pl. **-lises**, **-li** /-lʌɪ, -liː/. M16. [Late L f. Gk *mētropolis*, f. *mētēr*, *mētr-* mother + *polis* city.] **1** *Eccl.* The see of a metropolitan bishop. M16. **2** The mother city or parent State of a colony, *spec.* an ancient Greek one. M16. **3a** The chief city of a country, a capital; any large busy city; *the metropolis*, such a city, (esp., in Britain, London) as distinct from its surrounding rural or provincial areas. L16. **b** A city as the centre of some specified activity. Usu. foll. by *of*. L17. **c** *Bot.* & *Zool.* The district in which a species, group, etc., is most represented. *rare*. E19.

2 J. A. ROEBUCK The best means of making the wants of the colonies known to . . the metropolis which founds them. 3a P. THEROUX The border town . . was so small it made Tapachula seem a metropolis. b J. BRYCE Rome is the metropolis of religion.

metropolitan /mɛtrəˈpɒlɪt(ə)n/ *n.* & *a.* Also **M-**. LME. [Late L *metropolitanus*, f. Gk *mētropolitēs*, f. *mētropolis*: see prec., -AN.] **A** *n.* **1** *Eccl.* (The title of) a bishop having the oversight of the bishops of a province, in the Western Church now approximately co-extensive with archbishop, in the Orthodox Church ranking above an archbishop and below a patriarch. LME. **2** A chief town, a metropolis. Now *rare*. M16. †**3** = METROPOLIS 3b. E17–E18. **4** A native or inhabitant of a metropolis; a person who has metropolitan or urbane ideas, manners, etc. L18. **5** A native or inhabitant of the mother city or parent State of a colony. M19.

4 A. BRIEN These sophisticated metropolitans, all of them Petersburg graduates.

B *adj.* **1** *Eccl.* Belonging to an ecclesiastical metropolis. Also, pertaining to or characteristic of a metropolitan. M16. **2a** Of, pertaining to, or constituting a metropolis or large city (esp., in Britain, London). Later also, (of a person, lifestyle, etc.) urbane, sophisticated, exciting. M16. **b** Designating or pertaining to a city underground railway system. M19. **c** Designating a type of early English pottery found in or near London. L19. **3** Of, pertaining to, or designating the parent State of a colony. E19.

2 V. S. NAIPAUL A busy, alert man, deep in the metropolitan excitements of London.

Special collocations: **metropolitan bishop** = sense A.1 above. **metropolitan county** *Hist.* each of six units of English local government centred on a large urban area (in existence from 1974 to 1986). **metropolitan magistrate** a paid professional magistrate in London (cf. STIPENDIARY).

metropolitanate *n.* = METROPOLITANSHIP M19. **metropolitanism** *n.* metropolitan spirit, ideas, or institutions M19. **metropolitani'zation** *n.* the process of giving a metropolitan character to a person or area M20. **metropolitanize** *v.t.* make metropolitan; convert into a metropolis: M19. **metropolitanship** *n.* the office or see of a metropolitan bishop M17.

metropolite /mɪˈtrɒp(ə)lʌɪt/ *n.* Also **M-**. L16. [Late L *metropolita* f. Gk *mētropolitēs*, f. *mētropolis* METROPOLIS: see -ITE[1].] **1** *Eccl.* = METROPOLITAN *n.* 1. L16. †**2** = METROPOLIS 3a. L16–M17.

metropolitical /mɛtrəpəˈlɪtɪk(ə)l/ *a.* Also **M-**. M16. [f. med.L *metropoliticus*, f. as prec.: see -AL[1].] **1** *Eccl.* = METROPOLITAN *a.* 1. M16. **2** = METROPOLITAN *a.* 2a, 3. E17.

metropolitically *adv.* in the capacity of a metropolitan bishop M17.

metrorrhagia /miːtrəˈreɪdʒɪə/ *n.* M19. [f. Gk *mētra* womb + -O- + -RRHAGIA.] *Med.* Abnormal uterine haemorrhage.

metrorrhagic *a.* M19.

metrostaxis /miːtrəˈstaksɪs/ *n.* L19. [f. Gk *mētra* womb + *-staxis*, f. *stazein* drip.] *Med.* Slight continuous uterine haemorrhage.

-metry /mɪtri/ *suff.* [Repr. Gk *-metria*, f. *-metrēs* measurer, f. *metron* METRE *n.*[1]: see -Y[3].] Used in wds adopted f. Gk and in Eng. wds modelled on these, usu. denoting the action, process, or science of measuring something (as *alkalimetry*, *chronometry*, *gasometry*), *spec.* (corresp. to ns. in *-meter*) by means of a particular instrument (as *barometry*).

metteur en scène /mɛtœːr ɑ̃ sɛn/ *n. phr.* Pl. ***metteurs en scène*** (pronounced same). E20. [Fr., lit. 'a person who puts on the stage'.] A producer of a play; a director of a film.

mettle /ˈmɛt(ə)l/ *n.* & *a.* Also †**metal**. M16. [Var. of METAL *n.* & *a.*] **A** *n.* **I 1** The quality of a person's disposition or temperament. M16. **2** A person's spirit or courage. L16. **3** The natural vigour or spirit of an animal, esp. a horse. L16.

1 J. CHEEVER We think we know each other's mettle intimately. 2 J. HUXLEY I feared . . I had not the mettle to cope with this whirlwind. 3 J. MARTINEAU They have horses of best descent and mettle.

†**II** See METAL *n.*

Phrases: **on one's mettle** inspired to do one's best. †**put a person off his** or **her mettle** undermine a person's courage. **put a person on his** or **her mettle** test a person's powers of endurance or resistance. **show one's mettle** reveal or demonstrate one's courage. **try a person's mettle** = *put a person on his or her metal* above.

B *adj.* **1** Of spirited temperament. *obs.* exc. *Sc.* L16. **2** See METAL *a.*

1 R. L. STEVENSON He is an honest and a mettle gentleman.

mettled *a.* (*a*) = METTLESOME; (*b*) having a temperament of a specified kind: L16. **mettlesome** *a.* full of mettle; spirited: M17.

Mettwurst /ˈmɛtvʊrst/ *n.* L19. [G.] A type of smoked German sausage.

meu /mjuː/ *n.* E16. [Irreg. f. as MEUM *n.*[2]] = MEUM *n.*[2]

meubles /mœbl/ *n.pl.* ME. [OFr. *mo(e)bles*, *muebles*, use as n.(pl.) of adj., f. L *mobilis* MOBILE *a.* Reintroduced f. Fr. in 18 in sense 2.] †**1**

Movable property or goods; *spec.* (*Sc. Law*) movable as opp. to heritable property; = MOVABLE *n.* 2. ME–L16. 2 (Items of) household furniture. L18.

meum /ˈmiːəm, ˈmeɪəm/ *n.*[1] *arch.* L16. [L, neut. of *meus* mine.] The principle that a person has sole rights to his or her own property and no rights to another's. Chiefly in *meum and tuum*, (the distinction between) what is mine or one's own and what is yours or another's.

meum /ˈmiːəm/ *n.*[2] M16. [L f. Gk *mēon*.] = SPIGNEL.

meunière /məːˈnjɛː, *foreign* mønjɛːr/ *a.* M19. [Fr. (*à la*) *meunière* lit. '(in the manner of) a miller's wife'.] *Cookery*. Esp. of fish: cooked or served in lightly browned butter with lemon juice and parsley. Usu. *postpositive*.

Meursault /məːˈsəʊ, ˈməː-, *foreign* mœrso (*pl. same*)/ *n.* M19. [A commune in the Côte d'Or, France.] A (usu. white) burgundy wine produced near Beaune.

meuse /mjuːs, -z/ *n.* & *v.* Now *dial.* Also **muse**. E16. [OFr. *musse*, *m(o)uce* (mod. dial. *muche*) hiding place, f. *musser*, *muchier* to hide (whence MITCH *v.*). Cf. MUSET.] A *n.* 1 A gap in a hedge or fence through which hares, rabbits, etc., pass, esp. as a means of escape; *fig.* a way out of a difficulty. E16. 2 The form (lair) of a hare. E17. B *v.i.* Go through a meuse. M17.

mevalonic /mɛvəˈlɒnɪk/ *a.* M20. [f. ME(THYL + VAL(ERIC *a.* + LACT)ON(E + -IC.] Biochem. *mevalonic acid*, a crystalline compound, $C_6H_{12}O_4$, which is a growth factor for some lactobacilli and a precursor of cholesterol in animals and carotenoids in plants; 3,5-dihydroxy-3-methylpentanoic acid.

mevalonate /mɪˈvalǝneɪt/ *n.* a salt or ester of mevalonic acid; *loosely* the acid itself or its anion: M20.

mew /mjuː/ *n.*[1] [OE *mǣw*, corresp. to OS *mēu* (MLG, MDu. *mēwe*, Du. *meeuw*), f. Gmc, whence also OHG *méh*, ON *már* (pl. *mávar*, *máfar*).] A gull. Also called *seamew*.

Comb.: **mew gull** (chiefly *N. Amer.*) the common gull, *Larus canus*.

mew /mjuː/ *n.*[2] ME. [(O)Fr. *mue*, f. *muer*: see MEW *v.*[1]] 1 A cage for hawks, esp. while moulting; in *pl.*, the building(s) housing a set of these. ME. 2†a A cage for confining animals, esp. poultry, for fattening. LME–M19. b A breeding-cage. Now *dial.* LME. 3†a A place of confinement. LME–E17. b A secret place; a den. Now *rare*. LME.

Phrases: **in mew** (*a*) (of a hawk) in the process of moulting; † (*b*) (of a person) in hiding or confinement.

mew /mjuː/ *n.*[3] & *int.* L16. [Imit.: rel. to MEW *v.*[2] Cf. MIAOW *n.*] 1 (Repr.) the characteristic cry of a cat, sea bird, etc. L16. †2 (A sound) expr. derision. E–M17.

1 *transf.*: DENNIS POTTER The sounds of his weeping grew from a pathetic little mew into a violent sob.

mew /mjuː/ *v.*[1] LME. [In branch I f. (O)Fr. *muer*, f. L *mutare*: see MUTATION *n.*; in branch II f. MEW *n.*[2]] I 1 *v.t.* & *i.* Of a bird, esp. a hawk: moult, shed (feathers). LME. †b Of a stag: cast (its horns). LME–L18. †2 *v.t.* & *i. fig.* Change or remove (clothing). LME–M17. II†3 *v.t.* Coop *up* (poultry etc.) for fattening. *rare*. LME–M17. 4 *v.t.* Confine, enclose; conceal. Now usu. foll. by *up*. LME. 5 *v.t.* Put (a hawk) in a cage at moulting time. M16.

mew /mjuː/ *v.*[2]*i.* ME. [Imit.: rel. to MEW *n.*[3] Cf. MIAOW.] 1 Of a cat, sea bird, etc.: make its characteristic cry. ME. 2 *transf.* Of a person: utter a similar sound esp. in distress or (formerly) derision; *fig.* whimper, whine. E17.

1 D. M. THOMAS A little black cat at her feet, mewing up at her pathetically.

Mewari /mɛˈwɑːri/ *n.* & *a.* L19. [f. *Mewar* (see below) + -I[2].] A *n.* The language spoken in Udaipur (formerly Mewar), a former State in NW India, now part of Rajasthan. L19. B *adj.* Of or pertaining to Udaipur (Mewar) or its inhabitants. E20.

Mewati /mɛˈwɑːti/ *n.* & *a.* L18. [Hind. *mevātī*, f. as MEO *n.*[1] & *a.*[1]] A *n.* Pl. same, **-s**. 1 A member of a people of the Mewat region in NW India (now called Alwar and part of Rajasthan) and neighbouring areas; a Meo; *spec.* one professing Islam. L18. 2 The Rajasthani dialect of this people. E20. B *attrib.* or as *adj.* Of or pertaining to the Mewati or their dialect. M19.

mewl /mjuːl/ *v.* & *n.* LME. [Imit. Cf. MIAUL.] A *v.i.* 1 Esp. of an infant: cry feebly, whimper. LME. 2 = MEW *v.*[2] I. E17. B *n.* A thin cry, a whimper. M19.

mews /mjuːz/ *n.* LME. [Pl. of MEW *n.*[2]] 1 Orig., the royal stables at Charing Cross in London, built on the former site of the royal hawk mews. Later *gen.*, any set of stable buildings grouped round an open yard or alley. Treated as *sing.* or *pl.* LME. 2 Such a set of buildings converted into accommodation for people. Also, (a dwelling in) a row of town houses built in the style of a mews. E19.

mewt /mjuːt/ *v.i. obs.* exc. *dial.* ME. [Imit.] = MEW *v.*[2]

Mex /mɛks/ *a.* & *n. US slang.* M19. [Abbrev.] A *adj.* = MEXICAN *a.* M19. B *n.* Pl. same. = MEXICAN *n.*; *spec.* = MEXICAN *dollar*. E20.

Mexican /ˈmɛksɪk(ə)n/ *n.* & *a.* E17. [Sp. *mexicano* (now *mej-*), f. *Mexico*, f. *Mexitli* one of the names of the Aztec god of war: see -AN.] A *n.* 1 A native or inhabitant of Mexico, a country in Southern N. America. E17. 2 Nahuatl. Also = *Mexican Spanish* below. E19. 3 = *Mexican dollar* below. E19. B *adj.* Of or pertaining to Mexico or its inhabitants. E17.

Special collocations & *comb.*: **Mexican-American** *a.* & *n.* (designating or pertaining to) a person of Mexican descent in the US. **Mexican brown** *slang* crude heroin. **Mexican dollar** the Mexican peso; a coin of this value. **Mexican embroidery** a kind of embroidery characterized by brightly coloured floral or geometric designs. **Mexican fruit fly** a Central American dipteran insect, *Anastrepha ludens*, a pest of mangoes and citrus fruit. **Mexican hairless** (**dog**) (an animal of) a breed of small dog, lacking hair except for tufts on the head and tail. **Mexican-Indian** *a.* & *n.* (designating or pertaining to) a member of any of the aboriginal peoples of Mexico. **Mexican orange** a Mexican shrub, *Choisya ternata*, of the rue family, grown for its fragrant white flowers. **Mexican overdrive** *US slang* (the neutral gear position used when) coasting downhill in a motor vehicle. **Mexican poppy** a prickly-leaved poppy, *Argemone mexicana*, a weed in many warm countries. *Mexican* SCAMMONY. **Mexican shilling** *Hist.* a silver coin formerly current in some states of the US. **Mexican Spanish** (of) the variety of Spanish used in Mexico. **Mexican stand-off** (orig. in poker) a situation in which there is no clear winner; an impasse. **Mexican tea** a strong-scented goosefoot, *Chenopodium ambrosioides*, used as a flavouring in Mexico and medicinally. **Mexican thistle** = *Mexican poppy* above. **Mexican War** the war of 1846–8 between the US and Mexico. *Mexican wave*: see WAVE *n.* 5e.

Mexicaniˈzation *n.* the action of Mexicanizing L19. **Mexicanize** *v.t.* & *i.* make or become Mexican in character, manners, ideas, etc. M19.

Mexicano /mɛksɪˈkɑːnəʊ/ *n.* & *a.* Also **m-**. E20. [Sp.: see prec.] A *n.* Pl. **-os**. Fem. **-a** /-ə/. A native or inhabitant of Mexico; a person of Mexican descent, *esp.* a Mexican-American. E20. B *attrib.* or as *adj.* Pertaining to or designating a Mexicano. M20.

mexiletine /mɛkˈsʌɪlətiːn/ *n.* L20. [f. ME(TH- + *xil-* alt. of XYL(ENE + ET(H + -INE[5].] *Pharm.* A cyclic derivative of propanol used to treat ventricular arrhythmia; 1-(2,6-dimethylphenoxy)-2-propanamine, $C_6H_3(CH_3)_2OCH_2CH(CH_3)NH_2$.

Meyerbeerian /mʌɪəˈbɪərɪən/ *a.* L19. [f. *Meyerbeer* (see below) + -IAN.] Characteristic of or resembling the work of the German operatic composer Giacomo Meyerbeer (1791–1864), noted esp. for long grand operas dealing with epic subjects in a spectacular way.

mézair /meɪˈzɛː, *foreign* mezɛːr (*pl. same*)/ *n.* M18. [Fr., f. It. *mezzaria* middle gait.] *Horsemanship.* A movement involving a series of levades with a short step between each.

meze /ˈmeɪzeɪ/ *n.* Pl. same, **-s**. E20. [Turk. = snack, appetizer, f. Pers. *maza* to taste, relish.] (Any of) a selection of hot and cold dishes served as an hors-d'oeuvre in the Middle East and eastern Mediterranean region.

Mezentian /mɪˈzɛnʃ(ə)n/ *a.* M19. [f. *Mezentius* (see below) + -AN.] Of an action etc.: cruelly binding, comparable to that of Mezentius, a mythical Etruscan king who had living people bound to corpses and left to starve.

SYD. SMITH That fatal and Mezentian oath which binds the Irish to the English Church.

mezereon /mɪˈzɪərɪən/ *n.* Also **-eum** /-ɪəm/. L15. [med.L = Arab. *māzaryūn*.] A Eurasian early-flowering woodland shrub, *Daphne mezereum* (family Thymelaeaceae), with fragrant purplish or rose-coloured flowers; the dried bark of the root of this, formerly used in liniments.

mezuza /məˈzuːzə/ *n.* Also **-ah**. Pl. **-zoth** /-zəʊt/. M17. [Heb. *mĕzūzāh* lit. 'doorpost' (*Deut.* 6:9).] A piece of parchment inscribed with Pentateuchal texts enclosed in a case and attached to the doorpost of a Jewish house in fulfilment of religious law.

mezz /mɛz/ *n. slang.* M20. [*Mezz* Mezzrow (1899–1972), US jazz clarinettist and drug user.] Marijuana.

Comb.: **mezzroll** a marijuana cigarette.

mezzadria /meddzaˈdriːa/ *n.* Also ***mezzeria*** /meddzeˈriːa/. L19. [It.] *Hist.* A system of feudal land tenure in Italy whereby a farmer paid the landowner a proportion (orig. half) of the farm's produce as rent.

mezzadro /medˈdzadro/ *n.*, pl. **-ri** /-ri/, a tenant farmer of this system M20.

mezza-majolica /mɛtsəməˈjɒlɪkə, -ˈdʒɒlɪkə/ *n.* M19. [It., f. *mezza* fem. of *mezzo* (see MEZZO *adv.*) + MAJOLICA.] A kind of Italian decorative pottery made between the 15th and 17th cents., less elaborate than true majolica.

mezzani /mɛdˈzɑːni/ *n.*. L19. [It., pl. of *mezzano*: see next.] Pasta in the form of medium-sized tubes; an Italian dish consisting largely of this and usu. a sauce.

mezzanine /ˈmɛzəniːn/ *n.* & *a.* E18. [Fr. f. It. *mezzanino* dim. of *mezzano* middle, medium, f. L *medianus* MEDIAN.] A *n.* 1 A low storey between two others in a building, usu. between the ground floor and the floor above. E18. b *Theatr.* A floor beneath the stage, from which the traps are worked. M19. c The lowest gallery in a theatre or cinema; a dress circle. *N. Amer.* E20. 2 A small window at the level of a mezzanine or attic. M18.

1c *New Yorker* I was in a movie house, fairly plush, in a sort of mezzanine, or balcony.

B *adj.* 1 Designating an intermediate floor, storey, etc. M19. 2 *Comm.* Designating unsecured, higher-yielding loans that are subordinate to bank loans and secured loans but rank above equity. L20.

2 *Observer* Before . . 1983, potential raiders looked to venture capitalists . . to provide mezzanine finance.

mezza voce /mɛtsə ˈvɒtʃi/ *adv.*, *n.*, & *a. phr.* L18. [It. *mezza* fem. of MEZZO *adv.* + *voce* voice.] *Mus.* (With) half of the possible vocal or instrumental power; restrained.

mezzeria *n.* var. of MEZZADRIA.

mezzo /ˈmɛtsəʊ/ *n.* & *a.* Pl. of n. **-os**. M19. [Abbrev.] = MEZZO-SOPRANO.

Times Irina Arkipovna has been singing leading mezzo roles at the Bolshoi for almost 20 years.

mezzo /ˈmɛtsəʊ/ *adv.* M18. [It. = middle, half, f. L *medius* MEDIUM.] *Mus.* Qualifying a direction: half, moderately, fairly.

mezzo forte moderately loud. **mezzo piano** moderately soft.

Mezzofanti /mɛtsəʊˈfanti, mɛdz-/ *n.* L19. [Giuseppe *Mezzofanti* (1774–1849), It. cardinal who mastered over fifty languages.] A person of exceptional linguistic ability.

G. M. HOPKINS We have a . . young sucking Mezzofanti among us who could have written in seven languages.

mezzofantic *a.* E20.

Mezzogiorno /mɛtsəʊˈdʒɔːnəʊ/ *n.* M20. [It., f. MEZZO *adv.* + *giorno* day.] The southern part of Italy, including Sicily and Sardinia.

mezzo-relievo /ˌmɛtsəʊrɪˈliːvəʊ/ *n.* Also **-rilievo** /-rɪˈljeɪvəʊ/. Pl. **-os**. L16. [It.: see MEZZO *adv.*, RELIEVO *n.*[1]] (A sculpture, moulding, carving, etc., in) half-relief (see RELIEF *n.*[2]).

mezzo-soprano /ˌmɛtsəʊsəˈprɑːnəʊ/ *n.* & *a.* M18. [It.: see MEZZO *adv.*, SOPRANO. Cf. MEZZO *n.* & *a.*] *Mus.* **A** *n.* Pl. **-os**. A female voice intermediate in compass between soprano and contralto; a singer with such a voice; a part written for such a voice. M18. **B** *adj.* Designating, pertaining to, or intended for a mezzo-soprano. E19.

mezzo termine /mɛttso ˈtɛrmine/ *n. phr.* Pl. ***mezzo termini*** /ˈtɛrmini/. M18. [It.: see MEZZO *adv.*] A middle term, measure, or period.

C. M. YONGE In writing up to that *mezzo termine* of our lives, I have been living it over again.

mezzotint /ˈmɛtsəʊtɪnt, ˈmɛzəʊ-/ *n.* & *v.* M18. [Anglicized f. next.] **A** *n.* **1** A half-tint. Now *rare* or *obs.* M18. **2** A method of engraving a copper or steel plate by roughening it and then partially scraping the surface away so that it produces tones and halftones. Also, a print produced by this process. E19.

2 M. R. JAMES An indifferent mezzotint is, perhaps, the worst form of engraving known.

Comb.: **mezzotint rocker** = CRADLE *n.* 9.

B *v.t.* Engrave in mezzotint. E19.

mezzotinter *n.* M18.

mezzotinto /mɛttsoˈtinto/ *n.* Now *rare.* M17. [It., lit. 'half-tint': see MEZZO *adv.*] †**1** = MEZZOTINT *n.* 1. M17–L18. **2** = MEZZOTINT *n.* 2. M17.

mganga /(ə)mˈgaŋgə/ *n.* Pl. ***mgangas***, ***waganga*** /wəˈgaŋgə/. M19. [Bantu.] In Tanzania and other parts of E. Africa: an indigenous African doctor, a witch-doctor.

mho /məʊ/ *n.* Pl. **mhos**. L19. [OHM spelt backwards.] *Electr.* The cgs unit of conductance, equal to the conductance of a body whose resistance is one ohm. Cf. SIEMENS 2b.

mi /miː/ *n.* Also **me**. LME. [f. L *mi(ra)*: see UT and cf. ALAMIRE, BEMI.] *Mus.* The third note of a scale in a movable-doh system; the note E in the fixed-doh system.

mi /mʌɪ/ *a.*[1] *colloq.* L18. [Abbrev.] = MINOR *a.* 1b.

mi *a.*[2] see MY *a.*

miacid /ˈmʌɪəsɪd/ *n.* & *a.* M20. [mod.L *Miacidae* (see below), f. *Miacis* genus name: see -ID[3].] *Palaeont.* **A** *n.* A small carnivorous mammal of the extinct family Miacidae, known from N. American Palaeocene and Eocene fossils. M20. **B** *adj.* Of, pertaining to, or designating this family. L20.

miai /ˈmiai/ *n.* L19. [Jap., f. *mi* seeing + *ai* mutually.] The first formal meeting of the prospective partners in a Japanese arranged marriage.

mia-mia /ˈmʌɪəmʌɪə/ *n. Austral.* M19. [Aborig. *miam miam*. See also MAIMAI.] An Aboriginal hut or shelter; *transf.* a temporary shelter built by a traveller.

mianserin /mʌɪˈansərɪn/ *n.* L20. [Origin uncertain: includes SER(OTON)IN.] *Pharm.* A tetracyclic compound, $C_{18}H_{20}N_2$, with serotonin-blocking properties, used to treat depression.

Miao /mɪˈaʊ/ *n.* & *a.* Also **Meo** /mɪˈəʊ/. E20. [Chin. *Miáo* lit. 'tribes, people'.] **A** *n.* Pl. same. A member of a people of the mountains of southern China and Indo-China; the language of this people. E20. **B** *attrib.* or as *adj.* Of or pertaining to the Miao or their language. E20.

Earlier **Miaotse** /mɪˈaʊtsi/ *n.* & *a.* (pl. of n. same) M19.

miaow /mɪˈaʊ/ *n.*, *v.*, & *int.* Also **meow**, **miaouw**. L16. [Imit. Cf. MEW *n.*[3] & *int.*, MIAUL, & Fr. *miaou.*] **A** *n.* & *int.* (Repr.) the characteristic cry of a cat; *fig.* (a sound) implying spite or maliciousness in the person addressed (cf. CAT *n.*[1] 2). L16.

E. BRADFORD 'He's always . . where the bar is.' She leaned forward. 'Miaouw!' DENNIS POTTER This is the way the world begins. Not with a bang, but with a miaow.

B *v.i.* Make this sound. M17.

miargyrite /mʌɪˈɑːdʒɪrʌɪt/ *n.* M19. [f. Gk *meiōn* less + *arguros* silver + -ITE[1].] *Min.* A monoclinic sulphide of silver and antimony, a minor ore of silver usu. occurring as small black prisms.

miarolitic /miːərəˈlɪtɪk/ *a.* L19. [f. It. (dial.) *miarolo* a variety of granite: see -LITE, -IC.] *Petrogr.* Characterized by or designating irregular cavities in igneous rocks into which crystals project.

mias /ˈmʌɪəs/ *n.* Now *rare* or *obs.* Pl. same. M19. [Dyak *maias*.] An orang-utan.

miasm /ˈmʌɪaz(ə)m/ *n.* M17. [In sense 1 f. Fr. *miasme*, in sense 2 f. G *Miasm*, both f. as next.] **1** = MIASMA. M17. **2** *Homoeopathy.* A supposed predisposition to a particular disease, which a person either inherits or acquires. M19.

miasma /mɪˈazmə, mʌɪ-/ *n.* Pl. **-mas**, **-mata** /-mətə/. M17. [Gk *miasma(t-)* defilement, pollution, rel. to *miainein* pollute.] **1** (An) infectious or noxious vapour, esp. from putrescent organic matter, which pollutes the atmosphere. M17. **2** *fig.* A polluting, oppressive, or foreboding atmosphere; a polluting or oppressive influence. M19.

1 R. WEST Open ditches exhaling miasma. J. G. FARRELL Fever-bearing mists and miasmas hung everywhere. 2 M. PUZO The swampy miasma of Southern religiosity. E. PAWEL Kafka . . felt himself once again drowning in academic miasma.

miasmal *a.* = MIASMATIC 1 M19. **miasmic** *a.* = MIASMATIC 1 E19. **miasmically** *adv.* M20.

miasmatic /mɪəzˈmatɪk, mʌɪ-/ *a.* M18. [f. as prec. + -IC.] **1** Of, pertaining to, caused by, or having the nature of a miasma. M18. **2** *Homoeopathy.* Of, pertaining to, or caused by a miasm. L20.

miaul /mɪˈɔːl/ *v.* M17. [Fr. *miauler*, of imit. origin.] **1** *v.i.* Of a cat: miaow, mew, yowl. Of a person: cry or yowl like a cat. M17. **2** *v.t.* Sing (a song etc.) in a manner derisively likened to the cry of a cat. M19.

1 *Punch* Like the bursting of atomic bombs, Cats call to cats and Toms miaul to Toms. 2 G. MEREDITH The boy . . concluded by miauling 'Amalia' in the triumph of contempt.

mic /mʌɪk/ *n. colloq.* Also **mic.** (point). M20. [Abbrev.] = MICROPHONE. Cf. MIKE *n.*[3]

mica /ˈmʌɪkə/ *n.* Pl. **-s**, (in sense 1) †**micae**. E18. [L = grain, crumb, perh. extended in use by assoc. w. *micare* shine.] *Min.* †**1** A small plate of talc, selenite, or other glistening crystalline substance found in the structure of a rock. E18–E19. **2** Any of a group of monoclinic minerals composed of hydrous aluminosilicates of sodium, potassium, magnesium, etc., which occur in minute glittering plates or scales in granite and other rocks, and in crystals separable into thin, transparent, usu. flexible laminae, and are used as thermal or electric insulators. L18.

2 **common mica** muscovite. **water mica** clear colourless mica. *white mica*: see WHITE *a.*

Comb.: **mica flap** the flap of a mica valve; **mica-schist**, **-slate** a slaty metamorphic rock composed of quartz and mica; **mica valve** a device consisting of a flap of mica hinged at the top, used (esp. in ventilator shafts etc.) to allow air to flow in one direction only;

micaceous /mʌɪˈkeɪʃəs/ *a.* containing or resembling mica; pertaining to or of the nature of mica: L18.

Micawber /mɪˈkɔːbə/ *n.* M19. [Wilkins *Micawber*, a character in Dickens's novel *David Copperfield*.] An idle optimist; a person who trusts in the future to provide.

A. TROLLOPE It may be that after all the hopes of the West-Australian Micawbers will be realized. *attrib.*: *Guardian* The Green Paper's hope that growth will provide comes dangerously near the Micawber tradition.

Micawberish *a.* resembling or characteristic of Micawber; idly optimistic, irresponsible: E20. **Micawberism** *n.* an attitude or the attitudes characteristic of Micawber; idle optimism: L19.

mice *n.pl.* see MOUSE *n.*

micelle /mɪˈsɛl, mʌɪˈsɛl/ *n.* Also **-lla** /-lə/, pl. **-llae** /-liː/. L19. [G *Micell*, f. as dim. of L *mica* crumb.] *Chem.* **1** Each of the minute ordered aggregates within the microfibrils of a crystal-like polymer; = CRYSTALLITE 2c. L19. **2** An ultramicroscopic aggregate in a colloid, consisting of some tens or hundreds of ions or molecules. E20.

micellar *a.* of, pertaining to, or composed of micelles L19. **micelli'zation** *n.* the formation of micelles M20.

Michael /ˈmʌɪk(ə)l/ *n.* ME. [Male forename. In sense 3 substitution for MICKEY *n.*[1] interpreted as the name.] **1** = MICHAELMAS. *obs.* exc. *Sc.* ME. **2** = MICKEY FINN. *US slang.* M20. **3** *take the Michael (out of)*, = *take the mickey (out of)* s.v. MICKEY *n.*[1] *slang.* M20.

Michaelangelesque *a.* var. of MICHELANGELESQUE.

Michaelis constant /mɪˈkeɪlɪs ˈkɒnst(ə)nt/ *n. phr.* M20. [Leonor *Michaelis* (1875–1949), German-born US chemist.] *Biochem.* That concentration of a given enzyme which catalyses the associated reaction at half the maximum rate.

Michaelmas /ˈmɪk(ə)lməs/ *n.* ME. [Contr. of *St Michael's mass*.] (The date, 29 September, of) the feast of St Michael, one of the quarter days in England, Ireland, and Wales.

Comb.: **Michaelmas daisy** (a flowering stem of) any of various late-flowering garden asters, forms and hybrids of *Aster novi-belgii*, *A. novae-angliae*, and other N. American species, with long panicles of lilac, white, crimson, etc., blooms; **Michaelmas sitting(s)** = *Michaelmas term* (b) below; **Michaelmas term** (*a*) a term in some universities beginning soon after Michaelmas; (*b*) the first of the terms or sessions of the High Court in England; **Michaelmas tide** the season of Michaelmas.

†**miche** *n.* L15–E16. [Perh. rel. to G *Micke* fork of a branch, Du. *mik* forked stick.] *Naut.* A forked shaft or wedge as a support.

¶ May survive in 1st elem. of MITCH-BOARD.

†**miche** *v.* var. of MITCH *v.*

Michelangelesque /ˌmʌɪkəlandʒəˈlɛsk/ *a.* Also **Michael-**. L18. [f. *Michelangelo* (see below) + -ESQUE.] Of, pertaining to, or after the manner of the Florentine sculptor, painter, architect, and poet, Michelangelo Buonarroti (1475–1564).

Michelsberg /ˈmɪk(ə)lzbəːg/ *a.* E20. [See below.] *Archaeol.* Designating or pertaining to a neolithic culture of Belgium, Germany, northern France, and Switzerland, illustrated esp. by pottery remains found at Michelsberg in Baden, Germany.

Michelson /ˈmʌɪk(ə)ls(ə)n/ *n.* E20. [A. A. *Michelson* (1852–1931), German-born US physicist.] *Physics.* Used *attrib.* and in *possess.* to designate (*a*) the Michelson–Morley experiment (see next); (*b*) an interferometer of the type used in this experiment.

Michelson–Morley /ˌmʌɪk(ə)ls(ə)nˈmɔːli/ *n.* E20. [f. prec. + E. W. *Morley* (1838–1923), US chemist and physicist.] *Physics.* Used *attrib.* to designate an experiment performed in 1887 in which a beam of light was divided and made to travel over two paths, parallel and perpendicular to the earth's motion, before being recombined, the behaviour of the resulting interference fringes showing that the speed of light was the same in both directions, contrary to the notion that the earth moves through an ether.

micher /ˈmɪtʃə/ *n. obs.* exc. *dial.* ME. [App. f. OFr. agent-n., f. as MITCH *v.*: see -ER[2].] †**1** A secret or petty thief. ME–E19. †**2** A person who skulks about with dishonest intent; a pander, a go-between. LME–M17. **3** A truant. M16.

michery *n.* pilfering, cheating LME.

Michigan /ˈmɪʃɪg(ə)n/ *n.* E19. [A State in the north-western US.] **1** Used *attrib.* to designate things from or associated with Michigan. E19. **2** A card-game similar to Newmarket. *US.* E20.

Michigander /mɪʃɪˈgandə/ *n.* a native or inhabitant of Michigan M19. **Michiganian** /mɪʃɪˈgeɪmɪən/ *n.* = MICHIGANDER E19.

Michurinism /mɪˈtʃʊərɪnɪz(ə)m/ *n.* M20. [f. *Michurin* (see below) + -ISM.] Belief in or advocacy of the views of the Russian horticulturist I. V. Michurin (1855–1935); Lysenkoism.

Michurinist *n.* & *a.* (*a*) *n.* an advocate of or believer in Michurinism; (*b*) *adj.* of or pertaining to Michurinism or Michurinists: M20.

mick /mɪk/ *n.*[1] & *a. slang.* Also **M-**. M19. [Pet-form of male forename *Michael*. Cf. MICKY *n.*[1], MIKE *n.*[2]] **A** *n.* **1** An Irishman. Usu. *derog.*

M19. **2** A Roman Catholic. *derog.* E20. **3** *mad mick*, a pick (for breaking up hard ground, rock, etc.). E20. **B** *attrib.* or as *adj.* Irish; Roman Catholic. Usu. *derog.* L19.

mick /mɪk/ *n.*[2] *Austral. slang.* E20. [Origin unkn.] In the game of two-up, the reverse side of a coin.

mickery /ˈmɪkəri/ *n. Austral.* Also **mickerie**. L19. [Aborig. *migri.*] A water-hole or excavated well, esp. in a dry river-bed; marshy ground.

mickey /ˈmɪki/ *n.*[1] *colloq.* Also **micky**. M20. [Origin unkn.] *take the mickey (out of)*, act in a satirical or teasing manner (towards). Cf. MICHAEL 3, MIKE *n.*[2] 3.

B. GELDOF The boarders would laugh and take the mickey because I was a day boy.

Comb.: **mickey-take** *v.* & *n.* (*a*) *v.i.* tease, mock; (*b*) *n.* an instance of mickey-taking.

mickey *n.*[2] var. of MICKY *n.*[1]

Mickey Finn /mɪki ˈfɪn/ *n.* & *v. slang* (orig. *US*). E20. [App. a pers. name, of unkn. origin.] **A** *n.* A strong alcoholic drink, *esp.* one deliberately adulterated with a sleep-inducing drug or a laxative; a drug or laxative used as such an adulterant. E20. **B** *v.t.* (W. hyphen.) Adulterate (a drink) with a Mickey Finn; make unconscious with a Mickey Finn. M20.

Mickey Mouse /mɪki ˈmaʊs/ *a. colloq.* M20. [A mouselike cartoon character created by the American cartoonist Walt Disney (1901–66).] Of inferior quality; ridiculous, trivial; (of music, art, etc.) trite, brash.

Citizen (*Ottawa*) There is absolutely nothing Mickey Mouse about tractor-pulling—it's a serious and well-organized sport.

Mickey-mousing /mɪkɪˈmaʊsɪŋ/ *n.* M20. [f. as prec. + -ING[1].] *Cinemat.* The matching of a film's action with appropriate simultaneous music.

mickle *a.* etc., var. of MUCKLE.

micklemote /ˈmɪk(ə)lməʊt/ *n.* Also **-gemote** /-gɪməʊt/. LOE. [f. *mickle* var. of MUCKLE *a.* + MOOT *n.*[1]] *Hist.* The great council or parliamentary assembly under the Anglo-Saxon kings.

micky /ˈmɪki/ *n.*[1] Also **mickey, M-**. M19. [Pet-form of male forename *Michael*: cf. MICK *n.*[1], MIKE *n.*[2] In sense 5 substitution for MIKE *n.*[1] interpreted as the name *Mike*.] **1** (A name for) an Irishman. *US slang.* M19. **2** A (usu. unbranded) bull calf. *Austral. slang.* L19. **3** = *noisy miner* s.v. NOISY *a.* I. *Austral. colloq.* E20. **4** A flask or bottle of liquor. Chiefly *Canad. colloq.* E20. **5** *do a micky*, go away, escape. *slang.* M20.

micky *n.*[2] var. of MICKEY *n.*[1]

micky-mick *n.* see MINGIMINGI.

Micmac /ˈmɪkmak/ *n.* & *a.* E18. [Fr. f. Micmac *mi:kəmax* pl. (*mi:kəmaw* sing.).] **A** *n.* Pl. same, **-s**. A member of a N. American Indian people of the Maritime Provinces and Newfoundland in Canada; the Algonquian language of this people. E18. **B** *attrib.* or as *adj.* Designating or pertaining to this people or their language. M18.

†mico *n.* Pl. **-os**. E17–M19. [Sp. f. Tupi *micó.*] A small S. American marmoset, *esp.* one of the genus *Callithrix.*

Micoquian /mɪˈkəʊkɪən/ *a.* & *n.* M20. [Fr. *Micoquien*, f. La *Micoque*, a place in the Dordogne, France: see -IAN.] *Archaeol.* **A** *adj.* Designating or pertaining to a stage of the Acheulean culture in central and western Europe, characterized by fine pointed hand-axes. M20. **B** *n.* The Micoquian culture. M20.

micrencephaly /mʌɪkrɛnˈsɛf(ə)li, -ˈkɛf-/ *n.* L19. [f. MICRO- + Gk *egkephalos* brain + -Y[3].] *Med.* The condition of having a small brain. Also, microcephaly.

micrify /ˈmʌɪkrɪfʌɪ/ *v.t.* M19. [f. MICRO- after MAGNIFY.] Make small; render insignificant.

micrite /ˈmɪkrʌɪt/ *n.* M20. [f. MICR(OCRYSTALLINE + -ITE[1].] *Petrogr.* Microcrystalline calcite present as an interstitial constituent or matrix material in some kinds of limestone; a limestone consisting chiefly of this.

micritic /mɪˈkrɪtɪk/ *a.* containing a high proportion of micrite M20.

micro /ˈmʌɪkrəʊ/ *n.* & *a. colloq.* M19. [Independent use of next.] **A** *n.* Pl. **-os**. **1** *Entomol.* A moth belonging to the Microlepidoptera. M19. **2** A microskirt. M20. **3** A microcomputer; a microprocessor. L20. **4** A microwave oven. Chiefly *US.* L20. **B** *adj.* **1** Microscopic; very small; small-scale; *Chem.* of microanalysis. Freq. contrasted w. *macro.* E20. **2** Microeconomic. M20.

micro- /ˈmʌɪkrəʊ, *esp. Med.* ˈmɪkrəʊ/ *comb. form.* Bef. a vowel also **micr-**. [Gk *mikro-* f. *mikros* small: see -O-.] **1** Used in wds adopted f. Gk and in Eng. wds modelled on these, and as a freely productive pref., w. the senses: (*a*) small, reduced in size, (of a garment) very short, as *microprocessor*; *Med.* involving arrested development or underdevelopment of a part, as *microcephaly*; (*b*) (in names of instruments, techniques, and disciplines) dealing with small effects or small quantities, involving the use of a microscope, revealed by a microscope, as *microanalyser*, *microelectronic*; (*c*) containing or pertaining to something in minute form, quantity, or degree, as *microphagous*, *microvascular*; (*d*) pertaining to or obtained by microphotography, microphotographically reduced in size, as *microbook*, *microtext*; (*e*) *Chem.* of or pertaining to microanalysis, as *microscale.* **2** Used in names of units of measurement to denote a factor of one-millionth (10^{-6}), as *microgram*, *microinch*; also redupl. to denote a factor of 10^{-12} (cf. PICO-), as *micromicrofarad.* (Symbol μ.)

micro'aerophil(e) *a.* & *n.* (*a*) *adj.* = MICROAEROPHILIC; (*b*) *n.* a microaerophilic organism: E20. **microaero'philic** *a.* (of a micro-organism) requiring little free oxygen, or oxygen at a lower partial pressure than that of atmospheric oxygen E20. **micro'ammeter** *n.* an ammeter for measuring currents of the strength of a few microamperes M20. **microamp** *n.* = MICROAMPERE M20. **microampere** *n.* one millionth of an ampere L19. **microa'natomist** *n.* an expert in or student of microanatomy M20. **microa'natomy** *n.* the anatomy of very small structures; histology; the histology *of* a thing: M20. **micro'aneurysm** *n.* (*Med.*) a very small aneurysm M20. **microangi'opathy** *n.* (a) disease of the small blood-vessels M20. **microatoll** *n.* a circular growth of coral a few metres in diameter with a central depression, such as is found in intertidal areas in warm seas and on the flats inside a coral reef M20. **microbalance** *n.* a balance for weighing masses of a fraction of a gram E20. **Microballoon** *n.* (proprietary name in US for) an artificial hollow microsphere M20. **micro'barograph** *n.* an instrument for measuring very small changes in atmospheric pressure, such as those resulting from a distant explosion E20. **micro'barom** *n.* a minute oscillation of atmospheric pressure with a period of the order of 5 seconds M20. **microbeam** *n.* a very narrow beam of radiation M20. **micro'benthic** *a.* of or belonging to the microbenthos L20. **microbenthos** *n.* the microfauna of the benthos, *spec.* bottom-dwelling marine organisms less than 0.1 mm long M20. **microbiota** *n.* the micro-organisms of an area, site, or object collectively M20. **microblade** *n.* (*Archaeol.*) a small blade of flint or other stone struck from a prepared core M20. **microbody** *n.* (*Cytol.*) a very small organelle, *esp.* a peroxisome M20. **microbore** *a.* designating (a heating system with) a central-heating pipe with a very narrow bore M20. **micro'burin** *n.* (*Archaeol.*) the piece of stone that is snapped off a notched blade as waste when making a microlith M20. **microburst** *n.* a sudden strong air current produced by the impact with the ground of a fast localized down-draught L20. **microbus** *n.* a small passenger vehicle with seats fitted as in a bus M20. **microcalo'rimeter** *n.* an instrument for measuring very small amounts of heat E20. **microcalori'metric** *a.* of or pertaining to microcalorimetry E20. **microcalo'rimetry** *n.* the use of a microcalorimeter; measurement of very small amounts of heat: E20. **microcapsule** *n.* a minute capsule used to contain drugs, dyes, etc. and render them temporarily inactive M20. **Microcard** *n.* (US proprietary name for) an opaque card bearing microphotographs of a number of pages of a book, periodical, etc. M20. **microcard** *v.t.* reproduce on Microcards M20. **micro'cellular** *a.* (esp. of synthetic substances) containing or characterized by minute cells or pores E20. **micro'chemical** *a.* of or pertaining to microchemistry M19. **microchemist** *n.* an expert in or student of microchemistry M20. **micro'chemistry** *n.* the branch of chemistry that deals with the reactions and properties of substances in minute quantities, e.g. in living tissue L19. **microcinemato'graphic** *a.* of, pertaining to, or involving microcinematography M20. **microcinema'tography** *n.* the cinematography of very small objects with the aid of a microscope M20. **microcircuit** *n.* a minute electric circuit, *esp.* an integrated circuit M20. **microcircuitry** *n.* microcircuits collectively; the branch of electronics that deals with microcircuits: M20. **microcirculation** *n.* circulation of the blood in the smallest blood-vessels M20. **micro'clastic** *a.* (*Geol.*) minutely clastic L19. **micro'coccal** *a.* caused by, of, or pertaining to a micrococcus or micrococci L19. **micro'coccus** *n.* a bacterium of the family Micrococcaceae of Gram-positive spherical organisms L19. **microcode** *n.* & *v.* (*Computing*) (*a*) *n.* microinstructions collectively; a single microinstruction; each of the bit patterns of which a microinstruction is composed; (*b*) *v.t.* = MICROPROGRAM *v.*: M20. **microcolony** *n.* a group of animals or plants, esp. bacteria, found in a microhabitat; a very small group of cells in culture: M20. **microcontinent** *n.* (*Geol.*) an oceanic, often submarine, plateau that is thought to be an isolated fragment of continental material M20. **microconti'nental** *a.* (*Geol.*) of, pertaining to, or of the nature of a microcontinent M20. **microcook** *v.t.* & *i.* (*US*) = MICROWAVE *v.* L20. **microcopy** *n.* & *v.* (*a*) *n.* a copy of a text that has been reduced in size by the use of microphotography; microcopied form (chiefly in *in microcopy*); (*b*) *v.t.* & *i.* make a microcopy (of): M20. **microcrack** *n.* a very small or fine crack M20. **microcracking** *n.* microcracks collectively; the occurrence or formation of microcracks: M20. **microcyst** *n.* a bacterial or myxamoeboid resting cell, *esp.* one with a thick cell wall L19. **microdegree** *n.* a millionth of a degree centigrade (kelvin) M20. **microdensi'tometer** *n.* a densitometer for measuring the density of very small areas of a photographic image M20. **microdensito'metric** *a.* of, pertaining to, or involving microdensitometry M20. **microdensi'tometry** *n.* the use of a microdensitometer; measurement of the density of very small areas of a photographic image: M20. **micro'diorite** *n.* (*Geol.*) a rock similar to diorite but fine-grained E20. **microdrama** *n.* a very short drama, *spec.* a television drama only a few minutes long M20. **micro-e'lectrode** *n.* an electrode with a very fine tip, e.g. for investigating the electrical properties of individual cells E20. **micro-electropho'resis** *n.* electrophoresis in which the migration of individual particles or cells is observed using a microscope M20. **micro-electropho'retic** *a.* of, pertaining to, or involving micro-electrophoresis M20. **micro-en'capsulate** *v.t.* enclose in a microcapsule M20. **micro-encapsu'lation** *n.* the process of enclosing in microcapsules M20. **micro-engi'neering** *n.* engineering on a very small scale, esp. combined with micro-electronics M20. **micro-environment** *n.* (chiefly *Biol.*) the immediate small-scale environment of a thing, esp. as a distinct part of a larger environment M20. **micro-environ'mental** *a.* (chiefly *Biol.*) of, pertaining to, or of the nature of a micro-environment L20. **micro-evolution** *n.* evolutionary change within a species or smaller group of plants or animals, usu. over a short period M20. **micro-evo'lutionary** *a.* of or pertaining to micro-evolution M20. **microfauna** *n.* (*Biol.*) (a) fauna made up of minute animals; (a) fauna found in a microhabitat: L19. **micro'faunal** *a.* (*Biol.*) of or pertaining to microfauna M20. **microfel'sitic** *a.* (*Geol.*) cryptocrystalline L19. **microfibril** *n.* (*Biol.*) a small fibril visible only under an electron microscope, *esp.* each of a group that together make up a fibril (such as a cellulose fibril in the wall of a plant cell) M20. **micro'fibrillar** *a.* (*Biol.*) composed of microfibrils M20. **microfilament** *n.* (*Cytol.*) any of the small rodlike structures, about 4–7 nanometres in diameter, that are present in the cytoplasm of many eukaryotic cells and are thought to have a structural function and to be involved with cell motility M20. **microfila'mentous** *a.* (*Cytol.*) of or pertaining to a microfilament or microfilaments L20. **microfi'laria** *n.* (*Zool.*) the minute larval form of a filaria L19. **microfloppy** *n.* & *a.* (*Computing*) (designating) a floppy disk with a diameter less than 5¼ inches, 13.3 cm (usu. 3½ inches, 8.9 cm) L20. **microflora** *n.* (*Biol.*) (a) flora made up of minute plants; (a) flora found in a microhabitat: M20. **microfracture** *n.* a very small or fine fracture in a material M20. **micro'fracturing** *n.* the state of having microfractures; the formation of microfractures: M20. **microfungus** *n.* a fungus in which no sexual process has been observed or in which the reproductive organs are microscopic L19. **microgamete** *n.* (*Biol.*) the smaller (usu. male) gamete in an organism where the male and female gametes differ in size L19. **microga'metocyte** *n.* (*Biol.*) a gametocyte that gives rise to microgametes E20. **microga'metophyte** *n.* (*Bot.*) a gametophyte that develops from a microspore; a male gametophyte: E20. **microgram** *n.* a millionth of a gram L19. **microgranite** *n.* (a) granite rock that is recognizable as crystalline only under a microscope L19. **microgra'nitic** *a.* of, pertaining to, or of the nature of a microgranite L19. **micro'gravity** *n.* very weak gravity, such as that in a spacecraft L20. **microgroove** *n.* a very narrow groove on a gramophone record M20. **micro'gyria** *n.* (*Med.*) abnormal smallness of the gyri of the brain L19. **microhabitat** *n.* (*Ecol.*) a habitat which is of small or limited extent and which differs in character from some surrounding more extensive habitat M20. **microhardness** *n.* the hardness of a very small area of a sample, as measured by an indenter E20. **microimage** *n.* an image so small that it cannot be read etc. unaided L20. **microinch** *n.* a millionth of an inch M20. **microin'ject** *v.t.* (chiefly *Biol.*) inject *into* a microscopic object such as an individual cell; inject something into (such an object): M20. **microin'jection** *n.* (*Biol.* & *Med.*) injection on a microscopic scale, esp. into an individual cell or part of a cell E20. **microlevel** *n.* the most detailed or elementary level of a hierarchy M20. **microlin'guistic** *a.* of or pertaining to microlinguistics M20. **microlin'guistics** *n.* the branch of linguistics that deals with the analysis of specific linguistic data, as contrasted with prelinguistics and metalinguistics M20. **microlitre** *n.* a millionth of a litre L19. **micro-machining** *n.* the process or technique of shaping objects on a very small scale esp. using laser or particle beams M20. **micro'mania** *n.* (a) persistent or exaggerated tendency to belittle oneself L19. **micro'maniac** *n.* a person with micromania E20. **microma'nipulate** *v.t.* manipulate on a microscopic scale or with a micromanipulator M20. **micromanipu'lation** *n.* the performance of extremely delicate operations (e.g. the isolation of single cells) under a microscope, esp. using a micromanipulator; an operation so performed: E20. **microma'nipulator** *n.* an instrument used to perform micromanipulations, allowing a micropipette etc. to be operated in the field of view of a microscope E20. **micro'mastia** *n.* [Gk *mastos* breast] the condition in a post-pubertal woman of having an abnormally small breast E20. **micro'mazia** *n.* [Gk *mazos* breast] = MICROMASTIA L19. **micromere** *n.* [Gk *meros* part] *Biol.* a small cell formed by unequal division of an ovum or embryo, e.g. in sea urchins, and appearing at the animal pole L19. **micromesh** *n.* material (esp. nylon) consisting of a very fine mesh M20. **micro'millimetre** *n.* (*a*) a millionth of a millimetre, a nanometre; †(*b*) a thousandth of a millimetre, a micrometre: L19. **micromodule** *n.* (*Electronics*) a miniaturized module consisting of a stack of interconnected micro-elements M20. **micro'molar** *a.* (*Chem.*) designating or involving amounts of the order of a micromole or concentrations of the order of one micromole per litre L20. **micromole** *n.* (*Chem.*) one millionth of a mole M20. **micro'nodular** *a.* (*Med.*) (esp. of a form of cirrhosis) characterized by the presence of small nodules M20. **micro'nuclear** *a.* (*Zool.*) of or pertaining to a micronucleus L19. **micro'nucleus** *n.* (*Zool.*) the smaller of two nuclei in ciliated protozoa, concerned esp. with reproduction L19. **micro'nutrient** *n.* (*Biol.*) any of the chemical elements which are required in trace amounts by organisms for normal growth and development M20. **micro-o'paque** *n.* & *a.* (designating) a type of microform produced on card or paper instead of film M20. **micro-oven** *n.* a microwave oven M20. **micro'perthite** *n.* (*Min.*) a form of perthite in which the lamallae are microscopic L19. **microper'thitic** *a.* (*Min.*) of, pertaining to, or of the nature of microperthite L19. **microphage** *n.* [Gk *phagein* eat] *Physiol.* a small phagocytic leucocyte L19. **microphagous** /mʌɪˈkrɒfəgəs/ *a.* [Gk *phagein* eat] *Biol.* feeding on minute particles or micro-organisms E20. **micropho'tometer** *n.* an instrument for making photometric measurements of very small areas L19. **microphoto'metric** *a.* of, pertaining to, or involving microphotometry M20. **micropho'tometry** *n.* the use of microphotometers M20. **microphyll** *n.* (*Bot.*) a very short leaf, as in a clubmoss, with a single unbranched vein and no leaf gaps in the stele M20. **micro'phyllous** *a.* having small leaves or (*spec.*) microphylls M19. **micropipette** *n.* a very fine pipette for measuring, transferring, or injecting very small quantities of liquid E20. **microplankton** *n.* plankton of small size, *spec.* between 50 micrometres and 0.5 millimetre E20. **micropore** *n.* a very small pore L19. **micropo'rosity** *n.* microporous condition M20. **micro'porous** *a.* containing or characterized by micropores; microcellular: L19. **microprism** *a.* (*Photogr.*) designating an area of the focusing screen of some reflex cameras which is covered with a grid of tiny prisms and splits up the image when the subject is not in focus; (of focusing) that makes use of such an area: M20. **microprobe** *n.* & *v.t.* (examine using) a microanalyser M20. **micropro'jection** *n.* the process of projecting an enlarged image of a microscopic specimen E20. **micropro'jector** *n.* an apparatus for microprojection M20. **micropropa,gation** *n.* the propagation of plants by growing plantlets in tissue culture and then planting them out L20. **micropterous** /mʌɪˈkrɒpt(ə)rəs/ *a.* [Gk *pteron* wing] *Entomol.* having small wings E19. **micropublication** *n.* (a) publication in microform L20. **micropublish** *v.t.* publish in microform (freq. as *micropublishing* vbl n.) M20. **micropulsation** *n.* a small oscillation in the strength of the earth's magnetic field M20. **microreader** *n.* an apparatus for producing an enlarged readable image from a microfilm or microprint M20. **microrecord** *n.* a documentary record in micrographically reduced form M20. **micro-scale** *n.* a small or microscopic scale; *Chem.* the scale of microanalysis: M20. **microsecond** *n.* one millionth of a second E20. **microsection** *n.* a very thin section of a specimen that can be mounted on a slide for microscopic examination L19. **microsegment** *n.* (*Phonet.*) a unit of sound enclosed between two open junctures M20. **microseism** *n.* †(*a*) a minor earthquake; (*b*) an imperceptible disturbance of the earth's crust detectable by a seismometer but not caused by an earthquake: L19. **micro'seismic** *a.* of, pertaining to, or of the nature of a microseism; (of data) obtained with a seismometer: L19. **microsleep** *n.* a transitory state of sleep, esp. in a person deprived of normal sleep; a period or occasion of such sleep: M20. **microslide** *n.* a slide prepared for microscopic examination E20. **microspecies** *n.* (*Taxon.*) a species differing only in minor characters from others of its group, often one of limited geographical range forming part of an aggregate species L19. **microspectropho'tometer** *n.* an instrument for the spectrophotometric investigation of individual cells or particles M20. **micro,spectrophoto'metric** *a.* of, pertaining to, or involving microspectrophotometry M20. **microspectropho'tometry** *n.* the use of microspectrophotometers M20. **microsphere** *n.* a minute sphere; *spec.* one obtained by cooling a solution of a proteinoid: L19. **micro'spheric** *a.* of, pertaining to, or of the nature of a microsphere L19. **microstate** *n.* a very small country M20. **microstrip** *n.* (*Electr.*) a transmission line for microwaves that consists of dielectric material coated on one side with a metallic film forming a conducting strip and on the other with a metallic coating that serves as an earth; material of this kind: M20. **microstylous** *a.* (*Bot.*) having a short style in association with long filaments L19. **microswitch** *n.* a switch which can be operated rapidly by a small movement M20. **microteaching** *n.* (*US*) the teaching of a small group for a short time as part of a training or refresher course for teachers M20. **microtechnique** *n.* a technique for handling, preparing, or investigating very small amounts of something L19. **microtext** *n.* (a) text that is micrographically reduced in size M20. **microtopo'graphic(al)** *adjs.* of or pertaining to microtopography M20. **microto'pography** *n.* surface features on a small or microscopic scale M20. **microtra'becula** *n.*, pl. **-lae**, *Cytol.* a filament of the microtrabecular lattice L20. **microtra'becular** *a.* (*Cytol.*) pertaining to or designating a lattice of protein filaments in the cytoplasm of cells which is concerned with the transport of molecules in the cell L20. **microtron** *n.* (*Physics*) a variant of the cyclotron in which electrons are accelerated by microwaves M20. **micro'tubular** *a.* (*Cytol.*) of, pertaining to, or of the nature of a microtubule M20. **'microtubule** *n.* (*Cytol.*) a small, relatively rigid tubule, present in numbers in the cytoplasm of many cells, thought to have a structural function and to be involved with cell motility M20. **microunit** *n.* (*Med.*) a millionth part of a unit, esp. of an international unit (e.g. of insulin) E20. **micro'vascular** *a.* of or pertaining to the smallest blood-vessels E20. **micro'villar** *a.* (*Cytol.*) of, pertaining to, or involving a microvillus or microvilli M20. **micro'villous** *a.* (*Cytol.*) = MICROVILLAR M20. **'microvillus** *n.* (*Cytol.*) any of a number of minute projections from the surface of some cells; a process similar to a villus but smaller: M20. **microwatt** *n.* one millionth of a watt E20. **microweld** *v.t.* join by a very small weld M20.

microanalyser /mʌɪkrəʊˈanəlʌɪzə/ *n.* Also *-lyzer. M20. [f. MICRO- + ANALYSER.] An instrument in which a beam of radiation (usu. electrons) is focused on to a minute area of a sample and the resulting secondary radiation (usu. X-ray fluorescence) is analysed to yield chemical information.

microanalysis /ˌmʌɪkrəʊəˈnalɪsɪs/ *n.* M19. [f. MICRO- + ANALYSIS.] *Chem.* Orig., the analysis of very small samples, or very small areas of an object. Now *spec.* the quantitative analysis of samples weighing only a few milligrams.

micro'analyst *n.* E20. **microana'lytical** *a.* E20.

microbe /ˈmʌɪkrəʊb/ *n.* L19. [Fr., f. as MICRO- + Gk *bios* life.] An extremely minute living organism, a micro-organism; *esp.* a bacterium that causes disease or fermentation.

mi'crobial *a.* of, pertaining to, or caused by microbes L19. **mi'crobially** *adv.* by or with microbes L20. **mi'crobian** *a.* (now *rare*) = MICROBIAL L19. **mi'crobic** *a.* = MICROBIAL L19. **mi,crobi'cidal** *a.* that kills microbes; of or pertaining to a microbicide or its action: L19. **mi'crobicide** *n.* & *a.* (*a*) *n.* a microbicidal agent; (*b*) *adj.* (now *rare*) microbicidal: L19.

microbiology /ˌmʌɪkrə(ʊ)bʌɪˈɒlədʒi/ *n.* L19. [f. MICRO- + BIOLOGY.] The branch of science that deals with micro-organisms.

microbio'logic *a.* E20. **microbio'logical** *a.* L19. **microbio'logically** *adv.* M20. **microbiologist** *n.* L19.

microcephalic /mʌɪkrə(ʊ)sɪˈfalɪk, -kɛˈfalɪk/ *a.* & *n.* M19. [f. MICRO- + -CEPHALIC.] Chiefly *Med.* & *Anthropol.* A *adj.* Having an abnormally small head or skull. M19. B *n.* A microcephalic person. L19.

micro'cephalism *n.* = MICROCEPHALY M19. **micro'cephalous** *a.* = MICROCEPHALIC *a.* M19. **micro'cephalus** *n.*, pl. **-li** /-lʌɪ, -liː/, (*a*) = MICROCEPHALIC *n.*; (*b*) = MICROCEPHALY: M19. **micro'cephaly** *n.* microcephalic condition M19.

microchip /ˈmʌɪkrə(ʊ)tʃɪp/ *n.* L20. [f. MICRO- + CHIP *n.*] A semiconductor chip, an integrated circuit, *esp.* one in which large-scale integration is employed.

microchiropteran /ˌmʌɪkrəʊkʌɪˈrɒpt(ə)rən/ *a.* & *n.* L19. [f. mod.L *Microchiroptera* (see below), f. as MICRO- + *Chiroptera*: see CHIROPTERAN.] A *adj.* Of or pertaining to the chiropteran suborder Microchiroptera, which comprises all bats other than megachiropterans, most of them insectivorous. L19. B *n.* A microchiropteran bat. L19.

microclimate /ˈmʌɪkrə(ʊ)ˌklʌɪmət/ *n.* E20. [f. MICRO- + CLIMATE.] The climate of a very small or restricted area, or of the immediate surroundings of an object, esp. where this differs from the climate generally.

F. POHL Outside..the microclimate of my little garden..the air was too thin and too dry.

microcli'matic *a.* E20. **micro'climatically** *adv.* L20.

microclimatology /ˌmʌɪkrə(ʊ)klʌɪməˈtɒlədʒi/ *n.* M20. [f. MICRO- + CLIMATOLOGY.] The branch of science that deals with microclimates.

microclimato'logical *a.* M20. **microclimatologist** *n.* M20.

microcline /ˈmʌɪkrə(ʊ)klʌɪn/ *n.* M19. [G *Mikroklin*, f. as MICRO- + Gk *klinein* to lean, slope (from its angle of cleavage differing only slightly from 90 degrees).] *Min.* A triclinic potassium feldspar characteristic of granites and pegmatites, similar to orthoclase but forming large translucent crystals of a green, pink, or brown colour.

microcomputer /ˈmʌɪkrə(ʊ)kɒmˌpjuːtə/ *n.* L20. [f. MICRO- + COMPUTER.] A small computer or computer system, usu. one built around a single microprocessor; a home or personal computer. Also, a microprocessor.

microcomputing *n.* computing using a microcomputer L20.

microcosm /ˈmʌɪkrə(ʊ)kɒz(ə)m/ *n.* Also in quasi-Gk form **microcosmos** /mʌɪkrə(ʊ)ˈkɒzmɒs/. ME. [Fr. *microcosme* or med.L *micro(s)cosmus* f. Gk *mikros kosmos* little world.] 1 The world of human nature (as opp. to all nature); humanity viewed as an epitome of the universe. ME. 2 A community or other complex unity regarded as presenting an epitome of the world, or as constituting a world in itself. M16. 3 A miniature representation (*of*). E17.

1 R. SCRUTON To step down from the world of national politics, into the microcosm of ordinary human relations. 2 S. RUSHDIE The street was his microcosm and afforded him all his delights and pains.

3 G. A. SHEEHAN Like many sports, the marathon is a microcosm of life.

microcosmic /mʌɪkrə(ʊ)ˈkɒzmɪk/ *a.* L18. [f. prec. + -IC.] Of or pertaining to a microcosm; of the nature of a microcosm.

microcosmic salt hydrated sodium ammonium hydrogen phosphate, $HNaNH_4PO_4{\cdot}4H_2O$, a crystalline compound originally obtained from human urine.

microcosmical *a.* (now *rare*) microcosmic L16. **microcosmically** *adv.* in relation to the microcosm L19.

microcrystal /ˈmʌɪkrə(ʊ)krɪst(ə)l/ *n.* L19. [f. MICRO- + CRYSTAL *n.*] A crystal visible only under a microscope.

microcrystalline /mʌɪkrə(ʊ)ˈkrɪstəlʌɪn/ *a.* L19. [f. MICRO- + CRYSTALLINE.] Formed of microscopic crystals.

microcrystalline wax a high-molecular-weight hydrocarbon wax obtained from the residual lubricating fraction of crude oil, used in making waxed paper, adhesives, and polishes.

microcrystaˈllinity *n.* M20.

microcyclic /mʌɪkrə(ʊ)ˈsʌɪklɪk, -ˈsɪk-/ *a.* E20. [f. MICRO- + CYCLIC.] *Bot.* Of a rust fungus: having a short life cycle.

microcyte /ˈmʌɪkrə(ʊ)sʌɪt, ˈmɪ-/ *n.* L19. [f. MICRO- + -CYTE.] *Med.* An unusually small red blood cell.

microcytic /mʌɪkrə(ʊ)ˈsɪtɪk/ *a.* of the nature of, pertaining to, or characteristic of a microcyte; characterized by the presence of microcytes: E20. **microcyˈtosis** *n.* the presence of microcytes in the blood L19.

microdot /ˈmʌɪkrə(ʊ)dɒt/ *n.* & *v.* M20. [f. MICRO- + DOT *n.*[1]] **A** *n.* **1** A photograph, esp. of printed or written matter, reduced to the size of a dot. M20. **2** A tiny capsule or tablet of LSD. L20. **B** *v.t.* Infl. **-tt-**. Make a microdot or microdots of. M20.

microdrive /ˈmʌɪkrə(ʊ)drʌɪv/ *n.* M20. [f. MICRO- + DRIVE *n.*] **1** A small stepping motor or motor-driven apparatus for manipulating microelectrodes. M20. **2** *Computing.* A peripheral storage device for holding a cartridge similar to a microfloppy but containing a continuous loop of tape. L20.

micro-economics /ˌmʌɪkrəʊiːkəˈnɒmɪks, -ɛk-/ *n.* M20. [f. MICRO- + ECONOMICS.] The branch of economics that deals with the small-scale economic factors; economics of the individual firm, product, consumer, etc., rather than the aggregate. Cf. MACRO-ECONOMICS.

micro-economic *a.* M20. **micro-eˈconomist** *n.* M20.

micro-electronics /ˌmʌɪkrəʊɪlɛkˈtrɒnɪks, -ɛl-/ *n.* M20. [f. MICRO- + ELECTRONICS.] The branch of technology that deals with the design, manufacture, and use of microcircuits. Also, micro-electronic devices or circuits.

micro-electronic *a.* M20.

micro-element /ˈmʌɪkrəʊˌɛlɪm(ə)nt/ *n.* M20. [f. MICRO- + ELEMENT *n.*] **1** *Bot.* = MICRONUTRIENT. M20. **2** *Electronics.* A thin flat miniaturized circuit made with standardized length and width for assembly into a micromodule. M20.

microfiche /ˈmʌɪkrə(ʊ)fiːʃ/ *n.* Pl. same, **-s**. M20. [f. MICRO- + Fr. *fiche* slip of paper, index card.] A flat piece of film, usually the size of a standard catalogue card, containing microphotographs of the pages of a book, periodical, etc. Cf. FICHE *n.*[2]

Comb.: **microfiche reader** a device for projecting a readable image of a microfiche on to a screen.

microfilm /ˈmʌɪkrə(ʊ)fɪlm/ *n.* & *v.* M20. [f. MICRO- + FILM *n.*] **A** *n.* (A length of) photographic film containing microphotographs of the pages of a book, periodical, etc. M20.

Comb.: **microfilm reader** a device for projecting a readable image on to a screen from microfilm.

B *v.t.* Record on microfilm. M20.

microfilmer *n.* (*a*) a camera for producing images on microfilm; (*b*) a person who operates such a camera: M20.

microform /ˈmʌɪkrə(ʊ)fɔːm/ *n.* M20. [f. MICRO- + FORM *n.*] Microphotographic form; a microphotographic reproduction on film or paper of a book, periodical, etc., requiring magnification to produce a readable image.

microglia /mʌɪkrə(ʊ)ˈglʌɪə, mɪ-/ *n.* (usu. treated as *pl.*). E20. [f. MICRO- + GLIA.] *Anat.* **1** *pl.* Glial cells derived from mesoderm that function as macrophages (scavengers) in the central nervous system and form part of the reticulo-endothelial system. E20. **2** *sing.* Tissue composed of such cells. M20.

microglial *a.* E20.

micrograph /ˈmʌɪkrə(ʊ)grɑːf/ *n.* L19. [f. MICRO- + -GRAPH.] **1** A picture or photograph of greatly reduced size. *rare.* L19. **2** An enlarged image of an object as seen through a microscope, obtained either by hand drawing or (now usu.) photographically. E20.

micrography /mʌɪˈkrɒgrəfi/ *n.* M17. [f. MICRO- + -GRAPHY.] **1** The description or delineation of objects visible only under a microscope. M17. **2** The technique of producing micrographs or of studying objects by means of them. E20.

micrographer *n.* a person who produces micrographs M19. **microˈgraphic** *a.* M19. **microˈgraphically** *adv.* by means of micrography or a micrograph L19. **microˈgraphics** *n.* the production of photographically reduced texts M20.

microinstruction /ˈmʌɪkrəʊɪnˌstrʌkʃ(ə)n/ *n.* M20. [f. MICRO- + INSTRUCTION.] *Computing.* Each of a sequence of instructions executed in response to a more comprehensive instruction; *spec.* one that corresponds to one of the smallest, most elementary operations in a computer and is produced in accordance with a microprogram.

Microlepidoptera /ˌmʌɪkrə(ʊ)lɛpɪˈdɒpt(ə)rə/ *n.pl.* M19. [f. MICRO- + LEPIDOPTERA.] The families of moths whose members are mostly smaller than those of interest to collectors. Cf. MACROLEPIDOPTERA.

microlepidopterist *n.* an expert in or student of Microlepidoptera M19. **microlepidopterous** *a.* M19.

microlight /ˈmʌɪkrə(ʊ)lʌɪt/ *a.* & *n.* L20. [f. MICRO- + LIGHT *a.*[1]] (Of, pertaining to, or designating) a small low-speed lightweight one- or two-seater aircraft of open construction, used for recreation and racing.

microlighting *n.* flying a microlight, as a pastime or hobby L20.

microlite /ˈmʌɪkrə(ʊ)lʌɪt/ *n.* M19. [f. MICRO- + -LITE.] **1** *Min.* A complex oxide of tantalum and niobium with sodium and calcium, crystallizing in the cubic system as yellow, brownish, or blackish translucent crystals. M19. **2** *Petrogr.* = MICROLITH 1. L19.

microlitic /mʌɪkrə(ʊ)ˈlɪtɪk/ *a.* (*Petrogr.*) of or pertaining to microlites; characterized by the presence of microlites: L19.

microlith /ˈmʌɪkrə(ʊ)lɪθ/ *n.* L19. [f. MICRO- + -LITH.] **1** *Petrogr.* A microscopic acicular crystal with determinable optical properties, such as occurs in the groundmass of some rocks. L19. **2** *Archaeol.* A small shaped stone tool with a sharpened edge that was used with a haft, characteristic of mesolithic cultures. E20.

microˈlithic *a.* of or pertaining to microliths; *Petrogr.* characterized by the presence of microliths; *Archaeol.* characterized by the use of microliths: L19.

micrologic /ˈmʌɪkrə(ʊ)ˌlɒdʒɪk/ *n.* M20. [f. MICRO- + LOGIC *n.*] Microelectronic logic.

micrology /mʌɪˈkrɒlədʒi/ *n.* M17. [Sense 1 f. Gk *mikrologia*, f. as MICRO- + *-logia* -LOGY; sense 2 f. MICRO- + -LOGY.] **1** The discussion or investigation of trivial things or petty affairs; hair-splitting. M17. **2** The branch of science which depends on the use of a microscope. Also, a treatise on microscopic organisms. M19.

microˈlogical *a.* M19. **micrologist** *n.* an expert in or student of the examination and description of microscopic objects M19.

micrometeoroid /mʌɪkrəʊˈmiːtɪərɔɪd/ *n.* M20. [f. MICRO- + METEOROID.] A microscopic particle in space or of extraterrestrial origin which is small enough not to suffer ablation in the earth's atmosphere.

micrometeor *n.* = MICROMETEOROID M20. **micrometeˈoric** *a.* micrometeoroidal M20. **micrometeorite** *n.* a micrometeoroid, *spec.* one that has entered the earth's atmosphere M20. **micrometeoˈritic** *a.* of the nature of a micrometeorite; pertaining to or produced by micrometeorites: M20. **micrometeoˈroidal** *a.* of the nature of a micrometeoroid; pertaining to or produced by micrometeoroids: L20.

micrometeorology /ˌmʌɪkrə(ʊ)miːtɪəˈrɒlədʒi/ *n.* M20. [f. MICRO- + METEOROLOGY.] The branch of science that deals with the meteorological characteristics of a small area and with small-scale meteorological phenomena.

micrometeoroˈlogical *a.* M20. **micrometeorologist** *n.* M20.

micrometer /mʌɪˈkrɒmɪtə/ *n.*[1] L17. [Fr. *micromètre*, f. as MICRO-: see -METER.] An instrument or gauge for measuring very small objects or differences in size; *esp.* one in which linear movement is produced by turning a screw of fine pitch whose angular position is read as linear position.

micrometer *n.*[2] see next.

micrometre /ˈmʌɪkrə(ʊ)ˌmiːtə/ *n.* Also ***-meter**. L19. [f. MICRO- + METRE *n.*[2]] A millionth of a metre; = MICRON. (Symbol μ.)

¶Rare bef. M20.

micrometrical /mʌɪkrə(ʊ)ˈmɛtrɪk(ə)l/ *a.* E18. [f. MICROMETER *n.*[1] after *metre*, *metric*: see -METRIC, -AL[1].] Pertaining to or of the nature of a micrometer; obtained by the use of a micrometer.

micrometric *a.* = MICROMETRICAL M19. **micrometrically** *adv.* by means of a micrometer M19. **micrometry** /-ˈkrɒmɪtri/ *n.* the measurement of very small objects; the use of a micrometer: M19.

microminiature /mʌɪkrə(ʊ)ˈmɪnɪtʃə/ *a.* M20. [f. MICRO- + MINIATURE *n.* & *a.*] Much reduced in size, as a result of microminiaturization; even smaller than a size regarded as miniature.

microminiaturiˈzation *n.* extreme miniaturization; *spec.* the development or use of techniques for making electronic components and devices of greatly reduced size: M20. **microminiaturize** *v.t.* produce in a very much smaller version M20.

micromotion /ˈmʌɪkrə(ʊ)ˌməʊʃ(ə)n/ *n.* E20. [f. MICRO- + MOTION.] Small movements of the body recorded cinematographically for purposes of work study etc. Usu. *attrib.*

micron /ˈmʌɪkrɒn/ *n.* L19. [Gk *mikron* neut. of *mikros* small.] = MICROMETRE.

Micronesian /mʌɪkrə(ʊ)ˈniːzjən, -ʒ(ə)n/ *n.* & *a.* M19. [f. *Micronesia* (see below), intended to mean 'region of small islands', f. MICRO- + Gk *nēsos* island + -IA[1], after *Polynesia*: see -AN.] **A** *n.* A native or inhabitant of Micronesia, a group of small islands in the western region of the N. Pacific which includes the Caroline, Mariana, Marshall, and Gilbert Islands. Also, the group of Austronesian languages spoken in Micronesia. M19. **B** *adj.* Of or pertaining to Micronesia, the Micronesians, or their group of languages. M19.

micronize /ˈmʌɪkrənʌɪz/ *v.t.* Also **-ise**. M20. [f. MICRON + -IZE, or back-form. f. *Micronizer* (proprietary name in the US).] Break up into very fine particles.

microniˈzation *n.* M20.

micro-organism /mʌɪkrəʊˈɔːg(ə)nɪz(ə)m/ *n.* L19. [f. MICRO- + ORGANISM.] An organism too small to be seen except with the aid of a microscope, as a bacterium or virus.

microphone /ˈmʌɪkrəfəʊn/ *n.* L17. [f. MICRO- + -PHONE.] **1** An instrument by which quiet sounds can be made louder. Now *rare.* L17. **2** An instrument for converting sound waves impinging on it into variations in electric voltage or current, which may then be amplified or transmitted for reconversion into sound (as in broadcasting and the telephone) or recorded; *esp.* one made as an independent unit. L19.

2 B. MOORE Some with cameras, some with microphones and sound equipment.

microphoned *a.* (*a*) containing or furnished with a microphone; (*b*) *rare* picked up and transmitted by a microphone: E20.

microphonic /mʌɪkrəˈfɒnɪk/ *n.* & *a.* M19. [f. prec. + -IC.] **A** *n.* **1** In *pl.* The branch of science that deals with the amplification of sound. *rare.* M19. **2a** *Electronics.* An undesired signal or modulation produced (e.g. in a valve) by mechanical vibration. Usu. in *pl.* E20. **b** *Physiol.* A microphonic signal generated in the cochlea of

For other words beginning with *micro-* see the entry for **micro-**

the ear. M20. B *adj.* 1 Of or pertaining to a microphone or the use of microphones. L19. 2 Characterized by or pertaining to the production of variations in electrical potential in response to sound waves or vibrations; (of an electrical signal) produced by sound waves or vibrations. L19.

mi'crophonism *n.* (*Electronics*) = MICROPHONY (b) M20. **mi'crophony** *n.* † (*a*) *rare* weakness of voice; (*b*) *Electronics* the production of microphonics: M19.

microphoto /'mʌɪkrə(ʊ),fəʊtəʊ/ *n. colloq.* Pl. **-os.** M20. [Abbrev.] = MICROPHOTOGRAPH 2.

microphotograph /mʌɪkrə(ʊ)'fəʊtəgrɑːf/ *n.* M19. [f. MICRO- + PHOTOGRAPH.] 1 A photograph reduced to microscopic size. M19. 2 A photograph of a microscopic object on a magnified scale; = PHOTOMICROGRAPH. M19.

microphoto'graphic *a.* M19. **microphoto'graphically** *adv.* by means of microphotography L19. **micropho'tography** *n.* the art or practice of making microphotographs M19.

microphthalmos /mʌɪkrɒf'θalməs/ *n.* M19. [f. MICRO- + Gk *ophthalmos* eye.] *Med.* Abnormal smallness of one or both eyes.

microphthalmia *n.* = MICROPHTHALMOS M19. **microphthalmic** *a.* of, pertaining to, or characterized by microphthalmos M19.

microphysics /'mʌɪkrə(ʊ),fɪzɪks/ *n.* L19. [f. MICRO- + PHYSICS.] The branch of physics that deals with bodies and phenomena on a microscopic or smaller scale, esp. with molecules, atoms, and subatomic particles.

micro'physical *a.* E20.

microphyte /'mʌɪkrə(ʊ)fʌɪt/ *n.* M19. [f. MICRO- + -PHYTE.] A microscopic plant, *esp.* a bacterium.

micro'phytal, microphytic /-'fɪtɪk/ *adjs.* L19.

microprint /'mʌɪkrə(ʊ)prɪnt/ *n.* M20. [f. MICRO- + PRINT *n.*] A photographic print of text reduced by microphotography; printed matter so reduced.

microprinting *n.* the production of microprint M20.

microprocessor /mʌɪkrə(ʊ)'prəʊsesə/ *n.* L20. [f. MICRO- + PROCESSOR.] A device that can function as the central processing unit of a computer and consists of one or occas. more integrated circuits or chips.

microprogram /'mʌɪkrə(ʊ),prəʊgram/ *n.* & *v.* M20. [f. MICRO- + PROGRAM *n.*] *Computing.* A *n.* A program that causes any machine instruction to be transformed into a sequence of microinstructions. M20. B *v.t.* Infl. **-mm-**. Use microprogramming with (a computer); bring about by means of a microprogram. M20.

micro'programmable *a.* able to be microprogrammed M20. **micro'programmer** *n.* a person who writes microprograms or is a specialist in microprogramming M20. **micro'programming** *n.* the technique of making machine instructions generate sequences of microinstructions in accordance with a microprogram rather than initiate the desired operations directly, so that by changing the microprogram the set of possible machine instructions can be varied M20.

micropsia /mʌɪ'krɒpsɪə/ *n.* M19. [f. MICRO- + Gk *-opsia* seeing.] *Ophthalm.* A condition of the eyes in which objects appear smaller than normal.

micropyle /'mʌɪkrə(ʊ)pʌɪl/ *n.* E19. [Fr., f. as MICRO- + Gk *pulē* gate.] 1 *Bot.* The opening in the integument of an ovule, through which the pollen-tube penetrates to the embryo sac. Also, the small pore in the ripe seed which represents this opening. E19. 2 *Zool.* A small opening in the egg of some animals, esp. insects, through which spermatozoa can enter. M19.

micropylar *a.* M19.

microradiography /,mʌɪkrə(ʊ)reɪdɪ'ɒgrəfi/ *n.* E20. [f. MICRO- + RADIOGRAPHY.] Radiography of the fine structure of an object.

micro'radiogram *n.* the original image obtained on a sensitive plate or film in microradiography E20. **micro'radiograph** *n.* a photographic enlargement of a microradiogram M20. **microradio'graphic** *a.* of or obtained by microradiography M20.

microscope /'mʌɪkrəskəʊp/ *n.* & *v.* M17. [mod.L *microscopium*, f. as MICRO- + -SCOPE.] A *n.* 1 An optical instrument, consisting of a lens or combination of lenses, which produces a magnified image of an object close to it so as to reveal details invisible to the naked eye (also called *light microscope, optical microscope*). Also, an instrument analogous to this in function but employing radiation other than visible light (e.g. electrons or X-rays). M17. 2 (Usu. **M-**.) *The* constellation Microscopium. M19.

1 *fig.*: *Economist* American motor insurance is now to be put under the microscope. *electron microscope*: see ELECTRON *n.*[2]

Comb.: *microscope slide*: see SLIDE *n.* 7(b).

B *v.t.* Magnify; *fig.* scrutinize minutely. *rare.* M19.

microscopist /mʌɪ'krɒskəpɪst, 'mʌɪkrəskəʊpɪst/ *n.* a person who habitually uses a microscope or who is skilled in its use M19. **microscopy** /mʌɪ'krɒskəpi/ *n.* the use of a microscope. M17.

microscopic /mʌɪkrə'skɒpɪk/ *a.* L17. [f. prec. + -IC.] 1 Having the function or power of a microscope. L17. 2 So small as to be invisible or indeterminate without the use of a microscope; extremely small (*lit.* & *fig.*). M18. 3 = MICROSCOPICAL 1. Now chiefly *fig.*, regarded in terms of small units, concerned with minute detail (opp. *macroscopic*). L18.

1 POPE Why has not Man a microscopic eye? 2 ANTHONY HUXLEY Water and soil teem with microscopic plants. *Daily Telegraph* Although the Foreign Ministers sat for two hours and 20 minutes . . progress was microscopic. 3 D. CECIL The microscopic concentration of a scientist conducting an important experiment.

microscopical /mʌɪkrə'skɒpɪk(ə)l/ *a.* M17. [f. as prec. + -ICAL.] 1 Of or pertaining to the microscope or its use. M17. 2 = MICROSCOPIC 2. Now *rare.* M18.

1 F. RUTLEY The present state of microscopical knowledge. B. UNSWORTH Microscopical and chemical analysis of paint samples.

microscopically *adv.* by means of a microscope; so minutely as to be visible only with a microscope; as seen under a microscope: M17.

Microscopium /mʌɪkrə'skəʊpɪəm/ *n.* E19. [mod.L, f. as MICROSCOPE.] (The name of) an inconspicuous constellation of the southern hemisphere, between Piscis Austrinus and Sagittarius; the Microscope.

microscreen /'mʌɪkrə(ʊ)skriːn/ *n.* M20. [f. MICRO- + SCREEN *n.*[1]] 1 A screen with a fine mesh. M20. 2 A small screen for displaying an image; *spec.* a liquid crystal display in the keyboard of a microcomputer. L20.

microsmatic /mʌɪkrɒz'matɪk/ *a.* L19. [f. MICRO- + Gk *osmē* smell + -ATIC.] *Zool.* Having poorly developed olfactory organs.

microsome /'mʌɪkrəsəʊm/ *n.* L19. [f. MICRO- + -SOME[3].] *Cytol.* Orig., a small granule in the cytoplasm of a cell. Now, a cytoplasmic particle consisting of a fragment of endoplasmic reticulum and attached ribosomes from a cell disrupted by ultracentrifugation; a ribosome in an intact cell.

micro'somal *a.* L19.

microsporangium /,mʌɪkrəʊspə'randʒɪəm/ *n.* Pl. **-ia** /-ɪə/. L19. [f. MICRO- + SPORANGIUM.] *Bot.* A sporangium containing microspores.

microspore /'mʌɪkrə(ʊ)spɔː/ *n.* M19. [f. MICRO- + SPORE.] *Bot.* The smaller of the two kinds of spores in heterosporous cryptogams, which develop into male gametophytes; the analogous structure (the immature pollen grain) in seed plants.

micro'sporocyte *n.* a mother cell that divides into four microspores E20. **microsporo'genesis** *n.* the development of microspores M20. **microsporoge'netic** *a.* of or pertaining to microsporogenesis L20. **microsporous** *a.* having small seeds; resembling or derived from a microspore: M19.

microsporidian /,mʌɪkrəʊspə'rɪdɪən/ *a.* & *n.* E20. [f. mod.L *Microsporidia* (see below), f. MICRO- + SPORE + Gk *-idion* dim. suff.: see -AN.] *Zool.* A *adj.* Of, pertaining to, or designating the sporozoan phylum Microspora or (formerly) the class Microsporidia, comprising protozoan parasites of arthropods and fishes. E20. B *n.* A protozoan of this phylum. E20.

microsporidi'osis *n.* nosema disease of bees E20.

microstructure /'mʌɪkrə(ʊ),strʌktʃə/ *n.* L19. [f. MICRO- + STRUCTURE *n.*] Structure on a microscopic or very small scale; fine structure.

micro'structural *a.* L19. **micro'structurally** *adv.* as regards microstructure M20.

microsurgery /mʌɪkrə(ʊ)'səːdʒ(ə)ri/ *n.* E20. [f. MICRO- + SURGERY.] Manipulation (as by injection, dissection, etc.) of individual cells with the aid of microscopy; surgery of such intricacy as to necessitate being performed using microscopy.

micro'surgical *a.* M20.

microtherm /'mʌɪkrə(ʊ)θəːm/ *n.* L19. [f. MICRO- + Gk *thermē* heat.] *Bot.* A plant requiring a cold habitat and low mean temperatures for successful growth.

microtine /'mʌɪkrə(ʊ)tʌɪn/ *a.* & *n.* E20. [mod.L *Microtinae* (see below), f. *Microtus* genus name, f. as MICRO- + Gk *ōt-*, *ous* ear: see -INE[1].] A *adj.* Of, pertaining to, or designating the mammalian subfamily Microtinae (family Muridae), which includes voles and lemmings. E20. B *n.* A rodent of this subfamily. M20.

microtome /'mʌɪkrə(ʊ)təʊm/ *n.* & *v.* M19. [f. MICRO- + -TOME.] A *n.* An instrument for cutting extremely thin sections for microscopic work. M19. B *v.t.* Cut in sections with a microtome. L19.

microtone /'mʌɪkrə(ʊ)təʊn/ *n.* E20. [f. MICRO- + TONE *n.*] A musical interval smaller than a semitone.

micro'tonal *a.* of or pertaining to a microtone or microtones; employing or producing microtones: M20. **microto'nality** *n.* the use of microtones M20. **microtonally** *adv.* M20.

microwave /'mʌɪkrə(ʊ)weɪv/ *n.* & *v.* M20. [f. MICRO- + WAVE *n.*] A *n.* 1 A short electromagnetic wave; now *spec.* one with a wavelength between about one millimetre and 30 centimetres (corresponding to a frequency between 300 GHz and 1 GHz), or one whose length is such that it is convenient to use hollow waveguides for its transmission. M20. 2 *ellipt.* A microwave oven; microwave cookery. L20.

B *attrib.* or as *adj.* Of or pertaining to microwaves, employing microwaves; (of food) heated or cooked in a microwave oven, suitable for microwave cooking. M20.

Television As the USSR covers such a vast area microwave links are used for TV and other communications. S. TOWNSEND My father . . went to the pub and had a microwave mince and onion pie. **microwave oven** an oven in which food is heated by passing microwaves through it, the resulting generation of heat inside the food facilitating rapid cooking.

C *v.* 1 *v.t.* Heat or cook in a microwave oven. L20. 2 *v.i.* Be suitable for or undergo microwave cooking. L20.

microwavable *a.* (of food and food containers) suitable for cooking or heating in a microwave oven L20.

micrurgy /'mʌɪkrəːdʒi/ *n.* E20. [f. MICRO- + *-urgy* after *metallurgy*.] The performance of delicate manipulations under a microscope, esp. on biological material such as individual cells.

mi'crurgical *a.* E20.

mictic /'mɪktɪk/ *a.* M20. [f. Gk *miktos* mixed + -IC.] *Biol.* Of, pertaining to, or produced by mixis; of mixed parentage or descent.

micturate /'mɪktjʊreɪt/ *v.i.* M19. [Back-form. f. next: see -ATE[3].] Urinate.

micturition /mɪktjʊ'rɪʃ(ə)n/ *n.* E18. [f. L *micturire*, f. *mi(n)ct-* pa. ppl stem of *meiere* urinate: see -ITION.] Urination.

mid /mɪd/ *n.*[1] *obs.* exc. *dial.* ME. [Absol. use of MID *a.*] The middle.

mid /mɪd/ *n.*[2] *slang.* L18. [Abbrev.] = MIDSHIPMAN.

mid /mɪd/ *attrib. a.* & *adv.* Superl. MIDMOST, (*arch.*) **middest**. [OE *midd* (recorded only in obl. forms *midde, middes*, etc.), corresp. to OFris. *midde*, OS *middi*, OHG *mitti*, ON *miðr*, Goth. *midjis*, f. Gmc, f. IE base (whence also L *medius*, Gk *mesos* MESO-).] A *adj.* (Freq. w. hyphen.) 1 That is the part or point in the middle of. Now chiefly of a period of time and in special collocations & *comb.* Freq. in phrs. after *in.* OE. **b** Introducing an advb. phr. In the middle of. M16. **2** Being in or occupying a middle position. LME. **3** *spec.* **a** *Phonet.* Of a sound: produced with (part of) the tongue in a middle position between high and low. M19. **b** Of a colour: occupying a middle position in a range of shades. E20.

1 F. W. L. ADAMS From mid-June to mid-October. W. D. HOWELLS The wind rises, and by mid-afternoon, blows half a gale. H. D. LLOYD The gas-company suspended its operations in mid-course. *Which?* This had a mid position allowing flow both to the radiators and hot water supply. J. NAGENDA She rushed off . . leaving Roger in mid-joke. M. BRETT Many pension funds were showing surpluses in the mid 1980s. **b** G. MEREDITH Light that Caught him mid-gallop, blazed him home. **2** KEATS In the mid-days of autumn.

Special collocations & comb.: **mid-age** middle age. **mid-aged** *a.* middle-aged. **mid-Atlantic** *n.* & *a.* (*a*) *n.* the middle of the Atlantic Ocean; (*b*) *adj.* having characteristics of or features appealing to people both of Britain and of America. **midbrain** the part of the brainstem which joins the forebrain to the hindbrain; = MESENCEPHALON. **mid-brow** *n.* & *a.* = *middlebrow* s.v. MIDDLE *a.* **mid-calf** *a.* & *n.* (reaching to) the point halfway down the calf of the leg. **mid-circle** *Geom.* †(*a*) the great circle equidistant from the poles of a sphere; (*b*) the circle passing through the midpoints of the sides of a triangle. **midcrop** a crop harvested between the main crops. **midcult** *colloq.* middlebrow culture. **mid-cycle** *a.* & *n.* (*Physiol.*) (occurring during) the middle of the menstrual cycle. **mid-earth** *arch. rare.* (*a*) the middle of the earth; (*b*) = *middle earth* (a) s.v. MIDDLE *a.* **Mideast** (chiefly *US*) = *Middle East* s.v. MIDDLE *a.* **mid-engined** *a.* (of a car) having the engine located centrally between the front and rear axles. **mid-European** *a.* & *n.* = *Middle-European* s.v. MIDDLE *a.* **mid-feather** a thin structure dividing or partitioning the interior of a furnace, flue, etc. **midgut** *Anat.* & *Zool.* the middle part of the gut, in vertebrates including the small intestine. **mid-heaven** (*a*) *Astron.* & *Astrol.* the meridian, or middle line of the heavens; *esp.* the point where the ecliptic meets the meridian; (*b*) the middle of the sky. **midiron** *Golf* (*a*) an iron with a medium degree of loft; (*b*) a number 2 iron. **midline** *Anat.* & *Zool.* a median line; the median plane or plane of bilateral symmetry. **midlittoral** *a.* & *n.* (*Ecol.*) (designating) the zone on the seashore which is both covered and uncovered by the neap tides. †**mid man** (*a*) a mediator, an umpire; (*b*) a male midwife. **mid-ocean** *n.* & *a.* (*a*) *n.* the middle of an ocean; (*b*) *adj.* situated or occurring in the middle of an ocean (*mid-ocean ridge*, a long mountainous seismically-active ridge, freq. with a central rift, rising from the abyssal plain in the middle of an ocean basin and marking the site of magmatic upwelling associated with sea-floor spreading). **mid-oceanic** *a.* situated in, occurring in, or pertaining to the middle of an ocean. **midpoint** the middle point. **midrib** (*a*) *Bot.* a large, usu. strengthened, vein along the midline of a leaf; (*b*) *Archaeol.* a central ridge on the blade of a weapon. **midsagittal** *a.* (*Anat.*) designating or situated in an anteroposterior median plane. **mid-sea** *n.* & *a.* (*literary*) (situated or occurring in) the open sea. **mid-shot** *Cinemat.* a medium shot. **mid-sky** *poet.* the middle of the sky. **midsole** a layer of material between the inner and outer soles of a shoe, for absorbing shock. **mid-spoon** *Golf* a wooden-headed club of medium size. **mid-square** *a.* (*Math.*) designating a method of generating a pseudorandom sequence of digits by squaring an arbitrary large number, taking the middle digits of the result and using these as the first digits of the series and as the number to be squared to provide the next digits, and so on. **midterm** *n.* & *a.* (occurring in) the middle of a period of office, an academic term, a pregnancy, etc. **midtown** *n.* & *a.* (chiefly *US*) (situated or occurring in) the middle of a town, esp. when forming a distinct area. **mid-Victorian** *a.* & *n.* (*a*) *adj.* pertaining to or characteristic of the middle of the Victorian period; (*b*) *n.* a person of the mid-Victorian period. **mid-water** the part of a body of water near neither the bottom nor the surface. **midweek** *n.* & *a.* (occurring in) the middle of the week. **Midwest** the middle of the western part of the US, the region adjoining the northern Mississippi. **Midwestern** *a.* of or pertaining to the Midwest. **Midwesterner** a native or inhabitant of the Midwest. **midwicket** *Cricket* (the position of) a fielder placed between mid-on and square-leg on a line bisecting the line joining the wickets. **mid-wing** *a.* (*Aeronaut.*) designating an aircraft having the main wings placed approximately halfway between the top and bottom of the fuselage.

B *adv.* In the middle. Long *obs.* exc. in *comb.*, as *mid-mounted* adj. OE.

†**mid** *prep.*[1] OE–LME. [OE *mid*, (Northumb.) *miþ*, corresp. to OFris. *mith*, OS *mid* (Du. *met*), G *mit*, ON *með*, Goth. *miþ*, cogn. w. Gk *meta* (see META-).] With.

¶Prob. survives in MIDWIFE *n.*

mid /mɪd/ *prep.*[2] Now *poet.* Also **'mid.** LME. [Aphet.] = AMID.

¶Rare bef. 19.

mid-air /*as n.* mɪd 'ɛː, *as adj.* 'mɪdɛː/ *n.* & *a.* Also **midair.** M17. [f. MID *a.* + AIR *n.*[1]] **A** *n.* Some part or section of the air above ground level or above another surface. Chiefly in *in mid-air.* M17.

L. CODY They stared at her, glasses arrested in midair.

B *attrib.* or as *adj.* Situated or occurring in mid-air. L18.

Guardian If something is not done soon about these near misses, there is bound to be a mid-air collision.

Midas /'mʌɪdəs/ *n.* M16. [L & Gk, a king of Phrygia whose touch was said to turn all things to gold, and to whom also Apollo gave asses' ears as a punishment for not appreciating his music.] **1** A person incapable of appreciating something; *Midas ear(s)*, *Midas-eared*, (having) an incapacity to appreciate something. M16. **2** A person whose actions always bring financial reward; *Midas touch*, the ability to turn one's actions to financial advantage. L18.

2 L. P. HARTLEY Candidates for your financial wizard-work, your Midas touch, are queuing up.

midas fly *n. phr.* see MYDAS FLY.

midday /*as n.*, mɪd'deɪ, *as adj.* 'mɪddeɪ/ *n.* & *a.* OE. [f. MID *a.* + DAY *n.*] **A** *n.* **1** The middle of the day, when the sun is at its highest point; noon. OE. †**b** *Eccl.* = SEXT 1. OE–LME. †**2** [Cf. Fr. *midi.*] The south. LME–E17.

1 E. TEMPLETON He never ate more than one course at midday when he was working.

B *attrib.* or as *adj.* Of or pertaining to midday; occurring at midday, (of a train etc.) leaving or arriving at midday. ME.

P. BOWLES Narrow alleys, where the shade was a blessing after the midday sun. E. KUZWAYO We had our mid-day meal together daily. *Scotsman* To catch the midday flight to Jersey.

midden /'mɪd(ə)n/ *n.* ME. [Of Scand. origin: cf. Da. *Mødding*, earlier *møgdyng*, f. *møg* MUCK *n.*[1] + *dynge* heap (cf. DUNG *n.*), Norw. dial. *mykjardunge*, *mitting.*] **1** A dunghill, a manure-heap; a refuse-heap. ME. **2** *Archaeol.* A prehistoric refuse-heap of shells and bones and often also discarded artefacts; *spec.* = KITCHEN *midden.* M19. **3** A receptacle for refuse, a dustbin; the place where dustbins are kept. *Sc. colloq.* L19.

1 *fig.*: *Expression!* My own enthusiasm for the arts, then, grew up in the fertilising midden of unselfconsciousness.

Comb.: **midden cock, fowl** = DUNGHILL *cock*, *fowl*; **middenstead** *arch.* & *dial.* the place where a midden or dunghill is formed.

midder /'mɪdə/ *n. slang.* E20. [f. MID(WIFERY + -ER[6].] Midwifery; a midwifery case.

middest *a.* see MID *a.*

middie *n.* var. of MIDDY *n.*[1]

middle /'mɪd(ə)l/ *attrib. a.* & *n.* [OE *middel* = OFris. *middel*, OS *middil-* (Du. *middel*), OHG *mittil* (G *mittel*), f. WGmc, f. Gmc base of MID *a.*: see -LE[1].] **A** *adj.* **1** Designating that member of a group or series or that part of a whole situated so as to have the same number of members or parts on each side; equidistant from the ends or boundaries of a thing; situated at the centre. OE. †**b** Average, mean. L17–L18. **2** = MID *a.* 1. Now *rare.* ME. **3** Of size, rank, quality, or (now rarely) position in space or time: intermediate; medium. Of a course of action, an opinion, etc.: mediating. Of a colour: = MID *a.* 3b. LME. **b** Middle-sized (now *rare*); (of wool) having medium-length staple. LME. **c** Of or pertaining to the middle classes. L18. **4** *Gram.* Of or designating (the voice of) a verb (esp. in Greek) which expresses reflexive or reciprocal action. M18. **5** Designating a language at an intermediate stage in its history, between the old and modern forms. M19. **6** *Geol.* Designating a subdivision of a formation or period intermediate between two others (upper and lower). M19.

1 GOLDSMITH He was at that middle time of life which is happily tempered with the warmth of youth. W. M. CRAIG In the same way you will get the middle line of the mouth. J. TYNDALL The middle portion of the glacier. *Punch* My middle sister, Emily. **2** J. MACCULLOCH The two months of middle summer. **3** N. ROWE The middle Space, a Valley low depress'd. BURKE An Administration, that having no scheme of their own, took a middle line. T. D. ACLAND The want of better education, accessible to the middle ranks on easy terms. E. PACE The immaturity that plagued middle-level intelligence officials. D. FRANCIS A man . . of middle height . . and middling grey hair.

Special collocations & comb.: *Middle Academy*: see ACADEMY 2. **Middle America** (*a*) the region comprising Central America, Mexico, and the Antilles; (*b*) the middle class in the US, esp. as a conservative political force. **Middle American** *a.* & *n.* (a native or inhabitant) of Middle America. **Middle Atlantic States** the States of New York, New Jersey, and Pennsylvania. **Middle Britain** the middle class in Britain, esp. as a conservative political force. **middlebrow** *n.* & *a.* (a person) claiming to be or regarded as only moderately intellectual or cultured. **middle C** *Mus.* the C near the middle of the piano keyboard, the note between the treble and bass staves, at about 260 hertz frequency. **middle common-room** a common-room in a university college for the use of graduate students who are not fellows; graduate students collectively. **middle course** a compromise between two extremes (*steer a middle course*: see STEER *v.*[1]). **middle deck** a ship's deck between the upper deck and the lower deck. **middle distance** (*a*) the part of a (painted or actual) landscape between the foreground and the background; (*b*) a race distance intermediate between that of a sprint and a long-distance race, now usu. 400, 800, or 1500 metres and their imperial equivalents (880 yards etc.). **middle distillate** a petroleum fraction that distils at intermediate temperatures (about 180° to 340°C), from which is obtained paraffin, diesel oil, and heating oil. *middle ear*: see EAR *n.*[1] **middle earth** (*a*) *arch.* the earth, as situated between heaven and hell or as supposedly occupying the centre of the universe; (*b*) the real world as distinct from fairyland; †(*c*) the middle of the earth. **Middle East** *the* area around the eastern Mediterranean, *esp.* those countries from Egypt to Iran inclusive. **Middle Eastern** *a.* of, pertaining to, situated in, or occurring in the Middle East. **middle eight** *colloq.* the eight bars in the middle of a conventionally structured popular tune, often of a different character from the other parts of the tune. *Middle English*: see ENGLISH *a.* & *n.* **Middle-European** *a.* of, pertaining to, or characteristic of central Europe or its people. **middle finger**: between the index finger and the third finger. **middle game** the central phase of a chess game when strategies are developed. **middle genus** *Logic* a genus which is itself a species of a higher genus. **middle ground** (*a*) *Naut.* a shallow place, as a bank or bar, esp. as a navigational obstruction; (*b*) = *middle distance* (a) above; (*c*) an area of moderation or compromise. **middle guard** (*a*) *Cricket* the position occupied by a batsman defending the middle stump with the bat; (*b*) *Amer. Football* a defensive lineman who plays between the defensive tackles. **middle income** an average income. **Middle Kingdom** (*a*) *Hist.* China, *spec.* its eighteen inner provinces; (*b*) *the* eleventh and twelfth Dynasties, which ruled Egypt from the 22nd to the 18th cents. BC. **middle lamella** *Bot.* the thin layer between two adjacent plant cell walls. **middle leg** *slang* the penis. **middle-length** *a.* of medium length. **middle life** (*a*) the middle of a person's life, middle age; (*b*) middle-class life. **middle linebacker** *Amer. Football*: who plays behind the middle of the defensive line. **middle management** the middle level of management in a business or company, esp. comprising departmental managers. **middle manager** a manager at the level of middle management. **middle name** (*a*) a name between a person's first name and surname; (*b*) *fig.* the outstanding characteristic of a person. **middle passage** *Hist.* the middle part of a slave's transportation from Africa to America, the sea passage. **middle period** the middle phase of a culture, artist's work, etc. **middle piece** the part of a horse's body between the forelegs and the hind legs. **Middle Pointed** *Archit.* (now *Hist.*) decorated Gothic. **middle price** *Stock Exch.* the average of the bid and offer prices of a particular stock. **middle rail** the rail of a door level with the hand, on which the lock is usually fixed. **middle-rank** *a.* of intermediate status or value. **middle-rate** *a.* mediocre. **middle rib** a cut of beef consisting of the ribs between the fore ribs and the chuck ribs. **middle-road** *a.* = *middle-of-the-road* below. **middle school** (*a*) a secondary school for children between the ages of 9 and 13; (*b*) the middle (esp. third and fourth) forms in a secondary school. **middle-sized** *a.* of medium size. *middle* SPOTTED *woodpecker.* **Middle States** = *Middle Atlantic States* above. **middlestead** *dial.* the central part of a barn where threshing formerly took place. *Middle Temple*: see TEMPLE *n.*[1] 6. *middle term*: see TERM *n.* **middle-tone** = *halftone* (c) s.v. HALF-. †**middle wall** a partition wall. **middle watch** the watch from midnight to 4 a.m.; the members of a ship's crew on deck duty during this. **middle-water** *a.* designating or pertaining to fishing carried out at a medium distance from land. **middle way** (*a*) = *middle course* above; (*b*) the eightfold path of Buddhism between indulgence and asceticism. **Middle West** = *Midwest* s.v. MID *a.* **Middle Western** *a.* = *Midwestern* s.v. MID *a.* **Middle White** (an animal of) a medium-sized white (orig. Yorkshire) breed of pig with prick ears. **middle wicket** = *midwicket* s.v. MID *a.* **middle world** *arch.* = *middle earth* (a) above. **middle years** the years in the middle of a person's life, middle age.

B *n.* **1** The middle point, part, or position. (Foll. by *of*.) OE. **b** A strip of unplanted ground between two rows of a planted crop. Usu. in *pl.* *US.* E19. †**2** The position of being among or surrounded by a group of people or within a town etc. Chiefly in *in the middle of*, in the midst of. OE–M18. **3a** A person's waist. OE. **b** The part of a side of bacon between the fore-end and the gammon cuts. L19. **4** A mean; a point of moderation or compromise. Now *rare.* ME. †**5** An intermediate cause or agency. *rare.* ME–L17. **6** *Naut.* = *middle ground* (a) above. E18. **7** *Gram.* The middle voice of a verb; a middle verb. M18. **8** *Cricket.* = *middle guard* (a) above. M19. **9** A brief essay of a literary kind esp. in a weekly journal, usu. placed between the leading articles and the reviews. M19. **10** A middle-class person. *colloq.* M20.

1 R. K. NARAYAN I noticed her sitting erect in the middle of the road. C. ANGIER Mr Peterman demanded to know why she had walked out in the middle of her act. T. PARKS There was just one .. polished-wood table in the middle and then cupboards about the walls. L. CODY It could have been the middle of the night. Z. TOMIN Make sure this story has a happy beginning, middle and end. 2 H. BROOKE [He] is come to rob me in broad day, and in the middle of my own people. 3 G. BORROW He has got it buckled round his middle beneath his pantaloons. 4 DEFOE To keep the safe middle between these extremes.

Phrases & comb.: **in the middle** *slang* in a difficult or dangerous position, in trouble. **in the middle of** †(*a*) see sense B.2 above; (*b*) in the process of *doing*. *knock into the middle of next week*: see KNOCK *v.* *law of excluded middle*: see EXCLUDE 5. **middle-of-the-road** *a.* (of a person, course of action, music, etc.) avoiding extremes, unadventurous. *pig, piggy, in the middle*: see PIG *n.*[1], PIGGY *n.* *play both ends against the middle*: see PLAY *v.* *principle of excluded middle*: see EXCLUDE 5. *turn sides to middle*: see SIDE *n.* UNDISTRIBUTED *middle*.

middleness *n.* (*rare*) the fact or condition of being of middle rank or quality E20.

middle /ˈmɪd(ə)l/ *v.* LME. [f. MIDDLE *n.*] †**1** *v.i.* Be at the middle point. Only in LME. †**2** *v.t.* w. *it.* Take a middle course. Only in M17. **3** *v.t.* Bisect. *rare.* E18. **4** *v.t. Naut.* Fold or double in the middle. M19. **5** *v.t.* Place in the middle. L19. **6** *v.t.* & *i. Football.* Pass (the ball) from one of the wings to midfield in front of the goal. L19. **7** *v.t.* Strike (a ball) with the middle of the bat or racket. M20.

middle age /mɪd(ə)l ˈeɪdʒ/ *n. phr.* & *a.* As adj. usu. **middle-age.** LME. [f. MIDDLE *a.* + AGE *n.*] **A** *n. phr.* **1** The age between youth and old age, now regarded as between about 45 and 60. LME. **2** *the Middle Ages*, (now *rare*) *the Middle Age*, the period of European history from the fall of the Roman Empire in the West (*c* 500) to the fall of Constantinople (1453), or (usu.) from *c* 1000 to *c* 1453. E17.

B *attrib.* or as *adj.* **1** Of or pertaining to the Middle Ages, medieval. Now *rare.* M19. **2** Of or pertaining to middle age. M20.

2 middle-age spread an increase in bodily girth, often associated with middle age.

middle-'ageing *a.* becoming middle-aged L19. **middle-'ager** *n.* (chiefly *US*) a middle-aged person M20.

middle-aged /mɪd(ə)lˈeɪdʒd/ *a.* E17. [f. prec. + -ED[2].] **1** In middle age, (now) aged between about 45 and 60. E17. **b** Characteristic of or considered appropriate to a person in middle age. M19. †**2** Of or pertaining to the Middle Ages; medieval. E17–M19.

1b middle-aged spread = *middle-age spread* s.v. MIDDLE AGE.

middle class /mɪd(ə)l ˈklɑːs/ *n. phr.* & *a.* As adj. usu. **middle-class.** M18. [f. MIDDLE *a.* + CLASS *n.*] **A** *n.* A class of society between an upper and lower or working class, including professional and business workers and their families; *sing.* & in *pl.*, the members of such a class. M18.

upper middle class: see UPPER *a.*

B *adj.* Of, pertaining to, or characteristic of the middle class; conservative. M19.

I. HISLOP Twee, prim and dull . . . Even her voice sounded middle-class. D. ROWE The prejudice that middle-class people can hold about the working class.

middle-classdom *n.* (the characteristics of) the middle classes as a whole M20. **middle-classness** *n.* the quality or state of being middle-class. L19.

middleman /ˈmɪd(ə)lman/ *n.* Pl. **-men** /-mɛn/. LME. [f. MIDDLE *a.* + MAN *n.*] †**1** A workman employed in the making of iron wire. Only in LME. †**2** A soldier in the fifth or sixth rank in a file of ten deep. Only in 17. **3** A person who takes a middle course. M18. **4a** A person who paddles or rows in the middle of a boat. *N. Amer.* M18. **b** The middle climber of a mountaineering team. L19. **c** Chiefly *Hist.* A man in the middle of a line of blackface minstrels who led the dialogue between songs. *US.* L19. **5** A person standing in an intermediate relation to two parties; *spec.* (*a*) a trader who handles a commodity between its producer and its consumer; (*b*) an intermediary. M18. **b** *Hist.* In Ireland, a person who leased land and sub-let it at a higher rate. L18.

middlemanship *n.* the system of employing middlemen M19.

middlemost /ˈmɪd(ə)lməʊst/ *a.* Now *rare.* ME. [f. MIDDLE *a.* + -MOST.] That is in the very middle or nearest the middle. (Now only of position.)

middler /ˈmɪd(ə)lə/ *n.* M16. [f. MIDDLE *a.* + -ER[1].] †**1** An intermediary, a mediator. M16–L17. **2** A worker who performs the middle one of three operations in the preparation of flax. M19.

middlescent /mɪdəˈlɛs(ə)nt/ *a.* & *n.* M20. [f. MIDDLE *a.* after *adolescent*.] **A** *adj.* Of or pertaining to middle age, middle-aged. M20. **B** *n.* A middle-aged person. M20.

middlescence *n.* middle age M20.

middleveld /ˈmɪd(ə)lvɛlt, -f-/ *n.* L19. [Partial tr. Afk. *middelveld.*] (A region of) veld situated at an intermediate altitude; *spec.* the region in the Transvaal, South Africa, between 900 and 1200 m (3000 and 4000 ft) above sea level.

middleweight /ˈmɪd(ə)lweɪt/ *n.* & *a.* L19. [f. MIDDLE *a.* + WEIGHT *n.*] **A** *n.* A weight at which boxing etc. matches are made, intermediate between welterweight and heavyweight, in the amateur boxing scale now being between 71 and 75 kg, though differing for professionals, wrestlers, and weightlifters, and according to time and place; a boxer etc. of this weight. L19. **B** *adj.* (Of a boxer etc.) that is a middleweight; of or pertaining to middleweights. E20.

Phrases: **junior middleweight** (of) a weight in professional boxing of between 66.7 and 69.8 kg; (designating) a boxer of this weight. **light middleweight** (of) a weight in amateur boxing of between 67 and 71 kg; (designating) a boxer of this weight.

middling /ˈmɪdlɪŋ/ *n.* LME. [Prob. orig. f. MID *a.* + -LING[1]; later, the adj. used absol.] **1** †**a** A middle or intermediate part. LME–E17. **b** A mediocre or average person or thing. Freq. in *among the middlings*, of a mediocre class. Chiefly *dial.* L19. **2** A medium-sized pin. *rare.* M16. **3** In *pl.* Goods, esp. flour, cotton, or minerals, which have been sorted according to quality into the second of three grades. M18. **4** = MIDDLE *n.* 3b. *US.* L18.

middling /ˈmɪd(ə)lɪŋ/ *a.* & *adv.* Orig. *Sc.* ME. [Prob. f. MID *a.* + -LING[2].] **A** *adj.* **1** Of medium or moderate size; moderately large. Now (*colloq.*) passing into sense 4. ME. **2**†**a** Intermediate between two things; moderate. LME–M18. **b** Middle-aged. *rare.* E17. **3** Designating the second of three grades into which certain goods are sorted according to quality. M16. **4** Moderately good; mediocre, second-rate. M17. **5** Designating or pertaining to the middle class. Now *rare.* L17.

1 J. RATHBONE He was a man of middling height. 4 D. FRANCIS Etty gave him middling horses to ride. *fair-to-middling*: see FAIR *a.*

B *adv.* **1** Moderately, fairly. *colloq.* E18. **2** Fairly well (esp. in health). *colloq.* E19.

middlingly *adv.* M18. **middlingness** *n.* M19.

middy /ˈmɪdi/ *n.*[1] *colloq.* Also **middie.** E19. [f. MID *n.*[2] + -Y[6].] **1** A midshipman. E19. **2** More fully *middy blouse.* A kind of loose blouse with a sailor collar. E20.

middy /ˈmɪdi/ *n.*[2] *Austral. slang.* M20. [f. MID *n.*[1] + -Y[6].] A medium-sized measure of beer or other liquor; a glass holding this quantity.

midear /mɪˈdɪə/ *n.* E20. [f. MY *a.* + DEAR *n.*, repr. an informal or dial. pronunc.] As a form of address: my dear.

midfield /*as n.* & *adv.* mɪdˈfiːld, *as adj.* ˈmɪdfiːld/ *n.*, *a.*, & *adv.* L19. [f. MID *a.* + FIELD *n.*] **A** *n.* The middle of the field. Now *esp.* (*Sport*) the middle of the field of play (freq. in *in midfield*); the players positioned in midfield collectively. L19.

left midfield: see LEFT *a.* *right midfield*: see RIGHT *a.*

B *attrib.* or as *adj.* Of or pertaining to the midfield, positioned in midfield. L19.

C *adv.* In midfield. M20.

Western Mail (Cardiff) Mackay persisted in playing Todd midfield—against the player's wishes.

'midfielder *n.* a player positioned in midfield M20.

midge /mɪdʒ/ *n.* [OE *mycġ(e)*, corresp. to OS *muggia* (Du. *mug*), OHG *mucca* (G *Mücke*), ON *mý* (Sw. *mygg*, *mygga*), f. Gmc, rel. to L *musca* fly, Gk *muia*.] **1** A small insect resembling a gnat; *spec.* in *Entomol.*, any of numerous small slender dipterans of the family Chironomidae, common in swarms near water, or (more fully *biting midge*) of the family Ceratopogonidae. OE. **b** A small or insignificant person. Chiefly *Sc.* & *north.* M18. **2** *Hist.* A kind of small one-horse fly. Cf. FLY *n.*[2] 3b. M19.

1 *fungus-midge, gall-midge, pear midge*, etc.

midgern /ˈmɪdʒ(ə)n/ *n.* Long *obs.* exc. *dial.* Also **-erum** /-ərəm/. [OE *miċġern* = OS *midgarni*, OHG *mittigarni*, f. Gmc base of MID *a.* + base of ON *gǫrn* bowel, gut: see YARN.] **1** Orig., the fat surrounding the entrails of an animal. Later, leaf-fat. OE. **2** = MIDRIFF 1. *rare.* LME.

midget /ˈmɪdʒɪt/ *n.* & *a.* M19. [f. MIDGE + -ET[1].] **A** *n.* **1** An extremely small person. M19. **2** A very small thing; *spec.* a small vehicle. M20. **B** *attrib.* or as *adj.* Very small, small-scale, tiny. L19.

Midi /miːˈdiː, *foreign* midi/ *n.*[1] & *a.* L19. [Fr.] **A** *n.* *The* south of France. L19. **B** *attrib.* or as *adj.* Of or pertaining to the south of France. M20.

midi /ˈmɪdi/ *n.*[2] M20. [f. MIDI-.] A garment of medium length, *esp.* a skirt or coat reaching to mid-calf.

MIDI /ˈmɪdi/ *n.*[3] Also **midi.** L20. [Acronym, f. *m*usical *i*nstrument *d*igital *i*nterface.] An electronic device by means of which electronic musical instruments, synthesizers, and computers can be interconnected and used simultaneously. Usu. *attrib.*

midi- /ˈmɪdi/ *comb. form.* M20. [f. MID *a.*, MIDDLE *a.*, after MAXI-, MINI-.] Forming chiefly ns. denoting something of medium size or length, esp. a garment reaching to mid-calf, as *midi-coat, midiskirt*.

midibus a medium-sized bus, seating about 25 passengers.

midinette /mɪdɪˈnɛt, *foreign* midinɛt (*pl. same*)/ *n.* E20. [Fr., f. *midi* midday + *dînette* light dinner.] A French, esp. a Parisian, shop-girl; *esp.* a milliner's assistant.

Midland /ˈmɪdlənd/ *a.* & *n.* In gen. senses also **m-**. LME. [f. MID *a.* + LAND *n.*[1]] A *adj.* 1 Situated in the middle of a country; central and inland; remote from the sea. LME. b *spec.* Of or pertaining to the midland counties of England. M18. c Of or pertaining to the midland area of the US or the regional type of American English spoken there. L19. 2 Designating or pertaining to the Mediterranean Sea. Now *literary*. L16.

1b *midland* HAWTHORN.

B *n.* 1 The middle part of a country. LME. 2 *spec.* In *pl.* & †*sing.* *The* inland counties of central England. E17. 3 The central area of the US, esp. regarded as a dialectal area of American English. L19.

Midlander *n.* a native or inhabitant of the English Midlands or the Midland of the US E17.

mid-leg /mɪdˈlɛɡ/ *n.* & *adv.* L16. [f. MID *a.* + LEG *n.*] A *n.* 1 The middle of the leg. L16. 2 *Entomol.* Each of the intermediate or second pair of legs of an insect. E19. B *adv.* To the middle of the leg. E19.

mid-life /*as n.* mɪdˈlʌɪf, *as adj.* ˈmɪdlʌɪf/ *n.* & *a.* Orig. *US.* L19. [f. MID *a.* + LIFE *n.*] A *n.* Middle age; the period between youth and old age. L19.

B *attrib.* or as *adj.* Existing or occurring in mid-life; middle-aged. M20.

mid-life crisis a crisis of confidence or identity occurring in mid-life, characterized by the feeling that one is growing old or that life is passing one by.

midmost /ˈmɪdməʊst/ *a.*, *n.*, *adv.*, & *prep.* [OE *midmest* f. Gmc, f. base repr. by OHG *in mittamen* in the middle + -EST[1]. Later alt. by assoc. w. -MOST: cf. FOREMOST.] A *adj.* That is in the very middle, with regard to position, age, etc. OE. B *absol.* as *n.* The midmost part, the middle. Now *arch.* & *poet.* LME. C *adv.* In the middle or midst. *poet.* E18. D *prep.* In the middle or midst of. *arch.* & *poet.* L19.

midnight /ˈmɪdnʌɪt/ *n.* & *a.* OE. [f. MID *a.* + NIGHT *n.*] A *n.* 1 The middle of the night; 12 o'clock at night. OE. 2 (A period of) intense darkness; deep gloom. L16.

2 R. KIPLING This is the midnight—let no star Delude us—dawn is very far. M. L. KING A tragic breakdown of . . standards, and the midnight of moral degeneration deepens.

B *attrib.* or as *adj.* Of, occurring at, or pertaining to midnight. LME.

Special collocations & *phrases*: *burn the midnight oil*: see OIL *n.* **midnight blue** (of) a very dark shade of blue. **midnight feast**: held at midnight, esp. secretly by children. **midnight mass**: celebrated at or shortly before midnight, esp. on Christmas Eve. **midnight sun** the sun as seen in the polar regions at midnight during summer (*land of the midnight sun*: see LAND *n.*[1]).

midnightly *adv.* (*rare*) at midnight, every midnight M19.

midnoon /mɪdˈnuːn, ˈmɪdnuːn/ *n.* L16. [f. MID *a.* + NOON *n.*] Midday; noon.

fig.: LYTTON A man of your years, At the midnoon of manhood.

mid-off /mɪdˈɒf/ *n.* M19. [f. MID *a.* + OFF *a.*] *Cricket.* (The position occupied by) a fielder near the bowler on the off side.

mid-on /mɪdˈɒn/ *n.* L19. [f. MID *a.* + ON *a.*] *Cricket.* (The position occupied by) a fielder near the bowler on the on side.

mid-range /mɪdˈreɪn(d)ʒ/ *n.* M20. [f. MID *a.* + RANGE *n.*[1]] 1 *Statistics.* The arithmetic mean of the largest and the smallest values in a sample or other group. M20. 2 The middle part of the range of audible frequencies. Also, a loudspeaker designed to reproduce such frequencies in particular with fidelity. M20.

Midrash /ˈmɪdraʃ, -rʌʃ/ *n.* Pl. **Midrashim** /mɪˈdraʃɪm, mɪdraˈʃɪm; mɪdrʌˈʃɪm/. E17. [Heb. *midrāš* commentary, f. *dāraš* study, expound.] An ancient homiletic commentary on a text from the Hebrew scriptures, characterized by non-literal interpretation and legendary illustration. Also, the mode of exegesis characteristic of such a commentary. Cf. HAGGADAH 2.

Miˈdrashic *a.* of or pertaining to a Midrash or Midrashim L19.

midriff /ˈmɪdrɪf/ *n.* [OE *midrhif* (= OFris. *midref*), f. as MID *a.* + *hrif* belly (= OFris. *hrif*, *href*, OHG *href*), of unkn. origin.] 1 The diaphragm. OE. †b *transf.* A partition. M17–M18. 2 The area of the front of the body between the chest and the waist; the part of a garment which covers this area. M20.

1 **shake** or **tickle the midriff** cause laughter. 2 JAN MORRIS They seem to have gone badly to seed, having . . heavy haunches and protruding midriffs.

mids /mɪdz/ *n.* & *prep.* Long *obs.* exc. *Sc.* ME. [f. MID *n.*[1] + -S[3], in advb. phrs. after *in* etc.: cf. MIDST.] A *n.* 1 The middle, the midst. Chiefly in *in (the) mids (of)*. ME. †2 A means. E16–E18. 3 A mean between two extremes; a middle course, a compromise. M16. †B *prep.* In the middle of, among. LME–E17.

mid-season /*as n.* mɪdˈsiːz(ə)n, *as adj.* ˈmɪdsiːz(ə)n/ *n.* & *a.* E17. [f. MID *a.* + SEASON *n.*] A *n.* †1 The time in the middle of the day; noon. *rare* (Shakes.). Only in E17. 2 The middle of the season. L19. B *attrib.* or as *adj.* Of or pertaining to the middle of the season; occurring in the middle of the season. L19.

midship /ˈmɪdʃɪp/ *n.* L15. [f. MID *a.* + SHIP *n.*] The middle part of a ship or boat.

Comb.: **midship beam** the longest beam in a ship, lodged in the midship frame; **midship frame** the timber or frame in a ship having the greatest breadth.

midshipman /ˈmɪdʃɪpmən/ *n.* Earlier †**midships-**. Pl. **-men**. E17. [f. MIDSHIP or (earlier) MIDSHIPS + MAN *n.*] In the British navy, an officer ranking above a naval cadet and below a sub-lieutenant; in the US navy, a naval cadet.

¶Mod. form recorded f. L17.

midshipmanship *n.* the position or office of midshipman L18.

midshipmite /ˈmɪdʃɪpmʌɪt/ *n.* *Naut.* *slang.* M19. [Alt., after MITE *n.*[2]] = MIDSHIPMAN.

midships /ˈmɪdʃɪps/ *n.* & *adv.* E17. [Prob. of LG origin (Du. *midscheeps*, f. *mid* MID *a.* + *scheeps* genit. of *schip* SHIP *n.*): cf. G *Mittschiffs* As adv. aphet. f. AMIDSHIPS.] †A *n.* = MIDSHIP. E17–M18. B *adv.* = AMIDSHIPS. M19.

†**midshipsman** *n.* see MIDSHIPMAN.

midst /mɪdst/ *n.*, *prep.*, & *adv.* LME. [f. as MIDS + *t* as in *against*, *amongst*, etc.: cf. AMIDST.] A *n.* 1 The middle point or part; the middle *of*; the position of being involved in or surrounded by something, or a number of people etc. Now chiefly in *in the midst of*, *in our* (*your*, *their*, etc.) *midst*. LME. †2 = MIDS *n.* 3. *Sc.* E17–L18.

1 J. WAIN The tiny station was in the midst of its . . half-hour of alertness. A. JUDD Philip noticed Edward standing in the midst of a group. J. DISKI Men from the local village . . would drop in to join the . . strangers in their midst. P. LOMAS In the midst of war a general . . presents himself . . as being more certain.

B *prep.* In the middle of; among. *arch.* L16.

SHELLEY Midst others of less note, came one frail Form, A phantom among men.

C *adv.* 1 In the middle place. Only in *first, last, and midst* & vars. (after Milton). M17. 2 In the midst (*of*). *poet.* L17.

1 MILTON On Earth joyn all yee Creatures to extoll Him first, him last, him midst.

midstead /ˈmɪdstɛd/ *n.* Long *obs.* exc. *dial.* Also **mead-**, **mere-**, (earliest) †**mese-**, & other vars. M16. [f. MESE *n.*[1] + STEAD *n.*, alt. after MEAD *n.*[2], MERE *n.*[2], etc.] = MESSUAGE.

midstream /*as n.* & *adv.* mɪdˈstriːm, *as adj.* ˈmɪdstriːm/ *n.*, *a.*, & *adv.* ME. [f. MID *a.* + STREAM *n.*] A *n.* The middle of a stream. ME.

change or *swap horses in midstream*: see HORSE *n.*

B *attrib.* or as *adj.* 1 Of or pertaining to the middle of a stream; situated or occurring in the middle of a stream. ME. 2 *Med.* Designating urine other than that first or last passed in an act of urinating. M20.

C *adv.* In the middle of a stream. L19.

midsummer /*as n.* mɪdˈsʌmə, *as adj.* ˈmɪdsʌmə/ *n.* & *a.* OE. [f. MID *a.* + SUMMER *n.*[1]] A *n.* The middle of summer; *spec.* the period about the summer solstice. OE. B *attrib.* or as *adj.* Of or pertaining to midsummer; occurring in midsummer. ME.

Special collocations & *comb.*: **Midsummer** or **Midsummer's Day** 24 June, one of the recognized quarter days in England and Wales. **midsummer madness** extreme folly or madness. *Midsummer's Day*: see *Midsummer Day* above.

midsummery *a.* of, pertaining to, or characteristic of midsummer M19.

midward /ˈmɪdwəd/ *a.*, *n.*, & *prep.* Long *arch.* *rare.* OE. [f. MID *a.* + -WARD.] A *adj.* †1 The middle of. OE–ME. 2 Occupying the middle. ME. †B *n.* The middle (part). OE–M16. C *prep.* In the middle of. ME.

midwater /mɪdˈwɔːtə/ *n.* & *a.* M17. [f. MID *a.* + WATER *n.*] A *n.* Water neither near the surface nor near the bottom. M17. B *attrib.* or as *adj.* Situated or occurring in midwater. M19.

midway /ˈmɪdweɪ, mɪdˈweɪ/ *n.*, *a.*, *adv.*, & *prep.* OE. [f. MID *a.* + WAY *n.*] A *n.* †1 The middle of the way or distance, the halfway point. OE–L18. 2 A middle course, a medium. Now *rare* or *obs.* LME. 3 A central avenue at an exhibition, fair, etc., along which the chief exhibits or amusements are placed. Also (*colloq.*), any cheap place of amusement. *N. Amer.* L19. B *adj.* 1 Situated in the middle of the way, occupying the middle. Chiefly *poet.* OE. †2 Medium, moderate. L16–L17. C *adv.* In the middle of the way or distance; halfway. Also (*US*) foll. by *of*. ME. D *prep.* In the middle of, halfway down, along, etc. *rare.* L18.

midwife /ˈmɪdwʌɪf/ *n.* Pl. **-wives** /-wʌɪvz/. ME. [Prob. f. MID *prep.*[1] + WIFE *n.*] 1 A person, esp. a woman, with experience or training in assisting women in labour and childbirth, now *spec.* a nurse holding additional qualifications for this task. ME. 2 *fig.* A person who or thing which helps to bring something into being. L16.

Comb.: **midwife toad** a European toad, *Alytes obstetricans*, the male of which carries the eggs on his hind legs until the young hatch.

midwifely *a.* (*rare*) of, pertaining to, or characteristic of a midwife E17.

midwife /ˈmɪdwʌɪf/ *v.* Also **-wive** /-wʌɪv/. LME. [f. the n.] 1 *v.i.* Act as a midwife. Chiefly as *midwifing* vbl n. *rare.* LME. 2 *v.t.* Act as midwife at the birth of. Now *rare.* M17. 3 *v.t.* *fig.* Help to bring into being. M17.

3 *New Statesman* John Gau . . midwived the deal that brought the concert to the BBC. I. WATSON A valuable contribution to midwifing a truly original idea.

midwifery /ˈmɪdwɪfri, mɪdˈwɪf(ə)ri/ *n.* L15. [f. prec. + -ERY.] The work or profession of a midwife; the branch of medicine that deals with this; obstetrics.

midwinter /*as n.* mɪdˈwɪntə, *as attrib. adj.* ˈmɪdwɪntə/ *n.* & *a.* OE. [f. MID *a.* + WINTER *n.*] A *n.* The middle of winter; *spec.* the period about the winter solstice. OE. B *attrib.* or as *adj.* 1 Of or pertaining to midwinter; occurring in midwinter. ME. 2 Cold as midwinter. *poet.* L19.

midwive *v.* var. of MIDWIFE *v.*

midwives *n.* pl. of MIDWIFE *n.*

Miehle /ˈmiːlə/ *n.* L19. [f. Robert *Miehle* (d. 1932), US printer.] (Proprietary name for) a flat-bed cylinder printing-press.

mielie *n.* var. of MEALIE.

mien /miːn/ *n.*[1] *literary.* E16. [Prob. aphet. f. DEMEAN *n.*, later assim. to Fr. *mine* look, aspect.] 1 The look or bearing of a person, as showing character, mood, etc. E16. 2 *make (a) mien*, pretend *to do*, make a show *of doing*. E18.

1 A. POWELL Tall, stately . . she possessed a very aristocratic mien.

mien /miːn/ *n.*[2] M20. [Chin. *mian* wheat flour. Cf. earlier CHOW MEIN.] Wheat flour noodles.

Miesian /ˈmiːzɪən/ *a.* & *n.* M20. [f. *Mies* (see below) + -IAN.] A *adj.* Of, pertaining to, or characteristic of the style of the German-American architect Ludwig Mies van der Rohe (1886–1969). M20. B *n.* A devotee or follower of this style. M20.

mietjie /ˈmiːki, -tʃi/ *n.* *S. Afr.* M19. [Afk., of imit. origin.] = KLAAS'S CUCKOO.

miff /mɪf/ *n.* & *v.* *colloq.* E17. [Perh. imit.: cf. early mod.G *muff* int. & n., expr. disgust.] A *n.* A fit of pique, a huff; a petty quarrel, a tiff. E17.

B *v.* 1 *v.i.* a Take offence. Foll. by *at*, *with*. *rare.* M18. b Foll. by *off*: (of a plant) deteriorate, fade. L19. 2 *v.t.* Put out of humour; offend, irritate. Chiefly as *miffed* ppl a. E19.

2 J. CARROLL They were miffed because they couldn't go to the match. *Listener* John Gielgud . . was

considerably miffed by having a horse fall on him during the battle scenes.

miffish *a.* = MIFFY M20.

miffy /ˈmɪfi/ *a. colloq.* L17. [f. prec. + -Y[1].] 1 Easily offended or irritated. L17. 2 Of a plant: delicate, not robust. M19.

mig /mɪɡ/ *n.*[1] Long *obs.* exc. *dial.* [OE *miċġe* (fem.), *migga* (masc.), rel. to ON *míga*, late L *mingere* urinate.] Urine; the drainings from manure.

MiG /mɪɡ/ *n.*[2] & *a.* M20. [Russ. *MIG*, f. A. I. *Mikoyan* + *i* and + M. I. *Gurevich*, Russ. aircraft designers.] (Designating) a type of Russian fighter aircraft.

might /mʌɪt/ *n.*[1] [OE *miht*, non-WS *mæht* = OFris. *mecht*, *macht*, OS, OHG *maht* (G *Macht*), Goth. *mahts*, f. Gmc, f. base also of MAY *v.*[1]: see -T[1].] 1 Ability, (effective) power (*to do*); efficacy. *obs.* exc. *poet.* OE. †b In *pl.* The active powers of feeling, thinking, etc. OE–L16. 2 Bodily strength (great or small). Now chiefly *rhet.* OE. 3 Great strength, imposing power; mightiness. Now chiefly *rhet.* OE. b Superior force or power to enforce one's will. Usu. contrasted w. *right*. ME. †4 = PRINCIPALITY 5. OE–M17. 5 A considerable quantity or amount *of*. *dial.* M19.

1 SHAKES. *Tr. & Cr.* To be wise and love Exceeds man's might. SHELLEY Liquors . . whose healthful might Could medicine the sick soul to happy sleep. 2 A. P. HERBERT She had lifted three paddles . . heaving with all her small might. 3 WORDSWORTH The might Of the whole world's good wishes with him goes. S. QUINN: Wilhelm III ascended to power with the determination to consolidate Prussian might. b B. JOWETT They went to war, preferring might to right.

Phrases: **with all one's might, with might and main** with all one's strength, to the utmost of one's ability.

mightful *a.* (*arch.*) mighty, powerful ME. **mightless** *a.* (*arch.*) powerless, impotent ME. †**mightly** *adv.* = MIGHTILY OE–M18.

might /mʌɪt/ *n.*[2] E20. [f. *might* pa. of MAY *v.*[1]] An instance of what is expressed by the auxiliary verb *might*; a possibility.

might *v.* see MAY *v.*[1]

might-be /ˈmʌɪtbi/ *n.* & *a.* M17. [f. *might* pa. of MAY *v.*[1] + BE.] A *n.* What might be; a (remote) possibility. M17. B *adj.* That might be; (remotely) possible. M20.

mightest *v.* see MAY *v.*[1]

might-have-been /ˈmʌɪt(h)əvbiːn/ *n.* M19. [f. *might* pa. of MAY *v.*[1] + HAVE *v.* + *been* pa. pple of BE.] What might have been; a thing or event which might have occurred; a person who might have been greater or more eminent.

E. H. GOMBRICH The historian has little use for questions of might-have-been. *Listener* It was instructive to have the opportunity of hearing this gifted might-have-been.

mightily /ˈmʌɪtɪli/ *adv.* OE. [f. MIGHTY *a.* + -LY[2].] 1 In a mighty manner; powerfully, strongly; with great effort. OE. 2 To a high degree; greatly, very much. Now *colloq.* LME.

1 AV *Jonah* 3:8 Let man and beast . . cry mightily vnto God. D. STUART Her mother and father had worked mightily, with the pick and shovel. J. WINTERSON The Lord is working mightily. 2 W. OWEN Graves was mightily impressed.

mightiness /ˈmʌɪtɪnɪs/ *n.* ME. [f. MIGHTY *a.* + -NESS.] 1 The state or condition of being mighty, powerfulness, great strength. ME. 2 With possess. adj. (as *your* etc. *mightiness*): a title of respect given to a personage of exalted rank. Now only in *High Mightiness*, (*a*) *Hist.* an honorific designation of a member of the States General of the Netherlands; (*b*) *iron.* a form of address or mode of reference to a person considered to be high and mighty. L16.

mightn't *v.* see MAY *v.*[1]

mighty /ˈmʌɪti/ *a.* & *adv.* [OE *mihtiġ* = OFris. *mechtig*, *machtig*, OS *mahtig*, OHG *mahtīg* (G *mächtig*), f. Gmc base of MIGHT *n.*[1]: see -Y[1].] A *adj.* 1 Possessing might or power; powerful, potent, strong. Freq. *rhet.*, possessing a transcendent or imposing degree of power. OE. 2 Huge, massive, bulky. ME. 3a Considerable; very great in amount, extent, or degree. Now *colloq.* L16. b *attrib.* Thoroughgoing; being or having the quality of the n. indicated to a high degree. L17.

1 DRYDEN Mighty Caesar, thund'ring from afar, Seeks on Euphrates' Banks the Spoils of War. W. COWPER On every mind some mighty spell she cast. WORDSWORTH And hear the mighty waters rolling evermore. LONGFELLOW The smith, a mighty man is he, With large and sinewy hands. M. FOOT So mighty a figure as Lloyd George, who had taken command of No. 10 Downing Street in war and peace. 2 H. JAMES Flying buttresses thrown forth like an array of mighty oars. 3 *Beano* Don't disturb me . . I've a mighty lot of studying to do. b G. BORROW He is a mighty liberal.

Phrases: *high and mighty*: see HIGH *a.*, *adv.* & *n.* **mighty (me)!** *Sc.* & *dial.* expr. surprise or mild exasperation.

B *n. collect. pl. The* class of mighty people. ME. AV *2 Sam.* 1:19 How are the mightie fallen!

C *adv.* Very; greatly, extremely. Now *colloq.* ME.

P. MANN I've got a mighty important announcement to make.

migma /ˈmɪɡmə/ *n.* M20. [Gk = mixture.] *Geol.* (A) magma containing solid material.

migmatite /ˈmɪɡmətʌɪt/ *n.* E20. [f. Gk *migmat-*, MIGMA: see -ITE[1].] *Geol.* A rock composed of two intermingled but distinguishable components, usu. a granitic rock within a metamorphic host rock.

migˈmatic *a.* composed of migmatite E20. **migmatitic** /-ˈtɪtɪk/ *a.* = MIGMATIC M20. **migmatiˈzation** *n.* the process by which a migmatite is formed M20. **migmatized** *a.* converted into a migmatite M20.

mignardise /ˈmiɲardiːz (*pl. same*), ˈmɪnjədʌɪz/ *n.* E17. [Fr., f. *mignard* delicate, dainty, rel. to next: see -ISE[1].] 1 Affected delicacy of behaviour or appearance; an affectation. E17. 2 A variety of crochet formed by working fine ribbon or braid into the design. L19.

mignon /ˈmiːnjɒn, *foreign* miɲɔ̃ (*pl. same*)/ *a.* & *n.* Fem. **-onne** /-ɒn, *foreign* -ɔn/. M16. [Fr.: see MINION *n.*[1] & *a.*] A *adj.* Delicately formed; prettily small or delicate. M16.

filet mignon: see FILET *n.*[1] 1.

B *n.* A pretty child or young person. E19.

mignonette /mɪnjəˈnɛt/ *n.* E18. [Fr. *mignonnette* dim. of MIGNON: see -ETTE.] 1 A kind of light fine narrow pillow-lace. Also *mignonette lace*. E18. 2 Any of several plants of the genus *Reseda* (family Resedaceae), with small greenish or whitish flowers in spikelike racemes; spec. *R. odorata*, cultivated for its fragrant flowers. Also (more fully *wild mignonette*), a related plant of chalky ground, *R. lutea*. L18. b A colour resembling that of the flowers of the mignonette; greyish green or greenish white. L19. c A perfume derived from or resembling that of the flowers of the mignonette. L19.

mignonne *a.* & *n.* see MIGNON.

migod /mɪˈɡɒd/ *int.* M20. [f. MY *a.* + GOD *n.*, repr. an informal pronunc.] Expr. astonishment or shock, outrage, pain, or anger: my God!

migraine /ˈmiːɡreɪn, ˈmʌɪ-/ *n.* See also MEGRIM *n.*[1] LME. [(O)Fr. f. late L *hemicrania* f. Gk *hēmikrania*, f. *hēmi-* half, HEMI- + *kranion* skull.] A recurrent throbbing headache, usu. affecting one side of the head, often accompanied by nausea or disturbed vision; the illness or condition characterized by such headaches.

¶*Megrim* was the commoner form 16–19.

migraineur /miːɡreɪˈnəː/ *n.* a person subject to attacks of migraine L20. **migrainous** *a.* pertaining to or of the nature of migraine; subject to attacks of migraine: L19.

migrant /ˈmʌɪɡr(ə)nt/ *a.* & *n.* L17. [L *migrant-* pres. ppl stem of *migrare* MIGRATE: see -ANT[1].] A *adj.* That migrates. L17. B *n.* 1 A person who or animal which migrates. M18. b An immigrant; a new settler in Australia. *Austral.* E20. 2 *Bot.* A plant whose distribution has changed or extended. E20.

migrate /mʌɪˈɡreɪt, ˈmʌɪɡreɪt/ *v.i.* E17. [L *migrat-* pa. ppl stem of *migrare*: see -ATE[3].] 1 Move from one place to another. Now *rare* in *gen.* sense. E17. 2 *Biol.* Of an animal, flock, etc.: go from one region or habitat to another; *esp.* pass regularly between habitats according to the seasons, or as part of the life cycle. E18. b Of a plant: undergo a change in or extension of its distribution. L19. 3 Of a person, a people, etc.: move from one country or place of residence to settle in another. L18. 4 Chiefly *Biol.* & *Chem.* Of a cell, atom, molecule, etc.: move in a non-random manner from one position or region to another or in a particular direction. L19.

2 A. C. CLARKE Whales migrate north from the polar feeding grounds to have their calves in the tropics. 3 B. C. BRODIE The agricultural labourer is tempted . . to migrate to a manufacturing town. 4 H. DOWNEY The monocytes migrate into inflamed tissues. J. C. WARE Ions . . migrate independently in a solution and at different rates.

migrative /ˈmʌɪɡrətɪv/ *a.* migratory M19. **migrator** *n.* a person who migrates; an animal, esp. a bird, which migrates: L18.

migration /mʌɪˈɡreɪʃ(ə)n/ *n.* E17. [L *migratio(n-)*, f. as prec.: see -ATION.] 1 The action or an act of moving from one place to another. Now *rare* in *gen.* sense. E17. 2 The migrating of a person, a people, etc., from one country or place of residence to settle in another; an instance of this. M17. 3 The action, phenomenon, or an instance of animals, birds, etc., migrating. M17. b *Bot.* Change in or extension of the distribution of a plant. E20. 4 Chiefly *Biol.* & *Chem.* The non-random movement from one place to another of a cell, atom, molecule, etc. L19.

migrational *a.* L19.

migratory /ˈmʌɪɡrət(ə)ri, mʌɪˈɡreɪt(ə)ri/ *a.* E18. [f. MIGRATE + -ORY[2].] 1 Characterized by or given to (esp. periodical or seasonal) migration. E18. 2 Of or pertaining to migration. M18.

1 J. A. HAMMERTON A migratory fish which comes to the islands in autumn. W. LIPPMANN The inevitable and desirable human resistance to a migratory existence. **migratory locust** any of various locusts which periodically increase suddenly in numbers, undergo mass migrations, and devastate vegetation; spec. *Locusta migratoria*, widespread in the Old World tropics. 2 *Bird Watching* The staggering migratory feats of the Arctic tern.

migratorial /mʌɪɡrəˈtɔːrɪəl/ *a.* (*rare*) migratory M19.

mihrab /ˈmiːrɑːb/ *n.* E19. [Arab. *miḥrāb*.] 1 A niche, chamber, or slab in a mosque, indicating the direction of Mecca. E19. 2 A niche motif on an oriental prayer rug, resembling the shape of a mihrab in a mosque. E20.

mijnheer *n.* var. of MYNHEER.

Mikado /mɪˈkɑːdəʊ/ *n.* Pl. **-os**. E18. [Jap., f. *mi* august + *kado* gate: cf. *the Sublime* PORTE.] 1 *Hist.* The emperor of Japan. E18. 2 In full *Mikado pheasant*. A rare pheasant of the mountains of Taiwan, *Syrmaticus mikado*, having deep purple plumage with white markings. E20.

mikan /ˈmɪkɑːn/ *n.* M20. [Jap.] In Japan: a satsuma.

mike /mʌɪk/ *n.*[1] & *v.*[1] *slang.* E19. [Origin unkn.] A *n.* A rest; a period of idleness; an act of shirking. E19.

do or **have a mike** be idle, escape from or evade work.

B *v.i.* Shirk work; idle away one's time; go *off* to avoid a task. M19.

mike /mʌɪk/ *n.*[2] In senses 1, 2 **M-**. L19. [Pet-form of male forename *Michael*: cf. MICK *n.*[1], MICKY *n.*[1] In sense 3 substitution for MICKEY *n.*[1] interpreted as the name *Mick(e)y*.] 1 (A name for) an Irishman. *rare*. L19. 2 *for the love of Mike!*: expr. exasperation or surprise. *colloq.* E20. 3 *take the mike* (*out of*) = *take the mickey* (*out of*) s.v. MICKEY *n.*[1] *slang*. M20.

mike /mʌɪk/ *n.*[3] & *v.*[2] *colloq.* E20. [Abbrev.] A *n.* A microphone. E20. B *v.t.* Place a microphone in (a place) or close to (a person, instrument, or amplifier). Also foll. by *up*. M20.

mike /mʌɪk/ *n.*[4] *slang.* L20. [Abbrev.] A microgram, *spec.* of lysergic acid diethylamide (LSD).

Mikimoto pearl /mɪkɪˈməʊtəʊ ˈpəːl/ *n. phr.* M20. [See below.] A pearl cultured by means of a technique perfected by the Japanese pearl-farmer Kokichi Mikimoto (1858–1954).

mikva /ˈmɪkvə/ *n.* Also **-vah**, **-veh**. M19. [Yiddish *mikve* f. Heb. *miqweh* lit. 'collection, mass, esp. of water'.] A bath in which certain

Jewish ritual purifications are performed; the action of taking such a bath.

mil /mɪl/ *n.* In branch I also (earlier) **mille**. L17. [In branch I f. L *mille* thousand; in branch II f. as MILL *n.*[2]; in branch III abbrev. (cf. MILL *n.*[3]).] **I 1** See PER MIL. L17. **II 2a** A proposed coin of the value of one thousandth of a pound sterling. M19. **b** In Cyprus and Hong Kong (and formerly in Palestine and Egypt), a coin with a value equivalent to one thousandth of the basic monetary unit. E20. **3** A unit of length equal to one thousandth of an inch, used esp. in measuring the diameter of wire. L19 **4** Either of two units of angular measure: (*a*) 1/1600 of a right angle (3.375 minutes of arc); (*b*) 1/1000 of a radian (approx. 3.438 minutes of arc). E20. **III 5** Chiefly *Pharm.* = MILLILITRE. E20. **6** = MILLIMETRE. L20.

milady /mɪˈleɪdi/ *n.* L18. [Fr., f. Eng. *my lady*: cf. MILORD.] (A form of address used in speaking to) an English noblewoman or great lady.

milage *n.* var. of MILEAGE.

Milan /mɪˈlan/ *a.* LME. [It. *Milano*.] Designating any of various products, esp. textile fabrics and steel-work, made or originating in Milan, the chief city of Lombardy in N. Italy; Milanese.

Milanese /mɪləˈniːz/ *n.* & *a.* L15. [f. as prec. + -ESE.] **A** *n.* Pl. same. **1** A native or inhabitant of the Italian city of Milan. L15. **2** The dialect of Italian spoken in Milan. M17. **3** *The* territory of the old duchy of Milan. *obs.* exc. *Hist.* E18. **4** = *Milanese silk* below. E20.

B *adj.* Of or pertaining to Milan, its inhabitants, or its dialect. E17.

Milanese silk a fine warp-knit fabric with interlocking stitches, made from silk or (now) rayon etc.

milch /mɪltʃ/ *a.* & *v.* ME. [Repr. 2nd elem. of OE *þrimilċe* May (when cows could be milked thrice daily), f. Gmc base of MILK *n.*] **A** *adj.* **1** Of a mammal: giving or kept for milk. ME. **†2** Of a woman, esp. a wet-nurse: lactating. ME–E18. **†3** Milky. LME–E17.

1 milch cow (*a*) a cow giving or kept for milk; (*b*) *fig.* (*colloq.*) a ready source of regular income or profit; *spec.* a person from whom money is easily drawn. **3** *fig.*: SHAKES. *Haml.* The instant burst of clamour that she made . . Would have made milch the burning eyes of heaven.

B *v.t.* Milk. L16.

milcher *n.* an animal that yields milk E19.

mild /mʌɪld/ *a.*, *adv.*, & *n.* [OE *milde* = OFris. *milde*, OS *mildi*, OHG *milti* (Du., G *mild*), ON *mildr*, Goth. *-mildeis*, *milds*, f. Gmc, f. IE base also of L *mollis*, Gk *malakos* soft.] **A** *adj.* **1 a** Of a person having power, as a ruler: gracious, merciful, kind, indulgent; not harsh or severe. *arch.* OE. **b** Of a rule, regime, punishment, etc.: not (so) strict or severe. L16. **2** Of a person: gentle in character, manners, behaviour, etc.; not easily provoked. Of behaviour, language, etc.: conciliatory, inoffensive. OE. **b** Of an animal: tame, gentle; not wild or fierce. Now *rare* or *obs.* ME. **c** Of physical exercise, a fight, etc.: not (very) violent. Of amusement or recreation: moderate, gentle, not boisterous. M19. **d** Of a person or action: feeble; lacking in energy, vigour, etc. L19. **3** Of weather, etc.: not rough or stormy, not sharp or severe; calm, fine; moderately warm. Of a climate: temperate. LME. **4 a** Of a medicine: operating gently; not producing violent effects. Of food, tobacco, etc.: not sharp, strong, or too hot in taste; not pungent. LME. **b** Of (an attack of) an illness: not severe or acute. M18. **5** Of light, or a luminous body: shining softly. M17. **6** Of soil, wood, etc.: soft, easy to work. *dial.* M19.

1a J. ROGERS It teaches us . . to adore him as a mild and merciful Being. J. A. HERAUD This mild prince . . is deservedly popular. **b** ADAM SMITH The penalties imposed by this milder statute. H. ADAMS The rule of the Benedictines was always mild. **2** R. ELLMANN Though mild in disposition, John Wilde was strenuous in argument. E. WILSON The stories of Turgenev, which seem mild enough . . today. **c** A. BAIN There should also be social amusements of a mild character. C. ACHEBE A mild scuffle began right in front of me.

Special collocations & comb.: **mild beer**: not strongly flavoured with hops (opp. *bitter*). **mild-hearted** *a.* tender-hearted, gentle, merciful. **mild steel**: containing only a small percentage of carbon, of great strength and toughness, but not readily tempered or hardened.

B *adv.* Mildly. *poet.* OE.

C. WESLEY Mild he lays his Glory by, Born—that Man no more may die.

C *n.* (A drink of) mild beer. L19.

mildish *a.* tending to mildness, fairly mild E19. **mildness** *n.* ME.

milden /ˈmʌɪld(ə)n/ *v.* E17. [f. prec. + -EN[5].] **1** *v.t.* Make mild or milder. E17. **2** *v.i.* Become mild or milder. M19.

mildew /ˈmɪldjuː/ *n.* & *v.* [OE *mildēaw*, *meledēaw* = OS *milidou* (Du. *meeldauw*), OHG *militou* (G, w. assim. to *Mehl* MEAL *n.*[1], *Mehltau*), f. Gmc, f. base also of L *mel*, Gk *meli* honey, + base of DEW *n.*] **A** *n.* **†1** = HONEYDEW 1, 2. OE–M17. **2** A destructive growth on plants consisting of minute fungi and usu. appearing as a thin whitish coating; a similar growth on paper, leather, wood, etc., when exposed to damp. Also, an attack or form of the disease. ME.

2 POWDERY *mildew*.

B *v.* **1** *v.t.* Taint with mildew. M16. **2** *v.i.* Become tainted with mildew. M17.

mildewy *a.* resembling, of the nature of, or tainted with mildew M19.

mildly /ˈmʌɪldli/ *adv.* OE. [f. MILD *a.* + -LY[2].] In a mild manner. Also (modifying an adj.), somewhat, slightly.

Spectator A mildly mixed-up little boy. **to put it mildly** without any exaggeration (freq. *iron.*, implying understatement).

milds /mʌɪldz/ *n.* Now *Sc.* & *north.* Also **miles** /mʌɪlz/. [OE *melde* weak fem., cogn. w. OHG *melda*, *melde* (mod.G *Melde*), also with different ablaut grades *malta*, *molto*, MLG, Du. *melde*.] Any of several weeds of the goosefoot family; *esp.* fat-hen, *Chenopodium album*.

mile /mʌɪl/ *n.* [OE *mīl* (fem.) = MDu. *mīle* (Du. *mijl*), OHG *mīl(l)a* (G *Meile*), f. WGmc, f. L *mil(l)ia* pl. of *mil(l)e* thousand.] **1** Orig., the Roman unit of distance of 1,000 paces, equal to approx. 1,618 yards; also, a unit of distance (varying widely according to period and locality) derived from this. Now (also *statute mile*), a standard unit of length and distance equal to 1,760 yards (approx. 1.609 kilometres). OE. **b** *loosely* & *hyperbol.* A great distance, amount, or interval. Freq. in *pl.* (advb.), by a great distance, amount, or interval. L16. **c** A race over a distance of one mile. E20. **†2** The time it might take to travel a mile. ME–L16.

1b E. M. DELAFIELD I should have thought he'd be miles better than no one. J. PORTER She *was* on the scrounge. . . You could spot it a mile off. *Independent* People will run a mile when faced with an . . American wanting to talk.

Phrases: GEOGRAPHICAL *mile*. *measured mile*: see MEASURED 2. NAUTICAL *mile*. *not a hundred miles from*: see HUNDRED *a.* *Roman mile*: see ROMAN *a.* *run a mile*: see RUN *v.* **stick out a mile** be extremely obvious.

Comb.: **milecastle** any of a series of forts erected by the Romans at intervals along a military wall, esp. Hadrian's Wall across northern England; **mile-eater** *colloq.* a fast driver or traveller; **mile-mark** a milestone or other object placed to indicate the distance of a mile from a given point; **milepost** a post or stone serving as a mile-mark.

mileage /ˈmʌɪlɪdʒ/ *n.* Also **milage**. M18. [f. prec. + -AGE.] **1 a** A travel allowance at a fixed rate per mile. M18. **b** A rate per mile charged for the use of railway vehicles carrying goods or passengers over another company's line. M19. **2 a** A distance in miles; *spec.* (*a*) the number of miles of road made, used, or travelled; (*b*) the number of miles a vehicle can travel per litre, gallon, etc., of fuel. M19. **b** *fig.* Benefit, profit, advantage; scope for investigation. M19.

1a *Guardian* The newspaper . . declined to pay mileage for the use of cars on the firm's business. **2a** *Time* Taxes . . on the purchase of cars with poor gas mileage. *Lancaster Guardian* Austin Montego . . has 34,097 mileage. **b** B. T. BRADFORD He's such an opportunist he'll find a way to get mileage out of this. *Notes & Queries* There is still plenty of mileage in Hassett's approach, as her book proves.

miler /ˈmʌɪlə/ *n.* E19. [f. MILE *n.* + -ER[1].] **1** As 2nd elem. of comb.: a walk or journey of a specified number of miles. *colloq.* E19. **2** An athlete or horse specializing or competing in races over a distance of one mile. L19.

miles *n.* var. of MILDS.

miles gloriosus /ˌmiːleɪz glɔːrɪˈəʊsəs, ˌmʌɪliːz/ *n.* *literary.* Pl. ***milites gloriosi*** /ˌmiːlɪteɪz glɔːrɪˈəʊsiː, ˌmʌɪlɪtiːz glɔːrɪˈəʊsʌɪ/. E20. [The title of a Latin comedy by Plautus (*c*250–184 BC).] A boastful soldier.

Milesian /mʌɪˈliːʃɪən, -ʃ(ə)n, mɪ-/ *n.*[1] & *a.*[1] M16. [f. L *Milesius* f. Gk *Milēsios*: see -AN.] **A** *n.* A native or inhabitant of ancient Miletus, a city in Asia Minor. M16. **B** *adj.* Of or pertaining to Miletus or its inhabitants. E17.

Milesian /mʌɪˈliːʃɪən, -ʃ(ə)n, mɪ-/ *a.*[2] & *n.*[2] L16. [f. *Milesius* (see below) + -AN.] **A** *adj.* Of or pertaining to Milesius, a mythical Spanish king whose sons were said to have conquered the ancient kingdom of Ireland about 1300 BC, or to his people; Irish. L16. **B** *n.* A member of the people descended from the companions of Milesius; an Irish person. L17.

milestone /ˈmʌɪlstəʊn/ *n.* & *v.* M18. [f. MILE *n.* + STONE *n.*] **A** *n.* A pillar set up by a road to mark a distance in miles; *fig.* an event marking a significant stage in a life, history, etc. M18.

Art & Artists This exhibition represents a milestone in a young artist's career.

B *v.t.* Mark (stages etc.) as if by milestones. E20.

milfoil /ˈmɪlfɔɪl/ *n.* ME. [OFr. *milfoil* (mod. MILLEFEUILLE) f. L *milefolium*, *millef-*, f. L *mile*, *mille* a thousand + *folium* leaf (see FOIL *n.*[1]), after Gk *muriophullon* (f. *murios* myriad + *phullon* leaf).] **1** Any of various plants of the genus *Achillea*, of the composite family, with feathery finely divided leaves; *esp.* yarrow, *A. millefolium*. ME. **2** In full *water milfoil*. Any of various aquatic plants constituting the genus *Myriophyllum* (family Haloragaceae), which have whorled finely pinnate leaves and spikes of inconspicuous flowers. L16.

milia *n.* pl. of MILIUM *n.*[1]

miliaceous /mɪlɪˈeɪʃəs/ *a.* *rare.* L17. [f. MILIUM *n.*[1] + -ACEOUS.] *Med.* Miliary.

†miliad *n.* *rare.* E17–M18. [Irreg. f. L *milia* pl. of *mille* thousand: see -AD[1].] A group of one thousand.

miliaria /mɪlɪˈɛːrɪə/ *n.* E19. [mod.L, f. as MILIARY *a.*[2]] *Med.* A rash accompanying profuse sweating; *esp.* = PRICKLY *heat*.

miliary *n.* & *a.*[1] var. of MILLIARY.

miliary /ˈmɪlɪəri/ *a.*[2] L17. [L *miliarius* pertaining to millet, f. MILIUM millet: see -ARY[1].] **1** Resembling a millet-seed, or an aggregation of millet-seeds; granular. L17. **2** *Med.* Characterized by spots or lesions resembling millet-seeds; *miliary tuberculosis*, acute generalized tuberculosis. M18.

Milice /milis/ *n.* Also **m-**. M17. [Fr. f. L *militia* warfare.] **†1** Military service. *rare.* Only in M17. **2** In France: a militia, an army; *spec.* (*Hist.*) a force employed by the Vichy government of 1940–44 to repress internal dissent. L17.

¶Rare bef. M20.

milicien /milisjɛ̃ (*pl. same*)/ *n.* a member of the Milice M20.

miliciano /miliˈθjano/ *n.* Pl. **-os** /-ɒs/. Fem. **-na** /-na/. M20. [Sp.] *Hist.* A member of the irregular Republican force formed during the Spanish Civil War of 1936–9.

milieu /ˈmiːljəː, mɪˈljəː, *foreign* miljø/ *n.* Pl. **-ieus, -ieux** /-əːz, *foreign* -ø/. M19. [Fr., f. *mi* (f. L *medius* MID *a.*) + LIEU place.] **1** An environment; (esp. social) surroundings. M19. **2** *transf.* A group of people with a shared (cultural) outlook; a social class or set. M20. **b** (Also **M-**.) In France: (a group or organization belonging to) the criminal underworld. L20.

1 DYLAN THOMAS Will an artistic milieu make his writing any better. **2** P. BOWLES The American milieu in Tangier was peculiarly hermetic. **b** *Times* They have to keep an eye on . . the serious underworld, the *milieu*.

Comb.: **milieu therapy** *Psychol.* a form of group psychotherapy which relies on the social environment evolved by the staff and patients in the treatment unit.

miling /ˈmʌɪlɪŋ/ *n.* E20. [f. MILE *n.* + -ING[1].] The action of running a mile (as an athletic event).

milioline /ˈmɪlɪəlʌɪn/ *a.* & *n.* L19. [f. mod.L *Miliola* (see below), dim. of L *milium* millet: see -INE[1].] *Zool.* & *Palaeont.* A *adj.* Of, pertaining to, or designating the foraminiferan genus *Miliola* or to the suborder Miliolina. L19. B *n.* A milioline foraminifer. L19.

miliolite /ˈmɪlɪəlʌɪt/ *n.* M19. [f. as prec. + -ITE[1].] *Geol.* & *Palaeont.* A fossil milioline foraminifer; (in full *miliolite limestone*) a fine-grained limestone consisting largely of these.

militaire /militɛːr/ *n.* Pl. pronounced same. M18. [Fr.] In France, a soldier.

militancy /ˈmɪlɪt(ə)nsi/ *n.* M17. [f. next: see -ENCY.] The condition or fact of being militant, esp. in pursuing a political or social end.

C. PANKHURST Those of you who can express your militancy by going to the House of Commons and refusing to leave without satisfaction.

Also **militance** *n.* M20.

militant /ˈmɪlɪt(ə)nt/ *a.* & *n.* LME. [(O)Fr., or L *militant-* pres. ppl stem of *militare*: see MILITATE *v.*, -ANT[1].] A *adj.* 1 Engaged in warfare. LME. †2 Of a banner, standard, etc.: military. L15–E17. 3 Combative. E17. 4 Aggressively active in pursuing a political or social end. E20.

1 E. YOUNG This is a militant state, nor must man unbuckle his armour, till he puts on his shroud. *the Church militant*: see CHURCH *n.* 3. 3 E. BOWEN Her weariness and distraction brought the partisan in him to its most militant. J. L. ESPOSITO A militant reformist movement.

B *n.* 1 A person engaged in warfare. E17. 2 A person who is militant in pursuing a political or social end. E20.

militantly *adv.* E17.

militaria /mɪlɪˈtɛːrɪə/ *n.pl.* M20. [f. MILITARY *a.* & *n.* + -IA[2].] Military articles of historical interest.

militarise *v.* var. of MILITARIZE *v.*

militarism /ˈmɪlɪtərɪz(ə)m/ *n.* M19. [Fr. *militarisme*, f. *militaire*: see MILITARY, -ISM.] Military attitudes or ideals; the attachment of (undue) importance to military values and military strength; the policy of maintaining a strong military capability.

T. PARKER The high calling of professional militarism. *Sanity* We don't want militarism . . because we experienced one of the bloodiest battles of the Second World War.

militarist /ˈmɪlɪt(ə)rɪst/ *n.* & *a.* E17. [f. MILITARY + -IST.] A *n.* A soldier, a warrior; a person who studies military science; a person having military or militaristic attitudes and ideals. E17.

B *adj.* = MILITARISTIC *a.* M20.

A. E. STEVENSON Much of the world has come to think of us as militarist and . . a menace to peace.

milita'ristic *a.* characterized by militarism E20. **milita'ristically** *adv.* L20.

militarize /ˈmɪlɪt(ə)rʌɪz/ *v.t.* Also **-ise**. L19. [f. MILITARY + -IZE.] Make military or warlike; equip with military resources; imbue with militarism.

militari'zation *n.* L19.

military /ˈmɪlɪt(ə)ri/ *a.* & *n.* LME. [(O)Fr. *militaire* or L *militaris*, f. *milit-*, *miles* soldier + *-aris* -ARY[1].] A *adj.* 1 Of, pertaining to, or characteristic of a soldier or soldiers or armed forces; used, performed, or brought about by a soldier or soldiers or armed forces; appropriate to a soldier or armed forces. LME. 2 *spec.* Living as a soldier; belonging to an army or one of the other armed services. L16.

1 J. STEINBECK Cyrus developed an excellent military mind. C. S. FORESTER Phillips was in uniform . . but that was the only thing that was military about him. A. STORR Military organization is based upon a strict rank order and absolute obedience. W. BOYD It was not a civil but a military matter. *Today* The Band of the Welsh Guards . . usually plays stirring military marches. 2 *Trailer Life* During World War II American military men were able to foil the enemy by resorting to American vernacular.

Special collocations: **military academy** an institution for training army cadets. **military age** the age at which a person becomes liable for military service. **military attaché** an army officer serving with an embassy or attached as an observer to a foreign army. **military band** a band of musicians attached to a military unit. **military braid** a broad braid such as is worn on soldiers' uniforms. **military brush** = *military hairbrush* below. **military chest** an army's treasury. **military college** = *military academy* above. **Military Cross** a decoration instituted in 1915 and awarded to officers for gallantry in combat; abbrev. *MC*. **military drum** a side or snare drum. **military engineering**: dealing with the construction of bridges, fortifications, etc., and the laying and destruction of mines. **military hairbrush** a hairbrush without a handle. *military honours*: see HONOUR *n.* **military hospital**: for the treatment of soldiers, esp. in the field. **military law** (an ordinance or rule forming part of) the law governing an army. **Military Medal** a decoration of similar distinction to the Military Cross, instituted in 1916 for enlisted soldiers; abbrev. *MM*. **military orchid, orchis** a European orchid, *Orchis militaris*, with pinkish-grey, helmet-shaped flowers, now very rare in Britain. **military police** a corps responsible for police and disciplinary duties in the armed forces. **military policeman, police officer**: belonging to the military police. **military school** = *military academy* above. **Military Secretary** an army staff officer who acts as personal and confidential secretary to the commander-in-chief or certain other specified officers. **military service** (*a*) *Hist.* the service in war due from a vassal to his feudal superior; (*b*) service in the armed forces. **military tenure** *Hist.* a feudal tenure under which a vassal owed his superior certain defined services in war. *military tribune*: see TRIBUNE *n.*[1] 1. **military two-step** *Dancing* a variation of the two-step, with military gestures such as saluting.

B *n.* 1 *The* armed forces; soldiers generally. Treated as *sing.* or *pl.* M18. 2 A military man, *esp.* an army officer. M18.

1 A. S. NEILL People whose houses were occupied by the military . . learned that soldiers are . . more destructive than children. LADY BIRD JOHNSON A lot more understanding of what the military puts up with.

militarily *adv.* (*a*) in a military or warlike manner; (*b*) from a military point of view: M17. **militariness** *n.* M19. **militaryism** *n.* militarism L19.

militate /ˈmɪlɪteɪt/ *v.* L16. [L *militat-* pa. ppl stem of *militare* serve as a soldier, f. *milit-*, *miles* soldier: see -ATE[3].] 1 *v.i.* Of evidence, a fact, a circumstance: have force or effect *against* (rarely †*for*, *in favour of*). L16. †b Conflict, be inconsistent *with*. M18–M19. 2 *v.i.* a Serve as a soldier; take part in warfare. Now *rare*. E17. †b Contend, strive. M17–M19. c Advocate or employ militant action in pursuit of a political or social end. M20. 3 *v.t.* Dispute, debate (a question). Now *rare*. M18.

1 P. BOWLES It's crude. I don't think that militates against its success. 2a BURKE The supply of her armies militating in so many distant countries. b GIBBON The invisible powers of heaven . . seemed to militate on the side of the pious emperor. c V. WOOLF Tell me all about Mrs Pankhurst and the suffrage. Why did you militate?

militation /mɪlɪˈteɪʃ(ə)n/ *n. rare.* LME. [med.L *militatio(n-)*, f. as prec.: see -ATION.] Strife, conflict.

milites gloriosi *n. phr.* pl. of MILES GLORIOSUS.

militia /mɪˈlɪʃə/ *n.* L16. [L = military service, warfare, war, f. *milit-*, *miles* soldier.] †1 A system of military discipline, organization, and tactics; a manner or means of conducting warfare. L16–L17. 2 A military force, a body of soldiers; *spec.* a military force raised from the civilian population, as distinguished from mercenaries or professional soldiers; an auxiliary military force drawn from the civilian population in order to supplement the regular forces in an emergency; *collect.* the members of such a militia. L16. 3 The body of people, usu. men, legally liable to military service, without enlistment. *US*. L18.

2 C. MERIVALE A genuine militia, chosen from the citizens themselves. *Westminster Gazette* The Militia must in future be 'more soldierly'. D. JACOBSON The call-up of new recruits and reservists into the militia. *Times* They feared reprisals from left-wing militias. *attrib.*: MERLE COLLINS Come out, militia members, this is the time to defend your country.

Comb.: **militiaman** a member of a militia; **militiawoman** a female member of a militia.

milium /ˈmɪlɪəm/ *n.*[1] Pl. **milia** /ˈmɪlɪə/. LME. [L = millet.] 1 = MILLET *n.*[1] Now only as mod.L genus name. LME. 2 *Med.* A condition of the sebaceous glands in which small, hard, pale keratinous nodules are formed on the skin. Also, such a nodule. M19.

Milium /ˈmɪlɪəm/ *n.*[2] Also **m-**. M20. [Origin unkn.] (Proprietary name for) a type of insulating fabric.

milk /mɪlk/ *n.* & *a.* [OE (Anglian) *milc*, (WS) *meol(o)c* = OFris. *melok*, OS *miluk* (Du. *melk*), OHG *miluh* (G *Milch*), ON *mjólk*, Goth. *miluks*, f. Gmc, f. IE base also of L *mulgere* (see EMULSION), Gk *amelgein*.] A *n.* 1 An opaque white or bluish-white fluid secreted by the mammary glands of female mammals for nourishing their young. Also, the milk of cows, goats, sheep, etc., used as food for humans. OE. †b Lactation; the milk-yielding condition induced by childbirth. E16–L17. 2 A milky juice or latex secreted by certain plants, e.g. coconut milk. LOE. 3 *fig.* a [esp. w. allus. to *1 Cor.* 3:2, *Heb.* 5:12.] Nourishment appropriate to the earliest stages of development; something easy and pleasant to learn. Freq. in *milk for babes*. LME. b Something pleasant and (supposedly) nourishing. LME. 4 A culinary, pharmaceutical, cosmetic, or other preparation of herbs, drugs, etc., resembling milk. LME. †5 The milt of a fish. LME–E18. 6 *ellipt.* A milkman. *colloq.* L19.

1 P. S. BUCK Out of the woman's great brown breast the milk gushed forth for the child. M. PYKE Milk is an excellent food for man, and . . an equally good food for bacteria. L. CODY One cup of coffee, milk and no sugar. *buttermilk*, *certified milk*, *condensed milk*, *dried milk*, *evaporated milk*, *scald milk*, *skim(med) milk*, *whole milk*, etc. 3a A. WILSON The undiluted milk of the Nazarene gospel. A. MASON All knowledge, all speculation, all endeavour, were reduced to this children's milk. 4 *cleansing milk*, *virgin's milk*, etc.

Phrases etc.: ALMOND *milk*. *bread and milk*: see BREAD *n.*[1] **Bristol milk** †(*a*) *slang* sherry; (*b*) *spec.* a style of medium sherry. CERTIFIED *milk*. COCONUT *milk*. **come** or **go home with the milk** arrive home early in the morning. **cry over spilt milk** lament an irrecoverable loss or irreparable error. *devil's milk*: see DEVIL *n.* *go home with the milk*: see *come home with the milk* above. *in-milk*: see IN-[1]. **in the milk** (of grain) having a milky consistency due to incomplete development. **milk and honey** [w. allus. to the biblical description of the promised land] abundance, comfort, prosperity. **milk and water** (*a*) milk diluted with water; †(*b*) the colour of this, a bluish white; also, a kind of cloth of this colour; (*c*) *fig.* feeble, insipid, or mawkish discourse, thought, sentiment, etc. **milk-and-water** *a.* (*a*) resembling milk diluted with water; (*b*) feeble, insipid, mawkish. *milk for babes*: see sense 3a above; **milk of human kindness** [w. allus. to Shakespeare's *Macb.*] compassion, humanity. **milk of almonds** = ALMOND *milk*. **Milk of Magnesia** (proprietary name for) a white suspension of magnesium hydroxide in water, taken as an antacid or a laxative. **milk of sulphur** a suspension of amorphous powdered sulphur in water; precipitated sulphur obtained from this. *moose milk*: see MOOSE *n.*[1] **mother's milk** (*a*) the milk of a particular child's own mother; (*b*) *fig.* something wholesome or nourishing; something proper or appropriate to a person; (*c*) *slang* any of various alcoholic drinks. **out of the milk** (of grain) beginning to mature. *pigeon's milk*: see PIGEON *n.*[1] **pure milk** something of the purest or finest quality. *rice milk*: see RICE *n.*[2] *sugar of milk*: see SUGAR *n.* & *a.* **the milk in the coconut** *colloq.* a puzzling fact or circumstance. *tiger milk*: see TIGER *n.* *top of the milk*: see TOP *n.*[1]

Comb.: **milk bank**: storing human milk; **milk-bar** a snack bar selling milk drinks and other refreshments; **milk-blooded** *a.* (*arch.*) cowardly, spiritless; **milk-bush** any of various shrubs and trees with a milky sap, *esp.* (*a*) *Austral.* = *caustic bush* s.v. CAUSTIC *a.*; (*b*) *S. Afr.* = MELKBOS (b); **milk cap** any of various fungi of the genus *Lactarius*, which yield a milky latex when broken (*saffron milk cap*: see SAFFRON *a.*); **milk chocolate** †(*a*) a beverage made from chocolate and milk; (*b*) (a) chocolate for eating, made with milk; **milk-coffee** coffee made with milk, white coffee; **milk-cow** (now *dial.*) a cow yielding milk or kept for milking; **milk drop** a small delicate grey or white toadstool of leaf litter, *Mycena galopus*, which yields a latex when broken; **milk-duct** *Anat.* any of several ducts which convey milk from the mammary glands through the nipple to the exterior; **milkfish** a large fork-tailed silver marine fish, *Chanos chanos*, cultured for food in SE Asia and the Philippines; **milk float** a low-bodied (now usu. electric) vehicle for delivering milk; **milk-glass** a semi-translucent glass, whitened by the addition of various ingredients; also called *opaline*; **milk-house** a dairy, a place for storing or selling milk; **milk-leg** a painful swelling, usu. of the legs, which may occur after childbirth; **milk line** *Embryol.* (the line occupied by) a ridge of thickened ectoderm along either side of a mammalian embryo, on which, in females, the mammary glands later form; **milk-livered** *a.* (*arch.*) cowardly; **milk-loaf** a loaf of bread made with milk; **milkmaid** (*a*) a girl or woman who milks cows etc., or is employed in a dairy; (*b*) *dial.* (in *pl.*) any of several plants; *esp.* lady's smock, *Cardamine pratensis*; **milkman** a man who sells or delivers milk; **milk name** a name given to a Chinese child at one month old, later superseded by more formal names but occasionally used, esp. as an endearment; **milk-parsley** a tall umbelliferous plant of fens, *Peucedanum palustre*, having a milky juice when young; **milk powder** a preparation of dehydrated milk; **milk pudding**: made with rice, sago, tapioca, etc., baked with milk in a dish; **milk punch** a drink made of spirits mixed with milk and occas. other ingredients; **milk purslane** any of several small N. American spurges, esp. *Euphorbia maculata*; **milk ridge** *Embryol.* = *milk line* above; **milk room** a room in a house or dairy in which milk is stored; **milk round**, (*N. Amer.*) **route**, **run** (*a*) a route on which milk is regularly collected from farmers or delivered to customers; (*b*) *transf.* a regular trip or tour involving calls at several places; **milk shake** a frothy drink made from milk, flavouring, etc., mixed by shaking or whisking etc.; **milk-sick** *a.* affected with milk-sickness; **milk-sickness** *US* a disease of cattle and sheep in the western US, caused by ingestion of certain plants and sometimes communicated to humans in meat or dairy produce; **milk snake** a harmless, usu. brightly marked N. American colubrid snake, *Lampropeltis triangulum*, formerly supposed to suck milk from cows; **milkstone** (*a*) (now *rare* or *obs.*) any of various white stones, e.g. flint pebbles; (*b*) a hard deposit formed in or on dairy equipment by precipitation from milk; **milk stout** a kind of sweet stout made with lactose; **milk sugar** lactose; **milk-thistle** (*a*) a thistle with white-veined leaves, *Silybum marianum*; (*b*) [from the milky juice] = *sowthistle* s.v. SOW *n.*[1]; **milk-toast** *US* toast softened in milk; **milk tooth** a temporary tooth in a young mammal; **milk train** a train chiefly transporting milk, usu. very early in the morning; **milk-tree** any of several trees having a milky juice; *esp.* the cow-tree, *Brosimum utile*; **milk-tube, vessel** *Bot.* a laticiferous tube; **milk-vetch** = ASTRAGALUS; *esp.* = *liquorice vetch* s.v. LIQUORICE 3; **milk-walk** (*a*) a milkman's regular round for the sale of milk; (*b*) a dairy business; **milk-warm** *a.* approximately as warm as milk newly drawn from the cow; **milkwood (tree)** any of several trees having a milky sap; *spec.* (*a*) *Austral.* any of several trees of the family Apocynaceae, esp. *Alstonia scholaris*; (*b*) *S. Afr.* any of several trees of the family Sapotaceae; *esp.* (more fully *white milkwood*) *Sideroxylon inerme* and (more fully *red milkwood*) *Mimusops obovata*.

B *adj.* Milk-white. *rare.* LME.

milken *a.* (now *rare*) (*a*) consisting of or having much milk; (*b*) resembling milk, esp. in colour; †(*c*) *fig.* mild, gentle: LME. **milkful** *a.* (*obs.* exc. *dial.*) containing much milk, replete with milk L16. **milkless** *a.* having no milk E17. **milkness** *n.* (*obs.* exc. *Sc.*) (*a*) the collective yield of milk from (an animal of) a dairy of milking cattle; (*b*) *gen.* dairy produce: L15.

milk /mɪlk/ *v.* [OE *milcian*, f. as prec.] **I 1** *v.t.* Draw milk from (a mammal, esp. a cow, a goat, a sheep, etc.). OE. **b** Extract or draw (milk). Usu. in *pass.* Now *rare.* LME. †**c** Obtain milk from by sucking. *rare* (Shakes.). Only in E17. **2** *v.i.* Secrete or yield milk. Formerly of women, now only of cows, goats, sheep, etc. OE. †**3** *v.t.* Suckle. LME–L16. **4** *v.t.* Put milk into or on to. *colloq.* L19.

1 *Medical & Physical Journal* This cow being troublesome . . he had . . milked her himself. R. SUTCLIFF The goats were led from door to door to be milked into jugs. **4** J. WAINWRIGHT She milked and sugared both mugs of tea.

II *transf.* & *fig.* †**5** *v.t.* Create. *rare.* Only in LME. **6** *v.t.* Deprive or defraud of money etc.; exploit, turn into a source of (freq. illicit) profit, advantage, information, etc.; extract all possible advantage from. E16. **7** *v.t.* Elicit, draw *out*; drain *away*, *out of*; extract or extort (money, advantage, information, etc.) from a person, a business, etc. E17. **8** *v.t.* Extract sap, venom, etc., from. M18. **9** *v.t.* Intercept (a telegram, telephone message, etc.); tap (a telephone or telegraph wire, etc.). *slang.* L19. **10** *Theatr.* Exploit (a scene, a situation, a line, etc.) to elicit an extreme or extended reaction; contrive to elicit an extreme or extended reaction from (an audience). E20.

6 M. RICHLER He's pulled in for milking pay phones. *Daily Telegraph* A former Lloyd's underwriter . . deliberately milked the company . . of more than £40,000. **7** J. WAINWRIGHT The parents and guardians—the people from whom he milked money. G. SWIFT An almost successful embezzler . . being discovered after years milking the company funds. C. MCCULLOUGH All they care about is what they can milk out of him. **10** K. TYNAN The same dead desire to milk laughs from lines which have ceased to be funny. *Daily Telegraph* A . . versatile comedienne, who can milk the last drop of comedy out of any situation.

Phrases: **milk dry** *fig.* completely drain away the resources of (a person or thing). **milk the bull** or **ram** *fig.* engage in an enterprise doomed to failure.

milker *n.* (*a*) a person who or thing which milks a cow etc.; (*b*) an animal, esp. a cow, yielding milk or kept for milking: ME.

milkie *n.* var. of MILKY *n.*

milking /ˈmɪlkɪŋ/ *n.* LME. [f. MILK *v.* + -ING[1].] **1** The action of MILK *v.* LME. **2** The quantity of milk drawn from a cow etc., or from a dairy, at one time. M16.

1 *deep-milking*: see DEEP *adv.*

Comb.: **milking machine** a device for the automatic milking of cows, using intermittent suction via a cup on each teat; **milking-parlour** a shed specially equipped for milking cows; **milking shorthorn** (an animal of) a breed of shorthorn developed specially for producing milk.

milko /ˈmɪlkəʊ/ *n. slang.* Pl. **-os.** E20. [f. MILK *n.* + -O.] A milkman.

milko /ˈmɪlkəʊ/ *int.* E20. [f. MILK *n.* + O *int.*] (A milkman's call) indicating that milk is available.

milksop /ˈmɪlksɒp/ *n.* LME. [f. MILK *n.* + SOP *n.*[1]] †**1** *sing.* & in *pl.* Bread and milk; milky food. LME–E17. †**2** An infant still on a milk diet. Only in LME. **3** A spiritless man or youth. LME.

milksoppy *a.* spiritless, insipid L19.

milkweed /ˈmɪlkwiːd/ *n.* L16. [f. MILK *n.* + WEED *n.*[1]] **1** Any of certain plants with milky juice, *esp.* sowthistle, *Sonchus oleraceus*, and sun spurge, *Euphorbia helioscopia*. Now *dial.* L16. **2** Any of various N. American plants of the genus *Asclepias* (family Asclepiadaceae), which have a copious milky juice and seeds plumed with long silky hairs; esp. *A. syriaca.* E19. **3** In full *milkweed butterfly*: = MONARCH *n.* 3. L19.

Comb.: **milkweed beetle** any of several red and black N. American beetles of the genus *Tetraopes*; **milkweed bug** either of two red and black N. American bugs of the family Lygaeidae, *Oncopeltus fasciatus* and *Lygaeus kalmi*; *milkweed butterfly*: see sense 3 above.

milk-white /ˈmɪlkwʌɪt/ *n.* & *a.* OE. [f. MILK *n.* + WHITE *n.*, *a.*] (Of) pure white; white like milk.

milkwort /ˈmɪlkwəːt/ *n.* L16. [f. MILK *n.* + WORT *n.*[1]] **1** Any of several small plants of the genus *Polygala* (family Polygalaceae), having racemes of small irregular blue, pink, or white flowers, and formerly supposed to increase the milk of nursing mothers; *esp.* (more fully *common milkwort*) *P. vulgaris* and (more fully *heath milkwort*) *P. serpyllifolia.* L16. **2** In full *sea milkwort.* A plant of brackish turf, *Glaux maritima*, of the primrose family, with small pink axillary flowers. L16. **3** = SPURGE *n.* Now *dial.* M17.

milky /ˈmɪlki/ *n. slang.* Also **milkie.** L19. [f. MILK *n.* + -Y[6].] A milkman.

milky /ˈmɪlki/ *a.* LME. [f. MILK *n.* + -Y[1].] **1** Resembling milk, esp. in colour. Also, (of a gem, glass, liquid, etc.) cloudy, resembling milk in water. LME. **2a** Of or consisting of milk. *rare.* LME. **b** Containing or mixed with milk; having much milk; *poet.* yielding milk. M17. **c** *Bot.* Full of white or pale-coloured juice. M18. **3** *transf.* & *fig.* **a** Of a person, an action, an attribute, etc.: mild, gentle; timorous, weak, compliant; *slang* cowardly. E17. **b** Of a sound: soft, pleasant. *poet.* E20.

1 T. H. HUXLEY The liquid becomes milky as the carbonic gas . . bubbles through. R. WEST The . . bowl of blue and white porcelain shone with the proper clean milky radiance. **2b** W. C. BRYANT Argos, richly stocked In milky kine. **3a** BYRON They made . . me (the milkiest of men) a satirist. G. GREENE I'm not milky . . I just don't want another killing.

milkily *adv.* (*rare*) L19. **milkiness** *n.* (*a*) the state or condition of resembling milk; (*b*) cloudy whiteness of the sky etc.; nebulosity; (*c*) *fig.* mildness, gentleness; weakness: L17.

Milky Way /mɪlkɪ ˈweɪ/ *n. phr.* LME. [f. MILKY *a.* + WAY *n.*, tr. L *via lactea.*] **1** *The* faintly luminous band encircling the heavens and containing the countless stars of the main disc of the galaxy to which the earth belongs. LME. **b** A galaxy, spec. *the* galaxy to which the earth belongs. M19. **2** *fig.* †**a** The region of a woman's breast. *poet.* E17–E18. **b** A path etc. brilliant in appearance, or leading to heaven. M17.

mill /mɪl/ *n.*[1] [OE *mylen* f. WGmc f. late L *molinum*, *-ina*, f. L *mola* grindstone, mill, rel. to *molere* grind (see MEAL *n.*[1]). For loss of final *n* cf. ELL *n.*[1]] **1 a** A building designed and fitted with machinery for grinding corn into flour, orig. chiefly worked by wind or water power. OE. **b** An apparatus for grinding corn. M16. **2** A machine working in the manner of a corn-mill, not necessarily used for grinding; a machine performing a specified operation on a material in the process of manufacture. Also, a building fitted with such machinery; a building etc. where a specified industrial or manufacturing process is carried out. LME. **b** *spec.* An apparatus or a machine for grinding or reducing a solid substance to powder, shreds, pulp, etc. Also, a building fitted with machinery for this purpose. M16. **c** A machine which performs its work by rotary motion, *esp.* a lapidary's machine for cutting, polishing, or engraving gems. E17. **d** A machine for stamping gold and silver coins. M17. **e** An apparatus for juicing or expressing the liquid from fruit, vegetables, plants, etc., by grinding or crushing. L17. **3** A fist-fight; boxing-match. *slang.* E19. **4a** A treadmill. M19. **b** A prison, a guard-house. *slang.* M19. **5** A circling movement of cattle. *US.* L19. **6** *Mining.* An excavation in rock, transverse to the workings, supplying filler. L19. **7** A typewriter. *US slang.* E20. **8** The engine of an aircraft or motor vehicle. *slang.* E20.

1a *flouring mill*, *grist-mill*, etc. *floating mill*, *horse-mill*, *water-mill*, *windmill*, etc. **b** P. S. BUCK With this ox tied to his mill he could grind the grain. **2** R. K. NARAYAN Years ago there were two weaving mills at the end of the street. I. MCEWAN Back again on Monday to toil in the mills, factories, timber yards and quaysides of London. *cotton-mill*, *reversing mill*, *silk-mill*, *steel-mill*, etc. **b** H. BELLOC Black pepper . . ground large . . in fresh granules from a proper wooden mill. *coffee-mill*, *pepper-mill*, *powder-mill*, *salt-mill*, etc. **5** E. HOUGH He did all he could to break the 'mill' and get the cattle headed properly. **8** *Custom Car* The basic set-up is a 302 Mustang mill with early Jag suspension.

Phrases: GASTRIC *mill*. *glacier mill*: see GLACIER. **go (pass** etc.**) through the mill** experience difficulty, hardship, suffering, etc. *grist for, to, the mill*: see GRIST *n.*[1] 2. *pass through the mill*: see *go through the mill* above. **put through the mill** cause to experience difficulty, hardship, suffering, etc. *run of the mill*: see RUN *n.* *trouble at* (*the* or *t'*) *mill*: see TROUBLE *n.*

Comb.: **mill band** a continuous belt for the wheels of mill machinery; **mill bill** a steel adze fixed in a wooden handle, used for dressing and cracking millstones; **mill-clack** a clapper in a mill; a heraldic representation of this; **mill-dam** (*a*) a dam built across a stream to interrupt the flow and raise the level of the water so as to make it available for turning a wheel; (*b*) the area covered by water held in check by such a dam; **mill-dog** *Canad.* a kind of clamp for securing logs in a sawmill; **mill-dust** fine floury dust thrown out during the grinding of corn; **mill finish** the finish of paper not subjected to any extra processing after manufacture; **mill-hand** a worker in a mill or factory; **mill-head** a reservoir of pent-up water which, when released, turns a water-mill; **mill-hopper** a hopper for corn ready for grinding; **mill-horse**: used for turning or working a mill; **mill-house** a building in which milling is carried on; **mill-ink** = *mill-rind* below; **mill-lands** *Hist.*: attached or appertaining to a corn-mill, esp. in Scotland; **millman** a man in charge of or employed in a mill; **mill-pick** an iron tool for producing a corrugated surface on a millstone; a heraldic representation of this; **mill-post** (*a*) *Hist.* a post supporting a windmill; (*b*) in *pl.* (*joc.*), thick or fat legs; **mill-power** (a unit for measuring) water power for driving a mill; **mill privilege**, **right** *US* the privilege or right of using water for driving a mill; **mill-rind** the iron supporting the upper millstone of a corn-mill and carrying the eye which rests on the end of the mill spindle; a heraldic representation of this; **mill-ring** (*a*) the space in a mill between the runner and the frame surrounding it; (*b*) the meal scattered around a millstone, regarded as a perquisite of the miller; **mill-run** (*a*) a (standard) period of operation of a mill; (*b*) timber sawn to standard specifications; **mill-sail** a sail on a windmill; **mill-scale** *Metall.* iron oxide deposited on iron or steel during hot working; **mill seat** a site suitable for a water-mill; **mill-shaft** (*a*) a metal shaft used for driving machinery in a mill; (*b*) a tall chimney on a manufacturing mill; **mill site** *US* = *mill seat* above; **mill-stream** a mill-race; **mill tail** the water downstream from a mill which has passed through the mill-wheel; **†mill-tooth** a grinding or molar tooth; **mill town**: characterized by the presence of a manufacturing mill or mills; **mill-weir** = *mill-dam* above; **mill-wheel** a wheel, esp. a water-wheel, used to drive a mill; a heraldic representation of this; **mill-work** (the designing or construction of) machinery used in a mill or factory.

mill /mɪl/ *n.*[2] L18. [Abbrev. of L *millesimum* thousandth part, after CENT *n.*[1] Cf. MIL.] 1 One-thousandth of a dollar, a money of account in N. America. L18. 2 One-thousandth of a pound, proposed as a coin in Great Britain, and employed in Cyprus and Egypt. L19.

millage *n.* (*US*) [-AGE] the rate of taxation in mills per dollar to which a given area, group, etc., is liable L19.

mill /mɪl/ *n.*[3] *colloq.* M20. [Abbrev.: cf. MIL 6.] Chiefly *Photogr.* = MILLIMETRE.

Practical Photography Good old thirty-five mill It's a great film format to work with.

mill /mɪl/ *n.*[4] *colloq.* Also **mill.** (point). Pl. same. M20. [Abbrev.] = MILLION.

J. ARCHER How do you imagine I felt when we were overdrawn seven mill.

mill /mɪl/ *v.*[1] M16. [f. MILL *n.*[1] Cf. MULL *v.*[1]] **I** 1 *v.t.* Thicken (cloth etc.) in a fulling-mill. M16. 2 *v.t.* Grind (corn) in a mill; produce (flour) by grinding. Usu. in *pass.* L16. **b** Pound or grind to powder; crush to fragments. L18. **c** Hull (seeds) in a mill. M19. **d** Cut (butter, curd, soap, etc.) into small shreds for mixing or blending. M20. 3 *v.t.* Beat or whip (chocolate, cream, etc.) to a froth. Also foll. by *up*. M17. 4 *v.t.* Beat, strike; fight, overcome. Also, smash, break. *slang.* L17. **b** *v.i.* Fight, box. *slang.* M19. 5 *v.t.* †**a** Stamp (coins) by means of a mill. *rare.* Only in L17. **b** Flute the edge of (a coin or any piece of flat metal); produce regular grooves or similar markings on the edge of (a coin). E18. 6 *v.t.* Subject to a manufacturing process in a mill; saw in a sawmill; cut (metal) with a rotating tool. L17.

2 DELIA SMITH Rye is more commonly milled into various grades of flour for bread-making. 3 DICKENS A second milled and frothed the chocolate. 4b *London Daily News* An ageing journeyman boxer who had spent years milling in small halls.

II 7 *v.i.* Of a whale: turn around, reverse direction. M19. 8 *v.i.* Move continuously round, *spec.* in a circular mass, in or among a crowd, or aimlessly or confusedly. Also foll. by *about*, *around*. L19. 9 *v.t.* Turn (an idea) *over* in one's mind. E20.

8 O. HENRY The aroused cattle milled around the . . corral in a plunging mass. R. PARK They lost their bearings and milled aimlessly around. B. MOORE A hundred invited guests milling on the lawn.

millable *a.* suitable for milling E20.

mill /mɪl/ *v.*[2]*t.* *arch. slang.* M16. [Perh. a use of prec.] Rob (a house, shop, etc.). Also, steal.

millboard /ˈmɪlbɔːd/ *n.* E18. [Alt. of *milled board* s.v. MILLED *a.*] 1 A kind of strong pasteboard, orig. made of a pulp of old rope, sacking, paper, and other coarse matter milled or rolled with high pressure, used for bookbinding etc.; a piece of this. E18. 2 A specially prepared board for sketching. M19.

mille *n.* see MIL *n.*

†millecuple *a.* M17–M18. [Irreg. f. L *mille* thousand, after DECUPLE *a.*] Thousandfold.

milled /mɪld/ *a.* E17. [f. MILL *v.*[1] + -ED[1].] †1 Polished by some mechanical process. *rare.* Only in E17. 2 **a** Of a coin: (*a*) struck in a mill; (*b*) having the edge fluted or grooved by milling. M17. †**b** Of knitwear: ribbed. L17–E19. **c** Marked with transverse grooves or ribs; *esp.* (of the head of a screw etc.) serrated to afford a hold for adjustment. E18. 3 Pressed, fulled. M17. 4 Flattened by rolling or beating. L17. 5 Whipped or beaten to a froth. M18. 6 Ground, hulled, juiced, powdered, pressed, shredded, etc., in a mill. E19.

4 : **milled board** = MILLBOARD.

millefeuille /milfœːj, miːlˈfəːj/ *n.* Pl. pronounced same. L19. [Fr., lit. 'a thousand leaves'.] A rich confection of thin layers of puff pastry and a filling of jam, cream, etc.

millefiore /ˌmiːlɪfɪˈɔːri/ *n.* M19. [It., f. *mille* thousand + *fiore* flowers.] A kind of ornamental glass made by fusing together a number of glass rods of different sizes and colours and cutting the mass into sections which exhibit ornamental figures of varying pattern, usually embedded in colourless transparent glass to make paperweights etc. Also *millefiore glass*.

mille-fleurs /milflœːr/ *n.* M19. [Fr., lit. 'a thousand flowers'.] 1 A perfume distilled from flowers of different kinds. M19. 2 A pattern of flowers and leaves used in tapestry, on porcelain, etc. Usu. *attrib.* E20.

millegrain /ˈmɪlɪgreɪn/ *n.* & *a.* Also **milli-**. M20. [f. Fr. *mille* thousand + GRAIN *n.*[1]] (Designating) a gem setting of beaded or crenellated metal.

millenarian /mɪlɪˈnɛːrɪən/ *a.* & *n.* M17. [f. late L *millenarius*: see MILLENARY, -ARIAN.] **A** *adj.* Of or pertaining to the millennium; believing in the millennium or a millennium. M17.

A. MILLER I even harbored the millenarian suspicion that with our generation history might have come to an end.

B *n.* A person who believes in the millennium or a millennium. L17.

millenarianism *n.* = MILLENARISM M19.

millenarism /ˈmɪlɪnərɪz(ə)m/ *n.* M17. [f. MILLENARY + -ISM.] *Chr. Ch.* The doctrine of or belief in the coming of the millennium.

millenarist /ˈmɪlɪnərɪst/ *n.* & *a.* M19. [f. MILLENARY + -IST.] *Chr. Ch.* **A** *n.* = MILLENARY *n.* 2. M19. **B** *adj.* = MILLENARY *a.* 1. L19.

millenary /mɪˈlɛnəri, ˈmɪlɪnəri/ *n.* & *a.* M16. [f. late L *millenarius* consisting of a thousand, commander of a thousand, f. *milleni* a thousand each, f. *mille* a thousand: see -ARY[1]. In sense A.2 f. eccl.L *millenarii* millenarian heretics.] **A** *n.* 1 A total sum of one thousand; *esp.* a continuous period of one thousand years. M16. **b** (A celebration of) a thousandth anniversary. L19. 2 *Chr. Ch.* A believer in the millennium. M16.

1 *sabbatical millenary*: see SABBATICAL *a.*

B *adj.* 1 *Chr. Ch.* Of or pertaining to the millennium, or believers in the millennium. L16. 2 Consisting of or pertaining to a thousand, esp. a thousand years. E17.

2 **millenary petition** *Hist.* a petition presented by Puritan ministers (represented as one thousand) to James I in 1603, requesting changes in ecclesiastical ceremony etc.

millenism *n.* var. of MILLENNISM.

millenium *n.* var. of MILLENNIUM.

millennia *n.pl.* see MILLENNIUM.

millennial /mɪˈlɛnɪəl/ *a.* & *n.* M17. [f. MILLENNIUM + -AL[1].] **A** *adj.* 1 *Chr. Ch.* Of or pertaining to the millennium. M17. 2 Consisting of or pertaining to a thousand years. E19. **B** *n.* (A celebration of) a thousandth anniversary. L19.

millennialism *n.* = MILLENARISM E20. **millennialist** *n.* & *a.* (*a*) *n.* = MILLENARY *n.* 2; (*b*) *adj.* = MILLENARY *a.* 1: M19.

millennian /mɪˈlɛnɪən/ *n.* & *a.* M17. [f. MILLENNIUM + -AN] **A** *n.* *Chr. Ch.* A believer in the millennium. M17. **B** *adj.* 1 *Chr. Ch.* Of or pertaining to the millennium. E19. 2 Belonging to a period of a thousand years. M19.

millennism /ˈmɪlənɪsm/ *n.* *rare.* Also **millenism.** L17. [f. MILLENNIUM + -ISM.] *Chr. Ch.* = MILLENARISM.

†millennist *n.* = MILLENARY *n.* 2 M17–L18.

millennium /mɪˈlɛnɪəm/ *n.* Also **millenium.** Pl. **-iums, -ia** /-ɪə/. M17. [mod.L, f. L *mille* thousand, after *biennium* (see BIENNIAL).] 1 A period of one thousand years. Also, a thousandth anniversary. M17. 2 *Chr. Ch.* *The* period of one thousand years during which (according to one interpretation of *Rev.* 20:1–5) Christ will reign in person on earth. M17. 3 A period of peace, happiness, prosperity, and ideal government. E19.

1 *Scientific American* The millenniums preceding the 17th century. *Sunday Times* The distilled wisdom of millennia of human experience. *sabbatical millennium*: see SABBATICAL *a.* 3 A. STORR If only society were better organized . . , men would live in peace . . and the millenium would be at last realised. *Marxism Today* Who . . will draft this constitution? And with what in mind? To usher in a socialist millennium?

millepede *n.* var. of MILLIPEDE.

millepore /ˈmɪlɪpɔː/ *n.* M18. [mod.L *Millepora* (see below), f. L *mille* thousand + *porus* passage, PORE *n.*] *Zool.* Any of a group or order (Milleporina) of colonial hydrozoans which secrete coral-like calcareous skeletons covered with minute pores through which the polyps protrude; *esp.* a hydrozoan of the genus *Millepora*.

miller /ˈmɪlə/ *n.*[1] ME. [Prob. (w. assim. to MILL *n.*[1]) f. MLG, MDu. *molner*, *mulner* (Du. *molnaar*, *mulder*) = OS *mulineri*, corresp. to OHG *mulināri* (G *Müller*), ON *mylnari*, f. late L *molinarius*, f. *molina* MILL *n.*[1]: see -ER[1].] 1 A person who grinds corn in a mill; the proprietor or tenant of a corn-mill. Cf. MILLWARD. ME. **b** A person who operates any mill. Freq. w. specifying wd. M19. 2 A fish: a kind of ray. *rare.* E17. 3 Any of various white or white-powdered insects; *esp.* (also *miller-moth*) a noctuid moth, *spec.* a pale grey and white noctuid, *Acronicta leporina*. M17. 4 A pugilist. Formerly also, a murderer. *slang.* L17. 5 Any of various birds with distinctive white plumage or markings, as (*a*) a male hen-harrier; (*b*) a whitethroat. Chiefly *dial.* L19.

1b *cloth-miller*, *saw-miller*, etc.

Comb. & phrases: FLOURY *miller*; *miller-moth*: see sense 3 above; **miller's soul** = *miller-moth* above; **miller's thumb** (*a*) any of various small freshwater sculpins of the genus *Cottus*, *esp.* the European bullhead, *C. gobio*; (*b*) *dial.* any of various small hedge-birds, as the goldcrest and the long-tailed tit.

millering *n.* the work or trade of a miller L18.

Miller /ˈmɪlə/ *n.*[2] L19. [W. H. *Miller* (1801–80), Eng. scientist.] *Cryst.* Used *attrib.* with ref. to a method for specifying the position and orientation of a crystal plane or face in terms of the reciprocals of its intercepts with the three crystal axes.

Miller index each of the three integers which together specify a crystal plane in this method.

Millerian /mɪˈlɪərɪən/ *a.* of, pertaining to, or designating Miller's method for specifying crystal planes L19.

Miller effect /ˈmɪlər ɪˌfɛkt/ *n. phr.* M20. [f. J. M. *Miller* (1882–1962), US physicist.] *Electronics.* The feedback effect whereby capacitance in the output of a valve or transistor increases its input impedance.

Millerite /ˈmɪlərʌɪt/ *n.*[1] *US.* M19. [f. William *Miller* (see below) + -ITE[1].] A believer in the doctrines of William Miller (d. 1849), an American preacher who interpreted the Scriptures as foretelling the imminent coming of Christ and the end of the world.

Millerism *n.* the doctrines of William Miller M19.

millerite /ˈmɪlərʌɪt/ *n.*[2] M19. [f. as MILLER *n.*[2] + -ITE[1].] *Min.* Native nickel sulphide, crystallizing in the hexagonal system usu. as brassy or bronze crystals.

millesimal /mɪˈlɛsɪm(ə)l/ *n.* & *a.* E18. [f. L *millesimus* thousandth + -AL[1].] **A** *n.* A thousandth (part). E18. **B** *adj.* Thousandth; consisting of thousandth parts. M18.

millet /ˈmɪlɪt/ *n.*[1] LME. [(O)Fr., dim. of (dial.) *mil* f. L *milium*.] A cereal grass, *Panicum miliaceum*, widely grown in warm countries, with small spikelets arranged in a loose panicle; the grain of this plant. Also (w. specifying wd), any of various other drought-resistant usu. small-seeded cereal grasses grown esp. in warm countries of the world.

bulrush millet, foxtail millet, Hungarian millet, wood millet, etc.

Comb.: **millet-grass** = *wood millet* above; **millet-seed** *n.* & *a.* (*a*) *n.* the seed or grain of millet; (*b*) *adj.* (of grains of sand) almost spherical as a result of abrasion by the wind.

millet /ˈmɪlɛt/ *n.*[2] E20. [Turk. = nation, group of co-religionists, f. Arab. *milla(t)* religion.] *Hist.* A part of the population of the Ottoman Empire that owed allegiance to a particular religious leader, esp. a non-Muslim one.

milli- /ˈmɪli/ *comb. form.* [f. L *mille* thousand + -I-.] Used in names of units of measurement to denote a factor of one-thousandth (10^{-3}), as *millicurie, millimole, milliwatt;* also occas. combined with *micro-* to denote a factor of 10^{-9} (corresp. to NANO-), as *millimicroampere, millimicromole.* Abbrev. *m.*

millibar *n.* (*Meteorol.*) the usual unit of barometric pressure, equal to a thousandth of a bar (100 pascals) E20. **milliosmole** /mɪlɪˈɒzməʊl/ *n.* (*Physical Chem.*) an amount of an osmotically effective ion in solution equal to a milligram divided by the atomic mass of the ion M20.

milliammeter /mɪlɪˈamɪtə/ *n.* E20. [f. MILLI- + AMMETER.] An instrument for measuring electric currents of the order of milliamperes.

milliamp /ˈmɪlɪamp/ *n. colloq.* E20. [Abbrev.] = next.

milliampere /mɪlɪˈampɛː/ *n.* L19. [f. MILLI- + AMPERE.] *Electr.* One-thousandth of an ampere.

milliamperage *n.* current expressed in or of the order of milliamperes E20.

Millian /ˈmɪlɪən/ *a.* & *n.* M19. [f. *Mill* (see below) + -IAN. Cf. MILLITE.] **A** *adj.* Of or pertaining to the English utilitarian philosopher and political theorist John Stuart Mill (1806–73) or his theories. M19. **B** *n.* A follower of Mill or his theories. M20.

milliard /ˈmɪlɪɑːd/ *n.* L18. [Fr., f. *mille* thousand.] A thousand million.

milliar'daire *n.* (now *rare*) [after MILLIONAIRE] a person possessing a thousand million pounds, dollars, etc. E20.

milliary /ˈmɪlɪəri/ *n.* & *a.* Also **miliary**. E17. [L *milliarius*, f. *mille* thousand: see MILE, -ARY[1].] **A** *n.* A stone or mark set up by the ancient Romans as a point of departure in measuring distances of a thousand paces; a milestone. E17. **B** *adj.* Of or pertaining to the ancient Roman mile of a thousand paces; marking a mile. M17.

millième /ˈmiljɛm/ *n.* Also **-ieme**. E20. [Fr. = thousandth.] A monetary unit of Egypt and Sudan, equal to one-thousandth of a pound. Cf. MILLIME.

milligram /ˈmɪlɪgram/ *n.* Also **-gramme**. E19. [f. MILLI- + GRAM *n.*[2]] One-thousandth of a gram.

millilitre /ˈmɪlɪliːtə/ *n.* Also ***-liter**. E19. [f. MILLI- + LITRE.] A thousandth of a litre.

¶Now identical with a cubic centimetre (cf. LITRE).

millime /ˈmɪliːm/ *n.* M20. [Fr. MILLIÈME.] A monetary unit of Tunisia, equal to one-thousandth of a dinar.

millimetre /ˈmɪlɪmiːtə/ *n.* Also ***-meter**. E19. [f. MILLI- + METRE *n.*[2]] A thousandth of a metre, equal to 0.03937 inch.

Daily Telegraph Solidarity is indispensable and without it we won't move a millimetre forward. **millimetre of mercury** = TORR.

millimetric /mɪlɪˈmɛtrɪk/ *a.* (*a*) of the order of a millimetre in (wave)length; pertaining to or involving electromagnetic radiation having a wavelength of 1 to 10 millimetres; (*b*) minute: E20.

milliner /ˈmɪlɪnə/ *n.* & *v.* LME. [f. MILAN + -ER[1].] **A** *n.* **1** (**M-**.) A native or inhabitant of the Italian city of Milan. Now *rare* or *obs.* LME. **2** Orig., a seller of fancy wares and accessories, esp. such as were originally made in Milan. Now, a person who makes or sells women's hats. M16. **B** *v.i.* Make women's hats. Chiefly as *millinering* vbl n. E19.

millinerial /mɪlɪˈnɪərɪəl/ *a.* of or pertaining to a milliner or millinery M19. **millinery** *n.* (*a*) articles made or sold by a milliner; (*b*) the trade or business of a milliner: L17.

milling /ˈmɪlɪŋ/ *n.* LME. [f. MILL *v.*[1] + -ING[1].] **1** The action of MILL *v.*[1] LME. **2** The series of grooves on the edge of a coin, the grooved edge of a coin. E19.

Comb.: **milling machine** *spec.* a machine in which an object fixed to a carriage is subjected to the action of a rotating tool.

million /ˈmɪljən/ *n.* & *a.* (in mod. usage also classed as a *determiner*), (*cardinal numeral*). LME. [(O)Fr., prob. f. (O)It. †*millione* (now *milione*), f. *mille* thousand + augm. suff. *-one* -OON.] **A** *n.* **I** Pl. now usu. same after a numeral and often after a quantifier, otherwise **-s**; as *sing.* usu. preceded by *a*, or in emphatic use *one*. **1** A thousand times a thousand units *of* a specified category or group (now almost always definite, as *a million of the, those*, etc., *one million of its, his mother's*, etc.); a thousand times a thousand persons or things identified contextually, as pounds or dollars, years in dates, chances (in giving odds), units in oil production, etc.; *pl.* after a quantifier, multiples of a thousand times a thousand such persons or things. Usu. treated as *pl.* LME. **b** In *pl.* without specifying wd: several million; *hyperbol.* very large numbers. (Foll. by *of*.) LME. **c** A quantity equal to this, a very large amount. Now chiefly in *a million of money*. LME. **d** *The* multitude, the bulk of the population. E17. **2** A thousand times a thousand as an abstract number, the symbol(s) or figure(s) representing this (1,000,000 in arabic numerals); in *pl.* after a numeral, that number of multiples of a thousand times a thousand as an abstract number, the symbol(s) or figure(s) representing any such number (as 5,000,000). LME.

1 R. P. WARD By loans . . and other speculations, he achieved his million. *Manchester Examiner* He could count his soldiers by the million. D. H. LAWRENCE In the world beyond, how easily we might spare a million or two of humans. W. FAULKNER The whole million of them we have lost. W. S. CHURCHILL More than a million of the Local Defence Volunteers. F. FORSYTH Six million of his fellow Jews. I. MCEWAN Tens of millions have been saved in social security payments. **a million to one chance** a very low probability. **a — in a million, one in a million** a very valuable or unusual person or thing (of the type specified or understood). **gone a million** *Austral.* & *NZ colloq.* completely lost, in a hopeless state. *one in a million*: see *a — in a million* above. **b** A. BULLOCK He persisted in regarding Molotov . . as responsible for the murder of millions. S. BELLOW A huge tree . . old, arthritic . . but still capable of putting forth millions of leaves.

II 3 In *pl.* (treated as *sing.*). = GUPPY *n.*[1] Also *millions fish*. E20.

B *adj.* After an article, possessive, etc.: a thousand times a thousand (a cardinal numeral represented by 1,000,000 in arabic numerals); *hyperbol.* a very great many. After a numeral or quantifier: multiples of a thousand times a thousand. LME.

A. S. NEILL A million men say grace before meals . . and probably 999,999 men say it mechanically. M. ANGELOU A heckler had asked why sixteen million Africans allowed three million whites to control them. S. RUSHDIE She would never marry Haroun Harappa, no, not in a million years. *Scotsman* My Dad's car goes a *million* times faster than your Dad's car. (**like**) **a million dollars** excellent, splendid, magnificent.

Comb.: Forming compound numerals (cardinal or ordinal) with numerals below a million, as *1,600,000* (read *one million six hundred thousand*), *1,000,080* (read *one million and eighty*). Special combs., as **million-dollar** *a.* worth or costing a million dollars; *fig.* expensive-looking, splendid, attractive; **million-seller** a record, book, etc., of which a million copies have been sold; *millions fish*: see sense A.3 above.

millionism *n.* (*rare*) millionairedom M19. **millionist** *n.* (*rare*) a millionaire M19.

millionaire /mɪljəˈnɛː/ *n.* & *a.* E19. [Fr. *millionnaire*, f. as prec. Cf. next.] **A** *n.* A person whose assets are worth at least a million pounds, dollars, etc.; a person of great wealth. E19.

Millionaires' Row (a name for) a street containing the residences of very rich people.

B *attrib.* or as *adj.* **1** Having assets worth at least a million pounds, dollars, etc. M19. **2** *Geogr.* Designating a city with a population of more than a million. M20.

millionairedom *n.* the condition of being a millionaire L19. **millionaireship** *n.* the position or state of a millionaire E20. **millionairess** *n.* a female millionaire L19. **millionairish** *a.* characteristic of a millionaire L19.

millionary /ˈmɪljənəri/ *a.* & *n.* Now *rare.* E19. [f. MILLION + -ARY[1], after Fr. *millionnaire*: see prec.] **A** *adj.* = MILLIONAIRE *a.* 1. E19. **B** *n.* = MILLIONAIRE *n.* M19.

millioned /ˈmɪljənd/ *a.* Now *rare.* L16. [f. MILLION + -ED[2].] **1** Numbering a million. L16. **2** Possessing millions of pounds, dollars, etc. M18.

millionfold /ˈmɪljənfəʊld/ *n.* & *a.* M19. [f. MILLION + -FOLD.] **A** *n.* Pl. same. A million times the number or quantity: used advb. M19.

R. A. PROCTOR The radius . . might be increased a millionfold. L. MUMFORD The . . power of the writer whose works might be . . reprinted in age after age was increased potentially many millionfold.

B *adj.* A million times as many or as much. M19.

millionth /ˈmɪljənθ/ *a.* & *n.* L17. [f. MILLION + -TH[2], after HUNDREDTH.] **1** *adj.* & *n.* (The person or thing) that is number one million in a series. L17. **2** *n.* Each of a million equal parts into which something is or may be divided, a fraction which when multiplied by one million gives one. M19.

1 J. WAIN For the millionth time . . I can easily see why . . she had ideas once about going on the stage. **millionth part** = sense 2 above. 2 J. C. MAXWELL Your sum of Vital energy is not the millionth of an erg.

millipede /ˈmɪlɪpiːd/ *n.* Also **mille-**. E17. [L *millepeda* woodlouse, f. *mille* thousand + *ped-*, *pes* foot.] **1** Any of numerous herbivorous terrestrial arthropods of the class Diplopoda, having an elongated body with many segments, most of which bear two pairs of legs. E17. **2** A terrestrial isopod; a woodlouse. Now *rare.* M17. **3** = CENTIPEDE. *rare.* E18.

milliprobe /ˈmɪlɪprəʊb/ *n.* M20. [f. MILLI- + PROBE *n.*] An instrument for analysing small amounts of material; *spec.* a form of spectrophotometer used esp. to study fragile or precious objects, in which a narrow beam of accelerated particles (usu. protons) is directed at the specimen and the resulting fluorescence analysed.

millisecond /ˈmɪlɪsɛk(ə)nd/ *n.* E20. [f. MILLI- + SECOND *n.*[1]] A thousandth of a second.

Millite /ˈmɪlʌɪt/ *a.* & *n.* L19. [f. as MILLIAN + -ITE[1].] = MILLIAN.

millivolt /ˈmɪlɪvəʊlt, -vɒlt/ *n.* M19. [f. MILLI- + VOLT *n.*[1]] *Electr.* One-thousandth of a volt.

milli'voltmeter *n.* an instrument for measuring voltages of the order of millivolts E20.

mill-ken /ˈmɪlkɛn/ *n. slang. obs.* exc. *Hist.* M17. [f. MILL *v.*[2] + KEN *n.*[2]] A thief, a housebreaker.

mill-mountain /ˈmɪlmaʊntɪn/ *n.* Now *rare* or *obs.* M17. [Origin unkn.] Fairy flax, *Linum catharticum*.

millocracy /mɪˈlɒkrəsi/ *n.* Now *Hist.* or *joc.* M19. [f. MILL *n.*[1]: see -CRACY.] The body of mill-owners regarded as a dominant or ruling class.

'millocrat *n.* M19.

Millon /ˈmɪlən/ *n.* L19. [A. N. E. *Millon* (1812–67), Fr. chemist.] *Chem.* **1** *Millon's base*, a yellow powder, $Hg_2NOH{\cdot}2H_2O$, which is a mercury-substituted derivative of ammonia. L19. **2 a** *Millon's reagent*, a clear solution of mercuric nitrate containing some nitrous acid, used in Millon's test. L19. **b** *Millon('s) test, reaction*, an analytical test for phenolic compounds (e.g. oestrogens and (esp.) proteins containing tyrosine), which give a pink or reddish precipitate with Millon's reagent. L19.

millpond /ˈmɪlpɒnd/ *n.* L17. [f. MILL *n.*[1] + POND *n.*] **1** A pool of water retained by a mill-dam for driving a water-mill. L17. **2** The Atlantic

Ocean, esp. as separating Britain and N. America. *joc.* L19.

1 like a millpond (of a stretch of water) very calm.

mill-pool /ˈmɪlpuːl/ *n.* OE. [f. MILL *n.*[1] + POOL *n.*[1]] A millpond.

mill-race /ˈmɪlreɪs/ *n.* L15. [f. MILL *n.*[1] + RACE *n.*[1]] The current of water that drives a mill-wheel; a channel in which water runs to a water-mill.

Mills /mɪlz/ *n.* E20. [Sir William *Mills* (1856–1932), Eng. engineer.] *Mills bomb, grenade*, a type of hand-grenade serrated on the outside to form shrapnel on explosion.

Mill's Methods /mɪlz ˈmɛθədz/ *n. phr. pl.* L19. [J. S. *Mill*: see MILLIAN.] *Logic.* The five canons of inductive inquiry for discovering and establishing the validity of causal relations between phenomena.

millstone /ˈmɪlstəʊn/ *n.* OE. [f. MILL *n.*[1] + STONE *n.*] **1** Either of a pair of circular stones which grind corn by the rotation of the upper stone on the lower one. OE. **b** *Her.* A charge representing a millstone. L17. **2** *fig.* A heavy burden; an oppressive force. E18.

1 NETHER *millstone*. **see far into a millstone** (usu. *iron.*) be extraordinarily acute. **2** F. WELDON 109 Holden Road was a millstone rather than an asset. B. GELDOF The problems of Ethiopia and its hapless peoples, caught between the millstones of natural disaster and international politics.

Comb.: **millstone grit** *Geol.* any hard siliceous rock suitable for making millstones; *spec.* (freq. **M- G-**) a coarse sandstone of the British Carboniferous, lying immediately below the coal-measures.

†millward *n.* OE–L19. [f. MILL *n.*[1] + WARD *n.*] Orig., the keeper of a (manorial) mill. Later, a miller.

millwright /ˈmɪlrʌɪt/ *n.* LME. [f. MILL *n.*[1] + WRIGHT *n.*] A person who designs or builds mills or mill machinery.

millwrighting *n.* the trade of a millwright E19.

milo /ˈmʌɪləʊ/ *n.* L19. [Sesotho *maili*.] A drought-resistant variety of sorghum grown esp. in the central US. Also *milo maize*.

milometer /mʌɪˈlɒmɪtə/ *n.* M20. [f. MILE *n.* + -OMETER.] An instrument for measuring the number of miles travelled by a vehicle.

milord /mɪˈlɔːd/; *foreign* milɔːr (*pl. same*)/ *n.* Also **†milor.** L16. [f. *my lord*. In sense 2 Fr. f. Eng.: cf. MILADY, next.] **†1** A nobleman, a lord. *Sc.* Only in L16. **2** An English nobleman in Europe; an Englishman travelling in Europe in aristocratic style; a wealthy Englishman. E17.

milordo /mɪˈlɔːdəʊ/ *n.* Pl. **-di** /-di/. M18. [It. f. as prec.] An English nobleman in Italy; a wealthy Englishman travelling in Italy.

Milori /mɪˈlɔːri/ *n.* Also **m-.** L19. [A. *Milori*, 19th-cent. French dye manufacturer.] **1** *Milori green*, chrome green. L19. **2** *Milori blue*, a very pure Prussian blue. L19.

milpa /ˈmɪlpə/ *n.* M19. [Mex. Sp.] In Central America and Mexico, a small cultivated field, usu. of corn or maize.

Comb.: **milpa system** a system of cultivation involving cyclic burning off, forest re-establishment, and cultivation.

Milquetoast /ˈmɪlktəʊst/ *n.* & *a.* Chiefly *N. Amer.* Also **m-.** M20. [Caspar *Milquetoast*, a cartoon character created by H. T. Webster in 1924.] (A person who is) timid or unforthcoming.

milreis /ˈmɪlreɪs/ *n.* Pl. same. L16. [Port., f. *mil* thousand + REI *n.* + -S[1]] *Hist.* A former monetary unit of Portugal and Brazil equal to 1,000 reis, replaced in Portugal by the escudo in 1911 and in Brazil by the cruzeiro in 1942.

Milroy's disease /ˈmɪlrɔɪz dɪˌziːz/ *n. phr.* E20. [W. F. *Milroy* (1855–1942), US physician.] *Med.* A hereditary condition characterized by lymphoedema of the extremities, usu. the lower legs.

milt /mɪlt/ *n.* & *v.* As n. also **melt** /mɛlt/. [OE *milt(e*, corresp. to OFris., MDu. *milte* (Du. *milt*), OHG *milzi* (G *Milz*), ON *milti*, f. Gmc, perh. rel. to base of MELT *v.*] **A** *n.* **1** The spleen (now chiefly, that of a domestic animal). OE. **2** The semen of a male fish; the testes of a male fish. L15.

Comb.: **miltwaste** (now *rare* or *obs.*) the rustyback fern, *Ceterach officinarum*.

B *v.t.* & *i.* Of a male fish: fertilize with or emit milt. *rare.* L17.

milter *n.* a male fish, esp. in spawning time E17.

Milton /ˈmɪlt(ə)n/ *n.* M18. [See MILTONIC.] A person whose great innate ability is frustrated by lack of opportunity. Chiefly in *mute inglorious Milton*.

¶After a line in T. Gray's *Elegy Written in a Country Church-yard*.

miltonia /mɪlˈtəʊnɪə/ *n.* M19. [mod.L (see below), f. Charles Fitzwilliam, Viscount *Milton* (1786–1857), Eng. politician and horticulturist + -IA[1].] Any of various epiphytic orchids of the tropical S. American genus *Miltonia*, bearing large brilliantly coloured flowers.

Miltonian /mɪlˈtəʊnɪən/ *a.* & *n.* E18. [f. as next + -IAN.] **A** *adj.* = MILTONIC *a.* E18. **B** *n.* An admirer, student, or imitator of Milton. M19.

Miltonic /mɪlˈtɒnɪk/ *a.* & *n.* E18. [f. *Milton* (see below) + -IC.] **A** *adj.* Of, pertaining to, or characteristic of the English poet John Milton (1608–74) or his (esp. epic) style, language, or imagery. E18. **B** *n.* **†1** Miltonic language. *rare.* Only in E18. **2** In *pl.* Verses by or (usu.) typical of Milton. L18.

Miltonically *adv.* M19.

Miltonise *v.* var. of MILTONIZE.

Miltonism /ˈmɪlt(ə)nɪz(ə)m/ *n.* E19. [f. as MILTONIC + -ISM.] A Miltonic mode of expression; Miltonic language or style.

Miltonist /ˈmɪlt(ə)nɪst/ *n.* M17. [f. as MILTONIC + -IST.] An admirer or student of the English poet John Milton (1608–74) or his writing.

Miltonize /ˈmɪlt(ə)nʌɪz/ *v.* Also **-ise.** L18. [f. as MILTONIC + -IZE.] **1** *v.t.* Give a Miltonic character to. *rare.* L18. **2** *v.i.* Imitate the literary style of Milton. E20.

Miltown /ˈmɪltaʊn/ *n.* M20. [Origin unkn.] *Pharm.* (Proprietary name for) the drug meprobamate.

miltsiekte /ˈmɪltsɪktə/ *n. S. Afr.* L19. [Afk., f. *milt* spleen + *siekte* sickness.] = ANTHRAX 2.

miltz /mɪlts/ *n.* E20. [G *Milz* MILT *n.*] In Jewish cookery, the spleen of an animal.

mim /mɪm/ *a.* Orig. & chiefly *Sc.* & *dial.* L16. [Imit. of the pursing of the mouth. Cf. MIMP.] Affectedly modest or demure; primly silent or quiet.

Comb.: **mim-mouthed** *a.* affectedly reticent.

mimness *n.* E19.

Mimamsa /mɪˈmɑːmsə/ *n.* L18. [Skt *mīmāṃsā* profound thought, consideration, investigation, f. *man* think, consider.] A leading system of Hindu philosophy, based on the interpretation of Vedic ritual and text.

mimbar /ˈmɪmbɑː/ *n.* Also **min-** /mɪn-/. M19. [Arab. *minbar*, f. *nabara* raise.] A small set of steps in a mosque from which the *khutba* is delivered.

mime /mʌɪm/ *n.* & *v.* E17. [L *mimus* f. Gk *mimos*.] **A** *n.* **I 1** A mimic; a jester. Now chiefly *spec.*, a practitioner of the technique of mime (see sense 4 below); also *mime artist*. E17. **2** *Class. Hist.* A performer in a mime (see sense 3 below). L18.

1 C. J. CORNISH Those . . famous mimes, the Indian mynahs. *New Yorker* The chalkfaced mime Jousts with the crowd.

II 3 *Class. Hist.* A simple farcical drama characterized by mimicry and the ludicrous representation of familiar types of character. E17. **4** The art or technique of expressing or conveying action, character, or emotion without words and using only gestures, movement, etc., or (*spec.* in *Ballet*) using a fixed set of these; an expression of action etc. or a performance using such means. M20.

4 *Westworld* (*Vancouver*) Within minutes, each group presented a mime, so well performed that they could have been practising for hours.

B *v.* **1** *v.t.* & *i.* Use mime to express or convey (action, character, or emotion) or in the acting of (a play or part). E17. **b** Of a singer: mouth the words of (a song etc.) along with a soundtrack. M20. **2** *v.t.* Imitate, mimic. M18.

1 J. CLAVELL She . . put her hand to her head pretending pain, mimed being drunk and sleeping like a stone. A. CARTER She rubbed her stomach, pointed to her mouth . . clearly miming an invitation to supper.

mimer *n.* a mime or mimic, a buffoon, a jester; a person who mimes: M18.

mimeo /ˈmɪmɪəʊ/ *n.* & *v.* M20. [Abbrev. of MIMEOGRAPH *n.*] **A** *n.* Pl. **-os.** A copy of a document, newspaper, etc., reproduced by means of a mimeograph. M20. **B** *v.t.* = MIMEOGRAPH *v.* M20.

mimeograph /ˈmɪmɪəgrɑːf/ *n.* & *v.* L19. [Irreg. f. Gk *mimeomai* I imitate + -GRAPH.] **A** *n.* A duplicating machine for producing copies from a stencil; a copy produced in this way. L19. **B** *v.t.* Reproduce (text or diagrams) by means of a mimeograph. L19.

mimesis /mɪˈmiːsɪs, -mʌɪ-/ *n.* M16. [Gk *mimēsis*, f. *mimeisthai*: see MIMETIC.] **1** Chiefly *Rhet.* Imitation of another person's words or actions. M16. **b** The representation of the real world in art, poetry, etc. M20. **2** *Biol.* = MIMICRY 2. Now *rare.* M19. **3** *Sociol.* The deliberate imitation of the behaviour of one group of people by another as a factor in social change. M20.

mimester /ˈmʌɪmstə/ *n. rare.* L19. [f. MIME *v.* + -STER.] = MIME *n.* 1.

mimetic /mɪˈmɛtɪk/ *a.* M17. [Gk *mimētikos*, f. *mimeisthai* imitate, f. *mimos* MIME *n.*: see -IC.] **1** Having an aptitude for mimicry or imitation, habitually practising mimicry or imitation. M17. **2** Pertaining to, characterized by, or of the nature of imitation; *spec.* representing the real world in art, literature, etc.; of or pertaining to mimesis. M17. **3** = MIMIC *a.* 3. M18. **4 a** *Biol.* Characterized by or of the nature of mimicry. M19. **b** *Med.* Of a disease: resembling another disease. *rare.* M19. **c** *Cryst.* Of a crystal: having a high degree of apparent symmetry due to twinning or malformation. L19.

†mimetical *a.* (*rare*) = MIMETIC 1 E17–M18.

mimetically *adv.* M17.

mimetism /ˈmɪmɪtɪz(ə)m/ *n. rare.* L19. [Irreg. f. MIMETIC + -ISM.] = MIMICRY.

mimetite /ˈmɪmɪtʌɪt, ˈmʌɪ-/ *n.* M19. [f. Gk *mimētēs* imitator + -ITE[1].] *Min.* Lead chloroarsenate, a hexagonal mineral resembling pyromorphite and usu. found as yellow to brown crusts or needle-like crystals.

mimi *n.* see MEEMIE.

mimiambi /mɪmɪˈambʌɪ, mʌɪ-/ *n.pl.* E18. [L f. Gk *mimiamboi* pl., f. *mimos* MIME *n.* + *iambos* IAMBUS.] *Class. Pros.* Mimes written in iambic or scazontic verse.

mimiambic /mɪmɪˈambɪk, mʌɪ-/ *a.* & *n.* E18. [mod.L *mimiambicus*, f. as prec.: see -IC.] *Class. Pros.* **A** *adj.* Of or pertaining to mimiambi, (of a poet) writing mimiambi. E18. **B** *n.* In *pl.* = MIMIAMBI. M19.

mimic /ˈmɪmɪk/ *a.* & *n.* L16. [L *mimicus* f. Gk *mimikos*, f. *mimos* MIME *n.*: see -IC.] **A** *adj.* **1** Tending to practise or having an aptitude for mimicry or imitation. Formerly also, being or resembling a mime or jester. L16. **2** Of, pertaining to, or of the nature of mimicry or imitation. E17. **3** *attrib.* That is a copy of; having an (esp. amusing or ludicrous) imitative resemblance to. E17.

1 W. COWPER 'Sweet Poll!' his doting mistress cries, 'Sweet Poll!' the mimic bird replies. **3** G. ORWELL At the international level sport is frankly mimic warfare.

B *n.* **1** A person practising or skilled in mimicry or imitation, esp. of another's manner, voice, etc., in order to amuse. L16. **b** A poor or feeble imitation. E17. **2** Mimicry; imitation. *rare.* M17. **3** *Biol.* An animal or plant which exhibits mimicry. M19. **b** *Entomol.* = VICEROY. M20.

1 M. FOOT A marvellous mimic; he could have made another career as a music-hall comedian. **2** W. GASS She would throw her head back in the mimic of gargantuan guffaws, soundless and shaking. **3** V. B. WIGGLESWORTH The mimic will begin to lose its protective advantage if it becomes too numerous.

mimical *a.* = MIMIC *a.* E17. **mimically** *adv.* E17.

mimic /ˈmɪmɪk/ *v.t.* Infl. **-ck-**. L17. [f. MIMIC *n.*] **1** Imitate or copy (a person, gesture, action, etc.), esp. to amuse or ridicule; imitate or copy minutely or servilely. Also, represent in mime. L17. **2** Of a thing: have a close resemblance to; have the appearance of; *spec.* in *Med.*, (of a drug) produce an effect very similar to (the effect of another substance or agency). M18. **3** *Biol.* Have a mimetic resemblance to (something else) in form or colour. M19.

1 DEFOE The devil is known to mimic the methods, as well as the actions of his maker. L. STEPHEN The absurdity of mimicking a man who was his junior. R. KIPLING 'This is disgraceful,' said Maisie, mimicking Mrs. Jennett's tone. TOLKIEN You should have been the king's jester and earned your bread, and stripes too, by mimicking his counsellors. G. GREENE The purser mimicked the action of a man drinking and pointed towards me. **3** *Müllerian mimic*: see MÜLLERIAN *a.*[2]

mimicker *n.* M19.

mimicry /ˈmɪmɪkri/ *n.* L17. [f. MIMIC *n.* + -RY.] **1** The action, practice, or art of mimicking; an act, instance, or example of this. L17. **2** *Biol.* A close external resemblance which (part of) one living creature (or occas. a nest or other structure) bears to (part of) another, or to some inanimate object. M19.

1 BARONESS ORCZY The mimicry was so perfect, the tone of the voice so accurately produced. DENNIS POTTER When she told them what the wicked old witch said . . her own face twisted and snarled in chilling mimicry. D. FRASER With his gift of mimicry, he also caught the great man's manner perfectly. **in mimicry of** in imitation of. **2** R. DAWKINS A remarkable perfection of mimicry on the part of the cuckoo eggs. MERTENSIAN *mimicry*. *Müllerian mimicry*: see MÜLLERIAN *a.*[2]

miminy-piminy /ˌmɪmɪnɪˈpɪmɪni/ *a.* E19. [Fanciful formation: cf. MIM, NIMINY-PIMINY.] Ridiculously affected or overrefined; finical.

mimographer /mʌɪˈmɒɡrəfə/ *n.* M17. [f. L *mimographus* f. Gk *mimographos*, f. *mimos* MIME *n.*: see -GRAPHER.] *Class. Hist.* A writer or composer of mimes.

mimosa /mɪˈməʊzə, -sə/ *n.* & *a.* M18. [mod.L (see below), app. f. L *mimus* MIME *n.* + *-osa* fem. of *-osus* -OSE[1] (named from its being as sensitive as an animal).] **A** *n.* **1** Any of various tropical or subtropical leguminous shrubs, trees, lianes, etc., of the genus *Mimosa*, chiefly with bipinnate leaves and small pink or white flowers in ball-like clusters; *esp.* the sensitive plant, *Mimosa pudica*. Also, any of certain, chiefly Australian, trees of the related genus *Acacia*; *esp.* (the blossom of) the silver wattle, *A. dealbata*. Also *mimosa tree*. M18. **2** In full *mimosa-bark*. The bark of various Australian acacias, used in tanning. Also called *wattle-bark*. M19. **3** A bright yellow colour resembling that of the flowers of the silver wattle. E20. **4** A cocktail consisting of orange juice and champagne. M20. **B** *adj.* Of the colour mimosa, bright yellow. E20.

mimp /mɪmp/ *v.*, *n.*, & *a.* Chiefly *Sc.* & *dial.* E18. [Imit. Cf. MIM.] **A** *v.* †**1** *v.t.* Purse *up* (the mouth). Only in E18. **2** *v.i.* Speak or act in an affected manner. M19. **B** *n.* A pursing of the lips. L18. **C** *adj.* Prim, precise, affected. L19.

mimsy /ˈmɪmzi/ *a.* Also **mimsey**. M19. [In sense 1, nonsense wd invented by Lewis Carroll. In sense 2, f. MIM: cf. *clumsy*, *flimsy*.] **1** Unhappy. M19. **2** Prim, affected. L19.

1 L. CARROLL All mimsy were the borogoves. **2** J. CANNAN The lawns . . torn up and replaced by a mimsy pseudo-Elizabethan rose-garden.

mimulus /ˈmɪmjʊləs/ *n.* M18. [mod.L (see below), app. dim. of L *mimus* MIME *n.*] Any of various moisture-loving plants of the chiefly American genus *Mimulus*, of the figwort family, with chiefly bright yellow, sometimes red-blotched flowers like those of antirrhinums; *esp.* the monkey flower, *M. guttatus*.

min /mɪn/ *n.*[1] L19. [Abbrev.] = MINUTE *n.*

Min /mɪn/ *a.* & *n.*[2] E20. [See below.] **A** *adj.* Of or pertaining to the district of Min in Fukien province, SE China, or to the group of Chinese dialects spoken there. E20. **B** *n.* The Min group of Chinese dialects. M20.

mina /ˈmʌɪnə/ *n.*[1] Pl. **-nae** /-niː/, **-nas**. L16. [L f. Gk *mna*, prob. ult. f. Akkadian.] *Hist.* **1** An ancient monetary unit formerly used in Greece and Greek-speaking countries, equal to 100 drachmas. L16. **2** An ancient unit of weight formerly used in Western Asia, Greece, and Egypt, approx. equal to 1 lb (0.4536 kg). E17. **3** = MANEH. M18.

mina *n.*[2] see MYNAH.

minable *a.* var. of MINEABLE.

minacious /mɪˈneɪʃəs/ *a.* M17. [f. L *minac-*, *-ax* (f. *minari* threaten) + -OUS.] Menacing, threatening.

minaciously *adv.* L17. **minaciousness** *n.* M19.

minacity /mɪˈnasɪti/ *n.* M17. [f. (as) prec. + -ITY, after *tenacious*, *tenacity*.] (A) tendency to use threats; menace.

minae *n.pl.* see MINA *n.*[1]

Minaean /mɪˈniːən/ *n.* & *a.* Also **Minean**. E17. [f. L *Minaeus*, f. Arab. *Maʿīn* + -AN.] **A** *n.* **1** A native or inhabitant of Maʿin, an ancient kingdom of southern Arabia. E17. **2** = MINAIC *n.* M20. **B** *adj.* Of or pertaining to the Minaeans or their language. M19.

Minaic *a.* & *n.* (*a*) *adj.* = MINAEAN *a.*; (*b*) *n.* the Semitic language of the Minaeans: L19.

Minamata disease /mɪnəˈmɑːtə dɪˌziːz/ *n. phr.* M20. [*Minamata*, a town in Japan.] *Med.* Chronic poisoning by alkyl mercury compounds (from industrial waste), characterized by (usu. permanent) impairment of brain functions such as speech, sight, and muscular coordination.

minar /mɪˈnɑː/ *n.* M17. [Pers. & Urdu *minār* f. Arab. *manār*: see next.] In India and the Far East: a lighthouse; a tower, a turret.

minaret /ˈmɪnərɛt, mɪnəˈrɛt/ *n.* L17. [Fr., or Sp. *minarete*, It. *minaretto*, f. Turk. *minâre* f. Arab. *manāra* lighthouse, minaret, f. *nāra* to shine.] **1** A tall tower or turret connected with a mosque and surrounded by one or more projecting balconies from which a muezzin calls at hours of prayer. L17. **2** *transf.* An object or structure shaped like this. M19.

minareted *a.* having or characterized by minarets M19.

minargent /mɪˈnɑːdʒ(ə)nt/ *n.* L19. [f. ALU)MIN(IUM + Fr. *argent* silver.] A silver-coloured alloy consisting of cupro-nickel with some tungsten and aluminium, used in jewellery.

minarichi *n.* var. of MINNERICHI.

minatory /ˈmɪnət(ə)ri/ *a.* & *n.* M16. [Late L *minatorius*, f. L *minat-* pa. ppl stem of *minari* threaten: see -ORY[2].] **A** *adj.* Expressing or conveying a threat; threatening, menacing. M16.

G. VIDAL Letitia gave a laugh . . not unlike the minatory rattle of a leper's bell. P. ACKROYD He talks in minatory terms to the ghost of the . . boy he had once been, and berates him.

†**B** *n.* A threat, a menace. *rare.* L16–L17.

minatorily *adv.* M17. **minatoriness** *n.* M20.

minauderie /mɪˈnɔːdəri, *foreign* minodri (*pl. same*)/ *n.* M18. [Fr., f. *minauder* simper, flirt, f. *mine* MIEN *n.*[1]] Coquetry, flirtation; a coquettish manner or air.

minaudière /minodjɛːr/ *n.* Pl. pronounced same. E18. [Fr.: cf. prec.] †**1** A coquettish woman. E18–E19. **2** A small handbag without a handle, a clutch-bag. M20.

†**minaway** *n.* Chiefly *Sc.* L17–L19. [Fr. *menuet*.] = MINUET *n.*

minbar *n.* var. of MIMBAR.

mince /mɪns/ *v.* & *n.* Also (now *dial.*) **minch** /mɪn(t)ʃ/. LME. [OFr. *mincier* (dial. *minchier*) f. Proto-Romance, f. L MINUTIA.] **A** *v.* **1** *v.t.* Cut up or grind (esp. meat) into very small pieces. LME. †**b** Carve (a plover). L15–M19. **c** Cut (a person) up into small pieces. E17. **2** *v.t.* Subdivide (*up*) minutely. LME. †**3** *v.t.* Diminish, take away from. Chiefly *Sc.* L15–L19. **4a** *v.t.* & †*i.* Lessen or diminish (something) in representation; minimize. Now *rare.* M16. **b** *v.t.* Restrain (one's words etc.) within the bounds of politeness or decorum. Usu. in neg. contexts. L16. **5** *v.t.* & *i.* Utter or speak in an affectedly refined or precise manner. M16. **6** *v.i.* Walk with short steps and an affected preciseness or daintiness. M16. **b** *v.t.* Perform or enact in an affectedly precise or dainty manner. E17.

1 *Country Living* Mince the rest of the meat with the . . pork. **4b** T. S. ELIOT I didn't mince my words, I said to her myself. **6** V. WOOLF Three white pigeons . . minced with tiny steps on their little pink feet. DENNIS POTTER He minces out with an ogling smile.

Comb. & *phrases*: **minced meat** (*a*) meat cut up or ground into very small pieces; (*b*) *rare* = MINCEMEAT 3; **minced pie** = *mince pie* (a) below; **mince matters** = *mince the matter* (b) below; **mince pie** (*a*) a usu. small round pie containing mincemeat, traditionally eaten esp. at Christmas; (*b*) *rhyming slang* an eye (usu. in *pl.*); **mince the matter** †(*a*) make light of the matter in question; (*b*) use polite expressions to indicate disapproval etc. (usu. in neg. contexts).

B *n.* **1** Minced meat. E19. **2** An instance of mincing speech; a mincing walk. E20. **3** = *mince pie* (b) above. Usu. in *pl. rhyming slang.* M20.

mincer *n.* (*a*) a machine which or (*rare*) a person who minces meat etc.; (*b*) a person who speaks or walks in an affectedly dainty manner: L16. **mincing** *vbl n.* the action of the vb. M16. **mincing** *a.* that minces; affectedly refined or precise in speech or movement: M16. **mincingly** *adv.* L16. **mincingness** *n.* M19.

mincemeat /ˈmɪnsmiːt/ *n.* M17. [Alt. of *minced meat* s.v. MINCE *v.*] **1** *make mincemeat of*, defeat decisively or easily. M17. †**2** = *minced meat* (a) s.v. MINCE *v.* E–M18. **3** A mixture of currants, raisins, sugar, suet, chopped apples, candied peel, spices, etc. M19.

Mincha /ˈmɪnxɑː/ *n.* Also **-ah**. E19. [Heb. *minḥāh* lit. 'gift, offering'.] The Jewish daily afternoon worship.

minchen /ˈmɪn(t)ʃ(ə)n/ *n.* Long *obs.* exc. *Hist.* [OE *mynecenu* fem. of *munuc* MONK *n.*[1]] A nun.

minchery *n.* a nunnery M17.

minchiate /mɪnˈkjɑːteɪ/ *n.* M18. [It.] *Hist.* A card-game derived from tarot, formerly played in Tuscany, western Italy.

mind /mʌɪnd/ *n.*[1] [OE *ġemynd* corresp. to OHG *gimunt*, Goth. *gamunds* memory, f. Gmc, f. base of Y- + wk grade of ablaut series f. IE base meaning 'revolve in the mind, think'.] **I** Memory. †**1** The faculty of memory. OE–LME. **2** Remembrance, recollection, memory. Chiefly in phrs. OE. **3** That which is remembered *of* a person or thing; the memory *of*. Long *obs.* exc. *Sc.* OE. **4** †**a** The action of commemorating; (a) commemoration; a memorial. OE–L15. **b** *spec.* (chiefly *RC Ch.*). The commemoration of a deceased person by a requiem mass or (later more widely) special prayers held on the day of the death or funeral in any month or year following. *obs.* exc. in *month's mind*, *year's mind*. *arch.* OE. †**5** Mention, record. Chiefly in *make mind of*, *that*. Only in ME.

2 A. CLARKE Hard to hold the difference in mind. *Times Lit. Suppl.* Poets must flick in and out of mind As if we had no other kind Of knowing. *Proverb*: Out of sight, out of mind.

II Thought; purpose, intention. **6**†**a** The action or state of thinking about something; the thought *of*. Chiefly in *have mind of*, think of, give heed to. OE–L16. **b** Attention, heed. Usu. in neg. contexts w. *pay*. *N. Amer. colloq.* & *dial.* E20. **7a** Purpose, intention. *obs.* exc. in phrs. ME. **b** An inclination, a wish; a liking. Freq. in phrs. LME. **8** The direction of a person's thoughts, desires, inclinations, or energies. Freq. in phrs. ME. **9** A person's opinion, judgement, or view. Chiefly in phrs. LME. **10** A (usu. specified) disposition, character, or way of thinking and feeling. LME. †**b** A particular feeling or attitude towards something. L15–E17. **11** The state of a person's thoughts and feelings. E16.

6b P. HIGHSMITH Clara, knowing its harmlessness, paid it no mind. K. KESEY McMurphy didn't pay the guy any mind and went on arguing. **7b** D. DU MAURIER Entertained when he had the mind to do so. J. MAY We buried the furnace so we can . . make more iron when we've a mind to. J. NAGENDA We could all do it if we were of a mind to. **8** D. EDEN At first her mind had not been on Fergus. R. LARDNER I'll stop talking . . and keep my mind on the game. J. WAIN Took his mind off the two things he wanted . . to forget. E. KUZWAYO My mind would drift back to

Thaba'Nchu. 9 POPE Pray let me know your mind in this. M. W. MONTAGU I don't doubt you'll be of my mind. 10 SHAKES. *Two Gent.* Fear not; he bears an honourable mind And will not use a woman lawlessly. R. G. COLLINGWOOD The philosophy of craft . . was one of the greatest . . achievements of the Greek mind. **b** AV *Acts* 12:20 Herode bare an hostile mind intending warre. 11 W. SHENSTONE How, with one trivial glance, Might she ruin the peace of my mind! J. WAIN That ought to set Ned's mind at ease.

III Mental or psychic faculty. **12a** The seat of awareness, thought, volition, and feeling; cognitive and emotional phenomena and powers as constituting a controlling system, *spec.* as opp. *matter*; the spiritual as distinguished from the bodily part of a human being. ME. **b** A person or a group of people collectively as the embodiment of mental faculties. L16. **c** A controlling or directing spiritual being or agency. E17. **13** *spec.* The intellect, intellectual powers, esp. as distinguished from the will and emotions. ME. **14** The healthy or normal condition of the mental faculties. Freq. in phrs. LME.

12a C. WORDSWORTH His mind was filled with gloomy forebodings. J. GALSWORTHY His lively, twisting mind . . had recorded with amusement the confusion. G. F. KENNAN The example of the Russian revolution . . was in everybody's mind. P. PARISH The effects of L.S.D. on the mind are unpredictable. C. ANGIER She had built up an idea of England in her mind. A. ARONSON Rembrandt's interest in . . men's and women's minds in moments of uncontrolled passion. **b** W. J. MICKLE The same ungenerous minds . . who advised the rejection of Columbus. *Daily Telegraph* This cleavage of the European mind. 13 W. COWPER Possessor of a soul refined, An upright heart, and cultivated mind. 14 LD MACAULAY He was drunk . . or out of his mind. J. WAIN No one in his right mind will refuse . . if it is free.

Phrases: *a load off a person's mind*: see LOAD *n. at the back of one's mind*: see BACK *n.*[1] *balance of mind*: see BALANCE *n. bear in mind*: see BEAR *v.*[1] **be in two minds** be undecided. *blow a person's mind*: see BLOW *v.*[1] *bring to mind*: see BRING *v. call to mind*: see CALL *v.* **cast one's mind back** think back *to*; recall an earlier time. **change of mind** a change or alteration of one's opinion, plans, etc. **change one's mind** change or alter one's purpose, opinion, plans, etc. **close** or **shut one's mind (to)** refuse to consider (changes, new ideas, etc.), be unreceptive (to). **come to mind** (of a thought, idea, etc.) suggest itself. *cross one's mind*: see CROSS *v. enter one's mind*: see ENTER *v.* 1b. **give a bit** or **piece of one's mind** scold, reproach. **give one's mind to** apply oneself to, concentrate on. **have a (good) mind** (*a*) be strongly inclined or tempted (*to, to do*); (*b*) (*arch.*) foll. by *to*: have a liking for. **have a mind of one's own** be capable of independent opinions. **have half a mind** = *have a (good) mind* above. **have in mind** plan, intend. *have mind of*: see sense 6 above. *hearts and minds*: see HEART *n.* **in my mind** = *to my mind* (a) below. **†in (the) mind** disposed or inclined (*to do*). **know one's own mind** form and adhere to a decision or purpose without vacillating; be decisive. **lose one's mind** become insane. *make up one's mind*: see *make up* (j) s.v. MAKE *v.* **mind over matter** the power of the mind asserted over the physical universe. **month's mind** (*a*) see sense 4b above; (*b*) (*obs.* exc. *dial.*) an inclination, a fancy. *mortal mind*: see MORTAL *a.* 2. **of one mind** in agreement, of the same opinion. **†of (the) mind** = *in (the) mind* above. *one's mind's eye*: see EYE *n.* **on one's mind** occupying or esp. troubling one's thoughts. *open mind*: see OPEN *a.* **open one's mind (to)** consider readily (changes, new ideas, etc.), be receptive (to). PRESENCE *of mind.* **put in mind** remind (a person) *of*. **put out of one's mind** deliberately forget. **read a person's mind** discern a person's thoughts. *shut one's mind (to)*: see *close one's mind (to)* above. **speak one's mind** give one's candid opinion. *split mind*: see SPLIT *ppl a. the life of the mind*: see LIFE *n. the mind's eye*: see EYE *n. things of the mind*: see THING *n.*[1] *time out of mind*: see TIME *n. tiny mind*: see TINY *a.* **to my** etc. **mind** (*a*) in my etc. opinion; (*b*) to my etc. liking.

Comb.: **mind-bender** *slang* a person who or thing which influences or alters one's mood; *spec.* a hallucinogenic drug; **mind-bending** *a.* (*slang*) (esp. of a drug) influencing or altering the mind; **mind-bendingly** *adv.* (*slang*) in a mind-bending manner; **mind-blowing** *a.* (*slang*) (*a*) (of a drug etc.) inducing hallucinations; (*b*) confusing; shattering; **mind-blowingly** *adv.* (*slang*) in a mind-blowing manner; **mind-boggling** *a.* overwhelming, startling; **mind-bogglingly** *adv.* in a mind-boggling manner, to a mind-boggling extent; **mind-cure** the supposed curing of a disease by the mental powers of the healer; **mind-curer**, **curist** a person who practises mind-cure; **mind-expanding** *a.* psychedelic; **mind-game** a game designed to test or exercise the intellect; **mind-healer** = *mind-curer* above; **mind-healing** = *mind-cure* above; **mind-read** *v.t.* apparently discern the thoughts of (another person); **mind-reader** a person capable of mind-reading; **mind-set** (*a*) habits of mind formed by previous events or an earlier environment; (*b*) *loosely* a frame of mind, a mental attitude; **mind-transference** telepathy.

mind /mɪnd/ *n.*[2] Now *rare.* M19. [MIr., mod. *mionn.*] *Archaeol.* An Irish lunula.

mind /mʌɪnd/ *v.* ME. [f. MIND *n.*[1]] **1** *v.t.* Remind (*of, that, to do*). Now *rare* exc. *Sc.* ME. **†b** Serve as a reminder of. L16–E17. **2** *v.t.* Remember, recollect. Also w. refl. pron. as indirect obj. Now *arch.* & *dial.* exc. *Sc.* LME. **b** *v.i.* & *refl.* Foll. by *of.*: remember, recollect. Now *arch.* & *dial.* L17. **3** *v.t.* **†a** Mention, record. LME–M16. **b** Remember or mention in one's prayers, pray for. Long *obs.* exc. *Sc. dial.* LME. **4** *v.t.* Bear in mind; take care to remember, make certain, *that*. Usu. in *imper.* LME. **5** *v.t.* Apply oneself to, concern oneself diligently with, (business, one's affairs, etc.). LME. **†b** Care for, like, value. M17–M18. **6** *v.t.* Perceive, notice, be aware of. *obs.* exc. *dial.* L15. **7** *v.t.* Plan, contemplate, intend, (†an action etc., †*that, to do*). *obs.* exc. *dial.* E16. **8a** *v.t.* Attend to, heed, esp. with the intention of obeying. Now chiefly *N. Amer.* M16. **b** *v.i.* Pay attention; take note. Usu. in *imper.* w. emphatic force or qualifying a statement. *colloq.* E19. **9** *v.t.* & *i.* Object (to), be annoyed (by); be troubled or concerned (by). Usu. in neg. & interrog. contexts. E17. **10a** *v.t.* Be careful or attentive about; be wary concerning, be on one's guard against (now usu. in *imper.*). L17. **b** *v.i.* Look out, be careful. Usu. foll. by *out*. Usu. in *imper. colloq.* L17. **11** *v.t.* Take charge of or look after (esp. a child, shop, etc.) temporarily. Also, guard, protect. L17.

1 R. BURNS There's not a bonie bird that sings, But minds me o' my Jean. TENNYSON They mind us of the time When we made bricks in Egypt. 2 MRS H. WOOD I mind me that something was said about that paper. C. MACKENZIE Nobody in the islands could mind such a storm of rain. **b** THACKERAY I mind me of a time that's gone. 4 T. HARDY Mind you make a good impression upon him. 5 G. BERKELEY If some certain persons minded piety more than politics. **b** SMOLLETT His heir . . minded nothing but fox-hunting. 8a A. LURIE Her little brothers always ganged up on her . . and wouldn't mind what she said. **b** E. WAUGH Suppose you were just a crook. . . I don't say you are, mind, but supposing. J. BRAINE They bought it from a bankrupt woolman. . . Mind you, they don't use half of it. M. SPARK Foreigners always talk like that, mind you. 9 J. PORTER 'Tea, Mr Dover?' 'I don't mind if I do' said Dover, passing his cup. D. ATHILL I greatly minded making a fool of myself. C. P. SNOW I don't mind him having a look. 10a MRS H. WARD 'Mind what you're about,' cried Purcell, angrily. J. BETJEMAN And mind the terrier when you call. **b** H. JAMES Take care . . they'll see you, if you don't mind. *American Speech* Children whizzing around on bicycles . . shouting 'Mind out!'. 11 T. HARDY A boy who was minding a gingerbread stall. C. STEAD They were being minded by Louisa.

Phrases etc.: **don't mind me, us**, etc., *iron.* don't worry about me, us, etc.; do as you please. **do you mind?** *ellipt.* do you mind not doing that?, please do not do that. **mind one's eye** be on one's guard. *mind one's hits*: see HIT *n.* 3. *mind one's own* BUSINESS. *mind one's P's and Q's*: see P, P I. *mind one's step*: see STEP *n.*[1] **mind the shop** [cf. sense II above] have temporary charge of affairs. **mind-your-own-business** a dwarf creeping plant of the nettle family, *Soleirolia soleirolia*, cultivated in greenhouses and as a house-plant. NEVER (*you*) *mind.*

minded /ˈmʌɪndɪd/ *a.* L15. [f. MIND *n.*[1] + -ED[2].] **1** Intending, disposed, inclined, (*to do*). L15. **†2** Having a specified disposition towards a person or thing. E16–L17. **3** As 2nd elem. of comb.: **a** Having a specified kind of mind. E16. **b** Inclined or well able to think in a specified way. E17. **c** Interested in or enthusiastic about a specified thing. E20.

1 R. L. STEVENSON He . . can speak like a book when so minded. M. SPARK I wasn't minded to take on a girl of twenty-two. 3a *absent-minded, bloody-minded, feeble-minded, high-minded*, etc. **b** *Daily Chronicle* Monotonous even to the most . . statistically-minded. J. JONES Invaded and taken over by . . mystically minded people. **c** *Guardian* A bowling-green for the sports-minded customer.

Mindel /ˈmɪnd(ə)l/ *a.* & *n.* E20. [A river in southern Germany.] *Geol.* (Designating or pertaining to) a Pleistocene glaciation in the Alps preceding the Riss, possibly corresponding to the Elsterian of northern Europe.

minder /ˈmʌɪndə/ *n.* LME. [f. MIND *n.*[1], *v.* + -ER[1].] **†1** A person with a good memory. *rare.* Only in LME. **2** A person employed to have charge of or look after a specified thing; *spec.* a person employed to look after a child outside the home (as at a crèche) for a fixed part of the day. Chiefly as 2nd elem. of comb. LME. **b** A child who is looked after at a crèche etc. *rare.* M19. **3** In early use (*slang*), a person employed to protect a criminal; a thief's assistant. Later *gen.*, a person employed to protect anyone, esp. a famous person or an inexperienced political candidate in an election campaign. E20.

2 R. DINNAGE The children had been dumped with various minders. *child-minder, dog-minder, machine-minder*, etc. 3 L. GRIFFITHS If there's a threat . . you have to call on your minder. *Independent* Living in luxury, surrounded by minders and assistants.

Mindererus /mɪndəˈrɪərəs/ *n.* Now *rare* or *obs.* Also **m-**. L18. [Latinized form of the name of R. M. *Minderer* (d. 1621), Ger. physician.] Pharm. *spirit(s) of Mindererus*, a solution of ammonium acetate, formerly used as a febrifuge.

mindful /ˈmʌɪn(d)fʊl, -f(ə)l/ *a.* ME. [f. MIND *n.*[1] + -FUL.] **1** Taking heed or care; being conscious or aware. Freq. foll. by *of, that, to do.* ME. **2** Inclined or intending *to do. rare.* M16.

mindfully *adv.* LME. **mindfulness** *n.* M16.

mindless /ˈmʌɪndlɪs/ *a.* OE. [f. MIND *n.*[1] + -LESS.] **1** Unintelligent, stupid; (of an activity etc.) not requiring thought or skill. OE. **2** Thoughtless, heedless, careless, (*of*). LME.

mindlessly *adv.* M19. **mindlessness** *n.* M17.

†mindly *a.* LME. [f. MIND *n.*[1] + -LY[1].] **1** Mindful, conscious. Only in LME. **2** Of or pertaining to the mind; mental. LME–M19.

mine /mʌɪn/ *n.* ME. [(O)Fr. (perh. f. *miner* MINE *v.*) or directly f. MINE *v.*] **1** An excavation or a system of excavations in the earth for the extraction of metal, metallic ore, coal, salt, etc. ME. **b** *fig.* An abundant source or supply. M16. **†c** *transf.* A subterranean cavity. Only in E17. **2** A mineral; ore. Now only *spec.*, iron ore. ME. **3** *Mil.* **a** A subterranean passage dug under an enemy position (esp. the wall of a besieged fortress) in order to gain entrance or (later esp. with the use of an explosive) to collapse a wall or fortification. Also, the explosive charge placed in such a passage. LME. **b** A receptacle containing explosive placed in or on the ground or in the water with the purpose of destroying enemy personnel, ships, etc. Freq. w. specifying wd. LME. **4** A firework propelling crackers into the air. Now *rare.* M18. **5** A tunnel or network of tunnels made in the interior of a leaf by an insect larva. M19.

1 B. BYARS Friends were working the mine, digging out turquoise. B. MOORE The great moonlit slag heaps of the Gorodok mines. *coalmine, diamond mine, salt mine, tin mine*, etc. **b** D. H. LAWRENCE The courage of our own feelings . . becomes a mine of practical truth. B. GILROY They . . found her a mine of information. 3b B. MASON His jeep passed over a mine; wreckage was strewn over a wide area. *limpet mine, magnetic mine, pressure mine*, etc.

Comb.: **mine-car** a wheeled container used in a mine for the underground transport of coal etc.; **mine-detector** an instrument for detecting the presence of explosive mines; **mine-dump** *S. Afr.* a large mound or hill of mining waste at the surface of a mine, esp. a gold-mine, or former mine; **minefield** (*a*) an area laid with explosive mines; (*b*) *fig.* a situation or subject presenting unseen hazards; **mine-hunt** *v.i.* hunt or sweep for mines; **mine-hunter** = *minesweeper* below; **mine-iron** = *mine-pig* below; **minelayer** a ship or aircraft equipped to lay explosive mines; **mine-laying** *n.* & *a.* (*a*) *n.* the operation of laying explosive mines; (*b*) *adj.* that lays explosive mines; **mine-pig** pig-iron made from mine or ore; **mine-pit** a pit or shaft in a mine; **mine shaft**: giving access to a mine; **mine-sinker** a device for keeping a mine submerged; **mine-stone** ore, *esp.* iron ore;

minesweeper a ship for clearing away floating and submarine mines; **mine-sweeping** *n.* & *a.* (*a*) *n.* the operation of clearing away floating or submarine mines; (*b*) *adj.* that clears away floating or submarine mines; **mine tin**: worked out of the lode; **mine-town** = *mining town* s.v. MINING *vbl n.* whose population consists chiefly of miners; **mine-work** = sense 1 above.

mine /mʌɪn/ *possess. a.* (in mod. usage also classed as a *determiner*) & *pron.*, *1 sing.* [OE *mīn* = OFris., OS,OHG *mīn*. (Du. *mijn*, G *mein*), ON *minn*, Goth. *meins*, f. Gmc, f. IE locative form of base of ME *pron.* + adj. suff.] A *adj.* = MY *a.* Used *attrib.* bef. a vowel or *h* (*arch.*) or as the first of two or more possess. adjs. qualifying the same following n. Also (*arch.*) used w. emphatic force following any n. Cf. THINE *a.* OE.

SWIFT A little below the level of mine eyes. C. A. BRISTED There, reader mine! Is that last page grave . . enough for you? J. CONRAD I venture to ask that mine and Mr Razumov's intervention should not become public. P. G. WODEHOUSE I entered the saloon bar and requested mine host to start pouring.

B *pron.* [absol. use of the adj.: cf. THINE *pron.*] 1 My one(s), that or those belonging or pertaining to me. Formerly also *spec.*, my property; my affair. OE. 2 *of mine*, belonging or pertaining to me. LME.

1 J. RHYS Talking about cats you don't know how I miss mine. I. MURDOCH It is our duty, yours and mine. J. SIMMS The frog had been given to me: it was mine. B. GILROY 'Life is sweet' . . 'Not mine It's not worth a single cent.'

mine /mʌɪn/ *v.* ME. [(O)Fr. *miner*, perh. orig. Proto-Gallo-Romance deriv. of Celt. wd repr. by Ir. *méin*, Gael. *mèinn* ore, mine, Welsh *mwyn* ore, †mine. Cf. MINERAL *n.*] 1 *v.i.* a Dig in the earth. Also, make subterranean passages. Long *rare* or *obs.* ME. b *v.t.* Dig or burrow in (the earth); make (a hole, passage, one's way) underground by digging; *transf.* make a hollow or groove in. LME. c *v.t.* In *pass.* Provided with subterranean passages. E19. 2a *v.t.* & *i.* Chiefly in ancient warfare: dig a passage under the foundations of (a wall, fort, etc.), esp. in order to cause collapse or gain entrance. Now *rare* or *obs.* ME. b *v.t.* Lay explosive mines under or in. M17. 3 *v.t. fig.* Ruin or destroy slowly, undermine. LME. 4 *v.t.* Extract (metals, ore, coal, etc.) from a mine. LME b *fig.* Extract (information, an idea, etc.) from an abundant source or supply. M20. 5 *v.t.* & *i.* Dig in (the earth, a place, etc.) for metal, ore, coal, etc. Freq. foll. by *for*. LME. b *fig.* Delve into or *into* (an abundant source or supply) to extract information, an idea, etc. L19. 6 *v.t.* Exhaust (soil or land) by excessive cultivation. M20.

1b SIR W. SCOTT Condemned to mine a channell'd way, O'er solid sheets of marble grey. 2b K. DOUGLAS The verges . . in the road were mined with anti-personnel . . mines. O. MANNING We started mining Norwegian waters. 4 A. MOOREHEAD Gold had to be mined by machinery. *Scientific American* Oil left in the ground after pumping can be mined. *deep-mined*: see DEEP *adv.* 5 SIR W. SCOTT Nature had assigned to him . . a serf, to mine for the gold. W. W. SMYTH The . . rich coalfield . . mined as early as 1302. b G. GREENE By mining into layers of personality hitherto untouched. *Lochaber News* The . . cast mined every rich seam of comedy.

mineable /ˈmʌɪnəb(ə)l/ *a.* Also **minable**. L16. [f. MINE *v.* + -ABLE.] Able to be mined.

Minean *n.* & *a.* var. of MINAEAN.

Minenwerfer /ˈmiːnənvɛrfər, -wəːfə/ *n.* Also **m-**. E20. [G, f. *Minen* (pl.) mines + *Werfer* lit. 'thrower', f. *werfen* to throw.] *Hist.* A German trench mortar of the war of 1914–18.

miner /ˈmʌɪnə/ *n.* ME. [OFr. *minëor*, *minour* (mod. *mineur*), f. *miner*: see MINE *v.*, -ER[2], -OR. In sense 4, alt. of MYNAH.] 1 A person who works in a mine. ME. 2 A person who excavates subterranean passages in order to destroy an enemy position, esp. with the aid of an explosive charge. Cf. (*Royal*) *Sappers and Miners* s.v. SAPPER. ME. 3 A burrowing insect or larva; *esp.* = *leaf-miner* s.v. LEAF *n.*[1] E19. 4 Any of various Australian honeyeaters of the genus *Manorina*. M19.

Phrases: *bell-miner*: see BELL *n.*[1] **miner's disease** = *miner's lung* below. *miner's inch*: see INCH *n.*[1] 1C. **miner's lettuce** a kind of spring beauty, *Montia perfoliata*, sometimes eaten as a salad. **miner's lung** pneumoconiosis due to inhalation of coal dust. **miner's right** *Austral.* & *NZ* a licence to dig for gold etc. on private or public land. *noisy miner*: see NOISY *a.* 1.

†minera *n.* M17–M18. [med.L f. OFr. *min(i)ere*: see MINERAL *n.*] The matrix in which a metal or precious stone was supposed to grow. Also, the ore of a metal.

mineragraphy /mɪnəˈraɡrəfi/ *n.* E20. [f. MINERA(L *n.* + -GRAPHY.] = MINERALOGRAPHY.

mineraˈgraphic *a.* M20.

mineral /ˈmɪn(ə)r(ə)l/ *n.* LME. [OFr., or med.L *minerale* use as n. of neut. sing. of *mineralis*, f. *minera* ore f. OFr. *min(i)ere* mine, perh. ult. f. Proto-Gallo-Romance deriv. whence perh. also MINE *n.*, *v.*: see -AL[1].] 1 A substance obtained by mining; *esp.* one other than a native metal, an ore. LME. †b The art or industry of mining. L15–L16. †c A mine. L16–E17. 2 A (naturally occurring) substance that is neither animal nor vegetable; an inorganic substance (now freq., one required in the diet). LME. †b An inorganic substance used as a drug. M16–M18. 3 A solid, usu. naturally occurring, inorganic substance of homogeneous composition and distinctive chemical and physical properties. E19. 4 An artificial mineral water or other effervescent drink. Usu. in *pl.* L19.

Comb.: **mineral dressing** treatment of ore so as to remove gangue and concentrate the valuable constituents; **mineral rod** a divining-rod for finding mineral veins.

mineral /ˈmɪn(ə)r(ə)l/ *a.* LME. [OFr., or med.L *mineralis*: see prec., -AL[1].] 1 Of a material substance: neither animal nor vegetable in origin; inorganic. LME. 2a Of the nature of a mineral; obtained or obtainable by mining. L16. b Impregnated with minerals. Formerly also, (of colour) indicating such impregnation. M17. †3 Of or pertaining to mines or mining. Of a person: skilled in mining. L16–E18.

Special collocations: **mineral black** a black pigment made from graphite or slate. **mineral blue** a Prussian blue made lighter by the addition of alumina. **mineral brown** a brown pigment coloured with iron oxide. *mineral chameleon*: see CHAMELEON *n.* 5. **mineral charcoal** a fibrous substance like charcoal found between layers of coal; = FUSAIN 2. **mineral coal** †(*a*) a variety of coal in which there are no traces of vegetable structure; (*b*) native coal (as distinct from charcoal). **mineral green** Scheele's green, copper arsenite. **mineral grey** a pale blue-grey pigment obtained in the making of ultramarine from lapis lazuli. **mineral jelly** petroleum jelly. **mineral oil** petroleum; a distillation product of petroleum. **mineral pitch** asphalt. **mineral purple** (*a*) a dark red pigment containing iron oxide; (*b*) purple of Cassius. **mineral soil**: in which the organic constituents are small in proportion to the inorganic ones. *mineral tallow*: see TALLOW *n.* 2. **mineral tar** = MALTHA 2. **mineral violet** = MANGANESE *violet*. **mineral water** (*a*) water found in nature with some dissolved mineral salts present; a kind of such water; (*b*) an artificial (esp. effervescent) imitation of this, *esp.* soda water; (*c*) any effervescent non-alcoholic drink. **mineral wax** a fossil resin, *esp.* ozocerite. **mineral wool** a fine matted fibrous substance made from inorganic material, used for packing, insulation, etc. **mineral yellow** any of various inorganic yellow pigments; *esp.* a lead oxychloride.

mineralise *v.* var. of MINERALIZE.

mineralist /ˈmɪn(ə)rəlɪst/ *n.* E17. [f. MINERAL *n.* + -IST.] †1 A follower of Paracelsus in his use of minerals in medicines. Only in E17. 2 A mineralogist. M17.

mineralize /ˈmɪn(ə)rəlʌɪz/ *v.* Also **-ise**. M17. [f. MINERAL *n.*, *a.* + -IZE.] 1 *v.t.* Change wholly or partly into a mineral substance; change (a metal) into an ore. Chiefly as *mineralized* ppl a. M17. b *v.i.* Undergo such a change. *rare.* M19. 2 *v.t.* Add a mineral or minerals to; impregnate with inorganic substances; make into mineral water. Chiefly as *mineralized* ppl a. L18. 3 *v.i.* Seek for or study minerals. Now *rare.* L18. 4 *v.t.* In *pass.* Of a vein, deposit, etc.: contain ore or minerals to a specified extent. L19.

mineralizable *a.* L19. **mineraliˈzation** *n.* the process or action of mineralizing something; the state of being mineralized: M18. **mineralizer** *n.* (chiefly *Geol.*) (*a*) a substance that combines with a metal to form an ore, as oxygen, sulphur, arsenic, etc.; (*b*) a volatile constituent which controls or promotes the formation of minerals from a magma; a substance which promotes the artificial synthesis of a mineral: L18.

mineralocorticoid /mɪn(ə)rələˈkɔːtɪkɔɪd/ *n.* M20. [f. MINERAL *n.* + -O- + CORTICOID.] *Biochem.* Any of various corticosteroids (e.g. aldosterone) which are involved esp. with maintaining the salt balance in the body.

mineralography /mɪn(ə)rəˈlɒɡrəfi/ *n.* E20. [f. MINERAL *n.* + -OGRAPHY.] *Min.* The branch of science that deals with the physical and chemical microstructure of minerals, esp. of polished sections as studied with a reflecting microscope.

mineraloˈgraphic *a.* of or using mineralography E20.

mineralogy /mɪnəˈralədʒi/ *n.* L17. [f. MINERAL *n.* + -LOGY.] 1 The branch of science that deals with minerals. L17. 2 (A description of) the distribution of minerals in a region, or within a (type of) rock. L18.

mineraˈlogic *a.* (now chiefly *US*) = MINERALOGICAL E19. **mineraˈlogical** *a.* of, pertaining to, or used in mineralogy L18. **mineraˈlogically** *adv.* as regards mineralogy E19. **mineralogist** *n.* M17.

mineraloid /ˈmɪn(ə)rəlɔɪd/ *n.* E20. [f. MINERAL *n.* + -OID.] *Min.* A mineral which has an amorphous rather than crystalline structure.

minerval /mɪˈnəːv(ə)l/ *n.* E17. [L, f. *Minerva* (earlier *Men-*) the Roman goddess of handicrafts, wisdom (cf. Skt *manasvin* wise), and later also of war f. earlier form rel. to Skt *manas* mind, Gk *menos* courage, fury, f. base of MIND *n.*[1]] A gift given in gratitude by a pupil to a teacher.

Minervois /minɛrˈvwɑː/ *n.* E20. [See below.] A wine produced in the district of Minervois, in the department of Aude in southern France.

minery /ˈmʌɪnəri/ *n.* Now *rare* or *obs.* M16. [med.L *mineria*, *-aria*, f. *minare* to mine.] 1 A place where mining is carried out, a mine. M16. †b Materials for mining. Only in L17. †2 The art or industry of mining. Only in L18.

minestra /mɪˈnɛstrə/ *n.* L17. [It.] In Italy: soup, *esp.* minestrone.

minestrone /mɪnɪˈstrəʊni/ *n.* L19. [It.] A thick soup containing vegetables, beans, and pasta.

minette /mɪˈnɛt/ *n.* L19. [Fr.] *Geol.* 1 A dark porphyritic igneous rock consisting chiefly of biotite and alkaline feldspars. L19. 2 In full *minette ore*. A low-grade oolitic iron ore found mainly in Luxembourg and Lorraine. E20.

minever *n.* var. of MINIVER.

Ming /mɪŋ/ *n.* & *a.* L18. [Chin., lit. 'bright, clear'.] 1 (Designating or pertaining to) a dynasty ruling in China from the 14th to the 17th cent., between the Mongol and the Manchu dynasties. L18. 2 (Designating) porcelain ware made in China during this period, characterized by elaborate designs and vivid colours. L19. 3 (Designating or being of) any of various colours, esp. green or blue, characteristic of this porcelain. E20.

ming /mɪŋ/ *v. obs.* exc. *dial.* [Late OE (*ġe*)*myn*(*e*)*gian* f. WGmc (cf. OHG *bi-munigōn*), f. Gmc.] 1 *v.t.* Remind (a person); warn. Foll. by *of*, *on*, *that*, *to do*. LOE. 2 *v.t.* Bring into remembrance; commemorate; mention. Formerly also *simply*, remember. LOE. †3 *v.i.* Give an account; relate. Only in LME.

minge /mɪn(d)ʒ/ *n. dial.* & *coarse slang*. E20. [Origin unkn.] The female genitals. Also, women regarded collectively as a means of sexual gratification.

mingei /mɪŋˈɡeɪ/ *n.* M20. [Jap., f. *min* people + *gei* arts.] Japanese folk-art; traditional Japanese handicraft.

mingimingi /ˈmɪŋɪˌmɪŋi/ *n.* Also (*dial.*) **micky-mick** /ˈmɪkɪmɪk/. L19. [Maori.] Either of two New Zealand evergreen shrubs,

Cyathodes juniperina and *C. fasciculata* (family Epacridaceae), with tiny green flowers and red or white berries.

mingle /ˈmɪŋg(ə)l/ *v.* & *n.* Also (earlier) †**mengle**. LME. [Frequent. of MENG: see -LE³.] **A** *v.* **1** *v.t.* & *i.* Mix, blend, combine in a mixture. Freq. foll. by *with*. LME. †**b** *v.t.* Join in (conversation, friendship, etc.) *with* another person. E–M17. †**c** *v.t. fig.* Put together so as to make one. *rare* (Shakes.). Only in E17. **2** *v.t.* †**a** Mix up so as to confuse. Only in M16. **b** Form or make up by mixing various ingredients. Now *rare*. E17. **3** *v.i.* Of a person: move about at a social function, talking with others; circulate, mix; associate *with*. Also, join or participate *in*. E17.

1 W. STYRON Blood mingled with the water, turning it a muddy crimson. M. PUZO He found a bundle of newly washed clothes . . and mingled his own clothes with these. M. MEYER Applause . . was mingled with hissing. A. BROOKNER A look in which superiority mingled with forbearance. *mingle eyes*: see EYE *n.* 3 *Law Times* He is very anxious to avoid any appearance of mingling in party disputes. J. C. OATES She must mingle, must ease into a conversation. A. T. ELLIS Women who . . prefer to mingle only with those . . as attractive as themselves.

B *n.* The action of mingling; the state of being mingled; a mingled mass, a mixture. Now *rare*. M16.

SWIFT To represent persons . . without any mingle of my own interest. T. BOSTON A mingle of many different seeds.

Comb.: **mingle-mangle** a mixture, *esp.* a confused one.

minglement *n.* the action of mingling; (a) mixture: L17. **mingler** *n.* L16.

Mingrelian /mɪŋˈgriːlɪən/ *n.* & *a.* M17. [f. *Mingrelia* (see below) + -AN.] **A** *n.* **1** A member of a people inhabiting Mingrelia, an area of the Kutais region of the Caucasus. M17. **2** The S. Caucasian language of this people. L17. **B** *adj.* Of or pertaining to this people. L18.

mingy /ˈmɪndʒi/ *a. colloq.* E20. [Perh. f. M(EAN *a.*¹ + ST)INGY *a.*²] Mean, stingy, niggardly; depressingly small.

mingily *adv.* M20.

mini /ˈmɪni/ *n.* M20. [Abbrev.: cf. MINI-.] **1** A minicar; a minicab; *spec.* (**M-**) (proprietary name for) a distinctive small car first made in Britain in 1959. M20. **2** A miniskirt; a minidress. M20. **3** A minicomputer. L20.

mini /ˈmɪni/ *a. colloq.* M20. [Abbrev. of MINIATURE *a.*: cf. next.] Very small, tiny.

Punch Leg make-up . . gives sitting-down confidence to the wearer of the miniest skirt. **Mini Disc** a recordable magneto-optical disc resembling a small compact disc; abbrev. *MD*; (cf. *minidisc* s.v. MINI-).

mini- /ˈmɪni/ *comb. form.* M19. [f. MINI(ATURE *a.* (reinforced by MINIMUM): cf. MAXI-.] Forming chiefly ns. denoting something small, short, or minor of its kind.

minibar a selection of mostly alcoholic drinks placed in a hotel room for the use of a guest, a charge being added to the room bill for those used. **mini-break** a very short vacation. **mini-budget** a small usu. interim budget. **minibus** a small bus for up to about twelve passengers. **minicab** a car like a taxi but available only by phone. **minicell** *Biol.* a miniature cell, without nuclear material, produced by cell division in a particular strain of the bacterium *Escherichia coli*. **mini-coat** a short coat. **minicomputer** a computer of size and storage capacity greater than a microcomputer but smaller than a mainframe (usu. housed in one or a few cabinets). **minidisc** *Computing* a small data storage disc (cf. DISKETTE, *Mini Disc* s.v. MINI *a.*). **minidress** a very short dress. **minifloppy (disc)** *Computing* a small floppy disc 5¼ inches (13.3 cm) in diameter. **minigene** *Biol.* a short (usu. coding) sequence of DNA. **minigolf** = *miniature golf* s.v. MINIATURE *a.* **minihole** *Astron.* a very small black hole. *mini-moke*: see MOKE *n.*² **Minipiano, m-** (proprietary name for) a small piano. **minipill** a contraceptive pill containing a progestogen alone (not oestrogen). **mini-roundabout** a small traffic roundabout, indicated by road markings or a very low island. **mini-rugby** a simplified version of rugby with only nine players in a team. **miniseries** (orig. *US*) a usu. short television series dealing with a single complete theme or plot. **miniskirt** a very short skirt. **mini-summit** an interim meeting of heads of government, usu. on a particular issue. **minitrack** *n.* a system for tracking the position of a satellite by the phase difference between radio signals received by two aerials on the ground (usu. *attrib.*).

miniaceous /mɪnɪˈeɪʃəs/ *a.* Now *rare* or *obs.* L17. [f. L *miniaceus*, f. MINIUM: see -ACEOUS.] Of the colour of cinnabar; vermilion.

miniate /ˈmɪnɪeɪt/ *v.t.* M17. [L *miniat-* pa. ppl stem of *miniare* rubricate, illuminate, f. MINIUM: see -ATE³.] Colour or paint with vermilion; rubricate, illuminate, (a manuscript).

miniature /ˈmɪnɪtʃə/ *n.* & *a.* L16. [It. *miniatura* f. med.L, f. *miniare* MINIATE: see -URE. Cf. MINI-.] **A** *n.* **1** An image or representation on a small scale. Also occas., a minutely finished production. L16. **b** A thing that is much smaller or briefer than usual; *spec.* (*a*) *Chess* a problem involving seven or fewer pieces; a game decided in a small number of moves; (*b*) a very small bottle of spirits; (*c*) a short piece of music. E20. **2** The art or action, orig. that of a medieval illuminator, of painting portraits on a small scale and with minute finish, usu. on ivory or vellum; a portrait of this kind. M17. **3** The rubrication or illumination of a manuscript; a picture in an illuminated manuscript; (an) illuminated design. M17.

1 DRYDEN Tragedy is the miniature of human life. b P. CUTTING Ben and I crept up to my room to share a miniature of cherry brandy. J. MARQUAND A miniature of a man, as small as . . the dwarfed trees. 2 HUGH WALPOLE Painters in Enamel and Miniature. N. PEVSNER Miniatures painted minutely on parchment. A. LURIE He was tall and thin, with a short pointed beard like a man in an Elizabethan miniature.

Phrases: **in miniature** on a small scale; in a brief or abridged form.

B *adj.* Represented, designed, etc., on a small scale; much smaller than normal; tiny. E18.

SCOTT FITZGERALD A miniature picture theatre with four rows of overstuffed chairs. *miniature camera, poodle, railway*, etc. **miniature golf** a game in which a club is used to putt a small ball into a succession of holes on a green etc.

miniaturist *n.* an illuminator of manuscripts; a painter of miniatures: M19.

miniature /ˈmɪnɪtʃə/ *v.t.* E18. [f. prec.] **1** Represent or describe in miniature. E18. **2** Reduce to miniature dimensions. L19.

miniaturize /ˈmɪnɪtʃərʌɪz/ *v.t.* Also **-ise**. M20. [f. MINIATURE *n.* & *a.* + -IZE.] Produce in a smaller version; make small.

miniaturiˈzation *n.* the process or an instance of miniaturizing something M20.

Minié /ˈmɪnɪeɪ/ *n.* & *a.* M19. [Claude-Étienne *Minié*, French army officer (1804–79).] *Mil. Hist.* (Designating) an elongated bullet designed by Minié or a rifle adapted for firing this bullet.

minifundium /mɪnɪˈfʌndɪəm/ *n.* Pl. **-ia** /-ɪə/. Also **-io** /-ɪəʊ/, pl. **-ios**. M20. [mod.L, or Sp. *minifundio* smallholding: cf. LATIFUNDIUM.] In Latin America: a small farm or property, *esp.* one that is too small to support a single family. Usu. in *pl.*

minifundism *n.* an economic system based on minifundia M20. **minifunˈdist(a)** *n.* a person who owns or works on a minifundium M20.

minify /ˈmɪnɪfʌɪ/ *v.t.* L17. [Irreg. f. L *minor* less, *minimus* least, after MAGNIFY.] **1** Underestimate the size or importance of. L17. **2** Reduce or lessen in size or importance. M19.

minifiˈcation *n.* E20.

minikin /ˈmɪnɪkɪn/ *n.* & *a.* M16. [Du. *minneken*, f. *minne* love + *-ken* -KIN.] **A** *n.* **1** A small or insignificant person or thing. Also *spec.*, (a term of endearment for) a slight young girl or woman (now *dial.*). M16. **2** A thin string of gut used for the treble string of a lute or viol. Also *minikin string*. Long *rare*. M16. **3** A kind of small pin. Also *minikin pin*. E18. **B** *adj.* **1** Orig., dainty, elegant, sprightly. Now (*derog.*), affected, mincing. M16. **2** Of a thing: diminutive; miniature; tiny. L16. †**3** Of a voice: shrill. Only in E17. †**4** Designating a kind of baize. E17–E18.

Special collocations: **minikin pin** = sense A.3 above. **minikin string** = sense A.2 above.

minim /ˈmɪnɪm/ *n.* & *a.* LME. [As n., repr. various ellipt. uses in med.L of L *minimus* least, smallest, superl. of *parvus* small (see MINOR *a.* & *n.*). As adj. directly f. L *minimus*.] **A** *n.* **1** *Mus.* A symbol for a note with the time value of half a semibreve or two crotchets, having a hollow head and a straight stem; a note of this length. LME. **2** (**M-**.) A friar belonging to the mendicant order founded by St Francis of Paola (1416–1507). M16. **3** The least possible portion (*of*). Formerly also, an atom, a minute particle. L16. **4** A person, animal, or thing of the smallest size or importance. Usu. *derog.* L16. **5** A single downstroke of a pen. L16. **6** A unit of liquid capacity in apothecaries' measure, equal to about one drop of liquid; the sixtieth part of a fluid drachm. E19. **7** A very small (usu. bronze) Roman coin. L19. **B** *adj.* Smallest, extremely small. M17.

minima *n.* pl. of MINIMUM *n.*

minimal /ˈmɪnɪm(ə)l/ *a.* M17. [f. L *minimus* (see prec.) + -AL¹.] **1** Extremely small; of a minimum amount, quantity, or degree; very slight, negligible. M17. **2** *Ling.* Of a set or (usu.) pair of forms: distinguished by only one feature. M20. **3** *Art.* Characterized by the use of simple or primary forms, structures, etc., often geometric and massive. M20. **4** *Mus.* Characterized by the repetition of short phrases which change very gradually as the music proceeds. L20.

1 A. DAVIS News media . . following a conscious policy of minimal or no coverage. *USA Today* Strongest winds were 80 mph, making it a minimal hurricane. 2 H. A. GLEASON Calling *bill* and *pill* a minimal pair we assume that they differ by only one phoneme.

Special collocations: **minimal free form** *Ling.* the smallest form which can be used by itself as an utterance. **minimal pair** *Ling.* a pair of words distinguished by a single phoneme.

miniˈmality *n.* (*Ling.*) the quality or character of being minimal M20. **minimalize** *v.t.* = MINIMIZE L20. **minimally** *adv.* M20.

minimalist /ˈmɪnɪm(ə)lɪst/ *n.* & *a.* E20. [f. prec. + -IST, or (in senses A.1, B.1) f. Fr. *minimaliste*, tr. Russ. *men'shevik* MENSHEVIK.] **A** *n.* **1** (Also **M-**.) Orig. (*Hist.*), a Menshevik. Later also, any person advocating small or moderate reforms or policies. E20. **2** An advocate or practitioner of minimal art; a composer of minimal music. M20. **B** *adj.* **1** Orig. (*Hist.*), Menshevik. Later also, advocating moderate policies. E20. **2** Of or pertaining to minimal art or music. M20.

minimalism *n.* the advocacy or practice of a minimalist approach, *esp.* one which reduces governmental functions and intervention to a minimum M20. **minimaˈlistic** *a.* of or pertaining to minimalism, minimalist M20.

minimax /ˈmɪnɪmaks/ *n.* & *a.* M20. [f. MINI(MUM + MAX(IMUM.] *Math.* **A** *n.* The smallest of a set of maxima. M20. **B** *attrib.* or as *adj.* Of, pertaining to, or of the nature of a minimax; *spec.* in *Game Theory*, designating (*a*) a strategy that minimizes the greatest loss or risk to which a participant in a game etc. will be liable; (*b*) the theorem that for a finite zero-sum game with two players, the smallest maximum loss that a player can choose to risk is equal to the greatest minimum guaranteeable gain. Cf. MAXIMIN. M20.

minimax /ˈmɪnɪmaks/ *v.* M20. [f. prec.] *Math.* **1** *v.t.* Make equal to a minimax value. M20. **2** *v.i.* Adopt or employ a minimax strategy. M20.

minimi *n.* pl. of MINIMUS *n.*

minimise *v.* var. of MINIMIZE.

minimism /ˈmɪnɪmɪz(ə)m/ *n.* E19. [f. as MINIM *n.* + -ISM.] **1** Absorption in minute details. Now *rare* or *obs.* E19. **2** *Theol.* The policy or practice of minimizing the substance of a dogma, esp. that of papal infallibility. L19.

minimize /ˈmɪnɪmʌɪz/ *v.* Also **-ise**. E19. [f. L *minimus* (see MINIM) + -IZE.] **1** *v.t.* Reduce to the smallest possible amount, extent, or degree. E19. **2** *v.t.* & *i.* Estimate (a thing) at the lowest possible amount, value, significance, etc.; underestimate or play down (a problem, dogma, etc.); treat (a thing) as negligible. L19. **3** *v.i.* Attain a minimum value. L20.

1 *Which?* There's more than one . . layout for the carpet to minimise wastage. 2 *Christian World* Let no one think . . Jesus ever minimised the . . sinfulness of

sin. A. HUTSCHNECKER Pride made him minimize his inner terror.

minimi'zation *n.* E19. **minimizer** *n.* M19.

minimum /'mɪnɪməm/ *n.* & *a.* M17. [L, use as n. of neut. of *minimus*: see MINIM *n.* & *a.*] **A** *n.* Pl. **minima** /'mɪnɪmə/. †1 The smallest portion into which matter is divisible; an atom. Also, the hypothetical smallest possible portion of time or space. M17–M18. 2 The smallest amount or quantity possible, usual, attainable, etc. L17. 3 *Math.* The least value which a variable or a function may have; the smallest element in a set; a point at which a continuously varying quantity ceases to decrease and begins to increase; the value of a quantity at such a point. M18. 4 The lowest amount of a varying quantity (e.g. temperature, pressure, sunspot activity, etc.) attained or recorded within a particular period. E19.

Comb.: **minimum thermometer**: which records the lowest temperature attained since it was last set.

B *adj.* That is a minimum; that is the lowest possible, usual, attainable, etc. E19.

Special collocations: *minimum free form* Ling. = MINIMAL *free form.* **minimum lending rate** *Econ.* the minimum percentage at which a central bank will discount bills (abolished in Britain in 1981).

minimus /'mɪnɪməs/ *n.* & *a.* L16. [L: see MINIM.] **A** *n.* Pl. **-mi** /-mʌɪ/. A very small or insignificant creature. L16. **B** *adj.* Designating the youngest of several pupils with the same surname or the last to enter a school. (Appended to a surname and used esp. in public schools.) Cf. MINOR *a.* 1b. L18.

¶See also GLUTEUS *minimus.*

mining /'mʌɪnɪŋ/ *vbl n.* E16. [f. MINE *v.* + -ING[1].] The action of MINE *v.*; *esp.* the art or industry of extracting metals, coal, etc., from a mine.

coal-mining, gold-mining, hydraulic mining, etc.

Comb.: **mining-hole** a hole bored to receive a blasting charge in mining; **mining town**: chiefly inhabited by miners.

mining /'mʌɪnɪŋ/ *ppl a.* M16. [f. MINE *v.* + -ING[2].] That mines.

mining bee any of various solitary bees of the family Andrenidae, many of which nest in tunnels in the ground, sometimes grouped in colonies.

minion /'mɪnjən/ *n.*[1] & *a.* E16. [Fr. *mignon* repl. OFr. *mignot*: cf. MIGNON.] **A** *n.* 1a A lover; (chiefly *derog.*) a mistress. Formerly also as a form of address. Now *rare* or *obs.* E16. **b** A favourite of a monarch, prince, or other powerful person; *derog.* a servile agent, a slave. Now also, a follower, an attendant, an assistant, etc. E16. **c** A favourite child, servant, animal, etc. Also as a form of address. Now *derog.* M16. †2 A small kind of ordnance. M16–L19. 3 A size of type between nonpareil and brevier. M17. †4 A kind of peach. Also more fully *minion peach.* L17–M18.

B *adj.* 1 Dainty, elegant, fine, pretty, neat. Now *rare.* E16. 2 Dearly loved, favourite, pet. Now *rare.* E18.

Special collocations: †**minion peach** = sense A.4 above.

minion /'mɪnjən/ *n.*[2] *rare.* E17. [Fr. f. L MINIUM.] †1 = MINIUM. E–M17. 2 Calcined iron ore used in cement or mortar. L18.

miniscule *n.* & *a.* see MINUSCULE.

minish /'mɪnɪʃ/ *v. arch.* ME. [OFr. *menu(i)sier*, ult. f. L MINUTIA: cf. MINCE *v.* & *n.*] **I** *v.t.* 1 = DIMINISH 1, 2. ME. **b** Break up *into* (parts etc.). *rare.* LME. 2 Disparage, belittle. *rare.* LME. 3 Take away, remove. L15. **II** *v.i.* 4 = DIMINISH 6. ME. †5 Take something away. LME–E16.

minister /'mɪnɪstə/ *n.* ME. [(O)Fr. *ministre* f. L *minister*, f. *minus* less, adv. corresp. to *minor* MINOR *a.*, parallel in formation to correl. *magister* MASTER *n.*[1]] 1a A person acting under the authority or as an agent of another; *spec.* †(*a*) a law officer; †(*b*) a subordinate officer, an underling. Now *rare.* ME. **b** A person or thing employed or used to achieve a purpose or intention, convey a gift, etc. Foll. by *of.* Now *rare* exc. as passing into sense 2. LME. 2 *Eccl.* a A person, esp. an ordained one, with a certain liturgical ministry or function; a member of the clergy, esp. in a Protestant Church, responsible for leading or coordinating preaching, public worship, and pastoral care in a particular church, chapel, community, etc.; a pastor. ME. **b** A functionary or official of a religion other than Christianity. Long *rare.* LME. **c** *RC Ch.* (The title of) the superior of certain religious orders. Also *minister general.* LME. 3†a A servant, an attendant. LME–L18. **b** A person who ministers to the wants of another. *arch.* E19. 4 *Polit.* (Also **M-**.) a A person appointed to act for a head of State etc. in a particular government department; a person in charge of a government department; a Secretary of State. E17. **b** A diplomatic agent officially representing a State or sovereign in a foreign country, *esp.* one ranking below an ambassador. E18. 5 A fish: = *horn pout* s.v. HORN *n.* & *a. US.* M19.

1a S. JOHNSON The community, of which the magistrate is only the minister. **b** H. P. LIDDON The Angels are ministers of the Divine Will. 2a GEO. ELIOT Something between the Catholic priest and the dissenting minister. L. M. MONTGOMERY That's the way the ministers say it in church. R. A. KNOX You will want human ministers to dispense the sacraments. **minister of religion** (esp. in official use) a member of the clergy of any denomination. 4a M. E. G. DUFF The King . . immediately dismissed his Ministers. *Daily Mirror* At a Cabinet meeting some Ministers . . complained that the Chancellor had got it all wrong. *Foreign Minister*: see FOREIGN. **Minister of State** a minister in the British Government, *esp.* one holding a rank below that of a head of department. **Minister of the Crown** a minister or head of a department in the British Government. *minister premier*: see PREMIER *a.* 1. **Minister without Portfolio** a minister in the British Government, with Cabinet rank but not in charge of a specific department. *premier minister*: see PREMIER *a.* 1. *Prime Minister*: see PRIME *a.*

ministership *n.* the office or position of a minister M16. †**ministral** *a.* (*rare*) pertaining to a minister or agent E18–M19.

minister /'mɪnɪstə/ *v.* ME. [(O)Fr. *ministrer* f. L *ministrare*, f. *minister*: see prec.] 1 *v.i. Chr. Ch.* Serve or officiate at a service; act as a minister. ME. 2 *v.i.* Serve, esp. at table; attend to or *to* the needs of another; assist, be useful, (*to* a person, cause, etc.); be conducive or contribute *to* something. LME. 3 *v.t.* Provide, supply, impart, (something necessary or helpful). Formerly also, administer (justice, a sacrament, etc.). *arch.* LME.

2 **ministering angel** a kind-hearted person, esp. a woman, who nurses or comforts others. 3 A. P. STANLEY The story . . was able to minister true consolation.

ministerial /mɪnɪ'stɪərɪəl/ *a.* & *n.* M16. [Fr. *ministériel* or late L *ministerialis*, f. L *ministerium* MINISTRY, but app. interpreted as deriv. of MINISTER *n.*: see -IAL.] **A** *adj.* 1 Pertaining to the office, function, or character of a minister of religion. M16. 2 Pertaining to or entrusted with the execution of the law or the commands of a superior. L16. 3 Subsidiary or instrumental in achieving a purpose etc. E17. 4 Of or pertaining to a Minister of State or a government department; supporting the Government against the Opposition. M17.

3 DE QUINCEY We may admit arts of style and ornamental composition as the ministerial part of rhetoric. 4 H. MARTINEAU Parliament was to be dissolved on the first ministerial reverse.

B *n. Hist.* An executive household officer under the feudal system. E19.

ministerialism *n.* support for the Government M19. **ministerialist** *n.* a supporter of the Government L18. **ministerially** *adv.* in the manner or capacity of a minister E17.

ministrable /'mɪnɪstrəb(ə)l/ *a.* & *n.* E20. [Fr., f. as MINISTER *v.*: see -ABLE.] *Polit.* (A person who is) likely or expected to become a minister.

ministrant /'mɪnɪstr(ə)nt/ *a.* & *n.* M16. [L *ministrant-* pres. ppl stem of *ministrare*: see MINISTER *v.*, -ANT[1].] **A** *adj.* That ministers. M16. **B** *n.* A person who ministers. E19.

ministrate /'mɪnɪstreɪt/ *v.t.* Long *rare.* L15. [L *ministrat-*: see next, -ATE[3].] Administer.

ministration /mɪnɪ'streɪʃ(ə)n/ *n.* ME. [OFr., or L *ministratio(n-)*, f. *ministrat-* pa. ppl stem of *ministrare* MINISTER *v.*: see -ATION.] 1 The action or an act of serving or ministering, esp. in religious matters; in *pl.*, the services of a minister of religion etc. ME. †2 The action of administering a sacrament, justice, an estate, etc.; administration. ME–L16. †3 Agency, instrumentality. LME–M16. 4 The action of supplying, providing, or giving something. Foll. by *of.* L15.

ministrative /'mɪnɪstrətɪv/ *a.* M19. [App. f. MINISTER *v.* + -ATIVE.] Pertaining to or of the nature of ministration; affording service or assistance.

ministrator /'mɪnɪstreɪtə/ *n. rare.* LME. [L, f. *ministrare*: see MINISTER *v.*, -ATOR.] A person who ministers or administers. Formerly also, the executor of a will.

ministrer /'mɪnɪstrə/ *n.* LME. [f. MINISTER *v.* + -ER[1].] A person who ministers or serves.

ministress /'mɪnɪstrɪs/ *n.* L15. [f. MINISTER *n.* + -ESS[1].] A female minister. Chiefly *fig.*

M. AKENSIDE Beauty sent from heaven, The lovely ministress of truth and good.

ministry /'mɪnɪstri/ *n.* LME. [L *ministerium*, f. MINISTER *n.*] 1 The action of ministering; ministration. Now *rare* exc. as passing into sense 2a. LME. †**b** A particular kind of ministration; a function, an office. LME–M17. **c** The condition or fact of being an agent or instrument; agency, instrumentality. Now *rare.* L16. 2 *Eccl.* a The functions or a particular function proper or pertaining to a minister, priest, etc.; the action or an act of religious ministration. LME. **b** *collect.* The clergy; the ministers of a Church, esp. the Established Church. Now *rare.* M16. **c** The period of tenure of a particular minister. E17. **d** *The* clerical profession or calling; the office of minister of a church or congregation. E19. 3 *collect.* The body of executive officers responsible for the functions of government or the law; now *spec.* the ministers responsible for the administration of a country or State. Also, the period of government under one Prime Minister. LME. 4 (Also **M-**.) A government department headed by a minister; the building occupied by a government department. L19.

1 TENNYSON My idea of heaven is the perpetual ministry of one soul to another. **c** A. PHELPS Heroic believers become such by the ministry of heroic pains. 2a J. SWAN A certain Priest . . was suspended from his ministry. **b** ANDREW THOMSON Patronage . . was the most effective instrument of placing a hireling ministry in the pulpits. **d** D. CUPITT Being intended for the ministry he entered Strasburg University to study theology. 4 *Ministry of Agriculture, Ministry of Defence, Ministry of the Interior,* etc.

minium /'mɪnɪəm/ *n.* LME. [L.] 1 Cinnabar, esp. as a red pigment; vermilion. *obs.* exc. *Hist.* LME. 2 Any red earth. Long *rare* or *obs.* E17. 3 = *red lead* s.v. RED *a.* M17.

miniver /'mɪnɪvə/ *n.* Also **-nev-**. L16. [AN *menuver* f. (O)Fr. *menu vair*, f. *menu* little (see MENU) + VAIR.] 1 A kind of fur (now plain white) used as a lining and trimming in ceremonial dress. L16. 2 Orig., the animal from which this fur was (supposedly) obtained. Now only (*dial.*), a stoat or ermine in its white winter coat. M17.

minivet /'mɪnɪvɪt/ *n.* M19. [Origin unkn.] Any of various brightly coloured cuckoo shrikes of the genus *Pericrocotus*, of tropical Asia.

mink /mɪŋk/ *n.* & *a.* LME. [Origin uncertain: rel. to Sw. *menk*, *mänk*: cf. LG *mink* otter.] **A** *n.* 1 The skins or dark brown fur of the mink (see sense 2 below); a garment made of this fur. LME. 2 Either of two semi-aquatic mammals of the genus *Mustela* that resemble stoats, *M. vison*, native to N. America and farmed for its fur, and the European *M. intreola.* E17. 3 A dark brown colour. M20. **B** *attrib.* or as *adj.* Made of the fur of the mink. Also, of the colour mink. E20.

minke /'mɪŋkə, -ki/ *n.* M20. [Norw., perh. f. *Meincke* a 19th-cent. whaling gunner, who mistook it for the larger blue whale.] In full *minke whale.* A small baleen whale, *Balaenoptera acutorostrata.* Also called *piked whale, lesser rorqual.*

Minkowski /mɪŋˈkɒfski/ *n.* E20. [Hermann *Minkowski* (1864–1909), Russian-born Ger. mathematician.] *Physics.* Used *attrib.* with ref. to various concepts occurring in or arising from the work of Minkowski, esp. his theory that the universe has four orthogonal dimensions (the three spatial dimensions and time).

minnarichi *n.* var. of MINNERICHI.

Minnelied /ˈmɪnəliːt/ *n.* Pl. ***-lieder*** /-liːdə(r)/. L19. [G, f. *Minne* love + *Lied* song.] A love-song written by a minnesinger, or in the style of the minnesingers.

minneola /mɪnɪˈəʊlə/ *n.* M20. [*Minneola*, a town in Florida, USA.] A thin-skinned, deep reddish variety of tangelo.

minnerichi /mɪnəˈrɪtʃi/ *n.* *Austral.* Also **mi(n)na-**. E20. [Aborig.] The red mulga, *Acacia cyperophylla*.

Minnesinger /ˈmɪnəsɪŋə/ *n.* Also **m-**. E19. [G, f. *Minne* love + †*Singer* (mod. *Sänger*) singer.] A German lyric poet or singer of the 12th to 14th cents.

Minnesong /ˈmɪnəsɒŋ/ *n.* M19. [G *Minnesang*, f. *Minne* love + *Sang* song.] A song of a minnesinger; the corpus of such songs. Cf. MINNELIED.

Minnesota /mɪnɪˈsəʊtə/ *n.* M20. [f. as next.] *Minnesota Multiphasic Personality Inventory*, a personality test made up of over 500 items, the responses to which are graded for various personality traits in accordance with criteria calculated from groups of normal subjects and subjects with clinically diagnosed psychiatric disorders. Abbrev. *MMPI*.

Minnesotan /mɪnɪˈsəʊtən/ *n.* & *a.* L19. [f. *Minnesota* (see below) + -AN.] (A native or inhabitant) of Minnesota, a State in the north central US.

minnie /ˈmɪni/ *n.*[1] *Sc.* & *north. colloq.* E16. [Origin uncertain: perh. childish alt. of *mammy*.] Mother.

Minnie /ˈmɪni/ *n.*[2] *slang.* Also **m-**. E20. [Abbrev. of MINENWERFER.] *Mil. Hist.* (A bomb discharged by) a German trench mortar in the war of 1914–18.
moaning minnie: see MOANING *ppl a.*

minnow /ˈmɪnəʊ/ *n.* LME. [Perh. repr. OE wd cogn. w. OHG *muniwa* (tr. L *capito* a large-headed fish) but infl. by OFr. *menuise*, f. Proto-Romance wd meaning 'small objects': cf. MINUTIA.] **1** A small freshwater cyprinid fish, *Phoxinus phoxinus*, common in streams, lakes, and ponds in Europe. Also *loosely*, any small (esp. cyprinid) fish; *dial.* a stickleback. LME. **b** A small or insignificant person or thing. L16. **2** *Angling.* A minnow attached to a hook for use as bait; an artificial bait resembling this. E17.
1b *Sunday Times* The airline is still a minnow by the standards of the big flag carriers.
Comb.: **minnow-fisher** a person who fishes for minnows or with minnows as bait.

Minoan /mɪˈnəʊən/ *a.* & *n.* L19. [f. (L) *Minós*, Gk *Minōs*, legendary king of Crete to whom a palace excavated at Knossos was attributed + -AN.] **A** *adj.* Of or pertaining to the Bronze Age civilization of Crete (*c*3000–1100 BC) or its people, culture, or language. L19. **B** *n.* **1** A native or inhabitant of the Minoan world. E20. **2** The language or scripts associated with the Minoan civilization. M20.

Min of Ag /mɪn əv ˈag/ *n. phr. colloq.* M20. [Abbrev.] *The* Ministry of Agriculture, Fisheries, and Food in the British Government.

minol /ˈmʌɪnɒl/ *n.* M20. [Prob. f. MINE *n.* + -OL.] An explosive consisting of a mixture of ammonium nitrate, TNT, and aluminium powder.

minor /ˈmʌɪnə/ *a.* & *n.* ME. [L, compar. of *parvus* small, rel. to *minuere* lessen. Of Franciscan friars f. OFr. *menour* in *freres menours* lit. 'lesser brothers', med.L *fratres minores*.] **A** *adj.* **1** Lesser; designating or pertaining to the lesser or relatively lesser of or *of* two things, classes, etc.; opp. *major*. Also, comparatively unimportant or insignificant; (of an operation) relatively simple or small scale. In earliest use (**M-**), designating a Franciscan friar. ME. **b** Designating the younger of two pupils with the same surname or the second to enter a school. (Appended to a surname and used esp. in public schools.) Cf. MINIMUS *a.* L18. **2** Of less than full age; below the age of majority. Now *rare.* L15. **3** *Logic.* (Of a term) functioning as the subject of the conclusion in a syllogism; (of a premiss) containing the minor term of a syllogism. L16. **4** That constitutes the minority. M17. **5** *Mus.* (Of an interval) smaller by a semitone than the correlative major interval; (of a scale) with semitones above the second, fifth, and seventh notes; (of a key) based on a minor scale, tending to produce a melancholy effect. L17.
1 D. CARNEGIE He praised my work, assured me that he only wanted a minor change. F. ASTAIRE Harriet had a prominent role, but . . Betty and Lucille were still playing minor parts.
B *n.* **1** (**M-**.) *ellipt.* A Franciscan friar. ME. **2** *Logic.* A minor term or premiss. LME. **3** A person who has not yet attained his or her majority. Cf. INFANT *n.*[1] 2. E17. **4** A minor interval, key, scale, etc. (*Mus.*); a minor theatre, a minor work; a minor company or organization. L18. **5** Any of various noctuid moths chiefly of the genus *Proclus*. Usu. w. specifying wd. M19. **6** In a university etc.: (a qualification in) a subject or course secondary to one's main subject or course. L19. **7** *Bridge.* (A card in) a minor suit. E20.
3 L. DUNCAN We're minors, aren't we? Not one of us is eighteen yet.
Special collocations & phrases: *harmonic minor*: see HARMONIC *a.* **in a minor key** (of a novel, life, etc.) understated, uneventful. MELODIC *minor.* **minor axis** *Geom.* the axis of an ellipse which passes through the centre at right angles to the major axis. *minor canon*: see CANON *n.*[2] 2. **minor determinant** *Math.* a determinant whose matrix is formed from that of another determinant by deleting one or more rows and columns. **minor league** *N. Amer.* a league of professional clubs in baseball, football, etc., other than the major leagues. **minor orders** *Chr. Ch.* the degrees of the ordained ministry below those of bishop, priest, deacon, and (formerly, in the West) subdeacon. **minor piece** *Chess* a knight, a bishop. *minor planet*: see PLANET *n.*[1] *Minor Prophet*: see PROPHET. **minor suit** *Bridge* the suit of diamonds or clubs. *minor* TRANQUILLIZER. *quint minor*: see QUINT *n.*[2] TERES *minor. tierce minor*: see TIERCE *n.*[1] 4. *tonic minor*: see TONIC *a.* 4. URSA *Minor.* VARIOLA *minor.*

minor /ˈmʌɪnə/ *v.i.* Chiefly *N. Amer.* M20. [f. prec.] Foll. by *in*: study or qualify in as a subsidiary subject at a university, college, etc.

minorate /ˈmʌɪnəreɪt/ *v.t.* Pa. pple & ppl a. **-ated**, (earlier) †**-ate**. LME. [med.L *minorat-* pa. ppl stem of *minorare* diminish, f. MINOR *a.* & *n.*: see -ATE[3].] Diminish, depreciate.
†**minoration** *n.* a lessening, a diminution LME–M19. †**minorative** *a.* & *n.* (*a*) *adj.* that diminishes or lessens, gently laxative; (*b*) *n.* a gentle laxative: M16–M18.

Minorca /mɪˈnɔːkə/ *n.* M19. [f. as next.] A variety of the domestic fowl with black, white, or blue glossy plumage.

Minorcan /mɪˈnɔːk(ə)n/ *a.* & *n.* M18. [f. *Minorca*, Sp. *Menorca* (see below) + -AN.] **A** *adj.* Of or pertaining to Minorca, the easternmost of the Balearic Islands in the western Mediterranean. M18. **B** *n.* A native or inhabitant of Minorca. L18.

Minoress /ˈmʌɪnərɪs/ *n. obs.* exc. *Hist.* LME. [OFr. *menouresse*, f. *menour*: see MINOR *a.* & *n.*, -ESS[1].] A Franciscan nun of the second order, a poor Clare.

Minorite /ˈmʌɪnərʌɪt/ *a.* & *n. arch.* M16. [f. MINOR *a.* & *n.* + -ITE[1]] **A** *adj.* Of the order of Friars Minor, Franciscan. M16. **B** *n.* **1** A Friar Minor, a Franciscan. M16. †**2** A person of minor rank or concerned with minor matters. M17–E19.

minority /mʌɪˈnɒrɪti, mɪ-/ *n.* & *a.* L15. [Fr. *minorité* or med.L *minoritas*, f. MINOR *a.* & *n.*: see -ITY.] **A** *n.* **1** The state of being a minor; the period of a person's life prior to attaining full age. L15. †**b** The condition or fact of being smaller, inferior, or subordinate. M16–E18. **2** The smaller number or part; a number which is less than half the whole number. Also *spec.*, (the number of votes cast for or by) the smaller party voting together in a deliberative assembly or electoral body. M18. **3** A small group of people differing from the rest of a community in ethnic origin, religion, language, or culture; a member of such a group. E20.
1 J. R. GREEN The long minority of Henry the Sixth who was a boy . . at his father's death. **2** H. WILSON The right of a minority to differ from the majority. D. FRANCIS He was one of the minority of men in morning suits. **3** *Equals* A campaign against racial hatred and the discrimination . . facing ethnic minorities. I. MURDOCH You're so keen on the rights of minorities, underprivileged groups or whatever jargon you use. *national minority*: see NATIONAL *a.*
B *attrib.* or as *adj.* Of, for, composed of, or appealing to a minority of people. M20.
Language The lack of trained personnel . . qualified to work with minority children. R. DAWKINS Zoology is still a minority subject in universities.
Comb.: **minority carrier** *Electronics* in a semiconductor, a charge carrier (electron or hole) of the kind carrying the smaller proportion of the electric current; **minority debt**: incurred by a person while under age; **minority government**: in which the governing party has most seats but still less than half the total; **minority movement** a movement to secure justice or proper representation for minorities; **minority report** a separate report presented by members of a committee etc. who disagree with the majority.

minot /mino/ *n. obs.* exc. *Hist.* Pl. pronounced same. L16. [Fr., f. *mine* a measure of 6 bushels.] A former French unit of capacity, normally equal to 3 French bushels (approx. 39.36 litres, 8.66 gallons).

Minotaur /ˈmʌɪnətɔː/ *n.* LME. [OFr. (mod. *Minotaure*) f. L *Minotaurus* f. Gk *minōtauros*, f. *Minōs* (see MINOAN) + *tauros* bull.] *Gk Mythol.* (A representation of) a monster with the body of a man and the head of a bull, which was kept in a Cretan labyrinth and fed with human flesh.

minoxidil /mɪˈnɒksɪdɪl/ *n.* L20. [f. A)MINO- + OX(IDE + *-il*, of unkn. origin.] *Pharm.* A pyrimidine derivative used to treat hypertension which can also promote hair growth when applied topically; 2,6-diamino-4-piperidino-pyridine-1-oxide, $C_9H_{15}N_5O$.

minster /ˈmɪnstə/ *n.* [OE *mynster* = OHG *munistri* (G *Münster*), MDu. *monster*, ON *mustari* rel. to eccl.L *monasterium* MONASTERY.] †**1** A monastery; a Christian religious house. OE–E16. **2** The church of a monastery; a church originating in a monastic establishment. Also, any large or important church, *esp.* a collegiate church or former collegiate church. Also *minster church.* OE. †**b** *transf.* A temple. ME–L16.
2 *Beverley Minster, York Minster*, etc.

minstrel /ˈmɪnstr(ə)l/ *n.* ME. [OFr. *menestral*, *-(e)rel*, *mini-* entertainer, handicraftsman, servant f. Prov. *menest(ai)ral* officer, attendant, employee, musician f. late L *ministerialis* official, officer, f. L *ministerium*: see MINISTRY, -AL[1].] †**1** A servant with a special function. *rare.* Only in ME. **2** Orig., a person employed by a patron to entertain with singing, story-telling, buffoonery, etc.; a jester. Now (*Hist.*), a medieval singer or musician, *esp.* one singing or reciting heroic or lyric poetry and providing musical accompaniment. ME. **3** *transf.* Any musician, singer, or poet. *poet.* & *rhet.* E18. **4** A member of a band of entertainers with blacked faces, performing songs and music ostensibly of Negro origin. Usu. in *pl.* M19.
4 *blackface minstrel, Negro minstrel, nigger minstrel.*
†**minstrelship** *n.* minstrelsy, the performance of music L15–E19.

minstrelsy /ˈmɪnstr(ə)lsi/ *n.* ME. [OFr. *menestralsie*, f. *menestrel*: see prec.] **1** The art or occupation of a minstrel; the practice of playing and singing. *arch.* ME. **2** A group or gathering of minstrels; *collect.* musicians, singers. ME. †**3** Musical instruments collectively; a musical instrument. LME–E16. **4** Minstrel poetry. E19.

mint /mɪnt/ *n.*[1] [OE *mynet*, corresp. (w. variation of gender) to OFris. *menote*, *munte*, OS *munita* (Du. *munt*), OHG *munizza*, *muniz* (G *Münze*), f. Gmc, f. L *moneta*: see MONEY *n.*] **1** A coin; money. Now *rare* or *obs.* OE. 2 A place where money is coined, usu. under the authority and direction of the State. LME. b *fig.* A place where something originates or is generated; a source, a fount, (*of*). M16. †3 Coinage. L15–E17. 4 A set of machines for coining. L16. 5 A vast sum of or *of* money. M17.

2b H. SACHEVERELL The Pulpit, and the Press, those Mints of Atheism. TENNYSON But thou and I are one in kind, As moulded like in Nature's mint. 5 M. M. R. KHAN How elegantly she dresses. . . Must have cost her husbands a mint.

Phrases: **in mint condition** (or **state**) freshly minted, as new.

Comb.: **mint-bill** *Hist.* a bill or promissory note given by an officer of the mint to an importer of bullion deposited for coining; **mint-mark** a mark on a coin indicating the mint at which it was struck; **mint par, parity (of exchange)** (*a*) the ratio between the gold equivalent of the currency units of two countries; (*b*) the rate of currency exchange between two countries based on this ratio; **mint master** (*a*) the superintendent of coinage at a mint; (*b*) a person who coins new ideas, words, etc.; **mint price** the standard price of bullion as recognized at a mint.

mint /mɪnt/ *n.*[2] & *a.*[1] [OE *minte* = OHG *minza* (G *Minze*), f. WGmc, f. L *ment(h)a* f. Gk *minthē*, *minthos*, prob. of Mediterranean origin.] A *n.* 1 (The leaves of) any of various aromatic often moisture-loving labiate plants of the genus *Mentha*, which bear lilac flowers and include spearmint, peppermint, and other culinary herbs; *spec.* spearmint, *Mentha spicata*, or another cultivated form. Formerly freq. in *pl.* in collect. sense. OE. b With specifying wd: any of various plants of allied genera, e.g. *Clinopodium* and (in N. America) *Pycnanthemum* and *Monarda*. ME. 2 A sweet or chocolate flavoured with an extract of such a plant, esp. peppermint. L19. 3 Mint-green colour. L20.

1 *bergamot mint*: see BERGAMOT *n.*[2] 3. *horsemint*: see HORSE *n.* PEPPERMINT. SPEARMINT. b *catmint*: see CAT *n.*[1]

B *attrib.* or as *adj.* Flavoured with, or containing mint; of the colour of mint. E19.

Special collocations & comb.: **mint cake** (*a*) a very thin sweet cake flavoured with chopped fresh mint; (*b*) a peppermint-flavoured sweet. **mint-green** *a.* of a pale green colour like that of mint. **mint julep** (chiefly *US*) an iced alcoholic drink flavoured with fresh mint. **mint sauce** (*a*) finely chopped mint in vinegar and sugar, usu. eaten with roast lamb; (*b*) *slang* money, cash. **mint-sling** *US* a drink containing some alcoholic beverage flavoured with mint. **mint tea, mint-water** a cordial distilled from mint.

mint /mɪnt/ *n.*[3] Long *obs.* exc. *dial.* LME. [Origin uncertain: perh. contr. of MINUTE *n.*] A small insect, a mite, a weevil.

mint /mɪnt/ *a.*[2] E20. [Ellipt. for *in mint condition* s.v. MINT *n.*[1]] In mint condition, as new.

mint /mɪnt/ *v.*[1] Now *arch.* & *dial.* [OE *myntan*, prob. ult. f. IE base of MIND *n.*[1]] †1 *v.i.* & *t.* Think. OE–ME. 2 *v.i.* & *t.* Intend; try; venture (*to do*). OE. 3 *v.t.* Attempt, aim, (a blow). OE. 4 *v.i.* Aim a blow; take aim in shooting; make a threatening movement. (Foll. by *at*, *to*.) ME. †b Make a movement to seize something. Foll. by *to*. E17–E19. 5 *v.i.* Make an attempt; aim *at*, aspire *to*. ME. 6 *v.t.* Mention, speak of. Long *rare*. LME.

mint /mɪnt/ *v.*[2]*t.* M16. [f. MINT *n.*[1]] 1 Make (coin) by stamping metal; *fig.* produce, invent, (a word, phrase, idea, etc.). Cf. COIN *v.*[1] M16. †2 Convert (bullion) into coin; *fig.* impress with a stamp or character. M16–M18.

2 H. BROOKE To have his soul melted and minted as mine has been.

mintage /ˈmɪntɪdʒ/ *n.* L16. [f. MINT *n.*[1] or *v.*[2] + -AGE.] 1 The action or process of minting money; *fig.* the coining of a new word, idea, etc. L16. 2 The product of a mint; a coin or coins originating from a specified source. Freq. *fig.* M17. 3 The cost of or duty paid for minting. M17. 4 *fig.* A stamp, an impression. M17.

1 H. J. S. MAINE Few literary theories of modern mintage have more to recommend them.

minted /ˈmɪntɪd/ *a.* L19. [f. MINT *n.*[2] + -ED[2]] Flavoured with mint.

minter /ˈmɪntə/ *n.* [OE *mynetere* = OS *muniteri* (MDu., Du. *munter*), OHG *munizzāri*, f. late L *monetarius*, f. *moneta*: see MONEY *n.*, -ARY[1].] †1 A money-changer. OE–ME. 2 A person who coins or stamps money. OE.

Minton /ˈmɪntən/ *n.* & *a.* M19. [See below.] (Designating) pottery made at Stoke-on-Trent, Staffordshire, England, from 1793 onwards, by Thomas Minton (1766–1836) and his successors.

minty /ˈmɪnti/ *a.*[1] L19. [f. MINT *n.*[2] + -Y[1].] Having much mint; suggestive of mint; having or resembling the flavour of mint.

minty /ˈmɪnti/ *a.*[2] & *n.* *US slang.* M20. [Origin unkn.] A *adj.* Of a man: effeminate; homosexual. Of a woman: of masculine behaviour or appearance; lesbian. M20. B *n.* A homosexual person. L20.

minuend /ˈmɪnjʊɛnd/ *n.* E18. [L *minuendus* (sc. *numerus* number) gerundive of *minuere* diminish: see -END.] *Math.* The number from which another number (the subtrahend) is to be subtracted.

minuet /mɪnjʊˈɛt/ *n.* & *v.* Also **men-** /mɛn-/. L17. [Fr. *menuet* use as n. of adj. *menuet* small, fine, delicate, dim. of *menu* small: see MENU, -ET[1].] A *n.* 1 A slow stately dance for two in triple time, fashionable in the 18th cent. L17. 2 A piece of music for this dance or in its rhythm, often forming a movement in a suite, sonata, or symphony. L17. B *v.i.* Dance a minuet. M19.

minuetto /minuˈetto, mɪnjʊˈɛtəʊ/ *n.* Pl. **-tti** /-t(t)i/, **-ttos** /-təʊz/. E18. [It.] = MINUET *n.*

minus /ˈmʌɪnəs/ *prep.*, *n.*, *adv.*, & *a.* L15. [L, use as adv. of neut. of *minor* adj.: see MINOR *a.* & *n.*] A *prep.* I 1 Made less by, reduced by, with the subtraction or deduction of, (a specified number, amount, or proportion); below zero by (a specified amount). Also (*colloq.*), lacking, deprived of, without. L15.

1 J. MARQUAND His left hand was . . minus three fingers. R. HOLMES A snowy night with a temperature of minus eighteen degrees. *Which?* The cost of replacing the items . . minus a deduction.

II 2 As the name of the mathematical symbol '−', signifying a negative quantity or quality, something subtracted, etc. (part of speech unfixed and ambiguous). L16.

2 *alpha minus*, *beta minus*, *gamma minus*: see ALPHA etc. *omega minus*: see OMEGA 2.

B *n.* 1 The mathematical symbol '−'. Also *minus sign*. M17. 2 A quantity subtracted; a negative quantity; a loss, a deficiency, a disadvantage. M17

2 *Daily Telegraph* The current account had been in deficit with a minus of £75 million. *American Speech* For almost every minus, there is a compensating plus.

C *adv.* (Charged) negatively. M18.

D *adj.* 1 Negatively charged. L18. 2 Of a quantity: negative, preceded by the minus sign; of the nature of a negative quantity or a deficit. Also (*colloq.*), lacking; insignificant; non-existent, absent. E19. 3 *Printing* & *Photogr.* (Followed by the name of a colour) designating a complementary colour, i.e. that of white light from which a specified colour has been removed. E20.

2 *Chronicle* He was considerably *minus* at the last Newmarket meeting. R. FRY My recommendation would generally prove a minus quantity. *Moneypaper* A tendency to exaggerate plus and minus points.

minuscule /ˈmɪnəskjuːl/ *n.* & *a.* Also **mini-** /ˈmɪni-/. E18. [Fr. f. L *minuscula* (sc. *littera* letter) fem. of *minusculus* rather less, dim. of MINOR *a.* & *n.*: see -CULE. Var. w. *-ni-* by assoc. w. MINI-.] A *n.* In *Palaeogr.*: a small letter, as opp. to a capital or uncial; (a manuscript in) a small cursive script developed from early Roman hands and written as between four notional lines (with ascenders and descenders). Formerly also (*Typogr.*), a small or lower-case letter. E18.

B *adj.* 1 a *Typogr.* Of a letter: small, lower-case. Now *rare* or *obs.* E18. b *Palaeogr.* Of a letter: small, not capital or uncial; of, written in, or concerning minuscules. M19. 2 Extremely small; unimportant. L19.

1b *Bodleian Library Record* Written in an elegant minuscule script of about the mid-twelfth century. 2 *New York Times* Such concentration on minuscule . . matters is a waste of time.

minuscular /mɪˈnʌskjʊlə/ *a.* (*Palaeogr.*) of the nature of a minuscule, composed of minuscules M18.

minute /ˈmɪnɪt/ *n.* & *v.* LME. [(O)Fr. f. late L use as n. of L *minuta* fem. of *minutus*: see next. In senses 1 and 2 of n. f. med.L *pars minuta prima* first minute part, the 1/60 of a unit in a system of sexagesimal fractions. In sense 4 of n. perh. f. med.L *minuta scriptura* a draft in small writing.] A *n.* 1 The sixtieth part of an hour. Also, any of the sixty lines or marks on the face of a clock etc., marking intervals of one minute. LME. b A short space of time; an instant; a (specified) moment. LME. c The distance one can travel in a minute by a stated or implied means. L19. 2 The sixtieth part of a degree of angular measurement. Also *minute of arc*. LME. 3†a A coin of very small value; a mite. LME–L16. b A small particular, a detail; a very small or unimportant thing. *obs.* exc. *dial.* L15. 4 a A rough draft; a note or memorandum giving instructions to an agent etc., or serving as a reminder or record of a transaction etc. Also (in *pl.*), a brief summary of the proceedings at a meeting. LME. b An official memorandum authorizing or recommending a course of action. M16. c *Sc. Law.* A memorandum relating to matters of procedure or evidence presented to a court by a party to a suit. M19.

Phrases: *arc minute*: see ARC *n.* **at the minute** at the present time. **just a minute** *int.* (*a*) requesting someone to wait a short time; (*b*) as a prelude to a query or objection. *last minute*, *last-minute*: see LAST *a.* *mad minute*: see MAD *a.* **the minute (that)** as soon as. *up to the minute*: see UP *adv.*[1] **wait a minute** *imper.* & *int.* = *just a minute* above.

Comb.: **minute bell**: tolled at intervals of a minute, esp. as a sign of mourning or distress; **minute-book**: containing systematic records of the transactions of a society, court, etc.; **minute-glass** a sand-glass that runs for a minute; **minute-gun**: fired at intervals of a minute, esp. at a funeral; **minute-hand** the long hand of a clock or watch, which indicates minutes; †**minute-jack** a fickle or changeable person; **minute steak** a thin slice of steak to be cooked quickly; **minute-wheel**: that moves the minute-hand of a clock or watch.

B *v.t.* 1 a Draft (a document, a scheme); record in a minute or the minutes; make a minute of the contents of (a document). M16. b Inform (someone) by means of a minute or memorandum; send minutes to (a person). E20. 2 Time to the nearest minute; time accurately. E17.

minuter *n.* a person who writes minutes or notes proceedings E19.

minute /mʌɪˈnjuːt/ *a.* LME. [L *minutus* pa. pple of *minuere* make small, diminish.] †1 Chopped small. *rare.* Only in LME. †2 Of an impost, tithe, etc.: lesser. L15–L17. 3 Very small; insignificant, petty. E17. 4 Of an investigation, record, inquirer, etc.: characterized by attention to detail; very precise, particular, or accurate. L17.

3 R. K. NARAYAN Such minute type that you would have to search for it with a magnifying glass. 4 L. STRACHEY A minute and detailed analysis . . followed, filling several pages.

minuteness *n.* M17.

minutely /ˈmɪnɪtli/ *a.* E17. [f. MINUTE *n.* + -LY[1].] Occurring, performed, etc., every minute.

minutely /ˈmɪnɪtli/ *adv.*[1] L16. [f. as prec. + -LY[2].] Every minute, minute by minute.

minutely /mʌɪˈnjuːtli/ *adv.*[2] L16. [f. MINUTE *a.* + -LY[2].] 1 Orig., into small pieces. Now, on a minute scale. L16. 2 In a minute manner, kind, or degree; with great precision or exactness. E18.

minuteman /ˈmɪnɪtman/ *n.* Chiefly *US.* Pl. **-men.** L18. [f. MINUTE *n.* + MAN *n.*] 1 *Hist.* A member of a class of militiamen of the American revolutionary period, who held themselves ready for instant military service. L18. b *transf.* & *fig.* In the US, a political watchdog or activist; a member of an organization concerned with specific political issues. E20. 2 (**M-**.) A type of US three-stage intercontinental ballistic missile. M20.

minuterie /mɪˈnjuːt(ə)ri/ *n.* M20. [Fr. = clockwork, timing mechanism, f. MINUTE *n.*: see -ERY.] (An electric light controlled by) a light switch incorporating a timing mechanism to turn it off automatically after a short time.

minutia /mɪˈnjuːʃɪə, mʌɪ-/ *n.* Pl. **-tiae** /-ʃiː, -ʃɪʌɪ/. M18. [L = smallness (in pl., trifles), f. *minutus* MINUTE *a.*] A precise detail; a small or trivial matter or object. Usu. in *pl.*

minutiose /-ʃɪəʊs/ *a.* dealing with minutiae M19. **minutious** *a.* characterized by attention to minutiae E19.

minutial /mɪˈnjuːʃɪəl/ *a. arch.* E17. [f. as prec. + -AL¹.] Of the nature of minutiae; pertaining to details.

minx /mɪŋks/ *n.* M16. [Origin unkn.] †**1** A pet dog. Only in M16. **2** A pert, sly, or flirtatious young woman; a hussy. Also, a prostitute. L16.

minxish *a.* having the character of a minx L19. **minxishly** *adv.* E20.

miny /ˈmʌɪni/ *a. rare.* E17. [f. MINE *n.* + -Y¹.] Of or pertaining to a mine or mines; mineral.

minyan /ˈmɪnjan/ *n.*¹ Pl. **-im** /-ɪm/. M18. [Heb. *minyān* lit. 'count, reckoning'.] The quorum of ten males over thirteen years of age required for traditional Jewish public worship.

Minyan /ˈmɪnɪən/ *a.* & *n.*² L16. [f. L *Minyae*, Gk *Minuai* Minyans (see below) + -AN. As adj. perh. also f. Gk *Minueios*, f. *Minuai*.] **A** *adj.* **1** Of or pertaining to a possibly historical ancient people said to have inhabited parts of central Greece, with whom the legends about Jason and the Argonauts are associated. L16. **2** Designating a type of very smooth grey pottery first found at Orchomenus in Boeostia and orig. attributed to the Minyans. E20. **B** *n.* A member of the Minyan people. E18.

minyanim *n.* pl. of MINYAN *n.*¹

Miocene /ˈmʌɪəsiːn/ *a.* & *n.* M19. [Irreg. f. Gk *meiōn* less + *kainos* new, recent (as containing remains of fewer modern species than the Pliocene).] *Geol.* **A** *adj.* Designating or pertaining to the fourth epoch of the Tertiary period or sub-era, after the Oligocene and before the Pliocene. M19. **B** *n.* The Miocene epoch; the series of rocks dating from this time, containing fossil evidence of numerous mammals and the first hominids. M19.

Mioˈcenic *a.* M19.

miogeocline /mʌɪəˈdʒiːəklʌɪn/ *n.* M20. [f. next.] *Geol.* = next.

miogeoˈclinal *a.* L20.

miogeosyncline /ˌmʌɪə(ʊ)dʒiːəˈsɪŋklʌɪn/ *n.* M20. [f. Gk *meiōn* less + GEOSYNCLINE.] *Geol.* A geosyncline containing little or no volcanic rock; *esp.* one situated between a larger, volcanic geosyncline (eugeosyncline) and a stable area of the crust (craton).

miogeosynˈclinal *a.* of, pertaining to, or of the nature of a miogeosyncline M20.

miombo /mɪˈɒmbəʊ/ *n.* Pl. **-os.** M19. [Bantu.] Any of several tropical African leguminous trees of the genus *Brachystegia*; open woodland dominated by such trees, esp. in Tanzania.

miosis /mʌɪˈəʊsɪs/ *n.* Also (earlier) **my-.** E19. [f. Gk *muein* shut the eyes + -OSIS.] *Med.* (Abnormal or excessive) contraction of the pupil of the eye.

mioˈsitic *a.* & *n.* = MIOTIC M19.

miotic /mʌɪˈɒtɪk/ *a.* & *n.* Also (earlier) **my-.** M19. [f. prec. + -OTIC.] **A** *adj.* Pertaining to, causing, or exhibiting miosis. M19. **B** *n.* An agent which produces miosis. M19.

mi-parti /miparti/ *a.* & *adv.* E17. [Fr., pa. pple of *mipartir* divide in half, f. *mi-* (f. L *medium* middle) + *partir* divide.] *Her.* (Divided) per pale.

Mipolam /ˈmɪpəlam/ *n.* Also **m-.** M20. [Arbitrary.] (Proprietary name for) plastic composed of polyvinyl chloride, used for chemically resistant piping and containers.

Miquelet /ˈmɪkəlɪt/ *n.* L17. [Fr. f. Sp. *miquelete*, *migue-*, f. Catal. *Miquel*, Sp. *Miguel* Michael.] *Hist.* Orig., a member of a body of Catalonian bandits active in the Pyrenees in the 17th cent.; a Spanish guerrilla soldier during the Peninsular war. Later also, a soldier of any of various local regiments of Spanish infantry, chiefly performing escort duties.

Comb.: **miquelet lock** a type of flintlock developed in Spain.

Mir /mɪə/ *n.*¹ E17. [Pers. & Urdu *mīr* leader, commander f. Arab. *ʾamīr*: see AMIR.] = AMIR, EMIR.

mir /mɪə/ *n.*² L19. [Russ.] A village community in pre-revolutionary Russia.

Mir /mɪə/ *n.*³ & *a.* E20. [f. *Mirabad* a town in the Sarawan district of Iran.] (Designating) a rare and fine quality Saraband rug woven in Mirabad.

mirabelle /mɪrəˈbɛl/ *n.* E18. [Fr.] **1** (A fruit from) a European variety of plum tree. E18. **2** (A) liqueur distilled from mirabelles, esp. those grown in Alsace, France. M20.

mirabile dictu /mɪˌrɑːbɪleɪ ˈdɪktuː/ *adv. phr.* M19. [L *mirabile* neut. of *mirabilis* (see MIRABLE) + *dictu* supine of *dicere* say.] Wonderful to relate.

mirabilia /mɪrəˈbɪlɪə/ *n.pl.* M20. [L, use as n. of neut. pl. of *mirabilis*: see MIRABLE, -IA².] Wonders, marvels, miracles.

mirabilite /mɪˈrabɪlʌɪt/ *n.* M19. [f. (*sal*) *mirabilis* s.v. SAL *n.*¹, f. as next: see -ITE¹.] *Min.* Native hydrated sodium sulphate (Glauber's salt), a monoclinic mineral found usu. as colourless prisms or massive deposits, esp. near salt springs or lakes, and in caves.

†**mirable** *a.* & *n.* ME. [L *mirabilis* wonderful, f. *mirari* to wonder: see MIRACLE, -ABLE.] **A** *adj.* Wonderful, marvellous. ME–E17.

SHAKES. *Tr. & Cr.* Not Neoptolemus so mirable.. could promise to himself A thought of added honour torn from Hector.

B *n.* A marvel, a wonder. Only in M17.

miracidium /mʌɪrəˈsɪdɪəm/ *n.* Pl. **-dia** /-dɪə/. L19. [f. Gk *meirakidion* dim. of *meirakion* boy, stripling: see -IDIUM.] *Zool.* A digenean trematode (fluke) in the ciliated free-swimming larval stage, in which form it passes from the definitive to the (first) intermediate host, forming a sporocyst. Cf. CERCARIA.

miracidial *a.* M20.

miracle /ˈmɪrək(ə)l/ *n.* & *v.* ME. [(O)Fr. f. L *miraculum* object of wonder, f. *mirari*, *-are* look at, wonder, f. *mirus* wonderful.] **A** *n.* **1** A marvellous event not ascribable to human or natural agency, and therefore attributed to the intervention of a supernatural agent, esp. (in Christian belief) God; *spec.* an act demonstrating control over nature, serving as evidence that the agent is either divine or divinely favoured. ME. **2** Now more fully *miracle play.* A medieval dramatic representation based on the life of Jesus or the legends of the saints. ME. **3** *transf.* A remarkable or marvellous phenomenon or event. Also (w. specifying wd), a remarkable development in a specified area. Freq. *hyperbol.* ME. **b** A person or thing of more than natural excellence; a surpassing specimen or example *of.* LME.

1 G. GREENE There were miracles too; a virgin wept salt tears and a candle.. burnt inexplicably for one week. B. MOORE Without a miracle, Christ did not rise from His tomb and ascend into heaven. 3 F. L. WHIPPLE To overcome gravity and carry men out into space.. is to me a true miracle. *London Daily News* The compact disc miracle could prove to be a very short-lived one. *attrib.*: *Times* The discoverer of the 'miracle' rice and wheat strains.. was awarded the Nobel Peace Prize. b J. LAWSON The Humming-Bird is the Miracle of all our wing'd Animals.

Phrases: **to a miracle** marvellously well.

Comb.: **miracle cure** (a drug, treatment, etc., said to effect) a remarkable or extraordinary cure; **miracle drug** a drug treating or curing previously untreatable or incurable illnesses and representing a breakthrough in medical science; **miracle fruit** (the fruit of) a W. African tree, *Synsepalum dulcificum* (family Sapotaceae), whose berries have the property of making sour or salt things taste sweet; **miracle man**: who performs miracles; *miracle play*: see sense 2 above.

B *v.* †**1** *v.refl.* Be revealed by a miracle. *rare* (Shakes.). Only in E17. **2** *v.i.* & *t.* Work miracles (on, for). *rare.* M17.

†**miracular** *a.* miraculous E18–E19. †**miraculist** *n.* (*a*) a miracle-worker; (*b*) a believer in miracles: M17–E19.

miraculize /mɪˈrakjʊlʌɪz/ *v.t.* Also **-ise.** E18. [f. L *miraculum* (see prec.) + -IZE.] Make miraculous; consider as miraculous.

miraculous /mɪˈrakjʊləs/ *a.* LME. [(O)Fr. *miraculeux* or med.L *miraculosus*, f. L *miraculum*: see MIRACLE, -ULOUS.] **1** Of the nature of a miracle; supernatural; produced or effected by a miracle. LME. †**b** Of or pertaining to a miracle or miracles. M16–M19. **2** *transf.* Resembling a miracle; extraordinary, remarkable; astonishing. L16. **b** Intoxicated, very drunk. *dial.* L19. **3** Of a thing or (formerly) a person: having the power to work miracles. L16.

1 R. INGALLS Vision.. had always struck her as miraculous. 2 J. F. LEHMANN All problems which we discussed in our letters seemed to settle themselves with miraculous ease. J. DISKI One of those miraculous London autumns that made winter seem improbable. 3 A. B. JAMESON The miraculous oil which flowed under her shrine. **miraculous berry** = *miracle fruit* s.v. MIRACLE *n.* **miraculous fruit** the fruit of a tropical African plant, *Thaumatococcus danielli* (family Marantaceae), with similar properties to the miracle fruit.

miraculously *adv.* in a miraculous manner; (as) by a miracle; in a miraculous degree: LME. **miraculousness** *n.* L16.

mirador /miraˈdor/ *n.* L17. [Sp., f. *mirar* look, observe.] In Spain: a watch-tower. Also, a turret or belvedere on the top of a Spanish house.

mirage /ˈmɪrɑːʒ, mɪˈrɑːʒ/ *n.* & *a.* E19. [Fr., f. *se mirer* be reflected or mirrored, f. L *mirare*: see MIRACLE, -AGE.] **A** *n.* **1** An optical illusion caused by atmospheric conditions (usu. the refraction of light in heated air); *esp.* the false appearance of a distant sheet of water in a desert or on a hot road. Also, the appearance in the sky of a reflected image of a distant object, a wavelike appearance of warmed air just above the ground. E19. **2** *fig.* An illusion, a fantasy. E19. **3** Any of various pale fashion colours; *esp.* pale blue, grey, or turquoise. E20.

1 R. RENDELL It was a mirage he had seen in that river village, a trick of the heat and light.

B *adj.* **1** Resembling a mirage. E20. **2** Of a pale colour, esp. blue, grey, or turquoise. M20.

miragy *a.* of, pertaining to, or of the nature of a mirage L19.

Miranda /mɪˈrandə/ *a.* M20. [f. *Miranda* versus Arizona, the case that led to the Supreme Court ruling on the matter.] *US Law.* Designating or pertaining to the duty of the police to inform a person taken into custody of his or her right to legal counsel and the right to remain silent under questioning.

mirbane /ˈməːbeɪn/ *n.* M19. [Fr., of unkn. origin.] In *essence* or *oil of mirbane*, nitrobenzene as used in perfumery.

Mirditë /ˈməːdɪtə/ *n.* & *a.* Pl. same. Also (*sing.*) **-ita, -ite** /-ʌɪt/. M19. [See below.] **A** *n.* A people inhabiting Mirditë, a region around the river Drin in Albania. M19. **B** *adj.* Of or pertaining to the Mirditë. E20.

mire /mʌɪə/ *n.*¹ ME. [ON *mýrr*, ult. f. Gmc base of MOSS *n.*] **1** A wet swampy area of land; a boggy place; *gen.* swampy ground, bog. ME. **b** *Ecol.* An ecosystem in which wet peat is the substrate for vegetation. M20. **2** Wet or soft mud; slush; dirt. ME.

1 S. NAIPAUL The track.. was a mire, impassable even for four-wheel drive vehicles. 2 *fig.*: P. TOYNBEE Still floundering and foundering in the same old mire of complexities and contradictions.

Phrases: **find oneself** (or **stick**) **in the mire** be in difficulties.

†**mirish** *a.* M17–E18.

†**mire** *n.*² Only in ME. [Perh. f. OE wd corresp. to MDu. *miere* (Du. *mier*), MLG *mire.*] An ant.

¶ Survives as 2nd elem. of PISMIRE.

mire /mʌɪə/ *v.* LME. [f. MIRE *n.*¹] **1** *v.t.* Plunge or sink (oneself) in (a) mire; *esp.* (in *pass.*) be or become stuck or embedded in (a) mire; *fig.* involve in difficulties. LME. **b** Of bog, mud, etc.: hold fast, entangle. L19. **2** *v.t.* Bespatter or soil with mire or filth; *fig.* defile. L15. **3** *v.i.* Sink in (a) mire; be bogged *down.* E17.

J. HELLER No turbulent.. hailstorms or thunderstorms to mire or discomfit them. *New Yorker* The milk cow was mired in a bog hole. b R. ADAMS A wide marsh that mired them to the knees. 2 M. ARNOLD Her palfrey's flanks were mired and bathed in sweat. 3 W. SEWALL The roads being soft . . I mired down.

mired /ˈmʌɪrɛd/ *n.* M20. [Contr. of *micro reciprocal degree*.] *Photogr.* A unit expressing the reciprocal of colour temperature, defined as 10^{-6} per kelvin.

mirepoix /mɪrpwa/ *n.* Pl. same. L19. [Fr. f. the Duc de *Mirepoix* (1699–1757), Fr. diplomat and general.] *Cookery.* A mixture of sautéed diced vegetables used in sauces etc. or served as a separate dish.

mirex /ˈmʌɪrɛks/ *n.* Orig. *US.* M20. [Origin unkn.] An organochlorine insecticide used esp. against ants.

mirid /ˈmɪrɪd, ˈmʌɪ-/ *n.* & *a.* M20. [mod.L *Miridae*, the family formerly called Capsidae, f. *Miris* genus name, f. L *mirus* wonderful, extraordinary: see -ID³.] A *n.* Any bug of the heteropteran family Miridae, which includes numerous plant pests; a plant-bug. M20. B *adj.* Of, pertaining to, or designating this family. M20.

mirific /mʌɪˈrɪfɪk/ *a.* Chiefly *joc.* (now *rare*). L15. [Fr. *mirifique* f. L *mirificus*, f. *mirus* wonderful: see -FIC.] Doing wonders; exciting wonder or astonishment; marvellous.
†**mirifical** *a.* E17–E19. **mirifically** *adv.* L19.

mirk *n.*, *a.*, *v.* vars. of MURK *n.*¹, *a.*, *v.*

mirky *a.* var. of MURKY.

mirl /məːl/ *v.*¹ *Sc.* M19. [Alt. of MIRR.] Move briskly; turn round, twirl.

mirl *v.*² var. of MURL.

mirligoes /ˈməːlɪgəʊz/ *n.pl. Sc.* L18. [Fanciful formation f. MIRL *v.*¹, after *vertigo*.] Dizziness vertigo.

mirliton /ˈməːlɪtɒn/ *n.* E19. [Fr. = reed pipe, of imit. origin.] 1 A musical instrument resembling a kazoo; any instrument in which a sound is given a nasal quality by means of a vibrating membrane. E19. 2 A chayote. *US.* E20.

miro /ˈmɪərəʊ/ *n.*¹ Pl. **-os**. M19. [Maori.] (The wood of) a New Zealand evergreen coniferous tree, *Prumnopitys ferruginea* (family Podocarpaceae), with large reddish-purple arils. Also *miro tree*.

miro /ˈmɪərəʊ/ *n.*² *NZ.* Also **miro-miro** /mɪərəʊˈmɪərəʊ/. Pl. **-os**. M19. [Maori.] Either of two New Zealand songbirds of the genus *Petroica* (family Eopsaltridae), the New Zealand tomtit, *P. macrocephala*, and the New Zealand robin, *P.* (formerly *Miro*) *australis*.

miroton /mirotɔ̃/ *n.* Pl. pronounced same. E18. [Fr.] A dish of small thin slices of meat, esp. made into ragout.

mirr /məː/ *v.i. Sc.* M18. [Norw. *mirra*.] Tingle, quiver, tremble.

mirrnyong /ˈməːnjɒŋ/ *n. Austral.* Also ***myrnyong***. L19. [Aborig.] A mound of shells, ashes, and other debris accumulated in a place used for cooking by Australian Aborigines; an Aboriginal kitchen-midden.

mirror /ˈmɪrə/ *n.* & *v.* ME. [OFr. *mirour* (mod. *miroir*, f. var. *mirëoir*) f. Proto-Romance f. L *mirat-* pa. ppl stem of *mirari*: see MIRACLE, -OR.] A *n.* I *lit.* 1 A smooth surface, formerly of polished metal, now usu. (exc. in some scientific instruments) of glass coated on one side with an amalgam, which reflects light rays to form an image; a looking-glass. ME. 2 A glass or crystal used in magic. *arch.* ME.

1 T. IRELAND She tried to catch her reflection in the mirror on the wall.

II *fig.* 3 A person or thing embodying a feature or characteristic deserving of imitation; a pattern, an exemplar; a model of excellence; a paragon. Freq. foll. by *of*. Now *rare*. ME. †**b** A person or thing embodying something to be avoided; a deterrent, a warning. *rare*. LME–M17. 4 A thing or (*poet.*) a person regarded as giving a faithful reflection or true description of something. LME.

3 L. STRACHEY In the eyes of Victoria he was the mirror of manly beauty. 4 R. CHRISTIANSEN The Poet's mind was no longer a mirror reflecting Nature.

III *transf.* 5 Something which reflects an image, *esp.* water. Usu. *poet.* LME. 6 *Archit.* A small round or oval ornament with a border. M19. 7 *Ornith.* A white spot on the black wingtip of a gull. E20.

Phrases: **by mirrors** (as if) by magic. *long mirror*: see LONG *a.*¹ *magic mirror*: see MAGIC *a. magnetic mirror*: see MAGNETIC *a.* **with mirrors** = *by mirrors* above.

Comb.: **mirror carp** an abnormal variety of the carp having just two or three rows of enlarged scales; **mirror embroidery** = *mirror-work* below; **mirror finish** a reflective surface; **mirror fugue** *Mus.* a fugue that can be played reversed or inverted; **mirror-glass** (glass used in) a mirror; **mirror image** an image etc. identical to its original but with the structure reversed; *loosely* an identical image, copy, etc.; **mirror nucleus, nuclide** *Nuclear Physics* either of two nuclides of the same atomic mass, each having as many protons as the other has neutrons; **mirror-plate** (*a*) a plate of glass suitable for a mirror; (*b*) a metal plate used for fixing a mirror etc. to a wall or base; **mirror scale** a graduated scale provided with an adjacent mirror so as to avoid parallax errors when taking readings; **mirror stage** *Psychol.* a stage in a child's development considered to be typified by its reacting to its reflection as if it were a real person; **mirror symmetry**: as of an object and its reflection; **mirror-work** small round pieces of mirror appliquéd on fabric; **mirror-writer** a person who practises mirror writing; **mirror writing** reversed writing (esp. characteristic of aphasia), like ordinary writing reflected in a mirror.

B *v.t.* †1 Be a model for in behaviour. Only in LME. 2 Reflect as in a mirror. L16. 3 Imitate, reproduce, represent. E19.

2 W. GOLDING The clear water mirrored the clear sky. 3 O. WILDE The gracious and comely form he had so skilfully mirrored in his art. SCOTT FITZGERALD Tom glanced around to see if we mirrored his unbelief.

mirrored *a.* (*a*) fitted with a mirror or mirrors; (*b*) having a reflective surface; (*c*) reflected (as) by a mirror: E19. **mirrorize** *v.t.* reflect (as) in a mirror L16. **mirror-like** *a.* resembling (that of) a mirror; smooth and reflective: L18. **mirrory** *a.* mirror-like L19.

mirth /məːθ/ *n.* [OE *myrigþ*, f. Gmc base also of MERRY *a.*: see -TH¹.] †1 Pleasurable feeling, enjoyment, gratification; happiness; (religious) joy. OE–L17. **b** A cause of joy. OE–LME. 2 Rejoicing; merrymaking; jollity, gaiety. ME. 3 A thing affording pleasure or amusement; a diversion, an (esp. musical) entertainment. Now *rare*. ME. 4 Merriment, hilarity, laughter. Formerly also, jocularity; ridicule. ME. †**b** A cause of hilarity. ME–E18.

2 W. IRVING The genial festival of Christmas, which . . lights up the . . home with mirth and jollity. 4 D. H. LAWRENCE Blue eyes . . swimming over with laughter-tears, their clear cheeks were flushed crimson with mirth. S. BELLOW Leventhal was smiling also, but without much mirth.

Comb.: **mirthquake** *colloq.* an extremely funny play, film, etc.

mirthsome *a.* mirthful, joyous E19.

mirthful /ˈməːθfʊl, -f(ə)l/ *a.* ME. [f. prec. + -FUL.] 1a Of a person, mood, etc.: joyful, full of merriment. ME. **b** Of a thing, place, time, etc.: characterized by or exhibiting mirth. LME. 2 Of a thing: amusing. ME.

mirthfully *adv.* LME. **mirthfulness** *n.* M19.

mirthless /ˈməːθlɪs/ *a.* LME. [f. as prec. + -LESS.] Joyless; sad, dismal.

mirthlessly *adv.* L19. **mirthlessness** *n.* E18.

MIRV /məːv/ *n.* & *v.* M20. [Acronym, f. *multiple independently-targeted re-entry vehicle*.] A *n.* A missile containing several independently guided warheads; a warhead carried by such a missile. M20. B *v.t.* Equip (a rocket, missile system, etc.) with a MIRV or MIRVs. M20.

miry /ˈmʌɪ(ə)ri/ *a.* LME. [f. MIRE *n.*¹ + -Y¹.] 1 Resembling or containing mire; swampy; muddy. LME. 2a Covered or bespattered with mire. L15. **b** *fig.* Dirty, defiled; despicable. L15.

miriness *n.* E17.

mirza /ˈmirzaː/ *n.* E17. [Pers. *mīrzā*, f. *mīr* prince (f. Arab. *ʾamīr* AMIR) + *zād* son.] In Iran: a royal prince (*Hist.*); a common honorific title for an official or a man of learning, or (*postpositively*, *Hist.*) a royal prince.

Mirzapur /ˈməːzəpʊə/ *n.* & *a.* L19. [A town in the State of Uttar Pradesh in northern India.] (Designating) a type of carpet manufactured in Mirzapur.

mis /mɪz/ *n.* & *a.* E20. [Abbrev.] A *n.* Misery. E20. B *adj.* Miserable. M20.

mis- /mɪs/ *pref.*¹ [OE *mis-* = OFris., OS *mis-*, OHG *missa-*, *missi-* (Du. *mis-*, G *miss-*), ON *mis-*, Goth. *missa-*, f. Gmc.] 1 Prefixed to vbs & vbl derivs. w. the sense 'amiss, badly, wrongly, mistakenly', as *misdirect*, *misguided(ly)*, *misleading(ly)*. 2 Prefixed to ns. of action, condition, and quality in the sense 'bad, wrong, faulty, perverse, misdirected', as *misalignment*, *mispronunciation*. 3 Prefixed to agent-ns. to form ns. w. the sense 'a person who or thing which mis—s', as *misuser*. 4 Prefixed to adjs. & derived advs. w. the sense 'wrongly, erroneously, perversely', as *misrepresentative*. 5 Expr. negation (of something good or desirable); = *dis-*, *in-*, *un-*. 6 Prefixed as an intensive to wds denoting something wrong or bad.

misˈact *v.t.* (long *rare*) act badly E17. **misaˈddress** *v.t.* address (a letter etc.) wrongly; address (remarks etc.) inappropriately or impertinently: M17. **misaˈdjustment** *n.* lack of adjustment E19. **misaˈffection** *n.* (now *rare* or *obs.*) (*a*) = DISAFFECTION 1; (*b*) a disease, a disorder: E17. **misaˈgree** *v.i.* (now *dial.*) disagree M16. **misˈaim** *v.t.* (*rare*) aim amiss L16. **misalloˈcation** *n.* (a) failure to allocate efficiently or fairly M20. **misaˈlly** *v.t.* (*rare*) ally or join inappropriately L17. **misappeˈllation** *n.* the action of using a wrong word in referring to something E19. **misaˈppreciate** *v.t.* fail to appreciate rightly E19. **misappreciˈation** *n.* (an) erroneous appreciation or valuation M19. **misaˈrranged** *a.* wrongly arranged M19. **misaˈrrangement** *n.* (a) bad or wrong arrangement L18. **misarticuˈlation** *n.* faulty articulation M20. **misaˈscription** *n.* (a) false ascription E20. **misaˈssign** *v.t.* (*rare*) assign erroneously M17. **misaˈward** *v.t.* (*rare*) award wrongly E17. **misbeˈgin** *v.t.* (*rare*) begin amiss or badly L16. **misbeˈstow** *v.t.* bestow wrongly or improperly M16. **misˈbode** *v.t.* (*rare*) forebode (something evil); chiefly as *misboding* vbl n. & ppl a.: E17. **misˈbound** *a.* (of a book) badly or wrongly bound E19. **misˈcasualty** *n.* (long *obs.* exc. *dial.*) a mischance, a mishap L16. **misˈcatalogued** *a.* wrongly catalogued M20. **mischaracteriˈzation** *n.* the action or an instance of mischaracterizing something M20. **misˈcharacterize** *v.t.* characterize wrongly L18. **misˈcharge** *v.t.* (now *rare*) charge wrongly or falsely L15. **misˈchoice** *n.* (a) wrong or improper choice L17. **misˈchoose** *v.t.* & *i.* make a wrong choice (of) ME. **misˈchristen** *v.t.* (*rare*) misname M17. **mis-ˈcipher** *v.t.* (*rare*) express wrongly in cipher M17. **mis-ciˈtation** *n.* (an) incorrect citation, (a) misquotation M17. **mis-ˈcite** *v.t.* cite incorrectly, misquote L16. **misclassifiˈcation** *n.* (an) incorrect classification E19. **misˈclassify** *v.t.* classify incorrectly M20. **misˈclosure** *n.* the deviation of the final surveyed position of a point from the initial one after a traverse has been carried out starting at the point and leading back to it M20. **misˈcode** *v.t.* code incorrectly M20. **misˈcolour** *v.t.* (*a*) give a wrong or improper colour to; (*b*) misrepresent, misinterpret, (a fact etc.): LME. **miscoˈmmunicate** *v.t.* communicate incorrectly or imperfectly M17. **miscommuniˈcation** *n.* (an instance of) incorrect or imperfect communication M20. **miscompreˈhend** *v.t.* misunderstand E19. **miscompreˈhension** *n.* misunderstanding M19. **miscompuˈtation** *n.* a wrong or faulty computation M17. **miscomˈpute** *v.i.* miscalculate L17. **misconˈjecture** *n.* (*rare*) (an) erroneous conjecture M17. **misconˈjunction** *n.* a wrong conjunction M19. **miscoˈnnection** *n.* a wrong connection, esp. when using a telephone M20. **misˈconsecrated** *a.* (*a*) consecrated to a wrong purpose; (*b*) improperly consecrated: M17. **misconˈvey** *v.refl.* convey a wrong impression of one's meaning M19. **misˈcook** *v.t.* (chiefly *Sc.*) cook badly; spoil in cooking; *fig.* mismanage: E16. **misˈcounsel** *v.t.* counsel or advise wrongly LME. **misˈcreed** *n.* (*poet.*, *rare*) a mistaken creed E19. **misdeˈcide** *v.i.* (*rare*) make a wrong decision E19. **misdeˈcision** *n.* (*rare*) wrong decision or judgement E19. **misdeclaˈration** *n.* (an) incorrect declaration, esp. in an official context E20. **misdeˈliver** *v.t.* (*a*) deliver to the wrong person or at the wrong place; (*b*) hand down improperly: M19. **misdeˈlivery** *n.* wrong delivery, delivery to the wrong person or at the wrong place L17. **misdeˈrive** *v.t.* (*a*) misdirect; (*b*) assign a wrong derivation to: M17. **misdeˈsert** *n.* (long *rare*) the condition of being undeserving L16. **misdeˈserve** *v.* (long *rare*) †(*a*) *v.i.* deserve ill; (*b*) *v.t.* fail to deserve: M17. **misdeˈvoted** *a.* (*rare*) improperly devoted; devoted to a wrong object: E17. †**misdiet** *v.*

& *n.* (*a*) *v.t.* feed a wrong diet to; (*b*) *n.* wrong diet, improper feeding: L15–E18. †**misdight** *a.* ill-clothed; badly prepared or provided; ill-treated: LME–E17. **misdistri'bution** *n.* wrong or faulty distribution E20. †**misdread** *n.* (*rare*, Shakes.) dread of evil: only in E17. **mis'drive** *v.t.* †(*a*) *rare* commit (a wrong); (*b*) drive in a wrong direction: ME. **mis'emphasis** *n.* incorrect emphasis E20. **mis'entry** *n.* (now *rare* or *obs.*) an erroneous entry E17. **mis'execute** *v.t.* execute or carry out improperly M17. **misexe'cution** *n.* improper execution M16. **misexplain** /mɪsɪk'spleɪn/ *v.t.* explain incorrectly L17. **mis'faith** *n.* (*rare*) disbelief; mistrust: LME. **mis'fame** *v.t.* (*rare*) spread a false report concerning, defame LME. **mis'feature** *n.* a distorted feature; a bad feature or trait: E19. **mis'file** *v.t.* file wrongly M20. **misfor'mation** *n.* malformation E19. **mis'formed** *a.* malformed, misshapen L16. **mis'function** *n.* = DYSFUNCTION M20. **mis'functional** *a.* = DYSFUNCTIONAL L20. †**misgraffed** *a.* (*rare*, Shakes.) badly grafted, *fig.* badly matched: only in L16. **mis'grounded** *a.* falsely grounded; ill-founded: L16. **mis'grown** *a.* grown out of shape; misshapen: E17. **mis'growth** *n.* a distorted or abortive growth M17. **mis'hook** *v.* & *n.* (*Cricket*) (*a*) *v.t.* hook (a ball) badly; (*b*) *n.* a bad hook: M20. **misim'pression** *n.* a wrong impression L17. **misin'fer** *v.t.* (long *rare*) (*a*) infer wrongly; (*b*) draw a wrong inference from: L16. **mis'key** *v.t.* & *i.* type (a character, word, etc.) wrongly on a keyboard, keypad, etc. L20. **mis'labelling** *n.* incorrect labelling M20. **mis'learn** *v.t.* learn badly or incorrectly L17. **mis'liver** *n.* (now *rare* or *obs.*) a person who leads an evil life LME. **mis'living** *n.* evil living ME. **mis'lodge** *v.t.* †(*a*) mislay; (*b*) lodge in a wrong place: L17. **mis'luck** *n.* & *v.i.* (chiefly *Sc.*) (meet with) misfortune E17. **mis'made** *a.* †(*a*) misshapen; (*b*) badly or wrongly made: LME. **mis'make** *v.t.* (*obs.* exc. *Sc.*) (*a*) make bad or badly; (*b*) *refl.* trouble oneself, put oneself out: ME. **mis'mark** *v.t.* (now *rare*) (*a*) *refl.* guess wrongly; (*b*) mark wrongly: LME. **mis'marriage** *n.* an unsuitable marriage E19. **mis'metre** *v.t.* spoil the metre of (verse etc.) LME. **mis'number** *v.t.* number incorrectly E17. **misob'servance** *n.* (*rare*) failure to observe rules or conditions properly LME. **mis'occupy** *v.t.* (*rare*) occupy or employ wrongly M16. **misper'form** *v.t.* perform improperly M17. **misper'formance** *n.* (an) improper performance L17. **misper'suade** *v.t.* (now *rare* or *obs.*) persuade wrongly or into error L16. **misper'suasion** *n.* (now *rare* or *obs.*) a misconception; a wrong conviction: L16. **mis'pleading** *n.* (now *rare*) wrong pleading; a mistake in pleading: M16. **mis'pointing** *n.* †(*a*) pointing with the wrong finger; (*b*) (now *rare*) incorrect punctuation: M16. **mis'praise** *v.t.* (now *rare*) (*a*) dispraise, blame; (*b*) praise wrongly: ME. **mis'prisal** *n.* (*rare*) contempt, disdain, scorn E17. **mis'proud** *a.* (*arch.*) wrongly or wickedly proud; arrogant: ME. **mis'rate** *v.t.* (now *rare*) estimate wrongly E17. †**misregard** *n.* lack of regard or care; neglect, contempt: M16–L17. **misre'late** *v.t.* relate or recount incorrectly E17. **mis'render** *v.t.* render or interpret incorrectly M17. **misre'peat** *v.t.* (now *rare* or *obs.*) repeat incorrectly E17. **misre'semblance** *n.* (long *rare*) (*a*) a lack of resemblance; (*b*) a bad likeness or portrait: E17. **mis'route** *v.t.* divert or reroute to the wrong destination or by a longer or more expensive route M20. **mis'script** *n.* an error in writing M19. **mis'see** *v.t.* see imperfectly, take a wrong view of L15. **mis'send** *v.t.* send to a wrong place or person; chiefly as *missent* ppl a.: LME. **mis'serve** *v.t.* (now *rare*) serve badly or unfaithfully ME. **mis'set** *v.t.* (*a*) misplace; (*b*) *Sc.* put in a bad mood: ME. **mis'style** *v.t.* (*rare*) style or term incorrectly E17. **mis'suit** *v.t.* suit badly E17. **mis'sworn** *a.* (chiefly *Sc.*) perjured, forsworn E16. **mis'term** *v.t.* apply a wrong term or name to L16. **mis'tutored** *a.* badly instructed or brought up M18. **mis'value** *v.t.* value wrongly E17. **misvocali'zation** *n.* the insertion of incorrect vowel-signs in forms of writing consisting mainly or entirely of consonants M20.

mis- /mɪs/ *pref.*[2] [OFr. *mes-* (mod. *més-*, *mes-*, *mé-*) f. Proto-Romance, ult. f. L *minus* (see MINUS): assim. to MIS-[1].] Occurring w. the sense 'bad(ly), wrong(ly)' and w. neg. force in a few wds adopted f. Fr., as *misadventure*, *mischief*, *misnomer*.

mis- *pref.*[3] (*comb. form*) see MISO-.

misadventure /mɪsəd'vɛntʃə/ *n.* ME. [OFr. *mesaventure*, f. *mesavenir* turn out badly (f. *mes-* MIS-[2] + *avenir* f. L *advenire*: see ADVENT), after *aventure* ADVENTURE *n.*] **1** Bad luck; a piece of bad luck; a mishap, a misfortune. ME. **2** *Law.* Homicide committed accidentally by a person in doing a lawful act, without any intention of hurt. Now chiefly in *death* or *homicide by misadventure*. E16.

1 M. FITZHERBERT After some misadventures.. Lloyd and Aubrey decided to abandon their projected ride.

†**misadventured** *a. rare* (Shakes.). Only in L16. [f. prec. + -ED[2].] Unfortunate.

misadventurous /mɪsəd'vɛntʃ(ə)rəs/ *a.* Now *rare.* LME. [Orig. f. OFr. *mesaventureux*, f. *mesaventure*: see MISADVENTURE, -OUS. Later f. MISADVENTURE + -OUS.] Unfortunate, unlucky.

misadvice /mɪsəd'vʌɪs/ *n.* Long *rare.* M17. [f. MIS-[1] 2 + ADVICE.] Wrong advice.

misadvise /mɪsəd'vʌɪz/ *v.t.* LME. [f. MIS-[1] 1 + ADVISE.] †**1** *refl.* Take bad advice; act unadvisedly. LME–E17. **2** Give incorrect advice to. M16.

2 W. HUNT Shipping companies had misadvised them on the practicability of the glacial route.

†**misadvised** *a.* illadvised, imprudent, injudicious; wrongly advised: LME–L18.

misalign /mɪsə'lʌɪn/ *v.t.* M20. [f. MIS-[1] 1 + ALIGN.] Give a wrong or imperfect alignment to.

misalignment *n.* E20.

misalliance /mɪsə'lʌɪəns/ *n.* M18. [f. MIS-[1] 2 + ALLIANCE *n.*, after Fr. MÉSALLIANCE.] An improper alliance, association, or union; *esp.* an unsuitable marriage.

misandry /mɪ'sandri/ *n.* E20. [f. MIS-[3] + ANDR(O- + -Y[3].] Hatred of men.

misanter *n.* var. of MISAUNTER.

misanthrope /'mɪz(ə)nθrəʊp, mɪs-/ *n.* & *a.* Also (earlier) in Gk & L forms †**misanthropos**, pl. **-poi**, †**-pus**, pl. **-pi**. M16. [Fr. f. mod.L *misanthropus* f. Gk *misanthrōpos*, f. as MIS-[3] + *anthrōpos* man.] **A** *n.* A hater of humankind; a person who distrusts people and avoids their company. M16. **B** *adj.* Misanthropic. M18.

misan'thropic *a.* pertaining to, resembling, or characteristic of a misanthrope; characterized by misanthropy: M18. **misan'thropical** *a.* misanthropic M17. **misan'thropically** *adv.* M19. **mi'santhropist** *n.* a misanthrope M17. **mi'santhropize** *v.i.* be a misanthrope M19.

misanthropy /mɪs'anθrəpi, mɪ'zan-/ *n.* M17. [Gk *misanthrōpia*, f. as MIS-[3] + *anthrōpos* man: see -IA[1].] Hatred of humankind; the character, nature, or condition of a misanthrope.

misapply /mɪsə'plʌɪ/ *v.t.* L16. [f. MIS-[1] 1 + APPLY.] Apply to a wrong person or object; make a wrong application of.

misappli'cation *n.* the action or an act of misapplying something, esp. money E17.

misapprehend /ˌmɪsaprɪ'hɛnd/ *v.t.* E17. [f. MIS-[1] 1 + APPREHEND.] Apprehend wrongly; fail to understand rightly, misunderstand.

misapprehension /ˌmɪsaprɪ'hɛnʃ(ə)n/ *n.* E17. [f. MIS-[1] 2 + APPREHENSION.] The action or an act of misapprehending something; an erroneous belief, a mistaken assumption.

J. TYNDALL An opinion, founded on a grave misapprehension. L. CODY It's a common misapprehension.. that the elderly lose their memories.

misapprehensive *a.* apt to misapprehend M17. **misapprehensively** *adv.* through misapprehension M19. **misapprehensiveness** *n.* M19.

misappropriate /mɪsə'prəʊprɪət/ *a. rare.* M19. [f. MIS-[1] 5 + APPROPRIATE *a.*] Inappropriate.

misappropriate /mɪsə'prəʊprɪeɪt/ *v.t.* M19. [f. MIS-[1] 1 + APPROPRIATE *v.*] Apply or assign to a wrong use; *spec.* apply (money belonging to another) dishonestly to one's own use, embezzle.

W. PLOMER He had misappropriated the funds entrusted to him.

ˌmisappropri'ation *n.* L18.

misattribution /ˌmɪsatrɪ'bjuːʃ(ə)n/ *n.* L19. [f. MIS-[1] 2 + ATTRIBUTION.] (An) attribution, esp. of a work of art or literature, to the wrong person.

New York Review of Books Such activities as sifting out fakes and correcting misattributions.

misa'ttribute *v.t.* attribute wrongly E20.

misaunter /mɪs'ɔːntə/ *n.* Long *obs.* exc. *Sc.* & *north.* Also **misanter** /mɪs'antə/. See also MISHANTER. ME. [Contr.] = MISADVENTURE.

misbecome /mɪsbɪ'kʌm/ *v.t.* Pa. t. **-became** /-bɪ'keɪm/; pa. pple **-become**. M16. [f. MIS-[1] 1 + BECOME.] Be unsuitable for, be unbecoming to.

misbecoming /ˌmɪsbɪ'kʌmɪŋ/ *a.* E17. [f. MIS-[1] 1 + BECOMING *a.*, or f. prec. + -ING[2]] Unsuitable, unbecoming.

SIR W. SCOTT A paroxysm of laughter has seized him at a misbecoming time and place.

misbecomingly *adv.* E17. **misbecomingness** *n.* (*a*) the quality or condition of being misbecoming; (*b*) an unbecoming characteristic: M17.

misbeget /mɪsbɪ'gɛt/ *v.t. rare.* Infl. as BEGET. ME. [f. MIS-[1] 1 + BEGET.] Beget unlawfully.

misbegotten /mɪsbɪ'gɒt(ə)n/ *a.* L15. [f. MIS-[1] 1 + *begotten* pa. pple of BEGET.] Unlawfully begotten; illegitimate; *fig.* ill-conceived; contemptible. Also used as a term of abuse.

misbehave /mɪsbɪ'heɪv/ *v.i.* & (now *rare*) *refl.* L15. [f. MIS-[1] 1 + BEHAVE.] Behave badly; conduct oneself improperly.

M. WARNOCK Having misbehaved, I was shut in the night nursery as a punishment.

misbehaviour *n.* L15.

misbeholden /mɪsbɪ'həʊld(ə)n/ *a.* Long *obs.* exc. *Sc.* & *north.* E17. [f. MIS-[1] 1 + *beholden* pa. pple of BEHOLD.] Unbecoming, indiscreet. Chiefly in *misbeholden word*.

misbelief /mɪsbɪ'liːf/ *n.* ME. [f. MIS-[1] 2, 5 + BELIEF.] **1** Erroneous or unorthodox religious belief; heresy. ME. **b** *gen.* (An) erroneous belief; (a) false opinion or notion. LME. †**2** Lack of belief; disbelief, incredulity. ME–M17.

misbelieve /mɪsbɪ'liːv/ *v.* ME. [f. MIS-[1] 1, 5 + BELIEVE.] **1** *v.i.* Believe falsely; hold an erroneous or unorthodox belief. Now chiefly as *misbelieving* ppl a. and in MISBELIEVER. ME. **2** *v.t.* Not believe; distrust (a person); disbelieve (a thing). *obs.* exc. *Sc.* LME.

misbeliever /mɪsbɪ'liːvə/ *n.* LME. [f. MIS-[1] 3 + BELIEVER.] A person who holds an erroneous or unorthodox belief; a heretic, an infidel.

misbeseem /mɪsbɪ'siːm/ *v.t. arch.* L16. [f. MIS-[1] 1 + BESEEM.] = MISBECOME.

misbirth /mɪs'bəːθ/ *n. rare.* M17. [f. MIS-[1] 2 + BIRTH *n.*[1]] A stillbirth; a premature birth with loss of the foetus.

misborn /mɪs'bɔːn/ *a.* Long *rare* or *obs.* OE. [f. MIS-[1] 1 + BORN *a.*] **1** Prematurely born; abortive; born deformed. OE. **2** Born illegitimately; base-born. L16.

miscalculate /mɪs'kalkjʊleɪt/ *v.i.* & *t.* L17. [f. MIS-[1] 1 + CALCULATE.] Calculate or reckon wrongly; misjudge.

LD MACAULAY The conspirators found that they had miscalculated. E. WAUGH They never contemplated.. military conquest.. and entirely miscalculated the spirit of the people.

miscalcu'lation *n.* (a) wrong or faulty calculation; a misjudgement: E18. **miscalculator** *n.* a person who miscalculates L19.

miscall /mɪs'kɔːl/ *v.t.* LME. [f. MIS-[1] 1 + CALL *v.*] **1** Call by a wrong or inappropriate name; misname. Freq. w. compl. LME. **b** Misread, mispronounce. *dial.* M19. **2** Call by a bad name; call (a person) names; abuse, malign. Now *arch.* & *dial.* LME.

1 R. ELLMANN What Wilde carelessly miscalled in print the *Sonata Impassionata*.

miscarriage /mɪs'karɪdʒ, 'mɪskarɪdʒ/ *n.* L16. [f. next + -AGE.] †**1 a** Misconduct, misbehaviour. L16–L17. **b** A misdemeanour, a misdeed. M17–E19. **2** Mismanagement, maladministration; failure (of an enterprise etc.); a blunder, a mistake. Now *rare* exc. in *miscarriage of justice* below. E17. †**b** Mishap, disaster. Only in 18. **3** The action of giving birth with loss of the foetus, esp. in the period before a live birth is possible; an instance of this; *spec.* a spontaneous abortion. M17. **4** The failure of a letter, freight, etc., to reach its destination. M17.

2 miscarriage of justice a failure of the judicial system to attain the ends of justice. 3 A. N. WILSON Bessie became pregnant again.. but had a miscarriage.

miscarry /mɪs'kari/ *v.* ME. [OFr. *mescarier*, f. as MIS-[1], CARRY *v.*] †**1** *v.i.* & *t.* in *pass.* Come to harm, misfortune, or destruction; (of a person) meet one's end; (of an inanimate object) be lost

For other words beginning with *mis-* see the entry for **mis-**

or destroyed. ME–M18. 2 *v.i.* & *refl.* Go wrong or astray; do wrong, misbehave. Long *rare*. ME. †3 *v.t.* Cause (a person) to go wrong; mislead, delude, seduce. LME–L17. 4 *v.i.* a Have a miscarriage. Also (now *rare*) foll. by *of* the foetus. E16. b Of a foetus: be born dead in a miscarriage. L16. 5 *v.i.* †a Of a plant, seed, etc.: be abortive or unproductive; fail. L16–M18. b Of a plan, business, etc.: go wrong; come to nothing; be unsuccessful. E17. c Of a person: fail in one's purpose or object; be unsuccessful. E17. 6 *v.i.* & †*t.* in *pass.* Of a letter etc.: fail to reach its proper destination; get into wrong hands. E17.

1 SHAKES. *Lear* Our sister's man is certainly miscarried. 4 *Daily Telegraph* In most other abnormalities associated with late motherhood, the woman miscarries. 5b H. HALLAM A similar proposition in the session . . seems to have miscarried in the Commons. c R. W. EMERSON If our young men miscarry in their first enterprises, they lose all heart.

miscast /mɪsˈkɑːst/ *v.* Pa. t. & pple **-cast**. LME. [f. MIS-[1] 1 + CAST *v.*] †1 *v.t.* Cast (one's eye) with evil intent. Only in LME. 2 *v.t.* & *i.* Miscalculate. Exc. *dial.* now only as *miscasting* vbl n. M16. 3 *v.t.* Give an unsuitable role to (an actor). Usu. in *pass.* E20.

miscegenation /ˌmɪsɪdʒɪˈneɪʃ(ə)n/ *n.* M19. [Irreg. f. L *miscere* MIX *v.* + *genus* race + -ATION.] The mixing of people of different racial types; *esp.* the interbreeding of Whites and non-Whites.

ˈmiscegenated *a.* produced by miscegenation; of mixed descent: M19.

miscellanea /mɪsəˈleɪnɪə/ *n.* L16. [L, neut. pl. of L *miscellaneus*: see MISCELLANEOUS.] As *pl.*, miscellaneous items, esp. literary compositions, collected together. As *sing.*, a miscellaneous collection, esp. of literary compositions; a miscellany.

†**miscellaneal** *a.* M17–E18. [f. L *miscellaneus*: see next, -AL[1].] Miscellaneous.

miscellaneous /mɪsəˈleɪnɪəs/ *a.* E17. [f. L *miscellaneus*, f. *miscellus* mixed, f. *miscere* MIX *v.*: see -EOUS.] 1 (With a sing. n.) consisting of members or elements of different kinds, of mixed composition or character; (with a pl. n.) of various kinds. E17. 2 Of a person: having various qualities or aspects; many-sided. M17.

1 DICKENS He was a sort of town-traveller for a number of miscellaneous houses. R. K. NARAYAN I received a miscellaneous collection of mail-catalogues, programmes . . and what not.

miscellaneously *adv.* with variety or diversity; in various ways, on miscellaneous subjects: M18. **miscellaneousness** *n.* E18.

miscellany /mɪˈsɛləni/ *n.* L16. [(Fr. *miscellanées* fem. pl. f.) L MISCELLANEA, with assim. to -Y[3].] 1 A mixture, a medley. L16. 2 In *pl.* Separate articles or studies on a subject, or compositions of various kinds, collected into one volume. (Freq. in titles of books.) Long *rare* or *obs.* E17. 3 A literary work or production containing miscellaneous pieces on various subjects. M17.

1 R. MACAULAY A miscellany of assorted amusements—Greek plays, . . playing cards, a chessboard, bottles and glasses. 3 *Times Lit. Suppl.* The variety of the contents of this military miscellany.

miscellanist *n.* a writer of miscellanies E19.

†**miscellany** *a.* E17–M18. [f. as MISCELLANEOUS, perh. after prec.] Miscellaneous.

mischance /mɪsˈtʃɑːns/ *n.* ME. [OFr. *mesch(e)ance*, f. *mescheoir*, f. *mes-* MIS-[2] + *cheoir* befall: see CHANCE *n.*] 1 Bad luck. Formerly also, disaster, calamity. ME. 2 A piece of bad luck; a mishap, an unlucky accident. Formerly also, an accidental injury or mutilation; a state of unhappiness, an evil fate. ME.

Phrases: **by (some) mischance** by an unlucky accident, by misfortune.

mischanceful *a.* (now *poet.*) unfortunate ME. **mischancy** *a.* (chiefly *Sc.*) unfortunate E16.

mischance /mɪsˈtʃɑːns/ *v.* Long *rare*. M16. [f. MIS-[1] 1 + CHANCE *v.*] 1 *v.i.* Happen unfortunately. M16. †2 *v.t.* in *pass.* Be unfortunate; have bad luck. M–L16.

mischanter *n.* var. of MISHANTER.

mischief /ˈmɪstʃɪf/ *n.* ME. [OFr. *mesch(i)ef* (mod. *méchef*), f. *meschever*, f. *mes-* MIS-[2] + *chever* come to an end (of), f. *chef* head.] 1 Evil plight or condition; misfortune; trouble, distress. Formerly also, need, want, poverty. Long *obs.* exc. *Sc.* ME. †b A misfortune, a calamity. ME–M17. †2 Wickedness. ME–E17. 3 An injury inflicted by a person or other agent; an evil arising out of or existing in certain conditions; an evil consequence. Now only in *pl.* exc. in *do a mischief to* below. LME. 4 Harm or evil considered as attributable to a particular agent or cause. L15. 5 A pathological condition. Formerly, a disease, an illness. M16. 6 A cause or source of harm or evil; *spec.* a person whose conduct or influence is harmful, or who causes petty annoyance or acts in a vexatious manner. L16. 7 *the mischief*, the devil: in exclamatory and imprecatory phrs. (cf. DEVIL *n.* 1). L16. 8 *Law.* A wrong or hardship which it is the object of a statute to remove or for which equity affords a remedy. E17. 9a Formerly, harmful character, influence, or intent. Now, playful or teasing mischievousness, playful malice. M17. b *The* most unfortunate aspect or vexatious circumstance (*of* an affair). M17. 10 Vexatious or annoying action or conduct; behaviour, esp. in a child, which is troublesome but not malicious, except in a playful or teasing way. L18.

3 S. SMILES The social mischiefs . . from a neglect of the purifying influence of women. 4 SIR W. SCOTT It was hardly possible two such . . rascals should colleague together without mischief. 7 R. KIPLING You 'eathen, where the mischief 'ave you been? J. M. SYNGE I am coughing away like the mischief to-day. SWIFT But Cupid, full of mischief, longs To vindicate his mother's wrongs. A. MENEN Suddenly his eyes looked mischief again. 10 B. POTTER Now run along, and don't get into any mischief.

Phrases: **do a mischief to** wound, injure or kill (oneself, another). **make mischief** create or promote discord, esp. by gossip. **mean mischief** intend to create or promote trouble or discord.

Comb.: **mischief-maker** a person who makes mischief; **mischief night** an evening, orig. 30 April, now 4 November or 31 October (Hallowe'en), on which children traditionally indulge in mischievous pranks.

mischiefful *a.* (now *dial.*) †(*a*) unfortunate, disastrous; (*b*) mischievous: ME.

mischief /ˈmɪstʃɪf/ *v.* *arch.* L15. [f. the n. Cf. next.] 1 *v.t.* Do physical harm to; inflict injury on. L15. 2 *v.i.* Suffer injury. Long *rare*. E16.

mischieve /mɪsˈtʃiːv/ *v.* ME. [OFr. *meschever*: see MISCHIEF *n.*] †1 *v.i.* Suffer injury; meet with misfortune. ME–E17. 2 *v.t.* Afflict or overwhelm with misfortune; destroy, ruin. *arch.* LME. 3 *v.t.* Do physical harm to, wound, hurt; injure, damage. Now *Sc.* LME. †4 *v.t.* Abuse, slander. M17–M18.

mischievous /ˈmɪstʃɪvəs/ *a.* ME. [AN *meschevous* f. OFr. *meschever*: see MISCHIEF *n.*, -OUS.] †1 Unfortunate, calamitous, disastrous; (of a person) miserable, needy, poverty-stricken. ME–M17. 2 Having harmful effects or results; inflicting damage or injury; having a harmful influence or intent. Now chiefly *Sc.* LME. 3 Disposed to or full of mischief; playfully troublesome or teasing; (of behaviour) of the nature of mischief. L17.

3 *Beano* Two mischievous little bear cubs are always landing in some sort of pickle. G. VIDAL Darius gave me a great, mischievous smile. V. S. NAIPAUL An unlikely bond between the two men was a mischievous sense of humour.

mischievously *adv.* †(*a*) unfortunately, disastrously; (*b*) with harmful effect, result, or intent; (*c*) playfully, teasingly: ME. **mischievousness** *n.* M16.

misch metal /mɪʃ ˈmɛt(ə)l/ *n. phr.* E20. [G *Mischmetall*, f. *mischen* to mix + *Metall* metal.] An alloy of cerium with other lanthanides, used esp. as an additive in iron, e.g. in making flints for cigarette lighters.

Mischsprache /ˈmɪʃʃpraːxə/ *n.* Pl. **-en** /-ən/. M20. [G.] = MIXED *language*.

mischty /ˈmɪstʃi/ *n.* *dial.* Also **-chy**. L19. [Alt.] Mischief.

miscible /ˈmɪsɪb(ə)l/ *a.* & *n.* L16. [med.L *miscibilis*, f. L *miscere* MIX *v.*: see -IBLE.] A *adj.* Able to be mixed (*with* something); *spec.* (of a liquid) capable of forming a true solution *with* another liquid, (of liquids) mutually soluble. L16.

T. THOMSON Alcohol has a strong affinity for water, and is miscible with it. *Armed Forces* A mono-propellant . . may comprise . . a combination of miscible liquids such as hydrazine, hydrazine nitrate and water.

B *n.* A miscible substance. *rare*. M17.

misciˈbility *n.* M18.

misconceit /mɪskənˈsiːt/ *n.* *arch.* LME. [f. MIS-[1] 2 + CONCEIT *n.*] = MISCONCEPTION.

misconceit /mɪskənˈsiːt/ *v.t.* *arch.* L16. [f. MIS-[1] 1 + CONCEIT *v.*] = MISCONCEIVE 2.

misconceive /mɪskənˈsiːv/ *v.* LME. [f. MIS-[1] 1 + CONCEIVE.] 1 *v.i.* Have a false conception, entertain wrong notions, (*of*). LME. 2 *v.t.* Form a false conception of; fail to understand rightly; devise or plan badly. L16.

2 *Times* His Lordship said that the action was obviously completely misconceived. *Shetland Times* Public apprehension about the health effects of radiation was misconceived.

misconceiver *n.* E17.

misconception /mɪskənˈsɛpʃ(ə)n/ *n.* M17. [f. MIS-[1] 2 + CONCEPTION.] A false view or opinion (*about*); the action or an act of misconceiving something.

Which? Some of their answers showed misconceptions about what drugs do.

misconduct /mɪsˈkɒndʌkt/ *n.* E18. [f. MIS-[1] 2 + CONDUCT *n.*[1]] 1 Bad management, mismanagement; *esp.* culpable neglect of duties. E18. 2 Improper or wrong behaviour. E18. †3 In *pl.* Instances of misconduct. E18–M19.

1 BURKE Whenever in any matter of money there is concealment, you must presume misconduct. 2 A. PRYCE-JONES His misery was said to be due to the misconduct . . of his wife.

misconduct /mɪskənˈdʌkt/ *v.t.* M18. [f. MIS-[1] 1 + CONDUCT *v.*] 1 Mismanage. M18. 2 *refl.* Misbehave. L19.

2 *Daily Telegraph* It is a criminal offence to misconduct yourself at the polls.

misconstruct /mɪskənˈstrʌkt/ *v.t.* Now *rare*. M17. [f. MIS-[1] + CONSTRUCT *v.*] 1 Misconstrue. Chiefly *Sc.* M17. 2 Construct badly. E19.

misconstruction /mɪskənˈstrʌkʃ(ə)n/ *n.* E16. [f. MIS-[1] 2 + CONSTRUCTION.] 1 The action of misconstruing something or someone. E16. 2 Faulty or bad construction. *rare*. E19.

misconstrue /mɪskənˈstruː/ *v.t.* LME. [f. MIS-[1] 1 + CONSTRUE *v.*] 1 Put a wrong construction on (a word, an action, etc.); mistake the meaning of (a person); take in a wrong sense. LME. 2 Infer wrongly. *rare*. E19.

1 E. BOWEN He had misjudged her attitude, misconstrued her motives.

miscontent /mɪskənˈtɛnt/ *n.* Long *rare*. L17. [f. MIS-[1] 2 + CONTENT *n.*[2]] Discontent.

miscontent /mɪskənˈtɛnt/ *a.* Now *arch.* & *dial.* L15. [f. MIS-[1] 4, 5 + CONTENT *pred. a.*] Not content; dissatisfied; ill-pleased.

miscontent /mɪskənˈtɛnt/ *v.t.* L15. [f. MIS-[1] 1, 5 + CONTENT *v.*] Dissatisfy, displease.

miscontentment *n.* (*arch.*) M16.

miscopy /mɪsˈkɒpi/, *as n. also* ˈmɪskɒpi/ *v.* & *n.* E19. [f. MIS-[1] 1 + COPY *v.*[1]] A *v.t.* Copy incorrectly. E19. B *n.* An error in copying. L19.

miscount /mɪsˈkaʊnt, ˈmɪskaʊnt/ *n.* L16. [f. MIS-[1] 2 + COUNT *n.*[1] Cf. OFr. *mescont(e)*.] A wrong count or reckoning; a miscalculation.

miscount /mɪsˈkaʊnt/ *v.* LME. [f. MIS-[1] 1 + COUNT *v.* Cf. OFr. *mesconter* (mod. (*se*) *mécompter*).] 1 *v.i.* Make a wrong calculation. LME. 2 *v.t.* Miscalculate, misreckon. M16.

2 SIR W. SCOTT After twice miscounting the sum, he threw the whole to his daughter.

miscreance /ˈmɪskrɪəns/ *n.* *arch.* LME. [OFr. *mescreance* (mod. *mécréance*), f. *mes-* MIS-[2] + CREANCE.] False belief or faith; misbelief.

miscreancy /ˈmɪskrɪənsi/ *n.* E17. [f. prec.: see -ANCY.] 1 = MISCREANCE. *arch.* E17. 2 Villainy, depravity. E19.

For other words beginning with *mis-* see the entry for **mis-**

miscreant /ˈmɪskrɪənt/ *a.* & *n.* ME. [OFr. *mescreant* (mod. *mécréant*) misbelieving, unbelieving, pres. pple of *mescroire* (mod. *mécroire*) disbelieve, f. *mes-* MIS-[2] + *croire* f. L *credere* believe: see -ANT[1].] A *adj.* 1 Misbelieving, heretical. *arch.* ME. 2 Depraved, villainous, base; rebellious, reprobate. L16.

2 POPE All the miscreant race of human kind.

B *n.* 1 A misbeliever, a heretic. *arch.* LME. 2 A wretch, a villain, a rascal; a moral reprobate. L16.

2 LYTTON He belongs to a horrible gang of miscreants, sworn against all order and peace.

miscreate /mɪskrɪˈeɪt/ *ppl a.* Now *rare* or *obs.* L16. [f. MIS-[1] 1 + CREATE *a.*] Miscreated.

miscreate /mɪskrɪˈeɪt/ *v.t. rare.* E17. [f. MIS-[1] 1 + CREATE *v.*] Create wrongly or badly.

miscreation *n.* (*a*) the action of the vb; (*b*) a miscreated or misshapen thing: M19. **miscreative** *a.* creating or forming wrongly or badly E19.

miscreated /mɪskrɪˈeɪtɪd/ *ppl a.* L16. [f. MIS-[1] 1 + *created* pa. pple of CREATE *v.*: see -ED[1].] Created or formed improperly or unnaturally; misshapen, deformed.

miscue /mɪsˈkjuː/ *n.*[1] & *v.*[1] L19. [f. MIS-[1] 2 (or stem of MISS *v.*[1]) + CUE *n.*[3]] A *n.* 1 *Billiards, Snooker*, etc. A failure to strike the ball properly with the cue. L19. 2 *transf.* & *fig.* An error resulting in some kind of failure. L19. B *v.i.* Make a miscue. L19.

miscue /mɪsˈkjuː/ *n.*[2] & *v.*[2] M20. [f. MIS-[1] 2 + CUE *n.*[2]] A *n.* An unexpected response or failure to respond to a phonetic or contextual cue in reading; an error, a slip. M20. B *v.* 1 *v.i.* Make an error in reading. M20. 2 *v.t.* Misread or misinterpret (a cue); cause (a cue) to be misread. M20.

misdate /mɪsˈdeɪt, *as n. also* ˈmɪsdeɪt/ *v.* & *n.* L16. [f. MIS-[1] 1 + DATE *v.*] A *v.t.* & *i.* Assign or affix a wrong date (to); date wrongly. L16. B *n.* A wrong date. *rare.* M19.

misdeal /mɪsˈdiːl, *as n. also* ˈmɪsdiːl/ *v.* & *n.* L15. [f. MIS-[1] 1 + DEAL *v.*] A *v.* Pa. t. & pple **-dealt** /-ˈdɛlt/. †1 *v.i.* Distribute unfairly. Only in L15. 2 *v.i.* Deal or act improperly. M16. 3 *v.i.* & *t.* Make a mistake in dealing (cards). M19. B *n.* A mistake in dealing cards; a misdealt hand. M19.

misdeed /mɪsˈdiːd/ *n.* [OE *misdǣd* = OHG *missitāt*, Goth. *missadeþs*, f. Gmc. base of MIS-[1], DEED *n.*] An evil deed; a wrongdoing; a crime.

R. K. NARAYAN He catalogued our sins and misdeeds.

misdeem /mɪsˈdiːm/ *v.* Now chiefly *arch.* & *poet.* ME. [f. MIS-[1] 1 + DEEM *v.*] 1 *v.i.* Form a wrong judgement (*of*); hold a mistaken opinion. ME. 2 *v.t.* Have a mistaken opinion or view of. LME. b Suppose mistakenly *that*. L16. c Wrongly suppose (a person or thing) to be something else; mistake (a thing) *for* another. M17. †3 *v.i.* & *t.* Form an unfavourable judgement (of), think ill (of or *of*). LME–M18. †4a *v.i.* Suspect evil. LME–L16. **b v.t.** Have a suspicion of; suspect (some evil). L15–E17.

1 H. F. CARY Farther on, If I misdeem not, Soldanieri bides. 2 J. R. LOWELL If ever with distempered voice or pen We have misdeemed thee, here we take it back.

misdemean /mɪsdɪˈmiːn/ *v.i.* & *refl.* L15. [f. MIS-[1] 1 + DEMEAN *v.*[1]] Misbehave, misconduct oneself.

misdemeanant /mɪsdɪˈmiːnənt/ *n.* E19. [f. prec. + -ANT[1].] A person convicted of a misdemeanour; *transf.* a person guilty of misconduct.

misdemeanour /mɪsdɪˈmiːnə/ *n.* Also ***-or.** L15. [f. MIS-[1] 2 + DEMEANOUR.] 1 Bad behaviour, misconduct. Now *rare.* L15. 2a An instance of this; a misdeed, an offence. L15. b *Law.* An indictable offence, formerly (in the US, still) distinguished from and less heinous than a felony. L15. 3 A person convicted of a misdemeanour; = MISDEMEANANT. Now *rare.* E19.

2a H. JAMES He had been guilty of a misdemeanour in succumbing to the attractions of the admirable girl. b I. MURDOCH Like a criminal who asks for other misdemeanours to be taken into account.

misdescribe /mɪsdɪˈskraɪb/ *v.t.* E19. [f. MIS-[1] 1 + DESCRIBE.] Describe inaccurately.

misdescription *n.* (an) inaccurate description M19. **misdescriptive** *a.* giving an inaccurate description (*of*) E20.

misdiagnose /mɪsˈdaɪəgnəʊz/ *v.t.* E20. [f. MIS-[1] 1 + DIAGNOSE.] Diagnose wrongly (a condition, an individual suffering from a condition).

misdiagnosis /ˌmɪsdaɪəgˈnəʊsɪs/ *n.* Pl. **-noses** /-ˈnəʊsiːz/. M20. [f. MIS-[1] 2 + DIAGNOSIS.] (A) wrong diagnosis.

misdial /mɪsˈdaɪəl/ *v.i.* & *t.* Infl. **-ll-**, ***-l-**. M20. [f. MIS-[1] 1 + DIAL *v.*] Dial (a telephone number etc.) wrongly.

misdirect /mɪsdaɪˈrɛkt, -dɪ-/ *v.t.* E17. [f. MIS-[1] 1 + DIRECT *v.*] Direct wrongly; give a wrong direction to; *spec.* send (a person, letter, etc.) to a wrong address.

R. MANNING Talents are too often misdirected or not fully developed. M. WESLEY She had come to the wrong house, had been misdirected.

misdirection /mɪsdaɪˈrɛkʃ(ə)n, -dɪ-/ *n.* M18. [f. MIS-[1] 2 + DIRECTION.] 1a Wrong direction or guidance; direction to a wrong address. M18. b Distraction, diversion of a person's attention, esp. by a conjuror or thief. M20. 2 A wrong direction, line, or course. M19.

misdivision /mɪsdɪˈvɪʒ(ə)n/ *n.* L19. [f. MIS-[1] 2 + DIVISION.] 1 (An instance of) incorrect division. L19. 2 *spec.* in *Cytol.* (An) abnormal (esp. transverse instead of longitudinal) division of a chromosome at meiosis or mitosis. M20.

misdo /mɪsˈduː/ *v.* Infl. as DO *v.* [OE *misdōn*, f. Gmc base of MIS-[1], DO *v.*] 1 *v.i.* Do evil or wrong; do harm or injury. Now *rare* or *obs.* OE. 2 *v.t.* a Do in error, make a mistake in doing. Now *rare* or *obs.* OE. b Do badly or improperly. M19. 3 *v.t.* Harm, injure, wrong. Long *rare.* ME. †4 *v.t.* Destroy, do away with. ME–E17.

1 DRYDEN I have misdone; and I endure the Smart. 2a T. KYD O poore Horatio, what hadst thou misdonne.

misdoer *n.* (now *rare*) a wrongdoer, a malefactor ME. **misdoing** *n.* (*a*) the action of the vb; (*b*) a misdeed: ME.

misdoubt /mɪsˈdaʊt/ *n.* Now chiefly *Sc.* & *dial.* L16. [f. MIS-[1] 6 + DOUBT *n.*] Apprehension of evil; *gen.* mistrust, suspicion.

†**misdoubtful** *a.* (*rare*) suspicious: only in L16. **misdoubtfully** *adv.* (long *rare*) L16.

misdoubt /mɪsˈdaʊt/ *v.* Now chiefly *Sc.* & *dial.* ME. [f. MIS-[1] 6 + DOUBT *v.*] 1 *v.t.* Have doubts as to the existence, truth, or reality of (a thing). Also foll. by (*but*) *that*. Earliest as *misdoubting* vbl n. ME. 2 *v.t.* Fear, suspect; be suspicious about. M16. b *v.refl.* & *i.* Suspect; be suspicious *of*. *obs.* or *arch.* M17. 3 *v.t.* Have doubts about the character, honesty, etc., of (a person); mistrust. L16. 4 *v.t.* Have misgivings or forebodings with regard to. L16.

2 M. DRAYTON Warn'd by Danger to misdoubt the worst. *Harper's Magazine* I misdoubt the ladies won't like it. 4 DICKENS I much misdoubt an amateur artist's success in this vast place.

misdraw /mɪsˈdrɔː/ *v.* Pa. t. **-drew** /-druː/; pa. pple **-drawn** /-drɔːn/. ME. [f. MIS-[1] 1 + DRAW *v.*] †1 *v.i.* Go astray. Only in ME. 2 *v.t.* Draw or draw up incorrectly. LME. †3 *v.t.* Entice, allure, mislead. LME–L16.

misdrawing *n.* a faulty drawing LME.

mise /miːz, maɪz/ *n.* LME. [OFr. = action of setting, expenses, wages, arbitration, f. *mis* pa. pple of *mettre* place, set, f. L *mittere* send, (later) put, place.] †1 In *pl.* Expenses, costs. LME–L15. 2 A grant, payment, or tribute made to secure a liberty or immunity. Now *rare.* L15. 3 *Law* (now *Hist.*). The issue in a writ of right. M16. 4 A settlement by agreement. E18.

misease /mɪsˈiːz/ *n. arch.* ME. [OFr. *mesaise*, f. *mes-* MIS-[2] + *aise* EASE *n.*] 1 Distress, trouble, misery; extreme suffering or discomfort. ME. †2 Lack of the means of living; poverty, need, want. ME–L15. 3 Uneasiness, disquiet. E20.

mise au point /miːz o pwɛ̃/ *n. phr.* Pl. ***mises au point*** (pronounced same). M20. [Fr.] A focusing or clarification of an obscure subject or problem.

miseducate /mɪsˈɛdjʊkeɪt/ *v.t.* E19. [f. MIS-[1] 1 + EDUCATE.] Educate wrongly or badly.

miseduˈcation *n.* E17.

mise-en-page /miːzɑ̃paːʒ/ *n.* Pl. ***mises-en-page*** (pronounced same). E20. [Fr. *mise en pages* page-setting, imposition.] The design of a printed page etc., including the layout of text and illustrations. Also, the composition of a picture.

mise en scène /miːz ɑ̃ sɛn/ *n. phr.* Also ***mise-en-scène.*** Pl. ***mises en scène*** (pronounced same). M19. [Fr.] 1 The staging of a play; the scenery and properties of a stage production. M19. 2 The setting or surroundings of an event or action. L19.

misemploy /mɪsɪmˈplɔɪ, -ɛm-/ *v.t.* E17. [f. MIS-[1] 1 + EMPLOY *v.*] Employ or use wrongly or improperly.

misemployment *n.* L16.

miser /ˈmaɪzə/ *a.*, *n.*, & *v.* L15. [L = wretched, unfortunate.] †A *adj.* 1 Miserly, niggardly. L15–M19. 2 Miserable, wretched. M16–E17.

B *n.* †1 A miserable or wretched person; a wretch. M16–M19. 2 A person who hoards wealth and lives miserably in order to do so. Also, an avaricious grasping person, a niggard. M16.

2 GOLDSMITH As some lone miser, visiting his store, Bends at his treasure, counts, recounts it o'er. V. WOOLF Like a miser, she has hoarded her feelings within her own breast.

C *v.t.* Hoard *up* in a miserly way. *rare.* L19.

miserhood *n.* (*rare*) miserliness M19.

miserabilism /ˈmɪz(ə)rəbɪlɪz(ə)m/ *n. rare.* L19. [mod.L *miserabilismus*, f. L *miserabilis* MISERABLE: see -ISM.] Pessimism, gloomy negativity.

miserabilist *n.* & *a.* (*a*) *n.* an advocate or adherent of miserabilism; (*b*) *adj.* of or pertaining to miserabilism or miserabilist: E20.

miserable /ˈmɪz(ə)rəb(ə)l/ *a.* & *n.* LME. [(O)Fr. *misérable* f. L *miserabilis* pitiable, f. *miserari* be pitiful, f. *miser*: see MISER *a.*, -ABLE.] A *adj.* I Of a person. 1 Existing in a state of external discomfort or distress; needy, poverty-stricken, wretchedly poor. Now *rare.* LME. 2 Miserly, mean, stingy. Now chiefly *Sc.*, *Austral.*, & *NZ.* L15. 3 Full of mental misery; wretchedly unhappy or uncomfortable. L16.

3 C. ANGIER She was miserable and agitated and quarrelling with everyone.

II 4 Of a thing: pitiable, deplorable. Now *rare.* LME. 5 Of a condition, an event, etc.: full of misery; causing wretchedness or extreme discomfort. L15. 6 Unworthy, inadequate; contemptible, mean. E16.

5 V. BRITTAIN Three miserable weeks of disappointment . . and anxiety, and depression. A. WESKER A cold, miserable, two-roomed flat, all on your own. D. FRANCIS It was an uncomfortable, miserable, thought. 6 *New Republic* The miserable pensions that are being paid to the widows of fallen soldiers. G. ORWELL The miserable little threepenny-bit.

B *n.* A miserable person; a person who is extremely unhappy or wretched. M16.

miseraˈbility *n.* (*rare*) M16. **miserableness** *n.* E16. **miserably** *adv.* LME.

misère /mɪˈzɛː, *foreign* mizɛːr (*pl. same*)/ *n.* E19. [Fr. = poverty, misery.] 1 *Cards.* A declaration by which the caller undertakes not to win any tricks. E19. 2 Misery; a miserable condition or circumstance. L19.

misereatur /mɪˌzɛrɪˈeɪtə/ *n.* LME. [L (= may (God) have mercy), 3rd person sing. pres. subjunct. of *misereri* (see next): its first wd.] *Eccl.* In the Western Church: = ABSOLUTION 1b.

miserere /mɪzəˈrɪəri, -ˈrɛː-/ *n.* ME. [L, imper. sing. of *misereri* have pity, have mercy, f. *miser* MISER *a.*] 1a Psalm 51 (50 in the Vulgate), beginning *Miserere mei Deus* 'Have mercy upon me, O God', one of the penitential psalms. ME. b A musical setting of this psalm. L18. 2 *transf.* A cry for mercy; a prayer in which mercy is sought. E17. †3 In full *miserere mei* [= on me]. Severe colic; ileus. E17–L18. 4 = MISERICORD 4. L18.

misericord /mɪˈzɛrɪkɔːd/ *n.* ME. [(O)Fr. *miséricorde* f. L *misericordia*, f. *misericors* pitiful, f.

miser, stem of *misereri* (see prec.) + *cord-*, *cor* heart.] 1 Compassion, pity, mercy. Also as *int. arch.* ME. 2 A dagger for dealing a death stroke. ME. 3 *Hist.* An apartment in a monastery in which certain relaxations of the rule were permitted. LME. 4 A shelving projection on the underside of a hinged seat in a choir stall, which, when turned up, gives support to someone standing. E16.

miserly /ˈmʌɪzəli/ *a.* L16. [f. MISER *n.* + -LY[1].] 1 Of, pertaining to, or characteristic of a miser; niggardly, stingy. L16. 2 Of a quantity: paltry, meagre. M20.

1 V. S. NAIPAUL A miserly and cruel man who counted every biscuit in the tin.

miserliness *n.* M17.

misery /ˈmɪz(ə)ri/ *n.* LME. [f. AN var. of (O)Fr. *misère* or f. L *miseria* f. *miser*: see MISER *a.*, -Y[3].] 1 The state of being in external discomfort or distress; wretchedness of outward circumstances. LME. 2a A distressing condition or circumstance; a cause or source of wretchedness. Now only in *pl.* LME. b A wretched person or place. L18. c A gloomy self-pitying person; a killjoy. *colloq.* E20. 3 The state of being wretchedly or profoundly unhappy; extreme sorrow or distress. E16. †4 Miserliness, niggardliness. M16–E17. 5 Bodily pain. *dial.* E19. 6 *Cards.* = MISÈRE I. *colloq.* M19.

1 J. RUSKIN The misery of unaided poverty. 2a H. CARPENTER He's one of those people who really feels the miseries of the world. c W. RUSSELL You can be a real misery sometimes, can't y'? 3 J. HERSEY The general blur of misery through which they moved.

Phrases: **misery me!** expr. self-pity, distress, or general wretchedness. **put out of his, her, its, misery** release from suffering or suspense. **the miseries** *colloq.* a fit of peevishness or depression.

Comb.: **misery guts** *colloq.* = sense 2c above.

mises au point, **-*en-page***, ***en scène*** *n. phrs.* pls. of MISE AU POINT etc.

misesteem /mɪsɪˈstiːm/ *n.* M19. [f. MIS-[1] 2 + ESTEEM *n.*] Want of esteem or respect; disrespect.

misesteem /mɪsɪˈstiːm/ *v.t. arch.* E17. [f. MIS-[1] I + ESTEEM *v.*] = MISESTIMATE *v.*

misestimate /mɪsˈɛstɪmət/ *n.* M19. [f. MIS-[1] 2 + ESTIMATE *n.*] A wrong estimate or valuation.

misestimate /mɪsˈɛstɪmeɪt/ *v.t.* M19. [f. MIS-[1] I + ESTIMATE *v.*] Estimate wrongly, have a false estimate of.

misestimation /ˌmɪsɛstɪˈmeɪʃ(ə)n/ *n.* E19. [f. MIS-[1] 2 + ESTIMATION.] (A) wrong or false estimation.

misexpress /mɪsɪkˈsprɛs, -ɛk-/ *v.refl.* E18. [f. MIS-[1] I + EXPRESS *v.*[1]] Express oneself wrongly or badly.

misexpression *n.* M17. **misexpressive** *a.* E19.

misfall /mɪsˈfɔːl/ *v.i.* Long *obs.* exc. *Sc.* ME. [f. MIS-[1] I + FALL *v.* Cf. MLG, MDu., Du. *misvallen*, MHG *missevallen*, G *missfallen*.] †1 Suffer misfortune, come to grief. Only in ME. 2 Of an event, chance, etc.: happen unfortunately, turn out badly. ME.

misfare /mɪsˈfɛː/ *n.* Long *rare.* ME. [f. MIS-[1] 2 + FARE *n.*[1]] A mishap; misfortune.

misfare /mɪsˈfɛː/ *v.i.* Long *obs.* exc. *Sc.* [OE *misfaran* = OFris. *misfara*, MHG *missevarn*, ON *misfara*, f. Gmc base of MIS-[1], FARE *v.*] 1 Fare badly, come to grief. OE. †2 Go wrong, transgress. OE–L16.

misfeasance /mɪsˈfiːz(ə)ns/ *n.* E17. [OFr. *mesfaisance*, f. pres. pple of *mesfaire* (mod. *méfaire*), f. *mes-* MIS-[2] + *faire* do: see -ANCE. Cf. MALFEASANCE.] *Law.* (A) transgression, (a) trespass; *spec.* (a) wrongful exercise of lawful authority.

misfeasor *n.* a person who commits a misfeasance M17.

†misfeign *v.i. rare* (Spenser). Only in L16. [f. MIS-[1] I + FEIGN *v.*] Feign with an intention to do wrong.

misfield /mɪsˈfiːld, *as n. also* ˈmɪsfiːld/ *v.* & *n.* L19. [f. MIS-[1] I + FIELD *v.*] *Cricket, Rugby Football*, etc. A *v.t.* & *i.* Field (a ball) badly. L19. B *n.* An instance of bad fielding of a ball. E20.

misfigure /mɪsˈfɪɡə/ *n. rare.* LME. [f. MIS-[1] 2 + FIGURE *n.*] Disfigurement, deformity.

misfigure /mɪsˈfɪɡə/ *v.t. obs.* exc. *dial.* M16. [f. MIS-[1] I + FIGURE *v.*] Disfigure, distort; disguise.

misfire /mɪsˈfʌɪə, *as n. also* ˈmɪsfʌɪə/ *v.* & *n.* M18. [f. MIS-[1] I + FIRE *v.* Cf. *miss fire* s.v. MISS *v.*[1]] A *v.i.* 1 Of a gun, a gun's charge: fail to discharge or explode. M18. 2 Of an internal-combustion engine: suffer failure of the fuel to ignite (correctly or at all). E20. 3 *fig.* Fail to have an intended effect; go wrong. M20.

2 *Classic Racer* The engine started misfiring during the fifth lap. 3 A. N. WILSON Either it was a mistake .. or .. a nasty practical joke which had hideously misfired.

B *n.* 1 A failure to discharge or explode; *fig.* a failure of intention. Cf. MISS-FIRE. M19. 2 Misfiring. E20.

1 *Rally Sport* After a lead came off the distributor .. they had to contend with a misfire.

misfit /ˈmɪsfɪt/ *n.* & *a.* E19. [f. MIS-[1] 2 + FIT *n.*[3]] A *n.* 1 A garment etc. which does not fit the person for whom it is meant. Also, a person who is unsuited to his or her environment, work, etc. E19. 2 *Physical Geogr.* A misfit stream (see sense B.2 below). E20.

1 G. B. SHAW Clothed in a seedy misfit which made him look lamentably down on his luck. M. DRABBLE Forever desiring, .. never achieving, an eternal misfit.

B *attrib.* or as *adj.* 1 That is a misfit. E20. 2 *Physical Geogr.* Designating or pertaining to a stream which, on the basis of its present-day flow, would have eroded a larger or a smaller valley than it has done. Cf. OVERFIT, UNDERFIT. M20.

misfit /mɪsˈfɪt/ *v.t.* & *i.* Infl. **-tt-**. M19. [f. MIS-[1] I + FIT *v.*[1], or f. prec.] Fail to fit, fit badly.

misfortunate /mɪsˈfɔːtʃ(ə)nət/ *a.* Now chiefly *Sc.* & *US.* E16. [f. MIS-[1] 4 + FORTUNATE *a.*] Unfortunate.

misfortune /mɪsˈfɔːtʃuːn, -tʃ(ə)n/ *n.* LME. [f. MIS-[1] 2 + FORTUNE *n.*] 1 Bad fortune, ill luck; an instance of this. LME. 2 A pregnancy outside marriage; an illegitimate child. Chiefly in *have* or *meet with a misfortune*, have an illegitimate child. *dial.* & *colloq.* E19.

1 J. B. MOZLEY Misfortune, adversity, soften the human heart. M. FLANAGAN You have had your own misfortunes, even disasters.

misfortuned *a.* (now *rare*) affected by misfortune, unfortunate LME. **misfortuner** *n.* (*rare*) an unfortunate person L18.

misgive /mɪsˈɡɪv/ *v.* Pa. t. **-gave** /-ˈɡeɪv/; pa. pple **-given** /-ˈɡɪv(ə)n/. E16. [f. MIS-[1] I, 5 + GIVE *v.*] 1 *v.t.* Of a person's mind, heart, etc.: incline (the person) to doubt or apprehension, fill with suspicion or foreboding, (*about*); cause to fear *that.* E16. b *v.i.* Of the mind, (*rare*) a person, etc.: have misgivings. E17. 2 *v.i.* Fail, go wrong; *spec.* (of a gun) misfire. Chiefly *Sc.* L16. 3 *v.t.* Give wrongly. Now *rare.* E17.

1 V. ACKLAND We were to set out on a honeymoon. My heart misgave me. 3 J. RUSKIN His swift correction of my misgiven Wordsworth's line.

misgiver *n.* (*rare*) a person who has misgivings E17.

misgiving /mɪsˈɡɪvɪŋ/ *n.* E17. [f. MISGIVE *v.* + -ING[1].] The action of MISGIVE *v.*; a feeling of mistrust, apprehension, or loss of confidence, (freq. in *pl.*).

R. K. NARAYAN They still had many misgivings about the expedition. C. THUBRON This religion of materialism filled me with misgiving.

misgo /mɪsˈɡəʊ/ *v.i. obs.* exc. *dial.* Infl. as GO *v.* ME. [f. MIS-[1] I + GO *v.*] 1 Go astray; go the wrong way. ME. 2 Go wrong in conduct or action; make a mistake; miscarry. ME.

misgotten /mɪsˈɡɒt(ə)n/ *a.* LME. [f. MIS-[1] I + GOTTEN *ppl a.*] 1 Wrongly obtained; ill-gotten. LME. 2 = MISBEGOTTEN. LME.

misgovern /mɪsˈɡʌv(ə)n/ *v.t.* LME. [f. MIS-[1] I + GOVERN.] Govern wrongly or badly; mismanage, misdirect. Now *spec.* direct and control the affairs of (a State etc.) wrongly or badly, mismanage the government of.

misgovernor *n.* a person who misgoverns a State etc. LME.

misgovernance /mɪsˈɡʌv(ə)nəns/ *n.* Now *rare* or *obs.* LME. [f. MIS-[1] 2 + GOVERNANCE.] †1 Misconduct, misbehaviour. LME–E17. †2 Mismanagement, misuse. LME–L17. 3 Misgovernment. LME.

misgoverned /mɪsˈɡʌv(ə)nd/ *a.* LME. [f. MISGOVERN + -ED[1].] †1 Characterized by misconduct; immoral. LME–E17. †2 Unruly; misdirected. L16–M17. 3 Badly ruled; mismanaged. M19.

misgovernment /mɪsˈɡʌv(ə)nm(ə)nt/ *n.* LME. [f. MIS-[1] 2 + GOVERNMENT.] †1 Unruly behaviour; misconduct. LME–M17. 2 Bad government of a country or State; maladministration. Also, disorder, anarchy. L16. †3 *gen.* Mismanagement. E17–L18.

misguidance /mɪsˈɡʌɪd(ə)ns/ *n.* M17. [f. MIS-[1] 2 + GUIDANCE.] Misdirection.

misguide /mɪsˈɡʌɪd/ *v.* LME. [f. MIS-[1] I + GUIDE *v.*] †1 *v.refl.* Go astray; conduct oneself or one's affairs badly. LME–M17. 2 *v.t.* Mismanage, misgovern. Also, treat badly; injure, spoil. *obs.* exc. *Sc.* L15. 3 *v.t.* & *i.* Misdirect, mislead. L15.

3 GOLDSMITH Vanity is more apt to misguide men than false reasoning.

misguider *n.* (now *rare*) L16.

misguided /mɪsˈɡʌɪdɪd/ *a.* L15. [f. prec. + -ED[1].] †1 Badly behaved, immoral. L15–E16. 2 Guided in a wrong direction; *spec.* misdirected or mistaken in action or thought. M17.

2 M. MEYER A .. tragedy of a lonely, misguided and tormented spirit. *Private Eye* The country has been brought to a halt by the .. misguided actions of .. malcontents.

misguidedly *adv.* M19. **misguidedness** *n.* E19.

mishandle /mɪsˈhand(ə)l/ *v.t.* LME. [f. MIS-[1] I + HANDLE *v.*[1]] Handle or treat badly, wrongly, or roughly; maltreat.

S. WEYMAN Solomon is old, and they may mishandle him. *Atlantic Monthly* The .. construction involved is so commonly mishandled in current American speech and print. E. PIZZEY He mishandled the cork. The champagne exploded over the table.

mishanter /mɪˈʃantə/ *n. Sc.* & *north.* Also **mischanter** /mɪsˈtʃantə/. M18. [Var. of MISAUNTER. Form. w. *-sch-* app. after *mischance.*] Misadventure, a mishap.

mishap /ˈmɪshap/ *n.* ME. [f. MIS-[1] 2 + HAP *n.*] 1 Bad luck, misfortune (now *rare*); harm, injury. ME. 2 An unlucky accident. ME.

1 *Independent* She skated impressively without mishap. 2 *Publishers Weekly* Miss Read begins her summer holiday with a mishap, a fall that nets her a broken arm and an injured ankle.

mishappen /mɪsˈhap(ə)n/ *v.i.* Now *rare.* ME. [f. MIS-[1] I + HAPPEN *v.*] (Of a person) meet with mishap or misfortune; (of an event etc.) happen unfortunately.

mishear /mɪsˈhɪə/ *v.* Pa. t. & pple **-heard** /-həːd/. OE. [f. MIS-[1] I + HEAR.] †1 *v.t.* Disobey. Only in OE. 2 *v.t.* & *i.* Hear incorrectly or imperfectly. OE.

mishit /mɪsˈhɪt, ˈmɪshɪt/ *n.* L19. [f. MIS-[1] 2 + HIT *n.*] In various sports: a faulty or bad hit of a ball.

mishit /mɪsˈhɪt/ *v.t.* Infl. **-tt-**. Pa. t. & pple **-hit.** E20. [f. MIS-[1] I + HIT *v.*] In various sports: hit (a ball) badly, strike a ball from (an opponent) badly.

mishla /ˈmɪʃlɔː/ *n.* Also **mush-** /ˈmʌʃ-/, **-law.** L17. [Miskito *mushla.*] A fermented liquor from plantain, cassava, maize, etc., made in eastern Central America.

mishmash /ˈmɪʃmaʃ/ *n.* & *v.* Also **mish-mash.** L15. [Redupl. of MASH *n.*[1]] A *n.* A confused mixture; a medley, a hodgepodge, a jumble. L15.

C. THUBRON He began to reminisce in a mishmash of German and English. J. IRVING It was a .. mishmash of the parts that were still serviceable.

B *v.t.* Make a mishmash of; throw into confusion. L17.

Mishnah /ˈmɪʃnə/ *n.* Also **-a.** E17. [Post-biblical Heb. *mišnāh* repetition, instruction.] The collection of precepts and customs which form the basis of the Talmud and is held to embody the contents of Jewish oral law. Also, a paragraph of this.

Mishnaic /mɪʃˈneɪk/ *a.* L19. **Mishnic** *a.* M19. **Mishnical** *a.* E18.

For other words beginning with *mis-* see the entry for **mis-**

misidentify /mɪsʌɪˈdɛntɪfʌɪ/ *v.t.* L19. [f. MIS-[1] 1 + IDENTIFY.] Identify erroneously.
misidentiˈfication *n.* E20.

misimprove /mɪsɪmˈpruːv/ *v.t.* Now *rare.* M17. [f. MIS-[1] 5 + IMPROVE *v.*[2]] 1 Use wrongly or badly; abuse. Latterly chiefly *US.* M17. 2 Make worse in attempting to improve. M19.
misimˈprovement *n.* (latterly chiefly *US*) failure to use properly, misuse M17.

misincline /mɪsɪnˈklʌɪn/ *v.t. rare.* M17. [f. MIS-[1] 1 + INCLINE *v.*] Incline in a wrong direction.
misinclined *a.* (*a*) wrongly inclined; (*b*) disinclined: E18.

misinform /mɪsɪnˈfɔːm/ *v.t.* LME. [f. MIS-[1] 1 + INFORM *v.*] Give wrong or misleading information to.
misinformant *n.* a person who gives wrong or misleading information M19. **misinforˈmation** *n.* (*a*) the action of misinforming someone; the condition of being misinformed; (*b*) wrong or misleading information: L16. **misinformative** *a.* giving wrong or misleading information E20. **misinformer** *n.* a misinformant M17.

misinstruct /mɪsɪnˈstrʌkt/ *v.t.* M16. [f. MIS-[1] 1 + INSTRUCT.] Instruct wrongly or badly.
misinstruction *n.* (an instance of) wrong or bad instruction M17.

misintelligence /mɪsɪnˈtɛlɪdʒ(ə)ns/ *n.* Now *rare.* M17. [f. MIS-[1] 2 + INTELLIGENCE *n.*] †1 Misunderstanding; disagreement, discord. M17–M18. 2 Wrong impression as to meaning or facts. L18. 3 Misinformation. E19. 4 Lack of intellect. M19.

misinterpret /mɪsɪnˈtəːprɪt/ *v.t.* M16. [f. MIS-[1] 1 + INTERPRET.] Interpret wrongly; draw a wrong inference from.
misinterpretable *a.* E17. **misinterpreˈtation** *n.* L16. **misinterpreter** *n.* L16.

misjoin /mɪsˈdʒɔɪn/ *v.t.* M16. [f. MIS-[1] 1 + JOIN *v.*] Join or connect wrongly or unsuitably.

misjoinder /mɪsˈdʒɔɪndə/ *n.* E19. [f. MIS-[1] 2 + JOINDER.] *Law.* Improper joinder of parties in an action; improper joinder of offences in a criminal prosecution.

misjudge /mɪsˈdʒʌdʒ/ *v.t.* & *i.* LME. [f. MIS-[1] 1 + JUDGE *v.*] Judge or assess wrongly; have or form a wrong opinion (of).
Bella How easy it is to misjudge from appearances. F. WELDON Sandy misjudged the speed of the incoming traffic.
misjudgement *n.* E16. **misjudger** *n.* (*rare*) L19.

miskal /ˈmɪskɑːl/ *n.* Also (earlier) †***mitigal.*** M16. [(Port. *matical*, Sp. *mitical* f.) Arab. *miṯkāl*, f. *ṯakala* weigh.] An Arabian unit of weight equal to about 4½ grams or ⅙ ounce.

misken /mɪsˈkɛn/ *v.t. Sc.* & *north.* LME. [f. MIS-[1] 1, 5 + KEN *v.*] = MISKNOW.

miskick /mɪsˈkɪk, *as n. also* ˈmɪskɪk/ *v.* & *n.* L19. [f. MIS-[1] 1 + KICK *v.*[1]] A *v.t.* & *i.* Kick (a ball etc.) badly or wrongly. L19. B *n.* An instance of miskicking, a bad kick. L19.

Miskito /mɪˈskiːtəʊ/ *a.* & *n.* Also **Mosquito** /mɒ-/. Pl. **-os.** L18. [Amer. Indian name.] A *adj.* Designating or pertaining to an American Indian people living on the Atlantic coast of Nicaragua and Honduras. L18. B *n.* A member of this people; their language. M20.

misknow /mɪsˈnəʊ/ *v.t.* Pa. t. **-knew** /-njuː/; pa. pple **-known** /-nəʊn/. ME. [f. MIS-[1] 1, 5 + KNOW *v.*] 1 Refuse to recognize or notice; affect ignorance of; disown. ME. 2 Not know or be aware of; be ignorant of. *obs.* exc. *Sc.* LME. 3 Fail to recognize; mistake the identity of. LME. 4 Have a wrong idea of; misapprehend, misunderstand. M16. †b *refl.* Have false ideas about oneself, one's position, etc. Chiefly *Sc.* M16–E17.
misknowledge *n.* †(*a*) failure to recognize or acknowledge; (*b*) lack of understanding: LME.

mislay /mɪsˈleɪ/ *v.t.* Pa. t. & pple **mislaid** /mɪsˈleɪd/. LME. [f. MIS-[1] 1 + LAY *v.*[1]] 1 Place or set wrongly; err in placing (a thing). Now *rare.* LME. 2 Accidentally put (a thing) in a place where it cannot readily be found; *euphem.* lose. E17.
2 N. MITFORD Cedric went . . to buy *Vogue*, having mislaid his own copy.

mislead /mɪsˈliːd/ *v.t.* Pa. t. & pple **misled** /mɪsˈlɛd/. [OE *mislǣdan*, f. MIS-[1] 1 + LEAD *v.*[1]] 1 Lead astray in action or conduct; cause to have an incorrect impression or belief. OE. †2 Mismanage. ME–L15. 3 Lead or guide in the wrong direction. L16.
1 M. FITZHERBERT His optimistic reports misled the politicians. *Daily Mail* British Coal bosses accused Mr. Scargill of deliberately misleading his members.
misleader *n.* LME.

misleading /mɪsˈliːdɪŋ/ *a.* M17. [f. prec. + -ING[2].] That leads someone astray, that causes error; imprecise, confusing, deceptive.
W. TREVOR My delicate appearance was misleading. *Which?* The Act will make it illegal to make misleading statements about ticket prices.
misleadingly *adv.* M19. **misleadingness** *n.* M19.

mislear /mɪsˈlɪə/ *v.t.* Long *obs.* exc. *dial.* Also **-lere.** [OE *mislǣran*, f. MIS-[1] 1 + LERE *v.*] Misteach; mislead, misguide.

misleared /mɪsˈlɪəd/ *a. Sc.* & *north.* Also **-lered.** L17. [f. prec. + -ED[1].] Unmannerly, ill-bred.

misled *v.* pa. t. & pple of MISLEAD.

mislike /mɪsˈlʌɪk/ *v.* & *n. arch.* [OE *mislīcian*, f. MIS-[1] 1 + LIKE *v.*[1]] A *v.* 1 *v.t.* Be displeasing to; displease, offend. OE. †2 *v.i.* Be displeased. Also, be troubled or uneasy. ME–M17. †3 *v.i.* Grow sickly or unhealthy; waste away. LME–E17. 4 *v.t.* Be displeased at; disapprove of; dislike. E16.
4 GLADSTONE They mistrust and mislike the centralisation of power.
B *n.* †1 Discomfort, trouble, unhappiness. Only in ME. 2 Distaste for, dislike *of.* Also, a dislike. M16. †3 Wasting away; sickliness, disease. M16–E17. †4 Disaffection, dissension. L16–M17.
misliker *n.* M16. **misliking** *n.* = MISLIKE *n.* ME.

mislippen /mɪsˈlɪp(ə)n/ *v.t. Sc.* & *north.* M16. [f. MIS-[1] 1 + LIPPEN *v.*] 1 Deceive; disappoint. M16. 2 Neglect, overlook. L16. 3 Suspect. E19.

mislocate /mɪslə(ʊ)ˈkeɪt/ *v.t.* E19. [f. MIS-[1] 1 + LOCATE *v.*] Assign an incorrect location or position to.
mislocation *n.* M17.

mismanage /mɪsˈmanɪdʒ/ *v.t.* & *i.* L17. [f. MIS-[1] 1 + MANAGE *v.*] Manage badly or wrongly.
M. MEYER Hansen was frequently drunk and mismanaged the estate.
mismanagement *n.* M17. **mismanager** *n.* a bad manager L17.

mismatch /mɪsˈmatʃ, ˈmɪsmatʃ/ *n.* E17. [Partly f. MIS-[1] 2 + MATCH *n.*[1], partly f. the vb.] A bad match; a discrepancy. Also, an unequal or unfair sporting contest.
Christian Science Monitor A basic mismatch between the capability of the utilities and a very demanding technology.

mismatch /mɪsˈmatʃ/ *v.t.* L16. [f. MIS-[1] 1 + MATCH *v.*[1]] Match badly, unsuitably, or incorrectly.

mismate /mɪsˈmeɪt/ *v.t.* E19. [f. MIS-[1] 1 + MATE *v.*[2]] Mismatch, mate badly or unsuitably. Chiefly as *mismated* ppl a.

mismeasure /mɪsˈmɛʒə/ *v.t.* M18. [f. MIS-[1] 1 + MEASURE *v.*] Measure or estimate incorrectly.
mismeasurement *n.* M19.

mismove /mɪsˈmuːv/ *n. US.* L19. [f. MIS-[1] 2 + MOVE *n.*] A wrong or faulty move.

misname /mɪsˈneɪm/ *v.t.* L15. [f. MIS-[1] 1 + NAME *v.*] †1 Call by an abusive name; insult. L15–M17. 2 Call by a wrong name; name wrongly or unsuitably. M16.
2 *Contemporary Review* The now misnamed Pacific Ocean.

misnome /mɪsˈnəʊm/ *v.t. rare.* E19. [Back-form. f. next.] Misname.

misnomer /mɪsˈnəʊmə/ *n.* & *v.* LME. [AN, use as n. of OFr. *mesnom(m)er*, f. *mes-* MIS-[2] + *nommer* f. L *nominare*, f. *nomen* name: see -ER[4].] A *n.* 1 A wrong name or designation. LME. 2 The use of a wrong name; a misapplication of a term. M17.
1 S. BRETT Hickton's rehearsal schedule (probably a misnomer for a process that was continuous). 2 B. GELDOF To call the place a camp would have been a misnomer.
B *v.t.* Misname, apply a misnomer to. Chiefly as *misnomered* ppl a. M18.

miso /ˈmiːsəʊ/ *n.* E18. [Jap.] Paste made from fermented soya beans and barley or rice malt, used in Japanese cookery.

miso- /ˈmɪsəʊ, ˈmʌɪsəʊ/ *comb. form.* Bef. a vowel also **mis-.** [Gk, f. base of *misein* to hate, *misos* hatred: see -O-.] Forming ns. and adjs. w. the sense 'hating, hatred of, a hater of'. Cf. PHILO-.
miˈsologist *n.* a hater of reason or discussion L19. **miˈsology** *n.* hatred of reason or discussion; hatred of learning or knowledge: M19. **misoˈneism** *n.* [Gk *neos* new] hatred of novelty L19. **misoˈneist** *n.* a hater of novelty L19. **miˈsosophy** *n.* hatred of wisdom E19.

misogamy /mɪˈsɒgəmi, mʌɪ-/ *n.* M17. [mod.L *misogamia*, f. Gk *misogamos* hating marriage, f. as MISO- + -GAMY.] Hatred of marriage.
misogamist *n.* a hater of marriage E18.

misogynist /mɪˈsɒdʒ(ə)nɪst, mʌɪ-/ *n.* E17. [f. Gk *misogunēs*, f. as MISO- + *gunē* woman: see -IST.] A hater of women.
M. MEYER He did not flirt, but was certainly no misogynist.
misogyˈnistic *a.* pertaining to or characteristic of misogynists or misogyny; misogynous: E19.

misogyny /mɪˈsɒdʒ(ə)ni, mʌɪ-/ *n.* M17. [mod.L *misogynia* f. Gk *misogunia*, f. as prec.: see -Y[3].] Hatred of women.
ˈ**misogyne** *n.* (now *rare*) = MISOGYNIST E19. **misoˈgynic** *a.* = MISOGYNOUS E19. **misogynism** *n.* = MISOGYNY M19. **misogynous** *a.* having a hatred of women; characterized by misogyny: L19.

misorder /mɪsˈɔːdə/ *n.* Now *rare.* LME. [f. MIS-[1] 2 + ORDER *n.*] 1 Lack or breach of order; confusion, disorder, misbehaviour. LME. b An instance of this. M16. †2 Bad or wrong order. M16–M17.

misorder /mɪsˈɔːdə/ *v.t.* Now *rare* or *obs.* LME. [f. MIS-[1] 1 + ORDER *v.*] †1 *refl.* Misbehave oneself; be disorderly or ill-behaved. LME–M18. 2 Put into disorder; confuse, disturb. L15.

misorient /mɪsˈɔːrɪɛnt, -ˈɒr-/ *v.t.* M20. [f. MIS-[1] 1 + ORIENT *v.*] Orient differently or variably; orient badly.
misorienˈtation *n.* M20.

misorientate /mɪsˈɔːrɪənteɪt, -ˈɒr-/ *v.t.* M20. [f. MIS-[1] 1 + ORIENTATE.] = prec.

misperceive /mɪspəˈsiːv/ *v.t.* E20. [f. MIS-[1] 1 + PERCEIVE *v.*] Perceive wrongly or incorrectly; mistake.
misperception *n.* (a) wrong or incorrect perception E18.

mispickel /ˈmɪspɪk(ə)l/ *n.* L17. [G.] *Min.* Arsenopyrite.

misplace /mɪsˈpleɪs/ *v.* M16. [f. MIS-[1] 1 + PLACE *v.*] I *v.t.* 1 Assign a wrong position to. Now *rare.* M16. 2 Put in the wrong place; mislay, lose. Also, put in the wrong hands. L16. 3 Bestow (one's affections etc.) on a wrong or inappropriate object; place (one's confidence etc.) misguidedly. Freq. as *misplaced* ppl a. M17.
2 W. COWPER The globe and sceptre in such hands misplaced. *Femina* The . . form had been misplaced by the company. 3 H. JACOBSON I am prepared to accept your . . misplaced enthusiasm.
†II *v.i.* 4 Use wrong or unsuitable words. *rare* (Shakes.). Only in E17.
misplacement *n.* M17.

misplay /mɪsˈpleɪ, ˈmɪspleɪ/ *n.* Chiefly *US.* M19. [f. MIS-[1] 2 + PLAY *n.*] A bad or forbidden play or move in a game; bad or wrong play.

misplay /mɪsˈpleɪ/ *v.t.* Chiefly *US.* M20. [f. MIS-[1] 1 + PLAY *v.*] Play wrongly, badly, or in contravention of the rules.

misprint /*as vb* mɪsˈprɪnt, *as n.* ˈmɪsprɪnt/. *v.* & *n.* L15. [f. MIS-[1] 1 + PRINT *v.*] A *v.* 1 *v.t.* Print incorrectly, print by mistake. L15. 2 *v.i.* Of a deer: leave footprints in a pattern different from the usual one. E20.
B *n.* A mistake in printing or in a printed work. E19.
A. PRICE The same story, only . . with more misprints, in the *Guardian.*

misprision /mɪsˈprɪʒ(ə)n/ *n.*[1] LME. [AN *mesprisioun* = OFr. *mesprison* error, wrong action or speech, f. *mesprendre* (mod. *méprendre*), f. *mes-* MIS-[2] + *prendre* take. Cf. MISPRIZE *v.*[2]] 1 *Law.* A wrongful act or omission; *spec.* a misdemeanour

For other words beginning with *mis-* see the entry for **mis-**

or failure of duty by a public official. Now *rare*. LME. 2 *Law*. In full *misprision of treason* or (now *Hist.*) *felony*. Orig., an offence similar to, but less serious than, treason or felony. Now, the crime of (deliberately) concealing one's knowledge of a treasonable act or (formerly) a felony. M16. 3 The mistaking of one thing for another; a misunderstanding, a mistake. L16.

misprision /mɪsˈprɪʒ(ə)n/ *n.*² *arch.* L16. [f. MISPRIZE *v.*¹, after prec.] Contempt, scorn. Also, failure to appreciate or recognize the value of something (usu. foll. by *of*).

misprize /mɪsˈprʌɪz/ *v.*¹ & *n.*¹ LME. [OFr. *mesprisier* (mod. *mépriser*), f. *mes-* MIS-² + *priser*, f. *pris-*: see PRIZE *v.*¹] A *v.t.* Despise, scorn. Also, fail to appreciate the value or good qualities of. LME. B *n.* = MISPRISION *n.*² *rare*. L16.

misprizer *n.* (*rare*) L16.

†**misprize** *v.*² & *n.*² L15. [OFr. *mespris* pa. pple of *mesprendre* commit a crime (mod. *se méprendre* be mistaken): see MISPRISION *n.*¹] A *v.* 1 *v.i.* Commit an offence, do wrong. Only in L15. 2 *v.t.* Mistake, misunderstand. L16–M17. B *n.* Mistake. *rare* (Spenser). Only in L16.

mispronounce /mɪsprəˈnaʊns/ *v.t.* L16. [f. MIS-¹ 1 + PRONOUNCE *v.*] Pronounce incorrectly.

ˌmispronunciˈation *n.* M16.

misproportioned /mɪsprəˈpɔːʃ(ə)nd/ *a.* M16. [f. MIS-¹ 1 + PROPORTIONED.] Badly or wrongly proportioned.

misproportion *n.* lack of proportion E19.

mispunctuate /mɪsˈpʌŋ(k)tʃʊeɪt, -tjʊ-/ *v.t.* & *i.* M19. [f. MIS-¹ 1 + PUNCTUATE *v.*] Punctuate incorrectly.

mispunctuˈation *n.* E19.

misquote /mɪsˈkwəʊt/ *n.* M19. [f. MIS-¹ 2 + QUOTE *n.*²] An incorrect quotation, a misquotation.

misquote /mɪsˈkwəʊt/ *v.t.* L16. [f. MIS-¹ 1 + QUOTE *v.*] Quote incorrectly.

misquoˈtation *n.* (*a*) inaccuracy in quoting; (*b*) an incorrect quotation: L18. **misquoter** *n.* M19.

misread /mɪsˈriːd/ *v.t.* Pa. t. & pple **misread** /mɪsˈrɛd/. E19. [f. MIS-¹ 1 + READ *v.*] Read or interpret (a text, a situation, etc.) wrongly.

misreader *n.* M19. **misreading** *n.* an incorrect reading, a misinterpretation M19.

misrecite /mɪsrɪˈsʌɪt/ *v.t.* L16. [f. MIS-¹ 1 + RECITE *v.*] Recite, relate, or describe incorrectly; give an inaccurate account of.

misrecital *n.* an incorrect recital or account M16.

misreckon /mɪsˈrɛk(ə)n/ *v.* E16. [f. MIS-¹ 1 + RECKON *v.*] 1 *v.t.* Reckon or calculate (an amount) incorrectly; make a wrong calculation in respect of (a certain number). E16. †2 *v.t.* Charge (a person) wrongly, *esp.* overcharge. M16–M17. 3 *v.i.* Make a wrong calculation; be out in one's reckoning. E17.

misrecollect /ˌmɪsrɛkəˈlɛkt/ *v.t.* & *i.* L18. [f. MIS-¹ 1 + RECOLLECT *v.*] Recollect wrongly or imperfectly.

misrecollection *n.* E19.

misregister /mɪsˈrɛdʒɪstə/ *n.* M20. [f. MIS-¹ 2 + REGISTER *n.*¹] *Printing*. The inaccurate positioning of printed matter on a sheet, *esp.* the misalignment of two or more colours in relation to each other.

misregistration /ˌmɪsrɛdʒɪˈstreɪʃ(ə)n/ *n.* M20. [f. MIS-¹ 2 + REGISTRATION.] Misalignment or faulty registration of images, esp. of the three fields that compose a colour television picture.

misremember /mɪsrɪˈmɛmbə/ *v.t.* & *i.* M16. [f. MIS-¹ 1 + REMEMBER *v.*] Remember wrongly or imperfectly; *dial.* forget.

misremembrance *n.* (*rare*) M16.

misreport /mɪsrɪˈpɔːt/ *n.* LME. [f. MIS-¹ 2 + REPORT *n.*] †1 Unfavourable repute. LME–L17. 2 A false or incorrect report. M16. 3 False or inaccurate reporting. Now *rare*. M16.

2 A. LANG If they are all misreports . . what is the value of anthropological evidence? 3 *Times Lit. Suppl.* Hepburn has cleared away a huge clutter of accumulated legend and misreport.

misreport /mɪsrɪˈpɔːt/ *v.* LME. [f. MIS-¹ 1 + REPORT *v.*] 1 *v.t.* Report incorrectly; give a false account of. LME. †2 *v.i.* Give a false report (*of*). E16–E17. †3 *v.t.* Speak ill of; slander. M16–E17.

1 H. LATIMER Christ himselfe was misreported, & falsely accused. DE QUINCEY His behaviour . . scandalously misreported by Bennet.

misreporter *n.* (now *rare*) M16.

misrepresent /ˌmɪsrɛprɪˈzɛnt/ *v.t.* M17. [f. MIS-¹ 1 + REPRESENT *v.*] 1 Represent wrongly or imperfectly; give a false representation or account of. M17. 2 Represent badly as an agent or representative, fail in acting as a representative of. *rare*. M19.

1 H. JAMES I'm not at all keen about marrying—your son misrepresented me.

ˌmisrepresenˈtation *n.* the action of the vb; (*a*) wrong or incorrect representation: M17. **misrepreˈsentative** *n.* a person who fails to represent others, a bad representative M19. **misrepreˈsentative** *a.* not (properly) representative (*of*) M18. **misrepresenter** *n.* a person who misrepresents L17.

misrule /mɪsˈruːl/ *n.* LME. [f. MIS-¹ 2 + RULE *n.*] †1 Disorderly conduct; ill-regulated living; excess. LME–E17. 2 Bad rule or government; misgovernment. Also, disorder, anarchy. LME.

Phrases: **Lord** or **Master of Misrule** (*a*) (*Hist.*) a person presiding over Christmas games and revelry in a wealthy household; (*b*) *transf.* a person, emotion, etc., that causes disorderly conduct; a ringleader.

misrule /mɪsˈruːl/ *v.t.* LME. [f. MIS-¹ 1 + RULE *v.*] †1 Manage or control badly. LME–E19. 2 Rule or govern badly. LME.

misruler *n.* (*rare*) †(*a*) a disorderly person; (*b*) a bad ruler: LME.

miss /mɪs/ *n.*¹ [OE *miss*, corresp. to MLG, MHG *misse* (Du. *mis*), ON *missa*, *missir*.] 1 Deprivation or loss of or *of* a person or thing. Now *rare*. OE. †b Observable lack. L17–E18. 2 (A feeling of) disadvantage or regret caused by the loss or absence *of* a person or thing. Chiefly in *have* or *find* (*a*) (*great*) *miss of*, *feel the miss of*, etc. Now *dial.* & *colloq.* ME. †3 Wrong, wrongdoing, offence; a wrong, a misdeed. Latterly *Sc.* ME–E19. 4 A failure to hit something aimed at. M16. b *Billiards* etc. A failure to hit the object ball, on account of which the opponent scores; *esp.* a deliberate failure which leaves the cue-ball in a safe position. M19. c An unsuccessful gramophone record. M20. 5 A failure to obtain or achieve something. Now *rare*. E17. 6 A failure to do or attend something: in *give* (*a thing*) *a miss*, omit to do or attend (something), avoid, leave alone. *colloq.* E20.

1 C. H. SPURGEON Temporal blessings are not trifles, for the miss of them would be a dire calamity. b DEFOE There was no miss of the usual Throng of People in the Streets. 3 G. CHAPMAN Some other way I might repair this shameful miss. 4 RIDER HAGGARD He has just killed half a dozen . . partridges without a miss. *Proverb*: A miss is as good as a mile. *near miss*: see NEAR *a.* **4b give a miss (in baulk)** deliberately fail to hit the object ball (in baulk). **score a miss** receive points from a miss by one's opponent. 5 R. L'ESTRANGE Aërius turn'd Heretique upon the misse of a Bishoprick. 6 J. CANNAN I'm afraid I've given church a miss this morning.

miss /mɪs/ *n.*² Also (esp. in titles) **M-**. M17. [Abbrev. of MISTRESS *n.*] 1 A kept woman, a mistress; a prostitute. *obs.* exc. *dial.* M17. 2 (**M-**.) Used as a title preceding the name of an unmarried woman or girl without a higher or honorific or professional title, or a married woman's maiden name retained for professional or other reasons. M17. b Used preceding the name of a country, group, etc. as a title of a young woman representing it, esp. in a beauty contest. E20. 3 A young unmarried woman; a girl, *esp.* one at school or who has lately left school. Now usu. *derog.*, with implication of silliness or sentimentality. M17. b A pert girl. E19. c In *pl.* (w. ref. to sizes or styles of articles of clothing): girls of from about 10 to 17 years of age; garments or garment sizes suitable for girls of this age. L19. 4 (Without proper name or article.) Used (without ref. to married status) as a conventional form of address or reference to a (young) woman, as a shop assistant or waitress, or (among children) a female teacher (corresp. to *sir*). Also (now *rare* or *obs.*), latterly regarded as *uneducated*, used as a designation of or form of address to the daughter of the house. L17. b An English governess in France. E20. 5 = MRS. *dial.* & *US*. L18.

1 M. CHARLTON I would rather chuse to see this child . . the wife of an honest man, than the Miss of a Nobleman. 2 W. F. HARVEY Saxon was introduced . . to Parke and Mrs. Parke and Miss Cornelius. J. BETJEMAN Now I'm engaged to Miss Joan Hunter Dunn. *Daily Telegraph* Miss Myrella Cohen, QC, 44, leaving the House of Lords with her husband, Lt-Col Mordaunt Cohen. b *Miss America*, *Miss World*, etc. 3 A. P. HERBERT Closing her blue eyes dreamily like some Victorian miss. b M. ALLINGHAM A sulky little miss if ever I saw one. c *Vogue* We pass through the Baby Linen on our way to the Misses. 4 BYRON Is it miss or the cash of mamma you pursue? J. B. PRIESTLEY 'Let's have coffee, shall we? Miss! Miss!' M. GEE Miss who was kind and taught drama.

Phrases: *junior miss*: see JUNIOR *a.* **Miss Ann(e)**, **Miss Annie** *US Black slang*, *derog.* (a name for) a young White woman, esp. the daughter of a landowner. *Miss Fixit*: see FIXIT 1. *Miss Lonelyhearts*: see LONELY *a.* **Miss Milligan** a kind of patience played with two packs of cards. *Miss Molly*: see MOLLY *n.*¹ 2. **Miss Nancy** *dial.* & *colloq.* (a name for) an unheroic or effeminate male. **Miss Right** the young woman who would make the ideal wife for a particular person, one's destined wife. **miss sahib** *Anglo-Ind.* the daughter of a mem-sahib, a European girl. **Miss Willmott's ghost** [Ellen Ann Willmott (1860–1934), Eng. horticulturist] a large ornamental sea holly, *Eryngium giganteum*, which turns white after it has flowered.

miss /mɪs/ *n.*³ M18. [Perh. a use of prec., or of MISS *n.*¹] *Cards*. In loo: an extra hand for which any of the players may discard his or her own.

miss /mɪs/ *n.*⁴ *colloq.* L19. [Abbrev.] = MISCARRIAGE 3.

miss /mɪs/ *v.*¹ [OE *missan* = OFris. *missa*, (M)LG, (M)Du. *missen*, (O)HG *missen*, ON *missa*, f. Gmc: see MIS-¹.] I *v.t.* & (*arch.*) *i.* foll. by *of*. Fail to hit, meet, etc. 1 Fail to hit or strike (esp. a target). OE. 2 Fail to obtain, receive, or attain to. ME. b Fail to capture or catch. L16. 3a Fail to achieve or accomplish. ME. b Fail *to do*; (now *Sc.* & *dial.*) have no success in *doing*. LME. 4a Lose or fail to hit on (the right path). Chiefly in *miss one's way*. LME. b Fail to obtain footing on (a step, plank, etc.). M16. 5 Fail to observe, hear, or perceive intellectually. L15. 6 Escape, avoid. Now *dial.* exc. w. specification of a margin, as *just*, *narrowly*, etc. E16. 7 Fail to make possible or intended contact with (a person). M16. 8a Fail to take advantage of (an opportunity etc.). E17. b Not be able or fortunate enough to witness, experience, etc.; be too late to catch (a train etc.) or to watch (an event, broadcast programme, etc.). E17.

1 D. FRANCIS Thanked the fates that the destructive lump of metal had missed my heart. F. CHICHESTER The compass showed that I was fifty-five degrees off course, headed to miss even Tasmania. C. SIMMONS Mr. Margin put the phone down hard, missing the cradle. *fig.*: J. R. GREEN Cromwell . . in his later years felt bitterly that Puritanism had missed its aim. 2 LD MACAULAY A project which . . had very narrowly missed of success. J. CONRAD He missed a larger fame only by the chances of the service. b J. G. WHITTIER They had missed of the old chief, but had captured his son. *Daily Chronicle* Jackson was missed off a 'balloon' in the long field. 3a DEFOE If he miss'd of his Business outward bound, he was to go up to China. b KEATS I was in pain, Lest I should miss to bid thee a good morrow. A. C. SWINBURNE With what excellent care . . this has been done, no one can miss of seeing. 4b J. JACKSON Till wee misse the bridge and fall into the ditch. 5 K. WATERHOUSE She was missing the whole . . point. J. WILCOX Mr. Pickens missed the turn off Flat Avenue. V. GORNICK Although my mother never seemed to be listening . . she missed nothing. 6 J. BUCHAN A stranger who had just missed death by an ace. E. WAUGH He narrowly missed being run down by a large . . car. 7 V. BRITTAIN In the crowd . . we had somehow missed each other. 8a T. M. LINDSAY Better to be imposed upon . . than to miss the chance of entertaining a brother Christian. C. THUBRON Beneath the city's surface, I felt, a vivid life was going on and I was missing it. Z. TOMIN I slept heavily, missing the early dusk. B. CONACHER I wouldn't have missed playing in the best league in the world. b M. SARTON You'd better go and pack now, or you'll miss that plane. J. HOWKER Because of them sitting there nattering . . we missed the six o'clock news.

II *v.i.* Fail. †9 Go wrong, make a mistake. Orig. *impers.* OE–M18. 10 Fail to hit the target; fail to take a catch. ME. †11 Come to an end, give out. ME–E16. †12 Be lacking. Foll. by indirect obj., *to.* LME–E19. 13 Fail to happen, come, etc. *obs.* exc. *Sc.* LME. 14 Of a person, a plan, etc.: be unsuccessful. Now *rare* or *obs.* L16. 15a Of a crop etc.: be unproductive, fail. *dial.* E17. b Of a woman: fail to menstruate at the normal time, miss a period. M20. c Of an animal: fail to conceive after mating. M20. 16 Of a motor vehicle or engine: undergo failure of ignition in one or more cylinders. E20.

9 R. ASCHAM If a childe misse .. in forgetting a worde, or in chaunging a good with a worse. 10 A. LOVELL In cutting off Heads, they .. never miss. 14 DRYDEN The bank above must fail before the venture miss.

III *v.t.* Be without. 17 Be without, lack; cease to have, lose. Also, do without. Now only (*colloq.*) in *be missing*, have lost, be without. ME. †b In *pass.* Be missing or absent. LME–L16. 18 Notice the absence or loss of. ME. 19 Perceive with regret the absence or loss of; feel the lack of. ME.

17 O. FELTHAM He hath good Materials for a foundation: but misseth wherewith to rear the walls. G. NAYLOR Dr. Buzzard's truck is missing both fenders. 18 S. RAVEN By the time Nancy had missed him .. it would be too late. 19 R. P. JHABVALA He is lonely and misses his family very much.

IV *v.t.* Omit. 20 Omit, leave out (esp. part of what one is reading, writing, etc.). Also foll. by *out.* ME. 21 Omit the performance of (a customary or expected action); fail to keep (an appointment); fail to attend (church, school, etc., a given spectacle, ceremony, etc.). M16.

20 G. VIDAL Burden's heart missed a beat. M. S. POWER He creeps up the stairs, missing the fifth and ninth which creak. K. GIBBONS The only one that can read is Starletta and she misses words. 21 H. FIELDING She .. rarely missed a ball, or any other public assembly. A. LIVELY Tommy has grown impatient with me for missing rehearsals.

Phrases etc.: *hit-and-miss*: see HIT *v.* **miss a trick** *colloq.* fail to take advantage of an opportunity or notice something important (usu. in neg. contexts). **missed abortion** the retention of a foetus in the womb for a period after it has died. **missed approach** *Aeronaut.* an approach that is discontinued for any reason. **miss fire** (of a firearm) fail to go off, misfire; *fig.* be unsuccessful. *miss one's guess*: see GUESS *n.* *miss one's tip*: see TIP *n.*[4] *miss plant*: see PLANT *n.* 7. **miss stays** *Naut.* fail in an attempt to go about from one tack to another. **miss the boat** or **bus** *colloq.* lose an opportunity.

With advs. in specialized senses: **miss out** *colloq.* miss or be deprived of an experience (foll. by *on*); (see also sense 20 above).

missable *a.* (*a*) *Golf* (of a stroke, esp. a putt) capable of missing the hole (opp. *holeable*); (*b*) able to be missed (more usual in *unmissable*): E20.

miss /mɪs/ *v.*[2]*t.* E19. [f. MISS *n.*[2]] Address as 'miss'.

missaid *v.* pa. t. & pple of MISSAY.

missal /ˈmɪs(ə)l/ *n.* & *a.* ME. [eccl.L *missale* neut. sing. of *missalis* adj., f. *missa* MASS *n.*[1] Adj. f. *missalis.*] A *n.* A book containing the service of the Mass for the whole year; *loosely* a Roman Catholic book of prayers, esp. when illuminated. ME.

B *adj.* Of or pertaining to the Mass. LME.

missal book a missal.

missay /mɪsˈseɪ/ *v. arch.* Pa. t. & pple **missaid** /mɪsˈsɛd/. ME. [f. MIS-[1] 1 + SAY *v.*[1]] 1 *v.t.* Speak ill of (a person); abuse, slander. ME. †2 *v.t.* Say with abusive or slanderous intent. ME–E17. †3 *v.i.* Speak abusively or slanderously (*of*). ME–L16. 4 *v.t.* Say wrongly or incorrectly. Now *rare.* ME. 5 *v.i.* Say what is not right or correct, tell an untruth. LME.

1 T. HEYWOOD Is she such a Saint, None can missay her? 3 SPENSER Her tongue .. brought forth speeches myld when she would have missayd. 5 BYRON Some of mosque, and some of church, And some, or I missay, of neither.

misseem /mɪsˈsiːm/ *v.* Now *rare.* ME. [f. MIS-[1] 1 + SEEM *v.*] 1 *v.t.* Be unbecoming to. ME. †2 *v.i.* Give a false appearance. *rare* (Spenser). Only in L16.

misseeming *a.* unbecoming, unseemly ME.

missel *n.* var. of MISTLE.

missense /ˈmɪs-sɛns/ *a.* M20. [f. MIS-[1] 2 + SENSE *n.*] *Genetics.* Of, pertaining to, or designating a mutation which causes the substitution of one amino acid for another at a particular point in a polypeptide or protein molecule.

miss-fire /mɪsˈfʌɪə, ˈmɪsfʌɪə/ *n.* E19. [f. *miss fire* s.v. MISS *v.*[1] Cf. MISFIRE *n.*] A failure to discharge or explode.

misshape /mɪsˈʃeɪp/ *n.* Now *rare.* LME. [f. MIS-[1] 2 + SHAPE *n.*] A physical deformity; a misshapen body or person.

misshape /mɪsˈʃeɪp/ *v.t.* Pa. t. & pple **-shaped,** (*arch.*) **-shapen** /-ˈʃeɪp(ə)n/. LME. [f. MIS-[1] 1 + SHAPE *v.*] Give a bad, ugly, or wrong shape to; deform.

misshaped *a.* misshapen, deformed E16. †**misshapedness** *n.* (*rare*) E17–E18.

misshapen /mɪsˈʃeɪp(ə)n/ *a.* LME. [f. MIS-[1] 1 + *shapen* pa. pple of SHAPE *v.*] Having a bad, ugly, or wrong shape; deformed, monstrous; distorted (*lit.* & *fig.*). Formerly also, morally monstrous or ugly.

J. STEINBECK She was misshapen; her belly, tight .. and distended. *New York Review of Books* Some federal courts have developed misshapen theories of a conspiracy.

misshapenly *adv.* E17. **misshapenness** /-n-n-/ *n.* L16.

†**misshapen** *v.t. rare.* LME–L18 [Prob. f. pa. pple of MISSHAPE *v.*: see -EN[6]. Perh. partly f. MIS-[1] 1 + SHAPEN *v.*[1]] Distort, make misshapen.

missie *n.* var. of MISSY *n.*

missikin /ˈmɪsɪkɪn/ *n. joc.* E19. [f. MISSY *n.* + -KIN.] A little 'miss' or young lady.

missile /ˈmɪsʌɪl/ *a.* & *n.* E17. [L *missilis* (adj.), f. *miss-* pa. ppl stem of *mittere* send (out); sense B.2 f. *missile* use as n. of neut. sing. of adj.: see -ILE.] A *adj.* 1 Of a projectile etc.: suitable for throwing at a target or for discharge from a machine. E17. 2 Of a weapon: that discharges arrows, bullets, etc. *rare.* E19.

B *n.* †1 In *pl.* [= L *missilia*]. Sweets, perfumes, etc., thrown as largesse by Roman emperors. *rare.* E–M17. 2 A weapon or other object suitable for throwing at a target or discharging from a machine. M17. b A destructive projectile that is self-propelling and directed by remote control or automatically. M20.

2 R. P. JHABVALA The children .. often threw stones and other missiles. b *cruise missile, Exocet missile, Pershing missile*, etc. BALLISTIC *missile. guided missile*: see GUIDE *v.*

Comb.: **missileman** a person engaged in the construction, design, flying, or operation of a missile.

missilery *n.* (*N. Amer.*) missiles collectively, a collection of missiles L19.

missing /ˈmɪsɪŋ/ *a.* E16. [f. MISS *v.*[1] + -ING[2].] Not present, not to be found; absent, lost; (of a person) whose whereabouts are unknown and who has not been traced or confirmed to be alive; *spec.* (of a soldier, sailor, etc.) not present after an action but not definitely known to have been killed, wounded, or taken prisoner.

R. K. NARAYAN He was busy searching for a missing son. R. C. HUTCHINSON A protracted wrangle with the laundry about a missing shirt. **be among the missing** *US colloq.* be away from home. **missing link** something lacking to complete a series; *spec.* a hypothetical animal assumed to be an evolutionary link between man and the anthropoid apes. **missing mass** the amount by which an observed or measured mass falls short of an expected or inferred mass; *esp.* in *Astron.*, the difference between the calculated mass of the universe, a cluster of galaxies, etc., and the sum of the masses of the observed objects in the system.

†**missingly** *adv.* (*rare*, Shakes.) with a sense of loss: only in E17.

missiology /mɪsɪˈɒlədʒi/ *n.* M20. [Irreg. f. MISSION *n.* + -OLOGY.] The branch of knowledge that deals with the methods, purpose, etc., of religious missions.

missioˈlogical *a.* M20. **missiologist** *n.* M20.

mission /ˈmɪʃ(ə)n/ *n.* L16. [Fr., or L *missio(n-)*, f. *miss-* pa. ppl stem of *mittere* send (out): see -ION.] 1 An act or instance of sending someone or (formerly, *rare*) something, or an instance of being sent, esp. to perform some function or service; *spec.* of †(*a*) Jesuits to seminaries abroad; (*b*) members of a religious organization to do missionary work abroad; (*c*) *Theol.* the second or third person of the Trinity by the first, or the third person by the second, in a form manifest to humankind; (*d*) people with authority to preach the Christian faith and administer the sacraments; (*e*) a body of people to a foreign country to conduct negotiations, establish political or commercial relations, etc. L16. 2 A body of people sent with any of the above purposes; a body of missionaries; a delegation. E17. b A body of people established by a religious organization to do work similar to missionary work in their own country, esp. among the poor or disadvantaged. Also *home mission, city mission*, etc. M19. 3 The purpose for which such a body is sent or established; the commission with which a messenger, envoy, or agent is entrusted, *esp.* the errand on which a political mission is sent; in *pl.*, organized missionary activities (also *foreign missions*). L17. b A duty or function enthusiastically accepted or assumed by a person; a person's vocation or work in life. E19. 4 A permanent establishment of missionaries in a country; a missionary post or station; a mission house. M18. b A religious centre established in a district for missionary, evangelical, or humanitarian work; *spec.* a Roman Catholic centre organized like a parish, in a predominantly non-Catholic country. L18. 5 A journey with a purpose, *spec.* to preach and extend the Christian faith. L18. b A military or scientific operation or expedition for a particular purpose, *esp.* the dispatch of an aircraft or spacecraft on an operational flight. E20. 6 An intensive course of preaching, services, and other religious activity organized to stimulate interest in the work of a parish or in the Christian faith. E19.

2 *Daily Telegraph* A joint mission from Northern Ireland to America to promote industrial investment. 3 J. CONRAD To escort that .. lady back .. as a personal mission of the highest honour. b G. B. SHAW I believe we have a sacred mission to spread British ideas. P. CAREY Mrs Dalton was a woman with a mission .. to demystify the treatment of mental illness. 4 SOUTHEY They .. To the nearest mission sped and ask'd the Jesuit's aid. 5 F. WYNDHAM She .. continued on her measured, purposeful mission to the umbrella shop. b *Scientific American* The lunar samples returned to the earth by the Apollo missions.

Comb.: **mission control** a group or organization responsible for directing a spacecraft and its crew; **mission furniture** *US* a plain, solid style of furniture modelled originally on the furniture of Spanish missions in N. America; **mission house** a building where a Christian mission is conducted; **mission oak** *US* mission furniture made of oak; **mission stiff** *US slang* a person who frequents missions; *esp.* a tramp who pretends to be religious so as to get free food and lodging.

missional *a.* (*rare*) missionary E20. **missionate** *v.i.* (*US*) conduct a mission, do missionary work E19. **missioˈneer** *v.i.* (long *rare*) = MISSIONATE E18. **missionist** *n.* a person who does missionary work E20. **missionize** *v.t.* & *i.* conduct a mission (to), do missionary work (among) E19.

mission /ˈmɪʃ(ə)n/ *v.* L17. [f. the n.] 1 *v.t.* Send on a mission; give (a person) a mission to perform. Usu. in *pass.* L17. 2 *v.t.* Conduct a religious mission among (a people) or in (a district). L18. 3 *v.i.* Conduct a mission. L19.

missionary /ˈmɪʃ(ə)n(ə)ri/ *a.* & *n.* M17. [mod.L *missionarius* (whence also Fr. *missionnaire*), f. L *missio(n-)*: see MISSION *n.*, -ARY[1].] A *adj.* 1 Of or pertaining to religious missions; sent on or engaged in a mission; characteristic of a person sent on or engaged in a religious mission. M17. 2 Sent out. Now *obs.* exc. *poet.* L17.

1 MAX-MÜLLER The three missionary religions, Buddhism, Mohammedanism, and Christianity. *Company* He obviously has a missionary zeal to clean and tidy up other people's lives. 2 S. DOBELL The night .. calling By missionary winds and twilight birds.

B *n.* 1 A person sent on or engaged in a religious mission, *esp.* one sent to propagate the (Christian) faith in a foreign country; a person engaged in missionary work. M17. 2 An agent, an emissary; *esp.* a person sent on a political mission. Now *rare* or *obs.* L17. †3 A missionary body or establishment. E–M18. 4 The sweet-brier, *Rosa rubiginosa*, introduced to New Zealand by missionaries and now an invasive weed. *NZ.* L19.

1 M. ANGELOU If more Africans had eaten more missionaries, the Continent would be in better shape. *home missionary, city missionary*, etc. *transf.*: *Listener* The latest missionary for F. R. Leavis's organic community.

Comb. & special collocations: **missionary box**: for the reception of contributions to the funds of a missionary society; **missionary position** *colloq.* the position for sexual intercourse in which the woman lies underneath the man and facing him.

missionarize *v.i.* do missionary work E19. **missionaryship** *n.* the position or status of a missionary M19.

missionary /ˈmɪʃ(ə)n(ə)ri/ *v.* M19. [f. the n.] 1 *v.i.* Act as a missionary, do missionary work. M19. 2 *v.t.* Preach to (a person), as or in the manner of a missionary. Usu. in *pass.* L19.

missioned /ˈmɪʃ(ə)nd/ *a.* Chiefly *poet.* L18. [f. MISSION *n.*, *v.*: see -ED^2, -ED^1.] Having a mission; sent on a mission or errand.

missioner /ˈmɪʃ(ə)nə/ *n.* M17. [f. MISSION *n.* + -ER^1.] A person sent on a mission, a missionary; *esp.* a Jesuit missionary. Now chiefly, a person who leads a parochial mission (in some dioceses, a permanent clerical officer).

missis /ˈmɪsɪs, -ɪz/ *n. dial. & colloq.* Also **missus**. L18. [Repr. an informal pronunc. of MISTRESS *n.*: cf. MRS.] 1 (Among servants) one's mistress; (among N. American Blacks, in British India and South Africa) a white female employer, *loosely* any (esp. White) woman. Chiefly as a form of address. L18. 2 The wife of the person speaking, addressed, or referred to. Cf. MISTER *n.*^{2} 3. E19. 3 Used as a form of address to an older woman, esp. one who is a stranger. M19.

1 P. ABRAHAMS I work for old missus when I was a child. 2 DENNIS POTTER We haven't got to the stage of interviewing the candidate's missis yet. *Daily Mirror* If you fancy taking the missis for a day out, you take her virtually free. 3 G. B. SHAW He won't get no cab until half-past eleven, missus.

Missisauga /mɪsɪˈsɔːgə/ *n. & a.* E18. [Ojibwa, lit. 'people of the Mississagi River' (in Ontario, Canada).] A *n.* Pl. **-s**, same. 1 A member of an Algonquian Indian people. E18. 2 (**m-**.) = MASSASAUGA. M19. B *adj.* Designating or pertaining to the Missisauga. M18.

missish /ˈmɪsɪʃ/ *a.* Chiefly *derog.* L18. [f. MISS *n.*^{2} + -ISH^1.] Resembling or characteristic of a miss, young lady, or schoolgirl; affectedly demure, squeamish, or sentimental.

missishness *n.* M19.

mississippi /mɪsɪˈsɪpi/ *n.* E18. [Fanciful application of *Mississippi*, a N. American river.] A game similar to bagatelle, in which balls are driven against cushions at the side of the table so as to go through arches at the end of the table.

Mississippian /mɪsɪˈsɪpɪən/ *n. & a.* L18. [f. *Mississippi* (see below) + -AN.] A *n.* 1 A native or inhabitant of Mississippi, a state of the US on the Gulf of Mexico. L18. 2 *Geol.* The Mississippian period; the system of rocks dating from this time. E20. B *adj.* 1 Of or pertaining to the state of Mississippi. M19. 2 *Geol.* Designating or pertaining to the period of the Palaeozoic era in N. America, following the Devonian and preceding the Pennsylvanian, and corresponding to the Lower Carboniferous in Europe. L19.

missive /ˈmɪsɪv/ *a. & n.* LME. [med.L *missivus* (in *litterae missivae*), f. L *miss-*: see MISSION *n.*, -IVE.] A *adj.* 1 *letter(s) missive, missive letter*, a letter or epistle sent from one person or body to another; *spec.* (*a*) a letter from a superior authority, esp. the monarch, conveying a command, recommendation, or permission; now chiefly, in the Church of England, a letter from the monarch to a dean and chapter nominating the person whom they are to elect bishop; (*b*) *Sc. Law* = sense B.2 below; (*c*) *US* (among Congregationalists) an official letter inviting churches to send delegates to a council. LME. †2 = MISSILE *a.*. M16–E19. †3 Sent on an errand or as a message. E17–M19. B *n.* 1 A written message, a letter; *spec.* = *missive letter* above. Now usu., a letter that is official or (*joc.*) long or serious. Orig. chiefly *Sc.* E16. 2 *Sc. Law.* A document in the form of a letter interchanged by the parties to a contract (usu. one to do with property). Also *missive of lease.* E16. †3 A messenger. *rare.* E–M17. †4 An object hurled or thrown; a missile. M17–E19.

missort /mɪsˈsɔːt, *as n. also* ˈmɪs-sɔːt/ *v. & n.* L16. [f. MIS-^{1} 1 + SORT *v.*] A *v.t.* Sort (esp. letters) badly; allot to a wrong place in sorting. L16. B *n.* An instance of missorting; a letter etc. missorted. L19.

missound /mɪsˈsaʊnd/ *v.* L15. [f. MIS-^{1} 1 + SOUND *v.*^{1}] 1 *v.i.* Of music: sound wrong, be played or sung badly. *rare.* L15. 2 *v.t.* Mispronounce. M16.

Missouri /mɪˈzʊəri, -s-/ *n. & a.* E18. [A river and state in the US.] A *n.* A member of a Sioux Indian people, first encountered by Europeans near the Missouri River. Also, the language of this people. E18. B *attrib.* or as *adj.* Of or pertaining to the Missouris or their language. M18.

Missourian /mɪˈzʊərɪən, -s-/ *n. & a.* E19. [f. as prec. + -AN.] A *n.* A native or inhabitant of the State of Missouri in the US. E19. B *adj.* Of or pertaining to Missouri. L19.

missourite /mɪˈzʊərʌɪt, -s-/ *n.* L19. [f. as prec. + -ITE^1.] *Geol.* A grey granular igneous rock composed mainly of pyroxene, leucite, and sometimes olivine.

miss-out /ˈmɪsaʊt/ *n. slang.* E20. [f. *miss out* s.v. MISS *v.*^{1}] 1 In *pl.* In gambling: loaded dice. E20. 2 A losing throw in craps. M20.

misspeak /mɪsˈspiːk/ *v.* Infl. as SPEAK *v.* ME. [f. MIS-^{1} 1 + SPEAK *v.*] †1 *v.i.* Speak wrongly or improperly; speak disrespectfully *of.* ME–E17. 2 *v.t.* Mispronounce. *rare.* L16. 3 *v.refl. & i.* Fail to convey the meaning one intends by one's words. Chiefly *US.* L19.

misspeech /mɪsˈspiːtʃ/ *n.* LME. [f. MIS-^{1} 2 + SPEECH *n.*] †1 Malicious speaking. LME–L15. 2 Incorrect speaking, mispronunciation. *rare.* L19.

misspell /mɪsˈspɛl *as n. also* ˈmɪs-spɛl/ *v. & n.* M17. [f. MIS-^{1} 1 + SPELL *v.*^{2}] A *v.t.* Pa. t. & pple **-spelled, -spelt.** Spell incorrectly. M17. B *n.* A misspelling. *rare.* L19.

misspelling *n.* (an instance of) bad spelling L17.

†**misspence** *n.* var. of MISSPENSE.

misspend /mɪsˈspɛnd/ *v.t.* Pa. t. & pple **-spent** /-spɛnt/. LME. [f. MIS-^{1} 1 + SPEND *v.*] Spend wrongly, badly, or wastefully. Now chiefly as *misspent* ppl a.

Sunday Express He is a wasteful jiver, suggesting a mis-spent youth.

misspender *n.* E17.

†**misspense** *n.* Also **-ce.** L16–L18. [f. MIS-^{1} 2 + SPENSE.] Improper or wasteful expenditure.

misspent *v.* pa. t. & pple of MISSPEND.

miss-stay *v.* var. of MISSTAY.

misstate /mɪsˈsteɪt/ *v.t.* M17. [f. MIS-^{1} 1 + STATE *v.*] State erroneously; make wrong statements about.

misstatement *n.* a wrong or erroneous statement L18.

misstay /mɪsˈsteɪ/ *v.i.* Also **miss-stay.** E19. [App. f. *miss stays* s.v. MISS *v.*^{1}] Of a ship: miss stays.

misstep /mɪsˈstɛp/ *n.* L18. [f. MIS-^{1} 2 + STEP *n.*^{1}] A wrong step, a slip. Chiefly *fig.*

A. LURIE A misstep, an error in tact or tone, which would have hurt our friendship. *Scientific American* For a mountain goat one misstep could be fatal.

misstep /mɪsˈstɛp/ *v.i.* Infl. **-pp-.** LME. [f. MIS-^{1} 1 + STEP *v.*] Take a wrong step; go astray.

missus *n.* var. of MISSIS.

missy /ˈmɪsi/ *n.* Also **missie.** L17. [f. MISS *n.*^{2} + -Y^6.] (An affectionate or playful or (occas.) contemptuous form of address to) a young girl, a miss.

missyish *a.* = MISSISH E19.

missy /ˈmɪsi/ *a.* Usu. *derog.* E19. [f. MISS *n.*^{2} + -Y^1.] = MISSISH.

Literary World With nothing to recommend him physically but a missy prettiness.

mississness *n.* M19.

mist /mɪst/ *n.*^{1} [OE = (M)LG, (M)Du. *mist*, Icel. *mistur*, Norw. dial., Sw. *mist*, f. Gmc, f. IE base repr. also by Gk *omikhlē* mist, fog.] 1 A diffuse cloud of minute water droplets suspended in the atmosphere on or near the ground, so as to limit visibility (but to a lesser degree than fog); the obscurity produced by this. Also, any condensed vapour that settles in fine droplets on a surface and obscures glass etc. OE. b A diffuse cloud of small particles; a haze or haziness produced by distance or (*fig.*) time etc. L18. c A grey colour suggestive of mist. E20. 2 Dimness of eyesight; a haze or film before the eyes caused by illness, the shedding of tears, etc. OE. 3 Any of various immaterial things conceived as obscuring a person's mental vision or outlook, or as veiling the real character or blurring the outlines of a thing. OE. †4 A state of obscurity or uncertainty; an atmosphere of doubt. M16–E18.

1 G. GREENE The mist from his breath obscured the pane. H. CARPENTER Often the view was blurred by a slight mist, for the weather was generally damp. *Scotch mist*: see SCOTCH *a.* b W. COWPER The rustling straw sends up a frequent mist Of atoms. *Tarzan Monthly* Treasure from a civilization that has been lost in the mists of time for centuries. 2 C. LAMB A juggler, who threw mists before your eyes. TENNYSON She did not weep But o'er her meek eyes came a happy mist. 3 J. BARZUN To glimpse . . truth through the mists of adolescent incoherence. 4 G. BURNET In this mist matters must be left till the great revelation of all secrets.

Comb.: **mist-blower** a device for spraying insecticide into the tops of trees; **mistbow** = *fog-bow* s.v. FOG *n.*^{2}; **mist-flower** a blue-flowered hemp agrimony, *Eupatorium caelestinum*, of the eastern US; **mist-net** *n. & v.* (*a*) *n.* a net made of very fine threads, used to trap birds etc. for ringing or examination; (*b*) *v.t.* trap in a mist-net; **mist propagation** a method of rooting plant cuttings in which high humidity is maintained in a greenhouse by an automatic system of watering with fine spray at regular intervals; **mist propagator** an installation for mist propagation.

mistful *a.* full of mist; obscured (as if) with mist: L16. **mistless** *a.* free from mist M19. **mistlike** *a. & adv.* like a mist L16.

†**mist** *n.*^{2} LME–M17. [Perh. a use of prec., infl. by *mystery, mystic* etc.] = MYSTERY *n.*^{1} 1.

mist /mɪst/ *v.* OE. [f. MIST *n.*^{1}] 1 *v.i.* Be or become misty; gather or appear in the form of a mist; (of the eyes, outlines, etc.) become dim or blurred. Now freq. foll. by *over, up.* OE. 2 *v.t.* Cover or obscure (as) with mist; envelop in mist; make (the eyes) dim with tears. Also foll. by *over, up.* LME. b Spray (a plant) with vaporized moisture. M20.

1 E. BOWEN Fluctuations in temperature . . make polish mist over. B. MOORE The room misted like a steam bath. T. HEALD 'Oh, Simon', she said, her eyes misting with tears. 2 W. GOLDING Rage misted my spectacles. R. INGALLS A fog had begun to mist over the landscape.

mistake /mɪˈsteɪk/ *n.* E17. [f. the vb.] 1 A misconception about the meaning of something; a thing incorrectly done or thought; an error of judgement. E17. b An instance of a woman's becoming pregnant unintentionally; an unplanned baby. *colloq.* M20. 2 Error, the condition of being mistaken or incorrectly done. Chiefly in *by mistake, in mistake for* below. L17.

1 J. T. MICKLETHWAITE It is a great mistake to think that a building looks better for being empty. F. CHICHESTER I . . was worried to find silly mistakes creeping into my calculations, mistakes like writing down a number wrongly. 2 SHELLEY Falsehood, mistake, and lust.

Phrases: †**a mistake of** a misconception as to. **and no mistake** *colloq.* without any doubt. **by mistake** erroneously, mistakenly. **in mistake for** in error for. **make no mistake** have no doubt (*about*). †**under a mistake** under a misapprehension.

mistake /mɪˈsteɪk/ *v.* Pa. t. **mistook** /mɪˈstʊk/; pa. pple **mistaken** /mɪˈsteɪk(ə)n/, (*dial.* & *non-standard*) **mistook.** ME. [ON *mistaka* take in error, (refl.) miscarry (Sw. *misstaga* be mistaken), f. as MIS-^{1} + *taka* TAKE *v.* Cf. OFr. *mesprendre* (see MISPRIZE *v.*^{2}), which has prob.

influenced the meaning.] 1 *v.i.* Transgress, do wrong. *obs.* exc. *Sc.* ME. †2 *v.t.* Take improperly or in error. LME–M17. 3 *v.t.* Make an error in the choice of (one's route, target, etc.). Formerly also, make an error regarding (a date, number, etc.); perform (an action) at a wrong time. *arch.* LME. 4 *v.t.* Attach a wrong meaning to the words or actions of (a person); misunderstand. LME. †b Have a wrong view of the character of (a person). L16–L17. 5 *v.t.* Have a misconception regarding (an opinion, statement, action, purpose, etc.); attach an erroneous meaning to. L15. †6 *v.t.* Suppose erroneously to be or *to be*. L15–M18. 7 *v.t.* a Be under a misconception about the identity of; take to be somebody or something else; estimate wrongly. Now chiefly in phrs. below. L16. b Foll. by *for*: identify wrongly as (some other person or thing). E17. 8 *v.i.* (*arch.*), & *t.* in *pass.* as *be mistaken* & (now *Sc.*) *refl.* Make a mistake; be in error, be under a misapprehension. L16.

3 E. YOUNG When blind ambition quite mistakes her road. 4 R. K. NARAYAN I was only trying to suggest... So please don't mistake me. 5 A. J. AYER My reasoning on this point was not in itself incorrect, but .. I mistook its purport. 6 T. FULLER Vincent of Coventrie was .. bred a Franciscan (though Learned Leland mistakes him a Carmelite). 7a **there's no mistaking** it is impossible not to recognize (a person or thing). **mistake one's man** judge wrongly or underestimate the character or capabilities of the person one is dealing with. b R. DAHL The doctor .. was so drunk that he mistook the fractured elbow for a dislocated shoulder. 8 T. HARDY A .. greatcoat, which, if he mistook not, was the very same garment as .. had adorned the chair. D. L. SAYERS You may think that the prisoner was mistaken .. about the time he left the flat.

mistakable *a.* able to be mistaken or misunderstood M17. **mistaker** *n.* M16. **mistakingly** *adv.* erroneously, mistakenly M17.

mistaken /mɪˈsteɪk(ə)n/ *a.* M16. [pa. pple of prec.] 1 Based on or resulting from a mistake, erroneous. M16. 2 Having a wrong opinion or judgement, being under a misapprehension. E17.

1 E. A. FREEMAN A mistaken feeling of loyalty hindered him. *American Speech* 'Ten gallon' has been arrived at by a mistaken translation of a Spanish word. *mistaken identity*: see IDENTITY 1. 2 W. S. JEVONS There ought not to be so many mistaken people vainly acting in opposition to his lessons.

mistakenly *adv.* M17. **mistakenness** /-n-n-/ *n.* M19.

misteach /mɪsˈtiːtʃ/ *v.t.* Pa. t. & pple **-taught** /-tɔːt/. LOE. [f. MIS-[1] 1 + TEACH *v.*] Teach badly, wrongly, or incorrectly.

misted /ˈmɪstɪd/ *a.* E17. [f. MIST *n.*[1], *v.*: see -ED[2], -ED[1].] Obscured by or hidden in mist; dulled, blurred.

mistell /mɪsˈtɛl/ *v.t.* Pa. t. & pple **-told** /-təʊld/. LME. [f. MIS-[1] 1 + TELL *v.*] †1 Number incorrectly; miscount. LME–M17. 2 Relate or recount incorrectly; (now *Sc.*) misinform. M16.

mistemper /mɪsˈtɛmpə/ *v.t.* Long *arch. rare.* LME. [f. MIS-[1] 1 + TEMPER *v.*[1]] Chiefly as *mistempered* ppl a. 1 Put in disorder; disturb, derange. LME. †2 Mix badly or unsuitably. E16–M17. †3 Temper (a weapon) for an evil purpose. Only in L16.

mister /ˈmɪstə/ *n.*[1] Now *arch.* & *dial.* ME. [AN *mester*, OFr. *mestier* (mod. MÉTIER), f. Proto-Romance contr. of L *ministerium*: see MYSTERY *n.*[2]] I†1 A trade; a profession, a craft. ME–E17. †2 A person's office or function; an employment, an occupation; a practice. Only in ME. †3 Skill in a profession. LME–L15. II 4 Need (†*of*), necessity; a state of difficulty or distress, *esp.* a lack of means. Long *obs.* exc. *Sc.* ME. †b A need, a lack. *Sc.* E16–E19. †5 A necessity; in *pl.* necessary articles, fittings, etc. Chiefly *Sc.* LME–E19.

Comb.: **mister man** (long *arch.*) †(*a*) a craftsman, a man having a particular occupation; (*b*) (by misanalysis) a kind or class of man; **mister wight** (long *arch.*) (*a*) a kind or class of person or creature; (*b*) (by misunderstanding) a particular person or creature.

mister /ˈmɪstə/ *n.*[2] Also (esp. in titles) **M-**. M16. [Weakened form of MASTER *n.*[1] originating from reduced stress in use before a name. Cf. MISTRESS *n.*] 1 Used as a title preceding the name of a man without a higher or honorific or professional title, or preceding any of various designations of office. Now usu. written MR exc. *joc.* or with offensive emphasis. M16. b The word 'mister' (Mr) as a title; a person addressed as 'Mr', a man without a title of nobility etc. M18. 2 (Without proper name.) Used as a form of address to an adult male stranger, *esp.* one of superior status. Now regarded as *uneducated.* M18. b Used as a form of address to a ship's mate. *colloq.* E20. 3 The husband of the person speaking, addressed, or referred to. M20.

1 A. PRICE The sergeant's '*Mister* Audley' and his slight disdain. b S. FOOTE Has his majesty dubb'd me a Knight for you to make me a Mister? P. MOYES We're all good friends .. We don't use no Mister and Missus. 2 E. LEONARD Mister, gimme a dollar.

†**mister** *v.*[1] Chiefly *Sc.* LME. [f. MISTER *n.*[1]] 1 *v.i.* a *impers.* in (*it*) *misters* etc., it is necessary or needful etc. (*to do*). LME–E19. b Find it necessary (*to do*). LME–L16. 2 *v.i.* Of a thing: be necessary or requisite. LME–E16. 3 *v.t.* & *i.* Have need of or *of*, require. LME–E18.

mister /ˈmɪstə/ *v.*[2]*t.* M18. [f. MISTER *n.*[2]] Address as 'Mr'.

mistery *n.* var. of MYSTERY *n.*[2]

misthink /mɪsˈθɪŋk/ *v. arch.* Pa. t. & pple **-thought** /-ˈθɔːt/. ME. [f. MIS-[1] 1 + THINK *v.*[2]] †1 *v.i.* Have sinful thoughts. ME–E17. 2 *v.i.* & *t.* Have mistaken thoughts; think mistakenly *that.* E16. 3 *v.t.* & *i.* w. *of.* Have an unfavourable opinion of. L16. 4 *v.t.* Think (a thought) to a person's detriment. E17.

misthought /mɪsˈθɔːt/ *n.* ME. [f. MIS-[1] 2 + THOUGHT *n.*[1]] Mistaken thought or opinion.

misthrive /mɪsˈθraɪv/ *v.i.* Now *rare.* Infl. as THRIVE *v.* M16. [f. MIS-[1] 1 + THRIVE *v.*] Be unsuccessful; fail to thrive.

mistico /ˈmɪstɪkəʊ/ *n.* Pl. **-o(e)s**. E19. [Sp., perh. ult. f. Arab. *musaṭṭah* armed vessel.] A Spanish coasting vessel having three upright masts.

mistified *a.* var. of MYSTIFIED *a.*[1]

mistigris /ˈmɪstɪɡrɪs/ *n.* L19. [Fr. *mistigri* jack of clubs.] A joker or other card played as a wild card in some versions of poker etc.; the highest trump in certain trick games. Also, a game in which such a card is used.

mistime /mɪsˈtaɪm/ *v.* LOE. [f. as MIS-[1] 1 + TIME *v.*] †1 Of an event: cause misfortune. Of a person: suffer misfortune. LOE–LME. 2 *v.t.* Do or say at a wrong time. LME. 3 Miscalculate or misstate the time of. M17.

mistimed *a.* †(*a*) unfortunate; (*b*) ill-timed, unseasonable; (*c*) *dial.* keeping irregular hours: L15.

mistitle /mɪsˈtaɪt(ə)l/ *v.t.* E17. [f. MIS-[1] 1 + TITLE *v.*] Give a wrong title or name to.

mistle /ˈmɪs(ə)l/ *n.* Also **missel**. [OE *mistel* = OHG *mistil* (G *Mistel*), Du. *mistel*, ON *mistil-*: ult. origin unkn.] †1 Mistletoe. Also, basil. OE–L17. 2 In full *mistle thrush*, (dial.) *mistle bird.* A large greyish Eurasian thrush, *Turdus viscivorus*, noted for eating the berries of mistletoe and other plants. E17.

mistletoe /ˈmɪs(ə)ltəʊ/ *n.* [OE *misteltān* (= ON *mistilteinn*), f. as prec. + *tān* twig (= Du. *teen* withe, OHG *zein* rod, ON *teinn* twig, spit).] A European plant, *Viscum album* (family Loranthaceae), which is parasitic on various trees (esp. apple and poplar), bears white glutinous berries, and is used in Christmas decorations. Also (in full *American mistletoe*), any of several N. American parasitic plants of the related genus *Phoradendron*, esp. *P. serotinum*.

W. IRVING The mistle-toe is still hung up in farm-houses .. at Christmas.

Comb.: **mistletoe bird** *Austral.* a small black, white, and crimson flower-pecker, *Dicaeum hirundinaceum*; **mistletoe cactus** any of various cacti of the mainly tropical American genus *Rhipsalis*, esp. *R. baccifera*, with white fruits resembling those of mistletoe.

mistook *v.* see MISTAKE *v.*

mistral /ˈmɪstr(ə)l, mɪˈstrɑːl/ *n.* E17. [Fr. f. Prov. f. L *magistralis* (sc. *ventus* wind): see MAGISTRAL. Cf. MAESTRALE.] A strong cold north-west wind which blows through the Rhône valley and southern France into the Mediterranean, mainly in winter.

mistranslate /mɪstransˈleɪt, -trɑːns-/ *v.t.* M16. [f. MIS-[1] 1 + TRANSLATE *v.*] Translate incorrectly.

mistranslation *n.* L17.

†**mistreading** *n.* L16–M18. [f. MIS-[1] 1 + TREADING *n.*] A misdeed, a transgression.

mistreat /mɪsˈtriːt/ *v.t.* LME. [f. MIS-[1] 1 + TREAT *v.*] Treat badly or wrongly.

A. HUTSCHNECKER How can I forgive her for abandoning me at age three and mistreating me physically?

mistreatment *n.* E18.

mistress /ˈmɪstrɪs/ *n.* & *a.* ME. [OFr. *maistresse* (mod. *maîtresse*), f. *maistre* MASTER *n.*[1] + *-esse* -ESS[1], with subsequent shortening of first vowel (cf. MISTER *n.*[2]). See also MRS.] A *n.* I 1†a A woman who has charge of a child or young person; a governess. Only in ME. b A female tutor or teacher, *esp.* one in a school; a woman who teaches a particular subject. ME. 2 A woman who employs others in her service; a woman in relation to her servants or slaves. Also, the female owner of an animal (cf. sense 11 below), a woman or girl whom an animal is accustomed to obey. LME. 3 The female head of a household, family, or other establishment; the female principal of a college. LME. b *The* wife of a farmer (in relation to his tenants), a minister, etc. Chiefly *Sc.* L17. 4 A woman having the power to control, use, or dispose of something at will. Chiefly *pred.*, foll. by *of*. LME. 5†a The female governor of a territory, State, or people. LME–L18. b A country, State, etc., which has supremacy or control over other countries etc. LME. †c The chief, the first. L15–E17. †6 A woman, goddess, or thing personified as female that has control over a person or is regarded as a guiding influence. LME–L17. †7 A female patron or inspirer. LME–E18. 8 A woman loved and courted by a man; a sweetheart. Now *arch.* & *dial.* LME. 9 A woman (other than a wife) with whom a man has a long-standing sexual relationship. LME. 10 A woman proficient in an art, study, or other branch of knowledge. Now *rare.* LME. 11 A female possessor or owner (*of*). Now *rare* or *obs.* exc. as passing into senses 2, 10. M16.

1b POPE When I was at School, my Mistress did ever extol me above the rest. SCHOOLMISTRESS. *French mistress, music mistress, sewing mistress*, etc. 2 J. M. SLOAN Jane Welsh was among the best of mistresses to her servants. 3 J. M. BARRIE Her mother's death made her mistress of the house and mother to her little brother. **Mistress of the Robes** (in the English royal household) a lady of high rank, charged with the care of the Queen's wardrobe. *Mistress of Girton College* etc. 4 A. POWELL She was perfectly calm, mistress, as ever, of the situation. 5b W. S. CHURCHILL At sea and on land England was mistress of the outer world. 6 SHAKES. *Lear* Mumbling of wicked charms, conjuring the moon To stand's auspicious mistress. 7 S. CENTLIVRE Want, the mistress of invention. 8 T. HARDY They were yet mere lover and mistress. 9 LD MACAULAY His Protestant mistresses gave less scandal than his Popish wife. 10 ADDISON I would advise all young Wives to make themselves Mistresses of Wingate's Arithmetick. D. LESSING Our Mrs. Van is a mistress of rules and regulations. 11 G. WASHINGTON Without a considerable reinforcement, Frederick county will not be mistress of fifteen families. J. AUSTEN Elinor .. more anxious to be alone than to be mistress of the subject.

II Used as a title or preceding a name. 12 Used *voc.* as a respectful form of address; madam, ma'am. Now *arch.* & *W. Indian.* LME. 13a Used as a title preceding the first name or surname of an unmarried woman or girl; = MISS *n.*[2] 2. *obs.* exc. *dial.* LME. b Used as a title preceding the surname (orig. also the first name) of a married woman; = MRS. Now *dial.* & *W. Indian* L15.

12 SHAKES. *L.L.L.* Studies my lady? Mistress, look on me. 13b D. DUNNETT Are ye there, Mistress Rossi?

III *techn.* 14 The jack in bowls. Cf. MASTER *n.*[1] 8. L16. 15 A lantern used in coalmines. M19.

B *attrib.* or as *adj.* That is a mistress: (of a thing personified as female or (formerly) with a

n. grammatically fem. in L or Fr.) chief, leading, commanding, great, powerful. L16.

T. JACKSON Rome . . the Mistresse-citie of the world.

Comb.: **mistresspiece** (long *rare*) [after MASTERPIECE] an oustanding example of female beauty or accomplishment.

mistresshood *n.* the condition or status of a mistress (of a household) L19. **mistressing** *vbl n.* paying court to or dallying with a mistress M17. **mistressless** *a.* L19.

mistress /ˈmɪstrɪs/ *v.t.* L16. [f. the n.] **1** Provide with a mistress. L16. **2** Call or address as 'mistress'. E19. **3** Become mistress of (an art). *rare*. M19. **4** Dominate as a mistress. E20.

Phrases: **mistress it** play the part of a mistress.

mistressly /ˈmɪstrɪsli/ *a.* M18. [f. MISTRESS *n.* + -LY[1].] **1** Belonging to the mistress of a household. *rare*. M18. **2** Resembling or characteristic of a woman proficient in an art. Cf. MASTERLY *a.* 2. Now *rare*. L18.

mistress-ship /ˈmɪstrɪsʃɪp/ *n.* LME. [f. MISTRESS *n.* + -SHIP.] †**1** The status of a woman to whom the title of mistress was used. Only in *your mistress-ship*. LME–M17. **2** The condition or status of mistress or head of a household etc.; the authority of a woman in the position of a mistress. L16. **3** Pre-eminent skill in an art etc. shown by a woman. Now *rare* or *obs.* E19. **4** The post of mistress in a school. L19.

mistrial /mɪsˈtraɪəl, ˈmɪstraɪəl/ *n.* E17. [f. MIS-[1] 2 + TRIAL *n.*] **1** A trial rendered invalid by some error, as a disqualification in a judge or juror. E17. **2** An inconclusive trial, as where the jury cannot agree. *US*. L19.

mistrust /mɪsˈtrʌst/ *n.* LME. [f. MIS-[1] 2 + TRUST *n.*] Lack of trust or confidence, suspicion, distrust, (foll. by *of*, *in*). Formerly also, doubt as to the truth or probability *of* a thing.

SHAKES. *Jul. Caes.* Mistrust of good success hath done this deed. A. STORR Beethoven's deafness increased his mistrust of other human beings.

mistrust /mɪsˈtrʌst/ *v.* LME. [f. MIS-[1] 1, 5 + TRUST *v.*, prob. after OFr. *mesfier* (mod. *méfier*).] **1** *v.t.* Have no confidence in, be suspicious of; doubt the truth, validity, or genuineness of. LME. **2** *v.t.* **a** Suspect *that*. Now *dial.* & *US*. LME. **b** Suspect the existence of or future occurrence of (harm etc.). Now *rare* or *obs.* M16. **3** *v.i.* Be distrustful, suspicious, or without confidence. LME.

1 E. M. FORSTER I rather mistrust young men who slip into life gracefully. J. KLEIN I would tend to mistrust my own abilities. **2a** O. W. HOLMES I mistrusted he didn't mean to come. **b** J. FLORIO They were all asleepe mistrusting no harme.

mistruster *n.* LME.

mistrustful /mɪsˈtrʌstfʊl, -f(ə)l/ *a.* E16. [f. MISTRUST *n.* + -FUL.] **1** Lacking in trust or confidence; distrustful, suspicious, (*of*). E16. †**2** Causing mistrust or suspicion. *rare* (Shakes.). Only in L16.

mistrustfully *adv.* L16. **mistrustfulness** *n.* M16.

mistrusting /mɪsˈtrʌstɪŋ/ *a.* M16. [f. MISTRUST *v.* + -ING[2].] Suspicious, mistrustful.

mistrustingly *adv.* M16.

mistrustless /mɪsˈtrʌs(t)lɪs/ *a.* Now *rare*. L16. [f. MISTRUST *n.* + -LESS.] Free from mistrust or suspicion; unsuspecting (*of*).

mistry /mɪsˈtraɪ/ *v.t.* M17. [f. MIS-[1] 1 + TRY *v.*] Try (a person or case) wrongly or badly, subject to a wrong or badly conducted trial.

mistryst /mɪsˈtraɪst, -trɪst/ *v. Sc.* & *north.* M17. [f. MIS-[1] 1 + TRYST *v.*] **1** *v.t.* & *i.* (w. *with*). Fail to keep an engagement with. M17. **2** *v.t.* In *pass.* Be perplexed, confused, or frightened. E19.

mistune /mɪsˈtjuːn/ *v.* LME. [f. MIS-[1] 1 + TUNE *v.*] †**1** *v.i.* Be out of tune. Only in LME. **2** *v.t.* Tune wrongly; put out of tune, make discordant; perform (music) out of tune. E16.

misty /ˈmɪsti/ *a.* [OE *mistiġ*, f. as MIST *n.*[1] + *-iġ*, -Y[1].] **1** Clouded, obscured, or accompanied by mist; consisting of mist. OE. **b** Clouded with fine particles resembling mist. M19. **c** Of the eyes: blurred with tears. Of a person: having misty eyes. M19. **2** *fig.* **a** Obscure, unintelligible; vague, indistinct; confused. LME. **b** Not illuminated by reason, truth, etc. Formerly also, marked by or causing ignorance. E16.

1c C. POTOK My father's eyes were misty . . and I cried a little. T. K. WOLFE You would even see engineers . . getting misty about those old days. **2a** C. GROSS The jurists had not yet shrouded the notion in misty complexity. M. S. POWER He became one of her sweet, misty memories.

mistily *adv.* ME. **mistiness** *n.* (*a*) misty condition; (*b*) vapour, haze, mist: LME.

mistype /mɪsˈtaɪp/ *v.* M20. [f. MIS-[1] 1 + TYPE *v.*[1]] **1** *v.t.* & *i.* Type (a letter, words, etc.) incorrectly. M20. **2** *v.t.* Wrongly assign to a particular type; misclassify. L20.

misunderstand /ˌmɪsʌndəˈstand/ *v.* Pa. t. & pple **-stood** /-ˈstʊd/. ME. [f. MIS-[1] 1 + UNDERSTAND.] **1** *v.t.* Fail to understand rightly (words, a statement, etc.), take in a wrong sense. ME. **2** *v.t.* Misinterpret the words or actions of (a person). ME. **3** *v.i.* Fail to understand. LME.

1 J. BRIGGS They had misunderstood the phrase 'washed raisins' and washed the raisins in soap. **2** DENNIS POTTER Please do not misunderstand me, ladies and gentlemen. E. KUZWAYO Very offhand, even to the point where she could easily be misunderstood as unkind or uncaring. **3** R. K. NARAYAN They might misunderstand if I said anything contrary to their views.

misunderstandable *a.* M19. **misunderstander** *n.* E16.

misunderstanding /ˌmɪsʌndəˈstandɪŋ/ *n.* LME. [f. MISUNDERSTAND *v.* + -ING[1].] **1** Failure to understand; mistake of the meaning; an instance of this, a misconception, a misinterpretation. LME. **2** An interruption of harmonious relations; dissension, disagreement; a slight disagreement or quarrel. M17.

misunderstood *v.* pa. t. & pple of MISUNDERSTAND.

misusage /mɪsˈjuːsɪdʒ/ *n.* Now *rare*. M16. [f. MIS-[1] 2 + USAGE.] †**1** Misconduct; corrupt practice, abuse. M–L16. **2** Ill usage; mistreatment. Formerly also in *pl.*, instances of this. M16. **3** Bad or wrong use, misuse. M16.

misuse /mɪsˈjuːs/ *n.* LME. [f. MIS-[1] 2 + USE *n.*] **1** Wrong or improper use, misapplication; *spec.* non-therapeutic use of a drug; an instance of this. LME. †**2** (An instance of) misconduct. E16–E17. **3** Ill treatment. *rare*. L16.

1 *Q* The word 'classic' is prone to wild misuse. P. LOMAS The misuse of power that can occur in the psychoanalyst's office.

misuse /mɪsˈjuːz/ *v.t.* LME. [f. MIS-[1] 1 + USE *v.*] **1** Use wrongly or improperly, apply to a wrong purpose; *spec.* take (a drug) for non-therapeutic purposes. LME. **2**†**a** Violate, abuse sexually. LME–M16. **b** Subject to ill treatment; maltreat. M16. †**3** Deceive, delude. LME–E17. †**4** *refl.* Misbehave. M16–E17. †**5** Speak evil of; abuse, deride. L16–M17. †**6** Speak falsely of, misrepresent. *rare* (Shakes.). Only in L16.

1 R. DEACON The Chinese experienced his treachery when . . he had . . misused their funds. **2b** J. GALSWORTHY Relating . . the innumerable occasions on which Fortune had misused her. **5** ROBERT BURTON Socrates was brought upon the stage by Aristophanes, and misused to his face. **6** SHAKES. *Sonn.* All my vows are oaths but to misuse thee.

misuser /mɪsˈjuːzə/ *n.*[1] M16. [f. prec. + -ER[1].] A person who misuses something or someone.

misuser /mɪsˈjuːzə/ *n.*[2] E17. [OFr. *mesuser*, inf. used as n.: see -ER [4].] *Law.* Unlawful use of a liberty or benefit such as may lead to its forfeiture.

misventure /mɪsˈventʃə/ *n. arch.* M16. [f. MIS-[1] 2 + VENTURE *n.*] A mischance, a misfortune. Also, a foolish or ill-starred venture.

†**miswandered** *a.* L16–E17. [f. MIS-[1] 1 + *wandered* pa. pple of WANDER *v.*] In which one has gone astray.

SPENSER His late miswandred wayes now to remeasure right.

†**misween** *v.* L16. [f. MIS-[1] 1 + WEEN.] **1** *v.i.* Have a wrong opinion (*that*). L16–M17. **2** *v.t.* Think wrongly of, misjudge. E17–M18.

†**misweening** *n.* misthinking; misjudgement; mistrust: L15–L16.

†**miswend** *v.* Pa. t. & pple **-went**. ME. [f. MIS-[1] 1 + WEND *v.*[1]] **1** *v.t.* Turn in a wrong direction; misapply; lead astray; pervert. Only in ME. **2** *v.t.* (in *pass.*) & *i.* Go astray (*lit.* & *fig.*); come to grief. ME–E18.

2 P. SIDNEY What? is thy Bagpipe broke, or are thy lambes miswent?

misword /mɪsˈwəːd/ *n.* Now *dial.* ME. [f. MIS-[1] 2 + WORD *n.*] A harsh, angry, or cross word.

L. P. HARTLEY Together they had got on very well—not a 'misword' between them.

misword /mɪsˈwəːd/ *v.t.* L17. [f. MIS-[1] 1 + WORD *v.*] Word or express incorrectly.

miswrite /mɪsˈraɪt/ *v.t.* Pa. t. **-wrote** /-ˈrəʊt/; pa. pple **-written** /-ˈrɪt(ə)n/. LOE. [f. MIS-[1] 1 + WRITE *v.*] Write incorrectly or by mistake.

miswriting *n.* an error in writing LME.

misy /ˈmɪsi/ *n. obs.* exc. *Hist.* M16. [L f. Gk *misu*.] In translations or echoes of Pliny: a yellow crystalline mineral, often identified as copiapite.

misyoke /mɪsˈjəʊk/ *v.i.* & *t.* M17. [f. MIS-[1] 1 + YOKE *v.*] Join or be joined in marriage unsuitably.

mit *n.* var. of MITT.

mit /mɪt/ *prep.* & *adv. joc.* & *colloq.* L19. [G = with.] With (me, us, etc.).

W. JAMES I . . suppose Mrs. Godkin will come *mit*.

mita /ˈmita/ *n.* E18. [Sp. f. Quechua *mitta*.] *Hist.* A group of Peruvian Indians used by the Spaniards in S. America as forced labour.

Mitanni /mɪˈtani/ *n.* & *a.* E20. [Mitannian or Hurrian.] **A** *n.* Pl. same. **1** A member of the predominant people of Mitanni, a largely Hurrian kingdom centred on the Habur and Upper Euphrates which flourished in the 15th and early 14th cents. BC. E20. **2** The language of this people, = MITANNIAN *n.* 2. M20. **B** *attrib.* or as *adj.* Of or pertaining to Mitanni, its people, or their language. E20.

Mitannian /mɪˈtanɪən/ *a.* & *n.* L19. [f. as prec. + -AN.] **A** *adj.* = MITANNI *a.* L19. **B** *n.* **1** A member of the Mitanni. E20. **2** The language of the Mitanni. E20.

Mitbestimmung /ˈmɪtbəʃtɪmʊŋ/ *n.* M20. [G = co-determination.] In Germany, the policy in industry of involving both workers and management in decision-making.

mitch /mɪtʃ/ *v. obs.* exc. *dial.* Also †**miche**. LME. [App. f. OFr. *muchier* hide, lurk. Cf. MEECH, MOOCH *v.*] †**1** *v.t.* Pilfer. LME–L16. **2** *v.i.* **a** Retire from view; lurk out of sight; skulk. M16. **b** Play truant. L16.

mitch-board /ˈmɪtʃbɔːd/ *n.* L19. [Perh. f. var. of MICHE *n.* + BOARD *n.*] *Naut.* A support for a boom, yard, etc., when not in use.

mitchel /ˈmɪtʃ(ə)l/ *n.* Now *rare* or *obs.* M17. [Origin unkn.] A usu. square paving stone, varying in size from fifteen inches (approx. 38 cm) to two feet (approx. 61 cm).

mitchella /mɪˈtʃɛlə/ *n.* L18. [mod.L (see below), f. John *Mitchell* (d. 1768), English-born Amer. botanist.] A N. American trailing evergreen plant, *Mitchella repens*, of the madder family. Also called *partridge-berry*.

Mitchell grass /ˈmɪtʃ(ə)l grɑːs/ *n. phr.* L19. [Sir Thomas Livingstone *Mitchell* (1792–1855), Scottish-born explorer.] Any of various Australian fodder grasses of the genus *Astrebla*.

mite /maɪt/ *n.*[1] [OE *mīte* = MLG, MDu. *mīte* (Du. *mijt*), OHG *mīza* gnat, f. Gmc.] Orig., any minute insect or arachnid, esp. a small parasite infesting hawks. Now, any small free-living often parasitic arachnid of the order Acari, which also includes ticks.

cheese mite, harvest mite, itch-mite, mange mite, etc.

Comb.: **mite(-borne) typhus** = *scrub typhus* s.v. SCRUB *n.*[1]

miticide *n.* a substance used to kill mites M20. **mity** *a.* full of or containing many mites L17.

mite /maɪt/ *n.*[2] LME. [MLG, MDu. *mīte* f. Gmc, prob. identical w. prec.] **1** *Hist.* Orig., a Flemish copper coin of very small value. Later, any very small unit of currency; *spec.* half a farthing. LME. **b** *one's mite*, *a widow's mite* (w. allus. to *Mark* 12:43) a person's modest contribution to a cause, charity, etc., *esp.* the most the giver can manage, the best one can do. M17. †**2** A very small weight; *spec.* the twentieth part of a grain. LME–E18. 3 A tiny amount, a little bit, a fragment; *fig.* (chiefly *a mite, one mite*) a jot, a whit, (advb.) somewhat, slightly, a little. Now *colloq.* LME. 4 A very small object or living creature, *esp.* a tiny child. L16.

1 AV *Mark* 12:42 A certaine poore widow .. threw in two mites, which make a farthing. b R. K. NARAYAN You must contribute your mite for the economic and political salvation of our country. 3 J. RAY The Ants .. drop upon them a small Mite of their stinging Liquor. M. ANGELOU His left hand was only a mite bigger than Bailey's. J. CARROLL Colman withdrew a mite, holding his smile down. *New Health* Turning back now seemed a mite unadventurous. 4 A. WEST The poor mite does all he can to keep out of your way.

Comb.: **mite society** *Hist.* a 19th-cent. society which collected funds for charity by small contributions.

mitella /mɪˈtɛlə/ *n.* L17. [L, orig. = headband, dim of *mitra*: see MITRE *n.*[1]] †1 *Med.* A sling for the arm. Only in L17. 2 A plant of the genus *Mitella*; = *mitrewort* s.v. MITRE *n.*[1] M18.

miter *n.*, *v.* see MITRE *n.*[1], *n.*[2], *v.*[1], *v.*[2]

mitered *a.* see MITRED.

mithan /ˈmɪθ(ə)n/ *n.* M19. [Khasi *mythun* (whence Assamese *methon*).] In the Indian subcontinent: = GAYAL.

mither *v.* var. of MOIDER.

Mithraeum /mɪˈθriːəm/ *n.* Pl. **-aea** /-iːə/. L19. [mod.L, f. L *Mithras*: see next.] *Antiq.* A sanctuary of the god Mithras; a chapel for the worship of Mithras.

Mithraic /mɪˈθreɪɪk/ *a.* L17. [(f. L *Mithras*, *Mithres* f. Gk *Mithras* f.) OPers., Avest. *Mithra* = Skt *Mitra*, one of the gods of the Vedic pantheon: see -IC.] Of or pertaining to Mithras, an ancient Persian god worshipped in much of northern and western Europe in the time of the Roman Empire, and later often identified with the sun.

Mithraicism /-sɪz(ə)m/ *n.* = MITHRAISM M19.

Mithraism /ˈmɪθrə-ɪz(ə)m/ *n.* E19. [f. as prec. + -ISM.] The worship of the god Mithras, the religion or cult of followers of Mithras.

Mithraist *n.* a worshipper of or believer in Mithras L19. **Mithraˈistic** *a.* = MITHRAIC *a.* E20.

mithridate /ˈmɪθrɪdeɪt/ *n.* E16. [med.L *mithridatum*, alt. of late L *mithridatium*, orig. neut. of *Mithridatius* adj., pertaining to Mithridates: see next, -ATE[1].] 1 *Hist.* (A medicine claimed to be) a universal antidote or preservative against poison and disease. E16. 2 *mithridate mustard*, penny cress, *Thlaspi arvense*. L16.

1 *fig.*: SOUTHEY A drop of the true elixir, no mithridate so effectual against the infection of vice.

Mithridatic /mɪθrɪˈdatɪk/ *a.* In sense 2 also **m-**. M17. [L *mithridaticus* f. Gk *Mithridatikos*, f. *Mithridatēs*: see below, -IC.] 1 Of, pertaining to, or resembling Mithridates VI, king of Pontus (d. 63 BC), who reputedly made himself immune to poisons by constantly using antidotes. M17. 2 Pertaining to or of the nature of mithridatism. M19.

mithridatism /ˈmɪθrɪdeɪtɪz(ə)m, mɪˈθrɪdətɪz(ə)m/ *n.* M19. [f. *Mithridates* (see prec.) + -ISM.] Immunity to a poison induced by administering gradually increased doses of the poison.

miˈthridatize *v.t.* make proof against a poison by the administration of gradually increasing doses of it M19.

mitigable /ˈmɪtɪgəb(ə)l/ *a.* L17. [med.L *mitigabilis*, f. *mitigare*: see MITIGATE, -ABLE.] Able to be mitigated.

†mitigal *n.* see MISKAL.

mitigant /ˈmɪtɪg(ə)nt/ *a.* & *n.* *rare.* M16. [L *mitigant-* pres. ppl stem of *mitigare*: see next, -ANT[1].] A *adj.* Mitigating, soothing. M16. B *n.* A soothing medicine; a lenitive. M19.

mitigate /ˈmɪtɪgeɪt/ *v.* LME. [L *mitigat-* pa. ppl stem of *mitigare*, f. *mitis* mild, gentle: see -ATE[3].] 1 *v.t.* Make milder in manner or attitude, make less hostile; mollify. Now *rare.* LME. 2 *v.t.* Give relief from (pain, suffering, etc.); lessen the suffering or trouble caused by (an evil or difficulty of any kind). LME. 3 *v.t.* Make (anger, hatred, etc.) less fierce or violent. L15. 4 *v.t.* Lessen the rigour or severity of (a law), make less oppressive; reduce the severity of (a punishment); make (a custom) more humane. M16. b Lessen the gravity of (an offence); palliate, extenuate. E18. 5 *v.t.* Moderate (the severity, rigour, etc., *of* something). Also, make (heat, cold, light, etc.) more bearable. L16. 6 *v.i.* Become mitigated; grow milder or less severe. *rare.* M17.

2 E. WAUGH I have to endure these sufferings .. and your presence will mitigate them. A. FRASER The King's eventual course of action did nothing to mitigate the conspirators' difficulties. J. HUXLEY The depths of obsessive despair which he so often tried to mitigate. 3 W. H. PRESCOTT The envoys .. interposed to mitigate the king's anger. 4 *Irish Press* Two fines of £100, mitigated to £2 each, were imposed. b LD MACAULAY He could see no mitigating circumstances, no redeeming merit. 5 A. BEVAN Even successful rebellion could not serve to mitigate the rigours of toil. A. BURGESS The sun, its heat mitigated by the strong sea-wind.

mitigator *n.* E17. **mitigatory** *a.* & *n.* (*a*) *adj.* that mitigates something; alleviating, palliative; (*b*) *n.* a mitigatory thing; a soothing remedy; a plea in extenuation: M17.

mitigation /mɪtɪˈgeɪʃ(ə)n/ *n.* LME. [(O)Fr., or L *mitigatio(n-)*, f. as prec.: see -ATION.] 1 The action of mitigating something; the fact or condition of being mitigated. LME. b A mitigating circumstance or provision. E18. †2 Softening, qualification, esp. of wording. L16–E18.

1 A. BRIEN He was found guilty. I refused to make any statement in mitigation. R. ELLMANN They decided to ask for mitigation of his sentence on medical grounds. b J. BUTLER Mitigations and reliefs are provided .. for most of the afflictions in human life.

Mitnagged /mɪtˈnagɛd/ *n.* Pl. **-im** /-ɪm/. E20. [Heb. *miṯnaggēd* opponent.] A religious opponent of the Hasidim; any Jew who is not a Hasid.

mitochondrion /mʌɪtəˈkɒndrɪən/ *n.* Pl. **-dria** /-drɪə/. E20. [f. Gk *mitos* thread + *khondrion*, dim. of *khondros* granule, lump (of salt).] *Biol.* An organelle that primarily functions to store and release energy through the Krebs cycle and is present (usu. in great numbers) in the cytoplasm of most cells.

mitochondrial *a.* of or pertaining to a mitochondrion or mitochondria E20. **mitochondrially** *adv.* by, in, or through mitochondria L20.

mitogen /ˈmʌɪtədʒ(ə)n/ *n.* M20. [f. next + -GEN.] *Biol.* A substance or agent that induces or stimulates mitosis.

mitogeˈnetic, -genic *adjs.* inducing or stimulating mitosis M20.

mitosis /mʌɪˈtəʊsɪs/ *n.* Pl. **-toses** /-ˈtəʊsiːz/. L19. [f. Gk *mitos* thread of a warp + -OSIS.] *Cytol.* The process of division by which a cell nucleus gives rise to two daughter nuclei identical to the parent in number and size of chromosomes; an instance of this. Cf. MEIOSIS.

mitotic /mʌɪˈtɒtɪk/ *a.* L19. [f. prec. + -OTIC.] *Cytol.* Of, pertaining to, characterized by, or exhibiting mitosis.

mitotically *adv.* by mitosis L19.

mitraille /mitrɑːj, mɪˈtreɪl/ *n.* L18. [(O)Fr. = small money, pieces of metal, alt. of OFr. *mitaille*, f. *mite* rel. to MITE *n.*[2]] Cannon-shot consisting of masses of small missiles from a cannon; *spec.* small shot fired from a *mitrailleuse*.

mitrailleur /mitrɑjœːr/ *n.* Pl. pronounced same. M19. [Fr., f. *mitrailler* fire mitraille, f. as prec., + *-eur* -OR.] = MITRAILLEUSE.

mitrailleuse /mitrɑjøːz/ *n.* Pl. pronounced same. L19. [Fr., fem. of prec.] A breech-loading machine-gun with several barrels that can discharge small missiles rapidly and simultaneously in large quantities or singly in quick succession.

mitral /ˈmʌɪtr(ə)l/ *a.* & *n.* E17. [mod.L *mitralis*, f. L *mitra* MITRE *n.*[1]: see -AL[1].] A *adj.* 1 Of, pertaining to, or resembling a mitre. E17. 2 *Anat.* & *Med.* Designating or pertaining to the left auriculo-ventricular valve of the heart, so called from its shape. Also called *bicuspid valve*. L17. B *ellipt.* as *n.* The mitral valve. M19.

mitre /ˈmʌɪtə/ *n.*[1] Also ***miter**. ME. [OFr. f. L *mitra* f. Gk *mitra* belt, turban, perh. of Asian origin.] 1 *Eccl.* A tall deeply-cleft head-dress worn by a bishop or abbot, esp. as a symbol of episcopal office, forming in outline the shape of a pointed arch, and often made of embroidered white linen or satin. ME. b *The* episcopal office or dignity. LME. c *Hist.* A kind of head-dress resembling a bishop's mitre worn by women in medieval times. L19. 2a *Antiq.* A headband worn by women in ancient Greece. Also, an Asian head-dress, regarded by the Romans as effeminate when worn by men. LME. †b A kind of turban worn by Asian peoples. L16–M17. 3 *Heb. Antiq.* The ceremonial turban of a high priest. Also (*rare*), the head-dress of an ordinary priest. LME. 4 Any of numerous marine gastropods, esp. of the genus *Mitra*, with a shell resembling a mitre in shape. Also *mitre-shell*. M18.

1b LD MACAULAY Baxter .. refused the mitre of Hereford.

Comb.: *mitre-shell*: see sense 4 above; **mitrewort** any of various plants of the N. American and Asian genus *Mitella* (family Saxifragaceae) (also called *bishop's cap*) or (*false mitrewort*) the related N. American genus *Tiarella*.

mitre /ˈmʌɪtə/ *n.*[2] Also ***miter**. L17. [Perh. transf. use of prec.] 1a In full *mitre-joint*. A right-angled joint of wood or some other material, in which the angle made by the joined pieces is bisected by the line of junction. L17. b Either of the shaped ends or edges which form such a joint; a 45° angle such as these ends or edges have. E18. 2 In full *mitre-square*. A bevel with the blade set at 45°, or with two blades set at 45° to one another, for bevelling mitre-joints. L17. 3 In full *mitre-wheel*. Either of a pair of bevelled cog-wheels with teeth set at 45° and right-angled axes. M19.

Comb.: **mitre-bevel** = sense 2 above; **mitre-block, board, box** a block or frame of wood with slits for guiding a saw when cutting mitre-joints; **mitre-cramp**: for securing a glued mitre-joint while it is drying; **mitre gear** either of a pair of bevel gears of equal length with right-angled shafts; *mitre-joint*: see sense 1 above; **mitre-plane**: with an oblique surface for making mitre-joints; **mitre shooting-board**: used in chamfering the edges of wood; *mitre-square*: see sense 2 above; *mitre-wheel*: see sense 3 above.

mitre /ˈmʌɪtə/ *v.*[1]*t.* Also ***miter**. ME. [f. MITRE *n.*[1]] Confer or bestow a mitre on (a bishop or abbot), raise to a rank to which the dignity of wearing a mitre belongs.

mitre /ˈmʌɪtə/ *v.*[2] Also ***miter**. M18. [f. MITRE *n.*[2]] 1 *v.t.* Join with a mitre-joint; make a mitre-joint in; cut or shape to a mitre. Freq. as *mitred* ppl a. M18. 2 *v.i.* Form a mitre, meet in a mitre-joint. E19.

1 P. D. JAMES They made the bed .. flicking the sheets into place and neatly mitring each corner. *DIY Today* They have produced coving corners, thus eliminating the need to mitre pieces of coving together. 2 J. S. FOSTER Two parallel slopes with slopes normal to these .. which mitre or intersect.

mitring *n.* (*a*) the action of the vb; (*b*) the shaped end of a piece prepared to be mitred with another: M18.

mitred /ˈmʌɪtəd/ *a.* Also ***mitered**. LME. [f. MITRE *n.*[1], *v.*[1]: see -ED[2], -ED[1].] 1 Wearing or entitled to wear a mitre. LME. 2 Formed like a mitre. M16.

Special collocations: **mitred abbey** *Hist.* an abbey ruled by a mitred abbot. **mitred abbot** *Hist.* an abbot entitled to wear a mitre (and before the Reformation to be a member of the House of Lords).

mitriform /ˈmʌɪtrɪfɔːm/ *a.* M19. [mod.L *mitriformis*, f. *mitra* MITRE *n.*[1]: see -FORM.] *Bot.* & *Zool.* Resembling or shaped like a mitre; conical, hollow, and open at the base.

mitry /ˈmʌɪtri/ *a.* M19. [f. MITRE *n.*[1] + -Y[1].] *Her.* Charged with mitres.

Mitsein /ˈmɪtzʌɪn/ *n.* M20. [G, use as n. of inf. *mitsein*, f. *mit* with + *sein* be.] *Philos.* The concept of a person's being in its relationship with others.

mitsumata /mɪtsʊˈmɑːtə/ *n.* L19. [Jap.] A yellow-flowered deciduous shrub, *Edgeworthia papyrifera* (family Thymelaeaceae), native to China and widely cultivated in Japan, where its bast fibre is used to make paper.

mitt /mɪt/ *n.* Also **mit**. M18. [Abbrev. of MITTEN.] 1 A knitted or lace covering for the hand, leaving the fingers and thumb exposed; a fingerless glove. M18. 2 = MITTEN 1. E19. b *Baseball.* A protective glove worn by the catcher or first baseman. L19. 3 A hand. Usu. in *pl. slang.* L19.

1 SIR W. SCOTT The black silk gloves, or mitts. *Practical Photography* The . . digits of a market trader jutting . . out of fingerless mitts. 3 M. LEITCH Young Terry came into the room holding a full mug in his massive mitt.

Phrases: **the frozen mitt** *slang* an unfriendly reception; intentionally unfriendly treatment. **the glad mitt** *slang* a warm or friendly reception; = *the glad hand* s.v. GLAD *a.* **the icy mitt** = *the frozen mitt* above. *tip one's mitt*: see TIP *v.*[1]

Comb.: **mitt camp** *US slang* a palmist's or fortune-teller's establishment, tent, etc.; **mitt joint** *US slang* (*a*) a gambling house; (*b*) = *mitt camp* above; **mitt-reader** *US slang* a palmist, a fortune-teller.

mitted *a.* provided with or wearing mitts or mittens L19.

Mittagessen /ˈmɪtaːkˌɛsən/ *n.* Also ***m-***. L19. [G.] In Germany and Austria: a midday meal, lunch.

Mittel-European /ˌmɪt(ə)ljʊərəˈpiːən/ *a.* & *n.* M20. [f. G *mittel-* middle + EUROPEAN, after G *mittel-europäisch*.] A *adj.* Of or pertaining to central Europe, = *Middle-European* adj. s.v. MIDDLE *a.* & *n.* M20. B *n.* A native or inhabitant of central Europe. M20.

Mittelschmerz /ˈmɪtəlʃmɛrts/ *n.* L19. [G = middle pain.] *Med.* Pain in the lower abdomen regularly experienced by some women midway between successive menstrual periods and often thought to coincide with ovulation.

mitten /ˈmɪt(ə)n/ *n.* ME. [(O)Fr. *mitaine* = Prov. *mitana* (cf. med.L *mitan(n)a* f. Proto-Romance form w. the sense 'skin-lined glove cut off at the middle', f. L *medietas* half.] 1 A covering for the hand with one section for all four fingers and another for the thumb, worn for warmth or protection. Also (now *dial.*), a thick winter glove. ME. 2 *slang.* a Handcuffs. In *pl.* L16. b A hand. Usu. in *pl.* E19. c A boxing glove. Usu. in *pl.* M19. 3 = MITT 1. M18.

Phrases: **get the mitten** *slang* (*a*) (of a lover, partner, etc.) be jilted or rejected; (*b*) be dismissed from office, get the sack. **give** or **hand (a person) the mitten** *slang* end a relationship with (a person); jilt, reject.

Comb.: **mitten crab** a Chinese crab, *Eriocheir sinensis*, with long silky hairs on the pincers of the male, introduced into western European estuaries.

mittened *a.* provided with or wearing mittens E19.

mittimus /ˈmɪtɪməs/ *n.* & *v.* LME. [L, lit. 'we send', the first wd of the writ in Latin.] A *n.* 1 *Law.* †a A writ to transfer records from one court to another. LME–E18. b A warrant committing a person to prison. L16. 2 A dismissal from office; a notice to quit. Chiefly in *get one's mittimus*, be dismissed. *colloq.* & *dial.* L16. 3 A magistrate. *joc. rare.* M17. B *v.t.* Commit to prison by a warrant. *rare.* M18.

Mitty /ˈmɪti/ *n.* M20. [f. Walter *Mitty*, hero of James Thurber's short story *The Secret Life of Walter Mitty*.] A person who indulges in daydreams, esp. of a life much more exciting and glamorous than his or her real life.

Mitty'esque *a.* M20.

mitzvah /ˈmɪtsvə/ *n.* Pl. **-voth** /-vəʊt/. M17. [Heb. *miṣwāh* commandment.] *Judaism.* A precept; a duty, an obligation. Also, a good deed. Cf. BAR MITZVAH, BAT MITZVAH.

mivvy /ˈmɪvi/ *n. slang.* M19. [Origin unkn.] 1 A marble. M19. 2 A woman; the landlady of a lodging-house. *derog. arch.* L19. 3 A person who is adept at something; a genius, a marvel. E20.

Miwok /ˈmiːwɒk, ˈmʌɪ-/ *n.* & *a.* L19. [Miwok = people.] A *n.* Pl. **-s**, same. A member of a Penutian Indian people of California; the language of this people. L19. B *attrib.* or as *adj.* Of or pertaining to the Miwok or their language. E20.

mix /mɪks/ *n.* L16. [f. the vb.] 1 *gen.* The act or result of mixing; a mixture; the state of being mixed; a number of ingredients mixed together or intended for mixing. L16. 2 A mix-up, a muddle. *colloq.* L19. 3 A commercially prepared mixture of ingredients from which something, as a cake, concrete, etc. can be made. E20. 4 *Cinemat., Television, Audio*, etc. The action or process of combining or merging film pictures or soundtracks; a transition between two pictures or sounds in which one fades out as the other fades in, a dissolve. E20. b A version of a recording in which the component tracks are mixed in a different way; a recording made by mixing other recordings. L20. 5 The proportion or combination of different components that make up a product, plan, policy, or other integrated whole. M20. 6 = MIXER 5. M20.

1 W. D. HOWELLS You'll be ruined. Oh, poor Mr. Welling! Oh, what a fatal, fatal—mix! B. EMECHETA Ezechial was a typical product of this cultural mix. 3 B. MACDONALD I could use automatic biscuit mix for the crust. 4b N. SEDAKA The mixes did not sound particularly Top 40ish. *rough mix*: see ROUGH *a.* 5 *Broadcast* The editorial mix is likely to include personality pages . . and cartoon strips. *Lancaster Guardian* Without schools, villages lost their mix of age groups.

Comb.: **mixdown** *Audio* the process of mixing down a multi-track sound recording etc.; an instance of this; a recording so produced. **mix-up** the state of being mixed up; *spec.* a state of confusion, a muddle, a mess; a misunderstanding; a fight.

mix /mɪks/ *v.* Pa. t. & pple **mixed**, **†mixt**. L15. [Back-form. f. MIXED.] 1 *v.t.* Put together or combine (two or more substances or things) so that the constituents of each are diffused among those of the other or others; mingle, blend. L15. b *fig.* Combine or blend (different principles, qualities, etc.). L16. c Prepare (a compound, cocktail, etc.) by combining various ingredients. L16. †d Add as an ingredient, intersperse. (Foll. by *to*.) E17–M18. 2 *v.t.* a Unite (a person, oneself) *with* another in dealings or acquaintance. Formerly also, join in sexual intercourse. Now *rare.* M16. b Unite (the eyes) in an interchange of glances. *rare* (Shakes.). L16. c Join and clasp (hands). *rare.* E18. 3 *v.i.* a Have sexual intercourse *with*. Now *rare.* E17. b Move socially *in*, †*among*; keep company *with*, socialize *with*. M17. c Be involved (*in*), participate (*in*). E19. d Be sociable. E19. 4 *v.i.* a Be mixed, admit of being mixed; combine, blend together; go (well or badly) *with*. M17. b Of the eyes: interchange glances. *poet.* L19. 5 *v.t.* & *i.* Cross in breeding. M18. 6 *Cinemat., Television*, etc. a *v.t.* Blend (two pictures or sounds) temporarily by fading one out as the other is faded in. E20. b *v.t.* Combine (two or more sound signals) into one, with or without modulation, in a mixer. E20. c *v.i.* Pass from one picture or sound to another by fading one out as the other is faded in. (Foll. by *from, to*.) M20. 7 *v.t. Audio.* Produce by combining a number of separate recordings or tracks. L20.

1 M. W. MONTAGU Their own hair . . they mix with a great deal of false. J. BAXTER Mix a small quantity of salt with the food. c A. CROSS Kate, mixing herself another martini. 3b B. EMECHETA You can keep to yourself, you don't have to mix with them. d M. SPARK In no great hurry for the flat, preferring hotel life where one need not mix. 4a GOLDSMITH Sending up a part of their substance by evaporation, to mix in this great alembic. R. DEACON Espionage and politics do not mix.

Phrases & comb.: **mix and match** select and combine complementary or coordinating items, as clothing, china, etc., so as to form a matching collection; (of an item) coordinate with other related items. **mix-and-match** *a.* & *n.* (*a*) *adj.* suitable for or selected by mixing and matching, complementary, coordinating, assorted; (*b*) *n.* an instance of mixing and matching, a combination of complementary or coordinating items. **mix-down** the action or an act of mixing down a multi-track recording; a recording made in this way. **mix it** *slang* start fighting; fight, cause trouble. **mix it up** *slang* fight vigorously. **mix one's drinks** drink different kinds of alcoholic liquor in close succession; become intoxicated by this means.

With advs. in specialized senses: **mix down** convert (a multi-track sound recording or multiple signal) to one consisting of fewer tracks or components. **mix in** join in, take part, be sociable. **mix up** (*a*) mix thoroughly; (*b*) combine unsuitably or confusingly; confuse, mistake; (*c*) in *pass.*, be involved *in* or associated *with* (esp. something shady or discreditable).

mixable *a.* M19. **mixible** *a.* (long *rare*) E17. **mixy** *a.* (*a*) adapted for mixing; (*b*) *colloq.* sociable: E20.

mixed /mɪkst/ *a.* Also **†mixt**. LME. [(O)Fr. *mixte* (spec. in AN law phr. *accioun mixte* action partly real, partly personal) f. L *mixtus* pa. pple of *miscere* mingle, mix, rel. to Gk *misgein*, *mignunai*: see -ED[1].] 1 *Law* (now *Hist.*). Of an action: of the nature of both a real and a personal action. LME. 2 Mingled or blended together; formed by the mingling or combining of different substances, individuals, etc. LME. 3 Consisting of different or dissimilar elements or qualities; not of one kind, not pure or simple. LME. 4 Containing people from various backgrounds; unrestricted. Also, containing people of doubtful character or status. E17. 5 For, involving, or comprising both sexes. M17. 6 Of a science: involving or dealing with matter, not pure or simply theoretical. Now *rare* or *obs.* M17. 7 *Phonet.* = CENTRAL *a.* 4. M19. 8 Mentally confused, muddled, esp. through drink. *colloq.* L19.

2 E. PIZZEY Get two bunches of mixed summer flowers. 3 L. MACNEICE None of our hearts are pure, we always have mixed motives. A. W. CARDINALL The area . . is peopled by mixed races. *Guardian* Unstreaming, or teaching children in mixed ability groups. *Shetland Times* The new far-reaching controls on fishing activity . . have had a mixed welcome. 4 S. MIDDLETON 'It's a decent district, isn't it?' 'Yes. A bit mixed at the bottom end.' 5 *Times* University House . . became the first ever mixed students' hostel.

Special collocations & comb.: **mixed angle** (*obs.* exc. *Hist.*): formed by the intersection of a straight line and a curve. **mixed bag** a diverse assortment of people, items, etc. **mixed bathing** simultaneous bathing in the same place by people of both sexes. **mixed bed** a flower-bed containing an assortment of plants. **mixed blessing** a thing having advantages but also disadvantages. **mixed blood** (*a*) descent from two or more races; (*b*) a person of mixed descent. **mixed border** a long flower-bed containing a wide variety of different plants. **mixed bunch** = *mixed bag* above. **mixed company** (*a*) company comprising both sexes; (*b*) company comprising people of different backgrounds or characters. **mixed crystal** *Physical Chem.* a homogeneous crystal formed of more than one crystalline substance. **mixed doubles** a game of doubles in tennis, badminton, etc., in which each pair of players comprises a member of either sex. **mixed economy** an economic system containing both private and State enterprise. **mixed farming** farming which combines the raising of livestock and arable cultivation. **mixed feelings** conflicting emotions; a combination of pleasure and dismay. **mixed grill** a dish consisting of several different grilled items of food. **mixed language** a language made up of a mixture of elements from two or more other languages; a creolized language. **mixed-manned** *a.* (of a military force) comprising people of more than one nationality. **mixed marriage** a marriage between people of different races or religions. **mixed media** (*a*) the use of a variety of mediums in an entertainment, work of art, etc.; (*b*) = *mixed technique* below. **mixed-media** *a.* = MULTI-MEDIA. **mixed metaphor** a combination of two or more inconsistent metaphors. **mixed number** *Math.*: consisting of an integer and a fraction. **mixed-pressure** *a.* (of a steam turbine) powered by both high- and low-pressure steam. **mixed school**: in which girls and boys are taught together. **mixed technique** a technique in painting in which tempera and oils are combined. **mixed-traffic** *a.* (of a locomotive) suitable for both passenger and freight haulage. **mixed-up** (*a*) involved, intermingled; (*b*) *colloq.* mentally or emotionally confused; socially maladjusted.

mixedly *adv.* (now *rare*) L16. **mixedness** *n.* M17.

mixen /ˈmɪks(ə)n/ *n.* Now *arch.* or *dial.* [OE f. Gmc, rel. to OS, OHG, *mist* (G *Mist*), Goth. *maihstus* dung, ult. f. Gmc base meaning 'make water' (cf. OE *miċġe*, *migga* urine, OE *mīgan*, LG *mīgen*, ON *miga* urinate).] 1 A place where dung and refuse are laid; a dunghill. Also, a heap of dung, compost, etc., used for manure. OE. 2 (A term of abuse or reproach for) a woman or child. *dial.* M18.

mixer /ˈmɪksə/ *n.* E17. [f. MIX *v.* + -ER[1].] 1 A person who blends or mixes liquids, materials, etc.; *spec.* a person who mixes drinks, a bartender. E17. 2 A machine or device for mixing; *spec.* an electrical appliance for mixing foods. L19. b A container for mixing drinks; a cocktail-shaker. L19. 3a A person in respect of his or her ability to mix socially with others; a sociable person. L19. b A social gathering to enable people to get to know one another. *N. Amer. colloq.* E20. 4a *Cinemat., Television*, etc. A device designed to receive two or more separate signals, e.g. from microphones, and combine them (usu. in variable proportions) in a single output. Also, a person who operates such a device, responsible for balancing signal sources and shifting between sources. E20. b *Electronics.* A device that produces an output signal containing frequencies equal to the sum and the difference of the frequencies of two input signals. M20. 5 A soft drink with which an alcoholic drink is diluted, as soda water etc.; an alcoholic drink used in cocktails. M20. 6 A troublemaker. *slang.* M20.

3a A. STORR A child who is a poor mixer and cannot stand up for himself. R. DEACON He was a good mixer in all classes of society. b *New Yorker* He had married a girl he met at a mixer.

Comb.: **mixer tap** a tap through which both hot and cold water can be drawn at the same time, in any proportion.

Mix-Hellene /mɪkshɛˈliːn/ *n.* M19. [Gk *mixhellēn*, f. as MIXO- + HELLENE.] *Class. Hist.* A person of mixed Greek and barbarian descent.

mixing /ˈmɪksɪŋ/ *vbl n.* E16. [f. MIX *v.* + -ING[1].] The action of MIX *v.*

Comb.: **mixing desk** a console where sound signals are mixed during recording or broadcasting; **mixing valve** a valve in which separate supplies of hot and cold water are mixed together; a mixer tap.

mixis /ˈmɪksɪs/ *n.* M20. [Gk = mixing, (sexual) intercourse.] *Biol.* Sexual reproduction, esp. with alternation of different nuclear phases.

mixite /ˈmɪksʌɪt/ *n.* L19. [f. A. *Mixa*, 19th-cent. Czech mining official + -ITE[1].] *Min.* A hexagonal hydrated basic arsenate of copper and bismuth, usu. occurring as green fibrous incrustations.

Mixmaster /ˈmɪksmɑːstə/ *n.* Also **m-**. M20. [f. MIX *v.* + MASTER *n.*[1]] (Proprietary name for) a type of electrical food-mixer; *transf.* & *fig.* a machine or device with whirring blades, a thing constantly on the move.

Comb.: **mixmaster universe** *Astron.* a cosmological model in which the universe is made isotropic by continual expansions and contractions along randomly distributed directions.

mixo- /ˈmɪksəʊ/ *comb. form.* [Repr. Gk *mixo-*, f. base of *mignunai* to mix (cf. MIX *v.*): see -O-.] Used in the sense 'mixed'.

mixohaline /-ˈheɪlʌɪn/ *a.* [Gk *halinos* of salt] brackish M20. **mixotrophic** /-ˈtrəʊfɪk, -ˈtrɒfɪk/ *a.* (*Biol.*) designating, pertaining to, or characterized by a combination of autotrophic and heterotrophic nutrition E20. **mixotrophically** /-ˈtrəʊf-, -ˈtrɒf-/ *adv.* (*Biol.*) by mixotrophic nutrition L20.

mixolimnion /mɪksəˈlɪmnɪən/ *n.* Pl. **-nia** /-nɪə/. M20. [f. prec. + Gk *limnion* dim. of *limnē* lake.] The upper, freely circulating layer of a meromictic lake.

mixologist /mɪkˈsɒlədʒɪst/ *n. US slang.* M19. [f. MIX *n.* or *v.* + -OLOGIST.] A person who is skilled at mixing drinks.

mixolydian /mɪksəˈlɪdɪən/ *a.* L16. [Gk *mixoludios* half-Lydian: see MIXO-, LYDIAN.] *Mus.* Designating that mode which has G for its final and D for its dominant, or which is represented on the piano by the white notes from G to G. Also, designating the highest in pitch of the ancient Greek modes.

mixoploid /ˈmɪksəplɔɪd/ *a.* & *n.* M20. [f. MIXO- + -PLOID.] *Biol.* A *adj.* Composed of cells which are of differing ploidy or have differing numbers of chromosomes. M20. B *n.* A mixoploid organism. M20.

mixoploidy *n.* mixoploid condition M20.

†**mixt** *n.* L16–E19. [L *mixtum* neut. of *mixtus* mixed.] Something consisting of different elements mixed together; *esp.* a chemical compound.

†**mixt** *a.* var. of MIXED.

†**mixt** *v.* see MIX *v.*

mixte /mikst/ *a.* & *n.* Pl. of n. pronounced same. L20. [Fr. = mixed.] (Designating) a bicycle or bicycle frame having no crossbar but instead two thin tubes running from the head of the steering column to either side of the rear axle.

Mixtec /ˈmiːstɛk/ *n.* & *a.* Also (earlier) **Mixteca** /miːˈstɛkə/; **Mixteco** /miːˈstɛkəʊ/, pl. **-os**. L18. [Sp., f. Nahuatl *mixtecah* person from a cloudy place.] A *n.* 1 A member of a people of Central America. L18. 2 The language of this people. M19. B *attrib.* or as *adj.* Of or pertaining to the Mixtecs or their language. E20.

Miˈxtecan *n.* & *a.* (of or pertaining to) the Mixtec language M20.

mixtie-maxtie *a.* & *n.* var. of MIXTY-MAXTY.

mixtilinear /mɪkstɪˈlɪnɪə/ *a.* E18. [f. L *mixtus* MIXED + LINEAR, after *rectilinear.*] Formed or bounded by both straight and curved lines.

†**mixtion** *n.* LME–M18. [(O)Fr. *mistion* f. L *mixtio(n-)*, f. *mixt-*: see next, -ION.] = MIXTURE.

mixture /ˈmɪkstʃə/ *n.* LME. [Fr., or its source L *mixtura*, f. *mixt-* pa. ppl stem of *miscere* mix: see -URE.] I 1 A product of mixing; something mixed; a combination. LME. 2 A medicinal or other preparation consisting of two or more ingredients mixed together; *spec.* a liquid medicine as opp. to pills, powder, or other solid medicine. M16. 3 A variegated fabric, usu. of soft colouring. E18. 4 *Mus.* In full *mixture stop.* An organ-stop with several ranks of pipes. L18. 5 A blend of tea, tobacco, snuff, etc. M19. 6 *Chem.* The product of the mechanical mixing of substances without chemical change, as opp. to a compound. Also *mechanical mixture.* M19. 7a In an internal-combustion engine, the vaporized or gaseous fuel together with air that forms the explosive charge in the cylinder. L19. b A combination of petrol with a small proportion of oil, used as a combined fuel and lubricant in some two-stroke engines. M20.

1 N. ALGREN The other women regarded her with a strange mixture of admiration and pity. I. FLEMING The usual mixture of tourists and businessmen and local people coming home. P. CUTTING They bombed a mixture of military and civilian targets. 2 *Longman's Magazine* I took a sip of the horrid mixture. **the mixture as before** (an instruction on a medicine bottle) the same dose as previously; *fig.* something repeated or already encountered. 3 *heather mixture, Oxford mixture*, etc. 7a *lean mixture*: see LEAN *a.*

II †8 Sexual intercourse. L15–E18. 9 The action or an act of adding an ingredient; the presence of a diverse element in the composition of something. Also, an amount or proportion added; an admixture. E16. 10a The action, process, or fact of mixing or combining; an instance of this. M16. b A mixed state or condition. L16. 11 *Chem.* The mechanical mixing of two or more substances without chemical change, as opp. to chemical combination. M18.

9 B. KEACH Adulterating the Word of God by the Mixture of their own Fancies. A. DICKSON The soil in which there is a great mixture of moss. 10a J. TYNDALL From the intimate mixture of air and water we obtain foam.

mixty-maxty /mɪkstɪˈmaksti/ *a.* & *n. Sc.* & *dial.* Also **mixtie-maxtie**. L18. [Varied redupl. of *mixt* MIXED: see -Y[6], -IE.] A *adj.* Incongruously mixed; jumbled together, muddled. L18. B *n.* Something incongruously mixed; a confused mass, a heterogeneous mixture. E19.

miz /mɪz/ *n.* E20. [Abbrev. of MISTRESS *n.*] 1 Used as a title preceding a woman's name: Mrs, Miss. *Southern US.* E20. 2 = MS. L20.

mizen /ˈmɪz(ə)n/ *n.* Also **mizzen**. LME. [Fr. *misaine* (now foresail, foremast) f. It. *mezzana* use as n. of fem. of *mezzano* middle.] *Naut.* 1 More fully *mizen-sail.* The lowest fore-and-aft sail on the mizen-mast of a full-rigged ship. Formerly also, a similarly shaped principal sail in certain small craft. LME. 2 In full *mizen-mast.* The mast aft of the mainmast in a ship of three or more masts. LME.

Comb.: *mizen-mast*: see sense 2 above; *mizen-sail*: see sense 1 above; **mizen top** a platform near the head of the mizen mast; **mizen topmast** the mast next above the lower mizen mast; **mizen topsail** the sail above the mizen sail, set on the mizen topmast; **mizen yard** the yard on which the mizen sail is extended.

mizmaze /ˈmɪzmeɪz/ *n.* M16. [Varied redupl. of MAZE *n.*[1]] 1 A labyrinth, a maze. M16. 2 Mystification, bewildering delusion; a state of confusion. Chiefly *dial.* E17.

Mizo /ˈmiːzəʊ/ *n.* & *a.* M19. [Lushai, lit. 'highlander', f. *mi* person + *zo* hill.] A *n.* Pl. same, **-os**. A member of a people inhabiting the territory of Mizoram in NE India. M19. B *adj.* Of or pertaining to these people. M19.

Mizpah /ˈmɪzpə/ *a.* L19. [Heb. *Miṣpāh* place-name in ancient Palestine.] Designating a ring, locket, etc., given as an expression or token of association or remembrance, orig. and esp. one with 'Mizpah' inscribed on it (w. allus. to *Gen.* 31:49).

mizzen *n.* var. of MIZEN.

mizzle /ˈmɪz(ə)l/ *n.*[1] L15. [f. MIZZLE *v.*[1]] Fine rain, drizzle.

mizzle /ˈmɪz(ə)l/ *n.*[2] *slang.* E20. [f. MIZZLE *v.*[2]] A disappearance, a vanishing act.

do a mizzle depart suddenly, vanish.

mizzle /ˈmɪz(ə)l/ *v.*[1]*i.* LME. [Prob. f. LG *miseln* = Du. dial. *miezelen*, WFlem. *mizzelen, mijzelen*, frequent. (see -LE[3]) of the LG base repr. by Du. dial. *miesregen* drizzle, *miezig*, LG *misig* drizzling.] Rain in very fine drops, drizzle. Usu. *impers.* in *it mizzles, it is mizzling*, etc.

M. R. MITFORD It did not absolutely rain, it only mizzled. K. TENNANT A cold wind and a grey, mizzling rain.

mizzle /ˈmɪz(ə)l/ *v.*[2]*i. slang.* L18. [Origin unkn.] Disappear suddenly; decamp, vanish, take oneself off.

mizzler *n.* M19.

mizzle /ˈmɪz(ə)l/ *v.*[3]*i.* M20. [Perh. f. MOAN *v.* + GRIZZLE *v.*[2]] Complain, whimper; whine fretfully.

mizzly /ˈmɪzli/ *a.* M16. [f. MIZZLE *n.*[1] or *v.*[1] + -Y[1].] Of the nature of mizzle; marked by mizzling rain; drizzly.

mm /(ə)m/ *int.* Also **m'm**. E20. [Imit.] Expr. hesitation or inarticulate interrogation, assent, reflection, or satisfaction. Cf. UM *int.*

mna /mnɑː/ *n.* E17. [Gk.] = MINA *n.*[1]

M'Naghten rules, M'Naughten rules *n. phrs. pl.* vars. of MCNAUGHTEN RULES.

mneme /ˈniːmiː/ *n.* E20. [Gk *mnēmē* memory.] *Psychol.* & *Physiol.* The capacity for retaining after-effects of experience or stimulation. Also = MEMORY *trace.*

mnemic *a.* pertaining to, of the nature of, or involving mneme E20. **mnemically** *adv.* (*rare*) E20. **mnemicness** *n.* (*rare*) M20.

mnemon /ˈniːmɒn/ *n. rare.* M20. [f. as prec. + -ON.] *Psychol.* A unit of memory.

mnemonic /nɪˈmɒnɪk, niː-/ *a.* & *n.* M18. [med.L *mnemonicus* f. Gk *mnēmonikos* f. *mnēmōn, mnemon-* mindful, f. *mna-* base of *mnasthai* remember: see -IC.] A *adj.* 1 Intended or designed to aid the memory; of or pertaining to mnemonics. Also, (of a formula, code, etc.) easy to remember or understand. M18. 2 Of or pertaining to memory. E19.

1 J. AUEL His drawing was no more than a mnemonic aid to remind them of a place they knew. *Computing Equipment* Mnemonic option coding (opposed to numeric menus), and on-screen help messages. 2 *Gentleman's Magazine* The mnemonic power of the late Professor Porson.

B *n.* 1 A mnemonic device, formula, or code. M19. 2 = MNEMONICS. M19.

mnemonical *a.* = MNEMONIC *a.* 1 M17. **mnemonically** *adv.* M19. **mnemonician** /-ˈnɪʃ(ə)n/ *n.* (*rare*) = MNEMONIST M19. **ˈmnemonize** *v.t.* express by a mnemonic formula M19.

mnemonics /nɪˈmɒnɪks, niː-/ *n.pl.* (usu. treated as *sing.*). E18. [Gk *mnēmonika* neut. pl. of *mnēmonikos*: see prec., -IC.] The art of improving or developing the memory, esp. by artificial aids; a system of precepts and rules intended to aid or improve the memory.

mnemonist /ˈniːmənɪst/ *n.* M19. [f. MNEMONIC: see -IST.] An expert in mnemonics; a teacher of memory training and improvement; a person who exhibits his or her powers of memory.

mnemotechny /ˈniːmətɛkni/ *n.* M19. [f. as MNEME + Gk *-tekhnia*, *teknē* art: see -Y³.] = MNEMONICS.

mnemotechnic *a.* = MNEMONIC *a.* M19. **mnemotechnics** *n.pl.* = MNEMONICS M19.

mo /məʊ/ *n.*¹ *colloq.* Pl. **mos.** L19. [Abbrev. of MOMENT *n.*] A very short time, a moment.

I. WATSON If you'll hang on a mo, I'll take you myself.

mo /məʊ/ *n.*² *Austral.* & *NZ colloq.* Pl. **mos.** L19. [Abbrev.] = MOUSTACHE.

mo /məʊ/ *adv.*, *n.*³, & *a. obs.* exc. *Sc.* & *north.* [OE *mā* = OFris. *mā(r*, *mēr*, OS, OHG *mēr* (MDu. *mee*, G *mehr*), ON *meir*, Goth. *mais*, f. Gmc compar. f. IE.] A *adv.* †1 In or to a greater degree, extent, or quantity. OE–E16. 2 Longer, further, again, besides. Chiefly in *any mo*, *ever mo*, *never mo*, *no mo.* OE. B *n.* †1 Something in addition; an additional quantity or amount. OE–ME. 2 A greater number; more individuals of the kind specified or implied. (Foll. by *of*, *than.*) OE. 3 Other individuals of the kind specified; others in addition to those mentioned. OE. C *adj.* = MORE *a.* OE.

-mo /məʊ/ *suff.* [The final syllable of terms derived from the abl. sing. masc. of L ordinal numerals.] Forming ns. denoting a book size by the number of leaves into which a sheet of paper has been folded, as *duodecimo*, *sextodecimo*, etc., also read or written as *12mo*, *16mo*, etc.

moa /ˈməʊə/ *n.* M19. [Maori.] A large flightless bird of the genus *Dinornis*, resembling an ostrich, formerly inhabiting New Zealand and now extinct.

Comb.: **moa-hunter** a member of an early Maori culture in New Zealand distinguished by the hunting of moas.

Moabite /ˈməʊəbʌɪt/ *a.* & *n.* ME. [L *Moabita* (Gk *Mōabitēs*, repr. Heb. *mô'ābî*), f. *Moab*: see below, -ITE¹.] A *adj.* Of or pertaining to Moab, an ancient region east of the Dead Sea, or its inhabitants. ME.

Moabite stone a monument erected by Mesha king of Moab, *c*850 BC, which has an early example of an inscription in the Moabite language.

B *n.* A member of a Semitic people living in Moab. LME.

Moabitess *n.* (*rare*) a Moabite woman M16. **Moabitish** *a.* of, pertaining to, or resembling the Moabites E17.

moan /məʊn/ *n.* ME. [Ult. f. Gmc base (perh. repr. in OE) whence also MEAN *v.*² Cf. MEAN *n.*²] 1 Complaint, lamentation; a complaint, a lament. ME. †b A state of grief or lamentation. E16–M17. 2a A long low mournful sound indicative of physical or mental suffering or physical pleasure. L17. b A low plaintive sound made by wind, water, etc. E19. 3 A grievance, a grumble; an airing of complaints. E20.

1 TENNYSON And oft I heard the tender dove, In firry woodlands making moan. 2a I. MURDOCH The rhythmical moan with which the . . sufferer tries to soothe the . . pain. C. JOHNSON I heard the squeaking of mattress springs, . . and at last a venereal moan. 3 *Camera Weekly* Another moan has been that the range of lenses . . is . . limited.

moan /məʊn/ *v.* LME. [f. the n.] 1 *v.t.* †a *refl.* Lament or bewail one's lot. LME–M17. b Complain of, lament for; bemoan, bewail. L15. 2 *v.t.* Condole with (a person); pity. *obs.* exc. *Sc.* LME. 3 *v.i.* a Lament. Now *arch.* & *poet.* M16. b Grumble, grouse, complain. *colloq.* E20. 4 *v.i.* a Make a low mournful sound indicative of physical or mental suffering or physical pleasure. E18. b Of wind, water, etc.: make a low plaintive sound. E19. 5 *v.t.* Utter with a moan or moans. E19.

1b THACKERAY She . . bitterly moaned the fickleness of her Matilda. 3a G. BRIMLEY Listen to the fierce Achilles moaning for his lost mistress. b A. HUTSCHNECKER He moaned about what a hard day he had had. *Woman's Own* Sitting around moaning has never been her style. 4b A. B. DAVIDSON You hear . . the forests moan. 5 *Reader's Digest* 'I had so many things planned for today,' she moaned.

moaner *n.* (*colloq.*) E20.

moanful /ˈməʊnfʊl, -f(ə)l/ *a.* Now *rare.* L16. [f. MOAN *n.* + -FUL.] (Of a person, an action, etc.) full of moaning or lamentation; expressing grief; (of a melody, song, etc.) plaintive, mournful.

moanfully *adv.* (long *rare*) E17.

moaning /ˈməʊnɪŋ/ *ppl a.* L18. [f. MOAN *v.* + -ING².] That moans.

moaning minnie *colloq.* (*a*) a kind of German trench mortar; a bomb from such a mortar; (*b*) an air-raid siren; (*c*) a moaner, a grouser.

moaningly *adv.* E19.

moar /mɔː/ *n.* M17. [Manx = Ir. & Gael. *maor.*] A government officer in the Isle of Man.

moat /məʊt/ *n.* & *v.* Also †**mote.** LME. [Var. of MOTE *n.*²] A *n.* 1 A deep and wide defensive ditch surrounding a town, castle, etc., and usually filled with water. LME. 2 A pond, a lake. *obs.* exc. *dial.* LME. B *v.t.* Surround with or as with a moat, ditch, or trench. LME.

mob /mɒb/ *n.*¹ L17. [Abbrev. of MOBILE *n.*²] 1 A disorderly or riotous crowd; a rabble. L17. 2 *The* ordinary people, *the* populace, *the* masses. L17. †3 Ordinary or disorderly people forming a crowd. L17–L18. 4 An assemblage of people; a multitude, a crowd, a group. L17. b A battalion, a regiment; a military unit. *Mil. slang.* E20. 5a A gang of thieves or pickpockets working together; a member of such a gang. *slang.* M19. b More fully *the mob.* An organized association of violent criminals; *spec.* (**M-**), a society similar to the Mafia, controlling organized crime in the US and elsewhere. *slang.* E20. 6 A flock or herd of animals. *Austral.* M19.

1 B. MASON A lawless mob . . looting and defying the police. J. NAGENDA I've just escaped death at the hands of a mob. 4 *transf.*: E. YOUNG 'Twill not make one amid a mob of thoughts. b J. HIGGINS Her husband's a major with your old mob. 5a *swell mob*: see SWELL *a.* 2. b *Guardian* The Mob from its Chicago headquarters runs the subcontinent. M. ATWOOD It was the mob who put Ellis up to making the bust. 6 B. WANNAN He met a drover leisurely following a mob of sheep.

Comb.: **mob-handed** *a.* & *adv.* (*colloq.*) in considerable numbers; **mob law** law imposed and enforced by a mob; **mobsman** a member of a mob; a mobster; **mob rule** rule imposed and enforced by a mob.

mobbism *n.* mobbish behaviour L18.

mob /mɒb/ *n.*² *obs.* exc. *Hist.* M17. [Var. of MAB.] †1 A prostitute, a promiscuous woman. *slang.* M–L17. †2 A négligé, a dishabille. M17–E18. 3 More fully *mob-cap.* A large indoor cap covering all the hair, worn by women in the 18th and early 19th cents. M18.

†**mob** *v.*¹ Infl. **-bb-.** M17. [f. MOB *n.*²: cf. earlier MOBLE. In sense 2 assoc. w. MOB *n.*¹] 1 *v.t.* Muffle the head of (a person); dress untidily. Also foll. by *up.* M17–M18. 2 *v.i.* & *t.* (w. *it*). Go in disguise to the unfashionable part of a theatre etc. L17–M19.

mob /mɒb/ *v.*² Infl. **-bb-.** E18. [f. MOB *n.*¹] 1 *v.t.* a Crowd round or press unduly upon in order to attack or admire; (of a mob) attack. E18. b Force (a person) *into* an action etc. or drive *from* a place by crowding round and being oppressive. Now *rare.* E18. c Of a group of birds: fly noisily and aggressively close to (a predator etc.). E20. 2 *v.i.* Form a mob, congregate in a mob. E18.

1a R. K. NARAYAN You will be mobbed and unable to leave the place. D. JOHNSON The American Embassy was being mobbed.

mobbed *a.* crowded, thronging M19. **mobber** *n.* M18. **mobbing** *n.* (*a*) the action of the vb; (*b*) *Sc. Law* violent or riotous action performed with others for a common illegal purpose: L18.

mobbie /ˈmɒbi, ˈməʊbi/ *n.* Also **mobby.** M17. [Carib *mabi* (drink made from) sweet potato. See also MAUBY.] 1 A West Indian alcoholic drink made either from sweet potatoes or from sugar, ginger, and other ingredients. M17. 2 The juice from apples and peaches, used in making brandy; apple and peach brandy. *US.* Now *rare.* E18.

mobbish /ˈmɒbɪʃ/ *a.* L17. [f. MOB *n.*¹ + -ISH¹.] Resembling or characteristic of a mob; disorderly, tumultuous. Formerly also, characteristic of or appealing to the mob or the ordinary people; common.

mobbishly *adv.* E18. **mobbishness** *n.* E20.

mobby *n.* var. of MOBBIE.

mobile /ˈməʊbɪl/ *n.*¹ Now *rare.* LME. [Fr. (in *premier mobile* etc.) f. L *mobile* neut. of *mobilis*: see MOBILE *a.*] 1 = PRIMUM MOBILE 1. Chiefly w. *first*, *grand*, *great*, etc. LME. 2 *Metaphysics.* A body in motion or capable of movement. L17.

mobile /ˈməʊbɪliː/ *n.*² *arch.* E17. [L *mobile* (*vulgus*) lit. 'the excitable crowd'.] In full (*rare*) *mobile vulgus* /ˈvʌlgʌs/. = MOB *n.*¹ 2.

mobile /ˈməʊbʌɪl/ *n.*³ M20. [f. MOBILE *a.*] 1 A decorative structure usu. consisting of hanging pieces of metal, plastic, etc., which can each move and turn freely. M20. 2 *Mus.* A musical composition consisting of separate units which can be arranged in a variety of ways. M20. 3 *ellipt.* a A mobile canteen. M20. b A mobile police patrol. L20.

1 M. GEE She brought me a mobile of . . fishes and hung it . . over my bed.

mobile /ˈməʊbʌɪl/ *a.* L15. [(O)Fr. f. L *mobilis*, f. *movere* MOVE *v.*: see -ILE.] 1 Capable of movement; movable; not fixed or stationary. L15. 2 Characterized by facility or versatility of movement; *spec.* (of facial features) expressive, that can easily change in expression. M19. 3 Of troops, a police patrol, etc.: that may be easily and rapidly moved from place to place. L19. 4 *Sociol.* (Of a person) able to move into different social levels or to change environment or field of employment; (of a society) not rigidly stratified, able to accommodate social or professional movement. E20. 5 Of a shop, library, or other facility: accommodated in a vehicle so as to be transportable and serve different places. M20.

1 J. G. WOOD The hind toe of each foot is very mobile. T. H. HUXLEY The mobile liquid passes into a compact rigid solid. 2 N. HAWTHORNE This idea filled her mobile imagination with agreeable fantasies. J. HIGGINS He was handsome . . with a mobile, intelligent mouth. 4 E. GELLNER Whether the rulers are . . able to run a mobile society . . in which rulers and ruled can merge. **downwardly mobile** tending to decline in social and professional status. **upwardly mobile** improving or ambitious to improve one's social and professional status. 5 *New Statesman* Feeding centres and mobile canteens.

Special collocations: **mobile home** a large transportable structure, as a large caravan, set up permanently and used as living accommodation. **mobile phone** = *mobile telephone* below. **mobile sculpture** a sculpture having moving parts. **mobile telephone** a telephone which needs no external wire and can be carried around, a portable radio telephone.

Mobilian /məʊˈbɪlɪən/ *n.* & *a.* M19. [Perh. f. *Mobile* a town in Alabama, USA + -IAN.] (Designating or pertaining to) a lingua franca or trade language formerly used in south-eastern N. America.

mobiliary /məʊˈbɪlɪəri/ *a.* L17. [Fr. *mobiliaire*, f. L *mobilis*: see MOBILE *a.*: see -ARY¹.] 1 Of a court or legal procedure in the Channel Islands: of or pertaining to movable property. L17. 2 Of or pertaining to household furniture. M19. 3 *Mil.* Of or pertaining to mobilization. L19.

mobilisation *n.*, **-ise** *v.* vars. of MOBILIZATION, -IZE.

mobilism /ˈməʊbɪlɪz(ə)m/ *n.* M20. [Fr. *mobilisme*, f. as MOBILE *a.*: see -ISM.] *Geol.* (Belief in) the theory that the continents undergo lateral movement and deformation.

mobilist *n.* & *a.* (*a*) *n.* a believer in the theory of continental drift; (*b*) *adj.* of or pertaining to mobilism or mobilists: L20.

mobility /məʊˈbɪlɪti/ *n.*¹ LME. [(O)Fr. *mobilité* f. L *mobilitas*, f. *mobilis*: see MOBILE *a.*, -ITY.] 1 Ability to move or to be moved; ease or freedom of movement. LME. 2 Ability or tendency to change easily or quickly; changeableness; *spec.* (of facial features) facility of change of expression, expressiveness. M16. 3 *Sociol.* The ability or potential to move between different social levels, fields of employment, etc. Also *social mobility.* L18. 4 *Physics* etc. a Freedom of movement of the particles of a fluid. E19. b The degree to which a charge carrier moves in a definite direction in response to an electric field, usu. expressed as the average speed (cm/sec) in a field of one volt per cm divided by the net number of charges on the carrier. L19.

1 J. BERNSTEIN Organs adapted for touching are endowed with the greatest mobility. W. S. CHURCHILL The accident which I suffered .. has greatly decreased my mobility. 2 M. HALE Daily observe in our selves a strange mobility .. in our Imaginative .. Faculty. 3 *upward mobility*: see UPWARD *a.*

Comb.: **mobility allowance** a social-security benefit payable to a disabled person to assist with the cost of travel.

mobility /məʊˈbɪlɪti/ *n.*[2] Now *rare*. L17. [f. MOBILE *n.*[2], MOB *n.*[1], after *nobility*.] *The* mob; *the* ordinary people.

mobilization /ˌməʊbɪlʌɪˈzeɪʃ(ə)n/ *n.* Also **-isation**. L18. [Fr. *mobilisation*, f. as next: see -ATION.] The action or process of mobilizing something or someone; the fact of being mobilized.

Economist The task of the planner is the more effective mobilisation of all economic resources. S. G. CHANEY Vitamin A is also apparently required for mobilization of iron from the liver. *Armed Forces* A dogfight between Israeli and Syrian aircraft was used as an excuse for Syrian mobilisation.

mobilizational *a.* L20.

mobilize /ˈməʊbɪlʌɪz/ *v.* Also **-ise**. M19. [Fr. *mobiliser*, f. as MOBILE *a.*: see -IZE.] 1 *v.t.* Make movable or capable of movement; bring into circulation. M19. b *Med.* Free or detach surgically. L19. c Make (a substance) able to be transported by or as a liquid. L19. 2 *v.t.* & *i.* Prepare (orig. troops, an army) for action or active service; make or become ready for action. M19.

2 W. S. CHURCHILL Would it not be helpful to call up the reserves and mobilize the TA? H. MACMILLAN Israel mobilised and .. invaded the Sinai peninsula. A. HUTSCHNECKER Active hope .. mobilizes an individual's vast energies.

mobilizable *a.* L19.

Möbius /ˈməːbɪəs/ *n.* E20. [August Ferdinand *Möbius* (1790–1868), Ger. mathematician.] *Möbius strip, band*, etc., a surface having only one side and one edge, formed by twisting one end of a rectangular strip through 180 degrees and joining it to the other end.

moble /ˈmɒb(ə)l/ *v.t.* Now *rare* or *obs.* E17. [Frequent. of MOB *v.*[1] (though recorded earlier): see -LE[3].] Muffle the head or face of (a person). Usu. foll. by *up*.

mobocracy /mɒbˈɒkrəsi/ *n.* M18. [f. MOB *n.*[1]: see -CRACY.] 1 Mob rule, government by a mob. M18. 2 The mob or ordinary people as a ruling body; a ruling mob. M18.

ˈmobocrat *n.* a person who advocates mobocracy, a demagogue L18. **moboˈcratic** *a.* L18.

mobster /ˈmɒbstə/ *n. slang.* E20. [f. MOB *n.*[1] + -STER, after *gangster*.] A member of a group of criminals; a gangster.

moc /mɒk/ *n. N. Amer. colloq.* M20. [Abbrev.] = MOCCASIN.

†**Moca** *n.* var. of MOKO *n.*[1]

mocamp /ˈməʊkamp/ *n.* M20. [f. MO(TOR *n.* + CAMP *n.*[2]] A camp-site which can accommodate tents, caravans, etc., and has various amenities.

moccasin /ˈmɒkəsɪn/ *n.* E17. [Virginia Algonquian *mockasin*, and in other N. American Indian langs.] 1 a A kind of soft leather shoe, worn by N. American Indians, trappers, etc. E17. b A soft informal shoe resembling this. L19. 2 A venomous N. American crotaline snake of the genus *Agkistrodon*; *spec.* (more fully *water moccasin*) the semi-aquatic *A. piscivorus* of the southern US (also called *cotton-mouth* (*moccasin*)). L18.

Comb.: **moccasin flower, plant** *N. Amer.* a lady's slipper orchid, esp. the pink-flowered *Cyripedium acaule*; **moccasin snake** = sense 2 above; **moccasin telegraph** *N. Amer.* a rapid and often surreptitious means of transmitting information; a bush telegraph.

moccasined *a.* wearing or provided with moccasins E19.

Mocha /ˈmɒkə/ *n.*[1] Also **m-**. L17. [Prob. f. as next.] 1 In full *Mocha stone*. Moss agate or a similar form of chalcedony with dendritic markings. L17. 2 (**m-**.) Any of various brown and grey geometrid moths of the genus *Cyclophora*. Also †*mocha stone*. L18. 3 A type of English pottery, made from the late 18th to the early 20th cent., with coloured patterned bands on a white or cream body. M19.

mocha /ˈmɒkə/ *n.*[2] & *a.* L18. [*Mocha*, a port in Yemen on the Red Sea.] A *n.* 1 a A fine quality coffee, orig. produced in Yemen. Also *mocha coffee*. L18. b A flavouring made from this, often with chocolate added, used in cakes etc. L19. c The colour of mocha coffee; a dark brown colour. L19. 2 A soft kind of sheepskin. L19.

B *adj.* Of mocha; *spec.* flavoured with mocha. L19.

mocha brown = sense A.1c above.

mochi /ˈmɒtʃi/ *n.* Pl. same. E17. [Jap.] A cake made from glutinous rice, steamed and pounded.

Mochica /məˈtʃiːkə/ *a.* & *n.* Also †**Moxa**. M19. [Sp., f. an Indian wd: cf. *Moche* an archaeological site and valley on the north-west coast of Peru.] A *adj.* Of or pertaining to a pre-Inca people living on the Peruvian coast, or their language. M19. B *n.* Pl. same. A member of this people; their language. L19.

¶Also called *Yunca*.

Mochican *a.* & *n.* M20.

mock /mɒk/ *n.* LME. [f. the vb or (sense 4) the adj.] 1 a A derisive action or speech. Now *rare*. LME. b Derision, mockery. *rare*. M16. 2 A thing to be derided; something deserving scorn. L15. 3 The action of mocking or imitating someone or something; an imitation, a sham. Now *rare*. M17. 4 In *pl.* Mock examinations. M20.

2 G. GREENE He has become the mock of all his contemporaries. 4 F. MOUNT Emma's done brilliantly in her mocks.

Phrases: **make (a) mock of** ridicule. **put a** or **the mock on** *Austral. slang* put a stop to.

Comb.: **mock-bird** *US* a mockingbird.

mockage *n.* (now *rare*) mockery, ridicule, derision; the fact or condition of being mocked; an object of mockery: L15.

mock /mɒk/ *attrib. a.* M16. [Partly f. the n., partly f. stem of the vb in comb. w. an object.] 1 Sham, imitation, esp. without intention to deceive; pretended, fake; *spec.* (of an examination) set to give practice for a specified more serious examination. M16. 2 In names of plants etc.: = FALSE *a.* 7. M16.

1 B. PYM It was quite an imposing façade, mock Palladian. ALAN BENNETT He's doing his mock A levels next week. RACHEL ANDERSON Humphrey .. rolled his eyes upward in mock disapproval.

Special collocations: **mock auction** (*a*) a Dutch auction; (*b*) an auction of worthless goods, in which false bids are made in order to elicit genuine bids from others. **mock auctioneer** the auctioneer at a mock auction. *mock* CROC. **mock goose** (now *rare*) leg of pork cooked to resemble goose. **mock lead** = BLENDE. **mock moon** = PARASELENE. **mock-nightingale** *dial.* the blackcap, *Sylvia atricapilla*. **mock olive** any of various Australian trees of the genus *Notelaea*, of the olive family, with succulent fruit and hard wood. **mock orange** (*a*) a philadelphus; (*b*) *Austral.* an evergreen shrub, *Pittosporum undulatum* (family Pittosporaceae), with fragrant flowers. **mock privet** = PHILLYREA. **mock sun** = PARHELION. **mock turtle soup** soup made from a calf's head etc. to resemble turtle soup.

mock /mɒk/ *v.* LME. [OFr. *mo(c)quer* (mod. *se moquer de* laugh at) deride, jeer, f. Proto-Romance base repr. also by It. dial. *moka*, Sp. *mueca* grimace, Port. *moca* derision.] 1 *v.t.* Hold up to ridicule; deride with scornful words or gestures; scoff at. LME. b Defy, flout. Now *rare*. M16. 2 *v.i.* a Use ridicule; act or speak so as to show scorn; jeer, scoff. (Foll. by *at*, †*with*.) LME. †b Jest, trifle. LME–E17. 3 *v.t.* Deceive, delude, befool; tantalize, disappoint. LME. 4 *v.t.* a Ridicule by imitation; mimic contemptuously. L16. †b Simulate, make a false pretence of. *rare* (Shakes.). L16–E17. 5 *v.t.* Foll. by *up*: make a mock-up of; imitate, contrive. E20.

1 T. GRAY These hated walls that seem to mock my shame. J. WILSON A fiend .. Come here to mock .. My dying agony. 2 G. HARRIS The jangling of the keys at his waist seemed to mock at him. 4a S. HASTINGS Mocking everything and everybody in her witty .. high-pitched way.

mockable *a.* E17. **mockingly** *adv.* in a mocking manner M16.

†**mockado** *n.* & *a.* M16. [App. alt. of It. †*mocaiardo* mohair. In sense A.2 a misunderstanding, assoc. w. *mock(ery)* etc.] A *n.* Pl. **-o(e)s**. 1 A wool velvet, usu. of inferior quality, formerly used for clothing. M16–M17. 2 Mockery. Only in M18. B *attrib.* or as *adj.* 1 Made of this fabric. L16–M17. 2 Inferior. L16–E17.

mocker /ˈmɒkə/ *n.*[1] LME. [f. MOCK *v.* + -ER[1].] 1 A person who mocks, derides, or scoffs. LME. 2 A person who deceives or deludes. Long *rare* or *obs.* M16. 3 A mockingbird. *US*. L18. 4 (A cause of) bad luck; a thing that thwarts a person. Chiefly in *put the mockers on*, (*a*) bring bad luck to; (*b*) put a stop to. *slang*. E20.

1 J. PARKER Even the mocker may find his way into the church. *transf.*: AV *Prov.* 20:1 Wine is a mocker, strong drinke is raging.

Comb.: **mockernut** a N. American hickory, *Carya tomentosa* (more fully *mockernut hickory*); the fruit of this, a large nut with a small kernel.

mocker /ˈmɒkə/ *n.*[2] & *v. Austral.* & *NZ slang*. M20. [Origin unkn.] A *n.* Clothing, dress. M20. B *v.t.* Dress *up*. Chiefly as *mockered-up* ppl a. M20.

mockery /ˈmɒk(ə)ri/ *n.* LME. [(O)Fr. *moquerie*, f. as MOCK *v.*: see -ERY.] 1 Derision, ridicule; a derisive utterance or action. LME. b A subject or occasion of derision or ridicule. M16. 2 Mimicry, imitation; a counterfeit or absurdly inadequate representation. L16. 3 (A) ludicrously futile action; something insultingly unfitting. E17.

1 V. S. PRITCHETT She laughed .. a high chilling laugh of mockery. b G. P. R. JAMES He made a mockery of the very acquirements he boasted of.

mocket /ˈmɒkɪt/ *n.* Long *obs.* exc. *dial.* M16. [Shortened alt. of MUCKENDER.] A bib, a handkerchief.

mock-heroic /mɒkhɪˈrəʊɪk/ *n.* & *a.* M17. [f. MOCK *a.* + HEROIC.] A *n.* An imitation in a burlesque manner of the heroic character or literary style; burlesquing heroic action. Usu. in *pl.* M17. B *adj.* Imitating in this way. M17.

mockingbird /ˈmɒkɪŋbəːd/ *n.* L17. [f. *mocking* pres. pple of MOCK *v.* + BIRD *n.*] Any of various long-tailed songbirds of the New World family Mimidae, spec. *Mimus polyglottos* of the southern US and Central America, noted for mimicking other birds' calls and other sounds. Also (*locally*), any of various other birds with imitative calls.

mock-up /ˈmɒkʌp/ *n.* E20. [f. MOCK *v.* + UP *adv.*[1]] 1 An experimental model or replica of a proposed aircraft, ship, or other construction. E20. 2 *transf.* & *fig.* A plan; an imitation. M20.

mocky /ˈmɒki/ *n.* & *a. US slang. derog.* M20. [Perh. f. Yiddish *makeh* a plague.] A *n.* A Jew. M20. B *attrib.* or as *adj.* Jewish. M20.

moco /ˈməʊkəʊ/ *n.* Pl. **-os**. M19. [Fr. Port. *mocó* f. Tupi.] The rock cavy, *Kerodon rupestris*.

mocock /məʊˈkɒk/ *n. N. Amer.* L18. [Amer. Indian.] A container like a basket made from birch bark.

moco-moco /məʊkəʊˈməʊkəʊ/ *n.* Also **mucka-mucka** /ˈmʌkəmʌkə/ & other vars. M18. [Galibi.] A tall aroid plant, *Montrichardia arborescens*, of Guyana and other parts of tropical America.

Mod /mɒd/ *n.*[1] L19. [Gael. *mòd* assembly, court f. ON *mót*: see MOOT *n.*[1]] A Highland meeting for Gaelic literary and musical competitions.

mod /mɒd/ *n.*[2] & *v. colloq.* M20. [Abbrev.] A *n.* A modification. M20. B *v.t.* Infl. **-dd-**. Modify. M20.

mod /mɒd/ *n.*[3] & *a.* M20. [Abbrev. of MODERN or MODERNIST.] A *n.* (Usu. **M-**.) A young person, esp. in the 1960s, belonging to or associated with a group aiming at stylishness and smart modern dress. Freq. contrasted w. *rocker*. M20.

B *adj.* Modern, sophisticated, stylish, esp. in dress. Also (**M-**), characteristic of or belonging to Mods. M20.

See also MOD CON.

mod /mɒd, 'mɒdjʊləʊ/ *prep.* M19. [Abbrev.] *Math.* = MODULO *prep.*

modacrylic /mɒdə'krɪlɪk/ *a.* & *n.* M20. [f. *modified* ppl a. of MODIFY + ACRYLIC.] (Designating or made of) a man-made fibre consisting of molecules with 35 to 85 per cent by mass of $CH_2CH(CN)$ units (derived from acrylonitrile).

modal /'məʊd(ə)l/ *a.* & *n.* M16. [med.L *modalis*, f. L *modus*: see MODE, -AL[1].] A *adj.* 1 *Logic.* Designating or pertaining to a proposition involving the affirmation of possibility, impossibility, necessity, or contingency, or in which the predicate is affirmed or denied of the subject with a qualification; (of an argument) containing a modal proposition as a premiss. M16. 2 *Law.* Of a legacy, contract, etc.: containing provisions defining the manner in which it is to take effect. Now *rare.* L16. 3 *Mus.* Of or pertaining to a musical mode; using a mode or modes. L16. 4 Of or pertaining to mode or form as contrasted with substance. E17. 5 *Gram.* a Of or pertaining to the mood of a verb; (of a verb) used in expressing a mood of another verb. L18. b Of a particle: denoting manner. L19. 6a *Statistics.* Of, pertaining to, or of the nature of a mode; (of a value etc.) that occurs most frequently in a sample or population. L19. b Representative, typical. M20. 7 *Petrogr.* Of or pertaining to the mode of a rock; as indicated by a mode. E20.

1 **modal logic** the branch of logic that deals with modal propositions. 5a E. H. GROUT The modal auxiliaries *may, might, can, could, must, ought*, . . give a cast to the whole sentence. 6a *Journal of Genetic Psychology* The modal age of the youngsters was 13. b R. K. MERTON The characteristic (modal) pattern for handling a standardized problem. **modal personality** an imaginary personality held to be typical of a particular society or group, esp. through possessing the modal characteristics of the population.

B *n.* 1 *Logic.* A modal proposition. L16. 2 *Gram.* A modal verb. M20.

modally *adv.* M17.

modalise *v.* var. of MODALIZE.

modalism /'məʊd(ə)lɪz(ə)m/ *n.* Also **M-**. M19. [f. prec. + -ISM.] *Chr. Theol.* The doctrine that the three persons of the Trinity are merely three different modes or aspects of the divine nature; Sabellianism.

modalist *n.* & *a.* (*a*) *n.* a person who holds or professes modalism; (*b*) *adj.* = MODALISTIC: M19. **moda'listic** *a.* of or pertaining to modalism or modalists L19.

modality /məʊ'dalɪtɪ/ *n.* E17. [med.L *modalitas*, f. as MODAL *a.*: see -ITY.] 1 *gen.* The quality or fact of being modal; a modal quality or circumstance; the modal attributes of something. E17. 2 *Logic.* a The fact of being a modal proposition or syllogism. Also, a qualification which makes a proposition modal. E17. b The feature of a judgement defined by its classification as problematic, assertoric, or apodictic. M19. 3 *Psychol.* a A category of sensation, a sense (as sight, hearing). Formerly also, a qualitative aspect of a particular category of sensation. L19. b An attribute or trait of personality. M20. 4 *Gram.* The property of a verb or verbal form that is represented or distinguished by its mood. E20. 5a *Med.* A method or technique of treatment, *esp.* one not involving drugs. M20. b In diplomacy, politics, etc.: a procedure, a method. M20. c A mode of action or behaviour. M20.

1 J. NORRIS We cannot conceive a circle as being distinct from extension whose modality it is. 3a G. HUMPHREY Sensory presentation of various modalities—auditory, kinaesthetic, and so on. 5a *Muscle & Fitness* Sensible modalities such as the application of ice and heat are what the joint . . needs to heal. b G. F. KENNAN The modalities of German unification must flow from the will of the German people. c N. PODHORETZ A Jewish survivalist . . tolerant of any modality of Jewish existence . . identifiably Jewish.

modalize /'məʊd(ə)lʌɪz/ *v.t.* Also **-ise**. M19. [f. MODAL + -IZE.] Chiefly *Logic.* Make modal.

modali'zation *n.* M20.

mod con /mɒd 'kɒn/ *n. phr. colloq.* M20. [Abbrev. of *modern convenience.*] An amenity, appliance, etc., typical of a well-equipped modern home; any gadget or labour-saving device. Usu. in *pl.*

Leicester Mercury A BMW with electrically-operated windows and other mod-cons.

mode /məʊd/ *n.* & *a.* LME. [In branch I, f. L *modus* measure etc., f. IE base repr. also by METE *v.* In branch II, f. Fr. *mode* fem. f. L *modus*, w. change of gender due to final *e*. See also MOOD *n.*[2]] A *n.* I 1 *Mus.* a Orig., a tune, an air. Later, a particular scheme or system of sounds, *spec.* (*a*) each of the ancient Greek scales (Dorian, Phrygian, Lydian, Ionian, etc.) in which music in the diatonic style was composed; any of the scales used in other (e.g. oriental) systems of music; (*b*) (in medieval church music) each of the scales in which plainsong was composed (derived from and named after, but not always corresponding to, the ancient Greek ones), beginning on different notes of the natural scale, and thus having the intervals differently arranged; (*c*) (in modern music) either of the two classes (*major* and *minor*) of keys, having the intervals differently arranged; formerly sometimes = KEY *n.*[1] 6. LME. b The proportion (3 or 2) of a long to a large or a breve to a long, determining rhythm. *obs.* exc. *Hist.* M17. 2 *Gram.* = MOOD *n.*[2] 2. Now *N. Amer.* LME. 3 *Logic.* a = MOOD *n.*[2] 1. M16. b The character of a proposition as either necessary, contingent, possible, or impossible; each of the four kinds into which propositions are divided as having one or another of these qualities. M19. 4 A way or manner in which something is done or takes place; a method of procedure; a means. M17. b A mode of expression. *rare.* L18. c *Physics.* Any of the distinct kinds or patterns of vibration that an oscillatory system can sustain. M19. d Any of a number of distinct ways in which a machine, computer system, etc., operates. M20. 5 A particular form, manner, or variety (of some quality, process, or condition). Now *rare* exc. in *mode of life* and similar uses. M17. b *Petrogr.* The quantitative mineral (as distinct from chemical) composition of a rock sample. Cf. NORM *n.* 3. E20. 6 *Philos.* A manner or state of being of a thing; a thing considered as possessing certain non-essential attributes. Also (now *rare*), an attribute or quality of a substance. L17.

4 M. MITCHELL With the old horse dead, their one mode of conveyance was gone. D. JACOBSON Such highflown display is now the only mode of self-expression open to her. d D. ADAMS The massive computer was now in total active mode. 5 POPE Modes of Self-love the Passions we may call. 6 J. A. FROUDE God is an all-perfect Being . . existence is a mode of perfection, and therefore God exists.

II 7 A prevailing fashion, custom, or style, esp. of a particular place or period; (*arch.*) *the* fashion in dress, etiquette, etc., prevalent in society at the time. M17. b Conventional usage in dress, manners, etc., esp. among people of fashion. L17. †c A fashionable person or thing. E18–E19. 8 A thin light glossy black silk, alamode. *obs.* exc. *Hist.* M18. 9 *Lace-making. sing.* & in *pl.* Fancy stitching or stitches used to fill enclosed spaces in a design. M19. 10 [Short for Fr. *gris mode* fashion grey.] Any of several shades of grey used in women's clothing. Now *rare.* L19. 11 *Statistics.* The value or range of values of the variable which occurs most frequently in a set of data etc. L19.

7 W. C. SMITH A sort of dandies in religion, Affecting the last mode. A. LURIE Historians of costume have put forward various explanations for the modes of the 1920s. b T. JEFFERSON These sentiments became a matter of mode.

Phrases: **all the mode** enjoying general but usually temporary popularity, fashionable at the time in question. **in (the) mode** in fashion or customary use, esp. in polite society. †**man of mode** = *man of fashion* s.v. FASHION *n.* 7.

Comb.: **mode-locked** *a.* (*Physics*) subjected to or resulting from mode-locking; **mode-locking** *Physics* a technique of establishing a fixed phase relationship between the modes of oscillation in a laser, resulting in the emission at nanosecond intervals of short trains of picosecond light pulses.

B *adj.* Made of the silk mode (*obs.* exc. *Hist.*). Also (*rare*), of the grey mode. L18.

modeless *a.* †(*a*) unmeasured; (*b*) having no mode: L16.

model /'mɒd(ə)l/ *n.* & *a.* L16. [Fr. †*modelle* (now *modèle*) f. It. *modello* f. Proto-Romance alt. of L MODULUS.] A *n.* I Representation of structure. †1 An architect's set of designs for a projected building; a similar set of drawings representing the proportions and arrangement of an existing building. Also, a plan of a town, garden, etc. L16–E18. †b A summary, an abstract. E17–M18. 2a *fig.* A person or thing resembling another, esp. on a smaller scale. Now *dial.* exc. in *the* (*very*) *model of.* L16. b A three-dimensional representation of an existing person or thing or projected structure, showing the proportions and arrangement of its component parts. E17. c An archetypal image or pattern. M18. d *Dentistry.* A cast of the teeth or oral cavity, used to construct dental appliances. M19. e A simplified description of a system, process, etc., put forward as a basis for theoretical or empirical understanding; a conceptual or mental representation of something. E20. f *Math.* A set of entities that satisfies all the formulae of a given formal or axiomatic system. M20. †3 A mould; something that envelops closely. *rare* (Shakes.). Only in L16. †4 A small portrait; (by confusion) a medallion. E–M17. 5 An object or figure in clay, wax, etc., for reproduction in a more durable material. Formerly also, a sketch for a painting. L17. 6 A plasterer's tool for moulding a cornice, having a pattern in profile which is impressed on the plaster by working the tool backwards and forwards. E19.

1 SHAKES. *2 Hen. IV* When we mean to build, We first survey the plot, then draw the model. 2a S. PATRICK These quiet places are . . little models of Heaven. b L. DURRELL He had a model of the perfect woman built in rubber. T. PYNCHON Some dainty pasteboard model, a city-planner's city, perfectly detailed. **working model**: constructed to imitate the movements of the machine which it represents. c T. REID Every work of art has its model framed in the imagination. e *Scientific American* A model designed to forecast next week's weather ignores these variables. *Rutherford model*: see RUTHERFORD 1. 3 SHAKES. *Hen. V* O England! model to thy inward greatness. 5 *South African Panorama* Mr Bhana creates these images by first making a clay model.

II Type of design. 7 The design, pattern, or structural type of a material or immaterial thing. L16. b A garment by a particular designer, of a particular season, etc.; a copy of such a garment. L19. c A motor vehicle etc. of a particular design or produced in a specified year; each of a series of varying designs of the same type of object. E20. †8 Scale of construction; allotted measure; the measure of a person's ability or capacity. Only in 17. 9 The curvature of the surface of a violin etc. M19.

7 F. BROOKE This Town is . . built very stately at the Italian model. J. R. GREEN The new faith . . borrowed from Calvin its model of Church government. *New Model*: see NEW *a.* b *Times* The Valentino collection is untypically small. . . Strikes have dogged the production of the models. c J. GRENFELL They got a new car. Well, it's not *new*, 1944 model. *Practical Motorist* Sales of Uno and Panda models rose. **Model T** an early model of car produced by the American Ford Company; *fig.* a person who or thing which is outmoded, mass-produced, etc. 8 H. HIBBERT Shall any reduce . . the thoughts and wayes of God to their narrow and straitned model?

III An object of imitation. 10 A person or work proposed or adopted for imitation; an exemplar. M17. b *Biol.* An animal or plant to which another bears a mimetic resemblance. L19. 11 A person employed to pose for an artist, sculptor, photographer, etc. Also, an actual person, place, etc., on which a fictional character, location, etc., is based. L17. b A person (without qualification, usu. a woman) employed to display clothes by wearing them. E20. c *euphem.* A prostitute. M20. 12 An exemplary person or thing; a perfect exemplar *of* some excellence. Also, a representative specimen *of* some quality etc. L18. 13a = *model dwelling* below. Usu. in *pl. colloq.* L19. **b** = *model lodging-house* below. *Sc. colloq.* L19.

10 C. ACHEBE A budding dictator might choose models far worse than the English gentleman of leisure. **11** W. S. MAUGHAM He could not afford a model but painted still life. P. AUSTER Alexander Selkirk (thought by some to be the model for Robinson Crusoe). **b** D. G. PHILLIPS The sleek tight-fitting trying-on robe of the professional model. G. BLACK He looked like a male model . . for expensive men's knitwear. **12** E. KUZWAYO She was a perfect model of womanhood. C. TOMALIN Gilbert Cannon, fair-haired, handsome, pipe-smoking, . . the very model of the successful young Georgian man of letters.

Comb.: **model-drawing** (the branch of study that deals with) drawing in perspective from solid figures; **model-room** a room for the storage or exhibition of models of machinery etc.; **model theory** the branch of mathematics that deals with the construction and properties of models of formal systems etc.

B *attrib.* or as *adj.* **1** Serving as an example; exemplary, ideally perfect. M19. **2** Designating a small-scale model of the (kind of) object specified. E20.

1 R. LARDNER A model young man, sober, industrious and 'solid'. J. IRVING Bees are a model society, a lesson in teamwork! **model dwelling** any of a set of (esp.) 19th-cent. working men's flats, supposedly offering unusually comfortable and healthy accommodation at low rents. **model lodging-house** (now *Sc.*) a large lodging-house or hostel, nominally of superior standards. **2** ARNOLD BENNETT He sailed model yachts for us. E. NESBIT Among his presents he had a model engine.

†**modelize** *v.t.* frame or construct according to a model; give a particular shape to; organize: L16–E19.

model /ˈmɒd(ə)l/ *v.* Infl. **-ll-**, ***-l-**. L16. [f. the n., after Fr. *modeler*.] **1** *v.t.* †**a** Draw a plan of; produce a preliminary version of. Also, give an outline or synopsis of. (Foll. by *forth*, *out*.) L16–L17. **b** Frame a model or miniature replica of. M17. **2** *v.t.* †**a** Foll. by *out*: produce (a facial expression) by studied effort. Only in E17. **b** Form in imitation of a particular model. Now usu. foll. by (*up*)*on* the model. L17. **c** Assimilate in form *to*. L17. †**d** Bring *into* a specified shape. E18–E19. **e** Give shape to, frame, fashion, (a document, argument, or other immaterial object). M18. **3** *v.t.* Produce (a figure or likeness) as a model in clay, wax, etc. M17. **b** Devise a (usu. mathematical) model or simplified description of (a phenomenon, system, etc.). M20. †**4** *v.t.* Organize (a group of people, a community, a government, etc.). M17–M19. †**5** *v.t.* Train in or mould to a particular mode of life or behaviour. M17–M18. **6** *v.t.* & *i.* In drawing, painting, etc.: form with or assume the appearance of natural relief, (cause to) appear three-dimensional. M19. **7** *v.i.* Produce or devise a model or models. M19. **8a** *v.i.* Pose or act as a model; be a fashion or photographic model. E20. **b** *v.t.* Display (clothes) as a model. E20.

1b LONGFELLOW Many a ship that sailed the main Was modelled o'er and o'er again. **2b** R. G. COLLINGWOOD Alexander's philosophy of nature is even more closely modelled on the *Critique of Pure Reason*. T. IRELAND She'd always modelled herself on her older sister. **3** R. INGALLS She was modelling a bust in clay. **b** *Nature* The first attempts to model the urban system were made by traffic engineers. **4** R. FIDDES God, who founded human society, may model it as he pleases. **5** G. FARQUHAR 'Tis an insupportable toil . . for women . . to model their husbands to good breeding. **7** O. W. HOLMES I rough out my thoughts in talk as an artist models in clay. **8a** T. CALLENDER She modelled for him for free. She was a good sitter.

modeler *n.* see MODELLER.

modeliar *n.* see MUDALIYAR.

modeling *n.* see MODELLING.

modelist *n.* see MODELLIST.

modeller /ˈmɒd(ə)lə/ *n.* Also ***modeler**. E17. [f. MODEL *v.* + -ER¹.] A person who models something or who makes models; *esp.* a person who forms models in clay, plaster, wax, etc.

financial modeller: see FINANCIAL *a.*

modelling /ˈmɒd(ə)lɪŋ/ *n.* Also ***modeling**. L16. [f. MODEL *v.* + -ING¹.] **1** The action of MODEL *v.* L16. **2** *spec.* The work of a fashion or photographic model. M20. **3** The devising or use of abstract or mathematical models. M20.

3 financial modelling: see FINANCIAL *a.*

modellist /ˈmɒd(ə)lɪst/ *n.* Now *rare.* Also ***modelist**. L17. [f. MODEL *n.* or *v.* + -IST.] A maker of models.

modello /mɒˈdɛləʊ, *foreign* moˈdɛllo/ *n.* Pl. **-lli** /-(l)li/, **-llos**. M20. [It.: see MODEL *n.*] A detailed sketch for a larger painting, prepared for a patron's approval. Also, a small model for a larger sculpture.

modem /ˈməʊdɛm/ *n.* & *v.* M20. [f. MO(DULATOR + DEM(ODULATOR.] **A** *n.* A combined modulator and demodulator, used esp. to connect a computer to a telephone line, for converting digital electrical signals to analogue or audio ones and vice versa. M20. **B** *v.i.* & *t.* Signal or send via a modem. L20.

modena /ˈmɒdɪnə/ *n.* & *a.* Also (esp. sense 2) **M-**. E19. [*Modena*: see MODENESE.] **1** More fully *modena-red*. (Of) a deep purple colour. E19. **2** (**M-**.) In full *Modena pigeon*. A stocky variety of the domestic pigeon with red legs. L19.

modenature /məˈdiːnətʃə/ *n.* M17. [Fr. *modénature* f. It. *modanatura*, f. *modano* moulding: see -URE.] *Archit.* The mouldings decorating a cornice.

Modenese /mɒdɪˈniːz/ *a.* & *n.* E19. [f. *Modena* (see below) + -ESE.] **A** *adj.* Of or pertaining to the N. Italian city of Modena or its inhabitants. E19. **B** *n.* Pl. same. A native or inhabitant of Modena. M19.

moderacy /ˈmɒd(ə)rəsi/ *n.* *rare.* E17. [f. MODERATE *a.* + -CY.] Moderation; (esp. political) moderateness.

moderant /ˈmɒd(ə)r(ə)nt/ *n.* *rare.* L19. [L *moderant-* pres. ppl stem of *moderari* MODERATE *v.*: see -ANT¹.] A moderating thing.

moderantism /ˈmɒd(ə)r(ə)ntɪz(ə)m/ *n.* L18. [Fr. *modérantisme*, f. *modérant* pres. pple of *modérer* MODERATE *v.*: see -ISM.] *Hist.* The doctrine and spirit of the moderate republican party during and after the French Revolution.

moderate /ˈmɒd(ə)rət/ *a.* & *n.* LME. [L *moderatus* pa. pple, f. as next: see -ATE².] **A** *adj.* **1a** Avoiding excess or extremes of conduct; observing, exhibiting, or acting with moderation; temperate in conduct or expression. LME. **b** Not extreme in opinion; not strongly partisan; (also **M-**) designating or pertaining to any of various political and ecclesiastical parties avoiding extreme views. M17. **2a** Of medium quantity, quality, size, or extent; fairly large or good; tolerable; *depreciative* mediocre, scanty. LME. **b** Of a process, condition, or agency: not intense, violent, or severe; intermediate in strength or degree; *spec.* (of a wind) registering in the low to medium figures on the Beaufort scale. LME. **c** Of a price, charge, etc.: reasonable, low. E20.

1a SHAKES. *Merch. V.* O love, be moderate, allay thy ecstacy. GIBBON In the reformation of religion, his first steps were moderate and cautious. *Graphic* Teetotallers and moderate drinkers will probably be at war on this point. **b** G. GORER The children of police officers regard their fathers' profession with enthusiasm; but . . their wives . . are usually more moderate. **2** E. B. PUSEY The rest are very moderate productions. **b** E. RAFFALD Bake them in a moderate oven. N. PEVSNER It is a moderate climate with no scorching heat nor paralysing cold. M. ANGELOU The record player was on to a moderate volume. **c** H. CARPENTER Unfurnished houses at a moderate rent seemed impossible to find.

B *n.* A person who holds moderate opinions in politics, religion, etc.; *Fr. Hist.* (also **M-**) a Girondist. M17.

Listener 'Moderates' . . are at present containing the extremists and hot-heads.

moderately *adv.* LME. **moderateness** *n.* L16.

moderate /ˈmɒdəreɪt/ *v.* Pa. pple **-ated**, †**-ate**. LME. [L *moderat-* pa. ppl stem of *moderari*, *-are* reduce, control: see -ATE³.] **1** *v.t.* Make less violent, severe, intense, or rigorous. Formerly also, reduce the amount of (a fine, charge, etc.). LME. **b** *v.i.* Become less violent, severe, intense, or rigorous. L17. **c** *v.t.* *Nuclear Physics.* Slow down (a neutron); slow down neutrons in (a reactor). Cf. MODERATOR 6c. M20. **2** *v.t.* †**a** Adjust in quantity or proportion. L15–M17. †**b** Exercise a controlling influence over; regulate, control. M16–E19. **c** *Educ.* Review (examination papers, results, candidates, etc.) in relation to an agreed standard so as to ensure consistency of marking. M20. **3a** *v.t.* In academic and ecclesiastical contexts: preside over (a deliberative body) or at (a debate etc.). L16. **b** *v.i.* Act as moderator, preside, now esp. in the Presbyterian Church in Scotland. L16. †**4a** *v.i.* Act as mediator or arbitrator. Also, take a mediating view. L16–M18. **b** *v.t.* Decide (a question) as an arbitrator. E17–M18.

1 T. LEDIARD I . . advise you to moderate your demands. T. CAPOTE A short-tempered man who has difficulty moderating his excessive vigour. **b** R. L. STEVENSON Although the wind had not yet moderated, the clouds were all . . blown away.

Phrases: **moderate (in) a call** *Sc.* (of a presbytery or its leader) preside over the formal invitation to a minister elect.

moderated *ppl a.* that has been moderated; *esp.* †(*a*) reasonably restricted and limited; (*b*) *Nuclear Physics* provided with or slowed down by a moderator: L16.

moderation /mɒdəˈreɪʃ(ə)n/ *n.* LME. [(O)Fr. *modération* f. L *moderatio(n-)*, f. as prec.: see -ATION.] **1**†**a** Limitation, restriction; a restricting proviso or clause. LME–E18. **b** The action of making something less violent, severe, intense, or rigorous. Formerly also, reduction of expenditure etc. Now *rare.* L15. †**c** Control, rule; a system of government. E16–E18. **d** *Nuclear Physics.* The action or process of slowing down neutrons by the use of a moderator. M20. **e** *Educ.* The action or process of moderating examination papers etc. M20. **2** The quality of being moderate, esp. in conduct, opinion, etc.; avoidance of excess or extremes, temperance. Formerly also, avoidance of severity, clemency. LME. **3** The action of presiding over a presbytery's formal invitation to a minister elect; a meeting for the purpose of formally inviting a minister elect. *Sc.* E18. **4** (**M-**.) In *pl.* The first public examination in certain faculties for the BA degree at Oxford University. Abbrev. MODS. M19.

2 B. JOWETT He is sensible that moderation is better than total abstinence. O. WILDE Moderation is a fatal thing. Nothing succeeds like excess. **in moderation** in a moderate manner or proportion.

moderationist *n.* an advocate of moderation; *spec.* a person who supports moderate drinking as opp. to total abstinence: M19.

moderatism /ˈmɒd(ə)rətɪz(ə)m/ *n.* L18. [f. MODERATE *a.* & *n.* + -ISM.] The principles or policy of a moderate political or ecclesiastical party; belief in moderation.

moderatist *n.* E18.

moderato /mɒdəˈrɑːtəʊ/ *adv.* E18. [It. = MODERATE *a.*] *Mus.* A direction: at a moderate pace or tempo.

moderator /ˈmɒdəreɪtə/ *n.* LME. [L, f. as MODERATE *v.*: see -OR.] †**1** A ruler, a governor. LME–M19. **2** A person who acts as an arbitrator between disputants; an arbiter. Also, a mediator. M16. **3** A Presbyterian minister elected to preside over an ecclesiastical body. M16. **4** *gen.* A person chosen to preside over a meeting or assembly and conduct its business. L16. **b** *spec.* A chairman of a television or radio discussion. *N. Amer.* M20. **5a** Orig., a public officer appointed to preside over the disputations or exercises for university degrees. Later, (*a*) at Cambridge, either of two officers responsible for the proper conduct of the mathematical tripos examination; (*b*) at Oxford, an examiner for Moderations. L16. **b** At Dublin University: an honours graduate. M19. **c** An examiner who moderates examination papers etc. M20. **6** A person who or thing which mitigates something or makes something moderate. E17. **b** A regulator to control the flow of oil to the wick of an oil-lamp; (also *moderator-lamp*) a lamp equipped with this. M19. **c** A substance that slows down neutrons passing through it; *spec.* one used in a nuclear reactor to control the rate of fission (fast neutrons being less efficient at causing fission). M20.

modera'torial *a.* pertaining to or characteristic of a moderator M19. **moderatorship** *n.* the function or office of moderator M17.

†moderatrix *n.* Pl. **-trices, -trixes.** L16–M18. [L, f. as prec.: see -TRIX.] A female moderator.
Earlier **†moderatrice** *n.* [Fr.]: only in M16.

modern /'mɒd(ə)n/ *a.* & *n.* LME. [(O)Fr. *moderne*, or its source late L *modernus*, f. L *modo* just now, after L *hodiernus* of today (f. *hodie* today).] A *adj.* **1** Of or pertaining to the present and recent times, as opp. to the remote past. LME. **†2** Currently holding office; now existing. *rare.* E16–M18. **3** Characteristic of the present and recent times; not old-fashioned or obsolete, in current fashion. L16. **b** Of a person: up-to-date in lifestyle, outlook, opinions, etc.; liberal-minded. Occas. *derog.* M18. **†4** Everyday, ordinary, commonplace. L16–E17. **5** *spec.* **a** Designating the form of a language currently used, or the form representing the most recent significant stage of development, as opp. to any earlier form. L17. **b** *Geol., Zool.*, etc. Belonging to a comparatively recent period in the history of the earth. E19. **c** *Typogr.* Of a typeface: having straight serifs and marked contrast between the thick and thin parts of the letters. E19. **d** Designating or pertaining to art and architecture marked by a departure from traditional styles and values. L19.

1 A. BULLOCK Ernest Bevin owed less to formal education than any Englishman to hold so high an office .. in modern times. *secondary modern school*: see SECONDARY *a.* 3 E. HEATH Tehran has developed into a modern city. M. M. KAYE It was no old-fashioned musket but a modern precision-made weapon. b S. RICHARDSON You .. are not a modern woman; have neither wings to your shoulders, nor gad-fly in your cap. T. PARKS My father was .. considered .. modern because he had introduced singing with a guitar on the chancel steps. 4 SHAKES. *A.Y.L.* The justice, .. Full of wise saws and modern instances. 5a *modern Greek, modern Hebrew, modern Irish*, etc.

Special collocations: **modern convenience** = MOD CON. **modern dance** a free expressive style of dancing distinct from classical ballet. *modern English*: see ENGLISH *a.* & *n.* **modern first edition** the first edition of a book published after *c*1900. **modern Greats** (at Oxford University) the school of philosophy, politics, and economics. **modern history**: *spec.* of the period after the Middle Ages or after the fall of the Western Roman Empire. **modern jazz** jazz as developed in the 1940s and 1950s, *esp.* bebop. **modern languages** European languages (esp. French and German) as a subject of study, as opp. to Latin and Greek. *modern Latin*: see LATIN *a.* & *n.* *modern* PENTATHLON. **modern school** (*a*) in some English public schools, a separately organized division of the school in which Greek and most Latin is excluded from the curriculum; (*b*) *Hist.* = *secondary modern school* s.v. SECONDARY *a.* **modern side** = *modern school* (a) above.

B *n.* **1** A person or thing belonging to the present time. Usu. in *pl.* L16. **2** A person with modern tastes or opinions. Usu. in *pl.* L19. **3** = *modern first edition* above. E20.

1 H. ALLEN Few moderns .. can resist .. patronising the past. *Country Life* The Walker Art Centre houses a world-famous collection of moderns. *Danish modern*: see DANISH *a.* *secondary modern*: see SECONDARY *a.* *Swedish modern*: see SWEDISH *a.*

modernly *adv.* (*a*) (now *rare*) in modern times; (*b*) in a modern manner; after the fashion of modern times: E17. **modernness** /-n-n-/ *n.* M18.

moderne /mə'dəːn, *foreign* mɔdɛrn/ *a.* & *n.* M20. [Fr. = modern.] (Designating or characterized by) a popularization of the art deco style marked by bright colours and austere geometric shapes, or (freq. *derog.*) any ultra-modern style.

moderner /'mɒd(ə)nə/ *n.* L16. [f. MODERN *a.* + -ER[1].] A modern person.

modernise *v.* var. of MODERNIZE.

modernism /'mɒd(ə)nɪz(ə)m/ *n.* M18. [f. MODERN *a.* + -ISM.] **1** A usage, mode of expression, peculiarity of style, etc., characteristic of modern times. M18. **2** Modern character or quality of thought, expression, technique, etc.; affinity for what is modern. M19. **3** *Theol.* A movement towards modifying traditional beliefs and doctrines in accordance with modern ideas, esp. in the Roman Catholic Church in the late 19th and early 20th cents. E20. **4** The methods, style, or attitude of modern artists, writers, architects, composers, etc.; *spec.* a style of painting etc. rejecting classical and traditional methods of expression. E20.

Modernismus /modɛr'nɪsmʊs, mɒdə'nɪzməs/ *n.* Freq. *derog.* M20. [G = prec.] Modernism in architecture, art, etc.

modernist /'mɒd(ə)nɪst/ *n.* & *a.* L16. [f. MODERN *a.* + -IST.] A *n.* **†1** A person who lives in modern times. Only in L16. **2** A supporter or follower of modern ways or methods; an adherent of modernism. E18. **3** *spec.* **a** *Theol.* A supporter or advocate of theological modernism. E20. **b** An artist, architect, writer, etc., whose work is characterized by modernism. E20. **c** A person who plays or appreciates modern jazz. M20. **B** *attrib.* or as *adj.* Of, pertaining to, or characteristic of modernists or modernism. M19.

moder'nistic *a.* of, pertaining to, or suggestive of modernism or modernists; having affinity for what is modern: E20. **moder'nistically** *adv.* L20.

modernity /mə'dəːnɪti/ *n.* E17. [f. as prec. + -ITY.] **1** The quality or condition of being modern; modernness of character. E17. **2** A modern thing. M18.

modernize /'mɒd(ə)nʌɪz/ *v.* Also **-ise.** M18. [Fr. *moderniser*, f. *moderne* MODERN *a.*: see -IZE.] **1** *v.t.* Make modern; give a modern character or appearance to; refashion in modern style; provide with modern equipment; adapt to modern ideas; rewrite in modern spelling or language. M18. **2** *v.i.* Adopt modern methods, equipment, ideas, style, etc.; rebuild or refashion something in modern style. M18.

modernizable *a.* M20. **moderni'zation** *n.* (*a*) the action or an act of modernizing; the state of being modernized; (*b*) a modernized version: L18. **modernizer** *n.* M18.

modest /'mɒdɪst/ *a.* M16. [(O)Fr. *modeste* f. L *modestus* keeping due measure, f. base of MODERATE *v.* + pa. ppl suff.] **1** Having a moderate or humble estimate of one's own abilities or merits; unassuming, diffident, bashful; not bold or forward. Of an action, attribute, etc.: proceeding from or indicating such qualities. M16. **b** *fig.* Of a thing: apparently shy of observation, not conspicuous. L18. **†2** Well-conducted, orderly; not harsh or domineering. L16–M17. **3** Decorous in manner and conduct; scrupulously avoiding impropriety or indecency; reserved in sexual matters. L16. **4** Not excessive, not exaggerated, moderate; limited, restrained, slight; unpretentious in size, quantity, appearance, etc.; undistinguished on the social or economic scale; not lavish or wealthy. E17.

1 J. F. LEHMANN Leonard .. sat in modest silence, with lowered eyes. B. PYM He was too modest to believe that Penelope could have fallen in love with him. b R. BURNS Wee, modest, crimson-tipped flow'r. 3 C. C. TRENCH There was nothing modest or delicate in her approach to sex. L. CODY She didn't think she was excessively modest, it was just that there were some things you got used to doing in private. 4 I. MCEWAN These were modest, achievable tasks. K. WATERHOUSE Colchester Place Mansions is an altogether more modest establishment—no more than a converted house. T. K. WOLFE This was a modest sum compared to what other people spent. H. R. LANDON The father had a very modest position as a bass-singer at the Mannheim court.

modestly *adv.* M16.

modesty /'mɒdɪsti/ *n.* & *a.* M16. [(O)Fr. *modestie* or L *modestia*, f. *modestus*: see prec., -Y[3].] A *n.* **†1** Moderation; reasonableness; self-control; mildness of rule. M16–M19. **2** The quality of being modest about oneself. M16. **†b** Deferential feeling. L16–M17. **c** The quality of being modest in size, quantity, appearance, etc.; unpretentious character. E20. **3** Modest behaviour, manner, or appearance. M16. **b** = *modesty piece* below. *arch.* M18. **4** Any of certain inconspicuous plants; *spec.* (*a*) thorow-wax; (*b*) a white-flowered creeping plant, *Whipplea modesta*, of the hydrangea family, native to the western US. M19.

1 GIBBON The modesty of Alaric was interpreted .. as a sure evidence of his weakness. 2 P. MEDAWAR 'Just here our capacities fail us,' he says, with a modesty not found in .. his successors. R. DEACON With typical modesty he gave most of the credit .. to a Zulu assistant. c *Blackwood's Magazine* The straitness of their surroundings, the modesty of their homes. 3 E. B. BROWNING He could not think highly of the modesty of any woman who could read Don Juan! *Mail on Sunday* She still has to bow to her Muslim background in modesty of dress.

B *attrib.* or as *adj.* Serving to prevent immodest exposure of the (female) body. Orig. in *modesty piece* below. E18.

New Scientist Carpenters .. taking down all those modesty boards from the front of typing tables. **modesty piece** *arch.* a piece of lace etc. covering the bosom, worn with a low-cut dress. **modesty skirt** a short skirt on a woman's swimming costume.

modi *n.pl.* see MODUS.

modiation /məʊdɪ'eɪʃ(ə)n/ *n.* Long *obs.* exc. *Hist.* M17. [Late L *modiatio(n-)*, ult. f. L MODIUS: see -ATION.] Measurement by volume; a levy assessed by volume.

modicity /mə'dɪsɪti/ *n. rare.* E17. [Fr. *modicité* f. med.L *modicitat-*, f. L *modicus*: see next, -ITY.] Moderateness.

modicum /'mɒdɪkəm/ *n.* L15. [L = little way, short time, neut. sing. of *modicus* moderate, f. *modus* MODE.] **1** A small quantity or portion; a limited amount. L15. **†2** A person of small stature; *derog.* a young woman. E–M17.

1 A. TROLLOPE With the cup of coffee comes a small modicum of dry toast. L. CODY Slinger, of course, has a modicum of native wit. *Evening Telegraph (Grimsby)* Fleming .. caused more than a modicum of unrest in the Mariners defence whenever he charged forward.

modifiable /'mɒdɪfʌɪəb(ə)l/ *a.* E17. [f. MODIFY + -ABLE.] Able to be modified.

modifia'bility *n.* M19. **modifiableness** *n.* L19.

modificable /'mɒdɪfɪkəb(ə)l/ *a. rare.* E18. [f. L *modificare* MODIFY: see -ABLE.] Modifiable.

modifica'bility *n.* E19.

modificand /'mɒdɪfɪkand/ *n. rare.* M19. [L *modificandus*, f. *modificare*: see MODIFY, -AND.] Chiefly *Gram.* A word etc. that is (to be) modified.

modification /ˌmɒdɪfɪ'keɪʃ(ə)n/ *n.* L15. [(O)Fr., or L *modificatio(n-)*, f. *modificat-* pa. ppl stem of *modificari, -are*: see MODIFY, -FICATION.] **1** *Sc. Law.* The action of assessing or awarding a payment; *esp.* (*Hist.*) the fixing of a parish minister's stipend. L15. **†2** *Philos.* **a** The bringing of a thing into a particular mode of existence; differentiation into a variety of forms. E16–M19. **b** The form of existence belonging to a particular object; a particular form into which a thing is differentiated; a mode of being. M17–M19. **3** The action or an act of making changes to something without altering its essential nature or character; partial alteration; orig. *spec.* the action of qualifying a statement etc. Also, the state of being so changed. E17. **b** *Biol.* The development of non-heritable changes in an organism, as opp. to *variation, mutation.* L19. **4** The result of such alteration; a modified form, a variety. M17. **b** *Biol.* The non-heritable changes produced in an organism in response to a particular environment. L19. **5** *Gram.* **a** Qualification or limitation of the sense of one word, phrase, etc., by another; an instance or the result of this. E18. **b** (An) alteration of a vowel by umlaut. M19.

3 J. TYNDALL It required but a slight modification of our plans. *Which?* Manufacturers are quick to respond with modifications. 4 W. A. MILLER Stearin may exist in three modifications, each of which has a different fusing point.

modificational *a.* of the nature of or arising from modification E20. **'modificative** *n.* & *a.* [med.L *modificativus*] (now *rare*) (*a*) *Gram.* a modifying word or clause; (*b*) *adj.* having the property of modifying: M17. **'modificator** *n.* (*rare*) = MODIFIER E19. **'modificatory** *a.* modifying; tending to modify: E19.

modifier /'mɒdɪfʌɪə/ *n.* L16. [f. next + -ER[1].] **1** *Sc. Law.* An official who assesses or awards a payment etc. L16. **2** A person who or thing which modifies or alters something, or produces variation. L17. **b** *Gram.* A word, phrase, or clause which modifies another; a phonetic sign or symbol which modifies a character. M19. **c** *Genetics.* A gene which modifies the phenotypic expression of a gene at another locus. E20.

modify /ˈmɒdɪfʌɪ/ *v.t.* LME. [(O)Fr. *modifier* f. L *modificari*, *-are*, f. *modus* MODE: see -FY.] **1** *Sc. Law.* Assess or decree the amount of (a payment, *Hist.* esp. a parish minister's stipend); award (a payment) *to*. LME. †**2** Limit, restrain; appease, assuage. LME–M16. **3** Make partial or minor changes to; alter without radical transformation. Orig. *esp.* qualify or moderate (a statement etc.), alter so as to make less severe; now freq., alter so as to improve. LME. †**4** *Philos.* Give (an object) its particular form of being or distinguishing characters; differentiate into a variety of forms. M17–L18. **5** *Gram.* **a** Limit or qualify the sense of (a word, phrase, etc.). E18. **b** Change (a vowel) by umlaut. M19.

3 J. LANG There is generally a light breeze to modify the heat. T. H. HUXLEY The agents which are now at work in modifying the crust of the earth. P. FITZGERALD Freddie . . did in fact modify her behaviour. *New York Times* The company has concentrated on modifying cars developed by Renault for the American market. *Which?* One of our tested sets . . can be modified to run off a . . battery.

modii *n.* pl. of MODIUS.

modillion /məˈdɪljən/ *n.* M16. [Fr. *modillon*, †*modiglion* f. It. *modiglione* f. Proto-Romance, ult. f. L *mutulus* MUTULE.] *Archit.* A projecting bracket placed in series under the corona of the cornice in the Corinthian, composite and Roman Ionic orders; *gen.* an ornamental bracket under eaves etc.

modillioned *a.* ornamented with modillions L20.

modiolus /məˈdʌɪələs/ *n.* Pl. **-li** /-lʌɪ, -liː/, **-luses**. In sense 2 also **-la** /-lə/, pl. **-lae** /-liː/. L17. [L = nave of a wheel, dim. of MODIUS.] **1** *Surg.* The crown of a trepan. Long *rare* or *obs.* L17. **2** A horse mussel of the genus *Modiolus* (formerly *Modiola*). Now only as mod.L genus name. L18. **3** *Anat.* The conical axis of the cochlea of the ear. E19.

modiolar *a.* (*Anat.*) of or pertaining to the modiolus of the ear M19.

modish /ˈməʊdɪʃ/ *a.* M17. [f. MODE + -ISH^{1}.] Conforming to or following the mode or prevailing fashion; fashionable.

L. STRACHEY Eugénie, cool and modish, floated in an infinitude of flounces. *Times Lit. Suppl.* Fashionable, even modish, it is competently written. F. RAPHAEL He was always prone to behave as fashion required. . . Modish debauchery never went against his grain.

modishly *adv.* M17. **modishness** *n.* L17.

Modistae /məˈdɪstʌɪ/ *n.pl.* E20. [L, f. *modus* MODE.] A group of later medieval grammarians who put forward a system of Latin grammar in which Priscian's word categories were integrated into the framework of scholastic philosophy.

modiste /mɒˈdiːst, *foreign* mɔdist (*pl. same*)/ *n.* M19. [Fr., f. *mode* fashion, MODE *n.* + *-iste* -IST.] A person who makes, designs, or deals in articles of fashion; *esp.* a fashionable milliner or dressmaker.

modistic /məˈdɪstɪk/ *a.*^{1} E20. [f. prec. + -IC.] Of or pertaining to fashion(s).

modistic /məˈdɪstɪk/ *a.*^{2} M20. [f. MODISTAE + -IC.] Of or pertaining to the Modistae.

modius /ˈməʊdɪəs/ *n.* Pl. **modii** /ˈməʊdɪʌɪ/. LME. [L.] **1** *Hist.* A Roman measure of corn, equal to about a peck; in the Middle Ages, a measure of capacity of varying size, often equated with a bushel. LME. **2** A tall cylindrical head-dress with which certain gods are represented in classical art. E19.

Modoc /ˈməʊdɒk/ *n.* & *a.* M19. [Prob. f. N. Amer. Ind. *Móatokni* southerners.] **A** *n.* Pl. **-s**, same. **1** A member of a Penutian Indian people of the Oregon–California border. M19. **2** The language of this people, resembling Klamath. L19. **B** *attrib.* or as *adj.* Of or pertaining to the Modoc or their language. M19.

modom /ˈmɒdəm/ *n. colloq.* E20. [Repr. an affectedly refined pronunc.] Madam.

Mods /mɒdz/ *n.pl. colloq.* M19. [Abbrev.] The examination Moderations at Oxford University (see MODERATION 4).

modular /ˈmɒdjʊlə/ *a.* & *n.* L18. [mod.L *modularis*, f. L MODULUS: see -AR^{1}.] **A** *adj.* **1** *Math.* Of or pertaining to a modulus or module. L18. **2** *Archit.* Of or pertaining to a module as a unit of length. *rare.* M19. **3** Employing or involving a module or modules as the basis of design, measurement, or construction; designed as part of a system so designed or constructed; (of an educational course) designed as a series of units or discrete sections; (of a facility, service, etc.) provided in a number of discrete stages. M20. **B** *ellipt.* as *n.* A thing of modular construction or design. M20.

moduˈlarity *n.* the property of being modular; use of modules in design or construction: M20. **modulariˈzation** *n.* the action or process of making something modular; construction on modular principles: M20. **modularize** *v.t.* make modular; construct on modular principles: M20. **modularly** *adv.* on modular principles M20.

modulate /ˈmɒdjʊleɪt/ *v.* M16. [L *modulat-* pa. ppl stem of *modulari* measure, adjust to rhythm, make melody, f. MODULUS: see -ATE^{3}.] **1** *v.t.* Intone (a song etc.). *rare.* M16. **2** *v.t.* Regulate, adjust, temper, vary conformably *to*; soften, tone down; *esp.* attune (the voice, sounds, etc.) to a certain pitch or key, vary or inflect in tone; give tune or melody to. E17. **3** *v.t.* & *i. Mus.* (Cause to) change from one key to another. (Foll. by *from*, *to*.) E18. **4** *v.t.* **a** Vary the amplitude, frequency, or some other characteristic of (an electromagnetic wave or other oscillation, a beam of particles, etc.) in accordance with the variations of a second signal, usu. of lower frequency; vary (a property of a signal) in this way. Also, apply a signal to (a device) so as to vary its output signal; impress (a signal) *on* (*to*) a carrier wave by modulation. E20. **b** *gen.* Exert a modifying or controlling influence on (a physical property, phenomenon, etc.). M20. **5** *v.i. Biol.* Of a cell: undergo modulation *into*. M20. **6** *v.i.* Converse on citizens' band radio. *US slang.* L20.

2 GIBBON The songs of triumph were modulated to psalms and litanies. A. RADCLIFFE She determined to modulate that nature to her own views. G. GREENE She spoke gently . . for it was difficult to modulate her husky voice. 4a J. H. REYNER The radio transmission of sound . . is usually accomplished by modulating a high-frequency carrier-wave. *Music* This is recorded first . . . The video information is then modulated on top. b *Scientific American* The steam flow is modulated by a control valve. *Nature* Speculations on how thunderstorm electrification might modulate rainfall.

modulative *a.* (*rare*) serving to modulate something M19. **modulatory** *a.* pertaining to or serving for modulation L19.

modulation /mɒdjʊˈleɪʃ(ə)n/ *n.* LME. [L *modulatio(n-)*, f. as prec.: see -ATION.] **1** Singing, making music; a tune; in *pl.*, notes, sounds. Now *rare.* LME. **2** The action of modulating something appropriately; variation of line, form, etc., with regard to artistic effect; a tempering or toning down. Formerly also, rhythmical movement. M16. **3** The action of inflecting the voice or an instrument musically; variation of tone or pitch; a particular inflection or intonation. M16. **4** *Archit.* The proportioning or regulating of the parts of an order by the module. M17. **5** *Mus.* **a** The action or process of passing from one key to another in the course of a piece; (a) change of key. L17. †**b** Composition, performance, or arrangement in a particular mode or key. Also, a chord or succession of notes. Only in 18. **c** *Hist.* Any of certain notes in each church mode, on which a phrase of melody had to begin and end. L19. **6** Melodious literary composition; harmonious treatment of language. M18. **7** The process of modulating a wave or beam, esp. in order to impress a signal on it; the extent to which a modulated carrier wave is varied; a waveform or signal so impressed. E20. **b** *gen.* The process of exerting a controlling or modifying influence on a physical property or phenomenon. M20. **8** *Biol.* Reversible variation in the activity or form of a cell in response to a changing environment. M20.

7 AMPLITUDE *modulation*. FREQUENCY *modulation*.

Comb.: **modulation frequency** the frequency of a wave used to modulate another wave; **modulation index** a coefficient representing the degree of modulation of a carrier wave; *spec.* the ratio of the difference between the maximum and minimum frequencies of a frequency-modulated carrier to the frequency of the modulating signal.

modulator /ˈmɒdjʊleɪtə/ *n.* E16. [f. MODULATE + -OR.] **1** A person who or thing which modulates something; *spec.* (*a*) a device that produces modulation of a wave; (*b*) a regulating mechanism. E16. **2** *Mus.* A chart used in the tonic sol-fa system, showing the relations of tones and scales. M19.

module /ˈmɒdjuːl/ *n.* L16. [Fr., or its source L MODULUS: see -ULE.] †**1** Allotted compass or scale; one's power or capabilities. L16–L17. †**2a** A plan, design, or model of a larger thing. L16–L17. **b** A mere image or counterfeit. *poet.* L16–E17. **3** A standard or unit for measuring. E17. **4a** *Archit.* In the classic orders, the unit of length by which proportions are expressed, usu. the diameter or semidiameter of the column at the base of the shaft. M17. **b** A length chosen as a basis for the dimensions of parts of a building, items of furniture, etc., so that all lengths are integral multiples of it. M20. **5** *Math.* **a** = MODULUS 2. *rare.* L19. **b** Orig., a set that is a subset of a ring and is closed under addition and subtraction. Now usu., a commutative additive group whose elements may be multiplied by those of a ring, the product being in the group and multiplication being associative and distributive. E20. **6** *Engin.* The pitch diameter of a gear wheel (in millimetres) divided by the number of teeth. E20. **7** (Now the predominant sense.) Each of a series of standardized parts or units from which a complex structure, e.g. a building or a piece of furniture is or can be assembled; *loosely* a more or less independent component part. M20. **b** *Astronaut.* A separable section of a spacecraft that can operate as an independent unit. M20. **c** *Computing* etc. Any of a number of distinct but interrelated units from which a program may be built up or into which a complex activity may be analysed. M20. **d** Any of a number of distinct units or periods of education or training which can be combined to make up a course. M20.

2b SHAKES. *John* But a clod And module of confounded royalty. 4b J. S. FOSTER In Great Britain the accepted module is 100mm. 7 A. TOFFLER Pressed-steel modules . . hoisted by crane and plugged into building frames. *Good Housekeeping* A . . Habitat sofa which fits together in modules. *fig.*: D. ATTENBOROUGH The basic architectural module on which the echinoderm body is built. b *lunar* (*excursion*) *module*: see LUNAR *a.* d *Lilith* Students can take a degree by selecting the modules they want.

moduli *n.pl.* see MODULUS.

modulo /ˈmɒdjʊləʊ/ *prep.* L19. [L, abl. of MODULUS.] *Math.* With respect to a modulus of (a given value).

modulus /ˈmɒdjʊləs/ *n.* Pl. **-li** /-lʌɪ, -liː/, **-luses**. M16. [L, dim. of *modus* MODE.] †**1** *Archit.* = MODULE *n.* 4a. M16–M17. **2** *Math.* **a** A number by which logarithms to one base must be multiplied in order to obtain the corresponding logarithms to another base. M18. **b** A constant multiplier, coefficient, or parameter. M19. **c** A measure of a quantity which depends on two or more other quantities; *esp.* the absolute value of a complex quantity. M19. **d** A number by which another number may be divided leaving a remainder. Cf. CONGRUENT 2b, RESIDUE 4. M19. **3** *Physics* & *Engin.* A numerical quantity representing some property of a substance, and equal to the ratio of the magnitude of a (usu. mechanical) cause to the magnitude of its effect on the substance; *spec.* = *modulus of elasticity* below. E19.

3 *bulk modulus*: see BULK *n.*^{1} & *a.* **modulus of elasticity**, **elastic modulus** the ratio of the stress acting on a substance to the strain produced (also YOUNG'S MODULUS). *modulus of* RIGIDITY.

modus /ˈməʊdəs/ *n.* Pl. ***modi*** /ˈməʊdʌɪ/, ***moduses***. L16. [L = MODE.] **1** *Law.* The qualification of the terms of a conveyance etc., or the consideration involved. Long *obs.* exc.

Hist. L16. 2 A mode; *esp.* the way in which something is done; a mode or manner of operation. Now chiefly in L phrs. (see below) or *ellipt.* = *modus operandi* below. L16. 3 A money payment, *spec.* (in full †*modus decimandi* [L = mode of tithing]) one in lieu of tithe. E17. 4 *Logic.* A mood: in *modus ponens*, *modus tollens* below. M19.

Phrases: *modus decimandi*: see sense 3 above. ***modus operandi*** /ɒpəˈrandiː, -dʌɪ/ [= mode of operating] (*a*) the way in which something operates; (*b*) the way in which a person sets about a task. ***modus ponens*** /ˈpəʊnɛnz/ [= mood that affirms] *Logic* (an argument employing) the rule that the consequent *q* may be inferred from the conditional statement *if p then q* and the statement *p*. ***modus tollens*** /ˈtɒlɛnz/ [= mood that denies] *Logic* (an argument employing) the rule that the negation of the antecedent *p* (i.e. *not-p*) may be inferred from the conditional statement *if p then q* and the consequence *not-q*. ***modus vivendi*** /vɪˈvɛndiː, -dʌɪ/ [= mode of living] a way of living or coping; *esp.* a working arrangement between parties in dispute or disagreement which enables them to carry on pending a settlement.

†mody *a.* Only in 18. [f. MODE + -Y[1].] Fashionable, modish.

moellon /ˈmwɛlɒn/ *n.* L19. [Fr.] = DEGRAS I.

moeritherium /mɪərɪˈθɪərɪəm/ *n.* E20. [mod.L (see below), f. Gk *Moiris*, a lake in Egypt near where remains were first discovered + *thērion* wild animal.] An extinct proboscidean mammal of the genus *Moeritherium*, known from fossil remains of Upper Eocene age.

Moeso-Goth /ˈmiːsəʊgɒθ/ *n.* E19. [mod.L *Moesogothi* pl., f. L *Moesi* people of Moesia: see GOTH.] A member of a Gothic tribe which inhabited Moesia, a region corresponding to modern Bulgaria and Serbia, in the 4th and 5th cents.

Moeso-ˈGothic *a.* & *n.* (*a*) *adj.* of or pertaining to the Moeso-Goths or their language; (*b*) *n.* the language of the Moeso-Goths: E19.

moeurs /mœːrs, mœːr/ *n.pl.* E20. [Fr., f. as MORES.] The behaviour, customs, or habits of a people or a group of people.

mofette /mɒˈfɛt/ *n.* E19. [Fr. f. Neapolitan It. *mofetta* = Sp. *mofeta*.] (An exhalation of gas from) a fumarole.

moffie /ˈmɒfi/ *n. slang* (chiefly *S. Afr.*). E20. [Perh. abbrev. and alt. of HERMAPHRODITE.] An effeminate man; a male homosexual; a male transvestite.

mofussil /məʊˈfʌsɪl/ *n.* & *a. Indian subcontinent.* Also **M-**. L18. [Urdu *mufassil* f. Pers. & Urdu *mufassal* f. Arab. *mufaṣṣal* pass. pple of *faṣṣala* divide, separate.] A *n.* The rural localities of a district as distinguished from the chief station or the town. L18. B *attrib.* or as *adj.* Of the mofussil; remote, provincial. M19.

mog /mɒg/ *n. slang.* E20. [Abbrev. of MOGGY.] A cat.

Mogadon /ˈmɒgədɒn/ *n.* M20. [Origin unkn.] (Proprietary name for) the drug nitrazepam; a tablet of this.

moggy /ˈmɒgi/ *n.* Also **-ie**. L17. [Var. of MAGGIE.] 1 A girl, a wench; an untidily dressed woman. *dial.* & *slang.* Now *rare* or *obs.* L17. 2 A calf, a cow. *dial.* E19. 3 A cat. *slang.* E20.

Moghul *n.* & *a.* var. of MOGUL *n.*[1] & *a.*

mogo /ˈməʊgəʊ/ *n.* Pl. **-os**. L18. [Aborig.] A stone hatchet used by Australian Aborigines.

†Mogor *n.* & *a.* var. of MOGUL *n.*[1] & *a.*

mogote /məˈgəʊti/ *n.* E20. [Sp. = hillock, heap, haystack.] *Physical Geogr.* A steep-sided hill of roughly circular cross-section characteristic of karst topography, esp. in Cuba. Cf. HUM *n.*[3]

mogra /ˈməʊgrə/ *n.* M17. [Hind. *mogrā* f. Skt *mudgara*.] Arabian jasmine, *Jasminum sambac*.

Mogul /ˈməʊg(ə)l/ *n.*[1] & *a.* Also **†Mogor**, **Moghul**, (now preferred for the empire) **Mughal** /ˈmʊg(ə)l, ˈmuː-/, (esp. in sense A.2) **m-**. L16. [Urdu *muġal* f. Pers. & Urdu *muġul* = MONGOL. Var. *-or* f. Port.] A *n.* 1 *Hist.* A Mongolian; *spec.* (*a*) a follower of Genghis Khan in the 13th cent.; (*b*) a member of the Muslim dynasty, descended from Tamerlane, which ruled an empire in India, based on Delhi, from the 16th to the 19th cent. L16. 2 An important or influential person; a powerful autocrat. *colloq.* L17. †3 = *Mogul plum* below. Only in E18. 4 A steam locomotive of 2-6-0 wheel arrangement. L19.

1 **the** (**Great** etc.) **Mogul** the Mughal emperor at Delhi. 2 A. MILLER The son of a Hollywood mogul.

B *adj.* 1 *Hist.* Mongolian; *spec.* of or pertaining to the Mughals or their empire in India. E17. †2 *Mogul plum*, a particular variety of large plum. M18–M19.

mogul /ˈməʊg(ə)l/ *n.*[2] M20. [Prob. f. southern G dial. *Mugel*, *Mugl*.] A bump on a ski slope.

Moguntine /məˈgʌntʌɪn/ *a.* Now *rare* or *obs.* L16. [f. L *Moguntia* Mainz + -INE[1].] Of or pertaining to the city of Mainz, Germany, esp. as an early centre of printing.

mohair /ˈməʊhɛː/ *n.* & *a.* L16. [Arab. *mukayyar* cloth of goat's hair, lit. 'select, choice', pass. pple of *kayyara* prefer, later assim. to HAIR *n.*: cf. MOIRE.] A *n.* 1 A fabric, yarn, or mixture made from the hair of the Angora goat or in imitation of this. L16. 2 A garment made of such material. M17. 3 The hair of the Angora goat. M18. B *attrib.* or as *adj.* Made or consisting of mohair. M17.

mohajir /məˈhɑːdʒɪə, mʊ-/ *n.* & *a.* M20. [Urdu f. Arab. *muhājir* emigrant, rel. to *hajara* (see HEGIRA).] A *n.* (A descendant of) a Muslim emigrant who left India for Pakistan at the time of partition in 1947 or subsequently. M20. B *n.* Of or pertaining to mohajirs. L20.

Mohammed *n.*, **Mohammedan** *a.* & *n.* vars. of MUHAMMAD, MUHAMMADAN.

moharra *n.* var. of MOJARRA.

Moharram *n.* var. of MUHARRAM.

Mohave /məˈhɑːvi/ *n.* & *a.* Also **Mojave**. M19. [Mohave *hàmakhá:v.*] A *n.* Pl. **-s**, same. A member of a Yuman Indian people living along the Colorado river in N. America; the language of this people. M19. B *attrib.* or as *adj.* Of or pertaining to the Mohaves or their language. M19.

Mohawk /ˈməʊhɔːk/ *n.* & *a.* See also MOHOCK. M17. [Narragansett *mohowawog* lit. 'man-eaters'.] A *n.* Pl. **-s**, same. 1 A member of an Iroquois Indian people, one of the five of the original Iroquois confederation, orig. inhabiting parts of upper New York State; the language of this people. M17. 2 *Skating.* A step from either edge of the skate to the same edge on the other foot in an opposite direction. Cf. CHOCTAW *n.* 2. L19. 3 A Mohican haircut. Chiefly *US.* L20. B *attrib.* or as *adj.* 1 Of or pertaining to the Mohawk or their language. M18. 2 Of a hairstyle: = MOHICAN *a.* 2. L20.

Mohegan *n.* & *a.* see MOHICAN.

mohel /ˈməʊ(h)(ə)l/ *n.* M17. [Heb. *mōhēl*.] A Jew who performs the rite of circumcision.

Mohican /məʊˈhiːk(ə)n, ˈməʊɪk(ə)n/ *a.* & *n.* Also (exc. sense A.2, & now the preferred form in other senses) **Mohegan** /-g(ə)n/. M17. [Mohegan.] A *adj.* 1 Designating or pertaining to an Algonquian Indian people formerly inhabiting part of Connecticut, or their language. M17. 2 Of a hairstyle: in which the head is shaved except for a strip of hair from the middle of the forehead to the back of the neck (similar to the depictions of a deer-hair topknot worn by Indian men in the novel by J. F. Cooper: see below). Cf. MOHAWK *n.* 3, *a.* 2. M20.

B *n.* A member of the Mohegan people; the language of this people. M17.

last of the Mohicans [title of a novel (1826) by J. F. Cooper (1789–1851)] *the* sole survivor(s) of a noble race or kind.

¶ Freq. confused with the Mahicans.

Mohini-attam /ˈməʊhɪnɪˌatəm/ *n.* M20. [f. *Mohini* supreme seductress of Hindu mythology (f. Skt *muh-* confuse, bewilder) + Tamil *āṭṭam* dance.] An Indian dance for women, orig. from Kerala in SW India, noted for its gentle and graceful style.

Moho /ˈməʊhəʊ/ *n.* Also **m-**. M20. [Abbrev.] *Geol.* The Mohorovičić discontinuity.

Mohock /ˈməʊhɒk/ *n.* M17. [Var. of MOHAWK.] †1 = MOHAWK *n.* I. M17–L18. 2 *Hist.* A member of a band of aristocratic ruffians who roamed the streets of London at night in the early 18th cent. E18.

mohohu *n.* var. of MOHOOHOO.

mohonono /məʊhəˈnəʊnəʊ/ *n.* Pl. **-os**. M19. [Silozi *muHonono*.] An evergreen tree with grey-green leaves, *Terminalia sericea* (family Combretaceae), native to southern Africa.

mohoohoo /məˈhuːhuː/ *n.* Also **mohohu**. M19. [Setswana.] In southern Africa: the white rhinoceros, *Ceratotherium simum*.

Mohorovičić discontinuity /məʊhəˈrəʊvɪtʃɪtʃ dɪsˌkɒntɪˈnjuːɪti/ *n. phr.* M20. [A. *Mohorovičić* (1857–1936), Yugoslav seismologist.] *Geol.* The discontinuity between the earth's crust and the mantle which is believed to exist at a depth of about 10–12 km (6–7½ miles) under the ocean beds and 40–50 km (25–30 miles) under the continents. Abbrev. MOHO.

Mohs /məʊz/ *n.* L19. [Friedrich *Mohs* (1773–1839), Ger. mineralogist.] Used *attrib.* and in *possess.* to designate a hardness scale devised by Mohs in which ten reference minerals, ranging from very soft (talc) to very hard (diamond), are assigned values of one to ten in order of increasing hardness. Also used w. numerals to represent hardness values on this scale.

mohur /ˈməʊhə/ *n.* L17. [Pers. & Urdu *muhr* seal, cogn. w. Skt *mudrā*.] *Hist.* A gold coin, originally Persian, used in India from the 16th cent. onward, and in the 19th cent. worth 15 rupees. Freq. more fully *gold mohur*. Also called *dinar*.

mohwa *n.* var. of MAHUA.

Moi /ˈməʊɪ/ *n.* & *a.* M19. [Moi.] A *n.* Pl. **-s**, same. A member of an aboriginal people inhabiting the highlands of southern Vietnam (also called *Montagnard*). Also, the language of this people. M19. B *attrib.* or as *adj.* Of or pertaining to the Moi or their language. M20.

moi /mwa/ *pers. pron. joc.* L20. [Fr. = me.] Me; I, myself.

moider /ˈmɔɪdə/ *v. dial.* Also **mither** /ˈmʌɪðə/, **moither** /ˈmɔɪðə/. L17. [Origin unkn.] 1 *v.t.* Confuse, perplex, bewilder; worry, bother, fatigue; pester. Usu. in *pass.* L17. 2 *v.i.* Work very hard, toil. *rare.* E19. 3 *v.i.* Be delirious; babble; wander about aimlessly, ramble. M19.

1 J. O'FAOLAIN 'I'm a bit moidered,' she apologized. N. BAGNALL He was so moithered by the new language . . that he felt he had to use it. 3 D. WINSOR That phrase . . kept moithering round my brain.

moidore /ˈmɔɪdɔː/ *n.* E18. [Port. *moeda d'ouro* coin of gold.] *Hist.* A Portuguese gold coin current in England in the first half of the 18th cent., then worth about 27 shillings.

moiety /ˈmɔɪɪti/ *n.* LME. [OFr. *moité*, (also mod.) *moitié* f. L *medietas*, *-tat-*, f. *medius* MID *a.*: see -ITY. Cf. MEDIETY.] 1 A half, either of two equal parts. LME. 2 Either of two (occas. more) parts (not necessarily equal) into which something is or can be divided. Also (now only w. qualifying adj.), a small part, a lesser share of something. L16. †3 One's wife or (less usu.) husband. *joc.* M18–E19. 4 *Anthropol.* Either of two primary social divisions of a tribe (esp. of Australian Aborigines). L19. 5 *Chem.* A group of atoms forming part of a molecule. M20.

1 H. MACMILLAN The opportunity of acquiring half the shares in the Regent Oil Company—the other moiety was held by Caltex. *Southern Star* (*Eire*) Starting the second moiety of the game, Aidan Twomey moved from centre. 2 SHAKES. *1 Hen. IV* Methinks my moiety, North from Burton here, In quantity equals not one of yours. 5 L. W. BROWDER Nucleotides of ribosomal RNA are also altered by the addition of methyl groups to the ribose moieties.

moil /mɔɪl/ *n.*[1] Now *arch.* & *dial.* E17. [f. the vb.] 1 Toil, drudgery. Freq. in *toil and moil*. E17. 2 Mud, mire. E19. 3 Turmoil, confusion; trouble, vexation. M19.

†moil *n.*[2] M17–E19. [Perh. alt. of MULE *n.*[1] (in

sense 'hybrid').] (Cider produced from) a variety of apple.

moil /mɔɪl/ *n.*[3] *dial.* M19. [f. Ir. *maol* or Welsh *moel* lit. 'bald'. Cf. earlier MOILED, MOILEY, MULL *n.*[3]] A hornless cow or bull.

moil /mɔɪl/ *v.* LME. [OFr. *moillier* wet, moisten, paddle in mud (mod. *mouiller*) f. Proto-Romance, f. L *mollis* soft.] **1** *v.t.* Wet, moisten; soil, bedaub. Now *arch.* & *dial.* LME. †**b** *fig.* Defile. *rare.* L16–M17. **2** *v.i.* Toil, work hard, drudge. Freq. in *toil and moil*. M16. **3** *v.t.* Weary, fatigue; harass, worry. Chiefly *refl.* & in *pass.* Now *rare* or *obs.* M16. **4** *v.i.* & *t.* Burrow (in). Long *obs.* exc. *dial.* M16. **5** *v.i.* Move around in agitation or confusion; swirl, mill about. M20.

moiled /mɔɪld/ *a. dial.* L18. [f. as MOIL *n.*[3] + -ED[2].] Of cattle: hornless.

moiley /ˈmɔɪli/ *n. Sc.* & *Ir.* E19. [f. as MOIL *n.*[3] + -Y[6]. Cf. earlier MULEY *n.* & *a.*[1]] = MOIL *n.*[3]

Moine /mɔɪn/ *n.* L19. [*the Moine* (Gael. *A' Mhòine*), an area near Loch Eriboll in NW Scotland.] Geol. *the Moine(s)*, a highly folded series of metamorphic rocks in NW Scotland and western Ireland, believed to have been deposited in Precambrian times and metamorphosed later. Also *Moine series*.

Moinian *a.* & *n.* (of, pertaining to, or designating) this series M20.

moire /mwɑː/ *n.* M17. [Fr., later form of *mouaire* MOHAIR.] A watered fabric (orig. mohair, now usu. silk). Also *moire antique*.

moiré /ˈmwɑːreɪ/ *a.* & *n.* E19. [Fr. pa. pple of *moirer* give a watered appearance to, f. as prec.] **A** *adj.* **1** Of silk: watered. Also, (of metal etc.) having a clouded appearance like watered silk. E19. **2** Designating or pertaining to a pattern of light and dark fringes observed when a pattern of lines, dots, etc., is visually superimposed on another similar pattern, or on an identical one slightly out of alignment with the first. M20. **B** *n.* **1** A variegated or clouded appearance like that of watered silk, esp. as an ornamental finish applied to metal; a moiré pattern or effect. E19. **2** = MOIRE. M19.

moirette /mwɑːˈrɛt/ *n.* L19. [f. MOIRE + -ETTE.] A textile fabric made to imitate moire.

moissanite /ˈmɔɪsənʌɪt, ˈmwas-/ *n.* E20. [f. H. *Moissan* (1852–1907), Fr. chemist + -ITE[1].] *Min.* A green (sometimes black or bluish) silicon carbide, which crystallizes in the hexagonal system, is a rare constituent of meteoric iron, and is made artificially as carborundum.

moist /mɔɪst/ *a.* & *n.* LME. [OFr. *moiste* (mod. *moite*), perh. f. Proto-Romance f. L *mucidus* mouldy, alt. by assoc. with *musteus* new, fresh, f. *mustum* MUST *n.*[1]] **A** *adj.* **1** Slightly wet; containing moisture; damp, humid. LME. **b** Of the eyes: wet with tears, ready to shed tears. Formerly also, rheumy (as a sign of old age). LME. **c** *Hist.* Designating a quality associated with wetness and regarded in medieval and later times as one of four qualities inherent in all things; having a preponderance of this quality. Cf. *cold*, *dry*, *hot*. LME. **d** Of a season, climate, etc.: rainy, having some or considerable rainfall. L15. †**2** Juicy, succulent; fresh, new. LME–E17. †**3** Bringing rain or moisture; containing water or other liquid. LME–E18. †**4** Liquid; watery. LME–E17. **5** Associated or connected with liquid; *poet.* accompanied by tears; *Med.* accompanied by a discharge of phlegm, pus, etc. M16.

1 F. NORRIS It had rained copiously, and the soil, still moist, disengaged a pungent aroma. T. KENEALLY He sucked a pebble to keep his mouth moist. I. MURDOCH A full-lipped mouth all moist with.. lipstick and tears. **b** SHAKES. *2 Hen. IV* Have you not a moist eye..And will you yet call yourself young? A. MASSIE Her eyes grew moist..with regret for the past. **d** DRYDEN Invoke the Pow'rs who rule the Sky, For a moist Summer.

Special collocations: *moist gangrene*: see GANGRENE *n.* I. *moist scall*: see SCALL *n.* **moist sugar** (now *rare*) unrefined or partially refined sugar.

†**B** *n.* Moisture; moist quality, moistness. LME–M18.

moistful *a.* (*rare*) moist LME. **moistify** *v.t.* (*rare*) moisten; *esp.* = MOISTEN IC: L18. **moistish** *a.* L16. **moistless** *a.* free from moisture, dry L16. **moistly** *adv.* †(*a*) drunkenly; (*b*) in a moist manner: E17. **moistness** *n.* (*a*) the quality or state of being moist; †(*b*) moisture: LME.

moist /mɔɪst/ *v.* ME. [f. (as) the adj.] †**1** *v.i.* Grow moist. ME–L15. **2** *v.t.* Moisten. *obs.* exc. *dial.* LME. †**b** *fig.* Soften (the heart etc.). LME–L16. **3** *v.i.* Drizzle. *US. rare.* E20.

moisten /ˈmɔɪs(ə)n/ *v.* L16. [f. MOIST *a.* + -EN[5].] **1** *v.t.* Make moist; wet superficially or moderately. L16. †**b** *fig.* = MOIST *v.* 2b. *rare.* L16–M17. **c** *spec.* Wet (the lips, throat, etc.) with drink. (Foll. by *with*.) E17. **2** *v.i.* Become moist. M19.

1 E. BOWEN The pianist moistened the tips of her fingers to flatten her hair. A. CARTER A little fountain of fresh water that moistened the shingle. **c** SIR W. SCOTT You have been moistening your own throat. *moisten one's clay*: see CLAY *n.* 3. **2** G. SWIFT He held Sophie..and I saw..his eyes moisten.

moistener *n.* E17.

moisture /ˈmɔɪstʃə/ *n.* LME. [OFr. *moistour* (mod. *moiteur*), f. *moiste* MOIST *a.*, with suffix-substitution: see -URE.] †**1** Moistness; the quality or state of being moist or damp. LME–L18. **2** Water or other liquid diffused in a small quantity as vapour, through a solid, or condensed on a surface. Also, tears moistening the eyes. LME. **b** The liquid part or constituent of a body; the humour or moist property inherent in plants and animals (cf. MOIST *a.* IC). Also *radical moisture*. *obs.* exc. *Hist.* LME. †**3** Liquid; drink. LME–M18.

2 C. MCCULLOUGH The last drop of moisture had long since evaporated. JAYNE PHILLIPS October, a clean moisture in the air.

Comb.: **moisture content** the proportional amount of moisture in any substance; **moisture cream** a cosmetic cream to keep the skin moist; **moisture meter** an instrument for indicating moisture content, esp. by measuring electrical resistivity.

moistureless *a.* E19.

moisturize /ˈmɔɪstʃərʌɪz/ *v.t.* Also **-ise**. M20. [f. prec. + -IZE.] Make moist; *esp.* (of a cosmetic) make (the skin) less dry. Freq. as *moisturizing* vbl n. & ppl a.

moisturizer *n.* a cosmetic preparation to keep the skin moist M20.

moisty /ˈmɔɪsti/ *a.* LME. [f. MOIST *a.* + -Y[1]. Cf. MUSTY *a.*[2]] Moist, damp. Now chiefly (in collocation w. *misty*) w. ref. to weather or climate.

C. M. YONGE It is not doing the place justice to study it on a misty, moisty morning.

moit /mɔɪt/ *n. dial., Austral.*, & *NZ.* M19. [Alt. of MOTE *n.*[1]] A particle of wood, stick, etc., caught in the wool of a sheep.

moither *v.* var. of MOIDER.

mojarra /məʊˈharə/ *n.* Also **moh-**. M19. [Amer. Sp.] Any of various small percoid fishes of the family Gerreidae, found in neotropical coastal waters.

Mojave *n.* & *a.* var. of MOHAVE.

mojo /ˈməʊdʒəʊ/ *n.*[1] *US local.* Pl. **-os**. E20. [Prob. of Afr. origin: cf. Gullah *moco* witchcraft, magic, Fulah *moco'o* medicine man.] Magic, voodoo; a charm or amulet.

mojo /ˈməʊdʒəʊ/ *n.*[2] *US slang.* M20. [Origin unkn.] Any narcotic drug; *esp.* morphine.

mokaddam /mɒˈkʌdʌm/ *n.* E17. [Arab. *mukaddam* pass. pple of *kaddama* put in front or at the head.] In the Indian subcontinent: a headman, a local chief.

moke /məʊk/ *n.*[1] *slang* & *dial.* M19. [Probably f. a pers. name.] **1** A donkey. M19. **b** A very poor horse. *Austral.* & *NZ.* L19. **2** A stupid person, a dolt. M19. **3** A Black. *US. derog.* & usu. considered *racially offensive*. M19.

moke /məʊk/ *n.*[2] M20. [Origin unkn.] In full *mini-moke*. A small motor vehicle resembling a Jeep.

moki /ˈmɒki/ *n.*[1] *NZ.* M19. [Maori.] Either of two edible percoid marine fishes, the grey and white *Latridopsis ciliaris* (family Latridae), and (in full *red moki*) the fish *Chironemus spectabilis* (family Chironemidae), which is reddish-brown with dark brown bars.

moki /ˈmɒki/ *n.*[2] M19. [Maori.] *NZ Hist.* A Maori raft made of bulrushes etc.

moki-moki *n.* see MOKO-MOKO.

Moko /ˈməʊkəʊ/ *n.*[1] Pl. **-os**, (in sense 1, also) same. Also (earlier) †**Moca**. L18. [Yoruba.] **1** A Yoruba-speaking member of a people of southern Nigeria. L18. **2** (**m-**.) **a** A variety of plantain grown in Trinidad (also *moko fig*). Chiefly in *moko disease*, = sense 2b. E20. **b** A bacterial disease affecting the banana and other plantains. L20.

moko /ˈməʊkəʊ/ *n.*[2] Pl. **-os**. M19. [Maori.] The system or a pattern of tattooing the face practised by Maoris.

moko-moko /məʊkəʊˈməʊkəʊ/ *n. NZ.* Pl. **-os**. In sense 1 also **moki-moki** /məʊkɪˈməʊki/ & other vars. L19. [Maori.] **1** = KORIMAKO. Now *rare*. L19. **2** A lizard of the genus *Lygosoma*. E20.

mokopuna /ˈmɒkɒpunə/ *n. NZ.* Pl. same. E20. [Maori.] In Maori culture: a grandchild; a descendant.

moksha /ˈmɒkʃə/ *n.* L18. [Skt *mokṣa*, f. *muc* set free, release.] *Hinduism* & *Jainism*. The final release of the soul from a cycle of incarnations; the bliss so attained. Also called *mukti*.

mol *n.* see MOLE *n.*[5]

mola /ˈməʊlə/ *n.*[1] Now *rare*. E17. [L.] **1** *Med.* = MOLE *n.*[4] E17. **2** *Entomol.* = MOLAR *n.* 2. E19.

mola /ˈməʊlə/ *n.*[2] M20. [Cuna.] A square of brightly coloured appliquéd cloth worn as a blouse by Cuna Indian women of the San Blas Islands, Panama.

molal /ˈməʊl(ə)l/ *a.* E20. [f. MOLE *n.*[5] + -AL[1].] *Physical Chem.* **1** = MOLAR *a.*[3] I. E20. **2** Of a solution: containing one mole, or a specified number of moles, of solute per kilogram of solution. Of a concentration: expressed in terms of these quantities. Cf. MOLAR *a.*[3] 2. E20.

moˈlality *n.* the molal concentration of a solution E20.

Molale /məʊˈlɑːli/ *n.* M19. [Penutian.] **A** *n.* Pl. same, **-s**. A member of a Penutian Indian people of Oregon; the language of this people. M19. **B** *attrib.* or as *adj.* Of or pertaining to the Molale or their language. M20.

†**molan** *n.* see MULLEN *n.*[1]

molar /ˈməʊlə/ *n.* & *a.*[1] As n. orig. only in L pl. form †**molares**. LME. [L *molaris* adj. = of a mill, n. = grindstone, molar tooth, f. *mola* mill: see -AR[1].] **A** *n.* **1** A molar or grinding tooth; a true molar (see below). LME. **2** *Entomol.* A molar process. Cf. MOLA *n.*[1] 2. L19.

1 false molar a premolar, a molar tooth which has replaced a deciduous tooth. **true molar** a molar tooth which is not preceded by a deciduous tooth.

B *adj.* **1** Of a tooth: serving to grind; *spec.* designating any of the back teeth of mammals. E17. **b** Of or pertaining to a molar tooth. M19. **2** *Med.* Of the nature of a mola or false conception. *rare.* E19. **3** *Entomol.* Designating or pertaining to any of the thick internal processes with a grinding surface found on and near the base of the mandibles of many insects. L19.

¶As n. not recorded in Anglicized form *molar* bef. 19.

molar /ˈməʊlə/ *a.*[2] M19. [f. L *moles* mass + -AR[1].] **1** Of or pertaining to mass; acting on or by means of large masses or units. Freq. contrasted w. *molecular*. M19. **2** *Psychol.* Of or pertaining to behaviour as a whole, or an integrated set of responses serving a common goal. Cf. MOLECULAR *a.* 4. E20.

molar /ˈməʊlə/ *a.*[3] E20. [f. MOLE *n.*[5] + -AR[1].] *Physical Chem.* **1** Of or pertaining to one mole of a substance; = MOLAL *a.* I. E20. **2** Of a solution: containing one mole, or a specified number of moles, of solute per litre of solution. Of a concentration: expressed in terms of these quantities. Cf. MOLAL *a.* 2. E20.

moˈlarity *n.* the molar concentration of a solution M20.

†**molares** *n.pl.* see MOLAR *n.* & *a.*[1]

molariform /məʊˈlarɪfɔːm/ *a.* M19. [mod.L *molariformis*, f. as MOLAR *n.* & *a.*[1]: see -FORM.] Chiefly *Zool.* Having the form of or resembling a molar tooth.

molarization /məʊlərʌɪˈzeɪʃ(ə)n/ *n.* Also **-isation**. M20. [f. MOLAR *n.* & *a.*[1] + -IZATION.] *Zool.* The assumption, during the course of evolution, of the characteristics of a molar tooth by a premolar or other tooth.

ˈmolarized *a.* showing the consequences of molarization L20.

molary /ˈməʊləri/ *a.* Now *rare*. E19. [Fr. *molaire* MOLAR *a.*[1]: see -ARY[2].] Adapted for grinding or pulverizing food; = MOLAR *a.*[1] 1.

†molass *n. Sc.* M16–M19. [f. as MOLASSES.] A liquor distilled from molasses.

molasse /məˈlas/ *n.* L18. [Fr. f. as next.] *Geol.* A thickly-bedded sedimentary deposit consisting of soft ungraded sandstones, marls, conglomerates, etc. Orig. *spec.* (**M-**) such a deposit of Miocene to Oligocene age in the region between the Alps and the Jura.

molasses /məˈlasɪz/ *n.* Also (earlier) **†mel-** & other vars. See also earlier MOLASS. L16. [Port. *melaço* f. late L *mellaceum* must, use as n. of neut. sing. of *mellaceus* of the nature of honey, f. L *mel*, *mell-* honey.] **1** Uncrystallized syrup drained from raw sugar in refining; *N. Amer.* golden syrup. L16. **†2** = MOLASS. *Sc.* M–L18.

1 *fig.*: *New York Times* The mournful molasses of his prose.

molassed *a.* containing much molasses M20. **molassied** /məˈlasɪd/ *a.* M19.

mold *ns.*, *vs.* see MOULD *ns.*, *vs.*

Moldavian /mɒlˈdeɪvɪən/ *n.* & *a.* E17. [f. *Moldavia* (see below) + -AN.] **A** *n.* **1** A native or inhabitant of Moldavia (Moldova) in eastern Europe, one of the two principalities from which Romania was formed and later a constituent republic of the USSR which is now independent. E17. **2** The Romanian language as spoken and written in Moldavia. M19. **B** *adj.* Of or pertaining to Moldavia or its inhabitants. M18.

¶Cf. MOLDOVAN.

moldavite /ˈmɒldəvʌɪt/ *n.* L19. [G *Moldawit*, f. *Moldau* the Vltava River in Bohemia: see -ITE[1].] *Geol.* Orig., the material (resembling obsidian) of tektites. Now, a tektite from the strewn field in Bohemia and Moravia.

molded *adjs.*, **molder** *n.*, *v.*, **molding** *ns.* see MOULDED *adjs.* etc.

Moldovan /mɒlˈdəʊv(ə)n/ *n.* & *a.* M19. [f. *Moldova* (see below) + -AN.] **A** *n.* Orig. = MOLDAVIAN *n.* 1. Now *spec.* a native or inhabitant of Moldova (Moldavia), a republic of the CIS. M19. **B** *adj.* Of or pertaining to Moldova (Moldavia) or its inhabitants. L20.

molcajete /mɔlkaˈxete, mɒlkəˈheɪteɪ/ *n.* L20. [Mex. Sp., f. Sp. *moler* grind + *cajete* pot, bowl.] A mortar for grinding spices and small seeds in.

Moldo-Wallachian /ˌmɒldəʊwəˈleɪkɪən/ *a.* M19. [f. MOLDAVIAN + -O- + WALLACHIAN.] Of or pertaining to both Moldavia and Wallachia, principalities of Romania united in 1859.

moldy *a.*[1], *a.*[2] see MOULDY *a.*[1], *a.*[2]

mole /məʊl/ *n.*[1] [OE *māl* corresp. to MLG *mēl*, OHG *meil*, *meila*, f. Gmc, whence also OE *mǣlan*, OHG *meilen* to stain.] **†1** *gen.* A discoloured spot, esp. on cloth, linen, etc. OE–L19. **2** A spot or blemish on the human skin; *spec.* a small, often slightly raised patch made dark by an abnormally high concentration of melanin. LME. **†3** *fig.* A blemish, a fault; a distinguishing or identifying mark. M17–M18.

mole /məʊl/ *n.*[2] & *a.* ME. [Prob. f. MDu. *mol*, *moll(e)*, (M)LG *mol*, *mul*.] **A** *n.* **1** Any of various small burrowing mammals (insectivores) of the family Talpidae; *esp.* the Eurasian *Talpa europaea*, with grey velvety fur, very small eyes, and very short strong forelimbs adapted for digging. Also (w. specifying wd), any of various other animals considered to resemble this. Formerly used as a type of blindness (erron. attributed to the mole in classical and later times). ME. **2** *fig.* **a** A person who works in darkness. E17. **†b** A person with defective (physical or mental) vision. Only in 17. **c** A secret agent who gradually achieves a position deep within the security defences of a country; a trusted person within an organization etc. who betrays confidential information. *colloq.* L20. **3a** The borer of a mole-plough. E19. **b** A remotely operated or automatic machine capable of tunnelling or crawling. M20. **4** In *pl.* Moleskin trousers. L19. **5** The grey colour of moleskin. E20.

1 *duck-mole*: see DUCK *n.*[1] **golden mole** any of various burrowing insectivores of the African family Chrysochloridae. **marsupial mole** a small burrowing Australian marsupial, *Notoryctes typhlops*, with pale yellow fur and no functional eyes. *star-nosed mole*: see STAR *n.*[1] & *a.*

Comb.: **mole-cast** a molehill; **mole-catcher** (*a*) a person whose business it is to catch moles; †(*b*) a detested or contemptible person; **mole-coloured** *a.* = sense B. below; *mole-cricket*: see CRICKET *n.*[1]; **mole drain** a drain made by a mole-plough; **mole-drain** *v.t.* drain (land) using a mole-plough; **mole-plough** a plough in which a pointed iron shoe attached to an upright support is drawn along beneath the surface, making a hollow (drainage) channel resembling a mole's burrow; **mole-rat** any of various subterranean rodents of the African family Bathyergidae and certain other Old World subfamilies; **mole snake** a non-venomous colubrid snake, *Pseudaspis cana*, native to southern and eastern Africa, which feeds on rats and mice.

B *adj.* Of the grey colour of moleskin. E20.

mole /məʊl/ *n.*[3] LME. [Sense 1 f. L *moles* mass; senses 2, 3 f. Fr. *môle* f. L.] **†1** A great mass, a large piece; bulk, mass. LME–E18. **2** A massive structure, esp. of stone, serving as a pier, breakwater, or causeway; the water area contained within such a structure; a man-made harbour, a port. M16. **†3** *Antiq.* A Roman form of mausoleum. M17–M19.

Comb.: **mole-head** the outward or seaward end of a mole.

mole /məʊl/ *n.*[4] LME. [L MOLA *n.*[1]] *Med.* An abnormal mass of tissue in the uterus; a false conception.

HYDATIDIFORM *mole*.

mole /məʊl/ *n.*[5] Also **mol**. E20. [G *Mol*, f. *Molekul* molecule.] *Physical Chem.* That amount of a given substance or species having a mass in grams numerically the same as its molecular or atomic weight, equivalent (in the International System of Units) to the quantity of specified molecules, ions, electrons, etc., that in number equals the number of atoms in 0.012 kg of the carbon isotope of mass 12.

Comb.: **mole fraction** the ratio of the number of moles of a component in a solution to the total number of moles of all components present.

mole /ˈmoli, ˈməʊli/ *n.*[6] M20. [Mex. Sp. f. Nahuatl *molli* sauce, stew.] A highly spiced Mexican sauce made chiefly from chilli and chocolate, served with meat.

mole /məʊl/ *v.t.* L18. [f. MOLE *n.*[2]] **1** Free (ground) from molehills or moles. Chiefly as *moling* vbl n. L18. **2** Burrow or form holes in, as a mole does; bring *out* by burrowing or delving (chiefly *fig.*). M19.

2 W. M. RAINE Tait would mole out quite enough evidence against him.

moling *vbl n.* the action of the vb; *esp.* the making of mole drains: M20.

†molebut *n. rare.* L16–M18. [Fr. *molebout*, prob. f. dial. *mole* f. L MOLA *n.*[1]; *-bout* rel. to BUTT *n.*[1]] The sunfish, *Mola mola*.

†molecula *n.* Pl. **-lae**. L17. [mod.L: see MOLECULE.] **1** = MOLECULE 1. L17–E19. **2** A small mass. Only in E18.

molecular /məˈlɛkjʊlə/ *a.* L18. [f. next + -AR[1].] **1** Of or pertaining to a molecule or molecules; consisting of molecules; acting or inherent in the molecules of a substance. L18. **b** Designating the branch of a science that deals with phenomena at the molecular level. L19. **2** *Biol.* Consisting, or believed to consist, of submicroscopic particles (cf. MOLECULE 3); finely granular. Now only in *molecular layer* below. E19. **3** *Philos.* Of a proposition, sentence, etc.: consisting of or analysable into simpler propositions, sentences, etc., connected by one or more conjunctions. L19. **4** Of or pertaining to a small part or detail of a subject, system, etc., rather than to the whole; small-scale; *esp.* (*Psychol.*) concerned with or pertaining to an elementary unit of behaviour such as a physiological response (cf. MOLAR *a.*[2] 2). E20.

Special collocations: **molecular biology** the branch of biology that deals with the structure and function of macromolecules essential to life (as nucleic acids, proteins, etc.). **molecular heat** the heat capacity of one gram-molecule of a substance. **molecular layer** *Anat.* (*a*) either of the two plexiform layers of the retina; (*b*) the outermost layer of the cortex of the cerebellum and cerebrum, containing a mass of nerve fibres with many synapses but relatively few cells. **molecular sieve** a crystalline substance, esp. a zeolite, with pores of molecular dimensions which allow the entry of molecules smaller than a certain size. **molecular weight** = *relative molecular mass* s.v. RELATIVE *a. relative molecular mass*: see RELATIVE *a.*

molecuˈlarity *n.* (*a*) molecular quality; molecular agencies generally; (*b*) *Chem.* the number of reacting molecules involved in a single step of a chemical reaction: M19. **molecularly** *adv.* in a molecular manner; as regards molecules; on a molecular scale: M19.

molecule /ˈmɒlɪkjuːl/ *n.* L18. [Fr. *molécule* f. mod.L *molecula* dim. of L *moles* MOLE *n.*[3]: see -CULE. Cf. earlier MOLECULA.] **1** Any of the extremely minute particles of which material substances are thought to consist. Now *spec.* (*Chem.*), the smallest fundamental unit of a chemical compound that can take part in the chemical reactions characteristic of that compound; a number of atoms chemically joined together. L18. **2** *gen.* A very small particle. L18. **†3** *Biol.* A minute but functional particle of tissue that is invisible or barely visible under a microscope. E–M19.

1 TSCHERMAK(*'s*) *molecule*.

molehill /ˈməʊlhɪl/ *n.* LME. [f. MOLE *n.*[2] + HILL *n.*] A small mound of earth thrown up by a mole in burrowing near the surface of the ground.

make a mountain (out) of a molehill attribute great importance to something, esp. a difficulty or grievance, which is really insignificant.

molehilly *a.* having many molehills M19.

molendinar /mɒlənˈdiːnə/ *a. rare. joc.* E19. [med.L *molendinarius*, f. *molendinum* mill: see -AR[1].] Of or pertaining to a mill or miller.

¶Chiefly in the writings of Sir Walter Scott.

molendinary /məˈlɛndɪn(ə)ri/ *a.* & *n.* (belonging to) a mill E19.

Moler /ˈməʊlə/ *n.* Also **m-**. E20. [Da., f. dial. *mo* loose chalky soil (= Norw., Sw. *mo* sandy heath) + *ler* loam, clay (also Norw., Sw.).] (Proprietary name for) a kind of diatomaceous earth used as a building material.

moleskin /ˈməʊlskɪn/ *n.* & *a.* M17. [f. MOLE *n.*[2] + SKIN *n.*] **A** *n.* **1** The skin of the mole used as fur. Also, another skin sheared so as to resemble this. M17. **2** A strong soft fine-piled cotton fustian the surface of which is shaved before dyeing. E19. **b** In *pl.* Outer garments, esp. trousers, made of this. M19. **B** *adj.* Made of moleskin. M19.

molest /məˈlɛst/ *n.* Long *arch.* ME. [OFr. *moleste* use as n. of L *molestus*: see next.] Trouble, hardship; molestation, injury.

molestful *a.* troublesome, annoying, painful L16.

molest /məˈlɛst/ *v.t.* LME. [OFr. *molester* or L *molestare*, f. *molestus* troublesome, perh. rel. to *moles* MOLE *n.*[3]] **†1** Cause trouble to; vex, annoy, inconvenience. LME–E18. **b** Of disease: afflict, affect. M16–L17. **2** Interfere or meddle with (a person) injuriously or with hostile intent. Now *esp.* attack or abuse sexually. L15. **b** Tamper with (a thing). Now *rare*. E17.

1 ADDISON The Colds of Winter, and the Heats of Summer, are equally incapable of molesting you. 2 E. CALDWELL More likely to be mugged or . . otherwise molested in downtown Zephyrfield. A. SILLITOE She would carry a bag of pepper to throw in the face of any man who might try to molest her.

molester *n.* M16. **molestive** *a.* tending to cause annoyance; intentionally troublesome or interfering: E20.

molestation /mɒlɛˈsteɪʃ(ə)n, məʊ-/ *n.* LME. [(O)Fr. f. med.L *molestatio(n-)*, f. L *molestat-* pa. ppl stem of *molestare*: see prec., -ATION.] **1** The action of molesting someone or (now *rare*) something; the condition of being molested; intentional annoyance, hostile interference; (esp. sexual) assault. Formerly also, vexation, distress. LME. **b** *Sc. Law*. The harassing of a person in his or her possession or occupation of lands. LME. **2** An instance of molesting or being molested; a cause of annoyance. Now *rare*. LME.

moley /ˈməʊli/ *n. slang.* M20. [Origin unkn.] A potato containing embedded razor blades, used as a weapon.

molimen /mə(ʊ)ˈlʌɪmən/ *n.* Now *rare* or *obs.* Pl. **molimina** /mə(ʊ)ˈlɪmɪnə/. M19. [L *molimen*, *-min-* effort, f. *moliri* make an effort.] *Med.* An effort by which the system endeavours to perform a natural function, esp. menstruation.

†**moliminous** *a.* M17. [f. as prec. + -OUS.] **1** Involving great effort or endeavour; laborious. M17–E18. **2** Massive, cumbrous; weighty, momentous. M–L17.

molinary /ˈməʊlɪn(ə)ri/ *a. rare.* L18. [f. late L *molina* mill + -ARY¹.] Of or pertaining to the grinding of corn.

molindone /ˈmɒlɪndəʊn/ *n.* M20. [f. MO(RPHO)L(INE + IND(OLE + -ONE.] *Pharm.* An indole derivative, $C_{16}H_{24}N_2O_2$, used in the treatment of schizophrenia and other psychoses.

moline /məˈlʌɪn/ *a.* M16. [Prob. f. AN, f. *molin* (mod.Fr. *moulin*) mill.] *Her.* Of or resembling the broadened and curved extremities of a mill-rind. Chiefly in *cross moline*, a cross having the end of each limb broadened and curved back in this way.

molinete /moliˈnete, məʊlɪˈneɪti/ *n.* M20. [Sp., lit. '(toy) windmill, little mill'.] *Bullfighting.* A kind of decorative pass in which the matador turns away in the direction opposite to that of the bull's charge.

Molinism /ˈmɒlɪnɪz(ə)m/ *n.*¹ *rare.* M17. [f. Luis de *Molina* (1535–1600), Sp. Jesuit + -ISM.] *Theol.* The doctrine that the efficacy of grace depends simply on the will which freely accepts.

Molinist *n.*¹ & *a.*¹ (*a*) *n.* a believer in the doctrine of Molinism; (*b*) *adj.* of or pertaining to Molinism or Molinists: M17.

Molinism /ˈmɒlɪnɪz(ə)m/ *n.*² *rare.* E18. [f. Miguel de *Molinos* (*c*1640–96), Sp. priest + -ISM.] *Theol.* Quietism.

Molinist *n.*² & *a.*² (*a*) *n.* a quietist; (*b*) *adj.* of or pertaining to quietism or quietists: M19.

molinology /mɒlɪˈnɒlədʒi/ *n.* M20. [f. late L *molina* mill + -OLOGY.] The branch of knowledge that deals with mills and milling.

molinoˈlogical *a.* L20. **molinologist** *n.* M20.

moll /mɒl/ *n.* & *v.* E17. [Pet-form of female forename *Mary*. Cf. MOLLY *n.*¹] **A** *n.* A girl, a woman; *esp.* a prostitute; a female pickpocket or thief; a criminal's female accomplice; the girlfriend of a gangster or criminal. E17.

T. MIDDLETON None of these common Molls neither, but discontented and unfortunate gentlewomen. A. T. ELLIS A cigarette held between her teeth so that she looked like a gangster's moll.

Comb.: **moll-buzzer** *slang* a pickpocket or thief whose victims are mainly women; **moll-heron** *dial.* a heron; **mollrowing** /-raʊɪŋ/ *slang* (*a*) going out with (disreputable) women, wenching; (*b*) (a) caterwauling; **moll-shop** *slang* a brothel; **moll-washer** *dial.* the pied wagtail.

B *v.t. slang.* †**1** *moll it up with*, go out with (a woman). Only in E19. **2** As *molled* ppl a. Accompanied by or going out with a woman. Also foll. by *up*. M19.

mollescent /mɒˈlɛs(ə)nt/ *a. rare.* E19. [L *mollescent-* pres. ppl stem of *mollescere* become soft, f. *mollis* soft: see -ESCENT.] Tending to become soft.

mollescence *n.* E19.

molleton /ˈmɒlɪtɒn/ *n.* L18. [Fr., f. *mollet* dim. of *mol* soft.] Swanskin (flannel).

†**molliable** *a.* L17–M18. [f. L *mollire* soften + -ABLE.] Able to be softened.

mollie *n.*¹, *n.*², *n.*³ vars. of MOLLY *n.*¹, *n.*², *n.*³

mollient /ˈmɒlɪənt/ *n.* & *a. rare.* E17. [L *mollient-* pres. ppl stem of *mollire* soften, f. *mollis* soft: see -ENT.] †**A** *n. Med.* A softening application, an emollient. Only in E17. **B** *adj.* Softening. E18.

†**mollifaction** *n. rare.* L16–E19. [f. MOLLIFY: see -FACTION.] = MOLLIFICATION.

mollification /ˌmɒlɪfɪˈkeɪʃ(ə)n/ *n.* LME. [L *mollificatio(n-)*, f. *mollificat-* pa. ppl stem of *mollificare*: see MOLLIFY, -ATION.] The action of mollifying someone or (now *rare*) something; an instance of this; (a) reduction in severity; (an) appeasement.

ˈ**mollificative** *a.* & *n.* (now *rare*) (*a*) *adj.* that causes mollification or softening; †(*b*) *n.* a medicine that softens: LME.

mollify /ˈmɒlɪfʌɪ/ *v.* LME. [Fr. *mollifier* or L *mollificare*, f. *mollis* soft: see -FY.] **1** *v.t.* Make soft or supple; make tender. Now *rare*. LME. **2** *v.t.* Soften in temper or disposition; allay the anger or indignation of; calm, pacify, appease. Freq. in *pass.* LME. †**b** *v.i.* Become softened in temper or disposition; relax one's severity, become less angry, relent. E16–E19. †**3** *v.t.* Enervate, enfeeble. L15–L16. **4** *v.t.* Reduce in violence or intensity; reduce in harshness, severity, or rigour; express more favourably. Now *rare*. L15.

2 G. SANTAYANA 'Always nagging,' muttered Mrs. Darnley, secretly mollified by feeling her son's arm round her waist. A. GUINNESS The Colonel looked crosser, so I added, 'Sir', which mollified him slightly. 4 DRYDEN Now mince the Sin, And mollifie Damnation with a Phrase. R. TRAVERS Had he mollified his hard nature and softened his savage sentiments.

mollifiable *a.* E17. **mollifier** *n.* L16. **mollifyingly** *adv.* in a mollifying manner E20.

Mollisol /ˈmɒlɪsɒl/ *n.* M20. [f. L *mollis* soft + -SOL.] *Soil Sci.* A soil of an order comprising temperate grassland soils with a dark, humus-rich surface layer containing high concentrations of calcium and magnesium.

mollities /mɒˈlɪʃiːz/ *n.* Now *rare.* E17. [L, f. *mollis* soft.] †**1** Effeminacy. Only in E17. **2** *Med.* Softening, softness, esp. of the brain or bones. M19.

mollitious /mɒˈlɪʃəs/ *a. rare.* E17. [f. as prec. + -ITIOUS¹.] Luxurious, sensuous.

†**mollitude** *n.* M17–M18. [L *mollitudo*, f. *mollis* soft: see -TUDE.] Softness, effeminacy.

mollock /ˈmɒlək/ *v.i. slang.* M20. [Prob. f. blend of MOLL, MULLOCK.] Pursue amorous adventures; copulate. Also, dally, lounge.

S. GIBBONS He's off a-mollocking somewheres in Howling.

mollusc /ˈmɒləsk/ *n.* Also *-**sk**. L18. [Fr. *mollusque* f. mod.L *mollusca* (see below) neut. pl. of L *molluscus*, f. *mollis* soft.] *Zool.* Any animal of the phylum Mollusca, members of which (as limpets, snails, cuttlefish, oysters, mussels, etc.) have soft bodies and (usu.) hard shells.

¶Orig. used more widely (after Linnaeus), including also echinoderms, annelids, and hydroids.

moˈlluscan *a.* & *n.* (*a*) *adj.* of, pertaining to, or characteristic of a mollusc or molluscs; (*b*) *n.* a mollusc: E19.

mollusca *n.pl.* see MOLLUSCUM.

molluscicide /məˈlʌskɪsʌɪd/ *n.* M20. [f. prec. + -I- + -CIDE.] A substance used to kill molluscs.

mollusciˈcidal *a.* M20.

molluscoid /məˈlʌskɔɪd/ *a.* M19. [Sense 1 f. MOLLUSC; sense 2 f. MOLLUSCUM: see -OID.] **1** *Zool.* Resembling a mollusc; like that of a mollusc. M19. **2** *Med.* = MOLLUSCOUS 2. *rare.* L19.

molluscous /məˈlʌskəs/ *a.* E19. [f. as prec. + -OUS.] **1** Of or pertaining to molluscs; of the nature of a mollusc. E19. **b** *fig.* Like a mollusc; flabby, invertebrate. L19. **2** *Med.* Of, pertaining to, or of the nature of molluscum. M19.

molluscum /məˈlʌskəm/ *n.* Pl. **-sca** /-skə/. E19. [mod.L, neut. of *molluscus*: see MOLLUSC.] *Med.* **1** Any of various skin disorders characterized by soft rounded swellings or nodules; *esp.* molluscum contagiosum (see below). E19. **2** A soft nodule characteristic of such a disorder. M19.

1 molluscum contagiosum /kɒnteɪdʒɪˈəʊsəm/ [L = contagious] a viral disorder characterized by groups of small smooth painless pinkish nodules with a central depression, that yield a milky fluid when squeezed. **molluscum sebaceum** /sɪˈbeɪʃəm/ [L = sebaceous] = KERATOACANTHOMA.

Comb.: **molluscum body** any of the characteristic ovoid bodies, thought to be degenerate epidermal cells, found in the nodules of molluscum contagiosum; a cytoplasmic inclusion in a degenerating epidermal cell.

mollusk *n.* see MOLLUSC.

Mollweide /ˈmɒlvʌɪdə/ *n.* E20. [Karl B. *Mollweide* (d. 1825), Ger. mathematician and astronomer.] Used in *possess.* and *attrib.* to designate a homalographic map projection in which the surface of the globe is represented by an ellipse, with lines of latitude represented by the major axis and straight lines parallel to it (spaced more closely towards the poles), and meridians represented by the minor axis and equally spaced elliptical curves.

molly /ˈmɒli/ *n.*¹ Also **mollie**, (in senses 1, 2) **M-**. E18. [Pet-form of female forename *Mary*. Cf. MOLL.] **1** A young woman or girl; a prostitute. *slang* & *dial.* E18. **2** (A name for) an effeminate or homosexual male; a milksop. Also *Miss Molly. slang.* E18. **3** A large fruit basket. L19.

Comb.: **mollycot** *dial.* a man who busies himself with domestic duties supposedly the concern of a woman; **molly cotton-tail** *US* a cotton-tail.

molly /ˈmɒli/ *n.*² Also **mollie**. M19. [Perh. abbrev. of MOLLYMAWK.] *Naut.* **1** The fulmar. M19. **2** A meeting of captains held on board one of several whaling ships in company. L19.

molly /ˈmɒli/ *n.*³ Also **mollie**. M20. [Abbrev. of *Mollienisia*, former mod.L genus name, irreg. f. Count F. N. *Mollien* (1758–1850), Fr. statesman: see -IA¹.] Any of several small live-bearing freshwater fishes of the genus *Poecilia*, found from the USA to northern S. America; esp. *P. sphenops*, which has been bred into many colour varieties and is popular as an aquarium fish.

molly /ˈmɒli/ *v.* L19. [f. MOLLY *n.*¹ or MOLLYCODDLE *v.*] **1** *v.i.* Of a man: do housework. *dial.* L19. **2** *v.t.* = MOLLYCODDLE *v.* E20.

mollycoddle /ˈmɒlɪkɒd(ə)l/ *v.* & *n.* M19. [f. MOLLY *n.*¹ + CODDLE *v.*² & *n.*] **A** *v.t.* Coddle, pamper. M19.

R. K. NARAYAN That boy grew up fearlessly . . at an age when other boys were being mollycoddled.

B *n.* A person (usu. male) who is mollycoddled; an effeminate man or boy, a milksop. M19.

G. B. SHAW You are a mollycoddle If you were a real man you would . . delight in beating him.

mollycoddler *n.* M19.

molly-dooker /ˈmɒlɪduːkə/ *n. Austral. slang.* M20. [f. MOLLY *n.*¹ or MAULEY + DUKE *n.* + -ER¹.] A left-handed person.

mollyhawk /ˈmɒlɪhɔːk/ *n.* L19. [Alt.] = MOLLYMAWK.

Molly Maguire /ˌmɒlɪ məˈgwʌɪə/ *n.* M19. [A typical Irish female name: members of the first society disguised themselves as women.] *Hist.* **1** A member of a secret society formed in Ireland in 1843 for the purpose of resisting eviction for the non-payment of rent. M19. **2** A member of a secret society formed by Pennsylvania miners to resist the mine-owners, suppressed in 1876. M19.

mollymawk /ˈmɒlɪmɔːk/ *n.* Also **-mauk**, **mallemuck** /ˈmalɪmʌk/, & other vars. L17. [Du. *mallemok*, f. *mal* foolish + *mok* gull.] A fulmar, petrel, or similar bird; *spec.* any of the smaller albatrosses of the genus *Diomedea*.

moloch /ˈməʊlɒk/ *n.* In sense 1 usu. **M-**. E17. [Late L f. Gk *Molokh* f. Heb. *mōlek*, a Canaanite idol to whom children were sacrificed as burnt offerings (*Lev.* 18:21), held to be alt. of *melek* king, by substitution of the vowels of *bōšet* shame.] **1** An object to which horrible sacrifices are made. E17. **2** A slow-moving spiny Australian lizard, *Moloch horridus*, of grotesque appearance. Also called *mountain devil*, *spiny lizard*, *thorny devil*. M19. **3** = *dusky titi* s.v. DUSKY *I*. L19.

Comb.: **moloch gibbon** = SILVERY *gibbon*.

molossi *n.* pl. of MOLOSSUS.

Molossian /mə'lɒsɪən/ *n.* & *a.* L16. [f. L *Molossia* (see below) = Gk *Molossia*, *Molossus*: see -AN.] *Hist.* **A** *n.* A native or inhabitant of Molossia, a district of Epirus, Greece. L16. **B** *adj.* Of or pertaining to Molossia; *esp.* designating a kind of mastiff. M17.

molossid /mə'lɒsɪd/ *n.* & *a.* M20. [mod.L *Molossidae* (see below), f. as next: see -ID[3].] *Zool.* **A** *n.* A bat of the family Molossidae, the members of which are heavily built with a tail extending well beyond the tail membrane. Cf. *free-tailed bat* s.v. FREE *a.* etc., *mastiff bat* s.v. MASTIFF *n.* M20. **B** *adj.* Of, pertaining to, or designating this family. M20.

Also **molossine** *n.* & *a.* M19.

molossus /mə'lɒsəs/ *n.* Pl. **-ssi** /-sʌɪ/. L16. [L = Gk *Molossos*: see MOLOSSIAN.] **1** *Pros.* A metrical foot consisting of three long syllables. L16. **2** *Hist.* More fully *molossus dog*. A Molossian mastiff. E17.

Molotov /'mɒlətɒf/ *n.* M20. [Vyacheslav Mikhailovich *Molotov* (1890–1986), Soviet Minister for Foreign Affairs 1939–49.] **1** In full *Molotov cocktail*. A makeshift incendiary grenade, consisting of a bottle or other breakable container filled with flammable liquid, and a means of ignition. M20. **2** *Molotov bread basket*, (in the war of 1939–45) a container carrying high explosive and scattering incendiary bombs. M20.

molt *n.*, *v.* see MOULT *n.*, *v.*

molten /'məʊlt(ə)n/ *a.* ME. [Strong pa. pple of MELT *v.*] †**1** (Of metal etc.) that has been melted and again solidified; (of an object) made of cast metal. ME–E18. †**2** Dissolved in a liquid; *loosely* partially liquefied. Only in ME. **3** Liquefied by heat; in a state of fusion. Chiefly (connoting a higher temperature than *melted*) of metal, rock, etc. LME. **b** *fig.* Fiery, passionate; liquid. E19.

3 N. CALDER A yellow-hot fountain of molten rock. R. THOMAS Nick carried his away . . as if it was a bowl of molten gold. b F. HARRISON The molten passion of Burke.

molten *v.* pa. pple: see MELT *v.*

molter *n.*, *v.* see MOULTER *n.*, *v.*[1]

molto /'mɒltəʊ/ *adv.* E19. [It. f. L *multus* much.] *Mus.* Very. (Modifying adjs. f. It.)

†**molton** *n.* & *a.* M16–M19. [South *Molton*, a town in Devon, England.] (Made of) a kind of coarse woollen cloth.

Molucca /mə'lʌkə/ *n.* L17. [*Molucca* Islands, or *Moluccas*, a group of islands in SE Asia, now part of Indonesia.] Used *attrib.* to designate things found in or associated with the Molucca Islands.

Molucca balm a cultivated labiate plant, *Moluccella laevis*, native to the eastern Mediterranean region. **Molucca bean** the nicker-nut. **Molucca crab** the horseshoe crab.

Moluccan *a.* & *n.* (*a*) *adj.* of or pertaining to the Molucca Islands, their inhabitants, or any of the Austronesian languages spoken by them; (*b*) *n.* a native or inhabitant of the Molucca Islands: M18. †**Moluccian** *n.* = MOLUCCAN *n.*: only in E17.

moly /'məʊli/ *n.*[1] M16. [L f. Gk *mōlu*, perh. rel. to Skt *mūla* root.] **1** *Gk Mythol.* A magical herb having a white flower and a black root, said by Homer to have been given by Hermes to Odysseus as a charm against the sorceries of Circe. M16. **2** Any of various plants that have been supposed to be identical with the moly of Homer; *spec.* a yellow-flowered southern European allium, *Allium moly*. L16.

moly /'mɒli/ *n.*[2] *colloq.* M20. [Abbrev.] Molybdenum; *esp.* molybdenum disulphide as an engine lubricant.

molybdate /mə'lɪbdeɪt/ *n.* L18. [f. MOLYBDIC + -ATE[1].] *Chem.* A salt containing oxyanions of hexavalent molybdenum; *esp.* a salt of the anion MoO_4^{2-}.

†**molybdena** *n.* L17–M19. [L *molybdaena* f. Gk *molubdaina* angler's plummet, f. *molubdos* lead.] Orig., an ore or salt of lead. Later, molybdenite; molybdenum.

molybdenite /mə'lɪbdənʌɪt/ *n.* L18. [f. prec. + -ITE[1].] A sulphide of molybdenum. Now *spec.* in *Min.*, molybdenum disulphide as a trigonal mineral usu. occurring as tabular bluish-grey crystals.

molybdenum /mə'lɪbdənəm/ *n.* E19. [f. MOLYBDENA + *-um* after other chemical elements (usu. in -IUM).] A brittle silvery-white chemical element, atomic no. 42, which is one of the transition metals and is used in steel to give strength and resistance to corrosion. (Symbol Mo.)

Comb.: **molybdenum blue** a deep-blue colloidal complex oxide or mixture of oxides of molybdenum produced when an acidic solution of a molybdate is reduced.

molybdic /mə'lɪbdɪk/ *a.* L18. [f. MOLYBDENA + -IC.] *Chem.* & *Min.* Containing or derived from molybdenum; of molybdenum, esp. when hexavalent (cf. MOLYBDOUS). Chiefly in *molybdic acid*, a parent acid of molybdates; a hydrated form of molybdenum trioxide (MoO_3) obtained from acid solutions of molybdates.

molybdite /mə'lɪbdʌɪt/ *n.* M19. [f. as prec. + -ITE[1].] *Min.* Molybdenum trioxide, crystallizing in the orthorhombic system and usu. occurring as yellow needles or incrustations.

molybdo- /mə'lɪbdəʊ/ *comb. form* of (*a*) Gk *molubdos* lead (now *rare*); (*b*) *Chem.* MOLYBDENUM: see -O-.

molybdomancy *n.* (*rare*) divination by observing motions in molten lead L19.

molybdophyllite /mɒ,lɪbdə'fɪlʌɪt/ *n.* E20. [f. prec. + Gk *phullon* leaf + -ITE[1].] *Min.* A colourless or pale green hexagonal hydrated silicate of lead and magnesium.

molybdous /mə'lɪbdəs/ *a.* Now *rare.* L18. [f. MOLYBDENA + -OUS.] *Chem.* Of molybdenum in a lower valency. Cf. MOLYBDIC.

molysite /'mɒlɪsʌɪt/ *n.* M19. [f. Gk *molusis* (for *molusma*) stain, f. *molunein* to stain: see -ITE[1].] *Min.* Ferric chloride as a hexagonal mineral, formed as a yellow to red sublimation product near fumaroles and rapidly hydrated by the air.

mom /mɒm/ *n.* *colloq.* (chiefly *N. Amer.*). L19. [Partly var. of MAM, MUM *n.*[3], partly abbrev. of MOMMA.] Mother; *spec.* a matriarchal American mother.

J. HELLER The hot dog, the Brooklyn Dodgers, Mom's apple pie. That's what everyone's fighting for.

Comb.: **mom-and-pop** *attrib. a.* (*US*) designating a small shop, store, etc., of a type often run by a married couple.

mombin /məm'biːn/ *n.* M19. [Amer. Sp. *mombin* f. Caribbean name.] (The fruit of) a W. Indian tree of the genus *Spondias* (family Anacardiaceae), *esp.* (more fully *yellow mombin*) *S. mombin* and (more fully *red mombin*) *S. purpurea*. Cf. *hog plum* s.v. HOG *n.*

mome /məʊm/ *n.*[1] *arch.* M16. [Origin unkn.] A blockhead, a fool.

mome *n.*[2] var. of MOMME.

moment /'məʊm(ə)nt/ *n.* ME. [(O)Fr. f. L *momentum* (i) movement, moving power, (ii) importance, consequence, (iii) moment of time, particle, f. *movere* MOVE *v.*: see -MENT.] **1** A very brief portion or period of time; a point in time, an instant. ME. **b** Usu. w. *the* or *possess.*: the instant that is appropriate or decisive for something or someone; the fitting moment; the momentary conjunction of circumstances, esp. as affording an opportunity. L18. **c** A (brief) period of time marked by a particular quality of experience. E20. **2a** In medieval measurement of time, the tenth part of a point (see POINT *n.*[1] 2e), the fortieth or fiftieth part of an hour. *obs.* exc. *Hist.* LME. **b** A second of time. Now only *Sc.* M17. **c** *Geol.* A period of geological time corresponding to a stratigraphical zone. M20. †**3** A small particle, an infinitesimal amount; a detail. LME–M18. **4** Importance, weight. Now only in *of* (*great, little, some*, etc.) *moment*. E16. †**5** A cause or motive of action; a determining influence or consideration. E17–M18. **6** A definite stage, period, or turning-point in a course of events. (Now distinguished from sense 1.) M17. **7** *Physics* etc. †**a** Momentum. Only in E18. **b** Any of various functions describing torsional effects, generally having the form of the product of a force and a distance; *spec.* the turning effect produced by a force; the magnitude of this, equal to the product of the force and the perpendicular distance from its line of action to the point about which rotation may occur. M19. **c** *Statistics.* Each of a series of quantities (*first, second*, etc., *moment*) that express the average or expected value of the first, second, etc., powers of the deviation of each component of a frequency distribution from some given value, usu. the mean or zero. L19. **8** An element of a complex conceptual entity. M19.

1 R. HUGHES All woke at the same moment as if by clockwork. G. VIDAL He returned, a moment later, breathless. L. DUNCAN The moment he heard his own voice . . he felt like an idiot. b A. BULLOCK His moment came in 1944. W. TREVOR Until the moment's right for you to take over. J. NAGENDA Lofty and romantic sentiments such as man and moment meeting. R. ELLMANN The moment had come to issue a book of his poems. c G. B. SHAW Why do you select my most tragic moments for your most irresistible strokes of humour. 4 JO GRIMOND A wheel flew off . . but otherwise nothing of moment happened. A. SCHLEE There are so many things of more moment than how I feel. 5 SHAKES. *Ant. & Cl.* I have seen her die twenty times upon far poorer moment. 6 C. BIGG Three great moments in that fateful process. 7b J. S. FOSTER Equilibrium . . is obtained when the . . moments of some forces acting on a member are balanced. *Forestry* A turning moment of 1 Nm is produced by a force of 1 kg acting over a length of 1 m.

Phrases & comb.: *at this moment in time*: see TIME *n.* DIPOLE *moment*. *first moment*: see sense 7c above. **for a moment** (*a*) *pred.* destined to last for only a moment; (*b*) *advb.* during a moment. **for the moment** (*a*) so far as the immediate future is concerned; (*b*) temporarily during the brief space referred to. **have one's** (or **its**) **moments** be impressive, successful, happy, etc., on occasions. *in the heat of the moment*: see HEAT *n.* *last moment*: see LAST *a.* **live for** (or **in**) **the moment** live without concern for the future. *magnetic moment*: see MAGNETIC *a.* **moment-hand** (*obs.* exc. *Sc.*) the seconds hand of a watch etc. **moment of inertia** (of a body about an axis) the sum of the products of the mass of each particle of the body and the square of the distance of each particle from the axis. **moment of truth** [Sp. *el momento de la verdad*] the time of the final sword-thrust in a bullfight; a crisis, a turning-point; a testing situation. **moment-to-moment** *a.* immediately and continually experienced, required, considered, etc. **not for a** (or **one**) **moment** emphatically not. **of the moment** of importance at the time in question. **one moment** *ellipt.* wait, listen, etc., for one moment. **on the moment** (now *rare*) immediately, instantly. *on the spur of the moment*: see SPUR *n.*[1] *psychological moment*: see PSYCHOLOGICAL *a.* *quadrupole moment*: see QUADRUPOLE *a.* *sacrament of the present moment*: see SACRAMENT *n.* *second moment*: see sense 7c above. **the moment** *ellipt.* at the moment when, as soon as ever. **this moment** (*a*) without a moment's delay, immediately; (*b*) just now, hardly a moment ago. **to the moment** with exact punctuality; for the exact time required. *weak moment*: see WEAK *a.*

momenta *n.* pl. of MOMENTUM.

momental /mə'mɛnt(ə)l/ *a.* E17. [Late L *momentalis*, f. L *momentum*: see MOMENT, -AL[1].] †**1** Having only the duration of a moment; momentary. E–M17. †**2** Important; of moment. *rare.* Only in E19. **3** *Math.* Of or pertaining to momentum. *rare.* L19.

momentaneous /məʊm(ə)n'teɪnɪəs/ *a.* LME. [f. late L *momentaneus*, f. L *momentum* MOMENT: see -OUS.] **1** Lasting for only a moment; momentary. LME. †**2** Occurring in a moment, instantaneous. M17–L18. †**3** *Math.* Infinitesimal. Only in E18.

momenta'neity *n.* transitory character; momentariness: E20. **momentaneously** *adv.* M18. **momentaneousness** *n.* E18.

†**momentany** *a.* E16–E18. [Fr. *momentané* f. as prec.: see -Y[5].] Pertaining to the moment, momentary; transitory; evanescent.

momentarily /'məʊm(ə)nt(ə)rɪli, məʊm(ə)n'tɛrɪli/ *adv.* M17. [f. next + -LY[2].] **1** For a moment, fleetingly. M17. **2** At the moment, instantly. Now *rare.* L18. **3** At every moment; moment by moment. *rare.* E19. **4** At any moment, very soon. *N. Amer.* E20.

momentary /ˈməʊm(ə)nt(ə)ri/ *a.* LME. [L *momentarius*, f. *momentum* MOMENT: see -ARY[1].] 1 Lasting only a moment; of a moment's duration; transitory. LME. 2 Of a living being: short-lived, ephemeral. *literary*. L16. 3 Recurring or operative at every moment. Now *rare*. M18. †4 Instant, instantaneous. L18–M19. †5 *Math.* Infinitesimal. E–M19.

1 E. WAUGH Hinsley's momentary irritation subsided. A. JUDD Tim's momentary glance did not even show recognition. 2 R. LLOYD Born like a momentary fly, To flutter, buzz about, and die. 3 T. WARTON The due clock swinging slow.. Measuring time's flight with momentary sound. 4 DISRAELI If anything occurred which required my momentary attention.

momentariness *n.* E19.

momently /ˈməʊm(ə)ntli/ *a. rare.* LME. [f. MOMENT + -LY[1].] 1 Enduring for a moment. LME. 2 Occurring at every moment. M17.

momently /ˈməʊm(ə)ntli/ *adv.* L17. [f. MOMENT + -LY[2].] 1 From moment to moment; every moment. L17. 2 At any moment. L18. 3 For the moment; for a single moment. M19.

momentous /mə(ʊ)ˈmɛntəs/ *a.* M17. [f. MOMENT + -OUS.] †1 Having motive force. Only in M17. 2a Of a thing: of moment; of great consequence or importance; important, weighty. M17. b Of a person: influential, important. Now *rare*. M17.

2a M. MEAD Never before.. has mankind had such momentous choices placed in his hands. M. MEYER A momentous day for Eurpoe, for it marked the outbreak of the Franco-Prussian War.

momentously *adv.* M18. **momentousness** *n.* L17.

momentum /məˈmɛntəm/ *n.* Pl. **-ta** /-tə/. E17. [L: see MOMENT.] †1 A turning motion; *Physics* = MOMENT *n.* 7b. *rare*. E17–M19. 2a *Physics*. The quantity of motion of a moving body, equal to the product of the mass and the velocity of the body. L17. b The effect of inertia in the continuance of motion; impetus gained by movement; *fig.* strength or continuity derived from an initial effort. L18. †3 *Math.* An infinitesimal increment. Only in M18. †4 Force of movement. M18–E19. 5 = MOMENT *n.* 8. E19.

2a *angular momentum*: see ANGULAR 2. b J. TYNDALL His momentum rolled him over and over down the incline. R. HAYMAN Tiredness vanished as the narrative gathered momentum. E. PAWEL Teenage friendships tend to develop their own momentum.

Comb.: **momentum space** *Physics* a three-dimensional space in which each particle of a physical system is represented by a point whose three Cartesian coordinates are numerically equal to the components of its momentum in the directions of the three coordinate axes.

Momi *n.* pl. of MOMUS.

momism /ˈmɒmɪz(ə)m/ *n.* Orig. *US*. Also **M-**. M20. [f. MOM + -ISM.] Excessive attachment to or domination by one's mother.

momma /ˈmɒmə/ *n.* E19. [Alt. of MAMMA *n.*[2] Cf. MOM, MOMMY.] 1 In the southern US, esp. before the abolition of slavery, a Black woman having the care of White children. Cf. MAMMY *n.*[1] 2. E19. 2 Mother (= MAMMA *n.*[2] 1). Also = MAMMA *n.*[2] 2. Chiefly *US*. L19.

momme /mɒm, ˈmɒmeɪ/ *n.* Also **mome**. Pl. **-s**, same. E18. [Jap. *monme*.] A Japanese unit of weight equal to 3.75 grams (about ⅙ ounce).

mommet, **mommetry** *ns.* see MAUMET, MAUMETRY.

mommy /ˈmɒmi/ *n. colloq.* (chiefly *US*). E20. [Alt. of MAMMY *n.*[1] Cf. MOM, MUMMY *n.*[2]] Mother.

mompei /ˈmɒmpeɪ/ *n.pl.* Also **mompe**. M20. [Jap. *monpe*.] Baggy working trousers worn in Japan.

momser *n.* var. of MAMZER.

Momus /ˈməʊməs/ *n. literary*. Pl. **Momuses**, **Momi** /ˈməʊmʌɪ/. L16. [L = Gk *Mōmos* the god of ridicule in Gk mythol.] A fault-finder, a carping critic.

momzer *n.* var. of MAMZER.

Mon /mɔːn, məʊn/ *n.*[1] & *a.* L18. [Mon.] A *n.* Pl. **-s**, same. A member of an Indo-Chinese people now inhabiting eastern parts of Myanmar (Burma) and western parts of Thailand but having their ancient capital at Pegu in the south of Myanmar; the Austro-Asiatic language of this people. Also called *Talaing*. Cf. PEGUAN. L18. B *attrib.* or as *adj.* Of or pertaining to the Mons or their language. E19.

¶See also MON-KHMER.

mon /mɒn/ *n.*[2] Pl. same. L19. [Jap.] A Japanese family crest or badge, often used in decorative design.

mon /mʌn/ *n.*[3] *colloq.* Also **mun**. L19. [Abbrev.] Money.

mon- *pref.* see MONO-.

mona /ˈməʊnə/ *n.* L18. [Sp., Port. *mona*, *-o*, It. *monna*: see MONKEY *n.*] A W. African guenon, *Cercopithecus mona*. Also *mona guenon*, *monkey*.

monachal /ˈmɒnək(ə)l/ *a.* Also **-cal**. L16. [(O)Fr. *monacal* or eccl.L *monachalis*, f. L *monachus* MONK *n.*[1]: see -AL[1].] Monastic; monkish.

monachise *v.* var. of MONACHIZE.

monachism /ˈmɒnəkɪz(ə)m/ *n.* L16. [f. L *monachus* MONK *n.*[1] + -ISM.] The mode or rule of life of a monk or nun; the monastic system or principle; monasticism.

monachize /ˈmɒnəkʌɪz/ *v. rare*. Also **-ise**. L19. [f. as prec. + -IZE.] 1 *v.i.* Live as a monk; become a monk. L19. 2 *v.t.* Cause to become a monk. L19.

monachiˈzation *n.* E19.

monacid /mɒˈnasɪd/ *a.* M19. [f. MONO- + ACID *a.*] *Chem.* Of a base etc.: (composed of molecules) able to combine with one monovalent acid radical.

monack *n.* var. of MOONACK.

monad /ˈmɒnad, ˈməʊ-/ *n.* & *a.* In sense 1 also (earlier) in L form **-as** /-as/, pl. **-ades** /-ədiːz/. M16. [Fr. *monade* or its source late L *monas*, *monad-* f. Gk, f. *monos* alone: see -AD[1].] A *n.* 1a (**M-**.) The Deity, God. M16. b The number one, unity; a unit. Now chiefly *Hist.*, w. ref. to ancient Greek philosophy, in which the numbers were regarded as being generated from the unitary one. E17. 2 *Philos.* Esp. in the philosophy of Leibniz: an indivisible unit of being (as a soul, an atom); an absolutely simple entity. M18. 3 *Biol.* A hypothetical simple organism, *esp.* one assumed as the first term in the genealogy of living beings, or regarded as associated with others to form an animal or vegetable body. M19. †4 *Chem.* A monovalent element or group. M–L19.

1b S. ROSEN Unity, or a non-articulated monad, is unspeakable and unthinkable. 2 L. MUMFORD A monad that can think and feel is more important than a galaxy of impassive stars.

B *attrib.* or as *adj.* That is a monad; monadic. M19.

moˈnadiform *a.* (*Biol.*) having the form of a monad or simple organism M19.

monadelphous /mɒnəˈdɛlfəs/ *a.* E19. [f. MONO- + Gk *adelphos* brother + -OUS.] *Bot.* Of stamens: united by the filaments so as to form one group. Of a plant: having the stamens so united.

monades *n.pl.* see MONAD.

monadic /mɒˈnadɪk/ *a.* L18. [Gk *monadikos*, f. *monad-*, *monas*: see MONAD, -IC.] 1 Composed of monads or units; pertaining to or of the nature of a monad; existing singly. L18. b *Philos.* Designating or pertaining to a predicate that is non-relational and applies to only one subject term; (of a proposition, fact, etc.) containing such a predicate. L19. 2 Of or pertaining to monadism. M19.

monadical *a.* = MONADIC *a.* 1 M17. **monadically** *adv.* L18.

monadism /ˈmɒnədɪz(ə)m, ˈməʊ-/ *n.* L19. [f. MONAD + -ISM.] *Philos.* The theory of the monadic nature of matter; the philosophical doctrine of monads, esp. as formulated by Leibniz.

monadist *n.* M19. **monaˈdistic** *a.* L19.

monadnock /məˈnadnɒk/ *n.* L19. [*Monadnock*, a hill in New Hampshire, USA.] *Physical Geogr.* A hill or mountain of erosion-resistant rock rising above a peneplain.

monadology /mɒnəˈdɒlədʒi, məʊ-/ *n.* M18. [Fr. *monadologie*, f. as MONAD: see -OLOGY.] The philosophical doctrine of monads.

monadoˈlogical *a.* L19. **monadoˈlogically** *adv.* M20.

monal /ˈmɒnɑːl/ *n.* Also **monaul** /mɒˈnɔːl/. M18. [Nepali *monāl*, Hind. *munāl*.] Any of several crested pheasants of the genus *Lophophorus*; *spec.* (also *Himalayan monal*) the Impeyan pheasant, *L. impeyanus*. Also *monal pheasant*.

Mona Lisa /məʊnə ˈliːzə/ *n.* & *a.* E20. [A portrait by Leonardo da Vinci: see GIOCONDA.] A *n.* A woman having an enigmatic smile or expression such as that of the woman in Leonardo's painting *Mona Lisa*; an enigma. E20. B *attrib.* or as *adj.* Of a smile etc.: enigmatic, reminiscent of the *Mona Lisa*. M20.

Mona marble /məʊnə ˈmɑːb(ə)l/ *n. phr.* E19. [f. *Mona* Roman name for Anglesey (Welsh *Ynys Môn*), island off the north coast of Wales.] A serpentine limestone from the metamorphic beds of Anglesey.

mon ami /mɔn ami/ *n. phr.* Also (fem.) ***mon amie***. Pl. ***mes amis*** (fem. ***mes amies***) /mez ami/. L18. [Fr.] As a form of address: my friend.

monamide /ˈmɒnəmʌɪd/ *n.* M19. [f. MONO- + AMIDE.] *Chem.* A compound whose molecule contains one amino group.

monamine *n.* var. of MONOAMINE.

monandrous /mɒˈnandrəs/ *a.* E19. [f. Gk *monandros* having one husband, f. as MONO- + *andr-* male: see -ANDROUS.] 1 *Bot.* Having a single stamen. E19. 2 *Zool.* Having one male mate. M19.

monandry /mɒˈnandri/ *n.* Also (earlier) †**mono-andry**. M19. [f. MONOGAMY after *polygamy*, *polyandry*.] 1 The practice or custom of mating with only one male, or of having only one husband at a time. M19. 2 *Bot.* The condition of having one stamen. E20.

monarch /ˈmɒnək/ *n.* & *v.* LME. [(O)Fr. *monarque* or late L *monarcha* f. Gk *monarkhēs*, more freq. *monarkhos*, f. *monos* alone: see MONO-, -ARCH.] A *n.* 1 Orig., a sole and absolute ruler of a State. Later also, any ruler bearing the title of king, queen, emperor, empress, or the equivalent. LME. 2 *transf.* & *fig.* A person or thing of great power or pre-eminence in a particular sphere. L16. 3 More fully *monarch butterfly*. A large migratory orange and black danaid butterfly, *Danaus plexippus*, native to the Americas and known as a vagrant in western Europe. Also called *milkweed butterfly*. L19. 4 = *monarch flycatcher* below. M20.

1 SHAKES. *Merch. V.* The quality of mercy.. becomes The throned monarch better than his crown. R. SCRUTON In the figure of the monarch there is.. all the majesty of state. *the Merry Monarch*: see MERRY *a.* 2 W. COWPER I am monarch of all I survey. BYRON Mont Blanc is the monarch of mountains.

B *v.i.* & *t.* (w. *it*). Behave like a monarch, act autocratically. *rare*. E17.

Comb.: *monarch butterfly*: see sense 3 above; **monarch flycatcher** a flycatcher of the Old World family Monarchidae, *esp.* one of the genus *Monarcha*.

monarchess *n.* (now *rare*) a female monarch L16.

monarch /ˈmɒnɑːk/ *a.* L19. [f. MONO- + Gk *arkhē* beginning, origin.] *Bot.* Of the primary xylem of the root: arising from one point of origin. Of a root: having such a xylem.

monarchal /məˈnɑːk(ə)l/ *a.* L16. [OFr., or med.L *monarchalis*, f. late L *monarcha* MONARCH *n.*: see -AL[1].] 1 Of, pertaining to, or characteristic of a monarch; befitting a monarch. L16. 2 = MONARCHICAL 4. L16. 3 = MONARCHICAL 1. L16.

monarchally *adv.* M19.

monarchial /məˈnɑːkɪəl/ *a.* E17. [f. MONARCH *n.* or MONARCHY: see -IAL, -AL[1].] 1 = MONARCHICAL 1. E17. †2 = MONARCHICAL 4. *rare*. E–M17. 3 = MONARCHAL *a.* 1. L18.

Monarchian /məˈnɑːkɪən/ *n.* & *a.* M18. [Late L *monarchiani* pl., f. *monarchia*: see MONARCHY, -AN.] *Eccl. Hist.* A *n.* A heretic in the 2nd and 3rd cents. who denied the doctrine of the

Trinity. M18. B *adj.* Of or pertaining to the Monarchians or their beliefs. M19.

¶Cf. PRAXEAN.

Monarchianism *n.* M19.

monarchic /məˈnɑːkɪk/ *a.* E17. [Fr. *monarchique* or med.L *monarchicus* f. Gk *monarkhikos*, f. *monarkhos*: see MONARCH *n.*, -IC.] 1 = MONARCHICAL 1. E17. †2 = MONARCHICAL 3. E17–E19. 3 = MONARCHAL 1. M17.

monarchical /məˈnɑːkɪk(ə)l/ *a.* L16. [f. as prec. + -ICAL.] 1 Of the nature of or having the characteristics of a monarchy; (of a State) ruled by a monarch; (of government) vested in a monarch. L16. 2 = MONARCHAL 1. L16. 3 Of or pertaining to monarchy; favouring monarchy as a form of government. E17. 4 Having the status, power, or functions of a monarch. Formerly also, autocratic. E17.

monarchically *adv.* L16.

monarchise *v.* var. of MONARCHIZE.

monarchism /ˈmɒnəkɪz(ə)m/ *n.* M19. [Fr. *monarchisme*, f. as MONARCHY: see -ISM.] The principles of monarchical government; advocacy of monarchy or the monarchical principle.

monarchist /ˈmɒnəkɪst/ *n.* & *a.* M17. [f. MONARCHY + -IST.] A *n.* 1 An advocate or supporter of monarchy. M17. 2 A polytheist believing in monarchy among the gods. *rare.* L17. B *adj.* Advocating or supporting monarchy; of or pertaining to monarchism or monarchists. E20.

monarchize /ˈmɒnəkʌɪz/ *v.* Also -ise. L16. [f. MONARCH *n.* + -IZE.] 1 *v.i.* & †*t.* w. *it.* Perform the office of monarch; rule as a monarch; rule absolutely. L16. 2 *v.t.* †a Make subservient to one monarch; rule over as a monarch. Only in E17. b Make a monarchy of. M17.

†Monarcho *n.* L16–M17. [It. (= *monarca* monarch), title assumed by an insane Italian who fancied himself emperor of the world.] (A title for) a person generally ridiculed for absurd pretensions.

monarcho-fascist /məˌnɑːkəʊˈfaʃɪst/ *a.* M20. [f. MONARCH(IST + -O- + FASCIST.] In Communist phraseology: designating or pertaining to a Fascist government with a monarch as titular head of State, esp. that established in Greece after the war of 1939–45.

monarchy /ˈmɒnəki/ *n.* ME. [(O)Fr. *monarchie* f. late L *monarchia* f. Gk *monarkhia* f. *monarkhos* MONARCH *n.*: see -Y³.] 1 A State ruled by a monarch. ME. †b The territory of a monarch. *rare.* M16–L17. 2 Undivided rule by a single person; absolute power; *fig.* pre-eminence, predominance. LME. 3 Rule by a monarch; a form of government with a monarch at the head. E17.

1 A. BULLOCK He was not concerned whether Greece became a monarchy or a republic. 2 W. CONGREVE Nobody can dispute Your Lordship's Monarchy in Poetry. J. B. MOZLEY Gregory VII.. claimed the monarchy of the world. 3 C. V. WEDGWOOD The conception of monarchy for which King Charles both lived and died.

Phrases: *constitutional monarchy*: see CONSTITUTIONAL *a.* 4. *Fifth Monarchy*: see FIFTH *a.*

monarda /məˈnɑːdə/ *n.* L18. [mod.L (see below), f. Nicolas *Monardes* (1493–1588), Sp. physician & botanist.] Any of various fragrant N. American labiate plants constituting the genus *Monarda*, which bear heads of showy tubular flowers (also called (*wild*) *bergamot*); *spec.* one grown for ornament, *esp.* Oswego tea, *Monarda didyma*.

monas *n.* see MONAD.

monaster /mɒˈnastə/ *n.* L19. [f. MONO- + ASTER.] *Cytol.* = ASTER *n.* 3.

monasterial /mɒnəˈstɪərɪəl/ *a.* Now *rare.* LME. [Late L *monasterialis*, f. eccl.L *monasterium*: see next, -AL¹.] Belonging to or of the nature of a monastery.

monastery /ˈmɒnəst(ə)ri/ *n.* LME. [eccl.L *monasterium* f. eccl.Gk *monastērion*, f. Gk *monazein* live alone, f. *monos* alone.] (A place of residence of) a community living under religious vows; a monastic establishment; *esp.* (the residence of) a community of monks living in seclusion.

monastic /məˈnastɪk/ *a.* & *n.* LME. [(O)Fr. *monastique* or late L *monasticus* f. Gk *monastikos*, f. *monazein*: see prec., -IC.] A *adj.* †1 Of or pertaining to a hermit; anchoritic. Only in LME. 2 Of or pertaining to people living in seclusion from the world under religious vows, as monks, nuns, friars, etc.; of or pertaining to a monastery or monasteries. M16. b Resembling or suggestive of monks or their way of life; (of existence) solitary and celibate. M17. 3 *Bookbinding.* Designating a method of finishing by tooling without gold. L19.

2 H. CARPENTER The bedroom is bare and looks a little like a monastic cell. b DONNE He sinkes the deepe Where harmlesse fish monastique silence keepe.

B *n.* A member of a monastic order; a monk. M17.

monastical *a.* †(*a*) = MONASTIC *a.* 1; (*b*) = MONASTIC *a.* 2: LME. **monastically** *adv.* E17. **monasticism** *n.* the monastic system or mode of life L18. **monasticize** *v.t.* make monastic in character; convert to monasticism: M19.

Monastral /mɒˈnastr(ə)l/ *n.* M20. [Origin unkn.] (Proprietary name for) any of various synthetic pigments of high fastness, of which there are two classes: (*a*) blue and green phthalocyanine derivatives; (*b*) red and violet quinacridone derivatives.

monatomic /mɒnəˈtɒmɪk/ *a.* M19. [f. MONO- + ATOMIC.] *Chem.* Containing one atom; consisting of single atoms rather than molecules. Also, monobasic, monovalent.

monaul *n.* var. of MONAL.

monaural /mɒnˈɔːr(ə)l/ *a.* L19. [f. MONO- + AURAL *a.*¹] 1 Of or pertaining to the use of one ear only. L19. 2 = MONOPHONIC *a.* 3. M20.

monaurally *adv.* M20.

monaxial /mɒnˈaksɪəl/ *a.* L19. [f. MONO- + AXIAL.] Chiefly *Bot.* & *Zool.* Having only one axis; developing along a single line.

monazite /ˈmɒnəzʌɪt/ *n.* M19. [f. Gk *monazein* be solitary (on account of its rarity) + -ITE¹.] *Min.* A commercially important monoclinic phosphate of cerium, lanthanum, other rare-earth elements, and thorium, occurring as small brownish crystals, often in detrital sands associated with granites and gneisses.

Monbazillac /mɒnˈbazɪlak, *foreign* mɔ̃bazijak/ *n.* Also **Mont-** /mɒnt-/. E20. [Fr. (see below).] A sweet, white dessert wine, similar to Sauternes, produced at Monbazillac (Dordogne), in SW France.

mon cher /mɔ̃ ʃɛːr/ *n. phr.* L17. [Fr.] As a form of address to a male: my dear, my dear fellow.

monchiquite /mɒnˈtʃiːkwʌɪt/ *n.* L19. [f. Serra de *Monchique*, a mountain range in southern Portugal + -ITE¹.] *Petrogr.* A lamprophyre containing small phenocrysts of olivine and augite, and usu. also biotite or an amphibole, in a glassy groundmass containing analcime.

Mond /mɒnd/ *n.* L19. [Ludwig *Mond* (1839–1909), German-born Brit. chemist.] *Chem.* Used *attrib.* to designate (the plant used in and the products of) certain processes devised by Mond, *spec.* (*a*) a method of manufacturing producer gas from coal using air and excess steam, with ammonia as a by-product; (*b*) a process for purifying nickel by thermal decomposition of nickel carbonyl obtained from crude nickel oxide by reduction with hydrogen followed by reaction with carbon monoxide.

mondain /mɔ̃dɛ̃/ *n.* & *a.* Also (fem.) ***mondaine*** /mɔ̃dɛn/. L19. [Fr.: see MUNDANE.] A *n.* Pl. pronounced same. A worldly or fashionable person. Cf. DEMI-MONDAINE. L19. B *adj.* Of the fashionable world; worldly. L19.

Monday /ˈmʌndeɪ, -di/ *n.*, *adv.*, & *a.* [OE *mōnandæġ* corresp. to OFris. *mōne(n)dei*, MLG, MDu. *mān(en)dach* (Du. *maandag*), OHG *mānatag* (G *Montag*), ON *mánadagr*, f. as MOON *n.*¹ + DAY *n.*] A *n.* The second day of the week, following Sunday. OE.

Black Monday (*a*) Easter Monday; (*b*) *School slang* the first school-day after a vacation; (*c*) *Stock Exch.* Monday, 19 October 1987, the day of a worldwide collapse of stock markets. **†Bloody Monday** *School slang* the first day of vacation, a day of punishment for offenders. *collop Monday*: see COLLOP *n.*¹ *Easter Monday*: see EASTER *n.* *Hock Monday*: see HOCK-. **Saint Monday** *arch. slang* Monday spent in idleness as a consequence of drunkenness on the Sunday. *Shrove Monday*: see SHROVE-. *Yellow Monday*: see YELLOW *a.*

B *adv.* On Monday. Now *colloq.* ME.

C *attrib.* or as *adj.* Of Monday; characteristic of Monday; taking place on Monday(s). L16.

Monday Club a right-wing Conservative club that originally held its meetings on Mondays. **Monday-clubber** a member of the Monday Club. **Monday-morning** *attrib. a.* characterized by or suggestive of lethargy or disinclination after a busy or eventful weekend. *Monday morning quarterback*: see QUARTERBACK *n.* 2.

Mondayish *a.* suffering from or marked by indisposition or lethargy resulting from a busy or eventful weekend (orig. *spec.* of clergymen) E19. **Mondayishness** *n.* M19. **Mondays** *adv.* (*colloq.*) on Mondays, each Monday L20.

monde /mɔ̃ːd, mɔːnd/ *n.* Earlier in BEAU MONDE. M18. [Fr. = world.] The world of fashionable or aristocratic people; such people collectively. Also, a person's particular circle or set.

BEAU MONDE. DEMI-MONDE. *grand monde*: see GRAND *a.*² HAUT MONDE. *tout le monde*: see TOUT *a.*, *n.*⁵, & *adv.*

mondial /ˈmɒndɪəl/ *a.* E20. [Fr., f. as prec.] Pertaining to, affecting, or involving the whole world; worldwide, universal.

mon Dieu /mɔ̃ djø/ *int.* M18. [Fr.] My God! (cf. GOD *n.* 5).

mondo /ˈmɒndəʊ/ *n.*¹ Pl. -os. E19. [Jap., app. f. *mon* gate.] More fully *mondo grass*. Any of various plants constituting the genus *Ophiopogon*, of the lily family, with short stems and mats of long grasslike leaves; esp. *O. japonicus*, native to Japan and Korea, which is grown as a carpeting plant. Also called *lily-turf*.

mondo /ˈmɒndəʊ/ *n.*² Pl. -os. E20. [Jap., f. *mon* asking + *dō* answering.] An instructional technique of Zen Buddhism consisting of rapid dialogue of questions and answers between teacher and pupil.

mondo /ˈmɒndəʊ/ *a.* & *adv. slang.* M20. [f. It. *Mondo Cane* lit. 'world for a dog', title of a film (1961) showing bizarre behaviour.] A *adj.* 1 Anarchic and tasteless. M20. 2 As an intensifier: considerable, much; huge. L20.

B *adv.* Very, extremely. L20.

Phrases: **mondo bizarro** very bizarre, tastelessly bizarre.

mondongo /mɒnˈdɒŋgəʊ/ *n.* Pl. -os. E17. [Sp. = tripe, black pudding: cf. MUNDUNGUS.] A Latin American or W. Indian dish composed of tripe.

Mondrian /ˈmɒndrɪən/ *n.* & *a.* M20. [Anglicized form of *Mondriaan* (see below).] (In or resembling) the geometrical abstract style of the Dutch painter Piet Mondriaan (1872–1944); (of) neo-plasticism.

monecious *a.* see MONOECIOUS.

Monégasque /mɒnɪˈgask, *foreign* mɔnegask (*pl. same*)/ *n.* & *a.* L19. [Fr.] A *n.* A native or inhabitant of Monaco, an independent principality forming an enclave on the Mediterranean coast of France. L19. B *adj.* Pertaining to or characteristic of Monaco or its inhabitants. L19.

Monel /ˈməʊn(ə)l/ *n.* Also **m-**. E20. [Ambrose *Monell* (d. 1921), US businessman.] In full *Monel metal*. Any of a group of alloys composed of about 68 per cent nickel and 30 per cent copper with small amounts of other elements, having a high tensile strength and good corrosion resistance.

monellin /ˈmɒnəlɪn/ *n.* L20. [f. *Monell* Chemical Senses Center, Philadelphia + -IN¹.] *Chem.* A sweet-tasting protein isolated from the berries of the tropical African plant *Dioscoreophyllum cumminsii* (family Menispermaceae).

moneme /ˈmɒniːm/ *n.* M20. [Fr. *monème*, f. as MONO-: see -EME.] *Ling.* = MORPHEME.

monensin /məˈnɛnsɪn/ *n.* M20. [f. mod.L *cinna)monens(is* (see below) + -IN¹.] *Vet. Med.*

An antibiotic and ionophore produced by the bacterium *Streptomyces cinnamonensis*, used as a feed additive to increase the meat yield of livestock.

monepiscopacy /mɒnɪˈpɪskəpəsi/ *n.* L19. [f. MONO- + EPISCOPACY.] Government of the Church by bishops who have sole authority within their dioceses, rather than share it with other bishops.

monepiscopal *a.* L19.

moneron /məˈnɪərɒn/ *n. obs.* exc. *Hist.* Pl. **-ra** /-rə/. Also Anglicized as **moner** /ˈməʊnə/, pl. **-s.** M19. [f. Gk *monērēs* single.] *Zool.* A member of a group of protozoa (in Haeckel's scheme) composed of organisms of the simplest form.

monetarism /ˈmʌnɪt(ə)rɪz(ə)m/ *n.* M20. [f. MONETARY + -ISM.] The doctrine or theory that economic stabilization is achieved by tight control of the money supply; control of the money supply according to this doctrine.

monetarist /ˈmʌnɪt(ə)rɪst/ *a.* & *n.* E20. [f. next + -IST.] **A** *adj.* Monetary; *esp.* in accordance with or advocating monetarism. E20. **B** *n.* An advocate or practitioner of monetarism. M20.

monetaˈristic *a.* pertaining to or of the nature of monetarism L20.

monetary /ˈmʌnɪt(ə)ri/ *a.* E19. [Fr. *monétaire* or late L *monetarius*, f. L *moneta* MINT *n.*[1]: see -ARY[1].] **1** Of or pertaining to coinage or currency. E19. **2** Of or pertaining to money, pecuniary. M19.

moneˈtarian *a.* (*rare*) monetary E18. **monetarily** *adv.* L19.

monetise *v.* var. of MONETIZE.

monetite /ˈməʊnɪtʌɪt/ *n.* L19. [f. *Moneta* island near Puerto Rico in the Caribbean + -ITE[1].] *Min.* A triclinic hydrogen phosphate of calcium occurring as translucent, pale yellow crystals.

monetize /ˈmʌnɪtʌɪz/ *v.t.* Also **-ise.** L19. [f. L *moneta* (see next) + -IZE.] Convert into the form of money; put (metal) into circulation as money; assess in terms of money.

monetiˈzation *n.* M19.

money /ˈmʌni/ *n.* Pl. **moneys, monies.** ME. [OFr. *moneie* (mod. *monnaie* change) f. L *moneta* mint (in Rome), money, orig. epithet of Juno, in whose temple the mint was housed.] **1** A current medium of exchange in the form of coins and (in mod. use) banknotes; coins and banknotes collectively. ME. **b** Any objects or material serving the same purposes as coin. LME. **c** One of the four suits in packs of playing-cards in Italy, Spain, and Spanish-speaking countries, and in tarot packs. L16. **2** Property, wealth, possessions, resources, etc., viewed as convertible into coin or banknotes or having value expressible in terms of these. ME. **b** (With demonstrative or possess. adj.) a sum applied to a particular purpose or in the possession of a particular person. Also, wages, salary; one's pay; remuneration, profit. ME. **3** (With *pl.*) A particular kind of coin, coinage, or currency. ME. **4** In *pl.* Sums of money; a sum of money. Now chiefly in legal and quasi-legal parlance. LME.

1 AV *1 Kings* 21:2 I will give thee the worth of it in money. J. RULE Ann watched her counting out her money. E. CALDWELL Opening the purse, he.. dropped the money into it. 2 J. GROSS He left Oxford forced to make his own way.. without money or influence. R. GUY He was white, looked like money, and claimed rights to property. R. ELLMANN Wilde.. was again short of money. N. HINTON They cost a fortune... He hasn't got that sort of money. *Proverb*: Time is money. **b** SHAKES. *Com. Err.* The money that you owe me for the chain. R. KIPLING Come back when your money's spent. *Bella* I asked her for the money back. H. GARNER Working for Malloy-Harrison.. the money was better than most. J. WINTERSON There was no money in vermin any more. *beer money, conscience money, danger money, dirt money, earnest money, glove money, hush money, pocket money, protection money, spending money*, etc. 4 BYRON But to steal The moneys of a slumbering man! *Daily Telegraph* The receivers of a company in liquidation were entitled to keep moneys loaned. P. AUSTER The publisher.. paid all fees, monies and royalties.

Phrases: *accept wooden money*: see WOODEN *a.* *a* (*good*) *run for one's money*: see RUN *n.* **at the money** = *for the money* below. **be everybody's money** (freq. in neg. contexts) (*a*) *arch.* be what everybody prefers or can afford to buy; (*b*) be to everyone's liking. *big money*: see BIG *a.* *black money*: see BLACK *a.* *buy money*: see BUY *v.* *coin money*: see COIN *v.*[1] *dirty money*: see DIRTY *a.* *easy money*: see EASY *a.* *even money*: see EVEN *a.* *folding money*: see FOLDING *ppl a.* **for money** in return or exchange for money. **for my money** (*a*) in my opinion; (*b*) — is my choice (or favourite) (*the man for my money*: see MAN *n.*). **for the money** at the price paid. *front money*: see FRONT *n.*, *a.*, & *adv.* *funny money*: see FUNNY *a.* *hard money*: see HARD *a.* *hot money*: see HOT *a.* **in the money** among the prize-winners; amply or sufficiently supplied with money; rich. *mad money*: see MAD *a.* **make money** acquire or earn money; *esp.* make a profit (*out of*). *make the money fly*: see FLY *v.* **marry (into) money** marry a wealthy spouse, marry a person with a wealthy family. **money for jam, money for old rope** a profitable return for little or no trouble; a very easy job; someone or something easy to profit from. *money of account*: see ACCOUNT *n.* *near money*: see NEAR *a.* *new money*: see NEW *a.* *not for love or money*: see LOVE *n.* *old money*: see OLD *a.* *paper money*: see PAPER *n.* & *a.* *plastic money*: see PLASTIC *a.* **put one's money on** bet on (a horse etc.); *fig.* favour or depend on, expect the success of. **put one's money where one's mouth is** produce, bet, or pay out money to support one's statements or opinions. *ready money*: see READY *a.* *real money*: see REAL *a.*[2] *see the colour of a person's money*: see COLOUR *n.* *smart money*: see SMART *a.* *take wooden money*: see WOODEN *a.* *throw good money after bad*: see THROW *v.* **throw money at** try to solve (a problem) by increased expenditure alone, without due consideration. *value for money*: see VALUE *n.* *white money*: see WHITE *a.* **your money or your life**: a formula attributed to highwaymen etc. in obtaining money from their victims.

Comb.: **money-back** *a.* (of a system, agreement, etc.) providing for the customer's money to be refunded if the goods or service provided are not satisfactory; **money-bag** a bag for holding money; **moneybags** *colloq.* (freq. *derog.*) a person chiefly remarkable as a possessor or lover of money; a wealthy person; **money-belt** a belt with a purse for carrying money; **money-bill** a bill in Parliament for granting supplies; †**money-bound** *a.* (*colloq.*) detained for lack of money; **money box** a box in which money is kept; *esp.* a closed box into which money is dropped through a slit; **money-broker** a money-dealer; **money centre** a place of pre-eminent importance in the financial affairs of a region or country; **money-changer** a person whose business it is to change money at a fixed or authorized rate; **money-clause** a clause (in a parliamentary bill) for granting supplies; *money cowrie*: see COWRIE 1; **money crop** *US* = *cash crop* s.v. CASH *n.*[1]; **money-dealer** a person who deals in money in the way of exchange, banking, lending, etc.; **money flower** honesty, *Lunaria annua*; *money-grubber*: see GRUBBER *n.* 3; **money-grubbing** *n.* & *a.* (given to or characterized by) the assiduous amassing of money by contemptible methods; **money illusion**: that money has a fixed value in terms of its purchasing power; **money-jobber, -jobbing** a dealer, dealing, in money or coin; **moneylender** a person whose business is lending money at interest; **moneylending** *n.* & *a.* (engaged in) the business of lending money at interest; **moneymaker** †(*a*) a person who coins money; †(*b*) a maker of counterfeit coin; (*c*) a person who gains or earns much money; a person skilled in or intent on making money; (*d*) a profitable thing, idea, etc., a money-spinner; **moneymaking** *n.* & *a.* (*a*) *n.* the acquiring of wealth; the making of profits; (*b*) *adj.* occupied in or intent on making money; profitable, lucrative; **money-man** *colloq.* a financier; a financial expert; **money market** (*a*) the market in short-term finance between banks and other financial institutions (sometimes including the foreign exchange market and the bullion market); these institutions collectively; (*b*) *US* = *money centre* above; **money matters** the financial side of things, financial affairs; **money-monger** *derog.* (*arch.*) a moneylender; **money-mongering** *derog.* (*arch.*) moneylending; **money order** an order for payment of a specified sum issued at a bank or post office and payable at another (in British use not bearing the name of a specified payee); **money-power** (*a*) the power to coin money, regulate its use, etc.; (*b*) the power exercised by money or by wealthy people, firms, etc.; *money scrivener*: see SCRIVENER 3; **money spider** a very small spider supposed to bring good luck in pecuniary matters to the person over whom it crawls; *spec.* a spider of the family Linyphiidae; **money-spinner** (*a*) a money spider; (*b*) a person who or (now more usu.) thing which makes a lot of money; something very profitable; **money-spinning** *a.* very profitable; **money supply** *Econ.* the total amount of money in circulation or in being in a country (as measured by various criteria); **moneywort** = CREEPING *Jenny*; *Cornish moneywort*, a creeping plant of the figwort family, *Sibthorpia europaea*, with small pink flowers.

moneyless *a.* LME.

money /ˈmʌni/ *v.t.* LME. [f. the n. or (sense 1) Fr. *monnayer*.] **1** Coin, mint. *rare.* LME. **2** Supply with money, give money to; (formerly) bribe. Long *rare.* LME. **3** Dispose of for money. *rare.* E17. **4** Foll. by *out*: state the price of; give the prices of items in (a tender or estimate). *Sc.* M19.

moneyed /ˈmʌnɪd/ *a.* Also **monied.** LME. [f. MONEY *n.*, *v.*: see -ED[2], -ED[1].] **1** Having or possessing (much) money; wealthy. LME. †**b** Supplied (*well* etc.) with money. L15–L17. **2** Consisting of money, derived from money. L18. **3** Of a corporation etc.: having power to deal in money. *US.* L19.

moneyer /ˈmʌnɪə/ *n.* LME. [OFr. *mon(n)ier*, *-oier* (mod. *monnayeur*) f. late L *monetarius*, f. L *moneta* MONEY *n.*: see -ER[1].] †**1 a** A money-changer. Only in LME. **b** A banker, a financier. E18–M19. **2** Chiefly *Hist.* A person who coins money; a coiner, a minter. LME.

money's-worth /ˈmʌnɪzwəːθ/ *n.* L16. [f. MONEY *n.* + -'S[1] + WORTH *n.*[1]] **1** An equivalent for the sum of money paid or to be paid; full value. Now chiefly with possess. pron. L16. **2** A thing that is worth money or is recognized as equivalent to money. Cf. earlier MONEY-WORTH. *arch.* E17.

1 D. CECIL Playgoers expected their moneysworth in those days. 2 H. J. STEPHEN An obligation to pay money or money's worth.

money-worth /ˈmʌnɪwəːθ/ *n.* LME. [f. MONEY *n.* + WORTH *n.*[1]] **1** = MONEY'S-WORTH 2. Now *rare* or *obs.* LME. **2** Worth in money, value when exchanged for money. E20.

mong /mʌŋ/ *n.*[1] Long *obs.* exc. *dial.* Also **mung.** [OE *ġemang*, f. Gmc base also of MENG. Aphet. early in ME.] **1** A mingling, a mixture. Formerly also, commerce. Long *rare.* OE. **2** A mixture of different kinds of grain or meal; = MASLIN *n.*[2] 1. ME. **3** A crowd, an assembly. ME.

Comb.: **mongcorn** a mixture of kinds of grain, esp. wheat and rye, sown together.

mong /mʌŋ/ *n.*[2] *Austral. slang.* M20. [Abbrev.] A mongrel.

'mong /mʌŋ/ *prep. poet.* ME. [Aphet.] Among.

mongan /ˈmɒŋg(ə)n/ *n.* L19. [Aborig.] A ringtailed possum, *Pseudocheirus herbertensis*, inhabiting the rainforest of NE Queensland.

monger /ˈmʌŋgə/ *n.* & *v.* [OE *mangere* (= OHG, ON *mangari*), f. *mangian* (= OS *mangon*, ON *manga*) deal, trade, f. Gmc, f. L *mango* dealer, trader: see -ER[1].] **A** *n.* A dealer, a trader (in some specified commodity). Exc. in long-established combs. usu. *derog.*, a person who promotes or carries on a petty or disreputable traffic in something specified. Usu. as 2nd elem. of comb. OE.

C. KINGSLEY My only fear is people will fancy me a verbal-inspiration-monger. V. WOOLF He's a priest, a mystery-monger. *cheesemonger, fishmonger, ironmonger, newsmonger, scandalmonger, scaremonger, warmonger, whoremonger*, etc.

B *v.t.* Deal or traffic in. Chiefly as *mongering* vbl n. (usu. as 2nd elem. of comb.) & ppl a. L18.

Mongo /ˈmɒŋgəʊ/ *n.*[1] & *a.* E20. [Mongo.] **A** *n.* Pl. **-os**, same. A member of a Bantu-speaking people living in Zaire; the language of this people. E20. **B** *attrib.* or as *adj.* Of or pertaining to the Mongos or their language. M20.

mongo /ˈmɒŋgəʊ/ *n.*[2] Pl. **-os**, same. M20. [Mongolian *möngö* silver.] A monetary unit of Mongolia, equal to one-hundredth of a tugrik.

Mongol /ˈmɒŋg(ə)l/ *a.* & *n.* In senses A.2, B.2 also **m-.** L17. [Mongolian, said to be f. *mong* brave. Cf. MOGUL.] **A** *adj.* **1** Of, pertaining to, or characteristic of Mongolia (see next), its people, or their language; Mongolian. L17. **2** Pertaining to or affected with Down's syndrome (see note below). L19. **B** *n.* **1** A member of an Asian people now chiefly inhabiting Mongolia, but formerly extending more widely; a

Mongolian. M18. 2 A person with Down's syndrome (see note below). L19.

¶The use of *mongol* and related words to refer to Down's syndrome is increasingly regarded as offensive.

Mongolian /mɒŋˈgəʊlɪən/ *a.* & *n.* In sense A.3 also **m-**. E18. [f. prec. + -IAN.] A *adj.* 1 Of or pertaining to the central Asian territory or modern republic of Mongolia; of or pertaining to the Mongols or their language. E18. 2 = MONGOLOID *a.* 1. E19. 3 Affected with Down's syndrome (see note s.v. MONGOL). M19.

Special collocations: **Mongolian eye**: having an epicanthus. **Mongolian fold** = EPICANTHUS. **Mongolian hotpot** an oriental dish consisting of thinly-sliced meat, vegetables, etc., cooked in simmering stock at the table. **Mongolian pheasant** a pheasant, *Phasianus colchicus*, of a subspecies with a broken white neck-ring, native to southern Russia and Mongolia, and introduced with other races into western Europe and elsewhere; also called *Kirghiz pheasant*. **Mongolian spot** a bluish or brownish spot which is present in the sacral region of most newborn Oriental babies (and occas. in others), and usu. disappears in infancy.

B *n.* 1 A native or inhabitant of Mongolia; a Mongol. M18. 2 = MONGOLOID *n.* 1. M19. 3 The language of Mongolia, usu. considered a member of the Altaic family (though its affiliations are now in doubt). M19.

Mongolic /mɒŋˈgɒlɪk/ *a.* & *n.* E19. [f. MONGOL + -IC.] A *adj.* 1 Of, pertaining to, or designating a group of Altaic languages including Mongolian, Kalmuck, and Buriat. E19. 2 Mongolian. M19. B *n.* The Mongolic language group. E19.

Mongolise *v.* var. of MONGOLIZE.

mongolism /ˈmɒŋg(ə)lɪz(ə)m/ *n.* Also **M-**. E20. [f. MONGOL + -ISM.] *Med.* = DOWN'S SYNDROME (see note s.v. MONGOL).

Mongolize /ˈmɒŋg(ə)lʌɪz/ *v.t. rare.* Also **-ise**. E19. [f. MONGOL + -IZE.] Make Mongolian in character, customs, etc.

Mongoliˈzation *n.* M19.

Mongoloid /ˈmɒŋg(ə)lɔɪd/ *a.* & *n.* In senses A.2, B.2 also **m-**. M19. [f. MONGOL + -OID.] A *adj.* 1 Resembling or having some of the characteristic physical features of Mongolians; *spec.* designating or pertaining to the division of humankind including the indigenous peoples of eastern Asia, SE Asia, and the Arctic region of N. America, and characterized by dark eyes with an epicanthic fold, pale ivory to dark skin, straight dark hair, and little facial and bodily hair. M19. 2 Affected with Down's syndrome (see note s.v. MONGOL). L19. B *n.* 1 A person of Mongoloid physical type. M19. 2 A person affected with Down's syndrome (see note s.v. MONGOL). M20.

mongoose /ˈmɒŋguːs/ *n.* Also †**mungoose**. Pl. **-gooses**. L17. [Marathi *mangūs*, *mun-* f. Telegu *mungisi*, Kannada *mungisa*.] 1 Any of various long-tailed short-legged carnivorous mammals of the family Viverridae (which also includes the civets and genets), native to southern Asia and Africa, and noted for the ability to kill venomous snakes. L17. 2 A nectar-eating lemur, *Lemur mongoz*, of Madagascar and the Comoro Islands. More fully *mongoose lemur*. M18.

1 *slender mongoose*: see SLENDER *a.*

mongrel /ˈmʌŋgr(ə)l/ *n.* & *a.* LME. [App. f. base meaning 'mix' (cf. MENG, MONG *n.*[1]) + -REL.] A *n.* 1 A dog whose sire and dam are of different breeds. Chiefly & now only, a dog of no definable breed resulting from various crossings. LME. †b As a term of abuse: a contemptible person, a cur. L16–M19. 2 A person of mixed descent; a person whose parents are of different nationalities or (formerly) differing social status. *derog.* M16. 3†a A person of mixed or undefined opinions; a person whose political allegiance etc. varies according to expediency. *derog.* M16–E18. b A thing of mixed or intermediate character; a cross, a hybrid. *derog.* E17. c An animal or plant resulting from the crossing of different types (usually, different breeds or varieties), esp. other than by design. L17.

1 R. CROMPTON It.. stood eager, alert, friendly, a mongrel unashamed. 2 J. G. EDGAR Men.. of every race, mongrels almost to a man. 3b CARLYLE Some cart, or dilapidated mongrel between cart and basket.

B *adj.* 1 Of a dog: that is a mongrel, of no definable breed. L16. †b Worthless, contemptible. E17–E18. c Of an animal or plant: produced by the crossing of different varieties etc. (Cf. sense A.3c above.) M17. 2 Of mixed origin, nature, or character; not referable to any definite species or type; being neither one thing nor the other. *derog.* L16. b Of a word, dialect, etc.: made up of elements from different languages. E17. 3 Of a person: of mixed descent, having parents or ancestors of different nationalities. *derog.* E17.

1b SHAKES. *Lear* A knave, a rascal.. and the son and heir of a mongrel bitch. c BOSWELL Their sheep being of a mongrel race. 2 P. SIDNEY Neither the admiration and commiseration, nor the right sportfulnes, is by their mungrell Tragy-comedie obtained. b E. O. M. DEUTSCH The Aramaic.. had become.. a mongrel idiom. 3 SOUTHEY To learn that law from Norman or from Dane, Saxon.. or whatever name Suit best your mongrel race!

mongreldom *n.* = MONGRELISM L19. **mongrelism** *n.* the condition or quality of being mongrel or hybrid L16. **mongreliˈzation** *n.* the action or process of mongrelizing someone or something; mongrelism: L19. **mongrelize** *v.t.* make mongrel in breed, race, composition, or character E17. **mongrelly** *a.* resembling a mongrel M19.

'mongst /mʌŋst/ *prep. poet.* L16. [Aphet.] Amongst.

monial /ˈməʊnɪəl/ *n.* ME. [OFr. *moinel* (mod. *meneau*), use as n. of *moi(e)nel* adj. = middle, f. *moien*: see MEAN *a.*[2], -AL[1]. Cf. MUNNION.] *Archit.* A mullion.

monic /ˈmɒnɪk/ *a.* M20. [f. MONO- + -IC.] *Math.* Of a polynomial: having the coefficient of the term of highest degree equal to one.

monicker *n.* var. of MONIKER.

monied *a.* var. of MONEYED.

monies *n.pl.* see MONEY *n.*

moniker /ˈmɒnɪkə/ *n. slang.* Also **-nn-**, **monicker**. M19. [Origin unkn.] A name, a nickname.

monilia /məˈnɪlɪə/ *n.* Pl. same, **-ias**, **-iae** /-ɪiː/. M18. [mod.L (see below), f. L *monile* necklace (w. allus. to the chains of spores): see -IA[1].] Any fungus now or formerly belonging to the genus *Monilia*, which formerly included certain pathogenic fungi now assigned to *Candida*.

monilial *a.* of, pertaining to, or caused by a monilia or monilias M20. **moniliasis** /mɒnɪˈlʌɪəsɪs/ *n.* pl. **-ases** /-əsiːz/, *Med.* = CANDIDIASIS E20.

moniliform /məˈnɪlɪfɔːm/ *a.* E19. [Fr. *moniliforme* or mod.L *moniliformis*, f. L *monile* necklace: see -FORM.] Chiefly *Anat.*, *Zool.*, etc. Of the form of or resembling a necklace or string of beads.

monimolimnion /mɒnɪməˈlɪmnɪən/ *n.* Pl. **-nia** /-nɪə/. M20. [f. Gk *monimos* stable + *limnion* dim. of *limnē* lake.] The lower, denser, non-circulating layer of water in a meromictic lake.

monish /ˈmɒnɪʃ/ *v.t.* Now *rare*. ME. [OFr. *monester* aphet. f. *amonester* ADMONISH.] 1 Admonish; *Eccl.* = MONITION *v.* ME. †2 Exhort to do; give warning of; call to mind. LME–M16.

monishment *n.* L15.

monism /ˈmɒnɪz(ə)m, ˈməʊ-/ *n.* M19. [mod.L *monismus*, f. Gk *monos* single: see -ISM.] A theory or system of thought which recognizes a single ultimate principle, being, force, etc., rather than more than one (cf. DUALISM 1, PLURALISM 2); *spec.* (*a*) a theory that denies the duality of matter and mind; (*b*) the doctrine that there is only one supreme being, as opp. to a belief in good and evil as conflicting powers.

neutral monism: see NEUTRAL *a.*

monist /ˈmɒnɪst/ *n.* M19. [f. Gk *monos* single + -IST.] A person who holds any of the doctrines of monism.

neutral monist: see NEUTRAL *a.*

monistic /məˈnɪstɪk/ *a.* M19. [f. prec. + -IC.] Of, pertaining to, or of the nature of monism; advocating any of the theories of monism.

monistically *adv.* L19.

monition /məˈnɪʃ(ə)n/ *n.* & *v.* LME. [(O)Fr. f. L *monitio(n-)*, f. *monit-* pa. ppl stem of *monere* advise, warn: see -ITION.] A *n.* 1 = ADMONITION. LME. 2 A warning of the presence or imminence of something (now *spec.* of some impending danger). LME. 3 An official or legal notice, *esp.* one calling on a person to do something specified; *spec.* (*Eccl.*) a formal notice from a bishop or ecclesiastical court admonishing a person not to commit an offence. LME. B *v.t. Eccl.* Warn by a monition. L19.

monitor /ˈmɒnɪtə/ *n.* E16. [L, f. *monit-*: see prec., -OR.] †1 An official letter conveying an admonition. *Sc.* E–M16. 2 A school pupil or (esp. *US*) college student assigned disciplinary or other special duties (formerly in some cases including teaching). M16. 3 A person who or thing which admonishes someone or gives advice or a warning as to conduct. E17. 4a A reminder, a warning. M17. b A person who monitors something; *spec.* a person employed to listen to and report on (esp. foreign) radio broadcasts. E20. c A television receiver used in a studio to display the picture from a particular camera; a VDU connected directly to the source of a video signal, esp. one from a computer. Also *monitor screen* etc. M20. d Any instrument or device for monitoring some process or quantity, as for detecting or measuring radioactivity. M20. e A loudspeaker used in a studio for listening to what is being recorded; any large or powerful speaker, *esp.* one used on stage by a band. Also more fully *monitor speaker*. M20. f A computer program which monitors the running of other programs or the operation of a system. M20. †5 = BACKBOARD *n.* 2(a). L18–M19. 6 More fully *monitor lizard*. Any of various large tropical Old World lizards constituting the genus *Varanus* and the family Varanidae (so called from being supposed to warn of the vicinity of crocodiles). E19. 7 *Hist.* [f. the name of an ironclad used in the US Civil War.] A warship having a low freeboard and one or more heavy guns, suitable esp. for shore bombardment. M19. 8 A clerestory in the roof of a railway-carriage, building, etc. Freq. *attrib. US*. L19. 9 A jointed nozzle used in hydraulic mining, which may be turned in any direction. L19.

2 W. S. MAUGHAM I was going to make you a monitor next term. 3 C. MORGAN I am happy to-night, for my monitor tells me.. to be happy. C. THUBRON Once authority had sanctioned violence, no monitor inside him had called a halt. 4a A. JOLLY Such emblematical rites.. are useful helps and monitors to our weak minds. c S. BRETT He caught sight of something on one of the monitors. It was a shot from a camera.. focused nowhere in particular. 6 *Komodo monitor*, *Nile monitor*, etc.

monitorship *n.* M17. **monitress** *n.* a female monitor M18. **monitrix** *n.* (*rare*) = MONITRESS E18.

monitor /ˈmɒnɪtə/ *v.t.* E19. [f. the n.] †1 Guide as a monitor. *rare*. Only in E19. 2a Check or regulate the technical quality of (a radio transmission, television signal, etc.). E20. b Listen to and report on (radio broadcasts, telephone conversations, etc.). M20. c *gen.* Observe, supervise, keep under review; measure or test at intervals, esp. for the purpose of regulation or control. M20.

2b *Times Review of Industry* The output from the analyser can be monitored with headphones. D. HASTON Three weeks in Kleine Scheidegg, monitoring weather forecasts twice a day. c *Scientific American* The radius of the mirror was monitored frequently. H. KISSINGER A cease-fire and standstill to be monitored by UN representatives.

monitorial /mɒnɪˈtɔːrɪəl/ *a.* E18. [Fr., or f. L *monitorius* MONITORY + -AL[1].] 1 = MONITORY *a.* E18. 2 Of, pertaining to, or performed by a monitor or monitors. E19.

monitory /ˈmɒnɪt(ə)ri/ *n.* & *a.* LME. [L *monitorius*, f. as MONITOR *n.*: see -ORY[2].] A *n.* 1 A letter containing an admonition or warning, *esp.* one issued by a bishop or pope. LME. †2 An admonition; a warning. M16–M18. B *adj.* Giving or conveying a warning; serving to admonish; admonitory. L15.

monk /mʌŋk/ *n.*[1] [OE *munuc* = OFris. *munek*, OS *munik* (Du. *monnik*), OHG *munih* (G

Mönch), ON *múnker*, f. Gmc f. pop.L var. of late L *monachus* f. late Gk *monakhos*, use as n. of adj. = single, solitary, f. *monos* alone.] **1** A member of a Christian community of men living apart from the world under vows of poverty, chastity, and obedience, according to the rule of a particular order, and devoted chiefly to religious duties and contemplation. Also, a member of a similar community of adherents of any other religion. OE. **2** Any of various animals or things whose form suggests the cowled figure of a monk; *spec.* (*a*) (also †*sea-monk*) = *monkfish* below; (*b*) *Printing* a blotch or area of excessive inking (cf. FRIAR 4). E17.

1 *black monk*: see BLACK *a.* *Pied Monk*: see PIED *a.* *white monk*: see WHITE *a.*

Comb.: *monk bond*: see BOND *n.*[2] 9; †**monk-craft** *derog.* = MONKERY; **monkfish** (*a*) a bottom-dwelling shark of the genus *Squatina*, with a somewhat flattened body and broad winglike pectoral fins; esp. *S. squatina* of eastern Atlantic and Mediterranean waters; (*b*) an angler-fish; †**monk-house** a monastery; **Monk-Latin** a corrupt form of Latin used by monks; †**monk-monger** *derog.* a favourer of monks or monasticism; **monk's bench** = *monks' table* below; **monk seal** any of various light-bellied seals of the genus *Monachus*, esp. *M. monachus* of the Mediterranean and adjacent seas; **monk's gun** a 16th-cent. wheel-lock gun, supposedly invented by the monk Schwarz, the alleged inventor of gunpowder; **monk's rhubarb** a kind of dock, *Rumex pseudoalpinus*, formerly grown as a pot-herb; **monk('s)-seam** *Naut.* a seam in which the selvages of sails are sewn flat one over the other; **monk('s) shoe** a low shoe with a strap passing over the instep, buckled at the side; **monk's table** a convertible wooden seat, the back of which is hinged to swing over and rest horizontally on the arms, thus forming a table.

monkdom *n.* the condition of a monk; monks collectively; the domain of monks: M19. **monkhood** *n.* the state or profession of a monk; the monastic life, monasticism; monks collectively: OE. **monkism** *n.* monasticism E18. **monkship** *n.* the monastic system; monks collectively: E17.

monk /mʌŋk/ *n.*[2] *slang.* M19. [Abbrev.] A monkey.

monkery /ˈmʌŋkəri/ *n.* Chiefly *derog.* E16. [f. MONK *n.*[1] + -ERY.] **1** A body or community of monks; a monastery. Also, monks collectively; the monks of a particular place. E16. **2** The state, condition, or profession of monks; monastic life, monasticism. M16. **3** In *pl.* Monkish practices, appurtenances, or paraphernalia. E17. **4** Conduct or practice characteristic of or attributed to (esp. medieval) monks; a monastic way of life marked by corruption and other abuses. M17. **5** The way of life of a tramp; a district frequented by tramps. *arch. slang.* L18.

monkey /ˈmʌŋki/ *n.* M16. [Origin uncertain: perh. f. LG dim. of Proto-Romance wd (whence Fr. †*monne*, It. *monna*, Sp., Port. *mono*, *-a*).] **I 1** Any of numerous primates of a group including the families Cebidae (capuchins etc.), Callitrichidae (marmosets, tamarins, etc.), and Cercopithecidae (baboons, macaques, etc.), *esp.* any of the long-tailed kinds. M16. **b** The fur of any of certain monkeys. L19. **2a** A person who performs comical antics; a mimic. L16. **b** A mischievous person, esp. a child; a rascal, a scamp. E17. **3** A sheep. *Austral.* L19. **4** *the monkey*, a kind of dance performed to rock music. M20.

1 *capuchin monkey*, *colobus monkey*, *green monkey*, *howler monkey*, *Japanese monkey*, *moustache(d) monkey*, *rhesus monkey*, *Sykes'(s) monkey*, *spider monkey*, etc. **2b** BYRON A little curly-headed, good-for-nothing, And mischief-making monkey from his birth.

II †**5** A kind of gun or cannon. Only in M17. **6** Any of various appliances; *spec.* a pile-driving machine consisting of a heavy hammer or ram working vertically in a groove (also *monkey engine*); the ram of such a machine. M18. **7** A receptacle for liquor; *esp.* a globular earthenware water-vessel with a straight upright neck. M19. **8** Five hundred pounds; five hundred dollars. *slang.* M19.

Phrases (chiefly *colloq.* & *slang*): **a barrel** (or **wagon-load**, **cart-load**, etc.) **of monkeys**: a type of something extremely cunning, mischievous, jolly, or disorderly. **cold enough to freeze the balls off a brass monkey** *coarse slang* extremely cold (see also *brass-monkey(s)* s.v. BRASS *a.*). *grease monkey*: see GREASE *n.* **have a** (or **the**) **monkey on one's back** (*slang*, orig. *US*) be addicted to a drug. **have** or **get one's monkey up** be angry. **make a monkey** (**out**) **of** *colloq.* humiliate by making appear ridiculous. **monkey on a stick** a toy consisting of the figure of a monkey able to slide up and down a stick, used as a type of restlessness or agitation. **monkey's allowance** harsh treatment and little pay. **not give** (or **care**) **a monkey's** (**fuck** etc.) *coarse slang* not care at all; be completely indifferent or unconcerned. **put** (**a person's**) **monkey up** annoy, anger. *softly softly catchee monkey*: see SOFTLY *adv.* 3. STUFFED *monkey*. **suck the monkey** drink liquor from the bottle, or from a coconut shell, or from a cask using a straw; *gen.* tipple. **three** (**wise**) **monkeys** a conventional sculptured group of three monkeys, one with its paws over its mouth ('speak no evil'), one with its paws over its eyes ('see no evil'), and one with its paws over its ears ('hear no evil'); used allusively to refer to people who choose to ignore or keep silent about wrongdoing etc. **where the monkey puts** (or **keeps**) **his nuts** *coarse slang* in the anus.

Comb.: **monkey-apple** (the fruit of) any of various tropical trees and shrubs, esp. (*a*) *Anisophyllea laurina* (family Anisophyllaceae) of W. Africa; (*b*) a neotropical plant of the genus *Annona* (family Annonaceae); **monkey bars** a piece of playground equipment consisting of a ladder mounted horizontally above the ground, for children to swing from; **monkey-board** a footboard at the back of a vehicle for a footman etc. to stand on; **monkey-boat** (*a*) a long narrow canal boat; (*b*) a small boat used as a tender; **monkey bread** (the fruit of) the baobab tree; **monkey bridge** *Naut.* a small raised platform above a bridge, deck-house, etc., on a ship; **monkey business** *colloq.* mischief, trickery, fooling about; **monkey-chaser** *US slang* (usu. considered *offensive*) a Black from the W. Indies or other tropical region; **monkey-eating eagle** a very large eagle, *Pithecophaga jefferyi*, native to the Philippines; *monkey engine*: see sense 6 above; **monkey-face** a face like a monkey's; a funny face; *W. Indian colloq.* a grimace; **monkey-faced** *a.* having a face like a monkey's; *monkey-faced owl* (US colloq.), the barn owl; **monkey flower** any of various plants of the genus *Mimulus*, of the figwort family, *esp.* the yellow-flowered N. American *M. guttatus*; **monkey gland** *colloq.* a gland or testicle from a monkey or another primate, grafted on to a man as a possible means of rejuvenation; **monkey-house** a building at a zoo etc. in which monkeys are kept; **monkey island** *Naut.* = *monkey bridge* above; **monkey-jacket** a short close-fitting jacket worn by sailors etc. or at a mess; **monkey-man** (*a*) *US slang* a weak and servile husband; (*b*) a man resembling a monkey; **monkey nut** a peanut; **monkey orchestra** a group of Meissen or other porcelain figures representing monkeys playing musical instruments; **monkey orchid, orchis** a rare orchid, *Orchis simia*, native to Europe and the Mediterranean region, the flower having a purple lip suggesting a monkey in shape; **monkey parade** *slang* a social gathering of young people out of doors; **monkey-pod** (**tree**) the rain-tree or saman, *Albizia saman*; **monkey-pot** any of certain Brazilian trees of the genus *Lecythis* (family Lecythidaceae); the woody seed-vessel of such a tree, formerly used as a trap for monkeys; **monkeypox** a virus disease of monkeys (transmissible to humans), similar to smallpox; **monkey-puzzle** (**tree**), **monkey-puzzler** a large evergreen pine, *Araucaria araucana*, native to Chile, having whorled branches densely covered with leaves; also called *Chile pine*; **monkey-rope** *S. Afr.* any of various climbing plants, esp. *Secamone alpinii* (family Asclepiadaceae); **monkey's fist** a thick knot made at the end of a rope to give it weight when it is thrown; **monkeyshine** *US slang* = *monkey trick* below (usu. in *pl.*); **monkey suit** *slang* a uniform; a formal dress suit, evening dress; **monkey trial** a trial of a teacher for teaching evolutionary theories, contrary to the laws of certain States of the US; *spec.* that of J. T. Scopes in Tennessee in 1925; **monkey trick** a mischievous, foolish, or underhand trick or act; an antic; (usu. in *pl.*); **monkey wrench** a wrench or spanner having an adjustable jaw; *throw a monkey wrench into the works* (colloq.), cause confusion or trouble; = *throw a spanner into the works* s.v. SPANNER *n.*[1]

monkey /ˈmʌŋki/ *v.* L18. [f. the n.] †**1** *v.t.* Make like a monkey. *rare.* Only in L18. **2** *v.t.* Ape the manners of, mimic; ridicule, mock. M19. **3** *v.i.* Play mischievous or foolish tricks; fool or mess *about* or *around*; tamper *with*. *colloq.* (orig. *US*). L19.

3 J. HILTON Bryant had been monkeying on Wall Street, and the result had been a warrant for his arrest. *Times* Any departure from tradition . . would be as serious as monkeying about with . . an old school tie.

monkeyfy /ˈmʌŋkɪfʌɪ/ *v.t.* Now *rare.* M18. [f. MONKEY *n.* + -FY.] Make like a monkey; make ridiculous-looking.

monkeyish /ˈmʌŋkɪɪʃ/ *a.* E17. [f. as prec. + -ISH[1].] Like a monkey; playful, mischievous; imitative.

monkeyishly *adv.* E20. **monkeyishness** *n.* E19.

monkeyism /ˈmʌŋkɪɪz(ə)m/ *n.* E19. [f. MONKEY *n.* + -ISM.] Behaviour like that of a monkey.

Mon-Khmer /ˈməʊnk(ə)mɛː/ *n.* & *a.* L19. [f. MON *n.*[1] & *a.* + KHMER.] (Designating or pertaining to) a group of Austro-Asiatic languages spoken in SE Asia, of which the most important are Mon and Khmer.

monkish /ˈmʌŋkɪʃ/ *a.* M16. [f. MONK *n.*[1] + -ISH[1].] **1** Of or pertaining to monks; monastic. M16. **b** Used, made, or performed by monks. E17. **c** That is a monk. L17. **2** Resembling a monk; suggestive of a monk or monks. L16. **3** Characteristic of monks or the monastic system; *esp.* (*derog.*) displaying corruption or other disreputable characteristics attributed to medieval monasticism. L16.

monkishly *adv.* M20. **monkishness** *n.* E19.

monkly /ˈmʌŋkli/ *a.* OE. [f. MONK *n.*[1] + -LY[1].] Of or pertaining to a monk or monks; monastic.

monkliness *n.* L19.

monkshood /ˈmʌŋkshʊd/ *n.* Also **monk's-hood**. L16. [f. MONK *n.*[1] + -'S[1] + HOOD *n.*[1]] **1** Any of numerous highly toxic plants of the genus *Aconitum*; *esp.* the European *A. napellus*, which bears purple flowers with a hood. L16. **2** Larkspur, *Consolida ambigua*. Now *rare* or *obs.* L16. †**3** *Anat.* The trapezius muscle. Only in 17.

Monmouth cap /ˌmɒnməθ ˈkap/ *n. phr. obs.* exc. *Hist.* L16. [*Monmouth*, a town in Gwent, Wales.] A flat round cap formerly worn by soldiers and sailors.

monniker *n.* var. of MONIKER.

mono /ˈmɒnəʊ/ *n.* & *a. colloq.* M20. [Abbrev.] **A** *n.* Pl. **-os**. **1** (A) monophonic recording or reproduction. M20. **2** = MONONUCLEOSIS. Chiefly *N. Amer.* M20. **3** *Photogr.*, *Television*, etc. = MONOCHROME *n.* 1b, 2b. L20. **B** *adj.* **1** = MONOPHONIC *a.* 3. M20. **2** *Photogr.*, *Television*, etc. = MONOCHROME *a.* 2. L20.

mono- /ˈmɒnəʊ/ *comb. form.* Bef. a vowel also **mon-**. [Gk f. *monos* alone, only, single: see -O-.] Used in wds adopted f. Gk and in Eng. formations modelled on these, and as a freely productive pref., w. the senses 'one, alone, single', 'having, involving, etc., one'; *Chem.* signifying the presence of a single atom, radical, etc., of a particular kind in a molecule etc. Cf. UNI-.

monobuoy *n.* a floating platform anchored in deep water offshore at which oil tankers and other large vessels can moor L20. **mono-cable** *n.* & *a.* (designating or involving) an aerial ropeway in which a single endless rope is used to support and move loads E20. **monoˈcarbonate** *n.* (now *rare* or *obs.*) a salt containing the carbonate anion, CO_3^{2-}; a carbonate (cf. BICARBONATE): M19. **monoˈcausal** *a.* in terms of or having a sole cause M20. **monoˈcellular** *a.* (*Biol.*) = UNICELLULAR M19. **monoˈcentric** *a.* (*Biol.*) having a single centre; *Cytol.* having a single centromere: L19. **monoˈcephalous** *a.* (*Bot.*) (of a plant) having only one head or umbel M19. **monochasial** /-ˈkeɪz-/ *a.* (*Bot.*) (of a cyme) that is a monochasium L19. **monochasium** /-ˈkeɪz-/ *n.*, pl. **-ia**, [Gk *khasis* chasm, separation] *Bot.* a cyme in which each flowering branch gives rise to one lateral branch, so that the inflorescence is helicoid or asymmetrical L19. **monochlaˈmydeous** *a.* [Gk *khlamud-*, *khlamus* cloak] *Bot.* having only one floral envelope; having a single perianth: M19. **monoˈchloride** *n.* a salt containing one chloride ion to each combining ion or radical M19. **monoˈchroic** *a.* (*rare*) = MONOCHROME *a.* 1 L19. **monociˈstronic** *a.* (*Genetics*) containing as much genetic information as is carried by a single cistron M20. **mono-coloured** *a.* (*rare*) of only one colour L18. **monoconˈdylian**, **monoconˈdylic** *adjs.* (*Zool.*) (of a skull) having one occipital condyle, as that of birds and reptiles (opp. DICONDYLIAN) L19. **monoconsoˈnantal** *a.* containing a single consonant M20. **monoˈcormic** *a.* [Gk *kormos* trunk (of a tree)] *Bot.* (esp. of a conifer) having a single main axis of growth L19. **monoˈcrotic** *a.* (*Med.*) (of the pulse) having a single detectable beat (opp. *dicrotic*) L19. **monocrystal** *n.* a single crystal M20. **mono'crystalline** *a.* consisting of monocrystals; constituting a monocrystal: M20. **mono'dentate** *a.* (*Chem.*) (of a ligand) having only one point of attachment to a central atom M20. **monodia'lectal** *a.* speaking only one dialect M20. **monodi'mensional** *a.* existing in or having only one dimension; linear: M20. **mono'disperse** *a.* (*Physical Chem.*) designating or pertaining to a colloid containing particles of uniform size E20. **monoener'getic** *a.* (*Physics*) (consisting of particles) of the same energy; emitting radiation all of one energy: M20. **monoetha'nolamine** *n.* a viscous high-boiling liquid, $H_2NCH_2CH_2OH$, used in making detergents; 2-aminoethanol: E20. **monofil** *n.* & *a.* = MONOFILAMENT E20. **monofilament** *n.* & *a.* (made up of) a single strand of man-made fibre M20. **mono'functional** *a.* (*Chem.*) having or corresponding to a single functional group per molecule M20. **monogerm** *a.* (*Agric.*) designating or pertaining to varieties of sugar beet in which each seed ball has its contents reduced to one fruit and so gives rise to only one seedling M20. **mono'glacial** *a.* designating a theory postulating only one glacial period during the Pleistocene M20. **mono'glacialism** *n.* the monoglacial theory M20. **mono'glacialist** *n.* & *a.* (*a*) *n.* a supporter of monoglacialism; (*b*) *adj.* of or pertaining to monoglacialism or monoglacialists: E20. **mono'glyceride** *n.* (*Biochem.*) a compound consisting of glycerol esterified at only one of its hydroxyl groups M19. **mono'hydrate** *n.* (*Chem.*) a hydrate containing one mole of water per mole of the compound M19. **monohy'drated** *a.* (*Chem.*) hydrated with one molecule of water per molecule of compound M19. **mono'lobular** *a.* (*Med.*) consisting of or affecting a single lobule or lobe L19. **monome'niscous** *a.* (of the eyes of invertebrates) having only one lens L19. **mono'mictic** *a.* (of a lake) having only one overturn each year M20. **monomine'ralic** *a.* (*Petrogr.*) composed of a single mineral E20. **monomor'phemic** *a.* (*Ling.*) consisting of a single morpheme M20. **mono'nucleotide** *n.* (*Biochem.*) any of the compounds formed from one molecule each of phosphoric acid, a sugar, and a heterocyclic base, that are the units of which nucleic acids are composed; a monomeric nucleotide: E20. **mono'petalous** *a.* (*Bot.*) (*a*) gamopetalous; (*b*) having one petal: L17. **monophone** *n.* (*rare*) *Phonet.* a single sound; *esp.* a phoneme having no allophones: L19. **monoph'thalmic** *a.* one-eyed M19. **mono'phyllous** *a.* (*Bot.*) having or consisting of one leaf M18. **monopro'pellant** *n.* & *a.* (employing) a substance used as rocket fuel without an additional oxidizing agent M20. **mo'nopterous** *a.* (*Bot.*) (of a seed) having one wing M19. **monopulse** *a.* designating (the mode of operation of) radar in which the direction and usu. the range of a target is determined from a single echo pulse M20. **mo'norchid** *n.* & *a.* (a person or animal) having only one testicle E19. **mo'norchidism** *n.* absence of one testicle M19. **mo'norchis** *n.*, pl. **monorchides** /-ɪdiːz/, = MONORCHID *n.* E18. **monose'mantic** *a.* (*Ling.*) (of a word or phrase) having only one meaning M20. **mono'sepalous** *a.* (*Bot.*) (*a*) = GAMOSEPALOUS; (*b*) having one sepal: M19. **monospe'cific** *a.* (*Biol.*) pertaining to or consisting of only one species; (of an antibody) specific to one antigen: M20. **monospore** *n.* & *a.* (*a*) *n.* an undivided spore; (*b*) *adj.* = MONOSPOROUS: L19. **mono'sporous** *a.* having a single spore; derived from a single spore: M19. **mono'static** *a.* (of radar) having a single aerial as both transmitter and receiver M20. **monostome** *n.* & *a.* (*Zool.*) (an animal) having only one mouth or sucker M19. **mono'stylous** *a.* (*Bot.*) having only one style M19. **mono-'substituted** *a.* (*Chem.*) formed by or displaying mono-substitution L19. **mono-substi'tution** *n.* (*Chem.*) substitution affecting only one of the atoms or positions in a molecular structure L19. **monosympto'matic** *a.* exhibiting or concerning a single dominant symptom L19. **monosy'naptic** *a.* (*Physiol.*) involving a single synapse M20. **monosy'stemic** *a.* (*Ling.*) that establishes a single overall system of language analysis M20. **monothetic** /-'θɛtɪk/ *a.* (*a*) *Philos.* (*rare*) that postulates a single essential element; (*b*) *Taxon.* (of a classification) having groups formed on the basis of a single characteristic, or a series of single characteristics: L19. **mono'thetically** *adv.* (*Taxon.*) on the basis of a single characteristic or a series of single characteristics M20. **monotower** *n.* & *a.* (designating) a crane whose jib is mounted on a single tower M20. **monotrochal** /mə'nɒtrək(ə)l/ *a.* [Gk *trokhos* wheel, ring] *Zool.* having a single band or ring of cilia L19. **monotrophic** /-'trəʊfɪk, -'trɒfɪk/ *a.* (*Ecol.*) feeding on one kind of food, or one host organism E20. **mono-un'saturated** *a.* (*Chem.*) (of a compound, esp. a fat) saturated except for one multiple bond M20. **mo'novular** *a.* (*Biol.*) monozygotic M20. **monoxenous** /mə'nɒksɪnəs/*a.* (*Biol.*) [Gk *xenos* stranger] (of a parasite) restricted to a single host species M20.

monoamine /mɒnəʊ'eɪmiːn/ *n.* Also **monamine** /mɒn'eɪmiːn/. M20. [f. MONO- + AMINE.] *Biochem.* Any compound having a single amine group in its molecule; *spec.* one which is a neurotransmitter (e.g. serotonin, noradrenaline).

Comb.: **monoamine oxidase** an enzyme which catalyses the oxidation (and hence the inactivation) of monoamine neurotransmitters; *monoamine oxidase inhibitor*, any of a class of antidepressant drugs which inhibit the activity of monoamine oxidase (so allowing accumulation of serotonin and noradrenaline in the brain).

monoami'nergic *a.* releasing or involving a monoamine as a neurotransmitter; (of a diet) rich in monoaminergic substances: M20.

†mono-andry *n.* see MONANDRY.

monoao *n.* var. of MANOAO.

monobasic /mɒnə(ʊ)'beɪsɪk/ *a.* M19. [f. MONO- + BASIC *a.*] *Chem.* Of an acid: having one replaceable hydrogen atom. Formerly also, monovalent.

monoblastic /mɒnə(ʊ)'blastɪk/ *a.* L19. [f. MONO- + Gk *blastos* sprout, bud + -IC.] 1 *Bot.* Having a single germinal layer. L19. 2 *Physiol.* Of or pertaining to monoblasts. L20.

'monoblast *n.* (*Physiol.*) a cell which develops into a monocyte E20.

monobloc /'mɒnə(ʊ)blɒk/ *a.* E20. [Fr., f. as MONO- + *bloc* BLOCK *n.*] Made as, contained in, or involving a single casting.

monobrominated /mɒnə(ʊ)'brəʊmɪneɪtɪd/ *a.* M19. [f. MONO- + BROMINATE + -ED[1].] *Chem.* Having one bromine atom added to or substituted in the molecule.

monocarpellary /mɒnə(ʊ)'kɑːpəl(ə)ri/ *a.* M19. [f. MONO- + CARPELLARY.] *Bot.* Having or consisting of a single carpel.

monocarpic /mɒnə(ʊ)'kɑːpɪk/ *a.* M19. [f. MONO- + Gk *karpos* fruit + -IC.] *Bot.* Of a plant: bearing fruit only once during its life cycle.

'monocarp *n.* a monocarpic plant M19.

monocarpous /mɒnə(ʊ)'kɑːpəs/ *a.* M18. [In sense 1 f. MONO- + CARPEL; in sense 2 f. as prec.: see -OUS.] *Bot.* 1 = MONOCARPELLARY. M18. 2 = MONOCARPIC. M19.

monoceros /mə'nɒs(ə)rəs/ *n.* ME. [OFr. f. L f. Gk *monokerōs*, f. *monos* MONO- + *keras* horn.] †1 A unicorn. ME–M18. †2 A fish having a single hornlike process, as a sawfish. Also, a narwhal. L16–E19. 3 (**M-**.) (The name of) an inconspicuous constellation on the celestial equator lying in the Milky Way between Canis Major and Canis Minor; the Unicorn. L18.

monochlorinated /mɒnə(ʊ)'klɔːrɪneɪtɪd/ *a.* M19. [f. MONO- + CHLORINATE + -ED[1].] *Chem.* Having one chlorine atom added to or substituted in each molecule.

monochord /'mɒnə(ʊ)kɔːd/ *n.* LME. [(O)Fr. *monocorde* f. late L *monochordon* f. Gk *monokhordon* use as n. of *monokhordos* having a single string, f. as MONO- + *khordē* string: see CORD *n.*[1] & *a.* In sense 3 f. MONO- + CHORD *n.*[1]] 1 A musical instrument consisting of a soundboard with a single string and often a movable bridge, orig. used esp. to teach the intervals of plainsong, now esp. for mathematical determination of musical intervals. LME. 2 *Hist.* A medieval musical instrument with several strings and bridges for the production of a combination of sounds. LME. 3 A harmonious combination of sound; *fig.* harmony, concord. Now *rare*. LME.

monochromasy /mɒnə(ʊ)'krəʊməsi/ *n.* E20. [f. MONO- + -CHROMASY.] *Ophthalm.* = MONOCHROMATISM 2.

monochromat /mɒnə(ʊ)'krəʊmat/ *n.* Also **-ate** /-eɪt/. E20. [Back-form. f. MONOCHROMATIC.] A person with monochromatism.

monochromate /mɒnə(ʊ)'krəʊmeɪt/ *v.t.* M20. [Back-form. f. MONOCHROMATOR.] = MONOCHROMATIZE. Chiefly as *monochromated*, *monochromating* ppl adjs.

monochromatic /mɒnə(ʊ)krə'matɪk/ *a.* E19. [f. MONO- + CHROMATIC *a.* Cf. MONOCHROME.] 1 Having or producing only one colour; *spec.* (of light) of one wavelength. Also, (of other radiation) of a single wavelength or energy throughout. E19. 2 Executed in monochrome. E19. 3 *Ophthalm.* Having or designating a form of colour-blindness in which all colours appear as shades of one colour. E20.

monochromatically *adv.* (*a*) in a monochromatic way; (*b*) without regard to colour: L19. **monochromaticity** /-'tɪsɪti/ *n.* monochromatic condition; extent of concentration at one wavelength or frequency: M20.

monochromatism /mɒnə(ʊ)'krəʊmətɪz(ə)m/ *n.* M19. [f. MONOCHROMATIC + -ISM.] 1 The quality or fact of being monochromatic. M19. 2 *Ophthalm.* Complete colour-blindness. M20.

monochromatist *n.* a painter in monochrome: only in L18.

monochromatize /mɒnə(ʊ)'krəʊmətʌɪz/ *v.t.* Also **-ise**. M20. [f. prec. + -IZE.] Make (radiation) monochromatic. Chiefly as *monochromatized*, *monochromatizing* ppl adjs.

monochromati'zation *n.* M20.

monochromator /'mɒnə(ʊ)krəmeɪtə, mɒnə(ʊ)'krɒmɪtə/ *n.* E20. [f. MONOCHROMATIC + -OR.] *Physics.* A device used to select radiation of (or very close to) a single wavelength or energy.

monochrome /'mɒnəkrəʊm, mɒnə(ʊ)'krəʊm/ *n.* & *a.* M17. [In sense 1 f. med.L *monochroma*; in senses 2, 3, f. Fr. f. Gk *monokhrōmos*: both ult. f. Gk *monokhrōmatos* of one colour, f. as MONO- + *khrōma(t-)* colour.] **A** *n.* 1 A painting executed in different shades of one colour. M17. **b** A photograph in shades of one colour; *esp.* a black and white photograph. M20. 2 Representation in one colour (esp. in *in monochrome*). Also, the state of being in one colour; a tract of one colour. M19. **b** *Photogr.*, *Television*, etc. Reproduction in black and white. E20. 3 A paint or glaze of a single colour. E20.

2 *fig.*: *Listener* A dramatic exaggeration . . inevitably crept into the gentle monochrome.

B *adj.* 1 Having only one colour; executed in one colour. M19. 2 *Photogr.*, *Television*, etc. Reproducing all colours as shades of grey; black and white; of or pertaining to such reproduction. E20.

mono'chromic *a.* = MONOCHROME *a.* 1 M19. **'monochromist** *n.* a painter in monochrome M17. **mono'chromous** *a.* = MONOCHROME *a.* 1 M19. **'monochromy** *n.* the art of painting in monochrome M19.

monochronic /mɒnə(ʊ)'krɒnɪk/ *a.* M19. [f. Gk *monokhronos* (f. as MONO- + *khronos* time) + -OUS.] Relating to a single period of time; synchronic.

monocle /'mɒnək(ə)l/ *n.* M19. [Fr. f. as MONOCULUS.] An eyeglass for one eye.

monocled *a.* wearing a monocle E20.

monoclinal /mɒnə(ʊ)'klʌɪn(ə)l/ *a.* & *n.* M19. [f. MONO- + Gk *klinein* to lean, slope + -AL[1].] *Geol.* **A** *adj.* 1 Designating or consisting of strata that slope in the same direction, esp. at the same angle. Orig. *US*. M19. 2 Of a fold: consisting of a single slope connecting strata that are parallel but out of line. L19. **B** *n.* = MONOCLINE. L19.

monoclinally *adv.* E20.

monocline /'mɒnə(ʊ)klʌɪn/ *n.* L19. [f. as prec.: cf. ANTICLINE.] *Geol.* 1 A monoclinal fold. L19. 2 A set of monoclinal strata. E20.

monoclinic /mɒnə(ʊ)'klɪnɪk/ *a.* M19. [f. as MONOCLINAL: see -IC.] *Cryst.* Designating or pertaining to a crystal system referred to three unequal axes, two of which intersect at right angles, the third or principal axis intersecting one of these at right angles and the other obliquely.

monoclinous /mɒnə(ʊ)'klʌɪnəs/ *a.* E19. [f. Fr. *monocline* or mod.L *monoclinus*, f. Gk MONO- + *klinē* bed: see -OUS.] *Bot.* Of a flower or flowering plant: having stamens and pistils in the same flower, hermaphrodite.

For other words beginning with *mono-* see the main alphabetic sequence of entries

monoclonal /mɒnə(ʊ)'kləʊn(ə)l/ *a.* E20. [f. MONO- + CLONAL.] *Biol.* Forming a single clone; derived asexually from a single individual or cell.
monoclonal antibody a pure specific antibody produced in large quantities from a cultured cell line.

monocoque /'mɒnə(ʊ)kɒk/ *n.* & *a.* E20. [Fr., f. *mono-* MONO- + *coque* eggshell.] A *n.* 1 An aircraft fuselage or other structure having an outer covering in the form of a rigid load-bearing shell, usu. without longerons or stringers. E20. 2 A motor vehicle underframe and body built as a single rigid structure (or in racing cars as a number of boxlike sections) throughout which the stresses are distributed. M20. B *attrib.* or as *adj.* Designating or based on a structure of this type. E20.

monocot /'mɒnə(ʊ)kɒt/ *n.* L19. [Abbrev.] *Bot.* = MONOCOTYLEDON.

monocotyledon /,mɒnə(ʊ)kɒtɪ'liːd(ə)n/ *n.* E18. [mod.L *monocotyledones* pl., f. as MONO- + COTYLEDON.] *Bot.* A flowering plant having one cotyledon; a member of the group Monocotyledoneae (or Monocotyledones) comprising such plants. Cf. DICOTYLEDON.
monocotyledonous *a.* L18.

monocracy /mə'nɒkrəsi/ *n.* M17. [f. MONO- + -CRACY.] Government by a single person, autocracy.

monocrat /'mɒnə(ʊ)krat/ *n.* L18. [f. Gk *monokratēs* ruling alone: see MONO-, -CRAT.] A partisan of monocracy or monarchy; *spec.* in *US Hist.*, (Thomas Jefferson's name for) a member of the Federalist party. Also (*rare*), a sole ruler, an autocrat.
mono'cratic *a.* (*rare*) L19.

monocular /mə'nɒkjʊlə/ *a.* & *n.* M17. [f. late L MONOCULUS + -AR[1].] A *adj.* 1 Having only one eye. M17. 2 Of or pertaining to one eye only; adapted to or using one eye. Cf. UNIOCULAR 2. M19. b Wearing a monocle. *rare.* E20. B *n.* 1 A one-eyed person. *rare.* L19. 2 A field-glass or microscope for use with one eye, usu. as opp. *binocular(s)*. M20.
monocu'larity *n.* monocular condition M19. **monocularly** *adv.* with one eye only L19. **'monocule** *n.* (*rare*) = MONOCULUS L18. **monoculist** *n.* (*rare*) a one-eyed person E17.

monoculi *n.* pl. of MONOCULUS.

monoculous /mə'nɒkjʊləs/ *a.* M17. [f. late L MONOCULUS: see -ULOUS.] One-eyed.

monoculture /'mɒnə(ʊ)kʌltʃə/ *n.* E20. [Irreg. f. MONO- + CULTURE *n.*, perh. after Fr.] 1 The cultivation or exploitation of a single crop, or the maintenance of a single kind of animal, to the exclusion of others. E20. 2 An area in which such a practice prevails. M20.
1 J. ARDAGH The monoculture of cheap wine was dangerous for the region's economy. 2 *fig.*: *Listener* Los Angeles's least endearing characteristic: the tendency to fragment into self-contained, specialised areas—social monocultures.
mono'cultural *a.* E20. **mono'culturist** *n.* a person who practises or advocates monoculture L20.

monoculus /mə'nɒkjʊləs/ *n.* Pl. **-li** /-lʌɪ, -liː/. ME. [Late L, f. Gk MONO- + L *oculus* eye, after Gk *monophthalmos*.] 1 A one-eyed person or creature. ME. 2 A cyclopoid. M18. 3 A bandage for one eye. *rare.* M19.

monocycle /'mɒnə(ʊ)sʌɪk(ə)l/ *n.* M19. [f. MONO- + CYCLE *n.*, after *bicycle, tricycle.*] A vehicle having one wheel, turned by pedalling; a unicycle.

monocyclic /mɒnə(ʊ)'sʌɪklɪk, -'sɪk-/ *a.* L19. [f. Gk MONO- + *kuklos* circle + -IC.] 1 *Bot.* a Of a set of floral parts (sepals, stamens, etc.): forming a single whorl. L19. b Annual. *rare.* E20. 2 *Zool.* Of an echinoderm: having only a single ring of basal plates, or of tentacles. L19. 3 *Chem.* (Composed of molecules) having a single ring of atoms. E20. 4 *Geol.* Having undergone a single cycle of erosion or of mountain-building. M20.

monocyst /'mɒnə(ʊ)sɪst/ *n.* M19. [f. MONO- + CYST.] *Med.* A structure consisting of a single cyst.
mono'cystic *a.* (*a*) *Med.* having or consisting of a single cyst; (*b*) *Zool.* designating or pertaining to a group of gregarines without body segmentation: L19. **mono'cystid** *n.* & *a.* (*Zool.*) (*a*) *n.* a monocystic gregarine; (*b*) *adj.* = MONOCYSTIC (b): L19.

monocyte /'mɒnə(ʊ)sʌɪt/ *n.* E20. [f. MONO- + -CYTE] A large phagocytic white blood cell with a single oval or kidney-shaped nucleus and clear greyish cytoplasm.
monocytic /-'sɪtɪk/ *a.* M20. **monocy'tosis** *n.* (*Med.* & *Vet. Med.*) abnormal increase in the number of monocytes in the blood E20.

monodactyl /mɒnə(ʊ)'daktɪl/ *a.* Also **-yle.** E19. [Gk *monodaktulos*, f. MONO- + *daktulos* finger.] *Zool.* = next.
monodactyly *n.* monodactylous condition L19.

monodactylous /mɒnə(ʊ)'daktɪləs/ *a.* M19. [f. prec. + -OUS.] *Zool.* Having only one finger, toe, or claw.

monodelph /'mɒnə(ʊ)dɛlf/ *n.* M19. [Fr. *monodelphe* f. mod.L *monodelphia* pl., f. Gk MONO- + *delphus* womb.] *Zool.* Any of the large group of mammals of which the females have a single uterus and vagina; a eutherian.
mono'delphian, mono'delphous *adjs.* M19.

monodic /mə'nɒdɪk/ *a.* E19. [Gk *monōdikos*, f. *monōdos*: see MONODY, -IC.] Chiefly *Mus.* Of, pertaining to, or of the nature of monody.
†**monodical** *a.*: only in M17. **monodically** *adv.* L19.

monodist /'mɒnədɪst/ *n.* M18. [f. MONODY + -IST.] 1 A person who writes or sings a monody. M18. 2 A person who composes in the monodic style. E20.

monodon /'mɒnədɒn/ *n.* M18. [mod.L (see below), f. Gk *monodont-*, *monodous*, f. MONO-: see -ODON, -ODONT.] *Zool.* The narwhal, *Monodon monoceros*. Now chiefly as mod.L genus name.

monodont /'mɒnədɒnt/ *a.* *rare.* M19. [Gk *monodont-*: see prec., -ODONT.] *Zool.* Having one persistent tusk or tooth.
mono'dontal *a.* designating or having a single tusklike tooth M19.

monodrama /'mɒnə(ʊ)drɑːmə, mɒnə(ʊ) 'drɑːmə/ *n.* L18. [f. MONO- + DRAMA.] A dramatic piece for a single performer. Now *esp.* an opera for one singer.
monodra'matic *a.* pertaining to or characteristic of a monodrama E19. **mono'dramatist** *n.* a writer of a monodrama E19.

monodromy /mə'nɒdrəmi/ *n.* L19. [f. Gk MONO- + *dromos* course + -Y[3].] *Math.* 1 The property that a curve described by rotation through four right angles is closed. L19. 2 The property that if a (complex) variable z returns to its original value by any path, the function $f(z)$ also returns to its original value. E20.
monodromic /mɒnə(ʊ)'drəʊmɪk/ *a.* (of a function) having a single value for each value of the variable L19.

monody /'mɒnədi/ *n.* E17. [Late L *monodia* f. Gk *monōidia*, f. *monōdos* singing alone, f. MONO- + *ōidē* ODE: see -Y[3].] 1 In Greek drama, an ode sung by a single voice, esp. by one of the actors in a tragedy (as distinct from the chorus); a mournful song or dirge. E17. 2 A poem in which a mourner bewails a person's death. M17. 3 Monotonous sound; monotony. M19. 4 *Mus.* = MONOPHONY 1; *spec.* a 17th-cent. style of writing for a solo voice or instrument accompanied by a figured bass. Also, a composition in this style. L19.

monoecious /mə'niːʃəs/ *a.* Also ***monec-.** M18. [f. mod.L *Monoecia*, a class in Linnaeus's sexual system, f. as MONO- + Gk *oikos* house: see -IOUS.] 1 *Bot.* Having male and female flowers separate but on the same plant. Also, (of a cryptogam) having both male and female organs on the same individual. M18. 2 *Zool.* Hermaphrodite. E19.
monoeciously *adv.* M19. **monoecism** /-sɪz(ə)m/ *n.* monoecious condition L19. **monoecy** /-si/ *n.* = MONOECISM M20.

monogamic /mɒnə'gamɪk/ *a.* M19. [f. (as) MONOGAMY + -IC.] Of or pertaining to monogamy; practising monogamy, monogamous.
monogamian /mɒnə(ʊ)'geɪmɪən/ *a.* (*rare*) = MONOGAMIC E19. **monogamically** *adv.* E20.

monogamist /mə'nɒgəmɪst/ *n.* & *a.* M17. [f. Gk *monogamos* marrying only once, f. MONO- + *gamos* marriage: see -IST.] A *n.* 1 A person who by custom or law is debarred from remarrying after the death of the first spouse. Opp. *digamist.* Now *rare.* M17. 2 A person who has only one living and undivorced spouse. Opp. *bigamist, polygamist.* M18. B *adj.* = MONOGAMISTIC. L19.
monoga'mistic *a.* of or pertaining to monogamists or monogamy; favouring monogamy: L19.

monogamous /mə'nɒgəməs/ *a.* L18. [f. (as) next + -OUS.] 1 *Zool.* Of an animal, esp. a bird: pairing with only one mate for the breeding season, or for life. L18. 2 Having or permitted to have only one living and undivorced spouse at one time. Opp. *bigamous, polygamous.* E19. 3 Refraining or debarred from remarriage after the death of the first spouse. Opp. *digamous.* Now *rare.* E19. 4 Of or pertaining to monogamy. L19.
monogamously *adv.* L19. **monogamousness** *n.* M20.

monogamy /mə'nɒgəmi/ *n.* E17. [Fr. *monogamie* f. eccl.L, Gk *monogamia*, f. Gk *monogamos*: see MONOGAMIST, -GAMY.] 1 The practice or principle of marrying only once, or of not remarrying after the death of the first spouse. Opp. *digamy.* Now *rare.* E17. 2 The condition, rule, or custom of being married to only one person at a time. Opp. *bigamy, polygamy.* E18. 3 *Zool.* The habit of animals, esp. birds, of living in pairs, or having only one mate. L18.

monogastric /mɒnə(ʊ)'gastrɪk/ *a.* M18. [f. MONO- + GASTRIC.] 1 *Anat.* Of a muscle: having a single 'belly' or thick fleshy part. M18. 2 *Zool.* Having only one stomach or digestive cavity. E19.

monogenean /,mɒnə(ʊ)dʒɪ'niːən, mɒnə(ʊ) 'dʒɛnɪən/ *n.* & *a.* M20. [f. mod.L *Monogenea* (see below), f. as MONO- + Gk *genea* race, generation: see -AN.] *Zool.* A *n.* A fluke of the class Monogenea, which comprises chiefly ectoparasitic species restricted to one host, usu. a fish. M20. B *adj.* Of or pertaining to the monogeneans. M20.

monogeneous /mɒnə(ʊ)'dʒiːnɪəs/ *a.* *rare.* M19. [f. MONO- + Gk *genē-*, *genos* kind, race + -OUS.] 1 *Biol.* = MONOGENOUS 2. M19. 2 *Zool.* = MONOGENEAN *a.* L19.

monogenesis /mɒnə(ʊ)'dʒɛnɪsɪs/ *n.* M19. [f. MONO- + -GENESIS.] 1 *Biol.* Generation from a single parent; asexual reproduction. Now *rare* or *obs.* M19. 2 *Biol.* (A theory proposing) the origin of a species (esp. *Homo sapiens*), or of all organisms, from a single ancestor or ancestral pair; monogeny. L19. 3 *Ling.* (A theory proposing) the common origin of all languages. M20.

monogenetic /mɒnə(ʊ)dʒɪ'nɛtɪk/ *a.* L19. [f. MONO- + GENETIC.] 1 *Geol.* Resulting from a single process of formation; derived from one source. L19. 2 *Biol.* Of or pertaining to monogenesis. L19. 3 *Zool.* Of a parasite: having a life cycle restricted to one host. L19.

monogenic /mɒnə(ʊ)'dʒɛnɪk/ *a.* M19. [f. MONO- + -GENIC or (sense 2) GENIC *a.*] 1 *Geol.* = MONOGENOUS 3. *rare.* M19. 2 *Biol.* & *Med.* Involving or controlled by a single gene. M20.
monogenically *adv.* L20.

monogenist /mə'nɒdʒɪnɪst/ *n.* & *a.* M19. [f. as MONOGENY + -IST.] A *n.* 1 A person who believes or maintains the theory of human monogeny. M19. 2 A person who maintains the unity of origin of living beings. M19. B *adj.* Of or pertaining to monogenism or monogenists. M19.
monegenism *n.* the theory or doctrine of monogeny M19. **monoge'nistic** *a.* of or pertaining to monogenists or monogenism M19.

monogenous /mə'nɒdʒɪnəs/ *a.* Now *rare.* M19. [f. as MONOGENEOUS.] 1 *Bot.* Endogenous. M19. 2 *Biol.* Having a single common origin; monophyletic. M19. 3 *Geol.* Of a clastic rock: derived from a single pre-existing rock. L19. 4 *Biol.* Designating asexual reproduction involving one parent. L19.

monogeny /mə'nɒdʒəni/ *n.* M19. [f. MONO- + Gk *genos* kind, race + -Y[3].] The (theoretical) common origin of the human species, esp. from one pair of ancestors. Also, the theory of such origination, monogenism.

monoglot /ˈmɒnə(ʊ)glɒt/ *a.* & *n.* M19. [Gk *monoglōttos*, f. MONO- + *glōtta* tongue.] A *adj.* 1 Speaking, writing, or understanding only one language. M19. 2 Written in only one language. L19. B *n.* A person who knows only one language. L19.

monogram /ˈmɒnəgram/ *n.* & *v.* E17. [Sense 1 f. L *monogrammus*; sense 2 f. Fr. *monogramme* f. late L *monogramma* f. Gk, f. as MONO-, -GRAM.] A *n.* †1 A picture drawn in lines without shading or colour; a sketch. E17–M19. 2 A device composed of two or more letters (esp. the initials of a person's name) interwoven together. L17.

2 R. DAHL Several of the spoons bore the monogram of Christ.

B *v.t.* Infl. **-mm-**. Decorate with or reproduce as a monogram. Chiefly as *monogrammed* ppl a., bearing a monogram. M19.

R. CHANDLER Monogrammed towels on a rack. *Sunday Times* Hand-made suits and shoes, HFII monogrammed on every shirt.

monograˈmmatic *a.* of, pertaining to, or in the style of a monogram. L18.

monograph /ˈmɒnəgrɑːf/ *n.* & *v.* E19. [f. MONO- + -GRAPH, to replace MONOGRAPHY.] A *n.* 1 A separate treatise on a single specialized topic, orig. in botany or zoology. E19. 2 = MONOGRAM *n.* 2. *rare.* M19.

1 D. PAGE Mr. Woodward's Monograph of Fossil Crustacea. B. WEBB Research for the monograph on the professional organisations of medical men has been my main occupation.

B *v.t.* Produce a monograph on; treat in a monograph. L19.

monographer /məˈnɒgrəfə/ *n.* L18. [f. mod.L *monographus* (see MONOGRAPHY) + -ER[1].] The author of a monograph.

monographic /mɒnə(ʊ)ˈgrafɪk/ *a.* M18. [In branch I f. MONO- + -GRAPHIC; in branch II f. MONOGRAPHY or MONOGRAPH + -IC.] I†1 Of a picture etc.: consisting of lines without shading or colour. (Cf. MONOGRAM *n.* 1.) M18–M19. 2 Representing a sphere in a single diagram. *rare.* M19. 3 = MONOGRAMMATIC. L19. II4 Of, pertaining to, or of the nature of a monograph. Cf. earlier MONOGRAPHICAL. E19.

monographical *a.* (*rare*) = MONOGRAPHIC 4 L18. **monographically** *adv.* M19.

monographist /məˈnɒgrəfɪst/ *n.* E19. [f. MONOGRAPHY or MONOGRAPH + -IST.] = MONOGRAPHER.

monography /məˈnɒgrəfi/ *n.* Now *rare* or *obs.* L18. [mod.L *monographia*, f. *monographus* writer of a specialized treatise, f. MONO- + *-graphus*: see -GRAPH, -Y[3].] = MONOGRAPH *n.* 1.

monogynous /məˈnɒdʒɪnəs/ *a.* E19. [f. as next + -OUS.] 1 *Bot.* Of a flower or flowering plant: having only one pistil, style, or stigma. E19. 2 Of or pertaining to monogyny; living in monogyny. L19.

monogyny /məˈnɒdʒɪni/ *n.* L19. [f. Gk MONO- + *gunē* woman, wife: see -Y[3].] The practice or custom of mating with only one female, or of having only one wife at a time.

monogynist *n.* a person who practises or advocates monogyny L19.

monohull /ˈmɒnə(ʊ)hʌl/ *n.* & *a.* M20. [f. MONO- + HULL *n.*[2]] (A boat) having a single hull.

monohybrid /mɒnə(ʊ)ˈhʌɪbrɪd/ *n.* & *a.* E20. [f. MONO- + HYBRID.] *Genetics.* (Designating or pertaining to) a hybrid that is heterozygous with respect to a single gene.

monohybridism *n.* (*rare*) monohybrid condition E20.

monohydric /mɒnə(ʊ)ˈhʌɪdrɪk/ *a.* M19. [f. MONO- + HYDRIC *a.*[1]] *Chem.* Containing a single hydroxyl group or (formerly) a single hydrogen atom in the molecule.

monoicous /mɒˈnɔɪkəs/ *a.* E19. [f. as MONOECIOUS: see -OUS.] *Bot.* Esp. of a cryptogam: monoecious.

monoid /ˈmɒnɔɪd/ *n.* M19. [Gk *monoeidēs* uniform, f. MONO- + *eidos* form: see -OID.] *Math.* 1 A surface having a conical point of the highest possible ($n-1$)th order. Now *rare.* M19. 2 A semigroup possessing an identity element. M20.

monoideism /ˌmɒnəʊʌɪˈdiːɪz(ə)m/ *n.* M19. [f. MONO- + IDEA + -ISM.] (Abnormal or hypnotic) concentration of the mind on one idea.

monoideˈistic *a.* E20.

monokaryon /mɒnə(ʊ)ˈkarɪən/ *n.* M20. [f. MONO- + Gk *karuon* nut.] *Biol.* A mononuclear cell, spore, or mycelium (in higher fungi that have a dikaryotic stage).

monokaryˈotic *a.* containing a monokaryon; composed of monokaryons: M20.

monokini /mɒnə(ʊ)ˈkiːni/ *n.* M20. [f. MONO- after BIKINI (as if f. BI-).] A scanty one-piece beach garment; *esp.* one equivalent to the lower part of a bikini, worn by women and girls.

monolatry /məˈnɒlətri/ *n.* L19. [f. MONO- + -LATRY.] The worship of one god, where other gods may be supposed to exist.

monolater, **monolatrist** *ns.* E20. **monolatrous** *a.* L19.

monolayer /ˈmɒnəleɪə/ *n.* M20. [f. MONO- + LAYER *n.*] 1 *Chem.* etc. A layer or film one molecule thick. M20. 2 *Biol.* & *Med.* A cell culture consisting of a layer one cell thick. M20.

monolingual /mɒnə(ʊ)ˈlɪŋgw(ə)l/ *a.* & *n.* M20. [f. MONO- + LINGUAL.] A *adj.* 1 Knowing or using only one language. M20. 2 Written in a single language. M20. B *n.* A person who knows only one language. M20.

monolingualism *n.* the state of knowing or using only one language M20.

monolinguist /mɒnə(ʊ)ˈlɪŋgwɪst/ *n.* E20. [f. MONO- + LINGUIST.] = MONOLINGUAL *n.*

monolith /ˈmɒn(ə)lɪθ/ *n.* & *a.* M19. [Fr. *monolithe* f. Gk *monolithos*, f. MONO- + *lithos* stone.] A *n.* 1 A single block of stone, *esp.* a large one shaped into a pillar or monument; *Engin.* a large block of concrete, brickwork, etc., sunk in water, e.g. in the building of a dock. M19. 2 A person or thing like a monolith, esp. in being massive, immovable, or solidly uniform; a large impersonal political or corporate body. M20.

2 W. H. AUDEN The monolith Of State. J. WAIN You just wouldn't expect to get a flow of words out of a monolith like that.

B *adj.* Monolithic (*lit.* & *fig.*). M19.

monolithal *a.* (*rare*) monolithic M19. **monolithism** *n.* monolithic quality, esp. of a totalitarian organization E20.

monolithic /mɒnəˈlɪθɪk/ *a.* E19. [f. (as) prec. + -IC.] 1 Formed of a single (large) block of stone; of the nature of a monolith. E19. 2 Of, pertaining to, or characterized by monoliths. M19. 3 *Archit.* Made of a solid unbroken mass (of concrete). L19. 4 *transf.* & *fig.* Like a monolith; massive; immovable, unwavering, unemotional; solidly uniform; (of an organization) large and autocratic or monopolistic. E20. 5 *Electronics.* Of a solid-state circuit: composed of active and passive components formed in a single chip. M20.

4 A. L. ROWSE The Fourth Symphony of Sibelius, the most monolithic of them all. *Nature* Would not the merging of the research councils create too monolithic a central sponsor? CLIVE JAMES For all its monolithic sense of purpose, the Soviet Union seems hopelessly barren.

monolithically *adv.* E20.

monolog *n.* see MONOLOGUE.

monological /mɒnəˈlɒdʒɪk(ə)l/ *a.* E19. [f. Gk *monologos* MONOLOGUE + -ICAL.] Of, pertaining to, or of the nature of a monologue. Also, given to monologues.

monologic *a.* pertaining to or of the nature of a monologue M19.

monologise *v.* var. of MONOLOGIZE.

monologist /məˈnɒlədʒɪst, ˈmɒn(ə)lɒgɪst/ *n.* Also **-guist** /-gɪst/. E18. [f. MONOLOGUE + IST.] 1 A person who talks in monologue or soliloquizes. Also, a person who monopolizes conversation. E18. 2 A person who performs monologues. M19.

monologize /məˈnɒlədʒʌɪz, ˈmɒn(ə)lɒgʌɪz/ *v.i.* Also **-gu-** /-g-/, **-ise**. E19. [f. MONOLOGUE + -IZE.] Talk in monologue; deliver a monologue.

monologue /ˈmɒn(ə)lɒg/ *n.* & *v.* E17. [Fr., f. as MONO- + -LOGUE: cf. late Gk *monologos* speaking alone.] A *n.* Also ***-log**. †1 A person who monopolizes conversation. Only in E17. 2 A scene in a drama in which one person speaks alone. Also, a dramatic composition for a single performer; a dramatic entertainment performed throughout by one person. M17. b The form or style of dramatic scenes or compositions for one person. M17. c A literary composition in the form of a soliloquy, *spec.* in Old English verse. M19. 3 A long speech or harangue delivered by one person in company or in conversation; talk or discourse of the nature of a soliloquy. M19.

2 E. HOLMES The opera began with a monologue. B. REID I learned monologues from her, and she saw that I had acting potential. b DRYDEN He also gives you an account of himself . . in monologue. 3 P. H. GIBBS He . . held everybody spellbound by a brilliant monologue on post-war problems. R. P. JHABVALA They weren't conversations . . they were monologues.

B *v.i.* = MONOLOGIZE. E19.

monologian /mɒnəˈləʊdʒɪən/ *n.* (*rare*) = MONOLOGIST E17. **monology** /məˈnɒlədʒi/ *n.* †(*a*) a monologue; (*b*) the habit of monologizing: E17.

monologuise *v.* var. of MONOLOGIZE.

monologuist *n.* var. of MONOLOGIST.

monologuize *v.* var. of MONOLOGIZE.

monomachy /məˈnɒməki/ *n.* Also in L form **monomachia** /mɒnə(ʊ)ˈmakɪə/. L16. [Late L *monomachia* f. Gk *monomakhia*, f. as MONO- + -MACHY.] A combat or contest between two; a single combat, a duel.

monomania /mɒnə(ʊ)ˈmeɪnɪə/ *n.* E19. [f. MONO- + -MANIA.] 1 A mental illness in which a person is dominated by one irrational set of ideas. E19. 2 An exaggerated enthusiasm for one subject; an obsession, a craze (*for*). M19.

monomaniac *n.* & *a.* (*a*) *n.* a person who has (a) monomania; (*b*) *adj.* = MONOMANIACAL: M19. **monomaniacal** /-məˈnʌɪək(ə)l/ *a.* pertaining to, characterized by, or exhibiting monomania M19. **monomaniacally** /-məˈnʌɪək(ə)li/ *adv.* M19.

†monome *n.* & *a.* E18–M19. [Fr., after *binome*: see BINOMIAL. Cf. MONOMIAL.] *Math.* = MONOMIAL *n.* 1.

monomer /ˈmɒnəmə/ *n.* E20. [f. MONO- + -MER.] *Chem.* A compound from which a dimer, trimer, polymer, etc., is or might be formed by the linking together of its molecules (with or without those of another compound).

monoˈmeric *a.* of the nature of a monomer, consisting of a monomer or monomers E20.

monomerous /məˈnɒm(ə)rəs/ *a.* E19. [f. as prec. + -OUS.] 1 *Entomol.* Consisting of only one segment. E19. 2 *Bot.* Of a flower: having one member in each whorl. L19.

monometallic /mɒnə(ʊ)mɪˈtalɪk/ *a.* L19. [f. MONO- + METALLIC, after *bimetallic*.] 1 Pertaining to, involving, or using a standard of currency based on one metal. L19. 2 Consisting of one metal only. E20.

monometallism /-ˈmɛt(ə)lɪz(ə)m/ *n.* the monometallic system or standard of currency L19. **monometallist** /-ˈmɛt(ə)lɪst/ *n.* & *a.* (*a*) *n.* an advocate of monometallism; (*b*) *adj.* favouring monometallism: L19.

monometer /məˈnɒmɪtə/ *n.* E19. [Late L (adj.) f. Gk *monometros* adj., f. MONO- + *metron* METRE *n.*[1]] *Pros.* A line consisting of one metrical foot.

monometric /mɒnə(ʊ)ˈmɛtrɪk/ *a.* M19. [f. MONO- + -METRIC.] 1 *Cryst.* = CUBIC *a.* 2b. Now *rare* or *obs.* M19. 2 Written in one metre. *rare.* L19.

monomial /məˈnəʊmɪəl/ *n.* & *a.* E18. [Irreg. f. MONO- after *binomial*.] A *n.* 1 *Math.* An expression consisting of one term only. E18. 2 = MONONYM. *rare.* L19. B *adj.* 1 *Math.* Consisting of one term only. E19. 2 Designating or pertaining to a term, esp. a taxonomic name, consisting of one word only; mononymic. L19.

monomino /məˈnɒmɪnəʊ/ *n.* Pl. **-os**. M20. [f. MONO- + DOMINO, by deliberate false analogy as though the latter were from DI-[2]. Cf. PENTOMINO.] *Math.* A square considered as a structural unit or as occupying a position in a grid.

monomolecular /ˌmɒnə(ʊ)məˈlɛkjʊlə/ *a.* L19. [f. MONO- + MOLECULAR.] *Chem.* 1 Involving a single molecule; (of a reaction) having a molecularity of one; unimolecular. L19. 2 Of a film or layer: one molecule thick. E20.

monomorphic /mɒnə(ʊ)ˈmɔːfɪk/ *a.* L19. [f. MONO- + Gk *morphē* form + -IC.] Having or existing in only one form; monomorphous; *esp.* in *Biol.*, (of a population or species) identical or homogeneous as regards morphology or genotype.

monomorphism /mɒnə(ʊ)ˈmɔːfɪz(ə)m/ *n.* M19. [f. as prec. + -ISM.] 1 *Biol.* Monomorphic condition. M19. 2 *Math.* A one-to-one homomorphism. M20.

monomorphous /mɒnə(ʊ)ˈmɔːfəs/ *a.* M19. [f. as prec. + -OUS.] Chiefly *Biol.* Having or characterized by only one form; (of an insect) hemimetabolous.

monomyarian /ˌmɒnə(ʊ)mʌɪˈɛːrɪən/ *a.* & *n.* M19. [f. mod.L *Monomyaria* former taxonomic name, f. as MONO- + Gk *mus* muscle: see -ARY[1], -AN.] A *adj.* Of a bivalve mollusc: having only one (posterior) adductor muscle. M19. B *n.* A monomyarian mollusc (e.g. an oyster). M19.
Also **monoˈmyary** *a.* & *n.* M19.

Monongahela /mənɒŋgəˈhiːlə/ *n. US.* Now *rare.* E19. [A river in Pennsylvania, USA.] (American) rye whiskey.

mononuclear /mɒnə(ʊ)ˈnjuːklɪə/ *a.* & *n.* L19. [f. MONO- + NUCLEAR.] Chiefly *Biol.* A *adj.* Having one nucleus. L19. B *n.* A mononuclear cell; *spec.* a monocyte. E20.

mononucleated /mɒnə(ʊ)ˈnjuːklɪeɪtɪd/ *a.* L19. [f. MONO- + NUCLEUS: see -ATE[2], -ED[1].] = MONONUCLEAR *a.*
Also **mononucleate** *a.* E20.

mononucleosis /ˌmɒnə(ʊ)njuːklɪˈəʊsɪs/ *n.* Pl. **-oses** /-ˈəʊsiːz/. E20. [f. MONONUCLEAR + -OSIS.] *Med.* An abnormally high proportion of mononuclear leucocytes (monocytes or lymphocytes), or of monocytes alone, in the blood; *esp.* (more fully *infectious mononucleosis*) glandular fever.

mononym /ˈmɒnənɪm/ *n.* L19. [f. MONO- + -NYM.] A term consisting of one word only.
monoˈnymic *a.* L19.

monoped /ˈmɒnəpɛd/ *n.* & *a.* E19. [f. MONO- + L *ped-*, *pes* foot.] = MONOPOD.

monophagous /məˈnɒfəgəs/ *a.* M19. [f. MONO- + -PHAGOUS. Cf. Gk *monophagos* that eats alone.] That eats only one kind of food.

monophagy /məˈnɒfədʒi/ *n.* E17. [Gk *monophagia* eating alone, f. as MONO- + -PHAGY.] 1 The eating of only one kind of food. E17. 2 Eating alone. M17.

monophasic /mɒnə(ʊ)ˈfeɪzɪk/ *a.* L19. [f. MONO- + PHASE *n.* + -IC.] Exhibiting a single phase; *esp.* (*Physiol.*) designating or pertaining to (a record of) a nerve impulse that is of the same sign throughout.
monophasically *adv.* by a technique yielding a monophasic record E20. **monophasicity** /-ˈzɪsɪti/ *n.* M20.

monophonemic /mɒnə(ʊ)fəˈniːmɪk/ *a.* M20. [f. MONO- + PHONEMIC.] *Ling.* Of or pertaining to a single phoneme; consisting of a single phoneme.
monophoneˈmatic *a.* = MONOPHONEMIC *a.* M20. **monophoneˈmatically** *adv.* M20.

monophonic /mɒnə(ʊ)ˈfɒnɪk/ *a.* E19. [f. MONO- + Gk *phōnē* sound + -IC.] †1 Of an alphabet: phonetic. Only in E19. 2 *Mus.* = HOMOPHONIC 1. Also, having a simple melodic line predominating over other parts. L19. 3 Of sound recording and reproduction: involving only one channel, so that the sound output seems to come from a single source; = MONAURAL *a.* 2. Opp. STEREOPHONIC. M20.
monophonically *adv.* M20.

monophonous /məˈnɒf(ə)nəs/ *a. rare.* M19. [f. as prec. + -OUS.] 1 = HOMOPHONOUS. M19. 2 *Mus.* Of a musical instrument: producing only one note at a time. Also, monophonic. L19.

monophony /məˈnɒfəni/ *n.* L19. [f. as prec.: see -PHONY.] 1 Music in which there is a single melodic line. L19. 2 Monophonic recording or reproduction. M20.

monophthong /ˈmɒnəfθɒŋ/ *n.* E17. [Gk *monophthoggos* adj., f. MONO- + *phthoggos* voice, sound.] *Phonet.* A single vowel sound, a vowel sound without any glide.
monophˈthongal *a.* consisting of a monophthong L18. **monophthongiˈzation** *n.* the process or state of being monophthongized L18. **monophthongize** *v.t.* & *i.* convert, undergo conversion, into a monophthong L19.

monophyletic /ˌmɒnə(ʊ)fʌɪˈlɛtɪk/ *a.* L19. [f. MONO- + Gk *phuletikos*, f. *phulē* tribe: see -IC.] *Biol.* (Of a group or taxon) descended from a common evolutionary ancestor or ancestral group; (of a classification) employing such taxa. Also *spec.*, holophyletic.
ˈmonophyly *n.* the state of being monophyletic M20.

monophyodont /mɒnə(ʊ)ˈfʌɪədɒnt/ *n.* & *a.* M19. [f. Gk *monophuēs* single (f. as MONO- + *phuē* growth) + -ODONT.] *Zool.* (Designating or pertaining to) an animal which grows only one set of teeth. Cf. DIPHYODONT.

Monophysite /məˈnɒfɪsʌɪt/ *n.* & *a.* L17. [eccl.L *Monophysita* f. eccl.Gk *monophusitēs*, f. as MONO- + *phusis* nature: see -ITE [1].] *Chr. Theol.* A *n.* A person who holds that there is only one inseparable nature in the person of Jesus, contrary to a declaration of the council of Chalcedon (AD 451). L17. B *adj.* Of or pertaining to the doctrine of the Monophysites or a Church professing this doctrine. L18.
¶The term has long been used loosely of those Eastern Churches which did not accept the Chalcedonian canons, i.e. chiefly the Coptic, Ethiopian, Armenian, and Jacobite Churches.
monophysitic /ˌmɒnə(ʊ)fɪˈsɪtɪk/ *a.* (*rare*) = MONOPHYSITE *a.* E19. **monophysitism** *n.* the doctrine of the Monophysites M19.

monopitch /ˈmɒnə(ʊ)pɪtʃ/ *n.* & *a.* M20. [f. MONO- + PITCH *n.*[2]] A *n.* Uniformity of vocal pitch. M20. B *adj.* Of a roof: having a single uniformly sloping surface. Of a building: having such a roof. M20.

monoplane /ˈmɒnəpleɪn/ *n.* E20. [f. MONO- + PLANE *n.*[4]] An aeroplane having only one wing across or (now usu.) on either side of the fuselage. Formerly also, the wing of such an aeroplane.

monoplegia /mɒnə(ʊ)ˈpliːdʒə/ *n.* L19. [f. MONO- + -PLEGIA.] *Med.* Paralysis restricted to one limb or region of the body.
monoplegic *a.* pertaining to or affected with monoplegia L19.

monoploid /ˈmɒnə(ʊ)plɔɪd/ *a.* & *n.* E20. [f. MONO- + -PLOID.] *Biol.* = HAPLOID *a.* & *n.*
monoploidy *n.* = HAPLOIDY M20.

monopod /ˈmɒnə(ʊ)pɒd/ *n.* & *a.* Also **-pode** /-pəʊd/. E19. [L *monopodius* adj., *-ium* n. f. late Gk *monopodios* adj., *-ion* n., f. as MONO- + *pod-*, *pous* foot.] A *n.* A creature or structure having only one foot; *spec.* (*a*) (usu. **-pode**) any of a mythical race of beings having only one foot, with which they shaded themselves from the sun; (*b*) a one-legged support for a camera etc. E19. B *adj.* Having only one foot. L19.

monopodium /mɒnə(ʊ)ˈpəʊdɪəm/ *n.* Pl. **-ia** /-ɪə/. E19. [f. as MONO- + PODIUM.] 1 A table or stand with a single support. Also, a support for an early 19th-cent. table, sideboard, etc., comprising an animal's head with a single foot. E19. 2 *Bot.* A single continuous growth axis which extends at its apex and produces successive lateral shoots. Cf. SYMPODIUM. L19.
monopodial *a.* (*Bot.*) pertaining to or of the nature of a monopodium L19. **monopodially** *adv.* (*Bot.*) in the manner of a monopodium L19.

monopodous /məˈnɒpədəs/ *a. rare.* L19. [f. Gk MONO- + *pod-*, *pous* foot + -OUS.] One-footed.

monopody /məˈnɒpədi/ *n.* M19. [mod.L *monopodia* f. Gk, f. as prec.: see -Y[3].] *Pros.* A measure consisting of a single metrical foot.

monopolar /mɒnə(ʊ)ˈpəʊlə/ *a.* E20. [f. MONO- + POLAR *a.*] Pertaining to or having a single pole; *esp.* designating or pertaining to medical techniques and apparatus involving the use of two electrodes, one of which acts as a neutral or reference electrode.

monopole /ˈmɒnəpəʊl/ *n.*[1] M16. [(O)Fr., or late L *monopolium* MONOPOLY.] †1 A monopoly. M16–L17. †2 A conspiracy. M–L16. 3 (**M-**.) (The designation of) champagne of a brand exclusive to a particular shipper. L19.
3 T. BURKE Two bottles of dry Monopole to be put on the ice.

monopole /ˈmɒnəpəʊl/ *n.*[2] M20. [f. MONO- + POLE *n.*[2]] 1 A single electric charge or (esp.) magnetic pole (also *magnetic monopole*), having a spherically symmetric field. M20. 2 A radio aerial consisting of a single conducting rod with an electrical connection at one end. M20.

monopolise *v.* var. of MONOPOLIZE.

monopolist /məˈnɒp(ə)lɪst/ *n.* & *a.* E17. [f. MONOPOLY or MONOPOLE *n.*[1] + -IST.] A *n.* A person who monopolizes something or who possesses a monopoly; a person who favours monopoly. E17. B *adj.* Enjoying or favouring a monopoly. M19.
monopolism *n.* the system of monopolies; support for a monopoly: L19.

monopolistic /mənɒpəˈlɪstɪk/ *a.* L19. [f. prec. + -IC.] Of, pertaining to, or characterized by a monopoly or a system of monopolies; of the nature of a monopoly.
monopolistically *adv.* E20.

monopolize /məˈnɒpəlʌɪz/ *v.t.* Also **-ise**. E17. [f. next or MONOPOLE *n.*[1] + -IZE.] Have or obtain a monopoly of; obtain exclusive possession or control of (a trade, commodity, etc.); get or keep entirely to oneself; dominate or prevent others from sharing in (a conversation, a person's attention, etc.).
P. G. WODEHOUSE One of those forceful characters which monopolize any stage on which they appear. R. LARDNER We'd better join the ladies or my wife will say I'm monopolizing you.
monopolizable *a.* L19. **monopoliˈzation** *n.* the action or process of monopolizing something or someone; the condition of being monopolized: E18. **monopolizer** *n.* E17.

monopoly /məˈnɒp(ə)li/ *n.* M16. [L *monopolium* f. Gk *monopōlion*, *-pōlia*, f. MONO- + *pōlein* sell.] 1 Exclusive possession or control of the trade in a commodity, service, etc.; the condition of having no competitor in one's trade or business; *Law* a situation in which one supplier or producer controls more than a specified fraction of the market. M16. b *spec.* An exclusive privilege (conferred by a monarch, State, etc.) of selling some commodity or trading with a particular place or country. L16. 2 *gen.* Exclusive possession, control, or exercise of something. Foll. by *of*, *on*. E17. 3 A thing which is the subject of a monopoly. M19. 4 A company etc. which has a monopoly. L19. 5 (**M-**.) (Proprietary name for) a board game in which the players engage in property dealings, the board representing streets etc. in a large city. M20.
1 BURKE You have, in this kingdom, an advantage in Lead, that amounts to a monopoly. b J. SINCLAIR The Public Revenue [of Russia] . . is likely to increase, particularly the . . monopoly of brandy. 2 A. E. STEVENSON We claim no monopoly on the ideals we assert. L. GRIFFITHS For two years I had a monopoly of conkers in the playground. 3 M. E. G. DUFF The culture . . of tobacco was made a Crown monopoly. 4 E. BELLAMY The absorption of business by ever larger monopolies continued. 5 J. GARDAM The sky darkened during supper and during Monopoly the rain began.
Comb.: **monopoly capitalism** a capitalist system typified by trade monopolies in the hands of a few people; **Monopoly money** imitation money used in the game of Monopoly; money having no real existence or value; inflated currency; **monopoly value** the value of something that is the subject of a monopoly; extra value arising from the holding of a monopoly.

monopolylogue /mɒnəˈpɒlɪlɒg/ *n. obs.* exc. *Hist.* E19. [f. MONO- + POLY- + -LOGUE.] An entertainment in which a single performer sustains many characters.
¶Chiefly w. ref. to the English actor Charles Mathews (1776–1835).

Monoprix /ˈmɒnə(ʊ)priː/ *n.* M20. [Fr., lit. 'one price'.] Any of a chain of stores in France in which cheap goods are sold (orig. all at the same price). Also *Monoprix store* etc.

monops /ˈmɒnɒps/ *a.* & *n.* *rare.* M19. [f. Gk MONO- + *ōps* eye.] (A being) having one eye.

monopsony /məˈnɒpsəni/ *n.* M20. [f. MONO- + Gk *opsōnein* buy provisions + -Y³.] *Econ.* A situation in which there is a sole or predominant consumer for a particular product.

monopsonist *n.* the consumer in a monopsony M20. **monopsoˈnistic** *a.* pertaining to or of the nature of a monopsony M20.

monopsychism /mɒnə(ʊ)ˈsʌɪkɪz(ə)m/ *n.* M19. [f. MONO- + PSYCHE *n.*¹ + -ISM.] (The theory proposing) the unity of all human souls.

monopteros /məˈnɒptərɒs/ *n.* Also (earlier) †**-on**, †**monopter**. L17. [Use as n. of L adj. f. Gk, = having one wing, f. MONO- + *pteron* wing. Earlier forms f. Gk & f. Fr. *monoptère*.] *Class. Antiq.* A temple consisting of a single circle of columns supporting a roof.

monopteral *a.* of the construction of a monopteros E19.

monoptic /məˈnɒptɪk/ *a.* M17. [f. MONO- + OPTIC *a.*] = MONOCULAR *a.*

monoptically *adv.* M20.

monoptote /ˈmɒnəptəʊt/ *n.* E17. [Late L *monoptotus* f. late Gk *monoptōtos* having one case, f. Gk MONO- + *ptōtos* falling, cogn. w. *ptōsis* case.] *Gram.* A noun occurring in a single oblique case (as L *astu*).

monorail /ˈmɒnə(ʊ)reɪl/ *a.* & *n.* L19. [f. MONO- + RAIL *n.*²] **A** *adj.* Having or using a single rail; designating or pertaining to a railway in which the track is a single rail. L19.

monorail camera a camera mounted on a rail which allows positional adjustment and may support additional components.

B *n.* A railway in which the track is a single rail, on or suspended from which vehicles run; a vehicle that runs in this way. E20.

monorheme /ˈmɒnə(ʊ)riːm/ *n.* M20. [f. MONO- + RHEME.] *Ling.* A single element or word with a phrasal meaning.

monorhine /ˈmɒnə(ʊ)rʌɪn/ *a.* L19. [f. MONO- + Gk *rhin-*, *rhis* nose.] *Zool.* Having only one nasal passage; *spec.* designating agnathan vertebrates.

monorhinal *a.* = MONORHINE L19. **monorhinous** *a.* = MONORHINE E20.

monorhyme /ˈmɒnə(ʊ)rʌɪm/ *n.* & *a.* Also (*arch.*) **-rime**. M18. [Fr. *monorime*, f. as MONO- + *rime* RHYME *n.*] *Pros.* **A** *n.* A poem or passage in which all the lines have the same rhyme; in *pl.*, lines having one rhyme. M18. **B** *adj.* Having a single rhyme. M19.

monorhymed *a.* = MONORHYME *a.* L19.

monosabio /monoˈsabjo, mɒnəʊˈsabɪəʊ/ *n.* Pl. **-os** /-ɔs, -əʊz/. L19. [Sp., f. *mono* monkey + *sabio* wise, trained.] *Bullfighting.* A picador's assistant in the ring.

monosaccharide /mɒnə(ʊ)ˈsakərʌɪd/ *n.* L19. [f. MONO- + SACCHARIDE.] *Biochem.* A sugar which cannot be hydrolysed to give simpler sugars.

Also **monosaccharose** *n.* E20.

monose /ˈmɒnəʊz, -s/ *n.* L19. [f. MONO- + -OSE².] *Biochem.* = prec.

monosemic /mɒnə(ʊ)ˈsiːmɪk/ *a.* L19. [f. Gk *monosēmos*, f. MONO- + *sēma* sign, mark: see -IC.] **1** *Pros.* Consisting of or equal to a single mora. *rare.* L19. **2** *Ling.* Having only one meaning. M20.

monosemy /ˈmɒnə(ʊ)siːmi, məˈnɒsɪmi/ *n.* M20. [f. MONO- + Gk *sēma* sign, mark + -Y³, after POLYSEMY.] *Ling.* The property of having only one meaning.

monosexual /mɒnə(ʊ)ˈsɛksjʊəl, -ʃʊəl/ *a.* M20. [f. MONO- + SEXUAL.] Of or pertaining to one sex only. Also, sexually attracted to individuals of one sex, not bisexual.

monosexuˈality *n.* E20.

monosign /ˈmɒnə(ʊ)sʌɪn/ *n.* M20. [f. MONO- + SIGN *n.*] A sign or word used with only one meaning at a time. Opp. PLURISIGN.

monoˈsignative *a.* (of a sign or word) used with only one meaning at a time M20.

monosiphonous /mɒnə(ʊ)ˈsʌɪf(ə)nəs/ *a.* M19. [f. Gk MONO- + *siphōn* tube, pipe + -OUS.] *Bot.* Of an alga: having fronds composed of a single strand of large elongated cells.

Also **monosiphonic** /-sʌɪˈfɒnɪk/ *a.* E20.

monoski /ˈmɒnəskiː/ *n.* & *v.* M20. [f. MONO- + SKI *n.*, *v.*] **A** *n.* A single ski on which a person stands with both feet. M20. **B** *v.i.* Use a monoski. M20.

monoskier *n.* M20.

monosodium /mɒnə(ʊ)ˈsəʊdɪəm/ *a.* M19. [f. MONO- + SODIUM *n.*] *Chem.* Designating compounds, chiefly salts, containing one sodium atom or ion for each combining radical or ion.

monosodium glutamate the white crystalline sodium salt of glutamic acid, used in foods as a flavour enhancer or (esp. in oriental cuisine) a condiment.

monosome /ˈmɒnəsəʊm/ *n.* E20. [f. MONO- + -SOME³.] *Cytol.* **1** An unpaired chromosome in a diploid chromosome complement; a diploid individual having such a chromosome. E20. **2** A single ribosome attached to a molecule of messenger RNA. M20.

monosomic /mɒnə(ʊ)ˈsəʊmɪk/ *a.* & *n.* E20. [f. prec. + -IC.] *Cytol.* **A** *adj.* Having or designating a diploid chromosome complement in which one (occas. more than one) chromosome lacks its homologous partner. E20. **B** *n.* A monosomic individual or variety. E20.

ˈmonosomy *n.* monosomic character or condition. M20.

monospermic /mɒnə(ʊ)ˈspəːmɪk/ *a.* L19. [f. as next + -IC.] **1** *Bot.* = next. L19. **2** *Biol.* Pertaining to or exhibiting monospermy. E20.

monospermous /mɒnə(ʊ)ˈspəːməs/ *a.* E18. [f. MONO- + Gk *sperma* seed, SPERM + -OUS.] *Bot.* Producing only one seed.

ˈmonosperm *n.* (*rare*) a monospermous plant L19. **monospermal** *a.* = MONOSPERMOUS M19.

monospermy /ˈmɒnə(ʊ)spəːmi/ *n.* E20. [f. as prec.: see -Y³.] *Biol.* Penetration of an ovum by a single sperm.

monostable /ˈmɒnə(ʊ)steɪb(ə)l/ *a.* M20. [f. MONO- + STABLE *a.*] Chiefly *Electronics.* Having only one stable position or state.

monostich /ˈmɒnə(ʊ)stɪk/ *n.* Also (earlier) in Gk form †**-stichon**. L16. [Late L *monostichum*, *-ium* f. Gk *monostikhon* use as n. of *monostikhos* adj., f. MONO- + *stikhos* row, line of verse.] *Pros.* A poem or epigram consisting of only one metrical line.

monostich /ˈmɒnə(ʊ)stɪk/ *a.* M17. [Gk *monostikhos*: see prec.] *Pros.* Consisting of a single line of verse.

†**monostichon** *n.* see MONOSTICH *n.*

monostichous /məˈnɒstɪkəs, mɒnə(ʊ)ˈstʌɪkəs/ *a.* M19. [f. Gk *monostikhos* (see MONOSTICH *n.*) + -OUS.] (Having parts) arranged in or consisting of a single layer or row; *Bot.* arranged in a single vertical row.

monostrophic /mɒnə(ʊ)ˈstrɒfɪk/ *a.* L17. [Gk *monostrophikos*, f. *monostrophos* adj., f. as MONO- + STROPHE: see -IC.] *Pros.* Consisting of repetitions of the same strophic arrangement.

†**monosyllaba** *n.* pl. of MONOSYLLABON.

monosyllabic /mɒnə(ʊ)sɪˈlabɪk/ *a.* M18. [f. MONO- + SYLLABIC. Cf. med.L *monosyllabicus*, Fr. *monosyllabique*.] **1** Of a word: consisting of one syllable. M18. **2** Consisting of monosyllables or of a monosyllable; *spec.* (of a language, e.g. Chinese) having a vocabulary wholly composed of monosyllables. M18. **3** Of a person: uttering only monosyllables. L19.

†**monosyllabical** *a.* (*rare*) = MONOSYLLABIC L17–L18. **monosyllabically** *adv.* in a monosyllable or monosyllables E19. **monosyllabicity** /-sɪləˈbɪsɪti/ *n.* M20.

monosyllabism /mɒnə(ʊ)ˈsɪləbɪz(ə)m/ *n.* E19. [f. next + -ISM.] The quality or condition of being monosyllabic; addiction to the use of monosyllables.

monosyllable /ˈmɒnə(ʊ)sɪləb(ə)l/ *n.* & *a.* M16. [f. MONO- + SYLLABLE *n.*, prob. after L MONOSYLLABON.] **A** *n.* A word of one syllable. M16.

A. TROLLOPE 'No.' She pronounced the monosyllable alone. **in monosyllables** in monosyllabic words; in simple direct words; curtly, bluntly; saying little but 'yes' or 'no'.

B *adj.* = MONOSYLLABIC *a.* 1, 2. Now *rare.* L16.

†**monosyllabon** *n.* Pl. **-ba**. L16–E18. [L f. Gk *monosullabon* neut. of *monosullabos* adj., f. *monos* MONO- + *sullabē* SYLLABLE *n.*] A monosyllable.

monosymmetrical /ˌmɒnə(ʊ)sɪˈmɛtrɪk(ə)l/ *a.* L19. [f. MONO- + SYMMETRICAL.] **1** Chiefly *Bot.* Divisible into exactly similar halves in one plane only; zygomorphic. L19. **2** *Min.* = MONOCLINIC. L19.

monosymmetric *a.* = MONOSYMMETRICAL L19. **monosymmetrically** *adv.* L19. **monoˈsymmetry** *n.* monosymmetrical condition L19.

monotechnic /mɒnə(ʊ)ˈtɛknɪk/ *a.* E20. [f. MONO- after POLYTECHNIC.] Dealing with or (of a college etc.) providing instruction in a single technical subject.

monotessaron /mɒnə(ʊ)ˈtɛsərən/ *n.* M19. [Erron. f. Gk MONO- after DIATESSARON.] = DIATESSARON 3.

monothalamic /ˌmɒnə(ʊ)θəˈlamɪk/ *a.* M19. [f. MONO- + Gk *thalamos* chamber + -IC.] **1** *Zool.* = next. M19. **2** *Bot.* Of a fruit: formed from a single flower. L19.

monothalamous /mɒnə(ʊ)ˈθaləməs/ *a.* E19. [f. as prec. + -OUS.] *Zool.* Of a shell, hollow organ, etc.: having only one chamber.

monotheism /ˈmɒnə(ʊ),θiːɪz(ə)m/ *n.* M17. [f. Gk MONO- + *theos* god + -ISM.] The doctrine or belief that there is only one God.

monotheist /ˈmɒnə(ʊ),θiːɪst/ *n.* & *a.* L17. [f. as prec. + -IST.] **A** *n.* A person who believes in only one God; an adherent of monotheism. L17. **B** *adj.* = MONOTHEISTIC. E19.

monotheˈistic *a.* of, pertaining to, believing in, or characterized by monotheism M19. **monotheˈistically** *adv.* E20.

Monothelite /məˈnɒθɪlʌɪt/ *n.* & *a.* Also **-lete** /-liːt/. LME. [med.L *monothelita* f. late Gk *monothelētēs*, f. Gk MONO- + *thelētēs* agent-n. f. *thelein* to will.] *Theol.* **A** *n.* A person who holds the (heretical) doctrine (first propounded in the 7th cent.) that Jesus had only one (divine) will. Cf. DYOTHELITE. LME. **B** *adj.* Of or pertaining to the Monothelites or Monothelitism. E17.

Monothelism *n.* (*rare*) = MONOTHELITISM L17. **Monotheˈlitic** *a.* = MONOTHELITE *a.* E18. **Monothelitism** *n.* the doctrine of the Monothelites M18.

monothematic /ˌmɒnə(ʊ)θɪˈmatɪk/ *a.* L19. [f. MONO- + THEMATIC.] Chiefly *Mus.* Having a single dominant theme or element.

monotint /ˈmɒnə(ʊ)tɪnt/ *n.* L19. [f. MONO- + TINT *n.*] Representation in one colour or tint (chiefly in *in monotint*). Also, a picture in one colour.

monotocardian /mɒnəʊtəˈkɑːdɪən/ *a.* & *n.* E20. [f. mod.L *Monotocardia* former taxonomic name, f. Gk MONO- + *ōtos*, *ous* auricle + *kardia* heart: see -AN.] **A** *adj.* Designating or pertaining to a group of prosobranch molluscs having only one auricle and one gill. E20. **B** *n.* A monotocardian mollusc. E20.

monotocous /məˈnɒtəkəs/ *a.* L19. [f. Gk *monotokos*, f. MONO- + *tok-*, *tiktein* bring forth: see -OUS.] **1** *Zool.* Normally bearing only one at a birth; uniparous. L19. **2** *Bot.* = MONOCARPIC. L19.

monotone /ˈmɒnətəʊn/ *n.* & *a.* M17. [mod.L *monotonus* adj. f. late Gk *monotonos*, f. MONO- + *tonos* TONE *n.*] **A** *n.* **1** A continuance or uninterrupted repetition of the same tone; an utterance or other sound continued or repeated without change of pitch. M17. **2** *fig.* A monotonous continuance or recurrence *of* something. M19. **3** Monotony or sameness of style in writing etc.; something composed in a monotonous style. L19. **4** = MONOTINT. L19.

1 C. AIKEN On the bare boards . . The rain drummed monotones. M. ANGELOU His replies to questions . . were generally given in a monotone. **2** J. RUSKIN Its [science's] history is a monotone of endurance and destruction.

B *adj.* **1** Unchanging or repetitious in pitch or tone. M18. **2** *Math.* = MONOTONIC *a.* 2. E20.

monotoned *a.* (*rare*) having only one tone L19. **monotonely** *adv.* (*Math.*) = MONOTONICALLY (b) M20.

monotone /ˈmɒnətəʊn/ *v.t.* M19. [f. the n.] Recite, speak, or sing in a monotone; intone on a single note.

monotonic /mɒnə(ʊ)ˈtɒnɪk/ *a.* L18. [f. as prec. + -IC.] **1** Of or pertaining to a monotone; uttered in a monotone. Also, capable of producing only a single tone. L18. **2** *Math.* Of a function or sequence: varying consistently so that it either never increases or never decreases. E20.

monotonical *a.* (*rare*) = MONOTONIC M18. **monotonically** *adv.* (*a*) in the manner of a monotone; (*b*) *Math.* in the manner of a monotonic function: L19. **monotonicity** /-ˈnɪsɪti/ *n.* M20.

monotonous /məˈnɒt(ə)nəs/ *a.* L18. [f. as prec. + -OUS.] **1** (Of sound, utterance, etc.) continuing on the same note; having little or no variation in tone, pitch, or cadence. L18. **2** Lacking in variety; uninteresting or tedious through continued sameness. E19. **3** *Math.* = MONOTONIC *a.* 2. L19.

2 LD MACAULAY The monotonous smoothness of Byron's versification. A. TOFFLER We are driving along a monotonous turnpike. E. HEATH The food was . . extraordinarily monotonous The only supplement to lentils . . were bunches of small green grapes.

monotonist *n.* (*rare*) a person who is monotonous or who delights in monotony M18. **monotonize** *v.t.* make monotonous E19. **monotonously** *adv.* (*a*) in a monotonous manner; with tiresome uniformity or lack of variation; (*b*) *Math.* = MONOTONICALLY (b): E19. **monotonousness** *n.* M19.

monotony /məˈnɒt(ə)ni/ *n.* E18. [Fr. *monotonie* f. late Gk *monotonia*, f. *monotonos* MONOTONE *a.*: see -Y³.] **1** Sameness of tone or pitch; lack of variety in cadence or inflection. Also, a monotonous sound, a monotone. E18. **2** (Now the usual sense.) Tedious sameness of effect; lack of interesting variety; dull or tedious routine. E18.

2 I. BANKS The monotony of this dull waste of grass. R. THOMAS The monotony of domestic life bored her. I. MORRISON This shot is so important in billiards that it should be practised to the point of monotony.

monotreme /ˈmɒnə(ʊ)triːm/ *n.* & *a.* M19. [f. Gk MONO- + *trēmat-*, *trēma* hole, perforation.] *Zool.* **A** *n.* Any of various oviparous mammals of the order Monotremata, having a common opening for the urogenital and digestive systems, now restricted to Australia and New Guinea and comprising the duck-billed platypus and the echidnas. M19. **B** *adj.* Of or pertaining to this order. L19.

mono'tremate *a.* & *n.* (a) monotreme M19. **mono'trematous** *a.* = MONOTREME *a.* M19.

monotriglyph /mɒnə(ʊ)ˈtrʌɪglɪf/ *n.* & *a.* E18. [L *monotriglyphus* f. Gk *monotrigluphos* adj., f. MONO- + *trigluphos* TRIGLYPH.] *Archit.* **A** *n.* A spacing between columns of the Doric order which allows the use of one triglyph in the frieze, between those over the columns. E18. **B** *adj.* Having only one triglyph in the space over an intercolumniation. L18.

monotri'glyphic *a.* = MONOTRIGLYPH *a.* M19.

monotropa /məˈnɒtrəpə/ *n.* L18. [mod.L (see below) f. Gk *monotropos* living alone, solitary, f. MONO- + *tropos* turn, direction, way, manner.] A plant of the genus *Monotropa* (family Pyrolaceae); *esp.* = INDIAN *pipe*.

monotropic /mɒnə(ʊ)ˈtrɒpɪk/ *a.* L19. [f. MONO- + Gk *tropos* turn + -IC.] **1** *Math.* = MONODROMIC. *rare.* L19. **2** *Physical Chem.* Exhibiting monotropy. L19.

monotropy /məˈnɒtrəpi/ *n.* E20. [f. MONO- + Gk *tropē* turning + -Y³.] *Physical Chem.* The existence of two polymorphs of a substance, one of which is stable and the other metastable under all known conditions.

Also **monotropism** *n.* E20.

monotype /ˈmɒnə(ʊ)tʌɪp/ *n.* L19. [f. MONO- + TYPE *n.*] **1** *Taxon.* A monotypic genus or other taxon. L19. **2** (A process for making) a single print taken from oil-colour or printers' ink painted on a sheet of glass or metal. L19. **3** (**M-**.) (Proprietary name for) a composing-machine consisting of two units, a caster, which produces type in individual characters, and a keyboard, which produces punched tape used to control the caster. Also *Monotype machine.* L19.

monotypic /mɒnə(ʊ)ˈtɪpɪk/ *a.* L19. [f. mod.L *monotypus*, f. as MONO- + -TYPE: see -IC.] **1** Of or having only one type; *spec.* in *Taxon.*, representing or designating a taxon which contains only one taxon of the next subordinate rank, esp. a genus which contains only one species. L19. **2** *Biol.* Of evolution: = ANAGENETIC. Now *rare* or *obs.* L19.

monotypous /məˈnɒtɪpəs/ *a.* Now *rare* or *obs.* M19. [f. as prec.: see -OUS.] = MONOTYPIC 1.

monovalent /mɒnə(ʊ)ˈveɪl(ə)nt/ *a.* M19. [f. MONO- + -VALENT.] **1** *Chem.* Having a valency of one. M19. **2** *Med.* **a** Being or containing an antigen from a single strain of a micro-organism. M20. **b** Of an antigen or antibody: having only one site at which attachment to (respectively) antibody or antigen can occur. M20.

monovalence, monovalency *ns.* L19.

monoxide /məˈnɒksʌɪd/ *n.* M19. [f. MONO- + OXIDE.] *Chem.* An oxide containing one atom of oxygen in the molecule or empirical formula.

monoxylon /məˈnɒksɪlən/ *n.* Pl. **-la** /-lə/. Also **monoxyle** /məˈnɒksɪl/, pl. **-s**. M16. [Gk *monoxulon* neut. of *monoxulos*, f. MONO- + *xulon* wood.] A canoe or boat made from one piece of wood.

mono'xylic, -'xylous *adjs.* (*a*) formed or made out of a single piece of wood; (*b*) using one piece of wood to make a boat, coffin, etc.: M19.

monozygotic /ˌmɒnə(ʊ)zʌɪˈgɒtɪk/ *a.* & *n.* E20. [f. MONO- + ZYGOTE + -IC.] **A** *adj.* Of twins, triplets, etc.: derived from a single ovum, identical. E20. **B** *n.* An individual monozygotic twin, triplet, etc. M20.

monozygosity *n.* the condition of being monozygotic E20. **mono'zygous** *a.* = MONOZYGOTIC *a.* M20.

Monroe doctrine /mənˈrəʊ ˌdɒktrɪn, ˈmʌnrəʊ/ *n. phr.* M19. [James *Monroe*, US president 1817–25.] A principle of US foreign policy that any intervention by external powers in the politics of the Americas is a potentially hostile act against the US.

Monroeism, Monroism *n.* adherence to the Monroe doctrine L19.

mons /mɒnz/ *n.* M20. [Abbrev.] = MONS PUBIS. Usu. *attrib.*

Monseigneur /mɔ̃sɛɲœːr, mɒnsɛˈnjəː/ *n.* Pl. ***Messeigneurs*** /mesɛɲœːr, mɛsɛnˈjəː/. E17. [Fr., f. *mon* my + *seigneur* lord.] **1** A French honorific title given to an eminent person, esp. a prince, cardinal, archbishop, or bishop. E17. †**2** = MONSIGNOR. E–M17.

Monsieur /məˈsjəː, *foreign* məsjø/ *n.* In sense 2 also **m-**. Pl. **Messieurs** /mɛˈsjəː, *foreign* mesjø/. E16. [Fr., f. *mon* my + *sieur* lord. See also MOSSOO, MOUNSEER.] **1** Used as a title (preceding the surname or other designation) of or as a respectful form of address to a French or French-speaking man or (more widely) a man of any non-British nationality (corresp. to English *Mr*), and in literal renderings of French speech. E16. **b** In *pl.* Used as pl. of MR. Now only in abbrev. form MESSRS. L18. **2** A man usually addressed or referred to as '*Monsieur*'; a Frenchman, orig. one of rank. Now *rare* or *obs.* E16. †**b** The French people. L17–E18. **3** *Hist.* (A title of) the second son or eldest brother of the King of France. M16.

1 SHAKES. *Mids. N. D.* Mounsieur Cobweb; good mounsieur, get you your weapons in your hand. N. FREELING That is quite correct, Monsieur le Juge. **b** THACKERAY Lady Agnes . . voted the two Messieurs Pendennis most agreeable men. **2** N. LUTTRELL At last the monsieurs struck, and are brought into Plymouth.

¶As a title freq. abbrev. *M.*

Monsignor /mɒnˈsiːnjə, mɒnsiːˈnjɔː/ *n.* Also **-gnore** /-ˈnjɔːreɪ/. Pl. **-gnori** /-ˈnjɔːri/. L16. [It. *Monsignor(e)* after Fr. MONSEIGNEUR.] An honorific title given to a Roman Catholic prelate, officer of the papal court and household, etc.

monsoon /mɒnˈsuːn/ *n.* L16. [Early mod.Du. *monssoen* (mod. *moesson*, infl. by Fr. forms) f. Port. *monção* (cf. OSp. *monzon*) f. Arab. *mawsim* season, fixed period, f. *wasama* to brand, mark.] **1** A seasonal wind which blows in southern Asia, esp. in the Indian Ocean, approximately from the south-west from April to October (in full *south-west, summer, wet,* or *rainy monsoon*), and from the north-east from October to April (in full *north-east, winter,* or *dry monsoon*). L16. **b** The rainfall which accompanies the south-west or summer monsoon; the rainy season. M18. **2** Any wind which reverses its direction seasonally, as the temperature varies between two areas, esp. between land and ocean. L17.

1 C. FRANCIS The monsoons regularly bring torrential rain. **b** R. K. NARAYAN When the monsoon set in, in October–November, the circus moved out of Malgudi. **the change of the monsoon** the period of stormy weather between the north-east and the south-west monsoons.

Comb.: **monsoon forest** a deciduous forest in a region of heavy seasonal rainfall.

monsoonal *a.* pertaining to or of the nature of a monsoon L19. **monsoonish** *a.* L19.

mons pubis /mɒnz ˈpjuːbɪs/ *n. phr.* L19. [L = mount of the pubes.] *Anat.* The rounded mass of fatty tissue on the lower abdomen, over the joint of the pubic bones; *esp.* that of a female (= MONS VENERIS).

monster /ˈmɒnstə/ *n.* & *a.* ME. [(O)Fr. *monstre* f. L *monstrum*, orig. a divine portent or warning, f. *monere* warn.] **A** *n.* **1** An animal, plant, or other thing, which deviates markedly from the normal type; *spec.* a congenitally malformed animal, a deformed foetus or neonate. ME. †**2** Something extraordinary or unnatural; a prodigy, a marvel. LME–E18. **3** An imaginary creature, usu. large and of frightening appearance, and often made up of incongruous elements. LME. **4** A person of inhuman and horrible cruelty or wickedness; an atrocious example *of* evil, a vice, etc. L15. **5** An animal of huge size; anything very large and unwieldy (and freq. also hideous). E16.

1 R. W. EMERSON The members have suffered amputation from the trunk, and strut about so many walking monsters. *Scientific American* If the exceptions are strongly counter to intuition, they are sometimes called monsters. **3** K. CROSSLEY-HOLLAND She was a monster with a hundred heads. *fig.*: N. ROWE Oh thou fell Monster, War. **4** E. BAKER He was watching the monster who was now whipping the little girl with a . . rope. S. HASTINGS A monster of selfishness . . 'roaring like a bull because everything is not just as he always has it'. C. ACHEBE The Emperor may be a fool but he isn't a monster. **5** TENNYSON The wallowing monster spouted his foam-fountains in the sea. H. BASCOM The large ugly printing press. . . The Editor-in-Chief . . seldom visits this clanging monster.

B *attrib.* or as *adj.* Of extraordinary size or extent; gigantic, huge, monstrous. M19.

R. CROMPTON Their jaws never ceased to move rhythmically around a couple of Monster Humbugs. J. STEINBECK Joe got up . . and ate a monster breakfast. R. INGALLS There you are, caught in a monster machine.

monster /ˈmɒnstə/ *v.t.* E17. [f. the n.] **1** Make a monster of. *rare.* E17. **2** Exhibit or point out as something remarkable. *rare.* E17. **3** Depict as monstrous; defame, disparage. Chiefly *Austral.* L20.

monstera /mɒnˈstɪərə/ *n.* E20. [mod.L (see below), app. f. L *monstrum* MONSTER *n.*, from the odd appearance of the leaves in some species.] Any of various climbing aroid plants constituting the tropical American genus *Monstera*, some species of which have perforated leaves; *esp.* the Swiss cheese plant, *M. deliciosa*.

monstrance /ˈmɒnstr(ə)ns/ *n.* ME. [med.L *monstrantia*, f. L *monstrant-* pres. ppl stem of *monstrare* show, f. *monstrum*: see MONSTER *n.*, -ANCE.] **1** Demonstration, proof. Long *rare.* ME. **2** *RC Ch.* An open or transparent receptacle, usu. of gold or silver, for the exposition of the consecrated Host or (occas.) relics. LME.

monstre sacré /mɔ̃str sakre/ *n. phr.* Pl. ***-s -s*** (pronounced same). M20. [Fr., lit. 'sacred monster'.] A striking, eccentric, or controversial public figure.

monstriferous /mɒnˈstrɪf(ə)rəs/ *a.* Long *rare* or *obs.* M16. [f. L *monstrum* MONSTER *n.* + -FEROUS.] Producing or bearing monsters.

monstrosity /mɒnˈstrɒsɪti/ *n.* M16. [Late L *monstrositas*, f. L *monstrosus*: see next, -ITY.] **1** An

For other words beginning with *mono-* see the entry for **mono-**

abnormality of growth; a part or organ that is abnormally developed. Also = MONSTER *n.* 1. M16. 2 A huge (imaginary) creature, a monster; a hideous or outrageous thing; *esp.* an unsightly building. M17. 3 The condition or fact of being monstrous. M17.

1 *fig.*: C. A. BRIGGS The word Jehovah . . is a linguistic monstrosity. 2 SIR T. BROWNE We shall tolerate flying Horses . . Harpies and Satyres: for these are monstrosities . . or else Poeticall fancies. J. C. OATES They have a roomy sprawling house, a late-Victorian monstrosity. 3 *Sunday Times* They can gloss over the monstrosity of their nature with obscene bourgeois good taste.

monstrous /ˈmɒnstrəs/ *a.* & *adv.* LME. [OFr. *monstreux* or L *monstrosus*, f. *monstrum* MONSTER *n.*: see -OUS.] A *adj.* †1 Strange, unnatural; odd in conduct or disposition. LME–M18. 2 Unnaturally or extraordinarily large; huge, enormous. Cf. sense 7 below. E16. 3 Abnormally formed; congenitally malformed. M16. 4 (Of a creature) of the nature of a monster; of large size and fearsome appearance; of or pertaining to a monster or monsters. M16. b Containing many monsters. Now *rare* or *obs.* M17. 5 Like or befitting a monster of wickedness; atrocious, horrible. M16. 6 Outrageously wrong or absurd. L16. 7 Very great; remarkable in extent, degree, etc. *colloq.* E18.

1 SHAKES. *Mids. N. D.* O monstrous! O strange! We are haunted. 2 R. L. STEVENSON Laying out vast projects, and planning monstrous foundations. R. DAHL His face was like a monstrous ball of dough. 3 E. WHITE A mingling of the law and the gospel; which like all unnatural unions, produced a monstrous birth. 4 MILTON Nature breeds, Perverse, all monstrous, all prodigious things . . Gorgons and Hydra's, and Chimera's dire. A. MASON A beaked and feathered face whose monstrous features slowly, as he gazed, dissolved into his own. 5 SHAKES. *John* Thou monstrous slanderer of heaven and earth! 6 J. I. M. STEWART An error too monstrous for contemplation. M. STOTT It seems monstrous to pay 23p for what used to cost 2d. 7 SWIFT We have a monstrous deal of snow. D. JOHNSON The temperature was monstrous.

B *adv.* Exceedingly, wonderfully, very. *colloq.* (now chiefly *US*). L16.

monstrously *adv.* L15. **monstrousness** *n.* L16.

†**monstruous** *a.* LME–E18. [f. L *monstruosus*, irreg. f. *monstrum* MONSTER *n.*: see -OUS.] Monstrous.

†**monstruosity** *n.* [Fr. *monstruosité*] LME–L18. †**monstruously** *adv.* M16–E18. †**monstruousness** *n.* M16–M17.

mons Veneris /mɒnz ˈvɛnərɪs/ *n. phr.* E17. [L = mount of Venus: cf. VENUS.] 1 *Palmistry.* The ball of the thumb. E17. 2 *Anat.* The rounded mass of fatty tissue on a female's lower abdomen, above the vulva. Cf. MONS PUBIS. L17.

montage /mɒnˈtɑːʒ, ˈmɒntɑːʒ/ *n.* E20. [Fr., f. *monter* to mount.] 1 *Cinemat.* & *Television.* The selection and arrangement of separate sections of film as a consecutive whole; the blending (by superimposition) of separate shots to form a single picture; a sequence or picture resulting from such a process. E20. 2 *gen.* The process or technique of producing a composite whole by combining several different pictures, pieces of music, or other elements, so that they blend with or into one another; the result of such a process; a miscellany, a pastiche. M20.

1 *attrib.*: *Listener* A montage sequence from a Russian silent film.

Montagnais /ˈmɒntənjeɪ, *foreign* mɔ̃taɲɛ/ *n.* & *a.* Also (earlier) †**-ois**. E18. [Fr. = mountaineer.] A *n.* Pl. same. A member of an Algonquian Indian people of eastern Canada; the language of this people. E18. B *attrib.* or as *adj.* Of or pertaining to the Montagnais or their language. E20.

¶ Cf. earlier MOUNTAINER 3, also MOUNTAINEER *n.* 1b.

montagnard /mɒntəˈnjɑːd, *foreign* mɔ̃taɲaːr (*pl. same*)/ *a.* & *n.* M19. [Fr., f. *montagne* MOUNTAIN: see -ARD.] A *adj.* Inhabiting a mountain region; of or pertaining to montagnards or (**M-**) the Montagnards. M19. B *n.* 1 *Fr. Hist.* (**M-**.) A member of 'the Mountain' (see MOUNTAIN 4). L19. 2 A native or inhabitant of a mountain region; a highlander; *spec.* (**M-**) a member of an aboriginal people living in the highlands of southern Vietnam (= MOI). M20.

montagne russe /mɔ̃taɲ rys/ *n. phr. Canad.* Pl. ***-s -s*** (pronounced same). M19. [Fr., lit. 'Russian mountain'.] A switchback, a scenic railway, a roller coaster.

†**Montagnois** *n.* & *a.* see MONTAGNAIS.

Montagu /ˈmɒntəgjuː/ *n.* M19. [George *Montagu* (1751–1815), Brit. naturalist.] Used *attrib.* or *possess.* to designate various animals described by Montagu.

Montagu's blenny a small blenny, *Coryphoblennius galerita*, of intertidal pools around the Mediterranean and NE Atlantic. **Montagu's harrier** a relatively small migratory Eurasian harrier, *Circus pygargus*. **Montagu shell** (the shell of) any of various small marine bivalves of the family Montacutidae, which live as commensals on echinoderms. **Montagu's sea-snail** a small fish of the NE Atlantic, *Liparis montagui*, which feeds on littoral crustaceans.

Montague /ˈmɒntəgjuː/ *n.* L19. [Pers. name, of unkn. origin.] *Hairdressing.* A flat curl, secured by a hairpin etc., worn at the front of the hair. Also *Montague curl.* Usu. in *pl.*

montan /ˈmɒnt(ə)n/ *a.* E20. [f. as MONTANE.] *montan wax*, a hard, brittle substance, consisting mainly of higher fatty acids and their esters, which is extracted from lignite or peat by organic solvents and used in polishes and as an electrical insulator.

Montaña /mɒnˈtaɲa/ *n.* M19. [Sp. = MOUNTAIN.] In Spanish-American countries: a forest of considerable extent; *spec.* the forested eastern foothills of the Andes in Peru etc.

Montanan /mɒnˈtanən, -ˈtɑː-/ *n.* M20. [f. *Montana* (see below) + -AN.] A native or inhabitant of the State of Montana, in the north-western US.

Also **Montanian** *n.* L19.

montane /ˈmɒnteɪn/ *a.* M19. [L *montanus*, f. *mont-*, *mons* mountain: see MOUNT *n.*[1], -ANE. See also MONTAN.] Of, pertaining to, or inhabiting mountainous country; *spec.* designating or pertaining to the belt of upland vegetation below the tree line.

Montanism /ˈmɒntənɪz(ə)m/ *n.* L16. [f. *Montanus* (see below) + -ISM.] *Eccl. Hist.* The tenets of a heretical millenarian and ascetic Christian sect that set great store by prophecy, founded in Phrygia by Montanus in the middle of the 2nd cent.

Montanist *n.* & *a.* (*a*) *n.* an adherent of Montanism; (*b*) *adj.* of or pertaining to Montanism or Montanists: L16. **Montaˈnistic** *a.* M17. **Montanize** *v.i.* conform to the tenets of Montanism L16.

†**montant** *n.* LME. [Fr., use as n. of pres. pple of *monter* mount: see -ANT[1]. See also MUNTIN.] 1 = MUNTIN. LME–M19. 2 A downright blow or thrust. *rare.* Only in L16.

Montbazillac *n.* var. of MONBAZILLAC.

montbretia /mɒn(t)ˈbriːʃə/ *n.* L19. [mod.L *Montbretia* former genus name, f. A. F. E. Coquebert de *Montbret* (1780–1801), Fr. botanist: see -IA[1].] Any of various cultivated hybrid plants of the genus *Crocosmia*, of the iris family, with bright orange-yellow trumpet-shaped flowers.

mont de piété /mɔ̃ də pjete/ *n. phr.* Pl. ***monts de piété*** (pronounced same). M19. [Fr. Cf. It. MONTE DI PIETÀ.] A State pawnbroking organization in France providing loans to the poor at low rates of interest. Cf. MONTE DI PIETÀ, *mount of piety* s.v. MOUNT *n.*[1]

monte /ˈmɒnti/ *n.* In branch I (esp. sense 2) also **-ty**. E19. [Sp. = mountain, pile of cards left after dealing.] I 1 A Spanish and Spanish-American gambling game usu. played with a pack of forty cards. Also (in full *three-card monte*), a form of three-card trick. E19. 2 A certainty; *spec.* a horse considered a safe bet to win a race. *Austral.* & *NZ colloq.* L19. II 3 In Spanish-American countries: a small wooded tract; (a region of) chaparral or scrub. M19.

Monte Carlo /mɒnti ˈkɑːləʊ/ *n.* & *a.* M20. [A town in Monaco, famous for its casino.] 1 (Designating or involving) any of various methods of estimating the solution to numerical problems by the random (or pseudorandom) sampling of numbers in a probabilistic simulation. M20. 2 *Monte Carlo fallacy*, the fallacy that the probability of a particular outcome to one of a series of repeated but independent chance events is inversely dependent on the previous outcomes (e.g., that repeated failure increases the probability of success on the next occasion). M20.

monte di pietà /ˌmonte di pjeˈtaː/ *n. phr.* Pl. ***monti di pietà*** /ˌmonti/. M17. [It. Cf. Fr. MONT DE PIÉTÉ.] A State pawnbroking organization in Italy providing loans to the poor at low rates of interest. Cf. MONT DE PIÉTÉ, *mount of piety* s.v. MOUNT *n.*[1]

Montefiascone /ˌmɒntɪfɪəˈskəʊni/ *n.* L17. [See below.] A sweet white wine made in the region of Montefiascone, a town in Latium, central Italy. Also *Montefiascone wine.*

monteith /mɒnˈtiːθ/ *n.* L17. [f. Sc. surname *Monteith*: in sense 1 app. f. a 17th-cent. Scotsman who wore a cloak with a scalloped bottom edge; in sense 2 f. Henry Monteith, 19th-cent. Sc. dyer.] 1 A large ornamental punch-bowl, often silver, with a scalloped rim. L17. 2 A cotton handkerchief with a pattern of white spots on a coloured background. *obs.* exc. *Hist.* L19.

monte-jus /ˈmɒntəʒuːs, *foreign* mɔ̃tʒys/ *n.* L19. [Fr., f. *monter* raise + *jus* juice.] In sugar-refining, an apparatus for raising the level of the liquid by means of air or steam pressure.

montelimar /mɒnˈtɛlɪmɑː/ *n.* E20. [*Montélimar*, a town in the department of Drôme in SE France.] A type of nougat orig. made in Montélimar.

Montem /ˈmɒntɛm/ *n. obs.* exc. *Hist.* M18. [f. L *ad montem* to the hill (w. ref. to a mound near Slough where the event was held).] A festival celebrated until 1844 by the scholars of Eton College, who processed in fancy dress to raise money for the expenses of the senior colleger at King's College, Cambridge.

Montenegrin /mɒntɪˈniːgrɪn/ *n.* & *a.* Also **-ine**. E19. [f. *Montenegro* (see below) + -IN(E[1].] A *n.* A native or inhabitant of Montenegro, a former kingdom on the Adriatic coast, later part of Yugoslavia. E19. B *adj.* Of or pertaining to Montenegro or its inhabitants. E19.

Montepulciano /ˌmɒntɪpʊlˈtʃɑːnəʊ/ *n.* L17. [See below.] A red Italian wine made in the region of Montepulciano, a town in Tuscany, western Italy.

montera /monˈtera/ *n.* Also (now *rare*) **-ro** /-rəʊ/, pl. **-os** /-ɒs/. E17. [Sp., f. *montero* mountaineer, hunter, f. *monte* MOUNT *n.*[1]] A Spanish cap, orig. worn for hunting, with a spherical crown and flaps able to be drawn over the ears. Now usu. *spec.*, the black hat worn by a bullfighter.

Monterey /mɒntəˈreɪ, ˈmɒntərəɪ/ *n.* L19. [A city in California, USA.] 1 *Monterey pine*, a tall pine, *Pinus radiata*, native to the south-western US, widely planted as an ornamental and timber tree. L19. 2 *Monterey cypress*, = MACROCARPA. L19. 3 *Monterey (Spanish) mackerel*, a mackerel, *Scomberomorus concolor*, found in warm parts of the Pacific. L19.

montero *n.* see MONTERA.

Montessori /mɒntɪˈsɔːri/ *n.* E20. [Maria *Montessori* (1870–1952), It. physician and educationalist.] Used *attrib.* to designate an educational system, esp. for young children, that seeks to develop natural interests and abilities rather than use formal methods.

Montessorian *a.* & *n.* (*a*) *adj.* of or pertaining to the Montessori educational system; (*b*) *n.* an advocate or follower of this system: M20. **Montessorianism** *n.* the Montessori educational system E20.

Monteverdian /mɒntɪˈvɜːdɪən/ *a.* M20. [f. *Monteverdi* (see below) + -AN.] Of or pertaining to the Italian baroque composer Claudio Monteverdi (1567–1643), his music, or his style of composition.

Montezuma's revenge /mɒntɪˌzuːməz rɪˈvɛn(d)ʒ/ *n. phr. slang.* M20. [f. *Montezuma* II

(1466–1520), last Aztec emperor of Mexico.] Diarrhoea suffered by visitors to Mexico.

Montgolfier /mɒnt'gɒlfɪə, *foreign* mɔ̃gɔlfje (*pl. same*)/ *n.* L18. [J. M. & J. E. *Montgolfier*, Fr. brothers, who built the first such balloon which flew in 1783.] *Hist.* An early form of hot-air balloon. Also *Montgolfier balloon.*

Montgomery /mənt'gɒm(ə)ri/ *n.* L19. [William F. *Montgomery* (1797–1859), Ir. gynaecologist.] *Anat.* 1 *Montgomery('s) glands, glands of Montgomery*, glands in the areola of a woman's nipple, thought to be accessory mammary glands. L19. 2 *Montgomery('s) tubercles, tubercles of Montgomery*, small swellings on the areola which contain the outlets of Montgomery's glands, esp. when enlarged in early pregnancy. L19.

month /mʌnθ/ *n.* [OE *mōnaþ* = OFris. *mōnath, mōn(a)d*, OS *mānoþ* (Du. *maand*), OHG *mānōd* (G *Monat*), ON *mánuðr*, Goth. *mēnōþs*, f. Gmc, rel. to MOON *n.*[1]] 1 A fraction of a year corresponding to the period of revolution of the moon; any of usu. twelve roughly equal periods into which a year is divided; *spec.* each of the twelve (January, February, March, etc.) in the calendar inherited by Western nations from the Romans. OE. 2 *Astron.* A period in which the moon makes a complete revolution relative to some point, either fixed or movable; *esp.* the period from one new moon to the next, equal to 29 days, 12 hours, 44 minutes, 2.7 seconds. OE. 3 A space of time either extending between the same dates in successive months of the calendar, or containing four weeks or 28 days; such a period (identified contextually) forming part of a term of imprisonment, leave, notice, etc., or of pregnancy (commonly reckoned to last nine months normally); in *pl.*, a long while. OE. **b** A month's pay. *colloq.* L18. †4 In *pl.* The menstrual discharge; a menstrual period. L16–L17.

1 R. K. NARAYAN On the first of the month you were sure of your money. W. TREVOR In the summer months, in June and July and August. 3 SHELLEY What you in one night squander were enough For months! G. GREENE Remember me . . . I'll see you again in a month or two. *Venue* I only got six months, deferred. Not bad with my form. b G. B. SHAW I'll go this very minute. You can keep my month.

Phrases: ANOMALISTIC *month. calendar month*: see CALENDAR *n. draconic month*: see DRACONIC *a.* 3. **from month to month** continuously or without interruption from one month to the next. *lunar month*: see LUNAR *a.* †**month about** during alternate months. **month after month** each month as a sequel to the preceding one, esp. in an unvarying sequence. **month by month** in each successive month, monthly without ceasing. **month of Sundays** an indefinitely long period (usu. in neg. contexts); also, used as a type of dullness. **month's man** a man hired for one month's work during harvest. *month's mind*: see MIND *n.*[1] 4b. *r month*: see R, R I. *solar month*: see SOLAR *a.*[1] *synodic month*: see SYNODIC 2. **this day month** at a time a month after the day indicated. *tropical month*: see TROPICAL *a.* I.

Comb.: **month clock**: that goes for a month between windings; **month-long** *a.* & *adv.* (lasting) for a whole month.

mother *n.* (w. preceding numeral) a person or thing lasting or aged the specified number of months L19.

monthly /'mʌnθli/ *a.* & *n.* L16. [f. prec. + -LY[1].] A *adj.* 1 Of or pertaining to a month; payable every month. L16. 2 Continued or enduring for a month. Now *rare* exc. with the notion of recurrence. L16. 3 Done, recurring, produced, etc., once a month or every month; *spec.* menstrual. E17.

1 G. GREENE The habit of drawing occasional expenses for . . the professor, and monthly salaries for himself. F. SWINNERTON Complete independence in daily, weekly, or monthly needs. **monthly nurse** a nurse who attends a mother during the first month after labour. 2 R. GREENE Minutes ioyes are monthlie woes. R. WHELAN He had wangled monthly extensions of his visa. 3 LYTTON She saw Evelyn opening the monthly parcel from London. A. N. WILSON *David Copperfield* was published in monthly parts. **monthly rose** the China rose, *Rosa chinensis*, formerly believed to flower every month.

B *n.* 1 A magazine etc. published once in each month. M19. 2 *sing.* & (usu.) in *pl.* The menstrual discharge; a menstrual period. *colloq.* L19.

monthly /'mʌnθli/ *adv.* E16. [f. MONTH + -LY[2].] Once a month; in each or every month; month by month.

monticellite /mɒntɪ'sɛlʌɪt/ *n.* M19. [f. T. *Monticelli* (1758–1846), It. mineralogist + -ITE[1].] *Min.* An orthorhombic mineral of the olivine group which is a calcium magnesium silicate and usu. occurs as yellowish crystals.

monticle /'mɒntɪk(ə)l/ *n.* L15. [f. as next: see -CLE.] = MONTICULE I.

monticule /'mɒntɪkjuːl/ *n.* L18. [Fr. f. late L *monticulus* dim. of *monti-, mons* MOUNT *n.*[1]: see -CULE. Cf. earlier MONTICLE.] 1 A small mountain or hill. L18. **b** *spec.* A small conical mound produced by a volcanic eruption. M19. 2 Chiefly *Palaeont.* A minute swelling or bump, esp. on a fossil shell. L19.

mon'ticulose *a.* (*Palaeont.*) covered with minute bumps M19.

monti di pietà *n. phr.* pl. of MONTE DI PIETÀ.

Montilla /mɒn'tiljə/ *n.* L18. [A town in S. Spain. Cf. AMONTILLADO.] A dry fortified Spanish wine resembling sherry, produced in the area around Montilla; a drink of this.

montmorillonite /mɒntmə'rɪlənʌɪt/ *n.* M19. [f. *Montmorillon*, a town in France + -ITE[1].] *Min.* Orig., a rose-red clay mineral. Now, any montmorillonoid; *spec.* an alumina-rich montmorillonoid containing some sodium and magnesium.

Comb.: **montmorillonite group** the group of clay minerals comprising the montmorillonoids.

montmorillonitic /ˌmɒntmərɪlə'nɪtɪk/ *a.* resembling or containing montmorillonite M20.

montmorillonoid /mɒntmə'rɪlənɔɪd/ *n.* & *a.* M20. [f. prec. + -OID.] *Min.* (Designating or pertaining to) any of a group of clay minerals which undergo reversible expansion on absorbing water and have a characteristic structure in which water molecules are situated between sheets composed of two layers of silicon atoms sandwiching one nominally of aluminium, the silicon and aluminium being variously replaced by other elements.

Montonero /mɒntə'nɛːrəʊ/ *n.* Pl. **-os**. L20. [Amer. Sp., f. Sp. *montón* heap, mass, crowd + *-ero* -EER.] A member of a left-wing Peronist urban guerrilla organization in Argentina.

Montpellier /mɒnt'pɛlɪeɪ, *foreign* mɔ̃pɛlje/ *n.* M19. [A town in the department of Hérault, southern France.] **1a** *Montpellier yellow*, = *mineral yellow* s.v. MINERAL *a.* M19. **b** *Montpellier green*, = VERDIGRIS *green.* M20. 2 *Montpellier butter*, a sauce made by pounding together mixed herbs, oil, egg yolks, butter, etc., usu. served with cold poultry or fish. L19.

Montrealer /mɒntrɪ'ɔːlə/ *n.* L19. [f. *Montreal* (Fr. *Montréal*) (see below) + -ER[1].] A native or inhabitant of the city of Montreal in S. Quebec, Canada.

monts de piété *n. phr.* pl. of MONT DE PIÉTÉ.

Montserratian /mɒn(t)sə'ratɪən/ *n.* & *a.* L19. [f. *Montserrat* (see below) + -IAN.] A *n.* A native or inhabitant of Montserrat, one of the Leeward Islands in the W. Indies. L19. B *adj.* Of or pertaining to Montserrat. L20.

montuno /mɒn'tuːnəʊ/ *n.* Pl. **-os**. M20. [Amer. Sp. = native to mountains, wild, untamed.] 1 A traditional male costume worn in Panama, consisting of white cotton short trousers and an embroidered shirt. M20. 2 An improvised passage in a rumba. M20.

monture /'mɒntʃə/ *n.* M19. [Fr., f. *monter* MOUNT *v.*: see -URE.] A mounting, a setting; the manner in which something is set or mounted.

monty *n.* see MONTE *n.*

monument /'mɒnjʊm(ə)nt/ *n.* & *v.* ME. [(O)Fr. f. L *monumentum*, *moni-*, f. *monere* remind: see -MENT.] A *n.* †1 A sepulchre, a burial place. ME–M17. 2 A written document, a record. Formerly also, a piece of information given in writing. LME. 3 A structure or edifice intended to commemorate a notable person, action, or event; a stone or other structure built over a grave or in a church etc. in memory of a dead person. Formerly also, a carved figure, a statue, an effigy. LME. 4 An enduring thing, *esp.* a thing that by its survival commemorates a person, action, period, or event; a structure or edifice surviving from a past age; an outstanding survival of an early literature. Freq. foll. by *of*. E16. **b** A thing surviving as a symbol of or witness to a process or activity. Foll. by *to*. M20. **5†a** A thing serving for identification; a thing that warns, a portent. L16–M17. **b** An indication or token (*of* a fact). Now *rare*. E17. **c** *US Law.* A fixed object referred to in a document as a means of locating a tract of land or its boundaries. E19.

2 BURKE All our monuments bear a strong evidence to this change [in the laws]. 3 E. LONGFORD Old Tom Picton was given . . a monument . . in St. Paul's Cathedral. W. MCILVANNEY That was a monument they were sittin' beside. To the men from the village. 4 W. S. MAUGHAM A painter's monument is his work. G. K. ANDERSON The most important monument of Old English epic literature . . is . . *Beowulf*. *fig.*: *London Review of Books* Brecht . . has become a cultural monument Is it then not time . . to consider blowing him up? *ancient monument*: see ANCIENT *a.* 4. b D. ROWE Psychiatric hospitals are monuments to the destruction of the human spirit. 5a SHAKES. *Tam. Shr.* Wherefore gaze this goodly company As if they saw some wondrous monument? b G. MATHESON They came to Aaron to ask a sign—a visible monument of the Divine Presence.

B *v.t.* = MONUMENTALIZE. E17.

monumental /mɒnjʊ'mɛnt(ə)l/ *a.* E17. [f. as prec. + -AL[1].] 1 Of, pertaining to, or serving as a monument or monuments. Formerly also, of or pertaining to the tomb, sepulchral. E17. †**b** Serving as a memento. *rare*. E–M17. 2 Having the physical aspect of a monument; (esp. of a work of art) comparable to a monument in size, permanence, etc. Now freq. *loosely*, vast, stupendous. E17. 3 Historically prominent and significant. M19.

1 G. CLARK With Christianity came literacy, coinage and monumental architecture. b SHAKES. *All's Well* He hath given her his monumental ring. 2 V. S. NAIPAUL The farm buildings (made monumental by the snowfall). V. GLENDINNING She could turn on Wells for his monumental male selfishness. 3 M. COREN He quoted from Macaulay's monumental speech.

Special collocations: **Monumental City** *US* the city of Baltimore, Maryland. **monumental mason** a maker of tombstones etc.

monumentalism *n.* a monumental style; building on a grand scale: E20. **monumen'tality** *n.* the quality of being monumental L19. **monumentalize** *v.t.* make a permanent record of (a person, thing, event, etc.), esp. by means of a monument M19. **monumentally** *adv.* by way of a monument or memorial; in a monumental way or degree; *loosely* greatly, extremely: M17.

mon vieux /mɔ̃ vjø/ *n. phr.* L19. [Fr.] Old friend, old man: used as an affectionate form of address.

-mony /məni/ *suff.* (not productive). Repr. L *-monia, -monium*, Fr. *-monie*, forming ns. chiefly of action or state from vbl stems, as *alimony, ceremony, matrimony, parsimony, sanctimony, testimony.*

monzonite /'mɒnzənʌɪt/ *n.* L19. [f. Mount *Monzoni* in the Tyrol, Italy + -ITE[1].] *Geol.* A granular igneous rock with a composition intermediate between syenite and diorite, *spec.* one containing approximately equal amounts of orthoclase and plagioclase.

monzonitic /mɒnzə'nɪtɪk/ *a.* pertaining to, of the nature of, or containing monzonite E20.

moo /muː/ *n.*[1] *slang.* M20. [Abbrev.] = MOOLAH.

moo /muː/ *v.*, *n.*[2], & *int.* M16. [Imit.] A *v.i.* Of a bovine animal: make its characteristic deep resonant vocal sound, low. Of a person: make a sound imitative or suggestive of this. M16.

J. RHYS The cows here moo at me.

B *n.* 1 (Repr.) the low of a bovine animal; an act of lowing. Also as *int.* M16. 2 A woman (*derog.*). Also, a cow. *slang.* M20.

1 O. NASH The cow is of the bovine ilk; One end is moo, the other, milk. B. REID When . . she finishes up alone on the stage, going 'Moo, Moo, Moo', you realize . . she will be a success as a cow. 2 J. SPEIGHT Course it's tax free . . you silly moo.

Comb.: **moo-cow** *nursery* a cow.

mooch /muːtʃ/ *v.* & *n.* Also **mouch**. LME. [Prob. f. OFr. *muchier* (Norman dial. *mucher*) hide, skulk (whence also MITCH *v.*).] A *v.* †1 *v.i.* Pretend to be poor. *rare*. Only in LME. 2 *v.i.* Play truant, esp. to pick blackberries. *dial.* E17. 3 *v.i.* Skulk, sneak; loiter or loaf *about*. Now *esp.* wander aimlessly, saunter desultorily, (*along, around, off*). *colloq.* M19. 4 *v.t.* Pilfer, steal. *colloq.* M19. 5 *v.t.* & *i.* Cadge, scrounge. (Foll. by *off*, *on* a person.) *colloq.* (chiefly *N. Amer.*). M19. 6 *v.i.* Fish with light tackle allowed to drift. *N. Amer. dial.* M20.

3 R. LEHMANN The rest of the time I mooch about and go to the pictures. P. KAVANAGH There was Joe Finnegan still mooching around like a man who had lost a shilling in the grass. 4 *Daily Telegraph* They .. would hotly assert that they never mooched a penny. 5 D. JOHNSON One of the endless train .. here to mooch lunch. 6 *Sun* (*Vancouver*) Most anglers troll, rather than mooch or strip-cast.

B *n.* 1 The action or an act of loafing or scrounging. *colloq.* M19. 2 The fruit of the blackberry. *dial.* M19. 3 A loiterer, a loafer. *colloq.* E20.

1 **be on the mooch** cadge, scrounge. **do a mooch, go for a mooch** loiter, wander.

moocha *n.* var. of MUCHI.

moocher /ˈmuːtʃə/ *n.* Also **moucher**. L17. [f. MOOCH *v.* + -ER[1].] †1 A transgressor. *rare*. Only in L17. 2 A person who plays truant, esp. to pick blackberries. *dial.* L18. 3 A loiterer, a loafer. *colloq.* M19. 4 A cadger, a scrounger. *colloq.* (chiefly *N. Amer.*). M19. 5 A person who fishes with light tackle allowed to drift. *N. Amer. dial.* M20.

moochin /ˈmuːxɪn/ *n.* *Anglo-Welsh colloq.* M20. [Anglicized f. Welsh *mochyn* pig.] An objectionable person.

DYLAN THOMAS Up you get, you moochin, or I'll take you home.

mood /muːd/ *n.*[1] & *a.* [OE *mōd* = OFris., OS *mōd* (Du. *moed*), OHG *muot* (G *Mut*), ON *móðr* anger, grief, Goth. *mōþs*, *mōd-* anger, emotion, f. Gmc.] A *n.* †1 Mind, heart, thought, feeling. OE–LME. †2 *spec.* a Fierce courage; pride. OE–L15. b Anger. ME–E17. c Passionate grief. Only in ME. 3 The temporary state of mind or feelings of a person or group. Freq. w. specifying wd. OE. b *spec.* A fit of unaccountable bad temper or depression, a bad mood, (usu. in *pl.*); in *pl.* also, changes of mood. M19. c *transf.* The atmosphere or pervading tone of a place, event, composition, etc.; *esp.* one inducing a certain state of mind or emotion. E20.

2b *peck mood*: see PECK *v.*[1] 1. 3 I. COMPTON-BURNETT Duncan remained silent, and his mood cast a gloom. E. TAYLOR Even if I want to paint again .. I don't want to be in the painting *mood*. W. MAXWELL He was in a cheerful mood. E. KUZWAYO The sudden change of mood among the members. *bad mood, good mood*, etc. **in a** (or **the**) **mood** disposed, inclined, (*for*, †*of*, *to do*). **in no mood** not disposed, disinclined, (*for*, *to do*). b TENNYSON Sir Torre .. being in his moods Left them. *Observer* A creature of moods and temperament. **be in** or **get into a mood** (**with**) be or become peevish or bad-tempered (towards). c *Outdoor Living* (*NZ*) You can choose a fence that enhances the general mood of your home. M. FOOT At the 1979 Conference the mood was set.

Comb.: **mood-altering** *a.* (of a drug) capable of inducing changes of mood; **mood drug** a mood-altering drug, *esp.* a stimulant; **mood-elevating** *a.* (of a drug) having a stimulant or antidepressant effect; **mood swing** *Psychol.* an abrupt and unaccountable change of mood.

B *attrib.* or as *adj.* Inducing or suggestive of a particular mood. L19.

H. KEMELMAN The organ had been playing mood music, a series of mournful cadenzas in a minor key.

mood /muːd/ *n.*[2] M16. [Alt. of MODE *n.* & *a.* by assoc. w. prec.] 1 *Logic.* Any of the classes into which each of the four figures of valid categorical syllogism is subdivided according to the quality (affirmative or negative) and quantity (universal or particular) of the constituent propositions. Also, the type of structure to which a syllogism belongs in respect of quality and quantity alone. Cf. MODE *n.* 3a. M16. 2 *Gram.* Any of the groups of forms in the conjugation of a verb which indicate whether the action of the verb is represented as fact or in some other manner, as a possibility, command, wish, etc.; the quality of a verb as represented or distinguished by a particular mood. Cf. ASPECT *n.* 9, TENSE *n.* 2. M16. †3 *Mus.* a In medieval music, the duration or time-value of a note in relation to another in the rhythm of a piece. Cf. MODE *n.* 1b. L16–L18. b = MODE *n.* 1a. L16–M19.

2 *imperative mood, optative mood, predicative mood, subjunctive mood*, etc.

moodooga *n.* var. of MUDUGA.

moody /ˈmuːdi/ *a.* & *n.* [OE *mōdiġ*, f. as MOOD *n.*[1] + -Y[1].] A *adj.* †1 Brave, bold, high-spirited. OE–M18. †2 Proud, haughty; stubborn, wilful. OE–LME. †3 Angry, given to anger. ME–L17. 4 Subject to or indulging in moods of bad temper, depression, etc.; sullen, melancholy. L16. 5 Counterfeit, false; risky. *slang*. M20.

4 T. SHARPE The Fellows dined in moody silence. D. DELILLO The boy is fourteen, often evasive and moody.

B *n.* 1 Bluff; nonsense, rubbish. Chiefly in (*a lot of*) *old moody*. *colloq.* M20. 2 A bad mood; in *pl.*, a fit of depression, low spirits. *colloq.* M20.

1 R. BUSBY The same old moody he'd heard a thousand times before. 2 *Observer* I can't stand people having the moodies.

moodily *adv.* OE. **moodiness** *n.* OE.

mooey /ˈmuːɪ/ *n.* *slang*. M19. [Romany *mooi*. Cf. MOW *n.*[2]] A mouth; a face.

Moog /məʊɡ, muːɡ/ *n.* Also **m-**. M20. [R. A. *Moog*, (1934–), US engineer, the inventor.] (Proprietary name for) an electronic keyboard instrument producing a variety of different sounds. Also *Moog synthesizer*.

mool /muːl/ *n.* *Sc.* & *north.* L16. [App. var. of MOULD *n.*[1]] (A clod of) earth; loose soil; *spec.* (the soil for) a grave; in *pl.*, the grave.

moolah /ˈmuːlə/ *n.* *slang* (orig. *US*). Also **moola**. M20. [Origin unkn. See also MOO *n.*[1]] Money.

mooley *n.* & *a.* var. of MULEY *n.* & *a.*[1]

mooli /ˈmuːli/ *n.* Also **muli**. M20. [Hind. *mūlī* f. Skt *mūlikā*, f. *mūla* root.] A long white radish, the root of *Raphanus sativus* var. *longipinnatus*, used in eastern cooking.

moolvi(e) *ns.* vars. of MOULVI.

moomba /ˈmuːmbə/ *n.* *Austral.* M20. [Aborig.] An annual pre-Lent festival held in Melbourne.

moon /muːn/ *n.*[1] [OE *mōna* = OFris. *mōna*, OS *māno* (Du. *maan*), OHG *māno* (G *Mond*), ON *máni*, Goth. *mēna*, f. Gmc wd rel. to base of MONTH, ult. f. IE base repr. also by L *metiri* MEASURE *v.*, the moon being used to measure time.] 1 *The* natural satellite of the earth; a secondary planet which orbits around the earth, visible (esp. at night) by the light of the sun which it reflects. (In some contexts regarded as a passive overseer or witness to (the actions of) humankind; in others, a type of something extravagant or unattainable.) OE. b A natural satellite of any planet. M17. 2 The moon as visible (chiefly with a specified phase or point reached) during any one lunar month. Also, the moon when visible at any particular time or place. OE. †b With ordinal numeral: a specified day after a new moon. *rare*. OE–E18. 3 The period from one new moon to the next; a lunar month; *gen.* a month. Now chiefly *poet.* or *joc.* (esp. in *many a moon, many moons* below). LME. b = HONEYMOON. E18. c (Pl. same, -**s**.) A month's imprisonment. *slang*. M19. 4 The period of time in any one night during which the moon is visible. Long *rare*. LME. 5 = MOONLIGHT *n.* 1. *poet.* LME. 6 A (round or crescent-shaped) representation of the moon; a moon-shaped object. LME. b The disc etc. representing the moon in a clock which exhibits its phases. M16. c *sing.* & in *pl.* The buttocks. *slang*. M18. d A moon-shaped mark or area; *spec.* a small area of greater translucence in porcelain. M19. †7 *Alch.* The metal silver. L15–M17. 8 = MOONSHINE *n.* 3; *spec.* whiskey. *US colloq.* E20.

1 SHAKES. *A.Y.L.* Pray you no more of this; 'tis like the howling of Irish wolves against the moon. MILTON While over head the Moon Sits Arbitress. R. S. THOMAS I looked from my top window and saw the moon. *Listener* To .. expect to see what you yourself would choose .. is .. asking for the moon. *New Statesman* Those politicians .. promise the moon. *USA Today* The Class of 2000 won't necessarily go to the moon, but they will do some sub-orbital flying. b *Scientific American* Umbriel is the darkest of the major Uranian moons. 2 H. NISBET The moon .. bathed everything .. as only Australian moons can do. R. INGALLS The starlight is bright to see by even when the moon isn't out. *crescent moon, harvest moon, hunter's moon, quarter-moon*, etc. 3 P. S. BUCK A moon of days passed and the thing was not yet complete. b BYRON We are .. to set off by ourselves to Halnaby for the Moon. c E. WALLACE Gunner's got three moon for bein' a suspected. 6 TENNYSON Pure quintessences of precious oils In hollow'd moons of gems. c S. BECKETT Placing her hands upon her moons, plump and plain. 8 B. KROETSCH Give these gentlemen some of that moon.

Phrases: *bark against* (or *at*) *the moon*: see BARK *v.*[1] *blue moon*: see BLUE *a.* *change of the moon*: see CHANGE *n.* 1b. *cry for the moon*: see CRY *v.* 2. *dark of the moon*: see DARK *n.*[1] *eclipse of the moon*: see ECLIPSE *n.* *full moon*: see FULL *a.* **many a moon, many moons** a very long time. *mean moon*: see MEAN *a.*[2] *mock moon*: see MOCK *a.* *new moon*: see NEW *a.* *new of the moon*: see NEW *n.* *old moon*: see OLD *a.* **over the moon** *colloq.* very happy or delighted. **shoot the moon** *colloq.* make a moonlight flit. *the glimpses of the moon*: see GLIMPSE *n.* 3. *the man in the moon*: see MAN *n.* *the moon's age*: see AGE *n.* 1. *zodiac of the moon*: see ZODIAC *n.* 1b.

Comb.: **moonball** *v.* & *n.* (*Tennis slang*) (deliver) a very high lob; **moonbeam** a ray of moonlight; **moon boot** a thickly-padded boot designed for low temperatures; **moon-bounce** the use of the moon as a reflector of (esp. UHF) radio waves from one ground station to another; **moon buggy** a vehicle designed for the use of astronauts on the moon; **moon-cake** a round cake eaten in China during the Moon Festival; **moon-clock** a clock showing the phases of the moon; **moon-curser, -cusser** (orig. *dial.*, chiefly *Hist.*) = WRECKER *n.*[1] 1; **moon-daisy** the ox-eye daisy, *Leucanthemum vulgare*; **moon-dial** a dial for showing the hours of the night by the moon; **moon-down** *N. Amer.* = *moonset* below; **moon-face** a round, full face; *spec.* in *Med.*, a rounded swollen face associated with certain hormonal imbalances, e.g. an excess of glucocorticoids; **moon-faced** *a.* having a moon-face; **Moon Festival** a mid-autumn festival in China and Hong Kong; **moonfish** any of various pale or silver-coloured marine fishes with round, usu. thin bodies, *esp.* (*a*) the opah; (*b*) a sunfish, *Mola mola*; (*c*) any of several N. American carangids, as the lookdown, *Selene vomer*; (*d*) an Indo-Pacific fish, *Monodactylus argenteus*; **moon flask** *Antiq.* a Chinese circular ceramic bottle with a flattened body; **moon-flower** any of several tropical plants with white flowers fragrant at night; esp. *Ipomoea alba*, of the bindweed family; **moongate** a circular Chinese gateway in a wall; **moon-madness** lunacy; **moon-man** †(*a*) a Gypsy; (*b*) an imagined dweller in the moon; (*c*) a lunar astronaut; **moon-month** a lunar month; **moon pool** a shaft through the bottom of a drill-ship or oil rig for lowering and raising equipment etc.; **moon probe** *Astronaut.* (a vehicle used for) an exploratory unmanned space flight made towards the moon; **moonquake** a tremor of the moon's surface; **moon rat** a gymnure; esp. *Echinosorex gymnurus* of Malaya, Sumatra, and Borneo, which is blackish with white markings; **moonrise** (the time of) the rising of the moon; **moon-rocket** (*a*) a rocket designed for flight to the moon; (*b*) a ride at a funfair imitating this; **moonscape** (a representation of) the surface or landscape of the moon; a wasteland resembling this; **moonseed** a N. American woody climbing plant, *Menispermum canadense* (family Menispermaceae), so called from its crescent-shaped seeds; **moonset** (the time of) the setting of the moon; **moon-shaped** *a.* shaped like the moon; *esp.* crescent-shaped; **moonshot** a launch of a spacecraft to or towards the moon; **moonstomp** *n.* & *v.* (perform) a dance characterized by heavy rhythmic stamping; **moonstruck** *a.* mentally distracted, dazed through the supposed influence of the moon; *arch.* lunatic; **moon-up** *N. Amer.* = *moonrise* above; **moonwalk** *v.* & *n.* (*a*) *v.i.* walk (as if) on the moon; (*b*) *n.* a walk (as if) on the moon; **moonwalker** a person who moonwalks; **moonwort** a dwarf fern, *Botrychium lunaria*, with sterile fronds divided into crescent-shaped segments; **moon-year** a lunar year.

moonish *a.* resembling, characteristic of, or influenced by the moon; *fig.* changeable, fickle: LME. **moonless** *a.* without a moon; not lit up by the moon: E16. **moonlike** *a.* resembling or characteristic of the moon LME.

Moon /muːn/ *n.*[2] M19. [Dr William *Moon* (1818–94), Eng. inventor.] In full *Moon('s) type.* An embossed type used in books for the blind.

Moon /muːn/ *n.*[3] E20. [Henry *Moon* (1845–92), Eng. surgeon.] Med. *Moon's (mulberry) molar, tooth,* = *mulberry molar* s.v. MULBERRY *n.*

moon /muːn/ *v.* E17. [f. MOON *n.*[1]] **I** 1 *v.t.* Expose to moonlight. *rare.* E17. 2 *v.t.* & *i.* Shine (upon) as a moon; give out (light) as a moon. *rare.* M19. 3 *v.i.* & *t.* Expose one's buttocks (*to*). *slang.* M20.

II 4 *v.i.* Move or look listlessly or aimlessly *about, along, around,* etc. *colloq.* M19. 5 *v.t.* Pass *away* (a period of time) in an aimless or listless manner. L19. b Act aimlessly or dreamily from infatuation for a person or thing (foll. by *over*); gaze adoringly *at. colloq.* E20.

4a THOMAS HUGHES I mooned up and down the High-street, staring at all the young faces. A. N. WILSON Tennyson mooned about in pubs, worried about whether there was life beyond the grave. b J. JOHNSTON I just couldn't bear . . sitting there all evening looking at you two mooning at each other. P. LIVELY Carrie's in the big greenhouse, mooning over the alpines. 5 W. C. SMITH Why had I mooned away the night?

mooner *n.* †(*a*) a kind of watchdog; (*b*) a person who idles or moons about: L16. **mooningly** *adv.* in a listless or aimless manner L19.

moonack /ˈmuːnak/ *n. US.* Now *rare* or *obs.* Also **-ax** /-aks/, **mon-** /ˈməʊn-/. M17. [Delaware *monachgeu* digger.] The woodchuck, *Marmota monax* (occas. as a semi-mythical animal of ill omen).

moon-blind /ˈmuːnblʌɪnd/ *a.* M17. [f. MOON *n.*[1] + BLIND *a.*] 1 Of a horse: suffering from moon-eye. M17. 2 Of a person: suffering night blindness, supposedly from sleeping exposed to the moon's rays. M19.

moon-blindness *n.* E18.

mooncalf /ˈmuːnkɑːf/ *n.* Pl. **-calves** /-kɑːvz/. M16. [f. MOON *n.*[1] + CALF *n.*[1], perh. after G *Mondkalb.*] 1†a A misshapen foetus; a monstrosity. M16–M19. b A person with a mental handicap; a born fool. *colloq.* E17. 2 A person who gazes at the moon or idles time away; an absent-minded person. Formerly also, a fickle person. E17. 3 An animal imagined to inhabit the moon. *rare.* E20.

mooneas /ˈmuːnjas, ˈmuːnɪas/ *n. Canad.* L19. [Cree *mooniyas.*] A newcomer, a tenderfoot; a White man, a European.

mooned /muːnd, *poet.* ˈmuːnɪd/ *a.* M16. [f. MOON *n.*[1], *v.*: see -ED[2], -ED[1].] †1 Lunatic, mad. *rare.* Only in M16. 2 Crescent-shaped; ornamented or marked with (crescent) moons. E17. 3 Accompanied or lit by the moon or moonlight. E17.

2 MILTON Th' Angelic Squadron . . sharpning in mooned hornes Thir Phalanx. 3 E. BLUNDEN Lingering along the blue stream's mooned curves.

moon-eye /ˈmuːnʌɪ/ *n.* E17. [f. MOON *n.*[1] + EYE *n.*; in sense 1 tr. late L *oculus lunaticus.*] 1 An inflammatory disease of horses causing intermittent blindness; an eye affected with this. E17. 2 Any of several freshwater fishes resembling herring, of the family Hiodontidae of eastern N. America, esp. *Hiodon tergisus.* Also, a cisco. M19.

moon-eyed /ˈmuːnʌɪd/ *a.* E17. [f. prec. + -ED[2].] 1a Of a horse: affected with moon-eye, moon-blind. E17. b Purblind; squint-eyed. *obs.* exc. *dial.* L17. †2 Having eyes adapted for seeing at night. L17–E19. 3 Drunk, intoxicated. *US slang.* M18. 4 Having round wide open eyes. L18.

moonga *n.* var. of MUGA.

Moonie /ˈmuːni/ *n. slang.* L20. [f. Sun Myung *Moon*, founder of the Unification Church in 1954 + -IE.] A member of the Unification Church.

moonjah *n.* var. of MUNJA.

moonlet /ˈmuːnlɪt/ *n.* L18. [f. MOON *n.*[1] + -LET.] 1 A half-moon of a fingernail. *rare.* L18. 2 A small moon. M19. 3 An artificial satellite. M20.

moonlight /ˈmuːnlʌɪt/ *n.* & *a.* ME. [f. MOON *n.*[1] + LIGHT *n.*] A *n.* 1 The light of the moon; this as visible at a particular time or place. ME. †2 A painting of a moonlit landscape. M–L18. 3 = MOONSHINE *n.* 3. Now *rare* or *obs.* E19. 4 An excursion or raid by moonlight; *spec.* = *moonlight flit* below (chiefly in *do a moonlight*). *colloq.* L19.

1 A. NOYES The road was a ribbon of moonlight. E. TAYLOR A misty moonlight furred the grass, like rime. DENNIS POTTER Moonlight filtering behind him made menacing shadows. **moonlight and roses** sentimentality, romance.

B *adj.* Moonlit; taking place or performed by the light of the moon. L16.

J. RULE She took me for a moonlight ride.

Special collocations & comb.: **moonlight flit, flitting** a hurried, usu. nocturnal, removal or change of abode, esp. in order to avoid paying rent. **moonlight lustre** a 19th-cent. porcelain lustre glaze with a marbled effect.

moonlight /ˈmuːnlʌɪt/ *v.i.* Pa. t. & pple **-lighted.** L19. [f. prec.] 1 Engage by night in a stealthy or illicit activity, esp. a raid. Chiefly as *moonlighting* vbl n. L19. 2 Make a moonlight flit. *colloq.* E20. 3 Do paid work, esp. at night, in addition to one's regular employment. Chiefly as *moonlighting* vbl n. Cf. SUNLIGHTING 2. *colloq.* M20.

3 A. S. DALE He began to work days at one job and moonlight at another. D. LESSING At weekends I cooked in a café, underpaid of course, it was moonlighting.

moonlighter *n.* L19.

moonlit /ˈmuːnlɪt/ *a.* M19. [f. MOON *n.*[1] + LIT *a.*] Lighted by the moon; bathed in moonlight.

moonraker /ˈmuːnreɪkə/ *n.* L18. [f. MOON *n.*[1] + RAKER *n.*[1]] 1 A native of the county of Wiltshire in SW England. *colloq.* L18. 2 *Naut.* A small square sail above the sky-sail. E19.

moonraking *n.* (*arch.*) pursuing idle thoughts M19.

moonshee *n.* var. of MUNSHI *n.*[1]

moonshine /ˈmuːnʃʌɪn/ *n.* & *v.* LME. [f. MOON *n.*[1] + SHINE *n.*] A *n.* 1 = MOONLIGHT *n.* 1. Now chiefly *poet.* & *W. Indian.* LME. b (A type of) something insubstantial or unreal (orig. in †*moonshine in the water*). Now *esp.* foolish or visionary talk, ideas, etc. LME. †2 A month. *rare* (Shakes.). Only in E17. 3 Smuggled spirit; *esp.* (*N. Amer.*) illicitly distilled liquor, esp. whiskey. L18. B *v.* 1 *v.t.* Cheat, deceive. Now *rare* or *obs.* E19. 2 *v.i.* Make liquor, esp. whiskey, illicitly. *N. Amer. colloq.* L19.

moonshiner *n.* (*a*) a smuggler; (*b*) *US* a distiller of moonshine: M19. **moonshiny** *a.* (*a*) moonlit; (*b*) of the colour of moonlight, resembling moonlight; (*c*) vain, unreal: E17.

moonsiff *n.* var. of MUNSIF.

moonstone /ˈmuːnstəʊn/ *n.* M17. [f. MOON *n.*[1] + STONE *n.*] Any of various milky, pearly, or opalescent varieties of albite and other minerals, used in jewellery; *Min.* a lustrous opalescent variety of orthoclase.

moonwards /ˈmuːnwədz/ *adv.* M19. [f. MOON *n.*[1] + -WARDS, -WARD.] Towards the moon.

Also **moonward** *adv.* L19.

moony /ˈmuːni/ *a.* L16. [f. MOON *n.*[1], *v.* + -Y[1].] 1 Of or pertaining to the moon; resembling or characteristic of the moon. L16. 2 *spec.* a Shaped like a crescent moon; lunate. Now *rare.* L16. b Shaped like a full moon; (esp. of a face) circular, round. M19. 3 Moonlit. Also, of the colour of moonlight. M17. 4 (Of a person) inclined to act in a listless or aimless manner; stupidly dreamy. M19. b Slightly drunk. *slang.* Now *rare* or *obs.* M19.

1 D. L. SAYERS Shining with a thin, moony radiance. 2a F. RAPHAEL He had large hands with moony nails. b M. GORDON I looked moony and ridiculous in the mirror. 3 YEATS Robed all in raiment moony white. C. MACKENZIE A gratefully warm and moony night. 4 STEVIE SMITH Intending to prove his thoughts were not moony With love, or any such stuff.

moonily *adv.* M19. **mooniness** *n.* L19.

moop *v.* var. of MOUP.

moor /mʊə, mɔː/ *n.*[1] [OE *mōr* = OS *mōr* marsh, (M)Du. *moer*, (M)LG *mōr* (G *Moor*), OHG *muor*, f. Gmc, perh. rel. to MERE *n.*[1]] 1 An open area of uncultivated land; *esp.* such an area covered in heather etc.; a heath. Also, an area of such land preserved for shooting. OE. 2 A marsh, a fen. Now *dial.* & *US.* ME. 3 The soil of which moorland consists; peat. *Sc.* & *dial.* L16.

1 J. GARDAM They sped across the moor among the dotted farms. D. AYERST With the 'glorious twelfth' only three days off politicians were deserting Westminster for the grouse moors. *Dartmoor, Exmoor, Otmoor,* etc.

Phrases: **the Moor** *slang* Dartmoor Prison on Dartmoor, SW England.

Comb.: **moor-band (pan)** an iron pan found in moorland or below a bog; **moor-bird** a grouse, *esp.* a red grouse; **moorburn** *Sc.* the seasonal burning of heather etc. on a moor to make way for new growth; **moor-coal** a friable variety of lignite; **moorcock** a male red grouse; (occas.) a blackcock; **moor-evil** *dial.* = *moor-sickness* below; **moorfowl** = *moor-bird* above; **moor game** (red) grouse; **moor-grass** (*a*) (more fully *purple moor-grass*) a coarse grass, *Molinia caerulea*, often dominant in moorland and heath; (*b*) *blue moor-grass*, a grass of limestone pasture esp. in northern England, *Sesleria caerulea*; **moor-hag** = *peat-hag* s.v. PEAT *n.*[1]; **moor-head** the highest part of a moor; **moor-ill** *dial.* = *moor-sickness* below; **moorlog** peat, esp. as dredged from the North Sea; **moorman** *n.*[1] (*a*) an official who has charge of a moor; (*b*) a person who lives on a moor; **moor-palm(s)** *dial.* (*a*) the catkins of any of several moorland willows, esp. *Salix repens*; (*b*) the flowering spikelets of cotton-grass, *Eriophorum vaginatum*; **moor-pan** = *moor-band* (*pan*) above; **moor-sick** *a.* (*dial.*) affected with moor-sickness; **moor-sickness** *dial.* [perh. alt. of ON compound f. *moðr* exhausted: cf. Norn *mu, mø*] a wasting disease of sheep and cattle, *esp.* liver fluke; **moorsman** a person who lives on moors; a person familiar with moors; **moorstone** (a slab or piece of) a coarse granite found esp. in Cornwall.

Moor /mʊə, mɔː/ *n.*[2] LME. [OFr. *More* (mod. *Maure*) f. L *Maurus* (med.L *Morus*) f. Gk *Mauros.*] 1 Orig. (now *Hist.*), a native or inhabitant of Mauretania, a region of N. Africa corresponding to parts of present-day Morocco and Algeria. Later, a member of a Muslim people of mixed Berber and Arab descent inhabiting NW Africa, esp. present-day Mauritania, who in the 8th cent. conquered Spain. Formerly also *gen.*, a Black person (cf. BLACKAMOOR). LME. 2 A Muslim; *spec.* an Indian or Ceylonese (Sri Lankan) Muslim. Now *arch. rare.* L16.

Comb.: **Moor macaque** a brownish-black macaque, *Macaca maurus*, of Sulawesi; **Moorman** *n.*[2] (now *arch. rare*) = sense 2 above; †**Moor's-head** (*a*) a horse's head of a darker colour than its body; (*b*) (a heraldic representation of) the head of a Moor; (*c*) a type of vessel lid used in distilling.

Mooress *n.* (now *arch. rare*) a female Moor E17.

moor /mʊə, mɔː/ *v.* & *n.*[3] L15. [Prob. f. (M)LG *mōren*; cf. OE *mǣrels, mārels* mooring-rope, MDu. vbs *māren, mēren, moeren* (Du. *meren*).] A *v.* 1 *v.t.* Secure (a ship, buoy, etc.) in a particular place with a cable or rope fastened to the shore or to an anchor. L15. 2 *v.i.* & *refl.* Secure one's ship etc. in a particular place; anchor. Also foll. by *up.* E17. 3 *v.i.* Of a ship: be made secure in a particular place. L17.

1 P. V. WHITE Judd . . had moored the raft to a tree on the opposite bank. 2 G. ANSON We carried our hawsers . . in order to moor ourselves nearer in shore. A. WEST We slid up the bank and moored for our picnic under a huge alder. 3 J. H. BENNET A . . quay, that enables small vessels to moor close to land.

B *n.* An act of mooring. M18.

moorage /ˈmʊərɪdʒ, ˈmɔː-/ *n.* M17. [f. MOOR *v.* + -AGE.] 1 The action or process of mooring a ship etc.; the condition of being moored; a place for mooring. M17. 2 Money paid for the use of moorings. L17.

Moorcroft /ˈmʊəkrɒft, ˈmɔː-/ *n.* & *a.* E20. [William *Moorcroft* (1872–1945), Eng. potter.] (Designating) a type of pottery produced in Cobridge, Staffordshire, characterized by powdered blue effects and flambé glazes.

moorhen /ˈmʊəhɛn, ˈmɔː-/ *n.* ME. [f. MOOR *n.*[1] + HEN *n.*] 1 An aquatic bird of the rail family, *Gallinula chloropus*, with chiefly brownish-black and grey plumage and a reddish bill extended into a plate on the forehead, found on or near fresh water in temperate and tropical regions (also called *waterhen*, (US) *common gallinule*). Also, any of various other rails, chiefly of the genus *Gallinula.* ME. 2 A female red grouse. ME.

mooring /ˈmʊərɪŋ, ˈmɔː-/ *n.* LME. [f. MOOR *v.* + -ING^1.] **1** The action of MOOR *v.*; an instance of this. LME. **2** A rope, anchor, etc., by or to which a ship, buoy, etc. is moored; *spec.* a set of permanent anchors and chains laid down for the mooring of a ship etc. Freq. in *pl.* M18. **3** The place in a river or harbour where a vessel can be moored. Us. in *pl.* M18.

Comb.: *mooring-mast*: see MAST *n.*^{1} 2; **mooring-post** (*a*) a post fixed into the ground for mooring a boat etc. to a landing-place; (*b*) a piece of wood in the deck of a large ship to which moorings are fastened; **mooring swivel** a swivel used to shackle two chains together in mooring.

moorish /ˈmʊərɪʃ, ˈmɔː-/ *a.*^{1} LME. [f. MOOR *n.*^{1} + -ISH^1.] †**1** Boggy, swampy; (of water) resembling that found in a bog or swamp; *fig.* spongy, soft. LME–E19. **2** Of, pertaining to, or having the characteristics of a moor; having much moorland. M16. **3** Inhabiting a moor; growing on moorland. E17.

Moorish /ˈmʊərɪʃ, ˈmɔː-/ *a.*^{2} LME. [f. MOOR *n.*^{2} + -ISH^1.] **1** Of or pertaining to the Moors; *spec.* characteristic or in the style of furniture and architecture produced by the Moors in Spain and N. Africa. LME. **2** Muslim. Now *arch. rare.* E17.

Special collocations: **Moorish gecko** a harmless gecko, *Tarentola mauritania*, of dry regions around the western Mediterranean; also called *tarentola*. **Moorish idol** a fish of the surgeon fish family, *Zanclus cornutus*, which occurs among coral reefs in the Indian and Pacific Oceans and has a deep body with black and white stripes.

moorland /ˈmʊələnd, ˈmɔː-/ *n.* & *a.* OE. [f. MOOR *n.*^{1} + LAND *n.*^{1}] **A** *n.* Orig., uncultivated land; *esp.* fenland. Now, an extensive area of heath or moor. OE. **B** *attrib.* or as *adj.* Of the nature of, pertaining to, or inhabiting moorland. M16.

Moorpark /ˈmʊəpɑːk, ˈmɔː-/ *n.* L18. [*Moor Park*, Hertfordshire, southern England, the house of Sir William Temple (1628–99), who cultivated the fruit.] A large orange-fleshed variety of apricot.

moor-pout /ˈmʊəpaʊt, ˈmɔː-/ *n.* E16. [f. MOOR *n.*^{1} + var. of POULT *n.*^{1}] A young grouse.

moorpunky /ˈmɔːpʌŋki/ *n.* M18. [Hind. *morpaṅkhī* lit. 'peacock-tailed'.] *Hist.* In the Indian subcontinent, a pleasure-boat with a shape suggestive of a peacock, formerly used on the Ganges.

†**Moors** *a.* & *n. Anglo-Ind.* M18–L19. [Perh. f. Du. †*Moorsch* (now *Moors*) MOORISH *a.*^{2}] = HINDUSTANI *n.* 1, *a.*

moory /ˈmʊəri/ *n.* Also **moree** /ˈmɔːriː/. L17. [Origin uncertain: perh. rel. to Port. *morim* shirting.] *Hist.* A kind of Indian cloth.

moory /ˈmʊəri, ˈmɔːri/ *a.* ME. [f. MOOR *n.*^{1} + -Y^1.] **1** Marshy, fenny; growing in a marsh or fen. ME. **2** = MOORISH *a.*^{1} 2. L18.

moose /muːs/ *n.*^{1} Pl. same. E17. [Abnaki *mos.*] An elk (*Alces alces*), *esp.* a N. American or Siberian elk.

Comb.: **moose berry** = (the fruit of) the moose bush; **moose-bird** *N. Amer.* the Canada jay; **moose bush** a N. American white-flowered shrub, *Viburnum alnifolium*, of the honeysuckle family; **moose fly** any of several N. American horseflies, *esp.* one of the genus *Chrysops*; **moose milk** *Canad.* (*a*) rum and milk; (*b*) home-made liquor; **moose pasture** *Canad.* land of no value; **moosewood** (*a*) striped maple, *Acer pensylvanicum*; (*b*) leatherwood, *Dirca palustris*; **moose-yard** *N. Amer.* an area in which the snow has been trodden down by moose remaining there during the winter months.

moose /muːs/ *n.*^{2} *US Mil. slang.* M20. [f. as MOUSMÉ.] A young Japanese or Korean woman; *esp.* the wife or mistress of a serviceman stationed in Japan or Korea.

moosh *ns.* see MUSH *n.*^{1}, *n.*^{4}, *n.*^{5}

moot /muːt/ *n.*^{1} Also †**mote**. [OE *mōt* f. Gmc, f. base also of MEET *v.*: cf. MDu. *moet*, (also mod.) *gemoet*, MHG *muoze* meeting, attack, ON *mót*, and MOD *n.*^{1} See also GEMOT.] **1** An assembly of people, *esp.* = GEMOT; a place where a meeting is held. Long *arch.* or *Hist.* OE. †**2** *gen.* A meeting, an encounter. OE–L15. †**3** Litigation; an action at law; a plea; accusation. OE–E17. †**4** Argument; discussion; talking. ME–L17. **5** The discussion of a hypothetical case by law students for practice; a hypothetical doubtful case that may be used for discussion; a moot court. M16.

Comb.: **moot court**: at which students argue imaginary cases for practice; **moot hall** (*a*) (*Hist.* exc. as a proper name) a council chamber; a town hall; (*b*) *Law* a hall where moot cases are discussed; **moot-hill** *Hist.*: on which people gathered for a moot.

moot /muːt/ *n.*^{2} E19. [Origin unkn. Rel. to earlier MOOTER *n.*^{2}] A piece of hard wood hooped with iron at each end, used in block-making. Also, a ring-gauge for shaping treenails cylindrically to the desired size.

moot /muːt/ *a.* M16. [f. attrib. use of MOOT *n.*^{1} (in sense 5).] **1** Open to argument; debatable, doubtful. Freq. qualifying *point*. M16. **2** *US Law.* Of a case, issue, etc.: of no practical significance or relevance; abstract, academic. M19.

1 P. G. WODEHOUSE The point was very moot, and for a moment he hesitated. G. DURRELL Whether he could have bitten us successfully . . was rather a moot point. J. UPDIKE Wright Morris's *About Fiction* tackles this moot subject with the . . resistant prose of his own fiction.

mootness *n.* (*US Law*) E20.

moot /muːt/ *v.*^{1} [OE *mōtian*, f. as MOOT *n.*^{1}] **1** †**a** *v.i.* Speak, converse; *Sc.* complain. OE–E17. **b** *v.t.* Say, utter, mention. *obs.* exc. *Sc.* LME. **2a** *v.i.* Argue, plead, discuss, dispute, esp. in a law case; *Law* debate a hypothetical case, take part in a moot. Now only as *mooting* vbl n. OE. †**b** *v.t.* Argue (a point, case, etc.). LME–E19. **3** *v.t.* Raise or bring forward for discussion. M17.

3 J. N. ISBISTER Ideas about the possibility of a Zionist state were beginning to be mooted. J. F. LEHMANN As the months went by . . the mooted job . . receded even further into improbability.

mootable *a.* M16.

moot /muːt/ *v.*^{2}*t.* *obs.* exc. *dial.* L15. [Origin unkn.] Dig up, dig up by the roots; dig out (*spec.* an otter).

moot /muːt/ *v.*^{3}*t.* M19. [f. MOOT *n.*^{2} Cf. earlier MOOTER *n.*^{2}] Shape (a treenail) to the desired size, shape by means of a moot.

mootah /ˈmuːtə/ *n. US slang.* Also **mooter**, **mota**, & other vars. M20. [Origin unkn.] Marijuana.

mooter /ˈmuːtə/ *n.*^{1} OE. [f. MOOT *v.*^{1} + -ER^1.] †**1** A speaker; a person who argues; a lawyer who argues cases in a court of justice, a pleader; a person who discusses a hypothetical legal case. OE–E19. **2** A person who raises a matter for discussion. M19.

mooter /ˈmuːtə/ *n.*^{2} M18. [Rel. to MOOT *n.*^{2}, *v.*^{3}: see -ER^1.] A person who moots treenails.

mooter *n.*^{3} var. of MOOTAH.

†**mop** *n.*^{1} ME. [Origin uncertain: perh. rel. to MOPE *n.*, *v.*] **1** A fool, a simpleton. Only in ME. **2** A baby, a toddler; a rag doll. LME–L16.

¶Survives as 1st elem. of MOPPET, MOPSY.

mop /mɒp/ *n.*^{2} Also (earlier) †**map**(**p**). L15. [Origin uncertain: perh. ult. conn. w. L *mappa* (see MAP *n.*^{1}). In branch II f. the vb.] **I 1** A long stick with a bundle of coarse yarn or cloth or a piece of foam rubber or similar absorbent material fastened to one end so as to soak up liquid easily, used in cleaning floors (also *floor-mop*) and nautically for laying on pitch; (in full *dish-mop*) a smaller form of this for washing dishes. L15. **2** A thick mass of something, esp. of or *of* hair. E19. **3** Any of various small instruments resembling a mop, as (*a*) a circular pad of cloth used in polishing silver with rouge; (*b*) a surgical instrument with a sponge at the end of a handle, for applying medicated fluids or removing purulent matter. M19.

1 B. REID A lady who was cleaning the floor with a bucket and mop. 2 R. CROMPTON Thomas's blue eyes, beneath a mop of curls. **mops and brooms** *slang* half-drunk. *Mrs Mop*: see MRS.

II 4 *mop-up*, the action or an act of mopping something up. E20. **5** A rub, wipe, or clean with a mop. L20.

Comb.: **mop-board** *US* a skirting-board; **mophead** (*a*) the head of a mop; (*b*) (a person with) a thick head of hair; **mopstick** the handle of a floor-mop; *mop-up*: see sense 4 above.

mop /mɒp/ *n.*^{3} *arch.* L16. [Rel. to MOP *v.*^{1}] A grimace, orig. *esp.* one made by a monkey. Chiefly in *mops and mows*.

†**mop** *n.*^{4} L16–M18. [Origin unkn.] A young whiting or gurnard. Also *whiting-mop*, *gurnard-mop*.

mop /mɒp/ *n.*^{5} L17. [Perh. f. a mop (MOP *n.*^{2}) carried by maidservants seeking employment.] *Eng. Hist.* An annual fair at which servants seeking to be hired assembled together. Also *mop fair*.

mop /mɒp/ *v.*^{1}*i.* *arch.* Infl. **-pp-**. M16. [Rel. to MOP *n.*^{3}] Make a grimace. Chiefly in *mop and mow*.

mop /mɒp/ *v.*^{2}*t.* Infl. **-pp-**. E18. [f. MOP *n.*^{2}] **1** Foll. by *up*: (*a*) wipe up (water etc.) with or as with a mop; absorb; (*b*) *slang* drink or eat greedily; (*c*) *colloq.* appropriate, use up, (profits, cash, etc.); (*d*) *colloq.* make an end of, slaughter, (esp. a straggler or remnant); *Mil.* complete the occupation of (a district etc.) by capturing or killing enemy forces left there. E18. **2** Rub, wipe, or clean with or as with a mop. M18. **3** Wipe (one's face, brow, etc.) to remove perspiration or tears; wipe (perspiration or tears) *from* one's face, brow, etc. M19.

1 RIDER HAGGARD As he mopped up the streaming blood with a sponge. *Royal Air Force Journal* The enemy was still fighting behind us but they would be mopped up in time. *Sun* (*Baltimore*) West Virginia communities began mopping-up operations . . after two surging creeks flooded homes. *Lean Living* He . . drifted away into the crowd mopping up a couple of Bloody Mary's as he went. *Country Living* She has mopped up surplus energy by having another son. M. BRETT The charge . . is . . 5 per cent, which will mop up the first year's income. 2 Z. TOMIN Joseph, the old barman, was mopping the table. *mop the floor with*: see FLOOR *n.* 3 E. M. FORSTER 'Oh, good!' exclaimed Mr. Beebe, mopping his brow. A. SILLITOE He mopped the tears from her eyes.

mopane /mɒˈpɑːni/ *n. S. Afr.* Also **mopani**. M19. [Bantu *mo-pane*.] A leguminous tree, *Colophospermum mopane*, of desert regions in southern Africa, bearing small green flowers and with leaves consisting of a pair of leaflets which fold together during intense heat.

Comb.: **mopane worm** a black spotted caterpillar which feeds on mopane leaves and is an item of diet.

mope /məʊp/ *n.* M16. [Perh. of Scand. origin (cf. OSw. *mopa* befool, Sw. dial. *mopa* sulk, Da. *maabe* be stupid or unconscious). In senses 2, 3 f. the vb. Cf. MOP *n.*^{1}] **1** A fool, a simpleton. M16. **2** A person who mopes. L17. **3** In *pl.* Depression of spirits. Usu. *the mopes*. E19.

mope /məʊp/ *v.* M16. [Rel. to prec.] **1** *v.i.* Be in an abstracted or stupefied state; act without conscious thought. Long *obs.* exc. *dial.* M16. **2** *v.i.* Remain in a listless, apathetic condition, without making any effort to rouse oneself; be gloomily dejected; behave sulkily. Also foll. by *about*, *around*, (advs. & preps.). L16. **3** *v.t.* Make gloomily dejected, cause to mope. Now only *refl.* and in *pass.*, = sense 2 above. E17.

2 D. WELCH The town seemed full of almost useless men moping at street corners. A. WEST I would mope about the apartment with my hands in my pockets. M. GORDON Get out into the open. Don't mope around. 3 E. GASKELL I've got quite moped and dismal.

Comb.: †**mope-eyed** *a.* short-sighted.

moped /ˈməʊpɛd/ *n.* M20. [Sw., f. 'trampcykel med *mo*tor och *ped*aler', pedal cycle with engine and pedals.] Orig., a motorized pedal cycle. Now usu., a light two-wheeled motor vehicle with a small engine, *spec.* one of not more than 50 cc.

moper /ˈməʊpə/ *n.* L19. [f. MOPE *v.* + -ER^1.] A person who mopes, = MOPE *n.* 2.

mopery /ˈməʊp(ə)ri/ *n. colloq.* E20. [f. MOPE *v.* + -ERY.] Mopish behaviour; a fit of moping.

mophrodite /ˈmɒfrədʌɪt/ *n.* Now *rare* or *obs.* E18. [Alt.] = HERMAPHRODITE *n.*

mopish /ˈməʊpɪʃ/ *a.* E17. [f. MOPE *v.* + -ISH^1.] Given to or characterized by moping; causing moping.

mopishly *adv.* M17. **mopishness** *n.* L16.

Moplah /ˈmɒplə/ *n.* L18. [Malayalam *mā-pilla*.]

Any of the Muslim inhabitants of Malabar, SW India.

mopoke /ˈməʊpəʊk/ *n. Austral.* & *NZ.* Also **morepork** /ˈmɔːpɔːk/. E19. [Imit. of the bird's call.] 1 Any of several nocturnal birds with a distinctive cry; *spec.* (*a*) = BOOBOOK; (*b*) the tawny frogmouth, *Podargus strigoides.* E19. 2 A stupid or boring person. M19.

mopper-up /mɒpərˈʌp/ *n.* E20. [f. MOP *v.*² + -ER¹ + UP *adv.*¹] Chiefly *Mil.* A person who mops up things or people; *esp.* a person who mops up an enemy area.

moppet /ˈmɒpɪt/ *n.* E17. [f. MOP *n.*¹ + -ET¹.] 1 A baby, a girl; a darling, a favourite; (freq. as an affectionate form of address). Also *contempt.* a gaily dressed or frivolous woman. E17. 2 *contempt.* A man. *arch.* E18.

moppie /ˈmɒpi/ *n. S. Afr.* M20. [Afk. f. Du. *mopje* ditty.] A street-song of the Cape Malays, usu. of a teasing nature.

moppy /ˈmɒpi/ *a.* E18. [f. MOP *n.*² + -Y¹.] Of hair, foliage, etc.: resembling a mop; thick and untidy.

mopsy /ˈmɒpsi/ *n.* L16. [f. MOP *n.*¹ + -SY.] 1 A pretty child, a darling, a sweetheart, (esp. as a form of address). Now *rare* exc. *dial.* L16. 2 A slattern, an untidy woman. L17.

mopus /ˈməʊpəs/ *n.*¹ *arch. slang.* L16. [Origin unkn.] In *pl.*, money. Formerly *sing.*, a halfpenny, a farthing.

mopus /ˈməʊpəs/ *n.*² *obs.* exc. *dial.* L17. [f. MOPE *n.*] = MOPE *n.* 1, 2.

mopy /ˈməʊpi/ *a.* E19. [f. MOPE *v.* + -Y¹.] = MOPISH.

moquette /mɒˈkɛt/ *n.* M19. [Fr., perh. f. as MOCKADO.] A heavy piled fabric used for carpets and upholstery.

mor /mɔː/ *n.* M20. [Da. = humus.] *Soil Sci.* Humus forming a discrete layer on top of the soil with little mineral soil mixed with it, characteristic of coniferous forests and generally strongly acid. Cf. MULL *n.*⁷

mora /ˈmɔːrə/ *n.*¹ Pl. **morae** /ˈmɔːriː/. M16. [L = delay.] 1 *Sc. Law.* Undue delay in the assertion of a claim etc. M16. †2 A short space of time; a delay. *rare.* M–L17. 3a A unit of metrical time equal to the duration of a short syllable. M19. b *Ling.* The minimal unit of duration of a speech sound. M20.

mora /ˈmɔːrə/ *n.*² Also **morra** /ˈmɒrə/. E18. [It., of unkn. origin.] An Italian game in which one player guesses the number of fingers being held up by another. Formerly also called *love*.

mora /ˈmɔːrə/ *n.*³ E19. [Abbrev. of Tupi *moiratinga* white tree, f. *moira* white + *tinga* tree.] A lofty leguminous tree, *Mora excelsa*, found in Guyana and Trinidad. Also *mora-tree*.

mora /ˈmɔːrə/ *n.*⁴ E19. [Hind. *morhā*, Marathi *morā*.] In the Indian subcontinent: a stool; a wicker chair.

mora /ˈmɔːrə/ *n.*⁵ M19. [Gk, f. *mor-*, *mer-* divide.] *Gk Hist.* Each of the (orig. six) divisions of which the Spartan army consisted.

moraine /məˈreɪn/ *n.* L18. [Fr. f. Savoyard It. *morena*, f. southern Fr. *mor(re)* muzzle, snout, f. Proto-Romance wd whence also MORION *n.*¹] 1 An area or bank of debris that a glacier or ice sheet has carried down and deposited; the material forming such a deposit. L18. 2 *Gardening.* A bed made largely of stones covered with fine chippings, designed to produce suitable conditions for alpine plants. E20.

1 *end moraine, lateral moraine, push moraine*, etc.

morainal *a.* morainic L19. **morainic** *a.* of, pertaining to, or of the nature of a moraine M19.

moral /ˈmɒr(ə)l/ *n.* LME. [Use as n. of MORAL *a.*, infl. also by late L *morale* neut. sing., *moralia* neut. pl., Fr. *moral*, *morale* (cf. MORALE).] 1 In *pl.* & †*sing.* Moral matters: the title of various books by classical writers, *spec.* St Gregory the Great's work on the moral exposition of the biblical Book of Job. LME. 2a The moral teaching or practical lesson of a story, event, etc. L15. b An exposition of the moral teaching or practical lesson contained in a literary work; that part of a work which applies or points the moral meaning. Now *rare.* M16. †c Import, significance. L16–M19. 3†a A symbolic figure. Only in L16. b A counterpart, a likeness. Chiefly in *the very moral of.* M18. 4 = MORALITY 4b. Long *obs.* exc. *Hist.* L16. 5 In *pl.* & †*sing.* Moral habits, conduct, or (formerly) qualities; habits of life with regard to right and wrong conduct; *spec.* sexual conduct; without qualification, good or right habits or conduct. E17. 6 In *pl.* (usu. treated as *sing.*). = MORALITY 5a. Now *rare.* M17. 7 A moral certainty. *slang* (now chiefly *Austral.*). M19. 8 = MORALE 2. Now *rare.* L19.

2a DICKENS There's a moral in everything. *Scientific American* As a general moral we conclude that war as man wages it finds no counterpart in nature. 5 A. BEVAN This may be sound economics. It could not be worse morals. *Weekly News (Cambridge)* He was concerned over the lack of morals . . among the town's young people.

moral /ˈmɒr(ə)l/ *a.* LME. [L *moralis* (rendering Gk *ēthikos* ETHIC *a.*), f. *mor-*, *mos* custom (pl. *mores* manners, morals): see -AL¹.] 1 Of or pertaining to human character or behaviour considered as good or bad; of or pertaining to the distinction between right and wrong, or good and evil, in relation to the actions, volitions, or character of responsible beings; ethical; (of knowledge, judgements, etc.) pertaining to the nature and application of this distinction. LME. b Of a feeling: arising from the contemplation of something as good or bad. M18. c Of a concept or term: involving ethical praise or blame. M19. 2 Treating of or concerned with right and wrong, or the rules of right conduct, as a subject of study. LME. 3†a Of a person, esp. a writer: enunciating moral precepts. LME–M18. b Of a literary work, a pictorial or dramatic representation, etc.: dealing with the rightness and wrongness of conduct; having the teaching of morality as a motive; conveying a moral. Formerly also, allegorical, emblematical. LME. 4 (Of a story etc.) conforming to morality, not ribald or vicious; (of persons, habits, conduct, etc.) morally good, conforming to accepted standards of conduct. LME. b *spec.* Virtuous with regard to sexual conduct. E19. 5a Of an action: subject to moral law; having the property of being right or wrong. Of rights, obligations, responsibility, etc.: founded on moral law, valid according to principles of morality. L16. b Of an agent, an agent's attributes: capable of moral action; capable of choosing between right and wrong. M18. 6 Pertaining to, affecting, or operating on the character or conduct, as distinguished from the intellectual or physical nature of human beings; *esp.* designating the incidental effect of an action or event (e.g. a victory or defeat) in producing confidence or discouragement, sympathy or hostility, etc. L16. 7 Designating probable evidence that rests on a knowledge of human nature or a person's character; designating any evidence which is merely probable and not demonstrative. Chiefly in *moral certainty* below. M17. 8 Qualifying a descriptive noun: that is such metaphorically, relative to moral character or condition. L17. 9 Of, pertaining to, or concerned with the morals of a person or a community. L18.

1 J. B. MOZLEY Eloquence, imagination, poetical talent, are no more moral goodness than riches are. G. GREENE His books . . represent a moral struggle. M. FLANAGAN It's not my habit to pass moral judgements. 2 *moral philosophy, science, theology*, etc. 3b SHAKES. *Timon* A thousand moral paintings . . That shall demonstrate these quick blows of Fortune's More pregnantly than words. 4 D. CECIL Profoundly moral in his outlook he thought that man lived to be virtuous. 5b W. PALEY The moral and accountable part of his terrestrial creation. 6 A. ALISON All the moral advantages of a victory were on the side . . of the French. D. J. WEST A paper . . seeking to prove the moral imbecility of habitual criminals. 8 GLADSTONE An undenominational system of religion, framed by or under the authority of the State, is a moral monster. A. E. STEVENSON The Bill of Rights is the moral spine of the nation. 9 M. L. KING This change in climate was created through the moral leadership of Mahatma Gandhi.

Special collocations: **moral certainty** a degree of probability so great as to admit of no reasonable doubt; a practical certainty. **moral courage** the kind of courage which enables a person to encounter odium, disapproval, or contempt rather than depart from the right course. **moral cowardice** unworthy fear of other people's disapproval or hostility. **moral fibre** = *moral courage* above (freq. in *lack of moral fibre*). *moral* INSPIRATION. **moral law** the body of requirements to which an action must conform to be right or virtuous; a particular requirement of this kind. **moral majority** (*a*) (with cap. initials) a right-wing movement in the US; (*b*) the majority of people, regarded as favouring firm moral standards. **moral play** (*obs.* exc. *Hist.*) a morality play. **moral pressure** persuasion in which a person's moral sense is appealed to. **moral psychology**: concerned with the psychological effect on behaviour of rules of conduct, esp. the sense of right and wrong. **Moral Re-Armament** (the theories or practice of) the Oxford Group Movement. **moral sciences** at Cambridge University, politics, philosophy, and economics. **moral sense** the ability to distinguish between right and wrong, esp. as a faculty of the human mind. **moral support** support or help the effect of which is psychological rather than physical. **moral turpitude** (an instance of) conduct considered depraved. **moral tutor** a tutor in a university, college, etc., appointed to have a particular concern for the moral welfare of a particular student or particular students. **moral victory** an indecisive result or an actual defeat which it is believed will produce the moral effects of an actual victory.

moral /ˈmɒr(ə)l/ *v.t.* & *i.* Infl. **-ll-**, ***-l-**. E17. [f. the n.] = MORALIZE *v.*

†**moraller** *n.* (*rare*, Shakes.) a moralizer: only in E17.

morale /məˈrɑːl/ *n.* M18. [Fr. *moral* (f. as MORAL *a.*), respelt to indicate stress. Cf. LOCALE.] 1 Morality, morals; moral teaching. Now *rare.* M18. 2 The mental and emotional attitude of a person or group with regard to confidence, hope, zeal, willingness, etc.; degree of contentment with one's lot or situation. M19.

2 E. ROOSEVELT Sight of a new uniform and . . fresh men at the front would restore their morale. Z. TOMIN She gave me a . . majestic half-smile. It boosted my morale.

Comb.: **morale-booster** an event, occurrence, or saying which raises morale.

moralise *v.* var. of MORALIZE.

moralism /ˈmɒr(ə)lɪz(ə)m/ *n.* E19. [f. MORAL *n.*, *a.* + -ISM.] 1 Fondness for moralizing; an act of moralizing. E19. 2 The practice of a natural system of morality; religion consisting of or reduced to moral practice. M19.

moralist /ˈmɒr(ə)lɪst/ *n.* E17. [f. MORAL *n.* + -IST.] 1 A person who practises morality. E17. 2 A teacher or student of morals; a moral philosopher. M17. 3 A person who lives by or teaches a natural system of ethics, independently of religion. M17.

2 *senior moralist*: see SENIOR *a.*

moraˈlistic *a.* pertaining to or characteristic of a moralist; fond of moralizing; characterized by moralism: M19. **moraˈlistically** *adv.* in a moralistic manner; by way of moral judgement: L19.

morality /məˈralɪti/ *n.* LME. [((O)Fr. *moralité* f.) late L *moralitas*, f. L *moralis*: see MORAL *a.*, -ITY.] †1 Ethical wisdom; knowledge of moral science. Only in LME. 2 In *pl.* Moral qualities or endowments. Now *rare.* LME. 3a Moral discourse or instruction, moralizing; a moral lesson or exhortation. LME. †b Moral sense or interpretation; the moral of a story, event, etc. LME–E17. 4†a A literary work or artistic representation inculcating a moral lesson; a moralizing commentary; a moral allegory. LME–M17. b A drama of a kind (popular in the 16th cent.) intended to inculcate a moral or spiritual lesson, the chief characters being personifications of abstract qualities. L18. 5a The doctrine or branch of knowledge that deals with right and wrong conduct and with duty and responsibility; moral philosophy, ethics. LME. b In *pl.* Points of ethics, moral principles or rules. E17. c A particular system of moral philosophy or moral conduct. L17. 6 The quality or fact of being moral; the degree of conformity of an idea, practice, etc., to moral law; moral goodness or rightness. L16. 7 Moral conduct;

esp. good moral conduct; behaviour conforming to moral law; moral virtue. L16.

4b HUGH WALPOLE The actors seemed like figures in a Morality. 5a SWIFT The learning of this people . . consisting only in morality, history, poetry, and mathematics. b F. NORRIS The trite moralities and ready-made aphorisms of the philanthropists. c E. A. FREEMAN The morality of the Gospel had a direct influence upon the politics of the age. C. ACHEBE He has no sense of political morality. J. GLOVER In our society . . morality derived from religious commands and prohibitions is declining, but still powerful. 6 J. S. MILL The morality of an action depends on its foreseeable consequences. J. M. MCPHERSON Opponents also questioned the expediency, morality, even the theology of the legal tender bill. 7 M. STOTT Concern for one's fellows seems to me the essence of morality.

Comb.: **morality play** = sense 4b above; **morality squad** *Canad.* a police unit dealing with infractions of legislation concerning prostitution, pornography, etc.

moralize /ˈmɒr(ə)lʌɪz/ *v.* Also **-ise**. LME. [(O)Fr. *moraliser* or med.L *moralizare*, f. late L *moralitas*: see prec., -IZE.] **1** *v.t.* Interpret morally or symbolically; explain the moral meaning of; make the subject of moral reflection. LME. †**2** *v.t.* Supply (a literary work) with a moral or a subject for moralizing; (of an incident, event, etc.) exemplify the moral of (a story, saying, etc.). L16–E18. **3** *v.t.* Give a moral quality to. L16. **4a** *v.i.* Indulge in moral reflection or talk; pass moral judgements (*on*); found a moral *on* an event etc. M17. **b** *v.t.* Change the condition or aspect of (a person or thing) by moral talk or reflection. Foll. by *into*, *out of*. E18. **5** *v.t.* Improve the morals of. M17.

1 *American Notes & Queries* Medieval . . mythographers normally moralize Narcissus as the man who wastes himself in pursuing worldly goods. 4a W. IRVING No one can moralize better after a misfortune has taken place. *Evening Times* (*Glasgow*) No attempt to moralize on a young man I have always found to be pleasant. 5 O. CHADWICK Can you moralize them and civilize them without having religion at the bottom of it?

moralizable *a.* E20. **moraliˈzation** *n.* [late L *moralizatio(n-)*] the action or an act of moralizing; moral interpretation; a moralizing commentary (*on* a text): LME. **moralizer** *n.* L16. **moralizing** *vbl n.* the action or an act of moralizing, *esp.* indulgence in moral reflection or talk LME. **moralizingly** *adv.* in a moralizing manner L18.

moralled /ˈmɒr(ə)ld/ *a.* E17. [f. MORAL *n.* + -ED[2].] Having morals (of a specified kind).

moralless /ˈmɒr(ə)l-lɪs/ *a.* L19. [f. MORAL *n.* + -LESS.] Without a moral or morals.

morally /ˈmɒr(ə)li/ *adv.* LME. [f. MORAL *a.* + -LY[2].] †**1** In a moral sense; with a moral meaning or purpose. *rare.* LME–E16. **2** In respect of moral character or conduct; from the point of view of morality or moral law; with reference to moral responsibility. LME. **3** In accordance with morality; virtuously. M16. **4** On grounds of moral evidence. M17.

2 M. SINCLAIR More than ever morally inert. D. OGILVY Morally, I find myself between the rock and the hard place. *Observer* I believe that the possession and use of nuclear weapons can be morally acceptable. 4 T. DREISER I am morally certain he uses money to get what he is after.

moralness /ˈmɒr(ə)lnɪs/ *n. rare.* M17. [f. MORAL *a.* + -NESS.] The quality or condition of being moral.

moran /ˈmɒr(ə)n/ *n.* Pl. same. L19. [Masai.] A member of the warrior group of the Masai people of E. Africa, which comprises the younger unmarried males.

morass /məˈras/ *n.* LME. [MLG *moras* & Du. *moeras* alt. (by assim. to *moer* MOOR *n.*[1]) of MDu. *maras* f. (O)Fr. *marais*: see MARISH *n.*] **1** A bog, a marsh, (now *literary*); a very wet or muddy area of ground. LME. **2** *fig.* A complicated or confused situation, place, etc., that it is difficult to escape from or make progress through. M19.

1 C. PRIEST The lane . . was an almost impassable morass of deep puddles and squelching mud. 2 M. DRABBLE She was aware of an emotional situation of unparalleled density and complexity, of some dark morass of intrigue.

Comb.: **morass-weed** *W. Indies* a hornwort, *Ceratophyllum demersum*.

¶Bef. M17 only *Sc.*

morassy *a.* of or pertaining to a morass; having the characteristics of a morass; found in a morass: L17.

Morasthite /ˈmɒrəsθʌɪt/ *n.* LME. [f. *Moresheth-Gath* (see below) + -ITE[1].] In biblical translations and allusions: a native or inhabitant of Moresheth-Gath, a town near the Philistine city of Gath.

the Morasthite: the prophet Micah.

morat /ˈmɔːrət/ *n.* E19. [med.L *moratum*, f. L *morus* mulberry: see -ATE[1].] *Hist.* A drink made of honey and flavoured with mulberries.

moration /məˈreɪʃ(ə)n/ *n. rare.* E17. [L *moratio(n-)*, f. *morat-*: see next, -ATION.] Delay, tarrying.

moratorium /mɒrəˈtɔːrɪəm/ *n.* Pl. **-iums**, **-ia** /-ɪə/. L19. [mod.L, use as n. of neut. sing. of late L *moratorius* that delays, f. *morat-* pa. ppl stem of *morari* to delay: see -ORIUM.] **1** *Law.* A legal authorization to a debtor to postpone payment for a certain time; the period of such a postponement. L19. **2** A postponement or deliberate temporary suspension of some activity etc. M20.

2 *Daily Telegraph* Could we not now have a moratorium on Dylan Thomas records? *Nature* A provision calling for a five-year moratorium on the killing of all ocean mammals.

moratory /ˈmɒrət(ə)ri/ *a.* L19. [Late L *moratorius*: see prec., -ORY[2].] *Law.* Authorizing postponement of payment; of or pertaining to postponement of payment.

moratto /məˈratəʊ/ *n.* Now *rare* or *obs.* Pl. **-os**. M18. [Ult. f. Sp.] A variety of pea. Also *moratto pea*.

Moravian /məˈreɪvɪən/ *n.*[1] & *a.*[1] M16. [f. med.L *Moravia*, f. the River *Morava*: see -AN.] **A** *n.* **1** A native or inhabitant of Moravia, a region around the River Morava, now part of the Czech Republic. M16. **2** A member or adherent of a Protestant Church holding Hussite doctrines, founded in Saxony in the early 18th cent. by emigrants from Moravia. M18. **B** *adj.* Of or pertaining to Moravia or the Moravians. E17.

Moravianism *n.* the religious system of the Moravians E19.

Moravian /məˈreɪvɪən/ *n.*[2] & *a.*[2] L16. [f. med.L *Moravia* Moray (see below) + -AN.] *Hist.* **A** *n.* A native or inhabitant of Moray in NE Scotland (in early use, one of the great divisions of the country, later, a county occupying part of the territory formerly so named). L16. **B** *adj.* Of or pertaining to Moray. L19.

moray /mɒˈreɪ, ˈmɒreɪ/ *n.* E17. [Port. *moréia* f. L MURAENA.] More fully *moray eel*. A voracious eel-like fish of the family Muraenidae, inhabiting warm-temperate and tropical coastal waters; spec. *Muraena helena*, a large eel of the Mediterranean and eastern Atlantic.

morbid /ˈmɔːbɪd/ *a.* M17. [L *morbidus*, f. *morbus* disease: see -ID[1].] **1** Of the nature of or indicative of disease; affected by disease, unhealthy. Formerly also, productive of disease. Now *rare* exc. in *morbid anatomy* below. M17. **2** Of a mental state, an idea, etc.: unwholesome, sickly; marked by exaggerated or inappropriate feelings of gloom, apprehension, or suspicion. Of a person: given to morbid feelings or fancies. M19.

1 **morbid anatomy** the anatomy of diseased organs and tissues. 2 G. GORDON Morbid lot, they're only happy when their friends have died. W. GOLDING Lewis himself had a deep, and one might think morbid, fear of dead bodies.

morbidly *adv.* E19. **morbidness** *n.* M17.

morbidezza /morbiˈdeddza, mɔːbɪˈdetsə/ *n.* E17. [It., f. *morbido* morbid, f. as prec.] **1** *Painting.* Lifelike delicacy in flesh tints. E17. **2** Delicacy, softness, esp. in musical performance; sensibility, smoothness; effeminacy, sickliness. L19.

morbidity /mɔːˈbɪdɪti/ *n.* E18. [f. MORBID + -ITY.] **1** The quality or condition of being diseased or ill; a pathological state or symptom; a morbid characteristic or idea. E18. **2** Prevalence of disease; the extent or degree of prevalence of disease in a district. L19.

1 *Independent* An important cause of both morbidity and mortality in pedal cyclists is major head injury.

morbific /mɔːˈbɪfɪk/ *a.* M17. [(Fr. *morbifique* f.) mod.L *morbificus*, f. *morbus* disease: see -FIC.] **1** Causing disease; pathogenic. M17. **2** Diseased; pertaining to or caused by disease. M17.

Also †**morbifical** *a.*: only in 17.

morbility /mɔːˈbɪlɪti/ *n.* Now *rare.* L19. [G *Morbilität*, f. L *morbus* disease: see -ILE, -ITY.] = MORBIDITY 2.

morbilli /mɔːˈbɪlʌɪ/ *n.pl.* M16. [med.L, pl. of *morbillus* pustule, spot characteristic of measles, dim. of L *morbus* disease.] *Med.* (The spots characteristic of) measles.

morbilliform /mɔːˈbɪlɪfɔːm/ *a.* L19. [f. med.L *morbillus* (see prec.) + -I- + -FORM.] *Med.* Resembling (that of) measles.

morbillivirus /mɔːˈbɪlɪˌvʌɪrəs/ *n.* M20. [f. as prec. + VIRUS.] Any of a group of paramyxoviruses including those of measles, rinderpest, and canine distemper.

morbillous /mɔːˈbɪləs/ *a.* L18. [f. med.L *morbillosus*, f. *morbillus*: see MORBILLI, -OUS.] *Med.* Of or pertaining to measles.

morbleu /mɔrblø/ *int.* M17. [Fr., alt. of *mort Dieu* god's death.] A comic oath, usu. attributed to French speakers.

morbose /ˈmɔːbəʊs/ *a.* Long *rare* or *obs.* L17. [f. as next: see -OSE[1].] Caused by or causing disease; diseased, unhealthy.

morbous /ˈmɔːbəs/ *a.* Long *rare.* LME. [f. L *morbosus*, f. *morbus* disease: see -OUS.] Causing disease; of or pertaining to disease, diseased.

morceau /mɔːˈsəʊ, *foreign* mɔrso/ *n.* Pl. **-eaux** /-əʊz, *foreign* -o/. M18. [Fr.: see MORSEL.] A short literary or musical composition.

morceau de salon /də salɔ̃/ [= of the salon] a well-known tune elaborated by variations etc.

morcellate /ˈmɔːsəleɪt/ *v.t.* L19. [f. MORCELLE(MENT + -ATE[3].] Divide into many pieces; *fig.* fragment. Chiefly as *morcellated* ppl a.

morceˈllation *n.* the action or process of morcellating something; *esp.* (*Med.*) the surgical breaking up of a tumour or other growth into small pieces: L19.

morcellement /mɔrsɛlmɑ̃/ *n.* M19. [Fr., f. *morceler* break in pieces, f. OFr. *morcel* MORSEL: see -MENT.] Division into many pieces; *spec.* (*Med.*) morcellation.

mordacious /mɔːˈdeɪʃəs/ *a.* Now *rare.* M17. [f. L *mordac-* (see MORDICANT) + -IOUS.] **1** (Of sarcasm or invective) biting, keen; characterized by or using biting sarcasm or invective. M17. †**2** Of a material substance: pungent; caustic. Only in L17. **3** Biting (with teeth or fangs); given to biting. L18.

mordacity /mɔːˈdasɪti/ *n.* E17. [Fr. *mordacité* or L *mordacitas*, f. as prec.: see -ACITY.] **1** Mordant quality. Now *esp.* mordancy. E17. **2** Propensity for biting. L17.

mordant /ˈmɔːd(ə)nt/ *n.*, *a.*, & *v.* LME. [(O)Fr. *mordant* (use as n. of) pres. ppl a. of *mordre* to bite f. Proto-Romance alt. of L *mordere*: see -ANT[1].] **A** *n.* †**1** A tag of metal, sometimes jewelled, at the end of the pendant of a girdle. LME–E16. **2** A substance enabling a dye or stain to become fixed in the fabric, tissue, etc., on which it is used, usu. applied beforehand. L18. **3** An adhesive compound for fixing gold leaf. E19. **4** A corrosive liquid used to etch the lines on a printing plate. L19.

B *adj.* **1** Of sarcasm etc.: caustic, incisive. LME. **2** Corrosive. Now *rare.* E17. **3a** Having the property of a mordant or fixative. E19. **b** Of a dye: becoming fixed on the fibre only if a mordant is applied. E20. **4** Pungent; biting. Of pain: acute, burning. M19.

1 O. SACKS His wit had always been sharp, but now became mordant.

C *v.t.* Impregnate or treat with a mordant. M19.

mordancy *n.* the quality of being biting in speech; sarcastic force; incisiveness: M17. **mordantly** *adv.* (*a*) bitingly, sarcastically; (*b*) in the manner of a mordant: M19.

mordent /ˈmɔːd(ə)nt/ *n.* E19. [G f. It. *mordente* use as n. of vbl adj. f. *mordere* to bite f. Proto-Romance: see MORDANT.] *Mus.* An ornament consisting of the rapid alternation of the note written with the one immediately below it. Also = PRALLTRILLER.

†**mordexim** *n. Anglo-Ind.* Also **-in** & other vars. L16–E19. [Port. f. Marathi *modachī*.] Cholera.

mordicant /ˈmɔːdɪk(ə)nt/ *a.* LME. [Late L *mordicant-* pres. ppl stem of *mordicare* bite, gripe, f. L *mordac-*, *mordax* biting, abrasive, f. *mordere* to bite: see -ANT[1].] Corrosive, biting, sharp.

mordication /mɔːdɪˈkeɪʃ(ə)n/ *n.* Now *rare.* LME. [((OFr. f.) late L *mordicatio(n-)*, f. *mordicat-* pa. ppl stem of *mordicare*: see prec., -ATION.] 1 A biting, burning, or pricking sensation. LME. †2 Corrosiveness. Only in LME.

mordida /morˈdida/ *n.* M20. [Central Amer. & Mex. Sp.] In Mexico and Central America: a bribe, an illegal exaction.

mordoré /mɔrdɔre/ *n.* L18. [Fr., f. as MOOR *n.*[2] + DORÉ.] A colour between brown and red; russet.

Mordvin /ˈmɔːdvɪn/ *n.* Pl. **-vins**, **-va** /-və/, same. M18. [Russ.] 1 A member of a people of Finnish descent inhabiting the region of the middle Volga, in western Russia; a native or inhabitant of the Russian republic of Mordvin. M18. 2 The Finno-Ugric language of this people. L19.

Mordˈvinian *a.* & *n.* (*a*) *adj.* of or pertaining to the Mordvins; (*b*) *n.* = MORDVIN: L19.

more /mɔː/ *n.*[1] *obs.* exc. *dial.* [OE *more*, *moru* = OS *morha*, MLG *more*, OHG *mor(a)ha* (MHG *mor(h)e*, *mörhe*, G *Möhre*), f. Gmc.] 1 The root of a tree or plant; the fibrous roots of a tap root; a tree stump. OE. †b A plant. *poet. rare* (Spenser). Only in L16. †2 *fig.* Origin, source. Only in ME.

more /ˈmɔːreɪ/ *n.*[2] E17. [L, abl. of *mos*: see MORES.] Fashion, custom: only in L advb. phrs.

more hispanico /hɪˈspanɪkəʊ/ in accordance with Spanish custom. ***more majorum*** /məˈdʒɔːrəm/ [genit. pl. of *majores* ancestors] in traditional manner. ***more meo*** /ˈmeɪəʊ/ in my own fashion. ***more suo*** /ˈsuːəʊ/ in his own fashion.

more /mɔː/ *a.* (in mod. usage also classed as a *determiner*), *n.*[3], *adv.*, & *prep.* [OE *māra* (fem., neut. *māre*) = OFris. *māra*, OS *mēro* (MDu. *mēre*, mod.Du. *meer*, *meerder*), OHG *mēro* (G *mehr*, with compar. suff. *mehrere* several), ON *meire*, Goth. *maiza*, f. Gmc deriv. of base of MO *adv.*, *n.*[3], & *a.* Serving as compar. of MANY, MUCH. Cf. also MOST.] A *adj.* 1a Greater in size, larger; (of a person or animal) taller, bigger; greater in number, quantity, or amount. Long only in *the more part.* Now *arch. rare.* OE. b With ns. of quality, condition, action, etc.: greater in degree or extent. *obs.* exc. as passing into sense 2 and in (*the*) *more's the pity.* OE. †c *spec.* Designating the greater or superior of two things, places, etc., of the same name. Also, designating the elder of two siblings. ME–L16. †d Greater in power, authority, or importance. Only in ME. e Qualifying the designation of a person: entitled to the designation in a greater degree. Long *obs.* exc. in *the more fool you* (*he* etc.) (passing into adv.). LME. 2 Additional to the quantity or number specified or implied; an additional amount or number of; further. Now *rare* exc. w. preceding or implied indef. or numeral adj., & in *without more ado.* ME. 3 Existing in greater quantity, amount, or degree; a greater quantity or amount of. ME. 4 More numerous. *arch.* M16. 5 A greater number of. L16.

1b J. LOUTHIAN And, for the more Verification, I and the said Witnesses have subscribed the same. 2 T. HARDY It was too dark to arrange more flowers that night. H. H. FINLAYSON Without more ado, the men reach for their spears. G. ORWELL I have three more chapters and an epilogue to do. W. S. CHURCHILL Not to cut any more coal or make any more steel. B. NICHOLS No more wine, George, thank you. 3 B. JOWETT Ten is two more than eight. *Bookman* Had he but shown a little more firmness. 4 RV *2 Kings* 6:16 They that be with us are more than they that be with them. 5 G. GREENE For more years than he could remember he had kept a record. G. GORDON He had more teeth filled than she had.

B *n.* 1a Something that is more; a greater quantity, amount, proportion, or degree. (Foll. by *of.*) OE. b As compl.: something of greater importance or significance. OE. †2 Ancestors, elders; people of high rank. ME–E17. 3 An additional quantity, amount, or number; something else in addition to what is specified. Chiefly w. preceding or implied indef. or numeral adj. ME. b The 'something more' that has been mentioned or implied in the context. *rhet.* & *poet.* L16. 4 *pl.* A greater number *of* the class specified; a greater number of people. E17.

1a MILTON Where more is meant than meets the ear. J. TYNDALL The more I saw of my guide the more I liked him. I. MCEWAN You know more about it than I do. b LD MACAULAY Honour and shame were scarcely more to him than light and darkness to the blind. 2 SHAKES. *Macb.* Both more and less have given him the revolt. 3 J. RUSKIN Of this, however, more in another place. V. PALMER Heard any more about that thousand? G. LYALL They'll want to know more. b M. ARNOLD Know, man hath all which Nature hath, but more. 4 A. WILSON I'm glad they've come in. The more the merrier.

C *adv.* 1 In addition; in repetition or continuance of what has taken place; again, longer; besides, (now only after a designation of quantity or number). OE. 2 In a greater degree, to a greater extent; *spec.* modifying an adj. or adv. to form the compar. (the normal mode of forming the compar. of adjs. & advs. with three or more syllables, and of most of those with two syllables; also (now *arch.* & *dial.*) used pleonastically bef. the compar. of an adj. or adv.). ME. 3 Being or having something specified to a greater measure or degree *than* another; more correctly said to be the one thing *than* the other. Also foll. by *of* and w. ellipsis of the *than* cl. ME. 4 Modifying a cl. Further, moreover. LME.

1 R. BRIDGES Never call me woman more. E. NESBIT There are one or two things more. B. PYM I looked forward to being alone once more. 2 TENNYSON But Paris was to me More lovelier than all the world beside. M. ARNOLD I too have wish'd, no woman more, This starting, feverish heart away. H. T. BUCKLE The fine arts are addressed more to the imagination; the sciences to the intellect. G. BORROW 'Are the Welsh . . as clannish as the Highlanders?' . . 'Yes, . . and a good deal more'. E. BLUNDEN The bronze moon was more quiet . . than the morning. R. LEHMANN I wish I saw you more. J. STEINBECK Then it was June, and the sun shone more fiercely. S. BEDFORD My brother has a system too, but yours is more interesting. P. D. JAMES She could hardly have been more wrong. A. BROOKNER The salon was more agreeable than her room would have led her to expect. 3 T. MEDWIN More dead than alive. H. T. BUCKLE The Puritans were more fanatical than superstitious. YEATS *The Shadowy Waters* . . is more of a ritual than a human story. M. AMIS They were enjoying a kiss—well, more of a snog really. 4 G. W. DASENT He was industrious, and more, he was handsome.

†D *prep.* = PLUS *prep.* M16–E18.

Phrases (of adj., n., & adv.): **and more**: used (chiefly after a statement of quantity or number) to indicate an indefinite or unspecified addition to what has been mentioned. **any more than**: excluding or denying the following cl. equally with one just mentioned. *do more harm than good*: see HARM *n.* **more and more** in an increasing degree, to an increasing extent. *more by token*: see TOKEN *a.* *more haste, less speed*: see HASTE *n.* *more like*: see LIKE *a.* etc. *more often than not*: see OFTEN *adv.* **more or less** as an estimate, approximately; in a greater or less degree; to a greater or less extent. **more so** to a greater extent (than the other specified). **more than —**: indicating that the wd so qualified is (in some obvious respect) inadequate to the intended meaning. *more than a match for*: see MATCH *n.*[1] *more than meets the eye*: see MEET *v.* *more than somewhat*: see SOMEWHAT *adv.* **neither more nor less than** exactly, precisely, (that) and nothing else. *no more*: see NO *adv.*[2] ONCE *more.* **or more**: added to approximate designations of quantity, to indicate that the actual amount is probably greater than that stated. (*the*) *more's the pity*: see PITY *n.* WHAT *is more.*

more /mɔː/ *v. obs.* exc. *dial.* ME. [f. MORE *n.*[1]] 1 *v.i.* Take root, become rooted. Chiefly *fig.* ME. †2 *v.t.* Root, implant; establish. ME–L16. 3 *v.t.* Uproot, root *up.* ME.

moree *n.* var. of MOORY *n.*

moreen /məˈriːn/ *n.* & *a.* M17. [Origin unkn. Cf. MORELLA *n.*[1], -EEN[1].] (Made of) a stout woollen or woollen and cotton material used for furnishing.

moreish /ˈmɔːrɪʃ/ *a. colloq.* Also **morish**. M18. [f. MORE *n.*[3] + -ISH[1].] Pleasant to eat, causing a desire for more.

morel /məˈrɛl/ *n.*[1] ME. [OFr. *morele*, mod. *-elle* (= med.L *morella*, *maur-*) prob. fem. of *morel* (mod. *moreau*) f. med.L *morellus*: see MORELLO.] Any of various kinds of nightshade; *spec.* = *petty morel* (a) below.

petty morel (*a*) black nightshade, *Solanum nigrum*; (*b*) *US* American spikenard, *Aralia racemosa.*

morel /məˈrɛl/ *n.*[2] E17. [App. f. Fr. †*morelle*, prob. f. med.L *morellus*: see MORELLO.] = MORELLO.

morel /məˈrɛl/ *n.*[3] Also **morille** /məˈriːj, *foreign* mɔriːj (*pl. same*)/. L17. [Fr. *morille* f. Du., rel. to OHG *morhila* (G *Morchel* fungus).] Any of various edible cup fungi of the genus *Morchella*, esp. *M. esculenta*, with a honeycombed pale brown and dark brown cap.

†**morella** *n.*[1] M17–E18. [Perh. f. MOIRE + -ELLA.] A kind of material formerly used for dresses, curtains, etc.

†**morella** *n.*[2] var. of MORELLO.

Morellian /məˈrɛlɪən/ *a.* & *n.* L19. [f. Giovanni *Morelli* (1816–91), It. art critic + -IAN.] A *adj.* Of, pertaining to, or characteristic of a method of systematic art criticism stressing the study of detail as a guide in the attribution of paintings. L19. B *n.* A follower of the Morellian method. M20.

Morellianism *n.* E20.

morello /mɒˈrɛləʊ/ *n.* Pl. **-os**. Also †**-lla**. M17. [App. f It. *morello* (fem. *-la*) blackish f. med.L *morellus*, *maur-* (of a horse) dark brown, dim. of L *Maurus* MOOR *n.*[2]: cf. MOREL *n.*[2]] A form of the sour cherry, *Prunus cerasus*, with a dark fruit; the fruit of this tree. Also *morello cherry.*

morena /mɒˈreɪnə/ *n.* M19. [Sotho.] In Lesotho (formerly Basutoland), southern Africa: (the title of) a chief; also used as a respectful form of address to any person.

moreness /ˈmɔːnɪs/ *n. rare.* LME. [f. MORE *a.* + -NESS.] 1 The condition of being or having more. LME. †2 Plurality. Only in 17.

Morenu /mɒˈreɪnuː/ *n.* M17. [Heb. *mōrēnū* lit. 'our teacher'.] (An honorific title conferred on) a rabbi or Talmudic scholar.

Moreote /ˈmɔːrɪəʊt/ *n.* & *a.* M19. [mod.Gk *Moreōtēs*, f. *Morea*, a name of the Peloponnese peninsula: see -OTE.] A *n.* A native or inhabitant of the Peloponnese peninsula, Greece. M19. B *adj.* Of or pertaining to the Moreotes. M19.

moreover /mɔːrˈəʊvə/ *adv.* Orig. as two wds. ME. [f. MORE *adv.* + OVER *adv.*] †1 More, in excess. ME–E16. 2 Besides, further. Used at the beginning of a cl., or parenthetically, to introduce a statement as additional to what has been said. Freq. preceded by *and.* ME. †3 Modifying a cl. In addition to the fact *that.* *rare* (Shakes.). Only in E17.

2 R. KIPLING There is, moreover, a written paper of the hours of the trains that go south. *Nature* One cannot communicate with the world outside; and moreover, one would inexorably be propelled towards the centre. R. WHELAN Moreover, by the time the attack was scheduled to begin . . it would be light enough to photograph.

morepork *n.* var. of MOPOKE.

mores /ˈmɔːreɪz, -riːz/ *n.pl.* L19. [L, pl. of *mos* manner, custom.] 1 The acquired customs and moral assumptions which give cohesion to a community or social group. L19. 2 *Zool.* The habits, behaviour, etc., of a group of animals of the same kind. E20.

1 G. GREER Perhaps the pop revolution . . has had a far-reaching effect on sexual *mores.*

Moresca /məˈrɛskə/ *n.* M19. [It., fem. of next. Cf. MORISCA.] An Italian folk-dance related to the English morris dance.

Moresco /məˈrɛskəʊ/ *a.* & *n.* M16. [It., f. *Moro* MOOR *n.*[2] + *-esco* -ESQUE. Cf. MORISCO.] **A** *adj.* Of or pertaining to the Moors; Moorish. M16. **B** *n.* Pl. **-o(e)s**. **1** A Moor, esp. in Spain. L16. †**2** Moorish Arabic. Only in 17. **3** = prec. E17.

Moresque /məˈrɛsk/ *a.* & *n.* LME. [Fr. f. It. *moresco*: see prec., -ESQUE.] **A** *adj.* Of painting, carving, architecture, etc.: Moorish in style or ornamental design. LME. **B** *n.* †**1** A morris dance. Only in M16. **2** (An example of) arabesque ornament. E18.

Moreton Bay /mɔːt(ə)n ˈbeɪ/ *n. phr.* M19. [See below.] Used *attrib.* to designate trees first found in the neighbourhood of Moreton Bay, Queensland, Australia.

Moreton Bay chestnut a leguminous tree, *Castanospermum australe*, with racemes of yellow flowers and large woody pods (cf. *black bean* (b) s.v. BLACK *a.*). **Moreton Bay fig** a fig tree, *Ficus macrophylla*, with large glossy leaves, often planted for shade in Australia. **Moreton Bay pine** the hoop pine, *Araucaria cunninghamii*.

†**morfound** *v.* & *n.* LME. [(O)Fr. *morfondre*, f. *morve* mucus + *fondre* melt, FOUND *v.*[2]] **A** *v.i.* & *t.* (*refl.* & in *pass.*). Of a horse or other animal: take a thorough chill, be benumbed with cold. LME–E18. **B** *n.* A disease of animals, resulting from taking cold after being too hot. E16–E18.

†**morfounder** *v.i.* & *t.* (*refl.* & in *pass.*) = MORFOUND *v.* E16–M18.

morgan /ˈmɔːg(ə)n/ *n.*[1] Now *dial.* M17. [Perh. rel. to female forename *Margaret*.] Any of several white-rayed plants of the composite family; *esp.* (*a*) stinking camomile, *Anthemis cotula*; (*b*) the ox-eye daisy, *Leucanthemum vulgare*.

Morgan /ˈmɔːg(ə)n/ *n.*[2] M19. [Justin *Morgan* (1747–98), Amer. teacher and owner of a stallion from which the breed descends.] A breed of light thickset horse developed in New England; an animal of this breed. Also *Morgan colt*, *horse*, etc.

morgan /ˈmɔːg(ə)n/ *n.*[3] E20. [T. H. *Morgan*: see MORGANISM.] *Genetics.* A unit of the effective distance on a chromosome between two linked genes, defined so that the distance in morgans between two genes is equal to the frequency of crossing over between them when they are close enough together for the effect of multiple crossing over to be negligible.

morganatic /mɔːgəˈnatɪk/ *a.* L16. [Fr. *morganatique*, G *morganatisch*, or their source med.L *morganaticus*, in *matrimonium ad morganaticam*, in which the last wd is prob. f. Gmc wd (whence G *Morgengabe*) = OE *morgengifu* (f. *morgen* MORN + base of GIVE *v.*), morning-gift, the husband's gift to the wife after consummation relieving him of further liability.] †**1** Designating a morning-gift. *rare.* Only in L16. **2** (Of a marriage) between a man (less commonly a woman) of high rank and a woman (or man) of lower rank, the spouse and children having no claim to the possessions or title of the person of higher rank; (of a spouse) married to a person of higher rank in this way. E18.

morganatically *adv.* M19.

morganise *v.* var. of MORGANIZE.

Morganism /ˈmɔːg(ə)nɪz(ə)m/ *n.* M20. [f. *Morgan* (see below) + -IST.] *Biol.* (now *Hist.*). Mendelian genetics as propounded by Thomas Hunt Morgan (1866–1945), US geneticist and zoologist, incorporating the theory of the gene now generally accepted.

Morganist *n.* a supporter or advocate of Morganism M20.

morganite /ˈmɔːg(ə)nʌɪt/ *n.* E20. [f. J. P. *Morgan* (1837–1913), US financier + -ITE[1].] *Min.* A pink transparent variety of beryl used as a gemstone.

morganize /ˈmɔːg(ə)nʌɪz/ *v.t.* *US.* Also **-ise**. M19. [f. William *Morgan* (d. 1826) of the US, who was alleged to have been murdered by Freemasons.] Assassinate secretly in order to prevent or punish disclosures.

morgay /ˈmɔːgeɪ/ *n.* L17. [Corn. *morgi*, f. *mor* sea + *ky*, *kei* dog.] A dogfish; *esp.* the lesser-spotted dogfish, *Scyliorhinus canicula*.

morgen /ˈmɔːg(ə)n/ *n.* E17. [Du. & G (see MORN), app. meaning 'the area of land that can be ploughed in a morning'.] A measure of land in the Netherlands and South Africa (and hence in parts of the US), equal to about 0.8 hectare or two acres. Also, in Norway, Denmark, and Germany, a measure of land now equal to about 0.3 hectare or two-thirds of an acre.

morgenstern /ˈmɔːg(ə)nstəːn/ *n.* M17. [G, f. *Morgen* MORN + *Stern* STAR *n.*[1]] *Hist.* A weapon consisting of a heavy ball attached either as the head of a club set with spikes or at the end of a chain. Also called *morning star*.

morgue /mɔrg/ *n.*[1] Pl. pronounced same. L16. [Fr., of unkn. origin.] A haughty demeanour; haughty superiority, pride.

P. ANDERSON The famous *morgue* and truculence of Wittgenstein, Namier or Popper, expressed their inner confidence of superiority.

¶Formerly Anglicized.

morgue /mɔːg/ *n.*[2] M19. [Fr., proper name of a Paris mortuary: prob. identical w. prec.] **1** = MORTUARY 4. M19. **2a** In a newspaper office, the collection of material assembled for the future obituaries of people still living. *colloq.* E20. **b** A repository of cuttings, photographs, and information in a newspaper office, film studio, etc. *colloq.* E20.

1 C. THUBRON The dressing room was like a morgue Exhausted bathers stretched inert under sheets.

moribund /ˈmɒrɪbʌnd/ *a.* & *n.* E18. [L *moribundus*, f. *mori* die.] **A** *adj.* **1** At the point of death; dying. E18. **2** *fig.* About to come to an end. Also, lacking inspiration, vitality, or vigour. M19.

1 J. P. HENNESSY The people they indicated as moribund did in truth die soon afterwards. 2 *Spectator* We all talk of the Turkish Empire as moribund. C. CONNOLLY A stagnant world and a moribund society.

B *absol.* as *n.* A dying person; *pl.* the dying. M19.

W. H. AUDEN We know no fuss or pain or lying Can stop the moribund from dying.

mori'bundity *n.* moribund condition M19.

moriche /mɒˈrɪtʃeɪ/ *n.* M19. [Carib *moriche*, *morichi*, *muriche* = Tupi *mburiti*.] A tall S. American palm, *Mauritia flexuosa*, used as a source of sago, fibre, and (from the sap) wine. Also *moriche palm*.

moriform /ˈmɔːrɪfɔːm/ *a.* *rare.* M19. [f. L *morum* mulberry + -I- + -FORM.] Chiefly *Med.* Having the shape or form of a mulberry.

morigerate /məˈrɪdʒ(ə)rət/ *a.* *rare.* LME. [L *morigeratus* pa. pple of *morigerari* comply with, humour, f. as MORIGEROUS: see -ATE[2].] †**1** Of a (specified) character or nature. Only in LME. **2** Compliant, obedient. M16.

morigeration /mərɪdʒəˈreɪʃ(ə)n/ *n.* Now *rare.* LME. [L *morigeratio(n-)* compliance, f. *morigerat-* pa. ppl stem of *morigerari*: see prec., -ATION.] Obedience, compliance; deference to superiors, obsequiousness.

morigerous /məˈrɪdʒ(ə)rəs/ *a.* Now *rare.* L16. [f. L *morigerus* (f. *mor-*, *mos* custom, humour + *gerere*, after *morem gerere* humour (a person)) + -OUS.] Obedient, compliant, submissive (*to*).

morille *n.* var. of MOREL *n.*[3]

morillo *n.* var. of MORRILLO.

morillon /mɒˈrɪlən/ *n.*[1] M17. [Fr. (OFr. *moreillon*), f. *mor* dark brown, whence *morel*: see MOREL *n.*[1]] A variety of vine producing early black grapes; a grape from such a vine.

morillon /mɒˈrɪlən/ *n.*[2] Now *rare* or *obs.* L17. [Fr.] A female or young goldeneye (formerly mistaken for a separate species).

morinda /məˈrɪndə/ *n.* L19. [mod.L (see below), f. L *morus* mulberry + *Indus* Indian.] Any of various small trees of the genus *Morinda*, of the madder family, native esp. to tropical Asia, with roots and bark which yield red and yellow dyes.

morindin /məˈrɪndɪn/ *n.* M19. [f. as prec. + -IN[1].] *Chem.* An orange-red glycoside pigment present in the root-bark of morindas and other plants. Cf. SOORANJEE.

morindone *n.* an orange-red anthraquinone derivative which is the aglycone of morindin M19.

moringa /məˈrɪŋgə/ *n.* M18. [mod.L (see below).] Any of various African and Asian trees of the genus *Moringa* (family Moringaceae); esp. *M. oleifera*, of NW India, the source of ben nut oil.

morion /ˈmɒrɪən/ *n.*[1] M16. [Fr. f. Sp. *morrión*, f. *morro* round object f. Proto-Romance Cf. MORAINE.] *Hist.* A kind of helmet, without beaver or visor, worn by soldiers in the 16th and 17th cents.

morion /ˈmɒrɪən/ *n.*[2] M18. [Fr. f. L *morio(n)* error for *mormorion*.] *Min.* A brown or black variety of quartz.

Moriori /mɒrɪˈɔːri/ *n.* Pl. same, **-s**. M19. [Polynesian.] A member of a now extinct Polynesian people dominant in the Chatham Islands and parts of New Zealand before their conquest by the Maoris in the early 19th cent.

Morisca /məˈrɪskə/ *n.* M20. [Sp., fem. of next. Cf. MORESCA.] A Spanish folk-dance related to the English morris dance.

Morisco /məˈrɪskəʊ/ *a.* & *n.* M16. [Sp., f. *Moro* MOOR *n.*[2] + *-isco* -ESQUE. Cf. MORESCO.] **A** *adj.* Of or pertaining to the Moors; Moorish. M16. **B** *n.* Pl. **-o(e)s**. **1** A Moor, esp. in Spain. M16. **2** Orig., a dance with Moorish elements and sharing some features with the morris dance. Now usu. = MORISCA. M16. †**b** A dancer of the Morisco. *rare* (Shakes.). Only in L16. **3** Arabesque art, ornament, etc. E18.

morish *a.* var. of MOREISH.

Morisonian /mɒrɪˈsəʊnɪən/ *n.* & *a.* M19. [f. *Morison* (see below) + -IAN.] *Chr. Ch.* **A** *n.* A follower of James Morison, Sc. minister and founder of a sect called the Evangelical Union; a member or adherent of the Evangelical Union. M19. **B** *adj.* Holding the doctrines of Morison or of the Evangelical Union. L19.

morkin /ˈmɔːkɪn/ *n.* Now *rare* or *obs.* LME. [AN *mortekine* alt. (infl. by -KIN) of OFr. *mortecine* f. late L *morticina* carrion, use as n. of neut. pl. of L *morticinus* that has died, f. *mort-*, *mors* death.] An animal killed by disease or accident.

Morlacco /mɔːˈlakəʊ/ *n.* Now *rare.* Pl. **-cchi** /-kiː/. L18. [It.: see next.] *Hist.* = MORLACH *n.*

Mor'lacchian *n.* & *a.* = MORLACH L18.

Morlach /ˈmɔːlak/ *n.* & *a.* Also †**-ck**. L18. [It. *Morlacco*, pl. *-cchi* (also Serbo-Croat *Morlak*, pl. *-laci*) f. late L *Morovlachus* f. Byzantine Gk *Mauroblaxos*, f. *mauros* black + *Blaxos* Vlach: cf. VLACH.] *Hist.* **A** *n.* A member of a Vlach people inhabiting an area formerly called Morlacchia, centred on the eastern Adriatic port of Ragusa (modern Dubrovnik), between the 12th and 15th cents. L18. **B** *adj.* Of, pertaining to, or characteristic of Morlacchia or its people. L18.

morling /ˈmɔːlɪŋ/ *n.* Now *rare.* LME. [App. formed after MORKIN by substitution of -LING[1] for -KIN.] **1** Wool taken from the skin of a dead sheep. LME. †**2** = MORKIN. M17–M18.

mormal /ˈmɔːm(ə)l/ *n.* Long *obs.* exc. *dial.* LME. [OFr. *mortmal*, f. *mort* dead + *mal* evil.] An inflamed sore, esp. on the leg.

mormaor /ˈmɔːmɛː/ *n.* Also **maormor** /ˈmɛːmɔː/. E19. [Gael. *mormaer* (mod. *mórmhaor*), f. *mòr* great + *maor* bailiff.] In ancient Scotland, a high steward of a province.

†**mormo** *n.* Pl. **-os**. E17–M18. [Gk *mormō* a hideous female monster.] A hobgoblin; an imaginary terror.

Mormon /ˈmɔːmən/ *n.* & *a.* M19. [The prophet reputed to be the author of the Book of Mormon (see below).] **A** *n.* A member or adherent of the Church of Jesus Christ of Latter-day Saints, a millenary Christian sect founded in 1830 by Joseph Smith (1805–44) who claimed to have discovered and translated by divine inspiration the 'Book of Mormon', a text accepted by Mormons as Scripture along with the Bible, relating the story of a group of Hebrews who migrated to America *c*600 BC. M19.

B *attrib.* or as *adj.* Of or pertaining to the Mormons. M19.

Mormon Bible (*a*) a translation of the Bible executed and used by the Mormons; (*b*) the Book of Mormon. **Mormon Church** the Church of Jesus Christ of Latter-day Saints. **Mormon City** Salt Lake City, Utah. **Mormon cricket** a bush-cricket, *Anabrus simplex*, of the western US which is destructive to cereal crops. **Mormon State** in the US, a State in which Mormons predominate, *spec.* Utah. **Mormon trail**: followed by Mormon migrants to Utah in 1847. **Mormon war**: *spec.* between Utah Mormons and federal troops in 1857–8.

Mormondom *n.* (*a*) the Mormons collectively; (*b*) the territory or practices of the Mormons: M19. **Mormo'ness** *n.* a female Mormon M19. **Mormonish** *a.* pertaining to or characteristic of the Mormons or their beliefs M19. **Mormonism** *n.* the doctrine and practices of the Mormons M19. **Mormonist** *n.* (*rare*) = MORMON *n.* M19. **Mormonite** *n.* & *a.* (now *rare*) = MORMON M19.

mormoopid /mɔːməʊˈɒpɪd/ *n.* & *a.* L20. [mod.L *Mormoopidae* (see below), f. Gk *mormō* MORMO + *ōps* eye, face: see -ID[3].] **A** *n.* Any small insectivorous bat of the family Mormoopidae of central and N. America, in which the nose-leaf is reduced or absent but the lips are elaborate and leaf-shaped. L20. **B** *adj.* Of, pertaining to, or designating this family. L20.

mormyrid /ˈmɔːmɪrɪd/ *n.* & *a.* L19. [mod.L *Mormyridae* (see below), f. *Mormyrus* genus name, f. Gk *mormuros*: see -ID[3].] *Zool.* **A** *n.* Any of various thick-bodied freshwater fishes of the African family Mormyridae, many of which possess an elongated snout that resembles an elephant's trunk or an electric organs; *esp.* = ELEPHANT-*snout fish*. L19. **B** *adj.* Of, pertaining to, or designating this family. M20.

mormyrus *n.* a mormyrid (now only as mod.L genus name) M18.

morn /mɔːn/ *n.* [OE *morgen*, *mor(g)n-* = OFris. *morgen*, *morn*, OS, OHG *morgan* (Du. *morgen*, G *Morgen*), f. Gmc. See also MORROW.] **1** The beginning of the day; dawn, sunrise. *poet.* OE. **b** The east. *poet.* M17. **2** The early part of the day; morning. Now chiefly *poet.* OE. **3** The following morning. Also, the day after today or the day mentioned; = MORROW 2. Now only *the morn*, tomorrow (as n. & advb.). Now *Sc.* & *north.* OE.

1 M. ARNOLD Thy high mountain platforms, Where Morn first appears. 2 L. G. GIBBON It went on from morn till night. 3 J. M. BARRIE The morn's the Sabbath.

Comb.: **morn star** (*obs.* exc. *poet.*) = MORNING STAR I.

mornless *a.* (*rare*) L18.

Mornay /ˈmɔːneɪ/ *n.* & *a.* Also **m-**. E20. [Perh. f. Philip de *Mornay* (d. 1623), French Huguenot writer.] (In full *Mornay sauce, sauce Mornay*) a rich white sauce flavoured with cheese; (designating) a dish served with this sauce.

morne /mɔːn/ *n.*[1] L15. [(O)Fr., f. *morner* blunt (a lance), f. *morne* blunted, dull, ult. f. Frank.] *Hist.* The blunted head of a tilting-lance.

morne /mɔːn/ *n.*[2] *rare.* L19. [Amer. Fr., perh. alt. of Sp. *morón*.] In the Americas: a small round hill.

morne /mɔːn/ *a. literary.* M19. [(O)Fr., f. Frank. base also of MORNE *n.*[1]] Dismal, dreary.

morné /ˈmɔːneɪ/ *a.* E18. [Fr., pa. pple of *morner* blunt: see MORNE *n.*[1]] *Her.* Of a lion rampant: having no tongue, teeth, or claws.

morning /ˈmɔːnɪŋ/ *n.* ME. [f. MORN + -ING[1], after EVENING.] **1** The process or fact of the approach of dawn; the time about sunrise. ME. **b** Daybreak; (the light of) dawn. Freq. personified. *poet.* L16. **2** The beginning or early part of the day, esp. from sunrise until noon; this time spent in a particular way or characterized by particular weather, conditions, experiences, etc. LME. **b** The part of the day extending to dinner-time. Now *obs.* exc. *Hist.* M18. **3** *fig.* The beginning or early part of anything compared to a day; the early part *of* one's life etc. L16. **4a** An alcoholic drink taken before breakfast. Chiefly *Sc.* E18. **b** A light meal taken at rising, some time before breakfast. *dial.* E19. **c** *ellipt.* = *morning paper* below. *colloq.* M20. **5** *ellipt.* As *int.* Good morning. *colloq.* L19.

1 W. CATHER He wandered about .. all night, till morning put out the fireflies and the stars. 2 W. COWPER My morning is engrossed by the garden. *Times Lit. Suppl.* A morning's browsing in a book shop. DENNIS POTTER A hint of steely night .. showed that morning was on its way. J. GARDAM The sun's well up now and I never saw such a morning. E. SEGAL One August morning .. he turned five. *Monday morning, Tuesday morning*, etc. 3 W. H. PRESCOTT A war which hung like a dark cloud on the morning of her reign. 4c *Daily Telegraph* The .. 12 mornings printed in major provincial towns and cities.

Phrases: **in a morning** *colloq.* = *of a morning* below. **in the morning** (*a*) (following a specified time) between midnight and noon, = *a.m.*; (*b*) during or in the course of the morning; (*c*) habitually in the morning; (*d*) tomorrow morning. *last morning*: see LAST *a.* **morning after** (*a*) *the morning after* (*the night before*), a morning on which a person has a hangover; (*b*) a hangover; *gen.* an unpleasant aftermath of pleasure; (*c*) *morning-after pill*, a contraceptive pill effective when taken some hours after sexual intercourse. **morning, noon, and night** incessantly, all day. **of a morning** *colloq.* habitually in the morning. *pride of the morning*: see PRIDE *n.*[1] **this morning** (during) the morning of today. **tomorrow morning** (during) the morning of tomorrow.

Attrib. & *comb.*: In the senses 'of or pertaining to morning', 'existing, taking place, etc., during the morning', '(intended to be) worn or used during the morning', 'operating, acting, or on duty during the morning', as *morning call, flight, gown, light, meal, shower, train*, etc. Special combs., as **morning coat** a coat having tails, and with the front edge sloping back from the waist down; **morning coffee**: taken at mid-morning or (occas.) at breakfast; **morning dress** a man's morning coat and striped trousers; **morning-gift** *Hist.* a gift from a husband to his wife on the morning following the consummation of their marriage; **morning glory** (*a*) any of various tropical American climbing plants belonging to the genus *Ipomoea* or related genera of the bindweed family, esp. *I. purpurea* and *I. violacea*, with large trumpet-shaped flowers which fade in the afternoon; (*b*) *US slang* a thing which fails to live up to its promise; *morning-gun*: see GUN *n.*; **morning line** a list of probable betting odds established by the bookmaker prior to a sporting event; **morning paper** a newspaper published for sale during the (early) morning; **morning prayer** (*a*) a prayer said in the morning; (*b*) the Anglican service of matins; the Roman Catholic service of lauds; **morning room** a room used as a sitting-room during the morning or early part of the day; **morning sickness** nausea occurring in the morning, esp. early in pregnancy; **morning tea**: taken before rising or at mid-morning; **morningtide** (now *poet.*) the morning, the early part of the day; **morning watch** † (*a*) the last of the three or four watches into which the night was divided by the Jews and Romans; (*b*) *Naut.* (the person or people keeping) the watch between 4 and 8 a.m.

morningless *a.* (*poet.*, *rare*) M19. **morningly** *adv.* (*rare*) in the morning; every morning: M16.

mornings /ˈmɔːnɪŋz/ *adv.* Now *colloq.* & *US.* E17. [Pl. of prec.: cf. EVENINGS (earlier uses of -S[3] being identified w. -S[1]).] In the morning, every morning.

morning star /ˈmɔːnɪŋ ˈstɑː/ *n. phr.* M16. [f. MORNING + STAR *n.*[1]] **1** A planet, esp. Venus, when visible in the east before sunrise. M16. **b** *fig.* Jesus Christ. Also, a person regarded as a precursor. M16. **2** *Hist.* = MORGENSTERN. L17.

Moro /ˈmɔːrəʊ/ *n.* Pl. **-os**. L19. [Sp. = MOOR *n.*[2]] A Muslim of the Philippines.

Moroccan /məˈrɒk(ə)n/ *a.* & *n.* E18. [f. next + -AN.] **A** *adj.* Of or pertaining to Morocco, a country in NW Africa with coastlines on the Mediterranean Sea and Atlantic Ocean. E18. **B** *n.* A native or inhabitant of Morocco. M19.

morocco /məˈrɒkəʊ/ *n.* & *a.* Also (the usual sp. in sense B.1) **M-**. M17. [It. *Marocco* Morocco, corresp. to Sp. *Marruecos*, Fr. *Maroc*, f. Arab. var. of *Marrākeš* Marrakesh. Cf. MAROQUIN.] **A** *n.* Pl. **-os**. Fine flexible leather made (orig. in Morocco) from goatskin tanned with sumac, used esp. in bookbinding and shoemaking; leather imitating this, made from sheepskin, lambskin, etc.; a variety or example of such leather. M17.

French morocco: see FRENCH *a.* *Levant morocco*: see LEVANT *a.*[2] I. *Niger morocco*: see NIGER *n.*[2] I. *Persian morocco*: see PERSIAN *a.* *red morocco*: see RED *a.*

B *attrib.* or as *adj.* **1** Of, pertaining to, or originating in Morocco; Moroccan. M17. **2** Made of morocco. E19.

1 morocco leather = sense A. above.

morology /məˈrɒlədʒi/ *n.* L16. [Gk *mōrologia*, f. *mōros* foolish: see -LOGY.] †**1** Foolish talking. L16–M17. **2** The (supposed) branch of knowledge that deals with fools and folly. *joc.* M19.

moro'logical *a.* (*joc.*) E17. **morologist** *n.* (*rare*) E18.

moron /ˈmɔːrɒn/ *n.* E20. [Gk *mōron* neut. of *mōros* foolish.] **1** *Med.* An adult with a mental age of between about eight and twelve. E20. **2** A stupid or slow-witted person; a fool. *colloq.* E20.

2 M. S. POWER It's nothing but a bloody waste of .. energy sending that damn moron to school.

mo'ronic *a.* E20. **mo'ronically** *adv.* M20. **moronism** *n.* M20. **mo'ronity** *n.* M20.

morose /məˈrəʊs/ *a.* LME. [Late L *morosus*, f. L *mor-*, *mos* manner: see MORAL *a.*, -OSE[1].] †**1** Slow, deliberate, time-consuming; painstaking, scrupulous. LME–L17. **2** (Of a person, a mood, an action) sullen, gloomy, unsocial; (of a thing, an idea, etc.) heavy, ponderous, oppressive. M16.

2 J. A. ALEXANDER Pleasures which a more morose religion would proscribe as dangerous. CONAN DOYLE The moody, morose, brooding creature. J. GALSWORTHY A silent, almost morose, inattention to each other. A. HUTSCHNECKER The need then was to rouse him out of his morose mood.

morosely *adv.* LME. **moroseness** *n.* M17. **mo'rosity** *n.* M16.

morosoph /ˈmɔːrəsɒf/ *n.* L17. [Fr. *morosophe* f. Gk *mōrosophos*, f. *mōros* foolish + *sophos* wise.] Orig., a wise fool, a jester. Now, a foolish pedant or would-be philosopher.

Also **mo'rosophist** *n.* (*rare*) E17.

morph /mɔːf/ *n.*[1] *US slang.* E20. [Abbrev.] = MORPHINE.

morph /mɔːf/ *n.*[2] M20. [f. MORPH(EME).] *Ling.* **1** = ALLOMORPH. M20. **2** A phoneme or series of phonemes forming a variant or a number of variants of a morpheme. M20.

morph /mɔːf/ *n.*[3] M20. [Gk *morphē* form.] *Biol.* A variant form of an animal or plant produced by genetic differences.

morph /mɔːf/ *v.t.* L20. [Extracted f. METAMORPHOSIS.] Alter or animate (a computerized image) by transformation of a digital representation. Chiefly as *morphing* vbl n.

-morph /mɔːf/ *suff.* [Repr. Gk *morphē* form.] Forming ns. w. the sense 'a thing having a particular form or character', as *allelomorph*, *endomorph*, *isomorph*, *polymorph*.

morphallaxis /mɔːfəˈlaksɪs/ *n.* Orig. †**morpholaxis**. L19. [f. Gk *morphē* form + *allaxis* exchange.] *Zool.* Regeneration by the transformation of existing body tissues. Opp. EPIMORPHOSIS.

morphallactic *a.* M20.

morpheme /ˈmɔːfiːm/ *n.* L19. [Fr. *morphème* f. Gk *morphē* form, after *phonème* PHONEME.] *Ling.* The smallest morphological unit of language, which cannot be analysed into smaller units. Also (now *rare*), a morphological element considered in its functional relations in a linguistic system.

Comb.: **morpheme alternant** = ALLOMORPH.

morphemic /mɔːˈfiːmɪk/ *a.* M20. [f. prec. + -IC.] *Ling.* Of or pertaining to morphemes; of the nature of a morpheme.

morphemically *adv.* M20.

morphemics /mɔːˈfiːmɪks/ *n.* M20. [f. MORPHEME + -ICS.] The branch of linguistics that deals with morphemes and word structure.

Morpheus /ˈmɔːfɪəs/ *n.* LME. [L, name of the god of dreams. See also MURPHY *n.*[1]] (The god of) dreaming or (*pop.*) sleep.

in the arms of Morpheus asleep.

Morphean *a.* (*a*) of or pertaining to Morpheus; (*b*) sleepy, drowsy: L17.

morphew /ˈmɔːfjuː/ *n.* Pl. same. Now *rare* or *obs.* LME. [med.L *morphea* (mod.L *morphoea*) f. It. *morfea*, of unkn. origin.] A blemish or scurf mark on the skin.

morphia /ˈmɔːfɪə/ *n.* E19. [f. as MORPHINE + -IA[1].] = MORPHINE.

morphic /ˈmɔːfɪk/ *a.* M19. [f. Gk *morphē* form + -IC.] *Biol.* 1 Of or pertaining to form or anatomical shape; morphological. M19. 2 Of or pertaining to animal or plant morphs. M20.

1 **morphic resonance** the (supposed) cooperative influence of similar entities (living or inanimate) in facilitating the genesis of a new entity of the same kind.

morphically *adv.* in relation to or as regards shape or form; morphologically: L19.

morphine /ˈmɔːfiːn/ *n.* E19. [f. MORPHEUS + -INE[5].] *Chem.* An alkaloid narcotic extracted from opium, used in medicine chiefly as a painkiller, and addictive on continued use.

morphinated /-fɪn-/ *a.* containing morphine L19. **morphined** *a.* (*rare*) drugged (as) with morphine L19. **morphinism** /-fɪn-/ *n.* addiction to or dependence on morphine or opium L19. **morphinist** /-fɪn-/ *n.* (now *rare*) a person addicted to morphine L19. **morphinoˈmania** *n.* = MORPHIOMANIA L19. **morphinoˈmaniac** *n.* = MORPHIOMANIAC L19.

morphiomania /mɔːfɪəˈmeɪnɪə/ *n.* L19. [f. MORPHIA + -O- + -MANIA.] Craving for morphine, morphine addiction.

morphiomaniac *n.* a person who craves morphine, a morphine addict L19.

morphism /ˈmɔːfɪz(ə)m/ *n.* M20. [f. MORPH *n.*[3] + -ISM.] *Biol.* The existence of morphs or variant forms of an animal or plant species.

-morphism /ˈmɔːfɪz(ə)m/ *suff.* [f. as MORPH *n.*[3] + -ISM.] Forming ns. w. the senses (*a*) the condition or property of having a particular form or character; (*b*) *Math.* 'a transformation or correspondence of a certain kind', as *heteromorphism, isomorphism.*

morpho /ˈmɔːfəʊ/ *n.* Pl. **-os**. M19. [mod.L (see below) f. Gk *Morphō* an epithet of Aphrodite.] Any of several large Central and S. American nymphalid butterflies of the genus *Morpho*, esp. one with iridescent blue wings. Also *morpho butterfly*.

morpho- /ˈmɔːfəʊ/ *comb. form.* [f. Gk *morphē* form or f. MORPH(EME: see -O-.] Forming ns. and adjs. w. the senses 'of or pertaining to form', 'having a particular form or character', *Ling.* 'of or pertaining to morphemes'.

morphograˈphemic *a.* (*Ling.*) of or pertaining to the written form of words M20. **morphoˈlexical** *a.* (*Ling.*) of or pertaining to lexical form M20. **morphophone** *n.* (*Ling.*) a unit representing the phonemes occurring in dialectally different pronunciations of morphemes M20. **morphoˈphonic** *a.* of or pertaining to morphophones M20. **morphoˈphonics** *n.* = MORPHOPHONOLOGY M20. **morphosynˈtactic** *a.* (*Ling.*) of or pertaining to morphosyntax M20. **morphosynˈtactically** *adv.* (*Ling.*) with regard to morphosyntax M20. **morphoˈsyntax** *n.* (*Ling.*) a branch of linguistics combining morphology and syntax and their interaction M20. **morphoˈtactic** *a.* (*Ling.*) of or pertaining to morphotactics M20. **morphoˈtactically** *adv.* (*Ling.*) with regard to morphotactics M20. **morphoˈtactics** *n.* the branch of linguistics that deals with the sequence of morphemes in a language (cf. LEXOTACTICS, PHONOTACTICS) M20.

morphodite /ˈmɔːfədʌɪt/ *n. colloq.* L19. [Abbrev. & alt.] = HERMAPHRODITE *n.*

morphoea /mɔːˈfiːə/ *n.* L19. [mod.L: see MORPHEW.] *Med.* Localized scleroderma in which the skin is replaced by connective tissue.

morphogen /ˈmɔːfədʒ(ə)n/ *n.* M20. [f. MORPHO- + -GEN.] *Biol.* A chemical agent able to cause or determine morphogenesis.

morphogenesis /mɔːfə(ʊ)ˈdʒɛnɪsɪs/ *n.* L19. [f. MORPHO- + -GENESIS.] 1 *Biol.* The origination and development of morphological characters; morphogeny. L19. 2 *Physical Geogr.* The formation of landscapes or landforms. M20.

morphogeˈnetic *a.* L19. **morphogeˈnetical** *a.* L20. **morphogeˈnetically** *adv.* as regards morphogenesis E20.

morphogenic /mɔːfə(ʊ)ˈdʒɛnɪk/ *a.* L19. [f. MORPHOGENESIS: see -GENIC.] *Biol.* Of the nature of a morphogen; morphogenetic.

morphogeny /mɔːˈfɒdʒəni/ *n.* L19. [f. MORPHO- + -GENY.] 1 *Biol.* = MORPHOGENESIS 1. L19. 2 *Physical Geogr.* = MORPHOGENESIS 2. E20.

morphographer /mɔːˈfɒgrəfə/ *n. rare.* L17. [f. MORPHO- + -GRAPHER.] †1 A person skilled in the delineation of form. Only in L17. 2 *Biol.* A morphologist. L19.

morphography /mɔːˈfɒgrəfi/ *n.* M19. [f. MORPHO- + -GRAPHY.] (The scientific description of) external form.

morphoˈgraphical *a.* L19.

†morpholaxis *n.* see MORPHALLAXIS.

morpholine /ˈmɔːfəliːn/ *n.* L19. [f. MORPHINE with insertion of -OL.] *Chem.* A cyclic amine, C_4H_9NO, which is a hygroscopic oil used as a solvent for resins and dyes and whose fatty-acid salts are emulsifying soaps used in floor polishes.

morphology /mɔːˈfɒlədʒi/ *n.* M19. [f. MORPHO- + -LOGY.] 1 *Biol.* The branch of biology that deals with the form of living organisms, and with relationships between their structures. M19. 2 *Ling.* The form (including change, formation, and inflection) of words in a language; the branch of linguistics that deals with this. M19. 3 *gen.* Shape, form, external structure or arrangement, esp. as an object of study or classification. Also, a particular form or structure. L19.

3 *social morphology*: see SOCIAL *a.*

morphoˈlogic *a.* = MORPHOLOGICAL L19. **morphoˈlogical** *a.* of, pertaining to, or derived from morphology M19. **morphoˈlogically** *adv.* M19. **morphologist** *n.* M19. **morphologiˈzation** *n.* (*Ling.*) (*a*) conversion of a phonetic or phonemic feature to a morphological one; (*b*) morphological reinterpretation of a phonological rule or process: L20. **morphologize** *v.t.* (*Ling.*) subject (a feature, rule, or process) to morphologization (usu. in *pass.*) L20.

morphomaniac /mɔːfə(ʊ)ˈmeɪnɪak/ *n.* E20. [f. MORPH(INE + -O- + -MANIAC.] = MORPHIOMANIAC.

morphometry /mɔːˈfɒmɪtri/ *n.* M19. [f. MORPHO- + -METRY.] The process of measuring the external shape and dimensions of landforms, living organisms, or other objects.

morphoˈmetric *a.* of or pertaining to morphometry or morphometrics M20. **morphoˈmetrical** *a.* = MORPHOMETRIC M19. **morphoˈmetrically** *adv.* M20. **morphoˈmetrics** *n.pl.* (*a*) (treated as *sing.*) morphometry (esp. of living organisms); (*b*) morphometric features or properties: M20.

morphon /ˈmɔːfɒn/ *n.* L19. [G, f. Gk *morphē* form + *on* being. Cf. -ON.] 1 *Biol.* A biological individual distinguished by morphological features. Now *rare* or *obs.* L19. 2 *Ling.* In stratificational grammar, = MORPHOPHONEME. M20.

morˈphonic *a.* M20.

morphoneme /ˈmɔːfəʊniːm/ *n.* M20. [Contr. f. as MORPHOPHONEME.] *Ling.* = MORPHOPHONEME.

morphoˈnemic *a.* M20.

morphonology /mɔːfəˈnɒlədʒi/ *n.* M20. [Contr. f. as MORPHOPHONOLOGY.] *Ling.* = MORPHOPHONOLOGY.

morphonoˈlogic, -ical *adjs.* M20.

morphophoneme /mɔːfə(ʊ)ˈfəʊniːm/ *n.* M20. [f. MORPHO- + PHONEME. Cf. MORPHONEME.] *Ling.* Any of the variant phonemes representing the same morpheme.

morphophoˈnemic *a.* of or pertaining to morphophonemes M20. **morphophoˈnemically** *adv.* as a morphophoneme; with regard to morphophonemics: M20. **morphophoˈnemics** *n.* = MORPHOPHONOLOGY M20.

morphophonology /ˌmɔːfəʊfəˈnɒlədʒi/ *n.* M20. [f. MORPHO- + PHONOLOGY.] *Ling.* The branch of linguistics that deals with the phonological representation of morphemes.

morphophonoˈlogical *a.* M20.

morphopoiesis /ˌmɔːfəʊpɔɪˈiːsɪs/ *n.* M20. [f. MORPHO- + POIESIS.] *Biol.* The formation of an organic structure from a limited number of subunits.

morphopoietic /-pɔɪˈɛtɪk/ *a.* assisting morphopoiesis; shape-determining: M20.

morphosis /mɔːˈfəʊsɪs/ *n.* Pl. **-phoses** /-ˈfəʊsiːz/. L17. [Gk *morphōsis* a shaping, f. *morphoun* to shape, f. *morphē* form: see -OSIS.] †1 Form, figure, configuration. Only in L17. 2 *Bot.* The manner of development of an organism, esp. as marked by structural change. M19.

morphotectonic /ˌmɔːfəʊtɛkˈtɒnɪk/ *a.* M20. [f. as next: see -IC.] *Geol.* Of or pertaining to morphotectonics.

morphotectonics /ˌmɔːfəʊtɛkˈtɒnɪks/ *n.* M20. [f. MORPHO(LOGY + TECTONICS.] *Geol.* The branch of geomorphology that deals with the tectonic origins of large topographic features of the earth's surface (as continents, mountain ranges, river basins). Also, the morphotectonic character or features of a region.

morphotropism /mɔːfə(ʊ)ˈtrəʊpɪz(ə)m/ *n.* E20. [f. as next: see -ISM.] *Cryst.* = next.

morphotropy /mɔːˈfɒtrəpi/ *n.* E20. [f. MORPHO- + -TROPY.] *Cryst.* The changes in crystal structure brought about by replacing one kind of atom or radical in a crystal by others; the branch of science that deals with these.

morphotropic /-ˈtrəʊpɪk, -ˈtrɒpɪk/ *a.* of, pertaining to, or exhibiting morphotropy L19.

morpion /ˈmɔːpɪən/ *n. rare.* L16. [Fr.] A crab-louse.

morra *n.* var. of MORA *n.*[2]

†morrice *a.*, *n.*, & *v.* var. of MORRIS *a.*[1], *n.*[2], & *v.*

morrillo /moˈriʎo, məˈriːljəʊ/ *n.* Also ***mori-***. Pl. **-os** /-ɒs, -əʊz/. M20. [Sp. = fleshy part of an animal's neck.] *Bullfighting.* The muscle at the back of a bull's neck, one of the targets for a bullfighter's lance.

morris /ˈmɒrɪs/ *n.*[1] L16. [Alt. of *merrills*: see MERRILL 1.] More fully *nine men's morris*. The game merrills.

morris /ˈmɒrɪs/ *attrib. a.*[1], *n.*[2], & *v.* Also **†morrice**. LME. [Var. of MOORISH *a.* Cf. Flem. *mooriske dans*, Du. *moors dans*.] **A** *adj.* 1 Designating (in *morris dance*) or (chiefly as below) pertaining to a traditional English dance by groups of people in fancy costume (usu. representing legendary or symbolic figures) with ribbons and bells or sticks. LME. 2 *morris-pike*, a type of pike supposed to be of Moorish origin. *obs.* exc. *Hist.* L15.

1 **morris bell** any of the (many) small metal bells attached to the clothing of a morris dancer. **morris dancer** a person who participates in morris dancing. **morris dancing** the action or practice of performing morris dances.

B *n.* 1 A morris dance. Now *rare.* E16. 2 A body of morris dancers. Now *rare.* E16.

C *v.i.* 1 Dance; *slang* be hanged. Now *rare.* E18. 2 Move away rapidly; decamp. Also foll. by *off. slang.* Now *rare.* M18.

Morris /ˈmɒrɪs/ *a.*[2] L19. [See below.] Designating a style of simple utilitarian furniture, or richly decorated fabric, wallpaper, etc., characterized by intricate patterns of birds, flowers, and leaves, designed or made by the English poet and craftsman William Morris (1834–96).

Morris chair a type of easy chair with open padded arms and an adjustable back.

Moˈrrisian *a.* of, pertaining to, or characteristic of William Morris, his principles, or his work L19. **Morrisite** *n.* an adherent or student of the utilitarian and aesthetic principles and practice of William Morris M20.

Morrison shelter /ˈmɒrɪs(ə)n ˌʃɛltə/ *n. phr.* M20. [Herbert S. *Morrison*, UK Secretary of State for Home Affairs and Home Security (1940–5) when the shelter was adopted.] *Hist.* A transportable indoor steel table-shaped air-raid shelter.

Morris tube /ˈmɒrɪs tjuːb/ *n. phr.* L19. [f. Richard *Morris* (d. 1891), Eng. inventor.] A small-bore rifle barrel that can be inserted in a large-bore rifle or shot-gun for shooting practice.

morrow /ˈmɒrəʊ/ *n.* Now *literary* & *dial.* ME. [Var. of MORN (OE *morgen*) with *-w-* as reflex of OE *-g-*.] 1 = MORNING 1, 2. Also *ellipt.* as *int.*, good morrow, good morning. *obs.* exc. *dial.* ME. 2 (Usu. w. *the.*) The following day; *the morrow* (advb.), on the following day. ME. 3 *fig.* The time immediately following a particular event. (Foll. by *of.*) L16.

1 R. S. THOMAS Twm went to bed and woke on the grey morrow. 2 B. T. WASHINGTON On the morrow I can begin a *new* day of work. 3 A. BULLOCK There was resentment, on the morrow of victory.

Comb.: **morrow-mass** (*obs.* exc. *Hist.*) the first mass of the day; **morrow-speech** (*obs.* exc. *Hist.*) a periodical assembly of a guild held on the day following a feast.

morrowless *a.* (*rare*) not subject to time; without end: L19.

morse /mɔːs/ *n.*[1] LME. [(O)Fr. *mors* f. L *morsus* bite, catch, f. *mors-* pa. ppl stem of *mordere* bite.] The clasp or fastening of a cope, freq. made of gold or silver and set with precious stones.

morse /mɔːs/ *n.*[2] Now *rare* or *obs.* L15. [Ult. f. Lappish *morša*, whence Finn. *mursu*, Russ. *morzh*.] A walrus.

Morse /mɔːs/ *n.*[3] & *v.*[1] M19. [Samuel F. B. *Morse* (1791–1872), US electrician and inventor of the recording telegraph.] *Telegr.* A *n.* 1 Used *attrib.* to designate (things pertaining to) the recording telegraph. M19. 2 In full *Morse code*. An alphabet or code, devised by Morse for use with the recording telegraph, in which the letters are represented by combinations of long and short light or sound signals. M19. B *v.i.* & *t.* Signal using Morse code. E20.

morse /mɔːs/ *v.*[2]*t.* *Sc. obs.* exc. *Hist.* M16. [Aphet. f. Fr. *amorcer* prime (a gun), prepare for (an operation).] †1 Grease (a firearm). Only in M16. 2 Prime (a gun). Chiefly as *morsing* vbl n. M16.

morsel /ˈmɔːs(ə)l/ *n.* & *v.* ME. [OFr. (mod. MORCEAU), dim. of *mors*: see MORSE *n.*[1], -EL[2].] A *n.* 1 A small piece, *esp.* one cut or broken from a mass; a fragment. ME. 2 A bite; a mouthful; a small piece of food. Now passing into sense 1. ME. 3 A choice dish, a dainty. LME. 4 A small meal; a snack. LME. 5 *fig.* A small person. *joc.* E17.

1 S. O'FAOLÁIN Sean . . dropped the . . record bit by bit into the fire, frowning as each morsel melted. 2 K. A. PORTER Frau Baumgartner took a morsel of food. 3 W. C. WILLIAMS Oranges, chocolate, and those precious morsels which his mother could not afford.

B *v.t.* Infl. **-ll-**, ***-l-**. 1 Divide into small pieces. L16. 2 Distribute (property etc.) in small quantities. Foll. by *out*. M19.

morseliˈzation *n.* (*rare*) the action or an act of morselizing something L19. **morselize** *v.t.* (*rare*) break up into small pieces L19.

Morse taper /mɔːs ˈteɪpə/ *n. phr.* Also **m-**. L19. [Prob. f. *Morse* Twist Drill Co. of Massachusetts, USA.] A taper on a shank or socket that is one of a standard series having specified dimensions and angles.

¶ *Morse* is a proprietary name in the US.

†morsure *n.* LME–E19. [(O)Fr. f. late L *morsura*, f. *mors-*: see MORSE *n.*[1], -URE.] The action or an act of biting; a bite.

mort /mɔːt/ *n.*[1] ME. [(O)Fr. f. L *mort-*, *mors* death. In sense 4 prob. f. as MORT *a.*] †1 Death, slaughter. ME–L16. 2 *Hunting.* The note sounded on a horn at the death of the deer. Chiefly in *blow a mort*. *arch.* L15. 3 A dead body, a corpse. Now *rare* or *obs.* L15. 4 The skin of a sheep or lamb that has died a natural death. Also *mort skin*. *dial.* L16.

Comb.: **mortcloth** (*arch.*, chiefly *Sc.*) (a fee paid for the use of) a funeral pall; *mort-skin*: see sense 4 above.

mort /mɔːt/ *n.*[2] L15. [Origin unkn.] A salmon in its third year.

mort /mɔːt/ *n.*[3] *dial.* L17. [Perh. f. ON *mergð* multitude, f. *margr* many, infl. by *mortal* in sense 'excessive(ly)'.] A large quantity or number, a great deal. Usu. foll. by *of*.

†mort *n.*[4] see MOT *n.*[1]

mort /mɔːt/ *a.* Long *obs.* exc. *dial.* LME. [(O)Fr. f. L *mortuus* pa. pple of *mori* die.] Dead.

mortadella /mɔːtəˈdɛlə/ *n.* Pl. **-llas**, **-lle** /-li/. E17. [It., irreg. f. L *murtatum* (sausage) seasoned with myrtle berries.] A large spiced pork sausage; Bologna sausage.

mortal /ˈmɔːt(ə)l/ *a.*, *adv.*, & *n.* LME. [OFr., Latinized var. of (O)Fr. *mortel*, or directly f. L *mortalis*, f. *mort-*, *mors* death: see -AL[1].] A *adj.* 1 Subject to death, destined to die. LME. †b Doomed to immediate death. E16–E17. 2 *transf.* Of or pertaining to humanity as subject to death; of or pertaining to material, temporal or earthly existence; associated with death. LME. 3a Causing death; fatal; *hyperbol.* very hurtful or damaging. (Foll. by *to*.) LME. b Of pain, grief, fear, etc.: intense; very serious. LME. c Pertaining to or accompanying death. LME. d Of a period of time or a region: characterized by many deaths. Now *rare* or *obs.* M17. e Destructive (*to* a thing). L17. 4 *Chr. Theol.* Of sin: entailing damnation; depriving the soul of divine grace; = DEADLY *a.* 4. Opp. *venial*. LME. 5a Of war, a battle, etc.: fought to the death. LME. b Of an enemy: relentless, implacable. LME. c (Of enmity, hatred, etc.) pursued to the death; unappeasable; having the character of such enmity. L15. 6 Conceivable, imaginable, (after *any*, *every*, *no*, etc.). Cf. EARTHLY *a.* 4. *colloq.* E17. 7 Extremely great, excessive. *colloq.* E18. 8 [ellipt. f. *mortal drunk* below] Very drunk. *colloq.* Chiefly *Sc.* & *north.* L18. 9 Long; tedious. *colloq.* E19.

1 A. MASON They were banished from the garden and . . became mortal: prey to sickness, destined to old age and death. 2 T. KEIGHTLEY The axe descending, terminated his mortal existence. **mortal mind** in Christian Science, the source in humans of all delusion and error, creating the illusion of bodily sensations, pain, and illness. *this mortal coil*: see COIL *n.*[1] 3a L. STRACHEY The Duchess of York had been attacked by a mortal disease. A. G. GARDINER I have . . seen a batsman receive a mortal blow from a ball. b A. HUTSCHNECKER An hour of mortal dread when . . I was facing a firing squad. 4 MERLE COLLINS Missing church on Sundays was a mortal sin. 5b LD MACAULAY Halifax . . was the constant and mortal enemy of French ascendency. c ADDISON A Tribe of Egoists for whom I have always had a mortal Aversion. 6 J. GARDAM He knew every mortal thing you did. 7 DICKENS I was a mortal sight younger then. 9 LYTTON And so on for 940 mortal pages.

B *adv.* Mortally; extremely, excessively. *arch.* Now *dial.* & *slang*. LME.

mortal drunk very drunk, = *dead drunk* s.v. DEAD *adv.*

C *n.* 1 A being subject to death; a human being, as contrasted with an immortal. LME. 2 *loosely*. A person. E18.

1 D. ROWE We are all fallible mortals. We all die. T. K. WOLFE God or Fate would refuse to be anticipated by a mere mortal. 2 **no mortal** nobody.

mortalism *n.* (*Chr. Theol.*) belief in the mortality of the soul M17. **†mortalist** *n.* (*Chr. Theol.*) an adherent of mortalism M17–M18. **mortalize** *v.* †(*a*) *v.i.* become mortal; (*b*) *v.t.* make mortal; consider or represent as mortal: L16.

mortality /mɔːˈtalɪti/ *n.* ME. [(O)Fr. *mortalité* f. L *mortalitas*, f. *mortalis*: see prec., -ITY.] 1 The condition of being mortal or subject to death; mortal nature or existence. ME. 2 Loss of life on a large scale; abnormal frequency of death, as by war or pestilence. LME. †b An individual's death or decease. L16–M18. c The number of deaths in a given area or period, esp. from a particular cause; the average frequency of death, the death rate, (also *mortality rate*). M17. 3 Deadliness, power to kill. Now *rare* or *obs.* LME. 4 *Chr. Theol.* The quality or fact of entailing damnation. M16.

1 T. CAPOTE A man insuring his life is not unlike . . a man signing his will; thoughts of mortality . . occur. F. WELDON She did not want to think of herself diluting down through the generations. She craved mortality. 2c S. KITZINGER The mortality for breast cancer has not been reduced in the last 40 years. *bill of mortality*: see BILL *n.*[3]

mortally /ˈmɔːt(ə)li/ *adv.* LME. [f. MORTAL *a.* + -LY[2].] 1 In such a manner or to such a degree that death or (*Chr. Theol.*) damnation ensues; so as to cause death or damnation. LME. 2 Intensely, bitterly, grievously; *colloq.* extremely, exceedingly, very. LME. 3 = HUMANLY 2. *rare*. E17.

R. DAHL Mortally wounded on the deck of his ship. O. SACKS In the last months of his life, when mortally ill. 2 R. L. STEVENSON Looking mortally sheepish. ALDOUS HUXLEY The . . young lady . . would be mortally offended. 3 J. WAINWRIGHT Faster than seemed mortally possible.

mortar /ˈmɔːtə/ *n.*[1] & *v.*[1] LOE. [Partly f. AN *morter*, (O)Fr. *mortier* f. L MORTARIUM (to which the Eng. sp. was finally assim.), partly f. LG. Cf. next.] A *n.* 1 A vessel of marble, brass, or other hard material, with a cup-shaped cavity in which ingredients for pharmacy, cookery, etc., are pounded with a pestle (cf. PESTLE *n.* 2 for its symbolic use). LOE. 2 A weight or yoke, esp. of wood, worn about the neck as an instrument of punishment. *obs.* exc. *Hist.* LME. 3 *transf.* a A cavity in which to pound or grind something. *rare*. LME. b Any of various mechanical pounding or grinding devices. M18. 4 A bowl of wax or oil with a floating wick, used esp. as a night-light. Later also, a kind of thick candle. *obs.* exc. *Hist.* LME. 5 A short piece of artillery with a large bore and trunnions on the breech, for firing missiles at high angles. Formerly also †*mortar piece*. M16. b *transf.* Any of various devices for firing a life-line, a firework, etc. M17.

1 E. RUTHERFORD Finely powdered in an agate mortar. P. MATTHIESSEN Women . . pound grain in stone mortars. 5 E. BLUNDEN A long-range trench mortar . . fired with weary iteration and accurate inaccuracy. B. ENGLAND A . . red star shell exploded in the sky. A mortar had been fired.

Comb.: **mortar-bed** (*a*) the part of a gun-carriage on which the gun rests; (*b*) the bed on which the ore is crushed in a stamp-mill; *mortar-piece*: see sense 3 above.

B *v.t.* Direct mortar fire on to; bombard with mortar bombs. E20.

A. JUDD You have been mortared . . . Your platoon is decimated.

mortar /ˈmɔːtə/ *n.*[2] & *v.*[2] ME. [AN *morter* = (O)Fr. *mortier* (see prec.) w. transference of meaning from the vessel to the substance produced in it, as already in L.] A *n.* 1 A mixture of lime or cement and sand mixed with water, used in building to bond stone and brick. Also, any of various other materials with the same use. ME. 2 Plaster etc. used to face brick, stone, wood, etc. LME.

1 *bricks and mortar*: see BRICK *n.*

B *v.t.* Fix, join, or plaster with mortar. LME.

mortarless *a.* M17. **mortary** *a.* of the nature of mortar, consisting of mortar E19.

mortarboard /ˈmɔːtəbɔːd/ *n.* M19. [f. MORTAR *n.*[2] + BOARD *n.*] 1 An academic cap of black cloth with a stiff flat square top. M19. 2 A small square board with a handle on the underside, for holding mortar in bricklaying etc.; = HAWK *n.*[2] L19.

mortarium /mɔːˈtɛːrɪəm/ *n.* Pl. **-ia** /-ɪə/. M19. [L: cf. MORTAR *n.*[1]] *Rom. Antiq.* A Roman vessel for pounding or grinding.

mort d'ancestor /mɔː ˈdansɪstə/ *n. phr.* LME. [AN *mordancestre*, *mort d'auncestre* lit. 'ancestor's death'.] *Law* (now *Hist.*). An assize brought by the rightful heir against a person who usurped an inheritance.

mortgage /ˈmɔːgɪdʒ/ *n.* & *v.* LME. [OFr., lit. 'dead pledge', f. *mort* dead + *gage* GAGE *n.*[1]] A *n.* 1 The charging of real or personal property by a debtor in favour of a creditor as security for a money debt (esp. one incurred by the purchase of the property), on the condition that the property be discharged on payment of the debt within a certain period; a deed effecting this; a debt secured by this; a loan resulting from this. LME. 2 *fig.* A pledge, a bond. LME.

1 V. S. PRITCHETT Chekhov borrowed four thousand roubles . . and got a ten-year mortgage. *What Mortgage* A mortgage is a means to . . get and keep a roof over your head. †**in mortgage** mortgaged. *puisne mortgage*: see PUISNE *a.* 3. *second mortgage*: see SECOND *a.*

Comb.: **mortgage rate** the rate of interest charged on a loan secured by mortgage; freq., a common rate of interest on such loans agreed among building societies etc.

B *v.t.* 1 Make over (property, esp. a house or land) by or through a mortgage. LME. 2 *fig.* Pledge (*to*); make liable; establish a claim to (an income etc.) in advance. Usu. in *pass.* L16.

1 R. K. NARAYAN He would get his house back from the man to whom he had mortgaged it. J. WILCOX If your house is mortgaged, the bank should have those records. 2 *Economist* The hoary argument that Canada is being mortgaged to Wall Street bankers.

mortgageable *a.* M19. **mortgaˈgee** *n.* the creditor in a mortgage, now usu. a bank or building society L16. **mortgager** *n.* = MORTGAGOR M17. **mortgagor**

/mɔːgɪˈdʒɔː/ *n.* a person who mortgages property; the debtor in a mortgage: L16.

mortice *n.* & *v.* var. of MORTISE.

mortician /mɔːˈtɪʃ(ə)n/ *n. N. Amer.* L19. [f. L *mort-*, *mors* death (cf. MORT *n.*[1]) + -ICIAN.] An undertaker; a person who arranges funerals.

mortier /mɔrtje/ *n.* Pl. pronounced same. E18. [Fr. Cf. MORTAR *n.*[2]] *Hist.* A cap formerly worn by high officials of France.

mortiferous /mɔːˈtɪf(ə)rəs/ *a.* Now *rare.* M16. [f. L *mortifer* (f. *mort-*, *mors* death) + -OUS.] Bringing or causing (physical or spiritual) death.

mortific /mɔːˈtɪfɪk/ *a. rare.* M17. [eccl.L *mortificus*, f. L *mort-*, *mors* death: see -FIC.] Deadly.

mortification /ˌmɔːtɪfɪˈkeɪʃ(ə)n/ *n.* LME. [(O)Fr. f. eccl.L *mortificatio(n-)*, f. *mortificat-* pa. ppl stem of *mortificare*: see next, -ATION.] **1** The action or practice of mortifying the flesh or its appetites. LME. **2** *Sc. Law.* The action or an act of disposing of property for religious or other charitable purposes; property given for such purposes. Cf. MORTMAIN. LME. **3** Gangrene, necrosis. LME. †**4** Deadening or destruction of vitality or activity; devitalization. LME–L18. †**5** Chemical alteration of the external form of a substance; destruction or neutralization of the activity of a chemical substance. E17–E18. **6** (A cause of) deep humiliation; severe disappointment, great vexation. M17.

1 L. CODY There's no virtue in any mortification, either of the flesh or the spirit. 3 J. G. FARRELL The dark hue of mortification had already spread over half the palm. 6 N. MONSARRAT His mortification and grief at failing in his resolve knew no bounds. N. ANNAN He had the mortification of being ordered to retire from the bench.

mortified /ˈmɔːtɪfʌɪd/ *a.* E16. [f. next + -ED[1].] That has been mortified; *spec.* (*a*) (now *rare*) subdued by self-denial, abstinence, or bodily discipline, ascetic; (*b*) gangrenous, necrotic; (*c*) deeply humiliated, wounded in the feelings.

mortifiedly *adv.* L16. **mortifiedness** *n.* M17.

mortify /ˈmɔːtɪfʌɪ/ *v.* LME. [(O)Fr. *mortifier* f. eccl.L *mortificare* kill, subdue (the flesh), f. L *mort-*, *mors* death: see -FY.] †**1** *v.t.* Deprive of life; kill. Also, make insensible. LME–L17. †**2** *v.t.* Destroy the vitality, vigour, or activity of; neutralize the effect or value of; deaden (pain); dull (colour). LME–E18. †**3** *v.t.* Chemically alter the external form of; deprive (a chemical substance) of activity. LME–E18. **4** *v.t.* Subdue, subjugate, (the body, an appetite, a passion) by self-denial, abstinence, or bodily discipline. LME. †**b** *v.i.* Practise self-mortification; be an ascetic. M16–M19. **5** *v.t. Sc. Law.* Dispose of (property) for religious or other charitable purposes. L15. †**6** *v.t.* & *i. Cookery.* Make or become tender by hanging, keeping, etc. L16–L18. **7** *v.i.* Become gangrenous or necrotic. L16. **8** *v.t.* Cause to feel deeply humiliated; wound the feelings of. L17.

4 G. SANTAYANA The suffering may be a means of mortifying and outgrowing your sins. 7 E. BOWEN A scratch . . in Henry's arm had mortified. 8 P. ROSE It mortified Effie that her husband left her constantly alone.

mortifier *n.* E17. **mortifying** *a.* that mortifies someone or something; involving or practising mortification; deeply humiliating or hurtful: L16. **mortifyingly** *adv.* M18.

mortise /ˈmɔːtɪs/ *n.* & *v.* Also **-ice.** LME. [OFr. *mortoise* (mod. *mortaise*) = Sp. *mortaja*, perh. f. Arab. *murtaj* locked, place of locking.] **A** *n.* A cavity or recess in a framework into which the end of some other part is fitted to form a joint; *spec.* in *Carpentry*, a (usu. rectangular) recess cut in the surface of a piece of timber etc. to receive a tenon. Also, a groove or slot in or through which to put a rope, an adjustable pin, etc. LME.

mortise and tenon, tenon and mortise a joint composed of a mortise and a tenon; the method of joining pieces of wood etc. with a mortise and a tenon.

Comb.: **mortise lock** a lock recessed into a mortise in the frame of a door, a window, etc.

B *v.t.* **1** Fasten, fix, or join securely; *spec.* in *Carpentry*, join with a mortise and tenon; fasten *into* or *to* by means of mortise and tenon. LME. **2** Cut a mortise in; cut *through* with a mortise. E17.

mortiser *n.* a machine for cutting mortises L19.

Mortlake /ˈmɔːtleɪk/ *n.* In sense 2 **m-**. L17. [A town in Surrey, England.] **1** Used *attrib.* to designate a kind of tapestry woven at Mortlake in the first half of the 17th cent. L17. **2** *Physical Geogr.* An oxbow lake. Now *rare.* E20.

mortmain /ˈmɔːtmeɪn/ *n.* LME. [AN & OFr. *mortemain* f. med.L *mortua manus* dead hand, f. fem. of L *mortuus* dead + *manus* hand, prob. w. allus. to impers. ownership.] *Law* (now *Hist.*). **1** The condition of lands or tenements held inalienably by an ecclesiastical or other corporation; lands or tenements so held. LME. †**2** A licence of mortmain, conveying the monarch's permission to vest property in a corporation. M16–M17.

1 *fig.*: G. GREENE Catholics are always said to be freed in the confessional from the mortmain of the past.

Comb.: **mortmain act** any of several acts imposing restrictions on the devising of property to charitable use, *esp.* that of 1736.

Morton /ˈmɔːt(ə)n/ *n.* L19. [T. G. *Morton* (1835–1903), US surgeon.] *Med.* Used in *possess.* to designate a painful condition of the foot caused by compression of a plantar nerve by a metatarsal.

Morton's foot, toe.

Morton's fork /mɔːt(ə)nz ˈfɔːk/ *n. phr.* L19. [John *Morton* (*c*1420–1500), Archbishop of Canterbury and minister of Henry VII.] The argument (used by Morton to extract loans) that the obviously rich must have money and the frugal must have savings; *transf.* a situation in which there are two choices or alternatives whose consequences are equally unpleasant.

†**mortrel** *n.* LME–M18. [OFr. *morterel*, *-uel.*] A kind of soup.

mortuary /ˈmɔːtjʊəri, -tʃʊ-/ *n.* & *a.* LME. [As n., f. AN *mortuarie* f. med.L *mortuarium* neut. sing. of L *mortuarius* (whence the Eng. adj.: cf. Fr. *mortuaire*), f. *mortuus* dead: see -ARY[1].] **A** *n.* **1** *Hist.* A customary gift formerly claimed by the incumbent of a parish from the estate of a deceased parishioner. LME. †**b** A fine payable to any of certain ecclesiastical dignitaries on the death of a priest within his jurisdiction. L16–L18. †**2** A funeral. LME–E17. †**3** A burial place, a sepulchre. Only in M17. **4** A place where dead bodies are kept for a time, either for purposes of examination or pending burial or cremation. M19.

4 *Shetland Times* Helicopters began lifting the bodies . . taking them ashore to the improvised mortuary.

B *adj.* **1** Of or pertaining to the burial or cremation of the dead. L15. **2** Of, pertaining to, or depending on death; relating to or reminiscent of death. M16.

1 D. MADDEN They trundled the solid lozenge of pale wood into the hospital's chilly mortuary chapel. 2 W. GOLDING The craft of the Egyptologist is too often mortuary . . and I think that mummies are . . disgusting.

morucho /moˈrutʃo/ *n.* Pl. **-os** /-ɔs/. M20. [Sp.] A half-breed bull reared in Spain.

morula /ˈmɔːr(j)ʊlə/ *n.*[1] Pl. **-lae** /-liː/. M19. [mod.L, dim. of *morum* mulberry.] **1** *Med.* A segmented growth such as occurs in yaws; a disease characterized by such growths. Now *rare* or *obs.* M19. **2** *Biol.* A solid cluster of cells formed by repeated division of a fertilized ovum, prior to its development into a blastula. L19.

morula *n.*[2] var. of MARULA.

morwong /ˈmɔːwɒŋ/ *n.* L19. [Prob. f. Aborig.] Any of several marine food fishes of the family Cheilodactylidae and esp. the genus *Nemadactylus*, found off the Australian coast and distinguished by elongated rays in the pectoral fin.

mosaic /məʊˈzeɪɪk/ *n.* & *a.*[1] LME. [OFr. *mosaicq*, *mu-* (mod. *mosaïque*) f. It. *mosaico*, †*mu-* f. med.L *mosaicus*, *mu-*, obscurely f. late Gk *mouseion*, *-sion* (see MUSEUM), whence late L (*opus*) *museum* and *musivum* (see MUSIVE).] **A** *n.* **1** The process of producing pictures or decorative patterns by cementing together small pieces of stone, glass, or other (usu. hard) material of various colours; pictures or patterns, or a constructive or decorative material, produced in this way. LME. **b** A piece of mosaic; a design in mosaic. L17. **2** *transf.* & *fig.* Something resembling mosaic or a mosaic in its diversity of composition; *spec.* a mosaic map or photograph. M17. **3** *Biol.* An individual (commonly an animal) composed of cells of two genetically different types. E20. **4** An array of small photo-emissive metal plates forming the target plate in a television camera tube; an array of piezoelectric transducers in an ultrasonic detector. E20. **5** Mosaic disease of plants. M20.

1 K. CLARK The floors were of mosaic with figures, like a Roman pavement. S. KITZINGER We shall be able, as if piecing together fragments of mosaic, to learn more and more. **b** J. HENNESSY The expenditure of £60,000 on a mosaic outside the council offices. 2 W. HOGARTH The pine-apple, which nature has . . distinguished by bestowing . . rich mosaic upon it. *Listener* Janacek . . building his structures from a mosaic of ideas. M. GEE Living like animals, the floor . . a mosaic of bottles and coke-cans and girly magazines. 5 *rugose mosaic*: see RUGOSE I.

B *adj.* **1** Pertaining to mosaic as a form of art; produced in mosaic: L16. **b** *transf.* & *fig.* Diverse in composition or appearance; resembling the colours or patterns of mosaic. M17. **2** *Embryol.* Of, pertaining to, or characterized by a mode of development in which regions in an embryo are predetermined by the corresponding regions in that embryo at an earlier stage of development. L19. **3** Designating a viral plant disease characterized by a mottled pattern of discoloration on the leaves. L19. **4** *Biol.* Having or composed of cells of two genetically different types. E20. **5** Of a composite photograph or map: made up of a number of separate photographs of overlapping areas. E20. **6** *Cryst.* Of (the structure of) a crystal: made up of small blocks of perfect lattices set at very slight angles to one another. M20.

1 P. CUTTING The bathhouse with its . . bright mosaic floors. **b** *Railway Magazine* The large diagrammatic mosaic control panel gives details of all the power supplies.

Special collocations: **mosaic gold** (*a*) tin disulphide (stannic sulphide), used as an imitation gold pigment; (*b*) an alloy of copper and zinc used in cheap jewellery and ornamental metalwork. **mosaic work** = sense A.1 above.

mosaically *adv.* E17.

Mosaic /məʊˈzeɪɪk/ *a.*[2] M17. [Fr. *mosaïque* or mod.L *Mosaicus*, f. as MOSES: see -IC.] Of or pertaining to Moses, the Hebrew prophet who in the Bible led the Israelites out of slavery in Egypt and passed on to them the Ten Commandments, and to whom the authorship of the Pentateuch was traditionally ascribed; of or pertaining to the writings and institutions attributed to Moses.

Mosaic law the ancient law of the Hebrews contained in the Pentateuch.

mosaic /məʊˈzeɪɪk/ *v.t.* Infl. **-ck-**. L18. [f. MOSAIC *n.* & *a.*[1]] **1** Decorate or pattern (as) with mosaics. L18. **2** Combine as if into a mosaic; produce by such combination. *rare.* M19.

Mosaical /məʊˈzeɪɪk(ə)l/ *a.* Now *rare.* M16. [f. as MOSAIC *a.*[2]: see -ICAL.] = MOSAIC *a.*[2]

†**Mosaical rod** a divining rod.

mosaicism /məʊˈzeɪɪsɪz(ə)m/ *n.* E20. [f. MOSAIC *n.* & *a.*[1] + -ISM.] *Biol.* The property or state of being composed of cells of two genetically different types. Cf. MOSAIC *n.* 3 & *a.*[1] 4.

mosaicist /məʊˈzeɪɪsɪst/ *n.* M19. [f. MOSAIC *n.* & *a.*[1] + -IST.] A person who makes or deals in mosaic; a worker in mosaic.

Mosaism /ˈməʊzeɪɪz(ə)m/ *n.* M19. [mod.L *Mosaismus*, f. as MOSES: see -ISM.] The religious system, laws, and ceremonies prescribed by Moses; adherence to the Mosaic system or doctrines.

Mosan /ˈməʊs(ə)n/ *n.* E20. [f. *mōs* lit. 'four' in various N. Amer. langs. + -AN.] An American Indian language group of the north-western US and western Canada.

Mosan /ˈməʊz(ə)n/ *a.* E20. [Fr., f. L *Mosa* Meuse: see -AN.] Of or pertaining to a style of decorative art developed in the Meuse valley in western Europe in the 11th to 13th cents.

mosasaur /ˈməʊsəsɔː/ *n.* M19. [mod.L *Mosasaurus* genus name, f. L *Mosa* the River Meuse, near which the first remains were found: see -SAUR.] Any of a group of large extinct marine lizards of the Cretaceous period.

mosaˈsaurian *a.* & *n.* (of, pertaining to, or of the nature of) a mosasaur M19. **mosaˈsaurus** *n.*, pl. **-ri** /-rʌɪ/, **-ruses**, a mosasaur of the genus *Mosasaurus* M19.

moscatello /mɒskəˈtɛləʊ/ *n.* Also †**-dello**. Pl. **-lli** /-liː/, **-los**. M16. [It.: see MUSCATEL.] = MUSCATEL 1, *spec.* from Italy.

moscato /məˈskɑːtəʊ/ *n.* Pl. **-os**. E20. [It.: see MUSCAT.] A sweet Italian dessert wine.

moschatel /mɒskəˈtɛl/ *n.* M18. [Fr. *moscatelle* f. It. *moscatella*, f. *moscato* musk.] An inconspicuous plant of shady places, *Adoxa moschatellina* (family Adoxaceae), with ternate leaves and a terminal head of musk-scented green flowers. Also called *town-hall clock(s)*.

Moscow mule /ˈmɒskəʊ ˈmjuːl/ *n. phr.* M20. [f. *Moscow*, the capital of Russia + MULE *n.*[1]] A cocktail based on vodka and ginger beer.

†**mose** *v.i. rare* (Shakes.). Only in L16. [Origin unkn.] Suffer from glanders.

Moselle /mə(ʊ)ˈzɛl/ *n.* Also **Mosel** /ˈməʊz(ə)l/. L17. [See below. *Moselle* is the Fr., *Mosel* the G name of the river.] A light dry white wine produced in the valley of the Moselle in Germany. Also more fully *Moselle wine*.

Moses /ˈməʊzɪz/ *n.* E16. [eccl.L *Moses*, *Moyses*, eccl.Gk *Mōsēs*, f. Heb. *Mōšeh*. In sense 4 prob. alt. of MIMOSA.] 1 A person resembling the Hebrew prophet Moses (see MOSAIC *a.*[2]), esp. in his character as lawgiver or leader. E16. b Used as an oath or expletive. Also *holy Moses*. M19. c A male Jew. *derog.* M19. 2 In full *Moses boat*. A broad flat-bottomed boat used in the W. Indies. Also, a kind of boat used in Massachusetts. *obs.* exc. *Hist.* E18. 3 *prickly Moses*, any of several wattles with needle-like phyllodes, esp. *Acacia ulicifolia* and *A. verticillata*. *Austral.* L19.

1 M. L. KING In nearly every territory . . a courageous Moses pleaded passionately for the freedom of his people.

Comb.: **Moses basket** a carry-cot or small portable cot for a baby, esp. of wickerwork; *Moses boat*: see sense 2 above.

mosey /ˈməʊzi/ *v.i. slang* (orig. *US*). E19. [Origin unkn.] Orig., go away quickly or promptly; make haste. Now, walk in a leisurely or aimless manner; wander, amble. Freq. foll. by adv.

M. BRADBURY What say we mosey up to the ranch house? S. BELLOW I went down in the slow white elevator and . . moseyed around in the lobby. B. T. BRADFORD You can mosey off for a while.

MOSFET /ˈmɒsfɛt/ *n.* M20. [Acronym, f. *m*etal *o*xide *s*emiconductor *f*ield-*e*ffect *t*ransistor.] *Electronics.* A field-effect transistor in which there is a thin layer of silicon oxide between the gate and the channel.

moshav /ˈməʊʃɑːv/ *n.* Pl. **-im** /-ɪm/. M20. [mod.Heb. *mōšāḇ* dwelling, colony.] In Israel, a group of agricultural smallholdings worked partly on a cooperative and partly on an individual basis.

moskeneer /mɒskəˈnɪə/ *v.t. slang.* L19. [Yiddish f. Heb. *maškōn* a pledge.] Pawn (an article) for more than the real value.

mosker /ˈmɒskə/ *n. slang.* L19. [f. MOSK(ENEER + -ER[1].] A person who pawns an article for more than its real value.

mosker /ˈmɒskə/ *v.i.* Long *obs.* exc. *dial.* E17. [Origin unkn.] Decay, rot; crumble *away*.

moskonfyt /ˈmɔskɔnfeɪt/ *n. S. Afr.* L19. [Afk., f. *mos* must + *konfyt* jam.] A thick syrup prepared from grapes.

Moslem *n.* & *a.*, **Moslemin** *n.* & *a.* vars. of MUSLIM, MUSLIMIN.

Mosleyite /ˈməʊzlɪʌɪt/ *n.* & *a.* M20. [f. *Mosley* (see below) + -ITE[1].] A *n.* A follower or adherent of the English politician Sir Oswald Mosley (1896–1980), founder of the British Union of Fascists, or his views. M20. B *adj.* Of, pertaining to, or resembling Mosley or his views. M20.

Mosotho *n.sing.* see SOTHO.

mosque /mɒsk/ *n.* LME. [Fr. *mosquée* f. It. *moschea* (whence also G *Moschee*), ult. f. Arab. *masjid* lit. 'place of prostration'.] 1 A Muslim place of worship. LME. 2 *The* body of Muslims collectively; *the* Islamic authorities. *rare.* L18.

mosquito /mɒˈskiːtəʊ, mə-/ *n.*[1] Pl. **-oes**. L16. [Sp., Port., dim. of *mosca* fly f. L *musca*.] Any of various slender biting dipteran insects, esp. of the genera *Culex*, *Anopheles*, and *Aedes*, the female of which punctures the skins of animals (including humans) with a long proboscis and sucks blood.

attrib.: R. P. JHABVALA They came back, sunburned and full of mosquito bites.

Comb.: **mosquito-bar** *US* a kind of mosquito-net; **mosquito bee** a very small stingless bee; **mosquito-boat** *US* a motor torpedo boat; **mosquito-boot**: worn to protect the foot from mosquitoes; *mosquito coil*: see COIL *n.*[2] 4f; **mosquito-curtain** = *mosquito-net* below; **mosquito fish** a fish that eats mosquito larvae and pupae; *spec.* a small toothcarp, *Gambusia affinis*, native to the eastern and southern US and introduced elsewhere for mosquito control; **mosquito fleet** a fleet of small fast manoeuvrable boats; **mosquito hawk** *N. Amer.* (*a*) the nighthawk *Chordeiles minor*; (*b*) a dragonfly; **mosquito-net** a fine net of gauze or lace to keep off mosquitoes; **mosquito-netting** a coarse fabric with open meshes, used for mosquito-nets.

mosquital *a.* of or pertaining to a mosquito or mosquitoes L19. **mosquitoey** *a.* infested with mosquitoes M19.

Mosquito *n.*[2] & *a.* var. of MISKITO.

moss /mɒs/ *n.* [OE *mos* = MLG, MDu. *mos* bog, moss (Du. *mos*), OHG *mos* (G *Moos*), f. Gmc wd rel. to ON *mosi* bog, moss & ult. to L *muscus* moss.] I 1 a A bog, a swamp; *esp.* a peat-bog. *Sc.* & *north.* OE. b Wet spongy soil. *Sc.* & *north.* L16. 2 In full *moss-crop*. Either of the two common kinds of cotton-grass, *Eriophorum vaginatum* and *E. angustifolium*. *Sc.* & *north.* L15.

II 3 A plant of the class Musci, comprising small bryophytes with scalelike leaves usu. spirally arranged and the spore-capsule usu. opening by a lid, which grow in crowded masses in bogs, on the surface of the ground, on stones, trees, etc.; *collect.* the mass formed by such a plant. Also, any of certain algae, lichens, pteridophytes, or flowering plants resembling moss in habit; *rare* seaweed. OE. 4 a An excrescence or incrustation resembling moss; *esp.* the covering of the calyx and pedicels of the moss rose. E17. †b A kind of sugar coating. E18–M19. c Hair. *slang.* M20. 5 In full *moss rose*. A cultivar of the cabbage rose, *Rosa centifolia*, with a mosslike covering of glands on the calyx and freq. also the pedicels. L18. 6 *ellipt.* Moss green. L19.

3 R. K. NARAYAN There was still one step . . slippery with moss. *bog-moss*, *Ceylon moss*, *clubmoss*, *hair moss*, *Iceland moss*, *running moss*, *sphagnum moss*, etc.

Comb.: **moss agate** a variety of agate containing brown or black mosslike dendritic forms; **moss-bag** *Canad.* a light board with a cloth flap attached to each side, used by Indians to carry a baby with the flaps laced together and a lining of moss; **moss-berry** the cranberry, *Vaccinium oxycoccos*; **moss campion** a pink-flowered, almost stemless campion, *Silene acaulis*, found in mountains and on northern coasts; **moss-cheeper** *dial.* (*a*) the meadow pipit, *Anthus pratensis*; (*b*) the reed bunting, *Emberiza schoeniclus*; *moss-crop*: see sense 2 above; **moss green** a green colour resembling that of moss; **moss-grown** *a.* overgrown with moss; *fig.* antiquated; **moss-hag** *Sc.* broken ground or a hole from which peat has been dug; **moss horn** *US* = MOSSY *horn*; **moss-house** a garden shelter lined or covered with moss; **moss-oak** ancient oak-wood preserved in a blackened state in peat-bogs etc.; bog-oak; **moss opal** a variety of opal containing dendritic markings like those of moss agate; **moss-peat** peat formed from mosses, esp. those of the genus *Sphagnum*; **moss pink** a low-growing phlox, *Phlox subulata*, of the central US, with pink, violet, etc., flowers; *moss rose*: see sense 5 above; **moss-stitch** alternation of plain and purl stitches in knitting; **moss-wood** the wood of trees found buried in peat-bogs.

mosslike *a.* resembling moss M17.

moss /mɒs/ *v.* LME. [f. the n.] 1 *v.i.* Become mossy. LME. 2 *v.t.* Cover with moss. L16. †3 *v.t.* Remove moss from (trees etc.). L17–E18. 4 *v.i.* Gather or collect moss. E18.

2 E. B. BROWNING When years had mossed the stone.

Mossad /mɒˈsad, ˈmɒsad/ *n.* M20. [Heb. *mōsād* institution.] 1 *Hist.* An underground organization formed in 1938 to bring Jews from Europe to Palestine. M20. 2 The principal intelligence service of Israel. L20.

moss-back /ˈmɒsbak/ *n. N. Amer.* L19. [f. MOSS *n.* + BACK *n.*[1]] 1 A large old fish. L19. 2 *Hist.* A person who hid during the American Civil War to avoid conscription for the Southern army. L19. 3 A person attached to antiquated notions; an extreme conservative. *colloq.* L19.

moss-backed *a.* (*colloq.*) very old-fashioned; extremely conservative: L19.

Mössbauer /ˈmɜːsbaʊə/ *n.* M20. [Rudolf L. *Mössbauer* (b. 1929), Ger. physicist.] *Physics.* Used *attrib.* to designate (spectroscopy involving) an effect in which an atomic nucleus bound in a crystal emits a gamma ray of sharply defined frequency which can be used as a probe of energy levels in other nuclei.

mossbunker /ˈmɒsbʌŋkə/ *n.* L18. [Du. *marsbanker*. Cf. MAASBANKER.] = MENHADEN.

mossed /mɒst/ *a.* M18. [f. MOSS *n.*, *v.*: see -ED[2], -ED[1].] Covered or overgrown with moss.

mosser /ˈmɒsə/ *n.* M17. [f. MOSS *n.*, *v.* + -ER[1].] 1 = MOSS-TROOPER. M17. 2 A person who works in cutting and preparing peats. M19. 3 A collector or gatherer of moss. L19.

Mossi /ˈmɒsi/ *n.* & *a.* M19. [Afr. name.] A *n.* Pl. same, **-s**. A member of a people of Burkina Faso in W. Africa. M19. B *adj.* Of or pertaining to the Mossi. M20.

mossie /ˈmɒsi/ *n.*[1] *S. Afr.* L19. [Afk. f. Du. *musje* dim. of *mus* sparrow: see -IE.] = *Cape sparrow* s.v. CAPE *n.*[1]

mossie /ˈmɒsi, ˈmɒzi/ *n.*[2] *slang.* Also **-zz-** /-z-/. M20. [Abbrev.: see -IE.] A mosquito.

mosso /ˈmɒsəʊ/ *adv.* L19. [It., pa. pple of *muovere* move.] *Mus.* A direction: rapidly, with animation.

mossoo /məˈsuː/ *n. joc.* & *derog. arch.* E19. [Repr. an Anglicized pronunc. of MONSIEUR. Cf. MOUNSEER.] A Frenchman.

moss-trooper /ˈmɒstruːpə/ *n.* M17. [f. MOSS *n.* + TROOPER.] A pillager or marauder of the Scottish Borders in the middle of the 17th cent.; any bandit or raider.

moss-trooping *n.* banditry, raiding E19.

mossy /ˈmɒsi/ *a.* In sense 1 also (earlier, *obs.* exc. *dial.*) **mosy** /ˈməʊzi/. LME. [f. MOSS *n.* + -Y[1].] I 1 Covered with something like moss; appearing as if covered with moss; resembling moss; downy, velvety; hairy. LME. 2 Overgrown or covered with moss, having much moss; surrounded by moss. M16. 3 †a Stupid, dull. *slang.* L16–E17. b Extremely conservative or reactionary; old-fashioned, out of date; old. *US slang.* E20.

1 J. WILKINS Bearing mossy flowers. 2 R. WEST A shed that let in rain through its mossy tiles.

II 4 Marshy, boggy; peaty. *Sc.* & *north.* E16.

Special collocations & *comb.*: **mossy-backed** *a.* = MOSS-BACKED. **mossy-cup oak** the bur-oak, *Quercus macrocarpa*. *mossy* CYPHEL. **mossy horn** *US* an old steer; an old cowboy. **mossy saxifrage** a white-flowered saxifrage of rocky places, *Saxifraga hypnoides*, with mosslike cushions of leafy shoots.

mossiness *n.* M16.

most /məʊst/ *a.* (in mod. usage also classed as a *determiner*), *n.*, & *adv.* [OE *māst* (late Northumb.) = OFris. *māst*, *maest*, OS *mēst* (Du. *meest*), (O)HG *meist*, ON *mestr*, Goth. *maists*, f. Gmc, f. bases of MO *adv.*, *n.*[3], & *a.*, -EST[1]. Serving as superl. of MANY, MUCH. Cf. also MORE *a.* etc. See also MOSTEST.] A *adj.* 1 a Greatest in size, largest; greatest in number, quantity, or amount. Long only in *the most part*. OE. †b With ns. of quality, condition, action, etc.: greatest in degree or extent; utmost; very great. OE–E18. c Greatest in power, authority, or importance. Long *obs.* exc. *Sc.* OE. †d Qualifying the designation of a person: entitled to the designation in the highest degree.

ME-L17. 2 The greatest number of; the majority of; nearly all of. OE. 3 Existing in the greatest quantity, amount, or degree; the greatest quantity or amount of. LME.

1a L. A. ECHARD The most imaginable fatigue. d W. WALKER He had been a most Mad-man had he stood against them. 2 J. CONRAD The calm gulf is filled on most days of the year by.. clouds. *Daily Telegraph* I walked (though most people motor) to Salcombe Regis. 3 J. RUSKIN The work.. which was begun with most patience.

Phrases: **for the most part** (*a*) usually, on the whole, in most cases; (*b*) as regards the greater or greatest part.

B *n.* 1 The greatest quantity, amount, proportion, or degree. (Foll. by *of*.) OE. 2 *pl.* The greatest or most important people. Usu. in assoc. w. *least*. Now only *poet.* in *most and least*, all without exception. ME. 3 *pl.* The greatest number, the majority, (*of*); *spec.* the majority of people. L15. 4 *The* best thing, *the* most exciting thing. Cf. *the greatest* s.v. GREAT *n. slang*. M20.

1 E. F. BENSON Some had gone to the writers.., and some to the College,.. but the most had gone to the fire. C. D. SIMAK 'All my neighbours have lost their leases?' 'The most of them'. N. SEDAKA Mom had to work throughout most of her childhood. 3 BURKE A number of fine portraits, most of them of persons now dead. Z. TOMIN It's the shock—you've had it worse than most.

Phrases: **at (the) most** as the greatest amount; as the best possible; on the most generous estimate. **make the most of** (*a*) employ to the best advantage; (*b*) treat with the greatest consideration. *most and least*: see sense B.2 above.

C *adv.* 1 In the greatest degree, to the greatest extent; *spec.* modifying an adj. or adv. to form the superl. (the normal mode of forming the superl. of adjs. & advs. with three or more syllables, and of most of those with two syllables; also (*arch.*) used pleonastically bef. the superl. of an adj. or adv.). OE. 2 Mostly; for the most part. Long *obs.* exc. *Sc.* OE. **b** As an intensive superl. qualifying adjs. and advs.: in the greatest possible degree, very. E16. 3 Almost, nearly. Now *dial.* & *US.* L16.

1 SHAKES. *Jul. Caes.* This was the most unkindest cut of all. T. HARDY Of all the phenomena.. those appertaining to comets had excited him most. M. SINCLAIR Just when I expected most to find you. V. WOOLF Humblest, most candid of women! *Washington Post* Who in the world would you most like to dine with? *most favoured nation*: see FAVOURED *a.*[2] *the Most High*: see HIGH *a.* **b** S. JOHNSON I am.. your Lordship's most humble.. servant. SCOTT FITZGERALD 'It most certainly is not.' Dick assured her. *Most Honourable*: see HONOURABLE 3b. *Most Reverend*: see REVEREND. 4 M. TWAIN Punching their fists most into each other's faces.

Comb.: **†mostwhat** *adv.* & *a.* (*a*) *adv.* for the most part; (*b*) *adj.* the greater part of; **†mostwhen** *adv.* most frequently, on most occasions; **mostwhere** *adv.* (*rare*) in most places.

-most /məʊst/ *suff.* [OE *-mest*, f. Gmc superl. suff. w. *-m-* + base of -EST[1], but long regarded as f. MOST *a.*] Forming superlative adjs. and advs. from wds denoting position in space, time, or serial order, viz. (*a*) preps., as *foremost*, *inmost*, *utmost*; (*b*) compars. in *-er*, as *furthermost*, *innermost*, *uttermost*; (*c*) positive adjs., as *backmost*, *topmost*.

mostest /ˈməʊstɪst/ *a.*, *n.*, & *adv. dial.* & *joc.* L19. [f. MOST + -EST[1].] = MOST.

E. TERRY It's mostest kind to write to me. *Time* Porter Foley, who could get there fustest with the mostest drinks. *Daily Herald* Here's the hostess with the mostest.

mostlings /ˈməʊstlɪŋz/ *adv. dial.* E19. [f. MOST + -LINGS.] Mostly, usually; almost, nearly.

mostly /ˈməʊstli/ *adv.* L16. [f. MOST *a.* + -LY[2].] 1 For the most part; on the whole; usually. L16. **†2** In the greatest degree, to the greatest extent; most. L17-E19.

1 H. JAMES One went through the vain motions, but it was mostly a waste of life. V. WOOLF She talked more about virginity than women mostly do.

mosy *a.* see MOSSY.

mot /mɒt/ *n.*[1] *slang.* Also **mott**, (earlier) **†mort**. M16. [Origin unkn.] 1 A girl, a woman. M16. 2 A prostitute; a promiscuous woman. M16.

mot /mo, məʊ, (*pl. same*); *in sense 1* mɒt/ *n.*[2] L16. [Fr. = word, saying f. Proto-Gallo-Romance alt. of pop.L *muttum* rel. to L *muttire* to murmur. Cf. MOTTO.] 1 Orig., a motto. Later (now *dial.*) a word, an opinion. L16. 2 A witty saying. E19.

2 A. POWELL Good talkers.. remembered chiefly for their comparatively elaborate *mots*.

Phrases: BON *mot*. ***mot d'ordre*** /mo dɔrdr, məʊ ˈdɔːdrə/, pl. ***-s -s*** (pronounced same), [Fr. = of command] a political slogan; a statement of policy; an oral directive. ***mot juste*** /mo ʒyst, məʊ ˈʒuːst/, pl. ***-s -s*** (pronounced same), [Fr. = exact, appropriate] the precisely appropriate expression.

¶Formerly fully Anglicized.

mota *n.* var. of MOOTAH.

motard /mɔtaːr/ *n.* Pl. pronounced same. M20. [Fr., f. *moto-* comb. form of *moteur* (cf. MOTO-): see -ARD.] A member of the French motor cycle police.

mote /məʊt/ *n.*[1] [OE *mot* = WFris., Du. *mot* sawdust, dust of turf (in MDu. *steenmot*, *turfmot*), of unkn. origin.] 1 A particle of dust; *esp.* one seen floating in a sunbeam; an irritating particle in the eye or throat; *fig.* (w. allus. to *Matt.* 7:3) a fault observed in another person by a person who ignores a greater fault of his or her own (usu. *mote in a person's eye* etc.: cf. *beam in one's eye* s.v. BEAM *n.*). OE. **b** A minute particle of foreign matter in food or drink. Now *Sc.* ME. **†c** Any minute particle; something very minute or trivial, a trifle; (in neg. contexts) a jot. ME-E18. **†d** = An atom. L16-E17. **†2** A blemish, a flaw. LME-E18. 3 Orig., a tuft of fibre. Now, a seed bearing such a tuft, as an imperfection in wool or cotton. L16. 4 A straw, a stalk of hay; a slender twig. Now *dial.* L16.

1 C. AIKEN Where are the human hearts that danced like motes In the sunshafts of your brilliance! L. DEIGHTON Black smoke.. bringing oily smears, motes of soot. L. VAN DER POST The mote in our neighbour's eye is invariably a reflection of the beam in our own.

mote /məʊt/ *n.*[2] *obs.* exc. *Hist.* See also MOAT *n.* ME. [OFr. *mot(t)e* clod, hillock, mound, castle, etc. (mod.Fr. *motte*: see MOTTE *n.*[2]).] 1 A mound, a hill, esp. as the seat of a camp, city, or building; an embankment. Also *mote-hill*. Cf. MOTTE *n.*[2] ME. 2 A barrow, a tumulus. E16.

mote /məʊt/ *n.*[3] *arch.* ME. [OFr. MOT *n.*[2]] A note of a hunting horn or bugle.

†mote *n.*[4] LME-M19. [L *motus*, f. *mot-*: see MOTION.] Motion (of a celestial object).

†mote *n.*[5] var. of MOOT *n.*[1]

mote /məʊt/ *aux. v.*[1] Long *arch.* Pres. & pa. (all persons) **mote**. [OE *mōt* (see MUST *v.*[1]): a WGmc and Goth. preterite-pres. vb.] 1 Expr. permission or possibility, or a wish: may. OE. **b** Might, could. LME. 2 Expr. necessity or obligation: must. OE.

1 E. FAIRFAX Within the postern stood Argantes stout To rescue her, if ill mote her betide. E. JONG 'The Goddess will do what She will' 'So mote it be,' said the Grandmaster.

mote /məʊt/ *v.*[2] E16. [f. MOTE *n.*[1]] **†1** *v.i.* & *t.* Find fault (with). *rare.* E16-L19. 2 *v.t.* Remove flecks or specks from (cloth). L17.

mote /məʊt/ *v.*[3]*i.* *colloq.* Now *rare.* L19. [Back-form. f. MOTOR *v.*] Drive or ride in a motor car.

moted /ˈməʊtɪd/ *a.* E19. [f. MOTE *n.*[1] + -ED[2].] Full of dust motes.

motel /məʊˈtɛl/ *n.* E20. [Blend of MOTOR *n.* & *a.* and HOTEL.] A roadside hotel catering primarily for motorists; *spec.* one comprising self-contained accommodation with adjacent parking space.

motelier *n.* the manager or owner of a motel M20.

moteless /ˈməʊtlɪs/ *a.* LME. [f. MOTE *n.*[1] + -LESS.] **†1** Without blemish, spotless. LME-M17. 2 Free from dust motes. L19.

moteling /ˈməʊtlɪŋ/ *n. rare.* E17. [f. MOTE *n.*[1] + -LING[1].] A little mote; a very small thing.

motet /məʊˈtɛt/ *n.* LME. [(O)Fr., dim. of MOT *n.*[2]: see -ET[1]. Cf. med.L *motetus*, *-um*, MOTTETTO.] A short choral composition, *esp.* one for liturgical use or setting a religious text. Formerly also, a melody, a song.

motey /ˈməʊti/ *a.* LME. [f. MOTE *n.*[1] + -Y[1]. See also MOTTY.] Full of motes or specks; spotty.

¶Rare bef. M18.

moth /mɒθ/ *n.*[1] [OE *moþþe* (also *mohþe*), obscurely rel. to synon. MLG, MDu. *motte* (Du. *mot*), (M)HG *motte*, ON *motti*.] 1a Orig., the larva of a clothes-moth. Later (more fully *clothes-moth*), a small lepidopteran insect (of the genera *Tinea* and *Tineola*) whose larvae are destructive to clothes and other fabrics. OE. **b** Any of the large group of insects (including clothes-moths) which together with butterflies constitute the order Lepidoptera and are distinguished from butterflies (in most instances) by nocturnal activity, hairlike or slender antennae that are not clubbed, thicker bodies, the usu. folded position of the wings when at rest, and duller colouring. M18. **†2** A worm, a maggot, a woodlouse; any small crawling thing. LME-M18. **†3** [tr. L *tinea*.] A disease of the scalp; ringworm. *rare.* LME-E17. 4 *fig.* A thing that causes gradual destruction or disappearance. Now *rare.* L16 5 A prostitute. *slang.* L19.

1b *codling-moth*, *emerald moth*, *gypsy moth*, *hawk moth*, *silk moth*, *vapourer moth*, etc.

Comb.: **moth-borer** the larval form of various moths which damage plants by boring into stems or other parts, esp. the sugar cane borer, *Diatraea saccharalis*; **moth fly** an insect of the family Psychodidae of tiny dipteran flies with hairy bodies and wings; an owl midge; **moth mullein** a mullein, *Verbascum blattaria*, with yellow flowers and smooth leaves, reputedly attractive to moths; **moth orchid** any of various freq. epiphytic orchids constituting the genus *Phalaenopsis*, chiefly of the Malay archipelago, with flat spreading petals suggesting a moth; **mothproof** *a.* & *v.t.* (make) resistant to damage by moths; **mothproofer** a substance for mothproofing clothes or textile fibres.

mothlike *a.* resembling (that of) a moth L18.

moth /məʊθ/ *n.*[2] M19. [Hind. *moth*, Bihari *moth* f. Skt *mokuṣṭa*.] More fully *moth bean*. A bean, *Phaseolus aconitifolius*, grown esp. in India as a vegetable, for fodder, etc.

moth /mɒθ/ *v.i.* E17. [f. MOTH *n.*[1]] **†1** Become moth-eaten. *Sc.* Only in 17. 2 Hunt for moths. Chiefly as *mothing* vbl n. E19.

mothball /ˈmɒθbɔːl/ *n.* & *v.* E20. [f. MOTH *n.*[1] + BALL *n.*[1]] **A** *n.* 1 A ball of camphor or naphthalene placed among stored fabrics to keep moths away. E20. 2 *fig.* In *pl.* A prolonged state of being in disuse or reserve or out of active service. Chiefly in *in*, *out of*, *mothballs*. M20.

2 A. E. STEVENSON Take the Paley Report out of mothballs, and review its recommendations. *Guardian* Apollo hardware put in mothballs.. could be brought out.

B *v.t.* Store among or in mothballs; take out of use or active service; put in storage for an indefinite time. M20.

Journal (*Newcastle-upon-Tyne*) On the doorstep of one of the company's presently mothballed quarries. *New Internationalist* Environmental protests have persuaded the Aquino Government to mothball the Bataan nuclear plant.

moth-eaten /ˈmɒθiːt(ə)n/ *a.* LME. [f. MOTH *n.*[1] + *eaten* pa. pple of EAT *v.*] 1 Damaged or destroyed by moths; (of a person) shabby. LME. 2 Antiquated, time-worn. M16.

1 L. DEIGHTON Koch was a small moth-eaten man. 2 *Pilot* The cross runway.. is pretty moth-eaten and is closed.

†moth-eat *v.t.* damage or destroy (as) by moths L16-E18.

mothed /mɒθt/ *a.* M19. [f. MOTH *n.*[1] + -ED[2].] Full of moths, moth-eaten.

mother /ˈmʌðə/ *n.*[1] & *a.* [OE *mōdor* = OFris., OS *mōdor* (Du. *moeder*), OHG *muotar* (G *Mutter*), ON *móðir*, f. Gmc, f. IE base also of L *mater*, Gk (Doric) *matēr*, (Attic, Ionic) *mētēr*, Old Ch. Slav. *mati* (*mater-*), OIr. *máthir* (Ir. *máthair*), Skt *mātr*, *mātar-*, Tocharian *mācar*. See also next.] **A** *n.* 1 A female parent of a human being (used as a form of address by a son or daughter, and sometimes a son- or daughter-in-law, and sometimes also familiarly by the father of a woman's child or children or by any husband); a woman who undertakes the responsibilities of a mother towards a child. Also, a female parent of an animal. OE. **b** As *int.*

Expr. surprise, dismay, etc. Freq. *my mother!* M19. 2 A female ancestor. Long *rare*. OE. 3 *fig.* A quality, institution, place, etc., that is likened to a mother in her aspect of giving birth or exercising protective care, or as an object of affectionate respect; a source; a main stock or stem. OE. 4 Used as a form of address to an elderly woman, esp. of little means or education. Also used (instead of 'Mrs') bef. the surname of such a person. *arch.* ME. 5 A woman who exercises control like that of a mother, or who is looked up to as a mother; a matron, a house-mother. LME. **b** The head or superior of a female religious community. Also used as a form of address. E17. **c** A woman who runs a brothel. *slang.* L18. **d** A female owner of a pet, esp. a dog. *colloq.* E20. †6 *Anat.* (In full *hard mother*) = DURA MATER; (in full *godly, meek, mild, soft mother*) = PIA MATER. LME–E17. 7†**a** The womb. LME–E18. **b** Hysteria. *arch.* L15. 8 Womanly or maternal qualities. L16. †9 A certain figure in geomancy. L16–L19. 10 Liquid left after a dissolved substance has been crystallized out. E17. 11 In full *artificial mother*. An apparatus for rearing chickens artificially. E19. 12 A cask or vat used in vinegar-making. M19. 13 A disc with grooves that is made from the plating of an electrotyped master matrix and is used to make a stamper for gramophone records. E20. 14**a** *ellipt.* = *mother-fucker* below. *N. Amer. coarse slang.* M20. **b** A thing very big of its kind. Chiefly in *big mother*. Cf. *the father (and mother) of a* s.v. FATHER *n. N. Amer. colloq.* L20.

1 TENNYSON Lambs are glad Nosing the mother's udder. A. CHRISTIE Mother and I . . feel it's only neighbourly to do what we can. *Woman's Own* Expectant mothers will be immunized. *adoptive mother, biological mother, birth mother, foster-mother, natural mother*, etc. 3 GOLDSMITH Nature, a mother kind alike to all. B. FRANKLIN The repeal of that mother of mischiefs, the Stamp Act. *South African Panorama* The cow . . is celebrated as mother and rescuer of the Hindu people. 4 A. CHRISTIE 'Don't you take on so, mother' that's what the sergeant said to me. 5 L. STRACHEY The Queen was hailed . . as the mother of her people. *Guardian* A new school and dormitory for the pages 'with a full-time mother and hot meals'. 14a J. UPDIKE You haven't seen the lab! . . We finally got the mother finished, all but some accessory wiring.

Phrases: *artificial mother*: see sense 11 above. **be mother** *colloq.* serve out food or drink; *spec.* be the person who pours the tea. **fits of the mother** *arch.* hysteria. *hard, godly mother*: see sense 6 above. **(just) like mother makes** or **used to make (it)** having the qualities of home cooking; exactly to one's taste. *meek, mild mother*: see sense 6 above. **Mother of God** the Virgin Mary. *mother of months*: see *mother of the months* below. **Mother of Parliaments** (*a*) England; (*b*) the British Parliament. †**mother of the maids** the head of the maids of honour in the royal household. **mother of (the) months** the moon. **mother of thyme** wild thyme, *Thymus praecox* subsp. *arcticus*. **mothers and fathers** a game in which children play at being mother and father. *my sainted mother*: see SAINTED 2. *Reverend Mother*: see REVEREND. *soft mother*: see sense 6 above. *surrogate mother*: see SURROGATE *a.* *the father and mother of a*: see FATHER *n.* *wife and mother*: see WIFE *n.*

B *attrib.* or as *adj.* (Freq. w. hyphen.) 1 That is a mother. ME. 2 Inherited or learned from one's mother; native. LME.

1 COLERIDGE The mother-falcon hath her nest above it. 2 G. BORROW You want two things, brother: mother sense, and gentle Rommany.

Special collocations & comb.: **mother-and-babe** *a.* = *mother-in-babe* below. **mother-and-baby home** a maternity home for unmarried mothers, usu. with pre- and post-natal services. **motherboard** a printed circuit board containing the principal components of a microcomputer etc., to which daughterboards may be connected. **Mother Bunch** †(*a*) *slang* water; (*b*) *colloq.* a stout or untidy old woman. *Mother Carey's Chicken*: see CHICKEN *n.*[1] **mother cell** *Biol.* a cell which undergoes division and gives rise to daughter cells; *spec.* a cell which undergoes meiotic division. *Mother Church*: see CHURCH *n.* **mother-city** (*a*) the city from which the founders of a colony came; (*b*) a city regarded as serving as a mother to someone. **mother-clove** the dried fruit of the clove tree, resembling a clove in appearance but less aromatic. **mother coal** mineral charcoal. **mother complex** *Psychol.* a complex about one's mother. **mother country** (*a*) a country in relation to its colonies or dependencies, the country from which the founders of a colony came; (*b*) the country of one's birth. **mother earth** the earth considered as the mother of its inhabitants and productions; the ground; earth, soil. **mother-figure** a person or thing endowed with some of the attributes of a mother; *esp.* an older woman who is seen as a source of nurture, support, etc. **mother-fucker** *coarse slang* (chiefly *N. Amer.*), an obnoxious or despicable person; a very unpleasant person or thing. **mother-fucking** *a.* (*coarse slang*, chiefly *N. Amer.*) despicable, obnoxious, very unpleasant. **Mother Goose rhyme** *N. Amer.* a nursery rhyme. **mother-grabbing** *a.* (*US slang*) = *mother-fucking* above. **mother hen** (*a*) a hen with chicks; (*b*) a person who sees to the needs of others, esp. in a fussy or annoying way. **mother-house** the founding house of a religious order. **Mother Hubbard** a kind of cloak; (chiefly *US*) a kind of loose-fitting garment. **mother image, mother imago** *Psychol.* the mental image of an idealized or archetypal mother. **mother-in-babe** *a.* designating a wooden bobbin with a hollow shank which contains another smaller bobbin. **mother-in-law**, pl. **mothers-in-law**, (*a*) the mother of one's spouse; †(*b*) a stepmother; (*c*) *mother-in-law's tongue*, a W. African plant, *Sansevieria trifasciata*, of the agave family, with long transversely banded leaves, grown as a house-plant. **motherland** a person's native country; a country as the source or producer of something. **mother language** = *mother tongue* below. **mother liquid, liquor** = sense 10 above. **mother-lode** *Mining* a principal vein of ore; *fig.* a principal or rich source. **mother love**: such as a mother feels for her child. **mother-loving** *a.* (*a*) that loves one's own mother; (*b*) *coarse slang* = *mother-fucking* above. **mother mould** a rigid mould which holds a sculptor's casting material. **mother naked** *a.* completely naked. *Mother Nature*: see NATURE *n.* **mother of thousands** (*a*) any of several creeping plants prolific in flowers; *esp.* ivy-leaved toadflax, *Cymbalaria muralis*; (*b*) mind-your-own-business, *Soleirolia soleirolii*. **mother plane** an aircraft which launches or controls another aircraft. **mother plant** a parent plant from which other plants have been derived. **mother queen** (*a*) a queen mother; (*b*) a queen bee. **mother right** (*a*) matriarchy; (*b*) the custom by which dynastic succession passes only in the female line. **mother's boy, mother's darling** a boy or man who is excessively influenced by or attached to his mother. **Mother's** (or **Mothers'**) **Day** (orig. *US*) a day on which mothers are particularly honoured: in N. America, the second Sunday in May; in Britain, Mothering Sunday. **mother's help** a person who helps a mother, mainly by looking after children. **mother ship** (*a*) a ship or airship escorting or having charge of a number of other, usu. smaller, craft; (*b*) an aircraft or rocket from which another aircraft or rocket is launched or controlled. **Mother Shipton** a noctuid moth, *Euclidimera mi*, with a wavy mark on each forewing said to resemble the face of a crone; also called *shipton moth*. **mother's mark** (now *rare*) a naevus. **mothers' meeting** orig., a meeting (usually weekly) of mothers connected with a parish or congregation, for the purpose of receiving instruction and advice; now usu. *fig.*, a group of people in conversation together, esp. when they should be doing something else. *mother's milk*: see MILK *n.* **mother's pet** (*a*) an indulged or spoiled child; (*b*) the youngest child of a family. **mother's ruin** *colloq.* gin. **mother's son** a man (chiefly in *every mother's son*, every man, everyone). **mother stone** (*a*) the matrix of a mineral; (*b*) a rock from which another is derived by structural or chemical change. **Mothers' Union** an Anglican organization for mothers to meet together regularly. *Mother Superior*: see SUPERIOR *a.* **mother tincture** *Homoeopathy* a pure undiluted tincture of a drug. **mother-to-be**, pl. **mothers-to-be**, an expectant mother. **mother tongue** (*a*) one's native language; (*b*) a language which has given rise to others. **mother water** = sense 10 above. **mother wit** a person's natural wit; common sense. **motherwort** any of various plants formerly believed valuable in diseases of the womb; *spec.* a labiate herb, *Leonurus cardiaca*.

motherkin(s) *n.* (an affectionate name for) one's mother L19. **motherling** *n.* = MOTHERKINS M19. **mothership** *n.* (long *rare*) motherhood; the conduct of a mother; motherly care: LME.

mother /ˈmʌðə/ *n.*[2] LME. [Prob. a use of MOTHER *n.*[1]: corresp. in form and sense to MDu. *moeder* (Du. *moer*), G *Mutter*, and in sense to Fr. *mère* (*de vinaigre*), Sp. & It. *madre*.] 1 Dregs, scum, orig. that of oil, later that rising to the surface of fermenting liquors. *obs.* exc. in *mother of grapes* = MARC *n.* 1. LME. 2 In full *mother of vinegar*. A ropy mucilaginous substance produced on the surface of alcoholic liquids during acetogenic fermentation, and used to initiate such fermentation in other alcoholic liquids. E17.

mother /ˈmʌðə/ *v.*[1] M16. [f. MOTHER *n.*[1]] 1 *v.t.* Be or become the mother of, give birth to; *fig.* be the source of, give rise to. M16. 2 *v.t.* Foll. by *on*, *upon*: attribute the maternity of (a child) to; *fig.* attribute the authorship of (a work) to; ascribe the origin of (something) to. M16. 3 *v.t.* Appear as, or acknowledge oneself as, the mother or source of. E17. 4 *v.t.* Take care of or protect as a mother; behave in a motherly way towards. M19. 5**a** *v.t.* Find a mother for (a lamb or calf); pick out from a flock the mother of (a particular lamb). Also foll. by *up*. M19. **b** *v.i.* Of a lamb or calf: attach itself to a ewe or cow as mother. Also foll. by *up*. M20.

1 *Scientific American* Through normal birth, she has just mothered a normal, contented baby. 2 *Blackwood's Magazine* Many venerable repartees were mothered on her. 4 G. BOURNE If he is wakeful, mother him for a short time.

motherer *n.* (*rare*) L19.

mother /ˈmʌðə/ *v.*[2]*i.* E18. [f. MOTHER *n.*[2]] Become mothery.

mothercraft /ˈmʌðəkrɑːft/ *n.* E20. [f. MOTHER *n.*[1] + CRAFT *n.*] The business of being a mother; knowledge of and skill in looking after and bringing up children.

mothered /ˈmʌðəd/ *a.*[1] M17. [f. MOTHER *n.*[1] + -ED[2].] Having a mother or mothers (of a specified number or kind).

†**mothered** *a.*[2] L17–E18. [f. MOTHER *n.*[2] + -ED[2].] Containing mother.

†**motherhead** *n.* ME. [f. MOTHER *n.*[1] + -HEAD.] 1 The state or condition of being a mother; motherly care. Only in ME. 2 An embodiment of maternal qualities. *rare.* Only in L19.

motherhood /ˈmʌðəhʊd/ *n.* & *a.* L16. [f. MOTHER *n.*[1] + -HOOD.] **A** *n.* 1 Motherly feeling or love. *rare.* L16. 2 The condition or fact of being a mother. E17. 3 *Anthropol.* A clan constituted by kinship through the mother. L19. **B** *attrib.* or as *adj.* Of an issue, report, etc.: protective, withholding the worst aspects. *N. Amer.* L20.

mothering /ˈmʌð(ə)rɪŋ/ *n.* M17. [f. MOTHER *n.*[1], *v.*[1] + -ING[1].] 1 The custom of visiting, communicating with, or giving presents to one's mother (formerly, one's parents) on the fourth Sunday in Lent. Now *rare* exc. in *Mothering Sunday*, that Sunday. M17. 2 The action of MOTHER *v.*[1]; motherly care or supervision. M19.

mothering /ˈmʌð(ə)rɪŋ/ *ppl a.* M19. [f. MOTHER *n.*[1], *v.*[1] + -ING[2].] 1 That acts as a mother. M19. 2 [Cf. *mother-fucking* s.v. MOTHER *n.*[1]] Despicable, obnoxious; very unpleasant. *US slang.* M20.

motherless /ˈmʌðəlɪs/ *a.*, *n.*, & *adv.* LOE. [f. MOTHER *n.*[1] + -LESS.] **A** *adj.* Having no mother; having a dead, absent, or unknown mother. LOE. **B** *n. collect. pl. The* class of motherless people or motherless children. *rare.* M17. **C** *adv.* Completely. Only in *stone motherless* (Austral. slang), completely and utterly (in an implied or specified state, esp. last in a race by a long distance). L19.

motherlessness *n.* L19.

motherlike /ˈmʌðəlʌɪk/ *a.* & *adv.* M16. [f. as prec. + -LIKE.] **A** *adj.* Resembling a mother; having the qualities of a mother; befitting or characteristic of a mother. M16. **B** *adv.* In a motherlike manner. L16.

motherly /ˈmʌðəli/ *a.* OE. [f. as prec. + -LY[1].] 1 Of or pertaining to a mother. *rare.* OE. 2 Befitting or characteristic of a mother. ME. 3 Resembling a mother; having the character, manner, or appearance of a mother. M16.

2 R. WEST When she picks up facts she kind of gives them a motherly hug. 3 I. MCEWAN A friendly, motherly woman . . insisted on fastening his seatbelt for him.

motherliness *n.* M17.

motherly /ˈmʌðəli/ *adv.* LME. [f. as prec. + -LY[2].] In a motherly manner.

mother-of-pearl /mʌð(ə)rəfˈpəːl/ *n.* Also (earlier) †**mother-pearl**. E16. [tr. Fr. †*mère* *perle*, corresp. to It., Sp. *madreperla*, Du. *paarlemoer*, G *Perlmutter*.] 1 A smooth shining iridescent substance forming the inner layer of the shell of a mollusc, esp. an oyster. E16. 2 A shellfish yielding mother-of-pearl. L16.

Comb.: **mother-of-pearl cloud** a kind of iridescent cloud occurring above the tropopause which is sometimes seen in high latitudes after sunset; **mother-of-pearl work** a kind of embroidery in which pieces of mother-of-pearl are sewn on velvet or silk.

mothery /ˈmʌð(ə)ri/ *a.* L17. [f. MOTHER *n.*[2] + -Y[1].] Of wine or vinegar: turbid with fermented matter, fetid.

mothy /ˈmɒθi/ *a.* L16. [f. MOTH *n.*[1] + -Y[1].] Infested with moths; characterized by the presence of moths; reminiscent or suggestive of a moth.

motif /məʊˈtiːf/ *n.* M19. [Fr.: see MOTIVE *n.*] 1 A distinctive, significant, or dominant idea or theme; *spec.* (*a*) *Art.* a distinctive feature, subject, or structural principle in a composition or design; (*b*) in literature or folklore, a particular or recurrent event, situation, theme, character, etc.; (*c*) *Mus.* a figure, a leitmotiv. M19. 2 An ornamental design or piece of decoration; *spec.* (*a*) an ornament of lace, braid, etc., sewn separately on a garment; (*b*) an ornament on a vehicle identifying the maker, model, etc. L19. 3 A motivation, a basis, (for an idea etc.). L19.

1 P. TILLICH Another motif of recent Existentialism .. is the escape into authority. M. SWANTON This 'Tree of Life' motif is .. rare in Celtic sculpture. H. CARPENTER The quest-motif .. as a framework for an account of a spiritual journey. *Music Teacher* The Brahmsian characteristics are so clear, the motifs, the harmonic shifts. 2 *Times* The banning of dangerous *motifs* mounted where the radiator cap used to be. W. TREVOR The patterned motif was repeated on either side of the hall door.

motile /ˈməʊtʌɪl/ *a.* & *n.* M19. [f. L *motus* motion + -ILE, after *mobile*.] A *adj.* 1 *Biol.* Capable of motion; characterized by motion. M19. 2 *Psychol.* Of, pertaining to, or characterized by responses that involve motor imagery; (of a person) responding to perceptions more readily in terms of motor or kinaesthetic imagery than in auditory or visual terms. L19. B *n. Psychol.* A motile person. L19.

motility /məʊˈtɪlɪti/ *n.* M19.

Motilon /məʊtɪˈləʊn/ *a.* & *n.* Also **-lone**. Pl. of n. **-lon**, **-lones** /-ˈləʊnz, -ˈləʊnɪz/. E20. [Sp. *Motilón*, of Amer. Indian origin.] Designating or pertaining to, a member of, a Carib people of Colombia; (of) the language of this people.

motion /ˈməʊʃ(ə)n/ *n.* & *v.* LME. [(O)Fr. f. L *motio(n-)*, f. *mot-* pa. ppl stem of *movere* MOVE *v.*: see -ION.] A *n.* 1 †a The action of moving or urging (a person) *to do* something, *that* something be done; a suggestion; an instigation, an instruction. LME–L18. b *Law.* A formal application made to a court for a ruling or order, esp. an interlocutory injunction. LME. c A formal proposition or proposal put before a committee, council, legislature, etc. M16. †2 a A motive, a reason; a ground or cause of action. LME–M17. b An inner prompting or impulse; a desire, an inclination; a stirring of the soul, an emotion. LME–M18. 3 A commotion, (an) agitation; irregular movement, shaking. LME. 4 The action, process, or condition of moving or being moved; an instance or variety of this. LME. b *Philos.* Any kind of change; becoming. *arch.* exc. as tr. Gk *kinēsis*. L17. 5 a The action of the body in walking, running, etc.; a manner of walking or stepping; gait, carriage. L16. †b The power of locomotion of an animate body; (strenuous) physical exercise. Only in 17. 6 An evacuation of the bowels. Also (*sing.* & in *pl.*), faeces. L16. †7 A puppet-show; a puppet (*lit.* & *fig.*). L16–L17. 8 a A change of posture; a visible bodily movement, a gesture. E17. b A step, gesture, or other movement of the body acquired by drill and training; *spec.* (*Mil.*) each of the successive actions constituting a prescribed exercise of arms. E17. c In *pl.* & †*sing.* Activities performed by a person or body of people in pursuit of a goal; *esp.* the movements of an army in the field. Now *rare* or *obs.* L17. 9 A piece of moving mechanism. Formerly also, the movement of a watch. E17. 10 *Mus.* †a Movement, tempo. L17–E18. b The melodic progression of a single part with reference to the intervals taken by it; the progression of two or more parts with relation to each other. M18.

1c B. MONTGOMERY They .. tabled a motion that .. each zone might act as it thought best. J. D. MACDONALD A motion that we dispense with the reading of the minutes. 3 T. PERCIVAL The mixtures .. have some little fermentative motion in them. G. CRABBE His groans now told the motions of the cart. 4 A. KOESTLER The moon's motion round the earth. A. TUTUOLA Leaves were bowing .. in slow motion. 8a TENNYSON Her eyes on all my motions with a mute observance hung. 9 G. F. FIENNES The axles went .. faster than the wheels, which wasn't so good for the motion.

Phrases: **go through the motions** (*a*) simulate by gestures or movements (an act *of*); (*b*) make a pretence, do something perfunctorily or superficially. *harmonic motion*: see HARMONIC *a.* **in motion** moving, not at rest. *local motion*: see LOCAL *a. lost motion*: see LOST *a.* **make a motion** (*a*) begin to move (*towards*, *to do*); (*b*) beckon, gesture to (a person *to do* something). *man in motion*: see MAN *n. oblique motion*: see OBLIQUE *a.* **of one's own motion** *arch.* of one's own accord. *perpetual motion*: see PERPETUAL *a. proper motion*: see PROPER *a.* **put** (or **set**) **in motion** set going or working. *similar motion*: see SIMILAR *a.* 2. *slow motion*: see SLOW *a.* & *adv. thermal motion*: see THERMAL *a.*

Comb.: **motion photography** cinematography; **motion picture** a cinema film; **motion sickness** nausea induced by motion, esp. travelling in a vehicle; **motion study**: of the movements involved in the most efficient performance of a task; **motion-work** the mechanism for moving the hands of a watch or clock.

B *v.* †1 *v.t.* a Approach (a person) with a request; petition or suggest to (a person). L15–M16. b Propose, move, (a thing, *to do*, *that*). E16–M19. c Propose or recommend (a person) for employment etc. L16–L17. †2 *v.i.* Make a proposal, bring forward a motion, offer a plan. *rare*. E16–M19. 3 *v.i.* †a Make a motion or movement as if *to do*. M18–E19. b Make a gesture for the purpose of directing or guiding a person. L18. 4 *v.t.* Direct or guide (a person) by a sign or gesture. L18.

1b I. NEWTON Thanks .. for motioning to get the experiment .. tried. W. ROW They motioned in the Committee that .. Hamilton should be general-major. 3b G. VIDAL Gracefully, he motioned for us to join him. C. GEBLER My uncle motioned with his fat hands. 4 J. BUCHAN I got my door open and motioned him in. J. HIGGINS He .. motioned them to sit on the sofa.

motionable *a.* (*rare*) capable of motion M19.

motional /ˈməʊʃ(ə)n(ə)l/ *a.* L17. [f. MOTION *n.* + -AL[1].] Of or pertaining to motion; characterized by (certain) motions; *Electr.* (of an impedance) arising from the motion of a conductor in a magnetic field.

motionally *adv.* as regards motion L20.

motionless /ˈməʊʃ(ə)nlɪs/ *a.* L16. [f. MOTION *n.* + -LESS.] Not moving; incapable of motion.

motionlessly *adv.* L19. **motionlessness** *n.* E19.

motitation /məʊtɪˈteɪʃ(ə)n/ *n. rare.* M17. [f. L *motitat-* pa. ppl stem of *motitare* frequent. of *movere* MOVE *v.*: see -ATION.] A quivering movement.

motivate /ˈməʊtɪveɪt/ *v.t.* M19. [f. MOTIVE *n.* + -ATE[3], after Fr. *motiver*, G *motivieren*.] 1 Supply or be a motive for (an action); provide (a person etc.) with a motive or incentive (*to do*); stimulate the interest of (a person) in an activity. M19. 2 Serve as a reason for, justify, (a decision etc.). L20.

1 M. INNES The action was motivated only by the .. fact that there was nothing else to do with him. *Rugby World* The club coach who has to motivate players. D. LODGE We need to .. motivate more working-class children to go to university. 2 *Nature* The publisher motivates the slim size of the volumes by claiming it makes them more likely to be read.

motivated *a.* that has been motivated; having a motive or motivation: M20. **motivative** *a.* serving to motivate (a thought, action, etc.), providing motivation M20. **motivator** *n.* a person who or thing which initiates or motivates action or behaviour M20.

motivation /məʊtɪˈveɪʃ(ə)n/ *n.* L19. [Partly f. MOTIVE *v.*, partly f. MOTIVATE: see -ATION.] 1 The action or an act of motivating something or someone. L19. 2 The (conscious or unconscious) stimulus, incentive, motives, etc., for action towards a goal, esp. as resulting from psychological or social factors; the factors giving purpose or direction to behaviour. Also, a motive. E20. 3 The state or condition of being motivated; the degree to which a person is motivated; enthusiasm, drive. M20. 4 (A) manner or means of movement. M20.

2 R. S. WOODWORTH The instincts are extraordinarily important in the study of motivation. *Scientific American* Other important motivations for attempting to synthesize speech. 3 M. N. COX The second basic requirement is adequate motivation to persist. *Woman's Home* It was his background that gave him the motivation to succeed.

Comb.: **motivation research** the psychological or sociological investigation of motives, esp. those influencing the decisions of consumers.

motivational *a.* M20. **motivationally** *adv.* M20.

motive /ˈməʊtɪv/ *n.* & *v.* LME. [(O)Fr. *motif* use as n. of adj.: see next.] A *n.* †1 A matter etc. moved or brought forward; a motion, a proposition. LME–M17. b An inward or spiritual prompting or impulse. LME–M17. 2 A factor or circumstance inducing a person to act in a certain way; an emotion, reason, goal, etc., influencing or tending to influence a person's volition. LME. b *spec.* the purpose or aim motivating a person committing a crime. L18. †3 A moving limb or organ. *rare* (Shakes.). L16–E17. †4 An instigator, an inciter. Only in 17. 5 A motif in art, literature, or music. M19. B *v.t.* = MOTIVATE. M17.

motive /ˈməʊtɪv/ *a.* LME. [(O)Fr. *motif*, *-ive* f. late L *motivus*, f. L *mot-* pa. ppl stem of *movere* MOVE *v.*: see -IVE.] 1 a Having the quality of causing or initiating movement; productive of or used in the production of physical or mechanical motion. LME. b Of nerves: = MOTOR *a.* I. *rare*. M17. †2 Capable of movement, mobile; moving. LME–E17. 3 That moves or tends to move a person to a particular course of action; motivating. E16.

1a *Nature* Convection in the lower mantle .. provides the motive force for continental drift. *fig.*: M. ARNOLD The French Revolution .. found .. its motive power in the intelligence of men. 3 E. H. SEARS Those .. whose motive principles are selfish. DISRAELI Public reputation is a motive power.

motiveless /ˈməʊtɪvlɪs/ *a.* E19. [f. MOTIVE *n.* + -LESS.] Having no motive, irrational.

M. ALLINGHAM This cruel and .. motiveless crime.

motivelessly *adv.* L19. **motivelessness** *n.* L19.

motivi *n.* pl. of MOTIVO.

motivic /ˈməʊtɪvɪk/ *a.* M20. [f. MOTIVE *n.* + -IC: cf. MOTIF.] *Mus.* Of or pertaining to a motif or motifs.

motiviert /motiˈviːrt/ *a.* E19. [G.] Motivated.

motivity /məʊˈtɪvɪti/ *n.* L17. [f. MOTIVE *a.* + -ITY.] The power to cause or initiate motion.

motivo /moˈtiːvo/ *n.* Pl. **-vi** /-vi/. M18. [It.: cf. MOTIVE *n.*, MOTIF.] *Mus.* A motif.

motley /ˈmɒtli/ *a.*, *n.*, & *v.* LME. [Origin uncertain: perh. ult. f. MOTE *n.*[1]] A *adj.* 1 Diversified in colour, multicoloured; variegated. LME. 2 (Composed of elements) of diverse or varying character, form, appearance, etc. L16.

1 SHAKES. *A.Y.L.* O that I were a fool!, I am ambitious for a motley coat. 2 *Daily Telegraph* A motley crew with no ranks .. and half of them without uniforms. *Sunday Express* A fairytale with .. a motley assortment of evil baddies.

B *n.* †1 A cloth of mixed colour. LME–E17. 2 A mixture of colours, variegation; an incongruous mixture. LME. 3 (The multicoloured costume of) a professional fool or jester. *obs.* exc. *Hist.* L16.

2 J. LE CARRÉ A motley of foreign registration stickers covering one door. 3 **wear motley** play the fool.

C *v.t.* Make motley; mix incongruously. LME.

motleyness *n.* E19.

motmot /ˈmɒtmɒt/ *n.* M19. [Amer. Sp.: imit.] Any of several mainly insectivorous passerine birds of the neotropical family Momotidae, some of which have a double racket-tail.

moto /ˈməʊtəʊ/ *n.*[1] M18. [It.] *Mus.* Movement, pace.

CON MOTO. **moto perpetuo** /pəˈpɛtjʊəʊ/, pl. **moti perpetui** /ˌməʊtiː pəˈpɛtjʊiː/ [= perpetual motion] a rapid instrumental composition consisting mainly of notes of equal value (cf. PERPETUUM MOBILE 2).

moto /ˈməʊtəʊ/ *n.*[2] Pl. **-os.** L20. [Abbrev. of MOTO-CROSS.] A moto-cross or BMX race.

moto- /ˈməʊtəʊ/ *comb. form.* [f. MOTOR *a.*: see -O-.] Motor.

moto-cross *n.* cross-country motor cycle racing M20. **moto'neurone** *n.* (*Biol.*) = *motor neurone* s.v. MOTOR *a.* E20. **moto'sensitive** *a.* (*rare*) composed of motor and sensory nerve fibres M19.

moton /ˈməʊtɒn/ *n.* LME. [Origin unkn.] *Hist.* A piece of armour used in the 15th cent., app. for protecting the armpit.

motor /ˈməʊtə/ *n.* & *a.* LME. [L = mover; later, partly f. *mot-* (see MOTIVE *a.*) + -OR, partly after Fr. *moteur.*] A *n.* 1 A person who or thing which causes motion. LME. 2 *Anat.* A muscle which produces the main force of a movement of part of the body. Also, motor nerve. Now *rare.* E19. 3a A machine for producing motive power from some other form of energy, esp. electrical energy; an engine, *esp.* that of a vehicle. M19. b *ellipt.* A motor car, a motor vehicle. L19. 4 *Psychol.* = MOTILE *n.* Now *rare.* L19.

1 G. SARTON God exists, for it is the necessary principle and end of everything, the first motor. *fig.*: H. ARENDT Violence proved an excellent motor to set the mob . . in motion. 3a *phonic motor*: see PHONIC *a.* 1. b *Princeton Alumni Weekly* Many motors early took the highroad.

B *attrib.* or as *adj.* 1 *Anat.* & *Physiol.* Designating or pertaining to neurones, nerves, or nerve fibres which initiate or convey impulses resulting in an action, esp. muscular contraction. Opp. SENSORY *a.* E19. 2 Of, pertaining to, or involving muscular movement. M19. 3 Causing or producing motion; motive. L19. 4 Of a vehicle, vessel, etc.: driven or powered by a motor. L19. 5 Of, pertaining to, or designed for use in motors, motor vehicles, or motoring. E20.

4 *motor-ambulance, -cab, -cruiser, -hearse, -launch, -mower, -tractor, -tricycle, -yacht,* etc. 5 *motor accident, garage, horn, industry, insurance, mechanic, traffic, transport,* etc.

Special collocations & comb.: **motor area** any part of the central nervous system which has a motor function; esp. = *motor cortex* below. **motor bicycle** (*a*) a motorcycle; (*b*) a moped. **motor bike** *colloq.* = *motorcycle* below. **motor-bike** *v.i.* travel on a motor-bike. **motor boat** a motor-driven boat or launch. **motor-boat** *v.i.* (*a*) travel in a motor boat; (*b*) *Electronics* (of an amplifier) exhibit motor-boating. **motor-boating** (*a*) travel in a motor boat; (*b*) *Electronics* oscillation in an amplifier of such low frequency that individual cycles may be heard as a characteristic sound, caused by feedback from output to input, often through a common voltage supply. **motor bus** a bus with an engine. **motor-bus** *v.i.* travel by (motor) bus. **motor camp** (orig. *US*) a camp-site catering for motorists, caravans, etc. **motor car** (*a*) = CAR 6; (*b*) *US* a rail car for freight or passengers propelled by its own motors. **motor caravan** a van equipped with beds, cooking facilities, etc., like a caravan. **motor coach** (*a*) = COACH *n.* 1C; (*b*) a passenger coach on an electrified railway equipped with its own motor. **motor-coaster** (*a*) a motorized vessel employed in sailing along a coast; (*b*) a type of big dipper at a funfair. **motor cop** *N. Amer. colloq.* a police officer on a motorcycle. **motor cortex** the part of the cerebral cortex in which originate the nerve impulses that initiate voluntary muscular activity. **motor court** *US* a motel. **motorcycle** a two-wheeled motor-driven road vehicle without pedal propulsion. **motorcyclist** a rider of a motorcycle. **motor-drive** (*a*) a drive or journey in a motor car; (*b*) driving power provided by a motor or engine. **motor generator** *Electr.* an apparatus consisting of a mechanically coupled electric motor and generator which may be used to control the voltage, frequency, or phase of a supply. **motor home** *N. Amer.* a very large vehicle equipped as a self-contained home. **motor hotel, motor inn, motor lodge** a motel. **motorman** a driver of a tram, underground train, etc. **motor mouth** *N. Amer. slang* a person who talks fast or incessantly. **motor nerve, motor neurone**: having a motor function; *motor neurone disease*, a progressive disease characterized by degeneration of motor neurones and wasting and weakness of muscles. **motor-racing** racing of motorized vehicles, esp. cars, as a sport. **motor root** the anterior or ventral root of spinal or certain cranial nerves, containing axons of motor neurones. **motor-sailer** a boat equipped with both sails and an engine. *motor scooter*: see SCOOTER *n.* 5b. **motor unit** a neuroanatomical unit comprising a single motor neurone and the muscle fibres on which it acts. **motor vehicle** a road vehicle powered by an internal-combustion engine. **motor wind** *Photogr.* a camera winding mechanism driven by a motor.

motored *a.* provided or equipped with a motor E20.

motor /ˈməʊtə/ *v.* L19. [f. the n.] 1 *v.t.* a Convey (a person or goods) in a motor vehicle. L19. b Travel over (a distance) in a motor vehicle. E20. 2 *v.i.* a Travel or drive in a motor vehicle. L19. b Travel in a motor-boat; use an engine in a sailing boat. M20.

1a J. COLVILLE Philip . . motored me to Trent Park. 2a J. BUCHAN Mayot had motored to Cirencester. *fig.*: *Sunday Times* The directors are buying enthusiastically. The shares are starting to motor.

motorable /ˈməʊt(ə)rəb(ə)l/ *a.* E20. [f. prec. + -ABLE.] Of a road or district: suitable for or usable by motor vehicles.

Motorail /ˈməʊtəreɪl/ *n.* M20. [Blend of MOTOR *n.* and RAIL *n.*[2]] A rail service in which cars are transported together with their drivers and passengers.

Motorama /məʊtəˈrɑːmə/ *n.* M20. [Blend of MOTOR *n.* and *-orama* after PANORAMA.] An exhibition of motor vehicles.

motorcade /ˈməʊtəkeɪd/ *n.* & *v.* Orig. *US.* E20. [f. MOTOR *n.* + CAVAL)CADE.] A *n.* A procession of motor vehicles. E20. B *v.i.* Travel in a motorcade. M20.

motordom /ˈməʊtədəm/ *n.* E20. [f. MOTOR *n.* + -DOM.] The world of motoring; the people who use motor vehicles; motor vehicles collectively.

motorial /məʊˈtɔːrɪəl/ *a.* Now *rare* or *obs.* M19. [App. f. MOTOR *n.* & *a.* + -IAL, after *sensorial.*] *Biol.* & *Physiol.* Of or pertaining to motion; *spec.* of or pertaining to a motor nerve; motor.

motoric /məˈtɔːrɪk/ *a.* M20. [f. MOTOR *n.* & *a.* + -IC.] 1 Of, pertaining to, or characterized by muscular movement. M20. 2 Of a musical piece or performance: marked by precision or repetitiveness suggestive of mechanized action. M20.

motoring /ˈməʊt(ə)rɪŋ/ *vbl n.* L19. [f. MOTOR *v.* + -ING[1].] The action of driving or travelling in a motor vehicle, esp. a car.

Comb.: **motoring cap, goggles, veil,** etc.: for wearing in an open car.

motorise *v.* var. of MOTORIZE.

motorism /ˈməʊtərɪz(ə)m/ *n.* E20. [f. MOTOR *n.* + -ISM.] The use or prevalence of motor vehicles; the world of motoring.

motorist /ˈməʊt(ə)rɪst/ *n.* L19. [f. MOTOR *n.* + -IST.] A person who drives or rides in a motor car.

motorium /məʊˈtɔːrɪəm/ *n.* L19. [mod.L, f. L *motorius* moving, f. *mot-* stem of *movere* move: cf. -ORY[1].] 1 *Psychol.* The centres in the brain concerned in the function of voluntary muscle; the system of the body capable of initiating and effecting muscular movement. L19. 2 *Zool.* A cytoplasmic structure forming the centre of the neuromotor apparatus of some ciliates. E20.

motorize /ˈməʊtəraɪz/ *v.t.* Also **-ise.** E20. [f. MOTOR *n.* + -IZE.] 1 *Psychol.* Apprehend in terms of movements or motor imagery. *rare.* E20. 2 Provide or equip with a motor or with motor vehicles. E20.

motori'zation *n.* (*a*) *Psychol.* (*rare*) the process of apprehending something in a motile manner; (*b*) the introduction, use, or possession of motor vehicles; the process of equipping with motor vehicles: E20.

motorless /ˈməʊtəlɪs/ *a.* L19. [f. MOTOR *n.* + -LESS.] 1 Not provided with or using a motor. L19. 2 Of a road etc.: having little or no traffic. L20.

motorway /ˈməʊtəweɪ/ *n.* E20. [f. MOTOR *n.* + WAY *n.*] A dual carriageway specially designed for fast long-distance traffic and subject to special regulations concerning its use.

Radio Times A motorway differs from all other types of road in that it has no crossroads, no traffic lights, no pedestrian crossings. *attrib.*: J. MANN She had pulled into the motorway café.

Comb.: **motorway madness** *colloq.* reckless driving on a motorway, esp. in fog.

motory /ˈməʊtəri/ *a.* Now *rare* or *obs.* L17. [Late L *motorius*, f. L MOTOR *a.*: see -ORY[2].] = MOTOR *a.* 2, 3.

motoscafo /motoˈskaːfo/ *n.* Pl. ***-fi*** /-fi/. M20. [It.] In Italy: a motor-boat; *esp.* one used to carry passengers on the Venetian canals.

Motown /ˈməʊtaʊn/ *n.* & *a.* M20. [Contr. of *Motor Town*, nickname of Detroit, Michigan, USA, an important car-manufacturing city.] (Designating, pertaining to, or in the style of) a kind of music blending soul and pop styles, made popular in the 1960s by Black musicians and singers recording for the Motown Record Company. Cf. TAMLA, TAMLA MOTOWN.

¶ Proprietary name.

mott *n.*[1] var. of MOT *n.*[1]

mott *n.*[2] var. of next.

motte /mɒt/ *n.*[1] *US.* Also **mott.** M19. [Amer. Sp. *mata* grove, plant f. Sp. = bush, clump.] A clump of trees in prairie country.

motte /mɒt/ *n.*[2] L19. [Fr. = mound: cf. MOTE *n.*[2]] *Antiq.* A large man-made earthen mound with a flattened top, usu. surmounted by a fort, castle, etc.

motte-and-bailey *a.* designating or pertaining to a kind of castle built in Britain by the Normans, consisting of a fort on a motte surrounded by a bailey.

mottetto /motˈtetto, mɒˈtɛtəʊ/ *n.* Pl. ***-tti*** /-t(t)i/, ***-ttos*** /-təʊz/. M17. [It., f. as MOTTO + *-etto* -ET[1]. Cf. MOTET.] A motet, *spec.* an Italian one.

mottle /ˈmɒt(ə)l/ *n.* & *a.* L17. [Prob. back-form. f. MOTLEY *a.*] A *n.* 1 Any of the spots, patches, or blotches of a mottled surface. L17. 2 An irregular arrangement of spots, patches, or blotches of colour. M19. B *adj.* = MOTTLED. Chiefly in comb., as *mottle-faced* adj. L17.

mottle /ˈmɒt(ə)l/ *v.t.* L18. [Back-form. f. next.] Mark or dapple with spots, patches, or blotches. Chiefly as *mottled* ppl a.

S. BELLOW Women's faces . . mottled with crying.

mottler *n.* M19. **mottling** *n.* (the production of) a mottled appearance M19.

mottled /ˈmɒt(ə)ld/ *a.* L17. [f. as MOTTLE *n.* + -ED[2].] Dappled with spots or blotches; marked with spots, streaks, or patches of different colour.

B. ASHLEY He looked up at the mottled sky. **mottled beauty** a geometrid moth, *Alcis repandata*, which occurs in various pale and dark brown forms. **mottled calf** a variegated leather used for bookbinding. **mottled iron** a soft kind of cast iron. **mottled umber** a geometrid moth, *Erannis defoliaria*, of which the female is wingless.

motto /ˈmɒtəʊ/ *n.* & *v.* L16. [It. f. Proto-Gallo-Romance wd whence also MOT *n.*[2]] A *n.* Pl. **-o(e)s.** 1 Orig., a sentence or phrase attached to an emblematical design to explain its significance. Later, a short sentence or phrase inscribed on an object, expressing a reflection or sentiment considered appropriate to its purpose or destination. Also, a maxim adopted as a rule of conduct. L16. b *Her.* A significant word or sentence usu. placed on a scroll, either below an achievement of arms or above the crest, usu. expressing a maxim, aspiration, etc. E17. c A verse or saying in a paper cracker etc. M19. 2 A short quotation or epigram placed at the beginning of a book, chapter, etc.; an epigraph. E18. 3 A sweet wrapped in fancy paper together with a saying or scrap of verse. Also *motto-kiss. US.* M19. 4 *Mus.* A recurrent phrase having some symbolical significance. L19.

1 W. S. CHURCHILL With the motto 'Trust the People' . . he appealed to the rank and file. S. J. PERELMAN Think in telegrams, that's my motto. U. HOLDEN With a Latin motto on the blazer pocket. b O. NEUBECKER Mottoes become an integral part of the coat of arms.

B *v.t.* Inscribe with a motto. M18.

mottramite /ˈmɒtrəmaɪt/ *n.* L19. [f. *Mottram* St Andrew's, a village in Cheshire + -ITE[1].] *Min.*

An orthorhombic basic vanadate of lead, zinc, and copper, occurring as green or brownish blades or black incrustations and forming a series with descloizite.

motty /ˈmɒti/ *a. Sc.* L16. [f. as MOTEY, repr. pronunc.] = MOTEY.

Motu /ˈməʊtuː/ *n.* & *a.* L19. [Melanesian.] **A** *n.* Pl. same. A member of a Melanesian people of Papua New Guinea inhabiting the area of Port Moresby; the language of this people. L19. **B** *attrib.* or as *adj.* Of or pertaining to the Motu or their language. L19.

Also **Motuan** *a.* & *n.* L19.

motuca /məˈtuːkə/ *n.* Also **-ka**. M19. [Port. f. Tupi *mutuca*.] A Brazilian tabanid horsefly, *Hadrus lepidotus*. Also *motuca fly*.

motu proprio /məʊtuː ˈprəʊprɪəʊ, ˈprɒp-/ *adv.* & *n. phr.* E17. [L.] **A** *adv. phr.* Of one's own volition, on one's own initiative, spontaneously. E17. **B** *n. phr.* Pl. ***motu proprios***. An edict issued by the Pope personally to the Roman Catholic Church, or to a part of it. M19.

mou /muː/ *n.* Also **mu**. Pl. same. M19. [Chin. *mǔ*.] A Chinese unit of area, varying locally but usu. equal to about 670 square metres.

mouch *v.* & *n.* var. of MOOCH.

moucharaby /muːˈʃarəbi/ *n.* L19. [Fr. f. Arab. *mašrabiyya*, f. *mašraba* pitcher, f. *šariba* to drink.] In N. Africa, an external balcony enclosed with latticework.

mouchard /muʃaːr/ *n.* Pl. pronounced same. E19. [Fr., f. fig. use of *mouche* fly: see next, -ARD.] A police spy, *esp.* a French one.

mouche /muːʃ/ *n.* L17. [Fr., lit. 'a fly', f. L *musca*.] **1** *Hist.* A small patch of black plaster worn on the face as an ornament or to conceal a blemish. L17. **2** A natural mark on the face resembling such a patch; a beauty spot. M19.

moucher *n.* var. of MOOCHER.

mouchette /muːˈʃɛt/ *n.* E20. [Fr.] *Archit.* A motif in curvilinear tracery shaped like a curved dagger.

mouchoir /muʃwaːr (*pl. same*), ˈmuːʃwɑː/ *n.* L17. [Fr.] A handkerchief.

moue /muː/ *n.* & *v.* M19. [Fr.: see MOW *n.*[2]] **A** *n.* A pouting expression, a pout. M19. **B** *v.* **1** *v.t.* Stare at. *rare.* E20. **2** *v.i.* Pout. M20.

mouflon /ˈmuːflɒn/ *n.* Also **-ff-**. L18. [Fr. f. It. *muflone* f. Proto-Romance.] **1** A wild mountain sheep, as an aoudad, a urial; *spec.* the Asiatic sheep *Ovis orientalis*, native to the Middle East and established also in Sardinia, Corsica, and central Europe, and thought to be the closest relative of the domestic sheep. L18. **2** The fur of the mouflon; woollen fabric made from this or a similar fur. E20.

mought *v.* see MAY *v.*[1]

mouillé /muje, ˈmuːjeɪ/ *a.* M19. [Fr., pa. pple of *mouiller* wet, moisten.] *Phonet.* Of a consonant, esp. *l*, *n*, or *r*: palatalized, softened.

moujik *n.* var. of MUZHIK.

moul /məʊl/ *v.*[1] *obs.* exc. *Sc.* & *north.* ME. [Ult. f. ON vb rel. to *mygla* grow mouldy.] **1** *v.i.* Grow or become mouldy. ME. **2** *v.t.* Make mouldy. LME.

†moul *v.*[2]*t. rare.* M16–E18. [Var. of MOULD *v.*[1], perh. after Fr. *mouler* to mould.] = MOULD *v.*[2] 4, 5, 6.

moulage /ˈmuːlɑːʒ/ *n.* E20. [Fr. = moulding, moulded reproduction, f. *mouler* to mould: see -AGE.] A cast or impression of a (part of a) person or thing; the material used for or the process of making a cast or taking an impression.

mould /məʊld/ *n.*[1] Also ***mold**. [OE *molde* = OFris. *molde*, (M)Du. *moude*, OHG *molta*, ON *mold*, Goth. *mulda*, f. Gmc base meaning 'pulverize, grind'. Cf. OE *myl*, MDu. *mul*, *mol* dust, MEAL *n.*[1] Cf. also MOOL *n.*] **1** Loose, broken, or friable earth; surface soil, esp. as readily broken up. Also in *pl.* (now chiefly *Sc.* & *dial.*), lumps or clods of earth. OE. **2** The ground regarded as a place of burial. Now only *poet.* & *dial.* OE. **†3** The ground regarded as a surface or as a solid stratum. OE–E17. **4** The world in which humans live; the earth. Also, the land of a particular region. *obs.* exc. *poet.* OE. **5** The upper soil of cultivated land, garden-soil, esp. if rich in organic matter. Freq. w. specifying wd. ME. **6** (The material of) the human body. *obs.* exc. *poet.* and in *man of mould* below. ME. **†b** The dust (DUST *n.* 2a) to which a human body is regarded as returning after death; a dead person's remains. LME–M17.

1 H. MAUNDRELL Vast naked Rocks without the least sign of Mould. J. CLARE In fresh-turn'd moulds which first beheld the sun. 2 WORDSWORTH They were not loth To give their bodies to the family mould. A. E. HOUSMAN The bed of mould Where there's neither heat nor cold. 3 M. DRAYTON Where now it lyes even levell'd with the mold. 4 SIR W. SCOTT The fairest knight on Scottish mold. 5 N. NICHOLLS The loose and fermenting mould of the garden and fields. G. J. ROMANES The amount of mould which worms are able to cast up. *leaf-mould* etc. 6 COVERDALE *Tobit* 8:6 Thou maydest Adam of the moulde of the earth. MILTON And leprous sin will melt from earthly mould. **man of mould** a mere mortal. b G. SANDYS Though wormes devoure mee, though I turne to mold.

Comb.: **mould-board**, (long *obs.* exc. *Sc.*) **mouldbred** the board or metal plate in a plough for turning over the furrow-slice.

mould /məʊld/ *n.*[2] Now *dial.* [OE *molda*, *molde* = MDu. *moude* rel. to Skt *mūrdhan* highest point, head.] The top or dome of the head; a fontanelle in an infant's head.

mould /məʊld/ *n.*[3] Also ***mold**. ME. [App. (w. metathesis) f. OFr. *modle* (mod. *moule*) f. L MODULUS.] **I** A pattern by which something is shaped. **1a** A pattern or template used by a mason, bricklayer, etc., as a guide in shaping mouldings etc. ME. **b** Any of various thin flexible pieces of wood used for making a pattern of the frames used in constructing a ship's hull. M18. **2a** A hollow form or matrix into which fluid material is poured or plastic material is pressed to harden into a required shape. Also, an impressed surface from which a cast can be taken. LME. **b** *Cookery.* A hollow vessel used to give a shape to puddings, jelly, etc. Freq. w. specifying wd. L16. **3** *transf.* & *fig.* **a** That which gives an essential shape and form to something. Esp. in *cast in a heroic* etc. *mould* below. M16. **†b** The body regarded as the form within its clothes. E–M17. **†4** An object of imitation; a model, a pattern. M16–E17. **5** A frame or body on or round which a manufactured article is made. M17. **6** A package of leaves of gold-beaters' skin between which gold leaf is placed for beating. E18. **7** In photo-engraving, the gelatin which receives the impression from the negative and from which the copper plate is taken. L19.

1 J. NICHOLSON To find the moulds necessary for the construction of a semicircular arch. b *temple mould*: see TEMPLE *n.*[3] 2. 2 J. BRONOWSKI The Chinese made the mould for a bronze casting. b *Sunday Express* Line a paté mould with the remaining 4oz streaky bacon. *dariole mould*, *jelly mould*, etc. 3a SHAKES. *Coriol.* My wife comes foremost, then the honour'd mould Wherein this trunk was fram'd. J. WESLEY Cast in the Mould of Sin I am. b SHAKES. *Macb.* New honours . . Like our strange garments, cleave not to their mould But with the aid of use. 4 W. LAMBARDE Having neither good arte . . nor yet approved patterne or Moald to imitate and follow.

II Imparted form; result of moulding. **8** The distinctive nature of a person, character, etc., as indicative of origin. ME. **9** *Archit.* A moulding, a group of mouldings. L15. **10a** The form or shape of something, esp. an animal body. E16. **b** Bodily form, body. Chiefly *poet.* L16. **11** Orig., plastic material. Later, that which is moulded or fashioned. *rare.* M16. **†12** The form, structural type, or model of a building, ship, etc. L16–L18. **†13** Style, fashion, mode. E–M17. **14** In full *mould-candle*. A candle made in a mould as distinct from one made by dipping a wick in melted tallow. E19. **15** *Geol.* A fossil impression of a convex structure. M19. **16** A pudding, jelly, etc., shaped in a mould. M19.

8 M. PRIOR Hans Carvel . . Married a lass of London mould. B. JOWETT He has a character of a finer mould. **10a** SIR W. SCOTT The buff-coat . . Mantles his form's gigantic mould. b WORDSWORTH Whom doth she behold? . . His vital presence? his corporeal mould? 11 MILTON The formless Mass, This worlds material mould, came to a heap. 12 M. MACKENZIE A Vessel . . of such a Mould as to draw little Water. 13 P. HEYLIN The houses of the new mould in London, are just after their fashion. 14 T. L. PEACOCK She . . would have burned like a short mould.

Phrases: **break the mould** *fig.* make impossible the repetition of a certain type of creation. **cast in a heroic** etc. **mould** of a heroic etc. character. *running mould*: see RUNNING *a.* *waste mould*: see WASTE *n.* *wove mould*: see WOVE *a.* & *n.*

Comb.: **mould-blowing** *Glass-making* the blowing of glass inside a mould to give it the required shape; *mould-candle*: see sense 14 above; **mould-loft** *Shipbuilding* & *Aeronaut.* a room on the floor of which the plans of a ship etc. are drawn at full size; **mould-made** *a.* (of paper) made on a type of machine producing sheets resembling sheets of handmade paper; **mould oil** *Building* an oil applied to formwork to prevent concrete adhering to it; **mould-runner** an operative in a pottery responsible for transferring a completed article to the drying-oven.

mould /məʊld/ *n.*[4] Also ***mold**. LME. [Prob. f. pa. pple of MOUL *v.*[1] Cf. MOULD *a.*] A woolly, furry, or staining growth of minute fungi, as that which forms on food, textiles, etc., esp. in moist warm air. Also *spec.*, = FEN *n.*[2] 2.

DICKENS Mildew and mould began to lurk in closets. ANTHONY HUXLEY Glistening droplets of fluid such as exude from moulds on decaying matter. *blue mould*, *potato mould*, *slime mould*, *sooty mould*, etc.

mould /məʊld/ *n.*[5] Long *obs.* exc. in IRON-MOULD. Also **mold**. L16. [Alt.] = MOLE *n.*[1]

mould /məʊld/ *a.* Long *obs.* exc. *dial.* ME. [pa. pple of MOUL *v.*[1] Cf. MOULD *n.*[4]] Mouldy.

mould /məʊld/ *v.*[1] Also ***mold**. LME. [f. MOULD *n.*[3]] **1** *v.t.* Mix or knead (dough etc.); shape (bread) into loaves. LME. **†2** *v.t.* Mix (ingredients) to form a paste. LME–M17. **b** *fig.* Mix *up*, blend (*with*). E18–M19. **3** *v.t.* Produce (an object) in a particular form, esp. *out of* or *from* a certain element, *on* or *upon* a certain pattern (*lit.* & *fig.*). L15. **†b** Foll. by *up*: go to form. Only in E17. **4** *v.t.* Shape (fluid or plastic material) into a required shape by pouring or pressing into a hollow form or matrix. Also foll. by *into*. Cf. earlier MOUL *v.*[2] L16. **5** *v.t.* *Shipbuilding.* Orig., give a particular form or structure to (a vessel). Later, provide a particular pattern for (timbers etc.) using moulds. L16. **6** *v.t.* Bring (material) into a particular shape or form; shape or model the character, style, or development of. Foll. by *into*, *to*. E17. **7** *v.i.* & (*rare*) *refl.* Assume a certain form; become shaped. E17. **8** *v.t.* Take a cast of. Now *rare* or *obs.* L17. **9** *v.t.* Of a garment: fit close to (the figure). L19.

3 ADDISON There is great art in moulding a question. SHELLEY Obscure clouds, moulded by the casual air. G. SWIFT His fingers were soiled with newsprint . . as though they were moulded from lead. b SHAKES. *Hen. VIII* All princely graces That mould up such a mighty piece as this is. 4 J. BRONOWSKI To take some clay and mould it into a ball. T. E. HULME I have no material clay to mould to the given shape. 6 MAX-MÜLLER His character was chiefly moulded by his intercourse with men. P. G. WODEHOUSE A weaker spirit whom she could mould to her will. 7 *Ecclesiologist* When the Norman man-at-arms had begun to mould into the English country gentleman.

moulda'bility *n.* ability to be moulded L19. **mouldable** *a.* able to be moulded E17. **mouldableness** *n.* (*rare*) L19.

mould /məʊld/ *v.*[2] Also ***mold**. L15. [f. MOULD *n.*[4] or f. MOUL *v.*[1] + *-d*.] **1** *v.t.* Orig., allow to become mouldy. Later, cause to contract mould. Now *rare*. L15. **2** *v.i.* Become mouldy or covered with mould. M16.

1 E. RAINBOWE Sloth moulding some, anxiety consuming others. 2 E. FIELD The little toy soldier is red with rust, And his musket moulds in his hands. *fig.*: SPENSER The man that moulds in ydle cell.

mould /məʊld/ *v.*[3] Also ***mold**. M16. [f. MOULD *n.*[1]] **1** *v.t.* Bury. Long *obs.* exc. *Sc.* M16. **2** *v.i.* & (*rare*) *t.* Moulder (*away*), crumble to pieces. Now *rare*. M16. **3** *v.t.* Cover (the stems and roots of plants) with soil; earth *up*. Now chiefly *US* & *dial.* E17.

moulded /ˈməʊldɪd/ *a.*[1] *rare.* Also ***molded**. M16. [f. MOULD *n.*[4], *v.*[2]: see -ED[2], -ED[1].] Mouldy.

moulded /ˈməʊldɪd/ *a.*[2] Also ***molded**. L16. [f. MOULD *n.*[3], *v.*[1]: see -ED[2], -ED[1].] Esp. of a particular shape or structure: that has been moulded; that has a mould or moulds.

moulded breadth, **width**, etc. the greatest breadth, width, etc., of a vessel.

moulder /ˈməʊldə/ *n.* Also ***molder**. ME. [f. MOULD *v.*[1] + -ER[1].] 1 A person who moulds something; a person who moulds dough, clay, etc.; a person who makes loaves, bricks, etc., by moulding. Also, a person employed in making moulds for casting. ME. 2 An instrument for moulding; a mould. Now *rare* or *obs.* E17.

1 *Times* Mr Sydney Lavington . . an unemployed moulder and caster. M. STOTT The chief moulders of public opinion are commercial interests.

moulder /ˈməʊldə/ *v.* Also ***molder**. M16. [Perh. f. MOULD *n.*[1] + -ER[5], but cf. Norw. dial. *muldra.*] 1 *v.i.* Decay to dust; rot *away*; crumble. M16. 2 *v.t.* Cause to decay to dust, rot away, or crumble. Now *rare* exc. *dial.* M17. 3 *v.i.* Esp. of an army: be diminished in number; dwindle (*away*). Now *rare* or *obs.* L17. 4 *v.i.* Move *off* in an aimless or lifeless manner. *rare.* M20.

1 E. SHANKS We shall moulder in the plains of France. T. HOOPER [Honey]Combs which have dried out and partly mouldered away. *fig.*: TENNYSON Never man . . So moulder'd in a sinecure as he. 2 WORDSWORTH Long after we . . are mouldered in our graves. *fig.*: DONNE How many men have we seene Molder and crumble away great Estates. 3 CLARENDON If he had sat still the other great army would have mouldered to nothing. 4 E. BOWEN I mouldered off by myself . . to watch the old clock.

mouldery *a.* (long *rare* exc. *dial.*) (esp. of soil) crumbly, friable E17.

moulding /ˈməʊldɪŋ/ *n.*[1] Also ***molding**. ME. [f. MOULD *v.*[1] + -ING[1].] 1 The action of MOULD *v.*[1]; an instance of this. ME. 2 A moulded object; *Archit.* an ornamental variety of outline in the cornices, capitals, etc., of a building (freq. w. specifying wd); a similar outline in ornamental woodwork; a strip of wood, metal, plastic, etc., with an ornamental variety of outline. LME.

2 M. MOORCOCK She noticed the terra-cotta mouldings, depicting monks of olden days. D. LODGE Lifting the heavy-looking mouldings reeking of hot resin, from the machine. *bed moulding*, *bird's beak moulding*, *dovetail moulding*, *hood moulding*, *waste moulding*, etc.

Comb.: **moulding-board** a board used in moulding, *esp.* one on which dough etc. is kneaded; **moulding-plane** a plane for shaping mouldings.

moulding /ˈməʊldɪŋ/ *n.*[2] Also ***molding**. M16. [f. MOULD *v.*[2] + -ING[1].] 1 The process of becoming mouldy. M16. †2 Mould, mouldy growth. Only in 17.

moulding /ˈməʊldɪŋ/ *n.*[3] Also ***molding**. L17. [f. MOULD *v.*[3] + -ING[1].] The action or an act of covering the stems and roots of plants with soil; earthing-*up*.

mouldwarp /ˈməʊldwɔːp/ *n.* Now chiefly *dial.* & *poet.* Also **mouldywarp** /ˈməʊldɪwɔːp/ & other vars. ME. [Prob. f. MLG *moldewerp* (whence Du. *muldvarp*) = OHG *multwurf*, f. WGmc, f. Gmc bases of MOULD *n.*[1], WARP *v.*] = MOLE *n.*[2]

mouldy /ˈməʊldi/ *n. Navy & RAF slang.* E20. [Origin unkn.] A torpedo.

mouldy /ˈməʊldi/ *a.*[1] Also ***moldy**. LME. [f. MOULD *n.*[4] + -Y[1].] 1a Overgrown or covered with mould; decaying, decayed. LME. b Of, consisting of, or resembling mould. *rare.* L16. 2 *transf.* & *fig.* Stale, out of date; wretched; dull, miserable, boring. Now chiefly *slang.* L16.

1a J. LINDLEY Books will not become mouldy in the neighbourhood of Russia leather. W. HENRY Covered over with . . moldy hay. b ADDISON The walls On all sides furr'd with mouldy damps. 2 *Spectator* The ancient joke about smelling the paper-knife is one of the mouldiest of witticisms. M. KENNEDY Do please come home soon, for it's mouldy without you. ALDOUS HUXLEY One feels a bit low and mouldy after those bouts of flu.

Special collocations & *comb.*: **mouldy fig** *slang* an admirer or performer of traditional jazz (as opp. to other kinds of jazz). **mouldy-fig** *a.* (*slang*) of, pertaining to, or characteristic of a 'mouldy fig'.

mouldily *adv.* (*rare*) M19. **mouldiness** *n.* L16.

mouldy /ˈməʊldi/ *a.*[2] Now *rare.* Also ***moldy**. E17. [f. MOULD *n.*[1] + -Y[1].] Of the nature of mould or fine soil.

moule /mul/ *n.* Pl. pronounced same. L19. [Fr.] *Cookery.* A mussel. Usu. in *pl.*

moules bonne femme etc. ***moules à la marinière***, ***moules marinière(s)*** /(a la) marinjɛːr/ [lit. 'in the marine manner'] mussels served in their shells and cooked in a wine and onion sauce.

Mouli /ˈmuːli/ *n.* Also **m-**. M20. [Abbrev. of MOULINETTE.] (Proprietary name for) a type of kitchen utensil for grinding or puréeing food.

moulin /ˈmuːlɪn, *foreign* mulɛ̃ (*pl. same*)/ *n.* M19. [Fr., lit. 'mill'.] 1 A deep, nearly vertical shaft in a glacier, formed by falling water. Also called *glacier mill.* M19. 2 A type of kitchen utensil for grinding or puréeing food. M20.

moulinet /muːlɪˈnɛt/ *n.* M17. [Fr., dim. of *moulin* mill: see -ET[1].] 1 A device for winding, hoisting, etc.; a winch. Now *rare* or *obs.* M17. †2 A kind of turnstile. Only in 18. 3 *Fencing.* A circular swing of a sword or sabre. L19.

Moulinette /muːlɪˈnɛt/ *n.* Also **m-**. M20. [f. as prec.: see -ETTE.] (Proprietary name for) a type of kitchen utensil for grinding or puréeing food.

moult /məʊlt/ *n.* Also ***molt**. E19. [f. MOULT *v.*] The action or an act of moulting. Freq. in *in the moult*, in a condition of moulting.

Times August, with many birds in the moult. R. F. CHAPMAN A pellet of faecal matter is deposited at the larva-pupa moult.

moult /məʊlt/ *v.* Also ***molt**. ME. [Corresp. (w. intrusive *l*) to MLG, MDu. *mūten*, OHG *mūzzōn* (G *mause(r)n*), f. WGmc, f. L *mutare* change: prob. already in OE (implied in *bimūtian* to exchange).] 1 *v.i.* Of hair etc.: fall out. Of feathers: be shed in the process of a bird's changing plumage. Also foll. by *off.* Long *rare.* ME. 2 *v.i.* Of a bird: shed feathers in the process of changing plumage. Of an animal: shed a shell, a skin, hair, etc., in the process of acquiring a new growth. LME. 3 *v.t.* Of a bird: shed (feathers) in the process of changing plumage. Of an animal: shed (a shell, a skin, hair, etc.) in the process of acquiring a new growth. M16.

2 *Scientific American* Crabs are most vulnerable to attack when they molt. *Cage & Aviary Birds* They begin to moult into adult colour at about five months old. *transf.*: B. BAINBRIDGE He was covered in strands of saffron-coloured fur. She had moulted all over him. 3 D. ATTENBOROUGH The feathers on which a bird's life is so dependent are regularly moulted and renewed.

moulted *ppl a.* (*a*) that has moulted; deprived of feathers, hair, etc., by moulting; (*b*) shed during moulting: LME. †**moulten** *ppl a.* = MOULTED (a): only in L16.

moulter /ˈməʊltə/ *n. rare.* Also ***molter**. LME. [f. MOULT *v.* + -ER[1].] A moulting bird.

moulter /ˈməʊltə/ *v.*[1]*t.* & *i.* Long *obs.* exc. *dial.* Also **molter**. M16. [Perh. alt. of MOULDER *v.*] = MOULDER *v.*

†**moulter** *v.*[2]*i.* & *t.* M17–E18. [Perh. f. MOULTER *n.*] Moult.

moulvi /ˈmuːlvi/ *n.* Also **maulvi** /ˈmaʊlvi/, **moolvi(e)**. E17. [Urdu *maulvī* f. Arab. *mawlawī* judicial (used as n.), f. *mawlā* MULLAH.] A Muslim doctor of the law, an imam; *gen.* (esp. in the Indian subcontinent, used as a form of address to) a learned person or teacher.

mouly /ˈməʊli/ *a.* Long *obs.* exc. *dial.* L15. [f. MOUL *v.*[1] + -Y[1].] Mouldy.

mound /maʊnd/ *n.*[1] ME. [(O)Fr. *monde* f. L *mundus* world.] †1 The world; the earth as the abode of humankind. Only in ME. 2 A globe forming part of royal regalia, usu. of gold and often surmounted by a cross; an orb; *Her.* this as a charge. M16.

mound /maʊnd/ *v.* & *n.*[2] E16. [Origin unkn.] A *v.t.* 1 Enclose, surround, with a mound or mounds. E16. 2 Heap up in a mound or mounds. M19.

1 SHELLEY Let hell unlock Its mounded oceans of tempestuous fire. TENNYSON A sand-built ridge Of heaped hills that mound the sea. 2 D. STOREY The pots they'd mounded in the sink for washing. C. CONRAN Mound the green beans on top in little pyramids.

B *n.* 1 A hedge, a fence, esp. as forming a boundary. Long *obs.* exc. *dial.* M16. 2 A fortification consisting of a raised bank of earth etc. (cf. MOUNT *n.*[1] 2); *gen.* an embankment, a dam. Now *rare.* M16. 3 An artificially constructed elevation of earth, stones, debris, etc.; *esp.* a pile of earth heaped up on a grave, a tumulus. Also *gen.*, a heap , a pile, esp. of objects of the same kind. E18. 4 A naturally occurring elevation resembling a heap or pile of earth; a small hill. E19. 5 *Baseball.* The slight elevation on which a pitcher stands. E20.

1 SPENSER This great gardin, compast with a mound. 2 J. THOMSON The circly Mound That runs around the Hill; the Rampart once Of Iron War. BURKE The mounds and dykes of the low fat Bedford level. 3 P. BOWLES She pushed herself further back into the mound of pillows. P. ROTH The little mounds of pebbles piled there by the pilgrims. W. RAEPER The train sped on . . past the grass-grown burial mound. 4 T. H. HUXLEY The volcanic beds which make up the mass of the mound. *Cornwall Review* St. Agnes Beacon is a great mound rising to 600 feet. **mound of Venus** = *mount of* VENUS. 5 *Billings (Montana) Gazette* Buddy Welch . . won't be on the mound . . this season, he'll be in the outfield.

Comb.: **mound ant** *Austral.* = *meat-ant* s.v. MEAT *n.*; **mound-bird** a megapode; **mound-builder** (*a*) a member of a prehistoric N. American Indian people whose culture was characterized by the erection of mounds; (*b*) a megapode; **moundsman** *Baseball* a pitcher.

moundy *a.* covered with mounds M19.

mounseer /maʊnˈsɪə/ *n. joc.* & *derog. arch.* M17. [Repr. an Anglicized pronunc. of MONSIEUR. Cf. MOSSOO.] A Frenchman.

mount /maʊnt/ *n.*[1] OE. [L *mont-*, *mons* mountain, reinforced in ME by forms f. (O)Fr. *mont.* In sense 6 also infl. by It. *monte.*] I 1 Orig., a mountain, a high hill. Later, an approximately conical hill of moderate height rising from a plain; a hillock. Now chiefly *poet.* and in names of particular mountains etc. OE. 2 *Mil.* A substantial defensive or protective work of earth etc. Formerly also = CAVALIER *n.* 1. *obs.* exc. *Hist.* M16. †3 An artificially constructed mound of earth, stones, debris, etc., esp. in a garden. L16–E19.

1 BROWNING Ye mounts Where I climb to 'scape my fellow. *Mount Everest*, *St Michael's Mount*, *the Mount of Olives*, etc. *Sermon on the Mount*: see SERMON *n.* 2 AV *Isa.* 29:3 I . . will lay siege against thee with a mount. 3 H. COGAN Behind their houses . . were two great Mounts of dead mens bones. S. JOHNSON Digging canals and raising mounts.

II 4 Any of various fleshy prominences on the palm of the hand regarded in palmistry as significant of the degree of influence exercised by a particular planet. LME. †5 A measure of quantity of plaster equal to 30 hundredweight (approx. 1524 kg). M16–E18. †6 A financial institution; *spec.* a bank. E17–M18.

4 : *mount of* VENUS. 6 **mount of piety** [tr.] = MONTE DI PIETÀ, MONT DE PIÉTÉ.

mount /maʊnt/ *n.*[2] LME. [f. MOUNT *v.* Perh. also infl. by Fr. *monte.*] †1 = AMOUNT *n.* LME–M17. 2 An act of mounting (*rare*); a manner of mounting. Also (orig. *slang*), an act of copulation. L15. 3 A support in or on which something is set or placed or to which something is fixed, esp. for the purpose of display; *spec.* (*a*) a margin surrounding a picture etc., a card or other backing to which a drawing etc. is fastened; (*b*) a glass slide to which an object is secured for viewing by microscope; (*c*) a setting for a gem; (*d*) a stamp-hinge or other device for the arrangement and display of stamps in an album etc.; (*e*) the frame or support of a fan made of pieces of wood, ivory, etc.; (*f*) *Photogr.* a fitting to support a camera lens, *esp.* one on a camera with interchangeable lenses. Also in *pl.*, ornamental metal edges, borders, etc., esp. of decorative furniture. M18. 4 A horse, bicycle, etc., on which a person is mounted; a horse etc. provided for a person's riding. *colloq.* M19. 5 An opportunity for riding, esp. as a jockey. M19. 6 A stuffed and mounted skin, esp. of a bird. M20.

4 E. Elmhirst Others merely give their mounts a kick in the ribs and gallop onwards. G. Harris There was hardly enough fodder for the soldiers' mounts. 5 *Illustrated London News* The custom is to pay at least twenty-five pounds for a mount in the Derby. 6 *British Birds* The female mount . . had a half-spread tail.

mount /maʊnt/ *v.* ME. [OFr. *munter*, (also mod.) *monter* f. Proto-Romance, f. L *mont-*, *mons* MOUNT *n.*[1] Cf. AMOUNT *v.*] **I** *v.i.* **1** Go or move upwards, ascend, (freq. foll. by *up*); (of the blood) rise into the cheeks. Also, extend in an upward direction. ME. **2** Get on a horse, bicycle, etc., for the purpose of riding. (Foll. by *on*, †*to*.) ME. †**3** Amount or be equal *to* a certain number, quantity, etc. LME–M18. **4** *fig.* **a** Rise or ascend to a higher level of rank, power, etc.; be or become elevated. LME. **b** Go back in time. Foll. by (*up*) *to*. L18. **5** Increase in amount or intensity; (of a sound) rise in pitch, grow louder. Freq. foll. by *up*. LME. **6** Get up *on* something serving to raise one from a lower to a higher level. M17. **7** Orig., ascend a stage, platform, etc.; appear as a performer. Later *spec.*, appear as a witness, give (false) evidence. *arch. slang.* M18.

1 C. Kingsley A body of gladiators . . planting their scaling-ladders . . mounted to the attack. A. Trollope The blood mounted all over his face. G. Greene A bank mounted steeply on either side of the train. 2 F. Norris Annixter mounted and rode into Bonneville. 3 Pope Bring then these blessings to a strict account; . . see to what they mount. 4a Wordsworth As high as we have mounted in delight In our dejection do we sink as low. b J. M. Jephson An antiquity which mounts up to the eighth century.

II *v.t.* †**8** Cause to ascend or rise; lift up or *up*; erect. ME–E19. †**9** *fig.* Elevate; raise to a higher level of rank, power, etc. M16–L18. **10** Set or place on an elevation. Now only foll. by *on*, *upon*. M16. **11a** Raise (guns) into position; place in a position ready for firing. Also (now *rare*), raise the muzzle of (a gun); place at a particular angle of elevation. M16. **b** Provide (a fort, ship, etc.) *with* guns (usu. in *pass.*). Also, (of a fort, ship, etc.) have (guns) in position. M17. **c** Place (a guard, watch, etc.) for the purpose of defence or observation. Now chiefly in *mount guard* s.v. GUARD *n.* E18. **12** Place (a person) on a horse, bicycle, etc., for the purpose of riding; help into the saddle, provide with a horse for riding; in *pass.*, be seated on horseback. E17. **13a** Fix in position for a particular purpose; bring into readiness for operation. E18. **b** Set or place in or on or fix to a support, esp. for the purpose of display; *spec.* (*a*) surround (a picture etc.) with a margin, fasten (a drawing etc.) on to a card or other backing; (*b*) set (a gem etc.) in gold etc.; (*c*) secure (an object) on a microscope slide; (*d*) prepare (a preserved specimen) for examination and viewing. Also, fit (esp. decorative furniture) with ornamental edges, borders, etc. E19. **14** Put on or show oneself as wearing (an article of clothing). *arch.* E19. **15** Stage, present for public viewing or display, (a play, exhibition, etc.). Also, put on, produce, (a radio or television programme). L19. **16** Take action to initiate or effect (esp. a military offensive). M20.

8 J. Clare Water-lilies mount their snowy buds. 9 F. Quarles Who mounts the meeke, and beates the lofty downe. 10 Dryden We bear thee on our Backs and mount thee on the Throne. M. Kingsley A cluster of outbuildings . . each mounted on poles. 11a Shakes. *John* By east and west let France and England mount Their battering cannon, charged to the mouths. *Shooting Life* To mount the gun in a position that might not suit you. b H. Latham Earthworks mounted with cannon. B. B. Schofield The German ships . . mounted 10 5.9-inch and 5 5-inch guns. 12 H. Belloc I don't suppose he rides, but I can't mount him anyhow. A. Harding Charles, mounted upon the same horse. 13a *Outing* (*US*) He mounted his rod, and tried casting in shallow water. b G. J. Hinde Spicules . . when mounted in Canada balsam are nearly transparent. G. Greene Photographs mounted on mauve silk in oval frames. 14 S. Lover It was time to . . mount fresh linen and cambric. 15 *Listener* The first town that . . asked us to mount a festival. H. Carpenter The Group Theatre . . mounted a couple of small-scale productions. 16 *New York Times* Warplanes of the Far East Air Forces mounted 1,283 sorties. *Listener* Governments mount big campaigns to secure an 'incomes policy'.

III *v.t.* **17a** Ascend, climb up, (a hill, slope, stairs, etc.). L15. **b** Rise on to (an obstruction etc.) in the course of progression, esp. accidentally. M20. **18** Get on (a horse, bicycle, etc.) for the purpose of riding. M16. **19** Esp. of an animal: get on for the purpose of copulation. L17. **20** Ascend and take a place in or on; get up on or into. L17.

17b *Morning Post* He just managed to avoid a crash . . , and in doing so he mounted the footpath. 20 C. Thirlwall Since he himself had mounted the throne. P. Abrahams He's very sure of himself, Rae thought as he mounted the pulpit. *Times* Sentenced to death for drug trafficking and soon to mount the gallows.

mount the ladder: see LADDER *n.* 1b.

mountable *a.* (earlier in UNMOUNTABLE) E17. **mounter** *n.* E17.

mountain /ˈmaʊntɪn/ *n.* ME. [OFr. *montaigne* (mod. *montagne*), f. Proto-Romance fem. sing. or neut. pl. of adj., f. L *mont-*, *mons* MOUNT *n.*[1]] **1** A large natural elevation of the earth's surface, *esp.* one high and steep in form (larger and higher than a hill) and with a summit of relatively small area. Also in *pl.*, such elevations constituting a region characterized by remoteness and inaccessibility. ME. †**b** A large artificially constructed hill or tumulus. M16–M17. **2a** A large heap or pile; a towering mass. Also, a huge quantity *of*. LME. **b** A large surplus stock, esp. of a commodity. Freq. w. specifying wd. Cf. LAKE *n.*[2] 2b. M20. **3** More fully *mountain wine*. A variety of Malaga wine. E18. **4** Fr. Hist. *the Mountain*, an extreme party in the National Convention during the French Revolution, led by Robespierre and Danton, so called because its members occupied the most elevated position in the hall; any of several later political groups or parties of extreme views. Cf. PLAIN *n.*[1] 7. E19. **5** (**M-**.) A steam locomotive of 4-8-2 wheel arrangement. L19.

2a S. Kauffmann Mountains of . . meaningless, commercial tripe. D. Francis The gaze of both men swept the mountain of paper. *Sunday Times* Try harder . . to overcome the mountain of debt. b *Times* A butter mountain of 1, 032, 000 tonnes and a milk lake of 845, 000 tonnes. *beef mountain*, *grain mountain*, etc.

Phrases etc.: BURNING *mountain*. *cat o' mountain*, *cat of the mountain*: see CATAMOUNTAIN. *make a mountain (out) of a* MOLEHILL. †**mountain of ice** an iceberg. **mountains high** (of the sea) in huge waves. *old man of the mountains*: see OLD MAN *n. phr.* *snow-on-the-mountain*: see SNOW *n.*[1] *the Mountain*: see sense 4 above. *Welsh mountain (sheep)*: see WELSH *a.*

Attrib. & comb.: In the senses 'of, belonging to, or characteristic of mountains, occurring among mountains', as *mountain air*, *road*, *stream*, etc.; 'that is a native or inhabitant of mountains, originating among mountains', as *mountain tiger*, *tribe*, etc. Special combs., as **mountain ash** (*a*) a small European tree of the rose family, *Sorbus aucuparia*, with pinnate leaves, white flowers, and scarlet berries, esp. characteristic of heathy or hilly districts (also called *rowan*); also, either of two related N. American trees, *S. americana* and *S. decora*; (*b*) *Austral.* any of several tall eucalypts, esp. *Eucalyptus regnans*; *mountain* AVENS; **mountain bat** a very small social bat, *Emballonura monticola*, of Borneo, Java, Sumatra, and the Philippines; **mountain beaver** a small burrowing rodent, *Aplodontia rufa*, of forests in the north-western US; also called *sewellel*; **mountain bike** a rugged lightweight bicycle with deeply treaded tyres; **mountain blackbird** the ring ouzel; **mountain blue** a blue or bluish-copper mineral, *esp.* (*a*) azurite; (*b*) chrysocolla; **mountain bluebird** *N. Amer.* a bluebird of western N. America, *Sialia currucoides*, distinguished by a blue (rather than red) breast; **mountain-building** the formation of mountains, esp. as a result of folding and thrusting of the earth's crust; **mountain cat** any of various wild cats of mountainous regions, as the bobcat, the lynx; **mountain chain** a connected series of mountains; *esp.* an aggregate of ranges of mountains having a common alignment; **mountain chicken** *colloq.* an edible W. Indian frog of the genus *Leptodactylus*, a crapaud; **mountain-climber** a person who climbs mountains, esp. as a sport; **mountain-climbing** the action or activity of climbing mountains, esp. as a sport; **mountain cock** = CAPERCAILLIE; **mountain cranberry** *US* (the fruit of) the cowberry, *Vaccinium vitis-idaea*; **mountain daisy** any of various plants of the genus *Celmisia*, of the composite family, with large daisy-like flowers, mostly confined to the mountains of New Zealand; *Mountain* DAMARA; **mountain devil** (*a*) = MOLOCH 2; (*b*) *Austral.* the honey-flower, *Lambertia formosa*; **mountain dew** *colloq.* whisky (esp. Scotch whisky), esp. when illicitly distilled; **mountain duck** (*a*) *Austral.* a chestnut-breasted shelduck, *Tadorna tadornoides*; (*b*) *NZ* the blue duck, *Hymenolaimus malacorhynchos* (also called *whio*); **mountain ebony** (the dark hard wood of) any of several leguminous trees of the genus *Bauhinia*, esp. the Asian *B. variegata* and the Australian *B. hookeri*; **mountain fern** a fern of mountain pastures, *Oreopteris limbosperma*, with lemon-scented fronds; **mountain fever** any of various malarial or typhoid fevers contracted in mountain regions; **mountain finch** (*a*) = BRAMBLING; (*b*) = *snow finch* s.v. SNOW *n.*[1]; **mountain flax** (*a*) any of various upland plants; *esp.* a New Zealand plant, *Phormium cookianum*, a smaller relative of the New Zealand flax, *P. tenax*; (*b*) = AMIANTHUS; **mountain-folding** the formation of mountains as a result of folding of the earth's crust; **mountain gazelle** a small gazelle, *Gazella gazella*, now confined to semidesert and scrub in the Arabian peninsula; **mountain goat** a goat of mountain regions; *esp.* a Rocky Mountain goat, *Oreamnos americanus*; **mountain gorilla**: of a threatened race occurring at higher altitudes in Zaire, Rwanda, and Uganda, with long hair and long teeth; **mountain green** (*a*) glauconite or (formerly) malachite, esp. used as a pigment; the colour of this; (*b*) a small W. Indian tree, *Spathelia simplex*, of the rue family, producing showy purple flowers at the top of an unbranched stem; **mountain hare** a hare, *Lepus timidus*, of northern Eurasia whose coat is brown in summer and white in winter; also called *Arctic hare*, *blue hare*; **mountain heath** an evergreen alpine shrub, *Phyllodoce caerulea*, of the heath family; **mountain hemlock** a large coniferous tree, *Tsuga mertensiana*, of western N. America; **mountain-high** *a.* (*hyperbol.*) very high; **mountain land** *Anglo-Ir.* & *US* open waste land with poor vegetation, esp. in a hilly or mountainous region; **mountain laurel** a N. American evergreen shrub, *Kalmia latifolia*, of the heath family, with glossy leaves and pink flowers; **mountain limestone** *Geol.* a thick massive Carboniferous limestone; **mountain linnet** = TWITE; **mountain lion** = PUMA; **mountain mahogany** *N. Amer.* (*a*) sweet birch, *Betula lenta*; (*b*) any of various shrubs of the genus *Cercocarpus*, of the rose family; **mountain man** (*a*) an inhabiter or frequenter of mountains or mountainous country; (*b*) *US* a trapper; a pioneer; **mountain maple** = MAPLE *bush*; **mountain mint** any of various N. American labiate plants of the genus *Pycnanthemum*, whose leaves smell of mint when crushed; *mountain* NYALA; **mountain oyster** a lamb's testicle, as food; *mountain pansy*: see PANSY *n.* 1; **mountain panther** (*a*) = *snow leopard* s.v. SNOW *n.*[1]; (*b*) = PUMA; **mountain parrot** = KEA; **mountain partridge** = *mountain quail* below; **mountain plover** a small N. American plover, *Charadrius montanus*; **mountain plum** (the fruit of) a small spiny neotropical tree, *Ximenia americana* (family Olacaceae); **mountain pride** = *mountain green* (b) above; **mountain quail** a brown and grey plumed quail, *Oreortyx picta*, of western N. America; **mountain railway** (*a*) a light railway for transport in mountain regions; (*b*) a miniature ascending railway designed for amusement; a scenic railway; a funicular railway; **mountain range** a line or group of mountains connected by elevated ground; **mountain rat** the bushy-tailed woodrat, *Neotoma cinerea*, of the western US; **mountain reedbuck** a small reedbuck, *Redunca fulvorufula*, of montane grassland in southern, eastern, and central Africa; **mountain rescue** an organization for rescuing mountaineers, climbers, etc., in distress; **mountain rice** any of various grasses of the genus *Oryzopsis*, esp. *O. hymenoides*, used as grain by N. American Indians; **mountain ringlet** a satyrid butterfly, *Erebia epiphron*, of upland in northern Britain and parts of Europe; **mountain sheep** a sheep of the mountain regions; *esp.* (*N. Amer.*) a bighorn; **mountain sickness** a malady caused by breathing the rarefied air at a great height, altitude sickness; **mountainside** the sloping surface of a mountain below the summit; **mountain slide** a landslip occurring on a mountainside; **mountain snow** a spurge, *Euphorbia marginata*, of the western US, so called from the broad white border of its bracts; also called *snow-on-the-mountain*; *mountain sorrel*: see SORREL *n.*[1]; *mountain spiderwort*: see *spiderwort* (a) s.v. SPIDER *n.*; **Mountain (Standard) Time** *N. Amer.* the standard time of parts of Canada and the US in or near the Rocky Mountains; **mountain system** a group of mountain ranges in a region, assumed to have been formed by the same geological processes; **mountain tea** *N. Amer.* the checkerberry, *Gaultheria* *procumbens*; a drink made from an infusion of its leaves; **mountain thrush** any of several Old World thrushes found in mountainous areas, esp. *Zoothera mollissima* of the Himalayas and SE Asia and *Turdus abyssinicus* of E. Africa; *Mountain Time*: see *Mountain Standard Time* above; **mountain tortoise** = *leopard-tortoise* s.v. LEOPARD *n.*; **mountain trout** any of various fishes of mountain streams related to or resembling trout; *esp.* (chiefly *Austral.*) any of various fishes of the family Galaxiidae of the southern hemisphere; *mountain* VISCACHA; *mountain wine*: see sense 3 above; **mountain witch** a brightly coloured Jamaican quail dove, *Geotrygon versicolor*, of forest undergrowth; **mountain zebra** a zebra, *Equus zebra*, which has predominantly black stripes and a white belly, found locally on the mountain grasslands of SW Africa.

mountained *a.* (*rare*, chiefly *poet.*) (*a*) situated on a mountain; elevated, lofty; †(*b*) heaped mountain-high; †(*c*) obstructed by mountains; (*d*) containing mountains: E17.

mountaineer /maʊntɪˈnɪə/ *n.* & *v.* E17. [f. MOUNTAIN + -EER.] **A** *n.* **1** A native, inhabitant, or frequenter of mountains. E17. **b** More fully *Mountaineer Indian*. A member of any of various N. American Indian peoples of mountainous regions of Canada, esp. (formerly) the Montagnais or the Naskapi. *obs.* exc. *Hist.* L18. **c** A poorly educated person from a remote rural area. *US colloq.* (*derog.*). L19. **2** *Fr. Hist.* A member of the Mountain (see MOUNTAIN 4). E19. **3** A person skilled or occupied in mountaineering. M19. **B** *v.i.* Be a mountain-climber, practise mountain-climbing, esp. as a sport. Chiefly as *mountaineering* vbl n. & ppl a. E19.

†**mountainer** *n. rare.* LME. [f. MOUNTAIN + -ER[1].] **1** An adherent of a school of thought etc. with a name associated with mountains, as a Montanist. LME–M18. **2** = MOUNTAINEER *n.* 1. L16–M18. **3** = MONTAGNAIS *n.* Only in E17.

mountainet /maʊntɪˈnɛt/ *n.* Now chiefly *arch.* & *poet.* Also **-ette**. L16. [f. MOUNTAIN + -ET[1], -ETTE.] A small mountain; a hillock, a mound.

mountainous /ˈmaʊntɪnəs/ *a.* LME. [f. MOUNTAIN + -OUS, partly after Fr. *montagneux*.] †**1** Situated among mountains. *rare.* LME–M17. **2** Characterized by mountains; having many mountains. E17. **3** Resembling a mountain or mountains; huge, enormous. E17. †**4** Inhabiting mountains; living in a remote mountain region; uncivilized. E17–E18. †**5** Derived from or characteristic of mountains. L17–E19.

2 *Holiday Which?* The . . volcanic landscape of the Auvergne, mountainous but not wild. 3 J. RUSKIN The white edges of the mountainous clouds. M. WARNER She was almost blind, and mountainous. 5 A. SEWARD Gales, mountainous and maritime, which blow around your delightful retreat.

mountainously *adv.* E17. **mountainousness** *n.* E18.

mountainward /ˈmaʊntɪnwəd/ *adv.* & *a.* M19. [f. MOUNTAIN + -WARD.] **A** *adv.* In the direction of mountains. M19. **B** *adj.* Directed towards mountains. L19.

Also **mountainwards** *adv.* M19.

mountainy /ˈmaʊntɪni/ *a.* E17. [f. MOUNTAIN + -Y[1].] **1** = MOUNTAINOUS 2. E17. **2** Belonging to, inhabiting or frequenting a mountain or mountains. Chiefly *Anglo-Ir.* L18.

1 J. AIKEN The jagged silhouette of the mountainy horizon. 2 J. M. SYNGE Your mountainy sheep eating cabbages in Jimmy's field. J. O'FAOLAIN Mountainy men were a race apart.

mountant /ˈmaʊnt(ə)nt/ *n.* L19. [f. MOUNT *v.* + -ANT[1], after Fr. *montant*. Cf. next.] An adhesive substance for mounting photographs etc. Also, a material for securing or embedding specimens for microscopy.

mountant /ˈmaʊnt(ə)nt/ *a.* Long *rare* or *obs.* E16. [Fr. *montant* pres. pple of *monter* MOUNT *v.*: see -ANT[1]. Cf. prec.] Mounting, rising.

mountebank /ˈmaʊntɪbaŋk/ *n.* & *a.* L16. [It. *montambanco*, *montimbanco*, f. *monta in banco* mount (imper.) on a bench: see BANK *n.*[2]] **A** *n.* **1** An itinerant quack, esp. a vendor of medicines, appealing to an audience from a raised platform and using stories, juggling, etc., and often the assistance of a professional clown or fool. *obs.* exc. *Hist.* and as passing into sense 2. L16. **2** A false pretender to skill or knowledge, a charlatan; a person incurring contempt or ridicule through efforts to acquire something, esp. social distinction and glamour. L16. †**3** = MOUNTEBANKERY. M17–E18. **4** = BATELEUR. Also *mountebank eagle.* L19.

B *attrib.* or as *adj.* Of, pertaining to, or characteristic of a mountebank. E17.

GLADSTONE Theatrical, not to say charlatan and mountebank, politics.

mountebankism *n.* (*rare*) mountebankery M17.

mountebank /ˈmaʊntɪbaŋk/ *v.* E17. [f. the n.] **1** *v.i.* & (usu.) *t.* w. *it.* Behave as a mountebank, play the mountebank. Chiefly as *mountebanking* vbl n. & ppl a. E17. †**2** *v.t.* Master or prevail over (a person) by persuasion characteristic of a mountebank. E17–E18. †**3** *v.t.* Introduce by mountebank methods (*into*); transform by mountebank trickery. M17–E18.

mountebankery /ˈmaʊntɪbaŋk(ə)ri/ *n.* E17. [f. as prec. + -ERY.] **1** An act characteristic of a mountebank. E17. **2** Behaviour or practice characteristic of a mountebank. L17.

mounted /ˈmaʊntɪd/ *a.* L16. [f. MOUNT *v.* + -ED[1].] **1** *gen.* That has mounted or been mounted. L16. **2** Esp. of a member of a police force, an army, etc.: riding or serving on horseback or bicycle. L16.

Mountie /ˈmaʊnti/ *n. colloq.* E20. [f. prec. + -IE.] **1** A member of the Royal Canadian (formerly North West) Mounted Police. E20. **2** A member of a similar police force outside Canada. M20.

mounting /ˈmaʊntɪŋ/ *n.* LME. [f. MOUNT *v.* + -ING[1].] **1** The action of MOUNT *v.* LME. **2** A thing serving as a mount, support, or setting. M16. †**3** *sing.* & in *pl.* A soldier's outfit or kit. L17–E18. **4** = MUNTIN. E19.

2 ROWLAND(*'s*) *mounting.*

Comb.: **mounting-block** a block of stone from which to mount on horseback.

mounting /ˈmaʊntɪŋ/ *a.* M16. [f. MOUNT *v.* + -ING[2].] **1** That mounts. M16. †**2** *Her.* Of a beast of the chase or a reptile: standing on the left hind foot with the forefeet in the air. L17–M18.

†**mountjack** *n.* see MANJAK.

Mountmellick /maʊntˈmɛlɪk/ *a.* L19. [A town in Ireland where orig. made.] Designating a type of white-work embroidery characterized by raised surfaces.

†**mounture** *n.* ME. [OFr. *monteüre* (mod. *monture*), f. *monter* MOUNT *v.*: see -URE.] **1** A horse etc. for riding. ME–E17. **2** A raised surface to mount on; a mound, a hillock. LME–E17. **3** = MOUNTING *n.* 2. L15–L16. **4** = ELEVATION 3c. Only in E17. **5** *Mil.* The angle at which a gun is elevated. Only in 17. **6** = HARNESS *n.* 7. Only in L18.

moup /muːp/ *v. Sc.* Also **moop**. E16. [Origin unkn.: senses perh. different wds.] **1** *v.t.* & *i.* Eat (food), esp. as with toothless gums. Also foll. by *up*. E16. **2** *v.i.* Associate *with*. L18.

mourn /mɔːn/ *n.* Long *rare* exc. *Sc.* & *dial.* ME. [f. MOURN *v.*] Grief, mourning; a murmuring sound expressing grief.

mourn /mɔːn/ *a.* Long *arch. rare.* Also **mourne**. ME. [Perh. f. Fr. *morne*, ult. f. Gmc, cogn. w. MOURN *v.*] Sad, mournful.

mourn /mɔːn/ *v.* [OE *murnan* corresp. to OS *mornan*, *mornian*, OHG *mornēn* be anxious, ON *morna* pine away, Goth. *maurnan* be anxious.] **I** *v.i.* **1** Feel or show grief or deep regret; lament a misfortune etc. Freq. foll. by *for*, *over*. OE. **b** *spec.* Feel or show grief for a dead person or a person's death (freq. foll. by *for*); show the conventional signs of grief for a period after a person's death, esp. by wearing mourning garments. ME. **c** Utter lamentations *to*. *rare.* M16. **d** Of an animal: pine. *obs.* exc. *Sc.* L16. †**2** Yearn *for*, *after*, *to do*; care *for*. OE–LME. **3** (Of a dove) make its natural low murmuring sound (*literary*); (of a person, esp. an infant) make a plaintive sound similar to this, moan, (long *dial.*). E16.

1 W. CONGREVE Some Here are, who seem to mourn at our Success! LYTTON Let us not waste them in mourning over blighted hopes. c T. GRAY I fruitless mourn to him that cannot hear. 3 SHELLEY The dove mourned in the pine, Sad prophetess of sorrows not her own.

II *v.t.* **4** Feel or show grief or deep regret for (a dead person, a person's death, a misfortune, etc.). LME. **5** Utter in a mournful manner. E17.

4 A. N. WILSON Both mourned a rural . . England which was vanishing forever. V. S. NAIPAUL The Parray woman lived on . . mourning her pundit son. B. GILROY They buried her. . . She had many friends to mourn her. 5 J. STEINBECK 'Where is our happiness gone?' Pablo mourned.

mourne *a.* var. of MOURN *a.*

mourner /ˈmɔːnə/ *n.*[1] LME. [f. prec. + -ER[1].] **1** A person who mourns; a participant in funeral rites, esp. for a friend or relation. LME. **b** A person employed or hired to attend a funeral or to utter formal lamentations for the dead. L17. **2** A penitent. *US.* M19.

mournful /ˈmɔːnfʊl, -f(ə)l/ *a.* LME. [f. MOURN *v.* + -FUL.] **1** Expressing mourning or grief; doleful, sad, dismal. LME. **2** Full of or oppressed with grief; grieving. Formerly also, making a show of grief. L16. **3** Causing mourning or grief; lamentable. *rare.* L16.

1 OUIDA The scene was bleak and mournful. CONAN DOYLE The dog's mournful eye passed from one . . to the other. 2 J. WESLEY Thou wilt the mournful Spirit chear. 3 SHAKES. *1 Hen. VI* The treacherous manner of his mournful death.

Special collocations: **mournful widow** = *mourning bride* s.v. MOURNING *ppl a.*

mournfully *adv.* E17. **mournfulness** *n.* M17.

mourning /ˈmɔːnɪŋ/ *n.*[1] ME. [f. MOURN *v.* + -ING[1].] **1** The action of MOURN *v.*; the expression of grief for a person's death, esp. formally by the wearing of black clothes. Also, the period during which such clothes are worn. ME. **2** An instance of this; a lament; a formal manifestation of grief for a person's death. Now *rare.* LME. **3** *sing.* & (now *Sc.* & *north.*) in *pl.* The (esp. black) clothes worn by a mourner. M17.

1 TENNYSON Bury the Great Duke To the noise of the mourning of a mighty nation. H. R. LANDON Theatres . . did not reopen until the official period of mourning ended. 2 AV *Gen.* 50:10 And he made a mourning for his father seuen dayes. 3 B. GUEST Mourning was never worn. Death was not a subject for sorrow.

Phrases etc.: *close mourning*: see CLOSE *a.* *deep mourning*: see DEEP *a.* *half-mourning*: see HALF-. **in mourning** (*a*) grieving for a person's death, wearing (esp. black) clothes as a token of grief for a person's death; (*b*) *slang* (of an eye) blacked in fighting. *second mourning*: see SECOND *a.*

Attrib. & *comb.*: In the sense 'used or worn as a token of grief at a person's death', as *mourning-brooch*, *envelope*, *jewellery*, *-ring*, etc. Special combs., as **mourning-band** (*a*) a strip of black crape etc. worn round the sleeve of a coat or a hat in token of bereavement; (*b*) *slang* a dirty edge to a fingernail; **mourning cloak** †(*a*) a cloak worn by a mourner attending a funeral, usu. hired from the undertaker; (*b*) *N. Amer.* = CAMBERWELL BEAUTY; **mourning coach** (chiefly *Hist.*) (*a*) a black coach used by a person in mourning; (*b*) a (usu. black) closed carriage for conveying mourners at a funeral; **mourning-paper** notepaper with a black edge; **mourning-piece** *US* a pictorial representation of a tomb etc. intended as a memorial of the dead.

†**mourning** *n.*[2] E16–M18. [Alt. of Fr. *mortechien* (of unkn. origin), after prec.] *mourning of the chine*, glanders.

mourning /ˈmɔːnɪŋ/ *ppl a.* OE. [f. MOURN *v.* + -ING[2].] That mourns.

mourning bride sweet scabious, *Scabiosa atropurpurea*. **mourning dove** a common grey-brown N. American pigeon, *Zenaida macroura*, with a plaintive call. **mourning iris** a cultivated iris, *Iris susiana*, with patches of purple-black on the flowers. **mourning warbler** a warbler, *Geothlypis philadelphia*, of Canada and the north-eastern US, with a grey head and yellow underparts. **mourning widow** (*a*) any of several cultivated plants with dark or dingy flowers; *esp.* dusky cranesbill, *Geranium phaeum*; (*b*) a widow-bird.

mourningly *adv.* LME.

mournival /ˈmɔːnɪv(ə)l/ *n.* M16. [Fr. *mornifle* (now) a slap, a taunt, ult. origin unkn.] **1** *Cards.* A set of four aces, kings, queens, or jacks, in one hand. *obs.* exc. *Hist.* M16. 2 *gen.* Any set of four. Long *arch. rare.* E17.

mousaka *n.* var. of MOUSSAKA.

mouse /maʊs/ *n.* Pl. **mice** /mʌɪs/, in sense 4 also **mouses**. [OE *mūs*, pl. *mȳs* = OFris., OS, OHG *mūs* (Du. *muis*, G *Maus*), ON *mús*, f. Gmc f. IE base repr. also by L *mus*, Gk *mus*.] **I 1** Any of various small rodents, mostly of the family Muridae, usu. having a pointed snout and relatively large ears and eyes, and typically living on seeds and nuts. Also, any of various animals resembling these, as a shrew, a vole. OE. **2a** A term of endearment esp. for a woman or child: darling, pet. Long *rare*. E16. **b** Orig., a person or thing likened to a mouse in being small or insignificant. Now, a quiet, timid, or retiring person. L16. **3** In full *mouse-colour*. A shade of grey with a yellowish-brown tint. Also, a light dull brown shade esp. of hair. E17. **4** Any of various objects regarded as resembling a mouse in shape or appearance; *spec.* (*a*) *Naut.* a small collar made with yarn round a wire or rope and intended to hold an eye etc. in place; (*b*) *Computing* a small hand-held device moved over a flat surface to produce a corresponding movement of a cursor or arrow on a VDU, usu. having fingertip controls for selecting a function or entering a command. M18. **5** A small humped cowry, *Cypraea mus*, cream with brown markings. E19. **6** A small greyish-brown noctuid moth, *Amphipyra tragopoginis*, which runs away when disturbed. Also more fully *mouse moth*. E19. **7** A lump or discoloured bruise, *esp.* one on or near the eye and caused by a blow; a black eye. *slang*. M19.

1a *deer mouse, field mouse, flying mouse, harvest mouse, house mouse, jumping mouse, marsupial mouse, pocket mouse, waltzing mouse, white mouse*, etc. 2a DICKENS Not low this morning I hope? You ought *not* to be, dear Mouse. b DOUGLAS CLARK He was an uncouth bully, she was a mouse, a nonentity. 4 *Mini-Micro Systems* Using the mouse to.. select, a user can bring a 'page' to the top of the screen.

II 8 A muscle. Long *obs.* exc. as passing into sense 9. OE. **9** *spec.* Any of various muscular parts of meat. Long *dial.* L16.

Phrases: **country mouse** *fig.* a person from a rural area unfamiliar with urban life, as distinguished from *town mouse* below. **mouse and man** every living thing. *play cat and mouse*: see CAT *n.*[1] **quiet as a mouse** very quiet. *strong, thick*, etc., *enough to trot a mouse on*: see TROT *v.* **town mouse** an inhabitant of a city familiar with urban life, as distinguished from *country mouse* above.

Comb.: **mousebird** any of various long-tailed fruit-eating birds of the African genus *Colius* (and family Coliidae), with soft hairlike plumage; also called *coly*; *mouse-colour*: see sense 3 above; **mouse-coloured** *a.* of mouse-colour; **mouse deer** = CHEVROTAIN; **mouse-dun** mouse-colour; **mouse-ear** any of various plants with softly hairy leaves resembling a mouse's ear; *esp.* (*a*) (more fully *mouse-ear hawkweed*) any of several stoloniferous plants of the genus *Pilosella*, allied to the hawkweeds; spec. *P. officinarum*, common in dry grassland; (*b*) (more fully *mouse-ear chickweed*) any of various small plants of the genus *Cerastium*, of the pink family, with white flowers resembling chickweed; (*c*) a forget-me-not, esp. *Myosotis scorpioides*; (*d*) (more fully *mouse-ear cress*) thale cress, *Arabidopsis thaliana*; **mouse-eared** *a.* having an appendage resembling a mouse's ear; *mouse-eared bat*, any of numerous bats of the genus *Myotis*, *esp.* the Eurasian *M. myotis*, brown with greyish-white undersides, a rare visitor to Britain; **mouse-fish** (*a*) = SARGASSUM *fish*; (*b*) a slim, brightly coloured Indo-Pacific fish, *Gonorhynchus gonorhynchus*, which burrows in sand on the seabed; **mouse-hare** = PIKA; **mouse-hawk** a bird of prey that catches mice; *spec.* the short-eared owl, *Asio flammeus*; **mouse-hole** *n.* & *v.* (*a*) *n.* a hole used or made by a mouse for habitation or passage; a very small hole; (*b*) *v.t.* & *i.* make a mouse-hole (in); make a narrow passage or tunnel (through); **mouse-hunt** *n.*[1] (*obs.* exc. *dial.*) an animal that hunts mice, *spec.* a weasel; **mouse-hunt** *n.*[2] a hunt for a mouse or mice; **mouse-lemur** any of various small Madagascan lemurs of the family Cheirogaleidae, esp. of the genus *Microcebus*; *mouse moth*: see sense 6 above; **mouse opossum** = MANICOU; **mouse pox** *Vet. Med.* infectious ectromelia; **mousetail** a plant of damp fields, *Myosurus minimus*, of the buttercup family, with a long spike of tiny flowers. **mousekin** *n.* (*rare*) = MOUSELING M19. **mouselet** *n.* (*rare*) †(*a*) = *reed dagger* s.v. REED *n.*[1]; (*b*) = MOUSELING: M19. **mouselike** *a.* resembling (that of) a mouse; *esp.* very small, very quiet: M19. **mouseling** *n.* a young or small mouse M19. **mouseship** *n.* (*rare*) (*a*) the condition of being a mouse; (*b*) (with possess. adj., as *your* etc. *mouseship*) a mock title of respect given to a mouse: E18.

mouse /maʊz, -s/ *v.* ME. [f. the n.] **1** *v.i.* Esp. of a cat or owl: hunt for or catch mice. ME. †**2** *v.t.* Esp. of a cat: claw at, tear, bite, (a mouse etc.). M16–M17. **b** Pull (a woman) about good-naturedly but roughly. Chiefly in *touse and mouse*. Only in 17. **3** *v.i.* Search industriously; prowl *about* (as if) in search of something. Also foll. by *around, along*. L16. **b** *v.t.* Foll. by *over*: study (a book) industriously. *US*. E19. **c** *v.t.* Search industriously for. Also foll. by *out*. *US*. M19. **4** *v.t.* *Naut.* Put a mouse (see MOUSE *n.* 4) on (a stay); secure (a hook) with a mouse. M18.

mouser /ˈmaʊzə, -s-/ *n.* LME. [f. MOUSE *n.*, *v.* + -ER[1].] An animal that catches mice; *esp.* a cat, an owl.

mousery /ˈmaʊs(ə)ri/ *n.* L19. [f. MOUSE *n.* + -ERY.] **1** A place where mice abound; a colony of mice. L19. **2** A place where mice are bred or kept. M20.

mousetrap /ˈmaʊstrap/ *n.* & *v.* LME. [f. MOUSE *n.* + TRAP *n.*[1]] **A** *n.* **1** A trap for catching mice; *fig.* a device for enticing a person to destruction or defeat. LME. **2** More fully *mousetrap cheese*. Cheese for baiting a mousetrap; poor quality cheese. M17. **3** A very small house. *joc.* M19.

1 T. MIDDLETON Like a mouse-trap baited with bacon. M. R. D. FOOT The agents taken in the Villa des Bois mousetrap.. were in the noisome Béleyme prison. 2 *Times* Farm cheddar that will dazzle the tastebuds accustomed to factory mousetrap.

B *v.t.* Infl. **-pp-**. Catch (as) in a mousetrap; entice (a person) to destruction or defeat. L19.

mousey *n.*, *a.* vars. of MOUSY *n.*, *a.*

mousie *n.* var. of MOUSY *n.*

mousle /ˈmaʊz(ə)l/ *v.t.* Long *arch. rare.* M17. [Frequent. of MOUSE *v.*: see -LE[3]. Cf. TOUSLE.] Pull about roughly.

mousmé /ˈmuːsmeɪ/ *n.* Also **musume** /ˈmuːsʊmeɪ/. L19. [Jap. *musume* daughter, girl.] An unmarried Japanese girl, *esp.* one serving tea.

mousquetaire /muːskəˈtɛː/ *n.* & *a.* E18. [Fr., f. *mousquet* MUSKET *n.*[2] + *-aire* -EER. Cf. MUSKETEER.] **A** *n.* **1** *Hist.* A French musketeer. E18. **2** = *mousquetaire glove* below. L19.

B *attrib.* or as *adj.* Of an article of clothing: in the style of that of a French musketeer. M19.

mousquetaire glove a glove with a long loose wrist.

moussaka /muːˈsɑːkə, muːsəˈkɑː/ *n.* Also **mousaka**. M20. [Ult. f. Arab. *musakkā* through Turk. Cf. Turk. *musakka*, mod.Gk *mousakas*, Romanian *musaca*, Albanian, Bulgarian *musaka*, etc.] A Greek and eastern Mediterranean dish made with minced beef or lamb, aubergine, etc., with a cheese sauce.

mousse /muːs/ *n.* & *v.* M19. [Fr. = moss, froth.] **A** *n.* **1** The aggregation of tiny bubbles in sparkling wine, as champagne etc. M19. **2** *Cookery*. A sweet or savoury dish made from a purée or other base stiffened with whipped cream, gelatin, egg whites, etc., and usu. served chilled. Freq. w. specifying wd. L19. **3** In full *chocolate mousse*. A brown emulsion of seawater and oil produced by the weathering of oil spills and resistant to dispersal; a mass of this substance. M20. **4** *Hairdressing*. A frothy preparation for applying to the hair to facilitate setting or colouring. L20.

2 *chocolate mousse, lemon mousse, salmon mousse*, etc.

B *v.t.* *Hairdressing*. Apply mousse to (hair); set or colour (hair) using mousse. L20.

mousseline /ˈmuːsliːn/ *n.* L17. [Fr.: see MUSLIN.] **1** French muslin; a dress of this material. Also = *mousseline-de-laine* below. L17. **2** In full *mousseline glass*. (A wineglass of) a very thin blown glassware with ornamentation resembling muslin or lace. M19. **3** *Cookery*. In full *mousseline sauce*. A rich frothy sauce of seasoned or sweetened eggs or cream. E20. **b** Any of various dishes with a light frothy texture and usu. prepared by whipping or beating; a mousse. E20.

Comb.: **mousseline-de-laine** /dəˈleɪn/ [Fr. = of wool] a fine dress-material of wool or now esp. wool and cotton; **mousseline-de-soie** /dəˈswɑː/ [Fr. = of silk] a thin silk fabric with a texture like that of muslin; *mousseline glass*: see sense 2 above; *mousseline sauce*: see sense 3 above.

mousseron /ˈmuːsərɒn/ *n.* M17. [Fr.: see MUSHROOM *n.*] An edible agaric, *Clitopilus prunulus*, with a flattish white cap, pink gills, and a mealy smell.

mousseux /musø, muːˈsəː/ *a.* & *n.* E19. [Fr., f. as MOUSSE.] **A** *adj.* Of wine: sparkling. E19. **B** *n.* Pl. same. A sparkling wine. M20.

Moussorgskian *a.* var. of MUSSORGSKIAN.

moustache /məˈstɑːʃ/ *n.* Also ***must-**. L16. [Fr. f. It. *mostaccio, mostacchio*: see MUSTACHIO.] **1** A (cultivated) growth of hair above the whole or either half (freq. in *pl.*, esp. in *pair of moustaches*) of a man's lip or extending from this on either side of the lip; a growth of hair above a woman's lip. Also, an artificial strip of hair worn in imitation of this. L16. **2** A growth of hairs or bristles, or a marking resembling a man's moustache, round the mouth of certain animals or birds. E17. **3** In full *moustache monkey*. A W. African guenon, *Cercopithecus cephus*, with a pronounced white bar below the nose. L18. **4** *old moustache* [tr. Fr. *vieille moustache*], an old soldier. *arch.* E19.

1 G. GREENE The old fellow with the moustaches.. was English. P. THEROUX I.. left the stubble on my upper lip for a moustache I planned to grow. *transf.*: A. UTTLEY They all sipped the milk, and.. wiped the creamy moustaches from their lips. *handlebar moustache, Hitler moustache, Kaiser* (*Bill*) *moustache, pencil(-line) moustache, Zapata moustache*, etc.

Comb.: **moustache cup** a cup with a partial cover to protect a moustache during drinking; **moustache-lifter** a device for lifting one's moustache when drinking, sleeping, etc.; *moustache monkey*: see sense 3 above; **moustache tern** the whiskered tern, *Chlidonias hybridus*.

moustacheless *a.* (*rare*) L19.

moustached /məˈstɑːʃt/ *a.* Also ***must-**. M19. [f. prec. + -ED[2].] Having a moustache.

moustached honeyeater, moustached tamarin, moustached warbler, etc. **moustached guenon, monkey** = MOUSTACHE *monkey*.

moustachial /məˈstɑːʃɪəl/ *a.* Also ***must-**. L19. [f. MOUSTACHE + -IAL.] Chiefly *Ornith.* Resembling a moustache; *spec.* designating a streak of colour running back from the sides of a bird's beak.

moustachio *n.*, **-ioed** *a.* vars. of MUSTACHIO, -IOED.

Mousterian /muːˈstɪərɪən/ *a.* & *n.* Also (now *rare*) **-stier-**. L19. [Fr. *moust(i)érien*, f. *Le Moustier* a cave in the department of Dordogne, SW France, where remains were found: see -IAN.] *Archaeol.* **A** *adj.* Designating or pertaining to a middle palaeolithic culture following the Acheulean and preceding the Aurignacian, typified by flints worked on one side only. L19. **B** *n.* (A person of) this culture. E20.

ˈ**Mousteroid** *a.* resembling the Mousterian culture M20.

†**moustic** *n.* *rare.* M17–E19. [Fr. *moustique* by metathesis f. Sp. MOSQUITO.] A mosquito.

Moustierian *a.* & *n.* see MOUSTERIAN.

Moustiers /ˈmuːstɪə, *foreign* mustje/ *n.* & *a.* M19. [*Moustiers*-Sainte-Marie (see below).] (Designating) a type of faience formerly made at Moustiers-Sainte-Marie, a small town in the department of Basses Alpes, SE France.

mousy /ˈmaʊsi/ *n.* *colloq.* (chiefly *joc.* & *nursery*). Also **-ey, -ie**. L17. [Dim. or pet-form of MOUSE *n.*: see -Y[6], -IE.] A little mouse.

mousy /ˈmaʊsi/ *a.* Also **-ey**. E19. [f. MOUSE *n.* + -Y[1].] **1** Of or pertaining to mice, mouselike; of the nature or appearance of a mouse; (esp. of the hair) greyish-brown in colour; *fig.* (of a person) shy, quiet, timid, ineffectual. E19. **2** Containing mice, infested with mice. L19.

1 D. LIVINGSTONE We inhaled.. the heavy mousy smell. M. WEST A small mousy fellow stood up. L. R.

BANKS Thin, pale, .. with this mousy hair. 2 M. SPARK Mrs. Hogg .. climbing to her mousy room.

mousily *adv.* E20. **mousiness** *n.* L19.

moutan /ˈmuːt(ə)n/ *n.* E19. [Chin. *mudan*.] A tree peony, *Paeonia suffruticosa*, with white pink-blotched flowers, native to China and Tibet and the parent of many garden varieties.

mouth /maʊθ/ *n.* [OE *mūþ* = OFris. *mūth*, later *mund*, ON *munnr*, *muðr*, Goth. *munþs*, f. Gmc f. IE, corresp. to L *mentum* chin.] **I 1 a** The opening in the head of a person or animal through which food is ingested and vocal sounds emitted, closed by the lips; the cavity immediately behind this, containing the teeth and tongue. Also, the opening through which any animal organism ingests food. OE. **b** A person viewed as a consumer of food. Freq. in *a mouth to feed* below. M16. **c** A horse's readiness to feel and obey the pressure of the bit (usu. w. qualifying adj., as *bad, good, hard*, etc.); a horse's ability to be guided by the bit. E18. **2** The flesh surrounding the opening of the mouth, considered as a part of the human face; the lips. OE. **3 a** The mouth as the instrument of speech or voice; a person's voice; a person who is speaking. Formerly also, a person's utterance. Now chiefly *rhet.* exc. in *out of a person's own mouth, hush one's mouth*, and other phrs. below. OE. **b** The barking or baying of a hound etc. Freq. in *give mouth* below. L16. **c** Extravagant, insolent, or boastful talk, a propensity for this, (freq. in *be all mouth*); empty bragging, impudence. M20. **4** A person who speaks on behalf of another or of others; a spokesman. Now *rare* or *obs.* M16. **5** A silly person; a dupe; (now chiefly *Sc.*) a noisy person; a talkative or indiscreet person. *slang*. L17.

1a *Encycl. Brit.* The cavity of the mouth forms the commencement of the alimentary canal. B. SCHULBERG Sammy had his mouth full of .. steak sandwich. *foot-and-mouth (disease)*: see FOOT *n. hoof-and-mouth disease*: see HOOF *n. plum-in-the-mouth*: see PLUM *n.* b P. S. BUCK There was only another mouth coming which must be fed. 2 TENNYSON And on her mouth A doubtful smile dwelt. DAY LEWIS A small, thin mouth .. and eyes set well apart. 3a ADDISON You don't now thunder in the capitol, With all the mouths of Rome to second you. M. PATTISON Learned .. his faith from the mouth of the Roman priest. b SHAKES. *Mids. N. D.* My hounds are .. match'd in mouth like bells.

II 6 The place where a river enters the sea; the entrance to a harbour, valley, etc. OE. **7** The opening for filling or emptying something of containing capacity. ME. **8 a** The surface opening of a pit, well, cave, etc. ME. **b** The crater of a volcano. E17. **9** The aperture in an artificial structure (esp. a beehive) permitting ingress and egress. LME. **10** The opening out of the end of a tube, passage, vessel, etc. L16. **11** The muzzle of a gun. L16. **12** The opening between the forked jaws of a pair of scissors, pincers, etc. L16. **13** The cutting or working edge of a tool. Now chiefly *Sc.* E17. **14** A mouthpiece. Now *rare* or *obs.* E17. **15 a** A hole in the stock of a plane admitting the passage of shavings. L17. **b** An aperture in a musical pipe for producing the sound. E18. **16** *Bot.* **a** The orifice of a corolla-tube. M18. **b** The opening produced by the dehiscence of the spore-capsule of mosses. M19. **17** *Zool.* The aperture of a univalve shell. L18.

6 LD MACAULAY The castle .. situated at the mouth of Loch Riddan. 7 SWIFT Wipe the Mouth of the Bottle. 8a SPENSER His deepe devouring jawes Wyde gaped, like the griesly mouth of hell. E. HEMINGWAY Anselmo came out of the mouth of the cave. 9 *Beekeeping* The skep should be placed over .. them, mouth downwards, then the bees encouraged to climb .. into it. 10 LONGFELLOW The valley .. opens upon the broad plain .. like the mouth of a trumpet. 11 SHAKES. *John* Their battering cannon, charged to the mouths.

Phrases: *a bone in her mouth*: see BONE *n.* **a mouth to feed** a dependent, *esp.* a child; a person who consumes food but does no useful work in return. *bad(-)mouth*: see BAD *a. big mouth*: see BIG *a. born with a silver spoon in one's mouth*: see SPOON *n.* **by word of mouth** by spoken words, orally. *down in the mouth*: see DOWN *adv. from hand to mouth*: see HAND *n. from the horse's mouth*: see HORSE *n.* **give mouth** (of a hound etc.) bark or bay vehemently, give tongue. *hand to mouth*: see HAND *n. have one's heart in one's mouth*: see HEART *n. hush one's mouth*: see HUSH *v.*[1] **in a person's mouth** when said by a person. **keep one's mouth shut** *colloq.* say nothing, not reveal a secret. *laugh on the other* (or *wrong*) *side of one's mouth*: see LAUGH *v. look a gift-horse in the mouth*: see HORSE *n. look as if butter would not melt in one's mouth*: see BUTTER *n.*[1] *make a person's mouth water*: see WATER *v.* **make a poor mouth** plead poverty. **make a wry mouth** grimace in disgust, derision, etc. *motor mouth*: see MOTOR *n.* & *a. not open one's mouth*: see OPEN *v.* **one's mouth waters** one's mouth runs with saliva at the sight of food; *fig.* one experiences desire or envy. **out of a person's own mouth** (w. ref. to *Luke* 19:22) using a person's actual words. *poor mouth*: see POOR *a. put one's money where one's mouth is*: see MONEY *n.* **put words into a person's mouth** (*a*) tell a person what to say; (*b*) represent a person as having uttered words previously stated. *roof of the mouth*: see ROOF *n.* 2c. *run off at the mouth*: see RUN *v. run one's mouth*: see RUN *v.* SCABBY *mouth. shoot off one's mouth*: see SHOOT *v.* **shut a person's mouth** *slang* prevent a person from revealing something. **shut one's mouth** *slang* stop talking (freq. in *imper.*). **stop a person's mouth** block or obstruct a person's mouth (as) with a gag or muzzle; *fig.* = *shut a person's mouth* above. *take the bread out of a person's mouth*: see BREAD *n.*[1] **take the words out of a person's mouth** say what a person was about to say. *the lion's mouth*: see LION *n. wash one's mouth out (with soap)*: see WASH *v.* **with one mouth** (now *rare*) with one voice or one consent; unanimously. *with open mouth*: see OPEN *a. word of mouth*: see WORD *n.*

Comb.: **mouth-breeder**, **-brooder** any of various fishes of the families Cichlidae and Ariidae which protect their eggs, and occas. their offspring, by carrying them in the mouth; **mouth-filling** *a.* bombastic; **mouth glue** (now *rare*) (*a*) glue, orig. a preparation of isinglass, used by moistening with the tongue; †(*b*) isinglass; **mouth guard** a guard worn to protect the mouth, esp. by rugby players; *mouth-harp*: see HARP *n.* 1c; **mouth music** (*a*) = *mouth-organ* below; (*b*) singing without distinct utterance of words; **mouth-organ** (*a*) a musical instrument operated by the mouth; *spec.* a thin rectangular box containing metal reeds, each tuned to a note, moved along the lips while the air is blown or sucked through; a harmonica; *dial.* a jew's harp; (*b*) *Zool.* an organ associated with the mouth, a mouthpart; **mouthpart** *Zool.* any of the (usu. paired) organs surrounding the mouth of an insect or other arthropod, adapted for feeding (usu. in *pl.*); **mouth ring** the ring forming the mouth of a bottle; **mouth root** *US* the plant goldthread, *Coptis trifolia*, with an astringent root reputed to cure sore mouths; **mouth rot** an oral canker which may affect snakes in captivity; **mouth-to-mouth** *a.* involving the contact of one individual's mouth with another's; *spec.* designating a method of artificial respiration in which a person breathes into a patient's lungs through the mouth; **mouthwash** a liquid antiseptic etc. for use in the mouth; *fig.* nonsense, twaddle; **mouth-watering** *a.* (of food) so appetizing as to make the mouth run with saliva; *fig.* exciting desire or envy.

mouthless *a.* OE.

mouth /maʊð, *in sense 4* maʊθ/ *v.* ME. [f. the n.] **I** *v.t.* **1** Pronounce, speak (words etc.), esp. pompously or with exaggerated clarity; rant, declaim. Also foll. by *out*. ME. **b** Articulate (words etc.) silently or whisperingly; shape (words etc.) without voicing. Freq. w. direct speech as obj. M20. **2** Put or take (esp. food) in the mouth; seize with the mouth; touch (a thing) with the mouth. LME. **3** Train the mouth of (a horse); accustom (a horse) to the use of the bit. M16. **4** Estimate the age of (a sheep) by examining the teeth. *Austral.* & *NZ*. M20.

1 BYRON Who Taught you to mouth that name of 'villain'? A. BIRRELL The pompous high-placed imbecile mouthing his platitudes. R. BROOKE Your flat clear voice beside me Mouthed cheerful clear flat platitudes. b M. WOODHOUSE 'Security patrol,' she mouthed, and pulled my head down next to hers. M. GEE He still kept reading . . , frowning and sometimes mouthing a word. 2 R. KIPLING A wolf .. can .. mouth an egg without breaking it. TED HUGHES He mouthed her teat. L. ERDRICH Tor mouthed a chewed cigar. 3 *Your Horse* She had been mouthed to be shown in-hand.

II *v.i.* **5** †**a** Speak, talk, (*together*). Only in LME. **b** Pronounce or speak one's words, esp. pompously or with exaggerated clarity; rant, declaim. E17. **c** Articulate words etc. silently or whisperingly; shape words etc. without voicing. Freq. foll. by *at*. M20. **6** Of a river: disembogue (*in, into*). L16. †**7** Join lips (*with*); kiss. *contempt.* Only in 17. **8** Grimace; make derisive grimaces and noises with the mouth. L18.

5b ADDISON I'll .. mouth at Caesar 'till I shake the Senate. W. E. GOSSE The poet tramped the grassy heights .. mouthing and murmuring as he went. **mouth off** *colloq.* talk loudly, express one's opinions forcefully (also foll. by *at*). c G. GREENE The sergeant mouthed at him; you didn't mention the word death before a child. I. MCEWAN He was waving and mouthing at the stranger to stand aside or sit down. 6 F. TROLLOPE The Ohio and Chesapeake canal .. there mouths into the Potomac. 7 SHAKES. *Meas. for M.* The Duke .. would mouth with a beggar though she smelt brown bread and garlic. 8 R. GOWER Retaining her calm demeanour as the mob shouted and mouthed around her.

mouthable *a.* E19. **mouther** *n.* a person who mouths; *esp.* a person given to boastful or declamatory speech: E19. **mouthingly** *adv.* in a mouthing manner E20.

mouthed /maʊðd/ *a.* ME. [f. MOUTH *n.*, *v.*: see -ED[2], -ED[1].] **1** Having a mouth (of a specified kind); provided with a mouth. ME. †**2** Gaping, having the mouth widely opened. L16–M17.

1 KEATS I .. sat me down, and took a mouthed shell. *big-mouthed, close-mouthed, deep-mouthed, foul-mouthed, open-mouthed*, etc. 2 SHAKES. *Sonn.* The wrinkles .. Of mouthed graves will give thee memory.

mouthful /ˈmaʊθfʊl, -f(ə)l/ *n.* LME. [f. MOUTH *n.* + -FUL.] **1** A quantity that fills the mouth; as much or as many as a mouth will hold or take in at one time. Also, a small quantity (*of* something). LME. **2** A long or complicated word or phrase to pronounce. *colloq.* L19.

1 L. WOOLF Trying to induce her to eat a few mouthfuls. *Sunday Times* We do not want a mouthful of elementary caveman's speech. **say a mouthful** *colloq.* (orig. *US*) make a striking or important statement; say something noteworthy. 2 M. GEE Miranda Buchanan-Couttes-Hughes. What a mouthful.

mouthpiece /ˈmaʊθpiːs/ *n.* L17. [f. MOUTH *n.* + PIECE *n.*] **1** A piece placed at or forming the mouth of something; *spec.* the part of a telephone into which one speaks. L17. **2** Something placed in the mouth; *spec.* (*a*) the part of a bit crossing a horse's mouth; (*b*) the part of a musical instrument, breathing apparatus, etc., placed between the lips. E18. **3** The mouth; something representing this. *rare*. M18. **4** A person, organization, etc., expressing views on behalf of another or others, a spokesman; *slang* a lawyer. E19. **5** A protector for the mouth; a respirator; a gumshield. L19.

1 *Which?* Putting your hand over the mouthpiece often doesn't work with modern phones. 2 D. DELILLO Murray relighted his pipe, sucking impressively at the mouthpiece. 4 P. B. YUILL The Abreys would get legal aid. The state would fix them up with a good mouthpiece. CLIVE JAMES The paper *Soviet Russia*, mouthpiece of the Central Committee, carried the full text. A. S. DALE Father Brown is Chesterton's Mr Pickwick, a mouthpiece for his own wit and wisdom.

mouthy /ˈmaʊði/ *a.* L16. [f. MOUTH *n.* + -Y[1].] **1** Railing, ranting, bombastic. L16. **2** Of a hound: giving tongue unnecessarily. M20.

1 *Sun* (*Baltimore*) I was kind of a big mouth. I wasn't a bully, just mouthy. J. C. OATES Brigit was always headstrong and mouthy.

mouthily *adv.* (*rare*) E20. **mouthiness** *n.* (*rare*) M19.

mouton /ˈmuːtɒn/ *n.* LME. [f. as MUTTON.] **1** *Hist.* A French gold coin, bearing the figure of the Lamb of God, current in the 14th and 15th cents. LME. **2** A spy quartered with an accused person with a view to obtaining incriminating evidence. *arch.* E19. **3** The dressed skin of a sheep cut and dyed to resemble beaver's or seal's fur. M20.

mouton enragé /mutɔ̃ ɑ̃raʒe/ *n. phr.* Pl. ***-s -s*** (pronounced same). M20. [Fr., lit. 'angry sheep'.] A normally calm person who has become suddenly enraged or violent.

moutonnéed /muːˈtɒneɪd/ *a.* L19. [f. Fr. *moutonnée*, f. *mouton* sheep (see MUTTON) + -ED[1].] *Physical Geogr.* Of a rock, hill, etc.: rounded like a sheep's back, esp. by glacial action. Cf. ROCHE MOUTONNÉE.

moutons enragés *n. phr.* pl. of MOUTON ENRAGÉ.

mouvementé /muvmɑ̃te/ *a.* E20. [Fr.] Animated, agitated, bustling, full of variety; *spec.* (of music) lively.

movable /ˈmuːvəb(ə)l/ *a.* & *n.* Also (now the usual form in *Law*) **moveable**. LME. [OFr. *movable*, f. *moveir* MOVE *v.*: see -ABLE.] A *adj.* †1 Quick or ready in movement; having a tendency to move. LME–E18. †2 Changeable, fickle, inconstant. LME–L17. 3 Able to be moved; not fixed in one place or posture; changing from one date to another every year. LME. 4 Of property: admitting of being removed or displaced, personal; *esp.* in *Sc. Law* (now *Hist.*) designating property which devolved on an executor for division among the next of kin as opp. to the heir at law (opp. *heritable*). LME. 5 *Semitic Gram.* Of a letter etc.: pronounced, not silent. Opp. *quiescent*. M19.

3 *movable* DOH. *movable feast*: see FEAST *n.* **movable kidney** = FLOATING *kidney*. **movable rib** = FLOATING *rib*. *movable sheva*: see SHEVA 1. **movable type** *Printing* (now chiefly *Hist.*) individually cast pieces of metal type.

B *n.* †1 *Ptolemaic Astron.* Each of the nine (or ten) concentric revolving spheres of the heavens. Chiefly in *first* or *highest movable*, = PRIMUM MOBILE. LME–L17. 2 In *pl.* Personal property; property admitting of being removed or displaced; *Sc. Law* (now *Hist.*) moveable as opposed to heritable property. LME. 3 An article of furniture that may be removed from the building in which it is placed. Formerly also, a portable personal object. Now usu. in *pl.* E16. †4 A thing able to be moved or set in motion; *spec.* a moving part of a watch. E17–L18. †5 A person given to movement or change. E–M17.

movaˈbility *n.* LME. **movableness** *n.* LME. **movably** *adv.* (*rare*) in a movable manner; so as to be movable: L17.

movant /ˈmuːv(ə)nt/ *n.* & *a.* *US Law.* L19. [f. MOVE *v.* + -ANT[1].] (Designating) a person who applies to or petitions a court of law or a judge with the intention of obtaining a ruling in his or her favour.

move /muːv/ *n.* LME. [f. the vb.] †1 A proposal, a motion. *rare.* Only in LME. 2a A moving or change of position of a piece in chess, draughts, or some other game; a player's turn to move. M17. b An action calculated to secure some end; an action which initiates or advances a process or plan, a step, a proceeding; a play in a game. E19. c An act of moving from a stationary position; an act of rising from a seated position; a beginning of movement or departure, a movement. E19. d A change of place of habitation, employment, etc. M19. 3 *on the move*, in the process of moving from one place to another, travelling, moving about; progressing. L18.

2b W. C. WILLIAMS My first move was to try and get a job on one of the newspapers. M. FOOT Months before David Owen made his formal move to leave the Labour Party. G. NAYLOR It challenged me more than other sports, with its infinite possibility of moves. c G. GREENE He said nothing and made no move towards the door. L. CODY Mr. Fourie nodded but made no move to shake hands. d M. ANGELOU Why are you going to New York? Is he happy about the move?

Phrases: **get a move on** *colloq.* hurry up, bestir oneself. *key move*: see KEY *n.*[1]

move /muːv/ *v.* ME. [AN *mover* = OFr. *moveir* (mod. *mouvoir*) f. L *movere*.] I *v.t.* 1 Change the place, position, or posture of; take from one place, position, or situation to another; remove, dislodge, displace; put or keep in motion; shake, stir, disturb. Also foll. by adv. or advb. phr. ME. b Take off or lift (a hat, a cap) from one's head, as a gesture of salutation. Now *rare.* L16. c Cause (the bowels) to be evacuated. E19. d *Comm.* Find purchasers for; sell a stock of. E20. e *Cricket.* Cause (the ball) to swerve. M20. 2 Affect with emotion; rouse or excite feeling in (a person); perturb; excite *to* anger, laughter, pity, tears, etc.; *spec.* (*a*) affect with tender or compassionate emotion; †(*b*) provoke to anger. ME. †b *refl.* Be perturbed; become excited or angry. ME–M16. 3a Operate as a motive or influence on the will or belief of (a person); prompt, actuate, or impel *to* an action, *to do*; in *pass.*, have an inward prompting, feel inclined. ME. b Urge (a person) *to* an action, *to do*; make a proposal or request, now only in a formal manner, to (a monarch, court, Parliament, etc., formerly any person, *for* a thing, *in* or *of* a matter, *that*). *arch.* LME. †4 Stir up, initiate (strife, war, etc.). ME–L17. 5 Excite or provoke (laughter, an emotion, appetite, etc.) in or *in* a person. LME. †6 Utter (sound), say. LME–L17. 7†a Put forward as a proposal, request, or complaint; propound (a question etc.), mention (a matter). LME–M18. †b *spec.* Plead (a cause or suit) in a court; bring (an action at law). LME–M17. c Propose (a question, resolution, etc.) formally in a deliberative assembly; propose (now only, in a formal manner) *that, to do.* LME. 8 With cognate obj.: dance, perform (a dance). Now *rare.* M17.

1 E. HOYLE When you castle your King, do not move the Pawns before him till forced to it. T. HARDY She moved her lips . . but could not speak. J. GALSWORTHY Sir Laurence Mont . . moved his legs with speed. E. WAUGH The lake was moved by strange tides. J. RULE I must have that phone moved out of the hall. J. FOWLES I . . moved the towel with my foot. R. INGALLS Two policemen walked by and moved a couple of the men. M. WARNOCK The essential characteristic of material objects . . that they can be moved about in space. R. P. JHABVALA The date of . . Founder's Day had been moved forward. 2 A. WILSON His dismal, little rabbit face might have moved any heart less hard than his wife's. V. BROME Passionate language came naturally to Freud whenever he was deeply moved. 3a J. H. NEWMAN God moves us in order to make the beginning of duty easy. J. BARZUN It is not commercial greed . . that moves one government official to butter up another. J. M. COETZEE Money . . to buy your way to Africa or Brazil, as the desire moves you. b CLARENDON If he desired any thing . . he would move the King in it. W. TEMPLE He would move the Parliament to have my Statue set up. SWIFT I . . begged him . . that he would move the Captains to take some Pity on us. 5 LD MACAULAY All the prejudices, all the exaggerations of both the great parties in the state, moved his scorn. 7b S. KINGSLEY I move to strike out the clause condemning the slave traffic. W. S. CHURCHILL The Resolution . . which I now, Mr. Speaker, have the honour to move. H. MACMILLAN The Opposition chose to move a vote of censure on the Government. D. CAUTE I move that we unlock the door and listen to what they have to say.

II *v.i.* 9 Go, advance, proceed; pass or be transferred from one place to another; change place, position, or posture; be in motion; exhibit physical activity, stir. Also foll. by adv. or advb. phr. ME. b Advance in time, make progress, develop; grow. LME. c Depart, start off. Now *colloq.* LME. d Dance. Now *rare.* L16. e Bow in salutation. Now *rare.* L16. f Of the bowels: evacuate faeces. L17. g Change one's place of residence, transfer to other working premises. E18. h Transfer a piece from one position to another in the course of a game of chess, draughts, etc. M18. i Of merchandise, a stock of goods, an edition or impression of a book, etc.: find purchasers, be sold (*off*). M18. j Go quickly. *colloq.* E20. k Dance or play music energetically or with a strong rhythm; be exciting or dynamic. *colloq.* M20. †10 Speak, treat, or argue *of*. ME–E16. 11 Exist, live; operate; be socially active *in* a particular sphere, *with* particular people etc. LME. 12 Take action, act, proceed, (*in, against*). LME. †13 Be excited, be stirred up, be initiated. LME–L16. †14 Proceed, emanate, originate *from*. LME–L17. †15 Incline, tend *to, to do*; incline *toward* (a proposal). LME–L17. 16 Be a motive or influence. Now *rare.* L16. 17 Make a request, proposal, or application *for*. M17.

9 MILTON Whether Heav'n move or Earth Imports not, if thou reck'n right. SWIFT The Door did not move on Hinges, but up and down like a Sash. S. TOWNSEND The shadows moved round from west to east. I. MURDOCH His hands moved weakly, gesturing the judgment away. W. GOLDING I could hear my mother moving about in the kitchen. *Shetland Times* The birds . . have not yet begun to move south. I. MCEWAN They were moving again, picking up speed. b *Spectator* The story moves far too slowly, and the long conversations . . are tiresome. G. VIDAL Events moved rapidly. J. GARDAM He says things are going to start moving again here soon. g H. E. BATES In the first week of May that year we moved into another house. DAY LEWIS After my mother's death we had moved from Ealing to Notting Hill. L. HELLMAN Dash and I moved to Hollywood for four or five months. 11 SCOTT FITZGERALD They moved with a fast crowd, all of them young and rich and wild. W. RAEPER MacDonald did not move in the most glittering circles of the day. 12 J. LUBBOCK I would urge parents to move in the matter. *Scientific American* Your legal counsel can take care of registration when preparing to move against an infringer.

Phrases: *move a peg*: see PEG *n.*[1] *move heaven and earth*: see HEAVEN *n.* **move house** change one's place of residence. **move it** *colloq.* hurry up, bestir oneself, (usu. in *imper.*). **move with the times** be up to date in one's way of thinking or living.

With advs. & preps. in specialized senses: **move about** keep changing one's place of residence. **move in** (*a*) take possession of a new place of residence, occupy new premises; begin a new job etc.; take up residence *with*, begin to live *with*; help (a person) to do this; (*b*) *move in on*, take up residence with (someone), esp. so as to cause inconvenience or annoyance; attach oneself to, put pressure on (a person); become involved in, take control of (a project etc.). **move into** become involved in, take control of; begin investing in. **move on** (*a*) go to a new place; advance, progress; *spec.* move from a place where one is considered by a police officer to have stood too long and to be causing an obstruction; (*b*) (of a police officer) cause or order (a pedestrian) to move on. **move out** leave a place of residence to live elsewhere, end one's occupancy of premises; help (a person) to do this. **move over** adjust one's position in a horizontal direction to make room for another (*lit.* & *fig.*). **move up** adjust one's position in an upward direction to make room for another (*lit.* & *fig.*).

Comb.: **move-in** the action or an act of moving into a new place of residence or new premises.

moveable *a.* & *n.* see MOVABLE.

moveless /ˈmuːvlɪs/ *a.* L16. [f. MOVE *v.* or *n.* + -LESS.] Having no movement or motion, not moving, motionless; immovable, fixed.

movelessly *adv.* E19. **movelessness** *n.* M17.

movement /ˈmuːvm(ə)nt/ *n.* LME. [OFr. (mod. *mouvement*) f. med.L *movimentum*, f. L *movere* MOVE *v.*: see -MENT.] 1 The action or process of moving; change of place, position, or posture; passage from one place or situation to another; activity. Also, an instance or kind of this; a particular act or manner of moving. LME. b *spec.* A change of position of a military force, *esp.* a change in the disposition of troops etc. for reasons of tactics or strategy. L18. c In *pl.* The actions or activities and whereabouts of a person or body of people. M19. d The conveying of cattle from one district to another, esp. as prohibited or restricted during an epidemic of cattle disease. M19. e The departure or arrival of an aircraft, public transport vehicle, etc. M20. 2 A mental impulse, an act of will. Now *rare.* LME. 3 The moving (as distinguished from the stationary) parts of a mechanism, esp. of a watch or clock; a particular part or group of parts in a mechanism serving some special purpose. L17. 4a The impression of motion in a work of art; harmonious variety in the lines and ornamentation of a building. L18. b Progression of incidents or development of plot in a poem or narrative; the literary quality of giving a sense of progression through abundance of incident etc. or of carrying the interest of a reader through the course of a work. M19. 5a The manner of transition from note to note or passage to passage in a piece of music; the manner of melodic progression, tempo; rhythmical or accentual character in music or prosody. L18. b A principal division of a longer musical work having a distinctive structure of its own and usu. ending with the players ceasing to play. L18. 6a A course or series of actions and endeavours on the part of a body of people towards some special end; a body engaged in such a course. Freq. w. specifying wd. E19. b The way in which events or conditions are moving at a particular time or in a particular sphere; a tendency, a trend. M19. 7 *Comm.* Activity in the market for some commodity; a rise or fall in price. L19. 8 A motion of the bowels. L19.

1 T. H. HUXLEY Movements of the land .. brought about by the comparatively sudden action of subterranean forces. G. VIDAL He bowed without movement: he suggested a bow without actually executing it. M. HUGHES The only movement was the flickering of the fire. A. ARONSON Delilah .. cutting off his hair with quick, nervous movements. *Lancet* Specimens were collected immediately after a bowel movement. **b** *pincer movement* etc. **5b** *Musical Quarterly* The second movement of Beethoven's Piano Sonata, op. 14, no. 2. **6a** R. MANNING Two of the most fruitful movements of this century . . : the anti-nuclear movement and feminism. *the Labour movement, the Oxford Movement*, etc. **b** M. ESSLIN The Theatre of the Absurd is thus part of the 'anti-literary' movement of our time.

Phrases: **in the movement** in the direction or according to the tendency prevalent at a particular period or in a particular sphere. **the Movement** (the characteristics of) a group of English poets in the nineteen-fifties.

¶Rare bef. 18: not in Shakes., AV, or Milton's poetry.

†movent *a.* & *n.* M17–M19. [L *movent-* pres. ppl stem of *movere* MOVE *v.*: see -ENT.] (A thing) that moves or is moved.

mover /'muːvə/ *n.* LME. [f. MOVE *v.* + -ER[1]. In sense 6 f. MOVE *n.*] **1** A person who or thing which sets or keeps something in motion; a machine or mechanical agency which imparts motion. LME. †**b** A cause (*of*). *rare*. Only in E17. **2a** A person who incites or instigates to action; a promoter or originator of an action etc.; *colloq.* an enterprising person, a person who gets things done. LME. **b** *spec.* A person who moves a proposition or proposal in a deliberative assembly. E17. **3** A person who or thing which moves or is in motion; now chiefly with adj., an animal which moves in the specified manner or at the specified speed. L16. **4** A person who moves from place to place; *spec.* a person migrating westwards. *US*. E19. **5** A remover of furniture and other household goods. *N. Amer.* M19. **6** *Chess.* With prefixed numeral: a problem in which the king is to be mated in the specified number of moves. L19.

1 C. G. WOLFF There is no throughgoing sense of a malevolent God or an indifferent cosmic mover. P. MONETTE He was tireless and unfailing, a mover of mountains. **2a** C. THIRLWALL The chief movers of the rebellion made their escape. **3** *Horse & Rider* He should be a good straight mover. **5** L. EDEL The movers arrive to take her things to the new apartment.

Phrases: **first mover** (*a*) = PRIME MOVER 1, 2; (*b*) = PRIMUM MOBILE 1. *mover and* SHAKER. PRIME MOVER.

movie /'muːvi/ *n.* Orig. *US*. E20. [Abbrev. of *moving picture* s.v. MOVING *a.*: see -IE.] **1** A motion picture, a film; a showing of a motion picture. E20. **2** *the movies*, motion pictures as an industry, an art form, or a form of entertainment. E20. **3** A cinema. *US*. E20.

Comb.: **movie camera** a cine camera; **movie-goer** a frequenter of the cinema, a film-goer; **movie house** a cinema; **movie palace** a (palatial) cinema; **movie star** a celebrated cinema actor or actress, a film star; **Movietone** (proprietary name for) an early system employed in the making of sound films.

moviedom *n.* = FILMDOM E20.

movieola *n.* var. of MOVIOLA.

moving /'muːvɪŋ/ *n.* ME. [f. MOVE *v.* + -ING[1].] The action of MOVE *v.*; an instance of this; *spec.* (*a*) a change of place, position, or posture; movement; †(*b*) power or faculty of motion; †(*c*) a bodily movement or gesture; (*d*) an inward prompting, an impulse.

Comb.: **moving day** (*a*) a day of a move to a new residence or new premises; (*b*) *Mil.* a day on which a regiment or troops are on the march; **moving-man** *N. Amer.* = MOVER 5.

moving /'muːvɪŋ/ *a.* LME. [f. MOVE *v.* + -ING[2].] **1** That moves; that passes from one place, position, or posture to another; capable of moving, able to be moved; not fixed or stationary, in motion. LME. **b** *fig.* Unstable, changeful. Now *rare*. M16. **2** That moves something or someone; that causes or produces motion; that originates, causes, instigates, or actuates something. L15. **b** *spec.* That touches or has power to touch the feelings; affecting. L16.

1 E. FITZGERALD The Moving Finger writes; and, having writ, Moves on. R. CROMPTON They leapt on to a moving train. G. LORD In the moving light of the yellow fire. **b** POPE The moving Toyshop of their heart. **2** A. PRYCE-JONES He was also the moving spirit of the Shakespeare Society. **b** J. AGATE He was .. in the death scene immensely moving. A. C. BOULT He made a moving speech of thanks to the orchestra.

Special collocations & comb.: **moving average** a succession of averages derived from successive segments (usu. of constant size and overlapping) of a series of values. **moving-coil** *a.* designating electrical instruments and apparatus in which a coil of wire is suspended in a magnetic field, so that either the coil moves when a current flows through it or else a current is generated when the coil is caused to move. **moving-iron** *a.* designating electrical instruments and apparatus in which a current in a fixed coil of wire causes the movement of a piece of iron within the coil. **moving map** a map carried in a ship, aircraft, etc., which is displayed so that as the craft moves its position always corresponds to a fixed point in the middle of the map. **moving pavement** a footway arranged as a conveyor belt for the carrying of passengers. **moving picture** †(*a*) a painting, drawing, etc., in which objects move or appear to move; (*b*) a continuous picture of events obtained by projecting a sequence of photographs taken at very short intervals, a motion picture, a cinematographic film. **moving plant** = *telegraph plant* s.v. TELEGRAPH *n.* **moving sidewalk** *N. Amer.* = *moving pavement* above. **moving stair**(**case**) an escalator. **moving-target** *a.* designating radar apparatus or techniques that indicate only those objects which are moving relative to the transmitter.

movingly *adv.* in a moving, touching, or affecting manner L16. **movingness** *n.* the quality of being moving, touching, or affecting M17.

Moviola /muːvɪ'əʊlə/ *n.* Also **movieola**. E20. [f. MOVIE + -OLA.] (Proprietary name for) a device whereby the picture and sound of a cinematographic film are reproduced on a small scale so that the film may be edited or checked.

mow /maʊ/ *n.*[1] Now chiefly *N. Amer.* & *dial.* [OE *mūga, mūha, mūwa* corresp. to ON *múgi* swath, (also *múgr*) crowd, of unkn. origin.] **1** A stack of hay, corn, beans, peas, etc.; a heap of grain or hay in a barn. OE. †**2** A heap, a pile; a mound, a hillock. LME–L17. **3** A place in a barn where hay or corn is heaped up. M18.

Comb.: **mowburn** *v.i.* become mowburnt; **mowburnt** *a.* (of hay, corn, etc.) spoilt by being stacked damp or too green; **mowhay** *dial.* a rick-yard.

mow /məʊ, maʊ/ *n.*[2] ME. [Prob. f. OFr. *moe*, (also mod.) *moue*) pouting, †mouth, †lip, or MDu. *mouwe* (perh. the source of the Fr.).] **1** A grimace; *esp.* a derisive grimace. Now *arch.* & *literary*. ME. **2** A jest. Long only *pred.* & after preps. in *pl.*, jest (as opp. to earnest), a laughing matter, (usu. in neg. contexts). *Sc.* LME.

1 *mops and mows*.

mow /məʊ/ *n.*[3] E20. [f. MOW *v.*[1]] **1** *Cricket.* A sweeping stroke to leg. E20. **2** An act or instance of mowing something, esp. a lawn. L20.

mow /məʊ/ *v.*[1] Pa. pple **mowed, mown** /məʊn/. [OE *māwan* (str.) corresp. to (wk) OFris. *mēa*, MDu. *maeien* (Du. *maaien*), OHG *māen* (G *mähen*), f. Gmc base also of MEAD *n.*[2], MEADOW.] **1** *v.t.* & *i.* Cut down (grass, corn, etc.) with a scythe or (now) a machine (also foll. by *down*); cut down the produce of (a field etc.) in this way. OE. **2** *transf.* & *fig.* **a** *v.t.* & (*rare*) *i.* Cut with a sweeping stroke like that of a scythe; destroy or kill indiscriminately or in great numbers. Also, defeat comprehensively. Now usu. foll. by *down*. ME. **b** *v.t.* Create (a passage), make (one's way), by indiscriminate killing. M17. **c** *v.t.* Shave. *joc.* Now *rare*. M17. **d** *v.t.* & *i.* *Cricket.* Hit (the ball) to leg with a sweeping stroke. M19.

1 T. F. POWYS A field of rich clover ready to be mown. J. GARDAM We'll mow all day and if need be through the night. M. ANGELOU Neighbours spoke to each other as they mowed their lawns. **2a** POPE 'Tis not in me .. To mow whole Troops, and make whole Armies fly. *Daily Mirror* S.S. troops waited to mow them down with machine-guns. *Independent* A suspected gang member .. was himself mown down by two gunmen.

mowable *a.* (now *rare*) E17.

mow /maʊ/ *v.*[2]*t.* Now *dial.* ME. [f. MOW *n.*[1]] Put (hay, corn, etc.) in stacks or heaps. Also foll. by *up*.

mow /məʊ, maʊ/ *v.*[3]*i.* Now *arch.* & *literary*. ME. [f. MOW *n.*[2]] Make mouths, grimace. Freq. in collocation w. *mock*, *mop*.

M. LOWRY Yvonne Griffaton's father .. came to mock and mow at her. W. H. AUDEN Mopped and mowed at, as their train worms through a tunnel.

mower /'məʊə/ *n.* ME. [f. MOW *v.*[1] + -ER[1].] **1** A person who mows grass etc. ME. **2** A mowing-machine; a lawnmower. M19.

1 mower's mite a harvest-mite.

mowing /'məʊɪŋ/ *n.* LME. [f. MOW *v.*[1] + -ING[1].] **1** The action of MOW *v.*[1] LME. **2** The quantity of grass etc. cut at one time; in *pl.*, grass etc. removed by mowing. M18. **3** Land on which grass is grown for hay; a hayfield. *US*. M18.

Comb.: **mowing-machine** an agricultural machine for mowing grass etc.; *mowing-machine bird*, the grasshopper warbler, *Locustella naevia*.

mown *v.* pa. pple: see MOW *v.*[1]

mowra *n.* var. of MAHUA.

moxa /'mɒksə/ *n.*[1] L17. [Jap. *mogusa* (disyllabic) contr. of *moe kusa* burning herb.] **1** A soft wool prepared from down from the young leaves of any of various Asiatic plants, as *Artemisia indica* or *Crossostephium artemisioides*, used esp. as in oriental medicine in the form of a cone or cylinder for burning next to the skin as a counterirritant, cauterizing agent, etc. Also, a plant so used. L17. **2** Any substance prepared for moxibustion. M19.

moxi'bustion *n.* [blend w. COMBUSTION] the therapeutic use of burning moxa or another substance next to the skin M19.

†Moxa *a.* & *n.*[2] var. of MOCHICA.

moxie /'mɒksi/ *n.* *N. Amer. slang.* M20. [*Moxie*, proprietary name for a soft drink.] Courage, force of character; energy; ingenuity, wit.

moya /mɔɪ'ɑː/ *int.* *Anglo-Ir.* Also **mauryah** /mɔː'jɑː/ & other vars. E20. [Ir. *mar dh'eadh* as if it were so.] Expr. deep scepticism.

moyen /'mɔɪən/ *n.*[1] Long *obs.* exc. *Sc.* LME. [OFr. *moien* (mod. *moyen*) use as n. of adj.: see MEAN *a.*[2] Cf. MEAN *n.*[1]] †**1** A mediator, an intermediary. LME–E17. †**2** A means, an agency; *sing.* & in *pl.*, means, resources. LME–L17. **3** *sing.* & in *pl.* Mediation, intercession; exercise of influence. LME. †**4** Instrumentality. LME–E18. †**5** A middle condition or quality; a mean. L15–L16.

†moyen *n.*[2] E16–E19. [OFr. *moienne* use as n. of fem. of *moien*: see prec.] A kind of cannon of middle size.

moyen-âge /mwɑːjɛn'ɑːʒ/ *a.* Also **moyen-age** & w. cap. initials. M19. [Fr. = the Middle Ages.] Of or pertaining to the Middle Ages, medieval.

Moygashel /'mɔɪgəʃ(ə)l/ *n.* M20. [A village in Co. Tyrone, N. Ireland.] (Proprietary name for) a type of Irish linen.

moz *n.* & *v.* var. of MOZZ.

Mozambican /məʊzam'biːk(ə)n/ *a.* & *n.* Also **-quan**. L19. [f. *Mozambique* (see below) + -AN.] **A** *adj.* Of or pertaining to Mozambique, a country on the east coast of Africa (formerly a Portuguese colony). L19. **B** *n.* A native or inhabitant of Mozambique. L20.

Mozambiquer *n.* (now *rare*) = MOZAMBICAN *n.* E19.

Mozarab /məʊ'zarəb/ *n.* E17. [Sp. *mozárabe* f. Arab. *musta'rib* lit. 'making oneself an Arab'.] *Hist.* In Muslim Spain: a person allowed to practise Christianity (on condition of owning allegiance to the Moorish king).

Mozarabic /məʊ'zarəbɪk/ *a.* L17. [f. as prec. + -IC.] *Hist.* Of or pertaining to the Mozarabs, or Christianity in Muslim Spain.

Mozartian /məʊt'sɑːtɪən/ *a.* & *n.* Also **-ean**. M19. [f. *Mozart* (see below) + -IAN, -EAN.] **A** *adj.* Of, pertaining to, or characteristic of the Austrian composer Wolfgang Amadeus Mozart (1756–91) or his music. M19. **B** *n.* An interpreter, student, or admirer of Mozart or his music. M20.

Mozartianly *adv.* in the manner or style of or appropriate to Mozart's music E20.

moze /məʊz/ *v.t.* Now *rare* or *obs.* E16. [Perh. f. MOSS *n.*] = GIG *v.*[1]

mozetta *n.* var. of MOZZETTA.

mozo /'moθo, 'məʊzəʊ/ *n.* Pl. **-os** /-ɔs, -əʊz/. M19. [Sp., lit. 'boy'.] In Spain and Spanish-speaking countries: a male servant or attendant, a groom, a labourer; *spec.* a bullfighter's attendant.

mozz /mɒz/ *n.* & *v.* *Austral. colloq.* Also **moz.** E20. [Abbrev. of MOZZLE.] **A** *n.* An inconvenience, a jinx, a malign influence. Chiefly in *put the mozz on*, = sense B. below. E20. **B** *v.t.* Inconvenience, jinx, deter. M20.

mozzarella /mɒtsə'rɛlə/ *n.* E20. [It., dim. of *mozza* a kind of cheese, f. *mozzare* cut off: see + -ELLA.] More fully *mozzarella cheese*. A white Italian cheese originally made in the Naples area from buffalo milk.

mozzetta /məʊ'zɛtə, -'tsɛtə/ *n.* Also **mozetta.** L18. [It., aphet. f. *almozzetta*, f. med.L *almucia* AMICE *n.*[1] + *-etta* -ET[1].] *RC Ch.* A short cape with a hood, worn by the Pope, cardinals, and some other ecclesiastics.

mozzie *n.* var. of MOSSIE *n.*[2]

mozzle /'mɒz(ə)l/ *n.* *Austral. colloq.* L19. [Heb. *mazzāl* star, luck.] Luck, fortune.

mph /(ə)mh/ *int.* L19. [Natural exclam. Cf. UMPH *int.*] Expr. disapproval, doubt, or qualified approval.

mpingo /(ə)m'pɪŋgəʊ/ *n.* Pl. **-os.** L20. [Kiswahili.] An E. African leguminous tree, *Dalbergia melanoxylon*, whose dense black wood is used for carving and in making musical (esp. woodwind) instruments; the wood of this tree. Also called *African blackwood*.

Mpongwe /(ə)m'pɒŋgweɪ/ *n.* & *a.* M19. [Bantu.] **A** *n.* Pl. **-s**, same. A member of a people living in Gabon, esp. in the region of the Gabon estuary; the Bantu language of this people. M19. **B** *attrib.* or as *adj.* Of or pertaining to the Mpongwe or their language. M19.

Mr /'mɪstə/ *n.* Also **Mr.** (point). Pl. served by MESSRS. LME. [Abbrev. of MASTER *n.*[1], (now) MISTER *n.*[2]] **1** Used as a title preceding the name of any man without a higher or honorific or professional title (formerly below the rank of knight and above some undefined level of social status, the limit of which has been continually lowered) or preceding any of various designations of office. LME. **b** Used with following adj. or n. to form a name for a man who is an exemplar or type of the class or quality specified or who is closely associated with the thing specified. E19. **c** A person addressed as 'Mr'; the word 'Mr' as a title (in correspondence). E19. †**2** *gen.* = MASTER *n.*[1] M16–L17.

1 *Times* Mr. Justice Foster had agreed to resume the hearing of the case. *Guardian* Mr Heath . . made his reputation at the Board of Trade. M. FOOT A reply given by the new Speaker, Mr Speaker Weatherill. *Mr Chairman, Mr Mayor, Mr President*, etc. **b** *Health & Strength* In that first contest there was only one Mr Universe title to win. *Listener* In 1953, Ford, Mr Industry himself, commissioned the first geodesic dome. J. WAMBAUGH I been too nice to you. . . Well, no more Mr. Nice Guy!

Comb.: **Mr Big** the head of an organization of criminals; any important man; *Mr Chad*: see CHAD *n.*[1]; **Mr Charley, Charlie** *derog.* an adult male Black; **Mr Clean** an honourable or incorruptible politician; *Mr Fixit*: see FIXIT 1; *Mr Lo*: see LO *n.*; *Mr Next-Door*: see *next door* s.v. NEXT *a.*; **Mr Right** the man who would make the ideal husband for a particular person, one's destined husband; *Mr Speaker*: see SPEAKER 2a.

mridangam /mrɪ'daŋəm/ *n.* Also **-ga** /-gə/. L19. [Tamil alt. of Skt *mṛdaṅga*.] A double-headed barrel-shaped drum, once made of clay, now usually of wood, with one head larger than the other, used in southern Indian music. Cf. MADAL.

Mrs /'mɪsɪz, -s/ *n.* Also **Mrs.** (point). Pl. same (also served by MESDAMES). E17. [Abbrev. of MISTRESS *n.* Cf. MISSIS.] †**1** *gen.* = MISTRESS *n.* Only in 17. **2** Used as a title preceding the surname of a married woman without a higher or honorific or professional title, sometimes with the forename(s) of herself or her husband intervening, or (more familiarly) the forename of the husband alone, (formerly distinctive of gentlewomen); a woman so designated. E17. **b** Used as a title preceding the name of an unmarried lady or girl, Miss. *obs.* exc. *Hist.* M17. **c** *ellipt.* The wife of the person speaking, addressed, or referred to; a person's wife; *the Mrs*, one's own wife. *colloq.* E20.

2 R. H. BARHAM Mrs. John Ingoldsby at the table. A. CHRISTIE 'Who was at breakfast?' 'Mrs. Fortescue, Miss Fortescue, Mrs. Val Fortescue. . . Mrs. Val and Miss Fortescue always eat a hearty breakfast.' *Daily Telegraph* Mrs. Anne Kerr, Labour M.P. for Rochester and Chatham. **c** R. BROOKE He passed through Fiji lately. . . Mrs, I gather, is not with him. F. ASTAIRE I walked back with him to his box, where his Mrs. was waiting. E. BULLINS I'll have the Mrs. call the doctor as soon as I get home.

Comb.: *Mrs* GRUNDY; *Mrs Justice*: see JUSTICE *n.*; *Mrs Lo*; **Mrs Mop(p)** (a nickname for) a charwoman; the typical charwoman; *Mrs Next-Door*: see *next door* s.v. NEXT *a.*; **Mrs Thing**: used in place of a married woman's name of which the speaker is uncertain.

Ms /mɪz/ *n.* Also **Ms.** (point). Pl. **Mses, Mss,** /'mɪzɪz/. M20. [Contr. of MRS, MISS *n.*[2] Cf. MIZ 2.] Used as a title preceding the surname of any woman regardless of her marital status, sometimes with her forename(s) intervening; a woman so designated.

msasa /(ə)m'sɑːsə/ *n.* E20. [Shona.] A leguminous tree, *Brachystegia spiciformis*, of central Africa (esp. Zimbabwe), with fragrant white flowers and pinnate leaves which are crimson and bronze in spring.

Mses, Mss *ns.pl.* see MS.

Mswahili *n.sing.* see SWAHILI.

mtepe /(ə)m'teɪpeɪ/ *n.* L19. [Kiswahili.] A sailing craft characterized by a square matting sail, used on the east coast of Africa.

mu /mjuː/ *n.*[1] ME. [Gk.] **1** The twelfth letter (M, μ) of the Greek alphabet. ME. **2** Pl. same. One micrometre (micron). Usu. denoted by μ. L19. **3** *Electronics.* The amplification factor of a valve. E20.

Comb. **mu-meson** (*obs.* exc. *Hist.*) = MUON.

¶Rare bef. L19.

mu *n.*[2] var. of MOU.

†**mucaginous** *a.* M17–E19. [f. med.L *mucagin-*, *mucago*, f. as MUCUS, + -OUS.] = MUCILAGINOUS.

mucate /'mjuːkeɪt/ *n.* E19. [f. MUCIC + -ATE[1].] *Chem.* A salt or ester of mucic acid.

mucedinous /mjuː'siːdɪnəs/ *a.* M19. [f. mod.L *mucedin-*, *mucedo* mould (f. *mucere* be mouldy) + -OUS.] *Bot.* Of the nature of or resembling mould.

much /mʌtʃ/ *a.* (in mod. usage also classed as a *determiner*), *pron.*, *n.*, & *adv.* Compar. served by MORE *a.* etc., superl. by MOST. ME. [Abbrev. of reflex of OE *micel*: see MUCKLE.] **A** *adj.* **1** Great in size, bulk, amount, or degree. Long *obs.* exc. in names of English villages, as *Much Wenlock*. ME. **2** A great quantity or amount of, existing or present in great quantity. (Preceding the n. without the indef. article *a(n)*; *arch.* after the def. article *the*). ME. †**b** A great number of. ME–E17. **c** Many. Now chiefly *US dial.* M16.

1 SWIFT I have heard them say, 'Much talkers, little walkers'. 2 R. KIPLING A pale yellow sun . . showed the much dirt of the place. A. P. HERBERT There wasn't much rain here—only a drizzle. W. RAEPER Edward Lear's first *Book of Nonsense* had been published, with much acclaim. *iron.*: *Observer* They went on in the same way. . . Much good did it do them. **b** AV *Num.* 20:20 And Edom came out against him with much people.

B *pron.* & *n.* A great deal, a great quantity, (*of*); *pred.* something or someone great or important. ME.

D. EDEN I won't say you've got Dietrich's legs, ducky, but they don't miss by much. K. AMIS There may not be much to be said for Charlie-boy here. G. CHARLES Though he dazzled me at the beginning, I knew after a time that he wasn't much really. C. SAGAN We know rather much about the past and almost nothing about the future. R. ELLMANN Much of his time went into reading in other fields.

C *adv.* **1** In a great degree; to a great extent; greatly. (Qualifying a vb or the whole predication; comparatives or words implying comparison; occas. w. the intervention of *the* before a comparative; (*obs.* exc. *US dial.*) positive or uncompared adjs. and advs.). ME. **2** Pretty nearly, approximately. Chiefly qualifying expressions denoting similarity. M16. **3** For a large part of one's time. L18.

1 J. CONRAD His mother wept very much after his disappearance. C. P. SNOW I suppose he was much the better trained. W. FAULKNER 'Been much busy?' Earl says. 'Not much,' I says. J. STEINBECK I know this land ain't much good. B. PYM This shabby part of London, so very much the 'wrong' side of Victoria Station. A. S. BYATT She thought Julia much changed. P. KAVANAGH Her daughter . . cut off the woman's disquisition on actors much to Patrick's delight. S. HASTINGS With two best-sellers in . . four years, Nancy was much in demand. *comb.*: SOUTHEY This so much-to-be-admired eternal Providence. *Irish Times* This highly exclusive, much-sought-after . . cul-de-sac. A. BROOKNER I am getting some much needed exercise. 2 MILTON The Booke . . which came out . . much about the time. M. KEANE Sylvester returned to his party which he found much as when he had left it. C. MCCULLOUGH He and his sister were much of a height. 3 C. DARWIN I have not been much away from home of late.

Phrases: *a bit much*: see BIT *n.*[2] *as much*: see AS *adv.* etc. *as much as the traffic will bear* or *stand*: see TRAFFIC *n.* 1. **by much** by a great deal. *how much*: see HOW *adv.* *know too much*: see KNOW *v.* *leave much to be desired*: see LEAVE *v.*[1] *make much of*: see MAKE *v.* **much as** even though, however much. *much cry and little wool*: see CRY *n.* *much* LESS. *much obliged*: see OBLIGE *v.* **much of a —** (in neg. contexts) a great —, a — of any noteworthy quality, a — in any great degree. *much of a* MUCHNESS. *much the same*: see SAME *a.* *much to seek*: see SEEK *v.* **not come to much** have little success. **not much** *colloq.* certainly not, far from it; *iron.* certainly, very much. *not much in it*: see IN *prep.* **not much on** *colloq.* not useful or effective for (a purpose); no good at (something). **not much to look at** of insignificant or unattractive appearance. *not much wiser*: see WISE *a.* & *n.*[2] **not up to much** *colloq.* not very good, of a low standard. *pretty much*: see PRETTY *adv.* *say much for*: see SAY *v.*[1] *see much of*: see SEE *v.* *set much by*: see SET *v.*[1] *so much*: see SO *adv.* etc. **think (it) much** *arch.* regard as important or onerous (*to do*). *think much of*: see THINK *v.*[2] THIS *much.* TOO *much.* *without so much as a by your leave*: see LEAVE *n.*[1]

Comb.: †**muchwhat** *adv.* greatly; nearly, almost; to a considerable degree.

muchacha /mʊ'tʃɑːtʃə/ *n.* L19. [Sp.: fem. of next.] In Spain and Spanish-speaking countries: a girl, a young woman; a female servant.

muchacho /mʊ'tʃɑːtʃəʊ/ *n.* Pl. **-os.** L16. [Sp.] In Spain and Spanish-speaking countries: a boy, a young man; a male servant.

muchi /'muːtʃi/ *n.* Also **moocha** /'muːtʃə/. L19. [Zulu *umutsha*.] A loincloth made of hide or animal tails worn as traditional dress in South Africa.

muchly /'mʌtʃli/ *adv.* Now *joc.* E17. [f. MUCH *a.* + -LY[2].] Much, exceedingly.

muchness /'mʌtʃnɪs/ *n.* LME. [f. MUCH *a.* + -NESS.] †**1** Large size or bulk. Also, size, magnitude (large or small). LME–M17. **2** Greatness in quantity, number, or degree. LME. **b** An instance of this. Now *rare.* L17.

Phrases: **much of a muchness** *colloq.* much of the same importance or value; very much the same or alike.

mucho /'mʊtʃəʊ, 'mʌ-/ *a.* (*determiner*) & *adv.* *joc.* & *colloq.* M20. [Sp. = much, many.] **A** *adj.* Much, many. M20. **B** *adv.* Very. L20.

muci- /'mjuːsi/ *comb. form* of MUCUS: see -I-. Cf. MUCO-.

muci'carmine *n.* (*Histol.*) a specific stain for mucin, consisting of carmine and aluminium chloride in water L19. **mu'ciferous** *a.* secreting or conveying mucus M19. **mucigel** *n.* (*Biochem.*) a mucilaginous gel secreted by plant roots and usu. associated with large numbers of bacteria L20. **mucigen** *n.* the substance in a mucus-secreting cell from which mucin is derived L19. **mu'cigenous** *a.* (*a*) producing or secreting mucus; (*b*) of the nature of mucigen: L19. **mu'ciparous** *a.* = MUCIGENOUS (a) M19.

mucic /'mjuːsɪk/ *a.* E19. [Fr. *mucique*, f. as MUCUS: see -IC.] Chem. *mucic acid*, a crystalline carboxylic acid obtained by oxidation of lactose or various plant gums, and used in the synthesis of pyrroles; 2,3,4,5-tetrahydroxyhexanedioic acid, $HOOC(CHOH)_4COOH$.

mucid /'mjuːsɪd/ *a.* *rare.* M17. [L *mucidus*, f. *mucere* be mouldy: see -ID[1].] Mouldy, musty, slimy.

mucification /ˌmjuːsɪfɪˈkeɪʃ(ə)n/ *n.* M20. [f. MUCI- + -FICATION.] *Physiol.* Transformation of epithelial cells into mucus-secreting cells.

ˈ**mucify** *v.i.* & *t.* (cause to) undergo mucification M20.

mucilage /ˈmjuːsɪlɪdʒ/ *n.* LME. [(O)Fr. f. late L *mucilago* musty juice, f. as MUCUS: see -AGE.] **1** A polysaccharide substance extractable as a viscous or gelatinous solution in water from roots, seeds, and other parts of certain plants, and used in medicines and adhesives. LME. **b** *transf.* A viscous mass, a pulp. L17. **c** An aqueous solution of a gum etc. used as an adhesive; glue, gum. Chiefly *N. Amer.* M19. **2** A viscous secretion or bodily fluid (as mucus, synovia). LME.

mucilaginous /mjuːsɪˈladʒɪnəs/ *a.* LME. [f. med.L *mucilaginosus*, f. late L *mucilagin-*, *-ago*: see prec., -OUS. Cf. (O)Fr. *mucilagineux*.] **1** Having the nature or properties of mucilage; of a soft, moist, and viscous quality or appearance. Also, pertaining to or characteristic of mucilage. LME. **2** Containing or secreting mucilage. L17.

mucilaginously *adv.* M19.

mucin /ˈmjuːsɪn/ *n.* M19. [f. MUCUS + -IN[1].] *Biol.* Orig., mucus. Now, any of various glycoproteins forming the main constituents of mucus.

mucinous /ˈmjuːsɪnəs/ *a.* M19. [f. prec. + -OUS.] *Med.* Mucous; mucoid.

muck /mʌk/ *n.*[1] ME. [Prob. of Scand. origin: cf. ON *myki*, *mykr* dung, Da. *møg*, *mug*, *mog*, *møk*, Norw. *myk*, f. Gmc wd meaning 'soft'.] **1** Mud, dirt, filth; *spec.* the dung of cattle, usu. mixed with decomposing vegetable refuse, used for manure; farmyard manure. ME. **b** *Soil Sci.* Soil material consisting of decayed plant remains, distinguished from peat as being more thoroughly decomposed and having a higher mineral content. Orig. *US.* M19. **c** Waste material removed during mining or civil engineering operations; *spec.* (*US*), surface material overlying a placer deposit. L19. **2a** *fig.* Worldly wealth, money. Now *rare.* ME. **b** Anything regarded as disgusting or worthless. *colloq.* L19. **c** Bad weather; rain, snow. *slang* & *dial.* M20. **d** Hostile anti-aircraft fire. *Air Force slang.* M20. **3** An untidy or dirty state, a mess. *colloq.* M18.

1 B. GILROY A window that had accumulated years of grime and muck. **2b** J. OSBORNE A nice drop of gin—some of the muck they give you nowadays—tastes like cheap scent. I. MURDOCH Do you want pornographic muck to circulate?

Phrases: *Lady Muck*: see LADY *n.* & *a.* *Lord Muck*: see LORD *n.* **make a muck of** *colloq.* do (something) badly; spoil, bungle, (an undertaking etc.).

Comb.: **muck-heap**, **muckhill** a manure-heap, a midden; **muck soil** = sense 1b above; **muck-spreader** a machine for spreading dung; **muck-spreading** the action of distributing dung over a field; **muck sweat** *colloq.* a profuse sweat; **muckworm** a worm or grub that lives in muck; *fig.* a miser; a guttersnipe.

muck /mʌk/ *n.*[2] M17. [The 2nd syll. of AMOK taken erron. as a n.] **1** = AMOK *n.* 2. *rare.* M17. **2** *run a muck*, run amok. L17.

muck /mʌk/ *v.* LME. [f. MUCK *n.*[1] Cf. ON *moka* shovel (manure).] **1** *v.t.* Free from muck; remove muck from (a stable, pig-pen, or other shelter for an animal). Now usu. foll. by *out.* LME. **b** *v.t.* Remove muck from the shelter of (an animal). Usu. foll. by *out.* M20. **c** *v.i.* Foll. by *out*: remove muck from a stable, pig-pen, etc. M20. **2** *v.t.* Cover with muck, manure. LME. **3** *v.t.* **a** = MESS *v.* 7a. Usu. foll. by *up.* M19. **b** = MESS *v.* 7b. Usu. foll. by *about, around.* L19. **4** *v.i.* **a** = MESS *v.* 6a. Usu. foll. by *about, around.* M19. **b** Foll. by *in*: share food, facilities, etc.; eat; share tasks, cooperate, participate, consort *with.* E20. **5** *v.i.* *euphem.* = FUCK *v.* 1. Chiefly in imprecations (see FUCK *v.* 3). E20.

1 J. BETJEMAN She can muck out the stables and clean Her snaffle. **b** *Times* She did manual work . . toiling in the fields, mucking out the chickens. **c** C. WATSON Used to stand work and willing to muck out. **3a** J. TEY You don't want that dazzling outfit of yours to be mucked up. **b** N. BAWDEN I don't like to see him muck his life up. **4a** *Notes & Queries* The gang of young people mucking about at nightfall. **b** *Daily Telegraph* He mucked in with the rest of us.

Comb.: **muck-about** *colloq.* a person who mucks about; an act of mucking about; **muck-up** *colloq.* a blunder, a fiasco; a mess, a muddle.

mucking *ppl a.* & *adv.* (*euphem.*) = FUCKING E20.

muck-a-muck /ˈmʌkəmʌk/ *n. N. Amer.* M19. [Chinook Jargon. Cf. MUCKY-MUCK.] **1** Among Indians of western N. America: food. M19. **2** = HIGH-MUCK-A-MUCK. *colloq.* E20.

mucka-mucka *n.* var. of MOCO-MOCO.

muckender /ˈmʌkəndə/ *n. obs.* exc. *dial.* LME. [Prob. f. Fr. *mouchoir*, f. *moucher* clear the nose f. pop.L: cf. mod.Prov. *moucadour*, Sp. *mocador*, *-dero*. For the intrusive *n* cf. *colander*. See also MOCKET.] A handkerchief. Formerly also, a table-napkin, a bib.

mucker /ˈmʌkə/ *n.*[1] ME. [f. MUCK *v.* + -ER[1].] **1** A person who or machine which removes or spreads manure. ME. †**2** A scavenger. L15–L18. **3** A miser. *obs.* exc. *dial.* M16. **4** *euphem.* = FUCKER. E20. **5** *mucker-in*, a person who mucks in. M20. **6** A friend, a companion, a mate. *slang.* M20.

6 A. JUDD Mucker of mine from Sandhurst was killed there.

mucker /ˈmʌkə/ *n.*[2] M19. [f. MUCK *n.*[1] + -ER[1].] **1** A heavy fall. Chiefly in *come* or *go a mucker*, fall, come to grief. *slang.* M19. **2** A person who or machine which removes mining waste. L19.

mucker /ˈmʌkə/ *n.*[3] *slang* (orig. *US*). L19. [Prob. f. G *Mucker* a sulky person.] A fanatic, a hypocrite; a coarse rough person.

muckerish *a.* E20.

mucker /ˈmʌkə/ *v.*[1]*t. obs.* exc. *dial.* LME. [Perh. f. MUCK *n.*[1] + -ER[5].] Hoard (money or goods). Also foll. by *up.*

†**muckerer** *n.* (*rare*) ME–M18.

mucker /ˈmʌkə/ *v.*[2] *slang.* M19. [f. MUCKER *n.*[2]] **1** *v.i.* Come to grief, fail. M19. **2** *v.t.* Ruin, spoil; squander, throw *away.* M19.

muckle /ˈmʌk(ə)l/ *a.* (in mod. usage also classed as a *determiner*), *pron.*, *n.*, & *adv.* Now *Sc.* & *dial.* Also **mickle** /ˈmɪk(ə)l/. [OE *mićel*, superseded in ME by forms f. cognate ON *mikeli*, f. Gmc. Cf. MUCH.] **A** *adj.* **1** Great; considerable in size, bulk, number, importance, or (passing into sense A.2) amount or degree. OE. **2** A great quantity or amount of; much. OE.

Comb.: **muckle-mouthed** *a.* (of a person) disfigured by a disproportionately large mouth; **muckle wheel** the large wheel of a spinning wheel.

B *pron.* & *n.* **1** A great quantity or amount; much. OE. †**2** Great or eminent people. Only in ME. †**3** Size, stature; bigness. LME–E17. **4a** A large sum or amount. Chiefly in *many a little* or *pickle makes a muckle.* L16. **b** (*mickle.*) [By confusion.] A small amount. Chiefly in *many a mickle makes a muckle.* L18.

Phrases: **make muckle of** make much of, cherish. *so muckle*: see SO *adv.* etc.

C *adv.* To a great extent or degree. OE.

muckleness *n.* greatness, largeness; size: ME.

muckluck *n.* var. of MUKLUK.

muckna /ˈmʌknə/ *n.* L18. [Hind. *makunā*, *makhnā* f. Tamil *mokka* blunt.] In the Indian subcontinent: a male elephant without tusks, or having only rudimentary tusks.

muckrake /ˈmʌkreɪk/ *n.* & *v.* L17. [f. MUCK *n.*[1] + RAKE *n.*[1]] **A** *n.* A rake for collecting or sifting through muck (*lit.* & *fig.*). L17.

B *v.* **1** *v.i.* Rake refuse together. Chiefly *fig.*, search for evidence of corruption or scandal in order to expose it, esp. among powerful or well-known people or institutions. L19. **2** *v.t.* Subject (a person or institution) to muckracking. *US.* E20.

1 *Investors Chronicle* It was a commendable bit of muck-raking, a sordid story of local government graft.

muckraker *n.* †(*a*) a miser; (*b*) a person who seeks out and exposes scandals etc. about prominent people; (*c*) a prurient inquirer into private morals: E17.

mucky /ˈmʌki/ *a.* & *v.* M16. [f. MUCK *n.*[1] + -Y[1].] **A** *adj.* **1** Covered with muck, dirty, muddy; involving muck. M16. †**b** Of money: filthy, corrupting. Of a person: miserly. M16–M17. **c** Of weather: bad, foul. Chiefly *dial.* E19. **d** Grimy, grubby; unpleasant, sordid; indecent, obscene. *colloq.* L19. **2** Consisting of or resembling muck. L16.

1 *Sunday Express* A mucky job in the garden. **mucky pup** a dirty or messy person, esp. a child. **d** D. ROWE I can't stand going to my friend's house—she lets it get so mucky. B. REID Good vulgarity is marvellous—it's just when it's a bit mucky I don't like it.

B *v.t.* Make dirty. *dial.* E19.

muckiness *n.* E18.

mucky-muck /ˈmʌkɪmʌk/ *n. N. Amer. slang.* E20. [Redupl. of prec., after MUCK-A-MUCK.] = HIGH-MUCK-A-MUCK.

muco- /ˈmjuːkəʊ/ *comb. form* of MUCUS or (in *Biochem.*) MUCOID *n.*, *a.*, MUCIN: see -O-. Cf. MUCI-.

mucocele, **-coele** *n.* (*Med.*) a distended structure containing mucus, as produced by the blockage of secretory ducts, the appendix, etc. E19. **mucoˈciliary** *a.* (*Anat.*) designating or pertaining to a system of cilia and mucous glands lining the respiratory passages and serving to expel extraneous particles M20. **mucocuˈtaneous** *a.* involving or pertaining to a mucous membrane and the skin L19. **mucoˈlytic** *n.* & *a.* (*Med.*) (an agent) able to disperse or break down mucus or its constituents M20. **mucoˈmembranous** *a.* (*Anat.*) of or pertaining to a mucous membrane, mucosal L19. **mucoˈpeptide** *n.* (*Biochem.*) = MUREIN M20. **mucoperiˈosteum** *n.* (*Anat.*) a periosteum closely associated or continuous with a mucous membrane E20. **mucoˈprotein** *n.* (*Biochem.*) = PROTEOGLYCAN E20. **mucoˈpurulent** *a.* (*Med.*) designating or characterized by mingled pus and mucus M19. **mucopus** *n.* (*Med.*) pus mingled with mucus L19. **mucoviscīˈdosis** *n.* (*Med.*) = *cystic* FIBROSIS M20.

mucoid /ˈmjuːkɔɪd/ *n.* E20. [f. MUCIN + -OID.] *Biochem.* A substance resembling mucin, esp. a proteoglycan.

mucoid /ˈmjuːkɔɪd/ *a.* M19. [f. MUCUS + -OID.] Resembling, involving, or of the nature of mucus.

Also **muˈcoidal** *a.* (*rare*) M19.

mucoitin /mjuːˈkəʊɪtɪn/ *n.* E20. [f. MUCO- after *chondroitin.*] *Biochem.* A mixture of partly sulphated glycosaminoglycans extracted from various mucins.

mucopolysaccharide /ˌmjuːkəʊpɒlɪˈsakərʌɪd/ *n.* M20. [f. MUCO- + POLYSACCHARIDE.] = GLYCOSAMINOGLYCAN.

¶Common in *Med.* & *Biol.*, though *glycosaminoglycan* is preferred in *Biochem.*

mucopolysacchariˈdosis *n.*, pl. **-doses** /-ˈdəʊsiːz/, any of various congenital disorders of mucopolysaccharide metabolism characterized by mental handicap, skeletal abnormalities, and other symptoms M20.

mucor /ˈmjuːkɔː/ *n.* M17. [L (in sense 2 as mod.L genus name), f. *mucere* be mouldy.] †**1** Mouldiness, mustiness; mould. M17–M19. **2** Orig., any mould fungus. Now *spec.* a mould of the genus *Mucor* or the order Mucorales, found on decaying organic matter and occasionally pathogenic in humans. E19.

mucoˈraceous *a.* of, pertaining to, or characteristic of the order Mucorales or (esp.) the family Mucoraceae of moulds M19.

mucormycosis /ˌmjuːkɔːmʌɪˈkəʊsɪs/ *n.* Pl. **-coses** /-ˈkəʊsiːz/. E20. [f. prec. + MYCOSIS.] *Med.* & *Vet. Med.* Phycomycosis; *esp.* infection with fungus of the genus *Mucor*, affecting the skin, ears, paranasal sinuses, and respiratory passages.

mucosa /mjuːˈkəʊsə/ *n.* Pl. **-sae** /-siː/ L19. [mod.L (*membrana*) *mucosa*, fem. of L *mucosus* MUCOUS.] *Anat.* A mucous membrane.

mucosal *a.* of or pertaining to a mucosa L19.

mucose /ˈmjuːkəʊs/ *a.* M18. [L *mucosus*: see MUCOUS, -OSE[1].] Slimy; covered with mucus.

mucosity /mjuːˈkɒsɪti/ *n.* Now *rare.* L17. [Fr. *mucosité*, f. as prec.: see -ITY.] A mucous secretion, a slimy covering.

mucous /ˈmjuːkəs/ *a.* M17. [f. L *mucosus* slimy, mucous f. as MUCUS: see -OUS.] Containing, secreting, consisting of, or resembling mucus; covered with mucus; characterized by the presence of mucus. Formerly also *gen.*, slimy.

mucous membrane a mucus-secreting membrane which lines the gut, respiratory passages, and other cavities in the body, and is continuous with the skin at the mouth, anus, and other external openings.

mucousness *n.* (*rare*) E18.

mucro /ˈmjuːkrəʊ/ *n.* Pl. **mucrones** /mjuːˈkrəʊniːz/, **mucros**. M17. [L *mucro(n-)* point.] A pointed part or organ; *esp.* (*Zool.* & *Bot.*) a short, sharp terminal point, process, or apex.

mucronate /ˈmjuːkrəneɪt/ *a.* L18. [L *mucronatus*, f. as prec.: see -ATE[2].] Terminating in a point; *esp.* (*Bot.*) abruptly terminated by a hard short point.

Also **mucronated** *a.* (now *rare* or *obs.*) M17.

mucrones *n.pl.* see MUCRO.

mucronulate /mjuːˈkrɒnjʊlət/ *a.* E19. [mod.L *mucronulatus*, f. *mucronula* dim. of MUCRO: see -ULE, -ATE[2].] *Bot.* Having a small mucro.

muculent /ˈmjuːkjʊl(ə)nt/ *a.* M17. [Late L *muculentus*, f. as MUCUS: see -ULENT.] Slimy; mucous.

mucus /ˈmjuːkəs/ *n.* M17. [L, cogn. w. Gk *mussesthai* blow the nose (cf. L *emungere*), *mukter* nose, nostril.] A viscid or slimy substance not miscible with water, containing mucin and other glycoproteins and secreted by the mucous glands and membranes of animals for protection, lubrication, etc. Also, a viscid substance secreted by or present in plants.

mud /mʌd/ *n.*[1] LME. [Prob. f. MLG *mudde* (LG *mudde*, *mod*, *mōde*, *mūde*: cf. Du. *modden* dabble in mud), MHG *mot* (G dial. *Mott*) bog, peat.] **1** Soft wet soil, sand, dust, or other earthy matter; mire, sludge. Also, hard ground produced by the drying of an area of this; *colloq.* soil. LME. **b** In *pl.* Tracts of mud on the margin of a tidal river. L19. **c** *spec.* in *Geol.* A semi-liquid or soft and plastic mixture of finely comminuted rock particles with water; a kind of this. L19. **d** A liquid (freq. a suspension of clay etc. in water) that is pumped down inside a drill pipe and up outside it during the drilling of an oil or gas well, to remove drill cuttings, cool and lubricate the bit, and prevent the collapse of the sides of the hole or leakage through them. E20. **2** *fig.* **a** Something regarded as worthless or polluting. M16. †**b** The lowest or worst part of anything; the dregs. L16–M19. **c** Coffee, esp. when strong and bitter; *US* opium. *slang.* E20.

1c T. H. HUXLEY Herculaneum was sealed up by a crust of volcanic mud.

Phrases: *as clear as mud*: see CLEAR *a.* *drag through the mud*: see DRAG *v.* **drilling mud** = sense 1d above. **fling mud** = *sling mud* below. **here's mud in your eye!** cheers! good health! **mud and stud** posts and laths filled in with mud, as a building-material for walls of cottages etc. **mud in your eye!** = *here's mud in your eye!* above. **one's name is mud** one is in disgrace or temporarily unpopular. *red mud*: see RED *a.* **sling mud** make disparaging or slanderous allegations, criticize maliciously. *stick in the mud*: see STICK *v.*[1] **throw mud** = *sling mud* above.

Comb.: **mud balance**: for measuring the density of drilling mud; **mudbank** a bank of mud in the bed of a river or on the bottom of the sea; **mud-bath** (*a*) a medicinal bath of heated mud, used esp. to relieve rheumatism etc.; (*b*) a muddy place or occasion; **mud box** *Naut.* a box containing a coarse filter used to trap sediment in bilge-water; **mud-brick** brick made with mud; **mudcat** *US* (*a*) any of several N. American catfish of muddy rivers, esp. in the Mississippi valley; †(*b*) *colloq.* a native or inhabitant of Mississippi; **mud-crab** *Austral.* a large edible swimming crab, *Scylla serrata*, of Indo-Pacific mangrove swamps; **mud dab** *N. Amer.* (*a*) = *winter flounder* s.v. WINTER *n.*; (*b*) = YELLOWFIN *sole*; **mud-dauber** (*a*) any of various sphecid wasps that deposit their eggs, together with live prey, in cells made of mud; (*b*) *US* = CLIFF *swallow* (cf. *mud swallow* below); *fig.* a travelling workman; **mud eel** an elongate creature of muddy water; *esp.* (*a*) a larval lamprey; (*b*) a salamander, *Siren lacertina*, of the south-eastern US; **mud engineer** a person responsible for the quality and supply of drilling mud; **mud fever** *Vet. Med.* erythema of a horse's feet; **mudflap** a piece of rubber, metal, etc., hung behind a vehicle wheel to catch mud, stones, etc., thrown up from the road; **mud-flat** (*a*) a stretch of muddy land left uncovered at low tide; (*b*) a mudbank in a non-tidal river; **mud-flinger**, **-flinging** = *mud-slinger*, *-slinging* below; **mud-flow** a fluid or hardened stream or avalanche of mud; the flow or motion of such a stream; **mud fluid** = sense 1d above; **mud flush** a flow of drilling mud; **mudguard** a curved strip or cover over a cycle or other vehicle wheel to reduce the splashing of mud etc. from the ground; **mudguarded** *a.* fitted with mudguards; **mudhead** (*a*) *slang* a stupid person; (*b*) a ceremonial clown among the Zuñi and Hopi peoples who wears a mud-daubed mask; **mud-hen** (chiefly *N. Amer.*) any of various rails or coots; **mud hog** = *mud pump* below; **mudhole** (*a*) a hole containing mud, esp. as forming a defect in a road; a waterhole dried so as to become mud; (*b*) a hole at the base of a boiler, condenser, etc., through which sediment can be removed; **mudhook** *slang* (*a*) an anchor; (*b*) a foot; a hand; **mud-hopper** = *mudskipper* below; **mud-laden** *a.* laden with mud; *mud-laden fluid*, = sense 1d above; **mud-lava** volcanic mud; **mud-line** the limit of wave action on a coastal seabed below which mud will settle permanently on the bottom; **mud-logger** an engineer who monitors drilling by mud-logging; **mud-logging** examination of the drilling mud coming out of a borehole for signs of oil or gas or other indications of the strata being drilled; **mud-lump** *US* a mound or cone of mud or silt formed in a river delta; **mud-mask** = *mud-pack* below; **mud minnow** a small carnivorous fish of muddy water in N. America; **mud-pack** a face-pack containing fuller's earth or some similar material; **mud pie** a mass of mud formed into the shape of a pie, esp. by a child; **mud pilot** a pilot who works in shallow water; **mudpout** *N. Amer.* = *mudcat* (a) above; **mud pump**: for circulating mud fluid; **mud puppy** *US* any of various large neotenous aquatic salamanders, esp. of the genus *Necturus*; an axolotl, a hellbender; **mud room** *N. Amer.* a cloakroom, *spec.* one in which wet or muddy footwear may be left; **mud-sill** (*a*) the lowest sill of a structure, usu. embedded in soil; (*b*) *US* the lowest class of society; a person of this class; **mudskipper** any of various small gobies of the genus *Periophthalmus* and related genera, of tropical Asian, Australasian, and African coasts, which are able to scramble over mud, along tree roots, etc., by means of stout pectoral fins; **mudslide** an avalanche of mud, rock, etc.; earthy material deposited by such an avalanche; **mud-slinger** a person given to abuse, slander, or malevolent criticism; **mud-slinging** (the employment of) abuse, slander, or malevolent criticism; **mud snail** either of two European pond snails of the genus *Lymnaea*, the slender-shelled *L. glabra* and (occas.) *L. truncalata*; **mud snake** a non-venomous black and red colubrid snake of the southern US, *Farancia abacura*; also called *hoop-snake*, *horn-snake*; **mudstone** *Geol.* any clayey or silty rock, usu. formed by hardening of mud, *esp.* a mixed clay and silt rock lacking the laminations of shale; **mud-sucker** an American goby, *Gillichthys mirabilis*, often used as bait; **mud swallow** *US* = CLIFF *swallow*; **mud-thrower**, **-throwing** = *mud-slinger*, *-slinging* above; **mud trout** = *brook trout* (b) s.v. BROOK *n.*; **mud-turtle** any small turtle of the American family Kinosternidae, of mud or muddy water; **mud volcano** (*a*) a crack or fissure discharging mud and freq. forming a hardened mound or cone; (*b*) = *mud-lump* above; **mud wall** a wall built of earth or clay or having clay as a substitute for mortar; **mud wasp** *US* = *mud dauber* (a) above; **mud wing** a mudguard, a mudflap; **mud-worm** a worm that lives in mud; *fig.* a contemptible person; **mudwort** any of several dwarf creeping plants of the genus *Limosella*, of the figwort family, esp. *L. aquatica*, growing in mud at the edge of ponds; **mud-wrestler** an exponent of mud-wrestling; **mud-wrestling** a kind of entertainment in which usu. female contestants wrestle in a mud-filled ring.

muddish *a.* somewhat muddy M17. **mudless** *a.* E17.

†**mud** *n.*[2] see MUID *n.*[2]

mud /mʌd/ *v.* Now *rare*. Infl. **-dd-**. L16. [f. MUD *n.*[1]] **1** *v.t.* Cloud (liquid) by stirring up mud or sediment. L16. **2** *v.t.* †**a** Bury in mud. *rare* (Shakes.). Only in E17. **b** In *pass.* Become stuck in mud. M19. **3** *v.t.* Cover or plaster with mud. M17. **b** Seal (porous strata) by depositing a layer of mud on the sides of a borehole. (Foll. by *off*, *up*.) E20. **4** *v.i.* Esp. of a fish: lie dormant, burrow, or hide in mud. M17.

mudalali /mʊdəˈlɑːli/ *n.* M19. [Malayalam *mutalāḷi*, f. *mutal* property.] In India and Sri Lanka (Ceylon): a proprietor, a businessman, a rich trader.

mudaliyar /mʊˈdɛlɪjɑː, ˈmʊdəlɪə/ *n.* Also (earlier) **modeliar**. M17. [Tamil *mutaliyār* pl. of *mutali* a chief.] In Sri Lanka (Ceylon): a headman, a chief; a chief military officer.

mudar /məˈdɑː/ *n.* Also **madar**. E19. [Hindi *madār*] Any of several shrubs of the genus *Calotropis* (family Asclepiadaceae), of tropical Asia and Africa; esp. *C. procera* and *C. gigantea*, whose bark yields a fibre and whose seed-floss is used like kapok. Also, a preparation of the root of any of these trees.

mudder /ˈmʌdə/ *n. slang* (chiefly *US*). E20. [f. MUD *n.*[1] + -ER[1].] A racehorse which runs well in wet or muddy conditions; a sportsman or sportswoman or a team able to perform well in wet or muddy conditions.

muddie /ˈmʌdi/ *n. Austral. colloq.* Also **muddy**. M20. [f. MUD *n.*[1] + -IE, -Y[6].] A mud-crab.

muddied /ˈmʌdɪd/ *a.* E17. [f. MUDDY *v.* + -ED[1].] Covered with mud; made muddy; (of water) turbid.

R. KIPLING The flannelled fools at the wicket or the muddied oafs at the goals.

muddify /ˈmʌdɪfʌɪ/ *v.t.* L18. [f. MUDDY *a.* + -FY.] Make muddy; muddle.

muddle /ˈmʌd(ə)l/ *n.* E19. [f. the vb.] **1** A muddled condition; confusion, disorder; mental confusion, bewilderment. Also, a result of muddling, a bungle, a mess. E19. **2** A confused assemblage, a jumble. M19.

1 *Jazz Monthly* A muddle unparalleled in the history of jazz record issues. P. AUSTER The brain is in a muddle. 2 K. ISHIGURO Wedged in between was a dense muddle of roots.

Phrases: **make a muddle of** mishandle, bungle (an undertaking etc.); disorder (objects etc.).

¶Perh. earlier in MUDDLE-HEADED.

muddledom *n.* the condition of muddle; prevalence of muddle: L19.

muddle /ˈmʌd(ə)l/ *v.* ME. [Perh. f. MDu. *moddelen* frequent. of *modden* dabble in mud (cf. MUD *n.*[1]): see -LE[3].] **1** *v.i.* **a** Bathe or wallow in mud or muddy water. *arch.* ME. **b** Grub or root in soil; (of a bird) dabble in water. Now *rare* exc. *Sc. dial.* E17. **2** *v.t.* **a** Make muddy or turbid, cloud. Now *rare*. L16. **b** Crush and mix (ingredients) to make a drink. *US*. L19. **3** *v.t.* Confuse, bewilder; fuddle or stupefy, esp. with alcoholic drink. L17. **4** *v.i.* **a** Foll. by *along*, *on*: progress or live life in a haphazard way. E18. **b** Busy oneself in a confused, unmethodical, and ineffective manner. (Foll. by *with*, *at*.) M19. **c** Foll. by *through*: attain one's end haphazardly and despite a lack of skill or foresight. M19. **5** *v.t.* Foll. by *away*: squander or fritter away (money, time, etc.) without purpose or result. E19. **6** *v.t.* **a** Fail to distinguish correctly, confuse *together*, mix *up*. M19. **b** Bungle, mismanage (an undertaking etc.); bring into disorder. (Foll. by *up*.) L19.

4a M. MOORCOCK I expect she's muddling along like the rest of us. c *Village Voice* In the absence of a national program, America muddles through to produce its energy. 6a P. GROSSKURTH She muddled up her Latin conjugations.

muddled *a.* †(*a*) made muddy or turbid, clouded; (*b*) confused, disorganized, disordered: E17. **muddledly** *adv.* E20. **muddlement** *n.* muddle, confusion, bewilderment M19. **muddler** *n.* (*a*) a person who or thing which muddles; (*b*) *spec.* (*US*) a small stick for crushing and mixing the ingredients for a drink: M19. **muddlingly** *adv.* in a muddling manner M19.

muddle-headed /mʌd(ə)lˈhɛdɪd/ *a. colloq.* M18. [f. MUDDLE *n.*, *v.* + HEAD *n.* + -ED[2].] Having an unclear mind; stupid, confused.

ˈ**muddle-head** *n.* (*a*) a confused or stupid person, a blockhead; (*b*) a disorganized vague mind: M19. **muddleheadedly** *adv.* E20. **muddle-headedness** *n.* M19.

muddly /ˈmʌd(ə)li/ *a. colloq.* E20. [f. MUDDLE *n.* + -Y[1].] Confused, muddled; confusing, bewildering.

muddliness *n.* L19.

muddy *n.*[1] var. of MUDDIE.

muddy /ˈmʌdi/ *a.* & *n.*[2] ME. [f. MUD *n.*[1] + -Y[1].] **A** *adj.* **1 a** Containing much mud; turbid or clouded with mud; covered or spattered with mud. ME. **b** Of the nature of mud, resembling mud. E17. **2** Morally corrupt, base; carnal. Now *rare*. LME. **3** Living or growing in mud. L16. **4** Not clear or pure; clouded, opaque, turbid; dull, dim. L16. **b** Of a musical sound: blurred, undefined. M20. **5** Gloomy; sullen. Now *rare*. L16. **6** Not clear in mind, confused, muddled;

(of literary style, thought, etc.) obscure, vague. E17. **b** Partly intoxicated. Now *rare* or *obs.* L18.

1a M. ROBERTS The lane is muddy and soft after the storms. B. MOORE Oh, look at your coat, it's all muddy. 4 J. CARLYLE We breakfasted . . on muddy coffee and scorched toast. M. HUGHES It makes your eyes look green instead of that funny muddy shade.

B *n. The* Missouri River (also *the Big Muddy*); *the* Mississippi River. *US.* E19.

muddily *adv.* M17. **muddiness** *n.* M17.

muddy /ˈmʌdi/ *v.* E17. [f. the adj.] **1** *v.t.* Make muddy; *fig.* make confused or obscure; taint. E17. **2** *v.i.* Become muddy or turbid. M19.

1 C. G. LELAND I only muddied the palms of my gloves, on which I fell. GROVER SMITH In the original play there is no such muddying of the facts. M. SCAMMELL Came a new misunderstanding to muddy their relationship.

Mudéjar /muːˈdeɪhɑː/ *a.* & *n.* Also **Mudejar**, **m-**. Pl. of n. **-res** /-rɛs/. M19. [Sp. f. Arab. *mudajjan* pass. pple of *dajjana* allow to stay.] (Of, pertaining to, or characteristic of) a subject Muslim during the reconquest of the Iberian peninsula from the Moors who was allowed to retain Islamic laws and religion in return for owing allegiance and paying tribute to a Christian monarch; *spec.* (designating) a partly Islamic, partly Gothic style of architecture and decorative art of the 12th to the 15th cents.

mudfish /ˈmʌdfɪʃ/ *n.* Pl. **-es** /-ɪz/, (usu.) same. E16. [f. MUD *n.*[1] + FISH *n.*[1]] Any of various fishes which live in marine, estuarine, or freshwater mud; *esp.* (*a*) a bowfin; (*b*) a lungfish; (*c*) a mud minnow; (*d*) a mud-sucker; (*e*) a mummichog; (*f*) a burrowing fish of New Zealand, *Neochanna apoda*.

mudim /ˈmuːdɪm/ *n.* Also ***-in*** /-ɪn/. E19. [Malay (now *mudin*, *modin*), prob. f. Arab. *mu'aḏḏin* muezzin.] A junior Muslim official in Malaysia or Indonesia, *spec.* a person who performs the operation of circumcision.

mudir /muːˈdɪə/ *n.* M19. [Turk. *mudır* f. Arab. *mudīr* act. pple of *'adāra* direct, manage.] In Turkey, the governor of a subdistrict. In Egypt and Sudan, the governor of a province.

mudirate *n.* = MUDIRIEH L19.

mudirieh /muːˈdɪərɪeɪ/ *n.* L19. [Arab. *mudīriyya*, f. as prec.] In Egypt: the territory or province of a mudir; the official headquarters of a mudir.

Mudjur /ˈmʊdʒʊə/ *n.* Also **Mujur**. E20. [See below.] (Designating) a type of prayer rug made in or associated with Mudjur, a small town in Turkey, usu. with a deep border and an arch motif.

mudlark /ˈmʌdlɑːk/ *n.* & *v.* L18. [f. MUD *n.*[1] + LARK *n.*[1]] **A** *n.* †**1** A hog. *slang.* L18–E20. **2** A person who scavenges for usable debris in the mud of a river or harbour. Also, a street urchin; *joc.* a messy person, esp. a child. *colloq.* L18. **3** A magpie-lark. *Austral.* L19. **4** = MUDDER. *slang.* E20. **B** *v.i.* Carry on the occupation of a mudlark. Also, play in mud. M19.

mudlarker *n.* = MUDLARK *n.* 2 E19.

mudra /ˈmʌdrə, ˈmuː-/ *n.* E19. [Skt *mudrā* seal, sign, token.] Any of a large number of symbolic hand gestures used in Hindu religious ceremonies and in Indian dance. Also, a movement or pose in yoga.

muduga /ˈmuːdʊgə, mʊˈduːgə/ *n.* Also **moodooga**. M19. [Telugu *mōdugu*.] = DHAK. Only in *muduga oil*, oil from the seeds of the dhak, used as an anthelmintic.

muesli /ˈmuːzli, ˈmjuːzli/ *n.* M20. [Swiss G.] A dish, originating in Switzerland, consisting of a cereal (usu. oats), fruit, nuts, etc., eaten with milk or cream, esp. for breakfast.

Comb.: **muesli belt** *joc.* a region supposed to be densely populated by (prosperous middle-class) health-food faddists.

muezzin /muːˈɛzɪn/ *n.* L16. [Arab. dial. var. of Arab. *mu'aḏḏin* act. pple of *'aḏḏana* call to prayer, f. *'uḏn* ear.] A Muslim crier who proclaims the hours of prayer from a minaret or the roof of a mosque.

muff /mʌf/ *n.*[1] Long *obs.* exc. *dial.* LME. [Imit. of an inarticulate sound.] An utterance, a sound. Usu. in neg. contexts, as *not say muff*.

muff /mʌf/ *n.*[2] L16. [Du. *mof* abbrev. of MDu. *moffel*, *muffel* (corresp. to Fr. *moufle*, It. *muffa*) f. med.L *muff(u)la* glove, of unkn. origin.] **1** A covering, usu. of cylindrical shape, into which both hands may be inserted from opposite ends to keep them warm. L16. **2a** The female external genitals. *slang.* L17. **b** A woman, a girl, *esp.* a promiscuous one; a prostitute. *slang* (orig. *US*). E20. **3** *Founding.* Any of various devices for controlling heat in a furnace. Cf. MUFFLE *n.*[4] M18. **4** Any of various warming or protective coverings resembling a muff for the hands. L18. **5** A tuft of feathers on the head, neck, or legs of a bird. M19.

4 ear-muff, foot-muff, etc.

Comb.: **muff cock** *Sc.* a woodcock; **muff coupling** a cylindrical shaft coupling to fit over the abutting ends of shafts; **muff diver** *slang* a person who performs cunnilingus; **muff pistol** a small 19th-cent. pocket pistol.

muff /mʌf/ *n.*[3] *colloq.* E19. [Origin unkn.: rel. to MUFF *v.*[2]] **1** A person without skill or aptitude for something, orig. *spec.* some sport; a person lacking in practical sense. E19. **2** A failure; anything done clumsily or bungled, esp. in a ball game. M19.

muffish *a.* M19. **muffishness** *n.* M19.

muff /mʌf/ *a.* M19. [f. MUFF *v.*[3]] Of glass: frosted.

muff /mʌf/ *v.*[1]*i.* Chiefly *dial. rare.* M17. [f. MUFF *n.*[1]] Utter a word or sound. Usu. in neg. contexts.

muff /mʌf/ *v.*[2] *colloq.* E19. [Origin unkn.: rel. to MUFF *n.*[3]] **1** *v.t.* w. *it.* Die. *slang.* Now *rare* or *obs.* E19. **2** *v.t.* Bungle; perform or play badly or clumsily; miss (a ball) in a ball game. *colloq.* M19. **3** *v.t.* & *i.* Fail (an examination). *colloq.* L19.

2 R. COBB I might have done very well, or I might have completely muffed it, got everything wrong. R. THOMAS 'That must make a change', Cass said, carefully, not wanting to muff her line. *Cricketer International* Archie . . muffs a hard hit shot and allows the day's first boundary.

muff /mʌf/ *v.*[3]*t.* M19. [Origin uncertain: cf. MUFFLE *v.*] = MUFFLE *v.* 5. Chiefly as *muffed* ppl a. Cf. MUFF *a.*

muffed /mʌft/ *a.* E19. [f. MUFF *n.*[2] + -ED[2].] Provided with or having a muff; *spec.* (of a bird) having a tuft of feathers on the head, neck, or legs.

muffetee /mʌfɪˈtiː/ *n.* E18. [App. irreg. f. MUFF *n.*[2]] **1** A muffler worn round the neck. *obs.* exc. *dial.* E18. **2** A wristlet worn for warmth. M18.

muffin /ˈmʌfɪn/ *n.* E18. [Origin unkn.] **1a** Orig. (now *dial.*), a cake of any of various kinds of (esp. sweet) bread. Now, a flat circular spongy cake of bread, often eaten toasted and buttered. In N. America more fully *English muffin*. E18. **b** A cake made with baking powder, cooked in a cup-shaped tin. *N. Amer.* M19. **2** A kind of earthenware or china plate. Orig. *US.* E19. **3** A person who muffs catches etc. *arch. US slang.* M19. **4** A young woman, *esp.* one who regularly partners a particular man at social occasions. *Canad. slang.* M19.

Comb.: **muffin-face** *slang* an expressionless countenance; **muffin-fight** *colloq.* = *muffin-worry* below; **muffin-man** *Hist.* a seller of muffins; **muffin-worry** *colloq.* a tea party.

muffi'neer *n.* (*a*) a small caster with a perforated top for sprinkling salt or sugar on muffins; (*b*) *rare* a covered dish to keep toasted muffins hot: E19.

muffle /ˈmʌf(ə)l/ *n.*[1] M16. [App. f. MUFFLE *v.*] **1** Something that muffles or covers the face or neck; a muffler. *rare.* M16. **2** A device for muffling or deadening sound. M18. **3** Muffling effect; muffled sound. L19.

muffle /ˈmʌf(ə)l/ *n.*[2] L16. [Fr. *moufle*. Cf. MUFFLE *n.*[4], MUFFLE *v.*] **1** = MITTEN *n.* 1, MITT 1. L16. †**2** A boxing glove; = MUFFLER 2a. M18–M19. **3** A pulley containing several sheaves. E19.

muffle /ˈmʌf(ə)l/ *n.*[3] E17. [Fr. *mufle*, of unkn. origin.] Orig. (*rare*), a proboscis. Now, the mobile part of the upper lip and nose of a rodent, ruminant, or other mammal.

muffle /ˈmʌf(ə)l/ *n.*[4] M17. [Fr. *moufle*, perh. transf. use of *moufle* mitten, thick glove. Cf. MUFFLE *n.*[2], MUFFLE *v.*] A receptacle in which a substance can be heated in a furnace without coming in contact with combustion products; an inner chamber in a kiln in which pottery etc. can be fired at a low temperature without contact with the heat source.

Comb.: **muffle kiln**: containing a muffle.

muffle /ˈmʌf(ə)l/ *v.t.* LME. [Perh. aphet. f. OFr. *enmoufler*, f. as EN-[1] + MUFFLE *n.*[2]] **1** Wrap, cover up, or enfold, esp. so as to conceal, subdue, or provide protection from the weather. Freq. foll. by *up*. LME. **b** *gen.* Cover, conceal, obscure; stifle, suppress. L16. †**2** Cover (the eyes) to prevent seeing; cover the eyes of; blindfold. Usu. in *pass.* M16–E18. **3** = GAG *v.*[1] 2. L16. **4** Wrap up (a thing) so as to deaden its sound. M18. **b** Limit the audibility of, deaden (a sound). Usu. in *pass.* M19. **5** Make (glass) semi-opaque by giving it a crinkled surface; frost. Cf. MUFF *v.*[3] E20.

1 S. LEACOCK I was muffled up, to avoid recognition, in a long overcoat with the collar turned up. G. SWIFT They came every morning . . muffled in the winter in little anoraks and scarves. b R. ELLIS Mystical emblems, Emblems muffled darkly. D. MACDONALD Reviewers had their doubts. But they adopted various strategies for muffling them. 4b E. L. DOCTOROW All the sounds of the city were muffled by the snow.

muffledly *adv.* in a muffled manner E20.

muffler /ˈmʌflə/ *n.* M16. [f. prec. + -ER[1].] **1a** *Hist.* A sort of kerchief or scarf worn by women in the 16th and 17th cents. to cover part of the face and the neck. M16. †**b** A bandage for blindfolding a person. L16–E17. **c** A wrap or scarf worn round the neck or throat for warmth; *gen.* anything used to wrap a part of the body. L16. **2a** A boxing glove; = MUFFLE *n.*[2] 2. M18. **b** A glove, a mitten. Cf. MUFFLE *n.*[2] 1. E19. **c** *Hist.* A leather muff used to bind the hands of a mentally disordered person. M19. **3** Something that deadens sound; *spec.* (*a*) in a piano, a pad of felt inserted between the hammers and the strings; (*b*) in a steam engine, a device for silencing the escape of steam. Also (chiefly *N. Amer.*), a silencer on a vehicle's exhaust system. M19.

1c V. NABOKOV Shovelling the snow in my shirt-sleeves, a voluminous black and white muffler around my neck. 3 G. E. EVANS Attaching . . *mufflers*—leather pads—to the striking side of the clappers. S. BRILL The day before the tail pipe and muffler had broken off.

muffling /ˈmʌflɪŋ/ *n.* M16. [f. MUFFLE *v.* + -ING[1].] **1** The action of MUFFLE *v.* M16. **2** (An item of) clothing worn for warmth. L18.

Comb.: **muffling-box** a device for silencing the escape of steam from a steam engine.

mufti /ˈmʌfti/ *n.*[1] L16. [Arab. *muftī* act. pple of *'aftā* decide a point of law, rel. to FATWA. Cf. next.] A Muslim cleric or legal expert empowered to give rulings on religious matters; in the Ottoman Empire a chief legal authority, esp. of a large city (also *Grand Mufti*).

mufti /ˈmʌfti/ *n.*[2] E19. [Perh. joc. use of prec.] **1** Plain clothes worn by a person having the right to wear a uniform, esp. a military uniform. Freq. in *in mufti*. E19. **2** A civilian; a person wearing mufti. *rare.* M19.

1 E. P. THOMPSON The soldiers . . were allowed to don mufti. A. GUINNESS He was dressed in mufti but introduced himself as an Anglican priest.

mug /mʌg/ *n.*[1] E16. [Prob. of Scand. origin (cf. Norw. *mugge*, Sw. *mugg* pitcher with a handle), ult. origin unkn. See also MUG *n.*[3]] **1** A (large) earthenware vessel or bowl; a pot, a jug, a ewer. *Sc.* & *north.* E16. **2** A drinking-vessel, usu. cylindrical and with a handle and used without a saucer. M17. **b** A mug with the drink it contains; the contents of a mug; a mugful. L17. **3** A kind of cooling drink. Now *rare* or *obs.* E19.

2 J. GLASSCO The tea came in thick ironstone mugs. M. M. R. KHAN A mug with a handle . . for morning coffee. b J. HOWKER He hadn't touched the mug of tea I'd made for him.

Comb.: **mug-house** (*a*) *arch.* a public house; *mug-house club* (Hist.), any of various political clubs of Hanoverian sympathies meeting at public houses; (*b*) *dial.* a pottery.

mugful *n.* the contents of a mug; as much as a mug will hold: M19.

mug /mʌɡ/ *n.*² & *a.*¹ Chiefly *Sc.* & *north.* L16. [Origin unkn.] A *n.* (An animal of) a breed of sheep with the face covered in wool, *esp.* (a) Wensleydale. L16. B *attrib.* or as *adj.* Of this breed. L16.

mug /mʌɡ/ *n.*³ *slang.* E18. [Perh. a use of MUG *n.*¹, from the practice of representing faces on mugs. See also MUG *n.*⁶] 1 The face, the mouth. Also, a grimace. E18. b A photograph or other likeness of a person's face, esp. in police or other official records. Cf. *mug shot* below. Orig. *US.* L19. 2 The action of throttling or strangling a person. Chiefly in *put the mug on.* M19.

1 M. LEITCH Not once had a flicker of amusement . . crossed that suffering mug. b L. CODY We've been showing them the books . . and some women picked out a mug.

Comb.: **mug book** *US* a book containing photographs of people's faces, esp. in police records; **mug shot** (orig. *US*) a photograph of a person's face, esp. in police or other official records (cf. sense 1b above).

Mug /mʌɡ/ *n.*⁴ & *a.*² *Anglo-Ind.* Now *rare.* M18. [Bengali *Mag(h)*, of unkn. origin.] A *n.* = ARAKANESE *n.* Also, a native or inhabitant of Chittagong on the Bay of Bengal. M18. B *attrib.* or as *adj.* = ARAKANESE *a.* L19.

mug /mʌɡ/ *n.*⁵ *Sc.* & *dial.* L18. [f. MUG *v.*¹] Fog, mist; light rain, drizzle.

¶Prob. earlier, as the root of MUGGISH.

mug /mʌɡ/ *n.*⁶ & *a.*³ *slang.* M19. [Perh. a use of MUG *n.*³] A *n.* 1 A stupid or incompetent person, a fool, a simpleton; a gullible person. M19. 2 A person, a fellow; *spec.* a person on the opposite side of the law to oneself; (chiefly *US*) a hoodlum, a thug. L19.

1 R. C. HUTCHINSON I'm not such a mug as to think that. P. BARKER He's got one mug working to keep him. He doesn't need two. **mug's game** a thankless task; a useless, foolish, or unprofitable activity. 2 *Observer* There were recognised . . putters up of jobs, what the mugs called master minds.

B *attrib.* or as *adj.* Of a person: stupid, incompetent; gullible. E20.

L. GRIFFITHS I despise mug punters, the kind of people who bet on every race.

mug /mʌɡ/ *n.*⁷ *arch. slang.* M19. [f. MUG *v.*⁵] 1 An examination. *rare.* M19. 2 A person who learns a subject by concentrated study. L19.

mug /mʌɡ/ *v.*¹*i.* Long *obs.* exc. *Sc.* & *dial.* Infl. **-gg-**. LME. [Prob. of Scand. origin: cf. ON *mugga* mist, drizzle, Norw., Sw. dial. *mugg* mould, mildew, prob. rel. to MUCUS. See also next.] Drizzle, rain lightly.

mug /mʌɡ/ *v.*²*i. slang* & *dial.* Infl. **-gg-**. E18. [Perh. a use of prec.] Pout, grow sullen; mope.

mug /mʌɡ/ *v.*³ Infl. **-gg-**. E19. [f. MUG *n.*³] 1 *v.t.* Strike in the face; thrash; assault; strangle. Also (now the usual sense), rob with violence, esp. in a public place. E19. 2 *v.i.* Pull a face, esp. in front of an audience, a camera, etc.; grimace. *slang.* M19. 3 *v.t.* Photograph the face of, esp. for police or other official records. *US slang.* L19. 4 *v.t.* Kiss, fondle. *slang* (chiefly *Austral.* & *NZ*). E20.

1 V. S. PRITCHETT He took the affair as if his person had been assaulted, as if he had been mugged. W. MCILVANNEY An old woman could be mugged in a park. 2 J. HELLER I mug and gesticulate right along with the people on the screen. 3 G. V. HIGGINS We brought him up to the marshal's office and mugged him and printed him.

mugging *n.* the action or an act of the vb; *spec.* (an instance of) the robbing of a person with violence, esp. in a public place: M19.

mug /mʌɡ/ *v.*⁴*t. slang* & *dial.* Infl. **-gg-**. M19. [f. MUG *n.*¹] Bribe with alcoholic drink; buy a drink for (a person).

mug /mʌɡ/ *v.*⁵ *slang.* Infl. **-gg-**. M19. [Origin unkn.] 1 *v.i.* Read or study in a concentrated manner. Freq. foll. by *up.* M19. 2 *v.t.* Learn (a subject) by concentrated study. Freq. foll. by *up.* L19.

1 W. H. AUDEN You need not mug up on dates. 2 P. SCOTT I suspect that he mugged it up before he came to Tradura.

mug /mʌɡ/ *v.*⁶*i. slang* (chiefly *Canad.* & *Naut.*). Infl. **-gg-**. M19. [Origin unkn.] Foll. by *up*: eat heartily; also, have a snack, any meal, or a hot drink.

Comb.: **mug-up** a snack, a meal, a hot drink.

muga /ˈmuːɡə/ *n.* Also **moonga** /ˈmuːŋɡə/. M19. [Assamese *mugā.*] A wild silk obtained from the cocoon of an Assamese saturniid silk moth, *Antheraea assamensis.*

attrib.: *muga silk, worm*, etc.

Muganda /mʊˈɡandə/ *n.* & *a.* M19. [Bantu, f. *mu* sing. pref. + *ganda.* Cf. BAGANDA, LUGANDA.] A *n.* Pl. BAGANDA *n.* A member of the Baganda people; a native or inhabitant of the former kingdom of Buganda, now part of Uganda. M19. B *attrib.* or as *adj.* Of or pertaining to a Muganda or the Baganda. M19.

mugearite /ˈmʌɡɪərʌɪt/ *n.* E20. [f. *Mugeary*, a village on the Isle of Skye, Scotland + -ITE¹.] *Petrogr.* A dark fine-grained trachyte which has oligoclase as the main feldspar and also contains olivine, orthoclase, and apatite.

mugearitic /mʌɡɪəˈrɪtɪk/ *a.* E20.

muggee /mʌˈɡiː/ *n.* L20. [f. MUG *v.*³ + -EE¹.] The victim of a mugging; a person who is robbed with violence, esp. in a public place.

Spectator Have muggees . . no right to be protected against muggers?

mugger /ˈmʌɡə/ *n.*¹ *dial.* M18. [f. MUG *n.*¹ + -ER¹.] A hawker of earthenware.

mugger /ˈmʌɡə/ *n.*² M19. [Hind. *magar.*] A broad-nosed Indian crocodile, *Crocodylus palustris*, venerated by many Hindus.

mugger /ˈmʌɡə/ *n.*³ M19. [f. MUG *v.*³ + -ER¹.] 1 A person who mugs another; *spec.* a person who robs someone with violence, esp. in a public place. M19. 2 A person who pulls a face or grimaces, esp. in front of an audience, a camera, etc. *slang.* L19.

mugger /ˈmʌɡə/ *n.*⁴ *slang.* L19. [f. MUG *v.*⁵ + -ER¹.] A person who studies in a concentrated manner.

mugger /ˈmʌɡə/ *n.*⁵ M20. [Origin unkn.] A nail, usu. of wrought iron, used for protecting the inner soles of mountaineering boots.

mugger /ˈmʌɡə/ *n.*⁶ & *v. slang.* M20. [Alt. of BUGGER *n.*¹, *v.*] A *n.* An unpleasant or undesirable person or thing, a person, a chap. Also, a negligible amount. M20. B *v.* 1 *v.t.* Curse, damn. Chiefly in imprecations in optative form. M20. 2 *v.i.* Foll. by *off*: go away. M20.

mugget /ˈmʌɡɪt/ *n. obs.* exc. *dial.* L15. [Origin unkn.] The intestines of a calf or sheep, esp. when cooked as food. Formerly also (*rare*), a dish made from this.

muggins /ˈmʌɡɪnz/ *n.* Pl. same, **-inses**. M19. [Perh. the surname *Muggins*, w. allus. to MUG *n.*⁶ Cf. JUGGINS.] 1 A fool, a simpleton; a dupe, a person who is outwitted. Also used as a name for a person who has acted foolishly, esp. oneself. *colloq.* M19. 2a A card-game resembling snap. M19. b A game of dominoes in which the players count by fives or multiples of five. M19.

1 *Daily Telegraph* The letter bomb was not meant for me personally. I was just the muggins who opened it. *Undercurrents* I didn't . . put a copyright on it, . . and Muggins has not received a penny in payment.

muggish /ˈmʌɡɪʃ/ *a.* Long *rare* or *obs.* M17. [Prob. f. MUG *n.*⁵ + -ISH¹. Cf. MUG *v.*¹] Damp, musty.

muggle /ˈmʌɡ(ə)l/ *n. slang* (orig. *US*). E20. [Origin unkn.] 1 *sing.* & (usu.) in *pl.*, treated as *sing.* or *pl.* Marijuana. E20. 2 A marijuana cigarette. E20.

muggler *n.* a marijuana addict M20.

Muggletonian /mʌɡ(ə)lˈtəʊnɪən/ *a.* & *n.* M17. [f. *Muggleton* (see below) + -IAN.] A *n.* A member of a Christian sect founded in England *c*1651 by Lodowicke Muggleton (d. 1691) and John Reeve, who claimed to be the two witnesses of *Rev.* 11:3–6; a believer in the personal inspiration of Muggleton and Reeve. M17. B *adj.* Of or pertaining to this sect. L18.

Muggletonianism *n.* (adherence to) the doctrines of this sect L19.

muggy /ˈmʌɡi/ *a.* M18. [f. MUG *n.*⁵ or *v.*¹ + -Y¹.] 1 Mouldy, moist, damp, wet. *obs.* exc. *dial.* M18. 2 Of air, atmosphere, etc.: oppressively damp, close, and warm. Also, (of a room etc.) close and stuffy through lack of ventilation. M18.

2 R. GITTINGS London was warm and muggy in the summer of 1816. J. I. M. STEWART The darkness was warm and muggy again.

Mughal *n.* & *a.* see MOGUL *n.*¹ & *a.*

mugient /ˈmjuːdʒɪənt/ *a. rare.* M17. [L *mugient-* pres. ppl stem of *mugire* to bellow: see -ENT.] Lowing, bellowing.

mugo /ˈmuːɡəʊ/ *n.* Pl. **-os.** M18. [Fr. *mugho*, It. *mugo.*] In full *mugo pine.* A dwarf pine, *Pinus mugo*, of the mountains of central and southern Europe.

muguet /myɡɛ/ *n.* L16. [Fr. f. med.L *muscatum* musk-scented, f. *muscus* MUSK *n.* Cf. next.] †1 Any of certain fragrant plants; *spec.* woodruff, *Galium odoratum.* L16–M17. 2 Lily of the valley, *Convallaria majalis*; a scent made from or resembling it. L16.

¶Formerly naturalized.

mugwort /ˈmʌɡwəːt/ *n.* OE. [f. base of MIDGE + WORT *n.*¹ In sense 2 perh. alt. of prec.] 1 An aromatic hedge plant, *Artemisia vulgaris*, of the composite family, with small flower-heads in leafy panicles and pinnatifid leaves. Also, any of various other plants of this genus. OE. 2 Crosswort, *Cruciata laevipes. rare.* L18.

mugwump /ˈmʌɡwʌmp/ *n.* & *a.* Chiefly *N. Amer.* M19. [Algonquian *mugquomp* great chief.] A *n.* 1 A great man, a boss. Chiefly *joc.* M19. 2 A person who holds aloof from party politics; *spec.* in *US Hist.* a Republican who in 1884 refused to support the Republican nominee for president. Also, a person who remains neutral or non-committal. L19. B *attrib.* or as *adj.* That is a mugwump; of or pertaining to mugwumps. L19.

mugwumpery *n.* behaviour or qualities characteristic of a mugwump L19. **mugwumpish** *a.* E20. **mugwumpism** *n.* behaviour characteristic of a mugwump; the principles or practice of mugwumps: L19.

Muhammad /mʊˈhaməd/ *n.* Also **Mohammed** /məʊˈhamed/. E17. [Arab. *Muḥammad.* See also MAHOMET.] (The name of) the Arabian prophet of Islam (*c*570–632), whose revelations constitute the Koran, regarded by Muslims as the final messenger sent by God to warn humankind against the consequences of rebelliousness against the divinely ordered way.

†**Muhammadism** *n.* the Muslim religion, Islam E17–M19.

Muhammadan /mʊˈhaməd(ə)n/ *a.* & *n.* Also **Mohammedan** /məʊˈhamɪd(ə)n/. L17. [f. prec. + -AN.] A *adj.* Of or pertaining to the prophet Muhammad; Muslim. L17.

Muhammadan blue a cobalt blue used as an underglaze colour on Chinese porcelain of the Ming dynasty.

B *n.* A follower or adherent of Muhammad; a Muslim. L18.

¶A term not used or favoured by Muslims.

Muhammadanism *n.* the Muslim religion, Islam E19.

Muharram /məˈhʌrəm/ *n.* Also **Mo-**. E19. [Arab. *muharram* inviolable.] The first month of the year in the Islamic calendar; an annual celebration in this month commemorating the deaths of the grandsons of Muhammad.

muhimbi /muːˈhɪmbi, muːˈwɪmbi/ *n.* E20. [Luo.] An E. African evergreen leguminous tree, *Cynometra alexandri*; the hard heavy timber of this tree.

muid /ˈmuːɪd, *foreign* mɥi/ *n.*¹ Long *obs.* exc. *Hist.* LME. [OFr. *mui* (mod. *muid*) f. L *modium* neut. of MODIUS. Cf. next.] A former French dry unit of capacity equivalent to several bushels, varying widely among localities and commodities. Formerly also, a liquid measure of varying capacity; a cask holding this.

muid /ˈmuːɪd/ *n.*² Now chiefly *S. Afr.* Also (earlier) †**mud.** L15. [Du. *mud(de)* = OS *muddi*, OHG *mutti*, G *Mutt*, f. WGmc f. L MODIUS. Cf.

MUID *n.*[1]] A Dutch or (now esp.) South African dry measure of capacity equal to approx. 117 litres (3.22 bushels).

muishond /ˈməʊshɒnt/ *n. S. Afr.* Pl. **-honds**, same, **-honde** /-hɒndə/. L18. [Afk. f. Du. dial., or directly f. MDu. *muushont* weasel (lit. 'mouse-dog').] A mongoose, a polecat, a skunk; *spec.* the zorilla, *Ictonyx striatus.*

muisvoël /ˈməʊsfʊəl/ *n. S. Afr.* Also **-vogel** /-fəʊg(ə)l/. E19. [Afk., f. *muis* mouse + *voël* bird.] = *mousebird* s.v. MOUSE *n.*

mujahidin /ˌmʊdʒɑːhɪˈdiːn/ *n.pl.* Also **-hedin, -deen.** M20. [Pers., Arab. *mujāhidīn* colloq. pl. of *mujāhid* a person who fights a jihad.] Guerrilla fighters in an Islamic country, esp. as supporting the cause of Islam.

mujtahid /mʊdʒˈtɑːhɪd/ *n.* E19. [Pers. f. Arab., act. pple of *ijtahada* strive.] Esp. in Iran (Persia): a person accepted in Shiism as an authority on the interpretation of Islamic law.

Mujur *n.* var. of MUDJUR.

mukhtar /ˈmʊktɑː/ *n.* E20. [(Turk. *muhtar* f.) Arab. *muktār* pass. pple of *iktāra* choose, elect.] In Turkey and some Arab countries: the head of the local government of a town or village; a minor provincial official.

mukim /ˈmuːkɪm/ *n.* Pl. same, **-s.** M19. [Malay, f. Arab. *mukīm* remaining, resident.] In Malaysia: the smallest administrative district, corresponding to a parish.

mukluk /ˈmʌklʌk/ *n.* Also **muckluck.** M19. [Eskimo (Yupik) *maklak* bearded seal.] A high boot made of sealskin, canvas, etc.

mukti /ˈmʌkti, ˈmʊkti/ *n.* L18. [Skt = release, f. *muc* set free, release.] *Hinduism & Jainism.* = MOKSHA.

muktuk /ˈmʌktʌk/ *n.* M19. [Eskimo (Inuit) *maktak.*] The skin and outer blubber of a whale, used as food by Eskimos.

mulatta /mjuːˈlatə/ *n.* E17. [Sp. *mulata* fem. of *mulato* MULATTO.] A female mulatto.

mulatto /mjuːˈlatəʊ/ *n.* & *a.* Pl. **-o(e)s.** L16. [Sp. & Port. *mulato* young mule, mulatto, irreg. f. *mulo* MULE *n.*[1]] A *n.* A person having one White and one Black parent; a person of mixed White and Black parentage. L16. B *adj.* 1 Of the colour of the skin of a mulatto; tawny. E17. 2 That is a mulatto; of or pertaining to mulattos. L17. 3 Designating a kind of mid-brown fertile soil. *US.* M18.

mulattress /mjuːˈlatrɪs/ *n.* E19. [Fr. *mulâtresse* fem. of *mulâtre* MULATTO: see -ESS[1].] A female mulatto.

mulberry /ˈmʌlb(ə)ri/ *n.* & *a.* [OE *mōrberie*, corresp. to Du. *moerbezie*, OHG *mōrberi*, *murb-* (MHG *mūlber*, G *Maulbeere*), f. L *morum* mulberry, *morus* mulberry tree + BERRY *n.*[1], with dissimilation of *r..r* to *l..r.*] A *n.* 1 Any of various trees of the genus *Morus* (family Moraceae), *esp.* (*a*) (more fully *black mulberry*) *Morus nigra*, grown for its purple, succulent fruit; (*b*) (more fully *white mulberry*) *Morus alba*, which has white insipid fruit and whose leaves are used to feed silkworms; the berry-like multiple fruit of these trees. Also, (the similar fruit of) any of various other plants, esp. (*dial.* & *US*) a blackberry or raspberry. OE. 2 In full *mulberry colour.* The dark red or purple colour of a mulberry. E19. 3 In full *Mulberry harbour.* A man-made usu. prefabricated harbour, orig. and esp. as used under this code-name in the Allied invasion of Europe in 1944. M20.

Comb.: **mulberry-bird** *Austral.* the southern figbird, *Sphecotheres vieilloti*; *mulberry colour*: see sense 2 above; **mulberry-coloured** *a.* of the dark red or purple colour of a mulberry; **mulberry molar** *Med.* a first molar with a small, nodular, pitted crown resulting from congenital syphilis; **mulberry tree** a tree which bears mulberries.

B *adj.* Mulberry-coloured. E19.

mulch /mʌl(t)ʃ/ *n.* & *v.* M17. [Prob. f. use as n. of MULSH.] A *n.* Partly rotted straw; a mixture of wet straw, leaves, etc., spread around (the roots of) a plant to enrich or insulate the soil. M17. B *v.t.* Treat or cover with mulch. E18.

mulching *n.* (*a*) the action of the vb; (*b*) a mulch: E19.

mulct /mʌlkt/ *n. arch.* L16. [L *mulcta*, *multa*: see next. Cf. Fr. †*mulcte*, †*multe.*] A fine imposed for an offence; a penalty of any kind.

T. L. PEACOCK Imposed a heavy mulct on every one of his servants. I. ZANGWILL Nor was this the only mulct which Providence exacted.

mulct /mʌlkt/ *v.t. literary.* Pa. t. & pple **mulct, mulcted.** L15. [Fr. †*mul*(*c*)*ter* f. L *mul*(*c*)*tare*, f. *mul*(*c*)*ta* fine, amercement.] 1 Punish (a person) by a fine; extract money from (a person) by fine or taxation. Formerly also, subject to a penalty of any kind. L15. 2 Deprive (a person) *of* money, goods, etc., esp. by duress or fraudulent means; swindle. Usu. in *pass.* M18. 3 Obtain by swindling. M20.

1 G. M. TREVELYAN No government dared to propose to mulct the taxpayer for such a purpose. C. P. SNOW The Revenue might mulct him with largish fines. 2 *Contemporary Review* Each tree is mulcted of her spreading boughs. 3 P. GALLICO A rapacious old moneybag who would never miss the few dollars mulcted of her.

mulctuary /ˈmʌlktjʊəri/ *a. rare.* E17. [f. MULCT *n.* after *tumultuary.*] That punishes by a fine. Formerly also, punishable by a fine.

mule /mjuːl/ *n.*[1] & *a.* [OE *mūl* prob. f. Gmc f. L, reinforced in ME by OFr. *mul*(*e*) f. L *mulus*, *mula.*] A *n.* 1 An animal born of a mating between a male ass and a mare or *loosely* between a female ass and a stallion (= HINNY *n.*[1]), used esp. as a draught animal and for bearing loads, and proverbially regarded as the epitome of obstinacy. OE. 2a A person considered to resemble a mule; *esp.* a stupid or obstinate person. LME. b A person acting as a courier for illicit drugs. *US slang.* M20. 3 A hybrid plant or animal. E18. 4 Any of various devices combining the characteristics of two distinct types; *spec.* (*a*) *Hist.* a kind of spinning-machine producing yarn on spindles, intermediate between earlier types; (*b*) *Numism.* a coin with obverse and reverse produced by dies not originally intended for use on the same coin; (*c*) (now *dial.*) a boat combining the characteristics of a coble and a fishing boat; (*d*) a small tractor or locomotive, usu. electrically powered, for towing canal boats, moving trailers, etc. L18. 5 *Naut.* A large triangular sail sometimes used on a ketch. M20.

1 W. VAN T. CLARK A good mule can work two horses into the ground. J. WYNDHAM Obstinate as a mule over that, he was. 2b L. D. ESTLEMAN He was just another mule running kilos for the big boys.

B *attrib.* or as *adj.* Hybrid. M18.

Comb. & *special collocations*: **mule-bird, mule canary** a cross between a canary and another finch, esp. a goldfinch; **mule chest** a chest with a drawer or drawers; **mule deer** a black-tailed deer of western N. America, *Odocoileus hemionus*, with long ears; **mule-driver** a person who drives a mule, or a team or train of mules; **mule-driving** the occupation or activity of a mule-driver; **mule-ear(ed) rabbit** = JACKRABBIT; **mule-headed** *a.* stubborn; **mule-killer** *US* (*a*) a kind of small cart drawn by a mule or mules; (*b*) a scorpion; **mule rabbit** *US* = *mule-ear(ed) rabbit* above; **mule-skinner** *N. Amer.* a mule-driver, esp. on the prairies; **mule-skinning** *N. Amer.* mule-driving, esp. on the prairies; **mule-whacker** *US* a mule-driver.

mule /mjuːl/ *n.*[2] LME. [Fr. *mule* (fem.) slipper, *mules* (pl.) chilblains.] 1 A chilblain, esp. on the heel; a sore on a horse's pastern. Long *obs.* exc. *Sc.* LME. 2 A kind of (esp. backless) slipper or light shoe. M16.

2 M. WESLEY Pink feathered mules on her feet.

muled /mjuːld/ *a.* E20. [f. MULE *n.*[1] + -ED[2].] *Numism.* Of a coin: having obverse and reverse produced by dies not originally intended for use on the same coin.

Mules /mjuːlz/ *n.* Chiefly *Austral.* M20. [J. H. W. *Mules* (d. 1946), Austral. sheep-farmer.] Used *attrib.* and in *possess.* to designate an operation developed by Mules to reduce blowfly strike in sheep by removing the folds of skin in the crotch most likely to be affected.

mulesed /mjuːlzd/ *a.* (of a sheep) treated by the Mules operation M20. **mulesing** *n.* the application of the Mules operation M20.

muleta /məˈleɪtə/ *n.* M19. [Sp.] *Bullfighting.* A red cloth fixed to a stick used by a matador during the *faena.*

muleteer /mjuːlɪˈtɪə/ *n.* M16. [Fr. *muletier*, f. *mulet* dim. of OFr. *mul*(*e*) MULE *n.*[1]: see -ET[1], -EER.] A mule-driver.

muley /ˈmjuːli/ *n.* & *a.*[1] Now chiefly *US.* Also **mooley** /ˈmuːli/, (earlier) **mulley** /ˈmʌli/. L16. [Perh. f. as MOILEY. Cf. MULL *n.*[3]] A *n.* 1 A hornless cow; a cow. Also *muley cow.* L16. 2 A long stiff saw with a rapid vertical reciprocating motion, guided by carriages instead of being stretched in a frame. Also *muley saw. US.* M19. B *adj.* Of cattle: hornless. M19.

muley /ˈmjuːli/ *a.*[2] Long *obs.* exc. *Sc.* E17. [f. MULE *n.*[2] + -Y[1].] Having chilblains, esp. on the heel.

muley /ˈmjuːli/ *a.*[3] L19. [f. MULE *n.*[1] + -Y[1].] Mulish, stubborn; sulky.

mulga /ˈmʌlgə/ *n. Austral.* M19. [Aborig.] 1 Any of several small acacia, esp. *Acacia aneura*, forming dense scrub in dry inland areas and sometimes used for fodder (also *mulga tree*); *the* land covered with such vegetation, (colloq.) *the* outback. M19. 2 A thing made of the wood of a mulga tree, *esp.* a club or shield. M19. 3 In full *mulga wire.* A rumour, a message, a (false) report; *the* grapevine. *slang.* L19.

1 *red mulga*: see RED *a.*

Comb.: **mulga parrot** a multicoloured parrot, *Psephotus varius*, of southern Australia; *mulga tree*: see sense 1 above; *mulga wire*: see sense 3 above.

muli *n.* var. of MOOLI.

muliebral /mjuːlɪˈiːbr(ə)l/ *a. rare.* M17. [f. L *muliebris* (see next) + -AL[1].] Of or pertaining to woman or womanhood.

muliebrity /mjuːlɪˈɛbrɪti/ *n. literary.* L16. [Late L *muliebritas*, f. L *muliebris*, f. *mulier* woman: see -ITY.] Womanhood; the characteristics or qualities of a woman (opp. *virility*); softness, effeminacy.

mulier /ˈmjuːlɪə/ *a.* & *n.* Long *rare* or *obs.* LME. [Repr. AN *mulieré* (AL *mulieratus*), f. *mulier*, OFr. *moiller* wife f. L *mulier* woman.] *Law.* A *adj.* Of a child: born in wedlock, legitimate; legitimated by the subsequent marriage of the parents. LME. B *n.* A legitimate child; a child born in wedlock. LME.

mulierose /ˈmjuːlɪərəʊs/ *a. rare.* E18. [L *mulierosus*, f. *mulier* woman: see -OSE[1].] Fond of women.

mulierosity /ˌmjuːlɪəˈrɒsɪti/ *n. rare.* E17. [L *mulierositas*, f. as prec.: see -OSITY.] (Excessive) fondness for women.

mulish /ˈmjuːlɪʃ/ *a.* M18. [f. MULE *n.*[1] + -ISH[1].] Characteristic of a mule; resembling a mule; stubborn, sulky.

Times The attitude of the exchange staff.. is often off-hand, uncomprehending and mulish. N. MARSH 'Come, sir,' he said as Warrender still looked mulish.

mulishly *adv.* M19. **mulishness** *n.* M18.

mull /mʌl/ *n.*[1] ME. [(M)Du. *mul*, *mol* cogn. w. OE *myl* dust, ON *moli* crumb, *mylja* crush, f. Gmc base also of MEAL *n.*[1] Cf. MOULD *n.*[1], MULL *n.*[7]] 1 Something reduced to small particles; dust, ashes, rubbish. *obs.* exc. *dial.* ME. 2 A suspension of a finely ground solid in a liquid, esp. as used in recording the infrared spectrum of the solid. M20.

mull /mʌl/ *n.*[2] *Sc.* ME. [Rel. to Gael. *maol*, OIr. *mael* (mod. *maol*), ON *múli* (perh. identical with *múli* snout) = OHG *mūl* (G *Maul*) snout.] A promontory, a headland. Freq. in place-names.

Mull of Kintyre etc.

mull /mʌl, mʊl/ *n.*[3] Long *obs.* exc. *dial.* M17. [Perh. f. as MOIL *n.*[3] Cf. MULEY *n.*] A heifer, a cow.

mull /mʌl/ *n.*[4] L17. [Abbrev. of MULMULL.] More fully *mull muslin.* A thin soft plain muslin, freq. used in bookbinding. Cf. SUPER *n.*[2]

Bookseller The mull or other spine-lining is attached.

mull /mʌl/ *n.*[5] *Sc.* L18. [Var. of MILL *n.*[1]] A snuffbox, orig. one having a grinder.

mull /mʌl/ *n.*[6] *colloq.* E19. [Origin uncertain: perh. f. MULL *v.*[1]] A muddle, a mess. Chiefly in *make a mull of.*

mull /mʌl/ *n.*[7] E20. [Da. *muld* MOULD *n.*[1], rel. to MULL *n.*[1]] *Soil Sci.* Humus which does not form a distinct top layer but is admixed with the underlying mineral soil, characteristic of grassland and hardwood forest and usu. not very acidic. Cf. MOR.

mull /mʌl/ *n.*[8] E20. [f. MULL *v.*[3]] Mulled wine.

mull /mʌl/ *v.*[1] LME. [f. MULL *n.*[1] Branch II perh. a different wd: cf. MILL *v.*[1] II.] **I 1** *v.t.* Grind to powder, pulverize; crumble. *obs.* exc. *dial.* LME. **2** *v.t.* Convert (solid material) into a mull (MULL *n.*[1] 2). M20.

II 3 *v.i.* Of a thought etc.: develop without active consideration. *colloq.* (chiefly *US*). M19. **4** *v.t.* Turn *over* in one's mind; *US* consider, ponder. L19.

4 A. MACLEAN I . . tried to mull things over in my now thoroughly befogged mind. *Science* The Germans . . were mulling a public recommendation from their safety advisory committee. J. WAINWRIGHT I . . stared into the darkness and mulled over what had been said.

†**mull** *v.*[2]*t. rare.* Only in 17. [Origin unkn.] Dull, stupefy.

mull /mʌl/ *v.*[3]*t.* E17. [Origin unkn.] Make (wine, beer, etc.) into a hot drink with sugar, spices, etc. Chiefly as *mulled* ppl a.

mull /mʌl/ *v.*[4]*t. colloq.* M19. [f. MULL *n.*[6]] Bungle, miss, muff, (a catch, ball, etc.).

mull /mʌl/ *v.*[5] M20. [Origin unkn.] **1** *v.t.* Moisten (leather) during manufacture to increase suppleness. M20. **2** *v.i.* Of leather: become more supple during manufacture through moistening. M20.

mullah /ˈmʌlə, ˈmʊlə/ *n.* E17. [Pers., Urdu *mullā*, Turk. *molla* f. Arab. *mawlā*.] (A title given to) a Muslim learned in Islamic theology and sacred law.

mullein /ˈmʌlɪn/ *n.* Also ***mullen**. LME. [OFr. *moleine* (mod. *molène*) f. a Gaulish base corresp. to Breton *melen*, Corn. & Welsh *melyn* yellow.] **1** Any of various tall plants of the genus *Verbascum*, of the figwort family, with long spiky racemes of usu. yellow flowers and often with densely woolly leaves; *esp.* (in full *great mullein*), *V. thapsus*. LME. †**2** Any of several plants resembling these in foliage; *esp.* Jerusalem sage, *Phlomis fruticosa*. L16–M18. **3** = *mullein moth* below. E19.

Comb.: **mullein moth** a pale brown and grey noctuid moth, *Cucullia verbasci*, whose larvae feed on mullein; **mullein pink** the rose campion, *Lychnis coronaria*; **mullein shark** = *mullein moth* above; **mullein tea** an infusion of mullein leaves, used medicinally; **mullein wave** a white geometrid moth with pale grey markings, *Scopula marginepunctata*.

mullen /ˈmʌlən/ *n.*[1] Long *obs.* exc. *dial.* Also (earlier) †**molan**. LME. [Origin unkn.] A horse's headstall; a horse's bridle.

mullen *n.*[2] see MULLEIN.

muller /ˈmʌlə/ *n.*[1] LME. [Perh. f. AN (cf. OFr. *moloir* adj.), f. *moldre* grind: cf. -ER[2].] **1** A stone, or piece of a similar substance, with a flat base or grinding surface used for grinding powders etc. on a slab. LME. **2** Any of various mechanical contrivances for grinding or crushing. M19.

mullered *a.* (*rare*) ground with a muller M19.

muller /ˈmʌlə/ *n.*[2] M19. [f. MULL *v.*[3] + -ER[1].] A person who or thing which mulls wine etc.; *spec.* a vessel in which wine etc. may be mulled.

Muller /ˈmʊlə/ *n.*[3] E20. [See below.] Used *attrib.* and in *possess.* to designate a set of bodily exercises published and promoted by the 19th-cent. Danish physical educationalist J. P. Muller.

Muller *n.*[4] var. of MÜLLER *n.*[1]

Müller /ˈmʊlə/ *n.*[1] Also **Muller**. L18. [A Ger. surname, app. that of its discoverer.] Min. *Müller('s) glass*, = HYALITE.

Müller /ˈmʊlə/ *n.*[2] M19. [Heinrich *Müller* (1820–64), Ger. anatomist.] *Anat.* Used *attrib.*, in *possess.*, and w. *of* to designate various structures of the eye described by Müller, esp. (*a*) any of the fibroid glial cells which form the supportive tissue of the retina; (*b*) any of certain involuntary muscles of the eye.

Müllerian /mʊˈlɪərɪən/ *a.*[1] L19. [f. J. *Müller* (1801–58), Ger. physiologist + -IAN.] Anat. *Müllerian duct*, either of a pair of ducts in a vertebrate embryo which, in the female, form the Fallopian tubes and other reproductive structures. Also called *paramesonephric duct*.

Müllerian /mʊˈlɪərɪən/ *a.*[2] Also **Mu-**. L19. [f. J. F. T. *Müller* (1821–97), Ger. zoologist + -IAN.] Zool. *Müllerian mimic(ry)*, (an animal exhibiting) a form of mimicry in which two or more noxious species develop similar patterns of coloration etc. as a protective device.

Müller-Lyer illusion /mʊləˈlʌɪər ɪˌl(j)uːʒ(ə)n/ *n. phr.* L19. [F. C. *Müller-Lyer* (1857–1916), Ger. sociologist and philosopher.] An optical illusion in which a line with an arrowhead pointing outwards at each end appears shorter than one of equal length with the arrowheads pointing inwards.

Müller-Thurgau /mʊləˈtʊəgaʊ/ *n.* M20. [H. *Müller-Thurgau* (1850–1927), Swiss viniculturist.] (The vine bearing) a white grape from a cross between Riesling and Sylvaner vines; fruity white wine made from these grapes.

mullet /ˈmʌlɪt/ *n.*[1] Pl. same, **-s**. LME. [OFr. *mulet*, f. L *mullus* red mullet f. Gk *mullos* rel. to *melos* black: see -ET[1].] Any of various edible, mainly marine fishes, esp. of the families Mullidae and Mugilidae; *US* a grey mullet.

grey mullet: see GREY *a.* **red mullet** a mullet of the family Mullidae; *spec.* a red or reddish-brown food fish, *Mullus surmuletus*, of the Mediterranean and NE Atlantic.

Comb.: **mullet-head** *US colloq.* (*a*) a freshwater fish with a large flat head; (*b*) a stupid person; **mullet-headed** *a.* (*US colloq.*) stupid.

mullet /ˈmʌlɪt/ *n.*[2] LME. [AN *molet*, OFr. *molette* rowel, dim. of *meule* millstone f. L *mola* grindstone: see -ET[1].] *Her.* A star with five (or more) straight points, as a charge or as a cadency mark for a third son.

mulley *n.* & *a.* see MULEY *n.* & *a.*[1]

mulligan /ˈmʌlɪg(ə)n/ *n. N. Amer. colloq.* In sense 2 also **M-**. E20. [App. f. the surname *Mulligan*.] **1** A stew made from odds and ends of food. E20. **2** *Golf.* An extra stroke awarded after a poor shot, not counted on the score card. M20.

mulligatawny /ˌmʌlɪgəˈtɔːni/ *n.* L18. [Tamil *milaku-tanni* lit. 'pepper-water'.] More fully *mulligatawny soup*. A highly seasoned soup orig. from India.

mulligrubs /ˈmʌlɪgrʌbz/ *n.pl.* Now *arch.* & *dial.* L16. [Origin unkn.] A state of depression; a fit of low spirits. Also, stomach-ache, colic.

mullion /ˈmʌljən/ *n.* M16. [Metathetic var. of MONIAL: cf. MUNNION.] **1** *Archit.* A vertical bar dividing the lights in a window, esp. in Gothic architecture. M16. **2** *Geol.* Each of a series of ribs or columns on a rock face, usu. formed by folding. L19.

2 *mullion structure*.

mullioned *a.* having mullions; constructed with mullions: M18.

mullipuff /ˈmʌlɪpʌf/ *n.* Long *obs.* exc. *dial.* E17. [f. MULLY *a.* + PUFF *n.*] A puffball fungus; *fig.* a contemptible person.

mullite /ˈmʌlʌɪt/ *n.* E20. [f. the island of *Mull*, Scotland + -ITE[1].] *Min.* A colourless orthorhombic aluminium silicate formed naturally or artificially from other aluminium silicates at high temperatures and used in refractory porcelains and bricks.

mullock /ˈmʌlək/ *n.* & *v.* LME. [f. MULL *n.*[1] + -OCK.] **A** *n.* **1** Rubbish, refuse. Now *Austral.* & *dial.* LME. **2** Rock which does not contain gold or from which gold has been extracted. *Austral.* & *NZ.* M19. **3** *fig.* Worthless information, nonsense. *Austral.* & *NZ.* M19.

Phrases: **poke mullock (at)** *Austral.* deride, ridicule, poke fun (at).

B *v.* **1** *v.t.* Litter (a place), esp. with refuse from gold-mining. *Austral.* M19. **2** *v.i.* Work quickly and carelessly. Usu. foll. by *over. Austral.* L19.

mullocky *a.* of the nature of mullock L19.

mulloway /ˈmʌləweɪ/ *n.* Also (earlier) †**mallowe**. M19. [Aborig. *malowe*.] A large sciaenid food and game-fish, *Argyrosomos hololepidotus*, of Australian coastal waters. Also called *jewfish*.

mully /ˈmʌli/ *a.* Long *obs.* exc. *dial.* L16. [f. MULL *n.*[1] + -Y[1].] Dusty, powdery.

mully-grub /ˈmʌlɪgrʌb/ *n. Austral.* M20. [App. f. MULLIGRUBS *n.pl.* after GRUB *n.*] A grub, a caterpillar; *esp.* a witchetty grub.

mulmull /ˈmʌlmʌl/ *n.* E17. [Hindi *malmal*.] A thin variety of muslin. Cf. MULL *n.*[4]

Mulozi *n.sing.* see LOZI.

mulsh /mʌlʃ/ *a.* Long *dial. rare.* LME. [Prob. rel. to MELSH.] Soft.

mult- *comb. form* see MULTI-.

†**multangle** *n.* E17–L18. [mod.L *multangulum* neut. sing. of *multangulus*, f. L MULTI- + *angulus* ANGLE *n.*[3]] A polygon.

multangular /mʌlˈtaŋgjʊlə/ *a.* & *n.* L17. [mod.L *multangularis*, f. L MULTI- + *angulus* ANGLE *n.*[3]: see -AR[1]. Cf. MULTI-ANGULAR.] **A** *adj.* Having many angles; polygonal. L17. **B** *n.* A polygon. *rare.* M18.

multarticulate /mʌltɑːˈtɪkjʊlət/ *a. rare.* L17. [f. MULT(I- + ARTICULATE *a.*] Chiefly *Zool.* Having many joints or articulations.

multeity /mʌlˈtiːɪti/ *n.* E19. [f. MULT(I- after *aseity*.] **1** The quality or condition of being many or of consisting of many individual parts. E19. **2** A thing consisting of many individual parts. M19.

multi- /ˈmʌlti/ *comb. form.* Bef. a vowel also **mult-**. [L, f. *multus* much, many: see -I-.] Many; more than one.

multi-'access *a.* pertaining to or involving the simultaneous use of a computer by operators at a number of terminals M20. **multi-'angular** *a.* = MULTANGULAR *a.* M19. **multi-ar'ticular** *a.* (*Med.*) affecting more than one joint L19. **multi-ar'ticulate** *a.* (chiefly *Zool.*) = MULTARTICULATE E19. **multi'axial** *a.* involving several or many axes M19. **multibillio'naire** *n.* a person whose assets are worth several or many billions of dollars, pounds, etc. E20. **multi'cellular** *a.* having, consisting of, or involving several or many cells M19. **multicellu'larity** *n.* the state of being multicellular E20. **multi'central** *a.* = MULTICENTRIC (a) M19. **multi'centric** *a.* (*a*) pertaining to, arising from, or having several or many centres; (*b*) *Cytol.* having more than two centromeres: M20. **multi'channel** *a.* employing or possessing several or many communication or television channels M20. **multi'circuit** *a.* supplying or containing several or many electric circuits E20. **multicolline'arity** *n.* (*Statistics*) the existence of a perfect or nearly perfect linear correlation between a set of variables when the regression of some dependent variable on them is being investigated M20. **multicolour** *n.* & *a.* (*a*) *n.* the condition of being of several or many colours; in *pl.*, several or many colours; (*b*) *adj.* = MULTICOLOURED: M19. **multicoloured** *a.* being of several or many colours M19. **multicore** *a.* (esp. of an electric cable) having several or many cores E20. **multi'costate** *a.* (*Bot.*) having more than one rib M19. **multi'cuspid**, **multi'cuspidate** *adjs.* having more than two cusps M19. **multi'cyclic** *a.* (*Geol.*) produced by or having undergone several cycles of erosion and deposition M20. **multi'dentate** *a.* (*a*) having many teeth; (*b*) *Chem.* (of a ligand) having more than one point of attachment to a central atom; polydentate: E19. **multidia'lectal** *a.* fluent in the use of several dialects of the same language M20. **multidia'lectalism** *n.* the condition of being multidialectal; facility in using, the use of, several dialects of the same language: L20. **multidi'mensional** *a.* having or pertaining to more than three dimensions L19. **multidimensio'nality** *n.* the property of being multidimensional M20. **multidi'mensionally** *adv.* in a manner that involves or requires more than three dimensions M20. **multidisci'plinary** *a.* combining or involving several or many separate academic disciplines M20. **multi'disciplined** *a.* concerned with several or many separate academic disciplines M20. **multi-e'lectrode** *a.* possessing or involving several electrodes; *spec.* (of a valve) having two or more sets of electrodes, associated with separate electron beams, within a single envelope E20. **multi-'ethnic** *a.* composed of or involving several ethnic groups M20. **multi'faceted** *a.* having several or many facets (chiefly *fig.*) L19. **multifactor** *a.* = MULTIFACTORIAL M20. **multifac'torial** *a.* involving or dependent on a

For other words beginning with *multi-* see the main alphabetic sequence of entries number of factors (esp. genes) or causes E20. **multifac'torially** *adv.* in a multifactorial manner M20. **multi'filament** *a.* containing or composed of several or many filaments; *spec.* (of yarn) made up of many fine threads: M20. **multiflash** *a.* (*a*) *Photogr.* made with two or more flash-bulbs which are operated in rapid succession; (*b*) designating or pertaining to a process or apparatus for desalinating seawater by repeated sudden boiling at successively lower pressures: M20. **multi'focal** *a.* & *n.* (*a*) *adj.* having or pertaining to several foci, or a range of focal lengths; (*b*) *n.* a multifocal lens; usu. in *pl.*, spectacles with multifocal lenses: E20. **multifoe'tation** *n.* (*a*) pregnancy with more than one foetus; (*b*) pregnancy with more than two foetuses: M19. **multi'foliate** *a.* (*Bot.*) having many (more than 7 or 9) leaflets M19. **multifont** *a.* (*Computing*) pertaining to or having the ability to read or print characters of several different fonts M20. **multifunction** *a.* = MULTIFUNCTIONAL M20. **multi'functional** *a.* having or fulfilling several or many functions M20. **multifunctio'nality** *n.* the state of being multifunctional L20. **multigene** *a.* (*Genetics*) designating or pertaining to a group of genes which act together to produce a gene product or phenotypic effect M20. **multige'neric** *a.* (*Biol.*) derived from or involving more than one genus M20. **multigerm** *a.* (*Agric.*) designating or pertaining to varieties of sugar beet in which each seed ball contains several fruits and so gives rise to several seedlings M20. **multigrade** *a.* (of engine oil) meeting the requirements of several standard grades M20. **multijugate** /mʌl'tɪdʒəɡət, mʌltɪ'dʒuːɡət/ *a.* [L *jugum* yoke, pair] *Bot.* having many pairs of leaflets M19. **multila'mellar** *a.* having or consisting of several or many lamellae L19. **multila'mellate, multila'mellous** *adjs.* = MULTILAMELLAR M19. **multi'laminar, multi'laminate** *adjs.* having or consisting of several or many laminae or layers L19. **multilayer** *a.* & *n.* (*a*) *adj.* composed of or occurring in several or many layers; (*b*) *n.* a structure or film composed of several or many layers, *spec.* of more than one monolayer: E20. **multi'layered** *a.* having several or many layers, multilayer M20. **multi'level** *a.* having, involving, or operating on several or many levels; *spec.* designating a method of direct selling in which buyers at each level of a hierarchy secure the participation of further buyers at a level below them: M20. **multi'levelled** *a.* having several or many levels, multilevel M20. **multi'lineal** *a.* having several or many lines; *spec.* designating a kinship system including relationships derived from the parents, grandparents, etc., of both father and mother: L18. **multi'linear** *a.* having, consisting of, or involving several or many lines L19. **multi'lobate, multi'lobed** *adjs.* having or consisting of several or many lobes M19. **multi'lobular** *a.* having, consisting of, or affecting more than one lobule L19. **multilo'cation** *n.* the fact of being or power to be in several or many places simultaneously M19. **multi'locular** *a.* having, consisting of, or characterized by several or many cells or chambers E19. **multi'mammate** *a.* having several pairs of mammae; *multimammate rat*, a tropical African rodent, *Mastomys natalensis*, freq. destructive to crops: E20. **multi'media** *a.* designating or pertaining to a form of artistic, educational, etc., communication using more than one medium M20. **multimillio'naire** *n.* a person whose assets are worth several or many millions of dollars etc. M19. **multi-'negative** *n.* an array of similar images in negative form for printing small items several at a time by photolithography E20. **multi'nuclear, multi'nucleate** *adjs.* having more than one nucleus L19. **multi-occu'pation** *n.* occupation, esp. tenancy, of a house by more than one family with shared cooking, washing, etc., facilities M20. **multi-'occupy** *v.t.* occupy, esp. tenant, (a house) with one or more other families and with shared cooking, washing, etc., facilities; house (people, esp. tenants) in such accommodation: M20. **multi'ovulate** *a.* (*Bot.*) containing several or many ovules M19. **multi-'partism** *n.* (belief in or advocacy of) a multi-party system M20. **multi-'partist** *a.* of or pertaining to multi-partism M20. **multi-'party** *a.* comprising (members of) several political parties; designating or pertaining to an electoral system in which the interests of the electorate are represented by three or more political parties: E20. **multi-'partyism** *n.* = MULTI-PARTISM M20. **multipath** *a.* (*Telecommunications*) involving (radio) signals that have travelled from a single source by several paths M20. **multi'personal** *a.* comprising several or many personalities E19. **multiphase** *a.* having or producing two or more phases; multiphased; *Electr.* polyphase: L19. **multiphased** *a.* occurring in several stages L20. **multi'phasic** *a.* designating a form of test or investigation designed to reveal various phases or aspects of personality, health, etc. (MINNESOTA *Multiphasic Personality Inventory*) M20. **multi'pinnate** *a.* (*Bot.*) several or many times pinnate L19. **multi'planar** *a.* consisting of or pertaining to a number of planes M19. **multiplane** *n.* & *a.* (*a*) *n.* an aeroplane or glider having two or more sets of wings, one above the other; (*b*) *adj.* involving or occupying several or many distinct planes or layers; *Cinemat.* designating a technique used to give an enhanced impression of perspective: E20. **multiplaned** *a.* having or occupying several or many planes E20. **multi-ply** *n.* & *a.* (*a*) *n.* plywood consisting of more than three layers; (*b*) *adj.* consisting of more than three strands, layers, or thicknesses: M20. **multipoint** *a.* having or serving several or many points; *spec.* (of a water-heater) serving a number of hot-water taps: E20. **multi-po'sition** *a.* able to be used or placed in several or many positions M20. **multi-'positive** *n.* an array of similar images in positive form for printing small items several at a time by photolithography M20. **multipo'tential** *a.* (*Biol.* & *Med.*) = PLURIPOTENTIAL E20. **multi'processing** *n.* (*Computing*) processing by a number of processors sharing a common memory and common peripherals M20. **multi'processor** *n.* a computer capable of performing multiprocessing M20. **multi'program** *a.* (*Computing*) designed for or pertaining to multiprogramming M20. **multi'programmed** *a.* = MULTIPROGRAM M20. **multi'programming** *n.* (*Computing*) the execution of two or more independent programs concurrently M20. **multi-'purpose** *a.* serving several or many purposes M20. **multi'radiate** *a.* having several or many rays M19. **multi'section** *n.* (*rare*) division into several or many parts M19. **multi'septate** *a.* (*Bot.*) having several or many septa or partitions M19. **multi'serial** *a.* arranged in several or many series or rows M19. **multi'serially** *adv.* in a multiserial manner L19. **multi'sided** *a.* having several or many sides, many-sided E20. **multi'sonant** *a.* (*rare*) producing many sounds M17. **multi'sonous** *a.* (*rare*) = MULTISONANT E20. **multi'spectral** *a.* operating in or involving several regions of the electromagnetic spectrum M20. **multi'spiral** *a.* having several or many spiral coils or convolutions M19. **multista'bility** *n.* the property or state of being multistable M20. **multi'stable** *a.* (of a system) composed of a number of interconnected subsystems each of which can achieve stability independently of the others M20. **multistage** *a.* (*a*) consisting of, occurring in, or involving several or many stages; (*b*) *Statistics* designating sampling carried out in a number of stages, the sample obtained at each stage being divided into smaller units and taken as the population for the next stage of sampling: E20. **multistage** *v.t.* make multistage E20. **multi'storey** *a.* (of a building, esp. a car park) having several or many (esp. similarly designed) storeys E20. **multi-'task** *a.* (*Computing*) involving multi-tasking; capable of multi-tasking: M20. **multi-'tasking** *n.* & *a.* (*Computing*) (*a*) *n.* the concurrent execution of a number of different tasks, as by interleaving or multiprocessing; (*b*) *adj.* capable of multi-tasking: M20. **multi-'threaded** *a.* (*Computing*) employing multi-threading L20. **multi-'threading** *n.* (*Computing*) a programming technique whereby several processes can use the same applications software concurrently without interference L20. **multi-'tier** *a.* having or comprising several or many tiers or layers M20. **multi-'use** *a.* serving several or many uses M20. **multi-'user** *a.* having several or many users; (of a computer system) able to be used by more than one person and accessed from more than one terminal concurrently: M20. **multi'variant** *a.* influenced by or taking account of several variables; *Statistics* multivariate: E20. **multi'variate** *a.* (*Statistics*) involving or having two or more variates or random variables E20. **multi'various** *a.* (now *rare*) manifold and diverse E17. **multi'voltine** *a.* (*Entomol.*) producing several generations in a year L19. **multiwall** *a.* having several or many walls; *spec.* (of a large bag etc.) made of several layers of strong paper usu. attached to one another along the bottom and the side folds: M20.

multicultural /mʌltɪ'kʌltʃ(ə)r(ə)l/ *a.* M20. [f. MULTI- + CULTURAL.] Designating or pertaining to a society consisting of several or many culturally distinct groups.

Times This multicultural, multi-lingual society . . is one of the most cosmopolitan in the world.

multiculturalism *n.* the characteristics of a multicultural society; a policy advocating the establishment of a multicultural society: M20. **multiculturally** *adv.* L20.

multifarious /mʌltɪ'fɛːrɪəs/ *a.* & *n.* L16. [f. L *multifarius* varied, diverse (f. as MULTI-) + -OUS.] A *adj.* 1 Having great variety or diversity; (with *n.pl.*) many and various. L16. 2 *Law* (now *Hist.*). Of a bill: that inappropriately or confusingly embraces two or more distinct matters. E19.

1 A. J. CRONIN The whole range of his multifarious duties found Llewellyn blandly expert and prepared. CLIVE JAMES The place is too multifarious to be captured by the pen.

B *n. Kantian Philos.* A manifold (see MANIFOLD *n.* 2). E19.

multifariously *adv.* M17. **multifariousness** *n.* L17.

multifid /'mʌltɪfɪd/ *a.* M18. [f. MULTI- + -FID. Cf. L *multifidus*.] *Bot.* & *Zool.* Divided into several or many parts by deep clefts or notches.

multifidly *adv.* M19.

multifidous /mʌl'tɪfɪdəs/ *a.* Now *rare.* M17. [f. as prec. + -OUS.] *Zool.* Multifid; (of an animal) having multifid feet.

multiflora /mʌltɪ'flɔːrə/ *n.* E19. [Late L, fem. of *multiflorus* MULTIFLOROUS.] In full *multiflora rose*. A Japanese rose, *Rosa multiflora*, with clusters of small white or pink flowers; any of the cultivated varieties developed from this.

multiflorous /mʌltɪ'flɔːrəs/ *a.* M18. [f. late L *multiflorus*, f. as MULTI- + *flor-*, *flos* flower: see -OUS.] *Bot.* Of a stalk: bearing more than three flowers.

Also **multifloral** *a.* L19.

multifold /'mʌltɪfəʊld/ *a.* E19. [f. MULTI- + -FOLD, after *manifold*.] Manifold.

multiform /'mʌltɪfɔːm/ *a.* & *n.* E17. [Fr. *multiforme* or L *multiformis*, f. as MULTI- + -FORM.] A *adj.* Having several or many forms; highly diversified in form; of many and various forms or kinds. E17.

T. DWIGHT The multiform brogue, which salutes the ears of a traveller in . . New-York. *Wireless World* Produced by progressive tooling and multiform methods.

B *n.* A multiform object; something exhibiting many and various forms. Also, multiform character, multiformity. M19.

multi'formity *n.* the condition or character of being multiform; diversity or variety of form: L16. **multi'formous** *a.* (*rare*) multiform M17.

Multigraph /'mʌltɪɡrɑːf/ *n.* Also **m-**. E20. [f. MULTI- + -GRAPH.] (Proprietary name for) a small printing machine using specially cast type fitted into grooves on a rotating cylinder.

multigravida /mʌltɪ'ɡravɪdə/ *n.* Pl. **-das, -dae** /-diː/. L19. [f. MULTI- after PRIMIGRAVIDA.] *Med.* & *Zool.* A female who has been pregnant at least twice, or is in at least her second pregnancy. Cf. PRIMIGRAVIDA.

'multigravid *a.* & *n.* (*a*) *adj.* pregnant for at least the second time; (*b*) *n.* = MULTIGRAVIDA: M20.

multihull /'mʌltɪhʌl/ *n.* & *a.* M20. [f. MULTI- + HULL *n.*[2]] (A boat) having more than one hull.

multi'hulled *a.* having more than one hull M20.

multilateral /mʌltɪ'lat(ə)r(ə)l/ *a.* L17. [f. late L *multilaterus* + -AL[1], or f. med.L *multilateralis*, f. as MULTI- + LATERAL.] 1 (Of a figure) having more than four sides; many-sided (*lit.* & *fig.*). L17. 2 Orig. (*Law*), made or entered on by two or more parties. Later more widely, involving three or more States as parties to an agreement, esp. in respect of trade and finance, or of possession of weapons; not unilateral. E19. 3 Chiefly *Hist.* Of a school: offering two or more distinct curricula for secondary education. M20.

1 J. F. CLARKE The whole poem represents the multilateral character of Hinduism. 2 *Times* The . . first effective system of multilateral arms control the world had ever known. A. J. AUGARDE The only way . . is for each nation unilaterally to disarm itself. It is unrealistic to wait for multilateral disarmament.

multilateralism *n.* the quality of being multilateral; adherence to multilateral principles and practice, esp. in respect of (*spec.* nuclear) disarmament: E20. **multilateralist** *n.* & *a.* (*a*) *n.* an adherent or advocate of multilateralism; (*b*) *adj.* of, pertaining to, or characteristic of multilateralism or multilateralists: M20. **multilaterali'zation** *n.* the action or result of multilateralizing something M20. **multilateralize** *v.t.* make multilateral M20. **multilaterally** *adv.* M19. **multilateralness** *n.* (long *rare*) E18.

multilingual /mʌltɪ'lɪŋɡw(ə)l/ *a.* & *n.* M19. [f. MULTI- + L *lingua* tongue + -AL[1].] A *adj.* Involving several or many languages; written, spoken, etc., in several or many languages; having several or many languages; speaking several or many languages fluently. M19.

For other words beginning with *multi-* see the main alphabetic sequence of entries

A. S. DALE His family was multilingual, well-read and very eccentric.

B *n.* A multilingual person. M20.

multilingualism *n.* the ability to speak several or many languages; the use of several or many languages: M20. **multilinguist** *n.* a multilingual person E20. **multilingually** *adv.* M20.

Multilith /ˈmʌltɪlɪθ/ *n.* Also **m-**. M20. [f. MULTI- + LITH(OGRAPH *n.*] (Proprietary name for) a small offset-lithographic printing machine.

multilithed *a.* printed by a machine of this kind M20.

multiloquent /mʌlˈtɪləkwənt/ *a. rare.* M17. [Late L *multiloquentia*, f. as MULTI- + LOQUENT.] Using many words, esp. habitually; characterized by the use of many words; talkative.

multiloquence *n.* the (habitual) use of many words, talkativeness M18.

multimer /ˈmʌltɪmə/ *n.* M20. [f. MULTI- + -MER.] *Chem.* An aggregate of molecules held together by relatively weak bonds, such as hydrogen bonds.

multiˈmeric *a.* L20.

multimeter /ˈmʌltɪmiːtə/ *n.* Also (US proprietary name) **M-**. E20. [f. MULTI- + -METER.] *Electr.* An instrument designed to measure voltage, current, and usu. resistance, often over several different ranges of value.

multimodal /mʌltɪˈməʊd(ə)l/ *a.* E20. [f. MULTI- + MODAL.] 1 *Statistics.* (Of a frequency curve or distribution) having several modes or maxima; (of a property) occurring with such a distribution. E20. 2 Characterized by several different modes of occurrence or activity. E20.

multimodalism (*rare*), **multimoˈdality** *ns.* the property or quality of being multimodal E20.

multinational /mʌltɪˈnaʃ(ə)n(ə)l/ *a.* & *n.* E20. [f. MULTI- + NATIONAL *a.*] A *adj.* 1 Comprising or pertaining to several or many nationalities or ethnic groups, etc. E20. 2 Of a company or other organization: operating in several or many countries. M20. B *n.* A multinational company etc. L20.

multinationally *adv.* M20.

multinomial /mʌltɪˈnəʊmɪəl/ *a.* & *n.* E17. [f. MULTI- after *binomial.*] *Math.* A *adj.* = POLYNOMIAL *a.* E17. B *n.* = POLYNOMIAL *n.* L17.

multinominal /mʌltɪˈnɒmɪn(ə)l/ *a.* M17. [f. L *multinominis* (f. as MULTI- + L *nomin-*, *nomen* name) + -AL[1].] Having several or many names; polyonymous.

multip /mʌlˈtɪp/ *n. slang.* M20. [Abbrev.] *Med.* = next.

multipara /mʌlˈtɪp(ə)rə/ *n.* Pl. **-ras, -rae** /-riː/. M19. [mod.L, fem. of *multiparus*: see next.] *Med.* & *Zool.* A female who has had more than one pregnancy resulting in viable offspring; a pregnant female with at least one previous delivery. Cf. PRIMIPARA.

multiparous /mʌlˈtɪp(ə)rəs/ *a.* M17. [f. mod.L *multiparus*, f. as MULTI- + -PAROUS: see -OUS.] 1 *Zool.* Pertaining to or characterized by giving birth to more than one young at a single birth. M17. 2 *Med.* & *Zool.* Of, pertaining to, or designating a female who is a multipara. M19. 3 *Bot.* Of a cyme: that has many axes. L19.

multiˈparity *n.* the condition of being multiparous L19.

multipartite /mʌltɪˈpɑːtʌɪt/ *a.* E18. [L *multipartitus*, f. as MULTI- + PARTITE.] Divided into several or many parts; having several or many divisions.

multiped /ˈmʌltɪpɛd/ *n.* & *a.* Now *rare.* Also **-pede** /-piːd/. LME. [L *multipeda*, f. as MULTI- + *ped-* *pes* foot.] A *n.* A creature with many feet. Formerly *spec.*, a woodlouse. LME. B *adj.* Having many feet. M18.

multipedous /mʌlˈtɪpɪdəs/ *a.* (esp. of locomotion) pertaining to or characteristic of many-footed animals E18.

multiple /ˈmʌltɪp(ə)l/ *a.*, *n.*, & *v.* M17. [Fr. f. late L *multiplus* alt. of cl.L MULTIPLEX.] A *adj.* 1 Consisting of or characterized by several or many parts, elements, or individual components; having several or many origins, results, actions, etc.; manifold. M17. b *Med.* Of a disease or symptom: affecting several parts, organs, etc. M19. 2 With *n.pl.* Many and various. M17. 3 *Math.* That is a multiple (see sense B.1 below). Formerly also, that is some multiple *of.* E18.

1 P. AUSTER The Agents perform a multiple function—part junk dealer, part manufacturer, part shopkeeper. 2 P. CUTTING She had multiple cuts on her hands and legs. B. CHATWIN Dr Frankfurter unwrapped the object from its multiple layers of tissue paper.

Special collocations & comb.: **multiple-access** *a.* = MULTI-ACCESS. **multiple allele, allelomorph** *Genetics*: located at a genetic locus known to have three or more alleles. **multiple-aspect** *a.* designating a colour-light railway signal able to display at least three aspects. **multiple birth** *Med.* the birth of more than one child after a multiple pregnancy. **multiple-choice** *a.* designating (a question in) an examination etc. presenting the candidate with several possible answers from which one is to be selected as correct. **multiple-disc** *a.* designating a kind of friction clutch consisting of a row of co-axial discs fixed alternately to the driving and the driven parts. **multiple exposure** *Photogr.* the exposure of the same frame of a film more than once; a multiple image resulting from this. **multiple factors** genes which interact to control the expression of a character. **multiple fission** *Biol.* division of a cell into more than two daughter cells. **multiple image** a composite image consisting of two or more superimposed or adjacent images, e.g. resulting from the combination of reflected light rays, television signals, etc., that have travelled by different paths, or the simultaneous use of several projectors in a cinema. *multiple* MYELOMA. **multiple personality** *Psychol.* a dissociative condition in which an individual's personality is apparently split into two or more distinct sub-personalities, each of which may become dominant at different times. **multiplepoinding** *Sc. Law* an action by the holder of personal property claimed by several people, causing the claimants to interplead. **multiple pregnancy** *Med.* a single pregnancy in which more than one foetus develops. **multiple proportion** the proportion existing between a quantity and some multiple of it, or between several multiples of it; *law of multiple proportions* (Chem.), the tendency of chemical elements to combine in integral proportions. **multiple ratio** the ratio existing between a quantity and some multiple of it, or between several multiples of it. **multiple resistance** *Pharm.*: of a micro-organism to the action of more than one antibiotic. **multiple-resistant** *a.* (*Pharm.*) exhibiting multiple resistance. **multiple sclerosis** a chronic progressive demyelinating disease, chiefly affecting young adults, in which sclerosis occurs in patches in the brain and spinal cord and usu. characterized by successive remissions and relapses leading to tremor, paresis, ataxia, and disturbed sight and speech; also called *disseminated sclerosis.* **multiple shift** *Industry* a double or treble shift of work. **multiple shop, multiple store** any of several or many shops selling the same type of goods and owned by one firm; a shop having branches in various places. **multiple star** *Astron.* a group of three or more associated stars rotating around a common centre. *multiple store*: see *multiple shop* above. *multiple superparticular*: see SUPERPARTICULAR *a.* **multiple switchboard** *Teleph.*: in which each subscriber's circuit is accessible to each operator. **multiple twin** *Cryst.* a twinned crystal composed of three or more components whose relative orientations are all governed by the same twin law. **multiple-twin** *a.* (*Teleph.*) designating a cable with a number of cores each of which consists of four wires arranged as two twisted pairs twisted together. **multiple-unit** *a.* & *n.* (designating or pertaining to) a train with a number of coaches provided with motors controllable by a single driver. **multiple-use** *a.* = MULTI-USE *a.*

B *n.* 1 *Math.* A quantity which is a product of a given quantity and some other, *esp.* one which results from multiplication of that quantity by an integer. L17. 2 *Kantian Philos.* A manifold (see MANIFOLD *n.* 2). M19. 3 *Teleph.* Each of the sections of a multiple switchboard, containing one jack for each subscriber. Also, a circuit in which the same connection may be made at different points. E20. 4 A multiple shop or store. M20. 5 An inexpensive work of art able to be mass-produced by industrial methods. M20.

1 **least** or **lowest common multiple** the smallest quantity that has two or more given quantities (and no others) as its factors. 3 **in multiple** (connected) between the same pairs of wires, so forming such a circuit. 5 P. DICKINSON A bronze . . paperweight . . had the look of one of a large issue of multiples.

C *v.t. Teleph.* Make (a circuit) accessible to operators at more than one point; provide or employ duplicates of (a device) for this purpose. E20.

multiplet /ˈmʌltɪplət/ *n.* E20. [f. MULTIPLE *a.* + -ET[1], after *doublet*, *triplet*, etc.] *Physics.* 1 A closely-spaced group of related spectral lines in a spectrum; a group of related atomic states or energy levels with slightly different energies. E20. 2 A group of subatomic particles that differ only in charge. Also, a series of such groups, each characterized by a different value of hypercharge (or strangeness) but having the same spin and parity. M20.

multiplex /ˈmʌltɪplɛks/ *n.*, *a.*, & *v.* LME. [L, f. as MULTI- + -PLEX[1].] A *n.* †1 *Math.* = MULTIPLE *n.* 1. LME–L17. 2 *Kantian Philos.* A manifold (see MANIFOLD *n.* 2). M19. 3 *Telecommunications.* A multiplex system or signal. M20. 4 A complex of two or more cinemas on a single site. L20.

B *adj.* †1 *Math.* = MULTIPLE *a.* 3. M16–L18. 2 Manifold; of many elements, having many interrelated features; multiple. L17. b *Telecommunications.* Designating or pertaining to the transmission of two or more independent signals or programmes (to be later separated and recovered) simultaneously over a single wire or channel. L19. c *Med.* = MULTIPLE *a.* 1b. L19. d Designating a cinema complex incorporating two or more cinemas on a single site. L20.

2 T. L. PEACOCK The whole complex and multiplex detail of the noble science of dinner. F. W. FARRAR Brief and scattered letters out of the multiplex correspondence of a varied life. T. KENEALLY I hated him in the core of each of my dazzling and multiplex cells.

C *v.t. Telecommunications.* Incorporate into a multiplex signal or system. E20.

multiplexer, -or *ns.* a device which multiplexes something M20. **multiˈplexity** *n.* the quality or condition of being multiplex, multiplex nature or structure; an instance of this: L20.

multipliable /ˈmʌltɪplʌɪəb(ə)l/ *a.* E17. [f. MULTIPLY *v.* + -ABLE.] Able to be multiplied.

multiplicable /ˈmʌltɪplɪkəb(ə)l/ *a.* L15. [OFr., or med.L *multiplicabilis*, f. L *multiplicare* MULTIPLY *v.*: see -ABLE.] Able to be multiplied; multipliable.

multiplicaˈbility *n.* (*rare*) L17.

multiplicand /ˌmʌltɪplɪˈkand, ˈmʌltɪplɪkand/ *n.* L16. [med.L *multiplicandus* (sc. *numerus* number) gerundive of L *multiplicare* MULTIPLY *v.*: see -AND.] *Math.* A quantity to be multiplied by another (the multiplier).

multiplicate /ˈmʌltɪplɪkət, mʌlˈtɪplɪkət/ *a.* & *n.* Now *rare.* LME. [L *multiplicatus* pa. pple of *multiplicare* MULTIPLY *v.*: see -ATE[2]. As n. f. MULTI- after *duplicate* etc.] A *adj.* Orig., multiplied, increased. Later, manifold, of many elements or parts, multiplex. LME.

B *n.* Any of several or many exactly corresponding copies of a document etc. M19.

in multiplicate in several or many exactly corresponding copies.

multiplication /ˌmʌltɪplɪˈkeɪʃ(ə)n/ *n.* LME. [OFr., or L *multiplicatio(n-)*, f. *multiplicat-* pa. ppl stem of *multiplicare* MULTIPLY *v.*: see -ATION.] 1 The action or an act of multiplying something; the condition of being multiplied. Now chiefly as passing into sense 3. LME. 2 Reproduction of people or animals; propagation of plants. LME. 3 *Math.* a The action or process of multiplying quantities; the process of finding the quantity produced by repeatedly adding one quantity as many times as there are units in a second quantity, or (in the case of fractions) of finding the same fraction of one quantity as a second quantity is of unity. LME. b The successive application of an operator; generation of a product. M19. †4 *Alch.* The action of multiplying metals. LME–L17. 5 *Bot.* Abnormal increase in the number of whorls or of organs in a whorl. M19.

3b *logical multiplication*: see LOGICAL *a.*

Comb.: **multiplication constant, factor** *Nuclear Physics* in nuclear fission, the ratio by which the number of neutrons increases during a period equal to the lifetime of a neutron; **multiplication sign** the sign × placed between two quantities which are to be multiplied together; **multiplication table** a list (written or recited) of products of two factors (esp. the integers 1 to 12) taken in pairs.

multiplicational *a.* (*rare*) M19.

multiplicative /ˈmʌltɪplɪkətɪv/ *a.* & *n.* M17. [Late L *multiplicativus*, f. L *multiplicat-*: see prec., -ATIVE.] A *adj.* Tending to multiply; having the quality or function of multiplying. M17. B *n.* A numeral expressing a factor of multiplication, as *duplex*, *fourfold*, etc. M18.

multiplicatively *adv.* L19.

multiplicator /ˈmʌltɪplɪkeɪtə/ *n.* M16. [Late L, f. L *multiplicat-*: see MULTIPLICATION, -ATOR.] 1 *Math.* = MULTIPLIER 3a. Now *rare* or *obs.* M16. 2 *Physics.* = MULTIPLIER 4. E19.

multiplicious /mʌltɪˈplɪʃəs/ *a.* Long *rare.* E17. [App. f. L *multiplic-*: see MULTIPLY *v.*, -IOUS.] Multiplex.

multiplicity /mʌltɪˈplɪsɪti/ *n.* LME. [Late L *multiplicitas*, f. L *multiplic-*, MULTIPLEX: see -ICITY.] 1 The quality or condition of being multiplex or manifold; manifold variety; an instance of this. LME. 2 A large number *of*; *collect.* large numbers *of*; a variety of kinds *of*. L16. 3 *Physics.* The number of components in a multiplet (that of a spectral line or energy level which is not split being counted as 1). E20. 4 *Med.* In full *multiplicity of infection*. The ratio of the number of infective virus particles to the number of susceptible cells. M20.

1 A. STORR One of the major obstacles . . is his multiplicity of ill-formulated definitions for the same thing. ISAIAH BERLIN Tolstoy . . saw the manifold objects and situations on earth in their full multiplicity. 2 L. CODY No chin visible under a multiplicity of woolly scarves and collars. W. RAEPER One symbol can have a multiplicity of meanings.

multiplier /ˈmʌltɪplʌɪə/ *n.* LME. [f. MULTIPLY *v.* + -ER[1].] †1 A person who transmutes base metals into gold or silver (as) by alchemy. Also, a maker of counterfeit coins, a coiner. LME–M16. 2 A person who or thing which multiplies or causes something to increase. LME. 3a *Math.* A quantity by which another is to be multiplied. M16. b *Econ.* A factor by which an increase in income, employment, etc., is a multiple of the change in investment or government expenditure producing it. M20. 4 *Physics.* An instrument used for multiplying or increasing by repetitive reinforcement the intensity of a force, current, etc., to an appreciable or measurable value. L18. 5 *Angling.* A kind of reel in which a mechanism causes the barrel to revolve several times to a single revolution of the handle. M19. 6 A calculating instrument for use in multiplication. L19.

Comb.: **multiplier effect**: able to be assessed in terms of the economic multiplier.

multiply /ˈmʌltɪplʌɪ/ *v.* ME. [(O)Fr. *multiplier* f. L *multiplicare*, f. *multiplic-*, MULTIPLEX: see -Y[2].] 1 *v.t.* Cause to become of great(er) number or quantity; increase or augment by accumulation or repetition. Now chiefly as passing into sense 5. ME. b Use or utter a great many (words etc.). *arch.* ME. †c Increase the intensity of; magnify. LME–E19. d Adduce a large number of (instances etc.). E18. †2 *v.t.* Increase (a family etc.) by reproduction or procreation; cause (the earth) to increase in population. ME–L18. b Breed (animals); propagate (plants). L15–M19. 3 *v.i.* Become of great(er) number or quantity; be increased or augmented by accumulation or repetition. ME. 4 *v.i.* Increase in number by reproduction or procreation. ME. 5 *Math.* a *v.t.* Operate on (a given quantity) with another so as to find a product having the same ratio to the first quantity as the second has to unity; combine (two quantities, expressions, etc.) *together* by multiplication. (Foll. by *by*, †*in*, †*into* the second quantity.) LME. b *v.t.* & *i.* Of a quantity: operate on (another quantity) as a multiplier. LME. c *v.i.* Perform the process of multiplication. L16. d *v.t.* Perform an operation on (two or more quantities, vectors, etc.) analogous to multiplication, to give a product. E18. †6 *v.t.* & *i. Alch.* Transmute base metals into (gold or silver); cause (gold or silver) to increase. LME–L17.

1 ADDISON Till into seven it multiplies its stream. GIBBON The activity of the emperor seemed to multiply his presence. TENNYSON Thus truth was multiplied on truth. b SWIFT They avoid nothing more than multiplying unnecessary Words. c J. CLEVELAND An Optique Glasse contracts the sight At one end, but when turn'd doth multiply 't. d ADDISON 'Tis unnecessary to multiply Instances of this nature. 2 W. COWPER When man was multiplied and spread abroad In tribes and clans. b E. BALFOUR A large Mango multiplied at Mergui. 3 H. E. MANNING As sin has multiplied in its extent, so it would seem also to have become more intense. G. SWIFT Stars which seemed to multiply as we looked at them. 4 DEFOE As for my Cats, they multiply'd. 5a *Journal of Zoology* Sink speed equals the glide angle multiplied by flight velocity. c D. LARDNER If we require the area, we have only to multiply by 3.

Comb.: **multiplying-glass** †(*a*) a magnifying glass; (*b*) (chiefly *Hist.*) a toy consisting of a faceted concave glass or lens giving numerous reflections of an observed object.

multiply /ˈmʌltɪpli/ *adv.* L19. [f. MULTIPLE *a.* + -LY[2].] In a multiple manner; in more than one way; more than once.

J. BERMAN Mental functioning is always multiply determined. S. BELLOW We were doubly, multiply, interlinked.

multipolar /mʌltɪˈpəʊlə/ *a.* M19. [f. MULTI- + POLAR *a.*] 1 Having or pertaining to many poles; *spec.* (*a*) *Anat.* (of a nerve cell) having several or many processes; (*b*) *Electr.* having more than one pair of magnetic poles in a system of field magnets; (*c*) *Cytol.* having or involving more than two spindle poles. M19. 2 Consisting of or divided into more than two (esp. political) alliances, parties, etc. M20.

2 *Times* A multipolar world, where major powers could compete and co-operate simultaneously.

multipolarity /ˌmʌltɪpəˈlarɪti/ *n.* M20. [f. prec. + -ITY.] 1 Multipolar quality or condition. M20. 2 *Physics.* The highest order of multipole associated with a state or phenomenon. M20.

multipole /ˈmʌltɪpəʊl/ *n.* & *a.* E20. [f. MULTI- + POLE *n.*[2]] A *n. Physics.* A system of 2^l monopoles (where the order l = 1, 2, 3,...) with no net charge or pole strength and no moment of a lower order than l. Also, a quadrupole (l = 2) or higher order system, the dipole (l = 1) being treated as a special case. E20. B *attrib.* or as *adj.* 1 *Physics.* Designating or pertaining to a multipole; *esp.* designating electromagnetic radiation of the kind produced by an electric multipole with a moment varying sinusoidally in magnitude. E20. 2 Of a switch: designed to close or open several circuits simultaneously. E20.

multipotent /mʌlˈtɪpət(ə)nt/ *a.* E17. [L *multipotent-*, f. as MULTI- + POTENT *a.*[2]] Having much power; very powerful. Chiefly *Biol.* & *Med.*, = MULTIPOTENTIAL.

multipresence /ˈmʌltɪprɛz(ə)ns/ *n.* E17. [f. MULTI- + PRESENCE.] The fact of being or power to be present in several or many places simultaneously.

multiracial /mʌltɪˈreɪʃ(ə)l/ *a.* E20. [f. MULTI- + RACIAL *a.*] Of, pertaining to, or comprising several or many racially differentiated peoples; *esp.* (of a State, society, etc.) comprising such peoples in more or less equal membership.

Economist He triumphantly created the first multiracial government in Africa. *Times Lit. Suppl.* The pleasant relief of a man living a multi-racial life away from the colour bar.

multiracialism *n.* multiracial condition or quality; the principles or practice of a multiracial State, society, etc.: M20. **multiracialist** *n.* an adherent or advocate of multiracialism M20. **multiracially** *adv.* M20.

multi-track /ˈmʌltɪtrak/ *a.*, *n.*, & *v.* L20. [f. MULTI- + TRACK *n.*] *Audio.* A *adj.* Designating, pertaining to, or resulting from the separate recording of several (usu. between 2 and 24) tracks of sound for subsequent mixing. L20. B *n.* (A) multi-track recording. L20. C *v.t.* Record as or mix from separate soundtracks. Freq. as *multi-tracked* ppl a., *multi-tracking* vbl n. L20.

multi-tracker *n.* a multi-track recording device L20.

multituberculate /ˌmʌltɪtjuːˈbəːkjʊlət/ *a.* & *n.* L19. [f. mod.L *Multituberculata* (see below), f. as MULTI- + TUBERCULATE *a.*] A *adj.* (Of a tooth) bearing several cusps arranged in two or three rows; designating, of, or pertaining to the order Multituberculata. L19. B *n.* Any of various mammals of the extinct order Multituberculata, having multituberculate molar teeth. E20.

multitude /ˈmʌltɪtjuːd/ *n.* ME. [(O)Fr. f. L *multitudo*, *-din-*, f. *multus* many: see -TUDE.] 1 The quality or state of being numerous. ME. 2 A large number *of* people or things; in *pl.*, large numbers *of*. ME. †b A great quantity *of*. LME–L18. 3 A large gathering of people; a mass of people collected in one place; a throng. LME. 4 *The* populace, *the* common people. M16.

2 C. BAX The sun is a glowing speck in a dazzling multitude of stars. B. PYM One of those ubiquitous tea-shops which cater for the multitudes of office-workers. M. FOOT Jennie, like a multitude of other Labour candidates, went down to defeat. b EARL OF CHATHAM All this disgraceful danger, this multitude of misery. 3 R. WHATELY A skilful orator's being able to rouse . . the passions of a multitude. J. BALDWIN A long-awaited conqueror . . before whom multitudes cried, Hosanna!

multitudinous /mʌltɪˈtjuːdɪnəs/ *a.* E17. [f. L *multitudin-*, *-tudo* MULTITUDE + -OUS.] 1a Existing in great numbers; very numerous; consisting of many individuals or elements. E17. b Existing in or exhibiting many forms; having many elements or features; arising from or involving a great number. M17. 2 Of an ocean etc.: vast. *literary.* E17. 3 Of or pertaining to the populace, or common people. *rare.* E17. 4 Thronged or crowded (*with*). *poet.* E19.

1a H. AINSWORTH When this multitudinous and confused assemblage had nearly filled the inclosure. C. AIKEN Cloud-palaces and kingdoms . . And multitudinous cities. b C. KINGSLEY The multitudinous moan and wail of the lost spirits. 2 SHAKES. *Macb.* This my hand will rather The multitudinous seas incarnadine. 3 SHAKES. *Coriol.* Pluck out The multitudinous tongue; let them not lick The sweet which is their poison. 4 SHELLEY Regard this Earth Made multitudinous with thy slaves.

multitudinism *n.* (now *rare*) the (esp. religious) principle placing the interests of a large number before those of individuals M19. **multitudinosity** /-ˈnɒsɪti/ *n.* multitudinousness M19. **multitudinously** *adv.* M19. **multitudinousness** *n.* the state or quality of being multitudinous M17.

multivalent /mʌltɪˈveɪl(ə)nt, *esp. Cytol.* mʌlˈtɪvəl(ə)nt/ *a.* & *n.* L19. [f. MULTI- + -VALENT.] A *adj.* 1a *Chem.* = POLYVALENT 1a. L19. b *Immunol.* Of an antigen or antibody: having several sites at which attachment to an antibody or antigen can occur. M20. 2 *Cytol.* That is (part of) a multivalent. E20. 3 Chiefly *Ling.* & *Literary Criticism.* Having or susceptible of many applications, interpretations, meanings, or values. M20. B *n. Cytol.* An association of three or more completely or partly homologous chromosomes during the first division of meiosis. E20.

multivalence, **-ency** *ns.* the state or condition of being multivalent L19.

multivallate /mʌltɪˈvaleɪt, -lət/ *a.* M20. [f. MULTI- + VALLATE *a.*] Chiefly *Archaeol.* Surrounded by more than one rampart.

multivaˈllation *n.* multivallate fortification M20.

multivalve /ˈmʌltɪvalv/ *a.* & *n.* M18. [f. MULTI- + VALVE *n.*] A *adj.* 1 *Biol.* Esp. of a shell or shelled animal: having several or many valves. M18. 2 *Electronics.* Having several or many thermionic valves. E20. B *n.* A multivalve shell; an animal having such a shell, as a chiton, an acorn-shell. M18.

multivalved, **multiˈvalvular** *adjs.* = MULTIVALVE *a.* 1 M18.

multiverse /ˈmʌltɪvəːs/ *n.* L19. [f. MULTI- + UNI)VERSE.] The universe considered as lacking order or a single ruling and guiding power.

multiversity /mʌltɪˈvəːsɪti/ *n.* Chiefly *US.* M20. [f. MULTI- + UNI)VERSITY.] A very large university comprising many different departments and activities.

multivibrator /ˌmʌltɪvʌɪˈbreɪtə/ *n.* E20. [f. MULTI- + VIBRATOR.] *Electronics.* A device

For other words beginning with *multi-* see the entry for **multi-**

consisting of two amplifying valves or transistors, each with its output connected to the input of the other, which produces an oscillatory signal rich in harmonics.

multivious /mʌlˈtɪvɪəs/ *a.* M17. [f. L *multivius*, f. as MULTI- + *via* way: see -IOUS.] Having many ways; going or leading in many directions.

multivocal /mʌlˈtɪvək(ə)l/ *a.* E19. [f. MULTI- + L *vocare* to call + -AL¹, after *univocal, equivocal.*] Susceptible of many interpretations or meanings.

multivoˈcality *n.* multivocal condition or quality L20.

multocular /mʌlˈtɒkjʊlə/ *a.* E18. [f. MULT(I- + L *oculus* eye + -AR¹, after *monocular.*] Having many eyes; (of a device) adapted for more than one eye.

multum /ˈmʌltəm/ *n. obs.* exc. *Hist.* E19. [Perh. a use of L *multum* much.] A preparation of opium, cocculus indicus, or other plant extracts, added to beer etc. to increase the intoxicating effect.

multum in parvo /mʌltəm ɪn ˈpɑːvəʊ/ *n. phr.* M18. [L = much in little.] A great deal in a small compass.

multungulate /mʌlˈtʌŋgjʊlət/ *a.* & *n. rare.* M19. [mod.L *multungulatus*, f. as MULTI- + UNGULATE.] *Zool.* (An ungulate animal) having more than two separate toes on each foot.

multure /ˈmʌltʃə/ *n.* Chiefly *Sc. obs.* exc. *Hist.* ME. [OFr. *mo(u)lture* (mod. *mouture*) f. med.L *molitura*, f. *molit-* pa. ppl stem of *molere* grind: see MILL *n.*¹, -URE.] A toll of grain or flour payable to the proprietor or tenant of a mill in return for grinding corn. Also, the right to exact this toll.

OUTSUCKEN *multure.*

multurer *n.* a person who pays multure L16.

†mulvel *n.* ME–M18. [AN *muluelle* (Latinized as *mulvellus*), OFr. *muluel*, prob. alt. of. *moruel* dim. of *morue*, med.L *morua* cod.] = COD *n.*²

mum /mʌm/ *n.*¹, *int.*, *a.*, & *adv.* LME. [Imit.] A *n.* 1 An inarticulate sound made with closed lips, esp. as an indication of inability or unwillingness to speak; a word. Now usu. in neg. contexts. Long *obs.* exc. *Sc.* LME. 2 Refusal to speak, silence. Now chiefly in *mum's the word*, enjoining silence or secrecy. *colloq.* M16. †3 A silent person. M17–E19.

B *int.* Hush! Silence! Not a word! LME.

C *adj.* & *adv.* Strictly silent(ly) or secret(ly), not saying a word. *colloq.* E16.

R. BRIDGES Don't stand there mum. *Honolulu Advertiser* UH head football coach.. was mum on a successor. *First Base* He has decided to be mum on this matter. **sit mum** be silent.

Comb.: **mumbudget** *n.*, *int.*, *a.*, *adv.*, & *v.* †(*a*) = MUM *n.*¹, *int.*, *a.*, & *adv.*; (*b*) *v.i.* (*dial.*) be silent, come silently or secretly, (chiefly in *come mumbudgeting*).

mum /mʌm/ *n.*² E17. [G *Mumme.*] Chiefly *Hist.* A kind of beer originally brewed in Brunswick.

mum /mʌm/ *n.*³ *colloq.* & *dial.* M17. [Partly var. of MAM, partly abbrev. of MUMMY *n.*² Cf. MOM.] Mother.

Spectator The Mum restricts her son-in-law's roles. *News on Sunday* The pre-school children of the young mums were taking part in a nursery. **be mum** = *be mother* s.v. MOTHER *n.*¹

Comb.: **mum-figure** *colloq.* = *mother-figure* s.v. MOTHER *n.*¹

mum /mʌm/ *n.*⁴ *colloq.* & *dial.* M19. [Repr. a pronunc.] = MA'AM *n.*

mum /mʌm/ *n.*⁵ L19. [Abbrev.] A chrysanthemum.

mum /mʌm/ *v.* Infl. **-mm-**. LME. [Imit. Cf. MLG *mummen*, Du. *mommen.*] †1 *v.t.* Silence; cause to be silent. LME–M17. †2 *v.i.* Make an inarticulate sound with closed lips, esp. indicating inability or unwillingness to speak; whisper; keep silence. LME–M17. 3 *v.i.* Act in a mime or dumb show; play as a mummer. LME.

mumble /ˈmʌmb(ə)l/ *v.* & *n.* ME. [f. MUM *v.* + -LE³. Cf. LG *mummelen*, Du. *mommelen, mumm-.*] A *v.* 1 *v.i.* Eat in a slow ineffective manner; chew or bite softly, (as) with toothless gums. ME. 2 *v.i.* Speak indistinctly or with the lips partly closed; mutter. ME. 3 *v.t.* Say in subdued or indistinct tones. ME. 4 *v.t.* Bite or chew (as) with toothless gums; eat without making much use of the teeth. L16. b *transf.* Fondle with the lips. M17. †5 *v.t.* Maul; handle roughly or clumsily. E17–M18.

1 F. MARRYAT The calf with gilded horns, who.. mumbles with the flowers of the garland. 2 G. LORD He was.. mumbling with pain. R. FRAME My father spoke quietly.., he mumbled almost. 3 P. G. WODEHOUSE She eyed the speaker sternly... 'Yes, Ma'am,' he mumbled sheepishly. F. TUOHY My brother mumbled something about a holiday, but he did not explain further. 4 P. V. WHITE He mumbled it on his tongue.. before attempting to swallow it.

B *n.* A mumbled indistinct utterance or sound. E20.

R. C. HUTCHINSON The distant mumble of a congregation at prayer. F. RAPHAEL They heard the mumble of thunder.

mumblement *n.* (*rare*) mumbling; a mumbled or muttered statement: L16. **mumbler** *n.* M16. **mumblingly** *adv.* in a mumbling manner M18.

mumble-the-peg /ˈmʌmb(ə)lðəpɛg/ *n.* Now *US.* Also **mumbledypeg** /ˈmʌmb(ə)ldɪpɛg/, **-ty-** /-tɪ-/, & other vars. E17. [f. the requirement that an unsuccessful player draw a peg out of the ground with the teeth.] A game in which each player in turn throws a knife from a series of positions, continuing until the blade fails to stick in the ground. Also called *knifey.*

mumbo-jumbo /mʌmbəʊˈdʒʌmbəʊ/ *n.* In sense 1 **Mumbo Jumbo.** Pl. **-os.** M18. [Perh. f. Mande *mama dyumbo.*] 1 (A representation of) a grotesque idol said to have been worshipped by certain W. African peoples. M18. 2 *transf.* a An object of unintelligent veneration. M19. b Obscure or meaningless talk or writing; nonsense; meaningless or ignorant ritual. L19.

mumbo-jumboism *n.* worship of a mumbo jumbo L19.

mumchance /ˈmʌmtʃɑːns/ *n.*, *a.*, & *adv.* Now *arch.*, *dial.*, & *literary.* E16. [MLG *mummenschanze, -scanze, -kanze* game of dice, masked serenade, f. *mummen* mask, disguise + *schanz* f. (O)Fr. *chëance* CHANCE *n.*] A *n.* †1 A dicing game resembling hazard. E16–M17. †2 Masquerade; mumming. M–L16. 3 A person who acts in dumb show; a person who has nothing to say. *obs.* exc. *dial.* L17. B *adj.* & *adv.* Silent(ly); tongue-tied. L17.

Mumetal /ˈmjuːmɛt(ə)l/ *n.* Also **m-**. E20. [f. MU *n.*¹ (after μ, symbol for permeability) + METAL *n.*] (Proprietary name for) an alloy of nickel containing approx. 17 per cent iron, 5 per cent copper, and 2 per cent chromium by weight, which has high magnetic permeability and is used esp. in transformer cores and magnetic shields.

mummer /ˈmʌmə/ *n.* & *v.* LME. [OFr. *momeur*, f. *momer* act in dumb show, rel. to *momon* mask, Sp. *momo* grimace, perh. of Gmc origin. Partly f. MUM *v.* + -ER¹.] A *n.* 1 A person who mutters or murmurs. *rare.* LME. 2 An actor in a (traditional) masked mime or dumb show; a participant in a mumming. LME. b A (poor) actor, a play-actor. *arch. slang.* L18. B *v.i.* Take part in a mumming. Chiefly as *mummering* vbl n. L19.

Mummerset /ˈmʌməsɛt/ *n.* M20. [Prob. f. prec. after *Somerset.*] An imaginary rustic county in the West of England; its dialect, a pseudo-rustic dialect used by actors.

mummery /ˈmʌm(ə)ri/ *n.* M16. [(O)Fr. *momerie*, f. *momer*: see MUMMER, -ERY.] 1 A performance by mummers. M16. 2 Ridiculous ceremonial; religious ritual regarded as silly or hypocritical. M16.

mummia /ˈmʌmɪə/ *n.* L15. [med.L *mumia* MUMMY *n.*¹] 1 = MUMMY *n.*¹ 1. Long *rare.* L15. †2 = MUMMY *n.*¹ 2. Only in E18.

mummichog /ˈmʌmɪtʃɒg/ *n. US.* Also **mummy-**. L18. [Narragansett *moamitteaug.*] A killifish; *esp.* the black and silver killifish, *Fundulus heteroclitus.*

mummied /ˈmʌmɪd/ *a.* E17. [f. MUMMY *v.*, *n.*¹: see -ED¹, -ED².] Mummified.

mummification /ˌmʌmɪfɪˈkeɪʃ(ə)n/ *n.* E19. [f. MUMMIFY + -FICATION.] 1 The process of mummifying; the condition of being mummified. E19. 2 *Med.* Drying and shrivelling of tissues. M19.

mummified /ˈmʌmɪfʌɪd/ *a.* M19. [f. MUMMIFY + -ED¹.] 1 That has been mummified. M19. 2 *Med.* Of tissue, an organ: shrivelled or dried up. L19. 3 Of a fruit: brown and dry due to brown rot disease. E20.

mummiform /ˈmʌmɪfɔːm/ *a.* M19. [f. MUMMY *n.*¹ + -I- + -FORM.] Resembling or shaped like a mummy.

mummify /ˈmʌmɪfʌɪ/ *v.t.* E17. [f. MUMMY *n.*¹ + -FY, after Fr. *momifier.*] Make into a mummy; preserve (a body) by embalming and drying.

mumming /ˈmʌmɪŋ/ *n.* LME. [f. MUM *v.* + -ING¹.] †1 Inarticulate murmuring; indistinct speech. LME–L16. 2 The action of disguising oneself, esp. during festivities; participation in a mummers' play; a performance of a (traditional) masked mime or dumb show. LME. 3 = MUMMERY 2. E16.

mum-mumble /mʌmˈmʌmb(ə)l/ *v.i.* & *t.* E20. [Redupl. of MUMBLE *v.*, perh. after MUM *v.*] Mumble, mutter.

mummy /ˈmʌmi/ *n.*¹ & *v.* LME. [OFr. *mumie*, (also mod.) *momie* f. med.L *mumia* f. Arab. *mūmiyā* pissasphalt, embalmed body, perh. f. Pers. *mūm* wax.] A *n.* I 1 A medicinal preparation (supposed to have been) extracted from mummified remains. (Prob. often identical with sense 1d below.) *obs.* exc. *Hist.* LME. 2 *Alch.* A sovereign remedy. Also, a vital essence (cf. BALSAM *n.* 4). L16–E18. 3 (A) pulpy substance or mass, pulp. Chiefly in *beat to a mummy* & similar phrs. Formerly also, dead flesh. L16. 4 A semi-liquid bituminous substance used as a brown pigment and (formerly) as a medicine (cf. PISSASPHALT). Also, a mixture of wax and pitch formerly used in the transplanting and grafting of trees. E17.

II 5 The body of a human being or animal embalmed (as in the ancient Egyptian fashion) as a preparation for burial. E17. 6 A human or animal body desiccated by exposure to sun or air. Also, an animal carcass embedded in prehistoric ice. E18. 7 An apple, plum, or other fruit made brown and desiccated by brown rot disease. E20.

5 B. BAINBRIDGE Wrapped in strips of cloth like an Egyptian mummy. *fig.*: L. STEPHEN The old theological dogmas had become mummies.

Comb.: **mummy bag** a sleeping-bag covering the head and body; **mummy brown** (of) a shade of brown resembling that of the pigment mummy; **mummy-case** a case of wood or papier mâché (usually decorated with hieroglyphics) enclosing an Egyptian mummy; **mummy-cloth** a cloth wrapping an Egyptian mummy; **mummy disease** a disease of mushrooms of uncertain cause, characterized by atrophy or distortion and hardening of the fruiting body; **mummy-pits** *arch.* catacombs in which Egyptian mummies were interred.

B *v.t.* Mummify; make into a mummy. E17.

mummy /ˈmʌmi/ *n.*² *colloq.* (orig. *dial.*). L18. [Repr. a pronunc. of MAMMY *n.*¹ Cf. MOMMY.] Mother.

mummy's boy = *mother's boy* s.v. MOTHER *n.*¹

mummychog *n.* var. of MUMMICHOG.

mump /mʌmp/ *n.* See also MUMPS. L16. [Symbolic of the movements of the mouth in grimacing. Cf. next.] †1 A grimace. L16–M17. 2 A block of peat. M20.

mump /mʌmp/ *v.*¹ L16. [f. as prec. Cf. Icel. *mumpa* take into the mouth, *mumpaskælur* grimace, Du. *mompen, -elen* mumble in speaking, G *mumpfeln, -en* mumble in eating.] 1 *v.t.* Say indistinctly; mumble, mutter. *obs.* exc. *Sc.* L16. 2 *v.i.* †a Grimace; grin. L16–M18. b Assume a demure, sanctimonious, or miserable expression; be silent and sullen; sulk, mope. Now *arch.* exc. *Sc.* E17. 3 *v.i.* & *t.* Mumble with the gums; turn (food) over and over in the mouth; munch, nibble. *obs.* exc. *Sc.* & *dial.* L16.

mump /mʌmp/ *v.*² Now *arch.*, *dial.*, & *slang.* M17. [Prob. f. Du. *mompen* cheat.] †1 *v.t.* Overreach, cheat, (*of*, *out of*). M17–L19. 2 *v.i.* Beg, go about begging; sponge (*on*). L17. b Of a police officer: accept small gifts or bribes from tradespeople. Chiefly as *mumping* vbl n. *slang*. L20. 3 *v.t.* Obtain by begging or sponging. L17.

mumper *n.* L17.

mumpish /ˈmʌmpɪʃ/ *a. colloq.* E18. [f. MUMP *n.* or *v.*[1] + -ISH[1].] Sullenly angry; sulky; depressed in spirits.

mumps /mʌmps/ *n.pl.* (usu. treated as *sing.*). L16. [Pl. of MUMP *n.*] 1 An acute contagious viral disease mainly of children, characterized by swelling of the parotid salivary glands and fever; infectious parotitis. Also foll. by *the*. L16. 2 A fit of melancholy or ill humour; *the* sulks. L16.

mumpsimus /ˈmʌmpsɪməs/ *n.* Now *literary*. M16. [Erron. for L *sumpsimus* in *quod in ore sumpsimus* 'which we have taken into the mouth' (in the Eucharist), in a story of an illiterate priest who, when corrected, replied 'I will not change my old mumpsimus for your new sumpsimus'.] 1 An obstinate adherent of old ways, in spite of clear evidence of their error; an ignorant and bigoted opponent of reform. Formerly also *loosely*, an old fogey. M16. 2 A traditional custom or notion obstinately adhered to although shown to be unreasonable. M16.

mums /mʌmz/ *n. colloq.* M20. [Abbrev. of MUMSY *n.*] Mother.

mumsy /ˈmʌmzi/ *n.* & *a. colloq.* Also **-sey, -sie**. L19. [f. MUM *n.*[3] + -SY.] A *n.* Mother. L19. B *adj.* Warmly maternal. M20.

mu-mu *n.* var. of MUU-MUU.

mun *n.* var. of MON *n.*[3]

mun /mʌn/ *aux. v. dial.* ME. [ON *muna*, f. Gmc base of MIND *n.*[1] Cf. MAUN *v.*] = MUST *v.*[1] II, III, IV.

munch /mʌn(t)ʃ/ *v.* & *n.* LME. [App. imit.: cf. *crunch, scrunch*.] A *v.t.* & *i.* Eat (food or fodder) with continuous and noticeable action of the jaws; eat audibly, esp. with evident enjoyment. LME.

R. C. HUTCHINSON A sheep stopped munching the close grass. C. P. SNOW Aunt Milly munched away impassively. R. DAHL Children taking bars of creamy chocolate out of their pockets and munching them greedily. **munch out** *US slang* indulge in snacks.

B *n.* 1 Something to eat; a meal. *dial.* & *joc.* E19. 2 An act of munching. L19.

muncher *n.* M18.

Munchausen /ˈmʌn(t)ʃaʊz(ə)n, mʌnˈtʃɔːz(ə)n/ *n.* & *v.* M19. [Baron *Munchausen* (in G form *Münchhausen*), hero of a pseudo-autobiographical narrative of impossible adventures, written in English by the German Rudolf Eric Raspe (1785).] A *n.* 1 An extravagantly untruthful pseudo-autobiographical story of marvellous adventure; a tall story. M19. 2 A narrator of such a story or stories. Also *Baron Munchausen*. M20. 3 *Munchausen('s) syndrome*, a mental illness in which the patient repeatedly feigns a dramatic or severe illness so as to obtain hospital treatment. M20. B *v.i.* Tell extravagantly untruthful pseudo-autobiographical stories of marvellous adventure. Chiefly as *Munchausening* vbl n. M19.

Munchausenism *n.* = MUNCHAUSEN *n.* I. M19.

muncheel /mʌnˈtʃiːl/ *n.* E19. [Tamil *mañcil* stage, Malayalam *mañjal* stage, day's journey, muncheel.] A conveyance, usu. for one person, used in SW India and consisting of a hammock slung between two poles, carried by bearers. Cf. MACHILA.

Munchi /ˈmʊn(t)ʃi/ *n.* & *a.* Also **-shi** /-ʃi/. Pl. of n. **-s**, same. M19. [Hausa.] = TIV.

munchie /ˈmʌn(t)ʃi/ *n. slang.* E20. [f. MUNCH *v.* + -IE.] Food; a snack (usu. in *pl.*).

Munda /ˈmʊndə/ *n.* & *a.* M19. [Munda *Mundā*.] A *n.* Pl. **-s**, same. 1 A member of an ancient Indian people of pre-Aryan stock surviving in NE India. M19. 2 The language group including the dialects of the Mundas, believed to belong to the Austro-Asiatic family. L19. B *attrib.* or as *adj.* Of or pertaining to the Mundas or their language. M19.

mundane /ˈmʌndeɪn, mʌnˈdeɪn/ *a.* LME. [(O)Fr. *mondain* f. late L *mondanus*, f. L *mundus* world: see -ANE.] 1 Of or pertaining to this world (i.e. the earth as contrasted w. heaven); worldly; earthly. Also, of or pertaining to everyday life, dull, routine. LME. 2 Of or pertaining to the cosmos or universe; cosmic. M17. 3 *Astrol.* Of or pertaining to the horizon as opp. to the ecliptic or zodiac. L17.

1 A. STORR Jung's own sacrifice of mundane goals was the abandonment of his academic career. RACHEL ANDERSON We all went gloriously off to fight our war, leaving behind our families to get on with their mundane lives. D. MADDEN Her daily life was very mundane. 2 J. B. MOZLEY The idea of God as the Supreme Mundane Being. **mundane egg** in Indian and other cosmogonies, a primordial egg from which the world was hatched. 3 *mundane house*: see HOUSE *n.*[1] 9a.

mundanely *adv.* E19. **mundaneness** *n.* E18.

mundanity /mʌnˈdanɪti/ *n.* E16. [Fr. *mondanité*, f. as prec.: see -ITY.] 1 A mundane concern or event. Usu. in *pl.* E16. 2 The quality or fact of being mundane; worldliness. M17.

1 *Times Lit. Suppl.* The glittering mundanities of her parents' circle. J. UGLOW A literalism in art and a commitment to describing the mundanities of life.

mundatory /ˈmʌndət(ə)ri/ *n.* & *a. rare.* L17. [Late L *mundatorius*, f. L *mundare* cleanse, f. *mundus* clean: see -ORY[1].] A *n.* 1 *Eccl.* A purificator. L17. 2 *gen.* A means or implement of cleansing. M19. B *adj.* Having the property or quality of cleansing. E18.

¶ Chiefly in Dicts.

†**mundify** *v.t.* LME. [(O)Fr. *mondifier* or late L *mundificare*, f. *mundus* clean: see -FY.] 1 *Med.* Free (the body, an ulcer, a wound, etc.) from pus or noxious matter; cleanse. LME–M19. 2 Cleanse, purify, (*lit.* & *fig.*). E16–E19.

†**mundification** *n.* the action of cleansing an ulcer, a wound, etc.; the state of being cleansed: LME–E19. †**mundificative** *a.* & *n.* (*a*) *adj.* having the power to cleanse (esp. an ulcer, a wound, etc.); (*b*) *n.* cleansing medicament: LME–E18. †**mundifier** *n.* a person who or thing which cleanses something; a cleansing medicament: LME–M18.

mundivagant /mʌnˈdɪvəg(ə)nt/ *a. rare.* M17. [f. L *mundus* world + -I- + *vagant-* pres. ppl stem of *vagare* roam: see -ANT[1].] Roaming, wandering round the world.

mundungus /mʌnˈdʌŋgəs/ *n.* Now *rare*. Also †**-go**. M17. [Alt. of Sp. MONDONGO.] †1 Offal, refuse. M17–M19. 2 Bad-smelling tobacco. M17.

mung /mʌŋ, muːŋ/ *n.*[1] E19. [Hindi *mūng*.] (The seed of) either of two widely cultivated tropical Asian legumes: (*a*) (more fully *mung bean*) the green gram, *Vigna radiata*; (*b*) the black gram, *V. mungo*.

mung *n.*[2] var. of MONG *n.*[1]

munga /ˈmʌŋgə/ *n. Austral., NZ, & Mil. slang.* E20. [App. f. Fr. *manger* eat.] Food; a meal.

mungo /ˈmʌŋgəʊ/ *n.*[1] Also †**-os**. Pl. **-os**. M18. [Var. of MONGOOSE.] †1 = MONGOOSE I. M18–M19. 2 In full *mungo-root*. A plant of the madder family, *Ophiorrhiza mungos*, regarded as an antidote to snake-bites in India and elsewhere. M18.

†**mungo** *n.*[2] Also **M-**. Pl. **-o(e)s**. M18–M19. [A Black character in Bickerstaffe's *The Paddock* (1768).] (A name for) a Black slave; a Black.

mungo /ˈmʌŋgəʊ/ *n.*[3] M19. [Perh. f. Sc. male forename *Mungo* (in parts of NE England often applied to dogs), w. allus. to *mung* MONG *n.*[1]] Fibre made from old woven or felted material that has been shredded; inferior cloth made with such fibre.

†**mungoose** *n.* var. of MONGOOSE.

mungy /ˈmʌŋgi/ *a.* Long *obs.* exc. *dial.* M17. [Perh. alt. of MUGGY *a.*, but recorded earlier.] †1 Dark, gloomy. Only in M17. 2 Mouldy, moist, = MUGGY *a.* I. M17. 3 Of weather etc.: muggy. E19.

muni /ˈmʊni/ *n.*[1] L18. [Skt *muni* lit. 'silent', f. *man* think.] *Hinduism* & *Jainism*. An inspired or holy man; a sage; an ascetic, a hermit.

muni /ˈmjuːni/ *n.*[2] *US colloq.* L20. [Abbrev. of MUNICIPAL (*bond*).] A municipal bond.

Munich /ˈmjuːnɪk/ *n.* M20. [Eng. name of *München* capital of Bavaria, S. Germany.] An example of misjudged or dishonourable appeasement such as or comparable to the ceding to Germany of the Sudetenland of N. Czechoslovakia, agreed by Germany, Great Britain, France, and Italy in Munich on 29 September 1938 (the Munich Agreement).

Municheer, Munichite *ns.* an advocate of such an appeasement policy M20.

municipal /mjʊˈnɪsɪp(ə)l/ *a.* & *n.* M16. [L *municipalis*, f. MUNICIPIUM, f. *municip-, -ceps*, f. *munia* civic offices + *capere* take: see -AL[1].] A *adj.* 1 Of or pertaining to the internal affairs of a State as distinguished from its foreign relations. Orig. & chiefly in *municipal law*. M16. b *transf.* Belonging to one place only; having narrow limits. *rare.* M17. 2 Of or pertaining to the local self-government or corporate government of a city or town; having such government; conducted by a municipality. E17. 3 *Rom. Hist.* Of or pertaining to a municipium; *contempt.* provincial. E17.

2 **municipal bond** (chiefly *US*) a security issued by a local authority or its agent, orig. to finance local projects. *municipal corporation*: see CORPORATION 2.

B *n.* †1 In *pl.* Municipal laws. Only in L16. 2 *Rom. Hist.* An inhabitant of a municipium. E18. 3 A municipal bond. Usu. in *pl. US colloq.* E20.

municipalism *n.* (*a*) devotion to one's municipality; municipal or local loyalty (as opp. to national patriotism); (*b*) preference for municipal as opp. to centralized action or control in government: M19. **municipalist** *n.* an advocate of the extension of the range of municipal action or control M19. **municipaliˈzation** *n.* the action of municipalizing something L19. **municipalize** *v.t.* bring under municipal ownership or control; grant local self-government to: E19. **municipalizer** *n.* = MUNICIPALIST E20. **municipally** *adv.* with regard to a municipality or municipal affairs M19.

municipality /mjʊˌnɪsɪˈpalɪti/ *n.* L18. [Fr. *municipalité*, f. *municipal*, f. as prec.: see -ITY.] 1 A town, city, or district having local self-government; the community of such a town etc. L18. 2 The governing body of a town, city, or district having local self-government. L18. 3 *Rom. Hist.* A municipium. E19.

municipia *n.* pl. of MUNICIPIUM.

municipio /mjuːnɪˈsɪpɪəʊ, -ˈtʃɪp-/ *n.* Pl. **-os**. L19. [Sp. & It., f. L *municipium*: see MUNICIPAL.] A Spanish, Latin American, or Italian municipality.

municipium /mjuːnɪˈsɪpɪəm/ *n.* Pl. **-pia** /-pɪə/. E18. [L: see MUNICIPAL.] *Rom. Hist.* A provincial city whose citizens had the privileges of Roman citizens.

municipy /mjʊˈnɪsɪpi/ *n. rare.* L16. [f. as prec.] A municipality.

munificence /mjʊˈnɪfɪs(ə)ns/ *n.* LME. [Fr., or L *munificentia*, f. as next: see -ENCE.] The quality of being munificent; splendid liberality in giving; great generosity.

munificent /mjʊˈnɪfɪs(ə)nt/ *a.* L16. [L *munificent-*, f. *munificus* adj., f. *munus* gift: see -FIC, -ENT.] Splendidly generous, bountiful.

E. WAUGH: MGM were consistently munificent and we left . . in effortless luxury. R. THOMAS She was awed by the munificent beauty of the gift.

munificently *adv.* L16. **munificentness** *n.* (*rare*) E18.

muniment /ˈmjuːnɪm(ə)nt/ *n.* LME. [(O)Fr. f. L *munimentum* fortification, (in med.L) title-deed, f. *munire* fortify, secure: see -MENT.] 1 A document (as a title-deed, charter, etc.) preserved as evidence of rights or privileges (usu. in *pl.*). In *pl.* also, archives. LME. †2 In *pl.* Things with which a person or place is provided; furnishings. L15–M19. 3 Anything serving as a defence or protection. Now *rare*. M16.

Comb.: **muniment deed** a title-deed.

muninga /mʊˈnɪŋgə/ *n.* M20. [Kiswahili *mninga*.] = KIAAT.

munition /mjʊˈnɪʃ(ə)n/ *n.* & *v.* LME. [(O)Fr. f. L *munitio(n-)*, f. *munit-* pa. ppl stem of *munire* fortify, secure: see -ION.] A *n.* †1 A granted right or privilege. Only in LME. †2 An apparatus. Only in L15. 3 *sing.* (now chiefly when *attrib.*) & in *pl.* Military weapons, ammunition, equipment, and stores; *colloq.* the production of these. Also more fully *munition(s) of war*. E16. †4 The action of fortifying or defending; (a) fortification (*lit.* & *fig.*). M16–E19. B *v.t.* Supply with munitions. L16.

munitio'neer *n.* (now *rare*) a worker in a munition factory E20. **munitioner** *n.* (*rare*) a supplier or maker of munitions M17. **munitio'nette** *n.* (*arch. colloq.*) a female worker in a munition factory E20. **munitionment** *n.* (*a*) provision with or supply of munitions; (*b*) munitions collectively: E20.

munity /'mju:nɪti/ *n.* Now *rare.* LME. [AN, OFr. *munité* or med.L *munitas* back-form. f. *immunitas* IMMUNITY.] A granted right or privilege.

munja /'mu:ndʒə, 'mʌn-/ *n.* Also **moonjah, munj** /mu:n(d)ʒ, mʌn(d)ʒ/. M19. [Hindi *munj*, Skt *munja.*] A grass of the Indian subcontinent, *Saccharum munja*, whose leaves provide fibre for ropes etc.

munjeet /mʌn'dʒi:t/ *n.* E19. [Hind. *mañjīṭ(h).*] A plant of the madder family, *Rubia cordifolia*, native to the Indian subcontinent; the roots of this plant, used to make a red dye.

munjistin /mʌn'dʒɪstɪn/ *n.* M19. [f. mod.L *Munjista* (former genus name of MUNJEET) + -IN[1].] *Chem.* A crystalline orange dye present in munjeet, madder, and other plants; 1, 3-dihydroxyanthraquinone-2-carboxylic acid.

munnion /'mʌnjən/ *n.* L16. [Var. of MONIAL w. assim. of *l* to preceding *n*: cf. MULLION.] *Archit.* A mullion.

Munro /mʌn'rəʊ/ *n.* Pl. **-os.** E20. [Sir H. T. *Munro*, who published a list of all such peaks in the Journal of the Scottish Mountaineering Club for 1891.] *Mountaineering.* A Scottish mountain of at least 3000 feet (approx. 914 metres); any such mountain in the British Isles.

Munsell /'mʌns(ə)l/ *n.* E20. [Albert H. *Munsell* (1858–1918), US painter.] Used *attrib.* with ref. to Munsell's system of classifying colours by means of numerical values for three properties, hue, value (lightness or brightness), and chroma.

munshi /'mu:nʃi:/ *n.*[1] Also **moonshee.** L18. [Pers. & Urdu *munšī* f. Arab. *munšī'* writer, author, act. pple of *'anša'a* write (a book).] In the Indian subcontinent: a secretary, an assistant; a language-teacher.

Munshi *n.*[2] & *a.* var. of MUNCHI.

munsif /'mu:nsɪf/ *n.* Also **moon-.** E19. [Pers. & Urdu, f. Arab. *munṣif* just, honest, f. Arab. *'anṣafa* treat justly.] *Hist.* In the Indian subcontinent: a judge.

Munsterlander /'mʊnstəlandə, 'mʌn-/ *n.* L20. [G *Münsterlander*, f. *Münsterland*, the region of Germany where the breeds originated: see -ER[1].] (An animal of) either of two similar German breeds of gun dog, one black and white (more fully *large Munsterlander*), the other smaller and usu. brown and white (more fully *small Munsterlander*, *Munsterlander spaniel*).

munt /mʊnt/ *n.* *S. Afr.* & *Zimbabwean* (*Rhodesian*) *slang. derog.* M20. [Bantu *umuntu* person, sing. of *abantu* (see BANTU).] A Black African.

muntin /'mʌntɪn/ *n.* E17. [Var. of MONTANT w. loss of *t.*] An upright post or bar. Now *spec.* a central vertical piece between two panes of glass.

muntjac /'mʌntdʒak/ *n.* Also **-jak.** L18. [Sundanese *minchek.*] Any of several small deer with short antlers of the Asian genus *Muntiacus*; esp. *M. reevesi*, which has been introduced into Britain and Europe. Also called *barking deer.*

Muntz metal /'mʌnts 'mɛt(ə)l/ *n. phr.* M19. [f. George Frederick *Muntz* (1794–1857), Eng. metallurgist.] Brass containing about 55 to 64 per cent of copper (often with 1 per cent or more of lead), used in casting and extrusion and formerly esp. in sheathing ship's hulls.

munyeroo /mʌnjə'ru:/ *n.* *Austral.* L19. [Aborig.] Either of two small succulent plants of the purslane family, *Calandrinia balonensis* and *Portulaca oleracea*; a paste made from the ground seeds of either plant, formerly used as food by Aborigines.

muon /'mju:ɒn/ *n.* M20. [Contr. of *mu-meson*: see MU *n.*[1], -ON.] *Particle Physics.* An unstable lepton similar to the electron but with a mass about 207 times greater, which is the chief constituent of cosmic radiation at the earth's surface.

Comb.: **muon number** a quantum number that is ±1 for muons and their neutrinos and 0 for other particles and is conserved in all known interactions.

mu'onic *a.* of, pertaining to, or involving a muon; (of an atom) having a negative muon orbiting the nucleus: M20.

muonium /mju:'əʊnɪəm/ *n.* M20. [f. prec. + -IUM, after *positronium.*] *Particle Physics.* A short-lived neutral system, analogous to an atom, consisting of a positive muon and an electron.

mura /'mjʊərə/ *n.* Pl. same. E20. [Jap.] A Japanese village or hamlet, esp. as an administrative unit.

muraena /mjʊ'ri:nə/ *n.* Also **murena.** M16. [L *muraena*, *murena* sea-eel, lamprey f. Gk *muraina*, f. *muros* sea-eel.] An eel-like fish. Now chiefly as mod.L genus name of the moray eel.

murage /'mjʊərɪdʒ/ *n.* LME. [OFr., in med.L *muragium*, f. Fr. *mur* wall: see MURE *n.*, -AGE.] 1 *Hist.* A tax levied for building or repairing the walls of a town; the right granted to a town for the levying of such a tax. LME. †2 The building of walls; a system of defensive walls. *rare.* LME–E17.

†**murager** *n.* see MURENGER.

mural /'mjʊər(ə)l/ *n.* L15. [(O)Fr. *muraille* f. Proto-Romance, repr. L *muralia* neut. pl. of *muralis* (see next) taken as fem. sing.: see -AL[1]. In senses 2, 3 f. MURAL *a.*] †1 A wall. L15–M16. †2 A fruit tree growing against and fastened to a wall. Only in L17. 3 A painting executed directly on a wall or (occas.) ceiling, esp. as part of a scheme of decoration. E20.

2 W. BOYD A huge lecture room with a dull mythological mural on three walls. R. P. JHABVALA The same motif was repeated in a mural behind the bar.

muralist *n.* a painter of murals; *spec.* a member of a Mexican school of mural painting active in the first half of the 20th cent.: E20.

mural /'mjʊər(ə)l/ *a.* LME. [(O)Fr. f. L *muralis*, f. *murus* wall: see -AL[1].] 1 *Rom. Antiq.* Designating a crown, garland, etc., awarded to the first soldier to scale the wall of a besieged town. Cf. VALLAR. LME. 2 Placed or executed on a wall; fixed to a wall. M16. 3 *gen.* Of or pertaining to a wall; resembling a wall. L16. 4 *Astron.* Designating or pertaining to a wall or walled arch set exactly in the plane of the meridian for the alignment of a large instrument. *obs.* exc. *Hist.* E18. 5 *Anat.* & *Med.* Of or pertaining to the wall of a body cavity or vessel. L19.

1 *transf.*: S. JOHNSON He toils without the hope of mural or civick garlands. 2 K. CLARK A large mural painting in the church of St Sulpice. 3 G. HARTWIG Bold mural coasts, rising precipitously from the deep sea.

murally *adv.* (*rare*) (*a*) with a mural crown, garland, etc.; (*b*) by means of a wall or walls; (*c*) on or from a wall or walls: M19.

muralled /'mjʊər(ə)ld/ *a.* E18. [f. MURAL *a.*, *n.* + -ED[2].] 1 Used for or made into a mural crown. *rare.* E18. 2 Decorated with murals. M20.

1 J. P. PHILIPS Ardent to deck his brows with mural'd gold, Or civic wreath of oak. 2 A. WEST Stella watched the shadows . . as they bobbed on the muralled wall.

muramic /mjʊ'ramɪk/ *a.* M20. [f. L *murus* wall + AM(INE + -IC.] Biochem. *muramic acid*, an amino-sugar, $C_9H_{17}NO_7$, present in the cell walls of bacteria and in bacterial spores.

Murano /mjʊ'rɑ:nəʊ/ *n.* L19. [See below.] Used *attrib.* to designate Venetian glass or other articles from or associated with the island of Murano near Venice.

D. HALLIDAY Johnson filled my glass from a tinselled Murano glass wine jar.

Mura'nese *a.* of or pertaining to Murano L19.

Muratorian /mjʊərə'tɔ:rɪən/ *a.* M19. [f. *Muratori* (see below) + -AN.] Designating (in *Muratorian fragment, canon*) the earliest Western canon of the New Testament, *c*170, edited by the Italian scholar L. A. Muratori (1672–1750).

murchana /'mʊətʃənɑ:/ *n.* L19. [Skt *mūrchanā* modulation.] Each of a set of fourteen octave scales in Indian music that start on one of the seven notes of one or other grama.

murder /'mə:də/ *n.* Also (now *arch.* & *dial.*) **murther** /'mə:ðə/. [OE *morþor* = Goth. *maurþr*, f. Gmc f. IE base also of OE, OS *morþ*, ON *morð*, (O)HG *mord*, Du. *moord*, reinforced in ME by OFr. *murdre* (mod. *meurtre*), f. Gmc.] 1 (An instance of) the unlawful premeditated killing of one human being by another, (a) criminal homicide with malice aforethought; (an instance of) the deliberate killing of a human being in a manner or circumstances tantamount to murder. In early use also, (an) instance of non-criminal homicide of a particularly reprehensible kind; *fig.* (a) mortal sin, (a) great wickedness. OE. †2 Terrible slaughter, destruction of life. ME–L16. 3 As *int.* Expr. the fear that oneself or another is in danger of murder; *joc.* expr. shock, dismay, etc. LME. 4 (An instance of) destruction or spoliation tantamount to murder; something extremely unpleasant or undesirable to experience. Freq. *hyperbol.* M19. b Something or someone excellent or marvellous. *US slang.* M20. 5 A game for a number of participants, involving a mock murder hunt in which one player in the role of detective has to discover the identity of another player taking the role of murderer. M20.

1 DRYDEN Slaughter grows murder when it goes too far. LD MACAULAY Murder by false testimony is therefore the most aggravated species of murder. A. CHRISTIE If I'd committed a murder, I wouldn't go . . and give myself up. *USA Today* He was acquitted of attempted murder. *Daily Telegraph* The detective who solves a murder by deducing the series of events that led to the crime. *Proverb*: Murder will out. *first-degree murder. second-degree murder. personified*: SHELLEY I met Murder in the way—He had a mask like Castlereagh. 3 R. CROMPTON Police! Help! Murder! Robbers! 4 A. J. LERNER She should be taken out and hung For the cold-blooded murder of the English tongue! A. ROSS An old hip injury. . . Not so bad when I'm just walking . . but murder climbing stairs. b M. SHULMAN A Benny Goodman record started to play. 'Oh, B.G.!' cried Noblesse . . 'Man, he's murder, Jack.'

Phrases: *blue murder*: see BLUE *a.* *get away with murder*: see GET *v.* *judicial murder*: see JUDICIAL *a.*

Comb.: **murder bag**: containing equipment for a detailed examination at the scene of a murder; **murder book, file**: for recording details of a police investigation of a murder; **murder game** = sense 5 above; **murder inquiry, investigation** a police investigation of a murder; **murder log**: recording details of a police investigation of a murder; **murderman** (*a*) a murderer; (*b*) a writer of murder stories; **murdermonger** (*a*) a person who commits murder as a profession; (*b*) a writer of murder stories; **murder mystery** (*a*) a mysterious murder; (*b*) a novel, play, etc., about a murder in which the murderer's identity is concealed by a complicated plot until the dénouement; **murder one** *US colloq.* (a charge of) first-degree murder; **murder rap** *slang* (orig. *US*) a charge of murder; **murder room** a room used as a centre for directing a police investigation into a murder; **murder squad** a division of a police force appointed to investigate murders.

murderish *a.* (*rare*) murderous M16.

murder /'mə:də/ *v.* Also (now *arch.* & *dial.*) **murther** /'mə:ðə/. [OE *ā-*, *for-*, *of*)*myrþrian* = OHG *murdran*, Goth. *maurþrjan*, f. Gmc; superseded in ME by a new formation on the n.] I *v.t.* 1 Kill (a human being) unlawfully, esp. wickedly or inhumanly; *spec.* kill (a human being) with a premeditated motive, kill with malice aforethought. OE. b *refl.* Commit suicide. *arch.* LME. 2 Put an end to or destroy in an act tantamount to murder (chiefly *hyperbol.*); spoil by bad execution, representation, etc. ME. 3 Slaughter in a terrible manner, massacre. LME. 4 Consume or spend (time) unprofitably. *arch.* E18. 5 Conclusively defeat (an opponent etc.), esp. at a game or sport. *slang.* M20.

1 I. MCEWAN He was going to find his daughter and murder her abductor. 2 G. GREENE A really dreadful woman singer murders the . . charm of 'You're the Top'. D. CAUTE In the Roundhouse . . they now murder language and with it reason. M. GEE You . . ate red kidney beans and raw garlic while a pianist murdered Gershwin. 3 TENNYSON They turn on the pursuer . . They murder all that follow. J. STEINBECK Killer whales attacked the sea-lions . . and murdered a great number of them. 5 *Observer* If the passing had

got much worse, a team of corporals' grandmothers would have murdered them.

II *v.i.* 6 Perform the act of murder; commit murder. M16.

6 J. HYDE These men will fight, lie, rob, murder for Mormonism if commanded. A. STORR A measure of sympathy is generally extended to . . the lover who murders from jealousy. **†murdering piece** = MURDERER 2.

murderable *a.* able to be murdered; provoking or inviting murder: E20. **murde'ree** *n.* (*a*) a person who is murdered; (*b*) a person whose character and disposition provoke or invite murder: E20. **murderess** *n.* a female murderer LME.

murderer /'mə:d(ə)rə/ *n.* Also (now *arch.* & *dial.*) **murth-** /'mə:ð-/. ME. [Partly f. MURDER *v.*, partly f. AN *mordreour*, *mur-*, f. *mordrer* MURDER *v.*: see -ER[1].] 1 A person who commits murder. ME. †2 A small anti-personnel cannon or mortar used esp. on board ship. L15–E18.

murderous /'mə:d(ə)rəs/ *a.* Also (now *arch.* & *dial.*) **murth-** /'mə:ð-/. M16. [f. MURDER *n.* + -OUS.] Orig. (now *rare*), guilty of murder. Now, capable of or intending murder; of the nature of murder; characteristic of or involving murder.

D. HEWETT The little semis . . defending their privacy . . with rows of murderous iron spikes. H. MACMILLAN To fall a victim to the murderous attack of a fanatical monk. D. ROWE A terrible rage . . drove us to a murderous fury with our gods.

murderously *adv.* (*a*) in a murderous manner; (*b*) *colloq.* extremely: E17. **murderousness** *n.* M17.

†mure *n.* ME–L17. [(O)Fr. *mur* f. L *murum* accus. of *murus* wall.] A wall.

mure /mjʊə/ *v.t. arch.* LME. [(O)Fr. *murer*, f. as prec.] †1 = IMMURE *v.* 1. LME–L18. 2 Block up (a door, gate, etc.). Usu. foll. by *up*. LME. b Wall up the doors of; stop (*up*) the means of access to. M16. 3 = IMMURE *v.* 2. Also foll. by *up*. E17.

1 T. URQUHART All other Abbies are strongly walled and mured about. U. VON TROIL This bath . . is mured in with a wall of basalt. 2 S. PARKER Mure up your school doors. 3 F. MARRYAT Not a little tired of being mured up in the cottage.

murein /'mjʊəri:n/ *n.* M20. [f. L *murus* wall + *-ein*, after PROTEIN.] *Biochem.* A structural polymer forming the cell walls of many bacteria, consisting of glycosaminoglycan chains interlinked with short peptides. Cf. MUCOPEPTIDE, PEPTIDOGLYCAN.

murena *n.* var. of MURAENA.

murenger /'mjʊərɪndʒə/ *n.* Long *obs.* exc. *Hist.* Also (earlier) **†murager**; **muringer**. ME. [AL *muragiarius*, f. med.L *muragium* MURAGE: see -ER[2]. For the intrusive *n* cf. *harbinger*, *messenger*, etc.] An officer responsible for keeping the walls of a city in repair.

murex /'mjʊərɛks/ *n.* Pl. **murices** /'mjʊərɪsi:z/, **murexes**. L16. [L, perh. rel. to Gk *muax* sea-mussel.] Any of various spiny-shelled predatory gastropod molluscs of the genus *Murex* and related genera, of tropical and temperate seas, from some of which the dye Tyrian purple was formerly obtained. Also *murex shell*.

murexide /mjʊ'rɛksʌɪd/ *n.* Also **-id** /-ɪd/. M19. [f. prec. + -IDE.] *Chem.* Ammonium purpurate, used as an indicator.

Muria /'mjʊərɪə/ *n.* & *a.* M19. [Gond.] A *n.* A member of a Gond hill people of Bastar in India. M19. B *adj.* Of or pertaining to this people. M19.

muriate /'mjʊərɪət, -ɪeɪt/ *n. arch.* L18. [Fr., f. *muriatique* MURIATIC: see -ATE[1].] *Chem.* = CHLORIDE.

muriate /'mjʊərɪeɪt/ *v.t. arch.* L17. [f. L *muria* brine + -ATE[3].] Pickle in brine; impregnate with a chloride or chlorides; combine with chlorine. Freq. as *muriated* ppl a.

muriatic /mjʊərɪ'atɪk/ *a. arch.* L17. [L *muriaticus* pickled in brine, f. *muria* brine: see -ATIC.] †1 Pertaining to, of the nature of, or containing brine or salt. L17–M19. 2 Obtainable from seawater; *Chem.* of chlorine; *muriatic acid*, hydrochloric acid. L17.

muricate /'mjʊərɪkət/ *a.* M17. [L *muricatus* shaped like a murex, f. *muric-*, MUREX: see -ATE[2].] *Bot.* & *Zool.* Having sharp points, studded with short rough projections. Formerly also, ending in a long sharp point, like the murex.

Also **muricated** *a.* E18.

murices *n.pl.* see MUREX.

muriculate /mjʊ'rɪkjʊlət/ *a.* M19. [mod.L *muriculatus*, f. *muriculus* small murex, f. *muric-*, MUREX: see -CULE, -ATE[2].] *Bot.* Minutely muricate.

murid /mjʊ'ri:d, mʊ-/ *n.* E19. [Arab. *murīd*.] A follower of a Muslim pir or holy man; a disciple in a Sufi order.

Muridism /mjʊ'ri:dɪz(ə)m/ *n.* M19. [f. MURID + -ISM.] *Hist.* An Islamic revival movement in the Caucasus in the 19th cent. advocating the rising of Muslims against their religious and political opponents, the Russians.

muriform /'mjʊərɪfɔ:m/ *a.* M19. [f. L *murus* wall + -I- + -FORM.] *Bot.* 1 Having cells regularly arranged like the courses of bricks in a wall. M19. 2 Of fungus spores: having both longitudinal and transverse septa. L19.

muri gallici *n. phr.* pl. of MURUS GALLICUS.

murine /'mjʊərʌɪn, -rɪn/ *a.* & *n.* E17. [L *murinus*, f. *mur-*, *mus* mouse: see -INE[1].] A *adj.* 1 Of, resembling, or characteristic of a mouse; *Zool.* of or pertaining to the family Muridae or the subfamily Murinae of Old World rodents, usu. having a long hairless tail, and including the rats and mice. E17. 2 *Vet. Med.* Affecting mice or rats. M20.

2 **murine typhus** a mild form of typhus transmissible to humans by rat fleas.

B *n.* A murine animal, a mouse, a rat. L19.

†muring *n.* E17–E18. [f. MURE *n.* + -ING[1].] Wall-building; the structure of a wall.

muringer *n.* var. of MURENGER.

murk /mə:k/ *n.*[1] Also **mirk**. Now chiefly *Sc.* & *literary*. [OE *mirce*, *myrce* f. Gmc, reinforced in ME f. Scand. (ON *myrkr* n. & adj. = OS *mirki* adj.). Cf. MURK *a.*] Darkness, gloom, (*lit.* & *fig.*); air obscured by fog, dense vapour, etc.

CARLYLE Aloft from the murk of commonplace rise glancings of a starry splendour. W. DE LA MARE I still in the thin clear murk of dawn Descry her gliding streams. B. GELDOF On foggy days Hoath Head looked like a huge ship looming out of the murk.

murksome *a.* (*rare*) dark, obscure L16.

murk /mə:k/ *n.*[2] Now *rare*. L17. [Perh. var. of MARC.] = MARC 1.

murk /mə:k/ *a.* Now chiefly *Sc.* & *literary*. Also **mirk**. [OE *mirce*, *myrce*, reinforced in ME; of Scand. origin (ON *myrkr*: see MURK *n.*[1]).] Dark, gloomy; obscured by fog, dense vapour, etc.; not clear to the sight, indistinct, dim; hard to understand; depressing; unenlightened.

ALLAN RAMSAY Murk despair Made me think life was little worth. HARTLEY COLERIDGE Clothes thee in weed of penance, murk and dun. C. S. CALVERLEY Murk night seemed lately fair-complexioned day. J. R. LOWELL The chimes peal muffled with sea-mists murk.

murkness *n.* (*a*) (now only *Sc.*) darkness (*lit.* & *fig.*); (*b*) *rare* obscurity of air caused by fog etc., mist: ME.

murk /mə:k/ *v.* Also **mirk**. ME. [f. prec. Perh. partly f. ON *myrkva* grow dark.] 1 *v.i.* Grow or appear dark or gloomy. Long *rare* or *obs.* ME. 2 *v.t.* Darken, obscure, (*lit.* & *fig.*). Now chiefly *Sc.* & *literary*. ME.

murky /'mə:ki/ *a.* Also **mirky**. ME. [f. MURK *n.*[1] + -Y[1].] 1 Dark, gloomy; obscured by fog, dense vapour, etc.; grimy; not clear to the sight, indistinct, dim. ME. 2 *fig.* Sinister, suspiciously obscure; morally bad; not easy to understand; indistinct; confused. M19.

1 SIR W. SCOTT The path was altogether indiscernible in the murky darkness which surrounded them. K. LINES It was murky that night, a mist squatting upon the battlefield. V. S. NAIPAUL His greenhouse . . was empty, its glass murky with dust and rain. 2 DICKENS As through the narrow crevice of one good deed in a murky life of guilt. *Times* A singularly murky interlude has now ended. D. DELILLO Relatives were a sensitive issue, part of the murky and complex past. J. WILCOX This was where . . memory failed him, or at least where it became murky.

murkily *adv.* M19. **murkiness** *n.* E19.

murl /mə:l/ *v.i.* & *t. Sc.* & *north.* Also **mirl**. L15. [Origin unkn.] Crumble; (cause to) decay.

murly /'mə:li/ *a. rare.* E17. [f. prec. + -Y[1].] Of earth: crumbly, friable.

Murmi /'mə:mi/ *n.* & *a.* E19. [Prob. f. Tibetan, lit. 'people of the frontier', f. *mur* at the frontier + *mi* man.] A *n.* Pl. **-s**, same. 1 = TAMANG *n.* 1. E19. 2 = TAMANG *n.* 2. L19. B *attrib.* or as *adj.* = TAMANG *a.* E20.

murmur /'mə:mə/ *n.* LME. [(O)Fr. *murmure* or L *murmur* rel. to *murmurare*: see next.] 1a A subdued continuous sound, as made by waves, a stream, etc. LME. b *Med.* A (normal or abnormal) rushing sound heard over the heart, blood-vessels, or other organ during auscultation. M19. c A condition in which the heart produces or is apt to produce such a sound. *colloq.* E20. 2 A subdued expression of discontent or anger; a muttered or indistinct complaint. Formerly also, discontent or anger expressed in a subdued or indistinct way. LME. †3 Rumour. E16–M18. 4 A softly spoken word or sentence; subdued or nearly inarticulate speech. L17.

1a E. BOWEN The continuous murmur inside the whorls of a shell. F. WYNDHAM The continual murmur of moving water around and below me. 2 W. STUBBS The murmurs of the people reached the king in Normandy. B. CHATWIN People . . wouldn't raise a murmur against the Party or State. **without a murmur** without protest or complaint. 3 SHAKES. *Twel. N.* 'Twas fresh in murmur . . That he did seek the love of fair Olivia. 4 GOLDSMITH What billing, exchanging stolen glances, and broken murmurs?

Comb.: **murmur diphthong** *Phonet.* a diphthong ending with a glide or semivowel; **murmur vowel** *Phonet.* a glide or semivowel, a schwa.

murmurish *a.* (*rare*) somewhat like a murmur M19. **murmurous** *a.* (*a*) characterized by a murmur or murmurs, full of murmurs; †(*b*) complaining: L15. **murmurously** *adv.* M19. **murmurousness** *n.* E20.

murmur /'mə:mə/ *v.* ME. [(O)Fr. *murmurer* f. L *murmurare* corresp. to Gk *mormurein*, Skt *marmara* rustling (n. & adj.), (with variation) OHG *murmurōn*, *-ulōn* (G *murmeln*), Du. *murmelen* babble.] 1 *v.i.* Complain in low tones; give vent to a muttered or indistinct complaint; grumble (*at*, *against*). ME. 2 *v.i.* Make, produce, or emit a subdued continuous sound. LME. 3 *v.t.* Complain or grumble about, criticize the actions of; accuse. *Sc.* Long *rare*. L15. 4 *v.i.* & *t.* Utter (sounds, words) in a low voice and indistinctly. E16.

1 GOLDSMITH Those veteran legions . . began to murmur, for not having received the rewards which they had expected. 2 I. MURDOCH The waterfall distinctly murmured. 4 SCOTT FITZGERALD The butler . . murmured something close to Tom's ear. V. WOOLF 'Kreemo,' murmured Mrs. Bletchley, like a sleep-walker. W. GOLDING The assembly murmured in subdued agreement.

murmurer *n.* a person who murmurs; *esp.* a person who complains about constituted authority: L15. **murmuring** *n.* the action of the vb; an instance of this, a subdued or indistinct expression of discontent or anger: LME. **murmuringly** *adv.* in a murmuring manner E17.

murmuration /mə:mjʊ'reɪʃ(ə)n/ *n.* LME. [Fr. f. L *murmuratio(n-)*, f. *murmurat-* pa. ppl stem of *murmurare* MURMUR *v.*: see -ATION.] 1 The action of murmuring; an instance of this, a murmur. Now chiefly *Sc.* & *literary*. LME. 2 A company of starlings. L15.

1 *Westminster Gazette* Plaints and murmurations . . for the grievances which they clamoured to have redressed. L. MACNEICE Murmuration of corn in the wind. 2 J. HEATH-STUBBS Scores of starlings, wheeling, . . the whole murmuration Turning like one bird.

¶In isolated use in sense 2 in L15, revived M20.

murnong *n.* var. of MURRNONG.

Murphy /'mə:fi/ *n.*[1] *joc.* & *colloq.* M18. [Alt.] = MORPHEUS.

murphy /'mə:fi/ *n.*[2] Also (esp. in senses 2, 3) **M-**. E19. [*Murphy*, an Ir. surname.] 1 A potato. *slang.* E19. 2 More fully *Murphy game*. A confidence trick in which the victim is duped by unfulfilled promises of money, sex, etc. *US slang.* M20. 3 *Murphy's law*, any of various aphoristic expressions of the apparent perverseness and unreasonableness of things. Also called *Sod's law*. *joc.* M20.

murphy /ˈməːfi/ *v.t. US slang.* Also **M-**. M20. [f. MURPHY *n.*²] Dupe or swindle by a confidence trick giving unfulfilled promises of money, sex, etc.

Murphy bed /ˈməːfɪ bɛd/ *n. phr. N. Amer.* E20. [f. *Murphy* (see below) + BED *n.*] Any of various types of folding bed, developed from an original design by the American manufacturer William Lawrence Murphy (1876–1959).

†murr *n.* LME–M18. [Perh. imit.] A severe form of catarrh; an attack of this.

murr /məː/ *v.i. obs.* exc. *dial.* M17. [Imit.] Make a harsh noise; *Sc.* purr.

murra /ˈmʌrə/ *n.* Now *rare.* Also **-rrha** L16. [L = Gk *morria.*] A substance, possibly fluorite, used in ancient Rome for making valuable vases, cups, etc.

murrain /ˈmʌrɪn/ *n.* & *a.* ME. [AN *moryn*, (O)Fr. *morine*, †*moraine*, f. stem of *mourir*, †*morir*, f. Proto-Romance alt. of L *mori* die.] **A** *n.* **1** (A) plague, (a) pestilence, *esp.* the potato blight during the Irish famine in the mid 19th cent. Formerly freq. in imprecations and exclamations. *arch.* ME. **2** An infectious disease of livestock; *spec.* babesiosis. LME. **†3** Flesh of animals killed by disease; dead flesh, carrion. LME–E17. **†4** Death, mortality, esp. by plague or pestilence. Also (*rare*), slaughter. LME–M17.

1 O. NASH A murrain on every bridesmaid and every usher!

†B *adj.* Ill-conditioned; contemptible; excessive. L16–E18.

murrained *a.* killed by murrain; infected with murrain: E19.

murram /ˈmʌrəm/ *n.* E20. [Afr. name.] A hard dry lateritic soil found in tropical Africa and used locally as road metal.

Murray /ˈmʌri/ *n.*¹ M19. [John *Murray* (1808–92), Brit. publisher.] Any of a series of guidebooks or railway timetables published by John Murray or his successors.

Murray /ˈmʌri/ *n.*² L19. [A river and large river-system of SE Australia.] **1** Used *attrib.* to designate plants or animals associated with the region of the Murray river-system. L19. **2** Med. *Murray Valley encephalitis, fever*, a severe form of epidemic encephalitis caused by a mosquito-borne virus. M20.

1 **Murray cod** a large carnivorous serranid food fish, *Maccullochella macquariensis*. **Murray lily** the Darling lily, *Crinum flaccidum*. **Murray pine** any of several cypress pines, esp. (*a*) *Callitris preissii* subsp. *murrayensis*; (*b*) the white pine, *C. columellaris*.

murre /məː/ *n.* Now chiefly *N. Amer.* L16. [Origin unkn.] A guillemot, an auk.

common murre *N. Amer.* the common guillemot, *Uria aalge*. **thick-billed murre** *N. Amer.* Brünnich's guillemot, *U. lomvia*.

murrelet /ˈməːlɪt/ *n.* L19. [f. prec. + -LET.] Any of several small auks of the N. Pacific of the genera *Brachyramphus* and *Synthliboramphus*.

murrey /ˈmʌri/ *n.* & *a. arch.* ME. [OFr. *moré* adj. & n., *morée* n., f. med.L *moratus, morata*, f. L *morum* mulberry: see -Y⁵.] **A** *n.* The colour of a mulberry, a purple-red, (also *murrey colour*). Also, cloth of this colour. ME. **B** *adj.* Of the colour of a mulberry, purple-red. ME.

murrha *n.* var. of MURRA.

murrhine /ˈmʌrɪn, -rʌɪn/ *a.* & *n.* L16. [L *murr(h)inus*, f. as MURRA: see -INE¹.] **A** *adj.* Made of or pertaining to murra. L16.

murrhine glass modern delicate glassware from the East with coloured metal particles embedded in it.

B *n.* A murrhine vase. L18.

murrnong /ˈməːnɒŋ/ *n. Austral.* Also **murnong** & other vars. M19. [Aborig., lit. 'fingers of a hand'.] A yellow-flowered plant similar to a dandelion, *Microseris scapigera*, of the composite family, with clusters of small tuberous roots, formerly eaten by Aborigines.

murther *n.*, *v.*, **murtherer** *n.*, **murtherous** *a.* see MURDER *n.* etc.

muru /ˈmuːruː/ *n.* M19. [Maori.] *NZ Hist.* Raiding and plundering by Maoris, esp. in reprisal for an offence.

murumuru /ˌmuːruːˈmuːruː, ˈmuːruːˌmuːruː/ *n.* M19. [Port. f. Carib *murumurú*.] An Amazonian palm, *Astrocaryum murumuru*, whose stem is covered with black spines.

murus gallicus /mjʊərəs ˈgalɪkəs/ *n. phr.* Pl. ***-ri -ci*** /-riː -kiː/. M20. [L, f. *murus* wall + *gallicus* Gallic.] *Archaeol.* A type of late Iron Age Celtic fort having stone walls bound by horizontally placed timber frames.

Murut /ˈmuːrət/ *n.* M19. [Bajau *belud* hill.] **A** *n.* Pl. same, **-s**. A member of a Dyak people originally inhabiting the hill country in the interior of N. Borneo, although now more widely spread; the language of this people. M19. **B** *attrib.* or as *adj.* Of or pertaining to the Murut or their language. M20.

musa /ˈmjuːzə/ *n.*¹ Pl. **musae** /ˈmjuːziː/, **musas**. L16. [mod.L (see below), f. Arab. *mawz(a).*] Orig., a banana plant. Now, any plant of the genus *Musa* (family Musaceae), which includes the tropical plantain, *M. paradisiaca*, and bananas.

muˈsaceous *a.* of or pertaining to the family Musaceae M19.

musa /ˈmjuːzə/ *n.*² Also **MUSA**. M20. [Acronym, f. *m*ultiple *u*nit *s*teerable *a*ntenna.] A radio aerial consisting of an array of elements giving a beam which can be varied in direction by varying the phase relations between the elements.

musae *n.pl.* see MUSA *n.*¹

†musaeum *n.* var. of MUSEUM.

musang /mjʊˈsaŋ/ *n.* L18. [Malay = wild cat.] A palm civet of the Asian genus *Paradoxurus*; esp. the common palm civet or toddy cat, *P. hermaphroditus*.

Musca /ˈmʌskə/ *n.* L18. [L *musca* fly.] (The name of) a small constellation of the southern hemisphere, lying in the Milky Way between the Southern Cross and the South Pole; the Fly.

muscadel *n.* var. of MUSCATEL.

Muscadet /ˈmʌskədeɪ, ˈmʊsk-/ *n.* E20. [Fr., f. *muscade* nutmeg, f. *musc* MUSK *n.*: see -ET¹.] (A) white wine made in the Loire valley near Nantes, France; a drink of this; the variety of grape from which this wine is made.

muscadin /myskadɛ̃ (*pl. same*); ˈmʊskədɪn, ˈmʌsk-/ *n.* L18. [Fr., lit. 'musk-comfit', a sweet.] *Hist.* A (Parisian) dandy; *contempt.* a member of a moderate party in the early years of the French Revolution, composed chiefly of young men of the upper middle class.

muscadine /ˈmʌskədɪn, -ʌɪn/ *n.* M16. [Prob. alt. of *muscadel*, MUSCATEL: see -INE⁴.] **1** In full *muscadine wine*. = MUSCATEL 1. *obs.* exc. *Hist.* M16. **2** In full *muscadine grape*. = MUSCAT 2. Also, (the musky-flavoured grape of) a wild N. American vine, *Vitis rotundifolia*. L16.

muscae /ˈmʌsiː/ *n.pl.* M18. [L, pl. of *musca* fly.] Chiefly *Med.* In full *muscae volitantes* /vɒlɪˈtantiːz/ [pres. pple of *volitare* fly about]. Specks which appear to float before the eyes, freq. due to particles in the vitreous humour of the eye.

muscardine /mʌˈskɑːdiːn/ *n.* M19. [Fr. (f. the fungus's resemblance to the sweet confection *musca(r)din*: see MUSCADIN).] Any of various fungal diseases of insects (esp. silkworms); a fungus causing any of these.

muscardined *a.* affected with muscardine L19.

muscari /mʌˈskɑːri, -ˈskɛːri/ *n.* L16. [mod.L (see below), perh. repr. dim. of Gk *moskos* musk, from the musky smell of the flowers.] Any of various small bulbous plants of the genus *Muscari*, of the lily family; *spec.* = *grape* HYACINTH.

muscarine /ˈmʌskəriːn, -ɪn/ *n.* Also **-in** /-ɪn/. L19. [f. mod.L *muscaria* specific epithet of fly agaric (see below), f. L *muscarius*, f. *musca* fly: see -INE⁵, -IN¹.] *Biochem.* A poisonous alkaloid, $C_9H_{21}NO_3$, found in fly agaric, *Amanita muscaria*, and other fungi.

muscarinic /mʌskəˈrɪnɪk/ *a.* resembling muscarine or its physiological actions; (of a receptor) capable of responding to muscarine: M20.

muscat /ˈmʌskat/ *n.* M16. [(O)Fr. f. Prov. (= It. MOSCATO), f. *musc* MUSK *n.*: see -AT¹.] **1** In full *muscat wine*. = MUSCATEL 1. M16. **2** In full *muscat grape*. Any of several varieties of grape with a musky taste or smell; a vine bearing a variety of such a grape. M17. **†3** A kind of peach or pear with a musky taste or smell. M17–M18.

muscatel /mʌskəˈtɛl/ *n.* Also **-del** /-dɛl/. LME. [OFr. *muscadel*, *-tel* (= It. MOSCATELLO) f. Prov. dim. of *muscat*: see prec., -EL².] **1** (A) strong sweet wine made from the muscat or similar grape; a drink of this. LME. **2** In full *muscatel grape*. = MUSCAT 2. E16. **†3** A variety of pear with a musky taste or smell. M16–M18. **4** In full *muscatel raisin*. A raisin from the muscatel grape. Usu. in *pl.* M17.

Muschelkalk /ˈmʊʃ(ə)lkalk/ *n.* M19. [G, lit. 'shelly limestone', f. *Muschel* MUSSEL + *Kalk* CHALK *n.*] *Geol.* (The limestone of) the Middle Triassic in Europe, esp. Germany.

muscicapine /mʌˈsɪkəpʌɪn/ *a.* L19. [f. mod.L *Muscicapa* (see below), f. L *musca* fly + *capere* catch: see -INE¹.] *Ornith.* Of, pertaining to, or designating the family Muscicapidae or the genus *Muscicapa* of Old World flycatchers.

muscicole /ˈmʌsɪkəʊl/ *a.* & *n.* L19. [f. L *muscus* moss + -I- + -COLE.] *Ecol.* **A** *adj.* Living among or in association with mosses. L19. **B** *n.* A muscicole organism. M20.

muˈscicolous *a.* = MUSCICOLE *a.* M19.

muscid /ˈmʌsɪd/ *a.* & *n.* L19. [mod.L *Muscidae* (see below), f. L *musca* fly: see -ID³.] **A** *adj.* Of, pertaining to, or designating the dipteran family Muscidae, which includes houseflies. L19. **B** *n.* A fly of this family. L19.

muscimol /ˈmʌskɪmɒl/ *n.* M20. [f. as MUSCARINE + IM(INE + -OL.] *Biochem.* A narcotic and hallucinogenic alkaloid found in fly agaric, *Amanita muscaria*, and other fungi; 3-hydroxy-5-aminomethylisoxazole, $C_4H_6N_2O_2$.

muscle /ˈmʌs(ə)l/ *n.*¹ Also **†-cule**. LME. [Fr. f. L *musculus*, f. *mus* mouse (from the fancied mouselike form of some muscles): see -CULE.] **1** *Anat.* & *Physiol.* Any of the fibrous bands or bundles of contractile tissue which act to produce movement in or maintain the position of parts of the human or animal body. LME. **2** The part of the body consisting of muscles; muscular tissue; the substance of which muscles are composed. L18. **3** (Muscular) power, strength; influence; force, violence; intimidation; manpower to exert muscular power; *slang* a person employed to use or threaten violence. E19.

1 *adductor muscle, ciliary muscle, flexor muscle, pectoral muscle*, etc. *flex one's muscles*: see FLEX *v.* 1. **not move a muscle** be perfectly motionless. 2 SKELETAL *muscle*. *smooth muscle*: see SMOOTH *a.* & *adv.* STRIATED *muscle*. STRIPED *muscle*. 3 S. BRILL The Fund had used its financial muscle for investments that were radically different. B. CALLAGHAN There was heavy-jowled Lambchops . . who hired himself out as muscle to the after-hours clubs.

Comb.: **muscle-bound** *a.* having the muscles stiff and enlarged, esp. as a result of too much exercise or training; lacking flexibility; **muscle car** *N. Amer. slang* a powerful car, *spec.* = *hot rod* (a) s.v. HOT *a.*; **muscle cell** each of the elongated contractile cells, containing ordered actin and myosin filaments, of which muscular tissue is composed; **muscle current** the flow of electrical current which occurs on connecting different points of a muscle; **muscle curve** a curve indicating amount of muscular contraction as recorded by a myograph; **muscle fibre** = *muscle cell* above; **muscle-flexing** *a.* demonstrating aggression or strength; **muscle force** the force or power of human agency; **muscle-man** *colloq.* (*a*) a person who employs or threatens violence on behalf of a professional criminal; (*b*) a person with highly developed muscles; **muscle power** = sense 3 above; **muscle pull** *N. Amer.* a pulled muscle; **muscle scar** a marking on a bone, shell, etc., indicating a point of attachment of a muscle; **muscle sense** kinaesthetic sense; **muscle shirt** *N. Amer.* a man's tight-fitting T-shirt; **muscle spindle** any of numerous small sensory organs within muscle which respond to extension and contraction of the muscle and aid coordination.

muscled *a.* endowed with muscle (chiefly w. qualifying adj. or adv., as *full-muscled, well-muscled,* etc.) M17. **muscleless** /-l-l-/ *a.* M19. **muscling** *n.* muscular structure or development, muscles, formerly *spec.* as delineated or represented in art E18. **muscly** *a.* composed of muscle; exhibiting great muscular development: L16.

muscle *n.*[2] see MUSSEL *n.*

muscle /ˈmʌs(ə)l/ *v.* E20. [f. MUSCLE *n.*[1]] 1 *v.t.* Move by the exercise of (muscular) power. *US dial.* & *colloq.* E20. 2 *v.t.* Coerce by violence or by economic or political pressure. *slang.* E20. 3 *v.i.* Foll. by *in*: intrude into the business or activities of another or others by force or fraud; enter forcibly or uninvited, (foll. by *on*). *slang.* E20. 4 *v.i.* Make one's way by the exercise of (muscular) power. M20.

1 J. DICKEY We muscled the canoe laboriously cross-river to land. 2 *New Republic* U.S. companies . . don't usually use pricing to muscle their competitors. 3 E. WAUGH You're muscling in on my territory. N. MARSH To muscle in where I'm not wanted. L. CODY She's always muscling in on his conversations.

muscology /mʌˈskɒlədʒi/ *n.* M19. [f. L *muscus* moss + -OLOGY.] The branch of biology that deals with bryophytes, esp. mosses; the mosses or bryophytes of a district.

muscologist *n.* E19.

muscose /ˈmʌskəʊs/ *a. rare.* E18. [L *muscosus*, f. *muscus* moss: see -OSE[1].] Mosslike.

muscous /ˈmʌskəs/ *a. rare.* M17. [f. as prec. + -OUS.] Mossy.

muscovado /mʌskəˈvɑːdəʊ/ *n.* Pl. **-os.** E17. [Port. *mascabado* (Sp. *menoscabado*) use as n. (sc. *açúcar*, Sp. *azúcar* sugar) of pa. pple of *mascabar* make badly: see -ADO.] More fully *muscovado sugar.* Raw or unrefined sugar obtained from the juice of the sugar cane by evaporation and draining off the molasses; an example or type of this.

Muscovite /ˈmʌskəvʌɪt/ *n.*[1] & *a.* M16. [mod.L *Muscovita*, f. *Muscovia*: see MUSCOVY, -ITE[1].] A *n.* A native or inhabitant of Moscow on the central Asian plain, now the capital of Russia, formerly of the principality of Muscovy; *Hist.* a native or inhabitant of Muscovy; *arch.* a Russian. M16. B *adj.* Of or pertaining to Moscow or (*Hist.*) Muscovy; *arch.* Russian. E17.

muscovite /ˈmʌskəvʌɪt/ *n.*[2] M19. [f. *Muscovy glass* (see next) + -ITE[1].] *Min.* A colourless, silver-grey, or yellowish potassium-containing mica which is a component of many types of rock and is used esp. in electrical insulation. Also called *common mica, white mica.*

muscoviti'zation *n.* conversion into muscovite E20. **muscovitized** *a.* converted into muscovite M20.

Muscovy /ˈmʌskəvi/ *n.* Also **m-.** L16. [Fr. †*Muscovie* (now *Mos-*) f. mod.L *Moscovia*, f. Russ. *Moskva* Moscow: see -Y[3]. Sense 2 by assoc. w. MUSK *n.*] 1 *Muscovy glass,* †*talc,* common mica, muscovite. L16. 2 In full *Muscovy duck.* A large duck, *Cairina moschata*, native to central and S. America but widely domesticated, with variable black or white plumage and (in the male) a red caruncle on the bill and face (also called *musk duck*). Also = *musk duck* (b) s.v. MUSK *n.* M17.

muscular /ˈmʌskjʊlə/ *a.* L17. [f. MUSCULOUS by substitution of -AR[1].] 1 Of or pertaining to muscle or the muscles; (of a disease etc.) affecting the muscles. L17. 2 Composed of, containing, or of the nature of muscle. Also, forming a constituent of muscle. L17. 3 Of a body, a limb, etc.: characterized by muscle, having well-developed muscles. M18.

3 *fig.*: LYTTON No mind becomes muscular without rude and early exercise.

Special collocations: **muscular Christian** a person believing in or living a life of muscular Christianity. **muscular Christianity** Christian life characterized by cheerful physical activity or robust good works, *spec.* as described in the writings of Charles Kingsley; Christianity without asceticism. *muscular* DYSTROPHY. **muscular feeling, muscular sensation, muscular sense** = *muscle sense* s.v. MUSCLE *n.*[1] **muscular stomach** the gizzard of a bird etc.

muscu'larity *n.* the quality or state of being muscular; the fact of consisting of muscle or having well-developed muscles; muscular strength or vigour: L17. **muscularize** *v.i.* & *t.* become or make muscular M19. **muscularly** *adv.* M19.

muscularis /mʌskjʊˈlɑːrɪs/ *n.* M19. [mod.L, use as n. (perh. sc. *lamina* layer) of *muscularis*, f. L *musculus* MUSCLE *n.*[1] + *-aris* -ARY[2].] *Anat.* A thin layer of smooth muscle fibres in various organs, as the stomach, the ureter; *spec.* (in full *muscularis mucosae* /mjuːˈkəʊsiː/), that associated with a mucous membrane, esp. in the gut.

musculation /mʌskjʊˈleɪʃ(ə)n/ *n. rare.* M19. [Fr., f. L *musculus* MUSCLE *n.*[1]: see -ATION.] 1 The function of muscular movement. M19. 2 The disposition or arrangement of muscles. L19.

musculature /ˈmʌskjʊlətʃə/ *n.* L19. [Fr., f. L *musculus* MUSCLE *n.*[1] + *-atus* -ATE[2]: see -URE.] (The arrangement of) the muscular system of a body; the arrangement of muscles in an organ or limb.

†**muscule** *n.* var. of MUSCLE *n.*[1]

†**musculite** *n.* Also (earlier) in mod.L form **-ites.** L17–E19. [mod.L *musculites*, f. *musculus* MUSSEL *n.*: see -ITE[1].] *Palaeont.* A fossil mussel shell.

musculo- /ˈmʌskjʊləʊ/ *comb. form.* [L, f. *musculus* MUSCLE *n.*[1]: see -O-.] Chiefly *Anat.* & *Physiol.* Forming adjs. w. the senses 'pertaining to or composed of muscle and —', 'pertaining to the muscular system and —', as *musculo-membranous, musculoskeletal, musculotendinous,* etc.

musculo'fascial *a.* of or pertaining to a muscle and its associated fasciae M20.

†**musculous** *a.* LME. [f. (O)Fr. *musculeux* or L *musculosus*, f. *musculus* MUSCLE *n.*[1]: see -ULOUS.] 1 = MUSCULAR 2. LME–M18. 2 = MUSCULAR 3. E17–L18. 3 = MUSCULAR 1. M17–M18.

muse /mjuːz/ *n.*[1] Also (esp. in sense 1) **M-.** LME. [(O)Fr., or L *musa* f. Gk *mousa.*] 1 *Class. Mythol.* Each of nine (occas. more) goddesses, the daughters of Zeus and Mnemosyne (Memory), regarded as the inspirers of learning and the arts, esp. of poetry and music; a representation of one of the Muses, usu. as a beautiful young woman. Usu. in *pl.* LME. b *The* Muse appropriate to the work in question (as if only one were recognized), *the* source of poetic inspiration. *poet.* E17. 2 The inspiring goddess or adored woman of a particular poet; a poet's particular genius, the character of a particular poet's style. LME. †3 A poem, a song. LME–E16. 4 A person inspired by a Muse, a poet. E17. 5 A type of poetry or music; *the Muse,* poetry; *the Muses,* the liberal arts. *literary.* L17.

2 L. GORDON Emily replaced Vivienne as Eliot's muse in *Ash Wednesday.*

Phrases: **tenth Muse** a muse of inspiration imagined as added to the nine of classical mythology.

muse /mjuːz/ *n.*[2] *arch.* L15. [f. MUSE *v.*[2]] An act or (formerly) the action of musing; a state or fit of abstraction.

muse *n.*[3] & *v.*[1] var. of MEUSE.

muse /mjuːz/ *v.*[2] Now *literary.* ME. [(O)Fr. *muser* †meditate, waste time, perh. ult. f. med.L *musum* muzzle.] I *v.i.* 1 Be absorbed in thought; meditate continuously in silence; ponder. ME. 2 Be affected with astonishment or surprise; wonder, marvel, (*at*). Now *poet. rare.* ME. 3 Gaze meditatively; look thoughtfully or intently. LME. †4 Murmur; grumble, complain. LME–L16.

1 L. M. MONTGOMERY In school I can look at her and muse over days departed. R. MACAULAY She mused, her chin resting on one strong hand. P. FITZGERALD He appeared to be musing on what had passed between them. 2 TENNYSON Then came the fine Gawain and wonder'd at her, And Lancelot later came and mused at her. 3 J. H. NEWMAN He began to eye and muse upon the great bishop. K. TYNAN He hopes to be amused by his bully companions, but the eyes constantly muse beyond them.

II *v.t.* 5 Ponder over, reflect on; contemplate, meditate; think to oneself; ask oneself meditatively (*how, what,* etc.); say or murmur meditatively. Now only w. cl. or direct speech as obj. LME. †6 Marvel at (a thing, *how* etc.); be surprised *that.* E16–M17.

5 M. ARNOLD Ah me, I muse what this young fox may mean! R. K. NARAYAN Ramani stood over him, musing indignantly: 'Fast asleep at eight o'clock.' D. WELCH 'I wonder what sort of letters you write?' she mused.

muser *n.* LME. **musing** *n.* (*a*) the action of the vb; thoughtful abstraction; (*b*) a fit of thoughtful abstraction, a meditation: ME. **musingly** *adv.* in a musing manner E17.

†**musea** *n.pl.* see MUSEUM.

museau /myzo/ *n.* Pl. ***-eaux*** /-o/. E19. [Fr. colloq., lit. 'muzzle, snout'.] A person's face.

musée /myze (*pl. same*), ˈmjuːzeɪ/ *n.* M17. [Fr. f. as MUSEUM.] a (French) museum.

musée imaginaire /imaʒinɛːr, ɪmadʒɪˈnɛː/ an imaginary collection of all the works of human artifice.

museful /ˈmjuːzfʊl, -f(ə)l/ *a. arch.* E17. [f. MUSE *n.*[2] + -FUL.] Absorbed in thought; thoughtful, pensive.

musefully *adv.* L19.

museless /ˈmjuːzlɪs/ *a. literary.* M17. [f. MUSE *n.*[1] + -LESS, after Gk *amousos.*] Without learning; uncultured. Also, uninspired.

musellim /mʊˈsɛlɪm/ *n.*. L17. [Turk. *mütesellim* deputy governor, tax officer f. Arab. *mutasallim* act. pple of *tasallama* receive.] *Hist.* A Turkish officer, the lieutenant of a pasha.

museography /mjuːzɪˈɒɡrəfi/ *n.* E20. [f. MUSEUM: see -OGRAPHY.] The systematic description of the contents of museums. Also = MUSEOLOGY.

museographer *n.* = MUSEOGRAPHIST L19. **museo'graphical** *a.* M20. **museographist** *n.* L18.

museology /mjuːzɪˈɒlədʒi/ *n.* L19. [f. MUSEUM: see -OLOGY.] The science or practice of organizing and managing museums.

museo'logical *a.* M20. **museologist** *n.* L19.

muset /ˈmjuːzɪt/ *n.* Long *obs.* exc. *dial.* L16. [OFr. *mucette, muss-* hiding place, dim. of *muce, musse* MEUSE *n.*: see -ET[1].] = MEUSE *n.* 1, 2.

musette /mjuːˈzɛt/ *n.* LME. [(O)Fr., dim. of *muse* bagpipe: see -ETTE.] 1 A kind of small bagpipe, *esp.* a small French bagpipe of the 18th cent. with a soft tone. LME. 2 A soft pastoral air imitating the sound of the musette; a dance performed to such music. E18. 3 A reed-stop in an organ producing a soft tone resembling that of the musette. E19. 4 A small and simple variety of oboe without a reed-cap. L19. 5 More fully *musette bag.* A type of lightweight knapsack used esp. by the military and by racing cyclists. E20.

museum /mjuːˈzɪəm/ *n.* Also †**musaeum.** Pl. **-eums,** †**-ea.** E17. [L = library, study f. Gk *mouseion* seat of the Muses, use as n. of neut. of *mouseios*, f. *mousa* MUSE *n.*[1]] 1 a *Ancient Hist.* A university building, *spec.* (**M-**) that erected at Alexandria by Ptolemy Soter. E17. †b *gen.* A building or apartment dedicated to the pursuit of learning or the arts; a scholar's study. M17–M18. 2 A building or portion of a building used for the storing, preservation, and exhibition of objects considered to be of lasting value or interest, as objects illustrative of antiquities, natural history, fine and industrial art, etc.; an institution responsible for such a building or collection. Also, a collection of objects in such a building. M17. 3 *transf.* & *fig.* A thing resembling a museum, a repository of (esp. historical) information; a collection. M18.

2 *Daily Telegraph* The Reading Room of the British Museum . ., that immense rotunda. C. FRONDEL Curator of Minerals and Gems in the American Museum of Natural History. *Village Voice* The Museum of Modern Art has been running a Will Rogers Retrospective. U. LE GUIN The palace, preserved as a museum of the ancient times of royalty. *New Society* One of those painted wagons . . that gypsies donate to folk museums. 3 THACKERAY Miss Blanche . . had quite a little museum of locks of hair in her treasure-chest. G. S. FRASER He served . . as a kind of living museum of the older Scots folk-song tradition.

Comb.: **museum piece** an object suitable for exhibition in a museum; *derog.* an old-fashioned or quaint person, machine, etc.

museumish *a.* (*colloq.*) resembling a museum or exhibits in a museum E20.

mush /mʌʃ/ *n.*[1] In sense 3 also **moosh** /mʊʃ, muːʃ/. L17. [App. var. of MASH *n.*[1]] 1 Porridge; *spec.* maize porridge, maize meal boiled in water until it thickens (freq. in *mush and milk*). Chiefly *N. Amer.* L17. 2 *gen.* A soft pulpy or formless mass; soft pulp; slush. Also (*dial.*), something reduced to or resembling a mass of powder. E19. b Feeble sentimentality, (sentimental) nonsense. M19. 3 The mouth, the face. *slang.* M19. 4 *Radio.* Noise or distortion in the form of a hissing or rushing sound, esp. as a result of interference between transmitters. E20. 5 The foam produced when a wave breaks. *Surfing slang.* M20.

2 W. H. AUDEN My mind works abominably slowly, in a vague mush of tepid ideas. F. HOYLE The ice was hard-frozen not a mere pile of mush. J. DAVIS Oh no! My legs are turning to jelly! My mind is turning to mush. P. D. JAMES She trudged through the mush of fallen leaves.

Comb.: **mush-head** *slang* a person lacking in firmness, a feebly sentimental person; **mush ice** partly frozen water, ice mixed with water.

mush /mʌʃ/ *n.*[2] *slang.* E19. [Abbrev. of MUSHROOM *n.*] 1 An umbrella. Chiefly in *mush-faker*, = *mushroom-faker* s.v. MUSHROOM *n. arch.* E19. 2 An owner-driver of a cab; a cab-driver who owns one, two, or three cabs. L19.

mush /mʌʃ/ *n.*[3] *N. Amer.* E20. [f. MUSH *v.*[2]] A journey made through snow with a dog-sledge.

mush /mʌʃ, mʊʃ/ *n.*[4] *Mil. slang.* Also **moosh** /mʊʃ, muːʃ/. E20. [Perh. f. MUSH *v.*[1]] A guardroom, a cell; a military prison.

mush /mʌʃ, mʊʃ/ *n.*[5] *slang.* Also **moosh** /mʊʃ, muːʃ/. M20. [Origin uncertain: perh. a use of MUSH *n.*[1] 3.] A man, a fellow. Also used as a form of address.

mush /mʌʃ/ *n.*[6] *slang.* M20. [Contr.] = MOUSTACHE.

mush /mʌʃ/ *v.*[1] L18. [App. orig. var. of MASH *v.*[2] Later directly f. MUSH *n.*[1]] 1 *v.t.* & *i.* Crush, pulverize, crumble; (now usu.) reduce to soft pulp. Chiefly *dial.* L18. 2 *v.i.* Of an aircraft: fly sluggishly, almost stalling or stalling repeatedly; lose or maintain altitude when a gain is expected. M20. 3 *v.i.* Sink *in* or *into* a soft surface. *colloq.* M20. 4 *v.t.* & *i.* Kiss, esp. in public. *slang.* M20.

mush /mʌʃ/ *v.*[2] *N. Amer.* M19. [Alt. of Fr. *marchez* (imper.) or *marchons* (3rd person pl. subjunct.), forms of *marcher* MARCH *v.*[2]] 1 *v.i.* Travel through snow with a dog-sledge; (of dogs) pull a sledge. M19. 2 *v.i.* In *imper.* Keep moving! go *on*! (a command to dogs pulling a sledge). L19. 3 *v.i.* Travel on foot through snow or ice. L19. 4 *v.t.* Urge on or drive (dogs) through snow. E20. 5 *v.t.* Transport by dog-sledge. M20.

musha /ˈmʌʃə/ *int. Anglo-Ir.* M19. [Ir. *muise* var. of *maiseadh*, i.e. *má* if, *is* is, *eadh* it, or alt. of *Muire* Mary (i.e. the Virgin Mary): cf. WISHA.] Expr. surprise or disbelief.

musher /ˈmʌʃə/ *n.*[1] *slang.* L19. [f. MUSH *n.*[2] + -ER[1].] = MUSH *n.*[2] 2.

musher /ˈmʌʃə/ *n.*[2] *N. Amer.* L19. [f. MUSH *v.*[2] + -ER[1].] A person who travels through snow on foot; a driver of a dog-sledge.

mushie /ˈmʌʃi/ *n. Austral. colloq.* Also **mushy**. M20. [Abbrev.: see -IE.] A mushroom.

mushla(w) *ns.* vars. of MISHLA.

mushrat /ˈmʌʃrat/ *n. N. Amer.* L19. [f. as MUSKRAT.] = MUSKRAT.

mushroom /ˈmʌʃruːm, -rʊm/ *n.* & *a.* Also **†-rump**. LME. [(O)Fr. MOUSSERON f. late L *mussirio(n-)*.] A *n.* 1 Orig., any fungus having a fleshy fruiting body, usu. rounded or caplike, on a stalk growing from the ground, freq. regarded as the type of rapid growth. Now usu., either of two edible agarics, *Agaricus campestris* (in full *field mushroom*), and *A. bisporus*, which is cultivated for eating; *gen.* any (esp. edible) fungus resembling these in general appearance. Cf. TOADSTOOL *n.* 1. LME. 2 *fig.* A person or family that has suddenly sprung into notice; an upstart; a city, an institution, etc., that is of sudden growth. L16. †b A contemptible person. L16–M18. 3 *transf.* A thing shaped like a mushroom; *spec.* (*a*) *arch. slang* an umbrella; (*b*) *arch. colloq.* = *mushroom hat* below; (*c*) *Archit.* a reinforced concrete pillar broadening out towards the top, with reinforcing rods passing into a slab forming part of the floor above; (*d*) a cloud (of smoke, fire, etc.) that spreads upwards and outwards; (*e*) a mushroom-shaped implement over which material is stretched in darning, embroidery, etc. E18. 4 A pale pinkish- or greyish-brown colour resembling that of a mushroom. L19.

1 *horse mushroom, parasol mushroom, St George's mushroom*, etc. 2 C. MARLOWE A night growne mushrump, Such a one as my Lord of Cornewall is. *Twentieth Century* The radio industry, as much a mushroom as any ingredient of the Industrial Revolution. S. BRETT He was one of those showbiz mushrooms who spring up overnight.

B *attrib.* or as *adj.* Resembling a mushroom; *spec.* (*a*) of rapid growth; of short duration; *arch.* upstart; (*b*) mushroom-coloured, pale pinkish- or greyish-brown. L16.

Special collocations & *comb.*: **mushroom anchor** a mooring-anchor having a saucer-shaped head on a central shaft. **mushroom city**: that has sprung up rapidly. **mushroom cloud** a cloud of smoke shaped like a mushroom, *spec.* such as forms above a nuclear explosion. **mushroom colour** = sense A.4 above. **mushroom-coloured** *a.* of mushroom colour. **mushroom-coral** any of various stony corals which resemble mushrooms or other fungi. **mushroom-faker** *arch. slang* an itinerant umbrella-mender. **mushroom growth** rapid growth like that of a mushroom; a thing that has grown up rapidly. **mushroom hat** a low-crowned circular hat, *esp.* such a lady's hat with a down-curving brim. *mushroom loaf*: see LOAF *n.*[1] **mushroom-ring** a fairy-ring. **mushroom spawn** *colloq.* the mycelium of a mushroom. **mushroom-stone** a (fossil) mushroom-coral. **mushroom town**: that has sprung up rapidly. **mushroom valve** a lift valve whose moving element somewhat resembles a mushroom in shape.

mushroomy *a.* (*colloq.*) resembling a mushroom M19.

mushroom /ˈmʌʃruːm/ *v.* M18. [f. the n.] I†1 *v.t.* Elevate (a person) in social position with great suddenness. *rare.* Only in M18. 2 *v.i.* Esp. of a bullet: expand and flatten like a mushroom. Occas. foll. by *out.* L19. 3 *v.i.* Rise like a mushroom; expand or spring up rapidly; increase rapidly. Also foll. by *up, out.* E20.

3 J. KOSINSKI A cloud of dust mushroomed above. S. KITZINGER Clubs mushroomed where swinging couples could go and find new partners. C. MCCULLOUGH Both the younger brothers had mushroomed in self-confidence. *Scotsman* Prices . . are mushrooming by more than 50 per cent a year.

II 4 *v.i.* Gather mushrooms. Chiefly as *mushrooming* vbl n. & ppl a. M19.

mushroomer *n.* a person who gathers mushrooms L19.

†mushrump *n.* & *a.* var. of MUSHROOM *n.* & *a.*

mushy *n.* var. of MUSHIE.

mushy /ˈmʌʃi/ *a. colloq.* M19. [f. MUSH *n.*[1] + -Y[1].] 1 Soft and slushy; pulpy; formless; lacking firmness or distinctiveness. M19. 2 Feebly sentimental, insipid. L19. 3 Of a wave: breaking slowly; foamy. *Surfing slang.* M20.

1 **mushy peas** cooked peas prepared in a semi-liquid state.

mushily *adv.* L19. **mushiness** *n.* L19.

music /ˈmjuːzɪk/ *n.* ME. [(O)Fr. *musique* f. L *musica* f. Gk *mousikē* use as n. (sc. *tekhnē* art) of fem. of *mousikos* of a Muse or the Muses, of the arts, f. *mousa* MUSE *n.*[1]: see -IC.] 1 The art or science of combining vocal or instrumental sounds with a view to beauty or coherence of form and expression of emotion. ME. 2a Melodic or harmonic vocal or instrumental sound; an example or kind of such sound. LME. b Pleasing sound produced by an agent or agency specified or understood, as the song of a bird, the murmur of running water, the cry of hounds on seeing the chase; something which it is a delight to hear; an example or kind of such sound. L16. c Melodic or harmonic vocal or instrumental sound as devised by a composer; musical composition. E17. 3 A piece of music composed or performed; a performance of music, a concert. Long *rare.* L16. 4 A company of musicians, a band. *obs.* exc. *Mil.*, now chiefly in *Master of the King's* or *Queen's Music*, (the title of) an officer appointed to supervise and conduct military music for the monarch. L16. 5 *collect.* & in †*pl.* Musical instruments. *obs.* exc. *dial.* E17. 6 The written or printed score of a musical composition; such scores collectively; the graphic representation of musical composition. M17.

2a R. INGALLS The music came from a portable phonograph. *New Yorker* An overextended . . sequence of procedures from traditional black and modern white musics. W. TREVOR The music of the accordion floated up to my window. *baroque music, classical music, country music, dance music, early music, incidental music, Indian music, light music, orchestral music, piano music, pop music, programme music, rock music, soul music, violin music, vocal music*, etc. b G. FLETCHER My love lay sleeping, where birdes musicke made. W. DAVENANT I shall now be kil'd, Even with the musick of her voice. *Hounds* Hounds hunted hard all day . . and the music was enjoyed by a large mounted field. 3 *Scrutiny* To compose *Pomp and Circumstance* and the other occasional musics that so alarm the purists. 6 E. TAYLOR Charles played the piano . . without music. *Listener* He plays the piano with panache, but cannot read music. *sheet music*: see SHEET *n.*[1]

Phrases: *absolute music*: see ABSOLUTE *a.* 5. *face the music*: see FACE *v.* 2b. **make (beautiful** or **sweet) music (together)** *slang* have sexual intercourse, have a sexual relationship. *music of the spheres*: see SPHERE *n.* 2. **music to one's ears** something very pleasant to hear. **music while you work** continuous light music played to workers, esp. in factories. *rough music*: see ROUGH *a. set to music*: see SET *v.*[1] 44. *sweet music*: see SWEET *a.* & *adv. Turkish music*: see TURKISH *a.*

Comb.: **music book** a book containing written or printed music scores; **music box** †(*a*) a barrel-organ; (*b*) *N. Amer.* = *musical box* s.v. MUSICAL *a.*; **music case** (*a*) *Printing* (chiefly *Hist.*) a case for a font of music type; (*b*) a case for sheet music; **music cassette** a tape cassette of pre-recorded music; abbrev. *MC*; **music centre** a stereophonic system combining disc-player, radio, and cassette tape recorder in a single unit, usu. with separate loudspeakers; **music drama** opera without formal arias etc. and governed by dramatic considerations; **music gallery** a gallery in a church or hall for the accommodation of musicians; **music-grinder** *arch.* an itinerant street musician; **music hall** a public hall or theatre used for musical performances, *spec.* for variety entertainment as singing, dancing, and novelty acts, of a type popular in the late 19th and early 20th cents.; the type of entertainment provided at such halls; **music-hallish, music-hally** *adjs.* suggestive of (a) music hall; **†music-house** (*a*) a room in a theatre etc. in which musicians sat to perform; (*b*) a public hall or room for musical performances; **music licence** a magistrates' licence to give vocal and instrumental entertainments in a public building or apartment; **music-paper** paper ruled for writing music on, manuscript paper; **music-roll** (*a*) a container for rolled-up sheet music; (*b*) a roll, usually of perforated paper, used in a player-piano or similar instrument; **music-room** a room in which music is performed; formerly *spec.*, a room at the side of a theatre-stage in which musicians sat to perform; **music-shell** any of various gastropods, esp. *Voluta musica*, characterized by lines and dots on the shell resembling written music; the shell of such a gastropod; **music stand** a rest or frame to support sheet music or a score; **music stool** a stool for a pianist etc., usu. with adjustable height; **music theatre** the combination of elements from music and drama in new forms distinct from traditional opera, esp. as designed for small casts; **music therapy** performing or listening to music as a form of therapy; **music type** *Printing* (chiefly *Hist.*) a font of type used for the typographic printing of music, as distinguished from printing from intaglio plates or lithographically; **music volute** = *music shell* above; **music-wire** steel wire such as is used for some stringed musical instruments.

musicless *a.* (*a*) lacking taste or ability in music; unmusical; (*b*) without music: E17.

music /ˈmjuːzɪk/ *v.* Infl. **-ck-, -c-.** E18. [f. the n.] 1 *v.t.* Influence by music; train in music. E18. 2 *v.i.* Produce music; entertain oneself with music. L18. 3 *v.t.* Set to music, describe musically. L19.

musica /ˈmjuːzɪkə/ *n.* [L = MUSIC *n.*] The L for 'music' occurring in various phrases used in Eng., esp. w. reference to early music.

musica ficta /ˈfɪktə/ [lit. 'feigned'] (early contrapuntal music characterized by) the introduction by a singer of conventional chromatically altered tones to avoid unacceptable intervals E19. ***musica figurata*** /fɪgjʊˈrɑːtə/ [lit. 'figured'] (*a*) contrapuntal music in which the different melodic strands move more or less independently; (*b*) plainsong with decorated melody: M18. ***musica plana*** /ˈplɑːnə/ [= plain] plainsong, canto fermo M20. ***musica reservata*** /rɛzəˈvɑːtə/ [lit.

'reserved'] early music characterized by clarity, balance, restraint, and expressiveness M20.

musical /ˈmjuːzɪk(ə)l/ *a.* & *n.* LME. [(O)Fr. f. med.L *musicalis*, f. as prec.: see -AL[1].] A *adj.* 1 Of or pertaining to music. LME. 2 Having the nature or characteristics of music; tuneful, melodious, harmonious; pleasing in sound, euphonious. LME. 3 Fond of or skilled in music. LME. †4 *Math.* = HARMONIC *a.* 4a. L16–E19. 5 Set to or accompanied by music; including music; that plays music. L17. 6 Amusing; ridiculous. *US colloq.* E19.

1 A. ARONSON Repeatedly Shakespeare uses musical images to distinguish sanity from insanity. E. FEINSTEIN She had genuine musical talent; a light voice, . . but true. 2 J. CONRAD The musical clink of broad silver pieces. D. H. LAWRENCE 'Tea is ready, mother,' she said in a musical, quiet voice. 3 V. CRONIN Ivan Rimsky-Korsakov . . too was musical, singing well and playing the violin.

Special collocations: **musical bow** a simple musical instrument consisting of a string stretched across the ends of a curved stick, the string being tapped or plucked, often using the mouth-cavity or a gourd etc. as a resonator. **musical box** a mechanical musical instrument consisting of a revolving toothed cylinder working on a resonant comblike metal plate. **musical bumps** a (usu. indoor) game to music in which players must sit down on the floor or ground whenever the music stops, the last to sit being eliminated from the game. **musical chairs** a (usu. indoor) game to music in which players must sit down on a chair whenever the music stops, the one who finds none (there always being fewer chairs than players) being eliminated from the game; *fig.* a series of changes of roles, esp. of little significance. **musical chime** a set of bells arranged to play a tune, a carillon. **musical clock** a clock which produces short tunes at regular intervals. **musical comedy** a light drama on stage or film, consisting of dialogue, songs, and dancing, connected by a slight plot. **musical director** *spec.* the conductor of the orchestra of a theatre. **musical dramatist** a composer of music dramas. **musical drive** an exhibition by a military unit in which horses pull along military equipment to the accompaniment of music. **musical glasses** (*a*) a set of glasses containing different amounts of liquid, played by finger-pressure on the moistened rims; (*b*) the glass harmonica. *musical instrument*: see INSTRUMENT *n.* 2. **musical ride** an exhibition of riding to music by a military unit. **musical saw** a bent handsaw played with a violin bow.

B *n.* †1 A musical instrument. Only in L15. †2 A musical performance. Only in L16. 3 A musical party. Now *rare.* E19. 4 A film or a theatrical piece (not opera or operetta) of which music is an essential element; a musical comedy. M20.

musiˈcality *n.* the quality or character of being musical M19. **musicaliˈzation** *n.* the action or process of musicalizing something E20. **musicalize** *v.t.* set (a novel, play, or poem) to music; express or render (an art other than music) in the style or manner of music: E20. **musically** *adv.* (*a*) in a musical manner; (*b*) as regards music: LME. **musicalness** *n.* musicality L17.

musicale /mjuːzɪˈkɑːl/ *n. US.* L19. [Fr. (*soirée*) *musicale* musical evening.] A musical party; a concert, esp. at a private address.

musicassette /ˌmjuːzɪkəˈsɛt/ *n.* M20. [f. MUSIC *n.* + CASSETTE.] = *music cassette* s.v. MUSIC *n.*

musician /mjuːˈzɪʃ(ə)n/ *n.* LME. [(O)Fr. *musicien*, f. as MUSIC *n.*: see -IAN.] A person skilled in the science or practice of music; a composer or professional performer of music, esp. of instrumental music.

musicianer *n.* (now *dial.*) = MUSICIAN M16. **musicianess** *n.* a female musician E19. **musicianly** *a.* (*a*) characteristic or worthy of a skilled musician; (*b*) skilled in music: M19. **musicianship** *n.* skilled as a musician M19.

musicker /ˈmjuːzɪkə/ *n.* Long *dial.* & *slang.* Also **musiker**. LME. [f. MUSIC *n.* + -ER[1].] = MUSICIAN.

musico /ˈmuːzɪkəʊ/ *n. rare.* Pl. **-os**. E19. [It. f. L *musicus*, f. *musica* MUSIC *n.*] = MUSICIAN.

musico- /ˈmjuːzɪkəʊ/ *comb. form.* [L, f. *musicus*, f. *musica* MUSIC *n.*: see -O-.] Involving music and (another art or science), musical and —; of or pertaining to music.

musico-draˈmatic *a.* of or pertaining to music and drama combined, of or pertaining to music-drama L19. **musicoˈgenic** *a.* (*Med.*) (of an epileptic attack) precipitated by hearing music; (of epilepsy) characterized by such attacks: M20. **musiˈcography** *n.* the science or art of writing music; musical notation: M19. **musico-ˈmania** *n.* an excessive fondness for music M19. **musicophile** *n.* a lover of music M20. **musico-ˈphobia** *n.* hatred of music E20.

musicology /mjuːzɪˈkɒlədʒi/ *n.* E20. [Fr. *musicologie*, or directly f. MUSIC *n.* + -OLOGY.] The branch of knowledge that deals with music as a subject of study rather than as a skill or performing art; *esp.* academic research in music.

musicoˈlogical *a.* of or pertaining to musicology E20. **musicoˈlogically** *adv.* with regard to musicology M20. **musicologist** *n.* E20.

musiker *n.* var. of MUSICKER.

†**musimon** *n.* var. of MUSMON.

musion /ˈmjuːsɪɒn/ *n. obs.* exc. *Hist.* L16. [Origin uncertain: perh. arbitrarily f. L *mus* mouse.] *Her.* A wild cat.

musique concrète /myzik kɔ̃krɛt, mjuːˈziːk kɒnˈkrɛt/ *n. phr.* M20. [Fr. = concrete music.] Electronic music constructed by the rearrangement of recorded natural sounds.

musive /ˈmjuːsɪv/ *a.* & *n.* Now *rare* or *obs.* E16. [Fr. *musif*, *-ive* f. late L *musivus* (in *opus musivum* mosaic work) f. late Gk *mouseion*, *mousion*: see MUSEUM, -IVE.] A *adj.* = MOSAIC *a.*[1] I. E16. B *n.* †1 = MOSAIC *n.* I. E–M17. †2 A Eurasian noctuid moth, *Ochropleura musiva*. Only in M19.

musk /mʌsk/ *n.* LME. [Late L *muscus* f. Pers. *mušk*, *mišk* perh. f. Skt *muṣka* scrotum (with ref. to the shape of the musk deer's musk-bag).] 1 A reddish-brown glandular secretion of the male musk deer, with a strong, persistent odour, used in perfumery. Also, any of various similar odorous substances secreted by other animals, esp. for scent marking. LME. b A substance designed to imitate musk. M17. c An aromatic odour resembling that of musk. M19. 2 An animal which secretes musk, as a civet; *spec.* a musk deer. L15. 3 Any of various plants smelling of musk; *esp.* (*a*) = *musk plant* below; (*b*) = *musk stork's-bill* s.v. STORK *n.*; (*c*) *Austral.* = *musk tree* below. Formerly also, any of certain varieties of apple, pear, etc., with a musky smell. E18.

Comb.: **musk-bag** the bag or gland in which musk is stored in the musk deer and other animals; **musk-ball** †(*a*) a receptacle for musk; (*b*) *Hist.* a ball of soap scented with musk; **musk beetle** a large green longhorn beetle, *Aromia moschata*, having a musky scent; †**musk-cat** (*a*) an animal which secretes musk, *esp.* a civet; (*b*) a fop; (*c*) a courtesan; †**musk-cod** (*a*) = *musk-bag* above; (*b*) a fop smelling of perfume; **musk deer** (*a*) any of several small hornless ruminants of forests in eastern Asia, of the family Moschidae, the males of which secrete the scent musk; *esp.* the Siberian *Moschus moschiferus*; (*b*) *occas.* a chevrotain, a mouse-deer; **musk duck** (*a*) = *Muscovy duck* s.v. MUSCOVY 2; (*b*) a duck, *Biziura lobata*, of southern Australia, the male of which has a musky odour and a pendulous lobe below the bill; **musk kangaroo** a very small arboreal rat-kangaroo, *Hypsiprymnodon moschatus*; **musk lorikeet** a small Australian parrot, *Glossopsitta concinna*, green with red markings; **musk mallow** a mallow of dry grassland, *Malva moschata*, with rose-purple flowers and palmately divided leaves; **musk melon** the fruit of the melon, *Cucumis melo*, *esp.* a variety with netted rind and aromatic flesh; the plant producing this; **musk orchid** an orchid of chalk grassland, *Herminium monorchis*, with small green flowers; **musk ox** a large, shaggy, horned goat-antelope, *Ovibos moschatus*, of the tundra, esp. in Canada and Greenland, the male of which emits a strong odour during rutting; †**musk parrakeet** = *musk lorikeet* above; **musk plant** a yellow-flowered mimulus, *Mimulus moschatus*, formerly grown for the musky smell of its leaves (not perceptible in modern varieties); **musk-rose** a rambling rose, *Rosa moschata*, with large fragrant white flowers; **musk shrew** any of various shrews of the genus *Crocidura*; *musk stork's-bill*: see STORK *n.*; **musk thistle** a thistle, *Carduus nutans*, with drooping sweet-scented heads; **musk tortoise** = *musk turtle* below; **musk tree** any of several Australian trees or shrubs with musk-scented leaves or timber; esp. *Olearia argyrophylla*, of the composite family; **musk turtle** any of several small N. American freshwater turtles of the genus *Sternotherus*, which emit a musky scent when disturbed; also called *stink-pot* (*terrapin*, *turtle*); **musk-wood** (*a*) (the wood of) either of two musky-scented W. Indian trees of the family Meliaceae, *Guarea trichilioides* and *Trichilia moschata*; (*b*) *Austral.* (the wood of) the musk tree, *Olearia argyrophylla*.

†**muskish** *a.* somewhat musky E17–E18. **musklike** *a.* resembling (that of) musk E19.

musk /mʌsk/ *v.* M17. [f. the n. Cf. earlier MUSKED.] 1 *v.t.* Perfume (as) with musk. Now *rare.* M17. 2 *v.i.* & *t.* Of an animal: deposit musk (on). E20.

musked /mʌskt/ *a.* Now *rare.* L16. [f. MUSK *n.*, *v.*: see -ED[2], -ED[1].] Flavoured or perfumed with musk; tasting or smelling like musk.

muskeg /ˈmʌskɛg/ *n. Canad.* E19. [Cree *maske:k.*] A swamp or bog consisting of a mixture of water and partly dead vegetation, freq. covered by a layer of sphagnum or other mosses; terrain characterized by such swamps.

muskeggy *a.* characterized by muskeg L19.

muskellunge *n.* var. of MASKINONGE.

musket /ˈmʌskɪt/ *n.*[1] Long *obs.* exc. *Hist.* LME. [ONFr. *musket*, *mousquet*, OFr. *mou(s)chet*, *moschet* (mod. *émouchet*), of unkn. origin.] The male of the sparrowhawk.

musket /ˈmʌskɪt/ *n.*[2] Also †**musquet**. L16. [Fr. *mousquet*, †*-ette* f. It. *moschetto*, *-etta* (formerly) bolt from a crossbow, f. *mosca* fly f. L *musca*: see -ET[1].] *Hist.* A gun (orig. a matchlock) of the kind used by infantry soldiers, usu. smooth-bored and fired from shoulder-level.

Comb.: **musket-arrow** a short arrow discharged from an early type of musket; **musket ball** a ball used as ammunition for a musket; **musket powder** the kind of gunpowder used for small arms; **musketproof** *a.* not readily penetrated by musket balls; **musket shot** (*a*) shot fired from a musket; a musket ball; (*b*) the range of a musket.

musketade *n.* a continued discharge of muskets; an attack with muskets: M17.

musketeer /mʌskɪˈtɪə/ *n.* Also †**musquet-**. L16. [f. prec. + -EER, after Fr. MOUSQUETAIRE etc.] *Hist.* A soldier armed with a musket. Also, a member of either of two bodies forming part of the household troops of the French king in the 17th and 18th cents.

Phrases: **three musketeers** [f. tr. of Fr. *les trois mousquetaires* by Alexandre Dumas père] three close associates, three inseparable friends.

Comb.: **musketeer gauntlet, glove** = MOUSQUETAIRE *glove*.

musketoon /mʌskɪˈtuːn/ *n.* Also †**musquet-**. M17. [Fr. *mousqueton* f. It. *moschettone*, f. *moschetto* MUSKET *n.*[2]: see -OON.] *Hist.* A kind of short musket with a large bore.

musketry /ˈmʌskɪtri/ *n.* Also †**musquet-**. M17. [Fr. *mousqueterie*, f. as MUSKET *n.*[2]: see -RY.] 1 *collect.* Muskets. M17. 2 The fire of muskets. M18. 3 *collect.* Troops armed with muskets. L18. 4 The art or technique of manipulating small arms. M19.

Muskhogean, -gee *ns.* & *adjs.* vars. of MUSKOGEAN, -GEE.

muskie *n.* var. of MUSKY *n.*

Muskogean /mʌskəˈgiːən, mʌˈskəʊgɪən/ *n.* & *a.* Also **-kh-**. L19. [f. next + -AN.] (Designating or pertaining to) an Indian language family of south-eastern N. America, including Creek, Seminole, Apalachee, Choctaw, and Chickasaw, or the peoples speaking a language of this family.

Muskogee /mʌˈskəʊgiː/ *n.* & *a.* Also **-kh-**. L18. [Creek *ma:skó:ki.*] A *n.* Pl. **-s**, same. A member of a N. American Indian people forming part of the Creek Indian confederacy; the Muskogean language of this people. L18. B *attrib.* or as *adj.* Of or pertaining to the Muskogees or their language. L18.

muskrat /ˈmʌskrat/ *n.* Pl. **-s**, same. E17. [f. Algonquian, assim. to MUSK *n.* and RAT *n.*[1] (cf. MUSHRAT, MUSQUASH). In sense 2 f. MUSK *n.* + RAT *n.*[1]] 1 a A large semi-aquatic N. American rodent, *Ondatra zibethicus*, resembling a beaver; also (in full *round-tailed muskrat*), a similar animal, *Neofiber alleni*, found in Florida. Also called *musquash*. E17. b An inhabitant of a low-lying district, esp. of the St Clair Flats in Michigan. *US colloq.* M19. c The skin or thick brown fur of a muskrat. L19. 2 Any of various somewhat ratlike animals having a musky odour, e.g. a musk shrew, a desman, a pilori, or a musk kangaroo. L17.

Comb.: **muskrat house** the winter dwelling of a muskrat, built from plant stems etc.

muskwa *n.* var. of MUSQUAW.

musky /ˈmʌski/ *n. N. Amer.* Also **muskie**. L19. [Abbrev. of *muskellunge* var. of MASKINONGE: see -Y[6], -IE.] = MASKINONGE.

musky /ˈmʌski/ *a.* E17. [f. MUSK *n.* + -Y[1].] Smelling or tasting of musk; having a taste or smell like that of musk, suggestive of musk; perfumed with musk.

muskiness *n.* the quality of being musky; a musky odour or taste: E18.

Muslim /ˈmʊzlɪm, ˈmʌz-, -s-/ *n.* & *a.* Also **Moslem** /ˈmɒzləm, ˈmʊzlɪm/. Pl. **-s**, (chiefly *collect.*) same, (now *rare*) **-limin** /-lɪmɪn/ (see also MUSLIMIN). E17. [f. Arab. *muslim* act. pple of *ʼaslama*: see ISLAM.] **A** *n.* A follower of the religion of Islam. E17.

Times Within the Soviet borders there are more than 40 million moslems. M. M. R. KHAN 'You aren't a Hindu?' 'No, .. I am a devout Muslim' *Black Muslim*: see BLACK *a.*

B *adj.* Of or pertaining to the Muslims or their religion. L18.

Daily Telegraph The guns open up across the old Sidon road where it separates Moslem and Christian Beirut. **Muslim League** a political organization founded in India in 1906 whose demands in 1940 for an independent Muslim State led to the establishment of Pakistan.

Muslimism *n.* the religious system of the Muslims, Islam L18.

Muslimin /ˈmʊzlɪmɪn, ˈmʌz-, -s-/ *n.* & *a.* Now *rare* or *obs.* Also **Moslemin** /ˈmɒzlɪmɪn, ˈmʊz-/. E19. [Pl. of prec. taken as sing.] **A** *n.* A Muslim. E19. **B** *attrib.* or as *adj.* Muslim. M19.

muslin /ˈmʌzlɪn/ *n.* & *a.* E17. [Fr. MOUSSELINE f. It. *mussolina*, *-ino*, f. *Moussulo* Mosul in Iraq, where formerly made: see -INE[1].] **A** *n.* **1** Fine delicately woven cotton fabric; an example of this. E17. **b** A dress or skirt made of this. L18. **2** Sails collectively. *Naut. slang.* E19. **3** In full *muslin moth*. A small European moth, *Diaphora mendica*, of the family Arctiidae, the male usu. being blackish and the female white with black markings, though both may be brownish cream. E19. **4** Fine cotton cloth of a plain weave. *US.* M19.

1 *book-muslin, butter muslin, mull muslin, Swiss muslin*, etc.

Phrases: *bit of muslin*: see BIT *n.*[2] 6.

B *attrib.* or as *adj.* Made of muslin. L17.

muslined *a.* draped with or dressed in muslin L19. **musliˈnet** *n.* & *a.* (of) a fabric resembling muslin M18.

musmon /ˈmʌsmɒn/ *n.* Also †**musi-**. E17. [L *musimo(n-)*, late Gk *mousmōn*.] = MOUFLON.

musnud /ˈmʌsnʌd/ *n.* M18. [Urdu & Pers. *masnad* f. Arab. = cushion, f. *sanada* lean against.] A seat made of cushions, *esp.* one used as a throne by an Indian prince.

muso /ˈmjuːzəʊ/ *n. colloq.* (orig. *Austral.*). Pl. **-os**. M20. [Abbrev. of MUSICIAN: see -O.] A musician; *esp.* a professional musician.

musquash /ˈmʌskwɒʃ/ *n. N. Amer.* E17. [Western Abnaki *mòskwas*.] **1** = MUSKRAT 1a. E17. **2** = MUSKRAT 1c. L19.

Comb.: **musquash house** = MUSKRAT *house*; **musquash-root** a N. American cowbane, *Cicuta maculata*; **musquash sealskin** imitation sealskin made from musquash.

musquaw /ˈmʌskwɔː/ *n. N. Amer.* Also **muskwa**. M19. [f. an Algonquian wd (cf. Cree *maskwa*).] The American black bear.

†**musquet** *n.*, **-teer** *n.*, etc., vars. of MUSKET *n.*[2] etc.

†**musrol** *n.* M16–M19. [Fr. *muserolle* f. It. *museruola*, f. *muso* muzzle.] The noseband of a bridle.

muss /mʌs/ *n.*[1] *obs.* exc. *dial.* L16. [Origin unkn.] A game in which small objects are thrown down to be scrambled for; a scramble.

muss /mʌs/ *n.*[2] & *v. dial.* & *N. Amer. colloq.* M19. [App. alt. of MESS *n.* Sense A.1 perh. same wd as prec.] **A** *n.* **1** A disturbance, a row. M19. **2** A state of untidiness; a muddle, a mess. M19. **B** *v.t.* Make untidy; crumple, ruffle; smear, mess; entangle, confuse. Also foll. by *up*. M19.

mussal /mʌˈsɑːl/ *n.* L17. [Urdu *mašʿal* f. Arab.] In the Indian subcontinent: a torch.

mussalchee /mʌˈsɑːltʃi/ *n.* Also ***masalchi***. E17. [Pers. & Urdu *mašʿalchī*, f. as prec. + Turk. *-çı* agentive suff.] In the Indian subcontinent: a torch-bearer; a menial servant.

mussel /ˈmʌs(ə)l/ *n.* Also (now *rare*) **muscle**. [OE *muscle*, *muxle*, *musle*, superseded by forms f. corresp. MLG *mussel*, MDu. *mosscele* (Du. *mossel*) = OHG *muscula* (G *Muschel*), all f. Proto-Romance alt. of L *musculus*: see MUSCLE *n.*[1]] Any of various bivalve molluscs belonging chiefly to the marine superfamily Mytilacea or to the freshwater superfamily Unionacea; *esp.* the common edible marine bivalve, *Mytilus edulis*, which has a dark grey, slightly elongated shell and adheres by a byssus, freq. in large aggregations.

horse mussel, pearl mussel, swan mussel, etc.

Comb.: **mussel-bank**, **-bed** a large aggregation of mussels, esp. on intertidal rocks; **mussel crab** a pea-crab, *Pinnotheres maculatus*, which lives as a commensal in the shell of the edible mussel; **mussel-cracker**, **-crusher** (chiefly *S. Afr.*) any of several fishes with powerful jaws, *esp.* (more fully *white mussel-cracker, -crusher*) *Cymatoceps nasutus* and (more fully *black* or *blue mussel-cracker, -crusher*) *Sparodon durbanensis*, both of the family Sparidae; **mussel digger** *US* (*a*) a grey whale; (*b*) a machine for digging mussel mud; **mussel duck** *dial.* a duck which feeds on mussels; *esp.* a scaup; †**mussel man** a person who gathers mussels for a living; **mussel mud**: containing many mussel shells; **mussel picker** *dial.* an oystercatcher; **mussel plum** a dark purple variety of plum; **mussel rake**: used for gathering mussels; **mussel scalp**, **scaup** a mussel-bed; **mussel-shell** (*a*) the shell of a mussel; † (*b*) *rare* a person who gapes like a mussel-shell.

musselled *a.* poisoned by eating mussels M19.

†**mussitate** *v.i.* E17–E18. [L *mussitat-* pa. ppl stem of *mussitare* frequent. of *mussare* mutter: see -ATE[3].] Mutter.

mussitation /mʌsɪˈteɪʃ(ə)n/ *n.* Now *rare*. M17. [Late L *mussitatio(n-)*, f. as prec.: see -ATION.] Muttering, murmuring; *Med.* movement of the lips without vocal sound.

Mussolini /mʊsəˈliːniː, mʌs-/ *n.* M20. [Benito *Mussolini* (1883–1945), prime minister of Italy and leader of the Fascist Party in Italy.] A dictator, a fascist.

Mussolinian *a.* of, pertaining to, or characteristic of Mussolini M20. **Mussolinism** *n.* the political principles or policy of Mussolini or of the Fascist Party in Italy E20.

Mussorgskian /mʊˈsɔːgskɪən/ *a.* Also **Mouss-**. M20. [f. *M(o)ussorgsky* (see below) + -AN.] Of, pertaining to, or characteristic of the Russian composer Modest Petrovich Mussorgsky (1839–81) or his music.

mussuck /ˈmʌsək/ *n.* E17. [Hind. *masak* f. Skt *maśaka*.] In the Indian subcontinent: a leather water-bag.

Mussulman /ˈmʌs(ə)lmən/ *n.* & *a.* L16. [Pers. *musulmān* (adj.) f. as MUSLIM. In sense A.2 f. G *Muselmann*.] **A** *n.* Pl. **-mans**, **-men**. **1** A Muslim. *arch.* L16. **2** *Hist.* Under the Third Reich, an inhabitant of a concentration camp or extermination camp exhausted to the point of fatalism and loss of initiative. M20. **B** *adj.* Muslim. *arch.* L17.

Mussulmanic /mʌs(ə)lˈmanɪk/ *a.* (*arch.*) Muslim E19. **Mussulmanism** *n.* (now *rare*) Islam M18. **Mussulwoman** *n.* (*joc.*, now *rare*) a female Muslim M17.

mussurana /mʊsəˈrɑːnə/ *n.* E20. [Port. *muçurana* f. Tupi *musúrana*, lit. 'rope'.] A non-venomous tropical American colubrid snake, *Clelia clelia*, usu. black in colour, which feeds on other snakes, being immune to their venom.

mussy /ˈmʌsi/ *a. dial.* & *N. Amer. colloq.* M19. [f. MUSS *n.*[2] + -Y[1].] Untidy, rumpled, tousled.

mussiness *n.* M19.

must /mʌst/ *n.*[1] [OE *must* = (O)HG *most* f. L *mustum* use as n. of neut. of *mustus* new, fresh.] **1** New wine; grape juice before or during fermentation; an example of this. OE. †**2a** Any juice or liquor undergoing or prepared for undergoing alcoholic fermentation. LME–E18. **b** The pulp of apples or pears after the juice has been pressed out in making cider or perry. *dial.* L17–L19. †**3** A variety of cider apple. M17–M18.

†**must** *n.*[2] *Sc.* L15–M19. [OFr., var. of *musc* MUSK *n.*] Musk.

must /mʌst/ *n.*[3] E17. [Back-form. f MUSTY *a.*[2]] Mustiness; mould.

must /mʌst/ *n.*[4] & *a.*[1] E17. [f. MUST *v.*[1]] **A** *n.* **1** The verb *must* as conveying command, expressing necessity, etc. E17. **2** A thing that cannot or should not be overlooked or missed; a necessity. *colloq.* L19.

2 J. WYNDHAM We had finished adding our own secondary wants to the list of musts. S. BELLOW Daddy—you have to read it. A must!

B *attrib.* or as *adj.* Essential, mandatory, obligatory. *colloq.* E20.

New Statesman Those women's periodicals .. which are still 'must-reading' for debutantes. *New Yorker* The Planning Commission .. has yet to act on either of these two must items.

must /mʌst/ *a.*[2] & *n.*[5] Also **-th**. L19. [Urdu *mast* f. Pers., lit. 'intoxicated'.] **A** *adj.* Of a male elephant or camel: in a state of dangerous frenzy (associated with the rutting season). L19. **B** *n.* The condition or state of being in such a state or frenzy. L19.

must /mʌst/ *aux. v.*[1] Pres. & pa. (all persons) **must**. Neg. **must not**, (*informal*) **mustn't** /ˈmʌs(ə)nt/. No other parts used. [OE *mōste* pa. t. of *mōt* MOTE *v.*[1] = OFris. *mōt*, OS *mōt*, *muot* (Du. *moet*), OHG *muoz* find room or opportunity, may, must (G *muss*), Goth. *gamōtan* find room, rel. to MLG *mōte*, OHG *muoza* (G *Musse*) leisure, f. Gmc.] †**I** As pa. t. of MOTE *v.*[1] **1** Expr. permission or possibility, or a wish: might, could. OE–LME. **2** Expr. necessity or obligation: had to, was (were) obliged to, it was necessary that (I, you, he, it, etc.) should. OE–L15.

II As pres. t. (indic. & subjunct.), often *ellipt.* with vb understood or supplied from the context. **3** Expr. necessity: am (is, are) obliged or required to; have (has) to; it is necessary that (I, you, he, it, etc.) should; am (is, are) commanded, requested insistently, or recommended to. Also *ellipt.* (*arch.*), must go. ME. **b** Expr. a fixed or certain futurity: am (is, are) fated or certain to (*be* or *do*), shall certainly or inevitably (*be* or *do*). LME. **c** Say (says) or feel (feels) that one has to. LME. **4** Expr. the inferred or presumed certainty of a fact: certainly am (is, are) or do (does); it cannot be otherwise than that (I, you, he, it, etc.) am (are, is) or do (does). M17.

3 TENNYSON Seeing he must to Westminster and crown Young Henry there. A. S. NEILL I must get estimates from the printers. J. BUCHAN Haraldsen is an invalid, .. and must keep quiet. P. ROTH Doing as I wished, not as I must. I. MURDOCH You must both have a sip of sherry. J. TROLLOPE Must you look so utterly suburban? b DRYDEN Crowds of dead, that never must return. A. LURIE What must it be like in the winter! c WORDSWORTH He is not content with a ring .., but he must have rings in the ears, rings on the nose—rings everywhere. 4 *Poetry Nation Review* What he is thinking, because he must be thinking, / I cannot tell. ANTHONY SMITH There must be few who have not been depressed.

III 5 *must have done*, (*a*) should necessarily have done; (*b*) should have had to do, should have been obliged to do; (*c*) certainly did, it is to be concluded that I (you, he, it, etc.) did. LME.

5 SWIFT Had this point been steadily pursued .. there must probably have been an end of faction. E. BOWEN In the woodwork .. was a hook from which a bird-cage must have hung. J. FOWLES There must been about a dozen.

IV As pa. t. of branch II. **6** Was obliged, had to; it was necessary that (I, he, it, etc.) should; (now *colloq.*) it foolishly happened that (I, he, it, etc.) did. Now only in oblique narration or virtual oblique narration reporting a reflection made at the time, and in conditional clauses. L17.

6 W. CATHER The Doctor had said the house must be absolutely quiet. R. P. JHABVALA In order to find .. spiritual enrichment .. they must set off for India.

Phrases: **if you must know**: used to introduce information provided against the judgement or inclination of the speaker. *I must love you and leave you*: see LOVE *v.* 1. **I must say** I cannot refrain from saying. *must needs, needs must*: see NEEDS *adv.* **must not** am (is, are) not allowed to, am (is, are) obliged not to. *the show must go on*: see SHOW *n.*[1] **you must know** or **understand** you ought to be informed, I would have you know.

Comb.: **must-be** the inevitable, what is fated to happen.

must /mʌst/ *v.*[2] *obs.* exc. *dial.* M16. [Back-form. f. MUSTY *a.*[2]] **1** *v.i.* Become mouldy or musty. M16. **2** *v.t.* Make mouldy or musty. *rare.* E18.

†must *v.*[3]*t.* *Sc.* M18–E19. [f. MUST *n.*[2]] Powder with must or hair-powder.

mustache *n.*, **mustached** *a.*, **mustachial** *a.* see MOUSTACHE etc.

mustachio /məˈstɑːʃɪəʊ, -ʃəʊ/ *n.* Now chiefly *arch.* & *joc.* Also **mous-**, **†-cho(e)**. Pl. **-os**. M16. [(Sp. *mostacho* f.) It. *mostaccio* (cf. med.L *mustacia*) based ult. on Gk *mustax, mustak-* upper lip, moustache.] **1** A moustache, now *esp.* a large one. M16. **†2** In *pl.* Hairs or bristles around the mouth of an animal; a cat's whiskers. Also, the awn or bristles of certain grasses; = BEARD *n.* 3. L16–L18.

mustachioed *a.* having a (large) moustache E19.

mustafina /mʌstəˈfiːnə/ *n.* E19. [App. f. MUSTEE + Sp. *fino, fina* FINE *a.*] A person with one parent a mustee and the other a White.

mustang /ˈmʌstaŋ/ *n.* & *a.* E19. [App. blending of Sp. *mestengo* (now *mesteño*) and *mostrenco* (both meaning) wild or masterless cattle; *mestengo* f. *mesta* (f. L *mixta* use as n. of fem. pa. pple of *miscere* mix) association of graziers who appropriated wild cattle.] **A** *n.* **1** The wild or half-wild horse of American plains, esp. of Mexico and California, descended from stock introduced by the Spanish. E19. **2** = *mustang grape* below. M19. **3** An officer in the US services who has been promoted from the ranks. Also occas., a volunteer officer as distinct from a regular-army officer. *slang.* M19.

B *attrib.* or as *adj.* That is a mustang; of or pertaining to a mustang or mustangs. E19.

mustang grape (the fruit of) a native vine, *Vitis candicans*, of the south-western US, bearing small red grapes.

mustanger *n.* (*Western US*) a person who catches or entraps mustangs M19.

mustard /ˈmʌstəd/ *n.* & *a.* ME. [OFr. *mo(u)starde* (mod. *moutarde*) = Prov., Catal., Port., It. *mostarda* Romanian *muştar*, f. Proto-Romance, f. L *mustum* MUST *n.*[1] (orig. the condiment prepared with grape must).] **A** *n.* **1** Powder made from the crushed seeds of certain plants (see sense A.2 below); paste made from this, used as a pungent condiment and (esp. formerly) in making poultices or plasters; an example or type of this paste. ME. **2** Any of the cruciferous plants used to make this; spec. *Sinapis alba* (in full *white mustard*), *Brassica nigra* (in full *black mustard*), and (in US) *B. juncea* (in full *brown mustard*). Also (w. specifying wd): any of various other (chiefly cruciferous) plants, resembling these in appearance, pungency, etc. ME. **3** The brownish-yellow colour of the condiment mustard. L19. **4** A thing providing piquancy or zest. *US slang.* E20. **5** *ellipt.* = *mustard gas* below; *Chem.* any of a group of compounds with alkylating properties, having a structure typified by that of mustard gas. E20.

1 (as) **keen as mustard** very keen, acute, or enthusiastic. *Dijon mustard*, *Tewkesbury mustard*, etc. **cut the mustard** *slang* (chiefly *N. Amer.*) succeed; come up to expectations, meet requirements. DURHAM *mustard.* **English mustard** *esp.* coarse-grained mustard. **French mustard** *esp.* mustard made with vinegar. *keen as mustard*: see *as keen as mustard* above. **2 mustard and cress** seedlings of cress, *Lepidium sativum*, and white mustard, used as a relish in salads. *garlic mustard, hedge mustard, tower mustard, wild mustard*, etc. **5** NITROGEN *mustard.*

Comb.: **†mustard-bowl** a wooden bowl in which mustard seed was pounded, proverbially referred to as the instrument for producing stage thunder; **mustard bush** *Austral.* an almost leafless shrub, *Apophyllum anomalum*, of the caper family, with yellow flowers and shoots which taste of mustard; **mustard colour** = sense A.3 above; **mustard-coloured** *a.* of mustard colour; **mustard gas** a colourless oily liquid, dichlorodiethylsulphide, $(ClCH_2CH_2)_2S$, which is a powerful poison and vesicant, acting directly on the skin, used in chemical warfare; **mustard oil** an oil obtained from mustard seed; **mustard plaster** a poultice or plaster made with mustard; **mustard-pot** a pot or cruet for mustard for the table; **mustard seed** (*a*) the seed of mustard; *grain of mustard seed*, a small thing capable of vast development [from the great height attained by black mustard in Palestine (*Matt.* 13:31)]; †(*b*) a mustard plant; (*c*) *US* very fine shot used for shooting birds with not much injury to the plumage; **mustard weevil** a weevil, *Ceutorhyncus contractus*, which damages the white mustard plant.

B *attrib.* or as *adj.* **1** Of the nature of mustard, pungent; prepared with mustard. L16. **2** Of the brownish-yellow colour of the condiment mustard. M19. **3** Very good, keen, enthusiastic; thorough. *slang.* E20.

3 *Daily Express* The Russians and the East Germans are mustard on the theory of numbers.

mustarder *n.* (*Hist.*) a maker of or dealer in mustard LME. **mustardy** *a.* resembling mustard; covered with mustard; containing mustard, tasting of mustard: M19.

mustee /mʌˈstiː/ *n.* Also **mestee** /mɛˈstiː/. L17. [Abbrev. of Sp. MESTIZO.] A person with one parent a White and the other a quadroon; an octoroon; *loosely* a person with parents of different races.

mustelid /ˈmʌstɪlɪd/ *n.* & *a.* E20. [mod.L *Mustelidae* (see below), f. *Mustela* genus name, f. L *mustela* weasel: see -ID[3].] **A** *n.* Any of various carnivorous mammals of the family Mustelidae, which includes weasels, stoats, badgers, mink, skunks, martens, and otters. Cf. next. E20. **B** *adj.* Of, pertaining to, or designating this family. M20.

musteline /ˈmʌstɪlɪn, -ʌɪn/ *a.* & *n.* M17. [L *mustelinus*, f. *mustela* weasel.] **A** *adj.* Of or like a weasel; *spec.* designating or pertaining to the mustelid subfamily Mustelinae, which includes the weasels, stoats, mink, and martens. M17. **B** *n.* A musteline animal. L19.

muster /ˈmʌstə/ *n.* LME. [OFr. *moustre* (later Latinized, mod. *montre*) repr. Proto-Romance n. f. L *monstrare* show.] **1 †a** The action or an act of showing something; manifestation; exhibition, display. LME–M17. **b** A flock of peacocks. *rare.* LME. **2** A pattern, a specimen, a sample, latterly only of certain commercial items. LME. **3a** An act of mustering soldiers, sailors, etc.; an assembling of people for inspection, verification of numbers, etc.; a roll-call. LME. **b** An act of mustering stock (cattle, sheep, etc.), a round-up of stock. *Austral.* & *NZ.* M19. **4** The number of persons or things mustered or assembled on a particular occasion; an assembly, a collection. LME. **5** A muster-roll. Formerly also, a census report. M16. **6** Foll. by *out*: (a) discharge from service. *US.* L19.

Phrases: **false muster** (chiefly *Hist.*) a fraudulent presentation at a muster, or a fraudulent inclusion in a muster-roll, of men who are not available for service. **in muster** mustered, assembled for inspection. **pass muster**, (earlier) **pass †(the) musters** (orig. *Mil.*) undergo muster or review without censure; bear examination or inspection, come up to the required standard, be accepted (*as* the possessor of certain qualities).

Comb.: **muster-book** a book in which military forces are registered; a book containing the names of the crew of a warship; **†muster file** a muster-roll; **muster-master** an officer responsible for (the accuracy of) a muster-roll, esp. of some portion of an army; **muster-mastership** *Hist.* the function or position of a muster-master; **muster-roll** (*a*) an official list of the soldiers in an army or the sailors in a ship's company; a register; (*b*) *Naut.* the reading of a muster-roll; a roll-call.

muster /ˈmʌstə/ *v.* ME. [OFr. *mo(u)strer* (later Latinized, mod. *montrer*) f. L *monstrare* show.] **†1a** *v.t.* Show, display, exhibit; show up, report, tell, explain. ME–E17. **b** *v.i.* Show, appear, be displayed; make a good, bad, etc. appearance. LME–L16. **2a** *v.t.* & *i.* Collect or assemble (*spec.* soldiers) for ascertainment or verification of numbers, inspection as to condition and equipment, exercise, display, introduction into service, or (also foll. by *up*) for battle. LME. **b** *v.t. gen.* Collect, get together; *esp.* bring forward from one's own stores, raise (a number or amount); *fig.* summon, gather up, marshal, (one's thoughts, courage, strength, etc.). Also foll. by *up*. L16. **c** *v.t.* & *i.* Collect together or round up (stock, as cattle, sheep, etc.) for counting, shearing, drafting, branding, etc. Also, round up stock from (a place). *Austral* & *NZ.* M19. **3** *v.i.* (Of an army etc.) come together for inspection, exercise, or preparation for service; assemble, gather together in a body. LME. **4** *v.t.* **a** Enlist, enroll. Foll. by *in, into* (service). Now only *US.* LME. **b** Foll. by *out*: discharge from service. *US.* M19. **5** *v.t.* **†a** Take a census of. M16–M17. **b** Now chiefly *Naut.* Call the roll of. L17. **6** *v.t.* Of an army etc.: comprise, number. M19.

2a C. MARLOWE Ile muster vp an army secretly. R. SUTCLIFF Muster the squadron and hold them in readiness. R. K. NARAYAN They were mustering themselves to attack the other group. J. A. MICHENER The Babylonians began to muster the Hebrews for the long march to slavery. b H. JAMES With what they could muster between them. E. BOWEN Mrs. Heccomb . . began to muster her parcels. K. CROSSLEY-HOLLAND Mustering his vast strength he dragged the whole quaking mound up the slope. V. GLENDINNING It would be equally easy to muster evidence for a negative view. B. BAINBRIDGE She doubted whether she could muster up the tears expected at such a moment. C. ACHEBE I simply couldn't muster anything you could call enthusiasm. c P. V. WHITE I will have all cattle . . that we are taking with us, mustered. K. S. PRICHARD They had been mustering all day on the wide plains of Murndoo station. 3 J. R. GREEN The royal army had already mustered in great force. R. HUGHES The children mustered for their soup and biscuit. *fig.*: R. L. STEVENSON The fogs that will begin to muster about sundown.

musterer *n.* (*Austral.* & *NZ*) a person who rounds up or musters stock M19.

musth *a.* & *n.* var. of MUST *a.*[2] & *n.*[5]

mustine /ˈmʌstiːn/ *n.* M20. [f. MUSTARD *n.* + -INE[5].] *Pharm.* A strongly cytoxic nitrogen mustard, bis(2-chloroethyl)methylamine $(ClCH_2CH_2)_2NCH_3$, used to treat certain neoplasms, esp. Hodgkin's disease.

†musty *a.*[1] *rare.* LME–E19. [f. MUST *n.*[1] + -Y[1].] Of or pertaining to must or new wine; not yet fermented, undergoing fermentation.

musty /ˈmʌsti/ *a.*[2] & *v.* E16. [Perh. alt. of MOISTY after MUST *n.*[1]] **A** *adj.* **1** Mouldy; having a smell or taste indicative or suggestive of mouldiness or decay; stale-smelling, fusty. E16. **2** Having lost newness, interest, or liveliness; antiquated, disused, old-fashioned. L16. **3** Ill-humoured, peevish, sullen. *obs.* exc. *dial.* E17.

1 POPE The musty wine, foul cloth, or greasy glass. DICKENS Unsavoury smells of musty hay. A. CARTER The dining room . . never lost a musty and unused smell. D. LEAVITT Her room was musty from the closed windows. 2 H. FIELDING None but a musty moralist . . would have condemned such behaviour. CHARLES CHURCHILL Read musty lectures on Benevolence.

†B *v.i.* & *t.* Become or make musty. M17–E18.

mustily *adv.* E17. **mustiness** *n.* E16.

muta /ˈmjuːtə/ *v.i.* (*imper.*). L19. [It., imper. of *mutare* change.] *Mus.* A direction: change instrument or tuning.

mutable /ˈmjuːtəb(ə)l/ *a.* & *n.* LME. [L *mutabilis*, f. *mutare* change: see -ABLE.] **A** *adj.* **1** Liable or subject to change or alteration. LME. **b** *Gram.* In a Celtic language: subject to mutation. E18. **2** Changeable in mind or disposition; fickle, variable. LME. **3** *Biol.* Able to undergo mutation; liable to undergo frequent mutation. E20.

1 W. S. MAUGHAM The contemplation of the . . stars . . stimulated him to contempt of all mutable things. 2 H. CARPENTER She is mutable: in fact she is faithless.

B *n.* **1** A thing able to be changed. *rare.* M17. **2** *Gram.* A mutable consonant. M18.

muta'bility *n.* LME. **mutableness** *n.* (now *rare*) mutability L15. **mutably** *adv.* M17.

mutagen /ˈmjuːtədʒ(ə)n/ *n.* M20. [f. MUTA(TION + -GEN.] *Biol.* An agent that causes mutation.

mutagenesis /mjuːtəˈdʒɛnɪsɪs/ *n.* M20. [f. MUTA(TION + -GENESIS.] *Biol.* The production or origination of mutations.

mutagenic /mjuːtəˈdʒɛnɪk/ *n.* M20. [f. MUTA(TION + -GENIC.] *Biol.* Causing or capable of causing mutation.

mutagenicity /-dʒəˈnɪsɪti/ *n.* the property of being mutagenic M20.

mutagenize /ˈmjuːtədʒənʌɪz/ *v.t.* Also **-ise**. M20. [f. MUTAGEN + -IZE.] *Biol.* Treat (cells or organisms) with mutagenic agents.

mutant /ˈmjuːt(ə)nt/ *n.* & *a.* E20. [L *mutant-* pres. ppl stem of *mutare* change: see -ANT[1].] *Biol.* A *n.* An individual, gene, or (formerly) population which has arisen by or undergone mutation; *esp.* in *Sci. Fiction*, an individual with freak or grossly abnormal anatomy, abilities, etc. E20. B *adj.* Having the attributes of a mutant; produced by mutation. E20.

mutarotation /mjuːtərəʊˈteɪʃ(ə)n/ *n.* L19. [f. L *mutare* change + ROTATION.] *Chem.* (A) change of optical activity with time, as exhibited by freshly prepared solutions of some compounds, esp. sugars.

mutarotate *v.i.* exhibit mutarotation M20. **mutarotational** *a.* pertaining to or of the nature of mutarotation L20.

mutase /ˈmjuːteɪz/ *n.* E20. [f. L *mutare* change + -ASE.] *Biochem.* 1 An enzyme which catalyses a dismutation reaction. E20. 2 An enzyme which catalyses the transfer of a phosphate group from one carbon atom to another in a molecule. M20.

mutassarif *n.* var. of MUTESSARIF.

mutate /ˈmjuːteɪt/ *a.* & *n.* M19. [L *mutatus* pa. pple of *mutare* change: see -ATE[2].] A *adj. Bot.* Changed. *rare.* M19. B *n.* 1 *Gram.* A form having a mutated vowel. *rare.* L19. 2 *Chess.* A problem in which White's playing of the key replaces one block by another. E20.

mutate /mjuːˈteɪt/ *v.* E19. [Back-form. f. next.] 1 *v.i.* Undergo change, be transmuted; undergo (esp. genetic) mutation. E19. 2 *v.t.* Cause to undergo (esp. genetic) mutation. L19.

1 W. H. AUDEN We had the luck to see / . . old Russia suddenly mutate / into a proletarian state. EDMOND HAMILTON I think they were human once—human colonists who mutated under radioactive influence.

mutation /mjuːˈteɪʃ(ə)n/ *n.* LME. [L *mutatio(n-)*, f. *mutat-* pa. ppl stem of *mutare* change: see -ATION.] 1 The action or process of changing; an alteration, a change. LME. †b Change in government, revolution. LME–M18. 2 *Mus.* In medieval solmization, the change from one hexachord to another involving a change of the syllable applied to a given note. L16. 3 *Gram.* a In a Celtic language, a change of initial consonant caused (historically) by the preceding word. M19. b = UMLAUT *n.* 1. L19. 4 *Biol.* a A change in genetic material, esp. one which gives rise to heritable variations in offspring; the process by which such changes arise. L19. b A distinct form produced by genetic change; a mutant. E20.

1 J. DIDION I had never thought of him having dinner with his family . . but time brings odd mutations.

Comb.: **mutation mink** a mink of a mutant strain with a fur colour different from the normal; fur or a garment made from the skin of such a mink; **mutation pressure** *Genetics* a tendency for recurring mutation (rather than selection) to alter the frequency of a particular allele within a population; **mutation rank** *Mus.* = *mutation stop* below; **mutation rate** *Genetics* the rate at which mutations occur in the genes of a given population, or in a given gene; **mutation stop** *Mus.* a stop whose pipes produce a tone other than the proper pitch or an octave of the key struck; **mutation theory** (*Biol.*, now *Hist.*) the theory that new species arise by sudden divergence from a parent type, rather than gradually (as by natural selection).

mutational *a.* (chiefly *Biol.*) E20. **mutationally** *adv.* as a result of mutation M20. **mutationist** *n.* (*Biol.*, now *Hist.*) an advocate of mutation theory (opp. *selectionist*) E20.

mutatis mutandis /mjuːˌtɑːtɪs mjuːˈtandɪs, muː-, -iːs/ *adv. phr.* L15. [L, lit. 'things being changed that have to be changed'.] Making the necessary changes; with due alteration of details.

J. BAYLEY Both gifts he shares, *mutatis mutandis*, with the American poets.

mutative /ˈmjuːtətɪv/ *a.* M18. [med.L *mutativus*, f. *mutat-*: see MUTATION, -IVE.] 1 Of or pertaining to change or mutation. M18. 2 Given to change, changeable. E19.

mutato nomine /mjuːˌtɑːtəʊ ˈnəʊmɪneɪ, muː-, nɒ-/ *adv. phr.* E17. [L.] The name being changed, with a change of name or names.

J. B. FRASER The words of Burns, *mutato nomine*, describe their country exactly.

mutator /mjuːˈteɪtə/ *n.* M17. [f. MUTATE *v.* + -OR.] †1 A person who changes something. *rare.* Only in M17. 2 *Biol.* In full *mutator gene*. A gene which increases the mutation rate of other genes. M20.

mutch /mʌtʃ/ *n.* LME. [MDu. *mutse* (Du. *muts*) corresp. to (M)HG *mütze*, shortened by-forms of MDu. *a(l)mutse* f. med.L *almucia* AMICE *n.*[2]] †1 A covering for the head during the night, a nightcap. *Sc.* LME–M19. 2 A cap or coif of linen etc. worn by (esp. old) women and young children. *Sc.* & *dial.* L16.

mutchkin /ˈmʌtʃkɪn/ *n. Sc.* LME. [Early mod.Du. *mudseken* (now *mutsje*) dim. of *mudde*: see MUD *n.*[1], -KIN.] A unit of capacity for liquids or dry substances equal to a quarter of the old Scots pint or approx. three-quarters of an imperial pint (0.43 litres).

mute /mjuːt/ *n.*[1] *arch.* LME. [OFr. *muete*, (also mod.) *meute* f. pop.L f. L *movere* MOVE *v.*] 1 A pack of hounds. LME. †2 The baying of a pack of hounds. Only in LME.

mute /mjuːt/ *a.* & *n.*[2] ME. [(O)Fr. *muet* dim. of OFr. *mu* f. L *mutus*. Orig. two syllables.] A *adj.* 1 Of a person: lacking the faculty of speech, dumb. ME. b Of an animal: naturally lacking the power of articulate speech. M17. 2 Refraining from or temporarily deprived of speech, not emitting articulate sound. LME. b Characterized by an absence of sound; quiet, still. E16. 3 Not expressed or accompanied by speech or vocal utterance. L16. 4 *Gram.* & *Phonet.* a Of a consonant: produced by an entire interruption of the passage of breath or by the complete closure of the organs of the mouth; stopped, plosive. Now *rare.* L16. b Of a letter: not pronounced, silent. M17. 5 *Astrol.* Of a sign of the zodiac: symbolized by a voiceless creature (viz. Cancer, Scorpio, Pisces). M17. 6 Of a hound: not giving tongue while hunting. L17. 7 Of a metal or mineral: that does not ring when struck. E19. 8 *Cinemat.* Designating a positive or negative film print having no synchronous soundtrack. M20.

1 DEAF MUTE. 2 C. BOWEN Mute with wonder I stood. M. WARNER Mamma had tried to talk to Rosa . . but she'd stayed mute. **stand mute** *Law* not plead (*stand mute of malice*, refuse to plead: *stand mute by visitation of God*, be unable to plead). b C. BRONTË Mute was the room. 3 F. BURNEY Fixed in mute wonder, . . her eyes almost bursting from their sockets. *Daily News* The mute agonies of the suffocating lobster. 6 **run mute** follow the chase without giving tongue.

Comb.: **mute button** a device on a telephone etc. that temporarily prevents a caller hearing anything said at the receiver's end; **mute swan** a common Eurasian swan, *Cygnus olor*, with white plumage and an orange-red and black bill with a swollen knob in front of the eyes.

B *n.* 1 *Phonet.* A mute or stopped consonant, a plosive. M16. 2 A person prevented by nature, mutilation, or employment from speaking; *spec.* (*a*) an actor in a mime; (*b*) *Hist.* a servant in an oriental country deprived usu. deliberately of the power of speech; †(*c*) *Law* a person refusing to plead to an indictment; (*d*) a professional attendant or mourner at a funeral. L16. 3 *Mus.* a A clip placed over the bridge of a violin etc. to deaden the resonance without affecting the vibration of the strings. E19. b A pad or cone inserted into the bell of a wind instrument to soften the sound. M19. 4 *Cinemat.* A mute film print. M20.

2 DEAF MUTE. 3b *Harmon mute, straight mute*, etc.

mutely *adv.* E17. **muteness** *n.* L16.

mute /mjuːt/ *v.*[1] & *n.*[3] *arch.* LME. [OFr. *meutir*, later *mutir* aphet. f. *esmeutir*, earlier *esmeltir* (mod. *émeutir*), perh. f. Frank. vb meaning 'smelt'. Cf. MDu. *smelt* bird's faeces.] A *v.i.* & *t.* Of a bird, esp. a hawk: discharge (faeces). LME. B *n.* The action of defecating by a bird, esp. a hawk; *sing.* & in *pl.* (a deposit of) faeces, droppings. L15.

muting *n.*[1] (*a*) the action of the vb; (*b*) *sing.* & (usu.) in *pl.*, faeces, droppings: L15.

mute /mjuːt/ *v.*[2] L17. [f. MUTE *a.*] †1 *v.i.* Of a pack of hounds: run without giving tongue. Only in L17. 2 *v.t.* Deaden or soften the sound of (a thing or person); *spec.* muffle the sound of (a musical instrument); *fig.* tone down, reduce in intensity, subdue. L19. b Silence (a thing or person); *spec.* suppress the volume of (a loudspeaker) or the output of (an amplifier or other circuit component). L19.

2 M. PEMBERTON A heavy Indian carpet muted the footsteps of the Emperor. A. BROOKNER Fierce colour . . muted by the surrounding greyness.

muting *n.*[2] (*a*) the action of the vb; (*b*) *Electr.* the automatic suppression of the output of an amplifier when the input signal falls below some predetermined level: L19.

muted /ˈmjuːtɪd/ *a.* M19. [f. prec. + -ED[1].] Made mute, silent; muffled, quiet; understated; (of a musical instrument) having a muffled tone, employing a mute; (of colour or lighting) subdued.

Publishers Weekly The muted inner dignity of these deeply religious black people. B. BREYTENBACH He hears the muted rumbling of the city. *Patches* Spring greens are muted and delicate.

mutedly *adv.* L19.

mutessarif /muːtəˈsɑːriːf/ *n.* Also **muta-**. L19. [Turk. *mutessarıf* f. Arab. *mutaṣarrif* use as n. of act. pple of *taṣarrafa* enjoy usufruct.] *Hist.* In the Ottoman Empire and Iraq: a governor of a province or sanjak.

mutha /ˈmʌðə/ *n. non-standard US.* M20. [Repr. pronunc.] = MOTHER *n.*[1], esp. sense 4.

Comb.: **muthafucka, -ing** *coarse slang* = *mother-fucker, -ing* s.v. MOTHER *n.*[1]

muti /ˈmuːti/ *n. S. Afr.* L19. [Zulu *umuthi* tree, plant, medicine.] Traditional African medicine; a medicinal or healing charm, healing magic.

mutic /ˈmjuːtɪk/ *a.* L18. [L *muticus*: see MUTICOUS.] 1 *Bot.* = next. Now *rare* or *obs.* L18. 2 *Entomol.* Lacking spines. M19.

muticous /ˈmjuːtɪkəs/ *a.* M19. [f. L *muticus* awnless + -OUS.] *Bot.* Having no point or awn.

mutilate /ˈmjuːtɪlət/ *a.* & *n.* E16. [L *mutilatus* pa. pple, f. as next: see -ATE[2].] A *adj.* 1 Mutilated. *obs.* exc. *poet.* E16. 2 *Biol.* Of an animal or plant: having some part common to related forms either absent or present only in an imperfect or modified state. M18. B *n. Biol.* A mutilate organism; *spec.* a cetacean or sirenian as lacking fully developed limbs. Now *rare* or *obs.* M19.

mutilate /ˈmjuːtɪleɪt/ *v.t.* M16. [L *mutilat-* pa. ppl stem of *mutilare*, f. *mutilus* maimed: see -ATE[3]. Cf. prec. (earlier).] 1 Deprive (a person or animal) of a limb or bodily organ; cut off, severely wound, (a limb or organ); maim, mangle. M16. 2 Make (a thing, esp. a document, book, etc.) imperfect by removing or severely damaging a part. M16.

1 C. THIRLWALL He was condemned to be mutilated, . . in his nose and ears. R. K. NARAYAN Two fellows . . were mutilated—one fellow lost an arm.

mutilative *a.* (*rare*) causing mutilation L19. **mutilator**, †**-er** *n.* L16.

mutilation /mjuːtɪˈleɪʃ(ə)n/ *n.* E16. [Late L *mutilatio(n-)*, f. as prec.: see -ATION. Cf. (O)Fr. *mutilation*.] 1 The action of mutilating a person or animal; the excision or maiming of a limb or bodily organ; an instance of this. E16. 2 The action of mutilating a thing; an instance of this. M17.

2 M. SPARK Angry authors' letters about the mutilation of their books.

mutillid /mjuːˈtɪlɪd/ *n.* & *a.* E20. [f. mod.L *Mutilla* genus name: see -ID[3].] A *n.* Any wasp of the family Mutillidae, which includes the velvet ants and other solitary fossorial parasitic species.

E20. B *adj.* Of, pertaining to, or designating this family. L20.

†**mutilous** *a.* M17–E18. [f. L *mutilus* maimed + -OUS.] Of a thing: mutilated, imperfect.

mutine /ˈmjuːtiːn, -tɪn/ *n.* & *a.* M16. [(O)Fr. *mutin*, f. *muete* (mod. *meute*) f. Proto-Romance: see MUTE *n.*[1], -INE[4].] †A *n.* 1 Popular disturbance or revolt, rebellion, mutiny. M16–E17. 2 A rebellious person, a mutineer. L16–E17. B *adj.* Mutinous, rebellious, unsubmissive (now *spec.* of a woman or girl). L16.

¶Adj. not recorded in 17 or 18: reintroduced f. Fr. in 19.

†**mutine** *v.* M16. [Fr. *mutiner*, f. as prec.] 1 *v.i.* Rebel, mutiny. M16–L17. 2 *v.t.* Incite to revolt. Only in E17.

mutineer /mjuːtɪˈnɪə/ *n.* & *v.* E17. [Fr. *mutinier*, f. as MUTINE *n.*: see -EER.] A *n.* A person who mutinies. E17. B *v.i.* Mutiny, rebel. L17.

mutinize /ˈmjuːtɪnʌɪz/ *v.* *arch.* Also **-ise**. E17. [f. MUTINE *n.* + -IZE.] 1 *v.i.* Mutiny. E17. 2 *v.t.* Cause mutiny in. M17.

mutinous /ˈmjuːtɪnəs/ *a.* L16. [f. MUTINE *n.* + -OUS.] 1 Of a person: tending to mutiny, rebellious; rebelling, insurgent. L16. †b Turbulent, contentious. L16–E17. c *transf.* & *fig.* Ungovernable, stormy; wilful, unsubmissive. E17. 2 Of the nature of or proceeding from mutiny; characterized by or expressing mutiny. L16.

1 I. MURDOCH Titus and Gilbert had been in a state of subdued revolt, they were mutinous. c R. G. PRESTON The mutinous Passions of Grief, Anger, and Sadness do . . distract thee. 2 O. MANNING The sense of mutinous anger had gone.

mutinously *adv.* L16. **mutinousness** *n.* E17.

mutiny /ˈmjuːtɪni/ *n.* M16. [f. MUTINE *v.* or *n.* + -Y[3].] †1 Discord, strife; a dispute, a quarrel. M16–M17. 2 Open revolt against constituted authority, now *spec.* on the part of a disciplined esp. military or naval body against its officers or leaders; disregard for discipline, rebellious conduct; an instance of this, a mutinous rebellion. L16.

2 C. FRANCIS He would have to take action to prevent discontent developing into mutiny. **Indian Mutiny, Sepoy Mutiny** *Hist.* revolt of Indian (esp. Bengali) troops against the British in 1857–8.

mutiny /ˈmjuːtɪni/ *v.i.* M16. [f. the n.] 1 Engage in mutiny; revolt *against*; refuse to obey orders of a superior, esp. in the military and naval services. M16. †2 Contend or strive *with*, quarrel. L16–E17.

1 *fig.*: F. M. FORD Nevertheless her mind mutinied and revolted.

mutism /ˈmjuːtɪz(ə)m/ *n.* E19. [Fr. *mutisme*, f. L *mutus*: see MUTE *a.*, -ISM.] The state or condition of being mute; inability or unwillingness to speak, esp. (*Psychol.*) for psychological rather than physiological reasons.

muton /ˈmjuːtɒn/ *n.* M20. [f. MUT(ATION + -ON.] *Biol.* The smallest element of genetic material which can undergo a distinct mutation, usu. identified as a single pair of nucleotides. Cf. RECON *n.*[2]

mutoscope /ˈmjuːtəskəʊp/ *n.* L19. [f. L *mutare* change + -O- + -SCOPE.] *Hist.* An apparatus in which a series of photographs of a scene in motion may be viewed by looking through an aperture and turning a handle at the side of the instrument.

mutt /mʌt/ *n.* *slang* (orig. *US*). L19. [Abbrev. of *mutton-head* s.v. MUTTON.] 1 A stupid, awkward, or incompetent person; *gen.* a person, a fellow. L19. 2 A dog, *esp.* a mongrel. *derog.* or *joc.* E20.

1 **Mutt and Jeff** [f. two cartoon characters, one tall and one short, created by H. C. Fisher (1884–1954)] (*a*) a stupid or ill-matched pair of men; (*b*) *rhyming slang* deaf. 2 A. LURIE A medium-sized dirty-white long-haired mutt, mainly Welsh terrier.

mutter /ˈmʌtə/ *n.*[1] M17. [f. the vb.] An act of muttering, a low indistinct utterance.

mutter /ˈmʌtə/ *n.*[2] *rare.* M19. [Hindi *matar.*] A variety of pea from the Indian subcontinent.

mutter /ˈmʌtə/ *v.* ME. [f. base repr. also by MUTE *a.*: see -ER[5]. Cf. G dial. *muttern.*] 1 *v.i.* Speak in low and barely audible tones with the mouth nearly closed. ME. b Speak covertly *against*, complain *at*, grumble. M16. c *transf.* Make a low rumbling sound. L18. 2 *v.t.* Utter or say (a thing, *that*) indistinctly in a low tone; *fig.* express or say in secret, complain (*that*). LME.

1 J. CONRAD Muttering cautiously with downcast eyes. b DEFOE Our men muttered a little at this; but I pacified them. c D. H. LAWRENCE Thunder muttered in different places. 2 J. B. PRIESTLEY Mrs. Mounder . . muttered something that nobody could catch. *Times* Politicians . . began to mutter that the partnership was getting . . too cosy. **mutter over** recite (words) in low indistinct tones, mumble.

mutterer *n.* M16. **muttering** *n.* (*a*) the action of the vb; (*b*) something muttered; a rumour: E16. **mutteringly** *adv.* in a muttering manner L17.

Mutti /ˈmʊti/ *n.* *colloq.* E20. [G, f. *Mutter* mother.] Among German-speaking people: mother.

M. A. VON ARNIM Mutti, she's a witch!

mutton /ˈmʌt(ə)n/ *n.* ME. [OFr. *moton* (mod. *mouton*) f. med.L *multo(n-)*, prob. of Gaulish origin: cf. (O)Ir. *molt* castrated ram, Gael. *mult*, Welsh *mollt*, Corn. *mols* wether, Breton *maout* sheep.] 1 The flesh of sheep used as food. ME. 2a A sheep, *esp.* one intended to be eaten. Now only *joc.* ME. b The carcass of a sheep. *arch.* E17. 3 The genitals of a woman; copulation; *collect.* prostitutes. *slang. obs.* exc. in *hawk one's mutton* below. E16. 4 In full *mutton candle*. A candle made of mutton fat. *obs.* exc. *Hist.* M19. 5 *Typogr.* In full *mutton quad, quadrat*. = EM *quad, quadrat*. L19.

Phrases: *dead as mutton*: see DEAD *a.* **hawk one's mutton** *slang* (of a woman) look for a lover; solicit. LACED *mutton*. **mutton dressed as lamb** *colloq.* an ageing or unattractive woman dressed or made up as if younger or more attractive. POOR MAN *of mutton*. **return to one's muttons** *joc.* [after Fr. *revenons à nos moutons*] return to the matter in hand. *shoulder-of-mutton fist, sail*: see SHOULDER *n.* *underground mutton*: see UNDERGROUND *a.*

Comb.: *mutton-candle*: see sense 4 above; **mutton chop** (*a*) a piece of mutton, *spec.* including the rib and half vertebra to which it is attached; (*b*) (in full *mutton chop whisker*) a side whisker shaped like this, narrow at the top and broad and rounded at the bottom; **mutton-fat** *a.* (*a*) made of mutton fat; (*b*) designating a creamy white type of jade valued highly by connoisseurs; **mutton-fisted** *a.* (*colloq.*) clumsy, heavy-handed, ham-fisted; **mutton-head** *colloq.* (orig. *US*) a dull stupid person; **mutton-headed** *a.* (*colloq.* orig. *US*) dull, stupid; **mutton-leg sleeve** = *leg-of-mutton sleeve* s.v. LEG *n.*; *mutton quad, quadrat*: see sense 5 above; **mutton snapper** a large snapper, *Lutjanus analis*, of the Caribbean and W. Atlantic, with a black blotch below the dorsal fin.

muttoned *a.* (of a sheep) having flesh (of a specified quality), covered with flesh M19. **muttony** *a.* having the quality of or resembling mutton M19.

mutton-bird /ˈmʌt(ə)nbəːd/ *n.* E19. [f. prec. + BIRD *n.*] 1 Any of various sea birds of southern oceans whose cooked flesh is said to resemble mutton in flavour: (*a*) *NZ* the sooty shearwater, *Puffinus griseus*; (*b*) *Austral.* the short-tailed shearwater, *P. tenuirostris*; (*c*) an Antarctic petrel of the genus *Pterodroma*. E19. 2 *mutton-bird scrub*, a shrub or small tree, *Senecio reinoldii*, of the composite family, with round leathery leaves and small yellow flowers. *NZ.* L19.

mutton-birder *n.* (*Austral.* & *NZ*) a person who catches mutton-birds for food or sport L19.

mutton-fish /ˈmʌt(ə)nfɪʃ/ *n.* Pl. **-es** /-ɪz/, (usu.) same. M18. [f. MUTTON + FISH *n.*[1]] 1 Any of various marine fishes of the Caribbean and W. Atlantic whose flesh is said to resemble mutton, *esp.* an eelpout. M18. 2 (The flesh of) an edible mollusc of the genus *Haliotis*, esp. *H. ruber*; an abalone, a paua. *Austral.* M19.

mutual /ˈmjuːtʃʊəl, -tjʊəl/ *a.* & *n.* L15. [(O)Fr. *mutuel*, f. L *mutuus* borrowed, mutual, cogn. w. *mutare* to change: see -AL[1].] A *adj.* 1 Of a feeling, action, etc.: experienced, expressed, or performed by each of the parties concerned towards or with regard to the other(s); reciprocal. L15. b Having the same feelings for each other; standing in a reciprocal relation to another. M16. c Pertaining to or characterized by some (implied) mutual action or relation; *spec.* designating a building society, insurance company, etc., owned by its members and dividing some or all of its profits between them. L18. d *Electr.* Of a quantity, property, etc.: dependent equally and symmetrically on two circuits or circuit elements, and representing an effect on either of a certain kind of change in the other. M19. 2 Respective, belonging to each respectively. M16. 3 Held in common or shared between two or more parties. L16. †4 Of a relationship etc.: intimate. E17–M18. †5 Responsive. M17–M19.

1 J. S. HUXLEY Mutual aid . . establishes minimum waste. V. BRITTAIN The mutual devotion between herself and Roland was very pleasant to see. P. DICKINSON Can't stand the sight of her. . . Feeling's mutual. 3 P. MONETTE We met . . at a mutual friend's apartment.

Special collocations: **mutual admiration society** a group of people prone to overestimate each other's merits. **mutual assured destruction** a US military scenario in which nuclear war is deterred by each side knowing that the other is capable of inflicting unacceptable damage if attacked; abbrev. *MAD*. **mutual characteristic** *Electronics* a characteristic curve representing the variation of anode current with grid voltage at constant anode voltage. **mutual conductance** *Electronics* the ratio of the change in the anode current of a valve to the change of grid voltage causing it, the anode voltage being constant. **mutual fund** *N. Amer.* a unit trust. **mutual inductance** *Electr.* the property of two circuits or devices by virtue of which a variation in the current flowing through one induces an electromotive force in the other; also called *transconductance*. *mutual* MASTURBATION.

B *ellipt.* as *n.* 1 A mutual friend. *rare.* E20. 2 A mutual fund, society, etc. L20.

¶Sense A.3 is sometimes regarded as incorrect.

mutualness *n.* E17.

mutualise *v.* var. of MUTUALIZE.

mutualism /ˈmjuːtʃʊəlɪz(ə)m, -tjʊə-/ *n.* M19. [f. MUTUAL + -ISM.] 1 The doctrine that individual and collective well-being is attainable only by mutual dependence; a system based on this, *spec.* one involving non-profit credit and voluntary association for the exchange of services. M19. 2 *Biol.* A condition of (obligate or facultative) symbiosis in which two organisms contribute mutually to the well-being of each other. L19.

mutualist /ˈmjuːtʃʊəlɪst, -tjʊə-/ *n.* & *a.* M19. [f. MUTUAL + -IST.] A *n.* 1 An advocate of mutualism. M19. 2 *Biol.* An organism which lives in a condition of mutualism with another. L19. B *attrib.* or as *adj.* Of or pertaining to mutualists or mutualism. E20.

mutuaˈlistic *a.* exhibiting or characteristic of mutualism L19. **mutuaˈlistically** *adv.* M20.

mutuality /mjuːtʃʊˈalɪti, -tjʊ-/ *n.* L16. [f. MUTUAL + -ITY.] 1 The quality or condition of being mutual; reciprocity. L16. b *Law.* A situation in which two parties are mutually bound to perform certain reciprocal duties. M19. c A system of organizing conditions of work by agreement between the worker involved and the employer. M20. 2 An interchange of acts of goodwill; an intimacy. E17.

mutualize /ˈmjuːtʃʊəlʌɪz, -tjʊə-/ *v.t.* Also **-ise**. E19. [f. MUTUAL + -IZE.] †1 Give and receive in return; exchange. *rare.* Only in E19. 2 Organize (a company etc.) on cooperative or mutual principles. E20.

mutualiˈzation *n.* E20.

mutually /ˈmjuːtʃʊəli, -tjʊə-/ *adv.* M16. [f. MUTUAL + -LY[2].] 1 With mutual action or feeling; in a mutual relation; reciprocally. Freq. in *mutually exclusive*. M16. †b In return; as one side of a reciprocal action. L16–E18. 2 In cooperation or companionship; by mutual agreement; jointly, in common. L16.

1 D. H. LAWRENCE They began mutually to mistrust each other. A. T. ELLIS My mother . . thought the two qualities went together and Lili said they . . were mutually exclusive. **mutually assured destruction** = *mutual assured destruction* s.v. MUTUAL *a.*

mutuary /ˈmjuːtʃʊəri, -tjʊə-/ *n.* M19. [L *mutuarius*, f. *mutuus* borrowed: see MUTUAL, -ARY[1].] *Law.* A borrower of a thing which is to be consumed and therefore to be returned in kind.

†mutuate *v.t.* M16–E18. [L *mutuat-* pa. ppl stem of *mutuari* borrow, f. *mutuus* borrowed: see MUTUAL, -ATE³.] Borrow.

mutuation /mjuːtʃʊˈeɪʃ(ə)n, -tju-/ *n.* Now *rare.* E17. [f. as prec. + -ATION.] An act of lending or borrowing.

mutuatitious /ˌmjuːtʃʊəˈtɪʃəs, -tjʊ-/ *a. rare.* E17. [f. L *mutuatitius*, f. as MUTUATE: see -ITIOUS¹.] Borrowed, taken from some other.

mutuel /ˈmjuːtʃʊəl, -tjʊəl; *foreign* mytɥɛl (*pl. same*)/ *n.* Chiefly *N. Amer.* E20. [Abbrev. of PARI-MUTUEL.] A totalizator, a *pari-mutuel*.

mutule /ˈmjuːtjuːl/ *n.* M17. [Fr. f. L *mutulus*.] *Archit.* A block projecting under a cornice in the Doric order.

Earlier **†mutulo** *n.*, pl. **-li**, [It.]: only in M16.

mutuum /ˈmjuːtʃʊəm, -tjʊəm/ *n. obs.* exc. *Sc.* & *US.* L15. [L = loan, use as n. of neut. of *mutuus* borrowed: see MUTUAL.] *Law.* A contract under which a thing is lent which is to be consumed and therefore is to be returned in kind.

muu-muu /ˈmuːmuː/ *n.* Also **mu-mu**. E20. [Haw. *mu'u mu'u* lit. 'cut off' f. the original absence of a yoke.] A woman's usu. brightly coloured and patterned loose-fitting dress, (as) worn in Hawaii.

muvule /mʊˈvuːli/ *n.* Also **mvule** /(ə)mˈvuːli/ & other vars. E20. [Luganda *muvule*, Kiswahili *mvule*.] In E. Africa: (the timber of) an iroko.

muvver /ˈmʌvə/ *n. nursery* & *dial.* L19. [Repr. a pronunc.] Mother.

mux /mʌks/ *v.* & *n. dial.* (chiefly *US*). E19. [Origin uncertain: cf. MUSS *v.*, MUCK *v.*] **A** *v.t.* = MUCK *v.* 3. E19. **B** *n.* = MUCK *n.*¹ 3. M19.

Muzak /ˈmjuːzak/ *n.* Also **m-**. M20. [Alt. of MUSIC *n.* Cf. KODAK.] (Proprietary name for) a system for transmitting background music by wire for playing in a public place; recorded light background music generally; *transf.* bland undemanding music.

attrib.: *Arena* Muzak versions of 'Walk on By' . . are piped around the restaurants.

Muzaked *a.* (*a*) supplied with Muzak; (*b*) played in a style resembling that of Muzak: M20.

muzhik /muːˈʒɪk/ *n.* Also **moujik**. M16. [Russ.] *Hist.* A Russian peasant.

muzz /mʌz/ *v.* & *n.* M18. [Origin uncertain: cf. MUG *v.*⁵, MUZZLE *v.*², MUZZY.] **A** *v.* **1** *v.i.* Study intently, work hard *over* a book etc. *slang.* M18. **2** *v.t.* Make confused or muzzy, fuddle. *colloq.* L18.

2 G. BLACK Drugs don't seem to have muzzed you.

B *n.* **1** A person who studies intently. *slang.* L18. **2** A state of mental confusion; muddle, blur. *colloq.* M19.

muzzed *a.* (*colloq.*) fuddled; *spec.* drunk, intoxicated: L18.

muzzle /ˈmʌz(ə)l/ *n.* LME. [OFr. *musel* (mod. *museau*) f. Proto-Gallo-Romance dim. of med.L *musum*, of unkn. origin.] **I 1** The projecting part of an animal's face, including the nose and mouth. LME. **b** The part of the human face including the nose and chin. *joc.* LME. **2** The open end of the barrel of a firearm. M16. **3** A piece of metal on the end of a plough-beam to which the draught-tackle is attached; a clevis. Now *Sc.* M16.

1 R. SUTCLIFF One of the hounds poked a friendly muzzle into her face. 2 P. CAMPBELL I have looked down the muzzle of a gun.

II 4 A guard usu. consisting of straps or wires, put over an animal's nose and mouth to prevent it biting or eating. LME. **b** *Hist.* An ornamental piece of armour covering a horse's nose. M19.

4 R. CROMPTON They ought to wear muzzles; they've got rabies.

Comb.: **muzzle-loader** a firearm loaded through the muzzle; **muzzle-loading** *a.* loaded through the muzzle; **muzzle velocity** the velocity at which a projectile leaves the muzzle of a firearm.

†muzzle *a.* L17–E19. [OFr. *meslé*: see MUZZLED *a.*²] = MUZZLED *a.*²

muzzle /ˈmʌz(ə)l/ *v.*¹ LME. [f. the n.] **I** *v.t.* **1** Put a muzzle on (an animal, an animal's mouth); prevent by means of a muzzle from biting etc. LME. **2†a** Muffle, veil, mask, (the face). *Sc.* LME–L16. **b** Muffle the sound of (a musical instrument or bell). Now *dial.* M17. **3** Restrain from speaking, impose silence on. Now *spec.* censor, deprive of freedom of speech, (an institution or person, esp. the press). M16. **4a** Bring the muzzle or snout close to; *slang* kiss (a person), caress with the mouth. L16. **†b** Root about or amongst. E17–M18. **5** *Naut.* Take in (a sail). L17. **6** Hit (a person) on the mouth; beat up, thrash. *slang.* M19.

3 P. HOWARD He tried to frighten the British Government into muzzling *The Times*. A. N. WILSON The only voice . . the Russian Government did not dare to muzzle.

II *v.i.* **7** Thrust out the muzzle or nose; feel, smell, or root about with the muzzle. L15.

muzzle /ˈmʌz(ə)l/ *v.*² *dial.* L18. [App. conn. w. MUZZ *v.* & MUZZY.] **1** *v.t.* Make muzzy or confused, fuddle. L18. **2** *v.i.* Drink to excess. E19.

muzzled /ˈmʌz(ə)ld/ *a.*¹ LME. [f. MUZZLE *n.*, *v.*¹: see -ED², -ED¹.] **†1** Muffled, veiled, masked. *Sc.* LME–L16. **2** Having a muzzle (of a specified kind); wearing a muzzle. E16.

†muzzled *a.*² M17–M19. [Prob. f. OFr. *meslé* pa. pple of *mesler* mingle, mix (see MEDDLE) + -ED². Cf. MUZZLE *a.*] Brindled, dappled, flecked.

muzzler /ˈmʌzlə/ *n.* M17. [f. MUZZLE *n.*, *v.*¹ + -ER¹.] **1** A person who muzzles an animal. M17. **2** A blow on the mouth. *slang.* E19. **3** A muzzle-loading gun. L19. **4** *Naut.* A head wind. L19.

muzzy /ˈmʌzi/ *a. colloq.* E18. [Origin unkn.: cf. MUZZ, MUZZLE *v.*², FUZZY 3.] **1a** Dull, spiritless; mentally hazy or confused; dazed, fuddled, esp. through drinking alcohol. E18. **b** Blurred, indistinct. L18. **2** Of a place or occasion: tedious, gloomy. E18.

1a B. CASTLE Muzzy with all the complicated insurance formulae I have been studying. M. KEANE A bit muzzy probably after all that port and brandy. b *Daily Telegraph* The muzzy pictures reaching our screens from the moon.

muzzily *adv.* E20. **muzziness** *n.* E19.

mvule *n.* var. of MUVULE.

Mwami /ˈmwɑːmi/ *n.* L19. [Rwanda *umwami* chief.] (The royal title of) any the former kings of Ruanda and Urundi (now Rwanda and Burundi) in central Africa.

my /mʌɪ, *unstressed* mɪ/ *possess. a.* (in mod. usage also classed as a *determiner*), *1 sing.* Also (informal) **m'**, (now repr. non-standard speech) **mi** /mɪ/. ME. [Reduced form of MINE *a.* (orig. bef. consonants except *h*). Cf. ME *a.* See also MAH.] **1** Of me; of myself; which belongs or pertains to me. ME. **b** (Before a title) that has the specified social status or relationship with regard to me; (before a personal name) that has a familial relationship with me. ME. **2** *voc.* Used affectionately before terms of endearment or (chiefly *literary*) relationship, and affectionately, compassionately, familiarly, or patronizingly before certain designations otherwise rarely used vocatively, as *my man, my girl, my good woman, my poor man*. ME. **3** As *int.* Expr. surprise or admiration. Also redupl. (*my, my!*) and *oh, my!* E19.

1 SCOTT FITZGERALD My name is Judy Jones. D. BARNES Oh God, when I think back to my past. E. O'NEILL My saying what I'm telling you now proves it. *Listener* I knew that I did not look my best in my mackintosh. I. MURDOCH I call it my office, but it was more like their office. C. RAYNER You are a very remarkable surgeon, sir . . to have saved my brother from bleeding to death. *my eye!, my foot!, my goodness!, my hat!, my heavens!, my word!*, etc. *my own*: see OWN *a.* & *pron.* b C. M. YONGE A little pair of socks . . for my Johnnie. *my lady*: see LADY *n. my lord*: see LORD *n.* 2 J. STEINBECK These cheap white girls are vicious, my friend. M. KEANE Muriel, my dear, you may take Cynthia up to her room. 3 M. DE LA ROCHE My, you boys can play. . . I'd sooner dance to your music than any of the big orchestras. R. DAHL Oh my, it's perfect! It's beautiful. *New Yorker* My my and here I am out where I can't even get a case of Scotch to celebrate.

Comb.: **my-dear** *v.t.* address as 'my dear'; **my-lady** *v.t.* address as 'my lady'; **my-lord** *v.t.* address as 'my lord'.

mya /ˈmʌɪə/ *n.* Pl. **myae** /ˈmʌiiː/, **myas**. L18. [mod.L (see below), prob. alt. of Gk *mus* mussel.] *Zool.* A soft-shelled burrowing bivalve of the genus *Mya*; a gaper. Now chiefly as mod.L genus name.

myal /ˈmʌɪəl/ *n.* & *attrib. a.* L18. [Perh. f. Hausa *maye* sorcerer.] (Of or pertaining to) myalism.

myalgia /mʌɪˈaldʒə/ *n.* M19. [f. MYO- + -ALGIA.] *Med.* Muscular pain.

myalgic *a.* pertaining to, involving, or affected with myalgia; *myalgic encephalomyelitis*, a prolonged form of encephalomyelitis usu. occurring after a viral infection, characterized by headaches, fever, localized muscular pain, and weakness (abbrev. *ME*; also called *postviral (fatigue) syndrome*): M19.

myalism /ˈmʌɪəlɪz(ə)m/ *n.* M19. [f. MYAL + -ISM.] A kind of sorcery or witchcraft similar to obeah, practised in the W. Indies and some other countries.

myalist *n.* a person who practises myalism M19.

myall /ˈmʌɪəl/ *n.*¹ & *a. Austral.* L18. [Aborig.] **A** *n.* **†1** Among Aborigines: a stranger. L18–M19. **2** An Aborigine living in a traditional manner. Cf. WARRIGAL *n.* 2. M19. **B** *attrib.* or as *adj.* **†1** Among Aborigines: strange. E–M19. **2** Living in a traditional Aboriginal manner. Also, uncivilized, wild. M19.

myall /ˈmʌɪəl/ *n.*² M19. [Aborig., perh. transf. use of source of prec.] Any of several Australian acacias, *esp.* (more fully *weeping myall*) *Acacia pendula*, with a hard scented wood; the wood of these trees, used as fencing timber etc.

myasthenia /mʌɪəsˈθiːnɪə/ *n.* M19. [f. MYO- + ASTHENIA.] *Med.* Abnormal muscular weakness; *spec.* = *myasthenia gravis* below.

Comb.: **myasthenia gravis** /ˈgrɑːvɪs, ˈgravɪs/ [L = severe, grave] a rare chronic autoimmune disease, commoner in adolescents and young women, characterized by muscular weakness without atrophy and caused by a defect in the action of acetylcholine at neuromuscular junctions.

myasthenic /-ˈθɛnɪk/ *a.* pertaining to, involving, or affected with myasthenia M19.

myatonia *n.* var. of MYOTONIA.

mycelium /mʌɪˈsiːlɪəm/ *n.* Pl. **-ia** /-ɪə/. M19. [f. Gk *mukēs* fungus + *-elium*, after *epithelium*.] *Bot.* The vegetative part of the thallus of a fungus, usu. consisting of a network of fine white filaments (hyphae); tissue of this kind.

mycelial *a.* consisting of, pertaining to, or characterized by mycelium L19. **mycelioid** *a.* = MYCELIAL M19.

Mycenaean /mʌɪsɪˈniːən/ *n.* & *a.* L18. [f. L *Mycenaeus*, f. *Mycenae* Mycenae (see below) + -AN.] **A** *n.* A native or inhabitant of Mycenae, an ancient Greek city in the Argive plain. Also, the Greek dialect used when Mycenae flourished. L18. **B** *adj.* Of or pertaining to Mycenae; *esp.* designating or pertaining to the civilization, culture, or art of which it was the centre. M19.

myceto- /mʌɪˈsiːtəʊ/ *comb. form* of Gk *mukēt-*, *mukēs* fungus: see -O-. Cf. MYCO-.

mycetocyte *n.* (*Entomol.*) any of the large cells found in some insects, sometimes aggregated into a mycetome, which contain yeasts or other symbiotic micro-organisms E20. **mycetophagous** /mʌɪsɪˈtɒfəgəs/ *a.* feeding on fungi or mushrooms, fungivorous E20. **mycetophilid** *a.* & *n.* (*a*) *adj.* designating or pertaining to the dipteran family Mycetophilidae of fungus gnats or midges; (*b*) *n.* a mycetophilid fly: L19. **myceto'zoan** *n.* a myxomycete, a slime mould, *spec.* as considered to belong to the animal kingdom and placed in the class Mycetozoa L19.

mycetoma /mʌɪsɪˈtəʊmə/ *n.* Pl. **-mas, -mata** /-mətə/. L19. [f. MYCETO- + -OMA.] *Med.* Any of various conditions due to fungal infection; *spec.* the tropical disease Madura foot.

mycetomatous *a.* affected with mycetoma L19.

mycetome /ˈmʌɪsɪtəʊm/ *n.* E20. [f. MYCETO- + -OME.] *Entomol.* An organ consisting of an aggregation of mycetocytes, present in some insects.

-mycin /ˈmʌɪsɪn/ *suff.* [f. MYCO- + -IN¹.] Forming the names of antibiotic compounds derived from fungi, the first elem. usu. being part of a Latin binomial name, as *actinomycin*, *erythromycin*, *streptomycin*, etc.

myco- /ˈmʌɪkəʊ/ *comb. form.* [Irreg. f. Gk *mukēs* fungus + -O-. Cf. MYCETO-.] Forming chiefly scientific wds relating to fungi, as *mycology*, *mycoplasma*, *mycosis*, etc.

myco'biont *n.* [-BIONT] the fungal component of a lichen (cf. PHYCOBIONT) M20. **mycophile** *n.* a person who is fond of eating wild mushrooms and toadstools M20. **myco'philic** *a.* fond of or feeding on wild mushrooms and toadstools M20. **mycoprotein** *n.* †(*a*) the supposed principal constituent of cytoplasm; (*b*) a protein of fungal origin, *esp.* one produced for human consumption: L19. **mycotoxi'cosis** *n.*, pl. **-coses** /-'kəʊsiːz/, a pathological condition caused by a mycotoxin M20. **mycotoxin** *n.* a toxic substance produced by a fungus M20.

mycobacterium /ˌmʌɪkə(ʊ)bak'tɪərɪəm/ *n.* Pl. **-ia** /-ɪə/. E20. [mod.L (see below), f. as MYCO- + BACTERIUM.] *Med.* & *Biol.* Any of various Gram-positive, aerobic, filament-forming bacteria of the genus *Mycobacterium* or the family Mycobacteriaceae, including the causative agents of tuberculosis and leprosy.

mycobacterial *a.* of, pertaining to, or caused by mycobacteria M20.

mycology /mʌɪ'kɒlədʒi/ *n.* M19. [f. MYCO- + -LOGY.] The scientific study of fungi. Also, the fungi of a district or region.

myco'logic *a.* = MYCOLOGICAL L19. **myco'logical** *a.* of or pertaining to mycology or fungi M19. **myco'logically** *adv.* L19. **mycologist** *n.* M19.

mycophagy /mʌɪ'kɒfədʒi/ *n.* M19. [f. MYCO- + -PHAGY.] The eating of fungi, esp. (by a person) of those species usually neglected or avoided.

'mycophage *n.* = MYCOPHAGIST M20. **mycophagist** *n.* a person who practises mycophagy; an animal that eats fungi: M19. **mycophagous** *a.* fungus-eating, mycetophagous E20.

mycoplasma /mʌɪkə(ʊ)'plazmə/ *n.* Pl. **-mas**, **-mata** /-mətə/. M20. [mod.L *Mycoplasma* genus name, f. as MYCO- + PLASMA.] *Biol.* Any of a group of pleomorphic, Gram-negative, chiefly parasitic micro-organisms without a cell wall, which are smaller than bacteria but, unlike viruses, capable of growth in artificial media. Also called *pleuropneumonia-like organism*.

mycoplasmal *a.* of, pertaining to, or caused by mycoplasmas M20. **mycoplas'mosis** *n.*, pl. **-moses** /-'məʊsiːz/, a disease, esp. one of animals, caused by mycoplasma M20.

mycorrhiza /mʌɪkə(ʊ)'rʌɪzə/ *n.* Pl. **-zae** /-ziː/, **-zas**. Also **mycorhiza**. L19. [f. MYCO- + Gk *rhiza* root.] *Bot.* A symbiotic or slightly pathogenic fungus growing in association with the roots of a plant, either on the surface or within the cortex.

mycorrhizal *a.* E20.

mycosis /mʌɪ'kəʊsɪs/ *n.* Pl. **-coses** /-'kəʊsiːz/. M19. [f. MYCO- + -OSIS.] *Med.* 1 A disease caused by fungal infection, as ringworm. M19. 2 *mycosis fungoides* /fʌŋ'gɔɪdiːz/ [mod.L = fungoid], a malignant, usu. protracted lymphoma mainly confined to the skin and resulting in dome-shaped tumours. L19.

mycotic /mʌɪ'kɒtɪk/ *a.* pertaining to or of the nature of mycosis; *mycotic aneurysm*, aneurysm due to fungal or (usu.) bacterial infection: L19.

mycotrophy /mʌɪ'kɒtrəfi/ *n.* E20. [f. MYCO- + -TROPHY.] *Bot.* The association of the roots of certain plants with mycorrhizae which apparently aid the uptake of nutrients.

mycotrophic /-'trəʊfɪk, -'trɒfɪk/ *a.* of, pertaining to, or characterized by mycotrophy E20.

mycterism /'mɪktərɪz(ə)m/ *n.* *rare.* Also (earlier) in L form †**-ismus**. M16. [Gk *muktērismos*, f. *muktērizein* sneer at, f. *muktēr* nose: see -ISM.] A gibe, a scoff; scoffing.

myctophid /'mɪktəfɪd/ *n.* & *a.* M20. [mod.L *Myctophidae* (see below), f. *Myctophum* genus name f. Gk *muktēr* nose + *ophis* snake: see -ID[3].] *Zool.* A *n.* Any member of the family Myctophidae of deep-water marine fishes, having luminous organs along their sides. Also called *lantern-fish*. M20. B *adj.* Of, pertaining to, or designating this family. M20.

mydas fly /'mʌɪdəs flʌɪ/ *n. phr.* Also (earlier) **midas**. L19. [f. mod.L *Mydas* genus name.] Any of various large insectivorous dipteran flies of the family Mydidae (Mydaidae).

mydriasis /mɪdrɪ'eɪsɪs/ *n.* E19. [L f. Gk *mudriasis*: see -IASIS.] *Ophthalm.* Excessive dilatation of the pupil of the eye.

mydriatic /mɪdrɪ'atɪk/ *a.* & *n.* (*a*) *adj.* of, pertaining to, or causing mydriasis; (*b*) *n.* a drug that causes mydriasis: M19.

myel- *comb. form* see MYELO-.

myelencephalon /mʌɪəlɛn'sɛf(ə)lɒn, -'kɛf-/ *n.* M19. [f. MYELO- + ENCEPHALON.] *Anat.* 1 The cerebrospinal axis or system. Now *rare* or *obs.* M19. 2 The medulla oblongata. L19.

myelence'phalic, **-cephalous** *adjs.* of or pertaining to the myelencephalon M19.

myelin /'mʌɪəlɪn/ *n.* Also †**-ine**. M19. [f. MYELO- + -IN[1], -INE[5].] †1 *Chem.* A phospholipid substance extracted from various animal and some plant tissues. M–L19. 2 A complex mixture of proteins and phospholipids which forms an insulating sheath around certain nerve fibres. L19.

Comb.: **myelin sheath** the insulating layer of myelin laid down, usu. spirally, around the axons of certain nerve fibres by Schwann cells, which increases the rapidity of impulse conduction.

myelinated *a.* (of a nerve fibre) enclosed in a myelin sheath L19. **myeli'nation** *n.* the process of becoming myelinated; the state of being myelinated: L19.

myelitis /mʌɪə'lʌɪtɪs/ *n.* M19. [f. MYELO- + -ITIS.] *Med.* 1 Inflammation of the spinal cord. M19. 2 Inflammation of the bone marrow, osteomyelitis. *rare.* E20.

1 *transverse myelitis*: see TRANSVERSE *a.*

myelitic /mʌɪə'lɪtɪk/ *a.* M19.

myelo- /'mʌɪələʊ/ *comb. form* of Gk *muelos*, *-on* marrow, spinal cord: see -O-. Bef. a vowel also **myel-**.

myelo'genesis *n.* (*Physiol.*) the formation of myelin, myelination E20. **myelo'genic** *a.* (*Med.*) originating in the bone marrow L19. **mye'logenous** *a.* (*Med.*) = MYELOGENIC; *spec.* designating a form of leukaemia: L19. **myelogram** *n.* (*Med.*) (*a*) a radiograph obtained by myelography; (*b*) (a list of) the relative numbers of the various cells in a sample of bone marrow: M20. **myelo'graphic** *a.* of or pertaining to myelography M20. **myelo'graphically** *adv.* by myelography M20. **mye'lography** *n.* (*Med.*) radiography of the spinal cord after injection of a contrast medium or air into the subarachnoid space M20. **myelomono'cytic** *a.* (*Med.*) (of leukaemia) characterized by the presence in the blood of monocytes and their myeloid precursor cells M20. **myelope'roxidase** *n.* (*Biochem.*) a greenish peroxidase occurring in granules in myelocytes and neutrophils M20. **myelopro'liferative** *a.* (*Med.*) characterized by or pertaining to the proliferation of cells of or derived from the bone marrow M20. **mye'losis** *n.*, pl. **-loses** /-'ləʊsiːz/, *Med.* (*a*) *rare* (the formation of) a tumour of the spinal cord; (*b*) the proliferation of blood-cell precursors in the bone marrow: L19.

myeloblast /'mʌɪələ(ʊ)blast/ *n.* E20. [f. MYELO- + -BLAST.] *Physiol.* An immature bone-marrow cell, the precursor of a myelocyte, appearing in the blood in certain diseases.

myelo'blastic *a.* of, pertaining to, or involving myeloblasts E20. **myelobla'stosis** *n.* the presence of abnormally large numbers of myeloblasts in the bone marrow and blood M20.

myelocele /'mʌɪələ(ʊ)siːl/ *n.*[1] Also **-coele**. L19. [f. MYELO- + -CELE.] *Med.* Spina bifida in which the spinal cord is exposed over part of its length, usu. without protrusion as a swelling; an area of neural tissue so exposed. Cf. MYELOMENINGOCELE.

myelocele *n.*[2] var. of MYELOCOELE *n.*[1]

myelocoele /'mʌɪələ(ʊ)siːl/ *n.*[1] Also **-cele**. L19. [f. MYELO- + Gk *koilos* hollow, cavity.] *Anat.* The central canal of the spinal cord.

myelocoele *n.*[2] var. of MYELOCELE *n.*[1]

myelocyte /'mʌɪələ(ʊ)sʌɪt/ *n.* M19. [f. MYELO- + -CYTE.] †1 The nucleus of a ganglionic nerve cell. M–L19. 2 *Physiol.* An immature bone-marrow cell derived from and smaller than a myeloblast, which gives rise to granulocytes and appears in the blood in certain diseases. L19.

myelocytic /mʌɪələ(ʊ)'sɪtɪk/ *a.* of or pertaining to a myelocyte or myelocytes; involving myelocytes: L19.

myeloid /'mʌɪəlɔɪd/ *a.* M19. [f. MYELO- + -OID.] Chiefly *Med.* Of, pertaining to, involving, or resembling (the cells of) bone marrow.

myeloma /mʌɪə'ləʊmə/ *n.* Pl. **-mas**, **-mata** /-mətə/. M19. [f. MYELO- + -OMA.] *Med.* A malignant tumour of bone-marrow cells. Also (more fully *multiple myeloma*), myelomatosis.

myelomatosis /ˌmʌɪələ(ʊ)mə'təʊsɪs/ *n.* Pl. **-toses** /-'təʊsiːz/. E20. [f. prec. + -OSIS.] *Med.* A malignant proliferation of plasma cells, which accumulate in the bone marrow, often associated with abnormal proteins in the blood and urine.

myelomeningocele /ˌmʌɪələ(ʊ)mɪ'nɪŋgəsiːl, -ndʒ-/ *n.* L19. [f. MYELO- + MENINGO- + -CELE.] *Med.* Spina bifida in which the spinal cord and its meninges protrude through the cleft, forming a rounded swelling; the tissue so protruding. Also called *meningomyelocele*. Cf. MYELOCELE *n.*[1]

myelon /'mʌɪəlɒn/ *n.* Now *rare* or *obs.* M19. [f. as MYELO-.] *Anat.* The spinal cord.

myenteric /mʌɪɛn'tɛrɪk/ *a.* L19. [f. MYO- + ENTERIC.] *Anat.* Designating or pertaining to a plexus of sympathetic and parasympathetic nerves situated between and supplying the two layers of muscle in the small intestine.

myenteric reflex an involuntary reaction of these muscles to stimulus, characterized by contraction of the intestine before the point of stimulation and relaxation after it.

mygale /'mɪgəli/ *n.* LME. [Late L f. Gk *mugalē*.] 1 A shrew. Long *rare*. LME. 2 *Zool.* A very large hairy mygalomorph spider of the American genus *Mygale*. M19.

mygalomorph /'mɪg(ə)ləmɔːf/ *a.* & *n.* E20. [mod.L *Mygalomorphae* (see below), f. as prec.: see -O-, -MORPH.] *Zool.* A *adj.* Of or pertaining to the suborder Orthognatha (formerly Mygalomorphae) of (mainly large) spiders, including bird spiders, American tarantulas, funnel-web spiders, and trapdoor spiders. E20. B *n.* A mygalomorph spider. M20.

myiasis /mʌɪ'eɪsɪs, 'mʌɪəsɪs/ *n.* Pl. **-ases** /-'eɪsiːz, -əsiːz/. M19. [f. Gk *muia* fly + -IASIS.] *Med.* Infestation with maggots; (a) disease caused by this.

Mylar /'mʌɪlɑː/ *n.* Also **m-**. M20. [Arbitrary.] (Proprietary name for) a polyester made by the condensation of ethylene glycol and terephthalic acid and used to make strong heat-resistant films.

mylodon /'mʌɪləd(ə)n/ *n.* M19. [mod.L *Mylodon* (see below), f. Gk *mulē*, *mulos* molar (lit. 'millstone') + -ODON.] A gigantic extinct ground sloth of the genus *Mylodon*, with more or less cylindrical teeth, found in deposits from the Pleistocene epoch in S. America.

mylodont *a.* & *n.* (pertaining to or characteristic of) a mylodon L19.

mylohyoid /mʌɪləʊ'hʌɪɔɪd/ *n.* & *a.* Also (earlier) in mod.L form **-hyoideus** /-hʌɪ'ɔɪdɪəs/. L17. [mod.L, f. Gk *mulē*, *mulos*: see prec., HYOID.] *Anat.* A *n.* The mylohyoid muscle. L17. B *adj.* Connected with the lower jaw and the hyoid bone. Chiefly in *mylohyoid muscle*, a flat triangular muscle in the floor of the mouth. E19.

mylohyoi'dean *a.* = MYLOHYOID *a.* M19.

mylonite /'mʌɪlənʌɪt/ *n.* L19. [f. Gk *mulōn* mill + -ITE[1].] *Petrogr.* A schist, esp. a banded one, resulting from the grinding or crushing of rocks.

mylonitic /mʌɪlə'nɪtɪk/ *a.* pertaining to or of the nature of a mylonite L19. **myloniti'zation** *n.* = MYLONIZATION E20. **mylonitize** *v.t.* = MYLONIZE E20. **myloni'zation** *n.* the formation of mylonite E20. **mylonize** *v.t.* convert into mylonite (chiefly as *mylonized* ppl a.) E20.

mynah /'mʌɪnə/ *n.* Also **myna**, (earlier) **mina**. M18. [Hindi *mainā*.] Any of various birds of SE Asia and the Indian subcontinent that are related to starlings, some of which can mimic the human voice; *esp.* (*a*) *Acridotheres tristis* (introduced in southern Africa, Australia, and elsewhere); (*b*) *Gracula religiosa* (more fully *hill mynah*); also (*Austral.*) = MINER 4. Also *mynah bird*.

mynheer /mʌɪn'hɛː, -'hɪə; mə'nɛː, -'nɪə/ *n.* Also **mijn-**, (*S. Afr.*) **meneer** /mə'nɪə/. M17. [Du. *mijnheer* (Afk. *meneer*), f. *mijn* my + *heer* lord, master.] 1 As a courteous form of address to or a title of a Dutch or Afrikaans man: sir, Mr. M17. 2 A Dutch or Afrikaans man, esp. a gentleman. E18.

myo- /'mʌɪəʊ/ *comb. form* of Gk *mus* (genit. *muos*) muscle: see -O-. Bef. a vowel also **my-**.

myoball *n.* (*Biol.*) a spheroidal syncytium cultured artificially from muscle cells, myotubes, or myoblasts L20. **myoblast** *n.* (*Embryol.*) a cell which with other similar cells gives rise to a muscle fibre L19. **myo'blastic** *a.* (*Embryol.*) of or pertaining to myoblasts L19. **myo'chemistry** *n.* the biochemistry of muscular action M20. **myo'clonic** *a.* pertaining to, affected with, or of the nature of myoclonus L19. **myo'clonus** *n.* (*Med.*) spasmodic jerky contraction of groups of muscles, esp. in the limbs L19. **myocoel** *n.* [Gk *koilos* hollow] *Embryol.* the cavity in the centre of an early embryonic myotome L19. **myocyte** *n.* (*Zool.*) a muscle cell; *esp.* (in some sponges) a contractile cell not part of an organized muscle: L19. **myoe'lastic** *a.* (*Anat.* & *Phonet.*) pertaining to or involving both muscular and elastic tissue E20. **myoe'lectric** *a.* designating, pertaining to, or (esp. of a prosthetic limb) operated by the electric currents associated with muscular action M20. **myoe'lectrically** *adv.* by means of myoelectric currents M20. **myoepi'thelial** *a.* (*Anat.* & *Zool.*) designating or pertaining to an epithelial cell containing contractile fibres, esp. in the body wall of coelenterates, and in the ducts of some mammalian glands L19. **myoepi'thelium** *n.* (*Anat.* & *Zool.*) (a) tissue composed of myoepithelial cells L19. **myofi'broma** *n.*, pl. **-mas, -mata** /-mətə/, *Med.* = MYOMA L19. **myofilament** *n.* (*Anat.* & *Zool.*) any of the ultramicroscopic threadlike aggregates of protein molecules, thick filaments of myosin and thin filaments of actin, present in contractile cells, esp. in the myofibrils of striated muscle M20. **myo'genesis** *n.* (*Embryol.*) the formation of muscular tissue L19. **myo'genic** *a.* produced by or arising in muscle tissue L19. **myogram** *n.* a chart or record made by a myograph L19. **myograph** *n.* an instrument for displaying or recording muscular contractions and relaxations; (now usu.) an electromyograph: M19. **myo'graphic** *a.* of or pertaining to a myograph M19. **myohaemo'globin** *n.* (*Biochem.*, now *rare*) = MYOGLOBIN E20. **myo-i'nositol** *n.* (*Biochem.*) an isomer of inositol which is present in animal and plant tissue and is a member of the vitamin B complex (also called *meso-inositol*) M20. **myo'kymia** *n.* [Gk *kuma* wave] *Med.* any of several benign disorders associated with fasciculation of muscle fibres E20. **myomere** *n.* (*Embryol.*) = MYOTOME L19. **myo'meric** *a.* (*Embryol.*) of or pertaining to myomeres L19. **myoneme** *n.* [Gk *nēma* thread] *Zool.* any of the contractile filaments in the cytoplasm of many protozoans L19. **myo'neural** *a.* = NEUROMUSCULAR E20. **myo'pathic** *a.* (*Med.*) of, pertaining to, or of the nature of myopathy M19. **my'opathy** *n.* (*Med.*) (a) disease of muscle tissue M19. **myoplasm** *n.* (*Anat.*) = SARCOPLASM E20. **myo'plasmic** *a.* = SARCOPLASMIC L20. **myosar'coma** *n.*, pl. **-mas, -mata** /-mətə/, *Med.* a malignant tumour of muscular tissue L19. **myo'septum** *n.*, pl. **-ta**, *Zool.* a membrane which separates adjacent myomeres in lower vertebrates and the embryos of higher vertebrates E20. **myotatic** /-'tatɪk/ *a.* [Gk *tatikos* exerting tension] *Physiol.* (of a muscular contraction, esp. a reflex) caused by stretching of the muscle L19. **myotube** *n.* (*Embryol.*) a cylindrical syncytial cell formed during the development of a muscle fibre from myoblasts M20.

myocardium /mʌɪə(ʊ)'kɑːdɪəm/ *n.* L19. [f. MYO-, after *pericardium*.] *Anat.* The muscular tissue of the heart.

myocardiac *a.* = MYOCARDIAL E20. **myocardial** *a.* of or pertaining to the myocardium L19. **myocar'ditis** *n.* inflammation of the myocardium M19.

Myochrysine *n.* see MYOCRISIN.

myocomma /mʌɪə(ʊ)'kɒmə/ *n.* Pl. **-mmas, -mmata** /-mətə/. L19. [f. MYO- + Gk *komma* segment, COMMA.] *Embryol.* Orig. = MYOTOME. Now = MYOSEPTUM.

Myocrisin /mʌɪə(ʊ)'krʌɪsɪn/ *n.* Also ***-chrysine**. M20. [Fr. *Myochrysine*, f. as MYO- + CHRYSO- + -INE[5].] *Pharm.* (Proprietary name for) sodium aurothiomalate, a gold-containing salt given intramuscularly to treat some cases of rheumatoid arthritis.

myofibril /mʌɪə(ʊ)'fʌɪbrɪl/ *n.* Also in L form **-fibrilla** /-fʌɪ'brɪlə/, pl. **-llae** /-liː/. L19. [f. MYO- + FIBRIL.] *Anat.* & *Zool.* Any of the numerous long cylindrical bundles of contractile myofilaments arranged in parallel in a striated muscle fibre.

myofi'brillar *a.* E20.

myogen /'mʌɪədʒ(ə)n/ *n.* L19. [f. MYO(SIN + -O- + -GEN.] *Biochem.* A mixture of albumins extracted from skeletal muscle plasma.

myoglobin /mʌɪə(ʊ)'gləʊbɪn/ *n.* E20. [f. MYO- + GLOBIN, after *haemoglobin*.] *Biochem.* A red iron-containing protein which carries and stores oxygen in muscle cells, and resembles a subunit of haemoglobin in structure.

myology /mʌɪ'ɒlədʒi/ *n.* M17. [f. MYO- + -LOGY.] **1** The scientific study of muscles, esp. of their anatomical arrangement. M17. **2** (A description of) the muscular anatomy of a particular animal or part of the body. L17.

myo'logical *a.* M19. **myologist** *n.* E19.

myoma /mʌɪ'əʊmə/ *n.* Pl. **-mas, -mata** /-mətə/. L19. [f. MYO- + -OMA.] *Med.* A benign tumour composed of muscular tissue.

myomatous *a.* pertaining to or of the nature of a myoma L19. **myo'mectomy** *n.* (an instance of) surgical removal of a myoma, esp. from the uterus L19.

myometrium /mʌɪə(ʊ)'miːtrɪəm/ *n.* E20. [f. MYO- + Gk *mētra* womb + -IUM.] *Anat.* The muscular layer which forms the bulk of the wall of the uterus.

myometrial *a.* M20.

myomorph /'mʌɪə(ʊ)mɔːf/ *n.* & *a.* L19. [mod.L *Myomorpha* (see below), f. Gk *muo-*, *mus* mouse + -MORPH.] *Zool.* **A** *n.* A rodent of the suborder Myomorpha, which includes the ratlike rodents (rats, most mice, voles, hamsters, dormice, jerboas, etc.). L19. **B** *adj.* Pertaining to or designating this suborder. M20.

myo'morphic *a.* L19.

myope /'mʌɪəʊp/ *n.* & *a.* E18. [Fr., f. L *myop-*, *myops* f. Gk *muōps*: see next.] **A** *n.* A short-sighted person. E18.

fig.: O. W. HOLMES Intellectual myopes, near-sighted specialists.

B *adj.* Myopic. L19.

myopia /mʌɪ'əʊpɪə/ *n.* E18. [mod.L f. late Gk *muōpia*, f. Gk *muōps* short-sighted, f. *muein* blink, shut (an eye): see -OPIA.] A condition in which distant objects appear blurred because their image is focused in front of the retina; short-sightedness (*lit.* & *fig.*), near-sightedness.

Also **myopism** *n.* E19. **myopy** *n.* (now *rare*) M19.

myopic /mʌɪ'ɒpɪk/ *a.* & *n.* E19. [f. prec. + -IC.] **A** *adj.* Of, pertaining to, or affected with myopia; short-sighted, near-sighted. E19.

A. PRYCE-JONES She was very fair, with huge myopic blue eyes. M. WEST Eyes scarcely visible behind thick myopic lenses. *fig.*: G. DURRELL They had been very myopic about the whole thing.

B *n.* = MYOPE *n.* L19.

myopical *a.* (*rare*) = MYOPIC *a.* M18. **myopically** *adv.* in the manner of a short-sighted person E20.

myosin /'mʌɪə(ʊ)sɪn/ *n.* M19. [f. MYO- + -OSE[2] + -IN[1].] *Biochem.* A protein which with actin forms the contractile filaments of muscle fibres.

myosis *n.* see MIOSIS.

myositis /mʌɪə(ʊ)'sʌɪtɪs/ *n.* E19. [Irreg. f. Gk *muos* genit. of *mus* muscle + -ITIS.] *Med.* (A condition characterized by) inflammation and degeneration of muscle tissue.

myosotis /mʌɪə(ʊ)'səʊtɪs/ *n.* E17. [L (see below) f. Gk *muosōtis*, f. *muos* genit. of *mus* mouse + *ōt-*, *ous* ear.] A plant of the genus *Myosotis*; a forget-me-not. Formerly also, mouse-ear hawkweed, *Pilosella officinarum*.

Also **'myosote** *n.* L19.

myotic *a.* see MIOTIC.

myotome /'mʌɪətəʊm/ *n.* M19. [f. MYO- + -TOME.] *Embryol.* & *Zool.* (Each segment of) a part of the embryonic mesoderm which gives rise to the skeletal muscles; esp. in fish and amphibians, each of a series of muscle blocks either side of the spine.

myotomy /mʌɪ'ɒtəmi/ *n. rare.* L17. [f. MYO- + -TOMY.] †**1** (An anatomical treatise on) the dissection of muscles. L17–M18. **2** Surgical division of a muscle; an instance of this. L19.

myo'tomic *a.* M19.

myotonia /mʌɪə(ʊ)'təʊnɪə/ *n.* Also **mya-**. L19. [f. MYO- + Gk *tonos* TONE *n.* + -IA[1].] *Med.* (A condition characterized by) an apparent inability to relax voluntary muscles after vigorous effort.

myotonia atrophica /ə'trɒfɪkə/ [L = atrophic] = DYSTROPHIA *myotonica*. **myotonia congenita** /kən'dʒenɪtə/ [L = congenital] a rare hereditary disease appearing in young children, characterized by myotonia without muscular wasting or other symptoms; also called *Thomsen's disease*.

myotonic /-'tɒnɪk/ *a.* of, pertaining to, or affected by myotonia L19.

myrcene /'məːsiːn/ *n.* L19. [f. mod.L *Myrcia* former genus name of bayberry + -ENE.] *Chem.* An oily liquid terpene found in essential oils of bayberry, hop, and other plants; 2-methyl-6-methylene-2,7-octadiene, $C_{10}H_{16}$.

myria- /'mɪrɪə/ *comb. form.* Also (*rare*) **myrio-** /'mɪrɪəʊ/; bef. a vowel **myri-**. E19. [f. Gk *murias*, *murios*, or *murioi*: see next.] **1** With the sense 'very numerous', as *myriapod*. **2** Used (not now in standard scientific use) in names of units of measurement to denote a factor of ten thousand (10^4), as *myriagram*, *myriametre*.

myria'metric *a.* (*Astron.*) consisting of or designating radio waves with a wavelength between 10 and 100 kilometres M20.

myriad /'mɪrɪəd/ *n.* & *a.* M16. [Late L *myriad-*, *-as* f. Gk *muriad-*, *-as*, f. *murios* countless, innumerable, pl. *murioi* ten thousand: see -AD[1].] **A** *n.* **1** Chiefly *Class. Hist.* A unit of ten thousand. M16. **2a** In *pl.* Countless numbers, hosts, (*of*). M16. **b** A countless number, a host, (*of*). E18.

2a C. CHAPLIN Broadway .. began to light up with myriads of coloured electric bulbs. A. C. CLARKE Yet though myriads sought forgetfulness, even more found satisfaction. **b** F. W. ROBERTSON A myriad of different universes.

B *adj.* **1a** With pl. n.: existing in myriads; of indefinitely great number; countless, innumerable. Chiefly *literary.* L18. **b** With sing. n.: consisting of myriads; having countless phases or aspects. Chiefly *literary.* E19. **2** Chiefly *Class. Hist.* Ten thousand. *rare.* L19.

1a *Chambers's Journal* For the trespasser, the dangers were myriad. S. J. PERELMAN The myriad twinkling lights of Los Angeles. **b** W. FAULKNER Her myriad and sunken face. R. C. ZAEHNER The myriad sum-total of ever-reincarnating souls.

myriadfold *a.* & *n.* (*literary*) (*a*) *n.* an infinitely large amount (used *advb.*); (*b*) *adj.* countless, innumerable; having innumerable aspects or features: E18. **myriadth** *a.* (chiefly *literary*) that is a very minute part of a whole E19.

myriapod /'mɪrɪəpɒd/ *a.* & *n.* E19. [mod.L *Myriapoda* (see below), f. as MYRIA- + -POD.] *Zool.* **A** *n.* An arthropod of the class Myriapoda, which comprises the centipedes and millipedes. E19. **B** *adj.* Having very many feet; *spec.* pertaining to or of the nature of a myriapod. E19.

myri'apodal, myri'apodan *adjs.* = MYRIAPOD *a.* L19. **myri'apodous** *a.* = MYRIAPOD *a.* M19.

myrica /mɪ'rʌɪkə/ *n.* E18. [L f. Gk *murikē*] **1** A tamarisk. E18. **2** Any of various shrubs of the genus *Myrica* (family Myricaceae), with fragrant leaves, *esp.* bog myrtle, *M. gale*, and (in the US) a bayberry, esp. *M. pennsylvanica*. M18.

myricin /mɪ'rʌɪsɪn, 'mʌɪrɪsɪn, 'mɪ-/ *n.* E19. [f. mod.L *Myrica* (*cerifera*) wax myrtle (a source of myricin): see prec., -IN[1].] *Chem.* A wax ester, myricyl palmitate, found in beeswax and some plant waxes.

myricyl /mɪ'rʌɪsʌɪl, -sɪl, 'mʌɪrɪs-, 'mɪ-/ *n.* M19. [f. as prec. + -YL.] *Chem.* = MELISSYL.

Comb.: **myricyl alcohol** = MELISSYL *alcohol*; **myricyl palmitate** = MYRICIN.

myringo- /mɪ'rɪndʒəʊ, -ŋg-/ *comb. form* of mod.L *myringa* eardrum: see -O-. Bef. a vowel **myring-**. Cf. TYMPANO-.

myrin'gitis /-dʒ-/ *n.* inflammation of the eardrum M19. **myringoplasty** *n.* (an instance of) surgical repair of the eardrum, esp. by grafting L19. **myringotome** *n.* a surgical instrument for perforating the eardrum L19. **myrin'gotomy** *n.* (an instance of) surgical incision into the eardrum to relieve pressure or drain fluid, esp. as a treatment for otitis media L19.

myrio- *comb. form* see MYRIA-.

myriologue /'mɪrɪəlɒg/ *n.* E19. [mod.Gk *muriologion* alt. of *moirologion*, f. cl.Gk *moira* fate: see -LOGUE.] An extemporaneous Greek or Turkish lament or funeral song, composed and sung by a woman.

myriologist /mɪrɪ'ɒlədʒɪst/ *n.* a singer or composer of a myriologue M19.

myriorama /mɪrɪə'rɑːmə/ *n.* E19. [f. *myrio-* var. of MYRIA-, after *panorama*.] A picture made of a number of separate sections able to be combined in numerous ways to form different scenes.

myristic /mʌɪˈrɪstɪk, mɪ-/ *a.* M19. [f. mod.L *Myristica* genus name, f. med.L (*nux*) *myristica* nutmeg, f. Gk *murizein* anoint: see -IC.] Chem. *myristic acid*, a straight-chain fatty acid found in oil of nutmeg and other vegetable and animal fats; tetradecanoic acid, $CH_3(CH_2)_{12}COOH$.

myristate *n.* a salt or ester of myristic acid M19. **myristicin** *n.* a toxic terpene obtained from volatile oils of nutmeg and mace M19. **myristin** *n.* a naturally occurring triglyceride, glyceryl trimyristate M19. **myristyl** *n.* a radical derived from myristic acid, either $C_{14}H_{29}$· (tetradecyl) or $C_{13}H_{27}CO$· M19.

myrmeco- /ˈməːmɪkəʊ, məːˈmiːkəʊ/ *comb. form* of Gk *murmēk-*, *murmēx* ANT *n.* (freq. taken to include termites).

myrmecochore *n.* [Gk *khōrein* spread] *Bot.* an oily seed adapted to facilitate dispersal by ants; a plant with such seeds: E20. **myrmecoˈchorous** *a.* (*Bot.*) that is a myrmecochore; pertaining to myrmecochores E20. **myrmecoˈlogical** *a.* of or pertaining to myrmecology L19. **myrmeˈcologist** *n.* an expert in or student of myrmecology E20. **myrmeˈcology** *n.* the scientific study of ants L19. **myrmeˈcophagid** *n.* & *a.* (*Zool.*) (*a*) *n.* an anteater of the family Myrmecophagidae; (*b*) *adj.* pertaining to or designating this family: L19. **myrmeˈcophagous** *a.* that eats ants; characterized by feeding on ants M19. **myrmecophile** *n.* a myrmecophilous insect L19. **myrmeˈcophilous** *a.* (*Bot.* & *Zool.*) pertaining to or exhibiting myrmecophily M19. **myrmeˈcophily** *n.* (*Bot.* & *Zool.*) the condition of living in association with ants, esp. (in an insect) of living in an ant colony or (in a plant) of being specially adapted to feed or shelter ants L19. **myrmecophyte** *n.* a myrmecophilous plant, an ant-plant L19.

myrmecobius /məːmɪˈkəʊbɪəs/ *n.* Also **M-**. M19. [mod.L, f. Gk *murmēkobios* lit. 'living like an ant', f. as MYRMECO- + *bioun* live.] = NUMBAT. Now chiefly as mod.L genus name.

myrmecoid /ˈməːmɪkɔɪd/ *a. rare.* M19. [f. MYRMECO- + -OID.] Antlike.

myrmekite /ˈməːmɪkʌɪt/ *n.* E20. [f. Gk *murmēkia* anthill, wart + -ITE¹.] *Petrogr.* Plagioclase intergrown with drops or wormlike forms of quartz.

myrmeˈkitic *a.* of the nature of or containing myrmekite E20. **myrmekitiˈzation** *n.* formation of or conversion into myrmekite E20.

myrmeleon /məːˈmiːlɪən/ *n.* M18. [mod.L, contr. of med.L *mirmicoleon* f. Gk *murmēkoleōn*, f. *murmēk-*, *murmēx* ant + *leōn* lion.] = *ant-lion* s.v. ANT *n.* Now *rare* or *obs.* exc. as mod.L genus name.

myrmicine /ˈməːmɪsʌɪn/ *a.* L19. [f. mod.L *Myrmicinae* (see below), f. *Myrmica* genus name, f. Gk *murmēk-*, *murmēx* ant: see -INE¹.] *Entomol.* Designating or pertaining to the subfamily Myrmicinae of stinging ants.

myrmidon /ˈməːmɪd(ə)n/ *n.* Also (esp. in sense 1) **M-**. LME. [L *Myrmidones* (pl.) f. Gk *Murmidones* (as according to legend orig. created f. *murmēkes* ants).] **1** A member of a warlike people of ancient Thessaly, whom, according to a Homeric story, Achilles led to the siege of Troy. LME. †**2** A bodyguard; a faithful follower or servant. E17–E19. **3** An unscrupulously faithful follower or hireling; a hired ruffian; a despicable attendant. M17.

3 myrmidon of the law, of justice *arch.* (*derog.*) a police officer, bailiff, or other inferior administrative officer of the law.

Myrmidonian /məːmɪˈdəʊnɪən/ *a.* (now *rare*) designating or pertaining to the Myrmidons E17.

myrnyong *n.* var. of MIRRNYONG.

myrobalan /mʌɪˈrɒbələn/ *n.* LME. [(O)Fr. *myrobolan* or its source L *myrobalanum* f. Gk *murobalanon*, f. *muron* balsam, unguent + *balanos* acorn, date, ben nut.] **1** The astringent plumlike fruit of any of various tropical trees of the genus *Terminalia* (family Combretaceae), esp. *T. chebula* and *T. bellirica*, used in tanning and dyeing; a tree bearing such a fruit. LME. **2** In full *myrobalan plum*. The fruit of the cherry plum, *Prunus cerasifera*. M17.

1 BELLERIC *myrobalan*. CHEBULE *myrobalan*.

myronic /mʌɪˈrɒnɪk/ *a.* M19. [f. Gk *muron* unguent, perfume + -IC.] Chem. *myronic acid*, a sulphur-containing acidic glycoside of which sinigrin, obtained from black mustard, is the potassium salt.

ˈ**myronate** *n.* a salt or ester of myronic acid; *potassium myronate* = SINIGRIN: M19.

myrosin /ˈmʌɪ(ə)rəsɪn/ *n.* M19. [f. prec. + *-s-* + -IN¹.] *Biochem.* An enzyme which catalyses the hydrolysis of sinigrin and other sulphur-containing glycosides.

myrrh /məː/ *n.*¹ [OE *myrra*, *myrre*, corresp. to OS *myrra* (Du. *mirre*), OHG *myrra* (G *Myrrhe*), ON *mirra*, f. Gmc = L *myrrha* f. Gk *murra*, of Semitic origin (cf. Arab. *murr* bitter, Aram. *mūrā*, Heb. *mōr*, Akkadian *murru*).] **1** A bitter aromatic resinous exudate from the stem of various Arabian and African trees of the genus *Commiphora* (family Burseraceae), esp. *C. abyssinica* and *C. myrrha*, formerly important in perfumery and as an ingredient of incense; *Pharm.* a tincture made from this. OE. †**2** = *myrrh tree* below. LME–M17.

Comb.: **myrrh tree** a tree that yields myrrh.

myrrhed *a.* (*rare*) mixed or sprinkled with myrrh L15. **myrrhy** *a.* smelling like or redolent of myrrh M19.

myrrh /məː/ *n.*² L16. [L *myrris* f. Gk *murris*.] = *sweet* CICELY.

myrrhophore /ˈməːrəfɔː, ˈmɪr-/ *n.* M19. [f. Gk *murra* MYRRH *n.*¹ + -O- + -PHORE.] A woman carrying spices to the sepulchre of Christ, as represented in art.

myrtaceous /məːˈteɪʃəs/ *a.* M19. [f. mod.L *Myrtaceae* (see below) fem. pl. of L *myrtaceus*, f. *myrtus*: see next, -ACEOUS.] *Bot.* Of or pertaining to the family Myrtaceae, of which the myrtle is the type.

myrtle /ˈməːt(ə)l/ *n.* LME. [med.L *myrtilla*, *-illus* (whence OFr. *myrtille*, *-il*), dim. of L *myrtus*, *-ta* f. Gk *murtos*.] †**1** The fruit or berry of the shrub *Myrtus communis* (see below). LME–M18. **2** Any of various evergreen shrubs of the genus *Myrtus* (family Myrtaceae), esp. *M. communis*, of southern Europe, with white sweet-scented flowers, used in perfumery. LME. **b** Any of various plants of this and other families resembling myrtle in appearance, fragrance, etc.; *spec.* (*US*) periwinkle, *Vinca minor*. Usu. w. specifying wd. L16. **3** *ellipt.* = *myrtle-green* below. L19.

2b *bog myrtle*, *candleberry myrtle*, *crape myrtle*, *honey myrtle*, *wax-myrtle*, etc.

Comb.: **myrtle-berry** (*a*) the fruit of a myrtle; (*b*) [cf. Fr. *myrtille*] the fruit of the bilberry, *Vaccinium myrtillus*; **myrtle bird** = *myrtle warbler* below; **myrtle green** a shade of deep green like that of myrtle leaves; **myrtle-of-the-river** a large evergreen shrub of the myrtle family, *Calyptranthes zuzygium*, of tropical America; **myrtle warbler** a warbler found in eastern N. America, now considered to be a race of the yellow-rumped warbler, *Dendroica coronata*; **myrtle wine** wine made from myrtle-berries.

myself /mʌɪˈsɛlf, mɪˈsɛlf/ *pron.* OE. [f. ME *pron.* + SELF *a.* (but long interpreted as MY *a.* + SELF *n.*). See also MESELF.] **I** Orig. *emphatic*. **1** In apposition to the subjective pronoun *I* or (less commonly) *me*: in my own person; for my part. OE. **2** (Not appositional.) **a** Subjective: I myself (in emphatic use now *arch.* & *rhet.*); (pred. after *be* & after *than, as*) I. ME. **b** Objective: me personally (*arch.* in emphatic use). ME.

1 J. STEINBECK If I keep oiling my rifle, I myself may be an officer one day. J. C. POWYS I can tell you myself of one person. G. GREENE Myself I don't care to go fifty yards from the waterfront. R. P. JHABVALA I had.. hoisted my trunk and bedding on to my shoulders and carried them up myself. **2a** S. RICHARDSON Enough to make a better man than myself.. run into madness. E. FITZGERALD Myself when young did eagerly frequent Doctor and Saint. J. CONRAD Being myself a quiet individual I take it that what all men are really after is.. peace. **b** G. BORROW Several of the ultra-popish bishops.. had denounced the Bible, the Bible Society, and myself. T. HARDY As for Steve and myself, we were deeply moved. J. BUCHAN My earliest recollections are not of myself, but of my environment. I. MURDOCH Crystal was.. like myself, unmarried.

II *refl.* **3** Refl. (direct, indirect, & after preps.) corresp. to the subjective pronoun *I*: (to, for, etc.) me personally, me. OE.

3 M. AMIS I wrapped myself in a sheet and climbed the stairs like a ghost. J. SIMMS I found myself wondering whether I should not try to talk to her.

Phrases: **be myself** (*a*) act in my normal unconstrained manner; (*b*) feel as well as I usually do (usu. in neg. contexts). **by myself** on my own.

Mysian /ˈmɪsɪən/ *n.* & *a.* M16. [f. L *Mysia*, Gk *Musia* Mysia (see below) + -AN.] **A** *n.* **1** A native or inhabitant of ancient Mysia in NW Asia Minor. M16. **2** The language of ancient Mysia. M20. **B** *adj.* Of or pertaining to ancient Mysia, its inhabitants, or its language. M19.

mysid /ˈmʌɪsɪd/ *n.* & *a.* M20. [f. next + -ID³.] *Zool.* **A** *n.* A small shrimplike usu. marine crustacean of the family Mysidae or the suborder Mysidacea; an opossum-shrimp. M20. **B** *adj.* Of, pertaining to, or designating this family or suborder. M20.

mysis /ˈmʌɪsɪs/ *n.* Also **M-**. M19. [mod.L *Mysis* (see below), of unkn. origin.] *Zool.* **1** A mysid shrimp of the genus *Mysis*. Now chiefly as mod.L genus name. M19. **2** *mysis-phase*, *-stage*, a stage in the life cycle of certain decapods in which they resemble a shrimp of the genus *Mysis*. M19.

Mysoline /ˈmʌɪsəliːn/ *n.* Also **m-**. M20. [Origin unkn.] *Pharm.* (Proprietary name for) primidone.

mysophobia /mʌɪsəˈfəʊbɪə/ *n.* L19. [f. Gk *musos* uncleanness + -PHOBIA.] Irrational fear of dirt or defilement.

Mysore /mʌɪˈsɔː, ˈmʌɪsɔː/ *n.* E20. [See below.] Coffee grown in or around Karnataka (formerly called Mysore), a State in southern India.

Mysorean /mʌɪsəˈriːən/ *n.* & *a.* L19. [f. *Mysore* (see prec.) + -AN.] *Hist.* **A** *n.* A native or inhabitant of Mysore (now Karnataka) in southern India. L19. **B** *adj.* Of or pertaining to Mysore. M20.

mysost /ˈmʌɪsɒst/ *n.* M19. [Norw., f. *myse* whey + *ost* cheese.] A Norwegian whey cheese, orig. made from goat's milk.

myst /mɪst/ *n.* L17. [L *mysta*, *mystes* f. Gk *mustēs*: see MYSTIC.] = MYSTES.

mystacial /mɪˈsteɪʃ(ə)l/ *a.* L18. [f. Gk *mustax*, *-tak-* (see MUSTACHIO) + -IAL.] Resembling or in the position of a moustache; moustachial.

mystae *n.* pl. of MYSTES.

mystagogic /mɪstəˈgɒdʒɪk/ *a.* M17. [Late L *mystagogicus*, Gk *mustagōgikos*, f. *mustagōgos*: see next, -IC.] Of or pertaining to a mystagogue or mystagogy; relating to instruction in mysteries.

mystagogical *a.* E17. **mystagogically** *adv.* M19.

mystagogue /ˈmɪstəgɒg/ *n.* M16. [Fr., or L *mystagogus* f. Gk *mustagōgos*, f. *mustēs* (see MYSTIC) + *agōgos* leading, f. *agein* to lead.] In ancient Greece, a person who gave preparatory instruction to candidates for initiation into the Eleusinian or other mysteries; *gen.* a person who introduces others to religious mysteries, a teacher of mystical doctrines, a creator or disseminator of mystical doctrines.

mystaˈgoguery *n.* the doctrines or practices of a mystagogue E20.

mystagogy /ˈmɪstəgɒdʒi/ *n.* L16. [L *mystagogia* f. Gk *mustagōgia*, f. *mustagōgos*: see prec., -Y³.] (An) initiation into mysteries; instruction preparatory to initiation into mysteries; the doctrines or practices of a mystagogue.

mysterial /mɪˈstɪərɪəl/ *a.* Now *rare.* LME. [Late L *mysterialis*, f. *mysterium* MYSTERY *n.*¹: see -IAL.] Mysterious. Formerly also, mystical.

mysteriarch /mɪˈstɪərɪɑːk/ *n.* M17. [eccl.L *mysteriarches* f. Gk *mustēriarkhes*, f. *mustērion* MYSTERY *n.*¹: see -ARCH.] A person who presides over mysteries.

mysterioso /mɪˌstɪərɪˈəʊzəʊ/ *a.* M20. [It. = mysterious.] *Mus.* Executed in a mysterious manner.

mysteriosophy /mɪˌstɪərɪˈɒsəfi/ *n.* L19. [f. Gk *mustērion* MYSTERY *n.*¹ + *sophia* wisdom: see -Y³.] A system of doctrine concerning mysteries.

mysterious /mɪˈstɪərɪəs/ *a.* L16. [f. Fr. *mystérieux*, f. *mystère* MYSTERY *n.*¹: see -IOUS.] **1** Full of mystery; wrapped in mystery; impossible or difficult to explain, solve, discover, or identify; of obscure origin, nature, or purpose. L16. 2 *spec.* Of a person: whose movements are secret or unknown; delighting in mystery; enigmatic. Formerly also, dealing with or versed in mysteries; using occult arts. E17. 3 That is due to a mystery. *rare.* M17.

1 W. COWPER God moves in a mysterious way His wonders to perform. J. STEINBECK The communications system on Cannery Row is mysterious to the point of magic. A. MILLER The mysterious deaths . . of the explorers who had broken into his tomb. J. BERMAN Eliot intuits a mysterious relationship between suffering and artistic creativity. 2 A. GRAY He wanted to seem mysterious to these boys, someone ageless with strange powers.

mysteriously *adv.* M17. **mysteriousness** *n.* M17.

†mysterise *v.* var. of MYSTERIZE.

mysterium tremendum /mɪˌstɪərɪəm trɪˈmɛndəm/ *n. phr.* E20. [L = tremendous mystery.] A great or overwhelming mystery, *esp.* the great or overwhelming mystery of God or of existence.

†mysterize *v.* Also **-ise**. M17. [f. MYSTERY *n.*[1] + -IZE.] 1 *v.t.* Interpret mystically. Only in M17. 2 *v.i.* Make mysteries of things. E–M19.

mystery /ˈmɪst(ə)ri/ *n.*[1] ME. [AN equiv. of OFr. *mistere* (mod. *mystère*), or immed. f. the source L *mysterium* f. Gk *mustērion* secret thing or ceremony, f. base also of *mustikos* secret, MYSTIC.] †1 Mystic presence; hidden or mystic meaning; hidden religious symbolism. ME–L17. 2 A religious belief based on divine revelation, *esp.* a doctrine of faith involving difficulties which human reason is incapable of solving. Also *gen.*, a hidden or secret thing; a thing beyond human knowledge or comprehension; a riddle, an enigma, a puzzle; a person or thing not understood. LME. 3 A religious ordinance or rite, *esp.* a Christian sacrament; in *pl.*, the Eucharist. LME. 4a A secret rite of an ancient religion or other occult society to which only the initiated are admitted. Usu. in *pl.* L15. b A secret of Freemasonry. Usu. in *pl.* M18. 5†a A personal secret. E16–E17. b An action or practice shrouded in secrecy; a technical operation in a trade or art, now esp. a trivial one. Cf. MYSTERY *n.*[2] L16. c A political or diplomatic secret; a secret of State. Usu. more fully *mystery of State*. Now *rare* or *obs.* E17. 6a The condition or property of being secret or obscure; mysteriousness. Also, mysteries collectively, mysterious matter. E17. b The behaviour or attitude of mind of a person who makes a secret of (esp. intrinsically unimportant) things. L17. 7 *Chr. Ch.* An incident in the life of Jesus or of a saint regarded as an object of commemoration or as having a mystical significance; *spec.* each of the events in the life of Jesus contemplated with the use of a rosary, a division of a rosary corresponding to such an event. M17. 8 A miracle play. M18. 9 A girl newly arrived in a town or city; a girl with no fixed address; a young or inexperienced prostitute. *slang.* M20. 10 A mystery story; a mystery novel etc. M20.

2 SWIFT The Mysteries of the Christian Religion. M. ANGELOU He remained a mystery in my childhood. N. CHOMSKY The neurophysiology of language remains almost a total mystery. B. CHATWIN Or debate with learned rabbis the mysteries of the Cabbala. **make a mystery of** treat as a secret; keep (a thing) secret in order to make an impression. 5b HANNAH MORE No man is allowed to set up in an ordinary trade till he has served a long apprenticeship to its mysteries. DISRAELI Harassed with all the mysteries of packing. 6a HENRY MILLER The world was full of wonder and mystery. T. O. ECHEWA Sun-glasses for mystery—eyes that saw without being seen. *bag of mystery*: see BAG *n.*

Comb.: **mystery-bag** = *bag of mystery* s.v. BAG *n.*; **mystery man** (*a*) a conjuror, a medicine man; (*b*) a man about whom little is known; **mystery novel** a novel about the detection of a crime etc., a novel in which a mystery is unravelled; **mystery play** (*a*) = sense 8 above; (*b*) a play about the detection of a crime etc., a play in which a mystery is unravelled; **mystery-religion** a religion centred on mysteries and mystic rites; **mystery ship** an armed and camouflaged merchantman used in the war of 1914–18 as a decoy or to destroy submarines; **mystery story** a detective or crime story, a story in which a mystery is unravelled; **mystery tour, trip** a pleasure trip for which there is no advance announcement of the place(s) to be visited; **mystery woman** a woman about whom little is known; **mystery writer** a writer of mystery stories.

mystery /ˈmɪst(ə)ri/ *n.*[2] Also **mistery**. LME. [med.L *misterium* (cf. MISTER *n.*[1]) contr. of L *ministerium* MINISTRY by assoc. w. *mysterium*: see prec.] †1a An occupation; an office rendered. LME–M16. †b A helpful thing. Only in L16. 2a A handicraft; a craft, an art; one's trade, profession, or calling. *arch.* LME. †b Skill, art. E–M17. 3 A trade guild or company. Now *arch.* or *Hist.* L15.

2a **art and mystery**: a formula employed in indentures binding apprentices to a trade.

mystes /ˈmɪstiːz/ *n.* Pl. ***mystae*** /ˈmɪstiː/. L17. [L f. Gk *mustēs*: see next. Cf. MYST.] A person initiated into mysteries.

mystic /ˈmɪstɪk/ *n.* & *a.* ME. [(O)Fr. *mystique* or L *mysticus* adjs. f. Gk *mustikos*, f. *mustēs* initiated person, f. *muein* close (the eyes, lips), initiate: see -IC. Cf. next.] A *n.* †1 Mystical meaning; mystical representation. Only in ME. 2 Chiefly *Chr. Ch.* Orig., an exponent of mystical theology, a person who maintains the validity and the supreme importance of mystical theology. Later, a person who seeks by contemplation and self-surrender to obtain union with or absorption into God, or who believes in the possibility of the spiritual apprehension of knowledge inaccessible to the intellect; a person who has mystical experiences. L17. 3 = MYSTES. *rare.* M19. B *adj.* 1a Chiefly *Chr. Ch.* Spiritually allegorical or symbolical; of the nature of, or characteristic of, a sacred mystery; pertaining to religious mysteries; (now *rhet.*) having direct spiritual significance, transcending human understanding. LME. b *spec.* Designating or pertaining to the branch of theology relating to direct communion of the soul with God. Now *rare.* M17. 2 Of or pertaining to ancient religious mysteries or other occult rites or practices; occult, esoteric. E17. †3 Secret, concealed. Only in 17. 4 Of hidden meaning or nature; enigmatic, mysterious. M17. 5 Inspiring an awed sense of mystery. M19.

mysticly *adv.* (*rare*) LME.

mystical /ˈmɪstɪk(ə)l/ *a.* L15. [f. as prec.: see -ICAL. Cf. prec.] 1a Chiefly *Chr. Ch.* Spiritually allegorical or symbolical; having direct spiritual significance, transcending human understanding. L15. b Designating or pertaining to the branch of theology relating to direct communion of the soul with God. Also, of, pertaining to, or characteristic of, mystics; relating to or of the nature of mysticism. E17. 2 Having an unseen, unknown, or mysterious origin, character, effect, or influence. Now *rare* or *obs.* L15. †b Of a person: obscure in speech or in style. L15–E17. 3 Of or pertaining to mysterious or occult rites or practices. L16. †4 Secret, concealed. Only in 17.

1a R. COKE These two individual persons . . are made one mystical person. E. B. PUSEY Jerome gives here the mystical meaning. b M. IGNATIEFF Paul . . retained a mystical reverence for the office of Tsar. A. STORR A mystical experience of unity with the universe. 3 P. BENSON Americans came to explore the mystical sights of Somerset.

mystiˈcality *n.* (*rare*) M19. **mystically** /ˈmɪstɪk(ə)li/ *adv.* E16. **mysticalness** *n.* (*rare*) E17.

mysticete /ˈmɪstɪsiːt/ *n.* Formerly also in L form **†-cetus**. L18. [mod.L *Mysticeti* (see below) f. Gk *mustikētos* (in old editions of Aristotle), for *ho mus to kētos* 'the mouse, the whale so called'.] *Zool.* A whale of the suborder Mysticeti of baleen or whalebone whales; *spec.* the Greenland right whale or bowhead, *Balaena mysticetus*.

mysticise *v.* var. of MYSTICIZE.

mysticism /ˈmɪstɪsɪz(ə)m/ *n.* M18. [f. MYSTIC + -ISM.] 1 Chiefly *Chr. Ch.* The beliefs or mental tendencies characteristic of mystics; belief in the possibility of union with or absorption into God by means of contemplation and self-surrender; belief in or reliance on the possibility of spiritual apprehension of knowledge inaccessible to the intellect. M18. 2 (Religious) belief characterized by self-delusion or dreamy confusion of thought; belief based on the assumption of occult qualities or mysterious agencies. M18.

mysticity /mɪˈstɪsɪti/ *n.* Now *rare.* M18. [f. MYSTIC + -ITY, after Fr. *mysticité*.] The quality of being mystic or mystical.

mysticize /ˈmɪstɪsʌɪz/ *v.t.* Also **-ise**. L17. [f. MYSTIC *a.* + -IZE.] Make mystical; introduce a mystical element into, give a mystic meaning to.

mystico- /ˈmɪstɪkəʊ/ *comb. form.* M19. [f. MYSTIC + -O-.] Forming adjs. w. the senses 'mystical and —', 'mystically —', as *mystico-allegoric*, *-religious*.

mystification /ˌmɪstɪfɪˈkeɪʃ(ə)n/ *n.* E19. [Fr., f. as MYSTIFY: see -FICATION.] 1 The action of mystifying a person; an instance of this. E19. 2 The condition or fact of being mystified. E19.

mystificator /ˈmɪstɪfɪˌkeɪtə/ *n. rare.* E19. [Fr. *mystificateur*, f. as MYSTIFY: see -FIC, -ATOR.] A mystifier.

mystificatory /ˌmɪstɪfɪˈkeɪt(ə)ri/ *a.* M19. [f. (as) prec.: see -ORY[2].] Mystifying.

mystified /ˈmɪstɪfʌɪd/ *a.*[1] *rare.* Also **mist-**. M18. [f. MIST *n.*[1] or MISTY *a.*: see -FY, -ED[1]. Spelling assim. to next.] Beclouded, befogged.

mystified /ˈmɪstɪfʌɪd/ *a.*[2] M19. [f. MYSTIFY + -ED[1].] That has been mystified; bewildered, puzzled, perplexed.

mystifier /ˈmɪstɪfʌɪə/ *n.* E19. [f. MYSTIFY + -ER[1].] A person who mystifies another or others; a person who or thing which causes perplexity or bewilderment.

mystify /ˈmɪstɪfʌɪ/ *v.* E19. [Fr. *mystifier*, irreg. f. *mystère* MYSTERY *n.*[1] or *mystique* MYSTIC: see -FY.] I *v.t.* 1 Bewilder, perplex; play on the credulity of; hoax. E19. 2 Wrap up or involve in mystery; make mystical; interpret mystically. E19. 3 Involve in obscurity; obscure the meaning or character of. E19. II *v.i.* 4 Cause bewilderment or perplexity. E19.

mystifyingly *adv.* in a mystifying manner M20.

mystique /mɪˈstiːk/ *n.* L19. [Fr.: see MYSTIC.] The atmosphere of mystery and veneration investing some doctrines, arts, professions, or people; a mysterious attraction; any professional skill or technique designed or able to mystify and impress the lay person.

G. ORWELL All the beliefs . . that characterize our time are really designed to sustain the mystique of the Party. *Times* There is a mystique about violins, especially old violins. J. GATHORNE-HARDY Nannies had their own mystique—their medical and superstitious lore. PARTICIPATION *mystique*.

myth /mɪθ/ *n.* M19. [mod.L *mythus*, late L *mythos* f. Gk *muthos*. Cf. MYTHOS, MYTHUS.] 1 A traditional story, either wholly or partially fictitious, providing an explanation for or embodying a popular idea concerning some natural or social phenomenon or some religious belief or ritual; *spec.* one involving supernatural persons, actions, or events; a similar newly created story. M19. 2 A widely-held (esp. untrue or discredited popular) story or belief; a misconception; a misrepresentation of the truth; an exaggerated or idealized conception of a person, institution, etc.; a person, institution, etc., widely idealized or misrepresented. M19. 3 Myths collectively or as a genre; the technique or habit of creating myths. M19.

1 A. H. SAYCE An attempt . . to extract a pseudo-history from the Greek myths. J. D. CRICHTON At the heart of the ritual action, was the myth. M. HUGHES The heroes and heroines of the old myths and sagas. *solar myth*: see SOLAR *a.*[1] & *n.*[2] 2 GEO. ELIOT Many silly myths are already afloat about me, in addition to the truth. J. W. FULBRIGHT The master myth of the cold war is that the Communist bloc is a monolith. B. EMECHETA One of the myths she had been brought up to believe: that the white man never lied. 3 J. PLAMENATZ Themes as old as poetry and as myth.

mytheme *n.* [-EME] an element of a myth regarded as a unit of structure L20. **mythless** *a.* E20.

mythi *n.* pl. of MYTHUS.

mythic /ˈmɪθɪk/ *a.* M17. [Late L *mythicus* f. Gk *muthikos*, f. *muthos* MYTH: see -IC.] Mythical; widely idealized or misrepresented; fantastic, bizarre.